**Herkimer County
Community College Library
Herkimer, New York
13350**

1. Books may be kept for three weeks and may be renewed once, except when otherwise noted.

2. Reference books, such as dictionaries and encyclopedias are to be used only in the Library.

3. A fine is charged for each day a book is not returned according to the above rule.

4. All injuries to books beyond reasonable wear and all losses shall be made good to the satisfaction of the Librarian.

5. Each borrower is held responsible for all books drawn on his card and for all fines accruing on the same.

THE AUTHORITY SINCE 1868

THE WORLD ALMANAC®

AND BOOK OF FACTS

2005

WORLD ALMANAC BOOKS

THE WORLD ALMANAC®
AND BOOK OF FACTS
2005

Editorial Director: William A. McGeveran Jr.
Director of Desktop Publishing: Elizabeth J. Lazzara
Managing Editor: Lori P. Wiesenfeld
Senior Editor: Kevin Seabrooke
Editor: Erik C. Gopel; **Associate Editor:** Vincent G. Spadafora
Desktop Publishing Associate: Michael Meyerhofer
Contributing Editors: Jennifer Dunham, Richard Hantula, Jane Hogan, Michael J. Holley, Geoffrey M. Horn, Mark LaFlaur, Jane Reynolds, Dr. Lee T. Shapiro, George W. Smith, Donald Young
Research: Lisa Haddock, Sarah Janssen, Rachael Mason, Andrew Steinitz
Cover: Bill SMITH STUDIO

WORLD ALMANAC EDUCATION GROUP
Chief Executive Officer, WRC Media Inc.: Martin E. Kenney Jr.
Publisher: Ken Park
Director–Purchasing and Production: Edward A. Thomas
Associate Editor: Ileana Parvulescu; **Desktop Publishing Assistant:** Sean Westmoreland
Director of Indexing Services: Marjorie B. Bank; **Index Editor:** Walter Kronenberg
Facts On File World News Digest: Marion Farrier, Editor in Chief; Jonathan Taylor, Managing Editor
World Almanac Reference Database@*FACTS.com*: Louise Bloomfield, Dennis La Beau

WORLD ALMANAC BOOKS
Vice President–Sales and Marketing: James R. Keenley
Marketing Manager: Sarah De Vos

We acknowledge with thanks the many helpful letters and e-mails from readers of THE WORLD ALMANAC. Because of the volume of mail, it is not possible to reply to each one. However, every communication is read by the editors, and all suggestions receive careful attention. THE WORLD ALMANAC's e-mail address is Walmanac@waegroup.com.

The first edition of THE WORLD ALMANAC, a 120-page volume with 12 pages of advertising, was published by the New York World in 1868. Annual publication was suspended in 1876. Joseph Pulitzer, publisher of the *New York World*, revived THE WORLD ALMANAC in 1886 with the goal of making it a "compendium of universal knowledge." It has been published annually since then. THE WORLD ALMANAC does not decide wagers.

PHOTOS: COVER: Bush, Dept. of Defense photo by R. D. Ward; Kerry, Kerry-Edwards 2004 Inc. from Sharon Ward; peace sign, hurricane, Acropolis, © Getty Images; pope, Reuters/Landov; U.S. soldiers, Dept. of Defense photo by Tech Sgt. Scott Reed, U.S. Air Force; Muslims praying, Photos.com. **Page 832:** "The Lord of the Rings™: The Return of the King" © MMIII, New Line Productions, Inc.™ The Saul Zaentz Company d/b/a Tolkien Enterprises under license to New Line Productions, Inc. All rights reserved. Photo by Pierre Vinet. Photo appears courtesy of New Line Productions, Inc.

WORLD ALMANAC BOOKS
A Division of World Almanac Education Group, Inc.
A WRC Media Company
512 Seventh Avenue
New York, NY 10018

CONTENTS

The World Almanac
and Book of Facts
2005

THE TOP TEN NEWS STORIES OF 2004

1. Fifteen months after the U.S.-led invasion of Iraq and ensuing overthrow of Saddam Hussein, the U.S. June 28 **transferred sovereignty to an interim Iraqi government, headed by Prime Min. Iyad Allawi.** Hussein, who had been captured by U.S. forces in Dec. 2003, was arraigned before an Iraqi court July 1 on 7 criminal charges including genocide and crimes against humanity. More than 160,000 U.S. troops remained in Iraq, seeking to stabilize the country in the face of continuing **attacks by both Sunni and Shiite insurgents.** Militants in Apr. launched a wave of kidnappings of foreigners, some of whom were beheaded. Later in Apr., photographs of the **abuse of Iraqi detainees** by U.S. forces at the Abu Ghraib prison touched off an international scandal. Questions about the **rationale for the war** were debated, as inspectors failed to find evidence that Iraq possessed weapons of mass destruction. As of Oct. 15, coalition troop deaths since the start of the invasion totaled over 1,227, including 1,088 Americans. According to Iraq Body Count, a group monitoring international press reports, more than 13,000 Iraqi civilians had been killed during the fighting as of mid-Oct.

2. Polls showed **Pres. George W. Bush (R) locked in a tight race for reelection against Sen. John Kerry (D, MA).** Kerry had pulled ahead of the Democratic pack and effectively secured nomination Mar. 2 by nearly sweeping "Super Tuesday" primaries and caucuses. On July 6 he tapped as his running mate Sen. **John Edwards** (D, NC), his last serious rival in the primaries. Former Vermont Gov. **Howard Dean**, an early front-runner, had failed to win any primaries. The Bush administration's war on terrorism—as waged in Iraq and elsewhere—and the economy were key issues in the Nov. 2 election, in which control of Congress was also at stake.

3. The U.S. and its allies continued to **fight against terrorism** amid ongoing attacks. The bipartisan National Commission on Terrorist Attacks Upon the United States July 22 released a final report in its **probe of the Sept. 11, 2001, attacks;** U.S. intelligence agencies and their congressional overseers drew criticism in the report, which outlined **missed chances to disrupt the terrorist plot** but did not cast blame on either the Clinton or Bush administrations. The commission recommended an extensive overhaul of the U.S. intelligence community and the formation of a coherent strategy aimed at thwarting the growth of Islamist terrorism. Al-Qaeda leader **Osama bin Laden** remained at large as of Oct.; he was believed alive and hiding along the Afghanistan-Pakistan border. Abroad, al-Qaeda was linked to the Mar. 11 **bombings of commuter trains in Madrid**, Spain, which killed 191 people, days before an election that the anti-war Socialist Worker's Party ultimately won. In Afghanistan, where a U.S.-led alliance in 2001 had ousted the Taliban government that harbored al-Qaeda, millions of voters cast ballots Oct. 9 in the nation's first-ever presidential election. Russia saw ongoing **violence linked to the Chechen insurgency;** in one incident, Chechen guerrillas Sept. 1 took some 1,200 people hostage at a school in the Russian republic of North Ossetia; after a lengthy battle Sept. 3 between Russian security forces and rebels some 330 civilians—half of them children—were left dead according to the government. Citing the threat of terrorism, Russian Pres. Vladimir Putin Sept. 13 announced **structural government changes** that would strengthen central state authority.

4. In **Sudan**, Arab militias called the *janjaweed*, allegedly with government backing, carried out a **campaign of mass killing and rapes** against blacks in the Darfur region. By mid-Oct. an estimated 70,000 people had been killed and 1.4 million displaced. The UN Sept. 18 threatened sanctions against Sudan's oil industry if the government did not end the violence.

5. A mild **U.S. economic recovery** was marked by months of **slow growth in employment. Oil prices** rose in the early fall to more than $50 a barrel. The federal **deficit** hit a record estimated at $413 billion for fiscal year 2004. The Federal Reserve raised **interest rates** 3 times in 4 months, beginning June 30; they were the first increases in 4 years.

6. **Massachusetts** May 17 started issuing **marriage licenses to same-sex couples,** becoming the first U.S. state to do so. Some local jurisdictions, including San Francisco, CA, also began issuing licenses. The **California** Supreme Court on Aug. 13, nullified the licenses. Pres. Bush backed a **constitutional amendment** banning same-sex marriages, but efforts to bring the proposal to a Senate vote failed July 14, 48-50, and the amendment Sept. 30 failed to garner the required 2/3 majority in the House, 227-186.

7. **Deadly hurricanes** Charley, Frances, Ivan, and Jeanne struck the Caribbean, Florida, and other U.S. states during Aug.-Sept. More than 100 people died in the U.S., where insured damage was over $18 billion. Hurricane Jeanne, while classified as a tropical storm, set off massive flooding on the island of Hispaniola starting Sept. 17. By mid-Oct., the death toll in Haiti had reached more than 3,000.

8. The pursuit of **nuclear programs by Iran and North Korea** aroused mounting concerns in the international community. Iran had reached an agreement in 2003 with France, Britain, and Germany to temporarily halt uranium enrichment, but the agreement started to crumble in June. The **International Atomic Energy Agency** Sept. 18 demanded that Iran stop all enrichment of uranium, but Iran refused, claiming its purpose was peaceful. North Korea, which in 2002 had announced resumption of its nuclear-weapons programs in violation of international agreements, participated in 2 rounds of 6-nation talks intended to end its nuclear programs, in Feb. and June, but no agreement was reached.

9. Former Pres. **Ronald Wilson Reagan died June 5** at his home in Los Angeles at the age 93, a decade after the 40th president had disclosed he was suffering from Alzheimer's disease. His body was flown to Washington, DC, where it lay in state in the Capitol; on June 11 current and former world leaders attended a state funeral at Washington's National Cathedral; Reagan was buried at his presidential library in Simi Valley, CA.

10. The Israeli-Palestinian conflict continued with Israel's **assassinations of two high-profile leaders** of the Palestinian militant group **Hamas:** founder Sheikh Ahmed Yassin on Mar. 22 and Yassin's replacement, Abdel Aziz al-Rantisi, on Apr. 17. Prime Min. Ariel Sharon's controversial plans to **unilaterally withdraw Jewish settlements in the Gaza Strip** while holding on to major West Bank settlements was endorsed by the U.S. but rejected May 2 by Sharon's Likud Party; the Israeli cabinet approved a modified plan the next month.

TOP NEWSMAKERS OF 2004

(as of Oct. 15, 2004; in alphabetical order)

Osama Bin Laden, b. 1957 in Riyadh, Saudi Arabia, one of about 50 children of a self-made billionaire contractor and devout Muslim of Yemeni descent. After graduating in 1979 from King Abdul Aziz Univ. in Jeddah, Saudi Arabia, with a degree in civil engineering, he joined the Muslim *mujahadeen* rebels fighting the Soviets in Afghanistan. There he helped finance the cause and recruited Muslim fighters from Pakistan and the Arab countries. During this time, he associated with the Egyptian Islamic Jihad terrorist group, and together they formed al-Qaeda in the late 1980s. Returning to Saudi Arabia in 1989, he worked in his family's construction firm, while also aiding anti-government activities. During the Persian Gulf War, he strongly opposed the presence of non-Muslim troops on Saudi soil, and was forced to leave the country; he moved his family and fortune to Sudan, where he set up companies to cover al-Qaeda operations and terrorist camps. Forced to leave Sudan in 1996, he settled in Afghanistan, sheltered by the rigid Islamic Taliban regime. He resumed al-Qaeda operations there, and in 1998 called for a holy war against Americans and Jews.

Bin Laden has been blamed for many deadly terrorist attacks, including the Sept. 11, 2001, attacks and, more recently, the Mar. 11, 2004, train bombings in Madrid, Spain. Despite the U.S. campaign in Afghanistan and a $50 million reward for his capture, Bin Laden as of mid-Oct. 2004 was believed to be in poor health but alive, hiding out somewhere near the Afghanistan-Pakistan border.

George Walker Bush, b. July 6, 1946, New Haven, CT. *See* profile, page 589.

Mel Gibson, b. Jan. 3, 1956, Peekskill, NY; emigrated to Australia at age 12. One of Hollywood's top actors and directors, Gibson in 2004 released the controversial but highly successful film *The Passion of the Christ*, which he directed and produced with about $30 million of his own money after Hollywood studios refused to pick it up. The film, which grossed more than $600 million worldwide, has been praised as a pious masterpiece and also criticized for being overly graphic and possibly anti-Semitic. While his father, Hutton, is an outspoken Holocaust denier, Gibson has repudiated those views. He has said he made *The Passion* because his traditionalist Roman Catholic faith helped him overcome substance abuse and suicidal depression.

Gibson studied theater at the National Institute of Dramatic Art in Sydney, Australia. After a few TV roles, he gained worldwide fame with the Australian-made *Mad Max* (1979) and made his U.S. film debut in *The Bounty* (1984). In 1985, he was named *People* magazine's first "Sexiest Man Alive." Among other films, he starred in the *Lethal Weapon* series (1987, 1989, 1992, 1998) and directed *The Man Without a Face (1993)* and *Braveheart (1995)*, which won Best Director and Best Picture, as well as *The Passion of the Christ*. In 1980, he married his wife Robyn; they have 7 children.

Hu Jintao, b. Dec. 21, 1942, in Jixi, Anhui Province, China. He studied hydroelectric engineering at Qinghua Univ. in Beijing, graduating in 1965, and joined the Communist Party of China (CPC) the same year. In 1982, he was named an alternate member of the China Central Committee, the youngest ever, and joined the Secretariat of the Communist Youth League, becoming its leader 2 years later. He was appointed to several other party posts. As party chief in Tibet, he responded to separatist protests with martial law measures in 1989. By 1992, Hu was a member of the Politburo Standing Committee in Beijing, and head of the Party school of the CPC Central Committee. There, he introduced new courses on market economics and governance.

In 2002, Hu was made general secretary of the CPC Central Committee, a step leading to his election by the National People's Congress to the presidency in Mar. 2003, succeeding Jiang Zemin; in Sept. 2004 Jiang stepped down as leader of China's military, handing that post to Hu as well. Hu often makes use of the phrase "yi ren wei ben" ("putting peo-

ple first") in describing his professed philosophy. Since taking power, he has allowed the publication of formerly secret Politburo documents, cooperated with other nations during the SARS crisis of 2002-2003, and tried to manage the booming Chinese economy.

John Kerry, b. Dec. 11, 1943, at Fitzsimons Army Hospital in Aurora, CO. As a child, Kerry lived in a number of European countries, while his father was a member of the U.S. Foreign Service. He graduated from Yale Univ. in 1966, with a B.A. in history. Shortly before graduating, he enlisted in the Navy and, after attending Officer Candidate School, was deployed in the Western Pacific in Feb. 1968 aboard the *USS Gridley*. Kerry then requested active duty in Vietnam, and began his 2nd tour of duty in Dec. 1968 as a swift boat captain. He was awarded 3 Purple Hearts, a Silver Star, and a Bronze Star for his service, and left Vietnam in Apr. 1969, after 4 months. After leaving, Kerry joined the Vietnam Veterans Against the War (VVAW) and on Apr. 22, 1971, at Senate committee hearings he spoke of reported atrocities by U.S. forces during the war. In 1970, Kerry married Julia Thorne, with whom he has 2 daughters; they divorced in 1988.

After running unsuccessfully for the House of Representatives from Massachusetts in 1972, Kerry entered law school at Boston College and was admitted to the bar in 1976. For several years he served as an assistant district attorney, developing separate units to prosecute white-collar and organized crime. He later entered private practice. In 1982, he was elected lieutenant governor of Massachusetts; in 1984, he was elected to the U.S. Senate. During his nearly 2 decades as a senator, Kerry worked to initiate the Iran-Contra hearings, and served on the Foreign Relations and other important committees. With fellow Vietnam vet. Sen. John McCain (R-AZ), Kerry pursued an official investigation of outstanding POW/MIA soldiers.

Kerry married Teresa Heinz, widow of Sen. H. John Heinz III (R-PA), in 1995. In Sept. 2003 he announced his candidacy for the presidency. He won the Iowa caucuses and New Hampshire primary decisively, and by early March he was the presumptive nominee. Kerry announced his selection of Sen. John Edwards (NC) as his running mate on July 6 and officially received the Democratic nomination July 29.

James McGreevey, b. Aug. 6, 1957, Jersey City, NJ, the son of a Marine Corps drill instructor and a nurse. He received a BA from Columbia Univ. in 1978, a law degree from Georgetown in 1981, and a master's in education from Harvard in 1982. McGreevey began his political career in 1982 as a county assistant prosecutor and was first elected to office for 2 terms as a State Assembly Democrat in 1990-91. He married Karen Schutz in 1991; their daughter was born in Oct. 1992. In 1991 he was elected mayor of Woodbridge, NJ, and he also served as a state senator from 1994 to 1997. He and Karen divorced in 1997. McGreevey married Dina Matos in Oct. 2000; they had one child.

McGreevey became New Jersey's 51st governor in Jan. 2002, after an unsuccessful run in 1997. For 2 years he grappled with budget deficits by cutting property taxes and raising taxes on businesses and the wealthy. He signed domestic partnership legislation for gays and enacted "smart gun" requirements to develop user-specific handguns. His tenure was marked by ethical questions involving political operatives, fund-raisers, and administration members. On Aug. 12, 2004, he announced he would resign the governorship effective Nov. 15, disclosing that he was "a gay American" and that he had had an extramarital affair with another man. The man was later identified as Golan Cipel, whom he had appointed as a state homeland security aide.

Michael Moore, b. Apr. 23, 1954, Flint, MI. Raised in nearby Davison, Moore was educated in parochial schools and briefly attended a seminary at 14. At 18, unhappy with a policy at his public high school, he won a seat on the Davi-

son School Board, making him one of the nation's youngest elected officials. After studying at the Univ. of Michigan at Flint, Moore was a writer and editor for *The Flint Voice;* he was editor-in-chief of *Mother Jones* magazine in 1986. He won fame in 1989 for his first film, *Roger & Me,* which portrays his attempts to show up General Motors CEO Roger Smith for closing down the company's Flint plant. He married Kathleen Glynn in 1991. In the 1990s, his projects included *Canadian Bacon, The Big One,* and television series *TV Nation* and *The Awful Truth.* Moore is also the author of several books: *Downsize This!, Stupid White Men,* and *Dude, Where's My Country?* A former Eagle Scout, hunter, and longtime member of the National Rifle Association, Moore won the Best Documentary Feature Academy Award in Mar. 2003 for his 2002 film *Bowling for Columbine,* which examined the gun control issue.

Moore gained notoriety in 2003 when he denounced the war in Iraq in his Oscar acceptance speech. *Fahrenheit 9/11,* his controversial film condemning the war in Iraq and the Bush administration, received the Palme d'Or at the Cannes Film Festival in May 2004 and went on to set documentary film box-office revenue records.

Barack Obama, b. Aug. 4, 1961, Honolulu, HI, His father, Barack Obama Sr., a Kenyan economist, and mother, S. Ann Dunham, an anthropologist from Kansas, divorced when Obama was 2 years old, and the father returned to Kenya. Obama lived in Indonesia until the age of 10, when he returned to Hawaii to attend the Punahou School, graduating in 1979. He received a B.A. in political science from Columbia Univ. in 1983. At Harvard Law School, Obama became the first African American editor of the *Harvard Law Review* and completed his J.D., magna cum laude, in 1991. In 1992, Obama married Michelle Robinson and returned to Chicago to oversee a voter registration and education campaign, concentrating on low-income and minority voters. While in private practice he also became a senior lecturer in constitutional law at the Univ. of Chicago Law School in 1993. A memoir, *Dreams from My Father,* was published in 1995. In 1996, Obama was elected to the Illinois State Senate; he was defeated in a primary race for Congress in 2000. In 2004, Obama won a heated primary race for the Democratic endorsement for Senate.

Obama entered the national consciousness after delivering an eloquent and stirring keynote address at the Democratic National Convention in which he referred to himself as a former "skinny kid with a funny name," and spoke in favor of unity, against what he saw as artificial cultural and political divides in the U.S. If elected in Nov. 2004, he would be the first black male Democrat in the Senate.

Vladimir Putin, b. Oct. 7, 1952, Leningrad (now St. Petersburg), Russia; studied law at Leningrad State Univ., graduating in 1975. He served as a foreign intelligence officer in the KGB for 15 years, spending the last 6 in communist E Germany. After the regime there collapsed in 1990, he retired and became an adviser to his college mentor Anatoly Sobchak, who had recently become the first democratically elected mayor of St. Petersburg. By 1994, Putin rose to dep. mayor, and was known as the "Grey Cardinal" for his quiet influence over the city. Putin moved to Moscow in 1996 to work on Pres. Boris Yeltsin's staff in the Kremlin; Yeltsin appointed him director of the Federal Security Service in 1998 and named him Prime Minister in Aug. 1999. Putin soon launched a military campaign against rebels in Chechnya, who had stepped up attacks on Russian targets. On Dec. 31, 1999, Yeltsin unexpectedly resigned and appointed Putin acting president. After winning the pres. election in Mar. 2000, he reasserted federal control over Russia's many republics and moved toward a closely regulated market economy. Although reelected in Mar. 2004, his tight control of the media and prosecution of wealthy Russian oligarchs have been criticized as anti-democratic.

While Putin's relations with Pres. Bush have been mostly positive, he stood with Germany and France in refusing to join the 2003 coalition invasion of Iraq. He and his wife, Ludmilla, have 2 daughters.

Dan Rather, b. Oct. 31, 1931, Wharton, TX; began his career in journalism in 1950 as a reporter for the Associated Press in Huntsville, TX, and covered news for United Press International and local radio stations. After graduating from Sam Houston State Teachers College in 1953 with a B.A. in journalism, he worked in Houston before joining CBS News in 1962. In 1963 he was the first journalist to report Pres. John F. Kennedy's assassination. He covered the Johnson and Nixon White Houses, the Vietnam War, was coeditor of *60 Minutes,* and served as weekend news anchor. In March 1981, he succeeded Walter Cronkite as anchor/managing editor of *CBS Evening* News, where he has reported many of the late 20th century's defining news stories with a signature homespun style. He has written 7 books, and is the recipient of many journalism awards, including a Peabody Award.

On Sept. 8, 2004, Rather reported on *60 Minutes II* that official documents purportedly written by Lt. Col. Killian, commander of Pres. George W. Bush's Air National Guard unit in the 1970s, showed gaps in the president's service record. Despite claims from experts and Killian's own family that the documents were forged, Rather and CBS News initially stood by the story. On Sept. 20, Rather and CBS acknowledged that the documents' authenticity could not be vouched for. In his statement, Rather called his initial belief in the documents a "mistake in judgment."

Donald Rumsfeld, b. July 9, 1932, Chicago, IL, and graduated from Princeton Univ. in 1954 with a BA in political science. After serving as a U.S. Navy aviator (1954-57), he worked briefly as a congressional aide in Washington, DC, then joined a Chicago investment-banking firm. In 1962, Rumsfeld won a seat in the U.S. House from Illinois; he was reelected 3 times. He worked on Richard Nixon's presidential campaign in 1968, and served under Nixon as director of the Office of Economic Opportunity and U.S. representative to NATO. After Nixon's resignation in 1974, he became Pres. Ford's chief of staff and then secretary of defense (1975-77)—the youngest in U.S. history. Between government positions he was CEO of 2 companies, and in 1998, he chaired a commission that advocated a missile defense program to counter the threat of attacks from "rogue nations."

In 2000, Rumsfeld became Pres. George W. Bush's defense secretary. He was an advocate for a force structure that would be flexible and responsive to global theaters with greater cooperation among the services. He was in his Pentagon office when a hijacked plane crashed into the building Sept. 11, 2001, and soon was coordinating military efforts in Afghanistan and Iraq. Pres. Bush rejected calls for his ouster in the wake of the Abu Graib prison scandal.

Martha Stewart, b. Martha Helen Kostyra, Aug. 3, 1941, in Nutley, NJ. Stewart is one of 6 children born to Edward and Martha Kostyra. Growing up in Nutley, Stewart learned gardening from her father and cooking, baking, canning, and sewing from her mother. Stewart modeled to put herself through Barnard College, earning a degree in history and architectural history. She worked on Wall Street and then as a caterer in Westport, CT. Her first book, *Entertaining* (1982. brought her national attention. After successful appearances on morning television programs, she developed her own syndicated show, "Martha Stewart Living" (1993-).

She developed her own product lines, and eventually founded Martha Stewart Living Omnimedia, her publishing and merchandising empire, which reached nearly $300 million in annual revenues in 2002. She has received 6 Daytime Emmy Awards, and "Martha Stewart Living" has been nominated for 29 Emmys. But Stewart was convicted on 4 counts of lying to federal investigators about her sale of ImClone stock at the end of 2001. Stewart began serving a 5-month sentence in a minimum-security prison at Alderson, WV, in Oct. 2004. She was married to Andrew Stewart for 29 years; the couple divorced in 1990. She is the mother of one daughter, Alexis (born 1965).

SPECIAL SECTION: HISPANIC AMERICANS

A Growing Minority

By Roberto Suro

A second-generation Hispanic-American, Roberto Suro is director of the Pew Hispanic Center, a Washington, DC-based research institute, and former foreign correspondent for Time *magazine, the* New York Times, *and other publications. A leading authority on U.S. Hispanics, he is the author of* Strangers Among Us: Latino Lives in a Changing America *(1998).*

Think of a teenager who is growing fast, changing in appearance and forming a distinct identity all at once. That, roughly speaking, is where the Hispanic population of the U.S. finds itself today—in a kind of demographic adolescence. It is already an important member of the American family, but its ultimate character and impact are still to be determined.

The growth became stunningly apparent when the 2000 Census reported that the Hispanic or Latino (I use the terms interchangeably) population had grown to 35.3 million, a 58% jump from 1990, and the growth continues. The Census Bureau projects a Hispanic population of 47.8 million by the end of this decade. If that holds, the number of Latinos will grow nearly 6 times faster than the rest of the population.

Growth Around the Country

As it grows the Latino population is changing in character, starting with the places it calls home. For decades, Latinos have been concentrated in a handful of big cities, but they are now scattering across the country as well. In 2000, the greater metropolitan areas of Los Angeles, New York, Chicago, and Miami alone were home to 1 in 3 Latinos, but extraordinarily fast growth was occurring elsewhere in places where the Hispanic presence had been negligible. Between 1980 and 2000, Atlanta experienced a 995% increase in its Latino population. In Portland, OR, it grew by 437%, in Washington, DC, by 346%, and in Tulsa, OK, by 303%.

For the most part, these new destinations attracted Latinos, especially immigrants, because they offered jobs and affordable housing. Indeed, fast-paced economic development on a local level and rapid growth of the Latino population have gone hand-in-hand in places where Spanish was rarely heard a few decades ago. This trend has continued and may even have accelerated during the economic downturn of 2001-2002 and its aftermath. Hispanic population growth has become a national phenomenon affecting virtually every corner of the country.

Newcomers and Old-Timers

Nevertheless, Hispanics remain a relatively small share of the population. In 2000 they were about 13% of the total, and even with projections of rapid growth they will make up only 20% by 2030. It is not sheer size that determines the impact of the Hispanic population, but the fact that this segment of the population is growing so fast while the rest is growing hardly at all. To understand the dynamics of that growth and its significance, it is important to break down the Hispanic population into 3 key components:

• The new immigrants: Although people from Latin America have come to the U.S. during other periods, **an unprecedented wave of migration from Spanish-speaking lands has been underway since the 1960s**, and it has gained considerable momentum since the early 1990s. Currently, the Census Bureau estimates that migration, both legal and unauthorized, adds nearly 700,000 Latinos to the population each year. Many factors help determine the size of that flow and whether it will continue at the same rate. But as a result of the influx thus far, the foreign-born constitute about 40% of the Hispanic population.

• The second generation: Like most immigrants through history, new Hispanic immigrants have tended to be young adults of child-bearing age. Moreover, they have proved highly fertile, with birth rates almost twice as high as among non-Hispanic whites. As a result, **there is now a huge second generation of Latinos**—about 12.5 million people— that is very young, with a median age of about 13. They are the children of immigrants, but are full-fledged, native-born U.S. citizens. They now make up about 30% of the Hispanic population, and are the fastest-growing component.

• The old stock: **Many Latinos lived in the U.S. before the current era of immigration began**, and many trace their ancestry to families that lived in places like Texas, California, and Puerto Rico before those lands became part of the U.S. This component accounts for about 30%.

For the past 3 decades or so, the new immigrants have transformed urban neighborhoods, spurred the rise of Spanish-language media, and prompted periodic, sometimes heated, debates on immigration policy. Like many other immigrants, the Latino newcomers have not simply broken off ties with their home countries, but instead share their earnings with families left behind. The individual amounts are small, averaging about $300, but they are sent faithfully by a sizeable share of the immigrant population. These so-called remittances, totaling around $30 billion a year, have become an important factor in the economies of many Latin American nations. Meanwhile, in the U.S. the steady, growing supply of Latino immigrant workers has become a mainstay of several industries, such as construction and food processing. But even as the immigrant influx continues, the impact of Latino population growth is changing because the very makeup of that population is changing.

Second-Generation Hispanics

The second generation is the demographic echo of all that immigration, and it is a booming echo. Between 2000 and 2030 it will grow by about 17.7 million. Over the next 25 years or so, the number of second-generation Latinos in U.S. schools will double and the number in the labor force will triple. Nearly one-fourth of all labor force growth will be from children of Latino immigrants. The flow of newcomers from abroad is likely to continue, but even so the effect of Latino population growth is now shifting. Over the next several decades, the largest impact is going to be felt first in the nation's schools and then in the economy, as this unique group of Americans comes of age.

Latinos of the second generation differ markedly from their immigrant parents in several ways. They are not only native-born U.S. citizens but also native-born English speakers. While nearly three-quarters of the adults in the immigrant generation predominately speak Spanish, all but a small fraction of the second generation have mastered English. Moreover, the second generation is getting much more education than the immigrant generation, with almost twice as large a share going to college. Nonetheless, children of Latino immigrants lag behind non-Hispanic youth in every measure of educational achievement. And, they are different from other Americans, even other Hispanics, who are farther removed from the immigrant experience. Nearly half of second-generation Hispanics are bilingual, and many retain a degree of identification with their parents' home countries.

Their influence will be greatly magnified by an extraordinary historical coincidence: They will be moving into the workforce just as the huge Baby Boom generation of non-Hispanics is moving out. Moreover, the Baby Boom did not produce a lot of children to take its place. According to Census Bureau projections, in 2004 there were 44 million non-Hispanics between 40 and 50, boomers heading toward retirement, but only 35 million who were 10 or younger to replace them. The gap will be filled by some 9 million Latinos 10 or younger. Latinos, especially the children of immigrants, will play key roles supplying the labor market and then supporting a very large elderly population.

So what will this generation be like when it grows up? In 2003 the Census Bureau made it official that the Latino population had surpassed African Americans to become the nation's largest minority group. Currently, Latinos have many of the characteristics associated with minority group status, such as more poverty and less education than the national average. But will Hispanics be a minority group in the traditional sense 20 or 30 years from now? Or, will they follow the course of other immigrants' offspring, who went through the melting pot experience and emerged into the middle class? Much will depend on how they fare in the schools and then in the workplace. Given their numbers, the whole nation has a stake in the outcome.

HISPANIC AMERICANS: A STATISTICAL PORTRAIT

Data released by the U.S. Census Bureau in 2004 showed that by 2003 Latinos had become the largest minority group in the U.S. Hispanics were also a fast-growing minority. While the total U.S. population roughly doubled from 131.7 million in 1940 to 290.8 million in 2003, the number of Latinos increased almost 30 times during the same period, from about 1.4 million to 39.9 million. Between 2000 and 2003, the now sizeable Latino population expanded by 13%—almost 4 times as fast as the nation as a whole, and 14 times faster than the population of non-Hispanic whites (which grew 0.9%).

Population Growth in the U.S, 1970-2020[1]

Source: U.S. Census Bureau; figures in millions

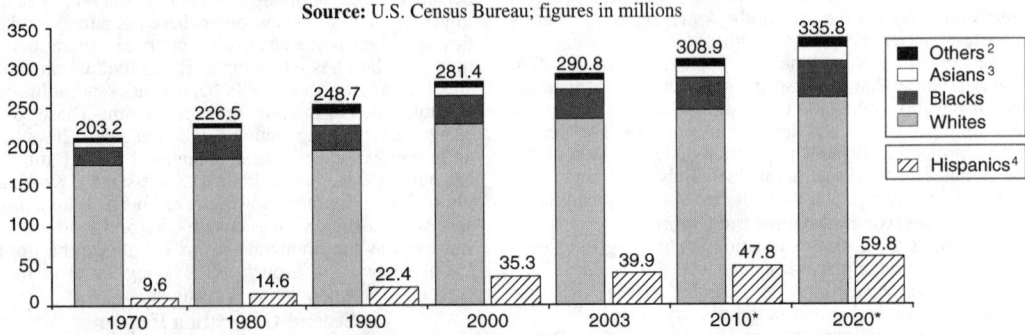

*Projected. (1) Totals may not add to 100% because of rounding. Because of changes in census questions and methods, data on race and Hispanic origin may not be wholly comparable over time. (2) Includes American Indians, Alaska Natives, and other races. From 2000 on, this category also includes Native Hawaiians, other Pacific Islanders, and persons reporting 2 or more races. (3) Figures for 1970-90 include Pacific Islanders. (4) May be of any race.

The Growing Hispanic Population

Source: U.S. Census Bureau

In 1970 the estimated 9.6 million Hispanic Americans made up 4.7% if the population, By 2020 the rapidly growing Hispanic population was expected to have expanded more than 6 times, to 59.8 million, or 17.8%, a sizable minority.

In 1930, after an upsurge in immigration from Mexico, the Census Bureau began counting "Mexicans" as a distinct category. In 1940 the Bureau broadened its survey to include "persons of Spanish mother tongue." In 1980, census takers began asking whether Americans were of "Spanish/Hispanic origin."

Statistics collected by the U.S. government treat race and Hispanic origin as separate concepts. This means that Hispanics cannot be included as a category when the population is broken down by race, as in the bars at left above for each year. But the bars at right show their growth in relation to the population as a whole. Latinos may be of any race, and people of any race may also describe themselves as Latinos. In 2002, Latinos who were white (either alone or in combination with other races) made up about 92% of the total, and Latinos who were black (either alone or in mixed-race combinations) comprised about 4%.

Population Groups by Age, 2003

Source: U.S. Census Bureau; resident population

Statistics show that the Hispanic population is relatively young, with 34% under 18 and 46% between the ages of 18 and 44.

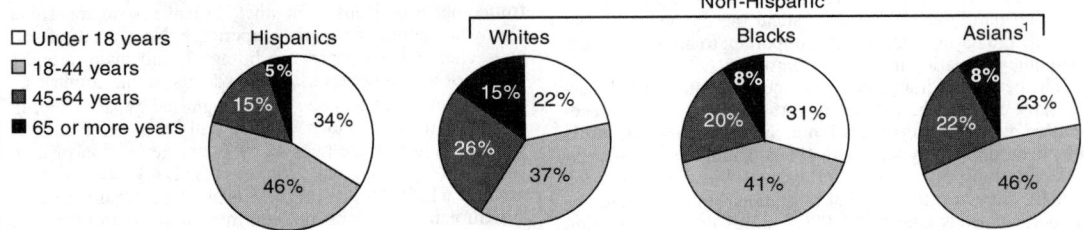

(1) Total does not add to 100% because of rounding.

Nativity and Place of Birth of the Latino Population, 2000

Source: U.S. Census Bureau; (in thousands)

Characteristic	All Hispanics[1]		Mexican	Puerto Rican	Cuban	Central American	South American
	Number	Percent					
Total population	35,238	100	20,900	3,404	1,250	1,812	1,420
Native[2]	21,081	59.8	12,223	3,356	394	439	333
Born in United States	19,414	55.1	12,045	2,032	380	417	312
State of residence	15,807	44.9	10,118	1,457	275	343	225
Different state	3,607	10.2	1,927	575	105	74	87
Born outside United States	1,667	4.7	178	1,325	14	22	21
Foreign born	14,158	40.2	8,677	47	856	1,372	1,087
Entered 1990 to March 2000	6,489	18.4	4,228	20	226	612	513
Naturalized citizen	3,940	11.2	1,930	20	517	360	400
Not a citizen	10,218	29.0	6,747	27	339	1,013	688

(1) Totals include Hispanic groups not shown separately. (2) Persons who were citizens at birth.

Legal and Illegal

The overwhelming majority of Hispanics living in the U.S. are either native-born or entered the U.S. legally. Millions of Hispanics, however, are undocumented or, as they are often called, illegal aliens. Estimates of the number of illegal Latino aliens are necessarily imprecise. A study published by the Pew Hispanic Center placed the number of undocumented Mexicans living in the U.S. in 2001 at about 4.5 million, and the number of illegals from Central America at 1.5 million.

Of the undocumented Mexicans, more than 78% had been living in the U.S. for at least 5 years, and more than 53% for at least 10 years. Many undocumented immigrants find seasonal employment in agriculture as migrant laborers. Other sectors with significant shares of undocumented workers include manufacturing, construction, and restaurants.

Hispanics by Origin, 2002
(in percent)
Source: U.S. Census Bureau

The largest percent of Hispanics today trace their origin to Mexico.

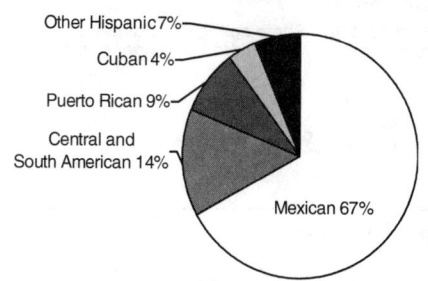

Other Hispanic 7%
Cuban 4%
Puerto Rican 9%
Central and South American 14%
Mexican 67%

Where Hispanic-Americans Live

The Latino population at present is highly concentrated. The 6 states with the highest percentages of Hispanics in 2002—New Mexico, California, Texas, Arizona, Nevada, and Colorado—are all located in the SW and W. Together they accounted for nearly 60% of all Hispanics in the U.S. About 3 of every 4 Latinos in this region were of Mexican ancestry.

Two other states with large Latino populations—Florida and New York—had much higher percentages of Latinos of Central or South American or Caribbean ancestry. In Florida, according to the 2000 Census, Cubans made up 31% of the Latino population. In New York, 37% of all Latinos were of Puerto Rican origin, and 16% were from the Dominican Republic.

Top 10 States by Percentage of Latino Population, 2002
Source: U.S. Census Bureau

Rank	State	Hispanic %	Hispanic Pop. (est.)	Total Pop. (est.)
1.	New Mexico...	42.9	796,171	1,855,059
2.	California.....	34.0	11,936,707	35,116,033
3.	Texas........	33.6	7,314,341	21,779,893
4.	Arizona	27.1	1,476,738	5,456,453
5.	Nevada	21.3	462,690	2,173,491
6.	Colorado	18.2	818,274	4,506,542

Rank	State	Hispanic %	Hispanic Pop. (est)	Total Pop. (est.)
7.	Florida.......	18.1	3,019,305	16,713,149
8.	New York.....	16.0	3,073,430	19,157,532
9.	New Jersey...	14.2	1,220,733	8,590,300
10.	Illinois	13.3	1,681,402	12,600,620
Totals:	Top 10 states .	24.9	31,799,791	127,949,072
	U.S.	13.4	38,761,301	288,368,698

Latino Population Percentage by State
Source: Population Reference Bureau; 2000

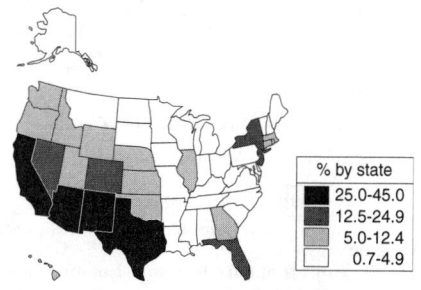

% by state
25.0-45.0
12.5-24.9
5.0-12.4
0.7-4.9

Latino Population Growth by State
Source: Population Reference Bureau; 1990-2000

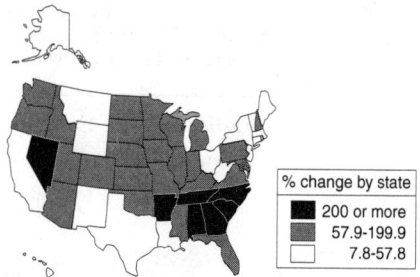

% change by state
200 or more
57.9-199.9
7.8-57.8

Places With the Highest Percentage of Hispanics, 2000
Source: U.S. Census Bureau; includes only places with 100,000 or more population.

Place and state	Total pop.	Hispanic pop.	% Hispanic	Place and state	Total pop.	Hispanic pop.	% Hispanic
East Los Angeles, CA*.	124,283	120,307	96.8	El Paso, TX	563,662	431,875	76.6
Laredo, TX	176,576	166,216	94.1	Santa Ana, CA......	337,977	257,097	76.1
Brownsville, TX	139,722	127,535	91.3	El Monte, CA........	115,965	83,945	72.4
Hialeah, FL..........	226,419	204,543	90.3	Oxnard, CA	170,358	112,807	66.2
McAllen, TX	106,414	85,427	80.3	Miami, FL...........	362,470	238,351	65.8

*East Los Angeles, California is a census-designated place and is not legally incorporated.

Hispanic Population of 10 Largest U.S. Cities, 2000
Source: U.S. Census Bureau; listed by city size.

Rank	Place and state	Total population Number	Hispanic population Number	Rank	% Hispanic	Rank	Place and state	Total population Number	Hispanic population Number	Rank	% Hispanic
1.	New York, NY	8,008,278	2,160,554	1	27.0	6.	Phoenix, AZ	1,321,045	449,972	6	34.1
2.	Los Angeles, CA	3,694,820	1,719,073	2	46.5	7.	San Diego, CA	1,223,400	310,752	9	25.4
3.	Chicago, IL	2,896,016	753,644	3	26.0	8.	Dallas, TX	1,188,580	422,587	8	35.6
4.	Houston, TX	1,953,631	730,865	4	37.4	9.	San Antonio, TX	1,144,646	671,394	5	58.7
5.	Philadelphia, PA	1,517,550	128,928	24	8.5	10.	Detroit, MI	951,270	47,167	72	5.0

Language and Religion

According to the 2000 Census, of the nearly 47 million Americans at least 5 years old who spoke a language other than English at home, about 60% spoke Spanish.

The 2002 National Survey of Latinos, conducted by the Pew Hispanic Center and the Kaiser Family Foundation, found that 17% of Hispanic adults spoke only Spanish at home while 12% spoke only English; the rest spoke both languages in varying proportions. On the job, however, just 4% spoke only Spanish, 7% more Spanish than English; 29% spoke both languages equally, while 27% spoke more English than Spanish, and 33% spoke only English.

When asked whether Latino immigrants needed to learn English in order to succeed in the United States, 89% of Latinos surveyed said yes.

A 2003 report from the Univ. of Notre Dame Institute for Latino Studies concluded that about 70% of Hispanics were Roman Catholic and about 23% Protestants.

Educational Attainment of the U.S. Population 25 Years of Age and Over, 2003

Source: U.S. Census Bureau

Group	Pop. (in thousands)	High school grad. or more	Some college or more	Bachelor's degree or more
Hispanics (of any race)...........	21,189	57.0%	29.6%	11.4%
Non-Hispanic whites.............	133,388	89.4%	56.4%	30.0%
Blacks.......................	20,527	80.0%	44.7%	17.3%
Asians.......................	7,691	87.6%	67.4%	49.8%
U.S. Total....................	185,183	84.6%	52.5%	27.2%

Employment and Income

The above statistics show that Hispanics in general have less education on the average than other U.S. population segments. Hispanics at present still also lag behind in employment and income. In the first quarter of 2004 the unemployment rate was 8.1% for Hispanics and 5.8% for non-Hispanics.

Compared with non-Hispanic whites, Hispanics were much more likely to have jobs as service employees, laborers, and farm workers, and much less likely to hold positions in managerial or professional occupations. Weekly wages in 2003 averaged $502 for Hispanics and $702 for non-Hispanics. Hispanic men had average earnings of $547 weekly, but women averaged only $436. Latinos who had not completed high school earned an average of $369 per week (about 9% more than their non-Hispanic counterparts), while Latinos with a college degree averaged $885 (14% less than non-Hispanics who had completed college).

Census Bureau statistics show that in 2001, 21.4% of Hispanic-Americans were living below the poverty level, compared to 7.8% of non-Hispanic whites. Among full-time year-round workers, 26.3% of Hispanic-Americans had annual earnings of $35,000 or more, compared to 53.8% of non-Hispanic whites.

Many Latinos work for employers who do not provide health insurance. Statistics compiled by the Pew Hispanic Center show that, as of 2000, 34% of Latinos under the age of 65 lacked health insurance, compared with 11% of non-Hispanic whites. Nearly 55% of foreign-born Latinos who were not U.S. citizens lacked any form of health insurance.

A growing number of Hispanics own their own businesses. The HispanTelligence research firm estimated in June 2004 that some 2,042,000 Hispanic-owned firms would generate revenues totaling $273.8 billion in 2004.

As shown below, only 14.2% of Hispanics, compared to 35.1% of non-Hispanic adults, have managerial or professional jobs. A larger percent of Hispanic women (18.1%) than Hispanic men (11.3%) have such occupations.

Occupations of the Employed U.S. Civilian Population 16 Years and Over

Source: U.S. Census Bureau; civilian population; 16 years and older; March 2002

Occupation group	Total		Hispanic origin and race Hispanic		Non-Hispanic, White		Non-Hispanic, Other	
	Number	Percent	Number	Percent	Number	Percent	Number	Percent
Total	135,154	100.0	16,160	100.0	97,772	100.0	21,222	100.0
Managerial and professional	42,427	31.4	2,288	14.2	34,269	35.1	5,869	27.7
Technical, sales, and administrative support	38,695	28.6	3,817	23.6	28,908	29.6	5,969	28.1
Service occupations	19,228	14.2	3,570	22.1	11,339	11.6	4,319	20.4
Precision production, craft, and repair	14,385	10.6	2,379	14.7	10,466	10.7	1,539	7.3
Operators, fabricators, and laborers	17,349	12.8	3,368	20.8	10,675	10.9	3,307	15.6
Farming, forestry, and fishing	3,070	2.3	738	4.6	2,114	2.2	218	1.0

Buying Power and Remittances

"Buying power" is the total personal income, after taxes, available for spending on goods and services. By that definition, Latino buying power which amounted to $221.9 billion in 1990, was expected to exceed $686 billion in 2004 and to approach $1 trillion in 2009, according to data compiled by the Selig Center for Economic Growth at the University of Georgia's Terry College of Business.

California ranked first in Latino buying power, an estimated $199 billion in 2004; this represented 18.2% of the total buying power in that state. Texas and California ranked 2nd and 3rd, followed by New York and Illinois.

An important characteristic of spending by Hispanics is the amount of money often sent to family members in their country of origin. These expenditures, or remittances, jumped from an estimated $10 billion in 1996 to $32 billion in 2002. According to the Inter-American Dialogue Task Force on Remittances, transfers of funds to Nicaragua in 2002 made up nearly 30% of that country's gross domestic product; corresponding figures were 15% for El Salvador and 12% for Honduras. The largest single share of remittances goes to Mexico—about one-third of the annual total.

Voting Power

Data compiled by the Tomás Rivera Policy Institute at the University of Southern California show that Latino voter turnout in presidential elections increased from 2,453,000 in 1980 to 5,934,000 in 2000. In Feb. 2004 the institute forecast a Latino turnout of about 6,700,000 in the 2004 presidential vote. Two states—California and Texas—account for more than half of all Hispanic registered voters. In Florida, a hotly contested state in recent elections, the proportion of registered Hispanics to all registered voters is approaching 1 in 8. Except for Cubans, most Hispanic-Americans are Democrats or independents.

According to the National Association of Latino Elected and Appointed Officials (NALEO), the number of elected Hispanic officeholders at all levels of government rose from 3,128 in 1984 to 4,853 in 2004; during the same period, the number of Hispanics in Congress increased from 9 to 22, all of them in the House of Representatives.

Top 10 States in Hispanic Percent of All Registered Voters, 2004
Source: Univision

Rank	State (electoral votes)	Hispanics Registered	% of Elig. Hispanic Reg.	Hispanic % of All Reg. Voters
1.	New Mexico (5)	259,000	56.1	32.5
2.	Texas (34)	2,035,000	60.0	21.7
3.	Arizona (10)	331,000	49.3	16.4
4.	California (55)	2,032,000	55.0	14.6
5.	Florida (27)	857,000	63.4	12.0
6.	Colorado (9)	213,000	57.0	10.7
7.	New York (31)	606,000	56.0	7.3
8.	Nevada (5)	59,000	47.2	7.1
9.	New Jersey (15)	218,000	61.4	5.4
10.	Illinois (21)	267,000	65.5	4.6

Party Affiliation of Latino Voters by Origin, 2004
Source: Pew Hispanic Center/Kaiser Family Foundation

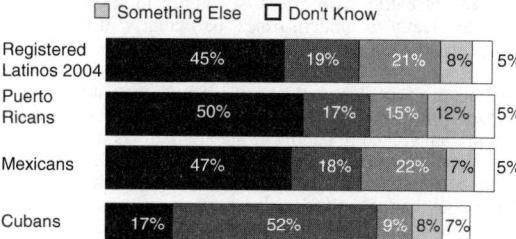

Legend: Democrats, Republicans, Independents, Something Else, Don't Know

	Democrats	Republicans	Independents	Something Else	Don't Know
Registered Latinos 2004	45%	19%	21%	8%	5%
Puerto Ricans	50%	17%	15%	12%	5%
Mexicans	47%	18%	22%	7%	5%
Cubans	17%	52%	9%	8%	7%

Leisure, Entertainment, and Sports

A study published by Rincón & Associates, a market research firm, estimates that in 2003 Hispanics spent $12.1 bil on entertainment. One magnet for entertainment dollars is recorded music: according to Nielsen SoundScan, albums in the Latin genre sold more than 27.4 million units in 2003, exceeding sales of jazz and classical recordings.

Although many Hispanics watch the same popular English-language programs as non-Hispanics (multiple showings of *American Idol* and *The Simpsons* ranked high among Latino viewers of network broadcasts in one typical week in spring 2004), millions of Hispanics tune in to the dominant Spanish-language network, Univision, to watch primetime soap operas, or telenovelas, such as *Amarte Es Mi Pecado* ("Loving You Is My Sin").

Nowhere in recent decades have Latino athletes earned greater fame and fortune than on the baseball diamond. Béisbol is a popular pastime in Mexico and among the Spanish-speaking countries of the Caribbean. By 2002, 26% of all Major League Baseball players were from Latin American countries or of Hispanic heritage. In Sept. 2004 the web site latinobaseball.com listed 1,117 Latinos who had played in the U.S. major leagues since 1900. Of these, 389 were from the Dominican Republic, 252 from Puerto Rico, 167 from Venezuela, and 149 from Cuba.

Top 5 Prime-Time TV Programs Among Hispanic-Americans
for week of 9/6/04-9/12/04
Source: Nielsen Media Research Inc.

Rank	Program	Network	Household Rating	Total Viewers	Rank	Program	Network	Household Rating	Total Viewers
1.	Mariana De La Noche WED	UNI	24.6	4,805,000	4.	Amarte Es Mi Pecado THU	UNI	23.9	4,175,000
2.	Amarte Es Mi Pecado WED	UNI	24.3	4,667,000	5.	Mariana De La Noche THU	UNI	23.8	4,199,000
3.	Mariana De La Noche TUE	UNI	23.9	4,503,000					

5 Top-Selling Latin Albums in the U.S., 2003
Source: Billboard

Rank	Title	Artist	Label	Units Sold
1.	Un Día Normal	Juanes	Surco/Universal Latino	293,274
2.	Almas del Silencio	Ricky Martin	Sony Discos	214,739
5.	4	A. B. Quintanilla III Presents Kumbia Kings	EMI Latin	164,986
4.	Mambo Sinuendo	Ry Cooder & Manuel Galbán	Perro Verde/Nonesuch/AG	146,147
5.	Hits Mix	Celia Cruz	Sony Discos	144,173

Highest-Paid Hispanic Players in Major League Baseball
(at the start of the 2004 season)
Sources: Associated Press; mlb.com; latinobaseball.com

Rank	Name	Born	Team	Annual Salary[1]
1.	Alex Rodriguez (3B)	New York, NY	NY Yankees	$21.7
2.	Manny Ramirez (LF)	Dominican Republic	Boston	$20.4
3.	Carlos Delgado (1B)	Puerto Rico	Toronto	$19.7
4.	Pedro Martinez (P)	Dominican Republic	Boston	$17.5
5.	Sammy Sosa (RF)	Dominican Republic	Chicago Cubs	$16.9
6.	Magglio Ordoñez (RF)	Venezuela	Chicago White Sox	$14.0

(1) in millions.

Top 5 Hispanic Daily Newspapers by Average Daily Circulation, 2003
Source: Advertising Age

Rank	Newspaper	City	Circ.
1.	La Opinión	Los Angeles, CA	126,628
2.	Hoy	New York, NY	109,598
3.	El Nuevo Herald	Miami, FL.	90,480
4.	Diario las Américas	Miami, FL.	61,285
5.	Al Día	Dallas, TX	53,258

Top 5 Hispanic Magazines by Paid Circulation, 2003
Source: Advertising Age

Rank	Magazine	Circ.	Frequency
1.	People en Español	425,127	Monthly
2.	RD Selecciones	331,239	Monthly
3.	Latina	308,439	Monthly
4.	Hispanic Magazine	270,829	Monthly
5.	Prevention en Español	240,158	Monthly

Doping in Sports: Steroids and Supplements

By Gary I. Wadler, M.D., FACP, FACSM

Dr. Gary Wadler is an Associate Professor of Clinical Medicine at NYU School of Medicine and a member of the World Anti-Doping Agency (WADA). He has served as medical adviser on doping to the White House Office of National Drug Control Policy and as a consultant to the Dept. of Justice on steroid abuse. He is lead author of the textbook Drugs and the Athlete *(1989).*

The term "doping" commonly refers to the practice of using prohibited drugs or methods in sports to gain an unfair athletic advantage. Since earliest times drugs of one sort or another have been used, and abused, to enhance performance. The word *dope* itself is likely derived from the Dutch word *dop*, an alcoholic beverage made from grape skins, used by traditional Zulu warriors to enhance their prowess in battle. The extent of doping in sports has increased greatly in modern times, particularly in recent decades, as new drugs are constantly being developed.

Detecting this abuse has never been an easy task. Scientists made a great leap forward in 1983 when, using new analytic technology, they identified 11 athletes from 9 countries involved in doping at the Pan Am Games in Caracas, Venezuela. Many other athletes, including 13 members of the U.S. track and field team, withdrew from the competition rather than submit to testing.

As the tests have become more sophisticated, so have the efforts to subvert them. The year 2004 marked a watershed moment in the ongoing effort to catch athletes using anabolic-androgenic steroids. After a syringe containing an unknown clear liquid was presented to authorities in June 2003 by a disgruntled track and field coach (later identified as Trevor Graham), scientists at the UCLA's Olympic Analytic Laboratory determined it to be a previously unknown anabolic steroid, tetrahydrogestrinone (THG), a "designer steroid" illicitly manufactured and undetectable utilizing standard methods because it disintegrated during traditional analysis.

> "The spirit of sport is the celebration of the human spirit, the body and the mind. Doping is contrary to the spirit of sport, erodes public confidence and jeopardizes the health and well-being of athletes."
> —from the WADA Athlete's Guide

Modifying the testing procedure to detect THG was promptly followed by indictments of the supplement distributor, BALCO (Bay Area Laboratory Co-operative) and its principals. Additionally, a vigorous investigation was undertaken by the U.S. Anti-Doping Agency. Fallout from the BALCO case affected the U.S. Olympic track and field team even before the 2004 Summer Games. Sprinter Toni Edwards, who qualified in the 100m and 200m, was given a 2-year ban. Calvin Harrison, who had been named to the pool for the 1,600-m relay, was also banned for 2 years. Sprinter Kelli White, who swept the 100m and 200m at the World Championships in 2003, was stripped of her medals and banned for 2 years in May 2004; White was cooperating in the ongoing BALCO investigations. These investigations gave rise to speculations that BALCO might have ties to some world famous athletes such as Marion Jones, Tim Montgomery, and Barry Bonds.

The identification of THG has raised concerns that some athletes may be using other yet-to-be identified anabolic-androgenic steroids and getting away with it. Their use may have serious short- and long-term effects on health, including masculinization of females, feminization of males, elevated cholesterol levels, damage to the heart and liver, and stunting of adolescent growth, as well as psychiatric disorders including severe mood swings and dependency, with depression upon withdrawal, possibly leading to suicide.

Anabolic-Androgenic Steroids

Anabolic-androgenic steroids are synthetic derivatives of the male hormone testosterone. First isolated and synthesized in 1935, these steroids were exploited for their anabolic (tissue building) properties. They were used by physicians to treat disorders such as malnutrition, anemias, cancer, growth disorders, and testosterone deficiency.

These steroids have been abused in sports for decades, by men and women alike, principally to build muscle and increase strength. Their abuse in 1988 by famed Canadian sprinter Ben Johnson brought wide attention to doping and anabolic-androgenic steroid abuse. But they have also been surreptitiously administered to more than 10,000 East German athletes and to elite Chinese swimmers. Their abuse by American athletes, both Olympic and professional, has been well documented. These types of abuses led to passage of the Anabolic Steroid Act of 1990, which categorized anabolic-androgenic steroids as controlled substances requiring detailed record keeping and special prescriptions.

Anabolic-androgenic steroids traditionally have been administered by injection or by mouth. The injectable forms are either water-soluble and relatively short acting or oil-based, lasting in the body for up to 9 months. The oral forms have fallen into disfavor principally because of their ease of detection by laboratory testing and their adverse effects on the liver. Recently, new transdermal delivery systems have been introduced permitting the substance to be delivered through the skin using patches, creams, and gels.

The attraction of anabolic-androgenic steroids stems from their capacity to increase lean body mass (muscle), decrease body fat, increase assertiveness/aggressiveness, and shorten recovery times. Anabolic steroid hormones work, in part, by stimulating receptor molecules in muscle cells, which activate specific genes to increase protein production. When combined with working out with weights (resistive exercise), this translates into increased muscle mass. Anabolic steroids also inhibit the cortisone-induced breakdown of protein that normally occurs after a heavy workout. This anti-catabolic effect leads to reduced recovery times, permitting more frequent and heavier workouts that translate into further muscle enhancment. Many of the effects of steroids are brought about through their direct actions in the brain. Once anabolic-androgenic steroids enter the brain, they are distributed to many regions, including the hypothalamus and limbic system, the system that is involved in many functions, including learning, memory, and mood regulation.

Recent stories of anabolic-androgenic steroid abuse have captured headlines around the world. In Major League Baseball, very conservatively, 5-7% of players tested positive for anabolic-androgenic steroids, in a limited "survey testing" program agreed to in a collective bargaining agreement.

Erythropoietin

Another potent drug, erythropoietin (EPO), has particular attraction to athletes in endurance sports, and, in fact, it was the most notable of abused drugs during the 2002 Salt Lake Olympic Games. Several cross-country skiers, including Larissa Lazutina of Russia, who would have had a record 10th career gold medal, tested positive for Darbopoietin, a long lasting EPO product, and were stripped of medals.

Erythropoietin, a hormone manufactured principally by the kidney, regulates the number of red blood cells circulating in the blood stream. Red blood cells contain hemoglobin, the molecule that transports oxygen from the lungs to all the body's tissues, including muscle. The capacity to carry oxygen to working muscle is critical for optimum endurance in sports such as cycling's Tour de France and the marathon.

In years past, endurance athletes willing to cheat would transfuse themselves with another's blood in order to increase the hemoglobin in their blood. Nowadays, weeks before an endurance event, some athletes have their own blood drawn and frozen. The resulting self-induced anemia causes the kidneys to produce more erythropoietin, so that new red blood cells are produced. Just prior to an endurance event, their previously frozen blood is thawed and transfused back into the athlete to guarantee a high level of circulating red blood cells.

In the 1980s synthetic erythropoietin was developed using recombinant DNA technology (rhEPO). The availability of rhEPO for persons with refractory anemias meant they rarely needed transfusions.

In the late 1980s, shortly after the introduction of rhEPO into Europe, there were about 30 deaths among the fittest athletes of 4 countries (Belgium, Netherlands, Denmark, and Sweden). These deaths were limited to 2 endurance sports (cycling and orienteering) and were thought most likely due to rhEPO abuse. When abused, rhEPO can markedly increase the number of circulating red blood cells, transforming the athlete's blood into a viscous substance that has difficulty traversing the blood vessels of the body. This can cause heart attacks, strokes, and death.

Doping with rhEPO reached a peak in the 1998 Tour de France cycling classic. Although difficult, testing for rhEPO was introduced at the 2000 Sydney Olympics. Since then, methods for its detection have improved and involve testing of urine specimens both in and out of competition.

Dietary Supplements

The use of dietary supplements has presented special challenges in sports. The Dietary Supplement and Health Education Act of 1994 (DSHEA) gave statutory definition to the term "dietary supplement." Included in the definition were "vitamins, minerals, amino acids, concentrates, metabolites, constituents, extracts or combinations." In contrast to drug makers, manufacturers of supplements are not permitted to claim that their products prevent, treat, ameliorate, or cure diseases. Typically, their claims include phrases such as "enhances energy utilization," "delays fatigue," "increases strength and endurance," "enhances healing," "contours body," "controls weight and fat loss."

Unlike drug makers, manufacturers of dietary supplements are not required to assure the pre-market safety, efficacy, or purity of their products. To ban a supplement, the Food and Drug Administration must show that it poses "a significant or unreasonable risk" at doses listed on the label. Of the many supplements available to athletes, two of the most well-known are ephedra and androstenedione.

Ephedra, or Ma Huang, is a powerful herb used in Chinese medicine for at least 5,000 years, and categorized as a dietary supplement under DSHEA. It is the herb from which ephedrine, once a particularly popular drug for asthma, allergies, and sinus disorders, was extracted. Until early 2004, when it was banned by the FDA, ephedra was widely available as a weight-loss product and "athletic enhancer."

The role of ephedra grew after passage of the Controlled Substances Act of 1970, when the powerful and widely abused stimulant amphetamine was reclassified as a controlled substance. Athletes learned that by combining ephedra (not a controlled substance) with caffeine and other over-the-counter stimulants they could achieve an amphetamine-like stimulatory effect without breaking federal law.

For many years the industry successfully resisted efforts to place limits on the availability of ephedra products. It was the ephedra-related death of Baltimore Oriole pitcher Steven Bechler from heat stroke in Feb. 2003 that finally provided sufficient impetus for the FDA to remove ephedra products from the shelves. Not surprisingly, the industry responded by replacing it with a related stimulant, synephrine, that is also classified as a dietary supplement under DSHEA.

Androstenedione is a steroid hormone that is converted into testosterone in the body; it has been called a "steroid precursor" or "prohormone." The abuse of "steroid precursors" has been even more widespread than anabolic-androgenic steroid abuse, since they do not need a prescription. Androstenedione ("andro") drew wide attention in 1998, when Mark McGwire hit a record-breaking 70 home runs while legally using the supplement.

Androstenedione provided a loophole to circumvent the Anabolic Steroid Act of 1990. However, in March 2004, the FDA advised 23 companies to stop manufacturing, marketing, and distributing products containing it. Major League Baseball banned "andro" on April 12, the same day that the FDA banned its sale. Nevertheless, analogs of androstenedione are not covered by the FDA regulatory action, and these analogs remain available.

Steroids and Youth

A 2003 National Institute on Drug Abuse study found that 3.5% of 12th graders had used anabolic-androgenic steroids at least once in their lives, as had 2.5% of 8th graders. A 2001 NCAA study concluded that more than 50% of NCAA athletes who used these drugs began while in high school.

WADA and USADA

Recognizing that doping undermines the ethical foundations of sport and threatens the health and well-being of athletes, the World Anti-Doping Agency (WADA) and U.S. Anti-Doping Agency (USADA) were established to address the subject of doping from multiple points of view.

WADA was created in 1999 as a shared initiative between sport and governments throughout the world promoting and coordinating the fight against doping through education, advocacy, research, testing, and leadership.

As of Oct. 2000, USADA, an independent, nonprofit organization, assumed full authority for testing, education, research, and adjudication for U.S. Olympic, Pan Am Games, and Paralympic athletes. As noted previously, USADA has been the lead agency in the sports-related aspects of the BALCO investigations.

At the heart of doping control is the complicated subject of drug testing—using laboratory science to eliminate the unfair competitive advantage that may accrue from performance-enhancing drugs. To be maximally effective, drug testing may be conducted either in or out of competition, depending on the specific drugs for which the test is done.

Year-round, announced, random drug testing is the gold standard for performance-enhancing drugs such as anabolic-androgenic steroids; to achieve their effects they must be taken for a significant period of time during training, in combination with weight training. Elite athletes are aware of the window of detectability for various anabolic-androgenic steroids, and some some try to cycle their use so as to minimize the risk of in-competition detection. In contrast, short-acting stimulants, such as amphetamine-type drugs, exert their maximal effect when used during competition, and that is the ideal time for testing for them.

Each professional sports league in the U.S. has a different testing protocol, except for the National Hockey League, which has none at all. Major League Baseball introduced testing for anabolic-androgenic steroids in 2003, but failed to develop an adequate testing program to effectively root out steroid abuse. Players are tested randomly only once a season and not at all during the off-season. Despite this significant flaw in the program, 5-7% of players tested positive for these drugs. The National Football League has the most comprehensive and effective anti-doping program, which is year-round. In Oct. 2003, the NFL tested 1,000 random urine samples for THG. Only 4 players, all from the Oakland Raiders, tested positive. Three players were fined 3 game checks based on their 2003 salaries; linebacker Bill Romanowski, who retired, also tested positive. Penalties as well as testing programs vary for different sports. Of course, regardless of the sport, it is imperative that the rights of athletes are protected at all times and that they are accorded a fair and thorough investigation.

The Future

Historically, most drugs that have been abused in sports, except for designer drugs such as THG, were developed for their therapeutic potential. Detecting instances of doping is likely to become increasingly complex as new therapeutic drugs and drug delivery systems are developed and are abused by those determined to cheat.

The findings of the Human Genome Project present daunting new challenges as gene therapy evolves as an integral part of medicine's therapeutic armamentarium in the years ahead. Unethical athletes and those around them are already reaching out to scientists working to develop therapeutic gene delivery systems for insulin-like growth factor (IGF-1) for patients afflicted with muscle wasting disorders, recognizing this technology's performance-enhancing potential. In the final analysis, the principle that sport is a contest of character, skill, and disciplined hard work, not a contest in pharmacology, must be inculcated in all athletes.

Islam

by Seyyed Hossein Nasr

Dr. Seyyed Hossein Nasr is University Professor of Islamic Studies at George Washington University and has written over 30 books on Islam and other topics.

The name of the religion of Islam comes from the Arabic word for peace and submission. Islam is a religion based on surrender to God the One who in Arabic is called Allah, a name also used by Christian Arabs for God. The oneness of God is the central doctrine, summarized in the first testament of the Islamic faith *La ilaha illa'Llah,* "there is no divinity but God." The second testament states that the Prophet of Islam, Muhammad, is the "messenger of God," or *Muhammadun rasul Allah.*

It is enough to state these two testimonies before two Muslim witnesses to become a Muslim. But Islam also believes that God sent many prophets before the Prophet of Islam, going back to Adam, and it reveres the great prophets of Judaism and Christianity such as Moses and Christ, calling Abraham, the father of monotheism, a *muslim,* that is, one who is in perfect surrender to God.

Islam in fact sees itself as the third major manifestation of Abrahamic monotheism, and the last religion to be revealed in this period of history, Muslims believe this period will come to an end with events involving a messianic figure called the Mahdi and Christ himself, in whose second coming Muslims, like traditional Christians, believe. Muslims also believe in the immortality of the soul and the responsibility of men and women before God for their actions in this world and, like many Christians, they believe in heaven, purgatory, and hell.

Basics of Islam

The **basic practices** of Islam are:

(1) **Daily canonical prayers** obligatory for all Muslim men and women, to be performed five times a day in the direction of Mecca. On Friday there are congregational prayers performed by the worshipers together usually but not necessarily, in a mosque.

(2) **Total fasting** from dawn to dusk during the lunar month of Ramadan, obligatory for all adult males and females if they are not sick, traveling, pregnant, or breast feeding. At the end of Ramadan there is the great celebration called the Eid—one of the two major religious holidays in Islam; the second is the end of the annual pilgrimage.

(3) **Pilgrimage to Mecca** in Saudi Arabia (*hajj*), which is obligatory once in a lifetime if one has the financial means.

(4) The **religious tax** to be paid annually to the Islamic public treasury or other charitable causes.

These practices, plus the required **testaments of faith** in the One God with Muhammad as his prophet, make up the "five pillars" of Islam.

Islam is not centrally organized as is Catholicism. Islamic religious functionaries called *imams* are people learned in religious law who lead congregational prayers in mosques and perform other religious duties, but they are not ordained. Various Muslim countries have official religious authorities such as *muftis,* usually chosen with the consent of political authorities, but their power is not the same as that of bishops and similar authorities in Christian churches.

The basic reality of Islam is the **Quran,** which Muslims consider to be the verbatim Word of God revealed during a 23-year period to the Prophet of Islam, Muhammad. When the Quran is recited ritually anywhere in the world, it must be done in the original Arabic. The Quran is the ultimate source of everything Islamic, from metaphysics and theology to sacred history, to ethics and law, to art. It is complemented by the sayings of Prophet of Islam called *Hadith,* collected in canonical works early in Islamic history.

Islam possesses a **religious law** called *al-Shari 'ah* which is as central to Islam as theology is to Christianity. The *Shari 'ah* is rooted in the Quran and *Hadith.* But other principles, such as analogy (comparing a new legal situation with an analogous one already established by the Quran and Hadith) and consensus of the religious scholars and the community

as a whole, called the *ummah,* are also used by various schools, so long as they do not contradict the Quran or the *Hadith.*

Over the centuries four major **schools of law** developed and have continued in the Sunni world (the majority denomination). Each school is dominant in different regions, for example the Maliki school in North Africa; the Hanafi school in Turkey, Pakistan, and Muslim India; the Shafi 'i school in Egypt, Indonesia, and Malaysia; and the Hanbali school in Syria and Saudi Arabia. There are also several Shi'ite schools of law; the most important is the Ja'fari, associated with the main branch of Shi'ism.

The *Shari 'ah,* which in many ways is like the *Halakhah* in Judaism, covers all aspects of life. More particularly it is divided into what concerns acts of worship and what concerns transactions, including social, economic, and political ones. Muslims believe that God is the ultimate law-giver and that human beings cannot devise laws that oppose divine laws. The *Shari'ah* is not, however, a fixed and rigid body of law. Rather it is like a tree whose roots are firm but whose branches grow in every season.

Islam also has an **inner spiritual path** called *al-Tariqah,* which like the *Shari'ah* goes back to the origin of Islamic revelation and the Prophet. This inner dimension of Islam came to be known as **Sufism**. Over the centuries the teachings of Sufism became organized within various Sufi orders, which survive to this day. Throughout Islamic history, Sufism has played a central role in Islamic thought and the arts. It has had a crucial role in the spread of Islam among the Turks, as well as in China, India, the Malay world, Africa, and eastern and southern Europe.

Sunnis and Shi'ites

While the Prophet Muhammad was alive, there was but one Islamic society, without any branches or divisions. Upon his death, most Muslims (Sunnis) accepted Abu Bakr as the true successor to Muhammad, while a smaller number (Shi'ah) believed that 'Ali ibn Abi Talib, the son-in law and first cousin of the Prophet, should have become his successor. Sunnis today constitute some 85% of the worldwide Muslim population. The Shi'ites, although only some 15%, are, however, concentrated in the central lands of Islam. Several countries—Iran, Iraq, Bahrain, Azerbaijan, and Lebanon—have Shi'ite majorities among their Muslims. There are also notable Shi'ite populations in India, Pakistan, Afghanistan, Syria, Turkey, and the Persian Gulf states.

Beginnings

Today there are over 1.2 billion Muslims who share the beliefs and practice of Islam as well as a history going back over 1,400 years to the founding of the religion in Mecca in A.D. 610. Then, according to Islamic belief, a man from Mecca from the tribe of Quraysh and named **Muhammad** was chosen as God's messenger. For over 12 years the Prophet preached the message of Islam in Mecca; then in 622, in the face of persecution, he migrated with most of his followers to Medina. This date marks the beginning of the Islamic calendar.

In Medina the Prophet integrated various groups to create the first Islamic community. Gradually, the community grew stronger, despite several attacks by Meccans. Tribes from all over Arabia come to accept Islam, and in 628 Muslims led by the Prophet reclaimed Mecca. The Prophet returned, however, to Medina; it became the capital of Arabia, which he integrated into a single society for the first time. It was also in Medina that he died in 632, at the age of 63.

From 632 to 661, four of the companions of the Prophet, Abu Bakr, 'Umar, 'Uthman, and 'Ali, ruled as his vice-regents or *khalifahs* (caliphs). They were men of great piety and religious authority as well as being political leaders of the Islamic community.

World's Largest Muslim Populations, estimated, mid-2005						
Rank	Country	Muslim population	% of total pop.	Rank	Country	Muslim population	% of total pop.
1.	Indonesia	171,600,000*	76.2	11.	Iraq	25,600,000	96.5
2.	Pakistan	154,600,000	95.5	12.	Afghanistan	25,400,000	97.9
3.	India	134,100,000	12.2	13.	Ethiopia	25,300,000	34.1
4.	Bangladesh	132,900,000	87.1	14.	Sudan	25,000,000	71.4
5.	Turkey	71,300,000	97.3	15.	Saudi Arabia	23,600,000	92.2
6.	Iran	67,700,000	95.8	16.	Yemen	21,300,000	99.0
7.	Egypt	63,500,000	84.8	17.	Uzbekistan	20,500,000	76.4
8.	Nigeria	54,700,000	42.0	18.	China	19,800,000	1.5
9.	Algeria	31,900,000	96.9	19.	Syria	17,200,000	92.1
10.	Morocco	31,000,000	98.6	20.	Malaysia	11,600,000	45.9

*Includes about 50 million persons classified as Muslim by the Indonesian government, but sometimes classified as New Religionists.
Source: Government sources; World Christian Database, www.worldchristiandatabase.org.

The borders of this community had by now expanded far beyond Arabia to include much of the Persian Empire, which had been defeated in the battle of Qadisiyyah in 636, and the former Byzantine provinces of Palestine and Syria as well as Egypt. But 'Ali was assassinated by a dissident, and it was Mu'awiyyah, governor of Syria and an opponent of 'Ali, who founded the first Muslim empire, called the **Umayyad**, with its capital in Damascus. The caliphs of this dynasty did not hold the religious prestige of the first four "rightly guided caliphs," but they were able to expand their empire from China to France and laid the basis for the foundation of classical Islamic civilization.

The Islamic World

The Umayyads, who were opposed by most non-Arab Muslims, were defeated in 750 and a new Sunni caliphate called the **Abbasid** gained power. It built Baghdad as its capital and heralded an age of great cultural and scientific activity that was to transform the later history of science and thought, not only in the Islamic world but also in the West. Greek texts were translated into Arabic, which became the world's most important scientific language for some seven centuries.

In the 10th century the **Fatimids**, who were Shi'ites, developed a rival caliphate, with their capital in Cairo, which they founded. Meanwhile, the Turks, who had migrated from the Altai mountains of Asia into Central Asia and northern Persia, founded many local dynasties. The most powerful among them, the **Seljuqs**, ruled over much of Western Asia, including eastern Turkey, but preserved the Abbasid caliphate as symbol of unity and source for legitimacy. The Seljuks laid the ground for the coming of the Ottomans and the final defeat of the Byzantine Empire.

From 1096, when the first Crusade occurred, the heart of the Islamic world was deeply immersed in a series of wars against European Christians who sought to conquer Palestine. The Crusaders captured Jerusalem and ruled over the Holy Land for almost a century, until Salah al-Din (Saladin), regained Jerusalem in 1187.

In 1258 the devastating Mongol invasion reached Iraq and the Abbasid caliphate was brought to an end. Henceforth, for some two centuries the central lands of the Islamic world were ruled by local dynasties, the most powerful of which was the **Ottomans**. By the 15th century the Ottomans had established an empire stretching from southeastern Europe through Turkey to the Arab world. Later they would incorporate Egypt and North Africa up to Western Algeria into their domain. Two other major Muslim empires came to vie with the Ottomans: the **Safavid**, which unified greater Persia, and the **Mogul** in India.

Outside the central lands of Islam, Islamic rule had been established in much of Spain and all of Morocco (called al-Maghrib by Muslims), which, from the 8th century onward, experienced a golden age of art, culture, and thought in a climate in which Muslims, Jews, and Christians lived with each other, for the most part, in a remarkably harmonious manner. This ended by 1492, when Ferdinand and Isabella conquered Granada, the last Muslim stronghold, and forced all Jews and Muslims to either leave Spain or convert to Catholicism. However, Muslim rule left its indelible mark

upon Spanish culture and, through the Spanish conquest of the New World, upon Central and South America.

Islam spread farther south in sub-Saharan Africa, and by the 13th century there were major Muslim empires in West Africa. The slave trade, followed by European colonization, weakened and finally subdued local Islamic power in Africa, but Islam continued to grow. On the other side of the world, Islam began to spread among the Malay people through travelers to that region. The Philippines were being ruled by a Muslim sultan in the 16th century when the Spaniards invaded it and killed the sultan and many of his people; those who remained Muslim fled to the south, where they are still fighting for local autonomy.

Modern Times

In the central lands of Islam, the empires of the Ottomans, Safavids, and Moguls weakened in the 18th century. India was gradually colonized by the British, who in 1857 put an official end to Mogul rule. (After Indian independence in 1947, Pakistan was established as an Islamic state; it was later divided into Pakistan and Bangladesh). The **Qajar** dynasty came to power in 1795 in Persia and ruled there until 1921 (it was replaced by the Western-oriented Pahlavi dynasty, overthrown in the Islamic Revolution of 1979). But the Qajars were politically weak and lost substantial territory to British power and, in much of Central Asia, to the Czarist armies of Russia.

As for the Ottomans, they sided with Germany in World War I and not only lost nearly all of their remaining empire in Europe but also the Arab territories. These were colonized by the British and the French, except for Arabia, which fell into the hands of the Saudi dynasty, and Egypt, by then nominally independent. As for Palestine, it was claimed by the British as a protectorate. With the rise in Zionism, it became bitterly contested between Arabs and Jews, leading in 1948 to the expulsion of many Palestinians from certain areas and the establishment of the state of Israel; the conflict endures to this day. In Turkey itself in 1924, the Ottoman caliphate was officially dissolved and the modern secular Turkish state created by Kamal Ataturk.

After World War II most Islamic countries gained independence, and with the fall of the Soviet Union, most, but not all, of the Muslim states under its control became independent. Also as a result of the breakdown of Yugoslavia in the 1990s, Bosnia gained its independence, while Kosovo remains under United Nations jurisdiction. Today there are some 52 members of the Organization of Islamic Countries (OIC).

Relations with Other Religions

Because of its geography and also on the basis of the teachings of Islam with respect to "the people of the Book," Islam has had a diverse and often creative relation with other religions during its history. It encountered Judaism and Christianity in its place of birth, as well as in Syria, Iraq, Egypt, and other places. It met Zoroastrianism and Manichaeism in Persia, Buddhism and Hinduism in India, and later Taoism and Confucianism in China. It also had direct contact with native African religions from early on.

Classical works of Islamic thought often speak of other religions, and Muslim scholars are considered to be pioneers in the study of what is today called comparative religion. Al-

though there were some bitter persecutions, by and large religious minorities fared better in the Islamic world than they did in the medieval Christian West. Muslim governments of the time usually allowed minorities to practice their religion fully, and in some cases, as in Andalusia, Persia, and the Ottoman Empire, religious minorities were prominent in business, culture, and sometimes political fields. The exclusivism and combative attitude toward Jews and Christians displayed by some Muslims today is to a large extent a reaction to the colonial experience, the partition of Palestine, and other fairly recent events.

Islam and the West

Today, Islamic society in many places is in the throes of a crisis brought about both by its internal weaknesses and by its domination by the West during the past two centuries. During all its earlier history, traditional Islam had been dominant, despite losses of territories such as Andalusia and the Tartar kingdom. Islamic civilization had even been able to absorb the shock of the Mongol invasion and turn the descendents of Genghis Khan, such as Tamerlane, into Muslim heroes. But in the 19th and 20th centuries, it became dominated by a civilization which it could neither defeat nor Islamicize.

In reaction to this situation, some Muslims believed it was necessary to return to the original purity and what they saw as austerity of early Islam. Others believed the Islamic world should modernize itself and imitate the West. And yet others believed the domination of Muslims by outsiders was a sign of the end of the world and the coming of the Mahdi. All these reactions found followers and have had their own history. And all have reappeared in new forms during the last half century, when, in the eyes of many Muslims, Islamic countries have become nominally independent but economically and culturally even more colonized than before.

The most important puritanical and so-called reformist movement of the 18th century was Wahhabism, which arose in southern Arabia. It preached a harsh interpretation of Islamic Law, was opposed to Sufism and Shi'ism, and also rejected a millennium of Islamic theology, philosophy, and art. This movement gained power when the Saudi Arabian kingdom was established. Other so-called reformist movements came into being later in the 20th century, such as the Muslim Brotherhood that arose in Egypt, and the Jama'at-i Islami of Pakistan. Wahhabism became significant outside of Arabia only during the 2nd half of the 20th century, because of the wealth that poured into Saudi Arabia from the sale of oil and the subsequent possibility of exporting Wahhabism—opposed by Orthodox Muslims, Shi'ites and Sunnis alike—into (especially) India, Pakistan, and Afghanistan. Meanwhile, newer forms of modernism, although religiously less popular than before, have continued to wield political power because they have been supported by the West. Waves of Mahdiism are also once again manifesting themselves, parallel to the messianic currents that can be observed in contemporary Judaism and Christianity.

The puritanical and reformist movement came to be called *fundamentalist* in the West after the Iranian Revolution of 1979, which established the Islamic Republic of Iran. This is an unfortunate term which lumps together people of very different views. There is no doubt that Islam has always believed that the law of society should be the *Shari'ah* or the Islamic Divine Law as applied to different circumstances; the kingdom of God and of Caesar were never separated in Islam. During the colonial period the application of *Shari'ah* was discarded or marginalized. Today, most Muslims who are activists, and commonly called fundamentalists, want to have their lives governed again by the Divine Law and have a government which reflects Islamic values. However, that does not necessarily mean the rule of the clergy. It means the development of political institutions on the basis of Islamic principles and with the awareness of existing conditions. Moreover, the vast majority of Muslims wish to attain these ends only by peaceful means, although this is far from easy. Most Muslim countries are undemocratic, governed by political and military "elites" not supported by their own people, and in many cases supported by Western powers as long as they cater to Western interests.

During the past two or three decades a number of groups have chosen the path of militancy and violence, with the aim of curtailing the power of the West in the Islamic world and returning society to what they consider to be its Islamic foundations. Those groups usually use the term *jihad* in an effort to legitimatize their activities. Actually, *jihad* means "exertion" and "effort in the path of God," and its significance is for the most part spiritual and religious, the "greater *jihad*," according to the Prophet, being struggle against one's own rebellious nature and negative passions. *Jihad* can also mean to exert one's effort to defend one's faith, homeland, family, and so forth, and those cases could at times lead to war. However, such outward *jihad* can be carried out only under strict conditions set out in the Divine Law. Some militant groups claim to use *jihad* in the latter sense, but usually without the sanction of the authorities in Islamic Law. A small number of groups have taken up terrorism, which, because of its killing of innocent people, is clearly banned by Islamic Law. Even in a formally declared war, Muslim soldiers are forbidden under Islamic Law to kill innocent people.

Today's Muslims

During the last few years, as a result of many events whose consequences have become intertwined, foremost among them the Arab-Israeli conflict and the terrorist attacks of September 11, the mass media in the West sometimes portrayed Islam as a violent religion opposed to other religions and strongly anti-Western. Actually the vast majority of Muslims have nothing to do with terrorism or violence of any kind, and have often been the objects of attacks themselves in many parts of the world. They live the life of traditional believers based on surrender to God, prayer, fasting, alms-giving, and seeking to gain inner peace. Faith in the one God is still very strong in Islam, and the Islamic intellectual and artistic traditions, as well as the inner path to God associated usually with Sufism, are all alive.

Most Muslims believe that they have much more in common with Jews and Christians than with any other religious group and that what unites the followers of various religious traditions is much greater than what divides them. Also most Muslims are not anti-Western, but oppose Western interests in the Islamic world if these interests happened to be against those of Muslims themselves. They wish to live and develop their own societies on the basis of their own world view, interests, and ideals without external pressure, in the same way that the West was to do during the various stages of its historical development.

FOR FURTHER READING

Ahmen, Nazeer. *Islam in Global History,* 2 vols. Chicago: Kazi Publications, 2000.
Cleary, Thomas. *The Essential Koran.* Edison, NJ: Castle Books, 1998.
Eaton, Charles le Gai. *Islam and the Destiny of Man.* Albany: State University of New York, 1985.
Lings, Martin. *Muhammad: His Life Based on the Earliest Sources.* New York: Inner Traditions, 1983.
Murata, Sachiko, and William Chittick. *The Vision of Islam.* New York: Paragon House, 1994.
Nasr, Seyyed Hossein. *Ideals and Realities of Islam.* Chicago: ABC International Group, 2001.
Nasr, Seyyed Hossein. *The Heart of Islam.* San Francisco, Harper, 2004.
Schimmel, Annemarie. *Islam: An Introduction.* Albany: State University of New York, 1992.

The Obesity Epidemic

By Vice Adm. Richard H. Carmona, M.D.

Vice Adm. Richard H. Carmona, MD, M.P.H., FACS, is the U.S. Surgeon General.

In 2002, when Pres. George W. Bush nominated me to serve as surgeon general, he told the American people that I would focus on disease prevention and health promotion. The president was acknowledging what health experts have been saying for years: we have been approaching health and health care the wrong way. The numbers tell us there is no greater imperative in health care than switching from a treatment-oriented society to a prevention-oriented society.

For decades, we have been doing very little about our unhealthy eating habits, lack of physical activity, and other poor choices that negatively impact our health. These attitudes and behaviors explain why there are over 125 million Americans suffering from a preventable chronic health problem.

Tobacco use is still the single most preventable cause of death and disease in the U.S., causing over 440,000 deaths each year. But today, obesity-related illness is the fastest-growing killer of Americans; it was expected to cost more than 400,000 lives in 2004. Deaths due to poor diet and physical inactivity have risen by 1/3 over the past decade, and these habits may soon overtake tobacco use as the leading preventable cause of death.

A Growing Problem

Nearly 2 out of 3 of all adult Americans are overweight or obese. That's a 50% increase from just a decade ago. We simply must invest more in prevention, from the time it's easiest: childhood. Over the past 20 years, the rate of overweight young children has doubled, and among adolescents it has tripled. Today 15% of American kids are overweight or obese. That's more than 9 million children—one in every 7 kids—who are at increased risk of weight-related chronic diseases.

These facts are just the beginning of a chain reaction of dangerous health problems, many of which were once associated only with adults. Today pediatricians are diagnosing an increasing number of children with type 2 diabetes—which used to be known as adult-onset diabetes—as well as with high blood pressure, and generally poorer health. Research indicates that unless we change our eating habits and increase the amount of physical activity, one-third of all children born in 2000 will develop type 2 diabetes during their lifetime. Tragically, people with this disease are at increased risk of developing heart disease, stroke, kidney disease, and blindness. These complications are likely to appear much earlier in life for those who develop type 2 diabetes in childhood or adolescence.

Because of the increasing rates of obesity, unhealthy eating habits, and physical inactivity, the current generation may be the first that will be less healthy and have a shorter life expectancy than their parents. The economic costs of obesity are staggering — second only to the cost of tobacco use. The annual cost of obesity is now estimated at more than $117 billion in direct and indirect costs.

I've traveled the nation talking to students as part of my "50 Schools in 50 States" initiative. I've met kids of every race and ethnicity, background, and upbringing. One thing is constant: too many of them are living unhealthy lifestyles. You can tell just by looking at them. I love seeing their bright smiling faces, full of hope and happiness. But what they don't know about excess weight could end up killing them later in life. Unless we do something now, they will grow up to be unhealthy adults, condemned to a lifetime of overweight and its co-morbidities.

Causes of Obesity

There is no single cause of all human obesity, so research is exploring prevention and treatment approaches that encompass behavioral, sociocultural, socioeconomic, environmental, physiologic, and genetic factors.

As the obesity epidemic has deepened, we have gained a deeper appreciation of gaps in the public's knowledge about what constitutes healthy behavior. Too many Americans lack the educational foundation to grasp concepts such as calorie intake and expenditure or the role of carbohydrates, fats, proteins, and micronutrients in maintaining a healthy weight. Even the seemingly simple things that we can all do to stay healthy and safe, such as getting regular medical check-ups and eating healthy foods, can be struggles for many families. The reality is that to be able to do these things, we must be health literate.

Every morning, while they're sitting at the breakfast table, people read the newspaper and the information on the cereal box. During the day they read the nutritional information on packaged foods. But do they really understand what they're reading? The labels list grams of fat. But do people know how many grams of fat they should eat in a day? How many is too many? Or too few? (The average adult who consumes 2,000 calories a day should normally take in no more than 65 grams of fat, and should take in at least 45 grams to ensure adequate nutritional intake; a slice of bologna or cup of milk has 8 grams.) These are seemingly simple questions, but we're not giving Americans simple answers.

Media coverage of the obesity epidemic has been widespread. Americans know there is a problem. So they're trying to figure out how much food they should feed their children. How much is too much? How much is too little? What constitutes a healthy diet? Even many educated Americans don't know what a calorie is, or how to burn it. Studies show that people of all ages, races, incomes, and education levels are challenged by low health literacy.

A compounding factor is that most patients hide any confusion from their doctors, because they're too ashamed or intimidated to ask for help about how much to eat, how much to exercise. Not everyone is a scientist or a health care professional, and we can't expect everyone to understand what it takes professionals years of training to learn.

What to Do

We must work together to close the gap between what health professionals know and what the American public understands about physical activity and healthy eating. Low health literacy adds as much as $58 billion per year to health care costs. Each year, 7 of 10 Americans who die succumb to a chronic disease that could have been prevented or delayed by eating well, being physically active, and not smoking. These steps are simple—how we communicate them should be simple as well.

Parents need information so that they can teach their children to make good food decisions, such as eating 5 to 9 servings of fruits and vegetables a day. Educators are testing ways to promote physical activity on the part of students—not just playing sports, but playing more outside, even something as simple as walking more often. Medical and nursing students are learning how to communicate their knowledge in ways their patients will understand.

What's called for is improved health education from elementary school through college, increased focus on health literacy in medical schools, and more creative public health information campaigns.

The U.S. Department of Health and Human Services is taking steps to improve American's health literacy, including surgeon general's communications written in plain language that people can understand and a new education campaign to promote physical activity and good eating habits. The U.S. has the best health care system in the world. At the dawn of the 21st century, medical discovery is advancing at an unprecedented rate. Yet Americans have not kept pace in adopting health behaviors to live longer, healthier lives.

I will do everything in my power to increase Americans' health literacy while I have the privilege of serving as surgeon general. Health literacy can save lives, save money, and improve the health and well being of millions of Americans. Better information and understanding are the keys to building a healthier nation and a healthier world.

For more information, visit www.surgeongeneral.gov

Movies and the Numbers Game:
How Statistics Don't Tell the Real Story about Our Favorite Films

By Leonard Maltin

Leonard Maltin has been editing his annual paperback reference Leonard Maltin's Movie Guide *since 1969, and has appeared on TV's* Entertainment Tonight *since 1982. He has written a number of other books on film topics, and teaches at the Univ. of Southern California. He publishes a quarterly newsletter for old-movie buffs, and presides over a website, www.leonardmaltin.com*

In the summer of 2004, *Shrek 2* became the most successful animated feature-film of all time. . . Or did it?

Mark Twain famously remarked (quoting Benjamin Disraeli) that there are "lies, damn lies, and statistics." He made that wisecrack long before the advent of movie box-office figures, or movies themselves, for that matter, but he might have been anticipating the kind of manipulation that box-office numbers now inspire.

Of course, this kind of chicanery isn't limited to the world of movies; political wheeler-dealers bend poll results to their advantage all the time, as do advertisers and promoters of all stripes. Even in the world of sports, where it would seem a home run is a home run and a hole in one a clearly defined event, experts point out that changes in the composition of bats and golf clubs may give today's athletes an edge over the heroes of yesterday.

What bothers me, as a movie lover, is the self-delusion that accompanies this brand of Hollywood hype, and the amnesia it attempts to conjure up in the minds of the public.

Is *Shrek 2* the most successful animated feature of all time? That depends on how you define success. Did it make the most money in the shortest span of time? Yes. Did it entertain its audience? Apparently so. (I was in the minority.) Will it stand the test of time, like *Snow White and the Seven Dwarfs* or *Cinderella* or *Lady and the Tramp*? It's too soon to tell—and that's my point.

Unlike many consumer products, movie tickets are purchased on blind faith. A customer can't get his money back after he's watched the film, even if he hates it. This is one way box-office numbers don't reveal the big picture.

In the summer of 2003, there was enormous interest in *Hulk*, the big-budget, big-screen adaptation of Stan Lee and Jack Kirby's Marvel comic book and the 1970s television show it spawned. The director was Ang Lee, who enjoyed international success with his groundbreaking action film *Crouching Tiger, Hidden Dragon*. Universal Pictures' marketing machine went into overdrive, and on opening weekend, *Hulk* took in a whopping $74 million.

There was just one problem: people didn't like the movie, to put it mildly. Poisonous word-of-mouth spread so quickly that *Hulk* took what was (at that time) the biggest second-weekend nosedive in box-office history. If you took just the opening weekend statistic—a $74 million opening—you could position *Hulk* as a blockbuster hit. But in this case nobody was fooled for long.

Inflation Hype

There's another problem with the Numbers Game: the numbers themselves keep changing. When moviegoers lined up to see Walt Disney's *Snow White and the Seven Dwarfs* in 1937, they may have paid as little as ten cents to see it. When I became an avid moviegoer in the 1960s, admission prices for kids were still just 35 to 50 cents. Even at Radio City Music Hall in New York City, you could get in for 99 cents if you arrived before noon.

Adjusting for ticket prices, let alone inflation, is not something today's Hollywood is anxious to do, because the results might not flatter their shiny new movies. In Los Angeles, where I live, prices have jumped not once but twice just in the few years between *Shrek* and *Shrek 2* . . . but you won't find an asterisk alongside trade advertising boasting about the newer film's box-office numbers. (When *The Godfather* opened in 1972, first-run theaters in New York City boosted their admission prices by one dollar—but that fact was blithely ignored in the trade ads Paramount took out boasting about the film's "record breaking" numbers its opening week).

Similarly, a publicity biography of filmmaker Chris Columbus calls him the most successful comedy director of all time. With films like *Home Alone* and *Mrs. Doubtfire* to his

credit, not to mention the first two Harry Potter films, there is no question of his box-office supremacy. But does that really make him the "most successful" in movie history? More so than Billy Wilder, or Preston Sturges, or Charlie Chaplin? They made people laugh, too.

It's not that I resent box-office success. Despite what seems to be an ever-widening gulf between popularity and what some would define as excellence, there are still films that prove those attributes needn't be mutually exclusive. Peter Jackson's *The Lord of the Rings* is a notable example of a film—in this case, a trio of films—that won critical acclaim and awards as well as audience approval.

Changing Times

Then there is the matter of perspective. Posterity takes a different view of films than contemporary criticism or even ticket sales would indicate. A survey of the 1950s and 60s drives this point home.

Ask almost anyone to name the best films of the 1950s, and titles like *Singin' in the Rain,* and *The Searchers* are likely to come up. John Ford's *The Searchers* (1956), starring John Wayne is arguably the best performance of his career, has been cited as a touchstone by many of today's foremost filmmakers, yet it failed to earn even one Oscar nomination. It did rank tenth on the year's list of top moneymakers, but some of the films ahead of it, like *The Eddy Duchin Story, I'll Cry Tomorrow,* and *War and Peace,* offer some idea of how tastes have changed in half a century.

Audiences and moviemakers alike took musicals for granted in the 1950s, so *Singin' in the Rain* (1952) wasn't seen as anything more than another good example of the genre. It too rated tenth in box-office rankings that year, topped by two films starring Dean Martin and Jerry Lewis (*Sailor Beware* and *Jumping Jacks*), and several examples of the epic-scale movies that lured audiences away from their television sets—*Quo Vadis, Ivanhoe,* and *The Greatest Show on Earth.* Like *The Searchers, Singin' in the Rain* came away from the Oscar derby empty-handed.

Cecil B. DeMille's gloriously corny circus yarn *The Greatest Show on Earth* has been referred to as the worst movie ever to win a Best Picture Academy Award. I respectfully disagree, but there is no question that its qualities pale alongside *Singin' in the Rain* or another enduring 1952 classic, *High Noon.*

Directors like Samuel Fuller, Budd Boetticher, Nicholas Ray, Don Siegel, and Douglas Sirk are heroes to today's film buffs, yet when their films came out in the 1950s and 60s they rarely won awards, and often slipped under the critics' radar. That's because they did some of their best work in the guise of soap operas, westerns, melodramas, and science-fiction. Films like *Shock Corridor, Seven Men from Now, Johnny Guitar, Invasion of the Body Snatchers,* and *All That Heaven Allows* seemed slightly tawdry alongside big-league movies like *Ben-Hur.*

Who is to say which of today's films will be cherished or studied in the years ahead? Will anyone care which of them topped the weekend box-office charts?

In 2004, Steven Spielberg put his heart into a contemporary, Frank Capra-esque fairy tale starring Tom Hanks. *The Terminal* opened opposite a raunchy comedy called *Dodgeball* and came in second. Today's youthful moviegoers prefer cheap laughs to sweetness and sentiment, but who is to say how history will judge the two films?

After all, in 1982, the Academy of Motion Picture Arts and Sciences had five films to choose from for Best Picture. The winner was Richard Attenborough's *Gandhi*. One of the other contenders lost the prize, but made its way into the annals of popular culture: *E.T. The Extra Terrestrial.*

So which film was the more successful? That's all in the eye of the beholder.

WORLDPLAY

By Cathy Millhauser

Cathy Millhauser's crosswords appear in numerous publications, including the New York Times *and* Wall Street Journal, *and in an original collection,* Humorous Crosswords.

A larger format of the puzzle is available at: www.worldalmanac.com/puzzle. For help with clues, see the *World Almanac* pages listed below.

ACROSS

1 Alloy in brass
5 Pen name of H. H. Munro
9 Saddam Hussein was seized in one, Dec. 2003
13 New Zealand director: P. Jackson; Taiwanese director: ____
14 Archbishop of New York
15 City in northeastern France
16 Rose feat?
18 "Candle in the Wind" singer John
19 Parent company of Stouffer's
20 Bio in a few words?
22 Verdi opera
24 Winning 2004 Le Mans car
25 Caelum constellation's likenesses
28 Raiders-over-Vikings Super Bowl number
32 Mt. Waialeale, Hawaii, gets the most of it
33 Chronology info about cloning?
35 Type of venomous insect
36 Lima to Caracas dir.
37 Political cartoonist Oliphant
38 Number showing a decreased crime rate?
43 Joni Mitchell's "_____ Sides Now"
44 Title for President Fox's wife
45 Piquant New Jersey export
47 30th or 40th anniversary gifts, e.g.
49 Roofing on Diana's wondrous temple
50 Chart of, say, causes of death?
54 Boy Pharaoh, Boy Pharaoh
58 1992 Literature Nobelist Walcott
59 Diagram showing vehicle sales?
61 Zola title roles
62 He passed baton to Coe in 1982
63 Noted art deco designer
64 Hydrogen's has one proton
65 1995 earthquake site in Japan
66 Title word in the sequel to the big-grossing "Raiders" film (1981)

DOWN

1 Newscaster Paula
2 1976 Wimbledon rival of Bjorn
3 Hoopsters that ousted the Knicks in 2004
4 "Unalienable" preceder
5 South Carolina did it in 1860
6 "...score and seven years _____"
7 Oscar-winning Malden
8 World's second-most-populated country
9 QB Reich did this for Bills in 1993
10 Part of ABM
11 Feature of a graphical user interface
12 Unit of force equaling .000072 poundal
15 Seattle landmark
17 Blue-and-white Bulldogs
21 Fossil ___ (energy source of concern)
23 Eubie Blake's *Shuffle _____*
25 Olympic sport like kayak
26 Arrive at, as Einstein did with his relativity theory
27 6:00 A.M. EST on 3/22/05 in Lancaster, PA
29 Greenhouse effect contributor
30 U.S. word in a French almanac
31 Domain of Queen Beatrix: abbr.
32 Scott Joplin output
34 Hat for painter of "Haystacks"
39 Iditarod competitor
40 1932 circus film on the National Registry
41 Theoretical shout from a World Almanac quiz answer
42 1987 Breeders' Cup winner
43 Michigan crop color
46 This was pulled on *Friends* in 2004
48 What Ford cut Nixon
50 *Show Boat* author Ferber
51 Felix Unger descriptor
52 Fleming Bond novel
53 It replaced the punt in Kerry
55 Kiribati crop
56 California temperatures: from −45 _____ 134
57 Oates' 1970 National Book Award novel
60 Actor Hunter

(For answers, see page 1007)

Where to find the answers:

ACROSS: 1 p. 134, 5 p. 268, 9 p. 24, 13 p. 283, 14 p. 738, 15 p. 466 (map), 16 p. 900, 18 p. 275, 19 p. 477, 20 p. 242, 22 p. 270, 24 p. 954, 25 p. 356, 28 p. 920, 32 p. 186, 33 p. 28, 35 p. 181, 36 p. 464 (map), 37 p. 252, 38 p. 161, 43 p. 275, 44 p. 802, 45 p. 429, 47 p. 386, 49 p. 505, 50 p. 77, 54 p. 519, 58 p. 316, 59 p. 236, 61 p. 269, 62 p. 878, 63 p. 249, 64 p. 336, 65 p. 208, 66 p. 300.

DOWN: 1 p. 245, 2 p. 950, 3 p. 903, 4 p. 560, 5 p. 434, 6 p. 571, 7 p. 328, 8 p. 848, 9 p. 859, 10 p. 226, 11 p. 396, 12 p. 347, 15 p. 451, 17 p. 935, 21 p. 169, 23 p. 270, 25 p. 860, 26 p. 520, 27 pp. 371 & 497, 29 p. 175, 30 —, 31 p. 535, 32 p. 270, 34 p. 250, 39 p. 967, 40 p. 298, 41 p. 148, 42 p. 960, 43 p. 425, 46 p. 813, 48 p. 588, 50 p. 266, 51 p. 49, 52 p. 266, 53 p. 231, 55 p. 792, 56 p. 188, 57 p. 321, 60 p. 282.

OCTOBER 16-31, 2003

National

Congress Acts on Bush's $87 Bil Iraq Funding Request—The Senate, 87-12, and the House, 303-125, **Oct. 17** approved measures to provide $87 bil for Iraq as requested by the Bush administration. Of that, about $20 bil was for the country's security and reconstruction, and the rest for U.S. military operations there. The Senate version required that $10 bil be treated as a loan to Iraq, but the White House **Oct. 21** threatened to veto the final bill if it retained the loan provision, arguing that Iraq was already heavily in debt. On **Oct. 29**, members of the House-Senate conference committee agreed to drop the Senate provision, and the full House approved the conference committee version **Oct. 31**. (The Senate approved the bill Nov. 3 and the president's signature was expected to follow.)

A donors' conference on Iraq, in Madrid, Spain, concluded **Oct. 24** with pledges of about $13 bil received, much of it in the form of loans rather than grants. With the expected addition of $20 bil from the U.S. the total still fell short of the $55 bil the World Bank estimated Iraq needed over the next 4 years.

Senate Passes Bill Opposing "Partial-Birth" Abortion"—The Senate **Oct. 21** approved, 64-34, a bill that would ban a type of late-term abortion commonly known as partial-birth abortion. The House had already approved the bill. Critics said they would challenge the law in court after Pres. George W. Bush signed it.

International

Iraq Violence Continues—Three U.S. servicemen died in Karbala **Oct. 16** in a fight with guards of a Shiite cleric. An American colonel was killed **Oct. 26** when missiles struck Baghdad's Rashid Hotel, where he was staying. The barrage wounded 16 others; Deputy Defense Sec. Paul Wolfowitz, on an inspection tour of Iraq, was staying at the hotel but escaped harm. A deputy mayor of Baghdad was assassinated **Oct. 26**.

A series of explosions rocked the capital **Oct. 27**, killing at least 34. The most deadly, near the headquarters of the International Committee of the Red Cross, killed at least 15, including one Red Cross worker. The attacks, 4 of which occurred at police stations, coincided with the onset of the month-long Islamic holiday of Ramadan. At an **Oct. 28** news conference, Pres. George W. Bush acknowledged that Iraq was "a dangerous place," placing the blame largely on remnants of the deposed regime and on "foreign terrorists" from Syria and Iran. He vowed that the U.S. would "stay the course," while stating that there was no present need for more U.S. troops. The UN announced **Oct. 30** that it was pulling its staff out of Baghdad and evaluating safety concerns; UN staff remained in northern Iraq.

UN Passes Iraq Resolution—The UN Security Council **Oct. 16** unanimously passed a U.S.- and British-backed resolution endorsing a U.S.-led multinational force in Iraq. The measure urged UN members to support the Iraq occupation with troops and money and called on the Iraq Governing Council to present, by Dec. 15, a timetable for preparing a new constitution. Russia, France, and Germany indicated dissatisfaction that the resolution did not accelerate the pace for a transfer of power or provide a stronger UN rule, and said they would not commit troops or new funds. But the unanimous resolution was seen as a victory for the U.S. government and a sign of lessened tension between the U.S. and some of its traditional European allies over Iraq.

Bush Visits Asian Nations—Pres. Bush **Oct. 16** began a weeklong trip to Asia; he said he would seek "to make sure that the people who are suspicious of our country understand our motives are pure." In Japan, **Oct. 17**, he thanked Prime Min. Junichiro Koizumi for Japan's pledge of $1.5 bil to help rebuild Iraq. Addressing the Philippines Congress in Manila **Oct. 18**, Bush said that Iraq, like the Philippines, could become a successful democracy

In an **Oct. 19** meeting with Chinese Pres. Hu Jintao, in Bangkok, Thailand, Pres. Bush proposed to offer North Korea a 5-nation security guarantee, providing the latter dropped its nuclear-weapons program. At the annual Asian summit in Bangkok, **Oct. 20**, he deplored remarks by Prime Min. Mahathir Mohamad of Malaysia, asserting that Jews "rule the world by proxy." (Mahathir made his comments **Oct. 16** opening a conference of Islamic nations in Malaysia; he later retired as prime minister **Oct. 31**, after 22 years in power.) On **Oct. 21** Asian summit participants vowed to take "all essential actions to dismantle, fully and without delay, transnational terrorist groups." On the island of Bali, **Oct. 22**, Bush met with Pres. Megawati Sukarnoputri of Indonesia and urged that Indonesia remain "pluralistic and democratic." Bush addressed the Australian parliament **Oct. 23** and was heckled by 2 members.

Israeli, Palestinian Strife Continues—Israeli planes and helicopter gunships struck in Gaza **Oct. 20**; at least 10 people died in several raids, and about 100 were injured. Although militants were targeted, the raids resulted in at least some civilian casualties, and were criticized by some Israelis. In addition, Israeli Chief of Staff Lt. Gen. Moshe Yaalon, the country's highest-ranking soldier, publicly criticized government policy toward Palestinians, according to news reports **Oct. 29**; he said travel restrictions and curfews imposed on Palestinians were increasing hatred of Israel and strengthening terrorism.

Russian Oil Tycoon Arrested—Mikhail Khodorkovsky, head of the Russian oil giant Yukos and believed to be the richest man in Russia, was arrested **Oct. 25** by government security agents and charged with tax evasion and fraud. Khodorkovsky was a vocal opponent of the government and had announced his intention to help fund opposition parties. On **Oct. 30** Russian prosecutors froze shares of Yukos stock held by Menatep, a bank controlled by Khodorkovsky. Yukos claimed the action was illegal, and on **Oct. 31** Russian Prime Min. Mikhail Kasyanov, viewed as the most powerful pro-business figure in the government, said he was "deeply concerned" about the action.

2 CIA Operatives Killed in Afghanistan—The CIA said **Oct. 28** that 2 of its operatives in Afghanistan had been killed Oct. 25. The agency said the operatives were tracking terrorists in southeastern Afghanistan.

General

Pope Celebrates Jubilee—John Paul II **Oct. 16** celebrated the 25th anniversary of his papacy at a Mass in St. Peter's Square in Rome. The frail pope, 83, asked Catholics to pray for him to have the strength to continue as their leader. Thousands attended the mass, paying tribute to a man who had served longer than all but 3 other popes in the church's history. On **Oct. 19**, in a ceremony in St. Peter's, the pope beatified Mother Teresa of Calcutta, revered for her work on behalf of the poor. In another ceremony **Oct. 21**, he created 30 new cardinals, including one American, Philadelphia Archbishop Justin Rigali. One other new cardinal was named in secret; he was believed to be living in China, where he might be endangered if his name were disclosed.

Wildfires Devastate Southern California—One of the worst series of forest fires ever recorded in southern California laid waste to more than 700,000 acres, and destroyed about 3,000 homes in late October. Driven by hot dry Santa Ana winds, one fire in the San Bernardino National Forest had forced thousands to flee **Oct. 24**. By **Oct. 26**, 10 separate blazes, roughly circling Los Angeles and extending nearly to San Diego, were out of control. Firefighters struggled to stop flames coming down the mountains toward suburbs of L.A. and the coastal town of Malibu. By **Oct. 31** the death toll stood at 22, including 2 in Mexico and one firefighter. Gov. Gray Davis **Oct. 29** toured the Lake Arrowhead area, where 50,000 people had been evacuated; by then, 12,000 firefighters were on the front lines. Cooler and damper conditions on **Oct. 30** brought hope for relief.

Florida Marlins Win World Series—The Florida Marlins, a wild-card team, captured baseball's World Series

Oct. 25, defeating the New York Yankees, 2-0, in the 6th and deciding game. Josh Beckett shut out the heavily favored Yankees in New York, giving up only 5 hits. Beckett was named MVP. The Marlins had previously won the World Series in 1997.

The Marlins Oct. 15 had defeated the Chicago Cubs 9-6 to win the National League Pennant in the deciding 7th game, coming from behind both in the game and in the series. The Yankees Oct. 16 had won the 7th game of their series with the Boston Red Sox, coming from behind and then breaking a tie in the bottom of the 11th inning, to post a 6-5 victory for the American League pennant.

Bank of America, FleetBoston Announce Merger—The Bank of America and FleetBoston announced their merger Oct. 27; the new combined institution would be the 2nd-largest U.S. bank in assets, and the largest in retail banking, with 33 mil customers. Bank of America would pay an estimated $48 bil in stock for FleetBoston. The merger was completed Apr. 1.

NOVEMBER 2003

National

Bush Gets $87.5 Bil for Iraq—The Senate Nov. 3 approved by voice vote the $87.5 bil that Pres. George W. Bush had sought for U.S. military forces in Iraq and for helping to rebuild the country. The House had given its approval, 298-121, on Oct. 31. The final version did not contain a requirement, originally supported by the Senate, that part of the reconstruction expenditures be in the form of a loan rather than a grant. Bush signed the bill Nov. 6.

3 States Elect New Governors—Republicans picked up 2 governorships in elections held Nov. 4. In Kentucky, Rep. Ernie Fletcher (R) defeated state Atty. Gen. Ben Chandler (D). In losing the governorship for the first time in 3 decades, the Democrats had been handicapped by scandals in the administration of Gov. Paul Patton. In Mississippi, Haley Barbour, former chair of the Republican National Committee, defeated Gov. Ronnie Musgrove (D). On the same day Philadelphia Mayor John Street (D) won easy reelection.

In Louisiana, Lt. Gov. Kathleen Blanco (D) was elected Nov. 15 to succeed outgoing Gov. Mike Foster (R), who was ineligible for a 3rd term; she defeated Bobby Jindal (R).

On Nov. 17, Arnold Schwarzenegger (R) was sworn in as governor of California, succeeding Gray Davis (D), recalled from office in October by voters, who chose the famous actor to replace him. The GOP now held 28 of the nation's 50 governorships.

Dean Gains Big Union Support—Former Gov. Howard Dean (VT), a leading contender for the Democratic presidential nomination, got the endorsement Nov. 6 of the 1.6-million-member Service Employees International Union. The American Federation of State, County and Municipal Employees, with 1.4 million members, also endorsed him, Nov. 12. On Nov. 8 Dean announced that he would not accept federal matching funds for his campaign, thus would not be subject to spending limits; Pres. Bush, as in 2000, had already chosen to forego federal funds.

Kerry Shakes Up Campaign Staff—On Nov. 10, Sen. John Kerry (MA), trailing Dean in polls in New Hampshire, fired his campaign manager, Jim Jordan, and replaced him with Mary Beth Cahill, chief of staff to Sen. Edward M. Kennedy (D, MA). Kerry's press secretary and deputy finance director quit the next day. Kerry said, Nov. 14, that he too would forego federal matching funds.

U.S. Economy Continues to Add Jobs—The Labor Dept. reported Nov. 7 that employment grew by 126,000 in October (later revised to 100,000), in the 3rd straight month of job creation after a 3-year decline. The unemployment rate edged downward to 6.0%, from 6.1% in September.

Senate Debates Judicial Nominees—Beginning Nov. 12, the Senate held a 40-hour nonstop session in which Republicans made an issue of the use of filibusters by Democrats to block votes on 4 of Bush's judicial nominees. Democrats said that they had approved all but a handful of Bush's 172 judicial nominees but that the nominees in question were too conservative; Republicans argued that Democrats were using ideo-

logical litmus tests. After the session ended Nov. 14, Republicans sought to end the filibuster against 3 of the nominees, but could not get the 60 votes needed.

Alabama's Chief Justice Removed from Office—An ethics panel voted unanimously Nov. 13 to remove Roy Moore as chief justice of the Alabama Supreme Court, after Moore refused to obey a federal court order to remove a tablet inscribed with the Ten Commandments from the state judicial building.

Massachusetts Court Backs Gay Marriage—The Massachusetts Supreme Judicial Court, in a controversial 4-3 decision Nov. 18, held that gay couples had a right to marry under the state constitution, which it said "forbids the creation of second-class citizens." The court—the first high state court to so rule—gave the legislature 6 months to provide for legal marriage between homosexuals. Gov. Mitt Romney (R) said he would seek to amend the state constitution to confine marriage to a union between a man and a woman.

August Blackout Blamed on Ohio Power Plant—A Nov. 19 report by government and industry officials blamed the Aug. 2003 blackout on malfunctioning computers and poorly trained employees at FirstEnergy, an Ohio utility. The inquiry found that the company had failed to perform basic maintenance of its transmission lines. Sec. of Energy Spencer Abraham said the blackout, which had affected parts of 8 Midwestern and Northeast states and Ontario, Canada, had been "largely preventable."

Mutual Funds Execs Charged—Gary Pilgrim and Harold Baxter, founders of the PBHG mutual fund group, were charged Nov. 20 with "market timing" and other actions contrary to their duty to the shareholders, in civil suits jointly filed by NY Atty. Gen. Eliot Spitzer and the SEC. The suits sought monetary restitution and a bar to further activity in the securities business by the two men, who had resigned from the fund Nov. 13. The charges were part of a growing scandal involving allegations that a number of mutual funds allowed executives or other favored individuals to enrich themselves by short-term trades unavailable to others, to the detriment of the funds.

Putnam Investments, the 5th-largest U.S. mutual funds group, had reached an accord Nov. 13 with the SEC to put in place safeguards against market timing by its executives and pay restitution; the mutual funds giant was still the object of investigation by the state of Massachusetts. On Nov. 25, Spitzer announced felony charges against executives of a firm that processed mutual-fund trade orders, the Phoenix-based Security Trust. The SEC also filed civil-fraud charges against the company and its executives; the company was to be dissolved by Mar. 31, 2004.

GDP Shows Big 3rd Quarter Gain—The Commerce Dept. reported Nov. 25 that the gross domestic product grew at a revised seasonally adjusted rate of 8.2% in the 3rd quarter of 2003, well above the 3rd quarter increase of 3.3%, and economists attributed the rapid growth in part to temporary factors including tax cuts and a boom in mortgage refinancing sparked by low interest rates.

Congress Approves Drug Coverage for Seniors—After an acrimonious struggle, Congress approved a measure providing long-awaited but limited prescription-drug coverage for the elderly. The House approved it, 220–215, Nov. 22; the Senate followed Nov. 25, 54–44. The compromise bill, endorsed by the AARP but opposed for varying reasons by most Democrats and some Republicans, was the biggest change in Medicare since its creation in 1965 and was widely considered a political victory for Bush, who supported it. After a $250 deductible Medicare, as of 2006, will cover 75% of drug costs up to $2,250 each year, then no coverage until another $3,600 is paid out of pocket, then 95% of the cost of each prescription. Persons with incomes under $12,124 a year are exempt from deductibles, coverage gap, and premiums; those with incomes over $80,000 pay higher premiums than before. Beneficiaries may choose a private plan instead, and these plans receive government subsidies under the new bill. Democrats charged that the bill contains giveaways to insurance and drug companies; some Republicans complained of the high cost. Bush signed the bill Dec. 8.

International

Iraq Attacks Escalate; U.S. Presses Self-Government—Attacks by Saddam Hussein loyalists and other unidentified insurgents in Iraq grew more deadly in November. Sixteen U.S. soldiers died and 20 were injured **Nov. 2** after guerrillas shot down a Chinook helicopter near Falluja, 30 miles west of Baghdad, with a surface-to-air missile. A 2nd missile narrowly missed hitting a 2nd Chinook. A Black Hawk helicopter exploded and crashed **Nov. 7** in Tikrit, killing the 6 American soldiers aboard.

In response, U.S. tanks, howitzers, and planes **Nov. 7-8** struck an area in Tikrit from which guerrilla attacks had been launched, and U.S. aircraft struck at 2 targets in Bagdad **Nov. 12**. Pres. George W. Bush declared **Nov. 3** that "America will never run" from Iraq, and in a **Nov. 6** speech, he called on Middle East states to embrace a democratic tradition and recognize that the ouster of Saddam Hussein was "a watershed event in the global democratic revolution."

U.S. hopes for a broader military force in Iraq were set back **Nov. 7** when Turkey withdrew its offer of troops, which Iraq's Governing Council had opposed.

In Nasiriya, **Nov. 12**, a truck and car crashed into a building housing Italian military police; 19 Italians and 13 Iraqis were killed and more than 100 people were wounded.

The senior U.S. commander in the Middle East, Gen. John Abizaid, said **Nov. 13** that the coalition faced 5,000 guerrilla fighters in Iraq who were getting better organized and financed. At least 17 U.S. soldiers were killed 2 days later when 2 Black Hawk helicopters collided over the northern city of Mosul and crashed. One soldier was missing and 5 others were injured. U.S. forces reacted by strikes against sites believed to have been staging areas for attacks. Bombs at 2 police stations near Baghdad killed 14 people.

U.S. officials **Nov. 14** confirmed that the administration now supported an acceleration of the move toward Iraqi self-government even before a new constitution, with a transitional assembly selecting interim leaders. Independence was to be restored in 2004; foreign troops, however, would remain. On **Nov. 26**, a leading Shiite, Grand Ayatollah Ali al-Sistani, denounced the U.S. plan, calling for a direct election, which would likely benefit the Shiite majority.

On **Nov. 27** Pres. Bush flew to Iraq under tight security to have Thanksgiving dinner in the mess hall at Baghdad International Airport with 600 soldiers of the First Armored Division and 82nd Airborne. The trip was known in advance only to a few and not announced to the public until the president had left Baghdad air space; he was accompanied by only a few select reporters and a small official entourage.

The month ended with a spate of violence, much of it aimed at non-American foreigners. Seven Spanish intelligence officers died south of Baghdad **Nov. 29** when their SUVs were attacked by rocket-propelled grenades and rifle fire. Separate attacks the same day also killed 2 Japanese diplomats and a Colombian oil worker, and 2 South Korean contractors were killed in an ambush **Nov. 30**. For all of November, guerrillas killed 104 coalition troops, including 79 Americans. When they came under attack in Samarra, **Nov. 30**, U.S. forces struck back, killing 54 Iraqi fighters according to U.S. military sources, although bodies were not recovered and Iraqi sources claimed many fewer were killed.

Bombings Rock Turkey—Twice during November, terrorists struck at Turkey, a largely Muslim nation that supported the U.S. invasion of Iraq. On **Nov. 15**, 2 truck bombs exploded outside 2 synagogues in Istanbul, killing 25 people and wounding more than 250; most had been attending Sabbath prayers. On **Nov. 20**, truck bombs exploded in Istanbul, at the British consulate and Turkish headquarters of the HSBC bank, killing 30 and injuring 450; the British consul general, Roger Short, was among those killed. An anonymous caller attributed the bank attack to al-Qaeda and the Islamic Front of the Raiders of the Great Orient, a Turkish group that had also claimed responsibility for the synagogue bombings.

A car bomb that exploded **Nov. 8** in a residential compound in Riyadh, Saudi Arabia, claimed 17 lives and wounded more than 120.

Bush Visits Britain—Pres. Bush arrived in London **Nov. 18** to begin a state visit to Britain. The next day he was welcomed by Queen Elizabeth II at Buckingham Palace; in a speech he urged Britain to stand with the U.S. in a long-term effort to defeat terrorism and bring democracy to Islamic nations of the Middle East. Bush's movements were sharply restricted for security reasons; the usual procession through the streets was scrubbed, and he did not address Parliament. At a meeting between Bush and Prime Min. Tony Blair **Nov. 20**, the 2 deplored the terrorist attacks that day in Turkey. The same day a crowd of anti-Bush protesters estimated by authorities at 100,000 to 110,000 marched through London streets.

President of Georgia Resigns—Pres. Eduard Shevardnadze resigned his office **Nov. 23**, after mass protests in Georgia. On **Nov. 20**, the Central Election Commission had certified that his supporters won the parliamentary election of **Nov. 2**, but international observers had reported instances of fraud. On **Nov. 22**, protestors had broken into Parliament, forcing Shevardnadze, the last foreign minister of the Soviet Union, to flee. His decade-long rule had been marked toward the end by national economic collapse and charges of official corruption.

General

U.S. Episcopal Church Consecrates Gay Bishop—The Rev. V. Gene Robinson was consecrated **Nov. 2** as bishop of New Hampshire, becoming the first openly gay prelate in the Episcopal Church U.S.A. The consecration went forward despite warnings from Anglican primates in Africa, Asia, and Latin America that it could cause a schism in the church. Rowan Williams, the archbishop of Canterbury, issued a statement **Nov. 2** that recognized the right of the American branch to choose its bishops, but expressed regret that the concerns of other church leaders had not been given consideration. On **Nov. 3**, Anglican leaders in Africa declared that they were in a state of "impaired communion" with the U.S. Episcopalians.

Man Admits Killing 48 Women in "Green River" Case—Gary Ridgway, a resident of a Seattle (WA) suburb, pleaded guilty **Nov. 5** to killing 48 young women, most of them prostitutes or runaways. Since the 1980s authorities had been seeking the so-called Green River Killer, who had strangled the women after having sex with them and left many of their bodies near the river. Ridgway confessed to the crimes in an agreement with prosecutors that spared him the death penalty; no other serial murderer in U.S. history had been convicted of so many killings. On Dec. 18, Ridgway was sentenced to 48 consecutive life terms.

2002 DC Sniper Convicted—A Virginia Beach (VA) jury **Nov. 17** found John Muhammad guilty in the sniper attacks that plagued the Washington, DC, area in fall 2002. Muhammad had been arrested along with a suspected teenage accomplice, Lee Malvo, currently on trial separately. He was convicted of 2 counts of capital murder, one for committing multiple murders over 3 years and one for killing Dean Meyers in Oct. 2002 to further a terrorist scheme aimed at extorting $10 mil. Muhammad was also found guilty of conspiracy to commit murder and illegal use of a firearm. Prosecutors relied on strong circumstantial evidence, including a rifle found in his car that ballistics tests showed had been used in 13 shootings. The jury **Nov. 24** recommended a death sentence, which was imposed by the judge **Mar. 9, 2004**.

Michael Jackson Arrested for Child Abuse—Law enforcement officials in Santa Barbara, CA, **Nov. 19** issued an arrest warrant for singer Michael Jackson on multiple counts of child molestation. They said that the pop star would be charged with "lewd and lascivious conduct" with a child under age 14. Allegations a decade earlier that he had molested a 13-year-old boy had been resolved out of court with a multimillion-dollar settlement. Jackson was booked at the Santa Barbara County Jail, **Nov. 20**, and released on $3 mil bail; he was formally charged **Dec. 18.** Jackson rejected the charge as unfounded.

DECEMBER 2003
National

Bush Lifts Tariffs on Steel Imports—Pres. George W. Bush reversed one of his trade policies **Dec. 4** when he lifted tariffs on imported steel, effective **Dec. 5**. His administration had imposed the tariffs in March 2002, and they were scheduled to be in effect for 3 years. However, the World Trade Organization Nov. 10 had upheld an earlier ruling declaring the tariffs illegal, and the European Union and a number of countries had threatened to retaliate against them.

South Dakota Congressman Resigns After Conviction—Rep. William Janklow (R, SD), a former governor of the state, was convicted **Dec. 8** of 2nd-degree manslaughter and other charges, and announced he would resign from Congress in January. In August, Janklow's car had struck and killed a motorcyclist.

Gore Endorses Dean for Democratic Nomination—Former Vice Pres. Al Gore **Dec. 9** endorsed Howard Dean for the Democratic presidential nomination. Gore, the party's presidential nominee in 2000, passed over another candidate, Sen. Joe Lieberman (CT), his 2000 running mate, and was criticized by some especially for having failed to notify Lieberman of his decision before it was made public. In **Dec. 9** speeches in New York and Iowa, Gore praised Dean for being the only leading Democratic contender who had consistently opposed the Iraq war. The 9 Democrats seeking the nomination debated that day in Durham, NH. On **Dec. 14**, Lieberman remarked, "If Howard Dean had his way, Saddam Hussein would be in power today, not in prison." On **Dec. 15**, Dean asserted, "The capture of Saddam Hussein has not made America safer." On **Dec. 23**, consumer advocate Ralph Nader, the Green Party presidential nominee in 1996 and 2000, said he would not seek the party's nomination for 2004.

Democrats Elected in San Francisco, Houston—In a nonpartisan election, businessman Gavin Newsom, a Democrat, won a runoff election for mayor of San Francisco **Dec. 9**, defeating Green Party member Matt Gonzalez, 53% to 47%; this was the best showing yet by a Green in a U.S. big-city mayoral election. Newsom was to succeed outgoing Mayor Willy Brown. In Houston, TX, **Dec. 6**, in another nonpartisan runoff, Bill White, a Democrat and former U.S. deputy energy secretary, won with 62% of the vote, defeating Cuban-born Orlando Sanchez, a Republican.

Supreme Court Upholds Campaign Finance Law—A 5-4 majority on the U.S. Supreme Court, **Dec. 10**, upheld the 2002 campaign-finance law as a constitutional approach to combating spending abuses in the political process. The 2002 Bipartisan Campaign Reform Act had been challenged on first-amendment grounds by a number of disparate organizations; they objected to the ban on unlimited "soft money" contributions to political parties and to a ban on certain advertising just prior to elections.

California Governor Declares Fiscal Crisis—Gov. Arnold Schwarzenegger (R, CA) **Dec. 18** declared that his state was in a fiscal crisis. This proclamation would allow him, he said, to cut spending by $150 mil without having to get the legislature's approval. California's bond ratings had been reduced to near junk-bond levels, and a state deficit of $15 bil was projected for 2004.

Terror Alert in U.S. Is Raised to 'High'—Tom Ridge, secretary of homeland security, announced **Dec. 21** that the U.S. antiterrorism alert status was being raised to "high" (orange) from "elevated" (yellow). Ridge said that the danger of a terrorist attack was "perhaps greater now than at any point since Sept. 11, 2001." He cited unspecific new intelligence information that suggested plans to strike during the holiday season.

On **Dec. 24**, Air France, responding to a U.S. request, canceled 6 flights between Paris and Los Angeles; U.S. officials reportedly suspected that passengers on the flights could have links to terrorism. On the same day the FBI circulated a warning to law enforcement organizations to be on the watch for almanacs, since they could be used by terrorists "to assist with target selection and pre-operational planning." Some media noted the warning humorously, since these general reference works, of which the largest-

selling is *The World Almanac and Book of Facts*, are read by millions of people each year.

On **Dec. 29**, the Department of Homeland Security announced a rule requiring armed air marshals on certain foreign carriers' flights entering U.S. airspace that intelligence suggested were at special risk of terrorist attack. When a British Airways plane landed at Dulles International Airport outside Washington, DC, **Dec. 31**, authorities held the passengers, interviewing some, and rescreened the luggage.

U.S. Bans Use of Weight-Reduction Pill—The Bush administration **Dec. 30** said it would prohibit use of Ephedra, an herbal supplement used by millions of Americans to lose weight or improve athletic performance. Tommy Thompson, secretary of Health and Human Services, said the supplement "was too risky to be used." Ephedra had been linked to heart attacks, strokes, and sudden deaths. In February 2003, Steve Bechler, a pitcher for the Baltimore Orioles, died after taking Ephedra tablets, and a medical examiner said that the supplement was a factor in his death.

Special Counsel to Investigate Leak of Agent's Name—Atty. Gen. John Ashcroft **Dec. 30** removed himself from any role in the investigation into the leaking of a CIA name to a journalist. At issue was whether anyone in the Bush administration had violated the law by revealing the name of the agent, Valerie Plame, to columnist Robert Novak, who published her name in July. The Justice Dept. said **Dec. 30** that a special counsel would head the investigation. Plame was the wife of Joseph Wilson, a former U.S. ambassador who had publicly cast doubt on an administration assertion of nuclear weapons links between Iraq and Niger.

Stock Values Rise Sharply in 2003—After losses for 3 years in a row, investors had much to cheer about **Dec. 31**, as major stock indexes showed large gains for 2003. The Dow Jones industrial average had risen 25% to 10,453.92. A broader measure, Standard & Poor's 500-stock index, posted a 26% gain, moving up to 1,111.92. The tech-heavy NASDAQ index advanced 50%, to 2003.37. Averages were still below their all-time highs of the late 1990s, however.

U.S. Economy at a Glance: Calendar Year 2003	
Unemployment rate.	6.0%
Consumer prices (change over 2003).	+1.9%
Trade deficit	$496.5 bil
Dow Jones closing (year end).	10,453.92
Dow Jones highest close (Dec. 31)	10,453.92
Dow Jones lowest close (Mar. 11)	7524.06
GDP (change over 2003)	+3.1%

International

U.S. Forces Strike Back in Iraq—U.S. forces continued the tactic of launching massive raids targeting insurgents resisting the occupation. On **Dec. 2**, 1,000 troops raided Hawija, west of Kirkuk, in an effort to capture an aide to former Pres. Saddam Hussein. At a meeting in Iraq **Dec. 6** with U.S. Sec. of Defense Donald Rumsfeld, Lt. Gen. Ricardo Sanchez said that attacks on U.S. forces were running below 20 a day, half the rate of a few weeks earlier.

Rumsfeld Visits Afghanistan—Amid reports of a growing number of attacks on U.S. forces in Afghanistan, Defense Sec. Rumsfeld met in Kabul **Dec. 4** with Pres. Hamid Karzai. Rumsfeld also met in Mazar-I-Sharif **Dec. 4** with 2 warlords who controlled regional military forces. In 2 U.S. air strikes that went wrong **Dec. 5** and 6, 15 Afghan children were among those killed.

Chinese Premier Visits U.S.—Premier Wen Jiabao of China visited the U.S. for the first time, **Dec. 7-10**. He met with Pres. George W. Bush and other administration officials at the White House, **Dec. 9**. During a joint news conference that day, Bush said the U.S. had warned the Taiwanese government against holding a planned referendum that would call on China to withdraw missiles aimed at the island. Administration officials said that Bush had also cautioned Wen against the use of force by China against Taiwan.

Russia's Ruling Party Wins Parliamentary Elections—United Russia, the political party led by Pres. Vladimir Putin, drew 37% of the popular vote **Dec. 7** in elections for the Duma, or lower house of parliament to win about half of the Duma seats. With allied parties it now had

a large majority, possibly enough to pass constitutional amendments. The Communist Party received 13% of the vote, a decline from 24% in 1999.

A suicide bomber killed over 45 people and injured about 150 in an explosion **Dec. 5** inside a crowded commuter train in Yessentuki, in southern Russia. A female suicide bomber killed herself and 5 others, and injured 13, in a bombing outside the National Hotel near Red Square **in Moscow, Dec. 9**.

Contracts Rule Passes Over Countries That Opposed Iraq War—On **Dec. 9**, the U.S. Defense Dept. made known that countries that had not supported the U.S.-led war in Iraq would not be allowed to bid on $18.6 bil in contracts for reconstruction projects there. Contracts would be limited to Iraq, the U.S., and 61 nations that supported the coalition war effort. Companies from other countries, including Canada, France, Germany, and Russia, would, however, be allowed to bid on subcontracts. Japan **Dec. 9** approved deployment of 600 troops to Iraq, while stating that they would use force only if attacked.

Martin Is Canada's New Prime Minister—Paul Martin, new leader of the Liberal Party, became Canada's 21st prime minister **Dec. 12**. His cabinet was sworn in the same day. He succeeded Jean Chrétien, who retired after a decade as the country's leader. Martin had been CEO of a shipping firm and finance minister in Chretien's cabinet. He said he wanted to improve relations with the U.S., strained by differences on the Iraq war. The opposition Conservative Party of Canada was established **Dec. 8** in a merger of the Canadian Alliance and the Progressive Conservative Party.

Saddam Hussein Captured by U.S. Forces—Saddam Hussein, the deposed Iraqi president, was captured by U.S. military forces **Dec. 13**. Acting on a tip from an unidentified individual, soldiers of the 4th Infantry Division found him in a raid on a small underground hideout near Ad Dawr, a village 9 miles southeast of Tikrit. The region had been loyal to Hussein during his tyrannical reign, which ended when he fled Baghdad in April 2003 as U.S. forces advanced.

Some 600 infantry troops as well as Special Forces soldiers, supported by tanks, artillery, and helicopters, had closed in on Saddam's hideout, a hole opening into a shaft just long enough for someone to lie down in. Bearded and reportedly disoriented, Saddam did not attempt to use a pistol in his possession; 2 rifles and $750,000 in U.S. money were found nearby. The hole was near 2 mud huts that contained clothing and a kitchen. Two other Iraqis were seized in the same raid.

Hussein's capture ended a massive 8-month manhunt. His 2 sons had been killed in July while resisting capture. In the hours after Hussein's arrest, his identify was verified through DNA testing. At a press conference **Dec. 14**, a video taken of Hussein after his capture was shown on TV, and several Iraqis were allowed to meet him, to help dispel any remaining doubts as to the captive's identity. The news triggered both pro- and anti-Hussein demonstrations within Iraq. Political leaders of many countries hailed the U.S. achievement. Hussein was taken to an undisclosed location.

Iraqi leaders urged that a war crimes tribunal (created a week earlier by the governing council) try Hussein. Pres. Bush said, **Dec. 15**, that he would work with the Iraqis to find a way to try Hussein "that will withstand international scrutiny." He said he favored the "ultimate penalty" for Huseein but that it was up to Iraqis to decide.

Documents found with Hussein led, **Dec. 15**, to the seizure by U.S. troops of several of his associates. U.S. officials said the same day that Hussein had denied that his regime had weapons of mass destruction and also denied directing the postwar insurgency.

> "Ladies and gentlemen, we got him."
> L. Paul Bremer, Dec. 14, 2003, U.S. civilian administrator in Iraq, at a news conference in Baghdad.

Violent Incidents Continue in Iraq—The capture of Saddam Hussein did not reduce the level of insurgent attacks and terrorist incidents in Iraq. An explosion outside a police station west of Baghdad **Dec. 14** killed 17 Iraqis and wounded 33. Bombs at 2 Baghdad police stations **Dec. 15** killed 8 and wounded more than 20. U.S. troops killed 17 Iraqis **Dec. 15** and **16** during violent clashes. They arrested

73 Iraqis **Dec. 16** at what appeared to be a meeting of insurgents. On **Dec. 25** and **26**, guerrillas launched rocket and bomb attacks across Iraq, killing 4 American soldiers and 6 Iraqi civilians. On **Dec. 31**, a car bomb killed 8 Iraqis and wounded 35, including 3 Americans, at the Nabil Restaurant in Baghdad.

President of Pakistan Survives 2 Assassination Attempts—Pakistani Pres. Pervez Musharraf survived 2 attempts to assassinate him in December. On **Dec. 14**, a bomb exploded at a bridge in Rawalpindi 30 seconds after his motorcade had crossed it. On **Dec. 25**, 2 suicide bombers drove into his motorcade in Rawalpindi and detonated bombs, killing themselves and 13 other people. More than 40 were wounded. Responding to criticism from opposition Islamic parties, Musharraf announced **Dec. 24** that by the end of 2004 he would step down as army chief. He also agreed to seek a vote of confidence from Parliament in order to serve the rest of his term.

Libya to Abandon Unconventional Arms Programs—Pres. Bush and British Prime Min. Tony Blair announced **Dec. 19** that Libya's Pres. Muammar al-Qaddafi had admitted seeking to develop nuclear, biological, and chemical weapons, and had agreed to abandon these efforts and accept international arms inspections. Libya had concealed facilities to produce nuclear fuel; its agreement to end its weapons programs came after 9 months of secret talks. Libya hoped that other countries would lift economic sanctions.

Suicide Bomber Kills 4 in Israel. 4 Israelis—3 soldiers and a civilian—died when a Palestinian suicide bomber detonated explosives at a bus stop in a suburb of Tel Aviv **Dec. 25**; 15 people were reported injured. The Popular Front for the Liberation of Palestine claimed responsibility for the attack, described as retaliation for the killing of 2 PFLP members a few days earlier. It was the first such bombings in Israel since early October, when a bomb at a restaurant in Haifa killed 21. Israeli officials claimed to have thwarted a number of attempted bombings during that period.

In a separate incident minutes before the Tel Aviv bombing, an Israeli helicopter gunship fired on a car in Gaza city, killing at least 5 Palestinians. Among those slain was a leader of Islamic Jihad said by officials to have been planning a "mega-terror attack" in Israel.

Italian Food Company Hit by Scandal—Parmalat, an Italian-based juice and dairy conglomerate, became the center of a major accounting scandal. Its chairman, Carlo Tanzi, was taken into custody **Dec. 27**, 3 days after the government took control of the troubled company. Tanzi reportedly admitted that the company's books overstated its assets by some $10 bil, although he denied ordering any cover-up. Other company executives were also arrested.

General

Influenza Spreads in the U.S.—By **Dec. 4**, Colorado reported more than 6,300 cases of influenza, with the deaths of 5 children. Health officials said an especially virulent strain, Fujian A, was to blame. Affecting mainly western states at first, the flu was significantly on the rise in 24 states by **Dec. 11**, and demand was outrunning the available supply of vaccine. The secretary for health and human services, Tommy Thompson, said that the government had managed to obtain 100,000 doses for adults and 150,000 for children; the doses would be made available to individuals in high-risk categories. Thompson said **Dec. 15** that the U.S. was purchasing 375,000 more doses. By **Dec. 24** the flu was classified as widespread in 45 states.

Teen Convicted in 2002 DC in Sniper Rampage—Lee Malvo, indicted for involvement in a month of sniper attacks in the Washington, DC, area that left 10 dead, was found guilty of 2 counts of capital murder by a jury in Chesapeake, VA, **Dec. 18**. On **Dec. 23** the jury recommended a sentence of life in prison without parole, which was officially imposed by the judge Mar. 10, 2004. Malvo was 17 at the time of the shooting spree in the fall of 2002. John A. Muhammad, his adult partner in the killings, had been convicted and sentenced to death in November. The Malvo jury found that the youth had pulled the trigger in the fatal shooting of FBI analyst Linda Franklin in Falls Church, VA. His lawyers had

contended that he was insane at the time of the shootings and had been brainwashed by Muhammad.

U.S. Holstein Found to Have "Mad Cow Disease"— The Bush administration announced **Dec. 23** that a Holstein in Washington State had tested positive for so-called mad-cow disease. The animal, first in the U.S. to be so identified, had been slaughtered. Mad cow disease, known technically as bovine spongiform encephalopathy (BSE), eats holes in the brains of cattle; it can be fatal in humans if they consume meat from an infected animal. The disease had claimed more than 100 lives since first being diagnosed in Britain in 1986.

The announcement had potentially serious economic consequences for the U.S. cattle industry. Japan and South Korea said **Dec. 23** that they would ban imports of American beef. By **Dec. 24**, Taiwan, Russia, and a number of other countries had joined the list. U.S. officials said **Dec. 28** that meat from the diseased cow, which had been born in Canada, was in a batch of ground beef shipped to 8 states and Guam. Officials said that only tissue from the brain, spinal cord, and part of the intestine would have been infected, and that these parts were not processed.

Earthquake in Ancient Iran City Kills Thousands— An earthquake struck the ancient city of Bam, in southeastern Iran, **Dec. 26**, killing more than 26,000 people and injuring thousands. In Bam, a city of 80,000, most people lived in mud-brick homes not capable of withstanding quakes, and a 2,000-year-old citadel, said to be the world's largest mud-brick structure, was largely destroyed.

JANUARY 2004
National

Bush Proposes Plan for Foreign Workers in U.S.— Pres. George W. Bush proposed **Jan. 7** to let foreign workers enter the U.S. and stay for up to 6 years, if they have jobs lined up that citizens will not take. Foreigners currently working without permits could also legalize their status under the plan. Immigrants already in the U.S. illegally could stay for up to 6 years if they have a job. The plan had strong support and strong opposition. Rep. Tom DeLay (R, TX), the House majority leader and a major critic of the plan, suggested **Jan. 7** that it would unfairly reward illegal behavior.

New Jobs Increase Only Slightly in December, Despite Economic Growth— The Labor Dept. reported **Jan. 9** that only 1,000 nonfarm jobs had been added in December, a sharp decline from 43,000 in November and 100,000 in October (revised figures). The unemployment rate fell from 5.9% to 5.7%, attributed at least partly to discouraged workers leaving the labor force. At the same time, the government reported **Jan. 30** that the economy had grown at an annual rate of 4% during the 4th quarter.

The International Monetary Fund warned **Jan. 7** that U.S. budget and international trade deficits could inhibit worldwide economic growth. The IMF said U.S. borrowing could push up interest rates in other countries.

Former Cabinet Member Criticizes Bush— Paul O'Neill, who was treasury secretary under Pres. George W. Bush until being dismissed in December 2002, provided harsh criticism of the president in *The Price of Loyalty*, a book by journalist Ron Suskind published **Jan. 13** but excerpted in the media earlier. O'Neill, who provided thousands of documents to Suskind, had been skeptical of the Bush tax cuts. He claimed the administration intended to oust Saddam Hussein from its earliest days, well before the Sept. 11, 2001, terrorist attacks, a contention the White House denied.

> *"The only way I can describe [the cabinet meeting] is that, well, the President is like a blind man in a roomful of deaf people. There is no discernible connection."*
>
> Ousted *former Bush Treas. Sec. Paul O'Neill*, in *The Price of Loyalty*, published Jan. 14. He later said he regretted the description.

Former Enron Executive Pleads Guilty— The former CFO of Enron pleaded guilty in federal district court in Houston **Jan. 14** to enriching himself at the company's expense and conspiring to inflate the stock's value. By the terms of his plea agreement, Andrew Fastow would serve 10 years in prison. He agreed to cooperate in investigations of

other former executives of the now-bankrupt energy services company. As part of the deal, Fastow agreed to forfeit $29 mil to settle fines and civil penalties; this included $23 mil in illegal profits. His wife, Lea Fastow, a former Enron assistant treasurer, pleaded guilty **Jan. 14** to attempting to hide one of her husband's transactions. She would serve 5 months in prison.

Kerry Wins 2 States as Nomination Race Heats Up— Sen. John Kerry (MA) won the first 2 contests in the race for the Democratic presidential nomination. The Iowa caucuses, held **Jan. 19**, selected delegates who would pick the national convention delegates. Kerry won 38% of the delegates, Sen. John Edwards (NC) 32%, ex-Gov. Howard Dean (VT) 18%, and Rep. Richard Gephardt (MO) 11%. Dean and Gephardt had been favored because they had union support and were best organized. Dean, shown on TV speaking to supporters after results were in, shouted defiantly that he would continue his campaign nationwide; his tone and exuberant yell drew criticism as excessive. Gephardt withdrew from the race Jan. 20.

New Hampshire held the first primary election, **Jan. 27**. Kerry and Dean, both from neighboring states, ran first and second with 39% and 26%, respectively. Gen. Wesley Clark (ret.) got 13%, Edwards 12%, and Sen. Joseph Lieberman (CT) 9%. Surveys of Democratic voters in both states showed widespread opposition to the Iraq war, but that did not always benefit Dean, who had made his outspoken opposition a key issue. Surveys showed many Democrats did not consider him sufficiently electable.

The Bush campaign said **Jan. 7** that it had raised $130.8 mil in contributions in 2003, a record for a presidential candidate in one year. On Jan. 15, former Sen. Carol Moseley Braun withdrew her presidential candidacy and endorsed Dean. On Jan. 28, Dean named Roy Neel, a friend of former Vice Pres. Al Gore, to be "chief executive officer" of his campaign; Joe Trippi, who had headed the campaign, quit in response.

Bush Gives State of the Union Address— Pres. Bush gave his annual State of the Union address to a joint session of Congress **Jan. 20**. He warned against harboring the "dangerous illusion" that the threat from terrorists no longer existed, and defended his decision to overthrow Saddam Hussein. At a time of continuing large federal budget deficits, he offered only modest spending proposals, but did call for making his tax cuts permanent.

International

More Steps Taken to Thwart Terrorism— Amid ongoing concerns about terrorist acts, British Airways **Jan. 1** and 2 canceled 2 flights from London to Washington. A Washington-London flight was canceled **Jan. 1**. Officials reportedly believed that hijackers were targeting those flights. More than a dozen flights had been canceled or diverted since the United States had raised its terrorism alert level to "high" in December. U.S. immigration officials announced **Jan. 5** that foreigners arriving with visas must be photographed and fingerprinted with a digital scanner. Visitors from 28 countries, mostly in Europe, who were not required to obtain visas for visits up to 90 days, would be exempt. On **Jan. 9**, the United States lowered its terrorist threat level from "high" to "elevated."

Afghan Council Approves Constitution— A grand council, known as the *loya jirga*, meeting in Kabul **Jan. 4**, approved a new constitution for Afghanistan. The country was formally named the Islamic Republic of Afghanistan, and all laws now would have to comport with Islamic beliefs. The government would include a popularly elected president, a legislature, and an independent judiciary.

Meanwhile, in incidents of violence, 2 bombs in Kandahar killed at least 15 people, many of them children, and injured dozens **Jan. 6**; officials blamed Taliban militants. Twelve civilian men were bound and executed on a remote road west of Kandahar **Jan. 6** in what authorities said appeared to be a Taliban action. Afghans said that an attack by a U.S. helicopter **Jan. 17** or **18** caused the deaths of 11 civilians; U.S. authorities, claimed that the only persons killed in the attack were 5 Taliban fighters. An explosion **Jan. 29**,

near a weapons cache outside Ghazni, killed 7 U.S. soldiers and wounded 3, with one soldier reported missing.

U.S. Military Death Toll in Iraq Reaches 500—The number of U.S. soldiers killed in the Iraqi conflict reached 500 on **Jan. 17**, including 346 in combat, according to the U.S. military. About 2,500 were wounded in action. Allied non-U.S. deaths totaled 90. On that day 3 were killed when their armored vehicle struck a bomb north of Baghdad. On **Jan. 8**, all 9 U.S. soldiers in a Black Hawk helicopter died when it crashed near Falluja after being hit by a missile. An explosion outside a Shiite Muslim mosque in Baqubah, **Jan. 9**, killed 5.

On **Jan. 8**, the U.S. announced the beginning of a rotation, to be completed by May, that would bring home 123,000 troops from Iraq and Kuwait and replace them with 110,000 others. The U.S. Defense Dept. said **Jan. 9** that it had designated ex-Pres. Saddam Hussein a prisoner of war.

The leading Shiite cleric, Grand Ayatollah Ali al-Sistani, called **Jan. 11** for direct elections to choose an interim government, putting himself at odds with the U.S. plan, which provided for provincial caucuses. L. Paul Bremer, the top U.S. civilian administrator, opposed his approach **Jan. 12**. U.S. officials looked to the UN to help mediate the dispute on forming a new government, and on **Jan. 27** UN Sec. Gen. Kofi Annan agreed to send a UN team to Iraq to look at whether early elections might be feasible, provided the U.S. and its coalition partners could guarantee their security.

Bush announced **Jan. 13** that Canada would be eligible to bid on some construction contracts in Iraq even though it had opposed the war. On **Jan. 18**, a truck bomb exploded at the U.S. occupation headquarters in Baghdad, killing at least 20 and wounding at least 60, mostly Iraqi civilians. Six U.S. soldiers died in 2 roadside bombings **Jan. 27**. On **Jan. 31**, 3 U.S. soldiers were killed southwest of Kirkuk when a bomb destroyed the vehicle in which they were riding. On the same day, a suicide bomber drove his car into a police station in Mosul, killing at least 9 and wounding 45.

Georgia Elects New President—On **Jan. 4**, less than 2 months after a popular uprising had toppled Pres. Eduard Shevardnadze, voters in Georgia chose his successor. Totals released **Jan. 5** showed that Mikhail Saakashvili, 36, a lawyer and former justice minister, had received 96% of the vote. After leaving the Shevardnadze government and accusing some of his former colleagues of corruption, Saakashvili had founded his own party. The new president was inaugurated **Jan. 25**.

Libya Ratifies Nuclear Test Ban Treaty—The Libyan regime of Col. Muammar al-Qaddafi **Jan. 14** ratified the Comprehensive Nuclear Test Ban Treaty. Libya acted a month after agreeing to dismantle its nuclear, biological, and chemical weapons programs. The treaty was not yet in effect; only 32 of a needed 44 countries had ratified it. Pres. Bush had said **Jan. 5** that he was continuing the status of a national emergency with Libya, under which Libya's U.S. assets were frozen and Libya was deemed a sponsor of terrorism. The Qaddafi Foundation, run by one of Qaddafi's sons, agreed **Jan. 9** to pay $170 mil in compensation for the 1989 bombing of a flight over Niger that killed 170.

Iraq Weapons Inspector Cites Error, Blames Intelligence—The chief U.S. weapons inspector in Iraq said, **Jan 23**, that he believed Iraq had no stockpiles of chemical and biological weapons at the time of the U.S. invasion. David Kay made the assertion as he resigned as chief inspector. On **Jan. 28**, he told the Senate Armed Services Committee, "we were almost all wrong" in believing Iraq had weapons of mass destruction, and said he did not believe analysts had been pressured to provide information that would bolster the case for war. Kay said he favored an outside independent investigation of the apparent intelligence failure.

In a report released **Jan. 8**, the Carnegie Endowment for International Peace had claimed that the Bush administration pressured analysts to exaggerate Iraq's weapons threat. Sec. of State Colin Powell acknowledged **Jan. 8** that he had no proof of a link between Saddam Hussein and al-Qaeda terrorists.

In England, a report released **Jan. 28** by Lord Hutton concluded that the government of Prime Min. Tony Blair had not willfully inflated the threat of WMDs to promote war, and castigated the BBC for making such charges. The Hutton report also found the government was not to blame for the suicide of David Kelly, a source for the BBC charges.

Jerusalem Bus Blast Kills 10—A suicide bomber detonated explosives on a bus in Jerusalem **Jan. 29**, killing 10 people beside himself. Over 45 others were injured, in the first such suicide bombing in Jerusalem since Sept. 2003. The bomber, a Palestinian, left a note saying the deed was retaliation for an Israeli raid the day before in the Gaza strip that left 8 or more Palestinians dead.

Despite the bus bombing, Israel went ahead **Jan. 29** with plans to release some 400 Palestinian prisoners as part of a deal negotiated with Hezbollah militants.

General

2 Unmanned U.S. Spacecraft Land on Mars—An unmanned U.S. spacecraft landed on Mars **Jan. 3**, and soon began sending dramatic photos of the landscape back to earth. Concluding a 7-month trip, the 400-pound Spirit landed almost precisely at its target position, in the Gusev Crater. Spirit, a robotic rover, was the 4th spacecraft to make a successful landing on Mars. By contrast, a British craft, Beagle 2, had been silent since its scheduled December 2003 landing. Photographs relayed from Spirit **Jan. 4**, via 2 other spacecraft orbiting the planet, showed rocks scattered across a flat plain. Scientists were looking for evidence that Mars once had water, which would increase the likelihood that the planet once harbored life. On **Jan. 21**, Spirit began transmitting erratically. Opportunity, a second U.S. rover, landed successfully **Jan. 24** on the opposite side of the planet. On **Jan. 25** it photographed bedrock emerging from soil with a pebbly texture.

Pres. George W. Bush **Jan. 14** advocated establishing a U.S. colony on the moon, where astronauts would live and work for extended periods and manned expeditions to Mars could be launched. NASA estimated the Moon project would cost $170 billion over 15 years; however, the administration anticipated only modest NASA budget increases over the next 5 years.

2 Teams Share College Football Title—Louisiana State defeated Oklahoma, 21-14, **Jan. 4** in the Sugar Bowl in New Orleans, the game that was intended to establish a single national championship team in Division 1-A. Under a system that took polls, computer calculations, and other factors into consideration, those 2 teams were matched. However, on **Jan. 1**, the University of Southern California defeated Michigan, 28-14, in the Rose Bowl, and on **Jan. 5** journalists voting in the Associated Press poll named USC (12-1) as the number 1 team. Voting the same day, coaches bound by BSC rules to support the Sugar Bowl winner voted LSU (13-1) number 1.

Pete Rose Admits Betting on Baseball—Pete Rose, one of baseball's greatest stars, admitted **Jan. 5** that he had gambled specifically on games involving his own team, the Cincinnati Reds. His autobiography, *My Prison Without Bars*, was published **Jan. 8**. Rose was permanently barred from baseball in 1989.

FEBRUARY 2004

National

Commission to Study Intelligence Breakdown—Bush administration officials said **Feb. 1** that a bipartisan commission would investigate why prewar intelligence reports that Iraq had weapons of mass destruction had apparently been wrong. On **Feb. 6** and **12**, Pres. George W. Bush named the 9 members of his commission, to be headed by U.S. Appeals Court Judge Laurence Silberman and former Sen. Charles Robb (D, VA); the commission was to report by Mar. 31, 2005.

Sec. of State Colin Powell indicated **Feb. 2** that he might not have recommended military action if he had not thought Iraq had WMDs, but said the war was still "the right thing to do." On **Feb. 3**, Britain began its own investigation of prewar intelligence. George Tenet, Director of Central Intelligence, conceded **Feb. 5** that the CIA had made misjudgments on Iraqi weapons, but denied that the agency

had come under pressure in shaping its assessments. During a *Meet the Press* TV interview, broadcast **Feb. 8**, Pres. Bush acknowledged that he might have been wrong in claiming before the war that Iraq had stockpiles of WMDs.

Bush Outlines 2005 Budget—On **Feb. 2**, Pres. Bush submitted to Congress a $2.4 tril budget proposal for the 2005 fiscal year, with a deficit of $364 bil. His estimated deficit for the current 2004 fiscal year was put at $521 bil, which would be a record in dollar terms, though not as a percent of GNP. The national debt was projected to reach $8.1 tril by the end of fiscal 2005. Bush proposed eliminating 65 federal programs and cutting many others, while urging that temporary tax cuts enacted during his administration be made permanent. Alan Greenspan, the Federal Reserve chairman, **Feb. 25** urged Congress not to cut deficits by raising taxes, but by cutting entitlement programs, including Social Security and Medicare.

Lethal Poison Forces Senate Buildings to Close—A suspicious powder was found **Feb. 2** on letter-opening machines in the mailroom of Sen. Bill Frist (R, TN), the Senate majority leader. The powder proved to contain ricin, which is lethal if inhaled or ingested. Three Senate office buildings were closed **Feb. 3** and reopened **Feb. 5**. An investigation was launched.

Kerry Leads Democrats—Sen. John Kerry (MA) continued to win primaries and caucuses in pursuit of the Democratic nomination for president. On **Feb. 3** he won in 5 states—Arizona, Delaware, Missouri, New Mexico, and Arizona, while Sen. John Edwards (NC) won the primary in South Carolina, his native state, and Gen. Wesley Clark (ret.) won narrowly over Edwards in Oklahoma. Sen. Joseph Lieberman, a centrist Democrat who had made his last stand in Delaware, withdrew **Feb. 3** after getting only 11% of the vote there. Kerry continued to win, in Michigan and Washington **Feb. 7**, in Maine **Feb. 8**, and in Virginia and Tennessee **Feb. 10**. Clark, who had hoped to win Tennessee, finished 3rd and withdrew from the race,

Kerry edged Edwards, 40% to 34%, in Wisconsin **Feb. 17**. Former Gov. Howard Dean of Vermont got 18% and announced **Feb. 18** that he was no longer actively seeking the presidency. In the last half of 2003, Dean had been seen as the front-runner, leading in polls and in money raised over the Internet, but he failed to win a single primary. He had been pounded by other candidates as too liberal and inexperienced to beat Pres. Bush in November, and several verbal missteps had also impaired his candidacy.

A coalition of 18 labor unions, including the Teamsters, endorsed Kerry **Feb. 17**, and on **Feb. 19** the AFL-CIO, representing 13 mil members, added its backing. Labor endorsements for Kerry were a disappointment for Edwards, whose campaign had focused on the theme that everyday Americans were not faring well. By month's end, Kerry had amassed about 700 of the 2,162 delegates needed for the nomination; Edwards had about 200. Two other candidates, Rep. Dennis Kucinich (OH) and the Rev. Al Sharpton, remained but were not considered serious contenders.

The Vietnam-era military service of Pres. Bush in the National Guard became an issue. On **Feb. 1**, Terrence McAuliffe, chairman of the Democratic National Committee, said Bush had been AWOL (absent without leave). Bush disputed the charge and on **Feb. 10, 11**, and **13** released military records. These showed he had performed services and received pay but did not prove whether he had attended sessions during a period from May 1972 to May 1973 when assigned to the Alabama Guard unit.

Ralph Nader, the consumer advocate who won about 3% of the national vote in 2000 as presidential candidate of the Green Party, said **Feb. 22** that he would run as an independent in 2004. Many Democrats opposed the move, arguing that the 97,000 votes he had gotten in Florida in 2000 had cost Vice Pres. Al Gore that state and the presidency. Meanwhile, Pres. Bush formally kicked off his campaign **Feb. 23** with a speech in which he criticized Kerry for allegedly flip-flopping on key issues.

Gay Marriage Advances, Stirs Opposition—The Massachusetts Supreme Court on **Feb. 4** ruled, 4-3, that the state could not, by approving civil unions, satisfy its 2003 decision

striking down a state ban on gay marriage. The state legislature, **Feb. 12**, ended an unsuccessful attempt to agree on an amendment to the state constitution that would ban gay marriage.

On **Feb. 12**, San Francisco began issuing marriage licenses to same-sex couples, notwithstanding a state law that defined marriage as a union between a man and a woman; within days, thousands of couples applied. On **Feb. 19**, San Francisco challenged the state law in court. The state supreme court Mar. 11 issued an interim stay blocking issuance of any more licenses to gay couples. Pres. Bush **Feb. 24** called for adoption of an amendment to the U.S. Constitution that would define marriage as a union of a man and a woman. He said, "a few judges and local authorities are presuming to change the most fundamental institution of civilization."

> *"The dissimilitude between the terms 'civil marriage' and 'civil union' is not innocuous; it is a considered choice of language that reflects a demonstrable assigning of same-sex, largely homosexual, couples to second-class status."*
>
> *Mass. Chief Justice Margaret Marshall*, writing for the court majority in a 4-3 decision, Feb. 4, that ruled out allowing "civil union" as a substitute for gay "marriage."

Jobs Continue to Lag—Democrats continued to criticize the Bush administration because the economic recovery did not include a surge in new jobs. The government reported **Feb. 6** that the unemployment rate in January had edged downward to 5.6% from 5.7%. In January, 112,000 new nonfarm jobs had been added, up from a revised total of 16,000 in December, but still far short of projected goals. Gregory Mankiw, chairman of the White House Council of Economic Advisers, aroused controversy **Feb. 9** when he said that outsourcing service jobs to low-wage workers overseas was "a plus for the economy in the long run."

Ex-Enron CEO Indicted for Fraud and Conspiracy—Jeffrey Skilling, former president and CEO of the Enron Corp., was indicted **Feb. 19** on federal charges of fraud, conspiracy, and insider trading. The indictment, in Houston, contended that he had disguised Enron's true financial performance while profiting from the sale of stock inflated by false earnings reports. He pleaded not guilty. A separate civil suit was filed the same day by the SEC.

Studies Detail Abuse of Children by Priests—Two reports released **Feb. 27** by the U.S. Conference of Catholic Bishops documented the sexual abuse of children by Roman Catholic priests in the U.S. from 1950 to 2002. One of the studies, by academics at the John Jay College of Criminal Justice, found that 4,392 priests had abused a total of at least 10,667 children. The data were based on information supplied by bishops on the basis of formal complaints. About 80% of the abuses were homosexual in nature. A 2nd report prepared by a National Review Board composed of lay Catholics appointed by bishops, strongly criticized some bishops for a lack of oversight, singling out Cardinal Bernard Law, the former archbishop of Boston; Cardinal Roger Mahoney of Los Angeles; and Cardinal Edward Egan of New York as examples.

International

Guerrillas Continue Attacks in Iraq— Two suicide attacks **Feb. 1** killed more than 100 people at the offices of the 2 leading Kurdish political parties in Erbil. At least 100 Iraqis were killed in 2 more suicide bombings, one on **Feb. 10** south of Baghdad that targeted applicants for the Iraqi police force, and the 2nd **Feb. 11** in Baghdad that killed people seeking work with the Iraqi army. At least 25 people were killed when insurgents attacked a police station in Fallujah **Feb. 14**. Other attackers at the same time freed 87 prisoners. UN Sec. Gen. Kofi Annan said **Feb. 19** that Iraq would not be able to conduct a direct national election before the scheduled June 30 transfer of sovereignty from the coalition forces.

Pakistani Scientist Shared Nuclear Technology—A scientist regarded as the key figure in the development of Pakistan's nuclear weaponry admitted **Feb. 4** that he had leaked that technology to other countries. Abdul Qadeer Khan admitted "errors in judgment" in providing designs and technology to Iran, Libya, and North Korea beginning in

1989; a report on Khan's conduct showed that he had made millions of dollars in the process. Pres. Pervez Musharraf of Pakistan pardoned Khan the next day and paid tribute to his role in developing Pakistan's bomb.

Bombing in Moscow Subway Kills 39—A female suicide bomber detonated an explosion from a suitcase, **Feb. 6,** on a subway car in Moscow. At least 39 people were killed and up to 200 injured. Pres. Vladimir Putin of Russia blamed Chechen "bandits."

Iran Elects Conservative Parliament—Islamic conservatives won a clear majority in parliamentary elections held **Feb. 20.** Some moderates boycotted the vote, protesting the ultra-conservative Guardian Council's decision to bar about 2,000 moderate candidates, including some 80 incumbents, from running. On **Feb. 1** about one-third of the parliament had resigned to protest the disqualifications.

President of Haiti Resigns as Rebels Advance—Pres. Jean-Bertrand Aristide left Haiti by air **Feb. 29** as rebels seeking his overthrow closed in on the capital, Port-au-Prince. Aristide left behind a country in chaos, with gunmen shooting in the streets amid widespread looting. The U.S. ordered Marines into Haiti, and French troops were also on the way.

The rebellion had gathered momentum in just a few weeks. The Gonaives Resistance Front **Feb. 5** seized Gonaives, the country's 4th-largest city. Aristide's opponents charged that he had rigged his successful re-election in 2000 and that his regime was corrupt. In the absence of an army, Aristide was supported by several thousand police officers and some armed civilians. Guy Philippe, a former police chief, took command of the insurgents **Feb. 18.** On **Feb. 22** the rebels seized Cap Haitien, the 2nd-largest city. Opposition leaders **Feb. 24** rejected a U.S. proposal for power sharing between the 2 sides.

General

Patriots Edge Carolina in Super Bowl XXXVIII—One of the most thrilling Super Bowl contests was decided **Feb. 1** with 4 seconds to play, when Adam Vinatieri kicked a 41-yard field goal for the New England Patriots. The Pats thus prevailed over the Carolina Panthers, 32-29. In the tumultuous 4th quarter, a total of 37 points were scored. Patriots quarterback Tom Brady was named Super Bowl MVP; he completed 32 of 48 passes for 354 yards and 3 touchdowns. The Patriots were 17-2 for the regular season and the playoffs, and won their last 15 games. In 2002, the Pats had also won the NFL title on a last-second kick by Vinatieri.

During a dance performance in the halftime show, produced by the cable TV network MTV, Justin Timberlake tore off part of Janet Jackson's top garment, exposing her right breast. The NFL and CBS (which telecast the Super Bowl), as well as many fans, deplored the incident. FCC Chairman Michael Powell **Feb. 11** said his agency was investigating whether federal laws had been violated. Jackson and Timberlake apologized, with the latter, **Feb. 2,** blaming it on a "wardrobe malfunction."

Human Stem Cells Cloned—South Korean scientists announced **Feb. 12** that they had successfully cloned human embryos and harvested their stem cells, a feat widely regarded as a major breakthrough. The aim of the research was not to pave the way to cloned human beings but to find a new source of embryonic stem cells, viewed by many researchers as the most promising avenue to a cure of diabetes, Parkinson's, and other serious diseases.

Explosion on Train Kills Hundreds in Iran—More than 300 people were killed **Feb. 18** when a runaway train carrying chemicals and fuel derailed in northeastern Iran. The subsequent fire and explosion injured hundreds more. The dead included officials and firefighters who had gone to the scene.

Film of Christ's Passion Draws Crowds and Controversy—A motion picture depicting the last 12 hours of Christ's life opened **Feb. 25** and quickly became a major box office hit. The film, *The Passion of the Christ,* produced and directed by actor Mel Gibson, depicted Christ's crucifixion and death in graphic detail, which was varyingly perceived as realistic and moving or excessively violent. The film was also criticized by some as wrongheaded and possibly anti-Semitic in its portrayal of Jews and their role in the death of Christ. Despite controversy, the film was popular and earned more than \$370 mil in theaters.

***Lord of the Rings* Wins 11 Oscars**—*The Lord of the Rings: The Return of the King* won 11 Oscars, including best picture, from the Academy of Motion Picture Arts and Sciences **Feb. 29.** Two earlier films—*Titanic* and *Ben-Hur*—had tied the record for 11 Oscars. The new movie, 3rd and last in a series based on the fantasy trilogy by J.R.R. Tolkien, was acclaimed for its technical wizardry, and Peter Jackson was named best director for the film. Charlize Theron was voted best actress for her portrayal of a serial killer in *Monster.* Sean Penn won best actor for *Mystic River,* in which he played the anguished father of a murdered daughter. Best supporting actor and actress awards went to Tim Robbins (*Mystic River*) and Renee Zellweger (*Cold Mountain*). Billy Crystal hosted the awards ceremonies.

MARCH 2004
National

Kerry Assured of Democratic Presidential Nomination—Sen. John Kerry (MA) emerged as the certain winner of the Democratic presidential nomination after he won 9 of the 10 primaries and caucuses held **Mar. 2.** He prevailed by wide margins in California, New York, and Ohio, and won narrowly in Georgia. Sen. John Edwards (NC) finished 2nd in those states. In all, Kerry had won 27 of 30 primaries and caucuses. Edwards, viewed as the only serious rival remaining, withdrew his candidacy **Mar. 3** and said he would work to get Kerry elected.

The debate between Republican and Democratic campaigns intensified. Kerry asserted **Mar. 8** that some foreign leaders had told him they wanted Pres. George W. Bush defeated for reelection, and the president's supporters demanded he identify them, which Kerry declined to do. A Bush TV commercial that debuted **Mar. 11** claimed Kerry would raise taxes by \$900 billion. Another GOP ad launched **Mar. 16** deplored Kerry's vote in Oct. 2003 against funding military operations in Iraq and Afghanistan; Kerry said his vote was a protest against Bush's failed policies.

Martha Stewart Convicted of Obstructing Justice—Martha Stewart, founder of Martha Stewart Living Omnimedia Inc. and one of the nation's most successful female entrepreneurs, was convicted **Mar. 5** of conspiracy and obstruction of justice. Peter Bacanovic, her former broker at Merrill Lynch, was convicted of similar charges in a U.S. district court in New York City.

Prosecutors contended that in December 2001 Bacanovic had told his assistant, Douglas Faneuil to tip off Stewart that ImClone founder Samuel Waksal and family members were selling their shares in the company before ImClone announced that its cancer drug Erbitux failed to win federal approval. Stewart allegedly ordered Bacanovic to sell her ImClone stock on that basis and then tried to cover up evidence of this. Faneuil and Stewart's assistant Ann Armstrong both testified for the prosecution.

WorldCom ex-CEO Charged, 2nd Ex-Official Pleads Guilty—Prosecutors in New York City **Mar. 2** charged Bernard Ebbers, former WorldCom CEO, with securities fraud, conspiracy, and false regulatory filings. The same day, Scott Sullivan, former WorldCom CFO, pleaded guilty to securities fraud and agreed to cooperate with prosecutors. Ebbers pleaded not guilty to all charges **Mar. 3.** The company's 2002 bankruptcy was the largest in U.S. history, costing investors \$180 billion.

U.S. Economy at a Glance: March 2004	
Unemployment rate.	5.7%
Consumer prices (change over 2003).	1.7%
Trade deficit (12 mo. through Mar.)	\$509.7 bil
Dow Jones closing, 1st quarter.	10,357.70
Dow Jones highest close, 1st quarter (Feb. 11) .	10,737.70
Dow Jones lowest close, 1st quarter (Mar. 24). .	10,048.23
1st quarter GDP growth (annual rate).	4.5%

U.S. Officials Testify on Sept. 11 Terror Attacks—The National Commission on Terrorist Attacks Upon the United States, a bipartisan commission investigating the Sept. 11, 2001, attacks, chaired by former NJ Gov. Thomas Kean,

conducted public hearings **Mar. 23-24**, following more lengthy private hearings. Appearing on **Mar. 23**, Sec. of State Colin Powell and Defense Sec. Donald Rumsfeld both said that better use of intelligence available at the time still would not have prevented the attacks.

The commission issued preliminary reports **Mar. 23**, noting that from April to July 2001 "alarming threats" came in about a possible al-Qaeda attack. CIA Director George Tenet testified **Mar. 24** that a lack of interagency cooperation had blunted a pre-Sept. 11 Bush administration effort to develop a comprehensive plan to thwart al-Qaeda.

Among witnesses attracting attention was Richard Clarke, chief of counterterrorism under Pres. Clinton and George W. Bush, who had left government service in 2003. In his testimony, **Mar. 24**, and a book, *Against All Enemies*, published **Mar. 22**, he contended that despite his urging, the Bush administration was preoccupied with Iraq, and long delayed approval of a program to deal with al-Qaeda prior to the Sept. 11 attacks; he also contended that the invasion of Iraq strengthened the radical Islamic movement worldwide.

A top administration official argued that while in the administration Clarke had praised Bush's counterterror efforts. National Security Adviser Condoleezza Rice, in interviews, disputed Clarke's version of events. The White House initially declined to have her testify publicly under oath, citing executive privilege, but under widespread pressure agreed **Mar. 30** to allow it. The White House also conceded that Bush and Vice Pres. Dick Cheney would appear privately before the whole panel.

> "Those entrusted with protecting you failed you, and I failed you. We tried hard, but that doesn't matter, because we failed. And for that failure, I would ask, once all the facts are out, for your understanding and for your forgiveness."
>
> Former counterterrorism chief Richard Clarke, testifying before the 9/11 commission, Mar. 24.

International

New Regime Seeks to End Chaos in Haiti—Following a month of insurrection during which perhaps 100 people died, Haiti came under control of a new interim government. Rebels entered Port-au-Prince, the capital, **Mar. 1**, a day after Pres. Jean-Bertrand Aristide fled into exile. UN peacekeepers from France and Canada also arrived, joining U.S. troops who were guarding the airport and presidential palace. Guy Philippe, the rebel commander, declared **Mar. 2** that he was in control of Haiti, but on **Mar. 3** he agreed to disarm his troops and leave Port-au-Prince.

Boniface Alexandre, the Supreme Court chief justice, was sworn in as interim president **Mar. 8**, and on the next day Gerard Latortue, an economist, was chosen as premier by a 7-member council. The death toll continued to rise, with revenge killings between factions claiming hundreds of lives.

Iraq Constitution Approved; Bombings Continue—In a step toward democracy, the Iraqi governing council approved a draft constitution on **Mar. 1**.

The draft constitution was intended to be in place until elections in late 2004 or early 2005. It provided for civilian control of the military and equal protection for both sexes and all religions. Islam was declared to be "a source" but not the primary source of law. The members of the council signed the constitution **Mar. 8** after 5 Shiite members dropped their complaints asserting that veto power was being given the Kurds.

Violence continued with 3 explosions in Baghdad and a single explosion in Karbala **Mar. 2** that killed more than 180 people; the victims were Shiite Muslim worshipers who had gathered to observe a holy day. A bomb carried by a 4th man failed to detonate in Baghdad, and he was captured. Iraqi police **Mar. 3** arrested 15 people in connection with the bombings.

On **Mar. 17**, a car bomb killed 7 and wounded 35 at the Mount Lebanon Hotel in Baghdad. As of **Mar. 19**, the first anniversary of the U.S.-led invasion of Iraq, 571 U.S. troops had been killed. A roadside bomb outside Fallujah, **Mar. 31** killed 5 U.S. military personnel. In a 2nd attack the same day in the so-called Sunni triangle, a stronghold for supporters of Saddam Hussein, 4 Americans working for a security company were killed when their SUVs were ambushed and

attacked with grenades; their corpses were dragged through the streets by a mob and 2 of them were hanged from a bridge, in an atrocity that gained wide attention.

Bombs in Madrid Kill 191, Prime Minister Ousted in Election—10 bombs exploded almost simultaneously on 4 commuter trains in Madrid, Spain, **Mar. 11**, killing 191 people and wounding 1,400. Most of the bombs had been placed in backpacks carried by passengers who debarked before they exploded. Police later that day found a van with detonators and an audiotape of Koran verses, and a group allied with al-Qaeda claimed responsibility that day. From 8 to 11 million people demonstrated in Madrid and other cities **Mar. 12** against the bombing.

The government of Prem. Jose Maria Aznar, which had supported the U.S.-led invasion of Iraq, initially blamed the Basque terrorist group ETA; critics charged that this view was motivated by fear that if al-Qaeda were responsible the government would be blamed in forthcoming elections for its pro-U.S. policy on the war. ETA denied responsibility, however, and mounting evidence pointed to Islamic terrorists linked to al-Qaeda, whose military spokesman in Europe **Mar. 13** said the bombings were in retribution for Spain's joining the U.S.-led coalition. By **Mar. 31**, 23 people had been arrested, as the investigation focused on a Moroccan Islamic extremist group.

The Socialist Workers Party scored an upset victory in Spain's parliamentary elections **Mar. 14**. The results ended 8 years in power for the Popular Party (PP) led by Aznar. The Socialists won 164 of 350 seats in Parliament to 148 for the PP, which had been leading in polls up until **Mar. 11** The incoming premier, Jose Luis Rodriguez Zapatero, had pledged to withdraw the 1,300 Spanish troops stationed in Iraq unless conduct of the occupation were to be turned over to the UN. Polls showed that most Spaniards opposed the war. Zapatero **Mar. 15** called the war and the postwar occupation "a disaster," and on **Mar. 17** he indicated he favored the Sen. John Kerry (MA) for U.S. president.

Putin Easily Reelected in Russia—Pres. Vladimir Putin **Mar. 14** won reelection as president of Russia, with 70% of the vote. The result had not been in doubt, and in fact Putin had announced his 2nd-term cabinet before the election. A Communist Party candidate got about 15%. Recent moves by Putin had left him with effectively no political opposition. International election monitors **Mar. 15** criticized heavy media bias in his favor and instances of irregularities.

Pakistan's Army Pursues "High-Value Target"—On **Mar. 16**, 7,000 Pakistani military forces began attacking some 500 enemy fighters in a rugged region near the Afghan border. The area was thought to be a bastion of support for the former Taliban regime in Afghanistan and for al-Qaeda. Pres. Pervez Musharraf said **Mar. 18** that the defenders, whose nationality was not clear, were fighting ferociously because they were guarding a "high-value target." No such top figure was found, but tunnels were discovered that might have provided an escape route.

Taiwan's President Reelected—Taiwan's Pres. Chen Shui-bian was re-elected **Mar. 20**, according to official returns, with about 50% of the vote. A referendum on calling for Taiwan to obtain antimissile systems if China did not withdraw missiles aimed toward it failed to attract sufficient support. The opposition Nationalist Party charged fraud in the presidential vote, and some called for a recount, but on **May 28**, after talks between political parties, such demands were dropped. On **Mar. 19**, the day before the election, both Chen and Vice Pres. Annette Lu were slightly wounded by gunshots while riding in an open vehicle in a motorcade.

Israelis Kill a Top Terrorist Leader—Sheikh Ahmed Yassin, founder and spiritual leader of the militant Palestinian organization Hamas, was killed by an Israeli missile **Mar. 22** as he left a mosque in Gaza City; 7 other Palestinians were also killed. Prime Min. Ariel Sharon said Yassin was the foremost terrorist leader responsible for bombings in Israel and the occupied territories; Palestinians took to the streets in Gaza and the West Bank to mourn Yassin and call for revenge. The next day, Hamas named Abdel Aziz Rantisi as a new leader. The U.S. expressed reservations about the killing of Yassin but on **Mar. 25** vetoed a UN resolution

condemning Israel for the assassination. On **Mar. 7**, 14 Palestinians were killed when Israeli troops attacked 2 Palestinian refugee camps in Gaza in a search for weapons.

Violence Claims Lives in Uzbekistan—More than 40 people were reportedly killed in a series of bombings and gun battles, **Mar. 28-31** in the central Asian nation of Uzbekistan. The attacks, including a suicide bombing in a bazaar, an assault on a police station, and an explosion at a bomb assembly factory, were blamed by the government on terrorists linked to al-Qaeda. Uzbekistan, a heavily Muslim country where militancy has been on the rise, allied itself with the U.S. in battling terrorism; at the same time, the government has been accused of using repressive measures against dissidents.

OPEC Cuts Production—OPEC ministers meeting **Mar. 31** in Vienna agreed to implement planned production cuts, ignoring concerns in some countries about crude oil prices, which were near their highest level in 13 years. Cuts totaling 1 million barrels a day were to begin April 1. As high gasoline prices continued to be a campaign issue in the U.S., Pres. Bush expressed disappointment but did not directly criticize the OPEC decision.

World Court Rules U.S. Should Review Death Sentences—The International Court of Justice, in The Hague, the Netherlands, ruled **Mar. 31** that U.S. courts must reexamine the death sentences imposed on 51 Mexicans who had been refused the right to speak with Mexican consular officials after being arrested. U.S. authorities were studying the ruling; it was unclear whether they would comply. The case was brought by Mexico, which also had sought, unsuccessfully, to have the World Court annul the sentences.

General

Government Warns of Obesity Dangers—Obesity could soon become the leading cause of preventable deaths in the U.S., according to a government report issued **Mar. 9**. The Centers for Disease Control estimated that in 2000 435,000 Americans died from smoking-related causes while a poor diet and failure to exercise claimed some 400,000 lives. The CDC reported **Mar. 5** that from 1971 to 2000 American women increased their caloric intake by 22%, while men increased their consumption by 7%.

Distant "Planetoid" Discovered Circling the Sun—Astronomers announced **Mar. 15** that an object with a diameter of 800 to 1,100 miles was circling the Sun far beyond the orbit of any known planet. Michael Brown of the California Institute of Technology called it a planetoid. The object, the farthest object ever seen circling the Sun, was smaller than any of the known planets. Officially named 2003 VB12, it was first discovered Nov. 14, 2003 at Cal Tech's Palomar Observatory and unofficially named Sedna after an Inuit goddess of the sea. Brown said it probably consisted of rock and ice. It was now 8 billion miles from Earth, but its elongated orbit takes it to a maximum distance of 84 billion miles. It takes 10,500 Earth years to make a complete revolution around the Sun.

APRIL 2004

National

308,000 New Jobs Added to Economy—The U.S. employment picture brightened in March, when 308,000 nonfarm jobs were created, according to data released **Apr. 2**. The unemployment rate stood at 5.7% in March, unchanged from February.

Corporate Fraud Case Ends in Mistrial—The prosecution of 2 top Tyco International executives ended in a mistrial **Apr. 2**. In a high-profile case, the 2 defendants, former CEO Dennis Kozlowski and former CFO Mark Swartz, were accused of defrauding the company of $600 million. In declaring a mistrial on the 12th day of jury deliberation, New York State Supreme Court Justice Michael Obus cited outside pressure on the jury, which had been seeking to reach verdicts on 32 separate counts, in a long trial that had begun in Sept. 2003. Efforts to reach agreement were reportedly complicated by one holdout juror sympathetic to the defense, whose name was publicized in the media.

Kerry Proposes Partial Tax Cut Repeal—Sen. John Kerry (MA), the prospective Democratic presidential nominee, declared in a speech **Apr. 7** that he would reduce the federal budget deficit by repealing the Bush tax cut for persons earning more than $200,000. He restated a proposal to reduce corporate taxes and said he would not seek to cut spending on national security, education, Social Security, or Medicare. Kerry noted that under the Bush administration the budget had gone from a $236 bil surplus in 2000 to a projected deficit approaching $500 bil in 2004.

Rice Testifies on Terror Attacks—Condoleezza Rice, the national security adviser, testified **Apr. 8** before the commission investigating the Sept. 11, 2001, terror attacks. She said that on Sept. 4, 2001, the administration had approved a plan to "eliminate" al-Qaeda. Rice was questioned closely about a briefing titled "Bin Laden Determined to Strike in U.S.", that went to Pres. George W. Bush on Aug. 6, 2001; it included an unconfirmed report that hijackers planned to seize a plane in order to demand release of prisoners held in connection with the 1993 World Trade Center bombing. Rice said the briefing contained mostly "historical information" and did not explicitly warn of attacks inside the U.S.

Atty. Gen. John Ashcroft, testifying **Apr. 13**, blamed pre-9/11 intelligence lapses on a legal "wall" that had been erected between the CIA, in intelligence-gathering, and the FBI, in criminal investigation. Testifying **Apr. 14**, CIA Director George Tenet said it would take 5 years for the CIA to become "the kind of clandestine service our country needs."

Bush Defends Iraq Policy at News Conference—For only the 3rd time, Pres. Bush held a prime-time news conference, **Apr. 13**. In a statement on Iraq, he said the U.S. would hold to its commitment to turn over sovereignty to an Iraqi government on June 30 and would use "decisive force" as needed to protect troops. Pressed to name any mistakes he had made in Iraq, Bush said that he would make no apologies and could not cite any specific mistakes. Referring to the Aug. 6, 2001, briefing prior to 9/11, he said he would have acted had the warnings been more specific.

> *"Now is the time and Iraq is the place in which the enemies of the civilized world are testing the will of the civilized world."*
> *Pres. George W. Bush,* at a White House press conference, Apr. 13.

Bush, Cheney Speak to 9-11 Panel—Pres. Bush and Vice Pres. Dick Cheney were questioned in the Oval Office for 3 hours, **Apr. 29**, by members of the commission investigating the Sept. 11 attacks. In the session, described by the president as "cordial," Bush and Cheney reportedly indicated that warnings prior to 9-11 had suggested that al-Qaeda was preparing to strike overseas. Bush and Cheney were not under oath and the meeting was not recorded electronically.

Names and Photos of Fallen U.S. Soldiers Shown on *Nightline*—The names and photos of the more than 700 U.S solders who died in Iraq since the beginning of the U.S.-led invasion were shown in an extended broadcast of ABC-TV's *Nightline*, **Apr. 30**. Some supporters of the U.S. intervention criticized the program as polemical, and one broadcast group barred airing of the program on its TV affiliates, a decision which itself drew protests. Anchor Ted Koppel said the broadcast was intended to honor the war dead and illustrate the cost of the war.

International

7 Countries Join NATO—A ceremony in Brussels, Belgium, **Apr. 2** marked the formal entry of 7 more nations into NATO. The new members included 3 former Soviet republics (Estonia, Latvia, Lithuania), a former Yugoslav republic (Slovenia), and 3 former Warsaw Pact members (Bulgaria, Romania, and Slovakia).

Terror Suspects Kill Themselves in Madrid—Four suspects in the March terror bombings in Madrid killed themselves with a bomb **Apr. 3** after police surrounded their apartment building in a suburb of the Spanish capital. Police had evacuated nearby tenants and engaged in a 2-hour gun battle before the suspects detonated the bomb. One of the dead men, a Tunisian named Sarhane Ben Abdelmajid Fakhet, was thought to be the ringleader in the Mar. 11 train bombings that had claimed 191 lives and wounded 1,400.

The apartment-house bombing killed one police officer and wounded 12. Currently, 15 suspects were in jail in connection with the terror attacks.

Insurgents in Iraqi Cities Rise Up Against Coalition—April proved to be the bloodiest month in Iraq since U.S.-led forces first entered Iraq in March 2003. Insurgents occupied parts of cities, and the ensuing urban warfare took a growing toll. A total of 127 U.S. military personnel were killed in action. The upsurge followed the arrest **Apr. 3** of an aide to radical Shiite cleric Moqtada al-Sadr as a suspect in the 2003 assassination of a Shiite leader, Ayatollah Abdel Majid al-Khoei.

Shiites demonstrating in Kufa **Apr. 4** against the arrest fought coalition forces from the U.S., Spain, and El Salvador. In the first coordinated hostile action by Shiites since the invasion of Iraq, they seized police stations and other sites in Baghdad, Najaf, Kufa, and Amara. Some U.S.-trained Iraqi police fled without offering resistance. Seven U.S. soldiers were killed in the Sadr City district of Baghdad **Apr. 4**.

On **Apr. 5**, Marines and Iraqi army troops surrounded and entered Fallujah, a hotbed of support for the former regime, to try to put down unrest there. By **Apr. 6** unrest had spread visibly to other cities, with Sunni and Shiite Muslims, longtime antagonists, sometimes fighting side by side. Sadr militiamen fought Italian troops in Nasiriyah **Apr. 6**. Twelve U.S. marines were killed that day during an attack on their base outside Baghdad. On **Apr. 7**, U.S. aircraft struck a mosque complex in Fallujah with a rocket and a bomb. Sadr's militia occupied Kut after Ukrainian troops pulled back. Kazakhstan said **Apr. 7** that it would pull out its 30 troops in May.

Although U.S. troops surrounded Najaf, Sadr **Apr. 16** refused to dissolve his militia. U.S. and Iraqi authorities **Apr. 19** reached a tenuous agreement suspending hostilities in Fallujah, while calling for insurgents to turn in heavy weapons in exchange for amnesty. A series of coordinated car bombings at police buildings in Basra, **Apr. 21**, killed more than 50, including about 20 schoolchildren. On **Apr. 23-24**, U.S. Marines killed about 30 insurgents in a firefight outside Fallujah. On **Apr. 29**, U.S. troops began pulling back from some positions, under an agreement handing control to an Iraqi general, with plans for Iraqi patrols of the city. The same day, 8 U.S. soldiers were killed by car bomb in a Baghdad suburb.

Over 40 foreigners were abducted by militants. Among them, 3 Japanese civilians were kidnapped **Apr. 8**; their captors threatened to kill them if 550 Japanese troops were not withdrawn from Iraq, but they were released **Apr. 15**, with the demand unmet. A U.S. employee of the Halliburton Corp. was kidnapped **Apr. 9** (he escaped from his captors May 2); Halliburton said **Apr. 12** that 6 other employees were missing. On **Apr. 12**, 11 employees of a Russian company were reported abducted, and 3 Czechs missing. Seven Chinese were freed **Apr. 12** after a day of captivity. On **Apr. 14** a militant group reported having killed one of 4 Italian men it had seized the day before.

Prime Min. Jose Luis Rodriguez Zapatero of Spain, a day after beginning his term, said **Apr. 18** that Spain's troops would be pulled out of Iraq as soon as possible. The next day, Honduras and the Dominican Republic announced that their small troop contingents would also be pulled out.

According to a *New York Times* story **Apr. 29**, a report by the Defense Intelligence Agency concluded, based on interviews with captives, that many of the bombings and guerrilla attacks were being coordinated by member of Saddam Hussein's secret service, who had been planning the insurgency even before the fall of Baghdad.

Photographs showing Iraqi prisoners forced into humiliating positions by gleeful American soldiers were circulated in newspapers and TV broadcasts around the globe beginning **Apr. 30**, provoking outrage, especially in the Arab world. Pres. Bush expressed "deep disgust" over the abuse and said an investigation was under way. (See further developments in May.)

Bush Backs Israeli Policy on Settlements—Pres. George W. Bush **Apr. 14,** after meeting in Washington, DC, with Israeli Prime Min. Ariel Sharon, expressed support for Sharon's proposal to withdraw Israeli settlements from Gaza. In a departure from past policy, he also supported Is-

rael's intention to retain major West Bank settlements as part of a final agreement with the Palestinians and endorsed the Israeli position that Palestinians who in 1948-49 had fled their homes did not have a right of return. U.S. policy had been to withhold positions on these issues.

On **Apr. 17**, Israeli forces assassinated Abdul Aziz al-Rantisi, new leader of the militant Hamas organization; he had led Hamas for less than a month after his predecessor's assassination. Rantisi, with 2 of his bodyguards, was killed in Gaza when missiles fired from an Israeli helicopter gunship struck their car. A White House statement advised Israel to weigh its actions carefully but did not condemn the attack, stating that Israel had the right to defend itself. On **Apr. 19**, King Abdullah of Jordan postponed a meeting with Bush, indicating displeasure with the president's statements with Sharon.

Oil-for-Food Probe Launched—UN Sec.-Gen. Kofi Annan named former U.S. Fed chairman Paul Volcker to head a 3-person committee to probe charges of corruption on the part of the Hussein regime and UN officials in the oil-for-food program, that had allowed the Iraqi government, under UN supervision, to sell oil and use the revenues to purchase needed civilian goods between 1997 and 2002. UN administrators, including Undersec. Benon Sevan, have been accused of taking large kickbacks in administering the program, and the U.S. General Accounting Office, **Apr. 17**, estimated that the Hussein regime had garnered more than $4 bil in cash through illegal kickbacks from customers and more than $5 bil by illegally selling oil outside the program.

Plans for Iraqi Caretaker Government Proceed—Plans for the formation of a temporary Iraqi government moved ahead. The UN envoy in Iraq, Lakhdar Brahimi, said **Apr. 14** that the country would be led by a president, prime minister, and 2 vice presidents. Pres. Bush **Apr. 19** named John Negroponte, U.S. ambassador to the UN, as ambassador to Iraq.

Al-Qaeda Offers Truce to Europe—A taped message purportedly from terrorist leader Osama bin Laden, broadcast **Apr. 14**, offered a "reconciliation initiative" to European countries that pulled troops out of the Muslim countries and abandoned alleged aggression joined to "the American plot against the big Muslim world." European nations in quick succession rejected any such agreement.

Bomber Strikes in Saudi Capital—A suicide bomber killed 4 others and himself, and injured about 150, when he detonated a bomb in his car in Riyadh, Saudi Arabia, **Apr. 21**. Six police officers had been killed in clashes with militants during the preceding 10 days.

Ex-NFL Player Killed in Afghanistan—Pat Tillman, who gave up a successful pro football career to join the U.S. Army Rangers, was killed in Afghanistan **Apr. 22**. Tillman, a safety with the Arizona Cardinals, had turned down a $3.6 million contract to enlist, saying it was his duty in the wake of the 9/11 terror bombings. He was killed while on patrol near the Pakistani border.

Violence in Southern Thailand Leaves Over 100 Dead—In the worst such incident in years, about 100 people were killed **Apr. 28** when armed insurgents stormed over a dozen police stations in southern Thailand; among the dead were about 30 killed in a police raid on a mosque near Pattani, reportedly used as cover by Muslim attackers. No group initially claimed responsibility. See further developments in May.

General

Connecticut Wins Both Men's and Women's Hoop Titles—For the first time, one school, the University of Connecticut, captured the men's and women's Division I collegiate basketball titles in the same year. The men's team (33-6) prevailed over Georgia Tech, 82-73, in the final game in San Antonio, TX, **Apr. 5**. Emeka Okafor scored 24 points and had 15 rebounds for the winners; he was named outstanding player of the Final 4. The Connecticut women (31-4) won the national title for the 5th time (all with coach Gene Auriemma), defeating Tennessee, 70-61, in New Orleans **Apr. 6**.

Train Explosion Takes Heavy Toll in North Korea—More than 160 people were killed, many of them schoolchildren, and more than 1,000 injured in a train explosion in North Korea **Apr. 22**, at a station near Ryongchon, not far

from the Chinese border. China, South Korea, and the U.S. provided relief aid, but North Korean officials Apr. 26 rejected a request from South Korea to let supplies be sent by truck across the demilitarized zone dividing the two nations.

Former Nets Star Acquitted of Serious Charges in Killing—After a 15-week trial a jury in Somerville, NJ, **Apr. 30** found former New Jersey Nets star Jayson Williams not guilty of aggravated manslaughter and two other serious charges in the Feb. 2002 shooting death of a chauffeur at his mansion. He was found guilty of covering up the incident, however, and the jury failed to reach a verdict on a charge of reckless manslaughter.

MAY 2004

National

Presidential Race Heated, With 6 Months to Go—Although the presidential election still lay 6 months in the future, campaigning in May was in high gear. With polls showing his job-approval ratings falling below 50%, Pres. George W. Bush began a bus tour of closely contested states. He spoke in several Michigan cities **May 3** and in Ohio cities **May 4**, referring to Kerry as inconsistent and weak on issues of national security. Resuming his tour **May 7**, he visited Iowa and Wisconsin. Sen. John Kerry (MA), the prospective Democratic nominee, in a Los Angeles speech **May 5**, called Bush's response to the Iraqi prison abuse scandal "slow and inappropriate." Citing the Iraqi prisoner abuse scandal and what he called "miscalculation" in prosecuting the war, Kerry called for, **May 6**, Sec. of Defense Donald Rumsfeld to resign. Both candidates were raising and spending record sums of money, mostly on TV ads.

Gas Price Tops $2 per Gallon at the Pump—Auto gas prices climbed sharply as the summer travel season approached. On **May 7**, oil prices hit a 13-year high of $40 a barrel on the New York Mercantile Exchange. The average nationwide price of gasoline reached $2 a gallon by mid-May and kept climbing. The Saudi oil minister asked other OPEC members **May 23** to increase oil production ceilings. (Members agreed June 3 to raise production quotas by 2 million barrels effective July 1.)

Gays Marry Legally in Massachusetts—For the first time in the U.S., on **May 17**, a state—Massachusetts—issued marriage licenses to same-sex couples. The state acted pursuant to court orders that it could not deny such licenses. Within days, thousands of couples, including some from other states, obtained licenses in Massachusetts.

9/11 Commission Faults New York Rescue Effort—The staff of the commission investigating the Sept. 11, 2001, terror attacks issued a report **May 18** that criticized aspects of the response and rescue effort to save lives. The report found that rivalry between New York City's police and fire departments had caused a breakdown of coordination and communication. It criticized the Port Authority of New York and New Jersey, which operated the 2 towers of the World Trade Center, for not having conducted evacuation drills and for not telling occupants that the doors to the roof were locked. The commission held hearings in the city **May 18-19**. Former Mayor Rudy Giuliani acknowledged **May 19** that "some terrible mistakes" had been made but he defended the overall response.

Major New Al-Qaeda Attack Feared in U.S.—Atty. Gen. John Ashcroft said **May 26** that the terrorist organization al-Qaeda was determined to launch another attack within the next few months, and was "almost ready" to do so. The existing intelligence, based on a high level of intercepted "chatter," reportedly did not suggest any specific target or method, but major-party political conventions in New York and Boston were thought to be among possible likely targets. Ashcroft also released photos of 7 people being sought as suspected al-Qaeda operatives.

Nichols Convicted, but Spared the Death Penalty—Terry Nichols, already serving a life term after a federal conviction in the 1995 terror bombing in Oklahoma City, was found guilty of 161 murders in a state court **May 26**. (Timothy McVeigh, apparently the chief architect of the crime, had been executed June 11, 2001). Prosecutors contended

that Nichols bought the ammonium nitrate fertilizer used in the bombing. The jury needed only 5 hours to reach a verdict on the charges—but deadlocked subsequently on a sentence, which meant Nichols again escaped the death penalty.

Court Upholds Oregon Assisted Suicide Law—A federal appeals court in San Francisco upheld the only assisted suicide law in the U.S. A 3-judge panel **May 26** upheld the Oregon "death with dignity" law in a split vote, concluding that the state had the right to decide this issue and criticizing Attorney Gen. John Ashcroft for seeking to block the law's enforcement. The measure allows incurably ill adults expected to die within 6 months to obtain lethal drugs from doctors.

World War II Memorial Dedicated—The World War II Memorial was dedicated **May 29** on the National Mall in Washington, DC. Some 70,000 elderly veterans of that epic conflict were among more than 100,000 persons attending the event, held on Memorial Day weekend. Only about 4 mil of the 16 mil who served in the war were still alive. Pres. Bush spoke at the dedication; also present were former presidents George H. W. Bush, a decorated World War II Navy pilot, and Bill Clinton. Former Sen. Robert Dole (R, KS), seriously wounded in the war, led the fund-raising effort for the 7.4-acre memorial, which cost $175 mil.

International

10 Countries Join EU—The European Union grew to 25 countries **May 1** with the admission of 10 new members. The growth was mostly in Eastern Europe, with the addition of Estonia, Latvia, Lithuania, Poland, Czech Republic, Slovakia, Hungary, and Slovenia. Two Mediterranean nations, Malta and Cyprus, also joined. The addition of several former Soviet bloc nations symbolically ended the "Iron Curtain" era that had divided Europe into 2 rival alliances.

Arab-Israeli Violence Continues—On **May 2**, 2 Palestinian gunmen were killed after they shot and killed a pregnant mother and her 4 daughters in Gaza. A bomb and a grenade, **May 11** and **13**, destroyed 2 armored personnel vehicles and killed 11 Israeli soldiers; at least 20 Palestinians died in fighting in connection with those incidents. On **May 13**, an Israeli helicopter fired into a refugee camp, killing 7 Palestinians. Israel **May 18** launched an offensive in the Rafah area, with about 40 Palestinians reported dead by the time the Israelis made a partial withdrawal on **May 21**. The UN Security Council **May 19**, 14-0, condemned the killing of civilians and urged Israel to stop destroying Palestinian homes. The U.S., which usually vetoes resolutions critical of Israel, abstained.

Nigerian Christians Massacre Muslims—Christian militants in Nigeria attacked the Muslim town of Yelwa on **May 2** and killed residents with firearms and machetes. The Nigerian Red Cross said **May 6** that 630 had died. On **May 18**, after rioting broke out, Pres. Olusegun Obasanjo declared a state of emergency.

Iraqi Prison Abuse Scandal Widens—The abuse of Iraqi prisoners by U.S. soldiers became a major scandal in **May** and the subject of several investigations. On **May 3**, Lt. Gen. Ricardo Sanchez, U.S. military commander in Iraq, reprimanded 6 commissioned and noncommissioned officers who supervised the prison at Abu Ghraib, in Baghdad, where many abuses occurred. A Mar. 9 classified report by Maj. Gen. Antonio Taguba, made public by the media **May 5**, said that "illegal abuse of detainees was intentionally perpetrated by several members" of the Army's 372nd Military Police Co. and 315th Military Intelligence Battalion. Abuses included punching and kicking detainees, keeping them naked for days, using unmuzzled dogs to menace them, and forcing them into sexually explicit positions for photographing. In interviews with Arab media outlets, Pres. George W. Bush deplored the mistreatment.

The International Committee of the Red Cross **May 6** said it had found widespread evidence of mistreatment of Iraqi prisoners in prisons across Iraq by coalition forces. On **May 7**, Pfc. Lynndie England of the 372nd MP Co. was charged in with mistreatment. She appeared in several published photographs, including one where she held a leash around the neck of a naked prisoner.

Sec. of Defense Donald Rumsfeld came under heavy fire testifying before congressional committees **May 7**, and there were calls for his resignation. Gen. Taguba told a Senate committee **May 11** that the abuses could be attributed to a failure of leadership from the brigade commander on down, and to a lack of discipline, training, and supervision. On **May 13** Sanchez issued guidelines barring certain forms of pressure, including sleep deprivation and the use of "stress positions." Testifying before the Senate committee **May 19**, Sanchez and Gen. John Abizaid, U.S. commander in the Middle East, accepted responsibility for misconduct by U.S. forces. On **May 24**, Pentagon officials said Sanchez would be replaced by a higher-ranking officer, but denied a connection to the prisoner abuse reports. A **May 5** Army report that came to light **May 25** said that U.S. mistreatment of prisoners in Iraq and Afghanistan was more widespread than previously known.

Spec. Jeremy Sivits pleaded guilty at a court-martial trial in Baghdad **May 19** to maltreating prisoners and dereliction of duty; his testimony also implicated others. He was given a bad conduct discharge and sentenced to a year in prison.

> *"That's not the way we do things in America."*
> *Pres. Bush,* May 10, commenting on photos showing U.S. soldiers abusing prisoners in Iraq.

U.S.-led Coalition Struggles to Assert Control; Interim Government Takes Shape—As the end-of-June deadline neared for the handover of control to an interim Iraqi government, the U.S.-led military coalition sought to dampen resistance without stirring up increased animosity. U.S. forces **May 6** seized the governor's office in Najaf, a stronghold of radical Shiite cleric Moktada al-Sadr, and installed a new Iraqi governor, as violence there continued. The U.S. military said **May 10** that it had destroyed al-Sadr's headquarters in Baghdad and killed about 16 of his followers. Meanwhile, on **May 10** U.S. forces and an Iraqi brigade jointly entered areas of the volatile city of Fallujah, where a cease-fire continued in place.

A videotape shown on the Internet **May 11** depicted the brutal beheading of Nick Berg, an American businessman imprisoned by Iraqi militants. He was decapitated by one of 5 masked men guarding him, identified on the screen as al-Qaeda leader Abu Musab al-Zarqawi, who read a statement linking the murder to abuses at Abu Ghraib. Berg's body was found near Baghdad **May 8**. Earlier, on **May 2**, in contrasting news, Thomas Hamill, an American civilian employee of a subsidiary of the Halliburton Co., had managed to safely flee his rebel guards after 3 weeks in captivity.

On **May 17**, the president of the Iraqi Governing Council, Ezzedine Salim, was assassinated in Baghdad by a suicide bomber; 6 others also died. At least 40 persons were killed **May 19** when U.S. forces attacked a gathering in Iraq's western desert. Survivors claimed the victims were part of a wedding party where there was ceremonial gunfire; the U.S. military disputed this claim.

Iraqi police and some Americans **May 20** raided the Baghdad home and headquarters of Ahmad Chalabi, a member of the Iraqi Governing Council. An exile for 4 decades before his 2003 return, Chalabi headed the Iraqi National Congress and had enjoyed great influence in the Bush administration. An INC official said **May 17** that the administration was now cutting off subsidies. Critics said Chalabi was the source of unreliable information about weapons of mass destruction; there also were reports that Chalabi had passed U.S. secrets to Iran, which he denied.

On **May 20**, U.S. troops pulled out of central Karbala, scene of intense fighting for over a week. In an overnight attack **May 22-23**, U.S. forces killed 36 enemy fighters around a mosque in the southern city of Kufa. On **May 27**, after a 7-week battle, U.S. forces, under a pact negotiated by Iraqi leaders, agreed to pull out from most positions in Najaf and nearby Kufa, in return for a cease-fire by Shiite militants loyal to the cleric al-Sadr. The agreement appeared to leave the radical forces there intact, though it called for those from other cities to leave. Iraqi officials also agreed to suspend an arrest warrant against al-Sadr for the murder of a rival cleric.

In a **May 24** speech, Pres. Bush outlined a general plan for transferring civilian authority to Iraqis by June 30 and helping to establish security, rebuild the infrastructure, promote international support, and move toward national elections in early 2005. He said, "I sent American troops to Iraq to make its people free, not to stay as an occupying power. Iraqis will write their own history, and find their own way."

On **May 28** the interim Iraqi government began to take shape with the unanimous approval by the Iraqi Governing Council of Iyad Alawi as prime minister. A prominent secular-minded Shiite and anti-Saddam exile reportedly having ties to the CIA, he was regarded as a compromise candidate.

Bomb Kills President of Chechnya—Pres. Akhmad Kadyrov of Chechnya was assassinated **May 9** when a bomb exploded near him in a stadium in Grozny, the rebellious republic's capital. Kadynov had been attending a celebration of the anniversary of the victory over Nazi Germany. The explosion killed 6 others and wounded about 50.

Sonia Gandhi Declines Prime Minister Post; a Sikh Succeeds to It—Sonia Gandhi, a member by marriage of the family that dominated Indian politics for 3 generations, declined **May 18** to accept office as prime minister. Her Indian National Congress party had won an upset victory in 4 rounds of parliamentary voting ending **May 10**. Congress Party members who have served as prime minister include Jawaharlal Nehru; his daughter, Indira Gandhi; and her son, Rajiv Gandhi. The latter 2 were both assassinated. Sonia, Rajiv's widow, had wide though not unanimous support within the party; she was a political neophyte.

The incumbent prime minister, Atal Bihari Vajpayee, had conceded **May 13** that his Bharatiya Janata Party lost the election. Pres. A.P.J. Abdul Kalam accepted his resignation, asking him to stay on until a new prime minister stepped in. On **May 19**, former Finance Min. Manmohan Singh was elected leader of the Congress party, and Kalam then named him prime minister. A Sikh, Singh was the first non-Hindu to lead an independent India. He was sworn in **May 22**.

Sonia's son Rahul Gandhi was elected to Parliament in his first bid for public office.

Gunmen Kill 22 in Saudi Arabia—Four armed militants scaled a fence and attacked a residential compound in Khobar, Saudi Arabia, **May 29**. They killed 22 and wounded 25, mostly workers in the oil industry from a number of countries. One American was killed. One gunman was wounded and captured, but the 3 others escaped.

General

Unbeaten Horse Wins Kentucky Derby, Preakness—For the first time since 1977, an unbeaten thoroughbred won both the Kentucky Derby and Preakness, the first two "jewels" in the Triple Crown of horse-racing. On **May 1**, in Louisville, Smarty Jones, who had won his previous 6 races, pulled away in the stretch on a sloppy track to win the Derby in 2 minutes, 4.06 seconds. He then won the Preakness Stakes in Baltimore **May 15** by a record margin of 11 1/2 lengths, in 1 minute, 55.59 seconds. (However, the highly favored Smarty Jones failed to win the Triple Crown when he took 2nd place in the Belmont Stakes in Elmont, NY, **June 5**, beaten in a last-minute surge by the winner, Birdstone.)

Randy Johnson Throws Perfect Game—Randy Johnson, veteran star pitcher for the Arizona Diamondbacks, pitched a perfect game **May 18** as his team defeated the Atlanta Braves, 2-0, in Atlanta. Johnson, 40, was the oldest of 17 pitchers in the history of Major League Baseball to achieve that honor. The left-hander had also tossed a no-hitter (but not a perfect game) for Seattle in 1990.

Top Qualifier Wins 500-Mile Auto Race—Buddy Rice, who had won the pole position as the fastest qualifier for the Indianapolis 500-Mile Race, drove to victory in the race itself **May 30**. The contest was cut to 180 laps from the usual 200 because of rain. Tony Kaanan, the 2nd-place finisher, was within 2 car lengths of Rice when the race was stopped. The co-owners of Rice's car were Bobby Rahal, the winning driver in 1986, and TV talk-show host David Letterman, who grew up in Indianapolis.

JUNE 2004
National

Democrats Pick Up House Seat in South Dakota—On **June 1**, for the 2nd time in 2004, the Democrats gained a seat in a U.S. House election to fill a vacancy. Stephanie Herseth, a lawyer, narrowly defeated Larry Diedrich, a former state legislator. Republicans now held 228 House seats and Democrats 206, with one independent.

Bush, Cheney Questioned in CIA Agent Leak Case—Federal prosecutors interviewed Pres. George W. Bush and Vice Pres. Richard Cheney about who may have leaked to columnist Robert Novak the name of a covert CIA agent. The agent was the wife of Joseph Wilson, a former ambassador, who had disputed an administration claim on Iraq's attempt to obtain uranium. The White House, **June 2**, confirmed that Bush had consulted a private attorney, whom he later retained, in connection with the investigation. Cheney was interviewed prior to **June 5**; prosecutors questioned Pres. Bush at the White House **June 24**.

CIA Director Resigns—Pres. Bush announced **June 3** that he had accepted the resignation, effective July 11, of George Tenet as director of Central Intelligence. Addressing CIA employees, Tenet said he wanted to spend more time with his family. He had served 7 years, a relatively long tenure, and had been credited with reforms, but had been strongly criticized for the agency's handling of the terrorist threat. He had also assured Bush, prior to the U.S. invasion, that Iraq had weapons of mass destruction. Tenet's deputy, John McLaughlin, was to serve as DCI pending a permanent replacement.

Ronald Reagan, 40th President, Dies at 93—Ronald Wilson Reagan, 40th president of the U.S., died at his home in Los Angeles **June 5**. He had been diagnosed with Alzheimer's disease in 1994 and had rarely been seen in public since then. With him at his death was his wife of 52 years, Nancy, and other family members.

More than 100,000 mourners filed past Reagan's coffin at his presidential library in Simi Valley, CA, before it was flown to Washington, DC, for a state funeral, **June 9**. In the capital, the coffin was transported by a horse-drawn caisson through the streets from near the White House to the U.S. Capitol. There, Reagan was eulogized by Vice Pres. Cheney. During the next 36 hours, tens of thousands filed past the coffin.

Another service was held at the National Cathedral in Washington **June 11**. Pres. George W. Bush and all 4 living former presidents were present. Both Pres. Bush and former Canadian Prime Min. Brian Mulroney gave eulogies. Former Prime Min. Margaret Thatcher of Britain was present, but her eulogy was delivered by videotape because she was not well enough to give it in person. Former Soviet leader Mikhail Gorbachev, former Pres. Lech Walesa of Poland, Prime Min. Tony Blair of Britain, and Chancellor Gerhard Schroeder of Germany were among other dignitaries present.

The Reagan family then returned to California, where the former president was laid to rest at his library at sunset, with eulogies by his 3 surviving children.

> "Ronald Reagan belongs to the ages now, but we preferred it when he belonged to us"
>
> Pres. Bush, June 11, in his eulogy for Reagan at the National Cathedral in Washington, DC, June 21.

9/11 Commission Staff Finds No Iraqi Link—The commission investigating the Sept. 11, 2001, terror attacks completed public hearings **June 16-17** and issued 3 preliminary staff reports. These reported finding "no credible evidence" that Iraq had cooperated with al-Qaeda in carrying out the attacks on the U.S. Iraq and al-Qaeda had reportedly been in contact, but the commission concluded there had been no "collaborative relationship." The commission said it did not believe reports that the lead hijacker, Mohamed Atta, had met with a senior Iraqi intelligence official in Prague, Czech Republic, in April 2001.

On the basis of interrogation of captured al-Qaeda leader Khalid Sheikh Mohammed, the commission concluded that he had promoted the idea of using airplanes against the U.S. as early as 1996. Terror mastermind Osama bin Laden reportedly decided to go forward with this idea in 1999, with

the date finally chosen only about 3 weeks beforehand. The staff concluded that the North American Aerospace Defense Command (NORAD) and the Federal Aviation Administration were unprepared for the attacks. It said that Vice Pres. Cheney had authorized Air Force fighters to shoot down hijacked airliners, but that it was not clear whether he had the approval of Pres. Bush. The 2 had difficulty communicating at first.

The commission concluded that the government of Saudi Arabia had not directly financed al-Qaeda, although the terror organization did raise a substantial amount of Saudi money. The commission estimated that the Sept. 2001 attacks cost $400,000 to $500,000.

Pres. Vladimir Putin of Russia said **June 18** that after the 2001 attacks Russia had given U.S. intelligence evidence that Iraq was planning attacks against the U.S.

Scandals Send 2 Political Leaders to Sidelines—Gov. John Rowland (R, CT) resigned **June 21**, effective July 1. He admitted that he had accepted free work on a vacation cottage from contractors who worked for the state and that his aides had paid for some of the work. A state House committee was drafting an impeachment article charging Rowland with obstructing its investigation. Witnesses told the committee that he had received expensive gifts and favors from contractors and aides. Lt. Gov. M. Jodi Rell (R) succeeded Rowland.

Jack Ryan, an investment banker who was the GOP nominee for the U.S. Senate in Illinois, withdrew as a candidate **June 25** after court papers showed that his ex-wife, TV actress Jeri Ryan, alleged he had taken her to sex clubs.

Clinton's Book and Moore's Documentary Enter the Political Arena—The presidential contest between Pres. Bush and Sen. John Kerry (MA), the prospective Democratic nominee, remained close, according to public opinion polls. The 2 campaigns were raising and spending record amounts of money, mostly on TV ads. A third contender, consumer advocate Ralph Nader, spent much of his time seeking ballot access in as many states as possible.

For a time in June the Kerry campaign appeared overshadowed by the publication of *My Life,* the autobiography of former Pres. Bill Clinton, a popular Democratic icon. Published **June 22** by Knopf, the title immediately rose to the top on best-seller lists.

Fahrenheit 9/11, the latest documentary film by Michael Moore, opened nationally on **June 25**. A biting anti-Bush polemic which focused on the invasion of Iraq, the film drew largely favorable reviews, though some found fault with it for exaggerations or factual errors. It broke box-office records for a documentary during its first few days.

Earlier, on **June 16**, a group of 26 retired top military officers, ambassadors, and other officials issued a statement denouncing Bush's foreign policy. Meanwhile, Sen. John McCain (R, AZ), a popular centrist reportedly wooed by Kerry as a possible running mate, campaigned with Bush in Washington state **June 18**.

Supreme Court Rebuffs President on Enemy Combatants—In cases decided **June 28**, the Supreme Court rebuffed a position of the Bush administration that the government could detain terror suspects indefinitely and interrogate them without access to courts or lawyers. In *Hamdi v. Rumsfeld* the court ruled, 8-1, that Congress had given the president the authority to hold U.S. citizens as enemy combatants, but that the plaintiff, Yaser Esam Hamdi, a U.S. citizen held for two years without charges, could argue in court that he was being held illegally. Justice Sandra Day O'Connor wrote for the majority that "a state of war is not a blank check for the president when it comes to the rights of the nation's citizens." In *Rasul v. Bush* and *Al Odah v. United States,* a 6-3 Supreme Court majority agreed that detainees held at Guantánamo Bay, Cuba, could use U.S. courts to argue that they were being held illegally.

In Shift, Fed Raises Interest Rate—On **June 30**, for the first time in 4 years, the Federal Reserve raised its benchmark interest rate, from a historic low 1% to 1.25% for overnight loans; at the same time the Fed said that inflation remained low and that rates in the future would rise at a "measured" pace.

U.S. Economy at a Glance: June 2004	
Unemployment rate	5.6%
Consumer prices (change over 2003)	3.3%
Trade deficit (12 mo. through June).	$536.6 bil
Dow Jones closing, 2nd quarter	10,435.38
Dow Jones highest close, 2nd quarter (Apr. 6) . .	10,570.81
Dow Jones lowest close, 2nd quarter (May 17). .	9,906.91
2nd quarter GDP growth (annual rate)	3.3%

International

Prices Peak, Then Decline—Oil prices jumped sharply **June 1**, following the May 29 attack in Saudi Arabia in which 22 people, mostly oil-industry workers, were killed. Crude oil prices hit $42.33 a barrel, the highest ever reported, before falling back. The Organization of Petroleum Exporting Countries voted **June 3** to increase output by 2 million barrels, or 8.5%, a day, beginning July 1. By **June 28**, oil had declined to below $38 a barrel, and the price of self-serve regular gasoline in the U.S. had fallen to an average of $1.94 a gallon, 13 cents below its recent peak.

Bush Meets with Pope, European Leaders—Pres. George W. Bush met in Rome **June 4** with Pope John Paul II. In a statement, the pope reiterated Vatican opposition to the war in Iraq and concern about strife in the Middle East. Bush met **June 4** with Prem. Silvio Berlusconi of Italy and **June 5** in Paris with Pres. Jacques Chirac of France. On **June 6**, the 60th anniversary of the Allied D-Day landing on the beaches of German-occupied Normandy, Bush attended a memorial service in Arromanches, France. Other attendees included Chirac, Queen Elizabeth II, Prime Min. Tony Blair of Britain, and Pres. Vladimir Putin of Russia. For the first time at one of these international D-Day observances, Germany was represented by its chancellor, currently Gerhard Schroeder. Thousands of soldiers killed in the 1944 invasion lay buried in nearby cemeteries.

Israeli Cabinet Backs a Gaza Withdrawal—Prime Min. Ariel Sharon of Israel won approval **June 6** for a revised plan to withdraw all Jewish settlements in Gaza and 4 small ones in the West Bank. His cabinet supported the plan 14-7, but only after he had dismissed 2 ministers to insure victory. In all, about 8,000 settlers would be affected. The opposition Labor Party said **June 6** that it would support the withdrawal in parliament.

Leaders of Industrial Nations Meet in U.S.—Leaders of the world's 8 major industrial nations met at Sea Island, GA, **June 8-10** at their annual summit. In their "Broader Middle East and North Africa Initiative," released **June 9**, they supported democratic reform, calling on nations in the region to promote reform from within, involve civic and business leaders in the process, and show willingness to make a long-term effort. Several leaders rebuffed efforts by Pres. Bush and Prime Min. Blair to obtain a NATO commitment to aid Iraq.

Investigations of Prison-Abuse Scandal Continue—Pres. Bush **June 10** indicated he was unsure whether he had seen 2 memoranda dealing with how to handle captured enemy combatants. The 2 memos, from the Defense and Justice departments, provided a relatively loose interpretation of the UN convention against torture and allowed for broad presidential powers in superseding treaties and laws. Bush said any orders he issued were consistent with the law and treaty obligations.

Sec. of Defense Donald Rumsfeld admitted **June 17** that he had ordered the name of a detainee omitted from a prison roster at the request of CIA Director George Tenet; the captive, being held in Baghdad, was thought to be a senior member of a terror group. On **June 22**, the administration released classified documents relating to policies toward detainees. In one, dated Feb. 7, 2002, Bush held that provisions of the Geneva conventions did not apply to al-Qaeda. He also asserted the constitutional authority to deny Geneva's protections to fighters captured in Afghanistan who did not follow the rules of combat. Bush aides **June 22** disavowed a 2002 Justice Dept. memo saying that torture might be legally defensible.

Saudi Terrorists Behead American Civilian—A terror group in Saudi Arabia **June 12** kidnapped Paul Johnson, an American employed by Lockheed Martin Corp., and beheaded him **June 18**. Later that day Saudi security forces shot and killed the group's leader, Abdelaziz al-Muqrin, and 3 of his comrades. The Saudis said **June 19** that 12 members of the group had been arrested.

Raids in a Russian Republic Take Heavy Toll—Guerrillas raided the city of Nazran and 2 smaller towns in the Russian region of Ingushetia during the night of **June 21-22**, killing 97; 105 were wounded. About half of the dead were government and law-enforcement officials. Ingushetia borders on the rebellious republic of Chechnya, but many of the raiders were thought to be Ingush.

U.S.-Led Coalition Transfers Power to Iraqis—On **June 28**, two days ahead of schedule, the U.S.-led coalition formally transferred political power in Iraq to an interim government that would run the country, with U.S. support, until elections were held. Only a few dozen people were present at the low-key ceremony, after which L. Paul Bremer III, the top U.S. civilian representative in Iraq, left the country. On **June 30** the new interim government took legal custody of Saddam Hussein and 11 of his aides, though they remained in physical custody of U.S. forces for security reasons. Hussein appeared before an Iraqi court that day and was to be arraigned July 1.

On **June 1** UN envoy Lakhdar Brahimi had appointed 33 members of the interim government, to be led by Iyad Allawi as prime minister. The ministers, included 6 women, represented all major religious and ethnic groups. Also on **June 1**, the U.S.-created Iraqi governing council voted to dissolve itself. Before doing so, it pushed through its choice for president, Sheikh Ghazi Ajil al-Yawar, a Sunni Muslim, who was not the favorite of Brahimi or Bremer.

Allawi said **June 4** that an early withdrawal of foreign troops would be a disaster. He and Sec. of State Colin Powell agreed **June 6** to cooperate closely to seek passage of a UN resolution establishing the conditions for the transfer of authority and providing that coalition forces could take "all necessary means" to protect the country. In a significant diplomatic victory for the U.S. and the interim government, the resolution won approval by the Security Council, 15-0, on **June 8**.

Violence against the coalition and civilian population continued during June, although, in one hopeful sign the radical Shiite cleric Moktada al-Sadr, **June 16**, did order his followers to stop fighting. Among other incidents, 5 U.S. troops were killed in a firefight in the Sadr City slum in Baghdad **June 4**, and 4 civilian contractors, 2 Americans and 2 Poles, were killed **June 5** in a rocket attack. Attacks on a police station and a military base **June 6** killed 19 Iraqis. A mortar **June 8** killed 6 Polish, Slovak, and Latvian soldiers; the same day, a bomb in the Kurdish city of Mosul killed 10 and wounded 25. The bombing of pipelines **June 14, 15,** and **16** forced the temporary closing of Iraq's main oil export terminal. Two car bombers in and near Baghdad killed 41 Iraqis **June 17**. Kim Sun-Il, a South Korean translator, was beheaded **June 22** by kidnappers, after South Korea rejected their demand for that country to pull its troops out of Iraq.

In a series of apparently coordinated attacks, insurgents struck **June 24** at Iraqi security forces and U.S. troops in 5 cities. More than 100 people, including many policemen and 3 Americans, were killed and hundreds wounded. Bombings in Mosul, targeting a hospital and police positions, took more than 60 lives. There was heavy fighting in Baquoba, where gunman seized the main police station.

At the NATO summit conference in Istanbul, **June 28**, the leaders declared that they would offer NATO's assistance to Iraq for the training of security forces. However, France and Germany indicated that no such training by their troops would take place in Iraq. Speaking in Istanbul, Turkey, **June 29**, Bush urged the Muslim world to put aside hatred of the West and embrace democracy.

Liberals Lose Majority in Canadian Parliament—The Liberal Party in Canada, led by incumbent Prime Min. Paul Martin, lost ground in the national parliamentary election held **June 28**. They won just 135 seats, falling well short of a majority. The Conservatives were left with 99 seats, the Bloc Quebecois with 54, and the labor-aligned New Democratic Party with 19 (there was 1 independent). The strained transfer of leadership to Martin from ex-Prime Min. Jean Chretien had left wounds among Liberals. While Conservative leader

Stephen Harper failed to make sufficient inroads with his program of lower taxes and more military spending, Martin acknowledged that the election had been a rebuff to Liberals, who went on to form a minority government; he declared that "as a party and as a government we must do better."

General

Colt's Bid for Racing's Triple Crown Fails—The attempt **June 5** by Smarty Jones, a horse that had never lost, to win horse racing's Triple Crown failed by a length. The winner in the Belmont Stakes was Birdstone, a 36-1 long shot. Smarty Jones had won the Kentucky Derby and Preakness. Running for the 9th time, he led much of the way but was overtaken in the stretch at Elmont, NY, and finished 2nd. Birdstone's time was 2 minutes, 27.50 seconds. No horse had taken the Triple Crown since Affirmed in 1978. Jockey Edgar Prado rode Birdstone.

Tampa Bay Wins First Hockey Title—The Tampa Bay Lightning, who had joined the National Hockey League in 1999, won their first National Hockey League championship **June 7**, defeating the Calgary Flames, 2-1, in Tampa, in the 7th game of their title series. Ruslan Fedotenko scored both goals for the winners. Brad Richards, who led all post-season players in scoring with 12 goals and 26 points, was named most valuable player in the playoffs.

Detroit Pistons Upset L.A. Lakers for NBA Title—The Detroit Pistons won the National Basketball Association championship **June 15**, defeating the Los Angeles Lakers in Auburn Hills, MI, 100-87. The Pistons, the Eastern Division champions, were underdogs, but prevailed 4 games to 1 against the Lakers, led by superstars Shaquille O'Neal and Kobe Bryant. Pistons guard Chauncey Billups, who had averaged 21 points a game in the finals, was named the series' most valuable player. The Pistons were coached by Larry Brown, the first coach ever to win both the NBA and NCAA titles, the latter at Kansas.

Goosen Wins U.S. Open Golf Title 2nd Time—Retief Goosen won the U.S. Open golf title for the 2nd time in 4 years **June 20** in Southampton, NY, with a 4-under-par total of 276.

Spacecraft Begins Saturn Orbit—After nearly 7 years in space, the *Cassini* spacecraft became the first ever to orbit the comparatively little known planet Saturn, starting at 9:12 pm Pacific Time on **June 30**. It was hoped that the craft would complete at least 74 orbits of the planet over a period of four years, A planned highlight of the $3.3 bil U.S.-European mission was a thorough scrutiny of Saturn's planet-sized moon Titan.

JULY 2004

National

Job Growth Slows—The government reported **July 2** that 112,000 new nonfarm jobs had been created in June. This total was lower than in recent months, but brought the total of new jobs since August 2003 to 1.5 million; the unemployment rate was 5.6%, compared to 6.1 percent in August 2003.

Founder of Bankrupt Enron Corporation Indicted—Kenneth Lay, founder and former CEO of the now-bankrupt Enron Corp., was indicted in a U.S. district court in Houston **July 7**. Lay **July 8** pleaded not guilty to the 11 criminal counts, which included conspiracy, bank fraud, securities fraud, and wire fraud.

Cable TV Company's Founder Convicted—John Rigas, founder of Adelphia Communications, a cable television company, and a son, Timothy Rigas, were convicted **July 8** of conspiracy, bank fraud, and securities fraud. A jury in U.S. District Court in New York City concurred with charges that they had hidden more than $2 bil in company debt and stolen more than $100 mil from Adelphia. The jury deadlocked **July 9** on similar charges against Michael Rigas, another son of John Rigas. A 4th defendant and former company official, Michael Mulcahey, was acquitted on all charges against him.

Senators Say Intelligence Agencies Were Wrong on Iraq Weapons—A U.S. Senate committee **July 9**, speaking unanimously, asserted that the CIA and other U.S. intelli-

gence agencies had produced false and misleading prewar information about Iraq's weapons programs. The report from the 17-member Senate Select Committee on Intelligence did, however, applaud the CIA for expressing doubt that al-Qaeda had significant ties with the Iraqi regime of Pres. Saddam Hussein.

The Senate report concluded that a National Intelligence Estimate (NIE) issued by the CIA in Oct. 2002 had overstated claims that Iraq possessed chemical and biological weapons. It found no basis for the claim that Iraq was reconstituting its nuclear weapons program, and the CIA was rebuked for having a bias toward reaching dire conclusions. The report did not, however, find that administration officials pressured analysts to produce conclusions buttressing the case for war against Iraq.

The report criticized intelligence agencies for not placing agents in Iraq after the inspectors left in 1998, and for relying too much on defectors. Sen. Pat Roberts (R, KS), chairman of the committee, said **July 9** that U.S. and foreign agencies had succumbed to a "groupthink" leading to "a global intelligence failure."

Constitutional Bar to Same-Sex Marriages Stalls—Supporters of an amendment to the U.S. Constitution that would forbid same-sex marriages were rebuffed in the Senate **July 14**. On a procedural motion requiring 60 yes votes, supporters of the amendment failed to gain a simple majority, losing 48-50. The amendment's author, Sen. Wayne Allard (R, CO), had argued for its passage **July 9**, saying, "Traditional marriage is under assault." Sen. John McCain (R, AZ) argued **July 14** that the amendment was antithetical to Republican Party philosophy. Democrats said the GOP was playing politics.

Martha Stewart Sentenced—Martha Stewart, convicted in March of lying to federal agents, was sentenced **July 16** to 5 months in prison. Judge Miriam Goldman Cedarbaum, in U.S. District Court in New York, also sentenced Stewart to 5 months of house arrest and 19 months of probation, and fined her $30,000 and court fees. Stewart's broker, Peter Bacanovic, was also sentenced to 5 months.

Former National Security Adviser Investigated—Samuel (Sandy) Berger, a national security adviser for Pres. Bill Clinton, admitted **July 19** to having removed classified documents from the National Archives, but said he had done so inadvertently. Berger had been reviewing Clinton-era documents for possible submission to the independent commission investigating the 2001 terror attacks. Berger **July 20** resigned as a campaign adviser to Sen. John Kerry.

9/11 Commission Urges Shakeup in U.S. Intelligence—The commission that investigated the Sept. 11, 2001, terror attacks on the U.S. released its final report **July 22**. The 567-page document summarized what was known about the events of that day and about the organization of the attacks by the al-Qaeda international terrorist network, as well as about government agencies' preparedness and response, which were found wanting. It called for sweeping reforms, including a restructuring of U.S. intelligence operations, now scattered among 15 agencies, under the supervision and budget control of a national intelligence director.

The FBI, CIA, Defense Dept., National Security Council, and oversight committees in the U.S. Congress were among entities that came under sharp criticism. The commission did not single out either the Clinton or Bush administrations for particular blame, and said it was impossible to say whether "any single step or series of steps" would have averted the attacks. The commission concluded, however, that "none of the measures adopted by the U.S. government from 1998 to 2001 disturbed or even delayed the progress of the al Qaeda plot, pointing to "failures of imagination, policy, capabilities, and management."

The report warned of the possibility of even more catastrophic attacks. Thomas Kean, the commission's chairman and a former Republican governor of New Jersey, said at a press conference **July 22** that the offensive against al-Qaeda and improvements in homeland security had made the country more secure, but that nevertheless, "we are not safe."

The bipartisan commission, consisting of 5 Republicans and 5 Democrats, and co-chaired by former U.S. Rep. Lee

Hamilton (D, IN), was created in large measure as the result of demands from survivors of the 9/11 victims for a thorough investigation.

Democrats Nominate Sen. John Kerry for President—In a carefully scripted national convention in Boston, **July 26-29**, a united Democratic Party nominated U.S. Sen. John Kerry of Massachusetts for president; he garnered all but a few holdout votes in a roll call begun late on the night of **July 28**. The next night he accepted the nomination in a speech stressing foreign affairs, national security, and his military service in Vietnam, while pledging to "restore trust and credibility to the White House." On **July 28**, Sen. John Edwards of North Carolina had accepted the party's nomination for vice president in a speech that set the theme "hope is on the way." Other speakers at the convention included former presidents Jimmy Carter and Bill Clinton (introduced by his wife, Sen. Hillary Rodham Clinton) and the keynote speaker, Barack Obama, candidate for the Senate from Illinois and a rising Democratic star.

Kerry had announced **July 6** his choice of Edwards to run on the ticket for vice president. The Kerry and Edwards families met the press **July 7** at an estate near Pittsburgh owned by Kerry's wife, Teresa Heinz Kerry. Beginning **July 8**, they campaigned together for 4 days. Edwards, a lawyer who had made a fortune winning huge settlements for victims in product-liability and medical-malpractice cases, was ending his first Senate term; in choosing him, Kerry passed over more experienced prospects. Edwards, Kerry's last serious rival in the presidential primaries, had attracted wide support as a charismatic speaker and campaigner.

A *CNN/USA Today* Gallup poll of registered voters from **Aug. 4** found the Kerry-Edwards ticket now tied with the Bush-Cheney ticket at 48%. An ABC News/*Washington Post* poll from **Aug. 3** found Kerry ahead 50% to 44%, with 2% support going to independent Ralph Nader.

> *"I defended this country as a young man and I will defend it as president."*
>
> *Sen. John Kerry* (D, MA), in his speech at the Democratic National Convention accepting his party's nomination for the presidency, July 29.

International

Saddam Hussein Arraigned in Iraqi Court—Ex-Pres. Saddam Hussein of Iraq was arraigned before an Iraqi judge **July 1** for crimes he allegedly committed during his long rule. The court was set up in one of his former palaces. Hussein questioned the authority of the court and denied any responsibility for the gas attack on the Kurdish village of Halabja in 1988, killing more than 5,000 people, saying he had first heard about it from the media. Hussein said he could not be considered guilty of invading Kuwait in 1990 because Kuwait was a part of Iraq. Eleven of his aides were also arraigned on various charges **July 1**.

New Iraqi Government Deals With Militias—Prem. Iyad Allawi of Iraq said **July 4** he was seeking to reach an amnesty agreement with Moqtada al-Sadr, the Shiite cleric who had revolted against the U.S. occupation. Allawi said his government would grant amnesty to other militias that gave up their weapons. The Iraqi government **July 7** gave Allawi the power to impose martial law where insurgents were active. Allawi said **July 18** that the government would let al-Sadr's newspaper reopen; U.S. authorities had shut it down.

U.S. planes **July 5** bombed a house in Fallujah linked to the Jordanian terrorist Abu Musab al-Zarqawi, killing at least 10. In insurgent activity, 5 American soldiers were killed in a mortar attack **July 8**; 2 car bombs **July 14** and **15** each killed 10 people; and militants **July 14** assassinated the governor of Ninevah province. U.S. planes bombed Fallujah again **July 18**, killing at least 12. A high Iraqi defense official was assassinated **July 18**. Three U.S. soldiers were killed **July 20**, and the American death toll since hostilities began now stood at about 900. In Baqouba, a hotbed of the insurgency, a car bomb exploded on **July 28** in a shopping area and killed 68 Iraqis. A police station was the apparent target; 56 were wounded.

A Filipino diplomat reported **July 7** that a Filipino hostage had been kidnapped by militants who demanded that the Philippines withdraw their 51 peacekeeping troops from Iraq. The Philippines government complied with this demand, withdrawing the last of their troops **July 19**, a month earlier than planned, and the hostage was freed **July 20**.

A Bulgarian hostage was beheaded **July 13**. Among other abductions, insurgents **July 21** kidnapped 7 truck drivers from different countries and threatened to kill them one by one if their Kuwaiti company did not leave Iraq. An Egyptian diplomat was kidnapped **July 23** but freed 3 days later.

U.S. Pilot Guilty in Deaths of 4 Canadians—A U.S. military court **July 6** found a U.S. Air Force pilot, Maj. Harry Schmidt, guilty of dereliction of duty in the 2002 deaths of 4 Canadian soldiers in Afghanistan, struck by a bomb from an F-16 jet flown by Schmidt. The Canadians were conducting a live-fire exercise, which he mistook for firing from Taliban. The judge said Schmidt had disobeyed an order to withhold fire. In 2003, Schmidt's copilot, Maj. William Umbach, was reprimanded and allowed to retire.

British Intelligence Faulted on Iraqi Weapons Claims—A British government committee concluded **July 14** that British intelligence prior to the Iraq war had been "seriously flawed" and—given that no weapons of mass destruction were found—had been proven wrong. The committee, headed by Lord Butler, said Iraq had no significant stocks of chemical or biological weapons or plans for using them. The report, however, said there was no proof that Prime Min. Tony Blair and others had manipulated prewar intelligence. The report found no evidence of cooperation between Iraq and al-Qaeda, but on another matter, concluded that Iraqi agents *had* visited Niger in 1999 and had reportedly tried to buy uranium. Blair told the House of Commons **July 14** that he accepted responsibility for any intelligence errors made, but that "no one lied, no one made up intelligence" and that going to war had been the right thing to do.

World Court Says Israeli Wall Violates International Law—The International Court of Justice ruled **July 9**, 14-1, that a 437-mile wall being built by Israel and impinging partly on Palestinian territory violated international law. The U.S. justice cast the dissenting vote. The court, in an unenforceable opinion, ordered Israel to tear down or reroute the barrier, erected to thwart Palestinian suicide attacks. Critics claimed the barrier would help Israel seize more land and complicate the formation of a Palestinian state. The Israeli Supreme Court had already ruled June 30 that 20 miles of the wall must be rerouted. The UN General Assembly voted 150-6, **July 20**, to demand that Israel remove the barrier in Palestinian territory.

Palestinian Leaders Clash—On **July 16**, Palestinian extremists kidnapped 2 Palestine Authority officials, including the police chief of Gaza, and 4 French aid workers, and held them for a day. Palestinian Pres. Yasir Arafat **July 17** dismissed the chief, who had been denounced by the kidnappers for stealing PA funds. He then placed a relative, Moussa Arafat, in overall charge of security in the Gaza Strip and, amid cries of cronyism, Prime Min. Ahmed Qurei temporarily resigned (later reversing himself). Militants denounced Moussa Arafat and destroyed his offices, **July 18**. Yasir Arafat, **July 19**, put a less controversial figure in charge of security in both Gaza and the West Bank.

UN Calls for Disarmament of Sudan Militia—The UN Security Council **July 30** adopted a U.S.-drafted resolution, cosponsored by Britain, France, Germany, Spain, Chile, and Romania, demanding that Sudan disarm within 30 days and prosecute the Arab Janjaweed militia, held responsible for rape, pillaging, and massacres that had killed an estimated 50,000 black Africans in the Dharfur region and driven another million from their lands into refugee camps. The 13-0 vote, with abstentions from China and Pakistan, came after the U.S. agreed to delete the specific threat of "sanctions" but referred to a section of the UN charter permitting punitive measures.

Pakistan Seizes Suspect in 1998 Embassy Bombings—Pakistan announced **July 29** that it had captured a Tanzanian al-Qaeda member sought by the U.S. in connection with the

bombing of U.S. embassies in Kenya and Tanzania in 1998. The suspect, Ahmed Khalfan Ghailani, had been arrested **July 25** in Gujrat, along with 15 others, and was reportedly providing "very valuable" information. The U.S. had put a $25 mil price on his head.

General

Russian, 17, Wins Women's Wimbledon Tennis Title—Maria Sharapova of Russia, 17, won the women's singles tennis title at Wimbledon, England, **July 3**. She defeated Serena Williams, the 2002 and 2003 champion, 6-1, 6-4. Sharapova, who had come to the U.S. at the age of 7, was the first Russian to win the Wimbledon women's title. On **July 4**, Roger Federer of Switzerland retained his men's title, defeating Andy Roddick of the U.S., 4-6, 7-5, 7-6, 6-4.

Hamilton Wins British Open Golf Title in Playoff—Todd Hamilton, an American who had never before won one of golf's 4 major tournaments, won the British Open in Troon, Scotland, **July 18** in a 4-hole playoff. He defeated Ernie Els of South Africa by one stroke.

Armstrong Wins 6th Straight Tour de France—Lance Armstrong of the U.S. won the Tour de France, the world's premier bicycle race, for the 6th consecutive year **July 25**. No one had ever won the contest more than 5 times. He won by 6 minutes and 19 seconds.

AUGUST 2004

National

Financial Institutions Are Reported Terror Targets—Security was increased **Aug. 1** around 5 buildings of financial institutions in New York City, Newark, NJ, and Washington, DC. Tom Ridge, secretary of homeland security, said these facilities, including the New York Stock Exchange, had been a focus of planning for terror attacks. The *New York Times* reported **Aug. 2** that an al-Qaeda member, Muhammad Naeem Noor Khan, had been arrested in Pakistan **July 13** and that his electronic files contained evidence of surveillance of the 5 buildings.

U.S. and Pakistani officials acknowledged **Aug. 6** that Khan had been engaged in a sting operation that resulted in the capture of al-Qaeda members; exposure of his name ended his usefulness. White House national security adviser Condoleezza Rice said **Aug. 8** that Khan's name had been given to reporters on background but that the administration had not identified him publicly.

British authorities **Aug. 17** charged 8 British subjects, among 12 seized **Aug. 3**, with plotting terror attacks in the U.S. One of the accused reportedly had reconnaissance plans for 4 of the buildings Ridge mentioned.

Bush Reacts to 9/11 Commission Proposals—Pres. George W. Bush **Aug. 2** gave qualified support to the principal proposals made by the commission that investigated the 2001 terror attacks. He said he favored the appointment of a national intelligence director (NID) and establishment of a National Counterterrorism Center, but unlike the commission, wanted them located outside the executive office of the president. Bush said his approach would shield the director and center from political influence. Bush also did not support giving the NID authority over the budget and personnel of 15 intelligence agencies.

Voters, Judges Act on Gay Marriage Issue—Gay-rights advocates suffered a setback **Aug. 3** when 71% of the voters in Missouri approved an amendment to the state constitution forbidding same-sex marriages. On **Aug. 12**, the California Supreme Court, in a 5-2 decision, invalidated more than 4,000 same-sex marriage licenses issued in San Francisco in February and March. It found unanimously that city authorities, backed by Mayor Gavin Newsom (D), had improperly granted the licenses. Voters had approved a state law defining marriage as the union of a man and a woman.

Vietnam Vets Attack Kerry's War Record—The Vietnam War record of Sen. John Kerry, the Democratic presidential nominee, became the center of angry charges and countercharges that flew for weeks, and appeared to damage Kerry's poll ratings. An organization called Swift Boat Veterans for Truth claimed in TV ads that Kerry had lied about his wounds in order to win medals. The ads, which began running **Aug. 4** in 3 states, were financed by soft money contributions, including $100,000 from Bob Perry, a Houston (TX) real-estate developer and Bush supporter. Sen. John McCain (R, AZ) **Aug. 5** called the ads "dishonest and dishonorable." Bush did not specifically condemn the ads but, **Aug. 24**, called for an end to all attack ads by tax-exempt independent so-called 527 groups, some of which have launched heavily funded ads critical of Bush. Kerry said **Aug. 19** that Navy records documented his medal awards and that he still carried shrapnel in his leg from a wound. *The Washington Post* reported **Aug. 19** that Larry Thurlow, a Kerry accuser who claimed there was no enemy fire when Kerry rescued a comrade, had himself won a medal with a citation describing enemy fire on that occasion.

A second ad by the veterans' group, first released **Aug. 20**, excoriated Kerry's 1971 antiwar testimony before a Senate committee, where he passed on stories suggesting widespread atrocities "on a day–to–day basis" by U.S. troops in Vietnam. Kerry forces charged that words were taken out of context in the ad. He filed a complaint with the Federal Election Commission **Aug. 20**, charging that the Swift Boat Veterans were coordinating their efforts with the Bush campaign, violating campaign finance law; the administration denied any connection. Benjamin Ginsberg, national counsel for the Bush campaign, did admit having given legal advice to the Swift Boat veterans, and resigned his post **Aug. 25**.

Bush Nominates New CIA Director—Pres. Bush **Aug. 10** announced his choice to succeed George Tenet as Director of Central Intelligence. He nominated Rep. Porter Goss (R, FL), who had been a clandestine operative for the CIA before being elected to Congress, where he chaired the House Permanent Select Committee on Intelligence. Despite charges by some Democrats that Goss was too partisan for the job, he was confirmed by the Senate in a 77-17 vote **Sept. 22**.

New Jersey Governor Reveals Homosexual Affair, Announces Resignation—Gov. James McGreevey (D) of New Jersey announced **Aug. 12**, that he had engaged in a "consensual" affair with another man. The man was later identified as Israeli citizen Golan Cipel, whom the governor had hired for a time as his homeland security adviser (at a salary of $110,000 a year). McGreevey, elected in 2001, said he would resign, effective Nov. 15; he spoke at a press conference in Trenton, with his 2nd wife at his side. Cipel, who had resigned from the security post, claimed through a lawyer **Aug. 13** that the governor had sexually harassed him. McGreevey's press secretary denied the allegation. Republicans urged the governor to resign by Sept. 3 so that the office could be up for election in November, but McGreevey did not do so.

> *"And so my truth is that I am a gay American."*
> NJ Gov. James McGeevey, Aug. 12, announcing that he was resigning his office.

Price of Oil Hits New Highs as Job Growth Slows—The price of oil mounted to a high of $48.70 a barrel on the NY Mercantile Exchange by **Aug. 19**. Other figures released **Aug. 6** showed poor job growth, with only 32,000 nonfarm jobs created in July; however, the unemployment rate edged downward to 5.5%. On **Aug. 10**, the Federal Reserve Board raised short-term interest rates by a quarter point, the 2nd increase in 2 months.

Reports Rebuke Officers, Officials for Prison Abuses—Two reports were issued on the mistreatment of prisoners seized by the U.S. military since the 2001 terror attacks. A 4-member panel headed by former Defense Sec. James Schlesinger found **Aug. 24** that mistreatment in Iraq, Afghanistan, and Guántanamo Bay, Cuba, could be traced to institutional and personal failures at high levels. Schlesinger, **Aug. 24**, likened the atmosphere at Abu Ghraib prison in Iraq to that in the film comedy *Animal House* and blamed Sec. of Defense Donald Rumsfeld and Lt. Gen. Ricardo Sanchez, then the highest-ranking U.S. military officer in Iraq, for failing to take corrective action. An Army investigation concluded **Aug. 25** that military intelligence units had played a major part in the Abu Ghraib abuses; it

recommended disciplinary action against 2 officers and assigned blame to 54 individuals in all.

GOP Convenes in New York—The Republican National Convention opened **Aug. 30** at Madison Square Garden in New York, under tight security. An estimated 400,000 anti-Bush demonstrators staged a mostly orderly protest, **Aug. 29**, marching to Union Square, where speakers included activist Rev. Jesse Jackson and filmmaker Michael Moore. Though denied a permit to assemble on the Great Lawn at Central Park, several groups gathered there afterward. Sporadic demonstrations continued on **Aug. 30-31**, erupting into occasional clashes with police and hundreds of arrests. Inside the convention hall, 2 prominent Republican moderates, Sen. John McCain (AZ) and former New York City Mayor Rudolph Giuliani, were among the speakers, **Aug. 30**; both extolled the Bush administration for its war on terrorism and linked the Iraq War to that effort. Major speakers on **Aug. 31** included First Lady Laura Bush, who portrayed her husband as having wrestled with an agonizing decision to go to war, and Austrian-born California Gov. Arnold Schwarzenegger, who praised Bush's leadership and portrayed the U.S. as a land of promise for immigrants.

International

Venezuelan President Survives Recall Referendum—Pres. Hugo Chavez Frias prevailed **Aug. 15** over an attempt to remove him from office. According to official figures announced **Aug. 16**, 58% of those voting rejected recalling him. Although denounced for leading a corrupt regime, Chavez had gained popularity because of his social programs for the poor and because of a sharp rise in oil prices, benefiting Venezuela as a top oil exporter.

Najaf Siege Leads to Agreement—The situation in Iraq deteriorated **Aug. 5** when radical Shiite leader Moktada al-Sadr, who had previously reached a truce with U.S. forces, called again for his followers to rise in revolt. They clashed with coalition troops in Sadr City, inside Baghdad, and in several southern cities. On **Aug. 7** U.S. Marines pushed into Najaf, Sadr's base. The U.S. military claimed **Aug. 11** that it had killed about 500 of Sadr's fighters, and Marines reportedly killed more than 60 Sadr fighters in Najaf **Aug. 17**. The Grand Ayatollah Ali al-Sistani, who had flown to London **Aug. 6** for heart surgery, returned **Aug. 25** and reached a tentative agreement **Aug. 27** with Sadr. The agreement, accepted by the interim Iraqi government, allowed Sadr's forces to leave Najaf provided that U.S. marines ended their 3-week siege.

In other incidents, car bombs set outside 4 Christian churches in Baghdad, **Aug. 1**, killed 11 people and wounded 47. The execution of a Turkish hostage by his radical captors was shown on an Internet videotape **Aug. 2**. On **Aug. 20**, 2 French journalists were abducted by Islamic radicals, who demanded that France repeal its law prohibiting Muslim headscarves in schools; the French rejected the demand. On **Aug. 31** Nepalese officials announced that Iraqi militants had killed 12 Nepalis captured just over a week earlier; it was the largest mass killing of captives yet, in the insurgency that followed the toppling of Saddam Hussein. A web site associated with a group calling itself Jaish Ansar al-Sunna posted gruesome still images and video of the militants murdering their victims.

Terror Suspected in 2 Russian Air Crashes —Two Russian passenger jetliners crashed within a few minutes of each other **Aug. 24** after they took off from Domodedovo airport in Moscow. One of the planes, bound for Volgograd, crashed 125 miles south of Moscow, killing all 44 aboard. The other, heading for the Black Sea, crashed 600 miles south of the capital, killing all 46 aboard. The crashes occurred 5 days before a presidential election in the rebellious province of Chechnya; Kremlin-backed candidate Alu Alkhanov won 74% of the vote in **Aug. 29** elections. The previous president had been assassinated in May. On **Aug. 27-28**, investigators found traces of explosives at both crash sites; terrorism was suspected. On **Aug. 31**, 10 people, including a suicide bomber, were killed in an explosion in a Moscow subway.

Bombing Kills 16 in Israel—Two suicide bombers set off almost simultaneous blasts on buses in the southern Israeli city of Beer Sheeva, **Aug. 31**, killing 16 people in addition to themselves.

General

Olympic Games Return to Greece—The Summer Games of the 28th Olympiad of the modern era returned to Greece in August. The games originated in ancient Greece, which had also hosted them when they were revived in 1896. A record total of 202 countries and 10,500 athletes took part in opening ceremonies in Athens **Aug. 13**. In the end, the U.S. won 103 medals (35 gold), while Russia won 92 (27 gold), and China 63 (32 gold).

Paul Hamm (U.S.) fell on the vault during the men's all-around gymnastics competition, but finished brilliantly on the high bar to narrowly edge Kim Dae Eun and Yang Tae Young, both of South Korea. Later, a mathematical error was discovered in the scores, which indicated Yang should have won. Hamm's gold medal was not taken from him, but 3 judges were suspended. Another American, Carly Patterson, won the women's all-around gymnastics gold medal.

Michael Phelps (U.S.) won 6 gold and 2 bronze medals in swimming—in butterfly, freestyle, individual medley, and relay events. By winning 8 medals, he broke Mark Spitz's record total of 7 in the 1972 swimming events, though all of Spitz's were gold. Natalie Coughlin (U.S.) won 5 swimming medals (2 gold, 2 silver, and 1 bronze). Chinese men and women dazzled in diving, winning 6 of 8 events.

The men's marathon went to Stefano Baldini of Italy, followed by Meb Keflezighi (U.S.) and Vanderlei de Lima (Brazil). De Lima had been leading with 4 miles to go when a spectator pushed him into the crowd. The women's marathon went to Mizuki Noguchi of Japan.

After fierce competition, 2 American men prevailed in the track and field sprints—Justin Gatlin in the 100 meters and Shawn Crawford in the 200. Jeremy Wariner (U.S.) took the 400. Hicham El Guerrouj of Morocco, widely hailed as the world's best middle-distance runner, finally won an Olympic gold in the 1500 meters, after 2 previous unsuccessful tries; he also took the 5000. Kelly Holmes of Britain won the women's 800 and 1500. Fani Halkia of Greece thrilled the crowd with an upset victory in the women's 400 hurdles. Roman Sebrle of the Czech Republic took the men's decathlon, and Carolina Kluft of Sweden won the women's heptathlon.

The U.S. men's basketball "Dream Team," consisting only of NBA players, lost 3 times and settled for bronze. Argentina defeated Italy for the gold, 84-69. The American women's basketball team, however, won gold after defeating Australia 74-63. Mariel Zagunis won the first American gold medal in fencing in 100 years, taking the gold in the women's sabre. Andre Ward brought the U.S. a gold in boxing for the first time since 1996, prevailing in the light-heavyweight division.

Israel won its first gold medal ever, when Gal Fridman prevailed in a windsurfing event, the men's mistral. American women won a gold in soccer, defeating Brazil, 2-1, in the final. Iraq, competing in the Olympics for the first time since the fall of Saddam Hussein, made a strong bid in men's soccer, placing 4th; the gold went to Argentina.

The games closed **Aug. 29**.

Hurricane Charley Tears Across Florida—Hurricane Charley ripped across Florida **Aug. 13–14**, causing at least 27 deaths. The hurricane had first struck Jamaica **Aug. 12** and then Cuba earlier on **Aug. 13**, killing 5 persons in all. Gaining momentum, it hit Florida's West Coast at the islands of Sanibel and Captiva and at the town of Punta Gorda, carrying winds of up to 145 mph. The eye of the storm came near Orlando before passing north. Charley destroyed or damaged 16,000 homes, damaged farm crops, and left a million households without electricity. Pres. Bush declared 25 Florida counties federal disaster areas, freeing up funds for the recovery. Charley returned to land **Aug. 14**, entering South Carolina with winds reduced to 75 mph.

SEPTEMBER 2004

National

Republican Convention Renominates Bush and Cheney—Pres. George W. Bush and Vice Pres. Richard Cheney were renominated **Sept. 1** by delegates to the Republican National Convention, held in New York City. In a fiery convention keynote address, that day, Sen. Zell Miller (GA), a Democrat who has broken with his party, declared that on issues of freedom and security, Sen. John Kerry (MA), the Democratic presidential nominee, had been "more wrong, more weak, and more wobbly" than any other national figure. Cheney, accepting his nomination **Sept. 1**, also attacked the Democratic nominee, arguing that he lacked the "ability and decisiveness" to defend the U.S.

Bush, in his acceptance speech **Sept. 2**, emphasized the war against terrorism, promising to build "a safer world and a more hopeful America." He hailed the liberation of more than 50 million people in Afghanistan and Iraq under his leadership. On the domestic front, Bush reiterating previous positions, called for making his tax cuts permanent and allowing personal savings accounts as options for a portion of contributions to Social Security.

After the conventions ended **Sept. 2,** most polls showed Bush holding a clear advantage over Kerry. A CNN/Gallup/*USA Today* poll released **Sept. 6** found that Bush led Kerry, 52% to 45%. A *Newsweek* poll conducted **Sept. 9-10** showed Bush leading Kerry, 49% to 43%.

> *"I believe the most solemn duty of the American president is to protect the American people. If America shows uncertainty or weakness in this decade, the world will drift toward tragedy. This will not happen on my watch."*
>
> Pres. Bush in his speech at the Republican National Convention, Sept. 2, accepting his party's nomination for the presidency.

Pres. Clinton Undergoes Heart Operation—Former Pres. Bill Clinton underwent quadruple bypass surgery on Sept. 6, in a 4-hour procedure at New York Presbyterian Hospital in New York City. Clinton, who was diagnosed with blockages after reporting chest pains, appeared to be making satisfactory progress in recovery from the operation but was expected to be limited in making campaign efforts on behalf of Kerry.

Iraq Becomes Major Issue in Election Campaign—Issues relating to terrorism and the war in Iraq dominated debate between the major-party presidential candidates. Sen. Kerry charged **Sept. 6** that Iraq was "the wrong war in the wrong place at the wrong time." Speaking of the threat posed by terrorists, Vice Pres. Cheney warned **Sept. 7** that "if we make the wrong choice, then the danger is that we'll get hit again and we'll be hit in a way that will be devastating." In a speech at New York Univ. **Sept. 20**, Kerry said the invasion had created a crisis "of historic proportions." He blamed the president for "colossal failures of judgment" in his approach to the war and reconstruction, and called for greater effort to attract UN and international support. Pres. Bush **Sept. 20** defended his record and argued that Kerry's proposals already were contained in plans made public by the administration.

Bush and Kerry faced each other **Sept. 30** at the University of Miami, in the first of 3 scheduled debates. Kerry attacked Bush vigorously on foreign policy, while Bush accused Kerry of lacking a consistent position on Iraq. Polls taken after the debate suggested more viewers thought Kerry had won the debate than Bush, whose performance appeared lackluster to many. Analysts generally considered that the race between Bush and Kerry was now close; two more presidential debates were scheduled.

9/11 Commission Proposals Receive Support—Legislators began to act on some of the proposals made in Aug. by the commission that investigated the **Sept. 11, 2001**, terror attacks. On **Sept. 7**, Sens. John McCain (R, AZ) and Joseph Lieberman (D, CT) introduced a bill to enact all 41 commission recommendations. Senate Majority Leader Bill Frist (R, TN) said **Sept. 8** that Pres. Bush had already moved to implement 36 of the proposals. Modifying his position, Bush agreed **Sept. 8** that the proposed new national intelligence

director should have full budgetary authority over the entire intelligence community, and that the position should be outside the executive office of the president.

CBS Report on Bush Military Record Is Alleged to Be Based on Forged Documents—CBS **Sept. 8** reported on its news program and on *60 Minutes* that newly discovered documents bolstered claims that Pres. Bush had failed to meet his responsibilities while a member of the National Guard in the 1970s. However, within days serious doubts were cast on the validity of the documents, supposedly typewritten memos from the files of the late Lt. Col. Jerry Killian, which described pressure to "sugarcoat" Lt. Bush's record because his father was a congressman and indicated that Bush had disobeyed an order to appear for a physical. Examination of the documents showed that they appeared to have been produced on a computer, and experts consulted by CBS prior to airing of the report said they could not vouch for them. Killian's former secretary, Marian Carr Knox, said **Sept. 14** that she had not typed the memos, although she said they reflected Killian's concerns at the time.

Texas Air National Guard Lt. Col. Bill Burkett (ret.), a Bush critic who gave the documents to CBS, did not reveal their genesis. Joe Lockhart, a leading aide to Sen. Kerry, conceded **Sept. 20** that he had contacted Burkett at the request of CBS producer Mary Mapes. CBS News Pres. Andrew Heyward admitted the same day, "CBS News cannot prove that the documents are authentic," and CBS News anchor Dan Rather apologized on the air for what he called "an error made in good faith." CBS **Sept. 22** established an independent panel headed by former PA Gov. Dick Thornburgh and former AP head Louis D. Boccardi to investigate the affair.

Ban on Purchase of Assault Weapons Expires—Congress did not renew the 1994 law that banned the manufacture and sale of 19 semiautomatic assault weapons and allowed it to expire on **Sept. 13**. Pres. Bush had said he favored renewing the ban, which included the AK-47 and the Uzi submachine gun, but he did not make efforts in its behalf. Critics of the ban contended that manufacturers had been able to produce nearly identical weapons legally. Sen. John Kerry charged **Sept. 13** that Bush "chose his powerful friends in the gun lobby over police officers and families that he had promised to protect."

Oil Price Hits $50 a Barrel—The price of oil hit an unwelcome milestone **Sept. 28**, topping $50 a barrel in intraday trading on the New York Mercantile Exchange. The threat of civil war in oil-rich Nigeria, instability in Iraq, and the effects of Hurricane Ivan in the Gulf of Mexico helped spur the rate hike. Meanwhile, the jobs situation improved, with unemployment edging downward in August to 5.4%, according to a government report issued **Sept. 3**. Some 144,000 non-farm jobs were created, and the July figure was revised upward to 73,000.

U.S. Economy at a Glance: September 2004	
Unemployment rate	5.4%
Dow Jones closing, 3rd quarter	10,080.27
Dow Jones highest close, 3rd quarter (Sept. 7)	10,342.79
Dow Jones lowest close, 3rd quarter (Aug. 12)	9,814.59

International

Hundreds Killed After Terrorists Seize Russian School— At least 330 people, half of them children, were killed and hundreds more were wounded after Chechen terrorists occupied a school in the city of Beslan, in the Russian republic of North Ossetia, **Sept. 1**. In all, 1,200 people, mostly children ages 6 to 16 who were attending the first day of school, were held under oppressive conditions by a group demanding withdrawal of Russian troops from Chechnya. On **Sept. 2**, the captors released 31 women, children, and infants. On **Sept. 3**, a bomb placed by the terrorists exploded in the gymnasium where hostages were being held. As hostages began to flee, the terrorists opened fire, which prompted Russian security forces surrounding the school to return fire. During a 13-hour battle, 11 members of Russia's special forces were killed. Of the 32 terrorists, 31 were killed and one was captured.

Speaking to the Russian people **Sept. 4**, Pres. Vladimir Putin said that after the controlling ideology of the Soviet regime disappeared in the early 1990s, "We stopped paying due attention to issues of defense and security."

Violence Continues in Iraq—With a scheduled nation-wide election just 4 months away, parts of Iraq remained in turmoil. On **Sept. 7** the death toll for U.S. military personnel since the 2003 invasion reached 1,000, with nearly 7,000 wounded. Attacks by insurgents remained at a high level, with Iraqi civilian casualties also mounting.

Among other incidents, a suicide car bomber **Sept. 4** killed 14 Iraqi police officers and 3 civilians in Kirkuk. The same day, 12 policemen and 5 national guardsmen were killed during a joint operation with U.S. forces south of Baghdad. A car bomb near Fallujah **Sept. 6** killed 7 U.S. Marines and 3 Iraqi national guardsmen. Three Polish soldiers were killed in an ambush **Sept. 12**.

After a suicide attack on a U.S. vehicle in Baghdad **Sept. 12**, U.S. helicopters fired on the vehicle where a crowd had gathered, killing 13 people, including a TV journalist; military officials said they needed to take action against the vehicle to "prevent looting and harm to the Iraqi people." U.S. planes bombed what was believed to be a meeting place for militants in Fallujah **Sept. 13**; 20 people were reportedly killed. A car bomb exploded in Baghdad **Sept. 14**, killing 47 Iraqis, many of whom were applying to join the police.

U.S. air attacks south of Fallujah **Sept. 16-17** killed more than 50 people according to local reports. A bomb exploding amid national guard recruits in Kirkuk, **Sept. 18**, killed 19. Fighting between anti-U.S. Shiite cleric Moqtada al-Sadr and U.S. forces resumed in Baghdad **Sept. 21**. A bomb in that city **Sept. 22** killed 11 and wounded 54. On **Sept. 25**; 7 Iraqis applying for the national guard were killed in Baghdad, and the U.S. military reported that 4 marines and a soldier had been killed. On **Sept. 30**, as U.S. troops handed out candy at a ceremony inaugurating a sewage treatment plant, 3 bombs went off, killing more than 40 people, including about 35 children.

A group believed to be led by Abu Musab al-Zarqawi posted videos on the internet **Sept. 20-21** depicting the beheading of 2 American civilians who had been kidnapped **Sept. 16**. The group had said that the men, Eugene Armstrong and Jack Hensley, would die unless the United States freed all Iraqi women that it was holding in prisons. The same group was holding a British citizen. Another group claimed **Sept. 19** that 3 captive Kurds had been killed. Two Italian women, kidnapped **Sept. 7** during raid on their Baghdad office, were released **Sept. 28**. Details of the release and conditions were unclear, with some reports saying ransom was paid.

A classified CIA intelligence report issued in July and made public **Sept. 16** foresaw the possibility of civil war in Iraq. Bush said **Sept. 21** that the CIA was "just guessing" as to what might happen; he noted that the report had sketched a range of possible outcomes. Iraq's interim Prime Min. Iyad Allawi, addressing a joint session of Congress **Sept. 23**, said that elections in Iraq would be held on schedule in January. He and Bush, after meeting at the White House, gave a positive picture of the overall situation in Iraq.

UN Urged to Stop Genocide in Sudan—Sec. of State Colin Powell told the Senate Foreign Relations Committee **Sept. 9** that Sudan's government and Arab militias had committed genocide against the black people of the Darfur region. Over the past 18 months some 50,000 people had been killed and hundreds of thousands left homeless, after Arab militias raided their towns and villages. Pres. Bush **Sept. 9** urged the UN and the international community to put a stop to the violence. A UN Security Council resolution **Sept. 18** called for Sudan to put an end to the killings.

Putin Proposes Government Changes—Russian Pres. Putin **Sept. 13** proposed major changes in the Russian political system said to be aimed at strengthening the nation's resistance to terrorism. He said that the heads of the Russian Federation's 89 administrative regions should hereafter be appointed by the federation president rather than being chosen in a public election. In addition, all 450 members of the State Duma, the lower house of the national legislature, would be chosen from party lists, based on the nationwide vote. Currently only half of the Duma members were chosen in that way, while the rest were elected in individual districts. The proposed changes would require legislative approval. Pres. Bush, while supporting Putin's struggle against terrorism, said **Sept. 15** that he was concerned that his approach "could undermine democracy in Russia."

Iran Rejects Plea to End Its Enrichment of Uranium—The board of the International Atomic Energy Agency **Sept. 18** asked Iran to stop its enrichment of uranium, which was a step toward producing fuel for either nuclear reactors or bombs. Iran had said that its program was for peaceful purposes only, and on **Sept. 19** it rejected any limit on its right to enrich uranium under the Nuclear Nonproliferation Treaty. Iran confirmed **Sept. 21** that it had begun to convert yellowcake uranium into a gas used in the enrichment.

Israel Launches Gaza Assault—On **Sept. 30**, Israeli tanks and armored vehicles moved into Jabaliya refugee camp, a hotbed for militants, in northern Gaza, in response to persistent Palestinian rocket fire. At least 28 Palestinians and 3 Israelis were killed in ensuing skirmishes.

General

3 More Hurricanes Lash Florida; 1,500 Are Killed in Haiti—Florida and the Caribbean took a beating in September from 3 more hurricanes, bringing to 4 the total that had swept through the region in less than 2 months. (Not since Texas in 1886 had a single state sustained 4 hurricanes in one year.) Two weeks after Hurricane Charley moved north from Florida, Hurricane Frances hit the Turks and Caicos Islands **Sept. 1**, then moved to the Bahamas **Sept. 2**, causing widespread damage. Florida officials **Sept. 2** ordered 2.5 million residents to evacuate, and Pres. George W. Bush **Sept. 4** declared the entire state of Florida a federal disaster zone. On **Sept. 5**, Frances entered the U.S. north of Palm Beach and cut across Florida to the northwest, before entering the Gulf of Mexico; more than 30 people in the U.S. were killed. Damage in Florida from Frances and Charley combined was put at more than $10 billion.

On **Sept. 7** Hurricane Ivan struck Grenada with 125 mph winds, killing about 40 people; it was upgraded **Sept. 9** to a category 5 hurricane, the highest classification, with 160 mph sustained winds. Ivan hit the U.S. shore between Mobile, AL, and Pensacola, FL, **Sept. 16**; it set off tornadoes as far north as Maryland—about 30 in Virginia alone—and caused widespread flooding. The death toll for Ivan was put at over 50 in the U.S. and 70 in the Caribbean; insured damages in the U.S. were estimated at $3 bil–$6 bil.

Jeanne, the most lethal of the 4 storms, reached the island of Hispaniola **Sept. 16**. About 20 people died in the Dominican Republic, while on Haiti at least 1,500 lost their lives. Haitians continued to suffer health problems from a lack of food and safe drinking water. Jeanne finally hit the east coast of Florida, north of West Palm Beach, **Sept. 26**; by the next day it reached southwestern Georgia. A total of 6 people in the U.S. died as a result of Hurricane Jeanne.

Rape Charge Against Basketball Star Dismissed—The judge in the sexual assault case against pro basketball star Kobe Bryant dismissed a rape charge against him **Sept. 1** at the request of prosecutors, who said that the alleged victim had decided not to testify. Bryant played for the Los Angeles Lakers. The alleged assault had occurred in 2003 in Eagle, CO. A medical exam of the woman after she was with Bryant in his room revealed DNA samples from Bryant. Her blood was on his T-shirt. Bryant asserted that his relations with her had been consensual.

Two Russian Women in U.S. Tennis Open Final—In an unexpected finale in the women's singles competition at the U.S. Open in New York City **Sept. 11**, Svetlana Kuznetsova, the 9th seed, defeated Elena Dementieva, the 6th seed, 6-3, 7-5. Both women were from Russia. On **Sept. 12**, Roger Federer of Switzerland, the top seed, defeated Lleyton Hewitt of Australia, 6-0, 7-6, 6-0. Federer had won 2 of the other 3 2004 Grand Slam events, the Australian and Wimbledon titles.

OCTOBER 1-15

National

More Debates Enliven Close Election Contest—Debates between candidates for national office continued to hold the public's attention, and the presidential race appeared close, according to polls. Surveys taken in the days after the **Sept. 30** presidential debate showed that Sen. John Kerry, the Democratic nominee, had outperformed Pres. George W. Bush.

The vice-presidential candidates debated **Oct. 5** in Cleveland. Vice Pres. Richard Cheney strongly defended the U.S. invasion of Iraq, while criticizing his opponent's attendance record in the Senate and his winning of huge settlements for clients as a trial attorney. Sen. John Edwards (D, NC) questioned Cheney's relationship with the Halliburton Corp., which Cheney once headed, while also citing the company's huge no-bid contract to provide services in Iraq

The Iraq controversy deepened **Oct. 6**, when Charles Duelfer, the top American arms inspector in Iraq, said in a 1,000-page report that the Saddam Hussein regime had destroyed its chemical weapons stockpiles soon after the 1991 Persian Gulf War. He said, however, that Hussein had sought to preserve the capacity to reconstitute weapons of mass destruction after sanctions were lifted.

The 2nd presidential debate, in St. Louis **Oct. 8**, was a town hall format where undecided voters questioned the candidates, who were free to move about the stage. Bush and Kerry clashed on a number of domestic and international issues. Bush claimed that Kerry was not credible as an advocate of fiscal conservatism and that his spending proposals would cost $2.2 trillion. Kerry rejected this figure, and charged that Bush had squandered budget surpluses that he had inherited in order to give a huge tax cut to the wealthy. When Kerry said that Bush had gone to war without the support of many U.S. allies, an angry Bush responded, referring to the British prime minister, "You tell Tony Blair we're going alone."

Pres. Bush and Sen. Kerry faced off in their final debate **Oct. 13** in Tempe, AZ. Bush continued to paint his rival as a tax-and-spend liberal, while Kerry repeated an earlier statement that Bush squandered a $5.6 trillion surplus. The two men spent the night returning to topics they had presented in previous debates and stump speeches, including abortion, gay marriage, and the role of religion in their lives.

Job Recovery Continues to Lag—The second Bush-Kerry debate came hours after a report **Oct. 8** that employment grew by only 96,000 jobs in September. Although an economic recovery was continuing, Bush would be the first president since Herbert Hoover in 1932 to run for reelection with fewer Americans employed than when he started. Another economic issue was the price of oil, which hit new highs almost daily in early October, moving to around $54 a barrel.

The federal deficit hit the $413 billion mark in 2004, the largest budget deficit in U.S. history, though it was smaller than had been anticipated. According to Treasury estimates issued **Oct. 14**, in total dollars, the government collected $1.88 trillion in revenue, and spent about $2.29 trillion.

International

Supporters of Rebel Cleric Turn In Their Arms to Iraqi Police—In an agreement announced **Oct. 9**, fighters supporting rebel Shiite cleric Moktada al-Sadr agreed to turn in their heavy weapons to Iraqi police. In return, Americans would end their attacks on Sadr City, the Baghdad slum that provided much of the cleric's support. The militiamen began surrendering weapons **Oct. 11**.

On **Oct. 1**, U.S. and Iraqi forces pushed into the center of insurgent-controlled Samarra. More than 5,000 troops, including 3,000 Americans, joined in the operation. About 100 guerrillas were reported killed. The Americans and Iraqis **Oct. 3** completed their conquest of insurgent-occupied neighborhoods. On **Oct. 12**, U.S. troops and airplanes attacked Sunni insurgents in several locations, in a push timed to conclude before the beginning of the Ramadan holy month. A number of mosques thought to harbor terrorists were raided. Insurgent attacks **Oct. 12** and **13** killed 6 U.S. soldiers.

Three suicide bombs exploded **Oct. 4**, 2 in Baghdad and one in Mosul, killing 26 and wounding more than 100. A video delivered to Abu Dhabi TV **Oct. 8** depicted the beheading of British hostage Kenneth Bigley. He had been kidnapped in September along with 2 Americans who had also been beheaded.

Insurgents made their way into the American-controlled, high-security Green Zone in Baghdad killing 5 and wounding 20 with a pair of bomb blasts **Oct. 14**. It was the first attack of its kind in the fortified zone. Witnesses said that the pair of insurgents carried backpacks that possibly contained the explosives and spent time at a café before detonating their bombs. The event led to a security review of the compound by U.S. forces. Marines launched a series of air and ground attacks **Oct. 14** on the insurgent stronghold of Fallujah after peace talks between city representatives and government officials were suspended.

Sporadic Bombings Continue in Pakistan; Hostage Freed—An explosion in a Shiite mosque in Sialkot, Pakistan, **Oct. 1**, killed at least 23 people. The attack was thought to be in retaliation for the announced killing, **Sept. 27**, of Amjad Hussain Farooqi, described as a top figure in the al-Qaeda terrorist organization. A car bomb in Multan **Oct. 7** killed 40. On **Oct. 14**, Pakistani commandos stormed an Islamic militant hideout, rescuing 1 Chinese hostage and killing 5 kidnappers. Another Chinese hostage died in the rescue.

Bombs Across Israeli Border in Egypt Kill 33—On **Oct. 7**, 3 bombs exploded at tourist resorts in Taba, Egypt, on the Gulf of Aqaba, just across the international boundary with Israel. At least 33 were killed and about 150 injured. Most of the victims were Israelis. One section of the Taba Hilton Hotel was reduced to rubble. Two other bombs exploded in bungalow communities along Egypt's Sinai coast.

On **Oct. 1**, at least 100 Israeli tanks joined by hundreds of soldiers, rolled into the Jabaliva refugee camp in Gaza City, and 2 Israeli missile strikes there killed 8 Palestinians and wounded 17. Dozens of Palestinians were killed in the next 2 weeks. On Oct. 15, the Israeli Defense Ministry announced a pullback, saying it wanted to ease the burden on innocent Palestinian civilians as the Muslim holy month of Ramadan began.

Afghanistan Holds Presidential Election—Afghanistan, 3 years after liberation from the rule of extreme Islamic fundamentalists, held its first presidential election **Oct. 9**. Anticipated attacks by insurgents to disrupt the voting failed to materialize. Afghan and international observers largely discounted charges of election fraud. Pres. Hamid Karzai was favored to win; a complete vote tally was expected to take weeks.

Australian Voters Reelect Prime Minister Howard—John Howard, the Australian prime minister who supported the war in Iraq and sent troops to join the U.S.-led coalition, was easily reelected **Oct. 9**. His center-right Liberal Party ran well ahead of the Labor Party led by Mark Latham. Observers said that the booming economy was the principal reason for Howard's victory.

"Enemy Combatant" Returns to Saudi Family—Yaser Esam Hamdi, a U.S. citizen captured in Afghanistan, labeled an enemy combatant, and held in solitary confinement for nearly 3 years without being charged was returned to his family in Saudi Arabia **Oct. 11** after agreeing to give up his U.S. citizenship.

General

Production of One Flu Vaccine Suspended—British regulators **Oct. 5** suspended production of flu vaccine at the Liverpool plant of Chiron, an Emeryville, CA, company. Contamination of the vaccine was cited as the reason. The action resulted in about a 50% reduction in vaccine available for use in the U.S. American health officials asked that flu shots be given on a priority basis to those who needed them most, including children under age 2, the ill, and those over age 65.

Kenyan Environmentalist Wins Nobel Peace Prize—On **Oct. 8**, for the first time, the Nobel Peace Prize went to an African woman. The recipient was Dr. Wangari Maathai, an assistant minister of the environment who had been jailed by a previous Kenya regime. She founded the Green Belt Movement in 1977 and organized women to plant 30 million trees.

Notable Supreme Court Decisions, 2003-2004

During the Supreme Court's 2003-2004 term, which ended June 29, 73 decisions were announced, of which 17, or about 23%, were decided by 5-4 votes. That percentage compared with 20% in 2003-03 and 28% in 2001-02. Chief Justice William H. Rehnquist and Justices Antonin Scalia and Clarence Thomas tended to vote as a conservative bloc, often finding themselves at odds with the court's liberal wing—Justices Ruth Bader Ginsburg, Stephen G. Breyer, John Paul Stevens, and David H. Souter. Justices Sandra Day O'Connor and Anthony M. Kennedy were considered swing votes, though the majority of their votes were with the conservatives in close cases. Following are some of the major rulings of the term.

Antiterrorism Powers: The Supreme Court June 28 ruled, 6-3, that terrorism detainees being held indefinitely at the U.S. naval base at Guantanamo Bay, Cuba, could use U.S. courts to challenge their detentions and claim violations of international law *[Rasul v. Bush, Al Odah v. United States]*. The court also ruled, 6-3, that U.S. citizen Yaser Esam Hamdi could challenge his incommunicado detention in a South Carolina military brig, where he had been held as an enemy combatant since his 2001 capture in Afghanistan. However, the court upheld, 5-4, the president's authority to designate U.S. citizens like Hamdi as enemy combatants *[Hamdi v. Rumsfeld]*. In a 3rd ruling, the court voted, 5-4, to set aside the challenge of another designated enemy combatant, U.S. citizen Jose Padilla, on procedural grounds *[Rumsfeld v. Padilla]*.

Church and State: The court Feb. 24 ruled, 7-2, that a Washington State scholarship program did not violate the First Amendment's guarantee of the free exercise of religion by denying aid to otherwise qualified students who were training to become clergy. *[Locke v. Davey]*. The court June 14 ruled, 8-0, against an atheist father who objected to the recitation of the Pledge of Allegiance, with its phrase "one nation under God," at his daughter's public school. A 5-justice majority found that the man, Dr. Michael Newdow, did not have legal standing to pursue his suit because he did lacked the required custody of his daughter *[Elk Grove Unified School District v. Newdow]*.

Election Issues: The court Dec. 10, 2003, upheld, 5-4, the 2 main parts of a landmark 2002 campaign finance law: a ban on unregulated "soft money" contributions to the national parties by individuals, corporations, and unions; and restrictions on late-campaign attack ads by corporations, unions, and other outside groups *[McConnell v. Federal Election Commission]*. On Apr. 23, the court, 5-4, upheld a 2002 redistricting plan for Pennsylvania's U.S. House delegation, finding there was no available standard by which it could be judged an unconstitutionally partisan gerrymander. However, the court left open the possibility that a workable standard for evaluating such cases could be honed in the future *[Vieth v. Jubelirer]*.

Freedom of Information: The court June 24 ruled, 7-2, that lower courts had not given due consideration to a request by Vice Pres. Richard Cheney to block disclosure of records of an energy policy task force he had headed. Justice Antonin Scalia Mar. 18 had issued an unusual 21-page memorandum rejecting a motion by a litigant in the case that had sought his recusal because of personal ties between him and Cheney *[Cheney v. U.S. District Court]*.

Criminal Law: The court June 24 ruled, 5-4, that sentences in criminal cases could be increased beyond statutory guidelines only by juries on the basis of conclusions reached beyond a reasonable doubt, and not by judges alone. *[Blakely v. Washington]*. On June 28 it ruled, 5-4, that police could not deliberately interrogate suspects before reading them their legal rights in order to then more easily elicit a repeated confession that could be introduced in court *[Missouri v. Seibert]*.

Civil Rights: The **court** Feb. 24 ruled, 6-3, that the 1967 Age Discrimination in Employment Act did not allow lawsuits by younger workers claiming discrimination in favor of older workers *[General Dynamics Land Systems v. Cline]*. The court May 17 ruled, 5-4, that disabled individuals could sue states under the Americans With Disabilities Act for failing to provide adequate physical access to state courthouses, despite the states' usual 11th Amendment immunity from private lawsuits in federal court *[Tennessee v. Lane]*.

Indian Tribal Powers: The court April 19 voted, 7-2, to uphold an American Indian tribe's sovereign authority to prosecute members of another tribe, even if the federal government was prosecuting the defendant for the same act *[United States v. Lara]*.

Human Rights: The court June 29 ruled, 6-3, that under the 1789 Alien Tort Claims Act, foreigners could file lawsuits in U.S. courts seeking damages for serious human rights abuses committed outside the country *[Sosa v. Alvarez-Machain, U.S. v. Alvarez-Machain]*.

The 2004 Nobel Prizes

The 2004 Nobel Prize winners were announced Oct. 4-11. Each prize is worth about $1.32 million.

Chemistry: Israelis Aaron Ciechanover and Avram Hershko and American Irwin Rose divided the prize for explaining how cells regulate protein degradation. Proteins to be broken down are given a molecular label (ubiquitin) and then destroyed. When the process does not work properly, we fall ill. Their breakthrough opened the way to developing drugs that could treat cervical cancer, cystic fibrosis, and other illnesses.

Economics: Norwegian Finn E. Kydland and American Edward C. Prescott split the prize "for their contributions to dynamic macroeconomics: the time consistency of economic policy and the driving forces behind business cycles." Their theories have made key contributions to monetary and fiscal policy in many countries.

Literature: Austrian feminist and social critic Elfriede Jelinek was recognized "for her musical flow of voices and counter-voices in novels and plays that with extraordinary linguistic zeal," the Swedish Academy stated. She made her debut with *Lisas Schatten (Lisa's Shade)* in 1967. Other works include the novel *Das Klavierspielerin* (1983; translated into English as *The Piano Teacher* in 1988) and the drama *Was geschah, nachdem Nora ihren Mann verlassen hatte oder Stützen der Gesellschaften* (1980; *What Happened After Nora left Her Husband, or Pillars of Societies*).

Peace: Wangari Maathai of Kenya was recognized for her contribution to sustainable development, democracy, and peace. She founded the Green Belt Movement in 1977; through it, she has mobilized poor women to plant 30 million trees. The movement also promotes education, family planning, nutrition, and the fight against corruption. Maathai is the first woman from Africa to win the prize.

Physics: Americans David J. Gross, H. David Politzer, and Frank Wilczek each took a third of the award "for the discovery of asymptotic freedom in the theory of the strong interaction." The three discovered that the dominant force (known as the *strong* or *color force*) within an atom's nucleus weakens when quarks are close together. When quarks are farther apart, the force is stronger—like the stretching of a rubber band.

Physiology or Medicine: Richard Axel and Linda B. Buck, both of the U.S., split the honor for their research on how humans recognize and remember some 10,000 different smells. The two discovered a family of 1,000 genes (about 3% of all an individual's total number) that program an equivalent number of olfactory receptor types. Each type of receptor recognizes a limited number of odors, and it sends information to a specific micro domain, called a glomerulus, in the brain's olfactory bulb. Cells with the same type of receptor send information to the same *glomerulus*. From there, the information is sent to other parts of the brain, where memory patterns are formed.

Offbeat News Stories, 2004

They Call Me "They." A Branson, MO, man had his name legally changed from Andrew Wilson to "They" in Sept. 2004. The 43-year-old inventor took the new name to make a point, of sorts. "'They do this' or 'They're to blame for that.' Who is this 'they' that everyone talks about? 'They' accomplish such great things. Somebody had to take responsibility," the inventor said in an Associated Press story. They holds 14 patents, including one for Ground Effect Lighting, which creates a neon glow under vehicles.

What'll They Think of Next? Press reports from around the globe noted the following product and service "innovations" in 2004:

–From Japan's *Mainichi Daily News* English language Web site: horse flesh, oyster and goat ice cream (three distinct flavors, thankfully) are now served as novelty flavors at Ice Cream City in Tokyo. Want some? Nay!

–A Virginia couple's Avian Fashions company offers reuseable Lycra and Velcro diapers for household birds, which allow the birds to travel without "embarrassment" and, like the starship *Enterprise*, "to boldly go…"

–Intel Corp. in June unveiled the The Intel Wireless Technology Surfboard, a one-of-kind 9-foot-board surfboard with a built-in laptop computer that could be used in the water or on the beach. A wireless connection supports "surfing" the internet.

–Worn out from a day of New York City tourism? Visit Metronaps in the Empire State Building. For $13.95 you can take a 20-minute nap in a special audio and vibration equipped "chair-pod."

What'll They Outsource Next? Some McDonald's restaurants around the U.S. were experimenting with a system where orders from drive-thru customers are answered by a call center in Colorado. The employee there records the order and sends it by computer network to the kitchen at the local restaurant. A McDonald's owner in Minneapolis who uses it says the system improves accuracy and saves an average of 20 seconds per order. Meanwhile, in a growing trend, priests in India are saying Masses for the dead or for other intentions requested by parishioners in North America, the *New York Times* reported June 13. Nowadays the intentions are often sent by e-mail. The system allows Western churches with more money but fewer priests to support churches in poorer places with their offerings.

It's About Motion. The Roanoke Ballet Theater Apr. 15 debuted "NASCAR Ballet," timed to coincide with the Advance Auto Parts 500 NASCAR race the same weekend in nearby Martinsville, VA. Dancers, choreographed by executive artistic director Jenny Mansfield, rounded an oval-shaped banked and barriered stage, occasionally crashing into one another to the sound of recorded new age music and the revving of engines. There were also video screens of sportcasters calling the 90-minute "race." The dancers wore race-suit like unitards patched with logos of the ballet's sponsors, though far fewer than on real NASCARs.

Artistic "Lisence?" When the new $26 mil Livermore, CA, Public Library opened in May 2004, one of its major attractions was a mosaic mural designed and installed by Miami-based artist Maria Alquilar. The only trouble is that 11 of the 175 famous names in the artwork were spelled wrong—including Shakespeare ("Shakespere"), Michelangelo ("Michaelangelo"), van Gogh ("van Gough"), and Einstein ("Eistein"). Alquilar has defended the $40,000 art work, saying the spellings were "interpretive," but whether it was imagination or just plain bad spelling, the city council paid $6,000 plus expenses to get the spellings corrected.

Measuring Happiness. Researchers at Dartmouth Coll. and Warwick Univ. worked out an economic scale to measure people's happiness under different circumstances. A successful marriage, for example, contributes so much to a person's contentment that it would be equivalent to $100,000 annually. Their equations indicated that increasing sexual activity (from once a month to once a week) could offer big happiness payoffs, equal to $50,000 added to one's annual salary. The researchers also concluded that unemployment decreases happiness beyond just the loss of wages, and that happiness over a lifetime is "U-shaped," meaning that people are happiest when very young and very old, with a low-point at around 40.

Leaving the Borough of Kings? New York Dept. of Transportation officials turned down Brooklyn Borough President Marty Markowitz's request for a sign reading "Leaving Brooklyn: Oy Vey!" to be placed on the Williamsburg Bridge into Manhattan. The DOT felt the Yiddish phrase, meaning "oh, woe," would be more distracting than helpful to drivers. Markowitz only meant for the common Brooklyn (Kings County) expression to "put a smile on people's faces." An earlier request for a similar sign on the Verrazano Narrows Bridge (between Staten Island and Brooklyn)—"Leaving Brooklyn: Fuhgeddaboudit!"—was also rejected by the DOT for "a lack of directional information."

Gorilla Goes Ape Over Surgery. Koko, a 33-year old gorilla who lives in Woodside, CA, was able to tell her handlers that her mouth hurt. Koko–who can use 1,000 words in American Sign Language and understands more than 2,000–told her handlers that she preferred dental surgery over taking pain medication, news reports said in early Aug. The 300-lb. ape made the decision after her handlers gave her an operation doll, like those used with children. The procedure was a complete success.

No Barking Zone. New York City attorney David Fink was fined $8,500 for barking like a dog, among other improprieties, at a hearing before Manhattan State Supreme Court Justice Charles Ramos. During the hearing, a witness testified that he had received intimidating "mad-dog lawyer" letters from Fink, the attorney handling the lawsuit against him. The next day, when the witness was questioned again about the letters, Fink, who was standing by, began barking like a dog, interrupting testimony. A lawyer for the defense said, "Mr. Fink was barking up the wrong tree."

And We Thought *The World Almanac* Was Big. At a whopping 5 feet by 7 feet and weighing 130 pounds, the 112-page *Bhutan: A Visual Odyssey Across the Last Himalayan Kingdom*, created by Michael Hawley of the MIT Media Lab, is the heavyweight champion of the book world. The photographic image for each page is nearly 2 gigabytes in size and a single book requires a roll of paper longer than a football field. It costs about $2,000 to produce a copy of the book, which sells for $10,000 and can only be ordered through Amazon.com. Proceeds go to the charity Friendly Planet, founded by Hawley, which will use the money to fund educational programs in Bhutan.

Notable Quotes: The Lighter Side

"A lot of presidential memoirs are dull and self-serving. I hope mine is interesting and self-serving."
—*Former Pres. Bill Clinton*, June 14, on his memoir *My Life.*

"Thank goodness they're both called John."
—*Teresa Heinz Kerry*, May 17, on verbally mixing up her late husband, Sen. John Heinz, with her husband Sen. John Kerry.

"That's cool . . . but I don't know who Cary Grant is."
—*Actor Frankie Muniz*, 18, Mar. 22, on being called "the Cary Grant of kid stars."

"But you know, never again. I mean . . . it was mad."
—*London resident Ashley Revell*, 32, Apr. 26, on betting his life savings ($135,300) on a single spin of a Las Vegas roulette wheel. He won.

"It sends a signal . . . At 80 years old, you're not dead."
—*Former Pres. George H.W. Bush*, May 24, on his latest parachute jump with the Army.

"It's enough fun that the money's just icing on the cake. But there seems to be a lot of icing."
—*Jeopardy! champ Ken Jennings*, July 26, who by then had won over $1 million in appearances on the show.

"You're fired."
—*Donald Trump*, to unlucky contestants on *The Apprentice.*

Notable Quotes in 2004

See also boxes in Chronology of Events.

Iraq Conflict

"Let freedom reign!"
—*Pres. George W. Bush*, in note handed to Nat. Security Advisor Condoleeza Rice after he was informed during a summit meeting June 28 that sovereignty had been given over to the Iraqi government.

"It turns out we were all wrong."
—Outgoing U.S. weapons inspector *David Kay* Jan. 28 testifying before the Senate Arms Services Committee about the widespread belief before the U.S.-led invasion that Iraq had weapons of mass destruction.

"I have not seen smoking-gun, concrete evidence about the connection, but I think the possibility of such connections did exist, and it was prudent to consider them at the time we did."
—*Secy. of State Colin Powell*, Jan. 8, on connections between Saddam Hussein and al-Qaeda.

"There's a reason why we sign these treaties—to protect my son in the military. That's why we have these treaties, so that when Americans are captured, they're not tortured."
—*Sen. Joseph Biden*, June 21, to Attorney Gen. John Ashcroft, during testimony about a Justice Dept. memo in which lawyers argued the U.S. was not bound by treaties against torture while interrogating al-Qaeda suspects.

Presidential Election

"Yeeaagh!"
—*Presidential hopeful Howard Dean*, Feb. 2, to supporters after his 3rd-place finish in the Iowa caucuses.

"I actually did vote for the $87 billion before I voted against it."
—*Democratic pres. candidate John Kerry*, Mar. 29, responding to Republican campaign ads criticizing his 2003 vote against funds for the Iraq war.

"Being lectured by the president on fiscal responsibility is a little bit like Tony Soprano talking to me about law and order in this country."
—*Sen. Kerry* in the 3rd presidential debate, Oct. 13.

"America can do better, and help is on the way."
—*Democratic pres. candidate John Kerry*, Aug. 9, accepting his nomination at the Dem. National Convention.

"He talks about a grand idea . . . we're going to solve the problem in Iraq by holding a summit. And what is he going to say to those people that show up at the summit? Join me in the 'wrong war at the wrong time at the wrong place.' "
—*Pres. Bush* in the 2nd presidential debate Oct. 8, referring to Kerry's plan and earlier critical comments about Bush's handling of the war in Iraq.

"The first lesson is this. Take it from me: every vote counts."
—*Former Vice Pres. Al Gore*, Aug. 9, on lessons he learned during his 2000 presidential campaign.

Other News

"We believe the 9/11 attacks revealed four kinds of failures: in imagination, policy, capabilities, and management. . . . [S]ince the plotters were flexible and resourceful, we cannot know whether any single step or series of steps would have defeated them."
—*Report from the National Commission on Terrorist Attacks Upon the United States*, released July 22.

"March 11, 2004, now occupies a place in the history of infamy."
—*Prime Min. Jose Maria Aznar* of Spain, Mar. 22, on the train bombings in Madrid that killed 191 people.

"Call it civil war. Call it ethnic cleansing. Call it genocide. . . . The reality is the same. There are people in Darfur who desperately need the help of the international community."
—*Secy. of State Colin Powell*, Sept. 20, calling on the UN to take action in war-torn Sudan.

"I want to say personally and directly I'm sorry. . . . This was an error made in good faith."
—*CBS anchorman Dan Rather*, Oct. 4, admitting that the network could not vouch for the authenticity of allegedly forged documents it had used on a *60 Minutes* report criticizing Pres. Bush's service record in the National Guard.

"You've got to stop beating up your women because you can't get a job because you didn't want to get an education and now you're [earning] minimum wage."
—*Bill Cosby*, July 12, speaking of black men at the Rainbow/PUSH Coalition and Citizenship Education Fund's annual conference.

"This is my brand-new wife."
—*Comedian Rosie O'Donnell*, Mar. 8, after marrying her girlfriend, Kelli Carpenter, in San Francisco, to protest a proposed constitutional amendment banning gay marriage.

"Although I truly believe this encounter between us was consensual, I recognize now that she did not and does not view this incident the same way I did."
—*LA Lakers star Kobe Bryant*, Sept. 13, in a statement released after a Colorado judge dropped his rape case.

"I am sorry if anyone was offended by the wardrobe malfunction during the halftime performance at the Super Bowl."
—*Singer Justin Timberlake*, Feb. 2, on the incident, during which Janet Jackson's breast was exposed on live television.

WORLD ALMANAC EDITORS' PICKS
Most Memorable Quotes of the Last 100 Years

The editors of The World Almanac have ranked the following as the most memorable quotes by Americans in the last 100 years.

1. "That's one small step for man, one giant leap for mankind."
   —Neil Armstrong, the first person to set foot on the moon (July 20, 1969)

2. "Yesterday, December 7, 1941—a date which will live in infamy…"
   —Pres. Franklin D. Roosevelt, message to Congress after Japanese attack on Pearl Harbor

3. "Ask not what your country can do for you—ask what you can do for your country."
   —Pres. John F. Kennedy, inaugural address (Jan. 20, 1961)

4. "I have a dream that my four little children will one day live in a nation where they will not be judged by the color of their skin but by the content of their character."
   —Rev. Dr. Martin Luther King Jr., speech at Lincoln Memorial during March on Washington (Aug. 28, 1963)

5. "Mr. Gorbachev, tear down this wall!"
   —Pres. Ronald Reagan, at Brandenburg Gate, West Berlin, Germany (June 12, 1987)

6. "Genius is one percent inspiration and ninety-nine percent perspiration."
   —Thomas Edison, Life (1932)

7. "Today I consider myself the luckiest man on the face of the earth."
   —Baseball player Lou Gehrig, giving his farewell speech (July 4, 1939)

8. "I shall return."
   —Gen. Douglas MacArthur, on leaving the Philippines to Japanese invaders (Mar. 12, 1942)

9. "In the future, everyone will be world-famous for fifteen minutes."
   —Pop artist Andy Warhol (1968)

10. "God, give us grace to accept with serenity the things that cannot be changed, courage to change the things which should be changed, and the wisdom to distinguish the one from the other."
    —Reinhold Niebuhr, The Serenity Prayer (1943)

11. "Rose is a rose is a rose, is a rose."
    —Gertrude Stein, Sacred Emily (1913)

12. "It ain't over 'til it's over."
    —Yogi Berra, as NY Mets manager in National League pennant race (1973)

Major Actions of the 108th Congress

The 108th Congress convened Jan. 7, 2003, with both chambers under Republican control. In the House of Representatives, Republicans held 229 seats and Democrats 205, with 1 independent aligned with the Democrats, for a total of 435 voting members. Among the 100 senators, Republicans held a 51-48 majority, with 1 independent allied with the Democrats. The House had 55 new members, and the Senate 11. A record 14 women held Senate seats, and 59 women served as full voting members of the House. Among House members were 37 African-Americans and a record 24 Hispanics; no blacks or Hispanics held seats in the Senate.

Leadership. The speaker of the House was J. Dennis Hastert (R, IL). Other high-ranking House members included Majority Leader Tom DeLay (R, TX) and Minority Leader Nancy Pelosi (D, CA), the highest-ranking woman in the history of the U.S. Congress. The longest continuously serving member of the House was John Dingell (D, MI), in office since 1955. In the Senate, Bill Frist (R, TN) was majority leader and Tom Daschle (D, SD) minority leader. The president pro tempore was Ted Stevens (R, AK), who entered the Senate in 1968. The longest-serving senator of either party was Robert Byrd (D, WV), who took office in 1959.

Ethics. Rep. Bill Janklow (R, SD) resigned his House seat Jan. 20, 2004, after he was convicted of manslaughter and reckless driving for killing a motorcyclist in a traffic accident. On June 1, Stephanie Herseth (D) was elected to fill the vacancy.

The House ethics committee, or Committee on Standards of Official Conduct, cited Majority Leader Tom DeLay for violating House rules on several occasions. The panel admonished him, Sept. 30, 2004, for having offered to endorse the son of Rep. Nick Smith (R, MI) in a primary election in hopes of gaining Smith's support in a close vote; the committee also found fault with Smith and Rep. Candice Miller (R, MI). On Oct. 6 the ethics panel admonished DeLay for misconduct in 2 other matters: first, for asking federal aviation officials to track down Democratic Texas legislators who had fled the state capital to prevent a quorum on a redistricting measure Texas Republicans favored; second, for taking part in a golf fundraiser sponsored by an energy company that created "an improper appearance."

Unfinished Business. The House recessed Oct. 9 and the Senate suspended its work Oct. 11 so that members could return to their home districts for 3 full weeks of campaigning before the Nov. 2 election. Uncompleted at the time of recess were 9 of 13 major government spending bills and measures that would fund highway and mass transit programs, reauthorize the 1996 welfare reform law, limit medical liability claims and class-action lawsuits, promote U.S. energy independence, and overhaul the nation's bankruptcy and immigration laws. A stopgap funding measure cleared by Congress Sept. 29 and signed by Pres. Bush Sept. 30 was expected to keep the government running until Congress reconvened for a lame-duck session in mid-November. (Republican strategists raised the possibility, however, that Congress might meet shortly before election day to pass a bill restructuring the U.S. intelligence community, if House and Senate conferees could iron out their differences over recommendations made by the 9-11 Commission.)

For Further Information. Following is a summary of major actions taken by the 108th Congress through Oct. 11, 2004. Measures that have become law are identified by their Public Law (PL) number. Detailed legislative information may be accessed via the Internet at http://thomas.loc.gov.

2003

War Funding. Supplemental appropriation for fiscal year ending Sept. 30, 2003, provides $78.5 billion in "emergency spending" for Iraq war and other items. Passed by the House Apr. 12 by voice vote; passed by the Senate Apr. 12 by unanimous consent vote; signed by Pres. Bush Apr. 16 (PL 108-11).

Emergency supplemental appropriation for fiscal year ending Sept. 30, 2004, provides $87 billion for military operations and reconstruction in Iraq and Afghanistan. Passed by the House Oct. 31, 298-121; passed by the Senate Nov. 3 by voice vote; signed by Pres. Bush Nov. 6 (PL 108-106).

National Debt. Increases public debt limit by $984 billion to a record $7.4 trillion. Deemed passed by the House Apr. 11 without direct vote; passed by the Senate May 23, 53-44; signed by Pres. Bush May 27 (PL 108-24).

HIV/AIDS. Authorizes the U.S. to spend $15 billion over 5 years to combat the global HIV/AIDS epidemic. Passed by the House May 1, 375-41; passed by the Senate by voice vote May 16; signed by Pres. Bush May 27 (PL 108-25).

Tax Cuts. Provides $330 billion in tax reductions, including a $148 billion cut in taxes on dividends and capital gains through 2007. Passed by the House May 23, 231-200; passed by the Senate May 23, 51-50 (with Vice Pres. Cheney casting tie-breaking vote); signed by Pres. Bush May 28 (PL 108-27).

Abortion. Bans a procedure known as intact dilation and extraction, or "partial-birth abortion." Passed by the House Oct. 2, 281-142; passed by the Senate Oct. 21, 64-34; signed by Pres. Bush Nov. 5 (PL 108-105).

Medicare Overhaul. Adds a prescription drug benefit (as of 2006) and opens the federal health insurance program to federally subsidized competition from private insurers. Passed by the House Nov. 22, 220-215; passed by the Senate Nov. 25, 54-44; signed by Pres. Bush Dec. 8 (PL 108-173).

2004

Federal Agency Funding. Provides $373 billion for departments of Agriculture, Commerce, Education, Health and Human Services, Justice, State, Transportation, Treasury, Veterans Affairs, and other agencies for 2004 fiscal year. Passed by the House Dec. 8, 2003, 242-176; passed by the Senate Jan. 22, 2004, 65-28; signed by Pres. Bush Jan. 23 (PL 108-199).

Fetal Protection. Makes it a crime to injure or kill a child in utero; law confers legal status on the fetus, but exempts actions taken by a pregnant woman toward her own unborn child or any legal, consensual medical procedure, including abortion. Passed by the House Feb. 26, 254-163; passed by the Senate Mar. 25, 61-38; signed by Pres. Bush Apr. 1 (PL 108-212).

Federal Marriage Amendment. Would have amended the Constitution to bar same-sex marriage; fell short of required 2/3 majority in both chambers. Failed in the House Sept. 30, 227-186; failed in the Senate on cloture vote July 14, 48-50.

Project BioShield. Guarantees $5.6 billion over 10 years to encourage drug firms to develop countermeasures against chemical, biological, and radiological terrorism. Passed by the House July 14, 414-2; passed by the Senate May 19, 99-0; signed by Pres. Bush July 21 (PL 108-276).

Defense Spending. Appropriates $417.5 billion for Defense Department operations, including a $25 billion emergency fund for activities in Iraq and Afghanistan. Passed by the House July 22, 410-12; passed by the Senate July 22, 96-0; signed by Pres. Bush Aug. 5 (PL 108-287).

Tax Cuts. At a 10-year cost of about $146 billion, extends provisions that were due to expire at the end of 2004, including a $1,000 per child tax credit and other middle-class tax breaks. Passed by the House Sept. 23, 339-65; passed by the Senate Sept. 23, 92-3; signed by Pres. Bush Oct. 4 (PL 108-311).

Military Draft. Would have reinstated compulsory military service. Defeated by the House Oct. 5, 402-2.

Corporate Taxes. Provides an estimated $143 billion in tax breaks over 10 years to U.S. manufacturers; repeals an export subsidy the World Trade Organization said violated global trade rules. Passed by the House Oct. 7, 280-141; passed by the Senate Oct. 11, 69-17.

OBITUARIES

A

Abbas, Mohammed Abul, 55 or 56, Palestinian guerrilla leader considered the mastermind of the 1985 hijacking of the Italian cruise ship *Achille Lauro*; Baghdad, Iraq, Mar. 8, 2004.

Abel, Elie, 83, foreign correspondent, later dean of the Columbia Graduate School of Journalism; Rockville, MD, July 23, 2004.

Adair, Red, 89, Texan who was the world's best-known oil-well firefighter; Houston, TX, Aug. 7, 2004.

Adams, Brock, 77, congressman and senator who was Pres. Carter's transportation secretary (1977-79); Stevensville, MD, Sept. 10, 2004.

Adams, Eddie, 71, photojournalist best known for his 1969 Pulitzer Prize-winning photo of a South Vietnamese general shooting a Vietcong prisoner; New York, NY, Sept. 19, 2004.

Aiken, Joan, 79, author of popular children's books including *The Wolves of Willoughby Chase* (1962); Petsworth, England, Jan. 4, 2004.

Aliyev, Heydar, 80, president of post-Soviet Azerbaijan from 1993 to Oct. 2003; Cleveland, OH, Dec. 12, 2003.

Avedon, Richard, 81 fashion photographer known for his stark, artistic portraits of the rich and famous; San Antonio, TX, Oct. 1, 2004.

B

Bank, Aaron, 101, U.S. Army officer known as the father of the Green Berets; Dana Point, CA, Apr. 1, 2004.

Barnes, Peter, 73, British playwright who satirized his nation's class system in *The Ruling Class* (1968), made into a 1972 film; London, England, July 1, 2004.

Barnett, Etta Moten, 102, actress and singer who in 1934 became the first black woman to sing at the White House; Chicago, IL, Jan. 2, 2004.

Bartley, Robert L., 66, influential long-time editorial-page editor of the *Wall Street Journal* (1972-2002); New York, NY, Dec. 10, 2003.

Bates, Alan, 69, British actor acclaimed for such plays as *Look Back in Anger* (1956) and such films as *Zorba the Greek* (1966); London, England, Dec. 27, 2003.

Beene, Geoffrey, 77, leading fashion designer, known for his innovative use of materials; New York, NY, Sept. 28, 2004.

Bergstrom, Sune, 88, Swedish biochemist; shared the 1982 Nobel Prize for medicine for research into prostaglandins; Stockholm, Sweden, Aug. 15, 2004.

Bernstein, Elmer, 82, prolific film composer whose scores included *The Man With the Golden Arm* (1955) and *Ghostbusters* (1984); Ojai, CA, Aug. 18, 2004.

Berry, Jan, 62, member of the duo Jan and Dean that produced a string of "surf-music" hits in the 1960s; Los Angeles, CA, Mar. 26, 2004.

Blankers-Koen, Fanny, 85, Dutch athlete; only woman ever to win 4 gold medals in track and field at one Olympics (1948); Amsterdam, the Netherlands, Jan. 25, 2004.

Bloch, Richard, 78, co-founder, with his brother, Henry, of H&R Block, largest preparer of U.S. tax returns; Kansas City, MO, July 21, 2004.

Boorstin, Daniel J., 89, Pulitzer Prize-winning cultural historian who served as the Librarian of Congress from 1975 to 1987; Washington, DC, Feb. 28, 2004.

Brando, Marlon, 80, dynamic and influential Hollywood actor; won best actor Oscars for *On the Waterfront* (1954) and *The Godfather* (1972); he rejected his second Oscar, blaming Hollywood for mistreating Native Americans; Los Angeles, CA, July 1, 2004.

Brown, Roosevelt, 71, Hall of Fame offensive tackle for the NFL's New York Giants in the 1950s and 60s; Columbus, NJ, June 9, 2004.

Bucher, Lloyd, 76, commander of the U.S. Navy spy ship *Pueblo*, seized in 1968 by North Korea, where he and his crew endured 11 months of captivity; San Diego, CA, Jan. 28, 2004.

Burchfield, Robert, 81, British lexicographer who, from 1957 to 1984, oversaw the preparation of a 6,000-page supplement to the *Oxford English Dictionary*; Abingdon, England, July 5, 2004.

Burford, Anne (Gorsuch), 62, director of the Environmental Protection Agency under Pres. Reagan; forced to resign in 1983 for refusing to hand over toxic-waste documents to Congress; Aurora, CO, July 18, 2004.

C

Cahill, Joe, 84, a founder of the Provisional Irish Republican Army; later a champion of the peace process; Belfast, N Ireland, July 23, 2004.

Caminiti, Ken, 41, former 3rd baseman and 1996 NL MVP; admitted after retiring in 2001 to using steroids to improve his game; Bronx, NY, Oct. 10, 2004.

Cantalupo, Jim, 60, chairman and CEO of McDonald's Corp.; Orlando, FL, Apr. 19, 2004.

Carney, Art, 85, actor who played sewer worker Ed Norton in the 1950s TV series "Honeymooners," and won a 1975 best actor Oscar for *Harry and Tonto*; Chester, CT, Nov. 9, 2003.

Cartier-Bresson, Henri, 95, pioneering French photojournalist and one of the preeminent photographers of his time; Cereste, France, Aug. 3, 2004.

Charles, Ray, 73, popular musician who surmounted early-onset blindness to become an esteemed pianist, singer, and songwriter; Beverly Hills, CA, June 10, 2004.

Chiang Kai-Shek, Madame (Soong Mei-ling), 105, widow of Chinese Nationalist leader Chiang Kai-Shek and highly influential in the 1930s and 1940s, when she mobilized U.S. support for her husband; New York, NY, Oct. 24, 2003.

Child, Julia, 91, French-cooking expert who, as a TV personality and author, did more than anyone else to popularize French cuisine in the U.S.; Montecito, CA, Aug. 13, 2004.

Chodorov, Jerome, 93, playwright and screenwriter who coauthored the 1940 hit Broadway comedy *My Sister Eileen*; Nyack, NY, Sept. 12, 2004.

Cooke, Alistair, 95, engaging British-turned-American journalist whose "Letter From America" aired on BBC radio for 58 years; he hosted *Masterpiece Theater* on U.S. public TV from 1971 to 1992; New York, NY, Mar. 29, 2004.

Cooper, Gordon, 77, one of NASA's original 7 astronauts; made 2 space trips but never got to the Moon; Ventura, CA, Oct. 4, 2004.

Corelli, Franco, 82, Italian tenor who dominated opera stages from the 1950s until his 1976 retirement; Milan, Italy, Oct. 29, 2003.

Counsilman, Doc, 83, legendary Indiana Univ. swimming coach who wrote the 1968 classic *The Science of Swimming*; Bloomington, IN, Jan. 4, 2004.

Cox, Archibald, 92, Harvard law professor and Watergate special prosecutor fired by Pres. Nixon in 1973 in the "Saturday Night Massacre"; Brooksville, ME, May 29, 2004.

Crain, Jeanne, 78, glamorous Hollywood actress of the 1940s and 50s; starred in such films as *State Fair* (1945) and *Pinky* (1949); Santa Barbara, CA, Dec. 14, 2003.

Crick, Francis, 88, British molecular biologist; co-discoverer (1953) of the structure of DNA, for which he shared a 1962 Nobel Prize; San Diego, CA, July 29, 2004.

D

Dangerfield, Rodney, 82, comedian best known for his "no respect" catch-phrase and one-liners; featured on TV (*The Tonight Show*) and film (*Caddyshack*); Los Angeles, CA, Oct. 5, 2004.

Danziger, Paula, 59, author of *The Cat Ate My Gymsuit* (1974), the Amber Brown series and other best-selling children's books; New York, NY, July 8, 2004.

Dash, Samuel, 79, chief counsel for the House Judiciary Committee during the Watergate hearings; Washington, DC, May 29, 2004.

Davis, Marvin, 79, billionaire oilman and real estate developer who owned 20th Century Fox film studio for part of the 1980s; Beverly Hills, CA, Sept. 25, 2004.

Dee, Frances, 96, Hollywood leading lady of the 1930s and 1940s, married to co-star Joel McCrea; Norwalk, CT, Mar. 4, 2004.

de la Hunty, Shirley Strickland, 78, Australian track and field athlete whose 7 Olympic medals were the most won by an Australian athlete; Perth, Australia, Feb. 17, 2004.

Dellinger, Dave, 88, eldest of the Chicago Seven protesters arrested at the 1968 Democratic presidential convention; convicted on rioting charges; Montpelier, VT, May 25, 2004.

Derrida, Jacques, 74, French philosopher who was a founding father of deconstructionism; Paris, France, Oct. 8, 2004.

Dodd, Clement S. ("Sir Coxsone"), 72, Jamaican record producer credited with launching the career of reggae giant Bob Marley; Kingston, Jamaica, May 4, 2004.

Dumas, Charles, 66, first high jumper to clear 7 feet, which he did in 1956, the year he won an Olympic gold medal; Inglewood, CA, Jan. 5, 2004.

Dunne, John Gregory, 71, novelist, journalist; often collaborated with wife Joan Didion; brother of writer Dominick Dunne; New York, NY, Dec. 30, 2003.

E

Ebb, Fred, 76, lyricist who with composer John Kander wrote for such classic musicals as *Cabaret* (1966) and *Chicago* (1975); New York, NY, Sept. 11, 2004.

Eckerd, Jack, 91, founder of a Florida-based drugstore empire; Clearwater, FL, May 19, 2004.

Ederle, Gertrude, 98, first woman to swim the English Channel (1926); Wyckoff, NJ, Nov 30, 2003.

Elam, Jack, 84, character actor who played villains in such classic westerns as *High Noon* (1952); Ashland, OR, Oct. 20, 2003.

F

Fassie, Brenda, 39, black pop singer from South Africa; one of Africa's best-known entertainers; near Johannesburg, South Africa, May 9, 2004.

Ferré, Luis A., 99, governor of Puerto Rico, 1969-73, and leading advocate of statehood for the island; San Juan, PR, Oct. 21, 2003.

Fitzsimmons, Lowell "Cotton", 72, winner of 832 games in 21 seasons as an NBA coach; Phoenix, AZ, July 24, 2004.

Fong, Hiram L., 96, first Asian American elected to the U.S. Senate; Honolulu, HI, Aug. 18, 2004.

Fordice, Kirk, 70, millionaire construction firm owner who served 2 terms (1992-2000) as Mississippi's first Republican governor since Reconstruction; Jackson, MS, Sept. 7, 2004.

Frame, Janet, 79, New Zealand novelist and poet whose work drew upon her painful experiences as a mental patient; Dunedin, New Zealand, Jan. 29, 2004.

G

Gades, Antonio, 67, flamenco dancer and choreographer known for such films as *Blood Wedding* (1980); Madrid, Spain, July 20, 2004.

Genevieve, 83, French chanteuse who was a regular on the *Tonight Show* with Jack Paar; Los Angeles, CA, Mar. 14, 2004.

Ghiaurov, Nicolai, 74, Bulgarian regarded as one of the finest operatic basses of his time; Modena, Italy, June 2, 2004.

Gibson, Don, 75, country singer and songwriter; hits included "I Can't Stop Loving You" (1957); Nashville, TN, Nov. 17, 2003.

Goldsmith, Jerry, 75, composer of music for *Patton* (1970), and *The Omen* (1976, for which he won an Oscar) and *Gunsmoke* and *Barnaby Jones* on TV; Beverly Hills, CA, July 21, 2004.

Goldsmith, Olivia, 54, author of the best-selling women's revenge-fantasy novel *The First Wives Club* (1992); New York, NY, Jan. 15, 2004.

Golub, Leon, 82, representational artist known for his paintings of monumental human figures committing violent acts; New York, NY, Aug. 8, 2004.

Graham, Otto, 82, quarterback who led pro football's Cleveland Browns to 10 championship games (and 7 titles) in 10 seasons with the team (1946-55); Sarasota, FL, Dec. 17, 2003.

Gray, Spalding, 62, actor noted for his dramatic monologues, including *Swimming to Cambodia*, made into a 1987 film; missing since Jan. 10; body recovered Mar, 7, 2004, from New York City's East River; a suspected suicide.

Gunn, Thom, 74, British poet and prize-winning collection *The Man With Night Sweats* (1992) mourned friends who died of AIDS; San Francisco, CA, Apr. 25, 2004.

H

Hagen, Uta, 84, grande dame of the American theater who originated the role of Martha in *Who's Afraid of Virginia Woolf?* (1962) and was a noted acting teacher; New York, NY, Jan. 14, 2004.

Hatfield, Bobby, 63, tenor half of the "blue-eyed soul" duo the Righteous Brothers, who were inducted into the Rock and Roll Hall of Fame in Mar. 2003; Kalamazoo, MI, Nov. 5, 2003.

Hemmings, David, 62, British actor who played a fashion photographer in the seminal 1960s film *Blow Up*; Bucharest, Romania, Dec. 3, 2003.

Hicks, Louise Day, 87, leader in the 1960s and 70s of the fight against busing to desegregate Boston's public schools; Boston, MA, Oct. 21, 2003.

Hirsch, Elroy (Crazylegs), 80, NFL Hall of Famer who was a halfback-play receiver for the Los Angeles Rams in the 1950s; Madison, WI, Jan. 28, 2004.

Hoff, Syd, 76, longtime cartoonist for the *New Yorker*; also wrote and illustrated dozens of children's books; Miami Beach, FL, May 12, 2004.

Hotter, Hans, 94, German singer noted for his bass-baritone roles in Wagner operas; Grünwald, Germany, Dec. 8, 2003.

Hounsfield, Sir Godfrey, 84, British engineer who developed the first practical CAT scanner; shared the 1979 Nobel Prize for medicine; Kingston upon Thames, England, Aug. 12, 2004.

I

Izetbegovic, Alija, 78, leader of Bosnia's Muslims during Bosnia's 1992-95 war of independence from Yugoslavia; Sarajevo, Bosnia & Herzegovina, Oct. 19, 2003.

J

Jacquet, Illinois, 81, tenor saxophonist and bandleader; came to the fore in the early 1940s in Lionel Hampton's band; New York, NY, July 22, 2004.

James, Art, 74, longtime TV game show host and announcer; Palm Springs, CA, Mar. 28, 2004.

James, Rick, 56, flamboyant funk rock artist whose signature tune was "Super Freak" (1981); Los Angeles, CA, Aug. 6, 2004.

Johnson, Samuel Curtis, 76, longtime head of S.C. Johnson & Son Inc., one of the leading U.S. family-owned businesses; Racine, WI, May 22, 2004.

Jones, Elvin, 76, jazz drummer; a charter member of the John Coltrane Quartet, which revolutionized jazz in the early 1960s; Englewood, NJ, May 18, 2004.

Jones, Reginald H., 86, chairman and CEO of General Electric Co (1972-81) and an economic adviser to 4 U.S. presidents; Greenwich, CT, Dec. 23, 2003.

Juliana, Princess, 94, queen of the Netherlands from 1948 until 1980, when she abdicated in favor of her eldest daughter, Beatrix; Baarn, the Netherlands, Mar. 20, 2004.

K

Keeshan, Bob, 76, children's TV's Captain Kangaroo for more than 3 decades and, before that, the original Clarabell the Clown on the *Howdy Doody Show*; Windsor, VT, Jan. 23, 2004.

Kenner, Hugh, 80, literary critic best known for his interpretations of the works of Ezra Pound and James Joyce; Athens, GA, Nov. 24, 2003.

Kerr, Clark, 92, economist, labor mediator, and educator who, as president of the University of California system (1958-67), turned it into a model for public universities; El Cerrito, CA, Dec. 1, 2003.

King, Alan, 76, veteran stand-up comedian; also well known as an actor, film and theater producer; New York, NY, May 9, 2004.

Kleiber, Carlos, 74, reclusive Swiss-based conductor of opera and symphonic music; July 13, 2004, location not released.

Klestil, Thomas, 71, president of Austria since July 1992, when he succeeded the controversial Kurt Waldheim; Vienna, Austria, July 6, 2004.

Klinger, Georgette, 88, skin care expert who introduced European facial techniques to the U.S. in the 1940s; New York, NY, Jan. 9, 2004.

Koenig, Cardinal Franz, 98, influential Roman Catholic prelate during his tenure as archbishop of Vienna (1956-85); Vienna, Austria, Mar. 13, 2004.

Kübler-Ross, Elisabeth, 78, Swiss-born psychiatrist whose book *On Death and Dying* (1969) helped revolutionize the care of the terminally ill; Scottsdale, AZ, Aug. 24, 2004.

Kupcinet, Irv, 91, gossip columnist and late-night TV talk-show host who was a Chicago institution; Chicago, IL, Nov. 10, 2003.

L

Lacy, Steve, 69, soprano saxophonist, composer, and bandleader, protégé of jazz master Thelonious Monk; Boston, MA, June 4, 2004.

Lange, Hope, 70, actress who earned an Oscar nomination as a troubled teen in *Peyton Place* (1957) and 2 Emmys for the 1960s series *The Ghost and Mrs. Muir*; Santa Monica, CA, Dec. 19, 2003.

Lauder, Estee, 97, creator of the cosmetics empire that bore her name; a leading philanthropist and socialite; New York, NY, Apr. 24, 2004.

Lee, Anna, 91, actress who played matriarch Lila Quartermaine in the TV soap *General Hospital*—from a wheelchair since being paralyzed in a 1979 auto accident; Los Angeles, CA, May 14, 2004.

Leigh, Janet, 77, Hollywood actress best-known and Oscar-nominated for her chilling role in *Psycho* (1960); Beverly Hills, CA, Oct. 3, 2004.

Lewis, Edward B., 81, Nobel Prize-winning geneticist who discovered the genes controlling the development of fertilized eggs into embryos; Pasadena, CA, July 21, 2004.

Lopez Portillo, Jose, 83, president of Mexico, 1976-82; presided over a corrupt administration that led Mexico to the brink of economic collapse; Mexico City, Mexico, Feb. 17, 2004.

Loudon, Dorothy, 70, actress who won a 1977 Tony for her role as sadistic headmistress Miss Hannigan in the musical *Annie*; New York, NY, Nov. 15, 2003.

M

Manchester, William, 82, historian and author of biographies of Winston Churchill, Douglas MacArthur, and John F. Kennedy; Middletown, CT, June 1, 2004.

Manfredi, Nino, 83, Italian actor who made a mark in such comic films as Franco Brusati's *Bread and Chocolate* (1973); Rome, Italy, June 4, 2004.

Mara, Ratu Sir Kamisese, 83, politician who guided Fiji to independence from Britain in 1970 and served as its first prime minister; Suva, Fiji, Apr. 18, 2004.

May, Billy, 87, trumpeter, bandleader, and arranger best known for his work with Frank Sinatra; San Juan Capistrano, CA, Jan. 22, 2004.

McCambridge, Mercedes, 87, Oscar-winning actress (in 1950, for *All the King's Men*); provided the creepy voice of the possessed girl in *The Exorcist* (1963); La Jolla, CA, Mar. 2, 2004.

McGraw, Tug, 59, colorful left-handed relief pitcher for the New York Mets and Philadelphia Phillies who in 1980 closed out the only World Series ever won by the Phillies; Nashville, TN, Jan. 5, 2004.

McGrory, Mary, 85, widely read political columnist whose columns on the Watergate scandal earned her a 1975 Pulitzer Prize; Washington, DC, Apr. 21, 2004.

McWhirter, Norris, 78, co-founder and longtime editor of the *Guinness Book of Records*; Kington Langley, England, Apr. 19, 2004.

Meyer, Russ, 82, filmmaker known for soft-core "sexploitation" films like *Faster, Pussycat! Kill! Kill!* (1965) and *Vixen!* (1968); Los Angeles, CA, Sept. 18, 2004.

Miller, Ann, 84, tap dancer and actress; a staple of Hollywood musicals in the 40s and 50s; later captivated Broadway audiences in *Sugar Babies* (1979-82); Los Angeles, CA, Jan. 22, 2004.

Milosz, Czeslaw, 93, Polish poet, essayist, and translator; a 1980 Nobel laureate; Krakow, Poland, Aug. 14, 2004.

Miner, Jan, 86, actress best known for portraying Madge the Manicurist in Palmolive dish detergent commercials (1966-92); Bethel, CT, Feb. 15, 2004.

Mitchelson, Marvin M., 76, celebrity divorce lawyer who pioneered the concept of "palimony"; Beverly Hills, CA, Sept. 18, 2004.

RONALD REAGAN

Ronald Reagan, 93, 40th president of the U.S., died June 5, 2004, at his home in Los Angeles, CA, from complications of Alzheimer's disease.

The ceremonies following his death evoked strong emotions, and more than 200,000 people waited hours to pass by his closed coffin lying at the Ronald Reagan Presidential Library, in Simi Valley, CA (where he was later buried), and in state in the Capitol. The news coverage focused on the charisma and positive achievements of the former lifeguard, screen actor, conservative spokesman, California governor, and U.S. president, who occupied the White House for 2 terms, from 1981 to 1989. He was recognized for his optimistic spirit, as well as for what most considered a key role in ending the Cold War and (though it was anathema to many) in shifting the domestic political landscape toward the right. Despite the encomiums, Reagan remained a highly controversial figure, and critics have continued to point to flaws in his record, such as unprecedented federal budget deficits and the Iran-contra scandal (involving the secret sale of arms to Iran to finance support for right-wing Nicaraguan guerrillas). To many, he led the country in the wrong direction, and some questioned whether he did contribute to the ending of the Cold War. Many commentators, even among those strongly opposed to his policies, nevertheless agreed with the assessment of the *New York Times*, that Reagan was "one of the most important presidents of the 20th century."

Born in Tampico, IL, Feb. 6, 1911, Reagan grew up in Dixon, IL, and graduated from Eureka College. After reporting sports events on radio, he got a screen test in Hollywood and appeared in many movies. His first political activity came as president of the Screen Actors Guild; during this time his views evolved in a pronouncedly anti-Communist and conservative direction. As a spokesman for conservative causes for the General Electric Corp., he gained a national following, buttressed in 1964 by an impassioned speech in behalf of Sen. Barry Goldwater, the Republican nominee for president. Twice elected governor of California (1966, 1970), Reagan sought to put into practice his philosophy in support of smaller government, less regulation, and lower taxes. After 2 unsuccessful tries for the GOP nomination for president, he won the nomination in 1980 and was elected president, unseating the incumbent, Jimmy Carter. He was reelected in 1984 over former Vice Pres. Walter Mondale.

Reagan's efforts to rein in government were frustrated by difficult economic times and a Democrat-controlled House of Representatives. He reduced, raised, and then reduced taxes as circumstances seemed to warrant. He committed the nation to a major military buildup to overcome the threat posed by the Soviet Union and its allies. During his 2nd term he and the new Soviet leader, Mikhail Gorbachev, explored ways to end the cold war, and in 1987 they signed the Intermediate-Range Nuclear Forces Treaty, banning an entire class of weapons.

Reagan was diagnosed with Alzheimer's disease in 1994 and disclosed the diagnosis in a letter to the American public. He remained mostly in seclusion from then on. He was survived by his wife, Nancy, and 3 of his 4 children.

Mydans, Carl, 97, *Life* magazine photographer who shot some of the most memorable images of World War II; Larchmont, NY, Aug. 16, 2004.

O

O'Neal, Ron, 66, actor who starred as a flamboyant drug dealer in the 1972 "blaxploitation" film *Superfly*; Los Angeles, CA, Jan. 14, 2004.

P

Paar, Jack, 85, edgy host of TV's *Tonight Show* (1957-62); he essentially invented the late-night celebrity chat format that became a TV staple; Greenwich, CT, Jan. 27, 2004.

Petrie, Daniel, 83, director esteemed for his TV work and such memorable films as *A Raisin in the Sun* (1961); Los Angeles, CA, Aug. 22, 2004.

Pople, Sir John A., 78, British mathematician turned chemist; won a 1998 Nobel Prize for development of computational methods in quantum chemistry; Chicago, IL, Mar. 15, 2004.

R

Ramone, Johnny (John Cummings), 55, guitarist and songwriter considered the driving force behind the pioneering punk rock group the Ramones; Los Angeles, CA, Sept. 15, 2004.

Randall, Tony, 84, actor best known as obsessively neat Felix Unger in TV's *The Odd Couple* (1970-75); he also founded a repertory company designed to restore classical theater to Broadway; New York, NY, May 17, 2004.

Reagan, Ronald, 93, 40th president of the U.S. (see separate box).

Reeve, Christopher, 52, actor best known for playing Superman in 4 feature films and for his activism on behalf of spinal cord research, following a 1995 riding accident that left him paralyzed; Mt. Kisco, NY, Oct. 10, 2004.

Reuther, Victor, 92, one of 3 brothers who led the United Auto Workers labor union during its heyday in the mid-20th century; Washington, DC, June 3, 2004.

Rockefeller, Laurance S., 94, middle brother of the 5 grandsons of billionaire oilman John D. Rockefeller; a pioneering venture capitalist, also a noted conservationist and philanthropist; New York, NY, July 11, 2004.

Roth Jr., William V., 82, Delaware Republican who served 5 terms in the Senate (1971-2001) and gave his name to the Roth IRA; Washington, DC, Dec. 13, 2003.

S

Sagan, Françoise, 69, French writer who won world renown as a teenager with her first novel, *Bonjour Tristesse* (1954); Honfleur, France, Sept. 24, 2004.

Sanford, Isabel, 86, first black actress to win an Emmy for best actress in a comedy series, for *The Jeffersons* (1975-85); Los Angeles, CA, July 9, 2004.

Scavullo, Francesco, 82, photographer who shot *Cosmopolitan* magazine's "Cosmo girl" covers from 1965 to 1997; New York, NY, Jan. 6, 2004.

Schott, Marge, 75, longtime owner of the Cincinnati Reds baseball team; repeatedly in trouble for objectionable remarks; Cincinnati, OH, Mar. 2, 2004.

Simon, Paul, 75, Illinois newspaper publisher who served 2 Senate terms (1985-97) and ran unsuccessfully for the 1998 Democratic presidential nomination; Springfield, IL, Dec. 9, 2003.

Singleton, Penny, 95, actress who played the comic strip character Blondie on radio and in the movies; Los Angeles, CA, Nov. 12, 2003.

Smith, Elliott, 34, singer-songwriter known for his dark, introspective songs—including 1998 Oscar nominee "Miss Misery," from *Good Will Hunting*; Los Angeles, CA, Oct. 21, 2003.

Smith, Jeff, 65, cookbook author and TV chef; appeared on PBS as the Frugal Gourmet until clouded by a 1997 sex scandal; Seattle, WA, July 7, 2004.

Snodgress, Carrie, 57, actress best known as the frustrated homemaker in the film *Diary of a Mad Housewife* (1970); Los Angeles, CA, Apr. 1, 2004.

Spahn, Warren, 82, National League pitcher (mostly for the Braves) whose 363 career wins were the most by a lefty in Major League Baseball; Broken Arrow, OK, Nov. 24, 2003.

Stark, Ray, 88, Hollywood producer and power broker; West Hollywood, CA, Jan. 17, 2004.

Stepanek, Mattie (J.T.), 13, inspirational poet and advocate for people like himself suffering from muscular dystrophy; Washington, DC, June 22, 2004.

Sterling, Jan, 82, glamorous film noir star of the 1940s through 1960s; Los Angeles, CA, Mar. 27, 2004.

Straight, Michael, 87, onetime editor and publisher of the *New Republic* who, in a 1983 memoir, revealed he had spied for the Soviet Union in the late 1930s; Chicago, IL, Jan. 4, 2004.

Straus, Roger W., 87, longtime head of the publishing firm Farrar, Straus & Co. or later Farrar, Straus & Giroux; New York, NY, May 25, 2004.

Sweeney, Charles W., 84, pilot of the B-29 Superfortress bomber that dropped the atom bomb on Nagasaki, Japan, in 1945; Boston, MA, July 16, 2004.

T

Thulin, Ingrid, 77, Swedish actress who graced 8 Ingmar Bergman films, including *Wild Strawberries* (1957) and *Cries and Whispers* (1972); Stockholm, Sweden, Jan. 7, 2004.

Tillman, Pat, 27, former NFL safety for the Arizona Cardinals; left football to join the Army Rangers; killed during ambush by Afghan insurgents; SW Afghanistan, Apr. 22, 2004.

Tisch, Laurence A., 80, financier and philanthropist who with his brother, Preston, built the Loews Corp. conglomerate; headed the CBS TV network from 1986 to 1995; New York, NY, Nov. 15, 2003.

U

Ustinov, Sir Peter, 82, award-winning British actor, director, writer, raconteur, and all-around character; Genolier, Switzerland, Mar. 28, 2004.

W

Washington, Walter E., 88, first black chief executive of a major U.S. city, and Washington's first elected mayor (1975-79) in more than a century; Washington, DC, Oct. 27, 2003.

Whipple, Fred, 97, Harvard astronomer known for his theories about the composition of comets; Cambridge, MA, Aug. 31, 2004.

Wilkins, Maurice, 88, British Nobel laureate (1962), who, with Crick and Watson, helped discover the structure of DNA; London, Oct. 5, 2004.

Winfield, Paul, 62, one of the first Oscar-nominated black actors (in 1973, for *Sounder*); portrayed such figures as Rev. Martin Luther King Jr. and Thurgood Marshall in TV dramas; Los Angeles, CA, Mar. 2, 2004.

Wray, Fay, 96, actress best known as the damsel carried to the top of the Empire State Building in the 1933 film *King Kong*; New York, NY, Aug. 8, 2004.

Historical Anniversaries

1905 — 100 Years Ago

Imperial guards at **Winter Palace in St. Petersburg**, Russia, fire into a crowd of unarmed petitioners, killing more than 100 on Jan. 22, "**Bloody Sunday**." The massacre led to widespread strikes and riots.

The world's **1st rotary club** is founded, Feb. 23 in Chicago.

Theodore Roosevelt is inaugurated Mar. 4 for his first full term as U.S. president.

An **earthquake** measuring 8.6 on the Richter scale kills nearly 20,000 people Apr. 4 in and around Kangra, India.

The **Industrial Workers of the World** (nicknamed "Wobblies") forms in Chicago June 27.

Mutiny breaks out on the Russian battleship *Potemkin* June 27-28, stemming from sailors' refusal to eat rotten meat.

A **yellow fever epidemic**, the last in the U.S., sweeps New Orleans July-Oct., infecting some 3,000 and killing more than 400.

On Sept. 1, **Alberta** and **Saskatchewan** become Canada's 8th and 9th provinces.

Russia and Japan sign the Treaty of Portsmouth in New Hampshire Sept. 5, following negotiations mediated by Pres. Theodore Roosevelt, and bring **an end to the Russo-Japanese War**. (In 1906, Roosevelt received a Nobel Peace Prize for his mediation.)

Norway's parliament votes June 7 to dissolve the union between Norway and Sweden; the 2 countries reach an agreement Sept. 23 to maintain a neutral frontier.

In response to revolutionary political pressures, Czar Nicholas II of Russia on Oct. 30 issues the so-called **October Manifesto**, nominally allowing certain civil rights and creating a legislature. It is followed by general strikes in support of reform, and a peasants' revolt.

Arthur Griffith, an Irish nationalist, organizes the political party **Sinn Fein** ("We Ourselves") Nov. 28, with the goal of independence for all of Ireland.

Art. Henri Matisse's *The Green Line*; Pablo Picasso's *Family of Saltimbanques*. Die Brücke expressionist movement begins in Germany; Fauvism takes shape in Paris.

Literature. E. M. Forster's *Where Angels Fear to Tread*, Baroness Orczy's *The Scarlet Pimpernel*, Mark Twain's *King Leopold's Soliloquy*, Edith Wharton's *The House of Mirth*. Jules Verne dies Mar. 24.

Movies. The first movie house (nickelodeon) designed exclusively to show films opens in Pittsburgh in June. Using child actors, Thomas Edison produces *The Little Train Robbery*, a parody of Edwin S. Porter's *Great Train Robbery* (1903).

Looking Back 100 Years		
	Then[1]	Now[2]
Total population	83,822,000	288,368,698
Foreign born	13.6%	11.5%
Male	51.3%	49.1%
Women in labor force	18.8%	59.5%
Median age	22.9	35.3
Number of states	45	50
Center of population	6 mi. SE of Columbus, IN	2.8 mi. E of Edgar Springs, MO
Average annual wage	$550	$33,000
Unemployment rate	4.3%	6.0%
President	Theodore Roosevelt	George W. Bush
(1) Data from 1905 except for women in labor force, median age, and center of population (1900). (2) Data for 2004 except for % male, women in labor force, median age, unemployment rate (2003); center of population (2000).		

Music. Debussy's *La Mer*; Gustav Mahler's *Symphony 7*; Richard Strauss's *Salome*.

Nonfiction. George Santayana's *The Life of Reason*; Max Weber's *The Protestant Ethic and the Spirit of Capitalism*.

Popular Songs. Jean Havez's "Everybody Works But Father"; "How'd You Like to Spoon With Me?" recorded by Corinne Morgan and the Haydn Quartette.

Science and Technology. Albert Einstein publishes his first scientific papers, enunciating his "special theory of relativity"; Robert Koch is awarded the Nobel Prize in physiology or medicine for "inventions and discoveries relating to tuberculosis."

Sports. Ty Cobb makes his major league baseball debut in August with the Detroit Tigers. The New York Giants defeat the Philadelphia Athletics in 5 games to take the second World Series. Harvard loses to Haverford, 1-0, in the first official intercollegiate soccer game in the U.S.

Theatre. George Bernard Shaw's play *Mrs. Warren's Profession*, about a prostitute, is closed down in NYC, Oct. 31, after one performance, at the insistence of morals watchdog Anthony Comstock; James M. Barrie's *Pantaloon/Alice Sit-by-the-Fire*, starring John, Lionel, and Ethel Barrymore, opens on Dec. 25 in NYC.

Miscellaneous. The **Cullinane Diamond**, world's largest gem-quality diamond at over 3,100 carats (more than a pound), is discovered in South Africa and bestowed upon Britain's King Edward VII.

1955 — 50 Years Ago

Congress grants Pres. Dwight Eisenhower authority to used armed force to defend **Formosa** (Taiwan) in case of any attack by mainland (Communist) China.

Winston Churchill, age 80, resigns as prime minister of Britain.

After buying the idea from Richard and Maurice "Mac" McDonald, Ray Kroc opens **the first McDonald's** restaurant, Apr. 15 in Des Plaines, IL.

West Germany is recognized by most nations as a sovereign state May 5, ending its postwar status as an occupied country, and joins NATO four days later.

The Soviet Union and 7 other Eastern European countries, May 14, sign the **Warsaw Pact**, a mutual defense treaty intended to counterbalance NATO.

On May 31, the U.S. Supreme Court rules that public schools must be integrated "**with all deliberate speed**," implementing its 1954 milestone decision in Brown v. Board of Education of Topeka.

Disneyland opens its gates July 17 in Anaheim, CA, attracting nearly 30,000 visitors its first day.

Leaders of the U.S., Britain, France, and the Soviet Union hold a **summit in Geneva**, Switzerland, July 18-25, seeking to ease Cold War tensions.

Up to 200 people die in Atlantic coastal flooding stretching from South Carolina to Massachusetts Aug. 20 as a result of **Hurricane Diane**.

After a bloody military rebellion, **Juan Perón** is forced to resign the presidency of Argentina Sept. 19.

Pres. Dwight Eisenhower suffers a heart attack, Sept. 24, while on vacation in Denver.

Rosa Parks is arrested in Montgomery, AL, Dec. 1 for refusing to give up her seat on a city bus. A successful **boycott** of the Montgomery city bus system, led by the **Rev. Dr. Martin Luther King Jr.**, begins on Dec. 5, and gives momentum to the civil rights movement.

The 2 largest U.S. labor organizations, the American Federation of Labor (AFL) and Congress of Industrial Organizations (CIO), merge Dec. 5, creating the **AFL-CIO**.

Art. Willem de Kooning's *Easter Monday*; Jackson Pollock's *Search*; Andy Warhol's 'Shoe' paintings.

Literature. Mackinlay Kantor's *Andersonville*; Vladimir Nabokov's *Lolita*; Flannery O'Connor's *A Good Man Is Hard to Find and Other Stories*; J.R.R. Tolkien's *The Return of the King*; Sloan Wilson's *The Man in the Gray Flannel Suit*. Allen Ginsberg reads his poem "Howl" at a San Francisco gallery. Wallace Stevens dies Aug. 2; Thomas Mann dies Aug. 12.

Movies. *Davy Crockett, King of the Wild Frontier* (compiled from 1954 TV miniseries), starring Fess Parker; *Marty* starring Ernest Borgnine; *Mister Roberts* starring Henry Fonda, James Cagney, and Jack Lemmon; *Rebel Without a Cause* starring James Dean, Natalie Wood, and Sal Mineo; *The Seven Year Itch* starring Marilyn Monroe. *On the Waterfront* wins best film at Oscar ceremonies for 1954 films, with Marlon Brando winning as Best Actor. James Dean dies in car crash at age 24.

Music. Darius Milhaud's *Symphony No. 6*; Walter Piston's *Symphony No. 5*; Igor Stravinsky's *Canticum Sacrum*.

Nonfiction. James Baldwin's *Notes of a Native Son*; Jim Bishop's *The Day Lincoln Was Shot*; Walter Lippmann's *Essays in the Public Philosophy*.

Popular Songs. Pat Boone, "Ain't That a Shame"; McGuire Sisters, "Mr. Sandman"; Bill Haley and His Comets, "Rock Around the Clock"; Les Baxter, "Unchained Melody."

Science and Technology. Albert Einstein dies at 76 on Apr. 18. The longest total solar eclipse of the 20th century (7 min. 8 sec.) is visible from Southeast Asia June 20.

Sports. Rocky Marciano knocks out Archie Moore in the 9th round to retain his world heavyweight championship Sept. 21; Brooklyn Dodgers win the World Series over the New York Yankees in 7 games; Detroit Red Wings take the Stanley Cup after 7 games against the Montreal Canadiens. Denton T. "Cy" Young dies Nov. 4.

Theatre. *Bus Stop* by William Inge with Kim Stanley, Anthony Ross, and Elaine Stritch; Tennessee Williams's *Cat on a Hot Tin Roof* starring Barbara Bel Geddes and Burl Ives; *Damn Yankees* with Gwen Verdon and Stephen Douglass; Cole Porter's *Silk Stockings* starring Don Ameche.

TV. *Captain Kangaroo* and *The Mickey Mouse Club* debut on TV Oct. 3.

Miscellaneous. The New York state legislature bans the sale of comic books containing explicit crime and horror to anyone under 18.

1980 – 25 Years Ago

President Jimmy Carter announces economic **sanctions** on the USSR Jan. 4, and U.S. withdrawal from the Moscow **Summer Olympic Games** Jan. 20, in protest against the Soviet invasion of Afghanistan (Dec. 1979).

A Soviet **Vostok** rocket explodes on the launch pad in Plesetsk, Russia, Mar. 18, killing 50.

Oscar Arnulfo Romero, archbishop of **El Salvador**, is assassinated Mar. 24 as he says Mass.

Zimbabwe achieves independence from Britain, Apr. 18.

Eight Americans are killed and 5 injured Apr. 24 in a failed attempt to rescue **U.S. embassy hostages** being held by militants in Iran. Sec. of State Cyrus Vance, who opposed the mission, resigns on Apr. 26, to be succeeded by Edmund Muskie.

After lying dormant since 1857, **Mt. St. Helens** in southwestern Washington erupts May 18 and again May 25 and June 12, causing more than 50 deaths.

Ted Turner's Cable News Network (**CNN**), the first 24-hour all-news cable network, begins broadcasting June 1.

Former Nicaraguan strongman Anastasio **Somoza** Debayle is assassinated, Sept. 17 in Paraguay.

Mohammad Reza Pahlavi, former **shah of Iran**, dies Oct. 26, in exile in Egypt.

Poland's **Solidarity** union forms Aug. 14, as about 17,000 shipyard workers in Gdansk strike under leader Lech Walesa.

Asserting sovereignty over a large area of disputed territory, **Iraq invades Iran** Sept. 22, beginning an 8-year war that killed an estimated 1 million people.

Ronald Reagan carries 44 states Nov. 4 to defeat incumbent Jimmy Carter for the presidency.

The so-called **Gang of Four** go on trial Nov. 20 in China, for allegedly seeking to overthrow the government.

An **earthquake** shakes the southern provinces of **Italy** Nov. 24, leaving hundreds of thousands homeless and about 3,000 dead.

Former Beatle **John Lennon is shot** dead outside his apartment building in New York City, Dec. 8.

Art. Anselm Kiefer's *Brünnhilde Sleeps* and *Your Golden Hair, Margarete*; Roy Liechtenstein's *Landscape*.

Literature. Samuel Beckett's *Company*; E.L. Doctorow's *Loon Lake*; Umberto Eco's *The Name of the Rose*; James Michener's *The Covenant*; Walker Percy's *The Second Coming*; A *Confederacy of Dunces* by John Kennedy Toole; writers Henry Miller and Jean-Paul Sartre die.

Movies. *Airplane*, starring Robert Hays and Julie Hagerty; *Caddyshack* starring Chevy Chase, Rodney Dangerfield, Ted Knight, and Bill Murray; *Coal Miner's Daughter* starring Sissy Spacek and Tommy Lee Jones; George Lucas's *Star Wars: Episode V—The Empire Strikes Back*, starring Mark Hamill, Harrison Ford, Carrie Fisher, and Alec Guinness; Robert Redford's *Ordinary People* starring Donald Sutherland, Timothy Hutton, and Mary Tyler Moore; Martin Scorsese's *Raging Bull* starring Robert DeNiro; Stanley Kubrick's *The Shining* starring Jack Nicholson.

Music. Pierre Boulez's *Notations*; Philip Glass's *Satyagraha*; Karlheinz Stockhausen's *Donnerstag*.

Nonfiction. Justin Kaplan's *Walt Whitman*; Henry Kissinger's *The White House Years*; Carl Sagan's *Cosmos*.

Popular Songs. Bob Seger's "Against the Wind"; Pink Floyd's "Another Brick in the Wall"; Blondie's "Call Me"; Lipps Inc.'s "Funkytown"; Michael Jackson's "Rock with You"; "Sailing" by Christopher Cross; Kenny Loggins's "This Is It."

Science and Technology. Scientists led by geologist Walter Alvarez find evidence that an asteroid may have caused the disappearance of dinosaurs some 65 million years ago. The Supreme Court rules June 16 that genetically engineered organisms can be patented.

Sports. The Winter Olympic Games are held Feb. 14-23 at Lake Placid, NY; the Summer Olympic Games are held in Moscow in July, boycotted by some 60 nations, including the U.S., in protest against the Soviet Union's Dec. 1979 invasion of Afghanistan. Olympian Jesse Owens dies at the age of 66.

Theatre. *42nd Street* starring Jerry Orbach and Tammy Grimes; Peter Shaffer's *Amadeus* starring Tim Curry and Ian McKellen; *Barnum* starring Glenn Close and Jim Dale; Mark Medoff's *Children of a Lesser God*; Lanford Wilson's *Fifth of July* starring Christopher Reeve; Neil Simon's *I Ought to Be in Pictures*.

Miscellaneous. The U.S. Military Academy, Air Force Academy, Naval Academy, and Coast Guard Academy graduate their first classes that include women May 28. The "Who Shot J.R." episode of *Dallas* airs Nov. 21 and is the highest-rated TV program to date in percent of viewers (53.3% of total audience, later surpassed by the last episode of M*A*S*H, which drew 60.2% in 1983).

UNITED STATES GOVERNMENT

EXECUTIVE BRANCH	LEGISLATIVE BRANCH	JUDICIAL BRANCH
PRESIDENT	**CONGRESS**	**Supreme Court of the United States**
Vice President	**Senate House**	Courts of Appeals
Executive Office of the President	Architect of the Capitol	District Courts
White House Office	U.S. Botanic Garden	Territorial Courts
Office of the Vice President	General Accounting Office	Court of International Trade
Council of Economic Advisers	Government Printing Office	Court of Federal Claims
Council on Environmental Quality	Library of Congress	Tax Court
National Security Council	Congressional Budget Office	Court of Appeals for Veterans Claims
Office of Administration		Administrative Office of the Courts
Office of Management and Budget		Federal Judicial Center
Office of National Drug Control Policy		Sentencing Commission
Office of Policy Development		
Office of Science and Technology Policy		
Office of the U.S. Trade Representative		

The Bush Administration

As of Oct. 2004; mailing addresses are for Washington, DC, except for the Pentagon.

Terms of office of the president and vice president: Jan. 20, 2001, to Jan. 20, 2005.

President — By law, Pres. George W. Bush receives an annual salary of $400,000 (taxable) and an annual expense allowance of $50,000 (nontaxable). This does not include amounts available for expenditures within the Executive Office of the President, including $3,850,000 for necessary expenses for the White House and amounts for travel and entertainment.
website: www.whitehouse.gov/president; *E-mail:* president@whitehouse.gov

Vice President — By law, Vice Pres. Dick Cheney receives an annual salary of $203,000 (taxable), plus $90,000 for official entertainment expenses (nontaxable).
website: www.whitehouse.gov/vicepresident; *E-mail:* vice.president@whitehouse.gov

The Cabinet Department Heads
(Salary: $175,700 per year)

Secretary of State — Colin L. Powell
Secretary of the Treasury — John W. Snow
Secretary of Defense — Donald H. Rumsfeld
Attorney General — John Ashcroft
Secretary of the Interior — Gale Norton
Secretary of Agriculture — Ann M. Veneman
Secretary of Commerce — Donald L. Evans
Secretary of Labor — Elaine L. Chao
Secretary of Health and Human Services — Tommy Thompson
Secretary of Housing and Urban Development — Alphonso Jackson
Secretary of Transportation — Norman Y. Mineta
Secretary of Energy — Spencer Abraham
Secretary of Education — Roderick R. Paige
Secretary of Veterans Affairs — Anthony Principi
Secretary of Homeland Security — Tom Ridge

The White House Staff
1600 Pennsylvania Ave. NW 20500
website: www.whitehouse.gov

Chief of Staff to the President — Andrew H. Card Jr.
Asst. to the President & Deputy Chief of Staff — Joseph W. Hagin II
Asst. to the President & Deputy Chief of Staff — Harriet Miers
Assistants to the President:
  Counsel to the President — Alberto R. Gonzalez
  Deputy Counsel to the President — David Leitch
  Domestic Policy Council — Margaret Spellings
  Homeland Security Advisor — John Gordon
  Presidential Personnel — Dina Powell
  Press Secretary — Scott McClellan
  Legislative Affairs — David Hobbs
  Communications — Dan Bartlett
  National Economic Council — Stephen Friedman, dir.
  Intergovernmental Affairs — Ruben S. Barrales
  National Security — Condoleezza Rice
  Staff Secretary — Brett Kavanaugh
  Political Affairs — Matt Schlapp
  Public Liaison — Lezlee Westine
  Cabinet Secretary — Brian Montgomery
  Director of Presidential Scheduling — Bradley Blakeman
  Director of Speechwriting — Michael Gerson
Chief of Staff to the First Lady — Andrea Ball
  E-mail: first.lady@whitehouse.gov

Senior Advisor to the President — Karl Rove
Director of Advance — Greg Jenkins
Management, Admin., & Oval Office Operations — Linda Gambatesa
Faith-Based and Community Initiatives — Jim Towey
Office of National AIDS Policy — Carol Thompson, act. dir.

Executive Agencies

Council of Economic Advisers — Dr. N. Gregory Mankiw, chair; *website:* www.whitehouse.gov/cea
Office of Administration — Tim Campen, dir.; *website:* www.whitehouse.gov/oa
Office of Science & Technology Policy — Dr. John H. Marburger; *website:* www.ostp.gov
Office of Natl. Drug Control Policy — John P. Walters, dir.; *website:* www.whitehousedrugpolicy.gov
Office of Management and Budget — Joshua B. Bolten, dir.; *website:* www.whitehouse.gov/omb
U.S. Trade Representative — Robert B. Zoellick; *website:* www.ustr.gov
Council on Environ. Quality — James L. Connaughton, chair; *website:* www.whitehouse.gov/ceq

Department of State
2201 C St. NW 20520
website: www.state.gov

Secretary of State — Colin L. Powell
Deputy Secretary — Richard L. Armitage
Chief of Staff — Lawrence Wilkerson
U.S. Ambassador to the United Nations — John Danforth
U.S. Agency for Intl. Dev. — Andrew S. Natsios
Under Sec. for Political Affairs — Marc Grossman
Under Sec. for Management — Grant S. Green Jr.
Under Sec. for Global Affairs — Paula J. Dobriansky
Under Sec. for Economic, Business, & Agricultural Affairs — Alan P. Larson
Under Sec. for Arms Control & International Security Affairs — John R. Bolton
Under Sec. for Public Diplomacy & Public Affairs — Patricia de Stacy Harrison, act.
Policy Planning Director — Mitchell B. Reiss
Chief of Protocol — Donald B. Ensenat
Inspector General — Anne Sigmund, act.
Legal Adviser — William H. Taft IV
Counterterrorism — J. Cofer Black
War Crimes Issues — Pierre-Richard Prosper
Director General of the Foreign Service & Director of Human Resources — W. Robert Pearson

Assistant Secretaries for:
  Administration — Willliam A. Eaton
  African Affairs — Constance Newman
  Arms Control — Stephen G. Rademaker
  Civil Rights — Barbara Pope
  Consular Affairs — Maura Harty
  Democracy, Human Rights, & Labor — Michael Kozak, act.
  Diplomatic Security — Francis X. Taylor
  East Asian & Pacific Affairs — James A. Kelly
  Economic & Business Affairs — Earl Anthony Wayne
  Educational & Cultural Affairs — Patricia de Stacy Harrison
  European & Eurasian Affairs — Elizabeth A. Jones
  Intelligence & Research — Tom Fingar
  International Narcotics & Law Enforcement Affairs — Robert Charles
  International Organization Affairs — Kim Holmes
  Legislative Affairs — Paul V. Kelly
  Near Eastern Affairs — William Joseph Burns
  Nonproliferation — John Stern Wolf
  Oceans, International Environmental, & Scientific Affairs — John F. Turner
  Political-Military Affairs — Lincoln P. Bloomfield
  Population, Refugees, & Migration — Arthur E. Dewey
  Public Affairs — Richard A. Boucher
  Resource Management — Christopher B. Burnham
  South Asian Affairs — Christina B. Rocca
  Verification & Compliance — Paula A. DeSutter
  Western Hemisphere Affairs — Roger F. Noriega

Department of the Treasury
1500 Pennsylvania Ave. NW 20220
website: www.ustreas.gov

Secretary of the Treasury — John W. Snow
Deputy Sec. of the Treasury — Samuel W. Bodman
Chief of Staff — Christopher Smith
Executive Secretary — Paul W. Curry
Under Sec. for Domestic Finance — Brian C. Roseboro
Under Sec. for International Affairs — John B. Taylor
General Counsel — Arnold I. Havens
Inspector General —Dennis S. Schindel, act.
Inspector General for Tax Administration — Pam Gardiner, act.
Treasurer of the U.S. — vacant
Assistant Secretaries for:
  Economic Policy — Mark Warshawsky
  Financial Institutions — Wayne A. Abernathy
  Financial Markets— Timothy Bitsberger, act.
  Fiscal Affairs — Donald Hammond
  International Affairs — Randy K. Quarles
  Legislative Affairs — John Duncan
  Management — Jesus Delgado-Jenkings, act.
  Public Affairs — Rob Nichols
  Tax Policy — Gregory Jenner, act.
  Terrorism & Financial Intelligence (Terrorist Financing)— Juan C. Zarate
Bureaus:
  Alcohol and Tobacco Tax and Trade — Arthur J. Libertucci, dir.
  Comptroller of the Currency — John Hawke Jr., compt.
  Engraving & Printing — Tom Ferguson, dir.
  Financial Crimes Enforcement Network — William Fox, dir.
  Financial Management Service — Richard Gregg, comm.
  Internal Revenue Service — Mark W. Everson, comm.
  U.S. Mint — Henrietta Holmsman Fore
  Office of Thrift Supervision — James Gilleran
  Public Debt — Van Zeck, comm.

Department of Defense
The Pentagon, Arlington, VA 20301
website: www.dod.gov

Secretary of Defense — Donald H. Rumsfeld
Deputy Secretary — Paul D. Wolfowitz
Under Sec. Comptroller/CIO — Tina W. Jonas
Under Sec. for Acquis. and Technol. — Michael Wynne, act.
Under Sec. for Intelligence — Dr. Stephen A. Cambone
Under Sec. for Personnel & Readiness — David S. C. Chu
Under Sec. for Policy — Douglas J. Feith
Assistant Secretaries for:
  Network & Info Integration— Linton Wells II
  Principal Deputy UnderSecretary (Personnel & Readiness)— Charles S. Abeil

Health Affairs — William Winkenwerder Jr., MD
International Security Affairs — Peter W. Rodman
International Security Policy — Dr. J. D. Crouch II
Legislative Affairs — Powell A. Moore
Public Affairs — Lawrence Di Rita, act.
Reserve Affairs — Thomas F. Hall
Special Operations & Low-Intensity Conflict — Thomas W. O'Connell
Program Analysis & Evaluation — Ken Krieg
Inspector General — Joseph E. Schmitz
General Counsel — William J. Haynes II
Intelligence Oversight — George B. Lotz II
Operational Test & Evaluation — Thomas P. Christie, dir.
Chairman, Joint Chiefs of Staff — Gen. Richard B. Myers
Secretary of the Army — Les Brownlee, act.
Secretary of the Navy — Gordon R. England
Commandant of the Marine Corps — Gen. Michael W. Hagee
Secretary of the Air Force — James G. Roche

Department of Justice
Constitution Ave. & 10th St. NW 20530
website: www.usdoj.gov

Attorney General — John Ashcroft
Deputy Attorney General — James B. Comey
Associate Attorney General — Robert D. McCallum Jr.
Office of Dispute Resolution — Jeffrey M. Senger
Solicitor General — Paul D. Clement, act.
Office of Inspector General — Glenn Fine
Assistants:
  Antitrust Division — R. Hewitt Pate
  Civil Division — Peter D. Keisler
  Civil Rights Division — R. Alexander Acosta
  Criminal Division — Christopher Wray
  Environ. & Nat. Resources Division — Thomas Sansonetti
  Justice Programs — Deborah Daniels
  Legal Counsel — Dan Levin, act.
  Legislative Affairs — William E. Moschella
  Legal Policy — Daniel J. Bryant
  Tax Division — Eileen O'Connor
Executive Secretariat — Kathie Harting
Office of Public Affairs — Mark Corallo
Office of Information & Privacy — Richard L. Huff/Daniel J. Metcalfe
Community Oriented Policing Services — Carl R. Peed
Federal Bureau of Investigation — Robert S. Mueller III
Bureau of Alcohol, Tobacco, Firearms, and Explosives— Carl J. Truscott.
Exec. Off. for Immigration Review — Kevin D. Rooney, dir.
Bureau of Prisons — Harley G. Lappin
Community Relations Service — Sharee M. Freeman, dir.
Drug Enforcement Admin. — Karen P. Tandy
Office of Intelligence Policy & Review — James Baker
Office of Professional Responsibility — H. Marshall Jarrett, counsel
Exec. Off. for U.S. Trustees — Lawrence Friedman, dir.
Foreign Claims Settlement Comm. — Mauricio J. Tamargo
Exec. Office for U.S. Attorneys — Mary Beth Buchanan, dir.
Pardon Attorney — Roger C. Adams
U.S. Parole Commission — Edward F. Reilly Jr.
U.S. Marshals Service — Benigno G. Reyna
U.S. Natl. Cen. Bureau of INTERPOL — James M. Sullivan
Office of Intergovernmental and Public Liaison — Greg Harris, act.
Office of Tribal Justice — Tracy Toulou
Violence Against Women Office — Diane Stewart
National Drug Intelligence Center — Michael T. Horn, dir.

Department of the Interior
1849 C St. NW 20240
website: www.doi.gov

Secretary of the Interior — Gale Norton
Deputy Secretary — J. Steven Griles
Assistant Secretaries for:
  Fish, Wildlife, & Parks — Craig Manson
  Indian Affairs — Aurene M. Martin
  Land & Minerals — Rebecca W. Watson
  Policy, Management, & Budget — P. Lynn Scarlett
  Water & Science — Bennett Raley
Bureau of Land Management — Kathleen Clarke
Bureau of Reclamation — John W. Keys III
Fish & Wildlife Service — Steven A. Williams
Geological Survey — Charles Groat
Minerals Management Service — R.M. "Johnnie" Burton

National Park Service — Fran P. Mainella, dir.
Surf. Mining Reclam. & Enforcement — Jeffrey Jarrett
Communications — Tina Kreisher, dir.
Congressional & Legislative Affairs — David L. Bernhardt
Solicitor — William G. Myers
External Affairs — Kit Kimball
Exec. Secretariat & Regulatory Affairs — Fay Iudicello

Department of Agriculture
1400 Independence Ave. SW 20250
website: www.usda.gov

Secretary of Agriculture — Ann M. Veneman
Deputy Secretary — James R. "Jim" Moseley
Under Secretaries for:
  Farm & Foreign Agric. Services — J. B. Penn
  Food, Nutrition, & Consumer Services — Eric M. Bost
  Food Safety — Elsa A. Murano
  Marketing & Regulatory Progs. — William T. Hawks
  Natural Resources & Environment — Mark E. Rey
  Research, Education, & Economics — Joseph Jen
  Rural Development — Gilbert Gonzalez, act.
Assistant Secretaries for:
  Administration — John Surina, act.
  Civil Rights — Vernon Parker
  Congressional Relations — Mary Waters
General Counsel — Nancy S. Bryson
Inspector General — Phyllis Fong
Chief Financial Officer — Patricia Healy, act.
Chief Information Officer — Scott Charbo
Chief Economist — Keith Collins
Communications — Alisa Harrison, dir.

Department of Commerce
1401 Constitution Ave. NW 20230
website: www.commerce.gov

Secretary of Commerce — Donald L. Evans
Deputy Secretary — Ted Kassinger
Chief of Staff — Lisi Kaufman
General Counsel — Jane Dana, act.
Under Sec. for Oceans & Atmosphere — Vice Admiral Conrad Lautenbacher (ret.)
Under Sec. for Industry & Security — Kenneth Juster
Under Sec. for International Trade — Grant Aldonas
Under Sec. for Economics and Statistics Admin. — Kathleen Cooper
Under Sec. for U.S. Patent & Trademark Office — Jon W. Dudas
Under Sec. for Technology — Phil Bond
Assistant Secretaries:
  Chief Financial Officer & Asst. Secretary for Admin. — Otto Wolff
  Economic Development Admin. — David Sampson
  Export Admin. — Peter Lichtenbaum
  Export Enforcement — Julie Myers
  Import Administration — Jim Jochun
  Legislative and Intergovernmental Affairs — Bret Palmer, act.
  Market Access & Compliance — William Lash
  National Telecomm. Information Administration — Michael D. Gallagher
  Oceans & Atmosphere — James Mahoney
  Manufacturing and Services — Albert Frina
  U.S. & Foreign Commercial Service — Rhonda Keenum, dir.
Bureau of the Census — Charles Louis Kincannon, dir.
Natl. Institute of Standards & Tech. — Arden Bement, dir.
Minority Business Dev. Agency — Ronald Langston, dir.
Public Affairs — Ron Bonjean, dir.
Policy and Strategic Planning—David Bohigian, dir.
Business Liason—Dan McCardell, dir.

Department of Labor
200 Constitution Ave. NW 20210
website: www.dol.gov

Secretary of Labor — Elaine L. Chao
Deputy Secretary — Steven J. Law
Chief of Staff — Andrew Siff
Assistant Secretaries for:
  Admin. & Management — Patrick Pizzella
  Congressional & Intergov. Affairs — Kristine Iverson
  Employment & Training — Emily Stover DeRocco
  Employment Standards — Victoria Lipnic
  Occupational Safety & Health — John Henshaw
  Mine Safety & Health — David Lauriski
  Employee Benefits Security Admin. — Ann Combs

Policy — David Gray, act.
Public Affairs — Lisa Kruska, act.
Veterans Employment & Training — Frederico Juarbe Jr.
Solicitor of Labor — Howard M. Radzely, act.
Bureau of International Affairs — Arnold Levine
Women's Bureau — Shinae Chun
Inspector General — Gordon S. Heddell
Bureau of Labor Statistics — Kathleen P. Utgoff

Department of Health and Human Services
200 Independence Ave. SW 20201
website: www.os.dhhs.gov

Secretary of Health & Human Services — Tommy Thompson
Deputy Secretary — Claude A. Allen
Chief of Staff — Scott Whitaker
Centers for Disease Control and Prevention— Julie Louise Gerberding, M.D., Ph.D, dir.
Health Care Research & Quality— Carolyn M. Clancy, M.D., dir.
National Institutes of Health— Elias Zerhouni, M.D., dir.
Assistant Secretaries for:
  Aging — Josefina Carbonell
  Children & Families — Wade F. Horn
  Health — Richard Carmona, M.D.
  Legislation — Jennifer Young
  Administration & Management — Ed Sontag
  Planning & Evaluation — Michael O'Grady, Ph.D
  Public Affairs — Kevin Keane
General Counsel — Alex Azar II
Inspector General — Dara Corrigan, act.
Office for Civil Rights — Richard M. Campanelli
Surgeon General — Richard Carmona, M.D.
Centers for Medicare and Medicaid Services — Mark McClellan, M.D., Ph.D
Faith-based and Community Initiatives— Robert J. Polito, dir.

Department of Housing and Urban Development
451 7th St. SW 20410
website: www.hud.gov

Secretary of Housing & Urban Development — Alphonso Jackson
Deputy Secretary — Roy A. Bernardi
Chief of Staff — Camille T. Pierce
Assistant Secretaries for:
  Community Planning & Development — vacant
  Congressional & Intergov. Relations — Steven B. Nesmith
  Fair Housing & Equal Opportunity — Carolyn Y. Peoples
  Administration — Vickers B. Meadows
  Housing & Federal Housing Comm. — John C. Weicher
  Policy Development & Research — Dennis Shea
  Public & Indian Housing — Michael Liu
Public Affairs — Cathy M. MacFarlane
General Counsel — vacant
Inspector General — Kevin M. Donohue
Chief Financial Officer — Carin M. Barth
Government National Mortgage Assn. — Ronald Rosenfeld
Off. of Federal Housing Enterprise Oversight — Armando Falcon

Department of Transportation
400 7th St. SW 20590
website: www.dot.gov

Secretary of Transportation — Norman Y. Mineta
Deputy Secretary — Kirk K. Kan Tine
Under Secretary for Policy — Jeffrey N. Shane
General Counsel —Jeffrey A. Rosen
Assistant Secretaries for:
  Administration — Vincent T. Taylor
  Aviation & International Affairs — Karan K. Bhatia
  Budget & Programs — Phyllis F. Scheinberg, act.
  Governmental Affairs — Nicole Nason
  Public Affairs — Robert Johnson
  Transportation Policy — Emil H. Frankel
Bureau of Transportation Statistics — Rick Kowalewski, act.
Federal Aviation Admin. — Marion C. Blakey
Federal Highway Admin. — Mary E. Peters
Federal Motor Carrier Safety Admin. — Annette M. Sandberg
Federal Railroad Admin. — Betty Monro, act.
Maritime Admin. — Capt. William G. Schubert
Natl. Highway Traffic Safety Admin. — Dr. Jeffrey W. Runge

Federal Transit Admin. — Jennifer L. Dorn
Research & Special Programs Admin. — Samuel G. Bonasso, act.
Inspector General — Kenneth M. Mead
St. Lawrence Seaway Devel. Corp. — Albert S. Jacquez

Department of Energy
1000 Independence Ave. SW 20585
website: www.energy.gov

Secretary of Energy — Spencer Abraham
Deputy Secretary — Kyle McSlarrow
Under Secretary — David Garman, act.
Chief of Staff — Joseph McMonigle
General Counsel — Lee Otis
Inspector General — Gregory Friedman
Assistant Secretaries for:
 Administration & Human Resource Management — Richard Farrell
 Congressional & Intergov. Affairs — vacant
 Defense Programs — vacant
 Energy Efficiency & Renewable Energy — David Garman
 Environment, Safety, & Health — John Shaw
 Environmental Management — vacant
 Fossil Energy — Carl Michael Smith
 International Affairs — vacant
 Oversight & Performance Assurance — Glenn Podonsky
Nuclear Energy — Bill Magwood
Energy Information Admin. — Guy F. Caruso
Economic Impact & Diversity — Theresa Speake
Hearings & Appeals — George Breznay, dir.
Science & Technology — Walter L. Warnick, dir.
Civilian Radioactive Waste Management — Margaret Chu
National Nuclear Security Admin. — Linton Brooks
Chief Financial Officer — Susan Grant
Energy Advisory Board — Craig R. Reed
Office of Public Affairs — Jeanne Lopatto

Department of Education
400 Maryland Ave. SW 20202
website: www.ed.gov

Secretary of Education — Roderick R. Paige
Deputy Secretary — Eugene W. Hickok
Under Secretary — Edward McPherson
Chief of Staff — Anne Radice
Councelors to the Sec. — Susan Sclafani, Ronald Tomalis
Inspector General — John P. Higgins Jr.
General Counsel — Brian W. Jones
Assistant Secretaries for:
 Adult & Vocational Education — Susan Sclafani
 Management and Chief Info. Officer — William Leidinger
 Civil Rights — vacant
 Institute of Education Sciences — Grover J. Whitehurst
 Elementary & Secondary Educ. — Raymond Joseph Simon
 Intergov. & Interagency Affairs — Laurie M. Rich
 Legislative & Congressional Affairs — Karen A. Johnson
 Postsecondary Education — Sally L. Stroup
 Special Educ. & Rehab. Services — vacant
Bilingual Education & Minority Language Affairs — Maria Hernandez Ferrier
Rehab. Services Admin. — Joanne M. Wilson, comm.

Department of Veterans Affairs
810 Vermont Ave. NW 20420
website: www.va.gov

Secretary of Veterans Affairs — Anthony Principi
Deputy Secretary — Gordon H. Mansfield
Assistant Secretaries for:
 Congressional Affairs — Pamela Iovino, act.
 Management — William A. Moorman, act.
 Human Resources & Admin. — Tim McClain
 Policy & Planning — Claude Kicklighter
 Public & Intergovernmental Affairs — Cynthia R. Church
Inspector General — Richard J. Griffin
Under Sec. for Benefits — Daniel L. Cooper
Under Sec. for Health — Jonathan Berlin, M.D., Ph.D, act.
Under Sec. for Memorial Affairs — John W. Nicholson
General Counsel — Tim McClain
Board of Veterans Appeals — Eligah Dane Clark, chair
Board of Contract Appeals — Gary Krump, chair
Small & Disadvantaged Business Utilization — Scott S. Denniston, dir.
Veterans Service Organization Liaison — Allen F. Kent

Department of Homeland Security
20528 (no street address used)
website: www.dhs.gov/dhspublic

Secretary of Homeland Security — Tom Ridge
Deputy Secretary — Adm. James Loy
Under Sec. for Border & Trans. Sec. — Asa Hutchinson
Under Sec. for Emergency Preparedness & Response — Michael Brown
Under Sec. for Info. Analysis & Infrastructure Protection — Frank Libutti
Under Sec. for Management — Janet Hale
Under Sec. for Science & Tech. — Dr. Charles E. McQueary
Assistant Secretaries for:
 Public Affairs — Susan K. Neely
 Bur. of Immigration & Customs Enforcement — Michael J. Garcia
 Infrastructure Protection — Robert P. Liscouski
 Policy & Planning of BTS — C. Stewart Verdery
State and Local Gov. Coordination — Josh Filler
U.S. Coast Guard Commandant — Adm. Thomas H. Collins
U.S. Secret Service — W. Ralph Basham, dir.
Inspector General — Clark Kent Ervin, act.
Bur. of Citizenship & Immigration Services — Eduardo Aguirre Jr., dir.
Office of Natl. Capital Region Coordination — Michael F. Byrne, dir.
Officer for Civil Rights & Civil Liberties — Daniel W. Sutherland
General Counsel — Joe D. Whitley
Chief Privacy Officer — Nuala O'Connor Kelly
Chief Information Officer — Steven I. Cooper
Chief Financial Officer — Bruce Marshall Carnes
Chief Human Capital Officer — Ronald J. James
Customs & Border Protection — Robert C. Bonner, comm.
National Cyber Security Division — Amit Yoran, dir.

Notable U.S. Government Agencies
Source: *The U.S. Government Manual*; National Archives and Records Administration; World Almanac research
All addresses are Washington, DC, unless otherwise noted; as of Oct. 2004
* = independent agency

Bureau of Alcohol, Tobacco, Firearms and Explosives — Carl J. Truscott, dir. (Dept. of Justice, 650 Mass. Ave NW, 20226). **website:** www.atf.gov
Bureau of the Census — Charles Louis Kincannon, dir. (Dept. of Commerce, 4700 Silver Hill Rd., 20233). **website:** www.census.gov
Bureau of Citizenship & Immigration Services — Eduardo Aguirre Jr., dir. (Dept. of Homeland Security, 425 I St. NW, 20536). **website:** http://uscis.gov
Bureau of Economic Analysis — J. Steven Landefeld, dir. (Dept. of Commerce, 1441 L St. NW, 20230). **website:** www.bea.gov
Bureau of Indian Affairs — David W. Anderson, asst. sec. (Dept. of the Interior, 1849 C St. NW, 20240). **website:** www.doi.gov/bureau-indian-affairs.html
Bureau of Prisons — Harley G. Lappin, dir. (Dept. of Justice, 320 First St. NW, 20534). **website:** www.bop.gov

Centers for Disease Control & Prevention — Dr. Julie L. Gerberding, dir. (Dept. of HHS, 1600 Clifton Rd., Atlanta, GA 30333). **website:** www.cdc.gov
***Central Intelligence Agency** — Porter Goss, dir. (Wash., DC 20505). **website:** www.cia.gov
***Commission on Civil Rights** — Mary Frances Berry, chair (624 9th St. NW, 20425). **website:** www.usccr.gov
***Commodity Futures Trading Commission** — Sharon Brown-Hruska, act. chair (3 Lafayette Centre, 1155 21st St. NW, 20581). **website:** www.cftc.gov
***Consumer Product Safety Commission** — Hal Stratton, chair (4330 East-West Hwy., Bethesda, MD 20814). **website:** www.cpsc.gov
***Environmental Protection Agency** — Mike Leavitt, adm. (Ariel Rios Bldg., 1200 Pennsylvania Ave. NW, 20460). **website:** www.epa.gov

*Equal Employment Opportunity Commission — Cari M. Dominguez, chair (1801 L St. NW, 20507). **website:** www.eeoc.gov

*Export-Import Bank of the United States — Philip Merrill, pres. and chair (811 Vermont Avenue NW, 20571). **website:** www.exim.gov

*Farm Credit Administration — Nancy C. Pellett, chair, Farm Credit Administration Board (1501 Farm Credit Drive, McLean, VA 22102). **website:** www.fca.gov

Federal Aviation Administration — Marion C. Blakey, adm. (Dept. of Trans., 800 Independence Ave. SW, 20591). **website:** www.faa.gov

Federal Bureau of Investigation — Robert S. Mueller III, dir. (Dept. of Justice, 935 Pennsylvania Ave. NW, 20535). **website:** www.fbi.gov

*Federal Communications Commission — Michael K. Powell, chair (445 12th St. SW, 20554). **website:** www.fcc.gov

*Federal Deposit Insurance Corporation — Donald E. Powell, chair (550 17th St. NW, 20429). **website:** www.fdic.gov

*Federal Election Commission — Bradley A. Smith, chair (999 E St. NW, 20463).**website:** www.fec.gov

*Federal Emergency Management Agency — Michael D. Brown, under sec. (500 C St. SW, 20472). **website:** www.fema.gov

*Federal Energy Regulatory Commission — Patrick Henry Wood III, chair (888 1st St. NE, 20426). **website:** www.ferc.gov

Federal Highway Administration — Mary E. Peters, adm. (Dept. of Trans., 400 7th St. SW, 20590). **website:** www.fhwa.dot.gov

*Federal Maritime Commission — Steven R. Blust, chair (800 N. Capitol St. NW, 20573). **website:** www.fmc.gov

*Federal Mine Safety & Health Review Commission — Michael F. Duffy, chair (601 New Jersey Ave. NW, 20001). **website:** www.fmshrc.gov

*Federal Reserve System — Alan Greenspan, chair, Board of Governors (20th St. & Constitution Ave. NW, 20551). **website:** www.federalreserve.gov

*Federal Trade Commission — Deborah Platt Majoras, chair (600 Pennsylvania Ave. NW, 20580). **website:** www.ftc.gov

Fish & Wildlife Service — Steven A. Williams, dir. (Dept. of the Interior, 1849 C St. NW, 20240). **website:** www.fws.gov

Food and Drug Administration — Lester M. Crawford, act. comm. (Dept. of HHS, 5600 Fishers Lane, Rockville, MD 20857). **website:** www.fda.gov

Forest Service — Dale N. Bosworth, chief (Dept. of Agriculture, 1400 Independence Ave. SW, 20250). **website:** www.fs.fed.us

Government Accountability Office — (cong. agency) David Michael Walker, comptroller gen. (441 G St. NW, 20548). **website:** www.gao.gov

*General Services Administration — Stephen A. Perry, adm. (1800 F St. NW, 20405). **website:** www.gsa.gov

Government Printing Office — (cong. agency) Bruce R. James, public printer (732 N. Capitol St. NW, 20401). **website:** www.gpoaccess.gov

*Inter-American Foundation — Frank Yturria, chair (901 N Stuart St., 10th floor, Arlington, VA 22203). **website:** www.iaf.gov

Internal Revenue Service — Mark W. Everson, comm. (Dept. of Treas., 1111 Constitution Ave. NW, 20224). **website:** www.irs.gov

Library of Congress — (cong. agency) Dr. James H. Billington, Librarian of Congress (101 Indep. Ave. SE, 20540). **website:** www.loc.gov

*National Aeronautics and Space Administration — Sean O'Keefe, adm. (300 E St. SW, 20546). **website:** www.nasa. gov

*National Archives & Records Administration — John W. Carlin, archivist (700 Pennsylvania Ave. NW, 20408). **website:** www.nara.gov

*National Endowment for the Arts — Dana Gioia, chair (1100 Pennsylvania Ave. NW, 20506). **website:** www.arts.gov

*National Endowment for the Humanities — Bruce Cole, chair (1100 Pennsylvania Ave. NW, 20506). **website:** www.neh.fed.us

National Institutes of Health — Dr. Elias Zerhouni, dir. (Dept. of HHS, 9000 Rockville Pike, Bethesda, MD 20892). **website:** www.nih.gov

*National Labor Relations Board — Robert J. Battista, chair (1099 14th St. NW, 20570). **website:** www.nlrb.gov

National Oceanic and Atmospheric Administration — Vice Adm. Conrad C. Lautenbacher Jr., admin. (Dept. of Commerce, 14th & Constitution Ave. NW, 20230). **website:** www.noaa.gov

National Park Service — Fran B. Mainella, dir. (Dept. of the Interior, 1849 C St. NW, 20240). **website:** www.nps.gov

*National Railroad Passenger Corp. (Amtrak) — David Gunn, pres. and CEO (60 Mass. Ave. NE, 20002). **website:** www.amtrak.com

*National Science Foundation — Dr. Arden L. Bement Jr., act. dir., National Science Foundation; Dr. Warren M. Washington, chair, National Science Board (4201 Wilson Blvd., Arlington, VA 22230).**website:** www.nsf.gov

*National Transportation Safety Board — Ellen Engleman Connors, chair (490 L'Enfant Plaza SW, 20594). **website:** www.ntsb.gov

*Nuclear Regulatory Commission — Nils J. Diaz, chair (11555 Rockville Pike, Rockville, MD 20852). **website:** www.nrc.gov

Occupational Safety & Health Administration — John L. Henshaw, asst. sec. (Dept. of Labor, 200 Constitution Ave. NW, 20210).**website:** www.osha.gov

*Occupational Safety & Health Review Commission — W. Scott Railton, chair (1120 20th St. NW, 20036). **website:** www.oshrc.gov

*Office of Government Ethics — Marilyn L. Glynn, act.dir. (1201 New York Ave. NW, Suite 500, 20005). **website:** www.usoge.gov

*Office of Personnel Management — Kay Coles James, dir. (1900 E St. NW, 20415-0001). **website:** www.opm.gov

*Office of Special Counsel — Scott J. Bloch, spec. counsel (1730 M St. NW, Suite 300, 20036). **website:** www.osc.gov

*Peace Corps — Gaddi H. Vasquez, dir. (1111 20th St., NW, 20526). **website:** www.peacecorps.gov

*Postal Rate Commission — George A. Omas, chair (1333 H St. NW, Suite 300, 20268). **website:** www.prc.gov

*Securities and Exchange Commission — William H. Donaldson, chair (450 5th St. NW, 20549). **website:** www.sec.gov

*Selective Service System — Jack Martin, act. dir. (National Headquarters, 1515 Wilson Blvd., Arlington, VA 22209-2425). **website:** www.sss.gov

*Small Business Administration — Hector V. Barreto, adm. (409 Third St. SW, 20416). **website:** www.sba.gov

Smithsonian Institution — (quasi-official agency) Lawrence M. Small, sec. (PO Box 37012, SI Building, Rm. 153, MRC 010, 20013). **website:** www.si.edu

*Social Security Administration — Jo Anne B. Barnhart, comm. (6401 Security Blvd., Baltimore, MD 21235). **website:** www.ssa.gov

Surgeon General — Dr. Richard Carmona (Dept. of HHS, 5600 Fishers Ln., Rm. 18-66, Rockville, MD 20857). **website:** www.surgeongeneral.gov

*Tennessee Valley Authority — Glenn L. McCullough Jr., chair, Board of Directors (400 W. Summit Hill Dr., Knoxville, TN 37902). **website:** www.tva.gov

*Trade and Development Agency — Thelma J. Askey, dir. (1000 Wilson Blvd. Ste. 1600, Arlington, VA 22209). **website:** www.tda.gov

United States Coast Guard — Adm. Thomas H. Collins, commandant (Dept. of Homeland Security, 2100 2nd St. SW, 20593). **website:** www.uscg.mil

United States Customs and Border Protection — Robert C. Bonner, comm. (Dept. of Homeland Security, 1300 Pennsylvania Ave. NW, 20229). **website:** www.customs.gov

United States Geological Survey — Charles G. Groat, dir. (Dept. of the Interior, 12201 Sunrise Valley Dr., Reston, VA 20192). **website:** www.usgs.gov

*United States International Trade Commission — Stephen Koplan, chair (500 E St. SW, 20436). **website:** www.usitc.gov

United States Mint — Henrietta Holsman Fore, dir. (Dept. of Treas., U.S. Mint Headquarters, 801 9th St., NW, 20002). **website:** www.usmint.gov

*United States Postal Service — John E. Potter, Postmaster General (475 L'Enfant Plaza SW, 20260). **website:** www.usps.com

United States Secret Service — W. Ralph Bashman, dir. (Dept. of Homeland Security, 245 Murray Dr., Bldg. 410, 20223). **website:** www.secretservice.gov

CABINETS OF THE U.S.

The U.S. Cabinet and Its Role

The heads of major executive departments of government constitute the Cabinet. This institution, not provided for in the U.S. Constitution, developed as an advisory body out of the desire of presidents to consult on policy matters. Aside from its advisory role, the Cabinet as a body has no formal function and wields no executive authority. Individual members exercise authority as heads of their departments, reporting to the president.

In addition to the heads of federal departments as listed below, the Cabinet commonly includes other officials designated by the president as of Cabinet rank.

The officials so designated by Pres. George W. Bush include: Vice Pres. Dick Cheney, Chief of Staff to the President Andrew H. Card Jr., Environmental Protection Agency Acting Administrator Michael O. Leavitt, Office of Management and Budget Director Joshua B. Bolten, Office of National Drug Control Policy Director John P. Walters, and United States Trade Representative Robert B. Zoellick.

The Cabinet meets at times set by the president. Members of Pres. Bush's Cabinet listed in this chapter are as of Oct. 15, 2004.

Secretaries of State

The Department of Foreign Affairs was created by act of Congress on July 27, 1789, and the name changed to Department of State on Sept. 15, 1789.

President	Secretary	Home	Apptd.	President	Secretary	Home	Apptd.
Washington	Thomas Jefferson	VA	1789	Harrison, B.	James G. Blaine	ME	1889
	Edmund Randolph	VA	1794		John W. Foster	IN	1892
	Timothy Pickering	PA	1795	Cleveland	Walter Q. Gresham	IN	1893
Adams, J.	Timothy Pickering	PA	1797		Richard Olney	MA	1895
	John Marshall	VA	1800	McKinley	Richard Olney	MA	1897
Jefferson	James Madison	VA	1801		John Sherman	OH	1897
Madison	Robert Smith	MD	1809		William R. Day	OH	1898
	James Monroe	VA	1811		John Hay	DC	1898
Monroe	John Quincy Adams	MA	1817	Roosevelt, T.	John Hay	DC	1901
Adams, J.Q.	Henry Clay	KY	1825		Elihu Root	NY	1905
Jackson	Martin Van Buren	NY	1829		Robert Bacon	NY	1909
	Edward Livingston	LA	1831	Taft	Robert Bacon	NY	1909
	Louis McLane	DE	1833		Philander C. Knox	PA	1909
	John Forsyth	GA	1834	Wilson	Philander C. Knox	PA	1913
Van Buren	John Forsyth	GA	1837		William J. Bryan	NE	1913
Harrison, W.H.	Daniel Webster	MA	1841		Robert Lansing	NY	1915
Tyler	Daniel Webster	MA	1841		Bainbridge Colby	NY	1920
	Abel P. Upshur	VA	1843	Harding	Charles E. Hughes	NY	1921
	John C. Calhoun	SC	1844	Coolidge	Charles E. Hughes	NY	1923
Polk	John C. Calhoun	SC	1845		Frank B. Kellogg	MN	1925
	James Buchanan	PA	1845	Hoover	Frank B. Kellogg	MN	1929
Taylor	James Buchanan	PA	1849		Henry L. Stimson	NY	1929
	John M. Clayton	DE	1849	Roosevelt, F.D.	Cordell Hull	TN	1933
Fillmore	John M. Clayton	DE	1850		E.R. Stettinius Jr.	VA	1944
	Daniel Webster	MA	1850	Truman	E.R. Stettinius Jr.	VA	1945
	Edward Everett	MA	1852		James F. Byrnes	SC	1945
Pierce	William L. Marcy	NY	1853		George C. Marshall	PA	1947
Buchanan	William L. Marcy	NY	1857		Dean G. Acheson	CT	1949
	Lewis Cass	MI	1857	Eisenhower	John Foster Dulles	NY	1953
	Jeremiah S. Black	PA	1860		Christian A. Herter	MA	1959
Lincoln	Jeremiah S. Black	PA	1861	Kennedy	Dean Rusk	NY	1961
	William H. Seward	NY	1861	Johnson, L.B.	Dean Rusk	NY	1963
Johnson, A.	William H. Seward	NY	1865	Nixon	William P. Rogers	NY	1969
Grant	Elihu B. Washburne	IL	1869		Henry A. Kissinger	DC	1973
	Hamilton Fish	NY	1869	Ford	Henry A. Kissinger	DC	1974
Hayes	Hamilton Fish	NY	1877	Carter	Cyrus R. Vance	NY	1977
	William M. Evarts	NY	1877		Edmund S. Muskie	ME	1980
Garfield	William M. Evarts	NY	1881	Reagan	Alexander M. Haig Jr.	CT	1981
	James G. Blaine	ME	1881		George P. Shultz	CA	1982
Arthur	James G. Blaine	ME	1881	Bush, G.H.W.	James A. Baker 3rd	TX	1989
	F.T. Frelinghuysen	NJ	1881		Lawrence S. Eagleburger	MI	1992
Cleveland	F.T. Frelinghuysen	NJ	1885	Clinton	Warren M. Christopher	CA	1993
	Thomas F. Bayard	DE	1885		Madeleine K. Albright	DC	1997
Harrison, B.	Thomas F. Bayard	DE	1889	Bush, G.W.	Colin L. Powell	NY	2001

Secretaries of the Treasury

The Treasury Department was organized by act of Congress on Sept. 2, 1789.

President	Secretary	Home	Apptd.	President	Secretary	Home	Apptd.
Washington	Alexander Hamilton	NY	1789	Van Buren	Levi Woodbury	NH	1837
	Oliver Wolcott	CT	1795	Harrison, W.H.	Thomas Ewing	OH	1841
Adams, J.	Oliver Wolcott	CT	1797	Tyler	Thomas Ewing	OH	1841
	Samuel Dexter	MA	1801		Walter Forward	PA	1841
Jefferson	Samuel Dexter	MA	1801		John C. Spencer	NY	1843
	Albert Gallatin	PA	1801		George M. Bibb	KY	1844
Madison	Albert Gallatin	PA	1809	Polk	Robert J. Walker	MS	1845
	George W. Campbell	TN	1814	Taylor	William M. Meredith	PA	1849
	Alexander J. Dallas	PA	1814	Fillmore	Thomas Corwin	OH	1850
	William H. Crawford	GA	1816	Pierce	James Guthrie	KY	1853
Monroe	William H. Crawford	GA	1817	Buchanan	Howell Cobb	GA	1857
Adams, J.Q.	Richard Rush	PA	1825		Phillip F. Thomas	MD	1860
Jackson	Samuel D. Ingham	PA	1829		John A. Dix	NY	1861
	Louis McLane	DE	1831	Lincoln	Salmon P. Chase	OH	1861
	William J. Duane	PA	1833		William P. Fessenden	ME	1864
	Roger B. Taney	MD	1833		Hugh McCulloch	IN	1865
	Levi Woodbury	NH	1834	Johnson, A.	Hugh McCulloch	IN	1865

President	Secretary	Home	Apptd.
Grant	George S. Boutwell	MA	1869
	William A. Richardson	MA	1873
	Benjamin H. Bristow	KY	1874
	Lot M. Morrill	ME	1876
Hayes	John Sherman	OH	1877
Garfield	William Windom	MN	1881
Arthur	Charles J. Folger	NY	1881
	Walter Q. Gresham	IN	1884
	Hugh McCulloch	IN	1884
Cleveland	Daniel Manning	NY	1885
	Charles S. Fairchild	NY	1887
Harrison, B.	William Windom	MN	1889
	Charles Foster	OH	1891
Cleveland	John G. Carlisle	KY	1893
McKinley	Lyman J. Gage	IL	1897
Roosevelt, T.	Lyman J. Gage	IL	1901
	Leslie M. Shaw	IA	1902
	George B. Cortelyou	NY	1907
Taft	Franklin MacVeagh	IL	1909
Wilson	William G. McAdoo	NY	1913
	Carter Glass	VA	1918
	David F. Houston	MO	1920
Harding	Andrew W. Mellon	PA	1921
Coolidge	Andrew W. Mellon	PA	1923
Hoover	Andrew W. Mellon	PA	1929
	Ogden L. Mills	NY	1932
Roosevelt, F.D.	William H. Woodin	NY	1933
	Henry Morgenthau, Jr.	NY	1934
Truman	Fred M. Vinson	KY	1945
	John W. Snyder	MO	1946
Eisenhower	George M. Humphrey	OH	1953
	Robert B. Anderson	CT	1957
Kennedy	C. Douglas Dillon	NJ	1961
Johnson, L.B.	C. Douglas Dillon	NJ	1963
	Henry H. Fowler	VA	1965
	Joseph W. Barr	IN	1968
Nixon	David M. Kennedy	IL	1969
	John B. Connally	TX	1971
	George P. Shultz	IL	1972
	William E. Simon	NJ	1974
Ford	William E. Simon	NJ	1974
Carter	W. Michael Blumenthal	MI	1977
	G. William Miller	RI	1979
Reagan	Donald T. Regan	NY	1981
	James A. Baker 3rd	TX	1985
	Nicholas F. Brady	NJ	1988
Bush, G.H.W.	Nicholas F. Brady	NJ	1989
Clinton	Lloyd Bentsen	TX	1993
	Robert E. Rubin	NY	1995
	Lawrence H. Summers	CT	1999
Bush, G.W.	Paul H. O'Neill	PA	2001
	John W. Snow	PA	2003

Secretaries of Defense

The Department of Defense, originally designated the National Military Establishment, was created on Sept. 18, 1947. It is headed by the secretary of defense, who is a member of the president's Cabinet. The departments of the army, of the navy, and of the air force function within the Defense Department, and since 1947 the secretaries of these departments have not been members of the president's Cabinet.

President	Secretary	Home	Apptd.
Truman	James V. Forrestal	NY	1947
	Louis A. Johnson	WV	1949
	George C. Marshall	PA	1950
	Robert A. Lovett	NY	1951
Eisenhower	Charles E. Wilson	MI	1953
	Neil H. McElroy	OH	1957
	Thomas S. Gates Jr.	PA	1959
Kennedy	Robert S. McNamara	MI	1961
Johnson, L.B.	Robert S. McNamara	MI	1963
	Clark M. Clifford	MD	1968
Nixon	Melvin R. Laird	WI	1969
	Elliot L. Richardson	MA	1973
	James R. Schlesinger	VA	1973
Ford	James R. Schlesinger	VA	1974
	Donald H. Rumsfeld	IL	1975
Carter	Harold Brown	CA	1977
Reagan	Caspar W. Weinberger	CA	1981
	Frank C. Carlucci	PA	1987
Bush, G.H.W.	Richard B. Cheney	WY	1989
Clinton	Les Aspin	WI	1993
	William J. Perry	CA	1994
	William S. Cohen	ME	1997
Bush, G.W.	Donald H. Rumsfeld	IL	2001

Secretaries of War

The War Department (which included jurisdiction over the navy until 1798) was created by act of Congress on Aug. 7, 1789, and Gen. Henry Knox was commissioned secretary of war under that act on Sept. 12, 1789.

President	Secretary	Home	Apptd.
Washington	Henry Knox	MA	1789
	Timothy Pickering	PA	1795
	James McHenry	MD	1796
Adams, J.	James McHenry	MD	1797
	Samuel Dexter	MA	1800
Jefferson	Henry Dearborn	MA	1801
Madison	William Eustis	MA	1809
	John Armstrong	NY	1813
	James Monroe	VA	1814
	William H. Crawford	GA	1815
Monroe	John C. Calhoun	SC	1817
Adams, J.Q.	James Barbour	VA	1825
	Peter B. Porter	NY	1828
Jackson	John H. Eaton	TN	1829
	Lewis Cass	MI	1831
	Benjamin F. Butler	NY	1837
Van Buren	Joel R. Poinsett	SC	1837
Harrison, W.H.	John Bell	TN	1841
Tyler	John Bell	TN	1841
	John C. Spencer	NY	1841
	James M. Porter	PA	1843
	William Wilkins	PA	1844
Polk	William L. Marcy	NY	1845
Taylor	George W. Crawford	GA	1849
Fillmore	Charles M. Conrad	LA	1850
Pierce	Jefferson Davis	MS	1853
Buchanan	John B. Floyd	VA	1857
	Joseph Holt	KY	1861
Lincoln	Simon Cameron	PA	1861
	Edwin M. Stanton	PA	1862
Johnson, A.	Edwin M. Stanton	PA	1865
	John M. Schofield	IL	1868
Grant	John A. Rawlins	IL	1869
	William T. Sherman	OH	1869
	William W. Belknap	IA	1869
	Alphonso Taft	OH	1876
	James D. Cameron	PA	1876
Hayes	George W. McCrary	IA	1877
	Alexander Ramsey	MN	1879
Garfield	Robert T. Lincoln	IL	1881
Arthur	Robert T. Lincoln	IL	1881
Cleveland	William C. Endicott	MA	1885
Harrison, B.	Redfield Proctor	VT	1889
	Stephen B. Elkins	WV	1891
Cleveland	Daniel S. Lamont	NY	1893
McKinley	Russel A. Alger	MI	1897
	Elihu Root	NY	1899
Roosevelt, T.	Elihu Root	NY	1901
	William H. Taft	OH	1904
	Luke E. Wright	TN	1908
Taft	Jacob M. Dickinson	TN	1909
	Henry L. Stimson	NY	1911
Wilson	Lindley M. Garrison	NJ	1913
	Newton D. Baker	OH	1916
Harding	John W. Weeks	MA	1921
Coolidge	John W. Weeks	MA	1923
	Dwight F. Davis	MO	1925
Hoover	James W. Good	IL	1929
	Patrick J. Hurley	OK	1929
Roosevelt, F.D.	George H. Dern	UT	1933
	Harry H. Woodring	KS	1937
	Henry L. Stimson	NY	1940
Truman	Robert P. Patterson	NY	1945
	Kenneth C. Royall[1]	NC	1947

(1) Last member of the Cabinet with this title. The War Department became the Department of the Army and became a branch of the Department of Defense in 1947.

Secretaries of the Navy
The Navy Department was created by act of Congress on Apr. 30, 1798.

President	Secretary	Home	Apptd.
Adams, J.	Benjamin Stoddert	MD	1798
Jefferson	Benjamin Stoddert	MD	1801
	Robert Smith	MD	1801
Madison	Paul Hamilton	SC	1809
	William Jones	PA	1813
	Benjamin W. Crowninshield	MA	1814
Monroe	Benjamin W. Crowninshield	MA	1817
	Smith Thompson	NY	1818
	Samuel L. Southard	NJ	1823
Adams, J.Q.	Samuel L. Southard	NJ	1825
Jackson	John Branch	NC	1829
	Levi Woodbury	NH	1831
	Mahlon Dickerson	NJ	1834
Van Buren	Mahlon Dickerson	NJ	1837
	James K. Paulding	NY	1838
Harrison, W.H.	George E. Badger	NC	1841
Tyler	George E. Badger	NC	1841
	Abel P. Upshur	VA	1841
	David Henshaw	MA	1843
	Thomas W. Gilmer	VA	1844
	John Y. Mason	VA	1844
Polk	George Bancroft	MA	1845
	John Y. Mason	VA	1846
Taylor	William B. Preston	VA	1849
Fillmore	William A. Graham	NC	1850
	John P. Kennedy	MD	1852
Pierce	James C. Dobbin	NC	1853
Buchanan	Isaac Toucey	CT	1857
Lincoln	Gideon Welles	CT	1861
Johnson, A.	Gideon Welles	CT	1865
Grant	Adolph E. Borie	PA	1869
	George M. Robeson	NJ	1869
Hayes	Richard W. Thompson	IN	1877
	Nathan Goff Jr.	WV	1881
Garfield	William H. Hunt	LA	1881
Arthur	William E. Chandler	NH	1882
Cleveland	William C. Whitney	NY	1885
Harrison, B.	Benjamin F. Tracy	NY	1889
Cleveland	Hilary A. Herbert	AL	1893
McKinley	John D. Long	MA	1897
Roosevelt, T.	John D. Long	MA	1901
	William H. Moody	MA	1902
	Paul Morton	IL	1904
	Charles J. Bonaparte	MD	1905
	Victor H. Metcalf	CA	1906
	Truman H. Newberry	MI	1908
Taft	George von L. Meyer	MA	1909
Wilson	Josephus Daniels	NC	1913
Harding	Edwin Denby	MI	1921
Coolidge	Edwin Denby	MI	1923
	Curtis D. Wilbur	CA	1924
Hoover	Charles Francis Adams	MA	1929
Roosevelt, F.D.	Claude A. Swanson	VA	1933
	Charles Edison	NJ	1940
	Frank Knox	IL	1940
	James V. Forrestal	NY	1944
Truman	James V. Forrestal[1]	NY	1945

(1) Last member of Cabinet with this title. The Navy Department became a branch of the Department of Defense when the latter was created on Sept. 18, 1947.

Attorneys General

The Office of Attorney General was established by act of Congress on Sept. 24, 1789. It officially reached Cabinet rank in Mar. 1792, when the first attorney general, Edmund Randolph, attended his initial Cabinet meeting. The Department of Justice, headed by the attorney general, was created June 22, 1870.

President	Attorney General	Home	Apptd.
Washington	Edmund Randolph	VA	1789
	William Bradford	PA	1794
	Charles Lee	VA	1795
Adams, J.	Charles Lee	VA	1797
Jefferson	Levi Lincoln	MA	1801
	John Breckenridge	KY	1805
	Caesar A. Rodney	DE	1807
Madison	Caesar A. Rodney	DE	1807
	William Pinkney	MD	1811
	Richard Rush	PA	1814
Monroe	Richard Rush	PA	1817
	William Wirt	VA	1817
Adams, J.Q.	William Wirt	VA	1825
Jackson	John M. Berrien	GA	1829
	Roger B. Taney	MD	1831
	Benjamin F. Butler	NY	1833
Van Buren	Benjamin F. Butler	NY	1837
	Felix Grundy	TN	1838
	Henry D. Gilpin	PA	1840
Harrison, W.H.	John J. Crittenden	KY	1841
Tyler	John J. Crittenden	KY	1841
	Hugh S. Legare	SC	1841
	John Nelson	MD	1843
Polk	John Y. Mason	VA	1845
	Nathan Clifford	ME	1846
	Isaac Toucey	CT	1848
Taylor	Reverdy Johnson	MD	1849
Fillmore	John J. Crittenden	KY	1850
Pierce	Caleb Cushing	MA	1853
Buchanan	Jeremiah S. Black	PA	1857
	Edwin M. Stanton	PA	1860
Lincoln	Edward Bates	MO	1861
	James Speed	KY	1864
Johnson, A.	James Speed	KY	1865
	Henry Stanbery	OH	1866
	William M. Evarts	NY	1868
Grant	Ebenezer R. Hoar	MA	1869
	Amos T. Akerman	GA	1870
	George H. Williams	OR	1871
	Edwards Pierrepont	NY	1875
	Alphonso Taft	OH	1876
Hayes	Charles Devens	MA	1877
Garfield	Wayne MacVeagh	PA	1881
Arthur	Benjamin H. Brewster	PA	1882
Cleveland	Augustus Garland	AR	1885
Harrison, B.	William H. H. Miller	IN	1889
Cleveland	Richard Olney	MA	1893
	Judson Harmon	OH	1895
McKinley	Joseph McKenna	CA	1897
	John W. Griggs	NJ	1898
	Philander C. Knox	PA	1901
Roosevelt, T.	Philander C. Knox	PA	1901
	William H. Moody	MA	1904
	Charles J. Bonaparte	MD	1906
Taft	George W. Wickersham	NY	1909
Wilson	J.C. McReynolds	TN	1913
	Thomas W. Gregory	TX	1914
	A. Mitchell Palmer	PA	1919
Harding	Harry M. Daugherty	OH	1921
Coolidge	Harry M. Daugherty	OH	1923
	Harlan F. Stone	NY	1924
	John G. Sargent	VT	1925
Hoover	William D. Mitchell	MN	1929
Roosevelt, F.D.	Homer S. Cummings	CT	1933
	Frank Murphy	MI	1939
	Robert H. Jackson	NY	1940
	Francis Biddle	PA	1941
Truman	Thomas C. Clark	TX	1945
	J. Howard McGrath	RI	1949
	J.P. McGranery	PA	1952
Eisenhower	Herbert Brownell Jr.	NY	1953
	William P. Rogers	MD	1957
Kennedy	Robert F. Kennedy	MA	1961
Johnson, L.B.	Robert F. Kennedy	MA	1963
	N. de B. Katzenbach	IL	1964
	Ramsey Clark	TX	1967
Nixon	John N. Mitchell	NY	1969
	Richard G. Kleindienst	AZ	1972
	Elliot L. Richardson	MA	1973
	William B. Saxbe	OH	1974
Ford	William B. Saxbe	OH	1974
	Edward H. Levi	IL	1975
Carter	Griffin B. Bell	GA	1977
	Benjamin R. Civiletti	MD	1979
Reagan	William French Smith	CA	1981
	Edwin Meese 3rd.	CA	1985
	Richard Thornburgh	PA	1988
Bush, G.H.W.	Richard Thornburgh	PA	1989
	William P. Barr	NY	1991
Clinton	Janet Reno	FL	1993
Bush, G.W.	John Ashcroft	MO	2001

Secretaries of the Interior

The Department of the Interior was created by act of Congress on Mar. 3, 1849.

President	Secretary	Home	Apptd.	President	Secretary	Home	Apptd.
Taylor	Thomas Ewing	OH	1849	Wilson	Franklin K. Lane	CA	1913
Fillmore	Thomas M. T. McKennan	PA	1850		John B. Payne	IL	1920
	Alex H. H. Stuart	VA	1850	Harding	Albert B. Fall	NM	1921
Pierce	Robert McClelland	MI	1853		Hubert Work	CO	1923
Buchanan	Jacob Thompson	MS	1857	Coolidge	Hubert Work	CO	1923
Lincoln	Caleb B. Smith	IN	1861		Roy O. West	IL	1929
	John P. Usher	IN	1863	Hoover	Ray Lyman Wilbur	CA	1929
Johnson, A.	John P. Usher	IN	1865	Roosevelt, F.D.	Harold L. Ickes	IL	1933
	James Harlan	IA	1865	Truman	Harold L. Ickes	IL	1945
	Orville H. Browning	IL	1866		Julius A. Krug	WI	1946
Grant	Jacob D. Cox	OH	1869		Oscar L. Chapman	CO	1949
	Columbus Delano	OH	1870	Eisenhower	Douglas McKay	OR	1953
	Zachariah Chandler	MI	1875		Fred A. Seaton	NE	1956
Hayes	Carl Schurz	MO	1877	Kennedy	Stewart L. Udall	AZ	1961
Garfield	Samuel J. Kirkwood	IA	1881	Johnson, L.B.	Stewart L. Udall	AZ	1963
Arthur	Henry M. Teller	CO	1882	Nixon	Walter J. Hickel	AK	1969
Cleveland	Lucius Q.C. Lamar	MS	1885		Rogers C.B. Morton	MD	1971
	William F. Vilas	WI	1888	Ford	Rogers C.B. Morton	MD	1971
Harrison, B.	John W. Noble	MO	1889		Stanley K. Hathaway	WY	1975
Cleveland	Hoke Smith	GA	1893		Thomas S. Kleppe	ND	1975
	David R. Francis	MO	1896	Carter	Cecil D. Andrus	ID	1977
McKinley	Cornelius N. Bliss	NY	1897	Reagan	James G. Watt	CO	1981
	Ethan A. Hitchcock	MO	1898		William P. Clark	CA	1983
Roosevelt, T.	Ethan A. Hitchcock	MO	1901		Donald P. Hodel	OR	1985
	James R. Garfield	OH	1907	Bush, G.H.W.	Manuel Lujan	NM	1989
Taft	Richard A. Ballinger	WA	1909	Clinton	Bruce Babbitt	AZ	1993
	Walter L. Fisher	IL	1911	Bush, G.W.	Gale Norton	CO	2001

Secretaries of Agriculture

The Department of Agriculture was created by act of Congress on May 15, 1862. On Feb. 8, 1889, its commissioner was renamed secretary of agriculture and became a member of the Cabinet.

President	Secretary	Home	Apptd.	President	Secretary	Home	Apptd.
Cleveland	Norman J. Colman	MO	1889	Truman	Charles F. Brannan	CO	1948
Harrison, B.	Jeremiah M. Rusk	WI	1889	Eisenhower	Ezra Taft Benson	UT	1953
Cleveland	J. Sterling Morton	NE	1893	Kennedy	Orville L. Freeman	MN	1961
McKinley	James Wilson	IA	1897	Johnson, L.B.	Orville L. Freeman	MN	1963
Roosevelt, T.	James Wilson	IA	1901	Nixon	Clifford M. Hardin	IN	1969
Taft	James Wilson	IA	1909		Earl L. Butz	IN	1971
Wilson	David F. Houston	MO	1913	Ford	Earl L. Butz	IN	1974
	Edwin T. Meredith	IA	1920		John A. Knebel	VA	1976
Harding	Henry C. Wallace	IA	1921	Carter	Bob Bergland	MN	1977
Coolidge	Henry C. Wallace	IA	1923	Reagan	John R. Block	IL	1981
	Howard M. Gore	WV	1924		Richard E. Lyng	CA	1986
	William M. Jardine	KS	1925	Bush, G.H.W.	Clayton K. Yeutter	NE	1989
Hoover	Arthur M. Hyde	MO	1929		Edward Madigan	IL	1991
Roosevelt, F.D.	Henry A. Wallace	IA	1933	Clinton	Mike Espy	MS	1993
	Claude R. Wickard	IN	1940		Dan Glickman	KS	1995
Truman	Clinton P. Anderson	NM	1945	Bush, G.W.	Ann M. Veneman	CA	2001

Secretaries of Commerce and Labor

The Department of Commerce and Labor, created by Congress on Feb. 14, 1903, was divided by Congress Mar. 4, 1913, into separate departments of Commerce and Labor. The secretary of each was made a Cabinet member.

Secretaries of Commerce and Labor

President	Secretary	Home	Apptd.
Roosevelt, T.	George B. Cortelyou	NY	1903
	Victor H. Metcalf	CA	1904
	Oscar S. Straus	NY	1906
Taft	Charles Nagel	MO	1909

Secretaries of Labor

President	Secretary	Home	Apptd.
Wilson	William B. Wilson	PA	1913
Harding	James J. Davis	PA	1921
Coolidge	James J. Davis	PA	1923
Hoover	James J. Davis	PA	1929
	William N. Doak	VA	1930
Roosevelt, F.D.	Frances Perkins	NY	1933
Truman	L.B. Schwellenbach	WA	1945
	Maurice J. Tobin	MA	1949
Eisenhower	Martin P. Durkin	IL	1953
	James P. Mitchell	NJ	1953
Kennedy	Arthur J. Goldberg	IL	1961
	W. Willard Wirtz	IL	1962
Johnson, L.B.	W. Willard Wirtz	IL	1963
Nixon	George P. Shultz	IL	1969
	James D. Hodgson	CA	1970
	Peter J. Brennan	NY	1973
Ford	Peter J. Brennan	NY	1974
	John T. Dunlop	CA	1975
	W.J. Usery Jr.	GA	1976
Carter	F. Ray Marshall	TX	1977

President	Secretary	Home	Apptd.
Reagan	Raymond J. Donovan	NJ	1981
	William E. Brock	TN	1985
	Ann D. McLaughlin	DC	1987
Bush, G.H.W.	Elizabeth Hanford Dole	NC	1989
	Lynn Martin	IL	1991
Clinton	Robert B. Reich	MA	1993
	Alexis M. Herman	AL	1997
Bush, G.W.	Elaine L. Chao	KY	2001

Secretaries of Commerce

President	Secretary	Home	Apptd.
Wilson	William C. Redfield	NY	1913
	Joshua W. Alexander	MO	1919
Harding	Herbert C. Hoover	CA	1921
Coolidge	Herbert C. Hoover	CA	1923
	William F. Whiting	MA	1928
Hoover	Robert P. Lamont	IL	1929
	Roy D. Chapin	MI	1932
Roosevelt, F.D.	Daniel C. Roper	SC	1933
	Harry L. Hopkins	NY	1939
	Jesse Jones	TX	1940
	Henry A. Wallace	IA	1945
Truman	Henry A. Wallace	IA	1945
	W. Averell Harriman	NY	1947
	Charles Sawyer	OH	1948
Eisenhower	Sinclair Weeks	MA	1953
	Lewis L. Strauss	NY	1958
	Frederick H. Mueller	MI	1959

President	Secretary	Home	Apptd.	President	Secretary	Home	Apptd.
Kennedy	Luther H. Hodges	NC	1961	Carter	Juanita M. Kreps	NC	1977
Johnson, L.B.	Luther H. Hodges	NC	1963		Philip M. Klutznick	IL	1979
	John T. Connor	NJ	1965	Reagan	Malcolm Baldrige	CT	1981
	Alex B. Trowbridge	NJ	1967		C. William Verity Jr.	OH	1987
	Cyrus R. Smith	NY	1968	Bush, G.H.W.	Robert A. Mosbacher	TX	1989
Nixon	Maurice H. Stans	MN	1969		Barbara H. Franklin	PA	1992
	Peter G. Peterson	IL	1972	Clinton	Ronald H. Brown	DC	1993
	Frederick B. Dent	SC	1973		Mickey Kantor	CA	1996
Ford	Frederick B. Dent	SC	1974		William M. Daley	IL	1997
	Rogers C.B. Morton	MD	1975		Norman Y. Mineta	CA	2000
	Elliot L. Richardson	MA	1975	Bush, G.W.	Donald L. Evans	TX	2001

Secretaries of Housing and Urban Development

The Department of Housing and Urban Development was created by act of Congress on Sept. 9, 1965.

President	Secretary	Home	Apptd.	President	Secretary	Home	Apptd.
Johnson, L.B.	Robert C. Weaver	WA	1966	Carter	Patricia Roberts Harris	DC	1977
	Robert C. Wood	MA	1969		Moon Landrieu	LA	1979
Nixon	George W. Romney	MI	1969	Reagan	Samuel R. Pierce Jr.	NY	1981
	James T. Lynn	OH	1973	Bush, G.H.W.	Jack F. Kemp	NY	1989
Ford	James T. Lynn	OH	1974	Clinton	Henry G. Cisneros	TX	1993
	Carla Anderson Hills	CA	1975		Andrew M. Cuomo	NY	1997
				Bush, G.W.	Mel Martinez	FL	2001
					Alphonso Jackson	TX	2004

Secretaries of Transportation

The Department of Transportation was created by act of Congress on Oct. 15, 1966.

President	Secretary	Home	Apptd.	President	Secretary	Home	Apptd.
Johnson, L.B.	Alan S. Boyd	FL	1966	Reagan	Andrew L. Lewis Jr.	PA	1981
Nixon	John A. Volpe	MA	1969		Elizabeth Hanford Dole	NC	1983
	Claude S. Brinegar	CA	1973		James H. Burnley	NC	1987
Ford	Claude S. Brinegar	CA	1974	Bush, G.H.W.	Samuel K. Skinner	IL	1989
	William T. Coleman Jr.	PA	1975		Andrew H. Card Jr.	MA	1992
Carter	Brock Adams	WA	1977	Clinton	Federico F. Peña	CO	1993
	Neil E. Goldschmidt	OR	1979		Rodney E. Slater	AR	1997
				Bush, G.W.	Norman Y. Mineta	CA	2001

Secretaries of Energy

The Department of Energy was created by federal law on Aug. 4, 1977.

President	Secretary	Home	Apptd.	President	Secretary	Home	Apptd.
Carter	James R. Schlesinger	VA	1977	Bush, G.H.W.	James D. Watkins	CA	1989
	Charles Duncan Jr.	WY	1979	Clinton	Hazel R. O'Leary	MN	1993
Reagan	James B. Edwards	SC	1981		Federico F. Peña	CO	1997
	Donald P. Hodel	OR	1982		Bill Richardson	NM	1998
	John S. Herrington	CA	1985	Bush, G.W.	Spencer Abraham	MI	2001

Secretaries of Health, Education, and Welfare

The Department of Health, Education, and Welfare was created by Congress on Apr. 11, 1953. On Sept. 27, 1979, it was divided by Congress into the departments of Education and of Health and Human Services, with the secretary of each being a Cabinet member.

President	Secretary	Home	Apptd.	President	Secretary	Home	Apptd.
Eisenhower	Oveta Culp Hobby	TX	1953	Nixon	Robert H. Finch	CA	1969
	Marion B. Folsom	NY	1955		Elliot L. Richardson	MA	1970
	Arthur S. Flemming	OH	1958		Caspar W. Weinberger	CA	1973
Kennedy	Abraham A. Ribicoff	CT	1961	Ford	Caspar W. Weinberger	CA	1974
	Anthony J. Celebrezze	OH	1962		Forrest D. Mathews	AL	1975
Johnson, L.B.	Anthony J. Celebrezze	OH	1963	Carter	Joseph A. Califano Jr.	DC	1977
	John W. Gardner	NY	1965		Patricia Roberts Harris	DC	1979
	Wilbur J. Cohen	MI	1968				

Secretaries of Health and Human Services

President	Secretary	Home	Apptd.	President	Secretary	Home	Apptd.
Carter	Patricia Roberts Harris	DC	1979	Reagan	Otis R. Bowen	IN	1985
Reagan	Richard S. Schweiker	PA	1981	Bush, G.H.W.	Louis W. Sullivan	GA	1989
	Margaret M. Heckler	MA	1983	Clinton	Donna E. Shalala	WI	1993
				Bush, G.W.	Tommy Thompson	WI	2001

Secretaries of Education

President	Secretary	Home	Apptd.	President	Secretary	Home	Apptd.
Carter	Shirley Hufstedler	CA	1979	Bush, G.H.W.	Lauro F. Cavazos	TX	1989
Reagan	Terrel Bell	UT	1981		Lamar Alexander	TN	1991
	William J. Bennett	NY	1985	Clinton	Richard W. Riley	SC	1993
	Lauro F. Cavazos	TX	1988	Bush, G.W.	Roderick R. Paige	TX	2001

Secretaries of Veterans Affairs

The Department of Veterans Affairs was created on Oct. 25, 1988, when Pres. Ronald Reagan signed a bill that made the Veterans Administration into a Cabinet department, effective Mar. 15, 1989.

President	Secretary	Home	Apptd.	President	Secretary	Home	Apptd.
Bush, G.H.W.	Edward J. Derwinski	IL	1989	Clinton	Togo D. West Jr.	NC	1998
Clinton	Jesse Brown	IL	1993		Hershel W. Gober (acting)	AR	2000
				Bush, G.W.	Anthony Principi	CA	2001

Department of Homeland Security

The Department of Homeland Security was created by act of Congress on Nov. 25, 2002. Pres. George W. Bush in 2003 appointed Thomas Ridge of Pennsylvania as its first secretary.

CONGRESS

The One Hundred and Eighth Congress

The 108th Congress convened on Jan. 7, 2003, and was to be succeeded by the 109th Congress in Jan. 2005.

The Senate, as of Oct. 2004

Rep., 51; Dem., 48; Ind., 1; Total, 100.

Terms are for 6 years and end Jan. 3 of the year preceding the senator's name in the following table. *Asterisk denotes senators running for reelection Nov. 2004. Annual salary, $158,100; President Pro Tempore, Majority Leader, and Minority Leader, $175,700. To be eligible for the Senate, one must be at least 30 years old, a U.S. citizen for at least 9 years, and a resident of the state from which chosen. Congress must meet annually on Jan. 3, unless it has, by law, appointed a different day.

The address is U.S. Senate, Washington DC 20510; the telephone number is 202-224-3121; the website is www.senate.gov

Senate officials in 2004 were: President Pro Tempore, Ted Stevens (AK); Majority Leader, Bill Frist (TN); Majority Whip, Mitch McConnell (KY); Minority Leader, Tom Daschle (SD); Minority Whip, Harry Reid (NV).

D–Democrat; R–Republican; I–Independent

Term ends	Senator (Party); Service from[1]
Alabama	
2005	Richard Shelby* (R); 1/6/87
2009	Jeff Sessions (R); 1/7/97
Alaska	
2005	Lisa Murkowski* (R); 12/20/02
2009	Ted Stevens (R);12/24/68
Arizona	
2005	John McCain* (R); 1/6/87
2007	Jon Kyl* (R); 1/4/95
Arkansas	
2005	Blanche Lincoln* (D); 1/6/99
2009	Mark Pryor (D); 1/7/03
California	
2005	Barbara Boxer (D); 1993
2007	Dianne Feinstein (D); 11/10/92
Colorado	
2005	Ben Nighthorse Campbell (R); 1993
2009	Wayne Allard (R); 1/7/97
Connecticut	
2005	Christopher J. Dodd* (D); 1981
2007	Joe Lieberman (D); 1989
Delaware	
2007	Thomas R. Carper (D); 2001
2009	Joseph Biden (D); 1973
Florida	
2005	Bob Graham (D); 1/6/87
2007	Bill Nelson (D); 2001
Georgia	
2005	Zell Miller (D); 7/24/00
2009	Saxby Chambliss (R); 1/7/03
Hawaii	
2005	Daniel K. Inouye* (D); 1963
2007	Daniel K. Akaka (D); 4/28/90
Idaho	
2005	Mike Crapo* (R); 1/6/99
2009	Larry E. Craig (R); 1991
Illinois	
2005	Peter G. Fitzgerald (R); 1/6/99
2009	Richard J. Durbin (D); 1/7/97
Indiana	
2005	Evan Bayh* (D); 1/6/99
2007	Richard G. Lugar (R); 1977
Iowa	
2005	Chuck Grassley* (R); 1981
2009	Tom Harkin (D); 1985
Kansas	
2005	Sam Brownback* (R); 11/27/96
2009	Pat Roberts (R); 1/7/97

Term ends	Senator (Party); Service from[1]
Kentucky	
2005	Jim Bunning* (R); 1/6/99
2009	Mitch McConnell (R); 1985
Louisiana	
2005	John B. Breaux (D); 1/6/87
2009	Mary L. Landrieu (D); 1/7/97
Maine	
2007	Olympia J. Snowe (R); 1/4/95
2009	Susan M. Collins (R); 1/7/97
Maryland	
2005	Barbara Ann Mikulski* (D); 1/6/87
2007	Paul S. Sarbanes (D); 1977
Massachusetts	
2007	Edward M. Kennedy (D); 11/7/62
2009	John F. Kerry (D); 1/2/85
Michigan	
2007	Debbie Stabenow (D); 2001
2009	Carl Levin (D); 1979
Minnesota	
2007	Mark Dayton (D); 2001
2009	Norm Coleman (R); 1/7/03
Mississippi	
2007	Trent Lott (R); 1989
2009	Thad Cochran (R); 12/27/78
Missouri	
2005	Christopher (Kit) Bond* (R); 1/6/87
2009	Jim Talent (R); 11/23/02
Montana	
2007	Conrad Burns (R); 1989
2009	Max Baucus (D); 12/15/78
Nebraska	
2007	Ben Nelson (D); 2001
2009	Chuck Hagel (R); 1/7/97
Nevada	
2005	Harry Reid* (D); 1/6/87
2007	John Ensign (R); 2001
New Hampshire	
2005	Judd Gregg* (R); 1993
2009	John Sununu (R); 1/7/03
New Jersey	
2007	Jon S. Corzine (D); 2001
2009	Frank Lautenberg (D); 1/7/03
New Mexico	
2007	Jeff Bingaman (D); 1983
2009	Pete V. Domenici (R); 1973
New York	
2005	Charles E. Schumer* (D); 1/6/99
2007	Hillary Rodham Clinton (D); 2001
North Carolina	
2005	John Edwards (D); 1/6/99
2009	Elizabeth H. Dole (R); 1/7/03

Term ends	Senator (Party); Service from[1]
North Dakota	
2005	Byron L. Dorgan* (D); 12/14/92
2007	Kent Conrad (D); 1/6/87
Ohio	
2005	George V. Voinovich* (R); 1/6/99
2007	Mike DeWine (R); 1/4/95
Oklahoma	
2005	Don Nickles (R); 1981
2009	James M. Inhofe (R); 11/21/94
Oregon	
2005	Ron Wyden* (D); 2/6/96
2009	Gordon Smith (R); 1/7/97
Pennsylvania	
2005	Arlen Specter* (R); 1981
2007	Rick Santorum (R); 1/4/95
Rhode Island	
2007	Lincoln D. Chafee (R); 11/2/99
2009	Jack Reed (D); 1/7/97
South Carolina	
2005	Ernest Hollings (D); 11/9/66
2009	Lindsey Graham (R); 1/7/03
South Dakota	
2005	Tom Daschle* (D); 1/6/87
2009	Tim Johnson (D); 1/7/97
Tennessee	
2007	Bill Frist (R); 1/4/95
2009	Lamar Alexander (R); 1/7/03
Texas	
2007	Kay Bailey Hutchison (R); 6/5/93
2009	John Cornyn (R); 12/2/02
Utah	
2005	Robert F. Bennett* (R); 1993
2007	Orrin G. Hatch (R); 1977
Vermont	
2005	Patrick Leahy* (D); 1975
2007	James M. Jeffords (I); 1989
Virginia	
2007	George F. Allen (R); 2001
2009	John W. Warner (R); 1/2/79
Washington	
2005	Patty Murray* (D); 1993
2007	Maria Cantwell (D); 2001
West Virginia	
2007	Robert C. Byrd (D); 1959
2009	John D. Rockefeller IV (D); 1/15/85
Wisconsin	
2005	Russ Feingold* (D); 1993
2007	Herbert H. Kohl (D); 1989
Wyoming	
2007	Craig Thomas (R); 1/4/95
2009	Michael B. Enzi (R); 1/7/97

(1) Jan. 3, when not otherwise noted.

The House of Representatives, as of Oct. 2004

Rep., 227; Dem., 205; Ind., 1; Vacancies, 2; Total 435. * Asterisk denotes members running for reelection Nov. 2004.

Terms are for 2 years ending Jan. 3, 2005. Annual salary, $158,100; Speaker of the House, $203,000; Majority Leader and Minority Leader, $175,700. To be eligible for membership, a person must be at least 25 years of age, a U.S. citizen for at least 7 years, and a resident of the state from which he or she is chosen. The address is U.S. House of Representatives, Washington, DC 20515; the telephone number is 202-224-3121. The website is www.house.gov

House officials in 2004 were: Speaker, J. Dennis Hastert (IL); Majority Leader, Tom DeLay (TX); Majority Whip, Roy Blunt (MO); Minority Leader, Nancy Pelosi (CA); Minority Whip, Steny Hoyer (MD).

Note: As a result of the 2000 census, new districts were added in the following states: Arizona (2), California, Colorado, Florida (2), Georgia (2), Nevada, North Carolina, and Texas (2). The following states lost districts: Connecticut, Illinois, Indiana, Michigan, Mississippi, New York (2), Ohio, Oklahoma, Pennsylvania (2), and Wisconsin. Many other districts were redrawn.

D=Democrat; R=Republican; I=Independent

Dist.	Representative (Party)	Dist.	Representative (Party)	Dist.	Representative (Party)
Alabama		25.	Howard P. "Buck" McKeon* (R)	4.	Ander Crenshaw* (R)
1.	Jo Bonner* (R)	26.	David Dreier* (R)	5.	Ginny Brown-Waite* (R)
2.	Terry Everett* (R)	27.	Brad Sherman* (D)	6.	Cliff Stearns* (R)
3.	Mike Rogers* (R)	28.	Howard L. Berman* (D)	7.	John L. Mica* (R)
4.	Robert B. Aderholt (R)	29.	Adam B. Schiff* (D)	8.	Ric Keller* (R)
5.	Robert E. (Bud) Cramer Jr.* (D)	30	Henry A. Waxman* (D)	9.	Michael Bilirakis* (R)
6.	Spencer Bachus* (R)	31.	Xavier Becerra* (D)	10.	C. W. Bill Young* (R)
7.	Artur Davis* (D)	32.	Hilda L. Solis* (D)	11.	Jim Davis* (D)
Alaska		33.	Diane E. Watson* (D)	12.	Adam H. Putnam* (R)
	Don Young* (R)	34.	Lucille Roybal-Allard* (D)	13.	Katherine Harris* (R)
Arizona		35.	Maxine Waters* (D)	14.	vacant[1]
1.	Rick Renzi* (R)	36.	Jane Harman* (D)	15.	Dave Weldon* (R)
2.	Trent Franks* (R)	37.	Juanita Millender-McDonald* (D)	16.	Mark Foley* (R)
3.	John B. Shadegg* (R)	38.	Grace F. Napolitano* (D)	17.	Kendrick B. Meek* (D)
4.	Ed Pastor* (D)	39.	Linda T. Sánchez* (D)	18.	Ileana Ros-Lehtinen* (R)
5.	J. D. Hayworth* (R)	40.	Edward R. Royce* (R)	19.	Robert Wexler* (D)
6.	Jeff Flake* (R)	41.	Jerry Lewis* (R)	20.	Peter Deutsch (D)
7.	Raúl M. Grijalva* (D)	42.	Gary G. Miller* (R)	21.	Lincoln Diaz-Balart* (R)
8.	Jim Kolbe* (R)	43.	Joe Baca* (D)	22.	E. Clay Shaw Jr.* (R)
Arkansas		44.	Ken Calvert* (R)	23.	Alcee L. Hastings* (D)
1.	Marion Berry* (D)	45.	Mary Bono* (R)	24.	Tom Feeney* (R)
2.	Vic Snyder* (D)	46.	Dana Rohrabacher* (R)	25.	Mario Diaz-Balart* (R)
3.	John Boozman* (R)	47.	Loretta Sanchez* (D)	**Georgia**	
4.	Mike Ross* (D)	48.	Christopher Cox* (R)	1.	Jack Kingston* (R)
California		49.	Darrell E. Issa* (R)	2.	Sanford D. Bishop Jr.* (D)
1.	Mike Thompson* (D)	50.	Randy "Duke" Cunningham* (R)	3.	Jim Marshall* (D)
2.	Wally Herger* (R)	51.	Bob Filner* (D)	4.	Denise L. Majette (D)
3.	Doug Ose (R)	52.	Duncan Hunter* (R)	5.	John Lewis* (D)
4.	John T. Doolittle* (R)	53.	Susan A. Davis* (D)	6.	Johnny Isakson (R)
5.	Robert T. Matsui* (D)	**Colorado**		7.	John Linder* (R)
6.	Lynn C. Woolsey* (D)	1.	Diana DeGette* (D)	8.	Mac Collins (R)
7.	George Miller* (D)	2.	Mark Udall* (D)	9.	Charlie Norwood* (R)
8.	Nancy Pelosi* (D)	3.	Scott McInnis (R)	10.	Nathan Deal* (R)
9.	Barbara Lee* (D)	4.	Marilyn N. Musgrave* (R)	11.	Phil Gingrey* (R)
10.	Ellen O. Tauscher* (D)	5.	Joel Hefley* (R)	12.	Max Burns* (R)
11.	Richard W. Pombo* (R)	6.	Thomas G. Tancredo* (R)	13.	David Scott* (D)
12.	Tom Lantos* (D)	7.	Bob Beauprez* (R)	**Hawaii**	
13.	Fortney Pete Stark* (D)	**Connecticut**		1.	Neil Abercrombie* (D)
14.	Anna G. Eshoo* (D)	1.	John B. Larson* (D)	2.	Ed Case* (D)
15.	Michael M. Honda* (D)	2.	Rob Simmons* (R)	**Idaho**	
16.	Zoe Lofgren* (D)	3.	Rosa L. DeLauro* (D)	1.	C. L. "Butch" Otter* (R)
17.	Sam Farr* (D)	4.	Christopher Shays* (R)	2.	Michael K. Simpson* (R)
18.	Dennis A. Cardoza* (D)	5.	Nancy Johnson* (R)	**Illinois**	
19.	George Radanovich* (R)	**Delaware**		1.	Bobby L. Rush* (D)
20.	Calvin M. Dooley (D)		Michael N. Castle* (R)	2.	Jesse L. Jackson Jr.* (D)
21.	Devin Nunes* (R)	**Florida**		3.	William O. Lipinski (D)
22.	William M. Thomas* (R)	1.	Jeff Miller* (R)	4.	Luis V. Gutierrez* (D)
23.	Lois Capps* (D)	2.	Allen Boyd* (D)	5.	Rahm Emanuel* (D)
24.	Elton Gallegly* (R)	3.	Corrine Brown* (D)	6.	Henry J. Hyde* (R)

Dist.	Representative (Party)
7.	Danny K. Davis* (D)
8.	Philip M. Crane* (R)
9.	Janice D. Schakowsky* (D)
10.	Mark Steven Kirk* (R)
11.	Jerry Weller* (R)
12.	Jerry F. Costello* (D)
13.	Judy Biggert* (R)
14.	J. Dennis Hastert* (R)
15.	Timothy V. Johnson* (R)
16.	Donald A. Manzullo* (R)
17.	Lane Evans* (D)
18.	Ray LaHood* (R)
19.	John Shimkus* (R)

Indiana

Dist.	Representative (Party)
1.	Peter J. Visclosky* (D)
2.	Chris Chocola* (R)
3.	Mark E. Souder* (R)
4.	Steve Buyer* (R)
5.	Dan Burton* (R)
6.	Mike Pence* (R)
7.	Julia M. Carson* (D)
8.	John N. Hostettler* (R)
9.	Baron P. Hill* (D)

Iowa

Dist.	Representative (Party)
1.	Jim Nussle* (R)
2.	James A. Leach* (R)
3.	Leonard L. Boswell* (D)
4.	Tom Latham* (R)
5.	Steve King* (R)

Kansas

Dist.	Representative (Party)
1.	Jerry Moran* (R)
2.	Jim Ryun* (R)
3.	Dennis Moore* (D)
4.	Todd Tiahrt* (R)

Kentucky

Dist.	Representative (Party)
1.	Ed Whitfield* (R)
2.	Ron Lewis* (R)
3.	Anne M. Northup* (R)
4.	Ken Lucas (D)
5.	Harold "Hal" Rogers* (R)
6.	Ben Chandler* (D)[2]

Louisiana

Dist.	Representative (Party)
1.	David Vitter (R)
2.	William J. Jefferson* (D)
3.	W. J. (Billy) Tauzin (R)
4.	Jim McCrery* (R)
5.	Rodney Alexander* (R)
6.	Richard H. Baker* (R)
7.	Christopher John (D)

Maine

Dist.	Representative (Party)
1.	Thomas H. Allen* (D)
2.	Michael H. Michaud* (D)

Maryland

Dist.	Representative (Party)
1.	Wayne T. Gilchrest* (R)
2.	C. A. Dutch Ruppersberger* (D)
3.	Benjamin L. Cardin* (D)
4.	Albert Russell Wynn* (D)
5.	Steny H. Hoyer* (D)
6.	Roscoe G. Bartlett* (R)
7.	Elijah E. Cummings* (D)
8.	Chris Van Hollen* (D)

Dist.	Representative (Party)
	Massachusetts
1.	John W. Olver* (D)
2.	Richard E. Neal* (D)
3.	James P. McGovern* (D)
4.	Barney Frank* (D)
5.	Martin T. Meehan* (D)
6.	John F. Tierney* (D)
7.	Edward J. Markey* (D)
8.	Michael E. Capuano* (D)
9.	Stephen F. Lynch* (D)
10.	William D. Delahunt* (D)

Michigan

Dist.	Representative (Party)
1.	Bart Stupak* (D)
2.	Peter Hoekstra* (R)
3.	Vernon J. Ehlers* (R)
4.	Dave Camp* (R)
5.	Dale E. Kildee* (D)
6.	Fred Upton* (R)
7.	Nick Smith (R)
8.	Mike Rogers* (R)
9.	Joe Knollenberg* (R)
10.	Candice S. Miller* (R)
11.	Thaddeus G. McCotter* (R)
12.	Sander M. Levin* (D)
13.	Carolyn C. Kilpatrick* (D)
14.	John Conyers Jr.* (D)
15.	John D. Dingell* (D)

Minnesota

Dist.	Representative (Party)
1.	Gil Gutknecht* (R)
2.	John Kline* (R)
3.	Jim Ramstad* (R)
4.	Betty McCollum* (D)
5.	Martin Olav Sabo* (D)
6.	Mark R. Kennedy* (R)
7.	Collin C. Peterson* (D)
8.	James L. Oberstar* (D)

Mississippi

Dist.	Representative (Party)
1.	Roger F. Wicker* (R)
2.	Bennie G. Thompson* (D)
3.	Charles W. "Chip" Pickering* (R)
4.	Gene Taylor* (D)

Missouri

Dist.	Representative (Party)
1.	Wm. Lacy Clay* (D)
2.	W. Todd Akin* (R)
3.	Richard A. Gephardt* (D)
4.	Ike Skelton* (D)
5.	Karen McCarthy (D)
6.	Sam Graves* (R)
7.	Roy Blunt* (R)
8.	Jo Ann Emerson* (R)
9.	Kenny C. Hulshof* (R)

Montana

Dist.	Representative (Party)
	Dennis R. Rehberg (R)

Nebraska

Dist.	Representative (Party)
1.	vacant[3]
2.	Lee Terry* (R)
3.	Tom Osborne* (R)

Nevada

Dist.	Representative (Party)
1.	Shelley Berkley* (D)
2.	Jim Gibbons* (R)
3.	Jon C. Porter* (R)

Dist.	Representative (Party)
	New Hampshire
1.	Jeb Bradley* (R)
2.	Charles Bass* (R)

New Jersey

Dist.	Representative (Party)
1.	Robert E. Andrews* (D)
2.	Frank A. LoBiondo* (R)
3.	Jim Saxton* (R)
4.	Christopher H. Smith* (R)
5.	Scott Garrett* (R)
6.	Frank Pallone Jr.* (D)
7.	Mike Ferguson* (R)
8.	Bill Pascrell Jr.* (D)
9.	Steven R. Rothman* (D)
10.	Donald M. Payne* (D)
11.	Rodney P. Frelinghuysen* (R)
12.	Rush D. Holt* (D)
13.	Robert Menendez* (D)

New Mexico

Dist.	Representative (Party)
1.	Heather Wilson* (R)
2.	Steve Pearce* (R)
3.	Tom Udall* (D)

New York

Dist.	Representative (Party)
1.	Timothy H. Bishop* (D)
2.	Steve J. Israel* (D)
3.	Peter T. King* (R)
4.	Carolyn McCarthy* (D)
5.	Gary L. Ackerman* (D)
6.	Gregory W. Meeks* (D)
7.	Joseph Crowley* (D)
8.	Jerrold L. Nadler* (D)
9.	Anthony D. Weiner* (D)
10.	Edolphus Towns* (D)
11.	Major R. Owens* (D)
12.	Nydia M. Velázquez* (D)
13.	Vito Fossella* (R)
14.	Carolyn B. Maloney* (D)
15.	Charles B. Rangel* (D)
16.	José E. Serrano* (D)
17.	Eliot L. Engel* (D)
18.	Nita M. Lowey* (D)
19.	Sue W. Kelly* (R)
20.	John E. Sweeney* (R)
21.	Michael R. McNulty* (D)
22.	Maurice D. Hinchey* (D)
23.	John M. McHugh* (R)
24.	Sherwood L. Boehlert* (R)
25.	James T. Walsh* (R)
26.	Thomas M. Reynolds* (R)
27.	Jack Quinn (R)
28.	Louise McIntosh Slaughter* (D)
29.	Amo Houghton (R)

North Carolina

Dist.	Representative (Party)
1.	G.K. Butterfield* (D)[4]
2.	Bob Etheridge* (D)
3.	Walter B. Jones* (R)
4.	David E. Price* (D)
5.	Richard Burr (R)
6.	Howard Coble* (R)
7.	Mike McIntyre* (D)
8.	Robin Hayes* (R)

Dist.	Representative (Party)
9.	Sue Wilkins Myrick* (R)
10.	Cass Ballenger (R)
11.	Charles H. Taylor* (R)
12.	Melvin L. Watt* (D)
13.	Brad Miller* (D)

North Dakota

	Earl Pomeroy* (D)

Ohio

Dist.	Representative (Party)
1.	Steve Chabot* (R)
2.	Rob Portman* (R)
3.	Michael R. Turner* (R)
4.	Michael Oxley* (R)
5.	Paul E. Gillmor* (R)
6.	Ted Strickland* (D)
7.	David L. Hobson* (R)
8.	John A. Boehner* (R)
9.	Marcy Kaptur* (D)
10.	Dennis J. Kucinich* (D)
11.	Stephanie Tubbs Jones* (D)
12.	Patrick J. Tiberi* (R)
13.	Sherrod Brown* (D)
14.	Steven C. LaTourette* (R)
15.	Deborah Pryce* (R)
16.	Ralph Regula* (R)
17.	Tim Ryan* (D)
18.	Robert W. Ney* (R)

Oklahoma

Dist.	Representative (Party)
1.	John Sullivan* (R)
2.	Brad Carson (D)
3.	Frank D. Lucas* (R)
4.	Tom Cole* (R)
5.	Ernest J. Istook Jr.* (R)

Oregon

Dist.	Representative (Party)
1.	David Wu* (D)
2.	Greg Walden* (R)
3.	Earl Blumenauer* (D)
4.	Peter A. DeFazio* (D)
5.	Darlene Hooley* (D)

Pennsylvania

Dist.	Representative (Party)
1.	Robert A. Brady* (D)
2.	Chaka Fattah* (D)
3.	Phil English* (R)
4.	Melissa A. Hart* (R)
5.	John E. Peterson* (R)
6.	Jim Gerlach* (R)
7.	Curt Weldon* (R)
8.	James C. Greenwood (R)
9.	Bill Shuster* (R)
10.	Don Sherwood* (R)
11.	Paul E. Kanjorski* (D)
12.	John P. Murtha* (D)
13.	Joseph M. Hoeffel (D)

Dist.	Representative (Party)
14.	Michael F. Doyle* (D)
15.	Patrick J. Toomey (R)
16.	Joseph R. Pitts* (R)
17.	Tim Holden* (D)
18.	Tim Murphy* (R)
19.	Todd Russell Platts* (R)

Rhode Island

Dist.	Representative (Party)
1.	Patrick J. Kennedy* (D)
2.	James R. Langevin* (D)

South Carolina

Dist.	Representative (Party)
1.	Henry E. Brown Jr.* (R)
2.	Joe Wilson* (R)
3.	J. Gresham Barrett* (R)
4.	Jim DeMint (R)
5.	John M. Spratt Jr.* (D)
6.	James E. Clyburn* (D)

South Dakota

	Stephanie Herseth* (D)[5]

Tennessee

Dist.	Representative (Party)
1.	William L. Jenkins* (R)
2.	John J. Duncan Jr.* (R)
3.	Zach Wamp* (R)
4.	Lincoln Davis* (D)
5.	Jim Cooper* (D)
6.	Bart Gordon* (D)
7.	Marsha Blackburn* (R)
8.	John S. Tanner* (D)
9.	Harold E. Ford* Jr. (D)

Texas

Dist.	Representative (Party)
1.	Max Sandlin* (D)
2.	Jim Turner (D)
3.	Sam Johnson* (R)
4.	Ralph M. Hall* (R)
5.	Jeb Hensarling* (R)
6.	Joe Barton* (R)
7.	John Abney Culberson* (R)
8.	Kevin Brady* (R)
9.	Nick Lampson* (D)
10.	Lloyd Doggett* (D)
11.	Chet Edwards* (D)
12.	Kay Granger* (R)
13.	Mac Thornberry* (R)
14.	Ron Paul* (R)
15.	Rubén Hinojosa* (D)
16.	Silvestre Reyes* (D)
17.	Charles W. Stenholm* (D)
18.	Sheila Jackson Lee* (D)
19.	Randy Neugebauer* (R)[6]
20.	Charles A. Gonzalez* (D)
21.	Lamar S. Smith* (R)
22.	Tom DeLay* (R)
23.	Henry Bonilla* (R)

Dist.	Representative (Party)
24.	Martin Frost* (D)
25.	Chris Bell (D)
26.	Michael C. Burgess* (R)
27.	Solomon P. Ortiz* (D)
28.	Ciro D. Rodriguez (D)
29.	Gene Green* (D)
30.	Eddie Bernice Johnson* (D)
31.	John R. Carter* (R)
32.	Pete Sessions* (R)

Utah

Dist.	Representative (Party)
1.	Rob Bishop* (R)
2.	Jim Matheson* (D)
3.	Chris Cannon* (R)

Vermont

	Bernard Sanders* (I)

Virginia

Dist.	Representative (Party)
1.	Jo Ann Davis* (R)
2.	Edward L. Schrock (R)
3.	Robert C. Scott* (D)
4.	J. Randy Forbes* (R)
5.	Virgil H. Goode Jr.* (R)
6.	Bob Goodlatte* (R)
7.	Eric Cantor* (R)
8.	James P. Moran* (D)
9.	Rick Boucher* (D)
10.	Frank R. Wolf* (R)
11.	Tom Davis* (R)

Washington

Dist.	Representative (Party)
1.	Jay Inslee* (D)
2.	Rick Larsen* (D)
3.	Brian Baird* (D)
4.	Doc Hastings* (R)
5.	George R. Nethercutt Jr. (R)
6.	Norman D. Dicks* (D)
7.	Jim McDermott* (D)
8.	Jennifer Dunn (R)
9.	Adam Smith* (D)

West Virginia

Dist.	Representative (Party)
1.	Alan B. Mollohan* (D)
2.	Shelley Moore Capito (R)
3.	Nick Joe Rahall II* (D)

Wisconsin

Dist.	Representative (Party)
1.	Paul Ryan* (R)
2.	Tammy Baldwin* (D)
3.	Ron Kind* (D)
4.	Gerald D. Kleczka (D)
5.	F. James Sensenbrenner Jr.* (R)
6.	Tom Petri* (R)
7.	David R. Obey* (D)
8.	Mark Green* (R)

Wyoming

	Barbara Cubin* (R)

The following members of Congress are non-voting: Eleanor Holmes Norton (D), Washington D.C.; Eni F.H. Falemavaega (D), American Samoa; Madelaine Z. Brodallo (D), Guam; Aníbal Acevado-Vilá (D) resident commissioner, Puerto Rico; Donna M. Christensen (D), Virgin Islands.

(1) Porter Goss resigned his seat Sept. 23, 2004, to accept nomination as director of the CIA; the seat was to be filled by election on Nov. 2, 2004. (2) Ben Chandler was elected in a special election Feb. 17, 2004, to fill the seat vacated by Ernie Fletcher (R) who had resigned Dec. 8, 2003. (3) Doug Bereuter resigned his seat effective Aug. 31, 2004; the seat was to be filled by election on Nov. 2, 2004. (4) G.K. Butterfield won a special election July 4, 2004, to fill the seat vacated by the resignation of Frank W. Balance Jr. (D), June 11, 2004. (5) Stephanie Herseth won a special election June 1, 2004, to fill the seat vacated by William Janklow (R). Janklow was convicted of second-degree manslaughter, Dec. 2003, for his involvement in an Aug. 2003 automobile accident that killed a motorist. He resigned Jan. 20, 2004, 2 days before he was sentenced to 100 days in jail. (6) Randy Neugebauer won a special election June 3, 2003, to fill the seat vacated by the resignation of Larry Combest (R) May 31, 2003.

Floor Leaders in the U.S. Senate Since the 1920s

Majority Leaders

Name	Party	State	Tenure
Charles Curtis[1]	Rep.	KS	1925-1929
James E. Watson	Rep.	IN	1929-1933
Joseph T. Robinson	Dem.	AR	1933-1937
Alben W. Barkley	Dem.	KY	1937-1947
Wallace H. White	Rep.	ME	1947-1949
Scott W. Lucas	Dem.	IL	1949-1951
Ernest W. McFarland	Dem.	AZ	1951-1953
Robert A. Taft	Rep.	OH	1953
William F. Knowland	Rep.	CA	1953-1955
Lyndon B. Johnson	Dem.	TX	1955-1961
Mike Mansfield	Dem.	MT	1961-1977
Robert C. Byrd	Dem.	WV	1977-1981
Howard H. Baker Jr.	Rep.	TN	1981-1985
Robert J. Dole	Rep.	KS	1985-1987
Robert C. Byrd	Dem.	WV	1987-1989
George J. Mitchell	Dem.	ME	1989-1995
Robert J. Dole	Rep.	KS	1995-1996
Trent Lott	Rep.	MS	1996-2001[3]
Thomas A. Daschle	Dem.	SD	2001-2003[3]
Bill Frist	Rep.	TN	2003-

Minority Leaders

Name	Party	State	Tenure
Oscar W. Underwood[2]	Dem.	AL	1920-1923
Joseph T. Robinson	Dem.	AR	1923-1933
Charles L. McNary	Rep.	OR	1933-1944
Wallace H. White	Rep.	ME	1944-1947
Alben W. Barkley	Dem.	KY	1947-1949
Kenneth S. Wherry	Rep.	NE	1949-1951
Henry Styles Bridges	Rep.	NH	1951-1953
Lyndon B. Johnson	Dem.	TX	1953-1955
William F. Knowland	Rep.	CA	1955-1959
Everett M. Dirksen	Rep.	IL	1959-1969
Hugh D. Scott	Rep.	PA	1969-1977
Howard H. Baker Jr.	Rep.	TN	1977-1981
Robert C. Byrd	Dem.	WV	1981-1987
Robert J. Dole	Rep.	KS	1987-1995
Thomas A. Daschle	Dem.	SD	1995-2001[3]
Trent Lott	Rep.	MS	(3)
Bill Frist	Rep.	TN	2002-2003[3]
Thomas A. Daschle	Dem.	SD	2003-

Note: The offices of party (majority and minority) leaders in the Senate did not evolve until the 20th century. (1) First Republican to be designated floor leader. (2) First Democrat to be designated floor leader. (3) Starting Jan. 3, 2001, the Senate was split 50-50; with Al Gore (D) as outgoing vice pres. with the deciding vote, Thomas A. Daschle (D) became majority leader and Trent Lott (R) was minority leader. From Jan. 20, 2001, with Dick Cheney (R) installed as vice pres., the positions were reversed. From June 6, 2001, the switch of Sen. James Jeffords (VT) from Republican to Independent meant the Democrats had a majority; Daschle resumed as majority leader, Lott as minority leader. Lott resigned as party leader Dec. 20, 2002, and Bill Frist was elected to replace him in the 108th Congress; since Republicans now had a majority, Frist became majority leader as of Jan. 7, 2003, with Daschle as minority leader.

Speakers of the House of Representatives

(as of Oct. 2004)

Name	Party	State	Tenure
Frederick Muhlenberg	Federalist	PA	1789-1791
Jonathan Trumbull	Federalist	CT	1791-1793
Frederick Muhlenberg	Federalist	PA	1793-1795
Jonathan Dayton	Federalist	NJ	1795-1799
Theodore Sedgwick	Federalist	MA	1799-1801
Nathaniel Macon	Dem.-Rep.	NC	1801-1807
Joseph B. Varnum	Dem.-Rep.	MA	1807-1811
Henry Clay	Dem.-Rep.	KY	1811-1814
Langdon Cheves	Dem.-Rep.	SC	1814-1815
Henry Clay	Dem.-Rep.	KY	1815-1820
John W. Taylor	Dem.-Rep.	NY	1820-1821
Philip P. Barbour	Dem.-Rep.	VA	1821-1823
Henry Clay	Dem.-Rep.	KY	1823-1825
John W. Taylor	Dem.	NY	1825-1827
Andrew Stevenson	Dem.	VA	1827-1834
John Bell	Dem.	TN	1834-1835
James K. Polk	Dem.	TN	1835-1839
Robert M. T. Hunter	Dem.	VA	1839-1841
John White	Whig	KY	1841-1843
John W. Jones	Dem.	VA	1843-1845
John W. Davis	Dem.	IN	1845-1847
Robert C. Winthrop	Whig	MA	1847-1849
Howell Cobb	Dem.	GA	1849-1851
Linn Boyd	Dem.	KY	1851-1855
Nathaniel P. Banks	American	MA	1856-1857
James L. Orr	Dem.	SC	1857-1859
William Pennington	Rep.	NJ	1860-1861
Galusha A. Grow	Rep.	PA	1861-1863
Schuyler Colfax	Rep.	IN	1863-1869
Theodore M. Pomeroy	Rep.	NY	1869
James G. Blaine	Rep.	ME	1869-1875
Michael C. Kerr	Dem.	IN	1875-1876
Samuel J. Randall	Dem.	PA	1876-1881
Joseph W. Keifer	Rep.	OH	1881-1883
John G. Carlisle	Dem.	KY	1883-1889
Thomas B. Reed	Rep.	ME	1889-1891
Charles F. Crisp	Dem.	GA	1891-1895
Thomas B. Reed	Rep.	ME	1895-1899
David B. Henderson	Rep.	IA	1899-1903
Joseph G. Cannon	Rep.	IL	1903-1911
Champ Clark	Dem.	MO	1911-1919
Frederick H. Gillett	Rep.	MA	1919-1925
Nicholas Longworth	Rep.	OH	1925-1931
John N. Garner	Dem.	TX	1931-1933
Henry T. Rainey	Dem.	IL	1933-1935
Joseph W. Byrns	Dem.	TN	1935-1936
William B. Bankhead	Dem.	AL	1936-1940
Sam Rayburn	Dem.	TX	1940-1947
Joseph W. Martin Jr.	Rep.	MA	1947-1949
Sam Rayburn	Dem.	TX	1949-1953
Joseph W. Martin Jr.	Rep.	MA	1953-1955
Sam Rayburn	Dem.	TX	1955-1961
John W. McCormack	Dem.	MA	1962-1971
Carl Albert	Dem.	OK	1971-1977
Thomas P. O'Neill Jr.	Dem.	MA	1977-1987
James Wright	Dem.	TX	1987-1989
Thomas S. Foley	Dem.	WA	1989-1995
Newt Gingrich	Rep.	GA	1995-1999
J. Dennis Hastert	Rep.	IL	1999-

Political Divisions of the U.S. Senate and House of Representatives, 1901-2004

Source: *Congressional Directory*; Senate Library

Note: all figures reflect immediate post-election party breakdown; **boldface** denotes party in majority immediately after election.

Congress	Years	SENATE Total Sens.	Demo-crats	Repub-licans	Other parties	Vacant	HOUSE OF REPRESENTATIVES Total Members	Demo-crats	Repub-licans	Other parties	Vacant
57th	1901-03	90	29	**56**	3	2	357	153	**198**	5	1
58th	1903-05	90	32	**58**			386	178	**207**		1
59th	1905-07	90	32	**58**			386	136	**250**		
60th	1907-09	92	29	**61**		2	386	164	**222**		
61st	1909-11	92	32	**59**		1	391	172	**219**		
62nd	1911-13	92	42	**49**		1	391	**228**	162	1	
63rd	1913-15	96	**51**	44	1		435	**290**	127	18	
64th	1915-17	96	**56**	39	1		435	**231**	193	8	3
65th	1917-19	96	**53**	42	1		435	210[1]	**216**	9	
66th	1919-21	96	47	**48**	1		435	191	**237**	7	
67th	1921-23	96	37	**59**			435	132	**300**	1	2
68th	1923-25	96	43	**51**	2		435	207	**225**	3	
69th	1925-27	96	40	**54**	1	1	435	183	**247**	5	
70th	1927-29	96	47	**48**	1		435	195	**237**	3	
71st	1929-31	96	39	**56**	1		435	163	**267**	1	4

		SENATE					HOUSE OF REPRESENTATIVES				
Congress	Years	Total Sens.	Demo-crats	Repub-licans	Other parties	Vacant	Total Members	Demo-crats	Repub-licans	Other parties	Vacant
72nd	1931-33	96	47	**48**	1		435	216[2]	**218**	1	
73rd	1933-35	96	**59**	36	1		435	**313**	117	5	
74th	1935-37	96	**69**	25	2		435	**322**	103	10	
75th	1937-39	96	**75**	17	4		435	**333**	89	13	
76th	1939-41	96	**69**	23	4		435	**262**	169	4	
77th	1941-43	96	**66**	28	2		435	**267**	162	6	
78th	1943-45	96	**57**	38	1		435	**222**	209	4	
79th	1945-47	96	**57**	38	1		435	**243**	190	2	
80th	1947-49	96	45	**51**			435	188	**246**	1	
81st	1949-51	96	**54**	42			435	**263**	171	1	
82nd	1951-53	96	**48**	47	1		435	**234**	199	2	
83rd	1953-55	96	46	**48**	2		435	213	221	1	
84th	1955-57	96	**48**	47	1		435	**232**	203		
85th	1957-59	96	**49**	47			435	**234**	201		
86th	1959-61	98	**64**	34			436[3]	**283**	153		
87th	1961-63	100	**64**	36			437[4]	**262**	175		
88th	1963-65	100	**67**	33			435	**258**	176		1
89th	1965-67	100	**68**	32			435	**295**	140		
90th	1967-69	100	**64**	36			435	**248**	187		
91st	1969-71	100	**58**	42			435	**243**	192		
92nd	1971-73	100	**54**	44	2		435	**255**	180		
93rd	1973-75	100	**56**	42	2		435	**242**	192	1	
94th	1975-77	100	**60**	37	2		435	**291**	144	1	
95th	1977-79	100	**61**	38	1		435	**292**	143		
96th	1979-81	100	**58**	41	1		435	**277**	158		
97th	1981-83	100	46	**53**	1		435	**242**	192	1	
98th	1983-85	100	46	**54**			435	**269**	166		
99th	1985-87	100	47	**53**			435	**253**	182		
100th	1987-89	100	**55**	45			435	**258**	177		
101st	1989-91	100	**55**	45			435	**260**	175		
102nd	1991-93	100	**56**	44			435	**267**	167	1	
103rd	1993-95	100	**57**	43			435	**258**	176	1	
104th	1995-97	100	48	**52**			435	204	**230**	1	
105th	1997-99	100	45	**55**			435	207	**227**	1	
106th	1999-2001	100	45	**55**			435	211	**223**	1	
107th	2001-03	100	50	**50**[5]			435	212	**221**	2	
108th	2003-05	100	48	**51**	1		435	205	**229**	1	

(1) Democrats organized the House with help of other parties. (2) Democrats organized House because of Republican deaths. (3 Proclamation declaring Alaska a state issued Jan. 3, 1959. (4) Proclamation declaring Hawaii a state issued Aug. 21, 1959. (5) While the Senate was split 50-50, control was held by whichever party had an incumbent vice president. Republican Sen. James M. Jeffords (VT) changed his party designation to Independent on June 6, 2001, switching control of the Senate to Democrats from Republicans.

Congressional Bills Vetoed, 1789-2003

Source: Senate Library

President	Regular vetoes	Pocket vetoes	Total vetoes	Vetoes overridden	President	Regular vetoes	Pocket vetoes	Total vetoes	Vetoes overridden
Washington	2	—	2	—	Benjamin Harrison	19	25	44	1
John Adams	—	—	—	—	Cleveland[2]	42	128	170	5
Jefferson	—	—	—	—	McKinley	6	36	42	—
Madison	5	2	7	—	Theodore Roosevelt	42	40	82	1
Monroe	1	—	1	—	Taft	30	9	39	1
John Q. Adams	—	—	—	—	Wilson	33	11	44	6
Jackson	5	7	12	—	Harding	5	1	6	—
Van Buren	—	1	1	—	Coolidge	20	30	50	4
William Harrison	—	—	—	—	Hoover	21	16	37	3
Tyler	6	4	10	1	Franklin Roosevelt	372	263	635	9
Polk	2	1	3	—	Truman	180	70	250	12
Taylor	—	—	—	—	Eisenhower	73	108	181	2
Fillmore	—	—	—	—	Kennedy	12	9	21	—
Pierce	9	—	9	5	Lyndon Johnson	16	14	30	—
Buchanan	4	3	7	—	Nixon	26	17	43	7
Lincoln	2	4	6	—	Ford	48	18	66	12
Andrew Johnson	21	8	29	15	Carter	13	18	31	2
Grant	45	48	93	4	Reagan	39	39	78	9
Hayes	12	1	13	1	George H. W. Bush[3]	29	15	44	1
Garfield	—	—	—	—	Clinton[4]	36	1	37	2
Arthur	4	8	12	1	George W. Bush[5]	—	—	—	—
Cleveland[1]	304	110	414	2	**Total[3,4]**	**1,484**	**1,065**	**2,549**	**106**

— = 0. (1) First term only. (2) Second term only. (3) Excluded from the figures are 2 additional bills, which Pres. George H. W. Bush claimed to be vetoed but Congress considered enacted into law because the president failed to return them to Congress during a recess period. (4) Does not include line-item vetoes, which were ruled unconstitutional by the Supreme Court on June 25, 1998. (5) As of Oct. 2004.

Librarians of Congress

Librarian	Served	Appointed by President	Librarian	Served	Appointed by President
John J. Beckley	1802-1807	Jefferson	Herbert Putnam	1899-1939	McKinley
Patrick Magruder	1807-1815	Jefferson	Archibald MacLeish	1939-1944	F. D. Roosevelt
George Watterston	1815-1829	Madison	Luther H. Evans	1945-1953	Truman
John Silva Meehan	1829-1861	Jackson	L. Quincy Mumford	1954-1974	Eisenhower
John G. Stephenson	1861-1864	Lincoln	Daniel J. Boorstin	1975-1987	Ford
Ainsworth Rand Spofford	1864-1897	Lincoln	James H. Billington	1987-	Reagan
John Russell Young	1897-1899	McKinley			

U.S. SUPREME COURT

(data as of Oct. 2004)

Justices of the U.S. Supreme Court

The Supreme Court comprises the chief justice of the U.S. and 8 associate justices, all appointed for life by the president with advice and consent of the Senate. Names of chief justices are in **boldface**. Salaries: chief justice, $203,000; associate justice, $194,300. The U.S. Supreme Court Bldg. is at 1 First St. NE, Washington, DC 20543. The Court website is www.supremecourtus.gov

Members at start of 2004-2005 term (Oct. 4, 2004): Chief justice: William H. Rehnquist; assoc. justices: Stephen G. Breyer, Ruth Bader Ginsburg, Anthony M. Kennedy, Sandra Day O'Connor, Antonin Scalia, David H. Souter, John Paul Stevens, Clarence Thomas.

Name, apptd. from	Term	Yrs	Born	Died
John Jay, NY	1789-1795	5	1745	1829
John Rutledge, SC[1]	1789-1791	1	1739	1800
William Cushing, MA	1789-1810	20	1732	1810
James Wilson, PA	1789-1798	8	1742	1798
John Blair, VA	1789-1796	6	1732	1800
James Iredell, NC	1790-1799	9	1751	1799
Thomas Johnson, MD	1791-1793	1	1732	1819
William Paterson, NJ	1793-1806	13	1745	1806
John Rutledge, SC[2,3]	1795	—	1739	1800
Samuel Chase, MD	1796-1811	15	1741	1811
Oliver Ellsworth, CT	1796-1800	4	1745	1807
Bushrod Washington, VA	1798-1829	31	1762	1829
Alfred Moore, NC	1799-1804	4	1755	1810
John Marshall, VA	1801-1835	34	1755	1835
William Johnson, SC	1804-1834	30	1771	1834
Henry B. Livingston, NY	1806-1823	16	1757	1823
Thomas Todd, KY	1807-1826	18	1765	1826
Joseph Story, MA	1811-1845	33	1779	1845
Gabriel Duval, MD	1811-1835	22	1752	1844
Smith Thompson, NY	1823-1843	20	1768	1843
Robert Trimble, KY	1826-1828	2	1777	1828
John McLean, OH	1829-1861	32	1785	1861
Henry Baldwin, PA	1830-1844	14	1780	1844
James M. Wayne, GA	1835-1867	32	1790	1867
Roger B. Taney, MD	1836-1864	28	1777	1864
Philip P. Barbour, VA	1836-1841	4	1783	1841
John Catron, TN	1837-1865	28	1786	1865
John McKinley, AL	1837-1852	15	1780	1852
Peter V. Daniel, VA	1841-1860	19	1784	1860
Samuel Nelson, NY	1845-1872	27	1792	1873
Levi Woodbury, NH	1845-1851	5	1789	1851
Robert C. Grier, PA	1846-1870	23	1794	1870
Benjamin R. Curtis, MA	1851-1857	6	1809	1874
John A. Campbell, AL	1853-1861	8	1811	1889
Nathan Clifford, ME	1858-1881	23	1803	1881
Noah H. Swayne, OH	1862-1881	18	1804	1884
Samuel F. Miller, IA	1862-1890	28	1816	1890
David Davis, IL	1862-1877	14	1815	1886
Stephen J. Field, CA	1863-1897	34	1816	1899
Salmon P. Chase, OH	1864-1873	8	1808	1873
William Strong, PA	1870-1880	10	1808	1895
Joseph P. Bradley, NJ	1870-1892	21	1813	1892
Ward Hunt, NY	1872-1882	9	1810	1886
Morrison R. Waite, OH	1874-1888	14	1816	1888
John M. Harlan, KY	1877-1911	34	1833	1911
William B. Woods, GA	1880-1887	6	1824	1887
Stanley Matthews, OH	1881-1889	7	1824	1889
Horace Gray, MA	1881-1902	20	1828	1902
Samuel Blatchford, NY	1882-1893	11	1820	1893
Lucius Q.C. Lamar, MS	1888-1893	5	1825	1893
Melville W. Fuller, IL	1888-1910	21	1833	1910
David J. Brewer, KS	1889-1910	20	1837	1910
Henry B. Brown, MI	1890-1906	15	1836	1913
George Shiras Jr., PA	1892-1903	10	1832	1924
Howell E. Jackson, TN	1893-1895	2	1832	1895
Edward D. White, LA[1]	1894-1910	16	1845	1921
Rufus W. Peckham, NY	1895-1909	13	1838	1909
Joseph McKenna, CA	1898-1925	26	1843	1926
Oliver W. Holmes, MA	1902-1932	29	1841	1935
William R. Day, OH	1903-1922	19	1849	1923
William H. Moody, MA	1906-1910	3	1853	1917
Horace H. Lurton, TN	1909-1914	4	1844	1914
Charles E. Hughes, NY[1]	1910-1916	5	1862	1948
Willis Van Devanter, WY	1910-1937	26	1859	1941
Joseph R. Lamar, GA	1910-1916	5	1857	1916
Edward D. White, LA[2]	1910-1921	10	1845	1921
Mahlon Pitney, NJ	1912-1922	10	1858	1924
James C. McReynolds, TN	1914-1941	26	1862	1946
Louis D. Brandeis, MA	1916-1939	22	1856	1941
John H. Clarke, OH	1916-1922	5	1857	1945
William H. Taft, CT	1921-1930	8	1857	1930
George Sutherland, UT	1922-1938	15	1862	1942
Pierce Butler, MN	1922-1939	16	1866	1939
Edward T. Sanford, TN	1923-1930	7	1865	1930
Harlan F. Stone, NY[1]	1925-1941	16	1872	1946
Charles E. Hughes, NY[2]	1930-1941	11	1862	1948
Owen J. Roberts, PA	1930-1945	15	1875	1955
Benjamin N. Cardozo, NY	1932-1938	6	1870	1938
Hugo L. Black, AL	1937-1971	34	1886	1971
Stanley F. Reed, KY	1938-1957	19	1884	1980
Felix Frankfurter, MA	1939-1962	23	1882	1965
William O. Douglas, CT	1939-1975	36[4]	1898	1980
Frank Murphy, MI	1940-1949	9	1890	1949
Harlan F. Stone, NY[2]	1941-1946	5	1872	1946
James F. Byrnes, SC	1941-1942	1	1879	1972
Robert H. Jackson, NY	1941-1954	12	1892	1954
Wiley B. Rutledge, IA	1943-1949	6	1894	1949
Harold H. Burton, OH	1945-1958	13	1888	1964
Fred M. Vinson, KY	1946-1953	7	1890	1953
Tom C. Clark, TX	1949-1967	18	1899	1977
Sherman Minton, IN	1949-1956	7	1890	1965
Earl Warren, CA	1953-1969	16	1891	1974
John Marshall Harlan, NY	1955-1971	16	1899	1971
William J. Brennan Jr., NJ	1956-1990	33	1906	1997
Charles E. Whittaker, MO	1957-1962	5	1901	1973
Potter Stewart, OH	1958-1981	23	1915	1985
Byron R. White, CO	1962-1993	31	1917	2002
Arthur J. Goldberg, IL	1962-1965	3	1908	1990
Abe Fortas, TN	1965-1969	4	1910	1982
Thurgood Marshall, NY	1967-1991	24	1908	1993
Warren E. Burger, VA	1969-1986	17	1907	1995
Harry A. Blackmun, MN	1970-1994	24	1908	1999
Lewis F. Powell Jr., VA	1971-1987	16	1907	1998
William H. Rehnquist, AZ[1]	1971-1986	15	1924	
John Paul Stevens, IL	1975-		1920	
Sandra Day O'Connor, AZ	1981-		1930	
William H. Rehnquist, AZ[2]	1986-		1924	
Antonin Scalia, VA	1986-		1936	
Anthony M. Kennedy, CA	1988-		1936	
David H. Souter, NH	1990-		1939	
Clarence Thomas, VA	1991-		1948	
Ruth Bader Ginsburg, DC	1993-		1933	
Stephen G. Breyer, MA	1994-		1938	

(1) Later, chief justice, as listed. (2) Formerly assoc. justice. (3) Named as acting chief justice; confirmation rejected by the Senate. (4) Longest term of service.

> **IT'S A FACT:** When the Supreme Court first met in New York in 1790, Justice William Cushing arrived wearing the wig he had worn while on the Massachusetts bench. Outside, bystanders teased him for his appearance. Cushing ended up taking the advice of Thomas Jefferson, who said, "Discard that monstrous wig which makes the English judges look like rats peeping through bunches of oakum [twisted hemp and jute fibers from old ropes]."

STATE GOVERNMENT
Governors of States and Puerto Rico
As of Oct. 15, 2004.

State	Capital, ZIP Code	Governor	Party	Term years	Term expires	Annual salary
Alabama	Montgomery 36130	Bob Riley	Rep.	4	Jan. 2007	$96,361
Alaska	Juneau 99811	Frank Murkowski	Rep.	4	Dec. 2006	85,776
Arizona	Phoenix 85007	Janet Napolitano	Dem.	4	Jan. 2007	95,000
Arkansas	Little Rock 72201	Mike Huckabee	Rep.	4	Jan. 2007	77,028
California	Sacramento 95814	Arnold Schwarzenegger	Rep.	4	Jan. 2007	175,000
Colorado	Denver 80203	Bill Owens	Rep.	4	Jan. 2007	90,000
Connecticut	Hartford 06106	M. Jodi Rell	Rep.	4	Jan. 2007	150,000
Delaware	Dover 19901	Ruth Ann Minner	Dem.	4	Jan. 2005	114,000
Florida	Tallahassee 32399	Jeb Bush	Rep.	4	Jan. 2007	124,575
Georgia	Atlanta 30334	Sonny Perdue	Rep.	4	Jan. 2007	127,303
Hawaii	Honolulu 96813	Linda Lingle	Rep.	4	Dec. 2006	94,780
Idaho	Boise 83720	Dirk Kempthorne	Rep.	4	Jan. 2007	98,500
Illinois	Springfield 62706	Rod R. Blagojevich	Dem.	4	Jan. 2007	150,691
Indiana	Indianapolis 46204	Joseph E. Kernan	Dem.	4	Jan. 2005	95,000
Iowa	Des Moines 50319	Tom Vilsack	Dem.	4	Jan. 2007	107,482
Kansas	Topeka 66612	Kathleen Sebelius	Dem.	4	Jan. 2007	101,281
Kentucky	Frankfort 40601	Ernie Fletcher	Rep.	4	Dec. 2007	109,146
Louisiana	Baton Rouge 70804	Kathleen Babineaux Blanco	Dem.	4	Jan. 2008	95,000
Maine	Augusta 04333	John E. Baldacci	Dem.	4	Jan. 2007	70,000
Maryland	Annapolis 21401	Robert L. Ehrlich Jr.	Rep.	4	Jan. 2007	145,000
Massachusetts	Boston 02133	Mitt Romney	Rep.	4	Jan. 2007	135,000
Michigan	Lansing 48909	Jennifer M. Granholm	Dem.	4	Jan. 2007	177,000
Minnesota	St. Paul 55155	Tim Pawlenty	Rep.	4	Jan. 2007	120,303
Mississippi	Jackson 39205	Haley Barbour	Rep.	4	Jan. 2008	122,160
Missouri	Jefferson City 65102	Bob Holden	Dem.	4	Jan. 2005	120,087
Montana	Helena 59620	Judy Martz	Rep.	4	Jan. 2005	96,462[1]
Nebraska	Lincoln 68509	Mike Johanns	Rep.	4	Jan. 2007	85,000
Nevada	Carson City 89710	Kenny C. Guinn	Rep.	4	Jan. 2007	110,299
New Hampshire	Concord 03301	Craig Benson	Rep.	2	Jan. 2005	102,704
New Jersey	Trenton 08625	James E. McGreevey[3]	Dem.	4	Jan. 2006	157,000
New Mexico	Santa Fe 87503	Bill Richardson	Dem.	4	Jan. 2007	110,000
New York	Albany 12224	George E. Pataki	Rep.	4	Jan. 2007	179,000
North Carolina	Raleigh 27603	Mike Easley	Dem.	4	Jan. 2005	121,391
North Dakota	Bismarck 58505	John Hoeven	Rep.	4	Jan. 2005	87,216
Ohio	Columbus 43266	Bob Taft	Rep.	4	Jan. 2007	122,800
Oklahoma	Oklahoma City 73105	Brad Henry	Dem.	4	Jan. 2007	117,571[1]
Oregon	Salem 97310	Ted Kulongoski	Dem.	4	Jan. 2007	93,600
Pennsylvania	Harrisburg 17120	Edward G. Rendell	Dem.	4	Jan. 2007	144,416
Rhode Island	Providence 02903	Donald L. Carcieri	Rep.	4	Jan. 2007	105,194
South Carolina	Columbia 29211	Mark Sanford	Rep.	4	Jan. 2007	106,078
South Dakota	Pierre 57501	Mike Rounds	Rep.	4	Jan. 2007	100,215
Tennessee	Nashville 37243	Phil Bredesen	Dem.	4	Jan. 2007	85,000
Texas	Austin 78711	Rick Perry	Rep.	4	Jan. 2007	115,345
Utah	Salt Lake City 84114	Olene S. Walker	Rep.	4	Jan. 2005	101,600
Vermont	Montpelier 05609	James H. Douglas	Rep.	2	Jan. 2005	127,456
Virginia	Richmond 23219	Mark R. Warner	Dem.	4	Jan. 2006	124,855
Washington	Olympia 98504	Gary Locke	Dem.	4	Jan. 2005	142,286
West Virginia	Charleston 25305	Bob Wise	Dem.	4	Jan. 2005	95,000
Wisconsin	Madison 53707	Jim Doyle	Dem.	4	Jan. 2007	131,768
Wyoming	Cheyenne 82002	Dave Freudenthal	Dem.	4	Jan. 2007	105,000
Puerto Rico	San Juan 00936	Sila Calderón	PDP[2]	4	Jan. 2005	70,000

(1) Salary in effect in July 2005. (2) Popular Democratic Party. (3) Gov. James McGreevey resigned the governorship Aug. 13, 2004, effective Nov.15, at which time State Senate Pres. Richard Codey (D) was to assume office for duration of the term.

State Officials, Salaries, Party Membership
As of Oct. 15, 2004

Alabama
Governor — Bob Riley, R, $96,361
Lt. Gov. — Lucy Baxley, D, $12 per day, plus $50 per day expenses, plus $3,780 per mo expenses
Atty. Gen. — Troy King, R, $163,429
Sec. of State — Nancy L. Worley, D, $71,500
Treasurer — Kay Ivey, R, $71,500
Auditor — Beth Chapman, R, $71,500
Legislature: meets annually at Montgomery 1st Tues. in Mar., 1st year of term of office; 1st Tues. in Feb., 2nd and 3rd yr; 2nd Tues. in Jan., 4th yr. Members receive $10 per day salary, plus $50 per day and $2,280 per month for expenses.
Senate — Dem., 25; Rep., 10. Total, 35
House — Dem., 62; Rep., 40; 3 vacancies. Total, 105

Alaska
Governor — Frank Murkowski, R, $85,776
Lt. Gov — Loren D. Leman, R, $80,040
Atty. General — Gregg Renkes, R, $91,200
Legislature: meets annually in Jan. at Juneau for 120 days with a 10-day extension possible upon 2/3 vote. Members receive $24,012 annually, plus $204 per diem.
Senate — Dem., 8; Rep., 12. Total, 20
House — Dem., 12; Rep., 28. Total, 40

Arizona
Governor — Janet Napolitano, D, $95,000
Sec. of State — Jan Brewer, R, $70,000
Atty. Gen. — Terry Goddard, D, $90,000

Treasurer — David Petersen, R, $70,000
Legislature: meets annually in Jan. at Phoenix. Each member receives an annual salary of $24,000 plus a per diem.
Senate — Dem., 13; Rep., 17. Total, 30
House — Dem., 20; Rep., 39; 1 ind. Total, 60

Arkansas
Governor — Mike Huckabee, R, $77,028
Lt. Gov. — Winthrop P. Rockefeller, R, $37,229
Sec. of State — Charlie Daniels, D, $48,142
Atty. Gen. — Mike Beebe, D, $64,189
Treasurer — Gus Wingfield, D, $48,142
Auditor — Jim Wood, D, $48,142
General Assembly: meets odd years in Jan. at Little Rock. Members receive $14,067 annually.
Senate — Dem., 27; Rep., 8. Total, 35
House — Dem., 70; Rep., 30. Total, 100

California
Governor — Arnold Schwarzenegger, R, $175,000
Lt. Gov. — Cruz Bustamante, D, $131,250
Sec. of State — Kevin Shelley, R, $131,250
Controller — Steve Westly, D, $140,000
Treasurer — Phil Angelides, D, $140,000
Atty. Gen. — Bill Lockyer, D, $148,750
Legislature: meets at Sacramento on the 1st Mon. in Dec. of even-numbered years; each session lasts 2 years. Members receive $99,000 annually, plus $121 per diem. High-ranking legislators earn an extra $7,425 or more, depending on post.

Senate — Dem., 25; Rep., 14; 1 vacancy. Total, 40
Assembly — Dem., 48; Rep., 32. Total, 80

Colorado

Governor — Bill Owens, R, $90,000
Lt. Gov. — Jane Norton, R, $68,500
Sec. of State — Donetta Davidson, R, $68,500
Atty. Gen. — Ken Salazar, D, $80,000
Treasurer — Mike Coffman, R, $68,500
General Assembly: meets annually in Jan. at Denver. Members receive $30,000 annually plus $99 per diem for attendance at interim committee meetings.
Senate — Dem., 17; Rep., 18. Total, 35
House — Dem., 28; Rep., 37. Total, 65

Connecticut

Governor — M. Jodi Rell, R, $150,000
Lt. Gov. — Keith B. Sullivan, D, $110,000
Sec. of State — Susan Bysiewicz, D, $110,000
Treasurer — Denise Nappier, D, $110,000
Comptroller — Nancy S. Wyman, D, $110,000
Atty. Gen. — Richard Blumenthal, D, $110,000
General Assembly: meets annually odd years in Jan. and even years in Feb., at Hartford. Members receive $28,000 annually, plus $5,500 (senator), $4,500 (representative) per year for expenses.
Senate — Dem., 20; Rep., 15; 1 vacancy. Total, 36
House — Dem., 94; Rep., 56; 1 vacancy. Total, 151

Delaware

Governor — Ruth Ann Minner, D, $114,000
Lt. Gov. — John C. Carney Jr., D, $64,900
Sec. of State — Harriet Smith Windsor, D, $109,800
Atty. Gen. — M. Jane Brady, R, $120,800
Treasurer — Jack A. Markell, D, $97,400
General Assembly: meets annually the 2nd Tues. in Jan. and continues each Tues., Wed., and Thurs. until June 30, at Dover. Members receive $36,400 annually.
Senate — Dem., 13; Rep., 8. Total, 21
House — Dem., 12; Rep., 29. Total, 41

Florida

Governor — Jeb Bush, R, $124,575
Lt. Gov. — Toni Jennings, R, $119,390
Chief Financial Officer — Tom Gallagher, R, $123,331
Atty. Gen. — Charlie Crist, R, $123,331
Comm. of Agriculture — Charles Bronson, R, $123,331
Legislature: meets annually at Tallahassee. Members receive $29,916 annually, plus expense allowance.
Senate — Dem., 14; Rep., 26. Total, 40
House — Dem., 39; Rep., 81. Total, 120

Georgia

Governor — Sonny Perdue, R, $127,303
Lt. Gov. — Mark Taylor, D, $83,148
Sec. of State — Cathy Cox, D, $112,776
Atty. Gen. — Thurbert Baker, D, $125,871
General Assembly: meets annually at Atlanta on 2nd Mon. in Jan. Members receive $16,200 annually ($128 per diem and $7,000 annual expense reimbursement).
Senate — Dem., 26; Rep., 30. Total, 56
House — Dem., 103; Rep., 76; 1 ind. Total, 180

Hawaii

Governor — Linda Lingle, R, $94,780
Lt. Gov. — James R. Aiona Jr., R, $90,041
Atty. Gen. — Mark J. Bennett, R, $105,000
Comptroller — Russ K. Saito, R, $100,000
Dir. of Budget & Finance — Georgina K. Kawamura, $99,996
Legislature: meets annually on 3rd Wed. in Jan. at Honolulu. Members receive $32,000 annually; presiding officers $37,000.
Senate — Dem., 20; Rep., 5. Total, 25
House — Dem., 36; Rep., 15. Total, 51

Idaho

Governor — Dirk Kempthorne, R, $98,500
Lt. Gov. — Jim Risch, R, $26,750
Sec. of State — Ben Ysursa, R, $82,500
Treasurer — Ron Crane, R, $82,500
Atty. Gen. — Lawrence Wasden, R, $91,500
Legislature: meets annually the Mon. on or nearest Jan. 9 at Boise. Members receive $15,646 annually, plus $99 per day during session if required to maintain a 2nd residence, $38 if no 2nd residence; plus $50 per day when engaged in legislative business when legislature is not in session.
Senate — Dem., 7, Rep., 28. Total, 35
House — Dem., 16; Rep., 54. Total, 70

Illinois

Governor — Rod R. Blagojevich, D, $150,691
Lt. Gov. — Patrick Quinn, D, $115,235
Sec. of State — Jesse White, D, $132,963
Comptroller — Daniel Hynes, D, $115,235
Atty. Gen. — Lisa Madigan, D, $132,963
Treasurer — Judy Baar Topinka, R, $115,235

General Assembly: meets annually in Nov. and Jan. at Springfield. Members receive $57,619 annually.
Senate — Dem., 32; Rep., 26; 1 ind. Total, 59
House — Dem., 66; Rep., 52. Total, 118

Indiana

Governor — Joseph E. Kernan, D, $95,000
Lt. Gov. — Katherine L. Davis, D, $76,000
Sec. of State — Todd Rokita, R, $66,000
Atty. Gen. — Steve Carter, R, $79,400
Treasurer — Tim Berry, R, $66,000
Auditor — Connie Kay Nass, R, $66,000
General Assembly: meets annually on the Tues. after 2nd Mon. in Jan. at Indianapolis. Members receive $11,600 annually, plus $112 per day in session, $25 per day while not in session.
Senate — Dem., 18; Rep., 32. Total, 50
House — Dem., 51; Rep., 49. Total, 100

Iowa

Governor — Tom Vilsack, D, $107,482
Lt. Gov. — Sally Pederson, D, $76,689
Sec. of State — Chester J. Culver D, $87,990
Atty. Gen. — Tom Miller, D, $105,430
Treasurer — Michael L. Fitzgerald, D, $87,990
Auditor — David A. Vaudt, R, $87,990
Sec. of Agriculture — Patty Judge, D, $87,990
General Assembly: meets annually in Jan. at Des Moines. Members receive $21,381 annually, plus expense allowance.
Senate — Dem., 21; Rep., 29. Total, 50
House — Dem., 46; Rep., 54. Total, 100

Kansas

Governor — Kathleen Sebelius, D, $101,281
Lt. Gov. — John Moore, D, $98,000
Sec. of State — Ron Thornburgh, R, $78,680
Atty. Gen. — Phill Kline, R, $90,480
Treasurer — Lynn Jenkins, R, $78,680
Insurance Commissioner — Sandy Praeger, R, $78,680
Legislature: meets annually on the 2nd Mon. of Jan. at Topeka. Members receive $81.11 per day salary, plus $91 per day expenses in session, plus $6,480 total allowance.
Senate — Dem., 10; Rep., 30. Total, 40
House — Dem., 45; Rep., 80. Total, 125

Kentucky

Governor — Ernie Fletcher, R, $109,146
Lt. Gov. — Stephen Pence, R, $92,790
Sec. of State — Trey Grayson, R, $92,790
Atty. Gen. — Gregory Stumbo, D, $92,790
Treasurer — Jonathan Miller, D, $92,790
Auditor — Crit (Eugenia) Luallen, D, $92,790
Sec. of Economic Dev. — Gene Strong, $162,750
General Assembly: meets annually on the 1st Tues. after the 1st Mon. in Jan. at Frankfort. Members receive $166 per day, plus $100 per day expenses during session and $1,581 per month for expenses for interim.
Senate — Dem., 16; Rep., 22. Total, 38
House — Dem., 64; Rep., 35; 1 vacancy. Total, 100

Louisiana

Governor — Kathleen Babineaux Blanco, D, $95,000
Lt. Gov. — Mitch Landrieux, D, $85,000
Sec. of State — W. Fox McKeithen, R, $85,000
Atty. Gen. — Charles C. Foti Jr., D, $85,000
Treasurer — John Kennedy, D, $85,000
Legislature: meets in odd-numbered years at Baton Rouge starting last Mon. in Mar., for 60 legislative days of 85 calendar days; meets in even-numbered years on last Mon. in Apr. for 30 days of 45 calendar days. Members receive $16,800 annually, plus $121 per day expenses while in session and $500 per month as an unvouchered expense allowance.
Senate — Dem., 25; Rep., 14. Total, 39
House — Dem., 69; Rep., 36. Total, 105

Maine

Governor — John E. Baldacci, D, $70,000
Sec. of State — Dan A. Gwadosky, D, $81,952
Atty. Gen. — G. Steven Rowe, D, $89,502
Treasurer — Dale McCormick, D, $81,349
State Auditor — Gail M. Chase, D, $90,293
Legislature: meets in odd-numbered years at Augusta on first Wed. in Dec.; meets in even-numbered years on Wed. after first Tues. in Jan. Members receive $11,384 for first regular session, $8,655 for 2nd, plus a daily expense allowance.
Senate — Dem., 18; Rep., 17. Total, 35
House — Dem., 80; Rep., 65; unrolled, 2; Green, 1; 1 vacancy. Total, 151

Maryland

Governor — Robert L. Ehrlich Jr., R, $145,000
Lt. Gov. — Michael S. Steele, R, $120,833
Comptroller — William Donald Schaefer, D, $120,833
Atty. Gen. — J. Joseph Curran Jr., D, $120,833
Sec. of State — R. Karl Aumann, R, $84,583
Treasurer — Nancy Kopp, D, $120,833

General Assembly: meets 90 consecutive days annually beginning on 2nd Wed. in Jan. at Annapolis. Members receive $40,500 annually, plus expenses.
Senate — Dem., 33; Rep., 14. Total, 47
House — Dem., 98; Rep., 43. Total, 141

Massachusetts
Governor — Willard "Mitt" Romney[1], R, $135,000
Lt. Gov. — Kerry Healey[1], R, $120,000
Sec. of the Commonwealth — William F. Galvin, D, $120,000
Atty. Gen. — Thomas F. Reilly, D, $122,500
Treasurer — Tim P. Cahill, D, $120,000
State Auditor — A. Joseph DeNucci, D, $120,000
General Court (legislature): meets Jan. annually in Boston. Members receive $49,710 annually.
Senate — Dem., 33; Rep., 7. Total, 40
House — Dem., 137; Rep., 23. Total, 160
(1) Does not accept salary.

Michigan
Governor — Jennifer M. Granholm, D, $177,000
Lt. Gov. — John Cherry, D, $123,900
Sec. of State — Terry Lynn Land, R, $124,900
Atty. Gen. — Michael Cox, R, $124,900
Treasurer — Jay B. Rising, $153,000
Legislature: meets annually in Jan. at Lansing. Members receive $79,650 annually.
Senate — Dem., 16; Rep., 22. Total, 38
House — Dem., 47; Rep., 62; 1 vacancy. Total, 110

Minnesota
(DFL=Democratic-Farmer-Labor Party)
Governor — Tim Pawlenty, R, $120,303
Lt. Gov. — Carol Molnau, R, $78,197
Sec. of State — Mary Kiffmeyer, R, $90,227
Atty. Gen. — Michael Hatch, DFL, $114,288
Auditor — Patricia Anderson, R, $102,258
Legislature: meets for a total of 120 days within every 2 years, at St. Paul. Members receive $31,141 annually, plus expense allowance during session.
Senate — DFL, 35; Rep., 31; 1 ind. Total, 67
House — DFL, 52; Rep., 77; 5 vacancies. Total, 134

Mississippi
Governor — Haley Barbour, R, $122,160
Lt. Gov. — Amy Tuck, R, $60,000
Sec. of State — Eric Clark, D, $90,000
Atty. Gen. — Jim Hood, D, $108,960
Treasurer — Tate Reeves, R, $90,000
Auditor — Phil Bryant, R, $90,000
Legislature: meets annually in Jan. at Jackson. Members receive $10,000 per regular session, plus travel allowance, and $1,500 per month when not in session.
Senate — Dem., 28; Rep., 24. Total, 52
House — Dem., 75; Rep., 47. Total, 122

Missouri
Governor — Bob Holden, D, $120,087
Lt. Gov. — Joe Maxwell, D, $77,184
Sec. of State — Matt Blunt, R, $96,455
Atty. Gen. — Jeremiah W. Nixon, D, $104,332
Treasurer — Nancy Farmer, D, $96,455
State Auditor — Claire McCaskill, D, $96,455
General Assembly: meets annually at Jefferson City beginning 1st Wed. after 1st Mon. in Jan. Members receive $31,351 annually.
Senate — Dem., 14; Rep., 20. Total, 34
House — Dem., 73; Rep., 90. Total, 163

Montana
Governor — Judy Martz, R, $96,462*
Lt. Gov. — Karl Ohs, R, $66,724
Sec. of State — Bob Brown, R, $76,539*
Atty. Gen. — Mike McGrath, D, $85,762*
Legislative Assembly: meets odd years in Jan. at Helena. Members receive $76.80 per legislative day, plus $90.31 per day for expenses while in session.
Senate — Dem., 21; Rep., 29. Total, 50
House — Dem., 47; Rep., 53. Total, 100
*Salary increases effective July 2005.

Nebraska
Governor — Mike Johanns, R, $85,000
Lt. Gov. — David Heineman, R, $60,000
Sec. of State — John A. Gale, R, $65,000
Atty. Gen. — Jon Bruning, R, $75,000
Treasurer — Ron Ross, R, $60,000
State Auditor — Kate Witek, R, $60,000
Legislature: Unicameral body composed of 49 members who are elected on a nonpartisan ballot and are called senators; meets annually in Jan. at Lincoln. Members receive $12,000 annually, plus expenses.

Nevada
Governor — Kenny C. Guinn, R, $117,000
Lt. Gov. — Lorraine Hunt, R, $50,000
Sec. of State — Dean Heller, R, $80,000

Controller — Kathy Augustine, R, $80,000
Atty. Gen. — Brian Sandoval, R, $110,000
Treasurer — Brian Krolicki, R, $80,000
Legislature: meets at Carson City odd years starting on 1st Mon. in Feb. for 120 days. Members receive $130 per day salary, plus a total of $6,800 in expenses, while in session. Each legislator is allowed $1,000 in expenses during a special session.
Senate — Dem., 8; Rep., 13. Total, 21
Assembly — Dem., 23; Rep., 19. Total, 42

New Hampshire
Governor — Craig Benson, R, $102,704
Sec. of State — William M. Gardner, D, $89,128
Atty. Gen. — Kelly A. Ayotte, R, $99,317
Treasurer — Michael A. Ablowich, R, $89,128
General Court (Legis.): meets every year in Jan. at Concord. Members receive $200, presiding officers $250, biannually.
Senate — Dem., 6; Rep., 18. Total, 24
House — Rep., 268; Dem., 118; 14 vacancies. Total, 400

New Jersey
Governor — James E. McGreevey, D, $157,000
Sec. of State — Regena L. Thomas, D, $141,000
Atty. Gen. — Peter Harvey, D, $141,000
Treasurer — John E. McCormac, $141,000
Legislature: meets throughout the year at Trenton. Members receive $49,000 annually, except president of Senate and speaker of Assembly, who receive 1/3 more.
Senate — Dem., 22; Rep., 18. Total, 40
Assembly — Dem., 47; Rep., 33. Total, 80

New Mexico
Governor — Bill Richardson, D, $110,000
Lt. Gov. — Diane D. Denish, D, $85,000
Sec. of State — Rebecca Vigil-Giron, D, $85,000
Atty. Gen. — Patricia Madrid, D, $95,000
Treasurer — Robert E. Vigil, D, $85,000
Auditor — Domingo P. Martinez, D, $85,000
Commissioner of Public Lands — Patrick Lyons, R, $90,000
Legislature: meets starting on the 3rd Tues. in Jan. at Santa Fe; odd years for 60 days, even years for 30 days. Members receive $145 per day while in session.
Senate — Dem., 24; Rep., 18. Total, 42
House — Dem., 43; Rep., 27. Total, 70

New York
Governor — George E. Pataki, R, $179,000
Lt. Gov. — Mary O. Donohue, R, $151,500
Sec. of State — Randy A. Daniels, R, $120,800
Comptroller — Alan G. Hevesi, D, $151,500
Atty. Gen. — Eliot Spitzer, D, $151,500
Legislature: meets annually on the 1st Wed. after the 1st Mon. in Jan. at Albany. Members receive $79,500 annually, plus $138 per day expenses.
Senate — Dem., 25; Rep., 37. Total, 62
Assembly — Dem., 103; Rep., 47. Total, 150

North Carolina
Governor — Mike Easley, D, $121,391
Lt. Gov. — Beverly Perdue, D, $107,136
Sec. of State — Elaine F. Marshall, D, $107,136
Atty. Gen. — Roy Cooper, D, $107,136
Treasurer — Richard H. Moore, D, $107,136
General Assembly: meets odd years starting on the 3rd Wed. following the 2nd Mon. in Jan. at Raleigh. Members receive $13,951 annually and a $559 monthly expense allowance, plus travel and other allowances in session. Also meets in even years for a short session (about 6-8 weeks), usually in May.
Senate — Dem., 27; Rep., 23. Total, 50
House — Dem., 59; Rep., 61. Total, 120

North Dakota
Governor — John Hoeven, R, $87,216
Lt. Gov. — John S. Dalrymple III, R, $67,708
Sec. of State — Alvin A. Jaeger, R, $68,018
Atty. Gen. — Wayne Stenehjem, R, $74,668
Treasurer — Kathi Gilmore, D, $64,233
Legislative Assembly: meets odd years in Jan. at Bismarck. Members receive $250 per month salary, plus $125 per calendar day salary during session and $45 per day expenses, plus any additional state or local taxes on lodging, with a limit of $650 per month.
Senate — Dem., 16; Rep., 31. Total, 47
House — Dem., 28; Rep., 66. Total, 94

Ohio
Governor — Bob Taft, R, $122,800
Lt. Gov. — Jennette Bradley, R, $64,375
Sec. of State — J. Kenneth Blackwell, R, $90,725
Atty. Gen. — Jim Petro, R, $90,725
Treasurer — Joseph T. Deters, R, $90,725
Auditor — Betty D. Montgomery, R, $90,725
General Assembly: begins odd years at Columbus starting on 1st Mon. in Jan. Members receive $51,674 annually.
Senate — Dem., 11; Rep., 22. Total, 33
House — Dem., 37; Rep., 62. Total, 99

Oklahoma

Governor — Brad Henry, D, $117,571*
Lt. Gov. — Mary Fallin, R, $94,839*
Sec. of State — M. Susan Savage, D, $90,000
Atty. Gen. — Drew Edmondson, D, $109,731*
Treasurer — Robert Butkin, D, $94,839*
Auditor — Jeff A. McMahan, D, $94,839*
Legislature: meets annually the first Mon. in Feb. at Oklahoma City. In odd-numbered years, the session includes one day (1st Tues. after 1st Mon.) in Jan. Members receive $38,400 annually.
Senate — Dem., 27; Rep., 20; 1 vacancy. Total, 48
House — Dem., 53; Rep., 48. Total, 101
*Salary increases effective July 2005.

Oregon

Governor — Ted Kulongoski, D, $93,600
Sec. of State — Bill Bradbury, D, $72,000
Atty. Gen. — Hardy Myers, D, $77,200
Treasurer — Randall Edwards, D, $72,000
Legislative Assembly: meets odd years in Jan. at Salem. Members receive $1,283 monthly, $91 expenses per day during session, and when attending meetings during the interim, plus between $450 and $750 expense account during interim.
Senate — Dem., 15; Rep., 15. Total, 30
House — Dem., 25; Rep., 35. Total, 60

Pennsylvania

Governor — Edward G. Rendell, D, $144,416
Lt. Gov. — Catherine Baker Knoll, D, $121,309
Sec. of the Commonwealth — Pedro A. Cortés, D, $103,890
Atty. Gen. — Jerry Pappert, R, $120,154
Treasurer — Barbara Hafer, R, $120,154
General Assembly: convenes annually on the 1st Tues. in Jan. at Harrisburg. Members receive $64,638.05 annually, plus expenses.
Senate — Dem., 21; Rep., 29. Total, 50
House — Dem., 94; Rep., 109. Total, 203

Rhode Island

Governor — Donald L. Carcieri, R, $105,194
Lt. Gov. — Charles J. Fogarty, D, $88,584
Sec. of State — Matthew A. Brown, D, $88,584
Atty. Gen. — Patrick C. Lynch, D, $94,121
Treasurer — Paul J. Tavares, D, $88,584
General Assembly: meets annually in Jan. at Providence. Members receive $10,000 annually (plus mileage and cost-of-living increase).
Senate — Dem., 30; Rep., 6; 2 vacancies. Total, 38
House — Dem., 63; Rep., 11; 1 ind. Total, 75

South Carolina

Governor — Mark Sanford, R, $106,078
Lt. Gov. — R. Andre Bauer, R, $46,545
Sec. of State — Mark Hammond, R, $92,007
Comptroller — Richard A. Eckstrom, R, $92,007
Atty. Gen. — Henry McMaster, R, $92,007
Treasurer — Grady L. Patterson Jr., D, $92,007
General Assembly: meets annually on the 2nd Tues. in Jan. at Columbia. Members receive $10,400 annually, plus $130 per day for expenses.
Senate — Dem., 19; Rep., 27. Total, 46
House — Dem., 51; Rep., 72; 1 vacancy. Total, 124

South Dakota

Governor — Mike Rounds, R, $100,215
Lt. Gov. — Dennis M. Daugaard, R, $13,673
Sec. of State — Chris Nelson, R, $68,092
Treasurer — Vernon L. Larson, R, $68,092
Atty. Gen. — Larry Long, R, $85,094
Auditor — Rich Sattgast, R, $68,092
Comm. of School & Public Lands — Bryce Healy, D, $68,092
Legislature: meets annually beginning the 2nd Tues. in Jan. at Pierre, for 40-day session in odd-numbered years, and 35-day session in even-numbered years. Members receive $12,000 per 2-year term plus $110 per diem for days in session.
Senate — Dem., 9; Rep., 26. Total, 35
House — Dem., 21; Rep., 49. Total, 70

Tennessee

Governor — Phil Bredesen[1], D, $85,000
Lt. Gov. — John S. Wilder, D, $49,500
Sec. of State — Riley C. Darnell, D, $135,060
Treasurer — Steve Adams, D, $135,060
Comptroller — John Morgan, D, $135,060
Atty. Gen. — Paul Summers, D, $126,582
General Assembly: meets annually on the 2nd Tues. in Jan. at Nashville. Members receive $16,500 annual salary, plus $129 per day expenses while in session.
Senate — Dem., 18; Rep., 15. Total, 33
House — Dem., 54; Rep., 45. Total, 99
(1) Does not accept salary.

Texas

Governor — Rick Perry, R, $115,345
Lt. Gov. — David Dewhurst, R, $7,200
Sec. of State — Geoffrey Connor, R, $117,516
Comptroller — Carole Keeton Strayhorn, R, $92,217
Atty. Gen. — Greg W. Abbott, R, $92,217
Railroad Commissioners — Michael L. Williams, R, Chair; Victor G. Carrillo, R; Charles R. Matthews, R; $92,217
Legislature: meets odd years in Jan. at Austin. Members receive $7,200 annually, plus $125 per day expenses while in session.
Senate — Dem., 12; Rep., 19. Total, 31
House — Dem., 62; Rep., 88. Total, 150

Utah

Governor — Olene S. Walker, R, $101,600
Lt. Gov. — Gayle F. McKeachnie, R, $79,000
Atty. Gen. — Mark Shurtleff, R, $85,400
Auditor — Auston G. Johnson, R, $81,500
Treasurer — Edward T. Alter, R, $79,000
Legislature: convenes for 45 days on 3rd Mon. in Jan. each year at Salt Lake City. Members receive $120 per day, plus $38 a day expenses.
Senate — Dem., 7; Rep., 22. Total, 29
House — Dem., 19; Rep., 56. Total, 75

Vermont

Governor — James H. Douglas, R, $127,456
Lt. Gov. — Brian E. Dubie, R, $54,103
Sec. of State — Deborah L. Markowitz, D, $80,818
Atty. Gen. — William H. Sorrell, D, $96,752
Treasurer — Jeb (George B.) Spaulding, D, $80,818
Auditor — Elizabeth M. Ready, D, $80,818
General Assembly: meets in Jan. at Montpelier (annual and biennial session). Members receive $536 per week while in session plus $105 per day for special session, plus expenses.
Senate — Dem., 19; Rep., 11. Total, 30
House — Dem., 69; Rep., 74; Progressive, 4; 3 ind. Total, 150

Virginia

Governor — Mark R. Warner, D, $124,855
Lt. Gov. — Timothy M. Kaine, D, $36,321
Atty. Gen. — Jerry W. Kilgore, R, $110,667
Sec. of the Commonwealth — Anita A. Rimler, D, $135,311
Treasurer — Jody M. Wagner, D, $118,644
General Assembly: meets annually in Jan. at Richmond. Members receive $18,000 (senate), $17,640 (assembly) annually, plus expense and mileage allowances.
Senate — Dem., 16; Rep., 24. Total, 40
House — Dem., 37; Rep., 61; 2 ind. Total, 100

Washington

Governor — Gary Locke, D, $145,132
Lt. Gov. — Brad Owen, D, $75,856
Sec. of State — Sam Reed, R, $101,702
Atty. Gen. — Christine Gregoire, D, $131,938
Treasurer — Mike Murphy, D, $101,702
Auditor — Brian Sonntag, D, $101,702
Legislature: meets annually in Jan. at Olympia. Members receive $34,227 annually, plus $101 per diem while in session, and $101 per diem for attending meetings during interim.
Senate — Dem., 24; Rep., 25. Total, 49
House — Dem., 52; Rep., 46. Total, 98

West Virginia

Governor — Bob Wise, D, $95,000
Sec. of State — Joe Manchin III, D, $75,000
Atty. Gen. — Darrell McGraw, D, $80,000
Treasurer — John D. Perdue, D, $75,000
Comm. of Agric. — Gus R. Douglass, D, $75,000
Auditor — Glen B. Gainer III, D, $75,000
Legislature: meets annually in Jan. at Charleston, except after gubernatorial elections, when the legislature meets in Feb. Members receive $15,000 annually.
Senate — Dem., 24; Rep., 10. Total, 34
House — Dem., 69; Rep., 31. Total, 100

Wisconsin

Governor — Jim Doyle, D, $131,768
Lt. Gov. — Barbara Lawton, D, $65,579
Sec. of State — Douglas La Follette, D, $62,549
Treasurer — Jack Voight, R, $62,549
Atty. Gen. — Peggy A. Lautenschlager, D, $127,868
Legislature: meets in Jan. at Madison. Members receive $45,569 annually, plus $88 per day expenses.
Senate — Dem., 15; Rep., 18. Total, 33
Assembly — Dem., 40; Rep., 59. Total, 99

Wyoming

Governor — Dave Freudenthal, D, $105,000
Sec. of State — Joseph B. Meyer, R, $92,000
Atty. Gen. — Patrick J. Crank, R, $95,000
Treasurer — Cynthia Lummis, R, $92,000
State Auditor — Max Maxfield, R, $92,000
Legislature: meets odd years in Jan., even years in Feb., at Cheyenne. Members receive $125 per day while in session, plus $80 per day for expenses.
Senate — Dem., 10; Rep., 20. Total, 30
House — Dem., 15; Rep., 45. Total, 60

VITAL STATISTICS

Recent Trends in Vital Statistics

Source: National Center for Health Statistics, U.S. Dept. of Health and Human Services; latest years available

Highlights

Final U.S. data for 2002 reported by the National Center for Health Statistics show that birth rates in that year were the lowest of any year since national data was first collected in 1909. Provisional data showed an increase for 2003. The teen birth rate declined in 2002 for the 11th straight year, dropping to 43.0 births per 1,000 women aged 15-19 years; this was a 30% reduction since 1991. According to provisional 2003 data, marriage rates declined for 2003, while divorce rates fell by 0.2 points. Life expectancy for all Americans at birth was 77.2 years in 2001, an all-time high and an increase of nearly 2 years since 1990.

Births

An estimated 4,093,000 babies were born in the U.S. in 2003, according to provisional data, a rise from 4,022,000 births in 2002. The birth rate increased to 14.0 per 1,000 total population, up from 13.9 in 2002. The fertility rate (number of live births per 1,000 women aged 15-44 years) rose to an estimated 65.8 for 2003, up from the 2002 rate of 64.8.

Deaths

The number of deaths during 2003 was estimated at 2,423,000, down from 2,447,864 in 2002. The provisional data for 2003 showed a death rate of 8.3 per 1,000 population, slightly lower than the previous year. The infant mortality rate was 6.7 infant deaths per 1,000 live births in 2003, down from 6.9 in 2002.

Natural Increase

As a result of natural increase (the excess of births over deaths) by itself, an estimated 1,670,000 persons were added to the population in 2003 according to provisional data. The rate of increase (5.7 per 1,000 population) was up very slightly from the revised figure of 5.4 for 2002.

Marriages

An estimated 2,187,700 marriages were performed in 2003, compared to 2,254,000 in 2002. The provisional marriage rate for 2003 (7.5 per 1,000 population) was down from the 2002 rate of 7.8.

Divorces

The provisional 2003 data give a divorce rate of 3.8 per 1,000 population, down from 4.0 in 2002. Data are incomplete, however. The NCHS no longer includes divorce data for California, Hawaii, Indiana, Louisiana, and Oklahoma.

Births and Deaths in the U.S.

Source: National Center for Health Statistics, U.S. Dept. of Health and Human Services

Year	BIRTHS Total number	Rate	DEATHS Total number	Rate	Year	BIRTHS Total number	Rate	DEATHS Total number	Rate
1960	4,257,850	23.7	1,711,982	9.5	1996	3,891,494	14.4	2,314,690	8.6
1970	3,731,386	18.4	1,921,031	9.5	1997	3,880,894	14.2	2,314,245	8.5
1980	3,612,258	15.9	1,989,841	8.8	1998	3,941,553	14.3	2,337,256	8.5
1990	4,092,994	16.7	2,148,463	8.6	1999	3,959,417	14.2	2,391,399	8.6
1991	4,094,566	16.2	2,169,518	8.6	2000	4,058,814	14.4	2,403,351	8.5
1992	4,049,024	15.8	2,175,613	8.5	2001	4,025,933	14.1	2,416,425	8.5
1993	4,000,240	15.4	2,268,553	8.7	2002	4,021,726	13.9	2,447,864	8.5
1994	3,952,767	15.0	2,278,994	8.7	2003(P)	4,093,000	14.0	2,423,000	8.3
1995	3,899,589	14.6	2,312,132	8.7					

(P) = provisional data. **NOTE:** Statistics cover only events occurring within the U.S. and exclude fetal deaths. Rates per 1,000 population; enumerated as of Apr. 1 for 1960 and 1970; estimated as of July 1 for all other years. Beginning 1970 statistics exclude births and deaths occurring among nonresidents of the U.S. Data include revisions. Birth and death rates for years in the 1990s revised on basis of the 2000 Census.

Marriage and Divorce Rates, 1920-2003

Source: National Center for Health Statistics, U.S. Dept. of Health and Human Services

The U.S. marriage rate dipped during the Depression and peaked sharply just after World War II; the trend after that has been more gradual. The divorce rate has generally risen since the 1920s; it peaked at 5.3 per 1,000 in 1981, before declining somewhat. The graph below shows marriage and divorce rates per 1,000 population since 1920. (Recent divorce rates are calculated excluding data and populations from the non-reporting states California, Indiana, Louisiana, and Oklahoma; incomplete reporting from Oklahoma may lead to slight underestimation of marriage rate. Some data are provisional.)

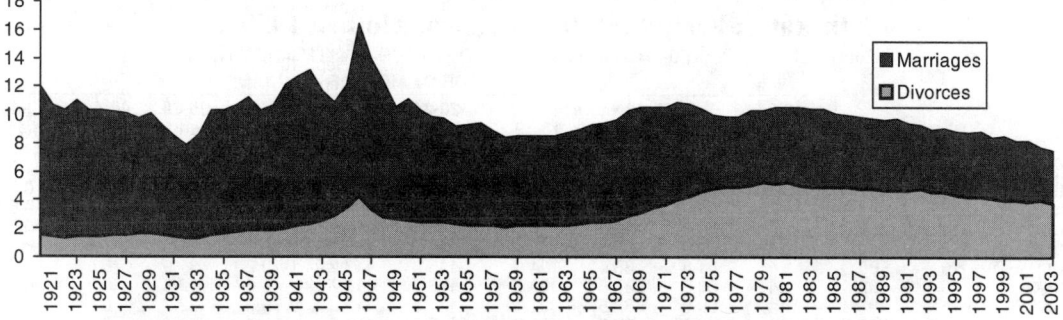

■ Marriages
□ Divorces

WORLD ALMANAC QUICK QUIZ

What was the number-one reason given by patients for emergency room visits in 2002?
(a) Chest pain and related symptoms
(b) Fever
(c) Shortness of breath
(d) Stomach pain, cramps, and spasms
For the answer, look in this chapter, or see page 1008.

Births and Deaths, by States, 2000-2002

Source: National Center for Health Statistics, U.S. Dept. of Health and Human Services

	LIVE BIRTHS						DEATHS					
	2002		2001		2000		2002		2001		2000	
	Number	Rate	Number	Rate	Number	Rate	Number	Rate	DEATHS	Rate	Number	Rate
Alabama......	58,967	13.1	60,454	13.5	63,299	14.2	46,055	1,026.5	45,316	1,014.0	45,062	1,027.0
Alaska	9,938	15.4	10,003	15.8	9,974	15.9	3,033	471.1	2,974	469.4	2,914	468.4
Arizona.......	87,837	16.1	85,597	16.1	85,273	16.6	42,807	784.5	41,058	773.7	40,500	829.5
Arkansas	37,437	13.8	37,010	13.7	37,783	14.1	28,517	1,052.3	27,759	1,030.1	28,217	1,095.2
California	529,357	15.1	527,759	15.3	531,959	15.7	234,660	668.2	234,044	676.4	229,551	682.5
Colorado......	68,418	15.2	67,007	15.1	65,438	15.2	29,209	648.1	28,294	638.5	27,288	659.7
Connecticut ...	42,001	12.1	42,648	12.4	43,026	12.6	30,129	870.7	29,827	868.4	30,129	913.8
Delaware	11,090	13.7	10,749	13.5	11,051	14.1	6,858	849.4	7,112	892.8	6,875	902.0
Dist. of Columbia	7,498	13.1	7,625	13.3	7,666	13.4	5,844	1,023.7	5,951	1,037.1	6,001	1,157.7
Florida	205,579	12.3	205,793	12.6	204,125	12.8	167,862	1,004.1	167,269	1,021.6	164,395	1,072.2
Georgia	133,300	15.6	133,526	15.9	132,644	16.2	65,463	764.7	64,485	767.2	63,870	804.1
Hawaii	17,477	14.0	17,072	13.9	17,551	14.5	8,802	707.0	8,394	684.1	8,290	703.0
Idaho	20,970	15.6	20,688	15.7	20,366	15.7	9,928	740.3	9,753	738.5	9,563	751.1
Illinois........	180,622	14.3	184,064	14.7	185,036	14.9	(1)	(1)	105,430	842.1	106,634	875.1
Indiana	85,081	13.8	86,459	14.1	87,699	14.4	55,352	898.7	55,198	900.9	55,469	928.1
Iowa	37,559	12.8	37,619	12.8	38,266	13.1	27,978	952.7	27,791	947.9	28,060	975.2
Kansas	39,412	14.5	38,869	14.4	39,666	14.8	25,015	921.1	24,647	912.1	24,717	927.2
Kentucky	54,233	13.3	54,658	13.4	56,029	13.9	41,218	1,007.1	39,861	979.7	39,504	991.2
Louisiana	64,872	14.5	65,352	14.6	67,898	15.2	42,055	938.2	41,757	934.1	41,138	940.3
Maine	13,559	10.5	13,759	10.7	13,603	10.7	12,695	980.7	12,421	967.0	12,354	981.6
Maryland	73,323	13.4	73,218	13.6	74,316	14.0	43,959	805.4	43,839	813.9	43,753	838.4
Massachusetts	80,645	12.5	81,077	12.7	81,614	12.9	56,949	886.0	56,754	886.6	56,681	913.6
Michigan......	129,967	12.9	133,427	13.3	136,171	13.7	87,798	873.6	86,424	863.7	86,953	876.7
Minnesota.....	68,025	13.6	67,562	13.6	67,604	13.7	38,557	768.1	37,735	757.0	37,690	780.7
Mississippi ...	41,518	14.5	42,282	14.8	44,075	15.5	28,852	1,004.7	28,259	988.2	28,654	1,028.1
Missouri	75,251	13.3	75,464	13.4	76,463	13.7	55,952	986.4	54,982	975.3	54,865	997.1
Montana......	11,049	12.1	10,970	12.1	10,957	12.1	8,514	936.2	8,265	912.9	8,096	911.8
Nebraska.....	25,383	14.7	24,820	14.4	24,646	14.4	15,737	910.1	15,174	882.2	14,992	897.5
Nevada.......	32,571	15.0	31,382	15.0	30,829	15.4	16,924	778.7	16,285	776.3	15,261	811.6
New Hampshire	14,442	11.3	14,656	11.6	14,609	11.8	9,847	772.3	9,815	779.4	9,697	797.5
New Jersey ...	114,751	13.4	115,795	13.6	115,632	13.7	73,971	861.1	74,710	877.8	74,800	911.7
New Mexico ...	27,753	15.0	27,128	14.8	27,223	15.0	14,365	774.4	14,129	771.7	13,425	768.1
New York	251,415	13.1	254,026	13.3	258,737	13.6	158,110	825.3	159,240	834.4	158,203	865.5
North Carolina .	117,335	14.1	118,185	14.4	120,311	14.9	72,103	866.6	70,934	864.4	71,935	928.5
North Dakota ..	7,757	12.2	7,629	12.0	7,676	12.0	5,890	928.9	6,048	950.1	5,856	930.6
Ohio	148,720	13.0	151,570	13.3	155,472	13.7	109,547	959.1	108,027	948.5	108,125	959.4
Oklahoma.....	50,387	14.4	50,118	14.4	49,782	14.4	35,548	1,017.5	34,682	999.6	35,079	1,037.8
Oregon.......	45,192	12.8	45,322	13.0	45,804	13.4	31,128	883.9	30,158	868.2	29,552	884.5
Pennsylvania ..	142,850	11.6	143,495	11.7	146,281	11.9	130,235	1,055.8	129,729	1,054.4	130,813	1,091.5
Rhode Island ..	12,894	12.1	12,713	12.0	12,505	11.9	10,250	958.2	10,021	945.7	10,027	1,006.6
South Carolina .	54,570	13.3	55,756	13.7	56,114	14.0	37,732	918.7	36,612	901.3	36,948	941.5
South Dakota ..	10,698	14.1	10,483	13.8	10,345	13.7	6,900	906.6	6,923	912.9	7,021	952.3
Tennessee....	77,482	13.4	78,340	13.6	79,611	14.0	56,606	976.4	55,151	959.2	55,246	998.4
Texas	372,450	17.1	365,410	17.1	363,414	17.4	159,273	731.3	152,779	714.9	149,939	735.4
Utah	49,182	21.2	47,959	21.0	47,353	21.2	13,117	566.3	12,662	555.7	12,364	571.2
Vermont	6,387	10.4	6,366	10.4	6,500	10.7	5,075	823.1	5,201	848.5	5,127	857.6
Virginia.......	99,672	13.7	98,884	13.7	98,938	14.0	57,197	784.2	56,280	782.0	56,282	807.4
Washington ...	79,028	13.0	79,570	13.3	81,036	13.7	45,318	746.7	44,642	744.9	43,941	756.2
West Virginia ..	20,712	11.5	20,428	11.3	20,865	11.5	21,014	1,166.2	20,967	1,164.2	21,114	1,171.5
Wisconsin.....	68,560	12.6	69,072	12.8	69,326	12.9	46,990	863.6	46,628	862.5	46,461	877.4
Wyoming	6,550	13.1	6,115	12.4	6,253	12.7	4,171	836.4	4,029	816.0	3,920	815.1
United States	4,021,726	13.9	4,025,933	14.1	4,058,814	14.4	2,447,864	848.9	2,416,425	848.5	2,403,351	873.1

Note: Birth rates are per 1,000 population. Death rates are per 100,000 population. Death rates for 2000 calculated using projections based on 1990 census; death rates for 2001 and birth rates for 2000 and 2001 calculated using census 2000 figures. (1) Illinois mortality data are not shown separately but are included in U.S. totals.

Birth Rates; Fertility Rates by Age of Mother, 1950-2002

Source: National Center for Health Statistics, U.S. Dept. of Health and Human Services

			AGE OF MOTHER								
	Birth rate[1]	Fertility rate[2]	10-14 years	15-19 years			20-24 years	25-29 years	30-34 years	35-39 years	40-44 years	45-49 years
				Total	15-17	18-19						
				Live births per 1,000 women by age group								
1950	24.1	106.2	1.0	81.6	40.7	132.7	196.6	166.1	103.7	52.9	15.1	1.2
1960	23.7	118.0	0.8	89.1	43.9	166.7	258.1	197.4	112.7	56.2	15.5	0.9
1970	18.4	87.9	1.2	68.3	38.8	114.7	167.8	145.1	73.3	31.7	8.1	0.5
1980	15.9	68.4	1.1	53.0	32.5	82.1	115.1	112.9	61.9	19.8	3.9	0.2
1990	16.7	70.9	1.4	59.9	37.5	88.6	116.5	120.2	80.8	31.7	5.5	0.2
1991	16.2	69.3	1.4	61.8	38.6	94.0	115.3	117.2	79.2	31.9	5.5	0.2
1992	15.8	68.4	1.4	60.3	37.6	93.6	113.7	115.7	79.6	32.3	5.9	0.3
1993	15.4	67.0	1.4	59.0	37.5	91.1	111.3	113.2	79.9	32.7	6.1	0.3
1994	15.0	65.9	1.4	58.2	37.2	90.2	109.2	111.0	80.4	33.4	6.4	0.3
1995	14.6	64.6	1.3	56.0	35.5	87.7	107.5	108.8	81.1	34.0	6.6	0.3
1996	14.4	64.1	1.2	53.5	33.3	84.7	107.8	108.6	82.1	34.9	6.8	0.3
1997	14.2	63.6	1.1	51.3	31.4	82.1	107.3	108.3	83.0	35.7	7.1	0.4
1998	14.3	64.3	1.0	50.3	29.9	80.9	108.4	110.2	85.2	36.9	7.4	0.4
1999	14.2	64.4	0.9	48.8	28.2	79.1	107.9	111.2	87.1	37.8	7.4	0.4
2000	14.4	65.9	0.9	47.7	26.9	78.1	109.7	113.5	91.2	39.7	8.0	0.5
2001	14.1	65.3	0.8	45.3	24.7	76.1	106.2	113.4	91.9	40.6	8.1	0.5
2002	13.9	64.8	0.7	43.0	23.2	72.8	103.6	113.6	91.5	41.4	8.5	0.5

(1) Live births per 1,000 population. (2) Live births per 1,000 women 15-44 years of age.

Numbers of Multiple Births in the U.S., 1990-2002

Source: National Center for Health Statistics, U.S. Dept. of Health and Human Services

The general upward trend in multiple births reflects greater numbers of births to older women and increased use of fertility drugs.

Year	Twins	Triplets	Quadruplets	Quintuplets and higher	Year	Twins	Triplets	Quadruplets	Quintuplets and higher
1990	93,865	2,830	185	13	1997	104,137	6,148	510	79
1992	95,372	3,547	310	26	1998	110,670	6,919	627	79
1993	96,445	3,834	277	57	1999	114,307	6,742	512	67
1994	97,064	4,233	315	46	2000	118,916	6,742	506	77
1995	96,736	4,551	365	57	2001	121,246	6,885	501	85
1996	100,750	5,298	560	81	2002	125,134	6,898	434	69

Nonmarital Childbearing in the U.S., 1970-2002

Source: National Center for Health Statistics, U.S. Dept. of Health and Human Services

Race of Mother	1970	1975	1980	1985	1990	1995	1996	1997	1998	1999	2000	2001	2002
Percent of live births to unmarried mothers													
All races	10.7	14.3	18.4	22.0	28.0	32.2	32.4	32.4	32.8	33.0	33.2	33.5	34.0
White	5.5	7.1	11.2	14.7	20.4	25.3	25.7	25.8	26.3	26.8	27.1	27.7	28.5
Black	37.5	49.5	56.1	61.2	66.5	69.9	69.8	69.2	69.1	68.9	68.5	68.4	68.2
American Indian or Alaska Native	22.4	32.7	39.2	46.8	53.6	57.2	58.0	58.7	59.3	58.9	58.4	59.7	59.7
Asian or Pacific Islander	—	—	7.3	9.5	13.2	16.3	16.7	15.6	15.6	15.4	14.8	14.9	14.9
Hispanic origin (selected states)[1,2]	—	—	23.6	29.5	36.7	40.8	40.7	40.9	41.6	42.2	42.7	42.5	43.5
White, non-Hispanic (selected states)[1]	—	—	9.6	12.4	16.9	21.2	21.5	21.5	21.9	22.1	22.1	22.5	23.0
Black, non-Hispanic (selected states)[1]	—	—	57.3	62.1	66.7	70.0	70.0	69.4	69.3	69.1	68.7	68.6	68.4
Births to unmarried mothers (1,000s)	399	448	666	828	1,165	1,254	1,260	1,257	1,294	1,309	1,347	1,349	1,366
Maternal age	**Percent distribution of live births to unmarried mothers**												
Under 20 years	50.1	52.1	40.8	33.8	30.9	30.9	30.4	30.7	30.1	29.3	28.0	26.6	25.4
20–24 years	31.8	29.9	35.6	36.3	34.7	34.5	34.2	34.9	35.6	36.4	37.4	38.2	38.6
25 years and over	18.1	18.0	23.5	29.9	34.4	34.7	35.3	34.4	34.3	34.3	34.6	35.2	34.7
	Live births per 1,000 unmarried women 15–44 years of age[3]												
All races and origins	26.4	24.5	29.4	32.8	43.8	45.1	44.8	44.0	44.3	44.4	45.2	45.0	43.7
White[4]	13.9	12.4	18.1	22.5	32.9	37.5	37.6	37.0	37.5	38.1	38.9	39.2	38.9
Black[4]	95.5	84.2	81.1	77.0	90.5	75.9	74.4	73.4	73.3	71.5	72.5	70.1	66.2
Hispanic origin (selected states)[1,2]	—	—	—	—	89.6	95.0	93.2	91.4	90.1	93.4	97.3	98.0	87.9
White, non-Hispanic	—	—	—	—	28.2	28.3	27.0	27.4	27.9	27.9	27.7	27.8	

— Data not available. (1) Data for Hispanics and non-Hispanics are affected by expansion of the reporting area for an Hispanic-origin item on the birth certificate and by immigration. The states in the reporting area increased from 22 in 1980, to 23 and the District of Columbia in 1983, 48 and DC by 1990, and 50 and DC by 1993. (2) Includes mothers of all races. (3) Rates computed by relating births to unmarried mothers, regardless of mother's age, to unmarried women 15–44 years of age. (4) For 1970 and 1975, birth rates are by race of child.

Top 20 Countries for U.S. Foreign Adoptions, 1991-2003

Source: Holt International Children's Service

Country	2003	2002	2001	2000	1999	1998	1997	1996	1995	1994	1993	1992	1991
China	6,859	5,053	4,681	5,053	4,101	4,206	3,597	3,333	2,130	787	330	206	61
Russia	5,209	4,939	4,279	4,269	4,348	4,491	3,816	2,454	1,896	1,530	746	324	0
Guatemala	2,328	2,219	1,609	1,518	1,002	911	788	427	449	436	512	418	329
South Korea	1,790	1,779	1,770	1,794	2,008	1,829	1,654	1,516	1,666	1,795	1,775	1,840	1,818
Kazakhstan	825	819	672	399	113	NA	NA	0	0	0	0	0	0
Ukraine	702	1,106	1,246	659	321	180	NA	1	4	164	273	55	0
India	472	466	543	503	499	478	349	380	371	412	331	352	445
Vietnam	382	766	737	724	709	603	425	354	318	220	110	22	37
Colombia	272	334	266	246	231	351	233	255	350	351	426	404	521
Haiti	250	187	192	131	96	121	144	68	49	61	51	16	49
Philippines	214	221	219	173	195	200	163	229	298	314	360	357	393
Romania	200	168	782	1,122	895	406	621	555	275	199	97	121	2,594
Bulgaria	198	260	297	214	221	151	148	163	110	97	133	91	9
Belarus	191	169	129	NA	NA	NA	NA	NA	NA	NA	NA	NA	NA
Ethiopia	135	105	158	95	103	96	82	44	63	54	30	37	15
Cambodia	124	254	407	402	249	249	66	32	10	3	1	15	60
Poland	97	101	86	83	97	77	78	62	30	94	70	109	92
Thailand	72	67	74	88	77	84	NA	55	53	47	69	86	131
Azerbaijan	62	NA	NA	NA	NA	NA	NA	NA	NA	NA	NA	NA	NA
Mexico	61	61	73	106	137	168	152	76	83	85	91	91	97

NA = Not available. Note: Totals are for U.S. government fiscal years.

10 Leading Causes of Infant Death in the U.S., 2001

Source: National Center for Health Statistics, U.S. Dept. of Health and Human Services

Cause	Number	Rate[1]	% change 2000-2001[2]
Congenital malformations, deformations, and chromosomal abnormalities	5,513	136.9	−3.3
Disorders relating to short gestation and low birthweight, not elsewhere classified	4,410	109.5	1.1
Sudden infant death syndrome	2,234	55.5	−10.8
Newborn affected by maternal complications of pregnancy	1,499	37.2	7.5
Newborn affected by complications of placenta, cord, and membranes	1,018	25.3	−3.4
Respiratory distress of newborn	1,011	25.1	2.0
Accidents (unintentional injuries)	976	24.2	11.5
Bacterial sepsis[3] of newborn	696	17.3	−8.5
Diseases of the circulatory system	622	15.4	−5.5
Intrauterine hypoxia and birth asphyxia	534	13.3	−14.2
All other causes	9,055	224.9	NA
All causes	**27,568**	**684.8**	**−0.9**

NA = Not applicable. (1) Infant deaths per 100,000 live births. (2) Refers to change in mortality rates from 2000 to 2001. (3) Toxic condition resulting from the spread of bacteria.

U.S. Infant Mortality Rates, by Race and Sex, 1960-2002[1]

Source: National Center for Health Statistics, U.S. Dept. of Health and Human Services

Year	ALL RACES Total	Male	Female	WHITE Total	Male	Female	BLACK Total	Male	Female
1960	26.0	29.3	22.6	22.9	26.0	19.6	44.3	49.1	39.4
1970	20.0	22.4	17.5	17.8	20.0	15.4	32.6	36.2	29.0
1980	12.6	13.9	11.2	11.0	12.3	9.6	21.4	23.3	19.4
1985	10.6	11.9	9.3	9.3	10.6	8.0	18.2	19.9	16.5
1987	10.1	11.2	8.9	8.6	9.6	7.6	17.9	19.6	16.0
1988	10.0	11.0	8.9	8.5	9.5	7.4	17.6	19.0	16.1
1989	9.8	10.8	8.8	8.1	9.0	7.1	18.6	20.0	17.2
1990	9.2	10.3	8.1	7.6	8.5	6.6	18.0	19.6	16.2
1991	8.9	10.0	7.8	7.3	8.3	6.3	17.6	19.4	15.7
1992	8.5	9.4	7.6	6.9	7.7	6.1	16.8	18.4	15.3
1993	8.4	9.3	7.4	6.8	7.6	6.0	16.5	18.3	14.7
1994	8.0	8.8	7.2	6.6	7.2	5.9	15.8	17.5	14.1
1995	7.6	8.3	6.8	6.3	7.0	5.6	15.1	16.3	13.9
1996	7.3	8.0	6.6	6.1	6.7	5.4	14.7	16.0	13.3
1997	7.2	8.0	6.5	6.0	6.7	5.4	14.2	15.5	12.8
1998	7.2	7.8	6.5	6.0	6.5	5.4	14.3	15.7	12.8
1999	7.1	7.7	6.4	5.8	6.4	5.2	14.6	15.9	13.2
2000	6.9	7.6	6.2	5.7	6.2	5.1	14.1	15.5	12.6
2001	6.8	7.5	6.1	5.7	6.2	5.1	14.0	15.5	12.5
2002[2]	7.0	NA	NA	5.8	NA	NA	14.3	NA	NA

NA = Not available. (1) Rates per 1,000 live births. (2) Preliminary data.

Years of Life Expected at Birth in U.S., 1900-2002

Source: National Center for Health Statistics, U.S. Dept. of Health and Human Services

Year[1]	ALL RACES Total	Male	Female	WHITE Total	Male	Female	BLACK Total	Male	Female
1900	47.3	46.3	48.3	47.6	46.6	48.7	NA	NA	NA
1910	50.0	48.4	51.8	50.3	48.6	52.0	NA	NA	NA
1920	54.1	53.6	54.6	54.9	54.4	55.6	NA	NA	NA
1930	59.7	58.1	61.6	61.4	59.7	63.5	NA	NA	NA
1940	62.9	60.8	65.2	64.2	62.1	66.6	NA	NA	NA
1950	68.2	65.6	71.1	69.1	66.5	72.2	NA	NA	NA
1960	69.7	66.6	73.1	70.6	67.4	74.1	NA	NA	NA
1970	70.8	67.1	74.7	71.7	68.0	75.6	64.1	60.0	68.3
1975	72.6	68.8	76.6	73.4	69.5	77.3	68.8	62.4	71.3
1980	73.7	70.0	77.5	74.4	70.7	78.1	68.1	63.8	72.5
1985	74.7	71.2	78.2	75.3	71.9	78.7	69.3	65.0	73.4
1987	75.0	71.5	78.4	75.6	72.2	78.9	69.1	64.7	73.4
1988	74.9	71.5	78.3	75.6	72.3	78.9	68.9	64.4	73.2
1989	75.1	71.7	78.5	75.9	72.5	79.2	68.8	64.3	73.3
1990	75.4	71.8	78.8	76.1	72.9	79.4	69.1	64.5	73.6
1991	75.5	72.0	78.9	76.3	72.9	79.2	69.3	64.6	73.8
1992	75.5	72.1	78.9	76.4	73.0	79.5	69.6	65.0	73.9
1993	75.5	72.1	78.9	76.3	73.0	79.5	69.2	64.6	73.7
1994	75.7	72.4	79.0	76.5	73.3	79.6	69.5	64.9	73.9
1995	75.8	72.5	78.9	76.5	73.4	79.6	69.6	65.2	73.9
1996	76.1	73.1	79.1	76.8	73.9	79.7	70.2	66.1	74.2
1997	76.5	73.6	79.4	77.1	74.3	79.9	71.1	67.2	74.7
1998	76.7	73.8	79.5	77.3	74.5	80.0	71.3	67.6	74.8
1999	76.7	73.9	79.4	77.3	74.6	79.9	71.4	67.8	74.7
2000	76.9	74.1	79.5	77.4	74.8	80.0	71.7	68.2	74.9
2001	77.2	74.4	79.8	77.7	75.0	80.2	72.2	68.6	75.5
2002[2]	77.4	74.7	79.9	77.8	75.3	80.3	72.5	68.9	75.7

NA = Not available. (1) Data prior to 1940 for death-registration states only. (2) Preliminary data.

U.S. Life Expectancy at Selected Ages, 2001

Source: National Center for Health Statistics, U.S. Dept. of Health and Human Services

Exact age in years	ALL RACES[1] Both sexes	Male	Female	WHITE Both sexes	Male	Female	BLACK Both sexes	Male	Female
0	77.2	74.4	79.8	77.7	75.0	80.2	72.2	68.6	75.5
1	76.7	74.0	79.3	77.1	74.5	79.6	72.2	68.6	75.4
5	72.8	70.1	75.4	73.2	70.6	75.7	68.3	64.8	71.5
10	67.9	65.2	70.4	68.3	65.6	70.8	63.4	59.8	66.6
15	52.9	60.2	65.5	63.3	60.7	65.8	58.5	54.9	61.7
20	58.1	55.5	60.6	58.5	56.0	60.9	53.7	50.3	56.8
25	53.4	50.9	55.7	53.8	51.3	56.1	49.1	45.8	52.0
30	48.6	46.2	50.9	49.0	46.6	51.2	44.5	41.4	47.2
35	43.9	41.5	46.0	44.2	41.9	46.3	39.9	36.9	42.5
40	39.2	37.0	41.3	39.5	37.3	41.6	35.5	32.5	38.0
45	34.7	32.5	36.6	34.9	32.8	36.9	31.2	28.4	33.6
50	30.3	28.2	32.1	30.5	28.4	32.3	27.1	24.4	29.3
55	26.0	24.0	27.7	26.1	24.2	27.8	23.3	20.8	25.3
60	21.9	20.1	23.4	22.0	20.2	23.5	19.7	17.5	21.5
65	18.1	16.4	19.4	18.2	16.5	19.5	16.4	14.4	17.9
70	14.6	13.1	15.7	14.6	13.2	15.7	13.5	11.7	14.7
75	11.5	10.2	12.4	11.5	10.2	12.3	10.8	9.3	11.7
80	8.8	7.7	9.4	8.7	7.7	9.3	8.6	7.3	9.2
85	6.5	5.7	6.9	6.4	5.6	6.7	6.7	5.7	7.0
90	4.8	4.2	5.0	4.6	4.1	4.8	5.1	4.5	5.3
95	3.6	3.2	3.7	3.4	3.0	3.4	3.9	3.6	4.0
100	2.7	2.5	2.8	2.4	2.3	2.5	3.0	2.9	3.0

(1) Includes races other than white and black.

The 10 Leading Causes of Death in the U.S., 2001

Source: National Center for Health Statistics, U.S. Dept. of Health and Human Services

	Number	Death rate[1]	% of deaths			Number	Death rate[1]	% of deaths
ALL CAUSES	2,416,425	848.5	100.0	5. Accidents		101,537	35.7	4.2
1. Heart disease	700,142	245.8	29.0	6. Diabetes mellitus		71,372	25.1	3.0
2. Cancer	553,768	194.4	22.9	7. Influenza and pneumonia		62,034	21.8	2.6
3. Stroke	163,538	57.4	6.8	8. Alzheimer's disease		53,852	18.9	2.2
4. Chronic lower respiratory				9. Kidney disease		39,480	13.9	1.6
diseases	123,013	43.2	5.1	10. Blood poisoning		32,238	11.3	1.3

(1) Per 100,000 population.

U.S. Abortions, by State, 1992-2000

Source: Alan Guttmacher Institute, New York, NY

	Reported abortions[1]			Rate per 1,000 women[2]			% change
	1992	1996	2000	1992	1996	2000	1996-2000[3]
U.S. TOTAL	1,528,930	1,360,160	1,312,990	25.7	22.4	21.3	−5
Alabama	17,450	15,150	13,830	18.1	15.5	14.3	−8
Alaska	2,370	2,040	1,660	16.6	14.2	11.7	−18
Arizona	20,600	19,310	17,940	23.4	19.2	16.5	−14
Arkansas	7,130	6,200	5,540	13.5	11.2	9.8	−12
California	304,230	237,830	236,060	41.8	32.8	31.2	−5
Colorado	19,880	18,310	15,530	23.6	19.9	15.9	−20
Connecticut	19,720	16,230	15,240	25.9	21.9	21.1	−4
Delaware	5,730	4,090	5,440	34.9	24.0	31.3	31
District of Columbia	21,320	15,220	9,800	134.6	104.5	68.1	−39
Florida	84,680	94,050	103,050	29.3	30.7	31.9	4
Georgia	39,680	37,320	32,140	23.7	20.8	16.9	−19
Hawaii	12,190	6,930	5,630	46.4	26.8	22.2	−17
Idaho	1,710	1,600	1,950	7.3	6.1	7.0	15
Illinois	68,420	69,390	63,690	25.2	25.3	23.2	−8
Indiana	15,840	14,850	12,490	12.0	11.1	9.4	−15
Iowa	6,970	5,780	5,970	11.3	9.3	9.8	5
Kansas	12,570	10,630	12,270	22.4	18.6	21.4	15
Kentucky	10,000	8,470	4,700	11.4	9.5	5.3	−44
Louisiana	13,600	14,740	13,100	13.5	14.5	13.0	−10
Maine	4,200	2,700	2,650	14.8	9.8	9.9	1
Maryland	31,260	31,310	34,560	26.2	26.2	29.0	11
Massachusetts	40,660	41,160	30,410	28.1	28.8	21.4	−26
Michigan	55,580	48,780	46,470	25.1	22.1	21.6	−2
Minnesota	16,180	14,660	14,610	15.6	13.7	13.5	−2
Mississippi	7,550	4,490	3,780	12.4	7.1	6.0	−17
Missouri	13,510	10,810	7,920	11.5	9.0	6.6	−27
Montana	3,300	2,900	2,510	18.5	15.4	13.5	−12
Nebraska	5,580	4,460	4,250	15.6	12.2	11.6	−4
Nevada	13,300	15,450	13,740	43.0	41.7	32.2	−23
New Hampshire	3,890	3,470	3,010	14.6	12.9	11.2	−13
New Jersey	55,320	63,100	65,780	30.5	34.9	36.3	4
New Mexico	6,410	5,470	5,760	17.7	14.1	14.7	4
New York	195,390	167,600	164,630	45.7	39.7	39.1	−2
North Carolina	36,180	33,550	37,610	22.2	19.5	21.0	8
North Dakota	1,490	1,290	1,340	10.7	9.2	9.9	7
Ohio	49,520	42,870	40,230	19.5	17.1	16.5	−3
Oklahoma	8,940	8,400	7,390	12.5	11.6	10.1	−13
Oregon	16,060	15,050	17,010	23.9	21.2	23.5	11
Pennsylvania	49,740	39,520	36,570	18.6	15.0	14.3	−5
Rhode Island	6,990	5,420	5,600	29.5	23.3	24.1	3
South Carolina	12,190	9,940	8,210	14.2	11.4	9.3	−18
South Dakota	1,040	1,030	870	6.9	6.5	5.5	−15
Tennessee	19,060	17,990	19,010	16.2	14.6	15.2	4
Texas	97,400	91,270	89,160	23.0	20.2	18.8	−7
Utah	3,940	3,700	3,510	9.2	7.5	6.6	−11
Vermont	2,900	2,300	-1,660	21.5	17.3	12.7	−27
Virginia	35,020	29,940	28,780	22.6	19.0	18.1	−5
Washington	33,190	26,340	26,200	27.7	20.9	20.2	−3
West Virginia	3,140	2,610	2,540	7.8	6.6	6.8	3
Wisconsin	15,450	14,160	11,130	13.5	12.2	9.6	−21
Wyoming	460	280	100	4.4	2.6	1.0	−64

(1) Rounded to the nearest 10.   (2) Aged 15-44 years old.   (3) Percentage change in the rate.

Contraceptive Use in the U.S.

Source: National Center for Health Statistics, U.S. Dept. of Health and Human Services; as of 1995; latest data available.

	Percent of women in each age group								Percent of women in each age group					
	15-44	15-19	20-24	25-29	30-34	35-39	40-44		15-44	15-19	20-24	25-29	30-34	35-39	40-44
Using any method	64.2	29.8	63.4	69.3	72.7	72.9	71.5	Diaphragm	1.2	0.0	0.4	0.6	1.7	2.2	1.9
Female								Condom	13.1	10.9	16.7	16.8	13.4	12.3	8.8
sterilization	17.8	0.1	2.5	11.8	21.4	29.8	35.6	Female							
Male								condom	0.0	—	0.1	—	—	—	—
sterilization	7.0	—	0.7	3.1	7.6	13.6	14.5	Periodic							
Pill	17.3	13.0	33.1	27.0	20.7	8.1	4.2	abstinence	1.5	0.4	0.6	1.2	2.3	2.1	1.8
Implant	0.9	0.8	2.4	1.4	0.5	0.2	0.1	Natural family							
Injectable	1.9	2.9	3.9	2.9	1.3	0.8	0.2	planning	0.2	—	0.1	0.2	0.3	0.4	0.2
Intrauterine								Withdrawal	2.0	1.2	2.1	2.6	2.1	2.3	1.4
device (IUD)	0.5	—	0.2	0.5	0.6	0.7	0.9	Other							
								methods[1]	1.0	0.3	0.9	1.2	1.3	0.9	1.8

(1) These include morning-after pill, foam, cervical cap, Today sponge, suppository, jelly or cream (without diaphragm), and other methods not shown separately.

U.S. Median Age at First Marriage, 1890-2003

Source: Bureau of the Census, U.S. Dept. of Commerce

Year[1]	Men	Women	Year[1]	Men	Women	Year[1]	Men	Women	Year[1]	Men	Women	Year[1]	Men	Women
2003 . . . 27.1		25.3	1997 . . 26.8		25.0	1991 . . 26.3		24.1	1970 . . . 23.2		20.8	1930 . . . 24.3		21.3
2002 . . . 26.9		25.3	1996 . . 27.1		24.8	1990 . . 26.1		23.9	1965 . . . 22.8		20.6	1920 . . . 24.6		21.2
2001 . . . 26.9		25.1	1995 . . 26.9		24.5	1985 . . . 25.5		23.3	1960 . . . 22.8		20.3	1910 . . . 25.1		21.6
2000 . . . 26.8		25.1	1994 . . 26.7		24.5	1980 . . 24.7		22.0	1950 . . . 22.8		20.3	1900 . . . 25.9		21.9
1999 . . . 26.9		25.1	1993 . . 26.5		24.5	1975 . . 23.5		21.1	1940 . . . 24.3		21.5	1890 . . . 26.1		22.0
1998 . . . 26.7		25.0	1992 . . 26.5		24.4									

(1) Figures after 1940 based on Current Population Survey data; figures for 1900-40 based on decennial censuses.

Cigarette Use in the U.S., 1985-2003

Source: Substance Abuse and Mental Health Services Administration (SAMHSA), U.S. Dept. of Health and Human Services
(percentage reporting use in the month prior to the survey; figures exclude persons under age 12)

	1985	1999	2000	2002	2003		1985	1999	2000	2002	2003
TOTAL.	**38.7**	**25.8**	**24.9**	**26.0**	**25.4**	**Race/Ethnicity**					
Sex						White	38.9	27.0	25.9	26.9	26.6
Male.	43.4	28.3	26.9	28.7	28.1	Black.	38.0	22.5	23.3	25.3	25.9
Female	34.5	23.4	23.1	23.4	23.0	Hispanic	40.0	22.6	20.7	23.0	21.4
Age group						**Education**[2]					
12-17	29.4	14.9	13.4	13.0	12.2	Non-high school graduate	37.3	39.9	32.4	35.2	35.3
18-25.	47.4	39.7	38.3	40.8	40.2	High school graduate	37.0	36.4	31.1	32.3	31.5
26-34.	45.7	24.9[1]	24.2[1]	25.2[1]	24.7[1]	Some college	32.6	32.5	27.7	29.0	28.9
35 and older	35.5	NA	NA	NA	NA	College graduate	23.0	18.2	13.9	14.5	14.0

NA = Not available. (1) Figures are for all persons aged 26 and older. (2) Estimates for Education are for persons aged 18 and older.

Drug Use in the General U.S. Population, 2003

Source: Substance Abuse and Mental Health Services Administration (SAMHSA), U.S. Dept. of Health and Human Services

According to the Substance Abuse and Mental Health Services Administration's 2003 National Survey on Drug Use and Health, an estimated 110 million Americans 12 years of age and older (46.4%) had used an illicit drug at least once during their lifetimes, 14.7% had used one during the previous year, and 8.2% had used one in the most recent month.

The rate of current illicit drug use (in the past month) in 2003 was 10.0% for men; for women it was 6.5%. An estimated 29.9% of Americans 12 or older (71.1 million) had used an illicit drug other than marijuana at least once in their life. There was little change in the overall rate of illicit drug use between 2002 and 2003.

The Substance Abuse and Mental Health Services Administration's Drug Abuse Warning Network (DAWN) reported 670,307 drug-related episodes in hospital emergency departments in the coterminous U.S in 2002, or 266 episodes per 100,000 population—almost unchanged from 2001. Cocaine was a factor in 33% of these. Alcohol in combination with illegal drug use was a factor in 34%. (Alcohol-related episodes were reported to DAWN only when alcohol was used in combination with a reportable drug.)

Drug Use: America's Middle and High School Students, 2003

Source: *Monitoring the Future,* Univ. of Michigan Inst. for Social Research and National Inst. on Drug Abuse

Use of illicit drugs by American young people dropped for a number of drugs in 2003, according to the University of Michigan's 29th annual survey of high school seniors and 13th annual survey of 8th and 10th graders. Use of Ecstasy, after climbing sharply since 1998, fell sharply for all grades surveyed. Marijuana and LSD also declined.

Alcohol use declined for all grade levels while remaining quite widespread: 19.7% of 8th graders had consumed alcohol in the past 30 days, 35.4% of 10th graders and 47.5% of 12th graders. Cigarette smoking, which had gone up in the mid-90s, continued its decline in recent years. For 8th graders, 10.2% had smoked in the past 30 days (down 0.5 points from 2002), while 16.7% of 10th graders (down 1.0 points) and 24.4% of 12th graders (down 2.3 points) had smoked in the past 30 days.

Compared to 2002, all 3 grade levels showed lower percentages of students who had used any illicit drug in the past 30 days. For 8th graders, 9.7% said they had used (a drop of 0.7 percentage points from the year before), and for 10th graders the percentage was down 1.3 points, with 19.5% saying they had used illicit drugs in the past 30 days. Students in the 12th grade showed a decline, with 24.1% of high school seniors admitting use in the most recent period, a drop of 1.3 points from 2002. For all grade levels, the percentages using any illicit drugs were substantially higher than in 1992, when 6.8% of 8th graders, 11.0% of 10th graders, and 14.4% of 12th graders had used illicit drugs.

Percentages of students in 2003 who had used an illicit drug at some time in the past year followed a similar pattern, with drops of about 1.7 and 2.8 points respectively for 8th and 10th graders, and 1.7 points for seniors compared to 2002. The 2003 percentages of those using drugs at some time in the past year were: 16.1% for 8th graders (compared to 12.9% in 1992), 32.0% for 10th graders (20.4% in 1992), and 39.3% for 12th graders (27.1% in 1992).

Marijuana remained the most commonly used illegal drug for all 3 grade levels. In 2003, the proportion of students who reported using marijuana the past year dropped by 2.1 points from 2002 for 10th graders. For both 8th graders and 12th graders, 30-day use of marijuana declined by a little less than a percentage point; in 2003, 12.8% of 8th graders and 34.9% of 12th graders had used marijuana in the past year, while 7.5% of 8th graders and 21.2% of 12th graders had used in the past 30 days. Use of marijuana on a daily basis went down 0.3 points for 10th graders, to 3.6% in 2003,while 1.0% of 8th graders (a 0.2 point drop from 2002) and 6.0% of 12th graders used marijuana daily.

Ecstasy declined significantly for all three grades. Of 8th graders, 0.7% had used the drug in the past 30 days, and 2.1 in the past year (drops of 0.7 and 0.8 points, respectively). For 10th graders, the numbers were 1.1% in the past 30 days (down 0.7 points) and 3.0% in the past year (down 1.8 points), while for seniors the 2003 figures were 1.3 in the past 30 days (down 1.1 points) and 4.5 in the past year (down 2.9 points). LSD use showed slight declines for all 3 grades in both the 30-day and annual categories; 0.6% of students in all 3 grades had used the drug in the past 30 days (drops of 0.1 points for all 3 grades). Use of hallucinogens other than LSD exhibited modest declines for all 3 grade levels both for use ever in one's lifetime and for use in the past year. Use of several categories of drugs remained basically unchanged in 2003; among these were heroin, narcotics other than heroin, and cocaine.

About 17,000 8th graders, 16,300 10th graders, and 15,200 seniors from 392 schools took part in the survey. The study did not take into account dropouts or absentees. This group tends to have higher rates of drug use overall.

Drug Use: America's High School Seniors, 1980-2003

Source: *Monitoring the Future*, Univ. of Michigan Inst. for Social Research and National Inst. on Drug Abuse

Class of:	1980	1985	1990	1995	1997	1998	1999	2000	2001	2002	2003	'02-'03 change[7]
Marijuana/hashish	60.3%	54.2%	40.7%	41.7%	49.6%	49.1%	49.7%	48.8%	49.0%	47.8%	46.1%	−1.7
Inhalants[1].......	17.3	18.1	18.5	17.8	16.9	16.5	16.0	14.2	13.0	11.7	11.2	−0.5
Amyl & butyl nitrites	11.1	7.9	2.1	1.5	2.0	2.7	1.7	0.8	1.9	1.5	1.6	0.1
Hallucinogens[2]..	15.6	12.1	9.7	12.7	15.1	14.1	13.7	13.0	14.7	12.0	10.6	−1.5
LSD	9.3	7.5	8.7	11.7	13.6	12.6	12.2	11.1	10.9	8.4	5.9	−2.5
PCP........	9.6	4.9	2.8	2.7	3.9	3.9	3.4	3.4	3.5	3.1	2.5	−0.6
Ecstasy	NA	NA	NA	NA	6.9	5.8	8.0	11.0	11.7	10.5	8.3	−2.2
Cocaine	15.7	17.3	9.4	6.0	8.7	9.3	9.8	8.6	8.2	7.8	7.7	−0.1
Crack.......	NA	NA	3.5	3.0	3.9	4.4	4.6	3.9	3.7	3.8	3.6	−0.2
Heroin[3]........	1.1	1.2	1.3	1.6	2.1	2.0	2.0	2.4	1.8	1.7	1.5	−0.2
Other opiates[4] ...	9.8	10.2	8.3	7.2	9.7	9.8	10.2	10.6	9.9	13.5	13.2	−0.4
Stimulants[4,5].....	26.4	26.2	17.5	15.3	16.5	16.4	16.3	15.6	16.2	16.8	14.4	−2.4
Sedatives[4]	14.9	11.8	7.5	7.6	8.7	9.2	9.5	NA	NA	NA	NA	NA
Barbiturates[4] ..	11.0	9.2	6.8	7.4	8.1	8.7	8.9	9.2	8.7	9.5	8.8	+0.7
Methaqualone[4].	9.5	6.7	2.3	1.2	1.7	1.6	1.8	0.8	1.1	1.5	1.0	−0.5
Tranquilizers[4]....	15.2	11.9	7.2	7.1	7.8	8.5	9.3	8.9	10.3	11.4	10.2	−1.2
Alcohol[6]	93.2	92.2	89.5	80.7	81.7	81.4	80.0	80.3	79.7	78.4	76.6	−1.8
Cigarettes.......	71.0	68.8	64.4	64.2	65.4	65.3	64.6	62.5	61.0	57.2	53.7	−3.5
Steroids	NA	NA	2.9	2.3	2.4	2.7	2.9	2.5	3.7	4.0	3.5	−0.5

NA = Not available. (1) Adjusted for underreporting of amyl and butyl nitrites. (2) Adjusted for underreporting of PCP. (3) Reflects use with or without injection. (4) Includes only drug use that was not under a doctor's orders. (5) Data for 1990-2002 are not directly comparable to prior years. (6) Data for 1994-2003 are not directly comparable to prior years. (7) In percent.

Alcohol Use by 8th and 12th Graders, 1980-2003

Source: *Monitoring the Future*, Univ. of Michigan Inst. for Social Research and National Inst. on Drug Abuse

	1980	1990	1992	1993	1994	1995	1996	1997	1998	1999	2000	2001	2002	2003
ALCOHOL[1]			*Percent using alcohol in the month before the survey*											
All 12th graders	72.0	57.1	51.3	51.0	50.1	51.3	50.8	52.7	52.0	51.0	50.0	49.8	48.6	47.5
Male.............	77.4	61.3	55.8	54.9	55.5	55.7	54.8	56.2	57.3	55.3	54.0	54.7	52.3	51.7
Female...........	66.8	52.3	46.8	46.7	45.2	47.0	46.9	48.9	46.9	46.8	46.1	45.1	45.1	43.8
White	75.4	63.8	56.8	55.6	54.0	54.5	54.8	56.4	57.7	56.3	55.1	55.3	54.0	52.3
Black	47.6	35.8	31.7	32.4	33.8	35.2	36.5	34.3	33.3	32.2	30.0	29.4	30.1	29.9
Hispanic..........	63.6	49.1	53.8	50.5	45.9	48.7	47.5	48.2	49.8	50.2	51.2	48.9	47.5	46.4
All 8th graders	—	—	26.1	26.2	25.5	24.6	26.2	24.5	23.0	24.0	22.4	21.5	19.6	19.7
Male.............	—	—	26.3	26.7	26.5	25.0	26.6	25.2	24.0	24.8	22.5	22.3	19.1	19.4
Female...........	—	—	25.9	26.1	24.7	24.0	25.8	23.9	21.9	23.3	22.0	20.6	20.0	19.8
White	—	—	26.6	27.1	25.3	25.4	26.6	26.7	24.8	24.7	24.7	23.2	21.5	20.1
Black	—	—	18.6	19.7	19.4	18.7	18.1	17.9	16.1	16.0	16.0	15.0	14.8	15.5
Hispanic..........	—	—	31.0	32.3	33.5	32.4	29.7	29.8	29.5	29.0	26.7	25.7	26.5	25.3
HEAVY ALCOHOL[2]			*Percent heavily using the 2 weeks before the survey*											
All 12th graders	41.2	32.2	27.9	27.5	28.2	29.8	30.2	31.3	31.5	30.8	30.0	29.7	28.6	27.9
Male.............	52.1	39.1	35.6	34.6	37.0	36.9	37.0	37.9	39.2	38.1	36.7	36.0	34.2	34.2
Female...........	30.5	24.4	20.3	20.7	20.2	23.0	23.5	24.4	24.0	23.6	23.5	23.7	23.0	22.1
White	44.3	36.6	32.1	31.3	31.5	32.3	33.4	35.1	36.4	35.7	34.6	34.5	33.7	32.4
Black	17.7	14.4	11.3	12.6	14.4	14.9	15.3	13.4	12.3	12.3	11.5	11.8	11.5	10.8
Hispanic..........	33.1	25.6	31.1	27.2	24.3	26.6	27.1	27.6	28.1	29.3	31.0	28.4	26.4	25.9
All 8th graders	—	—	13.4	13.5	14.5	14.5	15.6	14.5	13.7	15.2	14.1	13.2	12.4	11.9
Male.............	—	—	13.9	14.8	16.0	15.1	16.5	15.3	14.4	16.4	14.4	13.7	12.5	12.2
Female...........	—	—	12.8	12.3	13.0	13.9	14.5	13.5	12.7	13.9	13.6	12.4	12.1	11.6
White	—	—	12.7	12.6	12.9	13.9	15.1	15.1	14.1	14.3	14.9	13.8	12.7	11.8
Black	—	—	9.6	10.7	11.8	10.8	10.4	9.8	9.0	9.9	10.0	9.0	9.4	10.4
Hispanic..........	—	—	20.4	21.4	22.3	22.0	21.0	20.7	20.4	20.9	19.1	17.6	17.8	16.6

— Data not available. **Note:** *Monitoring the Future* study excludes high school dropouts (about 3-6% of the class group, according to a 1996 report) and absentees (about 16-17% of 12th graders and about 9-10% of 8th graders). High school dropouts and absentees have higher alcohol usage than those included in the survey. (1) In 1993 the alcohol question was changed to indicate that a "drink" meant "more than a few sips." (2) Five or more drinks in a row at least once in the prior 2-week period.

U.S. Motor Vehicle Accidents

Source: National Safety Council

Motor vehicle deaths in the U.S. in 2003 totaled 44,800, a 2% increase from 2002 (after a 1% hike from 2001 to 2002). Miles driven increased about 1% from 2002 to 2003, and the mileage death rate was up 1% from the previous year.

Among the estimated 196,700,000 licensed drivers in 2003, there were slightly more male drivers than female (98,600,000 male vs 98,100,000 female; 50.1% male), but males accounted for 62% of all miles driven. About 11,600,000 male drivers and 8,400,000 female drivers were involved in an accident in 2003. Male drivers were also involved in many more fatal accidents than female drivers; about 40,000 males compared to 14,000 females. The rate was also substantially higher for males (22 fatal accidents per billion miles driven) than for females (13).

About 57% of motor-vehicle deaths in 2003 happened during the day, when more people were driving. Based on mileage, however, night-time was far more dangerous, with a death rate more than 2.3 times that of day-time driving.

In 2002, about 35% of all traffic fatalities involved an intoxicated (blood alcohol concentration of 0.08 or greater) driver or nonoccupant. (In 1992 alcohol-related fatalities accounted for 47% of all traffic deaths.) Of the 17,419 alcohol-related traffic fatalities in 2003 (a 0.1% increase from 2001, but a 5% drop from 1992), an estimated 15,019 occurred in accidents where a driver or nonoccupant was intoxicated; the rest involved a driver or nonoccupant (pedestrian, bicyclist, etc.) who had been drinking but was not legally intoxicated. Alcohol was a factor in about 6% of all traffic accidents.

	Deaths 2003	% change from 2001	Rate 2003[1]
All motor vehicle accidents ...	44,800	+2	15.4
Collision between motor vehicles	19,900	+6	6.8
Collision with fixed object	13,000	−3	4.5
Pedestrian accidents........	5,600	−2	1.9
Noncollision accidents.......	5,200	0	1.8
Collision with pedal cycle	700	0	0.2
Collision with railroad train ...	300	0	0.1
Other collision (animal, animal-drawn vehicles)	100	0	(2)

(1) Deaths per 100,000 population. (2) Death rate was less than 0.05.

Improper Driving Reported in Accidents, 2000-2003

Source: National Safety Council

Type	Percentage of fatal accidents			Percentage of injury accidents			Percentage of all accidents		
	2003	2002	2000	2003	2002	2000	2003	2002	2000
Improper driving	**57.0**	**59.5**	**61.6**	**50.3**	**54.7**	**60.3**	**49.9**	**50.3**	**57.8**
Speed too fast or unsafe	24.9	21.9	18.6	17.2	12.6	16.3	13.1	10.1	13.6
Right of way	16.3	17.4	10.1	16.5	18.9	19.9	18.1	16.4	20.1
Failed to yield	8.0	10.1	4.6	12.8	14.3	15.0	10.6	11.4	12.7
Disregarded signal	5.3	4.0	8.2	2.9	3.3	1.3	5.7	3.4	2.2
Passed stop sign	3.0	3.3	3.8	0.8	1.3	3.6	1.8	1.6	5.3
Drove left of center.	5.9	5.7	0.7	0.8	0.9	1.1	0.8	0.7	1.0
Improper overtaking	0.5	1.0	0.9	1.2	0.5	2.0	1.7	0.8	2.4
Made improper turn	1.3	0.5	0.7	1.1	1.2	0.6	1.7	1.7	0.9
Followed too closely.	0.4	0.4	0.9	3.4	2.8	4.3	6.3	3.8	5.7
Other improper driving	7.7	12.5	9.0	10.1	17.9	16.1	8.2	16.8	14.1
No improper driving stated	**43.0**	**40.5**	**38.4**	**49.7**	**45.3**	**39.7**	**50.1**	**49.7**	**42.2**

Note: Based on reports from state traffic authorities. When a driver was under the influence of alcohol or drugs, the accident was considered a result of the driver's physical condition—not a driving error. For this reason, accidents in which the driver was reported to be under the influence are included under "no improper driving stated."

Principal Types of Accidental Deaths in the U.S., 1970-2003

Source: National Safety Council

Year	Motor vehicle	Falls	Poisoning	Drowning	Fires, flames, smoke	Suffocation: Ingestion of food, object	Firearms	Mechanical Suffocation
1970	54,633	16,926	5,299	7,860	6,718	2,753	2,406	NA
1980	53,172	13,294	4,331	7,257	5,822	3,249	1,955	NA
1985	45,901	12,001	5,170	5,316	4,938	3,551	1,649	NA
1990	46,814	12,313	5,803	4,685	4,175	3,303	1,416	NA
1991	43,536	12,662	6,434	4,818	4,120	3,240	1,441	NA
1992	40,982	12,646	7,082	3,542	3,958	3,182	1,409	NA
1993	41,893	13,141	8,537	3,807	3,900	3,160	1,521	NA
1994	42,524	13,450	8,994	3,942	3,986	3,065	1,356	NA
1995	43,363	13,986	9,072	4,350	3,761	3,185	1,225	NA
1996	43,649	14,986	9,510	3,959	3,741	3,206	1,134	NA
1997	43,458	15,447	10,163	4,051	3,490	3,275	981	NA
1998	43,501	16,274	10,801	4,406	3,255	3,515	866	NA
1999[1]	42,401	13,162	12,186	3,529	3,348	3,885	824	1,618
2000	43,354	13,322	12,757	3,482	3,377	4,313	776	1,335
2001[2]	43,788	15,019	14,078	3,281	3,309	4,185	802	1,370
2002[2]	44,100	15,300	16,100	3,000	2,800	4,400	800	1,500
2003[3]	44,800	16,200	13,900	2,900	2,600	4,300	700	1,200
Death rates per 100,000 population								
1970	26.8	8.3	2.6	3.9	3.3	1.4	1.2	NA
1980	23.4	5.9	1.9	3.2	2.6	1.4	0.9	NA
1985	19.3	5.0	2.2	2.2	2.1	1.5	0.7	NA
1990	18.8	4.9	2.3	1.9	1.7	1.3	0.6	NA
1991	17.3	5.0	2.6	1.8	1.6	1.3	0.6	NA
1992	16.1	5.0	2.7	1.4	1.6	1.2	0.6	NA
1993	16.3	5.1	3.4	1.5	1.5	1.2	0.6	NA
1994	16.3	5.2	3.5	1.5	1.5	1.2	0.5	NA
1995	16.5	5.3	3.4	1.7	1.4	1.2	0.5	NA
1996	16.5	5.6	3.5	1.5	1.4	1.2	0.4	NA
1997	16.2	5.8	3.8	1.5	1.3	1.2	0.4	NA
1998	16.1	6.0	4.0	1.6	1.2	1.3	0.3	NA
1999[1]	15.5	4.8	4.5	1.3	1.2	1.4	0.3	0.6
2000	15.7	4.8	4.6	1.3	1.2	1.6	0.3	0.5
2001[2]	15.4	5.3	4.9	1.2	1.2	1.5	0.3	0.5
2002[2]	15.3	5.3	5.6	1.0	1.0	1.5	0.3	0.5
2003[3]	15.4	5.6	4.8	1.0	0.9	1.5	0.2	0.4

NA = Not available. **Note:** There were 14,900 other accidental deaths in 2003. All figures include on-the-job deaths. (1) Data for 1999 and later not comparable with earlier data because of classification changes. (2) Revised data. (3) Preliminary data.

Risk Behaviors in High School Students, 2003

Source: CDC, *Youth Risk Behavior Surveillance—United States, 2003*

		Percent rarely or never wear seatbelts[1]			Percent rarely or never wear bicycle helmets[2]			Percent who rode with a driver who had been drinking alcohol[3]		
		Female	Male	Total	Female	Male	Total	Female	Male	Total
Race	Non-Hispanic White.	14.1	19.4	16.9	82.0	85.2	83.8	29.8	27.3	28.5
	Non-Hispanic Black.	15.6	25.6	20.6	94.3	95.0	94.6	29.8	31.8	30.9
	Hispanic.	15.8	24.2	20.2	87.9	91.4	90.1	40.0	32.8	36.4
Grade	9	17.6	22.9	20.4	80.3	86.4	83.9	30.2	26.4	28.2
	10	13.3	20.4	16.9	85.9	88.1	87.1	31.0	27.6	29.3
	11	15.5	21.4	18.5	86.8	87.6	87.3	30.7	30.3	30.5
	12	10.9	21.1	16.2	86.1	87.5	86.9	32.6	34.0	33.3
Total.		14.6	21.5	18.2	84.2	87.2	85.9	31.1	29.2	30.2

(1) When riding in a car or truck driven by someone else. (2) Among the 62.3% of students who rode bicycles during the 12 months preceding the survey. (3) In a car or truck one or more times during the 30 days preceding the survey.

► **IT'S A FACT:** Between 1912 and 2003, motor-vehicle deaths per 10,000 registered vehicles were reduced 94%, from 33 to about 2, according to the National Safety Council. In 1912, there were 950,000 vehicles registered and there were 3,100 fatalities. In 2003, there were 44,800 fatalities out of 240 million registered vehicles.

Sexual Activity of High School Students, 2003

Source: CDC, *Youth Risk Behavior Surveillance—United States, 2003*

		Ever had sexual intercourse			First sexual intercourse before age 13			Currently sexually active[1]			Responsible sexual behavior[2]		
		Female	Male	Total	Female	Male	Total	Female	Male	Total	Female	Male	Total
Race/Ethnicity	White[3]	43.0	40.5	41.8	3.4	5.0	4.2	33.1	28.5	30.8	56.5	69.0	62.5
	Black[3]......	60.9	73.8	67.3	6.9	31.8	19.0	44.2	54.0	49.0	63.6	81.2	72.8
	Hispanic....	46.4	56.8	51.4	5.2	11.6	8.3	35.8	38.5	37.1	52.3	62.5	57.4
Grade	9........	27.9	37.3	32.8	5.3	13.2	9.3	18.3	24.0	21.2	66.1	71.2	69.0
	10........	43.1	45.1	44.1	5.7	11.2	8.5	31.2	30.0	30.6	66.4	71.8	69.0
	11........	53.1	53.4	53.2	3.2	7.5	5.4	42.9	39.2	41.1	55.5	66.7	60.8
	12........	62.3	60.7	61.6	1.9	8.8	5.5	51.0	46.5	48.9	48.5	67.0	57.4
Total...............		45.3	48.0	46.7	4.2	10.4	7.4	34.6	33.8	34.3	57.4	68.8	63.0

(1) Sexual intercourse during the 3 months preceding the survey. (2) Used condom during last sexual intercourse. (3) Non-Hispanic.

Death Rates[1] for Suicide at Selected Ages, 1960, 1980, 2000

Source: *Health, United States, 2003*, National Center for Health Statistics, U.S. Dept. of Health and Human Services

	2000			1980			1960		
AGE	BOTH SEXES	MALE	FEMALE	BOTH SEXES	MALE	FEMALE	BOTH SEXES	MALE	FEMALE
15-24	10.2	17.1	3.0	12.3	20.2	4.3	5.2	8.2	2.2
25-44	13.4	21.3	5.4	15.6	24.0	7.7	12.2	17.9	6.6
45-64	13.5	21.3	6.2	15.9	23.7	8.9	22.0	34.4	10.2
65 and older.........	15.2	31.1	4.0	17.6	35.0	6.1	24.5	44.0	8.4
All ages	10.4	17.7	4.0	12.2	19.9	5.7	12.5	20.0	5.6

(1) Per 100,000 population.

Deaths in the U.S. Involving Firearms, by Age, 2001

Source: National Safety Council

	All ages	Under 5	5-14	15-19	20-24	25-44	45-64	65-74	75 & over
Total firearms deaths[1]	29,573	81	333	2,523	4,164	11,425	6,664	1,998	2,385
Male...................	25,480	46	249	2,270	3,796	9,659	5,532	1,754	2,174
Female................	4,093	35	84	253	368	1,766	1,132	244	211
Unintentional	802	15	57	110	96	268	172	33	51
Male..................	690	12	49	102	91	224	142	26	44
Female................	112	3	8	8	5	44	30	7	7
Suicides	16,869	0	90	838	1,292	5,594	5,106	1,758	2,191
Male..................	14,758	0	69	743	1,192	4,797	4,322	1,592	2,043
Female................	2,111	0	21	95	100	797	784	166	148
Homicides	11,348	66	180	1,525	2,675	5,286	1,298	192	126
Male..................	9,532	34	125	1,377	2,419	4,392	990	123	72
Female................	1,816	32	55	148	256	894	308	69	54
Undetermined[2]	231	0	6	24	40	98	41	10	12
Male..................	190	0	6	23	36	75	32	8	10
Female................	40	0	0	1	4	23	9	2	2

Note: There were 28,663 firearms deaths in 2000. (1) Total includes firearms deaths by legal intervention. These deaths totaled 323 in 2001. (2) "Undetermined" means that the intention involved (whether accident, suicide, or homicide) could not be determined.

Home Accident Deaths in the U.S., 1950-2003

Source: National Safety Council

Year	Total	Falls	Poisoning	Fires, burns[1]	Suffoc.: ingesting object	Suffoc.: mechanical	Firearms	Drowning	Natural heat/cold	All other
1950........29,000		14,800	2,550	5,000	(2)	1,600	950	(2)	(2)	4,100
1960........28,000		12,300	2,450	6,350	1,850	1,500	1,200	(2)	(2)	2,550
1970........27,000		9,700	4,100	5,600	1,800[3]	1,100[3]	1,400[3]	(2)	(2)	3,300[3]
1980........22,800		7,100	3,200	4,800	2,000	500	1,100	(2)	(2)	4,100[4]
1990........21,500		6,700	4,500	3,400	2,300	600	800	(2)	(2)	3,200
1995........27,200		8,400	7,000	3,500	1,500	800	900	900	(2)	4,200
1996........27,500		9,000	7,300	3,500	1,500	800	800	900	(2)	3,700
1997........27,700		9,100	7,800	3,200	1,500	800	700	900	(2)	3,500
1998........29,000		9,500	8,400	2,900	1,800	800	600	1,000	(2)	4,000
1999[3] 30,500		7,600	9,300	3,000	1,900	1,100	600	900	700	5,400
2000........29,200		7,100	9,800	2,700	2,100	1,000	500	1,000	400	4,600
2001[5] 33,200		8,600	11,300	3,000	2,000	1,100	600	900	400	5,300
2002[5] 35,300		8,600	13,000	2,500	2,200	1,300	500	900	300	6,000
2003[6] 33,100		9,000	11,200	2,300	2,200	1,000	400	700	300	6,000

(1) Includes deaths resulting from conflagration, regardless of nature of injury. (2) Included under "All other" category.   (3) Data for this year and later not comparable with earlier data because of classification changes. (4) Includes about 1,000 deaths attributed to summer heat wave. (5) Revised data. (6) Data are preliminary.

Worldwide Airline Fatalities, 1986-2003

Source: National Safety Council

Year	Aircraft accidents[1]	Passenger deaths	Death rate[2]	Year	Aircraft accidents[1]	Passenger deaths	Death rate[2]	Year	Aircraft accidents[1]	Passenger deaths	Death rate[2]
1986..	24	641	0.04	1992...	28	1,070	0.06	1998 ..	20	904	0.03
1987..	25	900	0.06	1993...	33	864	0.04	1999 ..	21	499	0.02
1988..	29	742	0.04	1994...	27	1,170	0.05	2000 ..	18	757	0.03
1989..	29	879	0.05	1995...	25	711	0.03	2001[3]..	13	577	0.02
1990..	27	544	0.03	1996...	24	1,146	0.05	2002[4]..	13	791	0.03
1991..	29	638	0.03	1997...	25	921	0.04	2003[5]..	6	334	0.01

(1) Involving 1 or more passenger fatalities and an aircraft with a maximum take-off mass greater than 2,250 kg. (2) Passenger deaths per 100 mil passenger kilometers. (3) Excluding accidents caused by terrorism or sabotage. (4) Revised data. (5) Preliminary.

U.S. Fires, 2003

Source: National Fire Protection Assn.

Fires

- Public fire departments responded to 1,584,500 fires in 2003, a decrease of 6.1% from 2002.
- There were 519,500 structure fires in 2003, a marginal increase of 0.1% from the 2002 figure.
- 77% of all structure fires, or 402,000 fires, occurred in residential properties.
- Fires in vehicles dropped 5.3% from the previous year, totaling 312,000 in 2003.
- There were 753,000 fires in outside properties, a decline of 10.3% from 2002.

Civilian deaths

- There were 3,925 civilian fire deaths in 2003. This was an increase of 16.1% from the year before.
- The number of civilian fire deaths in the home increased by 17.8%, to 3,145.
- 80% (3,145) of all fire deaths were caused by fires in the home.
- Home fires caused an average of one civilian death every 3 hours.

Civilian injuries

- There were an estimated 18,125 civilian fire injuries reported in 2003, a decrease of 1.6% from 2002.
- Residential properties were the site of 14,075 civilian fire injuries in 2003, and nonresidential structure fires accounted for 1,525 civilian injuries.
- Nationwide, a civilian was injured in a fire every half hour.

Property damage

- Direct property damage from fires amounted to an estimated $12,307,000,000 in 2003, an increase of 19.1% from 2002. This total figure includes the Southern California wildfires (cedar and old wildfires), with an estimated property loss of $2,040,000,000.
- Structure fires accounted for $8,678,000,000 of property damage.
- Property loss in residential properties came to $6,074,000,000 for 2003.

Intentionally set fires

- There were an estimated 37,500 intentionally set structure fires in 2003, a decrease of 15.7% from the 2002 number.
- Intentionally set structure fires resulted in 305 civilian deaths in 2003, a decrease of 12.9% from the year before. Property damage from intentionally set structure fires totaled $692,000,000, a drop of 24.7% from the 2002 figure.
- The number of intentionally set vehicle fires in 2003 was 30,500, a decrease of 25.6% from 2002. The 2003 intentionally set vehicle fires caused an estimated $132,000,000 in property damage, a decrease of 40.5% from 2002.

Physicians by Age, Sex, and Specialty, 2002

Source: American Medical Assn., as of Dec. 31, 2002

	Total Physicians[1]		Under 35 yrs		35-44 yrs		45-54 yrs		55-64 yrs	
	Male	Female	Male	Female	Male	Female	Male	Female	Male	Female
All Specialties..	638,182	215,005	80,847	58,361	139,774	70,278	160,621	52,223	114,565	20,101
Aerospace Medicine......	461	32	11	2	63	9	164	14	108	7
Allergy & Immunology	9,120	981	146	152	805	324	923	303	838	144
Anaesthesiology..........	28,756	7,855	3,236	1,116	9,821	2,861	9,342	2,300	4,673	1,135
Cardiovascular Disease...	20,088	1,882	1,699	352	5,316	723	6,751	684	4,079	164
Child Psychiatry.........	3,759	2,758	211	254	890	969	1,139	895	898	399
Colon/Rectal Surgery.....	1,084	113	67	18	300	66	361	26	228	4
Dermatology.............	6,506	3,482	660	867	1,303	1,318	1,788	915	1,775	308
Diagnostic Radiology	18,086	4,698	3,107	1,130	4,811	1,678	5,444	1,438	3,620	369
Emergency Medicine	20,429	5,098	4,210	1,705	5,387	1,660	6,670	1,287	3,157	369
Family Practice..........	63,194	23,317	7,773	7,603	13,616	8,351	18,192	5,649	7,786	1,320
Forensic Pathology	399	181	23	10	71	60	131	67	86	28
Gastroenterology	10,220	1,109	879	228	3,003	478	3,465	322	2,084	74
General Practice	11,297	2,249	34	15	446	202	1,818	686	2,819	731
General Preventive Med...	1,203	626	109	88	329	237	366	220	204	50
General Surgery..........	32,678	4,525	6,186	1,931	6,980	1,445	7,408	885	6,623	196
Internal Medicine	101,633	41,658	18,594	13,188	25,633	14,432	29,829	10,198	16,806	2,846
Medical Genetics	230	203	27	29	62	80	65	77	48	30
Neurological Surgery	4,770	238	642	73	1,076	78	1,230	74	1,029	10
Neurology...............	10,088	2,895	804	553	2,446	1,070	3,378	891	2,201	285
Nuclear Medicine	1,200	255	67	20	208	63	354	100	319	51
Obstetrics/Gynecology....	25,606	15,432	1,764	4,734	4,883	6,330	7,471	3,765	6,549	1,204
Occupational Medicine....	2,346	494	3	1	234	133	796	226	543	85
Ophthalmology..........	15,670	2,914	1,439	649	3,571	1,099	4,316	844	3,839	241
Orthopedic Surgery	22,329	882	3,345	290	5,363	316	5,932	221	4,893	37
Otolaryngology..........	8,839	987	1,236	301	2,161	391	2,181	237	2,000	40
Pathology-Anat./Clin......	12,575	5,604	888	803	2,423	1,670	3,557	1,774	2,961	942
Pediatric Cardiology......	1,241	459	141	93	401	210	327	83	216	43
Pediatrics	33,020	33,351	5,748	10,366	7,699	10,852	9,078	7,759	6,322	3,246
Physical Med./Rehab.	4,619	2,302	647	413	1,718	870	1,244	575	578	301
Plastic Surgery..........	5,822	713	407	137	1,494	260	1,733	238	1,491	63
Psychiatry..............	27,803	12,292	1,879	1,857	4,544	3,290	7,149	3,861	6,941	2,048
Public Health	1,231	600	1	2	70	57	327	177	329	108
Pulmonary Diseases	8,148	1,290	929	293	2,256	572	2,824	306	1,573	82
Radiation Oncology	3,215	968	406	167	934	354	877	268	676	144
Radiology...............	7,574	1,218	421	78	1,693	404	1,298	355	2,108	269
Thoracic Surgery	4,904	152	176	15	1,206	65	1,405	60	1,228	10
Transplantation Surgery...	75	8	—	—	31	5	32	3	6	—
Urology.................	10,048	383	1,026	144	2,244	135	2,481	92	2,656	8
Other Speciality	4,732	907	67	23	402	166	1,149	325	1,208	191
Unspecified	3,300	1,413	1,671	817	543	252	517	198	265	80

(1) Includes physicians 65 and older, "Inactive," "Address Unknown," and certain specialties with very few practitioners

U.S. Health Expenditures, 1960-2001

Source: *Health, United States, 2003,* National Center for Health Statistics, U.S. Dept. of Health and Human Services

	1960	1970	1980	1990	1995	1998	1999	2000	2001
					Amount in billions				
National health expenditures.	$26.7	$73.1	$245.8	$696.0	$990.1	$1,150.0	$1,219.7	$1,310.0	$1,424.5
					Percent distribution				
Health services and supplies	93.6	92.2	95.0	96.2	96.7	96.7	96.6	96.4	96.4
Personal health care.	87.6	86.5	87.3	87.6	87.4	87.8	87.3	86.8	86.8
Hospital care	34.4	37.8	41.3	36.5	34.7	32.9	32.3	31.8	31.7
Professional services.	31.3	28.3	27.4	31.2	32.0	32.7	32.5	32.4	32.5
Physician and clinical services	20.1	19.1	19.2	22.6	22.3	22.3	22.2	22.0	22.0
Other professional services	1.5	1.0	1.5	2.6	2.9	3.1	3.0	3.0	3.0
Dental services	7.4	6.4	5.4	4.5	4.5	4.6	4.6	4.6	4.6
Other personal health care	2.4	1.7	1.3	1.4	2.3	2.6	2.8	2.8	2.9
Nursing home and home health	3.4	6.1	8.2	9.4	10.6	10.7	10.0	9.6	9.3
Home health care	0.2	0.3	1.0	1.8	3.1	2.9	2.6	2.4	2.3
Nursing home care	3.2	5.8	7.2	7.6	7.5	7.7	7.3	7.2	6.9
Retail outlet sales of medical products	18.6	14.3	10.5	10.5	10.2	11.5	12.5	13.0	13.4
Prescription drugs.	10.0	7.5	4.9	5.8	6.1	7.6	8.6	9.3	9.9
Other medical products	8.5	6.8	5.6	4.7	4.0	4.0	3.9	3.7	3.5
Government administration and net cost									
of private health insurance	4.5	3.8	4.9	5.7	6.1	5.6	6.0	6.2	6.3
Government public health activities[1] . . .	1.5	1.9	2.7	2.9	3.2	3.3	3.4	3.4	3.3
Investment	6.4	7.8	5.0	3.8	3.3	3.3	3.4	3.6	3.6
Research	2.6	2.7	2.2	1.8	1.7	1.8	1.9	2.2	2.3
Construction	3.8	5.2	2.8	2.0	1.6	1.5	1.4	1.4	1.3
			Average annual percent change from previous year shown						
National health expenditures	—	10.6	12.9	11.0	7.3	5.1	6.1	7.4	8.7
Health services and supplies	—	10.4	13.2	11.1	7.4	5.1	6.0	7.1	8.7
Personal health care.	—	10.5	13.0	11.0	7.3	5.3	5.5	6.9	8.7
Hospital care	—	11.7	13.9	9.6	6.2	3.3	4.1	5.8	8.3
Professional services.	—	9.5	12.5	12.4	7.9	5.9	5.6	7.1	8.8
Physician and clinical services	—	10.1	12.9	12.8	7.0	5.2	5.2	6.9	8.6
Other professional services	—	6.6	17.1	17.5	9.5	7.6	3.3	5.8	9.1
Dental services	—	9.1	11.1	9.0	7.1	6.1	6.1	7.7	8.0
Other personal health care	—	7.2	10.0	11.4	18.9	9.6	11.3	9.1	11.5
Nursing home and home health	—	17.2	16.3	12.5	10.0	5.3	−0.6	3.0	5.2
Home health care	—	14.5	26.9	18.1	19.4	3.2	−3.7	−1.8	4.5
Nursing home care	—	17.4	15.4	11.5	7.2	6.1	0.5	4.7	5.5
Retail outlet sales of medical products	—	7.8	9.4	11.1	6.5	9.7	14.6	12.1	11.9
Prescription drugs.	—	7.5	8.2	12.8	8.6	12.8	19.7	16.4	15.7
Other medical products	—	8.1	10.6	9.2	3.8	4.6	4.9	2.7	2.4
Government administration and net									
cost of private health insurance	—	8.6	15.9	12.7	8.6	2.1	13.7	10.3	11.2
Government public health activities[1] . . .	—	13.2	17.4	11.6	9.2	6.5	7.7	7.7	5.3
Investment	—	12.9	7.9	8.0	4.3	5.5	7.3	16.2	9.0
Research	—	10.9	10.8	8.8	6.2	6.2	14.5	24.1	12.7
Construction	—	14.1	6.1	7.3	2.4	4.6	−0.9	5.8	3.2

Note: Numbers may not add to totals because of rounding. (1) Includes personal care services delivered by government public health agencies.

Ownership of Life Insurance in the U.S. and Assets of U.S. Life Insurance Companies, 1940-2002

Source: American Council of Life Insurers

(amounts in millions)

	PURCHASES OF LIFE INSURANCE				INSURANCE IN FORCE					
Year	Ordinary	Group	Industrial	Total	Ordinary	Group	Industrial	Credit	Total	Assets
1940	$6,689	$691	$3,350	$10,730	$79,346	$14,938	$20,866	$380	$115,530	$30,802
1950	17,326	6,068	5,402	28,796	149,116	47,793	33,415	3,844	234,168	64,020
1960	52,883	14,645	6,880	74,408	341,881	175,903	39,563	29,101	586,448	119,576
1970	122,820	63,690[1]	6,612	193,122[1]	734,730	551,357	38,644	77,392	1,402,123	207,254
1975	188,003	95,190[1]	6,729	289,922[1]	1,083,421	904,695	39,423	112,032	2,139,571	289,304
1980	385,575	183,418	3,609	572,602	1,760,474	1,579,355	35,994	165,215	3,541,038	479,210
1985	910,944	319,503[2]	722	1,231,169[2]	3,247,289	2,561,595	28,250	215,973	6,053,107	825,901
1990	1,069,660	459,271	220	1,529,151	5,366,982	3,753,506	24,071	248,038	9,392,597	1,408,208
1991	1,041,508	573,953[1]	198	1,615,659[1]	5,677,777	4,057,606	22,475	228,478	9,986,336	1,551,201
1992	1,048,135	440,143	222	1,488,500	5,941,810	4,240,919	20,973	202,090	10,405,792	1,664,531
1993	1,101,327	576,823	149	1,678,299	6,428,434	4,456,338	20,451	199,518	11,104,741	1,839,127
1994	1,056,976	560,232	257	1,617,465	6,429,811	4,443,179	18,947	189,398	11,081,335	1,942,273
1995	1,039,102	537,828	156	1,577,086	6,872,252	4,604,856	18,134	201,083	11,696,325	2,143,544
1996	1,089,137	614,565	130	1,703,832	7,407,682	5,067,804	18,064	210,746	12,704,296	2,327,924
1997	1,203,552	688,589	128	1,892,269	7,854,570	5,279,042	17,991	212,255	13,363,858	2,579,078
1998	1,324,565	739,508	106	2,064,179	8,505,894	5,735,273	17,365	212,917	14,471,449	2,826,522
1999[3] . . .	1,399,848	966,858	—	2,508,019	9,172,397	6,110,218	—	213,453	15,496,069	3,070,653
2000[3] . . .	1,593,907	921,001	—	2,681,234	9,376,370	6,376,127	—	200,770	15,953,267	3,181,736
2001[3] . . .	1,600,471	1,172,080	—	2,938,702	9,345,723	6,765,074	—	178,851	16,289,648	3,269,019
2002[3] . . .	1,752,941	1,013,728	—	2,888,817	9,311,729	6,876,075	—	158,534	16,346,338	3,380,000

— = Data not available. Ordinary purchases, ordinary in force, and group in force numbers were revised for 1994-97. (1) Includes Servicemen's Group Life Insurance, which amounted to $17.1 billion in 1970, $1.7 billion in 1975, and $166.7 billion in 1991. (2) Includes Federal Employees' Group Life Insurance of $10.8 billion. (3) For 1999 and later, category of "ordinary" is combined with data for "industrials." Also, totals for purchases from 1999 on include the category "Credit," not listed here.

Health Insurance Coverage,[1] by State, 1990, 2000, 2003

Source: Bureau of the Census, U.S. Dept. of Commerce

	2003 Not covered[2]	2003 % not covered	2000 Not covered[2]	2000 % not covered	1990 Not covered[2]	1990 % not covered		2003 Not covered[2]	2003 % not covered	2000 Not covered[2]	2000 % not covered	1990 Not covered[2]	1990 % not covered
AL..	629	14.2	582	13.3	710	17.4	MT..	177	19.4	150	16.8	115	14.0
AK .	122	14.2	117	18.7	77	15.4	NE..	195	11.3	154	9.1	138	8.5
AZ..	951	17.0	869	16.7	547	15.5	NV..	426	18.9	344	16.8	201	16.5
AR .	465	17.4	379	14.3	421	17.4	NH..	131	10.3	103	8.4	107	9.9
CA .	6,499	18.4	6,299	18.5	5,683	19.1	NJ ..	1,201	14.0	1,021	12.2	773	10.0
CO .	772	17.2	620	14.3	495	14.7	NM..	414	22.1	435	24.2	339	22.2
CT .	357	10.4	330	9.8	226	6.9	NY ..	2,866	15.1	3,056	16.3	2,176	12.1
DE .	91	11.1	72	9.3	96	13.9	NC..	1,424	17.3	1,084	13.6	883	13.8
DC .	79	14.3	78	14.0	109	19.2	ND..	69	10.9	71	11.3	40	6.3
FL..	3,071	18.2	2,829	17.7	2,376	18.0	OH..	1,362	12.1	1,248	11.2	1,123	10.3
GA .	1,409	16.4	1,166	14.3	971	15.3	OK..	701	20.4	641	18.9	574	18.6
HI ..	127	10.1	113	9.4	81	7.3	OR..	613	17.2	433	12.7	360	12.4
ID ..	253	18.6	199	15.4	159	15.2	PA ..	1,384	11.4	1,047	8.7	1,218	10.1
IL ..	1,818	14.4	1,704	13.9	1,272	10.9	RI...	108	10.2	77	7.4	105	11.1
IN ..	853	13.9	674	11.2	587	10.7	SC..	584	14.4	480	12.1	550	16.2
IA ..	329	11.3	253	8.8	225	8.1	SD..	91	12.2	81	11.0	81	11.6
KS .	294	11.0	289	10.9	272	10.8	TN ..	778	13.2	615	10.9	673	13.7
KY .	574	14.0	545	13.6	480	13.2	TX ..	5,374	24.6	4,748	22.9	3,569	21.1
LA..	912	20.6	789	18.1	797	19.7	UT ..	298	12.7	281	12.5	156	9.0
ME .	133	10.4	138	10.9	139	11.2	VT ..	58	9.5	52	8.6	54	9.5
MD .	762	13.9	547	10.4	601	12.7	VA ..	962	13.0	814	11.6	996	15.7
MA .	682	10.7	549	8.7	530	9.1	WA..	944	15.5	792	13.5	557	11.4
MI ..	1,080	10.9	901	9.2	865	9.4	WV..	296	16.6	250	14.1	249	13.8
MN .	444	8.7	399	8.1	389	8.9	WI ..	593	10.9	406	7.6	321	6.7
MS .	511	17.9	380	13.6	531	19.9	WY..	78	15.9	76	15.7	58	12.5
MO .	620	11.0	524	9.5	665	12.7	U.S..	44,961	15.6	39,804	14.2	34,719	13.9

(1) For population, all ages, including those 65 or over, an age group largely covered by Medicare. (2) In thousands.

Persons Not Covered by Health Insurance, by Selected Characteristics, 2003

Source: Bureau of the Census, U.S. Dept. of Commerce

	Number[1]	
Sex		
Male..........................	23,788	16.8%
Female	21,173	14.4
Race and Ethnicity		
White.........................	33,983	14.6
Non-Hispanic..	21,582	11.1
Black	7,080	19.6
Asian and Pacific Islander........	2,401	18.6
Hispanic[2]....................	13,237	32.7
Age		
Under 18 years	8,373	11.4
18 to 24 years	8,414	30.2
25 to 34 years	10,345	26.4
35 to 44 years	7,885	18.1
45 to 54 years	5,961	14.5
55 to 64 years	3,696	13.0
65 years and over	286	0.8
Nativity		
Native	33,146	13.1
Foreign born	11,815	34.5

	Number[1]	
Naturalized citizen	2,243	17.1%
Not a citizen	9,571	45.3
Region		
Northeast	6,919	12.9
Midwest	7,748	12.0
South	18,621	18.0
West........................	11,674	17.6
Household Income		
Less than $25,000	15,331	24.2
$25,000 to $49,999............	14,823	19.9
$50,000 to $74,999............	7,226	12.5
$75,000 or more	7,580	8.2
Education (18 years and older)		
No high school diploma	10,038	29.6
High school graduate only	13,272	19.5
Some college, no degree	6,512	15.7
Associate degree	2,083	12.3
Bachelor's degree or higher	4,683	8.7
TOTAL	**44,961**	**15.6**

(1) In thousands. (2) Persons of Hispanic origin may be of any race.

Health Coverage for Persons Under 65, by Characteristics, 1984, 1999-2001

Source: *Health, United States, 2003,* National Center for Health Statistics, U.S. Dept. of Health and Human Services

	PRIVATE INSURANCE 1984	1999[3]	2000	2001	MEDICAID[1] 1984	1999[3]	2000	2001	NOT COVERED[2] 1984	1999[3]	2000	2001
Age					Percent of each population group							
Under 18 years.............	72.6	68.8	67.0	66.7	11.9	18.1	19.4	21.2	13.9	11.9	12.4	11.0
18-44 years	76.5	72.0	70.9	70.6	5.1	5.7	5.6	6.3	17.1	21.0	22.0	21.7
45-64 years	83.3	79.3	78.7	78.6	3.4	4.4	4.5	4.7	9.6	12.2	12.7	12.3
Race and Hispanic origin[4,5]												
White, non-Hispanic.........	82.4	80.3	79.3	79.2	3.7	6.0	6.3	7.0	11.8	12.1	12.5	11.9
Black, non-Hispanic	59.4	58.2	57.0	57.6	19.1	18.7	19.3	20.3	19.7	19.4	20.0	19.2
All Hispanic	57.1	50.3	49.0	47.6	12.2	14.1	14.2	16.0	29.1	33.9	35.4	34.8
Percent of poverty level[4]												
Below 100%...............	33.0	26.1	25.8	25.6	30.5	36.8	37.2	39.0	34.7	34.4	34.2	33.3
100-149%.................	61.8	40.1	39.5	39.6	7.5	18.6	20.3	23.5	27.0	35.8	36.5	32.4
150-199%.................	77.2	59.4	58.4	57.0	3.1	9.8	10.8	13.3	17.4	27.7	27.3	26.4
200% or more..............	91.6	88.7	87.2	87.1	0.6	2.0	2.3	2.6	5.8	7.7	8.7	8.4
Geographic region[4]												
Northeast	80.7	77.1	76.5	76.5	8.5	10.1	10.5	10.8	10.1	12.2	12.1	11.6
Midwest	80.9	80.2	78.9	78.1	7.2	7.3	7.9	9.0	11.1	11.5	12.3	11.7
South	74.5	68.0	67.0	66.3	5.0	8.9	9.4	10.7	17.4	19.8	20.4	20.0
West......................	72.3	68.9	67.1	68.6	6.9	10.3	10.2	10.6	17.8	18.6	20.2	18.6

Note: Data based on household interviews of a sample of the civilian noninstitutionalized population. Percents do not add to 100 because other types of health insurance (e.g., Medicare, military) are not shown and persons with both private insurance and Medicaid appear in both columns. (1) Includes Medicaid or other public assistance. In 2001, the age-adjusted percent of the population under 65 covered by Medicaid was 7.9%; 1.2% were covered by state-sponsored health plans and 1.2% were covered by State Children's Health Insurance Program (SCHIP). (2) Includes persons not covered by private insurance, Medicaid or other public assistance, Medicare, or military plans. (3) In 1997 the questionnaire changed compared with previous years. (4) Age adjusted. (5) Changed reporting methods make percentages for race before 1999 not strictly comparable with those from 1999 on.

Enrollment in Health Maintenance Organizations (HMOs), 1976-2002

Source: *Health, United States, 2003*, National Center for Health Statistics, U.S. Dept. of Health and Human Services

	1976	1980	1990	1995	1996	1997	1998	1999	2000	2001	2002
				Number of enrolled in millions							
TOTAL...................	6.0	9.1	33.0	50.9	59.1	66.8	76.6	81.3	80.9	79.5	76.1
Model type[1]											
Individual practice assoc.[2]	0.4	1.7	13.7	20.1	26.0	26.7	32.6	32.8	33.4	33.1	31.6
Group[3]	5.6	7.4	19.3	13.3	14.1	11.0	13.8	15.9	15.2	15.6	15.0
Mixed	—	—	—	17.6	19.0	29.0	30.1	32.6	32.3	30.9	29.6
Federal program[4]											
Medicaid[5]	—	0.3	1.2	3.5	4.7	5.6	7.8	10.4	10.8	11.4	12.8
Medicare	—	0.4	1.8	2.9	3.7	4.8	5.7	6.5	6.6	6.1	5.4
				Percent of population enrolled in HMOs							
TOTAL...................	2.8	4.0	13.4	19.4	22.3	25.2	28.6	30.1	30.0	28.3	26.4
Geographic region											
Northeast	2.0	3.1	14.6	24.4	25.9	32.4	37.8	36.7	36.5	35.1	33.4
Midwest	1.5	2.8	12.6	16.4	18.8	19.5	22.7	23.3	23.2	21.7	20.6
South	0.4	0.8	7.1	12.4	15.2	17.9	21.0	23.9	22.6	21.0	19.8
West...................	9.7	12.2	23.2	28.6	33.2	36.4	39.1	41.4	41.7	40.7	38.2

— = Not available. **Note:** Data as of June 30 in 1976-80, Jan. 1 from 1990 onwards. HMOs in Guam included starting in 1994; Puerto Rico, 1998; Guam HMO enrollment was 34,000 in 2002 and Puerto Rico enrollment was 1,825,000 in 2002. Open-ended enrollment in HMO plans, amounting to 8 million on Jan. 1, 2002, included from 1994 onwards. (1) Enrollment may not equal total because some plans did not report these characteristics. (2) This type of HMO contracts with an association of physicians from various settings (a mixture of solo and group practices) to provide health services. (3) Group includes staff, group, and network model types. (4) Enrollment by Medicaid or Medicare beneficiaries, where the Medicaid or Medicare program contracts directly with the HMO to pay the premium. (5) Data for 1990 and later include enrollment in managed-care health insuring organizations.

Health Care Visits, by Selected Characteristics, 1997, 2001

Source: Centers for Disease Control and Prevention, National Center for Health Statistics. National Health Interview Survey, family core and sample adult questionnaires.

	No visits		1-3 visits		4-9 visits		10 or more visits	
	1997	2001	1997	2001	1997	2001	1997	2001
			Percent distribution					
All persons	16.5	16.5	46.2	45.8	23.6	24.4	13.7	13.3
Age								
Under 6 years...........	5.0	5.5	44.9	45.8	37.0	37.9	13.0	10.8
6–17 years.............	15.3	14.6	58.7	58.9	19.3	20.5	6.8	6.1
18–24 years............	22.0	25.4	46.8	44.7	20.0	19.5	11.2	10.5
25–44 years............	21.6	22.6	46.7	46.5	18.7	18.7	13.0	12.2
45–54 years............	17.9	17.1	43.9	44.9	23.4	23.6	14.8	14.4
55–64 years............	15.3	13.3	41.3	39.6	26.7	28.9	16.7	18.2
65–74 years............	9.8	8.1	36.9	35.8	31.6	33.5	21.6	22.6
75 years and over	7 7	5.8	31.8	28.2	33.8	38.1	26.6	27.9
Sex								
Male...................	21.3	21.3	47.1	46.5	20.6	21.6	11.0	10.7
Female.................	11.8	11.9	45.4	45.1	26.5	27.1	16.3	15.9
Race and Hispanic origin								
White, non-Hispanic.......	14.7	14.3	46.6	46.4	24.4	25.4	14.3	13.9
Black, non-Hispanic	16.9	16.4	46.1	46.4	23.1	24.0	13.8	13.1
Hispanic[1]	24.9	27.0	42.3	40.2	20.3	20.7	12.5	12.0
Geographic region								
Northeast	13.2	11.8	45.9	47.2	26.0	26.6	14.9	14.3
Midwest	15.9	14.9	47.7	47.2	22.8	24.0	13.6	13.9
South	17.2	17.7	46.1	45.2	23.3	24.4	13.5	12.8
West..................	19.1	20.5	44.8	44.1	22.8	22.8	13.3	12.7

NOTE: Covers visits to doctor's offices, emergency departments, and home visits. (1) Persons of Hispanic origin may be of any race.

Major Reasons Given by Patients for Emergency Room Visits, 2002

Source: National Center for Health Statistics, U.S. Dept. of Health and Human Services

Rank	Principal reason for visit	Number of visits (1,000)	Percent distribution
	ALL VISITS	110,155	100.0
1.	Stomach pain, cramps, and spasms	7,152	6.5
2.	Chest pain and related symptoms	5,637	5.1
3.	Fever	5,310	4.8
4.	Cough	3,016	2.7
5.	Shortness of breath	2,943	2.7
6.	Headache, pain in head..	2,844	2.6
7.	Back symptoms	2,713	2.5
8.	Symptoms referable to throat	2,483	2.3
9.	Vomiting..	2,422	2.2
10.	Pain, site not referable to a specific body system	2,176	2
11.	Lacerations and cuts—upper extremity	2,161	2
12.	Motor vehicle accident, type of injury unspecified	1,758	1.6
13.	Earache or ear infection..	1,748	1.6
14.	Accident, not otherwise specified	1,729	1.6
15.	Vertigo—dizziness..	1,578	1.4
16.	Injury, other and unspecified type—head, neck, and face................	1,468	1.3
17.	Low back symptoms	1,438	1.3
18.	Labored or difficult breathing (dyspnea)	1,387	1.3
19.	Skin rash	1,376	1.2
20.	Nausea	1,355	1.2
	ALL OTHER REASONS	57,462	52.2

Top 20 Reasons Given by Patients for Physicians' Office Visits, 2002

Source: National Center for Health Statistics, U.S. Dept. of Health and Human Services

Rank		Number of visits (1,000)	PERCENT DISTRIBUTION Total	Female	Male
	ALL VISITS	889,980[1]	100.0	100.0	100.0
1.	General medical examination.......	64,726	7.3	6.8	7.9
2.	Progress visit, not otherwise specified	40,983	4.6	3.9	5.6
3.	Cough	28,469	3.2	3.1	3.4
4.	Postoperative visit	22,083	2.5	2.4	2.6
5.	Prenatal examination, routine..........	19,582	2.2	3.7	–
6.	Symptoms referable to throat..........	18,515	2.1	2.2	2.0
7.	Hypertension	17,195	1.9	2.0	1.8
8.	Knee symptoms	14,803	1.7	1.7	1.7
9.	Well-baby examination	14,293	1.6	1.4	1.9
10.	Medication, other and unspecified kinds	14,076	1.6	1.6	1.6
11.	Stomach pain, cramps, and spasms	13,547	1.5	1.7	1.2
12.	Earache, or ear infection	13,160	1.5	1.4	1.5
13.	Back symptoms	12,902	1.4	1.4	1.6
14.	Vision dysfunctions..........	12,897	1.4	1.4	1.5
15.	Blood pressure test..........	12,630	1.4	1.5	1.3
16.	Fever	12,258	1.4	1.2	1.7
17.	Nasal congestion	12,149	1.4	1.2	1.5
18.	Skin rash..........	11,887	1.3	1.2	1.6
19.	Chest pain and related symptoms	11,189	1.3	1.4	1.1
20.	Diabetes mellitus	11,189	1.3	1.0	1.6
	ALL OTHER REASONS	511,446	57.5	57.8	57.0

(1) Based on 529,075,000 visits by women and 360,905,000 by men.

Drugs Most Frequently Prescribed in Physicians' Offices, 2002

Source: National Center for Health Statistics, U.S. Dept. of Health and Human Services; *Physicians' Desk Reference*; in thousands

Rank	Name of drug (principal generic substance)[1]	Times prescribed	% distribution	Therapeutic use
1.	Lipitor (atorvastatin calcium)..........	18,842	1.4	Lowers cholesterol
2.	Albuterol sulfate	15,442	1.1	Anti-inflammatory agent
3.	Amoxicillin..........	14,690	1.1	Antibiotic
4.	Synthroid..........	14,525	1.1	Thyroid hormone therapy
5.	Lasix (furosemide)..........	14,004	1.0	Diuretic, antihypertensive
6.	Celebrex (celecoxib)..........	13,763	1.0	Anti-inflammatory agent
7.	Tylenol (acetaminophen)..........	12,919	1.0	Analgesic (for pain relief)
8.	Vioxx (rofecoxib)[2]	12,650	0.9	Anti-inflammatory agent
9.	Augmentin..........	11,995	0.9	Antibiotic
10.	Norvasc (amlodipine besylate)	11,853	0.9	Lowers blood pressure
11.	Zyrtec	11,573	0.9	Antihistamine
12.	Zocor (simvastatin)	11,429	0.8	Lowers cholesterol
13.	A.S.A. (acetylsalicylic acid, aspirin)..........	10,670	0.8	Analgesic (for pain relief)
14.	Prednisone	10,422	0.8	Steroid, anti-inflammatory agent
15.	Allegra..........	10,420	0.8	Antihistamine
16.	Coumadin	10,090	0.7	Anticoagulant
17.	Atenolol..........	9,694	0.7	Beta blocker
18.	Claritin (loratadine)	9,208	0.7	Antihistamine
19.	Paxil	9,118	0.7	Antidepressant
20.	Prevacid	8,981	0.7	Acid/peptic disorders
	ALL OTHER	1,105,025	82.0	

(1) The trade or generic name used by the physician on the prescription or other medical records. The use of trade names is for identification only and does not imply endorsement by the Public Health Service or the U.S. Dept. of Health and Human Services. (2) Recalled by manufacturer 9/30/04 after new research showed that people taking the drug for 18 months or more were at an increased risk for heart attack and stroke.

Hospitals and Nursing Homes in the U.S., 2001

Source: *Hospital Statistics™ 2003* edition, Health Forum, LLC, An American Hospital Association Company, copyright 2003; *Health, United States, 2003*

For information on choosing a nursing home, go to the website www.medicare.gov/nursing/overview.asp

STATE	Hospitals[1]	% of beds occupied[1]	Nursing homes	% of beds occupied	STATE	Hospitals[1]	% of beds occupied[1]	Nursing homes	% of beds occupied
AL.......	107	59	228	91.2	MT......	53	65	103	78.1
AK.......	19	58	15	72.3	NE......	84	60	230	83.4
AZ.......	61	64	139	79.9	NV......	24	68	46	79.6
AR	83	58	250	74.5	NH......	28	61	83	90.4
CA	384	67	1,342	81.5	NJ......	78	69	364	87.1
CO	66	61	223	83.8	NM......	35	58	80	87.6
CT	35	74	254	91.9	NY......	212	77	669	93.9
DE	5	74	42	83.4	NC......	111	69	413	87.9
DC	10	73	21	91.3	ND......	40	58	87	92.9
FL.......	202	61	727	83.3	OH......	166	62	998	77.8
GA	147	62	361	91.3	OK......	108	58	379	69.1
HI	23	74	45	91.4	OR......	60	60	145	72.8
ID	40	54	84	72.5	PA......	205	68	766	87.5
IL	192	61	854	75.5	RI......	11	71	97	87.6
IN	110	57	560	73.8	SC......	62	71	179	88.6
IA	116	59	466	78.0	SD......	50	64	112	91.9
KS	133	53	380	80.4	TN......	123	55	349	88.9
KY	103	61	304	89.4	TX......	411	61	1,182	69.3
LA	125	57	332	77.5	UT......	42	56	92	72.8
ME	37	64	126	89.8	VT......	14	65	44	90.6
MD	49	73	251	83.1	VA......	87	69	277	86.4
MA	80	73	506	89.7	WA......	84	60	268	82.7
MI.......	145	65	434	83.8	WV......	57	63	139	90.6
MN	133	68	427	93.2	WI......	121	61	419	84.2
MS	96	60	199	89.9	WY......	24	54	39	82.2
MO......	117	60	545	70.5	U.S.	4,908	64	16,675	82.5

(1) Community hospitals (excludes federal hospitals, hospital units of institutions, facilities for the mentally retarded, and alcoholism and chemical dependency hospitals).

Expected New Cancer Cases and Deaths, by Sex, for Leading Sites, 2004

Source: American Cancer Society

The estimates of expected new cases are offered as a rough guide only. They exclude basal and squamous cell skin cancers and in situ carcinomas, except urinary bladder. Carcinoma in situ of the breast accounts for about 59,390 new cases annually, melanoma carcinoma in situ for about 40,780. More than 1 million cases of basal cell and squamous cell cancer, which are highly curable forms of skin cancer, occur annually.

EXPECTED NEW CASES

Both sexes		Women		Men	
Prostate	230,110	Breast	215,990	Prostate	230,110
Breast	217,440	Lung	80,660	Lung	93,110
Lung	173,770	Colorectal	73,320	Colorectal	73,620
Colorectal	146,940	Uterine corpus (endometrium)	40,320	Urinary bladder	44,640
Urinary bladder	60,240	Ovary	25,580	Melanoma-skin	29,900
ALL SITES	**1,368,030**	**ALL SITES**	**668,470**	**ALL SITES**	**699,560**

EXPECTED DEATHS

Both sexes		Women		Men	
Lung	160,440	Lung	68,510	Lung	91,930
Colorectal	56,730	Breast	40,110	Prostate	29,900
Breast	40,580	Colorectal	28,410	Colorectal	28,320
Pancreas	31,270	Ovary	16,090	Pancreas	15,440
Prostate	29,900	Pancreas	15,830	Non-Hodgkin's lymphoma	10,390
ALL SITES	**563,700**	**ALL SITES**	**272,810**	**ALL SITES**	**290,890**

U.S. Cancer Incidence for Top 15 Sites, 1992-2000

Source: Surveillance, Epidemiology, and End Results (SEER) Program, National Cancer Institute

	Rate[1]	Average yearly % change		Rate[1]	Average yearly % change		Rate[1]	Average yearly % change
ALL SITES	477.7	−0.7	Urinary bladder	20.4	−0.1	Oral cavity and pharynx	11.3	−2.0
Prostate	180.6	−3.1	Non-Hodgkin's			Pancreas	11.1	−0.4
Breast (female)	132.5	+0.8	lymphoma	19.1	0.0	Kidney and renal pelvis	10.8	+1.3
Lung	64.0	−1.2	Ovary	17.0	−0.8	Stomach	9.3	−1.3
Colon and rectum	54.5	−0.6	Melanoma of the skin	15.7	+2.5	Thyroid	6.4	+3.4
Corpus and uterus	24.5	−0.1	Leukemia	12.4	−1.3			

(1) Per 100,000 population; rates for prostate, breast, corpus and uterus, and ovary are sex-specific; rates age-adjusted to the 2000 population, and so not comparable with previously published rates; annual average for the 1992-2000 period.

U.S. Cancer Mortality for Top 15 Sites, 1992-2000

Source: Surveillance, Epidemiology, and End Results (SEER) Program, National Cancer Institute

	Rate[1]	Average yearly % change[2]		Rate[1]	Average yearly % change[2]		Rate[1]	Average yearly % change[2]
ALL SITES	206.5	−1.0	Ovary	9.0	−0.8	Liver and intrahepatic		
Lung	57.6	−0.8	Non-Hodgkin's lymphoma	8.5	0.0	bile duct	4.4	+2.1
Prostate	35.3	−3.4	Leukemia	7.8	−0.5	Urinary bladder	4.4	−0.3
Breast (female)	29.2	−2.4	Stomach	5.1	−2.8	Esophagus	4.3	+0.6
Colon and rectum	22.0	−1.7	Brain and other nervous			Kidney and renal pelvis	4.2	−0.3
Pancreas	10.6	−0.1	system	4.7	−0.7	Myeloma (bone marrow)	3.9	−0.3

(1) Per 100,000 population; rates age-adjusted to the 2000 population, and so not comparable with previously published rates; annual average for 8-year period; rates for prostate, breast, and ovary are sex-specific. (2) For 1992-2000.

Cardiovascular Diseases Statistical Summary, 2001

Source: American Heart Association

Prevalence — An estimated 64,400,000 Americans had one or more forms of heart and blood vessel disease in 2001.
- hypertension (high blood pressure) — 50,000,000
- coronary heart disease — 13,200,000
- stroke — 4,800,000
- congestive heart failure — 5,000,000

Mortality — 931,108 in 2001 (38.5% of all deaths).
- Someone died from cardiovascular disease every 34 seconds in the U.S. in 2001.

Congenital or inborn heart defects — Mortality from such heart defects was 4,109 in 2001.
Coronary heart disease (heart attack and angina pectoris) — caused 502,189 deaths in 2001.
- 13,200,000 Americans had a history of heart attack and/or angina pectoris.
- As many as 1,200,000 Americans had coronary attacks in 2001.

Congestive heart failure — killed 52,828 in 2001.
Stroke — killed 163,538 Americans in 2001.
Rheumatic heart disease — killed 3,489 in 2001.

Transplant Waiting List, Oct. 2004*

Source: United Network for Organ Sharing

Type of transplant	Patients waiting
Kidney	63,045
Liver	17,834
Pancreas	1,659
Kidney-pancreas	2,497
Intestine	202
Heart	3,397
Heart-lung	185
Lung	3,991
Total[1]	92,810

Transplants Performed, 2002

Source: United Network for Organ Sharing

Type of transplant	Number
Kidney	14,523
Liver	5,060
Pancreas	517
Kidney-pancreas	902
Intestine	44
Heart	2,111
Heart-lung	31
Lung	1,041
Multi-organ	315
Total	24,544

* As of Oct. 10, 2004. (1) This table shows the totals of patients waiting for each organ; some patients are waiting for more than one organ, so the total number waiting for organs is less than 92,810.

AIDS Deaths and New AIDS Cases in the U.S., 1985-2002

Source: *Health, United States, 2003;* National Center for Health Statistics, U.S. Dept. of Health and Human Services

	Percent Distribution	All Years[2]	1985	1990	1995	1999	2000	2001	2002	2002 rate[3]
TOTAL DEATHS[1]	—	501,669	6,981	31,988	52,254	18,454	17,347	17,402	16,371	NA
NEW AIDS CASES										
All races	—	831,112	8,159	41,448	70,412	44,580	40,282	41,450	42,745	15.0
All males, 13 years and over	100.0	676,609	7,504	36,179	56,689	34,013	30,135	30,663	31,644	28.0
Race White, non-Hispanic	47.7	322,920	4,746	20,825	26,028	12,691	11,314	11,054	11,221	13.9
Black, non-Hispanic	35.4	239,650	1,710	10,239	20,833	14,830	13,082	13,764	14,310	111.9
Hispanic[4]	15.6	105,628	992	4,743	9,111	6,043	5,275	5,318	5,543	39.3
American Indian or Alaska Native[5]	0.3	2,203	7	81	197	135	136	149	155	17.3
Asian or Pacific Islander[5]	0.8	5,666	49	264	489	295	291	348	381	8.2
Age 13-19 years	0.4	2,632	27	107	223	131	145	184	199	1.4
20-29 years	15.4	104,174	1,501	6,921	8,387	3,972	3,327	3,291	3,433	17.5
30-39 years	44.7	302,420	3,588	16,668	25,684	14,410	12,543	12,082	12,101	56.2
40-49 years	27.8	188,299	1,634	8,828	16,151	10,836	9,648	10,261	10,658	49.5
50-59 years	8.7	58,745	597	2,645	4,692	3,479	3,387	3,633	3,959	24.9
60 years and over	3.0	20,339	157	1,010	1,562	1,185	1,085	1,212	1,294	6.5
All females, 13 years and over	100.0	145,696	524	4,544	12,978	10,312	9,958	10,617	10,951	9.2
Race White, non-Hispanic	22.0	32,000	143	1,228	3,042	1,896	1,859	1,993	1,930	2.3
Black, non-Hispanic	61.2	89,130	280	2,557	7,586	6,711	6,489	6,963	7,339	50.0
Hispanic[4]	15.9	23,145	98	726	2,236	1,599	1,462	1,543	1,561	11.8
American Indian or Alaska Native[5]	0.3	509	2	9	38	40	70	42	42	4.5
Asian or Pacific Islander[5]	0.6	832	1	20	73	61	74	67	68	1.4
Age 13-19 years	1.4	1,995	5	67	157	166	170	171	203	1.5
20-29 years	20.6	29,996	178	1,117	2,676	1,886	1,750	1,717	1,819	9.6
30-39 years	43.6	63,504	232	2,087	5,934	4,234	3,973	4,145	3,991	18.7
40-49 years	24.1	35,168	45	780	3,059	2,789	2,857	3,147	3,377	15.3
50-59 years	7.0	10.243	26	274	818	916	867	999	1,150	6.9
60 years and over	3.3	4,790	38	219	334	321	341	438	411	1.5
All children, under 13 years	100.0	8,807	131	725	745	255	189	170	150	0.3
Race White, non-Hispanic	18.2	1,601	26	157	117	30	32	30	23	0.1
Black, non-Hispanic	61.6	5,422	87	390	483	171	122	111	99	1.2
Hispanic[4]	19.1	1,685	18	169	135	49	30	26	24	0.2
American Indian or Alaska Native[5]	0.4	31	0	5	2	2	1	0	0	0.0
Asian or Pacific Islander[5]	0.7	58	0	4	5	2	3	3	4	0.2
Age Under 1 year	36.9	3,249	54	298	258	87	61	47	46	1.1
1-12 years	63.1	5,558	77	427	487	168	128	123	104	0.2

NA = Not available. **Note:** The definition of AIDS cases for reporting purposes was expanded in 1985, 1987, and 1993, as more was learned about the spectrum of human immunodeficiency virus-associated diseases. Data exclude residents of U.S. territories. Figures were updated Dec. 31, 2002 to include delayed case reports and may differ from previous reports of *Health, United States.* (1) Based on preliminary figures presented at the National HIV Prevention Conference, July 2003. (2) Revised figures; includes cases and deaths prior to 1985 and for years not shown. Through Dec. 2002. (3) Rate is per 100,000 pop. (4) Persons of Hispanic origin may be of any race. (5) Excludes persons of Hispanic origin.

New AIDS Cases in the U.S., 1985-2002, by Transmission Category

Source: *HIV/AIDS Surveillance Report, 2002,* CDC, National Center for HIV, STD, and TB Prevention, Div. of HIV/AIDS Prevention

TRANSMISSION CATEGORY	Percent distribution	All years[1]	1985	1990	1995	1999	2000	2001	2002
All males 13 years and older	100	697,714	7,504	36,193	56,776	34,094	30,251	31,901	32,513
Men who have sex with men	55	384,784	5,348	23,658	30,944	15,632	13,648	13,265	14,545
Injecting drug use	22	151,367	1,103	6,923	13,376	6,893	5,554	5,261	5,121
Men who have sex with men and injecting drug use	8	54,224	661	2,943	4,185	1,929	1,587	1,502	1,510
Hemophilia/coagulation disorder	1	5,067	68	332	438	143	93	97	79
Heterosexual contact[2]	5	36,692	32	715	2,924	2,947	2,537	2,762	3,213
Sex with injecting drug user	1	10,412	25	454	871	634	514	549	519
Transfusion[3]	1	5,164	102	440	319	137	146	105	147
Undetermined[4]	9	60,420	190	1,182	4,590	6,413	6,686	8,909	7,898
All females 13 years and older	100	152,060	524	4,547	12,998	10,352	9,979	11,082	11,279
Injecting drug use	39	58,552	287	2,347	5,426	2,985	2,545	2,212	2,381
Hemophilia/coagulation disorder	<1	304	3	15	29	13	5	9	11
Heterosexual contact[2]	42	63,379	119	1,538	5,555	4,397	4,025	4,142	4,740
Sex with injecting drug user	15	22,939	82	1,030	1,923	1,135	976	937	985
Transfusion[3]	3	3,988	63	330	253	131	151	113	118
Undetermined[4]	17	25,837	52	317	1,735	2,826	3,253	4,606	4,029

Note: The definition of AIDS cases for reporting purposes was expanded in 1985, 1987, and 1993, as more was learned about the spectrum of human immunodeficiency virus-associated diseases. Data exclude residents of U.S. territories. (1) Includes cases prior to 1985 and for years not shown. (2) Includes persons who have had heterosexual contact with a person with human immunodeficiency virus (HIV) infection or at risk of HIV infection. (3) Receipt of blood transfusion, blood components, or tissue. (4) Includes persons for whom risk information is incomplete, persons still under investigation, men reported only to have had heterosexual contact with prostitutes, and interviewed persons for whom no specific risk is identified.

WORLD ALMANAC QUICK QUIZ
What age group accounts for the most deaths from firearms?
(a) 5-14　　　(b) 20-24　　　(c) 25-44　　　(d) 45-64
For the answer, look in this chapter, or see page 1008.

People Living with HIV, 2003

Source: UNAIDS/WHO working group on Global AIDS/HIV and STI Surveillance

Year-end 2003 estimates of persons infected with HIV, whether or not they had developed AIDs symptoms. Excludes countries where sufficient data were not available.

Country	Adults and Children with HIV	Percent of Adults with HIV	Country	Adults and Children with HIV	Percent of Adults with HIV
Algeria	9,100	0.1%	Kyrgyzstan	3,900	0.1
Angola	240,000	3.9	Laos	1,700	0.1
Argentina	130,000	0.7	Latvia	7,600	0.6
Armenia	2,600	0.1	Lebanon	2,800	0.1
Australia	14,000	0.1	Lesotho*	320,000	28.9
Austria	10,000	0.3	Liberia	100,000	5.9
Azerbaijan	1,400	<0.1	Libya	10,000	0.3
Bahamas	5,600	3.0	Lithuania	1,300	0.1
Bahrain	<600	0.2	Luxembourg	<500	0.2
Barbados	2,500	1.5	Madagascar	140,000	1.7
Belgium	10,000	0.2	Macedonia	<200	<0.1
Belize	3,600	2.4	Malawi*	900,000	14.2
Benin	68,000	1.9	Malaysia	52,000	0.4
Bolivia	4,900	0.1	Mali	140,000	1.9
Bosnia and Herzegovina	900	<0.1	Malta	<500	0.2
Botswana*	350,000	37.3	Mauritania	9,500	0.6
Brazil	660,000	0.7	Mexico	160,000	0.3
Brunei	<200	<0.1	Moldova	5,500	0.2
Bulgaria	<500	<0.1	Mongolia	<500	<0.1
Burkina Faso*	300,000	4.2	Morocco	15,000	0.1
Burundi	250,000	6.0	Mozambique	1,300,000	12.2
Cambodia	170,000	2.6	Myanmar**	330,000	1.2
Cameroon*	560,000	6.9	Namibia	210,000	21.3
Canada	56,000	0.3	Nepal	61,000	0.5
Central African Republic	260,000	13.5	Netherlands	19,000	0.2
Chad	200,000	4.8	New Zealand	1,400	0.1
Chile	26,000	0.3	Nicaragua	6,400	0.2
China	840,000	0.1	Niger	70,000	1.2
Colombia	190,000	0.7	Nigeria	3,600,000	5.4
Congo, Dem. Rep. of**	1,100,000	4.2	Norway	2,100	0.1
Congo, Rep. of	90,000	4.9	Oman	1,300	0.1
Costa Rica	12,000	0.6	Pakistan	74,000	0.1
Côte d'Ivoire	570,000	7.0	Panama	16,000	0.9
Croatia	<200	<0.1	Papua New Guinea	16,000	0.6
Cuba	3,300	0.1	Paraguay	15,000	0.5
Czech Republic	2,500	0.1	Peru	82,000	0.5
Denmark	5,000	0.2	Philippines	9,000	<0.1
Djibouti	9,100	2.9	Poland	14,000	0.1
Dominican Republic	88,000	1.7	Portugal	22,000	0.4
Ecuador	21,000	0.3	Romania	6,500	<0.1
Egypt	12,000	<0.1	Russian Federation	860,000	1.1
El Salvador	29,000	0.7	Rwanda*	250,000	5.1
Eritrea	60,000	2.7	Senegal*	44,000	0.8
Estonia	7,800	1.1	Serbia and Montenegro	10,000	0.2
Ethiopia	1,500,000	4.4	Singapore	4,100	0.2
Fiji	600	0.1	Slovakia	<200	<0.1
Finland	1,500	0.1	Slovenia	<500	<0.1
France	120,000	0.4	South Africa*	5,300,000	21.5
Gabon	48,000	8.1	Spain	140,000	0.7
Gambia	6,800	1.2	Sri Lanka	3,500	<0.1
Georgia	3,000	0.1	Sudan	400,000	2.3
Germany	43,000	0.1	Suriname	5,200	1.7
Ghana*	350,000	3.1	Swaziland**	220,000	38.8
Greece	9,100	0.2	Sweden	3,600	0.1
Guatemala	78,000	1.1	Switzerland	13,000	0.4
Guinea*	140,000	3.2	Syria	<500	<0.1
Guyana*	11,000	2.5	Tajikistan	<200	<0.1
Haiti	280,000	5.6	Tanzania*	1,600,000	8.8
Honduras	63,000	1.8	Thailand	570,000	1.5
Hong Kong	2,600	0.1	Togo	110,000	4.1
Hungary	2,800	0.1	Trinidad and Tobago	29,000	3.2
Iceland	<500	0.2	Tunisia	1,000	<0.1
India	5,100,000	0.9	Turkmenistan	<200	<0.1
Indonesia	110,000	0.1	Uganda*	530,000	4.1
Iran	31,000	0.1	Ukraine	360,000	1.4
Iraq	<500	<0.1	United Kingdom	51,000	0.2
Ireland	2,800	0.1	United States	950,000	0.6
Israel	3,000	0.1	Uruguay	6,000	0.3
Italy	140,000	0.5	Uzbekistan	11,000	0.1
Jamaica	22,000	1.2	Venezuela	110,000	0.7
Japan	12,000	<0.1	Vietnam	220,000	0.4
Jordan	600	<0.1	Yemen	12,000	0.1
Kazakhstan	16,500	0.2	Zambia	920,000	16.5
Kenya	1,300,000	6.7	Zimbabwe	1,800,000	24.6
Korea, South	8,300	<0.1 %	**GLOBAL TOTAL**	**37,800,000**	**1.1**

*A population-based survey with HIV prevalence measurement will be conducted in the near future. **New surveillance was conducted but the results were not available for inclusion in the estimation process.

HEALTH

Basic First Aid

Source: American Red Cross

NOTE: This information is not intended to be a substitute for formal training. It is recommended that you contact your local American Red Cross chapter to sign up for a First Aid/CPR/AED course.

It is important to get medical assistance as soon as possible, but knowing what to do until a doctor or other trained person gets to the scene can save a life, especially in cases of severe bleeding, stoppage of breathing, poisoning, and shock.

People with special medical problems, such as diabetes, cardiovascular disease, epilepsy, or allergies, are urged to wear some sort of emblem identifying the problem, as a safeguard against receiving medication that might be harmful or even fatal. Emblems may be obtained from Medic Alert Foundation, 2323 Colorado Ave., Turlock, CA 95382; 888-633-4298.

Animal bite — Wash wound with soap under running water and apply antibiotic ointment and dressing. When possible, the animal should be caught alive for rabies testing.

Asphyxiation — Call 9-1-1, or the local emergency number, then start rescue breathing.

Bleeding — Elevate the wound above the heart if possible. Apply direct pressure to the wound with sterile compress until bleeding stops. Call 9-1-1, or the local emergency number if bleeding is severe.

Burn — If mild, with skin unbroken and no blisters, flush with cool water until pain subsides. Apply a loose sterile dry dressing if necessary. If severe, call 9-1-1 or the local emergency number. Apply sterile compresses and keep patient comfortably warm until advanced medical assistance arrives. Do not try to clean burn or break blisters.

Chemical in eye — Call or have someone call 9-1-1 or the local emergency number. With the victim's head turned to the side, continuously flush the injured eye with water, letting the water run away from the other eye.

Choking — See **Abdominal Thrust**.

Convulsions — Place person on back on bed or rug. Loosen clothing. Turn head to side. Do not place a blunt object between the patient's teeth. If convulsions do not stop, get medical attention immediately.

Cut (minor) — Apply mild antiseptic and sterile compress after washing with soap under warm running water.

Fainting — If victim feels faint, lower him or her to the ground. Lay the victim down on his or her back. If there are no signs of a spinal injury or nausea, elevate the victim's legs approximately 12 inches. Loosen any restrictive clothing and check for any other signs of injury. Call 9-1-1 or the local emergency number if the victim remains unconscious for more than a few minutes.

Foreign body in eye — Try to remove the object by having the victim blink several times. If the object doesn't come out, try gently flushing the eye with water. Do not rub the eye. If the object still doesn't come out, the victim should receive professional medical attention.

Frostbite — Handle frostbitten area gently. Do not rub. Soak affected area in warm water (100–105° F). Do not allow frostbitten area to touch the container. Soak until frostbitten part looks red and feels warm. Loosely bandage with dry, sterile dressings. If fingers or toes are frostbitten, put sterile gauze between them.

Heat Stroke and Heat Exhaustion — Remove the victim from the heat. Loosen any tight clothing and apply cool, wet cloths to the skin. If the victim is conscious give him or her cool water, to drink slowly. Call 9-1-1 or the local emergency number if the victim becomes unconscious.

Hypothermia — Call 9-1-1 or the local emergency number. Move victim to a warm place. Remove wet clothing and dry victim, if necessary. Warm victim gradually by wrapping the person in warm blankets or clothing. Apply heat pads or other heat sources if available, but not directly to the body. Give the victim warm, non-alcoholic and decaffeinated liquids to drink.

Loss of Limb — If a limb is severed, it is important to properly protect the limb so that it can possibly be reattached. After the victim is cared for, the limb should be wrapped in a sterile gauze or clean material and placed in a clean plastic bag, garbage can or other suitable container. Pack ice around the limb on the OUTSIDE of the bag to keep the limb cold. Call ahead to the hospital to alert staff there of the situation.

Poisoning — Call 9-1-1 or the local emergency number and Poison Control Center (800-222-1222) and follow their directions. Do not give the victim any food or drink or induce vomiting, unless specified by the Poison Control Center.

Shock (injury-related) — Monitor breathing and consciousness. Help the victim rest as comfortably as possible. If uncertain as to his or her injuries, keep the victim flat on the back. Otherwise elevate feet and legs 12 inches. Maintain normal body temperature; if the weather is cold or damp, place blankets or extra clothing over and under the victim; if weather is hot, provide shade.

Snakebite — Call 9-1-1 or the local emergency number. Wash the injury. Keep the area still and at a lower level than the heart. Keep the victim quiet. If the victim cannot get professional medical help within 30 minute, consider using a snakebite kit if available.

Sprains and fractures — Apply ice to reduce swelling and pain. Do not try to straighten or move broken limbs. Apply a splint to immobilize the injured area if the victim must be transported. If you suspect a serious injury, call 9-1-1 or the local emergency number.

Sting from insect — If possible, remove stinger by scraping it away or using tweezers. Wash the area with soap and water; cover it to keep it clean. Apply a cold pack to reduce pain and swelling. Call 9-1-1 or the local emergency number immediately if body swells, patient collapses, or you know that the victim is allergic to the sting.

Unconsciousness — Call 9-1-1 or the local emergency number immediately. If the person has signs of circulation, place him or her in the recovery position (i.e., lying on his or her side, with head supported, so that the airway is open — but do not move if a spinal injury is suspected).

Abdominal Thrust (Heimlich Maneuver)

The recommended first aid for conscious choking victims is the abdominal thrust, commonly known as the Heimlich maneuver, after its creator, Dr. Henry Heimlich.

* Get behind the victim and wrap your arms around him or her about 1-2 inches above the navel.
* Make a fist with one hand and place it, with the thumb knuckle pressing inward at the abdomen.
* Grasp the fist with the other hand and give upward thrusts until object is removed or help arrives.

Rescue Breathing

* Determine consciousness by tapping the victim on the shoulder and asking loudly, "Are you okay?"
* Tilt the victim's head back so that the chin is pointing upward. Do not press on the soft tissue under the chin, as this might obstruct the airway. If you suspect that an accident victim might have neck or back injuries, open the airway by placing the tips of your index and middle fingers on the corners of the person's jaw, and your thumbs on the victim's cheekbones, to lift the jaw forward without tilting the head.
* Place your cheek and ear close to the victim's mouth and nose. Look at the chest to see if it rises and falls. Listen and feel for air to be exhaled for about 5 seconds.
* If there is no breathing, pinch the victim's nostrils shut with the thumb and index finger of your hand that is pressing on the victim's forehead. Another way to prevent leakage of air when the lungs are inflated is to press your cheek against the victim's nose.
* Blow air into the mouth by taking a deep breath and then sealing your mouth tightly around the victim's mouth. Initially, give 2 rescue (approx. 2 seconds each) breaths.
* Watch to see whether the victim's chest rises.
* Stop when the chest is expanded. Raise your mouth; turn your head to the side and listen for exhalation.
* Watch the chest to see if it falls. Check for signs of circulation, including movement or coughing in response to the rescue breaths. If there are signs of circulation, but no breathing, continue rescue breathing. If there are no signs of circulation, begin CPR.
* Repeat giving 1 breath every 5 seconds until the victim starts breathing or advanced medical help arrives and takes over. Recheck for breathing and movement about every minute.

Note: Infants (up to 1 year) and children (1 to 8 years) should be treated as described above, except for the following:

* Do not tilt the head as far back as an adult's head.
* Both the mouth and nose of an infant should be sealed by the mouth.
* Blow into the infant's mouth and nose once every 3 seconds with less pressure and volume than for a child.

Heart and Blood Vessel Disease

Sources: American Heart Association, 7272 Greenville Ave., Dallas, TX 75231-4596; phone: (800) 242-8721; Centers for Disease Control and Prevention; National Institutes of Health

Warning Signs

Of Heart Attack
- Uncomfortable pressure, fullness, squeezing, or pain in the center of the chest lasting 2 minutes or longer
- Pain may radiate to the shoulder, arm, neck, or jaw
- Sweating may accompany pain or discomfort
- Nausea and vomiting also may occur
- Shortness of breath, dizziness, or fainting may occur

The American Heart Association advises immediate action at the onset of these symptoms. More than half of heart attack victims die within 1 hour of the onset of symptoms.

Of Stroke
- Sudden numbness or weakness of face, arm or leg, especially on one side of the body
- Sudden confusion, trouble speaking or understanding
- Sudden trouble seeing in one or both eyes
- Sudden trouble walking, dizziness, loss of balance or coordination
- Sudden severe headache with no known cause

Prompt treatment of stroke can be a major factor in controlling the effects.

Some Major Risk Factors

Blood pressure—High blood pressure, or hypertension, increases the risk of stroke, heart attack, kidney failure, and congestive heart failure. It affects people of all races, sexes, ethnic origins, and ages. Various causes can trigger this **often symptomless** disease, and it is recommended that individuals have a blood pressure reading at least once every 2 years (more often if advised by a physician).

A blood pressure reading is really two measurements in one, with one written over the other, such as 122/78. The **upper number (systolic pressure)** represents the amount of pressure in the blood vessels when the heart contracts (beats) and pushes blood through the circulatory system. The **lower number (diastolic pressure)** represents the pressure in the blood vessels between beats, when the heart is resting. According to National Institutes of Health guidelines, a blood pressure reading below 120/80 is considered normal, and readings from 120/80 to 139/89 are considered either "normal" or "prehypertension."

High blood pressure is divided into 2 stages:
Stage 1 is 140-159 (systolic) over 90-99 (diastolic);
Stage 2 is 160+ (systolic) over 100+ (diastolic).

Individuals with diabetes or chronic kidney disease are considered to have high blood pressure if they have a reading of 130/80 or higher. The diagnosis can be based on either the systolic or the diastolic reading.

High blood pressure usually cannot be cured, but it can be controlled in a variety of ways, including lifestyle modifications and medication. Treatment always should be at the direction and under the supervision of a physician.

Cholesterol—Cholesterol is a waxy fat-like substance found in all cells of the body. It is produced by the body and also comes in some foods. The body needs some cholesterol, but excess levels increase the risk of heart disease. High cholesterol itself **does not cause symptoms**, so many people are unaware that they have a problem.

There are 2 kinds of cholesterol: **LDL (low-density lipoprotein)**, often called "bad" cholesterol, leads to narrowing of the arteries; **HDL (high-density lipoprotein)**, known as "good" cholesterol, helps reduce this risk.

National Institutes of Health guidelines classify total cholesterol levels (determined by a blood test) of less than 200 mg/dl as desirable, 200-239 as borderline high, and 240 and above as high. About 37 mil. Americans have a cholesterol level of 240 mg/dl or higher. LDL levels of less than 100 are considered optimal, 130-159 as borderline high, 160-189 as high, and 190 and over as very high. For HDL, levels of 60 mg/dl and above are considered protective against heart disease, while levels under 40 mg/dl are considered a major risk factor for heart disease.

Like high-blood pressure, high cholestrol can be controlled by life-style modification and medication, and should be treated under supervision of a physician.

Triglycerides, another form of fat in the blood, can also raise the risk of heart disease. Levels that are borderline high (150-199) or high (200 or more) may need treatment.

Diabetes—Diabetes is a major risk factor for heart disease; 2/3 to 3/4 of people with diabetes mellitus die of some form of heart or blood vessel disease. See also "Diabetes" in this chapter.

Smoking—Cigarette smokers have more than twice the risk of heart attack and 2-4 times the risk of sudden cardiac death as nonsmokers. Young smokers have a higher risk for early death from stroke. See also "Some Benefits of Quitting Smoking" in this chapter.

Obesity—Using a body mass index (BMI) of 25 and higher for overweight and 30 and higher for obesity, an estimated 131 mil. Americans age 20 and over are overweight and 62 mil. are obese. See also "Weight Guidelines for Adults" in this chapter.

Women and Cardiovascular Disease

The American Heart Association reports that heart disease and stroke, respectively, are the No. 1 and No. 3 killers of women over the age of 25 (cancer is the 2nd); one in 2.5 women eventually dies of some form of cardiovascular disease. Because heart disease was long viewed as a "man's" disease, many of the major cardiovascular studies were conducted only on men. Much recent attention has been directed toward understanding the influence of gender on cardiovascular disease risk and prevention, but important gaps in knowledge remain.

Women often present some of the same "classic" symptoms of heart attack that men feel, such as chest pain that spreads to the shoulders and arms, but they may more often report atypical chest pain or complain of abdominal pain, difficulty breathing (dyspnea), and nausea. Another problem in diagnosis is that women tend to have heart attacks later in life than men, so symptoms may more often be masked by other age-related diseases such as arthritis or osteoporosis. Even certain diagnostic tests and procedures such as the exercise stress test may not be as accurate in women, with the result that the disease process that leads to heart attack or stroke may not be detected early on, with potentially serious consequences.

Finding Your Target Heart Rate

Source: Carole Casten, EdD, *Aerobics Today;* Peg Jordan, RN, Aerobics and Fitness Assoc. of America

The target heart rate is the heartbeat rate a person should have during aerobic exercise (such as running, fast walking, cycling, or cross-country skiing) to get the full benefit of the exercise for cardiovascular conditioning.

First, determine the intensity level at which one would like to exercise. A sedentary person may want to begin an exercise regimen at the 60% level and work up gradually to the 70% level. Athletes and highly fit individuals must work at an 85% or higher level to receive benefits.

Second, calculate the target heart rate. One common way is by using the American College of Sports Medicine Method.

To obtain cardiovascular fitness benefits from aerobic exercise, it is recommended that an individual participate in an aerobic activity at least 3-5 times a week for 20-30 minutes per session, although cardiac patients and very sedentary individuals can obtain benefits with shorter periods (15-20 minutes). Generally, training changes occur in 4-6 weeks, but they can occur in as little as 2 weeks.

Using the American College of Sports Medicine Method to calculate one's target heart rate, an individual should subtract his or her age from 220, then multiply by the desired intensity level of the workout. Then divide the answer by 6 for a 10-second pulse count. (The 10-second pulse count is useful for checking whether the target heart rate is being achieved during the workout. One can easily check one's pulse—at the wrist or side of the neck—counting the number of beats in 10 seconds.)

For example, a 20-year-old wishing to exercise at 70% intensity would employ the following steps:

Maximum Heart Rate	$220 - 20 = 200$
Target Heart Rate	$200 \times .70 = 140$
10-second Pulse Count	$140/6 = 23$

To work at the desired level of intensity, this 20-year-old would strive for a target heart rate of 140 beats per minute, or a 10-second pulse count of 23.

Examples of Moderate[1] Amounts of Exercise

Source: *Physical Activity and Health: A Report of the Surgeon General*, U.S. Dept. of Health and Human Services, 1996

ACTIVITY	TIME[2]	ACTIVITY	TIME[2]	ACTIVITY	TIME[2]
Washing windows or floors	45-60	Bicycling 10 mi.	30	Basketball (playing a game)	15-20
Playing touch football	30-45	Dancing fast (social)	30	Bicycling 16 mi	15
Wheeling self in wheelchair	30-40	Raking leaves	30	Jumping rope	15
Walking 1¾ mi (20 min/mi)	35	Walking 2 mi (15 min/mi)	30	Running 1½ mi (10 min/mi).	15
Basketball (shooting baskets) . .	30	Swimming laps	20	Shoveling snow	15

Note: The activities are arranged from less vigorous, and using more time, to more vigorous, and using less time. (1) A "moderate" amount of physical activity uses about 150 calories (kcal), or 1,000 if done daily for a week. (2) Activities can be performed at various intensities; the suggested durations, in minutes; based on the expected intensity of effort.

Trends in Daily Use of Cigarettes, for U.S. 8th, 10th, and 12th Graders

Source: *Monitoring the Future*, Univ. of Michigan Inst. for Social Research and National Inst. on Drug Abuse
(percent who smoked daily in last 30 days; change 2002-2003 in percentage points)

	8th grade						10th grade						12th grade					
	1999	2000	2001	2002	2003	'02-'03 change	1999	2000	2001	2002	2003	'02-'03 change	1999	2000	2001	2002	2003	'02-'03 change
TOTAL.	8.1	7.4	5.5	5.1	4.5	−0.6	15.9	14.0	12.2	10.1	8.9	−1.2	23.1	20.6	19.0	16.9	15.8	−1.1
Sex.																		
Male.	7.4	7.0	5.9	5.4	4.4	−1.0	15.6	13.7	12.4	9.4	8.6	−0.8	23.6	20.9	18.4	17.2	17.0	−0.2
Female.	8.4	7.5	4.9	4.9	4.5	−0.4	15.9	14.1	11.9	10.8	9.0	−1.8	22.2	19.7	18.9	16.1	14.0	−2.2
College plans																		
None or under																		
4 yrs.	25.2	21.7	17.7	17.1	16.1	−0.9	32.1	28.8	27.3	22.9	22.1	−0.9	34.2	31.7	30.1	27.6	27.9	+0.3
Complete 4 yrs. .	5.9	5.6	3.9	3.9	3.2	−0.7	13.2	11.6	9.6	7.9	6.7	−1.2	19.5	16.6	15.5	13.8	12.1	−1.7
Region																		
Northeast.	7.2	6.9	6.1	3.7	2.9	−0.8	17.7	14.1	11.0	8.3	8.6	+0.2	23.2	22.8	21.9	18.4	16.4	−2.0
North central . . .	11.5	9.0	6.4	5.7	5.5	−0.2	19.6	16.3	13.2	11.5	10.2	−1.3	25.9	23.6	25.2	22.5	18.2	−4.4
South.	8.5	7.8	6.1	6.6	5.7	−0.9	16.3	15.7	14.3	11.3	10.1	−1.3	24.2	19.4	15.5	16.6	16.3	−0.3
West	3.8	4.9	2.6	2.9	2.4	−0.5	9.1	7.8	7.0	7.8	6.0	−1.8	17.3	16.9	13.4	9.5	11.8	+2.2
Race/Ethnicity[1]																		
White.	9.7	9.0	7.5	6.0	5.3	−0.8	19.1	17.7	15.5	13.3	11.4	−1.9	26.9	25.7	23.8	21.8	19.5	−2.3
Black.	3.8	3.2	2.8	2.8	2.9	+0.1	5.3	5.2	5.2	5.0	4.3	−0.7	7.7	8.0	7.5	6.4	5.4	−1.0
Hispanic.	8.5	7.1	5.0	4.4	3.7	−0.6	9.1	8.8	7.4	6.4	6.0	−0.4	14.0	15.7	12.0	9.2	8.0	−1.2

(1) For each of these groups, data for the specified year and previous year have been combined to increase sample size and thus provide a more reliable estimate.

Some Benefits of Quitting Smoking

Source: American Cancer Society, Inc., 1599 Clifton Road NE, Atlanta, GA 30329-4251; phone: (800) 227-2345

Within 20 Minutes
• Blood pressure drops to a level close to that before the last cigarette
• Temperature of hands and feet increases to normal

Within 8 Hours
• Carbon monoxide level in the blood drops to normal

Within 24 Hours
• Chance of heart attack decreases

Within 2 Weeks to 3 Months
• Circulation improves

• Lung function increases up to 30%

Within 1 to 9 Months
• Coughing, sinus congestion, fatigue, and shortness of breath decrease
• Cilia regain normal function in the lungs, increasing the ability to handle mucus, clean the lungs, and reduce infection

Within 1 Year
• Excess risk of coronary heart disease is half that of a smoker's

Within 5 Years
• Stroke risk is reduced to that of a non-smoker 5-15 years after quitting

Within 10 Years
• Lung cancer death rate about half that of a continuing smoker's
• Risk of cancer of the mouth, throat, esophagus, bladder, kidney, and pancreas decreases

Within 15 Years
• Risk of coronary heart disease is that of a nonsmoker's

Cancer Prevention

Source: American Cancer Society, 1599 Clifton Road NE, Atlanta, GA 30329-4251; phone: (800) 227-2345

PRIMARY PREVENTION: Modifiable determinants of cancer risk.

Smoking	Lung cancer mortality rates are about 22 times higher for current male smokers, and 12 times higher for current female smokers, than for those who have never smoked. Smoking accounts for about 30% of all cancer deaths in the U.S. Tobacco use is responsible for nearly 1 in 5 deaths in the U.S. Smoking is associated with cancer of the lung, mouth, nasal cavities, pharynx, larynx, esophagus, stomach, pancreas, liver, uterine cervix, kidney, bladder, and myeloid leukemia.
Nutrition and Diet	Risk for colon, rectum, breast (among postmenopausal women), kidney, prostate, and endometrial cancers increases in obese people. While a diet high in fat may be a factor in the development of certain cancers, particularly cancer of the colon and rectum, prostate, and endometrium, the link between obesity and cancer is more the result of an imbalance between caloric intake and energy expenditure than fat per se. Eating 5 or more servings of fruits and vegetables each day, and eating other foods from plant sources (especially grains and beans), may reduce risk for many cancers. Physical activity can help protect against some cancers, and help to maintain a healthy weight.
Sunlight	Many of the one million skin cancers that are diagnosed annually could have been prevented by protection from the sun's rays. Epidemiological evidence shows that sun exposure is a major factor in the development of melanoma and that the incidence rates are increasing around the world.
Alcohol	Heavy drinking, especially when accompanied by cigarette smoking or smokeless tobacco use, increases risk of cancers of the mouth, larynx, pharynx, esophagus, and liver. Studies have also noted an association between regular alcohol consumption and an increased risk of breast cancer.
Smokeless Tobacco	Use of chewing tobacco or snuff increases risk of cancers of the mouth and pharynx. The excess risk of cancer of the cheek and gum may reach nearly 50-fold among long-term snuff users.
Estrogen	Estrogen replacement therapy (ERT) to control menopausal symptoms can increase the risk of endometrial cancer. However, adding progesterone to estrogen (hormone replacement therapy, or HRT) helps to minimize this risk. Most studies suggest that long-term use (5 years or more) of HRT after menopause increases the risk of breast cancer, and recent studies suggest that risks from taking HRT exceed benefits. The benefits and risks of the use of HRT or ERT by menopausal women should be discussed carefully by the woman and her doctor.
Radiation	Excessive exposure to ionizing radiation can increase cancer risk. Medical and dental X rays are adjusted to deliver the lowest dose possible without sacrificing image quality. Excessive radon exposure in the home may increase lung cancer risk, especially in cigarette smokers. If levels are found to be too high, remedial actions should be taken.
Environmental Hazards	Exposure to various chemicals (including benzene, asbestos, vinyl chloride, arsenic, and aflatoxin) increases risk of various cancers. Risk of lung cancer from asbestos is greatly increased when combined with smoking.

Cancer-Detection Guidelines

SECONDARY PREVENTION: Steps to diagnose a cancer or precursor as early as possible after it has developed.

For people having periodic health examinations, a cancer-related checkup should include health counseling and, depending on a person's age, might include examinations for cancers of the thyroid, oral cavity, skin, lymph nodes, testes, and ovaries, as well as for some nonmalignant diseases. Special tests for certain cancer sites for individuals at average risk are recommended as outlined below:

Breast Cancer	Yearly mammograms starting at age 40 and continuing for as long as a woman is in good health.
	Breast clinical physical exams should be part of a periodic health exam, about every three years for women in their 20s and 30s and every year for women 40 and over.
	Women should report any breast change promptly to their healthcare providers. Breast self-exam is an option for women starting in their 20s.
	Women at increased risk (e.g., family history, genetic tendency, past breast cancer) should speak with their doctors about the benefits and limitations of starting mammography screening earlier, having additional tests (e.g., breast ultrasound or MRI), or having more frequent exams.
Cervical Cancer	Women should begin cervical cancer screening about 3 years after they begin having vaginal intercourse, but no later than when they are 21 years old. Screening should be done every year with the regular Pap test or every 2 years using the newer liquid-based Pap test.
	Beginning at age 30, women who have had 3 normal Pap test results in a row may get screened every 2 to 3 years. Women who have certain risk factors such as diethylstilbestrol (DES) exposure before birth, HIV infection, or a weakened immune system due to organ transplant, chemotherapy, or chronic steroid use should continue to be screened annually.
	Another reasonable option for women over 30 is to get screened every 3 years (but no more frequently) with either the conventional or liquid-based Pap test, *plus* the HPV DNA test.
	Women 70 years of age or older who have had 3 or more normal Pap tests in a row and no abnormal Pap test results in the last 10 years may choose to stop having cervical cancer screening. Women with a history of cervical cancer, DES exposure before birth, HIV infection or a weakened immune system should continue to have screening as long as they are in good health. Women who have had a total hysterectomy (removal of the uterus and cervix) may also choose to stop having cervical cancer screening, unless the surgery was done as a treatment for cervical cancer or precancer. Women who have had a hysterectomy without removal of the cervix should continue to follow the guidelines above.
Colorectal Cancer	Beginning at age 50, both men and women should follow one of these testing schedules: Yearly fecal occult blood test; or flexible sigmoidoscopy every five years; or yearly fecal occult blood test plus flexible sigmoidoscopy every 5 years; or colonoscopy every 10 years; or double-contrast barium enema every 5-10 years. **Note:** Persons known to be at increased risk for colorectal cancer (due to inflammatory bowel disease, personal or family history, etc.) need to begin screening at an early age and may need more frequent screening.
Endometrial Cancer	For women with or at high risk of hereditary nonpolyposis colon cancer (HNPCC), annual screening including endometrial biopsy should be obtained beginning at age 35.
Prostate Cancer	Both Prostate-Specific Antigen (PSA) and Digital Rectal Examination (DRE) should be offered annually, beginning at age 50, to men who have at least a 10-year life expectancy. Men at high risk, such as African-Americans and men who have a first-degree relative (father, brother, or son) diagnosed with prostate cancer at an early age, should begin testing at age 45. Health care professionals should give men the opportunity to openly discuss the benefits and risks of testing at annual checkups. Men should actively participate in the decision by learning about prostate cancer and the pros and cons of early detection and treatment of prostate cancer, so that they can make an informed decision about testing.
Skin Cancer	Adults should practice skin self-exam regularly. Suspicious lesions should be evaluated promptly by a physician.

Breast Cancer

Source: American Cancer Society, Inc., 1599 Clifton Road NE, Atlanta, GA 30329-4251; phone: (800) 227-2345

Each year more than 200,000 women and 1,000 men in the United States are diagnosed with breast cancer, and about 140,000 women and 400 men die from it. Breast cancer is the 2nd largest cause of cancer death for women in the U.S. (lung cancer ranks first), but mortality rates have been declining, especially among younger women, probably because of earlier detection and improved treatment.

The risk for breast cancer increases as a woman ages. It is also higher for women with a personal or family history, a long menstrual history (menstrual periods that started early and ended late in life), recent use of oral contraceptives (birth control pills), long-term use of postmenopausal hormone replacement therapy, and no children or no live birth until age 30 or older. Other risk factors for the disease include alcohol consumption and obesity. Inherited mutations such as in the BRCA1 and BRCA2 genes greatly increase a woman's risk for breast cancer, but these mutations probably account for less than 10% of all breast cancers. By far, the majority of women who develop breast cancer have no family history.

Breast cancer is often manifested first as an abnormality that appears on a mammogram, which is a special type of x-ray. Physical signs and symptoms that show up later, which may be detectable by a woman or her doctor, include a breast lump and, less commonly, breast thickening, swelling, distortion, or tenderness; skin irritation or dimpling; or pain, scaliness, or retraction of the nipple. Breast pain is more commonly associated with benign (noncancerous) conditions.

Studies show that **early detection** increases survival and treatment options. The American Cancer Society (ACS) recommends yearly mammograms starting at age 40. Breast clinical physical exams should be part of a periodic health exam, about every 3 years for women in their 20s and 30s and every year for women 40 and over. Women should report any breast change promptly to their health care providers. Breast self-exam is an option for women starting in their 20s. Women who may be at increased risk for the disease because of family history, genetic tendency, or past breast cancer should speak with their doctors about the benefits and limitations of starting mammography screening earlier, having additional tests (e.g. breast ultrasound or MRI), or having more frequent exams. Although most breast lumps that are detected are noncancerous, any suspicious lump needs to be biopsied.

Treatment for breast cancer may involve lumpectomy (local removal of a tumor), mastectomy (surgical removal of the breast), radiation therapy, chemotherapy, hormone therapy, immunotherapy, or some combination of these. For early-stage breast cancer, long-term survival rates following lumpectomy plus radiation therapy are similar to survival rates after modified radical mastectomy.

Numerous **drugs** that may **prevent** breast cancer or improve its treatment are being studied. One is **tamoxifen**, a synthetic hormone that blocks the action of estrogen in the breast. Already used for treating breast cancer, it has been shown to reduce the likelihood of developing the disease in women considered at higher than average risk, including women age 60 and older. Unfortunately, tamoxifen also has dangerous side effects, such as increased risk of uterine cancer and blood clots in the lungs. Research is also being done on another drug, **raloxifene**, which is approved for preventing osteoporosis in postmenopausal women. It is now being directly compared to tamoxifen in a large clinical study to evaluate its effect on breast cancer risk.

Diabetes

Source: American Diabetes Association, 1701 N Beauregard St., Alexandria, VA 22311; phone: (800) 342-2383

Diabetes is a chronic disease in which the body does not produce or properly use **insulin**, a hormone needed to convert sugar, starches, and other foods into energy necessary for daily life. Both genetics and environment appear to play roles in the onset of diabetes. This disease, which has no cure, is the 5th-leading cause of death by disease in the U.S. According to death certificate data, diabetes contributed to 213,000 deaths in 2000. It is estimated that there are 18.2 million Americans with diabetes, 5.9 million of whom are undiagnosed.

In 1997, the American Diabetes Association issued **new guidelines for diagnosing diabetes**. The recommendations include: lowering the acceptable level of blood sugar in a fasting glucose test from 140 mg of glucose/deciliter of blood to 126 mg/deciliter; testing all adults 45 years and older, and then every 3 years if normal; and testing at a younger age, or more frequently, in high-risk individuals. The American Diabetes Association supports studies that have proven that detection at an earlier stage and modest lifestyle changes will help prevent or delay complications.

There are 2 major types of diabetes:

Type 1 (formerly known as insulin dependent, or juvenile diabetes). The body produces very little or no insulin; disease most often begins in childhood or early adulthood. People with type 1 diabetes must take daily insulin injections to stay alive.

Type 2 (formerly known as non-insulin dependent, or adult-onset diabetes). The body does not produce enough or cannot properly use insulin. It is the most common form of the disease (90-95% of cases in people over age 20) and often begins later in life.

Warning Signs of Diabetes

Type 1 Diabetes (usually occurs suddenly):

frequent urination	unusual weight loss
unusual thirst	extreme fatigue
extreme hunger	irritability

Type 2 Diabetes (occurs less suddenly):

any type 1 symptoms	cuts/bruises slow to heal
frequent infections	tingling/numbness in hands or feet
blurred vision	recurring skin, gum, or bladder infections

Pre-Diabetes

Among U.S. adults 40-74 years of age, 41 million (40.1% of the population) have **pre-diabetes**, the state that occurs when a person's blood glucose levels are higher than normal but not high enough for a diagnosis of diabetes.

In a recent study, about 11% of people with pre-diabetes developed type 2 diabetes during each year of the study. Other studies show that most people with pre-diabetes develop type 2 diabetes in 10 years.

Complications of Diabetes

People often have diabetes many years before it is diagnosed. During that time, serious complications have a chance to develop. Potential complications include:

Blindness. Diabetes is the leading cause of blindness in people ages 20-74. Each year, from 12,000 to 24,000 people lose their sight because of diabetes.

Kidney disease. 10% to 21% of all people with diabetes develop kidney disease. In 2001, more than 2,813 people initiated treatment for end-stage renal disease (kidney failure) because of diabetes.

Amputations. Diabetes is the most frequent cause of non-traumatic lower limb amputations. The risk of a leg amputation is 15 to 40 times greater for a person with diabetes than for the average American. Each year, an estimated 80,000 people lose a foot or leg as a result of complications brought on by diabetes.

Heart disease and stroke. People with diabetes are 2 to 4 times more likely to have heart disease (more than 77,000 deaths due to heart disease annually). And they are 2 to 4 times more likely to suffer a stroke.

Alzheimer's Disease

Source: Alzheimer's Association, 225 N Michigan Ave., 17th Fl., Chicago, IL 60601-7633; phone: (800) 272-3900; www.alz.org

Alzheimer's disease, the most common form of dementia, is a progressive, degenerative disease of the brain in which nerve cells deteriorate and die for unknown reasons. Its first symptoms usually involve impaired memory and confusion about recent events. As the disease advances, it results in greater impairment of memory, thinking, behavior, and physical health.

The **rate of progression** of Alzheimer's varies, ranging from 3 to 20 years; the average length of time from onset of symptoms until death is 8 years. Eventually, affected individuals lose their ability to care for themselves and become susceptible to infections of the lungs, urinary tract, or other organs as they grow progressively debilitated.

Alzheimer's disease affects an estimated 4.5 million Americans, striking men and women of all ethnic groups. Although most people diagnosed with Alzheimer's are older than age 60, some cases occur in people in their 40s and 50s. An estimated 10% of the population over age 65 have Alzheimer's, and the disease affects almost half of those over 85. In the United States, annual costs of diagnosis, treatment, and long-term care are estimated at $100 billion.

Diagnosis involves a comprehensive evaluation that may include a complete health history, a physical examination, neurological and mental status assessments, and other testing as needed. Skilled health care professionals can generally diagnose Alzheimer's with about 90% accuracy. Other conditions that can cause similar symptoms include depression, drug interactions, nutritional imbalances, infections such as AIDS, meningitis, and syphilis, and other forms of dementia, such as those associated with stroke, Huntington's disease, Parkinson's disease, frontotemporal dementia, and vascular disease. Absolute confirmation of diagnosis requires a brain biopsy or autopsy.

Treatments for cognitive and behavioral symptoms are available, but no intervention has yet been developed that prevents Alzheimer's or reverses its course. Some research suggests that risk factors for heart disease, such as high blood pressure, elevated cholesterol, and excess body weight may also increase risk of developing Alzheimer's. Studies also suggest that staying physically and mentally active and socially connected may be associated with a lower risk for the disease.

Providing care for people with Alzheimer's is physically and psychologically demanding. Nearly 70% of affected individuals live at home, where family or friends care for them. In advanced stages of the disease, many individuals require care in a nursing home. Nearly half of all nursing home residents in the U.S. have Alzheimer's.

People with Alzheimer's need a safe, stable environment and a regular daily schedule offering appropriate stimulation. Physical exercise and social interaction are important, as is proper nutrition. Security is also a consideration, because many people with Alzheimer's tend to wander. An identification bracelet listing the person's name, address, and condition may help ensure the safe return of an individual who wanders.

Warning Signs of Alzheimer's Disease

- Recent memory loss that affects job performance
- Inability to learn new information
- Difficulty with everyday tasks such as cooking or dressing
- Inability to remember simple words
- Use of inappropriate words when communicating
- Disorientation of time and place
- Poor or decreased judgment
- Problems with abstract thinking
- Putting objects in inappropriate places
- Rapid changes in mood or behavior
- Increased irritability, anxiety, depression, confusion, and restlessness
- Prolonged loss of initiative

Acquired Immune Deficiency Syndrome
Source: Centers for Disease Control and Prevention; www.cdc.gov

AIDS (Acquired Immune Deficiency Syndrome) is caused by the human immunodeficiency virus (**HIV**). HIV kills or disables crucial cells of the immune system, progressively destroying the body's ability to fight disease.

HIV is commonly spread through unprotected sexual contact with an infected partner. It is also spread through contact with infected blood. Where modern screening techniques are used it is rare to contract HIV from transfusion, but it can be contracted when intravenous drug users share syringes with others. Though HIV can be spread through semen, vaginal fluids, and breast milk, there is no evidence it can be spread through saliva. The rate of transmission from a pregnant woman to her infant is about 25% without treatment, but can be reduced to less than 2% with treatment. Studies have indicated no evidence of HIV transmission through casual contact such as the sharing of food utensils, towels and bedding, telephones, or toilet seats.

Some people experience flu-like symptoms a short time after infection with HIV, and scientists estimate that about half of those infected with HIV develop more serious, often chronic symptoms within ten years. Even when symptoms are not present, HIV is active in the body, multiplying, infecting, and killing CD4+ T cells, or "T-helper cells," the crucial immune cells that signal other cells in the immune system to perform their functions.

The term **AIDS** applies to the most advanced stages of HIV infection. According to the official definition set by the Centers for Disease Control and Prevention (CDC), an HIV–infected person with fewer than 200 CD4+ T cells can be said to have AIDS. (Healthy adults usually have 1,000 or more). An HIV-infected person, regardless of T cell count, is diagnosed with AIDS if he or she develops one of 26 conditions that typically affect people with advanced HIV. Most of these conditions are "opportunistic infections" that occur when the immune system is so ravaged by HIV that the body cannot fight off certain bacteria, viruses and microbes.

Months or years prior to the onset of AIDS, many people experience such symptoms as swollen glands, lack of energy, fevers and sweats, and skin rashes. People with full-blown AIDS may develop infections of the intestinal tract, lungs, brain, eyes, and other organs, with a variety of symptoms, and may become severely debilitated. They also are prone to developing certain cancers, especially those caused by viruses, such as Kaposi's sarcoma, cervical cancer, and lymphoma. Children with AIDS may have delayed development or failure to thrive.

HIV is primarily **detected** by testing a person's blood for the presence of antibodies (disease-fighting proteins) to HIV. In about 5% of infected individuals, HIV antibodies may take more than 6 months after exposure to reach detectable levels, but in most cases the antibodies are detectable in about 6 weeks. HIV testing may also be performed on oral fluid and urine samples.

The **U.S. Food and Drug Administration** has approved a number of **drugs** that may slow down the growth of HIV in the body and treat the infections and cancers associated with AIDS. The first group of drugs used to treat HIV, called nucleoside analog reverse transcriptase inhibitors (NRTIs), include the drug zidovudine (commonly known as AZT). Non-nucleoside reverse transcriptase inhibitors (NNRTIs) have also been approved to treat HIV. A third class of drugs, called protease inhibitors, are also approved for HIV. In 2003 the FDA granted accelerated approval of Fuzeon for use with other anti-HIV drugs to treat advanced cases of infection. Fuzeon was the first among a new class of medications called fusion inhibitors; drugs in this class interfered with HIV's entry into cells by hindering the fusion of viral and cellular membranes.

Patients are typically given a combination of different drugs, because HIV can much more easily become resistant to a single drug. While these drugs extend the period between HIV infection and serious illness, they do not prevent the spread of the disease to others, and can have severe side effects.

Since there is no vaccine or cure for AIDS, the only **protection** is to avoid activities that carry a risk. When it cannot be known with certainty whether a sexual partner has HIV, the CDC recommends abstinence (the only certain protection), mutual monogamy with an uninfected partner, or correct and consistent use of male latex condoms.

Arthritis
Source: Arthritis Foundation, 1330 West Peachtree Street, Atlanta, GA 30309; phone: (800) 283-7800; www.arthritis.org

The term "arthritis" refers to more than 100 different diseases that cause pain, stiffness, swelling, and restricted movement in joints. The condition is usually chronic. The Centers for Disease Control and Prevention (CDC) estimates that nearly 70 million adults suffer from arthritis and/or chronic joint symptoms. The cause for most types of arthritis is unknown; scientists are studying the roles played by genetics, lifestyle, and the environment.

Symptoms of arthritis may develop either slowly or suddenly. A visit to the doctor is indicated when pain, stiffness, or swelling in a joint or difficulty in moving a joint persists for more than two weeks. To make a diagnosis of arthritis, the doctor records the patient's symptoms and examines joints, looking for any swelling or limited movement. In addition, the doctor checks for other signs often seen with arthritis, such as rashes, mouth sores, or eye involvement. Finally, the doctor may test the blood, urine, or joint fluid, or take X-rays of the joints.

Of the 3 most prevalent forms of arthritis, **osteoarthritis** is the most common, affecting more than 20 million Americans; it usually occurs after age 45. In this type, which is also called degenerative arthritis, the protective cartilage of joints is lost and changes occur in the bone, leading to pain and stiffness. It usually occurs in the fingers, knees, feet, hips, and back.

Fibromyalgia, another common arthritis condition, affects more than 2 million Americans and affects more women than men. In this form, widespread pain and tenderness occur in muscles and their attachments to the bone. Common symptoms include fatigue, disturbed sleep, stiffness, and psychological distress.

Rheumatoid arthritis, which also affects more than 2 million people in the U.S., is one of the most serious and disabling forms of the disease. In this type, which is also more common in women, inflammation of the joints leads to damage of the cartilage and bone. The areas of the body that can be affected are the hands, wrists, feet, knees, ankles, shoulders, neck, jaw, and elbows.

Other forms of arthritis and related conditions include lupus, gout, ankylosing spondylitis, and scleroderma; also related are bursitis and tendinitis, which may result from injuring or overusing a joint.

Medications to treat arthritis include drugs that relieve pain and swelling, such as analgesics, anti-inflammatory drugs, biologic response modifiers, glucocorticoids, or disease-modifying antirheumatic drugs, which tend to slow the disease process. Most treatment programs call for exercise, use of heat or cold, and joint-protection techniques, such as avoiding excess stress on joints, using assistive devices, and controlling weight. In some cases, surgery can help when other treatments fail.

Vioxx

The Merck Corporation voluntarily recalled the arthritis drug Vioxx Sept. 30, 2004, after tests of its effectiveness in preventing recurrence of polyps revealed that long-term use (18 months and over) may increase the risk of heart attack or stroke. Vioxx, which came onto the market in 1999 and was used by about 2 million people worldwide, is in a family of non-steroidal anti-inflammatory drugs known as COX-2 inhibitors. Following the recall, the FDA said it would closely monitor other COX-2 inhibitors, including Celebrex and Bextra, for possible side effects.

Stem Cells

Stem cells are unspecialized cells that, under certain conditions, give rise to specialized cells and, with the correct application, might one day be used on a wide scale to treat disease and regenerate damaged or destroyed tissue. Most research has focused on two types of stem cells, embryonic and adult. **Embryonic** stem cells are found only in embryos, while **adult** stem cells are found in many organs and tissues of the body. (Stem cells can also be obtained from fetuses and umbilical cords.) Embryonic stem cells are particularly promising because they are pluripotent (can turn into any kind of cell in the body) as opposed to adult stem cells, which typically turn only into the kinds of cells that make up the organ or tissue in which they are found. Researchers believe pluripotent cells may be useable to treat many diseases, including Parkinson's and Alzheimer's diseases, spinal cord injury, stroke, burns, heart disease, diabetes, osteoarthritis, and rheumatoid arthritis. But research on embryonic stem cells has been a subject of heated debate, since their extraction destroys the early-stage embryo from which they are derived.

Adult stem cells, such as blood-forming stem cells in bone marrow (called hematopoietic stem cells, or **HSCs**), are the only type of stem cell now commonly used to treat human diseases. Doctors have been transferring HSCs in bone marrow transplants for over 40 years. More advanced techniques of collecting, or "harvesting," HSCs are used to treat leukemia, lymphoma, and certain inherited blood disorders. However, these newer uses have been tested on a very limited number of patients. Some studies have found that adult stem cells appear to have a clinical potential for treating diabetes and other diseases, but other research has been less encouraging, so the promise of adult stem cells remains in debate in the scientific community.

Depression

Source: National Institute of Mental Health; Reviewed by: Michele Berk, Ph.D

Depression is a serious illness that affects thoughts, feelings, and the ability to function in everyday life. It strikes across all age groups, and often goes unrecognized or inadequately treated. A study released in 2003 by the National Institutes of Health estimated that 13-14 million Americans suffer from depression in any given year and that over 16% have depression at some point in life. Young people are among those at risk; the study found that in a one-year period, 3 times as many persons with depression were 18 to 29 years old as were 60 or older.

Nearly twice as many women as men suffer from a depressive illness in a given year. Although conventional wisdom holds that depression is most closely associated with menopause, in fact, the childbearing years are marked by the highest rates of depression, followed by the years prior to menopause. The influence of hormones on depression in women has been an active area of NIMH research.

In a given year, 1-2% of people over age 65 living in the community (outside of institutions) suffer from major depression. Depression frequently occurs with other physical illnesses, including heart disease, stroke, cancer, and diabetes. It is not a normal part of aging.

The **treatments** that are now available can alleviate symptoms, and with awareness growing, more people with depression are seeking the help they need. But many depressed people—and those around them—still fail to realize that they have an illness or could benefit from medical help. The 2003 NIH study also concluded that more than half of those seeking help do not get adequate treatment, often because they consult family practioners who do not deal aggressively enough with the problem.

Symptoms and Types of Depression

Symptoms of depression include the following:
• persistent sad mood
• loss of interest or pleasure in activities once enjoyed, including sex
• significant change in appetite or body weight
• difficulty sleeping or oversleeping
• physical slowing down or agitation
• loss of energy
• feelings of worthlessness or inappropriate guilt
• difficulty thinking or concentrating
• recurrent thoughts of death or suicide

A diagnosis of **major depressive disorder** (or **unipolar major depression**) is made if an individual has 5 or more of these symptoms during the same two-week period. Unipolar major depression typically comes to the fore in episodes that recur during a person's lifetime.

Bipolar disorder (or **manic-depressive illness**) is characterized by episodes of major depression as well as episodes of mania—abnormally and persistently elevated mood or irritability, accompanied by such symptoms as inflated self-esteem, less need for sleep, increased talkativeness, racing thoughts, distractibility, agitation, and excessive involvement in pleasurable activities that have a high potential for painful consequences. While sharing some of the features of major depression, bipolar disorder is a distinct illness.

Dysthymic disorder (or **dysthymia**), a less severe yet typically more chronic form of depression, is diagnosed when a depressed mood persists for at least two years in adults (one year in children or adolescents) and is accompanied by at least 2 other depressive symptoms. Many people with dysthymic disorder also experience major depressive episodes.

In contrast to the normal experiences of sadness, or passing moods, depression is extreme and persistent and can interfere significantly with an individual's ability to function. A recent study sponsored by the World Health Organization and the World Bank found unipolar major depression to be the leading cause of disability in the U.S. and worldwide.

Treatments for Depression

A variety of **medicines** are used to treat depression. These drugs influence the functioning of certain neurotransmitters in the brain, primarily serotonin and norepinephrine, known as monoamines. Older drugs—so-called tricyclic antidepressants (TCAs) and monoamine oxidase inhibitors (MAOIs)—affect the functioning of both of these neurotransmitters. But they can have strong side effects or, in the case of MAOIs, require dietary restrictions. Newer medications, such as the selective serotonin reuptake inhibitors (SSRIs), have fewer side effects. All of these medications can be effective, but some people respond to one type and not another.

NIMH research has shown that certain types of **psychotherapy**, particularly cognitive-behavioral therapy (CBT) and interpersonal therapy (IPT), can help relieve depression. CBT helps patients change the negative styles of thinking and behaving often associated with depression. IPT focuses on working through disturbed personal relationships that may contribute to depression. Studies of adults have shown that a combination of psychotherapy and antidepressant medication is most effective in treating moderate-to-severe depression.

Electroconvulsive therapy (ECT) has been found effective in treating 80-90% of cases of severe depression, particularly those that have not responded to other forms of treatment. ECT involves producing a seizure in the brain of a patient under general anesthesia by applying electrical stimulation through electrodes placed on the scalp. Memory loss and other cognitive problems are common, but typically short-lived, side effects.

For more information, start with the website www.nimh. nih.gov/publicat/depressionmenu.cfm

IT'S A FACT: Preliminary data in 2004 from a medical screening program funded by the Centers for Disease Control showed that nearly half of more than 1,000 screened rescue and recovery workers and volunteers who responded to the World Trade Center attacks of Sept. 11, 2001, have persistent respiratory problems, and more than half have symptoms of psychological stress.

Eating Disorders

Source: National Institute of Mental Health

Eating disorders involve serious disturbances in eating behavior, usually in the form of extreme and unhealthy reduction of food intake or severe overeating. They are not due to a failure of will; rather, they are real and treatable medical illnesses in which certain patterns of behavior get out of control. The **main types** are anorexia nervosa, bulimia nervosa, and binge-eating disorder. These disorders usually develop in adolescence or early adulthood and often occur with other illnesses such as depression, substance abuse, and anxiety disorders. They are much more common among females; only about 5 to 15% of anorexia or bulimia patients and 35% of binge eaters are male.

If not treated, eating disorders can lead serious complications, including heart conditions and kidney failure, which may lead to death.

Anorexia nervosa affects an estimated 0.5 to 3.7% of females during their lifetime. Symptoms include resistance to maintaining weight at even minimally normal levels, intense fear of gaining weight, exaggerated importance of body weight or shape in one's self image, and infrequent or absent menstrual periods. Anorexics see themselves as overweight even though they are dangerously thin. In response, they avoid food, and often takes other extreme measures to lose weight, such as compulsive exercise or purging by means of vomiting or laxatives and enemas. While some anorexics fully recover after a single episode, others may relapse frequently or experience chronic deterioration.

Bulimia nervosa affects an estimated 1.1 to 4.2% of females. It is characterized by recurrent uncontrolled binge-eating episodes followed by a compensatory behavior to prevent weight gain, such as self-induced vomiting, excessive exercise, or fasting. Persons with bulimia usually end up weighing within a normal range for their age and height, but they may fear gaining weight and feel intensely dissatisfied with their bodies. They often perform their behaviors in secret, feeling ashamed when they binge and relieved when they purge.

Binge-eating disorder (not officially approved as a psychiatric diagnosis) affects an estimated 2% to 5% of Americans in any given 6-month period. Like bulimia, a binge-eating disorder involves episodes of excessive eating during which the sufferer may lose all control, but individuals with this disorder do not compensate by purging, exercising, or fasting. Many are thus overweight, and the shame associated with the illness can lead to further bingeing.

Eating disorder sufferers may not admit they are ill and may resist treatment. Early diagnosis and a comprehensive treatment program are essential to recovery. Some patients may need immediate hospitalization. For anorexia, treatment usually follows 3 established steps: weight restoration (usually in an inpatient hospital setting), treatment of any accompanying psychological disturbances, and achieving long-term remission or recovery. Medications may be helpful in treating underlying depression or anxiety. Families are sometimes involved in the therapeutic process.

Schizophrenia

Source: National Institute of Mental Health; Reviewed by: Michele Berk, Ph.D

Schizophrenia is a chronic, severe, disabling brain disease that affects about 1% of the U.S. population, with more than 2 million Americans suffering from it in any given year. Although the disorder affects men and women with equal frequency, onset usually occurs earlier in men, mostly in their late teens or early 20s; women are generally affected in their 20s and early 30s. People with schizophrenia may have such symptoms as distorted perceptions of reality, hallucinations (especially hearing internal voices not heard by others), delusions (sometimes including believing that others are reading their minds, controlling their thoughts, or plotting to harm them), disordered thinking, and reduced emotional expressiveness. Suicide is a serious danger in people with schizophrenia, with a rate of approximately 10%.

There is **no known single cause** of schizophrenia. It is known that the disorder runs in families (the child of a sufferer, for example, has a 10% chance of developing schizophrenia), and scientists are studying several regions of the human genome to identify genes that may confer susceptibility. It is likely but not certain that the disorder is associated with an imbalance in the complex chemical systems of the brain. Studies of people with schizophrenia have found subtle abnormalities of their brain structure, although these abnormalities do not occur in every person with schizophrenia, and they are sometimes found in people who are not schizophrenic.

Because the causes of schizophrenia are not fully understood, **treatment** focuses on limiting the symptoms through the use of **antipsychotic drugs** supplemented by pshychosocial treatment. The majority of people with schizophrenia show substantial improvement while taking such medication, though some are not helped and a few do not need them. Antipsychotic medications are often effective in treating hallucinations and delusions. However, while drug treatment may reduce the frequency and intensity of psychotic episodes, it cannot be expected to prevent them. Antipsychotic medications may also have long-term side effects such as tardive dyskinesia (TD), characterized by involuntary movements in facial muscles and other parts of the body, although newer medications lower the risk of TD. Because of side effects and for other reasons, many people with schizophrenia do not adhere to treatment.

Once psychotic symptoms are under control through medication, **psychosocial therapy** can be effective in addressing behavioral problems, such as difficulty with communication, motivation, self-care, and establishing relationships with others. Contrary to a popular misconception, schizophrenia is not a "split-personality" disorder. Also, studies indicate that, except in cases where criminal violence or a substance-abuse problem existed before the onset of the disease, schizophrenics are not especially prone to violence. The **outlook** for patients has improved over the past 25 years. Although no totally effective therapy has yet been devised, many schizophrenics who adhere to treatment improve enough to lead independent, satisfying lives.

Organ and Tissue Donation

Source: U.S. Dept of Health and Human Services

Each year, over 20,000 Americans receive organ transplants that save or enhance their lives, but about 6,000 others die while waiting for a transplant. Over 80,000 people are on the waiting list for transplants, and there is an acute shortage of available organs to transplant. A similar situation exists with regard to tissue. In Apr. 2001, Health and Human Services Sec. Tommy G. Thompson announced a **Gift of Life Donation Initiative** aimed at encouraging organ donation. The HHS plan included enlisting the cooperation of major corporations, issuing a model donor card (which would identify its carrier as someone wishing to donate organs and/or tissue), and investigating donor registries as a way of ensuring that an individual's intent to donate is communicated.

Officials stress that individuals wishing to donate organs/tissues should inform their families, so that they know this when the issue is brought up by medical personnel. Prospective donors should also carry a signed organ donor card, and indicate their intentions on their driver's license. The organs that can be donated are the heart, kidneys, pancreas, lungs, liver, and intestines. The tissues are bone marrow, corneas, skin, heart valves, and connective tissue.

Officials stress that an agreement to donate one's organs after death will not affect the quality of medical care and that the process does not disfigure the body or prevent an open-casket funeral. There is no cost to the donor's family; all costs are borne by the recipient. A number of factors determine patients' priority in receiving an organ, such as blood and tissue type, medical urgency, location, and time on the waiting list. Organs and tissues cannot be bought or sold; this is illegal.

For more information, go to www.organdonor.gov/faq.html or call UNOS at 1-888-894-6361.

IT'S A FACT: In the U.S., there is an average of 13 cases of plague reported each year. This is the same disease that killed off over one-third of the European population during the "Black Death" in the 1300s and over 12 million people in China in the 1800s. Mostly caused by bites from infected animals or fleas carrying plague, it is actually a bacterial disease treatable with antibiotics. Today, it has a survival rate of about 85% when detected early.

Autism

Source: National Center on Birth Defects and Developmental Disabilities, Centers for Disease Control and Prevention; National Dissemination Center for Children With Disabilities

Autism is the common name for a group of so-called autism spectrum disorders (ASDs), certain developmental disabilities associated with an abnormality of the brain. These include autistic disorder, pervasive developmental disorder-not otherwise specified (PDD-NOS), and Asperger's syndrome. Autism is identified more commonly today than in the past; whether it is more common is not known. The National Dissemination Center for Children With Disabilities estimates that it affects 5 to 15 children per 1,000. Symptoms typically start to appear very early in childhood and last throughout life. Males are 4 times more likely than females to be autistic.

Autism covers a **wide range of behavior**; symptoms vary, and a symptom may appear strong in one person, mild or absent in another. In general, autistic people have unusual ways of learning, paying attention, and reacting; most have some problem with social and communications skills. They may prefer to be alone and have trouble understanding others' feelings. About 40% do not talk at all; others have echolalia, meaning they repeat what others say to them. Their voices may sound flat or they may seem unable to control how loudly or softly they talk. Some autistic people can speak well but have difficulty listening. Autistic people may tend to repeat certain behaviors and resist variations in daily routines. They may develop complex abilities more readily than simpler ones. For example, autistic children may be able to read very long words but not identify the sound the letter p makes.

The **cause** of autism is unknown; possible factors include neurological damage and biochemical imbalance in the brain. There is no known cure, but doctors believe early intensive training can help autistic children develop new skills and learn better how to talk, play, interact, and learn. Special education programs are available starting at age 3. While medicines have been effective in relieving some symptoms of autism, behavioral training is currently the most effective treatment.

For further information see www.cdc.gov/ncbddd/dddd autism.htm

Allergies and Asthma

Source: Asthma and Allergy Foundation of America, 1233 20th St., NW, Suite 402, Wash., DC 20036; phone: (800) 7-ASTHMA; www.aafa.org

One out of five Americans suffers from **allergies**. People with allergies have extra-sensitive immune systems that react to normally harmless substances. Allergens that may produce this reaction include plant pollens, dust mites, or animal dander; plants such as poison ivy; certain drugs, such as penicillin; and certain foods such as eggs, milk, nuts, or seafood.

The tendency to develop allergies is usually inherited, and allergies usually begin to appear in childhood, but they can show up at any age. Common allergies for infants include food allergies and eczema (patches of dry skin). Older children and adults may often develop allergic rhinitis (hay fever), a reaction to an inhaled allergen; common symptoms include nasal congestion, runny nose, and sneezing.

It is best to avoid contact with the allergen, if feasible. In some cases, medications such as antihistamines are used to decrease the reaction, and there are treatments aimed at gradually desensitizing the patient to the allergen. Other effective allergy treatments include decongestants, eye drops, and ointments.

Some people with allergies also have **asthma**, and allergens are a common asthma trigger. Asthma is a disease of chronic inflammation affecting the passages that carry air into and out of the lungs. It can develop at any age.

People with asthma have inflamed, supersensitive airways that tighten and become filled with mucus during an asthma episode. Wheezing, difficulty in breathing, tightening of the chest, and coughing are common symptoms. Asthma can progress through stages to become life-threatening if not controlled. Emergency **symptoms** include: no improvement minutes after initial treatment; struggling to breathe; hard time breathing, with patient hunched over and/or chest and neck pulled in with breathing; trouble walking or talking; stopping activity and not starting activity again; gray or blue lips or fingernails.

Besides common allergens, tobacco smoke, cold air, and pollution can trigger an asthma attack, as can viral infections or physical exercise that taxes the breathing. Of course, an accurate diagnosis by a physician is important. Although there is no cure for asthma or allergies, they can be controlled with medications and lifestyle changes.

Spending on Health in the 50 Most Populous Countries[1]

Source: *The World Health Report 2004*, The World Health Organization

Country	Spending on health as % of GDP	Per capita spending on health[2]	Country	Spending on health as % of GDP	Per capita spending on health[2]
Afghanistan	5.2	$8	Myanmar	2.1	197
Algeria	4.1	73	Nepal	5.2	12
Argentina	9.5	679	Nigeria	3.4	15
Australia	9.2	1,741	North Korea	2.5	22
Bangladesh	3.5	12	Pakistan	3.9	16
Brazil	7.6	222	Peru	4.7	97
Canada	9.5	2,163	Philippines	3.3	30
China	5.5	49	Poland	6.1	289
Colombia	5.5	105	Romania	6.5	117
Congo, Dem. Rep. of the	3.5	5	Russia	5.4	115
Egypt	3.9	46	Saudi Arabia	4.6	375
Ethiopia	3.6	3	South Africa	8.6	222
France	9.6	2,109	South Korea	6.0	532
Germany	10.8	2,412	Spain	7.5	1,088
Ghana	4.7	12	Sudan	3.5	14
India	5.1	24	Tanzania	4.4	12
Indonesia	2.4	16	Thailand	3.7	69
Iran	6.3	350	Turkey	5.0	109
Iraq	3.2	225	Uganda	5.9	14
Italy	8.4	1,584	Ukraine	4.3	33
Japan	8.0	2,627	United Kingdom	7.6	1,835
Kenya	7.8	29	**United States**	**13.9**	**4,887**
Malaysia	3.8	143	Uzbekistan	3.6	17
Mexico	6.1	370	Venezuela	6.0	307
Morocco	5.1	59	Vietnam	5.1	21

(1) Populations based on mid-2004 U.S. Census Bureau estimates. (2) At average exchange rates.

IT'S A FACT: Some people really do need their caffeine fix, according to a study published in the October 2004 issue of *Psychopharmacology*. Researchers at Johns Hopkins University concluded that as little as one cup of coffee per day can produce a caffeine addiction, with withdrawal symptoms that can include headache, fatigue, and even nausea.

Complementary and Alternative Medicine

Source: National Center for Complementary and Alternative Medicine, National Institutes of Health (NIH)

Complementary and alternative medicine (CAM) comprises a wide variety of healing philosophies, approaches, and therapies. It includes treatments and health care practices not widely taught in medical schools, not generally used in hospitals, and not usually reimbursed by health insurance companies. While some scientific evidence exists regarding some therapies, for most there are key questions that are yet to be answered through well-designed scientific studies—questions such as whether they are safe and whether they work for the diseases or medical conditions for which they are used. The National Institutes of Health cautions people not to seek alternative therapies without the consultation of a licensed health care provider.

The National Center for Complementary and Alternative Medicine (NCCAM), a part of the National Institutes of Health, distinguishes between **complementary medicine**, used together with conventional medicine (as, for instance, the use of aromatherapy to lessen discomfort after surgery) and **alternative medicine**, used in place of conventional medicine (as, for instance, adopting a special diet to treat cancer instead of using the conventional approaches of chemotherapy, radiation, or surgery). The list of what is considered to be CAM changes continually, as therapies proven to be safe and effective become adopted into conventional health care and as new approaches to health care emerge. Worldwide, only about 10-30% of health care is provided by conventional practitioners; the remaining 70-90% involves alternative practices. An estimated 1 in 3 Americans uses some form of alternative medicine.

The NCCAM classifies CAM in 5 categories:

Alternative medical systems are built upon complete systems of theory and practice. Often, these systems have evolved apart from and earlier than the conventional medical approach used in the U.S. Examples of alternative medical systems that have developed in Western cultures include homeopathic medicine and naturopathic medicine. Systems that have developed in non-Western cultures include traditional Chinese medicine and Ayurveda.

Mind-body medicine uses a variety of techniques designed to enhance the mind's capacity to affect bodily function and symptoms. Some techniques that were considered CAM in the past have become mainstream (for example, patient support groups and cognitive-behavioral therapy). Other mind-body techniques are still considered CAM, including meditation, prayer, mental healing, and therapies that use creative outlets such as art, music, or dance.

Biologically based therapies in CAM use substances found in nature, such as herbs, foods, and vitamins. Some examples include dietary supplements, herbal products, and other so-called "natural" but as yet scientifically unproven therapies (for example, using shark cartilage to treat cancer).

Manipulative and body-based methods in CAM are based on manipulation and/or movement of one or more parts of the body. Some examples include chiropractic or osteopathic manipulation and massage.

Energy therapies involve the use of energy fields. They are of two types:

—**Biofield therapies** are intended to affect energy fields that purportedly surround and penetrate the human body. The existence of such fields has not yet been proven. Some forms of energy therapy manipulate biofields by applying pressure and/or manipulating the body by placing the hands in, or through, these fields. Examples include qi gong, Reiki, and Therapeutic Touch.

—**Bioelectromagnetic-based therapies** involve the unconventional use of electromagnetic fields, such as pulsed fields, magnetic fields, or alternating current or direct current fields.

Top-Selling Medicinal Herbs in the U.S., 1999–2003[1]

Source: *Nutrition Business Journal*; dollars in millions

Top Herbs	1999	2000	2001	2002	2003	Top Herbs	1999	2000	2001	2002	2003
Noni/Morinda	$33	$87	$112	$187	$219	Ginseng	199	169	150	116	101
Echinacea	220	202	214	188	180	Black cohosh root	34	36	53	59	76
Garlic	183	170	177	173	176	Milk thistle	43	46	59	63	68
Saw palmetto	121	127	142	133	146	Other single herbs	1,212	1,177	1,085	1,300	1,396
Ginkgo biloba	311	246	213	163	129	Combination herbs	1,693	1,896	2,026	1,717	1,490
Green tea	23	39	68	74	110						
Soy	38	65	97	102	107	**Total**	**$4,110**	**$4,260**	**$4,397**	**$4,276**	**$4,197**

(1) Sales numbers do not include nonmedicinal use.

Alternative Health Services in the U.S., 2003

Source: *Nutrition Business Journal*

Health care practice	Practitioners Licensed	Lay or other	Total revenues[1]	Health care practice	Practitioners Licensed	Lay or other	Total revenues[1]
Chiropractic	69,800	3,800	$16,560	Homeopathy	1,200	6,000	$550
Massage Therapy	74,000	204,000	9,170	Nurses/MDs	664,000	42,000	200
Traditional Chinese medicine	13,600	16,000	3,940	Osteopathy	42,800	1,000	—
Acupuncture	18,100	5,400	2,520	Others	—	20,160	670
Naturopathy	2,800	3,400	720	**Total**	**886,300**	**301,760**	**34,330**

(1) In millions of dollars.

WORLD ALMANAC QUICK QUIZ
Rank these countries from most to least in per capita total health spending for the 50 most populous countries.
(a) United States   (b) Russia   (c) Japan   (d) Mexico
For the answer, look in this chapter, or see page 1008

Food Guide Pyramid

The Food Guide Pyramid was developed by the U.S. Dept. of Agriculture and was last revised in 2000. The Pyramid is an outline of what to eat each day. It is not meant as a rigid prescription, but as a general guide to help in choosing a healthful diet. It calls for eating a variety of foods to get needed nutrients and, at the same time, the right amount of calories to maintain or improve your weight.

The Pyramid focuses heavily on fat because most Americans' diets are too high in fat, especially saturated fat. Some nutritionists, however, argue the Pyramid puts too much stress on carbohydrates, such as bread and pasta, while underemphasizing the role of unsaturated fats and protein in a healthy diet. In Sept. 2003 the Dept. of Agriculture solicited comments on proposed revisions to the Pyramid that would take into greater account the sedentary lifestyle of most Americans and the dangers of obesity; possible changes under consideration include listing amounts in cups and ounces instead of servings and offering a range of calorie levels with appropriate levels of food intake for each.

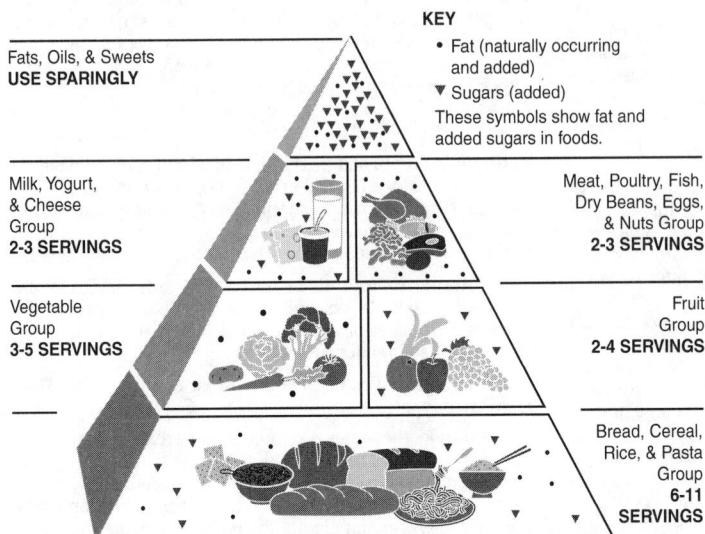

KEY
- Fat (naturally occurring and added)
- ▼ Sugars (added)

These symbols show fat and added sugars in foods.

Fats, Oils, & Sweets
USE SPARINGLY

Milk, Yogurt, & Cheese Group
2-3 SERVINGS

Meat, Poultry, Fish, Dry Beans, Eggs, & Nuts Group
2-3 SERVINGS

Vegetable Group
3-5 SERVINGS

Fruit Group
2-4 SERVINGS

Bread, Cereal, Rice, & Pasta Group
6-11 SERVINGS

What Counts as a Serving?

Bread, Cereal, Rice, and Pasta
1 slice of bread
1 ounce of ready to-eat cereal
½ cup of cooked cereal, rice, or pasta

Vegetable
1 cup of raw leafy vegetables
½ cup of other vegetables, cooked or chopped raw
¾ cup of vegetable juice

Fruit
1 medium apple, banana, orange
½ cup of chopped, cooked, or canned fruit
¾ cup of fruit juice

Milk, Yogurt, and Cheese
1 cup of milk or yogurt
1-1/2 ounces of natural cheese
2 ounces of process cheese

Meat, Poultry, Fish, Dry Beans, Eggs, and Nuts
2-3 ounces of cooked lean meat, poultry, or fish
½ cup of cooked dry beans or 1 egg counts as 1 ounce of lean meat.
2 tablespoons of peanut butter or ⅓ cup of nuts count as 1 ounce of meat.

Food and Nutrition

In a report issued in Sept. 2002, the Food and Nutrition Board of the National Academy of Sciences' Institute of Medicine recommended increased levels of physical activity and more flexible guidelines for eating. Adults and children should engage in moderately intense physical activity for an hour a day, the study said, a level twice the minimum goal set by the 1996 Surgeon General's report. Caloric intake should be geared to activity level, offering recommended calorie totals for individuals according to a scheme that takes into account height, weight, sex, and four different exertion levels (for example, a daily average of 1,800-2,000 calories was recommended for a 30-year-old woman weighing 111-150 pounds and 5 feet 5 inches tall with a sedentary lifestyle, while a very active woman, with other characteristics the same, might consume 2,500-2,800 calories a day).

The study said carbohydrates should make up 45-65% of an adult's calories, with fat providing 20-35% and protein 10-35%. The ranges were intended to allow people to accommodate their preferences while making healthy and realistic choices. Guidelines for children were similar, although the range for fat was slightly higher: it was recommended that 25-40% of a child's calories come from fat. Adults and children, it said, should have at least 130 grams of carbohydrates a day to provide necessary glucose for brain functions; most people, however, consume much more. The study contained the Food and Nutrition Board's first specific recommendations for daily intake of fiber [see below] and reaffirmed earlier recommended levels for protein, 0.8 grams per kilogram of body weight for adults. The report noted that mono- and polyunsaturated fats can play a positive role in the diet, while cautioning against saturated fats and excessive intake of added sugar.

The study was called *Dietary Reference Intakes for Energy, Carbohydrates, Fiber, Fat, Protein and Amino Acids (Macronutrients)*. Earlier Food and Nutrition Board reports had set Dietary Reference Intakes (DRIs) for vitamins and minerals. The DRIs, based on extensive scientific research, were intended to promote health at all stages of life, and not just guard against nutritional deficiencies.

PROTEIN

Proteins, composed of amino acids, are essential to good nutrition. They build, maintain, and repair the body. Best sources: eggs, milk, fish, meat, poultry, soybeans, nuts. High-quality proteins such as eggs, meat, or fish supply all 8 amino acids needed in the diet. Plant foods can be combined to meet protein needs as well: whole grain breads and cereals, rice, oats, soybeans, other beans, split peas, and nuts.

FATS

Fats provide energy by furnishing calories to the body, and they also carry vitamins A, D, E, and K. They are the most concentrated source of energy in the diet. Best sources of polyunsaturated and monounsaturated fats: margarine, vegetable/plant oils, nuts. Meats, cheeses, butter, cream, egg yolks, lard are concentrated sources of saturated fats.

CARBOHYDRATES

Carbohydrates provide energy for body function and activity by supplying immediate calories. The carbohydrate group includes sugars, starches, fiber, and starchy vegetables. Best sources: grains, legumes, potatoes, vegetables, fruits.

FIBER

The portion of plant foods that our bodies cannot digest is known as fiber. There are 2 basic types: *insoluble* ("roughage") and *soluble*. Insoluble fibers help move food materials through the digestive tract; soluble fibers tend to slow them down. Both types absorb water, thus prevent and treat constipation by softening and increasing the bulk of the undigested food components passing through the digestive tract. Soluble fibers have also been reported to be helpful in reducing blood cholesterol levels. Best sources: beans, bran, fruits, whole grains, vegetables. New recommendations from the Food and Nutrition Board call for men 50 and younger to have 38 grams of fiber a day and women to have

25 grams; 30 and 21 grams a day are proposed, respectively, for older men and women (because of reduced food intake). Fiber is also recommended for children and teenagers.

WATER

Water dissolves and transports other nutrients throughout the body, aiding the processes of digestion, absorption, circulation, and excretion. It helps regulate body temperature.

VITAMINS

Vitamin A—promotes good eyesight and helps keep the skin and mucous membranes resistant to infection. Best sources: liver, sweet potatoes, carrots, kale, cantaloupe, turnip greens, collard greens, broccoli, fortified milk.

Vitamin B_1 (thiamine)—prevents beriberi. Essential to carbohydrate metabolism and health of nervous system. Best sources: pork, enriched cereals, grains, soybeans, nuts.

Vitamin B_2 (riboflavin)—protects the skin, mouth, eyes, eyelids, and mucous membranes. Essential to protein and energy metabolism. Best sources: milk, meat, poultry, cheese, broccoli, spinach.

Vitamin B_6 (pyridoxine)—important in the regulation of the central nervous system and in protein metabolism. Best sources: whole grains, meats, fish, poultry, nuts, brewers' yeast.

Vitamin B_{12} (cobalamin)—needed to form red blood cells. Best sources: meat, fish, poultry, eggs, dairy products.

Niacin—maintains health of skin, tongue, digestive system. Best sources: poultry, peanuts, fish, enriched flour and bread.

Folic acid (folacin)—required for normal blood cell formation, growth, and reproduction and for important chemical reactions in body cells. Best sources: yeast, orange juice, green leafy vegetables, wheat germ, asparagus, broccoli, nuts.

Other B vitamins—biotin, pantothenic acid.

Vitamin C (ascorbic acid)—maintains collagen, a protein necessary for the formation of skin, ligaments, and bones. It helps heal wounds and mend fractures and aids in resisting some types of viral and bacterial infections. Best sources: citrus fruits and juices, cantaloupe, broccoli, brussels sprouts, potatoes and sweet potatoes, tomatoes, cabbage.

Vitamin D—important for bone development. Best sources: sunlight, fortified milk and milk products, fish-liver oils, egg yolks.

Vitamin E (tocopherol)—helps protect red blood cells. Best sources: vegetable oils, wheat germ, whole grains, eggs, peanuts, margarine, green leafy vegetables.

Vitamin K—necessary for formation of prothrombin, which helps blood to clot. Also made by intestinal bacteria. Best dietary sources: green leafy vegetables, tomatoes.

MINERALS

Calcium—works with phosphorus in building and maintaining bones and teeth. Best sources: milk and milk products, cheese, blackstrap molasses, some types of tofu.

Phosphorus—performs more functions than any other mineral, and plays a part in nearly every chemical reaction in the body. Best sources: cheese, milk, meats, poultry, fish, tofu.

Iron—Necessary for the formation of myoglobin, which is a reservoir of oxygen for muscle tissue, and hemoglobin, which transports oxygen in the blood. Best sources: lean meats, beans, green leafy vegetables, shellfish, enriched breads and cereals, whole grains.

Other minerals—chromium, cobalt, copper, fluorine, iodine, magnesium, manganese, molybdenum, potassium, selenium, sodium, sulfur, and zinc.

U.S. Per Capita Annual Consumption of Selected Foods, 1910-2002

Source: Economic Research Service, U.S. Dept. of Agriculture

	Whole milk[1]	Low-fat & skim milk[1]	Butter[2]	Margarine[2]	Red meat[2]	Poultry[2]	Fish & shellfish[2]
1910	25.18	7.05	18.4	1.6	125.9	16.0	11.2
1940	29.24	4.72	17.0	2.4	124.3	14.6	11.0
1970	25.48	5.78	5.4	10.8	145.1	40.1	11.7
2000	8.35	14.21	4.5	8.3	120.2	77.4	15.2
2002	7.73	14.16	NA	NA	120.5	81.0	15.6

NA = Not available. (1) Gallons. (2) Pounds.

Understanding Food Label Claims

Source: Food Labeling Education Information Center, Beltville, MD

The federal Nutrition Labeling and Education Act of 1990 provides that manufacturers can make certain claims on processed food labels only if they meet the definitions specified here:

SUGAR

Sugar free: less than 0.5g per serving

No added sugar; Without added sugar; No sugar added:

• No sugars added during processing or packing, including ingredients that contain sugars (for example, fruit juices, applesauce, or dried fruit).

• Processing does not increase sugar content above the amount naturally in the ingredients. (A functionally insignificant increase in sugars is acceptable from processes used for purposes other than increasing sugar content.)

• Food for which it substitutes normally contains added sugars.

Reduced sugar: at least 25% less sugar than reference food

CALORIES

Low calorie: 40 calories or less per serving; if the serving is 30g or less or 2 tablespoons or less, 40 calories or less per 50g of food

Calorie free: under 5 calories per serving

Reduced or Fewer calories: at least 25% fewer calories than reference food

FAT

Fat free: less than 0.5g of fat per serving

Saturated fat free: less than 0.5g of saturated fat per serving, and the level of trans fatty acids does not exceed 1% of total fat

Low fat: 3g or less per serving and, if the serving is 30g or less or 2 tbs or less, per 50g of the food

Low saturated fat: 1g or less per serving and not more than 15% of calories from saturated fatty acids

Reduced or Less fat: at least 25% less per serving than reference food

CHOLESTEROL

Cholesterol free: less than 2mg of cholesterol and 2g or less of saturated fat per serving

Low cholesterol: 20mg or less and 2g or less of saturated fat per serving and, if the serving is 30g or less or 2 tbs or less, per 50g of the food

Reduced or Less cholesterol: at least 25% less than reference food

SODIUM

Sodium free: less than 5mg per serving

Low sodium: 140 mg or less per serving and, if the serving is 30g or less or 2 tbs or less, per 50g of the food

Very low sodium: 35 mg or less per serving and, if the serving is 30g or less or 2 tbs or less, per 50g of the food

Reduced or Less sodium: at least 25% less per serving than reference food

FIBER

High fiber: 5g or more per serving. (Also, must meet low-fat definition, or must state level of total fat.)

Good source of fiber: 2.5g to 4.9g per serving

More or Added fiber: at least 2.5g more per serving than reference food

Nutritive Value of Food (Calories, Proteins, etc.)

Source: *Home and Garden Bulletin No. 72;* U.S. Dept. of Agriculture

FOOD	Measure	Grams	Food Energy (calories)	Protein (grams)	Fat (grams)	Saturated fats (grams)	Carbohydrate (grams)	Calcium (milligrams)	Iron (milligrams)	Sodium (milligrams)	Vitamin A (I.U.)	Ascorbic Acid (milligrams)
DAIRY PRODUCTS												
Cheese, cheddar, cut pieces	1 oz.	28	115	7	9	6.0	T	204	0.2	176	300	0
Cheese, cottage, small curd	1 cup	210	215	26	9	6.0	6	126	0.3	850	340	T
Cheese, cream	1 oz.	28	100	2	10	6.2	1	23	0.3	84	400	0
Cheese, Swiss	1 oz.	28	95	7	7	4.5	1	219	0.2	388	230	0
Half-and-half	1 tbsp.	15	20	T	2	1.1	1	16	T	6	70	T
Cream, sour	1 tbsp.	12	25	T	3	1.6	1	14	T	6	90	T
Milk, whole	1 cup	244	150	8	8	5.1	11	291	0.1	120	310	2
Milk, nonfat (skim)	1 cup	245	85	8	T	0.3	12	302	0.1	126	500	2
Milkshake, chocolate	10 oz.	283	355	9	8	4.8	60	374	0.9	314	240	0
Ice cream, hardened	1 cup	133	270	5	14	8.9	32	176	0.1	116	540	1
Sherbet	1 cup	193	270	2	4	2.4	59	103	0.3	88	190	4
Yogurt, fruit-flavored	8 oz.	227	230	10	2	1.6	43	345	0.2	133	100	1
EGGS												
Fried in margarine	1	46	90	6	7	1.9	1	25	0.7	162	390	0
Hard-cooked	1	50	75	6	5	1.6	1	25	0.6	62	280	0
Scrambled (milk added) in margarine	1	61	100	7	7	2.2	1	44	0.7	171	420	T
FATS & OILS												
Butter, salted	1 tbsp.	14	100	T	11	7.1	T	3	T	116	430	0
Margarine, salted	1 tbsp.	14	100	T	11	2.2	T	4	T	132	460	T
Olive oil	1 tbsp.	14	125	0	14	1.9	0	0	0	0	0	0
Salad dressing, blue cheese	1 tbsp.	15	75	1	8	1.5	1	12	T	164	30	T
Salad dressing, French, regular	1 tbsp.	16	85	T	9	1.4	1	2	T	188	T	T
Salad dressing, French, low calorie	1 tbsp.	16	25	T	2	0.2	2	6	T	306	T	T
Salad dressing, Italian	1 tbsp.	15	80	T	9	1.3	1	1	T	162	30	T
Mayonnaise	1 tbsp.	14	100	T	11	1.7	T	3	0.1	80	40	0
FISH, MEAT, POULTRY												
Clams, raw, meat only	3 oz.	85	65	11	1	0.3	2	59	2.6	102	90	9
Crabmeat, canned	1 cup	135	135	23	3	0.5	1	61	1.1	1,350	50	0
Fish sticks, frozen, reheated	1 fish stick	28	70	6	3	0.8	4	11	0.3	53	20	0
Salmon canned (pink), solids and liquid	3 oz.	85	120	17	5	0.9	0	167	0.7	443	60	0
Sardines, Atlantic, canned in oil, drained solids	3 oz.	85	175	20	9	2.1	0	371	2.6	425	190	0
Shrimp, French fried	3 oz.	85	200	16	10	2.5	11	61	2.0	384	90	0
Trout, broiled, with butter and lemon juice	3 oz.	85	175	21	9	4.1	T	26	1.0	122	230	1
Tuna, canned in oil	3 oz.	85	165	24	7	1.4	0	7	1.6	303	70	0
Bacon, broiled or fried crisp	3 slices	19	110	6	9	3.3	T	2	0.3	303	0	6
Ground beef, broiled, regular	3 oz.	85	245	20	18	6.9	0	9	2.1	70	T	0
Roast beef, relatively lean (lean only)	2.6 oz.	75	135	22	5	1.9	0	3	1.5	46	T	0
Beef steak, lean and fat	3 oz.	85	240	23	15	6.4	0	9	2.6	53	T	0
Beef & vegetable stew	1 cup	245	220	16	11	4.4	15	29	2.9	292	5,690	17
Lamb, chop, broiled loin, lean and fat	2.8 oz.	80	235	22	16	7.3	0	16	1.4	62	T	0
Liver, beef, fried	3 oz.	85	185	23	7	2.5	7	9	5.3	90	30,690	23
Ham, light cure, roasted, lean and fat	3 oz.	85	205	18	14	5.1	0	6	0.7	1,009	0	0
Pork, chop, broiled, lean and fat	3.1 oz.	87	275	24	19	7.0	0	3	0.7	61	10	T
Bologna	2 slices	57	180	7	16	6.1	2	7	0.9	581	0	12
Frankfurter, pork, cooked	1	45	145	5	13	4.8	1	5	0.5	504	0	12
Sausage, pork link, cooked	1 link	13	50	3	4	1.4	T	4	0.2	168	0	T
Veal, cutlet, braised or broiled	3 oz.	85	185	23	9	4.1	0	9	0.8	56	T	0
Chicken, drumstick, fried, bones removed	2.5 oz.	72	195	16	11	3.0	6	12	1.0	194	60	0
Chicken, roasted, half breast, without skin	3 oz.	86	140	27	3	0.9	0	13	0.9	64	20	0
Turkey, roasted, chopped light and dark meat	1 cup	140	240	41	7	2.3	0	35	2.5	98	0	0
Frankfurter, chicken, cooked	1	45	115	6	9	2.5	3	43	0.9	616	60	0
FRUITS & FRUIT PRODUCTS												
Apple, raw, 2-3/4 in. diam.	1	138	80	T	T	0.1	21	10	0.2	T	70	8
Apple juice	1 cup	248	115	T	T	T	29	17	0.9	7	T	2
Apricots, raw	3	106	50	1	T	T	12	15	0.6	1	2,770	11
Banana, raw	1	114	105	1	1	0.2	27	7	0.4	1	90	10
Cherries, sweet, raw	10	68	50	1	1	0.1	11	10	0.3	T	150	5
Cranberry juice cocktail, sweetened	1 cup	253	145	T	T	T	38	8	0.4	10	10	108
Fruit cocktail, canned, in heavy syrup	1 cup	255	185	T	T	T	48	15	0.7	15	520	5
Grapefruit, raw, medium, white	1/2	120	40	1	T	T	10	14	0.1	T	10	41
Grapes, Thompson seedless	10	50	35	T	T	0.1	9	6	0.1	1	40	5
Lemonade, frozen, unsweetened	6 oz.	244	55	1	1	0.1	16	20	0.3	2	30	77
Cantaloupe, 5-in. diam.	1/2	267	95	2	1	0.1	22	29	0.6	24	8,610	113
Orange, 2-5/8 in. diam.	1	131	60	1	T	T	15	52	0.1	T	270	70
Orange juice, frozen, diluted	1 cup	249	110	2	T	T	27	22	0.2	2	190	97
Peach, raw, 2-1/2 in. diam.	1	87	35	1	T	T	10	4	0.1	T	470	6
Raisins, seedless	1 cup	145	435	5	1	0.2	115	71	3.0	17	10	5
Strawberries, whole	1 cup	149	45	1	1	T	10	21	0.6	1	40	84
Tomatoes, raw	1	123	25	1	T	T	5	9	0.6	10	1,390	22
Watermelon, 4 by 8 in. wedge	1 piece	482	155	3	2	0.3	35	39	0.8	10	1,760	46
GRAIN PRODUCTS												
Bagel, plain	1	68	200	7	2	0.3	38	29	1.8	245	0	0
Biscuit, 2 in. diam., from home recipe	1	28	100	2	5	1.2	13	47	0.7	195	10	T
Bread, pita, enriched, white, 6-1/2 in. diam	1 pita	60	165	6	1	0.1	12	15	0.7	124	0	0
Bread, white, enriched	1 slice	25	65	2	1	0.3	12	32	0.7	129	T	T
Bread, whole-wheat	1 slice	28	70	3	1	0.4	13	20	1.0	180	T	T
Oatmeal or rolled oats, without added salt	1 cup	234	145	6	2	0.4	25	19	1.6	2	40	0
Bran flakes (40% bran), added sugar, salt, iron, vitamins	1 oz.	28	90	4	1	0.1	22	14	8.1	264	1,250	0
Corn flakes, added sugar, salt, iron, vitamins	1 oz.	28	110	2	T	T	24	1	1.8	351	1,250	15
Rice, puffed, added iron, thiamine, niacin	1 oz.	28	110	2	T	T	25	4	1.8	340	1,250	15
Wheat, shredded, plain, 1 biscuit or 2/3 cup	1 oz.	28	100	3	1	0.1	23	11	1.2	3	T	0
Bulgur, uncooked	1 cup	170	600	19	3	1.2	129	49	9.5	7	0	0
Cake, angel food, 1/12 of cake	1	53	125	3	T	T	29	44	0.2	269	0	0
Cupcake, 2-1/2 in. diam., with chocolate icing	1	35	120	2	4	1.8	20	21	0.7	92	50	T
Plain sheet cake with white, uncooked frosting, 1/9 of cake	1	121	445	4	14	4.6	77	61	1.2	275	240	T

FOOD	Measure	Grams	Food Energy (calories)	Protein (grams)	Fat (grams)	Saturated fats (grams)	Carbohydrate (grams)	Calcium (milligrams)	Iron (milligrams)	Sodium (milligrams)	Vitamin A (I.U.)	Ascorbic Acid (milligrams)
Fruitcake, dark, 1/32 of loaf	1	43	165	2	7	1.5	25	41	1.2	67	50	16
Cake, pound, 1/17 of loaf	1	29	110	2	5	3.0	15	8	0.5	108	160	0
Cheesecake, 1/12 of 9-in. diam. cake	1	92	280	5	18	9.9	26	52	0.4	204	230	5
Brownies, with nuts, from commercial recipe	1	25	100	1	4	1.6	16	13	0.6	59	70	T
Cookies, chocolate chip, from home recipe	4	40	185	2	11	3.9	26	13	1.0	82	20	0
Crackers, graham, 2-1/2 in. squares	2	14	60	1	1	0.4	11	6	0.4	86	0	0
Crackers, saltines	4	12	50	1	1	0.5	9	3	0.5	165	0	0
Danish pastry, round piece	1	57	220	4	12	3.6	26	60	1.1	218	60	T
Doughnut, cake type	1	50	210	3	12	2.8	24	22	1.0	192	20	T
Macaroni, firm stage (hot)	1 cup	130	190	7	1	0.1	39	14	2.1	1	0	0
Muffin, bran, commercial mix	1	45	140	3	4	1.3	24	27	1.7	385	100	0
Muffin, corn, from home recipe	1	45	145	3	5	1.5	21	66	0.9	169	80	T
Noodles, enriched, cooked	1 cup	160	200	7	2	0.5	37	16	2.6	3	110	0
Pie, apple, 1/6 of pie	1	158	405	3	18	4.6	60	13	1.6	476	50	2
Pie, cherry, 1/6 of pie	1	158	410	4	18	4.7	61	22	1.6	480	700	0
Pie, lemon meringue, 1/6 of pie	1	140	355	5	14	4.3	53	20	1.4	395	240	4
Pie, pecan, 1/6 of pie	1	138	575	7	32	4.7	71	65	4.6	305	220	0
Popcorn, air-popped, plain	1 cup	8	30	1	T	T	6	1	0.2	T	10	0
Pretzels, stick	10	3	10	T	T	T	2	1	0.1	48	0	0
Rolls, enriched, brown & serve	1	28	85	2	2	0.5	14	33	0.8	155	T	T
Rolls, frankfurter & hamburger	1	40	115	3	2	0.5	20	54	1.2	241	T	T
Tortillas, corn	1	30	65	2	1	0.1	13	42	0.6	1	80	0
LEGUMES, NUTS, SEEDS												
Beans, Black	1 cup	171	225	15	1	0.1	41	47	2.9	1	T	0
Beans, Great Northern, cooked	1 cup	180	210	14	1	0.1	38	90	4.9	13	0	0
Peanuts, roasted in oil, salted	1 cup	145	840	39	71	9.9	27	125	2.8	626	0	0
Peanut butter	1 tbsp.	16	95	5	8	1.4	3	5	0.3	75	0	0
Refried beans, canned	1 cup	290	295	18	3	0.4	51	141	5.1	1,228	0	17
Tofu	1 piece	120	85	9	5	0.7	3	108	2.3	8	0	0
Sunflower seeds, hulled	1 oz.	28	160	6	14	1.5	5	33	1.9	1	10	T
MIXED FOODS												
Chop suey with beef and pork, home recipe	1 cup	250	300	26	17	4.3	13	60	4.8	1,053	600	33
Enchilada	1	230	235	20	16	7.7	24	97	3.3	1,332	2,720	T
Pizza, cheese, 1/8 of 15 in.-diam. pie	1	120	290	15	9	4.1	39	220	1.6	699	750	2
Spaghetti with meatballs & tomato sauce	1 cup	248	330	19	12	3.9	39	124	3.7	1,009	1,590	22
SUGARS & SWEETS												
Candy, caramels	1 oz.	28	115	1	3	2.2	22	42	0.4	64	T	T
Candy, milk chocolate	1 oz.	28	145	2	9	5.4	16	50	0.4	23	30	T
Fudge, chocolate	1 oz.	28	115	1	3	2.1	22	22	0.3	54	T	T
Gelatin dessert, from prepared powder	1/2 cup	120	70	2	0	0.0	17	2	T	55	0	0
Candy, hard	1 oz.	28	110	0	0	0.0	28	T	0.1	7	0	0
Honey	1 tbsp.	21	65	T	0	0.0	17	1	0.1	1	0	T
Jams & preserves	1 tbsp.	20	55	T	T	0.0	14	4	0.2	2	T	T
Popsicle, 3 fl. oz.	1	95	70	0	0	0.0	18	0	T	11	0	0
Sugar, white, granulated	1 tbsp.	12	45	0	0	0.0	12	T	T	T	0	0
VEGETABLES												
Asparagus, spears, cooked from raw	4 spears	60	15	2	T	T	3	14	0.4	2	500	16
Beans, green, from frozen, cuts	1 cup	135	35	2	T	T	8	61	1.1	18	710	11
Broccoli, cooked from raw	1 spear	180	50	5	1	0.1	10	82	2.1	20	2,540	113
Cabbage, raw, coarsely shredded or sliced	1 cup	70	15	1	T	T	4	33	0.4	13	90	33
Carrots, raw, 7-1/2 by 1-1/8 in.	1	72	30	1	T	T	7	19	0.4	25	20,250	7
Cauliflower, cooked, drained, from raw	1 cup	125	30	2	T	T	6	34	0.5	8	20	69
Celery, raw	1 stalk	40	5	T	T	T	1	14	0.2	35	50	3
Collards, cooked from raw	1 cup	190	25	2	T	0.1	5	148	0.8	36	4,220	19
Corn, sweet, yellow, cooked from raw	1 ear	77	85	3	1	0.2	19	2	0.5	13	170	5
Eggplant, cooked, steamed	1 cup	96	25	1	T	T	6	6	0.3	3	60	1
Lettuce, iceberg, chopped	1 cup	55	5	1	T	T	1	10	0.3	5	180	2
Lettuce, looseleaf (such as romaine)	1 cup	56	10	1	T	T	2	38	0.8	5	1,060	10
Mushrooms, raw	1 cup	70	20	1	T	T	3	4	0.9	3	0	2
Onions, raw, chopped	1 cup	160	55	2	T	0.1	12	40	0.6	3	0	13
Peas, green, frozen, cooked	1 cup	160	125	8	T	0.1	23	38	2.5	139	1,070	16
Potatoes, baked, peeled	1	156	145	3	T	T	34	8	0.5	8	0	20
Potatoes, frozen, French fried (oven-heated)	10	50	110	2	4	2.1	17	5	0.7	16	0	5
Potatoes, mashed, milk added	1 cup	210	160	4	1	0.7	37	55	0.6	636	40	14
Potato chips	10	20	105	1	7	1.8	10	5	0.2	94	0	8
Potato salad	1 cup	250	360	7	21	3.6	28	48	1.6	1,323	520	25
Spinach, drained, cooked from raw	1 cup	180	40	5	T	0.1	7	245	6.4	126	14,740	18
Sweet potatoes, baked in skin, peeled	1	114	115	2	T	T	28	32	0.5	11	24,880	28
Vegetable juice cocktail, canned	1 cup	242	45	2	T	T	11	27	1.0	883	2,830	67
MISCELLANEOUS												
Beer, regular	12 fl. oz.	360	150	1	0	0.0	13	14	0.1	18	0	0
Gin, rum, vodka, whisky, 86 proof	1½ fl. oz.	42	105	0	0	0.0	T	T	T	T	0	0
Wine, table, white	3½ fl. oz.	102	80	T	0	0.0	3	9	0.3	5	(1)	0
Cola-type beverage	12 fl. oz.	369	160	0	0	0.0	41	11	0.2	18	0	0
Ginger ale	12 fl. oz	366	125	0	0	0.0	32	11	0.1	29	0	0
Coffee, brewed	6 fl. oz.	180	T	T	T	T	T	4	T	2	0	0
Tea, brewed	8 fl. oz.	240	T	T	T	T	T	0	T	1	0	0
Catsup	1 tbsp.	15	15	T	T	T	4	3	0.1	156	210	2
Mustard, prepared, yellow	1 tsp.	5	5	T	T	T	T	4	0.1	63	0	T
Olives, canned, green	4 medium	13	15	T	2	0.2	T	8	0.2	312	40	0
Pickles, dill, whole	1	65	5	T	T	T	1	17	0.7	928	70	4
Relish, finely chopped, sweet	1 tbsp.	15	20	T	T	T	5	3	0.1	107	20	1
Soup, tomato, prepared with milk	1 cup	248	160	6	6	2.9	22	159	1.8	932	850	68
Soup, chicken noodle, prepared with water	1 cup	241	75	4	2	0.7	9	17	0.8	1,106	710	T
Soup, green pea, prepared with water	1 cup	250	165	9	3	1.4	27	28	2.0	988	200	2
Soup, vegetarian, prepared with water	1 cup	241	70	2	2	0.3	12	22	1.1	822	3,010	1

T — Indicates trace. (1) Value not determined. **NOTE:** Values shown here for these foods may be from several different manufacturers and, therefore, may differ somewhat from the values provided by one source.

IT'S A FACT: The FDA gave its approval in June 2004 to a French company, Ricarimpex, to market and sell bloodsucking leeches as medical devices in the U.S. Although leeches are currently in use, particularly for reconstructive surgery and skin grafts, Ricarimpex was the first company to receive (or even ask for) FDA clearance to commercially market them for medicinal use. Companies already selling medical leeches to doctors and hospitals are also covered by the FDA decision.

Dietary Requirements

The Food and Nutrition Board of the National Academy of Sciences' Institute of Medicine, in reports published from 1997 to 2001, set **Dietary Reference Intakes (DRIs)** for vitamins and elements (often called minerals). The DRIs, based on recent scientific research, establish daily consumption values that aim to optimize health at all stages of life, not just to guard against nutritional deficiencies.

The DRIs include 4 categories of values. The **Recommended Dietary Allowance (RDA)** gives an intake that meets the nutrient requirements of almost all (97-98%) healthy individuals in a specified group. The **Estimated Average Requirement (EAR)** is the intake that meets the estimated nutrient need of half the individuals in a specified group, while the **Adequate Intake (AI)** is the value given when adequate scientific evidence is not available to calculate an EAR. For healthy breastfed infants, the AI is the mean intake; for other life stage groups the AI is thought to cover the needs of all individuals in the group, but lack of data or uncertainty in the data prevents the percentage of individuals covered from being specified with confidence. The **Tolerable Upper Intake Level (UL)** designates the maximum intake that is unlikely to pose risks of adverse health effects in almost all healthy individuals in a specified group; taking the nutrient above that level could be bad for one's health. RDAs and AIs may both be used as goals for individual intake.

The following two tables give the RDA or, where not available, the AI, followed by an asterisk(*).

Recommended Levels for Vitamins

Source: Food and Nutrition Board, National Academy of Sciences—Institute of Medicine, 2001

in milligrams per day (mg/d) or in micrograms per day (µg/d); asterisks denote levels defined as "adequate intake" (AI).

	Vitamin A (µg/d)[1]	Vitamin C (mg/d)	Vitamin D (µg/d)[2]	Vitamin E (mg/d)	Vitamin K (µg/d)	Thiamin (mg/d)	Riboflavin (mg/d)	Niacin (mg/d)[3]	Vitamin B6 (mg/d)	Folate (µg/d)[4]	Vitamin B12 (µg/d)	Pantothenic Acid (mg/d)	Biotin (µg/d)	Choline (mg/d)[5]
Infants														
0-6 mos	400*	40*	5*	4*	2.0*	0.2*	0.3*	2*	0.1*	65*	0.4*	1.7*	5*	125*
7-12 mos	500*	50*	5*	5*	2.5*	0.3*	0.4*	4*	0.3*	80*	0.5*	1.8*	6*	150*
Children														
1-3 yrs	300	15	5*	6	30*	0.5	0.5	6	0.5	150	0.9	2*	8*	200*
4-8 yrs	400	25	5*	7	55*	0.6	0.6	8	0.6	200	1.2	3*	12*	250*
Males														
9-13 yrs	600	45	5*	11	60*	0.9	0.9	12	1.0	300	1.8	4*	20*	375*
14-18 yrs	900	75	5*	15	75*	1.2	1.3	16	1.3	400	2.4	5*	25*	550*
19-30 yrs	900	90	5*	15	120*	1.2	1.3	16	1.3	400	2.4	5*	30*	550*
31-50 yrs	900	90	5*	15	120*	1.2	1.3	16	1.3	400	2.4	5*	30*	550*
51-70 yrs	900	90	10*	15	120*	1.2	1.3	16	1.7	400	2.46	5*	30*	550*
over 70 yrs	900	90	15*	15	120*	1.2	1.3	16	1.7	400	2.46	5*	30*	550*
Females														
9-13 yrs	600	45	5*	11	60*	0.9	0.9	12	1.0	300	1.8	4*	20*	375*
14-18 yrs	700	65	5*	15	75*	1.0	1.0	14	1.2	4007	2.4	5*	25*	400*
19-30 yrs	700	75	5*	15	90*	1.1	1.1	14	1.3	4007	2.4	5*	30*	425*
31-50 yrs	700	75	5*	15	90*	1.1	1.1	14	1.3	4007	2.4	5*	30*	425*
51-70 yrs	700	75	10*	15	90*	1.1	1.1	14	1.5	400	2.46	5*	30*	425*
over 70 yrs	700	75	15*	15	90*	1.1	1.1	14	1.5	400	2.46	5*	30*	425*
Pregnancy.....														
18 yrs. or less........	750	80	5*	15	75*	1.4	1.4	18	1.9	6008	2.6	6*	30*	450*
19-30 yrs.............	770	85	5*	15	90*	1.4	1.4	18	1.9	6008	2.6	6*	30*	450*
31-50 yrs.............	770	85	5*	15	90*	1.4	1.4	18	1.9	6008	2.6	6*	30*	450*
Lactation......														
18 yrs. or less........	1,200	115	5*	19	75*	1.4	1.6	17	2.0	500	2.8	7*	35*	550*
19-30 yrs.............	1,300	120	5*	19	90*	1.4	1.6	17	2.0	500	2.8	7*	35*	550*
31-50 yrs.............	1,300	120	5*	19	90*	1.4	1.6	17	2.0	500	2.8	7*	35*	550*

NOTE: For healthy breastfed infants, the AI is the mean intake. The AI for other life stage and gender groups is believed to cover needs of all individuals in the group, but lack of data or uncertainty in the data prevent being able to specify with confidence the percentage of individuals covered by this intake. (1) As retinol activity equivalents. (2) In the absence of adequate exposure to sunlight. (3) As niacin equivalents (NE). 1 mg of niacin = 60 mg of tryptophan; 0-6 months = preformed niacin (not NE). (4) As dietary folate equivalents (DFE). 1 DFE = 1 µg food folate = 0.6 µg of folic acid from fortified food or as a supplement consumed with food = 0.5 µg of a supplement taken on an empty stomach. (5) Although AIs have been set for choline, there are few data to assess whether a dietary supply of choline is needed at all stages of the life cycle, and it may be that the choline requirement can be met by endogenous synthesis at some of these stages. (6) Because 10-30% of older people may malabsorb food-bound B_{12}, it is advisable for those older than 50 years to meet their RDA mainly by consuming foods fortified with B_{12} or a supplement containing B_{12}. (7) In view of evidence linking folate intake with neural tube defects in the fetus, it is recommended that all women capable of becoming pregnant consume 400 µg from supplements or fortified foods in addition to intake of food folate from a varied diet. (8) It is assumed that women will continue consuming 400 µg from supplements or fortified food until their pregnancy is confirmed and they enter prenatal care, which ordinarily occurs after the end of the periconceptional period—the critical time for formation of the neural tube.

WORLD ALMANAC QUICK QUIZ

Rank these foods from most to least in protein content per serving.

(a) peanuts   (b) turkey   (c) beef steak   (d) bacon

For the answer, look in this chapter, or see page 1008

Recommended Levels for Elements (Minerals)

Source: Food and Nutrition Board, National Academy of Sciences—Institute of Medicine, 2001
in milligrams per day (mg/d) or in micrograms per day (µg/d); asterisks denote levels defined as "adequate intake" (AI).

	Calcium (mg/d)	Chromium (µg/d)	Copper (µg/d)	Fluoride (mg/d)	Iodine (µg/d)	Iron (mg/d)	Magnesium (mg/d)	Manganese (mg/d)	Molybdenum (µg/d)	Phosphorus (mg/d)	Selenium (µg/d)	Zinc (mg/d)
Infants												
0-6 mos	210*	0.2*	200*	0.01*	110*	0.27*	30*	0.003*	2*	100*	15*	2*
7-12 mos	270*	5.5*	220*	0.5*	130*	11	75*	0.6*	3*	275*	20*	3
Children												
1-3 yrs	500*	11*	340	0.7*	90	7	80	1.2*	17	460	20	3
4-8 yrs	800*	15*	440	1*	90	10	130	1.5*	22	500	30	5
Males												
9-13 yrs	1,300*	25*	700	2*	120	8	240	1.9*	34	1,250	40	8
14-18 yrs	1,300*	35*	890	3*	150	11	410	2.2*	43	1,250	55	11
19-30 yrs	1,000*	35*	900	4*	150	8	400	2.3*	45	700	55	11
31-50 yrs	1,000*	35*	900	4*	150	8	420	2.3*	45	700	55	11
51-70 yrs	1,200*	30*	900	4*	150	8	420	2.3*	45	700	55	11
over 70 yrs	1,200*	30*	900	4*	150	8	420	2.3*	45	700	55	11
Females												
9-13 yrs	1,300*	21*	700	2*	120	8	240	1.6*	34	1,250	40	8
14-18 yrs	1,300*	24*	890	3*	150	15	360	1.6*	43	1,250	55	9
19-30 yrs	1,000*	25*	900	3*	150	18	310	1.8*	45	700	55	8
31-50 yrs	1,000*	25*	900	3*	150	18	320	1.8*	45	700	55	8
51-70 yrs	1,200*	20*	900	3*	150	8	320	1.8*	45	700	55	8
over 70 yrs	1,200*	20*	900	3*	150	8	320	1.8*	45	700	55	8
Pregnancy												
18 yrs or less	1,300*	29*	1,000	3*	220	27	400	2.0*	50	1,250	60	12
19-30 yrs	1,000*	30*	1,000	3*	220	27	350	2.0*	50	700	60	11
31-50 yrs	1,000*	30*	1,000	3*	220	27	360	2.0*	50	700	60	11
Lactation												
18 yrs or less	1,300*	44*	1,300	3*	290	10	360	2.6*	50	1,250	70	13
19-30 yrs	1,000*	45*	1,300	3*	290	9	310	2.6*	50	700	70	12
31-50 yrs	1,000*	45*	1,300	3*	290	9	320	2.6*	50	700	70	12

Weight Guidelines for Adults

Source: *Clinical Guidelines on the Identification, Evaluation, and Treatment of Overweight and Obesity in Adults,*
National Heart, Lung, and Blood Institute, National Institutes of Health, 1998; *Health, United States, 2003*

Guidelines on identification, evaluation, and treatment of overweight and obesity in adults were released in June 1998 by the National Heart, Lung, and Blood Institute (NHLBI), in cooperation with the National Institute of Diabetes and Digestive and Kidney Diseases. The guidelines, based on research into risk factors in heart disease, stroke, and other conditions, define degrees of overweight and obesity in terms of **body mass index (BMI)**, which is based on weight and height and is strongly correlated with total body fat content. A BMI of 25-29 is said to indicate **overweight**; a BMI of 30 or above is said to indicate **obesity**. Weight reduction is advised for persons with a BMI of 25 or higher. (Previous guidelines have been less stringent.) Factors such as large waist circumference, high blood pressure or cholesterol, and a family history of obesity-related disease may increase risk.

Despite the advantages of controlling one's weight, the percentage of Americans who are overweight or obese has risen greatly in recent decades, according to data released by the National Center for Health Statistics. In 1999-2000, only 33.6% of adult Americans (20-74 years old) had a healthy weight (BMI of 18.5 to less than 25), while 64.5% were overweight or obese, and 30.9%, or nearly a third, were obese. In 1976-80, by contrast, 49.6% of adults had a healthy weight, and 47.4% were overweight or obese, with 15.1%—half the 1999-2000 figure—exhibiting obesity. (A small percentage of Americans have a BMI of under 18.5.)

Children and adolescents showed a similar pattern. In 1999-2000, 15.3% of children aged 6-11 were overweight or obese, compared with 6.5% in 1976-80. For adolescents (12-19 years in age), the numbers were 15.5% in 1999-2000, compared with 5.0% in the earlier period.

Health, United States, 2003, noted that the prevalence of diagnosed diabetes had increased markedly in recent years—to 6.5% of the adult population in 2002, up from 5.3% in 1997. The rise was attributed, in part, to the increase in overweight and obesity.

The table given here shows the BMI for certain heights and weights. For weight reduction tips, write to the NHLBI Information Center, PO Box 30105, Bethesda, MD 20824-0105. See also the NHLBI website: www.nhlbi.nih.gov/index.htm

Weight (lbs)

Height	HEALTHY						OVERWEIGHT					OBESE							
4'10"	91	96	100	105	110	115	119	124	129	134	138	143	148	153	158	162	167	172	177	181
4'11"	94	99	104	109	114	119	124	128	133	138	143	148	153	158	163	168	173	178	183	188
5'0"	97	102	107	112	118	123	128	133	138	143	148	153	158	163	168	174	179	184	189	194
5'1"	100	106	111	116	122	127	132	137	143	148	153	158	164	169	174	180	185	190	195	201
5'2"	104	109	115	120	126	131	136	142	147	153	158	164	169	175	180	186	191	196	202	207
5'3"	107	113	118	124	130	135	141	146	152	158	163	169	175	180	186	191	197	203	208	214
5'4"	110	116	122	128	134	140	145	151	157	163	169	174	180	186	192	197	204	209	215	221
5'5"	114	120	126	132	138	144	150	156	162	168	174	180	186	192	198	204	210	216	222	228
5'6"	118	124	130	136	142	148	155	161	167	173	179	186	192	198	204	210	216	223	229	235
5'7"	121	127	134	140	146	153	159	166	172	178	185	191	198	204	211	217	223	230	236	242
5'8"	125	131	138	144	151	158	164	171	177	184	190	197	203	210	216	223	230	236	243	249
5'9"	128	135	142	149	155	162	169	176	182	189	195	203	209	216	223	230	236	243	250	257
5'10"	132	139	146	153	160	167	174	181	188	195	202	209	216	222	229	236	243	250	257	264
5'11"	136	143	150	157	165	172	179	186	193	200	208	215	222	229	236	243	250	257	265	272
6'0"	140	147	154	162	169	177	184	191	199	206	213	221	228	235	242	250	258	265	272	279
6'1"	144	151	159	166	174	182	189	197	204	212	219	227	235	242	250	257	265	272	280	288
6'2"	148	155	163	171	179	186	194	202	210	218	225	233	241	249	256	264	272	280	287	295
6'3"	152	160	168	176	184	192	200	208	216	224	232	240	248	256	264	272	279	287	295	303
6'4"	156	164	172	180	189	197	205	213	221	230	238	246	254	263	271	279	287	295	304	312
BMI[1]	19	20	21	22	23	24	25	26	27	28	29	30	31	32	33	34	35	36	37	38

(1) The BMI numbers apply to both men and women. Some very muscular people may have a high BMI without health risks.

Where to Get Help

Source: Based on *Health & Medical Year Book*. © by Collier Newfield, Inc.; additional data, World Almanac research

Listed here are some of the major U.S. and Canadian organizations providing information about good health practices generally, or about specific conditions and how to deal with them. (Canadian sources are identified as such.) Where a toll-free number is not available, an address is given when possible.

Some entries conclude with an e-mail address for the organization and/or an address for its Internet site, where you can also obtain useful information. In addition to these selected sites, there is a vast array of medical information on the Internet; however, it is very important to be certain that the source of information is reliable and accurate. Always check with a physician before embarking on any new health-related undertaking.

General Sources

Centers for Disease Control and Prevention Voice Information System
800-311-3435
Recorded information about public health topics, such as AIDS and Lyme disease. Also, you can request to talk with a CDC expert or have information faxed to you.
Website: www.cdc.gov

National Health Information Center
800-336-4797; in Maryland, 301-565-4167
Phone numbers for more than 1,000 health-related organizations in the United States. Printed materials offered.
E-mail: info@nhic.org
Website: www.health.gov/NHIC

National Institutes of Health
301-496-4000
Free information, including the latest research findings, on many diseases.
E-mail: NIHinfo@OD.NIH.GOV
Website: www.nih.gov

Tel-Med
Check the phone book for local listings or call Tel-Med at 909-478-0330.
Recorded information on over 600 health topics. Online medical reference library in English and Spanish. Sponsored by local medical societies, health organizations, or hospitals.
E-mail: telmed@ix.netcom.com
Website: www.tel-med.com

Aging

National Association of Area Agencies on Aging's Eldercare Locator Line
800-677-1116
Information and assistance on a wide range of services and programs including adult day-care and respite services, consumer fraud, hospital and nursing home information, legal services, elder abuse/protective services, Medicaid/Medigap information, tax assistance, and transportation.
Hours 9 AM-8 PM EST M-F.
E-mail: eldercare_locator@aoa.gov
Website: www.eldercare.gov

National Institute on Aging
800-222-2225
Information and publications about disabling conditions, support groups, and community resources.
Hours: M-F 8:30-5:00 EST
E-mail: karpf@nia.nih.gov
Website: www.nia.nih.gov

AIDS

AIDSinfo
800-HIV-0440
Information on federally and privately sponsored clinical trials for patients with AIDS or HIV; treatment information ofr people with aids, their families and health care providers
E-mail: ContactUs@aidsinfo.nih.gov
Website: www.aidsinfo.nih.gov

Canadian AIDS Society
613-230-3580
Written materials and referrals.
Website: www.cdnaids.ca
E-mail: CASinfo@cdnaids.ca

Centers for Disease Control and Prevention National AIDS/HIV Hotline
800-342-AIDS 24 hours; in Spanish, 800-344-SIDA; for the hearing impaired, 800-AIDS-TTY
Information on the prevention and spread of AIDS, along with referrals.
E-mail: hivmail@cdc.gov
Website: www.cdc.gov/hiv/hivinfo/nah.htm

Alcoholism and Drug Abuse

Wellplace
800-821-4357, 24 hours
Referrals to local facilities
Website: www.wellplace.com

Alcoholics Anonymous
212-870-3400
Worldwide support groups for alcoholics. Check phone book for local chapters.
Websites: www.alcoholics-anonymous.org or www.AA.org

American Council on Alcoholism
800-527-5344
Treatment referrals and counseling for recovering alcoholics.
E-mail: aca2@earthlink.net
Website: www.aca-usa.org

National Clearinghouse for Alcohol and Drug Information
800-729-6686
Provides written materials on alcohol and drug-related subjects.
Website: www.health.org

National Council on Alcoholism and Drug Dependence Hopeline
800-622-2255
Advisory and referral service.
Website: www.ncadd.org
E-mail: national@ncadd.org

DrugHelp
Answers questions on substance abuse and provides referrals to treatment centers.
Website: www.drughelp.org

Alzheimer's Disease

Alzheimer's Association
800-272-3900
Gives referrals to local chapters and support groups; offers information on publications available from the association.
E-mail: info@alz.org
Website: www.alz.org

Alzheimer's Society of Canada
416-488-8772
Gives phone numbers for local support chapters. Publishes support materials.
E-mail: info@alzheimer.ca
Website: www.alzheimer.ca

Amyotrophic Lateral Sclerosis

ALS Association
818-880-9007
Information about ALS (Lou Gehrig's Disease) and referrals to ALS specialists, local chapters and support groups.
Website: www.alsa.org

Arthritis

Arthritis Foundation
800-283-7800
Information, publications, and referrals to local groups.
Website: www.arthritis.org

Arthritis Society (Canada)
393 University Ave., Suite 1700
Toronto, ON M5G 1E6
416-979-7228; in Ontario only, 800-321-1433
Phone numbers for local chapters.
E-mail: info@arthritis.ca
Website: www.arthritis.ca

National Institute of Arthritis and Musculoskeletal and Skin Diseases
877-226-4267 or 301-495-4484
Subject searches and resource referrals.
E-mail: niamsinfo@mail.nih.gov
Website: www.niams.nih.gov

Asthma and Allergies

See also *Lung Diseases*

Asthma and Allergy Foundation of America
800-7-ASTHMA
Information; education; links to support groups.
E-mail: info@aafa.org
Website: www.aafa.org

American Academy of Allergy, Asthma, and Immunology Referral Line
800-822-ASMA, 24 hours; 414-272-6071
Patient information and referrals for asthma and allergies.
E-mail: info@aaaai.org
Website: www.aaaai.org

Autism

Autism Society of America
301-657-0881 or 800-3AUTISM
Information about autism, referral to local chapters.
E-mail: info@autism-society.org
Website: www.autism-society.org

Blindness and Eye Care

Canadian National Institute for the Blind
416-486-2500 or contact your local chapter.
National office offers training and library with braille books and audiotapes. Local chapters provide core services: orientation in mobility, sight enhancement, counseling, referrals, career aid, technology services.
Website: www.cnib.ca

Foundation Fighting Blindness
888-394-3937; TDD 800-683-5555
Answers questions about retinal degenerative diseases; has written materials.
E-mail: info@blindness.org
Website: www.blindness.org

Library of Congress National Library Service for the Blind and Physically Handicapped
800-424-8567; in Washington, DC, 202-707-5100; for the hearing impaired, TDD 202-707-0744
Information on libraries that offer talking books and books in braille.
E-mail: nls@loc.gov
Website: www.loc.gov/nls

National Association for Parents of the Visually Impaired
800-562-6265 or 617-972-7441
Support and information for parents of individuals who are visually impaired.
E-mail: napvi@perkins.org
Website: www.napvi.org

Blood Disorders

Cooley's Anemia Foundation
800-522-7222
Information on patient care and support groups; makes referrals to local chapters.
E-mail: info@cooleysanemia.org
Website: www.thalassemia.org

Sickle Cell Disease Association of America
800-421-8453; 310-216-6363
Genetic counseling and information packet.
Website: www.sicklecelldisease.org
E-mail: scdaa@sicklecelldisease.org

Burns

Phoenix Society
800-888-2876; 616-458-2773
Counseling for burn survivors and information on self-help services for burn survivors and their families.
E-mail: info@phoenix-society.org
Website: www.phoenix-society.org

Cancer

American Cancer Society
800-ACS-2345
Publications and information about cancer and coping with cancer; makes referrals to local chapters for support services.
Website: www.cancer.org

Canadian Cancer Information Service
888-939-3333 or 416-961-7223
Information on prevention, treatment, drugs, clinical trials, local services.
E-mail: info@cis.cancer.ca
Website: www.cancer.ca

National Cancer Institute's Cancer Information Service
800-4-CANCER
Information about clinical trials, treatments, symptoms, prevention, referrals to support groups, and screening. Includes chat online information inquiries.
Website: cis.nci.nih.gov

Y-Me Breast Cancer Support Program
800-221-2141, 24 hours; 800-986-9505 Spanish, 24-hours
Information and literature on breast cancer, counseling, and referrals.
Website: www.y-me.org

Cerebral Palsy

Ontario Federation for Cerebral Palsy
Ontario only: 877-244-9686; 416-244-9686
Canada does not have a national cerebral palsy organization, but the provincial organizations offer information on housing, services, and coping with life, and each one will provide contact numbers for the others.
E-mail: info@ofcp.on.ca
Website: www.ofcp.on.ca

United Cerebral Palsy Associations
800-872-5827, (TTY) 202-973-7197; in Washington, DC, 202-776-0406
Written materials.
Website: www.ucpa.org

Child Abuse

See *Domestic Violence*

Children

American Academy of Pediatrics
847-434-4000
Child-care publications and materials; referrals to pediatricians.
E-mail: kidsdocs@aap.org
Website: www.aap.org

National Center for Missing and Exploited Children
800-843-5678; 703-274-3900. Operates 24 hours.
Hotline for reporting missing children and sightings of missing children.
Website: www.missingkids.org

Chronic Fatigue Syndrome

CFIDS Association of America
800-442-3437
Literature and a list of support groups.
E-mail: info@cfids.org
Website: www.cfids.org

Crisis

National Runaway Switchboard
800-621-4000
Crisis intervention and referrals for run-aways. Runaways can leave messages for parents, and vice versa. Operates 24 hours.
E-mail: info@nrscrisisline.org
Website: www.nrscrisisline.org

Cystic Fibrosis

Canadian Cystic Fibrosis Foundation
416-485-9149; 800-378-2233 in Canada only, Information and brochures; makes referrals to local chapters.
E-mail: info@cysticfibrosis.ca
Website: www.cysticfibrosis.ca

Cystic Fibrosis Foundation
800-FIGHT-CF or 301-951-4422
Answers questions and offers literature and referrals to local clinics.
E-mail: info@cff.org
Website: www.cff.org

Diabetes

American Diabetes Association
800-342-2383
Information about diabetes, nutrition, exercise, and treatment; offers referrals.
E-mail: askADA@diabetes.org
Website: www.diabetes.org

Canadian Diabetes Association
416-363-0177; 800-226-8464 in Canada only.
Information about diabetes and its management.
E-mail: info@diabetes.ca
Website: www.diabetes.ca

Juvenile Diabetes Foundation Hotline
800-533-2873
Answers questions, provides literature (some in Spanish). Offers referrals to local chapters, physicians, and clinics.
E-mail: info@jdf.org
Website: www.jdf.org

Digestive Diseases

Crohn's and Colitis Foundation of America
800-932-2423
Educational materials; offers referrals to local chapters, which can provide referrals to support groups and physicians.
E-mail: info@ccfa.org
Website: www.ccfa.org

Crohn's and Colitis Foundation of Canada
416-920-5035; in Canada only, 800-387-1479
Will send out educational materials upon request.
E-mail: ccfc@ccfc.ca
Website: www.ccfc.ca

Domestic Violence

Childhelp's USA National Child Abuse Hotline
800-4-A-CHILD
Crisis intervention, professional counseling, referrals to local groups and shelters for runaways, and literature. Operates 24 hours.
Website: www.childhelpusa.org

National Council on Child Abuse and Family Violence
800-799-7233, (TTY) 800-787-3244
Information and referrals.
Website: www.nccafv.org

Down Syndrome

National Down Syndrome Congress
800-232-6372; in Georgia, 770-604-9500
Answers questions on all aspects of Down syndrome. Provides referrals.
E-mail: info@ndsccenter.org
Website: www.ndsccenter.org

National Down Syndrome Society
800-221-4602; 212-460-9330 (NYC)
E-mail: info@ndss.org
Website: www.ndss.org

Drug Abuse

See *Alcoholism and Drug Abuse*

Dyslexia

International Dyslexia Association
800-ABCD-123; in Maryland, 410-296-0232
Information on testing, tutoring, and computers used to aid people with dyslexia and related disorders.
E-mail: info@interdys.org
Website: www.interdys.org

Eating Disorders

National Association of Anorexia Nervosa and Associated Disorders
847-831-3438
Written materials, referrals to health professionals treating eating disorders, telephone counseling, offers self-help groups and information on how to set up a self-help group.
E-mail: anad20@aol.com
Website: www.anad.org

Endometriosis

Endometriosis Association
800-992-ENDO, an answering machine for callers to request information; 414-355-2200
Website: www.endometriosisassn.org

Epilepsy

Epilepsy and Seizure Disorder Service at the Epilepsy Foundation of America
800-332-1000, Mon. through Thurs.
Information and referrals to local chapters.
Website: www.efa.org

Erectile Dysfunction

American Urological Association
866-746-4282. Information on various urological disorders and referrals.
E-mail: aua@auanet.org
Website: www.auanet.org

Food Safety and Nutrition

Meat and Poultry Hotline of the U.S. Department of Agriculture's Food, Safety, and Inspection Service
888-674-6854; TTY 800-256-7072
Information on prevention of food-borne illness and the proper handling, preparation, storage, labeling, and cooking of meat, poultry, and eggs.
E-mail: MPHotline.fsis@usda.gov
Website: www.foodsafety.gov

FDA Center for Food Safety and Applied Nutrition Outreach & Information Center
888-SAFE-FOOD
Information on how to buy and use food products and on their proper handling and storage, women's health, and cosmetics & colors. Callers may speak to food specialists, Mon. through Fri., 10 am to 4 PM (EST).
Website: www.cfsan.fda.gov

Headaches

National Headache Foundation
888-NHF-5552
Literature on headaches and treatment.
E-mail: info@headaches.org
Website: www.headaches.org

Heart Disease and Stroke

American Heart Association
800-242-8721
Information, publications, and referrals to organizations.
Website: www.americanheart.org

National Institute of Neurological Disorders and Stroke
800-352-9424, 301-496-5751; TTY 301-468-5981
Literature and information.
Website: www.ninds.nih.gov

National Stroke Association
800-787-6537
Information on support networks for stroke victims and their families; referrals to local support groups.
Website: www.stroke.org

Hospices

Children's Hospice International
800-242-4453, in Virginia, 703-684-0330
Information, referrals to children's hospices.
E-mail: info@chionline.org
Website: www.chionline.org

Hospice Education Institute Hospicelink
800-331-1620; in Maine, 207-255-8800
Information, referrals to local programs.
E-mail: info@hospiceworld.org
Website: www.hospiceworld.org

Huntington's Disease

Huntington's Disease Society of America
800-345-4372; in New York, 212-242-1968
Information and referrals to physicians and support groups.
E-mail: hdsainfo@hdsa.org
Website: www.hdsa.org

Kidney Diseases

Kidney Foundation of Canada
514-369-4806; in Canada only, 800-361-7494
Educational materials and general information.
Website: www.kidney.ca

National Kidney and Urologic Diseases Information Clearinghouse
301-654-4415, 800-981-5390
Information, referrals to organizations.
Website: www.kidney.niddk.nih.gov

National Kidney Foundation
800-622-9010, 212-889-2210
Information and referrals.
E-mail: info@kidney.org
Website: www.kidney.org

Lead Exposure

National Lead Information Center
800-424-LEAD
Recommendations (in English and Spanish) for reducing a child's exposure to lead. Referrals to state and local agencies.
Website: www.epa.gov/lead

Liver Diseases

American Liver Foundation
800-465-4837; 800-443-7872
Information on hepatitis, liver, and gallbladder diseases.
E-mail: info@liverfoundation.org
Website: www.liverfoundation.org

Lung Diseases

See also **Asthma and Allergies**

American Lung Association
Check the phone book for local listings or call the national office at 800-LUNG-USA for automatic connection to the office nearest you. Answers questions about asthma and lung diseases; publications and referrals.
Website: www.lungusa.org

Lung Line Information Service at the National Jewish Medical and Research Center
800-222-LUNG; outside the U.S.: 303-388-4461
Answers questions on asthma, emphysema, allergies, smoking, and other respiratory and immune system disorders.
E-mail: lungline@njc.org
Website: www.njc.org

Lupus

Lupus Foundation of America
800-558-0121; 202-349-1155
Sends information to those who leave name and address on answering machine.
E-mail: info@lupus.org
Website: www.lupus.org

Lyme Disease

Lyme Disease Foundation
860-525-2000
Written information; doctor referrals.
E-mail: lymefnd@aol.com
Website: www.lyme.org

Mental Health

Depression and Bipolar Support Alliance
800-826-3632
Support for patients and families, provides publications, and makes referrals to affiliated organizations.
E-mail: questions@dbsalliance.org
Website: www.dbsalliance.org

National Foundation for Depressive Illness
800-239-1265, 24 hours
Recorded message describing the symptoms of depression and offering an address for more information and physician referral.
Website: www.depression.org

National Institute of Mental Health
301-443-4513, toll free 866-615-6464; TTY 301-443-8431
Information on a range of topics, from children's mental disorders to schizophrenia, depression, eating disorders, and others.
E-mail: nimhinfo@nih.gov
Website: www.nimh.nih.gov

National Mental Health Association
800-969-6642
Referrals to mental health groups.
Website: www.nmha.org

Multiple Sclerosis

Multiple Sclerosis Society of Canada
416-922-6065, 800-268-7582 in Canada only.
Counseling, literature, and referrals to local chapters.
E-mail: info@mssociety.ca
Website: www.mssociety.ca

National Multiple Sclerosis Society
800-344-4867
Information about local chapters.
Website: www.nationalmssociety.org

Muscular Dystrophy

Muscular Dystrophy Association
800-572-1717
Written materials on 40 neuromuscular diseases, including muscular dystrophy. Will give information over the phone about such matters as MDA clinics, support groups, summer camps, and wheelchair purchase assistance.
E-mail: mda@mdausa.org
Website: www.mdausa.org

Nutrition

See *Food Safety and Nutrition*

Organ Donation

Living Bank
800-528-2971, 24 hours
A registry and referral service for people wanting to commit organs to transplantation or research.
E-mail: info@livingbank.org
Website: www.livingbank.org

Osteoporosis

National Osteoporosis Foundation
800-223-9994; in Washington, DC, 202-223-2226
Information packet available on request.
Website: www.nof.org

Pain

National Chronic Pain Outreach Association
540-862-9437
Information packet available on request.
Website: www.chronicpain.org

Parkinson's Disease

National Parkinson Foundation
800-327-4545; in Miami, 305-547-6666
Answers questions, makes physician referrals, and provides written information in English and Spanish.
E-mail: mailbox@parkinson.org
Website: www.parkinson.org

Parkinson Society Canada
800-565-3000, Canada only; 416-227-9700
Information; referrals to support groups.
E-mail: General.info@parkinson.ca
Website: www.parkinson.ca

Plastic Surgery

Plastic Surgery Information Service
888-475-2784
Referrals to board-certified plastic surgeons in the U.S. and Canada; general information.
Website: www.plasticsurgery.org

Polio

Post-Polio Health International
314-534-0475
Information on coping with the late effects of polio; referrals to other organizations.
E-mail: info@post-polio.org
Website: www.post-polio.org

Prostate Problems

American Foundation for Urologic Disease
800-828-7866, 410-689-3990
Information and publications.
Website: www.afud.org

Rare Disorders

National Organization for Rare Disorders
800-999-6673, 203-744-0100
Information on diseases and networking programs; referrals to organizations for specific disorders.
E-mail: orphan@rarediseases.org
Website: www.rarediseases.org

Rehabilitation

National Rehabilitation Information Center
800-34-NARIC; in Maryland, 301-459-5900; TTY 301-459-5984
Research referrals and information on rehabilitation issues.
E-mail: naricinfo@heitechservices.com
Website: www.naric.org

Scleroderma

United Scleroderma Foundation
800-722-4673
Referrals to local support groups and treatment centers, as well as information on scleroderma and related skin disorders.
E-mail: sfinfo@scleroderma.org
Website: www.scleroderma.org

Sexually Transmitted Diseases

See also *AIDS*

National STD Hotline
800-227-8922 or 800-242-2437; Spanish 800-344-7432
Information; confidential referrals.
E-mail: std-hivnet@ashastd.org
Website: www.ashastd.org

Sjogren's Syndrome

Sjogren's Syndrome Foundation
800-475-6473;
Provides an answering machine for callers to request treatment literature.
Website: www.sjogrens.org

Skin Problems

National Psoriasis Foundation
800-723-9166
Information and referrals.
E-mail: getinfo@psoriasis.org
Website: www.psoriasis.org

Speech and Hearing

American Speech-Language-Hearing Association Action Center
800-638-8255 (also TTY)
Materials on speech and language disorders and hearing impairment; referrals.
E-mail: actioncenter@asha.org
Website: www.asha.org

Canadian Hard of Hearing Association
800-263-8068, Canada only; TTY 613-526-2692; 613-526-1584
Publications; answers general questions.
E-mail: chhanational@chha.ca
Website: www.chha.ca

Dial a Hearing Screening Test
800-222-EARS
Answers questions on hearing problems. Makes referrals to local telephone numbers for a two-minute hearing test. Also to ear, nose, and throat specialists and to organizations that can provide specialized ear and hearing aid information. 9 AM–5 PM EST

Hearing Aid Helpline
800-521-5247, ext. 333
Information and distributes a directory of hearing aid specialists certified by the International Hearing Society.
Website: www.ihsinfo.org

National Center for Stuttering
800-221-2483; 212-532-1460
Information on stuttering in all age groups.
E-mail: martin.schwartz@nyu.edu
Website: www.stuttering.com

Stuttering Foundation of America
800-992-9392
Referrals to speech pathologists; resource lists, publications.
E-mail: info@stutteringhelp.org
Website: www.stutteringhelp.org

Spinal Injuries

National Spinal Cord Injury Association
800-962-9629; 301-214-4006
Peer counseling; referrals to local chapters and other organizations.
E-mail: info@spinalcord.org
Website: www.spinalcord.org

Stroke

See **Heart Disease and Stroke**

Sudden Infant Death Syndrome

American Sudden Infant Death Syndrome Institute
800-232-SIDS
Answers questions; literature; referrals to other organizations.
E-mail: prevent@sids.org
Website: www.sids.org

Tourette Syndrome

Tourette Syndrome Association
718-224-2999
Printed information.
E-mail: ts@tsa-usa.org
Website: tsa-usa.org

Urinary Incontinence

National Association for Continence
800-BLADDER, 843-377-0900
Information on bladder control, services available for incontinence, and assistive devices.
E-mail: memberservices@nafc.org
Website: www.nafc.org

Simon Foundation for Continence
800-23-SIMON
Support and literature on incontinence.
E-mail: Simoninfo@simonfoundation.org
Website: www.simonfoundation.org

Women's Health

National Women's Health Network
202-347-1140; 202-628-7814
Information and referrals on more than 70 women's health concerns.
E-mail: nwhn@nwhn.org
Website: www.nwhn.org

National Women's Health Resource Center
877-986-9472
A national clearinghouse for women's health information.
E-mail: vngethe@healthywomen.org
Website: www.healthywomen.org

ECONOMICS

Consumer Price Index

The Consumer Price Index (CPI) is a measure of the average change in prices over time of one or more kinds of basic consumer goods and services.

From Jan. 1978, the Bureau of Labor Statistics began publishing CPIs for 2 population groups: (1) a CPI for all urban consumers (CPI-U), which covers about 87% of the total population; and (2) a CPI for urban wage earners and clerical workers (CPI-W), which covers about 32% of the total population. The CPI-U includes, in addition to wage earners and clerical workers, groups such as professional, managerial, and technical workers, the self-employed, short-term workers, the unemployed, retirees, and others not in the labor force.

The CPI is based on prices of food, clothing, shelter, and fuels; transportation fares; charges for doctors' and dentists' services; drug prices; and prices of other goods and services bought for day-to-day living. The index currently measures price changes from a designated reference period, 1982-84, which equals 100.0. Use of this reference period began in Jan. 1988.

U.S. Consumer Price Indexes, 2003-2004

Source: Bureau of Labor Statistics, U.S. Dept. of Labor

(Data are semiannual averages of monthly figures. For all urban consumers; 1982-84 = 100; unless otherwise noted; % change not annualized)

	1st half 2003	% change 2nd half 2002 to 1st half 2003	2nd half 2003	% change 1st half 2003 to 2nd half 2003	1st half 2004	% change 2nd half 2003 to 1st half 2004
ALL ITEMS	183.3	1.3	184.6	0.7	187.6	1.6
Food, beverages	179.1	1.1	182.0	1.6	185.3	1.8
Housing	184.0	1.4	185.6	0.9	188.1	1.3
Apparel	121.4	−1.2	120.4	−0.8	121.0	0.5
Transportation	158.1	2.5	157.0	−0.7	161.5	2.9
Medical care	294.5	2.0	299.7	1.8	307.4	2.6
Recreation[1]	107.4	1.0	107.7	0.3	108.6	0.8
Education and communication[1]	109.2	0.2	110.4	1.1	111.0	0.5
Other goods, services	297.6	0.6	299.9	0.8	303.1	1.1
Services	215.0	1.7	218.0	1.4	221.1	1.4
SPECIAL INDEXES						
All items less food	184.2	1.4	185.1	0.5	188.1	1.6
Commodities less food	137.4	1.3	135.5	−1.4	138.1	1.9
Nondurables	164.8	2.9	165.7	0.5	170.7	3.0
Energy	135.7	14.9	137.3	1.2	146.8	6.9
All items less energy	190.0	1.7	191.2	0.6	193.5	1.2

(1) Dec. 1997 = 100.

U.S. Consumer Price Indexes (CPI-U),[1] Annual Percent Change, 1990-2003

Source: Bureau of Labor Statistics, U.S. Dept. of Labor

	1990	1991	1992	1993	1994	1995	1996	1997	1998	1999	2000	2001	2002	2003
ALL ITEMS	5.4	4.2	3.0	3.0	2.6	2.8	3.0	2.3	1.6	2.2	3.4	2.8	1.6	2.3
Food	5.8	2.9	1.2	2.2	2.4	2.8	3.3	2.6	2.2	2.1	2.3	3.2	1.8	2.2
Shelter	5.4	4.5	3.3	3.0	3.1	3.2	3.2	3.1	3.3	2.9	3.3	3.7	3.7	2.4
Rent, residential	5.6	6.1	2.5	2.3	2.5	2.5	2.7	2.9	3.2	3.1	3.6	4.5	4.0	2.9
Fuel and other utilities	3.5	3.3	2.2	3.0	1.0	0.7	3.1	2.6	−1.8	0.2	7.1	8.9	−4.4	7.6
Apparel and upkeep	4.6	3.7	2.5	1.4	−0.2	−1.0	−0.2	0.9	0.1	−1.3	−1.3	−1.8	−2.6	−2.5
Private transportation	5.2	2.6	2.2	2.3	3.1	3.7	2.7	0.7	−2.2	1.9	6.1	0.6	−0.8	3.2
New cars	1.8	3.8	2.5	2.4	3.4	2.2	1.7	0.2	−0.6	−0.3	−0.1	−0.5	−1.2	−1.5
Gasoline	14.1	−1.8	−0.2	−1.3	0.5	1.6	6.1	−0.1	−13.4	9.3	28.5	−3.6	−6.5	16.5
Public transportation	10.1	4.4	1.7	10.3	3.0	2.3	3.4	2.6	1.9	3.9	6.0	0.5	−1.5	0.9
Medical care	9.0	8.7	7.4	5.9	4.8	4.5	3.5	2.8	3.2	3.5	4.1	4.6	4.7	4.0
Entertainment, Recreation[2,3]	4.7	4.5	2.8	2.5	2.9	2.5	3.4	2.1	1.5	0.9	1.3	1.5	1.2	1.2
Education[3]	—	—	—	—	6.3	5.6	5.3	5.0	4.9	4.8	5.1	5.3	6.3	1.8
Commodities	5.2	4.2	2.0	1.9	1.7	1.9	2.6	1.4	0.1	1.8	3.3	1.0	−0.7	1.0

(1) The Consumer Price Index CPI-U measures average change in prices of goods and services purchased by all urban consumers. 1982-1984 = 100 unless otherwise noted. (2) The Bureau of Labor Statistics reclassified Entertainment as Recreation in 1997. (3) Dec. 1997 = 100.

Consumer Price Index, 1915-2004

Source: Bureau of Labor Statistics, U.S. Dept. of Labor

(1967 = 100. Annual averages of monthly figures, specified for all urban consumers.)

Prices as measured by the U.S. Consumer Price Index have risen steadily since World War II. What cost $1.00 in 1967 cost about 30 cents in 1915, 54 cents in 1945, and $5.62 by the first half of 2004.

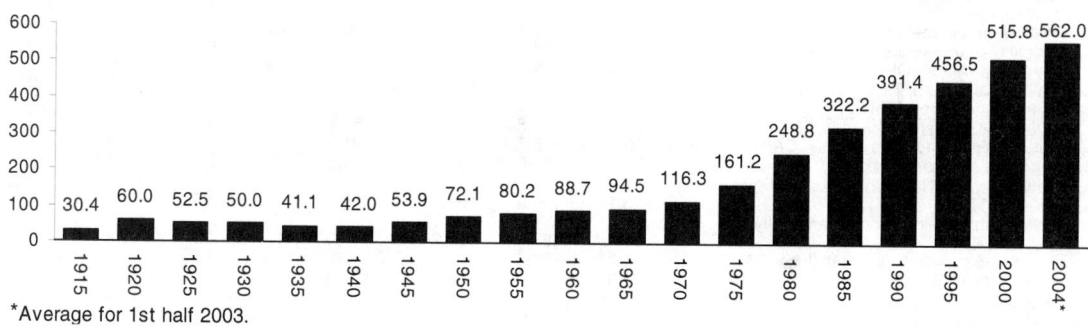

*Average for 1st half 2003.

U.S. Consumer Price Indexes for Selected Items and Groups, 1970-2003

Source: Bureau of Labor Statistics, U.S. Dept. of Labor

(1982-84 = 100, unless otherwise noted. Annual averages of monthly figures. For all urban consumers.)

	1970	1975	1980	1985	1990	1995	1998	1999	2000	2001	2002	2003
ALL ITEMS	38.8	53.8	82.4	107.6	130.7	152.4	163.0	166.6	172.2	177.1	179.9	184.0
Food and beverages	40.1	60.2	86.7	105.6	132.1	148.9	161.1	164.6	168.4	173.6	176.8	180.5
Food	39.2	59.8	86.8	105.6	132.4	148.4	160.7	164.1	167.8	173.1	176.2	180.0
Food at home	39.9	61.8	88.4	104.3	132.3	148.8	161.1	164.2	167.9	173.4	175.6	179.4
Cereals and bakery products	37.1	62.9	83.9	107.9	140.0	167.5	181.1	185.0	188.3	193.8	198.0	202.8
Meats, poultry, fish, and eggs	44.6	67.0	92.0	100.1	130.0	138.8	147.3	147.9	154.5	161.3	162.1	169.3
Dairy products	44.7	62.6	90.9	103.2	126.5	132.8	150.8	159.6	160.7	167.1	168.1	167.9
Fruits and vegetables	37.8	56.9	82.1	106.4	149.0	177.7	198.2	203.1	204.6	212.2	220.9	225.9
Sugar and sweets	30.5	65.3	90.5	105.8	124.7	137.5	150.2	152.3	154.0	155.7	159.0	162.0
Fats and oils	39.2	73.5	89.3	106.9	126.3	137.3	146.9	148.3	147.4	155.7	155.4	157.4
Nonalcoholic beverages	27.1	41.3	91.4	104.3	113.5	131.7	133.0	134.3	137.8	139.2	139.2	139.8
Other foods	39.6	58.9	83.6	106.4	131.2	151.1	165.5	168.9	172.2	176.0	177.1	178.8
Food away from home	37.5	54.5	83.4	108.3	133.4	149.0	161.1	165.1	169.0	173.9	178.3	182.1
Alcoholic beverages	52.1	65.9	86.4	106.4	129.3	153.9	165.7	169.7	174.7	179.3	183.6	187.2
Housing	36.4	50.7	81.1	107.7	128.5	148.5	160.4	163.9	169.6	176.4	180.3	184.8
Shelter	35.5	48.8	81.0	109.8	140.0	165.7	182.1	187.3	193.4	200.6	208.1	213.1
Rent of primary residence	46.5	58.0	80.9	111.8	138.4	157.8	172.1	177.5	183.9	192.1	199.7	205.5
Fuel and other utilities	29.1	45.4	75.4	106.5	111.6	123.7	128.5	128.8	137.9	150.2	143.6	154.5
Gas (piped) and electricity	25.4	40.1	71.4	107.1	109.3	119.2	121.2	120.9	128.0	142.4	134.4	145.0
Household furnishings & operations	46.8	63.4	86.3	103.8	113.3	123.0	126.6	126.7	128.2	129.1	128.3	126.1
Apparel	59.2	72.5	90.9	105.0	124.1	132.0	133.0	131.3	129.6	127.3	124.0	120.9
Men's and boys'	62.2	75.5	89.4	105.0	120.4	126.2	131.8	131.1	129.7	125.7	121.7	118.0
Women's and girls'	71.8	85.5	96.0	104.9	122.6	126.9	126.0	123.3	121.5	119.3	115.8	113.1
Footwear	56.8	69.6	91.8	102.3	117.4	125.4	128.0	125.7	123.8	123.0	121.4	119.6
Transportation	37.5	50.1	83.1	106.4	120.5	139.1	141.6	144.4	153.3	154.3	152.9	157.6
Private	37.5	50.6	84.2	106.2	118.8	136.3	137.9	140.5	149.1	150.0	148.8	153.6
New vehicles	53.0	62.9	88.4	106.1	121.4	139.0	143.4	142.9	142.8	142.1	140.0	137.9
Used cars and trucks	31.2	43.8	62.3	113.7	117.6	156.5	150.6	152.0	155.8	158.7	152.0	142.9
Gasoline	27.9	45.1	97.5	98.6	101.0	99.8	91.6	100.1	128.6	124.0	116.0	135.1
Public	35.2	43.5	69.0	110.5	142.6	175.9	190.3	197.7	209.6	210.6	207.4	209.3
Medical care	34.0	47.5	74.9	113.5	162.8	220.5	242.1	250.6	260.8	272.8	285.6	297.1
Entertainment/Recreation[1]	47.5	62.0	83.6	107.9	132.4	153.9	101.1	102.0	103.3	104.9	106.2	107.5
Other goods and services	40.9	53.9	75.2	114.5	159.0	206.9	237.7	258.3	271.1	282.6	293.2	298.7
Tobacco products	43.1	54.7	72.0	116.7	181.5	225.7	274.8	355.8	394.9	425.2	461.5	469.0
Personal care	43.5	57.9	81.9	106.3	130.4	147.1	156.7	161.1	165.6	170.5	154.7	153.5
Personal care products	42.7	58.0	79.6	107.6	128.2	143.1	148.3	151.8	153.7	155.1	174.7	178.0
Personal care services	44.2	57.7	83.7	108.9	132.8	151.5	166.0	171.4	178.1	184.3	188.4	193.2

(1) Dec. 1997 = 100; Entertainment was reclassified as Recreation in 1997.

Consumer Price Indexes by Region and Selected Cities, 2002-2003[1]

Source: Bureau of Labor Statistics, U.S. Dept. of Labor

(1982-84 = 100, unless otherwise noted; % change not annualized)

	Semiannual averages				Percent change from preceding semiannual average			
	2nd half 2002	1st half 2003	2nd half 2003	1st half 2004	2nd half 2002	1st half 2003	2nd half 2003	1st half 2004
U.S. CITY AVERAGE	180.9	183.3	184.6	187.6	1.1	1.3	0.7	1.6
Northeast urban	189.5	192.2	194.7	198.6	1.4	1.4	1.3	2.0
Size A—More than 1,500,000	191.2	194.0	196.9	200.7	1.5	1.5	1.5	1.9
Size B/C—50,000 to 1,500,000[2]	112.5	114.1	114.9	117.5	1.1	1.4	0.7	2.3
Midwest urban	175.9	177.8	178.8	118.4	1.2	1.1	0.6	1.5
Size A—More than 1,500,000	178.2	179.8	181.3	183.6	1.1	0.9	0.8	1.3
Size B/C—50,000 to 1,500,000[2]	111.5	113.0	113.5	115.5	1.1	1.3	0.4	1.8
Size D—Nonmetro. (less than 50,000)	169.9	172.0	171.8	174.3	1.4	1.2	-0.1	1.5
South urban	174.3	176.7	177.8	180.5	1.2	1.4	0.6	1.5
Size A—More than 1,500,000	175.7	178.4	179.6	182.1	1.3	1.5	0.7	1.4
Size B/C—50,000 to 1,500,000[2]	111.4	112.8	113.4	115.3	1.1	1.3	0.5	1.7
Size D—Nonmetro. (less than 50,000)	172.6	112.8	175.6	178.1	1.5	1.3	0.5	1.4
West urban	185.5	188.2	188.9	191.9	0.8	1.5	0.4	1.6
Size A—More than 1,500,000	188.1	191.0	191.4	194.3	1.0	1.5	0.2	1.5
Size B/C—50,000 to 1,500,000[2]	113.0	114.6	115.3	117.5	0.4	1.4	0.6	1.9
SELECTED AREAS								
Atlanta, GA	178.9	181.1	180.5	182.4	0.7	1.2	-0.3	1.1
Boston–Brockton–Nashua, MA–NH–ME–CT	198.7	201.9	205.9	208.6	2.2	1.6	2.0	1.3
Chicago–Gary–Kenosha, IL–IN–WI	182.2	183.8	185.3	187.2	1.2	0.9	0.8	1.0
Cleveland–Akron, OH	173.8	174.9	177.6	180.2	0.5	0.6	1.5	1.5
Dallas–Fort Worth, TX	173.3	176.1	176.4	177.8	0.7	1.6	0.2	0.8
Detroit–Ann Arbor–Flint, MI	180.3	182.2	182.9	184.2	1.5	1.1	0.4	0.7
Houston–Galveston–Brazoria, TX	160.7	162.8	164.6	168.7	1.8	1.3	1.1	2.5
L.A.–Riverside–Orange County, CA	183.3	186.7	187.2	191.5	1.2	1.9	0.3	2.3
Miami–Fort Lauderdale, FL	176.4	180.0	181.2	184.5	1.0	2.0	0.7	1.8
New York, NY–Northern NJ–Long Island, NY–NJ–CT–PA	193.1	196.4	199.2	203.1	1.3	1.7	1.4	2.0
Philadelphia–Wilmington–Atlantic City, PA–DE–NJ–MD	186.5	187.5	190.2	194.0	1.7	0.5	1.4	2.0
San Francisco–Oakland–San Jose, CA	193.7	196.8	196.1	198.2	0.7	1.6	-0.4	1.1
Seattle–Tacoma–Bremerton, WA	190.3	191.6	193.1	194.0	1.1	0.7	0.8	0.5
Washington–Baltimore, DC–MD–VA–WV[3]	113.9	115.6	116.9	118.3	1.6	1.5	1.1	1.2

(1) For all urban consumers. (2) Dec. 1996 = 100. (3) Nov. 1996 = 100.

Consumer Price Changes in Selected Countries, 1975-2003

Source: International Monetary Fund

(annual averages; some figures revised)

COUNTRY	1975-1980	1980-1985	1992-1993	1993-1994	1994-1995	1995-1996	1996-1997	1997-1998	1998-1999	1999-2000	2000-2001R	2001-2002	2002-2003
Canada.	8.7	7.4	1.8	0.2	2.2	1.6	1.6	1.0	1.7	2.7	2.5	2.2	2.8
France	10.5	9.6	2.1	1.7	1.8	2.0	1.2	0.7	0.5	1.7	1.6	1.9	2.1
Germany	4.1	3.9	4.1	3.0	1.8	1.5	1.8	1.0	0.6	1.5	2.0	1.4	1.0
Italy.	16.3	13.7	4.5	4.0	5.2	4.0	2.0	2.0	1.7	2.5	2.8	2.5	2.7
Japan	6.5	2.7	1.3	0.7	-0.1	0.1	1.7	0.6	-0.3	-0.7	-0.7	-0.9	-0.3
Spain	18.6	12.2	4.6	4.7	4.7	3.6	2.0	1.8	2.3	3.4	3.6	3.1	3.0
Sweden	10.5	9.0	4.6	2.2	2.5	0.5	0.5	-0.1	0.5	0.9	2.4	2.2	1.9
Switzerland.	2.3	4.3	3.3	0.8	1.8	0.8	0.5	0.1	0.7	1.5	1.0	0.6	0.6
United Kingdom	14.4	7.2	1.6	2.5	3.4	2.4	3.1	3.4	1.6	2.9	1.8	1.6	2.9
United States	8.9	5.5	3.0	2.6	2.8	3.0	2.3	1.6	2.2	3.4	2.8	1.6	2.3

R = Revised.

Index of Leading Economic Indicators

Source: The Conference Board

The index of leading economic indicators is used to project the U.S. economy's performance. The index is made up of 10 measurements of economic activity that tend to change direction in advance of the overall economy. The index has predicted economic downturns from 8 to 20 months in advance and recoveries from 1 to 10 months in advance; however, it can be inconsistent, and has occasionally shown "false signals" of recessions.

Components

Average weekly hours of production workers in manufacturing
Average weekly initial claims for unemployment insurance, state programs
Manufacturers' new orders for consumer goods and materials, adjusted for inflation
Vendor performance (slower deliveries diffusion index)

Manufacturers' new orders, nondefense capital goods industries, adjusted for inflation
New private housing units authorized by local building permits
Stock prices, 500 common stocks
Money supply: M-2, adjusted for inflation
Interest rate spread, 10-yr Treasury bonds less federal funds
Consumer expectations (researched by Univ. of Michigan)

U.S. Gross Domestic Product, Gross National Product, Net National Product, National Income, and Personal Income

Source: Bureau of Economic Analysis, U.S. Dept. of Commerce

(billions of current dollars; revised)

	1960	1970	1980	1990	2000	2001	2002	2003
Gross domestic product	526.4	1,038.5	2,789.5	5,803.1	9,817.0	10,128.0	10,487.0	11,004.0
Gross national product	529.5	1,044.9	2,823.7	5,837.9	9,855.9	10,171.6	10,514.1	11,059.2
Less: Consumption of fixed capital	55.6	106.7	343.0	682.5	1,187.8	1,281.5	1,303.9	1,353.9
Net national product	473.9	938.2	2,480.7	5,155.4	8,668.1	8,890.2	9,210.1	9,705.2
Less: Statistical discrepancy.	-0.9	7.3	41.4	66.2	-127.2	-89.6	-15.3	25.6
Equals: National income	474.9	930.9	2,439.3	5,089.1	8,795.2	8,979.8	9,225.4	9,679.6
Less: Corporate profits with inventory valuation and capital consumption adjustments	53.8	83.6	201.1	437.8	817.9	767.3	874.6	1,021.1
Taxes on production and imports less subsidies[1]	43.4	86.7	190.9	398.7	664.6	673.3	724.4	751.3
Contributions for government social insurance	16.4	46.4	166.2	410.1	702.7	731.1	748.3	773.2
Net interest and miscellaneous payments on assets.	10.6	39.1	181.8	442.2	559.0	566.3	532.9	543.0
Business current transfer payments (net)	1.9	4.5	14.4	39.4	87.1	92.8	80.9	77.7
Current surplus of government enterprises[1] . . .	0.9	0.0	-4.8	1.6	5.3	-1.4	2.8	9.5
Wage accruals less disbursements.	0.0	0.0	0.0	0.1	0.0	0.0	0.0	0.0
Plus: Personal income receipts on assets	37.9	93.5	338.7	924.0	1,387.0	1,380.0	1,334.6	1,322.7
Personal current transfer receipts.	25.7	74.7	279.5	595.2	1,084.0	1,193.9	1,282.7	1,335.4
Equals: Personal income	411.5	838.8	2,307.9	4,878.6	8,429.7	8,724.1	8,878.9	9,161.8

U.S. Gross Domestic Product

Source: Bureau of Economic Analysis, U.S. Dept. of Commerce

(billions of current dollars)

	1993	2003	2nd quarter 2004[1]		1993	2003	2nd quarter 2004[1]
Gross domestic product	6,657.4	11,004.0	11,657.5	Net exports of goods and services	-65.0	-498.1	-591.3
Personal consumption				Exports.	655.8	1,046.2	1,167.6
expenditures.	4,477.9	7,760.9	8,153.8	Goods	459.9	726.4	812.2
Durable goods	526.7	950.7	975.5	Services	195.9	319.8	355.4
Nondurable goods	1,379.4	2,200.1	2,354.6	Imports	720.9	1,544.3	1,758.9
Services	2,571.8	4,610.1	4,823.8	Goods	592.8	1,282.0	1,470.1
Gross private domestic				Services.	128.1	262.3	288.8
investment	953.4	1,665.8	1,920.7	**Government consumption**			
Fixed investment	932.5	1,667.0	1,861.7	**expenditures and gross**			
Nonresidential.	666.6	1,094.7	1,198.5	**investment**.	1,291.2	2,075.5	2,174.3
Structures	177.2	261.6	275.5	Federal	525.2	752.2	804.4
Equipment and software. . . .	489.4	833.1	923.1	National defense	362.9	496.4	541.2
Residential	266.0	572.3	663.2	Nondefense	162.4	255.7	263.2
Change in private inventories	20.8	-1.2	59.0	State and local	766.0	1,323.3	1,369.9

(1) Seasonally adjusted at annual rates.

Countries With Highest Gross Domestic Product and Per Capita GDP 2003[1]

Source: Central Intelligence Agency, *The World Factbook 2004*

Gross Domestic Product (in bil; est. 2003)

1. U.S.	$10,980	21. South Africa	$457
2. China[2]	6,449	22. Turkey	455
3. Japan	3,567	23. Argentina	433
4. India	3,022	24. Poland	427
5. Germany	2,271	25. Philippines	391
6. UK	1,664	26. Pakistan	318
7. France	1,654	27. Belgium	298
8. Italy	1,552	28. Egypt	294
9. Brazil	1,379	29. Saudi Arabia	286
10. Russia	1,287	30. Colombia	263
11. Canada	958	31. Bangladesh	259
12. Mexico	942	32. Ukraine	257
13. Spain	886	33. Austria	246
14. South Korea	855	34. Switzerland	240
15. Indonesia	758	35. Sweden	238
16. Australia	570	36. Greece	212
17. Taiwan	529	37. Malaysia	207
18. Iran	478	38. Vietnam	204
19. Thailand	476	39. Algeria	194
20. Netherlands	461	40. Portugal	182

Per Capita Gross Domestic Product (est. 2003)[3]

1. Luxembourg	$55,100	21. Sweden	$26,800
2. U.S.	37,800	22. Liechtenstein	25,000[5]
3. Norway	37,700	23. Singapore	23,700
4. San Marino	34,600[4]	24. Taiwan	23,400
5. Switzerland	32,800	25. U.A.E.	23,200
6. Denmark	31,200	26. Spain	22,000
7. Iceland	30,900	27. New Zealand	21,600
8. Austria	30,000	28. Qatar	21,500
9. Ireland	29,800	29. Greece	19,900
10. Canada	29,700	30. Israel	19,700
11. Belgium	29,000	31. Andorra	19,000[6]
12. Australia	28,900	32. Brunei	18,600[7]
13. Netherlands	28,600	33. Slovenia	18,300
14. Japan	28,000	34. Kuwait	18,100
15. UK	27,700	35. Portugal	18,000
16. Germany	27,600	36. South Korea	17,700
17. France	27,500	37. Malta	17,700
18. Finland	27,300	38. Bahrain	17,100
19. Monaco	27,000[5]	39. The Bahamas	16,800
20. Italy	26,800	40. Barbados	16,200

(1) U.S. data from *The World Factbook* may differ from data from the U.S. Bureau of Economic Analysis. International GDP estimates derive from purchasing power parity calculations, which involve the use of intl. dollar price weights applied to quantities of goods and services produced in a given economy. (2) Does not include Hong Kong, which had a GDP of $212 billion and a per capita GDP of $28,700 in 2003, or Macao, which had a GDP of $9.1 billion and a per capita GDP of $19,400 in 2003. (3) These territories or former territories (as well as Hong Kong, above note) had large per capita GDPs: Bermuda (UK, 2003) $36,000, Cayman Islands (UK, 2002) $35,000, Faroe Islands (Den., 2001) $22,000, Aruba (Neth., 2002) $28,000, Guam (U.S., 2000) $21,000, Greenland (Den., 2001) $20,000, Macao (China, 2001) $19,400, Gibraltar (UK, 1997) $17,500. (4) 2001 est. (5) 1999 est. (6) 2000 est. (7) 2002 est.

U.S. National Income by Industry[1]

Source: Bureau of Economic Analysis, U.S. Dept. of Commerce; in billions of current dollars; revised

	1998	1999	2000	2001	2002	2003
National income without capital consumption adjustment	7,661.4	8,122.9	8687.4	8,854.9	9,011.8	9,396.6
Domestic industries	7,640.1	8,089.2	8,648.5	8,811.2	8,984.7	9,341.5
Private industries	6,724.6	7,134.9	7,642.8	7,758.4	7,861.6	8,158.7
Agriculture, forestry, fishing, and hunting	78.5	73.6	70.1	69.3	66.9	75.8
Mining	72.6	69.3	93.8	101	79.1	94.9
Utilities	138.6	142.6	144.3	149.2	146	156.0
Construction	366.6	408.7	440.6	463.3	460.8	476.5
Manufacturing	1,112.1	1,150.3	1,228.5	1,094.1	1,074.8	1,113.1
Durable goods	672.5	695	744	617.8	615	639.2
Nondurable goods	439.5	455.3	484.5	476.2	459.8	473.9
Wholesale trade	505.4	537.1	563.8	557.7	554.2	569.6
Retail trade	591.1	626.8	665.3	689	708.2	725.8
Transportation and warehousing	235.3	247.4	261.2	251.9	248.5	259.9
Information	273.7	302.8	308.3	305.6	306.6	310.7
Finance, insurance, real estate, rental, leasing	1,328.5	1,396.3	1,529.3	1,643.7	1,672.3	1,740.8
Professional and business services	975.1	1072.2	1,151.6	1,171.3	1,205.2	1,226.4
Educ. services, health care, social assistance	582.7	615.8	664.6	719.2	774.9	824.8
Arts, entert., recreation, accommodation, food serv.	267.9	289.1	310.5	316.8	328.7	339.5
Other services, except government	196.6	202.9	215.8	226.2	235.4	244.9
Government	915.5	954.3	1,005.7	1,052.8	1,123.2	1,182.8
Rest of the world	21.3	33.8	38.9	43.6	27.0	55.1

(1) Figures may not add because of rounding. Total national income also includes income from outside the U.S.

U.S. National Income by Type of Income[1]

Source: Bureau of Economic Analysis, U.S. Dept. of Commerce; in billions of current dollars; revised

	1960	1970	1980	1990	2000	2001	2002	2003
National income[2]	474.9	930.9	2,439.3	5,089.1	8,795.2	8,979.8	9,225.4	9,679.6
Compensation of employees	296.4	617.2	1,651.8	3,338.2	5,782.7	5,942.1	6,069.5	6289
Wage and salary accruals	272.9	551.6	1,377.6	2754	4,829.2	4,942.8	4,976.3	5,103.6
Government	49.2	117.2	261.5	517.7	774.7	815.9	862.6	897.9
Supplements to wages and salaries	23.6	65.7	274.2	584.2	953.4	999.3	1,093.2	1,185.5
Employer contributions for employee pension and insurance funds	14.3	41.8	185.2	377.8	609.9	642.7	729.6	808.9
Employer contributions for government social insurance	9.3	23.8	88.9	206.5	343.5	356.6	363.6	376.6
Proprietors' income with inventory valuation and capital consumption adjustments	50.8	78.4	174.1	380.6	728.4	771.9	769.6	834.1
Farm	10.5	12.7	11.3	31.9	22.7	19.7	9.7	21.8
Nonfarm	40.3	65.7	162.8	348.7	705.7	752.2	759.9	812.3
Rental income of persons with capital consumption adjustments	17.1	21.4	30.0	50.7	150.3	167.4	170.9	153.8
Corporate profits with inventory valuation and capital consumption adjustment	53.8	83.6	201.1	437.8	817.9	767.3	874.6	1,021.1
Taxes on corporate income	22.8	34.8	87.2	145.4	265.2	204.1	183.8	234.9
Profits after tax with inventory valuation and capital consumption adjustments	31.0	48.9	113.9	292.4	552.7	563.2	690.7	786.2
Net dividends	13.4	24.3	64.1	169.1	377.9	370.9	390.0	395.3
Undistributed profits with inventory valuation and capital consumption adjustments	17.6	24.6	49.9	123.3	174.8	192.3	300.7	390.9
Net interest and miscellaneous payments	10.6	39.1	181.8	442.2	559	566.3	532.9	543

(1) Figures do not add, because of rounding and incomplete enumeration. (2) National income is the aggregate of labor and property earnings that arises in the production of goods and services. It is the sum of employee compensation, proprietors' income, rental income, adjusted corporate profits, and net interest. It measures the total factor costs of goods and services produced by the economy. Income is measured before deduction of taxes. Total national income figures include adjustments not itemized.

Selected Personal Consumption Expenditures in the U.S., 1995-2003[1]

Source: Bureau of Economic Analysis, U.S. Dept. of Commerce

(billions of dollars)

	1995	1998	1999	2000	2001	2002	2003
Personal consumption expenditures	4,975.8	5,879.5	6,282.5	6,739.4	7,055.0	7,376.1	7,760.9
Durable goods	611.6	750.2	817.6	863.3	883.7	916.2	950.7
Motor vehicles and parts	266.7	336.1	370.8	386.5	407.9	426.1	440.1
New autos	82.1	87.7	97.5	103.6	103.2	101.6	97.5
Tires, tubes, accessories, and other parts	37.8	43.9	47.0	49.0	49.1	50.7	53.2
Furniture and household equipment	228.6	273.1	293.9	312.9	312.1	319.9	328.0
Furniture, including mattresses and bedsprings	48.5	59.6	63.5	67.6	67.2	68.3	69.5
Kitchen and other household appliances	26.5	27.5	29.2	30.4	30.8	31.5	33.1
China, glassware, tableware, and utensils	23.4	27.2	29.3	31.0	31.0	31.8	32.2
Video and audio goods, including musical instruments	57.2	62.7	67.8	72.8	73.6	74.9	75.2
Computers, peripherals, and software	24.3	37.0	40.4	43.8	42.0	44.2	46.1
Ophthalmic products and orthopedic appliances	15.0	20.0	20.8	22.1	20.8	21.6	22.4
Wheel goods, sports and photographic equipment, boats, and pleasure aircraft	39.7	48.3	52.6	57.6	59.2	60.6	68.0
Jewelry and watches	38.4	43.9	48.1	50.6	49.2	51.0	53.6
Books and maps	23.2	28.8	31.5	33.7	34.6	36.9	38.5
Nondurable goods	1,485.1	1,683.6	1,804.8	1,947.2	2,017.1	2,080.1	2,200.1
Food	740.9	829.8	873.1	925.2	967.9	1,005.8	1,064.5
Food purchased for off-premise consumption	458.6	509.0	536.9	566.7	595.2	615.6	647.1
Purchased meals and beverages	274.0	311.9	326.9	348.8	362.8	380.0	406.5
Food furnished to employees (including military) and food produced and consumed on farms	8.3	9.0	9.3	9.7	9.9	10.2	10.9
Alcoholic beverages purchased for off-premise consumption	54.6	63.2	66.1	71.2	73.7	75.5	79.9
Clothing and shoes	241.7	270.9	286.3	297.7	297.7	302.1	307.2
Shoes	37.6	43.0	45.4	47.0	47.8	49.3	50.7
Women's and children's clothing and accessories except shoes	129.5	141.2	149.9	156.7	156.5	158.3	160.4
Men's and boys' clothing and accessories except shoes	74.7	86.6	91.0	94.0	93.4	94.6	96.1
Gasoline, fuel oil, and other energy goods	133.3	133.9	149.8	191.5	187.1	177.5	208.2
Gasoline and oil	120.2	122.4	137.9	175.7	171.6	163.4	191.3
Fuel oil and coal	13.1	11.5	11.9	15.8	15.4	14.1	16.9
Tobacco products	49.2	58.9	71.6	78.5	84.0	89.1	88.1
Toilet articles and preparations	45.9	52.6	53.9	55.0	54.4	54.2	53.2
Semidurable house furnishings	29.4	32.8	35.1	36.5	36.5	37.4	37.9
Cleaning and polishing preparations, misc. household supplies and paper products	48.8	55.9	59.2	61.6	64.5	66.6	69.1
Drug preparations and sundries	92.1	128.0	148.9	169.4	192.7	213.0	233.7
Nondurable toys and sport supplies	44.4	51.3	54.7	56.6	57.6	59.0	60.2
Stationery and writing supplies	16.3	17.7	18.5	19.0	18.3	18.1	17.7
Magazines, newspapers, and sheet music	27.5	32.1	33.5	35.0	35.0	35.3	36.6
Flowers, seeds, and potted plants	14.0	16.4	17.1	18.0	18.0	18.0	18.8
Services	2,879.1	3,445.7	3,660.0	3,928.8	4,154.3	4,379.8	4,610.1
Housing	764.4	894.6	948.4	1,006.5	1,073.7	1,144.8	1,188.4
Owner-occupied nonfarm dwellings—space rent	531.2	627.5	668.4	712.2	768.7	820.7	859.6
Tenant-occupied nonfarm dwellings—rent	186.6	209.0	219.0	227.5	240.7	258.7	262.3
Rental value of farm dwellings	9.4	9.9	10.2	10.7	11.4	11.8	11.9
Household operation	298.7	350.5	364.8	390.1	409.0	409.0	431.3
Electricity	91.0	97.1	97.2	102.3	108.0	111.7	116.1
Gas	31.2	32.7	33.4	41.0	48.6	40.8	51.2
Water and other sanitary services	39.3	46.2	48.8	50.8	52.8	55.2	58.2
Telephone and telegraph	85.0	110.3	118.4	125.1	128.4	128.3	129.8
Domestic service	13.8	17.1	16.1	17.4	16.9	16.8	18.5
Transportation	207.7	259.5	276.4	291.3	292.8	288.0	294.0
User-operated transportation	163.6	205.9	220.6	231.6	238.8	237.7	241.5
Purchased local transportation	10.1	11.8	11.9	12.2	12.5	12.4	12.6
Mass transit systems	7.1	8.3	8.6	9.1	9.2	9.0	8.8
Taxicab	3.0	3.5	3.3	3.1	3.2	3.4	3.7
Purchased intercity transportation	33.9	41.8	43.9	47.4	41.6	37.9	40.0
Railway	0.4	0.4	0.5	0.5	0.6	0.6	0.6
Bus	1.8	2.2	2.2	2.4	2.4	2.3	2.3
Airline	25.3	31.8	33.3	36.7	31.4	28.1	30.3
Medical care	797.9	921.4	961.1	1,026.8	1,113.8	1,210.3	1,301.1
Physicians	184.6	210.3	220.8	236.8	256.8	278.3	298.2
Dentists	45.4	54.1	57.4	61.8	66.8	72.2	75.0
Other professional services	126.6	149.4	153.3	161.6	175.5	189.7	205.1
Hospitals and nursing homes	380.5	435.9	453.6	482.6	525.3	574.0	616.8
Health insurance	60.7	71.6	76.1	84.0	89.4	96.1	106.0
Recreation	187.9	229.3	248.6	268.3	284.1	299.6	317.2
Admissions to specified spectator amusements	21.1	26.2	28.4	30.4	32.2	34.6	35.6
Personal care	61.2	75.0	80.7	87.0	90.4	92.9	95.1
Cleaning, storage, and repair of clothing and shoes	12.3	14.3	15.1	15.7	15.8	15.8	14.7
Barbershops, beauty parlors, and health clubs	26.8	33.6	35.6	38.4	40.1	41.6	43.7
Personal business	349.6	446.1	491.6	539.1	536.5	552.1	577.7
Brokerage charges and investment counseling	43.5	69.1	84.4	100.6	77.8	75.7	77.3
Bank service charges, trust services, and safe deposit box rental	37.2	50.2	58.3	64.2	69.1	75.5	82.5
Expense of handling life insurance and pension plans	72.9	82.7	85.2	96.1	91.9	84.8	91.5
Legal services	47.4	57.5	61.0	63.9	68.0	71.3	77.3
Funeral and burial expenses	12.4	13.8	14.0	14.0	14.6	14.6	15.7
Education and research	114.3	140.0	150.5	163.8	178.1	190.7	201.7
Higher education	62.9	75.0	80.0	86.4	95.1	103.9	112.2
Nursery, elementary, and secondary schools	27.0	31.0	32.7	34.6	36.5	38.3	39.5
Religious and welfare activities	120.4	146.0	154.5	172.3	186.5	202.9	211.2
Net foreign travel	−22.9	−16.6	−16.6	−16.2	−10.8	−10.4	−7.5
Foreign travel by U.S. residents	54.7	71.1	75.5	84.4	80.7	77.4	79.2
Less: Expenditures in the United States by nonresidents	77.6	87.7	92.1	100.7	91.5	87.9	86.7

NA = Not available. (1) Subtotals may not add to total, due to rounding.

U.S. Per Capita Money Income[1], 1970-2001

Source: Bureau of the Census, U.S. Dept. of Commerce

Year	Current dollars	2001 dollars	Year	Current dollars	2001 dollars	Year	Current dollars	2001 dollars	Year	Current dollars	2001 dollars
1970	$3,177	$12,543	1985	$11,013	$17,280	1996	$18,136	$20,372	1999	$21,181	$22,499
1975	4,818	13,972	1990	14,387	18,894	1997	19,241	21,162	2000	22,346	22,970
1980	7,787	15,844	1995	17,227	19,871	1998	20,120	21,821	2001	22,851	22,851

(1) "Money income" includes most direct sources of earning, but excludes company retirement contributions, capital gains, food stamps, rent vouchers and other items.

Distribution of U.S. Total Personal Income[1]

Source: Bureau of Economic Analysis, U.S. Dept. of Commerce; in billions of current dollars

Year	Personal income	Personal taxes and nontax payments	Disposable personal income	Personal outlays	Personal Savings Amount	Personal Savings As pct. of disposable income
1960	$411.5	$46.1	$365.4	$338.8	$26.7	7.3%
1965	555.7	57.7	498.1	455.1	43.0	8.6
1970	838.8	103.1	735.7	666.2	69.5	9.4
1975	1,335.0	147.6	1,187.4	1,061.9	125.6	10.6
1980	2,307.9	298.9	2,009.0	1,807.5	201.4	10.0
1985	3,526.7	417.4	3,109.3	2,829.3	280.0	9.0
1990	4,878.6	592.8	4,285.8	3,986.4	299.4	7.0
1995	6,152.3	744.1	5,408.2	5,157.3	250.9	4.6
2000	8,429.7	1,235.7	7,194.0	7,025.6	168.5	2.3
2001	8,724.1	1,237.3	7,486.8	7,354.5	132.3	1.8
2002	8,878.9	1,051.2	7,827.7	7,668.5	159.2	2.0
2003	9,161.8	1,001.9	8,159.9	8,049.3	110.6	1.4

(1) Personal income minus taxes/nontax payments=disposable income; disposable income minus outlays=savings. Figures may not add because of rounding.

Banks in the U.S.–Number, Deposits

Source: Federal Deposit Insurance Corp. (as of Dec. 31, 2002)

Comprises all FDIC-insured commercial and savings banks, including savings and loan institutions (S&Ls).

Year	ALL BANKS	Commercial banks[1] Natl.	Commercial banks[1] State	Commercial banks[1] Non-members	All savings	ALL DEPOSITS	Commercial banks[1] Natl.	Commercial banks[1] State	Commercial banks[1] Non-members	All savings
1935	15,295	5,386	1,001	7,735	1,173	$45,102[2]	$24,802	$13,653	$5,669	$978[2]
1940	15,772	5,144	1,342	6,956	2,330	67,494	35,787	20,642	7,040	4,025
1945	15,969	5,017	1,864	6,421	2,667	151,524	77,778	41,865	16,307	15,574
1950	16,500	4,958	1,912	6,576	3,054	171,963	84,941	41,602	19,726	25,694
1955	17,001	4,692	1,847	6,698	3,764	235,211	102,796	55,739	26,198	50,478
1960	17,549	4,530	1,641	6,955	4,423	310,262	120,242	65,487	34,369	90,164
1965	18,384	4,815	1,405	7,327	4,837	467,633	185,334	78,327	51,982	151,990
1970	18,205	4,621	1,147	7,743	4,694	686,901	285,436	101,512	95,566	204,367
1975	18,792	4,744	1,046	8,595	4,407	1,157,648	450,308	143,409	187,031	376,900
1980	18,763	4,425	997	9,013	4,328	1,832,716	656,752	191,183	344,311	640,470
1985	18,033	4,959	1,070	8,378	3,626	3,140,827	1,241,875	354,585	521,628	1,022,739
1990	15,158	3,979	1,009	7,355	2,815	3,637,292	1,558,915	397,797	693,438	987,142
1995	11,970	2,858	1,042	6,040	2,030	3,769,477	1,695,817	614,924	716,829	741,907
1998	10,463	2,456	994	5,324	1,689	4,386,298	2,137,946	810,471	733,027	704,855
1999	10,221	2,363	1,010	5,207	1,641	4,538,036	2,154,259	899,252	777,264	707,261
2000	9,905	2,230	991	5,094	1,590	4,914,808	2,250,464	1,032,110	894,000	738,234
2001	9,631	2,137	972	4,971	1,533	5,189,444	2,384,462	1,079,388	927,772	797,822
2002	9,354	2,077	950	4,861	1,439	5,568,508	2,565,771	1,152,380	971,730	878,627
2003	9,182	2,001	935	4,833	1,413	5,954,288	2,786,756	1,195,914	1,046,195	925,423

(1) "Nonmembers" are banks that are not members of the Federal Reserve System; "National" and "State" institutions are members.
(2) Figures for 1935 do not include data for S&Ls (not available).

50 Largest U.S. Bank Holding Companies[1]

Source: American Banker (as of Dec. 31, 2003)

Company Name	Total Assets (in thousands)	Company Name	Total Assets (in thousands)
Citigroup Inc., New York, NY	$1,264,032,000	SouthTrust Corp., Birmingham, AL	$52,128,326
J.P. Morgan Chase & Co., New York, NY	770,912,000	M&T Bank Corp., Buffalo, NY	49,826,081
Bank of America Corp., Charlotte, NC	736,487,404	Regions Financial Corp., Birmingham, AL	48,881,023
Wachovia Corp., Charlotte, NC	401,032,000	Mitsubishi Tokyo Financial Group	47,644,551
Wells Fargo & Co., San Francisco, CA	387,798,000	Charles Schwab Corp., San Francisco, CA	45,866,220
MetLife Inc., New York, NY	326,841,959	AmSouth Bancorp., Birmingham, AL	45,670,092
Bank One Corp., Chicago, IL	326,563,000	Sovereign Bancorp Inc., Wyomissing, PA	43,610,071
Washington Mutual Inc., Seattle, WA	235,442,148	Charter One Financial Inc., Cleveland, OH	42,713,133
FleetBoston Financial Corp., Boston, MA	200,356,000	Northern Trust Corp., Chicago, IL	41,450,173
U.S. Bancorp, Minneapolis, MN	189,286,000	BNP Paribas, Paris	39,233,786
SunTrust Banks Inc., Atlanta, GA	125,393,153	Popular Inc., San Juan, PR	36,426,000
National City Corp., Cleveland, OH	113,933,460	Deutsche Bank, Frankfurt	34,782,220
ABN Amro, Amsterdam	106,928,962	Marshall & Ilsley Corp., Milwaukee, WI	34,394,445
Countrywide Financial Corp., Calabasas, CA	97,957,619	Mellon Financial Corp., Pittsburgh, PA	34,048,947
HSBC Holdings PLC, London	92,958,123	Union Planters Corp., Memphis, TN	31,918,488
Bank of New York Co. Inc., New York, NY	92,404,942	Bank of Montreal, Montreal, Quebec	31,129,301
Fifth Third Bancorp, Cincinnati, OH	91,143,023	Huntington Bancshares Inc., Columbus, OH	30,565,542
BB&T Corp., Winston-Salem, NC	90,466,613	Zions Bancorp., Salt Lake City, UT	28,558,238
State Street Corp., Boston, MA	87,534,065	Compass Bancshares Inc., Birmingham, AL	27,032,300
KeyCorp, Cleveland, OH	84,146,964	Banknorth Group Inc., Portland, ME	26,461,796
Golden West Financial Corp., Oakland, CA	82,049,858	First Tennessee National Corp., Memphis, TN	24,507,953
Royal Bank of Scotland Group, Edinburgh	77,688,997	New York Community Bancorp Inc, Westbury, NY	23,503,762
PNC Fin. Services Group Inc., Pittsburgh, PA	68,193,348	National Commerce Fin. Corp., Memphis, TN	23,002,505
MBNA Corp., Wilmington, DE	59,126,089	GreenPoint Financial Corp., New York, NY	22,978,970
Comerica Inc., Detroit, MI	52,943,676	Commerce Bancorp Inc., Cherry Hill, NJ	22,744,869

(1) Includes foreign-owned banks with a strong presence in the U.S.

U.S. Bank Failures, 1934-2003

Source: Federal Deposit Insurance Corp.

Covers all FDIC-insured commercial and savings banks, including savings and loan institutions (S&Ls) 1980 and after.

Year	Closed or assisted	Year	Closed or assisted	Year	Closed or assisted	Year	Closed or assisted	Year	Closed or assisted	Year	Closed or assisted
1934...	9	1960...	1	1970...	7	1980...	22	1988...	465	1996...	6
1935...	26	1961...	5	1971...	7	1981...	40	1989...	534	1997...	1
1936...	69	1963...	2	1972...	2	1982...	119	1990...	382	1998...	3
1937...	77	1964...	7	1973...	6	1983...	99	1991...	271	1999...	8
1938...	74	1965...	5	1975...	13	1984...	106	1992...	181	2000...	7
1939...	60	1966...	7	1976...	17	1985...	180	1993...	50	2001...	4
1940...	43	1967...	4	1978...	7	1986...	204	1994...	15	2002...	11
1955...	5	1969...	9	1979...	10	1987...	262	1995...	8	2003...	3
1959...	3										

World's 50 Largest Banking Companies[1]

Source: *American Banker* (as of Dec. 31, 2002)

Company	Assets[2] (millions)	Company	Assets[2] (millions)
Mizuho Holdings, Japan	$1,135,553	Lloyds TSB Group PLC, UK	$406,886
Citigroup, U.S.	1,097,190	Rabobank Group, Netherlands	392,819
Sumitomo Mitsui Financial Group, Japan	872,962	Dexia, Belgium	367,874
UBS AG, Switzerland	852,190	Wells Fargo & Co., U.S.	349,259
Allianz AG, Germany	850,356	Wachovia Corp., U.S.	341,839
Deutsche Bank, Germany	791,674	Reasona Holdings Inc., Japan	332,892
J.P. Morgan Chase & Co., U.S.	758,800	Abbey National PLC, UK	331,121
HSBC Holdings PLC, U.K.	757,406	Banco Santander Central Hispano, Spain.	324,378
ING Group NV, Netherlands	751,711	BBV Argentaria, Spain	293,156
BNP Paribas, France	744,627	Intesa, Italy	280,733
Mitsubishi Tokyo Financial Group, Japan	742,896	Bank One Corp., U.S.	277,383
Bayerische Hypo-und Vereinsbanken AG, Germany	704,626	Washington Mutual Corp., U.S.	268,298
Credit Suisse Group, Switzerland	682,602	Nordea AB, Sweden	261,241
Royal Bank of Scotland Group, UK	663,279	Credit Lyonnais SA, France	256,729
Bank of America Corp., U.S.	660,458	Westdeutsche Landesbank Girozentrale, Germany .	249,810
Barclays PLC, UK	648,807	Almanij NV, Belgium	249,391
UFJ Holdings, Japan	590,898	Royal Bank of Canada, Canada	240,154
ABN Amro Holding NV, Netherlands	581,850	Eurohypo AG, Germany	237,166
HBOS PLC, UK	571,616	KBC Bank, Belgium	232,670
Credit Agricole SA, France	530,144	Danske Bank SA, Denmark.	230,579
Societe Generale, France	525,994	UniCredito Italiano SpA, Italy	223,674
Fortis, Netherlands	509,227	San Paolo Imi SpA, Italy	213,615
Axa, France	466,134	National Australia Bank, Australia	204,349
Commerzbank AG, Germany	437,407	Norddeutsche Landesbank, Germany.	206,675
Norinchukin Bank, Japan	433,630	FleetBoston Financial Corp., U.S.	190,453

(1) Includes bank holding companies and commercial and savings banks. (2) Currency conversion based on Exchange rates on Dec. 31 or at end of fiscal year.

Federal Deposit Insurance Corporation (FDIC)

The Federal Deposit Insurance Corporation (FDIC) is the independent deposit insurance agency created by Congress to maintain stability and public confidence in the nation's banking system. In its unique role as deposit insurer of banks and savings associations, and in cooperation with other federal and state regulatory agencies, the FDIC seeks to promote the safety and soundness of insured depository institutions in the U.S. financial system by identifying, monitoring, and addressing risks to the deposit insurance funds. The FDIC aims at promoting public understanding and sound public policies by providing financial and economic information and analyses. It seeks to minimize disruptive effects from the failure of banks and savings associations, and to ensure fairness in the sale of financial products and the provision of financial services.

To maintain its insurance funds, the FDIC assesses depository institutions insurance premiums twice a year. The amount of the premium is based on the institution's balance of insured deposits for the preceding two quarters and the institution's risk to the insurance fund. The Corporation may borrow from the U.S. Treasury, not to exceed $30 billion outstanding, but the agency has made no such borrowings since it was organized in 1933. The FDIC's Bank Insurance Fund was $34.1 billion (unaudited) and the Savings Association Insurance Fund stood at $12.4 billion (unaudited), as of June 30, 2004.

Federal Reserve Board Discount Rate

The discount rate is the rate of interest set by the Federal Reserve that member banks are charged when borrowing money through the Federal Reserve System. Includes any changes through Sept. 2004.

Effective date Rate	Effective date Rate	Effective date Rate	Effective date Rate	Effective date Rate
1980:	Oct. 12.... 9½	**1989:**	**1996:**	Apr. 18.... 4
Feb. 15 ... 13	Dec. 15 ...8½	Feb. 24....7	Jan. 31 ... 5	May 15 ... 3½
May 30 ... 12	**1984:**	**1990:**	**1998:**	June 27 ... 3¼
June 13 ... 11	April 9.... 9	Dec. 18....6½	Oct. 15 ... 4¾	Aug. 21 ... 3
July 28 ... 10	Nov. 21 ...8½	**1991:**	Nov. 17... 4½	Sept. 17... 2½
Sept. 26... 11	Dec. 24 ... 8	Apr. 30 ....5½	**1999:**	Oct. 2..... 2
Nov. 17 ... 12	**1985:**	Sept. 13 ... 5	Aug. 24 ... 4¾	Dec. 11 ... 1¼
Dec. 5 13	May 20.... 7½	Nov. 6.... 4½	Nov. 16 ... 5	**2002**
1981:	**1986:**	Dec. 20.... 3½	**2000:**	Nov. 6 .... ¾
May 5 14	March 7 ... 7	**1992:**	Feb. 2 ... 5¼	**2003**
Nov. 2 13	April 21... 6½	July 2 3	Mar. 21 ... 5½	Jan. 9[1]... 2¼, 2¾
Dec. 4 12	July 11.... 6	**1994:**	May 16 ... 6	June 25[1] .. 2, 2½
1982:	Aug. 21 ... 5½	May 17 .... ½	**2001:**	**2004**
July 20.... 11½	**1987:**	Aug. 16.... 4	Jan. 3 ... 5¾	Jun. 30 ... 2¼, 2¾
Aug. 2 11	Sept. 4 6	Nov. 15 .... 4¾	Jan. 31 ... 5	Aug. 10 ... 2½, 3
Aug. 16 ... 10	**1988:**	**1995:**	Mar. 20 ... 4½	Sept. 21... 2¾, 3¼
Aug. 27 ... 10	Aug. 9 ....6½	Feb. 1..... 5		

(1) The Federal Reserve approved a new system for lending directly to banks, effective Jan. 9, 2003. The discount rate was replaced with two new rates, the *primary credit rate* and *secondary credit rate*. The primary credit rate (listed first) is available to banks in generally sound financial condition. The secondary credit (listed second) rate is given to banks that do not qualify for the primary credit rate. Both are extended for very short terms, usually overnight. Under the new system, financially sound institutions are not required to exhaust all funds before borrowing from the Fed.

Federal Reserve System

The Federal Reserve System is the central bank for the U.S. The system was established on Dec. 23, 1913, originally to give the country an elastic currency, provide facilities for discounting commercial paper, and improve the supervision of banking. Since then, the system's responsibilities have been broadened. Over the years, stability and growth of the economy, a high level of employment, stability in the purchasing power of the dollar, and reasonable balance in transactions with other countries have come to be recognized as primary objectives of governmental economic policy.

The Federal Reserve System consists of the Board of Governors, the 12 District Reserve Banks and their branch offices, and the Federal Open Market Committee. Several advisory councils help the board meet its varied responsibilities.

The hub of the system is the 7-member **Board of Governors** in Washington, DC. The members of the board are appointed by the president and confirmed by the Senate, to serve 14-year terms. The president also appoints the chairman and vice chairman of the board from among the board members for 4-year terms that may be renewed. As of Oct. 2004 the board members were: Alan Greenspan, chair; Roger W. Ferguson Jr, vice chair; Edward M. Gramlich; Susan Schmidt Bies; Mark W. Olson; Ben S. Bernanke; and Donald L. Kohn.

The board is the policy-making body. In addition to those responsibilities, it supervises the budget and operations of the Reserve Banks, approves the appointments of their presidents, and appoints 3 of each District Bank's directors, including the chairman and vice chairman of each Reserve Bank's board.

The 12 **District Reserve Banks** and their branch offices serve as the decentralized portion of the system, carrying out day-to-day operations such as circulating currency and coin and providing fiscal agency functions and payments mechanism services. The 6 are in Boston, New York, Philadelphia, Cleveland, Richmond, Atlanta, Chicago, St. Louis, Minneapolis, Kansas City, Dallas, and San Francisco.

The system's principal function is monetary policy, which it controls using 3 tools: reserve requirements, the discount rate, and open market operations.

Uniform **reserve requirements**, set by the board, are applied to the transaction accounts and nonpersonal time deposits of all depository institutions. Responsibility for setting the **discount rate** (the interest rate at which depository institutions can borrow money from the Reserve Banks) is shared by the Board of Governors and the Reserve Banks. Changes in the discount rate are recommended by the individual boards of directors of the Reserve Banks and are subject to approval by the Board of Governors.

The most important tool of monetary policy is **open market operations** (the purchase and sale of government securities). Responsibility for influencing the cost and availability of money and credit through the purchase and sale of government securities lies with the **Federal Open Market Committee** (FOMC), which is composed of the 7 members of the Board of Governors, the president of the Federal Reserve Bank of New York, and 4 other Federal Reserve Bank presidents, who each serve 1-year terms on a rotating basis. The committee bases its decisions on economic and financial developments and outlook, setting yearly growth objectives for key measures of money supply and credit. The decisions of the committee are carried out by the Domestic Trading Desk of the Federal Reserve Bank of New York.

A Federal Advisory Council meets with the Federal Reserve Board 4 times a year to discuss business and financial conditions, as well as to make recommendations. It consists of 1 member from each Federal Reserve District, who is elected annually by the Board of Directors of each of the 12 Federal Reserve Banks. The council

The Consumer Advisory Council is a statutory body, including both consumer and creditor representatives, which advises the Board of Governors on its implementation of consumer regulations and other consumer-related matters.

Following the congressional passage of the Monetary Control Act of 1980, the Federal Reserve System's Board of Governors established the Thrift Institutions Advisory Council to provide information and perspectives on the special needs and problems of thrift institutions. This group is composed of representatives of mutual savings banks, savings and loan associations, and credit unions.

Website: www.federalreserve.gov

United States Mint

Source: United States Mint, U.S. Dept. of the Treasury

The United States Mint was created on Apr. 2, 1792, by an act of Congress, which established the U.S. national coinage system. Supervision of the mint was a function of the secretary of state, but in 1799 the mint became an independent agency reporting directly to the president. The mint was made a statutory bureau of the Treasury Department in 1873, with a director appointed by the president to oversee its operations.

The mint manufactures and ships all U.S. coins for circulation to Federal Reserve banks and branches, which in turn issue coins to the public and business community through depository institutions. The mint also safeguards the Treasury Department's stored gold and silver, as well as other monetary assets.

The composition of dimes, quarters, and half dollars, traditionally produced from silver, was changed by the Coinage Act of 1965, which mandated that these coins from here on in be minted from a cupronickel-clad alloy and reduced the silver content of the half dollar to 40%. In 1970, legislative action mandated that the half dollar and a dollar coin be minted from the same alloy.

The Eisenhower dollar was minted from 1971 through 1978, when legislation called for the minting of the smaller Susan B. Anthony dollar coin. The Anthony dollar, which was minted from 1979 through 1981, marked the first time that a woman, other than a mythical figure, appeared on a U.S. coin produced for general circulation. Authorized by the U.S. Dollar Coin Act of 1997 to replace the Susan B. Anthony dollar in 2000, is the Golden Dollar Coin. Golden in color, with a smooth edge and wide border, the obverse side depicts Sacagawea (a Shoshone woman who helped guide Lewis and Clark) and her infant son. The reverse

shows an American eagle and 17 stars, one for each of the states at the time of the Lewis and Clark expedition.

In commemoration of the bicentennials of the Louisiana Purchase and Lewis and Clark Exploration, the U.S. Mint released the Westward Journey Nickel Series in 2004-2005, featuring 4 new reverse designs. A modified portrait of Jefferson will appear on the obverse side of nickels released in 2005. The original nickel design will resume circulation in 2006.

Mint headquarters are in Washington, DC. Mint production facilities are in Philadelphia, Denver, San Francisco, and West Point, NY. In addition, the mint is responsible for the U.S. Bullion Depository at Fort Knox, KY.

Proof coin sets, silver proof coin sets, and uncirculated coin sets are available from the mint. The mint also produces ongoing series of national and historic medals in honor of significant persons, events, and sites.

Since 1982, the mint has produced the following congressionally authorized commemorative coins: 1982 George Washington half dollar; 1984 U.S. Olympic coins; 1986 U.S. Statue of Liberty coins; 1987 Bicentennial of the U.S. Constitution coins; 1989 U.S. Congressional coins; 1990 Eisenhower Centennial coin; 1991 United Services Organization 59th Anniversary coin; 1991 Korean War Memorial coin; 1991 Mount Rushmore Anniversary coins; 1992 U.S. Olympic coins; 1992 White House 200th Anniversary coin; 1992 Christopher Columbus Quincentenary coins; 1993 Bill of Rights coins; 1993 World War II 50th Anniversary coins; 1994 World Cup USA coins; Thomas Jefferson 250th Anniversary coin; U.S. Veterans coins (featuring the Prisoner of War coin, Vietnam Veterans Memorial coin, and Women in Military Service for America coin); Bicentennial of the U.S.

Capitol Commemorative Silver Dollar; 1995 Civil War Battlefield coins; 1995/1996 U.S. Olympic Games of the Atlanta Centennial Games; 1997 U.S. Botanic Garden Silver Dollar; 1997 Franklin Delano Roosevelt Gold coin; 1997 Gold and Silver Jackie Robinson Commemorative coins; 1997 National Law Enforcement Memorial Silver Dollar; Black Revolutionary War Patriots Silver Dollar; Robert F. Kennedy Silver Dollar; National Law Enforcement Officers Memorial Silver Dollar; 1999 Yellowstone National Park Silver Dollar; 1999 George Washington five-dollar gold coin; the Dolley Madison Silver Dollar; 2000 U.S. Leif Ericson Proof Silver Dollar; 2000 Icelandic Leif Ericson Proof Silver Krønur; the 2000 Library of Congress Commemorative Coin Program featuring the Proof Silver Dollar and the Proof Bi-metallic Gold and Platinum $10 coin; the 2001 American Buffalo Proof Siver Dollar; the 2001 U.S. Capitol Visitor Center Commemorative Coin Program, featuring the Half Dollar Clad Proof coin, the Proof Silver Dollar, and the Proof Gold $5 coin; the 2002 Olympic Winter Games Silver Dollar and Gold $5 coins, and 2002 West Point Bicentennial Commemorative Silver Dollar; the 2003 First Flight Centennial Commemorative coins (Gold, Silver, and Clad); the 2004 Lewis and Clark Bicentennial Silver Dollar; the 2004 Thomas A. Edison Commemorative Silver Dollar.

The congressionally authorized American Eagle gold, platinum, and silver bullion coins are available through dealers worldwide. The gold and platinum eagles are sold in one-ounce, half-ounce, quarter-ounce, and one-tenth-ounce sizes. The American eagle silver bullion coin contains one troy ounce of .999 fine silver and is priced according to the daily market value of silver. These coins also are available directly from the mint in proof condition, separately priced.

The mint offers free public tours and operates sales centers at the U.S. mints in Denver and Philadelphia; it also operates a sales center at Union Station, in Washington, DC.

Further information is available from the U.S. Mint, Customer Care Center, 801 9th St., NW, Washington, DC 20220.

Telephone number: (800) USA-MINT.

Website: www.usmint.gov

Denominations of U.S. Currency

Since 1969 the largest denomination of U.S. currency that has been issued is the $100 bill. As larger-denomination bills reach the Federal Reserve Bank, they are removed from circulation. Because some discontinued currency is expected to be in the hands of holders for many years, the description of the various denominations below is continued.

Amt.	Portait	Embellishment on Back	Amt.	Portait	Embellishment on Back
$1	Washington	Great Seal of U.S.	$100	B. Franklin	Independence Hall
2	Jefferson	Signers of Declaration	500	McKinley	Ornate denominational marking
5	Lincoln	Lincoln Memorial	1,000	Cleveland	Ornate denominational marking
10	Hamilton	U.S. Treasury	5,000	Madison	Ornate denominational marking
20	Jackson	White House	10,000*	Salmon Chase	Ornate denominational marking
50	Grant	U.S. Capitol	100,000*	Wilson	Ornate denominational marking

*For use only in transactions between Federal Reserve System and Treasury Department.

New Commemorative State Quarters, 1999-2008

Source: United States Mint, U.S. Dept. of the Treasury

Beginning in Jan. 1999, a series of 5 quarter dollars with new reverses are being issued each year through 2008, celebrating each of the 50 states. To make room on the reverse of the commemorative quarters for each state's design, certain design elements have been moved, thereby creating a new obverse design as well. The coins are being issued in the sequence the states became part of the Union (date each state entered the union is shown below).

1999	2000	2001	2002	2003
Delaware Dec. 7, 1787	Massachusetts Feb. 6, 1788	New York July 26, 1788	Tennessee June 1, 1796	Illinois Dec. 3, 1818
Pennsylvania Dec. 12, 1787	Maryland Apr. 28, 1788	North Carolina Nov. 21, 1789	Ohio Mar. 1, 1803	Alabama Dec. 14, 1819
New Jersey Dec. 18, 1787	South Carolina May 23, 1788	Rhode Island May 29, 1790	Louisiana Apr. 30, 1812	Maine Mar. 15, 1820
Georgia Jan. 2, 1788	New Hampshire June 21, 1788	Vermont Mar. 4, 1791	Indiana Dec. 11, 1816	Missouri Aug. 10, 1821
Connecticut Jan. 9, 1788	Virginia June 25, 1788	Kentucky June 1, 1792	Mississippi Dec. 10, 1817	Arkansas June 15, 1836
2004	**2005**	**2006**	**2007**	**2008**
Michigan Jan. 26, 1837	California Sept. 9, 1850	Nevada Oct. 31, 1864	Montana Nov. 8, 1889	Oklahoma Nov. 16, 1907
Florida Mar. 3, 1845	Minnesota May 11, 1858	Nebraska Mar. 1, 1867	Washington Nov. 11, 1889	New Mexico Jan. 6, 1912
Texas Dec. 29, 1845	Oregon Feb. 14, 1859	Colorado Aug. 1, 1876	Idaho July 3, 1890	Arizona Feb. 14, 1912
Iowa Dec. 28, 1846	Kansas Jan. 29, 1861	North Dakota Nov. 2, 1889	Wyoming July 10, 1890	Alaska Jan. 3, 1959
Wisconsin May 29, 1848	West Virginia June 20, 1863	South Dakota Nov. 2, 1889	Utah Jan. 4, 1896	Hawaii Aug. 21, 1959

Portraits on U.S. Treasury Bills, Bonds, Notes, and Savings Bonds

Denomination	Savings bonds	Treasury bills*	Treasury bonds*	Treasury notes*
$50	Washington		Jefferson	
75	Adams			
100	Jefferson		Jackson	
200	Madison			
500	Hamilton		Washington	
1,000	B. Franklin	H. McCulloch	Lincoln	Lincoln
5,000	P. Revere	J. G. Carlisle	Monroe	Monroe
10,000	J. Wilson	J. Sherman	Cleveland	Cleveland
50,000	C. Glass			
100,000		A. Gallatin	Grant	Grant
1,000,000		O. Wolcott	T. Roosevelt	T. Roosevelt
100,000,000				Madison
500,000,000				McKinley

*The U.S. Treasury discontinued issuing treasury bill, bond, and note certificates in 1986. Since then, all issues of marketable treasury securities have been available only in book-entry form, although some certificates remain in circulation.

U.S. Currency and Coin

Source: Financial Management Service, U.S. Dept. of the Treasury (June 30, 2004)

Amounts Outstanding and in Circulation

Currency	Total currency and coin	Total currency	Federal Reserve notes[1]	U.S. notes	Currency no longer issued
Amounts outstanding	$851,233,558, 787	$815,701,732,929	$815,194,147,995	$257,977,266	$249,607,668
Less amounts held by:					
Treasury.	310,662,840	24,162,840	23,969,825	7,505	185,510
Federal Reserve banks . . .	117,751,942,243	117,008,017,794	117,008,015,183	—	2,611
Amounts in circulation	$733,170,953,704	$698,669,552,295	$698,162,162,987	$257,969,761	$249,419,547

Coins[2]		Total	Dollars[3]	Fractional coins
Amounts outstanding		$35,531,825,858	$3,505,529,008	$32,026,296,850
Less amounts held by:				
Treasury.		286,500,000	257,570,000	28,930,000
Federal Reserve banks		743,924,449	199,012,195	544,912,254
Amounts in circulation		$34,501,401,409	$3,048,946,813	$31,452,454,596

(1) Issued on or after July 1, 1929. (2) Excludes coins sold to collectors at premium prices. (3) Includes $481,781,898 in standard silver dollars.

Currency in Circulation by Denominations

(June 30, 2004)

Denomination	Total currency in circulation	Federal Reserve notes[1]	U.S. notes	Currency no longer issued
$1	$7,909,856,694	$7,764,814,031	$143,503	$144,899,160
$2	1,363,309,136	1,231,029,046	132,267,518	12,572
$5	9,373,288,075	9,235,060,760	109,393,610	28,833,705
$10	14,532,239,980	14,510,699,020	6,300	21,534,660
$20	105,644,811,960	105,624,704,980	3,840	20,103,140
$50	58,795,968,850	58,784,472,250	500	11,496,100
$100	500,736,376,500	500,698,245,400	16,143,900	21,987,200
$500	142,602,500	142,407,500	5,500	189,500
$1,000	165,873,000	165,660,000	5,000	208,000
$5,000	1,765,000	1,710,000	—	55,000
$10,000	3,460,000	3,360,000	—	100,000
Partial notes[2]	600	—	90	510
TOTAL CURRENCY	**$698,669,552,295**	**$698,162,162,987**	**$257,969,761**	**$249,419,547**

(1) Issued on or after July 1, 1929. (2) Represents the value of certain partial denominations not presented for redemption.

Comparative Totals of Money in Circulation — Selected Dates

Date	Dollars (in millions)	Per capita[1]	Date	Dollars (in millions)	Per capita[1]
June 30, 2004	$733,171.0	$2,497.00	June 30, 1970	$54,351.0	$265.39
April 30, 2003	688.772.0	2,368.17	June 30, 1965	39,719.8	204.14
Mar. 31, 2002	641,909.0	2,238.45	June 30, 1960	32,064.6	177.47
Mar. 30, 2001	585,916.0	2,121.82	June 30, 1955	30,229.3	182.90
Mar. 31, 2000	562,949.0	2,050.00	June 30, 1950	27,156.3	179.03
Mar. 31, 1999	517,829.0	1,902.21	June 30, 1945	26,746.4	191.14
Mar. 31, 1998	474,979.0	1,762.42	June 30, 1940	7,847.5	59.40
Mar. 31, 1997	444,534.0	1,664.58	June 30, 1935	5,567.1	43.75
Mar. 31, 1996	416,280.0	1,573.15	June 30, 1930	4,522.0	36.74
Mar. 31, 1995	401,610.0	1,531.39	June 30, 1925	4,815.2	41.56
Mar. 31, 1990	257,664.4	1,028.71	June 30, 1920	5,467.6	51.36
June 30, 1985	185,890.7	778.58	June 30, 1915	3,319.6	33.01
June 30, 1980	127,097.2	558.28	June 30, 1910	3,148.7	34.07
June 30, 1975	81,196.4	380.08			

(1) Based on Bureau of the Census estimates of population. The requirement for a gold reserve against U.S. notes was repealed by Public Law 90-269, approved Mar. 18, 1968. Silver certificates issued on and after July 1, 1929, became redeemable from the general fund on June 24, 1968. The amount of security after those dates has been reduced accordingly.

New U.S. Currency Designs

On Mar. 25, 1996, the U.S. Treasury issued a redesigned $100 note incorporating many new and modified anti-counterfeiting features. It was the first of the U.S. currency series to be redesigned. A new $50 note was issued Oct. 27, 1997, a new $20 bill was released into circulation Sept. 24, 1998, and new $10 and $5 notes were issued May 24, 2000; a new $1 note with a more modest redesign was to come next. Old notes are being removed from circulation as they are returned to the Federal Reserve.

The new $100 bill has a larger portrait, moved off-center; a watermark (seen only when held up to the light) to the right of the portrait, depicting the same person (Benjamin Franklin); a security thread that glows red when exposed to ultraviolet light in a dark environment; color-shifting ink that changes from green to black when viewed at different angles, to appear in the numeral on the lower, front right-hand corner of the bill; microprinting in the numeral in the note's lower, front left-hand corner and on the portrait; and other features for security, machine authentication, and processing of the currency. The redesigned $5, $10, $20, and $50 bills incorporate the same features as the $100 bill, with the notable addition of a low-vision feature, a large (14-mm high, as compared to 7.8-mm on the old design), dark numeral on a light background on the back of the note. (The security thread glows yellow in the $50, green in the $20, orange in the $10, and blue in the $5. There is no color-shifting ink on the $5 note.)

On Oct. 9, 2003, the U.S. Treasury introduced a new $20 note, using background colors for the first time since 1905. The new note features subtle shades of green, blue, and peach. The notes have a security thread running vertically up one side, with "USA TWENTY" and a small U.S. flag; the thread glows green under UV light. Other security features include a watermark similar to the portrait of Andrew Jackson and color-shifting ink in the number "20" in the lower right corner on the note's face.

A new $50 note with background colors and similar security features was released Sept. 28, 2004.

More new currency information is available on the U.S. Treasury's website: www.ustreas.gov

Summary of Receipts, Outlays, and Surpluses or Deficits, 1936-2004

Source: Financial Management Service, U.S. Dept. of the Treasury; Congressional Budget Office

(millions of current dollars)

Fiscal Year[1]	Receipts	Outlays	Surplus or Deficit (−)[2]	Fiscal Year[1]	Receipts	Outlays	Surplus or Deficit (−)[2]
1936	$3,923	$8,228	$−4,304	1971	$187,139	$210,172	$−23,033
1937	5,387	7,580	−2,193	1972	207,309	230,681	−23,373
1938	6,751	6,840	−89	1973	230,799	245,707	−14,908
1939	6,295	9,141	−2,846	1974	263,224	269,359	−6,135
1940	6,548	9,468	−2,920	1975	279,090	332,332	−53,242
1941	8,712	13,653	−4,941	1976	298,060	371,779	−73,719
1942	14,634	35,137	−20,503	Transition quarter[3]	81,232	95,973	−14,741
1943	24,001	78,555	−54,554	1977	355,559	409,203	−53,644
1944	43,747	91,304	−47,557	1978	399,561	458,729	−59,168
1945	45,159	92,712	−47,553	1979	463,302	503,464	−40,162
1946	39,296	55,232	−15,936	1980	517,112	590,920	−73,808
1947	38,514	34,496	4,018	1981	599,272	678,209	−78,936
1948	41,560	29,764	11,796	1982	617,766	745,706	−127,940
1949	39,415	38,835	580	1983	600,562	808,327	−207,764
1950	39,443	42,562	−3,119	1984	666,457	851,781	−185,324
1951	51,616	45,514	6,102	1985	734,057	946,316	−212,260
1952	66,167	67,686	−1,519	1986	769,091	990,231	−221,140
1953	69,608	76,101	−6,493	1987	854,143	1,003,804	−149,661
1954	69,701	70,855	−1,154	1988	908,166	1,063,318	−155,151
1955	65,451	68,444	−2,993	1989	990,701	1,144,050	−153,319
1956	74,587	70,640	3,947	1990	1,031,308	1,251,776	−220,469
1957	79,990	76,578	3,412	1991	1,054,265	1,323,757	−269,492
1958	79,636	82,405	−2,769	1992	1,090,453	1,380,794	−290,340
1959	79,249	92,098	−12,849	1993	1,153,226	1,408,532	−255,306
1960	92,492	92,191	301	1994	1,257,451	1,460,553	−203,102
1961	94,388	97,723	−3,335	1995	1,351,495	1,515,412	−163,917
1962	99,676	106,821	−7,146	1996	1,452,763	1,560,094	−107,331
1963	106,560	111,316	−4,756	1997	1,578,955	1,600,911	−21,957
1964	112,613	118,528	−5,915	1998	1,721,421	1,652,224	+70,039
1965	116,817	118,228	−1,411	1999	1,827,302	1,704,942	+124,360
1966	130,835	134,532	−3,698	2000	2,025,060	1,788,143	+236,917
1967	148,822	157,464	−8,643	2001	1,991,044	1,863,769	+127,021
1968	152,973	178,134	−25,161	2002R	1,853,051	2,010,871	−157,820
1969	186,882	183,640	3,242	2003R	1,782,115	2,156,906	−374,791
1970	192,807	195,649	−2,842	2004E	1,879,799	2,292,352	−412,553

R = Revised. E = Estimated. (1) Fiscal years 1936 to 1976 end June 30; after 1976, fiscal years end Sept. 30. (2) May not equal difference between figures shown, because of rounding. (3) Transition quarter covers July 1, 1976-Sept. 30, 1976.

Budget Receipts and Outlays, 1789-1935

Source: U.S. Dept. of the Treasury; annual statements for years ending June 30 unless otherwise noted

(thousands of dollars)

Yearly Average	Receipts	Outlays	Yearly Average	Receipts	Outlays	Yearly Average	Receipts	Outlays
1789-1800[1]	$5,717	$5,776	1866-1870	$447,301	$377,642	1901-1905	$559,481	$535,559
1801-1810[2]	13,056	9,086	1871-1875	336,830	287,460	1906-1910	628,507	639,178
1811-1820[2]	21,032	23,943	1876-1880	288,124	255,598	1911-1915	710,227	720,252
1821-1830[2]	21,928	16,162	1881-1885	366,961	257,691	1916-1920	3,483,652	8,065,333
1831-1840[2]	30,461	24,495	1886-1890	375,448	279,134	1921-1925	4,306,673	3,578,989
1841-1850[2]	28,545	34,097	1891-1895	352,891	363,599	1926-1930	4,069,138	3,182,807
1851-1860	60,237	60,163	1896-1900	434,877	457,451	1931-1935	2,770,973	5,214,874
1861-1865	160,907	683,785						

(1) Average for period March 4, 1789, to Dec. 31, 1800. (2) Years from 1801 to 1842 end Dec. 31; average for 1841-1850 is for the period Jan. 1, 1841, to June 30, 1850.

Public Debt of the U.S.

Source: Bureau of Public Debt, U.S. Dept. of the Treasury; World Almanac research

Fiscal year	Debt (billions)	Debt per cap. (dollars)	Interest paid (billions)	% of federal outlays	Fiscal year	Debt (billions)	Debt per cap. (dollars)	Interest paid (billions)	% of federal outlays
1870	$2.4	$61.06	—	—	1984	$1,572.3	$6,640	$153.8	$18.1
1880	2.0	41.60	—	—	1985	1,823.1	7,598	178.9	18.9
1890	1.1	17.80	—	—	1986	2,125.3	8,774	190.2	19.2
1900	1.2	16.60	—	—	1987	2,350.3	9,615	195.4	19.5
1910	1.1	12.41	—	—	1988	2,602.3	10,534	214.1	20.1
1920	24.2	228	—	—	1989	2,857.4	11,545	240.9	21.0
1930	16.1	131	—	—	1990	3,233.3	13,000	264.8	21.1
1940	43.0	325	$1.0	10.5	1991	3,665.3	14,436	285.5	21.6
1950	256.1	1,688	5.7	13.4	1992	4,064.6	15,846	292.3	21.2
1955	272.8	1,651	6.4	9.4	1993	4,411.5	17,105	292.5	20.8
1960	284.1	1,572	9.2	10.0	1994	4,692.8	18,025	296.3	20.3
1965	313.8	1,613	11.3	9.6	1995	4,974.0	18,930	332.4	22.0
1970	370.1	1,814	19.3	9.9	1996	5,224.8	19,805	344.0	22.0
1975	533.2	2,475	32.7	9.8	1997	5,413.1	20,026	355.8	22.2
1976	620.4	2,852	37.1	10.0	1998	5,526.2	20,443	363.8	22.0
1977	698.8	3,170	41.9	10.2	1999	5,656.3	20,746	353.5	20.7
1978	771.5	3,463	48.7	10.6	2000	5,674.2	20,108	362.0	20.3
1979	826.5	3,669	59.8	11.9	2001	5,807.5	20,370	359.5	19.3
1980	907.7	3,985	74.9	12.7	2002	6,228.2	21,598	332.5	16.5
1981	997.9	4,338	95.6	14.1	2003	6,783.2	23,325	318.1	14.7
1982	1,142.0	4,913	117.4	15.7	2004[1]	7,379.1	25,182	321.6	14.0
1983	1,377.2	5,870	128.8	15.9					

Note: As of end of fiscal year. Through 1976, the fiscal year ended June 30. From 1977 on, the fiscal year ends Sept. 30. (1) Estimated.

U.S. Budget Receipts and Outlays, 1999-2004

Source: Financial Management Service, U.S. Dept. of the Treasury; Congressional Budget Office

As of Oct. 2004, the estimate from the Congressional Budget Office of the total U.S. budget deficit for the fiscal year 2004 was $413 billion, or 3.6% of GDP, an increase from the $374 billion deficit in 2003, and more than double the $158 billion deficit for 2002.

(in millions of current dollars; many figures do not add to totals because of independent rounding or omitted subcategories, including some subcategories with negative values.)

FISCAL YEAR:	1999[1]	2000[1]	2001[1]	2002[1]	2003[1]	2004[1,2]
NET RECEIPTS						
Individual income taxes	$879,480	$1,004,461	$994,339	$858,345	$793,699	$808,958
Corporation income taxes	184,680	207,288	151,075	148,044	131,778	189,370
Social insurance taxes and contributions:						
Federal old-age and survivors insurance	383,559	411,676	434,057	440,541	447,806	457,120
Federal disability insurance	60,910	68,907	73,463	74,780	76,036	77,624
Federal hospital insurance	132,268	135,528	149,650	149,049	147,186	150,589
Railroad retirement fund	4,143	4,336	4,272	4,177	3,954	—
Total employment taxes and contributions	580,880	620,447	661,442	668,548	674,982	689,359
Other insurance and retirement:						
Unemployment	26,480	27,641	27,812	27,620	33,366	39,453
Federal employees retirement	4,399	4,693	4,647	4,533	4,578	4,545
Non-federal employees	73	70	66	61	53	51
Total social insurance taxes and contributions	611,832	652,851	693,967	700,761	712,979	733,408
Excise taxes	70,412	68,866	66,232	66,989	67,522	69,851
Estate and gift taxes	27,782	29,010	28,400	26,507	21,959	24,831
Customs duties	18,336	19,913	19,616	18,602	19,862	21,083
Miscellaneous Receipts	34,781	42,669	37,664	33,803	34,317	32,299
Deposits of earnings by Federal Reserve Banks	25,917	32,293	26,124	23,683	21,878	19,652
Net Budget Receipts	**1,827,302**	**2,025,038**	**1,990,930**	**1,853,296**	**1,782,115**	**1,879,799**
NET OUTLAYS						
Legislative Branch	**2,612**	**2,913**	**3,029**	**3,230**	**3,428**	**3,880**
The Judiciary	**3,793**	**4,087**	**4,409**	**4,824**	**5,123**	**5,396**
Executive Office of the President:						
The White House Office	51	53	52	58	60	58
Office of Management and Budget	59	64	64	71	62	64
Total Executive Office	**416**	**284**	**280**	**496**	**388**	**3,309**
International Assistance Program:						
International security assistance	5,405	6,534	6,783	7,982	8,640	8,411
Multilateral assistance	1,857	1,759	2,166	2,187	2,115	2,640
Agency for International Development	2,337	2,622	2,764	3,682	4,024	4,322
International Development Assistance	2,410	2,953	2,895	3,752	4,284	4,618
Total International Assistance Program	**10,061**	**12,083**	**11,767**	**13,309**	**13,466**	**13,788**
Agriculture Department:						
Food stamp program	19,005	18,295	19,097	22,069	24,537	28,624
Farm Service Agency	19,508	33,353	22,974	17,519	18,344	11,345
Forest Service	3,423	3,978	4,225	5,438	5,147	5,481
Total Agriculture Department	**62,839**	**75,728**	**68,156**	**68,989**	**72,467**	**71,714**
Commerce Department:						
Bureau of the Census	1,131	4,214	1,025	628	612	681
Total Commerce Department	**5,036**	**7,931**	**5,017**	**5,322**	**5,680**	**5,853**
Defense Department—Military:						
Military personnel	69,503	75,950	73,977	86,802	106,746	113,576
Operation and maintenance	96,420	105,871	112,019	130,167	42,458	174,018
Procurement	48,824	51,616	54,991	62,511	67,925	76,217
Research, development, test, evaluation	37,362	37,608	40,462	44,388	53,102	60,756
Military construction	5,519	5,111	4,978	5,055	5,850	6,310
Total Defense Department—Military	**261,379**	**281,233**	**290,980**	**332,116**	**408,578**	**437,111**
Defense Department—Civil	**32,008**	**32,019**	**34,161**	**35,159**	**39,881**	**41,754**
Education Department	**32,435**	**33,308**	**35,959**	**46,285**	**57,399**	**62,814**
Energy Department	**16,054**	**15,010**	**16,420**	**17,772**	**19,385**	**19,974**
Health and Human Services Department:						
Public Health Service	25,554	28,281	32,667	36,597	41,239	44,419
Centers for Medicare and Medicaid Services[3]	390,181	413,124	450,751	243,001	532,746	586,515
Food and Drug Administration	951	1,023	1,075	1,127	1,397	1,380
National Institutes of Health	13,815	15,415	17,254	20,450	22,834	25,626
Total Health and Human Services Dept.	**359,700**	**382,627**	**426,444**	**466,104**	**508,405**	**543,215**
Homeland Security Department:						
Citizen and Immigration Services	—	—	—	—	1,297	476
U.S. Secret Service	—	—	—	—	1,152	1,320
Border and Transportation Security	—	—	—	—	17,208	13,875
U.S. Coast Guard	—	—	—	—	6,093	6,842
Total Homeland Security Department	**—**	**—**	**—**	**—**	**31,843**	**26,665**
Housing and Urban Development Department	**32,736**	**30,830**	**33,937**	**31,880**	**37,470**	**45,024**
Interior Department	**7,814**	**8,036**	**8,024**	**9,641**	**9,204**	**9,065**
Justice Department:						
Federal Bureau of Investigation	3,040	3,088	20,810	3,556	4,216	4,927
Drug Enforcement Administration	1,203	1,339	3,208	1,602	1,590	1,725
Immigration and Naturalization Service[4]	3,775	4,163	4,558	5,340	—	—
Federal Prison System	3,204	3,708	4,205	4,746	4,580	4,751
Total Justice Department	**18,318**	**19,561**	**20,810**	**24,197**	**21,529**	**28,950**
Labor Department:						
Unemployment Trust Fund	24,870	24,149	31,530	62,211	66,640	46,323
Total Labor Department	**32,459**	**31,354**	**39,280**	**64,252**	**69,171**	**56,784**
State Department	**6,463**	**6,849**	**7,446**	**9,453**	**9,257**	**10,947**
Transportation Department:						
Federal Aviation Administration	9,507	9,561	10,731	13,096	12,561	2,697
Total Transportation Department	**41,836**	**46,030**	**54,075**	**61,282**	**50,808**	**54,539**
Treasury Department:						
Internal Revenue Service	37,087	37,986	38,695	46,996	51,508	57,393
Interest on the public debt	353,511	362,118	359,508	332,537	318,149	321,566
Total Treasury Department	**386,703**	**390,813**	**389,944**	**374,516**	**366,756**	**374,797**

FISCAL YEAR:	1999[1]	2000[1]	2001[1]	2002[1]	2003[1]	2004[1,2]
Veterans Affairs Department	**43,169**	**47,087**	**45,043**	**50,881**	**56,892**	**59,550**
Environmental Protection Agency	6,752	7,236	7,390	7,451	8,065	8,335
General Services Administration	$–46	$25	$–8	$–271	$336	–403
National Aeronautics and Space Administration	13,665	13,442	14,094	14,429	14,552	15,186
Office of Personnel Management	47,515	48,660	50,915	52,512	54,135	56,535
Small Business Administration	58	–422	–569	492	1,559	4,077
Social Security Administration	**419,790**	**441,810**	**461,748**	**488,694**	**508,160**	**530,206**
Other independent agencies:						
Corporation for Natl. and Community Service	609	684	757	793	839	765
Corporation for Public Broadcasting	281	316	360	375	411	437
District of Columbia	–2,910	312	539	927	781	805
Equal Employment Opportunity Commission	255	290	289	324	315	324
Export-Import Bank of the U.S.	–159	–743	–1,749	–140	–3,428	–1,902
Federal Communications Commission	3,293	4,073	4,011	5,253	6,398	3,894
Federal Deposit Insurance Corporation	–5,025	–2,837	–1,220	–353	–732	–1,554
Legal Services Corporation	298	301	320	333	336	335
National Archives & Records Adm.	225	201	217	268	301	307
National Foundation on the Arts and Humanities	217	218	223	227	230	247
National Labor Relations Board.	182	198	220	230	231	242
National Science Foundation	3,285	3,487	3,691	4,187	4,735	5,118
Nuclear Regulatory Commission	37	33	31	40	48	71
Railroad Retirement Board	4,830	4,992	5,541	5,425	3,056	2,792
Securities and Exchange Commission	–255	–506	–330	–536	–532	–685
Smithsonian Institution	486	517	561	616	614	782
Tennessee Valley Authority	2	–307	–662	124	227	–413
Total other independent agencies	**6,943**	**10,526**	**12,581**	**15,874**	**11,634**	**5,847**
Undistributed offsetting receipts	–159,080	–172,844	–190,946	–201,149	–211,901	—
NET BUDGET OUTLAYS	**$1,704,942**	**$1,788,045**	**$1,863,909**	**$2,010,962**	**$2,156,906**	**$2,292,352**
Less net receipts	1,827,302	2,025,038	1,990,930	1,853,296	1,782,115	1,879,799
DEFICIT (-) OR SURPLUS (+)	**$+124,360**	**$+236,993**	**$+127,021**	**$–157,666**	**$–374,791**	**$–412,553**

— = Not available. (1) Fiscal year ends Sept. 30. (2) Figures for some agencies are preliminary. (3) Formerly the Health Care Financing Adm. (4) As of Jan. 2003, transferred to Homeland Security Dept.

State Finances: Revenue, Expenditures, Debt, and Taxes

Source: Census Bureau, U.S. Dept. of Commerce

(fiscal year 2002)

STATE	Revenue (millions)	Expenditures (millions)	Debt (millions)	Per capita debt	Per capita taxes	Per capita expenditures
Alabama	$14,942	$17,996	$6,405	$1,430	$1,453	$4,018
Alaska	5,019	7,402	5,308	8,281	1,700	11,548
Arizona	17,298	18,119	4,348	799	1,558	3,330
Arkansas	10,297	11,521	3,002	1,109	1,931	4,257
California	151,245	184,928	71,263	2,036	2,221	5,283
Colorado	11,809	16,823	5,419	1,204	1,538	3,738
Connecticut	16,993	20,117	20,784	6,009	2,611	5,816
Delaware	4,842	4,646	4,038	5,010	2,697	5,764
Florida	47,890	51,834	20,266	1,214	1,519	3,105
Georgia	24,847	30,053	8,243	965	1,612	3,517
Hawaii	5,869	7,446	5,656	4,558	2,756	6,000
Idaho	4,488	5,234	2,545	1,895	1,691	3,897
Illinois	41,095	49,131	34,761	2,762	1,786	3,904
Indiana	20,116	22,205	9,456	1,536	1,657	3,606
Iowa	11,130	12,721	3,713	1,265	1,705	4,333
Kansas	9,694	10,592	2,288	844	1,773	3,905
Kentucky	16,073	18,407	9,039	2,210	1,950	4,500
Louisiana	18,079	18,319	9,233	2,063	1,644	4,093
Maine	5,451	6,265	4,321	3,337	2,028	4,838
Maryland	20,788	23,317	12,309	2,258	1,985	4,278
Massachusetts	26,885	32,848	45,216	7,041	2,308	5,115
Michigan	43,950	49,184	21,947	2,185	2,177	4,897
Minnesota	22,439	26,693	6,408	1,275	2,632	5,312
Mississippi	11,052	12,742	4,160	1,451	1,649	4,445
Missouri	19,085	20,841	12,693	2,239	1,539	3,676
Montana	4,033	4,265	2,752	3,024	1,585	4,687
Nebraska	6,002	6,537	2,215	1,282	1,732	3,783
Nevada	6,888	7,348	3,668	1,693	1,821	3,391
New Hampshire	4,636	4,823	5,397	4,236	1,489	3,786
New Jersey	32,709	41,988	32,093	3,743	2,137	4,897
New Mexico	8,746	10,084	4,493	2,426	1,959	5,445
New York	104,534	119,199	89,856	4,696	2,261	6,230
North Carolina	31,524	33,124	11,128	1,340	1,871	3,988
North Dakota	3,017	3,020	1,673	2,639	1,762	4,764
Ohio	45,439	52,594	20,009	1,754	1,764	4,610
Oklahoma	13,134	14,727	6,477	1,856	1,734	4,220
Oregon	14,815	18,029	7,668	2,178	1,467	5,122
Pennsylvania	46,165	55,171	20,983	1,702	1,795	4,475
Rhode Island	4,891	5,767	5,856	5,483	1,992	5,400
South Carolina	16,997	20,009	10,116	2,465	1,483	4,876
South Dakota	2,491	2,772	2,308	3,036	1,285	3,647
Tennessee	17,952	20,029	3,628	627	1,347	3,459
Texas	60,588	70,274	24,008	1,104	1,319	3,233
Utah	8,468	10,107	4,729	2,039	1,693	4,358
Vermont	3,260	3,512	2,284	3,707	2,465	5,701
Virginia	23,577	28,044	13,785	1,892	1,754	3,848
Washington	23,813	30,378	13,552	2,234	2,082	5,007
West Virginia	9,130	9,409	4,537	2,514	1,968	5,213
Wisconsin	20,874	26,749	14,870	2,733	2,172	4,917
Wyoming	2,770	2,948	1,298	2,601	2,193	5,908
ALL STATES[1]	**$1,097,829**	**$1,280,290**	**$642,202**	**$2,234**	**$1,862**	**$4,455**

(1) Totals may not add because of rounding.

State and Local Government Receipts and Current Expenditures

Source: Bureau of Economic Analysis, U.S. Dept. of Commerce

(billions of current dollars; revised)

	1999	2000	2001	2002	2003
RECEIPTS	**$1,236.7**	**$1,319.5**	**$1,373.0**	**$1,411.9**	**$1,494.9**
Current tax receipts	840.4	893.2	915.8	926.5	969.2
Personal current taxes	214.5	236.6	242.7	220.1	226.1
Income taxes	195.5	217.3	223.1	199.6	204.6
Other	19.0	19.4	19.6	20.5	21.6
Taxes on production and imports	590.2	621.1	642.8	675.3	708.7
Sales taxes	301.6	316.6	321.1	329.1	343.9
Property taxes	242.8	254.6	269.3	291.5	305.0
Other	45.8	49.9	52.4	54.7	59.7
Taxes on corporate income	35.8	35.5	30.2	31.2	34.4
Contributions for government social insurance	9.8	11.0	13.6	14.5	15.0
Income receipts on assets	85.3	92.2	88.8	81.6	81.0
Interest receipts	78.4	84.0	80.3	73.2	71.3
Dividends	1.8	1.9	2.0	2.1	2.5
Rents and royalties	5.1	6.3	6.5	6.2	7.1
Current transfer receipts	290.8	315.4	350.8	385.9	425.9
Federal grants-in-aid	232.9	247.3	276.1	304.4	339.9
From business (net)	23.0	28.8	31.4	32.8	32.2
From persons	34.9	39.2	43.3	48.7	53.8
Current surplus of government enterprises	10.4	7.7	4.0	3.3	3.7
CURRENT EXPENDITURES	**1,186.3**	**1,269.5**	**1,368.2**	**1,436.9**	**1,498.1**
Consumption expenditures	858.9	917.8	969.8	1,016.5	1,058.5
Government social benefit payments to persons	252.4	271.7	305.2	331.9	350.3
Interest payments	74.6	79.5	85.5	87.4	88.9
Subsidies	0.4	0.5	7.7	1.0	0.3
Less: Wage accruals less disbursements	0.0	0.0	0.0	0.0	0.0
Net state and local government saving	50.4	50.0	4.8	−25.0	−3.2
Social insurance funds	1.7	2.0	2.6	1.6	1.1
Other	48.7	47.9	2.2	−26.6	−4.3
Addenda:					
Total receipts	1,276.6	1,363.2	1,421.6	1,463.7	1,546.4
Current receipts	1,236.7	1,319.5	1,373.0	1,411.9	1,494.9
Capital transfer receipts	39.9	43.7	48.6	51.8	51.5
Total expenditures	1,298.8	1,393.5	1,502.7	1,583.9	1,645.0
Current expenditures	1,186.3	1,269.5	1,368.2	1,436.9	1,498.1
Gross government investment	206.0	225.0	243.0	259.3	264.9
Net purchases of nonproduced assets	8.6	8.8	9.2	9.8	10.0
Less: Consumption of fixed capital	102.1	109.8	117.8	122.1	127.9
NET LENDING OR NET BORROWING (−)	**−22.3**	**−30.4**	**−81.1**	**−120.2**	**−98.7**

State and Local Government Current Expenditures, by Function

Source: Bureau of Economic Analysis, U.S. Dept. of Commerce

(billions of dollars)

	1980	1985	1990	1995	1998	1999	2000	2001
State and local	**$307.8**	**$447.0**	**$660.8**	**$902.5**	**$1,033.7**	**$1,105.8**	**$1,196.2**	**$1,292.6**
General public service	**26.3**	**39.3**	**59.4**	**83.6**	**100.3**	**107.6**	**117.1**	**124.3**
Executive and legislative	4.4	6.5	9.9	12.4	15.0	16.2	17.7	18.9
Tax collection and financial management	8.9	14.6	20.1	26.5	29.2	31.6	34.9	34.6
Net interest paid	−5.5	−8.0	−6.4	0.2		−1.1	−3.2	−2.5
Other	18.5	26.3	35.9	44.4	56.1	60.9	67.8	73.4
Public order and safety	**32.4**	**53.7**	**84.5**	**118.9**	**144.1**	**154.7**	**168.7**	**181.8**
Police	14.4	22.3	32.2	44.5	55.1	59.2	65.1	71.5
Fire	5.9	9.3	13.4	17.3	20.5	21.5	23.2	24.8
Law courts	5.7	9.2	14.9	20.6	25.2	27.2	29.5	31.2
Prisons	6.4	13.0	24.1	36.5	43.3	46.7	51.0	54.3
Economic affairs	**36.9**	**47.7**	**58.5**	**72.1**	**81.1**	**87.1**	**95.0**	**107.8**
General economic and labor affairs	7.1	7.4	10.1	12.0	13.8	14.5	15.5	16.2
Agriculture	1.9	1.8	3.7	4.1	4.4	5.0	5.7	5.6
Energy	−1.2	−3.2	−5.4	−6.6	−7.3	−8.0	−8.7	−2.1
Natural resources	2.8	4.2	5.9	8.3	8.6	9.1	9.9	10.7
Transportation	27.7	40.9	52.2	66.1	74.9	80.0	86.4	91.7
Highways	24.7	34.7	43.5	54.6	62.1	66.1	71.8	76.1
Air	−0.3	−0.6	−1.3	−1.7	−2.2	−2.4	−2.5	−2.3
Water	—	—	—	−0.1	−0.2	−0.2	−0.2	−0.3
Transit and railroad	3.3	6.8	10.0	13.3	15.3	16.4	17.4	18.2
Other	−1.4	−4.3	−8.1	−11.8	−13.3	−13.5	−13.8	−14.2
Housing and community services	**4.0**	**2.3**	**4.4**	**3.7**	**6.0**	**6.0**	**7.8**	**7.5**
Water	−0.4	−1.9	−2.4	−3.6	−4.8	−5.4	−5.5	−5.6
Sewerage	1.8	1.5	0.4	−0.7	−1.1	−1.2	−1.2	−1.4
Sanitation	2.4	2.8	4.5	5.3	6.0	6.4	7.0	7.0
Other	0.3	−0.1	1.9	2.7	6.0	6.2	7.5	7.4
Health	**41.2**	**62.3**	**106.2**	**179.6**	**196.7**	**215.6**	**236.5**	**268**
Recreation and culture	**4.1**	**6.5**	**9.4**	**12.2**	**13.9**	**14.7**	**16.1**	**16.8**
Education	**129.8**	**187.7**	**269.1**	**341.6**	**398**	**421**	**449.5**	**474.8**
Elementary and secondary	97.0	140.5	203.5	261.2	307.2	325.3	347.3	366.3
Higher	24.7	36.1	49.5	58.1	65.3	68.4	72.6	77.0
Libraries	1.6	2.5	3.7	4.7	5.8	6.2	6.6	6.9
Other	6.5	8.6	12.5	17.6	19.7	21.1	22.9	24.6
Income security	**33.0**	**47.4**	**69.1**	**90.8**	**93.6**	**99.1**	**105.5**	**111.6**
Disability	3.1	5.4	10.4	13.0	13.4	13.5	13.9	14.3
Welfare and social services	29.9	42.0	58.7	77.8	80.2	85.6	91.6	97.2

Top U.S. Charities by Donations, 2002[1]

Source: The Chronicle of Philanthropy

(in millions of dollars)

Rank/Organization	Private Support[2]	Total Income	Rank/Organization	Private Support[2]	Total Income
1. American National Red Cross (Washington, DC)	$1,736.4	$4,087.4	14. Stanford University (Palo Alto, CA)	$454.8	$2,511.8
2. Salvation Army (Alexandria, VA)	1,372.0	2,147.4	15. Boys and Girls Clubs of America (Atlanta, GA)	453.7	1,079.4
3. Gifts In Kind International (Alexandria, VA)	793.2	795.7	16. American Heart Association (Dallas, TX)	437.5	525.7
4. American Cancer Society (Atlanta, GA)	777.4	789.4	17. World Vision (Federal Way, WA)	437.1	553.0
5. Fidelity Investments Charitable Gift Fund (Boston, MA)	735.5	758.2	18. AmeriCares Foundation (New Canaan, CT)	412.7	413.5
6. Lutheran Services in America (St. Paul, MN)	723.3	8,030.8	19. Habitat for Humanity International (Americus, GA)	411.9	718.4
7. YMCA of the USA (Chicago, IL)	713.9	4,271.7	20. Cornell University (Ithaca, NY)	363.0	1,876.0
8. Nature Conservancy (Arlington, VA)	628.3	972.4	21. Campus Crusade for Christ International (Orlando, FL)	346.7	386.8
9. University of Southern California (Los Angeles, CA)	585.2	NA	22. Goodwill Industries International (Bethesda, MD)	337.8	2,055.2
10. Feed the Children (Oklahoma City, OK)	547.0	553.4	23. Food for the Poor (Deerfield Beach, FL)	320.8	351.9
11. United Way of New York City (New York, NY)	498.0	523.1	24. University of Pennsylvania (Philadelphia , PA)	319.7	2,714.4
12. America's Second Harvest (Chicago, IL)	485.1	487.9	25. The Johns Hopkins University (Baltimore, MD)	318.7	2,412.9
13. Harvard University (Cambridge, MA)	477.6	2,362.2			

(1) Preliminary. (2) Private support consists of donations from individuals, foundations, and corporations. Total income also includes government funding and fees charged.

Consumer Credit Outstanding, 2001-2003

Source: Federal Reserve System

(billions of dollars, revised)

Estimated amounts of credit outstanding as of end of year. Not seasonally adjusted.

	2001	2002	2003		2001	2002	2003
TOTAL	1,865.2	1,942.6	2,025.5	Finance companies	31.5	38.9	37.6
Major Holders				Credit unions	22.3	22.2	22.4
Commercial banks	558.4	587.2	636.4	Savings institutions	17.9	16.3	23.8
Finance companies	238.1	237.8	295.4	Nonfinancial business	50.6	48.8	26.5
Credit unions	189.6	195.7	205.9	Pools of securitized assets[1]	389.7	390.3	392.7
Fed. govt. and Sallie Mae	119.5	129.6	114.6	**Nonrevolving**	1,128.2	1,195.0	1,262.5
Savings institutions	71.1	68.7	77.9	Commercial banks	333.5	356.2	376.4
Nonfinancial business	88.8	86.5	70.3	Finance companies	206.6	198.8	257.8
Pools of securitized assets[1]	599.7	637.1	625.0	Credit unions	167.3	173.5	183.5
				Fed. government and Sallie Mae	119.5	129.6	114.6
Major Types of Credit[2]				Savings institutions	53.2	52.4	54.0
Revolving	737.0	747.5	763.1	Nonfinancial business	38.2	37.7	43.8
Commercial banks	224.9	231.0	260.1	Pools of securitized assets[1]	209.9	246.8	232.3

NA = Not applicable. (1) Outstanding balances of pools upon which securities have been issued; these balances are no longer carried on the balance sheets of the loan originators. (2) Includes estimates for holders that do not separately report consumer credit holding by type.

Global Stock Markets

Source: The Conference Board; not seasonally adjusted

Stock price indexes (1990[1]=100):	June 1, 1960	June 1, 1970	June 1, 1980	June 1, 1990	June 1, 2000	June 1, 2001	June 1, 2002	June 1, 2003	Jan. 1 2004	June 1 2004
United States	17.1	21.9	34.3	107.6	437.2	368.0	297.5	292.9	340.0	342.9
Japan	4.4	7.3	23.8	110.8	60.4	45.0	36.8	31.5	37.4	41.1
Germany	36.1	27.5	30.5	111.1	407.9	358.2	259.1	190.4	240.0	239.6
France	16.3	15.6	23.8	112.0	354.7	287.5	214.5	169.7	200.2	205.4
United Kingdom	8.2	11.6	24.9	108.2	279.9	252.0	209.1	182.1	202.0	205.9
Italy	28.9	20.6	15.9	117.3	309.0	254.1	196.7	181.1	201.3	206.5
Canada	14.8	25.0	60.3	103.6	298.0	226.1	208.9	204.1	249.1	249.8

(1) 12-month average.

U.S. Holdings of Foreign Stocks[1]

Source: Bureau of Economic Analysis, U.S. Dept. of Commerce

(billions of dollars)

	2001	2002	2003		2001	2002	2003
Europe	$942.2	$785.0	$1,101.7	**Latin America**	$59.3	$53.2	$84.3
Of which: United Kingdom	354.6	303.3	450.5	Of which: Argentina	0.7	0.6	0.9
Finland	51.3	42.4	57.1	Brazil	21.8	20.0	33.5
France	112.2	94.1	128.8	Mexico	26.3	23.9	36.7
Germany	72.2	58.1	76.5	**Other W. Hemisphere**	172.3	148.7	206.8
Ireland	28.4	23.0	30.8	Of which: Bermuda	118.9	98.3	133.3
Italy	33.7	27.5	36.9	Netherlands Antilles	14.5	10.7	14.7
Netherlands	112.8	89.9	119.9	**Other countries and territories**	178.6	147.1	248.4
Spain	32.5	26.8	35	Of which: Australia	37.1	30.4	44.8
Sweden	24.3	19.3	27.6	Hong Kong	30.2	21.8	33.8
Switzerland	75.6	65.5	89.6	Singapore	21.4	17.0	21.7
Canada	89.6	69.7	97.3				
Japan	170.7	140.5	233.7	**TOTAL HOLDINGS**	1,612.7	1,345.2	1,972.2

(1) As of year end.

Gold Reserves of Central Banks and Governments

Source: International Financial Statistics, IMF; million fine troy ounces

Year end	All countries[1]	United States	Belgium	Canada	France	Germany[2]	Italy	Japan	Nether-lands	Switzer-land	United Kingdom
1975	1,018.71	274.71	42.17	21.95	100.93	117.61	82.48	21.11	54.33	83.20	21.03
1980	952.99	264.32	34.18	20.98	81.85	95.18	66.67	24.23	43.94	83.28	18.84
1985	949.39	262.65	34.18	20.11	81.85	95.18	66.67	24.33	43.94	83.28	19.03
1990	939.01	261.91	30.23	14.76	81.85	95.18	66.67	24.23	43.94	83.28	18.94
1995	908.79	261.70	20.54	3.41	81.85	95.18	66.67	24.23	34.77	83.28	18.43
1996	906.10	261.66	15.32	3.09	81.85	95.18	66.67	24.23	34.77	83.28	18.43
1997	890.57	261.64	15.32	3.09	81.89	95.18	66.67	24.23	27.07	83.28	18.42
1998	966.15	261.61	9.52	2.49	102.37	118.98	83.36	24.23	33.83	83.28	23.00
1999	967.07	261.67	8.30	1.81	97.25	111.52	78.83	24.23	31.57	83.28	20.55
2000	952.09	261.61	8.30	1.18	97.25	111.52	78.83	24.55	29.32	77.79	15.67
2001	942.76	262.00	8.30	1.05	97.25	111.13	78.83	24.60	28.44	70.68	11.42
2002	930.56	262.00	8.29	0.60	97.25	110.79	78.83	24.60	27.38	61.62	10.09
2003	913.10	261.55	8.29	0.11	97.25	110.58	78.83	24.60	25.00	52.51	10.07

(1) Covers IMF members with reported gold holdings. For countries not listed above, see International Monetary Fund's *International Financial Statistics Report*. (2) West Germany prior to 1991.

Record One-Day Gains and Losses on the Dow Jones Industrial Average

Source: Dow Jones & Co., Inc.; as of Sept. 30, 2004

GREATEST POINT GAINS

Rank	Date	Close	Net Chg	% Chg
1.	3/16/2000	10630.60	499.19	4.93
2.	7/24/2002	8191.29	488.95	6.35
3.	7/29/2002	8711.88	447.49	5.41
4.	4/5/2001	9918.05	402.63	4.23
5.	4/18/2001	10615.83	399.10	3.91
6.	9/8/1998	8020.78	380.53	4.98
7.	10/15/2002	8255.68	378.28	4.80
8.	9/24/2001	8603.86	368.05	4.47
9.	10/1/2002	7938.79	346.86	4.57
10.	5/16/2001	11215.92	342.95	3.15

GREATEST POINT LOSSES

Rank	Date	Close	Net Chg	% Chg
1.	9/17/2001	8920.70	−684.81	−7.13
2.	4/14/2000	10305.77	−617.78	−5.66
3.	10/27/1997	7161.15	−554.26	−7.18
4.	8/31/1998	7539.07	−512.61	−6.37
5.	10/19/1987	1738.74	−508.00	−22.61
6.	3/12/2001	10208.25	−436.37	−4.10
7.	7/19/2002	8019.26	−390.23	−4.64
8.	9/20/2001	8376.21	−382.92	−4.37
9.	10/12/2000	10034.58	−379.21	−3.64
10.	3/7/2000	9796.03	−374.47	−3.68

GREATEST % GAINS

Rank	Date	Close	Net Chg	% Chg
1.	3/15/1933	62.10	8.26	15.34
2.	10/6/1931	99.34	12.86	14.87
3.	10/30/1929	258.47	28.40	12.34
4.	9/21/1932	75.16	7.67	11.36
5.	10/21/1987	2027.85	186.84	10.15
6.	8/3/1932	58.22	5.06	9.52
7.	2/11/1932	78.60	6.80	9.47
8.	11/14/1929	217.28	18.59	9.36
9.	12/18/1931	80.69	6.90	9.35
10.	2/13/1932	85.82	7.22	9.19

GREATEST % LOSSES

Rank	Date	Close	Net Chg	% Chg
1.	12/12/1914	54.00	−17.42	−24.39
2.	10/19/1987	1738.74	−508.00	−22.61
3.	10/28/1929	260.64	−38.33	−12.82
4.	10/29/1929	230.07	−30.57	−11.73
5.	11/6/1929	232.13	−25.55	−9.92
6.	12/18/1899	58.27	−5.57	−8.72
7.	8/12/1932	63.11	−5.79	−8.40
8.	3/14/1907	76.23	−6.89	−8.29
9.	10/26/1987	1793.93	−156.83	−8.04
10.	7/21/1933	88.71	−7.55	−7.84

Dow Jones Industrial Average, 1963-2003

High		YEAR		Low	High		YEAR		Low
Dec. 18	767.21	....1963....	Jan. 2	646.79	Jan. 6	1286.64	....1984...	July 24	1086.57
Nov. 18	891.71	....1964....	Jan. 2	766.08	Dec. 16	1553.10	....1985...	Jan. 4	1184.96
Dec. 31	969.26	....1965....	June 28	840.59	Dec. 2	1955.57	....1986...	Jan. 22	1502.29
Feb. 9	995.15	....1966....	Oct. 7	744.32	Aug. 25	2722.42	....1987...	Oct. 19	1738.74
Sept. 25	943.08	....1967....	Jan. 3	786.41	Oct. 21	2183.50	....1988...	Jan. 20	1879.14
Dec. 3	985.21	....1968....	Mar. 21	825.13	Oct. 9	2791.41	....1989...	Jan. 3	2144.64
May 14	968.85	....1969....	Dec. 17	769.93	July 16	2999.75	....1990...	Oct. 11	2365.10
Dec. 29	842.00	....1970....	May 6	631.16	Dec. 31	3168.83	....1991...	Jan. 9	2470.30
Apr. 28	950.82	....1971....	Nov. 23	797.97	June 1	3413.21	....1992...	Oct. 9	3136.58
Dec. 11	1036.27	....1972....	Jan. 26	889.15	Dec. 29	3794.33	....1993...	Jan. 20	3241.95
Jan. 11	1051.70	....1973....	Dec. 5	788.31	Jan. 31	3978.36	....1994...	Apr. 4	3593.35
Mar. 13	891.66	....1974....	Dec. 6	577.60	Dec. 13	5216.47	....1995...	Jan. 30	3832.08
July 15	881.81	....1975....	Jan. 2	632.04	Dec. 27	6560.91	....1996...	Jan. 10	5032.94
Sept. 21	1014.79	....1976....	Jan. 2	858.71	Aug. 6	8259.31	....1997...	Apr. 11	6391.69
Jan. 3	999.75	....1977....	Nov. 2	800.85	Nov. 23	9374.27	....1998...	Aug. 31	7539.07
Sept. 8	907.74	....1978....	Feb. 28	742.12	Dec. 31	11497.12	....1999...	Jan. 22	9120.67
Oct. 5	897.61	....1979....	Nov. 7	796.67	Jan. 14	11722.98*	....2000...	Mar. 7	9796.03
Nov. 20	1000.17	....1980....	Apr. 21	759.13	May 21	11337.92	....2001...	Sept. 21	8235.81
Apr. 27	1024.05	....1981....	Sept. 25	824.01	Mar. 19	10635.25	....2002...	Oct. 9	7286.27
Dec. 27	1070.55	....1982....	Aug. 12	776.92	Dec. 31	10453.90	....2003...	Mar. 11	7524.06
Nov. 29	1287.20	....1983....	Jan. 3	1027.04					

* Record high closing.

Milestones of the Dow Jones Industrial Average

(as of Sept. 30, 2004)

First close over...		First close over...		First close over...		First close over...	
100	Jan. 12, 1906	5500	Feb. 8, 1996	8400	Feb. 18, 1998	9300	July 16, 1998
500	Mar. 12, 1956	6000	Oct. 14, 1996	8300	Feb. 12, 1998	9500	Jan. 6, 1999*
1000	Nov. 14, 1972	6500	Nov. 25, 1996	8400	Feb. 18, 1998	9600	Jan. 8, 1999
1500	Dec. 11, 1985	7000	Feb. 13, 1997	8500	Feb. 27, 1998	9700	Mar. 5, 1999
2000	Jan. 8, 1987	7500	June 10, 1997	8600	Mar. 10, 1998	9800	Mar. 11, 1999
2500	July 17, 1987	8000	July 16, 1997	8700	Mar. 16, 1998	9900	Mar. 15, 1999
3000	April 17, 1991	8100	July 24, 1997	8800	Mar. 19, 1998	10000	Mar. 29, 1999
3500	May 19, 1993	8200	July 30, 1997	8900	Mar. 20, 1998	10100	Apr. 8, 1999
4000	Feb. 23, 1995	8100	July 24, 1997	9000	Apr. 6, 1998	10300	Apr. 12, 1999*
4500	June 16, 1995	8200	July 30, 1997	9100	Apr. 14, 1998	10400	Apr. 14, 1999
5000	Nov. 21, 1995	8300	Feb. 12, 1998	9200	May 13, 1998		

First close over...	
10500	Apr. 21, 1999
10700	Apr. 22, 1999*
10800	Apr. 27, 1999
11000	May 3, 1999*
11100	May 13, 1999
11200	July 12, 1999
11300	Aug. 25, 1999
11400	Dec. 23, 1999
11500	Jan. 7, 2000
11700	Jan. 14, 2000*

*9400, 10200, 10600, 10900, and 11600 are not listed because the Dow had risen another 100 points or more by the time the market closed for the day. The all-time record closing was 11722.98 on Jan. 14, 2000.

IT'S A FACT: While the stock market crash of 1929 that presaged the Great Depression is generally considered to have happened on Oct. 24 and Oct. 29, 1929, known respectively as "Black Thursday" and "Black Tuesday," the market lost only 11.9% of its value in the year 1929. The following 3 years were devastating. The Dow Jones plummeted from a high of 381.17 in September 1929 to 41.22 in July 1932, losing 89% of its value.

Components of the Dow Jones Averages
(as of Sept. 30, 2004)

Dow Jones Industrial Average

American International Group (AIG)
Alcoa
Altria Group
American Express Co.
Boeing Co.
Caterpillar
Citigroup

Coca-Cola
DuPont
Exxon Mobil Corp.
General Electric Co.
General Motors Corp.
Hewlett-Packard Co.
Home Depot
Honeywell International

IBM
Intel Corp.
J.P. Morgan Chase & Co.
Johnson & Johnson
McDonald's Corp.
Merck & Co.
Microsoft Corp.
Pfizer

Procter & Gamble Co.
SBC Communications
3M Company
United Technologies Corp.
Verizon Communications
Wal-Mart Stores
Walt Disney Co.

Dow Jones Utility Average

AES Corp.
American Electric Power Co.
CenterPoint Energy
Consolidated Edison

Dominion Resources
Duke Energy Corp.
Edison International
Exelon Corp.

FirstEnergy Corp.
NiSource
PG&E Corp.
Public Service Enterprise Group

Southern Co.
TXU
Williams Cos.

Dow Jones Transportation Average

Alexander & Baldwin
AMR (American Airlines) Corp.
Burlington Northern Santa Fe Corp.
C.H. Robinson Worldwide
CNF
Continental Airlines

CSX
Delta Air Lines
Expeditors International of Washington, Inc.
FedEx Corp.
GATX Corp.

J.B. Hunt Transportation Services
Norfolk Southern Corp.
Northwest Airlines Corp.
Roadway Corp.

Ryder System
Southwest Airlines Co.
Union Pacific Corp.
United Parcel Service
USF Corp.
Yellow Roadway Corp.

Record One-Day Gains and Losses on the Nasdaq Stock Market
Source: Nasdaq Stock Market; as of Sept. 30, 2004

	GREATEST POINT GAINS			GREATEST % GAINS			GREATEST POINT LOSSES			GREATEST % LOSSES	
Rank	Date	Change	Rank	Date	% Change	Rank	Date	Change	Rank	Date	% Change
1.	1/3/2001	324.83	1.	1/3/2001	14.17%	1.	4/14/2000	−355.49	1.	10/19/1987	−11.35%
2.	12/5/2000	274.05	2.	12/5/2000	10.48%	2.	4/3/2000	−349.15	2.	4/14/2000	−9.67%
3.	4/18/2000	254.41	3.	4/5/2001	8.92%	3.	4/12/2000	−286.27	3.	10/20/1987	−9.00%
4.	5/30/2000	254.37	4.	4/18/2000	8.12%	4.	4/10/2000	−258.25	4.	10/26/1987	−9.00%
5.	10/19/2000	247.04	5.	5/30/2000	7.94%	5.	1/4/2000	−229.46	5.	8/31/1998	−8.56%
6.	10/13/2000	242.09	6.	10/13/2000	7.87%	6.	3/14/2000	−200.61	6.	4/3/2000	−7.64%
7.	6/2/2000	230.88	7.	10/19/2000	7.79%	7.	5/10/2000	−200.28	7.	1/2/2001	−7.23%
8.	4/25/2000	228.75	8.	5/8/2002	7.78%	8.	5/23/2000	−199.66	8.	12/20/2000	−7.12%
9.	4/17/2000	217.87	9.	12/22/2000	7.56%	9.	10/25/2000	−190.22	9.	4/12/2000	−7.06%
10.	6/1/2000	181.59	10.	10/21/1987	7.34%	10.	3/29/2000	−189.22	10.	10/27/1997	−7.02%

Nasdaq Stock Market, 1971-2003

High	YEAR	Low	High	YEAR	Low	High	YEAR	Low	High	YEAR	Low
114.12	1971	99.68	208.29	1980	124.09	397.54	1988	329.00	1328.45	1996	978.17
135.15	1972	113.65	223.96	1981	170.80	487.60	1989	376.87	1748.62	1997	1194.39
136.84	1973	88.67	241.63	1982	158.92	470.30	1990	322.93	2200.63	1998	1357.09
96.53	1974	54.87	329.11	1983	229.88	586.35	1991	352.85	4090.61	1999	2193.13
88.00	1975	60.70	288.41	1984	223.91	676.95	1992	545.85	5048.62*	2000	2332.78
97.88	1976	78.06	325.53	1985	245.82	790.56	1993	645.02	2892.36	2001	1387.06
105.05	1977	93.66	411.21	1986	322.14	803.93	1994	691.23	2059.38	2002	1114.11
139.25	1978	99.09	456.27	1987	288.49	1072.82	1995	740.53	2009.88	2003	1271.47
152.29	1979	117.84									

* Record high closing, Mar. 10, 2000.

Milestones of the Nasdaq Stock Market
Source: Nasdaq Stock Market; as of Sept. 30, 2004

First close over...		First close over...		First close over...		First close over...	
100	Feb. 8, 1971	500	Apr. 12, 1991	2,500	Jan. 29, 1999	4,000	Dec. 29, 1999
200	Nov. 13, 1980	1,000	July 17, 1995	3,000	Nov. 3, 1999	4,500	Feb. 17, 2000
300	May 6, 1986	1,500	July 11, 1997	3,500	Dec. 3, 1999	5,000	Mar. 9, 2000
400	May 30, 1986	2,000	July 16, 1998				

Standard & Poor's 500 Index, 1992-2004
Source: *Facts On File World News Digest;* monthly closing levels; record high daily closing was 1527.46, Mar. 24, 2000.

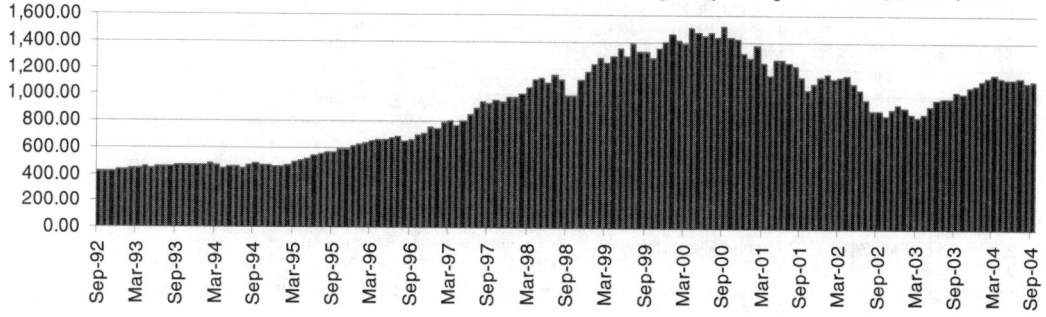

Most Active Common Stocks in 2003

New York Exchange Volume (millions of shares)		American Exchange Volume (millions of shares)		NASDAQ Volume (millions of shares)	
Lucent Technologies, Inc.	6,147.80	Nasdaq-100 Index Tracking Stock	2,652.6	Microsoft Corporation	16,782,267
Nortel Networks Corporation	3,943.00	SPDRS	2,157.7	Intel Corporation	14,711,830
Pfizer, Inc.	3,816.80	iShares MSCI-Japan	484.7	Cisco Systems, Inc.	14,664,944
General Electric Company	3,789.10	Semiconductor HOLDRS	435.0	Sun Microsystems, Inc.	13,230,334
Time Warner, Inc.	3,537.90	DIAMONDS (ETF)	386.8	Sirius Satellite Radio Inc.	12,530,653
EMC Corporation	2,807.40	Nabors Industries Ltd	378.2	Oracle Corporation	10,820,706
Citigroup, Inc.	2,742.50	Viragen, Inc	312.3	Applied Materials, Inc.	7,518,967
Motorola, Inc.	2,607.10	Devon Energy Corp	308.4	JDS Uniphase Corporation	7,375,780
Hewlett-Packard Company	2,471.80	Bema Gold Corp	289.2	Nextel Communications, Inc.	4,924,617
Texas Instruments Inc.	2,423.60	Boots and Coots Intern., Inc.	274.9	Dell Inc.	4,912,910

Average Yields of Long-Term Treasury, Corporate, and Municipal Bonds

Source: Office of Market Finance, U.S. Dept. of the Treasury; Federal Reserve System

Period	Treasury 30-year bonds[1]	New Aa corporate bonds[2]	New Aa municipal bonds[3]	Period	Treasury 30-year bonds[1]	New Aa corporate bonds[2]	New Aa municipal bonds[3]	Period	Treasury 30-year bonds[1]	New Aa corporate bonds[2]	New Aa municipal bonds[3]
1986				**1993**				**1999**			
June	7.57	9.39	7.87	June	6.81	7.48	5.63	Jun.	6.04	7.21	5.37
Dec.	7.37	8.87	6.87	Dec.	6.25	7.22	5.35	Dec.	6.35	7.55	5.95
1987				**1994**				**2000**			
June	8.57	9.64	7.79	June	7.40	8.16	6.11	June	5.93	7.75	5.80
Dec.	9.12	10.22	7.96	Dec.	7.87	8.66	6.80	Dec.	5.49	7.21	5.22
1988				**1995**				**2001**			
June	9.00	10.08	7.78	June	6.57	7.42	5.84	June	5.67	7.11	5.20
Dec.	9.01	10.05	7.61	Dec.	6.06	7.02	5.45	Dec.	5.48	6.80	5.25
1989				**1996**				**2002**			
June	8.27	9.24	7.02	June	7.06	8.00	6.02	June	5.65	6.57	5.09
Dec.	7.90	9.23	6.98	Dec.	6.55	7.45	5.64	Dec.	5.01	5.93	4.85
1990				**1997**				**2003**			
June	8.46	9.69	7.24	June	6.77	7.71	5.53	June	4.34	4.97	4.33
Dec.	8.24	9.55	7.09	Dec.	5.99	6.68	5.19	Dec.	5.11	5.62	4.65
1991				**1998**				**2004**			
June	8.47	9.37	7.13	Jun	5.70	6.43	5.12	June	5.45	6.01	5.05
Dec.	7.70	8.55	6.69	Dec	5.06	6.13	4.98				
1992											
June	7.84	8.45	6.49								
Dec.	7.44	8.12	6.22								

NA = Not available. (1) On Feb. 18, 2002, the U.S. treasury discontinued the 30-year constant maturity yield; rates thereafter are for 20-year yields. (2) Treasury series based on 3-week moving average of reoffering yields of new corporate bonds rated Aa by Moody's Investors Service with an original maturity of at least 20 years. Treasury discontinued yield index after Jan. 31, 2003. Rates thereafter are for Moody's seasoned Aaa corporate bonds as listed by Federal Reserve. (3) Index of new reoffering yields on 20-year general obligations rated Aa by Moody's Investors Service; discontinued by Treasury Jan. 31, 2003; rates thereafter are from Bond Buyer Index of general obligation, 20-year-to-maturity, mixed quality state and local bonds.

Performance of Mutual Funds by Type, 2004

Source: Thomson Financial, Rockville, MD, 800-232-2285

(data for periods ending Sept. 30, all figures are percents)

Fund Type/Fund Objective	AVERAGE ANNUAL RETURN 1-year	3-year	5-year	Fund Type/Fund Objective	AVERAGE ANNUAL RETURN 1-year	3-year	5-year
Diversified Stock				**Hybrid**			
Aggressive Growth	9.10	2.06	-2.45	Asset Allocation–Domestic	9.23	4.58	2.35
Equity Income	15.34	5.71	3.52	Asset Allocation–Global	11.39	7.17	3.90
Growth–Domestic	11.12	3.66	-1.16	Balanced–Domestic	9.13	4.41	2.68
Growth & Income	13.65	4.60	1.68	Balanced–Global	12.13	7.90	4.12
Mid Cap	15.39	8.76	5.33	**Bond**			
S&P 500 Index	11.70	3.25	-1.69	Corporate–High Yield	10.82	10.70	4.57
Small Cap	16.72	11.40	7.66	Corporate–Investment Grade	3.65	5.62	6.76
				Convertible	11.23	8.68	5.53
Specialty Stock				General Bd–Investment Grade	2.71	4.41	6.35
Sector–Energy/Natural Res	44.08	20.52	13.18	General Bd–Long	4.51	6.03	7.21
Sector–Financial Services	16.46	9.49	9.75	General Bd–Short & Interm.	4.57	6.28	6.12
Sector–Precious Metals	15.52	34.46	16.46	General Mortgage	2.78	3.93	5.65
Sector–Health/Biotechnology	9.63	1.51	9.24	**Global Income**	6.34	9.22	6.79
Sector–Other	-1.60	3.28	2.68	Loan Participation	4.27	4.95	4.14
Sector–Real Estate	24.98	19.53	17.98	Multi–Sector Bond	5.15	0.00	0.00
Sector–Tech/Communications	2.04	1.80	-11.40	US Government/Agency	2.76	4.16	6.21
Sector–Utilities	20.52	0.66	-0.02	US Government–Long	2.81	5.02	6.88
				US Government–Short & Interm	1.76	3.70	5.58
World Stock				US Treasury	1.94	5.71	7.76
Emerging Market Equity	25.15	24.59	7.52	**Municipal Bond**			
Global Equity	16.42	8.22	2.39	Municipal–High Yield	5.42	5.13	5.18
Non–US Equity	19.96	10.18	0.66	Municipal–Insured	3.33	4.71	5.84
Emerging Market Income	11.92	18.69	17.29	Municipal–National	3.23	4.43	5.36
				Municipal–Single State	3.57	4.59	5.55

The Richest 400

The Sept. 30, 2004, issue of *Forbes* contained the magazine's latest annual roster of the 400 wealthiest Americans. Here are the top ten (with Forbes's estimate of their net worth):

1. Bill Gates, $48 bil. (Microsoft)
2. Warren Buffett, $41 bil. (Berkshire Hathaway)
3. Paul Allen, $20 bil. (Microsoft)
4-8. Alice L. Walton, Helen R. Walton, Jim C. Walton, John T. Walton, S. Robson Walton, each $18 bil. (Wal-Mart heirs)
9. Larry Ellison, $18 bil. (Oracle)
10. Michael Dell, $13 bil. (Dell)

The total estimated net worth of all 400 came to $1 tril., up from $955 bil. in 2003, but below the $1.2 tril. total in 2000.

Chicago Board of Trade, Contracts Traded 1993, 2003

Source: Chicago Board of Trade

	1993	2003	% change 1993-2003		1993	2003	% change 1993-2003
FUTURES GROUP				Stock index	1,420	263,629	18,465.4
Agricultural	35,972,390	60,117,901	67.1	Metals	12,423	0	-100.0
Financial	105,989,406	298,052,099	181.2	**Total options**	36,531,698	80,521,459	120.4
Stock index	156,964	15,275,992	9,632.2	**COMBINED FUTURES AND OPTIONS**			
Metals	113,161	179,977	59.0	Agricultural	42,150,250	72,589,980	72.2
Total futures	142,241,377	373,669,290	162.7	Financial	136,322,817	365,837,850	168.4
OPTIONS GROUP				Stock index[1]	158,384	15,539,621	9,711.4
Agricultural	6,177,860	12,472,079	101.9	Metals	125,584	179,977	43.3
Financial	30,333,411	67,785,751	123.5	**GRAND TOTAL**	178,773,075	454,190,749	154.1

(1) Now called the Equity Index, and composed of 6 Dow Jones Indexes; not comparable to Stock Index shown for 1992.

U.S. Mutual Fund Shareholders[1]

Source: The Investment Company Institute

Shareholder Characteristics, 2004

Median age[2]	48
Median annual household income	$68,700
Median household financial assets[4]	$125,000
Median mutual fund assets	$48,000
Median number of funds owned	4
Employed[2]	77%
Married or living with a partner[2]	71%
Spouse or partner employed	75%
Four-year college degree or more[2]	57%

Owning:

Equity funds	80%
Bond funds	44%
Hybrid funds	34%
Money market funds	49%

Households owning mutual funds

Year	(in mil)[3]	Year	(in mil)[3]
1980	4.6	1998	44.4
1984	10.2	1999	48.4
1988	22.2	2000	51.7
1992	25.8	2001	56.3
1994	30.2	2002	54.2
1996	36.8	2003	53.3

(1) Except where noted, data include mutual funds both inside and outside employer-sponsored retirement plans. (2) Age of person responding to survey. (3) Data from 1980-88 exclude households owning mutual funds solely through employer-sponsored retirement plans. (4) Excluding primary residence.

Distribution of Financial Assets of U.S. Families[1]

Source: Federal Reserve System (by type of asset, in percent of family financial assets)

Type of financial asset	1989	1992	1995	1998	2001	Type of financial asset	1989	1992	1995	1998	2001
Transaction accounts	19.0	17.5	13.9	11.4	11.5	Retirement accounts	21.5	25.7	28.1	27.6	28.4
Certificates of deposit	10.2	8.0	5.6	4.3	3.1	Cash value of life insurance . . .	6.0	5.9	7.2	6.4	5.3
Savings bonds	1.5	1.1	1.3	0.7	0.7	Other managed assets	6.6	5.4	5.9	8.6	10.6
Bonds	10.2	8.4	6.3	4.3	4.6	Other	4.8	3.8	3.3	1.7	1.9
Stocks	15.0	16.5	15.6	22.7	21.6	Financial assets as a percentage					
Mutual funds (excluding money market funds)	5.3	7.6	12.7	12.4	12.2	of total assets	30.5	31.6	36.7	40.7	42.0

(1) Data from the triennial *Survey of Consumer Finances.*

Stock Ownership of U.S. Families, by Income & Age, 1989, 1995, 1998, & 2001[1]

Source: Federal Reserve System

(in percent, except as noted)

		Families having direct or indirect stock holdings[2]				Median value of portfolios (thousands of 2001 dollars)				Stock holdings as share of financial assets[3]			
		1989	1995	1998	2001	1989	1995	1998	2001	1989	1995	1998	2001
All families		31.7%	40.4%	48.9%	51.9%	$11.7	$16.9	$27.2	$34.3	27.8%	39.9%	53.9%	56.0%
Annual Income	Under $20	3.3	6.5	10.0	12.4	NA	4.3	5.4	7.0	13.6	14.2	20.4	36.9
(in thousands	$20-40	15.2	24.7	30.8	33.5	8.3	7.3	10.9	7.5	10.0	26.7	29.7	34.9
of dollars):	$40-60	28.6	41.5	50.2	52.1	6.3	7.2	13.1	15.0	16.7	28.4	37.9	46.4
	$60-80	44.0	54.3	69.3	75.7	8.0	14.6	20.4	28.5	21.7	35.6	45.7	51.7
	$80-90	57.6	69.7	77.9	82.0	13.1	28.9	49.0	64.6	26.1	41.3	50.4	57.4
	$90-100	76.9	80.0	90.4	89.6	53.7	69.3	146.5	247.7	34.3	45.4	62.5	60.4
By age of	Under 35	22.4	36.6	40.8	48.9	4.1	5.9	7.6	7.0	20.2	27.2	44.8	52.6
family head	35-44	39.0	46.4	56.7	59.5	7.1	11.6	21.8	27.5	29.3	39.5	54.6	57.3
(years):	45-54	41.8	48.9	58.6	59.2	18.1	30.0	41.4	50.0	33.5	42.6	55.7	59.1
	55-64	36.2	40.0	55.9	57.1	25.3	35.8	51.2	81.2	27.6	44.2	58.4	56.1
	65-74	26.7	34.4	42.7	39.2	27.9	39.3	61.0	150.0	26.0	35.8	51.3	55.1
	75 +	25.9	27.9	29.4	34.2	34.4	23.1	65.3	120.0	25.0	39.8	48.7	51.4

NA = Not available. ((1) Data from the triennial *Survey of Consumer Finances.* (2) Indirect holdings are those in mutual funds, retirement accounts, and other managed assets. (3) Among stock holding families.

Poverty Rate

Source: Bureau of the Census, U.S. Dept. of Commerce

The poverty rate is the proportion of the population whose income falls below the government's official poverty level, is adjusted each year for inflation. The national poverty rate was 12.5% in 2003, up from the 2002 rate of 12.1%, but below the 1990 rate of 13.5%. About 35.9 million people in the U.S. were in poverty in 2003, 1.5 million more than in 2002. In 2003 17.6% of children and 10.2% of people aged 65 and older were defined as poor.

Poverty Thresholds by Family Size, 1980-2003

Source: Bureau of the Census, U.S. Dept. of Commerce

	2003	2000	1990	1980		2003	2000	1990	1980
1 person	$9,393[1]	$8,794	$6,652	$4,186	3 persons	$14,393	$13,783	$10,419	$6,570
Under 65 years	9,573	8,959	6,800	4,284	4 persons	18,979	17,603	13,359	8,415
65 years and over	8,825	8,259	6,268	3,950	5 persons	22,887	20,819	15,792	9,967
2 persons	12,015[1]	11,239	8,509	5,361	6 persons	26,324	23,528	17,839	11,272
Householder under 65 . .	12,321	11,590	8,794	5,537	7 persons	30,289	26,754	20,241	12,761
Householder 65					8 persons	33,876	29,701	22,582	14,199
and over	11,1224	10,419	7,905	4,982	9 persons or more	40,751	35,060	26,848	16,896

(1) Weighted average; not used for computing poverty data.

Persons Below Poverty Level, 1960-2003
Source: Bureau of the Census, U.S. Dept. of Commerce

YEAR	Number below poverty level (in millions)				Percentage below poverty level				Avg. income cutoffs for family of 4 at poverty level[3]
	All races[1]	White	Black	Hispanic origin[2]	All races[1]	White	Black	Hispanic origin[2]	
1960	39.9	28.3	NA	NA	22.2	17.8	NA	NA	$3,022
1970	25.4	17.5	7.5	NA	12.6	9.9	33.5	NA	3,968
1980	29.3	19.7	8.6	3.5	13.0	10.2	32.5	25.7	8,414
1990	33.6	22.3	9.8	6.0	13.5	10.7	31.9	28.1	13,359
1991	35.7	23.7	10.2	6.3	14.2	11.3	32.7	28.7	13,924
1992	38.0	25.3	10.8	7.6	14.8	11.9	33.4	29.6	14,335
1993	39.3	26.2	10.9	8.1	15.1	12.2	33.1	30.6	14,763
1994	38.1	25.4	10.2	8.4	14.5	11.7	30.6	30.7	15,141
1995	36.4	24.4	9.9	8.6	13.8	11.2	29.3	30.3	15,569
1996	36.5	24.7	9.7	8.7	13.7	11.2	28.4	29.4	16,036
1997	35.6	24.4	9.1	8.3	13.3	11.0	26.5	27.1	16,400
1998	34.5	23.5	9.1	8.1	12.7	10.5	26.1	25.6	16,660
1999	32.3	21.9	8.4	7.4	11.8	9.8	23.6	22.8	17,029
2000	31.1	21.2	7.9	7.2	11.3	9.4	22.2	21.2	17,063
2001	32.9	22.7	8.1	8.0	11.7	9.9	22.7	21.4	18,104
2002	34.6	23.5	8.6	8.6	12.1	10.2	24.1	21.8	18,556
2003	35.9	24.3	8.8	9.1	12.5	10.5	24.4	22.5	18,979

NA = Not available. **NOTE:** Because of a change in the definition of poverty, data prior to 1980 are not directly comparable to data since 1980. (1) Includes other races not shown separately. (2) Persons of Hispanic origin may be of any race. (3) Figures for 1960-80 represent only nonfarm families.

Poverty by Family Status, Sex, and Race, 1986-2003
Source: Bureau of the Census, U.S. Dept. of Commerce
(No. in thousands)

	2003		2000		1995		1990		1986	
	No.	%[1]	No.	%[1]	No.	%[1]	No.	%[1]	No.	%[1]
TOTAL POOR	35,861	12.5	31,054	11.3	36,425	13.8	33,585	13.5	32,370	13.6
In families	25,684	10.4	22,015	9.6	27,501	12.3	25,232	12.0	24,754	12.0
Head of household	7,607	10.0	6,222	8.6	7,532	10.8	7,098	10.7	7,023	10.9
Related children	12,340	17.2	11,018	15.6	13,999	20.2	12,715	19.9	12,257	19.8
Unrelated individuals	9,713	20.4	8,503	18.9	8,247	20.9	7,446	20.7	6,846	21.6
In families, female householder, no husband present	12,413	30.0	10,425	27.9	14,205	36.5	12,578	37.2	11,944	38.3
Head of household	3,856	28.0	3,096	24.7	4,057	32.4	3,768	33.4	3,613	34.6
Related children	7,203	13.1	6,116	39.8	8,364	50.3	7,363	53.4	6,943	54.4
Unrelated female individuals	5,559	22.6	5,071	21.6	4,865	23.5	4,589	24.0	4,311	25.1
All other families	NA	NA	NA	NA	13,296	7.2	12,654	7.1	12,811	7.3
Head of household	NA	NA	NA	NA	3,475	6.1	3,330	6.0	3,410	6.3
Related children	NA	NA	NA	NA	5,635	10.7	5,352	10.7	5,313	10.8
Unrelated male individuals	4,154	18.0	3,548	16.0	3,382	18.0	2,857	16.9	2,536	17.5
TOTAL WHITE POOR[2]	24,272	10.5	21,242	9.4	24,423	11.2	22,326	10.7	22,183	11.0
In families	16,740	8.7	14,392	7.7	17,593	9.6	15,916	9.0	16,393	9.4
Head of household	5,058	8.1	4,151	6.9	4,994	8.5	4,622	8.1	4,811	8.6
Related children	7,624	13.9	6,838	12.3	8,474	15.5	7,696	15.1	7,714	15.3
Female householder, no spouse present	6,530	25.6	1,655	20	2,200	26.6	2,010	26.8	2,041	28.2
Unrelated individuals	7,225	18.6	6,402	17.2	6,336	19.0	5,739	18.6	5,198	19.2
TOTAL BLACK POOR[2]	8,781	24.4	7,862	22.0	9,872	29.3	9,837	31.9	8,983	31.1
In families	6,870	23.1	6,108	20.7	8,189	28.5	8,160	31.0	7,410	29.7
Head of household	1,986	22.3	1,685	19.1	2,127	26.4	2,193	29.3	1,987	28.0
Related children	11,162	33.6	3,417	30.4	4,644	41.5	4,412	44.2	4,039	42.7
Female householder, no spouse present	5,115	39.0	1,301	34.6	1,701	45.1	1,648	48.1	1,488	50.1
Unrelated individuals	1,781	29.5	1,708	28.0	1,551	32.6	1,491	35.1	1,431	38.5

NA = Not available. (1) Percentage of total U.S. population in each category who fell below poverty level and are enumerated here. For example, of all persons in families in 2003, 10.4%, or 25,684,000, were poor. (2) Data are for one race only. The Census Bureau revised race categories in 2002; 2003 figures are not directly comparable with previous years.

Persons in Poverty, by State, 2001-2003
Source: Bureau of the Census, U.S. Dept. of Commerce

	2002-03[1]	2001-02[1]		2002-03[1]	2001-02[1]		2002-03[1]	2001-02[1]
Alabama	14.7%	15.2%	Kentucky	14.3%	13.4%	Ohio	10.3%	10.1%
Alaska	9.2	8.7	Louisiana	17.2	16.9	Oklahoma	13.5	14.6
Arizona	13.5	14.1	Maine	12.5	11.9	Oregon	11.7	11.3
Arkansas	18.8	18.8	Maryland	8.0	7.3	Pennsylvania	10.0	9.5
California	13.1	12.8	Massachusetts	10.1	9.5	Rhode Island	11.3	10.3
Colorado	9.7	9.2	Michigan	11.5	10.5	South Carolina	13.5	14.7
Connecticut	8.2	7.8	Minnesota	6.9	6.9	South Dakota	12.1	10.0
Delaware	8.2	7.9	Mississippi	17.2	18.9	Tennessee	14.4	14.5
District of Columbia	16.9	17.6	Missouri	10.3	9.8	Texas	16.3	15.3
Florida	12.6	12.6	Montana	14.3	13.4	Utah	9.5	10.2
Georgia	11.5	12.1	Nebraska	10.2	10.0	Vermont	9.2	9.8
Hawaii	10.3	11.4	Nevada	9.9	8.0	Virginia	10.0	8.9
Idaho	10.8	11.4	New Hampshire	5.8	6.1	Washington	11.8	10.8
Illinois	12.7	11.5	New Jersey	8.3	8.0	West Virginia	17.1	16.6
Indiana	9.5	8.8	New Mexico	18.0	17.9	Wisconsin	9.2	8.2
Iowa	9.1	8.3	New York	14.2	14.1	Wyoming	9.4	8.8
Kansas	10.4	10.1	North Carolina	15.0	13.4	**U.S. Total**	**12.3**	**11.9**
			North Dakota	10.6	12.7			

(1) 2-year average.

IT'S A FACT: In 2003, the wealthiest foundation in the U.S. was the Bill and Melinda Gates Foundation, with assets of $26.8 bil. The top individual donor in 2003 was Joan B. Kroc, widow of McDonald's owner Ray Kroc, who died Oct. 12, 2003. Her contributions to charity totaled $1.91 bil. for the year.

U.S. Capital Gains Tax, 1960-2004

Source: George W. Smith IV, CPA, Partner, George W. Smith & Company, P.C.

The following shows changes in the maximum tax rate on net long-term capital gains for individuals since 1960.

Year	Max %	Year	Max %	Year	Max %	Year	Max %	Year	Max %
1960	25.0	1972	35.0[1]	1987	28.0	1997	20.0[4]	2001	20/18[6]
1970	29.5	1978	28.0	1988	33.0[2]	1999	20.0[5]	2003	20/15[7]
1971	32.5	1981	20.0	1990	28.0[3]				

(1) From 1972 to 1976, the interplay of minimum tax and maximum tax resulted in a marginal rate of 49.125%. (2) Statutory maximum of 28%, but "phase-out" notch increased marginal rate to 33%; interplay of all "phase-outs" could have increased the effective marginal rate to 49.5%. (3) The Budget Act of 1990 increased the statutory rate to 31% and capped the marginal rate at 28%; however, some taxpayers faced effective marginal rates of more than 34% because of the phase-out of personal exemptions and itemized deductions. (4) New rate is for those who, after July 28, 1997, sell capital assets held for more than 18 mos (12 mos for sales after Dec. 31, 1997). A 10% capital gains rate applies to individuals in the 15% income tax bracket. (Those who, after July 28, 1997, but before Jan. 1, 1998, sell capital assets held between 12 and 18 mos will be taxed at the old top rate of 28%. Those who sold capital assets after May 6, 1997, but before July 29, 1997, will be taxed at the 20% rate, so long as such assets were held for at least a year.) (5) The IRS Restructuring and Reform Act of 1998 repealed the more-than-18-month holding period for sales after Dec. 31, 1997. Beginning Jan. 1, 1998, capital assets need only be held 12 months to have the 20%/10% capital gains rates apply. (6) For capital assets bought after Dec. 31, 2000, and held for more than 5 years, the 20% minimum capital gains rate will be lowered to 18%. The 10% rate will be lowered to 8%, regardless of when the assets were bought. This provision was repealed in 2003. (7) The maximum capital gains rate for capital assets held more than one year and sold on or after May 6, 2003, was decreased to 15%. The 10% bracket was reduced to 5%. The capital gains rate for the sale of collectibles such as antiques remains at 28%, and the sale of certain depreciable real estate is taxed at a maximum of 25%.

2004 Federal Corporate Tax Rates

Taxable Income Amount	Tax Rate	Taxable Income Amount	Tax Rate	Taxable Income Amount	Tax Rate
Not more than $50,000	15%	$100,001 to $335,000	39%	$15,000,001 to $18,333,333	38%
$50,001 to $75,000	25%	$335,001 to $10,000,000	34%	More than $18,333,333	35%
$75,001 to $100,000	34%	$10,000,001 to $15,000,000	35%		

Personal service corporations (used by incorporated professionals such as attorneys and doctors) pay a flat rate of 35%.

Leading U.S. Businesses in 2003

Source: FORTUNE Magazine

(millions of dollars in revenues)

Advertising, Marketing
Omnicom Group	$8,621
Interpublic Group	6,114
Grey Global	1,307

Aerospace
Boeing	$50,485
Lockheed Martin	31,844
United Technologies	31,034
Northrop Grumman	28,686
Honeywell Intl.	23,103
Raytheon	18,109
General Dynamics	16,617
Textron	10,028
L-3 Communications	5,062
Goodrich	4,407

Airlines
AMR	$17,440
UAL	13,724
Delta Air Lines	13,303
Northwest Airlines	9,510
Continental Airlines	8,870
US Airways Group	6,846
Southwest Airlines	5,937
Alaska Air Group	2,445
America West Holdings	2,255
ExpressJet Holdings	1,311

Apparel
Nike	$10,697
VF	5,208
Jones Apparel Group	4,375
Liz Claiborne	4,241
Levi Strauss	4,091
Reebok International	3,485
Polo Ralph Lauren	2,439
Kellwood	2,398
Phillips Van Heusen	1,582
Warnaco Group	1,448

Automotive Retailing, Services
AutoNation	$19,381
United Auto Group	8,804
Sonic Automotive	7,598
Asbury Automotive Group	4,835
Group 1 Automotive	4,519
CarMax	3,970
Lithia Motors	2,514
Allete	1,728

Banks (Commercial)
Citigroup	$94,713
Bank of America Corp.	48,065
J.P. Morgan Chase & Co.	44,363
Wells Fargo	31,800
Wachovia Corp.	24,474
Bank One Corp.	21,454
U.S. Bancorp	15,354
FleetBoston	14,362

Beverages
Coca-Cola	$21,044
Coca-Cola Enterprises	17,330
Anheuser-Busch	14,147
Pepsi Bottling	10,265
Adolph Coors	4,000
PepsiAmericas	3,237
Constellation Brands	2,732
Brown-Forman	2,060
Coca-Cola Bottling	1,211

Building Materials, Glass
Owens Corning	$4,996
USG	3,666
Armstrong Holdings	3,259
Vulcan Materials	2,962
Martin Marietta Materials	1,748
Texas Industries	1,364

Chemicals
Dow Chemical	$32,632
DuPont	27,730
PPG Industries	8,756
Ashland	8,080
Rohm & Haas	6,421

Computer and Data Services
Electronic Data Systems	$21,596
Computer Sciences	11,347
First Data	8,544
Science Applications Intl.	6,457
Unisys	5,911
Affiliated Computer Svcs.	3,787

Computer Peripherals
EMC	$6,237
Lexmark International	4,755
Maxtor	4,086
Storage Technology	2,183
Symbol Technologies	1,530

Computers, Office Equipment
Intl. Business Machines	$89,131
Hewlett-Packard	73,061
Dell	41,444
Xerox	15,701
Sun Microsystems	11,434
Apple Computer	6,207
NCR	5,598

Computer Software
Microsoft	$32,187
Oracle	9,475
Computer Assoc. Intl.	3,116
Electronic Arts	2,482
PeopleSoft	2,267

Diversified Financials
General Electric	$134,187
Fannie Mae	53,767
American Express	25,866
Countrywide Financial	13,660
Marsh & McLennan	11,588

Electronics, Electrical Equip.
Emerson Electric	$13,999
Whirlpool	12,176
Eaton	8,061
SPX	5,130
Maytag	4,792

Energy
Duke Energy	$23,483
Williams	19,246
American Electric Power	15,441
El Paso	12,653
Reliant Resources	11,707

Engineering, Construction
Fluor	$8,836
Jacobs Engineering Grp.	4,616
Emcor Group	4,535
Peter Kiewit Sons'	3,375
Shaw Group	3,307

Entertainment
Time Warner	$43,877
Walt Disney	27,061
Viacom	26,585
Clear Channel Comm.	8,931
Regal Entertainment Group	2,490

Food
PepsiCo.	$26,971
ConAgra Foods	22,053
Sara Lee	18,291
General Mills	10,506
H.J. Heinz	9,328
Kellogg	8,812
Smithfield Foods	7,905
Campbell Soup	6,678
Land O'Lakes	5,978
Dole Food	4,608

Food and Drug Stores

Kroger	$53,791
Safeway	35,553
Albertson's	35,436
Walgreen	32,505
CVS	26,588
Publix Super Markets	16,848
Rite Aid	15,801

Food Production

Archer Daniels Midland	$30,708
Tyson Foods	24,549
Dean Foods	9,185
Farmland Industries	6,703
Chiquita Brands Intl.	2,770

Food Services

McDonald's	$17,141
Yum Brands	8,380
Darden Restaurants	4,655
Starbucks	4,076
Brinker International	3,285

Forest and Paper Products

International Paper	$25,200
Georgia-Pacific	20,255
Weyerhaeuser	19,873
Boise Cascade	8,245
MeadWestvaco	7,553

Furniture

Leggett & Platt	$4,388
Steelcase	2,587
Furniture Brands Intl.	2,368
La-Z-Boy	2,112
Hon Industries	1,756

General Merchandisers

Wal-Mart Stores	$258,681
Target	48,163
Sears Roebuck	41,124
J.C. Penney	32,923
Kmart Holding	26,032
Federated Dept. Stores	15,264
May Dept. Stores	13,343

Health Care

Medco Health Solutions	$34,265
UnitedHealth Group	28,823
HCA	21,808
WellPoint Health Networks	20,360
Cigna	18,808
Aetna	17,976
Anthem	16,771
Tenet Healthcare	14,582

Hotels, Casinos, Resorts

Marriott International	$9,198
Caesars Entertainment	4,669
Harrah's Entertainment	4,364
MGM Mirage	4,140
Hilton Hotels	3,853

Household and Personal Products

Procter & Gamble	$43,377
Kimberly-Clark	14,348
Colgate-Palmolive	9,903
Gillette	9,252
Avon Products	6,876
Estée Lauder	5,118
Clorox	4,171

Industrial and Farm Equip.

Caterpillar	$22,763
Deere	15,535
Illinois Tool Works	10,138
American Standard	8,568
Parker Hannifin	6,411

Insurance—Life, Health (Mutual)

TIAA-CREF	$26,016
New York Life Insurance	25,700
Mass. Mutual Life Ins.	21,076
Northwestern Mutual	17,060
Guardian Life of America	9,022

Insurance—Life, Health (Stock)

MetLife	$36,261
Prudential Financial	27,907
AFLAC	11,447
UnumProvident	10,400
John Hancock Fin. Svcs.	10,071

Insurance—Property, Casualty (Mutual)

State Farm Insurance Cos.	$56,065
Auto-Owners Insurance	4,211
Country Insurance & Financial Services	2,440
Sentry Insurance Group	2,088
Amica Mutual Insurance	1,539

Insurance—Property, Casualty (Stock)

American Intl. Group	$81,300
Berkshire Hathaway	63,859
Allstate	32,149
Hartford Financial Services	18,733
Liberty Mutual Ins. Group	16,914

Metals

Alcoa	$21,728
United States Steel	9,458
Nucor	6,266
AK Steel Holding	4,206
Phelps Dodge	4,143
International Steel Group	4,070

Mining, Crude-Oil Production

Occidental Petroleum	$9,326
Devon Energy	7,352
Unocal	6,539
Anadarko Petroleum	5,122
Burlington Resources	4,311

Motor Vehicles and Parts

General Motors	$195,645
Ford Motor	164,496
Delphi	28,096
Johnson Controls	22,646
Visteon	17,660

Network and Other Communications

Motorola	$27,058
Cisco Systems	18,878
Lucent Technologies	8,470
Avaya	4,338
Qualcomm	3,971

Package, Freight, and Mail Delivery

United Parcel Service	$33,485
FedEx	22,487
Brink's	4,051

Petroleum Refining

Exxon Mobil	$213,199
ChevronTexaco	112,937
ConocoPhillips	99,468
Valero Energy	37,969
Marathon Oil	37,137

Pharmaceuticals

Pfizer	$45,950
Johnson & Johnson	41,862
Merck	22,486
Bristol-Myers Squibb	20,671
Abbott Laboratories	19,681
Wyeth	15,851
Eli Lilly	12,583
Amgen	8,356
Schering-Plough	8,334
Forest Laboratories	2,246

Pipelines

Plains All Amer. Pipeline	$12,590
TransMontaigne	8,241
Kinder Morgan Energy	6,624
Enterprise Products	5,346
Enbridge Energy Partners	3,171

Publishing & Printing

Gannett	$6,711
Tribune	5,595
McGraw-Hill	4,839
R.R. Donnelley & Sons	4,787
New York Times	3,227
Knight-Ridder	2,946
Washington Post	2,839
Reader's Digest Assn.	2,475
American Greetings	1,996
Scholastic	1,958

Railroads

Union Pacific	$12,792
Burlington Northern Santa Fe	9,413
CSX	7,793
Norfolk Southern	6,468

Scientific, Photo., and Control Equip.

Eastman Kodak	$13,317
Agilent Technologies	6,056
Danaher	5,294
Thermo Electron	2,097
PerkinElmer	1,541

Securities

Morgan Stanley	$34,933
Merrill Lynch	27,745
Goldman Sachs Group	23,623
Lehman Brothers Holdings	17,287
Bear Stearns	7,395

Semiconductors and Other Electron.

Intel	$30,141
Solectron	11,700
Sanmina-SCI	10,361
Texas Instruments	9,834
Jabil Circuit	4,730

Specialty Retailers

Home Depot	$64,816
Costco Wholesale	42,546
Lowe's	31,263
Best Buy	22,673
Gap	15,854
TJX	13,328
Staples	13,181
Office Depot	12,359
Toys "R" Us	11,566
Circuit City Stores	9,954

Telecommunications

Verizon Communications	$67,752
SBC Communications	40,843
AT&T	34,529
Sprint	26,202
BellSouth	22,635
Comcast	21,263
AT&T Wireless Services	16,695
Qwest Communications	14,936
Nextel Communications	10,820
Alltel	8,190

Temporary Help

Manpower	$12,185
Kelly Services	4,325
Spherion	2,075
Robert Half Intl.	1,975
Volt Info. Sciences	1,610

Textiles

Mohawk Industries	$5,005
WestPoint Stevens	1,656

Tobacco

Altria Group	$60,704
R.J. Reynolds Tobacco	5,267
Universal	2,637

Toys, Sporting Goods

Mattel	$4,960
Hasbro	3,139

Transportation Equipment

Harley-Davidson	$4,904
Brunswick	4,129
Polaris Industries	1,606
Trinity Industries	1,433

Utilities: Gas and Electric

Exelon	$15,812
FirstEnergy	12,318
Edison International	12,156
Dominion Resources	12,078
Public Service Enterprise Group	11,340
Southern	11,251
PG&E Corp.	11,221
Consolidated Edison	9,827
CenterPoint Energy	9,772
AES	9,649

Waste Management

Waste Management	$11,574
Allied Waste Industries	5,583
Republic Services	2,518

Wholesalers (Diversified)

Genuine Parts	$8,449
W.W. Grainger	4,667
Fisher Scientific Intl.	3,564
Wesco International	3,287
Hughes Supply	3,253
World Fuel Services	2,662

25 U.S. Corporations with Largest Revenues in 2003

Source: FORTUNE Magazine

(millions of dollars)

Rank	Company	Revenues	Rank	Company	Revenues
1.	Wal-Mart Stores, Bentonville, AR	$258,681	14.	Berkshire Hathaway, Omaha, NE	$63,859
2.	Exxon Mobil, Irving, TX	213,199	15.	Altria Group, New York, NY	60,704
3.	General Motors, Detroit, MI	195,645	16.	McKesson, San Francisco, CA	57,129
4.	Ford Motor, Dearborn, MI	164,496	17.	Cardinal Health, Dublin, OH	56,830
5.	General Electric, Fairfield, CT	134,187	18.	State Farm Insurance, Bloomington, IL	56,065
6.	ChevronTexaco, San Ramon, CA	112,937	19.	Kroger, Cincinnati, OH	53,791
7.	ConocoPhillips, Houston, TX	99,468	20.	Fannie Mae, Washington, DC	53,767
8.	Citigroup, New York, NY	94,713	21.	Boeing, Chicago, IL	50,485
9.	IBM, Armonk, NY	89,131	22.	AmerisourceBergen, Chesterbrook, PA	49,657
10.	American Intl. Group, New York, NY	81,300	23.	Target, Minneapolis, MN	48,163
11.	Hewlett-Packard, Palo Alto, CA	73,061	24.	Bank of America, Charlotte, NC	48,065
12.	Verizon Communications, New York, NY	67,752	25.	Pfizer, New York, NY	45,950
13.	Home Depot, Atlanta, GA	64,816			

Fastest-Growing U.S. Franchises in 2003[1]

Source: *Entrepreneur* Magazine

Company	Type of Business	Minimum start-up cost[2]
Subway	Submarine sandwiches and salads	$86,000
Curves	Women's fitness and weight loss centers	35,600
The Quizno's Franchise Co.	Submarine sandwiches, soups, salads	208,400
7-Eleven Inc.	Convenience stores	Varies
Jackson Hewitt Tax Service	Tax preparation services	47,400
The UPS Store	Postal/business/communications services	145,800
McDonald's	Hamburgers, chicken, salads	506,000
Jani-King	Commercial cleaning	11,300
Dunkin' Donuts	Donuts and baked goods	255,700
Baskin-Robbins USA Co.	Ice cream and yogurt	145,700
Jiffy Lube Int'l. Inc.	Fast oil change	174,000
InterContinental Hotels Group	Hotels	Varies
Sonic Drive In Restaurants	Drive-in restaurants	710,000
Domino's Pizza LLC	Pizza, buffalo wings, breadsticks	141,400
Super 8 Motels Inc.	Economy motels	291,000
Kumon Math & Reading Centers	Supplemental education	8,000
Chem-Dry Carpet Drapery & Upholstery Cleaning	Carpet, drapery, and upholstery cleaning	23,600
ServiceMaster Clean	Commercial/residential cleaning and disaster restoration	26,600
RE/MAX Int'l. Inc.	Real estate	20,000
Snap-on Tools	Professional tools & equipment	17,600
Burger King Corp.	Hamburgers, fries, breakfast items	294,000
Jan-Pro Franchising Int'l. Inc.	Commercial cleaning	1,000
Merle Norman Cosmetics	Cosmetics studios	33,100
Papa John's Int'l. Inc.	Pizza	250,000
Jazzercise Inc.	Dance/exercise classes	2,600

(1) Ranked by number of new franchise units added. (2) Not including franchise fee, which varies.

Largest Corporate Mergers or Acquisitions in U.S.

Source: Securities Data Co.

(as of Sept. 2004; * denotes an announced merger or acquisition not yet complete; year = year effective or announced)

Company	Acquirer	Dollars (in billions)	Year	Company	Acquirer	Dollars (in billions)	Year
Time Warner	America Online, Inc.	$181.6	2001	NYNEX	Bell Atlantic	$30.8	1997
Warner-Lambert	Pfizer Inc.	88.8	2000	AT&T Broadband & Internet Services	Comcast Corp.	30.0	2001
Mobil Corp.	Exxon Corp.	86.4	1999	Electronic Data Syst.	shareholders	29.7	1996
Citicorp	Travelers Group Inc.	72.6	1998	First Chicago NBD	BANC ONE Corp.	29.6	1998
Ameritech Corp	SBC Communications Inc.	72.4	1999	RJR Nabisco	Kohlberg Kravis Roberts	29.4	1989
GTE Corp.	Bell Atlantic Corp.	71.3	2000	Pharmacia & Upjohn	Monsanto Co.	26.9	2000
Tele-Communications	AT&T	69.9	1999	Associates First Capital	shareholders	26.6	1998
AirTouch Communications	Vodafone Group PLC	65.8	1999	Conoco	Phillips Petroleum	24.8	2002
BankAmerica Corp.	NationsBank Corp.	61.6	1998	Lucent Technologies (AT&T)	shareholders	24.1	1996
Pharmacia Corp.	Pfizer, Inc	61.3	2003	Bestfoods	Unilever PLC	23.7	2000
Bank One Corp.	JP Morgan Chase	58.8	2004	Compaq Computer	Hewlett-Packard	23.5	2002
US West	Qwest Communication	56.3	2000	Amer. General Corp.	American Int'l. Group	23.4	2001
Amoco Corp.	British Petroleum Co. PLC	55.0	1998	AMFM, Inc.	Clear Channel Communications	22.7	2000
MediaOne Group	AT&T	51.9	2000	Pacific Telesis Group	SBC Communications, Inc.	22.4	1997
Liberty Media Group (AT&T)	shareholders	46.0	2001	General Re Corp.	Berkshire Hathaway Inc.	22.3	1998
Texaco	Chevron	43.3	2001	US Bancorp, MN	Firstar Corp.	21.1	2001
MCI Communications	WorldCom Inc.	41.4	1998	Ascend Communications	Lucent Technologies	21.1	1999
*AT&T Wireless Service	Cingular Wireless	41.0	2004	Network Solutions, Inc.	VeriSign, Inc.	20.8	2000
SDL Inc.	JDS Uniphase Corp.	41.0	2001	Waste Management	USA Waste Services	20.0	1998
CBS Corp.	Viacom	40.9	2000	Nabisco Holdings	Philip Morris	19.4	2000
Chrysler Corp.	Daimler-Benz AG	40.5	1998	AT&T Wireless Serv.	shareholders	18.8	2001
Wells Fargo & Co.	Norwest Corp.	34.4	1998	Capital Cities/ABC Inc	Walt Disney	18.3	1996
VoiceStream Wireless Corp.	Deutsche Telekom AG	34.1	2001	SunAmerica Inc.	American Int'l. Group	18.1	1999
ARCO	BP Amoco PLC	33.7	2000	Vivendi Universal	General Electric	14.0	2003
J.P. Morgan & Co.	Chase Manhattan	33.6	2000	John Hancock Financial Services	Manulife Financial	11.0	2003
US West Media Group	shareholders	31.7	1998				
Agilent Technologies	shareholders	31.2	2000				
Associates First Capital	Citigroup	31.0	2000				

Economic and Financial Glossary

Source: Reviewed by William M. Gentry, Graduate School of Business, Columbia University

Annuity contract: An investment vehicle sold by insurance companies. Annuity buyers can elect to receive periodic payments for the rest of their lives. Annuities provide insurance against outliving one's wealth.

Arbitrage: A form of hedged investment meant to capture slight differences in the prices of 2 related securities—for example, buying gold in London and selling it at a higher price in New York.

Balanced budget: A budget is balanced when receipts equal expenditures. When receipts exceed expenditures, there is a **surplus;** when they fall short of expenditures, there is a **deficit.**

Balance of payments: The difference between all payments, for some categories of transactions, made to and from foreign countries over a set period of time. A *favorable* balance of payments exists when more payments are coming in than going out; an *unfavorable* balance of payments obtains when the reverse is true. Payments may include gold, the cost of merchandise and services, interest and dividend payments, money spent by travelers, and repayment of principal on loans.

Balance of trade (trade gap): The difference between exports and imports, in both actual funds and credit. A nation's balance of trade is *favorable* when exports exceed imports and *unfavorable* when the reverse is true.

Bear market: A market in which prices are falling.

Bearer bond: A bond issued in bearer form rather than being registered in a specific owner's name. Ownership is determined by possession.

Bond: A written promise, or IOU, by the issuer to repay a fixed amount of borrowed money on a specified date and generally to pay interest at regular intervals in the interim.

Bull market: A market in which prices are on the rise.

Capital gain (loss): An increase (decrease) in the market value of an asset over some period of time. For tax purposes, capital gains are typically calculated from when an asset is bought to when it is sold.

Commercial paper: An extremely short-term corporate IOU, generally due in 270 days or less.

Convertible bond: A corporate bond (see below) that may be converted into a stated number of shares of common stock. Its price tends to fluctuate along with fluctuations in the price of the stock and with changes in interest rates.

Consumer price index (CPI): A statistical measure of the change in the price of consumer goods.

Corporate bond: A bond issued by a corporation. The bond normally has a stated life and pays a fixed rate of interest. Considered safer than the common or preferred stock of the same company.

Cost of living: The cost of maintaining a standard of living measured in terms of purchased goods and services. Inflation typically measures changes in the cost of living.

Cost-of-living adjustments: Changes in promised payments, such as retirement benefits, to account for changes in the cost of living.

Credit crunch (liquidity crisis): A situation in which cash for lending is in short supply.

Debenture: An unsecured bond backed only by the general credit of the issuing corporation.

Deficit spending: Government spending in excess of revenues, generally financed with the sale of bonds. A deficit increases the government debt.

Deflation: A decrease in the level of prices.

Depression: A long period of economic decline marked by low prices, high unemployment, and many business failures.

Derivatives: Financial contracts, such as options, whose values are based on, or *derived* from, the price of an underlying financial asset or indicator such as a stock or an interest rate.

Devaluation: The official lowering of a nation's currency, decreasing its value in relation to foreign currencies.

Discount rate: The rate of interest set by the Federal Reserve that member banks are charged when borrowing money through the Federal Reserve System.

Disposable income: Income after taxes that is available to persons for spending and saving.

Diversification: Investing in more than one asset in order to reduce the riskiness of the overall asset portfolio. By holding more than one asset, losses on some assets may be offset by gains realized on other assets.

Dividend: Discretionary payment by a corporation to its shareholders, usually in the form of cash or stock shares.

Dow Jones Industrial Average: An index of stock market prices, based on the prices of 30 companies, 28 of which are on the New York Stock Exchange.

Econometrics: The use of statistical methods to study economic and financial data.

Federal Deposit Insurance Corp. (FDIC): A U.S. government-sponsored corporation that insures accounts in national banks and other qualified institutions against bank failures.

Federal Reserve System: The entire banking system of the U.S., incorporating 12 Federal Reserve banks (one in each of 12 Federal Reserve districts), 25 Federal Reserve branch banks, all national banks, and state-chartered commercial banks and trust companies that have been admitted to its membership. The governors of the system greatly influence the nation's monetary and credit policies.

Full employment: The economy is said to be at full employment when everyone who wishes to work at the going wage-rate for his or her type of labor is employed, save only for the small amount of unemployment due to the time it takes to switch from one job to another.

Futures: A futures contract is an agreement to buy or sell a specific amount of a commodity or financial instrument at a particular price at a set date in the future. For example, futures based on a stock index (such as the Dow Jones Industrial Average) are bets on the future price of that group of stocks.

Golden parachute: Provisions in contracts of some high-level executives guaranteeing substantial severance benefits if they lose their position in a corporate takeover.

Government bond: A bond issued by the U.S. Treasury, considered a safe investment. These are divided into 2 categories—marketable and not marketable. *Savings bonds* cannot be bought and sold once the original purchase is made. Marketable bonds fall into several categories. *Treasury bills* are short-term U.S. obligations, maturing in 3, 6, or 12 months. *Treasury notes* mature in up to 10 years. *Treasury bonds* mature in 10 to 30 years. *Indexed bonds* are adjusted for inflation.

Greenmail: A company buying back its own shares for more than the going market price to avoid a threatened hostile takeover.

Gross domestic product (GDP): The market value of all goods and services that have been bought for final use during a period of time. It became the official measure of the size of the U.S. economy in 1991, replacing *gross national product (GNP)*, in use since 1941. GDP covers workers and capital employed within the nation's borders. GNP covers production by U.S. residents regardless of where it takes place. The switch aligned U.S. terminology with that of most other industrialized countries.

Hedge fund: A flexible investment fund for a limited number of large investors (the minimum investment is typically $1 million). Hedge funds use a variety of investment techniques, including those forbidden to mutual funds, such as short-selling and heavy leveraging.

Hedging: Taking 2 positions whose gains and losses will offset each other if prices change, in order to limit risk.

Individual retirement account (IRA): A self-funded tax-advantaged retirement plan that allows employed individuals to contribute up to a maximum yearly sum. With a *traditional* IRA, individuals contribute pre-tax earnings and defer income taxes until retirement. With a *Roth* IRA, individuals contribute after-tax earnings but do not pay taxes on future withdrawals (the interest is never taxed). *401(k) plans* are employer-sponsored plans similar to traditional IRAs, but having higher contribution limits.

Inflation: An increase in the level of prices.

Insider information: Important facts about the condition or plans of a corporation that have not been released to the general public.

Interest: The cost of borrowing money.

Investment bank: A financial institution that arranges the initial issuance of stocks and bonds and offers companies advice about acquisitions and divestitures.

Junk bonds: Bonds issued by companies with low credit ratings. They typically pay relatively high interest rates because of the fear of default.

Leading indicators: A series of 11 indicators from different segments of the economy used by the U.S. Commerce Department to predict when changes in the level of economic activity will occur.

Leverage: The extent to which a purchase was paid for with borrowed money. Amplifies the potential gain or loss for the purchaser.

Leveraged buyout (LBO): An acquisition of a company in which much of the purchase price is borrowed, with the debt to be repaid from future profits or by subsequently selling off company assets. A leveraged buyout is typically carried out by a small group of investors, often including incumbent management.

Liquid assets: Assets consisting of cash and/or items that are easily converted into cash.

Margin account: A brokerage account that allows a person to trade securities on credit. A **margin call** is a demand for more collateral on the account.

Money supply: The currency held by the public, plus checking accounts in commercial banks and savings institutions.

Mortgage-backed securities: Created when a bank, builder, or government agency gathers together a group of mortgages and then sells bonds to other institutions and the public. The investors receive their proportionate share of the interest payments on the loans as well as the principal payments. Usually, the mortgages in question are guaranteed by the government.

Municipal bond: Issued by governmental units such as states, cities, local taxing authorities, and other agencies. Interest is exempt from U.S.—and sometimes state and local—income tax. *Municipal bond unit investment trusts* offer a portfolio of many different municipal bonds chosen by professionals. The income is exempt from federal income taxes.

Mutual fund: A portfolio of professionally bought and managed financial assets in which you pool your money along with that of many other people. A share price is based on net asset value, or the value of all the investments owned by the funds, less any debt, and divided by the total number of shares. The major advantage, relative to investing individually in only a small number of stocks, is less risk—the holdings are spread out over many assets and if one or two do badly the remainder may shield you from the losses. *Bond funds* are mutual funds that deal in the bond market exclusively. *Money market mutual funds* buy in the so-called money market—institutions that need to borrow large sums of money for short terms. These funds often offer special checking account advantages.

National debt: The debt of the national government, as distinguished from the debts of political subdivisions of the nation and of private business and individuals.

National debt ceiling: Total borrowing limit set by Congress beyond which the U.S. national debt cannot rise. This limit is periodically raised by congressional vote.

Option: A type of contractual agreement between a buyer and a seller to buy or sell shares of a security. A **call** option contract gives the right to purchase shares of a specific stock at a stated price within a given period of time. A **put** option contract gives the buyer the right to sell shares of a specific stock at a stated price within a given period of time.

Per capita income: The total income of a group divided by the number of people in the group.

Prime interest rate: The rate charged by banks on short-term loans to large commercial customers with the highest credit rating.

Producer price index: A statistical measure of the change in the price of wholesale goods. It is reported for 3 different stages of the production chain: crude, intermediate, and finished goods.

Program trading: Trading techniques involving large numbers and large blocks of stocks, usually used in conjunction with computer programs. Techniques include *index arbitrage,* in which traders profit from price differences between stocks and futures contracts on stock indexes, and *portfolio insurance,* which is the use of stock-index futures to protect stock investors from potentially large losses when the market drops.

Public debt: The total of a nation's debts owed by state, local, and national government. Increases in this sum, reflected in public-sector deficits, indicate how much of the nation's spending is being financed by borrowing rather than by taxation.

Recession: A mild decrease in economic activity marked by a decline in real (inflation-adjusted) GDP, employment, and trade, usually lasting from 6 months to a year, and marked by widespread decline in many sectors of the economy.

Savings Association Insurance Fund (SAIF): Created in 1989 to insure accounts in savings and loan associations up to $100,000.

Seasonal adjustment: Statistical changes made to compensate for regular fluctuations in data that are so great they tend to distort the statistics and make comparisons meaningless. For instance, seasonal adjustments are made for a slowdown in housing construction in midwinter and for the rise in farm income in the fall after summer crops are harvested.

Short-selling: Borrowing shares of stock from a brokerage firm and selling them, hoping to buy the shares back at a lower price, return them, and realize a profit from the decline in prices.

Stagnation: Economic slowdown in which there is little growth in the GDP, capital investment, and real income.

Stock: *Common stocks* are shares of ownership in a corporation. For publicly held firms, the stock typically trades on an exchange, such as the New York Stock Exchange; for closely held firms, the founders and managers own most of the stock. There can be wide swings in the prices of this kind of stock. *Preferred stock* is a type of stock on which a fixed dividend must be paid before holders of common stock are issued their share of the issuing corporation's earnings. Preferred stock is less risky than common stock. *Convertible preferred stock* can be converted into the common stock of the company that issued the preferred. *Over-the-counter stock* is not traded on the major or regional exchanges, but rather through dealers from whom you buy directly. *Blue chip* stocks are so called because they have been leading stocks for a long time. *Growth* stocks are from companies that reinvest their earnings, rather than pay dividends, with the expectation of future stock price appreciation.

Supply-side economics: A school of thinking about economic policy holding that lowering income tax rates will inevitably lead to enhanced economic growth and general revitalization of the economy.

Takeover: Acquisition of one company by another company or group by sale or merger. A *friendly takeover* occurs when the acquired company's management is agreeable to the merger; when management is opposed to the merger, it is a *hostile* takeover.

Tender offer: A public offer to buy a company's stock; usually priced at a premium above the market.

Zero coupon bond: A corporate or government bond that is issued at a deep discount from the maturity value and pays no interest during the life of the bond. It is redeemable at face value.

Minerals

Source: U.S. Geological Survey, U.S. Dept. of the Interior, as of mid-2004; minerals.usgs.gov/minerals

Aluminum: the second most abundant metallic element in the earth's crust. Bauxite is the main source of aluminum. Guinea, Australia, and Jamaica have about 60% of the world's reserves. Main uses in the U.S. are transportation (35%), packaging (25%), and construction (15%).

Chromium: most of the world's production of chromite ore is in India, Kazakhstan, and South Africa. The metallurgical industry uses about 91% of the chromite consumed in the world; the chemical industry, 6%; and the refractory and foundry industry, 3%.

Cobalt: used in superalloys for jet engines; cemented carbides for cutting tools; batteries, catalysts, ceramics, and other chemical applications; permanent magnets, tool steels, and other alloys. Australia, Canada, Congo (Kinshasa), Cuba, Russia, and Zambia account for most of the world cobalt mine production.

Construction aggregates: construction sand and gravel and crushed stone are among the most accessible natural resources in the world. Construction sand and gravel are produced in every U.S. state, and crushed stone is mined in every state except Delaware. They are used in construction, agriculture, chemicals, and metallurgy and are produced worldwide.

Copper: main uses of copper and copper alloy products in the U.S. are in building construction (48%), electrical and electronic products (21%), consumer and general products (11%), industrial machinery and equipment (10%), and transportation (10%). The leading mine producers are Chile, the U.S. (in Arizona, Utah, and New Mexico), Indonesia, Peru, Australia, Russia, China, and Canada.

Gold: used in the U.S. in jewelry and the arts (92%), electrical and electronics (4%), dentistry (3%), and other industrial (1%). South Africa has about half of the world's resources; significant quantities are also present in the U.S. (mined in most western states and Alaska), Australia, Russia, Uzbekistan, Canada, and Brazil.

Gypsum: used in wallboard and plaster products, cement production, and agriculture. Leading producers are the U.S., Iran, Canada, Spain, China, and Mexico.

Iron ore: the source of primary iron for the world's iron and steel industries. Major producers include Brazil, Australia, China, India, Russia, Ukraine, and the U.S.

Lead: Australia, China, the U.S. (mostly in Alaska and Missouri), Peru, Canada, and Mexico are the world's largest producers of lead. The major end use in the U.S. is in lead acid storage batteries (84%). The U.S. produces and consumes about 20% of the world's lead. Most U.S. lead production (82%) is recycled material, and 97% of lead acid batteries (mostly automotive) are recycled.

Manganese: essential to iron and steel production. South Africa and Ukraine have over 80% and 10%, respectively, of the world's identified resources.

Nickel: vital to the stainless steel industry; and used to make superalloys. Leading producers are Russia, Australia, Canada, New Caledonia, and Indonesia.

Platinum-Group Metals: this group consists of 6 metals: platinum, palladium, rhodium, ruthenium, iridium, and osmium. They commonly occur together in nature and are among the scarcest of the metallic elements. In the U.S., the automotive and chemical industries use PGMs mainly as catalysts. They also are consumed in electrical and electronics, glass, dental, and medical industries. Russia and South Africa have most of the world's reserves.

Phosphate rock: used in fertilizers, animal feed supplements, chemicals, and food. Phosphorus is an essential element for plant and animal nutrition. The U.S., Morocco, China, Russia, and Tunisia are the world's leading producers.

Salt: used in chemicals, highway deicing, industry, agriculture, food, and water treatment. Leading producers are the U.S., China, Germany, India, and Canada.

Silver: used in photography, electrical and electronic products, sterlingware, electroplated ware, and jewelry in the U.S. Silver is mined in more than 60 countries. Alaska and Nevada produce more than 69% of U.S. silver.

Soda ash: a raw material for glass, chemicals, and detergents, it can be mined or produced synthetically. The U.S. is, by far, the world's leading producer of natural soda ash.

Sulfur: used in agricultural chemicals production, oil refining, metal mining, and many other industries. It is a byproduct of oil refining, natural gas processing, and nonferrous metal smelting. Leading producers are the U.S., Canada, Russia, China, and Japan.

Titanium: ilmenite and rutile are the major mineral sources of titanium. Titanium minerals are used to produce TiO_2 pigments (94%), titanium metal (3%), and other uses (3%) including alloys, ceramics, chemicals, and welding rod coatings. Major mining operations are in Australia, Canada, Norway, and South Africa. U.S. mine production is in Florida, Georgia, and Virginia.

Zinc: used as a protective coating on steel, as diecastings, as an alloying metal with copper to make brass, and as a component of chemical compounds in rubber and paints. Leading producers are China, Australia, Peru, Canada, the U.S. (in Alaska, Missouri, and Tennessee), and Mexico.

U.S. Reliance on Foreign Supplies of Minerals

Source: U.S. Geological Survey, U.S. Dept. of the Interior

Mineral	% Imported in 2003	Major sources (1999-2002)	Major Uses
Arsenic (trioxide)	100%	China, Chile, Mexico	Wood preservatives, nonferrous alloys
Asbestos	100	Canada	Roofing products, gaskets, friction products
Bauxite & alumina	100	Australia, Jamaica, Guinea, Suriname	Aluminum production, refractories, abrasives, chemicals
Columbium (niobium)	100	Brazil, Canada, Estonia, Germany	Steel making, superalloys
Fluorspar	100	China, South Africa, Mexico	Hydrofluoric acid, aluminum fluoride, steel making
Graphite (natural)	100	China, Mexico, Canada, Brazil	Refractories, brake linings, pencils, electrodes, motor brushes, high-modulus fibers
Indium	100	China, Canada, France, Russia	Coatings, solders, alloys, electrical components
Manganese	100	South Africa, Gabon, Australia, Mexico	Iron & steel making, batteries, agricultural chemicals
Mica, sheet (natural)	100	India, Belgium, China, Germany	Electronic & electrical equipment
Quartz crystal (industrial)	100	Brazil, Germany, Madagascar	Electronics, optical applications
Rare earths	100	China, France, Japan, Estonia	Catalysts, glass polishing, ceramics, magnets, metallurgy, phosphors
Rubidium	100	Canada	Inorganic chemicals, DNA separation, night-vision devices
Strontium	100	Mexico, Germany	Television picture tubes, ferrite magnets, pyrotechnics
Thallium	100	Belgium, Canada, France, Russia, United Kingdom	Electronics, alloys, glass
Vanadium	100	South Africa, Czech Republic, Canada, China	Steel making, catalysts
Yttrium	100	China, Japan, Germany, Netherlands	Television phosphors, fluorescent lights, oxygen sensors, ceramics
Gemstones	99	Israel, India, Belgium	Jewelry, carvings, gem & mineral collections
Platinum	96	South Africa, United Kingdom, Germany, Canada	Catalysts, jewelry, dental & medical alloys
Bismuth	95	Belgium, Mexico, China, United Kingdom	Pharmaceuticals, chemicals, alloys, metallurgical additives, solders, ammunition
Tin	91	Peru, China, Bolivia, Brazil, Indonesia	Solder, tin chemicals, tinplate, alloys
Stone (dimension)	86	Italy, Canada, India, Spain	Construction, monuments
Barite	81	China, India, Morocco	Oil & gas well-drilling fluids, chemicals
Diamond (natural industrial)	80	Switzerland, Russia, United Kingdom, Ireland	Abrasives, stone cutting, highway repair & construction
Potash	80	Canada, Russia, Belarus, Germany	Fertilizers, chemicals
Tantalum	80	Australia, Canada, China, Kazakhstan	Capacitors, superalloys, cemented carbide cutting tools
Cobalt	78	Finland, Norway, Russia, Canada	Chemicals, superalloys, cemented carbides, magnetic alloys
Rhenium	76	Chile, Kazakhstan, Germany	Superalloys, petroleum-reforming catalysts
Chromium	74	South Africa, Kazakhstan, Zimbabwe, Turkey, Russia	Steel, chemicals, refractories
Iodine	74	Chile, Japan, Russia	Animal feed, catalysts, heat stabilizers, pharmaceuticals, sanitation
Palladium	74	Russia, South Africa, United Kingdom, Belgium	Catalysts, dental, electronics, electrical
Titanium (sponge)	73	Japan, Kazakhstan, Russia	Aerospace, armor, chemical processing, power generation, medical devices
Titanium mineral concentrates	70	South Africa, Australia, Canada, Ukraine	Pigment, metal, welding-rod coatings, chemicals, ceramics
Tungsten	69	China, Russia, Canada	Cemented carbides, electrical & electronic components, tool steels, alloys
Zinc	57	Canada, Mexico, Peru	Galvanizing, zinc-base alloys, brass & bronze
Garnet (industrial)	56	Australia, India, China	Abrasive blasting media, waterjet cutting, water filtration, abrasive powders
Silver	56	Mexico, Canada, Peru, United Kingdom	Photography, electrical & electronic products, catalysts, brazing alloys, jewelry
Peat	55	Canada	Horticulture, agriculture
Silicon	54	Norway, South Africa, Russia, Canada	Iron & steel alloys, aluminum & aluminum alloys, specialty chemicals
Magnesium compounds	51	China, Australia, Canada, Austria	Refractory, environmental, chemical, agricultural applications

World Mineral Reserve Base

Source: U.S. Geological Survey, U.S. Dept. of the Interior; as of year-end 2003

Mineral	Reserve Base[1]	Mineral	Reserve Base[1]
Aluminum	.33,000 mil metric tons[2]	Nickel	.140 mil metric tons
Chromium	.1,800 mil metric tons[3]	Phosphate Rock	.50,000 mil metric tons
Cobalt	.13 mil metric tons	Platinum-Group Metals	.80,000 metric tons
Copper	.940 mil metric tons	Silver	.570,000 metric tons
Gold	.89,000 metric tons	Soda Ash (Natural)	.40,000 mil metric tons
Iron Ore	.330,000 mil metric tons	Titanium (ilmenite/rutile)	.830 mil metric tons[4]
Lead	.140 mil metric tons	Zinc	.460 mil metric tons
Manganese	.5,000 mil metric tons		

(1) Includes demonstrated reserves that are currently economic or marginally economic, plus some that are currently subeconomic. (2) Bauxite. (3) Chromite ore, gross weight, marketable product. (4) Titanium dioxide (TiO_2) content of ilmenite and rutile.

World Gold Production, 1975-2003[1]

Source: U.S. Geological Survey, U.S. Dept. of the Interior

(thousands of troy ounces)

Year	World prod.	Africa			North and South America				Other			
		South Africa	Ghana	Congo Dem. Rep.	United States	Canada	Mexico	Colombia	Australia	China	Philip- pines	Russia[2]
1975	38,476	22,938	524	116	1,052	1,654	145	309	527	NA	502,577	NA
1980	39,197	21,669	353	96	970	1,627	196	510	548	NA	753	8,425
1985	49,284	21,565	299	257	2,427	2,815	266	1,142	1,881	1,950	1,063	8,70
1990	70,207	19,454	541	299	9,458	5,447	311	944	7,849	3,215	791	9,710
1991	70,423	19,326	846	283	9,454	5,676	326	1,120	7,530	3,858	833	8,359
1992	73,530	19,743	998	225	10,617	5,189	318	1,033	7,825	4,501	730	8,232
1993	73,300	19,908	1,250	280	10,642	4,917	357	883	7,948	5,144	509	8,228
1994	72,500	16,650	1,400	357	10,500	4,710	447	668	8,237	4,240	870	8,173
1995	71,800	16,800	1,710	322	10,200	4,890	652	680	8,150	4,500	873	4,25
1996	73,600	16,000	1,580	264	10,500	5,350	787	710	9,310	4,660	970	3,960
1997	78,900	15,800	1,760	13	11,600	5,510	836	605	10,100	5,630	1,050	3,990
1998	80,300	15,000	2,330	5	11,800	5,320	817	605	10,000	5,720	1,090	3,690
1999	82,600	14,500	2,570	7	11,000	5,070	764	1,410	9,680	5,560	1,000	4,050
2000	83,300	13,900	2,320	2	11,300	5,020	848	1,190	9,530	5,790	1,170	4,600
2001	83,600	12,700	2,200	2	10,800	5,110	846	701	9,160	5,950	1,090	4,890
2002	82,900	12,800	2,230	2	9,580	4,870	663	669	8,780	6,170	1,290	5,410
2003	83,300	12,100	2,240	3	8,910	4,520	643	1,500	9,070	6,490	1,220	5,470

(1) Figures are rounded. (2) Figures for 1975-94 are for USSR as constituted prior to Dec. 1991; after 1994, Russia only. NA = Not available.

U.S. Nonfuel Minerals Production, 1997-2003

Source: U.S. Geological Survey, U.S. Dept. of the Interior

Production as measured by mine shipments, sales, or marketable production (including consumption by producers).

		1997	1998	1999	2000	2001	2002	2003
Beryllium (metal equivalent)	metric tons	231	243	200	180	100	80	85
Copper (recoverable content of ores, etc.)	thousand metric tons	1,940	1,860	1,600	1,450	1,340	1,140	1,120
Gold (recoverable content of ores, etc.)	metric tons	362	366	341	353	335	298	277
Iron ore, usable (includes byproduct material)	million metric tons	63.0	62.9	57.7	63.1	46.2	51.6	46.4
Lead (in concentrate)	thousand metric tons	448	481	503	449	454	440	449
Magnesium metal (primary)	thousand metric tons	125	106	W	W	W	W	W
Molybdenum (content of ore and concentrate)	metric tons	60,100	53,300	42,400	40,900	37,600	32,000	33,500
Silver (recoverable content of ores, etc.)	metric tons	2,180	2,060	1,950	1,860	1,740	1,420	1,240
Zinc (recoverable content of ores, etc.)	thousand metric tons	605	722	808	805	799	754	738
Asbestos	thousand metric tons	7	6	7	5	5	3	–
Barite (sold or used)	metric tons	692	476	434	392	400	420	468
Boron minerals (B_2O_2 equivalent)	thousand metric tons	604	587	618	546	536	518	560
Bromine	million kilograms	247	230	239	228	212	222	216
Cement (portland, masonry, etc.)	thousand metric tons	82,582	83,931	85,952	87,846	88,900	89,732	92,843
Clays	thousand metric tons	41,800	41,900	42,200	40,800	39,600	39,300	39,300
Diatomite	thousand metric tons	773	725	747	677	644	650	625
Feldspar	thousand metric tons	900[E]	820[E]	875[E]	790[E]	800[E]	790[E]	800[E]
Garnet (industrial)	metric tons	64,900	74,000	60,700	60,200	52,700	38,500	29,200
Gemstones (natural) million dollars	million dollars	25.0	14.3	16.1	17.2	14.9	12.6	12.5
Gypsum	thousand metric tons	18,600	19,000	22,400	19,500	16,300	15,700	16,600
Helium (extracted from natural gas)	million cubic meters	116	114	114	98	87	87[E]	87[E]
Helium (Grade A sold)	million cubic meters	107	114	117	127	132	127	124[E]
Iodine	thousand kilograms	1,320	1,490	1,620	1,470	1,290	1,420	1,080
Lime	thousand metric tons	19,700	20,100	19,700	19,500	18,900	17,900	19,200
Mica (scrap & flake)	thousand metric tons	112	87	95	101	98	81	76
Peat	thousand metric tons	661	685	731	792	736	642	634
Perlite (sold and used by producers)	thousand metric tons	706	685	677	672	588	521	493
Phosphate rock (marketable product)	thousand metric tons	45,900	44,200	40,600	38,600	31,900	36,100	35,000
Potash (K2O equivalent)	thousand metric tons	1,400	1,300	1,200	1,300	1,200	1,200	1,100
Pumice and pumicite	thousand metric tons	850[E]	872	1,000	1,050	920	956	914
Salt	thousand metric tons	40,600	40,800	44,400	43,300	42,200	37,700	41,100
Sand and gravel (construction)	thousand metric tons	952	1,070	1,110	1,120	1,130	1,130	1,130[E]
Sand and gravel (industrial)	thousand metric tons	28,500	28,200	28,900	28,400	27,900	27,300	27,500
Soda ash (sodium carbonate)	thousand metric tons	10,700	10,100	10,200	10,200	10,300	10,500	10,600
Sodium sulfate (natural)	thousand metric tons	318	290	NA	NA	NA	NA	NA
Stone (crushed)	million metric tons	1,410	1,510	1,530	1,550	1,590	1,520	1,490
Stone (dimension)	thousand metric tons	1,180	1,140	1,250	1,320	1,320	1,220	1,340
Sulfur (in all forms)	thousand metric tons	12,000	11,700	11,500	10,500	9,470	9,270	9,600
Talc	thousand metric tons	1,050	971	925	851	863	828	869
Titanium mineral concentrates[1]	thousand metric tons	400	400	300	300	300	300	300
Vermiculite concentrate	thousand metric tons	W	W	175[E]	150[E]	NA	NA	NA

(W) Withheld to avoid disclosing company proprietary data. (—) No production. (E) Estimated. (NA) Not available.

AGRICULTURE
U.S. Farms—Number and Acreage by State, 2000, 2003

Source: National Agricultural Statistics Service, U.S. Dept. of Agriculture

STATE	No. of farms (1,000) 2003	2000	Acreage in farms (mil.) 2003	2000	Acreage per farm 2003	2000	STATE	No. of farms (1,000) 2003	2000	Acreage in farms (mil.) 2003	2000	Acreage per farm 2003	2000
AL	45	47	8.9	9.0	198	191.5	NE	48.5	54	45.9	46.4	946	859.3
AK	0.61	0.58	0.9	0.92	1,475	1,586.2	NV	3	3	6.3	6.8	2,100	2,266.7
AZ	10.3	7.5	26.5	26.7	2,573	3,560	NH	3.4	3.1	0.45	0.42	132	135.5
AR	47.5	48	14.4	14.6	303	304.2	NJ	9.9	9.6	0.8	0.83	83	86.5
CA	78.5	87.5	27.1	27.8	345	317.7	NM	17.5	15.2	44.7	44	2,554	2,894.7
CO	31.4	29.5	31	31.6	987	1,071.2	NY	37	38	7.65	7.7	207	202.6
CT	4.2	3.9	0.36	0.36	86	92.3	NC	53.5	57	9.1	9.2	170	161.4
DE	2.3	2.6	0.53	0.58	230	223.1	ND	30.3	30.3	39.4	39.4	1,300	1,300.3
FL	44	44	10.2	10.3	232	234.1	OH	77.6	80	14.6	14.9	188	186.3
GA	49.3	50	10.8	11.1	219	222	OK	83.5	85	33.7	34	404	400
HI	5.5	5.5	1.3	1.44	236	261.8	OR	40	40	17.2	17.2	430	430
ID	25	24.5	11.8	11.9	472	485.7	PA	58.2	59	7.7	7.7	132	130.5
IL	73	78	27.5	27.7	377	355.1	RI	0.85	0.7	0.06	0.06	71	85.7
IN	59.5	64	15.04	15.5	253	242.2	SC	24.4	24	4.85	4.8	199	200
IA	90	95	31.7	32.8	352	345.3	SD	31.6	32.5	43.8	44	1,386	1,353.8
KS	64.5	64	47.2	47.5	732	742.2	TN	87	90	11.6	11.7	133	130
KY	87	90	13.8	13.6	159	151.1	TX	229	226	130.5	130	570	575.2
LA	27.2	29.5	7.85	8.1	289	274.6	UT	15.3	15.5	11.6	11.6	758	748.4
ME	7.2	6.8	1.37	1.27	190	186.8	VT	6.5	6.7	1.25	1.34	192	200
MD	12.1	12.4	2.06	2.1	170	169.4	VA	47.5	49	8.6	8.7	181	177.6
MA	6.1	6.1	0.52	0.57	85	93.4	WA	35.5	40	15.3	15.7	431	392.5
MI	53.3	52	10.09	10.4	189	200	WV	20.8	20.5	3.6	3.6	173	175.6
MN	80	79	27.7	28.6	346	362	WI	76.5	77	15.6	16.2	204	210.4
MS	42.8	43	11.11	11.1	260	258.1	WY	9.2	9.2	34.4	34.6	3,743	3,760.9
MO	106	109	30.2	30	285	275.2	**U.S.**	**2,127**	**2,172**	**939**	**942**	**441**	**434**
MT	28	27.6	60.1	56.7	2,146	2,054.3							

Farms and Land in Farms On the Decline

The number of farms in the United States in 2003 is estimated at 2.13 million, 0.4% fewer than in 2002. Total land in farms, at 938.8 million acres, decreased 1.55 mil. acres from 2002. The average size farm during 2003 was 441 acres, an increase of 1 acre from the previous year. The continuing decline in number of farms and land in farms reflects consolidation in farming operations and competition for agricultural land for other uses.

U.S. Farms, 1940-2003

Source: National Agricultural Statistics Service, U.S. Dept. of Agriculture

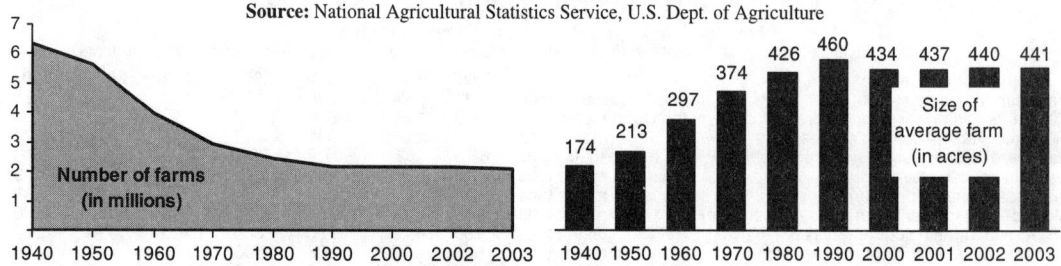

Number of farms (in millions). Size of average farm (in acres): 1940 174, 1950 213, 1960 297, 1970 374, 1980 426, 1990 460, 2000 434, 2001 437, 2002 440, 2003 441.

U.S. Federal Food Assistance Programs, 1990-2003[1]

Source: Food and Nutrition Service, U.S. Dept. of Agriculture
(in millions of dollars)

	1990	1995	1998	1999	2000	2001	2002	2003
Food stamps[2]	$15,491	$24,620	$18,893	$17,698	$17,029	$17,800	$20,687	$23,881
Puerto Rico nutrition asst.[3]	937	1,131	1,204	1,236	1,268	1,296	1,351	1,395
Natl. school lunch[4]	3,834	5,160	5,830	6,019	6,149	6,475	6,854	7,188
School breakfast[4,5]	596	1,048	1,272	1,345	1,393	1,450	1,567	1,651
WIC[6]	2,122	3,440	3,890	3,940	3,981	4,158	4,344	4,517
Summer food service[7]	164	237	263	268	267	272	263	257
Child/adult care[8]	813	1,464	1,553	1,621	1,684	1,738	1,853	1,925
Special milk[9]	19	17	17	16	15	16	16	14
Nutrition for the elderly[10]	142	148	141	140	137	152	152	3
Food distrib. to Indian reserv.[11]	66	65	72	76	72	69	69	69
Commodity supp. food prog.[11]	85	99	94	98	95	103	112	114
Food dist.–charitable inst.[12]	104	64	9	3	2	7	16	6
Emergency food assistance[13]	334	135	234	270	225	377	435	456
TOTAL[14]	**$24,707**	**$37,628**	**$33,472**	**$32,730**	**$32,317**	**$33,905**	**$37,719**	**$41,476**

(1) Data are for fiscal years (Oct. through Sept.). (2) Includes benefits and admin. expenses. (3) Puerto Rico participated in the Food Stamp Program from FY 1975 to July 1982, when it began a separate grant program. (4) Data are 9-month averages (summer months excluded). (5) Costs are cash payments (federal reimbursements to states). (6) Includes food benefits, nutrition services and admin. funds, Farmers' Market Nutrition Program, infrastructure, program evaluation, and technical assistance. (7) Includes cash payments, commodity costs, and admin. expenditures. (8) Includes cash payments, entitlement and bonus commodities, cash-in-lieu of commodities, sponsor admin. costs, start-up costs and audits. (9) Costs are cash payments based on an annually determined reimbursement rate and the actual cost of free milk. (10) Nutrition Services Incentive Program, formerly the Nutrition Program for the Elderly. Cash grants administered by the Agency on Aging; Food and Nutrition Service costs limited to value of commodities distributed. (11) FY 2003 costs are preliminary. Includes commodity distribution costs and admin. expenses. (12) Includes summer camps. (13) Food made available to hunger relief orgs. such as food banks and soup kitchens. Includes the Soup Kitchens/Food Banks Program (1989-96). (14) Totals may not add because of rounding.

Livestock on Farms in the U.S., 1900-2004

Source: National Agricultural Statistics Service, U.S. Dept. of Agriculture

(in thousands)

Year (On Jan. 1)	All cattle[1]	Milk cows	Sheep and lambs	Hogs and pigs[2]	Year (On Jan. 1)	All cattle[1]	Milk cows	Sheep and lambs	Hogs and pigs[2]
1900...	59,739	16,544	48,105	51,055	1991 ..	96,393	9,966	11,174	54,416
1910...	58,993	19,450	50,239	48,072	1992 ..	97,556	9,688	10,797	57,649
1920...	70,400	21,455	40,743	60,159	1993 ..	99,176	9,581	10,906	58,795
1930...	61,003	23,032	51,565	55,705	1994 ..	100,974	9,494	9,836	60,847
1940...	68,309	24,940	52,107	61,165	1995 ..	102,755	9,487	8,886	57,150
1950...	77,963	23,853	29,826	58,937	1996 ..	103,487	9,416	8,461	56,124
1955...	96,592	23,462	31,582	50,474	1997 ..	101,656	9,318	8,024	57,366
1960...	96,236	19,527	33,170	59,026	1998 ..	99,744	9,199	7,825	62,213
1965...	109,000	16,981	25,127	56,106	1999 ..	99,115	9,133	7,215	60,896
1970...	112,369	12,091	20,423	57,046	2000 ..	98,198	9,190	7,032	59,117
1975...	132,028	11,220	14,515	54,693	2001 ..	97,277	9,183	6,965	58,603
1980...	111,242	10,758	12,699	67,318	2002 ..	96,704	9,112	6,685	60,288
1985...	109,582	10,777	10,716	54,073	2003 ..	96,100	9,142	6,300	59,602
1990...	95,816	10,015	11,358	53,788	2004 ..	94,882	8,991	6,090	60,083

(1) From 1970, includes milk cows and heifers that have calved. (2) 1900-95, as of Dec. 1 of preceding year; 1996-2004 as of June 1 of same year.

U.S. Meat Production and Consumption, 1940-2003

Source: Economic Research Service, U.S. Dept. of Agriculture

(in millions of pounds)

Year	Beef Production	Beef Consumption[2]	Veal Production	Veal Consumption[2]	Lamb and mutton Production	Lamb and mutton Consumption[2]	Pork Production	Pork Consumption[2]	All red meats[1] Production	All red meats[1] Consumption[2]	All Poultry Production	All Poultry Consumption[2]
1940	7,175	7,257	981	981	876	873	10,044	9,701	19,076	18,812	NA	NA
1950	9,534	9,529	1,230	1,206	597	596	10,714	10,390	22,075	21,721	3,174	3,097
1960	14,728	15,465	1,109	1,118	769	857	13,905	14,057	30,511	31,497	6,310	6,168
1970	21,684	23,451	588	613	551	669	14,699	14,957	37,522	39,689	10,193	9,981
1980	21,643	23,560	400	420	318	351	16,617	16,838	38,978	41,170	14,173	13,525
1990	22,743	24,030	327	325	363	397	15,354	16,025	38,787	40,778	23,468	22,152
1991	22,917	24,115	306	305	363	397	15,999	16,392	39,585	41,209	24,701	23,272
1992	23,086	24,262	310	311	348	388	17,233	17,462	40,977	42,423	26,201	24,394
1993	23,049	24,006	285	286	337	381	17,088	17,408	40,759	42,081	27,328	25,097
1994	24,386	25,128	293	291	308	346	17,696	17,812	42,683	43,577	29,113	25,754
1995	25,222	25,534	319	319	285	346	17,849	17,768	43,675	43,967	30,393	25,944
1996	25,525	25,861	378	378	268	333	17,117	16,797	43,288	43,369	32,015	26,760
1997	25,490	25,611	334	333	260	332	17,274	16,823	43,358	43,099	32,964	27,261
1998	25,760	26,305	262	265	251	360	19,010	18,308	45,283	45,237	33,352	27,821
1999	26,493	26,937	235	235	248	358	19,308	18,946	46,284	46,476	35,252	29,584
2000	26,888	27,338	225	225	234	354	18,952	18,643	46,299	46,560	36,073	30,508
2001	26,212	27,026	205	204	227	368	19,160	18,492	45,804	46,089	38,942	30,823
2002	27,192	27,878	205	204	223	383	19,685	19,147	47,305	47,612	38,079	32,575
2003	26,339	26,999	202	204	203	367	19,966	19,435	46,710	47,005	38,477	33,129

(1) Meats may not add to total because of rounding. (2) Consumption (also called total disappearance) is estimated as: production plus beginning stocks, plus imports, minus exports, minus ending stocks. NA = Not available.

Eggs: U.S. Production, Price, and Value, 2002-2003[1]

Source: National Agricultural Statistics Service, U.S. Dept. of Agriculture

STATE	Eggs produced 2002	Eggs produced 2003 (mil)	Price per dozen[2] 2002	Price per dozen[2] 2003 (dollars)	Value of Production 2002	Value of Production 2003 (1,000 dollars)	STATE	Eggs produced 2002	Eggs produced 2003 (mil)	Price per dozen[2] 2002	Price per dozen[2] 2003 (dollars)	Value of Production 2002	Value of Production 2003 (1,000 dollars)
AL	2,281	2,190	1.560	1.620	296,530	295,650	NE	2,977	3,126	0.341	0.535	84,596	139,368
AR	3,333	3,384	1.070	1.220	297,193	344,040	NH	55	43	0.744	0.910	2,976	3,261
CA	6,257	5,439	0.392	0.623	204,232	282,375	NJ	534	556	0.512	0.630	22,784	29,190
CO	1,008	1,073	0.591	0.670	49,644	59,909	NY	1,100	1,048	0.489	0.645	44,825	56,330
CT	856	795	0.519	0.666	37,022	44,123	NC	2,518	2,523	1.090	1.150	228,718	241,788
FL	2,731	2,804	0.479	0.621	109,012	145,107	OH	7,940	7,642	0.447	0.588	295,765	374,458
GA	4,967	5,047	0.860	0.941	355,968	395,769	OK	951	933	0.832	0.927	65,936	72,074
HI	117.5	117.2	0.904	0.962	8,852	9,396	OR	760	783	0.536	0.667	33,947	43,522
ID	242	243	0.576	0.717	11,616	14,519	PA	6,520	6,754	0.514	0.659	279,273	370,907
IL	893	973	0.442	0.629	32,892	51,001	SC	1,380	1,373	0.626	0.762	71,990	87,186
IN	5,973	6,035	0.479	0.612	238,422	307,785	SD	568	761	0.332	0.500	15,715	31,708
IA	10,101	10,446	0.342	0.529	287,622	460,495	TN	300	290	1.270	1.320	31,750	31,900
KY	940	1,122	0.837	0.889	65,565	83,122	TX	4,774	4,745	0.687	0.784	273,312	310,007
LA	494	487	0.817	0.886	33,633	35,957	UT	894	866	0.42	0.520	31,290	37,527
ME	1,080	1,121	0.590	0.755	53,100	70,530	VT	58	53	0.623	0.818	3,037	3,613
MD	923	813	0.563	0.682	43,210	46,206	VA	734	744	0.988	1.180	60,433	73,160
MA	89	73	0.630	0.802	4,200	4,879	WA	1,369	1,307	0.486	0.646	55,445	70,360
MI	1,880	1,891	0.403	0.595	63,237	93,762	WV	262	270	1.400	1.510	30,450	33,975
MN	3,159	2,962	0.408	0.593	106,216	146,372	WI	1,158	1,137	0.511	0.587	49,312	55,618
MS	1,588	1,599	1.240	1.270	164,093	169,228	WY	3.6	3.6	0.486	0.620	146	186
MO	1,841	1,859	0.497	0.645	76,082	99,921	Other[3]	1,537	1,660	0.448	0.602	57,388	83,231
MT	104	107	0.460	0.650	3,987	5,796	U.S.[4]	87,252	87,196	0.589	0.731	4,281,416	5,315,311

(1) Estimates cover the 12-month period from Dec. 1 of the previous year through Nov. 30. (2) Average of all eggs sold by producers, including hatching eggs. (3) AK, AZ, KS, NM, NV, ND, and RI combined to avoid disclosure of individual operations; totals listed under "other." (4) Total states may not equal U.S. total because of rounding.

Grain, Hay, Potato, Cotton, Soybean, Tobacco Production, by State, 2003

Source: National Agricultural Statistics Service, U.S. Dept. of Agriculture

STATE	Barley (1,000 bu)	Corn, grain (1,000 bu)	Cotton (Upland) (1,000 b)	All hay (1,000 t)	Oats (1,000 bu)	Potatoes (1,000 cwt)	Soybeans (1,000 bu)	Tobacco (1,000 lb)	All wheat (1,000 bu)
Alabama	—	23,180	820	2,028	—	389	5,760	—	3,150
Alaska	135	—	—	29	34	168	—	—	—
Arizona	3,540	4,180	560	2,162	—	2,090	—	—	11,912
Arkansas	—	49,000	1,800	2,974	—	—	109,820	—	28,500
California	3,712	27,200	1,500	9,310	2,800	17,319	—	—	34,070
Colorado	8,938	120,150	—	3,610	975	26,198	—	—	78,160
Connecticut	—	NE	—	132	—	—	—	3,342	—
Delaware	1,239	19,926	—	38	—	864	6,408	—	1,927
Florida	—	3,198	130	638	—	9,400	360	11,000	492
Georgia	—	36,765	2,100	1,800	1,680	—	5,940	60,480	10,580
Hawaii	—	—	—	—	—	—	—	—	—
Idaho	47,520	7,000	—	4,950	1,625	123,180	—	—	87,300
Illinois	—	1,812,200	—	2,723	4,450	2,196	374,125	—	52,650
Indiana	—	786,940	—	2,110	1,050	925	203,300	8,400	29,670
Iowa	—	1,884,000	—	5,515	10,790	—	337,600	—	1,159
Kansas	456	300,000	100	7,000	4,550	1,026	57,040	—	480,000
Kentucky	600	147,960	—	6,375	—	—	53,320	229,840	20,460
Louisiana	—	67,000	1,015	1,102	—	—	25,160	—	5,740
Maine	1,755	NE	—	234	2,340	17,030	—	—	—
Maryland	2,166	50,430	—	539	—	1,104	15,910	2,175	5,365
Massachusetts	—	NE	—	171	—	770	—	1,396	—
Michigan	784	263,340	—	3,120	5,250	15,015	53,730	—	44,880
Minnesota	12,750	970,900	—	5,245	18,815	22,330	229,400	—	105,482
Mississippi	—	71,550	2,100	1,875	—	—	55,770	—	6,125
Missouri	—	302,400	710	8,168	1,206	1,882	143,260	2,600	53,070
Montana	31,590	2,380	—	4,635	1,980	3,339	—	—	137,530
Nebraska	200	1,124,200	—	7,600	6,570	9,860	179,600	—	83,720
Nevada	240	NE	—	1,429	—	3,320	—	—	549
New Hamp.	—	NE	—	113	—	—	—	—	—
New Jersey	135	6,893	—	267	—	702	2,992	—	1,092
New Mexico	—	8,640	75	1,281	—	2,132	—	—	4,200
New York	600	53,240	—	3,680	4,410	6,510	4,830	—	6,360
North Carolina	784	72,080	1,100	2,030	1,298	2,975	42,000	310,695	14,760
North Dakota	118,800	131,040	—	4,598	21,240	27,440	87,870	—	317,090
Ohio	348	478,920	—	3,974	3,960	1,290	162,640	9,010	68,000
Oklahoma	—	23,750	210	4,992	900	—	6,370	—	179,400
Oregon	3,840	5,100	—	3,629	1,500	20,991	—	—	53,540
Pennsylvania	3,965	102,350	—	4,070	6,490	3,915	15,375	7,880	7,095
Rhode Island	—	NE	—	17	—	150	—	—	—
South Carolina	—	22,575	330	884	1,120	—	11,760	63,000	7,215
South Dakota	2,915	427,350	—	7,210	15,640	340	113,130	—	116,241
Tennessee	—	82,530	875	4,726	—	—	45,920	72,870	13,500
Texas	—	194,700	4,250	12,388	6,300	6,528	5,040	—	96,600
Utah	2,800	2,015	—	2,490	492	335	—	—	5,585
Vermont	—	NE	—	470	—	—	—	—	—
Virginia	2,790	37,950	120	3,445	—	1,550	16,320	42,679	7,360
Washington	14,570	13,650	—	3,603	750	93,150	—	—	139,345
West Virginia	—	3,105	—	1,063	—	—	615	1,560	287
Wisconsin	1,925	367,650	—	4,380	15,410	32,800	46,200	4,277	12,300
Wyoming	7,125	6,450	—	2,330	1,058	—	—	—	4,065
UNITED STATES	276,087	10,113,887	17,795	157,123	144,649	459,045	2,417,565	831,204	2,336,526

NE = Not estimated; bu = bushels; b = bales (480-lbs); t = tons; cwt = hundredweight.

Production of Principal U.S. Crops, 1990-2003

Source: National Agricultural Statistics Service, U.S. Dept. of Agriculture

Year	Corn for grain (1,000 bu)	Oats (1,000 bu)	Barley (1,000 bu)	Sorghum for grain (1,000 bu)	All wheat (1,000 bu)	Rye (1,000 bu)	Flaxseed (1,000 bu)	Upland Cotton (1,000 b)	Cottonseed (1,000 t)
1990	7,934,028	357,654	422,196	573,303	2,729,778	10,176	3,812	15,505.4	5,968.5
1991	7,474,765	243,851	464,326	584,860	1,980,139	9,734	6,200	17,614.3	6,925.5
1992	9,476,698	294,229	455,090	875,022	2,466,798	11,440	3,288	16,219.5	6,230.1
1993	6,336,470	206,770	398,041	534,172	2,396,440	10,340	3,480	16,134.6	6,343.2
1994	10,102,735	229,008	374,862	649,206	2,320,981	11,341	2,922	19,662.0	7,603.9
1995	7,373,876	162,027	359,562	460,373	2,182,591	10,064	2,211	17,532.2	6,848.7
1996	9,293,435	155,273	395,751	802,974	2,285,133	9,016	1,602	18,413.5	7,143.5
1997	9,206,832	167,246	359,878	633,545	2,481,466	8,132	2,420	18,245.0	6,934.6
1998	9,758,685	165,981	352,125	519,933	2,547,321	12,161	6,708	13,475.9	5,365.4
1999	9,430,612	146,193	280,292	595,166	2,299,010	11,038	7,864	16,293.7	6,354.0
2000	9,915,051	149,545	318,728	470,526	2,232,460	8,386	10,730	16,799.2	6,435.6
2001[1]	9,506,840	117,024	249,420	514,524	1,957,043	6,971	11,455	19,602.4	7,452.2
2002[1]	9,007,659	118,628	226,573	369,758	1,619,001	6,955	12,569	16,530.3	6,419.3
2003	10,113,887	144,649	276,087	411,237	2,336,526	9,254	10,426	17,795.0	6,694.0

Year	Tobacco (1,000 lb)	All hay (1,000 t)	Beans, dry edible (1,000 cwt)	Peas, dry edible (1,000 cwt)	Peanuts[2] (1,000 lb)	Soybeans[3] (1,000 bu)	Potatoes (1,000 cwt)	Sweet potatoes (1,000 cwt)
1990	1,626,380	146,212	32,379	2,372	3,602,770	1,925,947	402,110	12,594
1991	1,664,372	152,073	33,765	3,715	4,926,570	1,986,539	417,622	11,203
1992	1,721,671	146,903	22,615	2,535	4,284,416	2,190,354	425,367	12,005
1993	1,613,319	146,799	21,913	3,292	3,392,415	1,870,958	428,693	11,053
1994	1,582,896	150,060	29,028	2,255	4,247,455	2,516,694	467,054	13,395
1995	1,268,538	154,166	30,812	4,765	4,247,455	2,176,814	443,606	12,906
1996	1,517,334	149,457	27,960	2,671	3,661,205	2,382,364	498,633	13,456
1997	1,787,399	152,536	29,370	5,752	3,539,380	2,688,750	467,091	13,327

Year	Tobacco (1,000 lb)	All hay (1,000 t)	Beans, dry edible (1,000 cwt)	Peas, dry edible (1,000 cwt)	Peanuts[2] (1,000 lb)	Soybeans[3] (1,000 bu)	Potatoes (1,000 cwt)	Sweet potatoes (1,000 cwt)
1998	1,479,867	151,780	30,418	5,934	3,963,440	2,741,014	475,771	12,382
1999	1,292,692	159,707	33,085	4,773	3,829,490	2,653,758	478,216	12,234
2000	1,052,999	151,921	26,409	3,474	3,265,505	2,757,810	513,621	13,794
2001[1]	991,223	156,764	19,583	3,763	4,276,704	2,890,682	437,888	14,637
2002[1]	878,592	150,962	29,974	4,242	3,320,490	2,749,340	459,802	12,865
2003	831,204	157,123	22,515	5,202	4,144,150	2,417,565	459,045	15,921

Year	Rice (1,000 cwt)	Sugarcane (1,000 t)	Sugar beets (1,000 t)	Pecans[4] (1,000 lb)	Apples (1,000 t)	Grapes (1,000 t)	Peaches (1,000 t)	Oranges[5] (1,000 bx)	Grapefruit[5] (1,000 bx)
1990	156,088	28,136	27,513	205,000	4,828.4	5,659.9	1,121.1	184,415	49,300
1991	159,367	30,252	28,203	299,000	4,853.4	5,555.9	1,347.8	178,950	55,500
1992	179,658	30,363	29,143	166,000	5,284.3	6,052.1	1,336.0	209,610	55,265
1993	156,110	31,101	26,249	365,000	5,342.4	6,023.2	1,330.1	255,760	68,375
1994	197,779	30,929	31,853	199,000	5,667.8	5,870.6	1,253.3	240,450	65,100
1995	173,871	30,944	27,954	268,000	5,292.5	5,922.3	1,150.8	263,605	71,050
1996	171,321	29,462	26,680	221,500	5,196.0	5,554.3	1,058.2	263,890	66,200
1997	182,992	31,709	29,886	335,000	5,161.9	7,290.9	1,312.3	292,620	70,200
1998	184,443	32,743	32,499	73,200	5,381.3	5,816.4	1,162.8	315,525	63,150
1999	206,027	35,299	33,420	203,100	5,223.3	6,234.8	1,216.7	224,580	61,200
2000	190,872	36,114	32,541	209,800	5,291.9	7,688.0	1,289.9	299,760	66,980
2001[1]	215,270	34,587	25,764	388,500	4,711.5	6,569.3	1,203.9	280,935	59,750
2002[1]	210,960	35,553	27,718	172,900	4,262.0	7,338.9	1,267.5	283,760	58,660
2003	199,157	34,368	30,605	282,100	4,306.7	6,572.7	1,259.5	267,040	50,080

(1) Revised. (2) Harvested for nuts. (3) Harvested for beans. (4) Utilized production only. (5) Crop year ending in year cited.

Total U.S. Government Agricultural Payments, by State, 1990-2003

Source: Economic Research Service, U.S. Dept. of Agriculture
(in thousands of dollars)

STATE	1990	1995	2000	2001	2002	2003
Alabama	$82,226	$54,140	$170,852	$230,126	$263,127	$219,214
Alaska	1,117	1,735	1,672	2,173	1,762	1,830
Arizona	43,349	9,456	107,066	99,254	70,241	135,261
Arkansas	312,696	383,783	900,648	832,135	450,038	819,994
California	252,333	239,809	667,466	586,699	461,041	645,272
Colorado	236,723	167,661	351,116	319,271	210,367	316,893
Connecticut	2,123	2,382	18,143	7,540	4,940	7,237
Delaware	3,213	3,150	25,028	24,963	11,944	17,096
Florida	37,155	55,778	56,741	107,311	82,651	109,824
Georgia	130,593	67,332	380,057	426,534	656,717	549,155
Hawaii	519	947	11,927	3,860	1,911	1,294
Idaho	133,431	89,482	261,297	207,636	165,391	151,620
Illinois	506,603	543,753	1,943,916	1,849,734	614,734	854,099
Indiana	244,170	246,026	938,464	925,249	334,330	438,053
Iowa	753,733	786,652	2,302,094	1,971,615	739,864	1,045,632
Kansas	834,746	422,226	1,231,923	1,068,601	456,622	807,415
Kentucky	81,610	67,382	448,473	293,367	138,254	145,219
Louisiana	154,631	164,251	451,831	434,012	253,108	422,076
Maine	6,982	14,114	13,851	7,794	13,740	11,494
Maryland	17,386	15,241	88,470	86,543	48,848	66,299
Massachusetts	3,023	2,490	10,973	10,129	6,064	11,439
Michigan	168,831	151,055	381,056	352,730	190,536	251,608
Minnesota	511,759	467,807	1,502,230	1,242,073	466,801	781,677
Mississippi	185,969	133,544	463,901	516,314	251,315	470,694
Missouri	299,065	256,629	869,390	817,027	398,355	506,049
Montana	299,599	189,809	490,002	475,972	261,998	353,350
Nebraska	624,646	507,302	1,406,971	1,297,564	537,903	722,620
Nevada	5,347	4,264	3,918	5,860	11,288	11,953
New Hampshire	1,856	1,216	4,768	2,774	3,642	4,762
New Jersey	15,744	5,491	22,481	16,399	6,446	12,041
New Mexico	63,840	55,134	79,495	93,560	73,726	92,390
New York	59,304	43,563	159,876	114,009	159,105	160,276
North Carolina	73,255	41,476	447,096	330,312	277,739	357,543
North Dakota	545,378	296,215	1,170,234	944,546	383,452	651,484
Ohio	197,006	167,351	678,104	681,519	280,826	395,322
Oklahoma	319,040	164,662	439,851	391,712	317,124	355,332
Oregon	89,137	52,145	137,401	104,725	80,081	106,595
Pennsylvania	41,414	41,096	147,848	103,435	129,275	182,426
Rhode Island	191	317	1,218	292	651	611
South Carolina	62,637	34,586	144,499	129,742	65,264	126,461
South Dakota	332,851	245,016	789,895	714,936	333,439	547,920
Tennessee	91,029	47,405	298,873	247,454	108,144	175,199
Texas	974,702	643,119	1,647,066	1,702,477	998,215	1,661,141
Utah	34,897	25,045	36,181	39,689	54,278	55,479
Vermont	5,793	4,334	26,093	7,863	36,294	28,479
Virginia	32,378	25,967	152,452	116,801	181,891	175,585
Washington	205,425	116,062	352,503	298,547	215,689	263,950
West Virginia	6,049	5,268	23,509	9,807	5,640	12,962
Wisconsin	181,243	184,350	603,213	414,981	332,068	475,696
Wyoming	31,283	31,432	34,302	50,171	65,792	51,042
UNITED STATES	**$9,298,030**	**$7,279,451**	**$22,896,433**	**$20,990,842**	**$11,365,194**	**$16,177,044**

Farm Business Real Estate Debt Outstanding, by Lender Groups,[1] 1960-2003

Source: Economic Research Service, U.S. Dept. of Agriculture

(in millions of dollars)

Dec. 31	Total farm real estate debt[2]	AMOUNTS HELD BY PRINCIPAL LENDER GROUPS				
		Farm Credit System[2]	Farm Services Agency[3]	Life insurance companies[4]	All operating banks	Other[5]
1960.............	$11,310	$2,222	$624	$2,652	$1,356	$4,456
1970.............	27,506	6,420	2,180	5,123	3,329	10,455
1980.............	89,692	33,225	7,435	11,998	7,765	27,813
1985.............	100,076	42,169	9,821	11,273	10,732	25,775
1990.............	74,732	25,924	7,639	9,704	16,288	15,169
1991.............	74,944	25,305	7,041	9,546	17,417	15,632
1992.............	75,421	25,408	6,394	8,765	18.757	16,095
1993.............	76,036	24,900	5,837	8,985	19,595	16,719
1994.............	77,680	24,597	5,465	9,025	21,079	17,514
1995.............	79,287	24,851	5,055	9,092	22,277	18,012
1996.............	81,657	25,730	4,702	9,468	23,276	18,481
1997.............	85,359	27,098	4,373	9,699	25,240	18,950
1998.............	89,615	28,888	4,073	10,723	27,168	18,763
1999.............	94,226	30,302	3,872	11,490	29,799	18,763
2000.............	91,109	29,692	3,418	11,053	29,757	17,188
2001.............	96,008	32,855	3,347	11,205	31,082	17,519
2002.............	103,356	37,815	3,181	11,421	33,060	17,880
2003[6].........	111,300	40,600	3,000	11,600	37,800	18,300

(1) Excludes operator households. (2) Includes data for joint stock land banks and real estate loans by Agricultural Credit Assn. (3) Includes loans made directly by Farm Services Agency for farm ownership, soil, and water loans to individuals, Native American tribe land acquisition, grazing associations, and half of economic emergency loans. Also includes loans for rural housing on farm tracts and labor housing. (4) American Council of Life Insurance members. (5) Estimated by ERS, USDA. Includes Commodity Credit Corporation storage and drying facility loans. (6) Preliminary.

U.S. Farm Marketings by State, 2002-2003

Source: Economic Research Service, U.S. Dept. of Agriculture

(in thousands of dollars)

STATE	RANK, 2003	2003 FARM MARKETINGS			2002 FARM MARKETINGS		
		Total	Crops	Livestock and products	Total	Crops	Livestock and products
Alabama	(25)	$3,415,298	$676,129	$2,739,169	$2,962,089	$583,811	$2,378,278
Alaska	(50)	50,896	23,316	27,580	50,679	22,773	27,906
Arizona	(29)	2,586,023	1,327,419	1,258,603	2,997,195	1,903,139	1,094,056
Arkansas	(12)	5,298,209	2,083,102	3,215,107	4,526,611	1,574,866	2,951,745
California	(1)	27,804,796	20,811,838	6,992,958	26,106,640	19,865,008	6,241,632
Colorado	(16)	4,964,311	1,288,642	3,675,669	4,880,517	1,378,928	3,501,589
Connecticut	(43)	484,832	320,175	164,657	468,489	314,125	154,364
Delaware	(40)	760,219	167,557	592,662	723,513	177,184	546,329
Florida	(9)	6,449,583	5,243,767	1,205,816	6,848,253	5,609,028	1,239,225
Georgia	(13)	5,246,328	2,024,456	3,221,872	4,472,045	1,582,309	2,889,736
Hawaii	(41)	549,353	463,539	85,814	509,143	424,354	84,789
Idaho	(21)	3,953,243	1,775,893	2,177,350	3,933,672	1,935,141	1,998,531
Illinois	(7)	8,289,958	6,490,106	1,799,851	7,486,125	5,923,828	1,562,297
Indiana	(14)	5,161,609	3,362,656	1,798,954	4,799,545	3,248,526	1,551,019
Iowa	(3)	12,633,200	6,560,188	6,073,014	10,833,860	5,759,106	5,074,754
Kansas	(5)	9,046,096	2,867,497	6,178,600	7,861,794	2,536,465	5,325,329
Kentucky	(24)	3,469,002	1,243,300	2,225,703	3,111,713	1,151,034	1,960,679
Louisiana	(33)	1,993,366	1,296,021	697,345	1,773,423	1,159,374	614,049
Maine	(42)	498,765	226,887	271,878	442,394	211,923	230,471
Maryland	(36)	1,466,500	619,888	846,612	1,431,766	621,423	810,343
Massachusetts	(47)	384,746	297,624	87,122	380,274	297,024	83,250
Michigan	(22)	3,820,824	2,421,523	1,399,301	3,390,072	2,130,372	1,259,700
Minnesota	(6)	8,587,959	4,515,789	4,072,171	7,478,126	3,833,272	3,644,854
Mississippi	(26)	3,411,004	1,246,445	2,164,558	2,962,343	1,012,645	1,949,698
Missouri	(15)	4,972,761	2,344,432	2,628,329	4,401,882	2,099,829	2,302,053
Montana	(34)	1,892,144	786,878	1,105,266	1,687,481	701,983	985,498
Nebraska	(4)	10,621,275	3,753,907	6,867,368	9,588,658	3,764,363	5,824,295
Nevada	(45)	395,801	141,474	254,327	366,242	155,085	211,157
New Hampshire	(48)	149,848	87,642	62,206	147,573	91,297	56,276
New Jersey	(39)	845,886	658,034	187,852	855,727	663,118	192,609
New Mexico	(32)	2,139,590	542,790	1,596,800	1,956,978	574,926	1,382,052
New York	(28)	3,139,376	1,224,758	1,914,618	3,104,484	1,234,324	1,870,160
North Carolina	(8)	6,916,349	2,758,504	4,157,845	6,602,899	2,658,886	3,944,013
North Dakota	(23)	3,777,519	2,907,322	870,197	3,222,630	2,498,974	723,656
Ohio	(17)	4,662,233	2,852,781	1,809,452	4,276,038	2,645,811	1,630,227
Oklahoma	(18)	4,526,113	1,022,107	3,504,006	3,730,952	837,492	2,893,460
Oregon	(27)	3,283,732	2,478,876	804,856	3,102,265	2,294,134	808,131
Pennsylvania	(19)	4,266,265	1,407,089	2,859,177	4,042,439	1,360,038	2,682,401
Rhode Island	(49)	57,224	48,555	8,669	46,087	39,787	6,300
South Carolina	(35)	1,644,455	754,455	890,001	1,452,079	691,852	760,227
South Dakota	(20)	4,017,915	1,898,701	2,119,214	3,779,495	1,719,982	2,059,513
Tennessee	(30)	2,338,653	1,267,803	1,070,850	1,999,858	1,086,785	913,073
Texas	(2)	15,341,961	5,030,521	10,311,440	12,664,912	4,577,242	8,087,670
Utah	(37)	1,138,154	258,421	879,733	1,057,178	249,426	807,752
Vermont	(44)	481,650	78,928	402,722	476,352	76,178	400,174
Virginia	(31)	2,227,292	695,131	1,532,161	2,172,890	721,763	1,451,127
Washington	(11)	5,345,292	3,818,220	1,527,072	5,208,955	3,713,638	1,495,317
West Virginia	(46)	389,540	72,550	316,990	378,486	78,289	300,197
Wisconsin	(10)	5,876,052	1,782,346	4,093,706	5,318,908	1,550,606	3,768,302
Wyoming	(38)	873,645	149,920	723,726	875,784	126,213	749,571
UNITED STATES		**$211,646,847**	**$106,175,899**	**$105,470,948**	**$192,947,507**	**$99,467,672**	**$93,479,835**

Average Prices Received by U.S. Farmers, 1940-2003

Source: National Agricultural Statistics Service, U.S. Dept. of Agriculture

Figures below represent dollars per 100 lb for hogs, beef cattle, veal calves, sheep, lamb, and milk (wholesale); dollars per head for milk cows; cents per lb for chickens, broilers, turkeys, and wool; cents per dozen for eggs; weighted calendar year prices for livestock and livestock products other than wool. For 1943-63, wool prices are weighted on marketing year basis. The marketing year was changed in 1964 from a calendar year to a Dec.-Nov. basis for hogs, chickens, broilers, and eggs.

Year	Hogs	Cattle (beef)	Calves (veal)	Sheep	Lambs	Milk cows	Milk	Chickens (excl. broilers)	Broilers	Turkeys	Eggs	Wool
1940...	5.39	7.56	8.83	3.95	8.10	61	1.82	13.0	17.3	15.2	18.0	28.4
1950...	18.00	23.30	26.30	11.60	25.10	198	3.89	22.2	27.4	32.8	36.3	62.1
1960...	15.30	20.40	22.90	5.61	17.90	223	4.21	12.2	16.9	25.4	36.1	42.0
1970...	22.70	27.10	34.50	7.51	26.40	332	5.71	9.1	13.6	22.6	39.1	35.4
1975...	46.10	32.20	27.20	11.30	42.10	412	8.75	9.9	26.3	34.8	54.5	44.8
1980...	38.00	62.40	76.80	21.30	63.60	1,190	13.05	11.0	27.7	41.3	56.3	88.1
1985...	44.00	53.70	62.10	23.90	67.70	860	12.76	14.8	30.1	49.1	57.1	63.3
1986...	49.30	52.60	61.10	25.60	69.00	820	12.51	12.5	34.5	47.1	61.6	66.8
1990...	53.70	74.60	95.60	23.20	55.50	1,160	13.74	9.3	32.6	39.4	70.9	80.0
1991...	49.10	72.70	98.00	19.70	52.20	1,100	12.27	7.1	30.8	38.4	67.8	55.0
1992...	41.60	71.30	89.00	25.80	59.50	1,130	13.15	8.6	31.8	37.7	57.6	74.0
1993...	45.20	72.60	91.20	28.60	64.40	1,160	12.84	10.0	34.0	39.0	63.4	51.0
1994...	39.90	66.70	87.20	30.90	65.60	1,170	13.01	7.6	35.0	40.4	61.4	78.0
1995...	40.50	61.80	73.10	28.00	78.20	1,130	12.78	6.5	34.4	41.6	62.4	104.0
1996...	51.90	58.70	58.40	29.90	82.20	1,090	14.75	6.6	38.1	43.3	74.9	70.0
1997...	52.90	63.10	78.90	37.90	90.30	1,100	13.36	7.7	37.7	39.9	70.3	84.0
1998...	34.40	59.60	78.80	30.60	72.30	1,120	15.41	8.0	39.3	38.0	65.5	60.0
1999...	30.30	63.40	87.70	31.10	74.50	1,280	14.38	7.1	37.1	40.8	62.2	38.0
2000...	42.30	68.60	104.00	34.30	79.80	1,340	12.40	5.7	33.6	40.7	61.8	33.0
2001[1]..	44.30	71.30	106.00	34.60	66.90	1,500	15.04	4.5	39.3	39.0	62.2	36.0
2002[1]..	33.40	66.50	96.40	27.90	73.80	1,600	12.18	4.8	30.5	36.5	58.9	53.0
2003...	37.20	79.70	102.00	34.90	94.40	1,340	12.55	4.8	34.6	36.0	73.1	74.0

Figures below represent cents per lb for cotton, apples, and peanuts; dollars per bushel for oats, wheat, corn, barley, and soybeans; dollars per 100 lb for rice, sorghum, and potatoes; dollars per ton for cottonseed and baled hay; weighted crop year prices. The marketing year is described as follows: apples, June-May; wheat, oats, barley, hay, and potatoes, July-June; cotton, rice, peanuts, and cottonseed, Aug.-July; soybeans, Sept.-Aug.; and corn and sorghum grain, Oct.-Sept.

Year	Corn	Wheat	Upland cotton*	Oats	Barley	Rice	Soybeans	Sorghum	Peanuts	Cottonseed	Hay	Potatoes	Apples
1940...	0.62	0.67	9.8	0.30	0.39	1.80	0.89	0.87	3.7	21.70	9.78	0.85	NA
1950...	1.52	2.00	39.9	0.79	1.19	5.09	2.47	1.88	10.9	86.60	21.10	1.50	NA
1960...	1.00	1.74	30.1	0.60	0.84	4.55	2.13	1.49	10.0	42.50	21.70	2.00	2.7
1970...	1.33	1.33	21.9	0.62	0.97	5.17	2.85	2.04	12.8	56.40	26.10	2.21	6.5
1975...	2.54	3.55	51.1	1.45	2.42	8.35	4.92	4.21	19.0	97.00	52.10	4.48	8.8
1980...	3.11	3.91	74.4	1.79	2.86	12.80	7.57	5.25	25.1	129.00	71.00	6.55	12.1
1985...	2.23	3.08	56.8	1.23	1.98	6.53	5.05	3.45	24.4	66.00	67.60	3.92	17.3
1986...	1.50	2.42	51.5	1.21	1.61	3.75	4.78	2.45	29.2	80.00	59.70	5.03	19.1
1990...	2.28	2.61	67.1	1.14	2.14	6.68	5.74	3.79	34.7	121.00	80.60	6.08	20.9
1991...	2.37	3.00	56.8	1.21	2.10	7.58	5.58	4.01	28.3	71.00	71.20	4.96	25.1
1992...	2.07	3.24	53.7	1.32	2.04	5.89	5.56	3.38	30.0	97.50	74.30	5.52	19.5
1993...	2.50	3.26	58.1	1.36	1.99	7.98	6.40	4.13	30.4	113.00	84.70	6.18	18.4
1994...	2.26	3.45	72.0	1.22	2.03	6.78	5.48	3.80	28.9	101.00	86.70	5.58	18.6
1995...	3.24	4.55	75.4	1.67	2.89	9.15	6.72	5.69	29.3	106.00	82.20	6.77	24.0
1996...	2.71	4.30	69.3	1.96	2.74	9.96	7.35	4.17	28.1	126.00	95.80	4.93	20.8
1997...	2.43	3.38	65.2	1.60	2.38	9.70	6.47	3.95	28.3	121.00	100.00	5.62	22.1
1998...	1.90	2.65	64.2	1.10	1.98	8.50	5.35	3.10	25.7	129.00	84.60	5.24	17.1
1999...	1.82	2.48	45.0	1.12	2.13	5.93	4.63	2.80	25.4	89.00	76.90	5.77	21.3
2000...	1.85	2.62	49.8	1.10	2.11	5.61	4.54	3.37	27.4	105.00	84.60	5.08	17.8
2001[1]...	1.97	2.78	29.8	1.59	2.22	4.25	4.38	4.25	23.4	90.50	96.50	6.99	22.9
2002[1]...	2.32	3.56	44.5	1.81	2.72	4.49	5.53	4.14	18.2	101.00	92.40	6.69	25.6
2003...	2.45	3.40	62.9	1.48	2.83	7.25	7.25	4.40	18.8	117.00	92.90	5.85	29.5

*Beginning in 1964, 480-lb net weight bales. NA = Not available. (1) Revised.

Value of U.S. Agricultural Exports and Imports, 1978-2003

Source: Economic Research Service, U.S. Dept. of Agriculture

(in billions of dollars, except percent)

Year[1]	Trade surplus	Agric. exports	% of all exports	Agric. imports	% of all imports	Year[1]	Trade surplus	Agric. exports	% of all exports	Agric. imports	% of all imports
1978.....	13.4	27.3	21	13.9	8	1991	16.4	39.3	10	22.9	5
1979.....	15.8	32.0	19	16.2	8	1992	18.3	43.1	10	24.8	5
1980.....	23.2	40.5	19	17.3	7	1993	17.7	42.9	10	25.1	4
1981.....	26.4	43.8	19	17.3	7	1994	19.2	46.2	10	27.0	4
1982.....	23.6	39.1	18	15.5	6	1995	26.0	56.3	10	30.3	4
1983.....	18.5	34.8	18	16.3	7	1996	26.8	60.3	10	33.5	4
1984.....	19.1	38.0	18	18.9	6	1997	21.0	57.2	9	36.1	4
1985.....	11.5	31.2	15	19.7	6	1998	14.9	51.8	8	36.9	4
1986.....	5.4	26.3	13	20.9	6	1999	10.7	48.4	8	37.7	4
1987.....	7.2	27.9	12	20.7	5	2000	12.2	51.2	7	39.0	3
1988.....	14.3	35.3	12	21.0	5	2001	14.3	53.7	8	39.4	4
1989.....	18.1	39.7	12	21.6	5	2002[2].....	11.2	53.1	8	41.9	4
1990.....	16.6	39.5	11	22.9	5	2003[3].....	12.2	59.5	9	47.3	4

(1) Fiscal year (Oct.-Sept.). (2) Revised. (3) Preliminary.

> ▶ **IT'S A FACT:** The U.S. produced 171.7 million pounds of honey from 2.6 million bee colonies in 2003. The top producing states were California (32.2 million pounds from 480,000 colonies), North Dakota (29.6 million pounds from 340,000 colonies), and Florida (14.9 million pounds from 210,000 colonies).

World Wheat, Rice, and Corn Production, 2003

Source: UN Food and Agriculture Organization; in metric tons

Country	Wheat	Rice[1]	Corn	Country	Wheat	Rice[1]	Corn
Algeria	2,970,000	300	1,000	Kyrgyzstan	1,013,718	18,342	398,541
Argentina	14,530,000	717,600	15,040,000	Laos	—	2,500,000	112,000
Australia	24,900,000	391,000	316,000	Lithuania	1,204,100	—	—
Austria	1,191,380	—	1,452,054	Madagascar	10,000	2,800,000	181,140
Azerbaijan	1,509,560	15,651	143,147	Malawi	1,000	86,882	1,900,975
Bangladesh	1,550,000	38,060,000	10,000	Malaysia	—	2,145,142	72,000
Belarus	1,100,000	—	20,000	Mexico	3,000,000	191,540	19,652,416
Belgium	1,640,364	13,194	554,743	Moldova	102,414	—	1,401,723
Botswana	550	10,198,900	10,000	Morocco	5,146,820	8,100	138,580
Brazil	5,899,800	400	47,809,300	Mozambique	1,000	200,439	1,248,000
Bulgaria	2,004,000	97,103	1,400,000	Nepal	1,344,000	4,155,000	1,441,000
Burundi	8,700	4,300,000	127,000	Netherlands	1,228,300	—	196,000
Cameroon	400	—	1,040,442	Nigeria	73,000	4,952,000	5,150,000
Canada	23,552,000	27,400	9,587,300	Pakistan	19,210,200	6,751,000	1,275,000
Chile	1,797,084	166,417,000	1,189,729	Peru	189,000	2,139,100	1,471,000
China	86,100,250	2,500,000	114,175,000	Philippines	—	14,031,000	4,478,173
Colombia	32,000	17,000	1,195,000	Poland	7,858,160	—	1,883,677
Congo, Dem. Rep.	12,000	1,403	1,100,000	Romania	2,479,052	1,500	9,576,985
Croatia	609,258	—	1,569,150	Russian Fed.	34,062,260	449,520	2,113,060
Cuba	—	715,800	360,000	Saudi Arabia	2,000,000	—	4,000
Czech Rep.	2,637,890	—	476,371	Serbia and Montenegro	1,369,208	—	3,825,539
Denmark	4,699,000	—	—	South Africa	1,600,000	3,200	9,714,254
Ecuador	14,994	1,235,967	677,479	Spain	6,290,100	855,000	4,300,800
Egypt	6,150,000	5,800,000	6,400,000	Sri Lanka	—	3,071,200	29,880
Ethiopia	1,400,000	15,500	3,000,000	Sweden	2,285,100	—	—
France	30,582,000	105,423	11,898,000	Syrian Arab Republic	4,912,993	—	240,000
Germany	19,296,100	—	3,415,000	Tanzania	71,000	640,189	2,430,000
Greece	1,631,700	175,000	2,205,700	Thailand	800	27,000,000	4,500,000
Guatemala	8,000	32,495	1,053,560	Tunisia	1,150,000	—	—
Hungary	2,919,000	10,000	4,534,000	Turkey	19,000,000	372,000	2,800,000
India	65,129,300	132,013,000	14,800,000	Turkmenistan	2,534,000	109,500	13,000
Indonesia	—	52,078,832	10,910,104	Uganda	12,000	120,000	1,200,000
Iran	12,900,000	3,300,000	1,800,000	Ukraine	3,600,000	84,000	6,900,000
Ireland	750,000	—	—	U.S.	63,589,820	9,033,610	256,904,560
Israel	170,000	—	60,000	United Kingdom	14,288,000	—	—
Italy	6,243,390	1,359,826	8,978,180	Uruguay	326,000	1,250,000	178,500
Japan	855,200	9,740,000	160	Uzbekistan	5,331,000	311,200	136,000
Jordan	42,500	—	10,700	Venezuela	152	700,611	1,504,800
Kazakhstan	11,518,500	200,000	438,000	Vietnam	—	34,518,600	2,933,700
Kenya	210,000	50,000	2,300,000	Zambia	100,000	12,000	1,161,000
Korea, North	145,000	2,284,000	1,725,000	Zimbabwe	130,000	600	802,664
Korea, South	10,000	6,068,000	70,000	**World***	**556,348,627**	**589,125,843**	**638,043,432**

— Production is small or nonexistent. *Because not all countries are reported on this table, country totals do not add to world totals.
(1) Rice paddy.

Wheat, Rice, and Corn—Exports/Imports of 10 Leading Countries, 2002, 1995

Source: UN Food and Agriculture Organization; in metric tons

TOP EXPORTERS

Wheat

2002		1995	
U.S.	24,245,829	U.S.	32,420,000
Australia	14,697,182	Canada	16,960,000
France	13,678,411	France	16,310,000
Canada	12,202,573	Australia	7,818,000
Russian Fed.	10,259,275	Argentina	6,913,286
Argentina	9,051,610	Germany	3,681,597
Ukraine	8,303,974	Hungary	2,764,541
Germany	5,872,406	U.K.	2,669,090
Kazakhstan	5,100,000	Kazakhstan	2,485,588
India	3,671,254	Denmark	1,540,179

Rice

2002		1995	
Thailand	7,337,561	Thailand	6,197,990
India	5,053,242	India	4,913,156
U.S.	3,266,872	U.S.	3,083,609
Viet Nam	3,240,932	Vietnam	1,988,000
China	2,067,839	Pakistan	1,852,267
Pakistan	1,684,326	Australia	541,848
Myanmar	900,000	Italy	523,898
Uruguay	652,386	Uruguay	462,471
Italy	593,454	Argentina	390,091
Egypt	464,402	Myanmar	353,800

Corn

2002		1995	
U.S.	47,685,821	U.S.	60,240,000
China	11,673,522	France	6,474,138
Argentina	9,483,591	Argentina	6,000,873
France	8,378,135	South Africa	1,508,450
Hungary	2,124,865	Hungary	600,950
South Africa	749,870	Canada	443,612
Germany	664,692	Belgium-Lux.	442,645
Ukraine	496,683	Zimbabwe	287,818
Brazil	280,975	Germany	244,000
Austria	268,468	Paraguay	203,430

TOP IMPORTERS

Wheat

2002		1995	
Italy	7,715,548	China	12,601,814
Brazil	6,572,241	Brazil	6,135,235
Spain	6,346,691	Japan	5,965,296
Algeria	5,998,039	Italy	5,078,844
Japan	5,862,826	Egypt	5,069,599
Egypt	5,574,748	Indonesia	4,054,203
Indonesia	4,306,650	Algeria	3,504,679
Iran	4,121,983	Iran	3,100,000
South Korea	3,861,349	Spain	2,757,498
Netherlands	3,812,363	Belgium-Lux.	2,719,024

Rice

2002		1995	
Japan	16,420,532	Indonesia	3,157,700
South Korea	9,112,503	China	1,645,837
Mexico	5,512,911	Iran	1,633,000
China	5,061,526	Bangladesh	995,946
Egypt	4,720,569	Brazil	870,506
Canada	4,017,178	South Korea	587,000
Spain	3,504,310	U. Arab Em.	540,888
Malaysia	2,408,114	Saudi Arabia	522,942
Colombia	2,098,679	Côte d'Ivoire	483,688
Netherlands	2,054,254	South Africa	466,154

Corn

2002		1995	
Japan	16,420,532	Japan	16,580,000
South Korea	9,112,503	China	11,702,350
Mexico	5,512,911	South Korea	9,035,169
China	5,061,526	Spain	2,912,371
Egypt	4,720,569	Mexico	2,686,921
Canada	4,017,178	Egypt	2,425,162
Spain	3,504,310	Malaysia	2,383,267
Malaysia	2,408,114	Belg.-Lux.	1,815,945
Colombia	2,098,679	Netherlands	1,589,800
Netherlands	2,054,254	U.K.	1,501,563

World Commercial Catch of Fish, Crustaceans, and Mollusks, by Major Fishing Areas, 1996-2001

Source: Food and Agriculture Organization of the United Nations (FAO)

(in thousands of metric tons; live weight)

AREA	1996	1997	1998	1999	2000	2001
Marine						
Pacific Ocean..................	63,452	62,657	57,047	63,631	65,524	63,298
Atlantic Ocean	25,237	26,385	25,606	25,648	26,049	26,386
Indian Ocean	8,432	8,777	8,940	9,100	9,284	9,204
Total Marine	**97,121**	**97,820**	**91,593**	**98,378**	**100,857**	**98,888**
Inland Waters						
Asia	19,501	21,104	22,431	24,397	25,577	26,861
Africa	1,950	2,018	2,134	2,245	2,406	2,414
Europe	838	821	856	901	886	821
N. America	564	600	597	627	618	618
S. America	448	465	477	524	556	579
Former USSR.................	412	388	432	507	498	412
Oceania	22	24	25	26	26	27
Total Inland.................	**23,323**	**25,032**	**26,520**	**28,720**	**30,070**	**31,320**
GRAND TOTAL.............	**120,444**	**122,852**	**118,113**	**127,098**	**130,927**	**130,207**

Note: Data for marine mammals and aquatic plants are excluded. Totals include areas or territories not shown. Details may not equal totals due to rounding.

Commercial Catch of Fish, Crustaceans, and Mollusks, for 20 Leading Countries, 1997-2002[1]

Source: Food and Agriculture Organization of the United Nations (FAO)

(in thousands of metric tons; live weight; ranked for 2002)

COUNTRY	2002	2001	2000	1999	1998	1997	COUNTRY	2002	2001	2000	1999	1998	1997
China	27,767	26,050	24,581	22,790	20,795	19,316	Philippines..	443	435	394	353	313	327
India.......	2,192	2,120	1,942	2,135	1,908	1,864	Egypt......	376	343	340	226	139	86
Indonesia ...	914	864	789	749	630	623	Taiwan.....	330	297	244	248	240	258
Japan......	828	802	763	759	767	807	S. Korea ...	297	294	293	304	327	392
Bangladesh .	787	713	657	593	575	486	Spain......	264	313	312	321	315	239
Thailand	645	724	738	694	595	540	France.....	250	252	267	265	268	287
Norway.....	554	511	491	476	411	368	Brazil......	246	208	177	141	104	88
Chile.......	546	566	392	274	293	272	Italy.......	184	218	214	207	206	191
Vietnam	519	519	511	467	413	405	U.K........	179	171	152	155	137	130
U.S.(2)	497	479	456	479	445	438	Canada	172	153	128	113	91	82

(1) Includes aquaculture. (2) Includes weight of clam, oyster, scallop, and other mollusk shells. This weight is not included in U.S. landings statistics shown elsewhere.

U.S. Commercial Landings of Fish and Shellfish, 1986-2002[1]

Source: U.S. Dept. of Commerce, Natl. Oceanic and Atmospheric Admin., Natl. Marine Fisheries Service

YEAR	Landings for human food		Landings for industrial purposes[2]		TOTAL	
	mil lb	mil dollars	mil lb	mil dollars	mil lb	mil dollars
1986.......	3,393	$2,641	2,638	$122	6,031	$2,763
1987.......	3,946	2,979	2,950	136	6,896	3,115
1988.......	4,588	3,362	2,604	158	7,192	3,520
1989.......	6,204	3,111	2,259	127	8,463	3,238
1990.......	7,041	3,366	2,363	156	9,404	3,522
1991.......	7,031	3,169	2,453	139	9,484	3,308
1992.......	7,618	3,531	2,019	147	9,637	3,678
1993.......	8,214	3,317	2,253	154	10,467	3,471
1994.......	7,936	3,751	2,525	95	10,461	3,846
1995.......	7,667	3,625	2,121	145	9,788	3,770
1996.......	7,474	3,355	2,091	132	9,565	3,487
1997.......	7,244	3,285	2,598	163	9,842	3,448
1998.......	7,173	3,009	2,021	119	9,194	3,128
1999.......	6,832	3,265	2,507	202	9,339	3,467
2000.......	6,912	3,398	2,157	152	9,069	3,550
2001.......	7,314	3,074	2,178	154	9,492	3,228
2002.......	7,205	2,940	2,192	152	9,397	3,092

Note: Data do not include products of aquaculture, except oysters and clams. (1) Statistics on landings are shown in round weight for all items except univalve and bivalve mollusks such as clams, oysters, and scallops, which are shown in weight of meats (excluding the shell). All data are preliminary. (2) Processed into meal, oil, solubles, and shell products or used as bait or animal food.

U.S. Domestic Landings, by Regions, 2001-2002[1]

Source: U.S. Dept. of Commerce, Natl. Oceanic and Atmospheric Admin., Natl. Marine Fisheries Service

REGION	2001		2002	
	1,000 lb	1,000 dollars	1,000 lb	1,000 dollars
New England	635,162	$646,447	583,915	$685,428
Middle Atlantic	217,975	172,503	206,697	170,134
Chesapeake................	617,244	174,968	495,675	172,320
South Atlantic..............	199,554	176,488	214,799	173,429
Gulf......................	1,605,564	798,319	1,716,140	692,717
Pacific Coast and Alaska	6,173,671	1,187,106	6,138,249	1,130,633
Great Lakes	18,818	17,844	17,848	15,544
Hawaii	23,870	54,561	23,841	52,113
TOTAL....................	**9,491,858**	**$3,228,236**	**9,397,164**	**$3,092,318**

(1) Landings reported in round (live) weight items except for univalve and bivalve mollusks (e.g., clams, oysters, scallops), which are reported in weight of meats (excluding shell). Landings for Mississippi River Drainage Area states not included (not available).

EMPLOYMENT

Employment and Unemployment in the U.S., 1900-2003

Source: Bureau of Labor Statistics, U.S. Dept. of Labor
(civilian labor force, persons 16 years of age and older; annual averages; in thousands)

Year[1]	Employed	Unemployed	Unemployment rate	Year[1]	Employed	Unemployed	Unemployment rate
1900[2]	26,956	1,420	5.0%	1989	117,342	6,528	5.3%
1910[2]	34,599	2,150	5.9	1990[3]	118,793	7,047	5.6
1920[2]	39,208	2,132	5.2	1991	117,718	8,628	6.8
1930[2]	44,183	4,340	8.9	1992	118,492	9,613	7.5
1940[2]	47,520	8,120	14.6	1993	120,259	8,940	6.9
1950	58,918	3,288	5.0	1994[4]	123,060	7,996	6.1
1955	62,170	2,852	4.4	1995	124,900	7,404	5.6
1960	65,778	3,852	5.5	1996	126,708	7,236	5.4
1965	71,088	3,366	4.5	1997[5]	129,558	6,739	4.9
1970	78,678	4,093	4.9	1998[5]	131,463	6,210	4.5
1975	85,846	7,929	8.5	1999[6]	133,488	5,880	4.2
1980	99,303	7,637	7.1	2000[7]	136,891	5,692	4.0
1985	107,150	8,312	7.2	2001[7]	136,933	6,801	4.7
1986	109,597	8,237	7.0	2002[7]	136,485	8,378	5.8
1987	112,440	7,425	6.2	2003[7]	137,736	8,774	6.0
1988	114,968	6,701	5.5				

(1) **Other unemployment rates (1905-1945):** 1905, 4.3; 1915, 8.5; 1925, 3.2; 1935, 20.3; 1936, 16.9; 1937, 14.3; 1938, 19.0; 1939, 17.2. 1945, 1.9; all for 14 years of age and older. (2) Persons 14 years of age and older. (3) Beginning in 1990, data incorporate 1990 census-based population controls, adjusted for estimated undercount. (4) Beginning in 1994, not strictly comparable with prior years, because of major redesign of the survey used. (5) Not strictly comparable with 1994-96 because of revisions in population controls used in household survey. (6) Data not strictly comparable with 1998 and earlier years because of further revisions in population controls used in household survey. (7) Beginning in 2000, not strictly comparable with earlier years because of revisions to the controls used in the survey.

Unemployment Insurance Data, by State, 2003

Source: Employment and Training Admin., U.S. Dept. of Labor; state programs only

STATE	Monetarily eligible claimants	First payments	Final payments	Initial claims	Benefits paid	Average weekly benefit	Employers subject to state law
AL	167,875	140,642	46,259	329,664	$288,747,453	$175.84	85,744
AK	55,606	49,493	21,728	98,757	123,484,456	193.04	16,682
AZ	146,884	115,857	60,467	241,812	348,412,482	173.26	109,279
AR	132,332	103,426	42,205	226,124	285,476,385	228.90	60,734
CA	1,751,698	1,379,996	693,780	2,954,617	5,761,404,774	246.37	1,027,244
CO	145,671	114,887	63,221	176,653	536,067,820	307.68	141,444
CT	234,932	155,146	61,148	258,980	677,483,607	286.19	96,329
DE	36,962	32,828	10,929	67,494	123,709,357	235.46	25,505
FL	430,541	326,174	169,036	630,201	1,108,827,973	225.02	420,450
GA	366,414	254,544	118,428	609,344	729,739,100	243.43	196,564
HI	40,013	29,809	8,712	80,026	123,615,031	312.21	29,035
ID	70,734	60,000	22,360	135,438	176,308,636	231.77	41,239
IL	514,792	455,182	205,121	855,658	2,340,075,870	280.94	279,594
IN	267,260	212,910	91,982	428,874	616,928,016	263.44	125,005
IA	131,459	113,570	33,690	199,123	361,166,887	260.12	68,642
KS	107,703	89,324	38,418	196,881	316,896,823	275.99	67,899
KY	178,466	135,856	39,747	332,426	448,011,672	249.62	82,983
LA	126,936	100,279	43,730	213,843	281,153,524	194.93	94,242
ME	55,488	32,592	12,906	74,372	122,016,728	231.13	39,430
MD	175,122	129,951	46,933	268,360	493,770,532	252.14	135,633
MA	328,808	280,144	137,827	507,842	1,689,459,544	356.58	174,922
MI	633,748	501,998	174,582	1,016,732	1,907,151,077	290.52	210,500
MN	210,385	169,854	68,030	323,050	794,504,355	322.15	132,925
MS	102,634	71,774	27,985	180,061	185,012,936	173.43	53,656
MO	262,959	182,972	79,483	443,788	591,918,712	205.62	130,937
MT	37,670	27,392	10,378	60,768	78,436,577	201.91	33,679
NE	62,476	46,204	21,252	83,454	127,352,461	216.16	45,458
NV	93,166	78,438	34,104	169,235	297,988,889	236.29	48,363
NH	34,422	23,035	7,937	54,951	112,358,250	258.60	39,020
NJ	412,163	367,278	195,806	593,073	1,999,066,371	333.67	272,205
NM	48,006	37,232	16,517	72,936	125,102,335	210.63	41,780
NY	762,257	599,055	364,275	1,212,889	2,870,751,766	271.55	476,724
NC	447,493	347,947	141,892	968,729	922,213,728	258.33	179,337
ND	19,990	15,578	5,575	31,610	44,634,049	222.30	18,802
OH	455,287	352,874	125,309	789,028	1,400,672,531	252.04	233,537
OK	101,874	76,897	35,298	167,338	271,370,608	229.45	75,474
OR	226,560	185,868	84,043	466,226	795,661,919	258.45	101,994
PA	671,295	566,022	212,711	1,246,993	2,523,135,443	291.84	270,784
RI	52,087	43,097	18,255	87,467	206,146,690	308.78	32,517
SC	201,288	148,646	58,756	400,832	401,842,703	210.05	90,341
SD	14,663	11,828	2,043	24,553	31,024,358	201.96	23,005
TN	232,322	200,848	83,824	428,209	558,679,492	210.24	110,286
TX	852,018	533,479	288,789	1,044,225	2,108,302,814	260.80	397,583
UT	75,995	57,362	25,944	95,026	206,657,019	269.38	57,102
VT	32,840	28,265	7,193	50,464	94,603,615	255.08	20,858
VA	229,364	165,621	68,815	428,675	585,651,548	276.09	166,574
WA	351,834	267,960	101,174	610,113	1,366,776,010	324.40	206,344
WV	68,504	54,558	15,575	92,530	177,089,796	219.87	37,057
WI	359,284	315,409	87,630	720,954	929,991,399	251.69	122,911
WY	30,728	15,612	5,192	26,413	46,516,049	238.07	19,549
DC	20,841	21,037	19,151	21,386	105,262,693	258.43	26,837
PR	106,351	106,183	58,352	179,447	228,114,540	106.62	50,300
VI	3,202	2,175	2,077	2,972	16,382,471	277.39	3,049
US	12,679,402	9,935,108	4,416,574	20,980,616	39,063,129,872	261.67	7,048,075

Unemployment Rates, by Selected Country, 1970-2003[1]

Source: Bureau of Labor Statistics, U.S. Dept. of Labor; civilian labor force, seasonally adjusted

Time period	U.S.	Australia	Canada	France	Germany[2]	Italy	Japan	Sweden	UK
1970	4.9	1.6	5.7	2.5	0.5	3.2	1.2	1.5	3.1
1975	8.5	4.9	6.9	4.2	3.4	3.4	1.9	1.6	4.6
1980	7.1	6.1	7.5	6.5	2.8	4.4	2.0	2.0	7.0
1981	7.6	5.8	7.6	7.6	4.0	4.9	2.2	2.5	10.5
1982	9.7	7.2	11.0	8.3	5.6	5.4	2.4	3.1	11.3
1983	9.6	10.0	11.9	8.6	6.9	5.9	2.7	3.5	11.8
1984	7.5	9.0	11.3	10.0	7.1	5.9	2.8	3.1	11.7
1985	7.2	8.3	10.7	10.5	7.2	6.0	2.6	2.8	11.2
1986	7.0	8.1	9.6	10.6	6.6	7.5	2.8	2.6	11.2
1987	6.2	8.1	8.8	10.8	6.3	7.9	2.9	2.2	10.3
1988	5.5	7.2	7.8	10.3	6.3	7.9	2.5	1.9	8.6
1989	5.3	6.2	7.5	9.6	5.7	7.8	2.3	1.6	7.2
1990	5.6	6.9	8.1	9.1	5.0	7.0	2.1	1.8	6.9
1991	6.8	9.6	10.3	9.6	5.6	6.9	2.1	3.1	8.8
1992	7.5	10.8	11.2	9.9	6.7	7.3	2.2	5.6	10.1
1993	6.9	10.9	11.4	11.3	8.0	10.2	2.5	9.3	10.5
1994	6.1	9.7	10.4	11.8	8.5	11.2	2.9	9.6	9.7
1995	5.6	8.5	9.4	11.3	8.2	11.8	3.2	9.1	8.7
1996	5.4	8.6	9.6	11.9	9.0	11.7	3.4	9.9	8.2
1997	4.9	8.6	9.1	11.8	9.9	11.9	3.4	10.1	7.0
1998	4.5	8.0	8.3	11.3	9.3	12.0	4.1	8.4	6.3
1999	4.2	7.2	6.8	10.6	8.5	11.5	4.7	7.1	6.0
2000	4.0	6.3	6.1	9.1	7.8	10.7	4.8	5.8	5.5
2001	4.7	6.7	6.4	8.5	7.9	9.6	5.1	5.0	5.1
2002	5.8	6.3	7.0	8.8	8.6	9.1	5.4	5.2	5.2
2003	6.0	6.1	6.9	9.3	9.3	8.8	5.3	5.8	v5.0

NOTE: Some data for 2002-2003 are preliminary. For the sake of comparisons, U.S. unemployment rate concepts were applied to unemployment data for other countries. Quarterly figures for France and Germany were calculated by applying annual adjustment factors to current published data and are less precise indicators of unemployment under U.S. concepts than the annual figures. (1) As a result of revisions in survey methodology, there are breaks in the data series for the U.S. (1994, 1997-2000), France (1992), Germany (1983, 1991), Italy (1986, 1991, 1993), and Sweden (1987); data prior to a survey change are not fully comparable to data after a survey change. (2) For former West Germany only, through 1990; from 1991 on figures are for unified Germany and not adjusted by the Bureau of Labor Statistics. (3) As a result of revisions in survey methodology, there are breaks in the data series for the U.S. (1994, 1997-2000), France (1992), Germany (1983, 1991), Italy (1986, 1991, 1993), and Sweden (1987); data prior to a survey change are not fully comparable to data after a survey change.

U.S. Unemployment Rates by Selected Characteristics, 2001-2004[1]

Source: Bureau of Labor Statistics, U.S. Dept. of Labor

	2001	2002	2003	Jan.	Feb.	Mar.	Apr.	May	June	July	Aug.
							2004				
Total (all civilian workers)	4.7	5.8	6.0	6.3	6.0	6.0	5.4	5.3	5.8	5.7	5.4
Men, 20 years and older	4.2	5.3	5.6	6.1	5.9	5.9	5.0	4.9	4.8	4.6	4.6
Women, 20 years and older	4.1	5.1	5.1	5.3	5.0	5.1	4.6	4.5	5.2	5.3	5.0
Both sexes, 16 to 19 years	14.7	16.5	17.5	17.5	17.1	16.9	16.3	17.4	19.9	18.2	15.5
White	4.2	5.1	5.2	5.6	5.4	5.4	4.8	4.7	5.1	4.8	4.7
Black	8.6	10.2	10.8	10.7	10.0	10.5	9.3	9.6	10.7	12.0	10.5
Hispanic origin	6.6	7.5	7.7	8.3	8.1	8.0	6.7	6.3	6.5	6.9	6.7
Asian	4.5	5.9	6.0	5.2	4.7	4.2	4.4	4.2	5.0	4.3	3.6
Married men, spouse present	NA	NA	NA	3.3	3.4	3.2	3.1	3.1	3.2	3.2	3.1
Married women, spouse present	NA	NA	NA	3.7	3.6	3.7	3.7	3.3	3.7	3.5	3.5
Women who maintain families	6.6	8.0	8.5	8.3	8.1	8.4	7.5	7.4	8.2	9.0	8.3
OCCUPATION											
Management, professional, and related occupations	2.3	3.0	3.0	3.0	2.7	2.7	2.6	2.8	2.9	3.1	2.9
Service occupations	5.8	6.6	6.6	8.0	7.5	7.4	6.3	6.0	6.8	6.1	6.7
Sales and office occupations	4.4	5.6	5.6	5.8	5.5	5.9	5.0	5.0	5.5	5.3	5.0
Natural resources, construction, and maintenance occupations	6.4	7.8	7.8	9.0	9.3	9.6	7.6	6.5	6.4	6.0	5.6
Production, transportation, and material moving cccupations	6.4	7.6	7.6	8.3	8.2	7.6	7.2	7.0	7.4	7.5	6.8
INDUSTRY											
Nonagricultural, private wage, and salary workers	5.0	6.2	6.3	6.7	6.4	6.4	5.7	5.5	5.8	5.5	5.3
Mining	4.2	6.3	6.7	5.8	5.0	4.4	6.4	4.3	5.0	5.4	1.9
Construction	7.1	9.2	9.3	11.3	11.6	11.3	9.5	7.4	7.0	6.4	6.0
Manufacturing	5.2	6.7	6.6	6.4	6.3	6.3	5.8	5.6	5.6	6.0	4.9
Durable goods	5.2	6.9	6.9	6.4	6.5	6.4	5.6	5.2	5.1	6.2	5.0
Non durable goods	5.2	6.2	6.1	6.3	6.0	6.1	6.2	6.2	6.3	5.7	4.8
Wholesale and retail trade	4.9	6.1	6.0	6.5	6.5	6.8	6.1	5.8	5.8	5.5	5.1
Transportation and utilities	4.3	4.9	5.3	4.6	5.5	5.4	4.5	4.4	4.3	4.3	4.4
Information	4.9	6.9	6.8	7.0	5.8	6.3	5.0	5.7	5.0	5.2	5.7
Financial activities	2.9	3.5	3.5	4.3	3.8	3.7	3.4	3.3	3.6	3.3	3.4
Professional and business services	6.1	7.9	8.2	8.7	7.7	7.9	6.0	6.5	6.5	6.2	6.7
Education and health services	2.8	3.4	3.6	3.7	3.4	3.2	3.3	3.2	4.2	4.0	3.7
Leisure and hospitality	7.5	8.4	8.7	10.0	8.9	9.0	7.9	8.1	9.6	7.8	8.4
Other services	4.0	5.1	5.7	5.3	5.8	5.9	5.6	5.1	5.4	5.6	5.6
Agriculture and related	11.2	10.1	10.2	15.1	14.2	12.7	8.3	7.4	7.6	10.0	7.0
Government	2.2	2.5	2.8	2.5	2.4	2.6	2.1	2.3	2.8	3.7	3.3
Self-employed and unpaid family workers	2.1	v2.6	2.7	2.8	2.5	2.5	2.3	2.7	2.8	2.6	2.9

(1) All monthly rates unadjusted, except for married men and women, which are seasonally adjusted. NA = Not available.

Employed Persons in the U.S., by Occupation and Sex, 2002 and 2003

Source: Bureau of Labor Statistics, U.S. Dept. of Labor

(in thousands)

	Total 16 years and older		Men 16 years and older		Women 16 years and older	
	2002	2003	2002	2003	2002	2003
Total	136,485	137,736	72,903	73,332	63,582	64,404
Management, professional, and related occupations	47,180	47,929	23,612	23,735	23,568	24,194
Management, business, and financial operations occupations	19,823	19,934	11,619	11,534	8,204	8,400
Management occupations	14,492	14,468	9,220	9,094	5,273	5,374
Business and financial operations occupations	5,330	5,465	2,399	2,440	2,931	3,026
Professional and related occupations	27,358	27,995	11,993	12,201	15,364	15,794
Computer and mathematical occupations	3,117	3,122	2,226	2,223	891	900
Architecture and engineering occupations	2,731	2,727	2,383	2,343	348	384
Life, physical, and social science occupations	1,287	1,375	741	783	545	592
Community and social services occupations	2,151	2,184	836	862	1,315	1,323
Legal occupations	1,473	1,508	776	811	697	697
Education, training, and library occupations	7,569	7,768	1,953	2,038	5,616	5,730
Arts, design, entertainment, sports, and media occupations	2,641	2,663	1,409	1,395	1,233	1,267
Healthcare practitioner and technical occupations	6,388	6,648	1,669	1,746	4,719	4,902
Service occupations	21,766	22,086	9,504	9,460	12,261	12,626
Healthcare support occupations	2,694	2,926	260	311	2,434	2,616
Protective service occupations	2,696	2,727	2,139	2,164	557	563
Food preparation and serving related occupations	6,968	7,254	3,077	3,151	3,891	4,104
Building and grounds cleaning and maintenance occupations	5,050	4,947	3,094	2,920	1,956	2,027
Personal care and service occupations	4,358	4,232	934	915	3,424	3,316
Sales and office occupations	35,408	35,496	12,821	12,851	22,587	22,645
Sales and related occupations	15,828	15,960	8,132	8,137	7,696	7,823
Office and administrative support occupations	19,580	19,536	4,690	4,714	14,890	14,823
Natural resources, construction, and maintenance occupations	13,562	14,205	12,874	13,541	688	665
Farming, fishing, and forestry occupations	1,040	1,050	788	819	252	231
Construction and extraction occupations	7,898	8,114	7,674	7,891	224	223
Installation, maintenance, and repair occupations	4,623	5,041	4,412	4,830	212	211
Production, transportation, and material moving occupations	18,569	18,020	14,091	13,745	4,478	4,274
Production occupations	10,081	9,700	6,863	6,696	3,218	3,004
Transportation and material moving occupations	8,488	8,320	7,228	7,049	1,260	1,270

NOTE: Beginning in Jan. 2000, data reflect revised population controls used in the household survey. Totals may not add because of independent rounding.

Elderly in U.S. Labor Force, 1890-2003

Source: Bureau of the Census, U.S. Dept. of Commerce

The percentage of men 65 years of age and older in the U.S. labor force steadily declined between 1890 and 1990 dropping 76% in 100 years, but more recently has increased slightly. The percentage of women 65 or older in the work force has always been much lower than that of men; after ranging from around 6% to 10% from 1890 to 1950, it has increased slightly to 8%-11% in recent decades.

(labor force participation rate; figs. for 1910 not available)

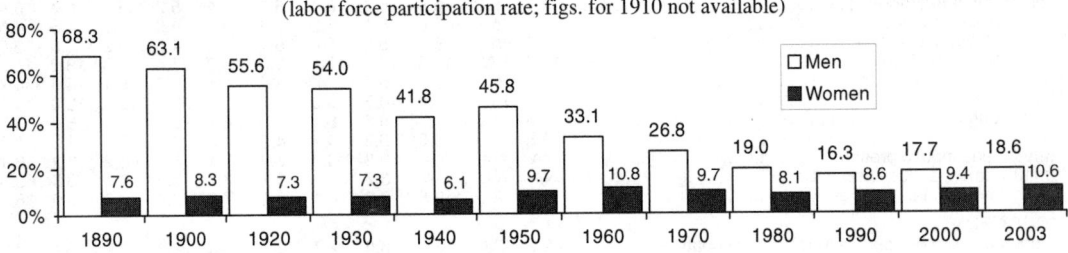

Projected Openings for Selected High-Paying Occupations, 2002-2012

Source: Bureau of Labor Statistics, U.S. Dept. of Labor

Job openings shown below represent the average number expected each year for workers in the U.S. who are entering these occupations for the first time. Numbers were released in spring 2004.

Occupation	Annual avg. job openings[1]	Median annual earnings[2]	Occupation	Annual avg. job openings[1]	Median annual earnings[2]
Registered nurses	110,119	$48,090	First-line office superv. or mgrs	40,909	$38,820
Postsecondary teachers	95,980	49,090	Accountants and auditors	40,465	47,000
Gen. & operations mgrs.	76,245	68,210	Carpenters	31,917	34,190
Sales representatives[3]	66,239	42,730	Auto mechanics/technicians	31,887	30,590
Truck drivers, heavy & tractor trailer	62,517	33,210	Police & Sheriff's patrol officers	31,290	42,270
Elementary school teachers	54,701	41,780	Lic. practical and voc. nurses	29,480	31,440
First-line retail superv. or mgrs.	48,645	29,700	Electricians	28,485	41,390
Secondary school teachers[4]	45,761	43,950	Management analysts	25,470	60,340
Gen. maintenance & repair wkrs	44,978	29,370	Computer systems analysts	23,735	62,890
Exec. secretaries, admin. assists.	42,444	33,410	Special education teachers	23,297	43,450

(1) As a result of growth and net replacement needs. (2) Median earnings are for 2002. (3) Wholesale and manufacturing, except technical and scientific products. (4) Except special and vocational education.

Civilian Employment of the Federal Government, March 2004

Source: Statistical Analysis and Services Division, U.S. Office of Personnel Management

(payroll in thousands of dollars)

	ALL AREAS		UNITED STATES		WASH., D.C., MSA[2]		OVERSEAS	
	Employ-ment*	Payroll*	Employ-ment	Payroll	Employ-ment	Payroll	Employ-ment	Payroll
TOTAL, all agencies[1]	2,704,959	$11,682,609	2,611,068	$11,329,888	331,722	$1,842,720	93,891	$352,721
Legislative Branch	30,348	157,216	30,340	157,144	29,326	150,971	8	72
Congress	17,154	85,751	17,154	85,751	17,154	85,751	—	—
U.S. Senate	6,766	33,476	6,766	33,476	6,766	33,476	—	—
House of Representatives	10,388	52,275	10,388	52,275	10,388	52,275	—	—
Architect of the Capitol	2,139	8,823	2,139	8,823	2,139	8,823	—	—
Congressional Budget Ofc	227	1,657	227	1,657	227	1,657	—	—
General Accounting Ofc	3,201	22,004	3,199	21,987	2,414	16,812	2	17
Government Printing Ofc	2,637	11,988	2,637	11,988	2,457	11,200	—	—
Library of Congress	4,409	23,339	4,403	23,284	4,376	23,180	6	55
U.S. Tax Court	249	1,757	249	1,757	249	1,757	—	—
Judicial Branch	34,399	166,915	33,962	165,064	1,926	11,277	437	1,851
Supreme Court	430	1,523	430	1,523	430	1,523	—	—
U.S. Courts	33,969	165,392	33,532	163,541	1,496	9,754	437	1,851
Executive Branch	2,640,212	11,358,478	2,546,766	11,007,680	300,470	1,680,472	93,446	350,798
Exec Ofc of the President	1,700	10,791	1,689	10,721	1,689	10,721	11	70
White House Office	404	2,022	404	2,022	404	2,022	—	—
Ofc of Vice President	24	143	24	143	24	143	—	—
Ofc of Mgmt & Budget	498	3,554	498	3,554	498	3,554	—	—
Ofc of Administration	211	1,264	211	1,264	211	1,264	—	—
Council Economic Advisors	30	169	30	169	30	169	—	—
Council Environmental Quality . . .	21	136	21	136	21	136	—	—
Ofc of Policy Development	28	161	28	161	28	161	—	—
National Security Council	56	400	56	400	56	400	—	—
Ofc of Natl Drug Control	107	760	107	760	107	760	—	—
Ofc of U.S. Trade Rep	200	1,404	189	1,334	189	1,334	11	70
Executive Departments	1,682,188	7,487,074	1,595,442	7,168,622	230,713	1,276,415	86,746	318,452
State	32,997	184,060	12,835	69,096	11,230	57,550	20,162	114,964
Treasury	126,408	532,777	125,763	530,362	15,191	96,376	645	2,415
Defense, Total	667,192	2,428,836	613,365	2,282,727	64,046	245,764	53,827	146,109
Defense, Mil Function	642,737	2,362,670	588,976	2,216,647	63,197	243,602	53,761	146,023
Defense, Civ Function	24,455	66,166	24,389	66,080	849	2,162	66	86
Dept of the Army	230,941	637,895	208,370	572,866	19,545	42,057	22,571	65,029
Army, Mil Function	206,487	571,730	183,982	506,787	18,696	39,895	22,505	64,943
Army, Civil Function	24,454	66,165	24,388	66,079	849	2,162	66	86
Corps of Engineers	24,355	65,913	24,289	65,827	750	1,910	66	86
Dept of the Navy	182,386	738,195	174,475	706,001	24,525	99,255	7,911	32,194
Dept of the Air Force	154,411	624,387	148,012	598,521	5,645	22,815	6,399	25,866
Defense Logist. Agency	21,753	106,161	20,986	101,791	1,648	11,329	767	4,370
Other Defense Activities	77,701	322,198	61,522	303,548	12,683	70,308	16,179	18,650
Justice	103,318	580,908	101,562	570,282	22,079	152,529	1,756	10,626
Interior	70,240	298,367	69,890	297,270	7,834	42,650	350	1,097
Agriculture	98,803	409,047	97,568	404,875	11,633	66,259	1,235	4,172
Commerce	37,126	192,338	36,369	188,513	20,142	120,222	757	3,825
Labor	16,009	91,812	15,971	91,611	5,433	34,552	38	201
Health & Human Services	60,632	332,174	60,387	330,693	27,842	170,077	245	1,481
Housing & Urban Dev	10,330	60,692	10,240	60,200	3,308	21,068	90	492
Transportation	57,668	461,903	57,311	459,297	9,416	68,330	357	2,606
Energy	15,140	99,380	15,129	99,295	5,066	37,152	11	85
Education	4,448	27,600	4,440	27,564	3,147	20,156	8	36
Veterans Affairs	232,818	1,157,519	229,276	1,143,807	7,081	44,388	3,542	13,712
Homeland Security	149,059	629,661	145,336	613,030	17,265	99,342	3,723	16,631
Independent Agencies	956,324	3,860,613	949,635	3,828,337	68,068	393,336	6,689	32,276
Bd of Gov, Fed Rsrv Sys	1,809	14,357	1,809	14,357	1,809	14,357	—	—
Environmtl Protect Agcy	17,762	110,509	17,710	110,210	6,008	39,847	52	299
Equal Employ Opp Comm	2,505	13,985	2,495	13,944	611	3,893	10	41
Federal Communic Comm	2,018	14,015	2,016	13,999	1,696	12,093	2	16
Federal Deposit Ins Corp	5,401	39,739	5,390	39,676	1,855	15,137	11	63
Federal Trade Comm	1,080	7,401	1,080	7,401	930	6,320	—	—
General Svcs Admin	12,710	71,394	12,642	71,071	4,576	27,660	68	323
Natl Aero & Space Admin	19,066	125,230	19,048	125,101	4,297	29,152	18	129
Natl Fnd Arts & Humanities	368	2,312	368	2,312	368	2,312	—	—
Nuclear Regulatory Comm	3,094	22,268	3,093	22,256	2,150	15,948	1	12
Peace Corps	1,109	5,174	700	3,492	562	2,968	409	1,682
Securities & Exch. Comm	3,579	29,639	3,579	29,639	2,061	16,845	—	—
Small Business Adm.	3,306	18,329	3,251	18,093	843	5,460	55	236
Smithsonian Inst.	5,001	21,828	4,977	21,628	4,565	19,656	24	200
Social Security Admin	64,794	292,763	64,333	290,926	1,671	8,680	461	1,837
Tennessee Valley Authority	13,178	89,377	13,178	89,377	6	47	—	—
U.S. Postal Service	773,695	2,836,334	769,927	2,820,886	19,140	82,136	3,768	15,448

NOTE: *Denotes figures that are preliminary or are based in whole or in part on figures for the previous month. (1) Totals include agencies not listed. (2) Metropolitan Statistical Area.

Fatal Occupational Injuries, 2003

Source: Bureau of Labor Statistics, U.S. Dept. of Labor

	FATALITIES			FATALITIES	
	Number	Percent		Number	Percent
TRANSPORTATION INCIDENTS	**2,357**	**42**	Caught in or compressed by equipment or		
Highway	1,350	24	objects	237	4
Collision between vehicles, mobile			Caught in running equipment or machinery	121	2
equipment	648	12	Caught in or crushed in collapsing		
Vehicle struck stationary object or equipment	341	7	materials	126	2
Worker struck by a vehicle	336	6	**FALLS**	**691**	**12**
Rail vehicle	43	1			
Water vehicle	68	1	**EXPOSURE TO HARMFUL SUBSTANCE**		
Aircraft	208	4	**OR ENVIRONMENTS**	**485**	**9**
ASSAULTS AND VIOLENT ACTS	**901**	**16**	Contact with electric current	246	4
Homicides	631	11	Contact with overhead powerlines	107	2
Shooting	487	9	Contact with temperature extremes	42	1
Stabbing	58	1	Exposure to caustic, noxious, or allergenic		
Self-inflicted injuries	218	4	substances	121	2
			Inhalation of substance	65	1
CONTACT WITH OBJECTS AND			Oxygen deficiency	73	1
EQUIPMENT	**911**	**16**	Drowning, submersion	52	1
Struck by object	530	10	**FIRES AND EXPLOSIONS**	**198**	**4**
Struck by falling object	322	6			
Struck by flying object	58	1	**TOTAL**	**5,559**	**100**

NOTE: Totals for categories may include subcategories not shown separately. Percentages based on incidence rate per total fatalities.

U.S. Occupational Illnesses, by Industry and Type of Illness, 2002

Source: Bureau of Labor Statistics, U.S. Dept. of Labor

(percent distribution)

	All private sector[1]	GOODS PRODUCING				SERVICE PRODUCING				
		Agri-culture[2]	Mining[3]	Con-struc-tion	Manu-facturing	Trans. pub. utilities[4]	Whole-sale	Retail	Finance[5]	Service
Total [1,436,194 cases]	100.0	100.0	100.0	100.0	100.0	100.0	100.0	100.0	100.0	100.0
Nature of injury or illness:										
Sprains, strains	43.0	33.4	40.0	36.8	37.7	48.6	47.2	41.2	36.3	48.7
Bruises, contusions	8.8	7.6	10.7	6.9	8.4	9.3	9.4	10.4	7.6	8.7
Cuts, lacerations	7.7	9.1	6.2	10.8	9.0	3.9	7.0	11.7	5.4	4.5
Fractures	6.9	9.1	16.1	10.6	7.0	6.2	7.1	6.3	8.1	5.4
Heat burns	1.5	0.4	1.2	1.0	1.7	0.4	0.6	3.1	0.6	1.3
Carpal tunnel syndrome	1.6	0.7	0.2	0.6	3.2	1.1	1.1	1.1	5.2	1.2
Tendonitis	0.6	1.1	—	0.5	1.1	0.5	0.5	0.5	1.3	0.6
Chemical burns	0.6	1.0	1.3	0.4	0.9	0.4	0.4	0.5	0.4	0.6
Amputations	0.6	1.2	1.7	0.6	1.5	0.5	0.6	0.3	0.2	0.2
Multiple traumatic injuries	3.7	4.7	4.4	4.0	3.7	4.2	4.0	2.8	3.9	3.6
Part of body affected by the injury or illness:										
Head	6.3	8.8	6.0	6.9	7.3	5.5	5.6	6.2	4.4	5.9
Eye	2.9	4.9	2.4	3.8	4.4	2.1	2.3	2.6	1.3	2.3
Neck	1.6	1.6	2.1	1.3	1.3	1.9	2.2	1.4	1.2	1.7
Trunk	36.3	31.8	35.8	33.2	33.8	39.8	38.8	35.6	30.3	38.9
Shoulder	5.8	5.5	5.1	4.8	6.6	7.4	5.9	5.1	4.1	5.8
Back	24.0	19.8	21.8	21.2	19.9	25.3	26.0	24.3	20.9	27.8
Upper extremities	22.9	22.8	22.0	24.4	31.6	16.2	19.4	25.1	23.6	18.0
Wrist	4.8	3.4	4.1	3.6	6.8	3.8	3.7	4.6	8.9	4.6
Hand, except finger	3.9	4.9	2.9	4.7	5.2	2.9	3.3	4.3	3.0	2.9
Finger	8.5	8.4	11.1	10.2	13.1	4.7	7.6	10.2	5.8	5.1
Lower extremities	21.2	22.2	24.4	24.1	17.6	23.6	23.1	21.1	22.0	20.7
Knee	7.9	7.0	9.0	9.1	6.7	8.7	7.6	7.1	8.1	8.4
Foot, except toe	3.2	3.4	3.5	3.8	2.9	3.6	4.0	3.6	3.1	2.5
Toe	1.0	0.9	0.4	1.3	1.0	0.8	1.1	1.5	0.9	0.7
Body systems	1.4	2.2	0.8	0.8	1.1	1.2	0.7	1.1	4.6	2.0
Multiple parts	9.7	8.8	8.9	8.4	6.6	11.2	9.5	8.9	13.7	12.2
Source of injury or illness:										
Chemicals and chemical products	1.4	2.5	7.3	0.8	2.0	0.9	1.0	1.3	1.4	1.6
Containers	13.4	8.7	5.2	5.3	12.5	18.1	22.9	22.6	9.0	7.5
Furniture and fixtures	3.6	0.9	0.3	1.7	2.7	2.0	2.7	5.7	5.5	4.9
Machinery	6.4	6.1	12.5	6.2	12.2	2.3	6.2	6.6	4.9	4.0
Parts and materials	10.3	6.9	20.4	22.9	17.5	8.7	11.4	5.8	4.6	3.3
Worker motion or position	15.4	13.9	5.1	12.6	19.3	16.0	13.2	13.5	22.9	15.0
Floors, walkways, ground surfaces	17.8	17.0	16.9	20.5	11.4	17.8	16.0	19.5	24.7	20.1
Tools, instruments, and equipment	6.5	7.8	7.8	11.1	6.9	4.6	4.5	7.0	5.5	5.2
Vehicles	8.3	10.0	5.3	6.0	4.9	18.5	14.2	6.3	7.7	6.8
Health care patient	4.9	—	—	—	—	0.8	0.1	—	0.6	18.3

Event or exposure leading to injury or illness:	All private sector[1]	GOODS PRODUCING Agri-culture[2]	Mining[3]	Con-struc-tion	Manu-facturing	SERVICE PRODUCING Trans. pub. utilities[4]	Whole-sale	Retail	Finance[5]	Service
Contact with objects and equipment . . .	26.5	30.2	42.2	35.1	34.1	21.2	27.0	28.3	17.3	18.1
Struck by object	13.3	16.4	24.6	19.7	14.7	10.2	13.4	15.8	8.3	9.1
Struck against object	7.0	6.2	7.3	7.5	7.4	6.7	7.0	7.8	7.0	5.9
Caught in equipment or object	4.4	5.6	9.4	4.2	9.3	2.5	5.0	3.3	1.3	2.1
Fall to lower level	6.1	7.7	7.8	13.7	3.6	7.8	6.2	4.5	7.5	4.5
Fall on same level	12.3	9.1	8.8	7.5	8.5	10.3	10.0	16.1	17.1	15.8
Slip, trip, loss of balance—without fall . .	3.4	2.4	1.6	2.9	2.8	3.8	2.9	3.8	3.6	3.7
Overexertion	26.5	15.9	27.0	20.7	24.6	27.4	29.9	26.4	19.8	30.8
Overexertion in lifting	14.5	8.7	10.0	10.9	12.7	13.8	18.2	17.4	11.5	15.5
Repetitive motion	4.1	2.2	0.4	1.8	8.4	3.0	2.4	3.2	9.7	3.2
Exposure to harmful substances	4.2	6.1	3.9	2.6	5.0	2.9	2.2	4.9	3.7	4.8
Transportation accidents	4.4	5.7	2.2	4.1	2.1	9.6	8.0	2.5	5.6	4.0
Fires and explosions	0.2	0.2	0.5	0.3	0.2	0.1	0.2	0.3	—	0.1
Assaults and violent acts by person . . .	1.3	0.2		0.1	0.1	0.4	0.3	0.9	1.0	3.7

NOTE: Dashes (—) indicate data are not available or do not meet publication guidelines. Because of rounding and classifications not shown, percentages may not add to 100. All injuries and illnesses reported involved days away from work. (1) Private sector includes all industries except government, but excludes farms with fewer than 11 employees. (2) Agriculture includes forestry and fishing, but excludes farms with fewer than 11 employees. (3) Data conforming to OSHA definitions for mining operators in coal, metal, and nonmetal mining are provided by the Mine Safety and Health Administration, U.S. Dept. of Labor. Independent mining contractors are excluded from the coal, metal, and nonmetal industries. Data for mining include establishments not governed by Mine Safety and Health Administration rules, such as those in oil and gas extraction. (4) Data for employers in railroad transportation are provided by the Federal Railroad Administration, U.S. Department of Transportation. (5) Finance includes insurance and real estate.

Hourly Compensation Costs[1], by Selected Country, 1975-2002

Source: Bureau of Labor Statistics, U.S. Dept. of Labor

(in U.S. dollars, compensation for production workers in manufacturing)

Country/Territory	1975	1985	1995	2002	Country/Territory	1975	1985	1995	2002
Australia	5.62	8.21	15.56	15.44	South Korea	0.32	1.23	7.29	9.04
Austria	4.51	7.58	25.32	20.83	Luxembourg	6.24	7.50	23.43	18.77
Belgium	6.41	8.97	27.62	22.79	Mexico	1.47	1.59	1.46	2.61
Brazil	—	—	—	2.58	New Zealand	3.09	4.30	9.79	8.65
Denmark	6.28	8.13	24.98	25.16	Norway	6.77	10.37	24.38	27.11
Finland	4.66	8.25	24.32	21.79	Portugal	1.54	1.49	5.17	5.12
France	4.52	7.52	19.38	17.27	Singapore	0.84	2.47	7.31	7.26
Germany[2]	6.29	9.50	30.25	24.31	Spain	2.53	4.66	12.80	12.02
Greece	1.69	3.66	8.95	—	Sri Lanka	0.28	0.28	0.48	0.49
Hong Kong SA[3]	0.76	1.74	4.91	5.85	Sweden	7.18	9.66	21.44	20.27
Ireland	3.07	6.00	13.78	15.54	Switzerland	6.09	9.66	29.31	24.11
Israel	2.03	3.65	9.48	10.85	Taiwan	0.38	1.50	5.91	5.81
Italy	4.67	7.63	16.04	15.07	United Kingdom	3.37	6.27	13.88	18.03
Japan	3.00	6.34	23.19	19.02	United States	6.36	13.01	17.19	21.37

— Data not available. (1) Compensation includes all direct pay (including bonuses, etc.), paid benefits, and for some countries, labor taxes. (2) 1975 and 1985 data are for area covered by the former West Germany. 1995 and 2002 are unified Germany. (3) Is now part of China.

Federal Minimum Hourly Wage Rates Since 1950

Source: Bureau of Labor Statistics, U.S. Dept. of Labor

The Fair Labor Standards Act of 1938 and subsequent amendments provide for minimum wage-coverage applicable to nonprofessional workers in specified nonsupervisory employment categories.

EFFECTIVE DATE	NONFARM WORKERS Under laws prior to 1966[1]	Percent of avg. earnings[2]	Under 1966 and later provis.[3]	FARM WORKERS[4]	EFFECTIVE DATE	NONFARM WORKERS Under laws prior to 1966[1]	Percent of avg. earnings[2]	Under 1966 and later provis.[3]	FARM WORKERS[4]
Jan. 25, 1950 . . .	$0.75	54	NA	NA	Jan. 1, 1976	$2.30	46	$2.20	$2.00
Mar. 1, 1956	1.00	52	NA	NA	Jan. 1, 1977	(5)	(5)	2.30	2.20
Sept. 3, 1961 . . .	1.15	50	NA	NA	Jan. 1, 1978	2.65	44	2.65	2.65
Sept. 3, 1963 . . .	1.25	51	NA	NA	Jan. 1, 1979	2.90	45	2.90	2.90
Feb. 1, 1967	1.40	50	$1.00	$1.00	Jan. 1, 1980	3.10	43	3.10	3.10
Feb. 1, 1968	1.60	54	1.15	1.15	Jan. 1, 1981	3.35	42	3.35	3.35
Feb. 1, 1969	(5)	(5)	1.30	1.30	Apr. 1, 1990	3.80[6]	35	3.80	3.80[6]
Feb. 1, 1970	(5)	(5)	1.45	(5)	Apr. 1, 1991	4.25[6]	38	4.25	4.25[6]
Feb. 1, 1971	(5)	(5)	1.60	(5)	Oct. 1, 1996	4.75[7]	37	4.75	4.75[7]
May 1, 1974	2.00	46	1.90	1.60	Sept. 1, 1997 . . .	5.15[7]	39	5.15	5.15[7]
Jan. 1, 1975	2.10	45	2.00	1.80					

NA = not applicable. (1) Applies to workers covered prior to 1961 Amendments and, after Sept. 1965, to workers covered by 1961 Amendments. Rates set by 1961 Amendments were: Sept. 1961, $1.00; Sept. 1964, $1.15; and Sept. 1965, $1.25. (2) Percent of gross average hourly earnings of production workers in manufacturing. (3) Applies to workers newly covered by Amendments of 1966, 1974, and 1977, and Title IX of Education Amendments of 1972. (4) Included in coverage as of 1966, 1974, and 1977 Amendments. (5) No change in rate. (6) Training wage for workers age 16-19 in first 6 months of first job: Apr. 1, 1990, $3.35; Apr. 1, 1991, $3.62. The training wage expired Mar. 31, 1993. (7) Under 1996 legislation, a subminimum training wage of $4.25 an hour was established for employees under 20 years of age during their first 90 consecutive calendar days of employment with an employer. For workers receiving gratuities, the minimum wage remained $2.13 per hour.

U.S Median Weekly Earnings, 2nd Quarter 2004*

Source: Bureau of Labor Statistics, U.S. Dept. of Labor

Age, Race, Hispanic or Latino ethnicity	Total		Men		Women	
	Number of workers (in thousands)	Median weekly earnings	Number of workers (in thousands)	Median weekly earnings	Number of workers (in thousands)	Median weekly earnings
ALL WORKERS, BY AGE						
16 years and over........................	101,300	$639	57,034	$714	44,266	$572
16 to 24 years	10,963	387	6,272	397	4,691	370
16 to 19 years	1,637	313	991	324	646	296
20 to 24 years	9,325	401	5,281	409	4,045	386
25 years and over........................	90,337	684	50,763	763	39,575	601
25 to 54 years	76,648	679	43,303	754	33,345	599
25 to 34 years	24,863	595	14,459	627	10,404	553
35 to 44 years........................	26,826	722	15,395	814	11,431	613
45 to 54 years........................	24,959	741	13,449	849	11,510	628
55 years and over........................	13,690	714	7,460	832	6,230	611
55 to 64 years........................	11,844	733	6,443	854	5,401	628
65 years and over........................	1,846	592	1,017	664	828	473
WHITE[1]						
16 years and over........................	82,756	655	47,688	729	35,067	583
16 to 24 years	9,177	391	5,344	398	3,833	379
25 years and over........................	73,579	703	42,344	781	31,234	612
25 to 54 years........................	61,980	698	35,917	769	26,063	611
55 years and over........................	11,599	729	6,427	862	5,171	618
BLACK OR AFRICAN AMERICAN[1]						
16 years and over........................	12,014	536	5,669	598	6,344	504
16 to 24 years	1,202	346	606	381	596	328
25 years and over........................	10,812	577	5,063	626	5,748	520
25 to 54 years........................	9,494	576	4,468	627	5,026	521
55 years and over........................	1,318	585	596	618	722	514
ASIAN[1]						
16 years and over........................	4,328	720	2,404	807	1,924	653
16 to 24 years	264	404	127	405	137	402
25 years and over........................	4,064	755	2,276	840	1,788	667
25 to 54 years	3,524	749	1,971	840	1,552	664
55 years and over........................	540	794	305	838	235	739
HISPANIC AND LATINO[2]						
16 years and over........................	14,324	451	9,163	477	5,160	414
16 to 24 years	2,233	346	1,439	353	794	330
25 years and over........................	12,091	484	7,724	502	4,367	439
25 to 54 years	10,951	481	7,063	499	3,888	436
55 years and over........................	1,139	508	661	558	478	472
Occupation						
Managerial, professional, and related occupations	36,217	$912	17,976	$1,073	18,241	$782
Management, business, and financial operations occupations...........................	14,828	952	8,183	1,134	6,645	810
Professional and related occupations........	21,389	882	9,793	1,046	11,596	768
Service occupations......................	13,847	409	7,012	474	6,835	369
Sales and office occupations	24,846	557	9,435	664	15,411	509
Sales and related occupations	9,899	616	5,601	753	4,298	465
Office and administrative support occupations..	14,947	525	3,835	585	11,112	516
Natural resources, construction, and maintenance occupations...........................	11,157	618	10,669	623	488	476
Farming, fishing, and forestry occupations.....	768	367	632	382	136	330
Construction and extraction occupations	6,090	595	5,963	596	127	509
Installation, maintenance, and repair occupations...........................	4,299	707	4,073	711	225	588
Production, transportation, and material moving occupations...........................	15,233	523	11,942	577	3,291	405
Production occupations	8,496	520	6,072	590	2,424	407
Transportation and material moving occupations	6,737	528	5,871	561	867	402

*Not seasonally adjusted; figures are for median usual weekly earnings of full-time wage and salary workers. (1) Persons who selected this race group only; persons who selected more than one race group are not included. (2) May be of any race.

Top-Paying U.S. Metropolitan Areas, by Average Annual Salary, 2002

Source: Bureau of Labor Statistics, U.S. Dept. of Labor

Rank	Metropolitan area	Average annual salary[1]	Rank	Metropolitan area	Average annual salary[1]
1.	San Jose, CA	$63,056	9.	Trenton, NJ........................	$47,969
2.	New York, NY	57,708	10.	Oakland, CA.......................	46,877
3.	San Francisco, CA	56,602	11.	Seattle–Bellevue–Everett, WA..........	46,093
4.	New Haven–Bridgeport–Stamford–Waterbury–Danbury, CT	51,170	12.	Boston–Worcester–Lawrence–Lowell–Brockton, MA–NH.................	45,685
5.	Middlesex–Somerset–Hunterdon, NJ	50,457	13.	Bergen–Passaic, NJ.................	45,185
6.	Jersey City, NJ	49,562	14.	Hartford, CT	44,387
7.	Newark, NJ	48,781	15.	Boulder–Longmont, CO	44,037
8.	Washington, DC–MD–VA–WV	48,430			

NOTE: Jacksonville, NC, recorded the **lowest average annual pay** among U.S. metropolitan areas in 2002—$22,269—followed by Brownsville–Harlingen–San Benito, TX ($22,892), McAllen–Edinburg–Mission, TX ($23,179), Yuma, AZ ($23,429), and Myrtle Beach, SC ($24,672). The nationwide metropolitan average was $38,423. (1) Data are preliminary and include workers covered by Unemployment Insurance and Unemployment Compensation for Federal Employees programs.

Average Hours and Earnings of U.S. Production Workers, 1969-2003[1]

Source: Bureau of Labor Statistics, U.S. Dept. of Labor
(annual averages)

	Weekly hours	Hourly earnings	Weekly earnings		Weekly hours	Hourly earnings	Weekly earnings		Weekly hours	Hourly earnings	Weekly earnings
1969...	37.5	$3.22	$120.75	1981...	35.2	7.43	261.54	1993 ...	34.3	$11.03	$378.40
1970...	37.0	3.40	125.80	1982...	34.7	7.86	272.74	1994 ...	34.5	11.32	390.73
1971...	36.8	3.63	133.58	1983...	34.9	8.19	285.83	1995 ...	34.3	11.64	399.53
1972...	36.9	3.90	143.91	1984...	35.1	8.48	297.65	1996 ...	34.3	12.03	412.74
1973...	36.9	4.14	152.77	1985...	34.9	8.73	304.68	1997 ...	34.5	12.49	431.25
1974...	36.4	4.43	161.25	1986...	34.7	8.92	309.52	1998 ...	34.5	13.00	448.04
1975...	36.0	4.73	170.28	1987...	34.7	9.13	316.81	1999 ...	34.3	13.47	462.49
1976...	36.1	5.06	182.67	1988...	34.6	9.43	326.28	2000 ...	34.3	14.00	480.41
1977...	35.9	5.44	195.30	1989...	34.5	9.80	338.10	2001 ...	34.0	14.53	493.20
1978...	35.8	5.87	210.15	1990...	34.3	10.19	349.29	2002 ...	33.9	14.95	506.07
1979...	35.6	6.33	225.35	1991...	34.1	10.50	358.06	2003 ...	33.7	15.35	517.36
1980...	35.2	6.84	240.77	1992...	34.2	10.76	367.83				

(1) Data refer to production workers in natural resources, mining and manufacturing, construction workers, and non-supervisory workers in the service industries. Figures may be revised.

Work Stoppages (Strikes and Lockouts) in the U.S., 1960-2003

Source: Bureau of Labor Statistics, U.S. Dept. of Labor; involving 1,000 workers or more

Year	Number of stoppages[1]	Workers involved[1] (thousands)	Work days idle[1] (thousands)	Year	Number of stoppages[1]	Workers involved[1] (thousands)	Work days idle[1] (thousands)
1960....	222	896	13,260	1986 ...	69	533	11,861
1965....	268	999	15,140	1987 ...	46	174	4,481
1970....	381	2,468	52,761	1988 ...	40	118	4,381
1971....	298	2,516	35,538	1989 ...	51	452	16,996
1972....	250	975	16,764	1990 ...	44	185	5,926
1973....	317	1,400	16,260	1991 ...	40	392	4,584
1974....	424	1,796	31,809	1992 ...	35	364	3,989
1975....	235	965	17,563	1993 ...	35	182	3,981
1976....	231	1,519	23,962	1994 ...	45	322	5,020
1977....	298	1,212	21,258	1995 ...	31	192	5,771
1978....	219	1,006	23,774	1996 ...	37	273	4,889
1979....	235	1,021	20,409	1997 ...	29	339	4,497
1980....	187	795	20,844	1998 ...	34	387	5,116
1981....	145	729	16,908	1999 ...	17	73	1,996
1982....	96	656	9,061	2000 ...	39	394	20,419
1983....	81	909	17,461	2001 ...	29	99	1,151
1984....	62	376	8,499	2002 ...	19	46	660
1985....	54	324	7,079	2003 ...	14	129	4,091

(1) Numbers cover stoppages that began in the year indicated. Workers are counted more than once if they are involved in more than 1 stoppage during the year. For work stoppages still open at the end of a calendar year, days idle include only the days for the calendar year.

Work Stoppages Involving 5,000 Workers or More Beginning in 2003

The numbers of workers idled and days of idleness because of strikes and lockouts in the U.S. rose in 2003, but were still low by historical standards. The number of stoppages declined. There were 14 major work stoppages beginning in 2003, idling 129,200 workers and resulting in 4.1 million workdays lost. There were only 5 stoppages in which more than 5,000 workers participated. The largest by far involved the United Food and Commercial Workers (UFCW) and Albertsons, Ralphs Grocery Company, and Vons, which lasted from Oct. 12, 2003, to Feb. 28, 2004. That stoppage involved more than 67,000 workers and accounted for 3,374,200 workdays lost in 2003 alone.

U.S. Union Membership, 1930-2003

Source: Bureau of Labor Statistics, U.S. Dept. of Labor

Year	Labor force[1] (thousands)	Union members[2] (thousands)	Percentage of labor force	Year	Labor force[1] (thousands)	Union members[2] (thousands)	Percentage of labor force
1930....	29,424	3,401	11.6	1989	103,480	16,960	16.4
1935....	27,053	3,584	13.2	1990	103,905	16,740	16.1
1940....	32,376	8,717	26.9	1991	102,786	16,568	16.1
1945....	40,394	14,322	35.5	1992	103,688	16,390	15.8
1950....	45,222	14,267	31.5	1993	105,067	16,598	15.8
1955....	50,675	16,802	33.2	1994	107,989	16,748	15.5
1960....	54,234	17,049	31.4	1995	110,038	16,360	14.9
1965....	60,815	17,299	28.4	1996	111,960	16,269	14.5
1970....	70,920	19,381	27.3	1997	114,533	16,110	14.1
1975....	76,945	19,611	25.5	1998	116,730	16,211	13.9
1980....	90,564	19,843	21.9	1999	118,963	16,477	13.9
1985....	94,521	16,996	18.0	2000	120,786	16,258	13.5
1986....	96,903	16,975	17.5	2001	122,482	16,387	13.4
1987....	99,303	16,913	17.0	2002[3]....	121,826	16,145	13.3
1988....	101,407	17,002	16.8	2003[4]....	122,358	15,776	12.9

(1) Does not include agricultural employment; from 1985, does not include self-employed or unemployed persons. (2) From 1930 to 1980, includes dues-paying members of traditional trade unions, regardless of employment status; after that includes employed only. From 1985, includes members of employee associations that engage in collective bargaining with employers. (3) Revised to incorporate changes to the class of worker status associated with the introduction of the 2002 Census industry and occupational classification systems into the Current Population Survey. (4) Data reflect revised population controls used in the household survey.

Union Affiliation and Median Weekly Earnings of Wage and Salary Workers in the U.S., 1996, 2003

Source: Bureau of Labor Statistics, U.S. Dept. of Labor

SEX AND AGE	1996				2003			
	TOTAL	Members of unions[1]	Represented by unions[2]	Non-union	TOTAL	Members of unions[1]	Represented by unions[2]	Non-union
Total, 16 years and older . . .	$490	$615	$610	$462	$620	$760	$755	$599
16 to 24 years	298	371	362	294	387	497	494	381
25 years and older	520	625	621	498	662	774	770	636
25 to 34 years	463	554	548	447	594	707	701	580
35 to 44 years	559	636	632	530	687	787	783	665
45 to 54 years	594	687	686	552	723	812	807	695
55 to 64 years	535	620	616	505	708	797	798	678
65 years and older	384	510	510	367	516	619	624	504
Men, 16 years and older . . .	557	653	651	520	695	805	802	667
16 to 24 years	307	375	369	303	398	498	493	392
25 years and older	599	669	668	580	744	821	821	724
25 to 34 years	499	591	587	485	628	737	732	613
35 to 44 years	632	683	683	617	775	841	839	759
45 to 54 years	698	718	721	682	834	865	865	822
55 to 64 years	643	667	664	633	827	834	842	821
65 years and older	477	589	593	424	612	713	720	603
Women, 16 years and older	418	549	543	398	552	696	691	523
16 to 24 years	284	358	339	280	371	495	494	366
25 years and older	444	560	555	420	584	709	704	562
25 to 34 years	415	497	495	405	546	661	657	525
35 to 44 years	463	561	556	439	590	706	703	574
45 to 54 years	481	620	616	445	609	736	731	589
55 to 64 years	420	524	523	395	601	748	743	576
65 years and older	334	417	413	321	435	517	531	422

Note: Data refer to the sole or principal job of full-time workers. Excluded are self-employed workers regardless of whether or not their businesses are incorporated. (1) Including members of an employee association similar to a union. (2) Including members of a labor union or employee association similar to a union, and others whose jobs are covered by a union or an employee-association contract.

Labor Union Directory

Source: Bureau of Labor Statistics, U.S. Dept. of Labor; AFL-CIO; World Almanac research.

(*) Independent union; all others affiliated with AFL-CIO.

Actors and Artistes of America, Associated (AAAA), 165 W. 46th St., Suite 500, New York, NY 10036; founded 1919; Theodore Bikel, Pres.; no individual members, 8 National Performing Arts Unions are affiliates; approx. 100,000 combined membership.

Actors' Equity Association, 165 W. 46th St., New York, NY 10036; founded 1913; Patrick Quinn, Pres. (since 2000); 40,000 active members; www.actorsequity.org

Air Line Pilots Association, 535 Herndon Pkwy., Herndon, VA 20170; founded 1931; Capt. Duane Woerth, Pres. (since 1999); 64,000+ members, 42 airlines; www.alpa.org

American Federation of Labor & Congress of Industrial Organizations (AFL-CIO), 815 16th St. NW, Washington, DC 20006; founded 1955; John J. Sweeney, Pres. (since 1995); 13 mil. members; www.aflcio.org

Automobile, Aerospace & Agricultural Implement Workers of America, International Union, United (UAW), 8000 E Jefferson Ave., Detroit, MI 48214; founded 1935; Ron Gettelfinger, Pres. (since 2002); 710,000 active (500,000 ret.) members, 950+ locals; www.uaw.org

Bakery, Confectionery, Tobacco Workers and Grain Millers International Union (BCTGM), 10401 Connecticut Ave., Kensington, MD 20895; founded 1886; Frank Hurt, Pres. (since 1992); 120,000 members; www.bctgm.org

Boilermakers, Iron Ship Builders, Blacksmiths, Forgers and Helpers, International Brotherhood of (IBBISB/BF&H), 753 State Ave., Suite 565, Kansas City, KS 66101; founded 1880; Newton B. Jones, Int'l Pres. (since 2003); 100,000+ members, 420 locals; www.boilermakers.org

Bricklayers and Allied Craftworkers, International Union of (BAC), 1776 Eye St. NW, Washington, DC 20006; founded 1865; John J. Flynn, Pres. (since 1999); 100,000 members, 200 locals; www.bacweb.org

***Carpenters and Joiners of America, United Brotherhood of,** 101 Constitution Ave., NW, Washington, DC 20001; founded 1881; Douglas J. McCarron, Pres. (since 1995); 520,000 members, 1,000 locals; www.carpenters.org

Communications Workers of America (IUE-CWA), 501 3rd St. NW, Washington, DC 20001; founded 1938; Morton Bahr, Pres. (since 1985); 700,000+ members, 1,200 locals. (Merged with the Intl. Union of Electronic, Electrical, Salaried, Machine, and Furniture Workers 10/1/00.); www.cwaunion.org

***Education Association, National,** 1201 16th St. NW, Washington, DC 20036; founded 1857; Reg Weaver, Pres. (since 2002); 2.7 mil. members, 14,000+ affiliates; www.nea.org

Electrical Workers, International Brotherhood of (IBEW), 1125 15th St. NW, Washington, DC 20005; founded 1891; Edwin D. Hill, Pres. (since 2001); 750,000 members, 1,019 locals; www.ibew.org

Engineers, International Union of Operating (IUOE), 1125 17th St. NW, Washington, DC 20036; founded 1896; Frank Hanley, Pres. (since 1990); 400,000 members, 170 locals; www.iuoe.org

Farm Workers of America, United (UFW), 29700 Woodford-Tehachapi Rd., PO Box 62, Keene, CA 93531; founded 1962; Arturo S. Rodríguez, Pres. (since 1993); 27,000+ members; www.ufw.org

***Federal Employees, Federal District 1, National Federation of (NFFE FD1, IAMAW, AFL-CIO),** 1016 16th St. NW, Washington, DC 20036; founded 1917; Richard N. Brown, Pres. (since 1998); 70,000 members, 200 locals; www.nffe.org

Fire Fighters, International Association of, 1750 New York Ave. NW, Washington, DC 20006; founded 1918; Harold Schaitberger, Pres. (since 2000); 263,000 members, 2,900 locals; www.iaff.org

Firemen and Oilers, National Conference of, 1023 15th St. NW, 10th Floor, Washington, DC 20035; founded 1898; George J. Francisco, Jr., Pres.; 26,000 members, 133 locals; www.ncfo.org

Flight Attendants, Association of, 501 3rd St. NW, Washington, DC 20001; founded 1945; Patricia A. Friend, Int'l Pres.; 46,000 members, 26 carriers; www.afanet.org

Food and Commercial Workers International Union, United (UFCW), 1775 K St. NW, Washington, DC 20006-1598; founded 1979 following merger; Joseph T. Hansen, Intl. Pres. (since 2004); 1.4 mil. members, 997 locals; www.ufcw.org

Glass, Molders, Pottery, Plastics & Allied Workers Intl. Union (GMP), 608 E Baltimore Pike, PO Box 607, Media, PA 19063; founded 1842; John P. Ryan, Pres.; 51,000 members, 290+ locals; www.gmpiu.org

Government Employees, American Federation of (AFGE), 80 F St. NW, Washington, DC 20001; founded 1932; John Gage, Pres. (since 2003); 600,000 members, 1,100 locals; www.afge.org

Graphic Communications International Union (GCIU), 1900 L St. NW, Washington, DC 20036; founded 1983; George Tedeschi, Pres. (since 2003); 150,000 members, 321 locals; www.gciu.org

Iron Workers, International Association of Bridge, Structural, Ornamental and Reinforcing, 1750 New York Ave. NW, Suite 400, Washington, DC 20006; founded 1896; Joseph Hunt, Gen. Pres. (since 2001); 127,000 members, 225 locals; www.ironworkers.org

Laborers' International Union of North America (LIUNA), 905 16th St. NW, Washington, DC 20006-1765; founded 1903; Terence M. O'Sullivan, Pres. (since 2000); 800,000 members, 500 locals; www.liuna.org

Letter Carriers, National Association of (NALC), 100 Indiana Ave. NW, Washington, DC 20001-2144; founded 1889; William H. Young, Pres. (since 2002); 301,000+ members, 2,600+ locals; www.nalc.org

Locomotive Engineers and Trainmen, Brotherhood of (BLET), 1370 Ontario St., Cleveland, OH 44113; founded 1863; Don M. Hahs, Pres. (since 2001); 59,000 members, 600+ divisions; www.ble.org

Longshore & Warehouse Union, International (ILWU), 1188 Franklin St., San Francisco, CA 94109-6800; founded 1937; James Spinosa, Pres. (since 2000); 42,000 members, 60+ locals; www.ilwu.org

Longshoremen's Association, International (ILA), 17 Battery Pl., Suite 930, New York, NY 10004; founded 1892; John M. Bowers, Pres. (since 1987); 65,000 members; www.ilaunion.org

Machinists and Aerospace Workers, International Association of (IAMAW), 9000 Machinists Pl., Upper Marlboro, MD 20772; founded 1888; R. Thomas Buffenbarger, Pres. (since 1997); 614,000 members, 1,174 locals; www.iamaw.org

Maintenance of Way Employees, Brotherhood of (BMWE), 26555 Evergreen Rd., Suite 200, Southfield, MI 48076; founded 1887; Freddie N. Simpson, Acting Pres. (since 2004); 45,000 members, 770 locals; www.bmwe.org

Marine Engineers' Beneficial Assn. (MEBA), 444 N. Capitol St. NW, Suite 800, Washington, DC 20001; founded 1875; Ron Davis, Pres. (since 2002); www.d1meba.org

Mine Workers of America, United (UMWA), 8315 Lee Highway, Fairfax, VA 22031; founded 1890; Cecil E. Roberts, Pres. (since 1995); 110,000 members, 600 locals; www.umwa.org

Musicians of the United States and Canada, American Federation of (AFM), 1501 Broadway, Suite 600, New York, NY 10036; founded 1896; Thomas F. Lee, Pres. (since 2001); 125,000 members, 250+ locals; www.afm.org

Newspaper Guild-Communications Workers of America (CWA), The, 501 3rd St. NW, Suite 250, Washington, DC 20001; founded 1933; Linda K. Foley, Pres. (since 1995); 34,000 members, 90 locals; www.newsguild.org

***Nurses Association, American (ANA),** 8515 Georgia Ave., Silver Spring, MD 20910; founded 1897; Barbara Blakeney, Pres.; 2.6 mil. members, 54 constituent state & territorial assns; www.nursingworld.org

Office and Professional Employees International Union (OPEIU), 265 W 14th St., Suite 610, New York, NY 10011; founded 1945 (AFL Charter); Michael Goodwin, Pres. (since 1994); 145,000 members, 200 locals; www.opeiu.org

PACE International Union, AFL-CIO, CLC (PACE), PO Box 1475, Nashville, TN 37202; founded 1884; Boyd D. Young, Pres. (since 1999); 320,000 members, 1,500 locals; www.paceunion.org

Painters and Allied Trades, International Union of (IUPAT), 1750 New York Ave. NW, Washington, DC 20006; founded 1887; James A. Williams, Gen. Pres.; 140,000 members, 425 locals; www.ibpat.org

Plasterers' and Cement Masons' International Association of the United States and Canada, Operative, 14405 Laurel Pl., Suite 300, Laurel, MD 20707; founded 1864; John J. Dougherty, Pres. (since 1996); 40,000 members, 100 locals; www.opcmia.org

Plumbing and Pipe Fitting Industry of the United States and Canada, United Association of Journeymen and Apprentices of the, 901 Massachusetts Ave. NW, PO Box 37800, Washington, DC 20013; founded 1889; Martin J. Maddaloni, Gen. Pres. (since 1997); 326,000 members, 321 locals; www.ua.org

***Police, National Fraternal Order of,** 1410 Donelson Pike, A-17, Nashville, TN 37217; Chuck Canterbury, Natl. Pres. (since 2003); 314,000 members, 2,100+ affiliates; www.grandlodgefop.org

Police Associations, International Union of, 1421 Prince St., Suite 400, Alexandria, VA 22314; AFL-CIO charter in 1979; Samuel Cabral, Pres. (since 1995); 80,000 members, 500 locals; www.iupa.org

***Postal Supervisors, National Association of,** 1727 King St., Suite 400, Alexandria, VA 22314-2753; Vincent Palladino, Pres. (since 1992); 35,000+ members, 400 locals; www.naps.org

Postal Workers Union, American (APWU), 1300 L St. NW, Washington, DC 20005; founded 1971; WIlliam Burrus, Pres. (since 2001); 333,000+ members, 1,600+ locals; www.apwu.org

Roofers, Waterproofers & Allied Workers, United Union of, 1660 L St. NW, Suite 800, Washington, DC 20036; founded 1906; John Martini, Intl. Pres.; 22,000 members; www.unionroofers.com

---
WORLD ALMANAC QUICK QUIZ

Rank these countries by 2003 unemployment rates from lowest to highest:

(a) Germany   (b) Japan
(c) United Kingdom   (d) United States

For the answer, look in this chapter , or see page 1008.

***Rural Letter Carriers' Association, National,** 1630 Duke St., 4th Fl., Alexandria, VA 22314; founded 1903; Dale Holton, Pres.; 100,000+ members; 50 state org; www.nrlca.org

Seafarers International Union of North America (SIU), 5201 Auth Way, Camp Springs, MD 20746; founded 1938; Michael Sacco, Pres. (since 1988); 80,000 members, 18 affiliates; www.seafarers.org

***Security, Police, and Fire Professionals of America (SPFPA),** 25510 Kelly Rd., Roseville, MI 48066; founded 1948; David L. Hickey, Pres. (since 2000); 12,000 members, 200 locals; www.spfpa.org

Service Employees International Union (SEIU), 1313 L St. NW, Washington, DC 20005; founded 1921; Andrew L. Stern, Pres. (since 1996); 1.6 million members, 350 locals; www.seiu.org

Sheet Metal Workers' International Association (SMWIA), 1750 New York Ave. NW, Washington, DC 20006; founded 1888; Michael J. Sullivan, Pres. (since 1999); 150,000 members, 194 locals; www.smwia.org

State, County, and Municipal Employees, American Federation of (AFSCME), 1625 L St. NW, Washington, DC 20036; Gerald W. McEntee, Pres. (since 1981); 1.4 mil. members, 3,617 locals; www.afscme.org

Steelworkers of America, United (USWA), 5 Gateway Center, Pittsburgh, PA 15222; founded 1936; Leo W. Gerard, Pres. (since 2001); 1.2 mil. members, 1,800 locals; www.uswa.org

Teachers, American Federation of (AFT), 555 New Jersey Ave. NW, Washington, DC 20001; founded 1916; Edward McElroy, Pres. (since 2004); 1.3 mil. members, 3,000 locals; www.aft.org

Teamsters, International Brotherhood of (IBT), 25 Louisiana Ave. NW, Washington, DC 20001; founded 1903; James P. Hoffa, Gen. Pres. (since 1999); 1.4 mil. members, 521 locals; www.teamsters.org

Television and Radio Artists, American Federation of, (AFTRA) 260 Madison Ave., 7th Fl., New York, NY 10016; founded 1937; John Connolly, Natl. Pres. (since 2001); 80,000 members, 33 locals; www.aftra.org

Theatrical Stage Employees, Moving Picture Technicians, Artists and Allied Crafts of the United States, Its Territories, and Canada, International Alliance of (IATSE), 1430 Broadway, 20th floor, New York, NY 10018; founded 1893; Thomas C. Short, Pres. (since 1994); 105,000+ members, 555+ locals; www.iatse-intl.org

Transit Union, Amalgamated (ATU), 5025 Wisconsin Ave. NW, Washington, DC 20016; founded 1892; Warren S. George, Pres. (since 2003); 180,000+ members, 273 locals; www.atu.org

Transportation-Communications International Union (TCU), 3 Research Place, Rockville, MD 20850; founded 1899; Robert A. Scardelletti, Pres. (since 1991); 100,000 members; www.tcunion.org

Transportation Union, United (UTU), 14600 Detroit Ave., Cleveland, OH 44107; founded 1969; Paul C. Thompson, Pres. (since 2004); 125,000 members, 680 locals; www.utu.org

Transport Workers Union of America, 1700 Broadway, New York, NY 10019; founded 1934; Sonny Hall, Int'l. Pres. (since 1993); 110,000 members, 92 locals; www.twu.org

***Treasury Employees Union, National (NTEU),** 1750 H St. NW, Washington, DC 20006; founded 1938; Colleen M. Kelley, Natl. Pres. (since 1999); 150,000+ represented, 270+ chapters; www.nteu.org

UNITE HERE, 275 7th Ave., New York, NY, 10001; formerly Union of Needletrades, Textiles and Industrial Employees (UNITE, founded 1900 as International Ladies' Garment Worker's Union) and Hotel Employees and Restaurant Employees International Union (HERE, founded 1891); unions merged 2004; 440,000+ members, Bruce Raynor, Gen. Pres. (since 2004); www.unitehere.org

***University Professors, American Association of (AAUP),** 1012 14th St. NW, Suite 500, Washington, DC 20005; founded 1915; Jane Buck, Pres.; 45,000 members, 500+ chapters; www.aaup.org

Utility Workers Union of America (UWUA), 815 16th St. NW, Washington, DC 20006; founded 1945; Donald Wightman, Pres. (since 1996); 43,000 members, 250 locals; www.uwua.org

TAXES

Federal Income Tax

Source: George W. Smith III, CPA, Managing Partner, George W. Smith & Company, P.C.

Congress enacted, and Pres. George W. Bush signed, a series of major tax bills in 2001, 2002, 2003, as shown below. On Oct. 4, 2004, Pres. Bush signed the Working Families Tax Relief Act, which extended several tax provisions expiring in 2003 and 2004 to later dates, some to Dec. 31, 2010.

Jobs and Growth Tax Relief Reconciliation Act of 2003

This 10-year, $350 billion package was the 3rd-largest tax cut in U.S. history.

Rate Reductions. The Tax Relief Act of 2001 had reduced top individual tax rates to 27%, 30%, 35%, and 38.6%. For 2003 and 2004, the new legislation further reduced the rates, to 25%, 28%, and 33%, with a mazimum rate of 35%. Unless Congress decides otherwise, the rates will revert to pre-2001 levels after 2010.

Child Tax Credit. The 2001 law had increased the maximum tax credit for each qualifying dependent child under age 17 from $500 to $600 initially, and up to $1,000 phased in over a 10-year period. The 2003 legislation advanced the credit for 2003 and 2004 to $1,000. To stimulate the economy, advance refunds of up to $400 per child, about 25 million checks, were mailed in July and Aug. 2003 to qualifying individuals. The Working Families Tax Relief Act extended the $1,000 credit to Dec. 31, 2005.

Dividend Income. Some of the toughest congressional debates involved cutting taxes on corporate dividends paid to individuals. Previously, dividends were taxed as normal income, so the tax rate could go as high as 38.6%. The 2003 law dropped the maximum rate to 15% for dividends paid after 2002. For taxpayers in the 10% and 15% tax brackets the rates were reduced to 5%. After 2008 dividends will be taxed at the rates they were prior to 2003.

Capital Gains. The maximum capital gains tax rate was reduced from 20% to 15% starting May 6, 2003. The lower 10% rate dropped to 5%. To qualify, the appreciated asset must be held for more than one year. This provision expires at the end of 2008. Higher capital gains rates on collectibles and certain real estate remained unchanged.

Deductions. Starting in 2003, the basic standard deduction for married couples filing jointly increased to twice the standard deduction for single filers. The 2004 legislation extends the increased standard deduction including the 10% and 15% tax brackets for married couples through 2010.

Business Assets. Section 179 of the tax code allowed a taxpayer to expense up to $25,000 of the cost of qualifying depreciable property such as machinery and equipment. In 2003, Congress increased the maximum to $100,000 through 2005. For 2004, the deduction was adjusted for inflation to $102,000 and begins to phase out if the annual cost of property exceeds $400,000.

Depreciation. Taxpayers can now elect an additional first-year depreciation of 50% for qualified property acquired after May 5, 2003, and before Jan. 1, 2005. A $4,600 deduction allowed under the 2002 law for certain new passenger automobiles in their first year of purchase was increased to $7,650.

Recent Federal Tax Rate Cuts			
	Pre-2001 Rates	After 2001 Cuts[1]	After 2003 Cuts[2]
Top Bracket ..	39.6%	38.6%	35%
Next	36%	35%	33%
Next	31%	30%	28%
Next	28%	27%	25%
Next	15%	15%	15%
Lowest	same	10%	10%
(1) Effective July 1, 2001. (2) Effective Jan. 1, 2003.			

Job Creation and Worker Assistance Act of 2002

This measure contained over $120 billion in current tax cuts and incentives.

Classroom Materials. Elementary and secondary school teachers, principals, and counselors who buy school books or other teaching materials and supplies with their own money were allowed to deduct up to $250 of these expenses and without itemizing. Teacher's classroom expense deduction was extended through 2005.

Operating Loss. Businesses and individuals with an operating loss in 2001 and 2002 were allowed to carry it back 5 years instead of 2; but after 2002 the 2-year rule again applied.

Depreciation. Businesses that purchase new qualifying property after Sept. 10, 2001, but before Sept. 10, 2004, were allowed to take a first-year depreciation deduction equal to 30% of the property's basis. This act also provided higher dollar deductions for new vehicles placed in service after Sept. 10, 2001, and before Sept. 10, 2004. The subsequent 2003 Tax Relief Act made additional changes.

Other Measures. The definition of qualified foster care payments excludable from income was expanded. Miscellaneous Income, Form 1099, may now be sent to recipients electronically. The new regulations also clarified when a taxpayer can qualify as head of household or surviving spouse if a child was kidnapped or missing.

The Economic Growth and Tax Relief Reconciliation Act of 2001 (Tax Relief Act)

This massive, 10-year tax package added 440 changes to the Internal Revenue Tax Code. In addition to changes mentioned above, here are some other highlights.

Dependent Care. The maximum expense eligible for the dependent care tax credit was increased from $2,400 to $3,000 for one qualifying child or other dependent incapable of self-care, and from $4,800 to $6,000 for 2 or more. The phase-out limitations for higher income also increased.

Adoption. The maximum adoption credit was increased to $10,390 per child for 2004, and the exclusion from income of employer-provided adoption assistance starts to phase out at $155,860 of adjusted gross income. Under the law a credit can be claimed for a special needs adoption whether or not the taxpayer has qualified adoption expenses.

Education. The legislation increased the maximum annual contributions allowed to a Coverdell Education Savings Account, formerly known as the Education IRA, from $500 to $2,000 per beneficiary for elementary and secondary education expenses, whether for a public, private, or religious school. Although contributions are not deductible, qualifying education distributions, including dividend and interest income earned, are not taxable. The phase-out maximum for joint filers ($190,000-$220,000) increases to twice that of single filers ($95,000-$110,000).

Student Loans. The income phase-out range for the interest deduction on student loans increased to $50,000-$65,000 for single taxpayers and $100,000-$130,000 for married taxpayers.

The legislation also repealed the 60-month time limitation for the number of months during which interest paid is deductible.

College. For 2004, the educational deduction increased to $4,000 for qualified college tuition and related expenses. Generally, any accredited public, nonprofit, or proprietary post-secondary institution is considered an eligible education institution. The expenses are deductible even if the taxpayer does not itemize. This deduction is repealed after 2005.

Joint Filers. The standard deduction available to married taxpayers filing a joint return will gradually increase until 2009, when the amount reaches 200% of that allowed for single taxpayers.

Higher Income. The phasing out of the personal exemption and Schedule A itemized deductions for higher income taxpayers will be reduced by $1/3$ in 2006 and 2007, $2/3$ for 2008 and 2009, and totally eliminated in 2010.

Recent Legislation, IRS Rulings, Other Tax Matters

Cell Phones. Cell phone expenses can be deducted as an employee business expense if used for the convenience of the employer and if their use is a condition of employment.

Alimony. The U.S. Tax Court in 2004 again ruled that a taxpayer could not deduct alimony payments made to a former spouse prior to divorce because the payments were voluntary and not legally required. Another Tax Court decision stated that payments to an individual pursuant to a written separation agreement, constituted alimony for federal tax purposes even though the separation agreement may not have been enforceable under state law.

Weight Loss. The Internal Revenue Service (IRS) now allows a medical deduction for costs of certain weight-loss programs. Participation must be for treatment of a physician-diagnosed disease including obesity. No deduction is allowed for purely cosmetic reasons or special diet foods.

Treadmills. According to the IRS, the cost of home exercise equipment qualifies as a tax-deductible medical expense if prescribed by a doctor to treat obesity or illness.

Eye Surgery. The cost of certain kinds of eye surgery (radial keratomy, lasik, etc.) to improve vision now is allowed as a medical deduction.

Smoking. Taxpayers can deduct two types of treatments for quitting cigarette smoking as a medical expense: (1) participation in a smoking-cessation program, and (2) prescription drugs to alleviate the effects of nicotine withdrawal. Over-the-counter products such as nicotine patches and chewing gum remain nondeductible.

Spouse's Half. A "tenancy by the entireties" is a form of co-ownership that applies only in the case of a married couple. The U.S. Circuit Court of Appeals, siding with the IRS, recently ruled that the IRS could levy on and sell property held by a delinquent taxpayer with a spouse.

Garage Sale. Revenues received from a garage sale usually do not result in taxable income. In most cases, the item that was sold cost more than the revenue received. Nor are losses deductible.

Day Camp. If both spouses work, the cost of summer day camp may qualify for the child care credit.

Divorce. Legal fees paid to collect taxable alimony or to seek tax advice during a divorce are deductible on Schedule A. Fees paid related to the settlement of assets are personal expenses and not deductible.

Happy Birthday. The IRS, Social Security Administration, and certain other government agencies recently decided that officially you "attain" your age on the day before your birthday. This could affect taxpayers born on Jan. 1 regarding credits for dependent care, adoption, child tax, earned income tax credit, and dependency exemptions.

Tax-Free Income. Rental income (for instance, for personal residences rented to players in a major golf tournament) is not taxable if the taxpayer's residence is rented for fewer than 15 days during the year. Expenses attributed to the rental income are not deductible.

Whoops. Penalties and fines paid to a governmental agency or department are not deductible. This includes parking and speeding tickets, also penalties for late filing of a tax return.

Frivolous Returns. An IRS news release states, "Taxpayers who file frivolous income tax returns face a $500 penalty and may be subject to civil penalties of 20-75% of the underpaid tax. Those who pursue frivolous tax cases in the courts may face a penalty of up to $25,000, in addition to the taxes, interest, and civil penalties that they may owe."

Tax Highlights

Hybrid Cars. Taxpayers who buy a hybrid gasoline-and-electric car certified by the IRS, qualify for a $1,500 deduction in 2004, down from $2,000 for 2003. Cars that qualify in 2004 include the Toyota Prius, Honda Insight, and Honda Civic Hybrid. The taxpayer must be the original owner for this one-time deduction to apply.

Medical Insurance. Medical insurance premiums paid for self-employed individuals, spouses, and dependents are a 100%, page-1, Form 1040 deduction in 2004. For more information call the IRS at 1-800-829-3676 and ask for their free Publication 535, Business Expenses.

Death Benefits. Qualified accelerated death benefits paid under a life insurance contract to terminally ill persons (certified as expected to die within 24 months) are excludable from gross income. A similar exclusion applies to the sale or assignment of insurance death benefits to another person. For 2004, accelerated death benefits paid to a chronically ill person under a long-term care rider are tax-free up to $230 per day. The dollar amount is indexed annually for inflation.

Sale of Residence. Married couples filing jointly who lived in their principal residence for at least 2 years during a 5-year period can exclude up to $500,000 in gain from the sale of their residence. This deduction is reusable every 2 years. Single taxpayers can exclude a gain up to $250,000. Married couples who do not share a principal residence but continue to file a joint return also may claim up to $250,000 for a qualifying sale or exchange of each spouse's principal residence.

Homeowners who have lived in their home fewer than 2 years and must sell because of a change in place of work can prorate the exclusion based on amount of time lived there.

House Closing Points. The IRS has ruled that taxpayers need not deduct points in the year of purchase of a home; they may amortize the points over the life of the loan.

Home Office. A deduction is allowed for taxpayers who set up an office at home to take care of the administrative or management side of their business, but the rules are complicated. The instructions on Form 8829, Expenses for Business Use of Your Home, provide guidance.

Domestic Workers. The annual threshold dollar amount for reporting and paying Social Security and federal unemployment taxes on domestic employees, including nannies and housekeepers, remains at $1,400 in 2004. Household workers under 18 are exempt unless household work is their principal occupation. Household employers must apply for an employer federal ID number and issue W-2 wage statements.

Mileage. The mileage allowance deduction for driving to obtain medical treatment or for automobile costs incurred in a job-related move increased in 2004 to 14 cents per mile. Cars used for volunteer work in charities remain at 14 cents per mile. Starting in 2004 the standard mileage rate for business use of autos, including leased cars, increased to 37.5 cents from 36 cents.

Investments. Investors can take a miscellaneous deduction on Schedule A for investment and custodial fees, trust administration fees, cost of investment advice, financial newspapers and reports, and other expenses incurred in managing their investment portfolio. However, they cannot deduct expenses for attending a convention, seminar, or similar meeting.

Innocent Spouse Relief. The IRS Reform Act of 1998 provides a separate liability section for taxpayers who are divorced, legally separated, or living apart for at least 12 months. In effect, this legislation prevents a spouse from being held liable for the other spouse's tax liability and misdeeds.

Children's Income. Parents may elect to include on their income tax return the dividend and interest income of a dependent child under age 14 whose unearned income is more than $800 and gross income is less than $8,000. Form 8814, Parent's Election to Report Child's Interest and Dividends, must be attached to the parents' tax return. The election is not available if estimated tax payments were made or any investments were sold in the child's name during the year.

Full-Time Student. A taxpayer may not claim a dependency exemption in 2004 for an individual who qualifies as a full-time student and is over age 23 at the end of the year, unless the child's gross income is less than $3,100.

Responsibility. If a dependent child with taxable income cannot file an income tax return, the parent, guardian, or other legally responsible person must file a return for the child.

Hobbies. Qualifying long-term gains for collectibles such as art, antiques, jewelry, stamps, and coins are taxed at a maximum 28%.

Filing and Payment Dates

Filing Dates. The due date for filing a 2004 Form 1040, 1040A, or 1040EZ U.S. Individual Income Tax Return is Fri., Apr. 15, 2005.

Estimated Taxes. Due dates for filing individual quarterly federal estimated tax payments, Form 1040-ES, for 2005 are: 1st quarter, Fri, Apr. 15; 2nd quarter, Wed., June 15; 3rd quarter, Thurs., Sept. 15; 4th quarter, Mon., Jan. 16, 2006. Different filing dates may apply for state and local quarterly estimated tax payments.

Refunds. Individuals can call the IRS toll-free at 1-800-829-4477 for a recorded message or visit the IRS web site at www.irs.gov to check on the status of their expected refund. Either way, taxpayers will need to have their expected refund amounts, social security number, and filing status available. Taxpayers may have refunds deposited directly into their bank accounts. The average refund received through Apr. 30, 2004, was $2,063, up 5% from a year earlier. The total dollar amount of refunds was $184.28 billion. About 89.3 million taxpayers received refunds by this time.

Need More Time? Individuals who cannot file their 2004 tax return by the due date may apply for a 4-month extension. Although the extension is automatic, Form 4868 must be filed no later than Apr. 15, 2005, to qualify. Extensions also may be obtained by calling 1-800-796-1074. The IRS estimates that 8.5 million individuals will file for the 4-month extension for 2004. An estimated 3 million taxpayers will request an additional 2-month extension through Oct. 17, 2005.

Payments. Taxpayers may use their VISA, MasterCard, Discover, or American Express credit cards for payments. To pay by credit card, call 1-888-2-PAY-TAX. There is a "convenience fee" charged by the credit card company based on the size of the payment. Estimated tax payments also can be paid this way or via the Internet, instead of filing Form 1040-ES payment vouchers.

Installment Payments. Depending on the amount of tax owed, taxpayers may apply for monthly installment payments by attaching Form 9465 to their tax return. There is a nominal filing fee if the request is approved.

Timely Postmark. When a taxpayer's return is mailed on time, the IRS must accept the postmark as the filing date even if the IRS receives it weeks later. The postmark of qualified couriers such as UPS and FedEx also is proof of timely mailing.

Caution: When the return is mailed after the filing due date, or after the extended due date, the IRS considers a return as filed on the date it is received by the IRS, not the date of postmark.

Statute of Limitations. Taxpayers have until Apr. 15, 2005, to file their 2001 federal tax return to claim a refund. After that date any tax or withholding refund for 2001, including the refundable earned income tax credit they may have coming, will be lost . . . forever.

Filing Penalties. The IRS can levy 2 potential penalties when a return is filed after the due date with a balance owing: one is for failing to file a timely return, the other is for failure to pay the tax when due. Interest will be charged on any unpaid tax balance.

Precaution. To protect the taxpayer's privacy, social security numbers no longer appear on mailing labels.

Services. Free IRS tax forms, information on tax legislation, or relevant court decisions, and other information and resources are available from the IRS via the following:

Tax Questions: 1-800-829-1040
Internet website: www.irs.gov
File Transfer Protocol: ftp.irs.gov
Fax: 1-703-368-9694
Forms/Publications: 1-800-829-3676

English/Spanish. The IRS provides videotaped instructions both in English and in Spanish at participating libraries. Many IRS publications and tax forms, including, instructions also are printed in Spanish. For more information, call 1-800-TAX-FORM and ask for the free IRS Publication 1SP, *Derechos del Contribuyente.*

Hearing Impaired. The IRS telephone service for hearing impaired persons is available for taxpayers with access to TDD equipment. The toll-free number is 1-800-829-4059.

Individual Income Tax Rates for Year 2004
Taxable Income

Tax Rate	Single	Married Filing Separately	Married Filing Jointly or Qualifying Widow(er)	Head of Household	Estates and Trusts
10%	$1 to $7,150	$1 to $7,150	$1 to $14,300	$1 to $10,200	$0 to $1,950
15%	$7,151 to $29,050	$7,151 to $29,050	$14,301 to $58,100	$10,201 to $38,900	$1,951 to $4,600
25%	$29,051 to $70,350	$29,051 to $58,625	$58,101 to $117,250	$38,901 to $100,500	$4,601 to $7,000
28%	$70,351 to $146,750	$58,626 to $89,325	$117,251 to $178,650	$100,501 to $162,700	$7,001 to $9,550
33%	$146,751 to $319,100	$89,326 to $159,550	$178,651 to $319,100	$162,701 to $319,100	More than $9,550
35%	More than $319,100	More than $159,550	More than $319,100	More than $319,100	

"Kiddie Tax." If a child under age 14 has net investment income exceeding $1,600 for 2004, the excess is taxed at the parents' top marginal tax rate.

Exemptions

Dollar Amounts. The personal exemption amount for each taxpayer, spouse, and dependent for 2004 is $3,100, up from $3,050 for 2003. These exemption amounts are adjusted each year for cost of living.

Phaseout. The exemption deduction for higher income taxpayers begins to be phased out when their income exceeds certain threshold dollar amounts. These threshold amounts are adjusted annually for cost of living. Each exemption is reduced by 2% for each $2,500 ($1,250 for married persons filing separately) or fraction thereof by which adjusted gross income for year 2004 exceeds the following:

Married filing jointly	$214,050
Qualifying widow(er)	$214,050
Head of household	$178,350
Single	$142,700
Married filing separately	$107,025

These exemptions are fully phased out when adjusted gross income is more than $122,500 ($61,250 for married filing separately) over the above threshold amount. These phase-out regulations will be completely repealed after 2010.

Standard Deduction

The standard deduction is a flat dollar amount that is subtracted from the adjusted gross income (AGI) of taxpayers who do not itemize deductions. The amount allowed depends on filing status and is adjusted annually for inflation.

2004 Standard Deduction Amount

Single	$4,850
Married filing jointly or qualifying widow(er)	$9,700
Married filing separately	$4,850
Head of household	$7,150

These figures are not applicable if an individual can be claimed as a dependent on another person's tax return.

Standard Deduction for Dependents. An individual reported as a dependent on another person's 2004 income tax return generally may claim on his or her own tax return only the greater of $800 or the sum of $250 plus earned income not to exceed the regular standard deduction. Earned income includes wages, salaries, commissions and tips, net profit from self-employment, and any part of a scholarship or fellowship grant that must be included in gross income.

Taxpayers who are 65 or older and/or blind may claim an additional standard deduction:

2004 Additional Standard Deduction Amount

Single or head of household, 65 or older OR blind	$1,250
Single or head of household, 65 or older AND blind	$2,400
Married filing jointly or qualifying widow(er), 65 or older OR blind (per person)	$950
Married filing jointly or qualifying widow(er), 65 or older AND blind (per person)	$1,900
Married filing separately, 65 or older OR blind	$950
Married filing separately, 65 or older AND blind	$1,900

Adjustments to Income

Traditional IRA. The maximum tax-deferred Individual Retirement Arrangement (IRA) deduction for a married couple filing jointly is $6,000 for 2004, but not to exceed total earned income if less than $6,000. Each spouse can contribute up to $3,000 annually even if one spouse had little or no income. Individuals age 50 or older can fund an additional "catch-up" amount of $500 through 2005. However, there are income limitations and phase-outs.

Withdrawals. There is a 10% early withdrawal penalty for IRA distributions before age 59½ unless it qualifies for one of the following exceptions:

• Distributions paid to the beneficiary after the death of the owner.
• Payments paid due to the disability of the owner.
• Part of a series of substantially equal periodic payments.
• Payments made to an employee following separation from employment after age 55. This exception does not apply if a qualified distribution from a pension plan is rolled into an IRA.

- Payment of certain unreimbursed medical expenses.
- Payment of certain qualifying higher education expenses.
- Payment of certain first-time home buyer acquisition costs (up to $10,000).

Roth IRA. Although contributions paid into a Roth IRA are not deductible, distributions of funds including investment earnings held in the account for 5 years or longer and distributed after age 59½ are free both of income tax and the 10% early withdrawal penalty at the time of distribution.

Funds paid from the Roth IRA after the 5-year exclusion period to an estate or decedent's beneficiary on or after an individual's death, including funds paid to an individual who is disabled, are tax and penalty free regardless of age.

Withdrawals from a Roth IRA held less than 5 years can be subject both to income tax and the 10% withdrawal penalty regardless of age. However, earnings withdrawn for "qualified higher education expenses" of the taxpayer, spouse, or any child or grandchild of the taxpayer or spouse are taxable but not subject to the early withdrawal penalty.

For more information on IRAs call the IRS at 1-800-829-3676 for a free copy of Publication 590, Individual Retirement Arrangements (IRA).

Itemized Deductions

If the total amount of itemized deductions is more than the standard deduction, taxpayers generally should itemize their deductions on Schedule A, Form 1040. The following examples are just a few of the deductions that may be itemized; some are subject to income limitations.

- **Medical expenses** that exceed 7.5% of the taxpayer's adjusted gross income. Medicines, birth control pills, and insulin qualify if prescribed by a doctor. Cosmetic surgery for congenital abnormality, for personal injury from an accident or trauma, or for a disfiguring disease is also allowed as a medical deduction.
- **Long-term care** insurance premiums as a medical expense, up to certain annual limits based on age. The amounts are adjusted annually for inflation. The maximum premium allowed in 2004 is: $260 if age 40 or less; $490 from 41 to 50; $980, 51 to 60; $2,600, 61 to 70, and $3,250 if over age 70. Any long-term benefits received under a qualifying policy are tax-free, subject to per diem restrictions.
- **Mortgage interest** paid on a primary residence or a second home. However, there are limitations on mortgages in excess of $1,000,000. Generally, borrowers can also deduct points paid on their principal-home mortgage loan. Interest on home equity loans is also deductible, but only covering the first $100,000 of equity debt. Credit card interest is not deductible.
- **Taxes.** State and local income taxes, real estate taxes, and personal property taxes, but not sales and transfer taxes.
- **Personal Losses.** Casualty and theft losses, subject to the $100 and 10% limitation rule for each occurrence.
- **Charitable contributions.** Taxpayers deducting individual contributions of $250 or more must obtain written substantiation from the charity. If the amount is $75 or more, the charity must provide a breakdown of the payment indicating how much was a deductible contribution and what (if any) was the nondeductible value of goods, meals, or services received.

Certain miscellaneous expenses are deductible, but only the amount that exceeds 2% of adjusted gross income. Miscellaneous deductions include investment expenses (not to exceed net investment income), union and professional dues, cost of tax preparation, safe-deposit box rental fees. Other deductible expenses include employment fees paid to agencies for resumes, postage, travel, and other out-of-pocket expenditures to look for a new job. The job search must be related to the individual's present occupation, and these expenses are deductible even if he or she does not get the job.

Miscellaneous expenses also include unreimbursed employee business expenses such as travel, automobile, telephone, and gifts. However, only 50% of the cost of customer meals and entertainment is deductible.

Threshold Reduction. Many itemized deductions otherwise allowed are further reduced by the smaller of these two figures: 3% of a taxpayer's 2004 adjusted gross income in excess of the threshold amount of $142,700 ($71,350 for married taxpayers filing separately) OR 80% of the amount of these itemized deductions otherwise allowable for the year. These dollar amounts are adjusted for cost-of-living increases each year.

This provision does not apply to medical expenses, investment interest expense, casualty losses, or gambling expenses.

The threshold reduction is phased out starting in 2006 by the Tax Relief Act of 2001 and completely repealed after 2009.

Moving Expenses. These are now a page 1, Form 1040 deduction. Taxpayers who change jobs or are transferred, usually can deduct part of their moving expenses, including travel and the cost of the moving of household goods, but not meals. Starting in 2004, the mileage rate for automobiles used in the move increased to 14 cents per mile. To take a deduction, the new job must be at least 50 miles farther from the former home than the old job. Employees must work full-time for at least 39 weeks during the first 12 months after they arrive in the general area of their new job.

Business Expenses

Business Equipment. The election to expense the cost of certain business machinery and other assets instead of depreciating them over a period of years is called a Section 179 Expense Election. The maximum annual dollar amount was increased for inflation in 2004 to $102,000.

Software. Off-the-shelf computer software now can be expensed.

Commercial Vehicles. The cost of heavy sport-utility vehicles (SUVs) and trucks weighing over 6,000 lbs. in 2004 qualify for the Section 179 tax provision.

Dues. Dues paid to social, athletic, luncheon, sporting, and country clubs, including airport and hotel clubs, are not deductible. Dues paid to the Chamber of Commerce, business economic clubs, and trade associations remain deductible.

Tax Credits

A tax *deduction* reduces a taxpayer's taxable income, whereas tax *credits* reduce in the amount of tax owed, dollar-for-dollar.

Adoption Credit. The adoption credit for qualified expenses increased in 2004. The phase-out of the credit begins at $155,860 of adjusted gross income. The credit limit is per person, not per year, and is adjusted annually for inflation.

Earned Income Credit. Lower-income workers who maintain a household may be eligible for a refundable earned income credit. The credit is based on total earned income such as wages, commissions, and tips. The Tax Relief Act of 2001 further simplified the rules by redefining earned income, extending the definition of qualifying children to include descendents of stepchildren, and eliminating the one-year residency requirement for foster children.

The phaseout range of the earned income credit increased for joint filers by an additional $1,000 starting in 2002, up to a maximum increase of $3,000 in 2008. Starting in 2009 the credit will be adjusted annually for the cost of living. After 2010 all these changes will expire.

Education Credits. The Hope Scholarship Credit applies to qualified tuition and expenses for the first 2 years of postsecondary education in a degree or certificate program at an eligible institution. However, it does not apply to room and board or cost of books. The credit can be as high as $1,500.

The Lifetime Learning Credit is available for taxpayers whose postsecondary education expenses are not eligible for the Hope credit. The credit is 20% of tuition and other qualifying expenses paid for by the taxpayer, spouse, or dependents. For 2004, taxpayers can deduct up to $2,000 ($10,000 of expenses x 20%) for all entitled students who are enrolled in an eligible educational institution.

The Lifetime Learning Credit is allowed only for years in which the Hope credit is not used. Neither credit may be taken in any year in which funds are withdrawn from a Coverdell education savings account for the same expenses. The credit begins to phase out for higher income levels.

These credits are deducted from the individual's federal income tax and reported on Form 8863, Education Credits (Hope and Lifetime Learning Credits). Any credit exceeding the individual's tax liability is nonrefundable.

Taxable Social Security Benefits

Earnings Limitations. In 2004, persons aged 62 to 65 lose $1 of their Social Security benefits for every $2 of earned income over $11,640. Persons who reach full age no longer are subject earnings limitations.

Taxable Benefits. Up to 50% of Social Security benefits may be taxable income if the person's total income is: over $25,000 but less than $34,000 for a single individual, head of household, qualifying widow(er), or a married person who is filing separately if spouses lived apart all year; or over $32,000 but less

than $44,000 for married individuals filing jointly. For higher incomes, 85% of Social Security benefits may become taxable.

Good News. *Social Security benefits are not taxable if they are the only income received during the year.*

Retirement Planning

The SIMPLE Plan. A popular retirement plan, the Savings Incentive Match Plan for Employees (SIMPLE), is available for businesses with 100 or fewer employees, including self-employed individuals. It is generally easier to implement and more cost-effective to administer than a traditional 401(k) plan.

Starting in 2004, employees can defer up to $9,000 in compensation, an increase of $1,000 from 2003. There is an additional $1,500 catch-up for individuals age 50 and over. The Tax Relief Act of 2001 increases the amount annually thereafter by $1,000 until $10,000 is reached in 2005. A SIMPLE retirement plan can operate either as an IRA or as a 401(k). The tax liability on these amounts is deferred until a future date when the taxpayer draws the money out of the account.

Profit-Sharing Plans. This plan limits the total employer and employee contributions to the lesser of 25% of compensation or $41,000.

Age 70½ Plus. The owner of a traditional IRA or a SIMPLE plan must begin receiving distributions from the IRA or SIMPLE by Apr. 1 of the calendar year following the year in which he or she reaches age 70½, even if the individual is not retired. However, any employee who works beyond age 70½ and is not a 5% or more owner of the business can continue to defer profit sharing and pension plan distributions.

Retired and Moved. States may not impose an income tax on retirement income if the person is no longer a resident.

Estate and Gift Taxes

Estate Exclusion. The Tax Relief Reconciliation Act of 2001 increased the estate tax exclusion from $675,000 to $1 million in 2002 and 2003, $1.5 mil. in 2004 and 2005, $2 mil. in 2006 through 2008, and $3.5 mil. in 2009.

Tax Rates. For 2001 the maximum tax rate on the value of an estate was 55%, reduced to 50% in 2002. Starting in 2004, the rate was further reduced to 48%, down 1% from 49% in 2003. The rates continue to decrease until 2009 when the maximum reaches 45%.

Repeal. All estate taxes are repealed for the year 2010. Unless new legislation is passed prior to 2011, the estate laws revert to 2001 with a $675,000 estate tax exclusion and a maximum tax rate of 55%.

Resident Alien. The estate of a resident alien is subject to the same rules as that of an American citizen. All property owned worldwide is subject to the U.S. estate tax rules and regulations.

Gifting. Citizens, resident and non-resident aliens can make tax-free gifts of up to $11,000 to as many individuals as he or she chooses; twice that amount with consent of the spouse even if only one spouse does the gifting.

Lifetime Gifting. A $1 mil. gift tax exclusion is the limit an individual is allowed to give to other individuals (not charities) during his or her lifetime before having to pay gift taxes. The annual $11,000 gifts are not included in the gift tax exclusion.

IRS Tax Audit

The IRS projects that well over 130 million individual income tax returns will be filed in the year 2004. The IRS said it audited 849,296 tax returns during 2003. Needless to say, the agency is very good at selecting returns that will yield additional taxes. If the IRS concludes that you owe more and you disagree with the findings, you can meet with a supervisor. If you still do not agree, you can appeal to a separate Appeals Office or to the U.S. Tax Court.

For more information about audits, call the IRS at 1-800-829-3676 for its free Publication 556, Examination of Returns, Appeal Rights, and Claims for Refund. Or visit www.irs.gov

Your Rights as a Taxpayer

Congress has enacted "taxpayer bill of rights" legislation and created an Office of the Taxpayer Advocate within the IRS, with authority to order IRS personnel to issue refund checks and meet deadlines for resolving disputes. Taxpayers Advocates can be contacted at 1-877-777-4778 (1-800-829-4059 for TTY/TDD). The IRS must pay legal fees if the taxpayer wins the case and the IRS cannot show it was "substantially justified" in pursuing it.

To confidentially report misconduct, waste, fraud, or abuse by an IRS employee, you can call 1-800-366-4484.

For more information ask for IRS Publication 1, Your Rights as a Taxpayer, by calling 1-800-TAX-FORM for a free copy.

Alternative Minimum Tax

The Alternative Minimum Tax (AMT) was established in 1969 to prevent people with very high incomes from using special tax breaks to pay little or no federal income tax. It was never indexed for inflation and, also because of various changes in the tax law, it affects more and more middle-income taxpayers every year. The IRS estimates that about 2.7 million individuals are now impacted by the tax, and it is projected that the number could reach more than 30 million by 2010.

The IRS provides a worksheet in the Form 1040A and 1040 instructions to help individuals determine whether they are subject to the AMT. Form 6251, Alternative Minimum Tax, is used to figure out how much tax you owe.

Federal Outlays to States Per Dollar of Tax Revenue Received

Source: The Tax Foundation

(figures for fiscal year 2002; revised; ranked highest to lowest)

State	Outlay	State	Outlay	State	Outlay	State	Outlay	State	Outlay
District of Columbia....	$6.17	Hawaii	$1.52	Arizona........	$1.20	Ohio	$1.02	California	$0.81
North Dakota...	2.03	Virginia	1.47	Maryland	1.20	Georgia	1.01	New York	0.81
New Mexico....	1.89	Oklahoma	1.47	Nebraska......	1.19	Oregon.......	1.00	Colorado.......	0.79
Mississippi.....	1.84	Kentucky......	1.46	Utah..........	1.14	Florida	1.00	Massachusetts..	0.79
Alaska.........	1.82	Louisiana......	1.44	Kansas........	1.14	Indiana........	0.99	Illinois..........	0.77
West Virginia...	1.74	Idaho.........	1.34	Vermont.......	1.12	Texas.........	0.92	Minnesota......	0.77
Montana	1.64	South Carolina..	1.32	Pennsylvania...	1.08	Washington	0.91	Nevada........	0.73
Alabama	1.61	Missouri.......	1.32	North Carolina ..	1.07	Michigan.......	0.90	New Hampshire .	0.68
South Dakota ..	1.59	Maine.........	1.31	Rhode Island ...	1.06	Wisconsin......	0.87	Connecticut	0.64
Arkansas......	1.53	Tennessee.....	1.24	Wyoming	1.05	Delaware	0.85	New Jersey.....	0.62
		Iowa..........	1.22						

Tax Burden in Selected Countries[1]

Source: Organization for Economic Cooperation and Development, 2003

Country[2]	Income tax	Social Security	Total payment[3]	Country[2]	Income tax	Social Security	Total payment[3]	Country[2]	Income tax	Social Security	Total payment[3]
Denmark	32%	11%	42%	Italy	18%	9%	27%	New Zealand .	21%	0%	21%
Germany	21	21	42	France......	13	14	27	Switzerland ..	10	11	21
Belgium.....	27	14	41	Hungary	13	13	26	Spain.......	12	6	19
Netherlands..	9	25	34	Iceland	25	0	25	Slovak Rep. .	6	13	19
Finland	25	6	31	Canada	18	7	25	Japan	6	12	17
Sweden.....	24	7	31	Australia	24	0	24	Portugal	6	11	17
Poland......	6	25	31	U.K.	16	8	24	Ireland......	11	5	16
Turkey......	15	15	30	**U.S**	**16**	**8**	**24**	Greece	0	16	16
Norway.....	21	8	29	Czech Rep...	12	13	24	Korea	2	5	7
Austria......	11	18	29	Luxembourg .	9	14	22	Mexico	3	2	4

(1) Does not include taxes not listed, such as sales tax or VAT. Rates shown apply to a single person with average earnings. (2) Ranked by total payment %. Ties ranked by income tax % where different. (3) Totals may not add due to rounding.

State Government Personal Income Tax Rates, 2004

Source: Reproduced with permission from *CCH State Tax Guide*, published and copyrighted by CCH Inc., 2700 Lake Cook Road, Riverwoods, IL 60015

Below are basic state tax rates on taxable income, for 2004 unless otherwise indicated. Alaska, Florida, Nevada, South Dakota, Texas, Washington, and Wyoming did not have state income taxes and are thus not listed. Tax rates apply in stages—for example, a single person in Arizona making $60,000 in taxable income would pay 2.87% on the first $10,000 of income, 3.2% on the next $15,000, etc. For further details, see notes at end of table.

Alabama
Single, Head of household, & Married filing separately
- $0 to $500 . . . . .2%
- $501 to $3,000 . . . . .4%
- $3,001 and over. 5%

Married filing jointly
- $0 to $1,000 . . . . .2%
- $1,001 to $6,000 . . . . . . .4%
- $6,001 and over. 5%

Arizona[1]
Single & Married filing separately
- $0 to $10,000. . . . . 2.87%
- $10,001 to $25,000 . . . . 3.2%
- $25,001 to $50,000 . . 3.74%
- $50,001 to $150,000 . . 4.72%
- $150,001 and over. . . 5.04%

Married filing jointly and Head of household
- $0 to $20,000. . . . . 2.87%
- $20,001 to $50,000 . . . . 3.2%
- $50,001 to $100,000 . . . 3.74%
- $100,001 to $300,000 . 4.72%
- $300,001 and over. . . . 5.04%

Arkansas[2,3]
Single, Head of household, Married filing jointly, & Married filing separately
- $0 to $3,299 . . . . .1%
- $3,300 to $6,699 . . . . . . 2.5%
- $6,700 to $9,999 . . . . . . 3.5%
- $10,000 to $16,699 . . . . 4.5%
- $16,700 to $27,899 . . . . .6%
- $27,900 and over. 7%

California[1, 2]
Single & Married filing separately
- $0 to $6,147. . . . . .1%
- $6,148 to $14,571 . . . . . . .2%
- $14,572 to $22,997 . . . . . .4%
- $22,998 to $31,925 . . . . . .6%
- $31,926 to $40,346 . . . . . .8%
- $40,347 and over. 9.3%

Head of household
- $0 to $12,300. . . . . .1%
- $12,301 to $29,143 . . . . . .2%
- $29,144 to $37,567 . . . . . .4%
- $37,568 to $46,494 . . . . . .6%
- $46,495 to $54,918 . . . . . .8%
- $54,919 and over. 9.3%

Married filing jointly
- $0 to $12,294. . . . . .1%
- $12,295 to $29,142 . . . . . .2%
- $29,143 to $45,994 . . . . . .4%
- $45,995 to $63,850 . . . . . .6%
- $63,851 to $80,692 . . . . . .8%
- $80,693 and over. 9.3%

Colorado
4.63% of federal taxable income.

Connecticut
Single & Married filing separately
- $0 to $10,000. . . . . .3%
- $10,001 and over. 5%

Head of household
- $0 to $16,000. . . . . .3%
- $16,001 and over. 5%

Married filing jointly
- $0 to $20,000. . . . . .3%
- $20,001 and over. 5%

Delaware
Single, Head of household, Married filing jointly, & Married filing separately
- $2,000 to $5,000 . . . . . . 2.2%
- $5,001 to $10,000 . . . . 3.9%
- $10,001 to $20,000 . . . . 4.8%
- $20,001 to $25,000 . . . . 5.2%
- $25,001 to $60,000 . . . 5.55%
- $60,001 and over. 5.95%

District of Columbia
Single, Head of household, Married filing jointly, & Married filing separately
- $0 to $10,000. . . . . .5%
- $10,001 to $30,000 . . . . 7.5%
- $30,001 and over. 9.3%

Georgia
Single
- $0 to $750 . . . . .1%
- $751 to $2,250 . . . . .2%
- $2,251 to $3,750 . . . . . . .3%
- $3,751 to $5,250 . . . . . . .4%
- $5,251 to $7,000 . . . . . . .5%
- $7,001 and over 6%

Head of household, Married filing jointly, or surviving spouse
- $0 to $1,000 . . . . .1%
- $1,001 to $3,000 . . . . . . .2%
- $3,001 to $5,000 . . . . . . .3%
- $5,001 to $7,000 . . . . . . .4%
- $7,001 to $10,000 . . . . . .5%
- $10,001 and over 6%

Married filing separately
- $0 to $500 . . . . .1%
- $501 to $1,500 . . . . .2%
- $1,501 to $2,500 . . . . . . .3%
- $2,501 to $3,500 . . . . . . .4%
- $3,501 to $5,000 . . . . . . .5%
- $5,001 and over 6%

Hawaii
Single & Married filing separately
- $0 to $2,000 . . . . .1.4%
- $2,001 to $4,000 . . . . . . .3.2%
- $4,001 to $8,000 . . . . . . .5.5%
- $8,001 to $12,000 . . . . . .6.4%
- $12,001 to $16,000 . . . . .6.8%
- $16,001 to $20,000 . . . . .7.2%
- $20,001 to $30,000 . . . . .7.6%
- $30,001 to $40,000 . . . . .7.9%
- $40,001 and over 8.25%

Head of household
- $0 to $3,000 . . . . .1.4%
- $3,001 to $6,000 . . . . . . .3.2%
- $6,001 to $12,000 . . . . . .5.5%
- $12,001 to $18,000 . . . . .6.4%
- $18,001 to $24,000 . . . . .6.8%
- $24,001 to $30,000 . . . . .7.2%
- $30,001 to $45,000 . . . . .7.6%
- $45,001 to $60,000 . . . . .7.9%
- $60,001 and over 8.25%

Married filing jointly
- $0 to $4,000 . . . . .1.4%
- $4,001 to $8,000 . . . . . . .3.2%
- $8,001 to $16,000 . . . . . .5.5%
- $16,001 to $24,000 . . . . .6.4%
- $24,001 to $32,000 . . . . .6.8%
- $32,001 to $40,000 . . . . .7.2%
- $40,001 to $60,000 . . . . .7.6%
- $60,001 to $80,000 . . . . .7.9%
- $80,001 and over 8.25%

Idaho[1, 2, 3]
Single & Married filing separately
- $0 to $1,104 . . . . .1.6%
- $1,105 to $2,207 . . . . . .3.6%
- $2,208 to $3,311 . . . . . .4.1%
- $3,312 to $4,415 . . . . . .5.1%
- $4,416 to $5,518 . . . . . .6.1%
- $5,519 to $8,278 . . . . . .7.1%
- $8,279 to $22,074 . . . . .7.4%
- $22,075 and over 7.8%

Head of household, Married filing jointly, or surviving spouse
- $0 to $2,208 . . . . .1.6%
- $2,209 to $4,414 . . . . . .3.6%
- $4,415 to $6,622 . . . . . .4.1%
- $6,623 to $8,830 . . . . . .5.1%
- $8,831 to $11,036 . . . . .6.1%
- $11,037 to $16,556 . . . .7.1%
- $16,557 to $44,148 . . . .7.4%
- $44,149 and over 7.8%

Illinois
3% of taxable net income

Indiana
3.4% of adjusted gross income

Iowa[2]
Single, Head of household, Married filing jointly, & Married filing separately
- $0 to $1,242 . . . . .0.36%
- $1,243 to $2,484 . . . . . .0.72%
- $2,485 to $4,968 . . . . . .2.43%
- $4,969 to $11,178 . . . . .4.5%

$11,179 to $18,630 . . .6.12%
$18,631 to $24,840. . . .6.48%
$24,841 to $37,260. . . .6.8%
$37,261 to $55,890 . . .7.92%
$55,891 and over 8.98%

Kansas
Single, Head of household, & Married filing separately
- $0 to $15,000 . . . . 3.5%
- $15,001 to $30,000. . . 6.25%
- $30,001 and over 6.45%

Married filing jointly
- $0 to $30,000. . . . . 3.5%
- $30,001 to $60,000. . . 6.25%
- $60,001 and over 6.45%

Kentucky
Single, Head of household, Married filing jointly, & Married filing separately
- $0 to $3,000 . . . . 2%
- $3,001 to $4,000. . . . . . . 3%
- $4,001 to $5,000. . . . . . . 4%
- $5,001 to $8,000. . . . . . . 5%
- $8,001 and over 6%

Louisiana[1]
Single, Head of household, & Married filing separately
- $0 to $12,500 . . . . 2%
- $12,501 to $25,000. . . . 4%
- $25,001 and over 6%

Married filing jointly
- $0 to $25,000 . . . . 2%
- $25,001 to $50,000. . . . 4%
- $50,001 and over 6%

Maine[2]
Single & Married filing separately
- $0 to $4,350 . . . . 2%
- $4,351 to $8,650. . . . . . 4.5%
- $8,651 to $17,350. . . . . . 7%
- $17,351 and over 8.5%

Head of household
- $0 to $6,550 . . . . 2%
- $6,551 to $13,000. . . . . 4.5%
- $13,001 to $26,050. . . . . 7%
- $26,051 and over 8.5%

Married filing jointly
- $0 to $8,700 . . . . 2%
- $8,701 to $17,350. . . . . 4.5%
- $17,351 to $34,700. . . . . 7%
- $34,701 and over 8.5%

Maryland
Single, Head of household, Married filing jointly, & Married filing separately
- $0 to $1,000 . . . . 2%
- $1,001 to $2,000. . . . . . . 3%
- $2,001 to $3,000. . . . . . . 4%
- $3,001 and over 4.75%

Massachusetts
- Short-term capital gains. . . 12%
- All other income. 5.3%

Michigan
3.9% of taxable income

Minnesota[2]
Single
- $0 to $19,440 . . . . 5.35%
- $19,441 to $63,860. . . . 7.05%
- $63,861 and over 7.85%

Head of household
- $0 to $23,940 . . . . 5.35%
- $23,941 to $96,180. . . 7.05%
- $96,181 and over 7.85%

Married filing jointly
- $0 to $28,420 . . . . 5.35%
- $28,421 to $112,910. . 7.05%
- $112,911 and over 7.85%

Married filing separately
- $0 to $14,210 . . . . 5.35%
- $14,211 to $56,460. . . . 7.05%
- $56,461 and over 7.85%

Mississippi
Single, Head of household, Married filing jointly, & Married filing separately
- $0 to $5,000. . . . . .3%
- $5,001 to $10,000. . . . . . .4%
- $10,001 and over. 5%

Missouri
Single, Head of household, Married filing jointly, & Married filing separately
- $0 to $1,000. . . . . 1.5%
- $1,001 to $2,000 . . . . . . .2%
- $2,001 to $3,000 . . . . . 2.5%
- $3,001 to $4,000 . . . . . . .3%
- $4,001 to $5,000 . . . . . 3.5%
- $5,001 to $6,000 . . . . . . .4%
- $6,001 to $7,000 . . . . . 4.5%
- $7,001 to $8,000 . . . . . . .5%
- $8,001 to $9,000 . . . . . 5.5%
- $9,001 and over. 6%

Montana[2,3]
Single, Head of household, Married filing jointly, & Married filing separately
- $0 to $2,199. . . . . .2%
- $2,200 to $4,399 . . . . . . .3%
- $4,400 to $8,899 . . . . . . .4%
- $8,900 to $13,299 . . . . . .5%
- $13,300 to $17,799 . . . . .6%
- $17,800 to $22,199 . . . . .7%
- $22,200 to $31,099 . . . . .8%
- $31,100 to $44,499 . . . . .9%
- $44,500 to $77,799 . . . . .10%
- $77,800 and over. 11%

Nebraska
Single
- $0 to $2,400. . . . . 2.56%
- $2,401 to $17,000 . . . . . 3.57%
- $17,001 to $26,500 . . . 5.12%
- $26,501 and over. 6.84%

Head of household
- $0 to $3,800. . . . . 2.56%
- $3,801 to $24,000 . . . . . 3.57%
- $24,001 to $35,000 . . . 5.12%
- $35,001 and over. 6.84%

Married filing jointly
- $0 to $4,000. . . . . 2.56%
- $4,001 to $30,000 . . . . . 3.57%
- $30,001 to $46,750 . . . 5.12%
- $46,751 and over. 6.84%

Married filing separately
- $0 to $2,000. . . . . 2.56%
- $2,001 to $15,000 . . . . . 3.57%
- $15,001 to $23,375 . . . 5.12%
- $23,376 and over. 6.84%

New Hampshire
5% on interest and dividends only

New Jersey
Single & Married filing separately
- $0 to $20,000. . . . . 1.4%
- $20,001 to $35,000 . . . 1.75%
- $35,001 to $40,000 . . . 3.5%
- $40,001 to $75,000 . . 5.525%
- $75,001 to 500,000 . . 6.37%
- $500,001 and over. . . . 8.97%

Head of household & Married filing jointly
- $0 to $20,000. . . . . 1.4%
- $20,001 to $50,000 . . . 1.75%
- $50,001 to $70,000 . . . 2.45%
- $70,001 to $80,000 . . . 3.5%
- $80,001 to $150,000 . 5.525%
- $150,001 to 500,000 . 6.37%
- $500,001 and over. . . . 8.97%

New Mexico[1]
Single
- $0 to $5,500. . . . . 1.7%
- $5,501 to $11,000 . . . . . 3.2%
- $11,001 to $16,000 . . . . 4.7%
- $16,001 to $26,000 . . . . . .6%
- $26,001 and over. 6.8%

Head of household
- $0 to $7,000. . . . . 1.7%
- $7,001 to $14,000 . . . . . 3.2%
- $14,001 to $20,000 . . . . 4.7%
- $20,001 to $33,000 . . . . . .6%
- $33,001 and over. 6.8%

Married filing jointly

$0 to $8,000	1.7%
$8,001 to $16,000	3.2%
$16,001 to $24,000	4.7%
$24,001 to $40,000	6%
$40,001 and over	6.8%

Married filing separately

$0 to $4,000	1.7%
$4,001 to $8,000	3.2%
$8,001 to $12,000	4.7%
$12,001 to $20,000	6%
$20,001 and over	6.8%

New York

Single & Married filing separately

$0 to $8,000	4%
$8,001 to $11,000	4.5%
$11,001 to $13,000	5.25%
$13,001 to $20,000	5.9%
$20,001 to $100,000	6.85%
$100,001 to $500,000	7.375%
$500,001 and over	7.7%

Head of Household

$0 to $11,000	4%
$11,001 to $15,000	4.5%
$15,001 to $17,000	5.25%
$17,001 to $30,000	5.9%
$30,001 to $125,000	6.85%
$125,001 to $500,000	7.375%
$500,001 and over	7.7%

Married filing jointly

$0 to $16,000	4%
$16,001 to $22,000	4.5%
$22,001 to $26,000	5.25%
$26,001 to $40,000	5.9%
$40,001 to $150,000	6.85%
$150,001 to $500,000	7.375%
$500,001 and over	7.7%

North Carolina

Single

$0 to $12,750	6%
$12,751 to $60,000	7%
$60,001 to $120,000	7.75%
$120,001 and over	8.25%

Head of household

$0 to $17,000	6%
$17,001 to $80,000	7%
$80,001 to $160,000	7.75%
$160,001 and over	8.25%

Married filing jointly

$0 to $21,250	6%
$21,251 to $100,000	7%
$100,001 to $200,000	7.75%
$200,001 and over	8.25%

Married filing separately

$0 to $10,625	6%
$10,626 to $50,000	7%
$50,001 to $100,000	7.75%
$100,001 and over	8.25%

North Dakota[2]

Single

$0 to $29,050	2.1%
$29,051 to $70,350	3.92%
$70,351 to $146,750	4.34%
$146,751 to $319,100	5.04%
$319,101 and over	5.54%

Head of Household

$0 to $38,050	2.1%
$38,901 to $100,500	3.92%
$100,501 to $162,700	4.34%
$162,701 to $319,100	5.04%
$319,101 and over	5.54%

Married filing jointly

$0 to $48,500	2.1%
$48,501 to $117,250	3.92%
$117,251 to $178,650	4.34%
$178,651 to $319,100	5.04%
$319,101 and over	5.54%

Married filing separately

$0 to $24,250	2.1%
$24,251 to $58,625	3.92%
$58,626 to $89,325	4.34%
$89,326 to $159,550	5.04%
$159,551 and over	5.54%

Ohio

Single, Head of household, Married filing jointly, & Married filing separately

$0 to $5,000	0.743%
$5,001 to $10,000	1.486%
$10,001 to $15,000	2.972%
$15,001 to $20,000	3.715%
$20,001 to $40,000	4.457%
$40,001 to $80,000	5.201%
$80,001 to $100,000	5.943%
$100,001 to $200,000	6.9%
$200,001 and over	7.5%

Oklahoma

Single & Married filing separately

$0 to $1,000	0.5%
$1,001 to $2,500	1%
$2,501 to $3,750	2%
$3,751 to $4,900	3%
$4,901 to $6,200	4%
$6,201 to $7,700	5%
$7,701 to $10,000	6%
$10,001 and over	6.65%

Head of household & Married filing jointly

$0 to $2,000	0.5%
$2,001 to $5,000	1%
$5,001 to $7,500	2%
$7,501 to $9,800	3%
$9,801 to $12,200	4%
$12,201 to $15,000	5%
$15,001 to $21,000	6%
$21,001 and over	6.65%

Oregon[2]

Single & Married filing separately

$0 to $2,600	5%
$2,601 to $6,500	7%
$6,501 and over	9%

Married filing jointly and Head of household

$0 to $5,200	5%
$5,201 to $13,000	7%
$13,001 and over	9%

Pennsylvania

3.07% of taxable compensation, net profits, net gains from the sale of property, rent, royalties, dividends, interest, etc.

Rhode Island

Generally, 25% of the federal income tax rates, including capital gains and other special rates for types of income in effect before enactment of the 2001 Economic Growth and Tax Relief Reconciliation Act

South Carolina[2,3]

Single, Head of household, Married filing jointly, & Married filing separately

$0 to $2,460	2.5%
$2,461 to $4,920	3%
$4,921 to $7,380	4%
$7,381 to $9,840	5%
$9,841 to $12,300	6%
$12,301 and over	7%

Tennessee

6% of interest and dividends

Utah

Single & Married filing separately

$0 to $863	2.3%
$864 to $1,726	3.3%
$1,727 to $2,588	4.2%
$2,589 to $3,450	5.2%
$3,451 to $4,313	6%
$4,314 and over	7%

Head of household & Married filing jointly

$0 to $1,726	2.3%
$1,727 to $3,450	3.3%
$3,451 to $5,176	4.2%
$5,177 to $6,900	5.2%
$6,901 to $8,626	6%
$8,627 and over	7%

Vermont[2,3]

Single

$0 to $28,400	3.6%
$28,401 to $68,800	7.2%
$68,801 to $143,500	8.5%
$143,501 to $311,950	9.0%
$311,951 and over	9.5%

Head of Household

$0 to $38,050	3.6%
$38,051 to $98,250	7.2%
$98,951 to $159,100	8.5%
$159,101 to $311,950	9.0%
$311,951 and over	9.5%

Married filing jointly

$0 to $47,450	3.6%
$47,451 to $114,650	7.2%
$114,651 to $174,700	8.5%
$174,701 to $311,950	9.0%
$311,951 and over	9.5%

Married filing separately

$0 to $23,725	3.6%
$23,726 to $57,325	7.2%
$57,326 to $87,350	8.5%
$87,351 to $155,975	9.0%
$155,976 and over	9.5%

Virginia

Single, Head of household, Married filing jointly, & Married filing separately

$0 to $3,000	2%
$3,001 to $5,000	3%
$5,001 to $17,000	5%
$17,001 and over	5.75%

West Virginia

Single, Head of household, & Married filing jointly

$0 to $10,000	3%
$10,001 to $25,000	4%
$25,001 to $40,000	4.5%
$40,001 to $60,000	6%
$60,001 and over	6.5%

Married filing separately

$0 to $5,000	3%
$5,001 to $12,500	4%
$12,501 to $20,000	4.5%
$20,001 to $30,000	6%
$30,001 and over	6.5%

Wisconsin[1, 2]

Single and Head of household

$0 to $8,610	4.6%
$8,611 to $17,220	6.15%
$17,221 to $129,150	6.5%
$129,151 and over	6.75%

Married filing jointly

$0 to $11,480	4.6%
$11,481 to $22,960	6.15%
$22,961 to $172,200	6.5%
$172,201 and over	6.75%

Married filing separately

$0 to $5,740	4.6%
$5,741 to $11,480	6.15%
$11,481 to $86,100	6.5%
$86,101 and over	6.75%

(1) Community property state in which one-half of the community income is usually taxable to each spouse. (2) Brackets indexed for inflation annually. (3) 2004 adjusted brackets not currently available. Bracketed rates listed are for 2003. **Colorado:** Alternative minimum tax imposed. Qualified taxpayers may pay alternative tax of 0.5% of gross receipts from sales. **Connecticut:** Resident estates and trusts are subject to the 5% income tax rate on all of their income. Additional state minimum tax imposed on resident individuals, trusts, and estates is equal to the amount by which the minimum tax exceeds the basic income tax (the lesser of (a) 19% of adjusted federal tentative minimum tax, or (b) 5.5% of adjusted federal alternative minimum taxable income). Separate provisions apply for non- and part-year resident individuals, trusts, and estates. **Idaho:** Each person (joint returns deemed one person) filing a return pays additional $10. **Illinois:** Additional personal property replacement tax of 1.5% of net income is imposed on partnerships, trusts, and S corporations. **Indiana:** Counties may impose an adjusted gross income tax on residents at .5%, .75%, or 1%, and at .25% on nonresidents or a county option income tax at rates ranging between .2% and 1%, with the rate on nonresidents equal to one-fourth of the rate on residents. **Iowa:** An alternative minimum tax of 6.7% of alternative minimum income if the minimum tax exceeds the taxpayer's regular income tax liability. The minimum tax is 75% of the maximum regular tax rate. **Maine:** Additional state minimum tax is imposed equal to the amount by which the state minimum tax (27% of adjusted federal tentative minimum tax) exceeds Maine income tax liability, other than withholding tax liability. **Michigan:** Persons with business activity allocated or apportioned to Michigan are also subject to a single business tax on an adjusted tax base. **Minnesota:** A 6.4% alternative minimum tax is imposed. **Montana:** Minimum tax, $1. **Nebraska:** The tax rates in the schedules are determined by multiplying the primary rate set by the legislature by the following factors for the brackets, from lowest to highest bracket. For tax years beginning on or after Jan. 1, 2003, the respective factors are: 0.6932, 0.9646, 1.3846, and 1.848. For tax years beginning before Jan. 1, 2003, the respective factors are: 0.6784, 0.9432, 1.3541, and 1.8054. The figure obtained for each bracket is rounded to the nearest hundredth of 1%. One rate schedule is to be established for each federal filing status (Sec. 77-2715.02). **New Mexico:** Qualified taxpayers may pay alternative tax of 0.75% of gross receipts from New Mexico sales. **New York:** A supplemental tax is imposed to recapture the tax table benefit. The supplemental tax is calculated in accordance with NY Tax Law Sec. 601(d). Special provisions apply for tax years beginning in 2003, 2004, 2005 because of the temporary increase in the state personal income tax rates for taxpayers at higher income levels. **Oklahoma:** Rates given are for taxpayers not deducting federal income tax. Rates for married individuals filing jointly, surviving spouses, and heads of households deducting federal income tax range from .50% of the first $2,000 to 10% of income over $24,000. For single individuals and married individuals filing separately deducting federal income tax, rates range from .50% of the first $1,000 to 10% of income over $16,000. **Vermont:** The tax amount in the schedules is increased by 24% of a taxpayer's federal tax liability for: additional taxes assessed due to early withdrawals from qualified retirement plans, individual retirement accounts, and medical savings accounts; recapture of the federal investment tax credit; or tax on qualified lump-sum distributions of pension income not included in federal taxable income. The amount of tax is decreased by 24% of the reduction in the taxpayer's federal liability due to farm income averaging. **West Virginia:** Minimum tax equal to the excess by which 25% of any federal minimum tax or alternative minimum tax for the taxable year exceeds the sum of the primary tax for West Virginia personal income tax purposes for the taxable year. **Wisconsin:** A permanant recycling surcharge is imposed on individuals, estates, partnerships, and trusts with at least $4 million in gross receipts, except those entities engaged only in farming, at the rate of the greater of $25 or .2% of net business income as allocated or apportioned to Wisconsin. The maximum surcharge is $9,800. An individual, estate, trust, or partnership engaged in farming with more than $1 million in gross receipts is subject to a surcharge of $25.

CRIME

Measuring Crime

The U.S. Dept. of Justice administers 2 statistical programs to measure the magnitude, nature, and impact of crime in the U.S. Because of a difference in focus and methodology, their results are not strictly comparable.

The **Uniform Crime Report (UCR)** program, conducted through the Federal Bureau of Investigation, was designed to provide statistics for law enforcement administration, operation, and management. It collects information on the crimes of homicide, forcible rape, robbery, aggravated assault, burglary, larceny-theft, motor vehicle theft, and arson, as they are reported to law enforcement authorities. A preliminary annual report is released by the Justice Dept. each spring, and a more final report on the same period is released in the following year.

The **National Crime Victimization Survey (NCVS)** is conducted annually by the Bureau of Justice Statistics through interviews with members of a nationally representative sample of households, who report on on their experience of crime. It complements the UCR by providing alternative information about crimes, including those not reported to police. In contrast to the UCR, it does not cover murder or arson.

Further explanation of the NCVS and UCR is available at: www.ojp.usdoj.gov/bjs/abstract/ntmc.htm

Uniform Crime Reports for 2003

Source: FBI, *Uniform Crime Reports*, 2003, preliminary

From 2002 to 2003, based on preliminary statistics, violent crime in the U.S. decreased by 3.2%, and property crime fell by 0.1%. In the violent crime category, robberies and forcible rape both fell by 1.9%, while murder increased by 1.3%. Aggravated assault declined by 4.1%.

Among property crimes reported in 2003, burglary increased 0.4%, motor vehicle theft was up 1.4%, and larceny-theft fell 0.5%. Reports of arson, which is also considered a property crime, but not included in the Crime Index, decreased by 6.9%.

Violent crime decreased in all major geographic regions, falling by 3.2% in the Northeast, 2.7% in the South, 7.0% in the Midwest, and 1.2% in the West. Property crimes fell by 2.7% in the Northeast and 2.2% in the Midwest, but were up by 0.5% in the South and 1.9% in the West.

Violent crime fell in cities in all population categories, except those with populations of 50,000 to 99,999, where it increased by 0.7%. Violent crime remained unchanged in metropolitan areas as a whole; in nonmetropolitan areas, violent crime fell by 4.2%.

Property crimes fell by 0.8% in cities with over 1 million people and by 3.4% in cities with populations of 250,000 to 499,999, but rose slightly in every other urban population group. In nonmetropolitan areas, the number of property crimes was unchanged.

In 2003, the UCR program temporarily suspended publication of the Crime Index, an aggregate total of offenses that include murder, forcible rape, aggravated assault, robbery, burglary, larceny theft, and motor-vehicle theft. Because the index had included both violent and property crimes and because property crimes predominate, the UCR program is developing an index that will differentiate between violent and property crimes.

National Crime Victimization Survey for 2003

Source: Bureau of Justice Statistics, U.S. Dept. of Justice

The NCVS estimated that there were about 24.2 million victimizations of Americans age 12 and up in 2003 (including those unreported), up from 23 million in 2002, but about the same level as 2001. The 2001-2003 totals represent the lowest numbers since the NCVS was initiated in 1973; in that year there were an estimated 44 million victimizations. According to this survey, the violent crime rate in 2003 fell by 2.2% from 2002, while the property crime rate rose by 2.6%. Murder increased by 1.3%. Crime rates have stabilized, after decreasing since 1994; between 1993 and 2003, violent crime, as reflected in NCVS statistics, fell 55%, and property crime 49%. According to NCVS estimates, only about half of all violent crimes and 38% of property crimes in 2003 were reported to the police.

Criminal Victimization, 2002-2003

Source: National Crime Victimization Survey, U.S. Dept. of Justice

Type of Crime	Number of victimizations		Victimization rates[1]		% change,
	2002	2003	2002	2003	2002-2003
All Crimes	23,036,030	24,212,800	NA	NA	NA
Personal Crimes	5,496,810	5,586,420	23.7	23.3	-1.7
Crimes of violence	5,341,410	5,401,720	23.1	22.6	-2.2
Rape	90,390	72,240	0.4	0.3	-25.0
Attempted rape	77,470	44,650	0.3	0.2	-33.3
Sexual assault	79,870	81,950	0.3	0.3	0
Robbery[2]	385,880	377,870	1.7	1.6	-5.9
With injury[2]	169,980	160,200	0.7	0.7	0
Aggravated assault[3]	990,110	1,101,110	4.3	4.6	7.0
Simple assault[4]	2,684,510	2,736,670	11.6	11.4	-1.7
Personal theft[5]	155,400	184,700	0.7	0.8	14.3
Property Crimes	17,539,220	18,626,380	159.0	163.2	2.6
Household burglary[2]	2,597,310	2,810,500	23.5	24.6	4.7
Motor vehicle theft[2]	780,630	763,500	7.1	6.7	-5.6
Theft[2]	13,039,920	13,718,840	118.2	120.2	1.7

NA = Not applicable (1) Per 1,000 persons age 12 or older or per 1,000 households. (2) Refers to completed crimes, and does not include attempted crimes. (3) Attack with a weapon or involving serious injury. (4) Attack without a weapon resulting in no injury, minor injury, or undetermined injury requiring less than 2 days' hospitalization. (5) Purse snatching and pocket picking.

Federal Bureau of Investigation

The Federal Bureau of Investigation was created July 26, 1908, and was referred to as Office of Chief Examiner. It became the Bureau of Investigation (Mar. 16, 1909), United States Bureau of Investigation (July 1, 1932), Division of Investigation (Aug. 10, 1933), and Federal Bureau of Investigation (July 1, 1935).

Director	Assumed office	Director	Assumed office	Director	Assumed office
Stanley W. Finch	July 26, 1908	J. Edgar Hoover	Dec. 10, 1924	John E. Otto, act.	May 26, 1987
A(lexander) Bruce Bielaski	Apr. 30, 1912	L. Patrick Gray, act.	May 3, 1972	William S. Sessions	Nov. 2, 1987
William E. Allen, act.	Feb. 10, 1919	William D. Ruckelshaus, act.	Apr. 27, 1973	Floyd I. Clarke, act.	July 19, 1993
William J. Flynn	July 1, 1919			Louis J. Freeh	Sept. 1, 1993
William J. Burns	Aug. 22, 1921	Clarence M. Kelley	July 9, 1973	Thomas J. Pickard, act.	June 25, 2001
J. Edgar Hoover, act.	May 10, 1924	William H. Webster	Feb. 23, 1978	Robert S. Mueller III	Sept. 4, 2001

Crime in the U.S., 1982-2002[1]

Source: FBI, *Uniform Crime Reports*, 2002, final statistics; additional data may be available at www.fbi.gov/ucr/ucr.htm

Year	Population[2]	Crime Index (total)	Violent crime[3]	Property crime[3]	Murder and non-negligent manslaughter[1]	Forcible rape	Robbery	Aggravated assault	Burglary	Larceny-theft
				NUMBER OF REPORTED OFFENSES						
1982—231,664,458		12,974,400	1,322,390	11,652,000	21,010	78,770	553,130	669,480	3,447,100	7,142,500
1983—233,791,994		12,108,630	1,258,087	10,850,543	19,308	78,918	506,567	653,294	3,129,851	6,712,759
1984—235,824,902		11,881,755	1,273,282	10,608,476	18,692	84,233	485,008	685,349	2,984,434	6,591,874
1985—237,923,795		12,430,357	1,327,767	11,102,590	18,976	87,671	497,874	723,246	3,073,348	6,926,380
1986—240,132,887		13,211,869	1,489,169	11,722,700	20,613	91,459	542,775	834,322	3,241,410	7,257,153
1987—242,288,918		13,508,708	1,483,999	12,024,709	20,096	91,111	517,704	855,088	3,236,184	7,499,851
1988—244,498,982		13,923,086	1,566,221	12,356,865	20,675	92,486	542,968	910,092	3,218,077	7,705,872
1989—246,819,230		14,251,449	1,646,037	12,605,412	21,500	94,504	578,326	951,707	3,168,170	7,872,442
1990—249,464,396		14,475,613	1,820,127	12,655,486	23,438	102,555	639,271	1,054,863	3,073,909	7,945,670
1991—252,153,092		14,872,883	1,911,767	12,961,116	24,703	106,593	687,732	1,092,739	3,157,150	8,142,228
1992—255,029,699		14,438,191	1,932,274	12,505,917	23,760	109,062	672,478	1,126,974	2,979,884	7,915,199
1993—257,782,608		14,144,794	1,926,017	12,218,777	24,526	106,014	659,870	1,135,607	2,834,808	7,820,909
1994—260,327,021		13,989,543	1,857,670	12,131,873	23,326	102,216	618,949	1,113,179	2,712,774	7,879,812
1995—262,803,276		13,862,727	1,798,792	12,063,935	21,606	97,470	580,509	1,099,207	2,593,784	7,997,710
1996—265,228,572		13,493,863	1,688,540	11,805,323	19,645	96,252	535,594	1,037,049	2,506,400	7,904,685
1997—267,783,607		13,194,571	1,636,096	11,558,475	18,208	96,153	498,534	1,023,201	2,460,526	7,743,760
1998—270,248,003		12,485,714	1,533,887	10,951,827	16,974	93,144	447,186	976,583	2,332,735	7,376,311
1999—272,690,813		11,634,378	1,426,044	10,208,334	15,522	89,411	409,371	911,740	2,100,739	6,955,520
2000—281,421,906		11,608,070	1,425,486	10,182,584	15,586	90,178	408,016	911,706	2,050,992	6,971,590
2001—285,317,559		11,876,669	1,439,480	10,437,189	16,037	90,863	423,557	909,023	2,116,531	7,092,267
2002—288,368,698		11,877,218	1,426,325	10,450,893	16,204	95,136	420,637	894,348	2,151,875	7,052,922
				PERCENT CHANGE: NUMBER OF OFFENSES						
2002/2001		(4)	−0.9	0.1	1.0	4.7	−0.7	−1.6	1.7	−0.6
2002/1998		−4.9	−7.0	−4.6	−4.5	2.1	−5.9	−8.4	−7.8	−4.4
2002/1993		−16.0	−25.9	−14.5	−33.9	−10.3	−36.3	−21.2	−24.1	−9.8
				RATE PER 100,000 INHABITANTS						
1982		5,600.5	570.8	5,029.7	9.1	34	238.8	289	1,488.0	3,083.1
1983		5,179.2	538.1	4,641.1	8.3	33.8	216.7	279.4	1,338.7	2,871.3
1984		5,038.4	539.9	4,498.5	7.9	35.7	205.7	290.6	1,265.5	2,795.2
1985		5,224.5	558.1	4,666.4	8.0	36.8	209.3	304	1,291.7	2,911.2
1986		5,501.9	620.1	4,881.8	8.6	38.1	226	347.4	1,349.8	3,022.1
1987		5,575.5	612.5	4,963.0	8.3	37.6	213.7	352.9	1,335.7	3,095.4
1988		5,694.5	640.6	5,054.0	8.5	37.8	222.1	372.2	1,316.2	3,151.7
1989		5,774.0	666.9	5,107.1	8.7	38.3	234.3	385.6	1,283.6	3,189.6
1990		5,802.7	729.6	5,073.1	9.4	41.1	256.3	422.9	1,232.2	3,185.1
1991		5,898.4	758.2	5,140.2	9.8	42.3	272.7	433.4	1,252.1	3,229.1
1992		5,661.4	757.7	4,903.7	9.3	42.8	263.7	441.9	1,168.4	3,103.6
1993		5,487.1	747.1	4,740.0	9.5	41.1	256	440.5	1,099.7	3,033.9
1994		5,373.8	713.6	4,660.2	9.0	39.3	237.8	427.6	1,042.1	3,026.9
1995		5,274.9	684.5	4,590.5	8.2	37.1	220.9	418.3	987	3,043.2
1996		5,087.6	636.6	4,451.0	7.4	36.3	201.9	391	945	2,980.3
1997		4,927.3	611	4,316.3	6.8	35.9	186.2	382.1	918.8	2,891.8
1998		4,620.1	567.6	4,052.5	6.3	34.5	165.5	361.4	863.2	2,729.5
1999		4,266.5	523	3,743.6	5.7	32.8	150.1	334.3	770.4	2,550.7
2000		4,124.8	506.5	3,618.3	5.5	32	145	324	728.8	2,477.3
2001		4,162.6	504.5	3,658.1	5.6	31.8	148.5	318.6	714.8	2,485.7
2002—		4,118.8	494.6	3,624.1	5.6	33.0	145.9	310.1	746.2	2,445.8
				PERCENT CHANGE: RATE PER 100,000 INHABITANTS						
2002/2001		−1.1	−2.0	−0.9	(4)	3.6	−1.7	−2.7	0.6	−1.6
2002/1998		−10.9	−12.9	−10.6	−10.5	−4.3	−11.8	−14.2	−13.5	−10.4
2002/1993		−24.9	−33.8	−23.5	−40.9	−19.8	−43.0	−29.6	−32.1	−19.4

(1) The murder and nonnegligent homicides that occurred as a result of the attacks of Sept. 11, 2001, are not included in this table. (2) Populations are Bureau of the Census provisional estimates as of July 1 for each year except 1990 and 2000, which are decennial census counts. (3) Violent crimes are offenses of murder, forcible rape, robbery, and aggravated assault. Property crimes are offenses of burglary, larceny-theft, and motor vehicle theft. (4) Less than one-tenth of 1 percent.

Law Enforcement Officers, 2002

Source: FBI, *Uniform Crime Reports*, 2002; later data may be available at www.fbi.gov/ucr/ucr.htm

The U.S. law enforcement community employed an average of 2.3 full-time officers for every 1,000 inhabitants as of Oct. 31, 2002.

Including full-time civilian employees, the overall law enforcement employee rate was 3.5 per 1,000 inhabitants, according to 13,981 city, college and university, county, and state police agencies. These agencies collectively offered law enforcement service covering a population of about 271 million, employing 665,555 officers and 291,947 civilians.

The law enforcement employee average for all cities nationwide was 3.1 per 1,000 inhabitants. The highest rate was 4.1 per 1,000 inhabitants, in cities with populations of 10,000 or fewer people. Suburban counties had the highest rate at an average 4.7, and rural counties had average rate of 4.2, respectively.

Regionally, the law enforcement employee rate in cities was 3.5 per 1,000 inhabitants in the Northeast and the South, 2.8 in the Midwest, and 2.4 in the West. Both nationally and in cities, males constituted 88.7% of all sworn employees. In rural counties, 92.1% of the officers were males, while in suburban counties males accounted for 86.9%.

Civilians made up 30.5% of all U.S. law enforcement employees. They represented 23.4% of the police employees in cities, 41% in suburban counties, and 39.3% in both rural counties. Females accounted for 62.1% of all civilian employees.

Fifty-six law enforcement officers in the U.S. and Puerto Rico were slain in the line of duty in 2002, 14 fewer than in 2001. Another 77 died from accidents occurring on duty, 1 less than in 2001. About 58,066 were assaulted while on duty, a 1.6% drop from 2001.

> **IT'S A FACT:** There were 100,102 women in state and federal prisons in mid-2003, making up 6.9% of the total U.S. prison population. Since 1995, the female prison population has grown at annual average rate of 5.2%. Male inmates numbered 1,360,818 in mid-2003, with an annual growth rate of 3.4% since 1995.

U.S. Crime Rates by Region, Geographic Division, and State, 2002

Source: FBI, *Uniform Crime Reports*, 2002; final statistics;
later data available at www.fbi.gov/ucr/ucr.htm
(rate per 100,000 population)

	Total rate	Violent crime[1]	Property crime[2]	Murder	Rape	Robbery	Aggra-vated assault	Burglary	Larceny-theft	Motor vehicle theft
U.S. TOTAL	**4,118.8**	**494.6**	**3,624.1**	**5.6**	**33.0**	**145.9**	**310.1**	**746.2**	**2,445.8**	**432.1**
Northeast	**2,889.0**	**416.5**	**2,472.6**	**4.1**	**23.6**	**148.7**	**240.1**	**457.8**	**1,714.0**	**300.8**
New England	**2,964.4**	**346.9**	**2,617.5**	**2.4**	**27.2**	**91.2**	**226.1**	**509.3**	**1,774.6**	**333.6**
Connecticut	2,997.2	311.1	2,686.1	2.3	21.1	117.3	170.4	493.8	1,857.9	334.4
Maine	2,656.0	107.8	2,548.2	1.1	29.1	20.9	56.8	538.1	1,899.7	110.4
Massachusetts	3,094.2	484.4	2,609.8	2.7	27.6	111.5	342.5	517.2	1,679.0	413.6
New Hampshire . . .	2,220.0	161.2	2,058.7	0.9	35.0	32.4	92.9	379.4	1,526.8	152.5
Rhode Island	3,589.1	285.2	3,303.8	3.8	36.9	85.6	158.8	599.7	2,248.3	455.8
Vermont	2,530.0	106.7	2,423.3	2.1	20.4	12.5	71.7	565.9	1,732.8	124.7
Middle Atlantic	**2,862.5**	**441.0**	**2,421.4**	**4.7**	**22.4**	**169.0**	**245.0**	**439.6**	**1,692.6**	**289.2**
New Jersey	3,024.2	374.5	2,649.7	3.9	15.7	161.9	193.0	511.0	1,722.7	416.0
New York	2,803.7	496.0	2,307.7	4.7	20.3	191.3	279.7	400.4	1,660.1	247.2
Pennsylvania	2,841.0	401.9	2,439.1	5.1	30.2	139.1	227.5	450.8	1,722.2	266.0
Midwest	**3,883.1**	**424.9**	**3,458.2**	**5.1**	**37.0**	**126.1**	**256.7**	**685.4**	**2,413.5**	**359.4**
East North Central . .	**3,880.9**	**453.0**	**3,427.9**	**5.8**	**38.4**	**145.2**	**263.5**	**704.6**	**2,348.8**	**374.6**
Illinois	4,016.4	620.7	3,395.6	7.5	34.1	200.6	378.5	643.8	2,395.9	356.0
Indiana	3,750.0	357.2	3,392.8	5.9	29.9	107.4	214.1	691.7	2,371.7	329.4
Michigan	3,874.1	540.3	3,333.8	6.7	53.4	117.9	362.3	706.1	2,132.9	494.7
Ohio	4,107.3	351.3	3,755.9	4.6	42.1	156.5	148.2	868.2	2,513.3	374.5
Wisconsin	3,252.7	224.9	3,027.8	2.8	22.7	86.6	112.7	513.2	2,267.2	247.3
West North Central . .	**3,888.2**	**358.9**	**3,529.3**	**3.2**	**33.7**	**81.3**	**240.7**	**640.4**	**2,565.3**	**323.6**
Iowa	3,448.2	285.6	3,162.6	1.5	27.1	39.8	217.2	634.8	2,329.5	198.3
Kansas	4,087.0	376.6	3,710.3	2.9	38.1	79.7	255.9	724.6	2,720.2	265.5
Minnesota	3,535.1	267.5	3,267.6	2.2	45.3	78.4	141.6	558.5	2,433.4	275.8
Missouri	4,602.4	538.7	4,063.8	5.8	25.8	123.8	383.2	753.1	2,819.2	491.5
Nebraska	4,256.7	313.9	3,942.8	2.8	26.8	78.6	205.7	597.3	2,974.8	370.6
North Dakota	2,406.2	78.2	2,328.0	0.8	25.7	9.1	42.6	353.7	1,813.7	160.5
South Dakota	2,278.7	177.4	2,101.3	1.4	47.4	15.4	113.1	398.7	1,595.0	107.6
South	**4,721.9**	**571.0**	**4,151.0**	**6.8**	**34.5**	**156.8**	**372.9**	**932.6**	**2,794.1**	**424.3**
South Atlantic	**4,686.1**	**601.4**	**4,084.7**	**6.7**	**32.0**	**167.8**	**394.8**	**906.5**	**2,735.7**	**442.5**
Delaware	3,939.0	599.0	3,340.0	3.2	44.3	142.9	408.5	663.3	2,298.2	378.6
District of Columbia	8,022.3	1,632.9	6,389.4	46.2	45.9	671.6	869.2	905.6	3,802.4	1,681.4
Florida	5,420.6	770.2	4,650.4	5.5	40.4	194.9	529.4	1,060.5	3,060.3	529.6
Georgia	4,507.2	458.8	4,048.4	7.1	24.6	156.9	270.1	863.7	2,740.4	444.3
Maryland	4,747.4	769.8	3,977.6	9.4	25.1	245.8	489.5	728.5	2,625.8	623.3
North Carolina	4,721.4	470.2	4,251.2	6.6	26.4	146.7	290.5	1,196.3	2,756.0	298.9
South Carolina	5,297.3	822.0	4,475.3	7.3	47.7	140.6	626.5	1,065.1	2,999.5	410.7
Virginia	3,140.3	291.4	2,848.9	5.3	25.2	95.4	165.5	435.4	2,160.1	253.3
West Virginia	2,515.2	234.3	2,280.9	3.2	18.2	36.5	176.4	537.1	1,527.5	216.3
East South Central . .	**4,229.6**	**479.9**	**3,749.7**	**6.8**	**35.8**	**126.4**	**311.0**	**935.0**	**2,474.3**	**340.3**
Alabama	4,465.2	444.2	4,020.9	6.8	37.1	132.9	267.5	949.0	2,762.3	309.6
Kentucky	2,902.6	279.0	2,623.6	4.5	26.6	74.8	173.1	680.6	1,729.2	213.8
Mississippi	4,159.2	343.3	3,815.9	9.2	39.2	116.9	178.0	1,030.5	2,453.8	331.6
Tennessee	5,018.9	716.9	4,302.0	7.2	39.5	162.4	507.8	1,056.5	2,787.7	457.8
West South Central .	**5,042.8**	**569.2**	**4,473.6**	**6.8**	**38.1**	**154.6**	**369.7**	**974.4**	**3,060.4**	**438.8**
Arkansas	4,157.5	424.4	3,733.1	5.2	27.8	93.1	298.2	857.1	2,624.6	251.4
Louisiana	5,098.1	662.3	4,435.7	13.2	34.1	158.9	456.1	1,011.7	2,973.7	450.3
Oklahoma	4,743.2	503.4	4,239.8	4.7	45.0	84.9	368.8	1,006.7	2,867.6	365.6
Texas	5,189.6	578.6	4,611.0	6.0	39.1	172.5	361.0	976.1	3,163.4	471.4
West	**4,418.8**	**508.2**	**3,910.6**	**5.7**	**34.3**	**146.0**	**322.2**	**751.5**	**2,534.0**	**625.1**
Mountain	**4,889.7**	**457.0**	**4,432.7**	**5.3**	**39.1**	**108.4**	**304.2**	**827.3**	**2,982.8**	**622.6**
Arizona	6,386.3	552.9	5,833.4	7.1	29.5	146.6	369.8	1,082.9	3,693.6	1,056.9
Colorado	4,347.8	352.4	3,995.4	4.0	45.8	79.4	223.2	702.9	2,778.0	514.4
Idaho	3,172.5	254.9	2,917.5	2.7	37.1	17.9	197.3	554.8	2,166.8	195.9
Montana	3,512.9	351.5	3,161.4	1.8	26.1	31.1	292.6	361.6	2,603.7	196.1
Nevada	4,497.5	637.5	3,860.0	8.3	42.7	235.5	351.0	871.9	2,183.5	804.5
New Mexico	5,077.8	739.5	4,338.2	8.2	55.4	118.9	557.1	1,058.4	2,878.9	400.9
Utah	4,452.4	236.9	4,215.5	2.0	40.7	49.2	145.0	653.0	3,229.1	333.4
Wyoming	3,580.9	273.5	3,307.4	3.0	29.7	18.6	222.2	490.9	2,667.5	149.0
Pacific	**4,226.2**	**529.1**	**3,697.1**	**5.8**	**32.3**	**161.4**	**329.6**	**720.5**	**2,350.5**	**626.2**
Alaska	4,309.7	563.4	3,746.3	5.1	79.4	76.0	402.9	607.0	2,755.4	383.8
California	3,943.7	593.4	3,350.3	6.8	29.0	185.0	372.6	679.0	2,038.1	633.2
Hawaii	6,043.7	262.0	5,781.7	1.9	29.9	97.2	133.0	1,021.9	3,963.7	796.0
Oregon	4,868.4	292.4	4,576.0	2.0	35.2	77.9	177.4	729.7	3,377.1	469.2
Washington	5,106.8	345.4	4,761.4	3.0	4.05	95.5	201.8	905.4	3,188.8	667.2
Puerto Rico	**2,352.6**	**349.1**	**2,003.5**	**20.1**	**6.2**	**232.7**	**90.1**	**641.1**	**1,027.3**	**335.2**

Note: Offense totals are based on all reporting agencies and estimates for unreported areas. Totals may not add because of rounding. (1) Violent crimes are murder, forcible rape, robbery, and aggravated assault. (2) Property crimes are burglary, larceny-theft, and motor vehicle theft. Data not included for property crime of arson.

Sentences vs. Time Served for Selected Crimes

Source: Bureau of Justice Statistics, *Truth in Sentencing in State Prisons,* 1999

The following is a comparison of the average maximum sentence lengths (excluding both life and death sentences) and the actual time served for selected state-court convictions.

Type of offense	Avg. sentence	Avg. time served[1]	Type of offense	Avg. sentence	Avg. time served[1]
All violent	7 years, 1 month	3 years, 3 months	Robbery	7 years, 8 months	3 years, 4 months
Homicide	15 years	7 years	Negligent manslaughter	8 years, 1 month	3 years, 5 months
Rape	9 years, 8 months	5 years, 1 month	Assault	5 years, 1 month	2 years, 4 months
Other sexual assault . .	6 years, 9 months	3 years, 3 months	Other	5 years, 7 months	2 years, 5 months

(1) Includes jail credit and prison time.

IT'S A FACT: Largely because of stricter sentencing laws, the number of federal and state prison inmates serving life sentences increased by 83% from 1992 to 2002; by 2002, there were 127,677 such lifers, accounting for almost 10% all sentenced prisoners, according to the Sentencing Project, a prison advocacy and research organization.

State and Federal Prison Population, Death Penalty, 2002-2003[1]

Source: Bureau of Justice Statistics, U.S. Dept. of Justice

As of June 30, 2003, there were 1,460,920 prisoners under the jurisdiction of federal or state adult correctional authorities, including those within these prison systems but held outside their facilities. The U.S. state and federal prison population grew 2.9%, which was less than the average annual growth of 3.2% since 1995, but represented the biggest growth in 4 years. As of mid-2003, these two systems housed 66% of the incarcerated population (1,380,776 out of 2,078,570). Jails, which are locally operated and typically hold persons awaiting trial and those with sentences of a year or less, held most of the remainder (691,301); juvenile and military facilities, territorial prisons, jails in Indian country, and facilities of the Bureau of Immigration and Customs Enforcement (formerly the INS) held the rest. The rate of incarceration in state and federal prisons was 480 per 100,000 U.S. residents, up from 411 at year-end 1995 (1 in every 109 men and 1 in every 1,639 women were sentenced prisoners under the jurisdiction of state or federal authorities). The number of persons under sentence of death at the end of 2002 dropped slightly from 3,577 to 3,557; 71 prisoners were executed in 2002—5 more than the previous year.

| | SENTENCED PRISONERS | | | DEATH PENALTY, 2002 | | |
	mid-2003	mid-2002	% change 2002-2003	Under sentence of death	Executions	Death penalty
U.S. TOTAL	1,460,920	1,419,937	2.9	3,557	71	—
Federal institutions	170,461	161,681	5.4	24	0	Yes
State institutions	1,290,459	1,258,256	2.6	3,533	71	38
Northeast	175,753	175,102	0.4	267	0	—
Connecticut	20,525	20,243	1.4	7	0	Yes
Maine	2,009	1,841	9.1	—	—	No
Massachusetts	10,511	10,620	−1.0	—	—	No
New Hampshire	2,483	2,476	0.3	0	0	Yes
New Jersey[2]	28,213	28,054	0.6	14	0	Yes
New York	65,914	67,131	−1.8	5	0	Yes
Pennsylvania	40,545	39,275	3.2	241	0	Yes
Rhode Island	3,569	3,694	−3.4	—	—	No
Vermont	1,984	1,768	12.2	—	—	No
Midwest	247,478	243,861	1.5	483	9	—
Illinois[2]	43,186	43,142	0.1	159	0	Yes
Indiana	22,576	21,425	5.4	36	0	Yes
Iowa[2]	8,395	8,172	2.7	—	—	No
Kansas[2]	9,009	8,758	2.9	5	0	Yes
Michigan	49,524	49,961	−0.9	—	—	No
Minnesota	7,612	6,958	9.4	—	—	No
Missouri	30,649	30,034	2.0	66	6	Yes
Nebraska	4,103	4,031	1.8	7	0	Yes
North Dakota	1,168	1,168	0.0	—	—	No
Ohio[2]	45,831	45,349	1.1	205	3	Yes
South Dakota	3,059	2,900	5.5	5	0	Yes
Wisconsin	22,366	21,963	1.8	—	—	No
South	581,901	561,411	3.6	1,884	61	—
Alabama	28,440	27,495	3.4	191	2	Yes
Arkansas	12,378	12,655	−2.2	40	0	Yes
Delaware	6,879	6,957	−1.1	14	0	Yes
Florida	80,352	73,553	—	366	3	Yes
Georgia	47,004	46,417	1.3	112	4	Yes
Kentucky	16,377	16,172	1.3	36	0	Yes
Louisiana	36,091	36,171	−0.2	86	1	Yes
Maryland	24,186	24,329	−0.6	15	0	Yes
Mississippi	20,542	19,287	6.5	66	2	Yes
North Carolina	33,334	32,755	1.8	206	2	Yes
Oklahoma[2]	23,004	23,435	−1.8	112	7	Yes
South Carolina	24,247	23,017	5.3	72	3	Yes
Tennessee[2]	25,409	24,277	4.7	95	0	Yes
Texas[2]	164,222	157,664	4.2	450	33	Yes
Virginia	34,733	32,739	—	23	4	Yes
West Virginia	4,703	4,488	4.8	—	—	No
West	285,327	277,882	2.7	899	1	—
Alaska	4,431	4,205	5.4	—	—	No
Arizona	30,741	29,103	5.6	120	0	Yes
California	163,361	160,315	1.9	614	1	Yes
Colorado	19,085	18,32	4.2	5	0	Yes
Hawaii	5,635	5,541	1.7	—	—	No
Idaho	5,825	5,802	0.4	20	0	Yes
Montana	3,440	3,515	−2.1	6	0	Yes
Nevada	10,527	10,426	1.0	83	0	Yes
New Mexico	6,173	5,929	4.1	2	0	Yes
Oregon	12,422	11,812	5.2	26	0	Yes
Utah	5,594	5,353	4.5	11	0	Yes
Washington	16,284	15,829	2.9	10	0	Yes
Wyoming	1,809	1,732	4.4	2	0	Yes

Note: The District of Columbia had transferred its sentenced felons to the Federal Bureau of Prisons, as of Dec. 31, and no longer operates a prison system. (1) All information applies to Dec. 31 of the year indicated. (2) Includes some inmates sentenced to one year or less.

Prison Situation Among the States and in the Federal System, Mid-2003

Source: *Prison and Jail Inmates at Midyear 2003*, Bureau of Justice Statistics, U.S. Dept. of Justice

10 largest prison populations, 2003	Number of inmates	10 highest incarceration rates, 2002	Prisoners per 100,000 residents[1]	10 largest % increases in prison population			
				Growth 2001-2002	% annual increase	Growth since 1995	% increase
Federal........	170,461	Louisiana	803	Vermont........	12.2	Wisconsin	110.4
Texas.........	164,222	Texas.........	692	Minnesota	9.4	West Virginia	92.9
California	163,361	Mississippi.....	688	Maine..........	9.1	North Dakota	91.5
Florida	80,352	Oklahoma......	645	Mississippi......	6.5	Montana........	91.0
New York	65,914	Alabama.......	612	Virginia	6.1	Vermont........	87.5
Michigan	49,524	South Carolina ...	561	Arizona........	5.6	Idaho	79.8
Georgia	47,004	Georgia	541	South Dakota....	5.5	Colorado.......	77.4
Ohio	45,831	Missouri........	537	Federal	5.4	South Dakota....	71.9
Illinois	43,186	Arizona........	502	Alaska	5.4	Federal	71.4
Pennsylvania ...	40,545	Michigan........	491	Indiana........	5.4	Utah...........	80.0

(1) Prisoners with sentences of more than 1 year. As of Dec. 31, 2002, the District of Columbia had transferred all sentenced felons to federal prison system.

Executions, by State and Method, 1977-2003

Source: Bureau of Justice Statistics, *Capital Punishment 2002*, Nov. 2003;
Death Penalty Information Center, NAACP Legal Defense and Education Fund, *Death Row, U.S.A.*

		Lethal injection	Electro-cution	Lethal gas	Firing squad	Hang-ing			Lethal injection	Electro-cution	Lethal gas	Firing squad	Hang-ing
TOTAL U.S.	885	718	151	11	2	3	Missouri.......	61	61	0	0	0	0
Federal govt. ...	3	3	0	0	0	0	Montana.......	2	2	0	0	0	0
Alabama.......	28	4	24	0	0	0	Nebraska......	3	0	3	0	0	0
Arizona........	22	20	0	2	0	0	Nevada	9	8	0	1	0	0
Arkansas	25	24	1	0	0	0	New Mexico....	1	1	0	0	0	0
California	10	8	0	2	0	0	North Carolina ..	30	28	0	2	0	0
Colorado.......	1	1	0	0	0	0	Ohio..........	8	8	0	0	0	0
Delaware	13	12	0	0	0	1	Oklahoma	69	69	0	0	0	0
Florida	57	13	44	0	0	0	Oregon.......	2	2	0	0	0	0
Georgia	34	11	23	0	0	0	Pennsylvania...	3	3	0	0	0	0
Idaho	1	1	0	0	0	0	South Carolina ..	28	23	5	0	0	0
Illinois	12	12	0	0	0	0	Tennessee.....	1	1	0	0	0	0
Indiana	11	8	3	0	0	0	Texas.........	313	313	0	0	0	0
Kentucky	2	1	1	0	0	0	Utah..........	6	4	0	0	2	0
Louisiana	27	7	20	0	0	0	Virginia	89	62	27	0	0	0
Maryland	3	3	0	0	0	0	Washington	4	2	0	0	0	2
Mississippi	6	2	0	4	0	0	Wyoming	1	1	0	0	0	0

Note: Table shows methods used since the 1976 reinstatement of the death penalty by the Supreme Court. Lethal injection was used in 80% of total executions. 17 states—Alabama, Arizona, Arkansas, California, Delaware, Florida, Georgia, Indiana, Kentucky, Louisiana, Mississippi, Nevada, North Carolina, South Carolina, Utah, Virginia, and Washington—have used 2 methods. 18 states had no executions during the period.

Total Estimated Arrests, 2002

Source: FBI, *Uniform Crime Reports*, 2002

Total, all arrests[1,2]	13,741,438	Vandalism	276,697
Murder and non-negligent manslaughter	14,158	Weapons; carrying, possessing, etc.	164,446
Forcible rape	28,288	Prostitution and commercialized vice	79,733
Robbery	105,774	Sex offenses (except forcible rape	
Aggravated assault	472,290	and prostitution).....................	95,066
Burglary	288,291	Drug abuse violations	1,583,813
Larceny-theft	1,160,085	Gambling	10,506
Motor vehicle theft	148,943	Offenses against the family and children	140,286
Arson	16,635	Driving under the influence	1,461,746
Violent crime[3]	**620,510**	Liquor laws	653,819
Property crime[4]	**1,613,954**	Drunkenness	572,735
Crime Index total[5]	**2,234,464**	Disorderly conduct.....................	669,938
Other assaults	1,288,682	Vagrancy............................	27,295
Forgery and counterfeiting	115,735	All other offenses......................	3,662,159
Fraud	337,404	Suspicion...........................	8,889
Embezzlement	18,552	Curfew and loitering law violations	141,252
Stolen property; buying, receiving, possessing	126,422	Runaways	125,688

(1) Does not include suspicion. (2) Because of rounding, the figures may not add to total. (3) Violent crimes are offenses of murder, forcible rape, robbery, and aggravated assault. (4) Property crimes are offenses of burglary, larceny-theft, and arson. (5) Includes arson.

Historic Assassinations Since 1865

1865—Apr. 14. U.S. Pres. Abraham Lincoln shot by John Wilkes Booth, a well-known actor with Confederate sympathies, at Ford's Theater in Washington, DC; died Apr. 15.

1881—Mar. 13. Alexander II, of Russia.—July 2. U.S. Pres. James A. Garfield shot by Charles J. Guiteau, a disappointed office seeker, in Washington, DC; died Sept. 19.

1894—June 24. Pres. Sadi Carnot of France, by Italian anarchist, Sante Caserio, in Lyon.

1898—Sept. 10. Empress Elizabeth of Austria, stabbed by Italian anarchist Luigi Luccheni.

1900—July 29. Umberto I, king of Italy.

1901—Sept. 6. U.S. Pres. William McKinley in Buffalo, NY; died Sept. 14. Leon Czolgosz executed for the crime.

1908—Feb. 1. King Carlos I of Portugal and his son Luis Felipe, in Lisbon.

1913—Feb. 23. Mexican Pres. Francisco I. Madero and Vice Pres. Jose Pino Suarez.—Mar. 18. George, king of Greece.

1914—June 28. Archduke Francis Ferdinand of Austria-Hungary and his wife in Sarajevo, Bosnia, by Gavrilo Princip.

1916—Dec. 30. Grigori Rasputin, powerful Russian monk.

1918—July 12. Grand Duke Michael of Russia, at Perm.—July 16. Nicholas II, abdicated as czar of Russia; his wife, the Czarina Alexandra; their son, Czarevitch Alexis; their daughters, Grand Duchesses Olga, Tatiana, Marie, Anastasia; and 4 members of their household, executed by Bolsheviks at Ekaterinburg.

1920—May 20. Mexican Pres. Gen. Venustiano Carranza in Tlaxcalantongo.

1922—Aug. 22. Michael Collins, Irish revolutionary.—Dec. 16. Polish Pres.Gabriel Narutowicz in Warsaw.

1923—July 20. Gen. Francisco "Pancho" Villa, ex-rebel leader, in Parral, Mexico.

1928—July 17. Gen. Alvaro Obregon, president-elect of Mexico, in San Angel, Mexico.

1932—May 6. Pres. Paul Doumer of France shot by Russian émigré, Pavel Gorgulov, in Paris.

1934—July 25. In Vienna, Austrian Chancellor Engelbert Dollfuss by Nazis.

1935—Sept. 8. U.S. Sen. Huey P. Long shot in Baton Rouge, LA, by Dr. Carl Austin Weiss; died Sept. 10.

1940—Aug. 20. Leon Trotsky (Lev Bronstein), 63, exiled Soviet war minister, near Mexico City.

1948—Jan. 30. Mohandas K. Gandhi, 78, shot in New Delhi, India, by Nathuram Vinayak Godse.—Sept. 17. Count Folke Bernadotte, UN mediator for Palestine, by Jewish extremists in Jerusalem.

1951—July 20. King Abdullah ibn Hussein of Jordan.—Oct. 16. Prime Min. Liaquat Ali Khan of Pakistan shot in Rawalpindi.

1956—Sept. 21. Pres. Anastasio Somoza of Nicaragua, shot in Leon; died Sept. 29.

1957—July 26. Pres. Carlos Castillo Armas of Guatemala, in Guatemala City by one of his own guards.

1958—July 14. King Faisal of Iraq, Crown Prince Abdullah, and July 15, Prem. Nuri as-Said, by rebels in Baghdad.

1959—Sept. 25. Prime Min. Solomon Bandaranaike of Ceylon, by Buddhist monk in Colombo.

1961—Jan. 17. Ex-Prem. Patrice Lumumba of the Congo, in Katanga Province.—May 30. Dominican dictator Rafael Leonidas Trujillo Molina, near Ciudad Trujillo.

1963—June 12. Medgar W. Evers, NAACP's Mississippi field secretary, shot dead by Byron De La Beckwith in Jackson, MS.—Nov. 2. Pres. Ngo Dinh Diem of South Vietnam, and his brother, Ngo Dinh Nhu, in a military coup.—Nov. 22. U.S. Pres. John F. Kennedy shot while riding in motorcade in Dallas, TX; accused gunman Lee Harvey Oswald was murdered by Jack Ruby while awaiting trial.

1965—Jan. 21. Iranian Prem. Hassan Ali Mansour in Tehran; 4 executed.—Feb. 21. Malcolm X, black nationalist, shot in New York City.

1966—Sept. 6. Prime Min. Hendrik F. Verwoerd of South Africa stabbed to death in parliament at Cape Town.

1968—Apr. 4. Rev. Dr. Martin Luther King Jr. fatally shot in Memphis, TN; James Earl Ray convicted of crime.—June 5. Sen. Robert F. Kennedy (D, NY) shot in Los Angeles; Sirhan Sirhan, convicted of crime.

1971—Nov. 28. Prime Min. Wasfi Tal of Jordan, in Cairo, by Palestinian guerrillas.

1973—Mar. 2. U.S. Amb. Cleo A. Noel Jr., U.S. Charge d'Affaires George C. Moore, and Belgian Charge d'Affaires Guy Eid killed by Palestinian guerrillas in Khartoum, Sudan.

1974—Aug. 19. U.S. Amb. to Cyprus, Rodger P. Davies, killed by sniper's bullet in Nicosia.

1975—Feb. 11. Pres. Richard Ratsimandrava, of Madagascar, shot in Tananarive.—Mar. 25. Saudi Arabian King Faisal shot by nephew Prince Musad Abdel Aziz, in Riyadh.—Aug. 15. Bangladesh Pres. Sheik Mujibur Rahman killed in coup.

1976—Feb. 13. Nigerian head of state, Gen. Murtala Ramat Mohammed, by self-styled "young revolutionaries."

1977—Mar. 16. Kamal Jumblat, Lebanese Druse chieftain, shot near Beirut.—Mar. 18. Congo Pres. Marien Ngouabi shot in Brazzaville.

1978—May 9. Former Italian Prem. Aldo Moro killed by Red Brigades terrorists who abducted him Mar. 16 in Rome and killed 5 bodyguards.—July 9. Former Iraqi Prem. Abdul Razak Al-Naif shot in London.

1979—Feb. 14. U.S. Amb. Adolph Dubs shot by Afghan Muslim extremists in Kabul.—Aug. 27. Lord Mountbatten, World War II hero, and 2 others killed when a bomb exploded on his fishing boat off the coast of Co. Sligo, Ire. IRA claimed responsibility.—Oct. 26. South Korean Pres. Park Chung Hee and 6 bodyguards fatally shot by Kim Jae Kyu, head of South Korean CIA, and 5 aides in Seoul.

1980—Apr. 12. Liberian Pres. William R. Tolbert slain in military coup.—Sept. 17. Former Nicaraguan Pres. Anastasio Somoza Debayle shot in Paraguay.

1981—Oct. 6. Egyptian Pres. Anwar al-Sadat shot by commandos while reviewing a military parade in Cairo; 7 others killed, 28 wounded; 4 convicted as assassins and executed.

1982—Sept. 14. Lebanese Pres.-elect Bashir Gemayel killed by bomb in east Beirut.

1983—Aug. 21. Philippine opposition leader Benigno Aquino Jr. shot by gunman at Manila International Airport.

1984—Oct. 31. Indian Prime Min. Indira Gandhi shot and killed by 2 Sikh bodyguards, in New Delhi.

1986—Feb. 28. Swedish Prem. Olof Palme shot by gunman on Stockholm street.

1987—June 1. Lebanese Prem. Rashid Karami killed when bomb exploded aboard a helicopter.

1988—Apr. 16. PLO military chief Khalil Wazir (Abu Jihad) gunned down by Israeli commandos in Tunisia.

1989—Aug. 18. Colombian presidential candidate Luis Carlos Galan killed by Medellín cartel drug traffickers at campaign rally in Bogotá.—Nov. 22. Lebanese Pres. Rene Moawad killed when bomb exploded next to his motorcade.

1990—Mar. 22. Presidential candidate Bernando Jamamillo Ossa shot by gunman at an airport in Bogotá.

1991—May 21. Rajiv Gandhi, former prime min. of India, killed by bomb during election rally in Madras.

1992—June 29. Mohammed Boudiaf, pres. of Algeria, shot by gunman in Annaba.

1993—May 1. Ranasinghe Premadasa, pres. of Sri Lanka, killed by bomb in Colombo.

1994—Mar. 23. Luis Donaldo Colosio Murrieta, Mexican presidential candidate, shot by gunman Mario Aburto Martinez. —Apr. 6. Burundian Pres. Cyprien Ntaryamira and Rwandan Pres. Juvenal Habyarimana killed, with 8 others, when their plane was apparently shot down.

1995—Nov. 4. Yitzhak Rabin, prime min. of Israel, shot by gunman Yigal Amir at peace rally in Tel Aviv.

1996—Oct. 2. Andrei Lukanov, former Bulgarian prime minister, shot outside his home by an unidentified gunman.

1998—Feb. 6. Claude Erignac, prefect of Corsica, shot in the back while walking to a concert, by two unidentified gunmen.—Apr. 26. Guatemalan Rom. Catholic Bishop Juan Gerardi Conedera, human rights champion, found beaten to death in Guatemala City; 4 persons convicted, June 8, 2001.

1999—Mar. 23. Paraguayan Vice-Pres. Luis Maria Argaña, ambushed and shot to death, along with his driver, by 4 unidentified assailants.—Apr. 9. Niger's Pres. Ibrahim Bare Mainassara, ambushed and killed by dissident soldiers.—Oct. 27. Armenia's Prime Min. Vazgen Sarkissian, along with 7 others, was shot to death during a session of Parliament.

2000—Jan. 15. Serbian paramilitary leader Zeljko Raznjatovic (alias Arkan), with 2 others, shot and killed by unidentified gunman in Belgrade hotel lobby; 4 suspects later charged with the killing.—June 8. Brig. Gen. Stephen Saunders, Britain's senior military representative in Greece, shot and killed by 2 men on motorcycle, while driving a car in an Athens suburb.

2001—Jan. 16. Congolese Pres. Laurent Kabila, shot to death by bodyguard at pres. palace in Kinshasa.—June 1. Nepal's King Birendra, Queen Aiswarya, and 7 other royals fatally shot by Crown Prince Dipendra, who also fatally wounded himself.—Sept. 9. Afghan Northern Alliance (anti-Taliban) guerrilla leader Ahmed Shah Massoud, injured in suicide-attack bombing in N. Afghanistan by 2 Arabs posing as journalists; died Sept. 15.—Oct. 14. Abdel Rahman Hamad, a leader of Palestinian militant group Hamas, shot dead by Israeli military snipers.—Oct. 17. Israeli tourism minister Rehavam Zeevi, fatally shot; Popular Front for the Liberation of Palestine (PFLP) claimed responsibility.

2002—May 6. Dutch right-wing politician Pim Fortuyn shot dead outside a radio station in Hilversum, Netherlands.—July 6. Afghan Vice-Pres. Haji Abdul Qadir, shot dead outside his office in Kabul.—July 23. Salah Sherhada, a founder of the armed wing of Hamas, killed with 14 others in an assassination air strike on Gaza City by an Israeli fighter jet.

2003—Mar. 12. Serbian Prime Min. Zoran Djindjic, shot dead by snipers outside government headquarters in Belgrade.—Apr. 10. Shiite Muslim cleric Abdul Majid al-Khoei attacked by crowd, hacked to death at Imam Ali mosque in Najaf, Iraq.—Apr. 17. Sergei Yushenkov, former Russian legislator and Liberal Party head, shot dead outside apartment in Moscow.—Aug. 29. Prominent Shiite Muslim cleric Bakir al-Hakim killed in car bombing at Imam Ali mosque in Najaf, Iraq.—Sept. 10. Swedish Foreign Min. Anna Lindh stabbed in dept. store in Stockholm; died Sept.11.

2004—Feb. 13. Former Chechen Pres. Zelimkhan Yandarbiyev killed after car exploded in Qatar.—Mar. 22. Sheik Ahmed Yassin, spiritual leader of Hamas, killed by Israeli missile attack in Gaza City.—Apr. 18. Hamas leader Dr. Abdel Aziz Rantisi killed by Israeli missile strike in Gaza City.—May 9. Bomb exploded at WWII memorial service in Grozny, Chechnya, killing the republic's president, Akhmad Kadyrov.—May 17. Car bomb exploded at Green Zone checkpoint in Baghdad, killing Iraqi Governing Council Pres. Ezzedine Salim.—June 12. Iraqi Dep. Foreign Min. Bassam Salih Kubba gunned down outside home in Baghdad.

Assassination Attempts

1912—Oct. 14. Former U.S. Pres. Theodore Roosevelt shot and wounded by demented man in Milwaukee, WI.

1933—Feb. 15. In Miami, FL, Joseph Zangara, anarchist, shot at Pres.-elect Franklin D. Roosevelt, but a woman seized his arm, and the bullet fatally wounded Mayor Anton J. Cermak, of Chicago, who died Mar. 6.

1944—July 20. Adolf Hitler was injured when a bomb, planted by a German officer, exploded in the dictator's headquarters. One aide was killed and 12 were injured in the explosion.

1950—Nov. 1. In an attempt to assassinate Pres. Harry Truman, 2 members of a Puerto Rican nationalist movement— Griselio Torresola and Oscar Collazo—tried to shoot their way into Blair House. Torresola was killed, and a White House policeman, Pvt. Leslie Coffelt, was fatally shot.

1970—Nov. 27. Pope Paul VI unharmed by knife-wielding assailant who attempted to attack him in Manila airport.

1972—May 15. Alabama Gov. George Wallace shot in Laurel, MD, by Arthur Bremer; seriously crippled.

1975—Sept. 5. Pres. Gerald R. Ford unharmed when a Secret Service agent grabbed a pistol aimed at him by Lynette (Squeaky) Fromme, a Charles Manson follower, in Sacramento.—Sept. 22. Pres. Ford again unharmed when Sara Jane Moore fired a revolver at him in San Francisco; a bystander helped deflect the shot.

1980—May 29. Civil rights leader Vernon E. Jordan Jr. shot and wounded in Ft. Wayne, IN.

1981—Jan. 16. Irish political activist Bernadette Devlin McAliskey and her husband shot and seriously wounded by 3 members of a Protestant paramilitary group in Co. Tyrone, Ire.—Mar. 30. Pres. Ronald Reagan, along with Press Sec. James Brady, Secret Service agent Timothy J. McCarthy, and Washington, DC, policeman Thomas Delahanty shot and seriously wounded by John W. Hinckley Jr. in Washington, DC.—May 13. Pope John Paul II and 2 bystanders shot and wounded by Mehmet Ali Agca, an escaped Turkish murderer, in St. Peter's Square, Rome.

1982—May 12. Pope John Paul II unharmed after guards overpowered a man with a knife, in Fatima, Portugal.

1984—Oct. 12. British Prime Min. Margaret Thatcher unharmed when a bomb, said to have been planted by the IRA, exploded at the Grand Hotel in Brighton, England, during a Conservative Party conference. Four died, including a member of Parliament.

1986—Sept. 7. Chilean Pres. Gen. Augusto Pinochet Ugarte escaped unharmed when motorcade was attacked by rebels.

1995—June 26. Egyptian Pres. Hosni Mubarak unharmed when gunmen fired on his motorcade in Addis Ababa, Ethiopia. Four died, including 2 Ethiopian police officers.

1997—Feb. 12. Colombian Pres. Ernesto Samper Pizano unharmed when a bomb exploded on a runway in Barranquilla as his plane was preparing to land.—Apr. 30. Tajik Pres. Imamali Rakhmanov injured when a grenade was thrown at him.

1998—Feb. 9. Georgian Pres. Eduard A. Shevardnadze unharmed when gunmen fired on his motorcade in Tbilisi, Georgia. Three died, including 2 bodyguards and 1 assailant.

2000—Sept. 18. Armed men attempted to assassinate Côte d'Ivoire military leader Gen. Robert Guei in a predawn raid.

2002—Apr. 14. Leading Colombian presidential candidate Alvaro Uribe Velez unharmed after bomb exploded under parked bus as his motorcade passed in Barranquilla; 3 bystanders were killed.—July 14. French Pres. Jacques Chirac, unharmed after Maxime Brunerie, a gunman with ties to neo-Nazi groups, fired at his open-top jeep during a Bastille Day parade in Paris.—Sept. 5. Afghan Pres. Hamid Karzai, unharmed after militant shot at car in Kandahar—Nov. 25. Turkmenistan Pres. Saparmurat Niyazov unharmed after gunmen open fire on his motorcade in Ashgabat.

2003—Dec. 14. Pakistani Pres. Pervez Musharraf unharmed after bomb detonates on bridge in Rawalpindi seconds after his motorcade crosses over.

2004—Mar. 19. Taiwanese Pres. Chen Shui-bian shot while campaigning in motorcade; minor injuries.—July 13. Separatists bombed motorcade of Sergei Abramov, Chenchya's acting pres.—Sept. 16. Rocket fired at helicopter carrying Afghan Pres. Hamid Karzai, nr. Gardez, Afghanistan.

Notable U.S. Kidnappings Since 1924

Robert Franks, 13, in Chicago, **May 22, 1924,** by 2 youths, Richard Loeb and Nathan Leopold, who killed boy. Demand for $10,000 ignored. Loeb died in prison; Leopold paroled 1958.

Charles A. Lindbergh Jr., 20 mos. old, in Hopewell, NJ, **Mar. 1, 1932;** found dead **May 12.** Ransom of $50,000 paid to man identified as Bruno Richard Hauptmann, 35, paroled German convict who entered U.S. illegally. Hauptmann was convicted after spectacular trial at Flemington, and electrocuted in Trenton, NJ, prison, **Apr. 3, 1936.**

William A. Hamm Jr., 39, in St. Paul, **June 15, 1933.** $100,000 paid. Alvin Karpis given life, paroled in 1969.

Charles F. Urschel, in Oklahoma City, **July 22, 1933.** Released **July 31** after $200,000 paid. George "Machine Gun" Kelly and 5 others sentenced to life.

Brooke L. Hart, 22, in San Jose, CA. Thomas Thurmond and John Holmes arrested after demanding $40,000 ransom. When Hart's body was found in San Francisco Bay, **Nov. 26, 1933,** a mob attacked the jail and lynched the 2 kidnappers.

June Robles, 6, in Tucson, AZ. Missing for 19 days after ransom note sent to parents. Found in an iron cage buried in the desert. No arrests made.

George Weyerhaeuser, 9, in Tacoma, WA, **May 24, 1935.** Returned home **June 1** after $200,000 paid. Kidnappers given 20 to 60 years.

Charles Mattson, 10, in Tacoma, WA, **Dec. 27, 1936.** Found dead **Jan. 11, 1937.** Kidnapper asked $28,000, but failed to contact for delivery.

Arthur Fried, in White Plains, NY, **Dec. 4, 1937.** Body not found. Two kidnappers executed.

Robert C. Greenlease, 6, taken from Kansas City, MO, school **Sept. 28, 1953,** held for $600,000. Body was found Oct. 7. Bonnie Brown Heady and Carl A. Hall pleaded guilty and were executed.

Peter Weinberger, 32 days old, Westbury, NY, **July 4, 1956,** for $2,000 ransom, not paid. Child found dead. Angelo John LaMarca, 31, convicted, executed.

Lee Crary, 8, in Everett, WA, **Sept. 22, 1957;** $10,000 ransom, not paid. He escaped after 3 days, led police to George E. Collins, who was convicted.

Frank Sinatra Jr., 19, from hotel room in Lake Tahoe, CA, **Dec. 8, 1963.** Released **Dec. 11** after his father paid $240,000 ransom. Three men sentenced to prison.

Barbara Jane Mackle, 20, abducted **Dec. 17, 1968,** from Atlanta, GA, motel; found unharmed 3 days later, buried in a coffin-like box 18 inches underground, after her father had paid $500,000 ransom; Gary Steven Krist sentenced to life, Ruth Eisenmann-Schier to 7 years.

Mrs. Roy Fuchs, 35, and 3 children held hostage 2 hours, **May 14, 1969,** in Long Island, NY, released after her husband, a bank manager, paid kidnappers $129,000 in bank funds; 4 men arrested, ransom recovered.

Virginia Piper, 49, abducted **July 27, 1972,** from her home in suburban Minneapolis; found unharmed near Duluth 2 days later after husband paid $1 million ransom.

Patricia "Patty" Hearst, 19, taken from her Berkeley, CA, apartment **Feb. 4, 1974.** "Symbionese Liberation Army" captors demanded her father, publisher Randolph Hearst, give millions to the area's poor. Implicated in a San Francisco bank holdup, **Apr. 15.** The FBI, **Sept. 18, 1975,** captured her and others; they were indicted on various charges. Patricia Hearst convicted of bank robbery, **Mar. 20, 1976;** released from prison under executive clemency, **Feb. 1, 1979.** In 1978, William and Emily Harris were sentenced to 10 years to life for the kidnapping; both were paroled in 1983.

J. Reginald Murphy, 40, an editor of *Atlanta* (GA) *Constitution,* kidnapped **Feb. 20, 1974;** freed **Feb. 22** after newspaper paid $700,000 ransom. William A. H. Williams arrested; most of the money recovered.

E. B. Reville, Hepzibah, GA, banker, and wife, Jean, kidnapped **Sept. 30, 1974.** Ransom of $30,000 paid. He was found alive; Jean Reville was found dead **Oct. 2.**

Jack Teich, Kings Point, NY, steel executive, seized **Nov. 12, 1974;** released **Nov. 19** after payment of $750,000.

Adam Walsh, 6, abducted from a Hollywood, FL, department store, **July 27, 1981.** Although his severed head was found 2 weeks later, his body was never recovered. John Walsh, Adam's father, became active in raising awareness about missing children.

Sidney J. Reso, oil company executive, seized **Apr. 29, 1992;** died **May 3;** Arthur D. Seale and wife, Irene, arrested **June 19.** Arthur Seale pleaded guilty, sentenced to life in prison; Irene Seale sentenced to 20-year prison term.

Polly Klaas, 12, Petaluma, CA, abducted at knife point, **Oct. 1, 1993,** during a slumber party at her home. Police arrested Richard Allen Davis on **Nov. 30;** he led them to her body, found **Dec. 4** in wooded area of Cloverdale, CA. Davis found guilty **June 18, 1996,** and sentenced to death **Sept. 26.**

Marshall I. Wais, 79, owner of 2 San Francisco steel companies, kidnapped **Nov. 19, 1996,** from his San Francisco home. Released unharmed the same day after $500,000 ransom paid; Thomas William Taylor and Michael K. Robinson arrested the same day.

Daniel Pearl, 38, reporter for *Wall Street Journal,* disappeared **Jan. 23, 2002,** while researching story in Karachi, Pakistan. British-born militant Ahmad Omar Saeed Sheikh **Feb. 14** admitted to organizing the kidnapping and said Pearl was dead. Sheikh and 3 others were convicted **July 15** of kidnapping and murder by a court in Hyderabad.

Elizabeth Smart, 14, was abducted from her home in Salt Lake City, UT, **June 5, 2002,** allegedly by Brian D. Mitchell and forced to live with Mitchell and wife Wanda for 9 months in various U.S. cities; found walking down street with captors in Sandy, UT, 15 miles from Smart family home, **Mar. 12, 2003.**

▶ **IT'S A FACT:** Before fingerprints (or DNA), the cumbersome Bertillon system was often used by police as a means of identification. Alphonse Bertillon created the system in 1879, while working as a police file clerk in France. He took 11 to 14 body measurements (from length of foot to width of jaw) and recorded the data on cards for use in later matching.

Notable Terrorist Incidents Worldwide, 1971-Sept. 2004

Note: Selected noteworthy incidents, excluding most assassinations, kidnappings, and military targets. Not including 2004 incidents in Iraq; see Chronology of the Year's Events.

Source: U.S. Dept. of State; *Facts On File World News Digest @ Facts.com*; World Almanac research

1971—Mar. 1. Senate wing of U.S. Capitol Building in Wash., DC, bombed by Weather Underground; no deaths.

1972—July 21. "Bloody Friday." Provisional IRA exploded 20+ bombs across Belfast, N. Ireland; 9 killed, hundreds injured.— Sept. 5. Members of Palestinian group Black September killed 2 Israeli athletes and seized 9 others at Olympic Village in Munich, W. Germany, during Summer Olympics. 9 hostages, 5 militants, 1 Ger. officer died in botched rescue.

1973—Dec. 17. Palestinian gunmen attacked Rome airport and bombed plane on tarmac; hijacked Lufthansa plane with 5 Italian hostages to Athens, then to Kuwait; 31 killed in all.

1974—June 17. Houses of Parliament in London, England, bombed by Provisional IRA; 11 injured.

1975—Jan. 27. Puerto Rican FALN nationalists bombed Fraunces Tavern in lower Manhattan; 4 killed, 53 injured.—Jan. 29. U.S. State Dept. building in Wash., DC, bombed by Weather Underground; no deaths.

1976—June 27. Palestinian and Baader-Meinhof militants forced Air France jet to land at Entebbe, Uganda. Israeli army rescued 103 hostages from airport terminal in battle with terrorists and Ugandan troops, July 3-4; 32 killed in all.

1978—Mar. 11. Palestinian militants landed on beach nr. Haifa, Israel; shot civilians and hijacked bus with hostages to Tel Aviv; exploded at roadblock; 43 killed.

1979—Nov. 4. Iranian radicals seized U.S. embassy in Tehran, taking 66 Americans hostage. 52 were held until Jan. 20, 1981.—Nov. 20. 200 Islamic terrorists seized Grand Mosque in Mecca, Saudi Arabia, and held hundreds of pilgrims hostage. Saudi forces retook mosque Dec. 4; about 250 died.

1983—April 18. Hezbollah suicide truck bomb at the U.S. embassy in Beirut, Lebanon, killed 63 people.—Oct. 9. N. Korean agents ambushed a S. Korean govt. delegation in Rangoon, Burma, killing 21.—Oct. 23. Hezbollah suicide truck bombings of U.S. and French military bases, Beirut, Lebanon; 242 Americans, 58 French killed.

1984—Apr. 12. 18 U.S. servicemen killed in bomb blast at restaurant near Air Force base in Torrejon, Spain.—Sept. 20. U.S. embassy annex near Beirut, Lebanon, bombed, killing approx. 20.

1985—June 14. Hezbollah members hijacked TWA Flight 847 with 153 passengers and crew to Beirut; 39 held for 17 days; 1 U.S. Navy sailor killed.—June 23. Air India Flight 182 destroyed by bomb off coast of Ireland; 329 killed. Blamed on Sikh terrorists.—Oct. 7. 4 Palestinians hijacked Italian cruise ship *Achille Lauro*; 1 passenger killed.—Nov. 23. EgyptAir Flight 648 from Athens to Cairo hijacked to Malta by Palestinian group Abu Nidal; 60 killed in rescue.—Dec. 27. Palestinian militants opened fire at El-Al airline counters at Rome and Vienna airports; 19 killed.

1986—Apr. 5. Nightclub in Berlin, W. Germany, bombed, 3 killed, incl. 2 U.S. servicemen; 200+ hurt. 3 Libyan embassy workers in Germany convicted in bombing.

1987—Apr. 17, 21. Bomb in Sri Lanka capital killed 100+; blamed on Tamil rebels who, 4 days later, attacked Sinhalese travelers on highway, killing 127.—June 19. Basque group ETA bombed supermarket garage in Barcelona, Spain; 21 killed, 45 injured.—Nov. 29. Bomb planted by N. Korean agents exploded on Korean Air Lines Flight 858 over Indian Ocean; 115 killed.

1988—Dec. 21. Pan Am Flight 103 exploded over Lockerbie, Scotland, killing all 259 aboard and 11 on the ground; Libya took responsibility for bombing in Aug. 2003.

1989—Sept. 19. French UTA Flight 722 from Congo to Paris destroyed by bomb in midair over Niger; 171 killed. Several Libyan officials convicted in absentia; no official admission.

1992—Mar. 17. Israeli embassy in Buenos Aires, Argentina, bombed; 28 killed, 200+ injured. Hezbollah suspected.

1993—Feb. 2. Truck bomb exploded in World Trade Center garage in New York City; 6 killed. Blast later linked to al-Qaeda.—Mar. 12-19. At least 11 bombs ripped through Bombay and Calcutta, India; 300+ killed.

1994—Feb. 25. U.S.-born Israeli settler Baruch Goldstein opened fire in mosque in Hebron, West Bank; about 30 Muslim worshippers killed.—July 18. Buenos Aires Jewish center bombed; 87 killed; blamed on Hezbollah.

1995—Mar. 20. 12 killed and over 5,000 injured when Japanese Aum Shinri-kyu cult members released Sarin nerve gas in several Tokyo subway cars.—Apr. 19. Murrah Federal Building in Oklahoma City bombed, killing 168 and injuring 500+. Timothy McVeigh and Terry Nichols convicted in bombing.—Nov. 13. U.S. miltary compound in Riyadh, Saudi Arabia, bombed by Islamic Movement of Change; about 40 killed.—Nov. 19. Suicide bomber drove into Egyptian embassy in Islamabad, Pakistan; at least 16 killed, 60 injured.

1996—Jan. 31. Tamil Tigers drove explosive-laden truck into Central Bank in Colombo, Sri Lanka; 90 killed.—Feb. 25. Hamas suicide bombers hit 2 buses in Jerusalem; 26 killed.— Mar. 4. Bomb outside Tel Aviv shopping mall killed 14, injured 130.—June 25. Bomb-laden fuel truck exploded outside Khobar Towers, a U.S. military complex in Dhahran, Saudi Arabia; killed 19.—June 27. Bomb exploded at Centennial Olympic Park in Atlanta, GA, during Summer Games; killed 2, injured 100+; suspect Eric Robert Rudolph arrested in 2003.— Dec. 3. Bomb exploded on subway train in Paris; 4 killed, 86 injured; blamed on Algerian extremists.

1997—Nov. 17. Gamaa al-Islamiya gunmen killed 58 tourists and 4 Egyptians in Valley of the Kings near Luxor, Egypt.

1998—Aug. 7. U.S. embassies in Nairobi, Kenya, and Dar-es-Salaam, Tanzania, bombed; 257 people killed; al-Qaeda blamed.—Aug. 15. IRA car bomb exploded outside courthouse in Omagh, N. Ireland; killed 29, injured 300+.—Oct. 18. National Liberation Army of Colombia blew up Ocensa oil pipeline; about 71 killed, 100+ injured.

1999—Sept. 9-16. 3 apt. buildings bombed in Moscow and Volgodansk, S. Russia; about 300 killed. Blamed on Chechen rebels.

2000—Oct. 12. U.S.S. *Cole* rammed by dingy full of explosives while docking in Aden, Yemen; 17 U.S. sailors killed, 39 injured. Blamed on al-Qaeda.

2001—Sept. 11. 19 al-Qaeda terrorists hijacked 4 U.S. domestic flights, including planes that crashed into World Trade Center towers and Pentagon. Total dead minus hijackers: 2,973.— Sept.-Nov. 7 letters tainted with deadly anthrax bacteria mailed through U.S. postal system killed 5; unsolved.

2002—Mar. 27. Suicide bombing at hotel in Netanya, Israel, during Passover celebration; 27 killed.—Oct 12. Resort in Bali, Indonesia, bombed; 202 dead; Jemaah Islamiah blamed.— Oct. 23. Chechen guerrillas seized theater in Moscow, held 700+ hostages; Russian authorities gassed theater; most guerrillas and about 128 hostages killed in incident.—Nov. 28. Suicide bombers destroyed Israeli-owned hotel near Mombasa, Kenya; 13 killed. At the same time, 2 missiles narrowly missed Israeli plane taking off from Mombasa airport; blamed on al-Qaeda.—Dec. 27. Chechen rebels plowed truck bomb into pro-Russian gov. headquarters in Grozny, Chechnya; 80 killed, 152 injured.

2003—Iraq: Aug. 19. UN headquarters in Baghdad bombed by truck, 22 killed, including UN envoy to Iraq.—Oct. 27. Suicide bombings at Intl. Red Cross and police stations; 40 killed. **Other areas:**—May 12. Truck bombing near gov. buildings hits Znamenskoye, Chechnya; 59 killed.—May 12-13. Al-Qaeda militants detonated car bombs at 3 residential complexes used by westerners in Riyadh, Saudi Arabia; 34 killed.—May 16. 5 explosions in Casablanca, Morocco; 41 killed, 100+ wounded. Blamed on al-Qaeda.—May 17-19. 5 suicide bombings in Israel; 17 killed; Hamas and al-Aqsa Martyrs brigade blamed.—Aug. 1. Truck bomb hit military hospital in Mozdok, Russia, near Chechnya; 50 killed; blamed on Chechen rebels.—Aug. 5. Car bomb hit Marriott hotel in Jakarta, Indonesia; 12 killed, 150 injured, blamed on Jemaah Islamiah.—Aug. 25. 2 bombs exploded in taxis in Mumbai (Bombay), India; 46 killed, 100+ injured; Islamic militants suspected.—Oct. 15. Bomb hit diplomat convoy in Gaza; 3 Americans killed.—Nov. 15. 2 synagogues in Istanbul, Turkey, bombed; 25 killed.— Nov. 20. British consulate and offices of HSBC, a British bank, bombed in Istanbul, Turkey; 27 killed incl. Br. cons. gen. Blamed on al-Qaeda.—Dec. 5. Suicide bombing on commuter train in Yessentuki, S Russia; 44 killed, 150 injured; blamed on Chechen rebels.—Dec. 9. Chechen suicide bombing outside National Hotel in Red Square, Moscow; 5 killed.

2004—Feb. 6. Bomb exploded on Moscow subway; 39 killed, 130 injured; Chechen rebels blamed.—Mar. 11. Al-Qaeda cell bombed 4 commuter trains during morning rush hour in Madrid, Spain; 191 killed, about 1,200 injured.—Mar. 28-29. Suicide bombings by Muslim militants hit Tashkent, Uzbekistan; 19 killed.—Apr. 21. Car bomb destroyed Saudi govt. security building in Riyadh; 4 killed, 148 injured.—May 29. Al-Qaeda militants stormed foreigner compound in Khobar, Saudi Arabia, taking hostages; 22 killed.—July 30. U.S. and Israeli embassies in Tashkent, Uzbekistan, bombed simultaneously; 2 killed.—Aug. 24. 2 Russian passenger planes crashed nearly simultaneously in diff. parts of Russia; 90 killed; blamed on Chechen rebels.—Sept. 1. Militants seized school in Beslan, in N Ossetia, Russia; held 1,000+ hostage for 3 days before Russian troops stormed school. About 330 killed, incl. 27 hostage-takers. Blamed on Chechen militants.—Sept. 9. Australian embassy in Jakarta, Indonesia, bombed; 9 killed; blamed on Jemaah Islamiah.

ENERGY

U.S. Energy Overview, 1960-2003

Source: Energy Information Administration, U.S. Dept. of Energy, *Annual Energy Review 2003;* in quadrillion Btu

	1960	1965	1970	1975	1980	1985	1990	1995	2000	2002	2003P
Production	**42.80**	**50.68**	**63.50**	**61.36**	**67.24**	**67.65**	**70.73**	**71.16**	**71.22**	**70.93**	**70.47**
Fossil fuels	39.87	47.24	59.19	54.73	59.01	57.54	58.53	57.44	57.25	56.92	56.44
Coal	10.82	13.06	14.61	14.99	18.60	19.33	22.46	22.03	22.62	22.70	22.31
Natural gas (dry)	12.66	15.78	21.67	19.64	19.91	16.98	18.33	19.08	19.66	19.50	19.64
Crude oil[1]	14.93	16.52	20.40	17.73	18.25	18.99	15.57	13.89	12.36	12.16	12.15
Natural gas plant liquids (NGPL)	1.46	1.88	2.51	2.37	2.25	2.24	2.18	2.44	2.61	2.55	2.34
Nuclear electric power	0.01	0.04	0.24	1.90	2.74	4.08	6.10	7.08	7.86	8.14	7.97
Hydroelectric pumped storage[2]	(3)	(3)	(3)	(3)	(3)	(3)	−0.04	−0.03	−0.06	−0.09P	−0.09
Renewable energy	2.93	3.40	4.08	4.72	5.49	6.03	6.13	6.69	6.16	5.96	6.15
Conventional hydroelectric power[4]	1.61	2.06	2.63	3.15	2.90	2.97	3.05	3.21	2.81	2.68P	2.78
Geothermal energy	(*)	(*)	0.02	0.07	0.11	0.20	0.34	0.29	0.32	0.33	0.31
Wood, waste, alcohol[5]	1.32	1.34	1.43	1.50	2.49	2.86	2.66	3.07	2.90	2.79	2.88
Solar	NA	NA	NA	NA	NA	(*)	0.06	0.07	0.07	0.06P	0.06
Wind	NA	NA	NA	NA	NA	(*)	0.03	0.03	0.06	0.11P	0.11
Imports	**4.19**	**5.89**	**8.34**	**14.03**	**15.80**	**11.78**	**18.82**	**22.26**	**28.97**	**29.41**	**31.02**
Coal	0.01	(*)	(*)	0.02	0.03	0.05	0.07	0.24	0.31	0.42	0.63
Natural gas	0.16	0.47	0.85	0.98	1.01	0.95	1.55	2.90	3.87	4.10	4.02
All crude oil and petroleum prods.[6]	4.00	5.40	7.47	12.95	14.66	10.61	17.12	18.88	24.53	24.68	26.21
Other[7]	0.02	0.01	0.02	0.08	0.10	0.17	0.08	0.24	0.26	0.20	0.17
Exports	**1.48**	**1.83**	**2.63**	**2.32**	**3.69**	**4.20**	**4.75**	**4.51**	**4.01**	**3.66**	**4.05**
Coal	1.02	1.38	1.94	1.76	2.42	2.44	2.77	2.32	1.53	1.03	1.12
Natural gas	0.01	0.03	0.07	0.07	0.05	0.06	0.09	0.16	0.25	0.52	0.70
All crude oil and petroleum prods.[6]	0.43	0.39	0.55	0.44	1.16	1.66	1.82	1.99	2.15	2.04	2.13
Other[7]	0.01	0.03	0.08	0.05	0.07	0.04	0.07	0.05	0.08	0.07	0.10
Consumption	**45.09**	**54.02**	**67.84**	**71.99**	**78.29**	**76.42**	**84.61**	**91.22**	**98.94**	**98.03**	**98.16**
Fossil fuels	42.14	50.58	63.52	65.36	69.98	66.22	72.46	77.49	85.00	84.10	84.34
Coal	9.84	11.58	12.27	12.66	15.42	17.48	19.17	20.09	22.58	21.98	22.71
Coal coke net imports	−0.01	−0.02	−0.06	0.01	−0.04	−0.01	0.01	0.06	0.07	0.06	0.05
Natural gas[8]	12.39	15.77	21.80	19.95	20.39	17.83	19.73	22.78	23.95	23.66	22.51
Petroleum[9]	19.92	23.25	29.52	32.73	34.20	30.92	33.55	34.55	38.40	38.40	39.07
Nuclear electric power	0.01	0.04	0.24	1.90	2.74	4.08	6.10	7.08	7.86	8.14	7.97
Hydroelectric pumped storage[2]	(3)	(3)	(3)	(3)	(3)	(3)	−0.04	−0.03	−0.06	−0.09P	−0.09
Renewable energy	2.93	3.40	4.08	4.72	5.49	6.03	6.13	6.67	6.16	5.96	6.15
Conventional hydroelectric power[4]	1.61	2.06	2.63	3.16	2.90	2.97	3.05	3.21	2.81	2.68P	2.78
Geothermal energy	(*)	(*)	0.01	0.07	0.11	0.20	0.34	0.29	0.32	0.33	0.31
Wood, waste, alcohol[5]	1.32	1.34	1.43	1.50	2.49	2.86	2.66	3.07	2.91	2.79	2.88
Solar energy	NA	NA	NA	NA	NA	(*)	0.06	0.07	0.07	0.06P	0.06
Wind energy	NA	NA	NA	NA	NA	(*)	0.03	0.03	0.06	0.11P	0.11

(1) Incl. lease condensate. (2) Total pumped storage facility production minus energy used for pumping. (3) Included in conventional hydroelectric power. (4) Starting in 1990, pumped storage is removed and expanded coverage of industrial use of hydroelectric power is included. (5) Substituted in 2000 for former "Biofuels" category; figures for 1960-99 were recalculated. Alcohol is ethanol blended into motor gasoline. (6) Incl. imports of crude oil for the Strategic Petroleum Reserve, which began in 1977. (7) Coal coke and small amts. of electricity transmitted across borders with Canada and Mexico. (8) Incl. supplemental gaseous fuels. (9) Petroleum products supplied, incl. natural gas plant liquids and crude oil burned as fuel. NA = Not available. P = preliminary. (*) = Less than 0.005 quadrillion Btu. **Note:** Some figures here have been revised. Some totals may not add because of rounding.

U.S. Energy Flow, 2003[1]

Source: Energy Information Administration, U.S. Dept. of Energy, *Annual Energy Review 2003*; in quadrillion Btu

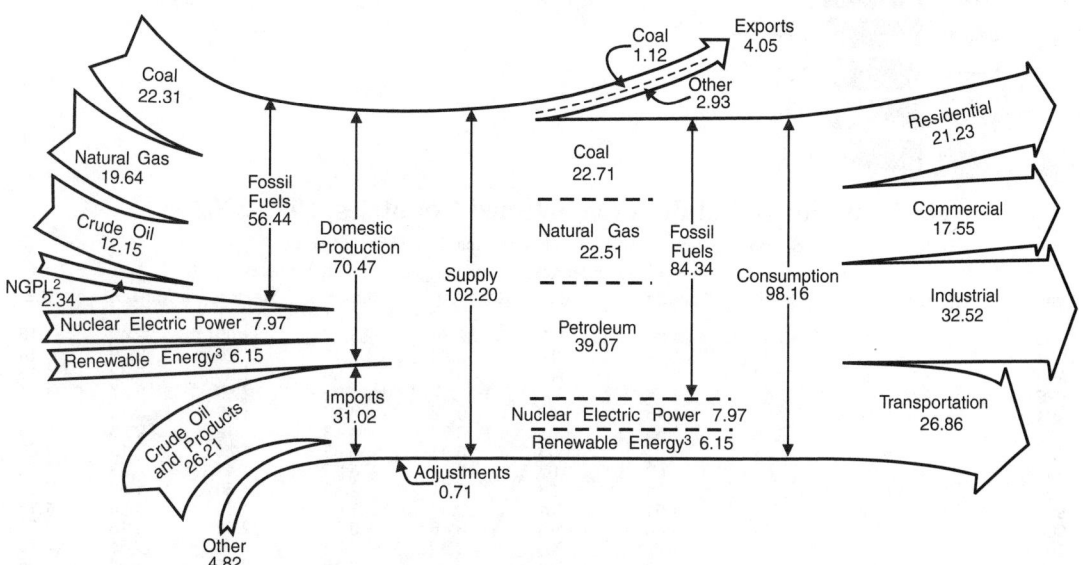

(1) Preliminary figures. (2) Natural Gas Plant Liquids. (3) Conv. hydroelectric power; wood, waste, and ethanol blended into gasoline; geothermal, solar, and wind. Some totals may not add due to rounding.

World Energy Consumption and Production Trends, 2002

Source: Energy Information Administration, U.S. Dept. of Energy, International Energy Database, Sept. 2004

The world's **consumption** of primary energy—petroleum, natural gas, coal, net hydroelectric, nuclear, geothermal, solar, wind, and wood and waste electric power, and other wood and waste—has increased from 397 quadrillion Btu in 2000 to 404 in 2001 and 412 in 2002.

The 30 countries of the Organization for Economic Cooperation and Development (OECD), which include some of the world's largest economies (United States, Japan, and Germany), continued to dominate global energy use. OECD nations accounted for 56% of the world's primary energy consumption in 2002.

World **production** of primary energy increased from 403 quadrillion Btu in 2001 to 405 quadrillion Btu in 2002. World production of petroleum in 2002 was almost 74 million barrels per day, or 153 quadrillion Btu; petroleum remained the most heavily used source of energy.

In 2002, 3 countries—U.S., Russia, and China—were the world's leading producers (39%) and consumers (41%) of energy. Russia and the U.S. alone supplied 29% of the world total. The U.S. alone accounted for 24% of the world's energy consumption. The U.S. consumed 38% more energy than it produced—an imbalance of 27 quadrillion Btu.

World's Major Consumers of Primary Energy, 2002

Source: Energy Information Administration, Dept. of Energy, International Energy Database, Sept. 2004; quadrillion Btu

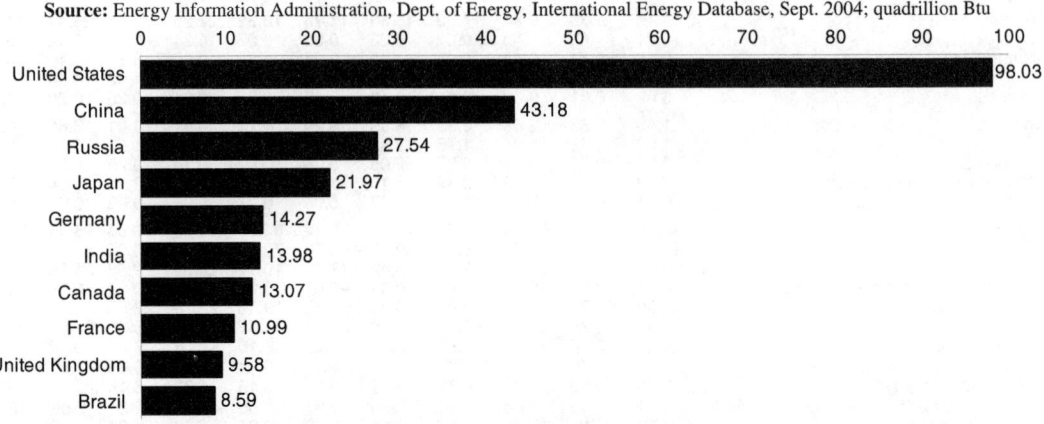

- United States: 98.03
- China: 43.18
- Russia: 27.54
- Japan: 21.97
- Germany: 14.27
- India: 13.98
- Canada: 13.07
- France: 10.99
- United Kingdom: 9.58
- Brazil: 8.59

World's Major Producers of Primary Energy, 2002

Source: Energy Information Administration, Dept. of Energy, International Energy Database, Sept. 2004; quadrillion Btu

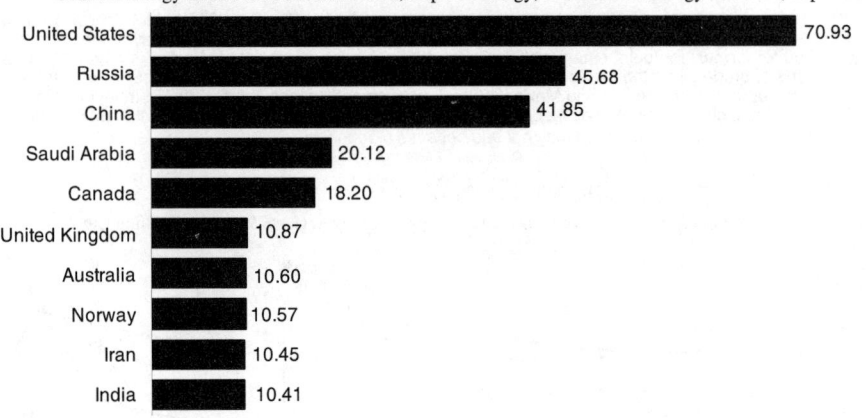

- United States: 70.93
- Russia: 45.68
- China: 41.85
- Saudi Arabia: 20.12
- Canada: 18.20
- United Kingdom: 10.87
- Australia: 10.60
- Norway: 10.57
- Iran: 10.45
- India: 10.41

Gasoline Retail Prices in Selected Countries, 1990-2003

Source: Energy Information Administration, U.S. Dept. of Energy
(average price of unleaded regular gas; dollars per gallon, including taxes)

Year	Australia	Brazil	Canada	China	Germany	Japan	Mexico	Taiwan	U.S.
1990	NA	$3.82	$1.87	NA	$2.65	$3.17	$1.00	$2.49	$1.16
1991	$1.96	2.91	1.92	NA	2.90	3.46	1.29	2.39	1.14
1992	1.89	2.92	1.73	NA	3.27	3.59	1.50	2.42	1.13
1993	1.73	2.40	1.57	NA	3.07	4.02	1.56	2.27	1.11
1994	1.84	2.80	1.45	$0.96	3.52	4.39	1.48	2.14	1.11
1995	1.95	2.16	1.53	1.03	3.96	4.43	1.12	2.23	1.15
1996	2.12	2.31	1.61	1.03	3.94	3.65	1.26	2.15	1.23
1997	2.05	2.61	1.62	1.07	3.54	3.27	1.47	2.23	1.23
1998	1.63	2.80	1.38	1.08	3.34	2.82	1.50	1.86	1.06
1999	1.72	NA	1.51	NA	3.42	3.27	1.80	1.86	1.17
2000	1.94	NA	1.86	NA	3.45	3.74	2.02	2.15	1.51
2001	1.71	NA	1.72	NA	3.40	3.35	2.21	2.01	1.46
2002	1.76	NA	1.70	NA	3.67	3.15	2.25	1.98	1.36
2003	2.20	NA	2.02	NA	4.58	3.47	2.09	2.16	1.59

NA = Not available.

Gasoline Retail Prices, U.S. City Average, 1974-2004

Source: Energy Information Administration, U.S. Dept. of Energy, *Monthly Energy Review*, Aug. 2004

(cents per gallon, including taxes)

AVERAGE	Leaded regular	Unleaded regular	Unleaded premium	All types[1]	AVERAGE	Leaded regular	Unleaded regular	Unleaded premium	All types[1]
1974	53.2	NA	NA	NA	1990	114.9	116.4	134.9	121.7
1975	56.7	NA	NA	NA	1991	NA	114.0	132.1	119.6
1976	59.0	61.4	NA	NA	1992	NA	112.7	131.6	119.0
1977	62.2	65.6	NA	NA	1993	NA	110.8	130.2	117.3
1978	62.6	67.0	NA	65.2	1994	NA	111.2	130.5	117.4
1979	85.7	90.3	NA	88.2	1995	NA	114.7	133.6	120.5
1980	119.1	124.5	NA	122.1	1996	NA	123.1	141.3	128.8
1981[2]	131.1	137.8	147.0[3]	135.3	1997	NA	123.4	141.6	129.1
1982	122.2	129.6	141.5	128.1	1998	NA	105.9	125.0	111.5
1983	115.7	124.1	138.3	122.5	1999	NA	116.5	135.7	122.1
1984	112.9	121.2	136.6	119.8	2000	NA	151.0	169.3	156.3
1985	111.5	120.2	134.0	119.6	2001	NA	146.1	165.7	153.1
1986	85.7	92.7	108.5	93.1	2002	NA	135.8	157.8	144.1
1987	89.7	94.8	109.3	95.7	2003	NA	159.1	177.7	163.8
1988	89.9	94.6	110.7	96.3	2004 (Jan.-June)	NA	181.9	200.2	186.1
1989	99.8	102.1	119.7	106.0					

Until unleaded gas became available in 1976, leaded was the only type used in automobiles. Average retail prices (in cents per gallon) for selected years preceding those in the table above were as follows: 1950: .27; 1955: .29; 1960: .31; 1965: .31; 1970: .36. (1) Also includes types of motor gasoline not shown separately. (2) In Sept. 1981, the Bureau of Labor Statistics changed the weights in the calculation of average motor gasoline prices. Starting in Sept. 1981, gasohol is included in average for all types, and unleaded premium is weighted more heavily. (3) Based on Sept. through Dec. data only. **NOTE:** Geographic coverage for 1974-77 is 56 urban areas; for 1978 and later, 85 urban areas. NA = Not applicable.

U.S. Petroleum Trade, 1976-2003

Source: Energy Information Administration, U.S. Dept. of Energy, *Monthly Energy Review*, Aug. 2004

(in thousands of barrels per day; average for the year)

Year	Imports from Persian Gulf[1]	Total imports	Total exports	Net imports[2]	Petroleum products supplied[3]	Year	Imports from Persian Gulf[1]	Total imports	Total exports	Net imports[2]	Petroleum products supplied[3]
1976	1,840	7,313	223	7,090	17,461	1990	1,966	8,018	857	7,161	16,988
1977	2,448	8,807	243	8,565	18,431	1991	1,845	7,627	1,001	6,626	16,714
1978	2,219	8,363	362	8,002	18,847	1992	1,778	7,888	950	6,938	17,033
1979	2,069	8,456	471	7,985	18,513	1993	1,782	8,620	1,003	7,618	17,237
1980	1,519	6,909	544	6,365	17,056	1994	1,728	8,996	942	8,054	17,718
1981	1,219	5,996	595	5,401	16,058	1995	1,573	8,835	949	7,886	17,725
1982	696	5,113	815	4,298	15,296	1996	1,604	9,478	981	8,498	18,309
1983	442	5,051	739	4,312	15,231	1997	1,755	10,162	1,003	9,158	18,620
1984	506	5,437	722	4,715	15,726	1998	2,136	10,708	945	9,764	18,917
1985	311	5,067	781	4,286	15,726	1999	2,464	10,852	940	9,912	19,519
1986	912	6,224	785	5,439	16,281	2000	2,488	11,459	1,040	10,419	19,701
1987	1,077	6,678	764	5,914	16,665	2001	2,761	11,871	971	10,900	19,649
1988	1,541	7,402	815	6,587	17,283	2002	2,269	11,530	984	10,546	19,761
1989	1,861	8,061	859	7,202	17,325	2003	2,501	12,264	1,027	11,238	20,034

(1) Bahrain, Iran, Iraq, Kuwait, Qatar, Saudi Arabia, and the United Arab Emirates. (2) Net imports are total imports minus total exports. (3) Basically includes domestic production and imports minus change in stocks, refinery imports, and exports. **Notes:** Beginning in Oct. 1977, imports for the Strategic Petroleum Reserves are included. U.S. geographic coverage includes the 50 states and the District of Columbia. U.S. exports include shipments to U.S. territories, and imports include receipts from U.S. territories. Figures in this table may not add because of rounding. Some figures are revised.

Energy Consumption, Total and Per Capita, by State, 2000

Source: Energy Information Administration, U.S. Dept. of Energy, State Energy Data Report 2000

Total Consumption

Rank/State	Trillion Btu	Rank/State	Trillion Btu
1. Texas	11,588.6	27. Colorado	1,199.9
2. California	8,518.7	28. Mississippi	1,143.8
3. Pennsylvania	4,779.9	29. Iowa	1,099.3
4. New York	4,620.0	30. Arkansas	1,083.7
5. Illinois	4,417.9	31. Oregon	1,079.7
6. Ohio	4,001.8	32. Kansas	1,035.7
7. Louisiana	3,965.2	33. Connecticut	863.0
8. Florida	3,943.8	34. West Virginia	744.0
9. Michigan	3,121.9	35. Utah	718.2
10. Indiana	2,777.6	36. Nevada	632.8
11. Georgia	2,769.9	37. Alaska	627.3
12. New Jersey	2,706.6	38. New Mexico	620.7
13. North Carolina	2,501.9	39. Montana	594.5
14. Virginia	2,303.6	40. Nebraska	583.5
15. Washington	2,173.8	41. Maine	561.2
16. Tennessee	2,025.9	42. Idaho	511.1
17. Alabama	1,977.3	43. Wyoming	417.1
18. Kentucky	1,868.2	44. North Dakota	365.4
19. Wisconsin	1,799.7	45. New Hampshire	329.1
20. Massachusetts	1,722.8	46. Delaware	302.6
21. Minnesota	1,688.0	47. Hawaii	264.8
22. Missouri	1,659.2	48. Rhode Island	250.4
23. Maryland	1,520.1	49. South Dakota	246.0
24. South Carolina	1,477.1	50. Dist. of Columbia	166.2
25. Oklahoma	1,400.5	51. Vermont	164.6
26. Arizona	1,215.8	**TOTAL U.S.**	**98,216.2**

Consumption Per Capita

Rank/State	Million Btu	Rank/State	Million Btu
1. Alaska	1,000.6	27. Nebraska	341.0
2. Louisiana	887.3	28. Georgia	338.4
3. Wyoming	844.7	29. Wisconsin	335.5
4. Montana	659.0	30. South Dakota	325.9
5. North Dakota	569.0	31. Virginia	325.4
6. Texas	555.8	32. New Jersey	321.7
7. Kentucky	462.2	33. Utah	321.6
8. Indiana	456.8	34. Nevada	316.7
9. Alabama	444.6	35. Oregon	315.6
10. Maine	440.1	36. Michigan	314.1
11. West Virginia	411.4	37. North Carolina	310.8
12. Oklahoma	405.9	38. Missouri	296.5
13. Arkansas	405.4	39. Dist. of Columbia	290.6
14. Mississippi	402.1	40. Maryland	287.0
15. Idaho	395.0	41. Colorado	279.0
16. Pennsylvania	389.2	42. Massachusetts	271.3
17. Delaware	386.1	43. Vermont	270.4
18. Kansas	385.3	44. New Hampshire	266.3
19. Iowa	375.7	45. Connecticut	253.4
20. Washington	368.8	46. California	251.5
21. South Carolina	368.2	47. Florida	246.8
22. Tennessee	356.1	48. New York	243.5
23. Illinois	355.7	49. Rhode Island	238.8
24. Ohio	352.5	50. Arizona	237.0
25. Minnesota	343.1	51. Hawaii	218.6
26. New Mexico	341.2	**TOTAL U.S.**	**349.0**

World Crude Oil and Natural Gas Reserves, Jan. 1, 2003

Sources: Energy Information Administration, U.S. Dept. of Energy, *U.S. Crude Oil, Natural Gas, and Natural Gas Liquids Reserves, Nov. 2003; Oil and Gas Journal (OGJ),* Dec. 2002; *World Oil (WO),* Aug. 2003

Region/Country	Crude oil (billion barrels) OGJ	WO	Natural gas (trillion cubic feet) OGJ	WO	Region/Country	Crude oil (billion barrels) OGJ	WO	Natural gas (trillion cubic feet) OGJ	WO
North America	215.3	45.4	255.8	262.1	**Middle East**	685.6	669.8	1,979.7	2,517.0
Canada............	180.0[1]	5.5	60.1	60. 1	Bahrain	0.1	NA	3.3	NA
Mexico	12.6	17.2	8.8	15.0	Iran	89.7	100.1	812.3	913.6
United States	22.7	22.7	186.9	186.9	Iraq	112.5	115.0	109.8	112.6
Central & South					Israel	(2)	NA	1.4	NA
America	98.6	75.9	250.1	244.4	Jordan	(2)	NA	0.2	NA
Argentina	2.9	2.8	27.0	23.4	Kuwait	96.5	98.9	52.7	56.6
Barbados	(2)	NA	(2)	NA	Oman.............	5.5	5.7	29.3	31.0
Bolivia............	0.4	0.9	24.0	28.1	Qatar	15.2	19.6	508.5	916.0
Brazil	8.3	9.8	8.1	8.4	Saudi Arabia	261.8	261.8	224.7	234.6
Chile.............	0.2	1.0	3.5	1.2	Syria	2.5	2.3	8.5	18.0
Colombia	1.8	1.6	4.5	4.2	United Arab Emirates .	97.8	63.0	212.1	204.1
Cuba.............	0.8	0.5	2.5	0.6	Yemen............	4.0	2.9	16.9	17.0
Ecuador	4.6	4.6	0.3	0.3	**Africa**	77.4	96.3	418.2	438.9
Guatemala	0.5	NA	0.1	NA	Algeria	9.2	13.0	159.7	170.0
Peru	0.3	1.0	8.7	8.6	Angola	5.4	8.9	1.6	4.0
Suriname	0.2	NA	0.0	NA	Benin	(2)	NA	(2)	NA
Trinidad and Tobago .	0.7	1.0	23.5	20.3	Cameroon	0.4	NA	3.9	NA
Venezuela	77.8	53.1	148.0	149.2	Congo (Brazzaville)...	1.5	1.5	3.2	4.2
Western Europe	18.3	17.0	191.6	175.7	Congo (Kinshasa)	0.2	NA	(2)	NA
Austria	(2)	(2)	0.8	0.8	Cote d'Ivoire (Ivory				
Croatia	1	(2)	1.2	1.2	Coast)	0.1	NA	1.1	NA
Denmark..........	1.3	1.8	3.0	4.2	Egypt	3.7	3.5	58.5	5.9
France	0.1	0.2	0.5	0.5	Equatorial Guinea	(2)	1.1	1.3	3.4
Germany	0.3	0.3	11.3	8.5	Ethiopia	(2)	NA	0.9	NA
Greece	(2)	NA	(2)	NA	Gabon	2.5	2.4	1.2	3.4
Ireland	0.0	NA	0.7	NA	Ghana	(2)	NA	0.8	NA
Italy..............	0.6	0.7	8.0	7.9	Libya	29.5	30.0	46.4	46.0
Netherlands	0.1	(2)	62.0	55.3	Madagascar.........	0.0	NA	0.0	NA
Norway............	10.3	9.0	77.3	74.7	Morocco...........	(2)	NA	(2)	NA
Spain	0.2	NA	0.1	NA	Mozambique	0.0	NA	4.5	NA
Turkey	0.3	0.3	0.3	0.3	Namibia	0.0	NA	2.2	NA
United Kingdom	4.7	4.5	24.6	22.2	Nigeria	24.0	32.0	124.0	178.5
Yugoslavia	0.1	NA	1.7	NA	Rwanda	0.0	NA	2.0	NA
Eastern Europe &					Somalia	0.0	NA	0.2	NA
Former U.S.S.R. ...	79.2	81.9	1,964.2	2,047.0	South Africa........	(2)	NA	(2)	NA
Albania	0.2	0.4	0.1	0.1	Sudan	0.6	0.7	3.0	4.0
Azerbaijan	7.0	NA	30.0	NA	Tanzania	0.0	NA	0.8	NA
Belarus...........	0.2	NA	0.1	NA	Tunisia...........	0.3	0.5	2.8	2.7
Bulgaria	(2)	(2)	0.2	(2)	**Asia & Oceania**	38.7	48.5	445.4	441.7
Czech Republic	(2)	(2)	0.1	0.1	Afghanistan	0.0	NA	3.5	NA
Estonia	0.0	NA	0.0	NA	Australia	3.5	3.7	90.0	85.0
Georgia	(2)	NA	0.3	NA	Bangladesh	0.1	NA	10.6	NA
Hungary	0.1	0.1	1.2	2.2	Brunei	1.4	1.1	13.8	8.3
Kazakhstan	9.0	NA	65.0	NA	Burma	0.1	0.3	10.0	15.7
Kyrgyzstan	(2)	NA	0.2	NA	China.............	18.3	23.7	53.3	46.7
Latvia	0.0	NA	0.0	NA	India..............	5.4	4.6	26.9	23.6
Lithuania..........	(2)	NA	0.0	NA	Indonesia..........	5.0	5.9	92.5	73.5
Moldova	0.0	NA	0.0	NA	Japan.............	0.1	NA	1.4	NA
Poland	(2)	0.1	5.8	5.9	Malaysia	3.0	4.3	75.0	88.0
Romania	1.0	1.1	3.6	4.2	New Zealand........	0.2	0.1	3.1	2.6
Russia	60.0	58.8	1,680.0	1,700.0	Pakistan...........	0.3	0.3	26.4	26.4
Slovakia	(2)	NA	0.5	NA	Papua New Guinea ...	0.2	0.4	12.2	13.5
Tajikistan	(2)	NA	0.2	NA	Philippines..........	0.2	0.2	3.8	3.9
Turkmenistan	0.5	NA	71.0	NA	Taiwan.............	(2)	NA	2.7	NA
Ukraine...........	0.4	NA	39.6	NA	Thailand...........	0.6	0.5	13.3	12.9
Uzbekistan	0.6	NA	66.2	NA	Vietnam	0.6	2.5	6.8	7.2
					World Total.........	**1,213.1**	**1,034.7**	**5,504.9**	**6,126.6**

NOTE: NA=Not available. Totals may not add because of rounding. Data for Kuwait and Saudi Arabia include one-half of the reserves in the Neutral Zone between Kuwait and Saudi Arabia. All reserve figures except those for the former USSR and natural gas reserves in Canada are *proved reserves.* Former USSR and Canadian natural gas figures include amounts understood as *proved,* and some *probable reserves.* Totals may not equal sum of components due to inclusion of small "other" amounts and independent rounding. (1) Figure for 2003 includes 174.8 billion barrels of bitumen that is contained in Alberta's oil sands. (2) Less than 50 million barrels of crude oil or less than 50 million cubic feet of natural gas.

Production of Crude Oil, by Major States, 2003

Source: Energy Information Administration, *Petroleum Supply Annual 2003*

(thousand barrels)

State	Total	State	Total	State	Total	State	Total
1. Texas[1].....	405,801	9. North Dakota..	29,406	17. Michigan.....	6,524	25. South Dakota .	1,237
2. Alaska[1]	355,582	10. Colorado.....	21,109	18. Ohio	5,647	26. Nevada......	493
3. California[1] ...	250,000	11. Montana	19,320	19. Florida.......	3,262	27. Tennessee ...	311
4. Louisiana[1] ...	90,111	12. Mississippi....	16,593	20. Nebraska	2,755	28. New York	144
5. New Mexico...	66,130	13. Utah	13,096	21. Kentucky.....	2,538	29. Missouri	82
6. Oklahoma ...	65,356	14. Illinois	11,696	22. Pennsylvania .	2,425	30. Arizona......	47
7. Wyoming	52,407	15. Alabama	7,877	23. Indiana	1,865	31. Virginia......	5
8. Kansas	33,944	16. Arkansas.....	7,226	24. West Virginia .	1,334	**US Total.....**	**2,073,453**

(1) Includes the following offshore production (thous. bbls.): Alaska (107,971), California (15,900), Louisiana (10,535), Texas (1,017).

U.S. Crude Oil Imports by Selected Country, 1988-2004

Source: Energy Information Administration, Petroleum Supply Monthly, Aug. 2004; ranked by 2004 totals
(thousand barrels per day)

	1988	1990	1995	1996	1997	1998	1999	2000	2001	2002	2003	2004[1]
Canada.	681	643	1,040	1,075	1,198	1,266	1,178	1,348	1,356	1,445	1,549	1,606
Mexico	674	689	1,027	1,207	1,360	1,321	1,254	1,313	1,394	1,500	1,569	1,593
Saudi Arabia*.	911	1,195	1,260	1,248	1,293	1,404	1,387	1,523	1,611	1,519	1,726	1,387
Venezuela*.	439	666	1,151	1,303	1,394	1,377	1,150	1,223	1,291	1,201	1,183	1,353
Nigeria*	607	784	621	595	689	689	623	875	842	589	832	1,094
Iraq*	343	514	0	1	89	336	725	620	795	459	481	651
Angola	203	236	360	344	425	465	357	295	321	321	363	287
Kuwait*.	80	79	213	235	253	300	246	263	327	216	208	266
United Kingdom	254	155	341	216	169	161	284	291	244	405	359	262
Algeria*.	58	63	27	8	6	10	25	1	11	30	112	197
Ecuador[4]	33	38	96	96	114	98	114	125	113	100	139	193
Norway.	62	96	258	293	288	221	263	302	281	348	181	169
Colombia	106	140	207	226	270	349	452	318	260	235	166	158
Gabon[3].	15	64	229	184	230	207	168	143	140	143	131	141
Russia[2].	0	1	14	18	3	9	21	7	0	85	151	119
Brazil	0	0	0	0	0	0	0	5	13	58	50	57
Trinidad and Tobago	71	76	62	58	56	53	40	56	51	68	67	56
Indonesia*	186	98	64	44	51	50	70	36	40	50	26	42
Australia.	59	47	16	25	31	31	31	49	34	51	27	17
China	82	77	53	57	48	42	13	33	13	20	13	12
Malaysia.	19	40	6	8	8	25	21	29	15	9	21	8
United Arab Emirates*	23	9	5	3	0	3	0	3	21	10	10	5
Total Arab-OPEC	**1,415**	**1,864**	**1,505**	**1,496**	**1,641**	**2,053**	**2,385**	**2,410**	**2,675**	**2,243**	**2,537**	**2,472**
Total Non-OPEC	**2,411**	**2,381**	**3,889**	**4,070**	**4,450**	**4,537**	**4,502**	**4,526**	**4,480**	**5,058**	**5,087**	**4,966**
Total OPEC	**2,696**	**3,514**	**3,341**	**3,438**	**3,775**	**4,169**	**4,228**	**4,544**	**4,848**	**4,083**	**4,578**	**4,962**
TOTAL	**5,107**	**5,894**	**7,230**	**7,508**	**8,225**	**8,706**	**8,731**	**9,071**	**9,328**	**9,140**	**9,655**	**9,927**

* Denotes OPEC members. (1) Jan.-July average. (2) May include oil from USSR states for 1988 and 1992. (3) Gabon withdrew from OPEC Dec. 31, 1994. Imports after Jan. 1, 1995, appear in Non-OPEC totals. (4) Ecuador withdrew from OPEC Dec. 31, 1992. Imports after Jan. 1, 1993, appear in Non-OPEC totals.

World Nuclear Power Summary, 2003

Source: International Atomic Energy Agency, Power Reactor Information System, Dec. 31, 2003

Country	Reactors in operation		Reactors under construction		Nuclear electricity supplied in 2003		Total operating experience[2]	
	No. of units	Total MW(e)	No. of units	Total MW(e)	TW(e).h[1]	% of nation's total	Years	Months
Argentina	2	935	1	692	7.03	8.59	50	7
Armenia	1	376	—	—	1.82	35.48	36	3
Belgium	7	5,760	—	—	44.61	55.46	191	7
Brazil	2	1,901	—	—	13.34	3.65	25	3
Bulgaria	4	2,722	—	—	16.04	37.71	129	2
Canada	16	11,323	—	—	70.29	12.53	486	11
China	8	5,977	3	2,610	41.59	2.18	39	1
Czech Republic	6	3,548	—	—	25.87	31.09	74	10
Finland	4	2,656	—	—	21.82	27.32	99	4
France	59	63,363	—	—	420.70	77.68	1,346	2
Germany	18	20,643	—	—	157.44	28.10	648	0
Hungary	4	1,755	—	—	11.01	32.69	74	2
India	14	2,550	8	3,622	16.37	3.30	223	5
Iran	—	—	2	2,111	—	—	0	0
Japan	53	44,139	3	3,696	230.08	25.01	1,123	7
Korea, North	—	—	1	1,040	—	—	0	0
Korea, South	19	15,850	1	960	123.28	40.01	220	8
Lithuania	2	2,370	—	—	14.30	79.89	36	6
Mexico	2	1,310	—	—	10.51	5.23	23	11
Netherlands	1	449	—	—	3.80	4.48	59	0
Pakistan	2	425	—	—	1.81	2.37	35	10
Romania	1	655	1	655	4.54	9.33	7	6
Russia	30	20,793	3	2,825	138.39	16.54	761	4
Slovakia	6	2442	2	776	17.86	57.35	100	6
Slovenia	1	656	—	—	4.96	40.45	22	3
South Africa	2	1,800	—	—	12.66	6.05	38	3
Spain	9	7,584	—	—	59.36	23.64	219	2
Sweden	11	9,451	—	—	65.50	49.62	311	1
Switzerland	5	3,220	—	—	25.93	39.73	143	10
Taiwan	6	4,884	2	2,600	37.37	21.50	134	1
Ukraine	13	11,207	4	3,800	76.70	45.93	279	10
United Kingdom	27	12,052	—	—	85.31	23.70	1,329	8
United States	104	98,298	—	—	763.74	19.86	2,871	8
TOTAL	**439**	**361,094**	**31**	**25,387**	**2,524.03**	**—**	**11,143**	**5**

(1) 1 terawatt-hour [TW(e).h] = 10^6 megawatt-hour [MW(e).h]. For an average power plant, 1 TW(e).h = 0.39 megatons of coal equivalent (input) and 0.23 megatons of oil equivalent (input). (2) Through Dec. 31, 2003.

Nations Most Reliant on Nuclear Energy, 2003

Source: International Atomic Energy Agency, Aug. 2004
(Nuclear electricity generation as % of total electricity generated)

Country	%	Country	%	Country	%	Country	%	Country	%
Lithuania.	79.7	Ukraine	45.9	Armenia	35.5	Japan	25.0	Canada	12.5
France	77.9	Slovenia	40.4	Hungary	32.7	United Kingdon	23.7	Romania	9.3
Slovakia	57.4	South Korea . .	40.0	Czech Republic	31.1	Spain	23.6	Argentina.	8.6
Belgium	55.5	Switzerland . . .	39.7	Germany	28.1	**United States**.	**19.9**	South Africa. . .	6.0
Sweden	49.6	Bulgaria.	37.7	Finland.	27.3	Russia.	16.5	Mexico	5.2

U.S. Nuclear Reactor Units and Power Plant Operations, 1980-2003

Source: Energy Information Administration, U.S. Dept. of Energy, Annual Energy Review 2003

	Number of reactor units							Total design capacity (million KWs)	Nuclear-based electricity generation (million net KW-hrs)	Nuclear portion of domestic electricity generation (percent)
	Licensed for operation		Construction permits		On order	Shutdowns	Total			
	Operable	In startup	Granted	Pending						
1980	71	1	82	12	3	0	168	162	251,116	11.0
1981	75	0	76	11	2	0	163	157	272,674	11.9
1982	78	2	60	3	2	1	144	134	282,773	12.6
1983	81	3	53	0	2	0	138	129	293,677	12.7
1984	87	6	38	0	2	0	132	123	327,634	13.6
1985	96	3	30	0	2	0	130	121	383,691	15.5
1986	101	7	19	0	2	0	128	119	414,038	16.6
1987	107	4	14	0	2	2	127	119	455,270	17.7
1988	109	3	12	0	0	0	123	115	526,973	19.5
1989	111	1	10	0	0	2	121	113	529,402	17.8
1990	112	0	8	0	0	1	119	111	576,974	19.0
1991	111	0	8	0	0	1	119	111	612,642	19.9
1992	109	0	8	0	0	2	117	111	618,841	20.1
1993	110	0	7	0	0	0	116	110	610,367	19.1
1994	109	0	7	0	0	1	116	110	640,492	19.7
1995	109	1	6	0	0	0	116	110	673,402	20.1
1996	109	0	6	0	0	1	116	110	674,729	19.6
1997	107	0	3	0	0	2	110	102	628,644	18.0
1998	104	0	3	0	0	3	107	99	673,702	18.6
1999	104	0	0	0	0	0	104	NA	728,198	19.7
2000	104	0	0	0	0	0	104	NA	753,893	19.8
2001	104	0	0	0	0	0	104	NA	768,826	20.6
2002	104	0	0	0	0	0	104	NA	780,220	20.2
2003	104	0	0	0	0	0	104	NA	763,744	19.8

NA = Not available.

Major U.S. Coal Producers, 2003[1]

Source: Energy Information Administration, U.S. Dept. of Energy

Rank	Company Name	Production (thousand short tons)	Percent of total production	Rank	Company Name	Production (thousand short tons)	Percent of total production
1.	Peabody Coal Co.	156,845	14.6	15.	Alpha Natural Resources., LLC	16,117	1.5
2.	Kennecott Energy & Coal Co.	115,001	10.7	16.	BHP Minerals Group	14,326	1.3
3.	Arch Coal, Inc.	107,731	10.1	17.	Pittsburg & Midway Coal Mining Co.	12,190	1.1
4.	RAG American Coal Holding, Inc.	63,306	5.9	18.	PacifiCorp	9,543	0.9
5.	CONSOL Energy Inc	58,499	5.5	19.	James River Coal Co.	9,357	0.9
6.	Vulcan Partners, L.P.	41,480	3.9	20.	Wexford Capital LLC	8,880	0.8
7.	A.T. Massey Coal Co., Inc.	39,719	3.7	21.	Peter Kiewit/Kennecott	8,092	0.8
8.	Horizon Natural Resources Inc.	32,742	3.1	22.	Transalta Centralia Mining LLC	6,232	0.6
9.	North American Coal Corp.	31,778	3.0	23.	Alcoa, Inc.	6,091	0.6
10.	Westmoreland Mining LLC	27,635	2.6	24.	Walter Industries, Inc.	6,045	0.6
11.	TXU Corp.	24,386	2.3	25.	TECO Energy, Inc.	5,742	0.5
12.	Black Beauty Coal Co.	19,895	1.9	26.	Andalex Resources Inc	5,231	0.5
13.	Robert Murray	19,407	1.8		**All Other Coal Producers**	**206,416**	**19.3**
14.	Alliance Coal, LLC	19,068	1.8		**U.S. TOTAL**	**1,071,753**	**100.0**

Note: The company is the firm controlling the coal, particularly the sale of the coal. (1) Preliminary.

Major U.S. Coal Mines, 2003[1]

Source: Energy Information Administration, U.S. Dept. of Energy

Rank	Mine Name/Company	Mine Type	State	Production (short tons)
1.	North Antelope Rochelle Complex/Powder River Coal Company	Surface	Wyoming	80,083,444
2.	Black Thunder/Thunder Basin Coal Company LLC	Surface	Wyoming	62,620,417
3.	Cordero Mine/Cordero Mining Co.	Surface	Wyoming	36,083,743
4.	Jacobs Ranch Mine/Jacobs Ranch Coal Company	Surface	Wyoming	35,491,218
5.	Antelope Coal Mine/Antelope Coal Company	Surface	Wyoming	29,533,072
6.	Eagle Butte Mine/RAG Coal West, Inc.	Surface	Wyoming	24,728,392
7.	North Rochelle/Triton Coal Company LLC	Surface	Wyoming	23,923,145
8.	Caballo Mine/Caballo Coal Company	Surface	Wyoming	22,743,284
9.	Belle Ayr Mine/RAG Coal West Inc.	Surface	Wyoming	17,844,826
10.	Buckskin Mine/Triton Coal Company	Surface	Wyoming	17,539,156
11.	Freedom Mine/The Coteau Properties Company	Surface	North Dakota	15,928,841
12.	Rosebud #6 Mine&Crusher & Conv/Western Energy Company	Surface	Montana	11,034,262
13.	Enlow Fork Mine/Consol Pennsylvania Coal Company	Underground	Pennsylvania	9,888,511
14.	Bailey Mine/Consol Pennsylvania Coal Company	Underground	Pennsylvania	9,391,318
15.	Navajo Mine/BHP Navajo Coal Company	Surface	New Mexico	8,937,403
16.	Spring Creek Coal Company/Spring Creek Coal Company	Surface	Montana	8,894,014
17.	Decker Mine/Decker Coal Co.	Surface	Montana	8,092,348
18.	Foidel Creek Mine/Twentymile Coal Company	Underground	Colorado	8,028,720
19.	Falkirk Mine/The Falkirk Mining Company	Surface	North Dakota	7,921,080
20.	Kayenta Mine/Peabody Western Coal Company	Surface	Arizona	7,780,490
21.	Jewett Mine/Northwestern Resources Company	Surface	Texas	7,460,693
22.	Sufco/Canyon Fuel Company LLC	Underground	Utah	7,125,797
23.	Lee Ranch Coal Co/Lee Ranch Coal Company	Surface	New Mexico	6,904,803
24.	Beckville Strip/TXU Mining Company LP	Surface	Texas	6,849,246
25.	McElroy Mine/McElroy Coal Company	Underground	West Virginia	6,791,716
26.	Emerald Mine #1/RAG Emerald Resources LP	Underground	Pennsylvania	6,619,501
	All Other Mines			**481,619,939**
	U.S. TOTAL			**1,071,752,573**

Note: The company is the firm operating the mine. (1) Preliminary.

ENVIRONMENT
Greenhouse Effect and Global Warming
Source: U.S. Environmental Protection Agency

The Earth absorbs incoming solar radiation and emits thermal radiation back into space, but some of this thermal radiation is trapped by atmospheric "greenhouse gases" that warm Earth's surface and atmosphere ("greenhouse effect"). Naturally occurring greenhouse gases include carbon dioxide (CO_2), water vapor, methane (CH_4), nitrous oxide (N_2O), and ozone (O_3). Mostly artificial greenhouse gases include chlorofluorocarbons (CFCs), hydrochlorofluorocarbons (HCFCs), hydrofluorocarbons (HFCs), perfluorocarbons (PFCs), and sulfur hexafluoride (SF6). (Several nongreenhouse gases—carbon monoxide [CO], oxides of nitrogen [NOx], and nonmethane volatile organic compounds [NMVOCs])—contribute indirectly to the greenhouse effect by producing greenhouse gases during chemical transformations and by influencing their atmospheric lifetimes.)

Levels of CO_2 are higher now than at any time in the past 400,000 years for which concentrations can be determined. They began rising over the past 2 centuries as a result of human activities such as the burning of fossil fuels (coal, oil, natural gas) and deforestation. During this time, atmospheric concentrations of CO_2, CH_4, and N_2O have risen about 30%, 149%, and 16%, respectively. Many scientists believe this buildup is a major cause of higher than normal average global temperatures since the 1990s. Over the 20th century Earth's average temperature rose about 1°F, and since the 1970s it has been rising faster. The hottest year on record was 1998, with 2002 and 2003 tied for 2nd-warmest. Some scientists believe the global temperature could rise by 2°F to 6°F over the 21st century. This could speed the melting of polar ice caps, inundate coastal lowlands, lead to stronger and more frequent hurricanes, and cause major changes in crop production and in natural habitat. A 2003 study released by the World Health Organization also cited problems such as increased malaria (caused by the expanded range of malaria-carrying mosquitoes) and malnutrition (caused by agricultural disruptions from climate change).

Delegates from over 150 nations adopted a proposal to limit emissions of CO_2, CH_4, N_2O, HFCs, PFCs, and SF_6 at a UN summit in Kyoto, Japan (Dec. 1997). Under the so-called Kyoto Protocol, the 38 participating industrial nations agreed to cut emissions by an average of 5.2% below 1990 levels by 2012 (a goal which many scientists said was far too modest). High-emissions nations could meet their targets by purchasing pollution credits from nations that exceed targets, and gain credits for "sinks," such as forests and croplands, that absorb CO_2 from the atmosphere. Developing nations that signed the accord were not bound.

For the protocol to take effect it had to be ratified by countries responsible for at least 55% of developed nations' greenhouse emissions in 1990. This threshold will be reached when the Russian Parliament ratifies the treaty as expected—it was approved Sept. 30, 2004, by the Russian cabinet. By Sept. 2004, 122 nations, excluding Russia, had ratified the treaty, not including the U.S. (which accounts for 36% of developed nations' emissions). Pres. Bill Clinton signed it in 1998 but did not send it to the Senate for ratification because of dim prospects for approval. Pres. George W. Bush opposed the treaty. A report submitted to the UN by his administration in May 2002 acknowledged a link between human activity and global warming, forecasting a 43% increase in U.S. greenhouse gas emissions from 2000 to 2020. The Bush Administration advocated a voluntary approach, including tax incentives for companies, rather than mandatory limits.

U.S. Greenhouse Gas Emissions from Human Activities, 1990-2002
Source: U.S. Environmental Protection Agency

GAS AND MAJOR SOURCE(S)	1990	1996	1997	1998	1999	2000	2001	2002
Carbon dioxide (CO_2)	5,002.3	5,498.5	5,577.6	5,602.5	5,676.3	5,859.0	5,731.8	5,782.4
Fossil fuel combustion	4,814.7	5,310.1	5,384.0	5,412.4	5,488.8	5,673.6	5,558.8	5,611.0
Methane (CH_4)	642.7	637	628.8	620.1	613.1	614.4	605.1	598.1
Landfills	210.0	208.8	203.4	196.6	197.8	199.3	193.2	193.0
Natural gas systems	122.0	127.4	126.1	124.5	120.9	125.7	124.9	121.8
Enteric fermentation[1]	117.9	120.5	118.3	116.7	116.6	115.7	114.3	114.4
Coal mining	81.9	63.2	62.6	62.8	58.9	56.2	55.6	52.2
Nitrous oxide (N_2O)	393.2	436.9	436.3	432.1	428.4	425.8	417.3	415.8
Agricultural soil management	262.8	288.1	293.2	294.2	292.1	289.7	288.6	287.3
Hydrofluorocarbons (HFCs), perfluorocarbons (PFCs), and sulfur hexafluoride (SF_6)[2]	90.9	114.9	121.7	135.7	134.8	139.1	129.7	138.2
TOTAL U.S. EMISSIONS	6,129.1	6,687.3	6,764.4	6,790.5	6,852.5	7,038.3	6,883.9	6,934.6
NET U.S. EMISSIONS[3]	5,171.3	5,632.1	5,943.5	6,084.7	6,176.8	6,348.2	6,194.1	6,243.8

Note: Emissions given in terms of equivalent emissions of carbon dioxide (CO_2), using units of teragrams of carbon dioxide equivalents (Tg CO_2 Eq.). (1) Digestive process of ruminent animals, such as cattle and sheep, producing methane as a byproduct. (2) These gases have extremely high global warming potential, and PFCs and SF_6 have long atmospheric lifetimes. (3) Total emissions minus carbon dioxide absorbed by forests or other means.

15 Major Nations Producing Carbon Dioxide Emissions, Ranked by 2002 Totals, 1980-2002
Source: U.S. Department of Energy
(million metric tons carbon equivalent)

Country	1980	1985	1990	1995	2000	2001	2002
United States	1,296.59	1,250.41	1,366.60	1,442.32	1,587.10	1,557.96	1,568.02
China	394.01	507.58	616.89	787.72	822.85	866.11	906.11
Russia[1]	837.21	958.58	1,037.47	433.26	420.89	423.54	415.16
Japan	261.18	246.13	269.89	298.63	322.53	322.27	321.67
India	82.67	120.41	161.80	236.48	271.67	275.49	279.87
Germany[2]	208.63	188.81	192.75	238.73	229.93	234.62	228.62
Canada	125.58	119.36	130.05	134.77	157.34	157.29	161.37
United Kingdom	168.16	160.98	163.66	152.60	151.48	155.52	150.77
Korea, South	35.16	44.69	63.82	109.28	114.96	117.60	122.88
Italy	103.31	102.56	113.24	118.45	122.43	122.50	122.36
Australia	54.67	61.49	72.37	79.59	97.78	106.68	111.92
France	136.02	108.56	102.00	100.69	112.09	112.36	111.08
Ukraine[3]	NA	NA	NA	121.80	97.64	102.56	105.89
South Africa	64.09	81.65	80.84	93.85	104.43	103.08	102.99
Mexico	64.67	74.62	83.96	86.91	102.50	100.08	98.87
WORLD TOTAL	5,082.65	5,353.00	5,901.28	6,029.22	6,515.83	6,607.66	6,690.73

(1) Numbers for 1980-90 are for the former Soviet Union. (2) Numbers for 1980-90 are for the former West Germany. (3) Included in Russia prior to 1995.

U.S. Greenhouse Gas Emissions, 2002

Source: U.S. Environmental Protection Agency

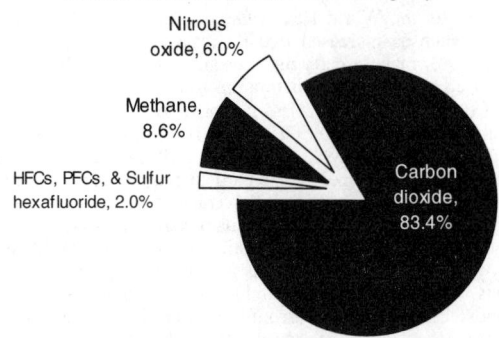

World Carbon Dioxide Emissions from the Use of Fossil Fuels, 2002

Source: U.S. Energy Information Administration

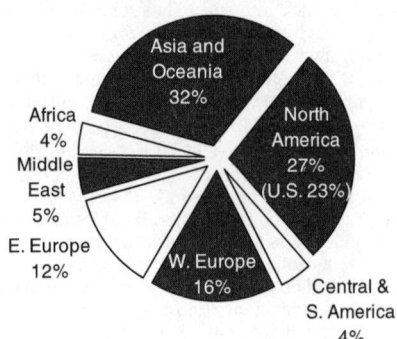

Average Global Temperatures, 1900-2003

Source: National Oceanic and Atmospheric Administration; in degrees Fahrenheit

1900-09 . . . . . 56.5	1930-39 . . . . .57.0	1960-69. . . . . 57.1	1990-99 . . . . . 57.6	2002. . . . . . . .57.9
1910-19 . . . . . 56.6	1940-49 . . . . .57.1	1970-79. . . . . 57.0	2000. . . . . 57.6	2003. . . . . . . .57.9
1920-29 . . . . . 56.7	1950-59 . . . . .57.1	1980-89. . . . . 57.4	2001. . . . . 57.8	

Toxics Release Inventory, U.S., 2001-2002

Source: U.S. Environmental Protection Agency

Releases of toxic chemicals into the environment, by manner of release and industry sector; pollutant transfers by destination of transfer. Totals below may not add because of rounding.

	2001 mil lb	2002 mil lb		2001 %	2002 %
Pollutant releases			**Top industries, total releases**		
Air releases	1,657	1,632	Metal mining	46	26
Surface water discharges	230	230	Electric utilities.	17	23
Underground injection	216	222	Primary metals	9	16
On-site land releases.	2,953	2,195	Chemicals	9	12
Off-site releases.	558	514	Hazardous waste/solvent recovery	4	4
TOTAL on- and off-site releases	**5,612**	**4,792**	Paper.	3	4
Pollutant transfers			All others	12	15
To recycling	1,695	1,986			
To energy recovery	840	804	**Top carcinogens, air/water/land releases**	**mil lb**	**mil lb**
To treatment.	280	276	Styrene	50	50
To publicly owned treatment works	340	347	Formaldehyde	21	19
Other transfers	2	1	Acetaldehyde.	13	14
Off-site to disposal	600	596	Dichloromethane	22	12
TOTAL.	**3,757**	**4,010**	Trichloroethylene.	9	8
			Ethylbenzene.	8	7

NA = Not available. **Note:** This information does not indicate whether (or to what degree) the public has been exposed to toxic chemicals.

Top 10 States, Total Toxics Releases, 2002

Source: U.S. Environmental Protection Agency

State	2002 mil lb	State	2002 mil lb	State	2002 mil lb	State	2002 mil lb
Alaska	548	Texas.	263	Utah.	175	Florida.	155
Nevada.	499	Ohio	254	Pennsylvania.	169	U.S. Total*	4,792
Arizona	329	Indiana	221	Tennessee.	156		

*Total includes District of Columbia, Puerto Rico, American Samoa, Guam, Northern Marianas, and the Virgin Islands.

Air Pollution

Source: World Bank, *World Development Indicators 2001*

Air pollution is a major threat to health and the environment. **Winter smog**—made up of soot, dust, and sulfur dioxide—is associated with increases in deaths. Prolonged exposure to **particulate pollution** can lead to chronic respiratory illnesses and exacerbate heart disease. It causes an estimated 500,000 premature deaths in the world each year.

Emissions of sulfur dioxide and nitrogen oxides lead to **acid rain,** which spreads over long distances, upsetting the chemical balance of soils, trees, and plants. Direct exposure to high levels of sulfur dioxide or acid deposition causes **defoliation**.

Where **coal** is a primary fuel, high levels of urban air pollution may result. If the coal has a high sulfur content, widespread acid deposition may result. Combustion of **petroleum** products is another important cause of air pollution.

Air Pollution in Selected World Cities[1]

Particulate matter in the following table refers to smoke, soot, dust, and liquid droplets from combustion that are in the air—specifically, to particulates less than 10 microns in diameter capable of reaching deep into the respiratory tract. The level of particulates, an important indicator of air quality, is significantly affected by the state of technology and pollution controls. **Sulfur dioxide** is a pollutant formed when fossil fuels containing sulfur are burned. **Nitrogen dioxide** is a poi-

sonous, pungent gas formed when nitric oxide combines with hydrocarbons and sunlight, producing a photochemical reaction. Nitrogen oxides are emitted by bacteria, nitrogenous fertilizers, aerobic decomposition of organic matter, biomass combustion, and, especially, burning fuel for vehicles and industrial activities.

Data in the following table are based on reports from urban monitoring sites. Annual means (measured in micrograms per cubic meter, mpcm) are average concentrations observed at various sites; resulting figures give a general indication of air quality, but results should be interpreted with caution. World Health Organization standards for acceptable air quality are 50 mpcm for sulfur dioxide and 40 mpcm for nitrogen dioxide; the WHO has set no guidelines for acceptable levels of suspended particulate matter.

City and Country	Particulate matter	Sulfur dioxide	Nitrogen dioxide	City and Country	Particulate matter	Sulfur dioxide	Nitrogen dioxide
Accra, Ghana	31	NA	NA	Milan, Italy	36	31	248
Amsterdam, Netherlands	37	10	58	Montreal, Canada	22	10	42
Athens, Greece	50	34	64	Moscow, Russia	27	109	NA
Bangkok, Thailand	82	11	23	Mumbai (Bombay), India	79	33	39
Barcelona, Spain	43	11	43	Nairobi, Kenya	49	NA	NA
Beijing, China	106	90	122	New York, NY	23	26	79
Berlin, Germany	25	18	26	Oslo, Norway	23	8	43
Cairo, Egypt	178	69	NA	Paris, France	15	14	57
Cape Town, South Africa	15	21	72	Prague, Czech Republic	27	14	33
Caracas, Venezuela	18	33	57	Quito, Ecuador	34	22	NA
Chicago, IL	27	14	57	Rio de Janeiro, Brazil	40	129	NA
Cordoba, Argentina	52	NA	97	Rome, Italy	35	NA	NA
Delhi, India	187	24	41	Seoul, South Korea	45	44	60
Kolkata (Calcutta), India	153	49	34	Sofia, Bulgaria	83	39	122
London, UK	23	25	77	Sydney, Australia	22	28	81
Los Angeles, CA	38	9	74	Tokyo, Japan	43	18	68
Manila, Philippines	60	33	NA	Toronto, Canada	26	17	43
Mexico City, Mexico	69	74	130	Warsaw, Poland	49	16	32

NA = Not available. (1) Data for particulates are for 1999 and come from the World Bank study, "The Human Cost of Air Pollution: New Estimates for Developing Countries;" data for sulfur dioxide and nitrogen dioxide are derived from WHO's Healthy Cities Air Management Information System and the World Resources Institute and were collected in 1998 or, if earlier, are the latest available.

Emissions of Principal Air Pollutants in the U.S., 1970-2003

Source: U.S. Environmental Protection Agency, Office of Air Quality Planning and Standards; in thousand tons; estimated

Source	1970	1975	1980	1985	1990	1995	2000	2001	2002	2003
Carbon monoxide	204,043	188,398	185,407	176,844	154,186	126,777	114,467	106,262	112,054	106,886
Nitrogen oxides[1]	26,883	26,377	27,079	25,757	25,529	24,956	22,598	21,549	21,102	20,728
Volatile org. compounds[1]	34,659	30,765	31,106	27,404	24,108	22,041	17,512	17,111	16,544	16,056
Particulate matter[2]	13,023	7,556	7,013	41,324	27,752	25,819	23,747	23,708	22,154	22,940
Sulfur dioxide	31,218	28,043	25,925	23,307	23,076	18,619	16,347	15,932	15,353	15,943
TOTAL[3]	**309,826**	**281,139**	**276,530**	**294,636**	**254,651**	**218,212**	**194,671**	**184,562**	**187,207**	**182,553**

(1) Ozone, a major air pollutant and the primary constituent of smog, is not emitted directly to the air but is formed by sunlight acting on emissions of nitrogen oxides and volatile organic compounds. (2) PM-10, particulates 10 microns or smaller in diameter. (3) Totals are rounded, as are components of totals.

Carbon Monoxide Emission Estimates, 1970-2003

Source: U.S. Environmental Protection Agency, Office of Air Quality Planning and Standards; in thousand tons

Source	1970	1975	1980	1985	1990	1995	2000	2001	2002	2003
Fuel combustion, elec. util.	237	276	322	291	363	372	484	485	499	530
Industrial processes[1]	10,610	8,304	7,700	5,894	5,572	5,631	3,628	3,782	3,830	3,900
Transportation	174,602	167,884	160,512	153,216	131,702	107,755	92,239	88,153	86,611	83,252
Fires	6,766	4,433	7,622	7,289	10,583	6,705	12,049	7,744	15,654	13,180
TOTAL[2]	**204,043**	**188,398**	**185,407**	**176,844**	**154,186**	**126,777**	**114,467**	**106,262**	**112,054**	**106,886**

(1) Includes industrial fuel combustion, chemical and allied manufacturing, metals processing, and petroleum and other industrial sectors. (2) Totals may not add because of rounding or because all categories are not listed.

Nitrogen Oxides Emission Estimates, 1970-2003

Source: U.S. Environmental Protection Agency, Office of Air Quality Planning and Standards; in thousand tons

Source	1970	1975	1980	1985	1990	1995	2000	2001	2002	2003
Fuel combustion, elec. util.	4,900	5,694	7,024	6,127	6,663	6,384	5,330	4,917	4,699	4,458
Industrial processes[1]	5,100	4,546	4,110	4,009	3,831	3,909	3,518	3,587	3,695	3,609
Transportation	15,276	15,029	14,846	14,508	13,373	12,989	12,560	11,930	11,452	11,484
TOTAL[2]	**26,883**	**26,377**	**27,079**	**25,757**	**25,529**	**24,956**	**22,598**	**21,549**	**21,102**	**20,728**

(1) Includes industrial fuel combustion, chemical and allied manufacturing, metals processing, and petroleum and other industrial sectors. (2) Totals may not add because of rounding or because all categories are not listed.

Particulate Matter (PM-10) Emissions, 1970-2003*

Source: U.S. Environmental Protection Agency, Office of Air Quality Planning and Standards; in thousand tons

Source	1970	1975	1980	1985	1990	1995	2000	2001	2002	2003
Fuel combustion, elec. util.	1,775	1,191	879	280	295	268	687	696	695	683
Industrial processes	8,310	4,267	3,433	1,199	1,199	1,132	931	967	855	957
Transportation	644	665	689	712	715	643	552	529	515	495
TOTAL[2]	**13,023**	**7,556**	**7,013**	**41,324**	**27,752**	**25,819**	**23,747**	**23,708**	**22,154**	**22,940**

*PM-10 refers to particulates equal or smaller than 10 microns in diameter, and so capable of entering deep into the respiratory tract. (1) Includes industrial fuel combustion, chemical and allied manufacturing, metals processing, and petroleum and other industrial sectors. (2) Totals include miscellaneous sources not determined.

 IT'S A FACT: Environmental officials began an ambitious project July 2004 to turn industrial salt ponds on the edge of San Francisco Bay into marshes, which they hope will attract wildlife. Using two massive water pipes, the salty water of the ponds, previously used for the commercial production of salt, will be flushed out with freshwater over a period of years. It is the biggest wetlands-restoration project on the West Coast.

IT'S A FACT: In 2004, for the second time in two years, water oxygen levels off the coast of Oregon fell dramatically, creating a "hypoxic dead zone," where fish or other marine life cannot survive. Caused by a natural upwelling of low-oxygen water from the deep, this phenomenon is new to the Oregon coast and researchers do not know why it occurred. Other dead zones have been documented around the world, but nearly all are artificial and are believed to be caused by pollution.

Air Quality of Selected U.S. Metropolitan Areas, 1993-2002

Source: U.S. Environmental Protection Agency, Office of Air Quality Planning and Standards

Data indicate the number of days metropolitan statistical areas failed to meet acceptable air-quality standards. All figures were revised based on new standards set in 1998.

Metropolitan statistical area	1993	1994	1995	1996	1997	1998	1999	2000	2001	2002
Atlanta, GA.	36	15	36	28	33	52	67	34	18	24
Bakersfield, CA	97	105	107	110	58	78	144	132	125	152
Baltimore, MD	48	40	36	28	30	51	40	19	32	42
Boston, MA–NH	2	6	7	4	7	8	10	1	12	16
Chicago, IL.	4	13	24	7	10	12	19	2	22	21
Dallas, TX.	12	24	29	10	27	33	25	22	16	15
Denver, CO	6	3	5	2	0	9	5	3	8	8
Detroit, MI.	5	11	14	13	11	17	20	15	27	26
El Paso, TX	7	6	3	6	2	6	5	4	9	13
Fresno, CA.	59	55	61	70	75	67	133	131	138	152
Houston, TX.	27	41	66	28	47	38	52	42	29	23
Las Vegas, NV–AZ.	3	3	3	14	4	5	8	2	1	6
Los Angeles–Long Beach, CA	134	139	113	94	60	56	56	87	88	80
Miami, FL	6	1	2	1	3	8	7	2	1	1
Minneapolis–St. Paul, MN–WI	0	2	5	0	0	1	1	2	2	1
New Haven–Meriden, CT.	12	13	14	8	19	9	19	9	15	25
New York, NY.	11	16	21	14	23	18	25	19	19	31
Orange County, CA	25	15	9	9	3	6	14	31	31	19
Philadelphia, PA–NJ	62	37	38	38	38	37	32	22	29	33
Phoenix–Mesa, AZ.	14	10	22	15	12	14	10	10	8	8
Pittsburgh, PA	14	22	27	12	21	39	40	29	52	53
Riverside–San Bernardino, CA	168	150	125	118	107	96	123	145	155	145
Sacramento, CA.	20	37	41	44	17	29	69	45	49	69
St. Louis, MO–IL	9	33	38	23	15	24	31	18	17	34
Salt Lake City–Ogden, UT	5	17	5	14	2	19	8	15	15	18
San Diego, CA	59	46	48	31	14	33	33	31	31	20
San Francisco, CA.	0	0	2	0	0	0	10	4	12	17
Seattle–Bellevue–Everett, WA.	0	3	2	6	1	3	6	7	3	6
Ventura, CA.	43	63	66	62	45	29	24	31	25	11
Washington, DC–MD–VA–WV.	52	22	32	18	30	47	39	11	22	34

Hazardous Waste Sites in the U.S., 2004

Source: U.S. Environmental Protection Agency, *National Priorities List,* Sept. 2004

State/Territory	Total proposed Gen	Fed	Total final Gen	Fed	Total	State/Territory	Total proposed Gen	Fed	Total final Gen	Fed	Total
Alabama	2	0	10	3	15	Nevada	0	0	1	0	1
Alaska	0	0	1	5	6	New Hampshire	1	0	18	1	20
Arizona	0	0	7	2	9	New Jersey	3	0	104	8	115
Arkansas	0	0	11	0	11	New Mexico	1	0	11	1	13
California	3	0	72	24	99	New York	2	0	86	4	92
Colorado	2	0	13	3	18	North Carolina	1	0	27	2	30
Connecticut	1	0	14	1	16	North Dakota	0	0	0	0	0
Delaware	0	0	13	1	14	Ohio	6	2	26	3	37
District of Columbia	0	0	0	1	1	Oklahoma	1	0	9	1	11
Florida	1	0	45	6	52	Oregon	0	0	9	2	11
Georgia	1	0	12	2	15	Pennsylvania	4	0	87	6	97
Hawaii	0	0	1	2	3	Rhode Island	0	0	10	2	12
Idaho	3	0	4	2	9	South Carolina	1	0	23	2	26
Illinois	5	1	36	4	46	South Dakota	0	0	1	1	2
Indiana	1	0	29	0	30	Tennessee	1	1	9	3	14
Iowa	1	0	12	1	14	Texas	2	0	38	4	44
Kansas	1	1	9	1	12	Utah	4	0	11	4	19
Kentucky	0	0	13	1	14	Vermont	1	0	10	0	11
Louisiana	3	0	12	1	16	Virginia	0	0	19	11	30
Maine	0	0	9	3	12	Washington	0	0	33	14	47
Maryland	1	0	9	9	19	West Virginia	0	0	7	2	9
Massachusetts	1	0	24	7	32	Wisconsin	1	0	38	0	39
Michigan	1	1	67	0	69	Wyoming	0	0	1	1	2
Minnesota	0	0	22	2	24	Guam	0	0	1	1	2
Mississippi	2	0	3	0	5	Puerto Rico	1	1	10	0	12
Missouri	0	0	23	3	26	Virgin Islands	0	0	2	0	2
Montana	1	0	14	0	15						
Nebraska	1	0	10	1	12	**Total**	**61**	**7**	**1,086**	**158**	**1,312**

Note: Gen = general superfund sites; Fed = federal facility sites.

WORLD ALMANAC QUICK QUIZ

Rank these countries from most to least in the amount of carbon dioxide they emitted in 2002.

   (a) Canada   (b) Russia   (c) United States   (d) France

For the answer look in this chapter, or see page 1008.

Renewable Water Resources

Source: Food and Agriculture Organization, United Nations

Globally, water supplies are abundant, but they are unevenly distributed among and within countries. In some areas, water withdrawals are so high, relative to supply, that surface water supplies are shrinking and groundwater reserves are being depleted faster than they can be replenished by precipitation. The U.S. has a total of 3,069.4 cubic kilometers of internal renewable water resources, or 10,837 cubic meters per capita. Totals for the world are 43,764 cubic kilometers, or 7,243 cubic meters per capita. These numbers, and those in the tables below, were published by the Food and Agriculture Organization in 2003; the tables draw upon studies done over a number of years and use 2000 population data.

Countries With Most Resources
(ranked by per capita resources)

Country	Totalcubic km	Cubic meters per capita
Iceland	170.0	609,319
Guyana	241.0	316,689
Suriname	122.0	292,566
Congo, Republic of	832.0	275,679
Papua New Guinea	801.0	166,563
Gabon	164.0	133,333
Solomon Islands	44.7	100,000
Canada	2,902.0	94,353
New Zealand	327.0	86,554
Norway	382.0	85,478

Countries With Least Resources*
(ranked by per capita resources, starting with the lowest)

Country/ Territory	Total cubic km	Cubic meters per capita
Kuwait	0.0	10
Gaza Strip, Palestine	0.1	52
United Arab Emirates	0.2	58
Bahamas	0.0	66
Qatar	0.1	94
Maldives	0.0	103
Libya	0.6	113
Saudi Arabia	2.4	118
Malta	0.1	129
Singapore	0.6	149

Some Endangered Animal Species

Source: Fish and Wildlife Service, U.S. Dept. of the Interior

Common name	Scientific name	Range
Albatross, Amsterdam	Diomedia amsterdamensis	Amsterdam Island, Indian Ocean
Antelope, giant sable	Hippotragus niger variani	Angola
Armadillo, giant	Pridontes maximus	Venezuela, Guyana to Argentina
Babirusa	Babyrousa babyrussa	Indonesia
Bandicoot, desert	Perameles eremiana	Australia
Bat, gray	Myotis grisescens	Central, southeastern U.S.
Bear, brown (grizzly)	Ursus arctos horribilis	Palearctic
Bison, wood	Bison bison athabascae	Canada, northwestern U.S.
Bobcat, Mexican	Felis rufus escuinapae	Central Mexico
Caiman, black	Melanosuchus niger	Amazon basin
Camel, Bactrian	Camelus bactrianus	Mongolia, China
Caribou, woodland	Rangifer tarandus caribou	Canada, Northwestern U.S.
Cheetah	Acinonyx jubatus	Africa to India
Chimpanzee, pygmy	Pan paniscus	Congo (formerly Zaire)
Condor, California	Gymnogyps californianus	U.S. (AZ, CA, OR), Mexico (Baja California)
Crane, whooping	Grus americana	Canada, Mexico, U.S. (Rocky Mts. to Carolinas)
Crocodile, American	Crocodylus acutus	U.S. (FL), Mexico, Caribbean Sea, Central and S America
Deer, Columbian white-tailed	Odocoileus virginianus leucurus	U.S. (OR, WA)
Dolphin, Chinese river	Lipotes vexillifer	China
Dugong	Dugong dugon	East Africa to southern Japan
Elephant, Asian	Elephas maximus	S central and southeastern Asia
Fox, northern swift	Vulpes velox hebes	Canada
Frog, Goliath	Conraua goliath	Cameroon, Equatorial Guinea, Gabon
Gorilla	Gorilla gorilla	Central and W Africa
Hartebeest, Tora	Alcelaphus buselaphus tora	Egypt, Ethiopia, Sudan
Hawk, Hawaiian	Buteo solitarius	U.S. (HI)
Hyena, brown	Hyaena brunnea	Southern Africa
Impala, black-faced	Aepyceros melampus petersi	Angola, Namibia
Kangaroo, Tasmanian forester	Macropus giganteus tasmaniensis	Australia (Tasmania)
Leopard	Panthera pardus	Africa and Asia
Lion, Asiatic	Panthera leo persica	Turkey to India
Manatee, West Indian	Trichechus manatus	Southeastern U.S., Caribbean Sea, Mexico
Monkey, spider	Ateles geoffroyi frontatus	Costa Rica, Nicaragua
Ocelot	Felis pardalis	U.S. (AZ, TX) to Central and S America
Orangutan	Pongo pygmaeus	Borneo, Sumatra
Ostrich, West African	Struthio camelus spatzi	W Sahara
Otter, marine	Lutra felina	Peru south to Straits of Magellan
Panda, giant	Ailuropoda melanoleuca	China
Panther, Florida	Felis concolor coryi	U.S. (FL)
Parakeet, golden	Aratinga guarouba	Brazil
Parrot, imperial	Amazona imperialis	West Indies (Dominica)
Penguin, Galapagos	Spheniscus menduiculus	Ecuador (Galapagos Islands)
Puma, eastern	Felis concolor couguar	Eastern N America (presumed extinct in wild)
Python, Indian	Python molurus molurus	Sri Lanka, India
Rat-kangaroo, brush-tailed	Bettongia penicillata	Australia
Rhinoceros, black	Diceros bicornis	Sub-Saharan Africa
Rhinoceros, northern white	Ceratotherium simum cottoni	Congo, Sudan, Uganda, Central African Rep.
Salamander, Chinese giant	Andrias davidianus	Western China
Sea-lion, Steller	Eumetopias jubatus	Alaska, Russia
Sheep, bighorn	Ovis canadensis	California
Squirrel, Carolina northern flying	Glaucomys sabrinus coloratus	U.S. (NC, TN)
Tiger	Panthera tigris	Asia
Tortoise, Galapagos	Geochelone elephantopus	Ecuador (Galapagos Islands)
Turtle, Plymouth red-bellied	Pseudemys rubriventris bangsi	U.S. (MA)
Whale, gray	Eschrichtius robustus	N Pacific Ocean
Whale, humpback	Megaptera novaeangliae	Oceania
Wolf, red	Canis rufus	U.S. (FL, NC, SC)
Woodpecker, ivory-billed	Campephilus principalis	Cuba
Yak, wild	Bos grunniens mutus	China (Tibet), India
Zebra, mountain	Equus zebra zebra	South Africa

U.S. List of Endangered and Threatened Species

Source: Fish and Wildlife Service, U.S. Dept. of Interior; as of Sept. 2004

Group	Endangered U.S.	Endangered Foreign	Threatened U.S.	Threatened Foreign	Total species[1]	Species with recovery plans	Group	Endangered U.S.	Endangered Foreign	Threatened U.S.	Threatened Foreign	Total species[1]	Species with recovery plans
Mammals	69	251	9	17	346	55	Crustaceans	18	0	3	0	21	13
Birds	77	175	14	6	272	78	**Animal subtotal**	390	516	129	40	1,075	416
Reptiles	14	64	22	15	115	33	Flowering plants	571	1	144	0	716	578
Amphibians	11	8	10	1	30	14	Conifers &						
Fishes	71	11	43	1	126	95	cycads	2	0	1	2	5	2
Clams	62	2	8	0	72	69	Ferns and allies	24	0	2	0	26	26
Snails	21	1	11	0	33	23	Lichens	2	0	0	0	2	2
Insects	35	4	9	0	48	31	**Plant subtotal**	599	1	147	2	749	608
Arachnids	12	0	0	0	12	5	**GRAND TOTAL**	989	517	276	42	1,824	1,022

(1) Some species are classified as both endangered and threatened. The table tallies these "dual status" species only once, as endangered, except for the olive ridley sea turtle, which is dual status but tallied as a U.S. threatened species. The other dual status species, all tallied as endangered, are: (U.S.) chinook salmon, gray wolf, green sea turtle, piping plover, roseate tern, sockeye salmon, steelhead, Steller sea lion; (non-U.S.) argali, chimpanzee, leopard, saltwater crocodile.

Classification

Source: *Funk & Wagnalls New Encyclopedia*

In biology, classification is the identification, naming, and grouping of organisms into a formal system. The 2 fields that are most directly concerned with classification are taxonomy and systematics. Although the 2 disciplines overlap considerably, taxonomy is more concerned with nomenclature (naming) and with constructing hierarchical systems, and systematics with uncovering evolutionary relationships. Two kingdoms of living forms, Plantae and Animalia, have been recognized since Aristotle established the first taxonomy in the 4th century BC. In addition, there are the following 3 kingdoms: Protista (one-celled organisms), Monera (bacteria and blue-green algae; also known as the kingdom Procaryotae), and Fungi. The 7 basic categories of classification (from most general to most specific) are: kingdom, phylum (or division), class, order, family, genus, and species. Below are 2 examples:

ZOOLOGICAL HIERARCHY

Kingdom	Phylum	Class	Order	Family	Genus	Species name	Common name
Animalia	Chordata	Mammalia	Primates	Hominidae	Homo	Homo sapiens	Human

BOTANICAL HIERARCHY

Kingdom	Division*	Class	Order	Family	Genus	Species name	Common name
Plantae	Magnoliophyta	Magnoliopsida	Magnoliales	Magnoliaceae	Magnolia	M. virginiana	Sweet Bay

* In botany, the division is generally used in place of the phylum.

Gestation, Longevity, and Incubation of Animals

Information reviewed by Ronald M. Nowak, author *Walker's Mammals of the World* (6th ed., Johns Hopkins University Press, 1999). Average longevity figures supplied by Ronald T. Reuther. These apply to animals in captivity; the potential life span of animals is rarely attained in nature. Figures on gestation and incubation are averages based on estimates.

ANIMAL	Gestation (days)	Average longevity (years)	Maximum longevity (yr-mo)	ANIMAL	Gestation (days)	Average longevity (years)	Maximum longevity (yr-mo)
Ass	365	12	47	Leopard	98	12	23
Baboon	187	20	45	Lion	100	15	30
Bear: Black	219	18	36-10	Monkey (rhesus)	166	15	37
Grizzly	225	25	50	Moose	240	12	27
Polar	240	20	45	Mouse (meadow)	21	3	4
Beaver	105	5	50	Mouse (dom. white)	19	3	6
Bison	285	15	40	Opossum (American)	13	1	5
Camel	406	12	50	Pig (domestic)	112	10	27
Cat (domestic)	63	12	28	Puma	90	12	20
Chimpanzee	230	20	60	Rabbit (domestic)	31	5	13
Chipmunk	31	6	10	Rhinoceros (black)	450	15	45-10
Cow	284	15	30	Rhinoceros (white)	480	20	50
Deer (white-tailed)	201	8	20	Sea lion (California)	350	12	34
Dog (domestic)	61	12	20	Sheep (domestic)	154	12	20
Elephant (African)	660	35	70	Squirrel (gray)	44	10	23-6
Elephant (Asian)	645	40	77	Tiger	105	16	26-3
Elk	250	15	26-8	Wolf (maned)	63	5	15-8
Fox (red)	52	7	14	Zebra (Grant's)	365	15	50
Giraffe	457	10	36-2				
Goat (domestic)	151	8	18				

Incubation time (days)

Chicken 21
Duck 30
Goose 30
Pigeon 18
Turkey 26

ANIMAL	Gestation (days)	Average longevity (years)	Maximum longevity (yr-mo)
Gorilla	258	20	54
Guinea pig	68	4	8
Hippopotamus	238	41	61
Horse	330	20	50
Kangaroo (gray)	36	7	24

Speeds of Animals

Source: Natural History magazine. © American Museum of Natural History

ANIMAL	mph	ANIMAL	mph	ANIMAL	mph
Cheetah	70	Cape hunting dog	45	Whippet	35.50
Pronghorn antelope	61	Coyote	43	Rabbit (domestic)	35
Wildebeest	50	Gray fox	42	Mule deer	35
Lion	50	Hyena	40	Jackal	35
Thomson's gazelle	50	Zebra	40	Reindeer	32
Quarterhorse	47.5	Mongolian wild ass	40	Giraffe	32
Elk	45	Greyhound	39.35	White-tailed deer	30

ANIMAL	mph	ANIMAL	mph	ANIMAL	mph
Wart hog	30	Wild turkey	15	Giant tortoise	0.17
Grizzly bear	30	Squirrel	12	Three-toed sloth	0.15
Cat (domestic)	30	Pig (domestic)	11	Garden snail	0.03
Black mamba snake	20	Chicken	9		
Six-lined race runner (lizard)	18	Spider (Tegenaria atrica)	1.17		

Note: Most of these measurements are for maximum speeds over approximate quarter-mile distances. Exceptions are the lion and elephant, whose speeds were clocked in the act of charging; the whippet, which was timed over a 200-yd course; the cheetah, timed over a 100-yd distance; and the black mamba, six-lined race runner, spider, giant tortoise, three-toed sloth, and garden snail, which were measured over various small distances.

Major Venomous Animals

Snakes

Asian pit viper — from 2 ft to 5 ft long; throughout Asia; reactions and mortality vary, but most bites cause tissue damage, and mortality is generally low.

Australian brown snake — 4 ft to 7 ft long; very slow onset of cardiac or respiratory distress; moderate mortality, but because death can be sudden and unexpected, it is the most dangerous of the Australian snakes; antivenom.

Barba Amarilla or fer-de-lance — up to 7 ft long; from tropical Mexico to Brazil; severe tissue damage common; moderate mortality; antivenom.

Black mamba — up to 14 ft long, fast-moving; S and C Africa; rapid onset of dizziness, difficulty breathing, erratic heartbeat; mortality high, nears 100% without antivenom.

Boomslang — less than 6 ft long; in African savannahs; rapid onset of nausea and dizziness, often followed by slight recovery and then sudden death from internal hemorrhaging; bites rare, mortality high; antivenom.

Bushmaster — up to 12 ft long; wet tropical forests of C and S America; few bites occur, but mortality rate is high.

Common or Asian cobra — 4 ft to 8 ft long; throughout southern Asia; considerable tissue damage, sometimes paralysis; mortality probably not more than 10%; antivenom.

Copperhead — less than 4 ft long; from New England to Texas; pain and swelling; very seldom fatal; antivenom seldom needed.

Coral snake — 2 ft to 5 ft long; in Americas south of Canada; bite may be painless; slow onset of paralysis, impaired breathing; mortalities rare, but high without antivenom and mechanical respiration.

Cottonmouth water moccasin — up to 5 ft long; wetlands of southern U.S. from Virginia to Texas. Rapid onset of severe pain, swelling; mortality low, but tissue destruction can be extensive; antivenom.

Death adder — less than 3 ft long; Australia; rapid onset of faintness, cardiac and respiratory distress; at least 50% mortality without antivenom.

Desert horned viper — in dry areas of Africa and western Asia; swelling and tissue damage; low mortality; antivenom.

European viper — 1 ft to 3 ft long; bleeding and tissue damage; mortality low; antivenom.

Gaboon viper — more than 6 ft long; fat; 2-in. fangs; south of the Sahara; massive tissue damage, internal bleeding; few recorded bites.

King cobra — up to 16 ft long; throughout southern Asia; rapid swelling, dizziness, loss of consciousness, difficulty breathing, erratic heartbeat; mortality varies sharply with amount of venom involved, but most bites involve nonfatal amounts; antivenom.

Krait — up to 5 ft long; in SE Asia; rapid onset of sleepiness; numbness; up to 50% mortality even with use of antivenom.

Puff adder — up to 5 ft long; fat; south of the Sahara and throughout the Middle East; rapid large swelling, great pain, dizziness; moderate mortality, often from internal bleeding; antivenom.

Rattlesnake — 2 ft to 6 ft long; throughout W Hemisphere; rapid onset of severe pain, swelling; mortality low, but amputation of affected digits is sometimes necessary; antivenom. Mojave rattler may produce temporary paralysis.

Ringhals, or spitting, cobra — 5 ft to 7 ft long; southern Africa; squirts venom through holes in front of fangs as a defense; venom is severely irritating, can cause blindness.

Russell's viper or tic-polonga — more than 5 ft long; throughout Asia; internal bleeding; bite reports common; moderate mortality rate; antivenom.

Saw-scaled or carpet viper — as much as 2 ft long; in dry areas from India to Africa; severe bleeding, fever; high mortality, causes more human fatalities than any other snake; antivenom.

Sea snakes — throughout Pacific, Indian oceans except NE Pacific; almost painless bite, variety of muscle pain, paralysis; mortality rate low, many bites not envenomed; some antivenoms.

Sharp-nosed pit viper or one hundred pace snake — up to 5 ft long; in S Vietnam, Taiwan, and China; the most toxic of Asian pit vipers; very rapid onset of swelling and tissue damage, internal bleeding; moderate mortality; antivenom.

Taipan — up to 11 ft long; in Australia and New Guinea; rapid paralysis with severe breathing difficulty; mortality nears 100% without antivenom.

Tiger snake — 2 ft to 6 ft long; S Australia; pain, numbness, mental disturbances with rapid paralysis; may be deadliest of all land snakes, but antivenom is quite effective.

Yellow or Cape cobra — 7 ft long; in S Africa; most toxic venom of any cobra; rapid onset of swelling, breathing and cardiac difficulties; mortality is high without treatment; antivenom.

Note: Not all bites by venomous snakes are actually envenomed. Any animal bite, however, carries the danger of tetanus, and anyone suffering a venomous snake bite should seek medical attention. Antivenoms do not cure; they are only an aid in the treatment of bites. Mortality rates above are for envenomed bites; low mortality, c. 2% or less; moderate, 2%-5%; high, 5%-15%.

Lizards

Gila monster — as much as 24 in. long, with heavy body and tail; in high desert in SW U.S. and N Mexico; immediate severe pain and transient low blood pressure; no recent mortality.

Mexican beaded lizard — similar to Gila monster, Mexican west coast; reaction and mortality rate similar to Gila monster.

Insects

Ants, bees, wasps, hornets, etc. Global distribution. Usual reaction is piercing pain in area of sting. Not directly fatal, except in cases of massive multiple stings. However, many people suffer allergic reactions — swelling and rashes — and a few may die within minutes from severe sensitivity to the venom (anaphylactic shock).

Spiders, Scorpions

Atrax spider — also known as funnel web spider; several varieties, often large; in Australia; slow onset of breathing, circulation difficulties; low mortality; antivenom.

Black widow — small, round-bodied with red hourglass marking; the widow and its relatives are found in tropical and temperate zones; severe musculoskeletal pain, weakness, breathing difficulty, convulsions; may be more serious in small children; low mortality; antivenom. The **redback** spider of Australia has the hourglass marking on its back, rather than on its front, but is otherwise identical to the black widow.

Brown recluse, or fiddleback, spider — small, oblong body; throughout U.S.; pain with later ulceration at place of bite; in severe cases fever, nausea, and stomach cramps; ulceration may last months; very low mortality.

Scorpion — crablike body with stinger in tail, various sizes, many varieties throughout tropical and subtropical areas; various symptoms may include severe pain spreading from the wound, numbness, severe agitation, cramps; severe reaction may include respiratory failure; low mortality, usually in children; antivenoms.

Tarantula — large, hairy spider found around the world; the American tarantula, and probably all other tarantulas, are harmless to humans, though their bite may cause some pain and swelling.

Sea Life

Cone-shell — mollusk in small, beautiful shell; in the S Pacific and Indian oceans; shoots barbs into victims; paralysis; low mortality.

Octopus — global distribution, usually in warm waters; all varieties produce venom, but only a few can cause death; rapid onset of paralysis with breathing difficulty.

Portuguese man-of-war — jellyfishlike, with tentacles up to 70 ft long; in most warm water areas; immediate severe pain; not directly fatal, though shock may cause death in rare cases.

Sea wasp — jellyfish, with tentacles up to 30 ft long, in the S Pacific; very rapid onset of circulatory problems; high mortality because of speed of toxic reaction; antivenom.

Stingray — several varieties of differing sizes; found in tropical and temperate seas and some fresh water; severe pain, rapid onset of nausea, vomiting, breathing difficulties; wound area may ulcerate, gangrene may appear; seldom fatal.

Stonefish — brownish fish that lies motionless as a rock on bottom in shallow water; throughout S Pacific and Indian oceans; extraordinary pain, rapid paralysis; low mortality; antivenom available, amount determined by number of puncture wounds; warm water relieves pain.

IT'S A FACT: Recreational fishing accounts for nearly 23% of the total take of over-fished populations in the U.S. inland and coastal waters, according to a study published Aug. 26 in the journal *Science*. It was commonly believed that recreational fishing only accounted for 2-3%, but after analyzing 22 years of state and federal data for recreational and commercial fishing, researchers found that the impact is much greater.

Major U.S. Public Zoological Parks

Source: *World Almanac* questionnaire, 2004; budget and attendance in millions; figures latest available

Zoo	Budget	Atten-dance	Acres	Species	Some major attractions/information
Arizona-Sonora Desert Museum (Tucson, AZ)	$6.0	0.5	100	300+	Desert Loop Trail, Hummingbird Aviary, Pollination Gardens (520) 883-2702; www.desertmuseum.org
Audubon Zoo (New Orleans)	NA	0.8	58	350+	Louisiana Swamp, Endangered Species, Safari Simulator (866) 744-7379; www.audubonzoo.org
Baltimore Zoo	NA	0.6	161	305	Children's zoo, African Watering Hole, Keeper Encounters (410) 396-7102; www.baltimorezoo.org
Bronx Zoo/Wildlife Conservation Park (N.Y.C.)	42.5	1.7	265	604	Tiger Mountain, Congo Gorilla Forest, Jungle World (718) 367-1010; www.bronxzoo.com
Brookfield Zoo (Chicago area)	48.0	2.0	216	479	Family Play Zoo, Living Coast, Habitat Africa, Tropic World (708) 485-0263; www.brookfieldzoo.org
Buffalo (NY) Zoological Society	5.0	0.4	23.5	195	River Otters, Polar Bear Exhibit, Vanishing Animals (716) 837-3900; www.buffalozoo.org
Cincinnati Zoo and Botanical Garden	18.0	1.2	75	3,500	Vanishing Giants, Jungle Trails, Manatee Springs (800) 94-HIPPO; www.cincinnatizoo.org
Cleveland Metroparks Zoo	14.0	1.3	168	579	Rainforest, Center for Zoological Medicine (216) 661-6500; www.clemetzoo.com
Columbus Zoo and Aquarium (Powell, OH)	27.9	1.3	588	758	Nocturnal building, Komodo dragons, orangutans (800) MONKEYS; www.columbuszoo.org
Dallas Zoo	12.0	0.6	95	330	Endangered Tiger Habitat, Wilds of Africa, Children's Zoo (214) 670-6826; www.dallaszoo.org
Denver Zoo	18.4	1.4	80	750	Komodo Dragon habitat, okapi, black rhino, Predator Ridge (303) 376-4800; www.denverzoo.org
Detroit Zoological Park (Royal Oak, MI)	12.8	1.3	125	581	Arctic Ring of Life, Wild Adventure, Natl. Amphibian Center (248) 398-0900; www.detroitzoo.org
The Houston Zoo	18.0	1.5	55	700+	Wortham World of Primates, koalas, komodo dragons (713) 533-6500; www.houstonzoo.org
Lincoln Park Zoological Gardens (Chicago)	17.0	3.0	35	208	Farm-in-the-Zoo, Kovler Lion House, Primate House (312) 742-2000; www.lpzoo.org
Los Angeles Zoo and Botanical Gardens	16.0	1.5	80	370	Dragons of Komodo, Chimpanzees of Mahale Mountains (323) 644-4200; www.lazoo.org
Louisville (KY) Zoo	10.0	0.8	134	402	Islands Exhibit, Gorilla Forest (502) 459-2181; www.louisvillezoo.org
Memphis (TN) Zoo	8.0	0.7	70+	500+	China Exhibit, Cat Country, Primate Canyon (901) 276-WILD; www.memphiszoo.org
Miami Metrozoo	9.0	0.5	300	325	Komodo dragons, meerkats, Dr. Wilde's Rainforest Museum (305) 251-0400; www.zsf.org
Milwaukee County Zoo	19.1	1.3	192	395	Apes of Africa, Siberian Tigers, Lake Wisconsin Exhibit (414) 771-3040; www.milwaukeezoo.org
Minnesota Zoo (Apple Valley)	16.6	1.0	485	400+	Meerkats of the Kalahari, Dolphin shows, Tiger Lair (800) 366-7811; www.mnzoo.org
The National Zoo (Washington, DC)	28.6	3.0	163	475	Giant pandas, Sumatran tigers, Great Cats Exchange (202) 673-4800; www.fonz.org
North Carolina Zoo	13.1	0.7	1,458	250	Australian Walkabout, chimpanzees, Dino Island Simulator (800) 488-0444; www.nczoo.org
Oklahoma City Zoological Park & Botanical Garden	10.5	0.7	110	600	Aquaticus, Cat Forest, Lion Overlook, Great EscApe (405) 424-3344; www.okczoo.com
Omaha's Henry Doorly Zoo	14.5	1.4	110	17,200	nocturnal exhibit, indoor rain forest, indoor desert (402) 733-8401; www.omahazoo.org
Oregon Zoo (Portland)	26.0	1.3	64	200	Africa Rainforest, Asian elephants, African savanna (503) 226-1561; www.oregonzoo.org
Philadelphia Zoo	19.1	1.2	42	330	PECO Primate Reserve, Reptile and Amphibian House (215) 243-1100; www.phillyzoo.org
Phoenix (AZ) Zoo	15.0	1.2	125	250	Arizona Trail, Discovery Trail, Africa Trail, Tropics Trail (602) 273-1341; www.phoenixzoo.org
Point Defiance Zoo & Aquarium (Tacoma, WA)	6.4	0.4	27	300	Polar bears, sharks, elephants, leopards, petting farm (253) 591-5337; www.pdza.org
Rio Grande Zoo (Albuquerque, NM)	11.0	0.7	64	220	Animals of Africa, Australia, and the Americas (505) 764-6200; www.cabq.gov/biopark
Riverbanks Zoo & Garden (Columbia, SC)	6.2	0.9	170	375+	Ndoki Forest, Koala Knockabout, African Plains, Birdhouse (803) 779-8717; www.riverbanks.org
St. Louis Zoo	37.2	3.0	90	810	Big Cat Country, Jungle of the Apes, Monsanto Insectarium (314) 781-0900; www.stlzoo.org
San Diego Wild Animal Park	NA	1.5	1,800	400	Condor Ridge, Heart of Africa (760) 747-8702; www.sandiegozoo.org
San Diego Zoo	NA	3.2	100	800+	Panda research station, Polar Bear Plunge, Gorilla Tropics (619) 231-1515; www.sandiegozoo.org
San Francisco Zoo	14.8	1.0	100	252	Gorilla World, Koala Crossing, Penguin Island, Lemur Forest (415) 753-7080; www.sfzoo.org
Toledo (OH) Zoo	15.0	1.0	62	700	Hippoquarium, Frogtown, Arctic Encounter, Africa! (419) 385-5721; www.toledozoo.org
Tulsa (OK) Zoo and Living Museum	2.1	0.5	86	15,000	Penguin Habitat, African Savanna (918) 669-6600; www.tulsazoo.org
Woodland Park Zoo (Seattle)	21.0	1.0	9	290	Baby Asian elephant, Tropical Rain Forest, Northern Trail (206) 684-4800; www.zoo.org
Zoo Atlanta	15.8	0.7	39	221	Gorillas of the Ford African Rain Forest, Orkin Children's Zoo (404) 624-5600; www.zooatlanta.org

Note: NA = Not available.

Major Canadian Public Zoological Parks

Source: *World Almanac* questionnaire, 2003; budget in millions of dollars (Canadian), attendance in millions; figures latest available.

Zoo	Budget	Atten-dance	Acres	Species	Some major attractions/information
Assiniboine Park Zoo (Winnipeg)	$3.0	0.3	90	360	Snow leopards, Siberian tigers, Bird of Prey Show *(204) 986-2327;* www.city.winnipeg.mb.ca
Calgary Zoo	NA	1.2	125	276	Botanical Garden, Prehistoric Park, Canadian Wilds *(403) 232-9300;* www.calgaryzoo.org
Granby Zoo (Quebec)	12.0	0.5	100	200	Exotic Animal collection, Shark Touch Tank *(877) 472-6299;* www.zoogranby.ca
Toronto Zoo	31.0	1.2	710	500	Gorilla Rainforest, African Savanna, polar bears *(416) 392-5900;* www.torontozoo.com

Top 50 American Kennel Club Registrations

Source: American Kennel Club, New York, NY; covers (new) dogs registered during calendar year shown

Breed	2003 Rank	2003 Number registered	2002 Rank	2002 Number registered	Breed	2003 Rank	2003 Number registered	2002 Rank	2002 Number registered
Labrador Retriever	1	144,934	1	154,616	Great Dane	27	8,949	28	8,975
Golden Retriever	2	52,530	2	56,124	English Springer Spaniel	28	8,860	27	9,128
Beagle	3	45,033	4	44,610	Weimaraner	29	8,763	29	8,774
German Shepherd	4	43,950	3	46,963	Brittany	30	7,751	30	7,846
Dachshund	5	39,473	5	42,571	West Highland White Terrier	31	7,408	31	7,814
Yorkshire Terrier	6	38,256	6	37,277	Collie	32	5,680	32	6,252
Boxer	7	34,136	7	34,340	Mastiff	33	5,655	34	5,797
Poodle	8	32,176	8	33,917	Australian Shepherd	34	5,626	35	5,789
Shih Tzu	9	26,935	10	28,294	Cavalier King Charles Spaniel	35	5,308	40	4,028
Chihuahua	10	24,930	9	28,466	Papillon	36	5,144	38	4,547
Miniature Schnauzer	11	22,288	11	23,926	Pekingese	37	4,769	33	5,822
Pug	12	21,340	14	21,774	Lhasa Apso	38	4,410	36	5,259
Pomeranian	13	20,808	12	23,061	Saint Bernard	39	4,298	37	5,188
Cocker Spaniel	14	19,036	15	20,655	Chinese Shar-Pei	40	4,100	39	4,437
Rottweiler	15	18,216	13	22,196	Chesapeake Bay Retriever	41	3,713	42	3,829
Bulldog	16	16,735	18	15,810	Cairn Terrier	42	3,707	43	3,812
Shetland Sheepdog	17	15,690	16	17,453	Scottish Terrier	43	3,559	44	3,516
Boston Terrier	18	14,727	17	15,983	Akita	44	3,246	41	3,987
Miniature Pinscher	19	13,162	19	15,230	Vizsla	45	3,181	46	3,106
Maltese	20	12,646	20	13,049	Newfoundland	46	3,135	45	3,121
German Shorthaired Pointer	21	12,269	22	12,174	Bernese Mountain Dog	47	3,132	51	2,567
Doberman Pinscher	22	11,553	23	11,829	Bullmastiff	48	2,943	47	2,900
Siberian Husky	23	10,660	21	12,350	Bloodhound	49	2,849	49	2,804
Pembroke Welsh Corgi	24	10,342	25	9,921	Airedale Terrier	50	2,771	48	2,841
Basset Hound	25	9,481	24	10,789					
Bichon Frise	26	9,410	26	9,706					

Breed Registration for Top 10 Pedigreed Cats, 1979-2003

Source: The Cat Fanciers' Association, Manasquan, NJ; ranked by new registrations, 2003.

Breed	2003	2000	1995	1990	1979	Breed	2003	2000	1995	1990	1979
Persian	20,431	25,524	44,735	60,661	25,819	Oriental	952	1,085	1,237	1,288	260
Maine Coon	4,385	4,539	4,332	2,727	401	American Shorthair	874	885	1,050	1,176	738
Exotic	2,720	2,094	1,610	1,311	289	Tonkinese	864	803	780	618	—
Siamese	1,921	2,131	3,025	3,860	3,607	Burmese	772	846	896	1,238	1,525
Abyssinian	1,417	1,683	2,469	2,702	1,524	**TOTAL**	**44,774**	**49,551**	**70,288**	**84,729**	**37,630**
Birman	1,057	998	990	969	258						

Trees of the U.S.

Source: American Forests, Washington, DC

Approximately 826 native and naturalized species of trees are grown in the U.S. The oldest living tree is believed to be a bristlecone pine tree in California named Methuselah, estimated to be 4,700 years old. The world's largest known living tree, the General Sherman giant sequoia in California, weighs more than 6,167 tons—as much as 41 blue whales or 740 elephants.
Listed here are 10 largest National Champion trees as listed by American Forests.

10 Largest National Champion Trees

Tree Type	Girth at 4.5 ft. (in.)	Height (ft.)	Crown Spread (ft.)	Total Points	Location
Giant sequoia (Gen. Sherman tree)	1,020	274	107	1,321	Sequoia National Park, CA
Coast redwood	950	321	75	1,290	Jedidiah Smith State Park, CA
Coast redwood	895	307	83	1223	Jedidiah Smith State Park, CA
Coast redwood	867	311	101	1203	Prairie Creek St. Pk., CA
Western redcedar	761	159	45	931	Olympic National Park, WA
Sitka spruce	668	191	96	833	Olympic National Park, WA
Common baldcypress	644	83	85	748	Cat Island, LA
Sitka spruce	629	204	93	856	Kloochy Creek Park, OR
Coast Douglas-fir	600	200	71	809	Olympic National Park, WA
Bluegum eucalyptus	586	141	126	759	Petrolia, CA
Coast Douglas fir	512	301	65	829	Jedidiah Smith State Park, CA

METEOROLOGY

National Weather Service Watches and Warnings

Source: National Weather Service, NOAA, U.S. Dept. of Commerce; *Glossary of Meteorology,* American Meteorological Society

The **National Weather Service** issues watches, warnings, and advisories for specific geographic areas to alert people to the possibility or imminent arrival of various forms of **severe weather**. A *Severe Thunderstorm* or *Tornado Watch* is issued for a specific area when a severe convective storm that usually covers a relatively small geographic area or moves in a narrow path is sufficiently intense to threaten life and/or property. Examples include thunderstorms with large hail, damaging winds, and/or tornadoes. Excessive *localized convective rains* are not classified as severe storms but are often the product of severe local storms. Such rainfall may result in phenomena that threaten life and property, such as *flash floods. Lightning* occurs with all thunderstorms and, along with flash floods, is a leading cause of storm deaths and injuries.

Severe Thunderstorm—a thunderstorm that produces a tornado, winds of at least 50 knots (58 mph), and/or hail at least $3/_4$ inch in diameter. A thunderstorm with winds of at least 35 knots (39 mph) and/or hail at least ½ inch in diameter is defined as approaching severe. A *Severe Thunderstorm Watch* is issued for a specific area where such storms are most likely to develop. A *Severe Thunderstorm Warning* indicates that a severe thunderstorm has been sighted or indicated by radar.

Tornado—a violent rotating column of air, usually pendant to a cumulonimbus cloud, with circulation reaching the ground. A tornado nearly always starts as a funnel cloud and may be accompanied by a loud roaring noise. On a local scale, it is the most destructive of all atmospheric phenomena. Tornado paths have varied in length from a few feet to more than 100 miles (avg. 5 mi); in diameter from a few feet to more than a mile (avg. 220 yd); average forward speed, 30 mph. Tornado watches and warnings follow the same criteria as those for thunderstorms.

Cyclone—an atmospheric circulation of winds rotating counterclockwise in the northern hemisphere and clockwise in the southern hemisphere. Tornadoes, hurricanes, and the lows shown on weather maps are all examples of cyclones of various size and intensity. Cyclones are usually accompanied by precipitation or stormy weather.

Subtropical Storm—a cyclone that develops over subtropical waters (N of 20° lat.) with one-minute sustained surface winds of 34 knots (39 mph) or more. It may form over warm or cold water, and can develop into a tropical storm or a hurricane.

Tropical Storm—a cyclone that develops over tropical waters (23.5° N-23.5° S lat.), with one-minute sustained surface winds within a range of 34 to 63 knots (39 to 73 mph). A *Tropical Storm Watch* is issued when tropical storm conditions may pose a threat to specified coastal areas within 36 hours. A *Tropical Storm Warning* is issued when tropical storm conditions are expeced in a specified costal area within 24 hours or less.

Hurricane—a severe cyclone originating over tropical ocean waters and having one-minute sustained surface winds of 64 knots (74 mph) or higher. (West of the international date line, in the western Pacific, such storms are known as *typhoons*.) The area of hurricane-force winds forms a circle or an oval, sometimes as wide as 300 mi in diameter. In the lower latitudes, hurricanes usually move west or northwest at 10 to 15 mph. When the center approaches 25° to 30° North Latitude, the direction of motion often changes to northeast, with increased forward speed. In the W Atlantic and E Pacific, hurricane season is June 1-Nov. 30. Hurricane watches and warnings follow the same criteria as those for tropical storms, and may remain in effect if dangerously high water and/or waves continue.

Winter Storm and Blizzard—A *Winter Storm Watch* is issued when conditions are favorable for hazardous winter weather, such as heavy snow, sleet, or freezing rain. A *Winter Storm Warning* is issued when hazardous winter weather conditions are imminent, and are usually issued for up to a 12-hour duration, which may be extended to 24 hours if needed. A *Blizzard Warning* is issued for winter storm conditions with winds of 35 mph or higher and sufficient falling and/or blowing snow to frequently reduce visibility to less than ¼ mi. for at least 3 hours.

Flood—Flooding takes many forms. *River Flooding:* This natural process occurs when rains, sometimes coupled with melting snow, fill river basins with too much water too quickly; torrential rains from decaying hurricanes or tropical systems can also be a major cause of river flooding. *Coastal Flooding:* Winds from tropical storms and hurricanes or intense offshore low pressure systems can drive ocean water inland and cause significant flooding. Coastal floods can also be produced by sea waves called *tsunamis,* sometimes referred to as tidal waves; these waves are produced by earthquakes or volcanic activity. *Flash Flooding:* Usually due to copious amounts of rain falling in a short time, flash flooding typically occurs within 6 hours of the rain event. Flash floods account for the majority of flood deaths in the U.S., and are the leading cause of deaths associated with thunderstorms. *Urban Flooding:* Urbanization significantly increases runoff over what would occur on natural terrain, making flash flooding in these areas extremely dangerous. Streets can become swift-moving rivers, and basements can become death traps as they fill with water. *Ice Jam Flooding:* Ice can accumulate at natural or artificial obstructions and stop the flow of water. As the water flow is stopped, water builds up and flooding can occur upstream. If the jam suddenly gives way, the gush of ice and water can cause serious downstream flash flooding.

Flash Flood or Flood Watch: means that flash flooding or flooding is possible within a designated area.

Flash Flood or Flood Warning: means that flash flooding or flooding has been reported or is imminent; all necessary precautions should be taken immediately.

National Weather Service Marine Warnings and Advisories

Small Craft Advisory—alerts mariners to sustained (exceeding 2 hours) weather and/or sea conditions, either present or forecast, potentially hazardous to small boats. Although "small craft" is not defined, hazardous conditions generally include winds of 18 to 33 knots and/or dangerous wave conditions. The advisory is also issued for lower wind speeds that may affect small craft operations. Criteria vary depending on region and type of marine environment. Upon receiving word of a Small Craft Advisory, the mariner should immediately obtain the latest marine forecast to determine the reason for the advisory.

Gale Warning—indicates that winds within the range 34 to 47 knots, not directly associated with a tropical storm, are forecast for the area.

Tropical Storm Warning—indicates that winds within the range of 34 to 63 knots associated with a tropical storm are forecast to occur within 24 hours or less.

Storm Warning—indicates that winds 48 knots or above, not directly associated with a tropical storm, are forecast for the area.

Hurricane Warning—indicates that winds 64 knots or greater associated with a hurricane are forecast for the area within 24 hours.

Special Marine Warning—indicates potentially hazardous weather conditions, usually of short duration (2 hours or less) and producing wind speeds of 34 knots or more, not adequately covered by existing marine warnings.

Primary sources of dissemination are commercial radio, TV, U.S. Coast Guard radio stations, and NOAA VHF-FM broadcasts. These NOAA broadcasts on 162.40 to 162.55 MHz can usually be received 20-40 mi from the transmitting antenna site, depending on terrain and quality of the receiver used. Where transmitting antennas are on high ground, the range may be somewhat greater, reaching 60 mi or more.

Monthly Normal Mean Temperatures, Normal Precipitation, U.S. Cities

Source: National Climatic Data Center, NESDIS, NOAA, U.S. Dept. of Commerce

Normals are averages covering a 30-year period. The temperature and precipitation normals given here are based on records for 1971-2000. Temperatures listed below represent means of the normal daily maximum and normal daily minimum temperatures for each month. For stations that did not have continuous records from the same site for the entire 30 years, the means have been adjusted to the record at the present site. (*) = city station. Other figures are for airport stations. T = temp. in Fahrenheit; P = precipitation in inches.

	Jan.		Feb.		Mar.		Apr.		May		June		July		Aug.		Sept.		Oct.		Nov.		Dec.	
Station	T	P	T	P	T	P	T	P	T	P	T	P	T	P	T	P	T	P	T	P	T	P	T	P
Albany, NY	22	2.7	25	2.3	35	3.2	47	3.3	58	3.7	66	3.7	71	3.5	69	3.7	61	3.3	49	3.2	39	3.3	28	2.8
Albuquerque, NM	36	0.5	41	0.4	48	0.6	56	0.5	65	0.6	75	0.7	79	1.3	76	1.7	69	1.1	57	1.0	44	0.6	36	0.5
Anchorage, AK	16	0.7	19	0.7	26	0.7	36	0.5	47	0.7	55	1.1	58	1.7	56	2.9	48	2.9	34	2.1	22	1.1	18	1.1
Asheville, NC	36	3.1	39	3.2	46	3.9	54	3.2	62	3.5	69	3.2	73	3.0	72	3.3	66	3.0	55	2.4	46	2.9	39	2.6
Atlanta, GA	43	5.0	47	4.7	54	5.4	62	3.6	70	4.0	77	3.6	80	5.1	79	3.7	73	4.1	63	3.1	53	4.1	45	3.8
Atlantic City, NJ	32	3.6	34	2.9	42	4.1	51	3.5	61	3.4	70	2.7	75	3.9	74	4.3	66	3.1	55	2.9	46	3.3	37	3.2
Baltimore, MD	32	3.5	36	3.0	44	3.9	53	3.0	63	3.9	72	3.4	77	3.9	75	3.7	67	4.0	55	3.2	46	3.1	37	3.4
Barrow, AK	–14	0.1	–16	0.1	–14	0.1	–1	0.1	20	0.1	35	0.3	40	0.9	39	1.0	31	0.7	15	0.4	–1	0.2	–11	0.1
Birmingham, AL	43	5.5	47	4.2	55	6.1	61	4.7	69	4.8	76	3.8	80	5.1	80	3.5	74	4.1	63	3.2	53	4.6	46	4.5
Bismarck, ND	10	0.5	18	0.5	30	0.9	43	1.5	56	2.2	65	2.6	70	2.6	69	2.2	58	1.6	45	1.3	28	0.7	15	0.4
Boise, ID	30	1.4	37	1.1	44	1.4	51	1.3	59	1.3	67	0.7	75	0.4	74	0.3	64	0.8	53	0.8	40	1.4	31	1.4
Boston, MA	29	3.9	32	3.3	39	3.9	48	3.6	59	3.2	68	3.2	74	3.1	72	3.4	65	3.5	54	3.8	45	4.0	35	3.7
Buffalo, NY	25	3.2	26	2.4	34	3.0	45	3.0	57	3.4	66	3.8	71	3.1	69	3.9	62	3.8	51	3.2	40	3.9	30	3.8
Burlington, VT	18	2.2	20	1.7	31	2.3	44	2.9	57	3.3	66	3.4	71	4.0	68	4.0	59	3.8	48	3.1	37	3.1	25	2.2
Caribou, ME	10	3.0	13	2.1	25	2.6	38	2.6	52	3.3	61	3.3	66	3.9	63	4.2	54	3.3	43	3.0	31	3.1	16	3.2
Charleston, SC	48	4.1	51	3.1	58	4.0	64	2.8	72	3.7	78	5.9	82	6.1	81	6.9	76	6.0	66	3.1	58	2.7	51	3.2
Charleston, WV	33	3.3	37	3.2	45	3.9	54	3.3	62	4.3	70	4.1	74	4.9	73	4.1	66	3.5	55	2.7	46	3.7	38	3.3
Chicago, IL	22	1.8	27	1.6	37	2.7	48	3.7	59	3.4	68	3.6	73	3.5	72	4.6	64	3.3	52	2.7	39	3.0	27	2.4
Cleveland, OH	26	2.5	28	2.3	38	2.9	48	3.4	59	3.5	68	3.9	72	3.5	70	3.7	63	3.8	52	2.7	42	3.4	31	3.1
Columbus, OH	28	2.5	32	2.2	42	2.9	52	3.3	63	3.9	71	4.1	75	4.6	74	3.7	67	2.9	55	2.3	44	3.2	34	2.9
Dallas–Ft. Worth, TX	44	1.9	49	2.4	57	3.1	65	3.2	73	5.2	81	3.2	85	2.1	84	2.0	78	2.4	67	4.1	55	2.6	47	2.6
Denver, CO	29	0.5	33	0.5	40	1.3	48	1.9	57	2.3	68	1.6	73	2.2	72	1.8	62	1.1	51	1.0	38	1.0	30	0.6
Des Moines, IA	20	1.0	27	1.2	38	2.2	51	3.6	62	4.3	71	4.6	76	4.2	74	4.5	65	3.2	53	2.6	38	2.1	25	1.3
Detroit, MI	25	1.9	27	1.9	37	2.5	48	3.1	60	3.1	69	3.6	74	3.2	72	3.1	64	3.3	52	2.2	41	2.7	30	2.5
Dodge City, KS	30	0.6	36	0.7	44	1.8	54	2.3	64	3.0	74	3.2	80	3.2	78	2.7	69	1.7	57	1.5	42	1.0	33	0.8
Duluth, MN	8	1.1	15	0.8	25	1.7	39	2.1	52	3.0	60	4.3	66	4.2	64	4.2	55	4.1	44	2.5	28	2.1	14	0.9
Fairbanks, AK	–10	0.6	–4	0.4	11	0.3	32	0.2	49	0.6	60	1.4	62	1.7	56	1.7	45	1.1	24	1.0	2	0.7	–6	0.7
Fresno, CA	46	2.2	51	2.1	56	2.2	61	0.8	69	0.4	76	0.2	81	0.0	80	0.0	75	0.3	65	0.7	53	1.1	45	1.3
Galveston, TX*	56	4.1	58	2.6	64	2.8	70	2.6	77	3.7	82	4.0	84	3.5	84	4.2	81	5.8	74	3.5	65	3.6	58	3.5
Grand Rapids, MI	22	2.0	25	1.5	35	2.6	46	3.5	58	3.4	67	3.7	71	3.6	69	3.8	61	4.3	50	2.8	38	3.4	28	2.7
Hartford, CT	26	3.8	29	3.0	38	3.9	49	3.9	60	4.4	69	3.9	74	3.7	72	4.0	63	4.1	52	3.9	42	4.1	31	3.6
Helena, MT	20	0.5	26	0.4	35	0.6	44	0.9	53	1.8	61	1.8	68	1.3	67	1.3	56	1.1	45	0.7	31	0.5	21	0.5
Honolulu, HI	73	2.7	73	2.4	74	1.9	76	1.1	77	0.8	80	0.4	81	0.5	82	0.5	82	0.7	80	2.2	78	2.3	75	2.9
Houston, TX	52	3.7	55	3.0	62	3.4	69	3.6	76	5.2	81	5.4	84	3.2	83	3.8	79	4.3	70	4.5	61	4.2	54	3.7
Huron, SD	14	0.5	21	0.6	33	1.7	46	2.3	58	3.0	68	3.3	73	2.9	72	2.1	61	1.8	48	1.6	31	0.9	19	0.4
Indianapolis, IN	27	2.5	31	2.4	42	3.4	52	3.6	63	4.4	72	4.1	75	4.4	74	3.8	66	2.9	55	2.8	43	3.6	32	3.0
Jackson, MS	45	5.7	49	4.5	57	5.7	63	6.0	72	4.9	79	3.8	81	4.7	81	3.7	76	3.2	64	3.4	55	5.0	48	5.3
Jacksonville, FL	53	3.7	56	3.2	62	3.9	67	3.1	73	3.5	79	5.4	82	6.0	81	6.9	78	7.9	69	3.9	62	2.3	55	2.6
Juneau, AK	26	4.8	29	4.0	34	3.5	41	3.0	48	3.5	54	3.4	57	4.1	56	5.4	50	7.6	42	8.3	33	5.4	29	5.4
Kansas City, MO	27	1.2	33	1.3	44	2.4	54	3.4	64	5.4	74	4.4	79	4.4	77	3.5	68	4.6	57	3.3	43	2.3	31	1.6
Knoxville, TN	38	4.6	42	4.0	50	5.2	58	4.0	66	4.7	74	4.0	78	4.7	77	2.9	71	3.0	59	2.7	49	4.0	41	4.5
Lander, WY	20	0.5	26	0.5	36	1.2	44	2.1	53	2.4	64	1.2	71	0.8	69	0.6	59	1.1	46	1.4	30	1.0	21	0.6
Lexington, KY	32	3.3	36	3.3	46	4.4	55	3.7	64	4.8	72	4.6	76	4.8	75	3.8	68	3.1	57	2.7	46	3.4	36	4.0
Little Rock, AR	40	3.6	45	3.3	53	4.9	61	5.5	70	5.1	78	4.0	82	3.3	81	2.9	74	3.7	63	4.3	52	5.7	43	4.7
Los Angeles, CA*	57	3.0	58	3.1	58	2.4	61	0.6	63	0.2	66	0.1	69	0.0	71	0.1	70	0.3	67	0.4	62	1.1	58	1.8
Louisville, KY	33	3.3	38	3.3	47	4.4	56	3.9	66	4.9	74	3.8	78	4.3	77	3.4	70	3.1	59	2.8	48	3.8	38	3.7
Marquette, MI*	12	2.6	15	1.9	24	3.1	36	2.8	50	3.1	59	3.2	64	3.0	62	3.6	54	3.7	43	3.7	29	3.3	17	2.4
Memphis, TN	40	4.2	45	4.3	54	5.6	62	5.8	71	5.2	79	4.3	83	4.2	81	3.0	75	3.3	64	3.3	52	5.8	43	5.7
Miami, FL	68	1.9	69	2.1	72	2.6	76	3.4	80	5.5	82	8.5	84	5.8	84	8.6	82	8.4	79	6.2	74	3.4	70	2.2
Milwaukee, WI	21	1.9	25	1.7	35	2.6	45	3.8	56	3.1	66	3.6	72	3.6	71	4.0	63	3.3	51	2.5	38	2.7	26	2.2
Minneapolis, MN	13	1.0	20	0.8	32	1.9	47	2.3	59	3.2	68	4.3	73	4.0	71	4.1	61	2.7	49	2.1	33	1.9	19	1.0
Mobile, AL	61	5.8	65	5.1	71	7.2	77	5.1	84	6.1	89	5.0	91	6.5	91	6.2	87	6.0	79	3.3	70	5.4	63	4.7
Moline, IL	21	1.6	27	1.5	39	2.9	51	3.8	62	4.3	71	4.6	75	4.0	73	4.4	65	3.2	53	2.8	39	2.7	26	2.2
Nashua, NH	23	3.9	26	3.1	35	4.1	46	3.9	57	3.7	66	3.9	71	3.7	69	3.8	61	3.6	49	3.9	39	4.2	28	3.7
Nashville, TN	37	4.0	41	3.7	50	4.9	59	3.9	67	5.1	75	4.1	79	3.8	78	3.3	71	3.6	60	2.9	49	4.5	41	4.5
Newark, NJ	31	4.0	34	3.0	42	4.2	52	3.9	63	4.5	72	3.4	77	4.7	76	4.0	68	4.0	56	3.2	46	3.9	36	3.6
New Orleans, LA	53	5.9	56	5.5	62	5.2	68	5.0	76	4.6	81	6.8	83	6.2	83	6.2	79	5.6	70	3.1	61	5.1	55	5.1
New York, NY*	33	3.6	35	2.8	42	3.9	52	3.7	62	4.2	72	3.6	77	4.4	76	4.1	69	3.8	58	3.3	48	3.7	38	3.5
Norfolk, VA	40	3.9	42	3.3	49	4.1	57	3.4	66	3.7	75	3.8	79	5.2	77	4.8	72	4.1	61	3.5	52	3.0	44	3.0
Oklahoma City, OK	37	1.3	42	1.6	51	2.9	60	3.0	68	5.4	77	4.6	82	2.9	81	2.5	73	4.0	62	3.6	49	2.1	40	1.9
Omaha, NE	22	0.8	28	0.8	39	2.1	51	2.9	62	4.4	72	4.0	77	3.9	75	3.2	65	3.2	53	2.2	38	1.8	26	0.9
Philadelphia, PA	32	3.5	35	2.7	43	3.8	53	3.5	64	3.9	72	3.3	78	4.4	76	3.8	69	3.9	57	2.8	47	3.2	37	3.3
Phoenix, AZ	54	0.8	58	0.8	63	1.1	70	0.3	79	0.2	89	0.1	93	1.0	91	0.9	86	0.8	75	0.8	62	0.7	54	0.9
Pittsburgh, PA	28	2.7	31	2.4	40	3.2	50	3.0	60	3.8	68	4.1	73	4.0	71	3.4	64	3.2	53	2.3	42	3.0	33	2.9
Portland, ME	22	4.1	25	3.1	34	4.1	44	4.3	54	3.8	63	3.3	69	3.3	67	3.1	59	3.4	48	4.4	38	4.7	28	4.2
Portland, OR	40	5.1	43	4.2	47	3.7	51	2.6	57	2.4	63	1.6	68	0.7	69	0.9	64	1.7	54	2.9	46	5.6	40	5.7
Providence, RI	29	4.4	31	3.5	39	4.4	49	4.2	59	3.7	68	3.4	73	3.2	72	3.9	64	3.7	53	3.7	44	4.4	34	4.1
Raleigh, NC	40	4.0	43	3.5	51	4.0	59	2.8	67	3.8	75	3.4	79	4.3	77	3.8	71	4.3	60	3.2	51	3.0	43	3.0
Rapid City, SD	22	0.4	27	0.5	35	1.0	45	1.9	55	3.0	65	2.8	72	2.0	71	1.6	61	1.1	48	1.4	33	0.6	25	0.4
Reno, NV	34	1.1	39	1.1	43	0.9	49	0.4	56	0.6	65	0.5	71	0.2	70	0.3	62	0.5	52	0.4	41	0.8	34	0.9
Richmond, VA	36	3.6	40	3.0	48	4.1	57	3.2	65	4.0	74	3.5	78	4.7	76	4.2	70	4.0	58	3.6	49	3.1	40	3.1
St. Louis, MO	30	2.1	35	2.3	46	3.6	57	3.7	67	4.1	77	3.8	80	3.9	78	3.0	70	3.0	58	2.8	45	3.7	34	2.9
Salt Lake City, UT	29	1.4	35	1.3	43	1.9	50	2.0	59	2.1	69	0.8	77	0.7	76	0.8	65	1.3	53	1.6	40	1.4	30	1.2
San Antonio, TX	51	1.7	55	1.8	63	1.9	69	2.6	76	4.7	81	4.3	84	2.0	84	2.6	79	3.0	71	3.9	60	2.6	53	2.0
San Diego, CA	58	2.3	59	2.0	60	2.3	63	0.8	65	0.2	67	0.1	71	0.0	73	0.1	72	0.2	68	0.4	62	1.1	58	1.3
San Francisco, CA	49	4.5	52	4.0	54	3.3	56	1.2	59	0.4	61	0.1	63	0.0	64	0.1	64	0.2	61	1.0	55	2.5	50	2.9
San Juan, PR	77	3.0	77	2.3	78	2.1	79	3.7	81	5.3	82	3.5	82	4.2	82	5.2	82	5.6	82	5.1	80	6.2	78	4.6
Santa Fe, NM	29	0.6	35	0.5	41	0.8	48	0.7	57	1.3	66	1.2	70	2.3	68	2.1	62	1.7	51	1.3	38	1.1	30	0.7
Savannah, GA	49	4.0	53	2.9	59	3.6	65	3.3	73	3.6	79	5.5	82	6.0	81	7.2	77	5.1	67	3.1	59	2.4	51	2.8
Seattle, WA	41	5.1	43	4.2	46	3.8	50	2.6	56	1.8	61	1.5	65	0.8	66	1.0	61	1.6	53	3.2	45	5.9	41	5.6
Spokane, WA	27	1.8	33	1.5	40	1.5	47	1.3	54	1.6	62	1.2	69	0.8	69	0.7	59	0.8	47	1.1	35	2.2	27	2.3
Springfield, MO	32	2.1	37	2.3	46	3.8	56	4.3	65	4.6	73	5.0	79	3.6	78	3.4	69	4.8	58	3.5	46	4.5	36	3.2
Tampa, FL	61	2.3	63	2.7	67	2.9	72	1.8	78	2.9	82	5.5	83	6.5	83	7.6	82	6.5	76	2.3	69	1.6	63	2.3
Washington, DC	34	3.6	36	2.8	44	3.9	54	3.3	64	4.3	73	3.6	78	4.2	76	3.9	69	4.1	57	3.4	47	3.3	38	3.2
Wilmington, DE	32	3.4	34	2.8	43	4.0	52	3.4	63	4.1	72	4.0	77	4.3	75	3.5	68	4.0	56	3.0	46	3.2	36	3.4

Normal High and Low Temperatures, Precipitation, U.S. Cities

Source: National Climatic Data Center, NESDIS, NOAA, U.S. Dept. of Commerce

The normal temperatures and precipitation data given here are based on records for the period 1971-2000. The extreme temperatures are based on records from time of each station's installation. (*) = city station. Other figures are for airport stations. Temperatures are Fahrenheit.

State	Station	NORMAL TEMPERATURE January Max.	January Min.	July Max.	July Min.	EXTREME TEMPERATURE Highest	EXTREME TEMPERATURE Lowest	AVG. ANNUAL PRECIPITATION (inches)
Alabama	Mobile	61	40	91	72	105	3	66.29
Alaska	Anchorage	22	9	65	52	85	−34	16.08
Alaska	Barrow	−8	−20	47	34	79	−56	4.16
Alaska	Juneau	31	21	64	49	90	−22	58.33
Arizona	Phoenix	65	43	104	81	122	17	8.29
Arkansas	North Little Rock	49	31	94	73	111	−6	49.19
California	Los Angeles*	66	49	75	63	110	23	13.15
California	San Francisco	56	43	71	55	106	20	20.11
Colorado	Denver	43	15	88	59	101	−19	15.81
Connecticut	Hartford	34	17	85	62	102	−26	46.16
Delaware	Wilmington	39	24	86	67	102	−14	42.81
District of Columbia	Washington–National	43	27	89	67	105	−5	39.35
Florida	Jacksonville	64	42	91	72	105	7	52.34
Florida	Miami	77	60	91	77	98	30	58.53
Georgia	Atlanta	52	34	89	71	105	−8	50.20
Georgia	Savannah	60	38	92	72	105	3	49.58
Hawaii	Honolulu	80	66	88	74	95	53	18.29
Idaho	Boise	37	24	89	60	111	−25	12.19
Illinois	Chicago	30	14	84	63	104	−27	36.27
Indiana	Indianapolis	35	19	86	65	104	−27	40.95
Iowa	Des Moines	29	12	86	66	108	−26	34.72
Kansas	Dodge City	41	19	93	67	110	−21	22.35
Kentucky	Lexington	40	24	86	66	103	−21	45.91
Kentucky	Louisville	41	25	87	70	106	−22	44.54
Louisiana	New Orleans	62	43	91	74	102	11	64.16
Maine	Caribou	19	0	76	55	96	−41	37.44
Maine	Portland	31	13	79	59	103	−39	45.83
Maryland	Baltimore	41	24	87	66	105	−7	41.94
Massachusetts	Boston	37	22	82	66	102	−12	42.53
Michigan	Detroit	31	18	83	64	104	−21	32.89
Michigan	Grand Rapids	29	16	82	61	100	−22	37.13
Michigan	Sault Ste. Marie*	22	5	76	52	98	−36	34.67
Minnesota	Duluth	18	−1	76	55	97	−39	31.00
Minnesota	Minneapolis-St. Paul	22	4	83	63	105	−34	29.41
Mississippi	Jackson	55	35	91	71	107	2	55.95
Missouri	Kansas City	36	18	89	68	109	−23	37.98
Missouri	St. Louis	38	21	90	71	107	−18	38.75
Montana	Helena	31	10	83	52	105	−42	11.32
Nebraska	Omaha	32	12	87	66	114	−23	30.22
Nevada	Reno	46	22	91	51	108	−16	7.48
New Hampshire	Concord	31	10	83	57	102	−37	37.60
New Jersey	Atlantic City	41	23	85	65	106	−11	40.59
New Mexico	Albuquerque	48	24	92	65	107	−17	9.47
New York	Albany	31	13	82	60	100	−28	38.60
New York	Buffalo	31	18	80	62	99	−20	40.54
New York	New York–Central Park*	38	26	84	69	106	−15	49.69
North Carolina	Raleigh	50	30	89	69	105	−9	43.05
North Dakota	Bismarck	21	−1	85	56	111	−44	16.84
Ohio	Cleveland	33	19	81	62	104	−20	38.71
Ohio	Columbus	36	20	85	65	102	−22	38.52
Oklahoma	Oklahoma City	47	26	93	71	110	−8	35.85
Oregon	Portland	46	34	79	57	107	−3	37.07
Pennsylvania	Philadelphia	39	26	86	70	104	−7	42.05
Pennsylvania	Pittsburgh	35	20	83	62	103	−22	37.85
Puerto Rico	San Juan	82	71	87	77	98	46	50.76
Rhode Island	Providence	37	20	83	64	104	−13	46.45
South Carolina	Charleston	59	37	91	73	105	6	51.53
South Dakota	Huron	25	4	86	61	112	−41	20.90
South Dakota	Rapid City	34	11	86	58	110	−31	16.64
Tennessee	Memphis	49	31	92	73	108	−13	54.65
Tennessee	Nashville	46	28	89	70	107	−17	48.11
Texas	Dallas-Fort Worth	54	34	95	75	109	17	34.73
Texas	Houston	62	41	94	74	109	17	47.84
Utah	Salt Lake City	37	21	91	63	107	−30	16.50
Vermont	Burlington	27	9	81	60	101	−30	36.05
Virginia	Norfolk	48	32	87	71	104	−3	45.74
Virginia	Richmond	45	28	88	68	105	−12	43.91
Washington	Seattle-Tacoma	46	36	75	55	100	0	37.07
Washington	Spokane	33	22	83	55	108	−25	16.67
West Virginia	Charleston	43	24	85	63	104	−16	44.05
Wisconsin	Milwaukee	28	13	81	63	103	−26	34.81
Wyoming	Lander	32	9	86	55	101	−37	13.42

Mean Annual Snowfall (inches) based on climate normals 1971-2000: Boston, MA, 41.8; Sault Ste. Marie, MI, 132.6; Albany, NY, 62.7; Burlington, VT, 83.1; Lander, WY, 102.9; Anchorage, AK, 69.5.

Wettest Spot: Mount Waialeale, HI, on the island of Kauai, is the rainiest place in the world and in the U.S., according to the National Geographic Society; it has an average annual rainfall of 460 inches.

Temperature Extremes: A temperature of 136° F observed at El Azizia (Al Aziziyah), near Tripoli, Libya, on Sept. 13, 1922, is generally accepted as the world's highest temperature recorded under standard conditions. The record high in the U.S. was 134° F in Death Valley, CA, July 10, 1913. A record low of −129°F was recorded at the Soviet Antarctica station of Vostok on July 21, 1983. The record low in the U.S. was −80° F at Prospect Creek, AK, Jan. 23, 1971.

Annual Climatological Data for-U.S. Cities, 2003

Source: National Climatic Data Center, NESDIS, NOAA, U.S. Dept. of Commerce

Station	Elev. (ft.)	Temperature °F Highest	Date	Lowest	Date	Precipitation[1] Total (in.)	Greatest in 24 hours	Date[1]	Sleet or snow Total (in.)	Greatest in 24 hours	Date	Fastest wind MPH	Date	No. of Days Prec. .01 in. or more	Snow, sleet 1 in. or more
Albany, NY	278	93	6/26	−12	1/28	46.32	1.74	10/26-10/27	88.5	12.5	12/06	41	12/11	159	19
Albuquerque, NM	5,305	104	7/14	11	12/29	6.35	1.15	10/07-10/08	4.8	2.0	12/12	51	11/22	40	2
Anchorage, AK	130	84	7/08	−14	12/02	16.68	1.62	10/02-10/03	77.6	7.3	12/19	54	3/13	114	21
Asheville, NC	2,171	89	8/27	5	1/24	59.46	3.08	7/21-7/22	17.4	4.0	4/10	46	1/23	152	6
Atlanta, GA	971	92	8/28	8	1/24	52.91	3.48	5/05-5/06	—	—	—	46	5/02	124	—
Atlantic City, NJ	114	94	8/30	2	2/14	48.32	2.92	6/07	41.8	16.0	2/16	43	11/13	142	9
Baltimore, MD	193	93	6/26	5	1/18	62.66	3.19	10/26-10/27	58.0	21.8	2/16	45	11/13	153	14
Barrow, AK	35	63	7/10	−43	1/06	5.80	0.62	9/09	60.2	4.7	9/09	46	12/29	92	15
Birmingham, AL	636	93	8/15	7	1/24	65.58	5.78	5/07-5/08	T	T	7/21	41	7/21	129	0
Bismarck, ND	1,651	106	8/17	−22	1/23	14.05	1.26	9/10	40.4	3.3	11/03	53	7/03	99	15
Boise, ID	2,858	108	7/22	16	12/30	10.11	.79	3/25-3/26	7.8	1.9	4/06	44	7/26	85	3
Boston, MA	19	93	8/22	0	2/16	44.37	2.00	10/12	77.7	23.6	2/17	39	12/06	139	11
Buffalo, NY	714	87	6/26	−3	3/03	37.16	1.16	12/24-12/25	92.4	9.1	1/19	46	11/13	170	25
Burlington, VT	345	96	6/24	−20	1/28	36.21	2.01	9/28	108.1	17.4	1/04	35	2/05	140	21
Caribou, ME	627	92	6/25	−22	2/27	42.64	2.77	12/15	136.0	27.1	12/15	38	2/03	165	31
Charleston, SC	45	95	7/09	17	1/24	50.99	2.80	3/20	T	T	1/23	38	6/03	125	0
Chicago, IL	655	95	8/25	−7	1/27	32.02	2.24	8/01	17.4	4.0	3/04	39	11/12	113	5
Cleveland, OH	802	92	8/21	−4	1/27	42.50	2.20	7/07-7/08	98.6	6.6	1/26	47	11/12	168	30
Columbus, OH	846	92	7/04	−5	1/27	49.03	3.72	8/29-8/30	49.4	8.9	2/16	44	7/08	167	15
Dallas-Ft. Worth, TX	559	109	8/06	17	1/24	24.55	2.67	9/11	—	—	—	45	6/11	71	—
Denver, CO	5,379	101	7/16	−7	2/07	13.92	2.43	6/18-6/19	—	—	—	47	4/15	73	—
Des Moines, IA	968	101	8/25	−8	2/07	32.91	3.55	11/03	41.1	5.7	2/15	48	1/12	100	12
Detroit, MI	628	92	7/04	−4	3/03	31.39	1.78	10/14	50.0	5.8	2/22	47	11/12	133	14
Duluth, MN	1,426	91	7/26	−18	3/05	24.96	1.90	9/18-9/19	74.6	8.5	4/04	46	4/16	117	23
Fairbanks, AK	461	86	7/20	−42	12/02	13.85	2.56	7/26-7/27	55.4	4.5	11/28	31	8/12	105	19
Fresno, CA	372	107	7/22	30	12/28	9.14	1.13	12/24-12/25	—	—	—	33	4/04	49	—
Grand Rapids, MI	785	92	8/21	−12	1/27	34.11	2.69	11/02	77.5	7.6	1/25	46	2/11	156	25
Hartford, CT	162	94	6/27	−6	3/07	55.91	4.05	9/28-9/29	73.8	15.0	2/17	39	11/14	147	19
Helena, MT	3,864	104	7/23	−13	2/24	9.34	0.64	6/19-6/20	—	—	—	45	10/29	92	—
Honolulu, HI	15	92	8/06	57	1/17	12.69	1.73	12/30-12/31	—	—	—	32	1/20	87	—
Houston, TX	118	104	8/07	28	1/18	45.74	5.67	11/16-11/17	0	0	—	37	8/11	96	0
Huron, SD	1,281	107	8/23	−24	1/23	16.42	2.02	6/24-6/25	32.5	5.8	11/03	51	2/11	85	8
Indianapolis, IN	794	93	8/27	−9	1/27	52.56	7.31	9/31-10/01	44.1	6.6	2/22-2/23	47	11/12	144	15
Jackson, MS	293	96	8/25	13	1/24	58.74	8.50	4/06-4/07	—	—	—	40	4/06	116	—
Jacksonville, FL	31	94	7/10	19	1/24	44.47	4.50	3/01-3/02	—	—	—	44	4/25	120	—
Kansas City, MO	1,005	106	8/21	−9	1/23	27.95	3.26	8/30-8/31	16.2	4.5	12/13	39	5/10	94	6
Knoxville, TN	979	92	8/27	4	1/24	58.66	4.35	5/05-5/06	—	—	—	44	6/11	151	—
Lander, WY	5,557	100	7/24	−16	2/24	10.26	0.89	6/23-6/24	94.9	14.5	2/02	64	2/16	60	22
Lexington, KY	977	93	7/08	−7	1/27	53.39	2.09	11/11-11/12	18.5	2.0	2/10	33	1/12	151	8
Los Angeles, CA	323	91	10/26	16	10/08	9.55	2.21	2/11-2/12	—	—	—	43	12/25	25	—
Louisville, KY	481	93	8/27	2	1/24	49.06	3.09	9/01-9/02	13.4	2.2	12/13	53	4/20	139	6
Marquette, MI	1,415	92	8/19	−30	3/03	35.31	3.07	5/11-5/12	191.8	14.1	2/03-2/04	—	—	159	50
Memphis, TN	283	98	8/18	10	1/24	51.98	3.62	5/16-5/17	—	—	—	48	7/22	117	—
Miami, FL	26	93	3/22	36	1/24	72.13	4.67	7/02	—	—	—	43	3/17	141	—
Milwaukee, WI	677	96	8/21	−5	1/23	22.30	1.40	12/09-12/10	32.6	6.1	3/04	41	5/11	122	9
Minn.-St. Paul, MN	871	97	8/24	−14	2/07	22.72	3.28	6/24-6/25	—	—	—	47	6/24	92	—
Mobile, AL	209	94	8/25	17	1/24	70.93	6.30	5/18	T	T	1/30	35	6/30	113	0
Moline, IL	604	97	8/26	−8	1/27	31.74	2.30	12/09-12/10	23.8	5.1	3/04	44	8/01	109	9
Nashville, TN	571	94	7/28	1	1/18	59.47	5.58	9/21-9/22	—	—	—	43	8/04	134	—
Newark, NJ	25	95	7/05	6	1/18	56.33	2.89	6/03-6/04	63.3	18.6	2/17	46	11/13	146	10
New Orleans, LA	4	95	8/10	25	1/24	66.28	5.16	11/27-11/28	—	—	—	40	6/30	117	—
New York, NY	158	93	6/26	7	1/28	58.42	2.81	6/03-6/04	58.1	16.3	2/17	32	11/13	142	12
Norfolk, VA	66	98	7/09	16	1/28	61.76	4.02	9/18	5.1	2.0	1/16	47	9/18	143	2
North Little Rock, AR	563	102	7/18	10	1/24	39.27	2.35	9/11-9/12	9.8	3.0	2/24	—	—	105	4
Oklahoma City, OK	1,281	106	7/20	9	2/24	22.63	2.04	8/30	6.9	2.6	2/09	43	6/11	77	3
Philadelphia, PA	10	97	6/26	8	1/18	47.98	2.06	2/21-2/22	43.9	16.0	2/16	46	11/13	149	11
Phoenix, AZ	1,103	117	7/16	32	12/29	6.82	1.65	2/13-2/14	—	—	—	47	7/29	28	—
Pittsburgh, PA	1,172	88	8/21	−4	1/27	41.04	1.80	8/30	70.2	8.8	2/16	48	6/08	178	19
Portland, ME	69	92	7/05	−17	2/14	38.25	1.63	10/15	66.4	8.8	1/04	37	12/15	128	21
Portland, OR	220	100	7/29	26	11/01	37.52	2.05	1/31	—	—	—	40	12/04	160	—
Providence, RI	50	92	7/05	−1	1/28	50.27	3.41	8/07-8/08	58.9	14.7	2/17	37	11/13	141	11
Raleigh, NC	427	95	7/09	10	1/24	50.01	2.31	8/15-8/16	5.1	2.3	1/23	33	4/10	135	3
Rapid City, SD	3,150	109	7/24	−17	2/24	10.97	0.90	4/30-5/01	—	—	—	52	12/17	94	—
Reno, NV	4,404	104	7/30	13	2/08	4.58	0.51	8/21	—	—	—	43	3/13	47	—
Richmond, VA	164	95	8/27	8	1/18	63.29	4.32	9/18	12.0	4.0	1/16	46	9/18	149	5
St. Louis, MO	707	104	8/21	1	1/24	46.06	3.78	6/25-6/26	23.5	4.0	2/23	40	3/19	120	8
Salt Lake City, UT	4,221	105	7/15	11	2/08	15.95	1.17	9/09-9/10	61.6	10.6	12/26	47	4/02	79	21
San Antonio, TX	818	103	8/08	15	1/19	28.45	2.81	9/04-9/05	0.2	0.1	2/25	38	11/18	96	0
San Diego, CA	78	88	10/26	40	12/28	9.18	1.48	2/25	—	—	—	30	12/25	30	—
San Francisco, CA	86	97	6/27	36	2/08	18.68	2.60	12/29	—	—	—	45	10/29	65	—
San Juan, PR	7	94	9/14	69	12/31	58.95	2.44	4/23	0	0	—	31	12/29	213	—
Sault Ste. Marie, MI	724	87	6/25	−21	3/03	30.39	1.71	8/03	—	—	—	33	12/01	154	—
Savannah, GA	48	96	7/09	17	1/24	47.71	3.05	4/07-4/08	T	T	1/23	32	5/02	134	0
Scottsbluff, NE	3,946	105	7/17	−15	2/24	10.46	.82	3/18	47.7	7.0	12/08	44	10/29	89	15
Seattle, WA	447	93	7/29	25	12/30	41.78	5.02	10/20	—	—	—	32	12/04	157	—
Spokane, WA	2,381	100	7/30	−5	11/22	14.41	1.08	5/30	32.5	8.2	11/20	48	11/19	112	10
Springfield, MO	1,277	100	8/21	−7	1/17	42.61	2.38	8/02-8/03	29.5	7.5	2/23	49	5/06	99	7
Tampa, FL	8	94	9/01	27	1/24	51.99	4.07	8/09-8/10	0	0	—	36	6/28	120	0
Washington, DC[3]	10	94	8/22	11	1/18	59.53	2.56	2/21-2/22	39.5	13.3	2/16	45	9/18	146	9
Wilmington, DE	92	93	6/26	6	1/28	55.33	3.73	6/19-6/20	43.5	17.0	2/16	47	11/13	149	10

Figures in italic means value also occurred on earlier date in 2003. (T) Trace. (—) Data not available or incomplete. (1) Where one date is shown, it is the starting date of the storm. (2) Sustained for at least 2 minutes, not peak gust. (3) As measured at Reagan Nat't. Airport.

Record Temperatures by State

Source: National Climatic Data Center, NESDIS, NOAA; U.S. Dept. of Commerce, through Dec. 2000

State	°F	LOWEST TEMPERATURE Latest date	Station	Approx. elevation in feet	°F	HIGHEST TEMPERATURE Latest date	Station	Approx. elevation in feet
Alabama	−27	Jan. 30,1966	New Market	760	112	Sept. 5,1925	Centerville	345
Alaska	−80	Jan. 23,1971	Prospect Creek Camp	1,100	100	June 27,1915	Fort Yukon	c. 420
Arizona	−40	Jan. 7,1971	Hawley Lake	8,180	128	June 29,1994	Lake Havasu City	505
Arkansas	−29	Feb. 13,1905	Pond	1,250	120	Aug. 10,1936	Ozark	396
California	−45	Jan. 20,1937	Boca	5,532	134	July 10,1913	Greenland Ranch	−178
Colorado	−61	Feb. 1,1985	Maybell	5,920	118	July 11,1888	Bennett	5,484
Connecticut	−32	Jan. 221961	Coventry	480	106	July 15,1995	Danbury	450
Delaware	−17	Jan. 17,1893	Millsboro	20	110	July 21,1930	Millsboro	20
Florida	−2	Feb. 13,1899	Tallahassee	193	109	June 29,1931	Monticello	207
Georgia	−17	Jan. 27,1940	CCC Camp F-16	1,000	112	Aug. 20,1983	Greenville	860
Hawaii	12	May 17,1979	Mauna Kea Obs. 111.2	13,770	100	Apr. 27,1931	Pahala	850
Idaho	−60	Jan. 18,1943	Island Park Dam	6,285	118	July 28,1934	Orofino	1,027
Illinois	−36	Jan. 5,1999	Congerville	635	117	July 14,1954	East St. Louis	410
Indiana	−36	Jan. 19,1994	New Whiteland	785	116	July 14,1936	Collegeville	672
Iowa	−47	Feb. 3,1996[1]	Elkader	770	118	July 20,1934	Keokuk	614
Kansas	−40	Feb. 13,1905	Lebanon	1,812	121	July 24,1936[1]	Alton (near)	1,651
Kentucky	−37	Jan. 19,1994	Shelbyville	730	114	July 28,1930	Greensburg	581
Louisiana	−16	Feb. 13,1899	Minden	194	114	Aug. 10,1936	Plain Dealing	268
Maine	−48	Jan. 19,1925	Van Buren	510	105	July 10,1911[1]	North Bridgton	450
Maryland	−40	Jan. 13,1912	Oakland	2,461	109	July 10,1936[1]	Cumberland Frederick	623 325
Massachusetts	−35	Jan. 12,1981	Chester	640	107	Aug. 2,1975	Chester New Bedford	640 120
Michigan	−51	Feb. 9,1934	Vanderbilt	785	112	July 13,1936	Mio	963
Minnesota	−60	Feb. 2,1996	Tower	1,460	114	July 6,1936[1]	Moorhead	904
Mississippi	−19	Jan. 30,1966	Corinth	420	115	July 29,1930	Holly Springs	600
Missouri	−40	Feb. 13,1905	Warsaw	700	118	July 14,1954[1]	Warsaw Union	705 560
Montana	−70	Jan. 20,1954	Rogers Pass	5,470	117	July 5,1937	Medicine Lake	1,950
Nebraska	−47	Dec. 22,1989	Oshkosh	3,379	118	July 24,1936[1]	Minden	2,169
Nevada	−50	Jan. 8,1937	San Jacinto	5,200	125	June 29,1994[1]	Laughlin	605
New Hampshire	−47	Jan. 29,1934	Mt. Washington	6,262	106	July 4,1911	Nashua	125
New Jersey	−34	Jan. 5,1904	River Vale	70	110	July 10,1936	Runyon	18
New Mexico	−50	Feb. 1,1951	Gavilan	7,350	122	June 27,1994	Waste Isolat. Pilot Plt.	3,418
New York	−52	Feb. 18,1979[1]	Old Forge	1,720	108	July 22,1926	Troy	35
North Carolina	−34	Jan. 21,1985	Mt. Mitchell	6,525	110	Aug. 21,1983	Fayetteville	213
North Dakota	−60	Feb. 15,1936	Parshall	1,929	121	July 6,1936	Steele	1,857
Ohio	−39	Feb. 10,1899	Milligan	800	113	July 21,1934[1]	Gallipolis (near)	673
Oklahoma	−27	Jan. 18,1930	Watts	958	120	June 27,1994[1]	Tipton	1,350
Oregon	−54	Feb. 10,1933[1]	Seneca	4,700	119	Aug. 10,1898[1]	Pendleton	1,074
Pennsylvania	−42	Jan. 5,1904	Smethport	c. 1,500	111	July 10,1936[1]	Phoenixville	100
Rhode Island	−25	Feb. 5,1996	Greene	425	104	Aug. 2,1975	Providence	51
South Carolina	−19	Jan. 21,1985	Caesars Head	3,115	111	June 28,1954[1]	Camden	170
South Dakota	−58	Feb. 17,1936	McIntosh	2,277	120	July 5,1936	Gannvalley	1,750
Tennessee	−32	Dec. 30,1917	Mountain City	2,471	113	Aug. 9,1930[1]	Perryville	377
Texas	−23	Feb. 8,1933[1]	Seminole	3,275	120	June 281994	Monahans	2,660
Utah	−69	Feb. 1,1985	Peter's Sink	8,092	117	Jul. 5,1985	Saint George	2,880
Vermont	−50	Dec. 30,1933	Bloomfield	915	105	July 4,1911	Vernon	310
Virginia	−30	Jan. 22,1985	Mountain Lake Bio. Station	3,870	110	July 15,1954	Balcony Falls	725
Washington	−48	Dec. 30,1968	Mazama Winthrop	2,120 1,755	118	Aug. 5,1961[1]	Ice Harbor Dam	475
West Virginia	−37	Dec. 30,1917	Lewisburg	2,200	112	July 10,1936[1]	Martinsburg	435
Wisconsin	−55	Feb. 4,1996	Couderay	1,300	114	July 13,1936	Wisconsin Dells	900
Wyoming	−66	Feb. 9,1933	Riverside R.S.	6,500	115	Aug. 8,1983	Basin	3,500

(1) Also on earlier dates at the same or other places.

Hurricane and Tornado Classifications

Source: National Weather Service, NOAA, U.S. Dept. of Commerce

The Saffir-Simpson Hurricane Scale is a 1-5 rating based on a hurricane's intensity. The scale is used to give an estimate of the potential property damage and flooding expected along the coast from a hurricane landfall. Wind speed is the determining factor in the scale. The Fujita (or F) Scale, created by T. Theodore Fujita, is used to classify tornadoes. The F Scale uses rating numbers from 0 to 5, based on the amount and type of wind damage.

Saffir-Simpson Scale (Hurricanes)

Category	Wind Speed	Severity	Storm Surge[1]
1	74-95 MPH	Weak	4-5 feet
2	96-110 MPH	Moderate	6-8 feet
3	111-130 MPH	Strong	9-12 feet
4	131-155 MPH	Very Strong	13-18 feet
5	above 155 MPH	Devastating	above 18 feet

(1) Above normal tides.

Fujita Scale (Tornadoes)

Rank	Wind Speed	Damage	Strength
F-0	40-72 MPH	Light	Weak
F-1	73-112 MPH	Moderate	Weak
F-2	113-157 MPH	Considerable	Strong
F-3	158-206 MPH	Severe	Strong
F-4	207-260 MPH	Devastating	Violent
F-5	above 261 MPH	Incredible	Violent

IT'S A FACT: Four hurricanes—Charley, Frances, Ivan, and Jeanne—hit Florida in August-September 2004. The last and only recorded instance of four hurricanes hitting the same state in one season was in 1886 in Texas.

Hurricane Names in 2005

Source: National Weather Service, NOAA, U.S. Dept. of Commerce

Atlantic hurricanes — Arlene, Bret, Cindy, Dennis, Emily, Franklin, Gert, Harvey, Irene, José, Katrina, Lee, Maria, Nate, Ophelia, Philippe, Rita, Stan, Tammy, Vince, Wilma.

Eastern Pacific hurricanes — Adrian, Beatriz, Calvin, Dora, Eugene, Fernanda, Greg, Hilary, Irwin, Jova, Kenneth, Lidia, Max, Norma, Otis, Pilar, Ramon, Selma, Todd, Veronica, Wiley, Xina, York, Zelda.

World Temperature and Precipitation

Source: World Meteorological Organization

Average daily maximum and minimum temperatures and annual precipitation are based on records for the period 1961-90. The record of extreme temperatures includes all available years of data for a given location and is usually for a longer period. Surface elevations are supplied by the WMO and may differ from city elevation figures in other sections of *The World Almanac*. NA = Not available.

Station	Surface elevation (feet)	Temperature °F AVERAGE DAILY January Max.	January Min.	July Max.	July Min.	EXTREME Max.	EXTREME Min.	Average annual precipitation (inches)
Algiers, Algeria	82	61.7	42.6	87.1	65.3	NA	NA	27.0
Athens, Greece	49	56.1	44.6	88.9	73.0	NA	NA	14.6
Auckland, New Zealand	20	74.8	61.2	58.5	46.4	NA	NA	49.4
Bangkok, Thailand	66	89.6	69.8	90.9	77.0	104	51	59.0
Berlin, Germany	190	35.2	26.8	73.6	55.2	107	-4	23.3
Bogotá, Colombia	8,357	67.3	41.7	64.6	45.5	75	21	32.4
Bombay (Mumbai), India	36	85.3	66.7	86.2	77.5	110	46	85.4
Bucharest, Romania	298	34.7	22.1	83.8	60.1	105	-18	23.4
Budapest, Hungary	456	34.2	24.8	79.7	59.7	103	-10	20.3
Buenos Aires, Argentina	82	85.8	67.3	59.7	45.7	104	22	45.2
Cairo, Egypt	243	65.8	48.2	93.9	71.1	118	34	1.0
Cape Town, South Africa	138	79.0	60.3	63.3	44.6	105	28	20.5
Caracas, Venezuela	2,739	79.9	60.8	81.3	66.0	96	45	36.1
Casablanca, Morocco	203	62.8	47.1	77.7	66.7	NA	NA	16.8
Copenhagen, Denmark	16	35.6	28.4	68.9	55.0	NA	NA	NA
Damascus, Syria	2,004	54.3	32.9	97.2	61.9	NA	NA	5.6
Dublin, Ireland	279	45.7	36.5	66.0	52.5	86	8	28.8
Geneva, Switzerland	1,364	38.3	27.9	76.3	53.2	101	-3	35.6
Havana, Cuba	164	78.4	65.5	88.3	74.8	NA	NA	46.9
Hong Kong, China	203	65.5	56.5	88.7	79.9	97	32	87.2
Istanbul, Turkey	108	47.8	37.2	82.8	65.3	105	7	27.4
Jerusalem, Israel	2,483	53.4	39.4	83.8	63.0	107	26	23.2
Lagos, Nigeria	125	90.0	72.3	82.8	72.1	NA	NA	59.3
Lima, Peru	43	79.0	66.9	66.4	59.4	NA	NA	0.2
London, England	203	44.1	32.7	71.1	52.3	99	2	29.7
Manila, Philippines	79	85.8	74.8	89.1	76.8	NA	NA	49.6
Mexico City, Mexico	7,570	70.3	43.7	73.8	53.2	NA	NA	33.4
Montreal, Canada	118	21.6	5.2	79.2	59.7	100	-36	37.0
Nairobi, Kenya	5,897	77.9	50.9	71.6	48.6	NA	NA	41.9
Paris, France	213	42.8	33.6	75.2	55.2	105	-1	25.6
Prague, Czech Republic	1,197	32.7	22.5	73.9	53.2	98	-16	20.7
Reykjavik, Iceland	200	35.4	26.6	55.9	46.9	76	-3	31.5
Rome, Italy	79	53.8	35.4	88.2	62.1	NA	NA	33.0
San Salvador, El Salvador	2,037	86.5	61.3	86.2	66.4	105	45	68.3
São Paulo, Brazil	2,598	81.1	65.7	71.2	53.1	NA	NA	57.4
Shanghai, China	23	45.9	32.9	88.9	76.6	104	10	43.8
Singapore	52	85.8	73.6	87.4	75.6	NA	NA	84.6
Stockholm, Sweden	171	30.7	23.0	71.4	56.1	97	-26	21.2
Sydney, Australia	10	79.5	65.5	62.4	43.9	114	32	46.4
Tehran, Iran	3,906	45.0	30.0	98.2	75.2	109	-5	9.1
Tokyo, Japan	118	49.1	34.2	83.8	72.1	NA	NA	55.4
Toronto, Canada	567	27.5	12.0	80.2	57.6	105	-26	30.8

Speed of Winds in the U.S.

Source: National Climatic Data Center, NESDIS, NOAA, U.S. Dept. of Commerce

In miles per hour; based on available records through 2003. Max. values for highest one-minute average, except where noted.

Station	Avg.	Max.	Station	Avg.	Max.	Station	Avg.	Max.
Albuquerque, NM	8.9	52	Honolulu, HI	11.3	46	Mt. Washington, NH[1]	35.1	231
Anchorage, AK[1]	7.1	75	Houston, TX	7.6	51	New Orleans, LA	8.2	69
Atlanta, GA	9.1	60	Indianapolis, IN	9.6	49	New York, NY[4]	9.3	40
Baltimore, MD	8.8	80	Jacksonville, FL	7.8	57	Omaha, NE	10.5	58
Bismarck, ND	10.2	64	Kansas City, MO	10.6	58	Philadelphia, PA[2]	9.5	73
Boston, MA[2]	12.4	54	Las Vegas, NV	9.2	56	Phoenix, AZ	6.2	51
Buffalo, NY	11.8	91	Lexington, KY	9.1	47	Pittsburgh, PA	9.0	58
Cape Hatteras, NC	10.9	60	Little Rock, AR[2]	7.8	65	Portland, OR	7.9	88
Casper, WY	12.7	81	Los Angeles, CA[2]	5.6	49	St. Louis, MO	9.6	52
Chicago, IL	10.3	58	Louisville, KY	8.3	56	Salt Lake City, UT[2]	8.8	71
Denver, CO	8.6	46	Memphis, TN	8.8	51	San Diego, CA[2]	7.0	56
Des Moines, IA[2]	10.7	76	Miami, FL[3]	9.2	86	San Francisco, CA[2]	8.7	47
Detroit, MI	10.2	53	Milwaukee, WI	11.5	54	Seattle, WA[2]	8.8	66
Hartford, CT	8.4	46	Minn.-St. Paul, MN	10.5	51	Spokane, WA[2]	8.9	59
Helena, MT[2]	7.7	73	Mobile, AL	8.8	63	Washington, DC[5]	9.4	49

(1) Short gust. (2) Calculated from minimum time during which one mile of wind passed station. (3) Highest velocity ever recorded in Miami area was 132 mph, at former station in Miami Beach in Sept. 1926. (4) Data for Central Park; Battery Place data through 1960, avg. 14.5, high 113. (5) Data from Ronald Reagan National Airport.

Tides and Their Causes

Source: U.S. Dept. of Commerce, Natl. Oceanic & Atmospheric Admin. (NOAA), Natl. Ocean Service (NOS)

The tides are a natural phenomenon involving the alternating rise and fall in the large fluid bodies of the earth caused by the combined gravitational attraction of the sun and moon. The combination of these 2 variable influences produces the complex recurrent cycle of the tides. Tides may occur in both oceans and seas, to a limited extent in large lakes, in the atmosphere, and, to a very minute degree, in the earth itself. The length of time between succeeding tides varies as the result of many factors.

The tide-generating force represents the difference between (1) the centrifugal force produced by the revolution of the earth around the common center-of-gravity of the earth-moon system and (2) the gravitational attraction of the moon acting upon the earth's overlying waters. The moon is about 400 times closer than the sun; so despite its smaller mass, the moon's tide-raising force is 2.5 times greater.

The tide-generating forces of the moon and sun acting tangentially to the earth's surface tend to cause a maximum accumulation of waters at 2 diametrically opposite positions on the surface of the earth and to withdraw compensating amounts of water from all points 90° removed from these tidal bulges. As the earth rotates beneath the maxima and minima of these tide-generating forces, a sequence of 2 high tides, separated by 2 low tides, ideally is produced each day (semidiurnal tide). Each ocean basin reacts differently to this tidal forcing.

Twice in each month, when the sun, moon, and earth are directly aligned, with the moon between the earth and sun (at new moon) or on the opposite side of the earth from the sun (at full moon), the sun and moon exert gravitational force in a mutual or additive fashion. The highest high tides and lowest low tides are produced at these times. These are called *spring* tides. At 2 positions 90° in between, the gravitational forces of the moon and sun—imposed at right angles—counteract each other to the greatest extent, and the range between high and low tides is reduced. These are called *neap* tides.

The inclination to the equator of the moon's monthly orbit and the inclination of the sun to the equator during the earth's yearly orbit produce a difference in the height of succeeding high tides and in the extent of depression of succeeding low tides that is known as the *diurnal inequality*. In most cases, this produces a so-called *mixed tide*. In extreme cases, these phenomena may result in only one high tide and one low tide each (*diurnal tide*). There are other monthly and yearly variations in the tide because of the elliptical shape of the orbits themselves.

U.S. convention distinguishes between Mean Higher High Water (MHHW), Mean High Water (MHW), Mean Tide Level (MTL), Mean Sea Level (MSL), Mean Low Water (MLW), and Mean Lower Low Water (MLLW). Diurnal range of tide is the difference in height between MHHW and MLLW. Mean range of tide is the difference between MHW and MLW.

The range of tide in the open ocean is generally less than the coastal regions, as the range of the incoming tide can be augmented by the continental shelves, as well as by bays and estuaries. In some shallow inlets and bays, the range may be diminished. In the Bay of Fundy in Nova Scotia, the range of tide, or difference between high and low waters, may reach 43½ feet or more (under spring tide conditions).

In every case, actual high or low tide can vary considerably from the average, as a result of weather conditions such as strong winds, abrupt barometric pressure changes, or prolonged periods of extreme high or low pressure.

Average Rise and Fall of Tides[1]

Place	Ft.	In.	Place	Ft.	In.	Place	Ft.	In.
Baltimore, MD	1	8	Hampton Roads, VA	2	10	St. John's, Nfld.	2	7
Boston, MA	10	4	Key West, FL	1	10	St. Petersburg, FL	2	3[2]
Charleston, SC	5	10	Mobile, AL	1	6[2]	San Diego, CA	5	9
Cristobal, Panama	1	1	New London, CT	3	1	Sandy Hook, NJ	5	2
Eastport, ME	19	4	Newport, RI	3	11	San Francisco, CA	5	10
Ft. Pulaski, GA	7	6	New York, NY	5	1	Seattle, WA	11	4
Galveston, TX	1	5[2]	Philadelphia, PA	6	9	Vancouver, B.C.	10	6
Halifax, N.S.	4	5[2]	Portland, ME	9	11	Washington, DC	3	2

(1) Mean ranges, except where noted. (2) Diurnal range.

El Niño and La Niña

Source: National Weather Service, NOAA, U.S. Dept. of Commerce

El Niño is a climatically significant disruption of the ocean-atmosphere system characterized by large-scale weakening of trade winds and warming of the surface layers in the central and E equatorial Pacific. The term *El Niño*, Spanish for "the Christ Child," was originally used by fishermen to refer to a warm ocean current appearing around Christmas off the W coasts of Ecuador and Peru and lasting several months. The term has come to be reserved for exceptionally strong, warm currents that bring heavy rains.

El Niño events generally occur at irregular intervals of 2 to 7 years, at an average of once every 3 to 4 years. They typically last 12 to 18 months. The intensity of El Niño events varies; some are strong such as the 1982-83 and 1997-98 events; others are considerably weaker, based on intensity and area encompassed by the abnormally warm ocean temperatures. The eastward extent of warmer than normal water varies from episode to episode.

El Niño influences weather around the globe, and its impacts are most clearly seen in the winter. During El Niño years, winter temperatures in the continental U.S. tend to be warmer than normal in the N and W coast states and cooler than normal in the SE. Conditions tend to be wetter than normal over central and southern California, the SW states and across much of the South, and drier than normal over the N portions of the Rocky Mountains and in the Ohio valley. Globally, El Niño brings wetter than normal conditions to Peru and Chile and dry conditions to Australia and Indonesia. It should be noted that El Niño is only one of a number of factors influencing seasonal variations of climate.

The opposite of El Niño is La Niña, with colder than normal sea surface temperatures in the equatorial Pacific. La Niña typically brings wetter, cooler conditions to the Pacific NW and drier, warmer conditions to much of the southern U.S. during winter.

El Niño and La Niña are opposite phases of the El Nino-Southern Oscillation (ENSO) cycle, an interannual shift in tropical sea level pressure between the E and W hemispheres. The events are monitored by satellites, and by buoys in the Pacific Ocean. Highly sophisticated numerical computer models of the ocean and atmosphere use this data to predict the onset and evolution of El Niño and La Niña.

Wind Chill Table

Source: National Weather Service, NOAA, U.S. Dept. of Commerce

Temperature and wind combine to cause heat loss from body surfaces. The following table shows that, for example, a temperature of 5° Fahrenheit, plus a wind of 10 miles per hour, causes a body heat loss equal to that in minus 10 degrees temperature with no wind. In other words, a 10-mph wind makes 5° feel like minus 10.

The National Weather Service issued new wind chill calculations in 2002. The top line of figures shows temperatures in degrees Fahrenheit. The column at far left shows wind speeds up to 45 mph. (Wind speeds greater than 45 mph have little additional chilling effect.) At wind chills in the shaded area, frostbite occurs in 15 minutes or less.

Calm	40	35	30	25	20	15	10	5	0	−5	−10	−15	−20	−25	−30	−35	−40	−45
5	36	31	25	19	13	7	1	− 5	−11	−16	−22	−28	−34	−40	−46	−52	−57	−63
10	34	27	21	15	9	3	−4	−10	−16	−22	−28	−35	−41	−47	−53	−59	−66	−72
15	32	25	19	13	6	0	−7	−13	−19	−26	−32	−39	−45	−51	−58	−64	−71	−77
20	30	24	17	11	4	−2	−9	−15	−22	−29	−35	−42	−48	−55	−61	−68	−74	−81
25	29	23	16	9	3	−4	−11	−17	−24	−31	−37	−44	−51	−58	−64	−71	−78	−84
30	28	22	15	8	1	−5	−12	−19	−26	−33	−39	−46	−53	−60	−67	−73	−80	−87
35	28	21	14	7	0	−7	−14	−21	−27	−34	−41	−48	−55	−62	−69	−76	−82	−89
40	27	20	13	6	−1	−8	−15	−22	−29	−36	−43	−50	−57	−64	−71	−78	−84	−91

Heat Index

The heat index is a measure of the contribution high humidity makes, in combination with abnormally high temperatures, to reducing the body's ability to cool itself. For example, the index shows that an air temperature of 100°Fahrenheit with a relative humidity of 50% has the same effect on the human body as a temperature of 120°. Sunstroke and heat exhaustion are likely when the heat index reaches 105. This index is a measure of what hot weather "feels like" to the average person.

| Relative Humidity | Air Temperature (°F) | | | | | | | | | | |
| | 70 | 75 | 80 | 85 | 90 | 95 | 100 | 105 | 110 | 115 | 120 |
	Apparent Temperature (°F)										
0%	64	69	73	78	83	87	91	95	99	103	107
10%	65	70	75	80	85	90	95	100	105	111	116
20%	66	72	77	82	87	93	99	105	112	120	130
30%	67	73	78	84	90	96	104	113	123	135	148
40%	68	74	79	86	93	101	110	123	137	151	
50%	69	75	81	88	96	107	120	135	150		
60%	70	76	82	90	100	114	132	149			
70%	70	77	85	93	106	124	144				
80%	71	78	86	97	113	136					
90%	71	79	88	102	122						
100%	72	80	91	108							

Ultraviolet (UV) Index Forecast

Source: National Weather Service, NOAA, U.S. Dept. of Commerce

The National Weather Service (NWS), Environmental Protection Agency (EPA), and Centers for Disease Control and Prevention (CDC) developed and began offering a UV index on June 28, 1994, in response to increasing incidence of skin cancer, cataracts, and other effects from exposure to the sun's harmful rays. The UV Index is now a regular element of NWS atmospheric forecasts.

UV Index number and forecast. The UV Index number, ranging from 0 to 10+, is an indication of the expected intensity of UV radiation reaching the earth's surface during the solar noon hour (11:30 AM-12:30 PM standard time). The lower the number, the less the radiation. The UV Index forecast is produced daily for 58 cities by the NWS Climate Prediction Center, and uses the following scale.

UV Index	Exposure	Minimum Precautions
0-2	Minimal	SPF 15 sun screen
3-4	Low	Sun screen and hat
5-6	Moderate	Sun screen, hat, UV sunglasses
7-9	High	Above; and avoid sun 10am - 4pm
10+	Very High	Same

The index number is based on several factors: latitude, day of year, time of day, total atmospheric ozone, elevation, and predicted cloud conditions. The index is valid for a radius of about 30 miles around a listed city; however, adjustments should be made for a number of factors.

Ozone. Ozone, a form of oxygen, the molecules of which consist of three atoms rather than two, blocks UV radiation. The more ozone, the lower the UV radiation at the surface.

Cloudiness. Cloud conditions affect the Index number. Clear skies allow 100% UV transmission to the surface, broken clouds allow about 73%, and overcast conditions allow 32%.

Reflectivity. Reflective surfaces intensify UV exposure. As an example, grass reflects 2.5% to 3% of UV radiation reaching the surface; sand, 20% to 30%; snow and ice, 80% to 90%; water, up to 100% (depending on reflection angle).

Elevation. At higher elevations, UV radiation travels a shorter distance to reach the surface so there is less atmosphere to absorb the rays. For every 4,000 ft. one travels above sea level, the UV Index increases by 1 unit. Snow and lack of pollutants intensify UV exposure at higher altitudes.

Latitude. The closer to the equator, the higher the UV radiation level.

SPF number. The UV Index is not linked in any way to the SPF number on suntan lotions and sunscreens. For an explanation of the SPF factor, contact the product's manufacturer or the Food and Drug Administration.

Further information. For precautions to take after learning the UV Index number, call the U.S. EPA hotline (800-296-1996) or your doctor. For questions on scientific aspects, call the NWS at 301-713-0622.

▶ **IT'S A FACT:** Based on temperature normals (30-year averages), the warmest time of year for New York City is July 20-22, with normal highs of 85° F, Chicago's warmest days are most likely to fall between July 16 and 29, with average highs of 84°. In Los Angeles, temperatures typically reach their highest around Aug. 5, with highs topping off at 86°. Following these dates in each location, temperatures tend to get cooler. The coldest days of the year, on average, fall around Jan. 21-22 in New York (low 25°), Jan. 8-21 in Chicago (low 14°), and Dec. 19-Jan. 8 in Los Angeles (low 48°).

Lightning

Source: National Weather Service

There are an estimated 25 million cloud-to-ground lightning bolts in the U.S. each year, killing an annual average of 73 people. This is a small number compared to deaths from fire (about 4,000 a year) and motor vehicle accidents (about 40,000), but still significant. By way of comparison with other weather phenomena, tornadoes cause an average of 68 deaths a year, and hurricanes an average of 16. Documented injuries from lightning in the U.S. number about 300 a year.

Lightning is a result of ice in storm clouds. As ice particles rise and sink in the cloud, numerous collisions between them cause a separation of electrical charge. Positively charged crystals rise to the top, while negatively charged crystals drop to lower parts. As the storm travels, a pool of positive charges gathers in the ground below and follows along, traveling up objects like trees and telephone poles. In a common form of lightning, the negatively charged area in the storm sends charges downward; these are attracted to positively charged objects, and a channel develops, with an electrical transfer that you see as lightning. Lightning can travel as far as miles away from the area of a storm.

The transfer of charges in lightning generates a huge amount of heat, sending the temperature in the channel to 30,000 degrees Fahrenheit and causing the air within it to expand rapidly; the sound of that expansion is thunder. Sound travels more slowly than light, so you usually see lightning before you hear thunder.

To (very roughly) gauge one's danger, use the 30-30 rule. In good visibility, count the time between a lightning flash and the crack of thunder. If it's less than 30 seconds the storm is within 6 miles and dangerous. Find shelter immediately. The threat of more lightning does not stop right away; you need to wait about 30 minutes after the last flash of the storm to be sure.

Most lightning deaths and injuries occur in the summer months when people are outdoors; when a storm threatens people need to move to a safe place promptly. Even while indoors, people are advised to stay away from windows and avoid contact with anything conducting electricity.

For more information about lightning, try the website www.lightningsafety.noaa.gov/overview.htm

Global Measured Extremes of Temperature and Precipitation Records

Source: National Climatic Data Center; based on latest available records data

Highest Temperature Extremes

Continent	Highest Temp. (deg F)	Place	Elevation (feet)	Date
Africa	136	El Azizia, Libya	367	Sept. 13, 1922
North America	134	Death Valley, CA (Greenland Ranch)	−178	July 10, 1913
Asia	129	Tirat Tsvi, Israel	−722	June 22, 1942
Australia	128	Cloncurry, Queensland	622	Jan. 16, 1889
Europe	122	Seville, Spain	26	Aug. 4, 1881
South America	120	Rivadavia, Argentina	676	Dec. 11, 1905
Oceania	108	Tuguegarao, Philippines	72	Apr. 29, 1912
Antarctica	59	Vanda Station, Scott Coast	49	Jan. 5, 1974

Lowest Temperature Extremes

Continent	Lowest Temp. (deg F)	Place	Elevation (feet)	Date
Antarctica	−129.0	Vostok	11,220	July 21, 1983
Asia	−90.0	Oimekon, Russia	2,625	Feb. 6, 1933
Asia	−90.0	Verkhoyansk, Russia	350	Feb. 7, 1892
Greenland	−87.0	Northice	7,687	Jan. 9, 1954
North America	−81.4	Snag, Yukon, Canada	2,120	Feb. 3, 1947
Europe	−67.0	Ust'Shchugor, Russia	279	Jan.[*]
South America	−27.0	Sarmiento, Argentina	879	June 1, 1907
Africa	−11.0	Ifrane, Morocco	5,364	Feb. 11, 1935
Australia	−9.4	Charlotte Pass, NSW	5,758	June 29, 1994
Oceania	12.0	Mauna Kea Observatory, HI	13,773	May 17, 1979

[*] Exact day and year unknown.

Greatest Measured Average Annual Precipitation Extremes

Continent	Highest Avg. (inches)	Place	Elevation (feet)	Years of Data
South America	523.6[1,2]	Lloro, Colombia	520[3]	29
Asia	467.4[1]	Mawsynram, India	4,597	38
Oceania	460.0[1]	Mt. Waialeale, Kauai, HI	5,148	30
Africa	405.0	Debundscha, Cameroon	30	32
South America	354.0[2]	Quibdo, Colombia	120	16
Australia	340.0	Bellenden Ker, Queensland	5,102	9
North America	256.0	Henderson Lake, British Columbia	12	14
Europe	183.0	Crkvica, Bosnia-Herzegovina	3,337	22

(1) The value given is continent's highest and possibly the world's, depending on measurement practices, procedures, and period of record variations. (2) The official greatest average annual precipitation for South America is 354 inches at Quibdo, Colombia. The 523.6 inch average at Lloro, Colombia (14 mi SE and at a higher elevation than Quibdo) is an estimate. (3) Approximate elevation.

Lowest Measured Average Annual Precipitation Extremes

Continent	Lowest Avg. (inches)	Place	Elevation (feet)	Years of Data
South America	0.03	Arica, Chile	95	59
Africa	<0.1	Wadi Halfa, Sudan	410	39
Antarctica	0.8[1]	Amundsen-Scott South Pole Station	9,186	10
North America	1.2	Batagues, Mexico	16	14
Asia	1.8	Aden, Yemen	22	50
Australia	4.05	Mulka (Troudaninna), South Australia	160[2]	42
Europe	6.4	Astrakhan, Russia	45	25
Oceania	8.93	Puako, Hawaii	5	13

(1) The value given is the average amount of solid snow accumulating in one year as indicated by snow markers. The amount of liquid content of the snow is undetermined. (2) Approximate elevation.

YEAR IN PICTURES

BUSH & CHENEY ▶
Pres. George Bush and his running mate, Vice-Pres. Dick Cheney, appear together at the Republican National Convention in New York, after Bush's speech accepting the party's presidential nomination, Sept. 2, 2004.

KERRY & EDWARDS ▲
At the Democratic National Convention in Boston, John Kerry (left) and John Edwards, the party's candidates for president and vice president, wave to delegates, following Kerry's acceptance speech on July 29.

◀ RISING STAR
Barack Obama, an Illinois state senator seeking a U.S. Senate seat in November, delivers a stirring keynote address July 27 at the Democratic National Convention.

AP/WIDE WORLD PHOTOS

PRIMARY SCREAM ▶
Former Vermont Gov. Howard Dean, delivering an intense speech to supporters Jan. 19 after a disappointing 3rd-place finish in the Iowa caucuses. Considered the Democratic frontrunner early on, he inspired a loyal following but failed to win broad support in the primaries.

AP/WIDE WORLD PHOTOS

GRAND OLD PARTY ▼
Sen. John McCain (R, AZ) appears with Pres. Bush at a campaign rally Aug. 10 in Pensacola, FL. Despite past differences with Bush, the nationally popular McCain (sounded out by Sen. John Kerry as a possible running mate) was campaigning for the president's reelection.

AP/WIDE WORLD PHOTOS

RONALD REAGAN PRESIDENTIAL LIBRARY

AP/WIDE WORLD PHOTOS

AP/WIDE WORLD PHOTOS

A NATION MOURNS ▲

The casket of former Pres. Ronald Reagan is carried from the National Cathedral in Washington, DC, after funeral services June 11 (right), as the Reagan family, at left, and other dignitaries look on. Reagan died at his Los Angeles home, June 5, at 93. Above: Pres. Reagan and Soviet leader Mikhail Gorbachev shake hands at their historic 1985 meeting in Geneva, Switzerland.

AP/WIDE WORLD PHOTOS

◄ MY LIFE

Former Pres. Bill Clinton signs copies of *My Life* at a New York City bookstore. Released June 22, the memoir sold over 400,000 copies on the first day—a record for a nonfiction book. Clinton made news later in the year when he underwent coronary bypass surgery Sept. 6.

9-11 COMMISSION ▶

Members of the National Commission on Terrorist Attacks Upon the U.S., chaired by former NJ Gov. Thomas Kean (far left), question witnesses at hearings. The final report, released July 22 and unanimously endorsed by the 10-member bipartisan panel, urged a reorganization of U.S. intelligence.

◀ HEAVY HITS

Residents of Punta Gorda, FL, after Hurricane Charley struck the state's west coast, Aug. 13-14. Frances, a weaker but bigger storm that hit Sept. 5-6, prompted the largest evacuation in Florida history. Hurricane Ivan raided the Gulf coast Sept. 16-17. The 3 storms caused over 100 deaths and over $12 billion in damages in the U.S. alone.

CIA CHIEF RESIGNS ▲

Amid controversy over a string of U.S. intelligence failures, CIA Director George Tenet resigned, effective July 11, citing personal reasons.

◀ MEMORIAL AT LAST

The long-awaited National World War II Memorial was dedicated on the Mall in Washington, DC, May 29, 59 years after the war's end.

◄ FAHRENHEIT 9/11
Writer-director Michael Moore's controversial film *Fahrenheit 9/11* offers a scathing criticism of the Bush administration. Released June 25, the film grossed more than $115 million domestically in 2 months, breaking box-office records for a documentary.

NJ GOVERNOR RESIGNS ►
At the statehouse in Trenton, NJ, Gov. James McGreevey announced Aug. 12 that he would resign in November. McGreevey said he had engaged in a "consensual affair" with a man, later identified as an Israeli national whom he had appointed to a high-level security post. Standing beside him: his wife, Dina, and mother, Virginia.

◄ STEWART SENTENCED
Homemaking entrepreneur Martha Stewart is escorted from Manhattan federal court by U.S. marshals July 16, after being sentenced to 5 months in prison and 5 months home confinement. She was convicted in March for obstructing an investigation into her 2001 sale of ImClone stock.

GAY MARRIAGE ►
Julie Goodridge (left) and Hillary Goodridge celebrate outside the Unitarian Universalist Church in Boston following their wedding May 17; they were among the first gay couples to marry after being plaintiffs in a suit that led to recognition of same-sex unions in Massachusetts.

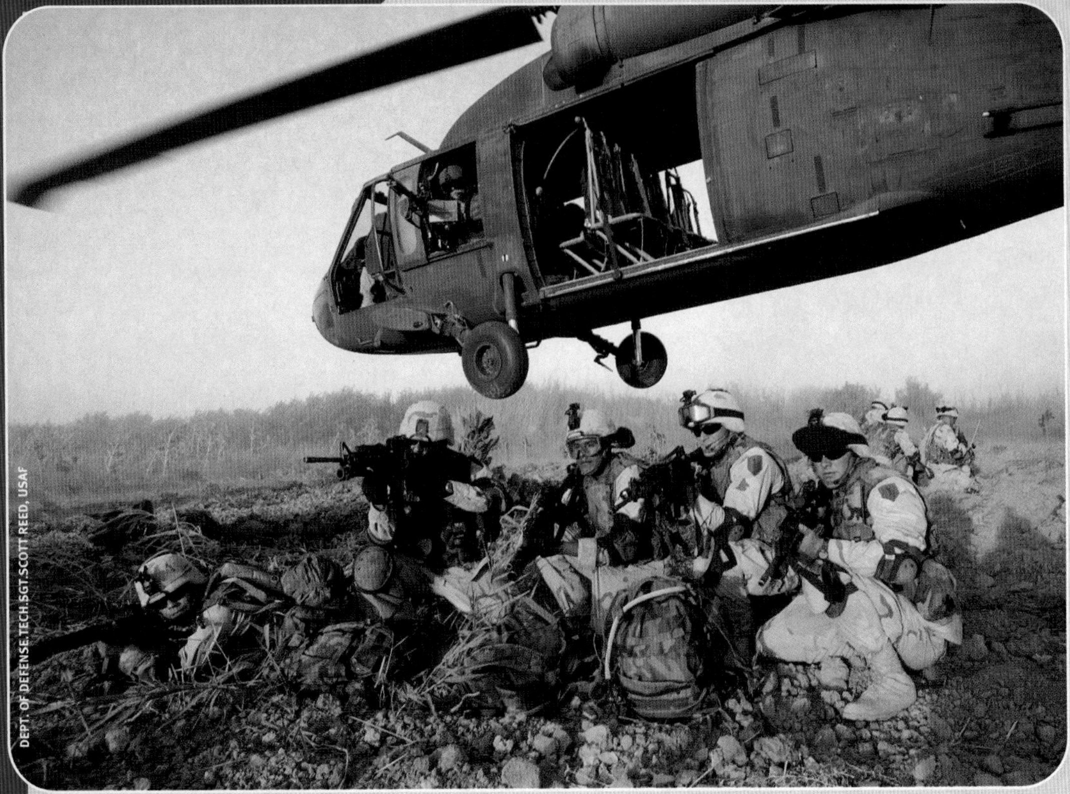
DEPT. OF DEFENSE.TECH.SGT.SCOTT REED, USAF

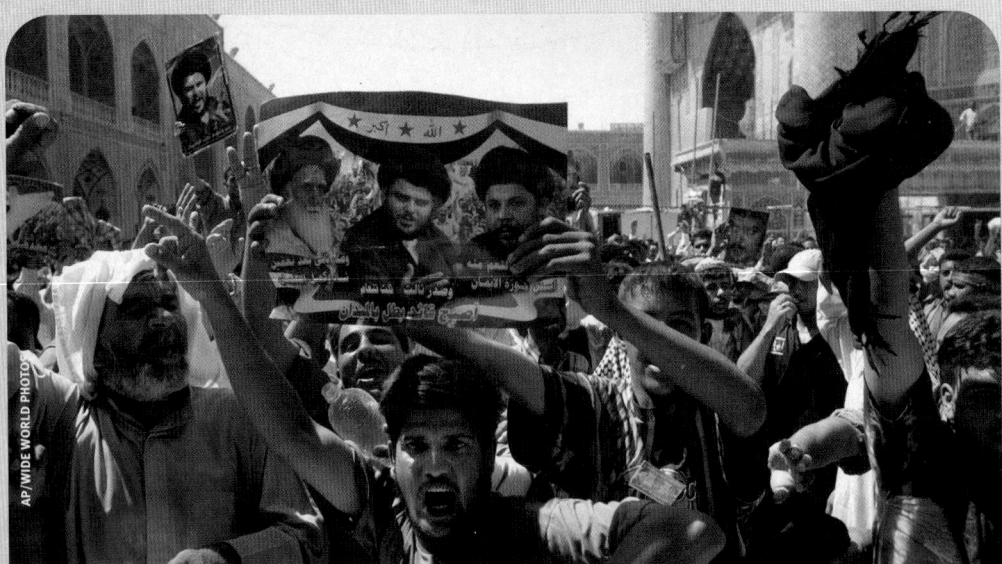

ON THE BATTLEFIELD ▲
Reconnaissance troops, members of a U.S. Quick Response force, brace themselves in a security posture, as a UH-60A Black Hawk helicopter flies overhead. These were among some 160,000 U.S.-led troops stationed in Iraq at midyear, as the U.S. continued efforts to bring stability to the war-torn nation. By mid-September, more than 1,000 Americans had been killed.

SADR STANDOFF ▼
Iraqis loyal to Moqtada al-Sadr hoist pictures of the radical Shiite cleric as they rally Aug. 16 at the sacred Imam Ali mosque complex in the southern city of Najaf. The complex was the scene of clashes between Sadr's militia and U.S. and Iraqi troops, during an August standoff.

AP/WIDE WORLD PHOTOS

HANDOVER IN IRAQ ▲

Interim Iraqi Prime Min. Iyad Allawi (center) looks on as U.S. Administrator Paul Bremer (right) and Iraqi Chief Justice Midhat Al-Mahmodi shake hands during the transfer of national sovereignty to Iraq, in a Baghdad ceremony held 2 days ahead of schedule, June 28.

SADDAM IN THE DOCK ▶

At his arraignment July 1 in an Iraqi courtroom, one of his former palaces on the outskirts of Baghdad, a defiant Saddam Hussein appears in public for the first time since his Dec. 2003 capture.

ATROCITIES OF WAR ▲

Above, charred bodies hang from a bridge over the Euphrates River in Fallujah, as Iraqis chant anti-American slogans Mar. 31; gunmen had ambushed and killed 4 U.S. security contractors, and a mob dragged their bodies through the streets. At right, one of the photos released in April that brought wide attention to instances of prisoner abuse by U.S. military police at Abu Ghraib prison in Iraq.

Farewells

RAY CHARLES ▲

ALISTAIR COOKE ▲

TONY RANDALL ▲

ISABEL SANFORD ▲

▲ MARLON BRANDO

ESTEE LAUDER ▲

◄ FRANCIS CRICK

JACK PAAR ▼

JULIA CHILD ▲

BOB KEESHAN
[CAPTAIN
KANGAROO] ►

◄ ARCHIBALD COX

DISASTERS

As of Sept. 30, 2004. Listings in this chapter are selective, and generally do not include acts of terrorism, war-related disasters, or disasters with relatively low fatalities.

Some Notable Shipwrecks Since 1854

(Figures indicate estimated lives lost. Does not include most wartime disasters.)

1854, Mar.—City of Glasgow; Brit. steamer missing in N Atlantic; 480.

1854, Sept. 27—Arctic; U.S. (Collins Line) steamer sunk in collision with French steamer *Vesta* near Cape Race; 285-351.

1856, Jan. 23—Pacific; U.S. (Collins Line) steamer missing in N Atlantic; 186-286.

1858, Sept. 23—Austria; German steamer destroyed by fire in N Atlantic; 471.

1863, Apr. 27—Anglo-Saxon; Brit. steamer wrecked at Cape Race; 238.

1865, Apr. 27—Sultana; Mississippi River steamer blew up near Memphis, TN; 1,450.

1869, Oct. 27—Stonewall; steamer burned on Mississippi River below Cairo, IL; 200.

1870, Jan. 25—City of Boston; Brit. (Inman Line) steamer vanished between New York and Liverpool; 177.

1870, Oct. 19—Cambria; Brit. steamer off N Ireland; 196.

1872, Nov. 7—Mary Celeste; U.S. half-brig sailed from New York for Genoa; found abandoned; loss of life unknown.

1873, Jan. 22—Northfleet; Brit. steamer foundered off Dungeness, England; 300.

1873, Apr. 1—Atlantic; Brit. (White Star) steamer off Nova Scotia; 585.

1873, Nov. 23—Ville du Havre; French steamer sank after collision with Brit. sailing ship *Loch Earn*; 226.

1875, May 7—Schiller; German steamer off Scilly Isles; 312.

1875, Nov. 4—Pacific; U.S. steamer sank after collision off Cape Flattery; 236.

1878, Sept. 3—Princess Alice; Brit. steamer sank after collision in Thames River; 700.

1878, Dec. 18—Byzantin; French steamer sank after collision in Dardanelles; 210.

1881, May 24—Victoria; steamer capsized in Thames River, Canada; 200.

1883, Jan. 19—Cimbria; German steamer sank in collision with Brit. steamer *Sultan* in North Sea; 389.

1887, Nov. 15—Wah Yeung; Brit. steamer burned at sea; 400.

1890, Feb. 17—Duburg; Brit. steamer wrecked, China Sea; 400.

1890, Sept. 19—Ertogrul; Turkish frigate off Japan; 540.

1891, Mar. 17—Utopia; Brit. steamer sank in collision with Brit. ironclad *Anson* off Gibraltar; 562.

1895, Jan. 30—Elbe; German steamer sank in collision with Brit. steamer *Craithie* in North Sea; 332.

1895, Mar. 11—Reina Regenta; Spanish cruiser foundered near Gibraltar; 400.

1898, Feb. 15—Maine; U.S. battleship blown up in Havana Harbor; 260.

1898, July 4—La Bourgogne; French steamer sank in collision with Brit. sailing ship *Cromartyshire* off Nova Scotia; 549.

1898, Nov. 26—Portland; U.S. steamer off Cape Cod; 157.

1904, June 15—General Slocum; excursion steamer burned in East River, New York City; 1,030.

1904, June 28—Norge; Danish steamer wrecked on Rockall Island, Scotland; 620.

1906, Aug. 4—Sirio; Italian steamer wrecked off Cape Palos, Spain; 350.

1908, Mar. 23—Matsu Maru; Japanese steamer sank in collision near Hakodate, Japan; 300.

1909, Aug. 1—Waratah; Brit. steamer, Sydney to London, vanished; 300.

1910, Feb. 9—General Chanzy; French steamer wrecked off Minorca, Spain; 200.

1911, Sept. 25—Liberté; French battleship exploded at Toulon; 285.

1912, Mar. 5—Principe de Asturias; Spanish steamer wrecked off Spain; 500.

1912, Apr. 14-15—Titanic; Brit. (White Star) steamer hit iceberg in N Atlantic; 1,503.

1912, Sept. 28—Kichemaru; Japanese steamer sank off Japanese coast; 1,000.

1914, May 29—Empress of Ireland; Brit. (Canadian Pacific) steamer collided with Norw. collier in St. Lawrence River; 1,014.

1915, May 7—Lusitania; Brit. (Cunard Line) steamer torpedoed and sunk by German submarine off Ireland; 1,198.

1915, July 24—Eastland; steamer capsized in Chicago River; 844.

1916, Feb. 26—Provence; French cruiser sank in Medit.; 3,100.

1916, Mar. 3—Principe de Asturias; Spanish steamer wrecked near Santos, Brazil; 558.

1916, Aug. 29—Hsin Yu; Chinese steamer sank off Chinese coast; 1,000.

1917, Dec. 6—Mont Blanc, Imo; French ammunition ship and Belgian steamer collided in Halifax Harbor; 1,600.

1918, Apr. 25—Kiang-Kwan; Chinese steamer sank in collision off Hankow; 500.

1918, July 12—Kawachi; Japanese battleship blew up in Tokayama Bay; 500.

1918, Oct. 25—Princess Sophia; Canadian steamer sank off Alaskan coast; 398.

1919, Jan. 17—Chaonia; French steamer lost in Straits of Messina, Italy; 460.

1919, Sept. 9—Valbanera; Spanish steamer lost off Florida coast; 500.

1921, Mar. 18—Hong Kong; steamer wrecked in South China Sea; 1,000.

1922, Aug. 26—Niitaka; Japanese cruiser sank in storm off Kamchatka, USSR; 300.

1924, June 12—USS Mississippi; U.S. battleship; explosions in gun turret, off San Pedro, CA; 48.

1927, Oct. 25—Principessa Mafalda; Italian steamer blew up, sank off Porto Seguro, Brazil; 314.

1928, Nov. 12—Vestris; Brit. steamer sank off Virginia; 113.

1934, Sept. 8—Morro Castle; U.S. steamer, Havana to New York, burned off Asbury Park, NJ; 134.

1939, May 23—Squalus; U.S. submarine sank off Portsmouth, NH; 26.

1939, June 1—Thetis; submarine sank, Liverpool Bay; 99.

1942, Feb. 18—Truxtun and **Pollux;** U.S. destroyer and cargo ship ran aground, sank off Newfoundland; 204.

1942, Oct. 2—Curacao; Brit. cruiser sank after collision with liner *Queen Mary;* 338.

1944, Dec. 17-18—3 U.S. Third Fleet destroyers sank during typhoon in Philippine Sea; 790.

1945, Jan. 30—Wilhelm Gustloff; Liner with German refugees, soldiers sunk by Soviet submarine in Baltic; 5,000-9,000.

1945, Apr. 16—Goya; Cargo ship carrying German refugees, soldiers sunk by Soviet submarine in Baltic; 6,000-7,000.

1945, May 3—Cap Arcona, Thielbek; German liners carrying concentration camp inmates sunk by British warplanes in Lubeck Bay; 7,000-8,000.

1947, Jan. 19—Himera; Greek steamer hit a mine off Athens; 392.

1947, Apr. 16—Grandcamp; French freighter exploded in Texas City, TX, harbor, starting fires; 576+.

1948, Dec. 15—Chinese army evacuation ship exploded and sank off S Manchuria; 6,000.

1948, Dec. 3—Kiangya; Chinese refugee ship wrecked in explosion S of Shanghai; 1,100+.

1949, Sept. 17—Noronic; Canadian Great Lakes Cruiser burned at Toronto dock; 130.

1952, Apr. 26—Hobson and **Wasp;** U.S. destroyer and aircraft carrier collided in Atlantic; 176.

1954, May 26—Bennington; U.S. carrier damaged by explosions off Rhode Island; 103.

1954, Sept. 26—Toya Maru; Japanese ferry sank in Tsugaru Strait, Japan; 1,172.

1956, July 26—Andrea Doria and **Stockholm;** Italian liner and Swedish liner collided off Nantucket; 51.

1957, July 14—Eshghabad; Soviet ship ran aground in Caspian Sea; 270.

1960, Dec. 19—Constellation; U.S. aircraft carrier caught fire in Brooklyn Navy Yard, NY; 49.

1961, Apr. 8—Dara; British liner exploded in Persian Gulf; 236.

1961, July 8—Save; Portuguese ship ran aground off Mozambique; 259.

1963, Apr. 10—Thresher; U.S. Navy atomic submarine sank in N Atlantic; 129.

1964, Feb. 10—Australian destroyer *Voyager* sank after collision with aircraft carrier *Melbourne* off New South Wales; 82.

1965, Nov. 13—Yarmouth Castle; Panamanian registered cruise ship burned and sank off Nassau; 89.

1967, July 29—Forrestal; U.S. aircraft carrier caught fire off N Vietnam; 134.

1968, Jan. 25—Dakar; Israeli submarine vanished in Medit.; 69.

1968, late May—Scorpion; U.S. nuclear submarine sank in Atlantic near Azores; 99 (located Oct. 31).

1969, June 2—Evans; U.S. destroyer cut in half by Australian carrier *Melbourne*, S China Sea; 74.

WORLD ALMANAC QUICK QUIZ

Can you rank the following famous disasters by estimated total death toll, from lowest to highest?

(a) 1984 Bhopal, India, toxic gas leak
(b) 1912 Titanic shipwreck
(c) 1755 Lisbon earthquake
(d) 1942 Cocoanut Grove fire in Boston

For the answer look in this chapter, or see page 1008.

1970, Mar. 4—Eurydice; French submarine sank in Mediterranean near Toulon; 57.
1970, Dec. 15—Namyong-Ho; South Korean ferry sank in Korea Strait; 308.
1974, May 1—Motor launch capsized off Bangladesh; 250.
1974, Sept. 26—Soviet destroyer sank in Black Sea; 200+.
1975, Nov. 10—Edmund Fitzgerald; U.S. cargo ship sank during storm on Lake Superior; 29.
1976, Oct. 20—George Prince and **Frosta;** ferryboat and Norwegian tanker collided on Mississippi R. at Luling, LA; 77.
1976, Dec. 25—Patria; Egyptian liner caught fire and sank in the Red Sea; 100.
1979, Aug. 14—23 yachts competing in Fastnet yacht race sank or abandoned during storm in S Irish Sea; 18.
1981, Jan. 27—Tamponas II; Indonesian passenger ship caught fire and sank in Java Sea; 580.
1981, May 26—Nimitz; U.S. Marine combat jet crashed on deck of U.S. aircraft carrier; 14.
1983, Feb. 12—Marine Electric; coal freighter sank during storm off Chincoteague, VA; 33.
1983, May 25—10th of Ramadan; Nile steamer caught fire and sank in Lake Nasser; 357.
1986, Apr. 20—ferry sank near Barisal, Bangladesh; 262.
1986, Aug. 31—Soviet passenger ship *Admiral Nakhimov* and Soviet freighter *Pyotr Vasev* collided in Black Sea; 398.
1987, Mar. 6—British ferry capsized off Zeebrugge, Belgium; 189.
1987, Dec. 20—Philippine ferry *Dona Paz* and oil tanker *Victor* collided in Tablas Strait; 4,341.
1988, Aug. 6—Indian ferry capsized on Ganges R.; 400+.
1989, Apr. 19—USS Iowa; explosion in gun turret; 47.
1989, Apr. 7—Komsolets; Soviet submarine; sank after fire off Norwegian coast; 42.
1989, Aug. 20—Brit. barge *Bowbelle* struck Brit. pleasure cruiser *Marchioness* on Thames R. in central London; 56.
1989, Sept. 10—Romanian pleasure boat and Bulgarian barge collided on Danube R.; 161.
1991, Apr. 10—Auto ferry and oil tanker collided outside Livorno Harbor, Italy; 140.
1991, Dec. 14—Salem Express; ferry rammed coral reef near Safaga, Egypt; 462.
1993, Feb. 17—Neptune; ferry capsized off Port-au-Prince, Haiti; 500+.
1993, Oct. 10—West Sea Ferry; capsized in Yellow Sea near W South Korea during storm; 285.
1994, Sept. 28—Estonia; ferry sank in Baltic Sea; 1,049.
1996, May 21—Bukoba; ferry sank in Lake Victoria (Africa); 500.
1997, Feb. 20—Tamil refugee boat sank off Sri Lanka; 165.
1997, Mar. 28—Albanian refugee boat sank in Adriatic Sea after being rammed by Italian navy warship *Sibilla*; 83.
1997, Sept. 8—Pride of la Gonâve; Haitian ferry sank off Montrouis, Haiti; 200+.

1998, Apr. 4—passenger boat capsized off coast near Ibaka beach, Nigeria; 280.
1998, Sept. 2—2 passenger boats capsized on Lake Kivu, near Bukavu, Congo; 200+.
1998, Sept. 18—ferry sank S of Manila; 97.
1999, Feb. 8—Harta Rimba; cargo ship sank off Indonesia; 280+.
1999, Mar. 26—passenger boat overturned off coast, Sierra Leone; 150+.
1999, Apr. 2—passenger ferry sank off coast of Nigeria; 100+.
1999, May 1—excursion boat sank in Lake Hamilton, AR; 13.
1999, May 8—passenger ferry capsized off Bangladesh; 200+.
1999, Nov. 24—Dashun; passenger ferry capsized near Yantai, China; 280.
2000, May 3—2 ferries capsized, Meghna R., Bangladesh; 72+.
2000, June 29—overloaded ferry capsized in storm off Sulawesi Island, Indonesia; 500+.
2000, Aug. 12—Kursk; Russian sub sank in Barents Sea; 118.
2000, Sept. 26—Express Samina; Greek ferry sank off Paros, Greece; 81+.
2001, Feb. 9—Ehime Maru; Japanese trawler sunk by surfacing U.S. submarine *Greeneville*, near Hawaii; 9.
2001, Dec. 22—North Korean spy ship sank after exchanging fire with Japanese coast guard; 15.
2001, Oct. 19—Indonesian fishing boat overloaded with asylum-seekers sank off Java's south coast; 350+.
2002, May 4—Bangladesh ferry sank, Meghna R.; 370+.
2002, May 26—barge struck Interstate highway bridge over Arkansas R. in Oklahoma; 13+.
2002, Sept. 26—overloaded Senegalese ferry capsized in ocean off The Gambia; 1,863.
2003, Mar. 23—overloaded ferry capsized in Lake Tanganyika off Burundi; 111+.
2003, Apr. 21—2 ferries capsized in storms in Bangladesh on Meghna and Buriganga rivers; 180+.
2003, Apr. 4—ferry sank near Chhatak in Bangladesh; 80+.
2003, July 8—overcrowded ferry sank near Chandpur in the Bangladesh River; c. 400.
2003, Oct. 15—Andrew J. Barberi; NYC ferry crashed into dock on approaching Staten Is.; 11.
2003, Nov. 25—Overloaded ferry sank on Lake Mayi Ndombe, Dem. Rep. of Congo; 130-200.
2004, Jan. 26—Convoi Lengi; ferry caught fire on Congo R. in Dem. Rep. of Congo; 200.
2004, Feb. 28—Bow Mariner; tanker carrying ethanol caught fire and exploded off Virginia coast; 21.
2004, Mar 6—Water taxi capsized in storm in Baltimore's Inner Harbor; 5.
2004, Mar. 11—ferry sank off Madagascar during cyclone; 113.
2004, May 24—Lightning Sun; ferry sank in Meghna river in Bangladesh; 60+.

Some Notable Aircraft Disasters Since 1937

Date	Aircraft	Site of accident	Deaths
1937, May 6	German zeppelin Hindenburg	Burned at mooring, Lakehurst, NJ	36[*]
1944, Aug. 23	U.S. Air Force B-24 Liberator bomber	Hit school, Freckleton, England	61[*]
1945, July 28	U.S. Army B-25	Hit Empire State Building, New York, NY	14[*]
1952, Dec. 20	U.S. Air Force C-124	Fell, burned, Moses Lake, WA	87
1953, Mar. 3	Canadian Pacific Comet Jet	Karachi, Pakistan	11[1]
1953, June 18	U.S. Air Force C-124	Crashed, burned near Tokyo	129
1955, Oct. 6	United Airlines DC-4	Crashed in Medicine Bow Peak, WY	66
1955, Nov. 1	United Airlines DC-6B	Exploded, crashed near Longmont, CO	44[2]
1956, June 20	Venezuelan Super-Constellation	Crashed in Atlantic off Asbury Park, NJ	74
1956, June 30	TWA Super-Const., United DC-7	Collided over Grand Canyon, AZ	128
1960, Dec. 16	United DC-8 jet, TWA Super-Const.	Collided over New York City	134[3]
1962, Mar. 16	Flying Tiger Super-Constellation.	Vanished in W Pacific	107
1962, June 3	Air France Boeing 707 jet	Crashed on takeoff from Paris	130
1962, June 22	Air France Boeing 707 jet	Crashed in storm, Guadeloupe, W.I.	113
1963, Feb. 1	Lebanese Middle East Airlines Vickers Viscount 754, Turkish Mil. Douglas C-47	Planes collided in mid-air over Ankara, Turkey, killing all 17 on planes, 87 on ground	104
1963, June 3	Chartered Northwest Airlines DC-7	Crashed in Pacific off British Columbia	101
1963, Nov. 29	Trans-Canada Airlines DC-8F	Crashed after takeoff from Montreal	118
1964, Mar. 1	Paradise Airlines Constellation	Crashed on approach in heavy weather	85
1965, May 20	Pakistani Boeing 720-B	Crashed at Cairo, Egypt, airport	121
1965, Sept. 17	Pan Am Boeing 707-121B	Crashed into mountains on approach to Montserrat, France	30
1966, Jan. 24	Air India Boeing 707 jetliner	Crashed on Mont Blanc, France-Italy	117
1966, Feb. 4	All-Nippon Boeing 727	Plunged into Tokyo Bay	133
1966, Mar. 5	BOAC Boeing 707 jetliner	Crashed on Mount Fuji, Japan	124
1966, Dec. 24	U.S. military-chartered CL-44	Crashed into village in South Vietnam	129[*]
1967, Apr. 20	Swiss Britannia turboprop	Crashed at Nicosia, Cyprus	126
1967, July 19	Piedmont Boeing 727, Cessna 310	Collided in air, Hendersonville, NC	82
1968, Apr. 20	S. African Airways Boeing 707	Crashed on takeoff, Windhoek, South-West Africa	122
1968, May 3	Braniff International Electra	Crashed in storm near Dawson, TX	85
1969, Mar. 16	Venezuelan DC-9	Crashed after takeoff from Maracaibo, Venezuela	155[4]
1969, Dec. 8	Olympic Airways DC-6B	Crashed near Athens in storm	93
1970, Feb. 15	Dominican DC-9	Crashed into sea on takeoff from Santo Domingo	102
1970, July 3	British chartered jetliner	Crashed near Barcelona, Spain	112
1970, July 5	Air Canada DC-8	Crashed near Toronto International Airport	108
1970, Aug. 9	Peruvian turbojet	Crashed after takeoff from Cuzco, Peru	101[*]
1970, Nov. 14	Southern Airways DC-9	Crashed in mountains near Huntington, WV	75[5]

Date	Aircraft	Site of accident	Deaths
1971, July 30	All-Nippon Boeing 727, Jap. AF F-86	Collided over Morioka, Japan	162[6]
1971, Sept. 4	Alaska Airlines Boeing 727	Crashed into mountain near Juneau, AK	111
1972, Aug. 14	East German Ilyushin-62	Crashed on takeoff, East Berlin.	156
1972, Oct. 13	Aeroflot Ilyushin-62	Crashed near Moscow	176
1972, Dec. 3	Chartered Spanish airliner	Crashed on takeoff, Canary Islands	155
1972, Dec. 29	Eastern Airlines Lockheed Tristar	Crashed on approach to Miami Intl. Airport.	101
1973, Jan. 22	Chartered Boeing 707	Burst into flames during landing, Kano Airport, Nigeria.	176
1973, Feb. 21	**Libyan jetliner**	**Shot down by Israeli fighter planes over Sinai.**	**108**
1973, Apr. 10	British Vanguard turboprop	Crashed during snowstorm at Basel, Switzerland.	104
1973, June 3	Soviet Supersonic TU-144	Crashed near Goussainville, France	14[7]
1973, July 11	Brazilian Boeing 707	Crashed on approach to Orly Airport, Paris	122
1973, July 31	Delta Airlines jetliner	Crashed, landing in fog at Logan Airport, Boston	89
1973, Dec. 23	French Caravelle jet.	Crashed in Morocco	106
1974, Mar. 3	Turkish DC-10 jet.	Crashed at Ermenonville near Paris	346
1974, Apr. 23	Pan American 707 jet	Crashed in Bali, Indonesia	107
1974, Dec. 1	TWA-727	Crashed in storm, Upperville, VA	92
1974, Dec. 4	Dutch-chartered DC-8	Crashed in storm near Colombo, Sri Lanka	191
1975, Apr. 4	Air Force Galaxy C-5A	Crashed near Saigon, S Viet., after takeoff (carrying orphans).	172
1975, June 24	Eastern Airlines 727 jet	Crashed in storm, JFK Airport, NY	113
1975, Aug. 3	Chartered 707	Hit mountainside, Agadir, Morocco	188
1976, Sept. 10	Brit. Airways Trident, Yug. DC-9	Collided near Zagreb, Yugoslavia	176
1976, Sept. 19	Turkish 727	Hit mountain, S Turkey	155
1976, Oct. 13	Bolivian 707 cargo jet	Crashed in Santa Cruz, Bolivia	100[8]
1977, Mar. 27	**KLM 747, Pan American 747**	**Collided on runway, Tenerife, Canary Islands**	**583[9]**
1977, Nov. 19	TAP Boeing 727.	Crashed on Madeira	130
1977, Dec. 4	Malaysian Boeing 737	Hijacked, then exploded in mid-air over Straits of Johore	100
1977, Dec. 13	U.S. DC-3	Crashed after takeoff at Evansville, IN	29[10]
1978, Jan. 1	Air India 747.	Exploded, crashed into sea off Bombay	213
1978, Sept. 25	Boeing 727, Cessna 172	Collided in air, San Diego, CA.	150
1978, Nov. 15	Chartered DC-8	Crashed near Colombo, Sri Lanka	183
1979, May 25	**American Airlines DC-10**	**Crashed after takeoff at O'Hare Intl. Airport, Chicago.**	**275[11]**
1979, Aug. 17	Two Soviet Aeroflot jetliners	Collided over Ukraine	173
1979, Nov. 26	Pakistani Boeing 707.	Crashed near Jidda, Saudi Arabia	156
1979, Nov. 28	New Zealand DC-10	Crashed into mountain in Antarctica	257
1980, Mar. 14	Polish Ilyushin 62.	Crashed making emergency landing, Warsaw	87[12]
1980, Aug. 19	Saudi Arabian Tristar	Burned after emergency landing, Riyadh	301
1981, Dec. 1	Yugoslavian DC-9	Crashed into mountain in Corsica	178
1982, Jan. 13	Air Florida Boeing 737	Crashed into Potomac R. after takeoff	78
1982, July 9	Pan Am Boeing 727.	Crashed after takeoff in Kenner, LA	153[13]
1983, Sept. 1	**S. Korean Boeing 747**	**Shot down after violating Soviet airspace**	**269**
1983, Nov. 27	Colombian Boeing 747	Crashed near Barajas Airport, Madrid	183
1985, Feb. 19	Spanish Boeing 727.	Crashed into Mt. Oiz, Spain	148
1985, June 23	Air-India Boeing 747	Crashed into Atlantic Ocean S of Ireland	329
1985, Aug. 2	Delta Air Lines L-1011	Crashed at Dallas-Ft. Worth Intl. Airport.	137
1985, Aug. 12	**Japan Air Lines Boeing 747**	**Crashed into Mt. Ogura, Japan**	**520[14]**
1985, Dec. 12	Arrow Air DC-8.	Crashed after takeoff in Gander, Newfoundland.	256[15]
1986, Mar. 31	Mexican Boeing 727	Crashed NW of Mexico City	166
1986, Aug. 31	Aeromexico DC-9	Collided with Piper PA-28 over Cerritos, CA.	82[16]
1987, May 9	Polish Ilyushin 62M	Crashed after takeoff in Warsaw, Poland	183
1987, Aug. 16	Northwest Airlines MD-82	Crashed after takeoff in Romulus, MI	156
1987, Nov. 28	S. African Boeing 747	Crashed into Indian Ocean near Mauritius	159
1987, Nov. 29	S. Korean Boeing 707	Exploded over Thai-Burmese border	155
1988, Mar. 17	Colombian Boeing 707	Crashed into mountainside near Venezuela border	137
1988, July 3	**Iranian A300 Airbus**	**Shot down by U.S. Navy warship *Vincennes* over Pers. Gulf**	**290**
1988, Dec. 21	**Pan Am Boeing 747**	**Bomb on board; exploded over Lockerbie, Scot.**	**270[17]**
1989, Feb. 8	U.S. Boeing 707.	Crashed into mountain in Azores Islands off Portugal	144
1989, June 7	Suriname DC-8	Crashed near Paramaribo Airport, Suriname	168
1989, July 19	United Airlines DC-10	Crashed while landing in Sioux City, IA.	111
1989, Sept. 19	**French DC-10**	**Bomb on board; exploded in air over Niger**	**171**
1990, Jan. 25	Avianca Air Boeing 707	Crashed on landing, JFK Airport, NY	73
1990, Feb. 14	Indian Airlines Airbus 320	Crashed and burned landing in Bangalore, India	91
1990, Oct. 2	Chinese airline Boeing 737, 707	Hijacked; 737 jet landing in Guangzhou, crashed into 707	132
1991, May 26	Lauda-Air Boeing 767-300.	Exploded over rural Thailand	223
1991, July 11	Nigerian DC-8	Crashed while landing at Jidda, Saudi Arabia.	261
1991, Oct. 5	Indonesian military transport	Crashed after takeoff from Jakarta	137*
1992, July 31	Thai Airbus A-300-310.	Crashed into mountain S. of Kathmandu, Nepal.	113
1992, Oct. 4	**El Al Boeing 747-200F**	**Crashed into 2 apartment bldgs., Amsterdam, Netherlands.**	**120***
1993, Feb. 8	Iran Air TU-154	Collided in air with military plane	132
1993, Mar. 5	Macedonian Pal Air Fokker 100.	Crashed after takeoff in snowstorm in Skopje, Macedonia	83
1994, Jan. 3	Aeroflot TU-154	Crashed and exploded after takeoff in Irkhutsk, Russia	125[18]
1994, Apr. 26	China Airlines Airbus A-300-600R	Crashed at Japan's Nagoya Airport	264
1994, June 16	China Northwest Airlines TU-154.	Crashed 10 min. after takeoff	160
1994, Sept. 8	USAir Boeing 737-300.	Crashed in Aliquippa, PA, near Pittsburgh Intl. Airport.	132
1994, Oct. 31	American Eagle ATR-72-210.	Crashed in field near Roselawn, IN.	68
1995, Aug. 11	Aviateca Boeing 737	Crashed into Chichontepec volcano, El Salvador	65
1995, Dec. 18	Zairian passenger jet	Crashed in Angola, location disputed	136
1995, Dec. 20	American Airlines Boeing 757	Crashed into mountain 50 mi N of Cali, Colombia	160
1996, Jan. 8	Antonova 32 cargo jet	Crashed into central market, Kinshasa, Zaire	350+*
1996, Feb. 6	Turkish Boeing 757	Crashed into Atlantic Ocean, off Dominican Republic.	189
1996, Apr. 25	T-43, a military version of a Boeing 737	Crashed into mountain near Dubrovnik, Croatia	35[19]
1996, May 11	ValuJet DC-9	Crashed into the Florida Everglades after takeoff	110
1996, July 17	Trans World Airlines Boeing 747	Exploded and crashed in Atlantic Ocean, off Long Isl., NY	230
1996, Aug. 29	Vnukovo TU-154	Crashed into mountain on Arctic island of Spitsbergen.	141
1996, Oct. 2	Aeroperu Boeing 757.	Crashed in Pacific after takeoff from Lima, Peru.	70
1996, Oct. 31	Brazilian TAM Fokker-100.	Crashed into houses in São Paulo, Brazil.	98[20]
1996, Nov. 7	Nigerian Boeing 727	Crashed into a lagoon 40 mi SE of Lagos, Nigeria	143
1996, Nov. 12	**Saudi Arabian Boeing 747, Kazakh Ilyushin-76 cargo plane**	**Collided in midair near New Delhi, India.**	**349[21]**
1996, Nov. 23	Ethiopian Boeing 767.	Hijacked, then crashed in Indian Ocean off the Comoros.	127

Date	Aircraft	Site of accident	Deaths
1997, Jan. 9	Comair Embraer 120	Crashed on approach into Detroit Metro. Airport	29
1997, Feb. 4	2 Sikorsky CH-53 transport helicopters	Collided in midair over northern Galilee, Israel	73
1997, May 8	China Southern Airlines Boeing 737	Crashed on approach into Shenzhen's Huangtian Airport	35
1997, July 11	Cubana de Aviación Antonov-24	Crashed into the Caribbean off SE Cuba	44
1997, Aug. 6	Korean Air Boeing 747-300	Crashed into jungle on Guam on approach into airport.	228
1997, Sept. 3	Vietnamese Airlines TU-134	Crashed on approach into Phnom Penh airport	64
1997, Sept. 14	U.S. C-141 cargo plane, Ger. TU-154	Collided in midair off SW Africa	33
1997, Sept. 26	Indonesian Airbus A-300	Crashed near Medan, Indonesia, airport	234
1997, Oct. 10	Austral Airlines DC-9-32	Crashed and exploded near Neuvo Berlin, Uruguay	74
1997, Dec. 6	Russian AN-124 transport cargo plane	Crashed into apartment complex near Irkutsk, Siberia	67*
1997, Dec. 15	Chartered TU-154 from Tajikistan	Crashed in desert near Sharja, U.A.E., airport	85
1997, Dec. 17	Chartered Yakovlev-42 from Ukraine	Crashed in mountains near Katerini, Greece	70
1997, Dec. 19	SilkAir Boeing 737-300	Crashed in Musi River, Sumatra, Indonesia	104
1998, Jan. 14	Afghan cargo plane	Crashed into mountain, SW Pakistan	50+
1998, Feb. 2	Cebu Pacific Air DC-9-32	Crashed into mountain near Cagayan de Oro, Philippines	104
1998, Feb. 16	China Airlines Airbus 300-622R	Crashed on approach to airport, Taipei, Taiwan	203[22]
1998, Apr. 20	Air France Boeing 727-200	Crashed into mountain after takeoff from Bogotá, Colombia	53
1998, Sept. 2	Swissair MD-11	Crashed into Atlantic Ocean off Halifax, Nova Scotia	229
1998, Sept. 25	Pauknair BAE146	Crashed into hillside in Morocco	38
1998, Oct. 11	Congo Air Lines Boeing 727	Shot down by rebels in Kindu, Congo	40
1998, Dec. 11	Thai Airways Airbus A310-200	Crashed short of runway at Surat Thani airport, S Thailand	101
1999, Feb. 24	China Southwest Airlines TU-154	Crashed on approach to Wenzhou airport, eastern China	61
1999, Sept. 1	LAPA Boeing 737-200	Crashed on takeoff from Jorge Newbery Airport, Buenos Aires	74[23]
1999, Oct. 31	EgyptAir Boeing 767-300	Crashed off Nantucket, MA	217
2000, Jan. 31	Alaska Airlines MD-83	Crashed into Pacific Ocean NW of Malibu, CA	88
2000, Apr. 19	Air Philippines Boeing 737-200	Crashed by Davao airport	131
2000, May 21	Chartered Jetstream 31	Crashed near Wilkes-Barre, PA	19
2000, July 25	Air France Concorde	Crashed into hotel after takeoff from Paris	113[24]
2000, Aug. 23	Gulf Air Airbus A320	Crashed into Persian Gulf near Manama, Bahrain	143
2000, Oct. 31	Singapore Airlines 747-400	Crashed immediately after takeoff, Taipei, Taiwan	81
2000, Oct. 31	Chartered Antonov 26	Exploded after takeoff in northern Angola	50
2000, Nov. 15	Chartered Antonov 24	Crashed after takeoff from Luanda, Angola	40+
2001, Jan. 27	Chartered Beechcraft King Air 200	Crashed after takeoff from Boulder, CO	10[25]
2001, Mar. 3	C23 Sherpa mil. transp.	Crashed in storm, central GA	21
2001, Apr. 7	M-17 helicopter	Crashed into mountain S. of Hanoi, Vietnam	16[26]
2001, July 3	Vladivostokavia Tu-154	Crashed on approach to landing at Irkutsk, Russia	145
2001, Sept. 11	**2 Boeing 767s, 2 Boeing 757s**	**See below**[27]	**265**[27]
2001, Oct. 4	Sibir Airlines Tupelov Tu-154	Crashed into Black Sea, struck by errant Ukrainian missile	78
2001, Oct. 8	Twin-engine Cessna, Scandinavian Airlines System (SAS) jetliner	Collided in heavy fog during takeoff from Milan, Italy	118*
2001, Nov. 12	**American Airlines Airbus A-300**	**Crashed after takeoff from JFK Airport, New York, NY**	**265***
2002, Jan. 28	Ecuadoran airline Boeing 727-100	Crashed in Andes mountains in southern Colombia	92
2002, Feb. 12	Iran Air Tours Tu-154	Crashed before landing in Khorramabad, Iran	119
2002, Apr. 15	Air China Boeing 767-200	Crashed into hillside amid rain and fog near Pusan, South Korea	122
2002, Apr. 18	4-seat Rockwell Commander	Crashed into Pirelli building, tallest skyscraper in Milan, Italy	3*
2002, May 4	EAS Airlines BAC 1-11-500	Crashed in suburb of Kano, Nigeria, shortly after takeoff	148+*
2002, May 7	China Northern MD-82	Plunged into Yellow Sea near Dalian, China, after fire in cabin	112
2002, May 25	China Airlines Boeing 747-200	Broke apart in mid-air and plunged into Taiwan Strait	225
2002, July 1	Bashkirian Airlines Tu-154, DHL (Ger. cargo) Boeing 757	Collided over S Germany	71
2002, July 4	Prestige Airlines Cargo Boeing B-707	Crashed short of runway in Bangui, Central African Rep.	25
2002, July 27	Ukraine Air Force Sukhoi SU-27	Crashed into spectators at airshow in Lviv, Ukraine	85
2002, Aug. 19	Russian Mi-26 helicopter	Troop-carrier hit by Chechen missile near Grozny	127
2002, Dec. 23	Aeromist Kharkiv Antonov AN-140	Crashed into mountain in fog approaching Isfahan, Iran	46
2003, Jan. 8	Air Midwest, Beechcraft 1900D	Crashed after takeoff at Charlotte, N.C.	21
2003, Jan. 8	Turkish Airlines Avro RJ-100	Crashed on landing in Diyarbakir, Turkey	75
2003, Jan. 9	TANS Airlines Fokker 28 Fellowship	Crashed into mountain near Chachopoyas, Peru	46
2003, Feb. 19	Iranian Guard Ilyushin IL-76	Troop-carrying plane crashed into mountain near Kerman, Iran	275
2003, Mar. 6	Air Algerie Boeing 737	Crashed on takeoff at Tamanrasset, Algeria	102
2003, May 8	**Congolese Army IL-76**	**On flight from Kinshasa door opened, people sucked out**	**60-170(?)**
2003, May 26	Ukrain.-Medit. Airlines Yak. 42D	Crashed into mountain in fog approaching Trabzon, Turkey	75
2003, July 8	Sudan Airways, Boeing 737-2J8C	Crashed into hillside after takeoff from Port Sudan Airport	116
2003, Aug. 24	Tropical Airways Let 410UVP-E	Crashed after takeoff in Haiti, because of overloading	21
2003, Nov. 29	Congolese Air Force Antonov 26	Crashed on takeoff attempt from Boendo, Dem. Rep. of Congo.	33
2003, Dec. 25	Union Transp. Africaines Boeing B-727	Crashed after takeoff from Cotonou, Benin	140
2004, Jan. 3	Flash Airlines Boeing B-737	Crashed after takeoff from Sharm el-Sheik, Egypt	148
2004, Jan. 13	Uzbekistan Airways Yakovlev YAK-40	Crashed on landing attempt in fog at Tashkent, Uzbekistan	37
2004, Jan. 17	Cessna 208B Grand Caravan	Crashed into L. Erie after takeoff from island nr. Can.	10
2004, Feb. 10	Iranian Kish Airline Fokker-50	Crashed on approach to Sharjah, UAE	43
2004, Mar. 21	Med-Trans Corp. Bell 407 helicopter	Crashed in Pyote, TX, enroute to Lubbock, TX	4
2004, May 15	Rico Linhas Aereas Embraer 120ER Brasilia	Crashed in Amazon jungle near Manaus, Brazil	33
2004, June 8	Gabon Express Hawker Siddeley HS-748	Crashed into sea after takeoff from Libreville, Gabon	19
2004, June 29	UN Mi-8 helicopter	Crashed in forest in Sierra Leone	24[28]
2004, Aug. 24	Volga-Aviaexpress Tupolev TU-134A-3, Sibir Airlines Tupolev TU-154B2	2 planes crashed after take off from Moscow, Russia; brought down by Chechen terrorists	90

*Including those on ground and in buildings. (1) First fatal crash of commercial jet. (2) Caused by bomb planted by John G. Graham in insurance plot to kill his mother, a passenger. (3) Incl. all 128 aboard planes and 6 on ground. (4) Killed 84 on plane and 71 on ground. (5) Incl. 43 Marshall Univ. football players and coaches. (6) Airliner-fighter crash; pilot of fighter parachuted to safety, was arrested for negligence. (7) First supersonic plane crash; killed 8 on ground. (8) Crew of 3 killed; 97 killed on the ground. (9) World's worst airline disaster. (10) Incl. Univ. of Evansville basketball team. (11) Incl. 2 on ground. Highest death toll in U.S. aviation history. (12) Incl. 22 members of U.S. boxing team. (13) Incl. 8 on ground. (14) Worst single-plane disaster. (15) Incl. 248 members of U.S. 101st Airborne Division. (16) Incl. 15 on ground. (17) Incl. 11 on ground. (18) Incl. 1 on ground. (19) Incl. U.S. Sec. of Commerce Ron Brown. (20) Incl. 2 on ground. (21) World's worst midair collision. (22) Incl. 6 on ground. (23) Incl. 10 on ground. (24) World's first Concorde crash; deaths incl. 5 on ground. (25) Incl. 7 players and staff of Oklahoma State Univ. men's basketball team. (26) Carried U.S. mil. personnel, searching for MIAs from Vietnam War. (27) 4 planes were hijacked and crashed, with all on board (265, incl. 19 hijackers) killed: American Airlines Flight 11, a Boeing 767-200, with 81 passengers,11 crew, crashed into Tower 1 of the World Trade Center in NYC; United Airlines Flight 175, a Boeing 767-200, with 56 passengers, 9 crew, crashed into Tower 2 of the World Trade Center; American Airlines Flight 77, a Boeing 757-200, with 58 passengers, 6 crew, crashed into the Pentagon outside Washington, DC; United Air Lines Flight 93, a Boeing 757-200, with 37 passengers, 7 crew, crashed near Shanksville, PA. About 2,600 people on ground died at the 2 World Trade Center towers, and 125 in the Pentagon. (28) Including 14 Pakistani UN Peacekeepers.

Some Notable Railroad Disasters Since 1925

Date	Location	Deaths	Date	Location	Deaths
1925, June 16	Hackettstown, NJ	50	1981, June 6	Bihar, India	800+
1925, Oct. 27	Victoria, MS	21	1982, Jan. 27	El Asnam, Algeria	130
1926, Sept. 5	Waco, CO	30	1982, July 11	Tepic, Mexico	120
1937, July 16	Nr. Patna, India	107	1983, Feb. 19	Empalme, Mexico	100
1938, June 19	Saugus, MT	47	1985, Feb. 23	Madhya Pradesh, India	50
1939, Aug. 12	Harney, NV	24	1985, Aug. 3	southern France	35
1939, Dec. 22	Near Magdeburg, Germany	132	1987, July 2	Kasumbalesha Shaba, Zaire	125
1939, Dec. 22	Near Friedrichshafen, Germany	99	1988, June 27	Paris train station, Gare de Lyon	57
1940, Apr. 19	Little Falls, NY	31	1988, Dec. 12	London, England	35
1940, July 31	Cuyahoga Falls, OH.	43	1989, Jan. 15	Maizdi Khan, Bangladesh	110+
1943, Aug. 29	Wayland, NY	27	1989, June 9	train collided with bus in S Russia	31
1943, Sept. 6	Frankford Junction, Philad. PA	79	1990, Jan. 4	Sindh Prov., Pakistan	210+
1943, Dec. 16	Between Rennert and Buie, NC.	72	1991, May 14	Shigaraki, Japan	42
1944, Jan. 16	León Prov., Spain	500	1993, Sept. 22	Big Bayou Conot, AL	47
1944, Mar. 2	Salerno, Italy	521	1994, Mar. 8	Nr. Durban, South Africa	63
1944, July 6	High Bluff, TN.	35	1994, Sept. 22	Tolunda, Angola	300
1944, Aug. 4	Near Stockton, GA.	47	1995, Aug. 20	Firozabad, India.	358
1944, Sept. 14	Dewey, IN	29	1996, Feb. 16	Silver Spring, MD	11
1944, Dec. 31	Bagley, UT.	50	1997, Mar. 3	Punjab State, Pakistan	125
1945, Aug. 9	Michigan, ND	34	1997, Mar. 31	Huarte Arakil, Spain	21
1946, Mar. 20	Aracaju, Mexico	185	1997, Apr. 29	Hunan, China	58
1946, Apr. 25	Naperville, IL	45	1997, May 4	Rwanda	100+
1947, Feb. 18	Gallitzin, PA	24	1997, Sept. 14	Central India	77
1949, Oct. 22	Nr. Dwor, Poland	200+	1998, June 3	Eschede, Germany	102
1950, Feb. 17	Rockville Centre, NY	31	1998, Feb. 19	Yaounde, Cameroon	100+
1950, Sept. 11	Coshocton, OH	33	1999, Mar. 15	Bourbonnais, IL	11
1950, Nov. 22	Richmond Hill, NY	79	1999, Mar. 24	Nairobi, Kenya	32+
1951, Feb. 6	Woodbridge, NJ.	84	1999, Aug. 2	Gauhati, India	285+
1952, Mar. 4	Nr. Rio de Janeiro, Brazil.	119	1999, Oct. 5	London, England	31
1952, July 9	Rzepin, Poland	160	2000, Jan. 4	Rena, Norway	35
1952, Oct. 8	Harrow, England	112	2000, July 28	São Paulo, Brazil	12
1953, Mar. 27	Conneaut, OH	21	2000, Nov. 11	Kaprun, Austria	155
1955, Apr. 3	Guadalajara, Mexico	300	2001, Feb. 28	Great Heck, England	13
1956, Jan. 22	Los Angeles, CA	30	2001, June 22	Cochin, India	64
1957, Sept. 1	Kendal, Jamaica	178	2001, Sept. 1	Indonesia	40
1957, Sept. 29	Montgomery, W Pakistan	250	2002, Feb. 20	South of Cairo, Egypt	373
1957, Dec. 4	London, England	90	2002, Apr. 18	Seville, FL	4
1958, May 8	Rio de Janeiro, Brazil.	128	2002, Apr. 23	Placentia, CA.	2
1958, Sept. 15	Elizabethport, NJ	48	2002, May 25	Muamba, Mozambique	196+
1960, Nov. 14	Pardubice, Czech.	110	2002, June 24	Igandu, Tanzania.	281+
1962, Jan. 8	Woerden, Netherlands	91	2002, Sept. 10	Bihar, India	118
1962, May 3	Tokyo, Japan	163	2002, Nov. 6	Nancy, France	12
1963, Nov. 9	Yokohama, Japan	120+	2003, Jan. 3	Maharashtra, India	18
1964, July 26	Porto, Portugal	94	2003, Feb. 1	NW Zimbabwe	46
1967, July 6	Madgeburg, Germany	94	2003, May 8	near Lake Balaton in Hungary	33
1970, Feb. 1	Buenos Aires, Argentina	236	2003, May 15	Ludhiana, India	36
1972, June 16	Vierzy, France	107	2003, June 3	Spain, Albacete province.	19
1972, July 21	Seville, Spain	76	2003, June 22	Rajapur, India	33
1972, Oct. 6	Saltillo, Mexico	208	2003, July 2	Andhra Pradesh, India.	22
1972, Oct. 30	Chicago, IL	45	2004, Feb. 18	Neyshabur, NE Iran.	300+
1974, Aug. 30	Zagreb, Yugoslavia	153	2004, Apr. 22	Ryongchon, North Korea.	161
1975, Feb. 28	London subway train	41	2004, July 22	Mekece, NW Turkey	36
1977, Jan. 18	Granville, Australia.	83			

Some Notable U.S. Tornadoes Since 1925

Date	Location	Deaths	Date	Location	Deaths
1925, Mar. 18	MO, IL, IN	689	1969, Jan. 23	MS.	32
1927, Apr. 12	Rock Springs, TX.	74	1971, Feb. 21	Mississippi delta	110
1927, May 9	AR, Poplar Bluff, MO	92	1973, May 26-27	South, Midwest (series)	47
1927, Sept. 29	St. Louis, MO	90	1974, Apr. 3-4	AL, GA, TN, KY, OH	315
1930, May 6	Hill, Navarro, Ellis Co., TX	41	1977, Apr. 4	AL, MS, GA	22
1932, Mar. 21	AL (series of tornadoes).	268	1979, Apr. 10	TX, OK.	60
1936, Apr. 5	MS, GA	455	1984, Mar. 28	NC, SC	57
1936, Apr. 6	Gainesville, GA	203	1985, May 31	NY, PA, OH, Ont. (series)	75
1938, Sept. 29	Charleston, SC.	32	1987, May 22	Saragosa, TX	29
1942, Mar. 16	Central to NE Mississippi	75	1989, Nov. 15	Huntsville, AL	18
1942, Apr. 27	Rogers and Mayes Co., OK.	52	1990, Aug. 28	Northern IL	25
1944, June 23	OH, PA, WV, MD	150	1991, Apr. 26	KS, OK	23
1945, Apr. 12	OK-AR	102	1992, Nov. 21-23	South, Midwest	26
1947, Apr. 9	TX, OK, KS	169	1994, Mar. 27-28	AL, TN, GA, NC, SC (series)	52
1948, Mar. 19	Bunker Hill and Gillespie, IL.	33	1995, May 6-7	Southern OK, northern TX.	23
1949, Jan. 3	LA and AR	58	1997, Mar. 1	Central AR.	26
1952, Mar. 21	AR, MO, TN (series)	208	1997, May 27	Jarrell, TX	27
1953, May 11	Waco, TX.	114	1998, Feb. 22-23	Central FL	42
1953, June 8	MI, OH	142	1998, Mar. 20	Northeast GA.	12
1953, June 9	Worcester and vicinity, MA	90	1998, Mar. 24	Eastern India	145
1953, Dec. 5	Vicksburg, MS	38	1998, Apr. 8	AL, GA, MS	39
1955, May 25	KS, MO, OK, TX.	115	1999, May 3-4	OK, KS	42
1957, May 20	KS, MO	48	2000, Feb. 14	Southwest GA	22+
1958, June, 4	NW Wisconsin	30	2000, July 14	Alberta.	11
1959, Feb. 10	St. Louis, MO	21	2000, Dec. 16	AL	12
1960, May 5, 6	Southeastern OK, AR	30	2001, Feb. 24	Pontotoc, MS.	8
1962, Mar. 31	Milton, FL.	17	2001, Nov. 23-24	AL, AR, MS (series)	13
1965, Apr. 11	IN, IL, OH, MI, WI.	271	2002, Apr. 27-28	IL, KY, MD, MO.	6
1966, Mar. 3	Jackson, MS	57	2002, Nov. 9-11	AL, MS, OH, PA, TN	36
1966, Mar. 3	MS, AL	61	2003, Mar. 20	GA	6
1967, Apr. 21	IL, MI	33	2003, May 4-11	TN, MO, KS, IL, OK, WV, AL.	48
1968, May 15	Midwest	71	2004, Apr. 20-21	IL, IN	8

Principal U.S. Mine Disasters Since 1900

Source: Bureau of Mines, U.S. Dept. of the Interior; Mine Safety and Health Admin., U.S. Dept. of Labor

(All are bituminous-coal mines unless otherwise noted.)

Date	Location	Deaths	Date	Location	Deaths
1900, May 1	Scofield, UT	200	1922, Nov. 6	Spangler, PA	77
1902, May 19	Coal Creek, TN	184	1922, Nov. 22	Dolomite, AL	90
1902, July 10	Johnstown, PA	112	1923, Feb. 8	Dawson, NM	120
1903, June 30	Hanna, WY	169	1923, Aug. 14	Kemmerer, WY	99
1904, Jan. 25	Cheswick, PA	179	1924, Mar. 8	Castle Gate, UT	171
1905, Feb. 26	Virginia City, AL	112	1924, Apr. 28	Benwood, WV	119
1907, Jan. 29	Stuart, WV	84	1926, Jan. 13	Wilburton, OK	91
1907, Dec. 6	Monongah, WV	361	1927, Apr. 30	Everettville, WV	97
1907, Dec. 19	Jacobs Creek, PA	239	1928, May 19	Mather, PA	195
1908, Nov. 28	Marianna, PA	154	1930, Nov. 5	Millfield, OH	82
1909, Nov. 13	Cherry, IL	259	1940, Jan. 10	Bartley, WV	91
1910, Jan. 31	Primero, CO	75	1947, Mar. 25	Centralia, IL	111
1910, May 5	Palos, AL	90	1951, Dec. 21	West Frankfort, IL	119
1910, Nov.8	Delagua, CO	79	1959, Jan. 22	Port Griffith, PA	12
1911, Apr. 8	Littleton, AL	128	1968, Nov. 20	Farmington, WV	78
1911, Dec. 9	Briceville, TN	84	1970, Dec. 30	Hyden, KY	38
1912, Mar. 26	Jed, WV	83	1972, May 2	Kellogg, ID[1]	91
1913, Apr. 23	Finleyville, PA	96	1976, Mar. 9	Oven Fork, KY	15
1913, Oct. 22	Dawson, NM	263	1981, Apr. 15	Redstone, CO	15
1914, Apr. 28	Eccles, WV.	181	1981, Dec. 8	Whitwell, TN	13
1915, Mar. 2	Layland, WV	112	1984, Dec. 19	Huntington, UT	27
1917, Apr. 27	Hastings, CO	121	1989, Sept. 13	Sturgis, KY	10
1917, June 8	Butte, MT[1]	163	2001, Sept. 23	Brookwood, AL	13
1919, June 5	Wilkes-Barre, PA[2]	92			

Note: World's worst mine disaster killed 1,549 workers in Manchuria, Apr. 25, 1942. (1) Metal mine. (2) Anthracite mine.

Some Notable Hurricanes, Typhoons, Blizzards, Other Storms

H.—hurricane; T.—typhoon

Date	Location	Deaths	Date	Location	Deaths
1888, Mar. 11-14	Blizzard, eastern U.S.	400	1974, June 11	Storm Dinah, Luzon Isl., Phil.	71
1900, Sept. 8	H., Galveston, TX	8,000+	1974, July 11	T. *Gilda*, Japan, S. Korea	108
1906, Sept. 19-24	H., LA, MS	350	1974, Sept. 19-20	H. *Fifi*, Honduras	2,000
1906, Sept. 18	T., Hong Kong	10,000+	1974, Dec. 25	Cyclone leveled Darwin, Austral.	50
1915, Aug. 16	H., Galveston, TX	275	1975, Sept. 13-27	H. *Eloise*, Caribbean, NE U.S.	71
1915, Sept. 29	H., LA	500	1976, May 20	T. *Olga*, floods, Philippines	215
1919, Sept. 14	Florida Keys through Gulf to TX	800-900	1978, Oct. 27	T. *Rita*, Philippines	c. 400
1926, Sept. 11-22	H., FL, AL	243	1979, Aug. 30 - Sept. 7	H. *David*, Caribbean, E U.S.	1,100
1926, Oct. 20	H., Cuba	600	1980, Aug. 4-11	H. *Allen*, Caribbean, TX	272
1928, Sept. 6-20	H., southern FL	2,500+	1981, Nov. 25	T. *Irma*, Luzon Isl., Philippines	176
1930, Sept. 3	H., Dominican Republic	2,000	1983, June	Monsoon, India	900
1935, Aug. 29-Sept. 10	H., Caribbean, southeastern U.S.	400+	1984, Sept. 2	T. *Ike*, S Philippines	1,363
1937, Sept. 2	T., "The Great Typhoon," Hong Kong	10,000+	1985, May 25	Cyclone, Bangladesh	10,000
1938, Sept. 21	H., Long Island, NY; New England	600	1985, Oct. 26-Nov. 6	H. *Juan*, SE U.S.	97
1940, Nov. 11-12	Blizzard, NE, Midwest U.S.	144	1987, Nov. 25	T. *Nina*, Philippines	650
1942, Oct. 15-16	H., Bengal, India	40,000	1988, Sept. 10-17	H. *Gilbert*, Caribbean, Gulf of Mex.	260
1947, Dec. 26	Blizzard, NYC, N Atlantic states	55	1989, Sept. 16-22	H. *Hugo*, Caribbean, SE U.S.	504
1952, Oct. 22	T., Philippines	440	1990, May 6-11	Cyclones, SE India	450
1954, Aug. 30	H. *Carol*, northeastern U.S.	68	1991, Apr. 30	Cyclone, Bangladesh	139,000
1954, Oct. 5-18	H. *Hazel*, E Canada, U.S.; Haiti	347	1991, Nov. 5	Tropical storm, Philippines	7,000+
1955, Aug. 12-13	H. *Connie*, NC, SC, VA, MD	43	1992, Aug. 24-26	H. *Andrew*, southern FL, LA	58
1955, Aug. 7-21	H. *Diane*, eastern U.S.	400	1993, Mar. 13-14	Blizzard, E U.S.	200
1955, Sept. 19	H. *Hilda*, Mexico	200	1993, June	Monsoon, Bangladesh	2,000
1956, Feb. 1-29	Blizzard, W Europe	1,000	1994, Nov. 8-18	Storm Gordon, Caribbean, FL	830
1957, June 25-30	H. *Audrey*, TX to AL	390	1995, Oct. 2-4	H. *Opal*, S Mexico, FL, AL	59
1958, Feb. 15-16	Blizzard, NE U.S.	171	1995, Nov. 2-3	T. *Angela*, Philippines	600+
1959, Sept. 17-19	T. *Sarah*, Japan, South Korea	2,000	1996, Jan. 7-8	Blizzard, NE U.S.	100
1959, Sept. 26-27	T. *Vera*, Honshu, Japan	4,466	1996, Aug. 22	Blizzard, Himalayas, N India	239
1960, Sept. 4-12	H. *Donna*, Caribbean, E U.S.	148	1996, Aug. 29- Sept. 6	H. *Fran*, Carib., NC, VA, WV	30
1961, Oct. 31	H. *Hattie*, Br. Honduras	400	1996, Sept. 9-10	H. *Hortense*, Caribbean	24
1962, Sept. 1	T. *Wanda*, Hong Kong	130-200	1996, Sept. 9	T. *Sally*, S China	114
1963, May 28-29	Windstorm, Bangladesh	22,000	1996, Nov. 6	Cyclone, Andhra Pradesh, India	1,000+
1963, Oct. 4-8	H. *Flora*, Caribbean	6,000	1996, Nov. 24-25	Ice storms, TX to MO	26
1964, June 30	T. *Winnie*, N Philippines	107	1996, Dec. 25	Tropical storm, E Malaysia	100+
1964, Sept. 5	T. *Ruby*, Hong Kong and China	735	1997, May 19	Cyclone, Bangladesh	108
1965, May 11-12	Windstorm, Bangladesh	17,000	1997, Aug. 18	Typhoon, Taiwan	24
1965, June 1-2	Windstorm, Bangladesh	30,000	1997, Oct. 8-10	H. *Pauline*, SW Mexico	230
1965, Sept. 7-12	H. *Betsy*, FL, MS, LA.	74	1998, Feb. 4-6	Blizzard, KY, WV	10+
1965, Dec. 15	Windstorm, Bangladesh	10,000	1998, June 9	Cyclone, Gujarat, India	1,320
1966, June 4-10	H. *Alma*, Honduras, SE U.S.	51	1998, Aug.	Monsoon, Bangladesh	326
1966, Sept. 24-30	H. *Inez*, Carib., FL, Mexico	293	1998, Sept. 21-23	H. *Georges*, Caribbean, FL Keys, U.S. Gulf Coast	600+
1967, July 9	T. *Billie*, SW Japan	347	1998, Oct. 27-29	H. *Mitch*, Honduras, Nicaragua, Guatemala, El Salvador	10,866+
1967, Sept. 5-23	H. *Beulah*, Carib., Mex., TX	54	1999, Sept. 4-17	H. *Floyd*, Baha., E seaboard, U.S	69+
1967, Dec. 12-20	Blizzard, SW U.S.	51	1999, Oct. 29	Cyclone, E India	9,392
1968, Nov. 18-28	T. *Nina*, Philippines	63	1999, Dec. 26-29	Gales, France, Switz., Germany	120
1969, Aug. 17-18	H. *Camille*, MS, LA	256	2000, Dec. 27	Winter storm, TX, OK, AR.	40+
1970, Sept. 15	T. *Georgia*, Philippines	300	2001, June 6-17	Tropical storm *Allison*, SE U.S.	47
1970, Oct. 14	T. *Sening*, Philippines	583	2001, July 30	T. *Toraji*, Taiwan	200
1970, Oct. 15	T. *Titang*, Philippines	526	2001, Oct. 8-9	H. *Iris*, Belize.	22
1970, Nov. 13	Cyclone, Bangladesh	300,000	2001, Nov. 2-5	H. *Michelle*, Cuba, Jamaica	17
1971, Aug. 1	T. *Rose*, Hong Kong	130	2001, Nov. 6-12	T. *Lingling*, S Philip., Vietnam	220+
1972, June 19-29	H. *Agnes*, FL to NY	118	2002, July 1-11	T. *Chata'an*, Micron., Philip., Jap.	70+
1972, Dec. 3	T. *Theresa*, Philippines	169	2002, Aug.-Sept.	T. *Rusa*, North & South Korea	115+
1973, June-Aug.	Monsoon rains, India	1,217	2003, Feb. 16-17	Blizzard, E seaboard U.S.	59
			2003, Sept. 2	T. *Dujuan*, S China	32

Date	Location	Deaths	Date	Location	Deaths
2003, Sept. 12	T. *Maemi*, South Korea	130	2004, Aug. 12-15	T. *Rananim*, E China	164
2003, Sept. 7-19	H. *Isabel*, NC, VA, MD		2004, Aug. 13-14	H.*Charley*, W, cent. Florida,	
	E seaboard, U.S.	40+		S. Carolina	36
2003, Dec. 17	Cyclone, southern India	50	2004, Aug. 24-Sept. 10	T. *Aere*, China, Taiwan, Philip.	67
2004, Jan. 26-Feb. 4	Cyclone *Elita*, Madagascar	29	2004, Sept. 5-6	H. *Frances*, Bahamas, Florida	35
2004, Mar. 7-19	Cyclone *Gafilo*, Madagascar	198	2004, Sept. 7-16	H. *Ivan*, Barbados, Grenada,	
2004, Apr. 8	Cyclone 22P, Fiji	22		Jamaica, Cuba, U.S. Gulf	
2004, May 18	T. *Nida*, Philippines	19+		Coast	115
2004, May 19	Cyclone, Myanmar	220	2004, Sept. 16-26	H. *Jeanne*, Dom. Rep., Haiti, Florida	1,500+

Some Notable Floods, Tidal Waves

Date	Location	Deaths	Date	Location	Deaths
1889, May 31	Johnstown, PA	2,209	1995, Jan. 30- Feb. 9	NW Europe	40
1903, June 15	Heppner, OR	325	1995, July	NE China	1,200
1911	Chang Jiang River, China	100,000	1995, Aug. 19	SW Morocco	136
1913, Mar. 25-27	OH, IN	732	1995, Dec. 25	KwaZulu Natal, South Africa	166
1915, Aug. 17	Galveston, TX	275	1996, Feb. 17	Biak Isl., Indonesia	105
1928, Mar. 13	Dam collapse, Saugus, CA	450	1996, April	Afghanistan	100+
1928, Sept. 13	Lake Okeechobee, FL	2,000	1996, June-July	S China	950+
1931, Aug.	Huang He River, China	3,700,000	1996, Aug. 7	Pyrenees Mts., Spain	71
1937, Jan. 22	OH, MS Valleys	250	1996, Dec.-1997, Jan.	NW U.S.	29
1939	N China	200,000	1997, Mar.	Ohio R. Valley	35
1946, Apr. 1	HI, AK	159	1997, July	Poland, Czech Republic	98
1947, Sept. 20	Honshu Island, Japan	1,900	1997, Nov.	Spanish-Portuguese border	31+
1951, Aug.	Manchuria	1,800	1997, Nov.	Bardera, Somalia	1,300+
1953, Jan. 31	W Europe	2,000	1998, Jan.	Kenya	86
1954, Aug. 17	Farahzad, Iran	2,000	1998, Feb.	California to Tijuana, Mexico	30+
1955, Oct. 7-12	India, Pakistan	1,700	1998, Mar.	SW Pakistan	300+
1959, Nov. 1	W Mexico	2,000	1998, July-Aug.	China	4,150
1959, Dec. 2	Frejus, France	412	1998, July-Sept.	Bangladesh	1,441
1960, Oct. 10	Bangladesh	6,000	1998, July 17	Papua New Guinea	3,000
1960, Oct. 31	Bangladesh	4,000	1999, Aug. 1-4	South Korea, Philippines,	
1962, Feb. 17	North Sea coast, Germany	343		Vietnam, Thailand	188+
1962, Sept. 27	Barcelona, Spain	445	1999, Sept.-Oct.	NE Mexico	350+
1963, Oct. 9	Dam collapse, Vaiont, Italy	1,800	1999, Oct.-Dec.	Central Vietnam	700+
1966, Nov. 3-4	Florence, Venice, Italy	113	1999, Feb. 6-11	Botswana	70+
1967, Jan. 18-24	E Brazil	894	1999, Dec.	Venezuela	9,000+
1967, Mar. 19	Rio de Janeiro, Brazil	436	2000, Feb.-Mar.	Madagascar	150+
1967, Nov. 26	Lisbon, Portugal	464	2000, Feb.-Mar.	Mozambique	700
1968, Aug. 7-14	Gujarat State, India	1,000	2000, May 17	Timor Island	50+
1968, Oct. 7	NE India	780	2000, Aug. 2	Himachal Pradesh, India	120+
1969, Jan. 18-26	Southern CA	100	2000, Aug. 2	Bhutan	200+
1969, Mar. 17	Mundau Valley, Alagoas, Braz.	218	2000, Sept. 19-30	India, Bangladesh	1,000+
1969, Aug. 20-22	Western VA	189	2000, Oct. 12-17	France, Brit., Italy, Switz.	35
1969, Sept. 15	South Korea	250	2001, Jan.-Feb.	Mozambique	84+
1969, Oct. 1-8	Tunisia	500	2001, Aug.-Nov.	S Vietnam and Cambodia	360+
1970, May 20	Central Romania	160	2001, Aug. 1-6	Taiwan	100+
1970, July 22	Himalayas, India	500	2001, Aug. 10-12	NE Iran	247
1971, Feb. 26	Rio de Janeiro, Brazil	130	2001, Aug.	Northern Thailand	170
1972, Feb. 26	Buffalo Creek, WV	118	2001, Nov. 9-10	Northern Algeria	711+
1972, June 9	Rapid City, SD	236	2001, Dec. 23-31	Rio de Janeiro	66
1972, Aug. 7	Luzon Isl., Philippines	454	2002, Jan. 30-Feb. 15	Java Isl., Indonesia	147
1972, Aug. 19-31	Pakistan	1,500	2002, Feb. 19	La Paz, Bolivia	65
1974, Mar. 29	Tubaro, Brazil	1,000	2002, Apr.-May	E Africa	150+
1974, Aug. 12	Monty-Long, Bangladesh	2,500	2002, early May	MO, IL, IN, WV, VA KY	20
1976, June 5	Teton Dam collapse, ID	11	2002, Apr.-Aug.	China	800+
1976, July 31	Big Thompson Canyon, CO	139	2002, July-Aug.	India, Nepal, Bangladesh	1,100+
1976, Nov. 1	East Java, Indonesia	136	2002, Aug.	Russia	110
1977, July 19-20	Johnstown, PA	68	2002, Aug.	Germany, Hungary, Austria,	
1977, Nov. 6	Toccoa, GA	39		Czech Rep.	100+
1978, June-Sept.	N India	1,200	2003, May 17-27	Sri Lanka	250
1979, Jan.-Feb.	Brazil	204	2003, Aug.-mid-Sept.	E India	200+
1979, July 17	Lomblem Isl., Indonesia	539	2003, early Nov.	Sumatra, Indonesia	65+
1979, Aug. 11	Morvi, India	15,000	2003, Dec. 10-		
1980, Feb. 13-22	Southern CA, AZ	26	Jan. 23, 2004	Sumatra, Indonesia	148
1981, Apr.	N China	550	2003, Dec. 19-		
1981, July	Sichuan, Hubei Prov., China	1,300	Jan. 7, 2004	Central Philippines	200
1982, Jan. 23	Nr. Lima, Peru	600	2004, Jan. 10-Mar. 8	Brazil	161
1982, May 12	Guangdong, China	430	2004, Apr. 4-6	Coahuila, N Mexico	37
1982, Sept. 17-21	El Salvador, Guatemala	1,300+	2004, Apr. 9-May 11	W Kenya	50
1984, Aug-Sept.	South Korea	200+	2004, Apr. 12-16	Djibouti City, Djibouti	53
1985, July 19	Dam collapse, N Italy	361	2004, May 23-25	Dom. Republic and Haiti	2,000
1987, Aug.-Sept.	N Bangladesh	1,000+	2004, June-Sept.	Bangladesh, India, Myanmar,	
1988, Sept.	N India	1,000+		Nepal	2,000+
1993, July-Aug.	Midwest	48	2004, June-Sept.	China	500
1994, July	GA, AL	32	2004, Aug. 8-12	NE Nigeria	65

Some Major Earthquakes

Source: Global Volcanism Network, Smithsonian Institution; U.S. Geological Survey, Dept. of the Interior; World Almanac research
Magnitude of earthquakes (Mag.) is measured on the Richter scale; each higher number represents a tenfold increase in energy.
Adopted in 1935, the scale is applied to earthquakes as far back as reliable seismograms are available.

Date	Location	Deaths	Mag.	Date	Location	Deaths	Mag.
526, May 20	Antioch, Syria	250,000	NA	1556, Jan. 24	Shaanxi, China	830,000	"
856	Corinth, Greece	45,000	NA	1667, Nov.	Shemaka, Caucasia	80,000	"
1057	Chihli, China	25,000	NA	1693, Jan. 11	Catania, Italy	60,000	"
1169, Feb. 11	Near Mt. Etna, Sicily	15,000[1]	"	1730, Dec. 30	Hokkaido, Japan	137,000	"
1268	Cilicia, Asia Minor	60,000	"	1737, Oct. 11	India, Calcutta	300,000	NA
1290, Sept. 27	Chihli, China	100,000	"	1755, June 7	N Persia	40,000	"
1293, May 20	Kamakura, Japan	30,000	"	1755, Nov. 1	Lisbon, Portugal	60,000	8.75*
1531, Jan. 26	Lisbon, Portugal	30,000	"	1783, Feb. 4	Calabria, Italy	30,000	NA

> ▶ **IT'S A FACT:** On May 23, 2004, the roof collapsed in a section of the newly built Terminal 2E at Charles De Gaulle airport near Paris, France, killing 4 people. The glass and steel structure was based on a tubular design traditionally used for underground tunnels, and had cost $900 million to build.

Date	Location	Deaths	Mag.	Date	Location	Deaths	Mag.
1797, Feb. 4	Quito, Ecuador	41,000	"	1981, July 28	S Iran	1,500	7.3
1822, Sept. 5	Asia Minor, Aleppo	22,000	NA	1982, Dec. 13	W Arabian Peninsula	2,800	6.0
1828, Dec. 28	Echigo, Japan	30,000	"	1983, Oct. 30	E Turkey	1,342	6.9
1868, Aug. 13-15	Peru, Ecuador	40,000	"	1985, Mar. 3	Chile	146	7.8
1875, May 16	Venezuela, Colombia	16,000	"	1985, Sept. 19	Michoacan, Mexico	9,500	8.1
1886, Aug. 31	Charleston, SC	60	6.6	1986, Oct. 10	El Salvador	1,000+	5.5
1896, June 15	Japan, sea wave	27,120	NA	1987, Mar. 6	Colombia-Ecuador	4,000+	7.0
1905, Apr. 4	Kangra, India	19,000	8.6	1988, Aug. 20	India-Nepal border	1,450	6.6
1906, Apr. 18-19	San Francisco, CA	503[2]	8.3	1988, Nov. 6	China-Burma border	1,000	7.3
1906, Aug. 17	Valparaiso, Chile	20,000	8.6	1988, Dec. 7	Soviet Armenia	55,000	7.0
1907, Oct. 21	Central Asia	12,000	8.1	1989, Oct. 17	San Francisco Bay area	63	6.9
1908, Dec. 28	Messina, Italy	83,000	7.5	1990, May 30	N Peru	115	6.3
1915, Jan. 13	Avezzano, Italy	29,980	7.5	1990, June 20	W Iran	40,000+	7.7
1918, Oct. 11	Mona Passage, P.R.	116	7.5	1990, July 16	Luzon, Philippines	1,621	7.8
1920, Dec. 16	Gansu, China	200,000	8.6	1991, Feb. 1	Pakistan, Afgh. border	1,200	6.8
1923, Sept. 1	Yokohama, Japan	143,000	8.3	1991, Oct. 19	N India	2,000	7.0
1925, Mar. 16	Yunnan, China	5,000	7.1	1992, Mar. 13, 15	E Turkey	4,000	6.2/6.0
1927, May 22	Nan-Shan, China	200,000	8.3	1992, June 28	S California	1	7.5/6.6
1932, Dec. 25	Gansu, China	70,000	7.6	1992, Dec. 12	Flores Isl., Indonesia	2,500	7.5
1933, Mar. 2	Japan	2,990	8.9	1993, July 12	off Hokkaido, Japan	200+	7.7
1933, Mar. 10	Long Beach, CA	115	6.2	1992, Sept. 1	SW Nicaragua	116	7.0
1934, Jan. 15	India, Bihar-Nepal	10,700	8.4	1992, Oct. 12	Cairo, Egypt	450	5.9
1935, Apr. 21	Taiwan (Formosa)	3,276	7.4	1993, Sept. 30	Maharashtra, S India	9,748[3]	6.3
1935, May 30	Quetta, India	50,000	7.5	1994, Jan. 17	Northridge, CA	61	6.8
1939, Jan. 25	Chillan, Chile	28,000	8.3	1994, Feb. 15	S Sumatra, Indon.	215	7.0
1939, Dec. 26	Erzincan, Turkey	30,000	8.0	1994, June 6	Cauca, SW Colombia	1,000	6.8
1946, Dec. 20	Honshu, Japan	1,330	8.4	1994, Aug. 19	N Algeria	164	6.0
1948, June 28	Fukui, Japan	5,390	7.3	1995, Jan. 16	Kobe, Japan	5,502	6.9
1949, Aug. 5	Pelileo, Ecuador	6,000	6.8	1995, May 27	Sakhalin Isl., Russia	1,989	7.5
1950, Aug. 15	Assam, India	1,530	8.7	1996, Feb. 3	SW China	200+	7.0
1953, Mar. 18	NW Turkey	1,200	7.2	1997, Feb. 27	W Pakistan	100+	7.3
1956, June 10-17	N Afghanistan	2,000	7.7	1997, Feb. 28	NW Iran	1,000+	6.1
1957, July 2	N Iran	1,200	7.4	1997, May 10	N Iran	1,560	7.5
1957, Dec. 13	W Iran	1,130	7.3	1998, Feb. 4, 8	Takhar province, NE Afghanistan	2,323	6.1
1960, Feb. 29	Agadir, Morocco	12,000	5.9	1998, May 22	Central Bolivia	105	6.5
1960, May 21-30	S Chile	5,000	9.5	1998, May 30	NE Afghanistan	4,700+	6.9
1962, Sept. 1	NW Iran	12,230	7.3	1998, June 27	Adana, Turkey	144	6.3
1963, July 26	Skopje, Yugoslavia	1,100	6.0	1999, Jan. 25	Armenia, Colombia	1,185+	6.0
1964, Mar. 27	Alaska	131	9.2	1999, Aug. 17	Western Turkey	17,200+	7.4
1966, Aug. 19	E Turkey	2,520	7.1	1999, Sept. 7	Athens, Greece	143	5.9
1968, Aug. 31	NE Iran	12,000	7.3	1999, Sept. 21	Taichung, Taiwan	2,474	7.6
1970, Jan. 5	Yunnan Prov., China	15,621	7.7	1999, Nov. 12	Duzce, Turkey	675+	7.2
1970, Mar. 28	W Turkey	1,100	7.3	2000, June 4	Sumatra, Indonesia	103	7.9
1970, May 31	N Peru	66,000	7.8	2001, Jan. 13	San Vicente, El Salvador	800+	7.6
1971, Feb. 9	San Fernando Val., CA	65	6.6	2001, Jan. 26	Gujarat, India	20,000+	7.9
1972, Apr. 10	S Iran	5,054	7.1	2001, Feb. 13	San Vicente, El Salvador	255	6.6
1972, Dec. 23	Managua, Nicaragua	5,000	6.2	2001, June 23	Arequipa, Peru	102	8.1
1974, Dec. 28	Pakistan (9 towns)	5,200	6.3	2002, Feb. 3	Central Turkey	44+	6.5
1975, Sept. 6	Turkey (Lice, etc.)	2,300	6.7	2002, Mar. 3	N Afghanistan	166	7.4
1976, Feb. 4	Guatemala	23,000	7.5	2002, Mar. 25-26	Nahrin, N Afghanistan	1,000+	6.1
1976, May 6	NE Italy	1,000	6.5	2002, Apr. 1	E New Guinea	36	5.0
1976, June 25	Irian Jaya, New Guinea	422	7.1	2002, Apr. 12	Hindu Kush, Afghanistan	50+	5.9
1976, July 27	Tangshan, China	255,000	8.0	2002, June 22	W Iran	261+	6.5
1976, Aug. 16	Mindanao, Philippines	8,000	7.8	2002, Oct. 31	S Italy	29	5.9
1976, Nov. 24	NW Iran-USSR border	5,000	7.3	2003, Jan. 22	Colima, Mexico	29	7.6
1977, Mar. 4	Romania	1,500	7.2	2003, Feb. 24	S Xinjiang prov., China	261	6.4
1977, Aug. 19	Indonesia	200	8.0	2003, May 1	E Turkey	177	6.4
1977, Nov. 23	NW Argentina	100	8.2	2003, May 21	N Algeria	2,200+	6.8
1978, Sept. 16	NE Iran	15,000	7.8	2003, Dec. 26	Bam, SE Iran	26,271	6.6
1979, Sept. 12	Indonesia	100	8.1	2004, Feb. 4	Papua, Indonesia	37	7.0
1979, Dec. 12	Colombia, Ecuador	800	7.9	2004, Feb. 14	NW Pakistan	24	5.5
1980, Oct. 10	NW Algeria	3,500	7.7	2004, Feb. 24	Al Hoceima, NE Morocco	629	6.4
1980, Nov. 23	S Italy	3,000	7.2	2004, May 28	N Iran	35	6.3
1981, June 11	S Iran	3,000	6.9				

*Estimated from earthquake intensity. NA = Not available. (1) Once thought to have been a volcanic eruption; evidence indicates a destructive earthquake and tsunami occurred on this date. (2) With subsequent fires, death toll rose to 700; some estimates are much higher. (3) Official death toll from Indian government. Other sources reported estimates of about 30,000 deaths.

Some Notable Fires Since 1930
(See also Some Notable Explosions Since 1920.)

Date	Location	Deaths	Date	Location	Deaths
1930, Apr. 21	Columbus, OH, penitentiary	320	1949, Apr. 5	Effingham, IL, hospital	77
1931, July 24	Pittsburgh, PA, home for aged	48	1950, Jan. 7	Davenport, IA, Mercy Hospital	41
1934, Dec. 11	Hotel Kerns, Lansing, MI	34	1953, Mar. 29	Largo, FL, nursing home	35
1938, May 16	Atlanta, GA, Terminal Hotel	35	1953, Apr. 16	Chicago, metalworking plant	35
1940, Apr. 23	Natchez, MS, dance hall	198	1957, Feb. 17	Warrenton, MO, home for aged	72
1942, Nov. 28	Cocoanut Grove, Boston	491	1958, Mar. 19	New York, NY, loft building	24
1942, Dec. 12	St. John's, Nfld., hostel	100	1958, Dec. 1	Chicago, parochial school	95
1943, Sept. 7	Gulf Hotel, Houston, TX	55	1958, Dec. 16	Bogotá, Colombia, store	83
1944, July 6	Ringling Circus, Hartford, CT	168	1959, June 23	Stalheim, Norway, resort hotel	34
1946, June 5	LaSalle Hotel, Chicago	61	1960, Mar. 12	Pusan, Korea, chemical plant	68
1946, Dec. 7	Winecoff Hotel, Atlanta	119	1960, July 14	Guatemala City, mental hospital	225
1946, Dec. 12	NY, NY, ice plant, tenement	37	1960, Nov. 13	Amude, Syria, movie theater	152

Date	Location	Deaths	Date	Location	Deaths
1961, Jan. 6	Thomas Hotel, San Francisco	20	1985, Apr. 21	Tabaco, Phil., movie theater	44
1961, Dec. 8	Hartford, CT, hospital	16	1985, Apr. 26	Buenos Aires, Argentina, hospital	79
1961, Dec. 17	Niteroi, Brazil, circus	323	1985, May 11	Bradford, England, soccer stadium	53
1963, May 4	Diourbel, Senegal, theater	64	1985, May 13	Philadelphia, MOVE hdqrtrs, row	
1963, Nov. 18	Surfside Hotel, Atlantic City, NJ	25		houses	11
1963, Nov. 23	Fitchville, OH, rest home	63	1986, Dec. 31	Puerto Rico, Dupont Plaza Hotel	96
1963, Dec. 29	Roosevelt Hotel, Jacksonville, FL	22	1987, May 6-June 2	N China, forest fire	193
1964, May 8	Manila, apartment bldg.	30	1987, Nov. 17	London, England, subway	30
1964, Dec. 18	Fountaintown, IN, nursing home	20	1988, Mar. 20	Lashio, Burma, 2,000 buildings	134
1965, Mar. 1	LaSalle, Quebec, apartment	28	1990, Mar. 25	Bronx, NY, social club	87
1965, Aug. 11-16	Watts riot fires, CA	30+	1991, Mar. 3	Addis Ababa, Ethiopia, munitions dump	260+
1966, Mar. 11	Numata, Japan, 2 ski resorts	31	1991, Sept. 3	Hamlet, NC, processing plant	25
1966, Oct. 17	New York, NY, bldg. (firefighters)	12	1991, Oct. 20-21	Oakland, Berkeley, CA, wildfire	24
1966, Dec. 7	Erzurum, Turkey, barracks	68	1993, Apr. 19	Waco, TX, cult compound	72
1967, Feb. 7	Montgomery, AL, restaurant	25	1994, May 10	Bangkok, Thailand, toy factory	213
1967, May 22	Brussels, Belgium, store	322	1994, July 4-10	Glenwood Springs, CO (firefighters)	14
1967, July 16	Jay, FL, state prison	37	1994, Dec. 10	Karamay, China, theater	300
1968, May 11	Vijayawada, India, wedding hall	58	1994, Nov. 2	Durunka, Egypt, burning fuel flood	500
1969, Dec. 2	Notre Dame, Can., nursing home	54	1995, Oct. 28	Baku, Azerbaijan, subway train	300
1970, Jan. 9	Marietta, OH, nursing home	27	1995, Dec. 23	Mandi Dabwali, India, school	500+
1970, Nov. 1	Grenoble, France, dance hall	145	1996, Mar. 19	Quezon City, Philippines, nightclub	150+
1970, Dec. 20	Tucson, AZ, hotel	28	1996, Mar. 28	Bogor, Indonesia, shopping mall	78
1971, Dec., 25	Seoul, South Korea, hotel	162	1996, Oct. 22	Caracas, Venezuela, jail	25
1972, May 13	Osaka, Japan, nightclub	116	1996, Nov. 20	Hong Kong, building	39
1972, July 5	Sherborne, England, hospital	30	1997, Feb. 23	Baripada, India, worship site	164
1973, June 24	New Orleans, LA, bar	32	1997, Apr. 15	Mina, Saudi Arabia, encampment	343
1973, Aug. 3	Isle of Man, Eng., amusement park	51	1997, June 7	Thanjavur, India, temple	60+
1973, Sept. 1	Copenhagen, Denmark, hotel	35	1997, June 13	New Delhi, India, movie theater	60
1973, Nov. 29	Kumamoto, Japan, dept. store	107	1997, July 11	Pattaya, Thailand, hotel	90
1973, Dec. 2	Seoul, South Korea, theater	50	1997, Sept. 29	Children's home, near Colina, Chile	30
1974, Feb. 1	São Paulo, Brazil, bank building	189	1998, Dec. 3	Manila, Philippines, orphanage	28
1974, June 30	Port Chester, NY, discotheque	24	1999, Mar. 24	France and Italy, Mont Blanc tunnel	40
1974, Nov. 3	Seoul, S. Korea, hotel, disco	88	1999, Oct. 30	Inchon, S. Korea, karaoke salon	55+
1975, Dec. 12	Mina, Saudi Arabia, tent city	138	2000, Mar. 17	Kanungu, Uganda, church	530
1976, Oct. 24	Bronx, NY, social club	25	2000, Oct. 20	Mexico City, Mexico, nightclub	20
1977, Feb. 25	Moscow, Russia, Rossiya hotel	45	2000, Dec. 25	Luoyang, China, shopping center	309
1977, May 28	Southgate, KY, nightclub	164	2001, Jan. 1	Volendam, Netherlands, cafe	10
1977, June 9	Abidjan, Ivory Coast, nightclub	41	2001, Mar. 6	Central China, school	41
1977, June 26	Columbia, TN, jail	42	2001, Mar. 26	Machakos, Kenya, school	64
1977, Nov. 14	Manila, Philippines, hotel	47	2001, Aug. 6	Madras, India, home for mentally ill	27
1978, Jan. 28	Kansas City, Coates House Hotel	16	2001, Aug. 18	Quezon City, Philippines, hotel	73
1978, Aug. 19	Abadan, Iran, movie theater	425+	2001, Sept. 1	Tokyo, Japan, nightclub	44
1979, July 14	Saragossa, Spain, hotel	80	2001, Oct. 24	Swiss Alps, St. Gotthard Tunnel	11
1979, Dec. 31	Chapais, Quebec, social club	42	2001, Dec. 29	Lima, Peru, fireworks accident	291
1980, May 20	Kingston, Jamaica, nursing home	157	2002, Mar. 11	Mecca, Saudi Arabia, girls' school	15
1980, Nov. 21	MGM Grand Hotel, Las Vegas	84	2002, June 16	Beijing, China, internet cafe	24
1980, Dec. 4	Stouffer Inn, Harrison, NY	26	2002, July 7	Donetsk region, Ukraine, coal mine	34+
1981, Jan. 9	Keansburg, NJ, boarding home	30	2002, July 20	Lima, Peru, disco	25+
1981, Feb. 10	Las Vegas Hilton	8	2002, July 31	Donetsk region, Ukraine, coal mine	20
1981, Feb. 14	Dublin, Ireland, discotheque	44	2003, Feb. 20	Warwick, RI, nightclub (pyrotechnics)	100
1982, Sept. 4	Los Angeles, apartment house	24	2003, Sept. 15	Riyadh, Saudi Arabia, prison	94
1982, Nov. 8	Biloxi, MS, county jail	29	2003, Nov. 24	Moscow, Russ., students' hostel	36
1983, Feb. 13	Turin, Italy, movie theater	64	2004, May 17	Honduras, prison in San Pedro Sula	104
1983, Dec. 17	Madrid, Spain, discotheque	83	2004, July 16	Kumbakonam, India, pvt. school	80+
1984, May 11	Great Adventure Amusement Pk., NJ	8	2004, Aug. 1	Asunción, Paraguay, market	400+

Some Notable Explosions Since 1920

(See also Principal U.S. Mine Disasters Since 1900.) **Note:** Many bombings related to political conflicts and terrorism are not included.

Date	Location	Deaths	Date	Location	Deaths
1920, Sept. 16	Wall Street, NY, NY, bomb	30	1965, Oct. 21	Bridge, Tila Bund, Pakistan	80
1921, Sept. 21	Chem. storage facility, Oppau, Ger.	561	1965, Oct. 30	Cartagena, Colombia	48
1924, Jan. 3	Food plant, Pekin, IL	42	1965, Nov. 14	Armory, Keokuk, IA	20
1927, May 18	Bath school, Lansing, MI	38	1967, Dec. 25	Apartment bldg., Moscow, USSR	20
1928, April 13	Dance hall, West Plains, MO	40	1968, Apr. 6	Sports store, Richmond, IN	43
1937, Mar. 18	New London, TX, school	311	1970, Apr. 8	Subway construction, Osaka, Japan	73
1940, Sept. 12	Hercules Powder, Kenvil, NJ	55	1971, June 24	Tunnel, Sylmar, CA	17
1942, June 5	Ordnance plant, Elwood, IL	49	1973, Feb., 10	Liquid gas tank, Staten Island, NY	40
1944, Apr. 14	Bombay, India, harbor	700	1975, Dec. 27	Coal mine, Chasnala, India	431
1944, July 17	Port Chicago, CA, pier	322	1976, Apr. 13	Lapua, Finland, munitions works	40
1944, Oct. 21	Liquid gas tank, Cleveland	135	1977, Nov. 11	Freight train, Iri, South Korea	57
1947, Apr. 16	Texas City, TX, pier	576	1977, Dec. 22	Grain elevator, Westwego, LA	35
1948, July 28	Farben works, Ludwigshafen, Ger.	184	1978, Feb. 24	Derailed tank car, Waverly, TN	12
1950, May 19	Munitions barges, S. Amboy, NJ	30	1978, July 11	Propylene tank truck, Spanish campsite	150
1956, Aug. 7	Dynamite trucks, Cali, Colombia	1,100	1980, Oct. 23	School, Ortuella, Spain	64
1958, Apr. 18	Sunken munitions ship, Okinawa, Japan	40	1982, Apr. 25	Antiques exhibition, Todi, Italy	33
1958, May 22	Nike missiles, Leonardo, NJ	10	1982, Nov. 2	Salang Tunnel, Afghanistan	1,000+
1959, Apr. 10	World War II bomb, Philippines	38	1984, Feb. 25	Oil pipeline, Cubatao, Brazil	508
1959, June 28	Rail tank cars, Meldrim, GA	25	1984, June 21	Naval supply depot, Severomorsk, USSR	200+
1959, Aug. 7	Dynamite truck, Roseburg, OR	13	1984, Nov. 19	Gas storage area, NE Mexico City	334
1959, Nov. 2	Jamuri Bazar, India, explosives	46	1984, Dec. 3	Chemical plant, Bhopal, India	3,849
1959, Dec. 13	2 apt. bldgs., Dortmund, Ger.	26	1984, Dec. 5	Coal mine, Taipei, Taiwan	94
1960, Mar. 4	Belgian munitions ship, Havana, Cuba	100	1985, June 25	Fireworks factory, Hallett, OK	21
1962, Oct. 3	Telephone Co. office, NY, NY	23	1988, Apr. 10	Pakistani army ammunitions dump	
1963, Jan. 2	Packing plant, Terre Haute, IN	17		near Rawalpindi and Islamabad	100
1963, Mar. 9	Dynamite plant, S. Africa	45	1988, July 6	Oil rig, North Sea	167
1963, Aug. 13	Explosives dump, Gauhaiti, India	32	1989, June 3	Gas pipeline, between Ufa, Asha, USSR	650+
1963, Oct. 31	State Fair Coliseum, Indianapolis, IN	73	1992, Mar. 3	Coal mine, Kozlu, Turkey	270+
1964, July 23	Bone, Algeria, harbor munitions	100	1992, Apr. 22	Sewer, Guadalajara, Mexico	190
1965, Mar. 4	Gas pipeline, Natchitoches, LA	17	1992, May 9	Coal mine, Plymouth, Nova Scotia	26
1965, Aug. 9	Missile silo, Searcy, AR	53	1993, Feb. 26	World Trade Center, NY, NY	6

Date	Location	Deaths	Date	Location	Deaths
1994, July 18	Jewish com. center, Buenos Aires, Arg...	100	2000, Aug. 20	Natural gas pipeline, Carlsbad, NM	10
1995, Apr. 19	Fed'l. office building, Oklahoma City	168	2000, Sept. 9	Truck explodes in Urumqi, China.......	60
1995, Apr. 29	Subway construction, South Korea	110	2000, Sept. 13	Bomb, Jakarta, Indonesia	15
1995, Nov. 13	Military facility, Riyadh, Saudi Arabia	7	2000, Sept. 19	Bomb, Islamabad, Pakistan	16
1996, Jan. 31	Bank, Colombo, Sri Lanka	53	2000, Oct. 12	U.S. destroyer, Yemen................	17
1996, Feb. 25	Jerusalem and Ashkelon, Israel	27	2001, Mar. 6	School, Wanzai County China	41
1996, Mar. 3-4	Jerusalem and Tel Aviv, Israel	33	2001, Apr. 21	Coal mine, Shaanxi, China	51
1996, June 25	U.S. military housing complex, near	19	2001, June 1	Dance club, Tel Aviv, Israel	21
	Dhahran, Saudi Arabia	19	2001, July 17	Coal mine, Guanxi, China............	76+
1996, July 24	Train, Colombo, Sri Lanka	86	2001, Aug. 19	Coal mine, Donetsk region, Ukraine	52
1996, Nov. 16	Russian military apartment, Dagestan		2001, Sept. 21	Chem. plant, Toulouse, France	29
	region, Russia	68	2002, Jan. 21	Volcanic lava causes gas station blast	
1996, Nov. 21	Building, San Juan, Puerto Rico........	29		in Goma, Dem. Rep. of the Congo ...	50+
1996, Nov. 27	Coal mine, Shanxi province, China	91+	2002, Jan. 27	Munitions dump, Lagos, Nigeria	1,000+
1996, Dec. 30	Train, Assam, India	59+	2002, Mar. 21	Car bomb near U.S. embassy, Lima,	
1997, Jan. 18	Near courthouse, Lahore, Pakistan	25		Peru	9
1997, Mar. 19	Ammunition depot, Jalalabad, Afgh.....	16	2002, Apr. 11	Truck nr. synagogue, Djerba, Tunisia ...	17
1997, July 8	Train, Punjab, India	36	2002, Apr. 21	Bomb, dept. store, Mindanao, Philip.....	14
1997, Nov. 19	Car, Hyderabad, India	23	2002, Apr. 26	Bomb at mosque, central Pakistan	12
1997, Dec. 2	Coal mine, Novokuznetsk, Siberia	68	2002, May 8	Bomb on bus outside hotel, Karachi, Pak.	14
1998, Jan. 17	Coal mine, Sokobanja, Serbia	29	2002, May 9	Land mine at parade, Kaspiisk, Russia ..	34+
1998, Feb. 14	Oil tankers (2), Yaounde, Cameroon....	120	2002, June 14	Car bomb outside U.S. consulate,	
1998, Feb. 14	17 bombs, Coimbatore, India..........	50		Karachi, Pak....................	12
1998, Mar. 5	Bus, Colombo, Sri Lanka	32	2002, June 18	Bomb on bus, Jerusalem, Israel	20
1998, Apr. 4	Coal mine, Donetsk, Ukraine	63	2002, July 5	Bomb in market, Larba, Algeria........	35+
1998, Aug. 7	Bomb, U.S. emb., Nairobi, Kenya	213	2002, Aug. 9	Explosion, Jalalabad, Afghanistan......	25+
	Bomb, U.S. emb., Dar-es-Salaam, Tanz .	11	2002, Sept. 5	Car bomb, Kabul, Afghanistan	30
1998, Aug. 15	Car bomb, Omagh, Ireland............	29	2002, Oct. 12	Bombings of nightclubs in Bali, Indon....	202
1998, Sept. 8	Two buses, Sao Paulo, Brazil	59	2003, Aug. 5	Car bomb at hotel in Jakarta, Indon.....	12
1998, Oct. 17	Oil pipeline, Jesse, Nigeria...........	700+	2003, Aug. 19	Truck bomb, UN headquarters, Baghdad	22
1999, May 16	Fuel truck, Punjab province, Pakistan ...	75	2003, Aug. 25	Bombs in 2 taxis, Mumbai, India	52
1999, July 29	Gold mine, Carletonville, S. Africa	17	2003, Aug. 29	Explosion at mosque in Najaf, Iraq	80+
1999, Sept. 10	Apartment building, Moscow	94	2003, Dec. 5	Bomb on train in Yessentuki, Russia.....	45
1999, Sept. 13	Apartment building, Moscow	118	2003, Dec. 23	Gas well explosion in Chongqing, China.	233
1999, Sept. 16	Apartment building, Moscow	18	2004, Jan. 19	Natural gas facility in Skikda, Algeria....	27
1999, Sept. 26	Fireworks factory, Celaya, Mexico	56	2004, Feb. 6	Bomb on subway car in Moscow, Russia	39
2000, Feb. 25	Bombs on 2 buses, Ozamis, Philip......	41	2004, Mar. 11	Madrid commuter trains bombed, Spain .	191
2000, Mar. 11	Coal mine, Krasnodon, Ukraine	80	2004, Apr. 17	Chemical factory in China	9+
2000, Apr. 16	Airport hangar, Congo, Dem. Rep. of....	100+	2004, May 6-7	Ammunition dump in Ukraine..........	5
2000, July 16	Oil pipeline, Warri, Nigeria	30	2004, May 11	Plastics factory in Glasgow, Scotland ...	4+
2000, Aug. 19	Train derailed in Nairobi, Kenya........	25	2004, July 19	Coal mine, Ukraine	31

Notable Nuclear Accidents

Oct. 7, 1957 — A fire in the Windscale plutonium production reactor N of Liverpool, England, released radioactive material; later blamed for 39 cancer deaths.

Jan. 3, 1961 — A reactor at a federal installation near Idaho Falls, ID, killed 3 workers. Radiation contained.

Oct. 5, 1966 — A sodium cooling system malfunction caused a partial core meltdown at the Enrico Fermi demonstration breeder reactor, near Detroit, MI. Radiation contained.

Jan. 21, 1969 — A coolant malfunction from an experimental underground reactor at Lucens Vad, Switzerland, released radiation into a cavern, which was then sealed.

Mar. 22, 1975 — Fire at the Brown's Ferry reactor in Decatur, AL, caused dangerous lowering of cooling water levels.

Mar. 28, 1979 — The worst commercial nuclear accident in the U.S. occurred as equipment failures and human mistakes led to a loss of coolant and a partial core meltdown at the Three Mile Island reactor in Middletown, PA.

Feb. 11, 1981 — 8 workers were contaminated when 100,000 gallons of radioactive coolant fluid leaked into containment building of TVA's Sequoyah 1 plant in Tennessee.

Apr. 25, 1981 — Some 100 workers were exposed to radiation during repairs of a nuclear plant at Tsuruga, Japan.

Jan. 6, 1986 — A cylinder of nuclear material burst after being improperly heated at a Kerr-McGee plant at Gore, OK. One worker died; 100 were hospitalized.

Apr. 26, 1986 — In the worst nuclear accident in the history of nuclear power, fires and explosions resulting from an unauthorized experiment at the Chernobyl nuclear power plant near Kiev, USSR (now in Ukraine), left at least 31 dead in the immediate aftermath and spread radioactive material over much of Europe. An estimated 135,000 people were evacuated from the region, some of which was uninhabitable for years. As a result of the radiation released, tens of thousands of excess cancer deaths (as well as increased birth defects) were expected.

Sept. 30, 1999 — Japan's worst nuclear accident ever occurred at a uranium-reprocessing facility in Tokaimura, NE of Tokyo, when workers accidentally overloaded a container with uranium, thereby exposing workers and area residents to extremely high radiation levels.

> On Dec. 24, 1984, in the worst industrial accident in history, more than 3,000 people were killed within hours when toxic gas leaked from a Union Carbide factory in Bhopal, India. An estimated 14,000 or more eventually died, and more than 100,000 suffered injuries.

Record Oil Spills

The number of tons can be multiplied by 7 to estimate roughly the number of barrels spilled; the exact number of barrels in a ton varies with the type of oil. Each barrel contains 42 gallons.

Name, place	Date	Cause	Tons
Ixtoc I oil well, S Gulf of Mexico	June 3, 1979	Blowout	600,000
Nowruz oil field, Persian Gulf...............................	Feb. 1983	Blowout	600,000 (est.)
Atlantic Empress & *Aegean Captain*, off Trinidad and Tobago ...	July 19, 1979	Collision	300,000
Castillo de Bellver, off Cape Town, South Africa	Aug. 6, 1983	Fire	250,000
Amoco Cadiz, near Portsall, France........................	Mar. 16, 1978	Grounding	223,000
Torrey Canyon, off Land's End, England	Mar. 18, 1967	Grounding	119,000
Sea Star, Gulf of Oman	Dec. 19, 1972	Collision...........	115,000
Urquiola, La Coruna, Spain	May 12, 1976.......	Grounding	100,000

Other Notable Oil Spills

Name, place	Date	Cause	Gallons
Persian Gulf	began Jan. 23, 1991 ..	Spillage by Iraq	130,000,000[1]
Braer, off Shetland Islands................................	Jan. 5, 1993.........	Grounding	26,000,000
Prestige, off N Spain	Nov. 13-19, 2002	Ship broke in half.......	22,600,000
Aegean Sea, off N Spain	Dec. 3, 1992	Unknown	21,500,000
Sea Empress, off SW Wales	Feb. 15, 1996	Grounding	18,000,000
World Glory, off South Africa	June 13, 1968	Hull failure	13,524,000
Exxon Valdez, Prince William Sound, AK	Mar. 24, 1989	Grounding	10,080,000

(1) Est. by Saudi Arabia. Some estimates as low as 25 mil gal.

AEROSPACE

Memorable Moments in Human Spaceflight

Sources: National Aeronautics and Space Administration; Congressional Research Service; World Almanac research

Listed are selected notable U.S. missions by the National Aeronautics and Space Administration (NASA), plus non-U.S. missions (shown with an asterisk), sponsored by the USSR or, later, the Commonwealth of Independent States. Dates are Eastern standard time. EVA = extravehicular activity. ASTP = Apollo-Soyuz Test Project. STS = Space Transportation System, NASA's name for the overall Shuttle program. Number of total flights by each crew member is given in parentheses when flight listed is not the first.

Launch Date	Mission[1]	Crew (no. of flights)	Duration (hr:min)	Remarks
4/12/61	*Vostok 1	Yuri A. Gagarin	1:48	**1st human orbital flight**
5/5/61	Mercury-Redstone 3	Alan B. Shepard Jr.	0:15	**1st American in space**
7/21/61	Mercury-Redstone 4	Virgil I. Grissom	0:15	Spacecraft sank, Grissom rescued
8/6/61	*Vostok 2	Gherman S. Titov	25:18	1st spaceflight of more than 24 hrs
2/20/62	Mercury-Atlas 6	John H. Glenn Jr.	4:55	**1st American in orbit;** 3 orbits
5/24/62	Mercury-Atlas 7	M. Scott Carpenter	4:56	Manual retrofire error caused 250-mi landing overshoot
8/11/62	*Vostok 3	Andrian G. Nikolayev	94:22	Vostok 3 and 4 made 1st group flight
8/12/62	*Vostok 4	Pavel R. Popovich	70:57	On 1st orbit, it came within 3 mi of Vostok 3
10/3/62	Mercury-Atlas 8	Walter M. Schirra Jr.	9:13	Landed 5 mi from target
5/15/63	Mercury-Atlas 9	L. Gordon Cooper	34:19	1st U.S. evaluation of effects of one day in space on a person; 22 orbits
6/14/63	*Vostok 5	Valery F. Bykovsky	119:06	Vostok 5 and 6 made 2nd group flight
6/16/63	*Vostok 6	Valentina V. Tereshkova	70:50	**1st woman in space;** passed within 3 mi of Vostok 5
10/12/64	*Voskhod 1	Vladimir M. Komarov, Konstantin P. Feoktistov, Boris B. Yegorov	24:17	1st 3-person orbital flight; 1st without space suits
3/18/65	*Voskhod 2	Pavel I. Belyayev, Aleksei A. Leonov	26:02	Leonov made **1st "space walk"** (10 min)
3/23/65	Gemini-Titan 3	Grissom (2), John W. Young	4:53	1st piloted spacecraft to change its orbital path
6/3/65	Gemini-Titan 4	James A. McDivitt, Edward H. White 2nd	97:56	White was 1st American to "walk in space" (36 min)
8/21/65	Gemini-Titan 5	Cooper (2), Charles Conrad Jr.	190:55	Longest-duration human flight to date
12/15/65	Gemini-Titan 6A	Schirra (2), Thomas P. Stafford	25:51	Completed 1st U.S. space rendezvous, with Gemini 7
12/4/65	Gemini-Titan 7	Frank Borman, James A. Lovell	330:35	Longest-duration Gemini flight
3/16/66	Gemini-Titan 8	Neil A. Armstrong, David R. Scott	10:41	**1st docking of one space vehicle with another;** mission aborted, control malfunction; 1st Pacific landing
6/3/66	Gemini-Titan 9A	Stafford (2), Eugene A. Cernan	72:21	Performed simulation of lunar module rendezvous
7/18/66	Gemini-Titan 10	Young (2), Michael Collins	70:47	1st use of Agena target vehicle's propulsion systems; 1st orbital docking
9/12/66	Gemini-Titan 11	Conrad (2), Richard F. Gordon Jr.	71:17	1st tethered flight; highest Earth-orbit altitude (850 mi)
11/11/66	Gemini-Titan 12	Lovell (2), Edwin E. "Buzz" Aldrin Jr.	94:34	Final Gemini mission; 5-hr EVA
4/23/67	*Soyuz 1	Komarov (2)	26:40	Crashed on reentry, killing Komarov
10/11/68	Apollo-Saturn 7	Schirra (3), Donn F. Eisele, R. Walter Cunningham	260:09	1st piloted flight of Apollo spacecraft command-service module only; live TV footage of crew
12/21/68	Apollo-Saturn 8	Borman (2), Lovell (3), William A. Anders	147:00	**1st lunar orbit** and piloted lunar return reentry (command-service module only); views of lunar surface televised to Earth
1/14/69	*Soyuz 4	Vladimir A. Shatalov	71:21	Docked with Soyuz 5
1/15/69	*Soyuz 5	Boris V. Volyanov, Aleksei S. Yeliseyev, Yevgeny V. Khrunov	72:54	Docked with 4; Yeliseyev and Khrunov transferred to Soyuz 4 via a spacewalk
3/3/69	Apollo-Saturn 9	McDivitt (2), D. Scott (2), Russell L. Schweickart	241:00	1st piloted flight of lunar module
5/18/69	Apollo-Saturn 10	Stafford (3), Young (3), Cernan (2)	192:03	1st lunar module orbit of Moon, 50,000 ft from Moon surface
7/16/69	Apollo-Saturn 11	Armstrong (2), Collins (2), Aldrin (2)	195:18	**1st lunar landing** made by Armstrong and Aldrin (7/20); collected 48.5 lb of soil, rock samples; lunar stay time 21:36:21
10/11/69	*Soyuz 6	Georgi S. Shonin, Valery N. Kubasov	118:43	1st welding of metals in space
10/12/69	*Soyuz 7	Anatoly V. Flipchenko, Vladislav N. Volkov, Viktor V. Gorbatko	118:40	Space lab construction test made; Soyuz 6, 7, and 8: 1st time 3 spacecraft, 7 crew members orbited the Earth at once
10/13/69	*Soyuz 8	Shatalov (2), Yeliseyev (2)	118:51	Part of space lab construction team
11/14/69	Apollo-Saturn 12	Conrad (3), Richard F. Gordon Jr. (2), Alan L. Bean	244:36	Conrad and Bean made **2nd Moon landing** (11/18); collected 74.7 lb of samples, lunar stay time 31:31
4/11/70	Apollo-Saturn 13	Lovell (4), Fred W. Haise Jr., John L. Swigert Jr.	142:54	Aborted after service module oxygen tank ruptured; crew returned in lunar module
6/1/70	*Soyuz 9	Nikolayev (2), Vitaliy I. Sevastyanov	424:59	Longest human spaceflight to date
1/31/71	Apollo-Saturn 14	A. Shepard (2), Stuart A. Roosa, Edgar D. Mitchell	216:01	Shepard and Mitchell made **3rd Moon landing** (2/3); collected 96 lb of lunar samples; lunar stay 33:31
4/19/71	*Salyut 12	(Occupied by Soyuz 11 crew)		**1st space station**
4/22/71	*Soyuz 10	Shatalov (3), Yeliseyev (3), Nikolay N. Rukavishnikov	47:46	**1st successful docking with a space station;** failed to enter space station
6/6/71	*Soyuz 11	Georgi T. Dobrovolskiy, V. Volkov (2), Viktor I. Patsayev	570:22	Docked and entered Salyut 1 space station; **crew died** during reentry from loss of pressurization
7/26/71	Apollo-Saturn 15	D. Scott (3), James B. Irwin, Alfred M. Worden	295:12	Scott and Irwin made **4th Moon landing** (7/30); 1st lunar rover use; 1st deep space walk; 170 lb of samples; 66:55 stay

Launch Date	Mission[1]	Crew (no. of flights)	Duration (hr:min)	Remarks
4/16/72	Apollo-Saturn 16	Young (4), Charles M. Duke Jr., Thomas K. Mattingly 2nd	265:51	Young and Duke made **5th Moon landing** (4/20); collected 213 lb of lunar samples; lunar stay 71:2
12/7/72	Apollo-Saturn 17	Cernan (3), Ronald E. Evans, Harrison H. Schmitt	301:51	Cernan and Schmitt made 6th and **last lunar landing** (12/11); collected 243 lb of samples; record lunar stay over 75 hrs
5/14/73[2]	Skylab 1	(Occupied by Skylab 2, 3, and 4 crews)		**1st U.S. space station**; fell out of orbit 7/11/79
5/25/73	Skylab 2	Conrad (4), Joseph P. Kerwin, Paul J. Weitz	672:49	1st Amer. piloted orbiting space station; crew repaired damage caused in boost
7/28/73	Skylab 3	Bean (2), Owen K. Garriott, Jack R. Lousma	1,427:09	Crew systems and operational tests; scientific activities; 3 EVAs, 13:44
11/16/73	Skylab 4	Gerald P. Carr, Edward G. Gibson, William Pogue	2,017:15	Final Skylab mission
7/15/75	*Soyuz 19 (ASTP)	Leonov (2), Kubasov (2)	143:31	U.S.-USSR joint flight; crews linked up in space (7/17), conducted experiments, shared meals, held a joint news conf.
7/15/75	Apollo (ASTP)	Vance Brand, Stafford (4), Donald K. Slayton	217:28	Joint flight with Soyuz 19
12/10/77	*Soyuz 26	Yuri V. Romanenko, Georgiy M. Grechko (2)	2,314:00	1st multiple docking to a space station (Soyuz 26 and 27 docked at Salyut 6)
1/10/78	*Soyuz 27	Vladimir A. Dzhanibekov	142:59	*See Soyuz 26*
3/2/78	*Soyuz 28	Aleksei A. Gubarev (2), Vladimir Remek	190:16	1st international crew launch; Remek was 1st Czech in space
4/12/81	Columbia (STS-1)	Young (5), Robert L. Crippen	54:21	**1st space shuttle** to fly into Earth's orbit
11/12/81	Columbia (STS-2)	Joe H. Engle, Richard H. Truly	54:13	1st scientific payload; 1st reuse of space shuttle
11/11/82	Columbia (STS-5)	Brand (2), Robert Overmyer, William Lenoir, Joseph Allen	122:14	1st 4-person crew
6/18/83	Challenger (STS-7)	Crippen (2), Frederick Hauck, Sally K. Ride, John M. Fabian, Norman Thagard	146:24	Ride was **1st U.S. woman in space**; 1st 5-person crew
6/27/83	*Soyuz T-9	Vladimir A. Lyakhov (2), Aleksandr Pavlovich Aleksandrov	3,585:46	Docked at Salyut 7; 1st construction in space
8/30/83	Challenger (STS-8)	Truly (2), Daniel Brandenstein, William Thornton, Guion Bluford, Dale Gardner	145:09	Bluford was **1st African-American in space**
11/28/83	Columbia (STS-9)	Young (6), Brewster Shaw Jr., Robert Parker, Garriott (2), Byron Lichtenberg, Ulf Merbold	247:47	1st 6-person crew; 1st Spacelab mission
2/3/84	Challenger (41-B)	Brand (3), Robert Gibson, Ronald McNair, Bruce McCandless, Robert Stewart	191:16	1st untethered EVA
2/8/84	*Soyuz T-10B	Leonid Kizim, Vladimir Solovyov, Oleg Atkov	1,510:43	Docked with Salyut 7; crew set space duration record of 237 days
4/3/84	*Soyuz T-11	Yury Malyshev (2), Gennady Strekalov (3), Rakesh Sharma	4,365:48	Docked with Salyut 7; Sharma 1st Indian in space
4/6/84	Challenger (41-C)	Crippen (3), Francis R. Scobee, George D. Nelson, Terry J. Hart, James D. van Hoften	167:40	1st in-orbit satellite repair
7/17/84	*Soyuz T-12	Dzhanibekov (4), Svetlana Y. Savitskaya (2), Igor P. Volk	283:14	Docked at Salyut 7; Savitskaya was 1st woman to perform EVA
8/30/84	Discovery (41-D)	Henry W. Hartsfield (2), Michael L. Coats, Richard M. Mullane, Steven A. Hawley, Judith A. Resnik, Charles D. Walker	144:56	1st flight of U.S. nonastronaut (Walker)
10/5/84	Challenger (41-G)	Crippen (4), Jon A. McBride, Kathryn D. Sullivan, Ride (2), Marc Garneau, David C. Leestma, Paul D. Scully-Power	197:24	1st 7-person crew
11/8/84	Discovery (51-A)	Hauck (2); David M. Walker, Dr. Anna L. Fisher, J. Allen (2), D. Gardner (2)	191:45	1st satellite retrieval/repair
4/12/85	Discovery (51-D)	Karol J. Bobko, Donald E. Williams, Jake Garn, C. Walker (2), Jeffrey A. Hoffman, S. David Griggs, M. Rhea Seddon	167:55	Garn (R, UT) was **1st U.S. senator in space**
6/17/85	Discovery (51-G)	Brandenstein (2), John O. Creighton, Shannon W. Lucid, Steven R. Nagel, Fabian (2), Prince Sultan Salman al-Saud, Patrick Baudry	169:39	Launched 3 satellites; Salman al-Saud was 1st Arab in space; Baudry was 1st French person on U.S. mission
10/3/85	Atlantis (51-J)	Bobko (3), Ronald J. Grabe, David C. Hilmers, Stewart (2), William A. Pailes	97:47	1st Atlantis flight
10/30/85	Challenger (61-A)	Hartsfield (3), Nagel (2), Buchli (2), Bluford (2), Bonnie J. Dunbar, Wubbo J. Ockels, Richard Furrer, Ernst Messerschmid	168:45	1st 8-person crew; 1st German Spacelab mission
1/12/86	Columbia (61-C)	R. Gibson (2), Charles F. Bolden Jr., Hawley (2), G. Nelson (2), Franklin R. Chang-Diaz, Robert J. Cenker, Bill Nelson	146:04	B. Nelson was 1st U.S. representative in space; material and astronomy experiments conducted
1/28/86	Challenger (51-L)	Scobee (2), Michael J. Smith, Resnik (2), Ellison S. Onizuka (2), Ronald E. McNair, Gregory B. Jarvis, Christa McAuliffe	—	**Exploded 73 sec after liftoff**; all aboard were killed
2/20/86	*Mir[2]	—	—	*Mir* **space station** with 6 docking ports launched
3/13/86	*Soyuz T-15	Kizim (3), Solovyov (2)	3,000:01	Ferry between stations; docked at *Mir*
2/5/87	*Soyuz TM-2	Romanenko (3), Aleksandr I. Laveikin	7,835:38	Romanenko set endurance record, since broken
7/22/87	*Soyuz TM-3	Aleksandr Viktorenko, Aleksandr Pavlovich Aleksandrov (2), Mohammed Faris	3,847:16	Docked with *Mir*; Faris 1st Syrian in space
12/21/87	*Soyuz TM-4	V. Titov (2), Muso Manarov, Anatoly Levchenko	8,782:39	Docked with *Mir*
6/7/88	*Soyuz TM-5	Viktor Savinykh (3), Anatoly Solovyev, Aleksandr Panayotov Aleksandrov	236:13	Docked with *Mir*
9/29/88	Discovery (STS-26)	Hauck (3), Richard O. Covey (2), Hilmers (2), G. Nelson (2), John M. Lounge (2)	97:00	1st shuttle flight since *Challenger* explosion 1/28/86

Launch Date	Mission[1]	Crew (no. of flights)	Duration (hr:min)	Remarks
5/4/89	Atlantis (STS-30)	D. Walker (2), Grabe (2), Thagard (2), Mary L. Cleave (2), Mark C. Lee	96:56	Launched Venus orbiter *Magellan*
10/18/89	Atlantis (STS-34)	Donald E. Williams (2), Michael J. McCulley, Lucid (2), Chang-Diaz (2), Ellen S. Baker	119:39	Launched Jupiter probe and orbiter *Galileo*
4/24/90	Discovery (STS-31)	McCandless (2), Sullivan (2), Loren J. Shriver (2), Bolden (2), Hawley (3)	121:16	**Launched Hubble Space Telescope**
10/6/90	Discovery (STS-41)	Richard N. Richards (2), Robert D. Cabana, Bruce E. Melnick, William M. Shepherd (2), Thomas D. Akers	98:10	Launched *Ulysses* spacecraft to investigate interstellar space and the Sun
5/18/91	*Soyuz TM-12	Anatoly Artsebarskiy, Sergei Krikalev (2) (to *Mir*), Helen Sharman	3,471:22	Docked with *Mir;* Sharman 1st from United Kingdom in space
3/17/92	*Soyuz TM-14	Viktorenko (3) (to *Mir*), Alexandr Kaleri (to *Mir*), Klaus-Dietrich Flade, Aleksandr Volkov (3) (from *Mir*), Krikalev (2) (from *Mir*)	3,495:11	First human CIS space mission; docked with *Mir* 3/19; Viktorenko and Kaleri to *Mir;* Volkov and Krikalev from *Mir;* Krikalev was in space 313 days
5/7/92	Endeavour (STS-49)	Brandenstein (4), Kevin C. Chilton, Melnick (2), Pierre J. Thuot (2), Richard J. Hieb (2), Kathryn Thornton (2), Akers (2)	213:30	1st 3-person EVA; satellite recovery and redeployment
9/12/92	Endeavour (STS-47)	R. Gibson (4), Curtis L. Brown Jr., Lee (2), Jay Apt (2), N. Jan Davis, Mae Carol Jemison, Mamoru Mohri	190:30	Jemison was 1st black woman in space; Lee and Davis 1st married couple to travel together in space; 1st Japanese Spacelab
6/21/93	Endeavour (STS-57)	Grabe (3), Brian J. Duffy (2), G. David Low (3), Nancy J. Sherlock, Peter J. K. Wisoff, Janice E. Voss	239:46	Carried Spacelab commercial payload module
12/2/93	Endeavour (STS-61)	Covey (3), Kenneth D. Bowersox (2), Claude Nicollier (2), Story Musgrave (5), Akers (3), K. Thornton (3), Hoffman (4)	259:58	Hubble Space Telescope repaired; Akers set new U.S. EVA duration record (29 hr, 40 min)
2/3/94	Discovery (STS-60)	Bolden (3), Kenneth S. Reightier Jr. (2), Davis (2), Chang-Diaz (3), Ronald M. Sega, Krikalev (3)	199:10	Krikalev was 1st Russian on U.S. shuttle
7/1/94	*Soyuz TM-19	Yuri I. Malenchenko, Talgat A. Musabayev, Merbold (2) (from *Mir*)	3,022:53	Docked with *Mir;* Merbold from *Mir*
9/9/94	Discovery (STS-64)	Richards (4), L. Blaine Hammond Jr. (2), Jerry M. Linenger, Susan J. Helms (2), Carl J. Meade (3), Lee (3)	262:50	Performed atmospheric research; 1st untethered EVA in over 10 years
2/3/95	Discovery (STS-63)	James D. Wetherbee (3), Eileen M. Collins, Bernard A. Harris (2), C. Michael Foale (3), Janice E. Voss (2), V. Titov (4)	198:29	*Discovery* and Russian space station rendezvous
3/2/95	Endeavour (STS-67)	Stephen S. Oswald (3), William G. Gregory, Samuel T. Durrance (2), Ronald Parise (2), Wendy B. Lawrence, Tamara E. Jernigan (3), John M. Grunsfeld	399:09	Shuttle data made available on the Internet; astronomy research conducted
3/14/95	*Soyuz TM-21	Thagard (2), Vladimir Dezhurov, Strekalov (5)	2,688[3]	Docked with *Mir* 3/16/95; Thagard was 1st Amer. on the Russ. spacecraft; Valery Polyakov returned to Earth, 3/22/95, after record stay in space (439 days)
6/27/95	Atlantis (STS-71)	R. Gibson (5), Charles J. Precourt (2), E. Baker (3), Gregory J. Harbaugh (2), Dunbar (4), Solovyev (4) (to *Mir*), Nikolai M. Budarin (to *Mir*), Thagard (5) (from *Mir*), Strekalov (from *Mir*), Dezhurov (from *Mir*)	269:47	**1st shuttle-*Mir* docking**; exchanged crew members with *Mir;* Thagard, with his stay on *Mir,* had spent 115 days in space
11/12/95	Atlantis (STS-74)	Kenneth D. Cameron (3), James D. Halsell Jr. (2), Chris Hadfield, Jerry L. Ross (5), William S. McArthur (2)	196:30	2nd shuttle-*Mir* docking (11/15-11/18); erected a 15-ft permanent docking tunnel to *Mir* for future use by U.S. orbiters
2/22/96	Columbia (STS-75)	Andrew M. Allen (3), Scott J. Horowitz, Chang-Diaz (5), Umberto Guidoni, Hoffman (5), Maurizio Cheli, Nicollier (3)	377:40	Lost an Italian satellite when its tether was severed; microgravity experiments performed; singe marks found on 2 O-rings
3/22/96	Atlantis (STS-76)	Chilton (3), Richard A. Searfoss (2), Sega (2), Michael R. Clifford (3), Linda Godwin (3), Lucid (5) (to *Mir*)	221:15	3rd shuttle-*Mir* docking (5 days); Lucid to *Mir*, 2-person EVA
9/16/96	Atlantis (STS-79)	Apt (4), Terry Wilcutt (2), WilliamReady (3), Akers (4), Carl E. Walz (3), Lucid (5) (from *Mir*), John E. Blaha (5) (to *Mir*)	243:19	Docked with *Mir* 9/18/96; exchanged crew members; **Lucid set U.S. and women's duration in space record (188 days)**
11/19/96	Columbia (STS-80)	Kenneth D. Cockrell (3), Kent V. Rominger (2), Jernigan (4), Thomas D. Jones (3), Musgrave (6)	423:53	Longest-duration shuttle flight; Musgrave was oldest person to fly in space; 2 science satellites deployed and retrieved
1/12/97	Atlantis (STS-81)	Michael A. Baker (4), Brent W. Jett (2), Wisoff (3), Grunsfeld (2), Marsha Ivins (4), Linenger (2) (to *Mir*), Blaha (5) (from *Mir*)	243:30	Docked with *Mir* 1/14-1/19/97; Linenger to *Mir;* Blaha from *Mir*, spent 128 days in space
2/11/97	Discovery (STS-82)	Bowersox (4), Horowitz (2), Joe Tanner (2), Hawley (4), Harbaugh (4), Lee (4), Steve Smith (2)	238:47	Increased capabilities of Hubble Space Telescope; 5 EVAs used to service it
5/15/97	Atlantis (STS-84)	Precourt (3), E. Collins (2), Jean-François Clervoy (2), Carlos Noriega, Ed Lu, Elena Kondakova, Foale (4) (to *Mir*), Linenger (2) (from *Mir*)	221:20	Docked with *Mir* 5/16-5/21; Foale to *Mir;* Linenger from *Mir*, 132 days in space, 2nd-longest time for an American; stay on *Mir* marked by troubles incl. fire 2/23
8/5/97	*Soyuz TM-26	Solovyev (5), Pavel Vinogradov	4,743:35	Docked with *Mir* 8/7/97; repaired damaged space station
8/7/97	Discovery (STS-85)	Brown (4), Rominger (3), Davis (3), Robert L. Curbeam Jr., Stephen K. Robinson, Bjarni V. Tryggvason	284:27	Deployed and retrieved satellite designed to study Earth's middle atmosphere; demonstrated robotic arm
9/25/97	Atlantis (STS-86)	Wetherbee (4), Michael J. Bloomfield, V. Titov (4), Scott Parazynski (2), Jean-Loup Chrétien (3), Lawrence (2), David A. Wolf (2) (to *Mir*), Foale (4) (from *Mir*)	236:24	Docked with *Mir* 9/27-10/3/97; delivered new computer to *Mir;* Wolf to *Mir;* Foale from *Mir;* stay on *Mir* marked by major collision with cargo ship 6/25

Launch Date	Mission[1]	Crew (no. of flights)	Duration (hr:min)	Remarks
1/22/98	Endeavour (STS-89)	Wilcutt (3), Joe F. Edwards Jr., Dunbar (5), Michael P. Anderson, James F. Reilly II, Salizhan Sharipov, Andrew Thomas (2) (to *Mir*), Wolf (2) (from *Mir*)	211:48	Docked with *Mir* 1/24-1/29/98; delivered water and cargo; Thomas to *Mir;* Wolf from *Mir,* 128 days in space
1/29/98	*Soyuz TM-27	Musabayev (2), Budarin (2), Leopold Eyharts	4,923:36	Docked with *Mir* 1/31/98
4/17/98	Columbia (STS-90)	Searfoss (3), Scott D. Altman, Richard M. Linnehan (2), Dafydd Rhys Williams, Kathryn P. Hire, Jay C. Buckey, James A. Pawelczyk	381:50	Studied effects of microgravity on the nervous systems of the crew and over 2,000 live animals; 1st surgery in space on animals meant to survive
6/2/98	Discovery (STS-91)	Precourt (4), Dominic L. Gorie, Lawrence (3), Chang-Diaz (6), Janet L. Kavandi, Valery Ryumin (4), A. Thomas (2) (from *Mir*)	235:53	Final docking mission with *Mir;* Thomas from *Mir,* 141 days in space
10/29/98	Discovery (STS-95)	Brown (5), Steven W. Lindsey (2), Parazynski (3), Robinson (2), Pedro Duque, Chiaki Mukai (2), Glenn (2)	213:44	Sen. John Glenn (D, OH), 77, was **oldest person to fly in space**; Duque was 1st Spaniard in space; experiments to study aging performed on Glenn
12/4/98	Endeavour (STS-88)	Cabana (4), Frederick W. Sturckow, Nancy J. Currie (3), Ross (6), James H. Newman (3), Krivalev (4)	283:18	**1st assembly of International Space Station (ISS)**; attached U.S.-built *Unity* connecting module to Russian-built *Zarya* control module; 1st crew to enter ISS
7/23/99	Columbia (STS-93)	E. Collins (3), Jeffrey S. Ashby, Hawley (5), Catherine G. Coleman (2), Michel Tognini (2)	118:50	Collins was 1st woman to command a space shuttle; deployed Chandra X-ray Observatory telescope
12/19/99	Discovery (STS-103)	Brown (6), Scott Kelly, S. Smith (3), Foale (5), Grunsfeld (3), Nicollier (4), Clervoy (3)	191:10	Replaced equipment on and upgraded Hubble Space Telescope; 3 EVAs
2/11/00	Endeavour (STS-99)	Kevin Kregel (3), Gorie (2), Kavandi (2), Janice E. Voss (5), Mohri (2), Gerhard P.J. Thiele	269:38	Used radar to make most complete topographic map of Earth's surface ever produced
5/19/00	Atlantis (STS-101)	Halsell (5), Horowitz (3), Helms (4), Yury Usachev (3), James S. Voss (4), Mary Ellen Weber (2), Jeffrey N. Williams	236:09	Serviced and resupplied ISS; boosted orbit of ISS to an altitude of about 238 mi; 1 EVA
9/8/00	Atlantis (STS-106)	Wilcutt (4), Altman (2), Lu (2), Richard A. Mastracchio, Daniel C. Burbank, Malenchenko (2), Boris V. Morukov	283:10	Prepared ISS for 1st permanent crew; 1 EVA by all 7 crew members
10/11/00	Discovery (STS-92)	Duffy (4), Pamela A. Melroy, Koichi Wakata (2), Leroy Chiao (3), Wisoff (4), Michael Lopez-Alegria (2), McArthur (3)	309:43	Installed framework structure on ISS, setting the stage for future additions; 4 EVAs
10/31/00	*Soyuz TM-204	Shepherd (4), Yuri Gidzenko (2), Krikalev (5)	—	Established **1st permanent manning of ISS** with 3-person crew for a 4-month stay
11/30/00	Endeavour (STS-97)	Jett (3), Bloomfield (2), Tanner (3), Marc Garneau (3), Noriega (2)	259:57	Delivered 17-ton solar arrays, batteries, and radiators to ISS; 3 EVAs
2/7/01	Atlantis (STS-98)	Cockrell (4), Ivins (5), Jones (4), Curbeam (2), Mark L. Polansky	309:20	Installed U.S. Destiny Laboratory Module on the ISS; 3 EVAs
3/8/01	Discovery (STS-102)	Wetherbee (5), James M. Kelly, Helms (4) (to ISS), James S. Voss (5) (to ISS), Paul Richards, Andrew S.W. Thomas (2), Usachev (4) (to ISS), Shepherd (4) (from ISS), Gidzenko (2) (from ISS), Krikalev (5) (from ISS)	307:49	Transported 2nd permanent crew (Voss, Helms, Usachev) to ISS and returned 1st crew to Earth; 2 EVAs
4/19/01	Endeavour (STS-100)	Rominger (5), John L. Phillips, Hadfield (2), Ashby (2), Parazynski (4), Guidoni (2), Yuri V. Lonchakov	285:30	Installed the Canadarm2, a robotic arm, and delivered supplies to ISS; 2 EVAs
7/12/01	Atlantis (STS-104)	Lindsey (3), Charles O. Hobaugh, Michael L. Gernhardt (4), Kavandi (3), Reilly (2)	259:58	Installed a Joint Airlock, with nitrogen and oxygen tanks to permit future spacewalks from the ISS; 3 EVAs
8/10/01	Discovery (STS-105)	Horowitz (4), Sturckow (2), Daniel Barry (3), Patrick G. Forrester, Culbertson (3) (to ISS), Dezhurov (2) (to ISS), Mikhail Tyurin (to ISS), Usachev, (4), Voss (5) (from ISS), Helms (5) (from ISS)	285:13	Transported Expedition 3 crew to ISS (Culbertson, Tyurin, Dezhurov) and returned Expedition 2 crew to Earth; 2 EVAs
12/5/01	Endeavour (STS-108)	Gorie (3), Mark Kelly, Godwin (4), Daniel Tani, Yury Onufrienko (2) (to ISS), Daniel Bursch (4) (to ISS), Walz (4) (to ISS), Culbertson (3) (from ISS), Dezhurov (2) (from ISS), Tyurin (from ISS)	283:36	Transported Expedition 4 crew to ISS (Onufrienko, Bursch, Walz) and returned Expedition 3 crew to Earth; deployed STARSHINE 2 satellite; 1 EVA
3/1/02	Columbia (STS-109)	Altman (3), Duane G. Carey, Grunsfeld (4), Currie (4), Linnehan (3), Newman (4), Michael J. Massimino	262:10	Installed powerful new camera and upgraded other equipment on Hubble Space Telescope; 5 EVAs
4/8/02	Atlantis (STS-110)	Bloomfield (3), Stephen N. Frick, Rex J. Walheim, Ellen Ochoa (4), Lee M.E. Morin, Ross (7), S. Smith (4)	259:42	Installed S0 Truss, backbone for expansion of ISS; Ross set records with 7th spaceflight, 9th spacewalk; 4 EVAs
6/5/02	Endeavour (STS-111)	Cockrell (5), Paul Lockhart, Chang-Diaz (7), Philippe Perrin, Valery Korzun (2) (to ISS), Peggy Whitson (to ISS), Sergei Treschev (to ISS), Onufrienko (2) (from ISS), Bursch (4) (from ISS), Walz (4) (from ISS)	332:35	Transported Expedition 5 crew to ISS (Korzun, Whitson, Treschev) and returned Expedition 4 crew to Earth; brought platform for ISS robot arm; 3 EVAs
10/7/02	Atlantis (STS 112)	Ashby (3), Melroy (2), Wolf (3), Sandy Magnus, Piers Sellers, Fyodor Yurchikhin	259:58	Installed S1 Truss to ISS; 3 EVAs
10/30/02	*Soyuz TMA-1	Sergei Zalyotin (2), Frank De Winne, Yuri Lonchakov (2)	—	1st launch of Soyuz TMA (Crew returned 11/10/02 on Soyuz TM-34 already docked at ISS)
11/23/02	Endeavour (STS 113)	Wetherbee (6), Lockhart (2), Lopez-Alegria (3), John Herrington, Bowersox (5) (to ISS), Budarin (3) (to ISS), Don Pettit (to ISS), Korzun (2) (from ISS), Whitson (from ISS), Treschev (from ISS)	330:47	Delivered Expedition 6 crew to ISS (Bowersox, Budarin, Pettit) and returned Expedition 5 crew to Earth; installed P1 Truss to ISS; 3 EVAs

Launch Date	Mission[1]	Crew (no. of flights)	Duration (hr:min)	Remarks
1/16/03	Columbia (STS 107)	Rick Husband (2), William McCool, Michael Anderson (2), David Brown, Kalbana Chawla (2), Laurel Clark, Ilan Ramon	382:20	**Entire crew lost when *Columbia* burned up during reentry**, 2/1/03 (*see below*)
4/26/03	*Soyuz TMA-2	Yuri Ivanovich Malenchenko (3), Edward Tsang Lu (3)	—	Delivered Expedition 7 crew to ISS (Malenchenko and Lu)
10/15/03	*Shenzhou 5	Yang Liwei	21:00	**1st Chinese manned spacecraft**
10/18/03	*Soyuz TMA-3	Alexander Kaleri (4), Michale Foale (6), Pedro Duque	—	Delivered Expedition 8 crew to ISS (Foale and Kaleri); Duque returned to Earth 10/27/03 with Expedition 7 crew on TMA-2
4/18/04	*Soyuz TMA-4	Gennady Padalka (2), Edward Fincke, Andre Kuipers	—	Transported Expedition 9 crew to ISS (Fincke and Padalka); Kuipers returned 4/29/04 with Expedition 8 crew on TMA.7-3
6/21/04	SpaceShipOne	Mike Melvill	0:90	**1st privately funded, manned spaceflight**[4]

Note: As of Sept. 2004, there have been 113 space shuttle flights, 87 since the 1986 *Challenger* explosion, but none since the 2003 loss of *Columbia*. Both totals include the final (28th) *Columbia* flight. There are 3 remaining shuttles: the *Discovery* (30 flights), the *Atlantis* (26), and the *Endeavour* (19); the *Challenger* completed 9 missions in all. Four Soviets have died during spaceflight: Vladimir Komarov was killed on *Soyuz 1* (1967) when parachute lines tangled during descent; the 3-person *Soyuz 11* crew (1971) was asphyxiated. Six Americans and an Israeli astronaut died aboard the *Columbia*; 7 Americans died in the *Challenger* explosion, and 3 astronauts—Virgil I. Grissom, Edward H. White, and Roger B. Chaffee—died in the Jan. 27, 1967, *Apollo 1* fire on the ground at Cape Canaveral, FL. (1) For shuttle flights, mission name is in parentheses following name of orbiter. (2) Space stations, such as the *Salyuts* and *Mir*, were used to house crews starting in 1971. (3) Approx. crew duration for Thagard's stay. Crew did not return together. (4) SpaceShipOne flew at least 100 km (62 mi) into space, 9/29/04, piloted by Mike Melvill, and 10/4/04, piloted by Brian Binnie, winning the $10 mil Ansari Prize for first private venture to accomplish this feat twice within 2 weeks.

Columbia Disaster Aftermath

After the loss of the space shuttle *Columbia* and its crew on Feb. 1, 2003, a special panel, the Columbia Accident Investigation Board, issued a report sharply criticizing the "organizational culture" of NASA, saying that complacency and a reduced focus on safety had contributed to the disaster. The specific cause, the board found, was a hole knocked in the heat shield on *Columbia*'s left wing by a chunk of foam insulation that had broken off from one of the large external fuel tanks and hit the wing at a speed of 545 mph. During reentry, hot gases entered the hole, melting *Columbia*'s structure and causing its breakup. Engineers had observed the chunk of foam and suggested that observations be made to see if it had caused damage, but none were undertaken. The board contended that a rescue mission could possibly have been mounted if the foam-caused damage had been investigated.

After the *Columbia* accident, the other space shuttles were grounded. Later, having analyzed the Investigation Board's recommendations, NASA began modifying the remaining shuttles, starting with *Discovery*. Technicians installed wiring for wing leading-edge sensors to register any impact and for a digital camera to monitor the external tank as it separates from the orbiter. Wiring was also installed to support a boom extension for *Discovery*'s robotic arm to give pilots the ability to inspect the outside areas of the craft's thermal protection system while in orbit. The external fuel tank was redesigned to prevent any debris of a critical size from impacting the orbiter.

Discovery was due to launch in spring 2005. Its mission will be to deliver supplies to the International Space Station, but the major focus of the first flight will be the evaluation of the orbiter's safety upgrades.

International Space Station

The International Space Station (ISS) is considered the largest cooperative scientific project in history.

16 cooperating nations: U.S., Russia, Canada, Belgium, Denmark, France, Germany, Italy, Netherlands, Norway, Spain, Sweden, Switzerland, United Kingdom, Japan, and Brazil

Impact of *Columbia* disaster: The grounding of U.S. space shuttles after the *Columbia* disaster in Feb. 2003 deprived the ISS of its main supply ships and put a temporary halt to the further assembly of the station. Since lower capacity Russian *Soyuz* and *Progress* craft were the only means of ferrying provisions and crew to and from Earth, the size of the crew aboard the ISS was reduced to 2. The crew conducted repair and maintenance operations during 2004.

The station when completed:
- mass of 1,040,000 lb
- 356' x 290', with almost an acre of solar panels
- internal volume roughly equivalent to passenger cabin of a 747 jumbo jet
- 6 laboratories; living space for up to 7 people

Examples of research conducted or planned:
- growing living cells in a gravity-free environment
- studying the effects on humans of long-term exposure to reduced gravity
- studying large-scale long-term changes in Earth's environment by observing Earth from orbit

Summary of Worldwide Successful Launches, 1957-2003

Source: National Aeronautics and Space Administration

Year	Total[1]	Russia[2]	U.S.	Japan	ESA[3]	China	France	India	U.K.	Germany	Canada	Israel
1957-59	24	6	18	—	—	—	—	—	—	—	—	—
1960-69	1,035	399	614	—	2	—	4	—	1	—	—	—
1970-79	1,366	1,028	247	18	5	8	14	1	6	3	4	—
1980-89	1,431	1,132	191	26	14	16	5	9	4	7	5	—
1990-99	1,045	542	300	23	55	33	16	11	7	6	4	—
2000-03	264	104	96	7	34	17	0	4	0	0	0	2
TOTAL......	5,165	3,211	1,466	74	110	74	39	26	18	16	13	1

(1) Includes launches sponsored by countries not shown. (2) Data for 1957-91 apply to the Soviet Union, 1992-96 to the Commonwealth of Independent States, after 1996 apply to Russia. (3) European Space Agency.

Notable Proposed Space Missions

Source: National Aeronautics and Space Administration

Planned Launch	Mission	Purpose
Dec. 2004..	Deep Impact	Rendezvous with comet Tempel 1 in July 2005; will crash a small probe into the comet to study the composition of the crater formed by the impact and the debris.
Aug. 2005..	Mars Reconnaissance Orbiter..	Arrive at Mars in Mar. 2006 to search for evidence that water persisted on the surface.
Jan. 2006..	New Horizons (Pluto)	After a gravity boost from Jupiter in 2007, fly by Pluto in 2015, then go on to explore one or more Kuiper Belt objects.
2007	Planck-Herschel Satellite	Study the origins of the universe and "dark matter"; collect data to study whether the universe is finite or infinite.
2009	Mars Science Laboratory	Roving, long-range, long-duration science lab to study the Martian surface.

Notable U.S. Planetary Science Missions

Source: National Aeronautics and Space Administration

Spacecraft	Launch date[1]	Mission	Remarks
Mariner 2	Aug. 27, 1962	Venus	Passed within 22,000 mi of Venus 12/14/62; contact lost 1/3/63 at 54 million mi
Ranger 7	July 28, 1964	Moon	Yielded over 4,000 photos of lunar surface
Mariner 4	Nov. 28, 1964	Mars	Passed behind Mars 7/14/65; took 22 photos from 6,000 mi
Ranger 8	Feb. 17, 1965	Moon	Yielded over 7,000 photos of lunar surface
Surveyor 3	Apr. 17, 1967	Moon	Scooped and tested lunar soil
Mariner 5	June 14, 1967	Venus	In solar orbit; closest Venus flyby 10/19/67
Mariner 6	Feb. 24, 1969	Mars	Came within 2,000 mi of Mars 7/31/69; collected data, photos
Mariner 7	Mar. 27, 1969	Mars	Came within 2,000 mi of Mars 8/5/69
Mariner 9	May 30, 1971	Mars	First craft to orbit Mars 11/13/71; sent back over 7,000 photos
Pioneer 10	Mar. 2, 1972	Jupiter	Passed Jupiter 12/4/73; exited the planetary system 6/13/83; transmission ended 3/31/97 at 6.39 billion mi
Pioneer 11	Apr. 5, 1973	Jupiter, Saturn	Passed Jupiter 12/3/74; Saturn 9/1/79; discovered an additional ring and 2 moons around Saturn; operating in outer solar system; transmission ended 9/95
Mariner 10	Nov. 3, 1973	Venus, Mercury	Passed Venus 2/5/74; arrived Mercury 3/29/74. 1st time gravity of 1 planet (Venus) used to whip spacecraft toward another (Mercury)
Viking 1	Aug. 20, 1975	Mars	Landed on Mars 7/20/76; did scientific research, sent photos; functioned 6 years
Viking 2	Sept. 9, 1975	Mars	Landed on Mars 9/3/76; functioned 3 years
Voyager 1	Sept. 5, 1977	Jupiter, Saturn	Encountered Jupiter 3/5/79, provided evidence of Jupiter ring; passed near Saturn 11/12/80; passed Pioneer 10 to become most distant human-made object 2/17/98
Voyager 2	Aug. 20, 1977	Jupiter, Saturn, Uranus, Neptune	Encountered Jupiter 7/9/79; Saturn 8/25/81; Uranus 1/24/86; Neptune 8/25/89
Pioneer Venus 1	May 20, 1978	Venus	Entered Venus orbit 12/4/78; spent 14 years studying planet; ceased operating 10/19/92
Pioneer Venus 2	Aug. 8, 1978	Venus	Encountered Venus 12/9/78; probes impacted on surface
Magellan	May 4, 1989	Venus	Landed on Venus 8/10/90; orbited and mapped Venus; monitored geological activity on surface; ceased operating 10/11/94
Galileo	Oct. 18, 1989	Jupiter	Used Earth's gravity to propel it toward Jupiter; encountered Venus Feb. 1990; encountered Jupiter 12/7/95; released probe to Jovian surface; encountered moons; disintegrated 9/21/03
Near Earth Asteroid Rendezvous (NEAR)	Feb. 17, 1996	Asteroid Eros	Rendezvoused with *Eros* 4/00; began orbiting and studying the asteroid; communication ceased 2/28/01
Mars Global Surveyor	Nov. 7, 1996	Mars	Began orbiting Mars 9/11/97; began mapping survey of entire surface 3/9/99; discovered magnetism on planet; observed Martian moon Phobos; found evidence of liquid water in past 6/22/00
Mars Pathfinder	Dec. 4, 1996	Mars	Landed on Mars 7/4/97; rover *Sojourner* made measurements of the Martian climate and soil composition, sending thousands of surface images; ceased operating 9/27/97
Cassini-Huygens	Oct. 15, 1997	Saturn	Began orbiting Saturn 6/30/04; 4-year mission to study planet's atmosphere, rings, and moons; *Huygens* probe sched. to land on moon Titan 1/14/05.
Lunar Prospector	Jan. 6, 1998	Moon	Began orbiting Moon 1/11/98; mapped abundance of 11 elements on Moon's surface; discovered evidence of water-ice at both lunar poles; made 1st precise gravity map of entire lunar surface; crashed into crater near Moon's south pole 7/31/99 to end mission
Stardust	Feb. 7, 1999	Comet Wild-2	Reached comet 1/2/04; gathered dust samples; sched. to return them to Earth in 2006.
2001 Mars Odyssey	Apr. 7, 2001	Mars	Reached Mars 10/24/01; primary mission to study climate and geologic history completed 8/04; began extended mission.
Genesis	Aug. 8, 2001	Sun	Orbited Sun, collected particles from solar wind. Capsule containing specimens crashed to Earth 9/8/04 after a failure to deploy its drag chute; some samples survived.
Mars Exploration Rovers	June 7 & July 10, 2003	Mars	Rovers *Spirit* and *Opportunity* landed on Mars Jan. 2004, began studying the geology of the planet, focusing on history of water
Rosetta	Mar. 2, 2004	Comet Churyumov-Gerasimenko	Rendezvous with comet in 2011 to study the object's nucleus and environment. Probe will make a soft-landing on surface.

(1) Coordinated Universal Time

Passenger Traffic at World Airports, 2003[1]

Source: Airports Council International

Airport Location (Name)	Passenger Arrivals and Departures	Airport Location (Name)	Passenger Arrivals and Departures
London, UK (Heathrow)	63,487,136	Munich, Germany (Munich)	24,193,304
Tokyo/Haneda, Japan (Tokyo Intl.)	62,876,269	Barcelona, Spain (El Prat)	22,747,817
Frankfurt, Germany (Rhein/Main)	48,351,664	Paris, France (Orly)	22,457,037
Paris, France (Charles De Gaulle)	48,220,436	Mexico City, Mexico (Mexico City)	21,693,595
Amsterdam, Netherlands (Schiphol)	39,960,400	Seoul, South Korea (Kimpo Intl.)	19,937,146
Madrid, Spain (Barajas)	35,854,293	Manchester, UK (Manchester)	19,901,157
Bangkok, Thailand (Bangkok Intl.)	30,175,379	Jakarta, Indonesia (Soekarno Hatta)	19,703,840
London, UK (Gatwick)	30,007,021	Palma De Mallorca, Spain (Palma de Mallorca)	19,178,941
Hong Kong, China (Hong Kong Intl.)	27,092,290	Osaka, Japan (Itami)	18,829,733
Tokyo, Japan (Narita)	26,537,406	Fukuoka, Japan (Fukuoka)	18,811,039
Rome, Italy (Fiumicino)	26,284,478	London, UK (Stansted)	18,716,691
Sydney, Australia (Kingsford Smith)	25,333,508	Sapporo, Japan (Chitose)	18,459,717
Toronto, Ontario (Lester B. Pearson Intl.)	24,739,312	Dubai, UAE (Dubai)	18,062,344
Singapore (Changi)	24,664,137	Melbourne, Australia (Melbourne)	17,738,139
Beijing, China (Beijing Capital Intl.)	24,363,860	Copenhagen, Denmark (Copenhagen)	17,643,641

(1) Excludes U.S. airports (see page 217), and airports not participating in Airports Council Intl. Airport Traffic Statistics collection.

Passenger Traffic at U.S. Airports, 2003

Source: Airports Council International-North America

Airport	Passenger Arrivals and Departures	Airport	Passenger Arrivals and Departures	Airport	Passenger Arrivals and Departures
Hartsfield Atlanta (ATL)	79,086,792	Houston (IAH)	34,154,574	Orlando (MCO)	27,319,223
Chicago O'Hare (ORD)	69,508,672	Minneapolis/St. Paul (MSP)	33,201,860	Seattle-Tacoma (SEA)	26,755,888
Los Angeles (LAX)	54,982,838	Detroit (DTW)	32,664,620	Philadelphia (PHL)	24,671,075
Dallas/Ft. Worth (DFW)	53,253,607	JFK-New York (JFK)	31,732,371	Boston Logan (BOS)	22,791,169
Denver (DEN)	37,505,138	Miami (MIA)	29,595,618	La Guardia-New York (LGA)	22,482,770
Phoenix Sky Harbor (PHX)	37,412,165	Newark (EWR)	29,431,061	Charlotte (CLT)	21,717,797
Las Vegas (LAS)	36,285,932	San Francisco (SFO)	29,313,271		

U.S. Scheduled Airline Traffic, 1990-2003

Source: Courtesy of Air Transport Association of America, Inc. Reprinted with permission.
Copyright ©2004 by Air Transport Association of America, Inc. All rights reserved.
(in thousands, except where otherwise noted)

	1990	1995	2000	2001*	2002*	2003*
Revenue passengers enplaned	465,600	547,800	666,200	622,100	612,877	646,523
Revenue passenger miles	457,926,000	540,656,000	692,757,000	651,700,000	641,102,000	655,850,000
Available seat miles	733,375,000	807,078,000	956,950,000	930,511,000	892,554,000	893,902,000
% of seating utilized	62.4	67.0	72.4	70.0	71.8	73.4
Cargo traffic (ton miles)	12,549,000	16,921,000	23,888,000	22,003,000	23,243,000	24,608,000
Passenger revenue	$58,453,000	$69,594,000	$93,622,000	$80,947,000	$73,577,000	NA
Net profit	−$3,921,000	$2,314,000	$2,486,000	−$8,275,000	−$11,312,415	−3,624,682
Employees[1]	545,809	546,987	679,967	671,969	601,355	570,868

NA = Not available. **1. Note: Not in thousands.** *Revenues and profit measures include aid payments from the U.S. government after Sept. 2001 terrorist attacks.

Leading U.S. Passenger Airlines, 2003

Source: Courtesy of Air Transport Association of America, Inc. Reprinted with permission.
©2004 by Air Transport Association of America, Inc. All rights reserved.
(in thousands)

Airline	Passengers	Airline	Passengers	Airline	Passengers	Airline	Passengers
American	88,151	America West	20,031	Skywest	10,719	Mesaba	5,702
Delta	84,076	Alaska	15,046	ATA	9,386	Hawaiian	5,597
Southwest	74,719	American Eagle	12,474	Atlantic Southeast	9,205	Frontier	5,061
United	66,018	AirTran	11,651	JetBlue	8,949	Horizon	4,934
Northwest	51,865	Continental Express	11,227	Atlantic Coast	8,390	Aloha	4,119
US Airways	41,250	Comair	10,935	Air Wisconsin	5,865	Spirit	4,105
Continental	38,474						

U.S. Airline Safety, Scheduled Commercial Carriers, 1985-2003

Source: Federal Aviation Administration

	Departures (millions)	Fatal accidents	Fatalities	Accident rate[2]		Departures (millions)	Fatal accidents	Fatalities	Accident rate[2]
1985	6.1	4	197	0.066	1995	8.1	2	166	0.025
1986[1]	6 9	2	5	0.014	1996	7.9	3	342	0.038
1987[1]	7.3	4	231	0.041	1997	9.9	3	3	0.030
1988[1]	7.3	3	285	0.027	1998	10.5	1	1[3]	0.009
1989	7.3	8	131	0.110	1999	10.9	2	12	0.018
1990	7.8	6	39	0.077	2000	11.0	3	92	0.027
1991	7.5	4	162	0.053	2001[1]	10.6	6	531	0.019
1992	7.5	4	33	0.053	2002	9.9	0	0	0.000
1993	7.7	1	1	0.013	2003[4]	9.8	2	22	0.020
1994[1]	7.8	4	239	0.051					

(1) Sabotage-caused accidents are included in the number of fatal accidents and fatalities, but not in the calculation of accident rates. (2) Fatal accidents per 100,000 departures. (3) On-ground employee fatality. (4) Preliminary figures.

Aircraft Operating Statistics

Source: Courtesy of Air Transport Association of America, Inc. Reprinted with permission. Copyright © 2003 by Air Transport Association of America, Inc. All rights reserved. Figures are averages for most commonly used models.

	No. of seats	Speed airborne (mph)	Flight length (mi)	Fuel (gal per hr)	Operating cost per hr		No. of seats	Speed airborne (mph)	Flight length (mi)	Fuel (gal per hr)	Operating cost per hr
B747-200/300*	370	520	3,148	3,625	$9,153	B727-200*	148	430	644	1,289	$4,075
B747-400	367	534	3,960	3,411	8,443	B727-100*	—	417	468	989	13,667
B747-100*	—	503	2,022	1,762	3,852	A320	146	454	1,065	767	2,359
B747-F*	—	506	2,512	3,593	7,138	B737-400	141	409	646	703	2,595
L-1011	325	494	2,023	1,981	8,042	MD-80	134	432	791	953	2,718
DC-10*	286	497	1,637	2,405	7,374	B737-700LR	132	441	879	740	1,692
B767-400	265	495	1,682	1,711	3,124	B737-300/700	132	403	542	723	2,388
B-777	263	525	3,515	2,165	5,105	A319	122	442	904	666	1,913
A330	261	509	3,559	1,407	3,076	A310-200*	—	455	847	1,561	8,066
MD-11*	261	515	2,485	2,473	7,695	B737-100/200	119	396	465	824	2,377
A300-600*	235	460	947	1,638	6,518	B717-200	112	339	175	573	3,355
B757-300	235	472	1,309	985	2,345	B737-500	110	407	576	756	2,347
B767-300ER*	207	497	2,122	1,579	4,217	DC-9	101	387	496	826	2,071
DC-8*	—	437	686	1,712	8,065	F-100	87	398	587	662	2,303
B757-200*	181	464	1,175	1,045	3,312	B737-200C	55	387	313	924	3,421
B767-200ER	175	487	1,987	1,404	3,873	ERJ-145	50	360	343	280	1,142
A321	169	454	1,094	673	1,347	CRJ-145	49	397	486	369	1,433
B737-800/900	151	454	1,035	770	2,248	ERJ-135	37	357	382	267	969
MD-90	150	446	886	825	2,716	SD 340B	33	230	202	84	644

* Data includes cargo operations.

WORLD ALMANAC QUICK QUIZ

Which of these airports around the world had the most passenger traffic in 2003?

(a) Chicago O'Hare   (b) Hartsfield Atlanta   (c) London Heathrow   (d) Amsterdam Schiphol

For the answer look in this chapter, or see page 1008.

Some Notable Aviation Firsts[1]

1903 — On Dec. 17, near Kitty Hawk, NC, brothers Wilbur and Orville Wright made the 1st human-carrying, powered flight. Each made 2 flights; the longest, about 852 ft, lasted 59 sec.

1907 — U.S. airplane manufacturing company formed by Glenn H. Curtiss.

1908 — 1st airplane passenger, Lt. Frank P. Lahm, rode with Wilbur Wright in a brief (6 min, 24 sec) flight.

1911 — 1st transportation of mail by airplane officially approved by the U.S. Postal Service began on Sept. 23. It lasted one week. In 1918, limited scheduled airmail service began. By 1921, scheduled transcontinental airmail service began between New York City and San Francisco.

1914 — 1st scheduled passenger airline service began. It operated between St. Petersburg and Tampa, FL.

1919 — 1st airline food, a basket lunch, was served as part of a commercial airline service.

1930 — Ellen Church became 1st flight attendant.

1939 — On Aug. 27, the German Heinkel He 178 made the 1st successful flight powered by a jet engine.

1947 — Mach 1, the sound barrier was broken by Amer. Chuck Yeager in a Bell X-1 rocket-powered aircraft.

1947 — Largest airplane ever flown, Howard Hughes's "Spruce Goose," flew 1 mi at an altitude of 80 ft.

1953 — Jacqueline Cochran became 1st woman to fly faster than sound.

1960 — Convair B-58, 1st supersonic bomber, was introduced.

1968 — The supersonic speed of Mach 2 was accomplished for 1st time, in a Tupolev Tu-144. The plane had an approximate maximum speed of 1,200 mph.

1970 — The Tupolev Tu-144, during commercial transport, exceeded Mach 2. It reached about 1,335 mph at 53,475 ft.

1976 — The Concorde began 1st scheduled supersonic commercial service.

1977 — The Gossamer Condor successfully demonstrated human-powered flight, completing figure-8 course of 1.15 miles.

1979 — The human-powered Gossamer Albatross crossed the English Channel in 2 hr, 49 min.

(1) Excludes notable around-the-world and international trips.

Some Notable Around-the-World and Intercontinental Trips

Aviator or Craft	From/To	Miles	Time	Date
Nellie Bly	New York/New York		72d 06h 11m	1889
George Francis Train	New York/New York		67d 12h 03m	1890
Charles Fitzmorris	Chicago/Chicago		60d 13h 29m	1901
J. W. Willis Sayre	Seattle/Seattle		54d 09h 42m	1903
J. Alcock-A.W. Brown [1]	Newfoundland/Ireland	1,960	16h 12m	June 14-15, 1919
2 U.S. Army airplanes	Seattle/Seattle	26,103	35d 01h 11m	1924
Richard E. Byrd, Floyd Bennett [2]	Spitsbergen (Nor.)/N. Pole	1,545	15h 30m	May 9, 1926
Amundsen-Ellsworth-Nobile Polar Expedition (in a dirigible)	Spitsbergen (Nor.)/over N. Pole to Teller, Alaska		80h	May 11-14,1926
E.S. Evans and L. Wells (*N.Y. World*)	New York/New York	18,410[3]	28d 14h 36m 05s	June 16-July 14, 1926
Charles Lindbergh[4]	New York/Paris	3,610	33h 29m 30s	May 20-21, 1927
Amelia Earhart, W. Stultz, L. Gordon	Newfoundland/Wales		20h 40m	June 17-18, 1928
Graf Zeppelin	Friedrichshafen, Ger./Lakehurst, NJ	6,630	4d 15h 46m	Oct. 11-15, 1928
Graf Zeppelin	Friedrichshafen, Ger./Lakehurst, NJ	21,700	20d 04h	Aug. 14-Sept. 4, 1929 July 1, 1931
Wiley Post and Harold Gatty (Monoplane Winnie Mae)	New York/New York	15,474	8d 15h 51m	
C. Pangborn-H. Herndon Jr.[5]	Misawa, Japan/Wenatchee, WA	4,458	41h 34m	Oct. 3-5, 1931
Amelia Earhart [6]	Newfoundland/Ireland	2,026	14h 56m	May 20-21, 1932
Wiley Post (Monoplane Winnie Mae)[7]	New York/New York	15,596	115h 36m 30s	July 15-22, 1933
Hindenburg Zeppelin	Lakehurst, NJ/Frankfort, Ger.		42h 53m	Aug. 9-11, 1936
Howard Hughes and 4 assistants	New York/New York	14,824	3d 19h 08m 10s	July 10-13, 1938 June 17-30, 1947
America, Pan American 4-engine Lockheed Constellation[8]	New York/New York	22,219	101h 32m	
Col. Edward Eagan	New York/New York	20,559	147h 15m	Dec. 13, 1948
USAF B-50 Lucky Lady II (Capt. James Gallagher) [9]	Ft. Worth, TX/Ft. Worth, TX	23,452	94h 01m	Mar. 2, 1949
Col. D. Schilling, USAF [10]	England/Limestone, ME	3,300	10h 01m	Sept. 22, 1950
C.F. Blair Jr.	Norway/Alaska	3,300	10h 29m	May 29, 1951
Canberra Bomber [11]	N. Ireland/Newfoundland	2073	04h 34m	Aug. 26, 1952
	Newfoundland/N. Ireland	2073	03h 25m	Aug. 26, 1952
3 USAF B-52 Strato-fortresses [12]	Merced, CA/CA	24,325	45h 19m	Jan. 15-18, 1957
USSR TU-114 [13]	Moscow/New York	5,092	11h 06m	June 28, 1959
Peter Gluckmann (solo)	San Francisco/San Francisco	22,800	29d	Aug. 22-Sept. 20, 1959
Robert & Joan Wallick	Manila/Manila	23,129	5d 06h 17m 10s	June 2-7, 1966
Trevor K. Brougham	Darwin, Australia/Darwin	24,800	5d 05h 57m	Aug. 5-10, 1972
Arnold Palmer	Denver/Denver	22,985	57h 7m 12s	May 17-19, 1976
Boeing 747[14]	San Francisco/San Francisco	26,382	57h 25m 42s	Oct. 28-31, 1977
Richard Rutan & Jeana Yeager[15]	Edwards AFB, CA	24,986	09d 03m 44s	Dec. 14-23, 1986
Concorde	New York/New York	1,114 mph	31h 27m 49s	Aug. 15-16, 1995
Col. Douglas L. Raaberg and crew, B1 bomber[16]	Dyess AFB, Abilene, TX/ Dyess AFB	6,250	36h 13m 36s	June 3, 1995
Linda Finch[17]	Oakland, CA/Oakland, CA	26,000	73d	Mar. 17-May 28, 1997
Bertrand Piccard, Brian Jones[18]	Switzerland/Egypt	29,054.6	19d 21h 55m	Mar. 1-21, 1999
Steve Fossett[19]	Australia/Australia	21,109.6	14d 20h 01m	June 19-July 4, 2002

(1) Nonstop transatlantic flight. (2) Claim of reaching N. Pole in dispute; if claim is untrue, then Amundsen-Ellsworth-Nobile were the first to fly over N. Pole. (3) Includes mileage by train and auto, 4,110; by plane, 6,300; by steamship, 8,000. (4) Solo transatlantic flight in the Ryan monoplane "Spirit of St. Louis." (5) Nonstop transpacific flight. (6) First woman's transoceanic solo flight. Earhart disappeared in the Pacific in 1937 while attempting an around-the-world flight. (7) First to fly solo around N circumference of the world and first to fly twice around the world. (8) Inception of regular commercial global air service. (9) First nonstop round-the-world flight, refueled 4 times in flight. (10) Nonstop jet transatlantic flight. (11) Transatlantic round trip on same day. (12) First nonstop global flight by jet planes; refueled in flight by KC-97 aerial tankers; average speed approx. 525 mph. (13) Nonstop between Moscow and New York. (14) Speed record around the world over both Earth's poles. (15) Circled Earth nonstop without refueling. (16) Refueled in flight 6 times. Tested B-1B bomber by bombing 3 pre-arranged target sites on 3 continents. (17) Followed the intended around-the-world flight route (1937) of Amelia Earhart. (18) First to circumnavigate the globe nonstop in a balloon. (19) First solo circumnavigation of the globe nonstop in a balloon; time, dates, and distance are for complete flight, which exceeded circumnavigation because winds prevented landing.

NATIONAL DEFENSE

Chief Commanding Officers of the U.S. Military

Chairman, Joint Chiefs of Staff
Gen. Richard B. Myers (USAF)
Vice Chairman
Gen. Peter Pace (USMC)

The **Joint Chiefs of Staff** consists of the Chairman and Vice Chairman of the Joint Chiefs of Staff; the Chief of Staff, U.S. Army; the Chief of Naval Operations; the Chief of Staff, U.S. Air Force; and the Commandant of the Marine Corps.

Army

Chief of Staff	Date of Rank
Gen. Peter J. Schoomaker	Oct. 4, 1997

Other Generals

Abizaid, John	June 27, 2003
Bell, Burwell B.	Dec. 2002
Brown, Bryan D.	Aug. 25, 2003
Byrnes, Kevin P.	Nov. 7, 2002
Casey, George W., Jr.	July 1, 2004
Cody, Richard	June 24, 2004
Hill, James T.	Aug. 18, 2002
Kern, Paul J.	Oct. 30, 2001
LaPorte, Leon	May 1, 2002
McNeill, Dan K.	June 3, 2004

Air Force

Chief of Staff	Date of Rank
Gen. John P. Jumper	Nov. 17, 1997

Other Generals

Cook, Donald G.	Dec, 17, 2001
Eberhart, Ralph E.	Aug. 1, 1997
Foglesong, Robert H.	Nov. 5, 2001
Handy, John W.	July 1, 2000
Hornburg, Hal M.	Aug. 1, 2000
Lord, Lance W.	Apr. 19, 2002
Martin, Gregory S.	June 1, 2000
Moseley, T. Michael	Oct. 1, 2002
Myers, Richard B.	Sept. 1, 1997
Wald, Charles F.	Jan. 1, 2003

Navy

Chief of Naval Operations	Date of Rank
Adm. Vernon E. Clark	Nov. 1, 1999

Other Admirals

Bowman, Frank L. (submariner)	Oct. 1, 1996
Doran, Walter F. (surface warfare)	May 4, 2002
Fallon, William J. (aviator)	Nov. 1, 2000
Fargo, Thomas B. (submariner)	Dec. 1, 1999
Giambastiani, Edmund P., Jr. (submariner)	Oct. 2, 2002
Johnson, Gregory G. (aviator)	Oct. 24, 2001
Mullen, Michael G. (surface warfare)	Aug. 28, 2003

Marine Corps

Commandant of the Marine Corps (CMC)	Date of Rank
Gen. Michael W. Hagee	Jan. 13, 2003

Other Generals

Nyland, William L.	Sept. 4, 2002
Pace, Peter	Sept. 8, 2000

Coast Guard

Commandant, with rank of Admiral	Date of Rank
Thomas H. Collins	May 30, 2002

Vice Commandant, with rank of Vice Admiral	
Thomas J. Barrett	May 30, 2002

Unified Combatant Commands Commanders-in-Chief

U.S. European Command, Stuttgart-Vaihingen, Germany —Gen. James L. Jones (USMC)
U.S. Pacific Command, Honolulu, HI — Adm. Thomas B. Fargo (USN)
U.S. Joint Forces Command, Norfolk, VA — Adm. Edmund P. Giambastiani
U.S. Special Operations Command, MacDill AFB, Florida — Gen. Bryan D. Brown (U.S. Army)
U.S. Transportation Command, Scott AFB, Illinois — Gen. John W. Handy (USAF)
U.S. Central Command, MacDill AFB, Florida — Gen. John Abizaid (U.S. Army)
U.S. Southern Command, Miami, FL — Gen. James T. Hill (U.S. Army)
U.S. Northern Command, Peterson AFB, Colorado — Gen. Ralph E. Eberhart (USAF)
U.S. Strategic Command, Offutt AFB, Nebraska — Adm. James O. Ellis Jr. (USN)

North Atlantic Treaty Organization (NATO) International Commands

NATO Headquarters: Chairman, NATO Military Committee — Gen. Harald Kujat (Germany)
Strategic Commands:
Allied Command Operations (ACO) — Gen. James L. Jones (USMC), Supreme Allied Commander, Europe
Allied Command Transformation (ACT) — Adm. Edmund P. Giambastiani (USN), Supreme Allied Commander Transformation
ACO Subordinate Commands:
Joint Force Command Brunnsum (JFC Brunnsum) — Gen. Gerhard W. Back (German Luftwaffe), Commander, Brunnsum
Joint Force Command Naples (JFC Naples) — Adm. Gregory G. Johnson (USN), Commander, Naples
Joint Headquarters Lisbon (JHQ Lisbon) — Vice Adm. H.G. Ulrich III (USN), Commander, Lisbon

Chairmen of the Joint Chiefs of Staff, 1949-2003

Gen. of the Army Omar N. Bradley, USA	8/16/49 –8/14/53	Gen. David C. Jones, USAF	6/21/78 – 6/18/82
Adm. Arthur W. Radford, USN	8/15/53 – 8/14/57	Gen. John W. Vessey Jr., USA	6/18/82 – 9/30/85
Gen. Nathan F. Twining, USAF	8/15/57 – 9/30/60	Adm. William J. Crowe, Jr., USN	10/1/85 – 9/30/89
Gen. Lyman L. Lemnitzer, USA	10/1/60 – 10/30/62	Gen. Colin L. Powell, USA	10/1/89 – 9/30/93
Gen. Maxwell D. Taylor, USA	10/1/62 – 7/3/64	Gen. John M. Shalikashvili, USA	10/1/93 – 9/30/97
Gen. Earle G. Wheeler, USA	7/3/64 – 7/2/70	Gen. Henry H. Shelton, USA	10/1/97 – 9/30/01
Adm. Thomas H. Moorer, USN	7/3/70 – 6/30/74	Gen. Richard B. Myers, USAF	10/1/01 –
Gen. George S. Brown, USAF	7/1/74 – 6/20/78		

Military Units, U.S. Army and Air Force

ARMY UNITS. Squad: In infantry usually 4-10 enlisted personnel under a staff sergeant. **Platoon:** In infantry 3-4 squads under a lieutenant. **Company:** Headquarters section and 3-4 platoons under a captain. (Company-size unit in the artillery is a battery; in the cavalry, a troop.) **Battalion:** Hdqts. and 3-5 companies under a lieutenant colonel. (Battalion-size unit in the cavalry is a squadron.) **Brigade:** Hdqts. and 3 or more battalions under a colonel. **Division:** Hdqts. and 3 brigades with artillery, combat support, and combat service support units under a major general. **Army Corps:** Two or more divisions with corps troops under a lieutenant general. **Field Army:** Hdqts. and 2 or more corps with field Army troops under a general.

AIR FORCE UNITS. Flight: Numerically designated flights are the lowest level unit in the Air Force. They are used primarily where there is a need for small mission elements to be incorporated into an organized unit. **Squadron:** A squadron is the basic unit in the Air Force. It is used to designate the mission units in operational commands. **Group:** The group is a flexible unit composed of 2 or more squadrons whose functions may be operational, support, or administrative in nature. **Wing:** An operational wing normally has 2 or more assigned mission squadrons in an area such as combat, flying training, or airlift. **Numbered Air Forces:** Normally an operationally oriented agency, the numbered air force is designed for the control of 2 or more wings with the same mission and/or geographical location. **Major Command:** A major subdivision of the Air Force that is assigned a major segment of the USAF mission. Major Command is composed of 3 or more numbered air forces.

Principal U.S. Military Training Centers

Air Force

Name, PO address	ZIP	Nearest city	Name, PO address	ZIP	Nearest city
Columbus AFB, MI	39701	Tupelo	Maxwell AFB, AL	36112	Montgomery
Goodfellow AFB, TX	76908	San Angelo	Sheppard AFB, TX	76311	Wichita Falls
Keesler AFB, MS	39534	Biloxi	All are Air Education and Training Command Bases.		
Lackland AFB, TX	78236	San Antonio			

Army

Name, PO address	ZIP	Nearest city	Name, PO address	ZIP	Nearest city
Aberdeen Proving Ground, MD	21005	Aberdeen	Fort Lee, VA	23801	Petersburg
Carlisle Barracks, PA	17013	Carlisle	Fort McClellan, AL	36205	Anniston
Fort Benning, GA	31905	Columbus	Fort Rucker, AL	36362	Dothan
Fort Bliss, TX	79916	El Paso	Fort Sill, OK	73503	Lawton
Fort Bragg, NC	28307	Fayetteville	Fort Leonard Wood, MO	65473	Waynesville
Fort Gordon, GA	30905	Augusta	Joint Readiness Training Center,		
Fort Huachuca, AZ	85613	Sierra Vista	Ft. Polk, LA	71459	Leesville
Fort Jackson, SC	29207	Columbia	National Training Center, Ft. Irwin, CA	92310	Barstow, CA
Fort Knox, KY	40121	Radcliff	The Judge Advocate General's Legal		
Fort Leavenworth, KS	66027	Leavenworth	Center and School, VA	22903	Charlottesville

Marine Corps

Name, PO address	ZIP	Nearest city	Name, PO address	ZIP	Nearest city
MCB Camp Lejeune, NC	28547	Jacksonville	MCAS Cherry Point, NC	28533	Havelock
MCB Camp Pendleton, CA	92055	Oceanside	MCAS Miramar, CA	92145	San Diego
MCB Kaneohe Bay, HI	96863	Kailua	MCAS New River, NC	28545	Jacksonville
MCAGCC Twentynine Palms, CA	92278	Palm Springs	MCAS Beaufort, SC	29904	Beaufort
MCCDC Quantico, VA	22134	Quantico	MCAS Yuma, AZ	85369	Yuma
MCRD Parris Island, SC	29905	Beaufort	MCMWTC Bridgeport, CA	93517	Bridgeport
MCRD San Diego, CA	92140	San Diego			

MCB = Marine Corps Base. MCAGCC = Marine Corps Air-Ground Combat Center. MCCDC = Marine Corps Combat Development Command. MCRD = Marine Corps Recruit Depot. MCAS = Marine Corps Air Station. MCMWTC = Marine Corps Mountain Warfare Training Center.

Navy

Name, PO address	ZIP	Nearest city	Name, PO address	ZIP	Nearest city
Naval Education & Training Ctr	32508	Pensacola, FL	Naval Submarine School	06349	Groton, CT
Naval Air Training Center	78419	Corpus Christi,TX	Naval Training Ctr., Great Lakes	60088	N. Chicago, IL
Training Command Fleet	92113	San Diego, CA	Naval War College	02841	Newport, RI
Naval Aviation Schools Command	32508	Pensacola, FL	Naval Air Tech. Training Ctr	32508	Pensacola, FL
Naval Education & Training Ctr	02841	Newport, RI	Fleet Antisubmarine Warfare	92147	San Diego, CA
Naval Post Graduate School	93943	Monterey, CA			

The Federal Service Academies

U.S. Military Academy, West Point, NY. Founded 1802. Awards BS degree and Army commission for a 5-year service obligation. For admissions information, write Admissions Office, Bldg. 606, USMA, West Point, NY 10996. www.usma.edu

U.S. Naval Academy, Annapolis, MD. Founded 1845. Awards BS degree and Navy or Marine Corps commission for a 5-year service obligation. For admissions information, write Candidate Guidance Office, Naval Academy, 117 Decatur Rd., Annapolis, MD 21402-5018. www.usna.edu

U.S. Air Force Academy, Colorado Springs, CO. Founded 1954. Awards BS degree and Air Force commission for a 6-year service obligation. For admissions information, write Registrar, U.S. Air Force Academy, CO 80840-5025. www.usafa.edu

U.S. Coast Guard Academy, New London, CT. Founded 1876. Awards BS degree and Coast Guard commission for a 5-year service obligation. For admissions information, write Director of Admissions, Coast Guard Academy, 31 Mohegan Ave., New London, CT 06320-8103. www.cga.edu

U.S. Merchant Marine Academy, Kings Point, NY. Founded 1943. Awards BS degree, a license as a deck, engineer, or dual officer, and a U.S. Naval Reserve commission. Service obligations vary according to options taken by the graduate. For admissions information, write Admission Office, U.S. Merchant Marine Academy, 300 Steamboat Rd., Kings Point, NY 11024. www.usmma.edu

Personal Salutes and Honors, U.S.

The U.S. **national salute,** 21 guns, is also the salute to a national flag. U.S. independence is commemorated by the salute to the Union—one gun for each state—fired at noon July 4, at all military posts provided with suitable artillery.

A 21-gun salute on arrival and departure, with 4 ruffles and flourishes, is rendered to the **president** of the United States, to a former president, and to a president-elect. The national anthem or "Hail to the Chief," as appropriate, is played for the president, and the national anthem for the others. A 21-gun salute on arrival and departure, with 4 ruffles and flourishes, also is rendered to the **sovereign or chief of state of a foreign country** or a member of a reigning royal family, and the national anthem of his or her country is played. The music is considered an inseparable part of the salute and immediately follows the ruffles and flourishes without pause. For the Honors March, generals receive the "General's March," admirals receive the "Admiral's March," and all others receive the 32-bar medley of "The Stars and Stripes Forever."

GRADE, TITLE, OR OFFICE	SALUTE (IN GUNS) Arriving	Leaving	Ruffles and flourishes	Music
Vice president of United States	19		4	Hail, Columbia
Speaker of the House	19		4	Honors March
U.S. or foreign ambassador	19		4	Nat. anthem of official
Premier or prime minister	19		4	Nat. anthem of official
Secretary of Defense, Army, Navy, or Air Force	19	19	4	Honors March
Other cabinet members, Senate president pro tempore, governor, or chief justice of U.S.	19		4	Honors March
Chairman, Joint Chiefs of Staff	19	19	4	
Army chief of staff, chief of naval operations, Air Force chief of staff, Marine commandant	19	19	4	Honors March
General of the Army, general of the Air Force, fleet admiral	19	19	4	
Generals, admirals	17	17	4	
Assistant secretaries of Defense, Army, Navy, or Air Force	17	17	4	Honors March
Chair of a committee of Congress	17		4	Honors March

OTHER SALUTES (on arrival only) include: 15 guns, with 3 ruffles and flourishes, for U.S. envoys or ministers and foreign envoys or ministers accredited to the U.S.; 15 guns, for a lieutenant general or vice admiral; 13 guns, with 2 ruffles and flourishes, for a major general or rear admiral (upper half) and for U.S. ministers resident and ministers resident accredited to the U.S.; 11 guns, with 1 ruffle and flourish, for a brigadier general or rear admiral (lower half) and for U.S. charges d'affaires and like officials accredited to the U.S.; 11 guns, no ruffles and flourishes, for consuls general accredited to the U.S.

U.S. Army, Navy, Air Force, Marine Corps, and Coast Guard Insignia

Source: Dept. of the Army, Dept. of the Navy, Dept. of the Air Force, U.S. Dept. of Defense

Army

General of the Armies — Gen. John J. Pershing (1860-1948), the only person to have held this rank in life, was authorized to prescribe his own insignia, but never wore in excess of four stars. The rank originally was established posthumously by Congress for George Washington in 1799, and he was promoted to the rank by joint resolution of Congress, approved by Pres. Gerald Ford, Oct. 19, 1976.

General of the Army — Five silver stars fastened together in a circle and the coat of arms of the United States in gold color metal with shield and crest enameled.

General	Four silver stars
Lieutenant General	Three silver stars
Major General	Two silver stars
Brigadier General	One silver star
Colonel	Silver eagle
Lieutenant Colonel	Silver maple leaf
Major	Gold maple leaf
Captain	Two silver bars
First Lieutenant	One silver bar
Second Lieutenant	One gold bar

Warrant Officers

Grade Five — Silver bar with 4 enamel silver squares
Grade Four — Silver bar with 4 enamel black squares
Grade Three — Silver bar with 3 enamel black squares
Grade Two — Silver bar with 2 enamel black squares
Grade One — Silver bar with 1 enamel black squares

Noncommissioned Officers

Sergeant Major of the Army (E-9) — Three chevrons above 3 arcs, with an American Eagle centered on the chevrons, flanked by 2 stars—one star on each side of the eagle. Also wears distinctive red and white shield collar insignia.

Command Sergeant Major (E-9) — Three chevrons above 3 arcs with a 5-pointed star with a wreath around the star between the chevrons and arcs.

Sergeant Major (E-9) — Three chevrons above 3 arcs with a 5-pointed star between the chevrons and arcs.

First Sergeant (E-8) — Three chevrons above 3 arcs with a lozenge between the chevrons and arcs.

Master Sergeant (E-8) — Three chevrons above 3 arcs.

Sergeant First Class (E-7) — Three chevrons above 2 arcs.

Staff Sergeant (E-6) — Three chevrons above 1 arc.

Sergeant (E-5) — Three chevrons.

Corporal (E-4) — Two chevrons.

Specialists

Specialist (E-4) — Eagle device only.

Other enlisted

Private First Class (E-3) — One chevron above one arc.
Private (E-2) — One chevron.
Private (E-1) — None.

Air Force

Insignia for Air Force officers are identical to those of the Army. Insignia for enlisted personnel are worn on both sleeves and consist of a star and an appropriate number of rockers. Chevrons appear above 5 rockers for the top 3 noncommissioned officer ranks, as follows (in ascending order): Master Sergeant, 1 chevron; Senior Master Sergeant, 2 chevrons; and Chief Master Sergeant, 3 chevrons. The insignia of the Chief Master Sergeant of the Air Force has 3 chevrons and a wreath around the star design.

Navy

The following stripes are worn on the lower sleeves of the Service Dress Blue uniform. They are of gold embroidery.

Rank	Insignia
Fleet Admiral*	1 two inch with 4 one-half inch
Admiral	1 two inch with 3 one-half inch
Vice Admiral	1 two inch with 2 one-half inch
Rear Admiral (upper half)	1 two inch with 1 one-half inch
Rear Admiral (lower half)	1 two inch
Captain	4 one-half inch
Commander	3 one-half inch
Lieutenant Commander	2 one-half inch with 1 one-quarter inch between
Lieutenant	2 one-half inch
Lieutenant (j.g.)	1 one-half inch with one-quarter inch above
Ensign	1 one-half inch
Warrant Officer-W-4	½" stripe with 1 break
Warrant Officer W-3	½" stripe with 2 breaks, 2" apart
Warrant Officer W-2	½" stripe with 3 breaks, 2" apart

Enlisted personnel (noncommissioned petty officers)—A rating badge worn on the upper left sleeve, consisting of a spread eagle, appropriate number of chevrons, and centered specialty mark.

*The rank of Fleet Admiral is reserved for wartime use only.

Marine Corps

Marine Corps' distinctive cap and collar ornament is the Marine Corps Emblem—a combination of the American eagle, a globe, and an anchor. Marine Corps and Army officer insignia are similar. Marine Corps enlisted insignia, although basically similar to the Army's, feature crossed rifles beneath the chevrons. Marine Corps enlisted rank insignia are as follows:

Sergeant Major of the Marine Corps (E-9) — Same as Sergeant Major (below) but with Marine Corps emblem in the center with a 5-pointed star on both sides of the emblem.

Sergeant Major (E-9) — Three chevrons above 4 rockers with a 5-pointed star in the center.

Master Gunnery Sergeant (E-9) — Three chevrons above 4 rockers with a bursting bomb insignia in the center.

First Sergeant (E-8) — Three chevrons above 3 rockers with a diamond in the middle.

Master Sergeant (E-8) — Three chevrons above 3 rockers with crossed rifles in the middle.

Gunnery Sergeant (E-7) — Three chevrons above 2 rockers with crossed rifles in the middle.

Staff Sergeant (E-6) — Three chevrons above 1 rocker with crossed rifles in the middle.

Sergeant (E-5) — Three chevrons above crossed rifles.

Corporal (E-4) — Two chevrons above crossed rifles.

Lance Corporal (E-3) — One chevron above crossed rifles.

Private First Class (E-2) — One chevron.

Private (E-1) — None.

Coast Guard

Coast Guard insignia follow Navy custom, with certain minor changes such as the officer cap insignia. The Coast Guard shield is worn on both sleeves of officers and on the right sleeve of all enlisted personnel.

For Further Information on the U.S. Armed Forces

Army — Office of the Chief of Public Affairs, Attention: Media Relations Division—MRD, Army 1500, Washington, DC 20310-1500. **Website:** www.army.mil

Navy — Chief of Information, 1200 Navy Pentagon, Washington, DC 20350-1200. **Website:** www.navy.mil

Air Force — Office of Public Affairs, 1690 Air Force, Pentagon, Washington, DC 20330-1690. **Website:** www.af.mil

Marine Corps — Marine Corps Headquarters , Division of Public Affairs, U.S. Marine Corps, Washington, DC 20380-1775. **Website:** www.usmc.mil

Coast Guard — Commandant (G-IPA), U.S. Coast Guard, 2100 Second St. SW, Washington, DC 20593-0001. **Website:** www.uscg.mil

Additional information on all the U.S. Armed Forces branches, as well as many other related organizations, can be accessed through DefenseLINK, the official Internet site of the Dept. of Defense: www.defenselink.mil

U.S. Army Personnel on Active Duty[1]

Source: Dept. of the Army, U.S. Dept. of Defense

(As of midyear, except where noted)

Date	Total strength[2]	Commissioned officers			Warrant officers		Enlisted personnel		
		Total	Male	Female[3]	Male[4]	Female	Total	Male	Female
1940	267,767	17,563	16,624	939	763	—	249,441	249,441	—
1942	3,074,184	203,137	190,662	12,475	3,285	—	2,867,762	2,867,762	—
1943	6,993,102	557,657	521,435	36,222	21,919	—	6,413,526	6,358,200	55,325
1944	7,992,868	740,077	692,351	47,726	36,893	10	7,215,888	7,144,601	71,287
1945	8,266,373	835,403	772,511	62,892	56,216	44	7,374,710	7,283,930	90,780
1946	1,889,690	257,300	240,643	16,657	9,826	18	1,622,546	1,605,847	16,699
1950	591,487	67,784	63,375	4,409	4,760	22	518,921	512,370	6,551
1955	1,107,606	111,347	106,173	5,174	10,552	48	985,659	977,943	7,716
1960	871,348	91,056	86,832	4,224	10,141	39	770,112	761,833	8,279
1965	967,049	101,812	98,029	3,783	10,285	23	854,929	846,409	8,520
1970	1,319,735	143,704	138,469	5,235	23,005	13	1,153,013	1,141,537	11,476
1975	781,316	89,756	85,184	4,572	13,214	22	678,324	640,621	37,703
1980 (Sept. 30) . .	772,661	85,339	77,843	7,496	13,265	113	673,944	612,593	61,351
1985 (Sept. 30) . .	776,244	94,103	83,563	10,540	15,296	288	666,557	598,639	67,918
1990 (Mar. 31) . . .	746,220	91,330	79,520	11,810	15,177	470	639,713	567,015	72,698
1995	521,036	72,646	62,250	10,396	12,053	599	435,807	377,832	57,975
1996 (May 31) . . .	493,330	68,850	58,875	9,975	11,456	660	408,511	351,669	56,842
1997 (May 31) . . .	487,297	67,986	58,270	9,716	11,021	719	403,072	342,817	60,255
1998	491,707	67,048	56,650	10,398	10,989	661	402,000	345,149	56,851
1999	479,100	66,613	56,952	9,661	10,767	757	388,211	329,803	58,408
2000	471,633	66,344	56,391	9,953	10,608	781	393,900	333,947	59,953
2001	478,918	64,809	54,570	10,239	10,575	795	398,983	336,264	62,719
2002	485,536	66,446	55,715	10,731	10,900	812	404,363	341,794	62,569
2003 (Sept. 30) . .	499,301	68,198	56,980	11,218	11,273	854	414,769	351,921	62,848
2004	500,203	69,307	NA	NA	NA	NA	414,325	NA	NA

NA = Not available. (1) Represents strength of the active Army, including Philippine Scouts, retired Regular Army personnel on extended active duty, and National Guard and Reserve personnel on extended active duty; excludes U.S. Military Academy cadets, contract surgeons, and National Guard and Reserve personnel not on extended active duty. (2) Data for 1940 to 1946 include personnel in the Army Air Forces and its predecessors (Air Service and Air Corps). (3) Includes women doctors, dentists, and Medical Service Corps officers for 1946 and subsequent years, women in the Army Nurse Corps for all years, and the Women's Army Corps and Women's Medical Specialists Corps (dietitians, physical therapists, and occupational specialists) for 1943 and subsequent years. (4) Act of Congress approved Apr. 27, 1926, directed the appointment as warrant officers of field clerks still in active service. Includes flight officers as follows: 1943, 5,700; 1944, 13,615; 1945, 31,117; 1946, 2,580.

U.S. Navy Personnel on Active Duty

Source: Dept. of the Navy, U.S. Dept. of Defense

(As of midyear, except where noted)

Date	Officers	Nurses	Enlisted	Officer Candidates	Total	Date	Officers	Nurses	Enlisted	Officer Candidates	Total
1940	13,162	442	144,824	2,569	160,997	1996	60,013	—	376,595	—	436,608
1945	320,293	11,086	2,988,207	61,231	3,380,817	1997	57,341	—	340,616	—	397,957
1950	42,687	1,964	331,860	5,037	381,538	1998 (Sept.) . .	55,007	—	326,196	—	381,203
1960	67,456	2,103	544,040	4,385	617,984	1999	55,726	—	322,372	—	378,098
1970	78,488	2,273	605,899	6,000	692,660	2000 (Oct.) . .	53,698	—	320,212	—	373,910
1980[1]	63,100	—	464,100	—	527,200	2001 (Aug.) . .	54,117	—	317,100	—	375,618
1990 (Sept.) .	74,429	—	530,133	—	604,562	2002	55,506	—	324,712	—	384,576
1993 (Mar.) . .	66,787	—	445,409	—	512,196	2003	55,852	—	324,927	—	380,779
1994 (Apr.) . .	64,430	—	418,378	—	482,808	2004	55,592	—	319,929	—	375,521
1995 (May) . .	61,075	—	402,626	—	463,701						

(1) Starting in 1980, "Nurses" are included with "Officers," and "Officer Candidates" are included with "Enlisted."

U.S. Air Force Personnel on Active Duty

Source: Air Force Dept., U.S. Dept. of Defense

(As of midyear)

Year[1]	Strength	Year[1]	Strength	Year[1]	Strength	Year[1]	Strength	Year[1]	Strength	Year[1]	Strength
1918	195,023	1942	764,415	1960	814,213	1991	510,432	1996	389,400	2001	351,935
1920	9,050	1943	2,197,114	1970	791,078	1992	470,315	1997	378,681	2002	369,721
1930	13,531	1944	2,372,292	1980	557,969	1993	444,351	1998	363,479	2003	373,116
1940	51,165	1945	2,282,259	1986	608,200	1994	426,327	1999	357,929	2004	379,887
1941	152,125	1950	411,277	1990	535,233	1995	400,051	2000	357,777		

(1) Prior to 1947, data are for U.S. Army Air Corps and Air Service of the Signal Corps.

U.S. Marine Corps Personnel on Active Duty

Source: Dept. of the Marines, U.S. Dept. of Defense

(As of midyear)

Year	Officers	Enlisted	Total	Year	Officers	Enlisted	Total	Year	Officers	Enlisted	Total
1940	1,800	26,545	28,345	1991	19,753	174,287	194,040	1998	17,984	154,648	172,632
1945	37,067	437,613	474,680	1992	19,132	165,397	184,529	1999	17,892	155,250	173,142
1950	7,254	67,025	74,279	1993	18,878	161,205	180,083	2000	17,897	154,744	172,641
1960	16,203	154,418	170,621	1994	18,430	159,949	178,379	2001	18,072	152,559	170,631
1970	24,941	234,796	259,737	1995	18,017	153,929	171,946	2002	18,472	154,913	173,385
1980	18,198	170,271	188,469	1996	18,146	154,141	172,287	2003	18,908	160,814	179,722
1990	19,958	176,694	196,652	1997	18,089	154,240	172,329	2004	19,052	157,150	176,202

> **IT'S A FACT:** Napoleon Bonaparte once said that the military "moves on its stomach." In 1795, he offered a prize of 12,000 francs to anyone who could find a way to preserve food for his troops, who were dying in larger numbers from malnutrition than from combat. In 1810, a baker named Nicolas Appert won the prize when he showed that heating jars of food and sealing them prevented spoiling. Thus Napoleon is often credited with beginning the canned food process.

U.S. Coast Guard Personnel on Active Duty

Source: U.S. Coast Guard, U.S. Dept. of Defense

(As of mid year)

Year	Total	Officers	Cadets	Enlisted	Year	Total	Officers	Cadets	Enlisted	Year	Total	Officers	Cadets	Enlisted
1970	37,689	5,512	653	31,524	1994	37,284	7,401	881	29,002	2000	35,712	7,154	863	27,695
1980	39,381	6,463	877	32,041	1995	36,731	7,489	841	28,401	2001	35,328	7,112	631	27,585
1985	38,595	6,775	733	31,087	1996	35,229	7,270	830	27,129	2002	37,166	7,267	694	29,205
1990	37,308	6,475	820	29,860	1997	34,717	7,079	868	26,770	2003	39,000	7,532	983	30,859
1992	39,185	7,348	919	30,918	1998	34,890	7,140	805	26,945	2004	40,151	7,835	1,030	31,286
1993	38,832	7,724	691	30,417	1999	35,266	7,135	880	27,251					

Women in the U.S. Armed Forces

Source: U.S. Dept. of Defense, U.S. Census Bureau

Women in the Army, Navy, Air Force, Marines, and Coast Guard are fully integrated with male personnel. Expansion of military women's programs began in the Department of Defense in fiscal year 1973.

Admission of women to the service academies began in the fall of 1976.

Under rules instituted in 1993, women were allowed to fly combat aircraft and serve aboard warships. Women remained restricted from service in ground combat units.

Between Apr. 1993 and July 1994, almost 260,000 positions in the armed forces were opened to women. By the mid-1990s, 80% of all jobs and more than 90% of all career fields in the military had been opened to women. In 1975, women made up 4.6% of the armed forces. This figure had grown to 14.9% by Sept. 2003, with about 217,000 women on active duty.

Women Active Duty Troops in 2003

Service	% Women
Army	15.2
Navy	14.5
Marines	6.0
Air Force	19.6
Coast Guard	10.7

Women on Active Duty, All Services: 1973-2004

Year	% Women	Year	% Women
1973	2.5	1993	11.6
1975	4.6	1997	13.6
1981	8.9	2000	14.4
1987	10.2	2003	14.9

African American Service in U.S. Wars

American Revolution. About 5,000 African Americans served in the Continental Army, mostly in integrated units, some in all-black combat units.

Civil War. Some 200,000 African Americans served in the Union Army; about 38,000 died, mainly from disease; and 22 won the Medal of Honor (the nation's highest award).

World War I. About 367,000 African Americans served in the armed forces, 100,000 in France.

World War II. Over 1 mil African Americans served in the armed forces; all-black fighter and bomber AAF units and infantry divisions gave distinguished service. (By 1954, armed forces were completely desegregated.)

Korean War. Approximately 3,100 African Americans lost their lives in combat.

Vietnam War. 274,937 African Americans served in the armed forces (1965-74); 5,681 were killed in combat.

Persian Gulf War. About 104,000 African Americans served in the Kuwaiti theater—20% of all U.S. troops, compared with 8.7% of all troops for World War II and 9.8% for Vietnam.

Iraq War. More than 100 African-American military deaths (as of Sept. 2004).

Defense Contracts, 2003

Source: U.S. Dept. of Defense

(in thousands of dollars)

Listed are the 50 companies or organizations receiving the largest dollar volume of prime contract awards from the U.S. Department of Defense during fiscal year 2003.

Company	Total[1]	Company	Total[1]	Company	Total[1]
Lockheed Martin	$21,927,183	FedEx Corp	$1,046,698	GM GDLS Defense Group	$635,104
Boeing	17,339,689	Bell Boeing Joing Program	986,978	Stewart & Stevenson	
Northrop Grumman	11,125,799	Bechtel Group, Inc.	910,400	Services	619,613
General Dynamics	8,235,493	Booz Allen Hamilton	807,991	Chugach Alaska Corp.	580,208
Raytheon	7,915,749	Boeing Sikorsky Comanche		URS Corporation	577,755
United Technologies	4,547,824	Team	799,280	Renco Group Inc.	575,303
Halliburton	3,920,877	The Titan Corporation	798,536	Engineered Support	
General Electric	2,842,131	Government of the United		Systems, Inc.	559,930
Science Applications Intl.	2,615,869	States	780,876	Jacobs Engineering Group	557,164
Computer Sciences	2,530,847	Electronic Data Systems	772,085	N.V. Koninklijke	
Humana	2,362,112	Veritas Capital Management		Nederlandsche	545,843
L-3 Communications Holding	2,085,738	LLC	766,887	Alliant Techsystems	542,125
BAE Systems PLC	1,927,583	Exxon Mobil	756,733	Aerospace Corporation	539,517
Health Net	1,756,489	Textron	722,530	Harris	517,280
Carlyle Group	1,670,174	Johnson Controls	719,370	Government of Canada	515,710
ITT Industries	1,234,819	Parsons Corp.	685,011	Massachusette Institute of	
Triwest Healthcare Alliance	1,200,418	Cardinal Health	652,408	Technology	514,230
Honeywell International	1,199,176	Oshkosh Truck	649,662	Anteon Intl. Corp.	508,530
North American Airlines	1,194,932	Dell Computer Corp.	641,795	IBM	468,803

(1) Totals include subsidiaries of each company.

Veterans Compensation and Pension Case Payments

Source: Office of Policy Planning and Preparedness, Dept. of Veterans Affairs

Fiscal year	Living veteran cases	Deceased veteran cases	Total cases	Total expenditures (dollars)	Fiscal year	Living veteran cases	Deceased veteran cases	Total cases	Total expenditures (dollars)
1900	752,510	241,019	993,529	$138,462,130	1995	2,668,576	661,679	3,330,255	$17,765,045,000
1910	602,622	318,461	921,083	159,974,056	1996	2,671,026	637,232	3,308,258	17,055,809,000
1920	419,627	349,916	769,543	316,418,030	1997	2,666,785	613,976	3,280,761	19,284,287,000
1930	542,610	298,223	840,833	418,432,809	1998	2,668,030	594,782	3,262,812	20,164,598,000
1940	610,122	239,176	849,298	429,138,465	1999	2,673,167	578,508	3,251,675	21,023,864,000
1950	2,368,238	658,123	3,026,361	2,009,462,298	2000	2,672,407	563,754	3,236,161	21,963,216,000
1960	3,008,935	950,802	3,959,737	3,314,761,383	2001	2,669,156	548,589	3,217,745	23,198,139,000
1970	3,127,338	1,487,176	4,614,514	5,253,839,611	2002	2,744,866	539,796	3,284,662	25,407,916,000
1980	3,195,395	1,450,785	4,646,180	11,046,637,368	2003	2,831,784	537,513	3,369,297	27,904,356,000
1990	2,746,329	837,596	3,583,925	14,674,411,000					

U.S. Veteran Population, 2004

Source: U.S. Dept. of Veterans Affairs; as of Sept. 2004

TOTAL VETERANS IN CIVILIAN LIFE[1] **24,737,000**		Total Korean conflict	3,423,000
Total wartime veterans[2] **18,425,000**		Korean conflict with service in WWII	282,000
		Korean conflict with no prior wartime service . . .	2,781,000
Total Gulf War	3,997,000	World War II	3,984,000
Gulf War with service in Vietnam era	339,000	**Total peacetime veterans**	**6,312,000**
Gulf War with no prior wartime service	3,659,000	Service between Vietnam era and Gulf War only . . .	3,463,000
Total Vietnam era	8,122,000	Service between Korean conflict and Vietnam	
Vietnam era with service in Korean conflict. . . .	240,000	era only	2,665,000
Vietnam era with no prior wartime service	7,423,000	Other peacetime	184,000

NOTE: Details may not add to total shown because of rounding. (1) There are an indeterminate number of Mexican Border period veterans. (2) The total for "wartime veterans" consists only of veterans from each listed war that had no prior wartime service. Figures are for U.S. veterans worldwide. Source: VetPop2001, VA Office of the Actuary

The Medal of Honor

The Medal of Honor is the highest military award for bravery that can be given to any individual in the United States. The first Army Medals were awarded on Mar. 25, 1863, and the first Navy Medals went to sailors and Marines on Apr. 3, 1863.

On Dec. 21, 1861, Pres. Abraham Lincoln signed into law a bill to create the Navy Medal of Honor. Lincoln later (July 14, 1862) approved a resolution providing for the presentation of Medals of Honor to enlisted men of the Army and Voluntary Forces, making it a law. The law was amended on March 3, 1863, to extend its provisions to include officers as well as enlisted men.

The Medal of Honor is awarded in the name of Congress to a person who, while a member of the armed forces, distinguishes himself or herself conspicuously by gallantry and intrepidity at the risk of life above and beyond the call of duty while engaged in an action against any enemy of the United States; while engaged in military operations involving conflict with an opposing foreign force; or while serving with friendly foreign forces engaged in an armed conflict against an opposing armed force in which the United States is not a belligerent party.

The deed performed must have been one of personal bravery or self-sacrifice so conspicuous as to clearly distinguish the individual above his or her comrades and must have involved risk of life. Incontestable proof of the performance of service is required, and each recommendation for award of this decoration is considered on the standard of extraordinary merit.

Prior to World War I, the 2,625 Army Medal of Honor awards up to that time were reviewed to determine which past awards met new stringent criteria. The Army removed 911 names from the list, most of them former members of a volunteer infantry group during the Civil War who had been induced to extend their enlistments when they were promised the medal. However, in 1977 a medal was restored to Dr. Mary Walker, and in 1989 medals were restored to Buffalo Bill Cody and 7 other Indian scouts.

Since then, Medals of Honor have been awarded for:

World War I 124	Korean War 131
Peacetime (1920-40) . . . 18	Vietnam War 245
World War II 464	Somalia 2

The figure for World War II includes 7 African-American soldiers who were awarded Medals of Honor (6 of them posthumously) in Jan. 1997. Previously, no black soldier had received the medal for World War II service; an Army inquiry begun in 1993 concluded that the prevailing political climate and Army practices of the time had prevented proper recognition of heroism on the part of black soldiers in that war. In June 2002, 22 Asian Americans received the award for World War II service.

The most recent recipient was Humbert "Rocky" Versace, who was awarded the medal posthumously on July 8, 2002. Versace spent 23 months as a prisoner of the Viet Cong, distinguishing himself by resisting interrogation and demanding humane treatment for his fellow captives. He was executed by his captors in Sept. 1965.

Active Duty U.S. Military Personnel Strengths, Worldwide, 2004

Source: U.S. Dept. of Defense

(as of Mar. 31, 2004)

TOTAL WORLDWIDE[1]	1,425,887	**EUROPE**		**EAST ASIA & PACIFIC**	
		Belgium	1,534	Australia.	205
U.S. TERRITORIES & SPEC. LOCATIONS		Bosnia and Herzegovina	2,931	Japan	40,045
U.S., 48 contiguous states . . .	958,215	Germany	75,603	Korea, South	40,258
Alaska	17,989	Greece	562	Philippines	144
Hawaii	35,810	Iceland	1,754	Singapore.	196
Guam	3,315	Italy.	13,354	Thailand	113
Puerto Rico	769	Macedonia, F.Y.R. of	104	Afloat	16,601
Transients	31,397	Netherlands	722	**Regional Total**[2]	**97,724**
Afloat	120,666	Portugal	1,077	
Regional Total[2]	**1,168,195**	Serbia (incl. Kosovo)	128	**NORTH AFRICA, NEAR EAST,**
		Spain	1,968	**& SOUTH ASIA***
OTHER WESTERN HEMISPHERE		Turkey	1,863	Afghanistan	NA
Canada.	147	United Kingdom	11,801	Bahrain.	1,496
Cuba (Guantánamo)	700	Afloat	2,534	Diego Garcia	491
Haiti	455	**Regional Total**[2]	**116,507**	Egypt	350
Honduras	413			Iraq[3]	211,028
Afloat	25	**SUB-SAHARAN AFRICA**		Qatar	3,432
Regional Total[2]	**2,201**	Djibouti	539	Saudi Arabia.	291
		Regional Total[2]	**770**	Afloat	592
FORMER SOVIET UNION				**Regional Total**[2]	**217,935**
TOTAL	**162**			

*Special Forces personnel involved in Operation Enduring Freedom in Afghanistan not reported by Dept. of Defense. (1) Total worldwide also includes undistributed personnel. (2) Most countries and areas with fewer than 100 assigned U.S. military members not listed; regional totals include personnel stationed in those countries and areas not shown. (3) Includes troops in surrounding areas.

IT'S A FACT: The U.S. Naval base at Guantánamo Bay, Cuba, is the oldest U.S. military base overseas, and the only one located in a Communist country. The U.S. began leasing the site from Cuba in 1903, and has occupied the base since then despite tensions with the Castro government, which by treaty cannot terminate the lease without U.S. consent.

Directors of the Central Intelligence Agency

In 1942, Pres. Franklin D. Roosevelt established the Office of Strategic Services (OSS); it was disbanded in 1945. In 1946, Pres. Harry Truman established the Central Intelligence Group (CIG) to operate under the National Intelligence Authority (NIA). A 1947 law replaced the NIA with the National Security Council and the CIG with the Central Intelligence Agency.

Director	Served	Appointed by President	Director	Served	Appointed by President
Adm. Sidney W. Souers	1946	Truman	George H. W. Bush	1976 -1977	Ford
Gen. Hoyt S. Vandenberg	1946 -1947	Truman	Adm. Stansfield Turner	1977-1981	Carter
Adm. Roscoe H. Hillenkoetter	1947-1950	Truman	William J. Casey	1981-1987	Reagan
Gen. Walter Bedell Smith	1950-1953	Truman	William H. Webster	1987-1991	Reagan
Allen W. Dulles	1953 -1961	Eisenhower	Robert M. Gates	1991-1993	Bush
John A. McCone	1961-1965	Kennedy	R. James Woolsey	1993 -1995	Clinton
Adm. William F. Raborn Jr.	1965-1966	Johnson	John M. Deutch	1995 -1997	Clinton
Richard Helms	1966 -1973	Johnson	George J. Tenet	1997 - 2004	Clinton
James R. Schlesinger	1973	Nixon	Porter Goss*	2004-	Bush
William E. Colby	1973 -1976	Nixon			

*Took office Sept. 2004.

Nations with Largest Armed Forces, by Active-Duty Troop Strength[1]

Source: *The Military Balance. 2003-2004* (International Institute for Strategic Studies, published by Oxford University Press, UK)

	Troop strength		Defense		Navy		Combat aircraft	
	Active troops	Reserve troops	expend.	Tanks (MBT)	Cruisers/ Frigates/	Sub-	FGA	Fighters
	(thousands)		($ bil)	(army only)	Destroyers	marines	(air force only)	
1. China	2,270	550	48.4	7,180	42F/21D	69	700	1,000
2. United States	1,414	1,259	329.6	7,620	27C/30F/49D*	72	3,513 aircraft	
3. India	1,298	535	13.1	3,398	16F/8D*	19	539	125
4. N. Korea	1,082	4,700	4.7	3,500	3F	26	525 FGA/FTR	
5. Russia	988	2,400	48.0	21,870	7C/10F/14D*	53	606	908
6. S. Korea	686	4,500	12.6	1,000	9F/6D	20	468 FGA/FTR	
7. Pakistan	620	513	2.5	2,368	8F	10	109	211
8. Iran	520	350	4.9	1,565	3F	3	186	74
9. Turkey	515	378	8.7	4,205	19F	13	483 aircraft	
10. Vietnam	484	3,000	2.3	1,315	6F	2	65	189
11. Myanmar	444	—	2.8	100	—	—	22	70
12. Egypt	443	254	3.1	4,395	10F/1D	4	131	333
13. Taiwan	370	1,657	7.5	926+	11D/21F	4	386	57
14. Syria	319	354	1.8	4,500	2F*	—	130	300
15. Thailand	306	200	1.7	333	12F	—	133	—
16. Ukraine	302	1,000	4.7	3,784	1C/2F	1	63	277
17. Indonesia	297	400	6.2	—	17F	2	59	12
18. Germany	296	390	31.5	2,398	12F/1D	12	376 aircraft	
19. Brazil	288	1,115	9.7	178	14F*	4	254+ aircraft	
20. France	260	100	38.0	614	12D/20F*	10	478 aircraft	
21. Ethiopia	253	—	0.4	270+	—	—	50	—
22. Japan	240	47	37.1	1,020	45D/9F*	16	60	180
23. Italy	217	65	24.2	1,183	1C/4D/12F*	6	263 aircraft	
24. United Kingdom	210	257	35.2	543	11D/20F	15	415 aircraft	
25. Saudi Arabia	199	—	21.0	1,055	7F	—	172	108
26. Morocco	196	150	1.3	744	2F	—	53	15
27. Mexico	193	300	5.3	—	3D/8F	—	107 aircraft	
28. Spain	178	329	8.3	552	16F*	6	186 aircraft	
29. Greece	178	6.1	6.2	1,723	2D/12F	8	418 aircraft	
30. Israel	162	425	9.4	3,950	—	3	379 aircraft	

MBT = main battle tank. FGA = fighter, ground attack; rgt = regiment; sqn = squadron (12-24 aircraft); wg = wing (72 fighter aircraft). *Denotes navies with aircraft carriers, as follows: United States 12, United Kingdom 3, France 1, India 1, Italy 1, Russian 1, Brazil 1, Spain 1, Thailand 1. (1) All figures are for Aug. 2003, except Defense Expenditure, which is for 2002. — = not available.

Nuclear Arms Treaties and Negotiations: A Historical Overview

Aug. 5, 1963—Limited Test Ban Treaty signed in Moscow by U.S., USSR, and Britain; prohibited testing of nuclear weapons in space, above ground, and under water.

Jan. 27, 1967—Outer Space Treaty banned the introduction of other weapons of mass destruction in space.

July 1, 1968—Nuclear Nonproliferation Treaty, with U.S., USSR, and Great Britain as major signers, limited spread of nuclear material for military purposes by agreement not to help nonnuclear nations get or make nuclear weapons. In 1995, the treaty was extended indefinitely. As of Sept. 2004, 189 countries had signed the treaty; Israel, India,

and Pakistan were not signatories. In Jan. 2003, N. Korea withdrew from the treaty.

May 26, 1972—Strategic Arms Limitation Treaty (SALT I) signed in Moscow by U.S. and USSR. This short-term agreement imposed a 5-year freeze on both testing and deployment of intercontinental ballistic missiles (ICBMs) as well as submarine-launched ballistic missiles (SLBMs). In the area of defensive nuclear weapons, the separate **ABM Treaty,** signed on the same occasion, limited antiballistic missiles to 2 sites of 100 antiballistic missile launchers in each country (amended in 1974 to 1 site in each country).

July 3, 1974—ABM Treaty Revision (protocol on anti-ballistic missile systems) and **Threshold Test Ban Treaty** on limiting underground testing of nuclear weapons to 150 kilotons were signed by U.S. and USSR in Moscow.

Sept. 1977—U.S. and USSR agreed to continue to abide by **SALT I**, despite its expiration date.

June 18, 1979—SALT II signed in Vienna by the U.S. and USSR, constrained offensive nuclear weapons, limiting each side to 2,400 missile launchers and heavy bombers; ceiling to apply until Jan. 1, 1985. Treaty also set a subceiling of 1,320 ICBMs and SLBMs with multiple warheads on each side. SALT II never reached the Senate floor for ratification because Pres. Jimmy Carter withdrew support following Dec. 1979 Soviet invasion of Afghanistan.

Dec. 8, 1987—Intermediate-Range Nuclear Forces (INF) Treaty signed in Washington, DC, by U.S. and USSR, eliminating all U.S. and Soviet intermediate- and shorter-range nuclear missiles from Europe and Asia. Ratified, with conditions, by U.S. Senate May 27, 1988; by USSR June 1, 1988. Entered into force June 1, 1988.

July 31, 1991—Strategic Arms Reduction Treaty (START I) signed in Moscow by USSR and U.S. to reduce strategic offensive arms by about 30% in 3 phases over 7 years. START I was the first treaty to mandate reductions by the superpowers. Treaty was approved by U.S. Senate Oct. 1, 1992.

With the Soviet Union breakup in Dec. 1991, 4 former Soviet republics became independent nations with strategic nuclear weapons—Russia, Ukraine, Kazakhstan, and Belarus. The last 3 agreed in principle in 1992 to transfer their nuclear weapons to Russia and ratify START I. The Russian Supreme Soviet voted to ratify, Nov. 4, 1992, but Russia decided not to provide instruments of ratification until the other 3 republics ratified START I and acceded to the Nuclear Nonproliferation Treaty (NPT) as nonnuclear nations.

By late 1994, all 3 nations had done so, and NPT entered into force on Dec. 5, 1994.

Jan. 3, 1993—START II signed in Moscow by U.S. and Russia, called for both sides to reduce their long-range nuclear arsenals to about one-third of their then-current levels within a decade and disable and dismantle launching systems. The U.S. ratified START II Jan. 26, 1996; Russia ratified it Apr. 13, 2000. On Sept. 26, 1997, the U.S. and Russia signed an agreement that would delay the dismantling of launching systems under START II to the end of 2007.

Sept. 24, 1996—Comprehensive Test Ban Treaty (CTBT) signed by U.S. and Russia. The CTBT banned all nuclear weapon tests and other nuclear explosions. It was intended to help prevent the nuclear powers from developing more advanced weapons, while limiting the ability of other states to acquire such devices. As of July 2004, the CTBT had been signed by 172 nations, including China, Russia, the U.S., the U.K., and France; ratified by 117, including France, Russia, and the U.K., but not the U.S. or China. Enters into force after 44 nuclear-capable states ratify it. As of Sept. 25, 2004, 32 of the 44 had done so.

Sept. 1997—ABM Treaty amended to allow greater flexibility in development of shorter-range nuclear weapons.

May 24, 2002—Nuclear Arms Reduction Pact (Treaty of Moscow) signed by U.S. and Russia in Moscow, committed both countries to cutting nuclear arsenals to 1,700 to 2,200 warheads each, down from about 6,000, by 2012. No intermediate timetable established, but joint committee set up for monitoring implementation; either side allowed to back out with 90 days notice. Ratified by U.S. Senate, Mar. 6, 2003.

June 2002—U.S. formally withdrew from the **ABM Treaty**, effective June 13, with the intent of developing a defensive missile system. Russia, June 14, announced its withdrawal from **START II**, stating that U.S. withdrawal from the ABM Treaty effectively invalidated START II.

Monthly Military Pay Scale[1]

Source: U.S. Dept. of Defense; effective Jan. 1, 2004

Years of Service:	<2	2	3	4	6	8	10	12	14	16	18	20	22	24	26
Grade							**Commissioned officers**								
O-10...	NA	NA	NA	NA	NA	NA	NA	NA	NA	NA	NA	$12,133	$12,133	$12,133	$12,133
O-9....	NA	NA	NA	NA	NA	NA	NA	NA	NA	NA	NA	10,955	11,112	11,340	11,738
O-8....	$7,751	$8,005	$8,173	$8,221	$8,430	$8,782	$8,864	$9,197	9$,293	$9,580	$9,996	10,379	10,635	10,635	10,635
O-7....	6,441	6,740	6,878	6,989	7,187	7,384	7,612	7,839	8,067	8,782	9,386	9,386	9,386	9,386	9,434
O-6....	4,774	5,244	5,588	5,588	5,610	5,850	5,882	5,882	6,216	6,807	7,154	7,501	7,698	7,898	8,285
O-5....	3,980	4,483	4,793	4,852	5,045	5,161	5,416	5,603	5,844	6,214	6,390	6,563	6,761	6,761	6,761
O-4....	3,434	3,975	4,240	4,299	4,545	4,809	5,138	5,394	5,572	5,674	5,733	5,733	5,733	5,733	5,733
O-3....	3,019	3,422	3,694	4,027	4,220	4,432	4,569	4,794	4,911	4,911	4,911	4,911	4,911	4,911	4,911
O-2....	2,608	2,971	3,422	3,537	3,610	3,610	3,610	3,610	3,610	3,610	3,610	3,610	3,610	3,610	3,610
O-1....	2,264	2,357	2,849	2,849	2,849	2,849	2,849	2,849	2,849	2,849	2,849	2,849	2,849	2,849	2,849
Commissioned officers with over 4 years' active duty service as enlisted member or warrant officer															
O-3E...	NA	NA	NA	4,027	4,220	4,432	4,569	4,794	4,984	5,093	5,241	5,241	5,241	5,241	5,241
O-2E...	NA	NA	NA	3,537	3,610	3,725	3,919	4,069	4,180	4,180	4,180	4,180	4,180	4,180	4,180
O-1E...	NA	NA	NA	2,849	3,042	3,155	3,269	3,382	3,537	3,537	3,537	3,537	3,537	3,537	3,537
Warrant officers															
W-5....	NA	NA	NA	NA	NA	NA	NA	NA	NA	NA	NA	5,361	5,544	5,729	5,914
W-4....	3,119	3,356	3,452	3,547	3,710	3,872	4,035	4,194	4,359	4,617	4,783	4,944	5,112	5,277	5,446
W-3....	2,849	2,968	3,089	3,129	3,257	3,403	3,596	3,786	3,989	4,141	4,292	4,357	4,424	4,570	4,716
W-2....	2,506	2,649	2,774	2,865	2,943	3,158	3,322	3,443	3,562	3,644	3,713	3,843	3,973	4,104	4,104
W-1....	2,213	2,394	2,515	2,594	2,802	2,928	3,040	3,165	3,247	3,322	3,444	3,536	3,536	3,536	3,536
Enlisted members															
E-9....	NA	NA	NA	NA	NA	NA	3,769	3,855	3,962	4,089	4,217	4,421	4,594	4,777	5,055
E-8....	NA	NA	NA	NA	NA	3,086	3,222	3,306	3,408	3,518	3,716	3,816	3,986	4,081	4,314
E-7....	2,145	2,341	2,431	2,550	2,642	2,801	2,891	2,980	3,140	3,220	3,296	3,342	3,498	3,599	3,855
E-6....	1,856	2,041	2,131	2,219	2,310	2,516	2,596	2,685	2,763	2,791	2,810	2,810	2,810	2,810	2,810
E-5....	1,700	1,814	1,901	1,991	2,131	2,251	2,340	2,368	2,368	2,368	2,368	2,368	2,368	2,368	2,368
E-4....	1,558	1,638	1,727	1,814	1,892	1,892	1,892	1,892	1,892	1,892	1,892	1,892	1,892	1,892	1,892
E-3....	1,407	1,496	1,586	1,586	1,586	1,586	1,586	1,586	1,586	1,586	1,586	1,586	1,586	1,586	1,586
E-2....	1,338	1,338	1,338	1,338	1,338	1,338	1,338	1,338	1,338	1,338	1,338	1,338	1,338	1,338	1,338
E-1>4..	1,193	1,193	1,193	1,193	1,193	1,193	1,193	1,193	1,193	1,193	1,193	1,193	1,193	1,193	1,193
E-1<4..	1,104	NA	NA	NA	NA	NA	NA	NA	NA	NA	NA	NA	NA	NA	NA

NA = Not applicable. (1) Basic pay is limited for O-7 to O-10 to $12,133 per month, and for O-6 and below to $10,683 per month. (2) E-1>4 = E-1 grade personnel with 4 or more months service. E-1<4 = E-1 grade personnel with less than 4 months service.

Casualties in Principal Wars of the U.S.

Source: U.S. Dept. of Defense, U.S. Coast Guard

Data prior to World War I are based on incomplete records in many cases. Casualty data are confined to dead and wounded personnel and, therefore, exclude personnel captured or missing in action who were subsequently returned to military control. Dash (—) indicates information is not available. off. = officers.

WAR	Branch of service	Number serving	CASUALTIES			
			Battle deaths	Other deaths	Wounds not mortal[7]	Total[13]
Revolutionary War..............	Total	—	**4,435**	—	**6,188**	**10,623**
1775-83	Army	184,000	4,044	—	6,004	10,048
	Navy	to	342	—	114	456
	Marines	250,000	49	—	70	119
War of 1812	Total	**286,730[8]**	**2,260**	—	**4,505**	**6,765**
1812-15	Army	—	1,950	—	4,000	5,950
	Navy	—	265	—	439	704
	Marines	—	45	—	66	111
Mexican War...................	Total	**78,789[8]**	**1,733**	**11,550**	**4,152**	**17,435**
1846-48	Army	—	1,721	11,550	4,102	17,373
	Navy	—	1	—	3	4
	Marines	—	11	—	47	58
	Coast Guard[12]	71 off.	—	—	—	—
Civil War						
Union forces	Total	**2,213,363[8]**	**140,415**	**224,097**	**281,881**	**646,392**
1861-65	Army	2,128,948	138,154	221,374	280,040	639,568
	Navy	—	2,112	2,411	1,710	6,233
	Marines	84,415	148	312	131	591
Confederate forces	Total	—	**74,524**	**59,297**	—	**133,821**
(estimate)[1]	Army	600,000	—	—	—	—
1863-66	Navy	to	—	—	—	—
	Marines	1,500,000	—	—	—	—
	Coast Guard[12]	219 off.	1	—	—	1
Spanish-American War..........	Total	**307,420**	**385**	**2,061**	**1,662**	**4,108**
1898	Army[3]	280,564	369	2,061	1,594	4,024
	Navy	22,875	10	0	47	57
	Marines	3,321	6	0	21	27
	Coast Guard[12]	660	0	—	—	—
World War I...................	Total	**4,743,826**	**53,513**	**63,195**	**204,002**	**320,710**
April 6, 1917 - Nov. 11, 1918	Army[4]	4,057,101	50,510	55,868	193,663	300,041
	Navy	599,051	431	6,856	819	8,106
	Marines	78,839	2,461	390	9,520	12,371
	Coast Guard	8,835	111	81	—	192
World War II	Total	**16,353,659**	**292,131**	**115,185**	**671,846**	**1,079,162**
Dec. 7, 1941 - Dec. 31, 1946[2]	Army[5]	11,260,000	234,874	83,400	565,861	884,135
	Navy[6]	4,183,466	36,950	25,664	37,778	100,392
	Marines	669,100	19,733	4,778	68,207	91,718
	Coast Guard	241,093	574	1,343	—	1,917
Korean War[9]..................	Total	**5,764,143**	**33,667**	**3,249**	**103,284**	**140,200**
June 25, 1950 - July 27, 1953	Army	2,834,000	27,709	2,452	77,596	107,757
	Navy	1,177,000	493	160	1,576	2,226
	Marines	424,000	4,267	339	23,744	28,353
	Air Force	1,285,000	1,198	298	368	1,864
	Coast Guard	44,143	—	—	—	—
Vietnam War[10]	Total	**8,752,000**	**47,393**	**10,800**	**153,363**	**211,556**
Aug. 4, 1964 - Jan. 27, 1973	Army	4,368,000	30,929	7,272	96,802	135,003
	Navy	1,842,000	1,631	931	4,178	6,740
	Marines	794,000	13,085	1,753	51,392	66,230
	Air Force	1,740,000	1,741	842	931	3,514
	Coast Guard	8,000	7	2	60	69
Persian Gulf War	Total	**467,939[11]**	**148**	**151**	**467**	**766**
1991	Army	246,682	98	105	—	203
	Navy	98,852	6	14	—	20
	Marines	71,254	24	26	—	50
	Air Force	50,751	20	6	—	26
	Coast Guard	400	—	—	—	—
Iraq War[14]	Total	**269,363**	**732**	**247**	**7,026**	**8,005**
2003-	Army	99,664	520	194	4,972	5,686
	Navy	61,018	15	6	127	148
	Marines	66,166	190	42	1,854	2,086
	Air Force	42,515	7	5	73	85
	Coast Guard	1,250	1	—	—	1

(1) Authoritative statistics for the Confederate forces are not available. An estimated 26,000-31,000 Confederate personnel died in Union prisons. (2) Data are for Dec. 1, 1941, through Dec. 31, 1946, when hostilities were officially terminated by presidential proclamation; few battle deaths or wounds not mortal were incurred after Japanese acceptance of Allied peace terms on Aug. 14, 1945. Numbers serving Dec. 1, 1941-Aug. 31, 1945, were: Total—14,903,213; Army—10,420,000; Navy—3,883,520; Marine Corps—599,693. (3) Number serving covers the period April 21-Aug. 13, 1898, while dead and wounded data are for the period May 1-Aug. 31, 1898. Active hostilities ceased on Aug. 13, 1898, but ratifications of the treaty of peace were not exchanged between the U.S. and Spain until April 11, 1899. (4) Includes Army Air Forces battle deaths and wounds not mortal, as well as casualties suffered by American forces in northern Russia to Aug. 25, 1919, and in Siberia to April 1, 1920. Other deaths covered the period April 1, 1917-Dec. 31, 1918. (5) Includes Army Air Forces. (6) Battle deaths and wounds not mortal include casualties incurred in Oct. 1941 due to hostile action. (7) Marine Corps data for Iraq War, World War II, the Spanish-American War, and prior wars represent the number of individuals wounded, whereas all other data in this column represent the total number (incidence) of wounds. (8) As reported by Commissioner of Pensions in his Annual Report for Fiscal Year 1903. (9) As a result of an ongoing Dept. of Defense review of available Korean War casualty record information, updates to previously reported figures for battle deaths and other deaths are reflected in this table. (10) Number serving covers the period Aug. 4, 1964-Jan. 27, 1973 (date of ceasefire). Includes casualties incurred in Mayaguez incident. Wounds not mortal exclude 150,332 persons not requiring hospital care. (11) Estimated. (12) Actually the U.S. Revenue Cutter Service, predecessor to the U.S. Coast Guard. (13) Totals do not include categories for which no data are listed. (14) Including deaths from May 1, 2003 (declared end of major combat) through Sept. 4, 2004. Military deaths through Apr. 30, 2003 only totaled 115 combat-related and 23 other. As of Sept. 24, 2004, there were 1,042 total military deaths. **NOTE:** As of Sept. 24, there have been 138 military deaths in Op. Enduring Freedom, mostly in Afghanistan and the Persian Gulf area.

Homeland Security

On Nov. 25, 2002, Pres. George W. Bush signed a measure creating a cabinet-level **Department of Homeland Security (DHS)**. It became operational on Jan. 24, 2003, headed by Sec. Tom Ridge, a former Pennsylvania governor (1995-2001).

The main **objectives** of the DHS are to prevent terrorist attacks within the U.S., reduce the vulnerability to attacks, and minimize the effects of such attacks should they occur. The DHS is responsible for border and transportation security, protecting critical infrastructure, coordinating emergency response activities, and overseeing research and development for homeland security efforts. The new department also responds to natural disasters.

Following the attacks of Sept. 11, 2001, Pres. Bush created a small-scale advisory office known as the Office of Homeland Security. When a congressional inquiry in the summer of 2002 revealed extensive failures in intelligence gathering and communication, sentiment grew in favor of creating a large agency that could coordinate anti-terrorism efforts. The final plan passed by Congress in Nov. 2002 called for the integration of 22 federal agencies from many different departments.

The DHS is organized into 5 directorates: Border and Transportation Security, Emergency Preparedness, Science and Technology, Information Analysis and Infrastructure Protection, and Management, the administrative arm of the department. The U.S. Coast Guard, Secret Service, and Bureau of Citizenship and Immigration Services (formerly part of the INS) became part of DHS as discrete entities, separate from the directorates. The fiscal year 2005 budget for DHS was $40.2 billion.

Emergency Preparedness

In Feb. 2003, the DHS launched its public service "Ready" campaign in association with the Ad Council and the Sloan Foundation. People are advised to take 3 steps.

1. Make a Kit. Make a home emergency supply kit with at least 3 days' worth of essential provisions for "sheltering-in-place," and assemble a lightweight version in case evacuation is necessary. Kits should include 1 gallon of water per person per day. Provide enough easily prepared canned or dried foods. In colder climates, supply warm clothes and a sleeping bag for each member of the family.

Kits should contain a first-aid kit, flashlight, battery-powered radio, extra batteries, toiletries, and any needed medical presciptions. They should include a filter mask (available in hardware stores) or other covering to use as a filter when breathing. Duct tape and heavy-duty garbage bags or plastic sheeting should be available in case it is necessary to seal windows and doors.

2. Make a Plan. Form a communication plan, with designated contacts for each family member. Provisions should be made both for staying in place and for evacuating.

Shelter-in-place. Designate in advance an interior room, or one with the fewest windows and doors, for shelter. In an emergency, if there is heavy debris in the air or authorities deem the air contaminated, close windows, doors, vents, and fireplace dampers, and turn off air conditioners, forced-air heating systems, exhaust fans, and clothes dryers. Take family members and emergency supplies to a selected room and seal doors and windows as needed. Follow TV or radio broadcasts, or the Internet, for further instructions.

Evacuation. Create an evacuation plan with a specific meeting place for family members. Keep at least half a tank of gas in the car at all times, and learn alternate driving routes, as well as alternate means of transportation in your area. If the air is contaminated, drive with the windows and vents closed and keep the air conditioning or heater off.

Work and School. Talk to schools and employers about emergency plans and how they will communicate with families in emergencies.

3. Be Informed. What to do depends partly on the nature of the threat.

Biological Threat. If a biological danger is reported, keep in contact with TV, radio, or the Internet for news and advice. If you become aware of a release of an unknown substance nearby, get away and cover your mouth and nose with layers of fabric that can filter the air but still allow breathing. Wash with soap and water, and seek medical attention.

Chemical Threat. In the event of a chemical attack, leave the contaminated area immediately, if you can safely do so. Signs of a chemical attack in the area may include people with symptoms such as watery eyes, twitching, choking, difficulty breathing, or loss of coordination. Listen to news reports. If you believe you may have been exposed to a chemical agent, remove clothes promptly and wash with soap and water. Do not scrub chemical into skin. Be sure to seek medical attention.

Explosions. If there is an explosion, take shelter from the blast under a desk or table. Leave the building or area when feasible; check for fire, and never use elevators.

Nuclear Blast. In case of a nuclear blast, take cover immediately, preferably below ground. Decide whether to shelter-in-place or evacuate; bear in mind that the more shielding and distance between you and the blast, and the less time of exposure, the more you reduce your risk.

Further Information: FEMA publishes a handbook, *Are You Ready? A Guide to Citizen Preparedness*, which can be obtained electronically at www.fema.gov/areyouready, or in print by calling 1-800-480-2520. You can also visit www.ready.gov or call 1-800-BE-READY.

Security Advisories

The Homeland Security Advisory System, established on Mar. 12, 2002, indicates the estimated threat level for a terrorist attack in the U.S.; state and local authorities may have separate alert systems and criteria.

Low (Green) Governments should refine and exercise pre-planned protective measures and train personnel, assess and update vulnerabilities, and take steps to reduce them.

Guarded (Blue) In addition to the above, authorities should check communications with emergency response and command locations, review emergency response procedures, and provide public information as needed.

Elevated (Yellow) Authorities should also increase surveillance of critical locations, coordinate emergency plans with nearby jurisdictions, implement response plans as appropriate.

High (Orange) Authorities should coordinate with federal, state, and local law enforcement agencies, or National Guard or other armed service; take additional precautions at public events, including possible cancellation; prepare to execute contingency procedures and move to alternate locations; restrict access to threatened facilities.

Severe (Red) Authorities should increase or redirect personnel to address critical emergency needs; assign or pre-position emergency response and specialty teams; monitor, redirect, or limit access to transportation systems; close public and government facilities

As of Oct. 2003, the national threat level had reached "high" 5 times: Sept. 10-24, 2002, around the anniversary of Sept. 11; Feb. 7-27, 2003, based on threats of attacks during the Haj pilgrimage in Mecca; Mar. 17-Apr. 16, 2003, during the Iraq War; and May 20-30, following bombings in Saudi Arabia and Morocco, and as a precaution for Memorial Day; Dec. 21, 2003-Jan. 15, 2004, based on threats specific to the holiday season. A 6th high alert warning was announced Aug. 1, 2004, but covered only specific financial targets in New York City, NY, northern NJ, and Washington, DC. As of Sept. 30, 2004, the nation was on "elevated" alert, except for the areas covered in the Aug. 1, 2004, alert. New York City was at "high" alert, as it had been since the system was established.

TRADE AND TRANSPORTATION

U.S. Trade With Selected Countries and Major Areas, 2003

Source: Office of Trade and Economic Analysis, U.S. Dept of Commerce

(in millions of dollars; countries ranked by amount of total trade with U.S.)

COUNTRY	Total Trade with U.S.	U.S. Exports to	Rank[1]	U.S. Imports from	Rank[1]	U.S. Trade Balance with	Rank[2]
Canada	$391,518.4	$169,923.7	1	$221,594.70	1	$–51,671.0	3
Mexico	235,471.8	97,411.8	2	138,060.00	3	–40,648.2	4
China	180,804.0	28,367.9	6	152,436.10	2	–124,068.2	1
Japan	170,040.9	52,004.3	3	118,036.60	4	–66,032.4	2
Federal Republic of Germany	96,944.6	28,831.9	5	68,112.70	5	–39,280.8	5
United Kingdom	76,622.9	33,827.9	4	42,795.00	6	–8,967.0	16
Korea, South	61,302.0	24,072.6	7	37,229.40	7	–13,156.8	12
Taiwan	49,047.3	17,447.9	9	31,599.40	8	–14,151.5	10
France	46,272.3	17,053.0	10	29,219.30	9	–12,166.3	13
Malaysia	36,354.3	10,914.1	16	25,440.20	11	–14,526.1	8
Italy	35,974.8	10,560.6	17	25,414.20	12	–14,853.7	7
Ireland	33,442.2	7,695.7	20	25,746.50	10	–18,050.9	6
Singapore	31,697.9	16,560.2	11	15,137.70	17	1,422.4	222
Netherlands	31,647.8	20,695.0	8	10,952.80	21	9,742.2	230
Brazil	29,121.3	11,211.0	15	17,910.30	14	–6,699.3	20
Belgium	25,376.9	15,236.1	12	10,140.80	24	5,095.2	228
Saudi Arabia	22,664.3	4,595.7	25	18,068.60	13	–13,472.9	11
Hong Kong	22,371.6	13,520.5	13	8,851.10	27	4,669.3	227
Thailand	21,013.8	5,835.3	23	15,178.50	16	–9,343.2	15
Venezuela	19,967.1	2,831.0	32	17,136.10	15	–14,305.1	9
Israel	19,660.7	6,892.1	21	12,768.60	19	–5,876.5	22
Australia	19,501.3	13,087.6	14	6,413.70	30	6,673.9	229
Switzerland	19,341.7	8,656.4	18	10,685.30	22	–2,028.9	33
Philippines	18,046.3	7,987.3	19	10,059.00	25	–2,071.7	32
India	18,035.0	4,979.7	24	13,055.30	18	–8,075.6	17
Sweden	14,342.6	3,223.4	30	11,119.20	20	–7,895.8	18
MAJOR AREA/GROUP							
North America	626,990.1	267,335.5	NA	359,654.6	NA	–92,319.2	NA
Western Europe	432,233.9	165,956.8	NA	266,277.1	NA	–100,320.3	NA
Euro Area	300,335.5	113,131.8	NA	187,203.7	NA	–74,071.90	NA
European Union (EU)	396,557.1	151,730.9	NA	244,826.2	NA	–93,095.30	NA
European Free Trade Association	26,841.1	10,380.3	NA	16,460.8	NA	–6,080.50	NA
Eastern Europe	25,425.6	7,105.8	NA	18,319.8	NA	–11,214.00	NA
Former Soviet Republics	14,810.9	4,094.7	NA	10,716.2	NA	–6,621.50	NA
OECD	430,176.8	165,070.6	NA	265,106.2	NA	–100,035.60	NA
Pacific Rim Countries	607,414.7	188,448.7	NA	418,966.0	NA	–230,517.20	NA
Asia/Near East	60,832.7	19,362.4	NA	41,470.3	NA	–22,107.90	NA
Asia/NICS	164,418.8	71,601.1	NA	92,817.7	NA	–21,216.60	NA
Asia/South	25,976.3	6,280.5	NA	19,695.8	NA	–13,415.30	NA
ASEAN	127,093.8	45,244.0	NA	81,849.8	NA	–36,605.80	NA
APEC	1,281,479.7	469,749.5	NA	811,730.2	NA	–341,980.70	NA
South/Central America	130,775.3	51,946.2	NA	78,829.1	NA	–26,882.80	NA
Twenty Latin American Republics	351,772.3	142,278.6	NA	209,493.7	NA	–67,215.20	NA
Central American Common Market	23,239.1	10,825.8	NA	12,413.3	NA	–1,587.50	NA
LAFTA	316,491.2	124,500.1	NA	191,991.1	NA	–67,491.10	NA
NATO	810,118.9	331,512.6	NA	478,606.3	NA	–147,093.70	NA
OPEC	85,623.3	17,279.4	NA	68,343.9	NA	–51,064.50	NA
WORLD TOTAL	**1,981,892.3**	**724,771.0**	**NA**	**1,257,121.3**	**NA**	**–532,350.30**	**NA**

(1) Rank shown is for column to the left. (2) Rank is by size of U.S. trade deficit; ranking includes the territories as well as nations. NA = Not applicable. **Note:** Details may not equal totals because of rounding or incomplete enumeration.

Definitions of areas used in the table, as provided by the source: **North America**—Canada, Mexico. **Western Europe**—Andorra, Austria, Belgium, Bosnia and Herzegovina, Croatia, Cyprus, Denmark, Faroe Islands, Finland, France, Germany, Gibraltar, Greece, Iceland, Ireland, Italy, Liechtenstein, Luxembourg, Macedonia, Malta and Gozo, Monaco, Netherlands, Norway, Portugal, San Marino, Serbia & Montenegro, Slovenia, Spain, Svalbard/Jan Mayen Island, Sweden, Switzerland, Turkey, United Kingdom, Vatican City. **Euro Area**—Austria, Belgium, Finland, France, Germany, Greece, Ireland, Italy, Luxembourg, Netherlands, Portugal, Spain. **EU**—(European Union) Austria, Belgium, Denmark, Finland, France, Germany, Greece, Ireland, Italy, Luxembourg, Netherlands, Portugal, Spain, Sweden, United Kingdom. **EFTA**—(European Free Trade Association) Iceland, Liechtenstein, Norway, Switzerland. **Eastern Europe**—Albania, Armenia, Azerbaijan, Belarus, Bulgaria, Czech Republic, Estonia, Georgia, Hungary, Kazakhstan, Kyrgyzstan, Latvia, Lithuania, Moldova, Poland, Romania, Russia, Slovakia, Tajikistan, Turkmenistan, Ukraine, Uzbekistan. **Former Soviet Republics**—Armenia, Azerbaijan, Belarus, Estonia, Georgia, Kazakhstan, Kyrgyzstan, Latvia, Lithuania, Moldova, Russia, Tajikistan, Turkmenistan, Ukraine, Uzbekistan. **OECD**—(Organization for Economic Cooperation & Development in Europe) Austria, Belgium, Denmark, Finland, France, Germany, Greece, Iceland, Ireland, Italy, Liechtenstein, Luxembourg, Monaco, Netherlands, Norway, Portugal, San Marino, Spain, Svalbard/Jan Mayen Island, Sweden, Switzerland, Turkey, United Kingdom. **Pacific Rim Countries/Territories**—Australia, Brunei, China, Indonesia, Japan, Macao, Malaysia, New Zealand, Papua New Guinea, Philippines, Singapore, South Korea, Taiwan. **Asia/Near East**—Bahrain, Iran, Iraq, Israel, Jordan, Kuwait, Lebanon, Oman, Qatar, Saudi Arabia, Syria, U.A.E., Yemen. **Asia/NICS**—(Newly Industrialized Countries) Hong Kong (special administrative region of China), Singapore, South Korea, Taiwan. **Asia/South**—Afghanistan, Bangladesh, India, Nepal, Pakistan, Sri Lanka. **ASEAN**—(Association of Southeast Asian Nations) Brunei, Cambodia, Indonesia, Malaysia, Philippines, Singapore, Thailand. **AC**—(Asia-Pacific Economic Cooperation) Australia, Brunei, Canada, Chile, China, Indonesia, Japan, Malaysia, Mexico, New Zealand, Papua New Guinea, Peru, Philippines, Russia, Singapore, South Korea, Taiwan, Thailand, Vietnam. **South/Central America**—Anguilla, Antigua and Barbuda, Argentina, Aruba, Bahamas, Barbados, Belize, Bermuda, Bolivia, Brazil, British Virgin Islands, Cayman Islands, Chile, Colombia, Costa Rica, Cuba, Dominica, Dominican Republic, Ecuador, El Salvador, Falkland Islands, French Guiana, Grenada, Guadeloupe, Guatemala, Guyana, Haiti, Honduras, Jamaica, Martinique, Montserrat, Netherland Antilles, Nicaragua, Panama, Paraguay, Peru, St. Kitts and Nevis, St. Lucia, St. Vincent and the Grenadines, Suriname, Trinidad and Tobago, Turks and Caicos Islands, Uruguay, Venezuela. **20 Latin American Republics**—Argentina, Bolivia, Brazil, Chile, Colombia, Costa Rica, Cuba, Dominican Republic, Ecuador, El Salvador, Guatemala, Haiti, Honduras, Mexico, Nicaragua, Panama, Paraguay, Peru, Uruguay, Venezuela. **Central American Common Market**—Costa Rica, El Salvador, Guatemala, Honduras, Nicaragua. **LAFTA**—(Latin American Free Trade Assn.) Argentina, Bolivia, Brazil, Chile, Colombia, Ecuador, Mexico, Paraguay, Peru, Uruguay, Venezuela. **NATO**—Belgium, Canada, Denmark, France, Germany, Greece, Iceland, Ireland, Italy, Liechtenstein, Luxembourg, Monaco, Netherlands, Norway, Portugal, San Marino, Spain, Svalbard/Jan Mayan Island, Sweden, Switzerland, Turkey, United Kingdom. **OPEC**—Algeria, Indonesia, Iran, Iraq, Kuwait, Libya, Nigeria, Qatar, Saudi Arabia, United Arab Emirates, Venezuela.

U.S. Exports and Imports by Principal Commodity Groupings, 2003

Source: Office of Trade and Economic Analysis, U.S. Dept. of Commerce

(millions of dollars)

Items	Exports	Imports	Items	Exports	Imports
TOTAL	$724,771	$1,257,121	Jewelry	$2,030	$7,499
Agricultural commodities	**59,561**	**47,453**	Lighting, plumbing	1,348	6,000
Animal feeds	3,878	636	Metal manufactures[1]	11,243	17,979
Cereal flour	1,672	2,497	Metalworking machinery	4,163	5,326
Coffee	5	1,612	Nickel	392	1,171
Corn	4,934	151	Optical goods	2,249	2,993
Cotton, raw and linters	3,376	28	Paper and paperboard	9,782	14,848
Hides and skins	1,643	74	Photographic equipment	3,329	5,029
Live animals	782	1,619	Plastic articles[1]	6,781	10,215
Meat and preparations	7,252	4,403	Platinum	470	2,619
Oils/fats, vegetable	1,140	1,348	Pottery	88	1,764
Rice	1,024	212	Power generating mach.	31,605	32,437
Soybeans	7,964	47	Printed materials	4,611	4,148
Sugar	6	534	Records/magnetic media	4,474	5,853
Tobacco, unmanufactured	1,038	690	Rubber articles[1]	1,417	2,357
Vegetables and fruits	8,115	11,475	Rubber tires and tubes	2,199	5,256
Wheat	3,935	123	Scientific instruments	28,029	23,660
Manufactured goods	**557,954**	**1,027,391**	Ships, boats	1,160	1,891
ADP equipment; office machines	28,842	80,812	Silver and bullion	177	801
Airplane parts	14,453	4,475	Spacecraft	142	188
Airplanes	24,649	12,235	Specialized industrial machinery	23,432	20,852
Aluminum	2,942	7,239	Television, VCR, etc.	16,853	71,168
Artwork/antiques	1,158	4,395	Textile yarn, fabric	10,458	17,259
Basketware, etc.	4,697	7,856	Toys/games/sporting goods	3,154	21,574
Chemicals - cosmetics	6,550	5,613	Travel goods	291	4,844
Chemicals - dyeing	4,130	2,482	Vehicles	60,907	172,611
Chemicals - fertilizers	2,339	2,130	Watches/clocks/parts	241	3,601
Chemicals - inorganic	5,580	7,388	Wood manufactures	1,576	9,286
Chemicals - medicinal	18,782	31,741	**Mineral fuels**	**13,768**	**153,298**
Chemicals - organic	20,140	32,741	Coal	1,610	1,172
Chemicals - plastics	21,068	12,158	Crude oil	159	101,795
Chemicals[1]	12,999	6,860	Liquified propane/butane	469	2,310
Clothing	4,959	68,166	Mineral fuels, other	2,573	1,648
Copper	1,232	3,158	Natural gas	1,390	18,503
Electrical machinery	69,868	82,427	Petroleum preparations	7,008	26,680
Footwear	495	15,602	**Selected commodities**	**19,915**	**29,198**
Furniture and bedding	3,607	24,356	Alcoholic bev.,distilled	551	3,696
Gem diamonds	336	12,932	Cigarettes	1,404	301
General industrial machinery	30,199	38,494	Cork, wood, lumber	3,390	7,279
Glass	2,509	2,335	Crude fertilizers	1,580	1,338
Glassware	673	1,904	Fish and preparations	3,082	10,927
Gold, nonmonetary	4,779	2,933	Metal ores; scrap	5,664	3,062
Iron and steel mill products	6,254	11,092	Pulp and waste paper	4,090	2,595

(1) Those not specified elsewhere. **NOTE:** Not all products are listed in each commodity group.

Trends in U.S. Foreign Trade, 1790-2003

Source: Office of Trade and Economic Analysis, U.S. Dept. of Commerce

In 1790, U.S. exports and imports combined came to $43 million and there was a $3 million trade deficit. In 2003, U.S. exports and imports combined amounted to nearly $2 trillion, and the trade deficit, which has generally been climbing in recent years (after a century of trade surpluses), reached $532 billion, the highest dollar total in history.

(in millions of dollars)

Year	Exports	Imports	Trade Balance	Year	Exports	Imports	Trade Balance	Year	Exports	Imports	Trade Balance
1790	$20	$23	$−3	1880	$836	$668	$168	1970	$42,681	$40,356	$2,325
1795	48	70	−22	1885	742	578	165	1975	107,652	98,503	9,149
1800	71	91	−20	1890	858	789	69	1980	220,626	244,871	−24,245
1805	96	121	−25	1895	808	732	76	1985	213,133	345,276	−132,143
1810	67	85	−19	1900	1,394	850	545	1990	394,030	495,042	−101,012
1815	53	113	−60	1905	1,519	1,118	401	1991	421,730	485,453	−63,723
1820	70	74	−5	1910	1,745	1,557	188	1992	448,164	532,665	−84,501
1825	91	90	1	1915	2,769	1,674	1,094	1993	465,091	580,659	−115,568
1830	72	63	9	1920	8,228	5,278	2,950	1994	512,626	683,256	−170,630
1835	115	137	−22	1925	4,910	4,227	683	1995	584,742	743,445	−158,703
1840	124	98	25	1930	3,843	3,061	782	1996	625,075	795,289	−170,214
1845	106	113	−7	1935	2,283	2,047	235	1997	689,182	870,671	−181,489
1850	144	174	−29	1940	4,021	2,625	1,396	1998	682,138	911,896	−229,758
1855	219	258	−39	1945	9,806	4,159	5,646	1999	695,797	1,024,618	−328,821
1860	334	354	−20	1950	9,997	8,954	1,043	2000	781,918	1,218,022	−436,104
1865	166	239	−73	1955	14,298	11,566	2,732	2001	729,100	1,140,999	−411,899
1870	393	436	−43	1960	19,659	15,073	4,586	2002	693,103	1,161,366	−468,263
1875	513	533	−20	1965	26,742	21,520	5,222	2003	724,771	1,257,121	−532,350

The North American Free Trade Agreement (NAFTA)

NAFTA, a free trade pact between the U.S., Canada, and Mexico, took effect Jan. 1, 1994. Major provisions are:

Agriculture—Tariffs on all farm products are to be eliminated over 15 years. Domestic price-support systems may continue provided they do not distort trade.

Automobiles—By 2003, at least 62.5% of an automobile's value must have been produced in North America for it to qualify for duty-free status. Tariffs are to be phased out over 10 years.

Banking—U.S. and Canadian banks may acquire Mexican commercial banks accounting for as much as 8% of the industry's capital. All limits on such ownership of banks end in 2004.

Disputes—Special judges have jurisdiction to resolve disagreements within strict timetables.

Energy—Mexico continues to bar foreign ownership of its oil fields but, starting in 2004, U.S. and Canadian companies can bid on contracts offered by Mexican oil and electricity monopolies.
Environment—The trade agreement cannot be used to overrule national and state environmental, health, or safety laws.
Immigration—All 3 countries must ease restrictions on the movement of business executives and professionals.
Jobs—Barriers to limit Mexican migration to U.S. remain unaffected by NAFTA.
Patent and copyright protection—Mexico strengthened its laws providing protection to intellectual property.

Tariffs—Tariffs on 10,000 customs goods are to be eliminated over 15 years. One-half of U.S. exports to Mexico are to be considered duty-free by 1999.
Textiles—A "rule of origin" provision requires most garments to be made from yarn and fabric that have been produced in North America. Most tariffs being phased out by 1999.
Trucking—Trucks were to have free access on crossborder routes and throughout the 3 countries by 1999, but the U.S. continued to impose restrictions on Mexican trucks. In 2001, an arbitration panel ruled that the U.S. restrictions were in violation of NAFTA. Pres. Bush in Nov. 2002 eased restrictions on Mexican trucks entering the U.S.

U.S. Trade With Mexico and Canada, 1993-2003

Source: Office of Trade and Economic Analysis, U.S. Dept. of Commerce
(U.S. exports to, imports from, Canada and Mexico in millions of dollars)

	With MEXICO				With CANADA		
Year	Exports	Imports	U.S. Trade Balance[1]	Year	Exports	Imports	U.S. Trade Balance[1]
1993	$41,581	$39,917	$1,664	1993	$100,444	$111,216	$–10,772
1994[2]	50,844	49,494	1,350	1994[2]	114,439	128,406	–13,968
1995	46,292	61,685	–15,393	1995	127,226	145,349	–18,123
1996	56,792	74,297	–17,506	1996	134,210	155,893	–21,682
1997	71,388	85,938	–14,549	1997	151,767	167,234	–15,467
1998	78,773	94,629	–15,857	1998	156,603	173,256	–16,653
1999	86,909	109,721	–22,812	1999	166,600	198,711	–32,111
2000	111,349	135,926	–24,577	2000	178,941	230,838	–51,897
2001	101,297	131,338	–30,041	2001	163,424	216,268	–52,844
2002	97,470	134,616	–37,146	2002	160,923	209,088	–48,165
2003	97,412	138,060	–40,648	2003	169,924	221,595	–51,671

(1) Totals may not add due to rounding. (2) NAFTA provisions began to take effect Jan. 1, 1994.

Foreign Exchange Rates, 1970-2003

Source: International Monetary Fund, Federal Reserve Board; Federal Reserve Board
(National currency units per dollar except as indicated; data are annual averages)

Note: As of 2002, the euro, the European Union's single currency, replaced the national currencies in the EU nations shown (Austria, Belgium, France, Gemany, Greece, Ireland, Italy, Netherlands, Portugal, and Spain), as well as in Finland and Luxembourg.

Year	Australia[1] (dollar)	Austria (schilling)	Belgium (franc)	Canada (dollar)	Denmark (krone)	France (franc)	Germany[2] (deutsche mark)	Greece (drachma)
1970	1.1136	25.880	49.680	1.0103	7.489	5.5200	3.6480	30.00
1975	1.3077	17.443	36.799	1.0175	5.748	4.2876	2.4613	32.29
1980	1.1400	12.945	29.237	1.1693	5.634	4.2250	1.8175	42.62
1985	0.7003	20.690	59.378	1.3655	10.596	8.9852	2.9440	138.12
1990	0.7813	11.370	33.418	1.1668	6.189	5.4453	1.6157	158.51
1995	0.7415	10.081	29.480	1.3724	5.602	4.9915	1.4331	231.66
1998	0.6294	12.379	36.299	1.4835	6.701	5.8995	1.7597	295.53
2000	0.5815	0.9232[3]	0.9232[3]	1.4855	8.095	0.9232[3]	0.9232[3]	365.92
2001	0.5169	0.8952[3]	0.8952[3]	1.5487	8.3323	0.8952[3]	0.8952[3]	0.8952[3]
2002	0.5437	0.9454[3]	0.9454[3]	1.5704	7.8862	0.9454[3]	0.9454[3]	0.9454[3]
2003	0.6520	1.1315[3]	1.1315[3]	1.4013	6.5800	1.1315[3]	1.1315[3]	1.1315[3]

Year	India (rupee)	Ireland[1] (pound)	Italy (lira)	Japan (yen)	Malaysia (ringgit)	Mexico (new peso)	Netherlands (guilder)	Norway (krone)
1970	7.576	2.3959	623	357.60	3.0900	—	3.5970	7.1400
1975	8.409	2.2216	653	296.78	2.4030	—	2.5293	5.2282
1980	7.887	2.0577	856	226.63	2.1767	—	1.9875	4.9381
1985	12.369	1.0656	1,909	238.54	2.4830	—	3.3214	8.5972
1995	32.427	1.6038	1,628.9	94.06	2.5044	6.4194	1.6057	6.3352
1998	41.259	1.4257	1,736.2	130.91	3.9244	9.1360	1.9837	7.5451
1999	43.055	1.0668	0.9386[3]	113.91	3.8000	9.5604	0.9386[3]	7.7992
2000	45.000	0.9232[3]	0.9232[3]	107.80	3.8000	9.4590	0.9232[3]	8.8131
2001	47.22	0.8952[3]	0.8952[3]	121.57	3.8000	9.337	0.8952[3]	8.9964
2002	48.63	0.9454[3]	0.9454[3]	125.22	3.8000	9.663	0.9454[3]	7.9839
2003	46.59	1.1315[3]	1.1315[3]	115.97	3.8000	10.791	1.1315[3]	7.0819

Year	Portugal (escudo)	Singapore (dollar)	South Korea (won)	Spain (peseta)	Sweden (krona)	Switzerland (franc)	Thailand (baht)	UK[1] (pound)
1970	28.75	3.0800	310.57	69.72	5.1700	4.3160	21.000	2.3959
1975	25.51	2.3713	484.00	57.43	4.1530	2.5839	20.379	2.2216
1980	50.08	2.1412	607.43	71.76	4.2309	1.6772	20.476	2.3243
1985	170.39	2.2002	870.02	170.04	8.6039	2.4571	27.159	1.2963
1990	142.55	1.8125	707.76	101.93	5.9188	1.3892	25.585	1.7847
1995	151.11	1.4174	771.27	124.69	7.1333	1.1825	24.915	1.5785
1998	180.10	1.6736	1,401.44	149.40	7.9499	1.4498	41.359	1.6564
2000	0.9232[3]	1.7250	1,130.90	0.9232[3]	9.1735	1.6904	40.210	1.5156
2001	0.8952[3]	1.7930	1,292.01	0.8952[3]	10.3425	1.6891	44.532	1.4396
2002	0.9454[3]	1.7908	1,250.31	0.9454[3]	9.7233	1.5567	43.019	1.5025
2003	1.1315[3]	1.7411	1,192.08	1.1315[3]	8.0822	1.3454	41.564	1.6341

(1) U.S. dollars per unit of national currency. (2) West Germany before 1991. (3) Euro Area member, figures in euros per dollar.

WORLD ALMANAC QUICK QUIZ

Can you rank these countries, highest to lowest, by dollar value of their imports from the U.S. in 2003?
(a) Canada   (b) Mexico   (c) United Kingdom   (d) China
For the answer look in this chapter, or see page 1008.

Foreign Direct Investment[1] in the U.S. by Selected Countries and Territories

Source: Bureau of Economic Analysis; U.S. Dept. of Commerce
(millions of dollars)

	1995	2000	2003
ALL COUNTRIES[2]	$54,368	$1,256,867	$1,378,001
Canada	6,481	114,309	105,255
Europe[3]	36,654	887,014	1,000,532
Austria	8	3,007	4,104
Belgium	38	14,787	10,678
Denmark	NA	4,025	2,860
Finland	0	8,875	5,700
France	1,217	125,740	143,341
Germany	14,155	122,412	148,774
Ireland	106	25,523	26,793
Italy	NA	6,576	6,695
Liechtenstein	NA	319	277
Luxembourg	NA	58,930	104,452
Netherlands	855	138,894	146,117
Norway	14	2,665	3,218
Spain	147	5,068	5,520
Sweden	NA	21,991	19,823
Switzerland	4,198	64,719	112,856
United Kingdom	9,676	277,613	230,374
South and Central America[3]	NA	13,384	20,636
Brazil	5	882	663
Mexico	146	7,462	6,680
Panama	0	3,819	8,383
Venezuela	NA	792	4,884
Other Western Hemisphere[3]	NA	40,307	48,921
Bahamas	0	1,254	1,120
Bermuda	166	18,336	5,914
Netherlands Antilles	NA	3,807	4,048
UK islands, Caribbean	64	15,191	28,949
Africa[3]	NA	2,700	2,187
South Africa	NA	704	376
Middle East[3]	500	6,506	7,931
Israel	NA	3,012	3,834
Kuwait	31	908	1,155
Lebanon	0	1	1
Saudi Arabia	NA	NA	NA
United Arab Emirates	NA	64	39
Asia and Pacific[3]	9,169	192,647	192,539
Australia	2,488	18,775	24,652
Hong Kong	252	1,493	1,981
Japan	3,758	159,690	159,258
Korea, South	1,257	3,110	2,337
Malaysia	57	310	208
New Zealand	NA	395	607
Philippines	NA	47	33
Singapore	863	5,087	-162
Taiwan	286	3,174	2,708
European Union[4]	32,436	814,033	855,669
OPEC[5]	504	4,330	8,828

(1) The book value of foreign direct investors' equity in, and net outstanding loans to, their U.S. affiliates. A U.S. affiliate is a U.S. business enterprise in which a single foreign direct investor owns at least 10% of the voting securities or the equivalent. (2) Total includes sources not reflected in regional subtotals. (3) Totals include countries or territories not shown. (4) The European Union in 2003 included Austria, Belgium, Denmark, Finland, France, Germany, Greece, Ireland, Italy, Luxembourg, the Netherlands, Portugal, Spain, Sweden, and the United Kingdom. (5) Organization of Petroleum Exporting Countries: Algeria, Indonesia, Iran, Iraq, Kuwait, Libya, Nigeria, Qatar, Saudi Arabia, United Arab Emirates, and Venezuela. NA = Not available.

U.S. Direct Investment[1] Abroad in Selected Countries and Territories

Source: Bureau of Economic Analysis, U.S. Dept. of Commerce
(millions of dollars)

	1990	2000	2003
ALL COUNTRIES[2]	$424,086	$1,316,247	1,788,911
Canada	67,033	132,472	192,409
Europe	211,194	687,320	963,087
Austria	889	2,872	5,139
Belgium	9,050	17,973	25,804
Czech Republic	NA	1,228	1,790
Denmark	1,597	5,270	7,329
Finland	551	1,342	2,271
France	18,874	42,628	47,914
Germany	27,259	55,508	80,163
Greece	288	795	1,106
Hungary	NA	1,920	2,843
Ireland	6,880	35,903	55,463
Italy	13,117	23,484	30,417
Luxembourg	1,390	27,849	66,919
Netherlands	22,658	115,429	178,933
Norway	3,815	4,379	8,325
Poland	NA	3,884	5,453
Portugal	598	2,664	3,480
Russia	NA	1,147	1,176
Spain	7,704	21,236	38,215
Sweden	1,600	25,959	28,905
Switzerland	25,199	55,377	86,435
Turkey	494	1,826	1,989
United Kingdom	68,224	230,762	272,640
Other	NA	7,885	10,378
South America[3]	23,760	84,220	69,942
Argentina	2,956	17,488	11,026
Brazil	14,918	36,717	29,915
Chile	1,368	10,052	9,986
Colombia	1,728	3,693	2,751
Ecuador	387	832	1,446
Peru	410	3,130	2,659
Venezuela	1,490	10,531	10,859
Central America[3]	17,719	73,841	71,507
Costa Rica	NA	1,716	1,831
Honduras	NA	399	270
Mexico	$9,398	$39,352	$61,526
Panama	7,409	30,758	6,497
Other	NA	1,618	1,382
Other Western Hemisphere[3]	30,113	108,515	162,574
Bahamas	3,309	NA	NA
Barbados	NA	2,141	1,766
Bermuda	21,737	60,114	84,609
Dominican Republic	NA	1,143	860
UK islands, Caribbean	4,800	33,451	54,507
Other	NA	11,665	20,832
Africa[3]	4,861	11,891	18,960
Egypt	1,465	1,998	3,018
Nigeria	161	470	2,082
South Africa	956	3,562	3,902
Middle East[3]	3,973	10,863	16,942
Israel	756	3,735	6,208
Saudi Arabia	1,981	3,661	4,217
United Arab Emirates	519	683	1,430
Asia and Pacific[3]	61,869	207,125	293,490
Australia	14,846	34,838	40,985
China	NA	11,140	11,877
Hong Kong	6,187	27,447	44,323
India	513	2,379	3,609
Indonesia	3,226	8,904	10,387
Japan	20,997	57,091	73,435
Korea, South	2,178	8,968	13,318
Malaysia	1,384	7,910	7,580
New Zealand	3,131	4,271	3,849
Philippines	1,629	3,638	4,700
Singapore	3,385	24,133	57,589
Taiwan	2,014	7,836	10,961
Thailand	1,585	5,824	7,393
European Union[4]	NA	609,674	844,698
Eastern Europe[5]	NA	14,989	20,524
OPEC[6]	NA	28,545	36,549

(1) The book value of U.S. direct investors' equity in, and net outstanding loans to, their foreign affiliates. A foreign affiliate is a foreign business enterprise in which a single U.S. investor owns at least 10% of the voting securities or the equivalent. (2) Total includes countries not reflected in regional totals. (3) Total includes countries not shown. (4) The members of the European Union in 2003 were Austria, Belgium, Denmark, Finland, France, Germany, Greece, Ireland, Italy, Luxembourg, the Netherlands, Portugal, Spain, Sweden, and the United Kingdom. (5) Eastern Europe is defined to include Albania, Armenia, Azerbaijan, Belarus, Bulgaria, Czech Republic, Estonia, Georgia, Hungary, Kazakhstan, Kyrgyzstan, Latvia, Lithuania, Moldova, Poland, Romania, Russia, Slovakia, Tajikistan, Turkmenistan, Ukraine, and Uzbekistan. (6) Organization of Petroleum Exporting Countries: Algeria, Indonesia, Iran, Iraq, Kuwait, Libya, Nigeria, Qatar, Saudi Arabia, the United Arab Emirates, and Venezuela. NA = not available.

U.S. International Transactions, 1970-2003

Source: Bureau of Economic Analysis, U.S. Dept. of Commerce; revised as of July 2003

(millions of dollars)

	1970	1975	1980	1985	1990	1995	2000	2003
Exports of goods, services, and income[1]	$68,387	$157,936	$344,440	$382,749	$700,455	$991,490	$1,421,429	$1,314,888
Merchandise, bal. of payments basis[2]	42,469	107,088	224,250	215,915	389,307	575,871	771,994	713,122
Services	14,171	25,497	47,584	73,155	147,824	218,739	298,986	307,381
Income receipts on U.S.-owned assets abroad	11,748	25,351	72,606	93,679	163,324	196,880	347,614	291,354
Imports of goods and services and income payments	−59,901	−132,745	−333,774	−484,037	−757,758	−1,086,539	−1,779,188	−1,778,117
Merchandise, balance of payments basis[2]	−39,866	−98,185	−249,750	−338,088	−498,337	−749,431	−1,224,408	−1,260,674
Services	−14,520	−21,996	−41,491	−72,862	−120,019	−147,036	−224,916	−256,337
Income payments on foreign-owned assets in the U.S.	−5,515	−12,564	−42,532	−73,087	−139,402	−190,072	−322,345	−252,573
Unilateral transfers, net	−6,156	−7,075	−8,349	−22,700	−34,588	−34,046	−55,684	−67,439
Capital acct. transactions, net	NA	NA	NA	NA	NA	NA	−809	−3,079
U.S.-owned assets abroad, net (increase)/financial outflow [−])	−9,337	−39,703	−86,967	−39,889	−74,011	−307,207	−569,798	−283,414
U.S. official reserve assets, net	2,481	−849	−8,155	−3,858	−2,158	−9,742	−290	1,523
U.S. government assets, other than official reserve assets, net	−1,589	−3,474	−5,162	−2,821	2,307	−549	−941	537
U.S. private assets, net	−10,229	−35,380	−73,651	−33,211	−74,160	−296,916	−568,567	−285,474
Foreign-owned assets in the U.S., net (increase/financial inflow [+])	6,359	17,170	62,612	146,383	140,992	451,234	1,046,896	829,173
Stat. discrepancy (sum of above items with sign reversed)	−219	4,417	20,886	17,494	24,911	−14,931	−62,846	−12,012
Memorandum: Balance on current account	2,331	18,116	2,317	−123,987	−91,892	−129,095	−413,443	−530,668

NA = Not available. (1) Excludes transfers of goods and services under U.S. military grant programs. (2) Excludes exports of goods under U.S. military agency sales contracts identified in Census export documents, excludes imports of goods under direct defense expenditures identified in Census import documents, and reflects various other adjustments.

Merchant Fleets of the World by Flag of Registry, 2004

Source: Maritime Administration, U.S. Dept. of Commerce

Self-propelled oceangoing vessels of 1,000 gross deadweight tons and over, as of Jan. 1, 2004 (tonnage in thousands)

		All Vessels		Tanker		Dry Bulk Carrier		Container		Other[1]	
		No.	Tons	No.	Tons	No.	Tons	No.	Tons	No.	Tons
By Flag	Panama	4,735	183,886	1,117	58,746	1,460	91,532	574	20,304	1,584	13,305
	Liberia	1,447	78,623	561	44,106	293	18,390	374	12,737	219	3,390
	Greece	734	51,508	300	30,134	295	18,634	47	2,235	92	504
	Bahamas	980	43,119	243	26,414	171	9,439	77	2,195	489	5,070
	Malta	1,207	41,088	261	16,494	473	19,869	50	1,179	423	3,546
	Cyprus	1,054	35,813	144	7,016	425	21,919	129	3,307	356	3,571
	Singapore	867	35,211	421	18,573	130	9,942	185	4,662	131	2,034
	Hong Kong	633	32,450	97	7,081	353	20,839	84	2,673	99	1,857
	Marshall Islands	406	27,700	186	19,058	89	5,738	74	1,662	57	1,241
	Norway (NIS)[2]	596	25,295	302	14,470	82	7,588	5	88	207	3,149
	China[3]	1,508	24,901	291	4,549	336	11,751	129	2,596	752	6,006
	United States	418	13,325	109	5,875	20	837	86	3,281	203	3,331
	Japan	562	12,526	238	6,625	144	4,626	15	474	165	800
	India	283	10,560	114	6,746	87	3,369	8	152	74	293
	Italy	426	9,718	225	4,739	36	2,605	24	821	141	1,553
	Korea (South)	498	9,489	154	1,905	100	5,839	51	794	193	951
	United Kingdom	358	9,435	83	1,880	17	1,609	120	4,773	138	1,174
	Isle of Man	225	9,400	122	6,958	19	1,561	17	363	67	517
	St. Vincent & the Grenadines	670	8,731	61	667	121	4,752	27	181	461	3,131
	Denmark (DIS)	253	8,539	76	3,389	2	76	78	4,705	97	368
	All Other	10,730	150,387	2,227	53,826	1,115	41,179	861	20,084	6,587	35,297
By Country[4]	Greece	2,973	155,857	805	63,613	1,349	78,265	198	7,455	621	6,524
	Japan	2,671	106,703	775	38,817	847	52,509	217	7,665	832	7,712
	Norway	1,108	48,208	456	29,934	169	11,047	16	502	467	6,725
	Germany	2,160	47,511	223	9,174	168	7,006	889	25,067	880	6,264
	China	2,133	46,210	319	7,542	617	25,956	219	4,700	978	8,011
	United States	973	45,188	396	32,304	101	5,035	91	3,128	385	4,721
	Hong Kong	464	30,200	99	10,788	217	16,358	38	1,468	110	1,586
	Korea (South)	763	24,880	228	8,128	175	13,004	98	2,213	262	1,535
	Singapore	698	23,090	316	13,801	120	5,080	141	3,150	121	1,059
	Taiwan	523	22,673	42	3,251	181	11,865	184	6,623	116	934
	United Kingdom	503	17,804	147	7,913	57	4,537	87	3,556	212	1,799
	Denmark	534	15,408	152	6,018	29	1,612	126	6,489	227	1,289
	Russia	1,655	14,801	403	8,223	117	1,822	24	329	1,111	4,426
	Saudi Arabia	95	12,039	78	11,751	1	2	-	-	16	285
	India	279	12,034	124	7,555	102	4,135	3	87	50	257
	Italy	455	11,570	235	5,382	53	3,651	12	298	155	2,240
	Malaysia	300	9,642	121	6,056	54	2,329	36	728	89	529
	Iran	125	8,640	35	5,713	45	2,051	8	213	37	662
	Turkey	528	8,628	92	1,487	131	5,118	32	359	273	1,664
	Switzerland	264	8,186	41	1,176	35	1,583	112	4,460	76	967
	All Other	9,444	152,431	2,245	60,626	1,200	49,131	484	10,775	5,517	31,899
TOTAL ALL SHIPS		28,650	821,703	7,332	339,251	5,768	302,096	3,015	89,267	12,535	91,089

(1) Includes roll-on/roll-off, passenger, breakbulk ships, partial container ships, refrigerated cargo ships, barge carriers, and specialized cargo ships. (2) NIS = Norwegian International Ship Registry. (3) Excluding Hong Kong. (4) Based on parent company nationality.

50 Busiest U.S. Ports, 2002

Source: Corps of Engineers, Dept. of the Army, U.S. Dept. of Defense
(ports ranked by tonnage handled; all figures in tons)

Rank	Port Name	Total	Domestic	Foreign	Imports	Exports
1.	South Louisiana, LA, Port of	216,396,497	124,908,067	91,488,430	34,577,409	56,911,021
2.	Houston, TX	177,560,719	62,372,636	115,188,083	80,026,921	35,161,162
3.	New York, NY and NJ	134,504,511	64,932,653	69,571,858	59,419,046	10,152,812
4.	Beaumont, TX	85,910,947	18,181,692	67,729,255	62,625,566	5,103,689
5.	New Orleans, LA	85,000,428	33,238,124	51,762,304	21,926,081	29,836,223
6.	Huntington - Tristate, WV, KY, OH	81,063,663	81,063,663	0	0	0
7.	Corpus Christi, TX	72,000,304	21,420,094	50,580,210	41,714,363	8,865,847
8.	Long Beach, CA	67,872,469	15,580,481	52,291,988	37,907,049	14,384,939
9.	Baton Rouge, LA	60,582,710	39,645,083	20,937,627	16,808,194	4,129,433
10.	Plaquemines, LA, Port of	59,110,736	35,826,872	23,283,864	13,725,168	9,558,696
11.	Texas City, TX	55,232,906	16,062,067	39,170,839	36,397,436	2,773,403
12.	Los Angeles, CA	52,216,048	6,808,260	45,407,788	31,627,547	13,780,241
13.	Pittsburgh, PA	52,050,661	52,050,661	0	0	0
14.	Valdez, AK	50,513,074	50,508,598	4,476	91	4,385
15.	Tampa, FL	48,384,970	31,815,180	16,569,790	8,343,457	8,226,333
16.	Lake Charles, LA	47,522,085	20,090,917	27,431,168	23,105,186	4,325,982
17.	Mobile, AL	46,021,599	21,871,248	24,150,351	15,661,508	8,488,843
18.	Duluth-Superior, MN and WI	44,160,834	29,699,830	14,461,004	624,222	13,836,782
19.	Baltimore, MD	38,822,710	15,188,610	23,634,100	18,256,065	5,378,035
20.	Philadelphia, PA	34,100,667	13,719,934	20,380,733	20,073,391	307,342
21.	St. Louis, MO and IL	32,601,491	32,601,491	0	0	0
22.	Pascagoula, MS	31,857,678	11,371,251	20,486,427	17,496,585	2,989,842
23.	Norfolk Harbor, VA	27,901,354	6,828,481	21,072,873	8,704,284	12,368,589
24.	Freeport, TX	27,163,872	5,079,632	22,084,240	19,778,106	2,306,134
25.	Portland, ME	27,131,856	1,986,833	25,145,023	24,970,592	174,431
26.	Portland, OR	26,635,044	11,203,936	15,431,108	4,065,740	11,365,368
27.	Paulsboro, NJ	26,382,576	8,284,374	18,098,202	17,775,692	322,510
28.	Marcus Hook, PA	25,207,395	9,626,723	15,580,672	15,561,662	19,010
29.	Charleston, SC	24,993,443	5,994,947	18,998,496	13,461,079	5,537,417
30.	Port Arthur, TX	22,675,808	7,458,017	15,217,791	11,687,188	3,530,603
31.	Richmond, CA	21,900,717	11,587,833	10,312,884	8,691,722	1,621,162
32.	Port Everglades, FL	21,279,754	12,582,424	8,697,330	6,707,601	1,989,729
33.	Savannah, GA	20,663,806	1,935,705	18,728,101	10,905,004	7,823,097
34.	Tacoma, WA	20,587,109	7,416,883	13,170,226	4,993,915	8,176,311
35.	Chicago, IL	20,402,907	18,777,496	1,625,411	1,059,317	566,094
36.	Boston, MA	20,353,642	7,109,959	13,243,683	12,471,484	772,199
37.	Seattle, WA	19,591,009	6,120,536	13,470,473	7,434,619	6,035,854
38.	Jacksonville, FL	17,905,831	8,228,941	9,676,890	8,688,528	988,362
39.	Detroit, MI	17,305,875	12,897,162	4,408,713	4,201,545	207,168
40.	Honolulu, HI	16,635,700	11,780,556	4,855,144	4,269,146	585,998
41.	Memphis, TN	16,400,555	16,400,555	0	0	0
42.	Anacortes, WA	15,362,650	12,790,686	2,571,964	1,711,572	860,392
43.	Two Harbors, MN	14,895,295	14,804,320	90,975	0	90,975
44.	Indiana Harbor, IN	13,839,001	13,325,649	513,352	471,753	41,599
45.	Cincinnati, OH	13,006,858	13,006,858	0	0	0
46.	Oakland, CA	12,454,506	2,994,905	9,459,601	4,020,827	5,438,774
47.	San Juan, PR	12,378,301	7,070,592	5,307,709	4,884,795	422,914
48.	Cleveland, OH	11,411,765	9,083,965	2,327,800	2,270,800	57,000
49.	Newport News, VA	11,300,962	6,192,716	5,108,246	1,142,937	3,965,309
50.	Toledo, OH	11,114,895	5,552,789	5,562,106	1,790,496	3,771,610

World Trade Organization (WTO)

Following World War II, the major world economic powers negotiated a set of rules for reducing and limiting trade barriers and settling trade disputes. These rules were called the General Agreement on Tariffs and Trade (GATT). Headquarters to oversee administration of the GATT were established in Geneva, Switzerland. Rounds of multilateral trade negotiations under the GATT were carried out periodically. The 8th round, begun in 1986 in Punta del Este, Uruguay, and dubbed the Uruguay Round, ended Dec. 15, 1993, when 117 countries completed a new trade-liberalization agreement. The name for the GATT was changed to the World Trade Organization (WTO), which officially came into being Jan. 1, 1995.

Leading Motor Vehicle Producers, 2003

Source: Automotive News Data Center and Marketing Systems GmbH

	Total	Passenger Cars	Trucks		Total	Passenger Cars	Trucks
United States	12,140,610	4,518,000	7,622,610	Iran	665,068	616,200	48,868
Japan	10,152,677	8,487,065	1,665,612	Sweden	549,073	444,119	104,954
Germany	5,499,710	5,145,403	354,307	Turkey	506,045	281,552	224,493
China	4,598,306	2,160,406	2,437,900	Czech Republic	439,845	431,864	7,981
France	3,614,933	3,201,494	413,439	South Africa	434,100	303,500	130,600
S. Korea	3,279,795	2,767,716	512,079	Australia	412,700	368,500	44,200
Spain	3,011,579	2,399,021	612,558	Malaysia	402,914	318,148	84,766
Canada	2,546,409	1,340,468	1,205,941	Poland	382,525	330,725	51,800
Brazil	1,870,679	1,520,062	350,617	Taiwan	375,437	264,837	110,600
United Kingdom	1,843,235	1,657,588	185,647	Indonesia	363,158	38,200	324,958
Mexico	1,585,261	914,343	670,918	Slovakia	243,983	243,900	83
Italy	1,318,589	1,026,454	292,135	Portugal	242,920	165,576	77,344
Russia	1,305,023	1,030,000	275,023	Netherlands	204,143	163,080	41,063
Belgium	940,371	825,136	115,235	Argentina	174,206	113,788	60,418
India	898,279	775,300	122,979				
Thailand	833,935	206,235	627,700	**World Total**[1]	**61,998,539**	**42,956,290**	**19,042,249**

(1) Total includes countries or territories not shown.

World Motor Vehicle Production, 1950-2003

Source: For 1950-1997, American Automobile Manufacturers Assn.; for 1998-2003: Automotive News Data Center and Marketing Systems GmbH
(in thousands)

Year	United States	Canada	W. Europe	Japan	Other	World total	U.S. % of world total
1950	8,006	388	1,991	32	160	10,577	75.7
1960	7,905	398	6,837	482	866	16,488	47.9
1970	8,284	1,160	13,049	5,289	1,637	29,419	28.2
1980	8,010	1,324	15,496	11,043	2,692	38,565	20.8
1985	11,653	1,933	16,113	12,271	2,939	44,909	25.9
1990	9,783	1,928	18,866	13,487	4,496	48,554	20.1
1991	8,811	1,888	17,804	13,245	5,180	46,928	18.8
1992	9,729	1,961	17,628	12,499	6,269	48,088	20.2
1993	10,898	2,246	15,208	11,228	7,205	46,785	23.3
1994	12,263	2,321	16,195	10,554	8,167	49,500	24.8
1995	11,985	2,408	17,045	10,196	8,349	49,983	24.0
1996	11,799	2,397	17,550	10,346	9,241	51,332	23.0
1997	12,119	2,571	17,773	10,975	10,024	53,463	22.7
1998	12,047	2,568	16,332	10,050	12,844	53,841	22.4
1999	13,107	3,042	17,603	9,985	14,050	57,787	22.7
2000	12,832	2,952	17,678	10,145	16,098	59,704	21.5
2001	11,518	2,535	17,825	9,777	16,170	57,705	19.7
2002	12,328	2,624	17,419	10,240	16,975	59,587	20.7
2003	12,141	2,546	17,356	10,153	19,803	61,999	19.6

Note: Data for 1998-2001 may not be fully comparable with earlier years because derived from different source.

New Passenger Cars Imported Into the U.S., by Country of Origin,[1] 1970-2003

Source: Bureau of the Census, Foreign Trade Division

	Japan	Germany[2]	Italy	United Kingdom	Sweden	France	South Korea	Mexico	Canada	Total[3]
1970	381,338	674,945	42,523	76,257	57,844	37,114	NA	NA	692,783	2,013,420
1975	695,573	370,012	102,344	67,106	51,993	15,647	NA	0	733,766	2,074,653
1980	1,991,502	338,711	46,899	32,517	61,496	47,386	NA	1	594,770	3,116,448
1981	1,911,525	234,052	21,635	12,728	68,042	42,477	NA	1	563,943	2,856,286
1982	1,801,185	259,385	9,402	13,023	89,231	50,032	NA	27	702,495	2,926,407
1983	1,871,192	239,807	5,442	17,261	114,726	40,823	NA	2	835,665	3,133,836
1984	1,948,714	335,032	8,582	19,833	114,854	37,788	NA	NA	1,073,425	3,559,427
1985	2,527,467	473,110	8,689	24,474	142,640	42,882	NA	13,647	1,144,805	4,397,679
1986	2,618,711	451,699	11,829	27,506	148,700	10,869	169,309	41,983	1,162,226	4,691,297
1987	2,417,509	377,542	8,648	50,059	138,565	26,707	399,856	126,266	926,927	4,589,010
1988	2,123,051	264,249	6,053	31,636	108,006	15,990	455,741	148,065	1,191,357	4,450,213
1989	2,051,525	216,881	9,319	29,378	101,571	4,885	270,609	133,049	1,151,122	4,042,728
1990	1,867,794	245,286	11,045	27,271	93,084	1,976	201,475	215,986	1,220,221	3,944,602
1991	1,762,347	171,097	2,886	14,862	62,905	1,727	186,740	249,498	1,109,248	3,612,665
1992	1,598,919	205,248	1,791	10,997	76,832	65	130,110	266,111	1,119,223	3,447,200
1993	1,501,953	180,383	1,178	20,029	58,742	23	122,943	299,634	1,371,856	3,604,361
1994	1,488,159	178,774	1,010	28,217	63,867	58	213,962	360,367	1,525,746	3,909,079
1995	1,114,360	204,932	1,031	42,450	82,593	14	131,718	462,800	1,552,691	3,624,428
1996	1,190,896	234,909	1,365	44,373	86,619	27	225,623	550,867	1,690,733	4,069,113
1997	1,387,812	300,489	1,912	43,691	79,780	67	222,568	544,075	1,731,209	4,378,295
1998	1,456,081	373,330	2,104	49,891	84,543	56	211,650	584,795	1,837,615	4,673,418
1999	1,707,277	461,061	1,697	68,394	83,399	186	372,965	639,878	2,170,427	5,639,616
2000	1,839,093	488,323	3,125	81,196	86,707	134	568,121	934,000	2,138,811	6,324,284
2001	1,790,346	494,131	2,580	82,487	92,439	92	633,769	861,853	1,855,789	6,065,138
2002	2,046,902	574,455	3,504	157,633	87,709	150	627,881	845,181	1,882,660	6,477,659
2003	1,770,355	561,482	2,943	207,158	119,773	298	692,863	680,214	1,811,892	6,127,485

(1) Excludes passenger cars assembled in U.S. foreign trade zones. (2) Figures prior to 1991 are for West Germany. (3) Includes countries not shown separately.

Domestic and Imported Retail Car Sales in the U.S., 1980-2003

Source: Ward's Communications

Year	Domestic	Imports Japan	Imports Germany	Imports Other Countries	Imports Total	Total U.S. Sales	Import Percent Total	Import Percent Japan	Import Percent Germany
1980	6,581,307	1,905,968	305,219	186,700	2,397,887	8,979,194	26.7	21.2	3.3
1981	6,208,760	1,858,896	282,881	185,502	2,327,279	8,536,039	27.3	21.8	3.3
1982	5,758,586	1,801,969	247,080	174,508	2,223,557	7,982,143	27.9	22.6	3.0
1983	6,795,295	1,915,621	279,748	191,403	2,386,772	9,182,067	26.0	20.9	3.0
1984	7,951,523	1,906,206	344,416	188,220	2,438,842	10,390,365	23.5	18.3	3.8
1985	8,204,542	2,217,837	423,983	195,925	2,837,745	11,042,287	25.7	20.1	3.8
1986	8,214,897	2,382,614	443,721	418,286	3,244,621	11,459,518	28.3	20.8	3.9
1987	7,080,858	2,190,405	347,881	657,465	3,195,751	10,276,609	31.1	21.3	3.4
1988	7,526,038	2,022,602	280,099	700,991	3,003,692	10,529,730	28.5	19.2	2.7
1989	7,072,902	1,897,143	248,561	553,660	2,699,364	9,772,266	27.6	19.4	2.5
1990	6,896,888	1,719,384	265,116	418,823	2,403,323	9,300,211	25.8	18.5	2.9
1991	6,136,757	1,500,309	192,776	344,814	2,037,899	8,174,656	24.9	18.4	2.4
1992	6,276,557	1,451,766	200,851	283,938	1,936,555	8,213,112	23.6	17.7	2.4
1993	6,741,667	1,328,445	186,177	261,570	1,776,192	8,517,859	20.9	15.6	2.2
1994	7,255,303	1,239,450	192,275	303,489	1,735,214	8,990,517	19.3	13.8	2.1
1995	7,128,707	981,506	207,482	317,269	1,506,257	8,634,964	17.4	11.4	2.4
1996	7,253,582	726,940	237,984	308,247	1,273,171	8,526,753	14.9	8.5	2.8
1997	6,916,769	726,104	297,028	332,173	1,355,305	8,272,074	16.4	8.8	3.6
1998	6,761,940	691,162	366,724	321,895	1,379,781	8,141,721	16.9	8.5	4.5
1999	6,979,357	757,568	466,870	494,489	1,718,927	8,698,284	19.8	8.7	5.4
2000	6,830,505	862,780	516,614	636,726	2,016,120	8,846,625	22.8	9.8	5.8
2001	6,324,996	836,685	522,659	738,285	2,097,629	8,422,625	24.9	9.9	6.2
2002	5,877,645	923,182	546,654	755,748	2,225,584	8,103,229	27.5	11.4	6.7
2003	5,527,430	817,038	543,823	722,190	2,083,051	7,610,481	27.4	10.7	7.1

(1) Includes cars manufactured in Canada and Mexico.

Passenger Car Production, U.S. Plants, 2002-2003

Source: Ward's AutoInfoBank

	2003	2002		2003	2002
TOTAL CARS	**4,510,469**	**5,018,777**	Alero	111,680	107,390
Mazda6	83,422	14,731	Aurora	1,786	7,217
Mazda 626	—	32,872	Intrigue	—	13,243
Mazda Total	**83,422**	**47,603**	**Oldsmobile Total**	**113,466**	**127,850**
Mercury Cougar	--	18,321	Bonneville	22,649	38,397
AUTOALLIANCE TOTAL¹	**83,422**	**65,924**	Grand Am	174,324	193,473
BMW Z3	—	11,634	Grand Prix	18,687	145,813
BMW Z4	56,589	11,554	Sunfire	52,393	83,463
BMW Total	**56,589**	**23,188**	**Pontiac Total**	**268,053**	**461,146**
Neon	1,859	12,054	Ion	138,008	35,000
Prowler	—	329	Saturn L	45,440	98,899
Sebring Convertible	46,158	50,020	Saturn S	—	110,457
Sebring Sedan	64,308	84,803	**Saturn Total**	**183,448**	**244,356**
Chrysler Total	**112,325**	**147,206**	**GM TOTAL**	**1,385,715**	**1,672,987**
Neon	150,957	156,988	Acura CL	4,201	13,625
Stratus Sedan	97,261	114,849	Acura TL	60,397	72,119
Viper	2,484	1,021	Acura Total	64,598	85,744
Dodge Total	**250,702**	**272,858**	Accord	380,946	336,231
CHRYSLER GROUP TOTAL	**363,027**	**420,064**	Civic	147,564	219,134
Focus	204,328	273,591	**Honda Total**	**528,510**	**555,365**
Mustang	154,937	171,262	**HONDA TOTAL**	**593,108**	**641,109**
Taurus	294,326	375,219	Stratus Coupe	18,056	17,783
Thunderbird	18,837	25,722	Dodge Total	18,056	17,783
Ford Total	**672,428**	**845,794**	Eclipse	39,287	74,616
Continental	—	12,703	Galant	59,572	99,850
Lincoln LS	39,579	41,078	**Mitsubishi Total**	**98,859**	**174,466**
Town Car	54,458	66,181	Chrysler Sebring Coupe	9,332	10,103
Lincoln Total	**94,037**	**119,962**	**MITSUBISHI TOTAL**	**126,247**	**202,352**
Sable	55,215	106,633	Altima	240,666	235,445
Mercury Total	**55,215**	**106,633**	Maxima	81,402	28
FORD TOTAL	**821,680**	**1,072,389**	**Nissan Total**	**322,068**	**235,473**
LeSabre	131,962	142,647	**NISSAN TOTAL**	**322,068**	**235,473**
Park Ave.	26,616	32,550	Corolla	157,561	137,642
Buick Total	**158,578**	**175,197**	Voltz*	1,733	8,108
CTS	59,250	47,072	**Toyota Total**	**159,294**	**145,750**
Deville	82,965	86,849	Pontiac Vibe	74,223	59,556
Eldorado	—	2,721	**NUMMI TOTAL²**	**233,517**	**205,306**
Seville	15,619	23,428	Subaru Legacy	89,243	93,125
XLR	1,731	—	**SUBARU TOTAL**	**89,243**	**93,125**
Cadillac Total	**159,565**	**160,070**	Avalon	49,250	75,250
Cavalier	282,424	264,937	Camry	356,829	311,610
Corvette	36,026	35,938	Solara	29,774	—
Malibu	184,155	203,493	**TOYOTA TOTAL**	**435,853**	**386,860**
Chevrolet Total	**502,605**	**504,368**			

* For export only. (1) Company is a joint venture between Ford and Mazda. (2) NUMMI (New United Motor Manufacturing, Inc.) is a joint venture between GM and Toyota.

U.S. Car Sales by Vehicle Size and Type, 1985-2003

Source: Ward's Communications; percent of total U.S. sales

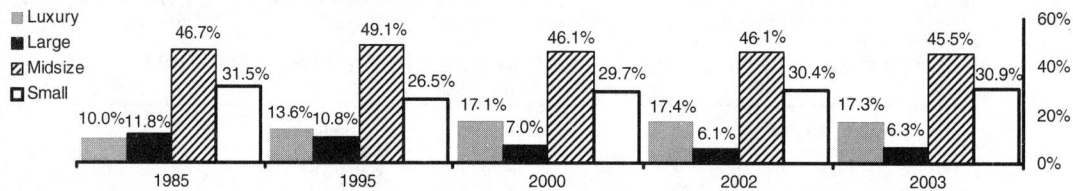

Top-Selling Passenger Cars in the U.S. by Calendar Year, 1997-2003

Source: Ward's Communications

2003

1. Toyota Camry	413,296	8. Ford Focus	229,353	15. Dodge Neon	120,101
2. Honda Accord	397,750	9. Nissan Altima	201,240	16. Volkswagen Jetta	117,867
3. Ford Taurus	300,496	10. Chevrolet Malibu	173,263	17. Saturn Ion	117,230
4. Honda Civic	299,672	11. Pontiac Grand Am	156,466	18. Buick Lesabre	114,572
5. Toyota Corolla	269,018	12. Ford Mustang	140,350	19. BMW 3- Series	111,944
6. Chevrolet Impaia	267,882	13. Pontiac Grand Prix	125,441	20. Oldsmobile Alero	99,123
7. Chevrolet Cavalier	256,550	14. Hyundai Elantra	120,858		

2002		2001		2000	
1. Toyota Camry	434,145	1. Honda Accord	414,718	1. Toyota Camry	422,961
2. Honda Accord	398,980	2. Toyota Camry	390,449	2. Honda Accord	404,515
3. Ford Taurus	332,690	3. Ford Taurus	353,560	3. Ford Taurus	382,035
4. Honda Civic	313,159	4. Honda Civic	331,780	4. Honda Civic	324,528
5. Toyota Corolla	254,360	5. Ford Focus	264,414	5. Ford Focus	286,166
6. Ford Focus	243,199	6. Toyota Corolla	245,023	6. Chevrolet Cavalier	236,803
7. Chevrolet Cavalier	238,225	7. Chevrolet Cavalier	233,298	7. Toyota Corolla	230,156
8. Nissan Altima	201,822	8. Chevrolet Impala	208,395	8. Pontiac Grand Am	214,923
9. Chevrolet Impala	198,918	9. Pontiac Grand Am	182,046	9. Chevrolet Malibu	207,376
10. Chevrolet Malibu	169,377	10. Chevrolet Malibu	176,583	10. Saturn S	177,355

Top-Selling Light Trucks in the U.S. by Calendar Year, 2001-2003

2003		2002		2001	
1. Ford F Series	806,887	1. Ford F Series	774,037	1. Ford F Series	865,152
2. Chevy Silverado	683,889	2. Chevy C/K Pickup/Silverado	648,040	2. Chevy C/K Pickup/Silverado	708,386
3. Dodge Ram Pickup	449,371	3. Ford Explorer	433,847	3. Ford Explorer	415,921
4. Ford Explorer	373,118	4. Dodge Ram Pickup	396,934	4. Dodge Ram Pickup	344,538
5. Chevy Trailblazer	261,334	5. Chevy Trailblazer	249,568	5. Ford Ranger	272,460
6. Dodge Caravan	233,394	6. Dodge Caravan	244,911	6. Dodge Caravan	242,036
7. Ford Ranger	209,117	7. Ford Ranger	226,094	7. Jeep Grand Cherokee	223,612
8. Jeep Grand Cherokee	207,479	8. Jeep Grand Cherokee	224,233	8. GMC Sierra	206,930
9. Chevy Tahoe	199,065	9. Chevy Tahoe	209,767	9. Chevy Tahoe	202,319
10. GMC Sierra	196,429	10. GMC Sierra	200,146	10. Ford Windstar	179,595

Sport Utility Vehicle Sales in the U.S., 1988-2003

Source: Ward's Communications

In 1988, 960,852 sport utility vehicles (SUVs) were sold in the United States, accounting for almost 19% of all light trucks and just over 6% of all sales of light vehicles (cars, SUVs, minivans, vans, pickup trucks, and trucks under 14,000 lbs.). In 2003, SUV sales increased 7.7% over the previous year to 4,534,194, or 27.3% of all light vehicles sold (49.8% of light trucks).

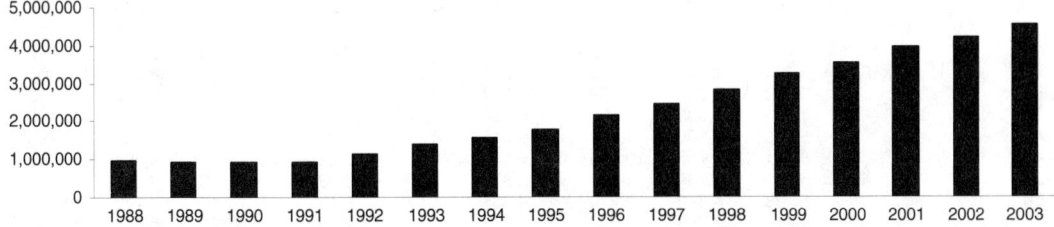

The Most Popular Colors, by Type of Vehicle, 2003 Model Year

Source: Du Pont Automotive Products

Luxury Cars		Full Size/Intermediate Cars		Compact/Sports Cars		Light Trucks	
Color	Percent	Color	Percent	Color	Percent	Color	Percent
Medium/Dark Gray	23.3	Silver	25.1	Silver	20.1	White	22.3
Silver	18.8	Light Brown	15.7	Black	13.6	Silver	17.0
White Metallic	17.8	Medium/Dark Gray	12.5	Medium/Dark Gray	11.9	Black	11.6
White	12.6	White	12.2	Medium/Dark Blue	11.1	Medium/Dark Blue	9.3
Black	10.9	Black	9.2	Medium Red	9.2	Medium/DarkGrey	8.8
Medium Red	3.9	Medium Red	6.6	White	9.0	Medium/Dark Green	7.0
Medium/Dark Blue	3.8	Medium/Dark Green	6.4	Light Brown	8.1	Light Brown	6.3
Gold	3.6	Medium/Dark Blue	5.5	Bright Red	6.3	Medium Red	6.2
Light Blue	3.1	Bright Red	2.0	Bright Blue	3.0	Bright Red	4.1
Light Brown	0.9	Gold	1.5	Yellow	2.6	Dark Red	1.8
Other	1.3	Other	3.3	Other	5.1	Other	5.6

U.S. Light-Vehicle Fuel Efficiency, 1975-2004

Source: Environmental Protection Agency, Office of Transportation and Air Quality, National Vehicle and Fuel Emissions Laboratory

After showing significant fuel-efficiency improvements from 1974 through 1985, both light-duty trucks (SUVs, minivans, vans, and light trucks) and cars have failed to show consistent fuel-efficiency gains since then. In addition, light-duty trucks, which are less fuel-efficient than cars, have come to occupy an increasing proportion of the total light vehicle market, rising from only 19% in 1975 to an estimated 48% by 2004. This increase has been a major factor in the leveling off in the fuel efficiency of the average light vehicle sold. The average fuel economy of all light vehicles sold for the model year 2004 was 20.8 miles per gallon.

YEAR	Cars (MPG*)	Light-duty Trucks (MPG*)	All Light Vehicles (MPG*)	YEAR	Cars (MPG*)	Light-duty Trucks (MPG*)	All Light Vehicles (MPG*)
1975	13.5	11.6	13.1	1998	24.4	17.8	20.9
1980	20.0	15.8	19.2	1999	24.1	17.5	20.6
1985	23.0	17.5	21.3	2000	24.1	17.7	20.7
1990	23.7	17.7	21.5	2001	24.3	17.6	20.7
1995	24.2	17.5	21.1	2002	24.5	17.6	20.6
1996	24.2	17.8	21.2	2003	24.7	17.8	20.7
1997	24.3	17.6	20.9	2004	24.6	17.9	20.8

*MPG value represents laboratory city and highway fuel efficiency combined in a 55%/45% ratio.

Cars Registered in the U.S., 1900-2002[1]

Source: U.S. Dept. of Transportation, Federal Highway Administration
(includes automobiles for public and private use)

Year	Cars Reg.	Year	Cars Reg.	Year	Cars Reg.	Year	Cars Reg.	Year	Cars Reg.
1900	8,000	1935	22,567,827	1970	89,243,557	1992	126,581,148	1998	131,838,538
1905	77,400	1940	27,465,826	1975	106,705,934	1993	127,327,189	1999	132,432,044
1910	458,377	1945	25,796,985	1980	121,600,843	1994	127,883,469	2000	133,621,420
1915	2,332,426	1950	40,339,077	1985	127,885,193	1995	128,386,775	2001	137,633,467
1920	8,131,522	1955	52,144,739	1990	133,700,497	1996	129,728,311	2002	135,920,677
1925	17,481,001	1960	61,671,390	1991	128,299,601	1997	129,748,704		
1930	23,034,753	1965	75,257,588						

(1) There were no publicly owned vehicles before 1925; statistics also exclude military vehicles for all years. Alaska and Hawaii data included since 1960.

IT'S A FACT: According to National Petroleum News, 2004 Station Count, there are 168,000 gas stations in the U.S. The number of retail outlets selling fuel to the public has declined from over 200,000 in 1994, mainly because of stricter environmental regulations, heavy competition, and lower profit margins.

Licensed Drivers, by Age, 1980-2002

Source: Federal Highway Administration, U.S. Dept. of Transportation

(in thousands)

AGE	1980 Male	1980 Female	1980 Total[1]	1990 Male	1990 Female	1990 Total[1]	2002 Male	2002 Female	2002 Total[1]
(under 16)	52	41	93	23	20	43	15	14	28
16	1,001	822	1,823	769	674	1,443	665	645	1,311
17	1,530	1,260	2,790	1,136	996	2,132	1,118	1,068	2,186
18	1,763	1,484	3,247	1,378	1,217	2,595	1,402	1,318	2,720
19	1,900	1,643	3,542	1,608	1,429	3,037	1,573	1,480	3,053
(19 and under)	6,246	5,249	11,496	4,913	4,336	9,249	4,772	4,526	9,298
20	1,930	1,706	3,636	1,691	1,538	3,229	1,639	1,563	3,202
21	1,961	1,772	3,733	1,694	1,555	3,249	1,669	1,608	3,276
22	1,998	1,813	3,811	1,701	1,561	3,262	1,703	1,646	3,348
23	2,062	1,876	3,938	1,767	1,631	3,398	1,708	1,653	3,362
24	2,047	1,868	3,915	1,951	1,807	3,758	1,706	1,645	3,351
(20-24)	9,998	9,034	19,032	8,804	8,093	16,897	8,425	8,115	16,540
25-29	9,865	9,060	18,925	10.239	9,656	19,895	8,728	8,372	17,100
30-34	9,010	8,359	17,369	10,507	10,071	20,578	9,737	9,378	19,115
35-39	7,113	6,583	13,696	9,684	9,371	19,055	10,189	9,937	20,126
40-44	5,828	5,306	11,134	8,610	8,295	16,905	10,614	10,584	21,199
45-49	5,311	4,765	10,076	6,642	6,378	13,020	9,942	9,998	19,939
50-54	5,351	4,739	10,090	5,376	5,108	10,484	8,736	8,789	17,524
55-59	5,198	4,572	9,770	4,855	4,583	9,438	7,148	7,142	14,290
60-64	4,439	3,793	8,232	4,738	4,497	9,235	5,371	5,378	10,749
65-69	3,631	2,949	6,580	4,266	4,109	8,375	4,254	4,284	8,538
(70 and over)	5,195	3,699	8,894	7,159	6,726	13,885	9,546	10,331	19,877
70-74	NA	NA	NA	NA	NA	NA	3,647	3,789	7,436
75-79	NA	NA	NA	NA	NA	NA	2,937	3,173	6,110
80-84	NA	NA	NA	NA	NA	NA	1,849	2,080	3,929
85 and over	NA	NA	NA	NA	NA	NA	1,113	1,289	2,401
TOTAL	77,187	68,108	145,295	85,792	81,223	167,015	97,461	96,834	194,296

(1)These totals may not add due to rounding. NA = not available.

Highway Speed Limits, by State

Source: Insurance Institute for Highway Safety

Under the National Highway System Designation Act, signed Nov. 28, 1995, by Pres. Bill Clinton, states were allowed to set their own highway speed limits, as of Dec. 8, 1995. Under federal legislation enacted in 1974 during the energy crisis, states had been, in effect, restricted to a National Maximum Speed Limit (NMSL) of 55 miles per hour (raised in 1987 to 65 mph on rural interstates).

Maximum posted speed limits, in miles per hour, are given by state in the table below. (Speeds shown in parentheses are for commercial trucks.) Most data current as of Sept. 2004. For more information visit the Insurance Institute for Highway Safety website at www.hwysafety.org

STATE	Rural Interstate	Urban[1] Interstate	Limited[2] Access Roads	Other Roads	STATE	Rural Interstate	Urban[1] Interstate	Limited[2] Access Roads	Other Roads
AL	70	65	65	65	MT	75 (65)	65	70[3]	70[3]
AK	65	55	65	55	NE	75	65	65	60
AZ	75	55	55	55	NV	75	65	70	70
AR	70 (65)	55	60	55	NH	65	65	55	55
CA	70 (55)	65	70	65	NJ	65	55	65	55
CO	75	65	65	65	NM	75	75	65	55
CT	65	55	65	55	NY	65	65	65	55
DE	65	55	65	55	NC	70	70	70	55
FL	70	65	70	65	ND	75	75	70	65
GA	70	65	65	65	OH	65	65	55	55
HI	60	50	45	45	OK	75	70	70	70
ID	75 (65)	75	65	65	OR	65 (55)	55	55	55
IL	65 (55)	55	65	55	PA	65	55	65	55
IN	65 (60)	55	55	55	RI	65	55	55	55
IA	65	55	65	55	SC	70	70	60	55
KS	70	70	70	65	SD	75	75	65	65
KY	65	65	65	55	TN	70	70	70	65
LA	70	70	70	65	TX	75 (65)[3]	70[3]	75 (65)[3]	60[4]
ME	65	65	65	60	UT	75	65	75	65
MD	65	65	65	55	VT	65	55	50	50
MA	65	65	65	55	VA	65	65	65	55
MI	70 (55)	65	70	55	WA	70 (60)	60	60	60
MN	70	65	65	55	WV	70	55	65	55
MS	70	70	70	65	WI	65	65	65	55
MO	70	60	70	65	WY	75	60	65	65

(1) Urban interstates are determined from U.S. Census Bureau criteria, which may be adjusted by state and local governments to reflect planning and other issues. (2) Limited access roads are multiple-lane highways with restricted access via exit and entrance ramps rather than intersections. (3) Speed limit is 65 mph at night (½ hour after sunset to ½ hour before sunrise). (4) Speed limit is 55 mph at night (½ hour after sunset to ½ hour before sunrise).

Selected Motor Vehicle Statistics

Source: Federal Highway Administration; U.S. Dept. of Transportation; Insurance Institute for Highway Safety
Driver's license age requirements, state gas tax, and safety belt laws as of August 2004; figures for 2002 where not specified.

STATE	Driver's license age requirements Regular[1]	Learner's Permit	State gas tax cents/ gal.	Safety belt use law[11]	Licensed drivers per 1,000 resident pop.	Regist. motor vehicles per 1,000 pop.	Licensed drivers per motor vehicle	Gals. of fuel used per vehicle	Miles per gal.	Annual miles driven per vehicle	Vehicle miles per licensed driver
Alabama	17	15	18	P	797	987	0.82	742	17.49	12,989	16,075
Alaska	16y, 6m*	14	8	S	746	964	0.79	596	13.24	7,891	10,194
Arizona	16	15y, 7m	18	S	672	722	0.94	841	15.49	13,030	13,994
Arkansas	16	14	21.7	S	725	691	1.06	1,081	14.86	16,062	15,308
California	17[2]	15	18	P	638	843	0.77	622	17.41	10,836	14,331
Colorado	17	15	22	S	702	477	1.50	1,228	16.48	20,248	13,755
Connecticut	16y, 6m[2]	16	25	P	772	842	0.93	624	17.16	10,706	11,678
Delaware	16y, 10m[2]	15y, 10m	23	P	710	835	0.87	724	18.19	13,165	15,488
Dist. of Col.	18[3]	16	20	P	542	416	1.37	816	18.30	14,932	11,466
Florida	18	15	13.9	S	763	835	0.93	670	19.07	12,774	13,996
Georgia	18	15	7.5	P	702	893	0.80	839	16.87	14,164	18,015
Hawaii	16y[2]	15y, 6m	16	P	654	717	0.93	539	18.47	9,956	10,908
Idaho	16[4]	14y, 6m	25	S	676	1,033	0.67	639	16.00	10,223	15,619
Illinois	18[2]	15	19	P	638	760	0.85	687	16.01	11,005	13,120
Indiana	18	15	15	P	685	920	0.76	797	16.06	12,803	17,181
Iowa	17[2]	14	20.1	P	679	1,127	0.61	642	14.53	9,318	15,479
Kansas	16	14	23	S	713	860	0.84	695	17.50	12,172	14,696
Kentucky	16y, 6m[5]	16	16.4	S	677	880	0.78	853	15.25	13,009	16,894
Louisiana	17[6]	15	20	P	707	817	0.88	799	14.80	11,828	13,665
Maine	16y, 6m[2]	15	22	S	733	747	1.00	915	16.63	15,220	15,523
Maryland	17y, 7m[7]	15y, 9m	23.5	P	646	712	0.92	791	17.48	13,827	15,242
Massachusetts	18	16	21	S	729	841	0.88	601	16.40	9,852	11,366
Michigan	17[2]	14y, 9m	19	P	699	849	0.84	716	16.38	11,735	14,255
Minnesota	17[2]	15	20	S	597	901	0.67	742	16.28	12,070	18,205
Mississippi	16[8]	15	18.4	Sa	648	681	0.97	1,103	16.90	18,636	19,570
Missouri	18	15	17	Sa	693	747	0.94	964	16.69	16,095	17,338
Montana	15[9]	14y, 6m	27	S	764	1,161	0.67	674	14.61	9,842	14,962
Nebraska	17	15	24.5	S	737	957	0.79	763	14.81	11,306	14,679
Nevada	16[2]	15y, 6m	24.7	S	672	576	1.19	1,031	13.91	14,340	12,298
New Hampshire	1y, 1m	15y, 6m	19.5	none	749	897	0.85	715	15.38	11,002	13,172
New Jersey	18y	16	10.5	P	665	779	0.87	737	14.19	10,458	12,245
New Mexico	16y, 6m[2]	15	18.5	P	671	829	0.83	892	16.61	14,815	18,321
New York	17[2]	16[10]	22.6	P	570	546	1.07	667	19.09	12,726	12,192
North Carolina	16y, 6m	15	22.1	P	714	739	0.98	854	17.69	15,106	15,630
North Dakota	16	14	21	S	727	1,101	0.67	738	14.23	10,504	15,910
Ohio	17[2]	15y, 6m	22	S	675	917	0.75	644	15.99	10,302	13,994
Oklahoma	16	15y, 6m	17	P	665	879	0.78	848	17.56	14,891	19,674
Oregon	17	15	24	P	728	872	0.85	662	17.01	11,266	13,488
Pennsylvania	17[2]	16	26.6	S	675	772	0.89	692	15.85	10,969	12,552
Rhode Island	17y, 6m[2]	16	30	Sa	674	725	0.94	588	17.85	10,496	11,300
South Carolina	16y, 6m	15	16	Sa	711	780	0.93	927	15.93	14,768	16,201
South Dakota	16	14	22	S	718	1,069	0.69	749	13.94	10,442	15,555
Tennessee	17	15	20	S	725	824	0.90	830	17.21	14,284	16,222
Texas	16y, 6[2]	15	20	P	605	673	0.92	991	15.21	15,072	16,764
Utah	17[7]	15y, 6m	24.5	Sa	661	797	0.84	748	17.77	13,298	16,056
Vermont	16y, 6m[2]	15	20	S	859	871	1.01	765	23.54	18,016	18,277
Virginia	18[2]	15, 6m	17.5	S	707	860	0.83	769	16.05	12,347	15,015
Washington	17[2]	15	23	P	722	879	0.83	623	16.49	10,265	12,502
West Virginia	17	15	25.35	S	735	812	0.94	744	18.37	13,674	15,098
Wisconsin	16y, 9[2]	15y, 6m	28.1	S	649	838	0.79	713	18.08	12,891	16,643
Wyoming	16	15	14	S	608	1,209	0.52	1,091	13.69	14,939	29,691
AVERAGE			19.13		674	796	0.86	749	16.60	12,437	14,698

NOTE: Many states are moving toward graduated licensing systems that phase in full driving privileges. During the learner's phase, driving generally is not permitted unless there is an adult supervisor. In an intermediate phase, young licensees not yet having unrestricted licenses may be allowed to drive unsupervised under certain conditions but not others. *As of 1/1/2005 (1) Unrestricted operation of private passenger car. (2) Applicants under age 18 (19 in VA) must have completed an approved driver education course (or home training in CT). (3) Learner's phase mandatory for all ages. Applicants under age 21 must complete a 6-month intermediate phase. (4) Applicants under age 17 must have completed an approved driver education course. (5) License holders under age 18 must complete a 4-hour course on safe driving within 1 yr. of receiving license (6) Applicants age 17 and older must have completed an educational program, but doesn't require behind-the-wheel training. (7) Initial applicants of any age must have completed an approved driver education course. (8) Applicants age 17 and older not subject to learner's permit and intermediate license requirements. (9) Applicants under age 16 must have completed an approved driver education course. (10) Driving in New York City is prohibited for all licensees under 18. (11) P = officer may stop vehicle for a violation (primary); S = an officer may issue seat belt citation only when vehicle is stopped for another moving violation (secondary). (a) Primary enforcement for children under a specified age: MS-8; MO-16; RI-18 (7/1/2005); SC, UT-19.

Road Mileage Between Selected U.S. Cities

	Atlanta	Boston	Chicago	Cincin-nati	Cleve-land	Dallas	Denver	Des Moines	Detroit	Houston
Atlanta, Ga.	...	1,037	674	440	672	795	1,398	870	699	789
Boston, Mass.	1,037	...	963	840	628	1,748	1,949	1,280	695	1,804
Chicago, Ill.	674	963	...	287	335	917	996	327	266	1,067
Cincinnati, Oh.	440	840	287	...	244	920	1,164	571	259	1,029
Cleveland, Oh.	672	628	335	244	...	1,159	1,321	652	170	1,273
Dallas Tex.	795	1,748	917	920	1,159	...	781	684	1,143	243
Denver, Col.	1,398	1,949	996	1,164	1,321	781	...	669	1,253	1,019
Detroit, Mich.	699	695	266	259	170	1,143	1,253	584	...	1,265
Houston, Tex.	789	1,804	1,067	1,029	1,273	243	1,019	905	1,265	...
Indianapolis, Ind.	493	906	181	106	294	865	1,058	465	278	987
Kansas City, Mo.	798	1,391	499	591	779	489	600	195	743	710
Los Angeles, Cal.	2,182	2,979	2,054	2,179	2,367	1,387	1,059	1,727	2,311	1,538
Memphis, Tenn.	371	1,296	530	468	712	452	1,040	599	713	561
Milwaukee, Wis.	761	1,050	87	374	422	991	1,029	361	353	1,142
Minneapolis, Minn.	1,068	1,368	405	692	740	936	841	252	671	1,157
New Orleans, La.	479	1,507	912	786	1,030	496	1,273	978	1,045	356
New York, N.Y.	841	206	802	647	473	1,552	1,771	1,119	637	1,608
Omaha, Neb.	986	1,412	459	693	784	644	537	132	716	865
Philadelphia, Pa.	741	296	738	567	413	1,452	1,691	1,051	573	1,508
Pittsburgh, Pa.	687	561	452	287	129	1,204	1,411	763	287	1,313
Portland Ore.	2,601	3,046	2,083	2,333	2,418	2,009	1,238	1,786	2,349	2,205
St. Louis, Mo.	541	1,141	289	340	529	630	857	333	513	779
San Francisco	2,496	3,095	2,142	2,362	2,467	1,753	1,235	1,815	2,399	1,912
Seattle, Wash.	2,618	2,976	2,013	2,300	2,348	2,078	1,307	1,749	2,279	2,274
Tulsa, Okla.	772	1,537	683	736	925	257	681	443	909	478
Washington, DC	608	429	671	481	346	1,319	1,616	984	506	1,375

	India-napolis	Kansas City	Los Angeles	Louis-ville	Memphis	Mil-waukee	Minne-apolis	New Orleans	New York	Omaha
Atlanta, Ga.	493	798	2,182	382	371	761	1,068	479	841	986
Boston, Mass.	906	1,391	2,979	941	1,296	1,050	1,368	1,507	206	1,412
Chicago, Ill.	181	499	2,054	292	530	87	405	912	802	459
Cincinnati, Oh.	106	591	2,179	101	468	374	692	786	647	693
Cleveland Oh.	294	779	2,367	345	712	422	740	1,030	473	784
Dallas, Tex.	865	489	1,387	819	452	991	936	496	1,552	644
Denver, Col.	1,058	600	1,059	1,120	1,040	1,029	841	1,273	1,771	537
Detroit, Mich.	278	743	2,311	360	713	353	671	1,045	637	716
Houston, Tex.	987	710	1,538	928	561	1,142	1,157	356	1,608	865
Indianapolis, Ind.	...	485	2,073	111	435	268	586	796	713	587
Kansas City, Mo.	485	...	1,589	520	451	537	447	806	1,198	201
Los Angeles, Cal.	2,073	1,589	...	2,108	1,817	2,087	1,889	1,883	2,786	1,595
Memphis, Tenn.	435	451	1,817	367	...	612	826	390	1,100	652
Milwaukee, Wis.	268	537	2,087	379	612	...	332	994	889	493
Minneapolis, Minn.	586	447	1,889	697	826	332	...	1,214	1,207	357
New Orleans, La.	796	806	1,883	685	390	994	1,214	...	1,311	1,007
New York, N.Y.	713	1,198	2,786	748	1,100	889	1,207	1,311	...	1,251
Omaha, Neb.	587	201	1,595	687	652	493	357	1,007	1,251	...
Philadelphia, Pa.	633	1,118	2,706	668	1,000	825	1,143	1,211	100	1,183
Pittsburgh, Pa.	353	838	2,426	388	752	539	857	1,070	368	895
Portland, Ore.	2,272	1,809	959	2,320	2,259	2,010	1,678	2,505	2,885	1,654
St. Louis, Mo.	235	257	1,845	263	285	363	552	673	948	449
San Francisco	2,293	1,835	379	2,349	2,125	2,175	1,940	2,249	2,934	1,683
Seattle, Wash.	2,194	1,839	1,131	2,305	2,290	1,940	1,608	2,574	2,815	1,638
Tulsa, Okla.	631	248	1,452	659	401	757	695	647	1,344	387
Washington, DC	558	1,043	2,631	582	867	758	1,076	1,078	233	1,116

	Phila-dephia	Pitts-burgh	Portland	St. Louis	Salt Lake City	San Francisco	Seattle	Toledo	Tulsa	Wash., DC
Atlanta, Ga.	741	687	2,601	541	1,878	2,496	2,618	640	772	608
Boston, Mass.	296	561	3,046	1,141	2,343	3,095	2,976	739	1,537	429
Chicago, Ill.	738	452	2,083	289	1,390	2,142	2,013	232	683	671
Cincinnati, Oh.	567	287	2,333	340	1,610	2,362	2,300	200	736	481
Cleveland Oh.	413	129	2,418	529	1,715	2,467	2,348	111	925	346
Dallas, Tex.	1,452	1,204	2,009	630	1,242	1,753	2,078	1,084	257	1,319
Denver, Col.	1,691	1,411	1,238	857	504	1,235	1,307	1,218	681	1,616
Detroit, Mich.	576	287	2,349	513	1,647	2,399	2,279	59	909	506
Houston, Tex.	1,508	1,313	2,205	779	1,438	1,912	2,274	1,206	478	1,375
Indianapolis, Ind.	633	353	2,272	235	1,504	2,293	2,194	219	631	558
Kansas City, Mo.	1,118	838	1,809	257	1,086	1,835	1,839	687	248	1,043
Los Angeles, Cal.	2,706	2,426	959	1,845	715	379	1,131	2,276	1,452	2,631
Memphis, Tenn.	1,000	752	2,259	285	1,535	2,125	2,290	654	401	867
Milwaukee, Wis.	825	539	2,010	363	1,423	2,175	1,940	319	757	758
Minneapolis, Minn.	1,143	857	1,678	552	1,186	1,940	1,608	637	695	1,076
New Orleans, La.	1,211	1,070	2,505	673	1,738	2,249	2,574	986	647	1,078
New York, N.Y.	100	368	2,885	948	2,182	2,934	2,815	578	1,344	233
Omaha, Neb.	1,183	895	1,654	449	931	1,683	1,638	681	387	1,116
Philadelphia, Pa.	...	288	2,821	868	2,114	2,866	2,751	514	1,264	133
Pittsburgh, Pa.	288	...	2,535	588	1,826	2,578	2,465	228	984	221
Portland, Ore.	2,821	2,535	...	2,060	767	636	172	2,315	1,913	2,754
St. Louis, Mo.	868	588	2,060	...	1,337	2,089	2,081	454	396	793
San Francisco	2,866	2,578	636	2,089	752	...	808	2,364	1,760	2,799
Seattle, Wash.	2,751	2,465	172	2,081	836	808	...	2,245	1,982	2,684
Tulsa, Okla.	1,264	984	1,913	396	1,172	1,760	1,982	850	...	1,189
Washington, DC	133	221	2,754	793	2,047	2,799	2,684	447	1,189	...

Air Distances Between Selected World Cities in Statute Miles

Point-to-point measurements are usually from City Hall.

	Bangkok	Beijing	Berlin	Cairo	Cape Town	Caracas	Chicago	Hong Kong	Honolulu	Lima
Bangkok..........	...	2,046	5,352	4,523	6,300	10,555	8,570	1,077	6,609	12,244
Beijing	2,046	...	4,584	4,698	8,044	8,950	6,604	1,217	5,077	10,349
Berlin	5,352	4,584	...	1,797	5,961	5,238	4,414	5,443	7,320	6,896
Cairo.............	4,523	4,698	1,797	...	4,480	6,342	6,141	5,066	8,848	7,726
Cape Town........	6,300	8,044	5,961	4,480	...	6,366	8,491	7,376	11,535	6,072
Caracas	10,555	8,950	5,238	6,342	6,366	...	2,495	10,165	6,021	1,707
Chicago	8,570	6,604	4,414	6,141	8,491	2,495	...	7,797	4,256	3,775
Hong Kong........	1,077	1,217	5,443	5,066	7,376	10,165	7,797	...	5,556	11,418
Honolulu..........	6,609	5,077	7,320	8,848	11,535	6,021	4,256	5,556	...	5,947
London............	5,944	5,074	583	2,185	5,989	4,655	3,958	5,990	7,240	6,316
Los Angeles	7,637	6,250	5,782	7,520	9,969	3,632	1,745	7,240	2,557	4,171
Madrid............	6,337	5,745	1,165	2,087	5,308	4,346	4,189	6,558	7,872	5,907
Melbourne	4,568	5,643	9,918	8,675	6,425	9,717	9,673	4,595	5,505	8,059
Mexico City.......	9,793	7,753	6,056	7,700	8,519	2,234	1,690	8,788	3,789	2,639
Montreal..........	8,338	6,519	3,740	5,427	7,922	2,438	745	7,736	4,918	3,970
Moscow	4,389	3,607	1,006	1,803	6,279	6,177	4,987	4,437	7,047	7,862
New York	8,669	6,844	3,979	5,619	7,803	2,120	714	8,060	4,969	3,639
Paris.............	5,877	5,120	548	1,998	5,786	4,732	4,143	5,990	7,449	6,370
Rio de Janeiro	9,994	10,768	6,209	6,143	3,781	2,804	5,282	11,009	8,288	2,342
Rome	5,494	5,063	737	1,326	5,231	5,195	4,824	5,774	8,040	6,750
San Francisco	7,931	5,918	5,672	7,466	10,248	3,902	1,859	6,905	2,398	4,518
Singapore.........	883	2,771	6,164	5,137	6,008	11,402	9,372	1,605	6,726	11,689
Stockholm	5,089	4,133	528	2,096	6,423	5,471	4,331	5,063	6,875	7,166
Tokyo	2,865	1,307	5,557	5,958	9,154	8,808	6,314	1,791	3,859	9,631
Warsaw	5,033	4,325	322	1,619	5,935	5,559	4,679	5,147	7,366	7,215
Washington, DC....	8,807	6,942	4,181	5,822	7,895	2,047	596	8,155	4,838	3,509

	London	Los Angeles	Madrid	Melbourne	Mexico City	Montreal	Moscow	New Delhi	New York	Paris
Bangkok..........	5,944	7,637	6,337	4,568	9,793	8,338	4,389	1,813	8,669	5,877
Beijing	5,074	6,250	5,745	5,643	7,753	6,519	3,607	2,353	6,844	5,120
Berlin	583	5,782	1,165	9,918	6,056	3,740	1,006	3,598	3,979	548
Cairo.............	2,185	7,520	2,087	8,675	7,700	5,427	1,803	2,758	5,619	1,998
Cape Town........	5,989	9,969	5,308	6,425	8,519	7,922	6,279	5,769	7,803	5,786
Caracas	4,655	3,632	4,346	9,717	2,234	2,438	6,177	8,833	2,120	4,732
Chicago	3,958	1,745	4,189	9,673	1,690	745	4,987	7,486	714	4,143
Hong Kong........	5,990	7,240	6,558	4,595	8,788	7,736	4,437	2,339	8,060	5,990
Honolulu..........	7,240	2,557	7,872	5,505	3,789	4,918	7,047	7,412	4,969	7,449
London............	...	5,439	785	10,500	5,558	3,254	1,564	4,181	3,469	214
Los Angeles	5,439	...	5,848	7,931	1,542	2,427	6,068	7,011	2,451	5,601
Madrid............	785	5,848	...	10,758	5,643	3,448	2,147	4,530	3,593	655
Melbourne	10,500	7,931	10,758	...	8,426	10,395	8,950	6,329	10,359	10,430
Mexico City.......	5,558	1,542	5,643	8,426	...	2,317	6,676	9,120	2,090	5,725
Montreal..........	3,254	2,427	3,448	10,395	2,317	...	4,401	7,012	331	3,432
Moscow	1,564	6,068	2,147	8,950	6,676	4,401	...	2,698	4,683	1,554
New York	3,469	2,451	3,593	10,359	2,090	331	4,683	7,318	...	3,636
Paris.............	214	5,601	655	10,430	5,725	3,432	1,554	4,102	3,636	...
Rio de Janeiro	5,750	6,330	5,045	8,226	4,764	5,078	7,170	8,753	4,801	5,684
Rome	895	6,326	851	9,929	6,377	4,104	1,483	3,684	4,293	690
San Francisco	5,367	347	5,803	7,856	1,887	2,543	5,885	7,691	2,572	5,577
Singapore.........	6,747	8,767	7,080	3,759	10,327	9,203	5,228	2,571	9,534	6,673
Stockholm	942	5,454	1,653	9,630	6,012	3,714	716	3,414	3,986	1,003
Tokyo	5,959	5,470	6,706	5,062	7,035	6,471	4,660	3,638	6,757	6,053
Warsaw	905	5,922	1,427	9,598	6,337	4,022	721	3,277	4,270	852
Washington, DC....	3,674	2,300	3,792	10,180	1,885	489	4,876	7,500	205	3,840

	Rio de Janeiro	Rome	San Francisco	Singapore	Stockholm	Tehran	Tokyo	Vienna	Warsaw	Wash., DC
Bangkok..........	9,994	5,494	7,931	883	5,089	3,391	2,865	5,252	5,033	8,807
Beijing	10,768	5,063	5,918	2,771	4,133	3,490	1,307	4,648	4,325	6,942
Berlin	6,209	737	5,672	6,164	528	2,185	5,557	326	322	4,181
Cairo.............	6,143	1,326	7,466	5,137	2,096	1,234	5,958	1,481	1,619	5,822
Cape Town........	3,781	5,231	10,248	6,008	6,423	5,241	9,154	5,656	5,935	7,895
Caracas	2,804	5,195	3,902	11,402	5,471	7,320	8,808	5,372	5,559	2,047
Chicago	5,282	4,824	1,859	9,372	4,331	6,502	6,314	4,698	4,679	596
Hong Kong........	11,009	5,774	6,905	1,605	5,063	3,843	1,791	5,431	5,147	8,155
Honolulu..........	8,288	8,040	2,398	6,726	6,875	8,070	3,859	7,632	7,366	4,838
London............	5,750	895	5,367	6,747	942	2,743	5,959	771	905	3,674
Los Angeles	6,330	6,326	347	8,767	5,454	7,682	5,470	6,108	5,922	2,300
Madrid............	5,045	851	5,803	7,080	1,653	2,978	6,706	1,128	1,427	3,792
Melbourne	8,226	9,929	7,856	3,759	9,630	7,826	5,062	9,790	9,598	10,180
Mexico City.......	4,764	6,377	1,887	10,327	6,012	8,184	7,035	6,320	6,337	1,885
Montreal..........	5,078	4,104	2,543	9,203	3,714	5,880	6,471	4,009	4,022	489
Moscow	7,170	1,483	5,885	5,228	716	1,532	4,660	1,043	721	4,876
New York	4,801	4,293	2,572	9,534	3,986	6,141	6,757	4,234	4,270	205
Paris.............	5,684	690	5,577	6,673	1,003	2,625	6,053	645	852	3,840
Rio de Janeiro	...	5,707	6,613	9,785	6,683	7,374	11,532	6,127	6,455	4,779
Rome	5,707	...	6,259	6,229	1,245	2,127	6,142	477	820	4,497
San Francisco	6,613	6,259	...	8,448	5,399	7,362	5,150	5,994	5,854	2,441
Singapore.........	9,785	6,229	8,448	...	5,936	4,103	3,300	6,035	5,843	9,662
Stockholm	6,683	1,245	5,399	5,936	...	2,173	5,053	780	494	4,183
Tokyo	11,532	6,142	5,150	3,300	5,053	4,775	...	5,689	5,347	6,791
Warsaw	6,455	820	5,854	5,843	494	1,879	5,689	347	...	4,472
Washington, DC....	4,779	4,497	2,441	9,662	4,183	6,341	6,791	4,438	4,472	...

NOTED PERSONALITIES

Widely Known Americans of the Present

Political leaders, journalists, other prominent living persons. As of Sept. 2004. Excludes most who fall in categories listed elsewhere in Noted Personalities, such as Writers of the Present and Entertainment Personalities of the Present, or in Sports Personalities. Includes some figures active in American life but not U.S. citizens.

Spencer Abraham, b 6/12/52 (East Lansing, MI), energy sec.
Roger Ailes, b 5/15/40 (Warren, OH), TV exec.
Madeleine K. Albright, b 5/15/37 (Prague, Czech.), former sec. of state.
Edwin "Buzz" Aldrin, b 1/20/30 (Montclair, NJ), former astronaut, 2nd person on the Moon.
Paul Allen, b 121/53 (Mercer Is., WA), co-founder of Microsoft.
Christiane Amanpour, b 1/12/58 (London, Eng.), TV journalist.
Richard K. Armey, b 7/7/40 (Cando, ND), former U.S. rep., House majority leader.
Neil Armstrong, b 8/5/30 (Wapakoneta, OH), former astronaut, 1st person on Moon.
John Ashcroft, b 5/9/42 (Chicago), former MO gov.; attorney general.
Bruce Babbitt, b 6/27/38 (Los Angeles), former AZ gov., interior sec.
F. Lee Bailey, b 6/10/33 (Waltham, MA), attorney.
Russell Baker, b 8/14/25 (Loudoun Co., VA), columnist.
Dave Barry, b 7/3/47 (Armonk, NY), humorist.
Marion Barry, b 3/6/36 (Itta Bena, MS), former Wash., DC, mayor.
Gary Bauer, b 5/4/46 (Covington, KY), political activist.
William Bennett, b 7/31/43 (Brooklyn, NY), author, former education secretary.
Lloyd Bentsen, b 2/11/21 (Mission, TX), former senator, treasury sec., vice-presid. nominee.
Samuel "Sandy" Berger, b 10/28/45 (Sharon, CT), former national security adviser.
Chris Berman, b 5/10/55 (Greenwich, CT), sportscaster.
Carl Bernstein, b 2/14/44 (Washington, DC), journalist, author.
Jeff Bezos, b 1/12/64 (Albuquerque, NM), founder and CEO of Amazon.com.
Joseph R. Biden Jr., b 11/20/42 (Scranton, PA), senator (DE).
James H. Billington, b 6/1/29 (Bryn Mawr, PA), librarian of Congress.
Wolf Blitzer, b 3/22/48 (Buffalo, NY), TV journalist.
Harold Bloom, b 7/11/30 (NYC), literary critic.
Michael R. Bloomberg, b 2/14/42 (Medford, MA), NYC mayor; financial information/media entrepreneur.
Roy Blunt, b 1/10/50 (Niangua, MO), U.S. House majority whip.
Julian Bond, b 1/14/40 (Nashville), civil rights leader.
David Bonior, b 6/6/45 (Detroit), former U.S. representative.
Barbara Boxer, b 11/11/40 (Brooklyn, NY), senator (CA).
Bill Bradley, b 7/28/43 (Crystal City, MO), former senator (NJ), basketball player, presid. candidate.
Ed Bradley, b 6/22/41 (Philadelphia), TV journalist.
James Brady, b 8/29/40 (Centralia, IL), former presid. press sec.; gun control advocate.
Carol Moseley Braun, b 8/16/47 (Chicago, IL), former senator, ambassador; 2004 presidential contender.

L. Paul Bremer III, b 9/30/41 (Hartford, CT), diplomat, former top U.S. civilian administrator in Iraq.
Jimmy Breslin, b 10/17/30 (Queens, NY), columnist, author.
Stephen Breyer, b 8/15/38 (San Francisco), Sup. Ct. justice.
David Broder, b 9/11/29 (Chicago Heights, IL), journalist.
Tom Brokaw, b 2/6/40 (Webster, SD), TV anchor.
David Brooks, b 1961 (NYC), columnist, political commentator.
Joyce Brothers, b 10/20/28 (NYC), psychologist.
Aaron Brown, b 11/10/48 (Hopkins, MN), CNN anchor.
Jerry (Edmund G.) Brown Jr., b 4/7/38 (San Francisco), Oakland mayor; former CA gov., pres. candidate.
Pat Buchanan, b 11/2/38 (Washington, DC), journalist, former presid. candidate.
Art Buchwald, b 10/20/25 (Mt. Vernon, NY), humorist.
William F. Buckley Jr., b 11/24/25 (NYC), columnist, author.
Warren Buffett, b 8/30/30 (Omaha), investor.
Dan Burton, b 6/21/38 (Indianapolis), U.S. representative.
Barbara Bush, b 6/8/25 (Rye, NY), former first lady.
Barbara Bush, b 11/25/81 (Dallas, TX), daughter of Pres. George W. Bush.
George H. W. Bush, b 6/12/24 (Milton, MA), former president.
George W. Bush, b 7/6/46 (New Haven, CT), U.S. president.
Jeb Bush, b 2/11/53 (Midland, TX), FL governor.
Jenna Bush, b 11/25/81(Dallas, TX), daughter of Pres. George W. Bush.
Laura Bush, b 11/4/46 (Midland, TX), first lady.
Robert Byrd, b 11/20/17 (N. Wilkesboro, NC), senator (WV), former majority leader.
Peter Camejo, b 12/31/39 (NYC), Green Party leader, 2004 vice presid. candidate.
Andrew Card, b 5/10/47 (Brockton, MA), White House chief of staff.
Tucker Carlson, b 5/16/69 (San Francisco), journalist, TV commentator.
Richard Carmona, b 11/22/49 (NYC), surgeon general.
Jimmy Carter, b 10/1/24 (Plains, GA), former president; won 2002 Nobel Peace Prize.
Rosalynn Carter, b 8/18/27 (Plains, GA), former first lady.
Stephen Carter, b 10/26/54 (Washington, DC), author, law prof.
James Carville Jr., b 10/25/44 (Fort Benning, GA), TV political commentator.
Steve Case, b 8/21/58 (Honolulu, HI), former AOL Time Warner chairman.
Oleg Cassini, b 4/11/13 (Paris, France), fashion designer.
Elaine Chao, b 3/26/53 (Taipei, Taiwan), labor sec.
Dick Cheney, b 1/30/41 (Lincoln, NE), U.S. vice president.
Lynne Cheney, b 8/14/41 (Casper, WY), political commentator, wife of Dick Cheney.
Noam Chomsky, b 12/7/28 (Philadelphia), linguist; activist.
Connie Chung, b 8/20/46 (Washington, DC), TV journalist.
Liz Claiborne, b 3/31/29 (Brussels, Belg.), fashion designer.

WORLD ALMANAC EDITOR'S PICKS
Most Famous in 50 Years

The editors of The World Almanac have ranked the following persons alive in mid-2004 as most likely to be remembered 50 years in the future. U.S. presidents were excluded from consideration.

1. Neil Armstrong, astronaut, first on the Moon
2. Bill Gates, software pioneer
3. Osama bin Laden, radical Muslim terrorist leader
4. Nelson Mandela, black South African leader
5. Mikhail Gorbachev, former Soviet leader
6. Saddam Hussein, former Iraqi dictator
7. James Watson, DNA pioneer
8. J.K. Rowling, children's book author

9. (Sir) Paul McCartney, Beatle
10. Pope John Paul II, pope since 1978
11. (Sir) Edmund Hillary, Everest conqueror
12. Muhammad Ali, champion boxer
13. Sandra Day O'Connor, first woman on U.S. Supreme Court
14. Queen Elizabeth II, long-reigning British monarch
15. Arthur Miller, *Death of a Salesman* playwright

Wesley Clark, b 12/23/44 (Chicago), retired general, former NATO commander in Europe; 2004 presid. contender.

Bill Clinton, b 8/19/46 (Hope, AR), former U.S. president.

Chelsea Clinton, b 2/27/80 (Little Rock, AR), daughter of former Pres. Clinton and Hillary Rodham Clinton.

Hillary Rodham Clinton, b 10/26/47 (Chicago), senator (NY), former first lady.

Johnnie L. Cochran Jr., b 10/2/37 (Shreveport, LA), attorney.

Bob Costas, b 3/22/52 (Queens, NYC), TV sports journalist.

Ann Coulter, b 12/8/61 (New Canaan, CT), political commentator, author.

Katie Couric, b 1/7/57 (Arlington, VA), TV journalist.

Walter Cronkite, b 11/4/16 (St. Joseph, MO), former TV news anchor.

Mario Cuomo, b 6/15/32 (Queens, NY), former NY gov.

Richard M. Daley, b 4/24/42 (Chicago), Chicago mayor.

John Danforth, b 9/5/36 (St, Louis, MO), former senator; Episcopal priest; U.S. ambassador to UN.

Thomas Daschle, b 12/9/47 (Aberdeen, SD), Senate minority leader.

Gray Davis, b 12/26/42 (NYC), former CA gov.; defeated in 2003 recall election.

Patti Davis, b 10/21/52 (LA county), daughter of Pres. Reagan.

Howard Dean, b 11/17/48 (NYC), former VT gov., 2004 pres. contender.

Oscar de la Renta, b 7/22/36 (Santo Domingo, Dominican Rep.), fashion designer.

Tom DeLay, b 4/8/47 (Laredo, TX), House majority leader.

Michael Dell, b 2/23/65 (Houston, TX), founder, chairman, and CEO of Dell computers.

Alan Dershowitz, b 9/1/38 (Brooklyn, NY), attorney.

Barry Diller, b 2/2/42 (San Francisco), TV exec.

Lou Dobbs, b 9/24/45 (Childress, TX), TV journalist.

Christopher Dodd, b 5/27/44 (Willimantic, CT), senator.

Elizabeth Hanford Dole, b 7/29/36 (Salisbury, NC), senator; former Red Cross pres., cabinet member, presid. contender.

Robert Dole, b 7/22/23 (Russell, KS), former Senate majority leader, presid. nominee.

Pete Domenici, b 5/7/32 (Albuquerque, NM), senator.

Sam Donaldson, b 3/11/34 (El Paso, TX), TV journalist.

Elizabeth Drew, b 11/16/35 (Cincinnati), journalist.

Matt Drudge, b 10/27/67 (Tacoma Park, MD), internet journalist.

Michael S. Dukakis, b 11/3/33 (Brookline, MA), former MA gov., presid. nominee.

Roger Ebert, b 6/18/42 (Urbana, IL), film critic.

Marian Wright Edelman, b 6/6/39 (Bennettsville, SC), children's rights advocate.

Elizabeth Anania Edwards, b. 7/3/49 (Jacksonville, FL), wife of John Edwards; attorney.

John Edwards, b 6/10/53 (Seneca, SC), senator; 2004 vice-presid. candidate.

Edward Egan, b 4/2/32 (Oak Park, IL), Roman Catholic cardinal, archbishop of New York.

Michael Eisner, b 3/7/42 (Mt. Kisco, NY), Disney Co. CEO.

Lawrence J. Ellison, b 8/17/44 (NYC), Oracle Corp. founder, CEO.

Don(ald) Evans, b 7/27/46 (Houston), commerce sec.

Rev. Jerry Falwell, b 8/11/33 (Lynchburg, VA), TV evangelist, religious educator.

Louis Farrakhan, b 5/11/33 (Roxbury, MA), Nation of Islam leader.

Russell Feingold, b 3/2/53 (Janesville, WI), senator.

Dianne Feinstein, b 6/22/33 (San Francisco), senator.

Geraldine Ferraro, b 8/26/35 (Newburgh, NY), former U.S. representative, vice-presid. nominee.

Carly Fiorina, b 9/6/54 (Austin, TX), CEO of Hewlett-Packard.

Bobby Fischer, b 3/9/43 (Chicago, IL), former chess champion.

Larry Flynt, b 11/1/42 (Salyersville, KY), publisher.

Shelby Foote, b 11/17/16 (Greenville, MS), historian.

Steve (Malcolm) Forbes Jr., b 7/18/47 (Morristown, NJ), publisher, former presid. contender.

Betty Ford, b 4/8/18 (Chicago), former first lady.

Gerald R. Ford, b 7/14/13 (Omaha), former president.

Steve Fossett, b 4/22/1944 (Jackson, TN), adventurer, balloonist.

Al Franken, b 5/21/51 (NYC), humorist, political writer.

John Hope Franklin, b 1/2/15 (Rentiesville, OK), historian.

Tommy R. Franks, b 6/17/45 (Wynnewood, OK), gen.,former commander in chief U.S. Central Command.

Betty Friedan, b 2/4/21 (Peoria, IL), author, feminist.

Milton Friedman, b 7/31/12 (Brooklyn, NY), economist.

Thomas Friedman, b 7/20/53 (Minneapolis), columnist, author.

Bill Frist, b 8/19/42 (Nashville, TN), Senate majority leader; physician.

John Kenneth Galbraith, b 10/15/08 (Iona Station, Ont., Canada), economist, author, former amb. to India.

Bill Gates, b 10/28/55 (Seattle), software pioneer; Microsoft exec.

Henry Louis Gates Jr., b 9/16/50 (Keyser, WV), scholar.

David Geffen, b 2/21/43 (Brooklyn, NY), entertainment exec.

Richard Gephardt, b 1/31/41 (St. Louis, MO), former House party leader; 2004 presid. contender.

Louis Gerstner, b 3/1/42 (Mineola, NY), retired IBM exec.

Ed Gillespie, b 1962 (Browns Mills, NJ), Republican National Committee chair.

Newt Gingrich, b 6/17/43 (Harrisburg, PA), former House Speaker.

Ruth Bader Ginsburg, b 3/15/33 (Brooklyn, NY), Sup. Ct. justice.

Rudolph Giuliani, b 5/28/44 (Brooklyn, NY), former NYC mayor.

John Glenn, b 7/18/21 (Cambridge, OH), former senator, astronaut.

Ellen Goodman, b 4/11/41 (Newton, MA), columnist.

Doris Kearns Goodwin, b 1/4/43 (Rockville Centre, NY), historian, TV commentator.

Berry Gordy, b 11/28/29 (Detroit), Motown founder.

Al Gore Jr., b 3/31/48 (Washington, DC), former senator, U.S. vice president, presid. candidate.

Tipper Gore, b 8/19/48 (Washington, DC), wife of Al Gore.

Porter Goss, b 11/26/38 (Waterbury, CT), CIA director; former CIA operative, U.S. representative (FL).

Rev. Billy Graham, b 11/7/18 (Charlotte, NC), evangelist.

Bob Graham, b 4/9/36 (Coral Gables, FL), U.S. senator, former FL gov; 2004 presidential contender.

(William) Franklin Graham III, b 7/14/52 (Asheville, NC), evangelist, son of Billy Graham.

Phil Gramm, b 7/8/42 (Ft. Benning, GA), former senator (TX), presid. contender.

Jennifer Granholm, b 2/5/59 (Vancouver, Can.), MI governor.

Richard Grasso, b 1946(?) (Queens, NY), former NYSE chair; quit when high pay aroused furor.

Andrew Greeley, b 2/5/28 (Oak Park, IL), Rom. Cath. priest, sociologist, writer.

Jeff Greenfield, b 6/10/43 (NYC), TV journalist.

Alan Greenspan, b 3/6/26 (NYC), Fed chairman.

Wilton Gregory, b 12/7/47 (Chicago), chairman, U.S. Conference of Catholic Bishops; bishop of Belleville, IL.

Andrew Grove, b 9/2/36 (Budapest, Hungary), Intel chairman.

Bryant Gumbel, b 9/29/48 (New Orleans), TV journalist.

Greg Gumbel, b 5/3/46 (New Orleans), sportscaster.

Chuck Hagel, b 10/4/46 (North Platte, NE), U.S. senator.

James Hahn, b 7/3/50 (Los Angeles), mayor of Los Angeles.

David Halberstam, b 4/10/34 (NYC), journalist, author.

Pete Hamill, b 6/24/35 (Brooklyn, NY), journalist, author.

Lee Hamilton, b 4/20/31 (Daytona Beach, FL), 9-11 Commission vice-chair; former U.S. rep. from Indiana.

Paul Harvey, b 9/4/18 (Tulsa, OK), radio journalist.

J. Dennis Hastert, b 1/2/42 (Aurora, IL), House Speaker.

Orrin Hatch, b 3/22/34 (Homestead Park, PA), senator (UT).

Hugh Hefner, b 4/9/26 (Chicago), publisher.

Jesse Helms, b 10/18/21 (Monroe, NC), former senator.

Leona Helmsley, b 7/4/20 (NYC), real estate exec, convicted on tax charges.

Heloise, b 4/15/51 (Waco, TX), advice columnist.

Tommy Hilfiger, b 3/24/51 (Elmira, NY), fashion designer.

Anita Hill, b 7/30/56 (Morris, OK), legal scholar, complainant against Clarence Thomas.

Christopher Hitchens, b 4/13/49 (Portsmouth, England), journalist, author.

James P. Hoffa, b 5/19/41, (Detroit), Teamsters Union head.

Richard Holbrooke, b 4/24/41 (Scarsdale, NY), former U.S. rep. to UN.

David Horowitz, b 1/10/39 (NYC), consumer advocate, columnist, author.

Steny H. Hoyer, b 6/14/39 (NYC), U.S. House minority whip.

Arianna Huffington, b 7/15/50 (Athens, Greece), political commentator.

H. Wayne Huizenga, b 12/29/39 (Evergreen Park, IL), entrepreneur, sports exec.

Brit Hume, b 6/22/43 (Wash. DC), TV journalist.

Kay Bailey Hutchison, b 7/22/43 (Galveston, TX), senator.

Henry J. Hyde, b 4/18/24 (Chicago), U.S. representative.

Lee Iacocca, b 10/15/24 (Allentown, PA), former auto exec.

Carl Icahn, b 1936 (Queens, NY), financier.

Jeffrey Immelt, b 2/19/56 (Cincinnati, OH), General Electric CEO.

Don Imus, b 7/23/40 (Riverside, CA), talk-show host.

Patricia Ireland, b 10/19/45 (Oak Park, IL), feminist leader.

Molly Ivins, b 8/30/44 (Monterey, CA), author, columnist.

Rev. Jesse Jackson, b 10/8/41 (Greenville, SC), civil rights leader, former presid. contender.

Peter Jennings, b 7/29/38 (Toronto, Can.), TV anchor.

Steve Jobs, b 2/24/55 (San Francisco), Apple Computer exec.; Pixar exec.

Jasper Johns, b 5/15/30 (Augusta, GA), artist.

Lady Bird Johnson, b 12/22/12 (Karnack, TX), former first lady.

Vernon E. Jordan Jr., b 8/15/35 (Atlanta), attorney, former presid. adviser, civil rights leader.

Donna Karan, b 10/2/48 (Queens, NY), fashion designer.

John R. Kasich, b 5/13/52 (McKees Rocks, PA), former U.S. representative (OH).

Jeffrey Katzenberg, b 12/21/50 (NYC), entertainment exec.

Thomas Kean, b 4/21/35 (NYC), 9-11 commission chair, Drew Univ. pres., former NJ gov.

Garrison Keillor, b 8/7/42 (Anoka, MN), author, broadcaster.

Jack Kemp, b 7/13/35 (Los Angeles), former vice-presid. nominee, HUD sec., pro football quarterback.

Anthony M. Kennedy, b 7/23/36 (Sacramento, CA), Sup. Ct. justice.

Edward M. Kennedy, b 2/22/32 (Brookline, MA), senator.

Joseph Robert ("Bob") Kerrey, b 8/27/43 (Lincoln, NE), former senator.

Teresa Heinz Kerry, b 10/5/38 (Mozambique), heiress, philanthropist; wife of John Kerry.

John Kerry, b 12/11/43 (Aurora, CO), senator (MA), 2004 presid. candidate.

Jack Kevorkian, b 5/26/28 (Pontiac, MI), physican, assisted-suicide activist; imprisoned on murder charges.

Coretta Scott King, b 4/27/27 (Marion, AL), civil rights leader, widow of Martin Luther King Jr.

Larry King, b 11/19/33 (Brooklyn, NY), TV talk show host.

Michael Kinsley, b 3/9/51 (Detroit), editor, pol. commenator.

Jeane J. Kirkpatrick, b 11/19/26 (Duncan, OK), political scientist, former ambassador to UN.

Henry Kissinger, b 5/27/23 (Fuerth, Germany), former sec. of state, nat. security adviser; won 1973 Nobel Peace Prize.

Calvin Klein, b 11/19/42 (Bronx, NY), fashion designer.

Philip H. Knight, b 2/24/38 (Portland, OR), founder and CEO of Nike.

Edward I. Koch, b 12/12/24 (NYC), former NYC mayor.

C. Everett Koop, b 10/14/16 (Brooklyn, NY), former surgeon general.

Ted Koppel, b 2/8/40 (Lancashire, England), TV journalist.

Dennis Kozlowski, b 11/16/46 (Irvington, NJ), former Tyco Int. CEO; acquitted of fraud charges.

Larry Kramer, b 6/25/35 (Bridgeport, CT), AIDS activist, writer.

William Kristol, b 12/23/52 (NYC), editor, columnist.

Steve Kroft, b 8/22/45 (Kokomo, IN), TV journalist.

Dennis Kucinich, b 10/8/46 (Cleveland, OH), U.S. representative, 2004 presidential contender.

Brian Lamb, b 10/9/41 (Lafayette, IN), cable TV exec., journalist.

Matt Lauer, b 12/30/57 (NYC), TV journalist.

Ralph Lauren, b 10/14/39 (Bronx, NY), fashion designer.

Bernard F. Law, b 11/4/31 (Torreon, Mexico), cardinal, former Rom. Cath. archbishop of Boston, figure in church scandal.

Kenneth L. Lay, b 4/15/42 (Tyrone, MO), former CEO of Enron, indicted on fraud charges.

Patrick Leahy, b 3/31/40 (Montpelier, VT), senator.

Norman Lear, b 7/27/22 (New Haven, CT), TV producer, political activist.

Jim Lehrer, b 5/19/34 (Wichita, KS), TV journalist, author.

Carl Levin, b 6/28/34 (Detroit), senator.

James Levine, b 6/23/43 (Cincinnati), conductor.

Monica Lewinsky, b 7/23/73 (San Francisco), former White House intern, key figure in White House scandal.

Joseph Lieberman, b 2/24/42 (Stamford, CT), senator, former vice presid. candidate; 2004 presid. contender.

Rush Limbaugh, b 1/12/51 (Cape Girardeau, MO), radio talk-show host.

Trent Lott, b 10/9/41 (Grenada, MS), senator, former Senate party leader.

Shannon Lucid, b 1/14/43 (Shanghai, China), NASA scientist, astronaut.

Richard G. Lugar, b 4/4/32 (Indianapolis), senator.

John Madden, b 4/10/36 (Austin, MN), sportscaster.

Roger Mahoney, b 2/27/36 (Hollywood, CA), Rom. Cath. cardinal, archbishop of Los Angeles.

Mary Matalin, b 8/19/53 (Chicago), political commentator.

Chris Matthews, b 12/18/45 (Philadelphia), TV journalist.

Terry McAuliffe, b 1957 (Syracuse, NY), Democratic national chairman.

John McCain, b 8/29/36 (Panama Canal Zone), senator (AZ); former presid. contender.

Scott McClellan, b 1968(?) (Austin, TX), White House press secretary.

Mitch McConnell, b 2/20/42 (Tuscumbia, AL), Senate majority whip

David McCullough, b 7/7/33 (Pittsburgh, PA), historian, biographer.

John McLaughlin, b 3/29/27 (Providence, RI), TV journalist.

George McGovern, b 7/19/22 (Avon, SD), former senator, presid. nominee.

Dr. Phil McGraw, b 9/1/50 (Vinita, OK), talk-show host, motivational speaker, author.

Robert S. McNamara, b 6/9/16 (San Francisco), former defense sec., World Bank head.

Russell Means, b 11/10/39 (Pine Ridge Indian Reserv., SD), Native American activist.

Kweisi Mfume, b 10/24/48 (Baltimore), civil rights leader, former U.S. representative.

Kate Michelman, b 8/4/42 (New Jersey), abortion-rights activist.

Zell Miller, b 2/24/32 (Young Harris, GA), former GA gov.; Dem. senator; gave fiery speech at 2004 Rep. Nat'l Convention.

Kate Millett, b 9/14/34 (St. Paul, MN), author, feminist.

Norman Mineta, b 11/12/31 (San Jose, CA), transportation sec.

George Mitchell, b 8/20/33, (Waterville, ME), former Senate majority leader; diplomat, Disney Co. chairman.

Walter Mondale, b 1/5/28 (Ceylon, MN), former vice pres., senator, presid. nominee.

Michael Moore, b 4/23/54 (Davison, MI), documentary filmmaker; author.

Bill Moyers, b 6/5/34 (Hugo, OK), TV journalist, author.

Robert S. Mueller III, b 8/7/44 (NYC), FBI director.

Rupert Murdoch, b 3/11/31 (Melbourne, Aust.), media exec.

Richard B. Myers, b 3/1/42 (Kansas City, MO), chairman of Joint Chiefs of Staff.

Ralph Nader, b 2/27/34 (Winsted, CT), consumer advocate, 2004 independent presid. candidate.

John Negroponte, b 7/21/39 (London, Eng.), U.S. amb. to Iraq, former U.S. rep. to UN.

Don Nickles, b 12/6/48 (Ponca City, OK), U.S. senator, former party whip.

Peggy Noonan, b 9/7/50 (Brooklyn, NY), columnist, speechwriter.

Oliver North, b 10/7/43 (San Antonio, TX), talk-show host, former Nat. Sec. Council aide, fig. in Iran-contra scandal.

Eleanor Holmes Norton, b 6/13/37 (Washington, DC), U.S. House delegate.

Gale Norton, b 3/11/54 (Wichita, KS), interior sec.

Robert Novak, b 2/26/31 (Joliet, IL), journalist.

Sam Nunn, b 9/8/38 (Perry, GA), former senator.

Barack Obama, b 8/4/61 (Hawaii), state senator, Dem. convention keynote speaker, U.S. Senate cand.

Sandra Day O'Connor, b 3/26/30 (El Paso, TX), Sup. Ct. justice.

Sean O'Malley, b 6/29/44 (Lakewood, OH), Rom. Cath. archbishop of Boston.

Paul O'Neill, b 12/4/35 (St. Louis, MO), former treasury sec.

Bill O'Reilly, b 9/10/49 (NYC), TV commentator, host.

Charles Osgood, b 1/8/33 (NYC), TV journalist, author.

Michael Ovitz, b 12/14/46 (Encino, CA), entertainment exec.

Clarence Page, b 6/2/47 (Dayton, OH), journalist, TV commentator.

Camille Paglia, b 4/2/47 (Endicott, NY), scholar, author.

Rod(erick) Paige, b 6/17/33 (Monticello, MS), education sec.

Leon F. Panetta, b 6/28/38 (Monterey, CA), former White House chief of staff, U.S. representative.

Rosa Parks, b 2/4/13 (Tuskegee, AL), civil rights activist whose actions sparked 1955 Montgomery bus boycott.

Richard Parsons, b 4/4/48 (NYC), Time Warner CEO.

George Pataki, b 6/24/45 (Peekskill, NY), NY gov.

Jane Pauley, b 10/31/50 (Indianapolis), TV journalist.

Nancy Pelosi, b 3/26/40 (Baltimore, MD), House minority leader.

Ross Perot, b 6/27/30 (Texarkana, TX), entrepreneur, former presid. nominee.

Colin Powell, b 4/5/37 (NYC), sec. of state; former national security adviser, Joint Chiefs of Staff chairman.

Anthony Principi, b 4/16/44 (Bronx, NY), sec. of veterans affairs.

Dan Quayle, b 2/4/47 (Indianapolis), former U.S. vice pres., senator, presid. contender.

Anna Quindlen, b 7/8/53 (Philadelphia), author, columnist.

Marc Racicot, b 7/24/48 (Thompson Falls, MT), former GOP national chair, former (MT) gov., 2004 Bush campaign mgr.

Dan Rather, b 10/31/31 (Wharton, TX), TV anchor.

Nancy Reagan, b 7/6/21 (NYC), former first lady.

Michael Reagan, b 3/18/45, talk-show host, adopted son of Pres. Reagan and his 1st wife.

Ron Reagan, b 5/20/58 (Los Angeles), journalist, TV talk show host, son of Pres. Reagan.

Sumner Redstone, b 5/27/23 (Boston), Viacom chairman, CEO.

Ralph Reed, b 6/24/61 (Portsmouth, VA), political adviser.

William H. Rehnquist, b 10/1/24 (Milwaukee), Sup. Ct. chief justice.

Robert B. Reich, b 6/24/46 (Scranton, PA), economist, former labor sec.

Harry Reid, b 12/2/39 (Searchlight, NV), Senate minority whip.

Janet Reno, b 7/21/38 (Miami, FL), former attorney gen.

Condoleezza Rice, b 11/14/54 (Birmingham, AL), national security advisor.

Ann Richards, b 9/1/33 (Lakeview, TX), former TX gov.

Bill Richardson, b 11/15/47 (Pasadena, CA), NM gov.; former energy sec., UN ambassador, U.S. representative.

Sally K. Ride, b 5/26/51 (Encino, CA), former astronaut, 1st U.S. woman in space.

Tom (Thomas Joseph) Ridge, b 8/26/45 (Munhall, PA), sec. of homeland security; former PA gov.

Geraldo Rivera, b 7/4/43 (NYC), TV journalist.

Cokie Roberts, b 12/27/43 (New Orleans), TV journalist.

Rev. Oral Roberts, b 1/24/18 (nr. Ada, OK), TV evangelist, educator.

Rev. Pat Robertson, b 3/22/30 (Lexington, VA), religious broadcasting exec, former presid. contender.

V. Gene Robinson, b 5/29/47 (Lexington, KY), first openly gay Episcopal bishop.

David Rockefeller, b 6/12/15 (NYC), banker.

John D. "Jay" Rockefeller 4th, b 6/18/37 (NYC), senator (WV), former WV gov.

Al Roker, b 8/20/54 (Queens, NY), TV weather person.

Mitt Romney, b 3/12/47 (Detroit), MA gov, former Olympics organizer.

Andy Rooney, b 1/14/19 (Albany, NY), TV commentator.

Charlie Rose, b 1/5/42 (Henderson, NC), TV journalist.
Karl Rove, b 12/25/50 (Denver) political consultant.
Louis Rukeyser, b 1/30/33 (NYC), TV journalist, financial analyst.
Donald Rumsfeld, b 7/9/32 (Chicago), defense sec.
Tim Russert, b 5/7/50 (Buffalo, NY), TV journalist.
Morley Safer, b 11/8/31 (Toronto, Can.), TV journalist.
William Safire, b 12/17/29 (NYC), columnist.
Ricardo Sanchez, b 1953 (Rio Grand City, TX), former top-ranking U.S. mil. commander in Iraq; named in prison scandal.
Diane Sawyer, b 12/22/45 (Glasgow, KY), TV journalist.
Antonin Scalia, b 3/11/36 (Trenton, NJ), Sup. Ct. justice.
Phyllis Schlafly, b 8/15/24 (St. Louis, MO) political activist.
Arthur Schlesinger Jr., b 10/15/17 (Columbus, OH), historian.
Bob Schieffer, b 2/25/37 (Austin, TX) TV news anchor.
Caroline Kennedy Schlossberg, b 11/27/57 (NYC), author, daughter of Pres. Kennedy.
Patricia Schroeder, b 7/30/40 (Portland, OR), former U.S. representative.
Rev. Robert Schuller, b 9/16/26 (Alton, IA), TV evangelist.
Charles Schumer, b 11/23/50 (Brooklyn, NY), senator.
Arnold Schwarzenegger, b 7/30/47 (Thal, Styria, Austria), actor, CA governor.
H. Norman Schwarzkopf, b 8/22/34 (Trenton, NJ), former military leader.
Willard Scott, b 3/7/34 (Alexandria, VA), TV weather person.
Allan H. ("Bud") Selig, b 7/30/34 (Milwaukee), baseball comm.
Richard Serra, b 11/2/39 (San Francisco), sculptor.
Donna E. Shalala, b 2/14/41 (Cleveland), former sec. of health and human services.
Gene Shalit, b 3/25/32 (NYC), TV film critic.
Rev. Al Sharpton, b 10/3/54 (Brooklyn, NYC), activist, civil rights leader; 2004 presid. contender.
Maria Shriver, b 11/6/55 (Chicago), TV journalist
George P. Shultz, b 12/13/20 (NYC), former sec. of state; other cabinet posts.
Russell Simmons, b 10/4/57 (Queens, NY), music producer, co-founder of Def Jam Records, founder and CEO of Rush Comm.
O. J. Simpson, b 7/9/47 (San Francisco), former football star, murder defendant.
Liz Smith, b 2/2/23 (Ft. Worth, TX), gossip columnist.
John Snow, b 8/2/39 (Toledo, OH), treasury sec, former CSX CEO.
George Soros, b 8/12/30 (Budapest, Hungary), financier, philanthropist.
David H. Souter, b 9/17/39 (Melrose, MA), Sup. Ct. justice.
Arlen Specter, b 2/12/30 (Wichita, KS), senator (PA).
Steven Spielberg, b 12/18/46 (Cincinnati, OH), movie director, producer.
Lesley Stahl, b 12/16/41 (Swampscott, MA), TV journalist.
Kenneth Starr, b 7/21/46 (Vernon, TX), former Whitewater independent counsel.
Shelby Steele, b 1/1/46 (Chicago), scholar, critic.
George Steinbrenner, b 7/4/30 (Rocky River, OH), NY Yankees owner.
Gloria Steinem, b 3/25/34 (Toledo, OH), author, feminist.
Frank Stella, b 5/12/36 (Malden, MA), painter.
George Stephanopoulos, b 2/10/61 (Fall River, MA), TV journalist, former presid. adviser.
David J. Stern, b 9/22/42 (NYC), NBA comm.
Howard Stern, b 1/12/54 (Roosevelt, NY), radio talk show host.
John Paul Stevens, b 4/20/20 (Chicago), Sup. Ct. justice.
Ted Stevens, b 11/18/23 (Indianapolis, IN), senator (AK), Senate president pro tempore.
Martha Stewart, b 8/3/41 (Nutley, NJ), homemaking adviser, entrepreneur, convicted of lying in stock-trading probe.

Arthur Ochs Sulzberger Jr., b 9/22/51 (Mt. Kisco, NY), newspaper publisher.
Lawrence H. Summers, b 11/30/54 (New Haven, CT), Harvard Univ. pres.
John H. Sununu, b 7/2/39 (Havana, Cuba), political commentator, former White House chief of staff.
John J. Sweeney, b 5/5/34 (NYC), AFL-CIO pres.
Paul Tagliabue, b 11/24/40 (Jersey City, NJ), NFL comm.
George Tenet, b 1/5/53 (Queens, NY), former CIA director.
Clarence Thomas, b 6/23/48 (Savannah, GA), Sup. Ct. justice.
Helen Thomas, b 8/4/20 (Winchester, KY), journalist.
Fred Thompson, b 8/19/42 (Sheffield, AL), former senator; actor.
Hunter S. Thompson, b 7/18/37 (Louisville, KY), journalist, author.
Tommy G. Thompson, b 11/19/41 (Elroy, WI), sec. of health and human services, former WI gov.
Margaret Truman (Daniel), b 2/17/24 (Independence, MO), author, daughter of Pres. Truman.
Donald Trump, b 6/14/1946 (NYC), real estate exec.; TV personality.
Ted Turner, b 11/19/38 (Cincinnati), TV exec, philanthropist.
Peter Ueberroth, b 9/2/37 (Chicago), sports & travel exec.
Jack Valenti, b 9/5/21 (Houston), movie industry exec.
Abigail Van Buren, b 7/4/18 (Sioux City, IA), advice columnist.
Gloria Vanderbilt, 2/20/24 (NYC), fashion designer, heiress.
Greta Van Susteren, b 6/11/54 (Appleton, WI), lawyer, TV commentator.
Ann M. Veneman, b 6/29/49 (Modesto, CA), agriculture sec.
Jesse Ventura, b 7/15/51 (Minneapolis), former wrestler, MN governor.
Paul Volcker, b 9/5/27 (Cape May, NJ), economist, former Fed chairman; chair of inquiry into UN Oil for Food scandal.
Mike Wallace, b 5/9/18 (Brookline, MA), TV journalist.
Barbara Walters, b 9/25/31 (Boston), TV journalist.
James Watson, b 4/6/28 (Chicago), biochemist, DNA pioneer, co-winner 1962 Nobel Prize.
Dr. Andrew Weil, b 6/8/42 (Philadelphia), health adviser.
Sanford I. Weill, b 3/16/33 (Brooklyn, NY), CEO of Citigroup.
Caspar Weinberger, b 8/18/17 (San Francisco), business exec, former defense sec., other cabinet posts.
Harvey Weinstein, b 3/19/52 (NYC), movie executive.
Jack Welch, b 11/19/35 (Peabody, MA), former General Electric CEO.
Jann Wenner, b 1/7/46 (NYC), publisher, founder Rolling Stone.
Cornel West, b 6/23/53 (Tulsa, OK), scholar, critic.
Ruth Westheimer, b 6/4/28 (Frankfurt am Main, Germany), human sexuality expert.
Christine Todd Whitman, b 9/26/46 (NYC), former EPA head, NJ gov.
Meg Whitman, b 8/4/56 (Cold Spring Harbor, NY), eBay pres. and CEO.
Elie Wiesel, b 9/30/28 (Sighet, Romania), scholar, author, 1986 Nobel Peace Prize winner.
L. Douglas Wilder, b 1/17/31 (Richmond, VA), former VA gov.
George Will, b 5/4/41 (Champaign, IL), journalist, author.
Brian Williams, b 1959 (Elmira, NY), TV journalist.
Jody Williams, b 10/9/50 (Brattleboro, VT), anti-landmine activist, 1997 Nobel Peace Prize winner.
Oprah Winfrey, b 1/29/54 (Kosciusko, MS), TV and media personality, businesswoman, actress.
Paul Wolfowitz, b 12/22/43 (NYC), deputy defense sec.
Bob Woodward, b 3/26/43 (Geneva, IL), journalist, author.
Paula Zahn, b 2/24/56 (Omaha, NE), TV journalist.
Robert B. Zoellick, b 7/25/53 (Naperville, IL), U.S. trade rep.
Mortimer Zuckerman, b 6/4/37 (Montreal, Quebec, Can.), publisher, columnist.

Widely Known World Personalities of the Present

Living Non-Americans only. Excludes current heads of state or government (see Nations chapter) and most others covered elsewhere, such as in Widely Known Americans, Entertainers and Writers lists, or Sports Personalities.

Crown Prince Abdullah, b 1924 (Riyadh, Saudi Ar.), de facto ruler of Saudi Arabia; heir to throne.
Gerry Adams, b 10/6/48 (Belfast, N. Ireland), Sinn Fein leader.
Prince Albert, b 3/14/58 (Monte Carlo, Monaco), crown prince of Monaco (son of Prince Rainier and Princess Grace).
Theo Albrecht, b 3/28/22 (Schonebeck, Ger.), German billionaire, CEO of Aldi.
Giulio Andreotti, b 1/14/19 (Rome, Italy), former Italian prime min.
Prince Andrew, b 2/19/60 (London, Eng.), Duke of York (2nd son of Queen Elizabeth II).
Kofi Annan, b 4/8/38 (Kumasi, Ghana), UN sec.-gen.; 2001 Nobel laureate.
Princess Anne, b 8/15/50 (London, Eng.), Princess Royal (daughter of Queen Elizabeth II).
Corazon Aquino, b 1/25/33 (Manila, Philip.), former pres. of Philippines.
Yasir Arafat, b 8/27/29 (Gaza Strip), head of Palestinian Authority; 1994 Nobel laureate.

Oscar Arias Sánchez, b 9/13/41 (Heredia, Costa Rica), former Costa Rican pres., peace negotiator, 1987 Nobel laureate.
Giorgio Armani, b 7/11/34 (Piacenza, Italy), fashion designer.
Ehud Barak, b 2/12/42 (Mishmar Ha-Sharon Kibbutz, Israel), former Israeli prime min.
Ahmed Ben Bella, b 1916(?) (Marnia, Algeria), 1st Algerian prime min.; revolutionary leader.
Boris Berezovsky, b 1/23/46 (Moscow, USSR), businessman, politician.
Tim Berners-Lee, b 6/8/55 (London, Eng.), World Wide Web inventor.
Benazir Bhutto, b 6/21/53 (Karachi, Pak.), former prime min. of Pakistan.
Osama bin Laden, b 1957(?) (Riyadh, Saudi Ar.), leader of al-Qaeda terrorist organization.
Hans Blix, b 6/28/28 (Uppsala, Sweden), UN weapons inspector.
Fernando Botero, b 1932 (Medellín, Col.), Colombian artist.
Boutros Boutros-Ghali, b 11/14/22 (Cairo, Egypt), former UN sec.-gen.

Richard Branson, b 7/18/50 (S. London, Eng.), British Virgin Records and Airways founder; explorer.

(Leonard) James Callaghan, b 3/27/12 (Portsmouth, Hampshire, Eng.), former British prime min.

Kim Campbell, b 3/10/47 (Port Alberni, British Columbia, Can.), former Canadian prime min.

Pierre Cardin, b 7/7/22 (Venice, Italy), fashion designer.

Princess Caroline, b 1/23/57 (Monte Carlo, Monaco), Monaco royal (older daughter of Prince Rainier and Princess Grace).

Violeta de Chamorro, b 10/18/29 (Rivas, Nicar.), former Nicaraguan pres.

Prince Charles, b 11/14/48 (London, Eng.), Prince of Wales (eldest son of Queen Elizabeth II); heir to British throne.

Jean Chrétien, b 1/11/34 (Shawinigan, Que., Can.), former Canadian prime min.

Christo (Javacheff), b 6/13/35 (Gabrovo, Bulg.), artist.

Joe (Charles Joseph) Clark, b 6/5/39 (High River, Alberta, Can.), former Canadian prime min.

King Constantine II, b 6/2/40 (Psychiko, Greece), former king of Greece.

Mairead Corrigan-McGuire, b 1/27/44 (Belfast, N. Ireland), British peace activist, 1976 Nobel laureate.

Francis Crick, b 6/8/16 (Northampton, Eng.), codiscoverer of DNA structure; 1962 Nobel laureate.

Dalai Lama (Tenzin Gyatso), b 7/6/35 (Taktser, Amdo, Tibet), Buddhist leader; 1989 Nobel laureate.

Jacques Derrida, b 7/15/30 (El Biar, Algeria), French deconstructionist philosopher.

Jean Claude Duvalier ("Baby Doc"), b 7/3/51 (Port-au-Prince, Haiti), former Haitian dictator.

Shirin Ebadi, b 1947 (Hamadan, Iran), human rights activist, 2003 Nobel laureate.

Bulent Ecevit, b 5/28/25 (Constantinople [Istanbul] Turkey), former Turkish premier.

Prince Edward, b 3/10/64 (London, Eng.), Earl of Essex (3rd son of Queen Elizabeth II).

Prince Felipe, b 1/30/68 (Madrid, Spain), heir to Spanish throne.

Sarah Ferguson, b 10/15/58 (London, Eng.), Duchess of York; ex-wife of Prince Andrew.

(Sir) David Frost, b 4/7/39 (Tenterden, Eng.), British journalist, interviewer.

Alberto Fujimori, b 7/28/38 (Lima, Peru), ousted pres. of Peru.

John Galliano, b 1960 (Gibraltar), fashion designer.

Valery Giscard d'Estaing, b 2/2/26 (Koblenz, Ger.), former French pres.

Jane Goodall, b 4/3/34 (London, Eng.), British anthropologist.

Mikhail Gorbachev, b 3/2/31 (Privolnoye, USSR), former Soviet pres.; 1990 Nobel laureate.

Jurgen Habermas, b 6/18/29 (Dusseldorf, Ger.), philosopher.

Prince Henry ("Harry") of Wales, b 9/15/84 (London, Eng.), son of Prince Charles; 3rd in line to British throne.

Vaclav Havel, b 10/5/36 (Prague, Czech.), former Czech pres.; playwright.

Stephen Hawking, b 1/8/42 (Oxford, Eng.), theoretical physicist; author.

Edward Heath, b 7/9/16 (St. Peters-in-Thanet, Kent, Eng.), former British prime min.

Sir Edmund Hillary, b 7/20/19 (Auckland, New Zeal.), 1st to reach summit of Mt. Everest, with Tenzing Norgay, 1953.

David Hockney, b 7/9/37 (Bradford, Eng.), artist.

Michael Howard, b 7/7/41 (Llanelli, Wales), British Conservative Party leader.

John Hume, b 1/18/37 (Derry, N. Ireland), Unionist politician; 1998 Nobel laureate.

Saddam Hussein, b 4/28/37 (Tikrit, Iraq), captured former Iraqi ruler.

Jiang Zemin, b 8/17/26 (Yangzhou, Jiangsu Prov., China), former pres. of China.

Pope John Paul II (Karol Wojtyla), b 5/18/20 (Wadowice, Pol.), head of Rom. Cath. church.

Kim Dae Jung, b 12/3/25 (near Mokpo, S. Korea), former S. Korean dissident, opposition leader, pres.; 2000 Nobelist.

Garry Kasparov, b 4/13/63 (Baku, Azerbaijan, USSR), former world chess champion.

Mikhail Khodorkovsky, b 6/26/63 (Moscow, USSR), oil oligarch; former head of Yukos; arrested in 2003.

F.W. (Frederik Willem) de Klerk, b 3/18/36 (Johannesburg, S. Africa), former S. African pres.; 1993 Nobel laureate.

Helmut Kohl, b 4/3/30 (Ludwigshafen, Ger.), former German chancellor.

Vladimir Kramnik, b 7/25/75 (Tuapse, Russia, USSR), world chess champion.

Hans Kung, b 3/19/28 (Sursee, Switz.), Rom. Cath. theologian.

Richard Leakey, b 12/19/44 (Nairobi, Kenya), Kenyan anthropologist.

Claude Lévi-Strauss, b 11/28/08 (Brussels, Belg.), French anthropologist, structuralist.

John Major, b 3/29/43 (Wimbledon, Eng.), former British prime min.

Nelson Mandela, b 7/18/18 (Transkei, S. Africa), former pres. of S. Africa; 1993 Nobel laureate.

Imelda Marcos, b 7/2/29 (Manila, Philip.), former first lady of Philippines.

Peter Max, b 10/19/37 (Berlin, Ger.), artist, designer.

Heather Mills McCartney b 1968 (Washington, Tyne and Wear, Eng.), model, land mine activist, wife of former Beatle Paul McCartney.

Jean-Marie Messier, b 12/13/56 (Grenoble, Fr.), former CEO of Vivendi Universal.

Empress Michiko, b 10/20/34 (Tokyo, Jap.), empress of Japan.

Slobodan Milosevic, b 8/20/41 (Pozarevac, Serbia, Yugoslavia), former Yugoslav pres.; on trial for war crimes.

Rev. Sun Myung Moon, b 1/6/20 (Kwangju Sangsa Ri, N. Korea), Unification Church founder.

Brian Mulroney, b 3/20/39 (Baie-Corneau, Quebec, Can.), former Canadian prime min.

Prince Naruhito, b 2/23/60 (Tokyo, Jap.), crown prince of Japan.

Benjamin Netanyahu, b 10/21/49 (Tel-Aviv, Israel), former Israeli prime min.

Queen Noor (Lisa Halaby), 8/23/51 (Washington, DC), American-born widow of Jordan's King Hussein.

Manuel Noriega, 2/11/34 (Panama City, Pan.), ousted Panamanian pres., jailed in Miami.

Mullah Muhammad Omar, b 1959 (Nodeh, Afghan.), former Afghan Taliban leader.

Yoko Ono, b 2/18/33 (Tokyo, Japan), widow of former Beatle John Lennon; musician.

Daniel Ortega Saavedra, b 11/11/45 (La Libertad, Nicar.), former Nicaraguan pres., Sandinista leader.

Camilla Parker Bowles, b 7/17/47 (London, Eng.), companion of Prince Charles.

Jean-Marie le Pen, b 6/20/28 (La Trinite-sur-Mer, Fr.), French right-wing politician

Shimon Peres, b 8/21/23 (Wolozyn, Pol.), former Israeli prime min.; 1994 Nobel laureate.

Javier Perez de Cuellar, b 1/19/20 (Lima, Peru), former UN sec.-gen.

Prince Philip, b 6/10/21 (Corfu, Greece), Duke of Edinburgh (husband of Queen Elizabeth II).

Augusto Pinochet Ugarte, b 11/25/15 (Valparaiso, Chile), former Chilean ruler.

Gerhard Richter, b 2/9/32 (Dresden, Ger.), artist.

Mary Robinson, b 5/21/44 (Ballina, Co. Mayo, Ireland), former Irish pres., UN High Commissioner for Human Rights.

Erno Rubik, b 7/13/44 (Budapest, Hung.), Rubik's Cube inventor.

Moqtada al-Sadr, b 1974 (Iraq), extremist Shiite cleric.

Yves Saint Laurent, b 8/1/36 (Oran, Algeria), fashion designer.

Carlos Salinas de Gortari, b 4/3/48 (Mexico City, Mex.), former Mexican pres.

Eduard Shevardnadze, b 1/25/28 (Mamati, Georgia, USSR), former Georgian pres.

Ayatollah Ali al-Sistani, b 8/4/30 (?) (Mashhad, Iran), major Iraqi Shiite religious leader.

Princess Stephanie, b 2/1/65 (Monte Carlo, Monaco), younger daughter of Prince Rainier and Princess Grace.

Jack Straw, b 8/3/46 (Buckhurst Hill, Essex, Eng.), British foreign sec.

Suharto, b 6/8/21 (Kemusa Argamulja, Java), former longtime Indonesian ruler.

Aung San Suu Kyi, b 6/19/45 (Rangoon, Burma), political activist, 1991 Nobel laureate, under effective house arrest.

Charles Taylor, b 1/28/48 (near Monrovia, Liberia), resigned 2003 as Liberian pres.

Valentina Tereshkova, b 3/6/37 (Maslennikovo, Russia, USSR), 1st woman in space.

Dame Margaret Thatcher, b 10/13/25 (Grantham, Eng.), former British prime min.

David Trimble, b 10/15/44 (Belfast, N. Ireland), former N. Ireland first minister, 1998 Nobel laureate.

John Napier Turner, b 6/7/29 (Richmond, Surrey, Eng.), former Canadian prime min.

Desmond Tutu, b 10/7/31 (Klerksdorp, Transvaal, S. Africa), former S. African archbishop; 1984 Nobel laureate.

Dominique de Villepin, b 11/14/53 (Rabat, Morocco), French foreign minister.

Kurt Waldheim, b 12/21/18 (St. Andra-Wordern, Austria), former UN sec.-gen. and Austrian pres.

Lech Walesa, b 9/29/43 (Popowo, Pol.), Solidarity leader; 1983 Nobel laureate.

Simon Wiesenthal, b 12/31/08 (Buczacz, Austr.-Hung.), pursuer of Nazi war criminals.

Prince William (of Wales), b 6/21/82 (London, Eng.), son of Prince Charles; 2nd in line to British throne.

Betty Williams, b 5/22/43 (Belfast, N. Ireland), British peace activist, 1976 Nobel laureate.

Rowan Williams, b 6/14/50 (Ystradgynlais, Wales), Archbishop of Canterbury.

Boris Yeltsin, b 2/1/31 (Butka, USSR), former Russian pres.

Muhammad Zahir Shah, b 10/15/14 (Kabul, Afghan.), former king of Afghanistan.

Ayman al-Zawahri, b 6/19/51 (Cairo, Egypt), reputed No. 2 al-Qaeda leader.

African-Americans of the Past

See also other categories.

Ralph David Abernathy, 1926-90, organizer, 1957, pres., 1968, Southern Christian Leadership Conf.

Crispus Attucks, c1723-70, leader of group of colonists that clashed with British soldiers in 1770 Boston Massacre.

Benjamin Banneker, 1731-1806, inventor, astronomer, mathematician, gazetteer.

Daisy Bates, 1920?-99, Arkansas, civil rights leader who fought for school integration.

James P. Beckwourth, 1798-c1867, western fur trader, scout; Beckwourth Pass in N California named for him.

Mary McCleod Bethune, 1875-1955, adviser to FDR and Truman; founder, pres., Bethune-Cookman College.

Henry Blair, 19th cent., pioneer inventor; obtained patents for a corn-planter, 1834, and cotton-planter, 1836.

Edward Bouchet, 1852-1918, first black to earn a PhD at a U.S. university (Yale, 1876).

Tom Bradley, 1917-98, first African-American mayor of L.A.

Sterling A. Brown, 1901-89, poet, literature professor; helped establish African-American literary criticism.

William Wells Brown, 1815-84, memoirist, ex-slave; first African American to publish a novel, 1853.

Ralph Bunche, 1904-71, first black to win the Nobel Peace Prize, 1950; undersecretary of the UN, 1950.

Stokely Carmichael (Kwame Toure), 1941-98, black power activist.

George Washington Carver, 1864-1943, botanist, chemist, and educator; transformed the economy of the South.

Charles Waddell Chesnutt, 1858-1932, author known for his short stories, such as in *The Conjure Woman (1899).*

Eldridge Cleaver, 1935-98, revolutionary social critic; former "minister of information" for Black Panthers; *Soul on Ice.*

James Cleveland, 1931-91, composer, musician, singer; first black gospel artist to appear at Carnegie Hall.

Countee Cullen, 1903-46, poet, prominent in the Harlem Renaissance of the 1920s; *The Black Christ.*

Benjamin O. Davis Jr., 1912-2002, leader of World War II black aviators, first African-American general in U.S. Air Force.

Benjamin O. Davis Sr., 1877-1970, first African-American general, 1940, in U.S. Army.

William L. Dawson, 1886-1970, Illinois congressman, first black chairman of a major U.S. House committee.

Aaron Douglas, 1900-79, "father of black American art."

Frederick Douglass, 1817-95, author, editor, orator, diplomat; edited abolitionist weekly *The North Star.*

St. Clair Drake, 1911-90, black studies pioneer, *Black Metropolis* (1945), with Horace R. Cayton.

Charles Richard Drew, 1904-50, physician, pioneered in development of blood banks.

William Edward Burghardt (W.E.B.) Du Bois, 1868-1963, historian, sociologist; an NAACP founder, 1909.

Paul Laurence Dunbar, 1872-1906, poet, novelist; won fame with *Lyrics of Lowly Life,* 1896.

Jean Baptiste Point du Sable, c1750-1818, pioneer trader and first settler of Chicago, 1779.

Medgar Evers, 1925-63, Mississippi civil rights leader; campaigned to register black voters; assassinated.

James Farmer, 1920-99, civil rights leader; founded Congress of Racial Equality.

Henry O. Flipper, 1856-1940, first African-American to graduate, 1877, from West Point.

Marcus Garvey, 1887-1940, founded Universal Negro Improvement Assn., 1911.

Ewart Guinier, 1911-90, trade unionist; first chairman of Harvard Univ.'s Dept. of African American Studies.

Prince Hall, 1735-1807, activist; founded black Freemasonry; served in American Revolutionary war.

Jupiter Hammon, c1720-1800, poet; first African-American to have his works published, 1761.

Lorraine Hansberry, 1930-65, playwright; won New York Drama Critics Circle Award, 1959; *A Raisin in the Sun.*

William H. Hastie, 1904-76, first black federal judge, appointed 1937; governor of Virgin Islands, 1946-49.

Matthew A. Henson, 1866-1955, member of Peary's 1909 expedition to the North Pole; placed U.S. flag at the pole.

Chester Himes, 1909-84, novelist; *Cotton Comes to Harlem.*

William A. Hinton, 1883-1959, physician, developed tests for syphilis; first black prof., 1949, at Harvard Med. School.

Charles Hamilton Houston, 1895-1950, lawyer, Howard University instructor, champion of minority rights.

Langston Hughes, 1902-67, poet, lyric writer, author; a major influence in 1920s Harlem Renaissance.

Daniel James Jr., 1920-78, first black 4-star general, 1975; commander, North American Air Defense Command.

Henry Johnson, 1897-1929, first American decorated by France in WW1 with the Croix de Guerre.

James Weldon Johnson, 1871-1938, poet, novelist, diplomat; lyricist for *Lift Every Voice and Sing.*

Barbara Jordan, 1936-96, congresswoman, orator, educator.; first black woman to win a seat in the Texas senate, 1966.

Ernest Everett Just, 1883-1941, marine biologist; studied egg development; author, *Biology of Cell Surfaces,* 1941.

Rev. Martin Luther King Jr., 1929-68, civil rights leader; led 1956 Montgomery, AL, boycott; founder, pres., Southern Christian Leadership Conference, 1957; Nobel laureate (1964); assassinated.

Lewis H. Latimer, 1848-1928, associate of Edison; supervised installation of first electric street lighting in NYC.

Mickey Leland, 1944-89, U.S. representative from Texas, 1978 until death; chairman of Congressional Black Caucus.

Henry Lewis, 1932-1996, (U.S.) conductor; first black conductor and musical director of major American orchestra.

Malcolm X (Little), 1925-65, Black Muslim, black nationalist leader; promoted black pride; assassinated.

Thurgood Marshall, 1908-93, first black U.S. solicitor general, 1965; first black justice of U.S. Sup. Ct., 1967-91.

Jan Matzeliger, 1852-89, invented lasting machine, patented 1883, which revolutionized the shoe industry.

Benjamin Mays, 1895-1984, educator, civil rights leader; headed Morehouse College, 1940-67.

Ronald McNair, 1950-86, physicist, astronaut; killed in *Challenger* explosion.

Dorie Miller, 1919-43, Navy hero of Pearl Harbor attack.

Elijah Muhammad, 1897-1975, founded Nation of Islam, 1931.

Huey P. Newton, 1942-89, co-founded Black Panther Party, 1966.

Pedro Alonzo Niño, navigator of Columbus's Niña, 1492.

Frederick D. Patterson, 1901-88, founder of United Negro College Fund, 1944.

Harold R. Perry, 1916-91, first black American Roman Catholic bishop in the 20th cent.

Adam Clayton Powell Jr., 1908-72, early civil rights leader, congressman, 1945-69.

Joseph H. Rainey, 1832-87, first black elected to U.S. House, 1869, from South Carolina.

A. Philip Randolph, 1889-1979, organized Brotherhood of Sleeping Car Porters, 1925; an organizer of 1941 and 1963 March on Washington movements.

Hiram R. Revels, 1822-1901, first African-American U.S. senator, elected in Mississippi, served 1870-71.

Norbert Rillieux, 1806-94; invented a vacuum pan evaporator, 1846, revolutionizing sugar-refining industry.

Paul Robeson, 1898-1976, actor, singer, civil rights activist; ostracized by conservatives in the 1950s.

Jackie Robinson, 1919-72, first African-American in major league baseball, 1947, and the Baseball Hall of Fame, 1962.

Carl T. Rowan, 1925-2000, reporter, columnist, author.

Bayard Rustin, 1910-87, an organizer of the 1963 March on Washington; exec. director, A. Philip Randolph Institute.

Peter Salem, at the Battle of Bunker Hill, June 17, 1775, shot and killed British commander Maj. John Pitcairn.

Carl Stokes, 1927-1996, first black mayor of a major American city (Cleveland), 1967-72.

Willard Townsend, 1895-1957, organized the United Transport Service Employees (redcaps), 1935.

Sojourner Truth, 1797-1883, born Isabella Baumfree; preacher, abolitionist; worked for black educ. opportunity.

Harriet Tubman, 1823-1913, Underground Railroad conductor, nurse and spy for Union Army in the Civil War.

Nat Turner, 1800-31, led most significant of more than 200 slave revolts in U.S., in Southampton, VA; hanged.

Booker T. Washington, 1856-1915, founder, 1881, and first pres. of Tuskegee Institute; *Up From Slavery.*

Harold Washington, 1922-87, first black mayor of Chicago.

Robert C. Weaver, 1907-97, first African-American appointed to cabinet; secretary of HUD.

Phillis Wheatley, c1753-84, poet; 2d American woman and first black woman to be published, 1770.

Walter White, 1893-1955, exec. sec., NAACP, 1931-55.

Roy Wilkins, 1901-81, exec. director, NAACP, 1955-77.

Daniel Hale Williams, 1858-1931, surgeon; performed one of first two open-heart operations, 1893.

Granville T. Woods, 1856-1910, invented third-rail system now used in subways, and automatic air brake.

Carter G. Woodson, 1875-1950, historian; founded Assn. for the Study of Negro Life and History.

Frank Yerby, 1916-91, first best-selling African-American novelist; *The Foxes of Harrow.*

Coleman A. Young, 1918-97, first Afr.-Amer. mayor of Detroit, 1974-93.

WORLD ALMANAC QUICK QUIZ

Which of the following were born in Canada?
(a) John Kenneth Galbraith   (b) Peter Jennings
(c) Tim Russert   (d) Dan Rather
For the answer look in this chapter, or see page 1008.

Architects and Some of Their Projects

Max Abramovitz, b 1908, Avery Fisher Hall, NYC; U.S. Steel Bldg. (now USX Towers), Pittsburgh, PA.

Henry Bacon, 1866-1924, Lincoln Memorial, Washington, DC.

Pietro Belluschi, 1899-1994, Juilliard School, Lincoln Center, Pan Am, now MetLife, Bldg. (with Walter Gropius), NYC.

Marcel Breuer, 1902-81, Whitney Museum of American Art (with Hamilton Smith), NYC.

Charles Bulfinch, 1763-1844, State House, Boston; Capitol (part), Washington, DC.

Gordon Bunshaft, 1909-90, Lever House, Park Ave, NYC; Hirshhorn Museum, Washington, DC.

Daniel H. Burnham, 1846-1912, Union Station, Washington DC; Flatiron Bldg., NYC.

Irwin Chanin, 1892-1988, theaters, skyscrapers, NYC.

David Childs, b 1941, Washington Mall Master Plan/Constitution Gardens, Washington, DC; WTC Freedom Tower, NYC.

Lucio Costa, 1902-98, master plan for city of Brasilia, with Oscar Niemeyer.

Ralph Adams Cram, 1863-1942, Cath. of St. John the Divine, NYC; U.S. Military Acad. (part), West Point, NY.

Norman Foster, b 1935, Commerzbank Headquarters, Frankfurt-am-Main, Ger.; London Millennium Bridge, London.

R. Buckminster Fuller, 1895-1983, U.S. Pavilion (geodesic domes), Expo 67, Montreal.

Frank O. Gehry, b 1929, Guggenheim Museum, Bilbao, Spain; Experience Music Project, Seattle, WA.

Cass Gilbert, 1859-1934, Custom House, Woolworth Bldg., NYC; Supreme Court Bldg., Washington, DC.

Bertram G. Goodhue, 1869-1924, Capitol, Lincoln, NE; St. Thomas's Church, St. Bartholomew's Church, NYC.

Michael Graves, b 1934, Portland Bldg., Portland, OR; Humana Bldg., Louisville, KY.

Walter Gropius, 1883-1969, Pan Am Bldg. (now MetLife Bldg.) (with Pietro Belluschi), NYC.

Lawrence Halprin, b 1916, Ghirardelli Sq., San Francisco; Nicollet Mall, Minneapolis; FDR Memorial, Washington, DC.

Peter Harrison, 1716-75, Touro Synagogue, Redwood Library, Newport, RI.

Wallace K. Harrison, 1895-1981, Metropolitan Opera House, Lincoln Center, NYC.

Thomas Hastings, 1860-1929, NY Public Library (with John Carrère), Frick Mansion, NYC.

James Hoban, 1762-1831, White House, Washington, DC.

Raymond Hood, 1881-1934, Rockefeller Center (part), Daily News, NYC; Tribune, Chicago, IL.

Richard M. Hunt, 1827-95, Metropolitan Museum (part), NYC; National Observatory, Washington, DC.

Helmut Jahn, b 1940, United Airlines Terminal, O'Hare Airport, Chicago.

William Le Baron Jenney, 1832-1907, Home Insurance (demolished 1931), Chicago, IL.

Philip C. Johnson, b 1906, AT&T headquarters (now 550 Madison Ave.), NYC; Transco Tower, Houston, TX.

Albert Kahn, 1869-1942, General Motors Bldg., Detroit, MI.

Louis Kahn, 1901-74, Salk Laboratory, La Jolla, CA; Yale Art Gallery, New Haven, CT.

Christopher Grant LaFarge, 1862-1938, Roman Catholic Chapel, West Point, NY.

Benjamin H. Latrobe, 1764-1820, Capitol (part), Washington, DC; State Capitol Bldg., Richmond, VA.

Le Corbusier, (Charles-Edouard Jeanneret), 1887-1965, Salvation Army Hostel and Swiss Dormitory, both Paris; master plan for cities of Algiers and Buenos Aires.

William Lescaze, 1896-1969, Philadelphia Savings Fund Society; Borg-Warner Bldg., Chicago.

Daniel Libeskind, b 1946, Jewish Museum Berlin; WTC Freedom Tower, NYC.

Maya Lin, b 1959, Vietnam Veterans Memorial, Washington, DC.

Charles Rennie Mackintosh, 1868-1928, Glasgow School of Art; Hill House, Helensburgh.

Bernard R. Maybeck, 1862-1957, Hearst Hall, Univ. of CA, Berkeley; First Church of Christ Scientist, Berkeley, CA.

Charles F. McKim, 1847-1909, Public Library, Boston; Columbia Univ. (part), NYC.

Charles M. McKim, b 1920, KUHT-TV Transmitter Bldg., Lutheran Church of the Redeemer, Houston, TX.

Richard Meier, b 1934, Getty Center Museum, Los Angeles, CA; High Museum of Art, Atlanta, GA.

Ludwig Mies van der Rohe, 1886-1969, Seagram Bldg. (with Philip C. Johnson), NYC; National Gallery, Berlin.

Robert Mills, 1781-1855, Washington Monument, Washington, DC.

Charles Moore, 1925-93, Sea Ranch, near San Francisco; Piazza d'Italia, New Orleans, LA.

Richard J. Neutra, 1892-1970, Mathematics Park, Princeton, NJ; Orange Co. Courthouse, Santa Ana, CA.

Oscar Niemeyer, b 1907, government buildings, Brasilia Palace Hotel, all Brasilia.

Gyo Obata, b 1923, Natl. Air & Space Museum, Smithsonian Inst., Washington, DC; Dallas-Ft. Worth Airport.

Frederick L. Olmsted, 1822-1903, Central Park, NYC; Fairmount Park, Philadelphia, PA.

I(eoh) M(ing) Pei, b 1917, East Wing, Natl. Gallery of Art, Washington, DC; Pyramid, The Louvre, Paris; Rock & Roll Hall of Fame and Museum, Cleveland, OH.

Cesar Pelli, b 1926, World Financial Center, Carnegie Hall Tower, NYC; Petronas Twin Towers, Malaysia.

William Pereira, 1909-85, Cape Canaveral; Transamerica Bldg., San Francisco, CA.

John Russell Pope, 1874-1937, National Gallery, Washington, DC.

John Portman, b 1924, Peachtree Center, Atlanta, GA.

George Browne Post, 1837-1913, NY Stock Exchange; Capitol, Madison, WI.

James Renwick Jr., 1818-95, Grace Church, St. Patrick's Cath., NYC.; Corcoran (Renwick) Gallery, Washington, DC.

Henry H. Richardson, 1838-86, Trinity Church, Boston, MA.

Kevin Roche, b 1922, Oakland Museum, Oakland, CA; Fine Arts Center, University of Massachusetts, Amherst.

James Gamble Rogers, 1867-1947, Columbia-Presbyterian Medical Center, NYC; Northwestern Univ., Evanston, IL.

John Wellborn Root, 1887-1963, Palmolive Bldg., Chicago; Hotel Statler, Washington, DC.

Paul Rudolph, 1918-97, Jewitt Art Center, Wellesley Colllege, MA; Art & Architecture Bldg., Yale Univ., New Haven, CT.

Eero Saarinen, 1910-61, Gateway to the West Arch, St. Louis, MO; Trans World Airlines Flight Center, NYC.

Louis Skidmore, 1897-1962, Atomic Energy Commission town site, Oak Ridge, TN; Terrace Plaza Hotel, Cincinnati, OH.

Clarence S. Stein, 1882-1975, Temple Emanu-El, NYC.

Edward Durell Stone, 1902-78, U.S. Embassy, New Delhi, India; (H. Hartford) Gallery of Modern Art, NYC.

Louis H. Sullivan, 1856-1924, Auditorium Bldg., Chicago, IL.

Richard Upjohn, 1802-78, Trinity Church, NYC.

Max O. Urbahn, 1912-95, Vehicle Assembly Bldg., Cape Canaveral, FL.

Robert Venturi, b 1925, Gordon Wu Hall, Princeton, NJ; Mielparque Nikko Kirifuri Resort, Japan.

Ralph T. Walker, 1889-1973, NY Telephone Bldg. (now NYNEX), IBM Research Lab, Poughkeepsie, NY.

Roland A. Wank, 1898-1970, Cincinnati Union Terminal, OH; head architect (1933-44), Tennessee Valley Authority.

Stanford White, 1853-1906, Washington Arch in Washington Square Park, first Madison Square Garden, NYC.

Frank Lloyd Wright, 1867-1959, Imperial Hotel, Tokyo; Guggenheim Museum, NYC; Marin County Civic Center, San Rafael; Kaufmann "Fallingwater" house, Bear Run, PA.; Taliesin West, Scottsdale, AZ.

William Wurster, 1895-1973, Ghirardelli Sq., San Francisco; Cowell College, UC Santa Cruz, CA.

Minoru Yamasaki, 1912-86, World Trade Center, NYC.

Artists, Photographers, and Sculptors of the Past

Artists are painters unless otherwise indicated.

Berenice Abbott, 1898-1991, (U.S.) photographer. Documentary of New York City, *Changing New York* (1939).

Ansel Easton Adams, 1902-84, (U.S.) photographer. Landscapes of the American Southwest.

Washington Allston, 1779-1843, (U.S.) landscapist. *Belshazzar's Feast.*

Albrecht Altdorfer, 1480-1538, (Ger.) landscapist.

Andrea del Sarto, 1486-1530, (It.) frescoes. *Madonna of the Harpies.*

Fra Angelico, c1400-55, (It.) Renaissance muralist. *Madonna of the Linen Drapers' Guild.*

Diane Arbus, 1923-71, (U.S.) photographer. Disturbing images.

Alexsandr Archipenko, 1887-1964, (U.S.) sculptor. *Boxing Match, Medranos.*

Eugène Atget, 1856-1927, (Fr.) photographer. Paris life.

John James Audubon, 1785-1851, (U.S.) *Birds of America.*

Hans Baldung-Grien, 1484-1545, (Ger.) *Todentanz.*

Ernst Barlach, 1870-1938, (Ger.) Expressionist sculptor. *Man Drawing a Sword.*

Frederic-Auguste Bartholdi, 1834-1904, (Fr.) *Liberty Enlightening the World, Lion of Belfort.*

Fra Bartolommeo, 1472-1517, (It.) *Vision of St. Bernard.*

Romare Bearden, 1911-88, (U.S.) collage and other media. *The Visitation.*

Aubrey Beardsley, 1872-98, (Br.) illustrator. *Salome, Lysistrata, Morte d'Arthur, Volpone.*

Max Beckmann, 1884-1950, (Ger.) Expressionist. *The Descent From the Cross.*

Gentile Bellini, 1426-1507, (It.) Renaissance. *Procession in St. Mark's Square.*

Giovanni Bellini, 1428-1516, (It.) *St. Francis in Ecstasy.*

Jacopo Bellini, 1400-70, (It.) *Crucifixion.*

George Wesley Bellows, 1882-1925, (U.S.) sports artist, portraitist, landscapist. *Stag at Sharkey's, Edith Clavell.*

Thomas Hart Benton, 1889-1975, (U.S.) American regionalist. *Threshing Wheat, Arts of the West.*

Gianlorenzo Bernini, 1598-1680, (It.) Baroque sculpture. *The Assumption.*

Albert Bierstadt, 1830-1902, (U.S.) landscapist. *The Rocky Mountains, Mount Corcoran.*

George Caleb Bingham, 1811-79, (U.S.) *Fur Traders Descending the Missouri.*

William Blake, 1752-1827, (Br.) engraver. *Book of Job, Songs of Innocence, Songs of Experience.*

Rosa Bonheur, 1822-99, (Fr.) *The Horse Fair.*

Pierre Bonnard, 1867-1947, (Fr.) Intimist. *The Breakfast Room, Girl in a Straw Hat.*

Gutzon Borglum, 1871-1941, (U.S.) sculptor. Mt. Rushmore Memorial.

Hieronymus Bosch, 1450-1516, (Flem.) religious allegories. *The Crowning With Thorns.*

Sandro Botticelli, 1444-1510, (It.) Renaissance. *Birth of Venus, Adoration of the Magi, Guiliano de'Medici.*

Margaret Bourke-White, 1906-71, (U.S.) photographer, photojournalist. WW2, USSR, rural South during the Depression.

Mathew Brady, c1823-96, (U.S.) photographer. Official photographer of the Civil War.

Constantin Brancusi, 1876-1957, (Romanian-Fr.) Nonobjective sculptor. *Flying Turtle, The Kiss.*

Georges Braque, 1882-1963, (Fr.) Cubist. *Violin and Palette.*

Pieter Bruegel the Elder, c1525-69, (Flem.) *The Peasant Dance, Hunters in the Snow, Magpie on the Gallows.*

Pieter Bruegel the Younger, 1564-1638, (Flem.) *Village Fair, The Crucifixion.*

Edward Burne-Jones, 1833-98, (Br.) Pre-Raphaelite artist-craftsman. *The Mirror of Venus.*

Alexander Calder, 1898-1976, (U.S.) sculptor. *Lobster Trap and Fish Tail.*

Julia Cameron, 1815-79, (Br.) photographer. Considered one of the most important portraitists of the 19th cent.

Robert Capa (Andrei Friedmann), 1913-54, (Hung.-U.S.) photographer. War photojournalist; invasion of Normandy.

Michelangelo Merisi da Caravaggio, 1573-1610, (It.) Baroque. *The Supper at Emmaus.*

Emily Carr, 1871-1945, (Can.) landscapist. *Blunden Harbour, Big Raven, Rushing Sea of Undergrowth.*

Carlo Carrà, 1881-1966, (It.) Metaphysical school. *Lot's Daughters, The Enchanted Room.*

Mary Cassatt, 1844-1926, (U.S.) Impressionist. *The Cup of Tea, Woman Bathing, The Boating Party.*

George Catlin, 1796-1872, (U.S.) American Indian life. *Gallery of Indians, Buffalo Dance.*

Benvenuto Cellini, 1500-71, (It.) Mannerist sculptor, goldsmith. *Perseus and Medusa.*

Paul Cézanne, 1839-1906, (Fr.) *Card Players, Mont-Sainte-Victoire With Large Pine Trees.*

Marc Chagall, 1887-1985, (Russ.) Jewish life and folklore. *I and the Village, The Praying Jew.*

Jean Simeon Chardin, 1699-1779, (Fr.) still lifes. *The Kiss, The Grace.*

Giorgio de Chirico, 1888-1978, (It.) painter, founded the metaphysical school. *Enigma of an Autumn Night.*

Frederick Church, 1826-1900, (U.S.) Hudson River school. *Niagara, Andes of Ecuador.*

Giovanni Cimabue, 1240-1302, (It.) Byzantine mosaicist. *Madonna Enthroned With St. Francis.*

Claude Lorrain (Claude Gellée), 1600-82, (Fr.) ideal-landscapist. *The Enchanted Castle.*

Thomas Cole, 1801-48, (U.S.) Hudson River school. *The Ox-Bow, In the Catskills.*

John Constable, 1776-1837, (Br.) landscapist. *Salisbury Cathedral From the Bishop's Grounds.*

John Singleton Copley, 1738-1815, (U.S.) portraitist. *Samuel Adams, Watson and the Shark.*

Lovis Corinth, 1858-1925, (Ger.) Expressionist. *Apocalypse.*

Jean-Baptiste-Camille Corot, 1796-1875, (Fr.) landscapist. *Souvenir de Mortefontaine, Pastorale.*

Correggio, 1494-1534, (It.) Renaissance muralist. *Mystic Marriages of St. Catherine.*

Gustave Courbet, 1819-77, (Fr.) Realist. *The Artist's Studio.*

Lucas Cranach the Elder, 1472-1553, (Ger.) Protestant Reformation portraitist. *Luther.*

Imogen Cunningham, 1883-1976, (U.S.) photographer, portraitist. Plant photography.

Nathaniel Currier, 1813-88, and **James M. Ives,** 1824-95, (both U.S.) lithographers. *A Midnight Race on the Mississippi, American Forest Scene—Maple Sugaring.*

John Steuart Curry, 1897-1946, (U.S.) Americana, murals. *Baptism in Kansas.*

Salvador Dalí, 1904-89, (Sp.) Surrealist. *Persistence of Memory, The Crucifixion.*

Honoré Daumier, 1808-79, (Fr.) caricaturist. *The Third-Class Carriage.*

Jacques-Louis David, 1748-1825, (Fr.) Neoclassicist. *The Oath of the Horatii.*

Arthur Davies, 1862-1928, (U.S.) Romantic landscapist. *Unicorns, Leda and the Dioscuri.*

Willem de Kooning, 1904-1997, (Dutch-U.S.) abstract expressionist. *Excavation, Woman I, Door to the River.*

Edgar Degas, 1834-1917, (Fr.) *The Ballet Class.*

Eugène Delacroix, 1798-1863, (Fr.) Romantic. *Massacre at Chios, Liberty Leading the People.*

Paul Delaroche, 1797-1856, (Fr.) historical themes. *Children of Edward IV.*

Luca Della Robbia, 1400-82, (It.) Renaissance terracotta artist. *Cantoria* (singing gallery), Florence cathedral.

Donatello, 1386-1466, (It.) Renaissance sculptor. *David, Gattamelata.*

Jean Dubuffet, 1902-85, (Fr.) painter, sculptor, printmaker. *Group of Four Trees.*

Marcel Duchamp, 1887-1968, (Fr.) Dada artist. *Nude Descending a Staircase, No. 2.*

Raoul Dufy, 1877-1953, (Fr.) Fauvist. *Chateau and Horses.*

Asher Brown Durand, 1796-1886, (U.S.) Hudson River school. *Kindred Spirits.*

Albrecht Dürer, 1471-1528, (Ger.) Renaissance painter, engraver, woodcuts. *St. Jerome in His Study, Melencolia I.*

Anthony van Dyck, 1599-1641, (Flem.) Baroque portraitist. *Portrait of Charles I Hunting.*

Thomas Eakins, 1844-1916, (U.S.) Realist. *The Gross Clinic.*

Alfred Eisenstaedt, 1898-1995, (Ger.-U.S.) photographer, photojournalist. Famous photo, V-J Day, Aug. 14, 1945.

Peter Henry Emerson, 1856-1936, (Br.) photographer. Promoted photography as an independent art form.

Jacob Epstein, 1880-1959, (Br.) religious and allegorical sculptor. *Genesis, Ecce Homo.*

Erté, 1892-1990, (Fr.) b. Romain de Tiertoff; painter, fashion and stage designer.

Jan van Eyck, c1390-1441, (Flem.) naturalistic panels. *Adoration of the Lamb.*

Roger Fenton, 1819-68, (Br.) photographer. Crimean War.

Anselm Feuerbach, 1829-80, (Ger.) Romantic Classicist. *Judgment of Paris, Iphigenia.*

John Bernard Flannagan, 1895-1942, (U.S.) animal sculptor. *Triumph of the Egg.*

Jean-Honoré Fragonard, 1732-1806, (Fr.) Rococo. *The Swing.*

Daniel Chester French, 1850-1931, (U.S.) *The Minute Man of Concord;* seated *Lincoln,* Lincoln Memorial, Washington, DC.

Caspar David Friedrich, 1774-1840, (Ger.) Romantic landscapes. *Man and Woman Gazing at the Moon.*

Thomas Gainsborough, 1727-88, (Br.) portraitist. *The Blue Boy, The Watering Place, Orpin the Parish Clerk.*

Alexander Gardner, 1821-82, (U.S.) photographer. Civil War; railroad construction; Great Plains Indians.

Paul Gauguin, 1848-1903, (Fr.) Post-impressionist. *The Tahitians, Spirit of the Dead Watching.*

Lorenzo Ghiberti, 1378-1455, (It.) Renaissance sculptor. Gates of Paradise baptistery doors, Florence.

Alberto Giacometti, 1901-66, (Swiss) attenuated sculptures of solitary figures. *Man Pointing.*

Giorgione, c1477-1510, (It.) Renaissance. *The Tempest.*

Giotto di Bondone, 1267-1337, (It.) Renaissance. *Presentation of Christ in the Temple.*

François Girardon, 1628-1715, (Fr.) Baroque sculptor of classical themes. *Apollo Tended by the Nymphs.*

Vincent van Gogh, 1853-90, (Dutch) *The Starry Night, L'Arlesienne, Bedroom at Arles, Self-Portrait.*

Edward Gorey, 1925-200, (U.S.) artist, illustrator. *The Doubtful Guest.*

Arshile Gorky, 1905-48, (U.S.) Surrealist. *The Liver Is the Cock's Comb.*

Francisco de Goya y Lucientes, 1746-1828, (Sp.) *The Naked Maja, The Disasters of War* (etchings).

El Greco, 1541-1614, (Sp.) *View of Toledo, Assumption of the Virgin.*

Horatio Greenough, 1805-52, (U.S.) Neo-classical sculptor.

Matthias Grünewald, 1480-1528, (Ger.) mystical religious themes. *The Resurrection.*

Frans Hals, c1580-1666, (Dutch) portraitist. *Laughing Cavalier, Gypsy Girl.*

Austin Hansen, 1910-96, (U.S.) photographer. Harlem, NY, life.

Childe Hassam, 1859-1935, (U.S.) Impressionist. *Southwest Wind, July 14 Rue Daunon.*

Edward Hicks, 1780-1849, (U.S.) folk painter. *The Peaceable Kingdom.*

Lewis Wickes Hine, 1874-1940, (U.S.) photographer. Studies of immigrants, children in industry.

Hans Hofmann, 1880-1966, (U.S.) early abstract Expressionist. *Spring, The Gate.*

William Hogarth, 1697-1764, (Br.) caricaturist. *The Rake's Progress.*

Katsushika Hokusai, 1760-1849, (Jpn.) printmaker. *Crabs.*

Hans Holbein the Elder, 1460-1524, (Ger.) late Gothic. *Presentation of Christ in the Temple.*

Hans Holbein the Younger, 1497-1543, (Ger.) portraitist. *Henry VIII, The French Ambassadors.*

Winslow Homer, 1836-1910, (U.S.) naturalist painter, marine themes. *Marine Coast, High Cliff.*

Edward Hopper, 1882-1967, (U.S.) realistic urban scenes. *Nighthawks, House by the Railroad.*

Horst P. Horst, 1906-99, (Ger.) fashion, celebrity photographer.

Jean-Auguste-Dominique Ingres, 1780-1867, (Fr.) Classicist. *Valpincon Bather.*

George Inness, 1825-94, (U.S.) luminous landscapist. *Delaware Water Gap.*

William Henry Jackson, 1843-1942, (U.S.) photographer. American West, building of Union Pacific Railroad.

Donald Judd, 1928-94, (U.S.) sculptor, major Minimalist.

Frida Kahlo, 1907-54, (Mex.) painter; *Self-Portrait With Monkey.*

Vasily Kandinsky, 1866-1944, (Russ.) Abstractionist. *Capricious Forms, Improvisation 38 (second version).*

Paul Klee, 1879-1940, (Swiss) Abstractionist. *Twittering Machine, Pastoral, Death and Fire.*

Gustav Klimt, 1862-1918, (Austrian) cofounder of Vienna Secession Movement, *The Kiss.*

Oscar Kokoschka, 1886-1980, (Austrian) Expressionist. *View of Prague, Harbor of Marseilles.*

Kathe Kollwitz, 1867-1945, (Ger.) printmaker, social justice themes. *The Peasant War.*

Gaston Lachaise, 1882-1935, (U.S.) figurative sculptor. *Standing Woman.*

John La Farge, 1835-1910, (U.S.) muralist. *Red and White Peonies, The Ascension.*

Sir Edwin (Henry) Landseer, 1802-73, (Br.) painter, sculptor. *Shoeing, Rout of Comus.*

Dorothea Lange, 1895-1965, (U.S.) photographer. Depression photographs, migrant farm workers.

Fernand Léger, 1881-1955, (Fr.) machine art. *The Cyclists.*

Leonardo da Vinci, 1452-1519, (It.) *Mona Lisa, Last Supper, The Annunciation.*

Emanuel Leutze, 1816-68, (U.S.) historical themes. *Washington Crossing the Delaware.*

Roy Lichtenstein, 1923-97, (U.S.) pop artist.

Jacques Lipchitz, 1891-1973, (Fr.) Cubist sculptor. *Harpist.*

Filippino Lippi, 1457-1504, (It.) Renaissance.

Fra Filippo Lippi, 1406-69, (It.) Renaissance. *Coronation of the Virgin, Madonna and Child With Angels.*

Morris Louis, 1912-62, (U.S.) abstract Expressionist. *Signa, Stripes, Alpha-Phi.*

René Magritte, 1898-1967, (Belgian) Surrealist. *The Descent of Man, The Betrayal of Images.*

Aristide Maillol, 1861-1944, (Fr.) sculptor. *L'Harmonie.*

Édouard Manet, 1832-83, (Fr.) forerunner of Impressionism. *Luncheon on the Grass, Olympia.*

Andrea Mantegna, 1431-1506, (It.) Renaissance frescoes. *Triumph of Caesar.*

Franz Marc, 1880-1916, (Ger.) Expressionist. *Blue Horses.*

John Marin, 1870-1953, (U.S.) Expressionist seascapes. *Maine Island.*

Reginald Marsh, 1898-1954, (U.S.) satirical artist. *Tattoo and Haircut.*

Masaccio, 1401-28, (It.) Renaissance. *The Tribute Money.*

Henri Matisse, 1869-1954, (Fr.) Fauvist. *Woman With the Hat.*

Michelangelo Buonarroti, 1475-1564, (It.) *Pietà, David, Moses, The Last Judgment,* Sistine Chapel ceiling.

Jean-Francois Millet, 1814-75, (Fr.) painter of peasant subjects. *The Gleaners, The Man With a Hoe.*

Joan Miró, 1893-1983, (Sp.) Exuberant colors, playful images. Catalan landscape, *Dutch Interior.*

Amedeo Modigliani, 1884-1920, (It.) *Reclining Nude.*

Piet Mondrian, 1872-1944, (Dutch) Abstractionist. *Composition With Red, Yellow and Blue.*

Claude Monet, 1840-1926, (Fr.) Impressionist. *The Bridge at Argenteuil, Haystacks.*

Henry Moore, 1898-1986, (Br.) sculptor of large-scale, abstract works. *Reclining Figure* (several).

Gustave Moreau, 1826-98, (Fr.) Symbolist. *The Apparition, Dance of Salome.*

James Wilson Morrice, 1865-1924, (Can.) landscapist. *The Ferry, Quebec, Venice, Looking Over the Lagoon.*

William Morris, 1834-1896, (Br.) decorative artist, leader of the Arts and Crafts movement.

Grandma Moses, 1860-1961, (U.S.) folk painter. *Out for the Christmas Trees, Thanksgiving Turkey.*

Edvard Munch, 1863-1944, (Nor.) Expressionist. *The Cry.*

Bartolome Murillo, 1618-82, (Sp.) Baroque religious artist. *Vision of St. Anthony, The Two Trinities.*

Eadweard Muybridge, 1830-1904, (Br.-U.S.) photographer. Studies of motion, *Animal Locomotion.*

Nadar (Gaspar-Félix Tournachon), 1820-1910, (Fr.) photographer, caricaturist, portraitist. Invented photo-essay.

Barnett Newman, 1905-70, (U.S.) abstract Expressionist. *Stations of the Cross.*

Isamu Noguchi, 1904-88, (U.S.) abstract sculptor, designer. *Kouros, BirdC(MU),* sculptural gardens.

Georgia O'Keeffe, 1887-1986, (U.S.) Southwest motifs. *Cow's Skull: Red, White, and Blue, The Shelton With Sunspots.*

José Clemente Orozco, 1883-1949, (Mex.) frescoes. *House of Tears, Pre-Columbian Golden Age.*

Timothy H. O'Sullivan, 1840-82, (U.S.) Civil War photographer.

Charles Willson Peale, 1741-1827, (U.S.) Amer. Revolutionary portraitist. *The Staircase Group,* U.S. presidents.

Rembrandt Peale, 1778-1860, (U.S.) portraitist. Thomas Jefferson.

Pietro Perugino, 1446-1523, (It.) Renaissance. *Delivery of the Keys to St. Peter.*

Pablo Picasso, 1881-1973, (Sp.) painter, sculptor. *Guernica; Dove; Head of a Woman; Head of a Bull, Metamorphosis.*

Piero della Francesca, c1415-92, (It.) Renaissance. *Duke of Urbino, Flagellation of Christ.*

Camille Pissarro, 1830-1903, (Fr.) Impressionist. *Boulevard des Italiens, Morning, Sunlight; Bather in the Woods.*

Jackson Pollock, 1912-56, (U.S.) abstract Expressionist. *Autumn Rhythm.*

Nicolas Poussin, 1594-1665, (Fr.) Baroque pictorial classicism. *St. John on Patmos.*

Maurice B. Prendergast, c1860-1924, (U.S.) Post-impressionist water colorist. *Umbrellas in the Rain.*

Pierre-Paul Prud'hon, 1758-1823, (Fr.) Romanticist. *Crime Pursued by Vengeance and Justice.*

Pierre Cecile Puvis de Chavannes, 1824-98, (Fr.) muralist. *The Poor Fisherman.*

Raphael Sanzio, 1483-1520, (It.) Renaissance. *Disputa, School of Athens, Sistine Madonna.*

Man Ray, 1890-1976, (U.S.) Dada artist. *Observing Time, The Lovers, Marquis de Sade.*

Odilon Redon, 1840-1916, (Fr.) Symbolist painter, lithographer. *In the Dream, Vase of Flowers.*

Rembrandt van Rijn, 1606-69, (Dutch) *The Bridal Couple, The Night Watch.*

Frederic Remington, 1861-1909, (U.S.) painter, sculptor. Portrayer of the American West, *Bronco Buster.*

Pierre-Auguste Renoir, 1841-1919, (Fr.) Impressionist. *The Luncheon of the Boating Party, Dance in the Country.*

Joshua Reynolds, 1723-92, (Br.) portraitist. *Mrs. Siddons as the Tragic Muse.*

Herb Ritts, 1952-2002, (U.S.) photographer. Nudes, celebrities.

Diego Rivera, 1886-1957, (Mex.) frescoes. *The Fecund Earth.*

Larry Rivers, 1923-2002, (U.S.) painter, sculptor, often realistic; Dutch Masters series.

Henry Peach Robinson, 1830-1901 (Br.) photographer. A leader of "high art" photography.

Norman Rockwell, 1894-1978, (U.S.) painter, illustrator. *Saturday Evening Post* covers.

Auguste Rodin, 1840-1917, (Fr.) sculptor. *The Thinker.*

Mark Rothko, 1903-70, (U.S.) abstract Expressionist. *Light, Earth and Blue.*

Georges Rouault, 1871-1958, (Fr.) Expressionist. *Three Judges.*

Henri Rousseau, 1844-1910, (Fr.) primitive exotic themes. *The Snake Charmer.*

Theodore Rousseau, 1812-67, (Swiss-Fr.) landscapist. *Under the Birches, Evening.*

Peter Paul Rubens, 1577-1640, (Flem.) Baroque. *Mystic Marriage of St. Catherine.*

Jacob van Ruisdael, c1628-82, (Dutch) landscapist. *Jewish Cemetery.*

Charles M. Russell, 1866-1926, (U.S.) Western life.

Salomon van Ruysdael, c1600-70, (Dutch) landscapist. *River With Ferry-Boat.*

Albert Pinkham Ryder, 1847-1917, (U.S.) seascapes and allegories. *Toilers of the Sea.*

Augustus Saint-Gaudens, 1848-1907, (U.S.) memorial statues. *Farragut, Mrs. Henry Adams (Grief).*

Andrea Sansovino, 1460-1529, (It.) Renaissance sculptor. *Baptism of Christ.*

Jacopo Sansovino, 1486-1570, (It.) Renaissance sculptor. *St. John the Baptist.*

John Singer Sargent, 1856-1925, (U.S.) Edwardian society portraitist. *The Wyndham Sisters, Madam X.*

George Segal, 1924-2000, (U.S.) sculptor of life-sized figures realistically depicting daily life.

Georges Seurat, 1859-91, (Fr.) Pointillist. *Sunday Afternoon on the Island of La Grande Jatte.*

Gino Severini, 1883-1966, (It.) Futurist and Cubist. *Dynamic Hieroglyph of the Bal Tabarin.*

Ben Shahn, 1898-1969, (U.S.) social and political themes. Sacco and Vanzetti series, *Seurat's Lunch, Handball.*

Charles Sheeler, 1883-1965, (U.S.) abstractionist.

David Alfaro Siqueiros, 1896-1974, (Mex.) political muralist. *March of Humanity.*

David Smith, 1906-65, (U.S.) welded metal sculpture. *Hudson River Landscape, Zig, Cubi* series.

Edward Steichen, 1879-1973, (U.S.) photographer. Credited with transforming photography into an art form.

Alfred Stieglitz, 1864-1946, (U.S.) photographer, editor; helped create acceptance of photography as art.

Paul Strand, 1890-1976, (U.S.) photographer. People, nature, landscapes.

Gilbert Stuart, 1755-1828, (U.S.) portraitist. George Washington, Thomas Jefferson, James Madison.

Thomas Sully, 1783-1872, (U.S.) portraitist. *Col. Thomas Handasyd Perkins, The Passage of the Delaware.*

William Henry Fox Talbot, 1800-77, (Br.) photographer. *Pencil of Nature,* early photographically illustrated book.

George Tames, 1919-94, (U.S.) photographer. Chronicled presidents, political leaders.

Yves Tanguy, 1900-55, (Fr.) Surrealist. *Rose of the Four Winds, Mama, Papa Is Wounded!*

Giovanni Battista Tiepolo, 1696-1770, (It.) Rococo frescoes. *The Crucifixion.*

Jacopo Tintoretto, 1518-94, (It.) Mannerist. *The Last Supper.*

Titian, c1485-1576, (It.) Renaissance. *Venus and the Lute Player, The Bacchanal.*

Jose Rey Toledo, 1916-94, (U.S.) Native American artist. Captured the essence of tribal dances on canvas.

Henri de Toulouse-Lautrec, 1864-1901, (Fr.) *At the Moulin Rouge.*

John Trumbull, 1756-1843, (U.S.) historical themes. *The Declaration of Independence.*

J(oseph) M(allord) W(illiam) Turner, 1775-1851, (Br.) Romantic landscapist. *Snow Storm.*

Paolo Uccello, 1397-1475, (It.) Gothic-Renaissance. *The Rout of San Romano.*

Maurice Utrillo, 1883-1955, (Fr.) Impressionist. *Sacre-Coeur de Montmartre.*

John Vanderlyn, 1775-1852, (U.S.) Neo-classicist. *Ariadne Asleep on the Island of Naxos.*

Diego Velázquez, 1599-1660, (Sp.) Baroque. *Las Meninas, Portrait of Juan de Pareja.*

Jan Vermeer, 1632-75, (Dutch) interior genre subjects. *Young Woman With a Water Jug.*

Paolo Veronese, 1528-88, (It.) devotional themes, vastly peopled canvases. *The Temptation of St. Anthony.*

Andrea del Verrocchio, 1435-88, (It.) Floren. sculptor. *Colleoni.*

Maurice de Vlaminck, 1876-1958, (Fr.) Fauvist landscapist. *Red Trees.*

Andy Warhol, 1928-87, (U.S.) Pop Art. *Campbell's Soup Cans, Marilyn Diptych.*

Antoine Watteau, 1684-1721, (Fr.) Rococo painter of "scenes of gallantry." *The Embarkation for Cythera.*

George Frederic Watts, 1817-1904, (Br.) painter and sculptor of grandiose allegorical themes. *Hope.*

Benjamin West, 1738-1820, (U.S.) realistic historical themes. *Death of General Wolfe.*

Edward Weston, 1886-1958, (U.S.) photographer. Landscapes of American West.

James Abbott McNeill Whistler, 1834-1903, (U.S.) *Arrangement in Grey and Black, No. 1: The Artist's Mother.*

Archibald M. Willard, 1836-1918, (U.S.) *The Spirit of '76.*

Grant Wood, 1891-1942, (U.S.) Midwestern regionalist. *American Gothic, Daughters of Revolution.*

Ossip Zadkine, 1890-1967, (Russ.) School of Paris sculptor. *The Destroyed City, Musicians, Christ.*

Business Leaders and Philanthropists of the Past

Giovanni Agnelli, 1921-2003, (It.) industrialist, principal shareholder of Fiat.

Walter Annenberg, 1908-2002, (U.S.) publisher, founder *TV Guide,* philanthropist.

Elizabeth Arden (F. N. Graham), 1884-1966, (U.S.) Canadian-born founder of cosmetics empire.

Philip D. Armour, 1832-1901, (U.S.) industrialist; streamlined meatpacking.

John Jacob Astor, 1763-1848, (U.S.) German-born fur trader, banker, real estate magnate; at death, richest in U.S.

Francis W. Ayer, 1848-1923, (U.S.) ad industry pioneer.

August Belmont, 1816-90, (U.S.) German-born financier.

James B. (Diamond Jim) Brady, 1856-1917, (U.S.) financier, philanthropist, legendary bon vivant.

Adolphus Busch, 1839-1913, (U.S.) German-born businessman; established brewery empire.

Asa Candler, 1851-1929, (U.S.) founded Coca-Cola Co.

Andrew Carnegie, 1835-1919, (U.S.) Scottish-born industrialist; philanthropist; founded Carnegie Steel Co.

Tom Carvel, 1908-89, (Gr.-U.S.) founded ice cream chain.

William Colgate, 1783-1857, (Br.-U.S.) Br.-born businessman, philanthropist; founded soap-making empire.

Jay Cooke, 1821-1905, (U.S.) financier; sold $1 billion in Union bonds during Civil War.

Peter Cooper, 1791-1883, (U.S.) industrialist, inventor, philanthropist; founded Cooper Union (1859).

Ezra Cornell, 1807-74, (U.S.) businessman, philanthropist; headed Western Union, established university.

Erastus Corning, 1794-1872, (U.S.) financier; headed N.Y. Central.

Charles Crocker, 1822-88, (U.S.) railroad builder, financier.

Samuel Cunard, 1787-1865, (Can.) pioneered trans-Atlantic steam navigation.

Marcus Daly, 1841-1900, (U.S.) Irish-born copper magnate.

W. Edwards Deming, 1900-93, (U.S.) quality-control expert who revolutionized Japanese manufacturing.

Walt Disney, 1901-66, (U.S.) pioneer in cinema animation; built entertainment empire.

Herbert H. Dow, 1866-1930, (U.S.) founder of chemical co.

James Duke, 1856-1925, (U.S.) founded American Tobacco, Duke Univ.

Eleuthere I. du Pont, 1771-1834, (Fr.-U.S.) gunpowder manufacturer; founded one of the largest business empires.

Thomas C. Durant, 1820-85, (U.S.) railroad official, financier.

William C. Durant, 1861-1947, (U.S.) industrialist; formed General Motors.

George Eastman, 1854-1932, (U.S.) inventor; manufacturer of photographic equipment.

Marshall Field, 1834-1906, (U.S.) merchant; founded Chicago's largest department store.

Harvey Firestone, 1868-1938, (U.S.) founded tire company.

Avery Fisher, 1906-94, (U.S.) industrialist, philanthropist, founded Fisher electronics.

Henry M. Flagler, 1830-1913, (U.S.) financier; helped form Standard Oil; developed Florida as resort state.

Malcolm Forbes, 1919-90, (U.S.) magazine publisher.

Henry Ford, 1863-1947, (U.S.) auto maker; developed first popular low-priced car.

Henry Ford 2nd, 1917-87, (U.S.) headed auto company founded by grandfather.

Henry C. Frick, 1849-1919, (U.S.) steel and coke magnate; had prominent role in development of U.S. Steel.

Jakob Fugger (Jakob the Rich), 1459-1525, (Ger.) headed leading banking, trading house, in 16th-cent. Europe.

Alfred C. Fuller, 1885-1973, (U.S.) Canadian-born businessman; founded brush company.

Elbert H. Gary, 1846-1927, (U.S.) one of the organizers of U.S. Steel; chaired board of directors, 1903-27.

Jean Paul Getty, 1892-1976, (U.S.) founded oil empire.

Amadeo Giannini, 1870-1949, (U.S.) founded Bank of America.

Stephen Girard, 1750-1831, (U.S.) French-born financier, philanthropist; richest man in U.S. at his death.

Leonard H. Goldenson, 1905-99, (U.S.) turned ABC into major TV network.

Jay Gould, 1836-92, (U.S.) railroad magnate, financier.

Hetty Green, 1834-1916, (U.S.) financier, the "witch of Wall St."; richest woman in U.S. in her day.

William Gregg, 1800-67, (U.S.) launched textile industry in S.

Meyer Guggenheim, 1828-1905, (U.S.) Swiss-born merchant, philanthropist; built merchandising, mining empires.

Armand Hammer, 1898-1990, (U.S.) headed Occidental Petroleum; promoted U.S.-Soviet ties.

Edward H. Harriman, 1848-1909, (U.S.) railroad financier, administrator; headed Union Pacific.

Henry J. Heinz, 1844-1919, (U.S.) founded food empire.

James J. Hill, 1838-1916, (U.S.) Canadian-born railroad magnate, financier; founded Great Northern Railway.

Conrad N. Hilton, 1888-1979, (U.S.) hotel chain founder.

Howard Hughes, 1905-76, (U.S.) industrialist, aviator, movie maker.

H. L. Hunt, 1889-1974, (U.S.) oil magnate.

Collis P. Huntington, 1821-1900, (U.S.) railroad magnate.

Henry E. Huntington, 1850-1927, (U.S.) railroad builder, philanthropist.

Walter L. Jacobs, 1898-1985, (U.S.) founder of the first rental car agency, which later became Hertz.

Howard Johnson, 1896-1972, (U.S.) founded restaurants.

Samuel Curtis Johnson, 1928-2004, (U.S.) headed S.C. Johnson & Sons.

Henry J. Kaiser, 1882-1967, (U.S.) industrialist; built empire in steel, aluminum.

Minor C. Keith, 1848-1929, (U.S.) railroad magnate; founded United Fruit Co.

Will K. Kellogg, 1860-1951, (U.S.) businessman, philanthropist; founded breakfast food co.

Richard King, 1825-85, (U.S.) cattleman; founded half-million-acre King Ranch in Texas.

William S. Knudsen, 1879-1948, (U.S.) Danish-born auto industry executive.

Samuel H. Kress, 1863-1955, (U.S.) businessman, art collector, philanthropist; founded "dime store" chain.

Ray A. Kroc, 1902-84, (U.S.) original CEO of McDonald's Corp.; oversaw company's vast expansion.

Alfred Krupp, 1812-87, (Ger.) armaments magnate.

William Levitt, 1907-94, (U.S.) industrialist, "suburb maker".

Thomas Lipton, 1850-1931, (Scot.) merchant, tea empire.

James McGill, 1744-1813, (Scot.-Can.) founded university.

Andrew W. Mellon, 1855-1937, (U.S.) financier, industrialist; benefactor of National Gallery of Art.

Charles E. Merrill, 1885-1956, (U.S.) financier; developed firm of Merrill Lynch.

John Pierpont Morgan, 1837-1913, (U.S.) most powerful figure in finance and industry at the turn of the cent.

Akio Morita, 1921-99, (Japan) co-founded Sony Corp.

Malcolm Muir, 1885-1979, (U.S.) created *Business Week* magazine; headed *Newsweek*, 1937-61.

Samuel Newhouse, 1895-1979, (U.S.) publishing and broadcasting magnate; built communications empire.

Aristotle Onassis, 1906-75, (Gr.) shipping magnate.

William S. Paley, 1901-90, (U.S.) built CBS communic. empire.

George Peabody, 1795-1869, (U.S.) merchant, financier, philanthropist.

James C. Penney, 1875-1971, (U.S.) businessman; developed department store chain.

William C. Procter, 1862-1934, (U.S.) headed soap co.

John D. Rockefeller, 1839-1937, (U.S.) industrialist; established Standard Oil.

John D. Rockefeller Jr., 1874-1960, (U.S.) philanthropist; established foundation; provided land for UN.

Laurance S. Rockefeller, 1910-2004, (U.S.) philanthropist, conservationist.

Meyer A. Rothschild, 1743-1812, (Ger.) founded international banking house.

Thomas Fortune Ryan, 1851-1928, (U.S.) financier; a founder of American Tobacco.

Edmond J. Safra, 1932-99, (U.S.) founded Republic National Bank of New York.

David Sarnoff, 1891-1971, (U.S.) broadcasting pioneer; established first radio network, NBC.

Richard Sears, 1863-1914, (U.S.) founded mail-order co.

Werner von Siemens, 1816-92, (Ger.) industrialist; inventor.

Alfred P. Sloan, 1875-1966, (U.S.) industrialist, philanthropist; headed General Motors.

A. Leland Stanford, 1824-93, (U.S.) railroad official, philanthropist; founded university.

Nathan Straus, 1848-1931, (U.S.) German-born merchant, philanthropist; headed Macy's.

Levi Strauss, c1829-1902, (U.S.) pants manufacturer.

Clement Studebaker, 1831-1901, (U.S.) wagon, carriage (maker).

Gustavus Swift, 1839-1903, (U.S.) pioneer meatpacker.

Gerard Swope, 1872-1957, (U.S.) industrialist, economist; headed General Electric.

Dave Thomas, 1932-2002, (U.S.) Wendy's founder.

James Walter Thompson, 1847-1928, (U.S.) ad executive.

Alice Tully, 1902-93, (U.S.) philanthropist, arts patron.

Theodore N. Vail, 1845-1920, (U.S.) organized Bell Telephone system; headed AT&T.

Cornelius Vanderbilt, 1794-1877, (U.S.) financier; established steamship, railroad empires.

Henry Villard, 1835-1900, (U.S.) German-born railroad executive, financier.

George Westinghouse, 1846-1914, (US) inventor, manufacturer; organized Westinghouse Electric Co., 1886.

Charles R. Walgreen, 1873-1939, (U.S.) founded drugstore chain.

DeWitt Wallace, 1889-1981, (U.S.) and **Lila Wallace,** 1889-1984, (U.S.) cofounders of *Reader's Digest* magazine.

Sam Walton, 1918-92, (U.S.) founder of Wal-Mart stores.

John Wanamaker, 1838-1922, (U.S.) pioneered department-store merchandising.

Aaron Montgomery Ward, 1843-1913, (U.S.) established first mail-order firm.

Thomas J. Watson, 1874-1956, (U.S.) IBM head, 1914-56.

John Hay Whitney, 1905-82, (U.S.) publisher, sportsman, philanthropist.

Charles E. Wilson, 1890-1961, (U.S.) auto industry exec., public official.

Frank W. Woolworth, 1852-1919, (U.S.) created 5 & 10 chain.

William Wrigley Jr., 1861-1932, (U.S.) founded Wrigley chewing gum company.

American Cartoonists

Reviewed by Lucy Shelton Caswell, Professor and Curator, Cartoon Research Library, Ohio State University

Scott Adams, b 1957, Dilbert.

Charles Addams, 1912-88, macabre cartoons.

Brad Anderson, b 1924, Marmaduke.

Sergio Aragones, b 1937, *MAD Magazine*.

Peter Arno, 1904-68, *The New Yorker*.

Tex Avery, 1908-80, animator, Bugs Bunny, Porky Pig.

George Baker, 1915-75, The Sad Sack.

Carl Barks, 1901-2000, Donald Duck comic books.

C. C. Beck, 1910-89, Captain Marvel.

Dave Berg, 1920-2002, *Mad Magazine*.

Jim Berry, b 1932, Berry's World.

Herb Block (Herblock), 1909-2001, political cartoonist.

George Booth, b 1926, *The New Yorker*.

Berkeley Breathed, b 1957, Bloom County.

Dik Browne, 1917-89, Hi & Lois, Hagar the Horrible.

Marjorie Buell, 1904-93, Little Lulu.

Ernie Bushmiller, 1905-82, Nancy.

Milton Caniff, 1907-88, Terry & the Pirates, Steve Canyon.

Al Capp, 1909-79, Li'l Abner.

Roz Chast, b 1954, *The New Yorker*.

Paul Conrad, 1924, political cartoonist.

Roy Crane, 1901-77, Captain Easy, Buz Sawyer.

Robert Crumb, b 1943, underground cartoonist.

Shamus Culhane, 1908-96, animator.

Jay N. Darling (Ding), 1876-1962, political cartoonist.

Jack Davis, b 1926, *MAD Magazine*.

Jim Davis, b 1945, Garfield.

Billy DeBeck, 1890-1942, Barney Google.

Rudolph Dirks, 1877-1968, The Katzenjammer Kids.

Walt Disney, 1901-66, produced animated cartoons, created Mickey Mouse, Donald Duck.

Steve Ditko, b 1927, Spider-Man.

Mort Drucker, b 1929, *MAD Magazine*.

Will Eisner, b 1917, The Spirit.

Jules Feiffer, b 1929, political cartoonist.

Bud Fisher, 1884-1954, Mutt & Jeff.

Ham Fisher, 1900-55, Joe Palooka.

Max Fleischer, 1883-1972, Betty Boop.

Hal Foster, 1892-1982, Tarzan, Prince Valiant.

Fontaine Fox, 1884-1964, Toonerville Folks.

Isadore "Friz" Freleng, 1905-95, animator, Yosemite Sam, Porky Pig, Sylvester and Tweety Bird.

Rube Goldberg, 1883-1970, Boob McNutt.

Chester Gould, 1900-85, Dick Tracy.

Harold Gray, 1894-1968, Little Orphan Annie.

Matt Groening, b 1954, Life in Hell, The Simpsons.

Cathy Guisewite, b 1950, Cathy.

Bill Hanna, 1910-2001, & **Joe Barbera,** b 1911, animators, Tom & Jerry, Yogi Bear, Flintstones.

Johnny Hart, b 1931, BC, Wizard of Id.

Oliver Harrington, 1912-95, Bootsie.

Alfred Harvey, 1913-94, created Casper the Friendly Ghost.

Jimmy Hatlo, 1898-1963, Little Iodine.

John Held Jr., 1889-1958, Jazz Age.

George Herriman, 1881-1944, Krazy Kat.

Harry Hershfield, 1885-1974, Abie the Agent.

Al Hirschfeld, 1903-2003, *N.Y. Times* theater caricaturist.

Burne Hogarth, 1911-96, Tarzan.

Helen Hokinson, 1900-49, *The New Yorker*.

Nicole Hollander, b 1939, Sylvia.

Chuck Jones, 1912-2002, animator, Bugs Bunny, Porky Pig.

Mike Judge, b. 1962, Beavis and Butt-head, King of the Hill.

Bob Kane, b 1916-98, Batman.

Bil Keane, b 1922, The Family Circus.

Walt Kelly, 1913-73, Pogo.

Hank Ketcham, 1920-2001, Dennis the Menace.

Ted Key, b 1912, Hazel.

Frank King, 1883-1969, Gasoline Alley.

Jack Kirby, 1917-94, Fantastic Four, The Incredible Hulk.

Rollin Kirby, 1875-1952, political cartoonist.

B(ernard) Kliban, 1935-91, cat books.

Edward Koren, b 1935, *The New Yorker*.

Harvey Kurtzman, 1921-93, *MAD Magazine*.

Walter Lantz, 1900-94, Woody Woodpecker.

Gary Larson, b 1950, The Far Side.

Mell Lazarus, b 1929, Momma, Miss Peach.

Stan Lee, b 1922, Marvel Comics.

David Levine, b 1926, *N.Y. Review of Books* caricatures.

Doug Marlette, b 1949, political cartoonist, Kudzu.

Don Martin, 1931-2000, *MAD Magazine*.

Bill Mauldin, 1921-2003, political cartoonist.

Jeff MacNelly, 1947-2000, political cartoonist, Shoe.

Winsor McCay, 1872-1934, Little Nemo.

John T. McCutcheon, 1870-1949, political cartoonist.

Aaron McGruder, b 1974, The Boondocks.

George McManus, 1884-1954, Bringing Up Father.

Dale Messick, b 1906, Brenda Starr.

Norman Mingo, 1896-1980, Alfred E. Neuman.

Bob Montana, 1920-75, Archie.

Dick Moores, 1909-86, Gasoline Alley.

Willard Mullin, 1902-78, sports cartoonist; Dodgers "Bum," Mets "Kid."

Russell Myers, b 1938, Broom Hilda.

Thomas Nast, 1840-1902, political cartoonist; Republican elephant and Democratic donkey.

Pat Oliphant, b 1935, political cartoonist.

Frederick Burr Opper, 1857-1937, Happy Hooligan.

Richard Outcault, 1863-1928, Yellow Kid, Buster Brown.

Brant Parker, b 1920, Wizard of Id.

Trey Parker, b 1969?, animator, co-creator of *South Park*.

Mike Peters, b 1943, cartoonist, Mother Goose & Grimm.
George Price, 1901-95, *The New Yorker.*
Antonio Prohias, 1921(?)-98, Spy vs. Spy.
Alex Raymond, 1909-56, Flash Gordon, Jungle Jim.
Forrest (Bud) Sagendorf, 1915-94, Popeye.
Art Sansom, 1920-91, The Born Loser.
Charles Schulz, 1922-2000, Peanuts.
Elzie C. Segar, 1894-1938, Popeye.
Joe Shuster, 1914-92, & **Jerry Siegel,** 1914-96, Superman.
Sidney Smith, 1887-1935, The Gumps.
Otto Soglow, 1900-75, Little King.
Art Spiegelman, b 1948, Raw, Maus.
William Steig, b 1907, *The New Yorker.*
Matt Stone, b 1971?, animator, co-creator of South Park.
Paul Szep, b 1941, political cartoonist.

James Swinnerton, 1875-1974, Little Jimmy, Canyon Kiddies.
Paul Terry, 1887-1971, animator of Mighty Mouse.
Bob Thaves, b 1924, Frank and Ernest.
James Thurber, 1894-61, *The New Yorker.*
Garry Trudeau, b 1948, Doonesbury.
Mort Walker, b 1923, Beetle Bailey.
Bill Watterson, b 1958, Calvin and Hobbes.
Russ Westover, 1887-1966, Tillie the Toiler.
Signe Wilkinson, b 1950, political cartoonist.
Frank Willard, 1893-1958, Moon Mullins.
J. R. Williams, 1888-1957, The Willets Family, Out Our Way.
Gahan Wilson, b 1930, *The New Yorker.*
Tom Wilson, b 1931, Ziggy.
Art Young, 1866-1943, political cartoonist.
Chic Young, 1901-73, Blondie.

Economists, Educators, Historians, and Social Scientists of the Past
For Psychologists see Scientists of the Past.

Brooks Adams, 1848-1927, (U.S.) historian, political theoretician; *The Law of Civilization and Decay.*
Henry Adams, 1838-1918, (U.S.) historian, autobiographer; *History of the United States of America, The Education of Henry Adams.*
Francis Bacon, 1561-1626, (Eng.) philosopher, essayist, and statesman; championed observation and induction.
George Bancroft, 1800-91, (U.S.) historian; wrote 10-volume *History of the United States.*
Jack Barbash, 1911-94, (U.S.) labor economist who helped create the AFL-CIO.
Henry Barnard, 1811-1900, (U.S.) public school reformer.
Charles A. Beard, 1874-1948, (U.S.) historian; *The Economic Basis of Politics.*
(St.) Bede (the Venerable), c673-735, (Br.) scholar, historian; *Ecclesiastical History of the English People.*
Ruth Benedict, 1887-1948, (U.S.) anthropologist; studied Indian tribes of the Southwest.
Sir Isaiah Berlin, 1909-97, (Br.) philosopher, historian; *The Age of Enlightenment.*
Louis Blanc, 1811-82, (Fr.) Socialist leader and historian.
Sarah G. Blanding, 1899-1985, (U.S.) head of Vassar College, 1946-64.
Leonard Bloomfield, 1887-1949, (U.S.) linguist; *Language.*
Franz Boas, 1858-1942, (U.S.) German-born anthropologist; studied American Indians.
Van Wyck Brooks, 1886-1963, (U.S.) historian; critic of New England culture, especially literature.
Edmund Burke, 1729-97, (Ir.) British parliamentarian and political philosopher; *Reflections on the Revolution in France.*
Nicholas Murray Butler, 1862-1947, (U.S.) educator; headed Columbia Univ., 1902-45; Nobel Peace Prize, 1931.
Joseph Campbell, 1904-87, (U.S.) author, editor, teacher; wrote books on mythology, folklore.
Thomas Carlyle, 1795-1881, (Sc.) historian, critic; *Sartor Resartus, Past and Present, The French Revolution.*
Edward Channing, 1856-1931, (U.S.) historian; wrote 6-volume *History of the United States.*
Henry Steele Commager, 1902-98, (U.S.) historian, educator; wrote *The Growth of the American Republic.*
John R. Commons, 1862-1945, (U.S.) economist, labor historian; *Legal Foundations of Capitalism.*
James B. Conant, 1893-1978, (U.S.) educator, diplomat; *The American High School Today.*
Benedetto Croce, 1866-1952, (It.) philosopher, statesman, and historian; *Philosophy of the Spirit.*
Bernard A. De Voto, 1897-1955, (U.S.) historian; wrote trilogy on American West; edited Mark Twain manuscripts.
Melvil Dewey, 1851-1931, (U.S.) devised decimal system of library-book classification.
Emile Durkheim, 1858-1917, (Fr.) a founder of modern sociology; *The Rules of Sociological Method.*
Charles Eliot, 1834-1926, (U.S.) educator, Harvard president.
Friedrich Engels, 1820-95, (Ger.) political writer; with Marx wrote the *Communist Manifesto.*
Irving Fisher, 1867-1947, (U.S.) economist; contributed to the development of modern monetary theory.
John Fiske, 1842-1901, (U.S.) historian and lecturer; popularized Darwinian theory of evolution.
Charles Fourier, 1772-1837, (Fr.) utopian socialist.
Giovanni Gentile, 1875-1944, (It.) philosopher, educator; reformed Italian educational system.
Sir James George Frazer, 1854-1941, (Br.) anthropologist; studied myth in religion; *The Golden Bough.*
Henry George, 1839-97, (U.S.) economist, reformer; led single-tax movement.
Edward Gibbon, 1737-94, (Br.) historian; *The History of the Decline and Fall of the Roman Empire.*
Francesco Guicciardini, 1483-1540, (It.) historian; *Storia d'Italia,* principal historical work of the 16th cent.
Thomas Hobbes, 1588-1679, (Eng.) philosopher, political theorist; *Leviathan.*

Richard Hofstadter, 1916-70, (U.S.) historian; *The Age of Reform.*
John Holt, 1924-85, (U.S.) educator and author.
John Maynard Keynes, 1883-1946, (Br.) economist; principal advocate of deficit spending.
Russell Kirk, 1918-94, (U.S.) social philosopher; *The Conservative Mind.*
Alfred L. Kroeber, 1876-1960, (U.S.) cultural anthropologist; studied Indians of North and South America.
Elisabeth Kubler-Ross,1926-2004, (Swiss) psychiatrist, author. *On Death and Dying.*
Christopher Lasch, 1932-94, (U.S.) social critic, historian; *The Culture of Narcissism.*
James L. Laughlin, 1850-1933, (U.S.) economist; helped establish Federal Reserve System.
Lucien Lévy-Bruhl, 1857-1939, (Fr.) philosopher; studied the psychology of primitive societies; *Primitive Mentality.*
John Locke, 1632-1704, (Eng.) philosopher and political theorist; *Two Treatises of Government.*
Thomas B. Macaulay, 1800-59, (Br.) historian, statesman.
Niccolò Machiavelli, 1469-1527, (It.) writer, statesman. *The Prince.*
Bronislaw Malinowski, 1884-1942, (Pol.) considered the father of social anthropology.
Thomas R. Malthus, 1766-1834, (Br.) economist; famed for *Essay on the Principle of Population.*
Horace Mann, 1796-1859, (U.S.) pioneered modern public school system.
Karl Mannheim, 1893-1947, (Hung.) sociologist, historian; *Ideology and Utopia.*
Harriet Martineau, 1802-76, (Eng.) writer, feminist; *Society in America*
Karl Marx, 1818-83, (Ger.) political theorist, proponent of Communism; *Communist Manifesto, Das Kapital.*
Giuseppe Mazzini, 1805-72, (It.) political philosopher.
William H. McGuffey, 1800-73, (U.S.) whose *Reader* was a mainstay of 19th-cent. U.S. public education.
George H. Mead, 1863-1931, (U.S.) philosopher, social psychologist.
Margaret Mead, 1901-78, (U.S.) cultural anthropologist; popularized field; *Coming of Age in Samoa.*
Alexander Meiklejohn, 1872-1964, (U.S.) Br.-born educator; championed academic freedom and experimental curricula.
James Mill, 1773-1836, (Sc.) philosopher, historian, economist; a proponent of utilitarianism.
Perry G. Miller, 1905-63, (U.S.) historian; interpreted 17th-cent. New England.
Theodor Mommsen, 1817-1903, (Ger.) historian; *The History of Rome.*
Ashley Montagu, 1905-99, (Eng.) anthropologist; *The Natural Superiority of Women.*
Charles-Louis Montesquieu, 1689-1755, (Fr.) social philosopher; *The Spirit of Laws.*
Maria Montessori, 1870-1952, (It.) educator, physician; started Montessori method of student self-motivation.
Samuel Eliot Morison, 1887-1976, (U.S.) historian; chronicled voyages of early explorers.
Lewis Mumford, 1895-1990, (U.S.) sociologist, critic; *The Culture of Cities.*
Gunnar Myrdal, 1898-1987, (Swed.) economist, social scientist; *Asian Drama: An Inquiry Into the Poverty of Nations.*
Joseph Needham, 1900-95, (Br.) scientific historian; *Science and Civilization in China.*
Allan Nevins, 1890-1971, (U.S.) historian, biographer; *The Ordeal of the Union.*
José Ortega y Gasset, 1883-1955, (Sp.) philosopher; advocated control by elite, *The Revolt of the Masses.*
Robert Owen, 1771-1858, (Br.) political philosopher, reformer; pioneer in cooperative movement.
Thomas (Tom) Paine, 1737-1809, (U.S.) political theorist, writer. *Common Sense.*
Vilfredo Pareto, 1848-1923, (It.) economist, sociologist.

Francis Parkman, 1823-93, (U.S.) historian; *France and England in North America.*

Elizabeth P. Peabody, 1804-94, (U.S.) education pioneer; founded 1st kindergarten in U.S., 1860.

William Prescott, 1796-1859, (U.S.) early American historian; *The Conquest of Peru.*

Pierre Joseph Proudhon, 1809-65, (Fr.) social theorist; father of anarchism; *The Philosophy of Property.*

François Quesnay, 1694-1774, (Fr.) economic theorist.

David Ricardo, 1772-1823, (Br.) economic theorist; advocated free international trade.

David Riesman, 1909-2002, (U.S.) sociologist, coauthor *The Lonely Crowd.*

Jean-Jacques Rousseau, 1712-78, (Fr.) social philosopher; the father of romantic sensibility; *Confessions.*

Edward Sapir, 1884-1939, (Ger.-U.S.) anthropologist; studied ethnology and linguistics of U.S. Indian groups.

Ferdinand de Saussure, 1857-1913, (Swiss) a founder of modern linguistics.

Hjalmar Schacht, 1877-1970, (Ger.) economist.

Joseph Schumpeter, 1883-1950, (Czech.-U.S.) economist, sociologist.

Elizabeth Seton, 1774-1821, (U.S.) nun; est. parochial school education in U.S.; first native-born American saint.

George Simmel, 1858-1918, (Ger.) sociologist, philosopher; helped establish German sociology.

Adam Smith, 1723-90, (Br.) economist; advocated laissez-faire economy, free trade; *The Wealth of Nations.*

Jared Sparks, 1789-1866, (U.S.) historian, educator, editor; *The Library of American Biography.*

Oswald Spengler, 1880-1936, (Ger.) philosopher and historian; *The Decline of the West.*

William G. Sumner, 1840-1910, (U.S.) social scientist, economist; laissez-faire economy, Social Darwinism.

Hippolyte Taine, 1828-93, (Fr.) historian; basis of naturalistic school; *The Origins of Contemporary France.*

A(lan) J(ohn) P(ercivale) Taylor, 1906-89, (Br.) historian; *The Origins of the Second World War.*

Nikolaas Tinbergen, 1907-88, (Dutch-Br.) ethologist; pioneer in study of animal behavior.

Alexis de Tocqueville, 1805-59, (Fr.) political scientist, historian; *Democracy in America.*

Francis E. Townsend, 1867-1960, (U.S.) led old-age pension movement, 1933.

Arnold Toynbee, 1889-1975, (Br.) historian; *A Study of History,* sweeping analysis of hist. of civilizations.

George Trevelyan, 1838-1928, (Br.) historian, statesman; favored "literary" over "scientific" history; *History of England.*

Barbara Tuchman, 1912-89, (U.S.) author of popular history books, *The Guns of August, The March of Folly.*

Frederick J. Turner, 1861-1932, (U.S.) historian, educator; *The Frontier in American History.*

Thorstein B. Veblen, 1857-1929, (U.S.) economist, social philosopher; *The Theory of the Leisure Class.*

Giovanni Vico, 1668-1744, (It.) historian, philosopher; regarded by many as first modern historian; *New Science.*

Izaak Walton, 1593-1683, (Eng.) wrote biographies; political-philosophical study of fishing, *The Compleat Angler.*

Sidney J., 1859-1947, and **Beatrice,** 1858-1943, **Webb,** (Br.) leading figures in Fabian Society and Labor Party.

Max Weber, 1864-1920, (Ger.) sociologist; *The Protestant Ethic and the Spirit of Capitalism.*

Emma Hart Willard, 1787-1870, (U.S.) pioneered higher education for women.

C. Vann Woodward, 1908-99, (U.S.) historian; *The Strange Career of Jim Crow.*

American Journalists of the Past
Reviewed by Dean Mills, Dean, Missouri School of Journalism
See also African-Americans, Business Leaders, Cartoonists, Writers of the Past.

Franklin P. Adams (F.P.A.), 1881-1960, humorist; wrote column "The Conning Tower."

Martin Agronsky, 1915-99, broadcast journalist; developed Agronsky & Company.

Joseph W. Alsop, 1910-89, and **Stewart Alsop,** 1914-74, Washington-based political analysts, columnists.

Brooks Atkinson, 1894-1984, theater critic.

Bartley, Robert L., 1937-2003, editorial-page editor for *Wall Street Journal.*

James Gordon Bennett, 1795-1872, editor and publisher; founded *NY Herald.*

James Gordon Bennett, 1841-1918, succeeded father, financed expeditions, founded afternoon paper.

Elias Boudinot, d 1839, founding editor of first Native American newspaper in U.S., *Cherokee Phoenix* (1828-34).

David Brinkley, 1920-2003, co-anchor of NBC's *Huntley-Brinkley Report,* host of ABC's *This Week With David Brinkley.*

Margaret Bourke-White, 1904-71, photojournalist.

Arthur Brisbane, 1864-1936, editor; helped introduce "yellow jounalism" with sensational, simply written articles.

Heywood Broun, 1888-1939, author, columnist; founded American Newspaper Guild.

Herb Caen, 1916-97, longtime columnist for *San Francisco Chronicle* and *Examiner.*

John Campbell, 1653-1728, published *Boston News-Letter,* first continuing newspaper in the American colonies.

Jimmy Cannon, 1909-73, syndicated sports columnist.

John Chancellor, 1927-96, TV journalist; anchored *NBC Nightly News.*

Harry Chandler, 1864-1944, *Los Angeles Times* publisher, 1917-41; made it a dominant force.

Marquis Childs, 1903-90, reporter and columnist for *St. Louis Post-Dispatch* and United Feature syndicate.

Craig Claiborne, 1920-2000, *NY Times* food editor and critic; key in internationalizing American taste.

Elizabeth Cochrane (Nellie Bly), pioneer woman journalist, investig. reporter, noted for series on trip around the world.

Charles Collingwood, 1917-85, CBS news correspondent, foreign affairs reporter, documentary host.

Alistair Cooke, 1908-2004, journalist, TV narrator, naturalized American citizen, "Letter from America" series.

Howard Cosell, 1920-95, TV and radio sportscaster.

Gardner Cowles, 1861-1946, founded newspaper chain.

Cyrus Curtis, 1850-1933, publisher of *Saturday Evening Post, Ladies' Home Journal, Country Gentleman.*

John Charles Daly, 1914-91, war correspondent; TV journalist; Voice of America head.

Charles Anderson Dana, 1819-97, editor, publisher; made *NY Sun* famous for its news reporting.

Elmer (Holmes) Davis, 1890-1958, *NY Times* editorial writer; radio commentator.

Richard Harding Davis, 1864-1916, war correspondent, travel writer, fiction writer.

Benjamin Day, 1810-89, published *NY Sun* beginning in 1833, introducing penny press to the U.S.

Frederick Douglass, 1817-95, ex-slave, social reformer, newspaper editor.

Finley Peter Dunne, 1867-1936, humorist, social critic, wrote "Mr. Dooley" columns.

Mary Baker Eddy, 1821-1910, founded Christian Science movement and *Christian Science Monitor.*

Rowland Evans Jr., 1921-2001, Washington columnist and commentator.

Fanny Fern (Sarah Willis Parton), 1811-1872, newspaper columnist, author.

Marshall Field III, 1893-1956, retail magnate, *Chicago Sun* founder.

Doris Fleeson, 1901-70, war correspondent, columnist.

James Franklin, 1697-1735, printer, pioneer journalist, publisher of *New England Courant* and *Rhode Island Gazette.*

Fred W. Friendly, 1915-98, radio, TV reporter, announcer, producer, executive, collaborator with Edward R. Murrow.

Margaret Fuller, 1810-50, social reformer, transcendentalist, critic and foreign correspondent for *NY Tribune.*

Frank E. Gannett, 1876-1957, founded newspaper chain.

William Lloyd Garrison, 1805-79, abolitionist; publisher of *The Liberator.*

Elizabeth Meriwether Gilmer (Dorothy Dix), 1861-1951, reporter, pioneer of the advice column genre.

Edwin Lawrence Godkin, 1831-1902, founder of *The Nation,* editor of *N.Y. Evening Post.*

Katharine Graham, 1917-2001, *Washington Post* publisher.

Sheilah Graham, 1904-89, Hollywood gossip columnist.

Horace Greeley, 1811-72, editor and politician; founded *NY Tribune.*

Meg Greenfield, 1930-1999, *Newsweek* columnist, editorial page editor *Washington Post.*

Gilbert Hovey Grosvenor, 1875-1966, longtime editor of *National Geographic* magazine.

John Gunther, 1901-70, *Chicago Daily News* foreign correspondent, author.

Sarah Josepha Buell Hale, 1788-1879, first female magazine editor, (Ladies' Magazine, later Godey's Lady's Book)

Benjamin Harris, 1673-1716, publisher (1690) of *Publick Occurrences,* 1st newspaper in the American colonies; suppressed after one issue.

William Randolph Hearst, 1863-1951, founder of Hearst newspaper chain and one of the pioneer yellow journalists.

Gabriel Heatter, 1890-1972, radio commentator.

John Hersey, 1914-98, foreign correspondent for *Time, Life,* and *The New Yorker;* author.

Marguerite Higgins, 1920-66, reporter, war correspondent.

Hedda Hopper, 1885-1966, Hollywood gossip columnist.

Roy Howard, 1883-1964, editor, executive, Scripps-Howard papers and United Press (later United Press International).

Chet (Chester Robert) Huntley, 1911-74, co-anchor of NBC's *Huntley-Brinkley Report.*

Ralph Ingersoll, 1900-85, editor, *Fortune, Time, Life* exec.

H. V. (Hans von) Kaltenborn, 1878-1965, radio commentator, reporter.

Murray Kempton, 1917-97, reporter, columnist for magazines and newspapers, including *NY Post.*

Dorothy Kilgallen, 1913-65, crime reporter; columnist.

John S. Knight, 1894-1981, editor, publisher; founded Knight newspaper group, which merged into Knight-Ridder.

Joseph Kraft, 1942-86, foreign policy columnist.

Arthur Krock, 1886-1974, *NY Times* political writer, Washington bureau chief.

Charles Kuralt, 1934-97, TV anchor and host of CBS "On the Road" featuring stories about life in the U.S.

Ann Landers, (Eppie Lederer), 1918-2002, advice columnist.

David Lawrence, 1888-1973, reporter, columnist, publisher; founded *U.S. News & World Report.*

Frank Leslie, 1821-80, engraver and publisher of newspapers and magazines, notably *Leslie's Illustrated Newspaper.*

Alexander Liberman, 1912-99, editorial director for Conde Nast magazines.

A(bbott) J(oseph) Liebling, 1904-63, foreign correspondent, critic, principally with *The New Yorker.*

Walter Lippmann, 1889-1974, political analyst, social critic, columnist, author.

Peter Lisagor, 1915-76, Washington bureau chief, *Chicago Daily News;* broadcast commentator.

David Ross Locke, 1833-88, humorist, satirist under pseudonym P.V. Nasby; owned *Toledo (Ohio) Blade.*

Elijah Parish Lovejoy, 1802-37, abolitionist editor in St. Louis and in Alton, IL; killed by proslavery mob.

Clare Booth Luce, 1903-87, war correspondent for *Life;* diplomat, playwright.

Henry R. Luce, 1898-1967, founded *Time, Fortune, Life, Sports Illustrated.*

C(harles) K(enny) McClatchy, 1858-1936 founder of McClatchy newspaper chain.

Sarah McClendon, 1910-2003, (U.S.) veteran White House correspondent.

Samuel McClure, 1857-1949, founder (1893) of *McClure's Magazine,* famous for its investigative reporting.

Anne O'Hare McCormick, 1889-1954, foreign correspondent, first woman on *NY Times* editorial board.

Robert R. McCormick, 1880-1955, editor, publisher, executive of *Chicago Tribune* and *NY Daily News.*

Dwight Macdonald, 1906-1982, reporter, social critic for *The New Yorker, The Nation, Esquire.*

Ralph McGill, 1893-1969, crusading editor and publisher of *Atlanta Constitution.*

Mary McGrory, 1918-2004, Washington, DC, columnist.

O(scar) O(dd) McIntyre, 1884-1938, feature writer, syndicated columnist concentrating on everyday life in New York City.

Don Marquis, 1878-1937, humor columnist for *NY Sun* and *N.Y. Tribune;* wrote "archy and mehitabel" stories.

Robert Maynard, 1937-97, first African-American editor and then owner of major U.S. paper, the *Oakland Tribune.*

Joseph Medill, 1823-99, longtime *editor of Chicago Tribune.*

H(enry) L(ouis) Mencken, 1880-1956, reporter, editor, columnist with *Baltimore Sun* papers; anti-establishment viewpoint.

Edwin Meredith, 1876-1928, founder of magazine company.

Frank A. Munsey, 1854-1925, owner, editor, and publisher of newspapers and magazines, including *Munsey's Magazine.*

Edward R. Murrow, 1908-65, broadcast reporter, executive; reported from Britain in WW2; hosted *See It Now, Person to Person.*

William Rockhill Nelson, 1841-1915, cofounder, editor, and publisher, *Kansas City Star.*

Adolph S. Ochs, 1858-1935, publisher; built *NY Times* into a leading newspaper.

Louella Parsons, 1881-1972, Hollywood gossip columnist.

Drew (Andrew Russell) Pearson, 1897-1969, investigative reporter and columnist.

(James) Westbrook Pegler, 1894-1969, reporter, columnist.

Shirley Povich, 1905-98, sports columnist.

Joseph Pulitzer, 1847-1911, *NY World* publisher; founded Columbia Journalism School, Pulitzer Prizes.

Joseph Pulitzer II, 1885-1955, longtime *St. Louis Post-Dispatch* editor, publisher; built it into major paper.

Ernie (Ernest Taylor) Pyle, 1900-45, reporter, war correspondent; killed in WW2.

Henry Raymond, 1820-69, cofounder, editor, *NY Times.*

Harry Reasoner, 1923-91, TV reporter, anchor.

John Reed, 1887-1920, reporter, foreign correspondent famous for coverage of Bolshevik Revolution.

Whitelaw Reid, 1837-1912, longtime editor, *NY Tribune.*

James Reston, 1909-95 *NY Times* political reporter, columnist.

Frank Reynolds, 1923-83, TV reporter, anchor.

(Henry) Grantland Rice, 1880-1954, sportswriter.

Jacob Riis, 1849-1914, reporter, photographer; exposed slum conditions in *How the Other Half Lives.*

Max Robinson, 1939-88, TV journalist, first African-American to anchor network news, 1978.

Harold Ross, 1892-1951, founder, editor, The *New Yorker.*

Mike Royko, 1932-97, Chicago newspaper columnist; wrote *Boss,* biography of Mayor Richard Daley.

(Alfred) Damon Runyon, 1884-1946, sportswriter, columnist; stories collected in *Guys and Dolls.*

John B. Russwurm, 1799-1851, cofounded (1827) nation's first black newspaper, *Freedom's Journal,* in NYC.

Adela Rogers St. Johns, 1894-1988, reporter, sportswriter for Hearst newspapers.

Harrison Salisbury, 1908-93, reporter, foreign correspondent; a Soviet specialist.

E(dward) W(lyllis) Scripps, 1854-1926, founded first large U.S. newspaper chain, pioneered syndication.

Eric Sevareid, 1912-92, war correspondent, radio newscaster, TV commentator.

William L. Shirer, 1904-93, broadcaster, foreign correspondent; wrote *The Rise and Fall of the Third Reich.*

Howard K. Smith, 1914-2002, broadcast journalist.

Red (Walter) Smith, 1905-82, sportswriter.

Edgar P. Snow, 1905-71, correspondent, expert on Chinese Communist movement.

Lawrence Spivak, 1900-94, co-creator, moderator, producer of *Meet the Press.*

(Joseph) Lincoln Steffens, 1866-1936, muckraking journalist.

I(sidor) F(einstein) Stone, 1907-89, one-man editor of *I.F. Stone's Weekly.*

Arthur Hays Sulzberger, 1891-1968, longtime publisher of *N.Y. Times.*

C(yrus) L(eo) Sulzberger, 1912-93, *N.Y. Times* foreign correspondent and columnist.

David Susskind, 1920-87, TV producer, public affairs talk-show host (*Open End*).

John Cameron Swayze, 1906-95, newscaster, anchor of *Camel News Caravan.*

Herbert Bayard Swope, 1882-1958, war correspondent and editor of *N.Y. World.*

Ida Tarbell, 1857-1944, muckraking journalist.

Isaiah Thomas, 1750-1831, printer, publisher, cofounder of revolutionary journal, *Massachusetts Spy.*

Lowell Thomas, 1892-1981, radio newscaster, world traveler.

Dorothy Thompson, 1894-1961, foreign correspondent, columnist, radio commentator.

Ida Bell Wells-Barnett, 1862-1931, African-American reporter, editor, anti-lynching crusader.

William Allen White, 1868-1944, editor, publisher; made *Emporia* (KS) *Gazette* known worldwide.

Walter Winchell, 1897-1972, reporter, columnist, broadcaster of celebrity news.

John Peter Zenger, 1697-1746, printer and journalist; acquitted in precedent-setting libel suit (1735).

Military and Naval Leaders of the Past
Reviewed by Alan C. Aimone, USMA Library

Creighton Abrams, 1914-74, (U.S.) commanded forces in Vietnam, 1968-72.

Alexander the Great, 356-323 B.C., (Maced.) conquered Persia and much of the world known to Europeans.

Harold Alexander, 1891-1969, (Br.) led Allied invasion of Italy, 1943, WW2.

Ethan Allen, 1738-89, (U.S.) headed Green Mountain Boys; captured Ft. Ticonderoga, 1775, Amer. Rev.

Edmund Allenby, 1861-1936, (Br.) in Boer War, WW1; led Egyptian expeditionary force, 1917-18.

Benedict Arnold, 1741-1801, (U.S.) victorious at Saratoga; tried to betray West Point to British, Amer. Rev.

Henry "Hap" Arnold, 1886-1950, (U.S.) commanded Army Air Force in WW2.

Ashurnasirpal II, 884-859 B.C., (Assyria) king, began Assyrian conquest of Middle East.

John Barry, 1745-1803, (U.S.) won numerous sea battles during Amer. Rev.

Belisarius, c505-565, (Byzant.) won remarkable victories for Byzantine Emperor Justinian I.

Pierre Beauregard, 1818-93, (U.S.) Confed. general, ordered bombardment of Ft. Sumter that began Civil War.

Gebhard von Blücher, 1742-1819, (Ger.) helped defeat Napoleon at Waterloo.

Napoleon Bonaparte, 1769-1821, (Fr.) defeated Russia and Austria at Austerlitz, 1805; invaded Russia, 1812; defeated at Waterloo, 1815.

Edward Braddock, 1695-1755, (Br.) commanded forces in French and Indian War.

Omar N. Bradley, 1893-1981, (U.S.) headed U.S. ground troops in Normandy invasion, 1944, WW2.

> **IT'S A FACT:** American WWI General John Pershing was known as "Black Jack," not because of any connection to the card game, but rather for his service with the 10th Cavalry Regiment (of the famed "Buffalo Soldiers") during the Spanish-American War. The 10th was one of two distinguished all-black cavalry regiments, both headed by white officers.

John Burgoyne, 1722-92, (Br.) general, defeated at Saratoga, Amer. Rev.

Julius Caesar, 100-44 B.C., (Rom.) general and politician; conquered N Gaul; overthrew Roman Republic.

Charlemagne, 742-814, (Fr.) king of the Franks, Holy Roman Emperor, conqured most of Western Europe.

El Cid (Rodrigo Diaz de Vivar), 1040-99, (Sp.) renowned knight, captured Valencia (1094); hero of Song of Cid epic.

Claire Lee Chennault, 1893-1958, (U.S.) headed Flying Tigers in WW2.

Mark W. Clark, 1896-1984, (U.S.) helped plan N. African invasion in WW2; commander of UN forces, Korean War.

Karl von Clausewitz, 1780-1831, (Pruss.) military theorist.

Lucius D. Clay, 1897-1978, (U.S.) led Berlin airlift, 1948-49.

Henry Clinton, 1738-95, (Br.) commander of forces in Amer. Rev., 1778-81.

Cochise, c1815-74, (Nat. Am.) chief of Chiricahua band of Apache Indians in Southwest.

Charles Cornwallis, 1738-1805, (Br.) victorious at Brandywine, 1777; surrendered at Yorktown, Amer. Rev.

Hernán Cortés, 1485-1547, (Sp.) led Spanish conquistadors in the defeat of the Aztec empire, 1519-28.

Crazy Horse, 1849-77, (Nat. Am.) Sioux war chief victorious at battle of Little Bighorn.

George Armstrong Custer, 1839-76, (U.S.) U.S. army officer defeated and killed at battle of Little Bighorn.

Moshe Dayan, 1915-81, (Isr.) directed campaigns in the 1967, 1973 Arab-Israeli wars.

Stephen Decatur, 1779-1820, (U.S.) naval hero of Barbary wars, War of 1812.

Anton Denikin, 1872-1947, (Russ.) led White forces in Russian civil war.

George Dewey, 1837-1917, (U.S.) destroyed Spanish fleet at Manila, 1898, Span.-Amer. War.

Karl Doenitz, 1891-1980, (Ger.) submarine com. in chief and naval commander, WW2.

Jimmy Doolittle, 1896-1993, (U.S.) led 1942 air raid on Tokyo and other Japanese cities in WW2.

Hugh C. Dowding, 1883-1970, (Br.) headed RAF, 1936-40, WW2.

Jubal Early, 1816-94, (U.S.) Confed. general, led raid on Washington, 1864, Civil War.

Dwight D. Eisenhower, 1890-1969, (U.S.) commanded Allied forces in Europe, WW2.

Erich von Falkenhayn, 1861-1922, (Ger.) minister of war, general, commander at Verdun in WW1.

David Farragut, 1801-70, (U.S.) Union admiral, captured New Orleans, Mobile Bay, Civil War.

John Arbuthnot Fisher, 1841-1920, (Br.) WW1 admiral, naval reformer.

Ferdinand Foch, 1851-1929, (Fr.) headed victorious Allied armies, 1918, WW1.

Nathan Bedford Forrest, 1821-77, (U.S.) Confed. general, led raids against Union supply lines, Civil War.

Frederick the Great, 1712-86, (Pruss.) led Prussia in Seven Years War.

Horatio Gates, 1728-1806, (U.S.) commanded army at Saratoga, Amer. Rev.

Genghis Khan, 1162-1227, (Mongol) unified Mongol tribes and subjugated much of Asia, 1206-21.

Geronimo, 1829-1909, (Nat. Am.) leader of Chiricahua band of Apache Indians.

Charles G. Gordon, 1833-85, (Br.) led forces in China, Crimean War; killed at Khartoum.

Ulysses S. Grant, 1822-85, (U.S.) headed Union army, Civil War, 1864-65; forced Lee's surrender, 1865.

Nathanael Greene, 1742-86, (U.S.) defeated British in Southern campaign, 1780-81, Amer. Rev.

Heinz Guderian, 1888-1953, (Ger.) tank theorist, led panzer forces in Poland, France, Russia, WW2.

Gustavus Adolphus, 1594-1632, (Swed.) King; military tactician; reformer; led forces in Thirty Years' War.

Douglas Haig, 1861-1928, (Br.) led British armies in France, 1915-18, WW1.

William F. Halsey, 1882-1959, (U.S.) defeated Japanese fleet at Leyte Gulf, 1944, WW2.

Hannibal, 247-183 B.C., (Carthag.) invaded Rome, crossing Alps, in Second Punic War, 218-201 B.C.

Sir Arthur Travers Harris, 1895-1984, (Br.) led Britain's WW2 bomber command.

Paul von Hindenburg, 1847-1934, (Ger.) chief of general staff, WW1; 2nd pres. of Weimar Republic.

Richard Howe, 1726-99, (Br.) commanded navy in Amer. Rev., 1776-78; June 1 victory against French, 1794.

William Howe, 1729-1814, (Br.) commanded forces in Amer. Rev., 1776-78.

Isaac Hull, 1773-1843, (U.S.) sunk British frigate Guerriere, War of 1812.

Thomas (Stonewall) Jackson, 1824-63, (U.S.) Confed. general, led Shenandoah Valley campaign, Civil War.

Joseph Joffre, 1852-1931, (Fr.) headed Allied armies, won Battle of the Marne, 1914, WW1.

Chief Joseph, c1840-1904, (Nat. Am.) chief of the Nez Percé, led his tribe across 3 states seeking refuge in Canada; surrendered about 30 mi from Canadian border.

John Paul Jones, 1747-92, (U.S.) commanded Bonhomme Richard in victory over Serapis, Amer. Rev., 1779.

Stephen Kearny, 1794-1848, (U.S.) headed Army of the West in Mexican War.

Albert Kesselring, 1885-1960, (Ger.) field marshal who led the defense of Italy in WW2.

Ernest J. King, 1878-1956, (U.S.) key WW2 naval strategist.

Horatio H. Kitchener, 1850-1916, (Br.) led forces in Boer War; victorious at Khartoum; organized army in WW1.

Henry Knox, 1750-1806, (U.S.) general in Amer. Rev.; first sec. of war under U.S. Constitution.

Lavrenti Kornilov, 1870-1918, (Russ.) commander-in-chief, 1917; led counter-revolutionary march on Petrograd.

Thaddeus Kosciusko, 1746-1817, (Pol.) aided Amer. Rev.

Walter Krueger, 1881-1967, (U.S.) led Sixth Army in WW2 in Southwest Pacific.

Mikhail Kutuzov, 1745-1813, (Russ.) fought French at Borodino, Napoleonic Wars, 1812; abandoned Moscow; forced French retreat.

Marquis de Lafayette, 1757-1834, (Fr.) fought in, secured French aid for Amer. Rev.

T(homas) E. Lawrence (of Arabia), 1888-1935, (Br.) organized revolt of Arabs against Turks in WW1.

William Daniel Leahy, 1875-1959, (U.S.) chief of staff to Pres. Roosevelt in WWII, Fleet Admiral.

Henry (Light-Horse Harry) Lee, 1756-1818, (U.S.) cavalry officer in Amer. Rev.

Robert E. Lee, 1807-70, (U.S.) Confed. general defeated at Gettysburg, Civil War; surrendered to Grant, 1865.

Curtis LeMay, 1906-90, (U.S.) Air Force commander in WW2, Korean War, and Vietnam War.

Lyman Lemnitzer, 1899-1988, (U.S.) WW2 hero, later general, chairman of Joint Chiefs of Staff.

James Longstreet, 1821-1904, (U.S.) aided Lee at Gettysburg, Civil War.

Erich Ludendorff, 1865-1937, (Ger.) general, victor at Tannenberg, WW1.

Maurice, Count of Nassau, 1567-1625, (Dutch) military innovator; led forces in Thirty Years' War.

Douglas MacArthur, 1880-1964, (U.S.) commanded forces in SW Pacific in WW2; headed occupation forces in Japan, 1945-51; UN commander in Korean War.

Erich von Manstein, 1887-1973, (Ger.) served WW1-2, planned inv. of France (1940), convicted of war crimes.

Carl Gustaf Mannerheim, 1867-1951, (Finn.) army officer and pres. of Finland 1944-46.

Francis Marion, 1733-95, (U.S.) led guerrilla actions in South Carolina during Amer. Rev.

Duke of Marlborough, 1650-1722, (Br.) led forces against Louis XIV in War of the Spanish Succession.

George C. Marshall, 1880-1959, (U.S.) chief of staff in WW2; authored Marshall Plan.

George B. McClellan, 1826-85, (U.S.) Union general, commanded Army of the Potomac, 1861-62, Civil War.

George Meade, 1815-72, (U.S.) commanded Union forces at Gettysburg, Civil War.

Billy Mitchell, 1879-1936, (U.S.) WW1 air-power advocate; court-martialed for insubordination, later vindicated.

Helmuth von Moltke, 1800-91, (Ger.) victorious in Austro-Prussian, Franco-Prussian wars.

Louis de Montcalm, 1712-59, (Fr.) headed troops in Canada, French and Indian War; defeated at Quebec, 1759.

Bernard Law Montgomery, 1887-1976, (Br.) stopped German offensive at Alamein, 1942, WW2; helped plan Normandy.

Daniel Morgan, 1736-1802, (U.S.) victorious at Cowpens, 1781, Amer. Rev.

Louis Mountbatten, 1900-79, (Br.) Supreme Allied Commander of SE Asia, 1943-46, WW2.

Joachim Murat, 1767-1815, (Fr.) led cavalry at Marengo, Austerlitz, and Jena, Napoleonic Wars.

Horatio Nelson, 1758-1805, (Br.) naval commander, destroyed French fleet at Trafalgar.

Michel Ney, 1769-1815, (Fr.) commanded forces in Switz., Aust., Russ., Napoleonic Wars; defeated at Waterloo.

Chester Nimitz, 1885-1966, (U.S.) commander of naval forces in Pacific in WW2.

George S. Patton, 1885-1945, (U.S.) led assault on Sicily, 1943, Third Army invasion of Europe, WW2.

Oliver Perry, 1785-1819, (U.S.) won Battle of Lake Erie in War of 1812.

John Pershing, 1860-1948, (U.S.) commanded Mexican border campaign, 1916, Amer. Expeditionary Force, WW1.

Henri Philippe Pétain, 1856-1951, (Fr.) defended Verdun, 1916; headed Vichy government in WW2.

George E. Pickett, 1825-75, (U.S.) Confed. general famed for "charge" at Gettysburg, Civil War.

Charles Portal, 1893-1971, (Br.) chief of staff, Royal Air Force, 1940-45, led in Battle of Britain.

Manfred Frieherr von Richthofen (Red Baron), 1892-1918, (Ger.) WW1 flying ace, led elite fighter squadron.

Hyman Rickover, 1900-86, (U.S.) father of nuclear navy.

Matthew Bunker Ridgway, 1895-1993, (U.S.) commanded Allied ground forces in Korean War.

Erwin Rommel, 1891-1944, (Ger.) headed Afrika Korps, WW2.

Gerd von Rundstedt, 1875-1953, (Ger.) supreme commander in West, 1942-45, WW2.

Saladin, 1138-93, (Kurdish Muslim) recaptured Jerusalem from Crusaders.

Aleksandr Samsonov, 1859-1914, (Russ.) led invasion of E Prussia, WW1, defeated at Tannenberg, 1914.

Antonio Lopez de Santa Anna, 1794-1876, (Mex.) defeated Texans at the Alamo; defeated in Mexican War.

Maurice, Count of Saxe, 1696-1750, (Fr.) general, War of Aust. Succession, War of Pol. Succession; noted tactician.

Scipio Africanus the Elder, 234?-183, (Rom.) hero of 2nd Punic War, defeated Hannibal, invaded N. Africa.

Winfield Scott, 1786-1866, (U.S.) hero of War of 1812; headed forces in Mexican War, took Mexico City.

Philip Sheridan, 1831-88, (U.S.) Union cavalry officer, headed Army of the Shenandoah, 1864-65, Civil War.

William T. Sherman, 1820-91, (U.S.) Union general, sacked Atlanta during "march to the sea," 1864, Civil War.

Carl Spaatz, 1891-1974, (U.S.) directed strategic bombing against Germany, later Japan, in WW2.

Raymond Spruance, 1886-1969, (U.S.) victorious at Midway Island, 1942, WW2.

Joseph W. Stilwell, 1883-1946, (U.S.) headed forces in the China, Burma, India theater in WW2.

J.E.B. Stuart, 1833-64, (U.S.) Confed. cavalry commander, Civil War.

Sun Tzu, 6th? cent. B.C., (Chin.) general, author of The Art of War.

Aleksandr Suvorov, 1729-1800, (Rus.) commanded Allied Russian and Austrian armies against Ottoman Turks in Russo-Turkish War.

Tamerlane, 1336-1405, (Turkoman Mongol) conqueror, established empire from India to Mediterranean Sea.

George H. Thomas, 1816-70, (U.S.) saved Union army at Chattanooga, 1863; won at Nashville, 1864, Civil War.

Semyon Timoshenko, 1895-1970, (USSR) defended Moscow, Stalingrad, WW2; led winter offensive, 1942-43.

Alfred von Tirpitz, 1849-1930, (Ger.) responsible for submarine blockade in WW1.

Henri de la Tour d'Auvergne, Viscount of Turenne, 1611-75, (Fr.) marshal, Thirty Years' War, Fronde, War of Devolution.

Sebastien Le Prestre de Vauban, 1633-1707, (Fr.) innovative military engineer and theorist.

Jonathan M. Wainwright, 1883-1953, (U.S.) forced to surrender on Corregidor, 1942, WW2.

George Washington, 1732-99, (U.S.) led Continental army, 1775-83, Amer. Rev.

Archibald Wavell, 1883-1950, (Br.) commanded forces in N and E Africa, and SE Asia in WW2.

Anthony Wayne, 1745-96, (U.S.) captured Stony Point, 1779, Amer. Rev.

Duke of Wellington, 1769-1852, (Br.) defeated Napoleon at Waterloo, 1815.

William I (The Conqueror), 1027-87, (Br.) victor Battle of Hastings 1066, became first Norman king of England.

James Wolfe, 1727-59, (Br.) captured Quebec from French, 1759, French and Indian War.

Isoroku Yamamoto, 1884-1943, (Jpn.) com. in chief of Japanese fleet and naval planner before and during WW2.

Georgi Zhukov, 1895-1974, (Russ.) defended Moscow, 1941, led assault on Berlin, 1945, WW2.

Philosophers and Religious Figures of the Past

Excludes most biblical figures. For Greeks and Romans, see also Historical Figures chapter.

Lyman Abbott, 1835-1922, (U.S.) clergyman, reformer; advocate of Christian Socialism.

Pierre Abelard, 1079-1142, (Fr.) philosopher, theologian, teacher; used dialectic method to support Christian beliefs.

Mortimer Adler, 1902-2001, (U.S.) philosopher, helped create "Great Books" program.

Felix Adler, 1851-1933, (U.S.) German-born founder of the Ethical Culture Society.

(St.) Anselm, c1033-1109, (It.) philosopher-theologian, church leader; "ontological argument" for God's existence.

(St.) Thomas Aquinas, 1225-74, (It.) preeminent medieval philosopher-theologian; *Summa Theologica*.

Aristotle, 384-322 BC, (Gr.) pioneering wide-ranging philosopher, logician, ethician, naturalist.

(St.) Augustine, 354-430, (N Africa) philosopher, theologian, bishop; *Confessions, City of God, On the Trinity*.

J. L. Austin, 1911-60, (Br.) ordinary-language philosopher.

Averroes (Ibn Rushd), 1126-98, (Sp.) Islamic philosopher, physician.

Avicenna (Ibn Sina), 980-1037, (Iran.) Islamic philosopher, scientist.

A(lfred) J(ules) Ayer, 1910-89, (Br.) philosopher; logical positivist; *Language, Truth, and Logic*.

Roger Bacon, c1214-94, (Eng.) philosopher and scientist.

Bahaullah (Mirza Husayn Ali), 1817-92, (Pers.) founder of Bahá'í faith.

Karl Barth, 1886-1968, (Swiss) theologian; a leading force in 20th-cent. Protestantism.

Thomas à Becket, 1118-70, (Eng.) archbishop of Canterbury; opposed Henry II; murdered by King's men.

(St.) Benedict, c480-547, (It.) founded the Benedictines.

Jeremy Bentham, 1748-1832, (Br.) philosopher, reformer; enunciated utilitarianism.

Henri Bergson, 1859-1941, (Fr.) philosopher of evolution.

George Berkeley, 1685-1753, (Ir.) idealist philosopher, churchman.

John Biddle, 1615-62, (Eng.) founder of English Unitarianism.

Jakob Boehme, 1575-1624, (Ger.) theosophist and mystic.

Dietrich Bonhoeffer, 1906-1945 (Ger.) Lutheran theologian, pastor; executed as opponent of Nazis.

William Brewster, 1567-1644, (Eng.) headed Pilgrims.

Emil Brunner, 1889-1966, (Swiss) Protestant theologian.

Giordano Bruno, 1548-1600, (It.) philosopher, pantheist.

Martin Buber, 1878-1965, (Ger.) Jewish philosopher, theologian; *I and Thou*.

Buddha (Siddhartha Gautama), c563-c483 BC, (Indian) philosopher; founded Buddhism.

John Calvin, 1509-64, (Fr.) theologian; a key figure in the Protestant Reformation.

Rudolph Carnap, 1891-1970, (U.S.) German-born analytic philosopher; a founder of logical positivism.

William Ellery Channing, 1780-1842, (U.S.) clergyman; early spokesman for Unitarianism.

Auguste Comte, 1798-1857, (Fr.) philosopher; originated positivism.

Confucius, 551-479 BC, (Chin.) founder of Confucianism.

John Cotton, 1584-1652, (Eng.) Puritan theologian.

Thomas Cranmer, 1489-1556, (Eng.) churchman; wrote much of *Book of Common Prayer*.

René Descartes, 1596-1650, (Fr.) philosopher, mathematician; "father of modern philosophy." *Discourse on Method, Meditations on First Philosophy*.

John Dewey, 1859-1952, (U.S.) philosopher, educator; instrumentalist theory of knowledge; helped inaugurate progressive education movement.

Denis Diderot, 1713-84, (Fr.) philosopher, encyclopedist.

John Duns Scotus, c1266-1308, (Sc.) Franciscan philosopher and theologian.

Mary Baker Eddy, 1821-1910, (U.S.) founder of Christian Science; *Science and Health*.

Jonathan Edwards, 1703-58, (U.S.) preacher, theologian; "Sinners in the Hands of an Angry God."

(Desiderius) Erasmus, c1466-1536, (Dutch) Renaissance humanist; *On the Freedom of the Will*.

Johann Fichte, 1762-1814, (Ger.) idealist philosopher.

Michel Foucault, 1926-84, (Fr.) structuralist philosopher, historian.

George Fox, 1624-91, (Br.) founder of Society of Friends.

(St.) Francis of Assisi, 1182-1226, (It.) espoused voluntary poverty; founded Franciscans.

al-Ghazali, 1058-1111, Islamic philosopher.

Georg W. F. Hegel, 1770-1831, (Ger.) idealist philosopher; *Phenomenology of Mind*.

Martin Heidegger, 1889-1976, (Ger.) existentialist philosopher; affected many fields; *Being and Time*.

Johann G. Herder, 1744-1803, (Ger.) philosopher, cultural historian; a founder of German Romanticism.

Thomas Hobbes, 1588-1679, (Eng.) philosopher, political theorist; *Leviathan*.

David Hume, 1711-76, (Sc.) empiricist philosopher; *Enquiry Concerning Human Understanding*.

Jan Hus, 1369-1415, (Czech.) religious reformer.

Edmund Husserl, 1859-1938, (Ger.) philosopher; founded the phenomenological movement.

Thomas Huxley, 1825-95, (Br.) philosopher, educator.

William Inge, 1860-1954, (Br.) theologian; explored mystic aspects of Christianity.

William James, 1842-1910, (U.S.) philosopher, psychologist; pragmatist; studied religious experience.

Karl Jaspers, 1883-1969, (Ger.) existentialist philosopher.

Joan of Arc, 1412-1431, (Fr.) national heroine and a patron saint of France; key figure in the Hundred Years' War.

Immanuel Kant, 1724-1804, (Ger.) philosopher; founder of modern critical philosophy; *Critique of Pure Reason.*

Thomas à Kempis, c1380-1471, (Ger.) monk, devotional writer; *Imitation of Christ* attributed to him.

Soren Kierkegaard, 1813-55, (Dan.) religious philosopher; pre-existentialist; *Either/Or, The Sickness Unto Death.*

John Knox, 1505-72, (Sc.) leader of the Protestant Reformation in Scotland.

Lao-Tzu, 604-531 BC, (Chin.) philosopher; considered the founder of the Taoist religion.

Gottfried von Leibniz, 1646-1716, (Ger.) rationalistic philosopher, logician, mathematician.

John Locke, 1632-1704, (Eng.) political theorist, empiricist philosopher; *Essay Concerning Human Understanding.*

(St.) Ignatius Loyola, 1491-1556, (Sp.) founder of the Jesuits; *Spiritual Exercises.*

Martin Luther, 1483-1546, (Ger.) leader of the Protestant Reformation, founded Lutheran church.

Jean-Francois Lyotard, 1924-98, (Fr.) postmodern philosopher, lecturer; *The Post-Modern Condition.*

Maimonides, 1135-1204, (Sp.) major Jewish philosopher.

Gabriel Marcel, 1889-1973, (Fr.) Rom. Catholic existentialist philosopher, dramatist, and critic.

Jacques Maritain, 1882-1973, (Fr.) Neo-Thomist philosopher.

Cotton Mather, 1663-1728, (U.S.) defender of orthodox Puritanism; founded Yale, 1701.

Philipp Melanchthon, 1497-1560, (Ger.) theologian, humanist; an important voice in the Reformation.

Maurice Merleau-Ponty, 1908-61, (Fr.) existentialist philosopher; *Phenomenology of Perception.*

Thomas Merton, 1915-68, (U.S.) Trappist monk, spiritual writer; *The Seven Storey Mountain.*

John Stuart Mill, 1806-73, (Br.) philosopher, economist; libertarian political theorist; *Utilitarianism.*

Muhammad, c570-632, (Arab) the prophet of Islam.

Dwight Moody, 1837-99, (U.S.) evangelist.

G(eorge) E(dward) Moore, 1873-1958, (Br.) philosopher; *Principia Ethica,* "A Defense of Common Sense."

Elijah Muhammad, 1897-1975, (U.S.) leader of the Black Muslim sect.

Heinrich Muhlenberg, 1711-87, (Ger.) organized the Lutheran Church in America.

John H. Newman, 1801-90, (Br.) Roman Catholic convert, cardinal; led Oxford Movement; *Apologia pro Vita Sua.*

Reinhold Niebuhr, 1892-1971, (U.S.) Protestant theologian.

Richard Niebuhr, 1894-1962 (U.S.) Protestant theologian.

Friedrich Nietzsche, 1844-1900, (Ger.) philosopher; *The Birth of Tragedy, Beyond Good and Evil, Thus Spake Zarathustra.*

Robert Nozick, 1938-2002, (U.S.) political philosopher; *Anarchy, State, and Utopia.*

Blaise Pascal, 1623-62, (Fr.) philosopher, mathematician; *Pensées.*

(St.) Patrick, c389-c461, (Br.) brought Christianity to Ireland.

(St.) Paul, ?-c67, a key proponent of Christianity; his epistles are first Christian theological writing.

Norman Vincent Peale, 1898-1993, (U.S.) minister, author; *The Power of Positive Thinking.*

C(harles) S. Peirce, 1839-1914, (U.S.) philosopher, logician; originated concept of pragmatism, 1878.

Plato, c428-347 BC, (Gr.) philosopher; wrote classic Socratic dialogues; argued for universal truths and independent reality of ideas or forms; *Republic.*

Plotinus, 205-70, (Rom.) a founder of neo-Platonism; *Enneads.*

W(illard) V(an) O(rman) Quine, 1908-2001, (U.S.) philosopher, logician; "On What There Is."

John Rawls, 1922-2002, (U.S.) politcial philosopher; *A Theory of Justice* (1971).

Josiah Royce, 1855-1916, (U.S.) idealist philosopher

Bertrand Russell, 1872-1970, (Br.) philosopher, logician; one of the founders of modern logic; a prolific popular writer.

Charles T. Russell, 1852-1916, (U.S.) founder of Jehovah's Witnesses.

Gilbert Ryle, 1900-76, (Br.) analytic philosopher; *The Concept of Mind.*

George Santayana, 1863-1952, (U.S.) philosopher, writer, critic; *The Sense of Beauty, The Realms of Being.*

Jean-Paul Sartre, 1905-80, (Fr.) philosopher, novelist, playwright. *Nausea, No Exit, Being and Nothingness.*

Friedrich von Schelling, 1775-1854, (Ger.) philosopher of romantic movement.

Friedrich Schleiermacher, 1768-1834, (Ger.) theologian; a founder of modern Protestant theology.

Arthur Schopenhauer, 1788-1860, (Ger.) philosopher; *The World as Will and Idea.*

Albert Schweitzer, 1875-1965, (Ger.) theologian, social philosopher, medical missionary.

Joseph Smith, 1805-44, (U.S.) founded Latter-Day Saints (Mormon) movement, 1830.

Socrates, 469-399 BC, (Gr.) influential philosopher immortalized by Plato.

Herbert Spencer, 1820-1903, (Br.) philosopher of evolution.

Baruch de Spinoza, 1632-77, (Dutch) rationalist philosopher; *Ethics.*

Billy Sunday, 1862-1935, (U.S.) evangelist.

Emanuel Swedenborg, 1688-1772, (Swed.) philosopher, mystic; *Principia.*

Pierre Teilhard de Chardin, 1881-1955, (Fr.) Jesuit priest, paleontologist, philosopher-theologian; *The Divine Milieu.*

Daisetz Teitaro Suzuki, 1870-1966, (Jpn.) Buddhist scholar.

(St.) Therese of Lisieux, 1873-97, (Fr.) Carmelite nun revered for everyday sanctity; *The Story of a Soul.*

Paul Tillich, 1886-1965, (U.S.) German-born philosopher and theologian; brought depth psychology to Protestantism.

John Wesley, 1703-91, (Br.) theologian, evangelist; founded Methodism.

Alfred North Whitehead, 1861-1947, (Br.) philosopher, mathematician; *Process and Reality.*

William of Occam, c1285-c1349 (Eng.) medieval scholastic philosopher; nominalist.

Roger Williams, c1603-83, (U.S.) clergyman; championed religious freedom and separation of church and state.

Ludwig Wittgenstein, 1889-1951, (Austrian) philosopher; major influence on contemporary language philosophy; *Tractatus Logico-Philosophicus, Philosophical Investigations.*

John Woolman, 1720-72, (U.S.) Quaker social reformer, abolitionist, writer; *The Journal.*

John Wycliffe, 1320-84, (Eng.) theologian, reformer.

(St.) Francis Xavier, 1506-52, (Sp.) Jesuit missionary, "Apostle of the Indies."

Brigham Young, 1801-77, (U.S.) Mormon leader after Smith's assassination; colonized Utah.

Huldrych Zwingli, 1484-1531, (Swiss) theologian; led Swiss Protestant Reformation.

Political Leaders of the Past

(U.S. presidents, vice presidents, Supreme Ct. justices, signers of Decl. of Indep. listed elsewhere.)

Abu Bakr, 573-634, Muslim leader, first caliph, chosen successor to Muhammad.

Dean Acheson, 1893-1971, (U.S.) sec. of state; architect of cold war foreign policy.

Samuel Adams, 1722-1803, (U.S.) patriot, Boston Tea Party firebrand.

Konrad Adenauer, 1876-1967, (Ger.) first West German chancellor.

Emilio Aguinaldo, 1869-1964, (Philip.) revolutionary; fought against Spain and the U.S.

Akbar, 1542-1605, greatest Mogul emperor of India.

Carl Albert, 1908-2000 (U.S.) House rep. from OK, Speaker, 1971-76.

Salvador Allende Gossens, 1908-1973, (Chilean) Marxist pres. 1970-73; ousted and died in coup.

Idi Amin, 1925-2003 (Uganda) Ugandan ruler from 1971 to 1979, blamed for hundreds of thousands of deaths.

Hafez al Assad, 1930-2000 (Syr.), Syrian ruler from 1970.

Herbert H. Asquith, 1852-1928, (Br.) liberal prime min.; instituted major social reform.

Atahualpa, ?-1533, Inca (ruling chief) of Peru.

Kemal Ataturk, 1881-1938, (Turk.) founded modern Turkey.

Clement Attlee, 1883-1967, (Br.) Labour party leader, prime min.; enacted natl. health, nationalized many industries.

Stephen F. Austin, 1793-1836, (U.S.) led Texas colonization.

Mikhail Bakunin, 1814-76, (Rus.) revolutionary; leading exponent of anarchism.

Arthur J. Balfour, 1848-1930, (Br.) foreign sec. under Lloyd George; issued Balfour Declaration backing Zionism.

Bernard M. Baruch, 1870-1965, (U.S.) financier, govt. adviser.

Fulgencio Batista y Zaldívar, 1901-73, (Cub.) Cuban pres. (1940-44, 1952-59), overthrown by Castro.

Lord Beaverbrook, 1879-1964, (Br.) financier, statesman, newspaper owner.

Menachem Begin, 1913-92, (Isr.) Israeli prime min., shared 1978 Nobel Peace Prize.

Eduard Benes, 1884-1948, (Czech.) pres. during interwar and post-WW2 eras.

David Ben-Gurion, 1886-1973, (Isr.) first prime min. of Israel, 1948-53, 1955-63.

Thomas Hart Benton, 1782-1858, (U.S.) Missouri senator; championed agrarian interests and westward expansion.

Aneurin Bevan, 1897-1960, (Br.) Labour party leader.

Ernest Bevin, 1881-1951, (Br.) Labour party leader, foreign minister; helped lay foundation for NATO.

Otto von Bismarck, 1815-98, (Ger.) statesman known as the Iron Chancellor; uniter of Germany, 1870.

James G. Blaine, 1830-93, (U.S.) Republican politician, diplomat; influential in Pan-American movement.

Léon Blum, 1872-1950, (Fr.) socialist leader, writer; headed first Popular Front government.

Simón Bolívar, 1783-1830, (Venez.) S. Amer. Revolutionary who liberated much of the continent from Spanish rule.

William E. Borah, 1865-1940, (U.S.) isolationist senator; helped block U.S. membership in League of Nations.

Cesare Borgia, 1476-1507, (It.) soldier, politician; an outstanding figure of the Italian Renaissance.

Willy Brandt, 1913-92, (Ger.) statesman, chancellor of West Germany, 1969-74; promoted East/West peace, *Ostpolitik.*

Leonid Brezhnev, 1906-82, (USSR) Soviet leader, 1964-82.

Aristide Briand, 1862-1932, (Fr.) foreign min.; chief architect of Locarno Pact and anti-war Kellogg-Briand Pact.

William Jennings Bryan, 1860-1925, (U.S.) Democratic, populist leader, orator; 3 times lost race for presidency.

Ralph Bunche, 1904-71, (U.S.) a founder and key diplomat of United Nations for more than 20 years.

John C. Calhoun, 1782-1850, (U.S.) political leader; champion of states' rights and a symbol of the Old South.

Robert Castlereagh, 1769-1822, (Br.) foreign sec.; guided Grand Alliance against Napoleon.

Camillo Benso Cavour, 1810-61, (It.) statesman; largely responsible for uniting Italy under the House of Savoy.

Nicolae Ceausescu, 1918-89, (Roman.) Communist leader, head of state 1967-89; executed.

Austen Chamberlain, 1863-1937, (Br.) statesman; helped finalize Locarno Treaties, both 1925.

Neville Chamberlain, 1869-1940, (Br.) Conservative prime min. whose appeasement of Hitler led to Munich Pact.

Chiang Kai-shek, 1887-1975, (Chin.) Nationalist Chinese pres. whose government was driven from mainland to Taiwan.

Chiang Kai-shek, Madame, 1898-2003, (Chin.) highly influential wife of Nationalist Chinese leader Chiang Kai-shek.

Winston Churchill, 1874-1965, (Br.) prime min., soldier, author; guided Britain through WW2.

Galeazzo Ciano, 1903-44, (It.) fascist foreign minister; helped create Rome-Berlin Axis, executed by Mussolini.

Henry Clay, 1777-1852, (U.S.) "The Great Compromiser," one of the most influential pre-Civil War political leaders.

Georges Clemenceau, 1841-1929, (Fr.) twice prem., Wilson's antagonist at Paris Peace Conference after WW1.

DeWitt Clinton, 1769-1828, (U.S.) political leader; responsible for promoting idea of the Erie Canal.

Robert Clive, 1725-74, (Br.) first administrator of Bengal; laid foundation for British Empire in India.

Jean Baptiste Colbert, 1619-83, (Fr.) statesman; influential under Louis XIV, created the French navy.

Bettino Craxi, 1934-2000, (It.) Italy's first post-WWII Socialist premier.

David Crockett, 1786-1836, (U.S.) frontiersman, congressman, died defending the Alamo.

Oliver Cromwell, 1599-1658, (Br.) Lord Protector of England, led parliamentary forces during Civil War.

Curzon of Kedleston, 1859-1925, (Br.) viceroy of India, foreign sec.; major force in post-WW1 world.

Édouard Daladier, 1884-1970, (Fr.) Radical Socialist politician, arrested by Vichy, interned by Germans until 1945.

Richard J. Daley, 1902-1976, (U.S.) Chicago mayor.

Georges Danton, 1759-94, (Fr.) leading French Rev. figure.

Jefferson Davis, 1808-89, (U.S.) pres. of the Confederacy.

Charles G. Dawes, 1865-1951, (U.S.) statesman, banker; advanced plan to stabilize post-WW1 German finances.

Alcide De Gasperi, 1881-1954, (It.) prime min.; founder of Christian Democratic party.

Charles De Gaulle, 1890-1970, (Fr.) general, statesman; first pres. of the Fifth Republic.

Deng Xiaoping, 1904-97, (Chin.) "paramount leader" of China; backed economic modernization.

Eamon De Valera, 1882-1975, (Ir.-U.S.) statesman; led fight for Irish independence.

Thomas E. Dewey, 1902-71, (U.S.) NY governor; twice loser in try for presidency.

Ngo Dinh Diem, 1901-63, (Viet.) South Vietnamese pres.; assassinated in government takeover.

Everett M. Dirksen, 1896-1969, (U.S.) Senate Republican minority leader, orator.

Benjamin Disraeli, 1804-81, (Br.) prime min.; considered founder of modern Conservative party.

Engelbert Dollfuss, 1892-1934, (Austrian) chancellor; assassinated by Austrian Nazis.

Andrea Doria, 1466-1560, (It.) Genoese admiral, statesman; called "Father of Peace" and "Liberator of Genoa."

Stephen A. Douglas, 1813-61, (U.S.) Democratic leader, orator; opposed Lincoln for the presidency.

Alexander Dubcek, 1921-92, (Czech.) statesman whose attempted liberalization was crushed, 1968.

John Foster Dulles, 1888-1959, (U.S.) sec. of state under Eisenhower, cold war policy-maker.

Abba Eban, 1915-2002, (Isr.) diplomat, foreign minister 1966-74.

Friedrich Ebert, 1871-1925, (Ger.) Social Democratic movement leader; 1st pres., Weimar Republic, 1919-25.

Sir Anthony Eden, 1897-1977, (Br.) foreign sec., prime min. during Suez invasion of 1956.

Ludwig Erhard, 1897-1977, (Ger.) economist, West German chancellor; led nation's economic rise after WW2.

Amintore Fanfani, 1908-99, (It.) six-time premier of Italy.

Joao Baptista de Figueiredo, 1918-99, (Braz.) president of Brazil, restored the nation's democracy.

Hamilton Fish, 1808-93, (U.S.) sec. of state, successfully mediated disputes with Great Britain, Latin America.

James V. Forrestal, 1892-1949, (U.S.) sec. of navy, first sec. of defense.

Francisco Franco, 1892-1975, (Sp.) leader of rebel forces during Spanish Civil War and longtime ruler of Spain.

Benjamin Franklin, 1706-90, (U.S.) printer, publisher, author, inventor, scientist, diplomat.

Louis de Frontenac, 1620-98, (Fr.) governor of New France (Canada); encouraged explorations, fought Iroquois.

J. William Fulbright, 1905-95, (U.S.) U.S. senator; leading figure in U.S. foreign policy during cold war years.

Hugh Gaitskell, 1906-63, (Br.) Labour party leader; major force in reversing its stand for unilateral disarmament.

Albert Gallatin, 1761-1849, (U.S.) sec. of treasury; instrumental in negotiating end of War of 1812.

Léon Gambetta, 1838-82, (Fr.) statesman, politician; one of the founders of the Third Republic.

Indira Gandhi, 1917-84, (In.) daughter of Jawaharlal Nehru, prime min. of India, 1966-77, 1980-84; assassinated.

Mohandas K. Gandhi, 1869-1948, (In.) political leader, ascetic; led movement against British rule; assassinated.

Giuseppe Garibaldi, 1807-82, (It.) patriot, soldier; a leader in the Risorgimento, Italian unification movement.

William E. Gladstone, 1809-98, (Br.) prime min. 4 times; dominant force of Liberal party from 1868 to 1894.

Paul Joseph Goebbels, 1897-1945, (Ger.) Nazi propagandist, master of mass psychology.

Barry Goldwater, 1909-98 (U.S.) conservative U.S. senator and 1964 Republican presid. nominee.

Klement Gottwald, 1896-1953, (Czech.) Communist leader; ushered Communism into his country.

Alexander Hamilton, 1755-1804, (U.S.) first treasury sec.; champion of strong central government.

Dag Hammarskjold, 1905-61, (Swed.) statesman; UN sec.-general.

Hassan II, King, 1929-99, (Moroc.), ruler of Morocco,1962-99.

John Hay, 1838-1905, (U.S.) sec. of state; primarily associated with Open Door Policy toward China.

Patrick Henry, 1736-99, (U.S.) major revolutionary figure, remarkable orator.

Édouard Herriot, 1872-1957, (Fr.) Radical Socialist leader; twice prem., pres. of National Assembly.

Theodor Herzl, 1860-1904, (Hung.) founded modern Zionism.

Heinrich Himmler, 1900-45, (Ger.) head of Nazi SS and Gestapo.

Paul von Hindenburg, 1847-1934, (Ger.) field marshal, WW1; 2nd pres. of Weimar Republic, 1925-34.

Adolf Hitler, 1889-1945, (Ger.) dictator; built Nazism, launched WW2, presided over the Holocaust.

Ho Chi Minh, 1890-1969, (Viet.) N Vietnamese pres., Vietnamese Communist leader.

Harry L. Hopkins, 1890-1946, (U.S.) New Deal administrator; closest adviser to FDR during WW2.

Edward M. House, 1858-1938, (U.S.) diplomat; confidential adviser to Woodrow Wilson.

Samuel Houston, 1793-1863, (U.S.) leader of struggle to win control of Texas from Mexico.

Cordell Hull, 1871-1955, (U.S.) sec. of state, 1933-44; initiated reciprocal trade to lower tariffs, helped organize UN.

Hubert H. Humphrey, 1911-78, (U.S.) Minnesota Democrat; senator; vice pres., pres. candidate.

Hussein, King, 1935-99 (Jordan), peacemaker; ruler of Jordan, 1952-99.

Jinnah, Muhammad Ali, 1876-1948, (Pak.) founder, first governor-general of Pakistan.

Benito Juarez, 1806-72, (Mex.) rallied his country against foreign threats, sought to create democratic, federal republic.

Constantine Karamanlis, 1907-98, (Gr.) Greek prime min. (1955-63, 1974-80); restored democracy; later president.

Frank B. Kellogg, 1856-1937, (U.S.) sec. of state; negotiated Kellogg-Briand Pact to outlaw war.

Robert F. Kennedy, 1925-68, (U.S.) attorney general, senator; assassinated while seeking presidency.

Aleksandr Kerensky, 1881-1970, (Russ.) headed provisional government after Feb. 1917 revolution.

Ayatollah Ruhollah Khomeini, 1900-89, (Iranian), religious-political leader; spearheaded overthrow of shah, 1979.

Nikita Khrushchev, 1894-1971, (USSR) prem., first sec. of Communist party; initiated de-Stalinization.

Kim Il Sung, 1912-94, (Korean) N Korean dictator, 1948-94.

Lajos Kossuth, 1802-94, (Hung.) principal figure in 1848 Hungarian revolution.

Pyotr Kropotkin, 1842-1921, (Russ.) anarchist; championed the peasants but opposed Bolshevism.

Kublai Khan, c1215-94, Mongol emperor; founder of Yüan dynasty in China.

Béla Kun, 1886-c1939, (Hung.) member of 3d Communist Internat.; tried to foment worldwide revolution.

Robert M. LaFollette, 1855-1925, (U.S.) Wisconsin public official; leader of progressive movement.

Fiorello La Guardia, 1882-1947, (U.S.) colorful NYC reform mayor.

Pierre Laval, 1883-1945, (Fr.) politician, Vichy foreign min.; executed for treason.

Andrew Bonar Law, 1858-1923, (Br.) Conservative party politician; led opposition to Irish home rule.

Vladimir Ilyich Lenin (Ulyanov), 1870-1924, (Russ.) revolutionary; founded Bolshevism; Soviet leader 1917-24.

Ferdinand de Lesseps, 1805-94, (Fr.) diplomat, engineer; conceived idea of Suez Canal.

Rene Levesque, 1922-87, (Can.) prem. of Quebec, 1976-85; led unsuccessful separartist campaign.

Maxim Litvinov, 1876-1951, (Pol.-Russ.) revolutionary, commissar of foreign affairs; favored cooperation with West.

Liu Shaoqi, c1898-1974, (Chin.) Communist leader; fell from grace during Cultural Revolution.

David Lloyd George, 1863-1945, (Br.) Liberal party prime min.; laid foundations for modern welfare state.

Henry Cabot Lodge, 1850-1924, (U.S.) Republican senator; led opposition to participation in League of Nations.

Huey P. Long, 1893-1935, (U.S.) Louisiana political demagogue, governor, U.S. senator; assassinated.

Rosa Luxemburg, 1871-1919, (Ger.) revolutionary; leader of the German Social Democratic party and Spartacus party.

J. Ramsay MacDonald, 1866-1937, (Br.) first Labour party prime min. of Great Britain.

Harold Macmillan, 1895-1986, (Br.) prime min. of Great Britain, 1957-63.

Joseph R. McCarthy, 1908-57, (U.S.) senator, extremist in searching out alleged Communists and pro-Communists.

Makarios III, 1913-77, (Cypriot) Greek Orthodox archbishop; first pres. of Cyprus.

Mao Zedong, 1893-1976, (Chin.) chief Chinese Marxist theorist, revolutionary, political leader; led Chinese revolution establishing his nation as Communist state.

Jean Paul Marat, 1743-93, (Fr.) revolutionary, politician; identified with radical Jacobins; assassinated.

José Martí, 1853-95, (Cub.) patriot, poet; leader of Cuban struggle for independence.

Jan Masaryk, 1886-1948, (Czech.) foreign min.; died by mysterious alleged suicide following Communist coup.

Thomas G. Masaryk, 1850-1937, (Czech.) statesman, philosopher; first pres. of Czechoslovak Republic.

Jules Mazarin, 1602-61, (Fr.) cardinal, statesman; prime min. under Louis XIII and queen regent Anne of Austria.

Giusseppe Mazzini, 1805-72, (It.), reformer dedicated to Risorgimento movement for renewal of Italy.

Tom Mboya, 1930-69, (Kenyan) political leader; instrumental in securing independence for Kenya.

Cosimo I de' Medici, 1519-74, (It.) Duke of Florence, grand duke of Tuscany.

Lorenzo de' Medici, the Magnificent, 1449-92, (It.) merchant prince, a towering figure in Italian Renaissance.

Catherine de Médicis, 1519-89, (Fr.) queen consort of Henry II, regent of France; influential in Catholic-Huguenot wars.

Golda Meir, 1898-1978, (Isr.) a founder of the state of Israel and prime min., 1969-74.

Klemens W. N. L. Metternich, 1773-1859, (Austrian) statesman; arbiter of post-Napoleonic Europe.

François Mitterrand, 1916-96, (Fr.) pres. of France, 1981-95.

Mobutu Sese Seko, 1930-97, (Zaire) longtime ruler of Zaire (now Congo) (1965-97); exiled after rebellion.

Guy Mollet, 1905-75, (Fr.) socialist politician, resistance leader.

Henry Morgenthau Jr., 1891-1967, (U.S.) sec. of treasury; fundraiser for New Deal and U.S. WW2 activities.

Gouverneur Morris, 1752-1816, (U.S.) statesman, diplomat. financial expert, helped plan decimal coinage.

Daniel Patrick Moynihan 1927-2003, (U.S.) senator, diplomat, social scientist and author.

Benito Mussolini, 1883-1945, (It.) leader of the Italian fascist state; assassinated.

Imre Nagy, c1896-1958, (Hung.) Communist prem.; assassinated after Soviets crushed 1956 uprising.

Gamal Abdel Nasser, 1918-70, (Egypt.) leader of Arab unification, 2nd Egyptian pres.

Jawaharlal Nehru, 1889-1964, (In.) prime min.; guided India through its early years of independence.

Kwame Nkrumah, 1909-72, (Ghan.) 1st prime min., 1957-60, and pres., 1960-66, of Ghana.

Frederick North, 1732-92, (Br.) prime min.; his inept policies led to loss of American colonies.

Julius K. Nyerere, 1923?-99, (Tanz.) founding father, 1st pres., 1962-85, of Tanzania.

Daniel O'Connell, 1775-1847, (Ir.) nationalist political leader; known as The Liberator.

Omar, c581-644, Muslim leader; 2nd caliph, led Islam to become an imperial power.

Thomas P. (Tip) O'Neill Jr., 1912-94, (U.S.) U.S. congressman, Speaker of the House, 1977-86.

Ignace Paderewski, 1860-1941, (Pol.) statesman, pianist; composer, briefly prime min., an ardent patriot.

Viscount Palmerston, 1784-1865, (Br.) Whig-Liberal prime min., foreign min.; embodied British nationalism.

Andreas George Papandreou, 1919-1996, (Gk.) leftist politician, served 2 times as prem. (1981-89, 1993-96).

Georgios Papandreou, 1888-1968, (Gk.) Republican politician; served 3 times as prime min.

Franz von Papen, 1879-1969, (Ger.) politician; major role in overthrow of Weimar Republic and rise of Hitler.

Charles Stewart Parnell, 1846-1891, (Ir.) nationalist leader; "uncrowned king of Ireland."

Lester Pearson, 1897-1972, (Can.) diplomat, Liberal party leader, prime min.

Robert Peel, 1788-1850, (Br.) reformist prime min., founder of Conservative party.

Eva (Evita) Perón, 1919-52 (Arg.) highly influential 2nd wife of Juan Perón.

Juan Perón, 1895-1974, (Arg.) dynamic pres. of Argentina (1946-55, 1973-74).

Joseph Pilsudski, 1867-1935, (Pol.) statesman; instrumental in reestablishing Polish state in the 20th cent.

Charles Pinckney, 1757-1824, (U.S.) founding father; his Pinckney plan largely incorporated into Constitution.

Christian Pineau, 1905-95, (Fr.) leader of French Resistance during WW2; French foreign min., 1956-58.

William Pitt, the Elder, 1708-78, (Br.) statesman; the "Great Commoner," transformed Britain into imperial power.

William Pitt, the Younger, 1759-1806, (Br.) prime min. during French Revolutionary wars.

Georgi Plekhanov, 1857-1918, (Russ.) revolutionary, social philosopher; called "father of Russian Marxism."

Raymond Poincaré, 1860-1934, (Fr.) 9th pres. of the Republic; advocated harsh punishment of Germany after WW1.

Pol Pot, 1925-98, (Camb.) leader of Khmer Rouge; ruled Cambodia, 1975-79; responsible for mass deaths.

Georges Pompidou, 1911-74, (Fr.) Gaullist political leader; pres. 1969-74.

Grigori Potemkin, 1739-91, (Russ.) field marshal; favorite of Catherine II.

Yitzhak Rabin, 1922-95, (Isr.) military, political leader; prime min. of Israel, 1974-77, 1992-95; assassinated.

Edmund Randolph, 1753-1813, (U.S.) attorney; prominent in drafting, ratification of constitution.

John Randolph, 1773-1833, (U.S.) Southern planter; strong advocate of states' rights.

Jeannette Rankin, 1880-1973, (U.S.) pacifist; first woman member of U.S. Congress.

Walter Rathenau, 1867-1922, (Ger.) industrialist, statesman.

Sam Rayburn, 1882-1961, (U.S.) Democratic leader; representative for 47 years, House Speaker for 17.

Paul Reynaud, 1878-1966, (Fr.) statesman; prem. in 1940 at the time of France's defeat by Germany.

Syngman Rhee, 1875-1965, (Korean) first pres. of S Korea.

Cecil Rhodes, 1853-1902, (Br.) imperialist, industrial magnate; established Rhodes scholarships in his will.

Cardinal de Richelieu, 1585-1642, (Fr.) statesman, known as "red eminence;" chief minister to Louis XIII.

Maximilien Robespierre, 1758-94, (Fr.) leading figure in French Revolution and Reign of Terror.

Nelson Rockefeller, 1908-79, (U.S.) Republican governor of NY, 1959-73; U.S. vice pres., 1974-77.

George W. Romney, 1907-95, (U.S.) auto exec.; 3-term Republican governor of Michigan.

Eleanor Roosevelt, 1884-1962, (U.S.) influential First Lady, humanitarian, UN diplomat.

Elihu Root, 1845-1937, (U.S.) lawyer, statesman, diplomat; leading Republican supporter of the League of Nations.

Dean Rusk, 1909-95, (U.S.) statesman; sec. of state, 1961-69.

John Russell, 1792-1878, (Br.) Liberal prime min. during the Irish potato famine.

Anwar al-Sadat, 1918-81, (Egypt.) pres., 1970-1981, promoted peace with Israel; Nobel laureate; assassinated.

António de Oliveira Salazar, 1889-1970, (Port.) longtime dictator.

José de San Martin, 1778-1850, S Amer. revolutionary; protector of Peru.

Eisaku Sato, 1901-75, (Jpn.) prime min.; presided over Japan's post-WW2 emergence as major world power.

Abdul Aziz Ibn Saud, c1880-1953, (Saudi Arabia) king of Saudi Arabia, 1932-53.

Robert Schuman, 1886-1963, (Fr.) statesman; founded European Coal and Steel Community.

Carl Schurz, 1829-1906, (U.S.) German-American political leader, journalist, orator, dedicated reformer.

Kurt Schuschnigg, 1897-1977, (Austrian) chancellor; unsuccessful in stopping Austria's annexation by Germany.

William H. Seward, 1801-72, (U.S.) anti-slavery activist; as U.S. sec. of state purchased Alaska.

Carlo Sforza, 1872-1952, (It.) foreign min., anti-fascist.

Sitting Bull, c1831-90, (Nat. Am.) Sioux leader in Battle of Little Bighorn over George A. Custer, 1876.

Alfred E. Smith, 1873-1944, (U.S.) NY Democratic governor; first Roman Catholic to run for presidency.

Margaret Chase Smith, 1897-1995, (U.S.) congresswoman, senator; 1st woman elected to both houses of Congress.

Jan C. Smuts, 1870-1950, (S. African) statesman, philosopher, soldier, prime min.

Paul Henri Spaak, 1899-1972, (Belg.) statesman, socialist leader.

Joseph Stalin, 1879-1953, (USSR) Soviet dictator, 1924-53; instituted forced collectivization, massive purges, and labor camps, causing millions of deaths.

Edwin M. Stanton, 1814-69, (U.S.) sec. of war, 1862-68.

Edward R. Stettinius Jr., 1900-49, (U.S.) industrialist, sec. of state who coordinated aid to WW2 allies.

Adlai E. Stevenson, 1900-65, (U.S.) Democratic leader, diplomat, Illinois governor, presidenial candidate.

Henry L. Stimson, 1867-1950, (U.S.) statesman; served in 5 administrations, foreign policy adviser in 30s and 40s.

Gustav Stresemann, 1878-1929, (Ger.) chancellor, foreign minister; strove to regain friendship for post-WW1 Germany.

Sukarno, 1901-70, (Indon.) dictatorial first pres. of the Indonesian republic.

Sun Yat-sen, 1866-1925, (Chin.) revolutionary; leader of Kuomintang, regarded as the father of modern China.

Robert A. Taft, 1889-1953, (U.S.) conservative Senate leader, called "Mr. Republican."

Charles de Talleyrand, 1754-1838, (Fr.) statesman, diplomat; the major force of the Congress of Vienna of 1814-15.

U Thant, 1909-74 (Bur.) statesman, UN sec.-general.

Norman M. Thomas, 1884-1968, (U.S.) social reformer; 6 times Socialist party presidential candidate.

Josip Broz Tito, 1892-1980, (Yug.) pres. of Yugoslavia from 1953, WW2 guerrilla chief, postwar rival of Stalin.

Palmiro Togliatti, 1893-1964, (It.) major Italian Communist leader.

Hideki Tojo, 1885-1948, (Jpn.) statesman, soldier; prime min. during most of WW2.

François Toussaint L'Ouverture, c1744-1803, (Haitian) patriot, martyr; thwarted French colonial aims.

Leon Trotsky, 1879-1940, (Russ.) revolutionary, founded Red Army, expelled from party in conflict with Stalin; assassinated.

Pierre Elliott Trudeau, 1919-2000, (Can.) longtime liberal prime minister of Canada, 1968-79, 1980-84; achieved native Canadian constitution.

Rafael L. Trujillo Molina, 1891-1961, (Dom.) dictator of Dominican Republic, 1930-61; assassinated.

Moise K. Tshombe, 1919-69, (Cong.) pres. of secessionist Katanga, prem. of Congo.

William M. Tweed, 1823-78, (U.S.) politicial boss of Tammany Hall, NYC's Democratic political machine.

Walter Ulbricht, 1893-1973, (Ger.) Communist leader of German Democratic Republic.

Arthur H. Vandenberg, 1884-1951, (U.S.) senator; proponent of bipartisan anti-Communist foreign policy.

Eleutherios Venizelos, 1864-1936, (Gk.) most prominent Greek statesman of early 20th cent.

Hendrik F. Verwoerd, 1901-66, (S. African) prime min.; rigorously applied apartheid policy despite protest.

George Wallace, 1919-98, (U.S.) former segregationist governor of Alabama and presid. candidate.

Robert Walpole, 1676-1745, (Br.) statesman; generally considered Britain's first prime min.

Daniel Webster, 1782-1852, (U.S.) orator, politician; advocate of business interests during Jacksonian agrarianism.

Chaim Weizmann, 1874-1952, (Russ.-Isr.) Zionist leader, scientist; first Israeli pres.

Wendell L. Willkie, 1892-1944, (U.S.) Republican who tried to unseat FDR when he ran for his 3d term.

Harold Wilson, 1916-95, (Br.) Labour party leader; prime min., 1964-70, 1974-76.

Emiliano Zapata, c1879-1919, (Mex.) revolutionary; major influence on modern Mexico.

Todor Zhivkov, 1911-98, (Bulg.) Communist ruler of Bulgaria from 1954 until ousted in a 1989 coup.

Zhou Enlai, 1898-1976, (Chin.) diplomat, prime min.; a leading figure of the Chinese Communist party.

Scientists of the Past
Revised by Peter Barker, Prof. & Chair, Dept. of the Hist. of Science, Univ. of Oklahoma
For pre-modern scientists see also Philosophers and Religious Figures of the Past and Historical Figures chapter.

Albertus Magnus, c1200-1280, (Ger.) theologian, philosopher; helped found medieval study of natural science.

Alhazen (Ibn al-Haytham), c965-ca.1040, mathematician, astronomer; optical theorist.

Andre-Marie Ampère, 1775-1836, (Fr.) mathematician, chemist; founder of electrodynamics.

John V. Atanasoff, 1903-95, (U.S.) physicist; co-invented Atanasoff-Berry Computer (1939-41), regarded in law as the original "automatic electronic digital computer".

Amedeo Avogadro, 1776-1856, (It.) chemist, physicist; proposed that equal volumes of gas contain equal numbers of molecules, permitting determination of molecular weights.

John Bardeen, 1908-91, (U.S.) double Nobel laureate in physics (transistor, 1956; superconductivity, 1972).

A. H. Becquerel, 1852-1908, (Fr.) physicist; discovered radioactivity in uranium (1896).

Alexander Graham Bell, 1847-1922, (U.S.) inventor; first to patent and commercially exploit the telephone (1876).

Daniel Bernoulli, 1700-82, (Swiss) mathematician; developed fluid dynamics and kinetic theory of gases.

Clifford Berry, 1918-1963, (U.S.) collaborated with Atanasoff on the ABC computer (1939-41).

Jöns Jakob Berzelius, 1779-1848, (Swed.) chemist; developed modern chemical symbols and formulas, discovered selenium and thorium.

Henry Bessemer, 1813-98, (Br.) engineer; invented Bessemer steel-making process.

Bruno Bettelheim, 1903-90, (Austrian-U.S.) psychoanalyst specializing in autistic and other disturbed children; *Uses of Enchantment* (1976).

Louis Blériot, 1872-1936, (Fr.) engineer; monoplane pioneer, first Channel flight (1909).

Franz Boas, 1858-1942, (Ger.-U.S.) founded modern anthropology; studied Pacific Coast tribes.

Niels Bohr, 1885-1962, (Dan.) atomic and nuclear physicist; founded quantum mechanics.

Max Born, 1882-1970, (Ger.) atomic and nuclear physicist; helped develop quantum mechanics.

Satyendranath Bose, 1894-1974, (Indian) physicist; forerunner of modern quantum theory for integral-spin particles.

Louis de Broglie, 1892-1987, (Fr.) physicist; proposed quantum wave-particle duality.

Robert Bunsen, 1811-99, (Ger.) chemist; pioneered spectroscopic analysis; discovered rubidium, caesium.

Luther Burbank, 1849-1926, (U.S.) naturalist; developed plant breeding into a modern science.

Vannevar Bush, 1890-1974, (U.S.) electrical engineer; developed differential analyzer, an early analogue computer; headed WWII Office of Scientific Res. and Dev.

Marvin Camras, 1916-95, (U.S.) inventor, electrical engineer; invented magnetic tape recording.

Alexis Carrel, 1873-1944, (Fr.) surgeon, biologist; developed methods of suturing blood vessels and transplanting organs.

Rachel Carson, 1907-64, (U.S.) marine biologist, environmentalist; *Silent Spring* (1962).

George Washington Carver, c1864-1943, (U.S.) agricultural scientist, nutritionist; improved and pioneered new uses for peanuts and sweet potatoes.

James Chadwick, 1891-1974, (Br.) physicist; discovered the neutron (1932); led British Manhattan Project group in U.S. (1943-45).

Albert Claude, 1898-1983, (Belg.-U.S.) a founder of modern cell biology; determined role of mitochondria.

Nicolaus Copernicus, 1473-1543, (Pol.) first modern astronomer to propose sun as center of the planets' motions.

Jacques Yves Cousteau, 1910-1997, (Fr.) oceanographer; co-inventor, with E. Gagnan, of the Aqualung (1943).

Seymour Cray, 1925-96, (U.S.) computer industry pioneer; developed supercomputers.

Francis Crick, (1916-2004), (Br.) biophysicist; co-discoverer of genetic code; shared 1962 Nobel Prize.

Marie, 1867-1934 (Pol.-Fr.) and **Pierre Curie,** 1859-1906, (Fr.) physical chemists; pioneer investigators of radioactivity, discovered radium and polonium (1898).

Gottlieb Daimler, 1834-1900, (Ger.) engineer, inventor; pioneer automobile manufacturer.

John Dalton, 1766-1844, (Br.) chemist, physicist; formulated atomic theory, made first table of atomic weights.

Charles Darwin, 1809-82, (Br.) naturalist; established theory of organic evolution; *Origin of Species* (1859).

Lee De Forest, 1873-1961, (U.S.) inventor of triode, pioneer in wireless telegraphy, sound pictures, television.

Max Delbruck, 1906-81, (Ger.-U.S.) founded molecular biology.

Rudolf Diesel, 1858-1913, (Ger.) mechanical engineer; patented Diesel engine (1892).

Theodosius Dobzhansky, 1900-75, (Russ.-U.S.) biologist; reconciled genetics and natural selection contributing to "modern synthesis" in evolution.

Christian Doppler, 1803-53, (Austrian) physicist; showed change in wave frequency caused by motion of source, now known as Doppler effect.

J. Presper Eckert Jr., 1919-95, (U.S.) co-inventor, with Mauchly, of the ENIAC computer (1943-45).

Thomas A. Edison, 1847-1931, (U.S.) inventor; held more than 1,000 patents, including incandescent electric lamp.

Paul Ehrlich, 1854-1915, (Ger.) medical researcher in immunology and bacteriology; pioneered antitoxin production.

Albert Einstein, 1879-1955, (Ger.-U.S.) theoretical physicist; founded relativity theory, replacing Newton's theories of space, time, and gravity. Proved E=mc² (1905).

John F. Enders, 1897-1985, (U.S.) virologist, helped discover vaccines against polio, measles, mumps and chicken pox.

Erik Erikson, 1902-94, (U.S.) psychoanalyst, author; theory of developmental stages of life, *Childhood and Society* (1950).

Leonhard Euler, 1707-83, (Swiss) mathematician, physicist; pioneer of calculus, revived ideas of Fermat.

Gabriel Fahrenheit, 1686-1736, (Ger.) physicist; improved thermometers and introduced Fahrenheit temperature scale.

Michael Faraday, 1791-1867, (Br.) chemist, physicist; discovered electrical induction and invented dynamo (1831).

Philo T. Farnsworth, 1906-71, (U.S.) inventor; built first television system (San Francisco, 1928).

Pierre de Fermat, 1601-65, (Fr.) mathematician; founded modern theory of numbers.

Enrico Fermi, 1901-54, (It.-U.S.) nuclear physicist; demonstrated first controlled chain reaction (Chicago, 1942).

Richard Feynman, 1918-88, (U.S.) theoretical physicist, author; founder of Quantum Electrodynamics (QED).

Alexander Fleming, 1881-1955, (Br.) bacteriologist; discovered penicillin (1928).

Jean B. J. Fourier, 1768-1830, (fr.) introduced method of analysis in math and physics known as Fourier Series.

Sigmund Freud, 1856-1939, (Austrian) psychiatrist; founder of psychoanalysis. *Interpretation of Dreams* (1901).

Erich Fromm, 1900-1980, (U.S.) psychoanalyst. *Man for Himself* (1947).

Galileo Galilei, 1564-1642, (It.) physicist; used telescope to vindicate Copernicus, founded modern science of motion.

Luigi Galvani, 1737-98, (It.) physiologist; studied electricity in living organisms.

Carl Friedrich Gauss, 1777-1855, (Ger.) math. physicist; completed work of Fermat and Euler in number theory.

Joseph Gay-Lussac, 1778-1850, (Fr.) chemist, physicist; investigated behavior of gases, discovered boron.

Josiah W. Gibbs, 1839-1903, (U.S.) theoretical physicist, chemist; founded chemical thermodynamics.

Robert H. Goddard, 1882-1945, (U.S.) physicist; invented liquid fuel rocket (1926).

George W. Goethals, 1858-1928, (U.S.) chief engineer who completed Panama Canal (1907-14).

William C. Gorgas, 1854-1920, (U.S.) physician; pioneer in prevention of yellow fever and malaria.

Stephen Jay Gould, 1941-2002, (U.S.) paleontologist, evolutionary biologist, writer.

Ernst Haeckel, 1834-1919, (Ger.) zoologist, evolutionist; early Darwinist, introduced concept of "ecology."

Otto Hahn, 1879-1968, (Ger.) chemist; with Meitner discovered nuclear fission (1938).

Edmund Halley, 1656-1742, (Br.) astronomer; predicted return of 1682 comet ("Halley's Comet") in 1759.

William Harvey, 1578-1657, (Br.) physician, anatomist; discovered circulation of the blood (1628).

Werner Heisenberg, 1901-76, (Ger.) physicist; developed matrix mechanics and uncertainty principle (1927).

Hermann von Helmholtz, 1821-94, (Ger.) physicist, physiologist; formulated principle of conservation of energy.

William Herschel, 1738-1822, (Ger.-Br.) astronomer; discovered Uranus (1781).

Heinrich Hertz, 1857-94, (Ger.) physicist; discovered radio waves and photo-electric effect (1886-7).

David Hilbert, 1862-1943, (Ger.) mathematician; contributed to algebra, calculus and foundational studies (formalism).

Edwin P. Hubble, 1889-1953, (U.S.) astronomer; discovered observational evidence of expanding universe.

Alexander von Humboldt, 1769-1859, (Ger.) naturalist, author; explored S America, created ecology.

Edward Jenner, 1749-1823, (Br.) physician; pioneered vaccination, introduced term "virus."

James Joule, 1818-89, (Br.) physicist; found relation between heat and mechanical energy (conservation of energy).

Carl Jung, 1875-1961, (Swiss) psychiatrist; founder of analytical psychology.

Sister Elizabeth Kenny, 1886-1952, (Austral.) nurse; developed treatment for polio.

Johannes Kepler, 1571-1630, (Ger.) astronomer; discovered laws of planetary motion.

Al-Khawarizmi, early 9th cent., (Arab.), mathematician; regarded as founder of algebra.

Robert Koch, 1843-1910 (Ger.) bacteriologist; isolated bacterial causes of tuberculosis and other diseases.

Georges Köhler, 1946-95, (Ger.) immunologist; with Cesar Milstein he developed monoclonal antibody technique.

Jacques Lacan, 1901-81, (Fr.) controversial influential psychoanalyst.

Joseph Lagrange, 1736-1813, (Fr.) geometer, astronomer; showed that gravity of earth and moon cancels creating stable points in space around them.

Jean B. Lamarck, 1744-1829, (Fr.) naturalist; forerunner of Darwin in evolutionary theory.

Pierre Simon de Laplace, 1749-1827, (Fr.) astronomer, physicist; proposed nebular origin for solar system.

Antoine Lavoisier, 1743-94, (Fr.) a founder of mod. chemistry.

Ernest O. Lawrence, 1901-58, (U.S.) physicist; invented the cyclotron.

Jerome Lejeune, 1927-94, (Fr.) geneticist; discovered chromosomal cause of Down syndrome (1959).

Louis 1903-72, and **Mary Leakey**, 1913-96, (Br.) early hominid paleoanthropologists; discovered remains in Africa.

Anton van Leeuwenhoek, 1632-1723, (Dutch) founder of microscopy.

Kurt Lewin, 1890-1947, (Ger.-U.S.) social psychologist; studied human motivation and group dynamics.

Justus von Liebig, 1803-73, (Ger.) founded quantitative organic chemistry.

Joseph Lister, 1827-1912, (Br.) physician; pioneered antiseptic surgery.

Hendrik Lorentz, 1853-1928 (Neth.), physicist, developed electron theory of matter, contrib. to relativity theory.

Konrad Lorenz, 1903-89, (Austrian) ethologist; pioneer in study of animal behavior.

Percival Lowell, 1855-1916, (U.S.) astronomer; predicted the existence of Pluto.

Louis, 1864-1948, and **Auguste Lumière**, 1862-1954, (Fr.) invented cinematograph and made first motion picture (1895).

Guglielmo Marconi, 1874-1937, (It.) physicist; developed wireless telegraphy.

John W. Mauchly, 1907-80, (U.S.) co-inventor, with Eckert, of computer ENIAC (1943-45).

James Clerk Maxwell, 1831-79, (Br.) physicist; unified electricity and magnetism; electromagnetic theory of light.

Maria Goeppert Mayer, 1906-72, (Ger.-U.S.) physicist; developed shell model of atomic nuclei.

Barbara McClintock, 1902-92, (U.S.) geneticist; showed that some genetic elements are mobile.

Lise Meitner, 1878-1968, (Austrian) co-discoverer, with Hahn, of nuclear fission (1938).

Gregor J. Mendel, 1822-84, (Austrian) botanist, monk; his experiments became the foundation of modern genetics.

Dmitri Mendeleyev, 1834-1907, (Russ.) chemist; established Periodic Table of the Elements.

Franz Mesmer, 1734-1815, (Ger.) physician; introduced hypnotherapy.

Albert A. Michelson, 1852-1931, (U.S.) physicist; invented interferometer.

Robert A. Millikan, 1868-1953, (U.S.) physicist; measured electronic charge.

Thomas Hunt Morgan, 1866-1945, (U.S.) geneticist, embryologist; established role of chromosomes in heredity.

Isaac Newton, 1642-1727, (Br.) natural philosopher; discovered laws of gravitation, motion; with Leibniz, founded calculus.

Robert N. Noyce, 1927-90, (U.S.) invented microchip.

J. Robert Oppenheimer, 1904-67, (U.S.) physicist; scientific director of Manhattan project.

Wilhelm Ostwald, 1853-1932, (Ger.) chemist, philosopher; main founder of modern physical chemistry.

Louis Pasteur, 1822-95, (Fr.) chemist; showed that germs cause disease and fermentation, originated pasteurization.

Linus C. Pauling, 1901-94, (U.S.) chemist; studied chemical bonds; campaigned for nuclear disarmament.

Jean Piaget, 1896-1980, (Swiss) psychologist; four-stage theory of intellectual development in children.

Max Planck, 1858-1947, (Ger.) physicist; introduced quantum hypothesis (1900).

Jules Henri Poincaré, 1854-1912 (Fr.), mathematician, founded algebraic topology, many other discoveries in math and physics

Walter S. Reed, 1851-1902, (U.S.) army physician; proved mosquitoes transmit yellow fever.

Theodor Reik, 1888-1969, (Austrian-U.S.) psychoanalyst, major Freudian disciple.

Bernhard Riemann, 1826-66, (Ger.) mathematician; developed non-Euclidean geometry used by Einstein.

Wilhelm Roentgen, 1845-1923, (Ger.) physicist; discovered X-rays (1895).

Carl Rogers, 1902-87, (U.S.) psychotherapist, author; originated nondirective therapy.

Ernest Rutherford, 1871-1937, (Br.) physicist; pioneer investigator of radioactivity, identified the atomic nucleus.

Albert B. Sabin, 1906-93, (Russ.-U.S.), developed oral polio livevirus vaccine.

Carl Sagan, 1934-96, (U.S.) astronomer, author.

Jonas Salk, 1914-95, (U.S.) developed first successful polio vaccine, widely used in U.S. after 1955.

Giovanni Schiaparelli, 1835-1910, (It.) astronomer; reported canals on Mars.

Erwin Schrödinger, 1887-1961, (Austrian) physicist; developed wave equation for quantum systems.

Glenn T. Seaborg, 1912-99, (U.S.) chemist, Nobel Prize winner (1951); codiscoverer of plutonium.

Harlow Shapley, 1885-1972, (U.S.) astronomer; mapped galactic clusters and position of Sun in our own galaxy.

B(urrhus) F(rederick) Skinner, 1904-89, (U.S.) psychologist; leading advocate of behaviorism.

Roger W. Sperry, 1913-94, (U.S.) neuorobiologist; established different functions of right and left sides of brain.

Benjamin Spock, 1903-98, (U.S.) pediatrician, child care expert; *Common Sense Book of Baby and Child Care*.

Charles P. Steinmetz, 1865-1923, (Ger.-U.S.) electrical engineer; developed basic ideas on alternating current.

Leo Szilard, 1898-1964, (Hung.-U.S.) physicist; helped on Manhattan project, later opposed nuclear weapons.

Edward Teller, 1908-2003, (Hung.-U.S.) physicist, aided on Manhattan project, had key role in development of H-bomb.

Nikola Tesla, 1856-1943, (Serb.-U.S.) invented a number of electrical devices including a.c. dynamos, transformers and motors.

William Thomson (Lord Kelvin), 1824-1907, (Br.) physicist; aided in success of transatlantic telegraph cable (1865); proposed Kelvin absolute temperature scale.

Alan Turing, 1912-54, (Br.) mathematician; helped develop basis for computers.

Rudolf Virchow, 1821-1902, (Ger.) pathologist; pioneered the modern theory that diseases affect the body through cells.

Alessandro Volta, 1745-1827, (It.) physicist; electricity pioneer.

Werner von Braun, 1912-77, (Ger.-U.S.) developed rockets for warfare and space exploration.

John Von Neumann, 1903-57, (Hung.-U.S.) mathematician; originated game theory; basic design for modern computers.

Alfred Russell Wallace, 1823-1913, (Br.) naturalist; proposed concept of evolution independently of Darwin.

John B. Watson, 1878-1958, (U.S.) psychologist; a founder of behaviorism.

James E. Watt, 1736-1819, (Br.) mechanical engineer, inventor; invented modern steam engine (1765).

Alfred L. Wegener, 1880-1930, (Ger.) meteorologist, geophysicist; postulated continental drift.

Norbert Wiener, 1894-1964, (U.S.) mathematician; founder of cybernetics.

Sewall Wright, 1889-1988, (U.S.) evolutionary theorist; helped found population genetics.

Wilhelm Wundt, 1832-1920, (Ger.) founder of experimental psychology.

Ferdinand von Zeppelin, 1838-1917, (Ger.) soldier, aeronaut, airship designer.

Social Reformers, Activists, and Humanitarians of the Past

Jane Addams, 1860-1935, (U.S.) cofounder of Hull House; won Nobel Peace Prize, 1931.

Susan B. Anthony, 1820-1906, (U.S.) a leader in temperance, anti-slavery, and woman suffrage movements.

Thomas Barnardo, 1845-1905, (Br.) social reformer; pioneered in care of destitute children.

Clara Barton, 1821-1912, (U.S.) organized American Red Cross.

Henry Ward Beecher, 1813-87, (U.S.) clergyman, abolitionist.

Amelia Bloomer, 1818-94, (U.S.) suffragette, social reformer.

William Booth, 1829-1912, (Br.) founded Salvation Army.

John Brown, 1800-59, (U.S.) abolitionist who led murder of 5 pro-slavery men, was hanged.

Frances Xavier (Mother) Cabrini, 1850-1917, (It.-U.S.) Italian-born nun; founded charitable institutions; first American canonized as a saint, 1946.

Carrie Chapman Catt, 1859-1947, (U.S.) suffragette.

Cesar Chavez, 1927-93, (U.S.) labor leader; helped establish United Farm Workers of America.

Clarence Darrow, 1857-1938, (U.S.) lawyer; defender of "underdog," opponent of capital punishment.

Dorothy Day, 1897-1980, (U.S.) founder of Catholic Worker movement.

Eugene V. Debs, 1855-1926, (U.S.) labor leader; led Pullman strike, 1894; 4-time Socialist presidential candidate.

Dorothea Dix, 1802-87, (U.S.) crusader for mentally ill.

Thomas Dooley, 1927-61, (U.S.) "jungle doctor," noted for efforts to supply medical aid to developing countries.

Marjory Stoneman Douglas, 1890-1998, (U.S.) writer and environmentalist; campaigned to save Florida Everglades.

William Lloyd Garrison, 1805-79, (U.S.) abolitionist.

Emma Goldman, 1869-1940, (Russ.-U.S.) published anarchist *Mother Earth*, birth-control advocate.

Samuel Gompers, 1850-1924, (U.S.) labor leader.

Michael Harrington, 1928-89, (U.S.) exposed poverty in affluent U.S. in *The Other America*, 1963.

Sidney Hillman, 1887-1946, (U.S.) labor leader; helped organize CIO.

Samuel G. Howe, 1801-76, (U.S.) social reformer; changed public attitudes toward the handicapped.

Helen Keller, 1880-1968, (U.S.) crusader for better treatment for the handicapped; deaf and blind herself.

Maggie Kuhn, 1905-95, (U.S.) founded Gray Panthers, 1970.

William Kunstler, 1919-95, (U.S.) civil liberties attorney.

John L. Lewis, 1880-1969, (U.S.) labor leader; headed United Mine Workers, 1920-60.

Karl Menninger, 1893-1990, (U.S.) with brother William founded Menninger Clinic and Menninger Foundation.

Lucretia Mott, 1793-1880, (U.S.) reformer, pioneer feminist.

Philip Murray, 1886-1952, (U.S.) Scottish-born labor leader.

Florence Nightingale, 1820-1910, (Br.) founder of modern nursing.

Emmeline Pankhurst, 1858-1928, (Br.) woman suffragist.

Walter Reuther, 1907-70, (U.S.) labor leader; headed UAW.

Jacob Riis, 1849-1914, (U.S.) crusader for urban reforms.

Margaret Sanger, 1883-1966, (U.S.) social reformer; pioneered the birth-control movement.

Earl of Shaftesbury (A. A. Cooper), 1801-85, (Br.) social reformer.

Elizabeth Cady Stanton, 1815-1902, (U.S.) woman suffrage pioneer.

Lucy Stone, 1818-93, (U.S.) feminist, abolitionist.

Mother Teresa of Calcutta, 1910-97, (Alban.) nun; founded order to care for sick, dying poor; 1979 Nobel Peace Prize.

Philip Vera Cruz, 1905-94, (Filipino-U.S.) helped to found the United Farm Workers Union.

William Wilberforce, 1759-1833, (Br.) social reformer; prominent in struggle to abolish the slave trade.

Frances E. Willard, 1839-98, (U.S.) temperance, women's rights leader.

Mary Wollstonecraft, 1759-97, (Br.) wrote *Vindication of the Rights of Women*.

Writers of the Present

Name (Birthplace)	Birthdate	Name (Birthplace)	Birthdate
Chinua Achebe (Ogidi, Nigeria)	11/16/30	Judy Blume (Elizabeth, NJ)	2/12/38
Richard Adams (Newbury, Eng.)	5/9/20	T. Coraghessan Boyle (Peekskill, NY)	12/2/47
Edward Albee (Washington, DC)	3/12/28	Ray Bradbury (Waukegan, IL)	8/22/20
Isabel Allende (Lima, Peru)	8/2/42	Barbara Taylor Bradford (Leeds, Eng.)	5/10/33
Dorothy Allison (Greenville, SC)	4/11/49	Dan Brown (Exeter, NH)	6/22/64
Martin Amis (Oxford, Eng.)	8/25/49	Rita Mae Brown (Hanover, PA)	11/28/44
Maya Angelou (St. Louis, MO)	4/4/28	Christopher Buckley (NYC)	1952
Piers Anthony (Oxford, Eng.)	8/6/34	James Lee Burke (Houston, TX)	12/5/36
Jeffrey Archer (Somerset, Eng.)	4/15/40	Robert Olen Butler (Granite City, IL)	1/20/45
Oscar Arias Sanchez (Heredia, Costa Rica)	9/13/41	A. S. Byatt (Sheffield, England)	8/24/36
John Ashbery (Rochester, NY)	7/28/27	Hortense Calisher (NYC)	12/20/11
Margaret Atwood (Ottawa, Ont.)	11/18/39	Ethan Canin (Ann Arbor, MI)	7/19/60
David Auburn (Chicago, IL)	1969	Peter Carey (Bacchus-Marsh, Victoria, Australia)	5/7/43
Louis Auchincloss (Lawrence, NY)	9/27/17	Michael Chabon (Washington, DC)	5/24/63
Jean Auel (Chicago, IL)	2/18/36	Sandra Cisneros (Chicago, IL)	12/20/54
Paul Auster (Newark, NJ)	2/3/47	Tom Clancy (Baltimore, MD)	4/12/47
Alan Ayckbourn (Hampstead, Eng.)	4/12/39	Mary Higgins Clark (NYC)	12/24/31
Nicholson Baker (Rochester, NY)	1/7/57	Arthur C. Clarke (Minehead, Eng.)	12/16/17
Russell Banks (Newton, MA)	3/28/40	Beverly Cleary (McMinnville, OR)	4/12/16
John Barth (Cambridge, MD)	5/27/30	Paulo Coelho (Rio de Janeiro, Brazil)	8/24/47
Ann Beattie (Washington, DC)	9/8/47	J(ohn) M(axwell) Coetzee (Capetown, S. Africa)	2/9/40
Saul Bellow (Lachine, Que.)	6/10/15	Billy Collins (NYC)	3/22/41
Peter Benchley (NYC)	5/8/40	Jackie Collins (London, Eng.)	10/4/41
John Berendt (Syracuse, NY)	12/5/39	Evan S. Connell (Kansas City, MO)	8/17/24
Thomas Berger (Cincinnati, OH)	7/20/24	Pat Conroy (Atlanta, GA)	10/26/45
Maeve Binchy (Dalkey, Ireland)	3/28/40	Robin Cook (NYC)	5/4/40

Name (Birthplace)	Birthdate
Patricia Cornwell (Miami, FL)	6/9/56
Harry Crews (Alma, GA)	6/6/35
Michael Crichton (Chicago, IL)	10/23/42
Michael Cunningham (Cincinnati, Ohio)	11/6/52
Don DeLillo (NYC)	11/20/36
Nelson DeMille (NYC)	8/23/43
Joan Didion (Sacramento, CA)	12/5/34
E. L. Doctorow (NYC)	1/6/31
Takako Doi (Hyogo, Jap.)	11/30/28
Rita Dove (Akron, OH)	8/28/52
Roddy Doyle (Dublin, Ireland)	5/58
John Gregory Dunne (Hartford, CT)	5/25/32
Umberto Eco (Alessandria, Italy)	1/5/32
Bret Easton Ellis (Los Angeles, CA)	3/7/64
James Ellroy (Los Angeles)	3/4/48
Louise Erdrich (Little Falls, MN)	7/6/54
Laura Esquivel (Mexico City, Mexico)	9/30/50
Lawrence Ferlinghetti (Yonkers, NY)	3/24/19
Helen Fielding (Morley, Yorkshire, Eng.)	1960
Ken Follet (Cardiff, Wales)	6/5/49
Dario Fo (San Giano, Italy)	3/26/26
Horton Foote (Wharton, TX)	3/14/16
Richard Ford (Jackson, MS)	2/16/44
Frederick Forsyth (Ashford, Eng.)	8/25/38
John Fowles (Leigh-on-Sea, Eng.)	3/31/26
Paula Fox (NYC)	4/22/23
Dick Francis (Tenby, Pembrokeshire, Wales)	10/31/20
Jonathan Franzen (Western Springs, IL)	8/17/59
Michael Frayn (London, Eng.)	9/8/33
Charles Frazier (Asheville, NC)	1950
Marilyn French (NYC)	11/21/29
Brian Friel (Omagh, County Tyrone, N. Ireland)	1/9/29
Carlos Fuentes (Panama City, Panama)	11/11/28
Ernest J. Gaines (Oscar, LA)	1/15/33
Gabriel Garcia Marquez (Aracataca, Colombia)	3/6/28
Frank Gilroy (Bronx, NY)	10/13/25
Gail Godwin (Birmingham, AL)	6/18/37
William Goldman (Highland Park, IL)	8/12/31
Nadine Gordimer (Springs, S. Africa)	11/20/23
Mary Gordon (Far Rockaway, Long Island, NY)	12/8/49
Sue Grafton (Louisville, KY)	4/24/40
Günter Grass (Danzig, now Gdansk, Poland)	10/16/27
Shirley Ann Grau (New Orleans, LA)	7/8/29
John Grisham (Jonesboro, AR)	2/8/55
John Guare (NYC)	2/5/38
Arthur Hailey (Luton, Eng.)	4/5/20
David Hare (St. Leonards, Sussex, Eng.)	6/5/47
Jim Harrison (Grayling, MI)	12/11/37
Robert Hass (San Francisco, CA)	3/1/41
Vaclav Havel (Prague, Czech.)	10/5/36
Seamus Heaney (Mossbawn, Cty. Derry, N. Ireland)	4/13/39
Mark Helprin (NYC)	6/28/47
Carl Hiaasen (S. Florida)	3/12/53
Oscar Hijuelos (NYC)	8/24/51
Tony Hillerman (Sacred Heart, OK)	5/27/25
S. E. Hinton (Tulsa, OK)	7/22/50
Alice Hoffman (NYC)	3/16/52
John Irving (Exeter, NH)	3/2/42
Kazuo Ishiguro (Nagasaki, Japan)	11/8/54
John Jakes (Chicago, IL)	3/31/32
P. D. James (Oxford, Eng.)	8/3/20
Erica Jong (NYC)	3/26/42
Garrison Keillor (Anoka, MN)	8/7/42
Thomas Keneally (Sydney, Austral.)	10/7/35
William Kennedy (Albany, NY)	1/16/28
Jamaica Kincaid (St. Johns, Antigua)	5/25/49
Stephen King (Portland, ME)	9/21/47
Barbara Kingsolver (Annapolis, MD)	4/8/55
Maxine Hong Kingston (Stockton, CA)	10/27/40
Galway Kinnell (Providence, RI)	2/1/27
Dean Koontz (Everett, PA)	7/9/45
Judith Krantz (NYC)	1/9/28
Maxine Kumin (Philadelphia, PA)	6/6/25
Milan Kundera (Brno, Czechoslovakia)	4/1/29
Tony Kushner (NYC)	7/16/56
David Leavitt (Pittsburgh, PA)	6/23/61
John Le Carré (Poole, Eng.)	10/19/31
Harper Lee (Monroeville, AL)	4/28/26
Ursula K. Le Guin (Berkeley, CA)	10/21/29
Madeleine L'Engle (NYC)	11/29/18
Elmore Leonard (New Orleans, LA)	10/11/25
Doris Lessing (Kermanshah, Persia)	10/22/19
Jonathan Lethem (Brooklyn, NY)	1964
Ira Levin (NYC)	8/27/29
David Lodge (South London, Eng.)	1/28/35
Alison Lurie (Chicago, IL)	9/3/26
Naguib Mahfouz (Cairo, Egypt)	12/11/11
Norman Mailer (Long Branch, NJ)	1/31/23
David Mamet (Chicago, IL)	11/30/47
Bobbie Ann Mason (nr. Mayfield, KY)	5/1/40
Peter Matthiessen (NYC)	5/22/27
Armistead Maupin (Washington, DC)	4/13/44
Ed McBain (real name Evan Hunter) (NYC)	10/15/26
Cormac McCarthy (Providence, RI)	7/20/33
Frank McCourt (Brooklyn, NY)	8/19/30
Colleen McCullough (Wellington, N.S.W.)	6/1/37
Alice McDermott (Brooklyn, NY)	6/27/53
Ian McEwan (Aldershot, England)	6/21/48
Thomas McGuane (Wyandotte, MI)	12/11/39
Terry McMillan (Port Huron, MI)	10/18/51
Larry McMurtry (Wichita Falls, TX)	6/3/36
Terrence McNally (St. Petersburg, FL)	11/3/39
John McPhee (Princeton, NJ)	3/8/31
Arthur Miller (NYC)	10/17/15
Toni Morrison (Lorain, OH)	2/18/31
Walter Mosley (Los Angeles, CA)	1/12/52
Bharati Mukherjee (Calcutta, India)	7/27/40
Alice Munro (Wingham, Ont.)	7/10/31
Haruki Murakami (Kyoto, Japan)	1/12/49
V. S. Naipaul (Chaguanas, Trinidad)	8/17/32
Joyce Carol Oates (Lockport, NY)	6/16/38
Edna O'Brien (Tuamgraney, Ir.)	12/15/30
Tim O'Brien (Austin, MN)	10/1/46
Kenzaburo Oe (Uchiko, Japan)	1/31/35
Michael Ondaatje (Colombo, Sri Lanka)	9/12/43
Cynthia Ozick (NYC)	4/17/28
Grace Paley (NYC)	12/11/22
Robert B. Parker (Springfield, MA)	9/17/32
Suzan-Lori Parks (Fort Knox, KY)	5/10/63
Marge Piercy (Detroit, MI)	3/31/36
Robert Pinsky (Long Branch, NJ)	10/20/40
Harold Pinter (Hackney, East London, Eng.)	10/10/30
Reynolds Price (Macon, NC)	2/1/33
Richard Price (Bronx, NY)	10/12/49
E. Annie Proulx (Norwich, CT)	8/22/35
Philip Pullman (Norwich, Eng.)	10/19/46
Thomas Pynchon (Glen Cove, Long Island, NY)	5/8/37
David Rabe (Dubuque, IA)	3/10/40
Ishmael Reed (Chattanooga, TN)	2/22/38
Ruth Rendell (London, England)	2/17/30
Anne Rice (New Orleans, LA)	10/4/41
Adrienne Rich (Baltimore, MD)	5/16/29
Nora Roberts (Washington, DC)	10/10/50
Philip Roth (Newark, NJ)	3/19/33
J.K. Rowling (Chipping Sodbury, Eng.)	7/31/65
Norman Rush (Oakland, CA)	1935
Salman Rushdie (Bombay, India)	6/19/47
Richard Russo (Johnstown, NY)	7/15/49
J. D. Salinger (NYC)	1/1/19
Jose Saramago (Azinhaga, Portugal)	11/16/22
Alice Sebold (Madison, WI)	1963
David Sedaris (Johnson City, NY)	12/26/56
Vikram Seth (Calcutta, India)	6/20/52
Sidney Sheldon (Chicago, IL)	2/11/17
Sam Shepard (Ft. Sheridan, IL)	11/5/43
Claude Simon (Tananarive, Madagascar)	10/10/13
Neil Simon (Bronx, NY)	7/4/27
Jane Smiley (Los Angeles, CA)	9/26/49
Aleksandr Solzhenitsyn (Kislovodsk, Russia)	12/11/18
Susan Sontag (NYC)	1/16/33
Wole Soyinka (Abeokuta, Nigeria)	7/13/34
Mickey Spillane (Brooklyn, NY)	3/9/18
Danielle Steel (NYC)	8/14/47
Richard Stern (NYC)	2/25/28
Mary Stewart (Sunderland, Eng.)	9/17/16
R(obert) L(awrence) Stine (Columbus, OH)	10/8/43
Tom Stoppard (Zlin, Czech.)	7/3/37
William Styron (Newport News, VA)	6/11/25
Wislawa Szymborska (Kornik, Poland)	7/2/23
Amy Tan (Oakland, CA)	2/19/52
Donna Tartt (Greenwood, MS)	12/23/63
Paul Theroux (Medford, MA)	4/10/41
Calvin Trillin (Kansas City, MO)	12/5/35
Scott F. Turow (Chicago, IL)	4/12/49
Anne Tyler (Minneapolis, MN)	10/25/41
John Updike (Shillington, PA)	3/18/32
Mario Vargas Llosa (Arequipa, Peru)	3/28/36
Gore Vidal (West Point, NY)	10/3/25
Paula Vogel (Washington, DC)	11/16/51
Kurt Vonnegut Jr. (Indianapolis, IN)	11/11/22
Derek Walcott (Castries, Saint Lucia)	1/23/30
Alice Walker (Eatonton, GA)	2/9/44
Robert James Waller (Rockford, IA)	8/1/39
Joseph Wambaugh (East Pittsburgh, PA)	1/22/37
Wendy Wasserstein (Brooklyn, NY)	10/18/50
Edmund White (Cincinnati, OH)	1/19/40
August Wilson (Pittsburgh, PA)	4/27/45
Lanford Wilson (Lebanon, MO)	4/13/37
Tom Wolfe (Richmond, VA)	3/2/31
Tobias Wolff (Birmingham, AL)	6/19/45
Herman Wouk (NYC)	5/27/15
Yevgeny Yevtushenko (Irkutsk, Russia)	7/18/33

Writers of the Past

See also Journalists of the Past, and Greeks and Romans in Historical Figures chapter.

Alice Adams, 1926-99, (U.S.) novelist, short-story writer. *Superior Woman.*

James Agee, 1909-55, (U.S.) novelist. *A Death in the Family.*

S(hmuel) Y(osef)Agnon, 1888-1970, (Is.) Hebrew novelist. *Only Yesterday.*

Conrad Aiken, 1889-1973, (U.S.) poet, critic. *Ushant.*

Anna Akhmatova, 1889-1966, (Russ.) poet. *Requiem.*

Louisa May Alcott, 1832-88, (U.S.) novelist. *Little Women.*

Sholom Aleichem, 1859-1916, (Russ.) Yiddish writer. *Tevye's Daughters, The Old Country.*

Vicente Aleixandre, 1898-1984, (Sp.) poet. *La destrucción o el amor, Dialogolos del conocimiento.*

Horatio Alger, 1832-1899, (U.S.) "rags-to-riches" books.

Jorge Amado, 1912-2001, (Brazil) novelist. *Dona Flor and Her Two Husbands, The Violent Land.*

Eric Ambler, 1909-98, (Br.) suspense novelist. *A Coffin for Dimitrios.*

Kingsley Amis, 1922-95, (Br.) novelist, critic. *Lucky Jim.*

Hans Christian Andersen, 1805-75, (Dan.) author of fairy tales. *The Ugly Duckling.*

Maxwell Anderson, 1888-1959, (U.S.) playwright. *What Price Glory?, High Tor, Winterset, Key Largo.*

Sherwood Anderson, 1876-1941, (U.S.) short-story writer. "Death in the Woods;" *Winesburg, Ohio.*

Reinaldo Arenas, 1943-1990, (Cuba) short-story writer, novelist. *Before Night Falls.*

Ludovico Ariosto, 1474-1533, (It.) poet. *Orlando Furioso.*

Matthew Arnold, 1822-88, (Br.) poet, critic. "Thrysis," "Dover Beach," "Culture and Anarchy."

Isaac Asimov, 1920-92, (U.S.) versatile writer, espec. of science-fiction. *I Robot.*

Miguel Angel Asturias, 1899-1974, (Guatemala) novelist. *El Señor Presidente.*

W(ystan) H(ugh) Auden, 1907-73, (Br.) poet, playwright, literary critic. "The Age of Anxiety."

Jane Austen, 1775-1817, (Br.) novelist. *Pride and Prejudice, Sense and Sensibility, Emma, Mansfield Park.*

Isaac Babel, 1894-1941, (Russ.) short-story writer, playwright. *Odessa Tales, Red Cavalry.*

James Baldwin, 1924-87, author, playwright. *The Fire Next Time, Blues for Mister Charlie.*

Honoré de Balzac, 1799-1850, (Fr.) novelist. *Le Père Goriot, Cousine Bette, Eugénie Grandet.*

James M. Barrie, 1860-1937, (Br.) playwright, novelist. *Peter Pan, Dear Brutus, What Every Woman Knows.*

Charles Baudelaire, 1821-67, (Fr.) poet. *Les Fleurs du Mal.*

L(yman) Frank Baum, 1856-1919, (U.S.) *Wizard of Oz* series.

Simone de Beauvoir, 1908-86, (Fr.) novelist, essayist. *The Second Sex, Memoirs of a Dutiful Daughter.*

Samuel Beckett, 1906-89, (Ir.) novelist, playwright. *Waiting for Godot, Endgame* (plays); *Murphy, Watt, Molloy* (novels).

Brendan Behan, 1923-64, (Ir.) playwright. *The Quare Fellow, The Hostage, Borstal Boy.*

Robert Benchley, 1889-1945, (U.S.) humorist.

Stephen Vincent Benét, 1898-1943, (U.S.) poet, novelist. *John Brown's Body.*

John Berryman, 1914-72, (U.S.) poet. *Homage to Mistress Bradstreet.*

Ambrose Bierce, 1842-1914, (U.S.) short-story writer, journalist. *In the Midst of Life, The Devil's Dictionary.*

Elizabeth Bishop, 1911-79, (U.S.) poet. *North and South—A Cold Spring.*

William Blake, 1757-1827, (Br.) poet, artist. *Songs of Innocence, Songs of Experience.*

Aleksandr Blok, 1880-1921, (Russ.) poet. "The Twelve", "The Scythians."

Giovanni Boccaccio, 1313-75, (It.) poet. *Decameron.*

Heinrich Böll, 1917-85, (Ger.) novelist, short-story writer. *Group Portrait With Lady.*

Jorge Luis Borges, 1900-86, (Arg.) short-story writer, poet, essayist. *Labyrinths.*

James Boswell, 1740-95, (Sc.) biographer. *The Life of Samuel Johnson.*

Pierre Boulle, (1913-94), (Fr.) novelist. *The Bridge Over the River Kwai, Planet of the Apes.*

Paul Bowles, 1910-99, (U.S.) novelist, short-story writer. *The Sheltering Sky.*

Anne Bradstreet, c1612-72, (U.S.) poet. *The Tenth Muse Lately Sprung Up in America.*

Bertolt Brecht, 1898-1956, (Ger.) dramatist, poet. *The Threepenny Opera, Mother Courage and Her Children.*

Charlotte Brontë, 1816-55, (Br.) novelist. *Jane Eyre.*

Emily Brontë, 1818-48, (Br.) novelist. *Wuthering Heights.*

Elizabeth Barrett Browning, 1806-61, (Br.) poet. *Sonnets From the Portuguese, Aurora Leigh.*

Joseph Brodsky, 1940-96, (Russ.-U.S.) poet. *A Part of Speech, Less Than One, To Urania.*

Robert Browning, 1812-89, (Br.) poet. "My Last Duchess," "Fra Lippo Lippi," *The Ring and The Book.*

Pearl S. Buck, 1892-1973, (U.S.) novelist. *The Good Earth.*

Mikhail Bulgakov, 1891-1940, (Russ.) novelist, playwright. *The Heart of a Dog, The Master and Margarita.*

John Bunyan, 1628-88, (Br.) writer. *Pilgrim's Progress.*

Anthony Burgess, 1917-93, (Br.) author. *A Clockwork Orange.*

Frances Hodgson Burnett, 1849-1924, (Br.-U.S.) novelist. *The Secret Garden.*

Robert Burns, 1759-96, (Sc.) poet. "Flow Gently, Sweet Afton," "My Heart's in the Highlands," "Auld Lang Syne."

Edgar Rice Burroughs, 1875-1950, (U.S.) "Tarzan" books.

William S. Burroughs, 1914-97, (U.S.) novelist. *Naked Lunch.*

George Gordon, Lord Byron, 1788-1824, (Br.) poet. *Don Juan, Childe Harold, Manfred, Cain.*

Pedro Calderon de la Barca, 1600-81, (Sp.) playwright. *Life Is a Dream.*

Italo Calvino, 1923-85, (It.) novelist, short-story writer. *If on a Winter's Night a Traveler.*

Luis Vaz de Camoes, 1524?-80 (Port.) poet. *The Lusiads.*

Albert Camus, 1913-60, (Fr.) writer. *The Stranger, The Fall.*

Elias Canetti, 1905-94, (Bulg.) novelist, essayist. *Auto-Da-Fe.*

Karel Capek, 1890-1938, (Czech.) playwright, novelist, essayist. *R.U.R. (Rossum's Universal Robots).*

Truman Capote, 1924-84, (U.S.) author. *Other Voices, Other Rooms, Breakfast at Tiffany's, In Cold Blood.*

Lewis Carroll (Charles Dodgson), 1832-98, (Br.) writer, mathematician. *Alice's Adventures in Wonderland.*

Giacomo Casanova, 1725-98, (It.) adventurer, memoirist.

Willa Cather, 1873-1947, (U.S.) novelist. *O Pioneers!, My Ántonia, Death Comes for the Archbishop.*

Constantine Cavafy, 1863-1933, (Gr.) poet. "Ithaka," "Sensual Pleasures."

Camilo Jose Cela, 1916-2001, (Sp.) novelist. *The Family of Pascual Duarte, The Hive.*

Miguel de Cervantes Saavedra, 1547-1616, (Sp.) novelist, dramatist, poet. *Don Quixote.*

Raymond Chandler, 1888-1959, (U.S.) writer of detective fiction. Philip Marlowe series.

Geoffrey Chaucer, c1340-1400, (Br.) poet. *The Canterbury Tales, Troilus and Criseyde.*

John Cheever, 1912-82, (U.S.) novelist, short-story writer. *The Wapshot Scandal,* "The Country Husband."

Anton Chekhov, 1860-1904, (Russ.) short-story writer, dramatist. *Uncle Vanya, The Cherry Orchard, The Three Sisters.*

G(ilbert) K(eith) Chesterton, 1874-1936, (Br.) critic, novelist, relig. apologist. Father Brown series of mysteries.

Kate Chopin, 1851-1904, (U.S.) writer. *The Awakening.*

Agatha Christie, 1890-1976, (Br.) mystery writer; created Miss Marple, Hercule Poirot; *And Then There Were None, Murder on the Orient Express, Murder of Roger Ackroyd.*

James Clavell, 1924-94, (Br.-U.S.) novelist. *Shogun, King Rat.*

Jean Cocteau, 1889-1963, (Fr.) writer, visual artist, filmmaker. *The Beauty and the Beast, Les Enfants Terribles.*

Samuel Taylor Coleridge, 1772-1834, (Br.) poet, critic. "Kubla Khan," "The Rime of the Ancient Mariner."

(Sidonie) Colette, 1873-1954, (Fr.) novelist. *Claudine, Gigi.*

Wilkie Collins, 1824-89, (Br.) Novelist. *The Moonstone.*

Joseph Conrad, 1857-1924, (Br.) novelist. *Lord Jim, Heart of Darkness, The Secret Agent.*

James Fenimore Cooper, 1789-1851, (U.S.) novelist. *Leatherstocking Tales, The Last of the Mohicans.*

Pierre Corneille, 1606-84, (Fr.) dramatist. *Medeé, Le Cid.*

Hart Crane, 1899-1932, (U.S.) poet. "The Bridge."

Stephen Crane, 1871-1900, (U.S.) novelist, short-story writer. *The Red Badge of Courage,* "The Open Boat."

E. E. Cummings, 1894-1962, (U.S.) poet. *Tulips and Chimneys.*

Roald Dahl, 1916-90, (Br.-U.S.) writer. *Charlie and the Chocolate Factory, James and the Giant Peach.*

Gabriele D'Annunzio, 1863-1938, (It.) poet, novelist, dramatist. *The Child of Pleasure, The Intruder, The Victim.*

Dante Alighieri, 1265-1321, (It.) poet. *The Divine Comedy.*

Robertson Davies, 1913-95, (Can.) novelist, playwright, essayist. Salterton, Deptford, and Cornish trilogies.

Daniel Defoe, 1660-1731, (Br.) writer. *Robinson Crusoe, Moll Flanders, Journal of the Plague Year.*

Charles Dickens, 1812-70, (Br.) novelist. *David Copperfield, Oliver Twist, Great Expectations, A Tale of Two Cities.*

Philip K. Dick, 1928-82, (U.S.) science fiction writer. *Do Androids Dream of Electric Sheep?*

James Dickey, 1923-1997, (U.S.) poet, novelist. *Deliverance.*

Emily Dickinson, 1830-86, (U.S.) lyric poet. "Because I could not stop for Death . . .," "Success is counted sweetest . . ."

Isak Dinesen (Karen Blixen), 1885-1962, (Dan.) author. *Out of Africa, Seven Gothic Tales, Winter's Tales.*

John Donne, 1573-1631, (Br.) poet, divine. *Songs and Sonnets.*

José Donoso, 1924-96, (Chil.) surreal novelist and short-story writer. *The Obscene Bird of Night.*

John Dos Passos, 1896-1970, (U.S.) novelist. *U.S.A.*

Fyodor Dostoyevsky, 1821-81, (Russ.) novelist. *Crime and Punishment, The Brothers Karamazov, The Possessed.*

Arthur Conan Doyle, 1859-1930, (Br.) novelist. Sherlock Holmes mystery stories.

Theodore Dreiser, 1871-1945, (U.S.) novelist. *An American Tragedy, Sister Carrie.*

John Dryden, 1631-1700, (Br.) poet, dramatist, critic. *All for Love, Mac Flecknoe, Absalom and Achitophel.*

Alexandre Dumas, 1802-70, (Fr.) novelist, dramatist. *The Three Musketeers, The Count of Monte Cristo.*

Alexandre Dumas (fils), 1824-95, (Fr.) dramatist, novelist. *La Dame aux Camélias, Le Demi-Monde.*

Lawrence Durrell, 1912-90, (Br.) novelist, poet. *Alexandria Quartet.*

Ilya G. Ehrenburg, 1891-1967, (Russ.) writer. *The Thaw.*

George Eliot (Mary Ann Evans or Marian Evans), 1819-80, (Br.) novelist. *Silas Marner, Middlemarch.*

T(homas) S(tearns) Eliot, 1888-1965, (Br.) poet, critic. *The Waste Land,* "The Love Song of J. Alfred Prufrock."

Stanley Elkin, 1930-95, (U.S.) novelist, short story writer. *George Mills.*

Ralph Ellison, 1914-94, (U.S.), writer. *Invisible Man.*

Ralph Waldo Emerson, 1803-82, (U.S.) poet, essayist. "Brahma," "Nature," "The Over-Soul," "Self-Reliance."

James T. Farrell, 1904-79, (U.S.) novelist. *Studs Lonigan.*

William Faulkner, 1897-1962, (U.S.) novelist. *Sanctuary, Light in August, The Sound and the Fury, Absalom, Absalom!*

Edna Ferber, 1887-1968, (U.S.) novelist, short-story writer, playwright. *So Big, Cimarron, Show Boat.*

Henry Fielding, 1707-54, (Br.) novelist. *Tom Jones.*

F(rancis) Scott Fitzgerald, 1896-1940, (U.S.) short-story writer, novelist. *The Great Gatsby, Tender Is the Night.*

Gustave Flaubert, 1821-80, (Fr.) novelist. *Madame Bovary.*

Ian Fleming, 1908-64, (Br.) novelist; James Bond spy thrillers. *Dr. No, Goldfinger.*

Ford Madox Ford, 1873-1939, (Br.) novelist, critic, poet. *The Good Soldier.*

C(ecil) S(cott) Forester, 1899-1966, (Br.) writer. Horatio Hornblower books.

E(dward) M(organ) Forster, 1879-1970, (Br.) novelist. *A Passage to India, Howards End.*

Anatole France, 1844-1924, (Fr.) writer. *Penguin Island, My Friend's Book, The Crime of Sylvestre Bonnard.*

Robert Frost, 1874-1963, (U.S.) poet. "Birches," "Fire and Ice," "Stopping by Woods on a Snowy Evening."

William Gaddis, 1922-98, (U.S.) novelist. *The Recognitions.*

John Galsworthy, 1867-1933, (Br.) novelist, dramatist. *The Forsyte Saga.*

Federico Garcia Lorca, 1898-1936, (Sp.) poet, dramatist. *Blood Wedding.*

Erle Stanley Gardner, 1889-1970, (U.S.) mystery writer; created Perry Mason.

Jean Genet, 1911-86, (Fr.) playwright, novelist. *The Maids.*

Kahlil Gibran, 1883-1931, (Lebanese-U.S.) mystical novelist, essayist, poet. *The Prophet.*

André Gide, 1869-1951, (Fr.) writer. *The Immoralist, The Pastoral Symphony, Strait Is the Gate.*

Allen Ginsberg, 1926-1997, (U.S.) Beat poet. "Howl."

Jean Giraudoux, 1882-1944, (Fr.) novelist, dramatist. *Electra, The Madwoman of Chaillot, Ondine, Tiger at the Gate.*

Johann Wolfgang von Goethe, 1749-1832, (Ger.) poet, dramatist, novelist. *Faust, Sorrows of Young Werther.*

Nikolai Gogol, 1809-52, (Russ.) short-story writer, dramatist, novelist. *Dead Souls, The Inspector General.*

William Golding, 1911-93, (Br.) novelist. *Lord of the Flies.*

Oliver Goldsmith, 1728-74, (Br.-Ir.) dramatist, novelist. *The Vicar of Wakefield, She Stoops to Conquer.*

Maxim Gorky, 1868-1936, (Russ.) dramatist, novelist. *The Lower Depths.*

Robert Graves, 1895-1985, (Br.) poet, classical scholar, novelist. *I, Claudius; The White Goddess.*

Thomas Gray, 1716-71, (Br.) poet. "Elegy Written in a Country Churchyard," "The Progress of Poesy."

Julien Green, 1900-98, (U.S.-Fr.) expatriate American, French novelist. *Moira, Each Man in His Darkness.*

Graham Greene, 1904-91, (Br.) novelist. *The Power and the Glory, The Heart of the Matter, The Ministry of Fear.*

Zane Grey, 1872-1939, (U.S.) writer of Western stories.

Jakob Grimm, 1785-1863, (Ger.) philologist, folklorist; with brother **Wilhelm,** 1786-1859, collected *Grimm's Fairy Tales.*

Alex Haley, 1921-92, (U.S.) author. *Roots.*

Dashiell Hammett, 1894-1961, (U.S.) detective-story writer; created Sam Spade. *The Maltese Falcon, The Thin Man.*

Knut Hamsun, 1859-1952, (Nor.) novelist. *Hunger.*

Thomas Hardy, 1840-1928, (Br.) novelist, poet. *The Return of the Native, Tess of the D'Urbervilles, Jude the Obscure.*

Joel Chandler Harris, 1848-1908, (U.S.) Uncle Remus stories.

Moss Hart, 1904-61, (U.S.) playwright. *Once in a Lifetime, You Can't Take It With You, The Man Who Came to Dinner.*

Bret Harte, 1836-1902, (U.S.) short-story writer, poet. *The Luck of Roaring Camp.*

Jaroslav Hasek, 1883-1923, (Czech.) writer, playwright. *The Good Soldier Schweik.*

John Hawkes, 1925-98, (U.S.) experimental fiction writer. *The Goose on the Grave, Blood Oranges.*

Nathaniel Hawthorne, 1804-64, (U.S.) novelist, short-story writer. *The Scarlet Letter,* "Young Goodman Brown."

Heinrich Heine, 1797-1856, (Ger.) poet. *Book of Songs.*

Robert Heinlein, 1907-88, (U.S.) science fiction writer. *Stranger in a Strange Land.*

Joseph Heller, 1923-99, (U.S.) novelist. Catch-22.

Lillian Hellman, 1905-84, (U.S.) playwright, author of memoirs. *The Little Foxes, An Unfinished Woman, Pentimento.*

Ernest Hemingway, 1899-1961, (U.S.) novelist, short-story writer. *A Farewell to Arms, For Whom the Bell Tolls.*

O. Henry (W. S. Porter), 1862-1910, (U.S.) short-story writer. "The Gift of the Magi."

George Herbert, 1593-1633, (Br.) poet. "The Altar," "Easter Wings."

Zbigniew Herbert, 1924-98, (Pol.) poet. "Apollo and Marsyas."

Robert Herrick, 1591-1674, (Br.) poet. "To the Virgins to Make Much of Time."

James Herriot (James Alfred Wight), 1916-95, (Br.) novelist, veterinarian. *All Creatures Great and Small.*

John Hersey, 1914-93, (U.S.) novelist, journalist. *Hiroshima, A Bell for Adano.*

Hermann Hesse, 1877-1962, (Ger.) novelist, poet. *Death and the Lover, Steppenwolf, Siddhartha.*

James Hilton, 1900-54, (Br.) novelist. *Lost Horizon.*

Oliver Wendell Holmes, 1809-94, (U.S.) poet, novelist. *The Autocrat of the Breakfast-Table.*

Gerard Manley Hopkins, 1844-89, (Br.) poet. "Pied Beauty," "God's Grandeur."

A(lfred) E. Housman, 1859-1936, (Br.) poet. *A Shropshire Lad.*

William Dean Howells, 1837-1920, (U.S.) novelist, critic. *The Rise of Silas Lapham.*

Langston Hughes, 1902-67, (U.S.) poet, playwright. *The Weary Blues, One-Way Ticket, Shakespeare in Harlem.*

Ted Hughes, 1930-98, (Br.) British poet laureate, 1984-98. *Crow, The Hawk in the Rain.*

Victor Hugo, 1802-85, (Fr.) poet, dramatist, novelist. *Notre Dame de Paris, Les Misérables.*

Zora Neale Hurston, 1903-60, (U.S.) novelist, folklorist. *Their Eyes Were Watching God, Mules and Men.*

Aldous Huxley, 1894-1963, (Br.) writer. *Brave New World.*

Henrik Ibsen, 1828-1906, (Nor.) dramatist, poet. *A Doll's House, Ghosts, The Wild Duck, Hedda Gabler.*

William Inge, 1913-73, (U.S.) playwright. *Picnic; Come Back, Little Sheba; Bus Stop.*

Eugene Ionesco, 1910-94, (Fr.) surrealist dramatist. *The Bald Soprano, The Chairs.*

Washington Irving, 1783-1859, (U.S.) writer. "Rip Van Winkle," "The Legend of Sleepy Hollow."

Christopher Isherwood, 1904-1986, (Br.) novelist, playwright. *The Berlin Stories.*

Shirley Jackson, 1919-65, (U.S.) writer. "The Lottery."

Henry James, 1843-1916, (U.S.) novelist, short-story writer, critic. *The Portrait of a Lady, The Ambassadors, Daisy Miller.*

Robinson Jeffers, 1887-1962, (U.S.) poet, dramatist. *Tamar and Other Poems, Medea.*

Samuel Johnson, 1709-84, (Br.) author, scholar, critic. *Dictionary of the English Language, Vanity of Human Wishes.*

Ben Jonson, 1572-1637, (Br.) dramatist, poet. *Volpone.*

James Joyce, 1882-1941, (Ir.) writer. *Ulysses, Dubliners, A Portrait of the Artist as a Young Man, Finnegans Wake.*

Ernst Junger, 1895-1998, (Ger.) novelist, essayist. *The Peace, On the Marble Cliff.*

Franz Kafka, 1883-1924, (Austro-Hung./Czech.) novelist, short-story writer. *The Trial, The Castle,* "The Metamorphosis."

George S. Kaufman, 1889-1961, (U.S.) playwright. *The Man Who Came to Dinner, You Can't Take It With You, Stage Door.*

Yasunari Kawabata, 1899-1972, (Japan.) novelist. *The Sound of the Mountains.*

Nikos Kazantzakis, 1883-1957, (Gk.) novelist. *Zorba the Greek, A Greek Passion.*

Alfred Kazin, 1915-98 (U.S.) author, critic, teacher. *On Native Grounds.*

John Keats, 1795-1821, (Br.) poet. "Ode on a Grecian Urn," "Ode to a Nightingale," "La Belle Dame Sans Merci."

Jack Kerouac, 1922-1969, (U.S.), author, Beat poet. *On the Road, The Dharma Bums,* "Mexico City Blues."

Joyce Kilmer, 1886-1918, (U.S.) poet. "Trees."

Rudyard Kipling, 1865-1936, (Br.) author, poet. "The White Man's Burden," "Gunga Din," *The Jungle Book.*

Jean de la Fontaine, 1621-95, (Fr.) poet. *Fables choisies.*

Pär Lagerkvist, 1891-1974, (Swed.) poet, dramatist, novelist. *Barabbas, The Sybil.*

Selma Lagerlöf, 1858-1940, (Swed.) novelist. *Jerusalem, The Ring of the Lowenskolds.*

Alphonse de Lamartine, 1790-1869, (Fr.) poet, novelist, statesman. *Méditations poétiques.*

Charles Lamb, 1775-1834, (Br.) essayist. *Specimens of English Dramatic Poets, Essays of Elia.*

Giuseppe di Lampedusa, 1896-1957, (It.) novelist. *The Leopard.*

William Langland, c1332-1400, (Eng.) poet. *Piers Plowman.*

Ring Lardner, 1885-1933, (U.S.) short-story writer, humorist.

Louis L'Amour, 1908-88, (U.S.) western author, screenwriter. *Hondo, The Cherokee Trail.*

D(avid) H(erbert) Lawrence, 1885-1930, (Br.) novelist. *Sons and Lovers, Women in Love, Lady Chatterley's Lover.*

Halldor Laxness, 1902-98, (Icelandic) novelist. *Iceland's Bell.*

Mikhail Lermontov, 1814-41, (Russ.) novelist, poet. "Demon," *Hero of Our Time.*

Alain-René Lesage, 1668-1747, (Fr.) novelist. *Gil Blas de Santillane.*

Gotthold Lessing, 1729-81, (Ger.) dramatist, philosopher, critic. *Miss Sara Sampson, Minna von Barnhelm.*

C(live) S(taples) Lewis, 1898-1963, (Br.) critic, novelist, religious writer. *Allegory of Love; The Lion, the Witch and the Wardrobe; Out of the Silent Planet.*

Sinclair Lewis, 1885-1951, (U.S.) novelist. *Babbitt, Main Street, Arrowsmith, Dodsworth.*

Li Po, 701-762 (China) poet. "Song Before Drinking," "She Spins Silk."

Vachel Lindsay, 1879-1931, (U.S.) poet. *General William Booth Enters Into Heaven, The Congo.*

Hugh Lofting, 1886-1947, (Br.) writer. Dr. Doolittle series.

Jack London, 1876-1916, (U.S.) novelist, journalist. *Call of the Wild, The Sea-Wolf, White Fang.*

Henry Wadsworth Longfellow, 1807-82, (U.S.) poet. *Evangeline, The Song of Hiawatha.*

Lope de Vega, 1562-1635, (Sp.) playwright. *Noche de San Juan, Maestro de Danzar.*

H(oward) P(hillips) Lovecraft, 1890-1937, (U.S.), novelist, short-story writer. "At the Mountains of Madness."

Amy Lowell, 1874-1925, (U.S.) poet, critic. "Lilacs."

James Russell Lowell, 1819-91, (U.S.) poet, editor. *Poems, The Biglow Papers.*

Robert Lowell, 1917-77, (U.S.) poet. "Lord Weary's Castle."

Joaquim Maria Machado de Assis, 1839-1908, (Brazil) novelist, poet. *The Posthumous Memoirs of Bras Cubas.*

Archibald MacLeish, 1892-1982, (U.S.) poet. *Conquistador.*

Bernard Malamud, 1914-86, (U.S.) short-story writer, novelist. "The Magic Barrel," *The Assistant, The Fixer.*

Stéphane Mallarmé, 1842-98, (Fr.) poet. *Poésies.*

Sir Thomas Malory, ?-1471, (Br.) writer. *Morte d'Arthur.*

Andre Malraux, 1901-76, (Fr.) novelist. *Man's Fate.*

Osip Mandelstam, 1891-1938, (Russ.) poet. *Stone, Tristia.*

Thomas Mann, 1875-1955, (Ger.) novelist, essayist. *Buddenbrooks, The Magic Mountain,* "Death in Venice."

Katherine Mansfield, 1888-1923, (Br.) short-story writer. "Bliss."

Christopher Marlowe, 1564-93, (Br.) dramatist, poet. *Tamburlaine the Great, Dr. Faustus, The Jew of Malta.*

Andrew Marvell, 1621-78, (Br.) poet. "To His Coy Mistress."

John Masefield, 1878-1967, (Br.) poet. "Sea Fever," "Cargoes," *Salt Water Ballads.*

Edgar Lee Masters, 1869-1950, (U.S.) poet, biographer. *Spoon River Anthology.*

W(illiam) Somerset Maugham, 1874-1965, (Br.) author. *Of Human Bondage, The Moon and Sixpence.*

Guy de Maupassant, 1850-93, (Fr.) novelist, short-story writer. "A Life," "Bel-Ami," "The Necklace."

François Mauriac, 1885-1970, (Fr.) novelist, dramatist. *Viper's Tangle, The Kiss to the Leper.*

Vladimir Mayakovsky, 1893-1930, (Russ.) poet, dramatist. *The Cloud in Trousers.*

Mary McCarthy, 1912-89, (U.S.) critic, novelist, memoirist. *Memories of a Catholic Girlhood.*

Carson McCullers, 1917-67, (U.S.) novelist. *The Heart Is a Lonely Hunter, Member of the Wedding.*

Herman Melville, 1819-91, (U.S.) novelist, poet. *Moby-Dick, Typee, Billy Budd, Omoo.*

George Meredith, 1828-1909, (Br.) novelist, poet. *The Ordeal of Richard Feverel, The Egoist.*

Prosper Mérimée, 1803-70, (Fr.) author. *Carmen.*

James Merrill, 1926-95, (U.S.) poet. *Divine Comedies.*

James Michener, 1907-97, (U.S.) novelist. *Tales of the South Pacific.*

Edna St. Vincent Millay, 1892-1950, (U.S.) poet. *The Harp Weaver and Other Poems.*

Henry Miller, 1891-1980, (U.S.) erotic novelist. *Tropic of Cancer.*

A(lan) A(lexander) Milne, 1882-1956, (Br.) author. *Winnie-the-Pooh.*

Czeslaw Milosz, 1911-2004, (Pol.) essayist, poet. "Esse," "Encounter."

John Milton, 1608-74, (Br.) poet, writer. *Paradise Lost, Comus, Lycidas, Areopagitica.*

Mishima Yukio (Hiraoka Kimitake), 1925-70, (Jpn.) writer. *Confessions of a Mask.*

Gabriela Mistral, 1889-1957, (Chil.) poet. *Sonnets of Death.*

Margaret Mitchell, 1900-49, (U.S.) novelist. *Gone With the Wind.*

Jean Baptiste Molière, 1622-73, (Fr.) dramatist. *Tartuffe, Le Misanthrope, Le Bourgeois Gentilhomme.*

Ferenc Molnár, 1878-1952, (Hung.) dramatist, novelist. *Liliom, The Guardsman, The Swan.*

Michel de Montaigne, 1533-92, (Fr.) essayist. *Essais.*

Eugenio Montale, 1896-1981, (It.) poet.

Brian Moore, 1921-99, (Ir.-U.S.) novelist. *The Lonely Passion of Judith Hearne.*

Clement C. Moore, 1779-1863, (U.S.) poet, educator. "A Visit From Saint Nicholas."

Marianne Moore, 1887-1972, (U.S.) poet.

Alberto Moravia, 1907-90, (It.) novelist, short-story writer. *The Time of Indifference.*

Sir Thomas More, 1478-1535, (Br.) writer, statesman, saint. *Utopia.*

Wright Morris, 1910-98 (U.S.) novelist. *My Uncle Dudley.*

Murasaki Shikibu, c978-1026, (Jpn.) novelist. *The Tale of Genji.*

Iris Murdoch, 1919-99 (Br.), novelist, philosopher. *The Sea, The Sea.*

Alfred de Musset, 1810-57, (Fr.) poet, dramatist. *La Confession d'un Enfant du Siècle.*

Vladimir Nabokov, 1899-1977, (Russ.-U.S.) novelist. *Lolita, Pale Fire.*

R.K. Narayan, 1906-2001, (India), novelist, *The Guide.*

Ogden Nash, 1902-71, (U.S.) poet of light verse.

Pablo Neruda, 1904-73, (Chil.) poet. *Twenty Love Poems and One Song of Despair, Toward the Splendid City.*

Patrick O'Brian, 1914-2000, (Br.) historical novelist. *Master and Commander, Blue at the Mizzen.*

Sean O'Casey, 1884-1964, (Ir.) dramatist. *Juno and the Paycock, The Plough and the Stars.*

Frank O'Connor (Michael Donovan), 1903-66, (Ir.) short-story writer. "Guests of a Nation."

Flannery O'Connor, 1925-64, (U.S.) novelist, short-story writer. *Wise Blood,* "A Good Man Is Hard to Find."

Clifford Odets, 1906-63, (U.S.) playwright. *Waiting for Lefty, Awake and Sing, Golden Boy, The Country Girl.*

John O'Hara, 1905-70, (U.S.) novelist, short-story writer. *From the Terrace, Appointment in Samarra, Pal Joey.*

Omar Khayyam, c1028-1122, (Per.) poet. *Rubaiyat.*

Eugene O'Neill, 1888-1953, (U.S.) playwright. *Emperor Jones, Anna Christie, Long Day's Journey Into Night.*

George Orwell (Eric Arthur Blair), 1903-50, (Br.) novelist, essayist. *Animal Farm, Nineteen Eighty-Four.*

John Osborne, 1929-95, (Br.) dramatist, novelist. *Look Back in Anger, The Entertainer.*

Wilfred Owen, 1893-1918 (Br.) poet. "Dulce et Decorum Est."

Dorothy Parker, 1893-1967, (U.S.) poet, short-story writer. *Enough Rope, Laments for the Living.*

Boris Pasternak, 1890-1960, (Russ.) poet, novelist. *Doctor Zhivago.*

Alan Paton, 1903-88, (S. Africa) novelist. *Cry, the Beloved Country.*

Octavio Paz, 1914-98, (Mex.) poet, essayist. *The Labyrinth of Solitude, They Shall Not Pass!, The Sun Stone.*

Samuel Pepys, 1633-1703, (Br.) public official, diarist.

S(idney) J(oseph) Perelman, 1904-79, (U.S.) humorist. *The Road to Miltown, Under the Spreading Atrophy.*

Charles Perrault, 1628-1703, (Fr.) writer. *Tales From Mother Goose (Sleeping Beauty, Cinderella).*

Petrarch (Francesco Petrarca), 1304-74, (It.) poet. *Africa, Trionfi, Canzoniere.*

Luigi Pirandello, 1867-1936, (It.) novelist, dramatist. *Six Characters in Search of an Author.*

Sylvia Plath, 1932-63, (U.S.) author, poet. *The Bell Jar.*

Edgar Allan Poe, 1809-49, (U.S.) poet, short-story writer, critic. "Annabel Lee," "The Raven," "The Purloined Letter."

Alexander Pope, 1688-1744, (Br.) poet. *The Rape of the Lock, The Dunciad, An Essay on Man.*

Katherine Anne Porter, 1890-1980, (U.S.) novelist, short-story writer. *Ship of Fools.*

Chaim Potok, 1929-2002, (U.S.) novelist. *The Chosen.*

Ezra Pound, 1885-1972, (U.S.) poet. *Cantos.*

Anthony Powell, 1905-2000, (Br.) novelist. *A Dance to the Music of Time* series.

J(ohn) B. Priestley, 1894-1984, (Br.) novelist, dramatist. *The Good Companions.*

Marcel Proust, 1871-1922, (Fr.) novelist. *Remembrance of Things Past.*

Aleksandr Pushkin, 1799-1837, (Russ.) poet, novelist. *Boris Godunov, Eugene Onegin.*

Mario Puzo, 1920-99, (U.S.) novelist. *The Godfather.*

François Rabelais, 1495-1553, (Fr.) writer. *Gargantua.*

Jean Racine, 1639-99, (Fr.) dramatist. *Andromaque, Phèdre, Bérénice, Britannicus.*

Ayn Rand, 1905-82, (Russ.-U.S.) novelist, moral theorist. *The Fountainhead, Atlas Shrugged.*

Terence Rattigan, 1911-77, (Br.) playwright. *Separate Tables, The Browning Version.*

Erich Maria Remarque, 1898-1970, (Ger.-U.S.) novelist. *All Quiet on the Western Front.*

Samuel Richardson, 1689-1761, (Br.) novelist. *Pamela; or Virtue Rewarded.*

Rainer Maria Rilke, 1875-1926, (Ger.) poet. *Life and Songs, Duino Elegies, Poems From the Book of Hours.*

Arthur Rimbaud, 1854-91, (Fr.) poet. *A Season in Hell.*

Edwin Arlington Robinson, 1869-1935, (U.S.) poet. "Richard Cory," "Miniver Cheevy," *Merlin.*

Theodore Roethke, 1908-63, (U.S.) poet. *Open House, The Waking, The Far Field.*

Romain Rolland, 1866-1944, (Fr.) novelist, biographer. *Jean-Christophe.*

Pierre de Ronsard, 1524-85, (Fr.) poet. *Sonnets pour Hélène, La Franciade.*

Christina Rossetti, 1830-94, (Br.) poet. "When I Am Dead, My Dearest."

Dante Gabriel Rossetti, 1828-82, (Br.) poet, painter. "The Blessed Damozel."

Edmond Rostand, 1868-1918, (Fr.) poet, dramatist. *Cyrano de Bergerac.*

Damon Runyon, 1880-1946, (U.S.) short-story writer, journalist. *Guys and Dolls, Blue Plate Special.*

John Ruskin, 1819-1900, (Br.) critic, social theorist. *Modern Painters, The Seven Lamps of Architecture.*

François Sagan, (Françoise quoirez) 1935-2004, (Fr.) novelist *Bonjour Tristesse.*

Antoine de Saint-Exupéry, 1900-44, (Fr.) writer. *Wind, Sand and Stars, The Little Prince.*

Saki, or H(ector) H(ugh) Munro, 1870-1916, (Br.) writer. *The Chronicles of Clovis.*

George Sand (Amandine Lucie Aurore Dupin), 1804-76, (Fr.) novelist. *Indiana, Consuelo.*

Carl Sandburg, 1878-1967, (U.S.) poet. *The People, Yes; Chicago Poems, Smoke and Steel, Harvest Poems.*

William Saroyan, 1908-81, (U.S.) playwright, novelist. *The Time of Your Life, The Human Comedy.*

Nathalie Sarraute, 1900-99, (Fr.) Nouveau Roman novelist. *Tropismes.*

May Sarton, 1914-95, (Belg.-U.S.) poet, novelist. *Encounter in April, Anger.*

Dorothy L. Sayers, 1893-1957, (Br.) mystery writer; created Lord Peter Wimsey.

Richard Scarry, 1920-94, (U.S.) author of children's books. *Richard Scarry's Best Story Book Ever.*

Friedrich von Schiller, 1759-1805, (Ger.) dramatist, poet, historian. *Don Carlos, Maria Stuart, Wilhelm Tell.*

Sir Walter Scott, 1771-1832, (Sc.) novelist, poet. *Ivanhoe.*

Jaroslav Seifert, 1902-86, (Czech.) poet.

Dr. Seuss (Theodor Seuss Geisel), 1904-91, (U.S.) children's book author and illustrator. *The Cat in the Hat.*

William Shakespeare, 1564-1616, (Br.) dramatist, poet. *Romeo and Juliet, Hamlet, King Lear, Julius Caesar,* sonnets.

Karl Shapiro, 1913-2000, (U.S.) poet. "Elegy for a Dead Soldier."

George Bernard Shaw, 1856-1950, (Ir.-Br.) playwright, critic. *St. Joan, Pygmalion, Major Barbara, Man and Superman.*

Mary Wollstonecraft Shelley, 1797-1851, (Br.) novelist, feminist. *Frankenstein. The Last Man.*

Percy Bysshe Shelley, 1792-1822, (Br.) poet. *Prometheus Unbound, Adonais,* "Ode to the West Wind," "To a Skylark."

Richard B. Sheridan, 1751-1816, (Br.) dramatist. *The Rivals, School for Scandal.*

Robert Sherwood, 1896-1955, (U.S.) playwright, biographer. *The Petrified Forest, Abe Lincoln in Illinois.*

Mikhail Sholokhov, 1906-84, (Russ.) writer. *The Silent Don.*

Georges Simenon (Georges Sims), 1903-89, (Belg.-Fr.) mystery writer; created Inspector Maigret.

Upton Sinclair, 1878-1968, (U.S.) novelist. *The Jungle.*

Isaac Bashevis Singer, 1904-91, (Pol.-U.S.) novelist, short-story writer, in Yiddish. *The Magician of Lublin.*

C(harles) P(ercy) Snow, 1905-80, (Br.) novelist, scientist. *Strangers and Brothers, Corridors of Power.*

Stephen Spender, 1909-95, (Br.) poet, critic, novelist. *Twenty Poems,* "Elegy for Margaret."

Edmund Spenser, 1552-99, (Br.) poet. *The Faerie Queen.*

Johanna Spyri, 1827-1901, (Swiss) children's author. *Heidi.*

Christina Stead, 1902-83, (Austral.) novelist, short-story writer. *The Man Who Loved Children.*

Richard Steele, 1672-1729, (Br.) essayist, playwright, began the *Tatler* and *Spectator. The Conscious Lovers.*

Gertrude Stein, 1874-1946, (U.S.) writer. *Three Lives.*

John Steinbeck, 1902-68, (U.S.) novelist. *The Grapes of Wrath, Of Mice and Men, The Winter of Our Discontent.*

Stendhal (Marie Henri Beyle), 1783-1842, (Fr.) novelist. *The Red and the Black, The Charterhouse of Parma.*

Laurence Sterne, 1713-68, (Br.) novelist. *Tristram Shandy.*

Wallace Stevens, 1879-1955, (U.S.) poet. *Harmonium, The Man With the Blue Guitar, Notes Toward a Supreme Fiction.*

Robert Louis Stevenson, 1850-94, (Br.) novelist, poet, essayist. *Treasure Island, A Child's Garden of Verses.*

Bram Stoker, 1845-1910, (Br.) writer. *Dracula.*

Rex Stout, 1886-1975, (U.S.) mystery writer; created Nero Wolfe.

Harriet Beecher Stowe, 1811-96, (U.S.) novelist. *Uncle Tom's Cabin.*

Lytton Strachey, 1880-1932, (Br.) biographer, critic. *Eminent Victorians. Queen Victoria, Elizabeth and Essex.*

August Strindberg, 1849-1912, (Swed.) dramatist, novelist. *The Father, Miss Julie, The Creditors.*

Jonathan Swift, 1667-1745, (Br.) satirist, poet. *Gulliver's Travels,* "A Modest Proposal."

Algernon C. Swinburne, 1837-1909, (Br.) poet, dramatist. *Atalanta in Calydon.*

John M. Synge, 1871-1909, (Ir.) poet, dramatist. *Riders to the Sea, The Playboy of the Western World.*

Rabindranath Tagore, 1861-1941, (In.) author, poet. *Sadhana, The Realization of Life, Gitanjali.*

Booth Tarkington, 1869-1946, (U.S.) novelist. *Seventeen.*

Peter Taylor, 1917-94, (U.S.) novelist. *A Summons to Memphis.*

Sara Teasdale, 1884-1933, (U.S.) poet. *Helen of Troy and Other Poems, Rivers to the Sea.*

Alfred, Lord Tennyson, 1809-92, (Br.) poet. *Idylls of the King, In Memoriam,* "The Charge of the Light Brigade."

William Makepeace Thackeray, 1811-63, (Br.) novelist. *Vanity Fair, Henry Esmond, Pendennis.*

Dylan Thomas, 1914-53, (Welsh) poet. *Under Milk Wood, A Child's Christmas in Wales.*

Henry David Thoreau, 1817-62, (U.S.) writer, philosopher, naturalist. *Walden,* "Civil Disobedience."

James Thurber, 1894-1961, (U.S.) humorist; "The Secret Life of Walter Mitty," *My Life and Hard Times.*

J(ohn) R(onald) R(euel) Tolkien, 1892-1973, (Br.) writer. *The Hobbit, Lord of the Rings* trilogy.

Leo Tolstoy, 1828-1910, (Russ.) novelist, short-story writer. *War and Peace, Anna Karenina,* "The Death of Ivan Ilyich."

Lionel Trilling, 1905-75 (U.S.) critic, author, teacher. *The Liberal Imagination.*

Anthony Trollope, 1815-82, (Br.) novelist. *The Warden, Barchester Towers,* the Palliser novels.

Ivan Turgenev, 1818-83, (Russ.) novelist, short-story writer. *Fathers and Sons, First Love, A Month in the Country.*

Amos Tutuola, 1920-97, (Nigerian) novelist. *The Palm-Wine Drunkard, My Life in the Bush of Ghosts.*

Mark Twain (Samuel Clemens), 1835-1910, (U.S.) novelist, humorist. *The Adventures of Huckleberry Finn, Tom Sawyer; Life on the Mississippi.*

Sigrid Undset, 1881-1949, (Nor.) novelist, poet. *Kristin Lavransdatter.*

Paul Valéry, 1871-1945, (Fr.) poet, critic. *La Jeune Parque, The Graveyard by the Sea.*

Paul Verlaine, 1844-96, (Fr.) Symbolist poet. *Songs Without Words.*

Jules Verne, 1828-1905, (Fr.) novelist. *Twenty Thousand Leagues Under the Sea.*

François Villon, 1431-63?, (Fr.) poet. *The Lays, The Grand Testament.*

Voltaire (F.M. Arouet), 1694-1778, (Fr.) writer of "philosophical romances"; philosopher, historian; *Candide.*

Robert Penn Warren, 1905-89, (U.S.) novelist, poet, critic. *All the King's Men.*

Evelyn Waugh, 1903-66, (Br.) novelist. *The Loved One, Brideshead Revisited, A Handful of Dust.*

H(erbert) G(eorge) Wells, 1866-1946, (Br.) novelist. *The Time Machine, The Invisible Man, The War of the Worlds.*

Eudora Welty, 1909-2001, (U.S.) Southern short story writer, novelist. "Why I Live at the P.O.," "The Ponder Heart."

Rebecca West, 1893-1983, (Br.) novelist, critic, journalist. *Black Lamb and Grey Falcon.*

Edith Wharton, 1862-1937, (U.S.) novelist. *The Age of Innocence, The House of Mirth, Ethan Frome.*

E(lwyn) B(rooks) White, 1899-1985, (U.S.) essayist, novelist. *Charlotte's Web, Stuart Little.*

Patrick White, 1912-90, (Austral.) novelist. *The Tree of Man.*

T(erence) H(anbury) White, 1906-64, (Br.) author. *The Once and Future King, A Book of Beasts.*

Walt Whitman, 1819-92, (U.S.) poet. *Leaves of Grass.*

John Greenleaf Whittier, 1807-92, (U.S.) poet, journalist. *Snow-Bound.*

Oscar Wilde, 1854-1900, (Ir.) novelist, playwright. *The Picture of Dorian Gray, The Importance of Being Earnest.*

Laura Ingalls Wilder, 1867-1957, (U.S.) novelist. *Little House on the Prairie* series of children's books.

Thornton Wilder, 1897-1975, (U.S.) playwright. *Our Town, The Skin of Our Teeth, The Matchmaker.*

Tennessee Williams, 1911-83, (U.S.) playwright. *A Streetcar Named Desire, Cat on a Hot Tin Roof, The Glass Menagerie.*

William Carlos Williams, 1883-1963, (U.S.) poet, physician. *Tempers, Al Que Quiere! Paterson,* "This Is Just to Say."

Edmund Wilson, 1895-1972, (U.S.) critic, novelist. *Axel's Castle, To the Finland Station.*

P(elham) G(renville) Wodehouse, 1881-1975, (Br.-U.S.) humorist. The "Jeeves" novels, *Anything Goes.*

Thomas Wolfe, 1900-38, (U.S.) novelist. *Look Homeward, Angel; You Can't Go Home Again.*

Virginia Woolf, 1882-1941, (Br.) novelist, essayist. *Mrs. Dalloway, To the Lighthouse, A Room of One's Own.*

William Wordsworth, 1770-1850, (Br.) poet. "Tintern Abbey," "Ode: Intimations of Immortality," *The Prelude.*

Richard Wright, 1908-60, novelist, short-story writer. *Native Son, Black Boy, Uncle Tom's Children.*

Elinor Wylie, 1885-1928, (U.S.) poet. *Nets to Catch the Wind.*

William Butler Yeats, 1865-1939, (Ir.) poet, playwright. "The Second Coming," *The Wild Swans at Coole.*

Émile Zola, 1840-1902, (Fr.) novelist. *Nana, Thérèsè Raquin.*

Poets Laureate

There is no record of the origin of the office of Poet Laureate of England. Henry III (1216-72) reportedly had a Versificator Regis, or King's Poet, paid 100 shillings a year. Other poets said to have filled the role include Geoffrey Chaucer (d 1400), Edmund Spenser (d 1599), Ben Jonson (d 1637), and Sir William d'Avenant (d 1668).

The first official English poet laureate was John Dryden, appointed 1668, for life (as was customary). Then came Thomas Shadwell, in 1689; Nahum Tate, 1692; Nicholas Rowe, 1715; Rev. Laurence Eusden, 1718; Colley Cibber, 1730; William Whitehead, 1757; Rev. Thomas Warton, 1785; Henry James Pye, 1790; Robert Southey, 1813; William Wordsworth, 1843; Alfred, Lord Tennyson, 1850; Alfred Austin, 1896; Robert Bridges, 1913; John Masefield, 1930; C. Day Lewis, 1968; Sir John Betjeman, 1972; Ted Hughes, 1984; Andrew Motion, 1999.

In U.S., appointment is by Librarian of Congress and is not for life: Robert Penn Warren, appointed 1986; Richard Wilbur, 1987; Howard Nemerov, 1988; Mark Strand, 1990; Joseph Brodsky, 1991; Mona Van Duyn, 1992; Rita Dove, 1993; Robert Hass, 1995; Robert Pinsky, 1997; Stanley Kunitz, 2000; Billy Collins, 2001; Louise Gluck, 2003; Ted Kooser, 2004.

Composers of Classical and Avant Garde Music

Carl Philipp Emanuel Bach, 1714-88, (Ger.) Cantatas, passions, numerous keyboard and instrumental works.

Johann Christian Bach, 1735-82, (Ger.) Concertos, operas, sonatas.

Johann Sebastian Bach, 1685-1750, (Ger.) *St. Matthew Passion, The Well-Tempered Clavier.*

Samuel Barber, 1910-81, (U.S.) *Adagio for Strings, Vanessa.*

Béla Bartók, 1881-1945, (Hung.) *Concerto for Orchestra, The Miraculous Mandarin.*

Amy Beach (Mrs. H. H. A. Beach), 1867-1944, (U.S.) *The Year's at the Spring, Fireflies, The Chambered Nautilus.*

Ludwig van Beethoven, 1770-1827, (Ger.) Concertos (*Emperor*), sonatas (*Moonlight, Pathetique*), 9 symphonies.

Vincenzo Bellini, 1801-35, (It.) *I Puritani, La Sonnambula, Norma.*

Alban Berg, 1885-1935, (Austrian) *Wozzeck, Lulu.*

Hector Berlioz, 1803-69, (Fr.) *Damnation of Faust, Symphonie Fantastique, Requiem.*

Leonard Bernstein, 1918-90, (U.S.) *Chichester Psalms, Jeremiah Symphony, Mass.*

Georges Bizet, 1838-75, (Fr.) *Carmen, Pearl Fishers.*

Ernest Bloch, 1880-1959, (Swiss-U.S.) *Macbeth* (opera), *Schelomo, Voice in the Wilderness.*

Luigi Boccherini, 1743-1805, (It.) Chamber music and guitar pieces.

Alexander Borodin, 1833-87, (Russ.) *Prince Igor, In the Steppes of Central Asia, Polovtzian Dances.*

Pierre Boulez, b 1925, (Fr.) *LeVisage* nuptial, *Edats/Multiple, Domaines.*

Johannes Brahms, 1833-97, (Ger.) Liebeslieder Waltzes, *Acad. Festival Overture,* chamber music, 4 symphonies.

Benjamin Britten, 1913-76, (Br.) *Peter Grimes, Turn of the Screw, A Ceremony of Carols, War Requiem.*

Anton Bruckner, 1824-96, (Austrian) 9 symphonies.

Dietrich Buxtehude, 1637-1707, (Dan.) Organ works, vocal music.

William Byrd, 1543-1623, (Br.) Masses, motets.

John Cage, 1912-92, (U.S.) *Winter Music, Fontana Mix.*

Emmanuel Chabrier, 1841-94, (Fr.) *Le Roi Malgré Lui, España.*

Gustave Charpentier, 1860-1956, (Fr.) *Louise.*

Frédéric Chopin, 1810-49, (Pol.) Mazurkas, waltzes, etudes, nocturnes, polonaises, sonatas.

Aaron Copland, 1900-90, (U.S.) *Appalachian Spring, Fanfare for the Common Man, Lincoln Portrait.*

Claude Debussy, 1862-1918, (Fr.) *Pelleas et Melisande, La Mer, Prelude to the Afternoon of a Faun.*

Gaetano Donizetti, 1797-1848, (It.) Elixir of Love, Lucia di Lammermoor, Daughter of the Regiment.

Paul Dukas, 1865-1935, (Fr.) *Sorcerer's Apprentice.*

Antonin Dvorak, 1841-1904, (Czech.) *Songs My Mother Taught Me, Symphony in E Minor (From the New World).*

Edward Elgar, 1857-1934, (Br.) *Enigma Variations, Pomp and Circumstance.*

Manuel de Falla, 1876-1946, (Sp.) *El Amor Brujo, La Vida Breve, The Three-Cornered Hat.*

Gabriel Fauré, 1845-1924, (Fr.) *Requiem, Elègie for Cello and Piano.*

Cesar Franck, 1822-90, (Belg.) Symphony in D minor, Violin Sonata.

George Gershwin, 1898-1937, (U.S.) *Rhapsody in Blue, An American in Paris, Porgy and Bess.*

Philip Glass, b 1937, (U.S.) *Einstein on the Beach, The Voyage.*

Mikhail Glinka, 1804-57, (Russ.) *A Life for the Tsar, Ruslan and Ludmilla.*

Christoph W. Gluck, 1714-87, (Ger.) *Alceste, Iphigènie en Tauride.*

Charles Gounod, 1818-93, (Fr.) *Faust, Romeo and Juliet.*

Edvard Grieg, 1843-1907, (Nor.) *Peer Gynt Suite,* Concerto in A minor for piano.

George Frideric Handel, 1685-1759, (Ger.-Br.) *Messiah, Water Music.*

Howard Hanson, 1896-1981, (U.S.) Symphonies No. 1 (Nordic) and No. 2 (Romantic).

Roy Harris, 1898-1979, (U.S.) Symphonies.

(Franz) Joseph Haydn, 1732-1809, (Austrian) Symphonies (*Clock, London, Toy*), chamber music, oratorios.

Paul Hindemith, 1895-1963, (U.S.) *Mathis der Maler.*

Gustav Holst, 1874-1934, (Br.) *The Planets.*

Arthur Honegger, 1892-1955, (Fr.) *Judith, Le Roi David, Pacific 231.*

Alan Hovhaness, 1911-2000, (U.S.) Symphonies, *Magnificat.*

Engelbert Humperdinck, 1854-1921, (Ger.) *Hansel and Gretel.*

Charles Ives, 1874-1954, (U.S.) *Concord Sonata,* symphonies.

Aram Khachaturian, 1903-78, (Russ.) Ballets, piano pieces, *Sabre Dance.*

Zoltán Kodaly, 1882-1967, (Hung.) *Háry János, Psalmus Hungaricus.*

Fritz Kreisler, 1875-1962, (Austrian) *Caprice Viennois, Tambourin Chinois.*

Edouard Lalo, 1823-92, (Fr.) *Symphonie Espagnole.*

Ruggero Leoncavallo, 1857-1919, (It.) *Pagliacci.*

Franz Liszt, 1811-86, (Hung.) 20 Hungarian rhapsodies, symphonic poems.

Edward MacDowell, 1861-1908, (U.S.) *To a Wild Rose.*

Gustav Mahler, 1860-1911, (Austrian) *Das Lied von der Erde;* 9 complete symphonies.

Pietro Mascagni, 1863-1945, (It.) *Cavalleria Rusticana.*

Jules Massenet, 1842-1912, (Fr.) *Manon, Le Cid, Thaïs.*

Felix Mendelssohn, 1809-47, (Ger.) *A Midsummer Night's Dream, Songs Without Words,* violin concerto.

Gian-Carlo Menotti, b 1911, (It.-U.S.) *The Medium, The Consul, Amahl and the Night Visitors.*

Claudio Monteverdi, 1567-1643, (It.) Opera, masses, madrigals.

Modest Moussorgsky, 1839-81, (Russ.) *Boris Godunov, Pictures at an Exhibition.*

Wolfgang Amadeus Mozart, 1756-91, (Austrian) Chamber music, concertos, operas (*Magic Flute, Marriage of Figaro*), 41 symphonies.

Jacques Offenbach, 1819-80, (Fr.) *Tales of Hoffmann.*

Carl Orff, 1895-1982, (Ger.) *Carmina Burana.*

Johann Pachelbel, 1653-1706, (Ger.) Canon and Fugue in D major.

Ignacy Paderewski, 1860-1941, (Pol.) Minuet in G.

Niccolò Paganini, 1782-1840, (It.) Caprices for violin solo.

Giovanni Palestrina, c1525-94, (It.) Masses, madrigals.

Krzystof Penderecki, b 1933, (Pol.) *Psalmus, Polymorphia, De natura sonoris.*

Francis Poulenc, 1899-1963, (Fr.) *Dialogues des Carmèlites.*

Mel Powell, 1923-98, (U.S.) *Duplicates: A Concerto for Two Pianos and Orchestra, Cantilena Concertante.*

Sergei Prokofiev, 1891-1953, (Russ.) *Classical Symphony, Love for Three Oranges, Peter and the Wolf.*

Giacomo Puccini, 1858-1924, (It.) *La Boheme, Manon Lescaut, Tosca, Madama Butterfly.*

Henry Purcell, 1659-95, (Eng.) *Dido and Aeneas.*

Sergei Rachmaninoff, 1873-1943, (Russ.) Concertos, preludes (Prelude in C sharp minor), symphonies.

Maurice Ravel, 1875-1937, (Fr.) *Bolèro, Daphnis et Chloè,* Piano Concerto in D for Left Hand Alone.

Nikolai Rimsky-Korsakov, 1844-1908, (Russ.) *Golden Cockerel, Scheherazade, Flight of the Bumblebee.*

Gioacchino Rossini, 1792-1868, (It.) *Barber of Seville, Otello, William Tell.*

Camille Saint-Saëns, 1835-1921, (Fr.) *Carnival of Animals (The Swan), Samson and Delilah, Danse Macabre.*

Alessandro Scarlatti, 1660-1725, (It.) Cantatas, oratorios, operas.

Domenico Scarlatti, 1685-1757, (It.) Harpsichord works.

Alfred Schnittke, 1934-98 (Sov.-Ger.) *Life With an Idiot.*

Arnold Schoenberg, 1874-1951, (Austrian) *Pelleas and Melisande, Pierrot Lunaire, Verklärte Nacht.*

Franz Schubert, 1797-1828, (Austrian) Chamber music (*Trout Quintet*), lieder, symphonies (Unfinished).

Robert Schumann, 1810-56, (Ger.) *Die Frauenliebe und Leben, Träumerei.*

Dimitri Shostakovich, 1906-75, (Russ.) Symphonies, *Lady Macbeth of the District Mzensk.*

Jean Sibelius, 1865-1957, (Finn.) Finlandia.

Bedrich Smetana, 1824-84, (Czech.) *The Bartered Bride.*

Karlheinz Stockhausen, b 1928, (Ger.) *Kontra-Punkte, Kontakte for Electronic Instruments.*

Richard Strauss, 1864-1949, (Ger.) *Salome, Elektra, Der Rosenkavalier, Thus Spake Zarathustra.*

Igor Stravinsky, 1882-1971, (Russ.) *Noah and the Flood, The Rake's Progress, The Rite of Spring.*

Toru Takemitsu, 1930-96, (Jpn.) *Requiem for Strings, Dorian Horizon.*

Peter I. Tchaikovsky, 1840-93, (Russ.) *Nutcracker, Swan Lake, The Sleeping Beauty.*

Georg Philopp Telemann, 1681-1767, (Ger.) church music, orchestral suites, chamber music.

Virgil Thomson, 1896-1989, (U.S.) Opera, film music, *Four Saints in Three Acts.*

Dmitri Tiomkin, 1894-1979, (Russ.-U.S.) film scores, including *High Noon.*

Sir Michael Tippett, 1905-98, (Br.) *A Child of Our Time, The Midsummer Marriage, The Knot Garden.*

Ralph Vaughan Williams, 1872-1958, (Eng.) *Fantasiz on a Theme by Thomas Tallis,* symphonies, vocal music.

Giuseppe Verdi, 1813-1901, (It.) *Aida, Rigoletto, Don Carlo, Il Trovatore, La Traviata, Falstaff, Macbeth.*

Heitor Villa-Lobos, 1887-1959, (Brazil) *Bachianas Brasileiras.*

Antonio Vivaldi, 1678-1741, (It.) Concerto grossos (*The Four Seasons*).

Richard Wagner, 1813-83, (Ger.) *Rienzi, Tannhäuser, Lohengrin, Tristan und Isolde.*

Carl Maria von Weber, 1786-1826, (Ger.) *Der Freischutz.*

Composers of Operettas, Musicals, and Popular Music

Richard Adler, b 1921, (U.S.) *Pajama Game; Damn Yankees.*

Milton Ager, 1893-1979, (U.S.) I Wonder What's Become of Sally; Hard-Hearted Hannah; Ain't She Sweet?

Arthur Altman, 1910-94, (U.S.) *All or Nothing at All.*

Leroy Anderson, 1908-75, (U.S.) Sleigh Ride, Blue Tango, Syncopated Clock.

Paul Anka, b 1941, (Can.) My Way; *Tonight Show* theme.

Harold Arlen, 1905-86, (U.S.) Stormy Weather; Over the Rainbow; Blues in the Night; That Old Black Magic.

Burt Bacharach, b 1928, (U.S.) Raindrops Keep Fallin' on My Head; Walk on By; What the World Needs Now Is Love.

Ernest Ball, 1878-1927, (U.S.) Mother Machree; When Irish Eyes Are Smiling.

Irving Berlin, 1888-1989, (U.S.) *Annie Get Your Gun; Call Me Madam;* God Bless America; White Christmas.

Leonard Bernstein, 1918-90, (U.S.) *On the Town; Wonderful Town; Candide; West Side Story.*

Eubie Blake, 1883-1983, (U.S.) *Shuffle Along;* I'm Just Wild About Harry.

Jerry Bock, b 1928, (U.S.) *Mr. Wonderful; Fiorello; Fiddler on the Roof; The Rothschilds.*

Carrie Jacobs Bond, 1862-1946, (U.S.) I Love You Truly.

Nacio Herb Brown, 1896-1964, (U.S.) Singing in the Rain; You Were Meant for Me; All I Do Is Dream of You.

Hoagy Carmichael, 1899-1981, (U.S.) Stardust; Georgia on My Mind; Old Buttermilk Sky.

George M. Cohan, 1878-1942, (U.S.) Give My Regards to Broadway; You're a Grand Old Flag; Over There.

Cy Coleman, b 1929, (U.S.) *Sweet Charity;* Witchcraft.

John Frederick Coots, 1895-1985, (U.S.) Santa Claus Is Coming to Town; You Go to My Head; For All We Know.

Noel Coward, 1899-1973, (Br.) *Bitter Sweet;* Mad Dogs and Englishmen; Mad About the Boy.

Neil Diamond, b 1941, (U.S.) I'm a Believer; Sweet Caroline.

Walter Donaldson, 1893-1947, (U.S.) My Buddy; Carolina in the Morning; Makin' Whoopee.

Vernon Duke, 1903-69, (U.S.) April in Paris.

Bob Dylan, b 1941, (U.S.) Blowin' in the Wind.

Gus Edwards, 1879-1945, (U.S.) School Days; By the Light of the Silvery Moon; In My Merry Oldsmobile.

Sherman Edwards, 1919-81, (U.S.) See You in September; Wonderful! Wonderful!

Duke Ellington, 1899-1974, (U.S.) Sophisticated Lady; Satin Doll; It Don't Mean a Thing; Solitude.

Sammy Fain, 1902-89, (U.S.) I'll Be Seeing You; Love Is a Many-Splendored Thing.

Fred Fisher, 1875-1942, (U.S.) Peg O' My Heart; Chicago.

Stephen Collins Foster, 1826-64, (U.S.) My Old Kentucky Home; Old Folks at Home, Beautiful Dreamer.

Rudolf Friml, 1879-1972, (Czech-U.S.) *The Firefly; Rose Marie; Vagabond King; Bird of Paradise.*

John Gay, 1685-1732, (Br.) *The Beggar's Opera.*

George Gershwin, 1898-1937, (U.S.) Someone to Watch Over Me; I've Got a Crush on You; Embraceable You.

Morton Gould, 1913-96, (U.S.) Fall River Suite, Holocaust Suite, Spirituals for Orchestra, Stringmusic.

Ferde Grofe, 1892-1972, (U.S.) Grand Canyon Suite.

Marvin Hamlisch, b 1944, (U.S.) The Way We Were; Nobody Does It Better; *A Chorus Line.*

Ray Henderson, 1896-1970, (U.S.) *George White's Scandals;* That Old Gang of Mine; Five Foot Two, Eyes of Blue.

Victor Herbert, 1859-1924, (Ir.-U.S.) *Mlle. Modiste; Babes in Toyland; The Red Mill; Naughty Marietta; Sweethearts.*

Jerry Herman, b 1933, (U.S.) *Hello Dolly; Mame.*

Brian Holland, b 1941, Lamont Dozier, b 1941, Eddie Holland, b 1939, (all U.S.) Heat Wave; Stop! In the Name of Love; Baby, I Need Your Loving.

Antonio Carlos Jobim, 1927-94, (Brazil) *The Girl From Ipanema; Desafinado; One Note Samba.*

Billy (William Martin) Joel, b 1949, (U.S.) Just the Way You Are; Honesty; Piano Man.

Scott Joplin, 1868-1917, (U.S.) Maple Leaf Rag; *Treemonisha.*

John Kander, b 1927, (U.S.) *Cabaret; Chicago; Funny Lady.*

Jerome Kern, 1885-1945, (U.S.) *Sally; Sunny; Show Boat.*

Carole King, b 1942, (U.S.) Will You Love Me Tomorrow?; Natural Woman; One Fine Day; Up on the Roof.

Burton Lane, 1912-1997, (U.S.) *Finian's Rainbow.*

Franz Lehar, 1870-1948, (Hung.) *Merry Widow.*

Jerry Leiber, & Mike Stoller, both b 1933, (both U.S.) Hound Dog; Searchin'; Yakety Yak; Love Me Tender.

Mitch Leigh, b 1928, (U.S.) *Man of La Mancha.*

John Lennon, 1940-80, & Paul McCartney, b 1942, (both Br.) I Want to Hold Your Hand; She Loves You.

Jay Livingston, 1915-2001 (U.S.) Mona Lisa; Que Sera, Sera.

Andrew Lloyd Webber, b 1948, (Br.) *Jesus Christ Superstar; Evita; Cats; The Phantom of the Opera.*

Frank Loesser, 1910-69, (U.S.) *Guys and Dolls; Where's Charley?; The Most Happy Fella; How to Succeed….*

Frederick Loewe, 1901-88, (Austrian-U.S.) *Brigadoon; Paint Your Wagon; My Fair Lady; Camelot.*

Henry Mancini, 1924-94, (U.S.) Moon River; Days of Wine and Roses; Pink Panther Theme.

Barry Mann, b 1939, & Cynthia Weil, b 1937, (both U.S.) You've Lost That Loving Feeling.

Jimmy McHugh, 1894-1969, (U.S.) Don't Blame Me; I'm in the Mood for Love; I Feel a Song Coming On.

Alan Menken, b 1949, (U.S.) *Little Shop of Horrors, Beauty and the Beast.*

Joseph Meyer, 1894-1987, (U.S.) If You Knew Susie; California, Here I Come; Crazy Rhythm.

Chauncey Olcott, 1858-1932, (U.S.) Mother Machree.

Jerome "Doc" Pomus, 1925-91, (U.S.) Save the Last Dance for Me; A Teenager in Love.

Cole Porter, 1893-1964, (U.S.) *Anything Goes; Kiss Me Kate; Can Can; Silk Stockings.*

Smokey Robinson, b 1940, (U.S.) Shop Around; My Guy; My Girl; Get Ready.

Richard Rodgers, 1902-79, (U.S.) *Oklahoma!; Carousel; South Pacific; The King and I; The Sound of Music.*

Sigmund Romberg, 1887-1951, (Hung.) *Maytime; The Student Prince; Desert Song; Blossom Time.*

Harold Rome, 1908-93, (U.S.) *Pins and Needles; Call Me Mister; Wish You Were Here; Fanny; Destry Rides Again.*

Vincent Rose, b 1880-1944, (U.S.) Avalon; Whispering; Blueberry Hill.

Harry Ruby, 1895-1974, (U.S.) Three Little Words; Who's Sorry Now?

Arthur Schwartz, 1900-84, (U.S.) *The Band Wagon;* Dancing in the Dark; By Myself; That's Entertainment.

Neil Sedaka, b 1939, (U.S.) Breaking Up Is Hard to Do.

Paul Simon, b 1942, (U.S.) Sounds of Silence; I Am a Rock; Mrs. Robinson; Bridge Over Troubled Waters.

Stephen Sondheim, b 1930, (U.S.) *A Little Night Music; Company; Sweeney Todd; Sunday in the Park With George.*

John Philip Sousa, 1854-1932, (U.S.) *El Capitan;* Stars and Stripes Forever.

Oskar Straus, 1870-1954, (Austrian) *Chocolate Soldier.*

Johann Strauss, 1825-99, (Austrian) *Gypsy Baron; Die Fledermaus;* waltzes: Blue Danube; Artist's Life.

Charles Strouse, b 1928, (U.S.) *Bye Bye, Birdie; Annie.*
Jule Styne, 1905-94, (Br.-U.S.) *Gentlemen Prefer Blondes; Bells Are Ringing; Gypsy; Funny Girl.*
Arthur S. Sullivan, 1842-1900, (Br.) *H.M.S. Pinafore; Pirates of Penzance; The Mikado.*
Deems Taylor, 1885-1966, (U.S.) *Peter Ibbetson.*
Harry Tobias, 1905-94, (U.S.) *I'll Keep the Lovelight Burning.*
Egbert van Alstyne, 1882-1951, (U.S.) In the Shade of the Old Apple Tree; Memories; Pretty Baby.
Jimmy Van Heusen, 1913-90, (U.S.) Moonlight Becomes You; Swinging on a Star; All the Way; Love and Marriage.
Albert von Tilzer, 1878-1956, (U.S.) I'll Be With You in Apple Blossom Time; Take Me Out to the Ball Game.
Harry von Tilzer, 1872-1946, (U.S.) Only a Bird in a Gilded Cage; On a Sunday Afternoon.
Fats Waller, 1904-43, (U.S.) Honeysuckle Rose; Ain't Misbehavin'.

Harry Warren, 1893-1981, (U.S.) You're My Everything; We're in the Money; I Only Have Eyes for You.
Jimmy Webb, b 1946, (U.S.) Up, Up and Away; By the Time I Get to Phoenix; Didn't We?; Wichita Lineman.
Kurt Weill, 1900-50, (Ger.-U.S.) *Threepenny Opera; Lady in the Dark; Knickerbocker Holiday; One Touch of Venus.*
Percy Wenrich, 1887-1952, (U.S.) When You Wore a Tulip; Moonlight Bay; Put On Your Old Gray Bonnet.
Richard A. Whiting, 1891-1938, (U.S.) Till We Meet Again; Sleepytime Gal; Beyond the Blue Horizon; My Ideal.
John Williams, b 1932, (U.S.) *Jaws; E.T.; Star Wars* series; *Raiders of the Lost Ark* series.
Meredith Willson, 1902-84, (U.S.) *The Music Man.*
Stevie Wonder, b 1950, (U.S.) You Are the Sunshine of My Life; Signed, Sealed, Delivered, I'm Yours.
Vincent Youmans, 1898-1946, (U.S.) *Two Little Girls in Blue; Wildflower; No, No, Nanette; Hit the Deck; Rainbow; Smiles.*

Lyricists

Howard Ashman, 1950-91, (U.S.) Little Shop of Horrors; The Little Mermaid.
Johnny Burke, 1908-84, (U.S.) Misty; Imagination.
Irving Caesar, 1895-1996, (U.S.) Swanee; Tea for Two; Just a Gigolo.
Sammy Cahn, 1913-93, (U.S.) High Hopes; Love and Marriage; The Second Time Around; It's Magic.
Leonard Cohen, b 1934, (Can.) Suzanne; Stranger Song.
Betty Comden, b 1919, (U.S.) and **Adolph Green,** 1915-2002, (U.S.) The Party's Over; Just in Time; New York, New York.
Hal David, b 1921, (U.S.) What the World Needs Now Is Love.
Buddy De Sylva, 1895-1950, (U.S.) When Day Is Done; Look for the Silver Lining; April Showers.
Howard Dietz, 1896-1983, (U.S.) Dancing in the Dark; You and the Night and the Music; That's Entertainment.
Al Dubin, 1891-1945, (U.S.) Tiptoe Through the Tulips; Anniversary Waltz; Lullaby of Broadway.
Fred Ebb, b 1936-2004, (U.S.) Cabaret; Zorba; Woman of the Year, Chicago.
Ray Evans, b 1915 (U.S.) Mona Lisa; Que Sera, Sera.
Dorothy Fields, 1905-74, (U.S.) On the Sunny Side of the Street; Don't Blame Me; The Way You Look Tonight.
Ira Gershwin, 1896-1983, (U.S.) The Man I Love; Fascinating Rhythm; S'Wonderful; Embraceable You.
William S. Gilbert, 1836-1911, (Br.) The Mikado; H.M.S. Pinafore; Pirates of Penzance.
Gerry Goffin, b 1939, (U.S.) Will You Love Me Tomorrow; Take Good Care of My Baby; Up on the Roof.

Mack Gordon, 1905-59, (Pol.-U.S.) You'll Never Know; The More I See You; Chattanooga Choo-Choo.
Oscar Hammerstein II, 1895-1960, (U.S.) Ol' Man River; Oklahoma!; Carousel.
E. Y. (Yip) Harburg, 1898-1981, (U.S.) Brother, Can You Spare a Dime; April in Paris; Over the Rainbow.
Sheldon Harnick, b 1924, (U.S.) Fiddler on the Roof, She Loves Me.
Lorenz Hart, 1895-1943, (U.S.) .) Isn't It Romantic; Blue Moon; Lover; Manhattan; My Funny Valentine.
DuBose Heyward, 1885-1940, (U.S.) Summertime.
Gus Kahn, 1886-1941, (U.S.) Memories; Ain't We Got Fun.
Alan J. Lerner, 1918-86, (U.S.) Brigadoon; My Fair Lady; Camelot; Gigi; On a Clear Day You Can See Forever.
Johnny Mercer, 1909-76, (U.S.) Blues in the Night; Come Rain or Come Shine; Laura; That Old Black Magic.
Bob Merrill, 1921-98, (U.S.) People; (How Much Is That) Doggie in the Window.
Jack Norworth, 1879-1959, (U.S.) Take Me Out to the Ball Game; Shine On Harvest Moon.
Mitchell Parish, 1901-93, (U.S.) Stardust; Stairway to the Stars.
Andy Razaf, 1895-1973, (U.S.) Honeysuckle Rose; Ain't Misbehavin'; S'posin'.
Leo Robin, 1900-84, (U.S.) Thanks for the Memory; Hooray for Love; Diamonds Are a Girl's Best Friend.
Paul Francis Webster, 1907-84, (U.S.) Secret Love; The Shadow of Your Smile; Love Is a Many-Splendored Thing.
Jack Yellen, 1892-1991, (U.S.) Down by the O-Hi-O; Ain't She Sweet; Happy Days Are Here Again.

Blues and Jazz Artists of the Past

Julian "Cannonball" Adderley, 1928-75, alto sax
Nat Adderley, 1931-2000, cornet
Henry "Red" Allen, 1908-67, trumpet
Louis "Satchmo" Armstrong, 1901-71, trumpet, singer, bandleader
Albert Ayler, 1936-70, tenor sax, alto sax
Mildred Bailey, 1907-51, singer
Chet Baker, 1929-88, trumpet, singer
Count Basie, 1904-84, bandleader, piano, composer
Sidney Bechet, 1897-1959, soprano sax, clarinet
Bix Beiderbecke, 1903-31, cornet, composer, piano
Bunny Berigan, 1908-42, trumpet
Barney Bigard, 1906-80, clarinet
Eubie Blake, 1883-1983, composer, piano
Art Blakey, 1919-90, drums, bandleader
Jimmy Blanton, 1921-42, bass
Charles "Buddy" Bolden, 1877-1931, cornet, pioneer bandleader
Lester Bowie, 1941-99, trumpet, composer, bandleader
Big Bill Broonzy, 1893-1958, blues singer, guitar
Clifford Brown, 1930-56, trumpet
Ray Brown, 1926-2002, bass
Don Byas, 1912-72, tenor sax
Charlie Byrd, 1925-99, guitarist; popularized bossa nova
Cab Calloway, 1907-94, bandleader, singer
Harry Carney, 1910-74, baritone sax, clarinet
Betty Carter, 1930-98, jazz singer
Sidney "Big Sid" Catlett, 1910-51, drums
Doc Cheatham, 1905-97, trumpet
Don Cherry, 1936-95, trumpet
Charlie Christian, 1916-42, guitar
Kenny "Klook" Clarke, 1914-85, drums
Buck Clayton, 1911-91, trumpet
Al Cohn, 1925-88, tenor sax
Cozy Cole, 1909-81, drums
John Coltrane, 1926-67, tenor sax, soprano sax, composer
Eddie Condon, 1905-73, guitar, bandleader
Tadd Dameron, 1917-65, piano, composer
Eddie "Lockjaw" Davis, 1921-86, tenor sax

Miles Davis, 1926-91, trumpet, composer
Wild Bill Davison, 1906-89, cornet
Paul Desmond, 1924-77, alto sax
Vic Dickenson, 1906-84, trombone
Willie Dixon, 1915-92, blues composer, bass
Johnny Dodds, 1892-1940, clarinet
Warren "Baby" Dodds, 1898-1959, drums
Eric Dolphy, 1928-64, alto sax, bass clarinet, flute
Jimmy Dorsey, 1904-57, alto sax, bandleader
Tommy Dorsey, 1905-56, trombone, bandleader
Billy Eckstine, 1914-93, singer, bandleader
Harry "Sweets" Edison, 1915-99, trumpet
Roy Eldridge, 1911-89, trumpet, singer
Duke Ellington, 1899-1974, piano, bandleader, composer
Bill Evans, 1929-80, piano
Gil Evans, 1912-88, composer, arranger, piano
Art Farmer, 1928-99, trumpet, flugelhorn
Ella Fitzgerald, 1917-96, singer
Tommy Flanagan, 1930-2001, piano
Erroll Garner, 1921-77, piano, composer
Stan Getz, 1927-91, tenor sax
Dizzy Gillespie, 1917-93, trumpet, composer, singer
Benny Goodman, 1909-86, clarinet, bandleader
Dexter Gordon, 1923-90, tenor sax
Stéphane Grappelli, 1908-97, violin
Bobby Hackett, 1915-76, trumpet, cornet
Lionel Hampton, 1908-2002, vibraphone, bandleader
W. C. Handy, 1873-1958, composer
Jimmy Harrison, 1900-31, trombone
Coleman Hawkins, 1904-69, tenor sax
Fletcher Henderson, 1898-1952, bandleader, arranger
Woody Herman, 1913-87, clarinet, alto sax, bandleader
Jay C. Higginbotham, 1906-73, trombone
Earl "Fatha" Hines, 1903-83, piano
Milt Hinton, 1910-2000, bass
Al Hirt, 1922-99, trumpet
Johnny Hodges, 1906-70, alto sax
Billie Holiday, 1915-59, singer
John Lee Hooker, 1917-2001, blues guitar, singer

Sam "Lightnin" Hopkins, 1912-82, blues singer, guitar
Howlin' Wolf, 1910-1976, blues singer, harmonica, guitar
Alberta Hunter, 1895-1984, singer
Mahalia Jackson, 1911-72, gospel singer
Milt Jackson, 1923-99, vibraphone
Elmore James, 1918-63, blues singer, guitar
Blind Lemon Jefferson, 1897-1930, blues singer, guitar
Bunk Johnson, 1879-1949, trumpet
J.J. Johnson, 1924-2001, trombone
James P. Johnson, 1891-1955, piano, composer
Robert Johnson, 1912-38, blues singer, guitar
Elvin Jones, 1927-2004, drums
Jo Jones, 1911-85, drums
Philly Joe Jones, 1923-85, drums
Thad Jones, 1923-86, cornet, bandleader, composer
Scott Joplin, 1868-1917, ragtime composer
Louis Jordan, 1908-75, singer, alto sax
Stan Kenton, 1911-79, bandleader, composer, piano
Barney Kessel, 1923-2004, guitar
Albert King, 1923-92, blues guitar
John Kirby, 1908-52, bandleader, bass
Rahsaan Roland Kirk, 1936-77, saxophones, composer
Gene Krupa, 1909-73, drums, bandleader
Scott LaFaro, 1936-61, bass
Huddie Ledbetter (Lead Belly), 1888-1949, folk and blues singer, guitar
John Lewis, 1920-2001, piano, Modern Jazz Quartet founder
Mel Lewis, 1929-90, drums, bandleader
Jimmie Lunceford, 1902-47, bandleader
Machito (Frank Grillo), 1912-84, Latin percussion, singer, bandleader
Shelly Manne, 1920-84, drums, bandleader
Jimmy McPartland, 1907-91, trumpet
Carmen McRae, 1920-94, singer
Glenn Miller, 1904-44, trombone, bandleader
Charles Mingus, 1922-79, bass, composer, bandleader
Thelonious Monk, 1917-82, piano, composer
Wes Montgomery, 1925-68, guitar
"Jelly Roll" Morton, 1885-1941, composer, piano
Bennie Moten, 1894-1935, piano, bandleader
Gerry Mulligan, 1927-96, baritone sax, composer
"Fats" Navarro, 1923-50, trumpet
Red Nichols, 1905-65, cornet, bandleader
Red Norvo, 1908-99, vibraphone, xylophone, bandleader
Arturo "Chico" O'Farrill, 1921-2001, Latin composer, arranger
King Oliver, 1885-1938, cornet, band leader
Sy Oliver, 1910-88, arranger, composer
Kid Ory, 1886-1973, trombone, bandleader
Oran "Hot Lips" Page, 1908-54, trumpet, singer
Charlie "Bird" Parker, 1920-55, alto sax, composer
Joe Pass, 1929-94, guitar
Art Pepper, 1925-82, alto sax
Oscar Pettiford, 1922-60, bass
Bud Powell, 1924-66, piano

Chano Pozo, 1915-48, Cuban percussion, singer
Louis Prima, 1911-78, singer, bandleader
Tito Puente, 1923-2000, Latin percussion, bandleader
Gertrude "Ma" Rainey, 1886-1939, blues singer
Don Redman, 1900-64, composer, arranger
Django Reinhardt, 1910-53, guitar
Buddy Rich, 1917-87, drums
Red Rodney, 1928-94, trumpet
Jimmy Rowles, 1918-96, piano
Jimmy Rushing, 1903-72, blues and jazz singer
Pee Wee Russell, 1906-69, clarinet
Zoot Sims, 1925-85, tenor sax
Zutty Singleton, 1898-1975, drums
Bessie Smith, 1894-1937, blues singer
Clarence "Pinetop" Smith, 1904-29, piano, singer; boogie woogie pioneer
Willie "The Lion" Smith, 1897-1973, piano, composer
Muggsy Spanier, 1906-67, cornet
Sonny Stitt, 1924-82, tenor sax, alto sax
Billy Strayhorn, 1915-67, composer, piano; Duke Ellington collaborator
Sun Ra, 1915?-93, bandleader, piano, composer
Art Tatum, 1910-56, piano
Art Taylor, 1929-95, drums
Jack Teagarden, 1905-64, trombone, singer
Mel Torme, 1925-99, singer ("the Velvet Fog")
Dave Tough, 1908-48, drums
Lennie Tristano, 1919-78, piano, composer
Joe Turner, 1911-85, blues singer
Sarah Vaughan, 1924-90, singer
Joe Venuti, 1904-78, violin
T-Bone Walker, 1910-75, blues guitar
Thomas "Fats" Waller, 1904-43, piano, singer, composer
Dinah Washington, 1924-63, singer
Grover Washington Jr., 1943-99, pop-jazz sax, composer
Ethel Waters, 1896-1977, jazz and blues singer
Muddy Waters, 1915-83, blues singer, songwriter
Julius Watkins, 1921-77, French horn
Chick Webb, 1902-39, bandleader, drums
Ben Webster, 1909-73, tenor sax
Junior Wells, 1934-98, blues singer, harmonica
Paul Whiteman, 1890-1967, bandleader
Charles "Cootie" Williams, 1910-85, trumpet, bandleader
Joe Williams, 1918-99, singer
Mary Lou Williams, 1910-81, piano, composer
Tony Williams, 1945-97, drums
John Lee "Sonny Boy" Williamson, 1914-48, blues singer, harmonica
Sonny Boy Williamson ("Rice" Miller), 1900?-65, blues singer, harmonica
Teddy Wilson, 1912-86, piano
Kai Winding, 1922-83, trombone
Jimmy Yancey, 1894-1951, piano
Lester "Pres" Young, 1909-59, tenor sax

Noted Country Music Artists of the Past and Present

Roy Acuff, 1903-92, fiddler, singer, songwriter; "Wabash Cannon Ball"
Alabama (Randy Owen, 1949- ; Jeff Cook, 1949- ; Teddy Gentry, 1952- ; Mark Herndon, 1955-) "Feels So Right"
Eddy Arnold, 1918- , singer, guitarist, the "Tennessee Plowboy"
Chet Atkins, 1924-2001, guitarist, composer, producer, helped create the "Nashville sound"
Gene Autry, 1907-98, first great singing movie cowboy; "Back in the Saddle Again"
Garth Brooks, 1962- , singer, songwriter, "Friends in Low Places"
Brooks & Dunn (Kix Brooks, 1955- ; Ronnie Dunn, 1953-) "Hard Workin' Man"
Boudleaux and Felice Bryant (Boudleau, 1920-87; Felice, 1925-2003), songwriting team; "Hey Joe"
Glen Campbell, 1936- , singer, instrumentalist, TV host; "Gentle on My Mind," "Rhinestone Cowboy"
Mary Chapin Carpenter, 1958- , singer, songwriter; "I Feel Lucky"
Carter Family (original members, "Mother" Maybelle 1909-78; A.P., 1891-1960, Sara, 1898-1979) "Wildwood Flower"
Johnny Cash, 1932-2003, singer, songwriter; "I Walk the Line," "Ring of Fire," "Folsom Prison Blues"
Patsy Cline, 1932-63, singer; "Walkin' After Midnight," "Crazy," "Sweet Dreams"
John Denver, 1943-97, singer, songwriter; "Rocky Mountain High"
Dixie Chicks (Natalie Maines, 1974- ; Martie Seidel, 1969- ; Emily Erwin Robison, 1972-) "Wide Open Spaces," "Fly"
Dale Evans (Lucille Wood Smith), 1912-2001, singer, actress, married Roy Rogers
Flatt & Scruggs (Lester Flatt, 1914-79; Earl Scruggs, 1924-), guitar-banjo duo and soloists; "Foggy Mountain Breakdown"
Red Foley, 1910-68, singer; "Chattanoogie Shoe Shine Boy"

Tennessee Ernie Ford, 1919-91, singer, TV host; "Sixteen Tons"
Lefty Frizzell, 1928-75, singer, guitarist; "Long Black Veil"
Vince Gill, 1957- , singer, songwriter; "When I Call Your Name"
Merle Haggard, 1937- , singer, songwriter; "Okie from Muskogee"
Emmylou Harris, 1947- , singer, songwriter, folk-country crossover artist; "If I Could Only Win Your Love"
Faith Hill, 1967-, singer, songwriter, married Tim McGraw; "Wild One," "This Kiss," "Breathe"
Alan Jackson, 1958- , singer, songwriter, "Where Were You (When the World Stopped Turning)"
Waylon Jennings, 1937-2002, singer, songwriter, "outlaw country" pioneer; "Luckenbach, Texas"
George Jones, 1931- , singer; "He Stopped Loving Her Today"
The Judds (Naomi, 1946- ; Wynonna, 1964-), mother-daughter duo; Wynonna also a solo act
Alison Krauss, 1971- , bluegrass fiddler, singer, bandleader; "When You Say Nothing at All"
Kris Kristofferson, 1936- , singer, songwriter, actor; "Me and Bobby McGee"
Brenda Lee, 1944- , singer; "I'm Sorry"
Patty Loveless, 1957- , singer, songwriter; "How Can I Help You Say Goodbye"
Lyle Lovett, 1957- , singer, songwriter, bandleader, actor; "Cowboy Man"
Loretta Lynn, 1935- , singer, songwriter; "Coal Miner's Daughter"
Kathy Mattea, 1959- , singer, songwriter; "Eighteen Wheels and a Dozen Roses"
Reba McEntire, 1955- , singer, songwriter, actress; "Whoever's in New England"
Tim McGraw, 1967- , singer; "It's Your Love," with wife, Faith Hill
Roger Miller, 1936-92, singer, songwriter; "King of the Road"
Ronnie Milsap, 1944- , singer, songwriter; "There's No Gettin' Over Me"

Bill Monroe, 1911-96, singer, songwriter, mandolin player, "father of bluegrass music"; "Mule Skinner Blues"

Patsy Montana, 1908-96, yodeling/singing cowgirl; "I Want to Be a Cowboy's Sweetheart"

Willie Nelson, 1933- , singer, songwriter, actor; "On the Road Again"

Mark O'Connor, 1961- , fiddler, country-classical crossover composer

Dolly Parton, 1946- , singer, songwriter, actress; "Dollywood" theme park; "Here You Come Again," "9 to 5"

Minnie Pearl, 1912-96, comedienne, Grand Ole Opry star

Charley Pride, 1938- , singer, 1st African-American country star; "Kiss an Angel Good Mornin'"

Jim Reeves, 1923-64, singer, songwriter; "Four Walls"

Charlie Rich, 1932-95, singer, songwriter called the "Silver Fox"; "The Most Beautiful Girl"

LeAnn Rimes, 1982- , singer; "Blue"

Tex Ritter, 1905-74, singer, songwriter; "Jingle, Jangle, Jingle"

Marty Robbins, 1925-82, singer, songwriter; "A White Sport Coat and a Pink Carnation"

Jimmie Rodgers, 1897-1933, singer, songwriter; "T for Texas"

Kenny Rogers, 1938- , singer, songwriter, actor; "The Gambler"

Roy Rogers (Leonard Slye), 1911-98, singer, actor, "King of the Cowboys," sang with Sons of the Pioneers.

Fred Rose, 1898-1954, songwriter, singer, producer; "Blue Eyes Cryin' in the Rain"

Ricky Skaggs, 1954- , singer, songwriter, bandleader; "Don't Cheat in Our Hometown"

Ralph Stanley, 1927- , singer, banjo player, "Man of Constant Sorrow"

George Strait, 1952- , singer, bandleader; "Ace in the Hole"

Merle Travis, 1917-83, singer, guitarist, songwriter; "Divorce Me C.O.D."

Randy Travis, 1959- , singer, songwriter; "Forever and Ever, Amen"

Ernest Tubb, 1914-84, singer, songwriter, guitarist; "Walking the Floor Over You"

Shania Twain, 1965- , singer, songwriter; "You're Still the One"

Conway Twitty, 1933-93, singer, songwriter; "Hello Darlin' "

Dottie West, 1932-91, singer, songwriter; "Here Comes My Baby"

Hank Williams Jr., 1949- , singer, songwriter; "Bocephus"; "All My Rowdy Friends (Have Settled Down)"

Hank Williams Sr., 1923-53, singer, songwriter; "Your Cheatin' Heart"

Bob Wills, 1905-75, Western Swing fiddler, singer, bandleader, songwriter; "New San Antonio Rose"

Tammy Wynette, 1942-98, singer; "Stand By Your Man"

Trisha Yearwood, 1964- , singer, songwriter; "How Do I Live"

Dwight Yoakam, 1957- , singer, songwriter, actor; "Ain't That Lonely Yet"

Dance Figures of the Past

Source: Reviewed by Gary Parks, Reviews editor, *Dance* magazine

Alvin Ailey, 1931-89, (U.S.) modern dancer, choreographer; melded modern dance and Afro-Caribbean techniques.

Frederick Ashton, 1904-88, (Br.) ballet choreographer; director of Great Britain's Royal Ballet, 1963-70.

Fred Astaire, 1899-1987, (U.S.) dancer, actor; teamed with dancer/actress

Ginger Rogers (1911-95) in movie musicals.

George Balanchine, 1904-83, (Russ.-U.S.) ballet choreographer, teacher; most influential exponent of the neoclassical style; founded, with Lincoln Kirstein, School of American Ballet and New York City Ballet.

Carlo Blasis, 1803-78, (It.) ballet dancer, choreographer, writer; his teaching methods are standards of classical dance.

August Bournonville, 1805-79, (Dan.) ballet dancer, choreographer, teacher; exuberant, light style.

Gisella Caccialanza, 1914-97, (U.S.) ballerina, charter member of Balanchine's American Ballet.

Enrico Cecchetti, 1850-1928, (It.) ballet dancer, leading dancer of Russia's Imperial Ballet; his technique was basis for Britain's Imperial Soc. of Teachers of Dancing.

Gower Champion, 1921-80, (U.S.) dancer, choreographer, director; with his wife **Marge,** b 1923, (U.S.) choreographed, danced in Broadway musicals and films.

John Cranko, 1927-73, (S. African) choreographer; created narrative ballets based on literary works.

Agnes de Mille, 1909-93, (U.S.) ballerina, choreographer; known for using American themes, she choreographed the ballet *Rodeo* and the musical *Oklahoma!*

Dame Ninette DeValois, 1898-2001, (Br.) choreographer, founding director London's Royal Ballet; *The Rake's Progress.*

Sergei Diaghilev, 1872-1929, (Russ.) impresario; founded Les Ballet Russes; saw ballet as an art unifying dance, drama, music, and decor.

Alexandra Danilova, 1903-97, (Russ.) ballerina; noted teacher at the School of American Ballet.

Isadora Duncan, 1877-1927, (U.S.) expressive dancer who united free movement with serious music; one of the founders of modern dance.

Fanny Elssler, 1810-84, (Austrian) ballerina of the Romantic era; known for dramatic skill, sensual style.

Michel Fokine, 1880-1942, (Russ.) ballet dancer, choreographer, teacher; rejected strict classicism in favor of dramatically expressive style.

Margot Fonteyn, 1919-91, (Br.) prima ballerina, Royal Ballet of Great Britain; famed performance partner of Rudolf Nureyev.

Bob Fosse, 1927-87, (U.S.) jazz dancer, choreographer, director; Broadway musicals and film.

Serge Golovine, 1924-98, (Fr.) ballet dancer with Grand Ballet du Marquis de Cuevas; choreographer.

Martha Graham, 1893-1991, (U.S.) modern dancer, choreographer; created and codified their own dramatic technique.

Martha Hill, 1901-95, (U.S.) educator; leading figure in modern dance; founded American Dance Festival.

Gregory Hines, 1946-2003, (U.S.) tap-dance innovator and master of improvisation.

Doris Humphrey, 1895-1958, (U.S.) modern dancer, choreographer, writer, teacher.

Robert Joffrey, 1930-88, (U.S.) ballet dancer, choreographer; cofounded with **Gerald Arpino,** b 1928, (U.S.), the Joffrey Ballet.

Kurt Jooss, 1901-79, (Ger.) choreographer, teacher; created expressionist works using modern and classical techniques.

Tamara Karsavina, 1885-1978, (Russ.) prima ballerina of Russia's Imperial Ballet and Diaghilev's Ballets Russes; partner of Nijinsky.

Nora Kaye, 1920-87, (U.S.) ballerina with Metropolitan Opera Ballet and Ballet Theater (now American Ballet Theatre).

Lincoln Kirstein, 1907-96 (U.S.) brought ballet as an art form to U.S.; founded, with George Balanchine, School of American Ballet and New York City Ballet.

Serge Lifar, 1905-86, (Russ.-Fr.) prem. danseur, choreographer; director of dance at Paris Opera, 1930-45, 1947-58.

José Limón, 1908-72, (Mex.-U.S.) modern dancer, choreographer, teacher; developed technique based on Humphrey.

Catherine Littlefield, 1908-51, (U.S.) ballerina, choreographer, teacher; pioneer of American ballet.

Léonide Massine, 1896-1979, (Russ.-U.S.) ballet dancer, choreographer; his "symphonic ballet" used concert music previously thought unsuitable for dance.

Kenneth MacMillan, 1929-92, (Br.) dancer, choreographer; directed Royal Ballet of Great Britain 1970-77.

Vaslav Nijinsky, 1890-50, (Russ.) prem. danseur, choreographer; leading member of Diaghilev's Ballets Russes; his ballets were revolutionary for their time.

Alwin Nikolais, 1910-93, (U.S.) modern choreographer; created dance theater utilizing mixed media effects.

Jean-George Noverre, 1727-1810, (Fr.) ballet choreographer, teacher, writer; "Shakespeare of the Dance."

Rudolf Nureyev, 1938-93, (Russ.) prem. danseur, choreographer; leading male dancer of his generation; director of dance at Paris Opera, 1983-89.

Ruth Page, 1903-91, (U.S.) ballerina, choreographer; danced and directed ballet at Chicago Lyric Opera.

Anna Pavlova, 1881-1931, (Russ.) prima ballerina; toured with her own company to world acclaim.

Marius Petipa, 1818-1910, (Fr.) ballet dancer, choreographer; ballet master of the Imperial Ballet; established Russian classicism as leading style of late 19th cent.

Pearl Primus, 1919-95, (Trinidad-U.S.) modern dancer, choreographer, scholar; combined African, Caribbean, and African-American styles.

Jerome Robbins, 1918-98, (U.S.) choreographer, director, dancer; *The King and I, West Side Story, Fiddler on the Roof; Gypsy.*

Bill (Bojangles) Robinson, 1878-1949, (U.S.) famed tap dancer; called King of Tapology on stage and screen.

Ruth St. Denis, 1877-1968, (U.S.) influential interpretive dancer, choreographer, teacher.

Ted Shawn, 1891-1972, (U.S.) modern dancer, choreographer; formed dance company and school with Ruth St. Denis; established Jacob's Pillow Dance Festival.

Marie Taglioni, 1804-84, (It.) ballerina, teacher; in title role of *La Sylphide* established image of the ethereal ballerina.

Antony Tudor, 1908-87, (Br.) choreographer, teacher; exponent of the "psychological ballet."

Galina Ulanova, 1910-98, (Russ.) revered ballerina with Bolshoi Ballet.

Agrippina Vaganova, 1879-1951, (Russ.) ballet teacher, director; codified Soviet ballet technique that developed virtuosity; called "queen of variations."

Mary Wigman, 1886-1973, (Ger.) modern dancer, choreographer, teacher; influenced European expressionist dance.

Opera Singers of the Past

Frances Alda, 1883-1952, (N.Z.) soprano
Pasquale Amato, 1878-1942, (It.) baritone
Marian Anderson, 1897-1993, (U.S.) contralto
Jussi Björling, 1911-60, (Swed.) tenor
Lucrezia Bori, 1887-1960, (It.) soprano
Maria Callas, 1923-77, (U.S.) soprano
Emma Calvé, 1858-1942, (Fr.) soprano
Enrico Caruso, 1873-1921, (It.) tenor
Feodor Chaliapin, 1873-1938, (Russ.) bass
Boris Christoff, 1914-93, (Bulg.) bass
Franco Corelli, 1921-2003, (It.) tenor
Giuseppe De Luca, 1876-1950, (It.) baritone
Fernando De Lucia, 1860-1925, (It.) tenor
Edouard De Reszke, 1853-1917, (Pol.) bass
Jean De Reszke, 1850-1925, (Pol.) tenor
Emmy Destinn, 1878-1930, (Czech.) soprano
Emma Eames, 1865-1952, (U.S.) soprano
(Carlo Broschi) Farinelli, 1705-82, (It.) castrato
Geraldine Farrar, 1882-1967, (U.S.) soprano
Eileen Farrell, 1920-2002, (U.S.) soprano
Kathleen Ferrier, 1912-53, (Eng.) contralto
Kirsten Flagstad, 1895-1962, (Nor.) soprano
Olive Fremstad, 1871-1951, (Swed.-U.S.) soprano
Amelita Galli-Curci, 1882-1963, (It.) soprano
Mary Garden, 1874-1967, (Br.) soprano
Nicolai Ghiaurov, 1929-2004, (Bulg.) bass
Beniamino Gigli, 1890-1957, (It.) tenor
Tito Gobbi, 1913-84, (It.) baritone
Giulia Grisi, 1811-69, (It.) soprano
Frieda Hempel, 1885-1955, (Ger.) soprano
Jerome Hines, 1921-2003, (U.S.) bass
Hans Hotter, 1909-2003, (Ger.) bass-baritone
Maria Jeritza, 1887-1982, (Czech.) soprano
Alexander Kipnis, 1891-1978, (Russ.-U.S.) bass
Dorothy Kirsten, 1910-1992, (U.S.) soprano
Alfredo Kraus, 1927-99, (Sp.) tenor

Luigi Lablache, 1794-1858, (It.) bass
Lilli Lehmann, 1848-1929, (Ger.) soprano
Lotte Lehmann, 1888-1976, (Ger.-U.S.) soprano
Jenny Lind, 1820-87, (Swed.) soprano
Maria Malibran, 1808-36, (Sp.) mezzo-soprano
Giovanni Martinelli, 1885-1969, (It.) tenor
John McCormack, 1884-1945, (Ir.) tenor
Nellie Melba, 1861-1931, (Austral.) soprano
Lauritz Melchior, 1890-1973, (Dan.) tenor
Zinka Milanov, 1906-89, (Yugo.) soprano
Lillian Nordica, 1857-1914, (U.S.) soprano
Giuditta Pasta, 1797-1865, (It.) soprano
Adelina Patti, 1843-1919, (It.) soprano
Peter Pears, 1910-86, (Eng.) tenor
Jan Peerce, 1904-84, (U.S.) tenor
Ezio Pinza, 1892-1957, (It.) bass
Lily Pons, 1898-1976, (Fr.) soprano
Rosa Ponselle, 1897-1981, (U.S.) soprano
Hermann Prey, 1929-98, (Ger.) baritone.
Elisabeth Rethberg, 1894-1976, (Ger.) soprano
Giovanni Battista Rubini, 1794-1854, (It.) tenor
Leonie Rysanek, 1926-1998, (Austrian) soprano
Bidú Sayão, 1902-99, (Braz.) soprano
Friedrich Schorr, 1888-1953, (Hung.) bass-baritone
Marcella Sembrich, 1858-1935, (Pol.) soprano
Eleanor Steber, 1916-90, (U.S.) soprano
Ferrucio Tagliavini, 1913-95, (It.) tenor
Luisa Tetrazzini, 1871-1940, (It.) soprano
Lawrence Tibbett, 1896-1960, (U.S.) baritone
Tatiana Troyanos, 1938-93, (U.S.) mezzo-soprano
Richard Tucker, 1913-75, (U.S.) tenor
Pauline Viardot, 1821-1910, (Fr.) mezzo-soprano
William Warfield, 1920-2002, (U.S.) bass-baritone
Leonard Warren, 1911-60, (U.S.) baritone
Ljuba Welitsch, 1913-96, (Bulg.) soprano
Wolfgang Windgassen, 1914-74, (Ger.) tenor

Rock and Roll, Rhythm and Blues, and Rap Artists

Titles in quotation marks are singles; others are albums.

Aaliyah: "More than a Woman"
Paula Abdul: "Straight Up"
***AC/DC (2003):** "Back in Black"
Bryan Adams: "Cuts Like a Knife"
***Aerosmith (2001):** "Sweet Emotion"
Christina Aguilera: "What a Girl Wants"
Alice In Chains: "Heaven Beside You"
***The Allman Brothers Band (1995):** "Ramblin' Man"
***The Animals (1994):** "House of the Rising Sun"
Paul Anka: "Lonely Boy"
Fiona Apple: "Criminal"
Ashanti: "Foolish"
The Association: "Cherish"
Frankie Avalon: "Venus"
The B-52s: "Love Shack"
Bachman Turner Overdrive: "Takin' Care of Business"
Backstreet Boys: "I Want it That Way"
Bad Company: "Can't Get Enough"
Erykah Badu: "On and On"
***La Vern Baker (1991):** "I Cried a Tear"
***Hank Ballard and the Midnighters (1990):** "Work With Me, Annie"
***The Band (1994):** "The Weight"
Barenaked Ladies: "One Week"
***The Beach Boys (1988):** "Good Vibrations"
Beastie Boys: "(You Gotta) Fight for Your Right (to Party)"
***The Beatles (1988):** *Sgt. Pepper's Lonely Hearts Club Band*
Beck: "Loser"
***The Bee Gees (1997):** "Stayin' Alive"
Pat Benatar: "Hit Me With Your Best Shot"
Ben Folds Five: "Brick"
***Chuck Berry (1986):** "Johnny B. Goode"
The Big Bopper: "Chantilly Lace"
Björk: "Human Behavior"
The Black Crowes: "Hard to Handle"
Black Sabbath: "Paranoid"
***Bobby "Blue" Bland (1992):** "Turn On Your Love Light"
Mary J. Blige: *My Life*
Blind Faith: "Can't Find My Way Home"
Blink-182: "All the Small Things"
Blondie: "Heart of Glass"
Blood, Sweat, and Tears: "Spinning Wheel"
Blues Traveler: "Run-Around"
Gary "U.S." Bonds: "Quarter to Three"
Bon Jovi: "Livin' on a Prayer"
***Booker T. and the M.G.'s (1992):** "Green Onions"
Earl Bostic: "Flamingo"
Boston: "More Than A Feeling"
***David Bowie (1996):** "Space Oddity"

Boyz II Men: "I'll Make Love to You"
Toni Braxton: "Un-Break My Heart"
***James Brown (1986):** "Papa's Got a Brand New Bag"
***Ruth Brown (1993):** "Lucky Lips"
***Jackson Browne (2004):** "Doctor My Eyes"
***Buffalo Springfield (1997):** "For What It's Worth"
***Jimmy Buffett:** "Margaritaville"
***Solomon Burke (2001):** "Over and Over (Huggin' and Lovin')"
Bush: "Glycerine"
***The Byrds (1991):** "Turn! Turn! Turn!"
Mariah Carey: "Vision of Love"
The Carpenters: "(They Long to Be) Close to You"
The Cars: "Shake It Up"
***Johnny Cash (1992):** "I Walk the Line"
***Ray Charles (1986):** "Georgia on My Mind"
Cheap Trick: "Surrender"
Chicago: "Saturday in the Park"
Chubby Checker: "The Twist"
***Eric Clapton (2000):** "Layla"
***The Clash (2003):** "Rock the Casbah"
***The Coasters (1987):** "Yakety Yak"
***Eddie Cochran (1987):** "Summertime Blues"
Joe Cocker: "With a Little Help From My Friends"
Coldplay: "Politik"
Collective Soul: "The World I Know"
Phil Collins: "Against All Odds"
***Sam Cooke (1986):** "You Send Me"
Coolio: "Gangsta's Paradise"
Alice Cooper: "School's Out"
***Elvis Costello and the Attractions (2003):** "Alison"
Counting Crows: "Mr. Jones"
***Cream (1993):** "Sunshine of Your Love"
Creed: "Arms Wide Open"
***Creedence Clearwater Revival (1993):** "Proud Mary"
***Crosby, Stills, and Nash (1997):** "Suite: Judy Blue Eyes"
Sheryl Crow: "All I Want to Do"
The Cure: "Boys Don't Cry"
The Crystals: "Da Doo Ron Ron"
Cypress Hill: "Insane in the Brain"
Danny and the Juniors: "At the Hop"
***Bobby Darin (1990):** "Splish Splash"
Spencer Davis Group: "Gimme Some Lovin' "
Deep Purple: "Smoke on the Water"
Def Leppard: "Photograph"
***The Dells (2004):** "Oh, What a Night"
Depeche Mode: "Strange Love"
Destiny's Child: "Survivor"
***Bo Diddley (1987):** "Who Do You Love?"

'Dion and the Belmonts (1989): "A Teenager in Love"
Celine Dion: "Because You Loved Me"
Dire Straits: "Money for Nothing"
DMX: "What's My Name"
'Fats Domino (1986): "Blueberry Hill"
Donovan: "Mellow Yellow"
The Doobie Brothers: "What a Fool Believes"
'The Doors (1993): "Light My Fire"
Dr. Dre: "Nothin' But a 'G' Thang"
'The Drifters (1988): "Save the Last Dance for Me"
Duran Duran: "Hungry Like the Wolf"
'Bob Dylan (1988): "Like a Rolling Stone"
'The Eagles (1998): "Hotel California"
'Earth, Wind, and Fire (2000): "Shining Star"
'Duane Eddy (1994): "Rebel-Rouser"
Missy Elliott: "Sock It 2 Me"
Emerson, Lake, and Palmer: "Lucky Man"
Eminem: "The Real Slim Shady"
En Vogue: "Hold On"
Enya: *Shepherd Moons*
The Eurythmics: "Sweet Dreams (Are Made of This)"
Everclear: "Father Of Mine"
'The Everly Brothers (1986): "Wake Up, Little Susie"
50 Cent (Curtis Jackson): *Get Rich Or Die Tryin'*
The Five Satins: "In the Still of the Night"
'The Flamingos (2001): "I Only Have Eyes for You"
'Fleetwood Mac (1998): *Rumours*
The Foo Fighters: "I'll Stick Around"
Foreigner: "Double Vision"
'The Four Seasons (1990): "Sherry"
'The Four Tops (1990): "I Can't Help Myself (Sugar Pie, Honey Bunch)"
'Aretha Franklin (1987): "Respect"
Nelly Furtado: "I'm Like a Bird"
Peter Gabriel: "Shock the Monkey"
Marvin Gaye (1987): "I Heard It Through the Grapevine"
Genesis: "No Reply at All"
Goo Goo Dolls: "Iris"
Grand Funk Railroad: "We're an American Band"
Grand Master Flash and the Furious Five: "The Message"
'The Grateful Dead (1994): "Uncle John's Band"
Macy Gray: "I Try"
'Al Green (1995): "Let's Stay Together"
Green Day: "Time of Your Life"
The Guess Who: "American Woman"
Guns N' Roses: "Sweet Child o' Mine"
'Bill Haley and His Comets (1987): "Rock Around the Clock"
Hall and Oates: "Kiss on My List"
Hanson: "MMMBop"
Juliana Hatfield: "Spin the Bottle"
'Isaac Hayes (2002): "Theme from 'Shaft'"
Heart: "Barracuda"
'Jimi Hendrix (1992): "Purple Haze"
Lauryn Hill: "Doo-Wop (That Thing)"
Hole: "Doll Parts"
The Hollies: "Long Cool Woman (In a Black Dress)"
'Buddy Holly (1986): "Peggy Sue"
'John Lee Hooker (1991): "Boogie Chillen"
Hootie and the Blowfish: *Cracked Rear View*
Whitney Houston: "I Will Always Love You"
'The Impressions (1991): "For Your Precious Love"
Indigo Girls: "Closer to Fine"
INXS: "Need You Tonight"
'The Isley Brothers (1992): "It's Your Thing"
'The Jackson Five (1997): "ABC"
Janet Jackson: *Rhythm Nation*
'Michael Jackson (2001): *Thriller*
'Etta James (1993): "At Last"
Tommy James & The Shondells: "Crimson and Clover"
Jane's Addiction: "Jane Says"
Ja Rule: *Venni, Vetti, Vecci*
Jay and the Americans: "This Magic Moment"
Jay-Z: "Can I Live"
'Jefferson Airplane (1996): "White Rabbit"
Jethro Tull: *Aqualung*
Joan Jett: "I Love Rock 'n' Roll"
Jewel: "You Were Meant for Me"
'Billy Joel (1999): "Piano Man"
'Elton John (1994): "Candle in the Wind"
'Little Willie John (1996): "Sleep"
'Janis Joplin (1995): "Me and Bobby McGee"
Journey: "Don't Stop Believin'"
K.C. and the Sunshine Band: "Get Down Tonight"
R. Kelly: "I Can't Sleep Baby (If I)"
Alicia Keys: "Fallin'"
Kid Rock: "Cowboy"
'B.B. King (1987): "The Thrill Is Gone"
Carole King: *Tapestry*
'The Kinks (1990): "You Really Got Me"

Kiss: "Rock 'n' Roll All Night"
'Gladys Knight and the Pips (1996): "Midnight Train to Georgia"
Korn: "Blind"
Lenny Kravitz: "Are You Gonna Go My Way?"
'Led Zeppelin (1995): "Stairway to Heaven"
'Brenda Lee (2002): "I'm Sorry"
'John Lennon (1994): "Imagine"
'Jerry Lee Lewis (1986): "Whole Lotta Shakin' Going On"
Lil' Kim: "No Matter What They Say"
Limp Bizkit: "Break Stuff"
Linkin Park: "One Step Closer"
Little Anthony and the Imperials: "Tears on My Pillow"
'Little Richard (1986): "Tutti Frutti"
Live: "Lightning Crashes"
L. L. Cool J: "Mama Said Knock You Out"
Jennifer Lopez: "Love Don't Cost a Thing"
'The Lovin' Spoonful (2000): "Summer in the City"
'Frankie Lymon and the Teenagers (1993): "Why Do Fools Fall in Love?"
Lynyrd Skynyrd: "Free Bird"
Madonna: "Material Girl"
'The Mamas and the Papas (1998): "Monday, Monday"
Aimee Mann: "Save Me"
Marilyn Manson: "Beautiful People"
'Bob Marley (1994): *Exodus*
'Martha and the Vandellas (1995): "Dancin' in the Streets"
The Marvelettes: "Please, Mr. Postman"
Matchbox 20: "Push"
Dave Matthews Band: "Don't Drink the Water"
'Curtis Mayfield (1999): "Superfly"
'Paul McCartney (1999): "Band on the Run"
Don McLean: "American Pie"
'Clyde McPhatter (1987): "A Lover's Question"
Meat Loaf: "Paradise by the Dashboard Light"
John (Cougar) Mellencamp: "Jack and Diane"
Men at Work: "Who Can It Be Now?"
Metallica: "Enter Sandman"
George Michael: "Faith"
'Joni Mitchell (1997): "Both Sides Now"
Moby: "Bodyrock"
The Monkees: "I'm a Believer"
Moody Blues: "Nights in White Satin"
'The Moonglows (2000): "Blue Velvet"
Alanis Morissette: "Ironic"
'Van Morrison (1993): "Brown-Eyed Girl"
Nelly: *Country Grammar*
'Ricky Nelson (1987): "Hello, Mary Lou"
Nine Inch Nails: "Closer"
Nirvana: *Nevermind*
No Doubt: *Rock Steady*
The Notorious B.I.G.: "Mo Money Mo Problems"
'N Sync: "Bye, Bye, Bye"
Oasis: "Wonderwall"
The Offspring: "Pretty Fly (for a White Guy)"
'Roy Orbison (1987): "Oh, Pretty Woman"
Ozzy Osbourne: "Crazy Train"
'Parliament/Funkadelic (1997): "One Nation Under a Groove"
Pearl Jam: "Jeremy"
'Carl Perkins (1987): "Blue Suede Shoes"
Peter, Paul, and Mary: "Leaving on a Jet Plane"
'Tom Petty and the Heartbreakers (2002): "Refugee"
Liz Phair: *Exile in Guyville*
Phish: "Sample in a Jar"
'Wilson Pickett (1991): "Land of 1,000 Dances"
Pink: *Missundazstood!*
'Pink Floyd (1996): *The Wall*
'Gene Pitney (2002): "Only Love Can Break a Heart"
'The Platters (1990): "The Great Pretender"
Poco: "Crazy Love"
'The Police (2003): "Every Breath You Take"
Iggy Pop: "Lust for Life"
'Elvis Presley (1986): "Love Me Tender"
The Pretenders: "Brass in Pocket"
'Lloyd Price (1998): "Stagger Lee"
'Prince (The Artist) (2004): "Purple Rain"
Procol Harum: "A Whiter Shade of Pale"
Public Enemy: "Fight the Power"
Puff Daddy and the Family: *No Way Out*
'Queen (2001): "Bohemian Rhapsody"
Radiohead: "Creep"
Rage Against the Machine: "Bulls on Parade"
'Bonnie Raitt (2000): "Something to Talk About"
'The Ramones (2002): "I Wanna Be Sedated"
'Otis Redding (1989): "(Sittin' on) the Dock of the Bay"
Red Hot Chili Peppers: "Under the Bridge"
'Jimmy Reed (1991): "Ain't That Loving You, Baby?"
Lou Reed: "Walk on the Wild Side"
R.E.M.: "Losing My Religion"
REO Speedwagon: "Can't Fight This Feeling"

Busta Rhymes: "What's It Gonna Be?"
*The Righteous Brothers (2003): "You've Lost That Lovin' Feelin'"
Johnny Rivers: "Poor Side of Town"
*Smokey Robinson and the Miracles (1987): "Shop Around"
*The Rolling Stones (1989): "Satisfaction"
The Ronettes: "Be My Baby"
Linda Ronstadt: "You're No Good"
Run-D.M.C.: "Raisin' Hell"
Rush: "Tom Sawyer"
Sade: "Smooth Operator"
Salt-N-Pepa: "Shoop"
*Sam and Dave (1992): "Soul Man"
*Santana (1998): "Black Magic Woman"
Seal: "Kiss From a Rose"
Neil Sedaka: "Breaking Up Is Hard to Do"
*Bob Seger (2004): "Old Time Rock & Roll"
The Sex Pistols: "Anarchy in the U.K."
Shaggy: "It Wasn't Me"
Shakira: "Whenever, Wherever"
Tupac Shakur: "How Do U Want It"
*Del Shannon (1999): "Runaway"
*The Shirelles (1996): "Soldier Boy"
Carly Simon: "You're So Vain"
*Paul Simon (2001): "50 Ways to Leave Your Lover"
*Simon and Garfunkel (1990): "Bridge Over Troubled Water"
Sisqo: "Thong Song"
*Sly and the Family Stone (1993): "Everyday People"
Smashing Pumpkins: "Today"
Patti Smith: "Because the Night"
Will Smith: "Gettin' Jiggy With It"
The Smiths: "This Charming Man"
Snoop Dogg: "Gin and Juice"
Sonic Youth: "Bull in the Heather"
Soundgarden: "Black Hole Sun"
Britney Spears: "Hit Me Baby One More Time"
Spice Girls: "Wannabe"
*Dusty Springfield (1999): "I Only Want to Be With You"
*Bruce Springsteen (1999): "Born to Run"
Squeeze (2001): "Tempted"
*Staple Singers (1999): "I'll Take You There"
*Steely Dan (2001): "Rikki Don't Lose That Number"
Steppenwolf: "Born to Be Wild"
*Rod Stewart (1994): "Maggie Mae"

Sting: "If You Love Somebody, Set Them Free"
Stone Temple Pilots: "Plush"
Styx: "Come Sail Away"
Sublime: "What I Got"
The Sugar Hill Gang: "Rapper's Delight"
Donna Summer: "Bad Girls"
*The Supremes (1988): "Stop! In the Name of Love"
*Talking Heads (2002): "Once in a Lifetime"
*James Taylor (2001): "You've Got a Friend"
*The Temptations (1989): "My Girl"
Three Dog Night: "Joy to the World"
TLC: "Waterfalls"
T. Rex: "Bang a Gong (Get It On)"
*Traffic (2004): Traffic
*Big Joe Turner (1987): "Shake, Rattle & Roll"
*Ike and Tina Turner (1991): "Proud Mary"
*Tina Turner: "What's Love Got to Do With It?"
The Turtles: "Happy Together"
U2: "With or Without You"
Usher: "You Make Me Wanna"
*Ritchie Valens (2001): "La Bamba"
Van Halen: "Running With the Devil"
Stevie Ray Vaughan: "Crossfire"
*The Velvet Underground (1996): "Sweet Jane"
*Gene Vincent[1] (1998): "Be-Bop-A-Lula"
Tom Waits: "Downtown Train"
The Wallflowers: "One Headlight"
Dionne Warwick: "I Say a Little Prayer"
*Muddy Waters (1987): "I Can't Be Satisfied"
Mary Wells: "My Guy"
The White Stripes: "Seven Nation Army"
*The Who (1990): *Tommy*
Lucinda Williams: *Car Wheels on a Gravel Road*
*Jackie Wilson (1987): "That's Why"
*Stevie Wonder (1989): "You Are the Sunshine of My Life"
Wu-Tang Clan: "Protect Ya Neck"
Weird Al Yankovic: Dare to Be Stupid
*The Yardbirds (1992): "For Your Love"
Yes: "Roundabout"
*Neil Young (1995): "Down by the River"
*The Young Rascals/The Rascals (1997): "Good Lovin' "
*Frank Zappa[1]/Mothers of Invention (1995): *Sheik Yerbouti*
*ZZ Top (2004): "Legs"

* Inducted into Rock and Roll Hall of Fame as performer between 1986 and 2004; year is in parentheses. (1) Only individual performer is in Rock and Roll Hall of Fame.

Entertainment Personalities of the Present

Living actors, musicians, dancers, singers, producers, directors, radio-TV performers.

Name	Birthplace	Birthdate	Name	Birthplace	Birthdate
Abbado, Claudio	Milan, Italy	6/26/33	Amos, Tori	Newton, NC	8/22/63
Abdul, Paula	San Fernando, CA.	6/19/62	Anderson, Gillian	Chicago, IL.	8/9/68
Abraham, F. Murray	Pittsburgh, PA	10/24/39	Anderson, Harry	Newport, RI	10/14/52
Adams, Bryan	Kingston, Ontario.	11/5/59	Anderson, Ian	Dunfermline, Scotland	8/10/47
Adams, Don	New York, NY	4/13/23	Anderson, Kevin	Gurnee, IL	1/13/60
Adams, Edie	Kingston, PA	4/16/29	Anderson, Loni	St. Paul, MN.	8/5/46
Adams, Mason	Brooklyn, New York, NY	2/26/19	Anderson, Lynn	Grand Forks, ND	9/26/47
Adjani, Isabelle	Paris, France	6/27/55	Anderson, Melissa Sue	Berkeley, CA	9/26/62
Ad-rock	South Orange, NJ	10/31/66	Anderson, Pamela.	Comox, Vancouver Isl., BC	7/1/67
Affleck, Ben.	Berkeley, CA	8/15/72	Anderson, Richard	Long Branch, NJ	8/8/26
Aghdashloo, Shohreh	Tehran, Iran.	1952	Anderson, Richard Dean	Minneapolis, MN	1/23/50
Aguilera, Christina	Staten Is., New York, NY.	12/18/80	Anderson, Wes	Houston, TX.	5/1/69
Agutter, Jenny	Taunton, Somerset, Eng.	12/20/52	Andersson, Bibi	Stockholm, Sweden.	11/11/35
Aiello, Danny.	New York, NY	6/20/33	Andress, Ursula	Bern, Switzerland.	3/19/36
Aiken, Clay	Raleigh, NC	11/30/78	Andrews, Anthony	London, England	1/12/48
Aimee, Anouk	Paris, France	4/27/32	Andrews, Julie	Walton-on-Thames, Surrey, England.	10/1/35
Albanese, Licia	Bari, Italy	7/22/13			
Alberghetti, Anna Maria	Pesaro, Italy	5/15/36	Andrews, Patty	Minneapolis, MN	2/16/20
Albert, Eddie	Rock Island, IL.	4/22/08	Aniston, Jennifer	Sherman Oaks, CA	2/11/69
Albert, Marv	Brooklyn, New York, NY	6/12/41	Anka, Paul	Ottawa, Ontario	7/30/41
Alda, Alan	New York, NY	1/28/36	Ann-Margret	Stockholm, Sweden.	4/28/41
Alexander, Jane	Boston, MA	10/28/39	Antonioni, Michelangelo	Ferrara, Italy	9/29/12
Alexander, Jason	Newark, NJ	9/23/59	Apple, Fiona	New York, NY	9/13/77
Allen, Debbie	Houston, TX	1/16/50	Applegate, Christina	Los Angeles, CA	11/25/71
Allen, Joan	Rochelle, IL	8/20/56	Archer, Anne	Los Angeles, CA	8/25/47
Allen, Karen	Carrollton, IL	10/5/51	Arkin, Adam.	Brooklyn, NY	8/19/56
Allen, Tim	Denver, CO	6/13/53	Arkin, Alan.	New York, NY	3/26/34
Allen, Woody	Brooklyn, NY	12/1/35	Arnaz, Desi, Jr.	Hollywood, CA.	1/19/53
Alley, Kirstie	Wichita, KS	1/12/51	Arnaz, Lucie	Hollywood, CA.	7/17/51
Allman, Gregg	Nashville, TN	12/8/47	Arness, James	Minneapolis, MN	5/26/23
Allyson, June	Bronx, New York, NY	10/7/17	Arnold, Eddy	Henderson, TN	5/15/18
Alonso, Maria Conchita	Cienfuegos, Cuba	6/29/57	Arnold, Tom.	Ottumwa, IA.	3/6/59
Alpert, Herb.	Los Angeles, CA	3/31/35	Arquette, David	Winchester, VA	9/8/71
Altman, Robert	Kansas City, MO	2/20/25	Arquette, Patricia	Chicago, IL.	4/8/68
Almodóvar, Pedro	Calzada de Calatrava, Spain	9/25/51	Arquette, Rosanna	New York, NY	8/10/59
			Arroyo, Martina	Harlem, New York, NY	2/2/37
Ambrose, Lauren	New Haven, CT.	2/20/78	Arthur, Beatrice	New York, NY	5/13/23
Ames, Ed	Malden, Boston, MA	7/9/27	Ashanti (Douglas)	Glen Cove, NY.	10/13/80
Amos, John.	Newark, NJ	12/27/41	Ashley, Elizabeth.	Ocala, FL.	8/30/39

Name	Birthplace	Birthdate
Asner, Ed	Kansas City, KS	11/15/29
Assante, Armand	New York, NY	10/4/49
Astin, John	Baltimore, MD	3/30/30
Atkins, Eileen	London, England	6/16/34
Atkins, Sharif	Pittsburgh, PA	1/29/75
Atkinson, Rowan	Newcastle-Upon-Tyne, England	1/6/55
Attenborough, Richard	Cambridge, England	8/29/23
Auberjonois, Rene	New York, NY	6/1/40
Austin, Patti	New York, NY	8/10/48
Autry, Alan	Shreveport, LA	7/31/52
Avalon, Frankie	Philadelphia, PA	9/18/39
Aykroyd, Dan	Ottawa, Ontario	7/1/52
Azaria, Hank	Forest Hills, Queens, NY	4/25/64
Aznavour, Charles	Paris, France	5/22/24
Babyface (Kenneth Edmonds)	Indianapolis, IN	4/10/59
Bacall, Lauren	Bronx, New York, NY	9/16/24
Bacon, Kevin	Philadelphia, PA	7/8/58
Badalucco, Michael	Brooklyn, NY	12/20/54
Bader, Diedrich	Alexandria, VA	12/24/66
Badu, Erykah	Dallas, TX	2/26/71
Baez, Joan	Staten Island, NY	1/9/41
Bain, Conrad	Lethbridge, Alberta	2/4/23
Baio, Scott	Brooklyn, NY	9/22/61
Baker, Anita	Toledo, OH	1/26/58
Baker, Carroll	Johnstown, PA	5/28/31
Baker, Diane	Hollywood, CA	2/25/38
Baker, Joe Don	Groesbeck, TX	2/12/36
Baker, Kathy	Midland, TX	6/8/50
Baker, Kenny	Birmingham, England	8/24/34
Bakula, Scott	St. Louis, MO	10/9/54
Baldwin, Alec	Massapequa, NY	4/3/58
Baldwin, Daniel	Massapequa, NY	10/5/60
Baldwin, Stephen	Massapequa, NY	5/12/66
Baldwin, William	Massapequa, NY	2/21/63
Bale, Christian	Pembrokeshire, Wales	1/30/74
Ballard, Kaye	Cleveland, OH	11/20/26
Bana, Eric	Melbourne, Australia	8/9/68
Bancroft, Anne	Bronx, New York, NY	9/17/31
Banderas, Antonio	Málaga, Spain	8/10/60
Banks, Elizabeth	Pittsfield, MA	2/10/75
Banks, Tyra	Los Angeles, CA	12/4/73
Bannon, Jack	Los Angeles, CA	6/14/40
Baranski, Christine	Buffalo, NY	5/2/52
Barbeau, Adrienne	Sacramento, CA	6/11/45
Bardem, Javier	Las Palmas, Canary Islands	3/1/69
Bardot, Brigitte	Paris, France	9/28/34
Barker, Bob	Darrington, WA	12/12/23
Barkin, Ellen	Bronx, New York, NY	4/16/55
Barrie, Barbara	Chicago, IL	5/23/31
Barry, Gene	New York, NY	6/14/19
Barrymore, Drew	Los Angeles, CA	2/22/75
Bartoli, Cecilia	Rome, Italy	6/4/66
Barton, Misha	London, Eng.	1/24/86
Baryshnikov, Mikhail	Riga, Latvia	1/28/48
Basinger, Kim	Athens, GA	12/8/53
Bass, Lance	Laurel, MS	5/4/79
Bassett, Angela	Harlem, New York, NY	8/16/58
Bassey, Shirley	Cardiff, Wales	1/8/37
Bateman, Jason	Rye, NY	1/14/69
Bateman, Justine	Rye, NY	2/19/66
Bates, Kathy	Memphis, TN	6/28/48
Battle, Kathleen	Portsmouth, OH	8/13/48
Baxter, Meredith	Los Angeles, CA	6/21/47
Bean, Orson	Burlington, VT	7/22/28
Bean, Sean	Sheffield, England	4/17/59
Beatty, Ned	Louisville, KY	7/6/37
Beatty, Warren	Richmond, VA	3/30/37
Beauvais, Garcelle	St. Marc, Haiti	11/26/66
Beck (Hansen)	Los Angeles, CA	7/8/70
Beck, Jeff	Wallington, Surrey, Eng.	6/24/44
Beck, John	Chicago, IL	1/28/43
Beckinsale, Kate	London, England	7/26/73
Bedelia, Bonnie	New York, NY	3/25/48
Begley, Ed, Jr.	Los Angeles, CA	9/16/49
Behar, Joy	Brooklyn, NY	10/7/43
Belafonte, Harry	Harlem, New York, NY	3/1/27
Bel Geddes, Barbara	New York, NY	10/31/22
Bell, Art	Camp Lejeune, NC	6/17/45
Bell, Catherine	London, England	8/14/68
Bello, Maria	Norristown, PA	4/18/67
Belmondo, Jean-Paul	Neuilly-sur-Seine, France	4/9/33
Belushi, Jim	Chicago, IL	6/15/54
Belzer, Richard	Bridgeport, CT	8/4/44
Benatar, Pat	Brooklyn, NY	1/10/53
Benedict, Dirk	Helena, MT	3/1/45
Benigni, Roberto	Misericordia, Italy	10/27/52
Bening, Annette	Topeka, KS	5/29/58
Benjamin, Richard	New York, NY	5/22/38
Bennett, Tony	Astoria, Queens, NY	8/3/26
Benson, George	Pittsburgh, PA	3/22/43
Benson, Robby	Dallas, TX	1/21/56
Berenger, Tom	Chicago, IL	5/31/50
Berfield, Justin	Ventura County, CA	2/25/86
Bergen, Candice	Beverly Hills, CA	5/9/46
Bergen, Polly	Knoxville, TN	7/14/30
Bergeron, Tom	Haverhill, MA	5/6/55
Bergman, Ingmar	Uppsala, Sweden	7/14/18
Berlinger, Warren	Brooklyn, NY	8/31/37
Berman, Lazar	Leningrad, Russia	2/26/30
Berman, Shelley	Chicago, IL	2/3/26
Bernard, Crystal	Dallas, TX	9/30/64
Bernhard, Sandra	Flint, MI	6/6/55
Bernsen, Corbin	N. Hollywood, CA	9/7/54
Berry, Chuck	St. Louis, MO	10/18/26
Berry, Halle	Cleveland, OH	8/14/66
Berry, Ken	Moline, IL	11/3/33
Bertinelli, Valerie	Wilmington, DE	4/23/60
Bertolucci, Bernardo	Parma, Italy	3/16/40
Biafra, Jello	Boulder, CO	6/17/58
Bialik, Mayim	San Diego, CA	12/12/75
Biggs, Jason	Pompton Plains, NJ	5/12/78
Bikel, Theodore	Vienna, Austria	5/2/24
Billingsley, Barbara	Los Angeles, CA	12/22/22
Binoche, Juliette	Paris, France	3/9/64
Birch, Thora	Beverly Hills, CA	3/11/82
Birney, David	Washington, DC	4/23/39
Bishop, Joey	Bronx, NY	2/3/18
Bisset, Jacqueline	Weybridge, England	9/13/44
Bissett, Josie	Seattle, WA	10/5/70
Björk (Gudmundsdottir)	Reykjavik, Iceland	11/21/65
Black, Clint	Long Branch, NJ	2/4/62
Black, Jack	Los Angeles, CA	4/7/69
Black, Karen	Park Ridge, IL	7/1/42
Blades, Ruben	Panama City, Panama	7/16/48
Blair, Janet	Altoona, PA	4/23/21
Blair, Linda	St. Louis, MO	1/22/59
Blair, Selma	Southfield, MI	6/23/72
Blake, Robert	Nutley, NJ	9/18/33
Blanchett, Cate	Melbourne, Australia	5/14/69
Bledsoe, Tempestt	Chicago, IL	8/1/73
Bleeth, Yasmine	New York, NY	6/14/68
Blethyn, Brenda	Ramsgate, Kent, England	2/20/46
Blige, Mary J.	Bronx, NY	1/11/71
Bloom, Claire	London, England	2/15/31
Bloom, Orlando	Canterbury, England	1/13/77
Blyth, Ann	Mt. Kisco, NY	8/16/28
Bochco, Steven	New York, NY	12/16/43
Bocelli, Andrea	Lajatico, Italy	9/22/58
Bogdanovich, Peter	Kingston, NY	7/30/39
Bogosian, Eric	Woburn, MA	4/24/53
Bologna, Joseph	Brooklyn, NY	12/30/38
Bolton, Michael	New Haven, CT	2/26/53
Bonet, Lisa	San Francisco, CA	11/16/67
Bonham Carter, Helena	London, England	5/26/66
Bon Jovi, Jon	Sayreville, NJ	3/2/62
Bono (Vox)	Dublin, Ireland	5/10/60
Boone, Debby	Hackensack, NJ	9/22/56
Boone, Pat	Jacksonville, FL	6/1/34
Boreanaz, David	Buffalo, NY	5/16/71
Borgnine, Ernest	Hamden, CT	1/24/17
Bosco, Philip	Jersey City, NJ	9/26/30
Bosley, Tom	Chicago, IL	10/1/27
Bosson, Barbara	Charleroi, PA	11/1/39
Bostwick, Barry	San Mateo, CA	2/24/45
Bottoms, Timothy	Santa Barbara, CA	8/30/51
Bowen, Julie	Baltimore, MD	3/3/70
Bowie, David	London, England	1/8/47
Bowles, Peter	London, England	10/16/36
Boxleitner, Bruce	Elgin, IL	5/12/50
Boy George	Bexleyheath, England	6/14/61
Boyle, Lara Flynn	Davenport, IA	3/24/70
Boyle, Peter	Philadelphia, PA	10/18/33
Bracco, Lorraine	Brooklyn, NY	10/2/55
Brady, Wayne	Orlando, FL	6/2/72
Braff, Zach	S. Orange, NJ	4/6/75
Branagh, Kenneth	Belfast, N. Ireland	12/10/60
Brandauer, Klaus Maria	Steiermark, Austria	6/22/44
Brandy (Norwood)	McComb, MS	2/11/79
Braschi, Nicoletta	Cesena, Italy	8/10/60
Bratt, Benjamin	San Francisco, CA	12/16/63
Braugher, Andre	Chicago, Il	7/1/62
Braxton, Toni	Severn, MD	10/7/66
Bremner, Ewen	Edinburgh, Scotland	1971
Brendon, Nicholas	Los Angeles, CA	4/12/71
Brennan, Eileen	Los Angeles, CA	9/3/35
Brenneman, Amy	Glastonbury, CT	6/22/64
Brenner, David	Philadelphia, PA	2/4/45
Brewer, Teresa	Toledo, OH	5/7/31

IT'S A FACT: Nicolas Cage is the nephew of director Francis Ford Coppola. Before Cage changed his name, he appeared in the 1982 film *Fast Times at Ridgemont High*, credited as Nicolas Coppola.

Name	Birthplace	Birthdate
Bridges, Beau	Hollywood, CA	12/9/41
Bridges, Jeff	Los Angeles, CA	12/4/49
Brightman, Sarah	Berkhamstead, England	8/14/60
Brimley, Wilford	Salt Lake City, UT	9/27/34
Brinkley, Christie	Malibu, CA	2/2/54
Broadbent, Jim	Lincolnshire, England	5/24/49
Brochtrup, Bill	Inglewood, CA	3/7/63
Broderick, Matthew	New York, NY	3/21/62
Brody, Adam	San Diego, CA	12/15/79
Brody, Adrien	New York, NY	4/14/73
Brolin, James	Los Angeles, CA	7/18/40
Brooks, Albert	Beverly Hills, CA	7/22/47
Brooks, Garth	Tulsa, OK	2/7/62
Brooks, James L.	North Bergen, NJ.	5/9/40
Brooks, Mel	Brooklyn, NY	6/28/26
Brosnan, Pierce	Navan, Co. Meath, Ireland	5/16/53
Brown, Blair	Washington, DC	4/23/46
Brown, Bobby	Roxbury, Boston, MA	2/5/69
Brown, Bryan	Panania, Australia	6/23/47
Brown, James	Barnwell, SC	5/3/33
Browne, Jackson	Heidelberg, Germany	10/9/48
Browne, Roscoe Lee	Woodbury, NJ	5/2/25
Brubeck, Dave	Concord, CA	12/6/20
Bryson, Peabo	Greenville, SC	4/13/51
Buckley, Betty	Ft. Worth, TX.	7/3/47
Buffett, Jimmy	Pascagoula, MS	12/25/46
Bujold, Genevieve	Montreal, Quebec	7/1/42
Bullock, Sandra	Arlington, VA	7/26/64
Bumbry, Grace	St. Louis, MO.	1/4/37
Bundchen, Gisele	Horizontina, Brazil	7/20/80
Burghoff, Gary	Bristol, CT	5/24/43
Burke, Delta	Orlando, FL	7/30/56
Burnett, Carol	San Antonio, TX	4/26/33
Burns, Edward	Woodside, Queens, NY.	1/29/68
Burrows, Darren E.	Winfield, KS.	9/12/66
Burstyn, Ellen	Detroit, MI	12/7/32
Burton, LeVar	Landstuhl, W Germany	2/16/57
Burton, Tim	Burbank, CA	8/25/58
Buscemi, Steve	Brooklyn, NY	12/13/57
Busey, Gary	Goose Creek, TX.	6/29/44
Busfield, Timothy	Lansing, MI	6/12/57
Butler, Brett	Montgomery, AL	1/30/58
Buttons, Red	Bronx, NY	2/5/19
Buzzi, Ruth	Westerly, RI.	7/24/36
Bynes, Amanda	Thousand Oaks, CA	4/3/86
Byrne, David	Dumbarton, Scotland.	5/14/52
Byrne, Gabriel	Dublin, Ireland	5/12/50
Caan, James	Bronx, NY	3/26/40
Caballe, Montserrat	Barcelona, Spain	4/12/33
Caesar, Sid	Yonkers, NY	9/8/22
Cage, Nicolas	Long Beach, CA	1/7/64
Cain, Dean	Mt. Clemens, MI	7/31/66
Caine, Michael	London, England	3/14/33
Caldwell, Sarah	Maryville, MO	3/6/24
Caldwell, Zoe	Hawthorne, Australia	9/14/33
Cameron, James	Kapuskasing, Ontario	8/16/54
Cameron, Kirk	Panorama City, CA	10/12/70
Camp, Hamilton	London, England	10/30/34
Campanella, Joseph	New York, NY	11/21/27
Campbell, Bruce	Royal Oak, MI	6/22/58
Campbell, Glen	Delight, AR	4/22/36
Campbell, Naomi	South London, England.	5/22/70
Campbell, Neve	Guelph, Ontario	10/3/73
Campion, Jane	Waikanae, New Zealand.	4/30/54
Cannell, Stephen J.	Pasadena, CA	5/2/41
Cannon, Dyan	Tacoma, WA	1/4/37
Capshaw, Kate	Ft. Worth, TX.	11/3/53
Cara, Irene	New York, NY	3/18/64
Cardellini, Linda	Redwood City, CA	6/25/75
Cardinale, Claudia	Tunis, Tunisia	4/15/39
Carey, Drew	Cleveland, OH	5/23/58
Carey Jr., Harry	Saugus, CA	5/16/21
Carey, Mariah	Huntington, NY	3/27/70
Cariou, Len	Winnipeg, Canada.	9/30/39
Carlin, George	Bronx, New York, NY	5/12/37
Carlisle Hart, Kitty	New Orleans, LA	9/3/10
Carlton, Vanessa	Milford, PA.	8/16/80
Carlyle, Robert	Glasgow, Scotland	4/14/61
Carmen, Eric	Cleveland, OH.	8/11/49
Caron, Leslie	Boulogne, France	7/1/31
Carpenter, John	Carthage, NY.	1/16/48
Carpenter, Mary Chapin	Princeton, NJ.	2/21/58
Carr, Vikki	El Paso, TX.	7/19/41
Carradine, David	Hollywood, CA.	12/8/36
Carradine, Ever.	Los Angeles, CA	8/6/74

Name	Birthplace	Birthdate
Carradine, Keith	San Mateo, CA	8/8/49
Carreras, Jose	Barcelona, Spain	12/5/46
Carrere, Tia	Honolulu, HI.	1/2/67
Carrey, Jim	Newmarket, Ontario.	1/17/62
Carroll, Diahann	Bronx, NY	7/17/35
Carroll, Pat	Shreveport, LA.	5/5/27
Carson, Johnny	Corning, IA.	10/23/25
Carson, Lisa Nicole	Brooklyn, NY	7/12/69
Carter, Dixie	McLemoresville, TN.	5/25/39
Carter, Jack	Brooklyn, New York, NY .	6/24/23
Carter, Lynda	Phoenix, AZ.	7/24/51
Carter, Nick	Jamestown, NY	1/28/80
Carter, Ron	Ferndale, MI.	5/4/37
Cartwright, Nancy	Kettering, OH.	10/25/59
Caruso, David	Forest Hills, Queens, NY.	1/17/56
Carvey, Dana	Missoula, MT.	6/2/55
Case, Sharon	Detroit, MI	2/9/71
Cash, Rosanne	Memphis, TN.	5/24/55
Cassidy, David	New York, NY	4/12/50
Castellaneta, Dan	Chicago, IL.	9/10/58
Castle-Hughes, Keisha	Donnybrook, W. Australia, Australia.	3/24/90
Cates, Phoebe	New York, NY	7/16/63
Cattrall, Kim.	Liverpool, England.	8/21/56
Cavanagh, Tom.	Ottawa, Canada.	10/26/68
Cavett, Dick.	Gibbon, NE	11/19/36
Cedric the Entertainer	Jefferson City, MO.	4/24/64
Chabert, Lacey	Purvis, MS	9/30/82
Chalke, Sarah	Ottawa, Ontario	8/27/76
Chamberlain, Richard	Beverly Hills, CA	3/31/34
Chan, Jackie	Hong Kong.	4/7/54
Channing, Carol	Seattle, WA	1/31/21
Channing, Stockard.	New York, NY	2/13/44
Chaplin, Geraldine	Santa Monica, CA	7/31/44
Chapman, Tracy	Cleveland, OH	3/30/64
Chappelle, Dave	Washington, DC.	8/24/73
Charisse, Cyd	Amarillo, TX.	3/8/21
Charo	Murcia, Spain.	1/15/41
Chase, Chevy	New York, NY	10/8/43
Chasez, Joshua (J.C.).	Washington, DC.	8/8/76
Cheadle, Don	Kansas City, MO.	11/29/64
Checker, Chubby	Spring Gulley, SC	10/3/41
Cher	El Centro, CA.	5/20/46
Chianese, Dominic	Bronx, NY	2/24/31
Chiba, Sonny.	Fukuoka, Kyushu, Japan.	1/23/39
Chiklis, Michael	Lowell, MA.	8/30/63
Cho, Margaret	San Francisco	12/5/68
Chong, Rae Dawn	Vancouver, British Columbia	2/28/61
Chong, Thomas.	Edmonton, Alberta.	5/24/38
Chow Yun-Fat	Hong Kong.	5/18/55
Christensen, Hayden.	Vancouver, British Columbia	4/19/81
Christensen, Helena	Copenhagen, Denmark.	12/25/68
Christie, Julie.	Chukua, Assam, India	4/14/40
Christopher, William	Evanston, IL.	10/20/32
Chuck D	New York, NY	8/1/60
Church, Charlotte	Llandaff, Cardiff, Wales.	2/21/86
Church, Thomas Haden	El Paso, TX.	6/17/61
Clapp, Gordon.	North Conway, NH.	9/24/48
Clapton, Eric	Surrey, England.	3/30/45
Clark, Anthony	Lynchburg, VA.	4/4/64
Clark, Dick.	Mt. Vernon, NY.	11/30/29
Clark, Petula	Ewell, Surrey, England	11/15/32
Clark, Roy	Meherrin, VA	4/15/33
Clarkson, Kelly	Burleson, TX.	4/24/82
Clarkson, Patricia	New Orleans, LA	12/29/59
Clay, Andrew Dice.	Brooklyn, NY	9/29/58
Clayburgh, Jill	New York, NY	4/30/44
Cleese, John	Weston-super-Mare, Eng..	10/27/39
Cliburn, Van	Shreveport, LA.	7/12/34
Clooney, George	Lexington, KY	5/6/61
Close, Glenn	Greenwich, CT.	3/19/47
Coen, Ethan	St. Louis Park, MN.	9/21/57
Coen, Joel	St. Louis Park, MN.	11/29/54
Cohen, Leonard	Montreal, Canada.	9/21/34
Cole, Gary	Park Ridge, IL	9/20/57
Cole, Natalie	Los Angeles, CA.	2/6/50
Cole, Olivia	Memphis, TN.	11/26/42
Cole, Paula	Manchester, CT.	4/5/68
Coleman, Dabney	Austin, TX	1/3/32
Coleman, Gary	Zion, IL.	2/8/68
Coleman, Ornette	Fort Worth, TX.	3/19/30
Collette, Toni	Blacktown, Australia	11/1/72
Collins, Joan	London, England	5/23/33
Collins, Judy	Seattle, WA	5/1/39

Name	Birthplace	Birthdate
Collins, Pauline	Exmouth, England	9/3/40
Collins, Phil	London, England	1/30/51
Collins, Stephen	Des Moines, IA	10/1/47
Colvin, Shawn	Vermillion, SD	1/10/56
Combs, Sean "P. Diddy"	Harlem, NY	11/4/69
Comden, Betty	Brooklyn, NY	5/3/19
Connelly, Jennifer	Catskill Mountains, NY	12/12/70
Connery, Sean	Edinburgh, Scotland	8/25/30
Connick, Harry, Jr.	New Orleans, LA	9/11/67
Connors, Mike	Fresno, CA	8/15/25
Conrad, Robert	Chicago, IL	3/1/35
Conroy, Frances	Monroe, GA	11/13/53
Constantine, Michael	Reading, PA	5/22/27
Conti, Tom	Paisley, Scotland	11/22/41
Conway, Tim	Willoughby, OH	12/15/33
Cook, Barbara	Atlanta, GA	10/25/27
Coolidge, Rita	Nashville, TN	5/1/45
Coolio	Los Angeles, CA	8/1/63
Cooper, Alice	Detroit, MI	2/4/48
Cooper, Jackie	Los Angeles, CA	9/15/21
Copperfield, David	Metuchen, NJ	9/16/56
Coppola, Francis Ford	Detroit, MI	4/7/39
Coppola, Sofia	New York, NY	5/12/71
Corbett, John	Wheeling, WV	5/9/61
Corbin, Barry	Lamesa, TX	10/16/40
Cord, Alex	Floral Park, NY	5/3/33
Corea, Chick	Chelsea, MA	6/12/41
Corgan, Billy	Elk Grove, IL	3/17/67
Corley, Pat	Dallas, TX	6/1/30
Cornell, Chris	Seattle, WA	7/20/64
Corwin, Jeff	Halifax, Nova Scotia	7/11/67
Cosby, Bill	Philadelphia, PA	7/12/37
Costas, Bob	Queens, New York, NY	3/22/52
Costello, Elvis	London, England	8/25/54
Costner, Kevin	Compton, CA	1/18/55
Courtenay, Tom	Hull, England	2/25/37
Cowell, Simon	London, England	10/7/59
Cox, Brian	Dundee, Scotland	6/1/46
Cox, Nikki	Los Angeles, CA	6/2/78
Cox, Ronny	Cloudcroft, NM	7/23/38
Cox Arquette, Courteney	Birmingham, AL	6/15/64
Coyote, Peter	New York, NY	10/10/42
Cranston, Bryan	San Fernando Valley, CA	3/7/56
Crawford, Cindy	DeKalb, IL	2/20/66
Crawford, Michael	Salisbury, England	1/19/42
Crespin, Regine	Marseilles, France	2/23/26
Crosby, David	Los Angeles, CA	8/14/41
Cross, Ben	London, England	12/16/47
Crouse, Lindsay	New York, NY	5/12/48
Crow, Sheryl	Kennett, MO	2/11/62
Crowe, Cameron	Palm Springs, CA	7/13/57
Crowe, Russell	Wellington, New Zealand	4/7/64
Crowell, Rodney	Houston, TX	8/17/50
Crudup, Billy	Manhasset, NY	7/8/68
Cruise, Tom	Syracuse, NY	7/3/62
Cruz, Penelope	Madrid, Spain	4/28/74
Crystal, Billy	Long Beach, NY	3/14/47
Culkin, Kieran	New York, NY	9/30/82
Culkin, Macaulay	New York, NY	8/26/80
Culkin, Rory	New York, NY	7/21/89
Cullum, John	Knoxville, TN	3/2/30
Culp, Robert	Oakland, CA	8/16/30
Cummings, Constance	Seattle, WA	5/15/10
Curry, Tim	Cheshire, England	4/19/46
Curtin, Jane	Cambridge, MA	9/6/47
Curtis, Jamie Lee	Los Angeles, CA	11/22/58
Curtis, Tony	New York, NY	6/3/25
Cusack, Joan	New York, NY	10/11/62
Cusack, John	Evanston, IL	6/28/66
Cyrus, Billy Ray	Flatwoods, KY	8/25/61
Dafoe, Willem	Appleton, WI	7/22/55
Dahl, Arlene	Minneapolis, MN	8/11/28
Dale, Jim	Rothwell, England	8/15/35
Dalton, Abby	Las Vegas, NV	8/15/32
Dalton, Timothy	Colwyn Bay, Wales	3/21/46
Daltrey, Roger	London, England	3/1/44
Daly, Carson	Santa Monica, CA	6/22/73
Daly, Timothy	New York, NY	3/1/56
Daly, Tyne	Madison, WI	2/21/46
Damon, Matt	Cambridge, MA	10/8/70
Damone, Vic	Brooklyn, NY	6/12/28
Danes, Claire	New York, NY	4/12/79
D'Angelo	Richmond, VA	2/11/74
D'Angelo, Beverly	Columbus, OH	11/15/54
Dangerfield, Rodney	Babylon, NY	11/22/21
Daniels, Anthony	Salisbury, England	2/21/46
Daniels, Charlie	Wilmington, NC	10/28/36
Daniels, Jeff	Athens, GA	2/19/55
Daniels, William	Brooklyn, NY	3/31/27
Danner, Blythe	Rosemont, PA	2/3/43
Danson, Ted	San Diego, CA	12/29/47
Danza, Tony	Brooklyn, New York, NY	4/21/51
Darby, Kim	Hollywood, CA	7/8/48
David, Larry	Brooklyn, NY	7/2/47
Davidson, John	Pittsburgh, PA	12/13/41
Davis, Ann B.	Schenectady, NY	5/5/26
Davis, Clifton	Chicago, IL	10/4/45
Davis, Geena	Wareham, MA	1/21/56
Davis, Hope	Englewood, NJ	3/23/64
Davis, Judy	Perth, Australia	4/23/55
Davis, Kristin	Boulder, CO	2/24/65
Davis, Mac	Lubbock, TX	1/21/42
Davis, Ossie	Cogdell, GA	12/18/17
Dawber, Pam	Farmington Hills, MI	10/18/51
Dawson, Richard	Gosport, Hampshire, Eng.	11/20/32
Dawson, Rosario	Bronx, New York, NY	5/9/79
Day, Doris	Cincinnati, OH	4/3/24
Day, Laraine	Roosevelt, UT	10/13/17
Day-Lewis, Daniel	London, England	4/29/57
Dean, Jimmy	Plainview, TX	8/10/28
Dearie, Blossom	E. Durham, NY	4/28/26
DeCarlo, Yvonne	Vancouver, BC	9/1/22
Dee, Ruby	Cleveland, OH	10/27/24
DeFranco, Buddy	Camden, NJ	2/17/23
DeGeneres, Ellen	Metairie, LA	1/26/58
DeHaven, Gloria	Los Angeles, CA	7/23/25
De Havilland, Olivia	Tokyo, Japan	7/1/16
Delaney, Kim	Philadelphia, PA	11/29/61
Delany, Dana	New York, NY	3/13/56
De la Rocha, Zack	Long Beach, CA	1/12/70
DeLaurentiis, Dino	Torre Annunziata, Italy	8/8/19
Delon, Alain	Sceaux, France	11/8/35
Del Toro, Benicio	Santurce, Puerto Rico	2/19/67
DeLuise, Dom	Brooklyn, NY	8/1/33
Demme, Jonathan	Baldwin, NY	2/22/44
De Mornay, Rebecca	Santa Rosa, CA	8/29/62
Dench, Judi	York, England	12/9/34
Deneuve, Catherine	Paris, France	10/22/43
De Niro, Robert	New York, NY	8/17/43
Dennehy, Brian	Bridgeport, CT	7/9/38
Denver, Bob	New Rochelle, NY	1/9/35
DePalma, Brian	Newark, NJ	9/11/40
Depardieu, Gerard	Chateauroux, France	12/27/48
Depp, Johnny	Owensboro, KY	6/9/63
Derek, Bo	Long Beach, CA	11/20/56
De Rossi, Portia	Melbourne, Victoria, Australia	1/31/73
Dern, Bruce	Winnetka, IL	6/4/36
Dern, Laura	Santa Monica, CA	2/10/67
Devane, William	Albany, NY	9/5/39
DeVito, Danny	Neptune, NJ	11/17/44
DeWitt, Joyce	Wheeling, WV	4/23/49
Dey, Susan	Pekin, IL	12/10/52
Diamond, Neil	Brooklyn, NY	1/24/41
Diaz, Cameron	San Diego, CA	8/30/72
DiCaprio, Leonardo	Hollywood, CA	11/11/74
Dick, Andy	Charleston, SC	12/21/65
Dickinson, Angie	Kulm, ND	9/30/31
Diddley, Bo	McComb, MS	12/30/28
Diesel, Vin	New York, NY	7/18/67
Diggs, Taye	Essex Co., NJ	1/2/72
Diller, Phyllis	Lima, OH	7/17/17
Dillman, Bradford	San Francisco, CA	4/14/30
Dillon, Matt	New Rochelle, NY	2/18/64
Dinklage, Peter	Mendham, NJ	6/11/69
Dion, Celine	Charlemagne, Quebec	3/30/68
Djalili, Omad	London, England	1965
Dobson, Kevin	Queens, New York, NY	3/18/43
Dogg, Snoop	Long Beach, CA	10/20/71
Doherty, Shannen	Memphis, TN	4/12/71
Dolenz, Mickey	Los Angeles, CA	3/8/45
Domingo, Placido	Madrid, Spain	1/21/41
Domino, Fats	New Orleans, LA	2/26/28
Donahue, Phil	Cleveland, OH	12/21/35
D'Onofrio, Vincent	Brooklyn, NY	6/30/59
Donovan (Leitch)	Glasgow, Scotland	5/10/46
Donovan, Tate	Tenafly, NJ	9/25/63
Dorn, Michael	Luling, TX	12/9/52
Dorough, Howie	Orlando, FL	8/22/73
Dotrice, Roy	Guernsey, England	5/26/23
Douglas, Kirk	Amsterdam, NY	12/9/16
Douglas, Michael	New Brunswick, NJ	9/25/44
Dourdan, Gary	Philadelphia, PA	12/11/66
Dow, Tony	Hollywood, CA	4/13/45
Down, Lesley-Ann	London, England	3/17/54
Downey, Robert, Jr.	New York, NY	4/4/65
Downey, Roma	Derry, Northern Ireland	5/6/60
Downs, Hugh	Akron, OH	2/14/21

Name	Birthplace	Birthdate	Name	Birthplace	Birthdate
Drescher, Fran	Flushing, Queens, NY	9/30/57	Feinstein, Michael	Columbus, OH	9/7/56
Dreyfuss, Richard	Brooklyn, NY	10/29/47	Feldon, Barbara	Pittsburgh, PA	3/12/41
Driver, Minnie	London, England	1/31/70	Feldshuh, Tovah	New York, NY	12/27/52
Dryer, Fred	Hawthorne, CA	7/6/46	Feliciano, Jose	Lares, Puerto Rico	9/10/45
Duchovny, David	New York, NY	8/7/60	Fenn, Sherilyn	Detroit, MI	2/1/65
Duff, Hilary	Houston, TX	9/28/87	Ferrell, Conchata	Charleston, WV	3/28/43
Duffy, Julia	Minneapolis, MN	6/27/51	Ferrell, Will	Irvine, CA	7/16/67
Duffy, Patrick	Townsend, MT	3/17/49	Ferrer, Mel	Elberon, NJ	8/25/17
Duhamel, Josh	Minot, ND	11/14/72	Feuerstein, Mark	New York, NY	6/8/71
Dukakis, Olympia	Lowell, MA	6/20/31	Fey, Tina	Upper Darby, PA	5/18/70
Duke, Patty	Elmhurst, NY	12/14/46	Fiedler, John	Platteville, WI	2/3/25
Dullea, Keir	Cleveland, OH	5/30/36	Field, Sally	Pasadena, CA	11/6/46
Dunaway, Faye	Bascom, FL	1/14/41	Fiennes, Joseph	Salisbury, England	5/27/70
Duncan, Lindsay	Edinburgh, Scotland	11/7/50	Fiennes, Ralph	Suffolk, England	12/22/62
Duncan, Sandy	Henderson, TX	2/20/46	Fierstein, Harvey	Brooklyn, NY	6/6/54
Dunham, Katherine	Glen Ellyn, IL	6/22/10	50 Cent	Queens, NY	7/6/76
Dunne, Griffin	New York, NY	6/8/55	Fincher, David	Denver, CO	5/10/62
Dunst, Kirsten	Point Pleasant, NJ	4/30/82	Finney, Albert	Salford, England	5/9/36
Durbin, Deanna	Winnipeg, Manitoba	12/4/21	Fiorentino, Linda	Philadelphia, PA	3/9/60
Durning, Charles	Highland Falls, NY	2/28/23	Firth, Colin	Grayshott, England	9/10/60
Dussault, Nancy	Pensacola, FL	6/30/36	Firth, Peter	Bradford, Yorkshire, Eng.	10/27/53
Dutton, Charles S.	Baltimore, MD	1/30/51	Fischer-Dieskau, Dietrich	Berlin, Germany	5/28/25
Duvall, Robert	San Diego, CA	1/5/31	Fishburne, Laurence	Augusta, GA	7/30/61
Duvall, Shelley	Houston, TX	7/7/49	Fisher, Carrie	Beverly Hills, CA	10/21/56
Dylan, Bob	Duluth, MN	5/24/41	Fisher, Eddie	Philadelphia, PA	8/10/28
Dylan, Jakob	New York, NY	12/9/69	Fitzgerald, Geraldine	Dublin, Ireland	11/24/13
Dysart, Richard	Brighton, MA	3/30/29	Flack, Roberta	Black Mountain, NC	2/10/39
Dzundza, George	Rosenheim, Germany	7/19/45	Flanagan, Fionnula	Dublin, Ireland	12/10/41
			Flavor Flav	New York, NY	3/16/59
Eads, George	Fort Worth, TX	3/1/67	Fleetwood, Mick	Redruth, Cornwall, Eng..	6/24/42
Easton, Sheena	Bellshill, Scotland	4/27/59	Fleming, Rhonda	Hollywood, CA	8/10/23
Eastwood, Clint	San Francisco, CA	5/31/30	Fletcher, Louise	Birmingham, AL	7/22/34
Ebert, Roger	Urbana, IL	6/18/42	Flockhart, Calista	Freeport, IL	11/11/64
Eden, Barbara	Tucson, AZ	8/23/34	Florek, Dann	Flat Rock, MI	5/1/50
Edwards, Anthony	Santa Barbara, CA	7/19/62	Foch, Nina	Leyden, Netherlands	4/20/24
Edwards, Blake	Tulsa, OK	7/26/22	Fogelberg, Dan	Peoria, IL	8/13/51
Edwards, Ralph	Merino, CO	6/13/13	Fogerty, John	Berkeley, CA	5/28/45
Ehle, Jennifer	Winston-Salem, NC	12/29/69	Foley, Dave	Etobicoke, Ontario	1/4/63
Eichhorn, Lisa	Reading, PA	2/4/52	Fonda, Bridget	Los Angeles, CA	1/27/64
Eikenberry, Jill	New Haven, CT	1/21/47	Fonda, Jane	New York, NY	12/21/37
Ekberg, Anita	Malmo, Sweden	9/29/31	Fonda, Peter	New York, NY	2/23/40
Ekland, Britt	Stockholm, Sweden	10/6/42	Fontaine, Joan	Tokyo, Japan	10/22/17
Electra, Carmen	Cincinnati, OH	4/20/72	Ford, Faith	Alexandria, LA	9/14/64
Elfman, Jenna	Los Angeles, CA	9/30/71	Ford, Glenn	Sainte-Christine, Quebec	5/1/16
Elizabeth, Shannon	Houston, TX	9/7/73	Ford, Harrison	Des Plaines, IL	7/13/42
Elizondo, Hector	New York, NY	12/22/36	Forman, Milos	Caslav, Czechoslovakia..	2/18/32
Elliott, Bob	Boston, MA	3/26/23	Forsythe, John	Penns Grove, NJ	1/29/18
Elliott, Chris	New York, NY	5/31/60	Foster, Jodie	Los Angeles, CA	11/19/62
Elliott, Sam	Sacramento, CA	8/9/44	Fox, James	London, England	5/19/39
Elvira	Manhattan, KS	9/17/51	Fox, Jorja	New York, NY	7/7/68
Eminem	St. Joseph, MO	10/17/72	Fox, Matthew	Crowheart, WY	7/14/66
Enberg, Dick	Mt. Clemens, MI	1/9/35	Fox, Michael J.	Edmonton, Alberta	6/9/61
Englund, Robert	Glendale, CA	6/6/49	Fox, Vivica A.	Indianapolis, IN	7/30/64
Enya	Gweedore, Ireland	5/17/61	Foxworth, Robert	Houston, TX	11/1/41
Ephron, Nora	New York, NY	5/19/41	Foxworthy, Jeff	Atlanta, GA	9/6/58
Ermey, R. Lee	Emporia, KS	3/24/44	Foxx, Jamie	Terrell, TX	12/13/67
Estefan, Gloria	Havana, Cuba	9/1/57	Frampton, Peter	Kent, England	4/22/50
Estevez, Emilio	New York, NY	5/12/62	Franciosa, Anthony	East Harlem, NY, NY	10/25/28
Estrada, Erik	New York, NY	3/16/49	Francis, Anne	Ossining, NY	9/16/30
Etheridge, Melissa	Leavenworth, KS	5/29/61	Francis, Connie	Newark, NJ	12/12/38
Evans, Linda	Hartford, CT	11/18/42	Franco, James	Palo Alto, CA	4/19/78
Evans, Robert	New York, NY	6/29/30	Franken, Al	New York, NY	5/21/51
Everett, Chad	South Bend, IN	6/11/36	Franklin, Aretha	Memphis, TN	3/25/42
Everett, Rupert	Norfolk, England	5/29/59	Franklin, Bonnie	Santa Monica, CA	1/6/44
Everly, Don	Brownie, KY	2/1/37	Franz, Dennis	Maywood, IL	10/28/44
Everly, Phil	Chicago, IL	1/19/39	Fraser, Brendan	Indianapolis, IN	12/3/68
Evigan, Greg	South Amboy, NJ	10/14/53	Freeman, Al, Jr.	San Antonio, TX	3/21/34
			Freeman, Mona	Baltimore, MD	6/9/26
Fabares, Shelley	Santa Monica, CA	1/19/44	Freeman, Morgan	Memphis, TN	6/1/37
Fabian (Forte)	Philadelphia, PA	2/6/43	French, Dawn	Holyhead, Wales	10/11/57
Fabio	Milan, Italy	3/15/61	Fricker, Brenda	Dublin, Ireland	2/17/45
Fabray, Nanette	San Diego, CA	10/27/20	Friedkin, William	Chicago, IL	8/29/39
Fairchild, Morgan	Dallas, TX	2/3/50	Frost, David	Tenterden, England	4/7/39
Faison, Donald	New York, NY	6/22/74	Fry, Stephen	London, England	8/24/57
Falana, Lola	Philadelphia, PA	9/11/43	Fuentes, Daisy	Havana, Cuba	11/17/66
Falco, Edie	Brooklyn, NY	7/5/63	Fuller, Robert	Troy, NY	7/29/34
Falk, Peter	New York, NY	9/16/27	Funicello, Annette	Utica, NY	10/22/42
Fallon, Jimmy	Brooklyn, NY	9/19/74	Furlong, Edward	Pasadena, CA	8/2/77
Farentino, James	Brooklyn, NY	2/24/38	Furtado, Nelly	Victoria, British Columbia.	12/2/78
Fargo, Donna	Mt. Airy, NC	11/10/49			
Farina, Dennis	Chicago, IL	2/29/44	Gabor, Zsa Zsa	Budapest, Hungary	2/6/17
Farr, Jamie	Toledo, OH	7/1/34	Gabriel, John	Niagara Falls, NY	5/25/31
Farrell, Mike	St. Paul, MN	2/6/39	Gabriel, Peter	Surrey, England	2/13/50
Farrell, Perry	Queens, NY	3/29/59	Gallagher, Peter	Armonk, NY	8/19/55
Farrelly, Bob	Cumberland, RI	6/17/58	Gallo, Vincent	Buffalo, NY	4/11/62
Farrelly, Peter	Phoenixville, PA	12/17/56	Galway, James	Belfast, N. Ireland	12/8/39
Farrow, Mia	Los Angeles, CA	2/9/45	Gandolfini, James	Westwood, NJ	9/18/61
Fatone, Joey	Brooklyn, New York, NY	1/28/77	Garagiola, Joe	St. Louis, MO	2/12/26
Faustino, David	Los Angeles, CA	3/3/74	Garber, Victor	London, Ont.	3/16/49
Fawcett, Farrah	Corpus Christi, TX	2/2/47	Garcia, Andy	Havana, Cuba	4/12/56

Name	Birthplace	Birthdate
Garfunkel, Art	Queens, New York, NY	11/5/41
Garland, Beverly	Santa Cruz, CA	10/17/26
Garner, James	Norman, OK	4/7/28
Garner, Jennifer	Houston, TX	4/17/72
Garofalo, Janeane	Newton, NJ	9/28/64
Garr, Teri	Lakewood, OH	12/11/49
Garrett, Betty	St. Joseph, MO	5/23/19
Garrett, Brad	Woodland Hills, CA	4/14/60
Garth, Jennie	Urbana, IL	4/3/72
Gatlin, Larry	Seminole, TX	5/2/48
Gavin, John	Los Angeles, CA	4/8/31
Gayle, Crystal	Paintsville, KY	1/9/51
Gaynor, Mitzi	Chicago, IL	9/4/31
Gazzara, Ben	New York, NY	8/28/30
Geary, Anthony	Coalville, UT	5/29/47
Geary, Cynthia	Jackson, MS	3/21/65
Gedda, Nicolai	Stockholm, Sweden	7/11/25
Gellar, Sarah Michelle	New York, NY	4/14/77
Gere, Richard	Philadelphia, PA	8/31/49
Gervais, Ricky	Reading, England	6/25/61
Getty, Estelle	New York, NY	7/25/23
Ghostley, Alice	Eve, MO	8/14/26
Giannini, Giancarlo	La Spezia, Italy	8/1/42
Gibb, Barry	Isle of Man, England	9/1/46
Gibb, Robin	Isle of Man, England	12/22/49
Gibbons, Leeza	Irmo, SC	3/26/57
Gibbs, Marla	Chicago, IL	6/14/31
Gibson, Deborah	Brooklyn, New York, NY	8/31/70
Gibson, Henry	Germantown, PA	9/21/35
Gibson, Mel	Peekskill, NY	1/3/56
Gibson, Thomas	Charleston, SC	7/3/62
Gifford, Frank	Santa Monica, CA	8/16/30
Gifford, Kathie Lee	Neuilly-sur-Seine, France	8/16/53
Gilbert, Sara	Santa Monica, CA	1/29/75
Gilbert, Melissa	Los Angeles, CA	5/8/64
Gilberto, Astrud	Salvador, Brazil	3/30/40
Gill, Vince	Norman, OK	4/12/57
Gillette, Anita	Baltimore, MD	8/16/36
Gilley, Mickey	Natchez, MS	3/9/36
Gilliam, Terry	Minneapolis, MN	11/22/40
Gilmour, David	Cambridge, England	3/6/44
Gilpin, Peri	Waco, TX	5/27/61
Ginty, Robert	New York, NY	11/14/48
Givens, Robin	New York, NY	11/27/64
Glaser, Paul Michael	Cambridge, MA	3/25/43
Gleeson, Brendan	Belfast, N. Ireland	11/9/55
Glenn, Scott	Pittsburgh, PA	1/26/42
Gless, Sharon	Los Angeles, CA	5/31/43
Glover, Crispin	New York, NY	9/20/64
Glover, Danny	San Francisco, CA	7/22/47
Glover, Julian	London, England	3/27/35
Glover, Savion	Newark, NJ	11/19/73
Godard, Jean Luc	Paris, France	12/3/30
Goldberg, Whoopi	New York, NY	11/13/55
Goldblum, Jeff	Pittsburgh, PA	10/22/52
Goldthwait, Bobcat	Syracuse, NY	5/26/62
Goldwyn, Tony	Los Angeles, CA	5/20/60
Gooding, Cuba, Jr.	Bronx, NY	1/2/68
Goodman, John	Affton, MO	6/20/52
Gordon-Levitt, Joseph	Los Angeles, CA	2/17/81
Gorme, Eydie	Bronx, NY	8/16/32
Gorshin, Frank	Pittsburgh, PA	4/5/34
Gosselaar, Mark-Paul	Panorama City, CA	3/1/74
Gossett, Louis, Jr.	Brooklyn, NY	5/27/36
Gould, Elliott	Brooklyn, NY	8/29/38
Gould, Harold	Schenectady, NY	12/10/23
Goulet, Robert	Lawrence, MA	11/26/33
Gowdy, Curt	Green River, WY	7/31/19
Grace, Topher	New York, NY	7/19/78
Graham, Heather	Milwaukee, WI	1/29/70
Grammer, Kelsey	St. Thomas, Virgin Isl.	2/21/55
Granger, Farley	San Jose, CA	7/1/25
Grant, Amy	Augusta, GA	11/25/60
Grant, Hugh	London, England	9/9/60
Grant, Lee	New York, NY	10/31/27
Graves, Peter	Minneapolis, MN	3/18/26
Gray, Linda	Santa Monica, CA	9/12/40
Gray, Macy	Canton, OH	9/9/70
Grayson, Kathryn	Winston-Salem, NC	2/9/22
Green, Al.	Forrest City, AR	4/13/46
Green, Seth	Overbrook Park, PA	2/8/74
Green, Tom	Pembroke, Ontario	7/30/71
Greene, Shecky	Chicago, IL	4/8/26
Greenwood, Bruce	Noranda, Quebec	8/12/56
Gregory, Cynthia	Los Angeles, CA	7/8/46
Gregory, Dick	St. Louis, MO	10/12/32
Grey, Jennifer	New York, NY	3/26/60
Grey, Joel	Cleveland, OH	4/11/32
Grier, David Alan	Detroit, MI	6/30/55
Grier, Pam	Winston-Salem, NC	5/26/49

Name	Birthplace	Birthdate
Griffin, Merv	San Mateo, CA	7/6/25
Griffith, Andy	Mount Airy, NC	6/1/26
Griffith, Melanie	New York, NY	8/9/57
Griffiths, Rachel	New Castle, Australia	2/20/68
Grimes, Tammy	Lynn, MA	1/30/34
Grint, Rupert	Hertfordshire, England	8/24/88
Grizzard, George	Roanoke Rapids, NC	4/1/28
Groban, Josh	Los Angeles, CA	2/27/81
Grodin, Charles	Pittsburgh, PA	4/21/35
Grohl, David	Warren, OH	1/14/69
Grosbard, Ulu	Antwerp, Belgium	1/9/29
Gross, Michael	Chicago, IL	6/21/47
Guest, Christopher	New York, NY	2/5/48
Guillaume, Robert	St. Louis, MO	11/30/37
Gumbel, Greg	New Orleans, LA	5/3/46
Guthrie, Arlo	Brooklyn, New York, NY	7/10/47
Guttenberg, Steve	Brooklyn, New York, NY	8/24/58
Guy, Buddy	Lettsworth, LA	7/30/36
Guy, Jasmine	Boston, MA	3/10/64
Gyllenhaal, Jake	Los Angeles, CA	12/19/80
Hackman, Gene	San Bernardino, CA	1/30/30
Hagerty, Julie	Cincinnati, OH	6/15/55
Haggard, Merle	Bakersfield, CA	4/6/37
Hagman, Larry	Fort Worth, TX	9/21/31
Haid, Charles	San Francisco, CA	6/2/43
Haines, Connie	Savannah, GA	1/20/22
Hale, Barbara	DeKalb, IL	4/18/22
Hall, Anthony Michael	West Roxbury, MA	4/14/68
Hall, Arsenio	Cleveland, OH	2/12/55
Hall, Daryl	Pottstown, PA	10/11/49
Hall, Deidre	Milwaukee, WI	10/31/47
Hall, Michael C.	Raleigh, NC	2/1/71
Hall, Monty	Winnipeg, Manitoba	8/25/21
Hall, Tom T.	Olive Hill, KY	5/25/36
Halliwell, Geri	Watford, England	8/6/72
Hamill, Mark	Oakland, CA	9/25/51
Hamilton, George	Memphis, TN	8/12/39
Hamilton, Linda	Salisbury, MD	9/26/56
Hamlin, Harry	Pasadena, CA	10/30/51
Hammer	Oakland, CA	3/29/63
Hammond, Darrell	Melbourne, FL	10/8/60
Hampshire, Susan	London, England	5/12/37
Hancock, Herbie	Chicago, IL	4/12/40
Hanks, Tom	Concord, CA	7/9/56
Hannah, Daryl	Chicago, IL	12/3/60
Hannigan, Alyson	Washington, DC	3/24/74
Hanson, Curtis	Reno, NV	3/24/45
Hanson, Isaac	Tulsa, OK	11/17/80
Hanson, Taylor	Tulsa, OK	3/14/83
Hanson, Zac	Tulsa, OK	10/22/85
Harden, Marcia Gay	La Jolla, CA	8/14/59
Hardison, Kadeem	New York, NY	7/24/66
Harewood, Dorian	Dayton, OH	8/6/50
Harmon, Angie	Highland Park, TX	8/10/72
Harmon, Mark	Burbank, CA	9/2/51
Harper, Jessica	Chicago, IL	10/10/49
Harper, Tess	Mammoth Springs, AR	8/15/50
Harper, Valerie	Suffern, NY	8/22/40
Harrelson, Woody	Midland, TX	7/23/61
Harrington, Pat	New York, NY	8/13/29
Harris, Barbara	Evanston, IL	7/25/35
Harris, Ed	Tenafly, NJ	11/28/50
Harris, Emmylou	Birmingham, AL	4/2/47
Harris, Julie	Grosse Pte. Park, MI	12/2/25
Harris, Neil Patrick	Albuquerque, NM	6/15/73
Harris, Rosemary	Ashby, England	9/19/30
Harris, Steve	Chicago, IL	12/3/65
Harrison, Gregory	Avalon, CA	5/31/50
Harry, Deborah	Miami, FL	7/1/45
Hart, Mary	Madison, SD	11/8/50
Hart, Melissa Joan	Sayville, NY	4/18/76
Hartley, Hal	Lindenhurst, NY	11/3/59
Hartley, Mariette	New York, NY	6/21/40
Hartman, David	Pawtucket, RI	5/19/35
Hartman Black, Lisa	Houston, TX	6/1/56
Hartnett, Josh	San Francisco, CA	7/21/78
Harvey, P.J.	Yeovil, Somerset, England	10/9/69
Harvey, Steve	Welch, WV	11/23/56
Hasselhoff, David	Baltimore, MD	7/17/52
Hatcher, Teri	Sunnyvale, CA	12/8/64
Hatfield, Juliana	Wiscasset, ME	7/27/67
Hathaway, Anne	Brooklyn, NY	11/12/82
Hauer, Rutger	Breukelen, Netherlands	1/23/44
Haver, June	Rock Island, IL	6/10/26
Havoc, June	Seattle, WA	11/8/16
Hawke, Ethan	Austin, TX	11/6/70
Hawn, Goldie	Washington, DC	11/21/45
Hayden, Melissa	Toronto, Ontario	4/25/23
Hayek, Salma	Coatzacoalcos, Mexico	9/2/66

Name	Birthplace	Birthdate
Hayes, Isaac	Covington, TN	8/20/42
Hayes, Sean	Glen Ellyn, IL	6/26/70
Haynes, Roy	Roxbury, Boston, MA	3/13/26
Hays, Robert	Bethesda, MD	7/24/47
Head, Anthony Stewart	North London, England	2/20/54
Heard, John	Washington, DC	3/7/46
Hearn, George	St. Louis, MO.	6/18/34
Heaton, Patricia	Bay Village, OH	3/4/58
Heche, Anne	Aurora, OH	5/25/69
Hedren, Tippi	Lafayette, MN	1/19/31
Helfgott, David	Melbourne, Australia	5/19/47
Helgenberger, Marg	Fremont, NE	11/16/58
Helmond, Katherine	Galveston, TX	7/5/34
Hemingway, Mariel	Mill Valley, CA	11/22/61
Hemsley, Sherman	Philadelphia, PA	2/1/38
Henderson, Florence	Dale, IN	2/14/34
Henderson, Skitch	Birmingham, England	1/27/18
Henley, Don	Gilmer, TX	7/22/47
Henner, Marilu	Chicago, IL	4/6/52
Hennessy, Jill	Edmonton, Alberta.	11/25/68
Henry, Buck	New York, NY	12/9/30
Herman, Pee-Wee	Peekskill, NY	8/27/52
Herrmann, Edward	Washington, DC	7/21/43
Hershey, Barbara	Hollywood, CA.	2/5/48
Hesseman, Howard	Lebanon, OR	2/27/40
Heston, Charlton	Evanston, IL	10/4/24
Hetfield, James	Downey, CA	8/3/63
Hewitt, Jennifer Love	Waco, TX.	2/21/79
Hicks, Catherine	Scottsdale, AZ	8/6/51
Hildegarde	Adell, WI	2/1/06
Hill, Arthur	Melfort, Sask	8/1/22
Hill, Dulé	Orange, NJ	5/3/74
Hill, Faith	Jackson, MS	9/21/67
Hill, Lauryn	South Orange, NJ	5/25/75
Hill, Steven	Seattle, WA	2/24/22
Hillerman, John	Denison, TX.	12/20/32
Hilton, Paris	New York, NY	2/17/81
Hines, Cheryl	Miami Beach, FL	9/21/65
Hingle, Pat	Denver, CO	7/19/24
Hirsch, Judd	New York, NY	3/15/35
Ho, Don	Kakaako, Oahu, HI.	8/13/30
Hoffman, Dustin	Los Angeles, CA	8/8/37
Hoffman, Philip Seymour	Fairport, NY	7/23/67
Hogan, Paul	Lightning Ridge, New South Wales, Australia	10/8/39
Holbrook, Hal	Cleveland, OH	2/17/25
Holder, Geoffrey	Port of Spain, Trinidad.	8/1/30
Holliday, Polly	Jasper, AL	7/2/37
Holliman, Earl	Delhi, LA	9/11/28
Holly, Lauren	Bristol, PA	10/28/63
Holm, Celeste	New York, NY	4/29/19
Holm, Ian	Ilford, England	9/12/31
Holmes, Katie	Toledo, OH	12/18/78
Hooks, Jan	Decatur, GA.	4/23/57
Hopkins, Anthony	Port Talbot, South Wales	12/31/37
Hopkins, Bo	Greenville, SC	2/2/42
Hopkins, Telma	Louisville, KY.	10/28/48
Hopper, Dennis	Dodge City, KS	5/17/36
Horne, Lena	Brooklyn, NY	6/30/17
Horne, Marilyn	Bradford, PA	1/16/34
Hornsby, Bruce	Williamsburg, VA.	11/23/54
Horsley, Lee	Muleshoe, TX	5/15/55
Horton, Robert	Los Angeles, CA	7/29/24
Hoskins, Bob.	Suffolk, England	10/26/42
Hounsou, Djimon	Benin	4/24/64
Houston, Whitney	Newark, NJ	8/9/63
Howard, Ken	El Centro, CA	3/28/44
Howard, Ron	Duncan, OK.	3/1/54
Howell, C. Thomas	Van Nuys, CA	12/7/66
Howes, Sally Ann	London, England	7/20/30
Hudson, Kate	Los Angeles, CA	4/19/79
Hughes, Barnard	Bedford Hills, NY.	7/16/15
Hulce, Tom	Whitewater, WI	12/6/53
Humperdinck, Engelbert	Madras, India.	5/2/36
Humphries, Barry	Melbourne, Australia	2/17/34
Hunt, Bonnie	Chicago, IL	9/22/64
Hunt, Helen	Culver City, CA	6/15/63
Hunt, Linda	Morristown, NJ	4/2/45
Hunter, Holly	Conyers, GA	3/20/58
Hunter, Tab	New York, NY	7/11/31
Hurley, Elizabeth	Hampshire, England	6/10/65
Hurt, John	Chesterfield, England	1/22/40
Hurt, Mary Beth	Marshalltown, IA	9/26/48
Hurt, William	Washington, DC	3/20/50
Hussey, Ruth	Providence, RI.	10/30/14
Huston, Anjelica	Santa Monica, CA	7/8/51
Hutton, Betty	Battle Creek, MI.	2/26/21
Hutton, Lauren	Charleston, SC	11/17/43
Hutton, Timothy	Malibu, CA	8/16/60
Hyman, Earle	Rocky Mount, NC	10/11/26

Name	Birthplace	Birthdate
Ian, Janis	New York, NY	4/7/51
Ice Cube	Los Angeles, CA	6/15/69
Ice-T	Newark, NJ	2/16/58
Idle, Eric	S. Shields, England	3/29/43
Idol, Billy	Middlesex, England.	11/30/55
Iglesias, Enrique	Madrid, Spain.	5/8/75
Iglesias, Julio.	Madrid, Spain.	9/23/43
Iler, Robert	New York, NY	3/2/85
Iman	Mogadishu, Somalia	7/25/55
Imbruglia, Natalie	Sydney, Australia.	2/4/75
Imperioli, Michael	Mount Vernon, NY	1/1/66
Imus, Don	Riverside, CA.	7/23/40
Ingram, James	Akron, OH	2/16/56
Innes, Laura	Pontiac, MI.	8/16/59
Ireland, Kathy	Glendale, CA	3/20/63
Irons, Jeremy	Isle of Wight, England	9/19/48
Irving, Amy	Palo Alto, CA	9/10/53
Irving, George S.	Springfield, MA	11/1/22
Irwin, Bill	Santa Monica, CA	4/11/50
Irwin, Steve	Beerwah, Queensland, Australia.	2/22/62
Ivey, Judith	El Paso, TX	9/4/51
Ivory, James	Berkeley, CA	6/7/28
Jackee (Harry)	Winston-Salem, NC	8/14/56
Jackman, Hugh	Sydney, Australia.	10/12/68
Jackson, Anne.	Allegheny, PA	9/3/26
Jackson, Glenda	Birkenhead, England	5/9/36
Jackson, Janet	Gary, IN	5/16/66
Jackson, Jermaine	Gary, IN	12/11/54
Jackson, Jonathan	Orlando, FL	5/11/82
Jackson, Joshua	Vancouver, Brit. Columbia	6/11/78
Jackson, Kate	Birmingham, AL.	10/29/48
Jackson, La Toya	Gary, IN	5/29/56
Jackson, Michael.	Gary, IN	8/29/58
Jackson, Peter	Wellington, New Zealand.	10/31/61
Jackson, Samuel L.	Chattanooga, TN	12/21/48
Jacobi, Derek	London, England	10/22/38
Jagger, Mick	Dartford, England.	7/26/43
James, Etta	Los Angeles, CA	1/25/38
James, Kevin.	Mineola, NY	4/26/65
Janis, Conrad	New York, NY	2/11/28
Janney, Allison	Boston, MA	11/19/60
Janssen, Famke	Amsterdam, Netherlands.	11/5/65
Jardine, Al	Lima, OH	9/3/42
Jarmusch, Jim	Akron, OH	1/22/53
Jarreau, Al.	Milwaukee, WI	3/12/40
Jarrette, Keith	Allentown, PA	5/8/45
Jay Z	Brooklyn, NY	12/4/69
Jeffreys, Anne	Goldsboro, NC.	1/26/23
Jett, Joan.	Philadelphia, PA	9/22/60
Jewel (Kilcher)	Payson, UT	5/23/74
Jewison, Norman	Toronto, Ontario.	7/21/26
Jillian, Ann.	Cambridge, MA	1/29/50
Jillette, Penn	Greenfield, MA.	3/5/55
Joel, Billy	Bronx, NY	5/9/49
Johansson, Scarlett	New York, NY	11/22/84
John, Elton	Pinner, Middlesex, Eng.	3/25/47
Johns, Glynis.	Durban, S Africa	10/5/23
Johnson, Arte	Benton Harbor, MI	1/20/34
Johnson, Beverly.	Buffalo, NY.	10/13/52
Johnson, Don	Flatt Creek, MO.	12/15/49
Johnson, Van	Newport, RI	8/25/16
Johnston, Bruce	Chicago, IL.	6/24/44
Johnston, Kristen	Washington, DC.	9/20/67
Jolie, Angelina.	Los Angeles, CA	6/4/75
Jones, Charlie	Ft. Smith, AR	11/9/30
Jones, Cherry	Paris, TN	11/21/56
Jones, Davy	Manchester, England.	12/30/45
Jones, Dean	Morgan City, AL.	1/25/31
Jones, Elvin.	Pontiac, MI.	9/9/27
Jones, Gemma	London, England	12/4/42
Jones, George	Saratoga, TX	9/12/31
Jones, Grace.	Spanishtown, Jamaica.	5/19/52
Jones, Jack.	Hollywood, CA.	1/14/38
Jones, James Earl	Arkabutla, MS	1/17/31
Jones, Jennifer	Tulsa, OK.	3/2/19
Jones, Mick	London, England.	6/26/55
Jones, Norah	New York, NY	3/30/79
Jones, Quincy	Chicago, IL.	3/14/33
Jones, Shirley	Smithton, PA	3/31/34
Jones, Star	Badin, NC	3/24/62
Jones, Tom	Pontypridd, Wales	6/7/40
Jones, Tommy Lee	San Saba, TX	9/15/46
Jonze, Spike	Rockville, MD.	10/22/69
Jourdan, Louis.	Marseilles, France	6/19/19
Jovovich, Milla.	Kiev, Ukraine	12/17/75
Judd, Ashley	Granada Hills, CA	4/19/68
Judd, Naomi	Ashland, KY.	1/11/46
Judd, Wynonna	Ashland, KY.	5/30/64

Name	Birthplace	Birthdate
Kaczmarek, Jane	Milwaukee, WI	12/21/55
Kanaly, Steve	Burbank, CA	3/14/46
Kane, Carol	Cleveland, OH	6/18/52
Kaplan, Gabe	Brooklyn, NY	3/31/45
Karlen, John	Brooklyn, NY	5/28/33
Karn, Richard	Seattle, WA	2/17/56
Karras, Alex	Gary, IN	7/15/35
Kasem, Casey	Detroit, MI	4/27/32
Kattan, Chris	Sherman Oaks, CA	10/19/70
Kavner, Julie	Burbank, CA	9/7/51
Kazan, Lainie	New York, NY	5/15/42
Keach, Stacy	Savannah, GA	6/2/41
Keaton, Diane	Santa Ana, CA	1/5/46
Keaton, Michael	Pittsburgh, PA	9/9/51
Keel, Howard	Gillespie, IL	4/13/19
Keener, Catherine	Miami FL	3/23/59
Keitel, Harvey	Brooklyn, NY	5/13/39
Keith, David	Knoxville, TN	5/8/54
Keith, Penelope	Sutton, Surrey, England	4/2/40
Kellerman, Sally	Long Beach, CA	6/2/37
Kelly, Jean Louisa	Worcester, MA	3/9/72
Kelly, R(obert)	Chicago, IL	1/8/67
Kennedy, George	New York, NY	2/18/25
Kennedy, Jamie	Upper Darby, PA	5/25/70
Kennedy, Jayne	Washington, DC	10/27/51
Kenny G	Seattle, WA	6/5/56
Kent, Allegra	Santa Monica, CA	8/11/37
Kercheval, Ken	Wolcottville, IN	7/15/35
Kerns, Joanna	San Francisco, CA	2/12/53
Kerr, Deborah	Helensburgh, Scotland	9/30/21
Keys, Alicia	New York, NY	1/25/81
Khan, Chaka	Great Lakes, IL	3/23/53
Kidder, Margot	Yellowknife, N.W.T.	10/17/48
Kidman, Nicole	Honolulu, HI	6/20/67
Kiel, Richard	Detroit, MI	9/13/39
Kilborn, Craig	Kansas City, KS	8/24/62
Kilmer, Val	Los Angeles, CA	12/31/59
Kimbrough, Charles	St. Paul, MN	5/23/36
Kimmel, Jimmy	Brooklyn, NY	11/13/67
King, B. B.	Itta Bena, MS	9/16/25
King, Carole	Brooklyn, NY	2/9/42
King, Larry	Brooklyn, NY	11/19/33
King, Perry	Alliance, OH	4/30/48
Kingsley, Ben	Scarborough, England	12/31/43
Kingston, Alex	London, England	3/11/63
Kinnear, Greg	Logansport, IN	6/17/63
Kinney, Kathy	Stevens Point, WI	11/3/53
Kinski, Nastassja	Berlin, W. Germany	1/24/60
Kirby, Bruno	New York, NY	4/28/49
Kirkland, Gelsey	Bethlehem, PA	12/29/52
Kirkpatrick, Chris	Clarion, PA	10/17/71
Kitt, Eartha	North, SC	1/17/27
Klein, Robert	Bronx, New York, NY	2/8/42
Kline, Kevin	St. Louis, MO	10/24/47
Klugman, Jack	Philadelphia, PA	4/27/22
Knight, Gladys	Atlanta, GA	5/28/44
Knight, Shirley	Goessel, KS	7/5/36
Knight, Wayne	New York, NY	8/7/55
Knightley, Keira	Teddington, England	3/26/85
Knopfler, Mark	Glasgow, Scotland	8/12/49
Knotts, Don	Morgantown, WV	7/21/24
Knowles, Beyoncé	Houston, TX	9/4/81
Knoxville, Johnny	Knoxville, TN	3/11/71
Konitz, Lee	Chicago, IL	10/13/27
Kopell, Bernie	New York, NY	6/21/33
Korman, Harvey	Chicago, IL	2/15/27
Kotto, Yaphet	New York, NY	11/15/37
Krakowski, Jane	Parsippany, NJ	10/11/68
Krause, Peter	Alexandria, MN	8/12/65
Kretschmann, Thomas	Dessau, E. Germany	9/8/62
Kristofferson, Kris	Brownsville, TX	6/22/36
Kudrow, Lisa	Encino, CA	7/30/63
Kunis, Mila	Kiev, Ukraine, Soviet Union	8/14/83
Kuriyama, Chiaki	Tsuchiura, Ibaraki, Japan	10/10/84
Kurtz, Swoosie	Omaha, NE	9/6/44
Kutcher, Ashton	Cedar Rapids, IA	2/7/78
Kwan, Nancy	Hong Kong	5/19/39
LaBelle, Patti	Philadelphia, PA	5/24/44
LaBeouf, Shia	Los Angeles, CA	6/11/86
Ladd, Cheryl	Huron, SD	7/12/51
Ladd, Diane	Meridian, MS	11/29/32
Lagasse, Emeril	Fall River, MA	10/15/59
Lahti, Christine	Royal Oak, MI	4/4/50
Laine, Cleo	Southall, England	10/28/27
Laine, Frankie	Chicago, IL	3/30/13
Lake, Ricki	Hastings-on-Hudson, NY	9/21/68
Lamas, Lorenzo	Santa Monica, CA	1/20/58
Lambert, Christopher	Great Neck, NY	3/29/57
Landau, Martin	Brooklyn, NY	6/20/28

Name	Birthplace	Birthdate
Landis, John	Chicago, IL	8/3/50
Lane, Diane	New York, NY	1/22/65
Lane, Nathan	Jersey City, NJ	2/3/56
lang, k.d.	Consort, Alberta	11/2/61
Lang, Stephen	Queens, New York, NY	7/11/52
Lange, Jessica	Cloquet, MN	4/20/49
Langella, Frank	Bayonne, NJ	1/1/40
Langford, Frances	Lakeland, FL	4/4/14
Lansbury, Angela	London, England	10/16/25
LaPaglia, Anthony	Adelaide, Australia	1/31/59
Laredo, Ruth	Detroit, MI	11/20/37
Larroquette, John	New Orleans, LA	11/25/47
LaSalle, Eriq	Hartford, CT	6/23/62
Lauper, Cyndi	Brooklyn, NY	6/20/53
Laurie, Piper	Detroit, MI	1/22/32
Lavigne, Avril	Napanee, Ontario	9/27/84
Lavin, Linda	Portland, ME	10/15/37
Law, Jude	London, England	12/29/72
Lawless, Lucy	Mount Albert, New Zealand	3/29/68
Lawrence, Carol	Melrose Park, IL	9/5/34
Lawrence, Joey	Montgomery, PA	4/20/76
Lawrence, Martin	Frankfurt, Germany	4/16/65
Lawrence, Steve	Brooklyn, NY	7/8/35
Lawrence, Vicki	Inglewood, CA	3/26/49
Leach, Robin	London, England	8/29/41
Leachman, Cloris	Des Moines, IA	4/30/26
Lear, Norman	New Haven, CT	7/27/22
Learned, Michael	Washington, DC.	4/9/39
Leary, Denis	Worcester, MA	8/18/57
LeBlanc, Matt	Newton, MA	7/25/67
LeBon, Simon	Bushey, England	10/27/58
Ledger, Heath	Perth, Australia	4/4/79
Lee, Ang	Pingtung, Taiwan	10/23/54
Lee, Brenda	Lithonia, GA	12/11/44
Lee, Christopher	London, England	5/27/22
Lee, Jason	Huntington Beach, CA	4/25/70
Lee, Michele	Los Angeles, CA	6/24/42
Lee, Spike	Atlanta, GA	3/20/57
Leeves, Jane	London, England	4/18/61
Legrand, Michel	Paris, France	2/24/32
Leguizamo, John	Bogotá, Colombia	7/22/64
Leibman, Ron	New York, NY	10/11/37
Leigh, Janet	Merced, CA	7/6/27
Leigh, Jennifer Jason	Hollywood, CA	2/5/62
Leighton, Laura	Iowa City, IA	7/24/68
Lennox, Annie	Aberdeen, Scotland	12/25/54
Leno, Jay	New Rochelle, NY	4/28/50
Leonard, Robert Sean	Westwood, NJ	2/28/69
Leoni, Tea	New York, NY	2/25/66
Leslie, Joan	Detroit, MI	1/26/25
Leto, Jared	Bossier City, LA	12/26/71
Letterman, David	Indianapolis, IN	4/12/47
Levine, James	Cincinnati, OH	6/23/43
Levine, Ted	Parma, OH.	5/29/58
Levinson, Barry	Baltimore, MD	4/6/42
Levy, Eugene	Hamilton, Ontario	12/17/46
Lewis, Al	New York, NY	4/30/10
Lewis, Huey	New York, NY	7/5/50
Lewis, Jason	Newport Beach, CA	6/25/71
Lewis, Jerry	Newark, NJ	3/16/26
Lewis, Jerry Lee	Ferriday, LA	9/29/35
Lewis, Juliette	San Fernando Valley, CA	6/21/73
Lewis, Richard	Brooklyn, NY	6/29/47
Li, Jet	Beijing, China	4/26/63
Light, Judith	Trenton, NJ	2/9/49
Lightfoot, Gordon	Orillia, Ontario	11/17/38
Lil' Kim	Brooklyn, NY	7/11/75
Linden, Hal	Bronx, New York, NY	3/20/31
Ling, Lisa	Sacramento, CA	8/30/73
Linkletter, Art	Moose Jaw, Saskatchewan	7/17/12
Linn-Baker, Mark	St. Louis, MO	6/17/54
Linney, Laura	New York, NY	2/5/64
Liotta, Ray	Newark, NJ	12/18/55
Lithgow, John	Rochester, NY	10/19/45
Little, Rich	Ottawa, Ontario	11/26/38
Little Richard	Macon, GA	12/5/32
Littrell, Brian	Lexington, KY	2/20/75
Liu, Lucy	Queens, NY	12/2/68
L. L. Cool J	St. Albans, Queens, NY	1/14/68
Lloyd, Christopher	Stamford, CT	10/22/38
Lloyd, Emily	North London, England	9/29/70
Lloyd Webber, Andrew	London, England	3/22/48
Locke, Sondra	Shelbyville, TN	5/28/47
Lockhart, June	New York, NY	6/25/25
Locklear, Heather	Westwood, CA	9/25/61
Loggia, Robert	Staten Island, NY	1/3/30
Loggins, Kenny	Everett, WA	1/7/48
Logue, Donal	Ottawa, Canada	2/27/66
Lohan, Lindsay	New York, NY	7/2/86
Lollobrigida, Gina	Subiaco, Italy	7/4/27

Name	Birthplace	Birthdate	Name	Birthplace	Birthdate
Lom, Herbert	Prague, Czechoslovakia	1/9/17	Martin, Jesse L.	Rocky Mount, VA	1/18/69
Lonergan, Kenneth	New York, NY	10/16/62	Martin, Kellie	Riverside, CA	10/16/75
Long, Nia	Brooklyn, NY	10/30/70	Martin, Ricky	San Juan, Puerto Rico	12/24/71
Long, Shelley	Ft. Wayne, IN	8/23/49	Martin, Steve	Waco, TX	8/14/45
Lopez, George	Mission Hills, CA	4/23/61	Martin, Tony	Oakland, CA	12/25/13
Lopez, Jennifer	Bronx, NY	7/24/70	Martins, Peter	Copenhagen, Denmark	10/27/46
Loren, Sophia	Rome, Italy	9/20/34	Mason, Jackie	Sheboygan, WI	6/9/34
Loring, Gloria	New York, NY	12/10/46	Mason, Marsha	St. Louis, MO	4/3/42
Louis-Dreyfus, Julia	New York, NY	1/13/61	Masterson, Christopher	Long Island, NY	1/22/80
Love, Courtney	San Francisco, CA	7/9/64	Masterson, Mary Stuart	New York, NY	6/28/66
Love, Mike	Baldwin Hills, CA	3/15/41	Mastrantonio, Mary		
Lovett, Lyle	Klein, TX	11/1/57	Elizabeth	Lombard, IL	11/17/58
Lovitz, Jon	Tarzana, CA	7/21/57	Masur, Kurt	Brieg, Germany	7/18/27
Loveless, Patty	Pikeville, KY	1/4/57	Masur, Richard	New York, NY	11/20/48
Lowe, Rob	Charlottesville, VA	3/17/64	Mathers, Jerry	Sioux City, IA	6/2/48
Lowell, Carey	Huntington, NY	2/11/61	Matheson, Tim	Glendale, CA	12/31/47
Lucas, George	Modesto, CA	5/14/44	Mathis, Johnny	San Francisco, CA	9/30/35
Lucci, Susan	Scarsdale, NY	12/23/46	Matlin, Marlee	Morton Grove, IL	8/24/65
Luckinbill, Laurence	Ft. Smith, AR	11/21/34	Matthews, Dave	Johannesburg, South Africa	1/9/67
Ludwig, Christa	Berlin, Germany	3/16/24	May, Elaine	Philadelphia, PA	4/21/32
Luhrmann, Baz	Sydney, Australia	9/17/62	Mayo, Virginia	St. Louis, MO	11/30/20
Lumet, Sidney	Philadelphia, PA	6/25/24	Mazursky, Paul	Brooklyn, NY	4/25/30
LuPone, Patti	Northport, NY	4/21/49	MCA	Brooklyn, NY	11/20/65
Lynch, David	Missoula, MT	1/20/46	McAdams, Rachel	London, Ontario, Canada	10/7/86
Lynley, Carol	New York, NY	2/13/42	McArdle, Andrea	Abington, PA	11/5/63
Lynn, Loretta	Butcher Hollow, KY	4/14/35	McBride, Patricia	Teaneck, NJ	8/23/42
Lynn, Vera	London, England	3/20/17	McCallum, David	Glasgow, Scotland	9/19/33
Lynne, Shelby	Quantico, VA	10/22/68	McCarthy, Andrew	Westfield, NJ	11/29/62
Lyonne, Natasha	Great Neck, NY	4/4/79	McCarthy, Jenny	Chicago, IL	11/1/72
			McCarthy, Kevin	Seattle, WA	2/15/14
Ma, Yo-Yo	Paris, France	10/7/55	McCartney, Paul	Liverpool, England	6/18/42
Maazel, Lorin	Neuilly-sur-Seine, France	3/6/30	McCarver, Tim	Memphis, TN	10/16/41
Mac, Bernie	Chicago, IL	10/5/58	McClanahan, Rue	Healdton, OK	2/21/34
MacArthur, James	Los Angeles, CA	12/8/37	McConaughey, Matthew	Uvalde, Texas	11/4/69
Macchio, Ralph	Huntington, NY	11/4/62	McCoo, Marilyn	Jersey City, NJ	9/30/43
MacCorkindale, Simon	Ely, England	2/12/52	McCormack, Eric	Toronto, Canada	4/18/63
MacDonald, Kelly	Glasgow, Scotland	2/23/76	McCormack, Mary	Plainsfield, NJ	2/8/69
MacDowell, Andie	Gaffney, SC	4/21/58	McCrane, Paul	Philadelphia, PA	1/19/61
MacGraw, Ali	Pound Ridge, NY	4/1/38	McDaniel, James	Washington, DC	3/25/58
MacGowan, Shane	Tunbridge, Kent, England	12/25/57	McDermott, Dylan	Waterbury, CT	10/26/61
MacLachlan, Kyle	Yakima, WA	2/22/59	McDiarmid, Ian	Carnoustie, Tayside,	
MacLaine, Shirley	Richmond, VA	4/24/34		Scotland	4/17/47
MacLeod, Gavin	Mt. Kisco, NY	2/28/31	McDonald, Audra	Berlin, Germany	7/3/70
MacNee, Patrick	London, England	2/6/22	McDonnell, Mary	Wilkes-Barre, PA	4/28/52
MacNeil, Cornell	Minneapolis, MN	9/24/22	McDormand, Frances	Illinois	6/23/57
MacNicol, Peter	Dallas, TX	4/10/54	McDowell, Malcolm	Leeds, England	6/13/43
MacPherson, Elle	Sydney, Australia	3/29/64	McEntire, Reba	McAlester, OK	3/28/55
Macy, Bill	Revere, MA	5/18/22	McFerrin, Bobby	New York, NY	3/11/50
Macy, William H.	Miami, FL	3/13/50	McGavin, Darren	Spokane, WA	5/7/22
Madden, John	Austin, MN	4/10/36	McGillis, Kelly	Newport Beach, CA	7/9/57
Madigan, Amy	Chicago, IL	9/11/50	McGoohan, Patrick	Astoria, Queens, NY	3/19/28
Madonna (Ciccone)	Bay City, MI	8/16/58	McGovern, Elizabeth	Evanston, IL	7/18/61
Madsen, Michael	Chicago, IL	9/25/58	McGovern, Maureen	Youngstown, OH	7/27/49
Maguire, Tobey	Santa Monica, CA	6/27/75	McGraw, Tim	Delhi, LA	5/1/67
Maher, Bill	New York, NY	1/20/56	McGregor, Ewan	Crieff, Scotland	3/31/71
Mahoney, John	Manchester, England	6/20/40	McGuire, Al	New York, NY	9/7/31
Majors, Lee	Wyandotte, MI	4/23/39	McKean, Michael	New York, NY	10/17/47
Malden, Karl	Gary, IN	3/22/12	McKechnie, Donna	Pontiac, MI	11/16/42
Malick, Terrence	Ottawa, IL	11/30/43	McKellen, Ian	Burnley, England	5/25/39
Malick, Wendie	Buffalo, NY	12/13/50	McKenzie, Benjamin	Austin, TX	9/12/78
Malina, Joshua	New York, NY	1/17/66	McLachlan, Sarah	Halifax, Nova Scotia	1/28/68
Malkovich, John	Christopher, IL	12/9/53	McLean, A.J.	West Palm Beach, FL	1/9/78
Malone, Dorothy	Chicago, IL	1/30/25	McMahon, Ed	Detroit, MI	3/6/23
Mamet, David	Chicago, IL	11/30/47	McNichol, Kristy	Los Angeles, CA	9/11/62
Manchester, Melissa	Bronx, NY	2/15/51	McPartland, Marian	Stough, England	3/20/20
Mandel, Howie	Toronto, Ontario	11/29/55	McRaney, Gerald	Collins, MS.	8/19/47
Mandrell, Barbara	Houston, TX	12/25/48	Meadows, Jayne	Wu Chang, China	9/27/20
Mangione, Chuck	Rochester, NY	11/29/40	Meara, Anne	Brooklyn, NY	9/20/29
Manheim, Camryn	Caldwell, NJ	3/8/61	Meat Loaf	Dallas, TX	9/27/51
Manilow, Barry	Brooklyn, NY	6/17/46	Mehta, Zubin	Bombay, India	4/29/36
Mann, Aimee	Richmond, VA	8/9/60	Mellencamp, John	Seymour, IN	10/7/51
Manoff, Dinah	New York, NY	1/25/58	Meloni, Christopher	Washington, DC.	4/2/61
Manson, Marilyn	Canton, OH	1/5/69	Mendes, Sam	Redding, England	8/1/65
Mantegna, Joe	Chicago, IL	11/13/47	Mendes, Sergio	Niteroi, Brazil	2/11/41
Marceau, Marcel	Strasbourg, France	3/22/23	Mercer, Marian	Akron, OH	11/26/35
Marcil, Vanessa	Indio, CA	10/15/69	Merchant, Natalie	Jamestown, NY	10/26/63
Margulies, Julianna	Spring Valley, NY	6/8/66	Merkerson, S. Epatha	Saginaw, MI	11/28/52
Marie, Constance	Hollywood, CA	9/9/69	Merrill, Dina	New York, NY	12/9/25
Marin, Cheech	Los Angeles, CA	7/13/46	Merrill, Robert	Brooklyn, NY	6/4/19
Marinaro, Ed	New York, NY	3/31/50	Messing, Debra	Brooklyn, NY	8/15/68
Markova, Alicia	London, England	12/1/10	Metcalf, Laurie	Carbondale, IL	6/16/55
Marriner, Neville	Lincoln, England	4/15/24	Michael, George	London, England	6/25/63
Marsalis, Branford	New Orleans, LA	8/26/60	Michaels, Al	Brooklyn, NY	11/12/44
Marsalis, Wynton	New Orleans, LA	10/18/61	Michaels, Lorne	Toronto, Canada	11/17/44
Marsh, Jean	London, England	7/1/34	Midler, Bette	Honolulu, HI	12/1/45
Marshall, Garry	Bronx, New York, NY	11/13/34	Midori	Osaka, Japan	10/25/71
Marshall, Penny	Bronx, New York, NY	10/15/42	Mike D	Brooklyn, NY	11/20/65
Marshall, Peter	Huntington, WV	3/30/27	Milano, Alyssa	Brooklyn, NY	12/19/72
Martin, Chris	Devon, England	3/22/77	Miles, Sarah	Ingatestone, England	12/31/41
Martin, Dick	Detroit, MI	1/30/22	Miles, Vera	near Boise City, OK	8/23/29

Name	Birthplace	Birthdate
Miller, Dennis	Pittsburgh, PA	11/3/53
Miller, Mitch	Rochester, NY	7/4/11
Miller, Penelope Ann	Santa Monica, CA	1/13/64
Mills, Donna	Chicago, IL	12/11/43
Mills, Hayley	London, England	4/18/46
Mills, John	Suffolk, England	2/22/08
Milner, Martin	Detroit, MI	12/28/27
Milnes, Sherrill	Downers Grove, IL	1/10/35
Milsap, Ronnie	Robinsville, NC	1/16/44
Mimieux, Yvette	Hollywood, CA	1/8/42
Minghella, Anthony	Isle of Wight, England	1/6/54
Ming-Na	Macao	11/20/63
Minnelli, Liza	Los Angeles, CA	3/12/46
Minogue, Kylie	Melbourne, Australia	5/28/68
Mirren, Helen	London, England	7/26/45
Mitchell, Brian	Seattle, WA	10/31/58
Mitchell, Elizabeth	Los Angeles, CA	3/27/70
Mitchell, Joni	Fort McLeod, Alberta	11/7/43
Moby	Harlem, New York, NY	9/11/65
Modine, Matthew	Loma Linda, CA	3/22/59
Moffat, Donald	Plymouth, England	12/26/30
Moffo, Anna	Wayne, PA	6/27/34
Molina, Alfred	London, England	5/24/53
Molinaro, Al	Kenosha, WI	6/24/19
Moll, Richard	Pasadena, CA	1/13/43
Moloney, Janel	Woodland Hills, CA	10/3/69
Monica (Arnold)	College Park, GA	10/24/80
Montalban, Ricardo	Mexico City, Mexico	11/25/20
Moody, Ron	London, England	1/8/24
Moore, Demi	Roswell, NM	11/11/62
Moore, Julianne	Fort Bragg, NC	12/3/60
Moore, Mandy	Nashua, NH	4/10/84
Moore, Mary Tyler	Brooklyn, NY	12/29/36
Moore, Melba	New York, NY	10/29/45
Moore, Michael	Flint, MI	4/23/54
Moore, Roger	London, England	10/14/27
Moore, Terry	Los Angeles, CA	1/7/29
Morales, Esai	Brooklyn, NY	10/1/62
Moranis, Rick	Toronto, Ontario	4/18/54
Moreau, Jeanne	Paris, France	1/23/28
Moreno, Rita	Humacao, PR	12/11/31
Morgan, Harry	Detroit, MI	4/10/15
Moriarty, Michael	Detroit, MI	4/5/41
Morissette, Alanis	Ottawa, Ontario	6/1/74
Morita, Pat	Isleton, CA	6/28/32
Morris, Garrett	New Orleans, LA	2/1/37
Morris, Howard	New York, NY	9/4/19
Morrison, Van	Belfast, N. Ireland	8/31/45
Morrissey	Manchester, England	5/22/59
Morrow, Rob	New Rochelle, NY	9/21/62
Morse, David	Beverly, MA	10/11/53
Morse, Robert	Newton, MA	5/18/31
Mortensen, Viggo	New York, NY	10/20/58
Mortimer, Emily	London, England	12/1/71
Morton, Joe	Brooklyn, NY	10/18/47
Morton, Samantha	Nottingham, Enlgand	5/13/77
Moses, William	Los Angeles, CA	11/17/59
Moss, Carrie-Anne	Vancouver, British Columbia	8/21/67
Moss, Kate	Croydon, Surrey, England	1/16/74
Mueller-Stahl, Armin	Tilsit, E. Prussia	12/17/30
Muldaur, Diana	Brooklyn, NY	8/19/38
Mulgrew, Kate	Dubuque, IA	4/29/55
Mull, Martin	Chicago, IL	8/18/43
Mullally, Megan	Los Angeles, CA	11/12/58
Mullan, Peter	Peterhead, Scotland	1960
Mulroney, Dermot	Alexandria, VA	10/31/63
Muniz, Frankie	Ridgewood, NJ	12/5/85
Munsel, Patrice	Spokane, WA	5/14/25
Murphy, Ben	Jonesboro, AR	3/6/42
Murphy, Brittany	Atlanta, GA	11/10/77
Murphy, Donna	Queens, NY	3/7/58
Murphy, Eddie	Brooklyn, NY	4/3/61
Murphy, Michael	Los Angeles, CA	5/5/38
Murray, Anne	Springhill, Nova Scotia	6/20/45
Murray, Bill	Wilmette, IL	9/21/50
Murray, Don	Hollywood, CA	7/31/29
Musburger, Brent	Portland, OR	5/26/39
Muti, Riccardo	Naples, Italy	7/28/41
Myers, Mike	Scarborough, Ontario	5/25/63
Nabors, Jim	Sylacauga, AL	6/12/30
Nagra, Parminder	Leicester, England	10/5/75
Nash, Graham	Blackpool, England	2/2/42
Naughton, James	Middletown, CT	12/6/45
Navarro, Dave	Santa Monica, CA	6/7/67
Neal, Patricia	Packard, KY	1/20/26
Nealon, Kevin	Bridgeport, CT	11/18/53
Neeson, Liam	Ballymena, N. Ireland	6/7/52
Neill, Sam	Ulster, N. Ireland	9/14/47
Nelligan, Kate	London, Ontario	3/16/51
Nelly	Austin, TX	11/2/74
Nelson, Craig T.	Spokane, WA	4/4/46
Nelson, Ed	New Orleans, LA	12/21/28
Nelson, Judd	Portland, ME	11/28/59
Nelson, Tracy	Santa Monica, CA	10/25/63
Nelson, Willie	Abbott, TX	4/30/33
Nero, Peter	Brooklyn, NY	5/22/34
Nesmith, Mike	Houston, TX	12/30/42
Nettleton, Lois	Oak Park, IL	8/16/29
Neuwirth, Bebe	Newark, NJ	12/31/58
Neville, Aaron	New Orleans, LA	1/24/41
Newhart, Bob	Oak Park, IL	9/5/29
Newman, Paul	Cleveland, OH	1/26/25
Newman, Randy	New Orleans, LA	11/28/43
Newton, Wayne	Norfolk, VA	4/3/42
Newton-John, Olivia	Cambridge, England	9/26/48
Nicholas, Denise	Detroit, MI	7/12/44
Nicholas, Fayard	Philadelphia, PA	10/20/14
Nichols, Mike	Berlin, Germany	11/6/31
Nicholson, Jack	Neptune, NJ	4/22/37
Nicks, Stevie	Phoenix, AZ	5/26/48
Nielsen, Connie	Copenhagen, Denmark	7/3/65
Nielsen, Leslie	Regina, Sask.	2/11/26
Nighy, Bill	Caterham, Surrey, Eng.	12/12/49
Nilsson, Birgit	Vastra Karup, Sweden	5/17/18
Nimoy, Leonard	Boston, MA	3/26/31
Nixon, Cynthia	New York, NY	4/9/66
Nolte, Nick	Omaha, NE	2/8/41
Noone, Peter	Manchester, England	11/5/47
Norman, Jessye	Augusta, GA	9/15/45
Norris, Chuck	Ryan, OK	3/10/40
North, Sheree	Hollywood, CA	1/17/33
Northam, Jeremy	Cambridge, Enlgand	12/1/61
Norton, Edward	Columbia, MD	8/18/69
Noth, Christopher	Madison, WI	11/13/54
Novak, Kim	Chicago, IL	2/13/33
Nuyen, France	Marseilles, France	7/31/39
Oates, John	New York, NY	4/7/49
Obradors, Jacqueline	San Fernando Valley, CA	10/6/66
O'Brian, Hugh	Rochester, NY	4/19/25
O'Brien, Conan	Brookline, MA	4/18/63
O'Brien, Margaret	Los Angeles, CA	1/15/37
Ocean, Billy	Fyzabad, Trinidad	1/21/50
O'Connor, Frances	Oxford, England	6/12/69
O'Connor, Sinead	Glenageary, Ireland	12/8/66
Odetta	Birmingham, AL	12/31/30
O'Donnell, Chris	Winnetka, IL	6/26/70
O'Donnell, Rosie	Commack, NY	3/21/62
O'Grady, Gail	Detroit, MI	1/23/63
O'Hara, Catherine	Toronto, Canada	3/4/54
O'Hara, Maureen	Dublin, Ireland	8/17/20
O'Herlihy, Dan	Wexford, Ireland	5/1/19
Oldman, Gary	South London, England	3/21/58
Olin, Ken	Chicago, IL	7/30/54
Olin, Lena	Stockholm, Sweden	3/22/55
Olmos, Edward James	E. Los Angeles, CA	2/24/47
Olsen, Ashley	Sherman Oaks, CA	6/13/86
Olsen, Mary-Kate	Sherman Oaks, CA	6/13/86
Olsen, Merlin	Logan, UT	9/15/40
Olson, Nancy	Milwaukee, WI	7/14/28
O'Malley, Mike	Boston, MA	10/31/69
O'Neal, Ryan	Los Angeles, CA	4/20/41
O'Neal, Tatum	Los Angeles, CA	11/5/63
O'Neill, Ed	Youngstown, OH	4/12/46
Ontkean, Michael	Vancouver, B.C.	1/24/46
Orbach, Jerry	Bronx, New York, NY	10/20/35
Orlando, Tony	New York, NY	4/3/44
Ormond, Julia	Epsom, England	1/4/65
Osbourne, Jack	London, England	11/8/85
Osbourne, Kelly	London, England	10/27/84
Osbourne, Ozzy	Birmingham, England	12/3/48
Osbourne, Ozzy	Birmingham, England	12/3/48
Osbourne, Sharon	London, England	10/10/52
O'Shea, Milo	Dublin, Ireland	6/2/26
Oslin, K.T.	Crossett, AR	5/15/42
Osment, Haley Joel	Los Angeles, CA	4/10/88
Osmond, Donny	Ogden, UT	12/9/57
Osmond, Marie	Ogden, UT	10/13/59
O'Toole, Annette	Houston, TX	4/1/53
O'Toole, Peter	Connemara, Ireland	8/2/32
Otto, Miranda	Brisbane, Australia	12/16/67
Owens, Buck	Sherman, TX	8/12/29
Oz, Frank	Herford, England	5/25/44
Ozawa, Seiji	Shenyang, China	9/1/35
Pacino, Al	East Harlem, NY	4/25/40
Packer, Billy	Wellsville, NY	2/25/40
Page, Bettie	Nashville, TN	4/22/23
Page, Jimmy	Heston, England	1/9/44
Page, Patti	Claremore, OK	11/8/27

Name	Birthplace	Birthdate
Paget, Debra	Denver, CO	8/19/33
Paige, Janis	Tacoma, WA	9/16/22
Palance, Jack	Lattimer, PA	2/18/20
Palin, Michael	Sheffield, England	5/5/43
Palmer, Betsy	East Chicago, IN	11/1/29
Palmer, Geoffrey	London, England	6/4/27
Palminteri, Chazz	Bronx, NY	5/15/51
Paltrow, Gwyneth	Los Angeles, CA	9/28/72
Pantoliano, Joe	Hoboken, NJ	9/12/51
Papas, Irene	Chiliomodion, Greece	9/3/26
Paquin, Anna	Wellington, New Zealand	7/24/82
Parker, Alan	London, England	2/14/44
Parker, Eleanor	Cedarville, OH	6/26/22
Parker, Fess	Ft. Worth, TX	8/16/25
Parker, Jameson	Baltimore, MD	11/18/47
Parker, Jean	Dear Lodge, MT	8/11/15
Parker, Mary-Louise	Fort Jackson, SC	8/2/64
Parker, Sarah Jessica	Nelsonville, OH	3/25/65
Parsons, Estelle	Marblehead, MA	11/20/27
Parton, Dolly	Sevierville, TN	1/19/46
Patinkin, Mandy	Chicago, IL	11/30/52
Patric, Jason	Queens, NY	6/17/66
Patton, Will	Charleston, SC	6/14/54
Paul, Adrian	London, England	5/29/59
Paul, Les	Waukesha, WI	1/9/15
Paulson, Sarah	Tampa, FL	12/17/75
Pavarotti, Luciano	Modena, Italy	10/12/35
Paxton, Bill	Fort Worth, TX	5/17/55
Pearce, Guy	Ely, England	10/5/67
Peet, Amanda	New York, NY	1/11/72
Pendergrass, Teddy	Philadelphia, PA	3/26/50
Penn, Arthur	Philadelphia, PA	9/27/22
Penn, Sean	Burbank, CA	8/17/60
Penny, Joe	London, England	9/14/56
Perez, Rosie	Brooklyn, NY	9/6/64
Perkins, Elizabeth	Queens, NY	11/18/60
Perlman, Itzhak	Tel Aviv, Israel	8/31/45
Perlman, Rhea	Brooklyn, NY	3/31/48
Perlman, Ron	New York, NY	4/13/50
Perrine, Valerie	Galveston, TX	9/3/43
Perry, Luke	Fredericktown, OH	10/11/66
Perry, Mathew	Williamstown, MA	8/19/69
Persoff, Nehemiah	Jerusalem, Israel	8/2/20
Pesci, Joe	Newark, NJ	2/9/43
Peters, Bernadette	Queens, NY	2/28/48
Peters, Brock	New York, NY	7/2/27
Peters, Roberta	Bronx, NY	5/4/30
Petersen, Wolfgang	Emden, Germany	3/14/41
Peterson, Oscar	Montreal, Quebec	8/15/25
Petty, Lori	Chattanooga, TN	3/23/63
Petty, Tom	Gainesville, FL	10/20/50
Pfeiffer, Michelle	Santa Ana, CA	4/29/58
Philbin, Regis	New York, NY	8/25/31
Phair, Liz	New Haven, CT	4/17/67
Phillippe, Ryan	New Castle, DE	9/10/74
Phillips, Lou Diamond	Subic Bay, Philippines	2/17/62
Phillips, Mackenzie	Alexandria, VA	11/10/59
Phillips, Michelle	Long Beach, CA	6/4/44
Phillips, Sian	Bettws, Wales, UK	5/14/34
Phoenix, Joaquin	San Juan, Puerto Rico	10/28/74
Pickett, Wilson	Prattville, AL	3/18/41
Pierce, David Hyde	Albany, NY	4/3/59
Pinchot, Bronson	New York, NY	5/20/59
Pink (Alecia Moore)	Doylestown, PA	9/8/79
Pinkett Smith, Jada	Baltimore, MD	9/18/71
Pirner, David	Green Bay, WI	4/16/64
Piscopo, Joe	Passaic, NJ	6/17/51
Pitt, Brad	Shawnee, OK	12/18/63
Plant, Robert	W. Bromwich, England	8/20/48
Pleshette, Suzanne	New York, NY	1/31/37
Plowright, Joan	Brigg, England	10/28/29
Plummer, Amanda	New York, NY	3/23/57
Plummer, Christopher	Toronto, Ontario	12/13/27
Poitier, Sidney	Miami, FL	2/20/27
Polanski, Roman	Paris, France	8/18/33
Pollack, Sydney	Lafayette, IN	7/1/34
Ponti, Carlo	Milan, Italy	12/11/12
Pop, Iggy	Muskegon, MI	4/21/47
Portman, Natalie	Jerusalem, Israel	6/9/81
Posey, Parker	Baltimore, MD	11/8/68
Post, Markie	Palo Alto, CA	11/4/50
Poston, Tom	Columbus, OH	10/17/21
Potente, Franka	Dulmen, Germany	7/22/74
Potts, Annie	Nashville, TN	10/28/52
Povich, Maury	Bethesda, MD	1/17/39
Powell, Jane	Portland, OR	4/1/28
Powers, Stefanie	Hollywood, CA	11/2/42
Prentiss, Paula	San Antonio, TX	3/4/39
Presley, Priscilla	Brooklyn, NY	5/24/45
Preston, Billy	Houston, TX	9/9/46

Name	Birthplace	Birthdate
Previn, Andre	Berlin, Germany	4/6/29
Price, Leontyne	Laurel, MS	2/10/27
Price, Molly	North Plainfield, NJ	12/15/66
Price, Ray	Perryville, TX	1/12/26
Pride, Charley	Sledge, MS	3/18/38
Priestley, Jason	Vancouver, Brit. Columbia	8/28/69
Prince (The Artist)	Minneapolis, MN	6/7/58
Prince, Faith	Augusta, GA	8/5/57
Principal, Victoria	Fukuoka, Japan	1/3/50
Prinze, Freddie, Jr.	Albuquerque, NM	3/8/76
Probst, Jeff	Wichita, KS	11/1/61
Proctor, Emily	Raleigh, NC	10/18/68
Prosky, Robert	Philadelphia, PA	12/13/30
Provine, Dorothy	Deadwood, SD	1/20/37
Pryce, Jonathan	Holywell, N. Wales	6/1/47
Pryor, Richard	Peoria, IL	12/1/40
Puck, Wolfgang	St. Veit, Austria	1/8/49
Pulliam, Keshia Knight	Newark, NJ	4/9/79
Pullman, Bill	Hornell, NY	12/17/53
Purcell, Sarah	Richmond, IN	10/8/48
Quaid, Dennis	Houston, TX	4/9/54
Quaid, Randy	Houston, TX	10/1/50
Queen Latifah	Newark, NJ	3/18/70
Quinn, Aidan	Chicago, IL	3/8/59
Quinn, Colin	Brooklyn, NY	8/15/59
Quinn, Martha	Albany, NY	5/11/59
Rachins, Alan	Cambridge, MA	10/3/42
Radcliffe, Daniel	London, England	7/23/89
Rae, Charlotte	Milwaukee, WI	4/22/26
Raffi	Cairo, Egypt	7/8/48
Rainer, Luise	Vienna, Austria	1/12/10
Raitt, Bonnie	Burbank, CA	11/8/49
Ramey, Samuel	Colby, KS	3/28/42
Ramone, Tommy	Budapest, Hungary	1/29/52
Randolph, Joyce	Detroit, MI	10/21/25
Raphael, Sally Jessy	Easton, PA	2/25/35
Rashad, Phylicia	Houston, TX	6/19/48
Ratzenberger, John	Bridgeport, CT	4/6/47
Raver, Kim	New York, NY	3/15/69
Rawls, Lou	Chicago, IL	12/1/35
Reddy, Helen	Melbourne, Australia	10/25/41
Redford, Robert	Santa Monica, CA	8/18/37
Redgrave, Lynn	London, England	3/8/43
Redgrave, Vanessa	London, England	1/30/37
Reed, Jerry	Atlanta, GA	3/20/37
Reed, Lou	Brooklyn, NY	3/2/42
Reed, Rex	Ft. Worth, TX	10/2/38
Reese, Della	Detroit, MI	7/6/31
Reeve, Christopher	New York, NY	9/25/52
Reeves, Keanu	Beirut, Lebanon	9/2/64
Reeves, Martha	Eufaula, AL	7/18/41
Regalbuto, Joe	Brooklyn, NY	8/24/49
Reid, Tara	Wyckoff, NJ	11/8/75
Reid, Tim	Norfolk, VA	12/19/44
Reid, Vernon	London, England	8/22/58
Reilly, Charles Nelson	New York, NY	1/13/31
Reilly, John C	Chicago, IL	5/24/65
Reiner, Carl	Bronx, NY	3/20/22
Reiner, Rob	Bronx, NY	3/6/47
Reinhold, Judge	Wilmington, DE	5/21/57
Reinking, Ann	Seattle, WA	11/10/49
Reiser, Paul	New York, NY	3/30/57
Reitman, Ivan	Komarno, Czechoslovakia	10/26/46
Remini, Leah	Brooklyn, NY	6/15/70
Resnik, Regina	New York, NY	8/30/22
Reynolds, Burt	Waycross, GA	2/11/36
Reynolds, Debbie	El Paso, TX	4/1/32
Reznor, Trent	Mercer, PA	5/17/65
Rhames, Ving	Harlem, New York, NY	5/12/59
Rhymes, Busta	Brooklyn, NY	5/20/72
Ribisi, Giovanni	Los Angeles, CA	12/17/74
Ricci, Christina	Santa Monica, CA	2/12/80
Richards, Denise	Downers Grove, IL	2/17/71
Richards, Keith	Dartford, Kent, England	12/18/43
Richards, Michael	Culver City, CA	7/24/49
Richardson, Ian	Edinburgh, Scotland	4/7/34
Richardson, Kevin	Lexington, KY	10/3/71
Richardson, Miranda	Lancashire, England	3/3/58
Richardson, Natasha	London, England	5/11/63
Richardson, Patricia	Bethesda, MD	2/23/51
Richie, Lionel	Tuskegee, AL	6/20/49
Richter, Andy	Grand Rapids, MI	8/28/66
Rickles, Don	Queens, NY	5/8/26
Rickman, Alan	Hammersmith, England	2/21/46
Riegert, Peter	New York, NY	4/11/47
Rigg, Diana	Doncaster, England	7/20/38
Rimes, LeAnn	Flowood, MS	8/28/82
Ringwald, Molly	Roseville, CA	2/18/68

Name	Birthplace	Birthdate
Ripa, Kelly	Stratford, NJ	10/2/70
Rivera, Chita	Washington, DC	1/23/33
Rivera, Geraldo	New York, NY	7/4/43
Rivers, Joan	Brooklyn, NY	6/8/33
Roach, Max	New Land, NC	1/10/25
Robbins, Tim	W. Covina, CA	10/16/58
Roberts, Doris	St. Louis, MO	11/4/29
Roberts, Eric	Biloxi, MS	4/18/56
Roberts, Julia	Smyrna, GA	10/28/67
Roberts, Pernell	Waycross, GA	5/18/28
Roberts, Tony	New York, NY	10/22/39
Robertson, Cliff	La Jolla, CA	9/9/25
Robertson, Dale	Harrah, OK	7/14/23
Robinson, Smokey	Detroit, MI	2/19/40
Rochon, Lela	Torrance, CA	4/17/64
Rock, Chris	South Carolina	2/7/66
Rock, The (Dwayne Johnson)	Hayward, CA	5/2/72
Rodgers, Jimmy	Camas, WA	9/18/33
Rodriquez, Johnny	Sabinal, TX	12/10/51
Rogan, Joe	Newark, NJ	8/11/67
Rogers, Kenny	Houston, TX	8/21/38
Rogers, Mimi	Coral Gables, FL	1/27/56
Rogers, Wayne	Birmingham, AL	4/7/33
Rohm, Elisabeth	Dusseldorf, Germany	4/28/73
Rollins, Henry	Washington, DC	2/13/61
Rollins, Sonny	Harlem, NY	9/7/30
Romano, Ray	Queens, NY	12/21/57
Romijn-Stamos, Rebecca	Berkeley, CA	11/6/72
Ronstadt, Linda	Tucson, AZ	7/15/46
Rooney, Mickey	Brooklyn, NY	9/23/20
Root, Stephen	Sarasota, FL	11/17/51
Rose, Axl	Lafayette, IN	2/6/62
Rose Marie	New York, NY	8/15/23
Roseanne	Salt Lake City, UT	11/3/52
Ross, Charlotte	Winnetka, IL	1/21/68
Ross, Diana	Detroit, MI	3/26/44
Ross, Katharine	Hollywood, CA	1/29/40
Rossdale, Gavin	London, England	10/30/67
Ross, Marion	Albert Lea, MN	10/25/28
Rossellini, Isabella	Rome, Italy	6/18/52
Rostropovich, Mstislav	Baku, Azerbaijan	3/27/27
Roth, David Lee	Bloomington, IN	10/10/55
Roth, Tim	London, England	5/14/61
Rotten, Johnny	London, England	1/31/56
Rourke, Mickey	Schenectady, NY	9/16/56
Routledge, Patricia	Birkenhead, England	2/17/29
Rowan, Kelly	Ottawa, Canada	1967
Rowlands, Gena	Cambria, WI	6/19/36
Rubinstein, John	Beverly Hills, CA	12/8/46
Rudner, Rita	Miami, FL	9/17/56
Ruehl, Mercedes	Queens, NY	2/28/48
Ruffalo, Mark	Kenosha, WI	11/22/67
Rupp, Debra Jo	Glendale, CA	2/24/51
Rush, Barbara	Denver, CO	1/4/27
Rush, Geoffrey	Toowoomba, Australia	7/6/51
Russell, Jane	Bemidji, MN	6/21/21
Russell, Ken	Southampton, England	7/3/27
Russell, Keri	Fountain Valley, CA	3/23/76
Russell, Kurt	Springfield, MA	3/17/51
Russel, Leon	Lawton, OK	4/2/41
Russell, Mark	Buffalo, NY	8/23/32
Russell, Nipsey	Atlanta, GA	10/13/24
Russell, Theresa	San Diego, CA	3/20/57
Russo, Rene	Burbank, CA	2/17/54
Rutherford, Ann	Toronto, Ontario	11/2/20
Ruttan, Susan	Oregon City, OR	9/16/50
Ryan, Meg	Fairfield, CT	11/19/61
Ryan, Roz	Detroit, MI	7/7/51
Rydell, Bobby	Philadelphia, PA	4/26/42
Ryder, Winona	Winona, MN	10/29/71
Sabato, Antonio, Jr.	Rome, Italy	2/29/72
Sade	Ibadan, Nigeria	1/16/59
Sagal, Katey	Hollywood, CA	1/19/53
Saget, Bob	Philadelphia, PA	5/17/56
Sagnier, Ludivine	La Celle-St.-Cloud, France	7/3/79
Sahl, Mort	Montreal, Quebec	5/11/27
Saint, Eva Marie	Newark, NJ	7/4/24
St. James, Susan	Hollywood, CA	8/14/46
St. John, Jill	Los Angeles, CA	8/19/40
St. Patrick, Mathew	Philadelphia, PA	3/17/69
Sajak, Pat	Chicago, IL	10/26/46
Saks, Gene	New York, NY	11/8/21
Sales, Soupy	Franklinton, NC	1/8/26
Salonga, Lea	Manila, Philippines	2/22/71
Samms, Emma	London, England	8/28/60
Sandler, Adam	Brooklyn, NY	9/9/66
Sands, Julian	West Yorkshire, England	1/15/58
San Giacomo, Laura	West Orange, NJ	11/14/61

Name	Birthplace	Birthdate
Santana, Carlos	Autlan, Mexico	7/20/47
Sarandon, Susan	New York, NY	10/4/46
Sarnoff, Dorothy	New York, NY	5/25/17
Sartain, Gailard	Tulsa, OK	9/18/46
Savage, Ben	Highland Park, IL	9/13/80
Savage, Fred	Highland Park, IL	7/9/76
Sawa, Devon	Vancouver, British Columbia	9/7/78
Saxon, John	Brooklyn, NY	8/5/35
Sayles, John	Schenectady, NY	9/28/50
Scaggs, Boz	Canton, OH	6/8/44
Scales, Prunella	Sutton Abinger, England	6/22/32
Scalia, Jack	Brooklyn, NY	11/10/51
Schallert, William	Los Angeles, CA	7/6/22
Scheider, Roy	Orange, NJ	11/10/35
Schell, Maria	Vienna, Austria	1/15/26
Schell, Maximilian	Vienna, Austria	12/8/30
Schenkel, Chris	Bippus, IN	8/21/23
Schiff, Richard	Bethesda, MD	5/27/55
Schiffer, Claudia	Rheinbach, Germany	8/25/70
Schneider, John	Mt. Kisco, NY	4/8/54
Schneider, Rob	San Francisco, CA	10/31/63
Schram, Bitty	New York, NY	7/17/68
Schreiber, Liev	San Francisco, CA	10/4/67
Schroder, Rick	Staten Island, NY	4/13/70
Schwarzenegger, Arnold	Thal, Austria	7/30/47
Schwarzkopf, Elisabeth	Jarotschin, Poland	12/9/15
Schwimmer, David	Astoria, Queens, NY	11/2/66
Sciorra, Annabella	New York, NY	3/24/64
Scofield, Paul	Hurstpierpoint, England	1/21/22
Scolari, Peter	New Rochelle, NY	9/12/54
Scorsese, Martin	Flushing, Queens, NY	11/17/42
Scott, Lizabeth	Scranton, PA	9/29/22
Scott, Ridley	South Shields, England	11/30/37
Scott, Seann William	Cottage Grove, MN	10/3/76
Scott-Heron, Gil	Chicago, IL	4/1/49
Scott Thomas, Kristin	Redruth, England	5/24/60
Scotto, Renata	Savona, Italy	2/24/35
Scram, Bitty	New York, NY	7/17/68
Scully, Vin	Bronx, NY	11/29/27
Seacrest, Ryan	Atlanta, GA	12/24/74
Seagal, Steven	Lansing, MI	4/10/51
Secor, Kyle	Tacoma, WA	5/31/58
Sedaka, Neil	Brooklyn, NY	3/13/39
Seeger, Pete	New York, NY	5/3/19
Segal, George	Great Neck, NY	2/13/34
Seidelman, Susan	Abington, PA	12/11/52
Seinfeld, Jerry	Brooklyn, NY	4/29/54
Sellecca, Connie	Bronx, NY	5/25/55
Selleck, Tom	Detroit, MI	1/29/45
Severinsen, Doc	Arlington, OR	7/7/27
Sevigny, Chloë	Springfield, MA	11/18/74
Sewell, Rufus	London, England	10/29/67
Seymour, Jane	Hillingdon, England	2/15/51
Shackelford, Ted	Oklahoma City, OK	6/23/46
Shaffer, Paul	Thunder Bay, Ontario	11/28/49
Shakira	Barranquilla, Colombia	2/2/77
Shalhoub, Tony	Green Bay, WI	10/9/53
Shandling, Garry	Chicago, IL	11/29/49
Shankar, Ravi	Benares, India	4/7/20
Shannon, Molly	Shaker Heights, OH	9/16/64
Sharif, Omar	Alexandria, Egypt	4/10/32
Shatner, William	Montreal, Quebec	3/22/31
Shaughnessy, Charles	London, England	2/9/55
Shaver, Helen	St. Thomas, Ontario	2/24/51
Shaw, Artie	New York, NY	5/23/10
Shea, John	N. Conway, NH	4/14/49
Shearer, Harry	Los Angeles, CA	12/23/43
Shearer, Moira	Dumfermline, Scotland	1/17/26
Shearing, George	London, England	8/13/19
Sheedy, Ally	New York, NY	6/13/62
Sheen, Charlie	Los Angeles, CA	9/3/65
Sheen, Martin	Dayton, OH	8/3/40
Sheindlin, Judge Judy	Brooklyn, NY	10/21/42
Shelley, Carole	London, England	8/16/39
Shepard, Sam	Ft. Sheridan, IL	11/5/43
Shepherd, Cybill	Memphis, TN	2/18/50
Sheridan, Nicollette	Worthing, England	11/21/63
Shields, Brooke	New York, NY	5/31/65
Shire, Talia	Lake Success, NY	4/25/46
Short, Bobby	Danville, IL	9/15/24
Short, Martin	Hamilton, Ontario	3/26/50
Show, Grant	Detroit, MI	2/27/62
Shue, Andrew	Washington, DE	2/20/67
Shue, Elisabeth	Wilmington, DE	10/6/63
Shyamalan, M. Night	Pondicherry, India	8/6/70
Siepi, Cesare	Milan, Italy	2/14/23
Sigler, Jamie-Lynn	Jericho, NY	5/15/81
Sikking, James B.	Los Angeles, CA	3/5/34
Sills, Beverly	Brooklyn, NY	5/25/29

Name	Birthplace	Birthdate	Name	Birthplace	Birthdate
Silver, Ron	New York, NY	7/2/46	Stiller, Ben	New York, NY	11/30/65
Silverman, Jonathan	Beverly Hills, CA	8/5/66	Stiller, Jerry	Brooklyn, NY	6/8/27
Silverman, Sarah	Bedford, NH.	12/70	Stills, Stephen	Dallas, TX	1/3/45
Silverstone, Alicia	Hillsborough, CA	10/4/76	Sting	Newcastle, England	10/2/51
Simmons, Gene	Haifa, Israel	8/25/49	Stipe, Michael	Decatur, GA	1/4/60
Simmons, Henry	Stamford, CT.	7/1/70	Stockwell, Dean	North Hollywood, CA	3/5/36
Simmons, Jean	London, England	1/31/29	Stoltz, Eric	Whittier, CA	9/30/61
Simmons, Richard	New Orleans, LA	7/12/48	Stone, Dee Wallace	Kansas City, KS.	12/14/48
Simon, Carly	Riverdale, NY	6/25/45	Stone, Oliver	New York, NY	9/15/46
Simon, Paul	Newark, NJ	10/13/41	Stone, Sharon	Meadville, PA.	3/10/58
Sinatra, Nancy	Jersey City, NJ	6/8/40	Stookey, Paul	Baltimore, MD	12/30/37
Sinbad.	Benton Harbor, MI.	11/10/56	Storch, Larry	New York, NY	1/8/23
Singleton, John	Los Angeles, CA	1/6/68	Storm, Gale	Bloomington, TX	4/5/22
Sinise, Gary	Blue Island, IL	3/17/55	Stowe, Madeleine	Eagle Rock, CA	8/18/58
Sirico, Tony	Brooklyn, NY	7/29/42	Strait, George	Pearsall, TX	5/18/52
Sisto, Jeremy	Grass Valley, CA	10/6/74	Strasser, Robin	New York, NY	5/7/45
Sizemore, Tom	Detroit, MI	9/29/64	Stratas, Teresa	Toronto, Ontario.	5/26/38
Skerritt, Tom	Detroit, MI	8/25/33	Strathairn, David	San Francisco, CA.	1/26/49
Skye, Ione	Hertfordshire, England	9/4/70	Strauss, Peter	Croton-on-Hudson, NY	2/20/47
Slater, Christian	New York, NY	8/18/69	Streep, Meryl	Summit, NJ	6/22/49
Slater, Helen	Massapequa, NY.	12/15/63	Streisand, Barbra	Brooklyn, NY	4/24/42
Slezak, Erika	Hollywood, CA.	8/5/46	Stringfield, Sherry	Colorado Springs, CO	6/24/67
Slick, Grace	Evanston, IL	10/30/39	Stritch, Elaine	Detroit, MI	2/2/26
Smirnoff, Yakov	Odessa, Ukraine	1/24/51	Stroman, Susan	Wilmington, DE	10/17/54
Smith, Allison	Bronx, NY	12/9/69	Struthers, Sally	Portland, OR	7/28/48
Smith, Jaclyn	Houston, TX	10/26/47	Stuart, Gloria	Santa Monica, CA	7/4/10
Smith, Keely	Norfolk, VA	3/9/32	Stuarti, Enzo	Rome, Italy.	3/3/25
Smith, Kevin	Red Bank, NJ	8/2/70	Studdard, Ruben	Birmingham, AL	9/12/78
Smith, Maggie	Ilford, England	12/28/34	Suchet, David	London, England	5/2/46
Smith, Patti	Chicago, IL	12/30/46	Sullivan, Erik Per	Worcester, MA.	7/12/91
Smith, Robert	Blackpool, England	4/21/59	Sullivan, Susan	New York, NY	11/18/42
Smith, Will	West Philadelphia, PA.	9/25/68	Sumac, Yma	Ichocan, Peru.	9/10/27
Smits, Jimmy	New York, NY	7/9/55	Summer, Donna	Dorchester, MA	12/31/48
Smothers, Dick	Governor's Island, NY.	11/20/38	Sutherland, Donald	St. John, New Brunswick.	7/17/34
Smothers, Tom	Governor's Island, NY.	2/2/37	Sutherland, Joan	Sydney, Australia.	11/7/26
Snipes, Wesley	Orlando, FL	7/31/62	Sutherland, Kiefer	London, England	12/21/66
Snyder, Tom	Milwaukee, WI.	5/12/36	Suvari, Mena	Newport, RI	2/9/79
Soderbergh, Steven	Atlanta, GA	1/14/63	Swank, Hilary	Bellingham, WA.	7/30/74
Somers, Suzanne	San Bruno, CA	10/16/46	Swayze, Patrick.	Houston, TX.	8/18/52
Sommer, Elke	Berlin, Germany	11/5/40	Swinton, Tilda	London, England	11/5/60
Sorbo, Kevin	Mound, MN	9/24/58	Swit, Loretta	Passaic, NJ	11/4/37
Sorvino, Mira	Tenafly, NJ	9/28/67	Sykes, Wanda	Portsmouth, VA	3/7/64
Sorvino, Paul	Brooklyn, NY	4/13/39	Szmanda, Eric.	Milwaukee, WI.	7/24/75
Soul, David	Chicago, IL	8/28/43			
Spacek, Sissy	Quitman, TX	12/25/49	T, Mr.	Chicago, IL.	5/21/52
Spacey, Kevin	S. Orange, NJ	7/26/59	Takei, George	Los Angeles, CA	4/20/37
Spade, David	Birmingham, MI	7/22/64	Tallchief, Maria	Fairfax, OK.	1/24/25
Spader, James	Boston, MA	2/7/60	Tamblyn, Amber	Santa Monica, CA	5/14/83
Spano, Joe	San Francisco, CA	7/7/46	Tamblyn, Russ	Los Angeles, CA	12/30/34
Spears, Britney	Kentwood, LA	12/2/81	Tarantino, Quentin	Knoxville, TN	3/27/63
Spector, Phil	Bronx, NY	12/26/40	Tautou, Audrey	Beaumont, France	8/9/78
Spelling, Aaron	Dallas, TX	4/22/28	Taylor, Billy	Greenville, NC	7/21/21
Spelling, Tori	Los Angeles, CA	5/16/73	Taylor, Buck	Hollywood, CA.	5/13/38
Spencer, John	New York, NY	12/20/46	Taylor, Elizabeth	London, England	2/27/32
Spielberg, Steven	Cincinnati, OH	12/18/46	Taylor, James	Boston, MA	3/12/48
Spiner, Brent	Houston, TX	2/2/49	Taylor, Rip	Washington, DC.	1/13/34
Springer, Jerry	London, England	2/13/44	Taylor, Rod	Sydney, Australia.	1/11/30
Springfield, Rick	Sydney, Australia	8/23/49	Taymor, Julie	Newton, MA.	12/15/52
Springsteen, Bruce	Freehold, NJ	9/23/49	Te Kanawa, Kiri	Gisborne, New Zealand.	3/6/44
Spurlock, Morgan	Parksburg, WV	11/7/70	Tebaldi, Renata.	Pesaro, Italy.	2/1/22
Stafford, Jo	Coalinga, CA	11/12/17	Teller	Philadelphia, PA	2/14/48
Stahl, Nick	Harlingen, TX	12/5/79	Temple Black, Shirley	Santa Monica, CA	4/23/28
Stahl, Richard	Detroit, MI	1/4/32	Tennant, Victoria	London, England	9/30/50
Stallone, Sylvester	New York, NY	7/6/46	Tennille, Toni	Montgomery, AL	5/8/43
Stamos, John	Cypress, CA	8/19/63	Tesh, John	Garden City, NY.	7/9/52
Stamp, Terence	Stepney, England	7/22/39	Tharp, Twyla	Portland, IN	7/1/41
Stang, Arnold	Chelsea, MA	9/28/25	Thaxter, Phyllis	Portland, ME	11/20/21
Stanton, Harry Dean	West Irvine, KY	7/14/26	Theron, Charlize	South Africa.	8/7/75
Stapleton, Jean	New York, NY	1/19/23	Thicke, Alan	Kirkland Lake, Ontario.	3/1/47
Stapleton, Maureen	Troy, NY	6/21/25	Thiessen, Tiffani	Long Beach, CA.	1/23/74
Starr, Ringo	Liverpool, England.	7/7/40	Thomas, Jay	Kermit, TX.	7/12/48
Steenburgen, Mary	Newport, AR	2/8/53	Thomas, Jonathan Taylor	Bethlehem, PA.	9/8/81
Stefani, Gwen	Anaheim, CA	10/3/69	Thomas, Marlo	Deerfield, MI	11/21/38
Stein, Ben	Washington, DC	11/25/44	Thomas, Michael Tilson	Hollywood, CA.	12/21/44
Stephens, James	Mt. Kisco, NY.	5/18/51	Thomas, Philip Michael.	Columbus, OH.	5/26/49
Stern, Daniel	Bethesda, MD	8/28/57	Thomas, Richard	New York, NY	6/13/51
Stern, Howard	Roosevelt, NY	1/12/54	Thomas, Sean Patrick.	Wilmington, DE	12/17/70
Sternhagen, Frances	Washington, DC	1/13/30	Thompson, Emma	London, England	4/15/59
Stevens, Andrew	Memphis, TN	6/10/55	Thompson, Jack	Sydney, Australia.	8/31/40
Stevens, Cat	London, England	7/21/48	Thompson, Lea	Rochester, MN.	5/31/61
Stevens, Connie	Brooklyn, NY	8/8/38	Thompson, Sada.	Des Moines, IA	9/27/29
Stevens, Rise	Bronx, NY	6/11/13	Thorne-Smith, Courtney	San Francisco, CA.	11/8/67
Stevens, Stella	Hot Coffee, MS	10/1/36	Thornton, Billy Bob	Hot Springs, AR.	8/4/55
Stevenson, Parker	Philadelphia, PA	6/4/52	Thurman, Uma	Boston, MA	4/29/70
Stewart, French	Albuquerque, NM	2/20/64	Tiegs, Cheryl.	Breckenridge, MN	9/25/47
Stewart, Jon	Trenton, NJ	11/28/62	Tierney, Maura	Boston, MA	2/3/65
Stewart, Patrick.	Mirfield, England	7/13/40	Tillis, Mel	Tampa, FL	8/8/32
Stewart, Rod	London, England	1/10/45	Tilly, Jennifer.	Harbor City, CA	9/16/58
Stiers, David Ogden	Peoria, IL.	10/31/42	Tilly, Meg.	Long Beach, CA.	2/14/60
Stiles, Julia	New York, NY	3/28/81	Timberlake, Justin	Memphis, TN	1/31/81

Name	Birthplace	Birthdate	Name	Birthplace	Birthdate
Todd, Richard	Dublin, Ireland	6/11/19	Ward, Simon	Kent, London, England	10/19/41
Tomei, Marisa	Brooklyn, NY	12/4/64	Warden, Jack	Newark, NJ	9/18/20
Tomlin, Lily	Detroit, MI	9/1/39	Warfield, Marsha	Chicago, IL	3/5/54
Tork, Peter	Washington, DC	2/13/42	Warner, Malcolm-Jamal	Jersey City, NJ	8/18/70
Torn, Rip	Temple, TX	2/6/31	Warren, Lesley Ann	New York, NY	8/16/46
Townsend, Robert	Chicago, IL	2/6/57	Warrick, Ruth	St. Joseph, MO	6/29/15
Townshend, Peter	Chiswick, England	5/19/45	Warwick, Dionne	East Orange, NJ	12/12/40
Travanti, Daniel J.	Kenosha, WI	3/7/40	Washington, Denzel	Mt. Vernon, NY	12/28/54
Travers, Mary	Louisville, KY	11/7/37	Watanabe, Ken	Koide, Niigata, Japan.	10/21/59
Travis, Nancy	Astoria, Queens, NY	9/21/61	Waters, John	Baltimore, MD	4/22/46
Travis, Randy	Marshville, NC	5/4/59	Waters, Roger	Great Bookham, England	9/6/44
Travolta, John	Englewood, NJ	2/18/54	Waterston, Sam	Cambridge, MA	11/15/40
Trebek, Alex	Sudbury, Ontario	7/22/40	Watson, Emily	London, England	1/14/67
Tritt, Travis	Marietta, GA	2/9/63	Watson, Emma	Oxford, England	4/15/90
Tucci, Stanley	Katonah, NY	1/11/60	Watts, Andre	Nuremberg, Germany	6/20/46
Tucker, Chris	Decatur, GA.	8/31/72	Watts, Naomi.	Shoreham, England.	9/28/68
Tucker, Michael	Baltimore, MD	2/6/44	Wayans, Damon	New York, NY	9/4/60
Tucker, Tanya	Seminole, TX.	10/10/58	Wayans, Keenen Ivory	Brooklyn, NY	6/8/58
Tune, Tommy	Wichita Falls, TX	2/28/39	Wayans, Marlon	New York, NY	723/72
Turlington, Christy.	Walnut Creek, CA	1/2/69	Wayans, Shawn	New York, NY	1/19/71
Turner, Janine	Lincoln, NE	12/6/62	Weathers, Carl	New Orleans, LA	1/14/48
Turner, Kathleen	Springfield, MO	6/19/54	Weaver, Dennis.	Joplin, MO	6/4/24
Turner, Tina	Brownsville, TN	11/26/39	Weaver, Fritz.	Pittsburgh, PA	1/19/26
Turturro, John	Brooklyn, NY	2/28/57	Weaver, Sigourney	New York, NY	10/8/49
Twain, Shania	Windsor, Ontario	8/28/65	Weiland, Scott	Santa Cruz, CA	10/27/67
Twiggy (Lawson).	London, England.	9/19/49	Weir, Peter	Sydney, Australia.	8/8/44
Tyler, Liv	New York, NY	7/1/77	Weisz, Rachel	London, England	3/7/71
Tyler, Steven.	Yonkers, NY	3/26/48	Weitz, Bruce	Norwalk, CT.	5/27/43
Tyson, Cicely	Harlem, NY	12/19/33	Welch, Raquel.	Chicago, IL.	9/5/40
			Weld, Tuesday	New York, NY	8/27/43
Uecker, Bob	Milwaukee, WI.	1/26/35	Weller, Peter	Stevens Point, WI	6/24/47
Uggams, Leslie	New York, NY	5/25/43	Wells, Kitty	Nashville, TN	8/30/19
Ullman, Tracey	Slough, England	12/30/59	Wendt, George	Chicago, IL.	10/17/48
Ullmann, Liv	Tokyo, Japan.	12/16/39	West, Adam.	Walla Walla, WA	9/19/28
Ulrich, Skeet	New York, NY	1/20/69	West, Shane	Baton Rouge, LA	6/10/78
Underwood, Blair	Tacoma, WA	8/25/64	Wettig, Patricia	Cincinnati, OH	12/4/51
Usher (Raymond IV)	Chattanooga,TN	10/14/78	Whalley, Joanne	Manchester, England.	8/25/64
			Wheaton, Wil.	Burbank, CA	7/29/72
Vaccaro, Brenda	Brooklyn, NY	11/18/39	Whitaker, Forest	Longview, TX.	7/15/61
Vale, Jerry.	Bronx, NY	7/8/32	White, Betty	Oak Park, IL.	1/17/22
Valente, Caterina	Paris, France.	1/14/31	White, Jack	Detroit, MI	7/9/75
Valley, Mark	Ogdensburg, NY	12/24/64	White, Jaleel	Pasadena, CA	11/27/76
Valli, Frankie	Newark, NJ	5/3/37	White, Vanna	N. Myrtle Beach, SC	2/18/57
Van Ark, Joan	New York, NY	6/16/43	Whitford, Bradley.	Madison, WI.	10/10/59
Vance, Courtney B.	Birmingham, MI	3/12/60	Whiting, Margaret	Detroit, MI	7/22/24
Van Damme, Jean-Claude	Brussels, Belgium	10/18/60	Whitman, Stuart	San Francisco, CA.	2/1/26
Van Der Beek, James.	Chesire, CT.	3/8/77	Whitmore, James	White Plains, NY	10/1/21
Van Doren, Mamie	Rowena, SD	2/6/31	Widmark, Richard	Sunrise, MN.	12/26/14
Vandross, Luther	New York, NY	4/20/51	Wiest, Dianne	Kansas City, MO	3/28/48
Van Dyke, Dick	West Plains, MO	12/13/25	Wilder, Gene	Milwaukee, WI	6/11/33
Van Dyke, Jerry	Danville, IL.	7/27/31	Wilkinson, Tom	Leeds, England	12/12/48
Van Halen, Eddie	Nijmegen, Netherlands	1/26/55	Williams, Andy.	Wall Lake, IA	12/3/27
Van Patten, Dick.	Queens, NY.	12/9/28	Williams, Armstong	Marion, SC.	2/5/59
Van Peebles, Mario	Mexico City, Mexico	1/15/57	Williams, Barry	Santa Monica, CA	9/30/54
Van Sant, Gus	Louisville, KY.	7/24/52	Williams, Billy Dee.	Harlem, NY	4/6/37
Van Zandt, Steven	Boston, MA	11/22/50	Williams, Cindy	Van Nuys, CA	8/22/47
Vardalos, Nia	Winnipeg, Manit, Can.	9/24/62	Williams, Esther	Los Angeles, CA	8/8/23
Vaughn, Robert.	New York, NY	11/22/32	Williams, Hal	Columbus, OH.	12/14/38
Vaughn, Vince	Minneapolis, MN	3/28/70	Williams, Hank, Jr.	Shreveport, LA.	5/26/49
Vedder, Eddie.	Evanston, IL.	12/23/64	Williams, JoBeth	Houston, TX.	12/6/48
Vega, Alexa	Miami, FL.	8/27/88	Williams, Kimberly.	Rye, NY.	9/14/71
Vereen, Ben	Miami, FL.	10/10/46	Williams, Lucinda	Lake Charles, LA	1/26/53
Verrett, Shirley	New Orleans, LA.	5/31/31	Williams, Michelle	Kalispell, MT	9/9/80
Vickers, Jon	Prince Albert, Sask.	10/29/26	Williams, Montel	Baltimore, MD	7/3/56
Vieira, Meredith.	Providence, RI.	12/30/53	Williams, Paul	Omaha, NE	9/19/40
Vigoda, Abe	New York, NY	2/24/21	Williams, Robin	Chicago, IL.	7/21/51
Vincent, Jan-Michael	Denver, CO.	7/15/44	Williams, Treat	Rowayton, CT	12/1/51
Vinton, Bobby	Canonsburg, PA	4/16/35	Williams, Vanessa.	Tarrytown, NY	3/18/63
Visnjic, Goran	Sibenik, Yugo. (Croatia)	9/9/72	Williamson, Kevin	New Bern, NC	3/14/65
Vitale, Dick	East Rutherford, NJ.	6/9/39	Williamson, Nicol.	Hamilton, Scotland.	9/14/38
Voight, Jon	Yonkers, NY	12/29/38	Willis, Bruce	Idar-Oberstein,	
Von Stade, Frederica	Somerville, NJ	6/1/45		W. Germany	3/19/55
Von Sydow, Max.	Lund, Sweden.	4/10/29	Wilson, Brian.	Hawthorne, CA.	6/20/42
Von Trier, Lars	Copenhagen, Denmark.	4/30/56	Wilson, Cassandra	Jackson, MS	12/4/55
			Wilson, Demond	Valdosta, GA.	10/13/46
Wagner, Jack	Washington, MO	10/3/59	Wilson, Elizabeth.	Grand Rapids, MI.	4/4/21
Wagner, Lindsay.	Los Angeles, CA	6/22/49	Wilson, Luke	Dallas, TX	9/21/71
Wagner, Robert	Detroit, MI	2/10/30	Wilson, Nancy	Chillicothe, OH.	2/20/37
Wahl, Ken	Chicago, IL	2/14/56	Wilson, Owen	Dallas, TX	11/18/68
Wahlberg, Mark	Dorchester, MA.	6/5/71	Windom, William	New York, NY	9/28/23
Wain, Bea	Bronx, NY	4/30/17	Winfrey, Oprah	Kosciusko, MS.	1/29/54
Waite, Ralph	White Plains, NY.	6/22/28	Winger, Debra.	Cleveland, OH	5/16/55
Waits, Tom	Pomona, CA	12/7/49	Winkler, Henry.	New York, NY	10/30/45
Walden, Robert.	New York, NY	9/25/43	Winningham, Mare	Phoenix, AZ.	5/16/59
Walken, Christopher	Astoria, Queens, NY	3/31/43	Winokur, Marissa Jaret	New York, NY	2/2/73
Wallace, Marcia	Creston, IA	11/1/42	Winslet, Kate	Reading, England	10/5/75
Wallach, Eli	Brooklyn, NY	12/7/15	Winter, Johnny	Beaumont,TX.	2/23/44
Walter, Jessica	Brooklyn, NY	1/31/40	Winters, Jonathan	Dayton, OH	11/11/25
Ward, Fred	San Diego, CA.	12/30/42	Winters, Shelley	East St. Louis, IL	8/18/22
Ward, Sela	Meridian, MS	7/11/56	Winwood, Steve	Birmingham, England	5/12/48

Name	Birthplace	Birthdate	Name	Birthplace	Birthdate
Wiseman, Joseph	Montreal, Quebec	5/15/18	Yankovic, Weird Al	Lynwood, CA	10/23/59
Withers, Jane	Atlanta, GA	4/12/26	Yanni	Kalamata, Greece	11/14/54
Witherspoon, Reese	Nashville, TN	3/22/76	Yarbrough, Glenn	Milwaukee, WI	1/12/30
Witt, Alicia	Worcester, MA	8/21/75	Yarrow, Peter	New York, NY	5/31/38
Wolf, Scott	Boston, MA	6/4/68	Yearwood, Trisha	Monticello, GA	9/19/64
Wonder, Stevie	Saginaw, MI.	5/13/50	Yoakam, Dwight	Pikesville, KY	10/23/56
Wong, Faye	Beijing, China	8/8/69	York, Michael	Fulmer, England	3/27/42
Woo, John.	Guangzhou, China	5/1/46	York, Susannah	London, England	1/9/41
Wood, Elijah	Cedar Rapids, IA	1/28/81	Young, Alan.	North Shields, England	11/19/19
Woodard, Alfre	Tulsa, OK	11/8/53	Young, Burt	New York, NY	4/30/40
Woods, James	Vernal, UT	4/18/47	Young, Neil	Toronto, Ontario.	11/12/45
Woodward, Edward	Croyden, England	6/1/30	Young, Sean	Louisville, KY	11/20/59
Woodward, Joanne	Thomasville, GA	2/27/30			
Wopat, Tom	Lodi, WI	9/9/51	Zane, Billy	Chicago, IL.	2/24/66
Wright, Martha	Seattle, WA	3/23/26	Zeffirelli, Franco	Florence, Italy	2/12/23
Wright, Max.	Detroit, MI	8/2/43	Zellweger, Renee	Katy, TX.	4/25/69
Wright, Steven	New York, NY	12/6/55	Zemeckis, Robert	Chicago, IL.	5/14/52
Wright, Teresa	New York, NY	10/27/14	Zerbe, Anthony	Long Beach, CA.	5/20/36
Wright Penn, Robin	Dallas, TX	4/8/66	Zeta-Jones, Catherine.	Swansea, Wales	9/25/69
Wyatt, Jane.	Campgaw, NJ	8/12/11	Zimbalist, Efrem, Jr.	New York, NY	11/30/18
Wyle, Noah	Hollywood, CA.	6/4/71	Zimbalist, Stephanie	New York, NY	10/8/56
Wyman, Bill.	London, England	10/24/36	Zimmer, Kim	Grand Rapids, MI.	2/2/55
Wyman, Jane	St. Joseph, MO	1/4/14	Zukerman, Pinchas	Tel Aviv, Israel	7/16/48
			Zuniga, Daphne.	San Francisco, CA.	10/28/62

Entertainment Personalities of the Past

See also other lists for some deceased entertainers not included here.

Name	Born	Died	Name	Born	Died	Name	Born	Died
Aaliyah	1979	2001	Baker, Josephine	1906	1975	Bixby, Bill	1934	1993
Abbott, Bud.	1895	1974	Baker, Stanley	1927	1976	Bjoerling, Jussi.	1911	1960
Abbott, George	1887	1995	Balanchine, George	1904	1983	Blackmer, Sidney.	1895	1973
Acuff, Roy	1903	1992	Ball, Lucille	1911	1989	Blackstone, Harry.	1885	1965
Adams, Joey	1911	1999	Balsam, Martin	1919	1996	Blake, Amanda.	1931	1989
Adams, Maude	1872	1953	Bancroft, George	1882	1956	Blaine, Vivian.	1921	1995
Adler, Jacob P	1855	1926	Bankhead, Tallulah.	1903	1968	Blanc, Mel	1908	1989
Adler, Luther	1903	1984	Banks, Leslie	1890	1952	Blocker, Dan	1928	1972
Adoree, Renee	1898	1933	Bara, Theda	1890	1955	Blondell, Joan	1909	1979
Agar, John	1921	2002	Barnes, Binnie	1903	1998	Blore, Eric	1888	1959
Aherne, Brian	1902	1986	Barnett, Etta Moten.	1902	2004	Blue, Ben	1901	1975
Ailey, Alvin	1931	1989	Barnum, Phineas T.	1810	1891	Blyden, Larry	1925	1975
Akins, Claude	1918	1994	Barrymore, Ethel	1879	1959	Bogarde, Dirk	1920	1999
Albertson, Frank	1909	1964	Barrymore, John.	1882	1942	Bogart, Humphrey	1899	1957
Albertson, Jack	1907	1981	Barrymore, Lionel	1878	1954	Boland, Mary	1880	1965
Alda, Robert	1914	1986	Barrymore, Maurice	1848	1905	Boles, John	1895	1969
Alexander, Ben	1911	1969	Bartel, Paul.	1938	2000	Bolger, Ray	1904	1987
Allen, Fred	1894	1956	Barthelmess, Richard.	1897	1963	Bond, Ward	1903	1960
Allen, Gracie	1906	1964	Bartholomew, Freddie	1924	1992	Bondi, Beulah	1892	1981
Allen, Mel	1913	1996	Bartok, Eva.	1926	1998	Bono, Sonny	1935	1998
Allen, Peter	1944	1992	Barty, Billy	1924	2000	Boone, Richard	1917	1981
Allen, Steve	1921	2000	Basehart, Richard.	1914	1984	Booth, Edwin	1833	1893
Allgood, Sara	1883	1950	Basie, Count.	1904	1984	Booth, Junius Brutus	1796	1852
Ameche, Don	1908	1993	Bates, Alan.	1934	2003	Booth, Shirley.	1898	1992
Ames, Leon.	1903	1993	Bates, Clayton (Peg Leg)	1907	1998	Borge, Victor	1909	2000
Amsterdam, Morey	1908	1996	Bates, Florence	1888	1954	Bow, Clara.	1905	1965
Anderson, Judith.	1897	1992	Bavier, Francis	1902	1989	Bowes, Maj. Edward	1874	1946
Anderson, Marian	1902	1993	Baxter, Anne.	1923	1985	Bowman, Lee	1914	1979
Andre the Giant.	1946	1993	Baxter, Warner	1889	1951	Brown, Les.	1912	2001
Andrews, Dana	1909	1992	Beatty, Clyde	1904	1965	Boxcar Willie	1931	1999
Andrews, Laverne	1913	1967	Beaumont, Hugh	1909	1982	Boyd, Stephen	1928	1977
Andrews, Maxine	1918	1995	Beavers, Louise	1902	1962	Boyd, William	1898	1972
Angeli, Pier	1933	1971	Beery, Noah, Sr..	1884	1946	Boyer, Charles	1899	1978
Anita Louise	1915	1970	Beery, Noah, Jr.	1913	1994	Bracken, Eddie	1915	2002
Arbuckle, Fatty			Beery, Wallace	1889	1949	Brady, Alice	1893	1939
(Roscoe)	1887	1933	Begley, Ed	1901	1970	Brand, Neville.	1921	1992
Arden, Eve	1908	1990	Bellamy, Ralph	1904	1991	Brando, Marlon	1924	2004
Arlen, Richard.	1900	1976	Belushi, John	1949	1982	Branigan, Laura	1957	2004
Arliss, George	1868	1946	Benaderet, Bea	1906	1968	Brazzi, Rossano.	1916	1994
Armetta, Henry	1888	1945	Bendix, William	1906	1964	Brennan, Walter	1894	1974
Armstrong, Louis.	1901	1971	Bennett, Constance	1904	1965	Brent, George	1904	1979
Arnaz, Desi	1917	1986	Bennett, Joan	1910	1990	Brett, Jeremy	1935	1995
Arnold, Edward	1890	1956	Bennett, Michael.	1943	1987	Brice, Fanny	1891	1951
Arquette, Cliff	1905	1974	Benny, Jack	1894	1974	Bridges, Lloyd	1913	1998
Arthur, Jean	1900	1991	Benzell, Mimi	1924	1970	Broderick, Helen	1891	1959
Ashcroft, Peggy	1907	1991	Beradino, John	1917	1996	Bronson, Charles	1921	2003
Astaire, Fred	1899	1987	Berg, Gertrude	1899	1966	Brooks, Foster	1912	2001
Astor, Mary	1906	1987	Bergen, Edgar	1903	1978	Brown, Joe E..	1892	1973
Atkins, Chet	1924	2001	Bergman, Ingrid	1915	1982	Brown, Les.	1912	2001
Atwill, Lionel	1885	1946	Berkeley, Busby	1895	1976	Bruce, Lenny	1925	1966
Auer, Mischa.	1905	1967	Berle, Milton	1908	2002	Bruce, Nigel	1895	1953
Aumont, Jean-Pierre.	1911	2001	Bernardi, Herschel	1923	1986	Bruce, Virginia	1910	1982
Austin, Gene.	1900	1972	Bernhardt, Sarah	1844	1923	Brynner, Yul	1915	1985
Autry, Gene.	1907	1998	Bernie, Ben.	1893	1943	Buchanan, Edgar	1903	1979
Axton, Hoyt	1938	1999	Berry, Jan.	1941	2004	Buchholz, Horst	1933	2003
Ayres, Lew	1908	1996	Bessell, Ted	1939	1996	Buñuel, Luis	1900	1983
			Bickford, Charles	1889	1967	Buono, Victor	1938	1982
Backus, Jim	1913	1989	Big Bopper, The	1930	1959	Burke, Billie	1885	1970
Bailey, Pearl	1918	1990	Bing, Rudolf	1902	1997	Burnette, Smiley.	1911	1967
Bainter, Fay	1892	1968	Bissell, Whit	1909	1996	Burns, George	1896	1996

> **IT'S A FACT:** Many years before making her first soufflé on TV, famed chef Julia Child (1912-2004) worked for the Office of Strategic Services (forerunner to the CIA) during World War II. She was stationed in Ceylon—an island nation off the coast of India, known today as Sri Lanka—where she performed clerical duties. In 1946, she moved with her husband to Paris, where she enrolled at the Cordon Bleu cooking school.

Name	Born	Died	Name	Born	Died	Name	Born	Died
Burr, Raymond	1917	1993	Connors, Chuck	1921	1992	Dix, Richard	1894	1949
Burton, Richard	1925	1984	Conrad, William	1920	1994	Dmytryk, Edward	1908	1999
Busch, Mae	1897	1946	Conried, Hans	1917	1982	Donahue, Troy	1936	2001
Bushman, Francis X.	1883	1966	Conte, Richard	1911	1975	Donat, Robert	1905	1958
Butterworth, Charles	1896	1946	Convy, Bert	1933	1991	Donlevy, Brian	1901?	1972
Byington, Spring	1893	1971	Conway, Tom	1904	1967	Dors, Diana	1931	1984
Cabot, Bruce	1904	1972	Coogan, Jackie	1914	1984	Dorsey, Tommy	1905	1956
Cabot, Sebastian	1918	1977	Cook, Elisha, Jr.	1904	1995	Douglas, Melvyn	1901	1981
Cagney, James	1899	1986	Cooke, Alistair	1908	2004	Douglas, Paul	1907	1959
Calhern, Louis	1895	1956	Cooke, Sam	1935	1964	Dove, Billie	1900	1998
Calhoun, Rory	1923	1999	Cooper, Gary	1901	1961	Downey, Morton, Jr.	1933	2001
Callas, Maria	1923	1977	Cooper, Gladys	1888	1971	Doyle, David	1929	1997
Calloway, Cab	1907	1994	Cooper, Melville	1896	1973	Drake, Alfred	1914	1992
Cambridge, Godfrey	1933	1976	Corby, Ellen	1913	1999	Draper, Ruth	1889	1956
Campbell, Mrs. Patrick	1865	1940	Corelli, Franco	1923	2003	Dresser, Louise	1881	1965
Candy, John	1950	1994	Corey, Jeff	1914	2002	Dressler, Marie	1869	1934
Cantinflas	1911	1993	Corio, Ann	1914	1999	Drew, Ellen	1915	2003
Cantor, Eddie	1892	1964	Cornell, Katharine	1893	1974	Drew, Mrs. John	1820	1897
Capra, Frank	1897	1991	Correll, Charles ("Andy")	1890	1972	Dru, Joanne	1923	1996
Carey, Harry	1878	1947	Costello, Dolores	1905	1979	Duchin, Eddy	1909	1951
Carey, Macdonald	1913	1994	Costello, Lou	1906	1959	Duff, Howard	1917	1990
Carle, Frankie	1903	2001	Cotten, Joseph	1905	1994	Duggan, Andrew	1923	1988
Carney, Art	1918	2003	Coward, Noel	1899	1973	Dumbrille, Douglass	1890	1974
Carpenter, Karen	1950	1983	Cox, Wally	1924	1973	Dumont, Margaret	1889	1965
Carradine, John	1906	1988	Crabbe, Buster	1908	1983	Duncan, Isadora	1878	1927
Carrillo, Leo	1880	1961	Crain, Jeanne	1925	2003	Dunn, James	1905	1967
Carroll, Leo G.	1892	1972	Crane, Bob	1928	1978	Dunne, Irene	1898	1990
Carroll, Madeleine	1906	1987	Crawford, Broderick	1911	1986	Dunnock, Mildred	1904	1991
Carroll, Nancy	1905	1965	Crawford, Joan	1904	1977	Durante, Jimmy	1893	1980
Carson, Jack	1910	1963	Cregar, Laird	1914	1944	Duryea, Dan	1907	1968
Carter, Benny	1907	2003	Crenna, Richard	1926	2003	Duse, Eleanora	1858	1924
Carter, Nell	1948	2003	Crews, Laura Hope	1880	1942	Dvorak, Ann	1912	1979
Caruso, Enrico	1873	1921	Crisp, Donald	1880	1974			
Casadesus, Gaby	1901	1999	Croce, Jim	1942	1973	Eagels, Jeanne	1894	1929
Casals, Pablo	1876	1973	Cronyn, Hume	1911	2003	Ebsen, Buddy	1908	2003
Cash, Johnny	1932	2003	Crosby, Bing	1903	1977	Eckstine, Billy	1914	1993
Cash, June Carter	1929	2003	Crothers, Scatman	1910	1986	Eddington, Paul	1927	1995
Cass, Peggy	1924	1999	Cruz, Celia	1925	2003	Eddy, Nelson	1901	1967
Cassidy, Jack	1927	1976	Cugat, Xavier	1900	1990	Edelman, Herb	1933	1996
Cassavetes, John	1929	1989	Cukor, George	1899	1983	Edwards, Cliff	1897	1971
Castle, Irene	1893	1969	Cullen, Bill	1920	1990	Edwards, Gus	1879	1945
Castle, Vernon	1887	1918	Cummings, Robert	1908	1990	Edwards, Vince	1928	1996
Caulfield, Joan	1922	1991	Currie, Finlay	1878	1968	Egan, Richard	1923	1987
Chaliapin, Feodor	1873	1938	Curtis, Keene	1923	2002	Eisenstein, Sergei	1898	1948
Champion, Gower	1919	1980	Curtis, Ken	1916	1991	Elam, Jack	1916	2003
Chandler, Jeff	1918	1961	Cushing, Peter	1913	1994	Ellington, Duke	1899	1974
Chaney, Lon	1883	1930				Elliot, Cass	1941	1974
Chaney, Lon, Jr.	1905	1973	Dailey, Dan	1914	1978	Elliott, Denholm	1922	1992
Chapin, Harry	1942	1981	Dandridge, Dorothy	1923	1965	Ellis, Mary	1897	2003
Chaplin, Charles	1889	1977	Daniell, Henry	1894	1963	Elman, Mischa	1891	1967
Chapman, Graham	1941	1989	Daniels, Bebe	1901	1971	Errol, Leon	1881	1951
Charles, Ray	1930	2004	Darin, Bobby	1936	1973	Evans, Dale	1912	2001
Chase, Ilka	1905	1978	Darnell, Linda	1921	1965	Evans, Edith	1888	1976
Chatterton, Ruth	1893	1961	Darwell, Jane	1879	1967	Evans, Maurice	1901	1989
Cherrill, Virginia	1908	1996	Da Silva, Howard	1909	1986	Ewell, Tom	1909	1994
Chevalier, Maurice	1888	1972	Davenport, Harry	1866	1949			
Child, Julia	1912	2004	Davies, Marion	1897	1961	Fadiman, Clifton	1904	1999
Clair, René	1898	1981	Davis, Bette	1908	1989	Fairbanks, Douglas	1883	1939
Clark, Bobby	1888	1960	Davis, Joan	1907	1961	Fairbanks, Douglas, Jr.	1909	2000
Clark, Dane	1913	1998	Davis, Sammy Jr.	1925	1990	Falkenburg, Jinx	1919	2003
Clark, Fred	1914	1968	Day, Dennis	1917	1988	Farley, Chris	1964	1997
Clayton, Jan	1917	1983	Dean, James	1931	1955	Farmer, Frances	1914	1970
Clift, Montgomery	1920	1966	Dee, Frances	1907	2004	Farnsworth, Richard	1920	2000
Cline, Patsy	1932	1963	Defore, Don	1917	1993	Farnum, Dustin	1870	1929
Clooney, Rosemary	1928	2002	Dekker, Albert	1905	1968	Farnum, William	1876	1953
Clyde, Andy	1892	1967	Del Rio, Dolores	1908	1983	Farrar, Geraldine	1882	1967
Cobain, Kurt	1967	1994	Demarest, William	1892	1983	Farrell, Charles	1901	1990
Cobb, Lee J.	1911	1976	DeMille, Agnes	1905	1993	Farrell, Eileen	1920	2002
Coburn, Charles	1877	1961	DeMille, Cecil B.	1881	1959	Farrell, Glenda	1904	1971
Coburn, James	1928	2002	Denison, Michael	1915	1998	Fassbinder, Rainer Werner	1946	1982
Coca, Imogene	1908	2001	Denning, Richard	1914	1998			
Cochran, Steve	1917?	1965	Dennis, Sandy	1937	1992	Fay, Frank	1897	1961
Coco, James	1930	1987	Denny, Reginald	1891	1967	Faye, Alice	1912	1998
Cody, Buffalo Bill	1846	1917	Denver, John	1943	1997	Fazenda, Louise	1895	1962
Cody, Iron Eyes	1907	1999	Derek, John	1926	1998	Feld, Fritz	1900	1993
Cohan, George M.	1878	1942	DeSica, Vittorio	1901	1974	Feldman, Marty	1933	1982
Cohen, Myron	1902	1986	Devine, Andy	1905	1977	Fell, Norman	1924	1998
Colbert, Claudette	1903	1996	Dewhurst, Colleen	1924	1991	Fellini, Federico	1920	1993
Cole, Nat "King"	1919	1965	De Wilde, Brandon	1942	1972	Fenneman, George	1919	1997
Collins, Ray	1890	1965	De Wolfe, Billy	1907	1974	Ferrer, Jose	1912	1992
Colman, Ronald	1891	1958	Diamond, Selma	1920	1985	Fetchit, Stepin	1898	1985
Columbo, Russ	1908	1934	Dietrich, Marlene	1901	1992	Fiedler, Arthur	1894	1979
Como, Perry	1912	2001	Digges, Dudley	1879	1947	Field, Betty	1918	1973
Conniff, Ray	1916	2002	Disney, Walt	1901	1966	Fields, Gracie	1898	1979

Name	Born	Died
Fields, W.C.	1879	1946
Fields, Totie	1931	1978
Finch, Peter	1916	1977
Fine, Larry	1902	1975
Firkusny, Rudolf	1912	1994
Fiske, Minnie Maddern	1865	1932
Fitzgerald, Barry	1888	1961
Flagstad, Kirsten	1895	1962
Fleming, Art	1924	1995
Fleming, Eric	1925	1966
Flippen, Jay C.	1900	1971
Flynn, Errol	1909	1959
Flynn, Joe	1925	1974
Foley, Red	1910	1968
Fonda, Henry	1905	1982
Fontaine, Frank	1920	1978
Fontanne, Lynn	1887	1983
Fonteyn, Margot	1919	1991
Ford, John	1895	1973
Ford, Paul	1901	1976
Ford, Tennessee Ernie	1919	1991
Ford, Wallace	1899	1966
Forrest, Helen	1918	1999
Fosse, Bob	1927	1987
Foster, Phil	1914	1985
Foster, Preston	1901	1970
Foxx, Redd	1922	1991
Foy, Eddie	1857	1928
Franchi, Sergio	1933?	1990
Francis, Arlene	1908	2001
Francis, Kay	1903	1968
Franciscus, James	1934	1991
Frankenheimer, John	1930	2002
Frann, Mary	1943	1998
Frawley, William	1893	1966
Frederick, Pauline	1885	1938
French, Victor	1934	1989
Friganza, Trixie	1870	1955
Frisco, Joe	1890	1958
Froman, Jane	1907	1980
Fuller, Samuel	1912	1997
Funt, Allen	1914	1999
Furness, Betty	1916	1994
Gabin, Jean	1904	1976
Gable, Clark	1901	1960
Gabor, Eva	1920	1995
Garbo, Greta	1905	1990
Garcia, Jerry	1942	1995
Gardenia, Vincent	1922	1992
Gardner, Ava	1922	1990
Garfield, John	1913	1952
Garland, Judy	1922	1969
Garson, Greer	1904	1996
Gassman, Vittorio	1922	2000
Gaye, Marvin	1939	1984
Gaynor, Janet	1906	1984
Gebel-Williams, Gunther	1934	2001
Geer, Will	1902	1978
George, Gladys	1900	1954
Gibb, Andy	1958	1988
Gibb, Maurice	1949	2003
Gibson, Hoot	1892	1962
Gielgud, John	1904	2000
Gilbert, Billy	1894	1971
Gilbert, John	1895	1936
Gilford, Jack	1907	1990
Gillette, William	1855	1937
Gingold, Hermione	1897	1987
Gish, Dorothy	1898	1968
Gish, Lillian	1893	1993
Gleason, Jackie	1916	1987
Gleason, James	1886	1959
Gluck, Alma	1884	1938
Gobel, George	1919	1991
Goddard, Paulette	1905	1990
Godfrey, Arthur	1903	1983
Godunov, Alexander	1949	1995
Goldwyn, Samuel	1882	1974
Gomez, Thomas	1905	1971
Goodman, Benny	1909	1986
Gorcey, Leo	1915	1969
Gordon, Gale	1906	1995
Gordon, Ruth	1896	1985
Gosden, Freeman ("Amos")	1899	1982
Gottschalk, Ferdinand	1869	1944
Gottschalk, Louis	1829	1869
Gould, Glenn	1932	1982
Gould, Morton	1913	1996
Grable, Betty	1916	1973
Graham, Martha	1894	1991
Graham, Virginia	1912	1998
Grahame, Gloria	1925	1981
Granger, Stewart	1913	1993
Grant, Cary	1904	1986
Granville, Bonita	1923	1988
Gray, Dolores	1924	2002
Gray, Spalding	1941	2004
Greco, Jose	1918	2001
Green, Adolph	1915	2002
Greene, Lorne	1915	1987
Greenstreet, Sydney	1879	1954
Greenwood, Charlotte	1890	1978
Greer, Jane	1924	2001
Gregory, James	1911	2002
Griffith, David Wark	1874	1948
Griffith, Hugh	1912	1980
Guardino, Harry	1925	1995
Guinness, Sir Alec	1914	2000
Guthrie, Woody	1912	1967
Gwenn, Edmund	1875	1959
Gwynne, Fred	1926	1993
Hackett, Buddy	1924	2003
Hackett, Joan	1934	1983
Hagen, Uta	1919	2004
Hale, Alan	1892	1950
Hale, Alan, Jr.	1918	1990
Haley, Bill	1925	1981
Haley, Jack	1899	1979
Hall, Huntz	1919	1999
Hall, Jon	1915	1979
Hamilton, Margaret	1902	1985
Hammerstein, Oscar	1847	1919
Hammerstein II, Oscar	1895	1960
Hampton, Lionel	1908	2002
Hardwicke, Cedric	1893	1964
Hardy, Oliver	1892	1957
Harlow, Jean	1911	1937
Harris, Phil	1904	1995
Harris, Richard	1930	2002
Harrison, George	1943	2001
Harrison, Rex	1908	1990
Hart, William S.	1870	1946
Hartman, Phil	1948	1998
Harvey, Laurence	1928	1973
Hatfield, Bobby	1940	2003
Hawkins, Jack	1910	1973
Hawkins, Screamin' Jay	1929	2000
Hawthorne, Nigel	1929	2001
Hayakawa, Sessue	1890	1973
Hayden, Sterling	1916	1986
Hayes, Gabby	1885	1969
Hayes, Helen	1900	1993
Hayes, Peter Lind	1915	1998
Hayward, Leland	1902	1971
Hayward, Louis	1909	1985
Hayward, Susan	1917	1975
Hayworth, Rita	1918	1987
Head, Edith	1907	1981
Healy, Ted	1896	1937
Heckart, Eileen	1919	2001
Heflin, Van	1910	1971
Heifetz, Jascha	1901	1987
Held, Anna	1873	1918
Hemingway, Margaux	1955	1996
Hemmings, David	1941	2003
Hendrix, Jimi	1942	1970
Henie, Sonja	1912	1969
Henreid, Paul	1908	1992
Henson, Jim	1936	1990
Hepburn, Audrey	1929	1993
Hepburn, Katharine	1907	2003
Hersholt, Jean	1886	1956
Hewett, Christopher	1922	2001
Hickey, William	1928	1997
Hickson, Joan	1906	1998
Hill, Benny	1925	1992
Hill, George Roy	1921	2002
Hiller, Wendy	1912	2003
Hines, Gregory	1946	2003
Hines, Jerome	1921	2003
Hirt, Al	1922	1999
Hitchcock, Alfred	1899	1980
Hobson, Valerie	1917	1998
Hodiak, John	1914	1955
Holden, Fay	1894	1973
Holden, William	1918	1981
Holiday, Billie	1915	1959
Holliday, Judy	1922	1965
Holloway, Sterling	1905	1992
Holly, Buddy	1936	1959
Holt, Jack	1888	1951
Holt, Tim	1918	1973
Homolka, Oscar	1898	1978
Hooker, John Lee	1917	2001
Hoon, Shannon	1967	1995
Hope, Bob	1903	2003
Hopkins, Miriam	1902	1972
Hopper, DeWolf	1858	1935
Hopper, Hedda	1885	1966
Hopper, William	1915	1970
Horowitz, Vladimir	1904	1989
Horton, Edward Everett	1886	1970
Houdini, Harry	1874	1926
Houseman, John	1902	1988
Hovis, Larry	1936	2003
Howard (Horwitz), Curly	1903	1952
Howard, Eugene	1881	1965
Howard, Joe	1867	1961
Howard, Leslie	1890	1943
Howard (Horwitz), Moe	1897	1975
Howard (Horwitz), Shemp	1895	1955
Howard, Tom	1885	1955
Howard, Trevor	1916	1988
Howard, Willie	1885	1949
Hudson, Rock	1925	1985
Hull, Henry	1890	1977
Hull, Josephine	1886	1957
Humphrey, Doris	1895	1958
Hunter, Jeffrey	1925	1969
Hunter, Kim	1922	2002
Hunter, Ross	1921	1996
Husing, Ted	1901	1962
Huston, John	1906	1987
Huston, Walter	1884	1950
Hutchence, Michael	1960	1997
Hutton, Jim	1934	1979
Hutton, Robert	1920	1994
Hyde-White, Wilfrid	1903	1991
Ingram, Rex	1895	1969
Iturbi, Jose	1895	1980
Ireland, Jill	1936	1990
Ireland, John	1915	1992
Irving, Henry	1838	1905
Ives, Burl	1909	1995
Jack, Wolfman	1938	1995
Jackson, Joe	1875	1942
Jackson, Mahalia	1911	1972
Jackson, Milt	1922	1999
Jaeckel, Richard	1926	1997
Jaffe, Sam	1891	1984
Jagger, Dean	1903	1991
Jam Master Jay	1965	2003
James, Dennis	1917	1997
James, Harry	1916	1983
James, Rick	1948	2004
Janis, Elsie	1889	1956
Jannings, Emil	1886	1950
Janssen, David	1930	1980
Jenkins, Allen	1900	1974
Jennings, Waylon	1937	2002
Jessel, George	1898	1981
Jeter, Michael	1952	2003
Johnson, Ben	1918	1996
Johnson, Celia	1908	1982
Johnson, Chic	1892	1962
Johnson, J.J.	1924	2001
Jolson, Al	1886	1950
Jones, Brian	1942	1969
Jones, Buck	1889	1942
Jones, Carolyn	1933	1983
Jones, Elvin	1927	2004
Jones, Henry	1912	1999
Jones, Spike	1911	1965
Joplin, Janis	1943	1970
Jordan, Richard	1938	1993
Jory, Victor	1902	1982
Joslyn, Allyn	1905	1981
Julia, Raul	1940	1994
Jump, Gordon	1932	2003
Jurado, Katy	1924	2002
Jurgens, Curt	1915	1982

Name	Born	Died	Name	Born	Died	Name	Born	Died
Kahn, Madeline	1942	1999	Levant, Oscar	1906	1972	McCrea, Joel	1905	1990
Kane, Helen	1910	1966	Levene, Sam	1905	1980	McDaniel, Hattie	1895	1952
Kanin, Garson	1912	1999	Levenson, Sam	1911	1980	McDowall, Roddy	1928	1998
Karloff, Boris	1887	1969	Lewis, Joe E.	1902	1971	McFarland, George	1928	1993
Karns, Roscoe	1893	1970	Lewis, Shari	1934	1998	"Spanky"		
Kaufman, Andy	1949	1984	Lewis, Ted	1892	1971	McGuire, Dorothy	1916	2001
Kaye, Danny	1913	1987	Liberace	1919	1987	McHugh, Frank	1899	1981
Kaye, Stubby	1918	1997	Lillie, Beatrice	1894	1989	McIntire, John	1907	1991
Kazan, Elia	1909	2003	Lind, Jenny	1820	1887	McKay, Gardner	1932	2001
Kean, Charles	1811	1868	Lindfors, Viveca	1920	1995	McKern, Leo	1920	2002
Kean, Mrs. Charles	1806	1880	Lindley, Audra	1918	1997	McLaglen, Victor	1883	1959
Kean, Edmund	1787	1833	Linville, Larry	1939	2000	McMahon, Horace	1907	1971
Keaton, Buster	1895	1966	Little, Cleavon	1939	1992	McNally, Stephen	1913	1994
Keeler, Ruby	1910	1993	Llewelyn, Desmond	1914	1999	McNeill, Don	1907	1996
Keeshan, Bob (Captain	1927	2004	Lloyd, Harold	1893	1971	McQueen, Butterfly	1911	1995
Kangaroo)			Lloyd, Marie	1870	1922	McQueen, Steve	1930	1980
Keith, Brian	1921	1997	Lockhart, Gene	1891	1957	Meadows, Audrey	1924	1996
Kellaway, Cecil	1894	1973	Logan, Ella	1913	1969	Medford, Kay	1920	1980
Kelley, DeForest	1920	1999	Lombard, Carole	1909	1942	Meek, Donald	1880	1946
Kelly, Emmett	1898	1979	Lombardo, Guy	1902	1977	Meeker, Ralph	1920	1989
Kelly, Gene	1912	1996	Long, Richard	1927	1974	Melba, Nellie	1861	1931
Kelly, Grace	1929	1982	Lopes, Lisa	1971	2002	Melchior, Lauritz	1890	1973
Kelly, Jack	1927	1992	Lopez, Vincent	1895	1975	Menjou, Adolphe	1890	1963
Kelly, Nancy	1921	1985	Lord, Jack	1920?	1998	Menken, Helen	1902	1966
Kelly, Patsy	1910	1981	Lorne, Marion	1888	1968	Menuhin, Yehudi	1916	1999
Kelton, Pert	1907	1968	Lorre, Peter	1904	1964	Mercouri, Melina	1925	1994
Kendall, Kay	1926	1959	Loudon, Dorothy	1933	2003	Mercury, Freddie	1946	1991
Kennedy, Arthur	1914	1990	Lovejoy, Frank	1912	1962	Meredith, Burgess	1909	1997
Kennedy, Edgar	1890	1948	Lowe, Edmund	1890	1971	Merman, Ethel	1908	1984
Kibbee, Guy	1886	1956	Loy, Myrna	1905	1993	Merrick, David	1911	2000
Kilbride, Percy	1888	1964	Lubitsch, Ernst	1892	1947	Merrill, Gary	1915	1990
Kiley, Richard	1922	1999	Ludden, Allen	1918	1981	Mifune, Toshiro	1920	1997
King, Alan	1927	2004	Lugosi, Bela	1882	1956	Milland, Ray	1905	1986
Kinski, Klaus	1926	1991	Lukas, Paul	1894	1971	Miller, Ann	1923	2004
Kirby, George	1923	1995	Lundigan, William	1914	1975	Miller, Glenn	1904	1944
Kirby, Durward	1912	2000	Lunt, Alfred	1892	1977	Miller, Marilyn	1898	1936
Kirsten, Dorothy	1910	1992	Lupino, Ida	1918	1995	Miller, Roger	1936	1992
Klemperer, Werner	1919	2000	Lymon, Frankie	1942	1968	Mills, Harry	1913	1982
Knight, Ted	1923	1986	Lynde, Paul	1926	1982	Minnevitch, Borrah	1903	1955
Kostelanetz, Andre	1901	1980	Lynn, Diana	1926	1971	Mineo, Sal	1939	1976
Kovacs, Ernie	1919	1962				Miner, Jan	1917	2004
Kramer, Stanley	1913	2001	MacDonald, Jeanette	1903	1965	Mingus, Charles	1922	1979
Kruger, Otto	1885	1974	Mack, Ted	1904	1976	Miranda, Carmen	1913	1955
Kubrick, Stanley	1928	1999	MacKenzie, Gisele	1927	2003	Mitchell, Cameron	1918	1994
Kulp, Nancy	1921	1991	MacLane, Barton	1902	1969	Mitchell, Thomas	1892	1962
Kurosawa, Akira	1910	1998	MacMurray, Fred	1908	1991	Mitchum, Robert	1917	1997
Kyser, Kay	1906	1985	MacRae, Gordon	1921	1986	Mix, Tom	1880	1940
			Macready, George	1909	1973	Monica, Corbett	1930	1998
Ladd, Alan	1913	1964	Madison, Guy	1922	1996	Monroe, Marilyn	1926	1962
Lahr, Bert	1895	1967	Magnani, Anna	1908	1973	Monroe, Vaughn	1911	1973
Lake, Arthur	1905	1987	Mancini, Henry	1924	1994	Montand, Yves	1921	1991
Lake, Veronica	1919	1973	Main, Marjorie	1890	1975	Montez, Maria	1917	1951
Lamarr, Hedy	1913	2000	Malle, Louis	1932	1995	Montgomery, Elizabeth	1933	1995
Lamas, Fernando	1915	1982	Mann, Herbie	1930	2003	Montgomery, George	1916	2000
Lamour, Dorothy	1914	1996	Mansfield, Jayne	1932	1967	Montgomery, Robert	1904	1981
Lancaster, Burt	1913	1994	Mantovani, Annunzio	1905	1980	Moore, Clayton	1914	1999
Lanchester, Elsa	1902	1986	Marais, Jean	1913	1998	Moore, Colleen	1900	1988
Lane, Pricilla	1917	1995	March, Fredric	1897	1975	Moore, Dudley	1935	2002
Landis, Carole	1919	1948	March, Hal	1920	1970	Moore, Grace	1901	1947
Landis, Jessie Royce	1904	1972	Marchand, Nancy	1928	2000	Moore, Garry	1914	1993
Landon, Michael	1936	1991	Marley, Bob	1945	1981	Moore, Victor	1876	1962
Lang, Fritz	1890	1976	Marshall, Brenda	1915	1992	Moorehead, Agnes	1906	1974
Langdon, Harry	1884	1944	Marshall, E.G.	1910	1998	Moreland, Mantan	1902	1973
Lange, Hope	1931	2003	Marshall, Herbert	1890	1966	Morgan, Dennis	1910	1994
Langtry, Lillie	1853	1929	Martin, Dean	1917	1995	Morgan, Frank	1890	1949
Lanza, Mario	1921	1959	Martin, Mary	1913	1990	Morgan, Helen	1900	1941
LaRue, Lash (Alfred)	1917	1996	Martin, Ross	1920	1981	Morgan, Henry	1915	1994
Lauder, Harry	1870	1950	Marvin, Lee	1924	1987	Morley, Robert	1908	1992
Laughton, Charles	1899	1962	Marx, Arthur (Harpo)	1888	1964	Morris, Chester	1901	1970
Laurel, Stan	1890	1965	Marx, Herbert (Zeppo)	1901	1979	Morris, Greg	1934	1996
Lawford, Peter	1923	1984	Marx, Julius (Groucho)	1890	1977	Morris, Wayne	1914	1959
Lawrence, Gertrude	1898	1952	Marx, Leonard (Chico)	1886	1961	Morrison, Jim	1943	1971
Lean, David	1908	1991	Marx, Milton (Gummo)	1893	1977	Morrow, Vic	1932	1982
Lee, Bernard	1908	1981	Mason, James	1909	1984	Mostel, Zero	1915	1977
Lee, Bruce	1940	1973	Massey, Daniel	1933	1998	Mowbray, Alan	1897	1969
Lee, Canada	1907	1952	Massey, Raymond	1896	1983	Mulhare, Edward	1923	1997
Lee, Gypsy Rose	1914	1970	Mastroianni, Marcello	1924	1996	Mulligan, Gerry	1927	1996
Lee, Anna	1913	2004	Matthau, Walter	1920	2000	Mulligan, Richard	1932	2000
Lee, Peggy	1920	2002	Mature, Victor	1916	1999	Muni, Paul	1895	1967
LeGallienne, Eva	1899	1991	Maxwell, Marilyn	1921	1972	Munshin, Jules	1915	1970
Lehmann, Lotte	1888	1976	Mayer, Louis B.	1885	1957	Murphy, Audie	1924	1971
Leigh, Vivien	1913	1967	Mayfield, Curtis	1942	1999	Murphy, George	1902	1992
Leighton, Margaret	1922	1976	Maynard, Ken	1895	1973	Murray, Arthur	1895	1991
Lemmon, Jack	1925	2001	Mazurki, Mike	1909	1990	Murray, Kathryn	1906	1999
Lennon, John	1940	1980	McCambridge, Mercedes	1916	2004	Murray, Mae	1885	1965
Lenya, Lotte	1898	1981	McCartney, Linda	1941	1998			
Leonard, Eddie	1870	1941	McClure, Doug	1935	1995	Nagel, Conrad	1896	1970
Leonard, Sheldon	1907	1997	McCormack, John	1884	1945	Naish, J. Carroll	1900	1973
LeRoy, Mervyn	1900	1987	McCrary, Tex	1910	2003	Naldi, Nita	1898	1961

Name	Born	Died	Name	Born	Died	Name	Born	Died
Nance, Jack	1943	1997	Porter, Eric	1928	1995	Rossellini, Roberto	1906	1977
Natwick, Mildred	1908	1994	Porter, Nyree Dawn	1940	2001	Rowan, Dan	1922	1987
Negri, Pola	1897	1987	Powell, Dick	1904	1963	Rubinstein, Artur	1887	1982
Nelson, Harriet (Hilliard)	1909	1994	Powell, Eleanor	1912	1982	Ruggles, Charles	1886	1970
Nelson, Ozzie	1906	1975	Powell, William	1892	1984	Russell, Gail	1924	1961
Nelson, Rick	1940	1985	Power, Tyrone	1913	1958	Russell, Harold	1914	2002
Nesbit, Evelyn	1885	1967	Preminger, Otto	1905	1986	Russell, Lillian	1861	1922
Newley, Anthony	1931	1999	Presley, Elvis	1935	1977	Russell, Rosalind	1911	1976
Newton, Robert	1905	1956	Preston, Robert	1918	1987	Rutherford, Margaret	1892	1972
Nicholas, Harold	1924	2000	Price, Vincent	1911	1993	Ryan, Irene	1903	1973
Nijinsky, Vaslav	1890	1950	Prima, Louis	1911	1978	Ryan, Robert	1909	1973
Nilsson, Anna Q.	1893	1974	Prinze, Freddie	1954	1977			
Niven, David	1910	1983	Prowse, Juliet	1936	1996	Sabu	1924	1963
Nolan, Lloyd	1902	1985	Puente, Tito	1923	2000	Sanford, Isabel	1917	2004
Normand, Mabel	1894	1930	Pyle, Denver	1920	1997	Sargent, Dick	1933	1994
Notorious B.I.G.	1972	1997				St. Cyr, Lili	1917	1999
Novarro, Ramon	1899	1968	Quayle, Anthony	1913	1989	St. Denis, Ruth	1877	1968
Nureyev, Rudolf	1938	1993	Questel, Mae	1908	1998	Sakall, S.Z.	1884	1955
			Quinn, Anthony	1915	2001	Sale (Chic), Charles	1885	1936
Oakie, Jack	1903	1978	Quintero, José	1924	1999	Sanders, George	1906	1972
Oakley, Annie	1860	1926				Savalas, Telly	1924	1994
Oates, Warren	1928	1982	Rabb, Ellis	1930	1998	Schildkraut, Joseph	1895	1964
Oberon, Merle	1911	1979	Rabbit, Eddie	1941	1998	Schipa, Tito	1889	1965
O'Brien, Edmond	1915	1985	Radner, Gilda	1946	1989	Schlesinger, John	1926	2003
O'Brien, Pat	1899	1983	Raft, George	1895	1980	Schnabel, Artur	1882	1951
O'Connell, Arthur	1908	1981	Rains, Claude	1890	1967	Schneider, Romy	1938	1982
O'Connell, Helen	1921	1993	Ralston, Esther	1902	1994	Scott, George C.	1927	1999
O'Connor, Carroll	1924	2001	Ramone, Dee Dee	1952	2002	Scott, Hazel	1920	1981
O'Connor, Donald	1925	2003	Ramone, Joey	1951	2001	Scott, Martha	1914	2003
O'Connor, Una	1880	1959	Ramone, Johnny	1951	2004	Scott, Randolph	1898	1987
O'Keefe, Dennis	1908	1968	Rampal, Jean-Pierre	1922	2000	Scott, Zachary	1914	1965
Oland, Warner	1880	1938	Tony Randall	1920	2004	Scott-Siddons, Mrs.	1843	1896
Olcott, Chauncey	1860	1932	John Randolph	1915	2004	Seberg, Jean	1938	1979
Oliver, Edna May	1883	1942	Rathbone, Basil	1892	1967	Seeley, Blossom	1892	1974
Olivier, Laurence	1907	1989	Ratoff, Gregory	1897	1960	Segovia, Andres	1893	1987
Olsen, Ole	1892	1963	Ray, Aldo	1926	1991	Selena	1971	1995
O'Neill, James	1849	1920	Ray, Johnnie	1927	1990	Sellers, Peter	1925	1980
O'Neill, Ron	1937	2004	Rayburn, Gene	1917	1999	Selznick, David O.	1902	1965
Orbison, Roy	1936	1988	Raye, Martha	1916	1994	Sennett, Mack	1884	1960
Ormandy, Eugene	1899	1985	Raymond, Gene	1908	1998	Senor Wences	1896	1999
O'Sullivan, Maureen	1911	1998	Reagan, Ronald	1911	2004	Serling, Rod	1924	1975
Ouspenskaya, Maria	1876	1949	Redding, Otis	1941	1967	Shakur, Tupac	1971	1996
Owen, Reginald	1887	1972	Redgrave, Michael	1908	1985	Shaw, Robert (actor)	1927	1978
			Reed, Donna	1921	1986	Shaw, Robert	1916	1999
Paar, Jack	1918	2004	Reed, Oliver	1938	1999	(conductor)		
Paderewski, Ignace	1860	1941	Reed, Robert	1932	1992	Shawn, Ted	1891	1972
Page, Geraldine	1924	1987	Reeves, George	1914	1959	Shean, Al	1868	1949
Pakula, Alan	1928	1998	Reeves, Steve	1926	2000	Shearer, Norma	1902	1983
Pallette, Eugene	1889	1954	Reinhardt, Max	1873	1943	Sheridan, Ann	1915	1967
Palmer, Lilli	1914	1986	Remick, Lee	1935	1991	Shore, Dinah	1917	1994
Palmer, Robert	1949	2003	Renaldo, Duncan	1904	1980	Shubert, Lee	1875	1953
Pangborn, Franklin	1894	1958	Rennie, Michael	1909	1971	Shull, Richard B.	1929	1999
Parks, Bert	1914	1992	Renoir, Jean	1894	1979	Siddons, Mrs. Sarah	1755	1831
Parks, Larry	1914	1975	Rettig, Tommy	1941	1996	Sidney, Sylvia	1910	1999
Pasternack, Josef A.	1881	1940	Reynolds, Marjorie	1923	1997	Signoret, Simone	1921	1985
Pastor, Tony	1837	1908	Rich, Charlie	1932	1995	Silverheels, Jay	1912	1980
(vaudevillian)			Richardson, Ralph	1902	1983	Silvers, Phil	1912	1985
Pastor, Tony			Riddle, Nelson	1921	1985	Sim, Alastair	1900	1976
(bandleader)	1907	1969	Riefenstahl, Leni	1902	2003	Simmons, Richard	1913	2003
Patti, Adelina	1843	1919	Ripperton, Minnie	1947	1979	Simone, Nina	1933	2003
Patti, Carlotta	1840	1889	Ritchard, Cyril	1898	1977	Sims, Irene	1930	2001
Patrick, Gail	1911	1980	Ritter, John	1948	2003	Sinatra, Frank	1915	1998
Pavlova, Anna	1885	1931	Ritter, Tex	1907	1974	Sinclair, Madge	1938	1995
Paycheck, Johnny	1938	2003	Ritter, Thelma	1905	1969	Singleton, Penny	1908	2003
Payne, John	1912	1989	Ritz, Al	1901	1965	Siskel, Gene	1946	1999
Pearl, Minnie	1912	1996	Ritz, Harry	1906	1986	Sitka, Emil	1914	1998
Peck, Gregory	1916	2003	Ritz, Jimmy	1903	1985	Sjostrom, Victor	1879	1960
Peerce, Jan	1904	1984	Robards, Jason	1922	2000	Skelton, Red	1913	1997
Pendleton, Nat	1899	1967	Robbins, Jerome	1918	1998	Skinner, Otis	1858	1942
Penner, Joe	1905	1941	Robbins, Marty	1925	1982	Smith, Alexis	1921	1992
Peppard, George	1928	1994	Robeson, Paul	1898	1976	Smith, Buffalo Bob	1917	1998
Perkins, Anthony	1932	1992	Robinson, Bill	1878	1949	Smith, C. Aubrey	1863	1948
Perkins, Carl	1932	1998	Robinson, Edward G.	1893	1973	Smith, Elliott	1969	2003
Perkins, Marlin	1905	1986	Roche, Eugene	1928	2004	Smith, Jeff	1939	2004
Peters, Jean	1926	2000	Rochester (E. Anderson)	1905	1977	Smith, Kate	1907	1986
Peters, Susan	1921	1952	Roddenberry, Gene	1921	1991	Smith, Kent	1907	1985
Phillips, John	1935	2001	Rodgers, Jimmie	1897	1933	Snodgress, Carrie	1946	2004
Phoenix, River	1970	1993	Rogers, Buddy	1904	1999	Snow, Hank	1914	1999
Piaf, Edith	1915	1963	Rogers, Fred	1928	2003	Solti, George	1912	1997
Pickens, Slim	1919	1983	Rogers, Ginger	1911	1995	Sondergaard, Gale	1899	1985
Pickford, Mary	1893	1979	Rogers, Roy	1911	1998	Sothern, Ann	1909	2001
Picon, Molly	1898	1992	Rogers, Will	1879	1935	Sousa, John Philip	1854	1932
Pidgeon, Walter	1897	1984	Roland, Gilbert	1905	1994	Sparks, Ned	1884	1957
Pinza, Ezio	1892	1957	Rolle, Esther	1920?	1998	Springfield, Dusty	1939	1999
Pitts, Zasu	1898	1963	Rollins, Howard	1950	1996	Stack, Robert	1919	2003
Plato, Dana	1964	1999	Roman, Ruth	1924	1999	Stander, Lionel	1908	1994
Pleasence, Donald	1919	1995	Romero, Cesar	1907	1994	Stanley, Kim	1925	2001
Pons, Lily	1904	1976	Rooney, Pat	1880	1962	Stanwyck, Barbara	1907	1990
Ponselle, Rosa	1897	1981	Rose, Billy	1899	1966	Steiger, Rod	1925	2002

Name	Born	Died	Name	Born	Died	Name	Born	Died
Sterling, Jan	1921	2004	Treacher, Arthur	1894	1975	Welles, Orson	1915	1985
Stern, Isaac	1920	2001	Tree, Herbert Beerbohm	1853	1917	Wellman, William	1896	1975
Stevens, Craig	1918	2000	Trevor, Claire	1909	2000	Werner, Oskar	1922	1984
Stevens, Inger	1934	1970	Truex, Ernest	1890	1973	West, Mae	1893	1980
Stevens, Mark	1916	1994	Truffaut, Francois	1932	1984	Weston, Jack	1924	1996
Stevenson, McLean	1929	1996	Tucker, Forrest	1919	1986	Whale, James	1889	1957
Stewart, James	1908	1997	Tucker, Richard	1913	1975	Wheeler, Bert	1895	1968
Stickney, Dorothy	1896	1998	Tucker, Sophie	1884	1966	White, Barry	1944	2003
Stokowski, Leopold	1882	1977	Turner, Lana	1920	1995	White, Jesse	1919	1997
Stone, Lewis	1879	1953	Turpin, Ben	1874	1940	White, Pearl	1889	1938
Stone, Milburn	1904	1980	Twelvetrees, Helen	1908	1958	Whiteman, Paul	1891	1967
Straight, Beatrice	1918	2001	Twitty, Conway	1933	1993	Whitty, May	1865	1948
Strasberg, Lee	1901	1982				Wickes, Mary	1910	1995
Strasberg, Susan	1938	1999	Urich, Robert	1947	2002	Wilde, Cornel	1918	1989
Strode, Woody	1914	1994	Ustinov, Peter	1921	2004	Wilder, Billy	1906	2002
Strummer, Joe	1952	2002				Wilding, Michael	1912	1979
Sturges, Preston	1898	1959	Valens, Ritchie	1941	1959	Williams, Bert	1877	1922
Sullavan, Margaret	1911	1960	Valentino, Rudolph	1895	1926	Williams, Guy	1924	1989
Sullivan, Barry	1912	1994	Vallee, Rudy	1901	1986	Williams, Hank Sr.	1923	1953
Sullivan, Ed	1902	1974	Van, Bobby	1928	1980	Wills, Bob	1905	1975
Sullivan, Francis L.	1903	1956	Vance, Vivian	1912	1979	Wills, Chill	1903	1978
Summerville, Slim	1892	1946	Van Cleef, Lee	1925	1989	Wilson, Carl	1946	1998
Swanson, Gloria	1899	1983	Van Fleet, Jo	1922	1996	Wilson, Dennis	1944	1983
Swarthout, Gladys	1904	1969	Varney, Jim	1949	2000	Wilson, Dooley	1894	1953
Switzer, Carl "Alfalfa"	1926	1959	Vaughan, Sarah	1924	1990	Wilson, Flip	1933	1998
			Veidt, Conrad	1893	1943	Wilson, Jackie	1934	1984
Talbot, Lyle	1904	1996	Velez, Lupe	1908	1944	Wilson, Marie	1917	1972
Talmadge, Norma	1893	1957	Vera-Ellen	1926	1981	Windsor, Marie	1919	2000
Tamiroff, Akim	1899	1972	Verdon, Gwen	1925	2000	Winfield, Paul	1941	2004
Tandy, Jessica	1909	1994	Vernon, Jackie	1925	1987	Winninger, Charles	1884	1969
Tanguay, Eva	1878	1947	Villechaize, Herve	1943	1993	Withers, Grant	1904	1959
Tati, Jacques	1908	1982	Vincent, Gene	1935	1971	Wong, Anna May	1907	1961
Taylor, Deems	1885	1966	Vicious, Sid	1958	1979	Wood, Natalie	1938	1981
Taylor, Dub	1907	1994	Vinson, Helen	1907	1999	Wood, Peggy	1892	1978
Taylor, Estelle	1899	1958	Von Stroheim, Erich	1885	1957	Wooley, Sheb	1921	2003
Taylor, Laurette	1887	1946	Von Zell, Harry	1906	1981	Woolley, Monty	1888	1963
Taylor, Robert	1911	1969				Worth, Irene	1916	2002
Terry, Ellen	1847	1928	Walker, Junior	1942	1995	Wray, Fay	1907	2004
Thalberg, Irving	1899	1936	Walker, Nancy	1922	1992	Wyler, William	1902	1981
Thaw, John	1942	2002	Walker, Robert	1918	1951	Wynette, Tammy	1942	1998
Thigpen, Lynne	1948	2003	Wallenda, Karl	1905	1978	Wynn, Ed	1886	1966
Thomas, Danny	1912	1991	Walsh, J. T.	1943	1998	Wynn, Keenan	1916	1986
Thomas, John Charles	1892	1960	Walsh, Raoul	1887	1980			
Thorndike, Sybil	1882	1976	Walston, Ray	1914	2001	Yankovic, Frank	1915	1998
Thulin, Ingrid	1926	2004	Walter, Bruno	1876	1962	York, Dick	1929	1992
Tibbett, Lawrence	1896	1960	Ward, Helen	1916	1998	Young, Clara Kimball	1890	1960
Tierney, Gene	1920	1991	Waring, Fred	1900	1984	Young, Gig	1913	1978
Tiny Tim	1923	1996	Warner, H. B.	1876	1958	Young, Loretta	1913	2000
Tippett, Sir Michael	1905	1998	Washington, Dinah	1924	1963	Young, Robert	1907	1998
Todd, Michael	1909	1958	Waters, Ethel	1896	1977	Young, Roland	1887	1953
Tomlinson, David	1917	2000	Waxman, Al	1935	2001	Youngman, Henny	1906	1998
Tone, Franchot	1903	1968	Wayne, David	1914	1995			
Torme, Mel	1925	1999	Wayne, John	1907	1979	Zanuck, Darryl F.	1902	1979
Toscanini, Arturo	1867	1957	Webb, Clifton	1891	1966	Zappa, Frank	1940	1993
Tracy, Lee	1898	1968	Webb, Jack	1920	1982	Zevon, Warren	1947	2003
Tracy, Spencer	1900	1967	Weems, Ted	1901	1963	Zinneman, Fred	1907	1997
Traubel, Helen	1903	1972	Weissmuller, Johnny	1904	1984	Ziegfeld, Florenz	1869	1932
Travers, Henry	1874	1965	Welk, Lawrence	1903	1992	Zukor, Adolph	1873	1976

Original Names of Selected Entertainers

EDIE ADAMS: Elizabeth Edith Enke
EDDIE ALBERT: Edward Albert Heimberger
ALAN ALDA: Alphonso D'Abruzzo
JASON ALEXANDER: Jay Greenspan
FRED ALLEN: John Sullivan
WOODY ALLEN: Allen Konigsberg
JUNE ALLYSON: Ella Geisman
JULIE ANDREWS: Julia Wells
EVE ARDEN: Eunice Quedens
BEATRICE ARTHUR: Bernice Frankel
JEAN ARTHUR: Gladys Greene
FRED ASTAIRE: Frederick Austerlitz
BABYFACE: Kenneth Edmonds
LAUREN BACALL: Betty Joan Perske
ERYKAH BADU: Erica Wright
ANNE BANCROFT: Anna Maria Italiano
GENE BARRY: Eugene Klass
PAT BENATAR: Patricia Andrejewski
TONY BENNETT: Anthony Benedetto
IRVING BERLIN: Israel Baline
JACK BENNY: Benjamin Kubelsky
JOEY BISHOP: Joseph Gottlieb
THE BIG BOPPER: Jiles Perry "J.P." Richardson
BONO (VOX): Paul Hewson
VICTOR BORGE: Borge Rosenbaum

DAVID BOWIE: David Robert Jones
BOY GEORGE: George Alan O'Dowd
FANNY BRICE: Fanny Borach
CHARLES BRONSON: Charles Buchinski
ALBERT BROOKS: Albert Einstein
MEL BROOKS: Melvin Kaminsky
GEORGE BURNS: Nathan Birnbaum
ELLEN BURSTYN: Edna Gilhooley
RICHARD BURTON: Richard Jenkins
RED BUTTONS: Aaron Chwatt
NICOLAS CAGE: Nicholas Coppola
MICHAEL CAINE: Maurice Micklewhite
MARIA CALLAS: Maria Kalogeropoulos
DIAHANN CARROLL: Carol Diahann Johnson
CEDRIC THE ENTERTAINER: Cedric Kyles
JACKIE CHAN: Chan Kwong-Sung
CYD CHARISSE: Tula Finklea
RAY CHARLES: Ray Charles Robinson
CHUBBY CHECKER: Ernest Evans
CHUCK D: Carlton Ridenhour
CHER: Cherilyn Sarkisian
PATSY CLINE: Virginia Patterson Hensley
LEE J. COBB: Leo Jacoby

CLAUDETTE COLBERT: Lily Chauchoin
ALICE COOPER: Vincent Furnier
DAVID COPPERFIELD: David Kotkin
HOWARD COSELL: Howard Cohen
ELVIS COSTELLO: Declan McManus
LOU COSTELLO: Louis Cristillo
PETER COYOTE: Peter Cohon
MICHAEL CRAWFORD: Michael Dumble-Smith
TOM CRUISE: Thomas Mapother IV
TONY CURTIS: Bernard Schwartz
VIC DAMONE: Vito Farinola
RODNEY DANGERFIELD: Jacob Cohen
BOBBY DARIN: Walden Robert Cassotto
DORIS DAY: Doris von Kappelhoff
YVONNE DE CARLO: Peggy Middleton
SANDRA DEE: Alexandra Zuck
JOHN DENVER: Henry John Deutschendorf Jr.
BO DEREK: Mary Cathleen Collins
DANNY DEVITO: Daniel Michaeli
ANGIE DICKINSON: Angeline Brown
BO DIDDLEY: Elias Bates
PHYLLIS DILLER: Phyllis Driver
DMX: Earl Simmons

IT'S A FACT: Actress Hedy Lamarr (1913-2000) in 1942 co-invented a frequency-hopping torpedo guidance system that used a piano roll to change between 88 frequencies. This method of communicating made it harder for enemies to jam remote-control signals. Filing under her married name, Hedy Keisler Markey, she was given a patent for her invention.

Earl TROY DONAHUE: Merle Johnson Jr.
KIRK DOUGLAS: Issur Danielovitch
MELVYN DOUGLAS: Melvyn Hesselberg
BOB DYLAN: Robert Zimmerman
BARBARA EDEN: Barbara Huffman
ELVIRA: Cassandra Peterson
EMINEM: Marshall Mathers
ENYA: Eithne Ni Bhraonian
DALE EVANS: Frances Smith
CHAD EVERETT: Raymond Cramton
DOUGLAS FAIRBANKS: Douglas Ullman
MORGAN FAIRCHILD: Patsy McClenny
JAMIE FARR: Jameel Farah
ALICE FAYE: Alice Jeanne Leppert
STEPIN FETCHIT: Lincoln Perry
W.C. FIELDS: William Claude Dukenfield
50 CENT: Curtis Jackson
BARRY FITZGERALD: William Shields
FLAVOR FLAV: William Drayton
JOAN FONTAINE: Joan de Havilland
JODIE FOSTER: Alicia Christian Foster
REDD FOXX: John Sanford
ANTHONY FRANCIOSA: Anthony Papaleo
ARLENE FRANCIS: Arlene Kazanjian
CONNIE FRANCIS: Concetta Franconero
GRETA GARBO: Greta Gustafsson
VINCENT GARDENIA: Vincent Scognamiglio
JOHN GARFIELD: Julius Garfinkle
JUDY GARLAND: Frances Gumm
JAMES GARNER: James Bumgarner
CRYSTAL GAYLE: Brenda Gayle Webb
KATHIE LEE GIFFORD: Kathie Epstein
WHOOPI GOLDBERG: Caryn Johnson
EYDIE GORME: Edith Gormezano
STEWART GRANGER: James Stewart
CARY GRANT: Archibald Leach
LEE GRANT: Lyova Rosenthal
JOEL GREY: Joe Katz
ROBERT GUILLAUME: Robert Williams
BUDDY HACKETT: Leonard Hacker
HAMMER: Stanley Kirk Burrell
JEAN HARLOW: Harlean Carpentier
REX HARRISON: Reginald Carey
LAURENCE HARVEY: Larushka Skikne
HELEN HAYES: Helen Brown
SUSAN HAYWARD: Edythe Marriner
RITA HAYWORTH: Margarita Cansino
PEE-WEE HERMAN: Paul Reubenfeld
CHARLTON HESTON: John Charlton Carter
WILLIAM HOLDEN: William Beedle
BILLIE HOLIDAY: Eleanora Fagan
JUDY HOLLIDAY: Judith Tuvim
BOB HOPE: Leslie Townes Hope
HARRY HOUDINI: Ehrich Weiss
LESLIE HOWARD: Leslie Stainer
HOWLIN' WOLF: Chester Burnett
ROCK HUDSON: Roy Scherer Jr. (later Fitzgerald)
ENGELBERT HUMPERDINCK: Arnold Dorsey
KIM HUNTER: Janet Cole
BETTY HUTTON: Betty Thornberg
ICE CUBE: O'Shea Jackson
ICE-T: Tracy Morrow
BILLY IDOL: William Broad
DAVID JANSSEN: David Meyer
JAY-Z: Shawn Carter
ANN JILLIAN: Anne Nauseda
ELTON JOHN: Reginald Dwight
DON JOHNSON: Donald Wayne
AL JOLSON: Asa Yoelson
JENNIFER JONES: Phylis Isley
TOM JONES: Thomas Woodward
SPIKE JONZE: Adam Spiegel
LOUIS JOURDAN: Louis Gendre
WYNONNA JUDD: Christina Ciminella
BORIS KARLOFF: William Henry Pratt
DANNY KAYE: David Kaminsky

DIANE KEATON: Diane Hall
MICHAEL KEATON: Michael Douglas
CHAKA KHAN: Yvette Stevens
CAROLE KING: Carole Klein
LARRY KING: Larry Zeiger
BEN KINGSLEY: Krishna Banji
NASTASSJA KINSKI: Nastassja Nakszynski
TED KNIGHT: Tadeus Wladyslaw Konopka
CHERYL LADD: Cheryl Stoppelmoor
VERONICA LAKE: Constance Ockleman
HEDY LAMARR: Hedwig Kiesler
DOROTHY LAMOUR: Mary Leta Dorothy Slaton
MICHAEL LANDON: Eugene Orowitz
MARIO LANZA: Alfredo Cocozza
QUEEN LATIFAH: Dana Owens
STAN LAUREL: Arthur Jefferson
STEVE LAWRENCE: Sidney Leibowitz
BRENDA LEE: Brenda Mae Tarpley
GYPSY ROSE LEE: Rose Louise Hovick
MICHELLE LEE: Michelle Dusiak
PEGGY LEE: Norma Egstrom
JANET LEIGH: Jeanette Morrison
VIVIEN LEIGH: Vivian Hartley
HUEY LEWIS: Hugh Cregg
JERRY LEWIS: Joseph Levitch
LIL' KIM: Kimberly Denise Jones
CAROLE LOMBARD: Jane Peters
JACK LORD: John Joseph Ryan
SOPHIA LOREN: Sophia Scicolone
PETER LORRE: Laszio Lowenstein
MYRNA LOY: Myrna Williams
BELA LUGOSI: Bela Ferenc Blasko
MOMS MABLEY: Loretta Mary Aitken
SHIRLEY MACLAINE: Shirley Beaty
ELLE MACPHERSON: Eleanor Gow
MADONNA: Madonna Louise Veronica Ciccone
LEE MAJORS: Harvey Lee Yeary
KARL MALDEN: Mladen Sekulovich
BARRY MANILOW: Barry Alan Pincus
JAYNE MANSFIELD: Vera Jane Palmer
MARILYN MANSON: Brian Warner
FREDRIC MARCH: Frederick Bickel
PETER MARSHALL: Pierre LaCock
WALTER MATTHAU: Walter Matuschanskayasky
DEAN MARTIN: Dino Crocetti
MEAT LOAF: Marvin Lee Aday
FREDDIE MERCURY: Frederick Bulsara
ETHEL MERMAN: Ethel Zimmerman
GEORGE MICHAEL: Georgios Panayiotou
RAY MILLAND: Reginald Truscott-Jones
ANN MILLER: Lucille Collier
HELEN MIRREN: Ilynea Lydia Mironoff
JONI MITCHELL: Roberta Joan Anderson
MOBY: Richard Melville Hall
MARILYN MONROE: Norma Jean Mortenson (later Baker)
YVES MONTAND: Ivo Livi
RON MOODY: Ronald Moodnick
DEMI MOORE: Demetria Guynes
GARRY MOORE: Thomas Garrison Morfit
RITA MORENO: Rosita Alverio
HARRY MORGAN: Harry Bratsburg
MR. T: Lawrence Tero
PAUL MUNI: Muni Weisenfreund
MIKE NICHOLS: Michael Igor Peschowsky
CHUCK NORRIS: Carlos Ray
NOTORIOUS B.I.G.: Christopher Wallace
HUGH O'BRIAN: Hugh Krampke
MAUREEN O'HARA: Maureen Fitzsimons
OZZY OSBOURNE: John Michael Osbourne
PATTI PAGE: Clara Ann Fowler
JACK PALANCE: Walter Palanuik
BERT PARKS: Bert Jacobson

MINNIE PEARL: Sarah Ophelia Cannon
BERNADETTE PETERS: Bernadette Lazzaro
EDITH PIAF: Edith Gassion
SLIM PICKENS: Louis Lindley
MARY PICKFORD: Gladys Smith
STEFANIE POWERS: Stefania Federkiewicz
PAULA PRENTISS: Paula Ragusa
ROBERT PRESTON: Robert Preston Meservey
PRINCE (THE ARTIST): Prince Rogers Nelson
DEE DEE RAMONE: Douglas Colvin
JOEY RAMONE: Jeffrey Hyman
JOHNNY RAMONE: John Cummings
TOMMY RAMONE: Tom Erdelyi
TONY RANDALL: Leonard Rosenberg
MARTHA RAYE: Margaret O'Reed
DONNA REED: Donna Belle Mullenger
DELLA REESE: Delloreese Patricia Early
BUSTA RHYMES: Trevor Smith Jr.
JOAN RIVERS: Joan Sandra Molinsky
EDWARD G. ROBINSON: Emmanuel Goldenberg
THE ROCK: Dwayne Johnson
GINGER ROGERS: Virginia McMath
ROY ROGERS: Leonard Franklin Slye
MICKEY ROONEY: Joe Yule Jr.
JOHNNY ROTTEN: John Lydon
LILLIAN RUSSELL: Helen Leonard
MEG RYAN: Margaret Hyra
WINONA RYDER: Winona Horowitz
SADE: Helen Folsad Abu
SOUPY SALES: Milton Hines
SUSAN SARANDON: Susan Tomaling
SEAL: Samuel Sealhenry
RANDOLPH SCOTT: George Randolph Crane
JANE SEYMOUR: Joyce Frankenberg
OMAR SHARIF: Michael Shalhoub
CHARLIE SHEEN: Carlos Irwin Estevez
MARTIN SHEEN: Ramon Estevez
BEVERLY SILLS: Belle Silverman
TALIA SHIRE: Talia Coppola
PHIL SILVERS: Philip Silversmith
SINBAD: David Atkins
"BUFFALO BOB" SMITH: Robert Schmidt
SNOOP DOGGY DOG: Calvin Broadus
ANN SOTHERN: Harriette Lake
ROBERT STACK: Robert Modini
BARBARA STANWYCK: Ruby Stevens
JEAN STAPLETON: Jeanne Murray
RINGO STARR: Richard Starkey
CONNIE STEVENS: Concetta Ingolia
STING: Gordon Sumner
JOE STRUMMER: John Graham Mellor
DONNA SUMMER: La Donna Gaines
RIP TAYLOR: Charles Elmer Jr.
ROBERT TAYLOR: Spangler Brugh
DANNY THOMAS: Muzyad Yakhoob, later Amos Jacobs
TINY TIM: Herbert Khaury
RIP TORN: Elmore Rual Torn Jr.
RANDY TRAVIS: Randy Traywick
SOPHIE TUCKER: Sophia Kalish
TINA TURNER: Annie Mae Bullock
TWIGGY: Leslie Hornby
CONWAY TWITTY: Harold Lloyd Jenkins
RUDOLPH VALENTINO: Rudolpho D'Antonguolla
FRANKIE VALLI: Frank Castelluccio
SID VICIOUS: John Simon Ritchie
JOHN WAYNE: Marion Morrison
CLIFTON WEBB: Webb Hollenbeck
RAQUEL WELCH: Raquel Tejada
GENE WILDER: Jerome Silberman
SHELLEY WINTERS: Shirley Schrift
STEVIE WONDER: Stevland Morris
JANE WYMAN: Sarah Jane Fulks
GIG YOUNG: Byron Barr
LORETTA YOUNG: Gretchen Michaels

ARTS AND MEDIA

Some Notable Movies, Sept. 2003 – Aug. 2004

Film	Stars	Director
50 First Dates	Adam Sandler, Drew Barrymore, Rob Schneider, Sean Astin	Peter Segal
Along Came Polly	Ben Stiller, Jennifer Aniston	John Hamburg
Anchorman: The Legend of Ron Burgundy	Will Ferrell, Christina Applegate	Adam McKay
Bad Santa	Billy Bob Thornton, Tony Cox, John Ritter, Bernie Mac, Lauren Graham	Terry Zwigoff
Barbershop 2: Back in Business	Ice Cube, Sean Patrick Thomas, Eve, Queen Latifah	Kevin Rodney Sullivan
Big Fish	Ewan McGregor, Albert Finney, Billy Crudup, Jessica Lange	Tim Burton
The Bourne Supremacy	Matt Damon, Franka Potente, Brian Cox, Julia Stiles	Paul Greengrass
Calendar Girls	Helen Mirren, Julie Walters	Nigel Cole
Cheaper by the Dozen	Bonnie Hunt, Steve Martin, Hilary Duff, Piper Perabo	Shawn Levy
Cold Mountain	Jude Law, Nicole Kidman, Renee Zellweger	Anthony Minghella
Collateral	Tom Cruise, Jamie Foxx	Michael Mann
The Day After Tomorrow	Dennis Quaid, Jake Gyllenhaal, Emmy Rossum	Roland Emmerich
DodgeBall: A True Underdog Story	Ben Stiller, Vince Vaughn, Christine Taylor	Rawson Marshall Thurber
The Dreamers	Michael Pitt, Eva Green, Louis Garrel	Bernardo Bertolucci
Dr. Suess' The Cat in the Hat	Mike Myers, Alec Baldwin, Kelly Preston, Dakota Fanning, Spencer Breslin	Bo Welch
Elf	Will Ferrell, James Caan, Zooey Deschanel	Jon Favreau
Ella Enchanted	Anne Hathaway, Hugh Dancy, Cary Elwes, Joanna Lumley	Tommy O'Haver
Eternal Sunshine of the Spotless Mind	Jim Carrey, Kate Winslet, Kirsten Dunst	Michel Gondry
Fahrenheit 9/11		Michael Moore
Garden State	Zach Braff, Ian Holm, Natalie Portman, Ron Liebman	Zach Braff
Girl with a Pearl Earring	Colin Firth, Scarlett Johansson	Peter Webber
Harry Potter and the Prisoner of Azkaban	Daniel Radcliffe, Emma Thompson, Rupert Grint, Robbie Coltrane, Gary Oldman, Alan Rickman, Maggie Smith,	Alfonso Cuaron
House of Sand and Fog	Jennifer Connelly, Ben Kingsley	Vadim Perelman
I, Robot	Will Smith, Bridget Moynahan, Bruce Greenwood	Alex Proyas
Intolerable Cruelty	George Clooney, Catherine Zeta-Jones, Geoffrey Rush	Joel Coen
Kill Bill Vol. 1, Vol. 2	Uma Thurman, David Carradine	Quentin Tarantino
The Last Samurai	Tom Cruise, Ken Watanabe, Timothy Spall	Edward Zwick
The Lord of the Rings: The Return of the King	Elijah Wood, Ian McKellen, Viggo Mortensen, Liv Tyler, Cate Blanchett, Orlando Bloom, Ian Holm	Peter Jackson
Lost in Translation	Bill Murray, Scarlett Johansson	Sofia Coppola
Love Actually	Hugh Grant, Alan Rickman, Emma Thompson	Richard Curtis
The Manchurian Candidate	Denzel Washington, Meryl Streep, Liev Schreiber, Jon Voight	Jonathan Demme
Master and Commander: The Far Side of the World	Russell Crowe, Paul Bettany, James D'Arcy	Peter Weir
The Matrix Revolutions	Laurence Fishburne, Jada Pinkett Smith, Keanu Reeves	Andy Wachowski, Larry Wachowski
Mona Lisa Smile	Julia Roberts, Kirsten Dunst, Julia Stiles	Mike Newell
Monster	Charlize Theron, Christina Ricci	Patty Jenkins
Mystic River	Sean Penn, Tim Robbins, Kevin Bacon, Laurence Fishburne	Clint Eastwood
The Passion of the Christ	James Caviezel, Monica Bellucci	Mel Gibson
Peter Pan	Jason Isaacs, Jeremy Sumpter, Rachel Hurd-Wood	P. J. Hogan
The Princess Diaries 2	Julie Andrews, John Rhys-Davies, Hector Elizondo, Anne Hathaway	Garry Marshall
Runaway Jury	John Cusack, Gene Hackman, Dustin Hoffman	Gary Fleder
The School of Rock	Jack Black, Joan Cusack	Richard Linklater
Shrek 2	Mike Myers, Eddie Murphy, Cameron Diaz	Andrew Adamson, Kelly Asbury, Conrad Vernon
Something's Gotta Give	Jack Nicholson, Diane Keaton, Keanu Reeves, Amanda Peet	Nancy Meyers
Spider-Man 2	Tobey Maguire, Kirsten Dunst, James Franco, Alfred Molina	Sam Raimi
The Station Agent	Peter Dinklage, Patricia Clarkson, Bobby Cannavale	Thomas McCarthy
The Stepford Wives	Nicole Kidman, Matthew Broderick, Glenn Close	Frank Oz
Troy	Brad Pitt, Eric Bana, Orlando Bloom, Brian Cox, Diane Kruger, Peter O'Toole	Wolfgang Petersen
Van Helsing	Hugh Jackman, Kate Beckinsale, Richard Roxburgh	Stephen Sommers
White Chicks	Shawn Wayans, Marlon Wayans	Keenen Ivory Wayans

TEN BOX-OFFICE FLOPS I LOVE
by Leonard Maltin—film critic, author *Leonard Maltin's Movie Guide*

King of the Hill (1993) with Jesse Bradford, Lisa Eichhorn, Adrien Brody; Steven Soderbergh's moving adaptation of the A.E. Hotchner memoir of growing up in the Depression. (PG-13)

The Ballad of Little Jo (1993) with Suzy Amis, Bo Hopkins, Ian McKellen; writer-director Maggie Greenwald's colorful story of a woman who learns the only way to survive in the Old West is to disguise herself as a man. (R)

Once Were Warriors (1994) with Rena Owen, Temuera Morrison; a stunning look at a family descended from the Maori tribe in New Zealand, and how one man's macho way of life all but ruins a family's existence. (R)

Marvin's Room (1996) with Meryl Streep, Diane Keaton, Leonardo DiCaprio, Robert DeNiro; a moving adaptation of Scott McPherson's play about estranged sisters brought together by their dying father. (PG-13)

Citizen Ruth (1996) with Laura Dern, Swoosie Kurtz, Kurtwood Smith; a stinging, often hilarious satire by Alexander Payne and Jim Taylor about a homeless woman who becomes a pawn for both sides in the abortion issue. (R)

The Mighty (1998) with Kieran Culkin, Elden Henson, Gena Rowlands; two teenage boys—one disabled, the other a social misfit—find that together they have strength rivaling the knights of old in this little gem of a film. (PG-13)

October Sky (1999) with Jake Gyllenhaal, Chris Cooper, Laura Dern; the true story of a boy whose life changed when he saw the Sputnik satellite in the sky, and became obsessed with building his own rocket. (PG)

The Dish (2000) with Sam Neill, Kevin Harrington, Patrick Warburton; a delightful comedy about a small Australian community that finds itself in the limelight because its satellite tracking station is crucial to a space mission. (PG-13)

Songcatcher (2000) with Janet McTeer, Aidan Quinn, Pat Carroll, Jane Adams; a fascinating story of a female musicologist who sets out to collect the folk songs of Appalachia, but learns a lot about herself in the process. (PG-13)

The Devil's Backbone (2001) with Eduardo Noriega, Marisa Paredes, Federico Luppi; an eerie, thoughtful ghost story set at a school for orphans during the Spanish civil war. (R)

See also the feature article Movies and the Numbers Game *by Leonard Maltin.*

50 Top-Grossing Movies, 2003

Source: *Variety*, box-office grosses in the U.S. and Canada during calendar year 2003

Rank	Title	Gross (millions)	Rank	Title	Gross (millions)
1.	Finding Nemo	$339.7	26.	Charlie's Angels: Full Throttle	$100.8
2.	Pirates of the Caribbean: Curse of the		27.	Dr. Seuss' The Cat in the Hat	99.5
	Black Pearl	305.4	28.	The Last Samurai	92.6
3.	Lord of the Rings: The Return of the King	298.1	29.	Legally Blonde 2: Red, White and Blonde	89.9
4.	The Matrix Reloaded	281.5	30.	Cheaper by the Dozen	89.4
5.	Bruce Almighty	242.6	31.	Something's Gotta Give	84.8
6.	X2: X-Men United	214.9	32.	Brother Bear	83.4
7.	Elf	171.2	33.	Master and Commander: The Far Side	
8.	Chicago	159.2		of the World	83.4
9.	Terminator 3: Rise of the Machines	150.4	34.	Freddy vs. Jason	82.2
10.	Bad Boys 2	138.4	35.	School of Rock	80.3
11.	The Matrix Revolutions	138.4	36.	The Texas Chainsaw Massacre	80.2
12.	Anger Management	133.8	37.	Old School	74.7
13.	Bringing Down the House	132.6	38.	Lord of the Rings: The Two Towers	73.1
14.	The Hulk	132.1	39.	The Haunted Mansion	70.8
15.	2 Fast 2 Furious	127.1	40.	Kill Bill Vol. 1	69.7
16.	Seabiscuit	120.2	41.	Holes	67.4
17.	S.W.A.T.	116.6	42.	Kangaroo Jack	66.7
18.	Spy Kids 3-D: Game Over	111.7	43.	The League of Extraordinary Gentlemen	66.5
19.	Freaky Friday	110.2	44.	Lara Croft Tomb Raider: The Cradle of Life	65.7
20.	Scary Movie 3	109.6	45.	Shanghai Knights	60.5
21.	The Italian Job	106.1	46.	Catch Me If You Can	59.7
22.	How to Lose a Guy in 10 Days	105.8	47.	Gothika	58.4
23.	American Wedding	104.4	48.	Open Range	58.3
24.	Daddy Day Care	104.2	49.	Love Actually	57.7
25.	Daredevil	102.5	50.	Bad Santa	57.6

National Film Registry, 1989-2003

Source: National Film Registry, Library of Congress

"Culturally, historically, or esthetically significant" American films placed on the registry. * = selected in 2003.

Abbott and Costello Meet Frankenstein (1948)
Adam's Rib (1949)
The Adventures of Robin Hood (1938)
The African Queen (1951)
Alien (1979)
All About Eve (1950)
All My Babies (1953)
All That Heaven Allows (1955)
All That Jazz (1979)
All Quiet on the Western Front (1930)
All the King's Men (1949)
An American in Paris (1951)
America, America (1963)
American Graffiti (1973)
A Movie (1958)
Annie Hall (1977)
Antonia: A Portrait of the Woman (1974)*
The Apartment (1960)
Apocalypse Now (1979)
Atlantic City (1980)*
The Awful Truth (1937)
The Bad and the Beautiful (1952)
Badlands (1973)
The Band Wagon (1953)
The Bank Dick (1940)
The Battle of San Pietro (1945)
Beauty and the Beast (1991)
Ben-Hur (1926)
The Best Years of Our Lives (1946)
Big Business (1929)
The Big Parade (1925)
The Big Sleep (1946)
The Birth of a Nation (1915)
The Black Pirate (1926)
Blacksmith Scene (1893)
The Black Stallion (1979)
Blade Runner (1982)
The Blood of Jesus (1941)
Bonnie and Clyde (1967)
Boyz N the Hood (1991)
Bride of Frankenstein (1935)
The Bridge on the River Kwai (1957)
Bringing Up Baby (1938)
Broken Blossoms (1919)
Butch Cassidy and the Sundance Kid (1969)*
Cabaret (1972)
Carmen Jones (1954)
Castro Street (1966)
Cat People (1942)
Chan Is Missing (1982)
The Cheat (1915)

The Chechahcos (1924)*
Chinatown (1974)
Chulas Fronteras (1976)
Citizen Kane (1941)
The City (1939)
City Lights (1931)
Civilization (1916)
Cologne: From the Diary of Ray and Esther (1939)
The Conversation (1974)
The Cool World (1963)
Cops (1922)
A Corner in Wheat (1909)
The Crowd (1928)
Czechoslovakia 1968 (1968)
David Holzman's Diary (1968)
The Day the Earth Stood Still (1951)
Dead Birds (1964)
The Deer Hunter (1978)
Destry Rides Again (1939)
Detour (1946)
Dickson Experimental Sound Film (1894-95)*
Dodsworth (1936)
The Docks of New York (1928)
Dog Star Man (1964)
Don't Look Back (1967)
Do the Right Thing (1989)
Double Indemnity (1944)
Dracula (1931)
Dr. Strangelove (or, How I Learned to Stop Worrying and Love the Bomb)(1964)
Duck Amuck (1953)
Duck Soup (1933)
Easy Rider (1969)
Eaux D'Artifice (1953)
El Norte (1983)
The Emperor Jones (1933)
The Endless Summer (1966)
E.T.: The Extra-Terrestrial (1982)
Evidence of the Film (1913)
The Exploits of Elaine (1914)
The Fall of the House of Usher (1928)
Fantasia (1940)
Fatty's Tintype Tangle (1915)
Film Portrait (1970)*
Five Easy Pieces (1970)
Flash Gordon serial (1936)
Footlight Parade (1933)
Force of Evil (1948)
The Forgotten Frontier (1931)
42nd Street (1933)

The Four Horsemen of the Apocalypse (1921)
Fox Movietone News: Jenkins Orphanage Band (1928)*
Frankenstein (1931)
Frank Film (1973)
Freaks (1932)
The Freshman (1925)
From Here to Eternity (1953)
From the Manger to the Cross (1912)
From Stump to Ship (1930)
Fuji (1974)
Fury (1936)
The General (1927)
Gerald McBoing Boing (1951)
Gertie the Dinosaur (1914)
Gigi (1958)
The Godfather (1972)
The Godfather, Part II (1974)
Gold Diggers of 1933 (1933)*
The Gold Rush (1925)
Gone With the Wind (1939)
GoodFellas (1990)
The Graduate (1967)
The Grapes of Wrath (1940)
Grass (1925)
The Great Dictator (1940)
The Great Train Robbery (1903)
Greed (1924)
Gun Crazy (1949)
Gunga Din (1939)
Harlan County, U.S.A. (1976)
Harold and Maude (1972)
The Heiress (1949)
Hell's Hinges (1916)
High Noon (1952)
High School (1968)
Hindenburg Disaster Newsreel Footage (1937)
His Girl Friday (1940)
The Hitch-Hiker (1953)
Hoosiers (1986)
Hospital (1970)
The Hospital (1971)
The House in the Middle (1954)
How Green Was My Valley (1941)
How the West Was Won (1962)
The Hunters (1957)*
The Hustler (1961)
I Am a Fugitive from a Chain Gang (1932)
The Immigrant (1917)
In the Heat of the Night (1967)
In the Land of the Head-Hunters aka In the Land of the War Canoes (1914)

Intolerance (1916)
Invasion of the Body Snatchers (1956)
It (1927)
It Happened One Night (1934)
It's a Wonderful Life (1946)
The Italian (1915)
Jammin' the Blues (1944)
Jam Session (1942)
Jaws (1975)
Jazz on a Summer's Day (1959)
The Jazz Singer (1927)
Killer of Sheep (1977)
King: A Filmed Record . . .Montgomery to
    Memphis (1970)
King Kong (1933)
The Kiss (1896)
Kiss Me Deadly (1955)
Knute Rockne, All American (1940)
Koyaanisqatsi (1983)
The Lady Eve (1941)
Lady Windermere's Fan (1925)
Lambchops (1929)
The Land Beyond the Sunset (1912)
Lassie Come Home (1943)
The Last of the Mohicans (1920)
The Last Picture Show (1972)
Laura (1944)
Lawrence of Arabia (1962)
The Learning Tree (1969)
Let's All Go to the Lobby (1957)
Letter From an Unknown Woman (1948)
The Life and Death of 9413—A
    Hollywood Extra (1928)
Life and Times of Rosie the Riveter
    (1980)
The Life of Emile Zola (1937)
Little Caesar (1930)
The Little Fugitive (1953)
Little Miss Marker (1934)
The Living Desert (1953)
The Lost World (1925)
Louisiana Story (1948)
Love Finds Andy Hardy (1938)
Love Me Tonight (1932)
Magical Maestro (1952)
The Magnificent Ambersons (1942)
The Maltese Falcon (1941)
The Manchurian Candidate (1962)
Manhattan (1921)
Manhattan (1979)
March of Time: Inside Nazi Germany—
    1938 (1938)
Marian Anderson: The Lincoln Memorial
    Concert (1939)
Marty (1955)
M*A*S*H (1970)
Master Hands (1936)
Matrimony's Speed Limit (1913)*
Mean Streets (1973)
Medium Cool (1969)*
Meet Me in St. Louis (1944)
Melody Ranch (1940)
Memphis Belle (1944)
Meshes of the Afternoon (1943)
Midnight Cowboy (1969)
Mildred Pierce (1945)
The Miracle of Morgan's Creek (1944)
Miss Lulu Bett (1921)
Modern Times (1936)
Modesta (1956)
Morocco (1930)
Motion Painting No. 1 (1947)
Mr. Smith Goes to Washington (1939)
Multiple Sidosis (1970)
The Music Box (1932)
My Darling Clementine (1946)
My Man Godfrey (1936)
The Naked Spur (1953)

Nanook of the North (1922)
Nashville (1975)
National Lampoon's Animal House (1978)
National Velvet (1944)*
Naughty Marietta (1935)*
Network (1976)
A Night at the Opera (1935)
The Night of the Hunter (1955)
Night of the Living Dead (1968)
Ninotchka (1939)
North by Northwest (1959)
Nostalgia (1971)*
Nothing but a Man (1964)
One Flew Over the Cuckoo's Nest (1975)
One Froggy Evening (1956)*
On the Waterfront (1954)
The Outlaw Josey Wales (1976)
Out of the Past (1947)
The Ox-Bow Incident (1943)
Pass the Gravy (1928)
Paths of Glory (1957)
Patton (1970)*
The Pearl (1948)
Peter Pan (1924)
Phantom of the Opera (1925)
The Philadelphia Story (1940)
Pinocchio (1940)
A Place in the Sun (1951)
Planet of the Apes (1968)
The Plow That Broke the Plains (1936)
Point of Order (1964)
The Poor Little Rich Girl (1917)
Porky in Wackyland (1938)
Powers of Ten (1978)
President McKinley Inauguration
    Footage (1901)
Primary (1960)
Princess Nicotine; or The Smoke Fairy
    (1909)*
The Prisoner of Zenda (1937)
The Producers (1968)
Psycho (1960)
The Public Enemy (1931)
Pull My Daisy (1959)
Punch Drunks (1934)
Raging Bull (1980)
Raiders of the Lost Ark (1981)
Rear Window (1954)
Rebel Without a Cause (1955)
Red River (1948)
Regeneration (1915)
Republic Steel Strike Riots Newsreel
    Footage (1937)
Return of the Secaucus 7 (1980)
Ride the High Country (1962)
Rip Van Winkle (1896)
The River (1937)
Road to Morocco (1942)
Roman Holiday (1953)
Rose Hobart (1936)
Sabrina (1954)
Safety Last (1923)
Salesman (1969)
Salomé (1922)
Salt of the Earth (1954)
Scarface (1932)
The Searchers (1956)
Serene Velocity (1970)
Seventh Heaven (1927)
Shadow of a Doubt (1943)
Shadows (1959)
Shaft (1971)
Shane (1953)
She Done Him Wrong (1933)
Sherlock, Jr. (1924)
Sherman's March (1986)
Shock Corridor (1963)
The Shop Around the Corner (1940)

Show Boat (1936)
Show People (1928)*
Singin' in the Rain (1952)
Sky High (1922)
Snow White (1933)
Snow White and the Seven Dwarfs (1937)
Some Like It Hot (1959)
The Son of the Sheik (1926)*
The Sound of Music (1965)
Stagecoach (1939)
A Star Is Born (1954)
Star Theatre (1901)
Star Wars (1977)
Steamboat Willie (1928)
Stranger Than Paradise (1984)
A Streetcar Named Desire (1951)
Stormy Weather (1943)
Sullivan's Travels (1941)
Sunrise (1927)
Sunset Boulevard (1950)
Sweet Smell of Success (1957)
Tabu (1931)
Tacoma Narrows Bridge Collapse (1940)
The Tall T (1957)
Tarzan and His Mate (1934)*
Taxi Driver (1976)
The Ten Commandments (1956)
The Tell-Tale Heart (1953)
Tevye (1939)
Theodore Case Sound Tests: Gus Visser
    and His Singing Duck (1925)
The Thief of Bagdad (1924)
The Thin Blue Line (1988)
The Thing From Another World (1951)
The Thin Man (1934)
This Is Cinerama (1952)
This Is Spinal Tap (1984)
Through Navajo Eyes (series) (1966)
Tin Toy (1988)*
To Be or Not To Be (1942)
To Fly (1976)
To Kill a Mockingbird (1962)
Tootsie (1982)
Topaz (1943-45)
Top Hat (1935)
Touch of Evil (1958)
Trance and Dance in Bali (1936-39)
The Treasure of the Sierra Madre (1948)
Trouble in Paradise (1932)
Tulips Shall Grow (1942)
Twelve O'Clock High (1949)
2001: A Space Odyssey (1968)
Verbena Tragica (1939)
Vertigo (1958)
The Wedding March (1928)*
Westinghouse Works 1904 (1904)
West Side Story (1961)
What's Opera, Doc? (1957)
Where Are My Children? (1916)
White Heat (1949)*
Why Man Creates (1968)
Why We Fight
    (Series/1943-45)
Wild and Wooly (1917)
The Wild Bunch (1969)
Wild River (1960)
Will Success Spoil Rock Hunter? (1957)
The Wind (1928)
Wings (1927)
Within Our Gates (1920)
The Wizard of Oz (1939)
Woman of the Year (1942)
A Woman Under the Influence (1974)
Woodstock (1970)
Yankee Doodle Dandy (1942)
Young Frankenstein (1974)*
Young Mr. Lincoln (1939)*
Zapruder Film (1963)

TOP MOVIE SONGS OF ALL TIME

In 2004, the American Film Institute published its list of top (American) movie songs of all time, based on a poll of jurors mostly from the film world. The top 10 are listed here.

Song	Movie (Year)	Song	Movie (Year)
1. Over the Rainbow	The Wizard of Oz (1939)	6. Mrs. Robinson	The Graduate (1967)
2. As Time Goes By	Casablanca (1942)	7. When You Wish Upon a Star	Pinocchio (1940)
3. Singin' in the Rain	Singin' in the Rain (1952)	8. The Way We Were	The Way We Were (1973)
4. Moon River	Breakfast at Tiffany's (1961)	9. Stayin' Alive	Saturday Night Fever (1977)
5. White Christmas	Holiday Inn (1942)	10. The Sound of Music	The Sound of Music (1965)

100 Best American Movies of All Time

Source: American Film Institute

Compiled in 1998 based on ballots sent to 1,500 figures, mostly from the film world. Criteria for judging included historical significance, critical recognition and awards, and popularity. The year each film was first released is in parentheses.

1. Citizen Kane (1941)
2. Casablanca (1942)
3. The Godfather (1972)
4. Gone With the Wind (1939)
5. Lawrence of Arabia (1962)
6. The Wizard of Oz (1939)
7. The Graduate (1967)
8. On the Waterfront (1954)
9. Schindler's List (1993)
10. Singin' in the Rain (1952)
11. It's a Wonderful Life (1946)
12. Sunset Boulevard (1950)
13. The Bridge on the River Kwai (1957)
14. Some Like It Hot (1959)
15. Star Wars (1977)
16. All About Eve (1950)
17. The African Queen (1951)
18. Psycho (1960)
19. Chinatown (1974)
20. One Flew Over the Cuckoo's Nest (1975)
21. The Grapes of Wrath (1940)
22. 2001: A Space Odyssey (1968)
23. The Maltese Falcon (1941)
24. Raging Bull (1980)
25. E.T.: The Extra-Terrestrial (1982)
26. Dr. Strangelove (1964)
27. Bonnie and Clyde (1967)
28. Apocalypse Now (1979)
29. Mr. Smith Goes to Washington (1939)
30. Treasure of the Sierra Madre (1948)
31. Annie Hall (1977)
32. The Godfather, Part II (1974)
33. High Noon (1952)
34. To Kill a Mockingbird (1962)
35. It Happened One Night (1934)
36. Midnight Cowboy (1969)
37. The Best Years of Our Lives (1946)
38. Double Indemnity (1944)
39. Doctor Zhivago (1965)
40. North by Northwest (1959)
41. West Side Story (1961)
42. Rear Window (1954)
43. King Kong (1933)
44. The Birth of a Nation (1915)
45. A Streetcar Named Desire (1951)
46. A Clockwork Orange (1971)
47. Taxi Driver (1976)
48. Jaws (1975)
49. Snow White and the Seven Dwarfs (1937)
50. Butch Cassidy and the Sundance Kid (1969)
51. The Philadelphia Story (1940)
52. From Here to Eternity (1953)
53. Amadeus (1984)
54. All Quiet on the Western Front (1930)
55. The Sound of Music (1965)
56. M*A*S*H (1970)
57. The Third Man (1949)
58. Fantasia (1940)
59. Rebel Without a Cause (1955)
60. Raiders of the Lost Ark (1981)
61. Vertigo (1958)
62. Tootsie (1982)
63. Stagecoach (1939)
64. Close Encounters of the Third Kind (1977)
65. The Silence of the Lambs (1991)
66. Network (1976)
67. The Manchurian Candidate (1962)
68. An American in Paris (1951)
69. Shane (1953)
70. The French Connection (1971)
71. Forrest Gump (1994)
72. Ben-Hur (1959)
73. Wuthering Heights (1939)
74. The Gold Rush (1925)
75. Dances With Wolves (1990)
76. City Lights (1931)
77. American Graffiti (1973)
78. Rocky (1976)
79. The Deer Hunter (1978)
80. The Wild Bunch (1969)
81. Modern Times (1936)
82. Giant (1956)
83. Platoon (1986)
84. Fargo (1996)
85. Duck Soup (1933)
86. Mutiny on the Bounty (1935)
87. Frankenstein (1931)
88. Easy Rider (1969)
89. Patton (1970)
90. The Jazz Singer (1927)
91. My Fair Lady (1964)
92. A Place in the Sun (1951)
93. The Apartment (1960)
94. Goodfellas (1990)
95. Pulp Fiction (1994)
96. The Searchers (1956)
97. Bringing Up Baby (1938)
98. Unforgiven (1992)
99. Guess Who's Coming to Dinner (1967)
100. Yankee Doodle Dandy (1942)

All-Time Top-Grossing American Movies[1]

Source: *Variety* magazine

Rank	Title (original release)	Gross[2]
1.	Titanic (1997)	$600.8
2.	Star Wars: Episode IV–A New Hope (1977)	461.0
3.	Shrek 2 (2004)	436.7
4.	E.T.: The Extra-Terrestrial (1982)	435.0
5.	Star Wars: Episode I–The Phantom Menace (1999)	431.1
6.	Spider-Man (2002)	403.7
7.	The Lord of the Rings: The Return of the King (2003)	377.0
8.	The Passion of the Christ (2004)	370.3
9.	Spider-Man 2 (2004)	368.4
10.	Jurassic Park (1993)	357.1
11.	The Lord of the Rings: The Two Towers (2002)	341.7
12.	Finding Nemo (2003)	339.7
13.	Forrest Gump (1994)	329.7
14.	The Lion King (1994)	328.5
15.	Harry Potter and the Sorcerer's Stone (2001)	317.6
16.	The Lord of the Rings: The Fellowship of the Ring (2001)	314.8
17.	Star Wars: Episode II–Attack of the Clones (2002)	310.7
18.	Star Wars: Episode VI–Return of the Jedi (1983)	309.2
19.	Independence Day (1996)	306.2
20.	Pirates of the Caribbean: The Curse of the Black Pearl (2003)	305.4
21.	The Sixth Sense (1999)	293.5
22.	Star Wars: Episode V– The Empire Strikes Back (1980)	290.3
23.	Home Alone (1990)	285.8
24.	The Matrix: Reloaded (2003)	$281.5
25.	Shrek (2001)	267.7
26.	Harry Potter and the Chamber of Secrets (2002)	262.0
27.	Dr. Seuss' How the Grinch Stole Christmas (2000)	260.0
	Jaws (1975)	260.0
29.	Monsters, Inc. (2001)	255.9
30.	Batman (1989)	251.2
31.	Men in Black (1997)	250.7
32.	Harry Potter and the Prisoner of Azkaban	247.8
33.	Toy Story 2 (1999)	245.9
34.	Bruce Almighty (2003)	242.7
35.	Raiders of the Lost Ark (1981)	242.4
36.	Twister (1996)	241.7
37.	My Big Fat Greek Wedding (2002)	241.4
38.	Ghostbusters (1984)	238.6
39.	Beverly Hills Cop (1984)	234.8
40.	Cast Away (2000)	233.6
41.	The Exorcist (1973)	232.7
42.	The Lost World: Jurassic Park (1997)	229.1
43.	Signs (2002)	228.0
44.	Rush Hour 2 (2001)	226.2
45.	Mrs. Doubtfire (1993)	219.2
46.	Ghost (1990)	217.6
47.	Aladdin (1992)	217.4
48.	Saving Private Ryan (1998)	216.2
49.	Mission: Impossible 2 (2000)	215.4
50.	X2: X-Men United (2003)	214.9

(1) Through Sept. 2, 2004. (2) Gross is in millions of absolute dollars based on box office sales in the U.S. and Canada. Rising ticket prices favor newer films. Revenues from re-releases are included.

Top-Selling Video Games, 2003

Source: The NPD Group / NPD Funworld / Point-of-Sale; ranked by units sold.

Platform, Title
1. Sony PlayStation 2, Madden NFL 2004
2. Nintendo Game Boy Advance, Pokemon Ruby
3. Nintendo Game Boy Advance, Pokemon Sapphire
4. Sony PlayStation 2, Need Speed: Underground
5. Nintendo GameCube, Zelda: The Wind Waker
6. Sony PlayStation 2, Grand Theft Auto: Vice City
7. Nintendo GameCube, Mario Kart: Double Dash
8. Sony PlayStation 2, Tony Hawk Underground
9. Sony PlayStation 2, Enter the Matrix
10. Sony PlayStation 2, Medal Honor Rising
11. Sony PlayStation 2, NCAA Football 2004
12. Microsoft Xbox, Halo
13. Sony PlayStation 2, True Crime: Streets LA
14. Sony PlayStation 2, Final Fantasy X-2
15. Sony PlayStation 2, NBA Live 2004

Most Popular Movie Videos/DVDs

Source: Alexander & Associates/Video Flash, New York, NY

Note: Year given to distinguish from other films with the same title.

ALL-TIME

Top Ten Rentals VHS[1]

1. Pretty Woman
2. Top Gun
3. The Little Mermaid
4. Home Alone
5. Ghost
6. The Lion King
7. Beauty and the Beast
8. Terminator II: Judgment Day
9. Forrest Gump
10. Aladdin

Top Ten Purchase Titles VHS[2]

1. The Lion King
2. Forrest Gump
3. Toy Story
4. Aladdin
5. Jurassic Park
6. Pocahontas
7. Beauty and the Beast
8. The Little Mermaid
9. Cinderella
10. 101 Dalmatians (1961)

DVD[3]

1. The Fast and the Furious
2. The Matrix
3. Gladiator (2000)
4. Shrek
5. The Lord of the Rings: The Fellowship of the Ring
6. Black Hawk Down
7. Training Day
8. The Ring (2002)
9. Sweet Home Alabama
10. Spider-Man (2002)

DVD[3]

1. The Lord of the Rings: The Fellowship of the Ring
2. Shrek
3. Harry Potter and the Sorcerer's Stone
4. Spider-Man (2002)
5. Monsters, Inc.
6. Gladiator (2000)
7. The Fast and the Furious
8. The Matrix
9. A Knight's Tale
10. Ice Age

2003

Top Ten Purchase Titles VHS

1. My Big Fat Greek Wedding
2. Sweet Home Alabama
3. Ice Age
4. Lilo and Stitch
5. Finding Nemo
6. Harry Potter and the Chamber of Secrets
7. Signs
8. Spider-Man (2002)
9. Harry Potter and the Sorcerer's Stone
10. Monsters, Inc.

Top Ten Rental Titles VHS

1. My Big Fat Greek Wedding
2. Sweet Home Alabama
3. The Ring (2002)
4. Signs
5. Bringing Down the House
6. 8 Mile
7. Finding Nemo
8. Maid in Manhattan
9. The Bourne Identity (2002)
10. The Lord of the Rings: The Two Towers

DVD

1. Finding Nemo
2. My Big Fat Greek Wedding
3. Lord of the Rings: The Two Towers
4. Harry Potter and the Chamber of Secrets
5. Signs
6. XXX (2002)
7. 8 Mile
8. Sweet Home Alabama
9. Pirates of the Caribbean: The Curse of the Black Pearl
10. The Matrix Reloaded

DVD

1. The Ring (2002)
2. Sweet Home Alabama
3. My Big Fat Greek Wedding
4. How to Lose a Guy in 10 Days
5. Bringing Down the House
6. Pirates of the Caribbean: The Curse of the Black Pearl
7. Signs
8. The Lord of the Rings: The Two Towers
9. The Bourne Identity (2002)
10. Catch Me if You Can

(1) March 1, 1987, to Dec. 31, 2003. (2) Feb. 16, 1988, to Dec. 31, 2003. (3) Jan. 1, 2000, to Dec. 31, 2003.

Top 50 Record Long-Run Broadway Plays[1]

Source: The League of American Theatres and Producers, Inc., New York, NY; www.IBDB.com

Title	Performances	Title	Performances	Title	Performances
1. Cats	7,485	18. Annie	2,377	35. Born Yesterday	1,642
2. *The Phantom of the Opera	6,933	Cabaret (revival)	2,377	36. Crazy For You	1,622
3. Les Misérables	6,680	20. Man of La Mancha	2,328	37. Ain't Misbehavin'	1,604
4. A Chorus Line	6,137	21. Abie's Irish Rose	2,327	38. The Best Little Whorehouse in	
5. Oh! Calcutta! (revival)	5,959	22. Oklahoma!	2,212	Texas	1,584
6. *Beauty and the Beast	4,260	23. Smokey Joe's Cafe	2,037	39. Mary, Mary	1,572
7. Miss Saigon	4,092	24. Pippin	1,944	40. Evita	1,567
8. *Rent	3,488	25. South Pacific	1,925	41. The Voice of the Turtle	1,557
9. 42nd Street	3,486	26. The Magic Show	1,920	42. Jekyll & Hyde	1,543
10. Grease (original)	3,388	27. Aida	1,852	43. Barefoot in the Park	1,530
11. *Chicago (revival)	3,259	28. Gemini	1,819	44. Dreamgirls	1,521
12. Fiddler on the Roof	3,242	29. Deathtrap	1,793	45. Mame	1,508
13. Life With Father	3,224	30. Harvey	1,775	46. Grease (revival)	1,505
14. Tobacco Road	3,182	31. Dancin'	1,774	47. Same Time, Next Year	1,453
15. *The Lion King	2,851	32. La Cage aux Folles	1,761	48. Arsenic and Old Lace	1,444
16. Hello, Dolly!	2,844	33. Hair	1,750	49. The Sound of Music	1,443
17. My Fair Lady	2,717	34. The Wiz	1,672	50. Me and My Girl	1,420

*Still running Sept. 12, 2004. (1) Number of performances through Sept. 12, 2004.

Broadway Season Statistics, 1959-2004

Source: The League of American Theatres and Producers, Inc., New York, NY

Season	Gross (mil $)	Attendance (mil)	Playing Weeks	New Productions	Season	Gross (mil $)	Attendance (mil)	Playing Weeks	New Productions
1959-1960	46	7.9	1,156	58	1982-1983	209	8.4	1,258	50
1960-1961	44	7.7	1,210	48	1983-1984	227	7.9	1,097	36
1961-1962	44	6.8	1,166	53	1984-1985	209	7.3	1,078	33
1962-1963	44	7.4	1,134	54	1985-1986	190	6.5	1,041	34
1963-1964	40	6.8	1,107	63	1986-1987	208	7.1	1,039	41
1964-1965	50	8.2	1,250	67	1987-1988	253	8.1	1,113	30
1965-1966	54	9.6	1,295	68	1988-1989	262	8.1	1,108	33
1966-1967	55	9.3	1,269	69	1989-1990	282	8.0	1,070	40
1967-1968	59	9.5	1,259	74	1990-1991	267	7.3	971	28
1968-1969	58	8.6	1,209	67	1991-1992	293	7.4	905	37
1969-1970	53	7.1	1,047	62	1992-1993	328	7.9	1,019	34
1970-1971	55	7.4	1,107	49	1993-1994	356	8.1	1,066	39
1971-1972	52	6.5	1,157	55	1994-1995	406	9.0	1,120	33
1972-1973	45	5.4	889	55	1995-1996	436	9.5	1,146	38
1973-1974	46	5.7	907	43	1996-1997	499	10.6	1,349	37
1974-1975	57	6.6	1,101	54	1997-1998	558	11.5	1,442	33
1975-1976	71	7.3	1,136	55	1998-1999	588	11.7	1,441	39
1976-1977	93	8.8	1,349	54	1999-2000	603	11.4	1,464	37
1977-1978	114	9.6	1,433	42	2000-2001	666	11.9	1,484	28
1978-1979	134	9.6	1,542	50	2001-2002	643	11.0	1,434	28
1979-1980	146	9.6	1,540	61	2002-2003	721	11.4	1,544	36
1980-1981	197	11.0	1,544	60	2003-2004	771	11.6	1,451	39
1981-1982	223	10.1	1,455	48					

Some Notable Non-Profit Theater Companies in the U.S

Source: Theatre Communications Group, Inc.

Actors Theatre of Louisville	Louisville	KY	La Jolla Playhouse	La Jolla	CA
Alabama Shakespeare Festival	Montgomery	AL	Lincoln Center Theater	New York	NY
Alley Theatre	Houston	TX	Long Wharf Theatre	New Haven	CT
Alliance Theatre Company	Atlanta	GA	Manhattan Theatre Club	New York	NY
American Conservatory Theater	San Francisco	CA	McCarter Theatre Center	Princeton	NJ
American Repertory Theatre	Boston	MA	Milwaukee Repertory Theater	Milwaukee	WI
Arena Stage	Washington	DC	North Shore Music Theatre	Beverly	MA
Arizona Theatre Company	Tucson	AZ	The Old Globe	San Diego	CA
Berkeley Repertory Theatre	Berkeley	CA	Oregon Shakespeare Festival	Ashland	OR
Center Stage	Baltimore	MD	Paper Mill Playhouse	Millburn	NJ
Center Theatre Group/Mark Taper Forum	Los Angeles	CA	Pittsburgh Public Theater	Pittsburgh	PA
Chicago Shakespeare Theater	Chicago	IL	The Public Theater	New York	NY
The Children's Theatre Company	Minneapolis	MN	Repertory Theatre of St. Louis	St. Louis	MO
Cincinnati Playhouse in the Park	Cincinnati	OH	Roundabout Theatre Company	New York	NY
The Cleveland Play House	Cleveland	OH	San Diego Repertory Theatre	San Diego	CA
Coconut Grove Playhouse	Miami	FL	San Jose Repertory Theatre	San Jose	CA
Denver Center Theatre Company	Denver	CO	Seattle Children's Theatre	Seattle	WA
Geffen Playhouse	Los Angeles	CA	Seattle Repertory Theatre	Seattle	WA
Geva Theatre Center	Rochester	NY	The Shakespeare Theatre	Washington	DC
Goodman Theatre	Chicago	IL	South Coast Repertory	Costa Mesa	CA
Guthrie Theater	Minneapolis	MN	Steppenwolf Theatre Company	Chicago	IL
Hartford Stage Company	Hartford	CT	Studio Arena Theatre	Buffalo	NY
Huntington Theatre Company	Boston	MA	TheatreWorks	Palo Alto	CA
Kansas City Repertory Theatre	Kansas City	MO	Trinity Repertory Company	Providence	RI
Laguna Playhouse	Laguna Beach	CA	Utah Shakespearean Festival	Cedar City	UT

U.S. Symphony Orchestras[1]

Source: American Symphony Orchestra League, 33 West 60th St., New York, NY 10023

Symphony Orchestra[2]	Music Director[3]	Symphony Orchestra[2]	Music Director[3]
Akron (OH)	Ya-Hui Wang	Madison (WI)	Douglas Reuh
Alabama (Birmingham)	Richard Westerfield	Memphis (TN)	David Loebel
American (New York, NY)	Leon Botstein	Milwaukee (WI)	Andreas Delfs
Arkansas (Little Rock)	David Itkin	Minnesota Orch. (Minneapolis)	Osmo Vänskä
Atlanta (GA)	Robert Spano	Mississippi (Jackson)	Louis Watson
Austin (TX)	Peter Bay	Music of the Baroque, (Chicago, IL)	Jane Glover
Baltimore (MD)	Jack Everly, Yuri Temirkanov	Monterey Symphony (Carmel, CA)	Kate Tamarkin
		Naples Philharmonic (FL)	Christopher Seaman
Baton Rouge Symphony (LA)	Timothy Muffitt	Nashville Symphony (TN)	Kenneth D. Schermerhorn
Boston (MA)	James Levine, desig.	National (Washington, DC)	Leonard Slatkin
Brooklyn Philharmonic Orch. (NY)	Robert Spano	New Haven (CT)	Jung-Ho Pak
Buffalo Philharmonic Orch. (NY)	JoAnn Falletta	New Jersey (Newark)	Neeme Järvi (desig.)
Cedar Rapids (IA)	Christian Tiemeyer	New Mexico (Albuquerque)	Guillermo Figureoa
Chamber Orch. of Philadelphia (PA)	Ignat Solzhenitsyn	New West Symphony (Thousand	
Charlotte Symphony (NC)	Christof Perick	Oaks, CA)	Mr. Boris Brott
Chattanooga Symphony and Opera		New York Philharmonic (NYC)	Lorin Maazel
Assn. (TN)	Robert E. Bernhardt	New York Pops (NYC)	Skitch Henderson
Chicago (IL)	Daniel Barenboim	North Carolina Symphony (Raleigh)	David Chambless Worters
Chicago Sinfonietta (IL)	Paul Freeman	Northeastern Pennsylvania	
Cincinnati (OH)	Paavo Järvi	Philharmonic (Avoca)	Clyde Mitchell
Cleveland Orch. (OH)	Franz Welser-Möst	Oklahoma City Philharmonic (OK)	Joel A. Levine
Colorado (CO)	Marin Alsop	Omaha Symphony (NE)	Victor Yampolsky
Dallas (TX)	Andrew Litton	Oregon Symphony (Portland)	Duane McDougall
Dayton Philharmonic Orch.(OH)	Neal Gittleman	Orlando Philharmonic Orch. (FL)	Hal France
Delaware (DE)	David Amato	Orpheus Chamber Orch. (NYC)	Graham Parker
Des Moines Symphony (IA)	Joseph S. Giunta	Pasadena Symphony Assoc. (CA)	Jorge Mester
Detroit (MI)	Neeme Järvi	Pacific Symphony (Santa Ana, CA)	Carl St. Clair
Elgin (IL)	Robert Hanson	Peter Nero and The Philly Pops (PA)	Peter Nero
Eos Orch. (NYC)	Jonathan Sheffer	Philadelphia Orchestra (PA)	Christoph Eschenbach
Evansville Philharmonic Orch. (IN)	Alfred Savia	Phoenix Symphony (AZ)	Hermann Michael
Florida Orchestra (Tampa)	Stefan Sanderling	Pittsburgh Symphony (PA)	Mariss Jansons
Florida West Coast (Sarasota)	Leif Bjaland	Portland (ME)	Toshiyuki Shimada
Fort Wayne Philharmonic (IN)	Edvard Tchivzhel	Puerto Rico (PR)	Guillermo Figueroa
Fort Worth (TX)	Miguel Harth-Bedoya	Rhode Island Philharmonic (RI)	Larry Rachleff
Grand Rapids Symphony (MI)	David Lockington	Richmond Symphony (VA)	Mark Russell Smith
Grant Park Orchestra and Chorus		Rochester Philharmonic Orch. (NY)	Christopher Seaman
(Chicago, IL)	Carlos Kalmar	St. Louis (MO)	Randy Adams
Greenville (SC)	Edvard Tchivzhel	St. Paul Chamber Orchestra (MN)	Andreas Delfs
Harrisburg Symphony Assn. (PA)	Stuart Malina	San Diego Symphony (CA)	Jaha Ling
Hartford (CT)	Edward Cumming	San Francisco Symphony (CA)	Michael Tilson Thomas
Honolulu (HI)	Dr. Samuel Wong	Santa Rosa Symphony (CA)	Jeffrey Kahane
Houston Symphony (TX)	Hans Graf	Seattle Symphony (WA)	Gerard Schwarz
Indianapolis (IN)	Mario Venzago	Shreveport (LA)	Kermit Poling
Jacksonville (FL)	Fabio Mechetti	Springfield (MA)	Kevin Rhodes
Kalamazoo (MI)	Raymond C. Harvey	Spokane (WA)	Fabio Mechetti
Kansas City Symphony (MO)	Frank Byrne	Syracuse (NY)	Daniel Hege
Knoxville (TN)	Lucas Richman	Toledo (OH)	Stefan Sanderling
Long Beach (CA)	Enrique Arturo Diemecke	Tucson (AZ)	George Hanson
Long Island Philharmonic	David S. Wiley	Utah Symphony and Opera (Salt	
Los Angeles Chamber Orch. (CA)	Jeffrey Kahane	Lake City)	Keith Lockhart
Los Angeles Philharmonic (CA)	Esa-Pekka Salonen	Virginia Symphony (VA)	JoAnn Falletta
Louisiana Philharmonic Orch. (New		Wichita (KS)	Andrew Sewell
Orleans)	Klauspeter Seibel	West Virginia (Charleston)	Grant Cooper
Louisville Orchestra (KY)	Uriel Segal	Youngstown (OH)	Isaiah Jackson

(1) Includes only orchestras with annual expenses $1.65 mil or greater. (2) If only place name is given, add Symphony Orchestra. (3) General title; listed is highest-ranking member of conducting personnel.

U.S. Opera Companies[1]

Source: OPERA America, 1156 15th Street NW, Suite 810, Washington, DC 20005; as of Sept. 2004.

Arizona Opera (Tucson/Phoenix); Joel Revzen, gen./art. dir.
Atlanta Opera (GA); Alfred Kennedy, exec. dir.
Austin Lyric Opera (TX); Richard Buckley, art. dir.
Baltimore Opera Company (MD); Michael Harrison, gen. dir.
Boston Lyric Opera (MA); Janice Mancini Del Sesto, gen. dir.
Central City Opera (Denver, CO); Pelham Pearce, gen. dir.
Chicago Opera Theater (IL); Brian Dickie, gen. dir.
Cincinnati Opera (OH); Nicholas Muni, art. dir.
Cleveland Opera (OH); Robert Chumbley, gen. dir.
Connecticut Grand Opera and Orchestra (Stamford, CT); Laurence Gilgore, gen. dir.
Connecticut Opera (Hartford); Willie Anthony Waters, gen./art. dir.
Dallas Opera (TX); Karen Stone, gen. dir.
Dayton Opera (OH); Thomas Bankston, art. dir.
Des Moines Metro Opera, Inc. (IA); Robert Larsen, art. dir.
Florentine Opera Company, Inc. (Milwaukee, WI); Dennis Hanthorn, gen. dir.
Florida Grand Opera (Miami, FL); Robert M. Heuer, gen. dir.
Fort Worth Opera Association (TX); Darren Woods, gen. dir.
Glimmerglass Opera (Cooperstown, NY); Joanne Cossa, gen. dir.
Hawaii Opera Theatre (Honolulu); Henry Akina, gen./art. dir.
Houston Grand Opera (TX); David Gockley, gen. dir.
Indianapolis Opera (IN); James Caraher, art. dir.
Kentucky Opera (Louisville); Deborah S. Sandler, gen. dir.
Knoxville Opera Company (TN); Francis Graffeo, gen. dir.
Los Angeles Opera (CA); Plácido Domingo, art. dir.
Lyric Opera of Chicago (IL); William Mason, gen. dir.
Lyric Opera of Kansas City (MO); Evan R. Luskin, gen. dir.
Metropolitan Opera (New York, NY); James Levine, art. dir.
Michigan Opera Theatre (Detroit); David DiChiera, gen. dir.
Minnesota Opera Company (Minneapolis); Kevin Smith, pres./gen. dir.

Nashville Opera Association (TN); Carol Penterman, exec. dir.
New Orleans Opera Association (LA); Robert Lyall, art. dir.
New York City Opera (NY); Paul Kellogg, gen./art. dir.
Opera Carolina (Charlotte, NC); James Meena, gen. dir.
Opera Colorado (Denver); James Robinson, art. dir.
Opera Columbus (OH); William Boggs, art. dir.
Opera Company of Philadelphia (PA); Robert B. Driver, art. dir.
OperaDelaware (Wilmington); Julie Van Blarcom, exec. dir.
Opera Memphis (TN); Michael Ching, art. dir.
Opera Omaha, Inc. (NE); Joan Desens, exec. dir.
Opera Pacific (Irvine, CA);John DeMain, art. dir.
Opera Theatre of Saint Louis (MO); Charles MacKay, gen. dir.
Orlando Opera (FL); Robert Swedberg, gen. dir.
Palm Beach Opera, Inc. (FL); Maria Nagid, interim dir.
Pittsburgh Opera (PA); Mark Weinstein, gen. dir.
Portland Opera (OR); Christopher Mattaliano, gen. dir.
San Diego Opera Association (CA); Ian D. Campbell, gen. dir.
San Francisco Opera (CA); Pamela Rosenberg, gen. dir.
Santa Fe Opera (NM); Richard Gaddes, gen. dir.
Sarasota Opera (FL); Victor DeRenzi, art. dir.
Seattle Opera (WA); Speight Jenkins, gen. dir.
Skylight Opera Theatre (Milwaukee, WI); Christopher Libby, man. dir.
Syracuse Opera (NY); Richard McKee art. dir.
Toledo Opera (OH); Renay Conlin, gen. dir.
Tri-Cities Opera Company (Binghamton, NY); Reed W. Smith, exec. dir.
Tulsa Opera (OK); Carol I. Crawford, gen. dir.
Utah Festival Opera (Logan); Michael Ballam, gen. dir.
Utah Symphony & Opera (Salt Lake City); Anne Ewers, gen. dir.
Virginia Opera (Norfolk); Peter Mark, art. dir.
Washington Opera (DC); Plácido Domingo, gen. dir.
West Virginia Symphony Orchestra (Charleston); Grant Cooper, art. dir.

(1) Includes only opera companies with budgets of $1 million or more.

Some Notable U.S. Dance Companies

Source: DanceUSA

Organization	City	State	Organization	City	State
Alabama Ballet	Birmingham	AL	Harem of the Queen	Washington	DC
Alban Elved Dance Company	Winston-Salem	NC	Houston Ballet Foundation	Houston	TX
Alvin Ailey American Dance Theater	New York	NY	Hubbard Street Dance Chicago	Chicago	IL
American Ballet Theatre	New York	NY	James Sewell Ballet	Minneapolis	MN
American Repertory Ballet Company	New Brunswick	NJ	Joe Goode Performance Group	San Francisco	CA
Aspen Santa Fe Ballet	Aspen	CO	Joffrey Ballet	Chicago	IL
	Santa Fe	NM	Kansas City Ballet	Kansas City	MO
AVAZ International Dance Theatre	Los Angeles	CA	Kathy Harty Gray Dance Theatre	Alexandria	VA
Axis Dance Company	Oakland	CA	Kim Robards Dance	Denver	CO
Ballet Austin	Austin	TX	Ko-Thi Dance Company	Milwaukee	WI
Ballet Hispanico of New York	New York	NY	Lar Lubovitch Dance Company	New York	NY
Ballet Memphis	Cordova	TN	Lily Cai Chinese Dance Company	San Francisco	CA
Ballet Tennessee	Chattanooga	TN	Limón Dance Company	New York	NY
BalletMet Columbus	Columbus	OH	Lizz Roman and Dancers	San Francisco	CA
Bebe Miller Company	New York	NY	Lori Belilove & Company	New York	NY
Betty Salamun's DANCECIRCUS	Milwaukee	WI	Luna Negra Dance Theater	Chicago	IL
Bill T. Jones/Arnie Zane Dance Company	New York	NY	Madison Ballet	Madison	WI
Boston Ballet	Boston	MA	Malashock Dance & Company	San Diego	CA
Bowen McCauley Dance	Arlington	VA	Margaret Jenkins Dance Company	San Francisco	CA
Buglisi/Foreman Dance	New York	NY	Mark Morris Dance Group	Brooklyn	NY
Carolyn Dorfman Dance Company	Union	NJ	Milwaukee Ballet	Milwaukee	WI
Chamber Dance Project	Sleepy Hollow	NY	Montgomery Ballet	Montgomery	AL
Charleston Ballet Theatre	Charleston	SC	Moving Arts Dance	Walnut Creek	CA
Chen & Dancers	New York	NY	Nai-Ni Chen Dance Company	Fort Lee	NJ
Chitresh Das Dance Company	San Francisco	CA	Nancy Karp and Dancers	San Francisco	CA
Cleo Parker Robinson Dance Ensemble	Denver	CO	New York City Ballet	New York	NY
Collage Dance Theatre	Los Angeles	CA	nicholasleichterdance	New York	NY
Colorado Ballet Company	Denver	CO	North Carolina Dance Theatre	Charlotte	NC
Company C	Walnut Creek	CA	Pacific Northwest Ballet	Seattle	WA
Contemporary Dance/Fort Worth	Fort Worth	TX	Parsons Dance Company	New York	NY
Crispin Spaeth Dance Group	Seattle	WA	Paul Taylor Dance Foundation	New York	NY
Csardas Dance Company	Medina	OH	Pittsburgh Ballet Theatre	Pittsburgh	PA
Cunningham Dance Foundation	New York	NY	Randy James Dance Works	Highland Park	NJ
Dance Consort: Mezzacappa-Gabrian	New York	NY	Richmond Ballet	Richmond	VA
Dance Institute of Washington	Washington	DC	Rincones & Company Dance Theater	Washington	DC
Dances Patrelle	New York	NY	Sandra Organ Dance Company	Houston	TX
Dayton Ballet	Dayton	OH	San Francisco Ballet	San Francisco	CA
Dayton Contemporary Dance Company	Dayton	OH	Snappy Dance Theatre	Cambridge	MA
Diavolo Dance Theater	Los Angeles	CA	Tap Fusion	New York	NY
Doug Varone & Dancers/DOVA, Inc.	New York	NY	Tennessee Children's Dance Ensemble	Knoxville	TN
EIKO & KOMA	New York	NY	Texas Ballet Theater	Ft. Worth	OK
Elisa Monte Dance	New York	NY	Troika Ranch	Brooklyn	NY
Felice Lesser Dance Theater	New York	NY	Tulsa Ballet Theatre	Tulsa	OK
Flamenco Vivo Carlota Santana	New York	NY	Urban Bush Women	Brooklyn	NY
Garth Fagan Dance	Rochester	NY	The Washington Ballet	Washington	DC
Gina Gibney Dance Inc.	New York	NY	Yu Wei Dance Collection	Philadelphia	PA

Some Notable Museums

This unofficial list of some of the largest (by budget) museums in the U.S. was compiled with the assistance of the American Association of Museums, a national association representing the concerns of the museum community. Association members also include zoos, aquariums, arboretums, botanical gardens, and planetariums, but these are not included in *The World Almanac* listing. See also Major U.S. Public Zoological Parks and Major Canadian Public Zoological Parks.

Museum	City	State	Museum	City	State
American Museum of Natural History	New York	NY	Museum of African American History	Detroit	MI
Amon Carter Museum of Western Art	Ft. Worth	TX	Museum of the American West	Los Angeles	CA
The Art Institute of Chicago	Chicago	IL	Museum of Contemporary Art	Los Angeles	CA
Brooklyn Museum of Art	Brooklyn	NY	Museum of Fine Arts	Boston	MA
Busch-Reisinger Museum	Cambridge	MA	Museum of Fine Arts	Houston	TX
California Academy of Sciences	San Francisco	CA	Museum of Modern Art	New York	NY
California Science Center	Los Angeles	CA	Museum of New Mexico	Santa Fe	NM
Carnegie Museums of Pittsburgh	Pittsburgh	PA	Museum of Science	Boston	MA
Chicago Historical Society	Chicago	IL	Mystic Seaport Museum	Mystic	CT
Children's Museum of Indianapolis	Indianapolis	IN	National Air & Space Museum	Washington	DC
Cincinnati Art Museum	Cincinnati	OH	National Baseball Hall of Fame and		
Cincinnati Museum Center	Cincinnati	OH	Museum, Inc.	Cooperstown	NY
Cleveland Museum of Art	Cleveland	OH	National Gallery of Art	Washington	DC
Colonial Williamsburg	Williamsburg	VA	National Museum of American History	Washington	DC
Corning Museum of Glass	Corning	NY	National Museum of the American Indian	Washington	DC
Dallas Museum of Art	Dallas	TX	National Museum of Natural History	Washington	DC
Denver Art Museum	Denver	CO	Nelson-Atkins Museum of Art	Kansas City	MO
Denver Museum of Nature and Science	Denver	CO	New York Historical Society	New York	NY
Detroit Institute of Arts	Detroit	MI	New York State Museum	Albany	NY
Exploratorium	San Francisco	CA	Peabody Essex Museum	Salem	MA
The Field Museum	Chicago	IL	Pennsylvania Historical & Museum		
Fine Arts Museums of San Francisco	San Francisco	CA	Commission	Harrisburg	PA
Franklin Institute	Philadelphia	PA	Philadelphia Museum of Art	Philadelphia	PA
The Frick Collection	New York	NY	Public Museum of Grand Rapids	Grand Rapids	MI
Harvard University Art Museums	Cambridge	MA	Rock & Roll Hall of Fame and Museum		
Henry F. Dupont Winterthur Museum	Winterthur	DE	Inc.	Cleveland	OH
Henry Ford Museum/Greenfield Village	Dearborn	MI	San Diego Museum of Art	San Diego	CA
High Museum of Art	Atlanta	GA	San Francisco Museum of Modern Art	San Francisco	CA
Houston Museum of Natural Science	Houston	TX	Science Museum of Minnesota	Saint Paul	MN
Jamestown-Yorktown Foundation	Williamsburg	VA	Scottsdale Museum of Contemp. Art	Scottsdale	AZ
Jewish Museum	New York	NY	St. Louis Science Center	St. Louis	MO
L.A. County Museum of Art	Los Angeles	CA	Toledo Museum of Art	Toledo	OH
Liberty Science Center, Liberty State Pk.	Jersey City	NJ	U.S. Holocaust Memorial Museum	Washington	DC
Maryland Science Center	Baltimore	MD	Univ. of Pennsylvania Museum of		
Mashantucket Pequot Museum and			Archaelogy and Anthropology	Philadelphia	PA
Research Center	Mashantucket	CT	Virginia Museum of Fine Arts	Richmond	VA
Metropolitan Museum of Art	New York	NY	Wadsworth Atheneum	Hartford	CT
Milwaukee Public Museum	Milwaukee	WI	Walker Art Center	Minneapolis	MN
Minneapolis Institute of Art	Minneapolis	MN	Whitney Museum of American Art	New York	NY

Best-Selling U.S. Magazines, 2003

Source: Audit Bureau of Circulations, Schaumburg, IL

General magazines, exclusive of comics; also excluding magazines that failed to file reports to ABC by press time. Based on total average paid circulation during the 6 months ending Dec. 31, 2003.

Publication	Paid circ.	Publication	Paid circ.	Publication	Paid circ.
1. AARP The Magazine...	22,052,328	35. Money	2,028,219	69. Vogue...............	1,260,026
2. AARP Bulletin	21,677,207	36. U.S. News & World		70. Country Home	1,247,563
3. Reader's Digest.......	11,044,694	Report.............	2,024,770	71. Popular Mechanics.....	1,238,965
4. TV Guide............	9,009,571	37. Entertainment Weekly ..	1,791,807	72. Cosmo Girl!	1,238,325
5. Better Homes and		38. ESPN The Magazine ...	1,759,697	73. PC Magazine	1,227,260
Gardens	7,606,820	39. Country Living	1,739,769	74. Star Magazine	1,206,984
6. National Geographic ...	6,602,650	40. VFW Magazine	1,710,550	75. Vanity Fair	1,182,831
7. Good Housekeeping ...	4,755,893	41. Men's Health	1,675,363	76. Boys' Life	1,182,623
8. Family Circle	4,641,656	42. Ebony..............	1,663,957	77. Family Handyman	1,140,997
9. Woman's Day	4,279,375	43. Familyfun	1,663,822	78. FHM (For Him	
10. Time	4,112,311	44. In Style.............	1,652,906	Magazine)	1,107,940
11. Ladies' Home Journal ..	4,102,373	45. Shape	1,640,871	79. PC World	1,103,699
12. People	3,603,115	46. Cooking Light.......	1,615,023	80. Weight Watchers	1,098,275
13. Westways	3,511,833	47. Endless Vacation......	1,596,898	81. Essence	1,071,253
14. Home & Away	3,309,306	48. Golf Digest..........	1,572,803	82. Scouting	1,059,132
15. Prevention	3,273,076	49. Teen People	1,571,272	83. American Hunter	1,056,569
16. Sports Illustrated	3,210,040	50. National Enquirer......	1,541,618	84. Michigan Living	1,040,139
17. Newsweek...........	3,122,407	51. Woman's World	1,538,030	85. Elle...............	1,030,555
18. Playboy	3,045,244	52. Field & Stream........	1,529,565	86. Kiplinger's Personal	
19. Cosmopolitan	2,918,062	53. Real Simple	1,500,246	Finance	1,028,275
20. O, The Oprah		54. Popular Science.......	1,463,565	87. Allure	1,014,384
Magazine	2,652,522	55. First For Women	1,448,515	88. Home	1,008,015
21. Via Magazine.........	2,641,159	56. Fitness............	1,431,157	89. Businessweek (North	
22. Guideposts	2,627,804	57. Game Informer		America)	991,757
23. Southern Living	2,608,632	Magazine	1,425,683	90. New Yorker	987,285
24. American Legion Mag. .	2,589,299	58. Sunset	1,425,020	91. This Old House	971,596
25. Maxim	2,504,932	59. Golf Magazine	1,410,783	92. Gourmet............	968,326
26. Redbook	2,392,427	60. American Rifleman	1,390,151	93. Travel + Leisure	965,977
27. Martha Stewart Living ..	2,364,920	61. Health	1,387,870	94. Reader's Digest Can.	
28. Seventeen...........	2,335,232	62. Car And Driver.......	1,369,286	English Edition.......	955,145
29. Glamour............	2,328,846	63. Self...............	1,314,270	95. Food & Wine	944,651
30. AAA Going Places.....	2,278,367	64. Stuff	1,312,270	96. Marie Claire	940,777
31. YM................	2,183,988	65. Us Weekly	1,308,772	97. Child..............	939,186
32. Parents	2,072,867	66. Bon Appetit	1,302,049	98. Traditional Home	938,901
33. Parenting Magazine ...	2,040,092	67. Rolling Stone	1,288,324	99. Outdoor Life	925,707
34. Smithsonian..........	2,030,651	68. Motor Trend	1,263,030	100. Forbes	920,752

Some Notable New Books, 2003

Source: List published by American Library Association, Chicago, IL, 2004, for books published in 2003

Fiction

Brick Lane, Monica Ali
The Inquisitor's Manual, Antonio Lobo Antunes
Any Human Heart, William Boyd
Alva and Irva: The Twins Who Saved a City, Edward Carey
Brownsville: Stories, Oscar Casares
Curious Incident of the Dog in the Night-Time, Mark Haddon
The Kite Runner, Khaled Hosseini
The Known World, Edward P. Jones
The Fortress of Solitude, Jonathan Lethem
Love, Toni Morrison
Star of the Sea, Joseph O'Connor
Drinking Coffee Elsewhere, ZZ Packer
The Cave, Jose Saramago

Poetry

Alabanza: New and Selected Poems, Martin Espada

Nonfiction

Wrapped in Rainbows: The Life of Zora Neale Hurston, Valerie Boyd
Naked in the Promised Land: A Memoir, Lillian Faderman
Beyond the River, Ann Hagedorn
Flat Broke with Children: Women in the Age of Welfare Reform, Sharon Hays
Mountains Beyond Mountains, Tracy Kidder
Michelangelo and the Pope's Ceiling, Ross King
Under the Banner of Heaven, Jon Krakauer
Random Family: Love, Drugs, and Coming of Age in the Bronx, Adrian Nicole LeBlanc
Food Inc.: Mendel to Monsanto—The Promises and Perils of the Biotech Harvest, Peter Pringle
Monster of God: The Man-Eating Predator in the Jungles of History and the Mind, David Quammen
Khrushchev: The Man and His Era, William Taubman
Triangle: The Fire That Changed America, David Von Drehle

Young Adults

Purple Hibiscus, Chimamanda Ngozi Adichie
The Goblin Wood, Hilari Bell
Fairie-Ality: The Fashion Collection From the House of Ellwand, Eugenie Bird
A Great and Terrible Beauty, Libba Bray
Faerie Wars, Herbie Brennan
Lucas, Kevin Brooks
True Confessions of a Heartless Girl, Martha Brooks
Staring Down the Dragon, Dorothea N. Buckingham
Sophie, Guy Burt
White Midnight, Dia Calhoun
Close to Shore: the Terrifying Shark Attacks of 1916, Michael Capuzzo
Prep, Jake Coburn
The Meaning of Consuelo, Judith Ortiz Cofer
Getting Away with Murder: True Story of the Emmett Till Case, Chris Crowe
King of the Mild Frontier: An Ill-Advised Autobiography, Chris Crutcher
Wonder When You'll Miss Me, Amanda Davis
A Northern Light, Jennifer Donnelly
Fight On! Mary Church Terrell's Battle for Integration, Dennis Brindell Fradin and Judith Bloom Fradin
Friction, E.R. Frank

Coal: A Human History, Barbara Freese
Fat Kid Rules the World, K.L. Going
Singing the Dogstar Blues, Alison Goodman
Runaway Girl: The Artist Louise Bourgeois, Jan Greenberg and Sandra Jordan
The Curious Incident of the Dog in the Night-Time: A Novel, Mark Haddon
September 11, 2001: Attack on New York City, Wilborn Hampton
Sweetblood, Pete Hautman
Across the Nightingale Floor: Tales of the Otori, Book One, Lian Hearn
A Stir of Bones, Nina Kiriki Hoffman
The Canning Season, Polly Horvath
Out of Order, A.M. Jenkins
The First Part Last, Angela Johnson
Target, Kathleen Jeffrie Johnson
Alice, I Think, Susan Juby
Buddha Boy, Kathe Koja
Jake, Reinvented, Gordon Korman
Uncommon Faith, Trudy Krisher
Boy Meets Boy, David Levithan
Shutterbug Follies, Jason Little
Burndive, Karin Lowachee
Birdland, Tracy Mack
The Earth, My Butt and Other Big Round Things, Carolyn Mackler
Drift, Manuel Luis Martinez
The Usual Rules, Joyce Maynard
Acceleration, Graham McNamee
Bloody Jack: Being an Account of the Curious Adventures of Mary "Jacky" Faber, Ship's Boy, L.A. Meyer
Inside the Alamo, Jim Murphy
Bottled Up: A Novel, Jaye Murray
Kissing Kate, Lauren Myracle
Out of Bounds: Seven Stories of Conflict and Hope, Beverly Naidoo
Breath, Donna Jo Napoli
Firebirds: An Anthology of Original Fantasy and Science Fiction, Sharyn November, ed.
The Interman, Jeff Parker
How Angel Peterson Got His Name and Other Outrageous Tales About Extreme Sports, Gary Paulsen
Trickster's Choice, Tamora Pierce
33 Snowfish, Adam Rapp
Pirates! Celia Rees
Stiff: The Curious Lives of Human Cadavers, Mary Roach
God Went to Beauty School, Cynthia Rylant
Persepolis: The Story of a Childhood, Marjane Satrapi
Dust, Arthur Slade
Milkweed, Jerry Spinelli
Sorcery & Cecelia, or The Enchanted Chocolate Pot: Being the Correspondence of Two Young Ladies of Quality Regarding Various Magical Scandals in London and the Country, Caroline Stevermer and Patricia C. Wrede
Blankets: An Illustrated Novel, Craig Thompson
Inside Out, Terry Trueman
Deep, Susanna Vance
Heir Apparent, Vivian Vande Velde
Zigzag, Ellen Wittlinger
Locomotion, Jacqueline Woodson
Sword of the Rightful King: A Novel of King Arthur, Jane Yolen
Dragon and Thief: A Dragonback Adventure, Timothy Zahn

Some Notable New Books for Children, 2003

Source: List published by American Library Association, Chicago, IL, 2004, for books published in 2003.

Younger Readers

Ella Sarah Gets Dressed, Margaret Chodos-Irvine
I Face the Wind, Vicki Cobb
Surprising Sharks, Nicola Davies
The Racecar Alphabet, Brian Floca
Diary of a Wombat, Jackie French
Little One Step, Simon James
What Do You Do With a Tail Like This? Steve and Page Jenkins
How I Became a Pirate, Melinda Long
Just a Minute: A Trickster Tale and Counting Book, Yuyi Morales
My Name Is Yoon, Helen Recorvits
One Is a Snail Ten Is a Crab: A Counting by Feet Book, April Pulley Sayre and Jeff Sayre
Don't Let the Pigeon Drive the Bus!, Mo Willems

Middle Readers

Silent Movie, Avi
Mack Made Movies, Don Brown
The Shape Game, Anthony Browne

George Washington's Teeth, Deborah Chandra and Madeleine Comora
Vote! Eileen Christelow
Granny Torrelli Makes Soup, Sharon Creech
Iqbal: A Novel, Francesco D'Adamo
The Tale of Despereaux: Being the Story of a Mouse, a Princess, Some Soup, and a Spool of Thread, Kate DiCamillo
The City of Ember, Jeanne DuPrau
Snowed In With Grandmother Silk, Carol Fenner
Bruh Rabbit and the Tar Baby Girl, Virginia Hamilton
Harvesting Hope: The Story of Cesar Chavez, Kathleen Krull
The Man Who Made Time Travel, Kathryn Lasky
Hana's Suitcase: A True Story, Karen Levine
Horse Hooves and Chicken Feet: Mexican Folktales, selected by Neil Philip
The Man Who Went to the Far Side of the Moon: The Story of Apollo 11 Astronaut Michael Collins, Bea Uusma Schyffert
Locomotion, Jacqueline Woodson

Older Readers

Colibri, Ann Cameron
Jack: The Early Years of John F. Kennedy, Ilene Cooper
Ben Franklin's Almanac: Being a True Account of the Good
   Gentleman's Life, Candace Fleming
In Defense of Liberty: The Story of America's Bill of Rights,
   Russell Freedman
Inkheart, Cornelia Funke
Olive's Ocean, Kevin Henkes
Keeper of the Night, Kimberly Willis Holt
The Merlin Conspiracy, Diana Wynne Jones
Theodore Roosevelt: Champion of the American Spirit, Betsy
   Harvey Kraft
Mosque, David Macaulay
Stop the Train! Geraldine McCaughrean
An American Plague: The True and Terrifying Story of the
   Yellow Fever Epidemic of 1793, Jim Murphy
Ruby Electric, Theresa Nelson
Run, Boy, Run, Uri Orlev
Cuba 15, Nancy Osa
East, Edith Pattou

The River Between Us, Richard Peck
The Wee Free Men: A Story of Discworld, Terry Pratchett
Remember the Lusitania! Diana Preston
Mortal Engines, Philip Reeve
Don't Hold Me Back: My Life and Art, Winfred Rembert
Harry Potter and the Order of the Phoenix, J.K. Rowling
The Tree of Life: A Book Depicting the Life of Charles Darwin,
   Naturalist, Geologist and Thinker, Peter Sis
The Amulet of Samarkand, Jonathan Stroud

All Ages

Tell Me a Picture, Quentin Black
Roller Coaster, Marla Frazee
The Man Who Walked Between the Towers, Mordicai Gerstein
There's a Frog in my Throat! 440 Sayings a Little Bird Told Me,
   Loreen Leedy and Pat Street
Kensuke's Kingdom, Michael Morpurgo
Blues Journey, Walter Dean Myers
Alice's Adventures in Wonderland: A Pop-up Adaptation of
   Lewis Carroll's Original Tale, Robert Sabuda
The Hidden Alphabet, Laura Vaccaro Seeger.

Best-Selling Books, 2003

Source: *Publishers Weekly*

Rankings are based on copies "shipped and billed" in 2003, minus returns through early 2004.

Fiction

1. *The Da Vinci Code*, Dan Brown
2. *The Five People You Meet in Heaven*, Mitch Albom
3. *The King of Torts*, John Grisham
4. *Bleachers*, John Grisham
5. *Armageddon*, Tim LaHaye and Jerry B. Jenkins
6. *The Teeth of the Tiger*, Tom Clancy
7. *The Big Bad Wolf*, James Patterson
8. *Blow Fly*, Patricia Cornwell
9. *The Lovely Bones*, Alice Sebold
10. *The Wedding*, Nicholas Sparks
11. *Shepherds Abiding*, Jan Karon
12. *The Dark Tower V: The Wolves of Calla*, Stephen King
13. *Safe Harbour*, Danielle Steel
14. *Babylon Rising*, Tim LaHaye and Greg Dinallo
15. *Trojan Odyssey*, Clive Cussler

Nonfiction

1. *The Purpose-Driven Life*, Rick Warren
2. *The South Beach Diet*, Arthur Agatston
3. *Atkins for Life*, Robert C. Atkins
4. *The Ultimate Weight Solution*, Dr. Phil McGraw
5. *Living History*, Hillary Rodham Clinton
6. *Lies: And the Lying Liars Who Tell Them*, Al Franken
7. *Guinness World Records 2004*, Guinness World Records
8. *Who's Looking Out for You?* Bill O'Reilly
9. *Dude, Where's My Country?* Michael Moore
10. *A Royal Duty*, Paul Burrell
11. *Good to Great*, Jim Collins
12. *Kate Remembered*, A. Scott Berg
13. *The Essential 55*, Ron Clark
14. *Treason*, Ann Coulter
15. *The World According to Mister Rogers*, Fred Rogers

Trade Paperbacks

1. *Dr. Atkins' New Carbohydrate Gram Counter*, Robert C. Atkins
2. *The Secret Life of Bees*, Sue Monk Kidd
3. *East of Eden*, John Steinbeck
4. *Seabiscuit*, Laura Hillenbrand

5. *Dr. Atkins' New Diet Revolution*, Robert C. Atkins
6. *Life of Pi*, Yann Martel
7. *Self Matters*, Phillip C. McGraw
8. *The Nanny Diaries*, Emma McLaughlin and Nicola Kraus
9. *The No. 1 Ladies' Detective Agency*, Alexander McCall
   Smith
10. *Trading Spaces Behind the Scenes*, Brian Kramer
11. *What to Expect When You're Expecting*, Heidi Murkoff,
   Arlene Eisenberg and Sandee Hathaway
12. *Fix-It and Forget-It Cookbook*, Dawn J. Ranck and Phyllis
   Pellman Good
13. *Cold Mountain*, Charles Frazier
14. *The Atkins Journal*, Robert C. Atkins
15. *The Hours*, Michael Cunningham

Almanacs, Atlases, & Annuals

1. *The World Almanac and Book of Facts 2004*, Edited by
   Ken Park
2. *The Old Farmer's Almanac 2004*
3. *J.K. Lasser's Your Income Tax 2004*, J.K. Lasser
4. *The Ernst & Young Tax Guide 2004*, Ernst & Young
5. *The World Almanac and Book of Facts 2003*, Edited by Ken
   Park
6. *The Old Farmer's Almanac 2003*
7. *AAA Europe TravelBook*
8. *AAA North American Road Atlas*
9. *What Color Is Your Parachute?* Richard Nelson Bolles

Mass Market

1. *Dr. Atkins' New Diet Revolution*, Robert C. Atkins
2. *The King of Torts*, John Grisham
3. *Seabiscuit*, Laura Hillenbrand
4. *Key of Light*, Nora Roberts
5. *Key of Knowledge*, Nora Roberts
6. *Key of Valor*, Nora Roberts
7. *Three Fates*, Nora Roberts
8. *Angels and Demons*, Dan Brown
9. *Red Rabbit*, Tom Clancy
10. *The Beach House*, James Patterson

Leading U.S. Daily Newspapers, 2003

Source: 2004 *Editor & Publisher International Yearbook*

(Circulation as of Sept. 30, 2003; m = morning, e = evening, d=all day)

As of Feb. 1, 2004, the number of U.S. daily newspapers had dropped to 1,456, for a net loss of 1 since Feb. 1, 2003. Average daily circulation as of Feb. 1, 2004, fell by 806, from 55,186,157 in the previous year to 55,185,351. The overall number of Sunday papers rose by 4, to 917. Average Sunday circulation as of Feb. 1, 2004, fell 285,604, or about 0.5%, from 58.8 million to 58.5 million.

Newspaper	Circulation
1. Arlington (VA) *USA Today* (m)	2,154,539
2. New York (NY) *Wall Street Journal* (m)	2,091,062
3. New York (NY) *Times* (m)	1,118,565
4. Los Angeles (CA) *Times* (m)	914,584
5. Washington (DC) *Post* (m)	732,872
6. New York (NY) *Daily News* (m)	729,124
7. Chicago (IL) *Tribune* (m)	680,879
8. New York (NY) *Post* (m)	652,426
9. Long Island (NY) *Newsday* (m)	580,069
10. Houston (TX) *Chronicle* (m)	553,018
11. San Francisco (CA) *Chronicle* (d)	512,640
12. Dallas (TX) *Morning News* (m)	510,133
13. Chicago (IL) *Sun-Times* (m)	481,798

Newspaper	Circulation
14. Boston (MA) *Globe* (m)	450,538
15. Phoenix (AZ) *Arizona Republic* (m)	432,284
16. Newark (NJ) *Star-Ledger* (m)	408,672
17. Minneapolis (MN) *Star Tribune* (m)	380,354
18. Philadelphia (PA) *Inquirer* (m)	376,493
19. Atlanta (GA) *Journal-Constitution* (m)	371,853
20. Cleveland (OH) *Plain Dealer* (m)	365,288
21. Detroit (MI) *Free Press* (m)	352,714
22. Portland (OR) *Oregonian* (d)	334,783
23. St. Petersburg (FL) *Times* (m)	334,742
24. San Diego (CA) *Union-Tribune* (m)	328,531
25. Miami (FL) *Herald* (m)	315,850
26. Orange County (CA) *Register* (m)	302,864

Newspaper	Circulation	Newspaper	Circulation
27. Baltimore (MD) *Sun*................ (m)	301,186	64. Rochester (NY) *Democrat and Chronicle*...(m)	173,900
28. Sacramento (CA) *Bee*............... (m)	289,905	65. Nashville (TN) *Tennessean* ....(m)	172,149
29. Denver (CO) *Post* .... (m)	288,937	66. West Palm Beach (FL) *Post*............(m)	168,147
30. Denver (CO) *Rocky Mountain News*.....(m)	288,889	67. Jacksonville (FL) *Times-Union*...........(m)	167,851
31. St. Louis (MO) *Post-Dispatch* .... (m)	285,869	68. Providence (RI) *Journal* ....(m)	167,609
32. San Jose (CA) *Mercury News*......... (m)	271,997	69. Neptune (NJ) *Asbury Park Press*.......(m)	167,284
33. Kansas City (MO) *Star* .... (m)	267,273	70. Raleigh (NC) *News & Observer*.........(m)	163,769
34. Orlando (FL) *Sentinel* .... (d)	257,222	71. Las Vegas (NV) *Review-Journal* ....(m)	160,391
35. New Orleans (LA) *Times-Picayune*.......(m)	253,610	72. Fresno (CA) *Bee*......................(m)	158,651
36. Columbus (OH) *Dispatch* .... (m)	252,564	73. Memphis (TN) *Commercial Appeal* ....(m)	157,820
37. Indianapolis (IN) *Star*............... (m)	249,891	74. Des Moines (IA) *Register* ....(m)	152,885
38. Milwaukee (WI) *Journal Sentinel*...... (m)	244,288	75. Seattle (WA) *Post-Intelligencer* ....(m)	150,851
39. Pittsburgh (PA) *Post-Gazette* .... (m)	242,546	76. Chicago (IL) *Daily Herald*...............(m)	150,364
40. Boston (MA) *Herald*................ (m)	241,457	77. Birmingham (AL) *News*..................(m)	148,938
41. Fort Lauderdale (FL) *Sun-Sentinel* ...... (m)	233,634	78. Philadelphia (PA) *Daily News*.............(m)	143,631
42. Seattle (WA) *Times*................. (m)	231,505	79. Westchester Co. (NY) *Journal News* ......(m)	142,873
43. Detroit (MI) *News* .... (e)	227,392	80. Honolulu (HI) *Advertiser*................(d)	142,025
44. Charlotte (NC) *Observer* .... (m)	226,849	81. Toledo (OH) *Blade* ....(m)	139,520
45. Tampa (FL) *Tribune* .... (m)	224,220	82. Tulsa (OK) *World* ....(m)	139,383
46. San Antonio (TX) *Express-News*........ (m)	222,536	83. Grand Rapids (MI) *Press* ....(e)	138,620
47. Los Angeles (CA) *Investors Business Daily* (m)	215,788	84. Salt Lake City (UT) *Tribune* ....(m)	134,985
48. Fort Worth (TX) *Star-Telegram* .... (m)	215,452	85. Akron (OH) *Beacon Journal* ....(m)	134,401
49. Louisville (KY) *Courier-Journal* .... (m)	213,176	86. Tacoma (WA) *News Tribune* ....(m)	128,511
50. Buffalo (NY) *News*.................. (d)	207,989	87. Dayton (OH) *Daily News* ....(m)	126,642
51. Oklahoma City (OK) *Daily Oklahoman* .... (m)	207,538	88. Los Angeles (CA) *La Opinion*.............(m)	124,692
52. Norfolk (VA) *Virginian-Pilot* .... (m)	201,141	89. Syracuse (NY) *Post-Standard* ....(m)	120,701
53. Omaha (NE) *World-Herald* .... (d)	192,075	90. Greensburg (PA) *Tribune-Review*.........(m)	119,646
54. St. Paul (MN) *Pioneer Press*.......... (m)	190,392	91. Wilmington (DE) *News Journal*............(d)	116,398
55. Richmond (VA) *Times-Dispatch* .... (m)	188,540	92. Knoxville (TN) *News-Sentinel*............(m)	114,593
56. Hartford (CT) *Courant*............... (m)	185,570	93. Columbia (SC) *State*v ....(m)	114,442
57. Riverside (CA) *Press-Enterprise* ...... (m)	183,974	94. Allentown (PA) *Morning Call*.............(m)	111,594
58. Little Rock (AR) *Democrat-Gazette*...... (m)	183,343	95. Albuquerque (NM) *Journal* ....(m)	109,693
59. Austin (TX) *American-Statesman* .... (m)	183,312	96. Lexington (KY) *Herald-Leader* ....(m)	106,941
60. Walnut Creek (CA) *Contra Costa Times*... (m)	182,541	97. Sarasota (FL) *Herald-Tribune*............(m)	105,636
61. Cincinnati (OH) *Enquirer*............. (m)	182,176	98. Daytona Beach (FL) *News-Journal* ....(m)	104,654
62. Bergen County (NJ) *Record* .... (m)	179,270	99. Worcester (MA) *Telegram & Gazette*......(m)	102,592
63. Los Angeles (CA) *Daily News*.......... (m)	178,360	100. Washington (DC) *Times*................(m)	102,255

Leading Canadian Daily Newspapers, 2003

Source: 2004 *Editor & Publisher International Yearbook*

(Circulation as of Sept. 30, 2003; all morning papers)

Newspaper	Circulation	Newspaper	Circulation
Toronto (ON) *Star*	463,840	Vancouver (BC) *Sun*...................	183,004
Toronto (ON) *Globe and Mail*............	317,411	Montreal (QC) *La Presse*	181,186
Montreal (QC) *Le Journal*...............	262,161	Vancouver (BC) *Province*	160,482
Toronto (ON) *National Post*	246,632	Montreal (QC) *Gazette*	140,503
Toronto (ON) *Sun*.....................	201,612	Ottawa (ON) *Citizen*	130,431

Top 20 News/Information Websites, July 2004

Source: comScore Media Metrix, Inc.

Rank	Visitors[1]	Rank	Visitors[1]
1. AIMTODAY.COM	25,873	11. Knight Ridder Digital.....................	6,984
2. Weatherbug.com Property	24,011	12. Tribune Newspapers	6,768
3. AOL NEWS	24,008	13. USATODAY Sites......................	6,090
4. The Weather Channel..................	23,801	14. Discovery.com Sites...................	5,476
5. Yahoo! News	23,085	15. ABCNEWS DIGITAL	5,332
6. CNN	19,667	16. BBC Sites	4,431
7. MSNBC	19,275	17. MSN Slate	4,223
8. ABOUT.COM.........................	18,015	18. FOXNEWS.COM	3,977
9. New York Times Digital.................	7,920	19. Google News	3,918
10. IBS Network	7,129	20. Advance Publications, Inc	3,736

(1) Number of unique visitors in thousands who visited website at least once in July 2004.

Top-Selling Albums of All-Time[1]

Source: Recording Industry Assn. of America, Washington, DC

Rank	Title, Artist	Sales (in millions)	Rank	Title, Artist	Sales (in millions)
1.	*Eagles/Their Greatest Hits 1971-1975*, Eagles...	28.0		*Jagged Little Pill*, Alanis Morissette.............	16.0
2.	*Thriller*, Michael Jackson...............	26.0		*No Fences*, Garth Brooks	16.0
3.	*The Wall*, Pink Floyd....................	23.0		*Boston*, Boston.......................	16.0
4.	*Led Zeppelin IV*, Led Zeppelin	22.0	18.	*Double Live*, Garth Brooks	15.0
5.	*Greatest Hits Volume I & Volume II*, Billy Joel....	21.0		*The Beatles 1962 - 1966*, The Beatles	15.0
6.	*Rumours*, Fleetwood Mac................	19.0		*Physical Graffiti*, Led Zeppelin	15.0
	Come On Over, Shania Twain...............	19.0		*Saturday Night Fever* (soundtrack), Bee Gees	15.0
	The Beatles, The Beatles.................	19.0		*Appetite For Destruction*, Guns 'N Roses	15.0
	Back In Black, AC/DC....................	19.0		*Dark Side of the Moon*, Pink Floyd..........	15.0
10.	*The Bodyguard* (soundtrack), Whitney Houston ..	17.0		*Born in the U.S.A.*, Bruce Springsteen	15.0
11.	*Greatest Hits*, Elton John....................	16.0	25.	*Bat Out of Hell*, Meat Loaf..................	14.0
	Hotel California, Eagles.....................	16.0		*Backstreet Boys*, Backstreet Boys	14.0
	The Beatles 1967-1970, The Beatles.........	16.0		*Supernatural*, Santana	14.0
	Cracked Rear View, Hootie & the Blowfish......	16.0		*Ropin' The Wind*, Garth Brooks..............	14.0

(1) As of Aug. 2003; sales figures represent RIAA multi-platinum certifications; albums ranked by latest sales certification.

▶ **IT'S A FACT:** Elvis Presley is the bestselling solo artist in U.S. history, with a total of 117.5 million albums sold. *Elvis' Christmas Album*, with more than 9 million sold, is Presley's top-selling album. "The King" has a total of 97 gold albums, with 55 going platinum and 25 enjoying multi-platinum status. Elvis has more gold and platinum singles than any other artist in history, with 51 gold, 27 platinum, and 7 multi-platinum.

Songs of the Century

Source: National Endowment for the Arts and the Recording Industry Association of America

A list of 365 "Songs of the Century" was compiled in 2001, based on ballots sent to musicians, critics, industry professionals, elected officials, and amateur music fans; the top 100 are listed below. Criteria for judging included historical significance and popularity of the song as well as the record and artist. (The list has attracted some controversy, because it is based on a relatively small number of returned ballots—about 200. The year each song was first released is in parentheses.

1. "Over the Rainbow," Judy Garland (1939)
2. "White Christmas," Bing Crosby (1942)
3. "This Land Is Your Land," Woody Guthrie (1947)
4. "Respect," Aretha Franklin (1967)
5. "American Pie," Don McLean (1971)
6. "Boogie Woogie Bugle Boy," The Andrews Sisters (1941)
7. *West Side Story* (album), original cast (1957)
8. "Take Me Out to the Ball Game," Billy Murray (1908)
9. "You've Lost That Lovin' Feelin'," The Righteous Brothers (1965)
10. "The Entertainer," Scott Joplin (1902)
11. "In the Mood," Glenn Miller Orchestra (1939)
12. "Rock Around the Clock," Bill Haley & The Comets (1955)
13. "When the Saints Go Marching In," Louis Armstrong (1938)
14. "You Are My Sunshine," Jimmie Davis (1940)
15. "Mack the Knife," Bobby Darin (1959)
16. "Satisfaction," The Rolling Stones (1965)
17. "Take the 'A' Train," Duke Ellington Orchestra (1941)
18. "Blueberry Hill," Fats Domino (1956)
19. "God Bless America," Kate Smith (1939)
20. "Stars and Stripes Forever," John Philip Sousa's Band (1896)
21. "I Heard It Through the Grapevine," Marvin Gaye (1968)
22. "Dock of the Bay," Otis Redding (1968)
23. "I Left My Heart in San Francisco," Tony Bennett (1962)
24. "Good Vibrations," The Beach Boys (1967)
25. "Stand By Me," Ben E. King (1961)
26. "Stormy Weather," Lena Horne (1943)
27. "Johnny B. Goode," Chuck Berry (1958)
28. "I Want to Hold Your Hand," The Beatles (1964)
29. "Midnight Train to Georgia," Gladys Knight & The Pips (1973)
30. "Imagine," John Lennon (1971)
31. "Rudolph the Red Nosed Reindeer," Gene Autry (1949)
32. "The Twist," Chubby Checker (1960)
33. "Happy Trails," Roy Rogers & Dale Evans (1951)
34. "Your Cheatin' Heart," Hank Williams (1953)
35. "Swing Low Sweet Chariot," Fisk Jubilee Singers (1909)
36. *The Sound of Music* (album), original cast (1960)
37. "'Round Midnight," Thelonius Monk (1948)
38. "What's Love Got to Do With It," Tina Turner (1984)
39. "Over There," The American Quartet (1917)
40. "Star Dust," Hoagy Carmichael (1928)
41. "Ain't Misbehavin'," Fats Waller (1929)
42. "Georgia on My Mind," Ray Charles (1960)
43. "Oh Pretty Woman," Roy Orbison (1964)
44. "Every Breath You Take," The Police (1983)
45. "My Girl," The Temptations (1965)
46. "Hotel California," The Eagles (1977)
47. "Happy Days Are Here Again," Ben Selvin Orchestra (1930)
48. "Stand By Your Man," Tammy Wynette (1968)
49. "Take Five," Dave Brubeck (1959)
50. "America the Beautiful," Louise Homer (1925)
51. "When a Man Loves a Woman," Percy Sledge (1966)
52. "Light My Fire," The Doors (1967)
53. "Stairway to Heaven," Led Zeppelin (1971)
54. "Sweet Georgia Brown," Ben Bernie Orchestra (1925)
55. "When You Wish Upon a Star," Cliff Edwards (1940)
56. "Yesterday"/"Act Naturally," The Beatles (1965)
57. "Louie Louie," The Kingsmen (1963)
58. "God Bless the Child," Billie Holiday (1941)
59. "Born in the USA," Bruce Springsteen (1975)
60. "The Girl from Ipanema," Stan Getz/Astrud Gilberto (1964)
61. "I Walk the Line," Johnny Cash (1956)
62. "The Star-Spangled Banner," John McCormick (1917)
63. "O Happy Day," The Edwin Hawkins Singers (1969)
64. "Great Balls of Fire," Jerry Lee Lewis (1957)
65. "What's Going On," Marvin Gaye (1971)
66. *Oklahoma* (album), original cast (1943)
67. "Zip-A-Dee-Doo-Dah," Johnny Mercer (1946)
68. "Don't Be Cruel"/"Hound Dog," Elvis Presley (1956)
69. "St. Louis Blues," W. C. Handy (1923)
70. "Yankee Doodle," Vess Ossman (1894)
71. "California Dreamin'," The Mamas & the Papas (1966)
72. "On the Road Again," Willie Nelson (1980)
73. "Auld Lang Syne," Frank Stanley (1907)
74. "Summertime," Sidney Bechet (1939)
75. "Theme from Shaft," Isaac Hayes (1971)
76. "Beat It," Michael Jackson (1983)
77. "Sentimental Journey," Les Brown Orchestra (1945)
78. "Blue Suede Shoes," Carl Perkins (1956)
79. "The Sound of Silence," Simon & Garfunkel (1965)
80. "Smells Like Teen Spirit," Nirvana (1992)
81. "It Had to Be You," Isham Jones Orchestra (1924)
82. "Minnie the Moocher," Cab Calloway (1931)
83. "Sixteen Tons," Tennessee Ernie Ford (1955)
84. "What a Wonderful World," Louis Armstrong (1967)
85. "Fire and Rain," James Taylor (1970)
86. "Y.M.C.A.," The Village People (1978)
87. "Heartbreak Hotel," Elvis Presley (1956)
88. "King of the Road," Roger Miller (1965)
89. "I Will Survive," Gloria Gaynor (1976)
90. "Ave Maria," Marian Anderson (1937)
91. "Begin the Beguine," Artie Shaw Orchestra (1938)
92. "Like a Rolling Stone," Bob Dylan (1965)
93. "Stop in the Name of Love," The Supremes (1965)
94. "Stayin' Alive," The Bee Gees (1978)
95. "1999," Prince (1982)
96. "Please Remember Me," Tim McGraw (1999)
97. *Porgy and Bess* (album), original cast (1935)
98. "Back in the Saddle Again," Gene Autry (1938)
99. "Shake, Rattle and Roll," Joe Turner (1954)
100. "In the Still of the Night," The Five Satins (1956)

Top-Grossing North American Concert Tours, 1985-2003

Source: Pollstar, Fresno, CA

Artist (Year)	Total gross[1]	Cities/ Shows	Artist (Year)	Total gross[1]	Cities/ Shows
1. The Rolling Stones (1994)	$121.2	43/60	11. Celine Dion (2003)	$80.5	1/145
2. Bruce Springsteen & The E. Street Band (2003)	115.9	30/47	12. Tina Turner (2000)	80.2	88/95
3. U2 (2001)	109.7	56/80	13. U2 (1997)	79.9	37/46
4. Pink Floyd (1994)	103.5	39/59	14. The Eagles (1994)	79.4	32/54
5. Paul McCartney (2002)	103.3	43/53	15. 'N Sync (2000)	76.4	64/86
6. The Rolling Stones (1989)	98.0	33/60	16. The New Kids on the Block (1990)	74.1	122/152
7. The Rolling Stones (1997)	89.3	26/33	17. Cher (2002)	73.6	84/93
8. The Rolling Stones (2002)	87.9	33/34	18. The Eagles (2003)	69.3	47/55
9. 'N Sync (2001)	86.8	36/43	19. Fleetwood Mac (2003)	69.0	86/71
10. Backstreet Boys (2001)	82.1	73/98	20. Cher (2003)	68.2	98/102
			Dave Matthews Band (2000)	68.2	43/63

(1) In millions. Not adjusted for inflation.

U.S. Commercial Radio Stations, by Format, 1997-2004[1]

Source: M Street Corporation, Littleton, NH © 2004; counts are for June of each year

Primary format	2004	2003	2002	2001	1999	1998	1997
1. Country	2,047	2,088	2,131	2,190	2,306	2,368	2,491
2. News/Talk	1,282	1,224	1,179	1,139	1,159	1,131	1,111
3. Oldies	813	807	813	786	766	799	755
4. Adult Contemporary (AC)	703	692	713	709	775	844	902
5. Spanish	665	628	603	574	536	493	474
6. Top 40	497	491	474	468	401	379	358
7. Sports	470	429	388	338	256	251	220
8. Adult Standards	460	497	547	569	595	561	551
9. Classic Rock	450	425	384	338	314	282	240
10. Hot AC	416	399	395	369	325	281	260
11. Religion (Teaching, Variety)	336	347	332	356	363	356	404
12. Soft AC	322	336	340	375	382	368	346
13. Rock	280	273	278	282	280	266	262
14. Black Gospel	273	253	254	264	257	238	208
15. Classic Hits	229	237	258	265	222	192	172
16. Southern Gospel	208	207	240	255	269	273	255
17. Modern Rock	165	169	147	140	136	145	137
18. R&B	159	189	193	183	166	171	169
18. Contemporary Christian	159	167	164	164	167	164	159
20. Urban AC	136	128	121	118	112	127	134
Off Air	104[2]	151[2]	110	113	96	102	143
Changing format/not available	4	1	5	3	3	3	2
TOTAL STATIONS	**10,649**	**10,605**	**10,569**	**10,516**	**10,444**	**10,292**	**10,207**

(1) Data for 2000 unavailable. (2) Represents commerical and non-commerical stations.

Sales of Recorded Music and Music Videos, by Units Shipped and Value, 1994-2003

Source: Recording Industry Assn. of America, Washington, DC
(in millions, net after returns)

FORMAT	1994	1995	1996	1997	1998	1999	2000	2001	2002	2003	% CHANGE 2002-2003
Compact disc (CD)											
Units shipped	662.1	722.9	778.9	753.1	847.0	938.9	942.5	881.9	803.3	745.9	−7.1%
Dollar value	8,464.5	9,377.4	9,934.7	9,915.1	11,416.0	12,816.3	13,214.5	12,909.4	12,044.1	11,232.9	−6.7%
CD single											
Units shipped	9.3	21.5	43.2	66.7	56.0	55.9	34.2	17.3	4.5	8.3	85.5%
Dollar value	56.1	110.9	184.1	272.7	213.2	222.4	142.7	79.4	19.6	35.9	84.04%
Cassette											
Units shipped	345.4	272.6	225.3	172.6	158.5	123.6	76.0	45.0	31.1	17.2	−44.7%
Dollar value	2,976.4	2,303.6	1,905.3	1,522.7	1,419.9	1,061.6	626.0	363.4	209.8	108.1	−48.5%
Cassette single											
Units shipped	81.1	70.7	59.9	42.2	26.4	14.2	1.3	−1.5	−0.5	NA	NA
Dollar value	274.9	236.3	189.3	133.5	94.4	48.0	4.6	−5.3	−1.6	NA	NA
LP/EP											
Units shipped	1.9	2.2	2.9	2.7	3.4	2.9	2.2	2.3	1.7	1.5	−11.5%
Dollar value	17.8	25.1	36.8	33.3	34.0	31.8	27.7	27.4	20.5	21.7	6.1%
Vinyl single											
Units shipped	11.7	10.2	10.1	7.5	5.4	5.3	4.8	5.5	4.4	3.8	−14.2%
Dollar value	47.2	46.7	47.5	35.6	25.7	27.9	26.3	31.4	24.9	21.5	−14.0%
Music video											
Units shipped	11.2	12.6	16.9	18.6	27.2	19.8	18.2	17.7	14.7	19.9	35.6%
Dollar value	231.1	220.3	236.1	323.9	508.0	376.7	281.9	329.2	288.4	399.9	38.7%
DVD audio											
Units shipped	—	—	—	—	—	—	—	0.3	0.4	0.4	0.8%
Dollar value	—	—	—	—	—	—	—	6.0	8.5	8.0	−5.3%
SACD											
Units shipped	—	—	—	—	—	—	—	—	—	1.3	NA
Dollar value	—	—	—	—	—	—	—	—	—	26.3	NA
DVD video*											
Units shipped	—	—	—	—	0.5	2.5	3.3	7.9	10.7	17.5	64.1%
Dollar value	—	—	—	—	12.2	66.3	80.3	190.7	236.3	369.6	56.4%
TOTAL UNITS	1,122.7	1,112.7	1,137.2	1,063.4	1,123.9	1,160.6	1,079.2	968.5	859.7	798.4	−7.2%
TOTAL VALUE	12,068.0	12,320.3	12,533.8	12,236.8	13,711.2	14,584.7	14,323.7	13,740.9	12,614.2	11,854.4	−6.0%

* While broken out for this chart, DVD Video Product is included in the Music Video totals.

Sales of Recorded Music and Music Videos, by Genre and Format, 1997-2003

Source: Recording Industry Assn. of America, Washington, DC
Breakdown is by percentage of sales revenue for all recorded music sold, ranked for 2003.

GENRE	2003	2002	2001	2000	1999	1998
Rock	25.2	24.7	24.4	24.8	25.2	25.7
Rap/Hip-Hop[1]	13.3	13.8	11.4	12.9	10.8	9.7
R&B/Urban[2]	10.6	11.2	10.6	9.7	10.5	12.8
Country	10.4	10.7	10.5	10.7	10.8	14.1
Pop	8.9	9.0	12.1	11.0	10.3	10.0
Religious[3]	5.8	6.7	6.7	4.8	5.1	6.3
Classical	3.0	3.1	3.2	2.7	3.5	3.3
Jazz	2.9	3.2	3.4	2.9	3.0	1.9
Soundtracks	1.4	1.1	1.4	0.7	0.8	1.7
Oldies	1.3	0.9	0.8	0.9	0.7	0.7
Children's	0.6	0.4	0.5	0.6	0.4	0.4

GENRE	2003	2002	2001	2000	1999	1998
New Age	0.5	0.5	1.0	0.5	0.5	0.6
Other[4]	7.6	8.1	7.9	8.3	9.1	7.9
FORMAT						
Compact disc (CD)	87.8	90.5	89.2	89.3	83.2	74.8
Singles (all types)	2.4	1.9	2.4	2.5	5.4	6.8
Cassette	2.2	2.4	3.4	4.9	8.0	14.8
Digital download[5]	1.3	0.5	0.2	NA	NA	NA
Music Videos/ Digital Video Disc (DVD)[6]	0.6	0.7	1.1	0.8	0.9	1.0
LPs	0.6	0.7	0.6	0.5	0.5	0.7

(1) Includes Rap (10.5% in 2002) and Hip-Hop (3.3% in 2002). (2) Includes R&B, blues, dance, disco, funk, fusion, Motown, reggae, soul. (3) Includes Christian, Gospel, Inspirational, Religious, and Spiritual. (4) "Other" includes Ethnic, Standards, Big Band, Swing, Latin, Electronic, Instrumental, Comedy, Humor, Spoken Word, Exercise, Language, Folk, and Holiday Music. (5) 2001 is the first year that data was collected on digital download purchases. (6) 2001 is the first year that music video/ DVD was recorded separately from audio DVD (not shown).

Multi-Platinum and Platinum Awards for Recorded Music and Music Videos, 2003

Source: Recording Industry Assn. of America, Washington, DC

To achieve platinum status, an **album** must reach a minimum sale of 1 mil units in LPs, tapes, and CDs, with a manufacturer's dollar volume of at least $2 mil based on one-third of the suggested retail list price for each record, tape, or CD sold. To achieve multi-platinum status, an album must reach a minimum sale of at least 2 mil units in LPs, tapes, and CDs, with a manufacturer's dollar volume of at least $4 mil based on one-third of the list price.

Singles must sell 1 mil units to achieve a platinum award (created in 1976) and 2 mil to achieve a multi-platinum award (created in 1984). In 1999, the Diamond Award, honoring sales of 10 million or more copes of an album or single, was introduced. EP singles count as 2 units. Double-CD sets count as 2 units. **Music videos** (long form) must sell 100,000 units to qualify for a platinum award and must sell more than 200,000 units for a multi-platinum award. **Video singles**, which must have a maximum running time of 15 minutes and no more than 2 songs per title, must sell 50,000 units to qualify for a platinum award and at least 100,000 units to qualify for a multi-platinum award.

Awards listed were for albums and singles released in 2003 and for music videos released at any time. Numbers in parentheses = millions sold. Alphabetized by artist's name.

Albums, Multi-Platinum

Away from the Sun, 3 Doors Down (2)
Get Rich or Die Tryin', 50 Cent (6)
Measure of A Man, Clay Aiken (2)
Dangerously in Love, Beyonce (2)
The Very Best of Cher, Cher (2)
Thankful, Kelly Clarkson (2)
One Heart, Celine Dion (2)
The Very Best of the Eagles, Eagles (2)
Fallen, Evanescence (3)
Closer, Josh Groban (2)
Beg for Mercy, G-Unit (2)
Shock 'N Y'all, Toby Keith (2)
Chocolate Factory, R. Kelly (2)
Meteora, Linkin Park (3)
Almas Del Silencio, Ricky Martin (2)
St. Anger, Metallica (2)
Speakerboxxx/The Love Below, Outkast (6)
Chicago, (motion picture soundtrack), Various (2)
In the Zone, Britney Spears (2)
Now That's What I Call Christmas!, Vol 2, Various (2)
Up! Shania Twain (10)

Albums, Platinum

Resurrection, 2 Pac
Y Tenerate Otra Vez, Pepe Aguilar
Proyecto Akwid, Akwid
Chapter II, Ashanti
Pandemonium! B2K
Let It Be...Naked, The Beatles
Love & Life, Mary J. Blige
Hotel Paper, Michelle Branch
Meet Me in Margaritaville, Jimmy Buffett
Jackpot, Chingy
The Very Best of Sheryl Crow, Sheryl Crow
Life for Rent, Dido
The Grand Champ, DMX
Metamorphosis, Hilary Duff
This Is Not a Test, Missy Elliott
Street Dreams, Fabolous
Faceless, Godsmack

Nuestro Destino Estaba Escrito, Intocable
Ah Via Musicom, Eric Johnson
The R. in R&B Collection, Volume I, R. Kelly
Kid Rock, Kid Rock
Take a Look in the Mirror, Korn
How the West Was Won, Led Zeppelin
La Bella Mafia, Lil' Kim
Chicken & Beer, Ludacris
American Life, Madonna
Some Devil, The Dave Matthews Band
Any Given Thursday, John Mayer
Heavier Things, John Mayer
Afterglow, Sarah McLachlan
The Long Road, Nickelback
2nd to None, Elvis Presley
The Essential Bruce Springsteen, Bruce Springsteen
14 Shades Of Grey, Staind
As Time Goes By...Great American Songbook, Vol. 2, Rod Stewart
Elephant, The White Stripes
Dance With My Father, Luther Vandross
Bad Boys II (soundtrack), Various
iWorship, Various
Listen to Your Lid II, Various
Lizzie McGuire (soundtrack), Various
NBA Livestyle 2003, Various
Now That's What I Call Music! Vol. 12, Various
Now That's What I Call Music! Vol. 13, Various
Now That's What I Call Music! Vol. 14, Various
Worship Together: I Could Sing of Your Love Forever, Various
Wow Worship Yellow, Various

Music Videos, Platinum

Best of Bowie, David Bowie
Mtv Unplugged 2.0, Dashboard Confessional
Top of the World: Live DVD, Dixie Chicks
Morning View Sessions, Incubus
Greatest Hits, Volume II (Disc 1), Alan Jackson

Live in Paris, Diana Krall
Live, Alison Krauss
Lennon Legend, John Lennon
Legend, Bob Marley & the Wailers
Any Given Thursday, John Mayer
The Dark Side of the Moon, Pink Floyd
Greatest Video Hits, Vol. 1, Queen
Meeting People Is Easy, Radiohead
Live, Rascal Flatts
Lovers Live, Sade
G3: Live in Concert, Joe Satriani
Because He Lives, Various
Hawaiian Homecoming, Various
I Do Believe, Various
Irish Homecoming, Various
Let Freedom Ring, Various
So Glad, Various
What A Time, Various

Music Videos, Multi-Platinum

DVD Anthology, The Beatles (13)
Coldplay Live 2003, Coldplay (5)
An Evening with the Dixie Chicks, Dixie Chicks (2)
The Closing of Winterland, Grateful Dead (2)
Live in Concert, Josh Groban (6)
HIStory on Film, Michael Jackson (3)
Video Greatest Hits/HIStory, Michael Jackson (2)
Live in New Orleans, Norah Jones (2)
Kiss Symphony - The DVD, Kiss (2)
Led Zeppelin, Led Zeppelin (10)
The Central Park Concert, Dave Matthews Band (4)
Binge & Purge (CD & video package), Metallica (15)
S&M, Metallica (6)
Live at the Garden, Pearl Jam (2)
Bring the Pain, Chris Rock (2)
Rush in Rio, Rush (3)
Supernatural Live, Santana (3)
Live on Broadway, Robin Williams (4)
Ryman Gospel Reunion, Various (2)
The Up In Smoke Tour, Various (5)

U.S. Households With Cable Television, 1977-2003

Source: Nielsen Media Research

Year	Basic cable subscribers	As % of households with TVs	Year	Basic cable subscribers	As % of households with TVs	Year	Basic cable subscribers	As % of households with TVs	Year	Basic cable subscribers	As % of households with TVs
1977	12,168,450	16.6	1984	37,290,870	43.7	1991	55,786,390	60.6	1998	67,011,180	67.4
1978	13,391,910	17.9	1985	39,872,520	46.2	1992	57,211,600	61.5	1999	68,537,980	68.0
1979	14,814,380	19.4	1986	42,237,140	48.1	1993	58,834,440	62.5	2000	69,297,290	67.8
1980	17,671,490	22.6	1987	44,970,880	50.5	1994	60,483,600	63.4	2001	72,958,180	69.2
1981	23,219,200	28.3	1988	48,636,520	53.8	1995	62,956,470	65.7	2002	73,525,150	68.9
1982	29,340,570	35.0	1989	52,564,470	57.1	1996	64,654,160	66.7	2003	73,365,880	68.0
1983	34,113,790	40.5	1990	54,871,330	59.0	1997	65,929,420	67.3			

Number of Cable TV Systems,[1] 1975-2004

Source: *Television and Cable Factbook*, Warren Communications News, Inc., Washington, DC; estimates as of Jan. 1

Year	Systems	Year	Systems	Year	Systems	Year	Systems	Year	Systems	Year	Systems
1975	3,506	1980	4,225	1985	6,600	1990	9,575	1995	11,218	2000	10,400
1976	3,681	1981	4,375	1986	7,500	1991	10,704	1996	11,119	2001	9,924
1977	3,832	1982	4,825	1987	7,900	1992	11,035	1997	10,950	2002	9,947
1978	3,875	1983	5,600	1988	8,500	1993	11,108	1998	10,845	2003	9,339*
1979	4,150	1984	6,200	1989	9,050	1994	11,214	1999	10,700	2004	8,869*

(1) The satellite-signal-receiving hardware, cable lines, and cable boxes that provide cable programming to homes within a geographic area. *Figures as of March

Top 20 Cable TV Networks, 2004

Source: *Cable Television Developments,* Natl. Cable Television Assn., April 2004; ranked by number of subscribers

Rank	Network[1]	Subscribers (mil)	Rank	Network[1]	Subscribers (mil)
1.	Discovery Channel (1985)	88.6	11.	The Weather Channel (1982)	87.5
2.	C-SPAN (Cable Satellite Public Affairs Network) (1979)	88.4	12.	Spike TV[2] (2003)	87.4
	USA Network (1980)	88.4	13.	ABC Family Channel[3] (2001)	87.1
4.	ESPN (1979)	88.3		TLC (The Learning Channel (1980)	87.1
5.	CNN (Cable News Network) (1980)	88.0	15.	ESPN2 (1993)	87.0
	TBS (Superstation) (1976)	88.0	16.	MTV (Music Television) (1981)	86.8
	TNT (Turner Network Television) (1988)	88.0	17.	Headline News (1982)	86.5
8.	A&E Network (1984)	87.6	18.	VH1 (Music First) (1985)	86.4
	LIFE (Lifetime Television) (1984)	87.6	19.	CNBC (1989)	86.1
	Nickelodeon (1979)	87.6		The History Channel (1995)	86.1

Note: Data include noncable affiliates. (1) Date in parentheses is year service began. (2) Formerly The Nashville Network (1983-2000); The National Network (2000-2003); The New TNN (2003). (3) Began 1977 as the Family Channel; FOX Family Channel (1998-2000).

U.S. Television Set Owners, 2004

Source: Nielsen Media Research; March 2004

Of the 108.4 million U.S. households that owned at least one TV set in 2004:

35% had 2 TV sets	91% had a VCR	68% received basic cable
42% had 3 or more TV sets		47% received premium cable

Some Television Addresses, Phone Numbers, Internet Sites

TELEVISION

ABC, Inc.—American Broadcasting Co.
500 S. Buena Vista St.
Burbank, CA 91521; (818) 460-7477
Website: abc.go.com

CBS—Columbia Broadcasting System
51 W. 52nd St.
New York, NY 10019; (212) 975-4321
Website: www.cbs.com

Fox—Fox Network
Fox Entertainment Group
1211 Avenue of the Americas
New York, NY 10036; (212) 852-7111
Website: www.fox.com

NBC—National Broadcasting Co.
30 Rockefeller Plaza
New York, NY 10112; (212) 664-4444
Website: www.nbc.com

PBS—Public Broadcasting Service
1320 Braddock Place
Alexandria, VA 22314; (703) 739-5000
Website: www.pbs.org

UPN—United Paramount Network
11800 Wilshire Blvd.
Los Angeles, CA 90025; (310) 575-7000
Website: www.upn.com

WB—WB Television Network
4000 Warner Blvd., Bldg. 34R
Burbank, CA 91522; (818) 977-5000
Website: www.thewb.com

CABLE

ABC FAMILY—ABC Family Channel
500 S. Buena Vista St.
Burbank, CA 91521; (818) 560-1000
Website: www.ABCfamily.go.com

A&E—Arts & Entertainment Network
235 E 45th St.
New York, NY 10017; (212) 210-1400
Website: www.aetv.com

AMC—American Movie Classics
200 Jericho Quadrangle
Jericho, NY 11753; (516) 803-4300
Website: www.amctv.com

APL—Animal Planet
One Discovery Place
Silver Spring, MD 20910-3354;
(240) 662-0000
Website: www.animalplanet.com

BET—Black Entertainment Television
1 BET Plaza, 1235 W St. NE
Washington, DC 20018; (202) 608-2000
Website: www.bet.com

CNBC—Consumer News and Business Channel
2200 Fletcher Ave.
Fort Lee, NJ 07024; (201) 585-2622
Website: moneycentral.msn.com/investor/home.asp

CNN—Cable News Network
One CNN Center
Atlanta, GA 30303; (404) 827-1500
Website: www.cnn.com

COMEDY—Comedy Central
1775 Broadway
New York, NY 10019; (212) 767-8600
Website: www.comedycentral.com

C-SPAN—Cable Satellite Public Affairs Network
400 N Capitol St. NW, Suite 650
Washington, DC 20001; (202) 737-3220
Website: www.c-span.org

DISN—The Disney Channel
3800 W Alameda Ave.
Burbank, CA 91505; (818) 569-7500
Website: www.disneychannel.com

DSC—The Discovery Channel
Discovery Communications
One Discovery Place
Silver Spring, MD 20910-3354;
(240) 662-0000
Website: www.discovery.com

ESPN—ESPN, Inc.
ESPN Plaza, 935 Middle St.
Bristol, CT 06010; (860) 766-2000
Website: www.espn.go.com

FOOD—Food Network
1180 Avenue of the Americas, 11th Floor
New York, NY 10036; (212) 398-8836
Website: www.foodnetwork.com

HBO—Home Box Office
1100 Avenue of the Americas
New York, NY 10036; (212) 512-1000
Website: www.hbo.com

HIST—The History Channel
235 E. 45th St.
New York, NY 10017; (212) 210-1375
Website: www.historychannel.com

LIFE—Lifetime
309 W 49th St.
New York, NY 10019; (212) 424-7000
Website: www.lifetimetv.com

MSNBC—Microsoft NBC News
1 MSNBC Plaza
Secaucus, NJ 07094; (201) 583-5000
Website: www.msnbc.com

MTV—Music Television
MTV Networks, Inc.
1515 Broadway
New York, NY 10036; (212) 258-8000
Website: www.mtv.com

NICK—Nickelodeon
MTV Networks, Inc.
1515 Broadway
New York, NY 10036; (212) 258-8000
Website: www.nick.com

Spike TV
MTV Networks
1515 Broadway, 37th Floor
New York, NY 10036; (212) 846-8000
Website: www.spiketv.com

TBS—Turner Broadcasting System
1050 Techwood Dr. NW
Atlanta, GA 30318
(404) 827-1700
Website: www.tbssuperstation.com

TLC—The Learning Channel
Discovery Communications
One Discovery Place
Silver Spring, MD 20910; (240) 662-2000
Website: tlc.discovery.com

TWC—The Weather Channel
300 Interstate North Parkway
Atlanta, GA 30339-2404; (770) 226-0000
Website: www.weather.com

USA—USA Network
USA Networks
1230 Avenue of the Americas
New York, NY 10020; (212) 413-5000
Website: www.usanetwork.com

▶ IT'S A FACT: After the TV quiz show *Jeopardy!* altered its 5-game limit for contestants at the start of the its 20th season in the fall of 2003, Utah software engineer Ken Jennings emerged as the show's all-time leading money-winner. He debuted on the show June 2, 2004. By Oct. 6, 2004, when the 21st regular season was set to continue after a hiatus for the Tournament of Champions, Jennings had won $1,635,061, with the chance of more to come. The previous *Jeopardy!* record was $1,155,102, reached by Brad Rutter of Lancaster, PA, in 2002.

Average U.S. Television Viewing Time, October 2003

Source: Nielsen Media Research (hours: minutes per week)

Group	Age	Total per week	M-F 7-10 AM	M-F 10 AM-4:00 PM	M-SUN 8-11 PM	SAT 7 AM-1 PM	M-F 11:30 PM-1 AM	Sunday 1-7:00 PM
Women	18+	35:17	2:22	5:13	9:38	0:55	1:38	1:36
	18-24	23:11	1:11	3:49	5:39	0:35	1:19	1:04
	25-54	33:46	2:20	4:35	9:13	0:55	1:42	1:32
	55+	42:50	2:55	6:47	11:52	1:00	1:40	1:56
Men	18+	31:25	1:21	3:32	8:59	0:49	1:38	1:51
	18-24	21:20	0:55	2:42	5:02	0:37	1:19	1:11
	25-54	30:25	1:35	3:05	8:48	0:50	1:43	1:50
	55+	38:18	2:18	4:52	11:16	0:53	1:40	2:11
Teens	12-17	19:19	0:43	1:30	5:38	0:46	0:42	1:07
Children	2-11	21:00	1:46	2:55	4:58	1:10	0:32	1:06
ALL VIEWERS		30:25	1:53	3:56	8:22	0:54	1:25	1:35

TV Viewing Shares, Broadcast Years 1990-2003[1]

Source: *Cable TV Facts*, Cable Advertising Bureau, New York, NY

	All Television Households[2]						All Cable Households[2]						Pay Cable Households[2]					
	'90	'95	'00	'01	'02	'03	'90	'95	'00	'01	'02	'03	'90	'95	'00	'01	'02	'03
Network Affiliates[3]	55	48	44	42	39	31	46	41	40	37	35	28	43	38	37	35	33	25
Indep. TV Stations[4] ...	20	22	12	11	11	12	16	17	9	8	8	9	16	17	9	8	8	8
Public TV Stations	3	3	3	3	3	3	3	3	2	2	2	2	2	2	2	2	2	2
Basic Cable[5]	21	30	46	49	49	52	32	42	55	57	56	58	30	41	55	57	56	58
Pay Cable	6	6	6	6	6	6	10	8	7	7	7	7	18	15	11	11	12	12

Note: After 1998, Fox affiliates switched from Independent classification to Network Affiliates. (1) Broadcast years represent the 12-month period October-September. (2) Share figures refer to percentage of the viewing audience for all television viewing, 24 hours/day. As a result of multiset use and rounding of numbers, share figures add to more than 100. (3) Includes CBS, NBC, ABC, and FOX. (4) Includes WB, UPN, and PAX. (5) Includes ad-supported cable and all other cable (non-pay and non-ad-supported channels).

Favorite Prime-Time Television Programs, 2003-2004

Source: Nielsen Media Research

Data are for regularly scheduled network programs in 2003-2004 season through May 26; ranked by average audience percentage. Average audience percentages, or ratings, are estimates of the percentage of all TV-owning households that are watching a particular program. Audience share percentages are estimates of the percentage of those watching TV that are tuned into a particular program. Tied programs are given the same rank.

Rank	Programs	Avg. Audience	Audience Share	Rank	Programs	Avg. Audience	Audience Share
1.	CSI: Crime Scene Investigation...	15.9	24	27.	Fear Factor..................	7.9	12
2.	American Idol-Tuesday	14.9	23		The Bachelorette.............	7.8	12
3.	American Idol-Wednesday.......	14.1	22		CBS Sunday Movie............	7.8	12
4.	Friends......................	13.6	22		Navy NCIS	7.8	12
5.	The Apprentice	13.0	20	28.	The West Wing	7.8	12
6.	E.R.	12.9	21		Judging Amy.................	7.7	13
7.	Survivor: All-Stars	12.4	20	32.	Still Standing................	7.7	12
8.	Survivor: Pearl Islands.........	12.1	19	34.	Las Vegas...................	7.6	11
9.	CSI: Miami..................	11.9	19		Frasier.....................	7.3	11
10.	NFL Monday Night Football......	11.5	19		King of Queens...............	7.3	11
11.	Everybody Loves Raymond......	11.2	17	35.	The Simple Life-Wednesday.....	7.3	11
12.	Without a Trace...............	11.1	18		Average Joe: Hawaii..........	7.1	11
13.	Law and Order...............	10.8	18	38.	The Guardian	7.1	11
14.	Will & Grace.................	10.4	16		JAG.......................	7.0	12
	Two and a Half Men...........	9.9	15		60 Minutes II	7.0	11
15.	My Big Fat Obnoxious Fiance	9.9	14	40.	Yes, Dear...................	7.0	11
17.	60 Minutes..................	9.4	16		Dateline NBC-Friday..........	6.9	12
18.	Cold Case	9.3	14		Average Joe: Adam Returns.....	6.9	11
19.	NFL Monday Showcase.........	9.1	14		Becker.....................	6.9	10
20.	Law and Order: SVU	8.7	14	43.	Scrubs.....................	6.9	10
	Crossing Jordan..............	8.6	14	47.	20/20-Friday	6.8	12
21.	Law and Order: Criminal Intent ...	8.6	13		Extreme Makeover-Wednesday ..	6.7	11
23.	The Bachelor................	8.5	13	48.	NYPD Blue..................	6.7	11
24.	Coupling....................	8.4	13		Joan of Arcadia..............	6.6	12
25.	Average Joe.................	8.2	13		Lyons Den	6.6	11
26.	Fox NFL Sunday-Post	8.0	14	50.	Simple Life	6.6	10

Favorite Syndicated Programs, 2003-2004

Source: Nielsen Media Research, Sept. 22, 2003- May 26, 2004

Average audience percentages, or ratings, are estimates of the percentage of TV-owning households watching a program.

Rank	Program	Avg. audience (%)	Rank	Program	Avg. audience (%)
1.	Wheel of Fortune...................	9.0	13.	ESPN NFL Regular Season 2	5.1
2.	Jeopardy	7.3	14.	Judge Judy......................	5.0
3.	ESPN NFL Regular Season	6.8	15.	Wheel of Fortune (weekend)	4.2
	Oprah Winfrey Show...............	6.8	16.	Warner Bros. Vol. 34	3.9
5.	Seinfeld (non-weekend)	6.1	17.	Live with Regis and Kelly	3.7
6.	Friends	6.0		That 70s Show	3.7
7.	MMN Home Team Baseball	5.9	19.	Inside Edition	3.6
8.	Entertainment Tonight..............	5.6		Millionaire	3.6
	Seinfeld (weekend)................	5.6	21.	Entertainment Tonight (weekend)	3.5
10.	Everybody Loves Raymond	5.5		Judge Joe Brown	3.5
11.	World Wrestling Entertainment	5.4		Warner Bros. Vol. 31	3.5
12.	Dr. Phil Show.....................	5.2		Will & Grace	3.5

All-Time Highest-Rated Television Programs

Source: Nielsen Media Research, Jan. 1961-Feb. 2004

Estimates exclude unsponsored or joint network telecasts (e.g., presidential addresses) or programs under 30 minutes long. Ranked by rating (percentage of TV-owning households tuned in to the program).

Rank	Program	Telecast date	Network	Rating (%)	Avg. households (in thousands)
1.	M*A*S*H (last episode)	2/28/83	CBS	60.2	50,150
2.	Dallas (Who Shot J.R.?)	11/21/80	CBS	53.3	41,470
3.	Roots-Pt. 8	1/30/77	ABC	51.1	36,380
4.	Super Bowl XVI	1/24/82	CBS	49.1	40,020
5.	Super Bowl XVII	1/30/83	NBC	48.6	40,480
6.	XVII Winter Olympics - 2nd Wed.	2/23/94	CBS	48.5	45,690
7.	Super Bowl XX	1/26/86	NBC	48.3	41,490
8.	Gone With the Wind-Pt. 1	11/7/76	NBC	47.7	33,960
9.	Gone With the Wind-Pt. 2	11/8/76	NBC	47.4	33,750
10.	Super Bowl XII	1/15/78	CBS	47.2	34,410
11.	Super Bowl XIII	1/21/79	NBC	47.1	35,090
12.	Bob Hope Christmas Show	1/15/70	NBC	46.6	27,260
13.	Super Bowl XIX	1/20/85	ABC	46.4	39,390
	Super Bowl XVIII	1/22/84	CBS	46.4	38,800
15.	Super Bowl XIV	1/20/80	CBS	46.3	35,330
16.	Super Bowl XXX	1/28/96	NBC	46.0	44,150
	ABC Theater (The Day After)	11/20/83	ABC	46.0	38,550
18.	Roots-Pt. 6	1/28/77	ABC	45.9	32,680
	The Fugitive	8/29/67	ABC	45.9	25,700
20.	Super Bowl XXI	1/25/87	CBS	45.8	40,030
21.	Roots-Pt. 5	1/27/77	ABC	45.7	32,540
22.	Super Bowl XXVIII	1/30/94	NBC	45.5	42,860
	Cheers (last episode)	5/20/93	NBC	45.5	42,360
24.	Ed Sullivan	2/9/64	CBS	45.3	23,240
25.	Super Bowl XXVII	1/31/93	NBC	45.1	41,990
26.	Bob Hope Christmas Show	1/14/71	NBC	45.0	27,050
27.	Roots-Pt. 3	1/25/77	ABC	44.8	31,900
28.	Super Bowl XXXII	1/25/98	NBC	44.5	43,630
29.	Super Bowl XV	1/25/81	NBC	44.4	34,540
	Super Bowl XI	1/9/77	NBC	44.4	31,610
31.	Super Bowl VI	1/16/72	CBS	44.2	27,450
32.	XVII Winter Olympics - 2nd Fri.	2/25/94	CBS	44.1	41,540
	Roots-Pt. 2	1/24/77	ABC	44.1	31,400
34.	Beverly Hillbillies	1/8/64	CBS	44.0	22,570
35.	Roots-Pt. 4	1/26/77	ABC	43.8	31,190
	Ed Sullivan	2/16/64	CBS	43.8	22,445
37.	Super Bowl XXIII	1/22/89	NBC	43.5	39,320
38.	Academy Awards	4/7/70	ABC	43.4	25,390
39.	Super Bowl XXXI	1/26/97	FOX	43.3	42,000
	Super Bowl XXXIV	1/30/00	ABC	43.3	43,620
41.	Thorn Birds-Pt. 3	3/29/83	ABC	43.2	35,990
42.	Thorn Birds-Pt. 4	3/30/83	ABC	43.1	35,900
43.	CBS NFC Championship	1/10/82	CBS	42.9	34,960
44.	Beverly Hillbillies	1/15/64	CBS	42.8	21,960
45.	Super Bowl VII	1/14/73	NBC	42.7	27,670

Highest-Rated TV Shows of Each Season, 1950-51 to 2003-2004

Source: Nielsen Media Research; regular series programs, Sept.-May season

Season	Program	Rating[1]	TV-owning households (in thousands)	Season	Program	Rating[1]	TV-owning households (in thousands)
1950-51	Texaco Star Theatre	61.6	10,320	1978-79	Laverne & Shirley	30.5	74,500
1951-52	Godfrey's Talent Scouts	53.8	15,300	1979-80	60 Minutes	28.2	76,300
1952-53	I Love Lucy	67.3	20,400	1980-81	Dallas	31.2	79,900
1953-54	I Love Lucy	58.8	26,000	1981-82	Dallas	28.4	81,500
1954-55	I Love Lucy	49.3	30,700	1982-83	60 Minutes	25.5	83,300
1955-56	$64,000 Question	47.5	34,900	1983-84	Dallas	25.7	83,800
1956-57	I Love Lucy	43.7	38,900	1984-85	Dynasty	25.0	84,900
1957-58	Gunsmoke	43.1	41,920	1985-86	Cosby Show	33.8	85,900
1958-59	Gunsmoke	39.6	43,950	1986-87	Cosby Show	34.9	87,400
1959-60	Gunsmoke	40.3	45,750	1987-88	Cosby Show	27.8	88,600
1960-61	Gunsmoke	37.3	47,200	1988-89	Roseanne	25.5	90,440
1961-62	Wagon Train	32.1	48,555	1989-90	Roseanne	23.4	92,100
1962-63	Beverly Hillbillies	36.0	50,300	1990-91	Cheers	21.6	93,100
1963-64	Beverly Hillbillies	39.1	51,600	1991-92	60 Minutes	21.7	92,100
1964-65	Bonanza	36.3	52,700	1992-93	60 Minutes	21.6	93,100
1965-66	Bonanza	31.8	53,850	1993-94	Home Improvement	21.9	94,200
1966-67	Bonanza	29.1	55,130	1994-95	Seinfeld	20.5	95,400
1967-68	Andy Griffith	27.6	56,670	1995-96	E.R.	22.0	95,900
1968-69	Rowan & Martin's Laugh-In	31.8	58,250	1996-97	E.R.	21.2	97,000
1969-70	Rowan & Martin's Laugh-In	26.3	58,500	1997-98	Seinfeld	22.0	98,000
1970-71	Marcus Welby, MD	29.6	60,100	1998-99	E.R.	17.8	99,400
1971-72	All in the Family	34.0	62,100	1999-2000	Who Wants to Be a Millionaire	18.6	100,800
1972-73	All in the Family	33.3	64,800	2000-01	Survivor II	17.4	102,200
1973-74	All in the Family	31.2	66,200	2001-02	Friends	15.3	105,500
1974-75	All in the Family	30.2	68,500	2002-03	CSI	16.1	106,700
1975-76	All in the Family	30.1	69,600	2003-04	CSI	15.9	108,400
1976-77	Happy Days	31.5	71,200				
1977-78	Laverne & Shirley	31.6	72,900				

(1) Rating is percent of TV-owning households tuned in to the program. Data prior to 1988-89 exclude Alaska and Hawaii.

WORLD ALMANAC EDITORS' PICKS
Favorite Sitcoms

The World Almanac staff ranked the following as favorite sitcoms of all time: (Animated comedies were not included.)

1.	Seinfeld	6.	M*A*S*H
2.	I Love Lucy	7.	The Honeymooners
3.	Cheers	8.	The Cosby Show
4.	All in the Family	9.	Frasier
5.	The Mary Tyler Moore Show	10.	The Odd Couple

100 Leading U.S. Advertisers, 2003

Source: Reprinted with permission from Ad Age (http://www.adage.com). © 2004, Crain Communications Inc.

(in millions of dollars)

Rank Advertiser	Ad spending	Rank Advertiser	Ad spending	Rank Advertiser	Ad spending
1. General Motors Corp.	3,430	35. General Mills.	956	67. Gap Inc.	486
2. Procter & Gamble Co.	3,323	36. Estee Lauder Cos.	906	68. AT&T Corp.	479
3. Time Warner	3,097	37. Hewlett-Packard Co.	899	69. Coca-Cola Co.	473
4. Pfizer	2,839	38. IBM Corp.	862	70. Albertson's	467
5. DaimlerChrysler	2,318	39. Best Buy Co.	838	71. Visa International	462
6. Ford Motor Co.	2,234	40. Wyeth	821	72. InterActiveCorp	461
7. Walt Disney Co.	2,129	41. Mars Inc.	813	73. Aventis	459
8. Johnson & Johnson	1,996	42. Bristol-Myers Squibb Co.	778	74. Kohl's Corp.	452
9. Sony Corp.	1,815	43. Anheuser-Busch Cos.	776	75. MasterCard International	440
10. Toyota Motor Corp.	1,683	44. Cendant Corp.	773	76. Bayer	435
11. Verizon Communications	1,674	45. ConAgra Foods	765	77. SABMiller	433
12. Sears, Roebuck & Co.	1,634	46. Yum Brands	761	78. Berkshire Hathaway	431
13. General Electric Co.	1,576	47. Diageo	748	79. Nextel Communications	424
14. GlaxoSmithKline	1,554	48. Federated Department Stores	707	80. Citigroup.	420
15. SBC Communications	1,511	49. Wal-Mart Stores	678	81. Kmart Corp.	413
16. McDonald's Corp.	1,368	50. American Express Co.	673	82. Campbell Soup Co.	412
17. Unilever	1,332	51. May Department Stores Co.	630	83. Doctor's Associates	408
18. Altria Group	1,311	52. Gillette Co.	612	84. AstraZeneca.	404
19. Nissan Motor Co.	1,301	53. Kroger Co.	612	85. Limited Brands	397
20. Merck & Co.	1,264	54. Schering-Plough Corp.	609	86. Intel Corp.	394
21. Viacom	1,249	55. Volkswagen	608	87. Reckitt Benckiser	393
22. L'Oreal	1,239	56. Sara Lee Corp.	583	88. Wendy's International	386
23. PepsiCo	1,212	57. Kellogg Co.	570	89. Mitsubishi Motors Corp.	382
24. Home Depot	1,150	58. Dell	565	90. BellSouth Corp.	376
25. Microsoft Corp.	1,147	59. Nike	559	91. Kimberly-Clark Corp.	348
26. Honda Motor Co.	1,144	60. Clorox Co.	553	92. Kia Motors Corp.	347
27. Nestle	1,113	61. Safeway	533	93. Cadbury Schweppes	341
28. U.S. Government	1,102	62. Burger King Corp.	525	94. Adolph Coors Co.	340
29. Target Corp.	1,083	63. Deutsche Telekom	518	United Parcel Service	340
30. Sprint Corp.	1,069	64. MCI	517	96. Hyundai Motor Co.	333
31. AT&T Wireless	1,035	65. Lowe's Cos.	504	97. Colgate-Palmolive Co.	332
32. News Corp.	1,032	66. Mattel	488	98. Philips Electronics	319
33. J.C. Penney Co.	1,025			99. SC Johnson	318
34. Novartis	967			100. Canon	317

U.S. Ad Spending by Top Categories, 2003

Source: Reprinted with permission from Ad Age (http://www.adage.com). © 2004, Crain Communications Inc.

(in millions of dollars)

Category	Total	Mag.	Bus. Pub.	News-paper	Out-door	Televison Net-work	Spot	Syndi-cated	Spanish Lang.	Cable	Radio	Inter-net
Automotive	18,393	2,118	78	6,271	339	2,713	4,819	129	218	1,058	434	216
Retail	16,205	1,235	129	6,685	291	1,951	2,684	237	256	873	750	1,115
Movies, media, advertising	8,319	1,196	343	2,301	231	1,299	728	157	67	589	353	1,055
Medicines & proprietary remedies	6,863	1,820	62	200	13	2,321	397	535	131	953	215	218
Food, beverages and confectionery	6,403	1,438	113	40	50	2,014	706	423	223	1,158	172	67
Financial services	6,236	735	183	1,482	193	1,008	496	190	32	802	200	916
Home furnishings, supplies, appliances	5,927	1,675	503	181	14	1,313	429	299	259	1,065	126	63
Telecommunications	5,592	255	103	1,924	107	1,030	669	132	175	530	372	296
Personal care	5,046	1,727	46	47	9	1,637	186	451	142	713	46	41
Airlines, hotels, car rental	4,691	789	294	1,607	264	294	446	49	31	463	119	334
Direct response companies	4,489	1,545	170	380	3	171	209	165	461	1,256	41	89
Restaurants and fast food	4,131	105	1	149	206	1,414	1,328	174	119	471	150	15
Computers, software, Internet	3,986	745	919	378	26	565	181	32	18	391	87	644
Insurance and real estate	3,279	292	66	1,200	196	365	443	91	33	316	119	158
Apparel	2,300	1,559	89	26	20	254	31	36	12	195	16	64
Government, politics and organizations	1,908	249	33	376	99	234	385	41	121	143	104	125
Beer, wine & liquor	1,810	437	16	56	156	522	146	38	67	239	64	69
Business & manufacturing equipment	1,740	266	810	145	21	227	37	12	0	94	55	74
Public Service Announcements	1,727	0	0	0	0	850	451	0	328	99	0	0
Sporting goods, toys and games	1,514	351	103	24	6	369	31	59	5	481	11	74
Pets, pet foods and supplies	461	103	1	3	1	168	33	40	0	97	2	14
Cigarettes, tobacco	377	290	6	9	1	26	17	10	3	13	3	1
Gas & oil	261	49	10	8	4	47	31	8	4	58	39	4
Miscellaneous	8,818	1,015	1,090	2,271	427	434	1,963	90	23	640	159	707
Total	120,476	19,994	5,165	25,763	2,674	21,224	16,843	3,396	2,727	12,696	3,636	6,358

AWARDS — MEDALS — PRIZES
The Alfred B. Nobel Prize Winners, 1901-2003

Alfred B. Nobel (1833-96) bequeathed $9 mil, the interest on which was to be distributed yearly to those judged to have most benefited humankind in physics, chemistry, medicine-physiology, literature, and promotion of peace. Prizes were first awarded in 1901. The 1st prize in economics was awarded in 1969, funded by Sweden's central bank. Each prize is now worth about 10 mil. Swedish kroner (about $1.35 mil). If year is omitted, no award was given. To find the 2004 winners, see Table of Contents.

Physics

2003 Vitaly L. Ginzburg, Alexei A. Abrikosov, Russ., Anthony J. Leggett, Br.
2002 Raymond Davis Jr., Riccardo Giacconi, U.S.; Masatoshi Koshiba, Jpn.
2001 Eric A. Cornell, Carl E. Wieman, U.S.; Wolfgang Ketterle, Ger.
2000 Jack S. Kilby, U.S.; Zhores I. Alferov, Russ.
1999 Gerardus 't Hooft and Martinus J. G. Veltman, Netherlands
1998 Robert B. Laughlin, Horst L. Störmer, Daniel C. Tsui, U.S.
1997 Steven Chu, William D. Phillips, U.S.; Claude Cohen-Tannoudji, Fr.
1996 David M. Lee, Douglas D. Osheroff, Robert C. Richardson, U.S.
1995 Martin Perl, Frederick Reines, U.S.
1994 Bertram N. Brockhouse, Can.; Clifford G. Shull, U.S.
1993 Joseph H. Taylor, Russell A. Hulse, U.S.
1992 Georges Charpak, Pol.-Fr.
1991 Pierre-Giles de Gennes, Fr.
1990 Richard E. Taylor, Can.; Jerome I. Friedman, Henry W. Kendall, U.S.
1989 Norman F. Ramsey, U.S.; Hans G. Dehmelt, Ger.-U.S.; Wolfgang Paul, Ger.
1988 Leon M. Lederman, Melvin Schwartz, Jack Steinberger, U.S.
1987 K. Alex Müller, Swiss; J. Georg Bednorz, Ger.
1986 Ernest Ruska, Ger.; Gerd Binnig, Ger.; Heinrich Rohrer, Swiss
1985 Klaus von Klitzing, Ger.
1984 Carlo Rubbia, It.; Simon van der Meer, Dutch
1983 Subrahmanyan Chandrasekhar, William A. Fowler, U.S.
1982 Kenneth G. Wilson, U.S.
1981 Nicolaas Bloembergen, Arthur Schaalow, U.S.; Kai M. Siegbahn, Swed.
1980 James W. Cronin, Val L. Fitch, U.S.
1979 Steven Weinberg, Sheldon L. Glashow, U.S.; Abdus Salam, Pakistani

1978 Pyotr Kapitsa, USSR; Arno Penzias, Robert Wilson, U.S.
1977 John H. Van Vleck, Philip W. Anderson, U.S.; Nevill F. Mott, Br.
1976 Burton Richter, Samuel C.C. Ting, U.S.
1975 James Rainwater, U.S.; Ben Mottelson, U.S.-Dan.; Aage Bohr, Dan.
1974 Martin Ryle, Antony Hewish, Br.
1973 Ivar Giaever, U.S.; Leo Esaki, Jpn.; Brian D. Josephson, Br.
1972 John Bardeen, Leon N. Cooper, John R. Schrieffer, U.S.
1971 Dennis Gabor, Br.
1970 Louis Neel, Fr.; Hannes Alfven, Swed.
1969 Murray Gell-Mann, U.S.
1968 Luis W. Alvarez, U.S.
1967 Hans A. Bethe, U.S.
1966 Alfred Kastler, Fr.
1965 Richard P. Feynman, Julian S. Schwinger, U.S.; Shinichiro Tomonaga, Jpn.
1964 Nikolai G. Basov, Aleksander M. Prochorov, USSR; Charles H. Townes, U.S.
1963 Maria Goeppert-Mayer, Eugene P. Wigner, U.S.; J. Hans D. Jensen, Ger.
1962 Lev. D. Landau, USSR
1961 Robert Hofstadter, U.S.; Rudolf L. Mossbauer, Ger.
1960 Donald A. Glaser, U.S.
1959 Owen Chamberlain, Emilio G. Segre, U.S.
1958 Pavel Cherenkov, Ilya Frank, Igor Y. Tamm, USSR
1957 Tsung-dao Lee, Chen Ning Yang, U.S.
1956 John Bardeen, Walter H. Brattain, William Shockley, U.S.
1955 Polykarp Kusch, Willis E. Lamb, U.S.
1954 Max Born, Br.; Walter Bothe, Ger.
1953 Frits Zernike, Dutch
1952 Felix Bloch, Edward M. Purcell, U.S.
1951 Sir John D. Cockcroft, Br.; Ernest T. S. Walton, Ir.
1950 Cecil F. Powell, Br.
1949 Hideki Yukawa, Jpn.
1948 Patrick M. S. Blackett, Br.
1947 Sir Edward V. Appleton, Br.

1946 Percy W. Bridgman, U.S.
1945 Wolfgang Pauli, U.S.
1944 Isidor Isaac Rabi, U.S.
1943 Otto Stern, U.S.
1939 Ernest O. Lawrence, U.S.
1938 Enrico Fermi, It.-U.S.
1937 Clinton J. Davisson, U.S.; Sir George P. Thomson, Br.
1936 Carl D. Anderson, U.S.; Victor F. Hess, Aus.
1935 Sir James Chadwick, Br.
1933 Paul A. M. Dirac, Br.; Erwin Schrodinger, Austria
1932 Werner Heisenberg, Ger.
1930 Sir Chandrasekhara V. Raman, Indian
1929 Prince Louis-Victor de Broglie, Fr.
1928 Owen W. Richardson, Br.
1927 Arthur H. Compton, U.S.; Charles T. R. Wilson, Br.
1926 Jean B. Perrin, Fr.
1925 James Franck, Gustav Hertz, Ger.
1924 Karl M. G. Siegbahn, Swed.
1923 Robert A. Millikan, U.S.
1922 Niels Bohr, Dan.
1921 Albert Einstein, Ger.-U.S.
1920 Charles E. Guillaume, Fr.
1919 Johannes Stark, Ger.
1918 Max K. E. L. Planck, Ger.
1917 Charles G. Barkla, Br.
1915 Sir William H. Bragg, Sir William L. Bragg, Br.
1914 Max von Laue, Ger.
1913 Heike Kamerlingh-Onnes, Dutch
1912 Nils G. Dalen, Swed.
1911 Wilhelm Wien, Ger.
1910 Johannes D. van der Waals, Dutch
1909 Carl F. Braun, Ger.; Guglielmo Marconi, It.
1908 Gabriel Lippmann, Fr.
1907 Albert A. Michelson, U.S.
1906 Sir Joseph J. Thomson, Br.
1905 Philipp E. A. von Lenard, Ger.
1904 John W. Strutt, Lord Rayleigh, Br.
1903 Antoine Henri Becquerel, Pierre Curie, Fr.; Marie Curie, Pol.-Fr.
1902 Hendrik A. Lorentz, Pieter Zeeman, Dutch
1901 Wilhelm C. Roentgen, Ger.

Chemistry

2003 Peter Agre, Roderick MacKinnon, U.S.
2002 John B. Fenn, U.S.; Koichi Tanaka, Japan; Kurt Wüthrich, Switzerland
2001 K. Barry Sharpless, U.S.; William S. Knowles, U.S., Ryoji Noyori, Japan
2000 Alan J. Heeger, U.S.; Alan G. MacDiarmid, NZ-U.S.; Hideki Shirakawa, Japan
1999 Ahmed H. Zewail, U.S.
1998 Walter Kohn, U.S.; John A. Pople, Br.
1997 Paul D. Boyer, U.S., & John E. Walker, Br.; Jens C. Skou, Dan.
1996 Harold W. Kroto, Br.; Robert F. Curl Jr., Richard E. Smalley, U.S.
1995 Paul Crutzen, Dutch; Mario Molina, Mex.-U.S.; Sherwood Rowland, U.S.
1994 George A. Olah, U.S.
1993 Kary B. Mullis, U.S.; Michael Smith, Br.-Can.
1992 Rudolph A. Marcus, Can.-U.S.
1991 Richard R. Ernst, Swiss
1990 Elias James Corey, U.S.
1989 Thomas R. Cech, Sidney Altman, U.S.
1988 Johann Deisenhofer, Robert Huber, Hartmut Michel, Ger.
1987 Donald J. Cram, Charles J. Pedersen, U.S.; Jean-Marie Lehn, Fr.
1986 Dudley Herschbach, Yuan T. Lee, U.S.; John C. Polanyi, Can.
1985 Herbert A. Hauptman, Jerome Karle, U.S.

1984 Bruce Merrifield, U.S.
1983 Henry Taube, Can.
1982 Aaron Klug, S. Afr.
1981 Kenichi Fukui, Jpn.; Roald Hoffmann, U.S.
1980 Paul Berg, Walter Gilbert, U.S.; Frederick Sanger, Br.
1979 Herbert C. Brown, U.S.; George Wittig, Ger.
1978 Peter Mitchell, Br.
1977 Ilya Prigogine, Belg.
1976 William N. Lipscomb, U.S.
1975 John Cornforth, Austral.-Br.; Vladimir Prelog, Yugo.-Swiss
1974 Paul J. Flory, U.S.
1973 Ernst Otto Fischer, Ger.; Geoffrey Wilkinson, Br.
1972 Christian B. Anfinsen, Stanford Moore, LWilliam H. Stein, U.S.
1971 Gerhard Herzberg, Canadian
1970 Luis F. Leloir, Arg.
1969 Derek H. R. Barton, Br.; Odd Hassel, Nor.
1968 Lars Onsager, U.S.
1967 Manfred Eigen, Ger.; Ronald G. W. Norrish, George Porter, Br.
1966 Robert S. Mulliken, U.S.
1965 Robert B. Woodward, U.S.
1964 Dorothy C. Hodgkin, Br.
1963 Giulio Natta, It.; Karl Ziegler, Ger.
1962 John C. Kendrew, Max F. Perutz, Br.

1961 Melvin Calvin, U.S.
1960 Willard F. Libby, U.S.
1959 Jaroslav Heyrovsky, Czech.
1958 Frederick Sanger, Br.
1957 Sir Alexander R. Todd, Br.
1956 Sir Cyril N. Hinshelwood, Br.; Nikolai N. Semenov, USSR
1955 Vincent du Vigneaud, U.S.
1954 Linus C. Pauling, U.S.
1953 Hermann Staudinger, Ger.
1952 Archer J. P. Martin, Richard L. M. Synge, Br.
1951 Edwin M. McMillan, Glenn T. Seaborg, U.S.
1950 Kurt Alder, Otto P. H. Diels, Ger.
1949 William F. Giauque, U.S.
1948 Arne W. K. Tiselius, Swed.
1947 Sir Robert Robinson, Br.
1946 James B. Sumner, John H. Northrop, Wendell M. Stanley, U.S.
1945 Artturi I. Virtanen, Fin.
1944 Otto Hahn, Ger.
1943 Georg de Hevesy, Hung.
1939 Adolf F. J. Butenandt, Ger.; Leopold Ruzicka, Swiss
1938 Richard Kuhn, Ger.
1937 Walter N. Haworth, Br.; Paul Karrer, Swiss
1936 Peter J. W. Debye, Dutch
1935 Frederic & Irene Joliot-Curie, Fr.
1934 Harold C. Urey, U.S.

1932 Irving Langmuir, U.S.
1931 Friedrich Bergius, Karl Bosch, Ger.
1930 Hans Fischer, Ger.
1929 Sir Arthur Harden, Br.;
Hans von Euler-Chelpin, Swed.
1928 Adolf O. R. Windaus, Ger.
1927 Heinrich O. Wieland, Ger.
1926 Theodor Svedberg, Swed.
1925 Richard A. Zsigmondy, Ger.
1923 Fritz Pregl, Austrian

1922 Francis W. Aston, Br.
1921 Frederick Soddy, Br.
1920 Walther H. Nernst, Ger.
1918 Fritz Haber, Ger.
1915 Richard M. Willstatter, Ger.
1914 Theodore W. Richards, U.S.
1913 Alfred Werner, Swiss
1912 Victor Grignard, Paul Sabatier, Fr.
1911 Marie Curie, Pol.-Fr.
1910 Otto Wallach, Ger.

1909 Wilhelm Ostwald, Ger.
1908 Ernest Rutherford, Br.
1907 Eduard Buchner, Ger.
1906 Henri Moissan, Fr.
1905 Adolf von Baeyer, Ger.
1904 Sir William Ramsay, Br.
1903 Svante A. Arrhenius, Swed.
1902 Emil Fischer, Ger.
1901 Jacobus H. van't Hoff, Dutch

Physiology or Medicine

2003 Paul C. Lauterbur, U.S.; Sir Peter
Mansfield, Br.
2002 Sydney Brenner, John E. Sulston,
Br.; H. Robert Horvitz, U.S.
2001 Leland H. Hartwell, U.S.; R. Timothy
(Tim) Hunt, Sir Paul M. Nurse, Br.
2000 Arvid Carlsson, Swed.; Paul Greengard,
U.S.; Eric R. Kandel, Aus-U.S.
1999 Günter Blobel, U.S.
1998 Robert F. Furchgott, Louis J.
Ignarro, Ferid Murad, U.S.
1997 Stanley B. Prusiner, U.S.
1996 Peter C. Doherty, Austral.;
Rolf M. Zinkernagel, Swiss
1995 Edward B. Lewis,
Eric F. Wieschaus, U.S.;
Christiane Nuesslein-Volhard, Ger.
1994 Alfred G. Gilman, Martin Rodbell, U.S.
1993 Phillip A. Sharp, U.S.;
Richard J. Roberts, Br.
1992 Edmond H. Fisher, Edwin G. Krebs,
U.S.
1991 Edwin Neher, Bert Sakmann, Ger.
1990 Joseph E. Murray,
E. Donnall Thomas, U.S.
1989 J. Michael Bishop,
Harold E. Varmus, U.S.
1988 Gertrude B. Elion, George H.
Hitchings, U.S; Sir James Black, Br.
1987 Susumu Tonegawa, Jpn.
1986 Rita Levi-Montalcini, It.-U.S.,
Stanley Cohen, U.S.
1985 Michael S. Brown,
Joseph L. Goldstein, U.S.
1984 Cesar Milstein, Br.-Arg.;
Georges J. F. Koehler, Ger.;
Niels K. Jerne, Br.-Dan.
1983 Barbara McClintock, U.S.
1982 Sune Bergstrom, Bengt Samuelsson,
Swed.; John R. Vane, Br.
1981 Roger W. Sperry, David H. Hubel,
Torsten N. Wiesel, U.S.
1980 Baruj Benacerraf, George
Snell, U.S.; Jean Dausset, Fr.
1979 Allan M. Cormack, U.S.;
Godfrey N. Hounsfield, Br.
1978 Daniel Nathans, Hamilton O.
Smith, U.S.; Werner Arber, Swiss
1977 Rosalyn S. Yalow, Roger C.L.
Guillemin, Andrew V. Schally, U.S.

1976 Baruch S. Blumberg,
Daniel Carleton Gajdusek, U.S.
1975 David Baltimore, Howard Temin,
U.S.; Renato Dulbecco, It.-U.S.
1974 Albert Claude, Lux.-U.S.;
George Emil Palade, Rom.-U.S.;
Christian Rene de Duve, Belg.
1973 Karl von Frisch, Ger.; Konrad Lorenz,
Ger.-Aus.; Nikolaas Tinbergen, Br.
1972 Gerald M. Edelman, U.S.;
Rodney R. Porter, Br.
1971 Earl W. Sutherland Jr., U.S.
1970 Julius Axelrod, U.S.; Sir Bernard
Katz, Br.; Ulf von Euler, Swed.
1969 Max Delbrück, Alfred D. Hershey,
Salvador Luria, U.S.
1968 Robert W. Holley, H. Gobind Khorana,
Marshall W. Nirenberg, U.S.
1967 Ragnar Granit, Swed.; Haldan
Keffer Hartline, George Wald, U.S.
1966 Charles B. Huggins,
Francis Peyton Rous, U.S.
1965 François Jacob, Andre Lwoff,
Jacques Monod, Fr.
1964 Konrad E. Bloch, U.S.;
Feodor Lynen, Ger.
1963 Sir John C. Eccles, Austral.; Alan
L. Hodgkin, Andrew F. Huxley, Br.
1962 Francis H. C. Crick, Maurice H. F.
Wilkins, Br.; James D. Watson, U.S.
1961 Georg von Bekesy, U.S.
1960 Sir F. MacFarlane Burnet, Austral.;
Peter B. Medawar, Br.
1959 Arthur Kornberg, Severo Ochoa, U.S.
1958 George W. Beadle, Edward L.
Tatum, Joshua Lederberg, U.S.
1957 Daniel Bovet, It.
1956 Andre F. Cournand,
Dickinson W. Richards Jr., U.S.;
Werner Forssmann, Ger.
1955 Alex H. T. Theorell, Swed.
1954 John F. Enders, Frederick C.
Robbins, Thomas H. Weller, U.S.
1953 Hans A. Krebs, Br.;
Fritz A. Lipmann, U.S.
1952 Selman A. Waksman, U.S.
1951 Max Theiler, U.S.
1950 Philip S. Hench, Edward C. Kendall,
U.S.; Tadeus Reichstein, Swiss
1949 Walter R. Hess, Swiss;
Antonio Moniz, Port.

1948 Paul H. Müller, Swiss
1947 Carl F. Cori, Gerty T. Cori, U.S.;
Bernardo A. Houssay, Arg.
1946 Hermann J. Muller, U.S.
1945 Ernst B. Chain, Sir Alexander
Fleming, Sir Howard W. Florey, Br.
1944 Joseph Erlanger, Herbert S. Gasser,
U.S.
1943 Henrik C. P. Dam, Dan.;
Edward A. Doisy, U.S.
1939 Gerhard Domagk, Ger.
1938 Corneille J. F. Heymans, Belg.
1937 Albert Szent-Gyorgyi, Hung.-U.S.
1936 Sir Henry H. Dale, Br.;
Otto Loewi, U.S.
1935 Hans Spemann, Ger.
1934 George R. Minot, William P.
Murphy, G. H. Whipple, U.S.
1933 Thomas H. Morgan, U.S.
1932 Edgar D. Adrian,
Sir Charles S. Sherrington, Br.
1931 Otto H. Warburg, Ger.
1930 Karl Landsteiner, U.S.
1929 Christiaan Eijkman, Dutch;
Sir Frederick G. Hopkins, Br.
1928 Charles J. H. Nicolle, Fr.
1927 Julius Wagner-Jauregg, Austrian
1926 Johannes A. G. Fibiger, Dan.
1924 Willem Einthoven, Dutch
1923 Frederick G. Banting, Can.;
John J. R. Macleod, Scot.
1922 Archibald V. Hill, Br.;
Otto F. Meyerhof, Ger.
1920 Schack A. S. Krogh, Dan.
1919 Jules Bordet, Belg.
1914 Robert Barany, Aus.
1913 Charles R. Richet, Fr.
1912 Alexis Carrel, Fr.
1911 Allvar Gullstrand, Swed.
1910 Albrecht Kossel, Ger.
1909 Emil T. Kocher, Swiss
1908 Paul Ehrlich, Ger.; Elie Metchnikoff, Fr.
1907 Charles L. A. Laveran, Fr.
1906 Camillo Golgi, It.; Santiago
Ramon y Cajal, Span.
1905 Robert Koch, Ger.
1904 Ivan P. Pavlov, Russ.
1903 Niels R. Finsen, Dan.
1902 Sir Ronald Ross, Br.
1901 Emil A. von Behring, Ger.

Literature

2003 J.M. Coetzee, S. Afr.
2002 Imre Kertész, Hung.
2001 Sir V.S. Naipaul, Br.
2000 Gao Xingjian, Chin.
1999 Günter Grass, Ger.
1998 Jose Saramago, Por.
1997 Dario Fo, It.
1996 Wislawa Szymborska, Pol.
1995 Seamus Heaney, Ir.
1994 Kenzaburo Oe, Jpn.
1993 Toni Morrison, U.S.
1992 Derek Walcott, W. Ind.
1991 Nadine Gordimer, S. Afr.
1990 Octavio Paz, Mex.
1989 Camilo José Cela, Span.
1988 Naguib Mahfouz, Egy.
1987 Joseph Brodsky, USSR-U.S.
1986 Wole Soyinka, Nig.
1985 Claude Simon, Fr.
1984 Jaroslav Siefert, Czech.
1983 William Golding, Br.
1982 Gabriel Garcia Marquez,
Colombian-Mex.
1981 Elias Canetti, Bulg.-Br.
1980 Czeslaw Milosz, Pol.-U.S.

1979 Odysseus Elytis, Gk.
1978 Isaac Bashevis Singer, U.S.
1977 Vicente Aleixandre, Span.
1976 Saul Bellow, U.S.
1975 Eugenio Montale, It.
1974 Eyvind Johnson, Harry Edmund
Martinson, Swed.
1973 Patrick White, Austral.
1972 Heinrich Böll, Ger.
1971 Pablo Neruda, Chil.
1970 Aleksandr I. Solzhenitsyn, USSR
1969 Samuel Beckett, Ir.
1968 Yasunari Kawabata, Jpn.
1967 Miguel Angel Asturias, Guat.
1966 Samuel Joseph Agnon, Isr.;
Nelly Sachs, Swed.
1965 Mikhail Sholokhov, USSR
1964 Jean Paul Sartre, Fr. (declined)
1963 Giorgos Seferis, Gk.
1962 John Steinbeck, U.S.
1961 Ivo Andric, Yugo.
1960 Saint-John Perse, Fr.
1959 Salvatore Quasimodo, It.
1958 Boris L. Pasternak, USSR (declined)
1957 Albert Camus, Fr.

1956 Juan Ramon Jimenez, Span.
1955 Halldor K. Laxness, Ice.
1954 Ernest Hemingway, U.S.
1953 Sir Winston Churchill, Br.
1952 Francois Mauriac, Fr.
1951 Par F. Lagerkvist, Swed.
1950 Bertrand Russell, Br.
1949 William Faulkner, U.S.
1948 T.S. Eliot, Br.
1947 Andre Gide, Fr.
1946 Hermann Hesse, Ger.-Swiss
1945 Gabriela Mistral, Chil.
1944 Johannes V. Jensen, Dan.
1939 Frans E. Sillanpaa, Fin.
1938 Pearl S. Buck, U.S.
1937 Roger Martin du Gard, Fr.
1936 Eugene O'Neill, U.S.
1934 Luigi Pirandello, It.
1933 Ivan A. Bunin, USSR
1932 John Galsworthy, Br.
1931 Erik A. Karlfeldt, Swed.
1930 Sinclair Lewis, U.S.
1929 Thomas Mann, Ger.
1928 Sigrid Undset, Nor.
1927 Henri Bergson, Fr.

1926 Grazia Deledda, It.
1925 George Bernard Shaw, Ir.-Br.
1924 Wladyslaw S. Reymont, Pol.
1923 William Butler Yeats, Ir.
1922 Jacinto Benavente, Span.
1921 Anatole France, Fr.
1920 Knut Hamsun, Nor.
1919 Carl F. G. Spitteler, Swiss

1917 Karl A. Gjellerup,
       Henrik Pontoppidan, Dan.
1916 Verner von Heidenstam, Swed.
1915 Romain Rolland, Fr.
1913 Rabindranath Tagore, Indian
1912 Gerhart Hauptmann, Ger.
1911 Maurice Maeterlinck, Belg.
1910 Paul J. L. Heyse, Ger.
1909 Selma Lagerlof, Swed.

1908 Rudolf C. Eucken, Ger.
1907 Rudyard Kipling, Br.
1906 Giosue Carducci, It.
1905 Henryk Sienkiewicz, Pol.
1904 Frederic Mistral, Fr.;
       Jose Echegaray, Span.
1903 Bjornsterne Bjornson, Nor.
1902 Theodor Mommsen, Ger.
1901 Rene F. A. Sully Prudhomme, Fr.

Peace

2003 Shirin Ebadi, Iran
2002 Jimmy Carter, U.S.
2001 UN; Kofi Annan, Ghana
2000 Kim Dae Jung, S. Kor.
1999 Doctors Without Borders
       (Médecins Sans Frontières), Fr.
1998 John Hume, David Trimble, N. Ir.
1997 Jody Williams, U.S.; International
       Campaign to Ban Landmines
1996 Bishop Carlos Ximenes Belo,
       José Ramos-Horta, Timorese
1995 Joseph Rotblat, Pol.-Br.;
       Pugwash Conference
1994 Yasir Arafat, Pal.; Shimon Peres,
       Yitzhak Rabin, Isr.
1993 Frederik W. de Klerk,
       Nelson Mandela, S. Afr.
1992 Rigoberta Menchú, Guat.
1991 Aung San Suu Kyi, Myanmarese
1990 Mikhail S. Gorbachev, USSR
1989 Dalai Lama, Tibet
1988 UN Peacekeeping Forces
1987 Oscar Arias Sanchez, Costa Rican
1986 Elie Wiesel, Rom.-U.S.
1985 Intl. Physicians for the Prevention
       of Nuclear War, U.S.
1984 Bishop Desmond Tutu, S. Afr.
1983 Lech Walesa, Pol.
1982 Alva Myrdal, Swed.; Alfonso
       Garcia Robles, Mex.
1981 Office of UN High Com. for Refugees
1980 Adolfo Perez Esquivel, Arg.
1979 Mother Teresa of Calcutta, Alb.-Ind.
1978 Anwar Sadat, Egy.;
       Menachem Begin, Isr.
1977 Amnesty International
1976 Mairead Corrigan,
       Betty Williams, N. Ir.

1975 Andrei Sakharov, USSR
1974 Eisaku Sato, Jpn.; Sean MacBride, Ir.
1973 Henry Kissinger, U.S.;
       Le Duc Tho, N. Viet. (Tho declined)
1971 Willy Brandt, Ger.
1970 Norman E. Borlaug, U.S.
1969 Intl. Labor Organization
1968 Rene Cassin, Fr.
1965 UN Children's Fund (UNICEF)
1964 Martin Luther King Jr., U.S.
1963 International Red Cross,
       League of Red Cross Societies
1962 Linus C. Pauling, U.S.
1961 Dag Hammarskjold, Swed.
1960 Albert J. Luthuli, S. Afr.
1959 Philip J. Noel-Baker, Br.
1958 Georges Pire, Belg.
1957 Lester B. Pearson, Can.
1954 Office of UN High Com. for Refugees
1953 George C. Marshall, U.S.
1952 Albert Schweitzer, Fr.
1951 Leon Jouhaux, Fr.
1950 Ralph J. Bunche, U.S.
1949 Lord John Boyd Orr of
       Brechin Mearns, Br.
1947 Friends Service Council, Br.; Amer.
       Friends Service Committee, U.S.
1946 Emily G. Balch, John R. Mott, U.S.
1945 Cordell Hull, U.S.
1944 International Red Cross
1938 Nansen International Office
       for Refugees
1937 Viscount Cecil of Chelwood, Br.
1936 Carlos de Saavedra Lamas, Arg.
1935 Carl von Ossietzky, Ger.
1934 Arthur Henderson, Br.
1933 Sir Norman Angell, Br.

1931 Jane Addams, Nicholas Murray
       Butler, U.S.
1930 Nathan Soderblom, Swed.
1929 Frank B. Kellogg, U.S.
1927 Ferdinand E. Buisson, Fr.;
       Ludwig Quidde, Ger.
1926 Aristide Briand, Fr.;
       Gustav Stresemann, Ger.
1925 Sir J. Austen Chamberlain, Br.;
       Charles G. Dawes, U.S.
1922 Fridtjof Nansen, Nor.
1921 Karl H. Branting, Swed.;
       Christian L. Lange, Nor.
1920 Leon V.A. Bourgeois, Fr.
1919 Woodrow Wilson, U.S.
1917 International Red Cross
1913 Henri La Fontaine, Belg.
1912 Elihu Root, U.S.
1911 Tobias M.C. Asser, Dutch;
       Alfred H. Fried, Austrian
1910 Permanent Intl. Peace Bureau
1909 Auguste M. F. Beernaert, Belg.;
       Paul H. B. B. d'Estournelles
       de Constant, Fr.
1908 Klas P. Arnoldson, Swed.;
       Fredrik Bajer, Dan.
1907 Ernesto T. Moneta, It.; Louis Renault,
       Fr.
1906 Theodore Roosevelt, U.S.
1905 Baroness Bertha von
       Suttner, Austrian
1904 Institute of International Law
1903 Sir William R. Cremer, Br.
1902 Elie Ducommun,
       Charles A. Gobat, Swiss
1901 Jean H. Dunant, Swiss;
       Frederic Passy, Fr.

Nobel Memorial Prize in Economic Science

2003 Robert F. Engle, U.S.; Clive W.J.
       Granger, Br.
2002 Daniel Kahneman, U.S. and Israel;
       Vernon L. Smith, U.S.
2001 George A. Akerlof, A. Michael
       Spence, Joseph E. Stiglitz, U.S.
2000 James J. Heckman,
       Daniel L. McFadden, U.S.
1999 Robert A. Mundell, Can.
1998 Amartya Sen, Indian
1997 Robert C. Merton, U.S.;
       Myron S. Scholes, Can.-U.S.
1996 James A. Mirrlees, Br.;
       William Vickrey, Can.-U.S.
1995 Robert E. Lucas Jr., U.S.
1994 John C. Harsanyi, John F. Nash,
       U.S.; Reinhard Selten, Ger.

1993 Robert W. Fogel,
       Douglass C. North, U.S.
1992 Gary S. Becker, U.S.
1991 Ronald H. Coase, Br.-U.S.
1990 Harry M. Markowitz, William F.
       Sharpe, Merton H. Miller, U.S.
1989 Trygve Haavelmo, Nor.
1988 Maurice Allais, Fr.
1987 Robert M. Solow, U.S.
1986 James M. Buchanan, U.S.
1985 Franco Modigliani, It.-U.S.
1984 Richard Stone, Br.
1983 Gerard Debreu, Fr.-U.S.
1982 George J. Stigler, U.S.
1981 James Tobin, U.S.
1980 Lawrence R. Klein, U.S.

1979 Theodore W. Schultz, U.S.;
       Sir Arthur Lewis, Br.
1978 Herbert A. Simon, U.S.
1977 Bertil Ohlin, Swed.;
       James E. Meade, Br.
1976 Milton Friedman, U.S.
1975 Tjalling Koopmans, Dutch-U.S.;
       Leonid Kantorovich, USSR
1974 Gunnar Myrdal, Swed.;
       Friedrich A. von Hayek, Austrian
1973 Wassily Leontief, U.S.
1972 Kenneth J. Arrow, U.S.;
       John R. Hicks, Br.
1971 Simon Kuznets, U.S.
1970 Paul A. Samuelson, U.S.
1969 Ragnar Frisch, Nor.;
       Jan Tinbergen, Dutch

Pulitzer Prizes in Journalism, Letters, and Music

Endowed by Joseph Pulitzer (1847-1911), publisher of the *New York World*, in a bequest to Columbia Univ. and awarded annually, in years shown, for work the previous year. Prizes are now $7,500 in each category, except Public Service (in Journalism), for which a medal is given. For letters and music, prizes in past years are listed; if a year is omitted, no award was given that year.

Journalism, 2004

Public Service: *NY Times*, for the work of David Barstow and Lowell Bergman on worker safety issues.
Breaking News Reporting: *LA Times* staff for coverage of the fall 2003 California wildfires.
Investigative Reporting: Michael D. Sallah, Mitch Weiss, and Joe Mahr of *The Blade*, Toledo, OH, for series on Vietnam War atrocities by elite U.S. Army platoon.
Explanatory Reporting: Kevin Helliker and Thomas M. Burton, *The Wall Street Journal*, for series on aneurysms.
Beat Reporting: Daniel Golden, *The Wall Street Journal*, for articles on admission preferences given to children of alumni and donors at universities.
National Reporting: *LA Times* staff for series on the economic impact of Wal-Mart.

International Reporting: Anthony Shadid of *The Washington Post* for coverage of U.S.-led war in Iraq.
Feature Writing: No award
Commentary: Leonard Pitts Jr., *The Miami Herald*, for columns focusing on controversial issues.
Criticism: Dan Neil, *LA Times*, for his reviews of automobiles
Editorial Writing: William Stall, *LA Times*, for editorials analyzing problems of California's government.
Editorial Cartooning: Matt Davies, *The Journal News*, White Plains, NY.
Breaking News Photog.: David Leeson and Cheryl Diaz Meyer, *The Dallas Morning News*, for photographs of the war in Iraq.
Feature Photog.: Carolyn Cole, *LA Times*, for photographs of Liberian civil war.

Letters

Fiction

1918—Ernest Poole, *His Family*
1919—Booth Tarkington, *The Magnificent Ambersons*
1921—Edith Wharton, *The Age of Innocence*
1922—Booth Tarkington, *Alice Adams*
1923—Willa Cather, *One of Ours*
1924—Margaret Wilson, *The Able McLaughlins*
1925—Edna Ferber, *So Big*
1926—Sinclair Lewis, *Arrowsmith* (refused prize)
1927—Louis Bromfield, *Early Autumn*
1928—Thornton Wilder, *Bridge of San Luis Rey*
1929—Julia M. Peterkin, *Scarlet Sister Mary*
1930—Oliver LaFarge, *Laughing Boy*
1931—Margaret Ayer Barnes, *Years of Grace*
1932—Pearl S. Buck, *The Good Earth*
1933—T. S. Stribling, *The Store*
1934—Caroline Miller, *Lamb in His Bosom*
1935—Josephine W. Johnson, *Now in November*
1936—Harold L. Davis, *Honey in the Horn*
1937—Margaret Mitchell, *Gone With the Wind*
1938—John P. Marquand, *The Late George Apley*
1939—Marjorie Kinnan Rawlings, *The Yearling*
1940—John Steinbeck, *The Grapes of Wrath*
1942—Ellen Glasgow, *In This Our Life*
1943—Upton Sinclair, *Dragon's Teeth*
1944—Martin Flavin, *Journey in the Dark*
1945—John Hersey, *A Bell for Adano*
1947—Robert Penn Warren, *All the King's Men*
1948—James A. Michener, *Tales of the South Pacific*
1949—James Gould Cozzens, *Guard of Honor*
1950—A. B. Guthrie Jr., *The Way West*
1951—Conrad Richter, *The Town*
1952—Herman Wouk, *The Caine Mutiny*
1953—Ernest Hemingway, *The Old Man and the* Sea
1955—William Faulkner, *A Fable*
1956—MacKinlay Kantor, *Andersonville*
1958—James Agee, *A Death in the Family*
1959—Robert Lewis Taylor, *The Travels of Jaimie McPheeters*
1960—Allen Drury, *Advise and Consent*
1961—Harper Lee, *To Kill a Mockingbird*
1962—Edwin O'Connor, *The Edge of Sadness*
1963—William Faulkner, *The Reivers*
1965—Shirley Ann Grau, *The Keepers of the House*
1966—Katherine Anne Porter, *Collected Stories*
1967—Bernard Malamud, *The Fixer*
1968—William Styron, *The Confessions of Nat Turner*
1969—N. Scott Momaday, *House Made of Dawn*
1970—Jean Stafford, *Collected Stories*
1972—Wallace Stegner, *Angle of Repose*
1973—Eudora Welty, *The Optimist's Daughter*
1975—Michael Shaara, *The Killer Angels*
1976—Saul Bellow, *Humboldt's Gift*
1978—James Alan McPherson, *Elbow Room*
1979—John Cheever, *The Stories of John Cheever*
1980—Norman Mailer, *The Executioner's Song*
1981—John Kennedy Toole, *A Confederacy of Dunces*
1982—John Updike, *Rabbit Is Rich*
1983—Alice Walker, *The Color Purple*
1984—William Kennedy, *Ironweed*
1985—Alison Lurie, *Foreign Affairs*
1986—Larry McMurtry, *Lonesome Dove*
1987—Peter Taylor, *A Summons to Memphis*
1988—Toni Morrison, *Beloved*
1989—Anne Tyler, *Breathing Lessons*
1990—Oscar Hijuelos, *The Mambo Kings Play Songs of Love*
1991—John Updike, *Rabbit at Rest*
1992—Jane Smiley, *A Thousand Acres*
1993—Robert Olen Butler, *A Good Scent From a Strange Mountain*
1994—E. Annie Proulx, *The Shipping News*
1995—Carol Shields, *The Stone Diaries*
1996—Richard Ford, *Independence Day*
1997—Steven Millhauser, *Martin Dressler: The Tale of an American Dreamer*
1998—Philip Roth, *American Pastoral*
1999—Michael Cunningham, *The Hours*
2000—Jhumpa Lahiri, *Interpreter of Maladies*
2001—Michael Chabon, *The Amazing Adventures of Kavalier & Clay*
2002—Richard Russo, *Empire Falls*
2003—Jeffrey Eugenides, *Middlesex*
2004—Edward P. Jones, *The Known World*

Drama

1918—Jesse Lynch Williams, *Why Marry?*
1920—Eugene O'Neill, *Beyond the Horizon*
1921—Zona Gale, *Miss Lulu Bett*
1922—Eugene O'Neill, *Anna Christie*
1923—Owen Davis, *Icebound*
1924—Hatcher Hughes, *Hell-Bent for Heaven*

1925—Sidney Howard, *They Knew What They Wanted*
1926—George Kelly, *Craig's Wife*
1927—Paul Green, *In Abraham's Bosom*
1928—Eugene O'Neill, *Strange Interlude*
1929—Elmer Rice, *Street Scene*
1930—Marc Connelly, *The Green Pastures*
1931—Susan Glaspell, *Alison's House*
1932—George S. Kaufman, Morrie Ryskind, and Ira Gershwin, *Of Thee I Sing*
1933—Maxwell Anderson, *Both Your Houses*
1934—Sidney Kingsley, *Men in White*
1935—Zoe Akins, *The Old Maid*
1936—Robert E. Sherwood, *Idiot's Delight*
1937—George S. Kaufman and Moss Hart, *You Can't Take It With You*
1938—Thornton Wilder, *Our Town*
1939—Robert E. Sherwood, *Abe Lincoln in Illinois*
1940—William Saroyan, *The Time of Your Life*
1941—Robert E. Sherwood, *There Shall Be No Night*
1943—Thornton Wilder, *The Skin of Our Teeth*
1945—Mary Chase, *Harvey*
1946—Russel Crouse and Howard Lindsay, *State of the Union*
1948—Tennessee Williams, *A Streetcar Named Desire*
1949—Arthur Miller, *Death of a Salesman*
1950—Richard Rodgers, Oscar Hammerstein 2nd and Joshua Logan, *South Pacific*
1952—Joseph Kramm, *The Shrike*
1953—William Inge, *Picnic*
1954—John Patrick, *Teahouse of the August Moon*
1955—Tennessee Williams, *Cat on a Hot Tin Roof*
1956—Frances Goodrich and Albert Hackett, *The Diary of Anne Frank*
1957—Eugene O'Neill, *Long Day's Journey Into Night*
1958—Ketti Frings, *Look Homeward, Angel*
1959—Archibald MacLeish, *J. B.*
1960—George Abbott, Jerome Weidman, Sheldon Harnick, and Jerry Bock, *Fiorello!*
1961—Tad Mosel, *All the Way Home*
1962—Frank Loesser and Abe Burrows, *How to Succeed in Business Without Really Trying*
1965—Frank D. Gilroy, *The Subject Was Roses*
1967—Edward Albee, *A Delicate Balance*
1969—Howard Sackler, *The Great White Hope*
1970—Charles Gordone, *No Place to Be Somebody*
1971—Paul Zindel, *The Effect of Gamma Rays on Man-in-the-Moon Marigolds*
1973—Jason Miller, *That Championship Season*
1975—Edward Albee, *Seascape*
1976—Michael Bennett, James Kirkwood, Nicholas Dante, Marvin Hamlisch, and Edward Kleban, *A Chorus Line*
1977—Michael Cristofer, *The Shadow Box*
1978—Donald L. Coburn, *The Gin Game*
1979—Sam Shepard, *Buried Child*
1980—Lanford Wilson, *Talley's Folly*
1981—Beth Henley, *Crimes of the Heart*
1982—Charles Fuller, *A Soldier's Play*
1983—Marsha Norman, *'night, Mother*
1984—David Mamet, *Glengarry Glen Ross*
1985—Stephen Sondheim and James Lapine, *Sunday in the Park With George*
1987—August Wilson, *Fences*
1988—Alfred Uhry, *Driving Miss Daisy*
1989—Wendy Wasserstein, *The Heidi Chronicles*
1990—August Wilson, *The Piano Lesson*
1991—Neil Simon, *Lost in Yonkers*
1992—Robert Schenkkan, *The Kentucky Cycle*
1993—Tony Kushner, *Angels in America: Millennium Approaches*
1994—Edward Albee, *Three Tall Women*
1995—Horton Foote, *The Young Man From Atlanta*
1996—Jonathan Larson, *Rent*
1998—Paula Vogel, *How I Learned to Drive*
1999—Margaret Edson, *Wit*
2000—Donald Margulies, *Dinner With Friends*
2001—David Auburn, *Proof*
2002—Suzan-Lori Parks, *Topdog/Underdog*
2003—Nilo Cruz, *Anna in the Tropics*
2004—Doug Wright, *I Am My Own Wife*

History (U.S.)

1917—J. J. Jusserand, *With Americans of Past and Present Days*
1918—James Ford Rhodes, *History of the Civil War*
1920—Justin H. Smith, *The War With Mexico*
1921—William Sowden Sims, *The Victory at Sea*
1922—James Truslow Adams, *The Founding of New England*
1923—Charles Warren, *The Supreme Court in United States History*
1924—Charles Howard McIlwain, *The American Revolution: A Constitutional Interpretation*
1925—Frederick L. Paxton, *A History of the American Frontier*
1926—Edward Channing, *A History of the U.S.*

1927—Samuel Flagg Bemis, *Pinckney's Treaty*
1928—V. L Parrington, *Main Currents in American Thought*
1929—Fred A. Shannon, *The Organization and Administration of the Union Army, 1861-65*
1930—Claude H. Van Tyne, *The War of Independence*
1931—Bernadotte E. Schmitt, *The Coming of the War, 1914*
1932—Gen. John J. Pershing, *My Experiences in the World War*
1933—Frederick J. Turner, *The Significance of Sections in American History*
1934—Herbert Agar, *The People's Choice*
1935—Charles McLean Andrews, *The Colonial Period of American History*
1936—Andrew C. McLaughlin, *The Constitutional History of the United States*
1937—Van Wyck Brooks, *The Flowering of New England*
1938—Paul Herman Buck, *The Road to Reunion, 1865-1900*
1939—Frank Luther Mott, *A History of American Magazines*
1940—Carl Sandburg, *Abraham Lincoln: The War Years*
1941—Marcus Lee Hansen, *The Atlantic Migration, 1607-1860*
1942—Margaret Leech, *Reveille in Washington*
1943—Esther Forbes, *Paul Revere and the World He Lived In*
1944—Merle Curti, *The Growth of American Thought*
1945—Stephen Bonsal, *Unfinished Business*
1946—Arthur M. Schlesinger Jr., *The Age of Jackson*
1947—James Phinney Baxter 3d, *Scientists Against Time*
1948—Bernard De Voto, *Across the Wide Missouri*
1949—Roy F. Nichols, *The Disruption of American Democracy*
1950—O. W. Larkin, *Art and Life in America*
1951—R. Carlyle Buley, *The Old Northwest: Pioneer Period 1815-1840*
1952—Oscar Handlin, *The Uprooted*
1953—George Dangerfield, *The Era of Good Feelings*
1954—Bruce Catton, *A Stillness at Appomattox*
1955—Paul Horgan, *Great River: The Rio Grande in North American History*
1956—Richard Hofstadter, *The Age of Reform*
1957—George F. Kennan, *Russia Leaves the War*
1958—Bray Hammond, *Banks and Politics in America—From the Revolution to the Civil War*
1959—Leonard D. White and Jean Schneider, *The Republican Era; 1869-1901*
1960—Margaret Leech, *In the Days of McKinley*
1961—Herbert Feis, *Between War and Peace: The Potsdam Conference*
1962—Lawrence H. Gibson, *The Triumphant Empire: Thunderclouds Gather in the West*
1963—Constance McLaughlin Green, *Washington: Village and Capital, 1800-1878*
1964—Sumner Chilton Powell, *Puritan Village: The Formation of a New England Town*
1965—Irwin Unger, *The Greenback Era*
1966—Perry Miller, *Life of the Mind in America*
1967—William H. Goetzmann, *Exploration and Empire: The Explorer and Scientist in the Winning of the American West*
1968—Bernard Bailyn, *The Ideological Origins of the American Revolution*
1969—Leonard W. Levy, *Origin of the Fifth Amendment*
1970—Dean Acheson, *Present at the Creation: My Years in the State Department*
1971—James McGregor Burns, *Roosevelt: The Soldier of Freedom*
1972—Carl N. Degler, *Neither Black nor White*
1973—Michael Kammen, *People of Paradox: An Inquiry Concerning the Origins of American Civilization*
1974—Daniel J. Boorstin, *The Americans: The Democratic Experience*
1975—Dumas Malone, *Jefferson and His Time*
1976—Paul Horgan, *Lamy of Santa Fe*
1977—David M. Potter, *The Impending Crisis*
1978—Alfred D. Chandler Jr., *The Visible Hand: The Managerial Revolution in American Business*
1979—Don E. Fehrenbacher, *The Dred Scott Case: Its Significance in American Law and Politics*
1980—Leon F. Litwack, *Been in the Storm So Long*
1981—Lawrence A. Cremin, *American Education: The National Experience, 1783-1876*
1982—C. Vann Woodward, ed., *Mary Chesnut's Civil War*
1983—Rhys L. Issac, *The Transformation of Virginia, 1740-1790*
1985—Thomas K. McCraw, *Prophets of Regulation*
1986—Walter A. McDougall, *The Heavens and the Earth*
1987—Bernard Bailyn, *Voyagers to the West*
1988—Robert V. Bruce, *The Launching of Modern American Science, 1846-1876*
1989—Taylor Branch, *Parting the Waters: America in the King Years, 1954-63*; and James M. McPherson, *Battle Cry of Freedom: The Civil War Era*
1990—Stanley Karnow, *In Our Image: America's Empire in the Philippines*
1991—Laurel Thatcher Ulrich, *A Midwife's Tale: The Life of Martha Ballard,* based on her diary, 1785-1812
1992—Mark E. Neely Jr., *The Fate of Liberty: Abraham Lincoln and Civil Liberties*

1993—Gordon S. Wood, *The Radicalism of the American Revolution*
1995—Doris Kearns Goodwin, *No Ordinary Time: Franklin and Eleanor Roosevelt: The Home Front in World War II*
1996—Alan Taylor, *William Cooper's Town: Power and Persuasion on the Frontier of the Early American Republic*
1997—Jack N. Rakove, *Original Meanings: Politics and Ideas in the Making of the Constitution*
1998—Edward J. Larson, *Summer for the Gods: The Scopes Trial and America's Continuing Debate Over Science and Religion*
1999—Edwin G. Burrows and Mike Wallace, *Gotham: A History of New York City to 1898*
2000—David M. Kennedy, *Freedom From Fear: The American People in Depression and War, 1929-1945*
2001—Joseph J. Ellis, *Founding Brothers: The Revolutionary Generation*
2002—Louis Menand, *The Metaphysical Club: A Story of Ideas in America*
2003—Rick Atkinson, *An Army at Dawn: The War in North Africa, 1942-1943*
2004—Steven Hahn, *A Nation Under Our Feet: Black Political Struggles in the Rural South from Slavery to the Great Migration*

Biography or Autobiography

1917—Laura E. Richards and Maude Howe Elliott, assisted by Florence Howe Hall, *Julia Ward Howe*
1918—William Cabell Bruce, *Benjamin Franklin, Self-Revealed*
1919—Henry Adams, *The Education of Henry Adams*
1920—Albert J. Beveridge, *The Life of John Marshall*
1921—Edward Bok, *The Americanization of Edward Bok*
1922—Hamlin Garland, *A Daughter of the Middle Border*
1923—Burton J. Hendrick, *The Life and Letters of Walter H. Page*
1924—Michael Pupin, *From Immigrant to Inventor*
1925—M. A. DeWolfe Howe, *Barrett Wendell and His Letters*
1926—Harvey Cushing, *Life of Sir William Osler*
1927—Emory Holloway, *Whitman: An Interpretation in Narrative*
1928—Charles Edward Russell, *The American Orchestra and Theodore Thomas*
1929—Burton J. Hendrick, *The Training of an American: The Earlier Life and Letters of Walter H. Page*
1930—Marquis James, *The Raven* (Sam Houston)
1931—Henry James, *Charles W. Eliot*
1932—Henry F. Pringle, *Theodore Roosevelt*
1933—Allan Nevins, *Grover Cleveland*
1934—Tyler Dennett, *John Hay*
1935—Douglas Southall Freeman, *R. E. Lee*
1936—Ralph Barton Perry, *The Thought and Character of William James*
1937—Allan Nevins, *Hamilton Fish: The Inner History of the Grant Administration*
1938—Divided between Odell Shepard, *Pedlar's Progress* (Bronson Alcott) and Marquis James, *Andrew Jackson*
1939—Carl Van Doren, *Benjamin Franklin*
1940—Ray Stannard Baker, *Woodrow Wilson, Life and Letters*
1941—Ola Elizabeth Winslow, *Jonathan Edwards*
1942—Forrest Wilson, *Crusader in Crinoline* (Harriet Beecher Stowe)
1943—Samuel Eliot Morison, *Admiral of the Ocean Sea* (Christopher Columbus)
1944—Carleton Mabee, *The American Leonardo: The Life of Samuel F. B. Morse*
1945—Russell Blaine Nye, *George Bancroft: Brahmin Rebel.*
1946—Linny Marsh Wolfe, *Son of the Wilderness* (John Muir)
1947—William Allen White, *Autobiography of William Allen White*
1948—Margaret Clapp, *Forgotten First Citizen: John Bigelow*
1949—Robert E. Sherwood, *Roosevelt and Hopkins*
1950—Samuel Flagg Bemis, *John Quincy Adams and the Foundations of American Foreign Policy*
1951—Margaret Louise Coit, *John C. Calhoun: American Portrait*
1952—Merlo J. Pusey, *Charles Evans Hughes*
1953—David J. Mays, *Edmund Pendleton, 1721-1803*
1954—Charles A. Lindbergh, *The Spirit of St. Louis*
1955—William S. White, *The Taft Story*
1956—Talbot F. Hamlin, *Benjamin Henry Latrobe*
1957—John F. Kennedy, *Profiles in Courage*
1958—Douglas Southall Freeman (Vols. I-VI) and John Alexander Carroll and Mary Wells Ashworth (Vol. VII), *George Washington*
1959—Arthur Walworth, *Woodrow Wilson: American Prophet*
1960—Samuel Eliot Morison, *John Paul Jones*
1961—David Donald, *Charles Sumner and the Coming of the Civil War*
1963—Leon Edel, *Henry James: Vols. 2-3*
1964—Walter Jackson Bate, *John Keats*
1965—Ernest Samuels, *Henry Adams*
1966—Arthur M. Schlesinger Jr., *A Thousand Days*
1967—Justin Kaplan, *Mr. Clemens and Mark Twain*
1968—George F. Kennan, *Memoirs (1925-1950)*
1969—B. L. Reid, *The Man From New York: John Quinn and His Friends*
1970—T. Harry Williams, *Huey Long*
1971—Lawrence Thompson, *Robert Frost: The Years of Triumph, 1915-1938*

1972—Joseph P. Lash, *Eleanor and Franklin*
1973—W. A. Swanberg, *Luce and His Empire*
1974—Louis Sheaffer, *O'Neill, Son and Artist*
1975—Robert A. Caro, *The Power Broker: Robert Moses and the Fall of New York*
1976—R.W.B. Lewis, *Edith Wharton: A Biography*
1977—John E. Mack, *A Prince of Our Disorder: The Life of T. E. Lawrence*
1978—Walter Jackson Bate, *Samuel Johnson*
1979—Leonard Baker, *Days of Sorrow and Pain: Leo Baeck and the Berlin Jews*
1980—Edmund Morris, *The Rise of Theodore Roosevelt*
1981—Robert K. Massie, *Peter the Great: His Life and World*
1982—William S. McFeely, *Grant: A Biography*
1983—Russell Baker, *Growing Up*
1984—Louis R. Harlan, *Booker T. Washington*
1985—Kenneth Silverman, *The Life and Times of Cotton Mather*
1986—Elizabeth Frank, *Louise Bogan: A Portrait*
1987—David J. Garrow, *Bearing the Cross: Martin Luther King Jr. and the Southern Christian Leadership Conference*
1988—David Herbert Donald, *Look Homeward: A Life of Thomas Wolfe*
1989—Richard Ellmann, *Oscar Wilde*
1990—Sebastian de Grazia, *Machiavelli in Hell*
1991—Steven Naifeh and Gregory White Smith, *Jackson Pollock: An American Saga*
1992—Lewis B. Puller Jr., *Fortunate Son: The Healing of a Vietnam Vet*
1993—David McCullough, *Truman*
1994—David Levering Lewis, *W.E.B. DuBois: Biography of a Race, 1868-1919*
1995—Joan D. Hedrick, *Harriet Beecher Stowe: A Life*
1996—Jack Miles, *God: A Biography*
1997—Frank McCourt, *Angela's Ashes: A Memoir*
1998—Katharine Graham, *Personal History*
1999—A. Scott Berg, *Lindbergh*
2000—Stacy Schiff, *Véra (Mrs. Vladimir Nabokov)*
2001—David Levering Lewis, *W.E.B. Du Bois: The Fight for Equality and the American Century, 1919-1963*
2002—David McCullough, *John Adams*
2003—Robert Caro, *The Years of Lyndon Johnson: Master of the Senate*
2004—William Taubman, *Khrushchev: The Man and His Era*

American Poetry

Before 1922, awards were funded by the Poetry Society.

1918—*Love Songs*, by Sara Teasdale.
1919—*Old Road to Paradise*, by Margaret Widdemer; *Corn Huskers*, by Carl Sandburg.
1922—Edwin Arlington Robinson, *Collected Poems*
1923—Edna St. Vincent Millay, *The Ballad of the Harp-Weaver; A Few Figs From Thistles; other works*
1924—Robert Frost, *New Hampshire: A Poem With Notes and Grace Notes*
1925—Edwin Arlington Robinson, *The Man Who Died Twice*
1926—Amy Lowell, *What's O'Clock*
1927—Leonora Speyer, *Fiddler's Farewell*
1928—Edwin Arlington Robinson, *Tristram*
1929—Stephen Vincent Benet, *John Brown's Body*
1930—Conrad Aiken, *Selected Poems*
1931—Robert Frost, *Collected Poems*
1932—George Dillon, *The Flowering Stone*
1933—Archibald MacLeish, *Conquistador*
1934—Robert Hillyer, *Collected Verse*
1935—Audrey Wurdemann, *Bright Ambush*
1936—Robert P. Tristram Coffin, *Strange Holiness*
1937—Robert Frost, *A Further Range*
1938—Marya Zaturenska, *Cold Morning Sky*
1939—John Gould Fletcher, *Selected Poems*
1940—Mark Van Doren, *Collected Poems*
1941—Leonard Bacon, *Sunderland Capture*
1942—William Rose Benet, *The Dust Which Is God*
1943—Robert Frost, *A Witness Tree*
1944—Stephen Vincent Benet, *Western Star*
1945—Karl Shapiro, *V-Letter and Other Poems*
1947—Robert Lowell, *Lord Weary's Castle*
1948—W. H. Auden, *The Age of Anxiety*
1949—Peter Viereck, *Terror and Decorum*
1950—Gwendolyn Brooks, *Annie Allen*
1951—Carl Sandburg, *Complete Poems*
1952—Marianne Moore, *Collected Poems*
1953—Archibald MacLeish, *Collected Poems*
1954—Theodore Roethke, *The Waking*
1955—Wallace Stevens, *Collected Poems*
1956—Elizabeth Bishop, *Poems, North and South*
1957—Richard Wilbur, *Things of This World*
1958—Robert Penn Warren, *Promises: Poems 1954-1956*
1959—Stanley Kunitz, *Selected Poems 1928-1958*
1960—W. D. Snodgrass, *Heart's Needle*
1961—Phyllis McGinley, *Times Three: Selected Verse From Three Decades*
1962—Alan Dugan, *Poems*

1963—William Carlos Williams, *Pictures From Breughel*
1964—Louis Simpson, *At the End of the Open Road*
1965—John Berryman, *77 Dream Songs*
1966—Richard Eberhart, *Selected Poems*
1967—Anne Sexton, *Live or Die*
1968—Anthony Hecht, *The Hard Hours*
1969—George Oppen, *Of Being Numerous*
1970—Richard Howard, *Untitled Subjects*
1971—William S. Merwin, *The Carrier of Ladders*
1972—James Wright, *Collected Poems*
1973—Maxine Winokur Kumin, *Up Country*
1974—Robert Lowell, *The Dolphin*
1975—Gary Snyder, *Turtle Island*
1976—John Ashbery, *Self-Portrait in a Convex Mirror*
1977—James Merrill, *Divine Comedies*
1978—Howard Nemerov, *Collected Poems*
1979—Robert Penn Warren, *Now and Then: Poems 1976-1978*
1980—Donald Justice, *Selected Poems*
1981—James Schuyler, *The Morning of the Poem*
1982—Sylvia Plath, *The Collected Poems*
1983—Galway Kinnell, *Selected Poems*
1984—Mary Oliver, *American Primitive*
1985—Carolyn Kizer, *Yin*
1986—Henry Taylor, *The Flying Change*
1987—Rita Dove, *Thomas and Beulah*
1988—William Meredith, *Partial Accounts: New and Selected Poems*
1989—Richard Wilbur, *New and Collected Poems*
1990—Charles Simic, *The World Doesn't End*
1991—Mona Van Duyn, *Near Changes*
1992—James Tate, *Selected Poems*
1993—Louise Glück, *The Wild Iris*
1994—Yusef Komunyakaa, *Neon Vernacular*
1995—Philip Levine, *The Simple Truth*
1996—Jorie Graham, *The Dream of the Unified Field*
1997—Lisel Mueller, *Alive Together: New and Selected Poems*
1998—Charles Wright, *Black Zodiac*
1999—Mark Strand, *Blizzard of One*
2000—C. K. Williams, *Repair*
2001—Stephen Dunn, *Different Hours*
2002—Carl Dennis, *Practical Gods*
2003—Paul Muldoon, *Moy Sand and Gravel*
2004—Franz Wright, *Walking to Martha's Vineyard*

General Nonfiction

1962—Theodore H. White, *The Making of the President 1960*
1963—Barbara W. Tuchman, *The Guns of August*
1964—Richard Hofstadter, *Anti-Intellectualism in American Life*
1965—Howard Mumford Jones, *O Strange New World*
1966—Edwin Way Teale, *Wandering Through Winter*
1967—David Brion Davis, *The Problem of Slavery in Western Culture*
1968—Will and Ariel Durant, *Rousseau and Revolution*
1969—Norman Mailer, *The Armies of the Night;* Rene Jules Dubos, *So Human an Animal: How We Are Shaped by Surroundings and Events*
1970—Eric H. Erikson, *Gandhi's Truth*
1971—John Toland, *The Rising Sun*
1972—Barbara W. Tuchman, *Stilwell and the American Experience in China, 1911-1945*
1973—Frances FitzGerald, *Fire in the Lake: The Vietnamese and the Americans in Vietnam;* Robert Coles, *Children of Crisis,* Volumes II & III
1974—Ernest Becker, *The Denial of Death*
1975—Annie Dillard, *Pilgrim at Tinker Creek*
1976—Robert N. Butler, *Why Survive? Being Old in America*
1977—William W. Warner, *Beautiful Swimmers*
1978—Carl Sagan, *The Dragons of Eden*
1979—Edward O. Wilson, *On Human Nature*
1980—Douglas R. Hofstadter, *Gödel, Escher, Bach: An Eternal Golden Braid*
1981—Carl E. Schorske, *Fin-de-Siecle Vienna: Politics and Culture*
1982—Tracy Kidder, *The Soul of a New Machine*
1983—Susan Sheehan, *Is There No Place on Earth for Me?*
1984—Paul Starr, *Social Transformation of American Medicine*
1985—Studs Terkel, *The Good War*
1986—Joseph Lelyveld, *Move Your Shadow;* J. Anthony Lukas, *Common Ground*
1987—David K. Shipler, *Arab and Jew*
1988—Richard Rhodes, *The Making of the Atomic Bomb*
1989—Neil Sheehan, *A Bright Shining Lie: John Paul Vann and America in Vietnam*
1990—Dale Maharidge and Michael Williamson, *And Their Children After Them*
1991—Bert Holldobler and Edward O. Wilson, *The Ants*
1992—Daniel Yergin, *The Prize: The Epic Quest for Oil*
1993—Garry Wills, *Lincoln at Gettysburg*
1994—David Remnick, *Lenin's Tomb: The Last Days of the Soviet Empire*
1995—Jonathan Weiner, *The Beak of the Finch: A Story of Evolution in Our Time*

1996—Tina Rosenberg, *The Haunted Land: Facing Europe's Ghosts After Communism*
1997—Richard Kluger, *Ashes to Ashes: America's Hundred-Year Cigarette War, the Public Health, and the Unabashed Triumph of Philip Morris*
1998—Jared Diamond, *Guns, Germs, and Steel: The Fates of Human Societies*
1999—John McPhee, *Annals of the Former World*
2000—John W. Dower, *Embracing Defeat: Japan in the Wake of World War II*
2001—Herbert P. Bix, *Hirohito and the Making of Modern Japan*
2002—Diane McWhorter, *Carry Me Home: Birmingham, Alabama, the Climactic Battle of the Civil Rights Revolution*

2003—Samantha Power, *A Problem From Hell: America and the Age of Genocide*
2004—Anne Applebaum, *Gulag: A History*

Special Citation in Letters
1944—Richard Rodgers and Oscar Hammerstein II, for *Oklahoma!*
1957—Kenneth Roberts, for his historical novels
1960—*The Armada*, by Garrett Mattingly
1961—*American Heritage Picture History of the Civil War*
1973—*George Washington, Vols. I-IV*, by James Thomas Flexner
1977—Alex Haley, for *Roots*
1978—E.B. White
1984—Theodore Seuss Geisel (Dr. Seuss)
1992—Art Spiegelman, for *Maus*

Music

1943—William Schuman, *Secular Cantata No. 2, A Free Song*
1944—Howard Hanson, *Symphony No. 4, Op. 34*
1945—Aaron Copland, *Appalachian Spring*
1946—Leo Sowerby, *The Canticle of the Sun*
1947—Charles E. Ives, *Symphony No. 3*
1948—Walter Piston, *Symphony No. 3*
1949—Virgil Thomson, *Louisiana Story*
1950—Gian-Carlo Menotti, *The Consul*
1951—Douglas Moore, *Giants in the Earth*
1952—Gail Kubik, *Symphony Concertante*
1954—Quincy Porter, *Concerto for Two Pianos and Orchestra*
1955—Gian-Carlo Menotti, *The Saint of Bleecker Street*
1956—Ernest Toch, *Symphony No. 3*
1957—Norman Dello Joio, *Meditations on Ecclesiastes*
1958—Samuel Barber, *Vanessa*
1959—John La Montaine, *Concerto for Piano and Orchestra*
1960—Elliott Carter, *Second String Quartet*
1961—Walter Piston, *Symphony No. 7*
1962—Robert Ward, *The Crucible*
1963—Samuel Barber, *Piano Concerto No. 1*
1966—Leslie Bassett, *Variations for Orchestra*
1967—Leon Kirchner, *Quartet No. 3*
1968—George Crumb, *Echoes of Time and The River*
1969—Karel Husa, *String Quartet No. 3*
1970—Charles W. Wuorinen, *Time's Encomium*
1971—Mario Davidovsky, *Synchronisms No. 6*
1972—Jacob Druckman, *Windows*
1973—Elliott Carter, *String Quartet No. 3*
1974—Donald Martino, *Notturno*
1975—Dominick Argento, *From the Diary of Virginia Woolf*
1976—Ned Rorem, *Air Music*
1977—Richard Wernick, *Visions of Terror and Wonder*
1978—Michael Colgrass, *Deja Vu for Percussion and Orchestra*
1979—Joseph Schwantner, *Aftertones of Infinity*
1980—David Del Tredici, *In Memory of a Summer Day*

1982—Roger Sessions, *Concerto for Orchestra*
1983—Ellen T. Zwilich, *Three Movements for Orchestra*
1984—Bernard Rands, *Canti del Sole*
1985—Stephen Albert, *Symphony, RiverRun*
1986—George Perle, *Wind Quintet IV*
1987—John Harbison, *The Flight Into Egypt*
1988—William Bolcom, *12 New Etudes for Piano*
1989—Roger Reynolds, *Whispers Out of Time*
1990—Mel Powell, *Duplicates: A Concerto for Two Pianos and Orchestra*
1991—Shulamit Ran, *Symphony*
1992—Wayne Peterson, *The Face of the Night, The Heart of the Dark*
1993—Christopher Rouse, *Trombone Concerto*
1994—Gunther Schuller, *Of Reminiscences and Reflections*
1995—Morton Gould, *Stringmusic*
1996—George Walker, *Lilacs*
1997—Wynton Marsalis, *Blood on the Fields*
1998—Aaron Jay Kernis, *String Quartet No. 2*
1999—Melinda Wagner, *Concerto for Flute, Strings and Percussion*
2000—Lewis Spratlan, *Life is a Dream, Opera in Three Acts: Act II, Concert Version*
2001—John Corigliano, *Symphony No. 2 for String Orchestra*
2002—Henry Brant, *Ice Field*
2003—John Adams, *On the Transmigration of Souls*
2004—Paul Moravec, *Tempest Fantasy*

Special Citation in Music
1974—Roger Sessions
1976—Scott Joplin
1982—Milton Babbitt
1985—William Schuman
1998—George Gershwin
1999—Edward Kennedy "Duke" Ellington

National Book Awards, 1950-2003

The National Book Awards (known as the American Book Awards from 1980 to 1986) are administered by the National Book Foundation and have been given annually since 1950. The prizes, each valued at $10,000, are awarded to U.S. citizens for works published in the U.S. in the 12 months prior to the nominations. In some years, multiple awards were given for nonfiction in various categories; in such cases, the history and biography (if any) or biography winner is listed. Selected additional awards in nonfiction are given in footnotes. Nonfiction winners in certain separate categories may not be shown.

Fiction

Year	Author, Title	Year	Author, Title
1950	Nelson Algren, *The Man With the Golden Arm*	1977	Wallace Stegner, *The Spectator Bird*
1951	William Faulkner, *The Collected Stories*	1978	Mary Lee Settle, *Blood Ties*
1952	James Jones, *From Here to Eternity*	1979	Tim O'Brien, *Going After Cacciato*
1953	Ralph Ellison, *Invisible Man*	1980	William Styron, *Sophie's Choice*
1954	Saul Bellow, *The Adventures of Augie March*	1981	Wright Morris, *Plains Song*
1955	William Faulkner, *A Fable*	1982	John Updike, *Rabbit Is Rich*
1956	John O'Hara, *Ten North Frederick*	1983	Alice Walker, *The Color Purple*
1957	Wright Morris, *The Field of Vision*	1984	Ellen Gilchrist, *Victory Over Japan*
1958	John Cheever, *The Wapshot Chronicle*	1985	Don DeLillo, *White Noise*
1959	Bernard Malamud, *The Magic Barrel*	1986	E.L. Doctorow, *World's Fair*
1960	Philip Roth, *Goodbye, Columbus*	1987	Larry Heinemann, *Paco's Story*
1961	Conrad Richter, *The Waters of Kronos*	1988	Pete Dexter, *Paris Trout*
1962	Walker Percy, *The Moviegoer*	1989	John Casey, *Spartina*
1963	J.F. Powers, *Morte d'Urban*	1990	Charles Johnson, *Middle Passage*
1964	John Updike, *The Centaur*	1991	Norman Rush, *Mating*
1965	Saul Bellow, *Herzog*	1992	Cormac McCarthy, *All the Pretty Horses*
1966	Katherine Anne Porter, *The Collected Stories*	1993	E. Annie Proulx, *The Shipping News*
1967	Bernard Malamud, *The Fixer*	1994	William Gaddis, *A Frolic of His Own*
1968	Thornton Wilder, *The Eighth Day*	1995	Philip Roth, *Sabbath's Theater*
1969	Jerzy Kosinski, *Steps*	1996	Andrea Barrett, *Ship Fever and Other Stories*
1970	Joyce Carol Oates, *Them*	1997	Charles Frazier, *Cold Mounatin*
1971	Saul Bellow, *Mr. Sammler's Planet*	1998	Alice McDermott, *Charming Billy*
1972	Flannery O'Connor, *The Complete Stories*	1999	Ha Jin, *Waiting*
1973	John Barth, *Chimera*	2000	Susan Sontag, *In America*
1974	Thomas Pynchon, *Gravity's Rainbow*	2001	Jonathan Franzen, *The Corrections*
1974	Isaac Bashevis Singer, *A Crown of Feathers*	2002	Julia Glass, *Three Junes*
1975	Robert Stone, *Dog Soldiers*	2003	Shirley Hazzard, *The Great Fire*
1976	William Gaddis, *JR*		

Nonfiction

Year	Author, Title
1950	Ralph L. Rusk, *Ralph Waldo Emerson*
1951	Newton Arvin, *Herman Melville*
1952	Rachel Carson, *The Sea Around Us*
1953	Bernard A. De Voto, *The Course of an Empire*
1954	Bruce Catton, *A Stillness at Appomattox*
1955	Joseph Wood Krutch, *The Measure of Man*
1956	Herbert Kubly, *An American in Italy*
1957	George F. Kennan, *Russia Leaves the War*
1958	Catherine Drinker Bowen, *The Lion and the Throne*
1959	J. Christopher Herold, *Mistress to an Age: A Life of Madame De Stael*
1960	Richard Ellman, *James Joyce*
1961	William L. Shirer, *The Rise and Fall of the Third Reich*
1962	Lewis Mumford, *The City in History: Its Origins, Its Transformations, and Its Prospects*
1963	Leon Edel, *Henry James: Vol. II: The Conquest of London; Vol. III: The Middle Years*
1964	William H. McNeill, *The Rise of the West: A History of the Human Community*
1965	Louis Fisher, *The Life of Lenin*
1966	Arthur M. Schlesinger, Jr., *A Thousand Days: John F. Kennedy in the White House*
1967	Peter Gay, *The Enlightenment, An Interpretation Vol I: The Rise of Modern Paganism*
1968	George F. Kennan, *Memoirs: 1925–1950*[1]
1969	Winthrop D. Jordan, *White Over Black: American Attitudes Toward the Negro, 1550-1812*[2]
1970	T. Harry Williams, *Huey Long*[3]
1971	James MacGregor Burns, *Roosevelt: The Soldier of Freedom*
1972	Joseph P. Lash, *Eleanor and Franklin: The Story of Their Relationship, Based on Eleanor Roosevelt's Private Papers*
1973	James Thomas Flexner, *George Washington, Vol. IV: Anguish and Farewell, 1793-1799*[4]
1974	John Clive, *Macaulay, The Shaping of the Historian*; Douglas Day, *Malcolm Lowry: A Biography*[5]
1975	Richard B. Sewall, *The Life of Emily Dickinson*[6]
1976	David Brion Davis, *The Problem of Slavery in the Age of Revolution, 1770-1823*

Year	Author, Title
1977	W.A. Swanberg, *Norman Thomas: The Last Idealist*[7]
1978	W. Jackson Bate, *Samuel Johnson*
1979	Arthur M. Schlesinger, Jr., *Robert Kennedy and His Times*
1980	Tom Wolfe, *The Right Stuff*
1981	Maxine Hong Kingston, *China Men*
1982	Tracy Kidder, *The Soul of a New Machine*
1983	Fox Butterfield, *China: Alive in the Bitter Sea*
1984	Robert V. Remini, *Andrew Jackson and the Course of American Democracy, 1833-1845*
1985	J. Anthony Lukas, *Common Ground: A Turbulent Decade in the Lives of Three American Families*
1986	Barry Lopez, *Arctic Dreams*
1987	Richard Rhodes, *The Making of the Atom Bomb*
1988	Neil Sheehan, *A Bright Shining Lie: John Paul Vann and America in Vietnam*
1989	Thomas L. Friedman, *From Beirut to Jerusalem*
1990	Ron Chernow, *The House of Morgan: An American Banking Dynasty and the Rise of Modern Finance*
1991	Orlando Patterson, *Freedom*
1992	Paul Monette, *Becoming a Man: Half a Life Story*
1993	Gore Vidal, *United States: Essays 1952-1992*
1994	Sherwin B. Nuland, *How We Die: Reflections on Life's Final Chapter*
1995	Tina Rosenberg, *The Haunted Land: Facing Europe's Ghosts After Communism*
1996	James Carroll, *An American Requiem: God, My Father, and the War That Came Between Us*
1997	Joseph J. Ellis, *American Sphinx: The Character of Thomas Jefferson*
1998	Edward Ball, *Slaves in the Family*
1999	John W. Dower, *Embracing Defeat: Japan in the Wake of World War II*
2000	Nathaniel Philbrick, *In the Heart of the Sea: The Tragedy of the Whaleship Essex*
2001	Andrew Solomon, *The Noonday Demon: An Atlas of Depression*
2002	Robert A. Caro, *Master of the Senate: The Years of Lyndon Johnson*
2003[8]	Carlos Eire, *Waiting for Snow in Havana: Confessions of a Cuban Boy*

(1) Science, Philosophy, and Religion: Jonathan Kozol, *Death at an Early Age.* (2) Arts & Letters: Norman Mailer, *The Armies of the Night: History as a Novel, The Novel as History.* (3) Arts & Letters: Lillian Hellman, *An Unfinished Woman: A Memoir.* (4) Contemp. Affairs: Frances FitzGerald, *Fire in the Lake: The Vietnamese and the Americans in Vietnam.* (5) Arts & Letters: Pauline Kael, *Deeper Into the Movies.* (6) Arts & Letters: Roger Shattuck, *Marcel Proust;* Lewis Thomas, *The Lives of a Cell: Notes of a Biology Watcher.* (7) Contemp. Thought: Bruno Bettelheim, *The Uses of Enchantment: The Meaning and Importance of Fairy Tales.*
(8) Other National Book Awards, 2003: Poetry: C.K. Williams, *The Singing.* Young People's Literature: Polly Horvath, *The Canning Season.* Medal for Distinguished Contribution to American Letters: Stephen King.

The Man Booker Prize for Fiction, 1969-2003

The Booker Prize for fiction, established in 1968, is awarded annually in October for what is judged the best full-length novel written in English by a citizen of the UK, the Commonwealth, or the Irish Republic. In 2002 sponsorship of the award was taken over by Man Group PLC, the name was changed to the Man Booker Prize, and the amount was increased from £20,000 to £50,000. The prize money for being named to the shortlist of 6 was also increased from £1,000 to £2,500.

1969—P. H. Newby, *Something to Answer For*
1970—Bernice Rubens, *The Elected Member*
1971—V. S. Naipaul, *In a Free State*
1972—John Berger, *G*
1973—J. G. Farrell, *The Siege of Krishnapur*
1974—Nadine Gordimer, *The Conservationist;* Stanley Middleton, *Holiday*
1975—Ruth Prawer Jhabvala, *Heat & Dust*
1976—David Storey, *Saville*
1977—Paul Scott, *Staying On*
1978—Iris Murdoch, *The Sea, The Sea*
1979—Penelope Fitzgerald, *Offshore*
1980—William Golding, *Rites of Passage*
1981—Salman Rushdie, *Midnight's Children*
1982—Thomas Keneally, *Schindler's Ark*
1983—J. M. Coetzee, *Life and Times of Michael K*
1984—Anita Brookner, *Hotel du Lac*
1985—Keri Hulme, *The Bone People*
1986—Kingsley Amis, *The Old Devils*

1987—Penelope Lively, *Moon Tiger*
1988—Peter Carey, *Oscar and Lucinda*
1989—Kazuo Ishiguro, *The Remains of the Day*
1990—A. S. Byatt, *Possession*
1991—Ben Okri, *The Famished Road*
1992—Michael Ondaatje, *The English Patient;* Barry Unsworth, *Sacred Hunger*
1993—Roddy Doyle, *Paddy Clarke Ha Ha Ha*
1994—James Kelman, *How Late It Was, How Late*
1995—Pat Barker, *The Ghost Road*
1996—Graham Swift, *Last Orders*
1997—Arundhati Roy, *The God of Small Things*
1998—Ian McEwan, *Amsterdam*
1999—J. M. Coetzee, *Disgrace*
2000—Margaret Atwood, *The Blind Assassin*
2001—Peter Carey, *True History of the Kelly Gang*
2002—Yann Martel, *Life of Pi*
2003—DBC Pierre, *Vernon God Little*

Newbery Medal Books, 1922-2004

The Newbery Medal is awarded annually by the Association for Library Service to Children, a division of the American Library Association, to the author of the most distinguished contribution to American literature for children.

Year Given	Book, Author
1922	*The Story of Mankind,* Hendrik Willem van Loon
1923	*The Voyages of Dr. Dolittle,* Hugh Lofting
1924	*The Dark Frigate,* Charles Boardman Hawes
1925	*Tales From Silver Lands,* Charles Joseph Finger
1926	*Shen of the Sea,* Arthur Bowie Chrisman

Year Given	Book, Author
1927	*Smoky, the Cowhorse,* Will James
1928	*Gay-Neck,* Dhan Gopal Mukerji
1929	*The Trumpeter of Krakow,* Eric P. Kelly
1930	*Hitty, Her First Hundred Years,* Rachel Field
1931	*The Cat Who Went to Heaven,* Elizabeth Coatsworth

Year Given	Book, Author
1932	*Waterless Mountain*, Laura Adams Armer
1933	*Young Fu of the Upper Yangtze*, Elizabeth Foreman Lewis
1934	*Invincible Louisa*, Cornelia Lynde Meigs
1935	*Dobry*, Monica Shannon
1936	*Caddie Woodlawn*, Carol Ryrie Brink
1937	*Roller Skates*, Ruth Sawyer
1938	*The White Stag*, Kate Seredy
1939	*Thimble Summer*, Elizabeth Enright
1940	*Daniel Boone*, James Daugherty
1941	*Call It Courage*, Armstrong Sperry
1942	*The Matchlock Gun*, Walter D. Edmonds
1943	*Adam of the Road*, Elizabeth Janet Gray
1944	*Johnny Tremain*, Esther Forbes
1945	*Rabbit Hill*, Robert Lawson
1946	*Strawberry Girl*, Lois Lenski
1947	*Miss Hickory*, Carolyn S. Bailey
1948	*Twenty-One Balloons*, William Pène Du Bois
1949	*King of the Wind*, Marguerite Henry
1950	*The Door in the Wall*, Marguerite de Angeli
1951	*Amos Fortune, Free Man*, Elizabeth Yates
1952	*Ginger Pye*, Eleanor Estes
1953	*Secret of the Andes*, Ann Nolan Clark
1954	*. . . And Now Miguel*, Joseph Krumgold
1955	*The Wheel on the School*, Meindert DeJong
1956	*Carry On, Mr. Bowditch*, Jean Lee Latham
1957	*Miracles on Maple Hill*, Virginia Sorensen
1958	*Rifles for Watie*, Harold Keith
1959	*The Witch of Blackbird Pond*, Elizabeth George Speare
1960	*Onion John*, Joseph Krumgold
1961	*Island of the Blue Dolphins*, Scott O'Dell
1962	*The Bronze Bow*, Elizabeth George Speare
1963	*A Wrinkle in Time*, Madeleine L'Engle
1964	*It's Like This, Cat*, Emily Cheney Neville
1965	*Shadow of a Bull*, Maja Wojciechowska
1966	*I, Juan de Pareja*, Elizabeth Borton de Trevino
1967	*Up a Road Slowly*, Irene Hunt
1968	*From the Mixed-Up Files of Mrs. Basil E. Frankweiler*, E. L. Konigsburg
1969	*The High King*, Lloyd Alexander
1970	*Sounder*, William H. Armstrong
1971	*The Summer of the Swans*, Betsy Byars
1972	*Mrs. Frisby and the Rats of NIMH*, Robert C. O'Brien
1973	*Julie of the Wolves*, Jean George
1974	*The Slave Dancer*, Paula Fox
1975	*M. C. Higgins the Great*, Virginia Hamilton
1976	*Grey King*, Susan Cooper
1977	*Roll of Thunder, Hear My Cry*, Mildred D. Taylor
1978	*Bridge to Terabithia*, Katherine Paterson
1979	*The Westing Game*, Ellen Raskin
1980	*A Gathering of Days*, Joan Blos
1981	*Jacob Have I Loved*, Katherine Paterson
1982	*A Visit to William Blake's Inn: Poems for Innocent and Experienced Travelers*, Nancy Willard
1983	*Dicey's Song*, Cynthia Voigt
1984	*Dear Mr. Henshaw*, Beverly Cleary
1985	*The Hero and the Crown*, Robin McKinley
1986	*Sarah, Plain and Tall*, Patricia MacLachlan
1987	*The Whipping Boy*, Sid Fleischman
1988	*Lincoln: A Photobiography*, Russell Freedman
1989	*Joyful Noise: Poems for Two Voices*, Paul Fleischman
1990	*Number the Stars*, Lois Lowry
1991	*Maniac Magee*, Jerry Spinelli
1992	*Shiloh*, Phyllis Reynolds Naylor
1993	*Missing May*, Cynthia Rylant
1994	*The Giver*, Lois Lowry
1995	*Walk Two Moons*, Sharon Creech
1996	*The Midwife's Apprentice*, Karen Cushman
1997	*The View From Saturday*, E. L. Konigsburg
1998	*Out of the Dust*, Karen Hesse
1999	*Holes*, Louis Sachar
2000	*Bud, Not Buddy*, Christopher Paul Curtis
2001	*A Year Down Yonder*, Richard Peck
2002	*A Single Shard*, Linda Sue Park
2003	*Crispin: The Cross of Lead*, Avi
2004	*The Tale of Despereaux: Being the Story of a Mouse, a Princess, Some Soup, and a Spool of Thread*, by Kate DiCamillo, illustrated by Timothy Basil Ering

Caldecott Medal Books, 1938-2004

The Caldecott Medal is awarded annually by the Association for Library Service to Children, a division of the American Library Association, to the illustrator of the most distinguished American picture book for children.

Year Given	Book, Illustrator
1938	*Animals of the Bible*, Dorothy P. Lathrop
1939	*Mei Li*, Thomas Handforth
1940	*Abraham Lincoln*, Ingri & Edgar Parin d'Aulaire
1941	*They Were Strong and Good*, Robert Lawson
1942	*Make Way for Ducklings*, Robert McCloskey
1943	*The Little House*, Virginia Lee Burton
1944	*Many Moons*, Louis Slobodkin
1945	*Prayer for a Child*, Elizabeth Orton Jones
1946	*The Rooster Crows*, Maude & Miska Petersham
1947	*The Little Island*, Leonard Weisgard
1948	*White Snow, Bright Snow*, Roger Duvoisin
1949	*The Big Snow*, Berta & Elmer Hader
1950	*Song of the Swallows*, Leo Politi
1951	*The Egg Tree*, Katherine Milhous
1952	*Finders Keepers*, Nicolas, pseud. (Nicholas Mordvinoff)
1953	*The Biggest Bear*, Lynd Ward
1954	*Madeline's Rescue*, Ludwig Bemelmans
1955	*Cinderella, or the Little Glass Slipper*, Marcia Brown
1956	*Frog Went A-Courtin'*, Feodor Rojankovsky
1957	*A Tree Is Nice*, Marc Simont
1958	*Time of Wonder*, Robert McCloskey
1959	*Chanticleer and the Fox*, Barbara Cooney
1960	*Nine Days to Christmas*, Marie Hall Ets
1961	*Baboushka and the Three Kings*, Nicolas Sidjakov
1962	*Once a Mouse*, Marcia Brown
1963	*The Snowy Day*, Ezra Jack Keats
1964	*Where the Wild Things Are*, Maurice Sendak
1965	*May I Bring a Friend?*, Beni Montressor
1966	*Always Room for One More*, Nonny Hogrogian
1967	*Sam, Bang, and Moonshine*, Evaline Ness
1968	*Drummer Hoff*, Ed Emberley
1969	*The Fool of the World and the Flying Ship*, Uri Shulevitz
1970	*Sylvester and the Magic Pebble*, William Steig
1971	*A Story A Story*, Gail E. Haley
1972	*One Fine Day*, Nonny Hogrogian
1973	*The Funny Little Woman*, Blair Lent
1974	*Duffy and the Devil*, Margot Zemach
1975	*Arrow to the Sun*, Gerald McDermott
1976	*Why Mosquitoes Buzz in People's Ears*, Leo & Diane Dillon
1977	*Ashanti to Zulu: African Traditions*, Leo & Diane Dillon
1978	*Noah's Ark*, Peter Spier
1979	*The Girl Who Loved Wild Horses*, Paul Goble
1980	*Ox-Cart Man*, Barbara Cooney
1981	*Fables*, Arnold Lobel
1982	*Jumanji*, Chris Van Allsburg
1983	*Shadow*, Marcia Brown
1984	*The Glorious Flight: Across the Channel with Louis Bleriot*, Alice and Martin Provensen
1985	*Saint George and the Dragon*, Trina Schart Hyman
1986	*The Polar Express*, Chris Van Allsburg
1987	*Hey, Al*, Richard Egielski
1988	*Owl Moon*, John Schoenherr
1989	*Song and Dance Man*, Stephen Grammell
1990	*Lon Po Po: A Red-Riding Hood Story From China*, Ed Young
1991	*Black and White*, David Macaulay
1992	*Tuesday*, David Wiesner
1993	*Mirette on the High Wire*, Emily Arnold McCully
1994	*Grandfather's Journey*, Allen Say
1995	*Smoky Night*, David Diaz
1996	*Officer Buckle and Gloria*, Peggy Rathmann
1997	*Golem*, David Wisniewski
1998	*Rapunzel*, Paul O. Zelinsky
1999	*Snowflake Bentley*, Mary Azarian
2000	*Joseph Had a Little Overcoat*, Simms Taback
2001	*So You Want to be President?*, David Small
2002	*The Three Pigs*, David Wiesner
2003	*My Friend Rabbit*, Eric Rohmann
2004	*The Man Who Walked Between the Towers*, Mordicai Gerstein

Miscellaneous Book Awards

(Awarded in 2004, unless otherwise noted)

Academy of American Poets Awards. Academy Fellowship (2003), $25,000 stipend: Li-Young Lee. James Laughlin Award, $5,000: Jeff Clark, *Music and Suicide*. Walt Whitman Award, $5,000: Geri Doran, *Resin*. Harold Morton Landon Translation Award, $1,000: Charles Martin, *Metamorphoses*; Anselm Hollo, *Pentii Saarikoski's Trilogy*. Lenore Marshall Poetry Prize, $25,000 (2003): Eamon Grennan, *Still Life With Waterfall*. Raiziss/de Palchi Translation Award (2003), $5,000: Andrew Frisardi, *The Selected Poems of Giuseppe Ungaretti*. Wallace Stevens Award, for mastery in the art of poetry, $150,000 (2003): Richard Wilbur.

American Academy of Arts and Letters. Academy Awards in Literature ($7,500 each): Henri Cole, Marilyn Hacker, Samuel Hynes, Arnost Lustig, Joe Ashby Porter, Louis D. Rubin, Paula Vogel, Greg Williamson. Michael Braude Award for Light Verse, $5,000: R.S. Gwynn. Benjamin H. Danks Award, $20,000: Doug Wright. E. M. Forster Award, $15,000: Robin Robertson. Sue Kaufman Prize for First Fiction, $2,500: Nell Freudenberger, *Lucky Girls*. Award of Merit for Poetry, $10,000: Rosanna Warren. Katherine Anne Porter Award, $20,000: Nicholson Baker. Richard and Hinda Rosenthal Foundation Award, $5,000: Olympia Vernon, *Eden*. Harold D. Vursell Memorial Award, $10,000: Judith Thurman. Morton Dawen Zabel Award, $10,000: Leonard Barkan. Rome Fellowships in Literature, one-year residence at the American Academy in Rome, for 2004-2005: Anthony Doerr (writer), Lisa Williams (poet).

Bollingen Prize in Poetry, by the Yale Univ. Library (2003): Adrienne Rich.

Edgar Awards, by the Mystery Writers of America: Grand Master award: Joseph Wambaugh. Best novel: *Resurrection Men*, Ian Rankin. Best first novel by an American author: *Death of a Nationalist*, Rebecca Pawel. Best paperback original: *Find Me Again*, Sylvia Maultash Warsh. Best Critical/Biographical: *Beautiful Shadow: A Life of Patricia Highsmith*, Andrew Wilson.

Golden Kite Awards, by Society of Children's Book Writers and Illustrators. Fiction: Jerry Spinelli, *Milkweed*. Nonfiction: Robert Byrd, *Leonardo: Beautiful Dreamer*. Picture-illustration:

Loren Long, *I Dream of Trains* (Angela Johnson, author). Picture book text: Amy Timberlake, *The Dirty Cowboy* (Adam Rex, illus.)

Le Prix Goncourt, by Académie Goncourt: Jacques-Pierre Amette, *La Maitresse de Brecht* (Brecht's Mistress).

Hugo Awards, by the World Science Fiction Convention. Novel: *Paladin of Souls,* Lois McMaster Bujold. Novella: *The Cookie Monster,* Vernor Vinge. Novelette: *Legions in Time,* Michael Swanwick. Short story: "A Study in Emerald," Neil Gaiman. John W. Campbell Award for Best New Writer: Jay Lake.

Coretta Scott King Award, by American Library Assn., for African American authors and illustrators of outstanding books for children and young adults. Author: Angela Johnson, *The First Part Last*. Illustrator: Ashley Bryan, *Beautiful Blackbird*.

Lincoln Prize, by Lincoln and Soldiers Institute at Gettysburg College, for contribution to Civil War studies, $ 30,000 and bust of Lincoln: Richard J. Carwardine, *Lincoln*. Special Lincoln Prize for extraordinary achievement, $20,000: John Y. Simon, editor, *The Papers of Ulysses S. Grant*.

National Book Critics Circle Awards. Fiction: Edward P. Jones, *The Known World*. Nonfiction: Paul Hendrickson, *Sons of Mississippi*. Criticism: Rebecca Solnit, *River of Shadows: Eadweard Muybridge and the Technological Wild West*. Biography/Autobiography: William Taubman, *Khrushchev: The Man and His Era*. Poetry: Susan Stewart, *Columbarium*. Nona Balakian Citation for Excellence in Reviewing: Scott McLemee. Ivan Sandrof Lifetime Achievement Award: Studs Terkel.

Nebula Awards, by the Science Fiction Writers of America. Novel: *The Speed of Dark,* Elizabeth Moon. Novella: *Coraline,* Neil Gaiman. Novelette: *The Empire of Ice Cream,* Jeffrey Ford. Short story: "What I Didn't See," Karen Joy Fowler.

PEN/Faulkner Award, for fiction, $15,000: John Updike, *The Early Stories*.

Whitbread Book of the Year Award, by Whitbread PLC: £25,000: Mark Haddon, *The Curious Incident of the Dog in the Night-Time*.

Journalism Awards, 2004

National Journalism Awards, by Scripps Howard Foundation, $5,000 each. Editorial writing: Tom Philp, *The Sacramento Bee* (CA). Human interest writing: Kelley Benham, *St. Petersburg Times* (FL). Environmental reporting (over 100,000 circ.): *The Washington Post* (David B. Ottaway and Joe Stephens); environmental reporting (under 100,000 circ.): *Naples Daily News* (FL). Public service reporting (over 100,000 circ.): *The Seattle Times* (Christine Willmsen and Maureen O'Hagan); public service reporting (under 100,000 circ.): *Argus Leader* (Sioux Falls, SD) (Stu Whitney and David Kranz). Commentary: John Kass, *Chicago Tribune*. Photojournalism: Brian Vander Brug, *Los Angeles Times*; editorial cartooning: Walt Handelsman, *Newsday* (Melville, NY); college cartooning: Nathaniel R. Creekmore, *The Babbler*, Lipscomb Univ. (Nashville, TN). Distinguished service to literacy: Rochelle Riley, *Detroit Free Press*; distinguished service to First Amendment: *Dayton Daily News* (OH). Business/economics reporting: Clint Riley, *The Record*, (Hackensack, NJ); web reporting: *Times Union* (TimesUnion.com), (Albany, NY) Electronic journalism—Small market radio: South Dakota Public Radio (Rapid City); large market radio: WBEZ, Chicago, *This American Life*; small market TV/cable: KTUU-TV, Anchorage, AK (Rhonda McBride); large market TV/cable: WCNC-TV, Charlotte, NC. (Stuart Watson). Journalism teacher of the year: Debashis Aikat, Univ. of NC, Chapel Hill.

National Magazine Awards, by American Society of Magazine Editors and Columbia Univ. Graduate School of Journalism. Gen. excel., circ. over 2 mil: *Newsweek*; 1 mil-2 mil: *Popular Science;* 500,000 to 1 mil: *Gourmet*; 250,000-500,000: *Budget Living*; 100,000-250,000: *Chicago Magazine*; under 100,000: *Aperture*. Personal service: *Men's Health*; leisure interests: *Consumer Reports*; feature writing: *The New Yorker*, fiction: *Esquire*; design: *Esquire*; photography: *City*; reporting: *Rolling Stone*; public interest: *The New Yorker*, profiles: *Esquire*; essays: *The New Yorker*, criticism/reviews: *Esquire*; columns/commentary: *New York*; single-topic issue: *The Oxford American*; gen. excellence online: CNET News.com (news.cnet.com).

George Foster Peabody Awards, by Univ. of Georgia. *Honor and Betrayal: Scandal at the Academy*, KMGH-TV, Denver, CO. *60 Minutes*, "All In the Family", CBS News, NY. *A Question of*

Fairness, NBC News, NY. *The NewsHour with Jim Lehrer,* "Jobless Recovery: Non-Working Numbers", MacNeil/Lehrer Productions, presented on PBS. *War Photographer,* Christian Frei Filmproductions, HBO/Cinemax Documentary Films, Swiss National Television, Suisseimage, presented on HBO. *The Elegant Universe with Brian Greene,* NOVA/WGBH (Boston) and Channel 4, presented on PBS. *Flag Wars,* P.O.V./American Documentary Inc., in assoc. with Independent Television Services (ITVS), Zula Pearl Films, and National Black Programming Consortium (NBPC), presented on PBS. *Two Towns of Jasper*, P.O.V./American Documentary Inc., in association with Independent Television Service (ITVS) and National Black Programming Consortium (NBPC), presented on PBS. *Chavez: Inside the Coup,* ZDF German TV in assoc. with the Irish Film Board. *Sisters in Pain,* WEKU-FM, Down to Earth Productions, presented on PBS. *To Live Is Better Than to Die,* Weijun Chen, HBO/Cinemax Documentary Films, TV2 Denmark, BBC, presented on Cinemax. *Know HIV/AIDS and Fight for Your Rights: Protect Yourself Campaigns, A Walk in Your Shoes: Living With HIV/AIDS, The Social History of HIV,* Viacom/MTV and the Kaiser Family Foundation. *Students Rising Above,* KRON-TV, San Francisco, CA. *Medicaid Dental Centers Investigation,* WCNC-TV, Charlotte, NC. *FRONTLINE,* "A Dangerous Business," WGBH/Frontline, *The New York Times*, and Canadian Broadcasting Corp., presented on PBS. *Great Performances:* "Degas and the Dance," Thirteen/WNET (NY), presented on PBS. *American Mavericks,* KSJN-FM/Minnesota Public Radio. *Mother Flew Away as a Kite,* TV Asahi Corporation. *Soldier's Girl,* Showtime. TRANSOM.ORG (online resource), Atlantic Public Media. *The Murder of Emmett Till,* American Experience/WGBH (Boston), presented on PBS. "Hoxie: the First Stand," Univ. of Memphis, TN.,and presented on PBS. *Evidence of Errors,* KHOU-TV, Houston, TX. *Building Homes: Building Problems,* WESH-TV, Winter Park, FL. *Israel's Secret Weapon,* BBC2. *Dora the Explorer,* MTV Networks/Nickelodeon. *The Wire,* HBO. *The Office,* BBC America. Individual Peabody Award: Bill Moyers.

Reuben Award, by National Cartoonists Society. For best cartoonist of 2003: Greg Evans.

The Spingarn Medal, 1915-2004

The Spingarn Medal has been awarded annually since 1915 (except in 1938) by the National Assoc. for the Advancement of Colored People for outstanding achievement by an African American.

1915 Ernest E. Just	1939 Marian Anderson	1960 Langston Hughes	1983 Lena Horne
1916 Charles Young	1940 Louis T. Wright	1961 Kenneth B. Clark	1984 Thomas Bradley
1917 Harry T. Burleigh	1941 Richard Wright	1962 Robert C. Weaver	1985 Bill Cosby
1918 William S. Braithwaite	1942 A. Philip Randolph	1963 Medgar W. Evers	1986 Dr. Benjamin L. Hooks
1919 Archibald H. Grimké	1943 William H. Hastie	1964 Roy Wilkins	1987 Percy E. Sutton
1920 W. E. B. Du Bois	1944 Charles Drew	1965 Leontyne Price	1988 Frederick D. Patterson
1921 Charles S. Gilpin	1945 Paul Robeson	1966 John H. Johnson	1989 Jesse Jackson
1922 Mary B. Talbert	1946 Thurgood Marshall	1967 Edward W. Brooke	1990 L. Douglas Wilder
1923 George W.Carver	1947 Dr. Percy L. Julian	1968 Sammy Davis Jr.	1991 Gen. Colin L. Powell
1924 Roland Hayes	1948 Channing H. Tobias	1969 Clarence M. Mitchell Jr.	1992 Barbara Jordan
1925 James W. Johnson	1949 Ralph J. Bunche	1970 Jacob Lawrence	1993 Dorothy I. Height
1926 Carter G. Woodson	1950 Charles H. Houston	1971 Leon H. Sullivan	1994 Maya Angelou
1927 Anthony Overton	1951 Mabel K. Staupers	1972 Gordon Parks	1995 John Hope Franklin
1928 Charles W. Chesnutt	1952 Harry T. Moore	1973 Wilson C. Riles	1996 A. Leon Higginbotham
1929 Mordecai W. Johnson	1953 Paul R. Williams	1974 Damon Keith	1997 Carl T. Rowan
1930 Henry A. Hunt	1954 Theodore K. Lawless	1975 Henry (Hank) Aaron	1998 Myrlie Evers-Williams
1931 Richard B. Harrison	1955 Carl Murphy	1976 Alvin Ailey	1999 Earl G. Graves Sr.
1932 Robert R. Moton	1956 Jack R. Robinson	1977 Alex Haley	2000 Oprah Winfrey
1933 Max Yergan	1957 Martin Luther King Jr.	1978 Andrew Young	2001 Vernon E. Jordan Jr.
1934 William T. B. Williams	1958 Daisy Bates and the	1979 Rosa L. Parks	2002 John Lewis
1935 Mary McLeod Bethune	Little Rock Nine	1980 Dr. Rayford W. Logan	2003 Constance Baker
1936 John Hope	1959 Edward Kennedy	1981 Coleman Young	Motley
1937 Walter White	(Duke) Ellington	1982 Dr. Benjamin E. Mays	2004 Robert L. Carter

Miscellaneous Awards, 2004

American Academy of Arts and Letters. Gold Medal for Graphic Art: Chuck Close. Gold Medal for Drama: John Guare. Medal for Spoken Language: former Pres. Bill Clinton. Award for Distinguished Service to the Arts: Beverly Sills. Arnold W. Brunner Memorial Prize in Architecture, $5,000: Hans Hollein. Academy Awards, $7,500 each, in Architecture: Preston Scott Cohen, James Corner, Marion Weiss, Michael Manfredi; in Art: Jacqueline Gourevitch, Spence Guerin, Faith Ringgold, Robert Stuart, John Walker; in Music: Miguel Chuaqui, Justin Dello Joio, Jorge Liderman, Richard Wilson. Jimmy Ernst Award in Art, $5,000: Stephen Pace. Walter Hinrichsen Award (Music): Stephen Blumberg. Charles Ives Fellowships in Music, $15,000: Kristin P. Kuster, Harold Meltzer. Charles Ives Scholarships in Music, $7,500 each: Judah E. Adashi, Judd Greenstein, Matthew Kajcienski, Tamar Muskal, Jeff Myers, Aaron Travers. Wladimir and Rhoda Lakond Award (Music), $5,000: Trent Johnson, Virginia Samuel. Goddard Lieberson Fellowships in Music, $15,000 each: Susan Botti, Evan Ziporyn. Richard Rodgers Awards for the Musical Theater, $100,000: *The Tutor*, Andrew Gerle and Maryrose Wood (production); *To Paint the Earth*, Daniel Frederick Levin and Jonathan Portera (staged reading); *Unlocked*, Sam Carner and Dick Gregor (staged reading). Richard and Hinda Rosenthal Foundation Award in Painting, $5,000: Chie Fueki. Willard L. Metcalf Award in Art, $10,000: Tara Donovan.

Congressional Gold Medal, by Congress. Dorothy Height.

Fields Medal, International Mathematical Union, every 4 years: (2002) Vladimir Voevodsky, Laurent Lafforgue.

Intel Science Talent Search (formerly given by Westinghouse). First ($100,000 schol.): Herbert Mason Hedberg, North Attleboro, MA; second ($75,000 schol.): Boris Alexeev, Athens, GA; third ($50,000 schol.): Ryna Karnik, Aloha, OR.

National Inventor of the Year Awards, by Intellectual Property Owners Assn. Jim Weber and Scott Leman of Caterpillar Inc.

John F. Kennedy Center for the Performing Arts Awards. (2003) James Brown, Carol Burnett, Loretta Lynn, Mike Nichols, Itzhak Perlman.

Library of the Year Award, by Gale Research, Inc., and *Library Journal*. San Jose Public Library and San Jose State University Library (CA).

National Humanities Medal (formerly Charles Frankel Prize), by National Endowment for the Humanities. $5,000 each: Robert Ballard, Joan Ganz Cooney, Midge Decter, Joseph Epstein, Elizabeth Fox-Genovese, Jean Fritz, Hal Holbrook, Edith Kurzweil, Frank Snowden, Jr, John Updike.

National Medal of the Arts, by the National Endowment for the Arts and the White House. *Austin City Limits* (PBS television program), Beverly Cleary, Rafe Esquith, Suzanne Farrell, Buddy Guy, Ron Howard, Mormon Tabernacle Choir, Leonard Slatkin, George Strait, Tommy Tune.

Presidential Medal of Freedom, by the White House. Robert L. Bartley, Edward Brooke III, Doris Day, Vartan Gregorian, Gilbert Melville Grosvenor, Gordon B. Hinckley, Pope John Paul II, Estee Lauder, Rita Moreno, Arnold Palmer, Arnall Patz, Norman Podhoretz, Walter Wriston.

Pritzker Architecture Prize, by the Hyatt Foundation, $100,000: Zaha Hadid, UK.

Teacher of the Year, by Council of Chief State School Officers and Scholastic, Inc.: Kathy Mellor, North Kingstown, RI.

Templeton Prize for Progress Toward Research or Discoveries about Spiritual Realities, by Templeton Foundation, £795,000 (about $1.465 million): George F.R. Ellis, Professor of Applied Mathematics, Univ. of Cape Town, South Africa.

Miss America Winners, for 1921-2005

1921	Margaret Gorman, Washington, DC	1954	Evelyn Margaret Ay, Ephrata, Pennsylvania
1922-23	Mary Campbell, Columbus, Ohio	1955	Lee Meriwether, San Francisco, California
1924	Ruth Malcolmson, Philadelphia, Pennsylvania	1956	Sharon Ritchie, Denver, Colorado
1925	Fay Lamphier, Oakland, California	1957	Marian McKnight, Manning, South Carolina
1926	Norma Smallwood, Tulsa, Oklahoma	1958	Marilyn Van Derbur, Denver, Colorado
1927	Lois Delander, Joliet, Illinois	1959	Mary Ann Mobley, Brandon, Mississippi
1933	Marion Bergeron, West Haven, Connecticut	1960	Lynda Lee Mead, Natchez, Mississippi
1935	Henrietta Leaver, Pittsburgh, Pennsylvania	1961	Nancy Fleming, Montague, Michigan
1936	Rose Coyle, Philadelphia, Pennsylvania	1962	Maria Fletcher, Asheville, North Carolina
1937	Bette Cooper, Bertrand Island, New Jersey	1963	Jacquelyn Mayer, Sandusky, Ohio
1938	Marilyn Meseke, Marion, Ohio	1964	Donna Axum, El Dorado, Arkansas
1939	Patricia Donnelly, Detroit, Michigan	1965	Vonda Kay Van Dyke, Phoenix, Arizona
1940	Frances Marie Burke, Philadelphia, Pennsylvania	1966	Deborah Irene Bryant, Overland Park, Kansas
1941	Rosemary LaPlanche, Los Angeles, California	1967	Jane Anne Jayroe, Laverne, Oklahoma
1942	Jo-Caroll Dennison, Tyler, Texas	1968	Debra Dene Barnes, Moran, Kansas
1943	Jean Bartel, Los Angeles, California	1969	Judith Anne Ford, Belvidere, Illinois
1944	Venus Ramey, Washington, D.C.	1970	Pamela Anne Eldred, Birmingham, Michigan
1945	Bess Myerson, New York City, New York	1971	Phyllis Ann George, Denton, Texas
1946	Marilyn Buferd, Los Angeles, California	1972	Laurie Lea Schaefer, Columbus, Ohio
1947	Barbara Walker, Memphis, Tennessee	1973	Terry Anne Meeuwsen, DePere, Wisconsin
1948	BeBe Shopp, Hopkins, Minnesota	1974	Rebecca Ann King, Denver, Colorado
1949	Jacque Mercer, Litchfield, Arizona	1975	Shirley Cothran, Fort Worth, Texas
1951	Yolande Betbeze, Mobile, Alabama	1976	Tawney Elaine Godin, Yonkers, New York
1952	Coleen Kay Hutchins, Salt Lake City, Utah	1977	Dorothy Kathleen Benham, Edina, Minnesota
1953	Neva Jane Langley, Macon, Georgia	1978	Susan Perkins, Columbus, Ohio

1979	Kylene Barker, Galax, Virginia		1992	Carolyn Suzanne Sapp, Honolulu, Hawaii
1980	Cheryl Prewitt, Ackerman, Mississippi		1993	Leanza Cornett, Jacksonville, Florida
1981	Susan Powell, Elk City, Oklahoma		1994	Kimberly Aiken, Columbia, South Carolina
1982	Elizabeth Ward, Russellville, Arkansas		1995	Heather Whitestone, Birmingham, Alabama
1983	Debra Maffett, Anaheim, California		1996	Shawntel Smith, Muldrow, Oklahoma
1984	Vanessa Williams*, Milwood, New York		1997	Tara Dawn Holland, Overland Park, Kansas
	Suzette Charles, Mays Landing, New Jersey		1998	Kate Shindle, Evanston, Illinois
1985	Sharlene Wells, Salt Lake City, Utah		1999	Nicole Johnson, Roanoke, Virginia
1986	Susan Akin, Meridian, Mississippi		2000	Heather Renee French, Maysville, Kentucky
1987	Kellye Cash, Memphis, Tennessee		2001	Angela Perez Baraquio, Honolulu, Hawaii
1988	Kaye Lani Rae Rafko, Monroe, Michigan		2002	Katie Harman, Gresham, Oregon
1989	Gretchen Carlson, Anoka, Minnesota		2003	Erika Harold, Urbana, Illinois
1990	Debbye Turner, Columbia, Missouri		2004	Ericka Dunlap, Orlando, Florida
1991	Marjorie Vincent, Oak Park, Illinois		2005	Deidre Downs, Birmingham, Alabama

* Resigned July 23, 1984.

Entertainment Awards

Tony (Antoinette Perry) Awards, 2004

Play: *I Am My Own Wife*, by Doug Wright
Musical: *Avenue Q*
Book of a musical: Jeff Whitty, *Avenue Q*
Actor, play: Jefferson Mays, *I Am My Own Wife*
Actress, play: Phylicia Rashad, *A Raisin in the Sun*
Actor, musical: Hugh Jackman, *The Boy From Oz*
Actress, musical: Idina Menzel, *Wicked*
Musical score: Robert Lopez and Jeff Marx, *Avenue Q*
Director, play: Jack O'Brien, *Henry IV*
Director, musical: Joe Mantello, *Assassins*
Play revival: *Henry IV*
Musical revival: *Assassins*

Featured actor, play: Brian F. O'Byrne, *Frozen*
Featured actress, play: Audra McDonald, *A Raisin in the Sun*
Featured actor, musical: Michael Cerveris, *Assassins*
Featured actress, musical: Anika Noni Rose, *Caroline, or Change*
Choreography: Kathleen Marshall, *Wonderful Town*
Costume design: Susan Hilferty, *Wicked*
Scenic design: Eugene Lee, *Wicked*
Lighting design: Jules Fisher and Peggy Eisenhauer, *Assassins*
Orchestrations: Michael Starobin, *Assassins*
Lifetime achievement: James M. Nederlander
Regional Theater: Cincinnati Playhouse in the Park

Tony Awards, 1948-2004

Year	Play	Musical	Year	Play	Musical
1948	*Mister Roberts*	No Award	1976	*Travesties*	*A Chorus Line*
1949	*Death of a Salesman*	*Kiss Me Kate*	1977	*The Shadow Box*	*Annie*
1950	*The Cocktail Party*	*South Pacific*	1978	*Da*	*Ain't Misbehavin'*
1951	*The Rose Tattoo*	*Guys and Dolls*	1979	*The Elephant Man*	*Sweeney Todd*
1952	*The Fourposter*	*The King and I*	1980	*Children of a Lesser God*	*Evita*
1953	*The Crucible*	*Wonderful Town*	1981	*Amadeus*	*42nd Street*
1954	*The Teahouse of the August Moon*	*Kismet*	1982	*The Life and Adventures of Nicholas Nickelby*	*Nine*
1955	*The Desperate Hours*	*The Pajama Game*	1983	*Torch Song Trilogy*	*Cats*
1956	*The Diary of Anne Frank*	*Damn Yankees*	1984	*The Real Thing*	*La Cage aux Folles*
1957	*Long Day's Journey Into Night*	*My Fair Lady*	1985	*Biloxi Blues*	*Big River*
1958	*Sunrise at Campobello*	*The Music Man*	1986	*I'm Not Rappaport*	*The Mystery of Edwin Drood*
1959	*J.B.*	*Redhead*			
1960	*The Miracle Worker*	(tie) *Fiorello!*, *The Sound of Music*	1987	*Fences*	*Les Miserables*
			1988	*M. Butterfly*	*Phantom of the Opera*
1961	*Becket*	*Bye, Bye Birdie*	1989	*The Heidi Chronicles*	*Jerome Robbins' Broadway*
1962	*A Man for All Seasons*	*How to Succeed in Business Without Really Trying*	1990	*The Grapes of Wrath*	*City of Angels*
			1991	*Lost in Yonkers*	*The Will Rogers Follies*
1963	*Who's Afraid of Virginia Woolf?*	*A Funny Thing Happened on the Way to the Forum*	1992	*Dancing at Lughnasa*	*Crazy for You*
			1993	*Angels in America: Millennium Approaches*	*Kiss of the Spider Woman*
1964	*Luther*	*Hello, Dolly!*	1994	*Angels in America: Perestroika*	*Passion*
1965	*The Subject Was Roses*	*Fiddler on the Roof*	1995	*Love! Valour! Compassion!*	*Sunset Boulevard*
1966	*Marat/Sade*	*Man of La Mancha*	1996	*Master Class*	*Rent*
1967	*The Homecoming*	*Cabaret*	1997	*The Last Night of Ballyhoo*	*Titanic*
1968	*Rosencrantz and Guildenstern Are Dead*	*Hallelujah, Baby!*	1998	*Art*	*The Lion King*
1969	*The Great White Hope*	*1776*	1999	*Side Man*	*Fosse*
1970	*Borstal Boy*	*Applause*	2000	*Copenhagen*	*Contact*
1971	*Sleuth*	*Company*	2001	*Proof*	*The Producers*
1972	*Sticks and Bones*	*Two Gentleman of Verona*	2002	*Edward Albee's The Goat or Who Is Sylvia?*	*Thoroughly Modern Millie*
1973	*That Championship Season*	*A Little Night Music*	2003	*Take Me Out*	*Hairspray*
1974	*The River Niger*	*Raisin*	2004	*I Am My Own Wife*	*Avenue Q*
1975	*Equus*	*The Wiz*			

2004 Selected Prime-Time Emmy Awards (for 2003-2004 season)

Drama series: *The Sopranos*, HBO
Comedy series: *Arrested Development*, FOX
Miniseries: *Angels in America*, HBO
Variety, music, or comedy series: *The Daily Show With Jon Stewart*, Comedy Central
Variety, music, or comedy special: *Elaine Stritch: At Liberty*, HBO
Made-for-television movie: *Something the Lord Made*, HBO
Lead actor, drama series: James Spader, *The Practice*, ABC
Lead actress, drama series: Allison Janney, *The West Wing*, NBC
Lead actor, comedy series: Kelsey Grammer, *Fraiser*, NBC
Lead actress, comedy series: Sarah Jessica Parker, *Sex and the City*, HBO
Lead actor, miniseries/movie: Al Pacino, *Angels in America*, HBO

Lead actress, miniseries/movie: Meryl Streep, *Angels in America*, HBO
Sup. actor, drama series: Michael Imperioli, *The Sopranos*, HBO
Sup. actress, drama series: Drea De Matteo, *The Sopranos*, HBO
Sup. actor, comedy series: David Hyde Pierce, *Fraiser*, NBC
Sup. actress, comedy series: Cynthia Nixon, *Sex and the City*, HBO
Sup. actor, miniseries/movie: Jeffrey Wright, *Angels in America*, HBO
Sup. actress, miniseries/movie: Mary-Louise Parker, *Angels in America*, HBO
Individual performance, variety series/music program: Elaine Stritch, *Elaine Stritch: At Liberty*, HBO
Reality/competition program: *The Amazing Race*, CBS
Bob Hope Humanitarian Award: Danny Thomas

2004 Selected Daytime Emmy Awards (for 2003-2004 season)

Drama series: *The Young and the Restless*, CBS
Actress: Michelle Stafford, *The Young and the Restless*, CBS
Actor: Anthony Geary, *General Hospital*, ABC
Sup. actress: Cady McClain, *As the World Turns*, CBS
Sup. actor: Rick Hearst, *General Hospital*, ABC
Younger actress: Jennifer Finnigan, *The Bold and the Beautiful*, CBS
Younger actor: Chad Brannon, *General Hospital*, ABC
Drama series directing team: *General Hospital*, ABC
Drama series writing team: *As the World Turns*, CBS
Preschool children's series: *Sesame Street*, PBS
Children's series: *Assignment Discovery*, ABC

Performer in children's series: Jeff Corwin, *Jeff Corwin Unleashed*, NBC
Performer in children's special: Gena Rowlands, *The Incredible Mrs. Ritchie*, Showtime
Game/audience participation show: *The Price Is Right*, CBS
Game show host: Bob Barker, *The Price Is Right*, CBS
Talk Show: *The Ellen DeGeneres Show*, syndicated
Talk show host: Wayne Brady, *The Wayne Brady Show*, synd.
Special class series: *When I Was a Girl*, WE
Lifetime Achievement Award: Rachel Ames, John Clarke, Jeanne Cooper, Eileen Fulton, Don Hastings, Anna Lee, Ray MacDonnell, Frances Reid, Helen Wagner, Ruth Warrick

Prime-Time Emmy Awards, 1952-2004

The National Academy of Television Arts and Science presented the first Emmy Awards in 1949. Through the years, award categories have changed, but since 1952, the Academy has recognized an outstanding comedy and drama each year.

Year Given	Comedy	Drama	Year Given	Comedy	Drama
1952	*Red Skelton Show*, NBC	*Studio One*, CBS	1975	*Mary Tyler Moore Show*, CBS	*Masterpiece Theatre: Upstairs, Downstairs*; PBS
1953	*I Love Lucy*, CBS	*Robert Montgomery Presents*, NBC	1976	*Mary Tyler Moore Show*, CBS	*Police Story*, NBC
1954	*I Love Lucy*, CBS	*The U.S. Steel Hour*, ABC	1977	*Mary Tyler Moore Show*, CBS	*Masterpiece Theatre: Upstairs, Downstairs*; PBS
1955	*Make Room for Daddy*, ABC	*The U.S. Steel Hour*, ABC	1978	*All in the Family*, CBS	*The Rockford Files*, NBC
1956	*Phil Silvers Show*, CBS	*Producer's Showcase*, NBC	1979	*Taxi*, ABC	*Lou Grant*, CBS
1957	*Phil Silvers Show*, CBS	*Requiem for a Heavyweight*, CBS[1]	1980	*Taxi*, ABC	*Lou Grant*, CBS
			1981	*Taxi*, ABC	*Hill Street Blues*, NBC
1958	*Phil Silvers Show*, CBS	*Gunsmoke*, CBS	1982	*Barney Miller*, ABC	*Hill Street Blues*, NBC
1959[2]	*Jack Benny Show*, CBS	(3)	1983	*Cheers*, NBC	*Hill Street Blues*, NBC
1960	*Art Carney Special*, NBC	*Playhouse 90*, CBS	1984	*Cheers*, NBC	*Hill Street Blues*, NBC
1961	*Jack Benny Show*, CBS	*Hallmark Hall of Fame: Macbeth*, NBC	1985	*The Cosby Show*, NBC	*Cagney & Lacey*, CBS
			1986	*Golden Girls*, NBC	*Cagney & Lacey*, CBS
1962	*Bob Newhart Show*, CBS	*The Defenders*, CBS	1987	*Golden Girls*, NBC	*L.A. Law*, NBC
1963	*Dick Van Dyke Show*, CBS	*The Defenders*, CBS	1988	*The Wonder Years*, ABC	*thirtysomething*, ABC
1964	*Dick Van Dyke Show*, CBS	*The Defenders*, CBS	1989	*Cheers*, NBC	*L.A. Law*, NBC
1965	*Dick Van Dyke Show*, CBS	*Hallmark Hall of Fame: The Magnificent Yankee*, NBC	1990	*Murphy Brown*, CBS	*L.A. Law*, NBC
			1991	*Cheers*, NBC	*L.A. Law*, NBC
1966	*Dick Van Dyke Show*, CBS	*The Fugitive*, ABC	1992	*Murphy Brown*, CBS	*Northern Exposure*, CBS
1967	*The Monkees*, NBC	*Mission: Impossible*, CBS	1993	*Seinfeld*, NBC	*Picket Fences*, CBS
1968	*Get Smart*, NBC	*Mission: Impossible*, CBS	1994	*Frasier*, NBC	*Picket Fences*, CBS
1969	*Get Smart*, NBC	*NET Playhouse*, NET	1995	*Frasier*, NBC	*NYPD Blue*, ABC
1970	*My World and Welcome to It*, NBC	*Marcus Welby, M.D.*, ABC	1996	*Frasier*, NBC	*ER*, NBC
			1997	*Frasier*, NBC	*Law & Order*, NBC
1971	*All in the Family*, CBS	*The Bold Ones: "The Senator,"* NBC	1998	*Frasier*, NBC	*The Practice*, ABC
			1999	*Ally McBeal*, Fox	*The Practice*, ABC
1972	*All in the Family*, CBS	*Masterpiece Theatre: Elizabeth R*, PBS	2000	*Will & Grace*, NBC	*The West Wing*, NBC
			2001	*Sex and the City*, HBO	*The West Wing*, NBC
1973	*All in the Family*, CBS	*The Waltons*, CBS	2002	*Friends*, NBC	*The West Wing*, NBC
1974	*M*A*S*H*, CBS	*Masterpiece Theatre: Upstairs, Downstairs*; PBS	2003	*Everybody Loves Raymond*, CBS	*The West Wing*, NBC
			2004	*Arrested Development*, Fox	*The Sopranos*, HBO

(1) "Best Single Program of the Year," shown on *Playhouse 90*, which was named "Best New Series." (2) Beginning in 1959, Emmys awarded for work in the season encompassing the previous and current year. (3) *Playhouse 90* (CBS) was best drama of 1 hour or longer; *Alcoa-Goodyear Theatre* (NBC) was best drama of less than 1 hour.

2004 Golden Globe Awards

(Awarded for work in 2003)

Film

Drama: *The Lord of the Rings: The Return of the King*
Musical/comedy: *Lost in Translation*
Actress, drama: Charlize Theron, *Monster*
Actor, drama: Sean Penn, *Mystic River*
Actress, musical/comedy: Diane Keaton, *Something's Gotta Give*
Actor, musical/comedy: Bill Murray, *Lost in Translation*
Sup. actress, drama: Renee Zellweger, *Cold Mountain*
Sup. actor, drama: Tim Robbins, *Mystic River*
Director: Peter Jackson, *The Lord of the Rings: The Return of the King*
Screenplay: Sofia Coppola, *Lost in Translation*
Foreign-language film: *Osama* (Afghanistan)
Original score: Howard Shore, *The Lord of the Rings: The Return of the King*
Original Song: "Into the West," from *The Lord of the Rings: The Return of the King*, Howard Shore, Fran Walsh, Annie Lennox

Cecil B. De Mille award for lifetime achievement: Michael Douglas

Television

Series, drama: *24*, Fox
Actress, drama: Frances Conroy, *Six Feet Under*, HBO
Actor, drama: Anthony LaPaglia, *Without a Trace*, CBS
Series, musical/comedy: *The Office*, BBC America
Actress, musical/comedy: Sarah Jessica Parker, *Sex and the City*, HBO
Actor, musical/comedy: Ricky Gervais, *The Office*, BBC Amer
Miniseries, movie made for TV: *Angels in America*, HBO
Actress, miniseries/movie: Meryl Streep, *Angels in America*, HBO
Actor, miniseries/movie: Al Pacino, *Angels in America*, HBO
Sup. actress, miniseries/movie: Mary-Louise Parker, *Angels in America*, HBO
Sup. actor, miniseries/movie: Jeffrey Wright, *Angels in America*, HBO

2004 People's Choice Awards

(Awarded for work in 2003)

Film

Picture: *Pirates of the Caribbean: The Curse of the Black Pearl*
Drama: *Lord of the Rings: The Two Towers*
Comedy: *Bruce Almighty*
Actor: Mel Gibson
Actress: Julia Roberts

Television

Drama: *CSI: Crime Scene Investigation*
Comedy: *Friends*

Male performer: Ray Romano, *Everybody Loves Raymond*
Female performer: Jennifer Aniston, *Friends*
New comedy: *Two and a Half Men*
New drama: *Joan of Arcadia*
Talk show host: Oprah Winfrey
Reality program: *Survivor: Pearl Islands*

Music

Male performer: Tim McGraw
Female performer: (tie) Faith Hill and Beyoncé Knowles
Group or band: Matchbox Twenty

Academy Awards (Oscars) for 1927-2003

Year	Picture	Actor	Actress	Sup. Actor[1]	Sup. Actress[1]	Director
1927-28	*Wings*	Emil Jannings, *The Way of All Flesh*	Janet Gaynor, *Seventh Heaven*			Frank Borzage, *Seventh Heaven;* Lewis Milestone, *Two Arabian Knights*
1928-29	*Broadway Melody*	Warner Baxter, *In Old Arizona*	Mary Pickford, *Coquette*			Frank Lloyd, *The Divine Lady*
1929-30	All Quiet on the Western Front	George Arliss *Disraeli*	Norma Shearer *The Divorcee*			Lewis Milestone *All Quiet on the Western Front*
1930-31	*Cimarron*	Lionel Barrymore *Free Soul*	Marie Dressler *Min and Bill*			Norman Taurog *Skippy*
1931-32	Grand Hotel	Fredric March *Dr. Jekyll and Mr. Hyde;* Wallace Beery *The Champ* (tie)	Helen Hayes *The Sin of Madelon Claudet*			Frank Borzage *Bad Girl*
1932-33	*Cavalcade*	Charles Laughton *The Private Life of Henry VIII*	Katharine Hepburn *Morning Glory*			Frank Lloyd *Cavalcade*
1934	It Happened One Night	Clark Gable *It Happened One Night*	Claudette Colbert *It Happened One Night*			Frank Capra *It Happened One Night*
1935	*Mutiny on the Bounty*	Victor McLaglen *The Informer*	Bette Davis *Dangerous*			John Ford *The Informer*
1936	*The Great Ziegfeld*	Paul Muni *Story of Louis Pasteur*	Luise Rainer *The Great Ziegfeld*	Walter Brennan *Come and Get It*	Gale Sondergaard *Anthony Adverse*	Frank Capra *Mr. Deeds Goes to Town*
1937	*Life of Emile Zola*	Spencer Tracy *Captains Courageous*	Luise Rainer *The Good Earth*	Joseph Schildkraut *Life of Emile Zola*	Alice Brady *In Old Chicago*	Leo McCarey *The Awful Truth*
1938	You Can't Take It With You	Spencer Tracy *Boys Town*	Bette Davis *Jezebel*	Walter Brennan *Kentucky*	Fay Bainter *Jezebel*	Frank Capra *You Can't Take It With You*
1939	*Gone With the Wind*	Robert Donat *Goodbye Mr. Chips*	Vivien Leigh *Gone With the Wind*	Thomas Mitchell *Stage Coach*	Hattie McDaniel *Gone With the Wind*	Victor Fleming *Gone With the Wind*
1940	Rebecca	James Stewart *The Philadelphia Story*	Ginger Rogers *Kitty Foyle*	Walter Brennan *The Westerner*	Jane Darwell *The Grapes of Wrath*	John Ford *The Grapes of Wrath*
1941	*How Green Was My Valley*	Gary Cooper *Sergeant York*	Joan Fontaine *Suspicion*	Donald Crisp *How Green Was My Valley*	Mary Astor *The Great Lie*	John Ford *How Green Was My Valley*
1942	Mrs. Miniver	James Cagney *Yankee Doodle Dandy*	Greer Garson *Mrs. Miniver*	Van Heflin *Johnny Eager*	Teresa Wright *Mrs. Miniver*	William Wyler *Mrs. Miniver*
1943	*Casablanca*	Paul Lukas *Watch on the Rhine*	Jennifer Jones *The Song of Bernadette*	Charles Coburn *The More the Merrier*	Katina Paxinou *For Whom the Bell Tolls*	Michael Curtiz *Casablanca*
1944	*Going My Way*	Bing Crosby *Going My Way*	Ingrid Bergman *Gaslight*	Barry Fitzgerald *Going My Way*	Ethel Barrymore *None But the Lonely Heart*	Leo McCarey *Going My Way*
1945	*The Lost Weekend*	Ray Milland *The Lost Weekend*	Joan Crawford *Mildred Pierce*	James Dunn *A Tree Grows in Brooklyn*	Anne Revere *National Velvet*	Billy Wilder *The Lost Weekend*
1946	The Best Years of Our Lives	Fredric March *The Best Years of Our Lives*	Olivia de Havilland *To Each His Own*	Harold Russell *The Best Years of Our Lives*	Anne Baxter *The Razor's Edge*	William Wyler *The Best Years of Our Lives*
1947	*Gentleman's Agreement*	Ronald Colman *A Double Life*	Loretta Young *The Farmer's Daughter*	Edmund Gwenn *Miracle on 34th Street*	Celeste Holm *Gentleman's Agreement*	Elia Kazan *Gentleman's Agreement*
1948	*Hamlet*	Laurence Olivier *Hamlet*	Jane Wyman *Johnny Belinda*	Walter Huston *Treasure of Sierra Madre*	Claire Trevor *Key Largo*	John Huston *Treasure of Sierra Madre*
1949	*All the King's Men*	Broderick Crawford *All the King's Men*	Olivia de Havilland *The Heiress*	Dean Jagger *Twelve O'Clock High*	Mercedes McCambridge *All the King's Men*	Joseph L. Mankiewicz *Letter to Three Wives*
1950	All About Eve	Jose Ferrer *Cyrano de Bergerac*	Judy Holliday *Born Yesterday*	George Sanders *All About Eve*	Josephine Hull *Harvey*	Joseph L. Mankiewicz *All About Eve*
1951	*An American in Paris*	Humphrey Bogart *The African Queen*	Vivien Leigh *A Streetcar Named Desire*	Karl Malden *A Streetcar Named Desire*	Kim Hunter *A Streetcar Named Desire*	George Stevens *A Place in the Sun*
1952	*The Greatest Show on Earth*	Gary Cooper *High Noon*	Shirley Booth *Come Back Little Sheba*	Anthony Quinn *Viva Zapata!*	Gloria Grahame *The Bad and the Beautiful*	John Ford *The Quiet Man*
1953	*From Here to Eternity*	William Holden *Stalag 17*	Audrey Hepburn *Roman Holiday*	Frank Sinatra *From Here to Eternity*	Donna Reed *From Here to Eternity*	Fred Zinnemann *From Here to Eternity*
1954	On the Waterfront	Marlon Brando *On the Waterfront*	Grace Kelly *The Country Girl*	Edmond O'Brien *The Barefoot Contessa*	Eva Marie Saint *On the Waterfront*	Elia Kazan *On the Waterfront*
1955	*Marty*	Ernest Borgnine *Marty*	Anna Magnani *The Rose Tattoo*	Jack Lemmon *Mister Roberts*	Jo Van Fleet *East of Eden*	Delbert Mann *Marty*
1956	Around the World in 80 Days	Yul Brynner *The King and I*	Ingrid Bergman *Anastasia*	Anthony Quinn *Lust for Life*	Dorothy Malone *Written on the Wind*	George Stevens *Giant*
1957	*The Bridge on the River Kwai*	Alec Guinness *The Bridge on the River Kwai*	Joanne Woodward *The Three Faces of Eve*	Red Buttons *Sayonara*	Miyoshi Umeki *Sayonara*	David Lean *The Bridge on the River Kwai*

Year	Picture	Actor	Actress	Sup. Actor[1]	Sup. Actress[1]	Director
1958	Gigi	David Niven *Separate Tables*	Susan Hayward *I Want to Live*	Burl Ives *The Big Country*	Wendy Hiller *Separate Tables*	Vincente Minnelli *Gigi*
1959	*Ben-Hur*	Charlton Heston *Ben-Hur*	Simone Signoret *Room at the Top*	Hugh Griffith *Ben-Hur*	Shelley Winters *Diary of Anne Frank*	William Wyler *Ben-Hur*
1960	*The Apartment*	Burt Lancaster *Elmer Gantry*	Elizabeth Taylor *Butterfield 8*	Peter Ustinov *Spartacus*	Shirley Jones *Elmer Gantry*	Billy Wilder *The Apartment*
1961	*West Side Story*	Maximilian Schell *Judgment at Nuremberg*	Sophia Loren *Two Women*	George Chakiris *West Side Story*	Rita Moreno *West Side Story*	Jerome Robbins, Robert Wise *West Side Story*
1962	Lawrence of Arabia	Gregory Peck *To Kill a Mockingbird*	Anne Bancroft *The Miracle Worker*	Ed Begley *Sweet Bird of Youth*	Patty Duke *The Miracle Worker*	David Lean *Lawrence of Arabia*
1963	*Tom Jones*	Sidney Poitier *Lilies of the Field*	Patricia Neal *Hud*	Melvyn Douglas *Hud*	Margaret Rutherford *The V.I.P.s*	Tony Richardson *Tom Jones*
1964	*My Fair Lady*	Rex Harrison *My Fair Lady*	Julie Andrews *Mary Poppins*	Peter Ustinov *Topkapi*	Lila Kedrova *Zorba the Greek*	George Cukor *My Fair Lady*
1965	*The Sound of Music*	Lee Marvin *Cat Ballou*	Julie Christie *Darling*	Martin Balsam *A Thousand Clowns*	Shelley Winters *A Patch of Blue*	Robert Wise *The Sound of Music*
1966	A Man for All Seasons	Paul Scofield *A Man for All Seasons*	Elizabeth Taylor *Who's Afraid of Virginia Woolf?*	Walter Matthau *The Fortune Cookie*	Sandy Dennis *Who's Afraid of Virginia Woolf?*	Fred Zinnemann *A Man for All Seasons*
1967	*In the Heat of the Night*	Rod Steiger *In the Heat of the Night*	Katharine Hepburn *Guess Who's Coming to Dinner*	George Kennedy *Cool Hand Luke*	Estelle Parsons *Bonnie and Clyde*	Mike Nichols *The Graduate*
1968	*Oliver!*	Cliff Robertson *Charly*	Katharine Hepburn *The Lion in Winter;* Barbra Streisand *Funny Girl* (tie)	Jack Albertson *The Subject Was Roses*	Ruth Gordon *Rosemary's Baby*	Sir Carol Reed *Oliver!*
1969	*Midnight Cowboy*	John Wayne *True Grit*	Maggie Smith *The Prime of Miss Jean Brodie*	Gig Young *They Shoot Horses, Don't They?*	Goldie Hawn *Cactus Flower*	John Schlesinger *Midnight Cowboy*
1970	Patton	George C. Scott *Patton* (refused)	Glenda Jackson *Women in Love*	John Mills *Ryan's Daughter*	Helen Hayes *Airport*	Franklin Schaffner *Patton*
1971	*The French Connection*	Gene Hackman *The French Connection*	Jane Fonda *Klute*	Ben Johnson *The Last Picture Show*	Cloris Leachman *The Last Picture Show*	William Friedkin *The French Connection*
1972	*The Godfather*	Marlon Brando *The Godfather* (refused)	Liza Minnelli *Cabaret*	Joel Grey *Cabaret*	Eileen Heckart *Butterflies Are Free*	Bob Fosse *Cabaret*
1973	*The Sting*	Jack Lemmon *Save the Tiger*	Glenda Jackson *A Touch of Class*	John Houseman *The Paper Chase*	Tatum O'Neal *Paper Moon*	George Roy Hill *The Sting*
1974	The Godfather Part II	Art Carney *Harry and Tonto*	Ellen Burstyn *Alice Doesn't Live Here Anymore*	Robert DeNiro *The Godfather Part II*	Ingrid Bergman *Murder on the Orient Express*	Francis Ford Coppola *The Godfather Part II*
1975	*One Flew Over the Cuckoo's Nest*	Jack Nicholson *One Flew Over the Cuckoo's Nest*	Louise Fletcher *One Flew Over the Cuckoo's Nest*	George Burns *The Sunshine Boys*	Lee Grant *Shampoo*	Milos Forman *One Flew Over the Cuckoo's Nest*
1976	*Rocky*	Peter Finch *Network*	Faye Dunaway *Network*	Jason Robards *All the President's Men*	Beatrice Straight *Network*	John G. Avildsen *Rocky*
1977	*Annie Hall*	Richard Dreyfuss *The Goodbye Girl*	Diane Keaton *Annie Hall*	Jason Robards *Julia*	Vanessa Redgrave *Julia*	Woody Allen *Annie Hall*
1978	The Deer Hunter	Jon Voight *Coming Home*	Jane Fonda *Coming Home*	Christopher Walken *The Deer Hunter*	Maggie Smith *California Suite*	Michael Cimino *The Deer Hunter*
1979	*Kramer vs. Kramer*	Dustin Hoffman *Kramer vs. Kramer*	Sally Field *Norma Rae*	Melvyn Douglas *Being There*	Meryl Streep *Kramer vs. Kramer*	Robert Benton *Kramer vs. Kramer*
1980	*Ordinary People*	Robert DeNiro *Raging Bull*	Sissy Spacek *Coal Miner's Daughter*	Timothy Hutton *Ordinary People*	Mary Steenburgen *Melvin & Howard*	Robert Redford *Ordinary People*
1981	*Chariots of Fire*	Henry Fonda *On Golden Pond*	Katharine Hepburn *On Golden Pond*	John Gielgud *Arthur*	Maureen Stapleton *Reds*	Warren Beatty *Reds*
1982	Gandhi	Ben Kingsley *Gandhi*	Meryl Streep *Sophie's Choice*	Louis Gossett Jr. *An Officer and a Gentleman*	Jessica Lange *Tootsie*	Richard Attenborough *Gandhi*
1983	*Terms of Endearment*	Robert Duvall *Tender Mercies*	Shirley MacLaine *Terms of Endearment*	Jack Nicholson *Terms of Endearment*	Linda Hunt *The Year of Living Dangerously*	James L. Brooks *Terms of Endearment*
1984	*Amadeus*	F. Murray Abraham *Amadeus*	Sally Field *Places in the Heart*	Haing S. Ngor *The Killing Fields*	Peggy Ashcroft *A Passage to India*	Milos Forman *Amadeus*
1985	*Out of Africa*	William Hurt *Kiss of the Spider Woman*	Geraldine Page *The Trip to Bountiful*	Don Ameche *Cocoon*	Anjelica Huston *Prizzi's Honor*	Sydney Pollack *Out of Africa*
1986	Platoon	Paul Newman *The Color of Money*	Marlee Matlin *Children of a Lesser God*	Michael Caine *Hannah and Her Sisters*	Dianne Wiest *Hannah and Her Sisters*	Oliver Stone *Platoon*
1987	*The Last Emperor*	Michael Douglas *Wall Street*	Cher *Moonstruck*	Sean Connery *The Untouchables*	Olympia Dukakis *Moonstruck*	Bernardo Bertolucci *The Last Emperor*
1988	*Rain Man*	Dustin Hoffman *Rain Man*	Jodie Foster *The Accused*	Kevin Kline *A Fish Called Wanda*	Geena Davis *The Accidental Tourist*	Barry Levinson *Rain Man*
1989	*Driving Miss Daisy*	Daniel Day-Lewis *My Left Foot*	Jessica Tandy *Driving Miss Daisy*	Denzel Washington *Glory*	Brenda Fricker *My Left Foot*	Oliver Stone *Born on the Fourth of July*
1990	Dances With Wolves	Jeremy Irons *Reversal of Fortune*	Kathy Bates *Misery*	Joe Pesci *Goodfellas*	Whoopi Goldberg *Ghost*	Kevin Costner *Dances With Wolves*
1991	*The Silence of the Lambs*	Anthony Hopkins *The Silence of the Lambs*	Jodie Foster *The Silence of the Lambs*	Jack Palance *City Slickers*	Mercedes Ruehl *The Fisher King*	Jonathan Demme *The Silence of the Lambs*
1992	*Unforgiven*	Al Pacino *Scent of a Woman*	Emma Thompson *Howards End*	Gene Hackman *Unforgiven*	Marisa Tomei *My Cousin Vinny*	Clint Eastwood *Unforgiven*

Year	Picture	Actor	Actress	Sup. Actor[1]	Sup. Actress[1]	Director
1993	Schindler's List	Tom Hanks *Philadelphia*	Holly Hunter *The Piano*	Tommy Lee Jones *The Fugitive*	Anna Paquin *The Piano*	Steven Spielberg *Schindler's List*
1994	Forrest Gump	Tom Hanks *Forrest Gump*	Jessica Lange *Blue Sky*	Martin Landau *Ed Wood*	Dianne Wiest *Bullets Over Broadway*	Robert Zemeckis *Forrest Gump*
1995	Braveheart	Nicolas Cage *Leaving Las Vegas*	Susan Sarandon *Dead Man Walking*	Kevin Spacey *The Usual Suspects*	Mira Sorvino *Mighty Aphrodite*	Mel Gibson *Braveheart*
1996	The English Patient	Geoffrey Rush *Shine*	Frances McDormand *Fargo*	Cuba Gooding Jr. *Jerry Maguire*	Juliette Binoche *The English Patient*	Anthony Minghella *The English Patient*
1997	Titanic	Jack Nicholson *As Good As It Gets*	Helen Hunt *As Good As It Gets*	Robin Williams *Good Will Hunting*	Kim Basinger *L.A. Confidential*	James Cameron *Titanic*
1998	Shakespeare in Love	Roberto Benigni *Life Is Beautiful*	Gwyneth Paltrow *Shakespeare in Love*	James Coburn *Affliction*	Judi Dench *Shakespeare in Love*	Steven Spielberg *Saving Private Ryan*
1999	American Beauty	Kevin Spacey *American Beauty*	Hilary Swank *Boys Don't Cry*	Michael Caine *The Cider House Rules*	Angelina Jolie *Girl, Interrupted*	Sam Mendes *American Beauty*
2000	Gladiator	Russell Crowe *Gladiator*	Julia Roberts *Erin Brockovich*	Benicio Del Toro *Traffic*	Marcia Gay Harden *Pollock*	Steven Soderbergh *Traffic*
2001	A Beautiful Mind	Denzel Washington *Training Day*	Halle Berry *Monster's Ball*	Jim Broadbent *Iris*	Jennifer Connelly *A Beautiful Mind*	Ron Howard *A Beautiful Mind*
2002	Chicago	Adrien Brody *The Pianist*	Nicole Kidman *The Hours*	Chris Cooper *Adaptation*	Catherine Zeta-Jones *Chicago*	Roman Polanski *The Pianist*
2003	The Lord of the Rings: The Return of the King	Sean Penn, *Mystic River*	Charlize Theron, *Monster*	Tim Robbins, *Mystic River*	Renée Zellweger, *Cold Mountain*	Peter Jackson, *The Lord of the Rings: The Return of the King*

(1) These awards not given until 1936.

OTHER 2003 OSCAR WINNERS: Animated film: *Finding Nemo.* Foreign film: *The Barbarian Invasions,* Canada. Original screenplay: Sofia Coppola, *Lost in Translation.* Adapted screenplay: Fran Walsh, Philippa Boyens, and Peter Jackson, *The Lord of the Rings: The Return of the King.* Cinematography: Russell Boyd, *Master and Commander: The Far Side of the World.* Art direction: Grant Major (art direction); Dan Hennah and Alan Lee (set decoration), *The Lord of the Rings: The Return of the King.* Film editing: Jamie Selkirk, *The Lord of the Rings: The Return of the King.* Original song: "Into the West," *The Lord of the Rings: The Return of the King,* music and lyrics by Fran Walsh, Howard Shore, and Annie Lennox. Original score: Howard Shore, *The Lord of the Rings: The Return of the King.* Costume design: Ngila Dickson and Richard Taylor, *The Lord of the Rings: The Return of the King.* Makeup: Richard Taylor, Peter King, *The Lord of the Rings: The Return of the King.* Sound mixing: Christopher Boyes, Michael Semanick, Michael Hedges, and Hammond Peek, *The Lord of the Rings: The Return of the King.* Documentary feature: Errol Morris and Michael Williams, *The Fog of War.* Documentary short subject: Maryann DeLeo, *Chernobyl Heart.* Short film, live: Aaron Schneider and Andrew J. Sacks, *Two Soldiers.* Short film, animated: Adam Elliot, *Harvie Krumpet.* Visual effects: Jim Rygiel, Joe Letteri, Randall William Cook, and Alex Funke, *The Lord of the Rings: The Return of the King.* Sound editing: Richard King, *Master and Commander: The Far Side of the World.* Honorary Oscar: Blake Edwards.

Other Film Awards

Year in parentheses is year awarded.

Cannes Film Festival Awards (2004), Feature Films—Palme d'Or (Golden Palm): *Fahrenheit 9/11,* Michael Moore, U.S., Grand Prize: *Old Boy,* Chan-Wook Park, South Korea, Best Actress: Maggie Cheung, France, *Clean,* Best Actor: Yuya Yagira, Japan, *Nobody Knows,* Best Director: Tony Gatlif, France, *Exils,* Best Screenplay: Agnès Jaoui and Jean-Pierre Bacri, France, *Comme une Image,* Special Jury Prize: Irma P. Hall, *The Ladykillers,* U.S., and *Tropical Malady,* Apichatpong Weerasethakul, Thailand, Camera d'Or (Golden Camera, first-time director): Keren Yedaya, Israel, *Or,* Special Mention Camera d'Or: *Lu Cheng (Passages),* China, Chao Yang, and *Bitter Dream,* Iran, Mohsen Amiryoussefi.

Short Films—Palme d'Or: *Trafic,* Catalin Mitulescu, Romania; Jury Prize: *Flatlife,* Jonas Geirnaert, Belgium.

Director's Guild of America Awards (2004), Feature film: Peter Jackson, *The Lord of the Rings: The Return of the King;* documentary: Nathaniel Kahn, *My Architect.*

Sundance Film Festival Awards (2004), Grand Jury Prize: (drama) *Primer,* Shane Carruth; (documentary) *Dig!* Ondi Timoner; Directing Award: (drama) Debra Granik, *Down to the Bone;* (documentary) Morgan Spurlock, *Supersize Me.* Waldo Salt Screenwriting Award: Larry Gross, *We Don't Live Here Anymore.* Freedom of Expression Award: (documentary) *Repatriation,* Kim Dong-won. Audience Award: (drama) *Maria Full of Grace,* Joshua Marston; (documentary) *Born Into Brothels,* Ross Kauffman and Zana Briski; (world) *Seducing Doctor Lewis,* Jean-François Pouliot. Cinematography Award: (drama) Nancy Schreiber, *November;* (documentary) Ferne Pearlstein, *Imelda.* Special Jury Awards: (documentary) *Farmingville,* Catherine Tambini and Carlos Sandoval; (drama) *Brother to Brother,* Rodney Evans; (dramatic performance) Vera Farmiga, *Down to the Bone.* Alfred P. Sloan Feature Film Award: *Primer,* Shane Carruth. International Filmmakers Awards: Gyorgy Palfi, Europe, *Taxidermia;* Andrucha Waddington, Latin America, *House of Sand;* Miranda July, U.S., *Me You and Everyone We Know.* Short Filmmaking: (Jury Prize) *When the Storm Came,* Shilpi Gupta; *Gowanus, Brooklyn,* Ryan Fleck.

2004 Academy of Country Music Awards

Entertainer of the Year: Toby Keith
Album of the Year: *Shock 'N Y'All,* Toby Keith; James Stroud, Toby Keith, producers; Dreamworks
Single of the Year: "It's Five O'Clock Somewhere," Alan Jackson and Jimmy Buffett; Keith Stegall, producer; Arista Nashville
Top Female Vocalist: Martina McBride
Top Male Vocalist: Toby Keith
Top Vocal Duo: Brooks & Dunn
Top Vocal Group: Rascal Flatts
Top New Artist Dierks Bentley

Video of the Year: "Beer for My Horses," Toby Keith and Willie Nelson; Mark Kalbfeld, producer; Michael Salomon, director
Song of the Year: "Three Wooden Crosses," Randy Travis; written by Douglas Johnson and Kim Williams; Mike Curb Music BMI, Sweet Radical Music BMI/Kim Williams Music ASCAP, Sony ATV Tunes ASCAP, publishers
Vocal Event of the Year: "It's Five O'Clock Somewhere," Alan Jackson and Jimmy Buffett; Keith Stegall, producer
Pioneer Award: Ray Price
Humanitarian Award: Martina McBride
Special Achievement Award: Willie Nelson

2004 MTV Video Music Awards

Video of the Year: Outkast, "Hey Ya!"
Best Male Video: Usher featuring Lil' Jon & Ludacris, "Yeah!"
Best Female Video: Beyoncé, "Naughty Girl"
Best Group Video: No Doubt, "It's My Life"
Best Rap Video: Jay-Z, "99 Problems"
Best Dance Video: Usher featuring Lil' Jon & Ludacris, "Yeah!"
Best Pop Video: No Doubt, "It's My Life"
Best Rock Video: Jet, "Are You Gonna Be My Girl"
Best Hip Hop Video: Outkast, "Hey Ya!"
Best New Artist: Maroon 5, "This Love"
Breakthrough Video: Franz Ferdinand, "Take Me Out"

Best R&B Video: Alicia Keys, "If I Ain't Got You"
Best Soundtrack From a Video Game: "Tony Hawk's Underground"
Best MTV2 Video: Yellowcard, "Ocean Avenue"
Best Direction: Mark Romanek for "99 Problems" (Jay-Z)
Best Choreography: Black Eyed Peas, "Hey Mama"
Best Art Direction: Outkast, "Hey Ya!"
Best Editing: Jay-Z, "99 Problems"
Best Cinematography: Jay-Z, "99 Problems"
Best Special Effects: Outkast, "Hey Ya!"
Viewers' Choice: Linkin Park, "Breaking the Habit"

Grammy Awards

Source: National Academy of Recording Arts & Sciences

Selected Grammy Awards for 2003
(awarded Feb. 8, 2004)

Record of the Year (single): "Clocks," Coldplay
Album of the Year: *Speakerboxxx/The Love Below,* OutKast
Song of the Year: "Dance With My Father," Richard Marx & Luther Vandross, songwriters (Luther Vandross)
New artist: Evanescence
Pop vocal perf., female: "Beautiful," Christina Aguilera
Pop vocal perf., male: "Cry Me a River," Justin Timberlake
Pop vocal perf., duo/group: "Underneath It All," No Doubt
Pop vocal album, traditional: *A Wonderful World,* Tony Bennett & k.d. lang
Pop instrumental album: *Mambo Sinuendo,* Ry Cooder & Manuel Galban
Pop vocal album: *Justified,* Justin Timberlake
Dance recording: "Come Into My World," Kylie Minogue
Rock vocal perf., female: "Trouble," Pink
Rock vocal perf., male: "Gravedigger," Dave Matthews
Rock vocal perf., duo/group: "Disorder in the House," Warren Zevon & Bruce Springsteen
Rock instrumental perf.: "Plan B," Jeff Beck
Hard rock perf.: "Bring Me to Life," Evanescence, featuring Paul McCoy
Metal perf.: "St. Anger," Metallica
Rock song: "Seven Nation Army," Jack White, songwriter (The White Stripes)
Rock album: *One by One,* Foo Fighters
R&B vocal perf., female: "Dangerously In Love 2," Beyoncé
R&B vocal perf., male: "Dance With My Father," Luther Vandross
R&B vocal perf., duo/group: "The Closer I Get to You," Beyoncé & Luther Vandross
R&B song: "Crazy in Love," Shawn Carter, Rich Harrison, Beyoncé Knowles, & Eugene Record, songwriters (Beyoncé featuring Jay-Z)
R&B album: *Dance With My Father,* Luther Vandross
R&B album, contemporary: *Dangerously in Love,* Beyoncé
Rap solo perf., female: "Work It," Missy Elliott
Rap solo perf., male: "Lose Yourself," Eminem
Rap vocal perf., duo/group: "Shake Ya Tailfeather," Nelly, P. Diddy, Murphy Lee
Rap album: *Speakerboxxx/The Love Below,* OutKast
Country vocal perf., female: "Keep on the Sunny Side," June Carter Cash
Country vocal perf., male: "Next Big Thing," Vince Gill
Country perf. with vocal, duo/group: "A Simple Life," by Ricky Skaggs & Kentucky Thunder
Country song: "It's Five O'Clock Somewhere," Jim "Moose" Brown & Don Rollins, songwriters (Alan Jackson & Jimmy Buffett)
Country album: *Livin', Lovin', Losin', Songs of the Louvin Brothers,* Various Artists
Bluegrass album: *Live,* Alison Krauss & Union Station
Jazz album, vocal: *A Little Moonlight,* Dianne Reeves
Jazz album, instr.: *Alegria,* Wayne Shorter
Jazz album, contemporary: *34th N Lex,* Randy Brecker
Blues album, contemporary: *Let's Roll,* Etta James
Blues album, traditional: *Blues Singer,* Buddy Guy
Folk album, contemporary: *The Wind,* Warren Zevon
Folk album, traditional: *Wildwood Flower,* June Carter Cash
Reggae album: *Dutty Rock,* Sean Paul
Latin pop album: *No Es Lo Mismo,* Alejandro Sanz
Producer, non-classical: The Neptunes
Classical album: *Mahler: Symphony No. 3; Kindertotenlieder,* Michael Tilson Thomas, conductor; Michelle DeYoung, mezzo soprano; Andreas Neubronner, producer (Vance George; Pacific Boychoir, San Francisco Girls Chorus & Women of the SFS Chorus; San Francisco Symphony)
Classical vocal perf.: *Schubert: Lieder With Orchestra,* Thomas Quasthoff, bass-baritone, and Anne Sofie von Otter, mezzo soprano (Claudio Abbado; Chamber Orchestra of Europe)
Opera album: *Janácek: Jenufa,* Bernard Haitink, conductor; Jerry Hadley, Karita Mattila, Eva Randová, Anja Silja & Jorma Silvasti, singers; Wolfram Graul, producer (Chorus of the Royal Opera House, Covent Garden; Orchestra of the Royal Opera House, Covent Garden)

Grammy Awards for 1958-2003

Record of the Year (single)	Year	Album of the Year
Domenico Modugno, "Nel Blu Dipinto Di Blu (Volare)"	1958	Henry Mancini, *The Music From Peter Gunn*
Bobby Darin, "Mack the Knife"	1959	Frank Sinatra, *Come Dance With Me*
Percy Faith, "Theme From a Summer Place"	1960	Bob Newhart, *Button Down Mind*
Henry Mancini, "Moon River"	1961	Judy Garland, *Judy at Carnegie Hall*
Tony Bennett, "I Left My Heart in San Francisco"	1962	Vaughn Meader, *The First Family*
Henry Mancini, "The Days of Wine and Roses"	1963	Barbra Streisand, *The Barbra Streisand Album*
Stan Getz, Astrud Gilberto, "The Girl From Ipanema"	1964	Stan Getz, Astrud Gilberto, *Getz/Gilberto*
Herb Alpert, "A Taste of Honey"	1965	Frank Sinatra, *September of My Years*
Frank Sinatra, "Strangers in the Night"	1966	Frank Sinatra, *A Man and His Music*
5th Dimension, "Up, Up and Away"	1967	The Beatles, *Sgt. Pepper's Lonely Hearts Club Band*
Simon & Garfunkel, "Mrs. Robinson"	1968	Glen Campbell, *By the Time I Get to Phoenix*
5th Dimension, "Aquarius/Let the Sunshine In"	1969	Blood Sweat and Tears, *Blood, Sweat and Tears*
Simon & Garfunkel, "Bridge Over Troubled Water"	1970	Simon & Garfunkel, *Bridge Over Troubled Water*
Carole King, "It's Too Late"	1971	Carole King, *Tapestry*
Roberta Flack, "The First Time Ever I Saw Your Face"	1972	George Harrison and friends, *The Concert for Bangla Desh*
Roberta Flack, "Killing Me Softly With His Song"	1973	Stevie Wonder, *Innervisions*
Olivia Newton-John, "I Honestly Love You"	1974	Stevie Wonder, *Fulfillingness' First Finale*
Captain & Tennille, "Love Will Keep Us Together"	1975	Paul Simon, *Still Crazy After All These Years*
George Benson, "This Masquerade"	1976	Stevie Wonder, *Songs in the Key of Life*
Eagles, "Hotel California"	1977	Fleetwood Mac, *Rumours*
Billy Joel, "Just the Way You Are"	1978	Bee Gees, *Saturday Night Fever*
The Doobie Brothers, "What a Fool Believes"	1979	Billy Joel, *52nd Street*
Christopher Cross, "Sailing"	1980	Christopher Cross, *Christopher Cross*
Kim Carnes, "Bette Davis Eyes"	1981	John Lennon, Yoko Ono, *Double Fantasy*
Toto, "Rosanna"	1982	Toto, *Toto IV*
Michael Jackson, "Beat It"	1983	Michael Jackson, *Thriller*
Tina Turner, "What's Love Got to Do With It"	1984	Lionel Richie, *Can't Slow Down*
USA for Africa, "We Are the World"	1985	Phil Collins, *No Jacket Required*
Steve Winwood, "Higher Love"	1986	Paul Simon, *Graceland*
Paul Simon, "Graceland"	1987	U2, *The Joshua Tree*
Bobby McFerrin, "Don't Worry, Be Happy"	1988	George Michael, *Faith*
Bette Midler, "Wind Beneath My Wings"	1989	Bonnie Raitt, *Nick of Time*
Phil Collins, "Another Day in Paradise"	1990	Quincy Jones, *Back on the Block*
Natalie Cole, with Nat "King" Cole, "Unforgettable"	1991	Natalie Cole, with Nat "King" Cole, *Unforgettable*
Eric Clapton, "Tears in Heaven"	1992	Eric Clapton, *Unplugged*
Whitney Houston, "I Will Always Love You"	1993	Whitney Houston, *The Bodyguard*
Sheryl Crow, "All I Wanna Do"	1994	Tony Bennett, *MTV Unplugged*
Seal, "Kiss From a Rose"	1995	Alanis Morissette, *Jagged Little Pill*
Eric Clapton, "Change the World"	1996	Celine Dion, *Falling Into You*
Shawn Colvin, "Sunny Came Home"	1997	Bob Dylan, *Time Out of Mind*
Celine Dion, "My Heart Will Go On"	1998	Lauryn Hill, *The Miseducation of Lauryn Hill*
Santana featuring Rob Thomas, "Smooth"	1999	Santana, *Supernatural*
U2, "Beautiful Day"	2000	Steely Dan, *Two Against Nature*
U2, "Walk On"	2001	Various Artists, *O Brother, Where Art Thou?*
Norah Jones, "Don't Know Why"	2002	Norah Jones, *Come Away With Me*
Coldplay, "Clocks"	2003	OutKast, *Speakerboxxx/The Love Below*

SCIENCE AND TECHNOLOGY
Science News of 2004

Life Sciences news and glossary entries reviewed by Prof. Maura C. Flannery, St. John's Univ., NYC.

The following were some of the more newsworthy developments in Science in the past year. (See also the chapters on Astronomy and Computers and the Internet.)

Life Science Developments

• **Stem cells** are unspecialized cells that, under certain conditions, can give rise to specialized cells which it is hoped can be used in the treatment of certain diseases. Embryonic stem cells are believed to have the greatest promise because they are pluripotent (can be used to replicate any cells), as opposed to adult stem cells or those taken from the umbilical cord. But research on embryonic stem cells has been a subject of heated debate, since their extraction destroys the early-stage embryo from which they are derived. Their use was an issue in the presidential race, with Democratic candidate Sen. John Kerry favoring a relaxation of the rules imposed in 2001 by Pres. George W. Bush that limited federally funded research to then existing stem cell lines.

• Among recent developments in stem cell research: a group of scientists from South Korea succeeded in **producing embryonic stem cells from cloned human cells** using eggs volunteered from 16 women, according to research announced online in February and published in *Science* Mar. 12, 2004. This development provided a strong indication that human cloning is technically possible. Scientists led by Woo Suk Hwang and Shin Yong Moon of Seoul National Univ. extracted the nucleus from an egg and replaced it with the nucleus of a cumulus cell—a type of cell from near the egg in a woman's ovary—from the same woman who had supplied the egg. Of the 66 cloned eggs produced in that way, 19 developed into blastocysts—an early stage in development. Stem cells were taken from the blastocysts and in one case developed into a viable reproducing colony, or "line," of stem cells.

• Researchers from Israel's Hadassah Univ. reported on June 30 that they had **used human embryonic stem cells to relieve symptoms of Parkinson's disease** in rats. The cells were transplanted into the brains of rats that suffered from symptoms comparable to Parkinson's. The symptoms diminished, and autopsies of the rats showed the stem cells had developed into dopamine-producing cells. A lack of the chemical dopamine is linked to Parkinson's.

• Scientists at the Reproductive Genetics Institute in Chicago **produced stem cell lines from human embryos** that had been intended for in vitro fertilization, but were not used for that procedure after screening showed that the embryos had genetic mutations linked to various diseases, according to an article in the June 4 issue of *New Scientist*. Scientists say that these stem cell lines, which include several with single-gene-mutation diseases, could offer a valuable tool for research on the diseases involved.

• Patients who underwent heart surgery and had adult stem cells (taken from their hip bones) injected into portions of their hearts fared better than those who did not, according to results of a 20-patient study by scientists at the Univ. of Pittsburgh School of Medicine in Pennsylvania. The research, presented on April 26, at a meeting of the American Association for Thoracic Surgery in Toronto, suggested that the **hearts of the patients receiving stem cells pumped blood more effectively** than those that did not. However, separate research on mice, published in the April 8 issue of *Nature*, called into question the effectiveness of heart repair through adult stem cells. (The issue of whether adult stem cells offer the potential benefits of embryonic stem cells has political implications; some have argued that embryonic stem cell research is unnecessary because adult stem cells can achieve the same ends.)

• Scientists from Duke Univ. in North Carolina presented a report at the International Association of Bone Marrow Transplantation Research meeting in February showing that **stem cells from umbilical cord blood, when transplanted into children suffering from rare diseases, can develop into heart muscle cells**. The clinical effectiveness of the cord blood in treating rare diseases has been known for some time, but only recent research has shown that it is the stem cells in the blood that make the difference, by specializing into needed tissues.

• Scientists in China, led by Xijun Ni of the Chinese Academy of Sciences in Beijing, **discovered a fossilized partial skull of a primate**—the zoological order to which monkeys, apes, and humans belong—dating back almost 55 million years, according to an article published in the Jan. 1 issue of *Nature*. The specimen, discovered in China's Hunan province, was considered the earliest skull from a "euprimate" (primate of modern aspect) ever found. The fossil established that primates were present in Asia during that period; primate fossils from North America and Europe had been previously found, but evidence from Asia was scarce. The researchers designated their find to a new species of the genus *Teilhardina*. The fossil came from a small animal estimated to weigh only about an ounce, and is believed to have subsisted on insects.

• Researchers at Harvard Univ. Medical School in Massachusetts reported in the Mar. 11 issue of *Nature* that female mammals—female mice, in particular—**produce new eggs throughout their lives**. The finding contradicted the prevailing wisdom that the store of eggs female mammals have at birth is their total allotment and that no new ones are created. Biologist Jonathan Tilly headed the study. If human females were also found to produce eggs throughout their lives, the discovery could lead to new developments in fertility.

• A collaborative of biologists from around the world, led by Richard Gibbs of the Baylor College of Medicine in Houston, TX, **sequenced the genome of the rat** and published their findings online and in the Apr. 1 issue of *Nature*. The brown Norway rat—commonly used in laboratories—was the third mammal to have its genome (the genetic material of an organism) sequenced, after humans and mice. Rats share many genes with humans (and mice), and scientists believe that knowledge of the rat genome could substantially aid medical research. Among other things, researchers eventually could be able to turn on or off specific genes in rats, and thereby gain a better understanding of the role those genes play in various diseases.

• Discoveries of fossils in the famous Burgess Shale in British Columbia, Canada, **shed light on evolution in arthropods** (creatures such as insects with exoskeletons) and butterflies, according to reports in *Nature* in April and May. The May 6 issue of the journal reported the discovery of a 505-million-year-old fossil of an arthropod in the act of molting—that is, shedding its exoskeleton. Present-day insects molt, and it had been thought that their ancient ancestors also did, but evidence had been lacking prior to this discovery. A separate discovery of 20-million-year-old butterflies caught in amber on the Caribbean island of Hispaniola was reported in *Nature* Apr. 1.

The finders cited this discovery as proof that substantial butterfly evolution occurred on the hypothetical southern continent of Gondwana, which is believed to have broken up to form Africa, Australia, South America, Antarctica, and India some 160-175 million years ago. However, this would have occurred far earlier than during the lives of the discovered butterflies, and some scientists believe that butterflies evolved later.

• Researchers associated with Harvard Univ. identified a **specific protein found in monkeys—TRIM5-alpha—that blocked infection by HIV**, the virus that causes AIDS, according to a report in *Nature* Feb. 26. The scientists, led by Joseph Sodroski of the Dana-Farber Cancer Institute (affiliated with Harvard), carried out their research on genetically engineered human and monkey cells grown in laboratories. Human cells have a version of the TRIM5-alpha protein, but it does not stop HIV as effectively as does the monkey protein. The precise way in which the monkey protein blocked HIV is not known, but scientists considered the discovery a major development. With additional understanding of how TRIM5-alpha works, it might be possible to develop new therapies to treat or prevent HIV infection.

• In the April 9 issue of *Science*, French archaeologists exploring a Stone Age grave on the island of Cyprus reported the **discovery of a skeleton of a cat near human remains** buried with various tools. The proximity and other circumstances suggest the two were buried together, raising the possibility that cats had been domesticated at that early date, some 9,500 years ago. Previously, it was believed that the Egyptians were the first to domesticate cats, about 4,000 years ago. One of the French researchers said this cat could either have been "pre-domesticated" (becoming something in between savage and domestic) or possibly fully domesticated. Dogs associated in a similar way with human burial sites have been found dating back to 11,000-12,000 BC in Israel.

• A group of biologists climbed some of the tallest trees in the world (including the world's tallest known tree, measured at 112.7 meters or 372 feet) to study inherent limits to the height trees can achieve, according to an article in *Nature* Apr. 22. The team, led by George Koch of Northern Arizona Univ. in Flagstaff, concluded that these redwoods, located in California's Humboldt Redwood State Park, **were limited to a maximum height** of about 130 meters (430 feet), based on an analysis of the stress that gravity and friction put on the system for transporting water to the upper reaches of the tree. Water moves up a tree through tissue called xylem that forms tubular canals running the length of the organism. As trees grow taller, gravity puts increasing stress on the xylem cells, which, according to the measurements of Koch and his team, reach their breaking point when the height reaches 120-130 meters (about 390-430 feet). Without water, the needles at the top of the tree cannot function as they should, and this stops the tree from growing taller.

• A team of geoscientists claimed in an article published in *Science* June 4 that they had located a crater left over from **a meteor that hit Earth** some 250 million years ago, **perhaps triggering a massive extinction of life forms** known as the Permian-Triassic extinction. Scientists believe that over 90% of the species of life on Earth died at that time. The team, led by Luann Becker of the Univ. of California at Santa Barbara, argued that the Bedout High—submerged off the coast of northwest Australia—is the central peak of an impact crater. Bedout rock samples obtained by oil drillers showed features of a massive impact, and radiometric dating puts the age of a sample at the right time for the Permian-Triassic extinction. Other scientists, however, expressed considerable doubt, and said that it was not definitively established that the Bedout structure was a crater.

• In a separate development, an international team of scientists, headed by Gerta Keller of Princeton Univ. in New Jersey, **called into question the notion that a massive asteroid strike off the Yucatan peninsula** (in Mexico) was solely responsible for the **extinction of the dinosaurs 65 million years ago.** The researchers, who published their observations in the *Proceedings of the National Academy of Sciences*, said that new measurements indicate the Chicxulub crater off Mexico was actually created some 300,000 years before the dinosaurs became extinct. The team argued that the Chicxulub impact event contributed to the extinction, but that a second, as yet unfound, impact actually finished off the dinosaurs. Many scientists, however, continue to believe that the Yucatan impact was responsible for the extinction of the dinosaurs on its own.

• Biologists in Japan, led by Tomohiro Kono of Tokyo Univ. of Agriculture, **produced a healthy mouse from two eggs**, neither fertilized by a sperm cell, according to their report in *Nature* April 22. In some species, unfertilized eggs can grow into full animals, a phenomenon called parthenogenesis. This occurs among some insects, fish, birds, and other animals, but never—until the work of the Japanese team—among mammals. (Unlike in natural occurrences of parthenogenesis, the mouse received chromosomes from eggs from two different females.) Kono and his colleagues inactivated a gene in one of the eggs that contributed to the makeup of the mouse and in doing so, caused the egg to behave more like a sperm cell. The **"mouse with two moms"** was called Kaguya, after a princess in a Japanese fairy tale. The team created only two healthy mice out of nearly 600 attempts.

• In a report published in *Science* June 11, scientists from the Max Planck Institute for Evolutionary Anthropology in Germany **described the language abilities of a very smart dog**, a border collie named Rico. This dog reportedly exhibited a kind of learning behavior called "fast mapping," generally seen only in humans. In fast mapping, a child may infer the meaning of a previously unknown word by a process of elimination—for example, correctly picking out a "banana" from a plate of fruit because words for the only other fruits on the plate are known. In a number of experiments, Rico was told to fetch an item he had never heard of from a group of familiar toys, and 7 times out of 10 he got it right. The dog successfully remembered about half of the objects a month later.

Physical Sciences

• Stephen Hawking, a world-renowned Cambridge Univ. physicist, **repudiated his long-held views** about what happens to information that falls in so-called black holes, speaking on July 21 at a conference of physicists in Dublin, Ireland. Hawking had stunned the world of physics some 30 years earlier arguing that black holes—places where gravity is so powerful that light cannot escape—could emit a form of radiation. At the same time, however, he had insisted that once objects entered a black hole, all information about them is lost, possibly going off into a parallel universe. Many physicists believed this loss of information could not actually occur, as it would contradict a basic tenet of quantum mechanics (the theory of how small particles behave).

The disagreement led to a bet between Hawking and the physicist John Preskill of the California Institute of Technology, with Preskill holding that information would not be lost. In announcing his new theory, Hawking conceded that his views had changed. He paid Preskill the agreed wager—an encyclopedia (*Total Baseball*) from which information could always be obtained. While he lost the bet, he claimed that in doing so he had solved a major problem of contemporary physics. Hawking's new theory involved esoteric mathematics, and opinions were divided among leading physicists as to whether his approach was valid.

• Two separate teams of scientists—one at the Univ. of Innsbruck in Austria and the other at the National Institute of Standards and Technology in Boulder, CO—reported in *Nature* June 17 that they had **succeeded in "teleporting" atoms.** In the context of modern physics, teleportation does not mean the instantaneous physical relocation of one thing to another place, but rather the transfer of "quantum states" from one object to another. This had previously been done with photons—light particles—but not with atoms. Both experiments reported in *Nature* employed "entanglement"—a mysterious aspect of quantum mechanics by which atoms or other particles can somehow influence each other's properties even when removed to a distance. The scientists involved did not see their accomplishments as paving the way toward object teleportation as exhibited on *Star Trek*, but as having possible practical applications for future computers and other devices.

• Scientists created a new state of matter called a **"fermionic condensate"** at a laboratory operated by the Univ. of Colorado at Boulder and the National Institute of Standards, according to a report in *Physical Review Letters* Jan. 30. The team, led by Deborah Jin, cooled about a half million potassium atoms to very near absolute zero, and then a magnetic field was applied. The magnetic field (adjusted to near a special "resonance" level) caused the atoms to pair up, producing the fermionic condensate. The "fermionic" part of the name refers to fermions, a category of particles characterized by the property that they are barred from sharing the same quantum state. Thus getting the fermions—inherently loner particles—to form a condensate was a substantial achievement. Jin said the experiment and further investigations of fermionic condensates could lead to a **better understanding of superconductivity.**

• Research by Russian scientists from the Joint Institute for Nuclear Research and American scientists from the Lawrence Livermore National Laboratory in California, **yielded two new elements**—elements 113 and 115—according to a report published in the Feb. 1 issue of *Physical Review C*. Scientists used a cyclotron to shoot a beam of

calcium atoms at a target of americium. Calcium atoms have an atomic number of 20 (for 20 protons in each nucleus) and americium has an atomic number of 95 (for 95 protons). In just a few cases—out of trillions of possible collisions—the atoms briefly fused to create atoms with an atomic number of 115. After about 90 milliseconds, element 115 decayed by emitting an alpha particle (a particle containing two protons and two neutrons) and became element 113. Element 113 further decayed to become atoms of lower atomic numbers. Element 115 lasted only a fraction of a second, but longer than some other previously discovered elements with slightly smaller atomic numbers. Scientists thought this relative longevity might signal that they were closing in on a hypothetical "island of stability" region where large atoms—provided they had enough neutrons—might last longer than many of the artificial elements so far created.

• Anton Zeilinger and colleagues at the Univ. of Vienna in Austria have shown that relatively large objects—molecules of 70 carbon atoms for instance—**can exhibit quantum behavior**. In experiments reported in *Nature* Feb. 19, the Austrian team demonstrated that this behavior could in effect be turned off—physicists use the term "decoherence" to describe a system's loss of quantum character—by the addition of heat. Specifically, the scientists looked at what happened when they shot their carbon-70 molecules ("C70 fullerenes") through a grating. According to quantum laws, the particles should have behaved like a wave and shown interference patterns. In classical (Newtonian) physics, by contrast, the particles would have behaved more like tiny bullets, spreading out in an even blur without interference. Zeilinger and his colleagues found that the fullerenes showed a characteristic quantum interference pattern when relatively cool (700 degrees Celsius or 1,300 degrees Fahrenheit), but became fuzzier when a laser beam was used to add energy and thus heat to the molecules. At 2,700 deg C (4,900 deg Fahrenheit), the fullerenes produced a "classical" blur.

• Thomas Gosnell, a scientist at the Lawrence Livermore National Laboratory, described a device he and colleagues were developing to **detect fissionable material** (usable for atomic bombs) that might be smuggled into the U.S. in cargo containers. Speaking at the American Physical Society meeting in Denver on May 2, Gosnell described a "nuclear car wash" that would operate by shooting a beam of neutrons into the containers. Any fissionable material would respond by emitting a distinctive "radiation signature" or gamma rays that could be easily detected. This would in effect irradiate the cargo, but scientists claim that most of it would remain non-radioactive by Dept. of Transportation standards. Use of the scanner on food shipments, however, might be problematic. Gosnell said that it would be possible within a year to

build a practical scanner ready for testing within a year. (Millions of containers enter the U.S. every year, and only a small number are currently inspected.)

• In a presentation Jan. 5 at a meeting of the American Astronomical Society in Atlanta, a team of astronomers said that results of an investigation of the so-called "red shift desert" era of the universe's history had revealed that **large galaxies formed not long after the Big Bang**. The research made use of the Gemini Observatory in Hawaii and was called the Gemini Deep Deep Survey. According to co-principal investigator Roberto Abraham, it had been thought that in the period under scrutiny, some 8 to 11 billion years ago, most of the galaxies existing were fairly small and filled with hot stars, and that they lacked an abundance of the heavier metallic elements that are formed by cycles of star births and supernovas. However, the team found that the galaxies they observed were relatively mature. "This glimpse back in time," Abraham said, "shows pretty clearly that we need to rethink what happened during this early epoch in galactic evolution."

• Objects in a vaccum can achieve motion according to Alexander Feigel, a physicist at Rockefeller Univ. in New York and the Weizmann Institute in Israel; and in the Jan. 16 issue of *Physical Review Letters* he showed how **vacuum energy could be used to actually set a particle into motion**. In Feigel's theory, if strong electric and magnetic fields were applied to a vacuum, the virtual photons that would wink in and out of existence in the vacuum could acquire an overall momentum in one direction, based on the directions of the electric and magnetic fields. An object then placed in the vacuum would acquire momentum going in the opposite direction, to balance the vacuum's momentum in accordance with the law that momentum is conserved. The momentum imparted to the object would cause it to move—apparently from nothing. According to the scientist's calculations, an object with water's density might move at a speed of about 0.2 millimeters (about 0.01 inches) an hour.

• Researchers at General Electric **made a switchable diode using a single carbon nanotube**—a tiny tube composed of carbon atoms—and described their device in the July 5 issue of *Applied Physics Letters*. Diodes are key elements in electrical circuits, controlling the direction of the electrical current. The scientists, led by Ji-Ung Lee, used electric fields to alter the properties of the nanotube so that it would function as a diode. Lee noted that other researchers had developed nanotube diodes previously, but they did not perform as efficiently as the GE device. Unlike the previous efforts, the performance of the GE diode was comparable to conventional diodes made from silicon. The diode could emit and detect light, which might prove useful for optical electronic equipment.

Science Glossary

This glossary covers some basic concepts, and others that come up frequently in the news, in biology, chemistry, geology, and physics. See also Astronomy, Computers and the Internet, Environment, Health, Meteorology, Weights and Measures.

Biology

Note: For classification terms such as *kingdom*, *phylum*, etc., see Environment chapter.

Amino acid: one of about 20 similar small molecules that are the building blocks of proteins.

Antibiotic: a drug made from a substance produced by a bacterium, fungus, or other organism that battles bacterial infections and diseases, killing the bacteria or halting their growth.

Autoimmunity: a condition in which an individual's immune system reacts against his or her own tissues; leads to diseases such as lupus, diabetes, inflammatory bowel disease, rheumatoid arthritis.

Bacterium (plural, bacteria): one of a large, varied class of microscopic and simple, single-celled organisms; bacteria live almost everywhere—some forms cause disease, while others are useful in digestion and other natural processes.

Biodiversity: richness of variety of life forms—both plant and animal—in a given environment.

Cell: the smallest unit of life capable of living independently, or with other cells; usually bounded by a membrane; may include a nucleus and other specialized parts.

Cholesterol: a fatty substance in animal tissues; it is produced by the liver in humans, and is found in foods such as butter, eggs, and meat, and is an essential body constituent.

Chromosome: one of the rod-like structures in the nuclei of cells that carry genetic material (DNA).

Cloning: the process of copying a particular piece of DNA to allow it to be sequenced, studied, or used in some other way; can also refer to producing a genetic copy of an organism.

DNA (deoxyribonucleic acid): the chemical substance that carries genetic information, which determines the form and functioning of all living things.

Ecosystem: an interdependent community of living organisms and their climatic and geographical habitat.

Enzyme: a protein that promotes a particular chemical reaction in the body.

Estrogen: one of a group of hormones that promote development of female secondary sex characteristics and the growth and health of the female reproductive system; males also produce small amounts of estrogen.

Evolution: the process of gradual change that may occur as a species adapts to its environment; natural selection is the process by which evolution occurs.

Fight-or-flight response: the physical response that occurs in all animals when they encounter a threat; bodies release hormones, such as cortisol and epinephrine, that speed up the heart rate and increase blood flow to the muscles, allowing animals to fight enemies or run away.

Gene: a portion of a DNA molecule that provides the blueprint for the assembly of a protein.

Gene pool: the collection and total diversity of genes in an interbreeding population.

Gene therapy: a treatment in which scientists try to implant functioning genes into a person's cells so the genes can produce proteins that the person lacks or that help the person fight disease.

Genetic sequencing: the process of determining the order of subunits within a gene or even the order of all genes for an organism.

Genome: the complete set of an organism's genetic material.

Hormone: a substance secreted in one part of an organism that regulates the functioning of other tissues or organs.

Meiosis: the process of cell division that results in gametes (sperm or egg cells), all of which contain half the number of chromosomes as their precursor.

Metabolism: the sum total of the body's chemical processes providing energy for vital functions, and enabling new material to be synthesized.

Mitosis: the process by which a cell divides its nucleus and other cell materials into two duplicate daughter cells with the same DNA.

Neuron: a nerve cell, of the type found in the brain or spinal cord, that sends electrical and chemical messages to other cells.

Nucleus (plural: nuclei): the center of an atom; or the portion of a cell containing the chemical directions for functioning.

Organism: a living being.

Phenotype: the observable properties and characteristics of an organism arising at least in part from its genetic makeup.

Pheromone: a chemical secreted by an animal to influence the behavior of other members of its own species.

Placebo effect: a phenomenon in which patients show improvements even though they have taken a medically inactive substance, called a placebo.

Protein: a complex molecule made up of one or more chains of amino acids; essential to the structure and function of all cells.

RNA (ribonucleic acid): a complex molecule similar to the genetic material DNA, but usually single-stranded; several forms of RNA translate the genetic code of DNA and use that code to assemble proteins for structural and biological functions in the body.

Species: a population of organisms that breed with each other in nature and produce fertile offspring; other definitions of species exist to accommodate the diversity of life on Earth.

Stem cell: a cell that can give rise to other types of cells; for instance, bone marrow stem cells divide and produce different types of blood cells.

Steroid: type of hormone that freely enters cells (other hormones bind to cell surfaces); different varieties can suppress immune response or influence stress reaction, blood pressure, or sexual development; includes testosterone- and estrogen-related compounds.

Testosterone: a hormone that stimulates the development and maintenance of male sexual characteristics and the production of sperm; women also produce small amounts of testosterone.

Virus: a microscopic, often disease-causing, organism made of genetic material surrounded by a protein shell; can only reproduce inside a living cell.

Chemistry

Acid: a class of compound that contrasts with bases. Acids taste sour, turn litmus red/pink, and often produce hydrogen gas in contact with some metals. Acids donate protons (hydrogen atoms minus the electron) in chemical reactions.

Base: a substance that yields hydroxyl ions (OH-) when dissolved in water; any of a class of compounds whose aqueous solutions taste bitter, feel slippery, turn litmus blue, and react with acids to form salts; also known as **alkaline.**

Carbon fiber: an extremely strong, thin fiber made by pyrolyzing (decomposing by heat) synthetic fibers, such as rayon, until charred; used to make high-strength composites.

Chlorofluorocarbon (CFC): one of a group of industrial chemicals that contain chlorine, fluorine, and carbon and have been found to damage Earth's ozone layer.

Element: a substance that cannot be chemically decomposed into simpler substances; the atoms of an element all have the same number of protons and electrons.

Isotope: an atom of a chemical element with the same number of protons in its nucleus as other atoms of that element, but with a different number of neutrons.

Molecule: the basic unit of a chemical compound, composed of two or more atoms bound together.

Osmosis: the transfer of a fluid from an area of higher concentration to an area of lower concentration, usually through a membrane.

Phase: any of the possible states of matter—solid, liquid, gas, or plasma—that change according to temperature and pressure.

Polymer: a huge molecule containing hundreds or thousands of smaller molecules arranged in repeating units.

Salt: a neutral compound produced by the reaction of an acid and a base.

Geology

Fault, tectonic: a crack or break in Earth's crust, often due to the slippage of tectonic plates past or over one another; usually geologically unstable.

Igneous: a type of rock formed by solidification from a molten state, especially from molten magma.

Magma: hot liquid rock material under Earth's crust, from which igneous rock is formed by cooling.

Metamorphic: in geology, the name given to sedimentary rocks or minerals that have recrystallized under the influence of heat and pressure since their original deposition.

Pangaea: a single super-continent that scientists believe broke apart about 170 million years ago to form the current continents.

Plate tectonics: theory that Earth's crust is made up of many separate rigid plates of rock that float on top of hot semi-liquid rock.

Sedimentary rock: rock formed by the buildup of material at the bottoms of bodies of water.

Physics

Absolute zero: the theoretical temperature at which all motion within a molecule stops, corresponding to −273.15° Celsius (−459.67° Fahrenheit).

Antimatter: matter that consists of antiparticles, such as antiprotons, that have an opposite charge from normal particles; when matter meets antimatter, both are destroyed and their combined mass is converted to energy. Antimatter is created in certain radioactive decay processes, but appears to be present in only small amounts in the universe.

Atom: the basic unit of a chemical element.

Atomic mass: the total mass of an atom of a given element; atoms of the same element with different atomic masses (different numbers of neutrons, not protons) are called isotopes.

Atomic number: the number of protons in an atom of a given element of the periodic table; the characteristic that sets atoms of different elements apart.

Bose-Einstein condensate: a "super-atom" comprised of thousands of atoms super-cooled to within a few billionths of a degree of absolute zero and thus condensed into the lowest energy state; atoms bound in the BEC behave synchronously, giving the BEC wavelike properties.

Boson: force-carrying particles including photons, gluons, and the W and Z particles; one of the two primary categories of particles in the Standard Model, the other being fermions.

Dark energy: a mysterious, undefined energy leading to a repulsive force pervading all of space-time; proposed by cosmologists as counteracting gravity and accelerating the expansion of the universe; predicted to make up 65% of the universe's composition.

Dark matter: hypothetical, invisible matter that some scientists believe makes up 90% of the matter in the universe; its existence was proposed to account for otherwise inexplicable gravitational forces observed in space.

Doppler effect: a change in the frequency of sound, light, or radio waves caused by the motion of the source emitting the waves or the motion of the person or instrument perceiving the waves.

Electron: negatively charged particle that is the least massive electrically charged fundamental particle; the most common charged lepton in the Standard Model.

Energy: capacity to perform work. Energy can take various forms, such as potential energy, kinetic energy, chemical energy, etc.

Entropy: A measure of disorder in a system. According to the Second Law of Thermodynamics, disorder or entropy can only increase in a closed system.

Fermion: any one of a number of matter particles including electrons, protons, neutrons, and quarks; one of the two primary categories of particles in the Standard Model, the other being bosons.

Field: the effects of forces (gravitational, electric, etc.) are visualized and described mathematically by physicists in terms of fields, which show the strength and direction of a force at a given position.

Fission: a nuclear reaction that occurs when the nuclei of large, unstable atoms break apart, releasing large amounts of energy.

Force: In classical physics, a force is something that causes acceleration in a body, and can be thought of as a push or pull.

Fusion: a nuclear reaction occurring when atomic nuclei collide at high temperatures and combine to form one heavier atomic nucleus, releasing enormous energy in the process.

Gravity: an attractive force between any 2 objects or particles, proportional to the mass (or energy) of the objects; strength of the force decreases with greater distance; the only fundamental force still unaccounted for by the Standard Model.

Half-life: the time it takes for half of a given amount of a radioactive element to decay.

Hertz: a measure of frequency, or how many times a given event occurs per second; applied to sound waves, electrical current, microchip clock speeds; abbreviated as Hz.

Inertia: the tendency of an object to resist a change in its state of motion (i.e., to stay at rest if it is at rest, or to continue moving at a constant speed if it is moving at a constant speed). Inertia is proportional to mass, so a heavier object has more inertia.

Laser: light consisting of a cascade of photons all having the same wavelength; *laser* stands for Light Amplification by Stimulated Emission of Radiation.

Neutrino: a tiny fundamental particle with no electrical charge and very small mass that moves very quickly through the universe; comes in three varieties, or flavors, called electron, muon, and tau.

Neutron: a neutral particle found in the nuclei of atoms.

Particle accelerator: a large machine with a long tunnel in which atoms smash into each other at high speeds; physicists use these machines to study subatomic particles.

Photon: the elementary unit, or quantum, of light or electromagnetic radiation, having no mass or electrical charge; one of the fundamental force-carrying particles, or bosons, described by the Standard Model.

Plasma: a high-energy state of matter different from solid, liquid or gas in which atomic nuclei and the electrons orbiting them separate from each other.

Proton: a positively charged subatomic particle found in the nuclei of atoms.

Quantum: a natural unit of some physically measurable property, such as energy or electrical charge.

Quark: a fermion and a fundamental matter particle that makes up neutrons and protons, forming atomic nuclei; there are 6 different "flavors" of quarks grouped in pairs; up and down, charm and strange, top and bottom.

Radiation: energy emitted as rays or particles; radiation includes heat, light, ultraviolet rays, gamma rays, X rays, cosmic rays, alpha particles, beta particles, and the protons, neutrons, and electrons of radioactive atoms.

Relativity, general theory of: a theory of space-time proposed by Albert Einstein in 1915; gravitational and other forces are transmitted through the effects of the curvature of space-time.

Relativity, special theory of: Einstein's theory of space and time: all laws of physics are valid in all uniformly moving frames of reference and the speed of light in a vacuum is always the same, so long as the source and the observer are moving uniformly (not accelerating).

Standard Model: prevailing theory of fundamental particles and forces of matter; matter particles are fermions: either leptons or quarks; force-carrying particles are bosons: either gluons, W or Z bosons or photons; gravity has not yet been worked into the model.

String theory: a theory that seeks to unify quantum mechanics and general relativity, positing that the basic constituents of matter can best be understood not as point objects but as tiny closed loops ("strings").

Subatomic particle: one of the small particles, such as electrons, neutrons, and protons, which make up an atom.

Superconductivity: the property of certain materials, usually metals and chemically complex ceramics, to conduct electricity without resistance, generally at very cold temperatures.

Thermodynamics: the branch of physics that describes how energy, heat, and temperature flow in physical systems.

Ultraviolet radiation: a form of light, invisible to the human eye, that has a shorter wavelength and greater energy than visible light but a longer wavelength and less energy than X rays.

Uncertainty principle: the theory that certain pairs of observable quantities—like energy and time, or position and momentum—cannot be measured with complete accuracy simultaneously; presented in 1927 by German physicist Werner Heisenberg; also known as indeterminacy principle.

Virtual particle: subatomic particles that rapidly pop into and out of existence and can exert real forces; usually occur in particle-antiparticle pairs and are rapidly annihilated.

Chemical Elements, Atomic Numbers, Year Discovered

Reviewed by Darleane C. Hoffman, Ph.D., Lawrence Berkeley National Laboratory and Department of Chemistry, Univ. of California, Berkeley.

See Periodic Table of the Elements on page 337 for atomic weights.

Element	Symbol	Atomic number	Year discov.	Element	Symbol	Atomic number	Year discov.	Element	Symbol	Atomic number	Year discov.
Actinium	Ac	89	1899	Gold	Au	79	BC	Promethium	Pm	61	1945
Aluminum	Al	13	1825	Hafnium	Hf	72	1923	Protactinium	Pa	91	1917
Americium	Am	95	1944	Hassium	Hs	108	1984	Radium	Ra	88	1898
Antimony	Sb	51	1450	Helium	He	2	1868	Radon	Rn	86	1900
Argon	Ar	18	1894	Holmium	Ho	67	1878	Rhenium	Re	75	1925
Arsenic	As	33	13th c.	Hydrogen	H	1	1766	Rhodium	Rh	45	1803
Astatine	At	85	1940	Indium	In	49	1863	Roentgenium	Rg	111	1995
Barium	Ba	56	1808	Iodine	I	53	1811	Rubidium	Rb	37	1861
Berkelium	Bk	97	1949	Iridium	Ir	77	1804	Ruthenium	Ru	44	1845
Beryllium	Be	4	1798	Iron	Fe	26	BC	Rutherfordium	Rf	104	1969
Bismuth	Bi	83	15th c.	Krypton	Kr	36	1898	Samarium	Sm	62	1879
Bohrium	Bh	107	1981	Lanthanum	La	57	1839	Scandium	Sc	21	1879
Boron	B	5	1808	Lawrencium	Lr	103	1961	Seaborgium	Sg	106	1974
Bromine	Br	35	1826	Lead	Pb	82	BC	Selenium	Se	34	1817
Cadmium	Cd	48	1817	Lithium	Li	3	1817	Silicon	Si	14	1823
Calcium	Ca	20	1808	Lutetium	Lu	71	1907	Silver	Ag	47	BC
Californium	Cf	985	1950	Magnesium	Mg	12	1829	Sodium	Na	11	1807
Carbon	C	6	BC	Manganese	Mn	25	1774	Strontium	Sr	38	1790
Cerium	Ce	58	1803	Meitnerium	Mt	109	1982	Sulfur	S	16	BC
Cesium	Cs	55	1860	Mendelevium	Md	101	1955	Tantalum	Ta	73	1802
Chlorine	Cl	17	1774	Mercury	Hg	80	BC	Technetium	Tc	43	1937
Chromium	Cr	24	1797	Molybdenum	Mo	42	1782	Tellurium	Te	52	1782
Cobalt	Co	27	1735	Neodymium	Nd	60	1885	Terbium	Tb	65	1843
Copper	Cu	29	BC	Neon	Ne	10	1898	Thallium	Tl	81	1861
Curium	Cm	96	1944	Neptunium	Np	93	1940	Thorium	Th	90	1828
Darmstadtium	Ds	110	1995	Nickel	Ni	28	1751	Thulium	Tm	69	1879
Dubnium			1970	Niobium[2]	Nb	41	1801	Tin	Sn	50	BC
(Hahnium)[1]	Db (Ha)	105		Nitrogen	N	7	1772	Titanium	Ti	22	1791
Dysprosium	Dy	66	1886	Nobelium	No	102	1958	Tungsten			1783
Einsteinium	Es	99	1952	Osmium	Os	76	1804	(Wolfram)	W	74	
Erbium	Er	68	1843	Oxygen	O	8	1774	Uranium	U	92	1789
Europium	Eu	63	1901	Palladium	Pd	46	1803	Vanadium	V	23	1830
Fermium	Fm	100	1953	Phosphorus	P	15	1669	Xenon	Xe	54	1898
Fluorine	F	9	1771	Platinum	Pt	78	1735	Ytterbium	Yb	70	1878
Francium	Fr	87	1939	Plutonium	Pu	94	1941	Yttrium	Y	39	1794
Gadolinium	Gd	64	1886	Polonium	Po	84	1898	Zinc	Zn	30	BC
Gallium	Ga	31	1875	Potassium	K	19	1807	Zirconium	Zr	40	1789
Germanium	Ge	32	1886	Praseodymium	Pr	59	1885				

Note: 111 elements are listed here. The discovery of element 111 with a mass number of 272 was reported by S. Hoffman *et al.* in 1995 and was approved by a Joint Working Party of the International Unions of Pure & Applied Chemistry (IUPAC) and Pure and Applied Physics (IUPAP) in 2003. The discoverers proposed the name Roentgenium with symbol Rg in early 2004 and it has been recommended to the IUPAC Bureau and Council by the Inorganic Chemistry Division of IUPAC and will probably be confirmed in late 2004. The discovery of element 112 by S. Hofman *et al.* in 1996 still awaits confirmation. Between 1999 and 2004, a multinational group and a Dubna/Lawrence Livermore National Laboratory group working in Dubna, Russia, have published evidence in refereed journals for observation of many isotopes of elements 112 through 116. These reports all await confirmation and are shown in italics in the periodic table. Reports of still heavier elements have not yet been published in refereed journals and are shown in parentheses. (1) The name Dubnium (Db) has been approved by IUPAC for element 105, but the name Hahnium (Ha) is used in most of the scientific literature before 1998 and is still sometimes used in the U.S. (2) Formerly Columbium.

Periodic Table of the Elements

Source: © 1996 Lawrence Berkeley National Laboratory

Parentheses indicate undiscovered elements.

Key:
- atomic number: 14
- atomic weight: 28.09
- symbol: Si
- name: Silicon

Group categories: alkali metals, alkaline earth metals, transitional metals, nonmetals, other metals, noble gases.

Group 1 (alkali)	2 (alk. earth)		transitional metals										13	14	15	16	17	18 (noble gases)
1 H 1.01 Hydrogen																		2 He 4.003 Helium
3 Li 6.94 Lithium	4 Be 9.01 Beryllium												5 B 10.81 Boron	6 C 12.01 Carbon	7 N 14.01 Nitrogen	8 O 15.999 Oxygen	9 F 18.998 Fluorine	10 Ne 20.18 Neon
11 Na 22.99 Sodium	12 Mg 24.31 Magnesium												13 Al 26.98 Aluminum	14 Si 28.09 Silicon	15 P 30.97 Phosphorus	16 S 32.06 Sulfur	17 Cl 35.45 Chlorine	18 Ar 39.95 Argon
19 K 39.10 Potassium	20 Ca 40.08 Calcium	21 Sc 44.96 Scandium	22 Ti 47.90 Titanium	23 V 50.94 Vanadium	24 Cr 51.996 Chromium	25 Mn 54.94 Manganese	26 Fe 55.85 Iron	27 Co 58.93 Cobalt	28 Ni 58.70 Nickel	29 Cu 63.55 Copper	30 Zn 65.37 Zinc		31 Ga 69.72 Gallium	32 Ge 72.59 Germanium	33 As 74.92 Arsenic	34 Se 78.96 Selenium	35 Br 79.90 Bromine	36 Kr 83.80 Krypton
37 Rb 85.47 Rubidium	38 Sr 87.62 Strontium	39 Y 88.91 Yttrium	40 Zr 91.22 Zirconium	41 Nb 92.91 Niobium	42 Mo 95.94 Molybdenum	43 Tc 98 Technetium	44 Ru 101.07 Ruthenium	45 Rh 102.91 Rhodium	46 Pd 106.40 Palladium	47 Ag 107.87 Silver	48 Cd 112.41 Cadmium		49 In 114.82 Indium	50 Sn 118.69 Tin	51 Sb 121.75 Antimony	52 Te 127.60 Tellurium	53 I 126.90 Iodine	54 Xe 131.30 Xenon
55 Cs 132.91 Cesium	56 Ba 137.33 Barium	57 La 138.91 Lanthanum	72 Hf 178.49 Hafnium	73 Ta 180.95 Tantalum	74 W 183.85 Tungsten	75 Re 186.21 Rhenium	76 Os 190.20 Osmium	77 Ir 192.22 Iridium	78 Pt 195.09 Platinum	79 Au 196.97 Gold	80 Hg 200.59 Mercury		81 Tl 204.37 Thallium	82 Pb 207.19 Lead	83 Bi 208.98 Bismuth	84 Po 209 Polonium	85 At 210 Astatine	86 Rn 222 Radon
87 Fr 223 Francium	88 Ra 226.03 Radium	89 Ac 227.03 Actinium	104 Rf 261 Rutherfordium	105 Db (Ha) 262 Dubnium (Hahnium)	106 Sg 266 Seaborgium	107 Bh 267 Bohrium	108 Hs 269 Hassium	109 Mt 268 Meitnerium	110 Ds 271 Darmstadtium	111 (Rg) 272 Roentgenium	112	113	114	115	116	(117)	(118)

Lanthanide series

58 Ce 140.12 Cerium	59 Pr 140.91 Praseodymium	60 Nd 144.24 Neodymium	61 Pm 145 Promethium	62 Sm 150.35 Samarium	63 Eu 151.96 Europium	64 Gd 157.25 Gadolinium	65 Tb 158.93 Terbium	66 Dy 162.50 Dysprosium	67 Ho 164.93 Holmium	68 Er 167.26 Erbium	69 Tm 168.93 Thulium	70 Yb 173.04 Ytterbium	71 Lu 174.97 Lutetium

Actinide series

90 Th 232.04 Thorium	91 Pa 231.04 Protactinium	92 U 238.03 Uranium	93 Np 237.05 Neptunium	94 Pu 244 Plutonium	95 Am 243 Americium	96 Cm 247 Curium	97 Bk 247 Berkelium	98 Cf 251 Californium	99 Es 252 Einsteinium	100 Fm 257 Fermium	101 Md 258 Mendelevium	102 No 259 Nobelium	103 Lr 262 Lawrencium

Discoveries and Innovations: Chemistry, Physics, Biology, Medicine

	Date	Discoverer	Nationality
Acetylene gas	1862	Berthelot	French
ACTH	1927	Evans, Long	U.S.
Adrenalin	1901	Takamine	Japan
Aluminum, electrolytic process	1886	Hall	U.S.
Aluminum, isolated	1825	Oersted	Danish
Anesthesia, ether	1842	Long	U.S.
Anesthesia, local	1885	Koller	Austrian
Anesthesia, spinal	1898	Bier	German
Aniline dye	1856	Perkin	English
Anti-rabies	1885	Pasteur	French
Antiseptic surgery	1867	Lister	English
Antitoxin, diphtheria	1891	Von Behring	German
Argyrol	1897	Bayer	German
Arsphenamine	1910	Ehrlich	German
Aspirin	1853	Gerhardt	French
Atabrine	1932	Mietzsch, et al.	German
Atomic numbers	1913	Moseley	English
Atomic theory	1803	Dalton	English
Atomic time clock	1948	Lyons	U.S.
Atomic time clock, cesium beam	1948	Essen	English
Atom-smashing theory	1919	Rutherford	English
Bacitracin	1943	Johnson, Meleneyl	U.S.
Bacteria, description	1676	Leeuwenhoek	Dutch
Bleaching powder	1798	Tennant	English
Blood, circulation	1628	Harvey	English
Blood plasma storage (blood banks)	1940	Drew	U.S.
Bordeaux mixture	1885	Millardet	French
Bromine from the sea	1826	Balard	French
Calcium carbide	1888	Wilson	U.S.
Calculus	1670	Newton	English
Camphor synthetic	1896	Haller	French
Canning (food)	1804	Appert	French
Carbon oxides	1925	Fisher	German
Chemotherapy	1909	Ehrlich	German
Chloamphenicol	1947	Burkholder	U.S.
Chlorine	1774	Scheele	Swedish
Chloroform	1831	Guthrie, S.	U.S.
Chlortetracycline	1948	Duggen	U.S.
Classification of plants and animals	1735	Linnaeus	Swedish
Cloning, DNA	1973	Boyer, Cohen	U.S.
Cloning, mammal	1996	Wilmut, et al.	Scottish
Cocaine	1860	Niermann	German
Combustion explained	1777	Lavoisier	French
Conditioned reflex	1914	Pavlov	Russian
Cortisone	1936	Kendall	U.S.
Cortisone, synthesis	1946	Sarett	U.S.
Cosmic rays	1910	Gockel	Swiss
Cyanamide	1905	Frank, Caro	German
Cyclotron	1930	Lawrence	U.S.
DDT (not applied as insecticide until 1939)	1874	Zeidler	German
Deuterium	1932	Urey, Brickwedde, Murphy	U.S.
DNA (structure)	1953	Crick	English
		Watson	U.S.
		Wilkins	English
Electric resistance, law of	1827	Ohm	German
Electric waves	1888	Hertz	German
Electrolysis	1852	Faraday	English
Electromagnetism	1819	Oersted	Danish
Electron	1897	Thomson, J.	English
Electron diffraction	1936	Thomson	English
		G.Davisson	U.S.
Electroshock treatment	1938	Cerletti, Bini	Italian
Erythromycin	1952	McGuire	U.S.
Evolution, natural selection	1858	Darwin	English
Falling bodies, law of	1590	Galileo	Italian
Gases, law of combining volumes	1808	Gay-Lussac	French
Geometry, analytic	1619	Descartes	French
Gold, cyanide process for extraction	1887	MacArthur, Forest	British
Gravitation, law	1687	Newton	English
HIV (human immuno-deficiency virus)	1984	Mortagnier	French
		Gallo	U.S.
Holograph	1948	Gabor	British
Human heart transplant	1967	Barnard	S. African
Indigo, synthesis of	1880	Baeyer	German
Induction, electric	1830	Henry	U.S.
Insulin	1922	Banting, Best, Macleod	Canadian, Scottish
Intelligence testing	1905	Binet, Simon	French
In vitro fertilization	1978	Steptoe, Edwards	English
Isoniazid	1952	Hoffmann-LaRoche	U.S.
		Domagk	German
Isotopes, theory	1912	Soddy	English
Laser	1957	Gould	U.S.
Light, velocity	1675	Roemer	Danish
Light, wave theory	1690	Huygens	Dutch
Lithography	1796	Senefelder	Bohemian
Logarithms	1614	Napier	Scottish
LSD-25	1943	Hoffman	Swiss
Mendelian laws	1866	Mendel	Austrian
Mercator projection (map)	1568	Mercator (Kremer)	Flemish
Methanol	1661	Boyle	Irish
Milk condensation	1853	Borden	U.S.
Molecular hypothesis	1811	Avogadro	Italian
Motion, laws of	1687	Newton	English
Neomycin	1949	Waksman,Lechevalier	U.S.
Neutron	1932	Chadwick	English
Nitric acid	1648	Glauber	German
Nitric oxide	1772	Priestley	English
Nitroglycerin	1846	Sobrero	Italian
Oil cracking process	1891	Dewar	U.S.
Oxygen	1774	Priestley	English
Oxytetracycline	1950	Finlay, et al.	U.S.
Ozone	1840	Schonbein	German
Paper, sulfite process	1867	Tilghman	U.S.
Paper, wood pulp, sulfate process	1884	Dahl	German
Penicillin	1928	Fleming	Scottish
practical use	1941	Florey, Chain	English
Periodic law and table of elements	1869	Mendeleyev	Russian
Physosstigmine synthesis	1935	Julian	U.S.
Pill, birth-control	1954	Pincus, Rock	U.S.
Planetary motion, laws	1609	Kepler	German
Plutonium fission	1940	Kennedy, Wahl, Seaborg, Segre	U.S.
Polymyxin	1947	Ainsworth	English
Positron	1932	Anderson	U.S.
Proton	1919	Rutherford	N. Zealand
Psychoanalysis	1900	Freud	Austrian
Quantum theory	1900	Planck	German
Quasars	1963	Matthews, Sandage	U.S.
Quinine synthetic	1946	Woodward, Doering	U.S.
Radioactivity	1896	Becquerel	French
Radiocarbon dating	1947	Libby	U.S.
Radium	1898	Curie, Pierre	French
		Curie, Marie	Pol.-Fr.
Relativity theory	1905	Einstein	German
Reserpine	1949	Jal Vaikl	Indian
Schick test	1913	Schick	U.S.
Silicon	1823	Berzelius	Swedish
Smallpox eradication	1979	World Health Org.	UN
Streptomycin	1944	Waksman, et al	U.S.
Sulfanilamide	1935	Bovet, Trefouel	French
Sulfanilamide theory	1908	Gelmo	German
Sulfapyridine	1938	Ewins, Phelps	English
Sulfathiazole	1939	Fosbinder, Walter	U.S.
Sulfuric acid	1831	Phillips	English
Sulfuric acid, lead	1746	Roebuck	English
Syphilis test	1906	Wassermann	German
Thiacetazone	1950	Belmisch, Mietzsch, Domagk	German
Tuberculin	1890	Koch	German
Uranium fission theory	1939	Hahn, Meitner, Strassmann	German
		Bohr	Danish
		Fermi	Italian
		Einstein, Pegram, Wheeler	U.S.
Uranium fission, atomic reactor	1942	Fermi, Szilard	U.S.
Vaccine, measles	1963	Enders	U.S.
Vaccine, meningitis (first conjugate)	1987	Gordon, et al., Connaught Lab	U.S.
Vaccine, polio	1954	Salk	U.S.
Vaccine, polio, oral	1960	Sabin	U.S.
Vaccine, rabies	1885	Pasteur	French
Vaccine, smallpox	1796	Jenner	English
Vaccine, typhus	1909	Nicolle	French
Vaccine, varicella	1974	Takahashi	Japan
Van Allen belts, radiation	1958	Van Allen	U.S.
Vitamin A	1913	McCollum, Davis	U.S.
Vitamin B	1916	McCollum	U.S.
Vitamin C	1928	Szent-Gyorgyi, King	U.S.
Vitamin D	1922	McCollum	U.S.
Vitamin K	1935	Dam, Doisy	U.S.
Xerography	1938	Carlson	U.S.
X ray	1895	Roentgen	German

Inventions

Invention	Date	Inventor	Nationality
Adding machine	1642	Pascal	French
Adding machine	1885	Burroughs	U.S.
Aerosol spray	1926	Rotheim	Norwegian
Airbag	1952	Hetrick	U.S.
Air brake	1868	Westinghouse	U.S.
Air conditioning	1902	Carrier	U.S.
Air pump	1654	Guericke	German
Airplane, automatic pilot	1912	Sperry	U.S.
Airplane, experimental	1896	Langley	U.S.
Airplane, hydro	1911	Curtiss	U.S.
Airplane jet engine	1939	Ohain	German
Airplane with motor	1903	Wright Bros.	U.S.
Airship	1852	Giffard	French
Arc welder	1919	Thomson	U.S.
Aspartame	1965	Schlatter	U.S.
Autogyro	1920	de la Cierva	Spanish
Automobile, differential gear	1885	Benz	German
Automobile, electric	1892	Morrison	U.S.
Automobile, exp'mtl.	1864	Marcus	Austrian
Automobile, gasoline	1889	Daimler	German
Automobile, gasoline	1892	Duryea	U.S.
Automobile magneto	1897	Bosch	German
Automobile muffler	1904	Pope	U.S.
Automobile self-starter	1911	Kettering	U.S.
Bakelite	1907	Baekeland	Belgium, U.S.
Balloon	1783	Montgolfier	French
Barometer	1643	Torricelli	Italian
Bicycle, modern	1885	Starley	English
Bifocal lens	1780	Franklin	U.S.
Bottle machine	1895	Owens	U.S.
Braille printing	1829	Braille	French
Bubble gum	1928	Diemer	U.S.
Burner, gas	1855	Bunsen	German
Calculating machine	1833	Babbage	English
Calculator, electronic pocket	1972	Merryman, Van Tassel	U.S.
Camera, Kodak	1888	Eastman, Walker	U.S.
Camera, Polaroid Land	1948	Land	U.S.
Car coupler	1873	Janney	U.S.
Carburetor, gasoline	1893	Maybach	German
Carding machine	1797	Whittemore	U.S.
Carpet sweeper	1876	Bissell	U.S.
Cash register	1879	Ritty	U.S.
Cassette, audio	1963	Philips Co.	Dutch
Cassette, videotape	1969	Sony	Japanese
Cathode-ray tube	1897	Braun	German
CAT, or CT, scan	1973	Hounsfield	English
Cellophane	1908	Brandenberger	Swiss
Celluloid	1870	Hyatt	U.S.
Cement, Portland	1824	Aspdin	English
Chronometer	1735	Harrison	English
Circuit breaker	1925	Hilliard	U.S.
Circuit, integrated	1959	Kilby, Noyce, Texas Instr.	U.S.
Clock, pendulum	1657	Huygens	Dutch
Coaxial cable system	1929	Affel, Espensched.	U.S.
Coffeemaker, automatic drip	1963	Bunn Corp.	U.S.
Compressed air rock drill	1871	Ingersoll	U.S.
Comptometer	1887	Felt	U.S.
Computer, automatic sequence	1944	Aiken, et al.	U.S.
Computer, electronic	1942	Atanasoff, Berry	U.S.
Computer, laptop	1987	Sinclair	English
Computer, mini	1960	Digital Corp	U.S.
Condenser microphone (telephone)	1916	Wente	U.S.
Contact lens, corneal	1948	Tuohy	U.S.
Contraceptive, oral	1954	Pincus, Rock	U.S.
Corn, hybrid	1917	Jones	U.S.
Cotton gin	1793	Whitney	U.S.
Cream separator	1878	DeLaval	Swedish
Cultivator, disc.	1878	Mallon	U.S.
Cystoscope	1878	Nitze	German
Diapers, disposable	1950	Donovan	U.S.
Diesel engine	1895	Diesel	German
Disc, compact	1972	RCA	U.S.
Disc player, compact	1979	Sony, Philips Co.	Japan, Dutch
Dishwasher	1893	Cochrane	U.S.
Disk, floppy	1970	IBM	U.S.
Disk, video	1972	Philips Co.	Dutch
Dynamite	1866	Nobel	Swedish
Dynamo, contin. current	1871	Gramme	Belgian
Electric battery	1800	Volta	Italian
Electric fan	1882	Wheeler	U.S.
Electrocardiograph	1903	Einthoven	Dutch
Electroencephalograph	1929	Berger	German
Electromagnet	1824	Sturgeon	English
Electron spectrometer	1944	Deutsch, Elliott, Evans	U.S.
Electron tube multigrid	1913	Langmuir	U.S.
Electroplating	1805	Brugnatelli	Italian
Electrostatic generator	1929	Van de Graaff	U.S.
Elevator brake	1852	Otis	U.S.
Elevator, push button	1922	Larson	U.S.
Engine, automatic transmission	1910	Fottinger	German
Engine, coal-gas 4-cycle	1876	Otto	German
Engine, compression ignition	1883	Daimler	German
Engine, electric ignition	1883	Benz	German
Engine, gas, compound	1926	Eickemeyer	U.S.
Engine, gasoline	1872	Brayton, Geo.	U.S.
Engine, gasoline	1889	Daimler	German
Engine, jet	1930	Whittle	English
Engine, steam, piston	1705	Newcomen	English
Engine, steam, piston	1769	Watt	Scottish
Engraving, half-tone	1852	Talbot	U.S.
Fiberglass	1938	Owens-Corning	U.S.
Fiber optics	1955	Kapany	English
Fiber optic wire	1970	Keck, Maurer Schulz	U.S.
Filament, tungsten	1913	Coolidge	U.S.
Flanged rail	1831	Stevens	U.S.
Flatiron, electric	1882	Seely	U.S.
Food, frozen	1923	Birdseye	U.S.
Freon	1930	Midgley, et al.	U.S.
Furnace (for steel)	1858	Siemens	German
Galvanometer	1820	Sweigger	German
Garbage bag, polyethylene	1950	Wasylyk	Canadian
Gas discharge tube	1922	Hull	U.S.
Gas lighting	1792	Murdoch	Scottish
Gas mantle	1885	Welsbach	Austrian
Gasoline (lead ethyl)	1922	Midgley	U.S.
Gasoline, cracked	1913	Burton	U.S.
Gasoline, high octane	1930	Ipatieff	Russian
Geiger counter	1913	Geiger	German
Glass, laminated safety	1909	Benedictus	French
Glider	1853	Cayley	English
Gun, breechloader	1811	Thornton	U.S.
Gun, Browning	1897	Browning	U.S.
Gun, magazine	1875	Hotchkiss	U.S.
Gun, silencer	1908	Maxim, H.P.	U.S.
Guncotton	1847	Schoenbein	German
Gyrocompass	1911	Sperry	U.S.
Gyroscope	1852	Foucault	French
Harvester-thresher	1818	Lane	U.S.
Heart, artificial	1982	Jarvik	U.S.
Helicopter	1939	Sikorsky	U.S.
Hydrometer	1768	Baume	French
Iron lung	1928	Drinker, Slaw	U.S.
Kaleidoscope	1817	Brewster	Scottish
Kevlar	1965	Kwolek, Blades	U.S.
Kinetoscope	1889	Edison	U.S.
Lamp, arc	1847	Staite	English
Lamp, fluorescent	1938	General Electric, Westinghouse	U.S.
Lamp, incandescent	1879	Edison	U.S.
Lamp, incand., gas	1913	Langmuir	U.S.
Lamp, klieg	1911	Kliegl, A. & J.	U.S.
Lamp, mercury vapor	1912	Hewitt	U.S.
Lamp, miner's safety	1816	Davy	English
Lamp, neon	1909	Claude	French
Lathe, turret	1845	Fitch	U.S.
Launderette	1934	Cantrell	U.S.
Lens, achromatic	1758	Dollond	English
Lens, fused bifocal	1908	Borsch	U.S.
Leyden jar (condenser)	1745	von Kleist	German
Lightning rod	1752	Franklin	U.S.
Linoleum	1860	Walton	English
Linotype	1884	Mergenthaler	U.S.
Liquid Paper	c.1951	Graham	U.S.
Lock, cylinder	1851	Yale	U.S.
Locomotive, electric	1851	Vail	U.S.
Locomotive, exp'mtl.	1802	Trevithick	English
Locomotive, exp'mtl.	1812	Fenton, et al.	English
Locomotive, exp'mtl.	1814	Stephenson	English
Locomotive, practical	1829	Stephenson	English
Locomotive, 1st U.S.	1830	Cooper, P.	U.S.
Loom, power	1785	Cartwright	English
Loudspeaker, dynamic	1924	Rice, Kellogg	U.S.
Machine gun	1862	Gatling	U.S.
Machine gun, improved	1872	Hotchkiss	U.S.
Machine gun (Maxim)	1883	Maxim, H.S.	U.S., Eng.
Magnet, electro	1828	Henry	U.S.
Magnetic Resonance Imaging (MRI)	1971	Damadian	U.S.
Mantle, gas	1885	Welsbach	Austrian
Mason jar	1858	Mason, J.	U.S.
Match, friction	1827	Walker, J.	English
Mercerized textiles	1843	Mercer, J.	English
Meter, induction	1888	Shallenberger	U.S.
Metronome	1816	Malezel	German
Microcomputer	1973	Truong, et al.	French

Invention	Date	Inventor	Nationality
Micrometer	1636	Gascoigne	English
Microphone	1877	Berliner	U.S.
Microprocessor	1971	Intel Corp.	U.S.
Microscope, compound	1590	Janssen	Dutch
Microscope, electronic	1931	Knoll, Ruska	German
Microscope, field ion	1951	Mueller	German
Microwave oven	1947	Spencer	U.S.
Minivan	1983	Chrysler	U.S.
Monitor, warship	1861	Ericsson	U.S.
Monotype	1887	Lanston	U.S.
Motor, AC	1892	Tesla	U.S.
Motor, DC	1837	Davenport	U.S.
Motor, induction	1887	Tesla	U.S.
Motorcycle	1885	Daimler	German
Movie machine	1894	Jenkins	U.S.
Movie, panoramic	1952	Waller	U.S.
Movie, talking	1927	Warner Bros.	U.S.
Mower, lawn	1831	Budding, Ferrabee	English
Mowing machine	1822	Bailey	U.S.
Neoprene	1930	Carothers	U.S.
Nylon	1937	Du Pont lab	U.S.
Nylon synthetic	1930	Carothers	U.S.
Oil cracking furnace	1891	Gavrilov	Russian
Oil filled power cable	1921	Emanueli	Italian
Oleomargarine	1869	Mege-Mouries	French
Ophthalmoscope	1851	Helmholtz	German
Pacemaker	1952	Zoll	U.S.
Paper	105	Ts'ai	Chinese
Paper clip	1900	Waaler	Norwegian
Paper machine	1809	Dickinson	U.S.
Parachute	1785	Blanchard	French
Pen, ballpoint	1888	Loud	U.S.
Pen, fountain	1884	Waterman	U.S.
Pen, steel	1780	Harrison	English
Pendulum	1583	Galileo	Italian
Percussion cap	1807	Forsythe	Scottish
Phonograph	1877	Edison	U.S.
Photo, color	1892	Ives	U.S.
Photo film, celluloid	1893	Reichenbach	U.S.
Photo film, transparent	1884	Eastman, Goodwin	U.S.
Photoelectric cell	1895	Elster	German
Photocopier	1938	Carlson	U.S.
Photographic paper	1835	Talbot	English
Photography	1816	Niepce	French
Photography	1835	Talbot	English
Photography	1835	Daguerre	French
Photophone	1880	Bell	U.S.-Scot.
Phototelegraphy	1925	Bell Labs	U.S.
Piano	1709	Cristofori	Italian
Piano, player	1863	Fourneaux	French
Pin, safety	1849	Hunt	U.S.
Pistol (revolver)	1836	Colt	U.S.
Plow, cast iron	1785	Ransome	English
Plow, disc	1896	Hardy	U.S.
Pneumatic hammer	1890	King	U.S.
Post-it note	1980	3M	U.S.
Powder, smokeless	1884	Vieille	French
Printing press, rotary	1845	Hoe	U.S.
Printing press, web	1865	Bullock	U.S.
Propeller, screw	1804	Stevens	U.S.
Propeller, screw	1837	Ericsson	Swedish
Pulsars	1967	Bell	English
Punch card accounting	1889	Hollerith	U.S.
Radar	1940	Watson-Watt	Scottish
Radio, magnetic detector	1902	Marconi	Italian
Radio, signals	1895	Marconi	Italian
Radio amplifier	1906	De Forest	U.S.
Radio beacon	1928	Donovan	U.S.
Radio crystal oscillator	1918	Nicolson	U.S.
Radio receiver, cascade tuning	1913	Alexanderson	U.S.
Radio receiver, heterodyne	1913	Fessenden	U.S.
Radio transmitter triode modulation	1914	Alexanderson	U.S.
Radio tube diode	1904	Fleming	English
Radio tube oscillator	1915	De Forest	U.S.
Radio tube triode	1906	De Forest	U.S.
Radio FM, 2-path	1933	Armstrong	U.S.
Rayon (acetate)	1895	Cross	English
Rayon (cuprammonium)	1890	Despeissis	French
Rayon (nitrocellulose)	1884	Chardonnet	French
Razor, electric	1917	Schick	U.S.
Razor, safety	1895	Gillette	U.S.
Reaper	1834	McCormick	U.S.
Record, cylinder	1887	Bell, Tainter	U.S.
Record, disc	1887	Berliner	U.S.
Record, long playing	1947	Goldmark	U.S.
Record, wax cylinder	1888	Edison	U.S.
Refrigerator car	1868	David	U.S.
Resin, synthetic	1931	Hill	English
Richter scale	1935	Richter	U.S.
Rifle, repeating	1860	Henry	U.S.
Rocket, liquid fuel	1926	Goddard	U.S.
Rollerblades	1980	Olson	U.S.
Rubber, vulcanized	1839	Goodyear	U.S.
Saccharin	1879	Remsen, Fahlberg	U.S.
Saw, circular	1777	Miller	English
Scotch tape	1930	Drew	U.S.
Seat belt	1959	Volvo	Swedish
Sewing machine	1846	Howe	U.S.
Shoe-lasting machine	1883	Matzeliger	U.S.
Shoe-sewing machine	1860	McKay	U.S.
Shrapnel shell	1784	Shrapnel	English
Shuttle, flying	1733	Kay	English
Sleeping-car	1865	Pullman	U.S.
Slide rule	1620	Oughtred	English
Smoke detector	1969	Smith, House	U.S.
Soap, hardware	1928	Bertsch	German
Spectroscope	1859	Kirchoff, Bunsen	German
Spectroscope (mass)	1918	Dempster	U.S.
Spinning jenny	c.1764	Hargreaves	English
Spinning mule	1779	Crompton	English
Steamboat, exp'mtl	1778	Jouffroy	French
Steamboat, exp'mtl	1785	Fitch	U.S.
Steamboat, exp'mtl	1787	Rumsey	U.S.
Steamboat, exp'mtl	1803	Fulton	U.S.
Steamboat, exp'mtl	1804	Stevens	U.S.
Steamboat, practical	1802	Symington	Scottish
Steamboat, practical	1807	Fulton	U.S.
Steam car	1770	Cugnot	French
Steam turbine	1884	Parsons	English
Steel (converter)	1856	Bessemer	English
Steel alloy	1891	Harvey	U.S.
Steel alloy, high-speed	1901	Taylor, White	U.S.
Steel, manganese	1884	Hadfield	English
Steel, stainless	1916	Brearley	English
Stereoscope	1838	Wheatstone	English
Stethoscope	1819	Laennec	French
Stethoscope, binaural	1840	Cammann	U.S.
Stock ticker	1870	Edison	U.S.
Storage battery, rechargeable	1859	Plante	French
Stove, electric	1896	Hadaway	U.S.
Submarine	1891	Holland	U.S.
Submarine, even keel	1894	Lake	U.S.
Submarine, torpedo	1776	Bushnell	U.S.
Superconductivity	1957	Bardeen, Cooper, Schreiffer	U.S.
Superconductivity in ceramics at high temp	1986	Bednorz Muller	German Swiss
Synthesizer	1964	Moog	U.S.
Tank, military	1914	Swinton	English
Tape recorder, magnetic	1899	Poulsen	Danish
Teflon	1938	Du Pont	U.S.
Telegraph, magnetic	1837	Morse	U.S.
Telegraph, quadruplex	1864	Edison	U.S.
Telegraph, railroad	1887	Woods	U.S.
Telegraph, wireless high frequency	1895	Marconi	Italian
Telephone[1]	1871	Meucci	U.S.-Italian
Telephone[1]	1876	Bell	U.S.-Scot.
Telephone answering machine (1st practical)	1954	Hashimoto	Japanese
Telephone, automatic	1891	Strowger	U.S.
Telephone, cellular	1947	Bell Labs	U.S.
Telephone, cordless[2]	1950	Gross	U.S.
Telephone, radio	1900	Poulsen, Fessenden	Danish
Telephone, radio	1906	De Forest	U.S.
Telephone, radio, long dist.	1915	AT&T	U.S.
Telephone, recording	1898	Poulsen	Danish
Telephone amplifier	1912	De Forest	U.S.
Telescope	1608	Lippershey	Neth.
Telescope	1609	Galileo	Italian
Telescope, astronomical	1611	Kepler	German
Teletype	1928	Morkrum, Kleinschmidt	U.S.
Television, color	1928	Baird	Scottish
Television, electronic	1927	Farnsworth	U.S.
Television, iconoscope	1923	Zworykin	U.S.
Television, mech. scanner	1923	Baird	Scottish
Tesla Coil	1891	Tesla	U.S.
Thermometer	1593	Galileo	Italian
Thermometer	1730	Reaumur	French
Thermometer, mercury	1714	Fahrenheit	German
Time recorder	1890	Bundy	U.S.
Tire, double-tube	1845	Thomson	Scottish
Tire, pneumatic	1888	Dunlop	Scottish
Toaster, automatic	1918	Strite	U.S.
Toilet, flush	1589	Harington	English
Tool, pneumatic	1865	Law	English
Torpedo, marine	1804	Fulton	U.S.
Tractor, crawler	1904	Holt	U.S.
Transformer, AC	1885	Stanley	U.S.
Transistor	1947	Shockley, Brattain, Bardeen	U.S.

Invention	Date	Inventor	Nationality
Trolley car, electric	1884-87	Van DePoele, Sprague	U.S.
Tungsten, ductile	1912	Coolidge	U.S.
Tupperware®	1945	Tupper	U.S.
Turbine, gas	1849	Bourdin	French
Turbine, hydraulic	1849	Francis	U.S.
Turbine, steam	1884	Parsons	English
Type, movable	1447	Gutenberg	German
Typewriter	1867	Sholes, Soule, Glidden	U.S.
Vacuum cleaner, electric	1907	Spangler	U.S.
Vacuum evaporating pan	1846	Rillieux	U.S.
Velcro	1948	de Mestral	Swiss
Video game ("Pong")	1972	Bushnell	U.S.

Invention	Date	Inventor	Nationality
Video home system (VHS)	1975	Matsushita, JVC	Japan
Washer, electric	1901	Fisher	U.S.
Welding, atomic hydrogen	1924	Langmuir, Palmer	U.S.
Welding, electric	1877	Thomson	U.S.
Windshield wiper	1903	Anderson	U.S.
Wind tunnel	1912	Eiffel	French
Wire, barbed	1874	Glidden	U.S.
Wrench, double-acting	1913	Owen	U.S.
X-ray tube	1913	Coolidge	U.S.
Zeppelin	1900	Zeppelin	German
Zipper, early model	1893	Judson	U.S.
Zipper, improved	1913	Sundback	Canadian

(1) While Alexander Graham Bell has traditionally been credited with invention of the telephone, which he patented, Antonio Meucci developed a working model before Bell. (2) Al Gross held a number of important early patents in the field of wireless communication; other people were also involved in the development of practical cordless telephones.

Top 30 Corporations Receiving U.S. Patents in 2003

Source: U.S. Patent and Trademark Office, U.S. Department of Commerce

Rank	Company	Number of patents
1.	International Business Machines Corp.	3,415
2.	Canon Kabushiki Kaisha	1,992
3.	Hitachi, Ltd	1,893
4.	Matsushita Electric Industrial Co., Ltd.	1,774
5.	Micron Technology, Inc.	1,707
6.	Intel Corporation	1,592
7.	Koninklijke Philips Electronics N.V.	1,353
8.	Samsung Electronics Co., Ltd.	1,313
9.	Sony Corporation	1,311
10.	Fujitsu Limited	1,302
11.	Hewlett-Packard Development Co., L.P.	1,292
12.	Mitsubishi Denki Kabushiki Kaisha	1,243
13.	Toshiba Corp.	1,184
14.	NEC Corp.	1,181
15.	General Electric Co.	1,139
16.	Advanced Micro Devices, Inc.	905

Rank	Company	Number of patents
17.	Fuji Photo Film Co., Ltd	804
18.	Seiko Epson Corp.	764
	Texas Instruments, Inc.	764
20.	Robert Bosch Gmbh	753
21.	Eastman Kodak Co.	748
22.	Siemens Aktiengesellschaft	660
23.	Honda Giken Kogyo Kabushiki Kaisha (Honda Motor Co., Ltd.)	647
24.	Infineon Technologies Ag	639
25.	Delphi Technologies Inc.	635
26.	Lucent Technologies Inc.	621
27.	Xerox Corp.	613
28.	Motorola, Inc.	610
29.	3M Innovative Properties Co.	572
30.	Sun Microsystems, Inc.	564

Breaking the Sound Barrier; Speed of Sound

The prefix **Mach** is used to describe supersonic speed. It was named for Ernst Mach (1838-1916), a Czech-born Austrian physicist. When a plane moves at the speed of sound, it is Mach 1. When the plane is moving at twice the speed of sound, it is Mach 2. Mach may be defined as the ratio of the velocity of a rocket or a jet to the velocity of sound in the medium being considered.

When a plane passes the sound barrier—flying faster than sound travels—listeners in the area hear thunderclaps, but the pilot of the plane does not hear them.

Sound is produced by vibrations of an object and is transmitted by alternate increase and decrease in pressures that radiate outward through a material media of molecules—somewhat like waves spreading out on a pond after a rock has been tossed into it.

The **frequency of sound** is determined by the number of times the vibrating waves undulate per second and is measured in cycles per second. The slower the cycle of waves, the lower the frequency. As frequencies increase, the sound is higher in pitch. The human ear is usually not sensitive to frequencies of fewer than 20 vibrations per second or greater than about 20,000 vibrations per second—although this range varies among individuals.

Intensity, or loudness, is the strength of the pressure of these radiating waves and is measured in decibels. (See Weights and Measures.)

The **speed of sound** is generally defined as 1,088 feet per second at sea level at 32° F. It varies in other temperatures and in different media. Sound travels faster in water than in air, and even faster in iron and steel.

Light; Colors of the Spectrum

Light, a form of electromagnetic radiation similar to radiant heat, radio waves, and X rays, is emitted from a source in straight lines and spreads out over larger areas as it travels; light per unit area diminishes as the square of the distance.

The English mathematician and physicist Sir Isaac Newton (1642-1727) described light as an **emission of particles**; the Dutch astronomer, mathematician, and physicist Christiaan Huygens (1629-95) developed the theory that light travels by a **wave motion**. It is now believed that these 2 theories are essentially complementary, and the development of quantum theory has led to results where light acts like a series of particles in some experiments and like a wave in others.

The **speed of light** was first measured in a laboratory experiment by the French physicist Armand Hippolyte Louis Fizeau (1819-96). Today the speed of light is known very precisely as 299,792.458 km per sec (or 186,282.396 mi per sec) in a vacuum; in water the speed of light is about 25% less, and in glass, 33% less.

Color sensations are produced through the excitation of the retina of the eye by light vibrating at different frequencies. The different colors of the spectrum may be produced by viewing a light beam that is refracted by passage through a prism, which breaks the light into its wavelengths.

Customarily, the **primary colors** are taken to be the 6 monochromatic colors that occupy relatively large areas of the spectrum: red, orange, yellow, green, blue, and violet. Scientists have differed, however, in how many and which primary colors they recognized. The color sensation of **black** is due to complete lack of stimulation of the retina, that of **white** to complete stimulation. The **infrared and ultraviolet rays**, below the red (long) end of the spectrum and above the violet (short) end respectively, are invisible to the naked eye. Heat is the principal effect of the infrared rays, and chemical action that of the ultraviolet rays.

WORLD ALMANAC QUICK QUIZ

Put these inventions in order, from earliest to latest:

(a) vacuum cleaner   (b) radar
(c) dynamite   (d) Scotch tape

For the answer look in this chapter, or see page 1008.

WEIGHTS AND MEASURES

Source: National Institute of Standards and Technology, U.S. Dept. of Commerce

The International System of Units (SI)

Two systems of weights and measures coexist in the U.S. today: the **U.S. Customary System** and the **International System of Units** (SI, after the initials of Système International). SI, **commonly identified with the metric system,** is actually a more complete, coherent version of it. Throughout U.S. history, the Customary System (inherited from, but now different from, the British Imperial System) has been generally used; federal and state legislation has given it, through implication, standing as the primary weights and measures system. The metric system, however, is the only system that Congress has ever specifically sanctioned. An 1866 law reads:

It shall be lawful throughout the United States of America to employ the weights and measures of the metric system; and no contract or dealing, or pleading in any court, shall be deemed invalid or liable to objection because the weights or measures expressed or referred to therein are weights or measures of the metric system.

Since that time, use of the metric system in the U.S. has slowly and steadily increased, particularly in the scientific community, in the pharmaceutical industry, and in the manufacturing sector—the last motivated by the practice in international commerce, in which the metric system is now predominantly used.

On Feb. 10, 1964, the National Bureau of Standards (now known as the National Institute of Standards and Technology) issued the following statement:

Henceforth it shall be the policy of the National Bureau of Standards to use the units of the International System (SI), as adopted by the 11th General Conference on Weights and Measures (October 1960), except when the use of these units would obviously impair communication or reduce the usefulness of a report.

On Dec. 23, 1975, Pres. Gerald R. Ford signed the Metric Conversion Act of 1975. It defines the metric system as being the International System of Units as interpreted in the U.S. by the secretary of commerce. The Trade Act of 1988 and other legislation declare the metric system the preferred system of weights and measures for U.S. trade and commerce, call for the federal government to adopt metric specifications, and mandate the Commerce Dept. to oversee the program. However, the metric system has still not become the system of choice for most Americans' daily use.

The following 7 units serve as the base units for the system: **length**—meter; **mass**—kilogram; **time**—second; **electric current**—ampere; **thermodynamic temperature**—kelvin; **amount of substance**—mole; and **luminous intensity**—candela.

Frequently Used Conversions

Boldface indicates exact values. For greater accuracy, use the "multiply by" number in parentheses. For more detailed tables, see page 344-347.

U.S. Customary to Metric

	If you have:	Multiply by:		To get:
Length	inches	**25.4**		millimeters
	inches	**2.54**		centimeters
	inches	**0.0254**		meters
	feet	0.3	**(0.3048)**	meters
	yards	0.9	**(0.9144)**	meters
	miles[1]	1.6	**(1.609344)**	kilometers
Area	sq. inches	6.5	**(6.4516)**	sq. cm.
	sq. feet	0.09	(0.09290341)	sq. meters
	sq. yards	0.84	(0.83612736)	sq. meters
	acres	0.4	(0.4046873)	hectares
	sq. miles	2.6	(2.58998811)	sq. kilometers
Weight	ounces (avdp)	28	**(28.349523125)**	grams
	pounds (avdp)	454	**(453.59237)**	grams
	pounds (avdp)	0.45	**(0.45359237)**	kilograms
	short tons[2]	0.91	**(0.90718474)**	metric tons
	long tons[3]	1	**(1.0160469088)**	metric tons
Liquid meas.	ounces	0.03	(0.02957353)	liters
	cups	0.24	(0.23658824)	liters
	pints	0.47	(0.473176473)	liters
	quarts	0.95	(0.946352946)	liters
	gallons	3.79	(3.785411784)	liters

Metric to U.S. Customary

	If you have:	Multiply by:		To get:
Length	millimeters	0.04	(0.03937)	inches
	centimeters	0.4	(0.3937)	inches
	meters	39	(39.37)	inches
	meters	3.3	(3.280840)	feet
	meters	1.1	(1.093613)	yards
	kilometers	0.6	(0.621371)	miles
Area	sq. cm.	0.16	(0.15500)	sq. inches
	sq. meters	10.8	(10.76391)	sq. feet
	sq. meters	1.2	(1.195990)	sq. yards
	hectares	2.5	(2.471044)	acres
	sq. kilometers	0.39	(0.386102)	sq. miles
Weight	grams	0.035	(0.03527396)	ounces (avdp)
	grams	0.002	(0.00220462)	pounds (avdp)
	kilograms	2.2	(2.204623)	pounds (avdp)
	metric tons	1.1	(1.102311)	short tons[2]
	metric tons	0.98	(0.9842065)	long tons[3]
Liquid meas.	liters	33.8	(33.81402)	ounces
	liters	4.2	(4.226752)	cups
	liters	2.1	(2.113376)	pints
	liters	1.1	(1.056688)	quarts
	liters	0.26	(0.264172)	gallons

(1) Statute mile. (2) A short ton is 2,000 pounds. (3) A long ton is 2,240 pounds.

Temperature Conversions

The left-hand column below gives a temperature according to the **Celsius** scale, and the right-hand gives the same temperature according to the **Fahrenheit** scale. The lowest number for each scale refers to what scientists call absolute zero, the temperature at which all molecular motion would be at its lowest level.

For temperatures not shown: To convert Fahrenheit to Celsius by formula, subtract 32 degrees and divide by 1.8; to convert Celsius to Fahrenheit, multiply by 1.8 and add 32 degrees.

Note: Although the term *centigrade* is still frequently used, the International Committee on Weights and Measures and the National Institute of Standards and Technology have recommended since 1948 that this scale be called *Celsius*.

Celsius	Fahrenheit	Celsius	Fahrenheit	Celsius	Fahrenheit	Celsius	Fahrenheit	Celsius	Fahrenheit
−273.15	−459.67	−45.6	−50	−1.1	30	30	86	66	150
−250	−418	−40	−40	0	32	32.2	90	70	158
−200	−328	−34.4	−30	4.4	40	35	95	80	176
−184	−300	−30	−22	10	50	37	98.6	90	194
−157	−250	−28.9	−20	15.6	60	37.8	100	93	200
−150	−238	−23.3	−10	20	68	40	104	100	212
−129	−200	−20	−4	21.1	70	43	110	121	250
−101	−150	−17.8	0	23.9	75	49	120	149	300
−100	−148	−12.2	10	25	77	50	122	150	302
− 73.3	−100	−10	14	26.7	80	54	130	200	392
− 50	− 58	− 6.7	20	29.4	85	60	140	300	572

Boiling and Freezing Points

Water boils at 212° F (100° C) at sea level. For every 550 feet above sea level, boiling point of water is lower by about 1° F. Methyl alcohol boils at 148° F. Average human oral temperature, 98.6° F. **Water freezes** at 32° F (0° C).

Mathematical Formulas

Note: The value of π (the Greek letter pi) is approximately 3.14159265 (equal to the ratio of the circumference of a circle to the diameter). The equivalence is typically rounded further to 3.1416 or 3.14.

To find the CIRCUMFERENCE of a:
Circle — Multiply the diameter by π.

To find the AREA of a:
Circle — Multiply the square of the radius (equal to ½ the diameter) by π.
Rectangle — Multiply the length of the base by the height.
Sphere (surface) — Multiply the square of the radius by π and multiply by 4.
Square — Square the length of one side.
Trapezoid — Add the 2 parallel sides, multiply by the height, and divide by 2.
Triangle — Multiply the base by the height, divide by 2.

To find the VOLUME of a:
Cone — Multiply the square of the radius of the base by π, multiply by the height, and divide by 3.
Cube — Cube the length of one edge.
Cylinder — Multiply the square of the radius of the base by π and multiply by the height.
Pyramid — Multiply the area of the base by the height and divide by 3.
Rectangular Prism — Multiply the length by the width by the height.
Sphere — Multiply the cube of the radius by π, multiply by 4, and divide by 3.

Playing Cards and Dice Chances

5-Card Poker Hands

Hand	Number possible	Odds against
Royal flush	4	649,739 to 1
Other straight flush	36	72,192 to 1
Four of a kind	624	4,164 to 1
Full house	3,744	693 to 1
Flush	5,108	508 to 1
Straight	10,200	254 to 1
Three of a kind	54,912	46 to 1
Two pairs	123,552	20 to 1
One pair	1,098,240	4 to 3 (1.37 to 1)
Nothing	1,302,540	1 to 1
TOTAL	**2,598,960**	

Bridge

The odds—against suit distribution in a hand of 4-4-3-2 are about 4 to 1, against 5-4-2-2 about 8 to 1, against 6-4-2-1 about 20 to 1, against 7-4-1-1 about 254 to 1, against 8-4-1-0 about 2,211 to 1, and against 13-0-0-0 about 158,753,389,899 to 1.

Dice
(probabilities on 2 dice)

Total	Odds against (single toss)	Total	Odds against (single toss)
2	35 to 1	8	31 to 5
3	17 to 1	9	8 to 1
4	11 to 1	10	11 to 1
5	8 to 1	11	17 to 1
6	31 to 5	12	35 to 1
7	5 to 1		

Large Numbers

No. of zeros	U.S.	British[1], French, German	No. of zeros	U.S.	British[1], French, German	No. of zeros	U.S.	British[1], French, German
6	million	million	30	nonillion	quintillion	54	septendecillion	nonillion
9	billion	milliard	33	decillion	1,000 quintillion	57	octodecillion	1,000 nonillion
12	trillion	billion	36	undecillion	sextillion	60	novemdecillion	decillion
15	quadrillion	1,000 billion	39	duodecillion	1,000 sextillion	63	vigintillion	1,000 decillion
18	quintillion	trillion	42	tredecillion	septillion	100	googol	googol
21	sextillion	1,000 trillion	45	quattuordecillion	1,000 septillion	303	centillion	—
24	septillion	quadrillion	48	quindecillion	octillion	600	—	centillion
27	octillion	1,000 quadrillion	51	sexdecillion	1,000 octillion	googol	googolplex	googolplex

(1) In recent years, it has become more common in Britain to use American terminology for large numbers.

Prime Numbers

A prime number is an integer other than zero or ±1 that is divisible only by ±1 and itself.

Prime Numbers Between 1 and 1,000

	2	3	5	7	11	13	17	19	23
29	31	37	41	43	47	53	59	61	67
71	73	79	83	89	97	101	103	107	109
113	127	131	137	139	149	151	157	163	167
173	179	181	191	193	197	199	211	223	227
229	233	239	241	251	257	263	269	271	277
281	283	293	307	311	313	317	331	337	347
349	353	359	367	373	379	383	389	397	401
409	419	421	431	433	439	443	449	457	461
463	467	479	487	491	499	503	509	521	523
541	547	557	563	569	571	577	587	593	599
601	607	613	617	619	631	641	643	647	653
659	661	673	677	683	691	701	709	719	727
733	739	743	751	757	761	769	773	787	797
809	811	821	823	827	829	839	853	857	859
863	877	881	883	887	907	911	919	929	937
941	947	953	967	971	977	983	991	997	(1,009)

Roman Numerals

I —	1	V —	5	IX —	9	XX —	20	LX —	60	CD —	400
II —	2	VI —	6	X —	10	XXX —	30	XC —	90	D —	500
III —	3	VII —	7	XI —	11	XL —	40	C —	100	CM —	900
IV —	4	VIII —	8	XIX —	19	L —	50	CC —	200	M —	1,000

Note: The numerals V, X, L, C, D, or M shown with a horizontal line on top denote 1,000 times the original value.

Common Fractions Reduced to Decimals

8ths	16ths	32nds	64ths		8ths	16ths	32nds	64ths		8ths	16ths	32nds	64ths		8ths	16ths	32nds	64ths	
			1	= 0.015625				17	= 0.265625				33	= 0.515625				49	= 0.765625
		1		= 0.03125			9	18	= 0.28125			17	34	= 0.53125			25	50	= 0.78125
			3	= 0.046875				19	= 0.296875				35	= 0.546875				51	= 0.796875
	1	2	4	= 0.0625		5	10	20	= 0.3125			18	36	= 0.5625		13	26	52	= 0.8125
			5	= 0.078125				21	= 0.328125				37	= 0.578125				53	= 0.828125
		3	6	= 0.09375			11	22	= 0.34375			19	38	= 0.59375			27	54	= 0.84375
			7	= 0.109375				23	= 0.359375				39	= 0.609375				55	= 0.859375
1	2	4	8	= 0.125	3	6	12	24	= 0.375	5	10	20	40	= 0.625	7	14	28	56	= 0.875
			9	= 0.140625				25	= 0.390625				41	= 0.640625				57	= 0.890625
		5	10	= 0.15625			13	26	= 0.40625			21	42	= 0.65625			29	58	= 0.90625
			11	= 0.171875				27	= 0.421875				43	= 0.671875				59	= 0.921875
	3	6	12	= 0.1875		7	14	28	= 0.4375		11	22	44	= 0.6875		15	30	60	= 0.9375
			13	= 0.203125				29	= 0.453125				45	= 0.703125				61	= 0.953125
		7	14	= 0.21875			15	30	= 0.46875			23	46	= 0.71875			31	62	= 0.96875
			15	= 0.234375				31	= 0.484375				47	= 0.734375				63	= 0.984375
2	4	8	16	= 0.25	4	8	16	32	= 0.5	6	12	24	48	= 0.75	8	16	32	64	= 1.0

> **IT'S A FACT:** In Sept. 1999, Jet Propulsion Laboratory engineers sent instructions to the *Mars Climate Orbiter* to fire its rockets to slow its approach toward Mars and put the craft into orbit. But the *Orbiter* flew too close to the planet and was lost. After an investigation, NASA concluded that the root cause of its getting too close was a measurement mix-up: the spacecraft's builder, Lockheed Martin Astronautics, had data in English units for thrust (pounds of force); these were entered into the craft's navigation computer, which assumed metric units (Newtons).

Metric System Prefixes

The following prefixes, in combination with the basic unit names, provide the multiples and submultiples in the metric system. For example, the unit name *meter*, with the prefix *kilo* added, produces *kilometer*, meaning "1,000 meters."

Prefix	Symbol	Multiples	Equivalent		Prefix	Symbol	Multiples	Equivalent
yotta	Y	10^{24}	septillionfold		deci	d	10^{-1}	tenth part
zetta	Z	10^{21}	sextillionfold		centi	c	10^{-2}	hundredth part
exa	E	10^{18}	quintillionfold		milli	m	10^{-3}	thousandth part
peta	P	10^{15}	quadrillionfold		micro	μ	10^{-6}	millionth part
tera	T	10^{12}	trillionfold		nano	n	10^{-9}	billionth part
giga	G	10^{9}	billionfold		pico	p	10^{-12}	trillionth part
mega	M	10^{6}	millionfold		femto	f	10^{-15}	quadrillionth part
kilo	k	10^{3}	thousandfold		atto	a	10^{-18}	quintillionth part
hecto	h	10^{2}	hundredfold		zepto	z	10^{-21}	sextillionth part
deka	da	10	tenfold		yocto	y	10^{-24}	septillionth part

Tables of Metric Weights and Measures

(**Note:** The metric system generally uses the term *mass* instead of *weight*. Mass is a measure of an object's inertial property, or the amount of matter it contains. Weight is a measure of the force exerted on an object by gravity or the force needed to support it. Also, the metric system does not make a distinction between "dry volume" and "liquid volume.")

Length

10 millimeters (mm)	= 1 centimeter (cm)
10 centimeters	= 1 decimeter (dm)
	= 100 millimeters
10 decimeters	= 1 meter (m)
	= 1,000 millimeters
10 meters	= 1 dekameter (dam)
10 dekameters	= 1 hectometer (hm)
	= 100 meters
10 hectometers	= 1 kilometer (km)
	= 1,000 meters

Area

100 square millimeters (mm^2)	= 1 square centimeter (cm^2)
10,000 square centimeters	= 1 square meter (m^2)
	= 1,000,000 square millimeters
100 square meters	= 1 are (a)
100 ares	= 1 hectare (ha)
	= 10,000 square meters
100 hectares	= 1 square kilometer (km^2)
	= 1,000,000 square meters

Volume

10 milliliters (mL)	= 1 centiliter (cL)
10 centiliters	= 1 deciliter (dL)
	= 100 milliliters
10 deciliters	= 1 liter (L)
	= 1,000 milliliters

10 liters	= 1 dekaliter (daL)
10 dekaliters	= 1 hectoliter (hL)
	= 100 liters
10 hectoliters	= 1 kiloliter (kL)
	= 1,000 liters

Volume (Cubic Measure)

1,000 cubic millimeters (mm^3)	= 1 cubic centimeter (cm^3)
1,000 cubic centimeters	= 1 cubic decimeter (dm^3)
	= 1,000,000 cubic millimeters
1,000 cubic decimeters	= 1 cubic meter (m^3)
	= 1 stere
	= 1,000,000 cubic centimeters
	= 1,000,000,000 cubic millimeters

Weight (Mass)

10 milligrams (mg)	= 1 centigram (cg)
10 centigrams	= 1 decigram (dg)
	= 100 milligrams
10 decigrams	= 1 gram (g)
	= 1,000 milligrams
10 grams	= 1 dekagram (dag)
10 dekagrams	= 1 hectogram (hg)
	= 100 grams
10 hectograms	= 1 kilogram (kg)
	= 1,000 grams
1,000 kilograms	= 1 metric ton (t)

Table of U.S. Customary Weights and Measures

Length

12 inches (in) . . . .= 1 foot (ft)
3 feet . . . .= 1 yard (yd)
5½ yards . . . .= 1 rod (rd), pole, or perch (16½ feet)
40 rods . . . .= 1 furlong (fur)
= 220 yards
= 660 feet
8 furlongs . . . .= 1 statute mile (mi)
= 1,760 yards
= 5,280 feet
3 miles . . . .= 1 league (land)
= 5,280 yards
= 15,840 feet
6076.11549 feet . . . .= 1 international nautical mile

Volume (Liquid Measure)

When necessary to distinguish the liquid pint or quart from the dry pint or quart, the word *liquid* or the abbreviation *liq* is used in combination with the name or abbreviation of the liquid unit.

4 gills (gi) . . . .= 1 pint (pt)
= 28.875 cubic inches
2 pints . . . .= 1 quart (qt)
= 57.75 cubic inches
4 quarts . . . .= 1 gallon (gal)
= 231 cubic inches
= 8 pints
= 32 gills

Volume (Dry Measure)

When necessary to distinguish the dry pint or quart from the liquid pint or quart, the word *dry* is used in combination with the name or abbreviation of the dry unit.

2 pints (pt) . . . .= 1 quart (qt)
= 67.2006 cubic inches
8 quarts . . . .= 1 peck (pk)
= 537.605 cubic inches
= 16 pints
4 pecks . . . .= 1 bushel (bu)
= 2,150.42 cubic inches
= 32 quarts

Area

Squares and cubes of units are sometimes abbreviated by using superscripts. For example, ft^2 means square foot, and ft^3 means cubic foot.

144 square inches . . . .= 1 square foot (ft^2)
9 square feet . . . .= 1 square yard (yd^2)
= 1,296 square inches
30 ¼ square yards . . . . . .= 1 square rod (rd^2)
= 272¼ square feet
160 square rods . . . .= 1 acre
= 4,840 square yards
= 43,560 square feet

640 acres . . . .= 1 square mile (mi^2)
1 mile square . . . .= 1 section (of land)
6 miles square . . . .= 1 township
= 36 sections
= 36 square miles

Cubic Measure

1 cubic foot (ft^3) . . . .= 1,728 cubic inches (in^3)
27 cubic feet . . . .= 1 cubic yard (yd^3)

Gunter's, or Surveyor's, Chain Measure

7.92 inches (in) . . . .= 1 link
100 links . . . .= 1 chain (ch)
= 4 rods
= 66 feet
80 chains . . . .= 1 statute mile (mi)
= 320 rods
= 5,280 feet

Avoirdupois Weight

When necessary to distinguish the avoirdupois ounce or pound from the troy ounce or pound, the word *avoirdupois* or the abbreviation *avdp* is used in combination with the name or abbreviation of the avoirdupois unit. The *grain* is the same in avoirdupois and troy weight.

27 $^{11}/_{32}$ grains . . . .= 1 dram (dr)
16 drams . . . .= 1 ounce (oz)
= 437 ½ grains
16 ounces . . . .= 1 pound (lb)
= 256 drams
= 7,000 grains
100 pounds . . . .= 1 hundredweight (cwt)*
20 hundredweights . . . . . .= 1 ton
= 2,000 pounds*

In *gross* or *long* measure, the following values are recognized.
112 pounds . . . .= 1 gross or long hundredweight*
20 gross or long
hundredweights. . . . . . .= 1 gross or long ton
= 2,240 pounds*

*When the terms *hundredweight* and *ton* are used unmodified, they are commonly understood to mean the 100-pound hundredweight and the 2,000-pound ton, respectively; these units may be designated *net* or *short* when necessary to distinguish them from the corresponding units in gross or long measure.

Troy Weight

24 grains . . . .= 1 pennyweight (dwt)
20 pennyweights . . . .= 1 ounce troy (oz t)
= 480 grains
12 ounces troy . . . .= 1 pound troy (lb t)
= 240 pennyweights
= 5,760 grains

Tables of Equivalents

In this table it is necessary to distinguish between the *international* and the *survey* foot. The international foot, defined in 1959 as exactly equal to 0.3048 meter, is shorter than the old survey foot by exactly 2 parts in 1 million. The survey foot is still used in data expressed in feet in geodetic surveys within the U.S. In this table the survey foot is indicated with capital letters.

When the name of a unit is enclosed in brackets, e.g., [1 hand], either (1) the unit is not in general current use in the U.S. or (2) the unit is believed to be based on custom and usage rather than on formal definition.

Equivalents involving decimals are, in most instances, rounded to the 3rd decimal place; exact equivalents are so designated.

Lengths

1 angstrom (Å) . . . .= 0.1 nanometer (exactly)
= 0.000 1 micrometer (exactly)
= 0.000 000 1 millimeter (exactly)
= 0.000 000 004 inch
1 cable's length . . . .= 120 fathoms (exactly)
= 720 FEET (exactly)
= 219 meters
1 centimeter (cm) . . . .= 0.3937 inch
1 chain (ch) (Gunter's
or surveyor's) . . . .= 66 FEET (exactly)
= 20.1168 meters
1 chain (engineer's) . . . .= 30.48 meters (exactly)
= 100 feet
1 decimeter (dm) . . . .= 3.937 inches
1 degree (geographical). . . . . .= 364,566.929 feet
= 69.047 miles (avg.)
= 111.123 kilometers (avg.)
of latitude . . . .= 68.708 miles at equator
= 69.403 miles at poles
of longitude . . . .= 69.171 miles at equator

1 dekameter (dam) . . . .= 32.808 feet
1 fathom . . . .= 6 FEET (exactly)
= 1.8288 meters
1 foot (ft) . . . .= 0.3048 meters (exactly)
= 0.015 chains (surveyors)
1 furlong (fur). . . . .= 660 FEET (exactly)
= $^1/_8$ statute mile (exactly)
= 201.168 meters
[1 hand] (height measure for
horses from ground to top
of shoulders) . . . .= 4 inches
1 inch (in) . . . .= 2.54 centimeters (exactly)
1 kilometer (km) . . . .= 0.621371 mile
= 3,280.8 feet
1 league (land) . . . .= 3 statute miles (exactly)
= 4.828 kilometers
1 link (Gunter's or surveyor's) . = 7.92 inches (exactly)
= 0.201 meter
1 link (engineer's) . . . .= 1 foot
= 0.305 meter

1 meter (m)	= 39.37 inches
	= 1.09361 yards
1 micrometer (μm)	= 0.001 millimeter (exactly)
	= 0.00003937 inch
1 mil	= 0.001 inch (exactly)
	= 0.0254 millimeter (exactly)
1 mile (mi) (statute or land) . . .	= 5,280 FEET (exactly)
	= 1.609344 kilometers (exactly)
1 international nautical mile (nmi)	= 1.852 kilometers (exactly)
	= 1.150779 statute miles
	= 6,076.11549 feet
1 millimeter (mm)	= 0.03937 inch
1 nanometer (nm)	= 0.001 micrometer (exactly)
	= 0.00000003937 inch
1 pica (typography)	= 12 points
1 point (typography)	= 0.013 837 inch (exactly)
	= 0.351 millimeter
1 rod (rd), pole, or perch	= 16½ FEET (exactly)
	= 5.029 meters
1 yard (yd)	= 0.9144 meter (exactly)

Areas or Surfaces

1 acre	= 43,560 square FEET (exactly)
	= 4,840 square yards
	= 0.405 hectare
1 are (a)	= 119.599 square yards
	= 0.025 acre
1 bolt (cloth measure):	
length	= 100 yards (on modern looms)
width	= 45 or 60 inches
1 hectare (ha)	= 2.471 acres
[1 square (building)]	= 100 square feet
1 square centimeter (cm²)	= 0.155 square inch
1 square decimeter (dm²).	= 15.500 square inches
1 square foot (ft²)	= 929.030 square centimeters
1 square inch (in²)	= 6.4516 square centimeters (exactly)
1 square kilometer (km²) .	= 247.104 acres
	= 0.386102 square mile
1 square meter (m²)	= 1.196 square yards
	= 10.764 square feet
1 square mile (mi²)	= 258.999 hectares
1 square millimeter (mm²)	= 0.002 square inch
1 square rod (rd²), sq. pole, or sq. perch	= 25.293 square meters
1 square yard (yd²)	= 0.836127 square meter

Capacities or Volumes

1 barrel (bbl), liquid	= 31 to 42 gallons*

*There are a variety of "barrels" established by law or usage. For example: federal taxes on fermented liquors are based on a barrel of 31 gallons; many state laws fix the "barrel for liquids" as 31½ gallons; one state fixes a 36-gallon barrel for cistern measurement; federal law recognizes a 40-gallon barrel for "proof spirits"; by custom, 42 gallons constitute a barrel of crude oil or petroleum products for statistical purposes, and this equivalent is recognized "for liquids" by 4 states.

1 barrel (bbl), standard for fruits, vegetables, and other dry commodities except dry cranberries	= 7,056 cubic inches
	= 1 barrel (bbl), standard for fruits
1 barrel (bbl), standard, cranberry	= 86 45/64 dry quarts
	= 2.709 bushels, struck measure
	= 5,826 cubic inches
1 board foot (lumber measure)	= a foot-square board 1 inch thick
1 bushel (bu) (U.S.) (struck measure)	= 2,150.42 cubic inches (exactly)
	= 35.239 liters
[1 bushel, heaped (U.S.)] . . .	= 2,747.715 cubic inches
	= 1.278 bushels, struck measure*

*Frequently recognized as 1¼ bushels, struck measure.

[1 bushel (bu) (British Imperial) (struck measure)]	= 1.032 U.S. bushels, struck measure
	= 2,219.36 cubic inches
1 cord (cd) firewood	= 128 cubic feet (exactly)
1 cubic centimeter (cm³)	= 0.061 cubic inch
1 cubic decimeter (dm³)	= 61.024 cubic inches
1 cubic inch (in³)	= 0.554 fluid ounce
	= 4.433 fluid drams
	= 16.387 cubic centimeters
1 cubic foot (ft³)	= 7.481 gallons
	= 28.317 cubic decimeters
1 cubic meter (m³)	= 1.308 cubic yards
1 cubic yard (yd³)	= 0.765 cubic meter
1 cup, measuring	= 8 fluid ounces (exactly)
	= ½ liquid pint (exactly)

[1 dram, fluid (fl dr) (British)] .	= 0.961 U.S. fluid dram
	= 0.217 cubic inch
	= 3.552 milliliters
1 dekaliter (daL)	= 2.642 gallons
	= 1.135 pecks
1 gallon (gal) (U.S.)	= 231 cubic inches (exactly)
	= 3.785 liters
	= 0.833 British gallon
	= 128 U.S. fluid ounces (exactly)
[1 gallon (gal) British Imperial]	= 277.42 cubic inches
	= 1.201 U.S. gallons
	= 4.546 liters
	= 160 British fluid ounces (exactly)
1 gill (gi)	= 7.219 cubic inches
	= 4 fluid ounces (exactly)
	= 0.118 liter
1 hectoliter (hL)	= 26.418 gallons
	= 2.838 bushels
1 liter (L) (1 cubic decimeter exactly)	= 1.057 liquid quarts
	= 0.908 dry quart
	= 61.024 cubic inches
1 milliliter (mL) (1 cu cm exactly)	= 0.271 fluid dram
	= 16.231 minims
	= 0.061 cubic inch
1 ounce, liquid (U.S.)	= 1.805 cubic inches
	= 29.574 milliliters
	= 1.041 British fluid ounces
[1 ounce, fluid (fl oz) (British)]	= 0.961 U.S. fluid ounce
	= 1.734 cubic inches
	= 28.412 milliliters
1 peck (pk)	= 8.810 liters
1 pint (pt), dry	= 33.600 cubic inches
	= 0.551 liter
1 pint (pt), liquid	= 28.875 cubic inches (exactly)
	= 0.473 liter
1 quart (qt), dry (U.S.)	= 67.201 cubic inches
	= 1.101 liters
	= 0.969 British quart
1 quart (qt), liquid (U.S.)	= 57.75 cubic in (exactly)
	= 0.946 liter
	= 0.833 British quart
[1 quart (qt) (British)]	= 69.354 cubic inches
	= 1.032 U.S. dry quarts
	= 1.201 U.S. liquid quarts
1 tablespoon	= 3 teaspoons*(exactly)
	= 4 fluid drams
	= ½ fluid ounce (exactly)
1 teaspoon	= 1/3 tablespoon*(exactly)
	= 11/3 fluid drams*

*The equivalent "1 teaspoon = 1⅓ fluid drams" has been found to correspond more closely with the actual capacities of teaspoons in use than the equivalent "1 teaspoon = 1 fluid dram" which is given by many dictionaries.

Weights or Masses

1 assay ton** (AT)	= 29.167 grams

**Used in assaying. The assay ton bears the same relation to the milligram that a ton of 2,000 pounds avoirdupois bears to the ounce troy; hence, the weight in milligrams of precious metal obtained from one assay ton of ore gives directly the number of troy ounces to the net ton.

1 bale (cotton measure)	= 500 pounds in U.S.
	= 750 pounds in Egypt
1 carat (c)	= 200 milligrams (exactly)
	= 3.086 grains
1 dram avoirdupois (dr avdp) . . .	= 27 11/32 (= 27.344) grains
	= 1.772 grams
1 gamma (g)	= 1 microgram (exactly), see below
1 grain	= 64.7989 milligrams
1 gram	= 15.432 grains
	= 0.035 ounce, avoirdupois
1 hundredweight, gross or long*** (gross cwt)	= 112 pounds (exactly)
	= 50.802 kilograms
1 hundredweight, net or short (cwt or net cwt)	= 100 pounds (exactly)
	= 45.359 kilograms
1 kilogram (kg)	= 2.20462 pounds
1 microgram (μg)	= 0.000001 gram (exactly)
1 milligram (mg)	= 0.015 grain
1 ounce, avoirdupois (oz avdp) .	= 437.5 grains (exactly)
	= 0.911 troy ounce
	= 28.3495 grams

1 ounce, troy (oz t)	= 480 grains (exactly) = 1.097 avoirdupois ounces = 31.103 grams
1 pennyweight (dwt)	= 1.555 grams
1 pound, avoirdupois (lb avdp) . .	= 7,000 grains (exactly) = 1.215 troy pounds = 453.59237 grams (exactly)
1 pound, troy (lb t)	= 5,760 grains (exactly) = 0.823 pound, avoirdupois = 373.242 grams
1 stone, (avdp)	= 14 pounds avdp (exactly) = 6.350 kilograms

1 ton, gross or long***(gross ton)	= 2,240 pounds (exactly) = 1.12 net tons (exactly) = 1.016 metric tons

***The gross or long ton and hundredweight are used commercially in the U.S. to only a limited extent, usually in restricted industrial fields. These units are the same as the British ton and hundredweight.

1 ton, metric (t)	= 2,204.623 pounds = 0.984 gross ton = 1.102 net tons
1 ton, net or short (sh ton)	= 2,000 pounds (exactly) = 0.893 gross ton = 0.907 metric ton

Electrical Units

The **watt** is the unit of power (electrical, mechanical, thermal, etc.). Electrical power is given by the product of the voltage and the current.

Energy is sold by the **joule,** but in common practice the billing of electrical energy is expressed in terms of the **kilowatt-hour,** which is 3,600,000 joules or 3.6 megajoules.

The **horsepower** is a nonmetric unit sometimes used in mechanics. It is equal to 746 watts.

The **ohm** is the unit of electrical resistance and represents the physical property of a conductor that offers a resistance to the flow of electricity, permitting just 1 ampere to flow at 1 volt of pressure.

Measures of Force and Pressure

Dyne = force necessary to accelerate a 1-gram mass 1 centimeter per second squared = 0.000072 poundal

Poundal = force necessary to accelerate a 1-pound mass 1 foot per second squared = 13,825.5 dynes = 0.138255 newtons

Newton = force needed to accelerate a 1-kilogram mass 1 meter per second squared

Pascal (pressure) = 1 newton per square meter = 0.020885 pound per square foot

Atmosphere (air pressure at sea level) = 2,116.102 pounds per square foot = 14.6952 pounds per square inch = 1.0332 kilograms per square centimeter = 101,323 newtons per square meter

Spirits Measures

Pony	= 0.5 jigger
Shot	= 0.666 jigger = 1.0 ounce
Jigger	= 1.5 shots
Pint	= 16 shots = 0.625 fifth
Fifth	= 25.6 shots = 1.6 pints = 0.8 quart = 0.75706 liter

Quart	= 32 shots = 1.25 fifths
Magnum	= 2 quarts = 2.49797 bottles (wine)

For champagne and brandy only:

Jeroboam	= 6.4 pints = 1.6 magnum = 0.8 gallon

For champagne only:

Rehoboam	= 3 magnums
Methuselah	= 4 magnums
Salmanazar	= 6 magnums
Balthazar	= 8 magnums
Nebuchadnezzar	= 10 magnums
Wine bottle (standard) .	= 0.800633 quart = 0.7576778 liter

Miscellaneous Modern Measures

Caliber—the diameter of a gun bore. In the U.S., caliber is traditionally expressed in hundredths of inches, e.g., .22. In Britain, caliber is often expressed in thousandths of inches, e.g., .270. Now it is commonly expressed in millimeters, e.g., the 5.56 mm M16 rifle. Heavier weapons' caliber has long been expressed in millimeters, e.g., the 155 mm howitzer. Naval guns' caliber refers to the barrel length as a multiple of the bore diameter. A 5-inch, 50-caliber naval gun has a 5-inch bore and a barrel length of 250 inches.

Decibel (dB)—a measure of the relative loudness or intensity of sound. A 20-decibel sound is 10 times louder than a 10-decibel sound; 30 decibels is 100 times louder; 40 decibels is 1,000 times louder, etc.

One decibel is the smallest difference between sounds detectable by the human ear. A 120-decibel sound is painful.

10 decibels	– a light whisper
20	– quiet conversation
30	– normal conversation
40	– light traffic
50	– typewriter, loud conversation
60	– noisy office
70	– normal traffic, quiet train
80	– rock music, subway
90	– heavy traffic, thunder
100	– jet plane at takeoff

Em—a printer's measure designating the square width of any given type size. Thus, an em of 10-point type is 10 points. An en is half an em.

Gauge—a measure of shotgun bore diameter. Gauge numbers originally referred to the number of lead balls just fitting the gun barrel diameter required to make a pound. Thus, a 16-gauge shotgun's bore was smaller than a 12-gauge shotgun's. Today, an international agreement assigns millimeter measures to each gauge, e.g.:

Gauge	Bore diameter (in mm)
6	23.34
10	19.67
12	18.52
14	17.60
16	16.81
20	15.90

Horsepower—the power needed to lift 550 pounds 1 foot in 1 second or to lift 33,000 pounds 1 foot in 1 minute. Equivalent to 746 watts or 2,546.0756 Btu/h.

Karat or carat—a measure of fineness for gold equal to $1/24$ part of pure gold in an alloy. Thus 24-karat gold is pure; 18-karat gold is ¼ alloy. The *carat* is also used as a unit of weight for precious stones; it is equal to 200 milligrams or 3.086 grains.

Knot—a measure of the speed of ships. A knot equals 1 nautical mile per hour.

Quire—25 sheets of paper

Ream—500 sheets of paper

Ancient Measures

Biblical

Cubit	= 21.8 inches
Omer	= 0.45 peck = 3.964 liters
Ephah	= 10 omers
Shekel	= 0.497 ounce = 14.1 grams

Greek

Cubit	= 18.3 inches
Stadion	= 607.2 or 622 feet
Obolos	= 715.38 milligrams
Drachma	= 4.2923 grams
Mina	= 0.9463 pound
Talent	= 60 mina

Roman

Cubit	= 17.5 inches
Stadium	= 202 yards
As, libra, pondus	= 325.971 grams = 0.71864 pound

ASTRONOMY

Edited by Lee T. Shapiro, Ph. D., Head of Education and Public Outreach, National Radio Astronomy Observatory

Celestial Events Summary, 2005

There are 4 **eclipses** in 2005: an annular-total solar eclipse, an annular partial solar eclipse, a partial lunar eclipse, and a penumbral lunar eclipse (which will pass unnoticed by almost all—see description in Eclipses, 2005). The eclipse path of the April annular-total solar eclipse reaches large regions of the western hemisphere, including the southern U.S. The eclipse path of the October annular eclipse reaches the North Atlantic Ocean, Europe, the Middle East, most of Africa, India, and much of the Indian Ocean. The partial lunar eclipse in October will be best seen in most of North America, in Australia, and in parts of Asia. The most likely viewing successes for **meteor showers** will be the Perseids in August and the Orionids in October.

The crescent **Moon,** with its light not overpowering, makes pretty pairings with the 2 brightest planets, Venus and Jupiter. Waxing crescent **pairings** are visible in the early evening soon after sunset, while waning crescent pairings are visible in the early morning rising shortly before sunrise. The waxing crescent Moon pairs with Venus the early part of each month June through December, while pairing with Jupiter in August and September. The waning crescent Moon pairs with Venus in early January and with Jupiter in December. Of special note are the quadruple grouping of the Moon, Venus, Mars, and Antares (often mistaken for Mars) in the morning in January, the occultation of the star Antares by the Moon in March, the very closing pairing of Venus and Mercury with Saturn nearby in June, the Moon tripled with Venus and Saturn in June, the Moon tripled with Venus and Mercury in July, and the Moon tripled with Venus and Jupiter in August and September.

For the **planets,** at the start of 2005 Saturn is up most of the night, Jupiter is up after midnight, Mars is low in the morning sky, while Venus and Mars are in the morning sky before sunrise. By May Venus has moved around to the evening sky joining Jupiter and Saturn; Mars remains in the morning sky. In early July, Saturn is leaving the evening sky, just as Mars is up for more than half the night. In August, Saturn reappears in the morning, while in early October Jupiter leaves in the early evening. In November, Jupiter joins Saturn in the morning, while Mars is now up all night long. The best opportunities for seeing Mercury occur in March (evening) and in December (morning).

Astronomical Positions and Constants

Two celestial bodies are in **conjunction** when they are due N and S of each other, either in **right ascension** (with respect to the N celestial pole) or in **celestial longitude** (with respect to the N ecliptic pole). Celestial bodies in conjunction will rise and set at nearly the same time. For the inner planets—Mercury and Venus—**inferior conjunction** occurs when either planet passes between Earth and the Sun, while **superior conjunction** occurs when either Mercury or Venus is on the far side of the Sun. Celestial bodies are in **opposition** when their Right Ascensions differ by exactly 12 hours, or when their Celestial Longitudes differ by 180°. In this case one of the 2 objects in opposition will rise while the other is setting. **Quadrature** refers to the arrangement where the coordinates of 2 bodies differ by exactly 90°. These terms may refer to the relative positions of any 2 bodies as seen from Earth, but one of the bodies is so frequently the Sun that mention of the Sun is omitted in that case.

When objects are in conjunction, the alignment is not perfect, and one is usually passing above or below the other. The geocentric angular separation between the Sun and an object is termed **elongation**. Elongation is limited only for Mercury and Venus; the greatest elongation for each of these bodies is approximately the time for longest observation. **Perihelion** is the point in an orbit that is nearest to the Sun, and **aphelion,** the point farthest from the Sun. **Perigee** is the point in an orbit that is nearest Earth, **apogee** the point that is farthest from Earth. An **occultation** of a planet or a star is an **eclipse** of it by some other body, usually the Moon. A **transit** of the Sun occurs when Mercury or Venus passes directly between Earth and the Sun, appearing to cross the disk of the Sun.

The following were adopted as part of the International Astronomical Union System of Astronomical Constants (1976): **Speed of light,** 299,792.458 km per sec., or about 186,282 statute mi per sec.; **solar parallax,** 8".794148; **Astronomical Unit (the mean distance between the Earth and the sun),** 149,597,870 km, or 92,955,807 mi; **constant of nutation,** 9".2025; and **constant of aberration,** 20".49552.

Celestial Events Highlights, 2005

(Coordinated Universal Time, or UTC—the standard time of the prime meridian)

January

Mercury visible low in the SE before sunrise, remains visible all month, passing Venus on the 15th.

Venus is low in the SE before sunrise. Don't confuse with Mercury, with which it is near all month.

Mars is rising low in the SE before sunrise, passes its "rival" Antares on the 7th.

Jupiter, rising around midnight, is prominent in the morning sky.

Saturn, at opposition, is up most of the night rising soon after sunset.

Moon passes Jupiter on the 4th and 31st, Mars on the 7th, Mercury and Venus on the 9th, Neptune on the 11th, Saturn on the 24th. Moon occults Antares on the 7th for the first of 13 times this year.

Watch for thin waning crescent Moon between Mars and Venus low in SE on the 8th.

Jan. 1—Pluto in Serpens Cauda the only divided constellation all year. Neptune in Capricornus and Uranus in Aquarius all year. Saturn in Gemini. Jupiter in Virgo. Mars in Scorpius. Venus in Ophiuchus. Sun in Sagittarius.

Jan. 2—Earth at perihelion, closest approach to the Sun.

Jan. 3—Quadrantid meteor shower, from midnight until dawn.

Jan. 4—Moon passes 0.4°S of Jupiter, occults Jupiter. (Like all occultations, visible only from some regions.)

Jan. 5—Mars enters Ophiuchus.

Jan. 6—Saturn passes 7° S of Pollux in the constellation of Gemini. Venus enters Sagittarius.

Jan. 7—Moon passes 3° S of Mars and 1.3° north of Antares in the constellation of Sagittarius, occults Antares. Mars passes 5° north of Antares.

Jan. 9—Moon passes 5° S of Mercury and 5° south of Venus.

Jan. 11—Moon passes 5° S of Neptune.

Jan. 13—Moon passes 4° S of Uranus. Saturn at opposition.

Jan. 14—Mercury passes 0.3° south of Venus. Saturn at closest approach to Earth.

Jan. 19—Sun enters Capricornus.

Jan. 23—Mercury at aphelion, farthest from the Sun.

Jan. 24—Moon passes 5° north of Saturn.

Jan. 31—Moon passes 0.9° S of Jupiter, occults Jupiter.

February

Mercury, gone for most of the month, reappears in the evening sky late in the month.

Venus is very low in the SE at the beginning of the month before sunrise disappearing in the glow of sunrise later.

Mars remains low in the SE before sunrise.

Jupiter, rising shortly before midnight, is prominent in the morning sky.

Saturn is up most of the night rising before sunset.

Moon passes Mars on the 4th, Saturn on the 20th, and Jupiter on the 27th. Watch for the bright waxing gibbous Moon close to Jupiter before sunrise on the 27th.

Feb. 1—Mars enters Sagittarius.

Feb. 2—Jupiter stationary, begins retrograde motion. Venus enters Capricornus.

Feb. 3—Neptune at conjunction.
Feb. 4—Moon passes 1.1° N of Antares, occults Antares.
Feb. 5—Moon passes 4° S of Mars.
Feb. 14—Mercury at superior conjunction, passing behind the Sun. Venus passes 1° S of Neptune.
Feb. 16—Sun enters Aquarius.
Feb. 20—Moon passes 5° N of Saturn.
Feb. 22—Venus at aphelion.
Feb. 24—Venus enters Aquarius.
Feb. 25—Uranus at conjunction.
Feb. 27—Moon passes 1.2° S of Jupiter, occults Jupiter.

March

Mercury, making a more noticeable appearance at mid-month, is in the evening sky until late in the month.
Venus is hidden in the glare of the Sun for the month as it passes behind the Sun from an Earthly perspective at the end of the month.
Mars remains low in the SE before sunrise.
Jupiter, rising a couple of hours after sunset, is prominent much of the night.
Saturn is high in the SE at sunset.
Moon passes Mars on the 4th, Neptune on the 8th, Mercury on the 11th, Saturn on the 19th, and Jupiter on the 26th. Lunar occultation of Antares on the 3rd, the first of 2 this month, should be visible from much of N America.
Mar. 3—Moon passes 0.8° N of Antares, occults Antares.
Mar. 6—Moon passes 5° S of Mars.
Mar. 8—Moon passes 5° S of Neptune. Mercury at perihelion.
Mar. 11—Moon passes 3° S of Mercury.
Mar. 12—Mercury at greatest eastern elongation of 18° (E of the Sun and setting after the Sun). Sun enters Pisces.
Mar. 18—Venus enters Pisces.
Mar. 19—Mercury stationary, begins retrograde motion. Moon passes 5° N of Saturn.
Mar. 20—Vernal Equinox at 7:33 A.M. EST (12:33 UTC); spring begins in N hemisphere, autumn S hemisphere. Venus enters Cetus. Mars enters Capricornus.
Mar. 22—Saturn stationary, resumes direct motion.
Mar. 26—Moon passes 1° S of Jupiter, occults Jupiter.
Mar. 27—Pluto stationary, begins retrograde motion. Sun barely touches constellation of Cetus.
Mar. 29—Mercury at inferior conjunction, between Earth and the Sun.
Mar. 30—Moon passes 0.7° N of Antares, occults Antares.
Mar. 31—Venus at superior conjunction, passing behind the Sun. Venus enters Pisces.

April

Mercury returns to the morning sky very low in the east before sunrise.
Venus remains hidden in the glare of the Sun.
Mars, low in SE before sunrise, passes Neptune on the 13th.
Jupiter, rising about sunset, is prominent all night.
Saturn, high in W at sunset, sets soon after midnight.
Moon passes Mars on the 3rd, Neptune on the 4th, Uranus on the 5th, Mercury on the 7th, Saturn on the 16th, and Jupiter on the 22nd. The solar eclipse on the 8th will be both annular and total; see details under Eclipses.
Apr. 2—Mercury at closest approach to Earth.
Apr. 3—Jupiter at opposition. Moon passes 4° S of Mars.
Apr. 4—Moon passes 5° S of Neptune.
Apr. 5—Moon passes 3° S of Uranus. Jupiter at closest approach to Earth.
Apr. 7—Moon passes 3° S of Mercury.
Apr. 8—Annular-total eclipse of the Sun, see details under Eclipses.
Apr. 11—Mercury stationary, resumes direct motion.
Apr. 13—Mars passes 1.2° S of Neptune.
Apr. 14—Jupiter at aphelion.
Apr. 15—Venus enters Aries.
Apr. 16—Moon passes 5° N of Saturn.
Apr. 18—Sun enters Aries.
Apr. 22—Moon passes 0.6° S of Jupiter, occults Jupiter.
Apr. 23—Mercury at aphelion.
Apr. 26—Mercury at greatest western elongation of 27° (W of the Sun, rises before the Sun). Moon passes 0.7° north of Antares, occults Antares.
Apr. 27—Mars enters Aquarius.

May

Mercury, very low in west northwest, disappears back into the glare of the Sun at the end of the month.
Venus, emerging from the glare of the Sun, is very low in the west-northwest after sunset.
Mars, getting higher in the SE before sunrise, passes Uranus on the 14th.
Jupiter, rising about sunset, is prominent all night.
Saturn, halfway up in the W at sunset, passes Pollux on the 31st.
Moon passes Neptune on the 1st and the 28th, Mars on the 2nd and the 31st, Uranus on the 3rd and 30th, Mercury on the 6th, Saturn on the 13th, and Jupiter on the 19th. The solar eclipse on the 8th will be both annular and totals; see details under Eclipses.
May 1—Moon passes 5° S of Neptune.
May 2—Moon passes 3° S of Mars.
May 3—Moon passes 3° S of Uranus.
May 4—Venus enters Taurus.
May 5—Eta Aquarid meteor shower from midnight until dawn this day and the next.
May 6—Moon passes 3° N of Mercury.
May 13—Moon passes 5° N of Saturn.
May 14—Sun enters Taurus. Mars passes 1.2° S of Uranus.
May 18—Venus passes 6° N of Aldebaran in the constellation Taurus.
May 19—Moon passes 0.4° S of Jupiter, occults Jupiter.
May 20—Neptune stationary, begins retrograde motion.
May 24—Moon passes 0.8° N of Antares, occults Antares.
May 28—Moon passes 5° S of Neptune.
May 30—Moon passes 3° S of Uranus.
May 31—Saturn passes 7° S of Pollux. Moon passes 0.55° S of Mars, occults Mars.

June

Mercury, moving to the early evening sky, passes Pollux on the 24th, Saturn on the 26th, and Venus on the 27th.
Venus, getting higher in the west northwest, passes Pollux on the 23rd, Saturn on the 25th. Look for very close pairing with Mercury on the 27th with Saturn also close.
Mars is in the SE at sunrise.
Jupiter is high in the S at sunset, setting soon after the middle of the night.
Saturn is getting low in the W at sunset.
Moon passes Venus on the 8th, Saturn on the 10th, Jupiter on the 16th, Neptune on the 25th, Uranus on the 26th, and Mars on the 29th. Watch for the thin waxing crescent Moon paired with Venus on the 8th and Saturn on the 9th.
June 3—Mercury at superior conjunction. Venus enters Gemini.
June 4—Mercury at perihelion.
June 5—Jupiter stationary, resumes direct motion.
June 7—Mars enters Pisces.
June 8—Moon passes 4° N of Venus.
June 10—Moon passes 5° N of Saturn.
June 13—Pluto at closest approach to Earth.
June 14—Venus at perihelion. Pluto at opposition.
June 15—Uranus stationary, begins retrograde motion.
June 16—Moon passes 0.4° S of Jupiter, occults Jupiter.
June 20—Moon passes 0.7° N of Antares, occults Antares.
June 21—Northern solstice at 2:46 P.M. EDT (6:46 UTC), summer begins in N hemisphere, winter in S hemisphere. Mars enters Cetus. Sun enters Gemini.
June 23—Venus passes 5° south of Pollux.
June 24—Mercury passes 5° south of Pollux.
June 25—Moon passes 5° south of Neptune. Venus passes 1.3° north of Saturn.
June 26—Mercury passes 1.4° north of Saturn. Venus enters Cancer. Moon passes 3° south of Uranus.
June 27—Mercury passes 0.08° south of Venus.
June 29—Moon passes 2° north of Mars.
June 30—Saturn enters Cancer. Mars enters Pisces

July

Mercury, in the early evening sky all month passes Venus on the 7th, with the very thin waxing crescent Moon lower in the sky.

Venus, bright and low in the west after sunset, passes Regulus on the 22nd.

Mars, getting higher in the morning sky; in S at sunrise.

Jupiter, in SW at sunset, is now setting before the middle of the night.

Saturn disappears in glow of sunset early in July.

Moon passes Mercury and Venus on the 8th, Jupiter on the 13th, Neptune on the 22nd, Uranus on the 24th, and Mars on the 27th. Watch for the thin waxing crescent Moon paired with Mercury and Venus on the 8th and then the waxing quarter Moon with Jupiter on the 13th.

July 5—Earth at aphelion.
July 7—Mercury passes 1.6° S of Venus.
July 8—Moon 5° N of Mercury and 3° N of Venus.
July 9—Mercury at greatest eastern elongation of 26°.
July 12—Venus enters Leo.
July 13—Moon passes 0.8° south of Jupiter, occults Jupiter.
July 17—Mars at aphelion.
July 18—Moon passes 0.6° N of Antares, occults Antares. Mercury at aphelion.
July 20—Sun enters Cancer.
July 22—Mercury stationary, begins retrograde motion. Moon passes 4° S of Neptune. Venus passes 1.2° N of Regulus in constellation Leo.
July 23—Saturn at conjunction.
July 24—Moon passes 2° south of Uranus.
July 27—Moon passes 4° north of Mars.

August

Mercury re-emerges from the glow of the Sun into the early morning sky during the second half of the month.

Venus, slowly getting higher in the west after sunset, draws ever closer to Jupiter through the month.

Mars, rising around midnight, is high in S at sunrise.

Jupiter, low in SW at sunset at the beginning of the month, is very low in WSW by the end of the month.

Saturn re-emerges from the glow of the Sun, in the east northeast before sunrise.

Moon passes Venus on the 8th, Jupiter on the 10th, Neptune on the 18th, Uranus on the 20th, Mars on the 25th, and Saturn on the 31st. Watch the thin waxing crescent Moon from the 7th through the 9th, moving from close to Venus to close to Jupiter, the three brightest objects in the night sky.

Aug. 2—Mars enters Cetus.
Aug. 3—Mercury at closest approach to Earth.
Aug. 6—Mercury at inferior conjunction.
Aug. 7—Mars enters Aries.
Aug. 8—Moon passes 1.2° N of Venus, occults Venus. Neptune at opposition and closest approach to Earth.
Aug. 10—Moon passes 1.3° S of Jupiter, occults Jupiter. Sun enters Leo.
Aug. 11—Venus enters Virgo.
Aug. 13—Quadrantid meteor shower from midnight until dawn.
Aug. 14—Moon passes 0.4° N of Antares, occults Antares.
Aug. 15—Mercury stationary, resumes direct motion.
Aug. 18—Moon passes 5° S of Neptune.
Aug. 20—Moon passes 2° S of Uranus.
Aug. 23—Mercury at greatest western elongation of 18°.
Aug. 25—Moon passes 6° N of Mars.
Aug. 31—Mercury at perihelion. Moon passes 5° N of Saturn. Uranus at closest approach to Earth.

September

Mercury soon leaves the morning sky returning to the glare of the Sun.

Venus, bright in the west southwest after sunset, passes Jupiter on the 2nd and Spica on the 5th.

Mars, rising a couple of hours before midnight, is high in the south southwest at sunrise.

Jupiter is very low in the west southwest at sunset.

Saturn is gradually getting higher in the morning sky before sunrise.

Moon passes Jupiter, Venus, and Spica on the 7th, Neptune on the 15th, Uranus on the 16th, Mars on the 22nd, and Saturn on the 28th. Watch the thin waxing crescent Moon grouped with the 2 brightest planets and the 15th brightest star on 6th and the 7th.

Sept. 1—Uranus at opposition.
Sept. 2—Venus passes 1.4° S of Jupiter.
Sept. 3—Pluto stationary, resumes direct motion.
Sept. 4—Mercury passes 1.1° N of Regulus.
Sept. 5—Venus passes 1.8° N of Spica in the constellation Virgo.
Sept. 7—Moon passes 1.8° S of Jupiter, 1.3° N of Spica, 0.6° S of Venus, occults Spica and Venus.
Sept. 10—Moon passes 0.2° N of Antares, occults Antares.
Sept. 15—Moon passes 5° S of Neptune.
Sept. 16—Sun enters Virgo. Moon passes 2° S of Uranus.
Sept. 18—Mercury at superior conjunction. Venus enters Libra.
Sept. 21—Jupiter passes 3° N of Spica.
Sept. 22—Moon passes 6° N of Mars. Autumnal Equinox at 6:23 P.M. EDT (22:23 UTC), autumn begins in N hemisphere, spring begins in S hemisphere.
Sept. 23—Mars enters Taurus.
Sept. 28—Moon passes 5° N of Saturn.

October

Mercury, returning to the evening sky, passes Jupiter on the 6th and Venus on the 7th.

Venus, bright in the SW after sunset, passes Antares on the 16th.

Mars, rising soon after sunset, is visible most of the night.

Jupiter, very low in the west southwest, soon disappears from the evening sky.

Saturn is high in the east southeast before sunrise.

Moon passes Venus on the 7th, Neptune on the 12th, Uranus on the 14th, Mars on the 19th, and Saturn on the 25th. Watch the thin waxing crescent Moon paired with Venus on the 6th and the 7th. Two eclipses this month, with an annular solar eclipse on the 3rd and a partial lunar eclipse on the 17th; see Eclipses.

Oct. 1—Mars stationary, begins retrograde motion.
Oct. 3—Annular eclipse of the Sun; see details under Eclipses
Oct. 4—Mercury passes 2° N of Spica. Venus at aphelion.
Oct. 6—Mercury passes 1.5° S of Jupiter.
Oct. 7—Moon passes 1.4° S of Venus. Venus enters Scorpius.
Oct. 8—Moon passes 0.2° N of Antares, occults Antares.
Oct. 9—Mars enters Aries.
Oct. 12—Moon passes 5° S of Neptune.
Oct. 14—Moon passes 3° S of Uranus. Mercury at aphelion.
Oct. 15—Venus enters Ophiuchus.
Oct. 16—Venus passes 1.6° N of Antares.
Oct. 17—Venus enters Scorpius.
Oct. 19—Moon passes 5° N of Mars.
Oct. 21—Venus enters Ophiuchus. Orionid meteor shower from midnight until dawn.
Oct. 22—Jupiter at conjunction.
Oct. 25—Moon passes 4° N of Saturn.
Oct. 26—Neptune stationary, resumes direct motion.
Oct. 30—Mars at closest approach to the Earth.
Oct. 31—Sun enters Libra. Moon passes 1.2° N of Spica, occults Spica.

November

Mercury, getting very low in the southwest evening sky, passes Antares twice on the 9th and the 18th, then disappears into the glare of the Sun.

Venus remains bright in the southwest after sunset.

Mars, passing opposition, is visible all night long.

Jupiter reappears in the morning sky very low in the east southeast before sunrise.

Saturn, rising a couple of hours before midnight, is high in the south before sunrise.

Moon passes Mercury on the 3rd, Venus on the 5th, Neptune on the 8th, Uranus on the 10th, Mars on the 15th, Saturn on the 22nd and Jupiter on the 29th.

Watch the thin waxing crescent Moon paired with Venus on the 5th.

Nov. 1—Venus enters Sagittarius.

Nov. 3—Mercury at greatest eastern elongation of 24°. Venus at greatest eastern elongation of 47°. Moon passes 1.3° south of Mercury.

Nov. 4—Moon passes 0.2° N of Antares, occults Antares.

Nov. 5—Moon passes 1.4° S of Venus.

Nov. 7—Mars at opposition.

Nov. 8—Moon passes 5° S of Neptune.

Nov. 9—Mercury passes 1.9° N of Antares.

Nov. 10—Moon passes 3° S of Uranus.

Nov. 14—Mercury stationary, begins retrograde motion.

Nov. 15—Moon passes 3° N of Mars.

Nov. 16—Uranus stationary, resumes direct motion.

Nov. 18—Mercury passes 3° N of Antares.

Nov. 22—Moon passes 4° N of Saturn. Saturn stationary, begins retrograde motion.

Nov. 23—Sun enters Scorpius.

Nov. 24—Mercury at inferior conjunction and closest approach to Earth.

Nov. 27—Mercury at perihelion.

Nov. 28—Moon passes 1.1° N of Spica, occults Spica.

Nov. 29—Moon passes 3° S of Jupiter.

Sun enters Ophiuchus.

Nov. 30—Jupiter enters Libra.

December

Mercury appears in the morning sky and passes Antares on the 20th.

Venus remains bright in the SW after sunset.

Mars, up in the E at sunset, sets a few hours after midnight.

Jupiter gradually higher in the morning sky in the SE.

Saturn, rising a few hours before midnight, is up for the rest of the night.

Moon passes Venus on the 4th, Neptune on the 6th, Uranus on the 7th, Mars on the 12th, Saturn on the 19th, Jupiter on the 27th, and Mercury on the 30th. Watch the thin waxing crescent Moon paired with Venus on the 3rd and 4th in the early evening and the thin waning crescent Moon paired with Jupiter on the 26th and 27th.

Dec. 4—Mercury stationary, resumes direct motion. Moon passes 2° S of Venus.

Dec. 6—Moon passes 4° S of Neptune.

Dec. 7—Moon passes 2° S of Uranus.

Dec. 10—Mars stationary, resumes direct motion.

Dec. 12—Moon passes 1.3° N of Mars, occults Mars. Mercury at greatest western elongation of 21°.

Dec. 14—Venus enters Capricornus.

Dec. 16—Pluto at Conjunction.

Dec. 17—Sun enters Sagittarius.

Dec. 19—Moon passes 4° N of Saturn.

Dec. 20—Mercury passes 6° N of Antares.

Dec. 21—Southern Solstice at 1:35 P.M. EST (18:35 UTC), winter begins in N hemisphere, summer begins in S hemisphere.

Dec. 23—Venus stationary, begins retrograde motion.

Dec. 25—Moon passes 0.9° N of Spica, occults Spica.

Dec. 27—Moon passes 4° S of Jupiter.

Dec. 29—Moon passes 0.2° N of Antares, occults Antares.

Dec. 30—Moon passes 5° S of Mercury.

Meteorites and Meteor Showers

When a chunk of material, ice or rock, plunges into Earth's atmosphere and burns up in a fiery display, the event is a **meteor**. While the chunk of material is still in space, it is a **meteoroid**. If a portion of the material survives passage through the atmosphere and reaches the ground, the remnant on the ground is a **meteorite**.

Meteorites found on Earth are classified into types, depending on their composition: **irons**, those composed chiefly of iron, a small percentage of nickel, and traces of other metals such as cobalt; **stones**, stony meteors consisting of silicates; and **stony irons**, containing varying proportions of both iron and stone.

Serious study of meteorites as non-earth objects began in the 20th century. Scientists use sophisticated chemical analysis, X rays, and mass spectrography in determining their origin and composition. Although most meteorites are now believed to be fragments of asteroids or comets, geochemical studies have shown that a few Antarctic stones came from the moon or from Mars, presumably ejected by the explosive impact of asteroids.

The **largest known meteorite**, estimated to weigh about 55 metric tons, is situated at Hoba West near Grootfontein, Namibia. The Manicouagan impact crater in Quebec, Canada, with an estimated diameter of 60 mi, is one of the largest crater structures still visible on the surface of the Earth. Although not visible to the eye, other still larger impact craters identified include the Vredefort crater in South Africa at 185 mi across and the Sudbury crater in Ontario, Canada, estimated at 125 mi across. The Bedout impact site off the NW coast of Australia gained attention in 2004, when scientists identified further evidence in support of the idea that it may be linked to the Permian extinction event 250 million years ago.

Sporadic meteors, which enter the atmosphere throughout the year, seem to originate from the asteroid belt. Other meteors that come in groups and tend to occur at the same time each year create **meteor showers**; these are the meteors associated with comets. As a comet orbits the Sun, the Sun slowly boils away some of the comet's material, and the comet leaves a trail of tiny particles which are dispersed along the comet's path. If Earth's orbit and this path intersect, then once a year, as Earth reaches that particular point in its orbit, there will be a meteor shower.

Meteor showers vary in strength, but usually the 3 best meteor showers of the year are the **Perseids**, around Aug. 12, the **Orionids**, around Oct. 21, and the **Geminids**, around Dec. 13. These showers feature meteors at the rate of about 60 per hour. Best observing conditions occur with the absence of moonlight, usually when the Moon's phase is between waning crescent Moon and waxing quarter Moon.

For most meteor showers the cometary debris is relatively uniformly scattered along the comet's orbit. However, in the case of the **Leonid** meteor shower, which occurs every year around Nov. 17-18, the cometary debris, from Comet Temple-Tuttle, seems to be bunched up in one stretch. Hence, most years when Earth crosses the orbit of this comet, the meteor shower produced is relatively weak. However, about every 33 years, Earth encounters the bunched-up debris. Sometimes the storm is a disappointment, as it was in 1899 and 1933; at other times it is a roaring success, as in 1833 and 1866. The Leonids stormed again recently producing rates between 1,000-3,000 meteors per hour in 2001. In **2005**, bright moonlight will interfere with most of the showers. Best chances are with the Perseids in August after the waxing quarter Moon sets and early morning for the Orionids in October. Typically, meteor showers are best observed after midnight, but the Geminids can be seen well before midnight as well as after.

 IT'S A FACT: British astronomer Edmund Halley (1656-1742), applying Newton's law of motion to the available data on comets, concluded that they travel in elliptical orbits around the sun, rather than being isolated or supernatural occurrences as was once believed, and he predicted the return in 1758 of a comet now named Halley's Comet. The comet returned as predicted, validating his theory, 16 years after his death.

Rising and Setting of Planets, 2005

In Coordinated Universal Time (0 in the *h* col. designates midnight)

Venus, 2005

Date	20° N Latitude Rise h m	20° N Latitude Set h m	30° N Latitude Rise h m	30° N Latitude Set h m	40° N Latitude Rise h m	40° N Latitude Set h m	50° N Latitude Rise h m	50° N Latitude Set h m	60° N Latitude Rise h m	60° N Latitude Set h m
Jan. 1	5 02	15 59	5 22	15 39	5 47	15 13	6 23	14 38	7 25	13 36
11	5 18	16 13	5 39	15 51	6 06	15 25	6 43	14 48	7 49	13 42
21	5 33	16 28	5 53	16 08	6 19	15 42	6 56	15 05	8 00	14 01
31	5 44	16 45	6 03	16 26	6 27	16 02	7 01	15 29	7 57	14 32
Feb. 10	5 53	17 02	6 09	16 46	6 30	16 25	6 58	15 57	7 45	15 11
20	5 58	17 18	6 12	17 05	6 28	16 49	6 50	16 27	7 25	15 52
Mar. 2	6 01	17 34	6 10	17 25	6 22	17 13	6 37	16 58	7 02	16 34
12	6 01	17 48	6 07	17 43	6 13	17 37	6 22	17 29	6 35	17 16
22	6 01	18 02	6 02	18 01	6 03	18 00	6 05	17 59	6 07	17 57
Apr. 1	5 59	18 15	5 56	18 19	5 52	18 23	5 47	18 29	5 38	18 38
11	5 59	18 29	5 51	18 37	5 42	18 46	5 29	18 59	5 09	19 20
21	5 59	18 43	5 47	18 55	5 33	19 10	5 13	19 30	4 41	20 03
May 1	6 01	18 59	5 46	19 14	5 27	19 34	5 00	20 01	4 16	20 47
11	6 07	19 15	5 48	19 34	5 24	19 58	4 51	20 32	3 53	21 30
21	6 15	19 32	5 54	19 53	5 27	20 20	4 48	20 59	3 38	22 10
31	6 26	19 48	6 03	20 10	5 34	20 40	4 53	21 22	3 34	22 40
June 10	6 40	20 02	6 17	20 25	5 48	20 54	5 06	21 36	3 46	22 56
20	6 56	20 14	6 34	20 35	6 06	21 03	5 26	21 43	4 14	22 54
30	7 12	20 22	6 52	20 42	6 28	21 06	5 53	21 41	4 51	22 41
July 10	7 27	20 27	7 11	20 43	6 50	21 03	6 22	21 32	5 34	22 19
20	7 42	20 29	7 29	20 41	7 13	20 57	6 52	21 18	6 17	21 52
30	7 55	20 28	7 46	20 36	7 36	20 46	7 21	21 00	6 58	21 23
Aug. 9	8 07	20 25	8 03	20 29	7 57	20 34	7 50	20 41	7 39	20 51
19	8 18	20 21	8 18	20 21	8 18	20 20	8 18	20 20	8 18	20 19
29	8 28	20 17	8 33	20 12	8 39	20 06	8 46	19 58	8 57	19 47
Sept. 8	8 39	20 13	8 48	20 04	8 59	19 53	9 14	19 37	9 37	19 14
18	8 51	20 10	9 04	19 57	9 20	19 40	9 42	19 18	10 18	18 42
28	9 02	20 09	9 20	19 52	9 41	19 30	10 10	19 00	10 59	18 11
Oct. 8	9 15	20 10	9 35	19 49	10 01	19 23	10 37	18 47	11 41	17 43
18	9 26	20 13	9 49	19 50	10 19	19 20	11 01	18 38	12 19	17 20
28	9 36	20 18	10 01	19 53	10 33	19 21	11 19	18 35	12 48	17 05
Nov. 7	9 42	20 22	10 08	19 57	10 40	19 25	11 28	18 37	13 01	17 04
17	9 44	20 26	10 09	20 01	10 40	19 29	11 26	18 44	12 54	17 15
27	9 38	20 25	10 01	20 01	10 31	19 32	11 13	18 50	12 31	17 32
Dec. 7	9 23	20 16	9 45	19 55	10 11	19 29	10 48	18 52	11 54	17 46
17	8 57	19 57	9 15	19 38	9 39	19 15	10 11	18 42	11 07	17 47
27	8 15	19 21	8 32	19 05	8 52	18 45	9 20	18 17	10 07	17 30

Mars, 2005

Date	20° N Latitude Rise h m	20° N Latitude Set h m	30° N Latitude Rise h m	30° N Latitude Set h m	40° N Latitude Rise h m	40° N Latitude Set h m	50° N Latitude Rise h m	50° N Latitude Set h m	60° N Latitude Rise h m	60° N Latitude Set h m
Jan. 1	3 56	14 57	4 14	14 38	4 38	14 14	5 10	13 42	6 06	12 47
11	3 48	14 44	4 08	14 24	4 33	13 59	5 08	13 24	6 08	12 24
21	3 40	14 33	4 01	14 12	4 27	13 46	5 04	13 09	6 09	12 04
31	3 32	14 24	3 53	14 02	4 20	13 35	4 58	12 57	6 06	11 49
Feb. 10	3 23	14 15	3 45	13 53	4 12	13 26	4 51	12 47	6 00	11 38
20	3 15	14 07	3 36	13 45	4 03	13 18	4 42	12 40	5 50	11 32
Mar. 2	3 05	13 59	3 26	13 38	3 52	13 12	4 30	12 35	5 35	11 30
12	2 55	13 52	3 15	13 32	3 40	13 07	4 15	12 32	5 16	11 32
22	2 44	13 45	3 03	13 27	3 26	13 03	3 59	12 31	4 53	11 36
Apr. 1	2 32	13 39	2 49	13 22	3 10	13 00	3 40	12 31	4 28	11 43
11	2 19	13 32	2 35	13 16	2 53	12 58	3 19	12 32	4 01	11 50
21	2 06	13 24	2 19	13 11	2 35	12 55	2 57	12 33	3 33	11 58
May 1	1 51	13 17	2 02	13 06	2 16	12 52	2 34	12 34	3 03	12 05
11	1 36	13 09	1 45	13 00	1 55	12 50	2 10	12 35	2 33	12 13
21	1 20	13 01	1 26	12 54	1 34	12 46	1 45	12 36	2 02	12 19
31	1 03	12 52	1 07	12 48	1 13	12 43	1 19	12 36	1 30	12 25
June 10	0 46	12 42	0 48	12 40	0 50	12 38	0 53	12 35	0 58	12 31
20	0 28	12 32	0 28	12 33	0 28	12 33	0 27	12 34	0 26	12 35
30	0 10	12 22	0 08	12 24	0 05	12 27	23 58	12 32	23 51	12 38
July 10	23 50	12 10	23 45	12 15	23 39	12 20	23 31	12 28	23 19	12 40
20	23 31	11 58	23 24	12 04	23 16	12 12	23 05	12 23	22 47	12 40
30	23 11	11 44	23 02	11 52	22 52	12 02	22 38	12 17	22 15	12 39
Aug. 9	22 50	11 28	22 40	11 38	22 27	11 51	22 10	12 07	21 43	12 34
19	22 27	11 11	22 16	11 22	22 02	11 36	21 42	11 56	21 11	12 26
29	22 02	10 50	21 50	11 03	21 34	11 18	21 13	11 40	20 38	12 15
Sept. 8	21 35	10 26	21 21	10 40	21 05	10 57	20 41	11 20	20 03	11 58
18	21 04	9 58	20 50	10 12	20 32	10 30	20 07	10 54	19 27	11 35
28	20 28	9 24	20 13	9 39	19 55	9 57	19 29	10 23	18 48	11 05
Oct. 8	19 47	8 44	19 32	8 59	19 13	9 18	18 47	9 44	18 05	10 26
18	19 00	7 57	18 45	8 12	18 27	8 31	18 01	8 57	17 18	9 40
28	18 09	7 06	17 54	7 20	17 36	7 39	17 11	8 04	16 29	8 46
Nov. 7	17 16	6 11	17 02	6 25	16 44	6 43	16 19	7 08	15 39	7 48
17	16 24	5 17	16 10	5 31	15 53	5 48	15 29	6 12	14 50	6 51
27	15 35	4 28	15 22	4 41	15 05	4 58	14 41	5 22	14 03	6 00
Dec. 7	14 51	3 44	14 38	3 57	14 21	4 14	13 57	4 38	13 19	5 16
17	14 12	3 05	13 58	3 19	13 41	3 37	13 17	4 01	12 37	4 40
27	13 37	2 32	13 23	2 47	13 05	3 05	12 39	3 31	11 58	4 12

Jupiter, 2005

Date	20° N Latitude Rise h m	Set h m	30° N Latitude Rise h m	Set h m	40° N Latitude Rise h m	Set h m	50° N Latitude Rise h m	Set h m	60° N Latitude Rise h m	Set h m
Jan. 1	0 28	12 15	0 33	12 11	0 39	12 05	0 46	11 58	0 57	11 46
11	23 49	11 38	23 54	11 34	0 03	11 28	0 11	11 20	0 23	11 08
21	23 12	11 01	23 17	10 56	23 23	10 50	23 31	10 42	23 43	10 30
31	22 33	10 22	22 38	10 17	22 44	10 11	22 52	10 03	23 05	9 51
Feb. 10	21 53	9 43	21 58	9 38	22 04	9 32	22 12	9 24	22 24	9 12
20	21 12	9 02	21 17	8 58	21 23	8 52	21 30	8 44	21 42	8 33
Mar. 2	20 30	8 21	20 34	8 16	20 40	8 11	20 47	8 04	20 58	7 53
12	19 46	7 39	19 51	7 35	19 56	7 29	20 02	7 23	20 12	7 13
22	19 02	6 56	19 06	6 52	19 10	6 48	19 16	6 42	19 25	6 32
Apr. 1	18 18	6 13	18 21	6 09	18 25	6 05	18 30	6 00	18 38	5 52
11	17 33	5 29	17 36	5 26	17 39	5 23	17 44	5 18	17 51	5 11
21	16 48	4 46	16 51	4 44	16 54	4 41	16 58	4 37	17 04	4 31
May 1	16 05	4 03	16 07	4 01	16 09	3 59	16 13	3 55	16 18	3 50
11	15 22	3 21	15 24	3 19	15 26	3 17	15 29	3 14	15 33	3 10
21	14 40	2 40	14 42	2 38	14 44	2 36	14 46	2 34	14 50	2 30
31	13 59	2 00	14 01	1 58	14 03	1 56	14 06	1 53	14 09	1 50
June 10	13 20	1 20	13 22	1 19	13 24	1 17	13 26	1 14	13 30	1 10
20	12 42	0 42	12 44	0 40	12 46	0 38	12 49	0 35	12 53	0 31
30	12 05	0 04	12 07	23 58	12 10	23 56	12 13	23 52	12 18	23 48
July 10	11 29	23 24	11 32	23 21	11 35	23 18	11 38	23 14	11 44	23 09
20	10 55	22 48	10 58	22 45	11 01	22 41	11 05	22 37	11 12	22 30
30	10 21	22 12	10 24	22 09	10 28	22 05	10 33	22 00	10 41	21 52
Aug. 9	9 48	21 37	9 52	21 34	9 56	21 29	10 02	21 23	10 11	21 14
19	9 16	21 03	9 20	20 59	9 25	20 54	9 32	20 47	9 43	20 36
29	8 44	20 30	8 49	20 25	8 55	20 18	9 03	20 10	9 15	19 58
Sept. 8	8 13	19 56	8 18	19 51	8 25	19 44	8 34	19 35	8 48	19 21
18	7 42	19 23	7 48	19 17	7 56	19 09	8 06	18 59	8 22	18 43
28	7 12	18 50	7 18	18 43	7 27	18 35	7 38	18 24	7 56	18 06
Oct. 8	6 41	18 18	6 49	18 10	6 58	18 01	7 11	17 48	7 30	17 29
18	6 11	17 46	6 20	17 37	6 30	17 27	6 44	17 13	7 05	16 52
28	5 41	17 13	5 50	17 04	6 01	16 53	6 16	16 38	6 39	16 15
Nov. 7	5 11	16 41	5 21	16 32	5 33	16 20	5 49	16 04	6 14	15 39
17	4 41	16 09	4 52	15 59	5 04	15 46	5 21	15 29	5 48	15 02
27	4 11	15 37	4 22	15 26	4 35	15 12	4 54	14 54	5 22	14 25
Dec. 7	3 41	15 04	3 52	14 53	4 06	14 38	4 25	14 19	4 56	13 49
17	3 10	14 31	3 22	14 19	3 36	14 04	3 57	13 44	4 28	13 12
27	2 38	13 58	2 51	13 46	3 06	13 30	3 27	13 09	4 00	12 36

Saturn, 2005

Date	20° N Latitude Rise h m	Set h m	30° N Latitude Rise h m	Set h m	40° N Latitude Rise h m	Set h m	50° N Latitude Rise h m	Set h m	60° N Latitude Rise h m	Set h m
Jan. 1	18 26	7 38	18 07	7 58	17 42	8 22	17 07	8 57	16 07	9 58
11	17 43	6 56	17 24	7 15	16 59	7 40	16 24	8 15	15 22	9 17
21	17 00	6 13	16 40	6 33	16 15	6 58	15 40	7 33	14 38	8 36
31	16 17	5 31	15 57	5 51	15 32	6 16	14 56	6 52	13 53	7 55
Feb. 10	15 35	4 49	15 15	5 09	14 49	5 34	14 13	6 10	13 10	7 14
20	14 53	4 07	14 33	4 27	14 07	4 53	13 31	5 29	12 27	6 33
Mar. 2	14 12	3 26	13 51	3 46	13 26	4 12	12 49	4 49	11 45	5 53
12	13 31	2 46	13 11	3 06	12 45	3 32	12 08	4 08	11 03	5 13
22	12 51	2 06	12 31	2 26	12 05	2 52	11 28	3 29	10 23	4 34
Apr. 1	12 12	1 27	11 52	1 48	11 26	2 13	10 50	2 50	9 45	3 55
11	11 34	0 49	11 14	1 09	10 48	1 35	10 12	2 12	9 07	3 17
21	10 57	0 11	10 37	0 32	10 11	0 57	9 35	1 34	8 30	2 39
May 1	10 21	23 31	10 00	23 51	9 35	0 20	8 58	0 57	7 54	2 01
11	9 45	22 55	9 25	23 15	8 59	23 40	8 23	0 20	7 19	1 23
21	9 09	22 19	8 49	22 39	8 24	23 04	7 48	23 40	6 45	0 46
31	8 34	21 43	8 15	22 03	7 50	22 28	7 14	23 04	6 12	0 09
June 10	8 00	21 08	7 40	21 28	7 16	21 53	6 41	22 28	5 39	23 29
20	7 26	20 34	7 07	20 53	6 42	21 17	6 07	21 52	5 07	22 52
30	6 52	19 59	6 33	20 18	6 09	20 42	5 35	21 16	4 36	22 16
July 10	6 18	19 25	6 00	19 44	5 36	20 07	5 02	20 41	4 04	21 39
20	5 45	18 50	5 26	19 09	5 03	19 32	4 30	20 05	3 33	21 02
30	5 11	18 16	4 53	18 34	4 30	18 57	3 57	19 30	3 02	20 25
Aug. 9	4 38	17 41	4 20	17 59	3 57	18 22	3 25	18 54	2 30	19 49
19	4 04	17 07	3 46	17 24	3 24	17 47	2 53	18 18	1 59	19 12
29	3 30	16 32	3 13	16 49	2 51	17 11	2 20	17 42	1 28	18 34
Sept. 8	2 56	15 57	2 39	16 14	2 17	16 36	1 47	17 06	0 56	17 57
18	2 21	15 21	2 04	15 38	1 43	16 00	1 13	16 30	0 23	17 20
28	1 46	14 46	1 30	15 02	1 09	15 23	0 39	15 53	23 46	16 42
Oct. 8	1 11	14 09	0 54	14 26	0 33	14 47	0 04	15 16	23 12	16 04
18	0 35	13 32	0 18	13 49	23 54	14 09	23 25	14 38	22 37	15 26
28	23 54	12 55	23 38	13 11	23 17	13 32	22 49	14 00	22 01	14 48
Nov. 7	23 16	12 17	23 00	12 33	22 40	12 54	22 11	13 22	21 24	14 09
17	22 38	11 39	22 22	11 55	22 01	12 15	21 33	12 43	20 46	13 31
27	21 58	10 59	21 42	11 16	21 22	11 36	20 53	12 04	20 06	12 51
Dec. 7	21 18	10 19	21 02	10 36	20 41	10 56	20 13	11 25	19 25	12 12
17	20 37	9 39	20 21	9 55	20 00	10 16	19 31	10 45	18 43	11 33
27	19 55	8 58	19 39	9 14	19 18	9 35	18 49	10 04	18 00	10 53

Brightest Stars

This table lists stars of greatest visual magnitude as seen in the night sky (the lower the number, the brighter the star). The common name of the star is in parentheses. Stars of variable magnitude are designated by v. Coordinates are for mid-2005. Greek letters in the star names indicate perceived degree of brightness within the constellation, alpha generally being the brightest, though there are some exceptions.

To find when the star is on the meridian, subtract Right Ascension of Mean Sun (see the table Greenwich Sidereal Time for 0^h UTC) from the star's Right Ascension, first adding 24h to the latter if necessary. Mark this result P.M. if less than 12h; if greater than 12, subtract 12h and mark the remainder A.M.

Star	Magnitude	Parallax "	Light-yrs	Right ascen. h m	Declination ° '
α Canis Majoris (Sirius)	−1.44v	0.379	8.6	6 45.1	−16 43
α Carinae (Canopus)	−0.62v	0.010	313	6 24.0	−52 42
α Bootis (Arcturus)	−0.05v	0.089	37	14 15.7	+19 11
α Centauri (Rigel Kentaurus)	−0.01	0.742	4.4	14 39.6	−60 50
α Lyrae (Vega)	0.03v	0.129	25.3	18 37.0	+38 47
α Aurigae (Capella)	0.08v	0.077	42	5 16.7	+46 00
β Orionis (Rigel)	0.18v	0.004	773	5 14.5	− 8 12
α Canis Minoris (Procyon)	0.40	0.286	11.4	7 39.3	+ 5 13
α Eridani (Achernar)	0.45v	0.023	144	1 37.7	−57 14
α Orionis (Betelgeuse)	0.45v	0.008	427	5 55.2	+ 7 24
β Centauri (Hadar)	0.61v	0.006	525	14 03.8	−60 22
α Aquilae (Altair)	0.76v	0.194	16.8	19 50.8	+ 8 52
α Crucis (Acrux)	0.77	0.010	321	12 26.6	−63 06
α Tauri (Aldebaran)	0.87v	0.050	65	4 35.9	+16 31
α Virginis (Spica)	0.98v	0.012	262	13 25.2	−11 10
α Scorpii (Antares)	1.06v	0.005	604	16 29.4	−26 26
β Geminorum (Pollux)	1.16v	0.097	33.7	7 45.3	+28 02
α Piscis Austrinis (Fomalhaut)	1.17	0.130	25.1	22 57.7	−29 37
β Crucis (Becrux)	1.25v	0.009	352	12 47.7	−59 41
α Cygni (Deneb)	1.25v	0.001	3230	20 41.4	+45 17
α Leonis (Regulus)	1.36	0.042	77	10 08.4	+11 58
ε Canis Majoris (Adhara)	1.50v	0.008	431	6 58.6	−28 58
α Geminorum (Castor)	1.58	0.063	52	7 34.6	+31 53
γ Crucis (Gacrux)	1.59v	0.037	88	12 31.2	−57 07
λ Scorpii (Shaula)	1.62v	0.005	703	17 33.6	−37 06
γ Orionis (Bellatrix)	1.64v	0.013	243	5 25.1	+ 6 21
β Tauri (Elnath)	1.65	0.025	131	5 26.3	+28 36
β Carinae (Miaplacidus)	1.67v	0.029	111	9 13.2	−69 43
ε Orionis (Alnilam)	1.69v	0.002	1340	5 36.2	− 1 12
α Gruis (Al Nair)	1.73v	0.032	101	22 08.2	−46 58
ζ Orionis (Alnitak)	1.74	0.004	817	5 40.7	− 1 56
γ Velorum (Al Suhail)	1.75v	0.004	840	8 09.5	−47 20
ε Ursae Majoris (Alioth)	1.76v	0.040	81	12 54.0	+55 58
ε Sagittarii (Kaus Australis)	1.79	0.023	145	18 24.2	−34 23
α Persei (Mirfak)	1.79v	0.006	592	3 24.3	+49 52
α Ursae Majoris (Dubhe)	1.81	0.026	124	11 03.7	+61 45
δ Canis Majoris (Wezen)	1.83v	0.002	1790	7 08.4	−26 24
η Ursae Majoris (Alkaid)	1.85v	0.032	101	13 47.5	+49 19
ε Carinae (Avior)	1.86v	0.005	632	8 22.5	−59 31
θ Scorpii	1.86	0.012	272	17 37.3	−43 00
β Aurigae (Menkalinan)	1.90v	0.040	82	5 59.5	+44 57
α Trianguli Australis (Atria)	1.91v	0.008	415	16 48.7	−69 02
γ Geminorum (Alhena)	1.93	0.031	105	6 37.7	+16 24
δ Velorum	1.93	0.041	80	8 44.7	−54 43
α Pavonis (Peacock)	1.94v	0.018	183	20 25.6	−56 44
α Ursae Minoris (Polaris)	1.97v	0.008	431	2 31.8	+89 16
β Canis Majoris (Mirzam)	1.98v	0.007	499	6 22.7	−17 57
α Hydrae (Alphard)	1.99v	0.018	177	9 27.6	− 8 40
α Arietis (Hamal)	2.01	0.049	66	2 07.2	+23 28
γ Leonis (Algieba)	2.01v	0.026	126	10 20.0	+19 50
β Ceti (Deneb Kaitos)	2.04v	0.034	96	0 43.6	−17 59
σ Sagittarii (Nunki)	2.05v	0.015	224	18 55.3	−26 18
θ Centauri (Menkent)	2.06	0.054	61	14 06.7	−36 22
α Andromedae (Alpheratz)	2.07v	0.034	97	0 08.4	+29 05
β Andromedae (Mirach)	2.07v	0.016	199	1 09.7	+35 37
κ Orionis (Saiph)	2.07v	0.005	721	5 47.8	− 9 40
β Ursae Minoris (Kochab)	2.07v	0.026	126	14 50.7	+74 09
β Gruis	2.07v	0.019	170	22 42.7	−46 53
α Ophiuchi (Rasalhague)	2.08	0.070	47	17 34.9	+12 34
β Persei (Algol)	2.09v	0.035	93	3 08.2	+40 57
γ Andromedae (Almaak)	2.10	0.009	355	2 03.9	+42 20
β Leonis (Denebola)	2.14	0.090	36.2	11 49.1	+14 34
γ Cassiopeiae	2.15v	0.005	613	0 56.7	+60 43
γ Centauri	2.20	0.025	130	12 41.5	−48 57
ζ Puppis (Naos)	2.21v	0.002	1400	8 03.6	−40 00
ι Carinae (Tureis)	2.21	0.005	692	9 17.1	−59 17
α Coronae Borealis (Alphecca)	2.22v	0.044	75	15 34.7	+26 43
λ Velorum (Suhail)	2.23v	0.006	573	9 08.0	−43 26
ζ Ursae Majoris (Mizar)	2.23	0.042	78	13 23.9	+54 56
γ Cygni (Sadr)	2.23v	0.002	1520	20 22.2	+40 15
γ Draconis (Eltanin)	2.24v	0.022	148	17 56.6	+51 29
δ Orionis (Mintaka)	2.25v	0.004	916	5 32.0	− 0 18
β Cassiopeiae (Caph)	2.28v	0.060	54	0 09.2	+59 09
ε Scorpii	2.29	0.050	65	16 50.2	−34 18
ε Centauri	2.29v	0.009	376	13 39.9	−53 28
δ Scorpii (Dschubba)	2.29v	0.008	401	16 00.3	−22 37
α Lupi	2.30v	0.006	548	14 41.9	−47 23
η Centauri	2.33v	0.011	308	14 35.5	−42 09
β Ursae Majoris (Merak)	2.34	0.041	79	11 01.8	+56 23
ε Bootis (Izar)	2.35	0.016	210	14 45.0	+27 05
κ Scorpii	2.39v	0.007	464	17 42.5	−39 02

Morning and Evening Stars, 2005

(Coordinated Universal Time)

	Morning	Evening		Morning	Evening
Jan.	Mercury Venus Mars Jupiter Saturn to Jan. 13 Pluto	Saturn from Jan. 13 Uranus Neptune	**Apr.**	Mercury Mars Jupiter to Apr. 3 Uranus Neptune Pluto	Venus Jupiter from Apr. 3 Saturn
Feb.	Mercury to Feb. 14 Venus Mars Jupiter Uranus from Feb. 25 Neptune from Feb. 3 Pluto	Mercury from Feb. 14 Saturn Uranus to Feb. 25 Neptune to Feb. 3	**May**	Mercury Mars Uranus Neptune Pluto	Venus Jupiter Saturn
			June	Mercury to June 3 Mars Uranus Neptune Pluto to June 14	Mercury from June 3 Venus Jupiter Saturn Pluto from June 14
Mar.	Mercury from Mar. 29 Venus to Mar.31 Mars Jupiter Uranus Neptune Pluto	Mercury to Mar. 29 Venus from Mar. 31 Saturn	**July**	Mars Saturn from July 23 Uranus Neptune	Mercury Venus Jupiter Saturn to July 23 Pluto

	Morning	Evening		Morning	Evening
Aug.	Mercury from Aug. 6	Mercury to Aug. 5			Uranus
	Mars	Venus			Neptune
	Saturn	Jupiter			Pluto
	Uranus	Neptune from Aug. 8	Nov.	Mercury from Nov. 24	Mercury to Nov. 24
	Neptune to Aug. 8	Pluto		Mars to Nov. 7	Venus
Sep.	Mercury to Sep. 18	Mercury from Sep. 18		Jupiter	Mars from Nov. 7
	Mars	Venus		Saturn	Uranus
	Saturn	Jupiter			Neptune
	Uranus to Sep. 1	Uranus from Sep. 1			Pluto
		Neptune	Dec.	Mercury	Venus
		Pluto		Jupiter	Mars
Oct.	Mars	Mercury		Saturn	Uranus
	Jupiter from Oct. 22	Venus		Pluto from Dec. 16	Neptune
	Saturn	Jupiter to Oct. 22			Pluto to Dec. 16

Greenwich Sidereal Time for 0^h UTC, 2005

(Add 12 hours to obtain Right Ascension of Mean Sun)

Date	d	h	m	Date	d	h	m	Date	d	h	m	Date	d	h	m
Jan. . .	1	6	43.0	Apr. . .	1	12	37.8	July . . .	10	19	12.1	Oct. . . .	8	1	06.9
	11	7	22.4		11	13	17.2		20	19	51.5		18	1	46.3
	21	8	01.8		21	13	56.7		30	20	30.9		28	2	25.8
	31	8	41.3	May . .	1	14	36.1	Aug. . . .	9	21	10.4	Nov. . . .	7	3	05.2
Feb. . .	10	9	20.7		11	15	15.5		19	21	49.8		17	3	44.6
	20	10	00.1		21	15	54.9		29	22	29.2		27	4	24.0
Mar. . .	2	10	39.5		31	16	34.4	Sept. . .	8	23	08.6	Dec. . . .	7	5	03.5
	12	11	19.0	June .	10	17	13.8		18	23	48.1		17	5	42.9
	22	11	58.4		20	17	53.2		28	0	27.5		27	6	22.3
					30	18	32.6								

Aurora Borealis and Aurora Australis

The **Aurora Borealis,** also called the **Northern Lights,** is a broad display of rather faint light in the northern skies at night. The **Aurora Australis,** a similar phenomenon, appears at the same time in southern skies. The aurora appears in a wide variety of forms. Sometimes it is seen as a quiet glow, almost foglike in character; sometimes as vertical streamers in which there may be considerable motion; sometimes as a series of luminous expanding arcs. There are many colors, with white, yellow, and red predominating.

The auroras are most vivid and most frequently seen at about 20° from the magnetic poles, along the northern coast of the N American continent and the eastern part of the northern coast of Europe. The Aurora Borealis has been seen as far S as Key West, and the Aurora Australis has been seen as far N as Australia and New Zealand. Such occurrences are rare, however.

The Sun produces a stream of charged particles, called the **solar wind.** These particles, mainly electrons and protons, approach Earth at speeds on the order of 300 mi per second. The solar wind also carries the Sun's magnetic field, which is huge. In fact it is so large it extends beyond the planets and so is called the **Interplanetary Magnetic Field** (IMF). Far past Pluto and the Kuiper Belt, the solar wind and the IMF lose their influence, and the boundary between them and interstellar space is called the **heliopause.** Interplanetary

Coronal mass ejections are large-scale, high-speed releases of as much as 10 billion tons of coronal material. Some of these particles are trapped by Earth's magnetic field, forming the **Van Allen belts**—2 donut-shaped radiation bands around Earth. Excess amounts of these charged particles, often produced by solar flares, follow Earth's magnetic lines of force toward Earth's magnetic poles. High in the atmosphere, collisions between solar and terrestrial atoms result in the glow in the upper atmosphere called the **aurora.** The glow may be vivid where the lines of magnetic force converge near the magnetic poles.

The auroral displays appear at heights ranging from 50 to about 600 mi and have given us a means of estimating the extent of Earth's atmosphere.

The auroras are often accompanied by **magnetic storms** whose forces, also guided by the lines of force of Earth's magnetic field, disrupt electrical communication. Sunspot activity has declined since its last maximum in 2001, and is expected to reach minimum in 2007, indicating this portion of the current solar cycle will be longer than the same portion of an average 11-year cycle. Strong coronal mass ejections can still occur as witnessed by the double coronal mass ejections that swept past the Earth on May 29, 2003, triggering 9 hours of severe geomagnetic storms and producing displays of the northern lights as far south as Virginia.

Largest Telescopes

Astronomers indicate the size of telescopes not by length or magnification, but by the diameter of the primary light-gathering component of the system—such as the lens or mirror. This measurement is a direct indication of the telescope's light-gathering power. The bigger the diameter, the fainter the objects you are enabled to see. For larger telescopes, the Earth's atmosphere limits the resolution of what you see. That is why the Hubble Space Telescope, which is outside the atmosphere, can have better resolution than larger telescopes on the Earth. **Refracting (lens) telescopes** are currently not made with lens diameters of more than 40 in. Mirror telescopes can be made less expensively than lens telescopes, so all modern large optical telescopes are made with mirrors. **Radio telescopes,** also reflecting telescopes, view at wavelengths not visible to optical telescopes or to the human eye. Radio telescopes are made larger than optical telescopes because larger diameters are required at longer wavelengths to obtain equivalent resolution. Arrays of telescopes are used to achieve even better resolution through a technique called interferometry. Originally developed for radio telescopes, the technique is now also used with optical and infrared telescopes.

Largest Refracting (lens) Optical Telescope: Yerkes Observatory—1 m (40 in), at Williams Bay, WI
Largest Reflecting (mirror) Optical/Infrared Telescope: Keck—9.8 m (32 ft), on Mauna Kea in Hawaii (segmented mirror; 2 equal-size telescopes)
Largest Infrared Interferometer: Four 8.2-m (27-ft) telescopes of the Very Large Telescope Interferometer (VLTI) with a 200-m (656-ft) baseline on Cerro Paranal in Chile
Largest Space Telescope: Hubble Space Telescope—2.4 m (94 in), in orbit around Earth
Largest Fully Steerable Radio Dish: Robert C. Byrd Green Bank Telescope—100 m x 110 m (328 ft x 361 ft), in West Virginia
Largest Single Radio Dish: Arecibo Observatory—305 m (1,000 ft), in Puerto Rico
Largest Radio Interferometer: Ten 25-m (82-ft) diameter telescopes of the Very Long Baseline Array (VLBA), dispersed from Hawaii to the Virgin Islands with a resolution equal to a radio dish of 8,600 km (5,000 mi), making it the highest resolution telescope in the solar system
Largest Millimeter Wavelength Interferometer: Sixty-four 12-m (39-ft) diameter telescopes of the Atacama Large Millimeter Array (ALMA), being built at 5,000 m (16,400 ft), will be the highest-altitude ground-based observatory

Constellations

Culturally, constellations are imagined patterns among the stars that, in some cases, have been recognized through millennia. Knowledge of constellations was once necessary in order to function as an astronomer. For today's astronomers, constellations are simply areas on the entire sky in which interesting objects await observation and interpretation.

Because Western culture has prevailed in establishing modern science, equally viable and interesting constellations and celestial traditions of other cultures are not well known outside their regions of origin. Even the patterns with which we are most familiar today have undergone considerable change over the centuries.

Today, **88 constellations** are officially recognized. Although many have ancient origins, some are "modern," devised out of unclaimed stars by astronomers a few centuries ago. Unclaimed stars were those too faint or inconveniently placed to be included in the more prominent constellations. Stars in a constellation are not necessarily near each other; they are just located in the same direction on the celestial sphere.

When astronomers began to travel to S Africa in the 16th and 17th centuries, they found an unfamiliar sky that showed numerous brilliant stars. Thus, we find constellations in the southern hemisphere that depict technological marvels of the time, as well as some arguably traditional forms, such as the "fly."

Many of the commonly recognized constellations had their **origins** in ancient Asia Minor. These were adopted by the Greeks and Romans, who translated their names and stories into their own languages, modifying some details in the process. After the declines of these cultures, most such knowledge entered oral tradition or remained hidden in monastic libraries. From the 8th century, the Muslim explosion spread through the Mediterranean world. Wherever possible, everything was translated into Arabic to be taught in the universities the Muslims established all over their newfound world.

In the 13th century, Alfonso X of Castile, an avid student of astronomy, had Ptolemy's *Almagest* translated into Latin. It thus became widely available to European scholars. In the process, the constellation names were translated, but the star names were retained in their Arabic forms. Thus the names of many stars—e.g., Altair, Alnitak, Mirfak—have Arabic roots, although linguistic adaptation and the inaccuracies of transliteration have wrought changes.

Until the 1920s, astronomers used curved boundaries for the constellation areas. As these were rather arbitrary at best, the International Astronomical Union adopted new constellation boundaries that ran due north-south and east-west, filling the sky much as the contiguous states fill up the area of the "lower 48" United States.

Common names of stars often referred to parts of the traditional figures they represented: Deneb, the tail of the swan; Betelgeuse, the armpit of the giant. Avoiding traditional names, astronomers may label stars by using Greek letters, generally to denote order of brightness. Thus, the "alpha star" would generally be the brightest star of that constellation. The "of" implies possession, so the genitive (possessive) form of the constellation name is used, as in Alpha Orionis, the first star of Orion (Betelgeuse). Astronomers usually use a 3-letter abbreviation for the constellation name, as indicated here.

Within these boundaries, and occasionally crossing them, popular "asterisms" are recognized: the so-called Big Dipper is a small part of the constellation Ursa Major, the big bear; the Sickle is the traditional head and mane of Leo, the lion; the three stars of the Summer Triangle are each in a different constellation, with Vega in Lyra the lyre, Deneb in Cynus the swan, and Altair in Aquila the eagle; the northeast star of the Great Square of Pegasus is Alpha Andromedae.

Name	Genitive Case	Abbr.	Meaning
Andromeda	Andromedae	And	Chained Maiden
Antlia	Antliae	Ant	Air Pump
Apus	Apodis	Aps	Bird of Paradise
Aquarius	Aquarii	Aqr	Water Bearer
Aquila	Aquilae	Aql	Eagle

Name	Genitive Case	Abbr.	Meaning
Ara	Arae	Ara	Altar
Aries	Arietis	Ari	Ram
Auriga	Aurigae	Aur	Charioteer
Boötes	Boötis	Boo	Herdsmen
Caelum	Caeli	Cae	Chisel
Camelopardalis	Camelopardalis	Cam	Giraffe
Cancer	Cancri	Cnc	Crab
Canes Venatici	Canum Venaticorum	CVn	Hunting Dogs
Canis Major	Canis Majoris	CMa	Greater Dog
Canis Minor	Canis Minoris	CMi	Littler Dog
Capricornus	Capricorni	Cap	Sea-goat
Carina	Carinae	Car	Keel
Cassiopeia	Cassiopeiae	Cas	Queen
Centaurus	Centauri	Cen	Centaur
Cepheus	Cephei	Cep	King
Cetus	Ceti	Cet	Whale
Chamaeleon	Chamaeleontis	Cha	Chameleon
Circinus	Circini	Cir	Compasses (art)
Columba	Columbae	Col	Dove
Coma Berenices	Comae Berenices	Com	Berenice's Hair
Corona Australis	Coronae Australis	CrA	Southern Crown
Corona Borealis	Coronae Borealis	CrB	Northern Crown
Corvus	Corvi	Crv	Crow
Crater	Crateris	Crt	Cup
Crux	Crucis	Cru	Cross (southern)
Cygnus	Cygni	Cyg	Swan
Delphinus	Delphini	Del	Dolphin
Dorado	Doradus	Dor	Goldfish
Draco	Draconis	Dra	Dragon
Equuleus	Equulei	Equ	Little Horse
Eridanus	Eridani	Eri	River
Fornax	Fornacis	For	Furnace
Gemini	Geminorum	Gem	Twins
Grus	Gruis	Gru	Crane (bird)
Hercules	Herculis	Her	Hercules
Horologium	Horologii	Hor	Clock
Hydra	Hydrae	Hya	Water Snake (female)
Hydrus	Hydri	Hyi	Water Snake (male)
Indus	Indi	Ind	Indian
Lacerta	Lacertae	Lac	Lizard
Leo	Leonis	Leo	Lion
Leo Minor	Leonis Minoris	LMi	Littler Lion
Lepus	Leporis	Lep	Hare
Libra	Librae	Lib	Balance
Lupus	Lupi	Lup	Wolf
Lynx	Lyncis	Lyn	Lynx
Lyra	Lyrae	Lyr	Lyre
Mensa	Mensae	Men	Table Mountain
Microscopium	Microscopii	Mic	Microscope
Monoceros	Monocerotis	Mon	Unicorn
Musca	Muscae	Mus	Fly
Norma	Normae	Nor	Square (rule)
Octans	Octantis	Oct	Octant
Ophiuchus	Ophiuchi	Oph	Serpent Bearer
Orion	Orionis	Ori	Hunter
Pavo	Pavonis	Pav	Peacock
Pegasus	Pegasi	Peg	Flying Horse
Perseus	Persei	Per	Hero
Phoenix	Phoenicis	Phe	Phoenix
Pictor	Pictoris	Pic	Painter
Pisces	Piscium	Psc	Fishes
Piscis Austrinus	Piscis Austrini	PsA	Southern Fish
Puppis	Puppis	Pup	Stern (deck)
Pyxis	Pyxidis	Pyx	Compass (sea)
Reticulum	Reticuli	Ret	Reticle
Sagitta	Sagittae	Sge	Arrow
Sagittarius	Sagittarii	Sgr	Archer
Scorpius	Scorpii	Sco	Scorpion
Sculptor	Sculptoris	Scl	Sculptor
Scutum	Scuti	Sct	Shield
Serpens	Serpentis	Ser	Serpent
Sextans	Sextantis	Sex	Sextant
Taurus	Tauri	Tau	Bull
Telescopium	Telescopii	Tel	Telescope
Triangulum	Trianguli	Tri	Triangle
Triangulum Australe	Trianguli Australis	TrA	Southern Triangle
Tucana	Tucanae	Tuc	Toucan
Ursa Major	Ursae Majoris	UMa	Greater Bear
Ursa Minor	Ursae Minoris	UMi	Littler Bear
Vela	Velorum	Vel	Sail
Virgo	Virginis	Vir	Maiden
Volans	Volantis	Vol	Flying Fish
Vulpecula	Vulpeculae	Vul	Fox

Eclipses, 2005

(in Coordinated Universal Time, standard time of the prime meridian)

There are 4 eclipses in 2005, an annular-total eclipse of the Sun, an annular eclipse of the Sun, a partial eclipse of the Moon, and a penumbral eclipse of the Moon.

Penumbral eclipses of the Moon have such little noticeable effect on the appearance of the Moon that most people are unaware of them even when looking at the Moon. An annular eclipse of the Sun occurs when, because of the elipticity of the orbits of the Moon and the Earth, the Moon is far enough away from the Earth, and the Earth close enough to the Sun, that the Moon's angular size is not quite large enough to block the Sun. A ring of the central disk of the Sun, or annulus, can then still be seen around the Moon even when the Moon is between the Earth and the Sun.

Occasionally the Moon is very close to the point where an annular eclipse rather than a total eclipse may occur. In such cases, the central phase of the eclipse may start as annular, then become solar, and near the end of the central phase again become total, as occurs in the April annular-total eclipse. Of course, all solar eclipses have partial phases, but a solar eclipse is called a partial solar eclipse only when it has no annular or total phase at all.

I. Annular-total eclipse of the Sun, April 8

This annular-total solar eclipse is visible from the S Pacific Ocean, all but the eastern part of S America, Central America, southern United States, the Caribbean, New Zealand, and a small part of Antarctica.

Circumstances of the Eclipse

Event	Date	h	m
Eclipse begins	Apr 8	17	51.2
Annular-total eclipse begins	8	18	53.5
Mid-eclipse	8	20	35.8
Annular-total eclipse ends	8	22	18.1
Eclipse ends	8	23	20.4

II. Penumbral eclipse of the Moon, April 24

Penumbral eclipses of the Moon are not very noticeable, since direct sunlight still reaches all portions of the daytime side of the Moon. Unlike total or partial eclipses of the Moon, during a penumbral eclipse there is no distinct shadow (the umbra) observable on the Moon. The beginning of the eclipse takes place over the western hemisphere, much of the Pacific Ocean, New Zealand, E Australia, E Indonesia, and most of Antarctica. The end of the eclipse takes place over the Pacific Ocean, New Zealand, Australia, Indonesia, E Asia, and the E Indian Ocean.

Circumstances of the Eclipse

Event	Date	h	m
Penumbral eclipse begins	Apr 24	7	49.8
Middle of eclipse	24	9	54.8
Penumbral eclipse ends	24	11	59.8

III. Annular eclipse of the Sun, October 3

This annular solar eclipse is visible from the N Atlantic Ocean, Europe, the Middle East, most of Africa, Greenland, Madagascar, India, and much of the Indian Ocean.

Circumstances of the Eclipse

Event	Date	h	m
Partial eclipse begins	Oct 3	7	35.5
Annular eclipse begins	3	8	42.4
Middle of eclipse	3	10	31.8
Annular eclipse ends	3	12	21.1
Partial eclipse ends	3	13	27.8

IV. Partial eclipse of the Moon, October 17

The beginning of the eclipse will be visible in most of the Pacific Ocean, N America except the E part, E Asia, Indonesia, Australia, New Zealand, and the eastern Indian Ocean. The end will be visible in most of the Pacific, western North America, most of Asia, Indonesia, Australia, New Zealand, and the E Indian Ocean.

Circumstances of the Eclipse

Event	Date	h	m
Partial eclipse begins	Oct. 17	11	34.0
Middle of eclipse	17	12	3.3
Partial eclipse ends	17	12	32.5

Total Solar Eclipses, 1990-2025

Total solar eclipses actually take place nearly as often as total lunar eclipses; they occur at a rate of about 3 every 4 years, while total lunar eclipses come at a rate of about 5 every 6 years. However, total lunar eclipses are visible over at least half of the Earth, while total solar eclipses can be seen only along a very narrow path up to a few hundred miles wide and a few thousand miles long. Observing a total solar eclipse is thus a rarity for most people. Unlike lunar eclipses, solar eclipses can be dangerous to observe. This is not because the Sun emits more potent rays during a solar eclipse, but because the Sun is always dangerous to observe directly and people are particularly likely to stare at it during a solar eclipse.

Date	Duration[1] m	s	Width (mi)	Path of Totality
1990, July 22	2	32	125	Finland, Soviet Union, Aleutian Islands
1991, July 11	6	53	160	Hawaii, Mexico, Central America, Colombia, Brazil
1992, June 30	5	20	182	S Atlantic Ocean
1994, Nov. 3	4	23	117	Peru, Bolivia, Paraguay, Brazil
1995, Oct. 24	2	9	48	Iran, India, SE Asia
1997, Mar. 9	2	50	221	Mongolia, Siberia
1998, Feb. 26	4	8	94	Galapagos Islands, Panama, Colombia, Venezuela
1999, Aug. 11	2	22	69	Europe, Middle East, India
2001, June 21	4	56	125	Atlantic Ocean, Africa, Madagascar
2002, Dec. 4	2	4	54	S Africa, Indian Ocean, Australia
2003, Nov. 23	1	57	338	Antarctica
2005, Apr. 8[h]	0	42	17	Pacific Ocean, northwestern S America
2006, Mar. 29	4	7	118	Atlantic Ocean, Africa, Asia
2008, Aug. 1	2	27	157	Arctic Ocean, Asia
2009, July 22	6	39	160	Asia, Pacific Ocean
2010, July 11	5	20	164	Pacific Ocean, southern S America
2012, Nov. 13	4	2	112	N Australia, Pacific Ocean
2013, Nov. 3[h]	1	40	36	Atlantic Ocean, Africa
2015, Mar. 20	2	47	304	N Atlantic Ocean, Arctic Ocean
2016, Mar. 9	4	10	96	Indonesia, Pacific Ocean
2017, Aug. 21	2	40	71	Pacific Ocean, U.S., Atlantic Ocean
2019, July 2	4	33	125	S Pacific Ocean, S America
2020, Dec. 14	2	10	56	S Pacific Ocean, S America, S Atlantic Ocean
2021, Dec. 4	1	55	282	Antarctica, S Atlantic Ocean
2023, Apr. 20[h]	1	16	31	Indian Ocean, New Guinea, Pacific Ocean
2024, Apr. 8	4	28	127	Pacific Ocean, Mexico, N America, Atlantic Ocean

h = indicates annular-total hybrid eclipse. (1) Duration refers to length of time at optimal viewing area.

Total Solar Eclipses in the U.S. in the 21st Century

During the 21st century Halley's Comet will return (2061-62), and there will be 8 total solar eclipses visible somewhere in the continental U.S. The first comes after a long gap; the last one was on Feb. 26, 1979, in the northwestern U.S.

Date	Path of Totality	Date	Path of Totality
Aug. 21, 2017	Oregon to South Carolina	Mar. 30, 2052	Florida to Georgia
Apr. 8, 2024	Mexico to Texas and up through Maine	May 11, 2078	Louisiana to North Carolina
Aug. 23, 2044	Montana to North Dakota	May 1, 2079	New Jersey to the lower edge of New England
Aug. 12, 2045	N California to Florida	Sept. 14, 2099	North Dakota to Virginia

Beginnings of the Universe

One of the dominating astronomical discoveries of the 20th century was the realization that the galaxies of the universe all seem to be moving away from us. It turned out that they are moving away not just from us but from one another—that is, the universe seems to be expanding. Scientists conclude that the universe must once, very long ago, have been extremely compact and dense. The explosion of matter that gave birth to the universe is called the **Big Bang**.

On the subatomic level, according to this theory, there were vast changes of energy and matter and the way physical laws operated during the first 5 minutes. After those minutes the percentages of the basic matter of the universe—hydrogen, helium, and lithium—were set. Everything was so compact and so hot that radiation dominated the early universe and there were no stable, un-ionized atoms. At first, the universe was opaque, in the sense that any energy emitted was quickly absorbed and then re-emitted by free electrons. As the universe expanded, density and temperature continued to drop. A few hundred thousand years after the Big Bang, the temperature dropped far enough that electrons and nuclei could combine to form stable atoms as the universe became transparent. Once that occurred, the radiation that had been trapped was free to escape.

In the 1940s, George Gamov and others predicted that astronomers should be able to see remnants of this escaped radiation. Astronomers were starting to search for this background radiation when physicists Arno Penzias and Robert Wilson, using a radio telescope, inadvertently beat them to the punch (the 2 were later awarded a Nobel Prize).

In 2003, NASA's Wilkinson Microwave Anisotropy Probe (WMAP), using highly sensitive amplifiers developed by the National Radio Astronomy Observatory (NRAO), made measurements of the temperature of this **cosmic microwave background** radiation to within millionths of a degree. From these measurements, scientists were able to deduce that our universe is 13.7 billion years old and the first generation stars began to form a mere 200 million years after the Big Bang.

A related mystery is that evidence suggests there is hidden matter and hidden energy that cannot be directly observed. This **dark matter** may be composed of gas, large numbers of cool, small objects, or even sub-atomic particles. The presence of dark matter is indicated by the rotation curves of galaxies and the dynamics of clusters of galaxies. Evidence for **dark energy** is derived from studies of distant Type Ia supernovae in far galaxies indicating the expansion of the universe is accelerating. The visible matter we see seems to constitute only about 4% of the total mass of the universe, while the rest of the mass of the universe is in the form of dark matter (23%) and dark energy (73%). Dark energy is a mysterious force that seems to work on the very fabric of the universe, spreading it apart.

The Solar System

The planets of the solar system, in order of mean distance from the Sun, are Mercury, Venus, Earth, Mars, Jupiter, Saturn, Uranus, Neptune, and Pluto (Pluto sometimes nearer than Neptune). Both Uranus and Neptune are visible through good binoculars, but Pluto is so distant and small that only large telescopes or long-exposure photographs can make it visible. All the planets orbit or revolve counterclockwise around the Sun.

Because Mercury and Venus are nearer to the Sun than is Earth, their motions about the Sun appear from Earth as wide swings first to one side of the Sun then to the other, though both planets move continuously around the Sun in almost circular orbits. When their passage takes them either between Earth and the Sun or beyond the Sun as seen from Earth, they are invisible to us. Because of the geometry of the planetary orbits, Mercury and Venus require much less time to pass between Earth and the Sun than around the far side of the Sun; so their periods of visibility and invisibility are unequal.

The planets that lie farther from the Sun than does Earth may be seen for longer periods and are invisible only when so located in our sky that they rise and set at about the same time as the Sun—and thus become overwhelmed by the Sun's brilliance. Though the giant planets emit their own energy, they are observed from Earth as a result of sunlight reflecting from their surfaces or cloud layers. However, on occasion, radio emissions from Jupiter exceed even those emitted by the Sun in intensity. Mercury and Venus, because they are between Earth and the Sun, show phases very much as the Moon does. The planets farther from the Sun are always seen as full, although Mars does occasionally present a slightly gibbous phase—like the Moon when not quite full.

The planets appear to move rapidly among the stars because of being closer. The stars are also in motion, some at tremendous speeds, but they are so far away that their motion does not change their apparent positions in the heavens sufficiently to be perceived. The nearest star is about 9,000 times farther away than Neptune, the most distant giant planet in our solar system. The count for identified moons in the solar system stood at 137 in mid-2004, but the discovery of new moons continued.

Planets and the Sun, by Selected Characteristics

Sun and Planets	Radius: at unit distance[1] "	Radius: at mean least distance[2] "	Radius: in mi mean radius	Volume[3]	Mass[3]	Density[3]	Sidereal period d	Sidereal period h	Sidereal period m	Sidereal period s	Gravity at surface[3]	Reflecting power Pct°	Daytime surface temp. °F
Sun	959.5	976	432,500	1,304,000	333,000	0.26	25	9	7		28.0		+9,941
Mercury	3.36	6.5	1,516	0.0562	0.0553	0.98	58	15	36		0.38	0.11	845
Venus	8.34	33.0	3,760	0.857	0.815	0.95	243		30R		0.90	0.65	867
Earth	8.78		3,959	1.000	1.000	1.00		23	56	4.2	1.00	0.37	59
Moon	2.40	986.2	1,080	0.0203	0.0123	0.61	27	7	43	40	0.16	0.12	260
Mars	4.67	12.8	2,106	0.151	0.107	0.71		24	37	22	0.38	0.15	−24
Jupiter	96.40	24.5	43,441	1,321	317.8	0.24		9	55	30	2.53	0.52	−162
Saturn	80.29	10.05	36,184	764	95.16	0.12		10	39	20	1.06	0.47	−218
Uranus	34.97	2.05	15,759	63.1	14.54	0.23		17	14	20R	0.90	0.51	−323
Neptune	33.95	1.2	15,301	57.7	17.15	0.30		16	6	40	1.14	0.41	−330
Pluto	1.65	0.08	742	0.007	0.002	0.32	6	9	17	30R	0.06	0.6	−369

(1) Angular radius, in seconds of arc, if object were seen at a distance of 1 astronomical unit. (2) Angular radius, in seconds of arc, when object is closest to Earth. (3) Earth = 1. R = Retrograde rotation.

Planet Superlatives

Largest, most massive planet	Jupiter	Most circular orbit	Venus
Fastest orbiting planet	Mercury	Slowest orbiting planet	Pluto
Fastest sidereal rotation	Jupiter	Slowest sidereal rotation	Venus
Longest (synodic) day	Mercury	Shortest (synodic) day	Jupiter
Rotational pole closest to ecliptic	Uranus	Hottest planet	Venus
Most moons	Jupiter	No moons	Mercury, Venus
Planet with largest moon	Jupiter	Planet with moon with most eccentric orbit	Neptune
Greatest average density	Earth	Lowest average density	Saturn
Tallest mountain	Mars	Deepest oceans	Jupiter
Strongest magnetic fields	Jupiter	Greatest amount of liquid, surface water	Earth

The Planets: Motion, Distance, and Brightness

Planet	Mean daily motion[1]	Orbital velocity mi per sec.[2]	Sidereal revolution days[3]	Synodic revolution days[4]	Distance from Sun in millions of mi Max.	Min.	Distance from Earth in millions of mi Max.	Min.	Light at[5] perihelion	aphelion
Mercury	14,732	29.75	87.97	115.9	43.4	28.6	137.9	48.0	10.56	4.59
Venus	5,768	21.76	224.7	583.9	67.7	66.8	162.2	23.7	1.94	1.89
Earth	3,548	18.50	365.256	—	94.5	91.4	—	—	1.03	0.97
Mars	1,887	15.00	686.98	779.9	154.9	128.4	249.4	33.9	0.52	0.36
Jupiter	299	8.12	4,332.6	398.9	507.4	460.1	602	366	0.041	0.034
Saturn	120	6.02	10,759.2	378.1	941.1	840.4	1,031	743	0.012	0.0098
Uranus	42	4.23	30,685.4	369.7	1,866	1,703	1,962	1,605	0.0030	0.0025
Neptune	22	3.37	60,189.0	367.5	2,824	2,762	2,913	2,676	0.0011	0.0011
Pluto	14	2.93	90,465.0	366.7	4,539	2,756	4,682	2,669	0.0011	0.00041

(1) Average angular motion measured in seconds of arc per day. (2) Speed of revolution around Sun. (3) Number of Earth days to orbit Sun with respect to background stars. (4) Number of Earth days to get back to the same position in its orbit around Sun, relative to Earth. (5) Light at perihelion and aphelion is solar illumination measured in units of mean illumination at Earth.

Planets of the Solar System

Note: AU = astronomical unit (92.96 mil mi, mean distance of Earth from the Sun); **d** = 1 Earth synodic (solar) day (24 hrs); **synodic day** = rotation period of a planet measured with respect to the Sun (the "true" day, i.e. the time from midday to midday, or from sunrise to sunrise); **sidereal day** = the rotation period of a planet with respect to the stars

Mercury

Distance from Sun	
Perihelion	28.6 mil mi
Semi-major axis	0.387 AU
Aphelion	43.4 mil mi
Period of revolution around Sun	87.97 d
Orbital eccentricity	0.2056
Orbital inclination	7.00°
Synodic day (midday to midday)	175.94 d
Sidereal day	58.65 d
Rotational inclination	0.01°
Mass (Earth = 1)	0.0553
Mean radius	1,516 mi
Mean density (Earth = 1)	0.984
Natural satellites	0
Average surface temperature	333°F

Mercury, the nearest planet to the Sun, is the 2nd-smallest of the 9 known planets. Its diameter is 3,032 mi; its mean distance from the Sun is 35,980,000 mi.

Mercury moves with great speed around the Sun, averaging about 30 mi per second to complete its circuit in about 88 Earth days. Mercury rotates upon its axis over a period of nearly 59 days, thus exposing all its surface periodically to the Sun. Because its orbital period is only about 50% longer than its sidereal rotation, the solar (synodic) day on Mercury, or the time from one sunrise to the next, is about 176 days, twice as long as a Mercurian year. It is believed that the surface passing before the Sun may reach a temperature of about 845° F, while the temperature on the nighttime side may fall as low as –300° F.

Uncertainty about conditions on Mercury and its motion arises from its short angular distance from the Sun as seen from Earth. Mercury is too much in line with the Sun to be observed against a dark sky, but is always seen during either morning or evening twilight.

Mariner 10 passed Mercury 3 times in 1974 and 1975. Less than half of the surface was photographed, revealing a degree of cratering similar to that of the Moon. The most imposing feature on Mercury, the Caloris Basin, is a huge impact crater more than 800 mi in diameter. Mercury also has a higher percentage of iron than any other planet. A very thin atmosphere of hydrogen and helium may be made up of gases of the solar wind temporarily concentrated by the presence of Mercury. The discovery of a weak but permanent magnetic field was a surprise to scientists. It has been held that both a fluid core and rapid rotation are necessary for the generation of a planetary magnetic field. Mercury may demonstrate the contrary; the field may reveal some-

thing about the history of Mercury. In 1991, radar mapping of Mercury revealed evidence of possible water ice near its north pole. Further evidence was provided by similar mappings of both the north and south pole in 1994 by the Arecibo radio telescope.

Venus

Distance from Sun	
Perihelion	66.8 mil mi
Semi-major axis	0.723 AU
Aphelion	67.7 mil mi
Period of revolution around Sun	224.70 d
Orbital eccentricity	0.0067
Orbital inclination	3.39°
Synodic day (midday to midday)	116.75 d (retrograde)
Sidereal day	243.02 d (retrograde)
Rotational inclination	177.4°
Mass (Earth = 1)	0.815
Mean radius	3,760 mi
Mean density (Earth = 1)	0.951
Natural satellites	0
Average surface temperature	867°F

Venus, slightly smaller than Earth, moves about the Sun at a mean distance of 67,240,000 mi in 225 Earth days. Its synodical revolution—its return to the same relationship with Earth and the Sun, which is a result of the combination of its own motion with that of Earth—is 584 days. As a result, every 19 months Venus is nearer to Earth than any other planet. Venus is covered with a dense, white, cloudy atmosphere that conceals whatever is below it. This same cloud reflects sunlight efficiently so that Venus is the 3rd-brightest object in the sky, exceeded only by the Sun and the Moon.

Spectral analysis of sunlight reflected from Venus's cloud tops has shown features that can best be explained by identifying material of the clouds as sulfuric acid. The *Mariner 2* space probe in 1962 confirmed a high surface temperature. *Mariner 2* was unable to detect the existence of a magnetic field even as weak as 1/100,000 of Earth's magnetic field.

Because Earth and Venus are about the same size and presumably formed at the same time by the same general process and from the same mixture of chemical elements, one is faced with the question: Why the difference? Measurements indicate that Venus has a surface temperature of over 865° F as a result of an extreme greenhouse effect. Due to the thick atmosphere, the temperature is essentially the same both day and night.

In 1967, the Soviet space probe, *Venera 4*, and the American *Mariner 5* arrived at Venus within a few hours of each other. *Venera 4* was designed to allow an instrument pack-

age to land gently on the surface, but it ceased to transmit information when its temperature reading went above 500° F, when it was still about 20 mi above the surface. The orbiting *Mariner 5*'s radio signals passed to Earth through Venus's atmosphere twice (once on the night side and once on the day side). The results were startling. Venus's atmosphere is nearly all carbon dioxide (96.5%), with 3.5% nitrogen and trace amounts of sulfur dioxide, carbon monoxide, argon, water, helium, and neon. It exerts a pressure at the surface more than 90 times Earth's normal sea-level pressure.

Radio astronomers determined the rotation period of Venus to be 243 days clockwise—in other words, contrary to the spin of the other planets and contrary to its own motion around the Sun. If it were exactly 243.16 days, Venus would present the same face toward Earth at every inferior conjunction. This rate and sense of rotation allows a solar day (sunrise to sunrise) on Venus of 116.8 Earth days. Any part of Venus will receive sunlight on its clouds for more than 58 days and then return to darkness for 58 days.

Mariner 10 passed Venus before traveling on to Mercury in 1974. The carbon dioxide found in abundance in the atmosphere is rather opaque to certain ultraviolet wavelengths, enabling sensitive cameras to photograph the cloud cover. Soviet spacecraft discovered that the clouds are confined in a 12-mi layer 30 to 42 mi above the surface.

In 1978, two U.S. *Pioneer* probes confirmed expected high surface temperatures and high winds aloft. Winds of about 200 mi per hour there may account for the transfer of heat into the night side despite the low rotation speed of the planet. However, at the surface, the winds are very slow. Soviet scientists obtained, in 1975 and later in 1982, 4 photos of surface rocks. The *Pioneer* orbiter confirmed the cloud pattern and its circulation shown by *Mariner 10*. Radar produced maps of the entire planet showing large craters, continent-size highlands, and extensive dry lowlands.

The Venus orbiter *Magellan* launched in 1989 used sophisticated radar techniques to observe Venus and map more than 99% of the surface. The spacecraft observed over 1,600 volcanoes and volcanic features, enabling creation of a 3-dimensional map. *Magellan* showed that more than 85% of the surface is covered by volcanic flows. Additionally, there are highly deformed mountain belts.

Craters more than 20 mi wide are believed to have been caused by impacting bodies. Theia Mons, a huge shield volcano, has a diameter of over 600 mi and a height of over 3.5 mi. (The largest Hawaiian volcano is only about 125 mi in diameter, but rises nearly 5.5 mi from the ocean floor.

Erosion is a very slow process on Venus due to the extreme lack of water, and features persist for long periods of time. There are indications of only restricted wind movement of dust and sand. No tectonic activity has been found similar to Earth's moving tectonic plates, but a system of global rift zones and numerous broad, low dome-like structures, called coronae, may be produced by the upwelling and subsidence of magma from the mantle. Volcanic surface features, such as vast lava plains, fields of small lava domes, and large shield volcanoes, are common. The few impact craters on Venus suggest that the surface is generally geologically young—less than 800 million years old.

A number of spacecraft missions to other planets have flown by Venus en route to their final destinations, including *Galileo* to Jupiter in 1989 and *Cassini* to Saturn in 1997. Approximately every 105-120 years, Venus and the Earth are in the proper positions so that Venus passes between the Earth and the Sun in a pair of transits 8 years apart. The second of the current pair of transits occurs in 2012.

Mars Probes

Twin NASA spacecraft—*Spirit* and *Opportunity*—launched in mid-2003 made successful bouncing, airbag-wrapped landings on Mars on Jan. 4 and Jan. 25, 2004, respectively. As of Sept. 2004, they were still laboriously exploring the Martian surface, able to travel over 100 yards in a day. The European Space Agency's *Mars Express*, also launched in mid-2003, arrived at Mars in December 2003. Although communication with its lander, *Beagle 2*, ended and the lander was presumably lost, the orbiter continued its prime mission of studying Mars in search of subsurface water.

Mars

Distance from Sun	
Perihelion	128.4 mil mi
Semi-major axis	1.524 AU
Aphelion	154.9 mil mi
Period of revolution around Sun	686.98 d (1.88 y)
Orbital eccentricity	0.0935
Orbital inclination	1.85°
Synodic day (midday to midday)	24h 39m 35s
Sidereal day	24h 37m 22s
Rotational inclination	25.19°
Mass (Earth = 1)	0.107
Mean radius	2,106 mi
Mean density (Earth = 1)	0.713
Natural satellites	2
Average surface temperature	−81° F

Mars's diameter is about 4,213 mi. Although Mars's orbit is nearly circular, it is somewhat more eccentric than the orbits of many of the other planets, and Mars is more than 26 mil mi farther from the Sun at its most distant point compared to its closest approach. Mars takes 687 Earth days to make one circuit of the Sun, traveling at about 15 mi a second. The planet rotates upon its axis in almost the same period of time as Earth—24 hours and 37 minutes. Mars's mean distance from the Sun is 142 mil mi, so its temperature is lower than that on Earth. In 1965, *Mariner 4* became the first spacecraft to fly by Mars, reporting that atmospheric pressure on Mars is between 1% and 2% of Earth's atmospheric pressure. As with Venus, the atmosphere is composed largely of carbon dioxide. The planet is exposed to an influx of cosmic radiation about 100 times as intense as that on Earth. Mars's orbit and its speed in relation to Earth's position and speed bring it fairly close to Earth about every 2 years. Every 15-17 years the close approaches are especially favorable for observation. In 2003, Mars came within 34,646,418 miles, its closest approach to Earth in nearly 60,000 years. Although early telescopic observations led some to believe the colors they saw were indications of vegetation, this would only be possible if Mars had abundant water and oxygen.

Mars's axis of rotation is inclined from a vertical to the plane of its orbit about the Sun by about 25°, so Mars has seasons as does Earth. White caps form about the poles, growing in the winter and shrinking in the summer. These are believed to be both water ice and carbon dioxide ice. It is the carbon dioxide that is seen to come and go with the seasons. The water ice is apparently in many layers with dust between them, indicating climatic cycles.

Mariners 6 and *7* in 1969 sent back many photographs showing cratering similar to the earlier views, but also other types of terrain. Some regions seemed featureless over large areas; others were chaotic, showing high relief without apparent organization into mountain chains or craters. *Mariner 9*, the first spacecraft to orbit Mars (1971), transmitted photos and other data showing that Mars resembles no other planet we know, yet there were features clearly of volcanic origin. One of these is Olympus Mons, a shield volcano whose caldera is more than 40 mi wide and whose outer slopes are 300 mi in diameter; it stands 15 mi above the surrounding plain—the tallest known mountain in the solar system. Some features may have been produced by faulting and stretching of the surface. Valles Marineris, extending nearly 2,500 mi, is an example on a colossal scale. Many craters seem to have been produced by impacting bodies that may have come from the nearby asteroid belt. Features near the S pole may have been produced by glaciers no longer present.

In 1976, the U.S. landed 2 *Viking* spacecraft on Mars. Though the landers had devices to perform chemical analyses of the soil in search of evidence of life; results were inconclusive. The orbiters returned pictures of topographic features that scientists believe can be explained only if Mars once had large quantities of flowing water.

Two U.S. spacecraft—*Mars Pathfinder* and *Mars Global Surveyor*—were launched to Mars in 1996. On July 4, 1997, *Pathfinder*, with its small movable robot named Sojourner, made a safe landing on Mars. Sojourner spent 3 months examining rocks near *Pathfinder*. Geological results from the *Pathfinder* indicate that in its beginning stages Mars melted

to a sufficient extent to separate into dense and lighter layers. It also appears that there was an era when the planet had large amounts of flooding waters on its surface.

The *Surveyor* did extensive mapping of the planet and reported the presence of a very weak magnetic field that may have been stronger in the distant past. *Surveyor* results support a view of the southern hemisphere of Mars covered with ancient craters like Earth's Moon. Interestingly, there is a significant difference in the northern hemisphere, which consists mainly of plains that are much younger and lower in elevation. The *Surveyor* produced a dramatic 3-D map that clearly shows this dramatic contrast. Pictures from the *Mars Global Surveyor* showed evidence for the presence of liquid water on Mars in recent times. The *Mars Odyssey* spacecraft, launched in 2001, detected evidence for the presence of water ice in the upper 3 feet of soil in a large area around the south pole.

In June 2003, the European Space Agency (ESA) launched the *Mars Express* spacecraft, its first probe to another planet. It reached Mars in December. Though its small lander, *Beagle 2,* was lost, the *Mars Express Orbiter* is performing remote sensing of Mars, including high resolution photography in a search for subsurface water.

Also in summer of 2003, NASA launched twin rovers, *Opportunity* and *Spirit*, to Mars, where they landed in Jan. 2004. Spirit landed about 15° south of the Martian equator at Gusev Crater, a bowl-shaped feature larger than Connecticut, which may have held a lake far in the past. *Opportunity* landed three weeks after *Spirit*, about halfway around Mars at Meridiani Planum, a smooth plain. Both rovers have found evidence that liquid water once existed in the regions they are exploring. They also exceeded their mission goals, with *Spirit* covering more than 2 miles and *Opportunity* holding the single-day travel record of over 300 feet. They have taken thousands of pictures, which will lead to better understanding of the history of Mars and when water may have been present there.

Mars has 2 satellites, discovered in 1877 by Asaph Hall. The outer satellite, Deimos, revolves around the planet in about 31 hours. The inner satellite, Phobos, whips around Mars in a little more than 7 hours, making 3 trips around the planet each Martian day. Since it orbits Mars faster than the planet rotates, Phobos rises in the W and sets in the E, opposite to what other bodies appear to do in the Martian sky. *Mariner* and *Viking* photos show these satellites to be irregularly shaped and pitted with numerous craters. Phobos also exhibits a system of linear grooves, each about 1/3 mi across and roughly parallel. Phobos measures about 11 by 17 mi and Deimos about 6.55 by 9.3 mi.

Of the tens of thousands of meteorites found on Earth, about a dozen may have originated on Mars. In 1996, a NASA research team concluded that a meteorite found in 1984 on an Antarctic ice field not only might be a rock blasted from the surface of Mars but also might contain evidence of life on Mars 3.5 bil years ago. The meteorite has been age-dated to about 4.5 bil years. The scientists theorize that 3.5 bil years ago, Mars may have been warmer and wetter, and microscopic life may have formed and left evidence in the rock, including possible fossilized microscopic organisms. It is thought that 16 mil years ago a huge asteroid or comet struck Mars, blasting material, including this rock, into space. The rock may have entered Earth's atmosphere about 13,000 years ago, landing in Antarctica. The evidence is intriguing, but not conclusive, in suggesting that Mars may have had microscopic life, at least far in the past.

Jupiter

Jupiter, largest of the planets, has an equatorial diameter of 88,846 mi, 11 times the diameter of Earth. Its polar diameter is more than 5,700 mi shorter. This noticeable oblateness is a result of the liquidity of the planet and its extremely rapid rate of rotation; a day is less than 10 Earth hours long. For a planet this size, this rotational speed is amazing. A point on Jupiter's equator moves at a speed of 22,000 mph, as compared with 1,000 mph for a point on Earth's equator. Jupiter is at an average distance of 484 mil mi from the Sun and takes almost 12 Earth years to make one complete circuit of the Sun.

Distance from Sun	
Perihelion	460.1 mil mi
Semi-major axis	5.204 AU
Aphelion	507.4 mil mi
Period of revolution around Sun	11.862 y
Orbital eccentricity	0.0489
Orbital inclination	1.304°
Synodic day (midday to midday)	9h 55m 33s
Sidereal day	9h 55m 30s
Rotational inclination	3.13°
Mass (Earth = 1)	317.8
Mean radius	43,441 mi
Mean density (Earth = 1)	0.24
Natural satellites	61
Average temperature*	−162°F

*i.e., temperature where atmosphere pressure equals 1 Earth atmosphere.

The major chemical constituents of Jupiter's atmosphere are molecular hydrogen (H_2—90%) and helium (He—10%). Minor constituents include methane (CH_4), ammonia (NH_3), hydrogen deuteride (HD), ethane (C_2H_6), and water (H_2O).

The temperature at the tops of clouds may be about –280° F. The gases become denser with depth, until they may turn into a slush or slurry. There is no sharp interface between the gaseous atmosphere and the hydrogen ocean that accounts for most of Jupiter's volume. *Pioneer 10* and *11*, passing Jupiter in 1973 and 1974, provided evidence for considering Jupiter almost entirely liquid hydrogen. Jupiter apparently has a liquid hydrogen ocean more than 35,000 mi deep. It likely has a rocky core about the size of Earth, but 13 times more massive.

Jupiter's magnetic field is by far the strongest of any planet. Electrical activity caused by this field is so strong that it discharges billions of watts into Earth's magnetic field daily. At lower layers, under enormous pressure, the liquid hydrogen takes on the properties of a metal. It is likely that this liquid metallic hydrogen is the source for both Jupiter's persistent radio noise and for its improbably strong magnetic field. Radio astronomy and information from the spacecraft passing in Jupiter's vicinity have revealed details of the overall structure of the huge magnetosphere surrounding Jupiter.

21 of Jupiter's 61 known satellites were found in 2003 through Earth-based observations. Four of the moons (in order from Jupiter), Io, Europa, Ganymede, and Callisto—all discovered by Galileo in 1610—are large and bright, rivaling Earth's Moon and Mercury in diameter, and may be seen through binoculars. They move rapidly around Jupiter, and it is easy to observe their change of position from night to night. The other satellites are much smaller, with 4 closer to Jupiter than Io, 5 between Ganymede and Callisto, and the rest farther out. None of them can be seen except through powerful telescopes. All but one of the 21 newly discovered moons appear to be in retrograde orbits. Indeed, 45 of the 46 outermost satellites revolve around Jupiter clockwise as seen from the north, contrary to the motions of most satellites in the solar system and to the direction of revolution of planets around the Sun. These moons may be captured asteroids. Jupiter's mass is more than twice the mass of all the other planets, moons, and asteroids put together.

Photographs from *Pioneer 10* and *11* were far surpassed by those of *Voyager 1* and *2*, both of which arrived at Jupiter in 1979. The Great Red Spot exhibited internal counterclockwise rotation and much turbulence was seen in adjacent material passing N or S of it. The satellites Amalthea, Io, Europa, Ganymede, and Callisto were photographed, some in great detail. Io has active volcanoes that probably have ejected material into a doughnut-shaped ring, or torus, enveloping its orbit about Jupiter. This is not to be confused with Jupiter's rings, the surprise of the *Voyager I* mission. Since then, ground-based telescopes have imaged Jupiter's rings in the infrared.

In 1994, 21 large fragments of Comet Shoemaker-Levy 9 collided with Jupiter. Moving at 134,000 mph, stretched out like a 21-car freight train, the fragments impacted one after another. Massive plumes of gas erupted, forming brilliant fire-

2004 Saturn Probes

Launched in Oct. 1997, the *Cassini* spacecraft, with its tag-along companion *Huygens*, reached the planet Saturn on July 1, 2004. *Cassini*, the first spacecraft to orbit Saturn, is intended to remain for many years, hopefully unlocking many of the planet's secrets, while the *Huygens* probe attempts to enter the atmosphere of Titan, Saturn's largest moon, and land on its surface. Previous Saturn probes—*Pioneer 11* and *Voyagers 1* and *2*—were all flybys.

Before orbiting Saturn, *Cassini* flew within 1,300 miles of Saturn's moon Phoebe and transmitted images back to Earth, which indicated a surface of water ice. Titan, the scheduled target of the Huygens probe on Dec. 24, 2004, is the 2nd-largest moon in the solar system (after Jupiter's Ganymede); it is larger in diameter than Pluto or Mercury and more massive than Pluto. It is also the only moon in the solar system with a significant atmosphere. But it does not have Earth's abundance of oxygen, and the surface temperature probably approaches −300° F. In mid-August, 2004, less than seven weeks after going into orbit around Saturn, Cassini discovered two tiny new moons, the smallest yet seen. (*See pictures, page 809.*)

balls and leaving dark blotches and smears behind. One of the largest chunks impacted with a force 100,000 times the power of the largest nuclear bomb ever detonated. It produced a plume 1,400 mi high and 5,000 mi wide and left a temporary dark discoloration larger than Earth.

The *Galileo* spacecraft went into orbit around Jupiter and released an atmospheric probe into the Jovian atmosphere in Dec. 1995. The probe, traveling at a speed of over 100,000 mph, plunged into Jupiter's atmosphere relaying information about it for 57.6 minutes. The probe revealed that Jupiter has thunderstorms many times larger than those occurring on Earth, and it also provided evidence that Jupiter's rings are composed of small dust grains blasted off the 4 innermost moons by meteoroid impacts.

Galileo continued an extended mission to study the 4 large moons. Its observations show extensive ongoing volcanic eruptions on Io, with the volcanoes hotter than Earth's volcanoes. Europa may have a 30-mi-deep salty, liquid ocean beneath its icy crust, perhaps a small metallic core, and a very tenuous atmosphere. Ganymede has it own magnetic field produced by a molten core perhaps of iron sulfide. Callisto has the oldest, most heavily cratered surface in the solar system, a very thin atmosphere of carbon dioxide, and possibly a subsurface liquid ocean. On Sept. 23, 2003, *Galileo* was intentionally plunged into Jupiter's atmosphere, destroying the spacecraft to prevent any accidental contamination of the possible subsurface ocean on Europa.

Saturn

Distance from Sun	
Perihelion	840.44 mil mi
Semi-major axis	9.582 AU
Aphelion	941.07 mil mi
Period of revolution around Sun	29.457 y
Orbital eccentricity	0.0565
Orbital inclination	2.485°
Synodic day (midday to midday)	10h 39m 23s
Sidereal day	10h 39m 22s
Rotational Inclination	26.73°
Mass (Earth = 1)	95.159
Mean radius	36,184 mi
Mean density (Earth = 1)	0.125
Natural satellites	33
Average temperature*	−218° F

*i.e., temperature where atmosphere pressure equals 1 Earth atmosphere.

Saturn, last of the planets visible to the unaided eye, is almost twice as far from the Sun as Jupiter. It is 2nd in size to Jupiter, but its mass is much smaller. Saturn's specific gravity is less than that of water. Its diameter is almost 74,900 mi at the equator while its polar diameter is almost 7,300 mi shorter—even more extreme than Jupiter. This noticeable oblateness is a result of the liquidity of the planet and its extremely rapid rate of rotation; a day is little more than 10 Earth hours long. Saturn's atmosphere is much like that of Jupiter, except that the temperature at the top of its cloud layer is at least 50° F colder. At about 300° F below zero, the ammonia would be frozen out of Saturn's clouds. The theoretical construction of Saturn resembles that of Jupiter; it likely has a small dense center surrounded by a layer of liquid and a deep atmosphere.

Until *Pioneer 11* passed Saturn in 1979, only 10 satellites of the planet were known from ground-based observations. *Pioneer 11* discovered 2 more, and 6 others were found in the *Voyager 1* and *2* flybys, which also yielded more information about Saturn's icy satellites. 12 more moons were reported in 2000, and another one in 2003. The *Cassini* spacecraft, in 2004, discovered two more moons. Like Jupiter, Saturn is

composed mostly of hydrogen (75%) and helium (25%), with traces of water, ammonia, methane, and rock.

Saturn's ring system begins about 4,000 mi above the visible disk of Saturn, lying above its equator and extending about 260,000 mi into space. The diameter of the ring system visible from Earth is about 170,000 mi; the rings are estimated to be about 700 feet thick. In 1973, radar observation showed the ring particles to be large chunks of material averaging a meter on a side. Later, *Voyager 1* and *2* observations showed the rings to be considerably more complex than had been believed.

Uranus

Distance from Sun	
Perihelion	1,703.4 mil mi
Semi-major axis	19.201 AU
Aphelion	1,866.4 mil mi
Period of revolution around Sun	84.01 y
Orbital eccentricity	0.0457
Orbital inclination	0.772°
Synodic day (midday to midday)	17h 14m 23s (retrograde)
Sidereal day	17h 14m 24s (retrograde)
Rotational inclination	97.77°
Mass (Earth = 1)	14.536
Mean radius	15,759mi
Mean density (Earth = 1)	0.230
Natural satellites	26
Average temperature*	−323° F

*i.e., temperature where atmosphere pressure equals 1 Earth atmosphere.

Voyager 2, after passing Saturn in 1981, headed for a rendezvous with Uranus, culminating in a flyby in 1986.

Uranus, discovered by Sir William Herschel on Mar. 13, 1781, lies 1.8 bil mi from the Sun, taking 84 years to make its circuit around our star. Uranus has a diameter of over 31,000 mi and spins once in some 17.4 hours, according to flyby magnetic data. One of the most fascinating features of Uranus is how far over it is tipped. Its N pole lies 98° from being directly up and down to its orbit plane. Thus, its seasons are extreme. When the Sun rises at the N pole, it stays up for 42 Earth years; then it sets, and the N pole is in darkness (and winter) for 42 Earth years.

Uranus has 26 known moons, which have orbits lying in the plane of the planet's equator. 5 moons are relatively large, while 16 are very small and were only discovered with the *Voyager 2* mission or in later observations. In the equatorial plane there is also a complex of 10 rings, 9 of which were discovered in 1978. Invisible from Earth, the 9 original rings were found by observers watching Uranus pass before a star. As they waited, they saw their photoelectric equipment register several short eclipses of the star; then the planet occulted the star as expected. After the star came out from behind Uranus, the star winked out several more times. Subsequent observations and analyses indicated the 9 narrow, nearly opaque rings circling Uranus. Evidence from the *Voyager 2* flyby showed the ring particles to be predominantly a yard or so in diameter.

In addition to photos of 10 very small satellites, *Voyager 2* returned detailed photos of the 5 large satellites. As in the case of other satellites newly observed in the *Voyager* program, these bodies proved to be quite different from one another and from any others. Miranda has grooved markings, reminiscent of Jupiter's Ganymede, but often arranged in a chevron pattern. Ariel shows rifts and channels. Umbriel is extremely dark, prompting some observers to regard its surface as among the oldest in the system. Titania has rifts and fractures, but not the evidence of flow found on Ariel. Oberon's main feature is its surface saturated with craters, unrelieved by

other formations. In 1986, 5 more small satellites, all in retrograde orbits, were found by re-examining *Voyager 2* images. The most recent discoveries have been made with the Hubble Space Telescope and the Subaru telescope.

Uranus likely does not have a rocky core, but rather a mixture of rocks and assorted ices with about 15% hydrogen and a little helium. The atmosphere is about 83% hydrogen, 15% helium, and 2% methane. In addition to its rotational tilt, Uranus's magnetic field axis is tipped an incredible 58.6° from its rotational axis and is displaced about 30% of its radius away from the planet's center.

Neptune

Distance from the Sun	
Perihelion	2,761.7 mil mi
Semi-major axis	30.047 AU
Aphelion	2,824.5 mil mi
Period of revolution around Sun	164.79 y
Orbital eccentricity	0.0113
Orbital inclination	1.769°
Synodic day (midday to midday)	16h 6m 37s
Sidereal day	16h 6m 36s
Rotational inclination	28.32°
Mass (Earth = 1)	17.147
Mean radius	15,301 mi
Mean density (Earth = 1)	0.297
Natural satellites	13
Average temperature*	−330° F

*i.e., temperature where atmosphere pressure equals 1 Earth atmosphere.

Neptune lies at an average distance of 2.8 bil mi from the Sun. It was the last planet visited in *Voyager 2*'s epic 12-year trek (1977-89) from Earth.

As with other giant planets, Neptune may have no solid surface, or exact diameter. However, a mean value of 30,600 mi may be assigned to a diameter between atmosphere levels where the pressure is about the same as sea level on Earth. Without a solid surface to view, it is challenging to determine a "true" rotation rate for a giant planet.

Astronomers use a determination of the rotation rate of the planet's magnetic field to indicate the internal rotation rate, which in the case of Neptune is 16.1 hours. Neptune orbits the Sun in 164.8 years in a nearly circular orbit. Neptune, discovered in 1846, will not have completed one full trip around the Sun since its discovery until 2010.

Voyager 2, which passed 3,000 mi from Neptune's N pole, found a magnetic field that is considerably asymmetric to the planet's structure, similar to, but not so extreme as, that found at Uranus. Neptune's magnetic field axis is tipped 46.9° from its rotational axis and is displaced more than 55% of its radius away from the planet's center. Neptune's atmosphere was seen to be quite blue, with quickly changing white clouds often suspended high above an apparent surface. There is a Great Dark Spot, reminiscent of the Great Red Spot of Jupiter. Observations with the Hubble Space Telescope have shown that the Great Dark Spot originally seen by *Voyager* has apparently dissipated, but a new dark spot has since appeared. Neptune's atmosphere is about 80% hydrogen, 19% helium, and 1% methane. Lightning and auroras have been found on other giant planets, while only the aurora phenomenon has been seen on Neptune.

Six new satellites were discerned around Neptune by *Voyager 2*; 5 of them orbit Neptune in a half day or less. In 2002 astronomers who had used large telescopes in Chile and Hawaii announced the discovery of 3 more satellites. In 2003, 2 more moons, which orbit farther from their parent planet than any other moons, were discovered.

Nereid, found in 1949, has the highest orbital eccentricity (0.75) of any moon. Its long looping orbit suggests that it was captured rather than having been there from the beginning. Largest of the 13 satellites of Neptune is Triton, the only large moon in a retrograde orbit, suggesting that it, too, was captured. Triton's large size, sufficient to raise significant tides on the planet, may one day, billions of years from now, cause Triton to come close enough to Neptune for it to be torn apart. Only about half of Triton has been observed, but its terrain shows cratering and a strange regional feature described as resembling the skin of a cantaloupe. Triton has a tenuous atmosphere of nitrogen with a trace of hydrocar-

bons and evidence of active geysers injecting material into it. At −390° F, the wintertime parts of Triton are the coldest regions yet found in the solar system.

Voyager 2 also confirmed the existence of 6 rings composed of very fine particles. There may be some clumpiness in the rings' structure. It is not known whether Neptune's satellites influence the formation or maintenance of the rings.

As with the other giant planets, Neptune is emitting more energy than it receives from the Sun. *Voyager* found the excess to be 2.7 times the solar contribution. Cooling from internal heat sources and from the heat of formation of the planets is thought to be responsible.

Pluto

Distance from Sun	
Perihelion	2,755.8 mil mi
Semi-major axis	39.236 AU
Aphelion	4,538.7 mil mi
Period of revolution around Sun	247.68 y
Orbital eccentricity	0.2444
Orbital inclination	17.16°
Synodic day (midday to midday)	6d 9h 17m (retrograde)
Sidereal day	6d 9h 18m (retrograde)
Rotational inclination	122.53°
Mass (Earth = 1)	0.0021
Mean radius	742.5 mi
Mean density (Earth = 1)	0.317
Natural satellites	1
Average surface temperature	−369°

Although Pluto on the average stays about 3.6 bil mi from the Sun, its orbit is so eccentric that its minimum distance of 2.76 bil mi is less than Neptune's distance from the Sun.

Pluto is currently the most distant planet, but for about 20 years of its orbit, Pluto is closer to the Sun than Neptune. Pluto takes 247.7 years to circumnavigate the Sun, a 3/2 resonance with Neptune.

About a century ago, a hypothetical planet was believed to lie beyond Neptune and Uranus because neither planet followed paths predicted by astronomers when all known gravitational influences were considered. In little more than a guess, a mass of 1 Earth was assigned to the mysterious body, and mathematical searches were begun. Amid some controversy about the validity of the predictive process, Pluto was discovered nearly where it had been predicted to lie, by Clyde Tombaugh at the Lowell Observatory in Flagstaff, AZ, in 1930.

At the U.S. Naval Observatory in Flagstaff, in 1978, James Christy obtained a photograph of Pluto that was distinctly elongated. Repeated observations of this shape and its variation were convincing evidence of the discovery of a satellite of Pluto, now named Charon. Later observations showed its diameter to be 737 mi across; it orbits Pluto at a distance of 12,200 mi and takes 6.39 days to move around the planet. In this same length of time, Pluto and Charon both rotate once around their axes. The Pluto-Charon system thus appears to rotate as virtually a rigid body. This information allows the mass of Pluto to be calculated as 0.0021 of Earth. This mass, together with a new diameter for Pluto of 1,485 mi, make its density about twice that of water. Theorists predict that Pluto has a rocky core, surrounded by a thick mantle of ice.

It is now clear that Pluto could not have influenced Neptune and Uranus to go astray. Besides being the smallest planet, Pluto is actually smaller than 7 of the solar system's moons. Although a 10th planet might be out there somewhere, theorists no longer believe there are unexplained perturbations in the orbit of Uranus or Neptune that might be caused by it. Astronomers have found over 600 asteroid-size objects, somewhat beyond Pluto, in a region called the Kuiper Belt, where some comets are believed to originate.

Because the rotational axis of the system is tipped more than 120°, there is only an interval of a few years every 125 years when Pluto and Charon alternately eclipse each other. Both worlds are roughly spherical and have comparable densities. Large regions on Pluto are dark, others light; Pluto has spots and perhaps polar caps. Although extremely cold, Pluto appears to have a thin nitrogen–carbon dioxide–methane atmosphere, at least while it is closer to the Sun. When Pluto occulted a star, the star's light faded in such a way as

to suggest it had passed through a haze layer lying above the planet's surface, indicating an inversion of temperatures and the possibility that Pluto has primitive weather.

A current controversy is the issue of Pluto's planet status. Pluto is clearly different from both the rocky terrestrial planets and the giant gaseous planets. Although some astronomers think Pluto most closely resembles the Kuiper Belt Objects

(see Solar System Debris, page 365) and should be grouped with them, Pluto is still officially labeled a planet. By way of comparison, Mercury, the 2nd-smallest planet, is about 2 times the radius of Pluto, while Pluto is about 1.5 times the radius of 2004 DW, the largest-known Kuiper Belt Object (discovered in 2004). Closest in size to Pluto is Neptune's largest moon, Triton, which is 1.13 times the radius of Pluto.

The Sun

The Sun, the controlling body of Earth's solar system, is a star often described as average. Yet, the Sun's mass and luminosity are greater than that of 90% of the stars in our Milky Way galaxy. On the other hand, most of the stars that can be easily seen on any clear night are bigger and brighter than the Sun. It is the Sun's proximity to Earth that makes it appear tremendously large and bright. The Sun is 400,000 times as bright as the full moon and gives Earth 6 mil times as much light as do all the other stars put together. A series of nuclear fusion reactions, where hydrogen nuclei are converted to helium nuclei, powers the Sun and produces the heat and light that make life possible on Earth.

The Sun has a diameter of 865,000 miles and, on average, is 92,976,000 miles from Earth. It is 1.408 times as dense as water. The light of the Sun reaches Earth in 499 seconds, or in slightly more than 8 minutes. The average solar surface temperature has been measured at a value of 5,778 K, or about 9,941° F. The interior temperature of the Sun is theorized to be about 28,300,000° F.

When sunlight is analyzed with a spectroscope, it is found to consist of a continuous spectrum composed of all the colors of the rainbow in order, crossed by many dark lines. The dark "absorption lines" are produced by gaseous materials in the outer layers of the Sun. More than 60 of the natural terrestrial elements have been identified in the Sun, all in gaseous form because of the Sun's intense heat.

Spheres and Corona

The radiating surface of the Sun is called the **photosphere**; just above it is the **chromosphere**. The chromosphere is visible to the naked eye only at total solar eclipses, appearing then to be a pinkish-violet layer with occasional great prominences projecting above its general level. With proper instruments, the chromosphere can be seen or photographed whenever the Sun is visible without waiting for a total eclipse. Above the chromosphere is the **corona**, also visible to the naked eye only at times of total eclipse. Instruments also permit the brighter portions of the corona to be studied whenever conditions are favorable. The pearly light of the corona surges mil of mi from the Sun. Iron, nickel,

and calcium are believed to be principal contributors to the composition of the corona, all in a state of extreme attenuation and high ionization that indicates temperatures nearly 2 mil° Fahrenheit.

Sunspots

There is an intimate connection between sunspots and the corona. At times of low sunspot activity, the fine streamers of the corona are longer above the Sun's equator than over the polar regions of the Sun; during periods of high sunspot activity, the corona extends fairly evenly outward from all regions of the Sun, but to a much greater distance in space. Sunspots are dark, irregularly shaped regions whose diameters may reach tens of thousands of miles. The average life of a sunspot group is 2 months, but some have lasted for more than a year.

Sunspots reach a low point, on average, every 11.3 years, with a peak of activity occurring irregularly between 2 successive minima. Launched in December 1995, the SOHO spacecraft was designed to provide several years of study of the Sun from an orbit around the Sun. The most recent solar maximum occurred in 2001; SOHO provided extraordinary views of the Sun's activity. The number of sunspots is now declining, heading towards solar minimum which should occur about 2006/2007.

Observations from SOHO show that magnetic arches, called prominences, extending tens of thousands of miles into the corona, may release enormous amounts of energy heating the corona. SOHO has also highlighted enormous releases of solar energy called coronal mass ejections. Coronal holes are regions where the corona appears dark in X rays. These are regions associated with open magnetic field lines, where the magnetic field lines project out into space instead of back towards the Sun, and it is in these regions where the high-speed solar wind originates. While studying the Sun, SOHO has also imaged 750 comets passing near the Sun, with more than 75% of these discoveries being made by amateurs viewing the images on the Internet. November 2003 saw the largest solar X-ray flare yet recorded on the Sun.

The Moon

Distance from Earth	
Perigee	225,744 mi
Semi-major axis	238,855 mi
Apogee	251,966 mi
Period of revolution	27.322 d
Synodic orbital period (period of phases)	29.53 d
Orbital eccentricity	0.0549
Orbital inclination	5.1450°
Sidereal day (rotation period	27.322 d
Rotational inclination	6.680°
Mass (Earth = 1)	0.0123
Mean radius	1,080 mi
Mean density (Earth = 1)	0.605
Average surface temperature	−100° F

The Moon completes a circuit around Earth in a period whose mean or average duration is 27 days, 7 hours, 43.2 minutes. This is the Moon's sidereal period. Because of the motion of the Moon in common with Earth around the Sun, the mean duration of the lunar month—the period from one New Moon to the next New Moon—is 29 days, 12 hours, 44.05 minutes. This is the Moon's synodic period.

The mean distance of the Moon from Earth is 238,855 mi. Because the orbit of the Moon about Earth is not circular but elliptical, however, the actual distance varies considerably. The maximum distance from Earth that the Moon may reach is 251,966 mi and the least distance is 225,744 mi. (All dis-

tances given here are from the center of one body to the center of the other.)

The Moon rotates on its axis in a period of time that is exactly equal to its sidereal revolution about Earth: 27.322 days. Thus the backside or farside of the Moon always faces away from Earth. But this does not mean that the backside is always dark. The farside of the Moon gets just as much direct sunlight as the nearside. At New Moon phase, the farside of the Moon is fully lit. With its long day and night, the daytime temperature can reach 2600° F, while the coldest nighttime temperature may reach −2800° F. This day-to-night contrast is exceeded only by that on Mercury.

The Moon's revolution about Earth is irregular because of its elliptical orbit. The Moon's rotation, however, is regular, and this, together with the irregular revolution, produces what is called "libration in longitude," which permits an observer on Earth to see first farther around the E side and then farther around the W side of the Moon. The Moon's variation N or S of the ecliptic permits one to see farther over first one pole and then the other of the Moon; this is called "libration in latitude." These two libration effects permit observers on Earth to see a total of about 60% of the Moon's surface over a period of time.

The hidden side of the Moon was first photographed in 1959 by the Soviet space vehicle *Lunik III*. The moon's farside does appear noticeably different from the nearside, in

that the farside has practically none of the large lava plains, called maria, so prominent on the nearside.

From 1969 through 1972, 6 American spacecraft brought 12 astronauts to walk on the surface of the Moon, and 3 additional missions either orbited and flew by the Moon. In 1998 NASA's *Lunar Prospector* spacecraft provided evidence for the presence of 300 million metric tons of water ice at the lunar poles. *Lunar Prospector* results also indicate that the Moon has a small core, supporting the idea that most of the mass of the Moon was ripped away from the early Earth when a Mars-size object collided with Earth.

Tides on Earth are caused mainly by the Moon, because of its proximity to Earth. The ratio of the tide-raising power of the Moon to that of the Sun is 11 to 5.

Harvest Moon and Hunter's Moon

The Harvest Moon, the full Moon nearest the autumnal equinox, ushers in a period of several successive days when the Moon rises soon after sunset. This phenomenon gives farmers in temperate latitudes extra hours of light in which to harvest their crops before frost and winter. The 2005 Harvest Moon falls on Sept. 18 UTC. Harvest Moon in the southern hemisphere temperate latitudes falls on Mar. 25.

The next full Moon after Harvest Moon is called the Hunter's Moon; it is accompanied by a similar but less marked phenomenon. In 2005, the Hunter's Moon occurs on Oct. 17 in the northern hemisphere and on Apr. 24 in the southern hemisphere.

Moon's Perigee and Apogee, 2005

(Coordinated Universal Time, standard time of the prime meridian)

Perigee					Apogee				
Date	Hour		Date	Hour	Date	Hour		Date	Hour
Jan. 10	10		July 21	20	Jan. 23	19		Aug. 4	22
Feb. 7	22		Aug. 19	6	Feb. 20	5		Sept. 1	3
Mar. 8	4		Sept. 16	14	Mar. 19	23		Sept. 28	15
Apr. 4	11		Oct. 14	14	Apr. 16	19		Oct. 26	10
Apr. 29	10		Nov. 10	00	May 14	14		Nov. 23	6
May 26	11		Dec. 5	5	June 11	6		Dec. 21	3
June 23	12				July 8	18			

Moon Phases, 2005

(Coordinated Universal Time, standard time of the prime meridian)

New Moon				Waxing Quarter				Full Moon				Waning Quarter		
Month	d	h	m	Month	d	h	m	Month	d	h	m	Month	d	h	m
Jan.	10	12	3	Jan.	17	6	57	Jan.	25	10	32	Jan.	3	17	46
Feb.	8	22	28	Feb.	16	0	16	Feb.	24	4	54	Feb.	2	7	27
Mar.	10	9	10	Mar.	17	19	19	Mar.	25	20	58	Mar.	3	17	36
Apr.	8	20	32	Apr.	16	14	37	Apr.	24	10	6	Apr.	2	0	50
May	8	8	45	May	16	8	57	May	23	20	18	May	1	6	24
June	6	21	55	June	15	1	22	June	22	4	14	May	30	11	47
July	6	12	2	July	14	15	20	July	21	11	00	June	28	18	23
Aug.	5	3	5	Aug.	13	2	38	Aug.	19	17	53	July	28	3	19
Sept.	3	18	45	Sept.	11	11	37	Sept.	18	2	1	Aug.	26	15	18
Oct.	3	10	28	Oct.	10	19	1	Oct.	17	12	14	Sept.	25	6	41
Nov.	2	1	25	Nov.	9	1	57	Nov.	16	0	57	Oct.	25	1	17
Dec.	1	15	1	Dec.	8	9	36	Dec.	15	16	15	Nov.	23	22	11
Dec.	31	3	12									Dec.	23	19	36

Searching for Planets

People have known of the existence of the 5 planets closest to the Sun since ancient times because they could be seen with the naked eye. However, the 3 farthest were discovered only since the invention of the telescope. The first, Uranus, was discovered in 1781 by the English astronomer William Herschel. Next, Neptune's existence and location were predicted through its action upon Uranus, by both John Couch Adams of England and Urbain Jean Joseph Le Verrier of France in 1845, leading to its discovery the following year. Finally, Pluto was discovered in 1930 by the American astronomer Clyde Tombaugh. Since then, many smaller objects have been found in the solar system, but none that are commonly classified as true planets.

During the last 10 years of the 20th century, astronomers did, however, begin to detect the presence of planets orbiting stars other than the Sun. As of yet, they have not seen those objects, but merely infer their existence by their effect on their parent star. The Sun is a typical star in many respects. With over 200 billion stars in the Milky Way, it seems plausible that many other stars might have planets.

Using the Doppler Effect to detect radial velocity changes in the motions of individual stars, astronomers are more likely to find high-mass planets in close and eccentric orbits around stars, because that situation produces larger and more noticeable changes. As of mid-2004, astronomers had found 122 planets in 107 star systems where the planets are less than 13 times the mass of Jupiter (which is 318 times the mass of Earth). About 30 star systems may have planets less massive than Jupiter. In August 2004 separate teams of astronomers reported detecting planets that compared with Neptune and Uranus in mass, except that they orbited much closer to their parent stars, taking less than 10 days to complete one orbit.

In addition to the radial velocity method, astronomers are now using an optical gravitational lensing means of detecting extrasolar planets. Three detections by this method have been confirmed by radial velocity measurements. The star Upsilon Andromedae seems to have 3 planets, with masses 0.69, 1.19, and 3.75 times the mass of Jupiter, yet 2 of the planets are closer to their star than Earth is to the Sun. Astronomers are puzzled as to how such large planets can exist so close to a star.

Solar System Debris: Asteroids, Comets, Kuiper Belt, and the Oort Cloud

Asteroids

Besides planets, many smaller objects orbit the sun. **Asteroids** or minor planets are found mainly between the orbits of Mars and Jupiter, but some may be found outside this region. Though most are very small, the largest asteroid, Ceres, discovered in 1801, is larger than most of the solar system's moons. It is smaller than any of the planets, but was initially assumed to be one. However, the next year Pallas was discovered, which led to a search for other such objects. This brought about the creation of a new classification—asteroids or minor planets. Some asteroids are gravitationally locked with Jupiter and the Sun so that they have roughly the same orbit as Jupiter but either 60° ahead or behind the planet. These are the **Trojan asteroids.** Many of the smaller moons

of the solar system, especially those in retrograde orbits, may be captured asteroids. Asteroids whose orbits either cross or come close to the Earth's orbit are labeled **Near Earth Asteroids** or NEAs. A handful of asteroids have actually been imaged, including 1998JM8 by the Arecibo and Goldstone radio telescopes, and Eros by the NEAR Shoemaker space probe, while the *Galileo* spacecraft imaged both Gaspra and Ida (including its moon Dactyl) on its way to Jupiter.

Comets

Comets are small icy bodies in orbit around the Sun. When they approach the Sun, the energy from the Sun boils off material from the icy nucleus, producing an enlarged head (or coma), and in many cases an extended tail. Because

of the proximity to the Sun and the expanded head and tail, comets are brighter when near the Sun. For large comets, the head may be a 100,000 mi across and the tail more than a million mi long, though both are mainly empty space.

Comets have been known since ancient times; centuries later, British astronomer Edmund Halley (1656-1742) realized that a group of historical reports were just repeated visits of the same object. Comets are the only astronomical objects named after their discoverers. In 1986, the European spacecraft *Giotto* took the first close-up images of a comet's nucleus, specifically of Comet Halley, showing it had a peanut-shaped nucleus whose longest dimension was about 10 mi.

In 1995, Alan Hale and Thomas Bopp independently discovered a comet that was then beyond the orbit of Jupiter. It was the farthest comet ever discovered by amateurs and one of the brightest of all time. It also holds the record for length of naked-eye visibility—19 months—and is the most photographed comet in history.

In Sept. 2001, NASA's *Deep Space 1* flew within 1,500 mi of the Comet Borrelly and took pictures of the 6-mi-long nucleus of the comet. On Jan. 2, 2004, NASA's *Stardust* spacecraft flew within 150 mi of Comet Wild 2 taking pictures and capturing thousands of tiny cometary particles, which are scheduled to be returned to Earth in early 2006. On July 4, 2005, NASA's *Deep Impact 2* was scheduled to drop an impact probe into Comet Tempel 1. It will plunge into the nucleus at nearly 23,000 mph, hopefully producing a soccer-field-size crater as much as 150 ft deep. The main spacecraft will record images.

Kuiper Belt; Sedna

The **Kuiper Belt** is a donut-shaped region that extends from 30 to 100 AU from the Sun and is thought to be the source for short-period comets such as Comet Halley or Comet Swift-Tuttle. The more than 800 objects found in this region in recent years are called Kuiper Belt Objects (KBOs). It is estimated that there are more than 70,000 objects 60 mi in diameter or larger within the Kuiper Belt. A sub-group called Plutinos have physical and orbital characteristics similar to Pluto, except that they are smaller. Not including Pluto, there are 7 KBOs larger than 500 mi in diameter.

In Nov. 2003 astronomers detected the most distant object yet seen within our solar system, 90 AU away. This object, a planetoid or KBO, was named **Sedna**, in honor of the Inuit goddess of the sea. Sedna may be as large as about 1,000 mi in diameter (still, however, not large enough to be generally considered a planet by astronomers). It has a very elliptical orbit, at its most distant about 880 AU from the Sun and at its closest about 76 AU. Its semimajor axis is 480 AU and it has an orbital period of 10,500 yrs, compared to Pluto's orbital period of 248 yrs. Sedna travels well beyond what is considered the traditional region of the Kuiper Belt and yet it is well short of being part of the Oort Cloud. It is likely that this large object originally formed among the giant planets or in the inner parts of the Kuiper Belt and was later ejected to its present location.

Oort Cloud

The Oort Cloud is a vast spherical shell hypothesized to exist around the Sun. Astronomer Jan Oort proposed its existence as the origin for long-period comets that enter the inner part of the solar system where the planets orbit. As of yet, our technology is not sufficient to detect any members of the Oort Cloud, other than those comets that have been observed that indicate the most distant parts of their orbits may reach out to 50,000 AU. Recent examples of such long-period comets are Comet Hale-Bopp and Comet Hyakutake.

Earth: Size, Computation of Time, Seasons

Distance from the Sun	
Perihelion	91.4 mil mi
Semi-major axis	1.0000 AU
Aphelion	94.5 mil mi
Period of revolution	365.256 d
Orbital eccentricity	0.0167
Orbital inclination	0.0°
Sidereal day (rotation period)	23h 56m 4.2s
Synodic day (midday to midday)	24h 0m 0s
Rotational inclination	23.45°
Mass (Earth = 1)	1.00
Mean radius	3,958.8 mi
Mean density (Earth = 1)	1.00
Natural satellites	1
Average surface temperature	59° F

Earth is the 5th-largest planet and the 3rd from the Sun. Its mass is 6,585,000,000,000,000,000,000 tons. Earth's equatorial diameter is 7,926 miles while its polar diameter is only 7,900 miles.

Size and Dimensions

Earth is considered a solid mass, yet it has a large, liquid iron, **magnetic core** with a radius of about 2,160 miles. Surprisingly, it has a solid **inner core** that may be a large iron crystal, with a radius of 760 miles. Around the core is a thick shell, or **mantle**, of dense rock. This mantle is composed of materials rich in iron and magnesium. It is somewhat plastic-like, and under slow steady pressure, it can flow like a liquid. The mantle, in turn, is covered by a thin **crust** forming the solid granite and basalt base of the continents and ocean basins. Over broad areas of Earth's surface, the crust has a thin cover of sedimentary rock such as sandstone, shale, and limestone formed by weathering and by deposits of sands, clays, and plant and animal remains.

The **temperature** inside the Earth increases about 1° F with every 100 to 200 feet in depth, in the upper 100 km of Earth, and reaches nearly 8,000-9,000° F at the center. The heat is believed to come from radioactivity in rocks, pressures within Earth, and the original heat of formation.

Atmosphere of Earth

Earth's atmosphere is a blanket composed of nitrogen, oxygen, and argon, in amounts of about 78%, 21%, and 1% by volume. Present in minute quantities are carbon dioxide, hydrogen, neon, helium, krypton, and xenon. Water vapor displaces other gases and varies from nearly zero to about 4% by volume. The atmosphere rests on Earth's surface with a weight equivalent to a layer of water 34 feet deep. For about 300,000 feet upward, the gases remain in the proportions stated. Gravity holds the gases to Earth. The weight of the air compresses it at the bottom so that the greatest density is at Earth's surface. Pressure and density decrease as height increases.

The lowest layer of the atmosphere extending up about 7.5 mi is the **troposphere**, which contains 90% of the air and the tallest mountains. This is also where most weather phenomena occur. The temperature drops with increasing height throughout this layer. The atmosphere for about 23 miles above the troposphere is the **stratosphere**, where the temperature generally increases with height. The stratosphere contains **ozone**, which prevents ultraviolet rays from reaching Earth's surface. Since there is very little convection in the stratosphere, jets regularly cruise in the lower parts to provide a smoother ride for passengers.

Above the stratosphere is the **mesosphere**, where the temperature again decreases with height for another 19 mi. Extending above the mesosphere to the outer fringes of the atmosphere is the **thermosphere**, a region where temperature once more increases with height to a value measured in thousands of degrees Fahrenheit. The lower portion of this region, extending from 50 to about 400 mi in altitude, is characterized by a high ion density and is thus called the **ionosphere**. Most meteors are in the lower thermosphere or the mesosphere at the time they are observed.

Longitude, Latitude

Position on the globe is measured by meridians and parallels. Meridians, which are imaginary lines drawn around Earth through the poles, determine **longitude**. The meridian running through Greenwich, England, is the **prime meridian** of longitude, and all others are either E or W. Parallels, which are imaginary circles parallel with the equator, determine **latitude**. The length of a degree of longitude varies as the cosine of the latitude. At the equator a degree of longitude is 69.171 statute mi; this is gradually reduced toward the poles. Value of a longitude degree at the poles is zero.

Latitude is reckoned by the number of degrees N or S of the **equator**, an imaginary circle on Earth's surface everywhere equidistant between the two poles. According to the International Astronomical Union ellipsoid of 1964, the length of a degree of latitude is 68.708 statute mi at the equator and varies slightly N and S because of the oblate form of the globe; at the poles it is 69.403 statute mi.

Definitions of Time

Earth rotates on its axis and follows an elliptical orbit around the Sun. The rotation makes the Sun appear to move across the sky from E to W. This rotation determines day and night, and the complete rotation, in relation to the Sun, is called the **apparent** or **true solar day**. A sundial thus measures **apparent solar time**. This length of time varies, but an average determines the mean solar day of 24 hours.

The mean solar day and **mean solar time** are in universal use for civil purposes. Mean solar time may be obtained from apparent solar time by correcting observations of the Sun for the **equation of time**. Mean solar time may be up to 16 minutes different from apparent solar time.

Sidereal time is the measure of time defined by the diurnal motion of the vernal equinox and is determined from observation of the meridian transits of stars. One complete rotation of Earth relative to the equinox is called the **sidereal day**. The **mean sidereal day** is 23 hours, 56 minutes, 4.091 seconds of mean solar time.

The interval required for Earth to make one absolute revolution around the Sun is a **sidereal** year; it consisted of 365 days, 6 hours, 9 minutes, and 9.5 seconds of mean solar time (approximately 24 hours per day) in 1900 and has been increasing at the rate of 0.0001 second annually.

The **tropical year**, upon which our calendar is based, is the interval between 2 consecutive returns of the Sun to the vernal equinox. The tropical year consisted of 365 days, 5 hours, 48 minutes, and 46 seconds in 1900. It has been decreasing at the rate of 0.530 second per century. The **calendar year** begins at 12 o'clock midnight precisely, local clock time, on the night of Dec. 31-Jan. 1. The day and the calendar month also begin at midnight by the clock.

On Jan. 1, 1972, the Bureau International des Poids et Mesures in Paris introduced **International Atomic Time** (TAI) as the most precisely determined time scale for astronomical usage. The fundamental unit of TAI in the international system of units is the second, defined as the duration of 9,192,631,770 periods of the radiation corresponding to the transition between 2 hyperfine levels of the ground state of the cesium 133 atom. **Coordinated Universal Time** (UTC), which serves as the basis for civil timekeeping and is the standard time of the prime meridian, is officially defined by a formula which relates UTC to mean sidereal time in Greenwich, England. (UTC has replaced GMT as the basis for standard time for the world.)

The Zones and Seasons

The 5 zones of Earth's surface are the Torrid, lying between the Tropics of Cancer and Capricorn; the N Temperate, between Cancer and the Arctic Circle; the S Temperate, between Capricorn and the Antarctic Circle; and the 2 Frigid Zones, between the Polar Circles and the Poles.

The inclination, or **tilt**, of Earth's axis, 23° 27′ away from a perpendicular to Earth's orbit of the Sun, determines the seasons. These are commonly marked in the N Temperate Zone, where spring begins at the vernal equinox, summer at the summer solstice, autumn at the autumnal equinox, and winter at the winter solstice. In the S Temperate Zone, the seasons are reversed. Spring begins at the autumnal equinox, summer at the winter solstice, etc.

The points at which the Sun crosses the equator are the **equinoxes**, when day and night are most nearly equal. The points at which the Sun is at a maximum distance from the equator are the **solstices**. Days and nights are then most unequal. However, at the equator, day and night are equal throughout the year.

In June, the North Pole is tilted 23° 27′ toward the Sun, and the days in the northern hemisphere are longer than the nights, while the days in the southern hemisphere are shorter

than the nights. In Dec., the North Pole is tilted 23° 27′ away from the Sun, and the situation is reversed.

The Seasons in 2005

In 2005 the 4 seasons begin in the northern hemisphere as shown. (Add 1 hour to Eastern Standard Time for Atlantic Time; subtract 1 hour for Central, 2 for Mountain, 3 for Pacific, 4 for Alaska, 5 for Hawaii-Aleutian. Also shown is Coordinated Universal Time.)

Seasons	Date	EST/EDT*	UTC
Vernal Equinox (spring)	Mar. 20	7:33	12:33
Northern Solstice (summer)	June 21	2:46*	6:46
Autumnal Equinox (autumn)	Sept. 22	18:23*	22:3
Southern Solstice (winter)	Dec. 21	13:35	18:35

Poles of Earth

The geographic (rotation) poles, or points where Earth's axis of rotation cuts the surface, are not absolutely fixed in the body of Earth. The pole of rotation describes an irregular curve about its mean position.

Two periods have been detected in this motion: (1) an annual period due to seasonal changes in barometric pressure, to load of ice and snow on the surface, and to other seasonal phenomena; (2) a period of about 14 months due to the shape and constitution of Earth. In addition, there are small but as yet unpredictable irregularities. The whole motion is so small that the actual pole at any time remains within a circle of 30 or 40 feet in radius centered at the mean position of the pole.

The pole of rotation for the time being is of course the pole having a latitude of 90° and an indeterminate longitude.

Magnetic Poles

Although Earth's magnetic field resembles that of an ordinary bar magnet, this magnetic field is probably produced by electric currents in the liquid currents of the Earth's outer core. The **north magnetic pole** of Earth is that region where the magnetic force is vertically downward, and the **south magnetic pole** is that region where the magnetic force is vertically upward. A compass placed at the magnetic poles experiences no directive force in azimuth (i.e., direction).

There are slow changes in the distribution of Earth's magnetic field. This slow temporal change is referred to as the secular change of the main magnetic field, and the magnetic poles shift due to this. The location of the N magnetic pole was first measured in 1831 at Cape Adelaide on the west coast of Boothia Peninsula in Canada's Northwest Territories (about latitude 70° N and longitude 96° W). Since then it has moved over 500 miles. It is now estimated to be at 83° N and 114°W, northwest of Ellef Ringnes Island in N Canada. Measurement for several decades by Canadian scientists indicates the motion of the pole has accelerated, now averaging about 25 mi per year.

The direction of the horizontal components of the magnetic field at any point is known as magnetic N at that point, and the angle by which it deviates E or W of true N is known as the magnetic declination.

A compass without error points in the direction of magnetic north. (In general, this is not the direction of the true rotational north pole.) If you follow the direction indicated by the N end of the compass, you will go along an irregular curve that eventually reaches the north magnetic pole (though not usually by a great-circle route). However, the action of the compass should not be thought of as due to any influence of the distant pole, but simply as an indication of the distribution of Earth's magnetism at the place of observation.

Rotation of Earth

The speed of rotation of Earth about its axis is slightly variable. The variations may be classified as:

(A) **Secular**. Tidal friction acts as a brake on the rotation and causes a slow secular increase in the length of the day, about 1 millisecond per century.

(B) **Irregular**. The speed of rotation may increase for a number of years, about 5 to 10, and then start decreasing. The maximum difference from the mean in the length of the day during a century is about 5 milliseconds. The accumulated difference in time has amounted to approximately 44

seconds since 1900. The cause is probably motion in the interior of Earth.

(C) **Periodic**. Seasonal variations exist with periods of 1 year and 6 months. The cumulative effect is such that each year, Earth is late about 30 milliseconds near June 1 and is ahead about 30 milliseconds near Oct. 1. The maximum seasonal variation in the length of the day is about 0.5 millisecond. It is believed that the principal cause of the annual variation is the seasonal change in the wind patterns of the northern and southern hemispheres. The semiannual varia-

tion is due chiefly to tidal action of the Sun, which distorts the shape of Earth slightly.

The secular and irregular variations were discovered by comparing time based on the rotation of Earth with time based on the orbital motion of the Moon about Earth and of the planets about the Sun. The periodic variation was determined largely with the aid of quartz-crystal clocks. The introduction of the cesium-beam atomic clock in 1955 made it possible to determine in greater detail than before the nature of the irregular and periodic variations.

Calculation of Rise Times

The Daily Calendar on pages 369-380 contain rise and set times for the Sun and Moon for the Greenwich Meridian at N latitudes 20°, 30°, 40°, 50°, and 60°. From day to day, the values for the Sun at any particular latitude do not change very much. This means that whatever time the Sun rises or sets at the 0° meridian, it will rise or set at the same time at the Standard Time meridian of your time zone. Standard Time meridians occur every 15° of longitude (15° E and W, 30° E and W, etc.). The corrections necessary to observe that event from your location will be to account for your distance from the Standard Time meridian and for your latitude. Thus, if your latitude is about 45°, sunrise on Jan. 1, 2000, is roughly halfway between 7:22 and 7:59 A.M. on the Standard Time meridian for your time zone. If you are 7.5° west of your Standard Time meridian, sunrise will be about ½ hour later than this; if 7.5° east, about ½ hour earlier.

The Moon, however, moves its own diameter, about one-half degree, in an hour, or about 13.2° in one complete turn of Earth—one day. Most of this is eastward against the background stars of the sky, but some is also N or S movement. All this motion considerably affects the times of rise or set, as you can see from the adjacent entries in the table. Thus, it is necessary to take your longitude into account in addition to your latitude. If you have no need for total accuracy, simply note that the time will be between the 4 values (see example below) you find surrounding your location and the dates of interest.

The process of finding more accurate corrections is called interpolation. In the example, linear interpolation involving simple differences is used. In extreme cases, higher order interpolation should be used. If such cases are important to you, it is suggested that you plot the times, draw smooth curves through the plots, and interpolate by eye between the relevant curves. Some people find this exercise fun.

Let's find the times of the moonset for the July Full Moon and sunrise the same day at Atlanta, GA.

First, where is Atlanta, GA? Find Atlanta's latitude and longitude in the "Latitude, Longitude, and Altitude of U.S. and Canadian Cities" table found in the World Exploration and Geography section of *The World Almanac*. You must also know the time zone in which the city is located, which you can estimate from the "International Time Zones" map in the map section of *The World Almanac*.

I.   Atlanta, GA: 33° 44′ 56″ N
     84° 23′ 17″ W

IA. Convert these values to decimals:
     56/60 = 0.93
     44 + 0.93 = 44.93
     44.93/60 = 0.75
     33 + 0.75 = 33.75 N
     17/60 = 0.28
     23 + 0.28 = 23.28
     23.28/60 = 0.39
     84 + 0.39 = 84.39 W

IB. Fraction Atlanta lies between 30° and 40°:
     33.75 − 30 = 3.75; 3.75/10 = 0.375

IC. Fraction world must turn between Greenwich and Atlanta:
     84.39/360 = 0.234

ID. Atlanta is in the Eastern Standard Time zone and the EST meridian is 75°; thus 84.39 is 84.39 − 75 = 9.39° W of the Eastern Standard Meridian. In 24 hours, there are 24 x 60 = 1,440 minutes; 1,440/360 = 4 minutes for every degree around Earth. So events happen 4 x 9.39 = 37.6 minutes later in Atlanta than at the 75° meridian. (If the location is E of the Standard Meridian, events happen earlier.)

IE. The values IB and IC are interpolates for Atlanta; ID is the time correction from local to Standard time for Atlanta. These values need never be calculated again for Atlanta.

IIA. To find the time of moonset we start from the table of Moon Phases, 2005. We see that July's Full Moon occurs on July 21. We need the Greenwich times for moonset at latitudes 30° and 40°, and for July 21 and 22, the day of the Full Moon and the next day. These values are found in the Astronomy Daily Calendar 2005; we then compute the difference between the two latitudes.

	30°	Diff.	40°
July 21	4:48	−0:33	4:15
July 22	6:04	−0:27	5:37

IIB. We want IB and the July 21 time difference:
     0.375 x −33 = −12.4

Add this to the July 21, 30° set time:
     4:48 + (−12.4) = 4:35.6
And for July 22:
     0.375 x −27 = −10.1
Add this to the July 22, 30° set time:
     6:04 + (−10.1) = 5:53.9
These 2 times are for the latitude of Atlanta, but for the Greenwich meridian.

IIC. To get the time for Atlanta meridian, take the difference between these 2 times just determined,
     5:53.9 − 4:35.6 = 78.3 minutes,
and calculate what fraction of this 24-hour change took place while Earth turned between Greenwich and Atlanta (See IC).
     78.3 x 0.234 = 18.3 minutes after 4:35.6
Thus 4:35.6 + 18.3 = 4:53.9 is the time the Full Moon will set in the local time of Atlanta.

IID. But this happens 37.6 minutes (See ID) later by EST clock time at Atlanta, thus
     4:53.9 + 37.6 = 5:31.5 EST
But this is summer, and daylight time is in effect;
     5:31.5 + 1:00 = 6:32 EDT is the set time for the Full Moon at Atlanta the morning of July 21, 2005.

IIIA. To find the time of sunrise we need the Greenwich times for sunrise at latitudes 30° and 40°. These values are found in the Astronomy Daily Calendar 2005; we then compute the difference between the two latitudes.

	30°	Diff.	40°
July 21	5:12	−0:23	4:49

IIIB. We want IB and the July 21 time difference:
     0.375 x −23 = −8.6
Add this to the July 21, 30° rise time:
     5:12 + (−8.6) = 5:03.4
This is the local time for the latitude of Atlanta.

IIIC. But this happens 37.6 minutes (See ID) later by EST clock time at Atlanta, thus
     5:03.4 + 37.6 = 5:41
But daylight time is in effect;
     5:41 + 1:00 = 6:41 is sunrise at Atlanta on July 21, 2005.

JANUARY 2005

1st Month   **31 days**

Coordinated Universal Time (Greenwich Mean Time)

NOTE: For each day, numbers on first line indicate Sun; numbers on second line indicate Moon.

Degrees are North Latitude.

Moon Phases: FM = Full Moon; LQ = Last (Waning) Quarter; NM = New Moon; FQ = First (Waxing) Quarter;

Sun's distance is in Astronomical Units

CAUTION: Must be converted to local time. For instructions see "Calculation of Rise Times," page 368.

Day of month, of week, of year	Sun on Meridian / Moon Phase h m s	Sun's Declination ° ′ / Distance	20° Rise Sun/Moon h m	20° Set Sun/Moon h m	30° Rise Sun/Moon h m	30° Set Sun/Moon h m	40° Rise Sun/Moon h m	40° Set Sun/Moon h m	50° Rise Sun/Moon h m	50° Set Sun/Moon h m	60° Rise Sun/Moon h m	60° Set Sun/Moon h m
1 SA	12 03 40	− 23 01	6 35	17 32	6 56	17 11	7 22	16 46	7 59	16 09	9 02	15 05
1		.9833	22 35	10 38	22 30	10 46	22 23	10 56	22 13	11 09	21 58	11 29
2 SU	12 04 08	− 22 56	6 36	17 33	6 56	17 12	7 22	16 46	7 58	16 10	9 02	15 07
2		.9833	23 22	11 10	23 26	11 13	23 25	11 17	23 25	11 22	23 24	11 29
3 MO	12 04 35	− 22 50	6 36	17 33	6 56	17 13	7 22	16 47	7 58	16 11	9 01	15 08
3	17 46 LQ	.9833	none	11 43	none	11 41	none	11 38	none	11 34	none	11 28
4 TU	12 05 03	− 22 44	6 36	17 34	6 57	17 14	7 22	16 48	7 58	16 12	9 00	15 10
4		.9833	0 18	12 18	0 23	12 10	0 30	12 00	0 39	11 48	0 53	11 28
5 WE	12 05 30	− 22 38	6 36	17 35	6 57	17 14	7 22	16 49	7 58	16 13	9 00	15 12
5		.9833	1 13	12 55	1 24	12 42	1 38	12 26	1 56	12 04	2 26	11 29
6 TH	12 05 56	− 22 31	6 37	17 35	6 57	17 15	7 22	16 50	7 58	16 15	8 59	15 14
6		.9833	2 12	13 38	2 29	13 20	2 50	12 56	3 19	12 24	4 08	11 31
7 FR	12 06 22	− 22 23	6 37	17 36	6 57	17 16	7 22	16 51	7 57	16 16	8 58	15 15
7		.9834	3 16	14 28	3 38	14 05	4 06	13 35	4 46	12 52	6 00	11 36
8 SA	12 06 48	− 22 15	6 37	17 37	6 57	17 17	7 22	16 52	7 57	16 17	8 57	15 17
8		.9834	4 24	15 27	4 50	15 00	5 24	14 25	6 13	13 34	7 55	11 51
9 SU	12 07 13	− 22 07	6 37	17 37	6 57	17 18	7 22	16 53	7 56	16 18	8 56	15 19
9		.9834	5 34	16 33	6 02	16 05	6 38	15 29	7 32	14 35	9 30	12 37
10 MO	12 07 37	− 21 58	6 37	17 38	6 57	17 18	7 22	16 54	7 56	16 20	8 54	15 21
10	12 03 NM	.9834	6 41	17 44	7 08	17 18	7 42	16 44	8 33	15 54	10 17	14 13
11 TU	12 08 01	− 21 49	6 38	17 39	6 57	17 19	7 21	16 55	7 55	16 21	8 53	15 23
11		.9835	7 41	18 55	8 04	18 33	8 34	18 05	9 17	17 25	10 33	16 13
12 WE	12 08 24	− 21 40	6 38	17 39	6 57	17 20	7 21	16 56	7 55	16 22	8 52	15 25
12		.9835	8 33	20 02	8 52	19 46	9 15	19 26	9 46	18 58	10 38	18 10
13 TH	12 08 47	− 21 30	6 38	17 40	6 57	17 21	7 21	16 57	7 54	16 24	8 50	15 28
13		.9836	9 19	21 05	9 31	20 55	9 47	20 43	10 08	20 26	10 40	19 59
14 FR	12 09 09	− 21 19	6 38	17 41	6 57	17 22	7 20	16 58	7 53	16 25	8 49	15 30
14		.9836	9 59	22 04	10 06	22 00	10 14	21 56	10 24	21 49	10 41	21 39
15 SA	12 09 30	− 21 09	6 38	17 41	6 57	17 23	7 20	16 59	7 53	16 27	8 48	15 32
15		.9837	10 36	23 00	10 37	23 02	10 38	23 05	10 39	23 08	10 41	23 14
16 SU	12 09 51	− 20 57	6 38	17 42	6 57	17 23	7 20	17 00	7 52	16 28	8 46	15 34
16		.9837	11 11	23 54	11 06	none	11 00	none	10 52	none	10 41	none
17 MO	12 10 11	− 20 46	6 38	17 43	6 56	17 24	7 19	17 02	7 51	16 30	8 44	15 37
17	06 57 FQ	.9838	11 46	none	11 36	0 02	11 23	0 11	11 07	0 24	10 41	0 45
18 TU	12 10 30	− 20 34	6 38	17 43	6 56	17 25	7 19	17 03	7 50	16 31	8 43	15 39
18		.9839	12 22	0 47	12 07	1 00	11 48	1 17	11 22	1 39	10 42	2 16
19 WE	12 10 48	− 20 22	6 38	17 44	6 56	17 26	7 18	17 04	7 49	16 33	8 41	15 41
19		.9839	13 01	1 41	12 41	1 59	12 16	2 22	11 42	2 54	10 44	3 48
20 TH	12 11 06	− 20 09	6 38	17 45	6 56	17 27	7 18	17 05	7 48	16 34	8 39	15 44
20		.9840	13 43	2 35	13 19	2 57	12 49	3 26	12 06	4 07	10 49	5 21
21 FR	12 11 23	− 19 56	6 38	17 45	6 55	17 28	7 17	17 06	7 47	16 36	8 37	15 46
21		.9841	14 28	3 29	14 02	3 55	13 28	4 28	12 39	5 16	11 02	6 52
22 SA	12 11 39	− 19 42	6 38	17 46	6 55	17 29	7 16	17 07	7 46	16 38	8 35	15 49
22		.9842	15 18	4 23	14 50	4 51	14 15	5 26	13 22	6 18	11 30	8 10
23 SU	12 11 54	− 19 28	6 38	17 46	6 55	17 29	7 16	17 08	7 45	16 39	8 33	15 51
23		.9843	16 10	5 15	15 43	5 42	15 08	6 18	14 16	7 10	12 27	9 00
24 MO	12 12 09	− 19 14	6 37	17 47	6 54	17 30	7 15	17 10	7 44	16 41	8 31	15 54
24		.9844	17 04	6 03	16 39	6 29	16 07	7 02	15 20	7 50	13 49	9 23
25 TU	12 12 23	− 18 59	6 37	17 48	6 54	17 31	7 14	17 11	7 43	16 43	8 29	15 56
25	10 32 FM	.9845	17 57	6 47	17 36	7 10	17 08	7 39	16 29	8 20	15 19	9 33
26 WE	12 12 36	− 18 45	6 37	17 48	6 53	17 32	7 14	17 12	7 42	16 44	8 27	15 59
26		.9846	18 50	7 28	18 33	7 47	18 11	8 10	17 41	8 43	16 50	9 38
27 TH	12 12 48	− 18 29	6 37	17 49	6 53	17 33	7 13	17 13	7 40	16 46	8 25	16 01
27		.9847	19 42	8 05	19 29	8 19	19 14	8 37	18 53	9 01	18 18	9 39
28 FR	12 12 59	− 18 14	6 37	17 50	6 52	17 34	7 12	17 14	7 39	16 48	8 23	16 04
28		.9848	20 32	8 39	20 25	8 49	20 16	9 00	20 04	9 16	19 45	9 40
29 SA	12 13 10	− 17 58	6 36	17 50	6 52	17 35	7 11	17 16	7 38	16 49	8 21	16 07
29		.9849	21 22	9 12	21 20	9 16	21 18	9 22	21 15	9 29	21 10	9 39
30 SU	12 13 19	− 17 41	6 36	17 51	6 51	17 36	7 10	17 17	7 36	16 51	8 18	16 09
30		.9851	22 13	9 44	22 17	9 43	22 21	9 42	22 27	9 41	22 37	9 39
31 MO	12 13 28	− 17 25	6 36	17 51	6 51	17 36	7 09	17 18	7 35	16 53	8 16	16 12
31		.9852	23 06	10 17	23 15	10 11	23 26	10 04	23 42	9 54	none	9 38

FEBRUARY 2005

2nd Month   **28 days**

Coordinated Universal Time (Greenwich Mean Time)

NOTE: For each day, numbers on first line indicate Sun; numbers on second line indicate Moon.

Degrees are North Latitude.

Moon Phases: FM = Full Moon; LQ = Last (Waning) Quarter; NM = New Moon; FQ = First (Waxing) Quarter;

Sun's distance is in Astronomical Units

CAUTION: Must be converted to local time. For instructions see "Calculation of Rise Times," page 368.

Day of month, of week, of year	Sun on Meridian / Moon Phase (h m s)	Sun's Declination ° ' / Distance	20° Rise Sun/Moon	20° Set Sun/Moon	30° Rise Sun/Moon	30° Set Sun/Moon	40° Rise Sun/Moon	40° Set Sun/Moon	50° Rise Sun/Moon	50° Set Sun/Moon	60° Rise Sun/Moon	60° Set Sun/Moon
1 TU	12 13 36	− 17 08	6 35	17 52	6 50	17 37	7 09	17 19	7 33	16 54	8 14	16 14
32		.9854	none	10 53	none	10 41	none	10 27	none	10 08	0 07	9 38
2 WE	12 13 44	− 16 51	6 35	17 53	6 50	17 38	7 08	17 20	7 32	16 56	8 11	16 17
33	07 27 LQ	.9855	0 02	11 32	0 16	11 15	0 34	10 54	1 00	10 26	1 43	9 39
3 TH	12 13 50	− 16 33	6 35	17 53	6 49	17 39	7 07	17 22	7 31	16 58	8 09	16 20
34		.9857	1 01	12 17	1 21	11 55	1 47	11 28	2 23	10 49	3 26	9 42
4 FR	12 13 56	− 16 16	6 34	17 54	6 48	17 40	7 06	17 23	7 29	16 59	8 06	16 22
35		.9858	2 05	13 10	2 30	12 44	3 01	12 11	3 47	11 23	5 17	9 51
5 SA	12 14 01	− 15 58	6 34	17 54	6 48	17 41	7 05	17 24	7 27	17 01	8 04	16 25
36		.9860	3 12	14 10	3 39	13 42	4 15	13 06	5 08	12 12	7 03	10 17
6 SU	12 14 05	− 15 39	6 34	17 55	6 47	17 41	7 03	17 25	7 26	17 03	8 01	16 28
37		.9862	4 18	15 17	4 46	14 50	5 23	14 14	6 16	13 21	8 12	11 26
7 MO	12 14 09	− 15 21	6 33	17 55	6 46	17 42	7 02	17 26	7 24	17 05	7 59	16 30
38		.9863	5 21	16 28	5 47	16 03	6 20	15 32	7 07	14 46	8 38	13 18
8 TU	12 14 11	− 15 02	6 33	17 56	6 46	17 43	7 01	17 28	7 23	17 06	7 56	16 33
39	22 28 NM	.9865	6 17	17 37	6 38	17 18	7 05	16 54	7 43	16 19	8 47	15 19
9 WE	12 14 13	− 14 43	6 32	17 56	6 45	17 44	7 00	17 29	7 21	17 08	7 54	16 36
40		.9867	7 06	18 44	7 22	18 31	7 41	18 14	8 08	17 51	8 50	17 14
10 TH	12 14 14	− 14 23	6 32	17 57	6 44	17 45	6 59	17 30	7 19	17 10	7 51	16 38
41		.9868	7 50	19 46	7 59	19 39	8 11	19 31	8 27	19 19	8 51	19 01
11 FR	12 14 14	− 14 04	6 31	17 57	6 43	17 46	6 58	17 31	7 18	17 12	7 49	16 41
42		.9870	8 29	20 45	8 33	20 45	8 37	20 44	8 43	20 43	8 51	20 42
12 SA	12 14 14	− 13 44	6 31	17 58	6 42	17 46	6 57	17 32	7 16	17 13	7 46	16 43
43		.9872	9 06	21 42	9 04	21 47	9 01	21 54	8 57	22 03	8 51	22 18
13 SU	12 14 13	− 13 24	6 30	17 58	6 42	17 47	6 55	17 34	7 14	17 15	7 43	16 46
44		.9874	9 42	22 37	9 34	22 49	9 24	23 03	9 11	23 22	8 51	23 53
14 MO	12 14 11	− 13 04	6 30	17 59	6 41	17 48	6 54	17 35	7 12	17 17	7 41	16 49
45		.9876	10 19	23 32	10 06	23 49	9 49	none	9 26	none	8 51	none
15 TU	12 14 08	− 12 43	6 29	17 59	6 40	17 49	6 53	17 36	7 11	17 18	7 38	16 51
46		.9878	10 58	none	10 39	none	10 16	0 10	9 45	0 39	8 52	1 27
16 WE	12 14 04	− 12 22	6 29	18 00	6 39	17 50	6 52	17 37	7 09	17 20	7 35	16 54
47	00 16 FQ	.9879	11 39	0 28	11 16	0 49	10 48	1 16	10 07	1 54	8 56	3 03
17 TH	12 14 00	− 12 01	6 28	18 00	6 38	17 50	6 50	17 38	7 07	17 22	7 32	16 57
48		.9881	12 24	1 23	11 58	1 48	11 25	2 20	10 37	3 06	9 05	4 37
18 FR	12 13 55	− 11 40	6 27	18 01	6 37	17 51	6 49	17 39	7 05	17 24	7 30	16 59
49		.9883	13 12	2 17	12 45	2 45	12 09	3 20	11 17	4 12	9 26	6 02
19 SA	12 13 49	− 11 19	6 27	18 01	6 36	17 52	6 48	17 41	7 03	17 25	7 27	17 02
50		.9886	14 04	3 10	13 36	3 38	13 00	4 14	12 07	5 07	10 13	7 02
20 SU	12 13 43	− 10 58	6 26	18 02	6 35	17 53	6 46	17 42	7 01	17 27	7 24	17 04
51		.9888	14 57	4 00	14 31	4 26	13 58	5 01	13 09	5 51	11 29	7 32
21 MO	12 13 36	− 10 36	6 25	18 02	6 34	17 53	6 45	17 43	6 59	17 29	7 21	17 07
52		.9890	15 51	4 45	15 28	5 09	14 59	5 40	14 17	6 24	12 59	7 44
22 TU	12 13 28	− 10 14	6 25	18 02	6 33	17 54	6 44	17 44	6 57	17 30	7 18	17 10
53		.9892	16 44	5 27	16 26	5 47	16 02	6 13	15 28	6 49	14 31	7 49
23 WE	12 13 20	− 9 52	6 24	18 03	6 32	17 55	6 42	17 45	6 55	17 32	7 16	17 12
54		.9894	17 37	6 05	17 23	6 21	17 05	6 41	16 41	7 08	16 01	7 51
24 TH	12 13 11	− 9 30	6 23	18 03	6 31	17 56	6 41	17 46	6 53	17 34	7 13	17 15
55	04 54 FM	.9896	18 28	6 40	18 19	6 51	18 08	7 05	17 53	7 23	17 30	7 52
25 FR	12 13 02	− 9 08	6 23	18 04	6 30	17 56	6 39	17 47	6 51	17 35	7 10	17 17
56		.9899	19 19	7 14	19 15	7 20	19 11	7 27	19 05	7 37	18 56	7 51
26 SA	12 12 52	− 8 46	6 22	18 04	6 29	17 57	6 38	17 48	6 49	17 37	7 07	17 20
57		.9901	20 10	7 46	20 12	7 47	20 14	7 48	20 18	7 49	20 23	7 51
27 SU	12 12 41	− 8 23	6 21	18 04	6 28	17 58	6 36	17 50	6 47	17 39	7 04	17 22
58		.9903	21 02	8 19	21 10	8 14	21 19	8 09	21 32	8 01	21 52	7 50
28 MO	12 12 30	− 8 01	6 21	18 05	6 27	17 58	6 35	17 51	6 45	17 41	7 01	17 25
59		.9906	21 57	8 54	22 10	8 44	22 26	8 31	22 49	8 15	23 27	7 49

MARCH 2005

3rd Month　　　　　　　　　　　　　　　　　　　　　　　　　　　　**31 days**

Coordinated Universal Time (Greenwich Mean Time)

NOTE: For each day, numbers on first line indicate Sun; numbers on second line indicate Moon.

Degrees are North Latitude.

Moon Phases: FM = Full Moon; LQ = Last (Waning) Quarter; NM = New Moon; FQ = First (Waxing) Quarter

Sun's distance is in Astronomical Units

CAUTION: Must be converted to local time. For instructions see "Calculation of Rise Times," page 368.

Day of month, of week, of year	Sun on Meridian Moon Phase h m s	Sun's Declination ° ´ Distance	20° Rise Sun Moon h m	20° Set Sun Moon h m	30° Rise Sun Moon h m	30° Set Sun Moon h m	40° Rise Sun Moon h m	40° Set Sun Moon h m	50° Rise Sun Moon h m	50° Set Sun Moon h m	60° Rise Sun Moon h m	60° Set Sun Moon h m
1 TU	12 12 18	− 7 38	6 20	18 05	6 26	17 59	6 33	17 52	6 43	17 42	6 58	17 27
60		.9908	22 55	9 31	23 13	9 16	23 37	8 57	none	8 31	none	7 49
2 WE	12 12 06	− 7 15	6 19	18 05	6 25	18 00	6 32	17 53	6 41	17 44	6 55	17 30
61		.9911	23 56	10 14	none	9 53	none	9 28	0 10	8 52	1 07	7 51
3 TH	12 11 54	− 6 52	6 18	18 06	6 24	18 00	6 30	17 54	6 39	17 45	6 52	17 33
62	17 36 LQ	.9913	none	11 03	0 19	10 38	0 49	10 06	1 33	9 21	2 55	7 56
4 FR	12 11 41	− 6 29	6 18	18 06	6 23	18 01	6 29	17 55	6 37	17 47	6 50	17 35
63		.9916	1 00	11 58	1 27	11 31	2 02	10 55	2 53	10 02	4 43	8 12
5 SA	12 11 28	− 6 06	6 17	18 06	6 22	18 02	6 27	17 56	6 35	17 49	6 47	17 38
64		.9918	2 05	13 01	2 33	12 32	3 10	11 56	4 05	11 01	6 07	8 59
6 SU	12 11 14	− 5 43	6 16	18 07	6 20	18 02	6 26	17 57	6 33	17 50	6 44	17 40
65		.9921	3 07	14 08	3 34	13 41	4 09	13 08	5 00	12 18	6 45	10 35
7 MO	12 10 59	− 5 20	6 15	18 07	6 19	18 03	6 24	17 58	6 31	17 52	6 41	17 43
66		.9924	4 04	15 16	4 28	14 54	4 57	14 26	5 40	13 46	6 57	12 32
8 TU	12 10 45	− 4 56	6 14	18 07	6 18	18 04	6 23	17 59	6 29	17 54	6 38	17 45
67		.9926	4 55	16 22	5 13	16 06	5 36	15 46	6 09	15 17	7 02	14 28
9 WE	12 10 30	− 4 33	6 13	18 08	6 17	18 04	6 21	18 01	6 27	17 55	6 35	17 48
68		.9929	5 40	17 26	5 53	17 16	6 08	17 03	6 29	16 46	7 03	16 18
10 TH	12 10 15	− 4 09	6 13	18 08	6 16	18 05	6 20	18 02	6 24	17 57	6 32	17 50
69	09 10 NM	.9932	6 21	18 26	6 27	18 23	6 35	18 18	6 46	18 12	7 03	18 02
11 FR	12 09 59	− 3 46	6 12	18 08	6 15	18 06	6 18	18 03	6 22	17 59	6 29	17 53
70		.9934	6 59	19 25	6 59	19 27	7 00	19 31	7 01	19 35	7 02	19 41
12 SA	12 09 43	− 3 22	6 11	18 09	6 13	18 06	6 16	18 04	6 20	18 00	6 26	17 55
71		.9937	7 36	20 22	7 30	20 31	7 24	20 41	7 15	20 56	7 02	21 19
13 SU	12 09 27	− 2 58	6 10	18 09	6 12	18 07	6 15	18 05	6 18	18 02	6 23	17 57
72		.9940	8 13	21 19	8 02	21 33	7 48	21 51	7 30	22 16	7 02	22 56
14 MO	12 09 10	− 2 35	6 09	18 09	6 11	18 08	6 13	18 06	6 16	18 03	6 20	18 00
73		.9942	8 51	22 15	8 35	22 35	8 15	22 59	7 47	23 34	7 02	none
15 TU	12 08 54	− 2 11	6 08	18 10	6 10	18 08	6 12	18 07	6 14	18 05	6 17	18 02
74		.9945	9 33	23 12	9 11	23 36	8 45	none	8 08	none	7 04	0 35
16 WE	12 08 36	− 1 47	6 08	18 10	6 09	18 09	6 10	18 08	6 12	18 07	6 14	18 05
75		.9948	10 17	none	9 52	none	9 20	0 06	8 35	0 50	7 10	2 13
17 TH	12 08 19	− 1 24	6 07	18 10	6 08	18 10	6 08	18 09	6 09	18 08	6 11	18 07
76	19 19 FQ	.9950	11 05	0 08	10 37	0 35	10 02	1 09	9 11	2 00	7 24	3 46
18 FR	12 08 02	− 1 00	6 06	18 10	6 06	18 10	6 07	18 10	6 07	18 10	6 08	18 10
77		.9953	11 56	1 03	11 28	1 31	10 51	2 07	9 58	3 01	7 59	4 59
19 SA	12 07 44	− 0 36	6 05	18 11	6 05	18 11	6 05	18 11	6 05	18 11	6 05	18 12
78		.9956	12 49	1 54	12 22	2 21	11 47	2 57	10 55	3 49	9 06	5 39
20 SU	12 07 26	− 0 12	6 04	18 11	6 04	18 11	6 04	18 12	6 03	18 13	6 02	18 15
79		.9958	13 43	2 41	13 18	3 07	12 47	3 39	12 02	4 26	10 34	5 55
21 MO	12 07 09	+ 0 11	6 03	18 11	6 03	18 12	6 02	18 13	6 01	18 15	5 59	18 17
80		.9961	14 36	3 24	14 16	3 46	13 50	4 14	13 13	4 53	12 07	6 01
22 TU	12 06 51	+ 0 35	6 02	18 12	6 02	18 13	6 00	18 14	5 58	18 16	5 56	18 20
81		.9964	15 29	4 03	15 13	4 21	14 53	4 43	14 25	5 14	13 39	6 04
23 WE	12 06 32	+ 0 59	6 02	18 12	6 00	18 13	5 59	18 15	5 56	18 18	5 53	18 22
82		.9967	16 21	4 39	16 10	4 53	15 56	5 09	15 38	5 30	15 08	6 04
24 TH	12 06 14	+ 1 22	6 01	18 12	5 59	18 14	5 57	18 16	5 54	18 19	5 49	18 24
83		.9969	17 12	5 13	17 07	5 21	17 00	5 31	16 51	5 44	16 36	6 04
25 FR	12 05 56	+ 1 46	6 00	18 12	5 58	18 14	5 55	18 17	5 52	18 21	5 46	18 27
84	20 58 FM	.9972	18 04	5 46	18 04	5 49	18 04	5 52	18 04	5 57	18 04	6 03
26 SA	12 05 38	+ 2 09	5 59	18 13	5 57	18 15	5 54	18 18	5 50	18 22	5 43	18 29
85		.9975	18 56	6 20	19 02	6 17	19 09	6 13	19 19	6 09	19 34	6 02
27 SU	12 05 20	+ 2 33	5 58	18 13	5 55	18 16	5 52	18 19	5 48	18 24	5 40	18 32
86		.9978	19 51	6 54	20 02	6 46	20 17	6 36	20 36	6 22	21 08	6 01
28 MO	12 05 01	+ 2 56	5 57	18 13	5 54	18 16	5 51	18 20	5 45	18 26	5 37	18 34
87		.9981	20 49	7 31	21 06	7 17	21 27	7 00	21 57	6 37	22 48	6 01
29 TU	12 04 43	+ 3 20	5 56	18 13	5 53	18 17	5 49	18 21	5 43	18 27	5 34	18 37
88		.9984	21 50	8 13	22 12	7 53	22 40	7 30	23 21	6 57	none	6 02
30 WE	12 04 25	+ 3 43	5 55	18 14	5 52	18 17	5 47	18 22	5 41	18 29	5 31	18 39
89		.9987	22 53	9 00	23 20	8 36	23 53	8 06	none	7 23	0 36	6 05
31 TH	12 04 07	+ 4 06	5 55	18 14	5 51	18 18	5 46	18 23	5 39	18 30	5 28	18 41
90		.9990	23 58	9 53	none	9 26	none	8 51	0 43	8 00	2 26	6 15

APRIL 2005

4th Month　　　　　　　　　　　　　　　　　　　　　　　　　　**30 days**

Coordinated Universal Time (Greenwich Mean Time)

NOTE: For each day, numbers on first line indicate Sun; numbers on second line indicate Moon.

Degrees are North Latitude.

Moon Phases: FM = Full Moon; LQ = Last (Waning) Quarter; NM = New Moon; FQ = First (Waxing) Quarter

Sun's distance is in Astronomical Units

CAUTION: Must be converted to local time. For instructions see "Calculation of Rise Times," page 368.

Day of month, of week, of year	Sun on Meridian / Moon Phase h m s	Sun's Declination ° ' / Distance	20° Rise Sun/Moon h m	20° Set Sun/Moon h m	30° Rise Sun/Moon h m	30° Set Sun/Moon h m	40° Rise Sun/Moon h m	40° Set Sun/Moon h m	50° Rise Sun/Moon h m	50° Set Sun/Moon h m	60° Rise Sun/Moon h m	60° Set Sun/Moon h m
1 FR	12 03 49	+ 4 30	5 54	18 14	5 49	18 19	5 44	18 24	5 37	18 32	5 25	18 44
91		.9993	none	10 53	0 26	10 25	1 03	9 48	1 58	8 53	4 01	6 48
2 SA	12 03 31	+ 4 53	5 53	18 15	5 48	18 19	5 42	18 25	5 35	18 33	5 22	18 46
92		.9995	1 00	11 58	1 28	11 30	2 04	10 55	2 57	10 02	4 52	8 09
3 SU	12 03 14	+ 5 16	5 52	18 15	5 47	18 20	5 41	18 26	5 32	18 35	5 19	18 49
93		.9998	1 57	13 04	2 23	12 40	2 55	12 10	3 41	11 25	5 08	10 00
4 MO	12 02 56	+ 5 39	5 51	18 15	5 46	18 20	5 39	18 27	5 30	18 37	5 16	18 51
94		1.0001	2 49	14 09	3 09	13 50	3 35	13 27	4 12	12 53	5 14	11 55
5 TU	12 02 39	+ 6 02	5 50	18 15	5 45	18 21	5 38	18 28	5 28	18 38	5 13	18 54
95		1.0004	3 34	15 12	3 49	14 59	4 08	14 43	4 34	14 21	5 15	13 44
6 WE	12 02 22	+ 6 24	5 49	18 16	5 43	18 22	5 36	18 29	5 26	18 40	5 10	18 56
96		1.0007	4 15	16 12	4 25	16 05	4 36	15 57	4 51	15 46	5 15	15 28
7 TH	12 02 05	+ 6 47	5 49	18 16	5 42	18 22	5 35	18 30	5 24	18 41	5 07	18 59
97		1.0010	4 53	17 10	4 57	17 09	5 01	17 09	5 06	17 08	5 15	17 07
8 FR	12 01 49	+ 7 10	5 48	18 16	5 41	18 23	5 33	18 31	5 22	18 43	5 04	19 01
98	20 32 NM	1.0013	5 30	18 07	5 27	18 12	5 24	18 19	5 20	18 29	5 14	18 44
9 SA	12 01 32	+ 7 32	5 47	18 16	5 40	18 24	5 31	18 32	5 20	18 44	5 01	19 03
99		1.0016	6 07	19 03	5 58	19 15	5 48	19 29	5 34	19 49	5 13	20 21
10 SU	12 01 16	+ 7 54	5 46	18 17	5 39	18 24	5 30	18 33	5 18	18 46	4 58	19 06
100		1.0019	6 45	20 01	6 31	20 18	6 13	20 39	5 50	21 10	5 13	22 00
11 MO	12 01 00	+ 8 16	5 45	18 17	5 38	18 25	5 28	18 34	5 15	18 48	4 55	19 08
101		1.0022	7 25	20 58	7 06	21 20	6 42	21 48	6 09	22 28	5 14	23 41
12 TU	12 00 45	+ 8 38	5 44	18 17	5 37	18 25	5 27	18 35	5 13	18 49	4 52	19 11
102		1.0024	8 08	21 56	7 45	22 22	7 15	22 54	6 33	23 43	5 18	none
13 WE	12 00 30	+ 9 00	5 44	18 18	5 35	18 26	5 25	18 36	5 11	18 51	4 49	19 13
103		1.0027	8 56	22 52	8 29	23 20	7 55	23 56	7 05	none	5 27	1 19
14 TH	12 00 15	+ 9 22	5 43	18 18	5 34	18 27	5 24	18 37	5 09	18 52	4 46	19 16
104		1.0030	9 46	23 45	9 18	none	8 42	none	7 48	0 49	5 51	2 45
15 FR	12 00 00	+ 9 43	5 42	18 18	5 33	18 27	5 22	18 38	5 07	18 54	4 43	19 18
105		1.0033	10 39	none	10 11	0 13	9 35	0 49	8 42	1 43	6 46	3 40
16 SA	11 59 46	+ 10 05	5 41	18 19	5 32	18 28	5 21	18 39	5 05	18 55	4 40	19 21
106	14 37 FQ	1.0035	11 33	0 34	11 07	1 01	10 34	1 35	9 46	2 25	8 09	4 03
17 SU	11 59 32	+ 10 26	5 40	18 19	5 31	18 28	5 19	18 40	5 03	18 57	4 38	19 23
107		1.0038	12 27	1 19	12 04	1 43	11 36	2 13	10 55	2 56	9 41	4 12
18 MO	11 59 18	+ 10 47	5 40	18 19	5 30	18 29	5 18	18 41	5 01	18 59	4 35	19 26
108		1.0041	13 20	2 00	13 02	2 20	12 39	2 44	12 07	3 18	11 13	4 16
19 TU	11 59 05	+ 11 08	5 39	18 19	5 29	18 30	5 16	18 42	4 59	19 00	4 32	19 28
109		1.0044	14 11	2 37	13 58	2 52	13 42	3 11	13 19	3 36	12 43	4 17
20 WE	11 58 52	+ 11 29	5 38	18 20	5 28	18 30	5 15	18 44	4 57	19 02	4 29	19 31
110		1.0046	15 03	3 11	14 55	3 22	14 45	3 34	14 32	3 51	14 11	4 17
21 TH	11 58 40	+ 11 49	5 38	18 20	5 27	18 31	5 14	18 45	4 55	19 03	4 26	19 33
111		1.0049	15 54	3 45	15 51	3 50	15 48	3 56	15 44	4 04	15 38	4 16
22 FR	11 58 28	+ 12 09	5 37	18 20	5 26	18 32	5 12	18 46	4 53	19 05	4 23	19 36
112		1.0052	16 46	4 18	16 49	4 17	16 53	4 17	16 59	4 16	17 08	4 15
23 SA	11 58 17	+ 12 30	5 36	18 21	5 25	18 32	5 11	18 47	4 51	19 06	4 20	19 38
113		1.0054	17 40	4 52	17 49	4 46	18 01	4 38	18 16	4 29	18 41	4 14
24 SU	11 58 06	+ 12 49	5 35	18 21	5 24	18 33	5 09	18 48	4 49	19 08	4 17	19 41
114	10 06 FM	1.0057	18 38	5 28	18 53	5 16	19 11	5 02	19 37	4 43	20 21	4 13
25 MO	11 57 55	+ 13 09	5 35	18 21	5 23	18 33	5 08	18 49	4 47	19 09	4 15	19 43
115		1.0060	19 39	6 08	20 00	5 51	20 25	5 30	21 02	5 01	22 08	4 13
26 TU	11 57 45	+ 13 29	5 34	18 22	5 22	18 34	5 07	18 50	4 46	19 11	4 12	19 46
116		1.0062	20 44	6 54	21 09	6 32	21 41	6 04	22 28	5 25	none	4 16
27 WE	11 57 36	+ 13 48	5 33	18 22	5 21	18 35	5 05	18 51	4 44	19 13	4 09	19 48
117		1.0065	21 50	7 47	22 18	7 21	22 54	6 47	23 48	5 58	0 01	4 23
28 TH	11 57 27	+ 14 07	5 33	18 22	5 20	18 35	5 04	18 52	4 42	19 14	4 06	19 51
118		1.0068	22 54	8 46	23 22	8 18	23 59	7 41	none	6 47	1 47	4 46
29 FR	11 57 18	+ 14 26	5 32	18 23	5 19	18 36	5 03	18 53	4 40	19 16	4 03	19 53
119		1.0070	23 53	9 51	none	9 22	none	8 46	0 53	7 52	2 54	5 53
30 SA	11 57 10	+ 14 44	5 31	18 23	5 18	18 37	5 01	18 54	4 38	19 17	4 01	19 55
120		1.0073	none	10 57	0 20	10 32	0 53	10 00	1 42	9 12	3 17	7 39

MAY 2005

5th Month　　　　　　　　　　　　　　　　　　　　　　**31 days**

Coordinated Universal Time (Greenwich Mean Time)

NOTE: For each day, numbers on first line indicate Sun; numbers on second line indicate Moon.

Degrees are North Latitude.

Moon Phases: FM = Full Moon; LQ = Last (Waning) Quarter; NM = New Moon; FQ = First (Waxing) Quarter

Sun's distance is in Astronomical Units

CAUTION: Must be converted to local time. For instructions see "Calculation of Rise Times," page 368.

Day of month, of week, of year	Sun on Meridian / Moon Phase (h m s)	Sun's Declination ° ' / Distance	20° Rise Sun/Moon	20° Set Sun/Moon	30° Rise Sun/Moon	30° Set Sun/Moon	40° Rise Sun/Moon	40° Set Sun/Moon	50° Rise Sun/Moon	50° Set Sun/Moon	60° Rise Sun/Moon	60° Set Sun/Moon
1 SU 121	11 57 03	+ 15 02	5 31	18 24	5 17	18 37	5 00	18 55	4 36	19 19	3 58	19 58
	06 24 LQ	1.0076	0 46	12 02	1 09	11 42	1 36	11 16	2 16	10 39	3 25	9 33
2 MO 122	11 56 56	+ 15 21	5 30	18 24	5 16	18 38	4 59	18 56	4 35	19 20	3 55	20 00
		1.0078	1 33	13 04	1 50	12 50	2 11	12 31	2 40	12 05	3 27	11 23
3 TU 123	11 56 50	+ 15 38	5 30	18 24	5 15	18 39	4 58	18 57	4 33	19 22	3 52	20 03
		1.0081	2 14	14 04	2 26	13 55	2 40	13 44	2 58	13 29	3 28	13 06
4 WE 124	11 56 44	+ 15 56	5 29	18 25	5 15	18 39	4 56	18 58	4 31	19 23	3 50	20 05
		1.0083	2 52	15 01	2 58	14 58	3 05	14 55	3 13	14 50	3 27	14 43
5 TH 125	11 56 39	+ 16 13	5 29	18 25	5 14	18 40	4 55	18 59	4 29	19 25	3 47	20 08
		1.0086	3 28	15 57	3 28	16 00	3 28	16 04	3 27	16 10	3 26	16 18
6 FR 126	11 56 35	+ 16 30	5 28	18 25	5 13	18 41	4 54	19 00	4 28	19 26	3 45	20 10
		1.0088	4 04	16 52	3 58	17 01	3 50	17 13	3 41	17 29	3 26	17 53
7 SA 127	11 56 31	+ 16 47	5 28	18 26	5 12	18 41	4 53	19 01	4 26	19 28	3 42	20 13
		1.0091	4 41	17 48	4 29	18 03	4 15	18 22	3 55	18 48	3 25	19 30
8 SU 128	11 56 27	+ 17 03	5 27	18 26	5 11	18 42	4 52	19 02	4 25	19 29	3 39	20 15
	08 45 NM	1.0093	5 19	18 46	5 02	19 06	4 41	19 31	4 13	20 07	3 26	21 09
9 MO 129	11 56 24	+ 17 20	5 27	18 27	5 11	18 43	4 51	19 03	4 23	19 31	3 37	20 18
		1.0096	6 01	19 43	5 40	20 07	5 13	20 38	4 34	21 23	3 28	22 49
10 TU 130	11 56 22	+ 17 35	5 26	18 27	5 10	18 43	4 50	19 04	4 21	19 32	3 34	20 20
		1.0098	6 47	20 40	6 22	21 07	5 50	21 42	5 03	22 34	3 35	none
11 WE 131	11 56 20	+ 17 51	5 26	18 27	5 09	18 44	4 49	19 05	4 20	19 34	3 32	20 23
		1.0100	7 37	21 35	7 09	22 04	6 34	22 40	5 41	23 34	3 51	0 22
12 TH 132	11 56 19	+ 18 06	5 25	18 28	5 09	18 44	4 48	19 06	4 18	19 35	3 29	20 25
		1.0102	8 29	22 27	8 01	22 54	7 25	23 29	6 31	none	4 32	1 32
13 FR 133	11 56 19	+ 18 21	5 25	18 28	5 08	18 45	4 47	19 07	4 17	19 37	3 27	20 27
		1.0105	9 23	23 14	8 56	23 39	8 22	none	7 31	0 21	5 46	2 07
14 SA 134	11 56 19	+ 18 36	5 24	18 29	5 07	18 46	4 46	19 07	4 16	19 38	3 25	20 30
		1.0107	10 17	23 56	9 53	none	9 23	0 10	8 39	0 56	7 16	2 21
15 SU 135	11 56 19	+ 18 50	5 24	18 29	5 07	18 46	4 45	19 08	4 14	19 39	3 22	20 32
		1.0109	11 10	none	10 50	0 17	10 25	0 44	9 50	1 21	8 48	2 26
16 MO 136	11 56 20	+ 19 04	5 24	18 29	5 06	18 47	4 44	19 09	4 13	19 41	3 20	20 34
	08 57 FQ	1.0111	12 02	0 34	11 47	0 51	11 28	1 12	11 02	1 41	10 18	2 28
17 TU 137	11 56 22	+ 19 18	5 23	18 30	5 05	18 48	4 43	19 10	4 11	19 42	3 18	20 37
		1.0113	12 53	1 09	12 43	1 21	12 30	1 36	12 13	1 57	11 46	2 28
18 WE 138	11 56 24	+ 19 32	5 23	18 30	5 05	18 48	4 42	19 11	4 10	19 44	3 15	20 39
		1.0115	13 43	1 42	13 38	1 49	13 32	1 58	13 24	2 10	13 12	2 28
19 TH 139	11 56 27	+ 19 45	5 23	18 31	5 04	18 49	4 41	19 12	4 09	19 45	3 13	20 41
		1.0117	14 34	2 14	14 35	2 17	14 36	2 19	14 37	2 22	14 39	2 27
20 FR 140	11 56 30	+ 19 57	5 22	18 31	5 04	18 50	4 41	19 13	4 08	19 46	3 11	20 43
		1.0119	15 27	2 47	15 33	2 44	15 41	2 40	15 52	2 34	16 09	2 26
21 SA 141	11 56 34	+ 20 10	5 22	18 31	5 03	18 50	4 40	19 14	4 06	19 48	3 09	20 46
	1	1.0121	16 23	3 22	16 35	3 14	16 50	3 03	17 11	2 48	17 46	2 25
22 SU 142	11 56 38	+ 20 22	5 22	18 32	5 03	18 51	4 39	19 15	4 05	19 49	3 07	20 48
		1.0123	17 23	4 01	17 41	3 46	18 03	3 29	18 35	3 04	19 30	2 25
23 MO 143	11 56 43	+ 20 33	5 21	18 32	5 02	18 51	4 38	19 16	4 04	19 50	3 05	20 50
	20 18 FM	1.0125	18 27	4 45	18 50	4 25	19 20	4 00	20 02	3 25	21 23	2 26
24 TU 144	11 56 48	+ 20 45	5 21	18 33	5 02	18 52	4 38	19 16	4 03	19 51	3 03	20 52
		1.0127	19 34	5 36	20 01	5 11	20 36	4 40	21 28	3 55	23 17	2 31
25 WE 145	11 56 54	+ 20 56	5 21	18 33	5 02	18 53	4 37	19 17	4 02	19 53	3 01	20 54
		1.0128	20 42	6 34	21 10	6 06	21 47	5 30	22 42	4 38	none	2 47
26 TH 146	11 57 01	+ 21 06	5 21	18 33	5 01	18 53	4 36	19 18	4 01	19 54	2 59	20 56
		1.0130	21 45	7 38	22 12	7 10	22 47	6 33	23 38	5 39	0 45	3 36
27 FR 147	11 57 07	+ 21 17	5 21	18 34	5 01	18 54	4 36	19 19	4 00	19 55	2 57	20 58
		1.0132	22 42	8 46	23 05	8 20	23 35	7 46	none	6 57	1 22	5 14
28 SA 148	11 57 15	+ 21 26	5 20	18 34	5 00	18 54	4 35	19 20	3 59	19 56	2 56	21 00
		1.0134	23 31	9 54	23 50	9 32	none	9 04	0 18	8 24	1 34	7 11
29 SU 149	11 57 22	+ 21 36	5 20	18 35	5 00	18 55	4 35	19 20	3 58	19 57	2 54	21 02
		1.0135	none	10 58	none	10 42	0 13	10 21	0 45	9 52	1 38	9 04
30 MO 150	11 57 31	+ 21 45	5 20	18 35	5 00	18 55	4 34	19 21	3 57	19 58	2 52	21 04
	11 47 LQ	1.0137	0 15	11 59	0 28	11 49	0 44	11 36	1 05	11 18	1 39	10 49
31 TU 151	11 57 39	+ 21 54	5 20	18 35	5 00	18 56	4 34	19 22	3 57	19 59	2 51	21 06
		1.0139	0 54	12 56	1 01	12 52	1 09	12 47	1 21	12 39	1 39	12 28

JUNE 2005

6th Month   **30 days**

Coordinated Universal Time (Greenwich Mean Time)

NOTE: For each day, numbers on first line indicate Sun; numbers on second line indicate Moon.

Degrees are North Latitude.

Moon Phases: FM = Full Moon; LQ = Last (Waning) Quarter; NM = New Moon; FQ = First (Waxing) Quarter

Sun's distance is in Astronomical Units

CAUTION: Must be converted to local time. For instructions see "Calculation of Rise Times," page 368.

Day of month, of week, of year	Sun on Meridian / Moon Phase / h m s	Sun's Declination ° ' / Distance	20° Rise Sun/Moon h m	20° Set Sun/Moon h m	30° Rise Sun/Moon h m	30° Set Sun/Moon h m	40° Rise Sun/Moon h m	40° Set Sun/Moon h m	50° Rise Sun/Moon h m	50° Set Sun/Moon h m	60° Rise Sun/Moon h m	60° Set Sun/Moon h m
1 WE	11 57 48	+ 22 02	5 20	18 36	4 59	18 56	4 33	19 23	3 56	20 00	2 49	21 08
152		1.0140	1 30	13 52	1 31	13 54	1 33	13 56	1 35	13 58	1 38	14 02
2 TH	11 57 58	+ 22 10	5 20	18 36	4 59	18 57	4 33	19 23	3 55	20 01	2 48	21 09
153		1.0142	2 05	14 47	2 01	14 54	1 55	15 03	1 48	15 16	1 38	15 35
3 FR	11 58 08	+ 22 18	5 20	18 37	4 59	18 57	4 32	19 24	3 54	20 02	2 46	21 11
154		1.0144	2 40	15 41	2 31	15 54	2 18	16 11	2 02	16 33	1 37	17 10
4 SA	11 58 18	+ 22 25	5 20	18 37	4 59	18 58	4 32	19 25	3 54	20 03	2 45	21 13
155		1.0145	3 18	16 37	3 03	16 56	2 44	17 19	2 18	17 51	1 38	18 46
5 SU	11 58 29	+ 22 32	5 20	18 37	4 59	18 58	4 32	19 25	3 53	20 04	2 44	21 14
156		1.0146	3 58	17 34	3 38	17 57	3 13	18 26	2 38	19 08	1 39	20 24
6 MO	11 58 40	+ 22 38	5 20	18 38	4 59	18 59	4 32	19 26	3 53	20 05	2 43	21 16
157	21 55 NM	1.0148	4 42	18 31	4 18	18 57	3 47	19 31	3 04	20 20	1 44	22 00
7 TU	11 58 51	+ 22 44	5 20	18 38	4 58	18 59	4 31	19 27	3 52	20 06	2 42	21 17
158		1.0149	5 30	19 27	5 03	19 55	4 28	20 31	3 38	21 24	1 57	23 20
8 WE	11 59 02	+ 22 50	5 20	18 38	4 58	19 00	4 31	19 27	3 52	20 07	2 41	21 18
159		1.0150	6 21	20 20	5 53	20 47	5 17	21 23	4 24	22 16	2 27	none
9 TH	11 59 14	+ 22 55	5 20	18 39	4 58	19 00	4 31	19 28	3 52	20 07	2 40	21 19
160		1.0152	7 15	21 08	6 47	21 34	6 12	22 07	5 20	22 55	3 30	0 07
10 FR	11 59 26	+ 23 00	5 20	18 39	4 58	19 01	4 31	19 28	3 51	20 08	2 39	21 21
161		1.0153	8 09	21 52	7 44	22 15	7 12	22 43	6 26	23 24	4 56	0 27
11 SA	11 59 38	+ 23 05	5 20	18 39	4 58	19 01	4 31	19 29	3 51	20 09	2 38	21 22
162		1.0154	9 02	22 31	8 41	22 50	8 14	23 13	7 36	23 45	6 27	0 35
12 SU	11 59 51	+ 23 09	5 20	18 40	4 58	19 01	4 31	19 29	3 51	20 09	2 38	21 23
163		1.0155	9 54	23 07	9 38	23 21	9 17	23 38	8 47	none	7 58	0 38
13 MO	12 00 03	+ 23 12	5 20	18 40	4 58	19 02	4 31	19 30	3 50	20 10	2 37	21 24
164		1.0156	10 45	23 41	10 33	23 50	10 18	none	9 58	0 02	9 25	0 39
14 TU	12 00 16	+ 23 16	5 20	18 40	4 58	19 02	4 31	19 30	3 50	20 10	2 37	21 24
165		1.0157	11 35	none	11 28	none	11 19	0 01	11 08	0 16	10 50	0 39
15 WE	12 00 29	+ 23 18	5 20	18 41	4 58	19 03	4 31	19 31	3 50	20 11	2 36	21 25
166	01 22 FQ	1.0158	12 24	0 13	12 23	0 17	12 21	0 22	12 18	0 28	12 14	0 38
16 TH	12 00 42	+ 23 21	5 21	18 41	4 59	19 03	4 31	19 31	3 50	20 11	2 36	21 26
167		1.0159	13 15	0 44	13 19	0 43	13 24	0 42	13 30	0 40	13 41	0 37
17 FR	12 00 54	+ 23 23	5 21	18 41	4 59	19 03	4 31	19 31	3 50	20 12	2 36	21 26
168		1.0159	14 08	1 18	14 18	1 11	14 30	1 03	14 46	0 52	15 12	0 36
18 SA	12 01 08	+ 23 24	5 21	18 41	4 59	19 03	4 31	19 32	3 50	20 12	2 36	21 27
169		1.0160	15 05	1 54	15 20	1 42	15 39	1 27	16 06	1 07	16 51	0 36
19 SU	12 01 20	+ 23 25	5 21	18 42	4 59	19 04	4 31	19 32	3 50	20 12	2 36	21 27
170		1.0161	16 07	2 34	16 27	2 17	16 54	1 55	17 31	1 25	18 39	0 36
20 MO	12 01 33	+ 23 26	5 21	18 42	4 59	19 04	4 31	19 32	3 50	20 13	2 36	21 28
171		1.0162	17 13	3 21	17 38	2 59	18 11	2 30	18 58	1 50	20 34	0 39
21 TU	12 01 46	+ 23 26	5 22	18 42	4 59	19 04	4 31	19 32	3 51	20 13	2 36	21 28
172		1.0162	18 21	4 16	18 49	3 50	19 25	3 16	20 20	2 26	22 20	0 49
22 WE	12 01 59	+ 23 26	5 22	18 42	5 00	19 04	4 32	19 32	3 51	20 13	2 36	21 28
173	04 14 FM	1.0163	19 28	5 19	19 56	4 51	20 32	4 14	21 26	3 19	23 20	1 19
23 TH	12 02 12	+ 23 26	5 22	18 42	5 00	19 04	4 32	19 33	3 51	20 13	2 36	21 28
174		1.0163	20 30	6 28	20 55	6 00	21 27	5 25	22 14	4 32	23 41	2 39
24 FR	12 02 25	+ 23 25	5 22	18 43	5 00	19 05	4 32	19 33	3 51	20 13	2 37	21 28
175		1.0164	21 24	7 38	21 45	7 14	22 10	6 44	22 46	6 00	23 47	4 35
25 SA	12 02 38	+ 23 24	5 22	18 43	5 00	19 05	4 32	19 33	3 52	20 13	2 37	21 28
176		1.0165	22 11	8 46	22 26	8 28	22 44	8 04	23 09	7 31	23 49	6 34
26 SU	12 02 50	+ 23 22	5 23	18 43	5 01	19 05	4 33	19 33	3 52	20 13	2 38	21 27
177		1.0165	22 53	9 50	23 02	9 38	23 12	9 23	23 27	9 01	23 50	8 26
27 MO	12 03 03	+ 23 20	5 23	18 43	5 01	19 05	4 33	19 33	3 53	20 13	2 39	21 27
178		1.0166	23 30	10 50	23 33	10 44	23 37	10 37	23 42	10 26	23 49	10 09
28 TU	12 03 15	+ 23 17	5 23	18 43	5 01	19 05	4 33	19 33	3 53	20 13	2 39	21 27
179	18 23 LQ	1.0166	none	11 47	none	11 47	24 00	11 47	23 55	11 47	23 49	11 47
29 WE	12 03 27	+ 23 14	5 24	18 43	5 02	19 05	4 34	19 33	3 54	20 13	2 40	21 26
180		1.0166	0 06	12 43	0 03	12 49	none	12 56	none	13 06	23 48	13 21
30 TH	12 03 39	+ 23 11	5 24	18 43	5 02	19 05	4 34	19 33	3 54	20 13	2 41	21 26
181		1.0167	0 42	13 38	0 33	13 49	0 23	14 03	0 09	14 23	23 48	14 55

JULY 2005

7th Month   **31 days**

Coordinated Universal Time (Greenwich Mean Time)

NOTE: For each day, numbers on first line indicate Sun; numbers on second line indicate Moon.

Degrees are North Latitude.

Moon Phases: FM = Full Moon; LQ = Last (Waning) Quarter; NM = New Moon; FQ = First (Waxing) Quarter

Sun's distance is in Astronomical Units

CAUTION: Must be converted to local time. For instructions see "Calculation of Rise Times," page 368.

Day of month, of week, of year	Sun on Meridian / Moon Phase (h m s)	Sun's Declination ° ' / Distance	20° Rise	20° Set	30° Rise	30° Set	40° Rise	40° Set	50° Rise	50° Set	60° Rise	60° Set
1 FR	12 03 51	+ 23 07	5 24	18 43	5 02	19 05	4 35	19 33	3 55	20 12	2 42	21 25
182		1.0167	1 18	14 33	1 05	14 50	0 48	15 11	0 25	15 40	23 50	16 30
2 SA	12 04 02	+ 23 03	5 25	18 43	5 03	19 05	4 35	19 33	3 56	20 12	2 43	21 24
183		1.0167	1 57	15 29	1 39	15 50	1 15	16 18	0 43	16 57	23 53	18 07
3 SU	12 04 13	+ 22 58	5 25	18 44	5 03	19 05	4 36	19 32	3 56	20 12	2 44	21 23
184		1.0167	2 40	16 25	2 17	16 51	1 48	17 23	1 06	18 10	none	19 43
4 MO	12 04 24	+ 22 53	5 25	18 44	5 04	19 05	4 36	19 32	3 57	20 11	2 46	21 22
185		1.0167	3 26	17 21	3 00	17 48	2 26	18 24	1 38	19 16	0 03	21 09
5 TU	12 04 35	+ 22 48	5 26	18 44	5 04	19 05	4 37	19 32	3 58	20 11	2 47	21 21
186		1.0167	4 16	18 14	3 48	18 42	3 12	19 18	2 19	20 12	0 26	22 07
6 WE	12 04 45	+ 22 42	5 26	18 44	5 05	19 05	4 38	19 32	3 59	20 10	2 48	21 20
187	12 02 NM	1.0167	5 09	19 04	4 41	19 31	4 05	20 05	3 12	20 54	1 18	22 33
7 TH	12 04 55	+ 22 36	5 26	18 44	5 05	19 05	4 38	19 31	4 00	20 10	2 50	21 19
188		1.0167	6 03	19 50	5 37	20 13	5 04	20 43	4 16	21 26	2 38	22 44
8 FR	12 05 04	+ 22 29	5 27	18 43	5 06	19 04	4 39	19 31	4 00	20 09	2 51	21 18
189		1.0167	6 57	20 30	6 34	20 50	6 06	21 15	5 25	21 50	4 10	22 48
9 SA	12 05 13	+ 22 22	5 27	18 43	5 06	19 04	4 39	19 31	4 01	20 09	2 53	21 16
190		1.0167	7 49	21 07	7 31	21 23	7 08	21 42	6 36	22 08	5 41	22 49
10 SU	12 05 22	+ 22 15	5 27	18 43	5 06	19 04	4 40	19 30	4 02	20 08	2 55	21 15
191		1.0167	8 40	21 41	8 26	21 52	8 10	22 05	7 46	22 22	7 09	22 49
11 MO	12 05 30	+ 22 07	5 28	18 43	5 07	19 04	4 41	19 30	4 03	20 07	2 56	21 13
192		1.0166	9 29	22 13	9 21	22 19	9 10	22 25	8 56	22 35	8 34	22 49
12 TU	12 05 38	+ 21 59	5 28	18 43	5 08	19 04	4 42	19 29	4 04	20 06	2 58	21 12
193		1.0166	10 18	22 44	10 15	22 45	10 11	22 45	10 05	22 46	9 57	22 48
13 WE	12 05 45	+ 21 51	5 28	18 43	5 08	19 03	4 42	19 29	4 05	20 06	3 00	21 10
194		1.0166	11 07	23 16	11 09	23 11	11 12	23 06	11 15	22 58	11 21	22 47
14 TH	12 05 52	+ 21 42	5 29	18 43	5 09	19 03	4 43	19 28	4 06	20 05	3 02	21 09
195	15 20 FQ	1.0165	11 58	23 50	12 06	23 40	12 15	23 28	12 28	23 11	12 48	22 46
15 FR	12 05 58	+ 21 33	5 29	18 43	5 09	19 03	4 44	19 28	4 08	20 04	3 04	21 07
196		1.0165	12 52	none	13 05	none	13 21	23 53	13 44	23 27	14 20	22 46
16 SA	12 06 03	+ 21 23	5 30	18 42	5 10	19 02	4 45	19 27	4 09	20 02	3 06	21 05
197		1.0164	13 50	0 27	14 08	0 12	14 31	none	15 04	23 48	16 01	22 47
17 SU	12 06 08	+ 21 13	5 30	18 42	5 10	19 02	4 45	19 27	4 10	20 02	3 08	21 03
198		1.0163	14 52	1 09	15 15	0 49	15 45	0 24	16 29	none	17 51	22 53
18 MO	12 06 13	+ 21 03	5 30	18 42	5 11	19 01	4 46	19 26	4 11	20 01	3 10	21 01
199		1.0163	15 58	1 59	16 25	1 34	17 00	1 03	17 52	0 17	19 43	23 09
19 TU	12 06 17	+ 20 52	5 31	18 42	5 11	19 01	4 47	19 25	4 12	20 00	3 12	20 59
200		1.0162	17 06	2 58	17 34	2 30	18 11	1 54	19 06	1 01	21 09	none
20 WE	12 06 21	+ 20 41	5 31	18 41	5 12	19 00	4 48	19 24	4 13	19 59	3 14	20 57
201		1.0161	18 11	4 03	18 38	3 35	19 12	2 59	20 03	2 04	21 45	0 01
21 TH	12 06 24	+ 20 30	5 31	18 41	5 12	19 00	4 49	19 24	4 15	19 57	3 16	20 55
202	11 00 FM	1.0161	19 10	5 14	19 33	4 48	20 02	4 15	20 43	3 26	21 56	1 46
22 FR	12 06 26	+ 20 18	5 32	18 41	5 13	19 00	4 49	19 23	4 16	19 56	3 18	20 53
203		1.0160	20 01	6 25	20 19	6 04	20 40	5 37	21 10	4 59	21 59	3 49
23 SA	12 06 28	+ 20 06	5 32	18 41	5 14	18 59	4 50	19 22	4 17	19 55	3 20	20 51
204		1.0159	20 46	7 33	20 58	7 18	21 12	6 59	21 31	6 33	22 00	5 48
24 SU	12 06 29	+ 19 54	5 33	18 40	5 14	18 58	4 51	19 21	4 18	19 54	3 22	20 49
205		1.0158	21 27	8 37	21 32	8 29	21 38	8 18	21 47	8 03	22 00	7 39
25 MO	12 06 29	+ 19 41	5 33	18 40	5 15	18 58	4 52	19 20	4 20	19 52	3 25	20 47
206		1.0157	22 05	9 37	22 04	9 35	22 03	9 32	22 01	9 29	21 59	9 22
26 TU	12 06 29	+ 19 28	5 33	18 40	5 15	18 57	4 53	19 20	4 21	19 51	3 27	20 44
207		1.0156	22 41	10 35	22 34	10 39	22 26	10 44	22 15	10 51	21 59	11 01
27 WE	12 06 29	+ 19 14	5 34	18 39	5 16	18 57	4 54	19 19	4 22	19 50	3 29	20 42
208		1.0155	23 18	11 32	23 06	11 41	22 51	11 54	22 30	12 11	21 59	12 37
28 TH	12 06 28	+ 19 01	5 34	18 39	5 17	18 56	4 55	19 18	4 24	19 48	3 31	20 40
209	03 19 LQ	1.0154	23 57	12 28	23 39	12 43	23 18	13 02	22 48	13 29	21 59	14 14
29 FR	12 06 26	+ 18 47	5 34	18 38	5 17	18 55	4 56	19 17	4 25	19 47	3 34	20 37
210		1.0153	none	13 24	none	13 44	23 49	14 10	23 10	14 47	22 02	15 52
30 SA	12 06 24	+ 18 32	5 35	18 38	5 18	18 55	4 56	19 16	4 26	19 45	3 36	20 35
211		1.0152	0 38	14 21	0 16	14 45	none	15 16	23 38	16 02	22 09	17 30
31 SU	12 06 21	+ 18 18	5 35	18 37	5 18	18 54	4 57	19 15	4 28	19 44	3 38	20 33
212		1.0151	1 23	15 17	0 58	15 44	0 25	16 19	none	17 11	22 26	19 00

AUGUST 2005

8th Month **31 days**

Coordinated Universal Time (Greenwich Mean Time)

NOTE: For each day, numbers on first line indicate Sun; numbers on second line indicate Moon.

Degrees are North Latitude.

Moon Phases: FM = Full Moon; LQ = Last (Waning) Quarter; NM = New Moon; FQ = First (Waxing) Quarter

Sun's distance is in Astronomical Units

CAUTION: Must be converted to local time. For instructions see "Calculation of Rise Times," page 368.

Day of month, of week, of year	Sun on Meridian / Moon Phase h m s	Sun's Declination ° ´ / Distance	20° Rise Sun/Moon h m	20° Set Sun/Moon h m	30° Rise Sun/Moon h m	30° Set Sun/Moon h m	40° Rise Sun/Moon h m	40° Set Sun/Moon h m	50° Rise Sun/Moon h m	50° Set Sun/Moon h m	60° Rise Sun/Moon h m	60° Set Sun/Moon h m
1 MO	12 06 17	+ 18 03	5 35	18 37	5 19	18 53	4 58	19 14	4 29	19 42	3 41	20 30
213		1.0150	2 12	16 11	1 45	16 39	1 09	17 15	0 17	18 09	23 08	20 08
2 TU	12 06 13	+ 17 48	5 36	18 36	5 20	18 52	4 59	19 13	4 31	19 41	3 43	20 28
214		1.0149	3 04	17 02	2 36	17 29	2 00	18 04	1 06	18 55	none	20 41
3 WE	12 06 08	+ 17 32	5 36	18 36	5 20	18 52	5 00	19 12	4 32	19 39	3 45	20 25
215		1.0147	3 58	17 48	3 31	18 13	2 57	18 44	2 07	19 30	0 22	20 54
4 TH	12 06 03	+ 17 16	5 36	18 35	5 21	18 51	5 01	19 10	4 34	19 38	3 48	20 23
216		1.0146	4 52	18 30	4 28	18 51	3 58	19 18	3 15	19 55	1 52	20 59
5 FR	12 05 57	+ 17 00	5 37	18 35	5 21	18 50	5 02	19 09	4 35	19 36	3 50	20 20
217	03 05 NM	1.0145	5 45	19 08	5 25	19 25	5 01	19 46	4 25	20 14	3 24	21 01
6 SA	12 05 51	+ 16 44	5 37	18 34	5 22	18 49	5 03	19 08	4 36	19 34	3 53	20 17
218		1.0143	6 36	19 42	6 21	19 55	6 03	20 09	5 37	20 30	4 54	21 01
7 SU	12 05 44	+ 16 27	5 37	18 34	5 23	18 48	5 04	19 07	4 38	19 33	3 55	20 15
219		1.0142	7 26	20 15	7 16	20 22	7 04	20 31	6 47	20 42	6 20	21 00
8 MO	12 05 36	+ 16 10	5 38	18 33	5 23	18 48	5 05	19 06	4 39	19 31	3 57	20 12
220		1.0140	8 15	20 46	8 10	20 48	8 04	20 51	7 56	20 54	7 44	20 59
9 TU	12 05 28	+ 15 53	5 38	18 33	5 24	18 47	5 06	19 04	4 41	19 29	4 00	20 09
221		1.0139	9 04	21 17	9 04	21 14	9 05	21 10	9 06	21 05	9 07	20 58
10 WE	12 05 19	+ 15 36	5 38	18 32	5 24	18 46	5 07	19 03	4 42	19 27	4 02	20 07
222		1.0137	9 53	21 49	9 59	21 41	10 06	21 31	10 16	21 18	10 32	20 57
11 TH	12 05 10	+ 15 18	5 39	18 31	5 25	18 45	5 08	19 02	4 44	19 26	4 05	20 04
223		1.0135	10 45	22 24	10 56	22 11	11 10	21 54	11 29	21 32	12 01	20 56
12 FR	12 05 00	+ 15 00	5 39	18 31	5 26	18 44	5 09	19 01	4 45	19 24	4 07	20 01
224		1.0133	11 40	23 04	11 56	22 45	12 17	22 22	12 46	21 50	13 36	20 56
13 SA	12 04 49	+ 14 42	5 39	18 30	5 26	18 43	5 10	18 59	4 47	19 22	4 09	19 58
225	02 38 FQ	1.0132	12 38	23 49	13 00	23 26	13 28	22 56	14 07	22 14	15 20	20 59
14 SU	12 04 38	+ 14 24	5 40	18 29	5 27	18 42	5 11	18 58	4 48	19 20	4 12	19 56
226		1.0130	13 41	none	14 07	none	14 40	23 40	15 29	22 50	17 09	21 08
15 MO	12 04 26	+ 14 05	5 40	18 29	5 27	18 41	5 12	18 57	4 50	19 18	4 14	19 53
227		1.0128	14 46	0 42	15 15	0 15	15 51	none	16 46	23 42	18 50	21 37
16 TU	12 04 14	+ 13 46	5 40	18 28	5 28	18 40	5 12	18 55	4 51	19 16	4 17	19 50
228		1.0126	15 51	1 42	16 19	1 14	16 56	0 37	17 50	none	19 46	22 58
17 WE	12 04 01	+ 13 27	5 41	18 27	5 29	18 39	5 13	18 54	4 53	19 14	4 19	19 47
229		1.0124	16 52	2 50	17 17	2 22	17 50	1 46	18 36	0 53	20 04	none
18 TH	12 03 48	+ 13 08	5 41	18 26	5 29	18 38	5 14	18 53	4 54	19 12	4 21	19 44
230		1.0122	17 47	4 00	18 07	3 36	18 33	3 05	19 09	2 21	20 10	0 56
19 FR	12 03 34	+ 12 49	5 41	18 26	5 30	18 37	5 15	18 51	4 56	19 11	4 24	19 42
231	17 53 FM	1.0120	18 35	5 10	18 50	4 51	19 08	4 28	19 32	3 55	20 11	2 58
20 SA	12 03 20	+ 12 29	5 41	18 25	5 30	18 36	5 16	18 50	4 57	19 09	4 26	19 39
232		1.0118	19 18	6 16	19 27	6 05	19 37	5 50	19 50	5 29	20 11	4 55
21 SU	12 03 05	+ 12 09	5 42	18 24	5 31	18 35	5 17	18 48	4 59	19 07	4 29	19 36
233		1.0116	19 58	7 20	20 00	7 15	20 02	7 08	20 06	6 59	20 11	6 45
22 MO	12 02 50	+ 11 49	5 42	18 23	5 31	18 34	5 18	18 47	5 00	19 05	4 31	19 33
234		1.0114	20 36	8 20	20 32	8 22	20 27	8 23	20 20	8 25	20 10	8 28
23 TU	12 02 34	+ 11 29	5 42	18 23	5 32	18 33	5 19	18 45	5 02	19 03	4 33	19 30
235		1.0112	21 14	9 19	21 04	9 27	20 51	9 36	20 35	9 49	20 09	10 09
24 WE	12 02 18	+ 11 09	5 42	18 22	5 33	18 32	5 20	18 44	5 03	19 01	4 36	19 27
236		1.0110	21 53	10 17	21 37	10 31	21 18	10 48	20 51	11 11	20 09	11 49
25 TH	12 02 01	+ 10 48	5 43	18 21	5 33	18 31	5 21	18 42	5 05	18 59	4 38	19 24
237		1.0108	22 35	11 15	22 14	11 34	21 48	11 58	21 12	12 32	20 11	13 30
26 FR	12 01 44	+ 10 27	5 43	18 20	5 34	18 29	5 22	18 41	5 06	18 56	4 41	19 21
238	15 18 LQ	1.0106	23 20	12 13	22 55	12 37	22 23	13 07	21 38	13 50	20 15	15 11
27 SA	12 01 27	+ 10 06	5 43	18 19	5 34	18 28	5 23	18 39	5 07	18 54	4 43	19 18
239		1.0104	none	13 11	23 40	13 37	23 05	14 12	22 14	15 02	20 27	16 48
28 SU	12 01 10	+ 9 45	5 43	18 19	5 35	18 27	5 24	18 38	5 09	18 52	4 45	19 15
240		1.0102	0 08	14 06	none	14 34	23 54	15 11	23 00	16 05	20 59	18 06
29 MO	12 00 52	+ 9 24	5 44	18 18	5 35	18 26	5 25	18 36	5 10	18 50	4 48	19 12
241		1.0099	0 59	14 58	0 31	15 26	none	16 02	23 58	16 55	22 05	18 49
30 TU	12 00 34	+9 03	5 44	18 17	5 36	18 25	5 26	18 35	5 12	18 48	4 50	19 09
242		1.0097	1 53	15 46	1 25	16 12	0 50	16 45	none	17 33	23 33	19 05
31 WE	12 00 15	+ 8 41	5 44	18 16	5 36	18 24	5 27	18 33	5 13	18 46	4 53	19 06
243		1.0095	2 47	16 29	2 22	16 52	1 50	17 20	1 04	18 01	none	19 11

SEPTEMBER 2005

9th Month   **30 days**

Coordinated Universal Time (Greenwich Mean Time)

NOTE: For each day, numbers on first line indicate Sun; numbers on second line indicate Moon.

Degrees are North Latitude.

Moon Phases: FM = Full Moon; LQ = Last (Waning) Quarter; NM = New Moon; FQ = First (Waxing) Quarter

Sun's distance is in Astronomical Units

CAUTION: Must be converted to local time. For instructions see "Calculation of Rise Times," page 368.

Day of month, of week, of year	Sun on Meridian Moon Phase h m s	Sun's Declination ° ′ Distance	20° Rise Sun Moon h m	20° Set Sun Moon h m	30° Rise Sun Moon h m	30° Set Sun Moon h m	40° Rise Sun Moon h m	40° Set Sun Moon h m	50° Rise Sun Moon h m	50° Set Sun Moon h m	60° Rise Sun Moon h m	60° Set Sun Moon h m
1 TH	11 59 56	+ 8 19	5 44	18 15	5 37	18 22	5 28	18 31	5 15	18 44	4 55	19 03
244		1.0092	3 40	17 08	3 19	17 27	2 52	17 50	2 14	18 21	1 06	19 13
2 FR	11 59 37	+ 7 58	5 45	18 14	5 38	18 21	5 29	18 30	5 16	18 42	4 57	19 00
245		1.0090	4 32	17 44	4 16	17 58	3 55	18 15	3 26	18 37	2 37	19 13
3 SA	11 59 18	+ 7 36	5 45	18 13	5 38	18 20	5 30	18 28	5 18	18 40	5 00	18 57
246	18 45 NM	1.0088	5 23	18 17	5 11	18 26	4 57	18 36	4 37	18 51	4 05	19 13
4 SU	11 58 58	+ 7 14	5 45	18 13	5 39	18 19	5 31	18 27	5 19	18 37	5 02	18 54
247		1.0085	6 12	18 49	6 06	18 52	5 58	18 57	5 47	19 03	5 30	19 11
5 MO	11 58 38	+ 6 51	5 45	18 12	5 39	18 18	5 31	18 25	5 21	18 35	5 04	18 51
248		1.0083	7 01	19 20	7 00	19 18	6 58	19 16	6 57	19 14	6 54	19 10
6 TU	11 58 18	+ 6 29	5 45	18 11	5 40	18 16	5 32	18 23	5 22	18 33	5 07	18 48
249		1.0080	7 50	19 52	7 55	19 45	8 00	19 37	8 07	19 26	8 18	19 09
7 WE	11 57 57	+ 6 07	5 46	18 10	5 40	18 15	5 33	18 22	5 24	18 31	5 09	18 45
250		1.0078	8 41	20 26	8 51	20 14	9 03	19 59	9 20	19 39	9 46	19 08
8 TH	11 57 37	+ 5 44	5 46	18 09	5 41	18 14	5 34	18 20	5 25	18 29	5 11	18 42
251		1.0075	9 35	21 03	9 50	20 46	10 09	20 24	10 35	19 55	11 19	19 07
9 FR	11 57 16	+ 5 22	5 46	18 08	5 41	18 13	5 35	18 19	5 27	18 27	5 14	18 39
252		1.0072	10 32	21 45	10 52	21 23	11 17	20 56	11 54	20 16	12 59	19 08
10 SA	11 56 55	+ 4 59	5 46	18 07	5 42	18 12	5 36	18 17	5 28	18 24	5 16	18 36
253		1.0070	11 32	22 34	11 56	22 08	12 28	21 35	13 15	20 47	14 46	19 13
11 SU	11 56 34	+ 4 36	5 47	18 06	5 42	18 10	5 37	18 15	5 30	18 22	5 18	18 33
254	11 37 FQ	1.0067	12 34	23 30	13 02	23 02	13 38	22 25	14 32	21 30	16 31	19 30
12 MO	11 56 13	+ 4 13	5 47	18 05	5 43	18 09	5 38	18 14	5 31	18 20	5 21	18 30
255		1.0064	13 38	none	14 06	none	14 43	23 27	15 39	22 32	17 46	20 26
13 TU	11 55 52	+ 3 50	5 47	18 04	5 43	18 08	5 39	18 12	5 33	18 18	5 23	18 27
256		1.0062	14 38	0 33	15 05	0 04	15 40	none	16 31	23 51	18 13	22 11
14 WE	11 55 30	+ 3 27	5 47	18 04	5 44	18 07	5 40	18 10	5 34	18 16	5 25	18 24
257		1.0059	15 34	1 40	15 57	1 14	16 26	0 40	17 07	none	18 21	none
15 TH	11 55 09	+ 3 04	5 47	18 03	5 45	18 05	5 41	18 09	5 36	18 14	5 28	18 21
258		1.0056	16 24	2 48	16 41	2 27	17 03	2 00	17 34	1 21	18 23	0 11
16 FR	11 54 48	+ 2 41	5 48	18 02	5 45	18 04	5 42	18 07	5 37	18 11	5 30	18 18
259		1.0054	17 08	3 55	17 20	3 39	17 34	3 20	17 53	2 53	18 23	2 08
17 SA	11 54 26	+ 2 18	5 48	18 01	5 46	18 03	5 43	18 05	5 39	18 09	5 33	18 15
260		1.0051	17 49	4 59	17 55	4 50	18 01	4 39	18 10	4 24	18 23	4 00
18 SU	11 54 04	+ 1 55	5 48	18 00	5 46	18 02	5 44	18 04	5 40	18 07	5 35	18 12
261	02 01 FM	1.0048	18 28	6 01	18 27	5 59	18 26	5 56	18 24	5 52	18 22	5 47
19 MO	11 53 43	+ 1 32	5 48	17 59	5 47	18 00	5 45	18 02	5 42	18 05	5 37	18 09
262		1.0045	19 07	7 01	18 59	7 06	18 50	7 11	18 39	7 19	18 21	7 30
20 TU	11 53 22	+ 1 08	5 48	17 58	5 47	17 59	5 46	18 00	5 43	18 02	5 40	18 06
263		1.0043	19 46	8 01	19 33	8 12	19 17	8 25	18 55	8 43	18 20	9 13
21 WE	11 53 00	+ 0 45	5 49	17 57	5 48	17 58	5 47	17 59	5 45	18 00	5 42	18 03
264		1.0040	20 28	9 01	20 09	9 17	19 46	9 38	19 13	10 07	18 21	10 56
22 TH	11 52 39	+ 0 22	5 49	17 56	5 48	17 57	5 48	17 57	5 46	17 58	5 44	18 00
265		1.0037	21 12	10 01	20 49	10 22	20 19	10 50	19 38	11 30	18 23	12 41
23 FR	11 52 18	−0 02	5 49	17 55	5 49	17 55	5 48	17 55	5 48	17 56	5 47	17 57
266		1.0034	22 00	11 00	21 34	11 26	20 59	11 59	20 10	12 47	18 31	14 24
24 SA	11 51 57	−0 25	5 49	17 54	5 49	17 54	5 49	17 54	5 49	17 54	5 49	17 54
267		1.0032	22 52	11 58	22 23	12 26	21 47	13 02	20 52	13 56	18 52	15 55
25 SU	11 51 36	−0 48	5 49	17 53	5 50	17 53	5 50	17 52	5 51	17 51	5 51	17 51
268	06 41 LQ	1.0029	23 45	12 52	23 17	13 21	22 41	13 57	21 47	14 52	19 47	16 52
26 MO	11 51 16	−1 12	5 50	17 53	5 50	17 52	5 51	17 51	5 52	17 49	5 54	17 48
269		1.0026	none	13 42	none	14 09	23 40	14 43	22 51	15 34	21 11	17 15
27 TU	11 50 56	−1 35	5 50	17 52	5 51	17 50	5 52	17 49	5 54	17 47	5 56	17 45
270		1.0023	0 40	14 27	0 14	14 51	none	15 21	none	16 05	22 45	17 23
28 WE	11 50 35	−1 58	5 50	17 51	5 52	17 49	5 53	17 47	5 55	17 45	5 58	17 41
271		1.0021	1 34	15 08	1 11	15 28	0 42	15 53	0 01	16 27	none	17 26
29 TH	11 50 15	−2 22	5 50	17 50	5 52	17 48	5 54	17 46	5 57	17 43	6 01	17 38
272		1.0018	2 26	15 44	2 08	16 00	1 45	16 19	1 12	16 45	0 17	17 26
30 FR	11 49 56	−2 45	5 51	17 49	5 53	17 47	5 55	17 44	5 58	17 41	6 03	17 35
273		1.0015	3 17	16 18	3 04	16 29	2 47	16 41	2 24	16 59	1 46	17 26

OCTOBER 2005

10th Month   **31 days**

Coordinated Universal Time (Greenwich Mean Time)

NOTE: For each day, numbers on first line indicate Sun; numbers on second line indicate Moon.

Degrees are North Latitude.

Moon Phases: FM = Full Moon; LQ = Last (Waning) Quarter; NM = New Moon; FQ = First (Waxing) Quarter

Sun's distance is in Astronomical Units

CAUTION: Must be converted to local time. For instructions see "Calculation of Rise Times," page 368.

Day of month, of week, of year	Sun on Meridian / Moon Phase (h m s)	Sun's Declination ° ' / Distance	20° Rise Sun/Moon	20° Set Sun/Moon	30° Rise Sun/Moon	30° Set Sun/Moon	40° Rise Sun/Moon	40° Set Sun/Moon	50° Rise Sun/Moon	50° Set Sun/Moon	60° Rise Sun/Moon	60° Set Sun/Moon
1 SA	11 49 36	− 3 08	5 51	17 48	5 53	17 45	5 56	17 42	6 00	17 38	6 06	17 32
274		1.0012	4 07	16 50	3 59	16 56	3 48	17 02	3 34	17 11	3 12	17 24
2 SU	11 49 17	− 3 32	5 51	17 47	5 54	17 44	5 57	17 41	6 01	17 36	6 08	17 29
275		1.0009	4 56	17 21	4 53	17 22	4 50	17 22	4 45	17 22	4 37	17 23
3 MO	11 48 59	− 3 55	5 51	17 46	5 54	17 43	5 58	17 39	6 03	17 34	6 10	17 26
276	10 28 NM	1.0006	5 46	17 53	5 48	17 48	5 51	17 42	5 55	17 34	6 02	17 21
4 TU	11 48 40	− 4 18	5 52	17 45	5 55	17 42	5 59	17 38	6 05	17 32	6 13	17 23
277		1.0004	6 37	18 27	6 45	18 16	6 55	18 04	7 08	17 47	7 30	17 20
5 WE	11 48 22	v4 41	5 52	17 45	5 56	17 41	6 00	17 36	6 06	17 30	6 15	17 20
278		1.0001	7 30	19 03	7 44	18 48	8 00	18 28	8 24	18 02	9 02	17 19
6 TH	11 48 05	− 5 04	5 52	17 44	5 56	17 39	6 01	17 34	6 08	17 28	6 17	17 17
279		.9998	8 26	19 44	8 45	19 24	9 09	18 58	9 43	18 22	10 41	17 20
7 FR	11 47 47	− 5 27	5 52	17 43	5 57	17 38	6 02	17 33	6 09	17 25	6 20	17 14
280		.9995	9 26	20 31	9 50	20 06	10 20	19 34	11 04	18 49	12 27	17 23
8 SA	11 47 30	− 5 50	5 53	17 42	5 57	17 37	6 03	17 31	6 11	17 23	6 22	17 11
281		.9992	10 28	21 25	10 55	20 57	11 30	20 21	12 22	19 28	14 14	17 34
9 SU	11 47 14	− 6 13	5 53	17 41	5 58	17 36	6 04	17 30	6 12	17 21	6 25	17 09
282		.9989	11 30	22 24	11 59	21 55	12 36	21 18	13 32	20 22	15 42	18 13
10 MO	11 46 58	− 6 36	5 53	17 40	5 59	17 35	6 05	17 28	6 14	17 19	6 27	17 06
283	19 01 FQ	.9986	12 31	23 28	12 59	23 01	13 35	22 26	14 28	21 34	16 20	19 43
11 TU	11 46 42	− 6 59	5 54	17 40	5 59	17 34	6 06	17 27	6 16	17 17	6 30	17 03
284		.9983	13 26	none	13 51	none	14 23	23 41	15 08	22 58	16 32	21 37
12 WE	11 46 27	− 7 21	5 54	17 39	6 00	17 33	6 07	17 25	6 17	17 15	6 32	17 00
285		.9980	14 17	0 34	14 37	0 11	15 02	none	15 36	none	16 35	23 33
13 TH	11 46 13	− 7 44	5 54	17 38	6 01	17 31	6 08	17 23	6 19	17 13	6 34	16 57
286		.9977	15 02	1 39	15 16	1 22	15 34	0 59	15 58	0 27	16 36	none
14 FR	11 45 59	− 8 06	5 54	17 37	6 01	17 30	6 09	17 22	6 20	17 11	6 37	16 54
287		.9974	15 43	2 43	15 51	2 31	16 01	2 16	16 14	1 56	16 35	1 23
15 SA	11 45 45	− 8 28	5 55	17 36	6 02	17 29	6 10	17 20	6 22	17 09	6 39	16 51
288		.9971	16 22	3 44	16 23	3 38	16 26	3 32	16 29	3 23	16 34	3 09
16 SU	11 45 32	− 8 50	5 55	17 36	6 03	17 28	6 11	17 19	6 23	17 07	6 42	16 48
289		.9969	16 59	4 43	16 55	4 45	16 50	4 46	16 43	4 48	16 33	4 51
17 MO	11 45 20	− 9 12	5 55	17 35	6 03	17 27	6 13	17 18	6 25	17 05	6 44	16 45
290	12 14 FM	.9966	17 38	5 43	17 28	5 50	17 15	6 00	16 58	6 13	16 32	6 33
18 TU	11 45 08	− 9 34	5 56	17 34	6 04	17 26	6 14	17 16	6 27	17 03	6 47	16 42
291		.9963	18 18	6 43	18 02	6 56	17 43	7 13	17 15	7 37	16 32	8 16
19 WE	11 44 57	− 9 56	5 56	17 33	6 05	17 25	6 15	17 15	6 28	17 01	6 49	16 39
292		.9960	19 02	7 43	18 41	8 03	18 14	8 27	17 37	9 02	16 34	10 02
20 TH	11 44 46	− 10 18	5 56	17 33	6 05	17 24	6 16	17 13	6 30	16 59	6 52	16 37
293		.9957	19 50	8 44	19 24	9 08	18 52	9 39	18 06	10 23	16 39	11 48
21 FR	11 44 36	− 10 39	5 57	17 32	6 06	17 23	6 17	17 12	6 32	16 57	6 54	16 34
294		.9955	20 41	9 44	20 13	10 11	19 37	10 46	18 44	11 38	16 52	13 29
22 SA	11 44 27	− 11 00	5 57	17 31	6 07	17 22	6 18	17 10	6 33	16 55	6 57	16 31
295		.9952	21 35	10 41	21 06	11 10	20 30	11 47	19 35	12 41	17 31	14 45
23 SU	11 44 18	− 11 22	5 58	17 31	6 07	17 21	6 19	17 09	6 35	16 53	6 59	16 28
296		.9949	22 30	11 34	22 03	12 02	21 28	12 37	20 36	13 30	18 47	15 20
24 MO	11 44 11	− 11 43	5 58	17 30	6 08	17 20	6 20	17 08	6 36	16 51	7 02	16 25
297		.9946	23 25	12 22	23 00	12 47	22 30	13 19	21 45	14 06	20 20	15 33
25 TU	11 44 04	− 12 03	5 58	17 29	6 09	17 19	6 21	17 06	6 38	16 49	7 04	16 23
298	01 17 LQ	.9944	none	13 04	23 58	13 26	23 32	13 53	22 56	14 31	21 53	15 37
26 WE	11 43 57	− 12 24	5 59	17 29	6 09	17 18	6 22	17 05	6 40	16 47	7 07	16 20
299		.9941	0 18	13 42	none	14 00	none	14 21	none	14 51	23 24	15 38
27 TH	11 43 52	− 12 44	5 59	17 28	6 10	17 17	6 23	17 04	6 41	16 45	7 10	16 17
300		.9939	1 09	14 17	0 54	14 30	0 35	14 45	0 08	15 06	none	15 38
28 FR	11 43 47	− 13 05	6 00	17 28	6 11	17 16	6 25	17 03	6 43	16 44	7 12	16 15
301		.9936	1 59	14 50	1 49	14 57	1 36	15 06	1 19	15 18	0 51	15 37
29 SA	11 43 43	− 13 25	6 00	17 27	6 12	17 15	6 26	17 01	6 45	16 42	7 15	16 12
302		.9933	2 49	15 21	2 44	15 23	2 37	15 26	2 29	15 30	2 15	15 36
30 SU	11 43 39	− 13 44	6 01	17 27	6 12	17 15	6 27	17 00	6 46	16 40	7 17	16 09
303		.9931	3 38	15 53	3 38	15 50	3 39	15 46	3 39	15 41	3 40	15 34
31 MO	11 43 37	− 14 04	6 01	17 26	6 13	17 14	6 28	16 59	6 48	16 39	7 20	16 07
304		.9928	4 29	16 26	4 34	16 17	4 42	16 07	4 51	15 54	5 07	15 33

NOVEMBER 2005

11th Month   **30 days**

Coordinated Universal Time (Greenwich Mean Time)

NOTE: For each day, numbers on first line indicate Sun; numbers on second line indicate Moon.

Degrees are North Latitude.

Moon Phases: FM = Full Moon; LQ = Last (Waning) Quarter; NM = New Moon; FQ = First (Waxing) Quarter

Sun's distance is in Astronomical Units

CAUTION: Must be converted to local time. For instructions see "Calculation of Rise Times," page 368.

Day of month, of week, of year	Sun on Meridian Moon Phase h m s	Sun's Declination ° ′ Distance	20° Rise Sun Moon h m	20° Set Sun Moon h m	30° Rise Sun Moon h m	30° Set Sun Moon h m	40° Rise Sun Moon h m	40° Set Sun Moon h m	50° Rise Sun Moon h m	50° Set Sun Moon h m	60° Rise Sun Moon h m	60° Set Sun Moon h m
1 TU	11 43 35	− 14 23	6 01	17 25	6 14	17 13	6 29	16 58	6 50	16 37	7 22	16 04
305		.9926	5 22	17 01	5 33	16 48	5 47	16 31	6 07	16 08	6 38	15 32
2 WE	11 43 34	− 14 43	6 02	17 25	6 15	17 12	6 30	16 56	6 51	16 35	7 25	16 01
306	01 25 NM	.9923	6 18	17 41	6 35	17 23	6 56	16 59	7 26	16 26	8 16	15 32
3 TH	11 43 34	− 15 01	6 02	17 24	6 15	17 11	6 31	16 55	6 53	16 33	7 27	15 59
307		.9920	7 17	18 27	7 39	18 04	8 07	17 34	8 48	16 51	10 01	15 34
4 FR	11 43 35	− 15 20	6 03	17 24	6 16	17 11	6 32	16 54	6 55	16 32	7 30	15 56
308		.9918	8 20	19 20	8 46	18 52	9 20	18 18	10 09	17 26	11 51	15 43
5 SA	11 43 37	− 15 39	6 03	17 24	6 17	17 10	6 34	16 53	6 56	16 30	7 33	15 54
309		.9915	9 24	20 18	9 52	19 50	10 29	19 13	11 24	18 17	13 30	16 11
6 SU	11 43 39	− 15 57	6 04	17 23	6 18	17 09	6 35	16 52	6 58	16 29	7 35	15 51
310		.9913	10 26	21 22	10 54	20 54	11 30	20 18	12 25	19 25	14 24	17 27
7 MO	11 43 42	− 16 15	6 04	17 23	6 19	17 09	6 36	16 51	7 00	16 27	7 38	15 49
311		.9910	11 23	22 27	11 49	22 03	12 22	21 31	13 09	20 46	14 41	19 17
8 TU	11 43 46	− 16 32	6 05	17 22	6 19	17 08	6 37	16 50	7 01	16 26	7 40	15 46
312		.9908	12 14	23 32	12 36	23 12	13 03	22 48	13 41	22 12	14 46	21 11
9 WE	11 43 51	− 16 49	6 05	17 22	6 20	17 07	6 38	16 49	7 03	16 24	7 43	15 44
313	01 57 FQ	.9905	13 00	none	13 16	none	13 36	none	14 03	23 39	14 47	23 00
10 TH	11 43 57	− 17 07	6 06	17 22	6 21	17 07	6 39	16 48	7 05	16 23	7 45	15 42
314		.9903	13 41	0 34	13 51	0 20	14 04	0 03	14 21	none	14 47	none
11 FR	11 44 03	− 17 23	6 07	17 21	6 22	17 06	6 41	16 47	7 06	16 21	7 48	15 39
315		.9900	14 19	1 34	14 23	1 27	14 28	1 17	14 35	1 04	14 46	0 44
12 SA	11 44 10	− 17 40	6 07	17 21	6 23	17 05	6 42	16 46	7 08	16 20	7 51	15 37
316		.9898	14 56	2 32	14 54	2 31	14 52	2 29	14 49	2 27	14 45	2 23
13 SU	11 44 19	− 17 56	6 08	17 21	6 23	17 05	6 43	16 45	7 10	16 18	7 53	15 35
317		.9896	15 33	3 30	15 25	3 35	15 16	3 41	15 03	3 49	14 44	4 02
14 MO	11 44 28	− 18 12	6 08	17 20	6 24	17 04	6 44	16 45	7 11	16 17	7 56	15 33
318		.9893	16 12	4 28	15 58	4 39	15 42	4 53	15 19	5 12	14 44	5 42
15 TU	11 44 37	− 18 27	6 09	17 20	6 25	17 04	6 45	16 44	7 13	16 16	7 58	15 30
319		.9891	16 53	5 27	16 35	5 44	16 11	6 05	15 39	6 35	14 45	7 24
16 WE	11 44 48	− 18 42	6 09	17 20	6 26	17 03	6 46	16 43	7 14	16 15	8 01	15 28
320	00 57 FM	.9889	17 39	6 28	17 16	6 50	16 46	7 17	16 04	7 57	14 48	9 10
17 TH	11 45 00	− 18 57	6 10	17 20	6 27	17 03	6 47	16 42	7 16	16 13	8 03	15 26
321		.9887	18 29	7 28	18 02	7 54	17 28	8 27	16 38	9 16	14 58	10 54
18 FR	11 45 12	− 19 12	6 11	17 20	6 28	17 03	6 49	16 41	7 18	16 12	8 06	15 24
322		.9885	19 22	8 27	18 54	8 56	18 18	9 32	17 23	10 26	15 24	12 24
19 SA	11 45 25	− 19 26	6 11	17 19	6 28	17 02	6 50	16 41	7 19	16 11	8 08	15 22
323		.9883	20 18	9 23	19 50	9 51	19 14	10 28	18 21	11 21	16 25	13 18
20 SU	11 45 39	− 19 40	6 12	17 19	6 29	17 02	6 51	16 40	7 21	16 10	8 10	15 20
324		.9881	21 14	10 14	20 48	10 40	20 16	11 14	19 28	12 03	17 54	13 39
21 MO	11 45 54	− 19 53	6 12	17 19	6 30	17 02	6 52	16 40	7 22	16 09	8 13	15 18
325		.9879	22 08	10 59	21 46	11 22	21 19	11 51	20 39	12 32	19 28	13 46
22 TU	11 46 10	− 20 06	6 13	17 19	6 31	17 01	6 53	16 39	7 24	16 08	8 15	15 17
326		.9877	23 00	11 39	22 43	11 58	22 22	12 21	21 51	12 54	21 00	13 49
23 WE	11 46 26	− 20 19	6 14	17 19	6 32	17 01	6 54	16 38	7 25	16 07	8 18	15 15
327	22 11 LQ	.9875	23 51	12 15	23 38	12 29	23 23	12 47	23 02	13 11	22 28	13 49
24 TH	11 46 43	− 20 31	6 14	17 19	6 33	17 01	6 55	16 38	7 27	16 06	8 20	15 13
328		.9873	none	12 48	none	12 57	none	13 09	none	13 25	23 52	13 49
25 FR	11 47 01	− 20 43	6 15	17 19	6 33	17 00	6 56	16 37	7 28	16 05	8 22	15 11
329		.9871	0 40	13 19	0 33	13 24	0 24	13 29	0 11	13 36	none	13 47
26 SA	11 47 20	− 20 55	6 15	17 19	6 34	17 00	6 57	16 37	7 30	16 04	8 24	15 10
330		.9870	1 29	13 50	1 27	13 50	1 24	13 49	1 21	13 48	1 16	13 46
27 SU	11 47 40	− 21 06	6 16	17 19	6 35	17 00	6 58	16 37	7 31	16 04	8 27	15 08
331		.9868	2 18	14 22	2 21	14 16	2 26	14 09	2 31	14 00	2 40	13 45
28 MO	11 48 00	− 21 17	6 17	17 19	6 36	17 00	7 00	16 36	7 33	16 03	8 29	15 07
332		.9866	3 09	14 57	3 18	14 45	3 29	14 32	3 44	14 13	4 09	13 44
29 TU	11 48 21	− 21 27	6 17	17 19	6 37	17 00	7 01	16 36	7 34	16 02	8 31	15 05
333		.9864	4 04	15 35	4 18	15 18	4 36	14 58	5 02	14 29	5 43	13 44
30 WE	11 48 43	− 21 37	6 18	17 19	6 37	17 00	7 02	16 36	7 35	16 02	8 33	15 04
334		.9863	5 03	16 19	5 22	15 57	5 47	15 30	6 23	14 51	7 26	13 45

DECEMBER 2005

12th Month   **31 days**

Coordinated Universal Time (Greenwich Mean Time)

NOTE: For each day, numbers on first line indicate Sun; numbers on second line indicate Moon.

Degrees are North Latitude.

Moon Phases: FM = Full Moon; LQ = Last (Waning) Quarter; NM = New Moon; FQ = First (Waxing) Quarter

Sun's distance is in Astronomical Units

CAUTION: Must be converted to local time. For instructions see "Calculation of Rise Times," page 368.

Day of month, of week, of year	Sun on Meridian / Moon Phase h m s	Sun's Declination ° ' / Distance	20° Rise Sun/Moon h m	20° Set Sun/Moon h m	30° Rise Sun/Moon h m	30° Set Sun/Moon h m	40° Rise Sun/Moon h m	40° Set Sun/Moon h m	50° Rise Sun/Moon h m	50° Set Sun/Moon h m	60° Rise Sun/Moon h m	60° Set Sun/Moon h m
1 TH	11 49 05	− 21 47	6 19	17 19	6 38	17 00	7 03	16 35	7 37	16 01	8 35	15 03
335	15 01 NM	.9861	6 05	17 09	6 30	16 43	7 01	16 10	7 47	15 23	9 16	13 51
2 FR	11 49 28	− 21 56	6 19	17 20	6 39	17 00	7 04	16 35	7 38	16 01	8 37	15 01
336		.9860	7 10	18 07	7 38	17 39	8 14	17 02	9 07	16 08	11 04	14 10
3 SA	11 49 52	− 22 05	6 20	17 20	6 40	17 00	7 05	16 35	7 39	16 00	8 39	15 00
337		.9858	8 15	19 11	8 43	18 43	9 20	18 06	10 15	17 11	12 19	15 08
4 SU	11 50 16	− 22 13	6 21	17 20	6 41	17 00	7 06	16 35	7 41	16 00	8 41	14 59
338		.9856	9 16	20 18	9 43	19 52	10 17	19 19	11 07	18 31	12 47	16 53
5 MO	11 50 41	− 22 21	6 21	17 20	6 41	17 00	7 06	16 35	7 42	15 59	8 43	14 58
339		.9855	10 10	21 24	10 33	21 03	11 02	20 37	11 43	19 58	12 55	18 50
6 TU	11 51 06	− 22 29	6 22	17 20	6 42	17 00	7 07	16 35	7 43	15 59	8 45	14 57
340		.9853	10 59	22 28	11 16	22 13	11 38	21 54	12 08	21 27	12 58	20 42
7 WE	11 51 32	− 22 36	6 22	17 21	6 43	17 00	7 08	16 35	7 44	15 59	8 46	14 57
341		.9852	11 41	23 29	11 53	23 20	12 07	23 08	12 27	22 53	12 58	22 27
8 TH	11 51 58	− 22 42	6 23	17 21	6 44	17 00	7 09	16 35	7 45	15 58	8 48	14 56
342	09 36 FQ	.9851	12 20	none	12 26	none	12 33	none	12 43	none	12 57	none
9 FR	11 52 25	− 22 48	6 24	17 21	6 44	17 00	7 10	16 35	7 46	15 58	8 49	14 55
343		.9849	12 56	0 27	12 56	0 24	12 56	0 20	12 56	0 15	12 57	0 07
10 SA	11 52 52	− 22 54	6 24	17 21	6 45	17 01	7 11	16 35	7 47	15 58	8 51	14 55
344		.9848	13 33	1 24	13 27	1 27	13 20	1 31	13 10	1 36	12 56	1 44
11 SU	11 53 19	− 22 59	6 25	17 22	6 46	17 01	7 12	16 35	7 48	15 58	8 52	14 54
345		.9847	14 10	2 20	13 58	2 29	13 44	2 41	13 25	2 56	12 55	3 20
12 MO	11 53 47	− 23 04	6 25	17 22	6 46	17 01	7 12	16 35	7 49	15 58	8 54	14 54
346		.9846	14 49	3 18	14 32	3 33	14 11	3 51	13 42	4 17	12 56	4 59
13 TU	11 54 15	− 23 08	6 26	17 22	6 47	17 01	7 13	16 35	7 50	15 58	8 55	14 53
347		.9844	15 33	4 16	15 11	4 36	14 43	5 02	14 05	5 38	12 58	6 41
14 WE	11 54 44	− 23 12	6 27	17 23	6 48	17 02	7 14	16 35	7 51	15 58	8 56	14 53
348		.9843	16 20	5 16	15 54	5 40	15 22	6 12	14 35	6 57	13 05	8 25
15 TH	11 55 12	− 23 16	6 27	17 23	6 48	17 02	7 15	16 36	7 52	15 58	8 57	14 53
349	16 15 FM	.9842	17 12	6 15	16 44	6 43	16 08	7 18	15 15	8 10	13 23	10 01
16 FR	11 55 42	− 23 19	6 28	17 24	6 49	17 02	7 15	16 36	7 53	15 59	8 58	14 53
350		.9841	18 07	7 12	17 39	7 41	17 02	8 17	16 09	9 11	14 09	11 10
17 SA	11 56 11	− 23 21	6 28	17 24	6 50	17 03	7 16	16 36	7 53	15 59	8 59	14 53
351		.9840	19 03	8 05	18 36	8 32	18 03	9 07	17 13	9 58	15 30	11 42
18 SU	11 56 40	− 23 23	6 29	17 24	6 50	17 03	7 17	16 37	7 54	15 59	9 00	14 53
352		.9840	19 58	8 52	19 35	9 17	19 06	9 48	18 23	10 32	17 04	11 53
19 MO	11 57 10	− 23 25	6 29	17 25	6 51	17 04	7 17	16 37	7 55	15 59	9 01	14 53
353		.9839	20 52	9 35	20 33	9 55	20 09	10 21	19 35	10 57	18 37	11 58
20 TU	11 57 39	− 23 26	6 30	17 25	6 51	17 04	7 18	16 38	7 55	16 00	9 01	14 54
354		.9838	21 43	10 12	21 29	10 28	21 11	10 48	20 47	11 15	20 07	11 59
21 WE	11 58 09	− 23 26	6 30	17 26	6 52	17 05	7 18	16 38	7 56	16 00	9 02	14 54
355		.9838	22 32	10 46	22 23	10 57	22 12	11 11	21 56	11 30	21 32	11 59
22 TH	11 58 39	− 23 26	6 31	17 26	6 52	17 05	7 19	16 39	7 56	16 01	9 03	14 55
356		.9837	23 20	11 18	23 16	11 24	23 11	11 32	23 05	11 42	22 54	11 58
23 FR	11 59 09	− 23 26	6 31	17 27	6 53	17 06	7 19	16 39	7 57	16 01	9 03	14 55
357	19 36 LQ	.9836	none	11 48	none	11 50	none	11 51	none	11 54	none	11 57
24 SA	11 59 39	− 23 25	6 32	17 27	6 53	17 06	7 20	16 40	7 57	16 02	9 03	14 56
358		.9836	0 09	12 19	0 10	12 16	0 11	12 11	0 13	12 05	0 17	11 56
25 SU	12 00 08	− 23 24	6 32	17 28	6 54	17 07	7 20	16 40	7 58	16 03	9 03	14 57
359		.9835	0 58	12 52	1 04	12 43	1 13	12 32	1 24	12 17	1 41	11 54
26 MO	12 00 38	− 23 22	6 33	17 29	6 54	17 07	7 20	16 41	7 58	16 03	9 04	14 58
360		.9835	1 50	13 27	2 02	13 13	2 17	12 56	2 37	12 32	3 11	11 54
27 TU	12 01 08	− 23 20	6 33	17 29	6 54	17 08	7 21	16 42	7 58	16 04	9 04	14 59
361		.9835	2 45	14 08	3 03	13 48	3 25	13 24	3 55	12 50	4 48	11 54
28 WE	12 01 37	− 23 17	6 34	17 30	6 55	17 09	7 21	16 42	7 58	16 05	9 04	15 00
362		.9834	3 45	14 54	4 08	14 30	4 36	14 00	5 18	13 17	6 34	11 58
29 TH	12 02 07	− 23 14	6 34	17 30	6 55	17 09	7 21	16 43	7 58	16 06	9 03	15 01
363		.9834	4 49	15 49	5 16	15 22	5 50	14 47	6 40	13 55	8 25	12 09
30 FR	12 02 36	− 23 11	6 34	17 31	6 55	17 10	7 22	16 44	7 59	16 07	9 03	15 02
364		.9834	5 55	16 51	6 24	16 23	7 01	15 46	7 56	14 50	10 01	12 45
31 SA	12 03 04	− 23 06	6 35	17 31	6 56	17 11	7 22	16 45	7 59	16 08	9 03	15 04
365	03 12 NM	.9834	7 00	17 59	7 28	17 32	8 03	16 57	8 56	16 05	10 48	14 15

CALENDAR

Julian and Gregorian Calendars; Leap Year; Century

The **Julian calendar**, under which all Western nations measured time until AD 1582, was authorized by Julius Caesar in 46 BC. It called for a year of 365¼ days, starting in January, with every 4th year being a **leap year** of 366 days. St. Bede, an Anglo-Saxon monk also known as the Venerable Bede, announced in AD 730 that the Julian year was 11 min, 14 sec too long, a cumulative error of about a day every 128 years, but nothing was done about this for centuries.

By 1582 the accumulated error was estimated at 10 days. In that year Pope Gregory XIII decreed that the day following Oct. 4, 1582, should be called Oct. 15, thus dropping 10 days and initiating the **Gregorian calendar**.

The Gregorian calendar continued a system devised by the monk Dionysius Exiguus (6th century), starting from the first year following the birth of Jesus Christ, which was inaccurately taken to be year 753 in the Roman calendar. Leap years were continued but, to prevent further displacements, centesimal years (years ending in 00) were made common years, not leap years, unless divisible by 400. Under this plan, **1600** and **2000** are leap years (as is **2004**); 1700, 1800, and 1900 are not.

The Gregorian calendar was adopted at once by France, Italy, Spain, Portugal, and Luxembourg. Within 2 years most German Catholic states, Belgium, and parts of Switzerland and the Netherlands were brought under the new calendar, and Hungary followed in 1587. The rest of the Netherlands, along with Denmark and the German Protestant states, made the change in 1699-1700.

The British government adopted the Gregorian calendar and imposed it on all its possessions, including the American colonies, in 1752, decreeing that the day following Sept. 2, 1752, should be called Sept. 14, a loss of 11 days. All dates preceding were marked OS, for Old Style. In addition, New Year's Day was moved to Jan. 1 from Mar. 25 (under the old reckoning, for example, Mar. 24, 1700, had been followed by Mar. 25, 1701). Thus George Washington's birthdate, which was Feb. 11, 1731, OS, became Feb. 22, 1732, NS (New Style). In 1753 Sweden also went Gregorian.

In 1793 the French revolutionary government adopted a calendar of 12 months of 30 days with 5 extra days in September of each common year and a 6th every 4th year. Napoleon reinstated the Gregorian calendar in 1806.

The Gregorian system later spread to non-European regions, replacing traditional calendars at least for official purposes. Japan in 1873, Egypt in 1875, China in 1912, and Turkey in 1925 made the change, usually in conjunction with political upheaval. In China, the republican government began reckoning years from its 1911 founding. After 1949, the People's Republic adopted the Common, or Christian Era, year count, even for the traditional lunar calendar, which is also retained. In 1918 the Soviet Union decreed that the day after Jan. 31, 1918, OS, would be Feb. 14, 1918, NS. Greece changed over in 1923. For the first time in history, all major nations had one calendar. The Russian Orthodox church and some other Christian sects retained the Julian calendar.

To convert from the Julian to the Gregorian calendar, add 10 days to dates Oct. 5, 1582, through Feb. 28, 1700; after that date add 11 days through Feb. 28, 1800; 12 days through Feb. 28, 1900; and 13 days through Feb. 28, 2100.

A **century** consists of 100 consecutive years. The 1st century AD may be said to have run from the years 1 through 100. The 20th century by this reckoning consisted of the years 1901 through 2000 and technically ended Dec. 31, 2000, as did the 2nd millennium AD. The 21st century thus technically began Jan. 1, 2001.

For a **Perpetual Calendar,** see pages 384-385.

Gregorian Calendar

Choose the desired year from the table below or from the Perpetual Calendar (for years 1803 to 2080). The number after each year designates which calendar to use for that year, as shown in the Perpetual Calendar—see pages 384-385. (The Gregorian calendar was inaugurated Oct. 15, 1582. From that date to Dec. 31, 1582, use calendar 6.)

1583-1802

Year	#	Year	#	Year	#	Year	#	Year	#	Year	#	Year	#	Year	#	Year	#	Year	#	Year	#
1583	7	1603	4	1623	1	1643	5	1663	2	1683	6	1703	2	1723	6	1743	3	1763	7	1783	4
1584	8	1604	12	1624	9	1644	13	1664	10	1684	14	1704	10	1724	14	1744	11	1764	8	1784	12
1585	3	1605	7	1625	4	1645	1	1665	5	1685	2	1705	5	1725	2	1745	6	1765	3	1785	7
1586	4	1606	1	1626	5	1646	2	1666	6	1686	3	1706	6	1726	3	1746	7	1766	4	1786	1
1587	5	1607	2	1627	6	1647	3	1667	7	1687	4	1707	7	1727	4	1747	1	1767	5	1787	2
1588	13	1608	10	1628	14	1648	11	1668	8	1688	12	1708	8	1728	12	1748	9	1768	13	1788	10
1589	1	1609	6	1629	2	1649	6	1669	3	1689	7	1709	3	1729	7	1749	4	1769	1	1789	5
1590	2	1610	6	1630	3	1650	7	1670	4	1690	1	1710	4	1730	1	1750	5	1770	2	1790	6
1591	3	1611	7	1631	4	1651	1	1671	5	1691	2	1711	5	1731	2	1751	6	1771	3	1791	7
1592	11	1612	8	1632	12	1652	9	1672	13	1692	10	1712	13	1732	10	1752	14	1772	11	1792	8
1593	6	1613	3	1633	7	1653	4	1673	1	1693	5	1713	1	1733	5	1753	2	1773	6	1793	3
1594	7	1614	4	1634	1	1654	5	1674	2	1694	6	1714	2	1734	6	1754	3	1774	7	1794	4
1595	1	1615	5	1635	2	1655	6	1675	3	1695	7	1715	3	1735	7	1755	4	1775	1	1795	5
1596	9	1616	13	1636	10	1656	14	1676	11	1696	8	1716	11	1736	8	1756	12	1776	9	1796	13
1597	4	1617	1	1637	5	1657	2	1677	6	1697	3	1717	6	1737	3	1757	7	1777	4	1797	1
1598	5	1618	2	1638	6	1658	3	1678	7	1698	4	1718	7	1738	4	1758	1	1778	5	1798	2
1599	6	1619	3	1639	7	1659	4	1679	1	1699	5	1719	1	1739	5	1759	2	1779	6	1799	3
1600	14	1620	11	1640	8	1660	12	1680	9	1700	6	1720	9	1740	3	1760	10	1780	14	1800	4
1601	2	1621	6	1641	3	1661	7	1681	4	1701	7	1721	4	1741	1	1761	5	1781	2	1801	5
1602	3	1622	7	1642	4	1662	1	1682	5	1702	1	1722	5	1742	2	1762	6	1782	3	1802	6

The Julian Period

How many days have you lived? To determine this, multiply your age by 365, add the number of days since your last birthday, and account for all leap years. Chances are your calculations will go wrong somewhere. Astronomers, however, find it convenient to express dates and time intervals in days rather than in years, months, and days. This is done by placing events within the Julian period.

The Julian period was devised in 1582 by the French classical scholar Joseph Scaliger (1540-1609), and it was named after his father, Julius Caesar Scaliger, not after the Julian calendar as might be supposed.

Scaliger began with a zero hour, or starting time, of noon on Jan. 1, 4713 BC (on the Julian calendar). This was the most recent time that 3 major chronological cycles began on the same day: (1) the 28-year solar cycle, after which dates in the Julian calendar (e.g., Feb. 11) return to the same days of the week (e.g., Monday); (2) the 19-year lunar cycle, after which the phases of the moon return to the same dates of the year; and (3) the 15-year indiction cycle, used in ancient Rome to regulate taxes. It will take 7,980 years to complete the period, the product of 28, 19, and 15.

Noon of Dec. 31, 2004, will be Julian Date (JD) 2,453,371; that many days will have passed since the start of the Julian period. The JD at noon of any date in 2005 may be found by adding to this figure the day of the year for that date, which can be obtained from the left half of the "How Far Apart Are Two Dates?" chart on the next page.

Julian Calendar

To find which of the 14 calendars of the Perpetual Calendar (pages 384-385) applies to any year under the Julian system, find the century for the desired year in the 3 leftmost columns below. Read across and find the year in the 4 top rows. Then read down. The number in the intersection is the calendar designation for that year. For some years and countries the Julian new year did not start Jan. 1; to find the correct Perpetual Calendar for Britain and its possessions, you can generally add one year for dates from Jan. 1-Mar. 24. For example, to look up Feb. 2, 1705, Old Style, use the year 1706.

Year (last 2 figures of desired year)

Century			01 02 03 04 05 06 07 08 09 10 11 12 13 14 15 16 17 18 19 20 21 22 23 24 25 26 27 28

Century			01	02	03	04	05	06	07	08	09	10	11	12	13	14	15	16	17	18	19	20	21	22	23	24	25	26	27	28
			29	30	31	32	33	34	35	36	37	38	39	40	41	42	43	44	45	46	47	48	49	50	51	52	53	54	55	56
			57	58	59	60	61	62	63	64	65	66	67	68	69	70	71	72	73	74	75	76	77	78	79	80	81	82	83	84
		00	85	86	87	88	89	90	91	92	93	94	95	96	97	98	99													
0	700 1400	12	7	1	2	10	5	6	7	8	3	4	5	13	1	2	3	11	6	7	1	9	4	5	6	14	2	3	4	12
100	800 1500	11	6	7	1	9	4	5	6	14	2	3	4	12	7	1	2	10	5	6	7	8	3	4	5	13	1	2	3	11
200	900 1600	10	5	6	7	8	3	4	5	13	1	2	3	11	6	7	1	9	4	5	6	14	2	3	4	12	7	1	2	10
300	1000 1700	9	4	5	6	14	2	3	4	12	7	1	2	10	5	6	7	8	3	4	5	13	1	2	3	11	6	7	1	9
400	1100 1800	8	3	4	5	13	1	2	3	11	6	7	1	9	4	5	6	14	2	3	4	12	7	1	2	10	5	6	7	8
500	1200 1900	14	2	3	4	12	7	1	2	10	5	6	7	8	3	4	5	13	1	2	3	11	6	7	1	9	4	5	6	14
600	1300 2000	13	1	2	3	11	6	7	1	9	4	5	6	14	2	3	4	12	7	1	2	10	5	6	7	8	3	4	5	13

How Far Apart Are Two Dates?

This table covers a range of 2 years. To use, **find the number for each date and subtract** the smaller from the larger. Example—for days from Feb. 10, 2005, to Dec. 15, 2006, subtract 41 from 714; the result is 673. For leap years, such as 2004, where Feb. 29 intervenes, one day must be then added; thus Feb. 4, 2003, and Mar. 13, 2004, were 403 days apart.

First Year

Date	Jan.	Feb.	Mar.	April	May	June	July	Aug.	Sept.	Oct.	Nov.	Dec.
1	1	32	60	91	121	152	182	213	244	274	305	335
2	2	33	61	92	122	153	183	214	245	275	306	336
3	3	34	62	93	123	154	184	215	246	276	307	337
4	4	35	63	94	124	155	185	216	247	277	308	338
5	5	36	64	95	125	156	186	217	248	278	309	339
6	6	37	65	96	126	157	187	218	249	279	310	340
7	7	38	66	97	127	158	188	219	250	280	311	341
8	8	39	67	98	128	159	189	220	251	281	312	342
9	9	40	68	99	129	160	190	221	252	282	313	343
10	10	41	69	100	130	161	191	222	253	283	314	344
11	11	42	70	101	131	162	192	223	254	284	315	345
12	12	43	71	102	132	163	193	224	255	285	316	346
13	13	44	72	103	133	164	194	225	256	286	317	347
14	14	45	73	104	134	165	195	226	257	287	318	348
15	15	46	74	105	135	166	196	227	258	288	319	349
16	16	47	75	106	136	167	197	228	259	289	320	350
17	17	48	76	107	137	168	198	229	260	290	321	351
18	18	49	77	108	138	169	199	230	261	291	322	352
19	19	50	78	109	139	170	200	231	262	292	323	353
20	20	51	79	110	140	171	201	232	263	293	324	354
21	21	52	80	111	141	172	202	233	264	294	325	355
22	22	53	81	112	142	173	203	234	265	295	326	356
23	23	54	82	113	143	174	204	235	266	296	327	357
24	24	55	83	114	144	175	205	236	267	297	328	358
25	25	56	84	115	145	176	206	237	268	298	329	359
26	26	57	85	116	146	177	207	238	269	299	330	360
27	27	58	86	117	147	178	208	239	270	300	331	361
28	28	59	87	118	148	179	209	240	271	301	332	362
29	29	—	88	119	149	180	210	241	272	302	333	363
30	30	—	89	120	150	181	211	242	273	303	334	364
31	31	—	90	—	151	—	212	243	—	304	—	365

Second Year

Date	Jan.	Feb.	Mar.	April	May	June	July	Aug.	Sept.	Oct.	Nov.	Dec.
1	366	397	425	456	486	517	547	578	609	639	670	700
2	367	398	426	457	487	518	548	579	610	640	671	701
3	368	399	427	458	488	519	549	580	611	641	672	702
4	369	400	428	459	489	520	550	581	612	642	673	703
5	370	401	429	460	490	521	551	582	613	643	674	704
6	371	402	430	461	491	522	552	583	614	644	675	705
7	372	403	431	462	492	523	553	584	615	645	676	706
8	373	404	432	463	493	524	554	585	616	646	677	707
9	374	405	433	464	494	525	555	586	617	647	678	708
10	375	406	434	465	495	526	556	587	618	648	679	709
11	376	407	435	466	496	527	557	588	619	649	680	710
12	377	408	436	467	497	528	558	589	620	650	681	711
13	378	409	437	468	498	529	559	590	621	651	682	712
14	379	410	438	469	499	530	560	591	622	652	683	713
15	380	411	439	470	500	531	561	592	623	653	684	714
16	381	412	440	471	501	532	562	593	624	654	685	715
17	382	413	441	472	502	533	563	594	625	655	686	716
18	383	414	442	473	503	534	564	595	626	656	687	717
19	384	415	443	474	504	535	565	596	627	657	688	718
20	385	416	444	475	505	536	566	597	628	658	689	719
21	386	417	445	476	506	537	567	598	629	659	690	720
22	387	418	446	477	507	538	568	599	630	660	691	721
23	388	419	447	478	508	539	569	600	631	661	692	722
24	389	420	448	479	509	540	570	601	632	662	693	723
25	390	421	449	480	510	541	571	602	633	663	694	724
26	391	422	450	481	511	542	572	603	634	664	695	725
27	392	423	451	482	512	543	573	604	635	665	696	726
28	393	424	452	483	513	544	574	605	636	666	697	727
29	394	—	453	484	514	545	575	606	637	667	698	728
30	395	—	454	485	515	546	576	607	638	668	699	729
31	396	—	455	—	516	—	577	608	—	669	—	730

Signs of the Zodiac

The **zodiac** is the apparent yearly path of the sun among the stars as viewed from earth, and was divided by the ancients into 12 equal sections or signs, each named for the constellation situated within its limits in ancient times. Astrologers claim that the temperament and destiny of each individual depend on the zodiac sign under which the person was born and the relationships between the planets at that time and throughout life.

Below are the 12 traditional signs and the traditional range of dates pertaining to each:

♈ **Aries** (Ram), March 21– April 19

♎ **Libra** (Balance), September 23– October 23

♉ **Taurus** (Bull), April 20– May 20

♏ **Scorpio** (Scorpion), October 24– November 21

♊ **Gemini** (Twins), May 21– June 21

♐ **Sagittarius** (Archer), November 22– December 21

♋ **Cancer** (Crab), June 22– July 22

♑ **Capricorn** (Goat), December 22– January 19

♌ **Leo** (Lion), July 23– August 22

♒ **Aquarius** (Water Bearer), January 20 – February 18

♍ **Virgo** (Maiden), August 23– September 22

♓ **Pisces** (Fishes), February 19 – March 20

Calendar for the Year 2005

	JANUARY								FEBRUARY								MARCH								APRIL					
S	M	T	W	T	F	S		S	M	T	W	T	F	S		S	M	T	W	T	F	S		S	M	T	W	T	F	S
						1				1	2	3	4	5				1	2	3	4	5							1	2
2	3	4	5	6	7	8		6	7	8	9	10	11	12		6	7	8	9	10	11	12		3	4	5	6	7	8	9
9	10	11	12	13	14	15		13	14	15	16	17	18	19		13	14	15	16	17	18	19		10	11	12	13	14	15	16
16	17	18	19	20	21	22		20	21	22	23	24	25	26		20	21	22	23	24	25	26		17	18	19	20	21	22	23
23	24	25	26	27	28	29		27	28							27	28	29	30	31				24	25	26	27	28	29	30
30	31																													

	MAY								JUNE								JULY								AUGUST					
S	M	T	W	T	F	S		S	M	T	W	T	F	S		S	M	T	W	T	F	S		S	M	T	W	T	F	S
1	2	3	4	5	6	7					1	2	3	4							1	2		1	2	3	4	5	6	
8	9	10	11	12	13	14		5	6	7	8	9	10	11		3	4	5	6	7	8	9		7	8	9	10	11	12	13
15	16	17	18	19	20	21		12	13	14	15	16	17	18		10	11	12	13	14	15	16		14	15	16	17	18	19	20
22	23	24	25	26	27	28		19	20	21	22	23	24	25		17	18	19	20	21	22	23		21	22	23	24	25	26	27
29	30	31						26	27	28	29	30				24	25	26	27	28	29	30		28	29	30	31			
																31														

	SEPTEMBER								OCTOBER								NOVEMBER								DECEMBER					
S	M	T	W	T	F	S		S	M	T	W	T	F	S		S	M	T	W	T	F	S		S	M	T	W	T	F	S
				1	2	3								1				1	2	3	4	5						1	2	3
4	5	6	7	8	9	10		2	3	4	5	6	7	8		6	7	8	9	10	11	12		4	5	6	7	8	9	10
11	12	13	14	15	16	17		9	10	11	12	13	14	15		13	14	15	16	17	18	19		11	12	13	14	15	16	17
18	19	20	21	22	23	24		16	17	18	19	20	21	22		20	21	22	23	24	26	26		18	19	20	21	22	23	24
25	26	27	28	29	30			23	24	25	26	27	28	29		27	28	29	30					25	26	27	28	29	30	31
								30	31																					

Federal Holidays and Other Notable Dates, 2005

Some dates may be subject to change. Some events omitted where date not scheduled as of Sept. 2004.

The days marked on the calendar above and shown below *in italics* are U.S. federal holidays, designated by the president or Congress and applicable to federal employees and the District of Columbia. Most U.S. states also observe these holidays, and many states observe others; practices vary from state to state. In most states the secretary of state's office can provide details.

January
1 *New Year's Day*; Rose, Cotton, and
   Fiesta bowls
3 Sugar Bowl
4 Orange Bowl
17 *Martin Luther King Jr. Day*
   (3rd Mon. in Jan.)
17-30 Australian Open tennis tournament
26 Australia Day, Australia

February
2 Groundhog Day
5 Constitution Day, Mexico
5-8 Carnival, Brazil
6 Super Bowl XXXIX (Jacksonville, FL)
8 Mardi Gras
9 Ash Wednesday; Chinese New Year
12 Lincoln's Birthday
13 NFL Pro Bowl
14 Valentine's Day
14-15 Westminster Dog Show
20 Daytona 500; NBA All-Star Game
21 *Washington's Birthday (observed),
   Presidents' Day, or Washington-
   Lincoln Day* (3rd Mon. in Feb.)
27 Academy Awards

March
5 Iditarod Trail Sled Dog Race begins
14 Commonwealth Day, Canada
17 St. Patrick's Day
20 First day of spring (Northern
   Hemisphere)
21 Benito Juárez's Birthday, Mexico
25 Good Friday
27 Easter

April
1 April Fool's Day
3 Daylight Saving Time begins in U.S.
4 NCAA men's basketball championship
5 NCAA women's basketball
   championship
7-10 Masters golf tournament
18 Patriots' Day; Boston Marathon
22 Earth Day
24 Passover (1st full day)

27 Administrative Professionals Day
28 Take Our Daughters and Sons
   to Work Day
29 Arbor Day, U.S.

May
1 May Day; Orthodox Easter
3 National Teacher Day, U.S.
5 Cinco de Mayo (Battle of Puebla
   Day), Mexico
7 Kentucky Derby
8 Mother's Day
15 Preakness Stakes; Buddha's
   Birthday, Korea, Hong Kong
21 Armed Forces Day
23 Victoria Day, Canada
23-June 5 French Open tennis
   tournament
30 *Memorial Day, or Decoration
   Day* (last Mon. in May)

June
11 Dragon Boat Festival, China;
   Belmont Stakes
16-19 U.S. Open golf tournament
14 Flag Day, U.S.
19 Father's Day
20-July 3 Wimbledon tennis
   tournament
21 First day of summer (Northern
   Hemisphere)

July
1 Canada Day
4 *Independence Day*
7–14 Running of the Bulls (Pamplona,
   Spain)
14 Bastille Day, France
14-17 British Open golf tournament

August
11-14 PGA Championship
29-Sept. 11 U.S. Open tennis
   tournament
30 St. Rose of Lima, Peru

September
5 *Labor Day*, U.S. (1st Monday in
   Sept.); Labor Day, Canada
11 Grandparents' Day, U.S.
16 Independence Day, Mexico
17 Citizenship Day, U.S.
19 St. Gennaro, Italy
22 First day of autumn (Northern
   Hemisphere)

October
3 German Unification Day, Germany;
   U.S. Supreme Court session begins
4 Rosh Hashanah (1st full day);
   Ramadan (1st full day)
10 *Columbus Day* (2nd Mon. in Oct.);
   Thanksgiving Day, Canada
12 Día de la Raza, Mexico
13 Yom Kippur
24 United Nations Day
30 Daylight Saving Time ends in U.S.
31 Halloween

November
1 All Saints' Day
2 Day of the Dead, Mexico
5 Guy Fawkes Day, UK
6 New York City Marathon
8 Election Day (observed in some states;
   1st Tues. after 1st Mon. in Nov.)
11 *Veterans Day*; Remembrance Day,
   Canada, UK
15 Shichi-Go-San (Seven-Five-Three),
   Japan
24 *Thanksgiving Day, U.S.* (4th Thurs. in
   Nov.)

December
10 Nobel Prizes awarded (announced
   in Oct.)
12 Virgin of Guadalupe Day, Mexico
21 First day of winter (Northern
   Hemisphere)
25 *Christmas Day*
26 Hanukkah (1st full day); Kwanzaa
   begins; Boxing Day, Australia,
   Canada, New Zealand, UK

WORLD ALMANAC QUICK QUIZ

Not factoring in Daylight Saving Time, if it were 1 PM in Washington, DC, what time would it be in Baghdad?
(a) 11 pm   (b) 9 PM   (c) 1 AM the following day   (d) 5 PM
For the answer look in this chapter, or see page 1008.

Perpetual Calendar

The number shown for each year indicates which Gregorian calendar to use. For 1583-1802, see "Gregorian Calendar" on page 381. For 1803-20, use numbers for 1983-2000, respectively. For Julian Calendar, see "Julian Calendar" on page 382.

Year	No.	Year	No.	Year	No.	Year	No.	Year	No.	Year	No.	Year	No.	Year	No.	Year	No.	Year	No.
1821	2	1847	6	1873	4	1899	1	1925	5	1951	2	1977	7	2003	4	2029	2	2055	6
1822	3	1848	14	1874	5	1900	2	1926	6	1952	10	1978	1	2004	12	2030	3	2056	14
1823	4	1849	2	1875	6	1901	3	1927	7	1953	5	1979	2	2005	7	2031	4	2057	2
1824	12	1850	3	1876	14	1902	4	1928	8	1954	6	1980	10	2006	1	2032	12	2058	3
1825	7	1851	4	1877	2	1903	5	1929	3	1955	7	1981	5	2007	2	2033	7	2059	4
1826	1	1852	12	1878	3	1904	13	1930	4	1956	8	1982	6	2008	10	2034	1	2060	12
1827	2	1853	7	1879	4	1905	1	1931	5	1957	3	1983	7	2009	5	2035	2	2061	7
1828	10	1854	1	1880	12	1906	2	1932	13	1958	4	1984	8	2010	6	2036	10	2062	1
1829	5	1855	2	1881	7	1907	3	1933	1	1959	5	1985	3	2011	7	2037	5	2063	2
1830	6	1856	10	1882	1	1908	11	1934	2	1960	13	1986	4	2012	8	2038	6	2064	10
1831	7	1857	5	1883	2	1909	6	1935	3	1961	1	1987	5	2013	3	2039	7	2065	5
1832	8	1858	6	1884	10	1910	7	1936	11	1962	2	1988	13	2014	4	2040	8	2066	6
1833	3	1859	7	1885	5	1911	1	1937	6	1963	3	1989	1	2015	5	2041	3	2067	7
1834	4	1860	8	1886	6	1912	9	1938	7	1964	11	1990	2	2016	13	2042	4	2068	8
1835	5	1861	3	1887	7	1913	4	1939	1	1965	6	1991	3	2017	1	2043	5	2069	3
1836	13	1862	4	1888	8	1914	5	1940	9	1966	7	1992	11	2018	2	2044	13	2070	4
1837	1	1863	5	1889	3	1915	6	1941	4	1967	1	1993	6	2019	3	2045	1	2071	5
1838	2	1864	13	1890	4	1916	14	1942	5	1968	9	1994	7	2020	11	2046	2	2072	13
1839	3	1865	1	1891	5	1917	2	1943	6	1969	4	1995	1	2021	6	2047	3	2073	1
1840	11	1866	2	1892	13	1918	3	1944	14	1970	5	1996	9	2022	7	2048	11	2074	2
1841	6	1867	3	1893	1	1919	4	1945	2	1971	6	1997	4	2023	1	2049	6	2075	3
1842	7	1868	11	1894	2	1920	12	1946	3	1972	14	1998	5	2024	9	2050	7	2076	11
1843	1	1869	6	1895	3	1921	7	1947	4	1973	2	1999	6	2025	4	2051	1	2077	6
1844	9	1870	7	1896	11	1922	1	1948	12	1974	3	2000	14	2026	5	2052	9	2078	7
1845	4	1871	1	1897	6	1923	2	1949	7	1975	4	2001	2	2027	6	2053	4	2079	1
1846	5	1872	9	1898	7	1924	10	1950	1	1976	12	2002	3	2028	14	2054	5	2080	9

The page also contains six sample reference calendars, each showing all twelve months (January through December), labelled:

- **1 — 2006**
- **2 — 2001/2007**
- **3 — 2002**
- **4 — 2003**
- **5 — 2009**
- **6 — 2010**

7 — 2005

JANUARY

S	M	T	W	T	F	S
						1
2	3	4	5	6	7	8
9	10	11	12	13	14	15
16	17	18	19	20	21	22
23	24	25	26	27	28	29
30	31					

FEBRUARY

S	M	T	W	T	F	S
		1	2	3	4	5
6	7	8	9	10	11	12
13	14	15	16	17	18	19
20	21	22	23	24	25	26
27	28					

MARCH

S	M	T	W	T	F	S
		1	2	3	4	5
6	7	8	9	10	11	12
13	14	15	16	17	18	19
20	21	22	23	24	25	26
27	28	29	30	31		

APRIL

S	M	T	W	T	F	S
					1	2
3	4	5	6	7	8	9
10	11	12	13	14	15	16
17	18	19	20	21	22	23
24	25	26	27	28	29	30

MAY

S	M	T	W	T	F	S
1	2	3	4	5	6	7
8	9	10	11	12	13	14
15	16	17	18	19	20	21
22	23	24	25	26	27	28
29	30	31				

JUNE

S	M	T	W	T	F	S
			1	2	3	4
5	6	7	8	9	10	11
12	13	14	15	16	17	18
19	20	21	22	23	24	25
26	27	28	29	30		

JULY

S	M	T	W	T	F	S
					1	2
3	4	5	6	7	8	9
10	11	12	13	14	15	16
17	18	19	20	21	22	23
24	25	26	27	28	29	30
31						

AUGUST

S	M	T	W	T	F	S
	1	2	3	4	5	6
7	8	9	10	11	12	13
14	15	16	17	18	19	20
21	22	23	24	25	26	27
28	29	30	31			

SEPTEMBER

S	M	T	W	T	F	S
				1	2	3
4	5	6	7	8	9	10
11	12	13	14	15	16	17
18	19	20	21	22	23	24
25	26	27	28	29	30	

OCTOBER

S	M	T	W	T	F	S
						1
2	3	4	5	6	7	8
9	10	11	12	13	14	15
16	17	18	19	20	21	22
23	24	25	26	27	28	29
30	31					

NOVEMBER

S	M	T	W	T	F	S
		1	2	3	4	5
6	7	8	9	10	11	12
13	14	15	16	17	18	19
20	21	22	23	24	25	26
27	28	29	30			

DECEMBER

S	M	T	W	T	F	S
				1	2	3
4	5	6	7	8	9	10
11	12	13	14	15	16	17
18	19	20	21	22	23	24
25	26	27	28	29	30	31

8

JANUARY

S	M	T	W	T	F	S
1	2	3	4	5	6	7
8	9	10	11	12	13	14
15	16	17	18	19	20	21
22	23	24	25	26	27	28
29	30	31				

FEBRUARY

S	M	T	W	T	F	S
			1	2	3	4
5	6	7	8	9	10	11
12	13	14	15	16	17	18
19	20	21	22	23	24	25
26	27	28	29			

MARCH

S	M	T	W	T	F	S
				1	2	3
4	5	6	7	8	9	10
11	12	13	14	15	16	17
18	19	20	21	22	23	24
25	26	27	28	29	30	31

APRIL

S	M	T	W	T	F	S
1	2	3	4	5	6	7
8	9	10	11	12	13	14
15	16	17	18	19	20	21
22	23	24	25	26	27	28
29	30					

MAY

S	M	T	W	T	F	S
		1	2	3	4	5
6	7	8	9	10	11	12
13	14	15	16	17	18	19
20	21	22	23	24	25	26
27	28	29	30	31		

JUNE

S	M	T	W	T	F	S
					1	2
3	4	5	6	7	8	9
10	11	12	13	14	15	16
17	18	19	20	21	22	23
24	25	26	27	28	29	30

JULY

S	M	T	W	T	F	S
1	2	3	4	5	6	7
8	9	10	11	12	13	14
15	16	17	18	19	20	21
22	23	24	25	26	27	28
29	30	31				

AUGUST

S	M	T	W	T	F	S
			1	2	3	4
5	6	7	8	9	10	11
12	13	14	15	16	17	18
19	20	21	22	23	24	25
26	27	28	29	30	31	

SEPTEMBER

S	M	T	W	T	F	S
						1
2	3	4	5	6	7	8
9	10	11	12	13	14	15
16	17	18	19	20	21	22
23	24	25	26	27	28	29
30						

OCTOBER

S	M	T	W	T	F	S
	1	2	3	4	5	6
7	8	9	10	11	12	13
14	15	16	17	18	19	20
21	22	23	24	25	26	27
28	29	30	31			

NOVEMBER

S	M	T	W	T	F	S
				1	2	3
4	5	6	7	8	9	10
11	12	13	14	15	16	17
18	19	20	21	22	23	24
25	26	27	28	29	30	

DECEMBER

S	M	T	W	T	F	S
						1
2	3	4	5	6	7	8
9	10	11	12	13	14	15
16	17	18	19	20	21	22
23	24	25	26	27	28	29
30	31					

9

JANUARY

S	M	T	W	T	F	S
	1	2	3	4	5	6
7	8	9	10	11	12	13
14	15	16	17	18	19	20
21	22	23	24	25	26	27
28	29	30	31			

FEBRUARY

S	M	T	W	T	F	S
				1	2	3
4	5	6	7	8	9	10
11	12	13	14	15	16	17
18	19	20	21	22	23	24
25	26	27	28	29		

MARCH

S	M	T	W	T	F	S
					1	2
3	4	5	6	7	8	9
10	11	12	13	14	15	16
17	18	19	20	21	22	23
24	25	26	27	28	29	30
31						

APRIL

S	M	T	W	T	F	S
	1	2	3	4	5	6
7	8	9	10	11	12	13
14	15	16	17	18	19	20
21	22	23	24	25	26	27
28	29	30				

MAY

S	M	T	W	T	F	S
			1	2	3	4
5	6	7	8	9	10	11
12	13	14	15	16	17	18
19	20	21	22	23	24	25
26	27	28	29	30	31	

JUNE

S	M	T	W	T	F	S
						1
2	3	4	5	6	7	8
9	10	11	12	13	14	15
16	17	18	19	20	21	22
23	24	25	26	27	28	29
30						

JULY

S	M	T	W	T	F	S
	1	2	3	4	5	6
7	8	9	10	11	12	13
14	15	16	17	18	19	20
21	22	23	24	25	26	27
28	29	30	31			

AUGUST

S	M	T	W	T	F	S
				1	2	3
4	5	6	7	8	9	10
11	12	13	14	15	16	17
18	19	20	21	22	23	24
25	26	27	28	29	30	31

SEPTEMBER

S	M	T	W	T	F	S
1	2	3	4	5	6	7
8	9	10	11	12	13	14
15	16	17	18	19	20	21
22	23	24	25	26	27	28
29	30					

OCTOBER

S	M	T	W	T	F	S
		1	2	3	4	5
6	7	8	9	10	11	12
13	14	15	16	17	18	19
20	21	22	23	24	25	26
27	28	29	30	31		

NOVEMBER

S	M	T	W	T	F	S
					1	2
3	4	5	6	7	8	9
10	11	12	13	14	15	16
17	18	19	20	21	22	23
24	25	26	27	28	29	30

DECEMBER

S	M	T	W	T	F	S
1	2	3	4	5	6	7
8	9	10	11	12	13	14
15	16	17	18	19	20	21
22	23	24	25	26	27	28
29	30	31				

10 — 2008

JANUARY

S	M	T	W	T	F	S
		1	2	3	4	5
6	7	8	9	10	11	12
13	14	15	16	17	18	19
20	21	22	23	24	25	26
27	28	29	30	31		

FEBRUARY

S	M	T	W	T	F	S
					1	2
3	4	5	6	7	8	9
10	11	12	13	14	15	16
17	18	19	20	21	22	23
24	25	26	27	28	29	

MARCH

S	M	T	W	T	F	S
						1
2	3	4	5	6	7	8
9	10	11	12	13	14	15
16	17	18	19	20	21	22
23	24	25	26	27	28	29
30	31					

APRIL

S	M	T	W	T	F	S
		1	2	3	4	5
6	7	8	9	10	11	12
13	14	15	16	17	18	19
20	21	22	23	24	25	26
27	28	29	30			

MAY

S	M	T	W	T	F	S
				1	2	3
4	5	6	7	8	9	10
11	12	13	14	15	16	17
18	19	20	21	22	23	24
25	26	27	28	29	30	31

JUNE

S	M	T	W	T	F	S
1	2	3	4	5	6	7
8	9	10	11	12	13	14
15	16	17	18	19	20	21
22	23	24	25	26	27	28
29	30					

JULY

S	M	T	W	T	F	S
		1	2	3	4	5
6	7	8	9	10	11	12
13	14	15	16	17	18	19
20	21	22	23	24	25	26
27	28	29	30	31		

AUGUST

S	M	T	W	T	F	S
					1	2
3	4	5	6	7	8	9
10	11	12	13	14	15	16
17	18	19	20	21	22	23
24	25	26	27	28	29	30
31						

SEPTEMBER

S	M	T	W	T	F	S
	1	2	3	4	5	6
7	8	9	10	11	12	13
14	15	16	17	18	19	20
21	22	23	24	25	26	27
28	29	30				

OCTOBER

S	M	T	W	T	F	S
			1	2	3	4
5	6	7	8	9	10	11
12	13	14	15	16	17	18
19	20	21	22	23	24	25
26	27	28	29	30	31	

NOVEMBER

S	M	T	W	T	F	S
						1
2	3	4	5	6	7	8
9	10	11	12	13	14	15
16	17	18	19	20	21	22
23	24	25	26	27	28	29
30						

DECEMBER

S	M	T	W	T	F	S
	1	2	3	4	5	6
7	8	9	10	11	12	13
14	15	16	17	18	19	20
21	22	23	24	25	26	27
28	29	30	31			

11

JANUARY

S	M	T	W	T	F	S
			1	2	3	4
5	6	7	8	9	10	11
12	13	14	15	16	17	18
19	20	21	22	23	24	25
26	27	28	29	30	31	

FEBRUARY

S	M	T	W	T	F	S
						1
2	3	4	5	6	7	8
9	10	11	12	13	14	15
16	17	18	19	20	21	22
23	24	25	26	27	28	29

MARCH

S	M	T	W	T	F	S
1	2	3	4	5	6	7
8	9	10	11	12	13	14
15	16	17	18	19	20	21
22	23	24	25	26	27	28
29	30	31				

APRIL

S	M	T	W	T	F	S
			1	2	3	4
5	6	7	8	9	10	11
12	13	14	15	16	17	18
19	20	21	22	23	24	25
26	27	28	29	30		

MAY

S	M	T	W	T	F	S
					1	2
3	4	5	6	7	8	9
10	11	12	13	14	15	16
17	18	19	20	21	22	23
24	25	26	27	28	29	30
31						

JUNE

S	M	T	W	T	F	S
	1	2	3	4	5	6
7	8	9	10	11	12	13
14	15	16	17	18	19	20
21	22	23	24	25	26	27
28	29	30				

JULY

S	M	T	W	T	F	S
			1	2	3	4
5	6	7	8	9	10	11
12	13	14	15	16	17	18
19	20	21	22	23	24	25
26	27	28	29	30	31	

AUGUST

S	M	T	W	T	F	S
						1
2	3	4	5	6	7	8
9	10	11	12	13	14	15
16	17	18	19	20	21	22
23	24	25	26	27	28	29
30	31					

SEPTEMBER

S	M	T	W	T	F	S
		1	2	3	4	5
6	7	8	9	10	11	12
13	14	15	16	17	18	19
20	21	22	23	24	25	26
27	28	29	30			

OCTOBER

S	M	T	W	T	F	S
				1	2	3
4	5	6	7	8	9	10
11	12	13	14	15	16	17
18	19	20	21	22	23	24
25	26	27	28	29	30	31

NOVEMBER

S	M	T	W	T	F	S
1	2	3	4	5	6	7
8	9	10	11	12	13	14
15	16	17	18	19	20	21
22	23	24	25	26	27	28
29	30					

DECEMBER

S	M	T	W	T	F	S
		1	2	3	4	5
6	7	8	9	10	11	12
13	14	15	16	17	18	19
20	21	22	23	24	25	26
27	28	29	30	31		

12 — 2004

JANUARY

S	M	T	W	T	F	S
				1	2	3
4	5	6	7	8	9	10
11	12	13	14	15	16	17
18	19	20	21	22	23	24
25	26	27	28	29	30	31

FEBRUARY

S	M	T	W	T	F	S
1	2	3	4	5	6	7
8	9	10	11	12	13	14
15	16	17	18	19	20	21
22	23	24	25	26	27	28
29						

MARCH

S	M	T	W	T	F	S
	1	2	3	4	5	6
7	8	9	10	11	12	13
14	15	16	17	18	19	20
21	22	23	24	25	26	27
28	29	30	31			

APRIL

S	M	T	W	T	F	S
				1	2	3
4	5	6	7	8	9	10
11	12	13	14	15	16	17
18	19	20	21	22	23	24
25	26	27	28	29	30	

MAY

S	M	T	W	T	F	S
						1
2	3	4	5	6	7	8
9	10	11	12	13	14	15
16	17	18	19	20	21	22
23	24	25	26	27	28	29
30	31					

JUNE

S	M	T	W	T	F	S
		1	2	3	4	5
6	7	8	9	10	11	12
13	14	15	16	17	18	19
20	21	22	23	24	25	26
27	28	29	30			

JULY

S	M	T	W	T	F	S
				1	2	3
4	5	6	7	8	9	10
11	12	13	14	15	16	17
18	19	20	21	22	23	24
25	26	27	28	29	30	31

AUGUST

S	M	T	W	T	F	S
1	2	3	4	5	6	7
8	9	10	11	12	13	14
15	16	17	18	19	20	21
22	23	24	25	26	27	28
29	30	31				

SEPTEMBER

S	M	T	W	T	F	S
			1	2	3	4
5	6	7	8	9	10	11
12	13	14	15	16	17	18
19	20	21	22	23	24	25
26	27	28	29	30		

OCTOBER

S	M	T	W	T	F	S
					1	2
3	4	5	6	7	8	9
10	11	12	13	14	15	16
17	18	19	20	21	22	23
24	25	26	27	28	29	30
31						

NOVEMBER

S	M	T	W	T	F	S
	1	2	3	4	5	6
7	8	9	10	11	12	13
14	15	16	17	18	19	20
21	22	23	24	25	26	27
28	29	30				

DECEMBER

S	M	T	W	T	F	S
			1	2	3	4
5	6	7	8	9	10	11
12	13	14	15	16	17	18
19	20	21	22	23	24	25
26	27	28	29	30	31	

13

JANUARY

S	M	T	W	T	F	S
					1	2
3	4	5	6	7	8	9
10	11	12	13	14	15	16
17	18	19	20	21	22	23
24	25	26	27	28	29	30
31						

FEBRUARY

S	M	T	W	T	F	S
	1	2	3	4	5	6
7	8	9	10	11	12	13
14	15	16	17	18	19	20
21	22	23	24	25	26	27
28	29					

MARCH

S	M	T	W	T	F	S
		1	2	3	4	5
6	7	8	9	10	11	12
13	14	15	16	17	18	19
20	21	22	23	24	25	26
27	28	29	30	31		

APRIL

S	M	T	W	T	F	S
					1	2
3	4	5	6	7	8	9
10	11	12	13	14	15	16
17	18	19	20	21	22	23
24	25	26	27	28	29	30

MAY

S	M	T	W	T	F	S
1	2	3	4	5	6	7
8	9	10	11	12	13	14
15	16	17	18	19	20	21
22	23	24	25	26	27	28
29	30	31				

JUNE

S	M	T	W	T	F	S
			1	2	3	4
5	6	7	8	9	10	11
12	13	14	15	16	17	18
19	20	21	22	23	24	25
26	27	28	29	30		

JULY

S	M	T	W	T	F	S
					1	2
3	4	5	6	7	8	9
10	11	12	13	14	15	16
17	18	19	20	21	22	23
24	25	26	27	28	29	30
31						

AUGUST

S	M	T	W	T	F	S
	1	2	3	4	5	6
7	8	9	10	11	12	13
14	15	16	17	18	19	20
21	22	23	24	25	26	27
28	29	30	31			

SEPTEMBER

S	M	T	W	T	F	S
				1	2	3
4	5	6	7	8	9	10
11	12	13	14	15	16	17
18	19	20	21	22	23	24
25	26	27	28	29	30	

OCTOBER

S	M	T	W	T	F	S
						1
2	3	4	5	6	7	8
9	10	11	12	13	14	15
16	17	18	19	20	21	22
23	24	25	26	27	28	29
30	31					

NOVEMBER

S	M	T	W	T	F	S
		1	2	3	4	5
6	7	8	9	10	11	12
13	14	15	16	17	18	19
20	21	22	23	24	25	26
27	28	29	30			

DECEMBER

S	M	T	W	T	F	S
				1	2	3
4	5	6	7	8	9	10
11	12	13	14	15	16	17
18	19	20	21	22	23	24
25	26	27	28	29	30	31

14 — 2000

JANUARY

S	M	T	W	T	F	S
						1
2	3	4	5	6	7	8
9	10	11	12	13	14	15
16	17	18	19	20	21	22
23	24	25	26	27	28	29
30	31					

FEBRUARY

S	M	T	W	T	F	S
		1	2	3	4	5
6	7	8	9	10	11	12
13	14	15	16	17	18	19
20	21	22	23	24	25	26
27	28	29				

MARCH

S	M	T	W	T	F	S
			1	2	3	4
5	6	7	8	9	10	11
12	13	14	15	16	17	18
19	20	21	22	23	24	25
26	27	28	29	30	31	

APRIL

S	M	T	W	T	F	S
						1
2	3	4	5	6	7	8
9	10	11	12	13	14	15
16	17	18	19	20	21	22
23	24	25	26	27	28	29
30						

MAY

S	M	T	W	T	F	S
	1	2	3	4	5	6
7	8	9	10	11	12	13
14	15	16	17	18	19	20
21	22	23	24	25	26	27
28	29	30	31			

JUNE

S	M	T	W	T	F	S
				1	2	3
4	5	6	7	8	9	10
11	12	13	14	15	16	17
18	19	20	21	22	23	24
25	26	27	28	29	30	

JULY

S	M	T	W	T	F	S
						1
2	3	4	5	6	7	8
9	10	11	12	13	14	15
16	17	18	19	20	21	22
23	24	25	26	27	28	29
30	31					

AUGUST

S	M	T	W	T	F	S
		1	2	3	4	5
6	7	8	9	10	11	12
13	14	15	16	17	18	19
20	21	22	23	24	25	26
27	28	29	30	31		

SEPTEMBER

S	M	T	W	T	F	S
					1	2
3	4	5	6	7	8	9
10	11	12	13	14	15	16
17	18	19	20	21	22	23
24	25	26	27	28	29	30

OCTOBER

S	M	T	W	T	F	S
1	2	3	4	5	6	7
8	9	10	11	12	13	14
15	16	17	18	19	20	21
22	23	24	25	26	27	28
29	30	31				

NOVEMBER

S	M	T	W	T	F	S
			1	2	3	4
5	6	7	8	9	10	11
12	13	14	15	16	17	18
19	20	21	22	23	24	25
26	27	28	29	30		

DECEMBER

S	M	T	W	T	F	S
					1	2
3	4	5	6	7	8	9
10	11	12	13	14	15	16
17	18	19	20	21	22	23
24	25	26	27	28	29	30
31						

> **IT'S A FACT:** Originally, the Roman week was 8 days long. This changed around 321 AD, after Christianity gained official recognition in the Roman Empire; a 7-day week was instituted, starting with Sunday.

Chronological Eras

Era	Year	Begins in 2005	Era	Year	Begins in 2005
Byzantine	7514	Sept. 14	Grecian (Seleucidae)	2317	Sept. 14 or Oct. 14
Jewish	5766	Oct. 3[1]	Diocletian	1722	Sept. 11
Roman (Ab Urbe Condita)	2758	Jan. 14	Indian (Saka)	1927	Mar. 22
Nabonassar (Babylonian)	2754	Apr. 23	Islamic/Muslim (Hijra)	1426	Feb. 9[2]
Japanese	17	Jan. 1	Chinese	4703	Feb. 9

(1) Year begins at sunset. (2) Year begins at moon crescent.

Chronological Cycles, 2005

Dominical Letter	B	Roman Indiction	13	Solar Cycle	26
Golden Number (Lunar Cycle)	11	Epact	XIX	Julian Period (year of)	6718

Chinese Calendar, Asian Festivals

Source: Chinese Information and Culture Center, New York, NY

The Chinese calendar (like the Jewish and Islamic calendars; see the Religion chapter) is a lunar calendar. It is divided into 12 months of 29 or 30 days (compensating for the lunar month's mean duration of 29 days, 12 hr, 44.05 min). This calendar is synchronized with the solar year by the addition of extra months at fixed intervals.

The Chinese calendar runs on a 60-year cycle. The cycles 1876-1935 and 1936-95, with the years grouped under their 12 animal designations, are printed below, along with the first 24 years of the current cycle. This cycle began in 1996 and will last until 2055. Feb. 9, 2005, marks the beginning of the year 4703 in the Chinese calendar, and is designated the Year of the Rooster. Readers can find the animal name for the year of their birth in the chart below. (Note: The first 3-7 weeks of each Western year belong to the previous Chinese year and animal designation.)

Both the Western (Gregorian) and traditional lunar calendars are used publicly in China and in North and South Korea, and 2 New Year's celebrations are held. In Taiwan, in overseas Chinese communities, and in Vietnam, the lunar calendar is used only to set the dates for traditional festivals, with the Gregorian system in general use.

The 4-day Chinese New Year, Hsin Nien, the 3-day Vietnamese New Year festival, Tet, and the 3-to-4-day Korean festival, Suhl, begin at the 2nd new moon after the winter solstice. The new moon in the Far East, which is west of the International Date Line, may be a day later than the new moon in the U.S. The festivals may start, therefore, anywhere between Jan. 21 and Feb. 19 of the Gregorian calendar.

Rat	Ox	Tiger	Hare (Rabbit)	Dragon	Snake	Horse	Sheep (Goat)	Monkey	Rooster	Dog	Pig
1876	1877	1878	1879	1880	1881	1882	1883	1884	1885	1886	1887
1888	1889	1890	1891	1892	1893	1894	1895	1896	1897	1898	1899
1900	1901	1902	1903	1904	1905	1906	1907	1908	1909	1910	1911
1912	1913	1914	1915	1916	1917	1918	1919	1920	1921	1922	1923
1924	1925	1926	1927	1928	1929	1930	1931	1932	1933	1934	1935
1936	1937	1938	1939	1940	1941	1942	1943	1944	1945	1946	1947
1948	1949	1950	1951	1952	1953	1954	1955	1956	1957	1958	1959
1960	1961	1962	1963	1964	1965	1966	1967	1968	1969	1970	1971
1972	1973	1974	1975	1976	1977	1978	1979	1980	1981	1982	1983
1984	1985	1986	1987	1988	1989	1990	1991	1992	1993	1994	1995
1996	1997	1998	1999	2000	2001	2002	2003	2004	2005	2006	2007
2008	2009	2010	2011	2012	2013	2014	2015	2016	2017	2018	2019

Special Months

Every year there are many thousands of special months, days, and weeks as a result of anniversaries, official proclamations, and promotional events, both trivial and serious. Here are a few of the special months:

January: National Hot Tea Month, National Mentoring Month, National Radon Action Month

February: Black History Month, American Heart Month, Library Lovers Month, National Condom Month, National Wildbird Feeding Month

March: Irish-American Heritage Month, Women's History Month, American Red Cross Month, National Frozen Foods Month

April: Alcohol Awareness Month, Keep America Beautiful Month, National Child Abuse Prevention Month

May: Clean Air Month, National Book Month, National Bike Month, Asian Pacific American Heritage Month

June: Children's Awareness Month, Gay and Lesbian Pride Month, National Rivers Month, National Safety Month

July: National Culinary Arts Month, National Hot Dog Month, Anti-Boredom Month, National Picnic Month

August: National Back to School Month, National Inventors' Month, Admit You're Happy Month, Women's Small Business Month

September: Baby Safety Month, Hispanic Heritage Month (Sept. 15-Oct. 15), National Cholesterol Education Month

October: National Domestic Violence Awareness Month, National Breast Cancer Awareness Month, Diversity Awareness Month

November: National American Indian Heritage Month, National Adoption Month, American Diabetes Month

December: Universal Human Rights Month, National Drunk and Drugged Driving Prevention Month, National Tie Month

Wedding Anniversaries

The traditional names for wedding anniversaries go back many years in social usage and have been used to suggest types of appropriate anniversary gifts. Traditional products for gifts are listed here in capital letters, with a few allowable revisions in parentheses, followed by common modern gifts in each category.

1st	PAPER, clocks	9th	POTTERY (CHINA), leather goods	25th	SILVER, sterling silver
2nd	COTTON, china	10th	TIN, ALUMINUM, diamond	30th	PEARL, diamond
3rd	LEATHER, crystal, glass	11th	STEEL, fashion jewelry	35th	CORAL (JADE), jade
4th	LINEN (SILK), appliances	12th	SILK, pearls, colored gems	40th	RUBY, ruby
5th	WOOD, silverware	13th	LACE, textiles, furs	45th	SAPPHIRE, sapphire
6th	IRON, wood objects	14th	IVORY, gold jewelry	50th	GOLD, gold
7th	WOOL (COPPER), desk sets	15th	CRYSTAL, watches	55th	EMERALD, emerald
8th	BRONZE, linens, lace	20th	CHINA, platinum	60th	DIAMOND, diamond

Birthstones

Source: Jewelry Industry Council

MONTH	Ancient	Modern	MONTH	Ancient	Modern
January	Garnet	Garnet	July	Onyx	Ruby
February	Amethyst	Amethyst	August	Carnelian	Sardonyx or Peridot
March	Jasper	Bloodstone or Aquamarine	September	Chrysolite	Sapphire
April	Sapphire	Diamond	October	Aquamarine	Opal or Tourmaline
May	Agate	Emerald	November	Topaz	Topaz
June	Emerald	Pearl, Moonstone, or Alexandrite	December	Ruby	Turquoise or Zircon

Standard Time, Daylight Saving Time, and Others

Source: National Imagery and Mapping Agency; U.S. Dept. of Transportation

See also Time Zone map, page 460.

Standard Time

Standard Time is reckoned from the Prime Meridian of Longitude in Greenwich, England. The world is divided into 24 zones, each 15 deg of arc, or one hour in time apart. The Greenwich meridian (0 deg) extends through the center of the initial zone, and the zones to the east are numbered from 1 to 12, with the prefix "minus" indicating the number of hours to be subtracted to obtain Greenwich Time. Each zone extends 7.5 deg on either side of its central meridian.

Westward zones are similarly numbered, but prefixed "plus," showing the number of hours that must be added to get Greenwich Time. Although these zones apply generally to sea areas, the Standard Time maintained in many countries does not coincide with zone time. A graphical representation of the zones is shown on the Standard Time Zone Chart of the World (WOBZC76) published by the National Imagery and Mapping Agency. This chart is available from the Federal Aviation Administration (FAA), 6501 Lafayette Avenue, Riverdale, MD 20737-1199; telephone: (800) 638-8972.

The U.S. and possessions are divided into 10 Standard Time zones. Each zone is approximately 15 deg of longitude in width. All places in each zone use, instead of their own local time, the time counted from the transit of the "mean sun" across the Standard Time meridian that passes near the middle of that zone. These time zones are designated as Atlantic, Eastern, Central, Mountain, Pacific, Alaska, Hawaii-Aleutian, Samoa, Wake Island, and Guam; the time in these zones is reckoned from the 60th, 75th, 90th, 105th, 120th, 135th, 150th, and 165th meridians west of Greenwich and the 165th and 150th meridians east of Greenwich. The time zone line wanders to conform to local geographical regions. The time in the various zones in the U.S. and U.S. territories west of Greenwich is earlier than Greenwich Time by 4, 5, 6, 7, 8, 9, 10, and 11 hours, respectively. However, Wake Island and Guam cross the International Date Line and are 12 and 10 hours later than Greenwich Time, respectively.

24-Hour Time

Twenty-four-hour time is widely used in scientific work throughout the world. In the U.S. it is also used in operations of the armed forces. In Europe it is frequently used by the transportation networks in preference to the 12-hour AM and PM system. With the 24-hour system the day begins at midnight, and times are designated 00:00 through 23:59.

International Date Line

The Date Line, approximately coinciding with the 180th meridian, separates the calendar dates. The date must be advanced one day when crossing in a westerly direction and set back one day when crossing in an easterly direction. The Date Line frequently deviates from the 180th meridian because of decisions made by individual nations affected. The line is deflected eastward through the Bering Strait and westward of the Aleutians to prevent separating these areas by date. The line is deflected eastward of the Tonga and New Zealand Islands in the South Pacific for the same reason. More recently it was deflected much farther eastward to include all of Kiribati. The line is established by international custom; there is no international authority prescribing its exact course.

Daylight Saving Time

Daylight Saving Time is achieved by advancing the clock one hour. Daylight Saving Time in the U.S. begins each year at 2 AM on the first Sunday in Apr. and ends at 2 AM on the last Sunday in Oct.

Daylight Saving Time was first observed in the U.S. during World War I, and then again during World War II. In the intervening years, some states and communities observed Daylight Saving Time, using whatever beginning and ending dates they chose. In 1966, Congress passed the Uniform Time Act, which provided that any state or territory that chooses to observe Daylight Saving Time must begin and end on the federal dates. Any state could, by law, exempt itself; a 1972 amendment to the act authorized states split by time zones to observe Daylight Saving Time in one time zone and standard time in the other time zone. Currently, Arizona, Hawaii, the eastern time zone portion of Indiana, Puerto Rico, the U.S. Virgin Islands, and American Samoa do not observe Daylight Saving Time.

Congress and the secretary of transportation both have authority to change time zone boundaries. Since 1966 there have been a number of changes to U.S. time zone boundaries. In addition, efforts to conserve energy have prompted various changes in the times that Daylight Saving Time is observed.

International Usage

Adjusting clock time so as to gain the added daylight on summer evenings is common throughout the world.

Canada, which extends over 6 time zones, generally observes Daylight Saving Time from the first Sunday of Apr. until the last Sunday of Oct. Saskatchewan remains on standard time all year. Communities elsewhere in Canada also may exempt themselves from Daylight Saving Time. Mexico, which occupies 3 time zones, observes Daylight Saving Time during the same period as most of Canada.

Member nations of the European Union (EU) observe a "summer-time period," the EU's version of Daylight Saving Time, from the last Sunday of Mar. until the last Sunday in Oct.

Russia, which extends over 11 time zones, maintains its Standard Time 1 hour fast for its zone designation. Additionally, it proclaims Daylight Saving Time from the last Sunday in Mar. until the 4th Sunday in Oct.

China, which extends across 5 time zones, has decreed that the entire country be placed on Greenwich Time plus 8 hours. Daylight Saving Time is not observed. Japan, which lies within one time zone, also does not modify its legal time during the summer months.

Many countries in the Southern Hemisphere maintain Daylight Saving Time, generally from Oct. to Mar.; however, most countries near the equator do not deviate from Standard Time.

WORLD ALMANAC QUICK QUIZ

Can you place these events or observances in chronological order as they appear in a calendar year?

   (a) Yom Kippur   (b) Mardi Gras
   (c) Boxing Day   (d) Bastille Day

For the answer look in this chapter, or see page 1008.

Standard Time Differences—World Cities

The time indicated in the table is fixed by law and is called the legal time or, more generally, Standard Time. Use of Daylight Saving Time varies widely. *Indicates morning of the following day. At 12:00 noon, Eastern Standard Time, the Standard Time (in 24-hour time) in selected cities is as follows:

Addis Ababa 20 00	Casablanca 17 00	Lisbon 17 00	Santiago 13 00
Amsterdam 18 00	Copenhagen 18 00	London 17 00	Sarajevo 18 00
Ankara 19 00	Dhaka 23 00	Madrid 18 00	Seoul 2 00*
Athens 19 00	Dublin 17 00	Manila 1 00*	Shanghai 1 00*
Auckland 5 00*	Edinburgh 17 00	Mecca 20 00	Singapore 1 00*
Baghdad 20 00	Geneva 18 00	Melbourne 3 00*	Stockholm 18 00
Bangkok 0 00*	Helsinki 19 00	Montevideo 14 00	Sydney 3 00*
Beijing 1 00*	Ho Chi Minh City ... 0 00*	Moscow 20 00	Taipei 1 00*
Belfast 17 00	Hong Kong 1 00*	Munich 18 00	Tashkent 22 00
Belgrade 18 00	Islamabad 22 00	Nagasaki 2 00*	Tehran 20 30
Berlin 18 00	Istanbul 19 00	Nairobi 20 00	Tel Aviv 19 00
Bogotá 12 00	Jakarta 0 00*	New Delhi 22 30	Tokyo 2 00*
Bombay (Mumbai) .. 22 30	Jerusalem 19 00	Oslo 18 00	Vladivostok 3 00*
Brussels 18 00	Johannesburg 19 00	Paris 18 00	Vienna 18 00
Bucharest 19 00	Kabul 21 50	Prague 18 00	Warsaw 18 00
Budapest 18 00	Karachi 22 00	Quito 12 00	Wellington 5 00*
Buenos Aires 14 00	Kathmandu 22 45	Rio de Janeiro 14 00	Yangon (Rangoon) .. 23 30
Cairo 19 00	Kiev 19 00	Riyadh 20 00	Yokohama 2 00*
Calcutta (Kolkata) ... 22 30	Lagos 18 00	Rome 18 00	Zurich 18 00
Cape Town 19 00	Lima 12 00	St. Petersburg 20 00	
Caracas 13 00			

Standard Time Differences—North American Cities

At 12:00 noon, Eastern Standard Time, the Standard Time in selected North American cities is as follows:

Akron, OH .... 12 00 Noon	*Fort Wayne, IN .... 12 00 Noon	Peoria, IL .... 11 00 AM
Albuquerque, NM ...... 10 00 AM	Frankfort, KY .... 12 00 Noon	*Phoenix, AZ .... 10 00 AM
Anchorage, AK .... 8 00 am	Havana, Cuba .... 12 00 Noon	Pierre, SD .... 11 00 AM
Atlanta, GA .... 12 00 Noon	Helena, MT .... 10 00 AM	Pittsburgh, PA .... 12 00 Noon
Austin, TX .... 11 00 AM	*Honolulu, HI .... 7 00 AM	*Regina, Sask .... 11 00 AM
Baltimore, MD .... 12 00 Noon	Houston, TX .... 11 00 AM	Reno, NV .... 9 00 AM
Birmingham, AL .... 11 00 AM	*Indianapolis, IN .... 12 00 Noon	Richmond, VA .... 12 00 Noon
Bismarck, ND .... 11 00 AM	Jacksonville, FL .... 12 00 Noon	Rochester, NY .... 12 00 Noon
Boise, ID .... 10 00 AM	Juneau, AK .... 8 00 AM	Sacramento, CA ...... 9 00 AM
Boston, MA .... 12 00 Noon	Kansas City, MO ...... 11 00 AM	St. John's, Nfld .... 1 30 PM
Buffalo, NY .... 12 00 Noon	*Kingston, Jamaica ..... 12 00 Noon	St. Louis, MO .... 11 00 AM
Butte, MT .... 10 00 AM	Knoxville, TN .... 12 00 Noon	St. Paul, MN .... 11 00 AM
Calgary, Alta .... 10 00 AM	Las Vegas, NV .... 9 00 AM	Salt Lake City, UT ..... 10 00 AM
Charleston, SC .... 12 00 Noon	Lexington, KY .... 12 00 Noon	San Antonio, TX ...... 11 00 AM
Charleston, WV ...... 12 00 Noon	Lincoln, NE .... 11 00 AM	San Diego, CA .... 9 00 AM
Charlotte, NC .... 12 00 Noon	Little Rock, AR .... 11 00 AM	San Francisco, CA .... 9 00 AM
Charlottetown, PEI ...... 1 00 PM	Los Angeles, CA ...... 9 00 AM	San Jose, CA .... 9 00 AM
Chattanooga, TN ..... 12 00 Noon	Louisville, KY .... 12 00 Noon	*San Juan, PR .... 1 00 PM
Cheyenne, WY .... 10 00 AM	Mexico City, Mexico ... 11 00 AM	Santa Fe, NM .... 10 00 AM
Chicago, IL .... 11 00 AM	Memphis, TN .... 11 00 AM	Savannah, GA .... 12 00 Noon
Cleveland, OH .... 12 00 Noon	Miami, FL .... 12 00 Noon	Seattle, WA .... 9 00 AM
Colorado Spr., CO ..... 10 00 AM	Milwaukee, WI .... 11 00 AM	Shreveport, LA .... 11 00 AM
Columbus, OH .... 12 00 Noon	Minneapolis, MN ...... 11 00 AM	Sioux Falls, SD .... 11 00 AM
Dallas, TX .... 11 00 AM	Mobile, AL .... 11 00 AM	Spokane, WA .... 9 00 AM
*Dawson, Yuk .... 9 00 AM	Montreal, Que .... 12 00 Noon	Tampa, FL .... 12 00 Noon
Dayton, OH .... 12 00 Noon	Nashville, TN .... 11 00 AM	Toledo, OH .... 12 00 Noon
Denver, CO .... 10 00 AM	Nassau, Bahamas ..... 12 00 Noon	Topeka, KS .... 11 00 AM
Des Moines, IA .... 11 00 AM	New Haven, CT .... 12 00 Noon	Toronto, Ont .... 12 00 Noon
Detroit, MI .... 12 00 Noon	New Orleans, LA ...... 11 00 AM	*Tucson, AZ .... 10 00 AM
Duluth, MN .... 11 00 AM	New York, NY .... 12 00 Noon	Tulsa, OK .... 11 00 AM
Edmonton, Alta .... 10 00 AM	Nome, AK .... 8 00 AM	Vancouver, BC .... 9 00 AM
El Paso, TX .... 10 00 AM	Norfolk, VA .... 12 00 Noon	Washington, DC ...... 12 00 Noon
Erie, PA .... 12 00 Noon	Oklahoma City, OK ..... 11 00 AM	Wichita, KS .... 11 00 AM
Evansville, IN .... 11 00 AM	Omaha, NE .... 11 00 AM	Wilmington, DE .... 12 00 Noon
Fairbanks, AK .... 8 00 AM	Ottawa, Ont .... 12 00 Noon	Winnipeg, Man .... 11 00 AM
Flint, MI .... 12 00 Noon	*Panama City, Panama ... 12 00 Noon	

Note: This same table can be used for Daylight Saving Time when it is in effect, but allowance must be made for cities that do not observe it; they are marked with an asterisk (*). Daylight Saving Time is one hour later than Standard Time.

WORLD ALMANAC QUICK QUIZ

Which of these is a traditional material for a 1st wedding anniversary gift?

(a) paper   (b) wood   (c) iron   (d) jade

For the answer look in this chapter, or see page 1008.

COMPUTERS AND THE INTERNET

About Personal Computers

Personal computers, or PCs, include nonportable home and office machines known as desktop computers along with a variety of smaller units used for so-called mobile computing. These smaller machines range in size from handhelds weighing several ounces to laptops, which may weigh, in the case of powerful "desktop replacement" units, 10 pounds or more. Handhelds used for personal-organization purposes are sometimes called personal digital assistants (PDAs). Many manufacturers refer to laptops, especially smaller and lighter models, as notebooks. Those equipped with a touch screen for handwritten input are called tablet PCs. Special software called the **operating system** enables you to operate the computer system's physical parts, or hardware. The most common operating systems used on PCs are Microsoft Windows, the Macintosh OS, and Linux for desktops and laptops and Microsoft's Pocket PC OS, the Palm OS, and the Symbian OS for handhelds.

The term "personal computer" is also used more narrowly to refer to desktops (and sometimes laptops) conforming to the standard developed by IBM for personal computers, which uses a microprocessor made by Intel, or a compatible processor, and an operating system, usually Windows or Linux, that can work with that processor.

The heart of a PC is its microprocessor, or **central processing unit** (CPU), contained on a chip of silicon. The microprocessor carries out arithmetic and logical operations specified by computer programs.

PCs have several places where data and instructions are kept, among them:

• **ROM** (Read Only Memory), a type of memory in which once information is written, it cannot be changed, but only read. ROM may be used to keep information that always needs to be available, such as the instructions for loading the operating system when you turn your computer on.

• **RAM** (Random Access Memory), where data and programs are temporarily kept when they are being worked on; its contents are lost when the computer is turned off.

• **Hard drive**, a hardware device used for long-term storage of data and programs; information placed on a hard disk will remain there until erased or deleted.

Hard drives are commonly found inside PCs, but "external" hard drives are also available that can be readily moved from place to place. Other portable devices for long-term storage of information and programs include floppy disks, CDs, DVDs, and a variety of small high-capacity devices that can be plugged into a PC's Universal Serial Bus (USB) port or **FireWire** port (also known as an IEEE 1394 port, after the specification established by the Institute of Electrical and Electronics Engineers).

Modern PCs usually accommodate one or more ways of connecting to other computers (and related devices) and to computer networks, including the Internet. The connection may be "wired" or, especially with mobile computers, wireless. Typical examples of wired links include an Ethernet connection to a local computer network and a modem connection via a telephone line.

Some handhelds have cellular telephone connection capability. Among the other well-known wireless connection technologies found in PCs are **Bluetooth**, usable only for extremely short distances (up to 35 feet), and Wi-Fi (or WiFi, for "WIreless FIdelity"), which works for up to several hundred feet. Looming on the horizon is WiMax (Worldwide Interoperability for Microwave Access), based on the IEEE 802.16 standard. Still under development, it promises extremely fast transmission of data over distances up to 30 miles.

Commonly used measures for the **capacity or power** of a PC include the **speed** of the microprocessor, expressed in megahertz (MHz), millions of cycles per second, or in gigahertz (GHz), billions of cycles per second; the size of the **RAM**, expressed in megabytes, or millions of bytes; and the size of the **hard drive**, expressed in gigabytes, or billions of bytes. Generally speaking, the bigger these numbers are, the more capable the machine. In mid-2004, average-priced desktop PCs (i.e., in the $800-$1,500 range) typically offered 256 or 512 megabytes of RAM, processor speeds greater than 2 gigahertz, and hard drives with 80 to 160 gigabytes storage capacity. (A caveat: technological improvements mean these numbers will be outdated fairly quickly.)

Computer Milestones

Devices for performing calculations are nothing new— the abacus, a frame with wires on which beads are moved back and forth (still used today in some parts of the world), traces its origins back to ancient times. But the marvels of electronic miniaturization that are modern PCs are a relatively recent development. They are the descendents of vacuum-tube devices introduced in the early 20th century.

Among early **landmark events in computer history** are:
• In 1623, the **1st mechanical calculator**, capable of adding, subtracting, multiplying, and dividing, was developed by the German mathematician Wilhelm Schikard; the only 2 models Schikard made, however, were destroyed in a fire.
• In 1642, French mathematician Blaise Pascal built the 1st of more than 4 dozen copies of an adding and subtracting machine that he invented.
• In 1790, French inventor Joseph Marie Jacquard devised a new control system for looms. He "programmed" the loom, communicating desired weaving operations to the machine via patterns of holes in paper cards.
• The British mathematician and scientist Charles Babbage used the Jacquard punch-card system in his design for a sophisticated, programmable **"Analytical Engine"** that contained some of the basic features of today's computers. Babbage's conception was beyond the capabilities of the technology of his time, and the machine remained unfinished at his death in 1871.
• The 1890 U.S. census was expedited by the rapid processing of huge amounts of data with an **electrical punch-card tabulating machine** developed by American inventor Herman Hollerith, whose company in 1924 became International Business Machines (**IBM**).
• On the eve of World War II researchers experimented with ways to speed up computation, since calculators using solely mechanical components were too slow. One approach was to use **electromechanical relays**, which basically are electrically controlled switches. In 1940, Bell Laboratories mathematician George Stibitz completed the 1st electromechanical relay-based calculator. In the same year Stibitz provided the 1st demonstration of remote operation of a computer, using a teletype to transmit problems to his machine and to receive the results.
• In 1941, German engineer Konrad Zuse completed the relay-based Z3, the 1st fully functional digital computer to be controlled by a program. In 1944, the **1st large-scale automatic digital computer**, the Mark I, built by IBM and Harvard Professor Howard Aiken, went into operation; this relay-based machine was 55 feet long and 8 feet high.
• Efforts were also under way to develop **fully electronic machines**, using vacuum tubes, which can operate much more quickly than relays. Between 1937 and 1942 the 1st rudimentary vacuum-tube calculator was built by the physicist John Vincent Atanasoff and his assistant Clifford Berry at Iowa State College (now University).
• More substantial electronic machines were the Colossus, developed by the British in 1943 to break German codes, and the **Eniac** (for Electronic Numerical Integrator and Computer), a 30-ton room-sized computer with over 18,000 vacuum tubes, built by physicist John Mauchly and engineer J. Presper Eckert at the University of Pennsylvania for the U.S. Army and completed in 1946. The Colossus was a special-purpose machine; its capabilities were powerful (for its time) but limited. Eniac was a general-purpose machine and could be programmed to do different tasks, although programming could take a couple of days, since cables had to be plugged in and switches set by hand.

IT'S A FACT: The world's fastest supercomputer is Japan's Earth Simulator. Programmed to simulate weather patterns and other massive systems such as the effects of earthquakes, it can perform 35 trillion calculations in a second. It's almost twice as fast as the next fastest, Thunder, located at Lawrence Livermore National Laboratory in California.

• In 1951, Eckert and Mauchly's **Univac** ("Universal Automatic Computer") became the 1st computer commercially available in the U.S.; the 1st customer: the Census Bureau. CBS-TV used a Univac in 1952 to predict election results.

The invention of the **transistor** in 1947 and the **integrated circuit** in 1958 paved the way for the development of the **microprocessor** (an entire computer processing unit on a chip), the 1st commercial example of which was the Intel 4004 in 1971. These advances allowed computers to become smaller, speedier, more reliable, and more powerful. In 1965 engineer and Intel cofounder Gordon Moore predicted that the number of transistors that could be put on a computer chip would double every year (revised in 1975 to every 18 months). "Moore's Law" has largely held true.

• In 1975, the **1st widely marketed personal computer**, the MITS Altair 8800, was introduced in kit form, with no keyboard and no video display, for under $400. In the same year **Microsoft** was founded by Bill Gates and Paul Allen.

• In 1976, the **1st PC word-processing program**, the Electric Pencil, was written.

• In 1977, the **Apple II** was introduced by Apple Computer, which had been formed the previous year by Steven Jobs and Stephen Wozniak. Capable of displaying text and graphics in color, the machine enjoyed phenomenal success.

• In 1981, **IBM** unveiled its **"Personal Computer,"** which used Microsoft's DOS (disk operating system).

• In 1984, Apple Computer introduced the 1st **Macintosh**. The easy-to-use Macintosh came with a proprietary operating system and was the 1st popular computer to have a GUI (graphical user interface) and a mouse—features originally developed by the Xerox Corporation.

• In 1990, Microsoft released **Windows** 3.0, the 1st workable version of its own GUI.

• In 1991, **Linux**, based on the Unix operating system used in high-power computers, was invented for the PC by Helsinki Univ. student Linus Torvalds and made available for free.

• In 1996, the **Palm Pilot**, the 1st widely successful handheld computer and personal information manager, arrived.

• In 1997, the IBM computer Deep Blue beat world chess champion Garry Kasparov in a 6-game match, 3.5-2.5.

• In 2001, Apple introduced a new Unix-based operating system called OS X for the Macintosh.

• By early 2002, according to computer industry research firm Gartner Dataquest, **1 billion personal computers** (PCs), including desktop and laptop machines of all types, had been shipped by manufacturers since 1975, when the 1st commercially successful PC went on sale. The next billion were expected to ship within 5 or 6 years.

As of early 2004, Apple had only about 3% of the overall U.S. personal computer market, with machines using the Microsoft Windows operating system accounting for almost all the rest.

About the Internet

The **Internet** is a vast and rapidly growing computer network of computer networks. In 1994, a total of 3 million people (most of them in the U.S.) made use of it; by early 2004, estimates of the number of users worldwide ranged as high as 945 million (Computer Industry Almanac Inc.). According to Nielsen//NetRatings, as of early 2004 more than 140 million people in the U.S. were going online each month. According to the marketing communications firm Global Reach, English was the native language of nearly 36% of the 729 million people the firm estimated were online in early 2004; the 2nd-most-common language was Chinese, with more than 14%.

Denmark was the country with the highest level of "e-readiness" in 2004, according to an annual ranking by IBM and the Economist Intelligence Unit (associated with the magazine *The Economist*). E-readiness is a measure of a country's openness to Internet-related business opportunities; it takes into account such factors as infrastructure, support services, adoption by businesses and consumers, and social, cultural, and legal conditions. Nordic countries occupied 4 of the top 5 positions on the list. Britain was 2nd, Sweden 3rd, Norway 4th, and Finland 5th. The U.S. was 6th. The Computer Industry Almanac Inc. estimated that in 2004, Denmark had 682 Web surfers per 1,000 residents, compared to 628 per 1,000 for the U.S.

The Internet is not owned or funded by any one institution, organization, or government. It has no CEO and is not a commercial service. Its development is guided by the Internet Society (ISOC), composed of volunteers. The ISOC appoints the Internet Architecture Board (IAB), which oversees issues of standards, network resources, etc.

Internet Developments

The Internet grew out of a series of developments in the academic, governmental, and information technology communities. Here are some **major historical highlights**:

• In 1969, ARPANET, an experimental 4-computer network, was established by the Advanced Research Projects Agency (ARPA) of the U.S. Defense Dept. so that research scientists could communicate. By 1971, ARPANET linked about 2 dozen computers ("hosts") at 15 sites, including MIT and Harvard. By 1981, there were over 200 hosts.

• In 1978, the first **spam**, or junk e-mail, message was sent over ARPANET.

• During the 1980s, more and more computers using different operating systems were connected. In 1983, the military

portion of ARPANET was moved onto the MILNET, and ARPANET was disbanded in 1990.

• In the late 1980s, the National Science Foundation's NSF-NET began its own network and allowed everyone to access it. It was, however, mainly the domain of "techies," computer-science graduates, and professors.

• In 1988, Internet Relay Chat (IRC) was developed by Finnish student Jarkko Oikarinen, enabling people to communicate via the Internet in "real time." It 1st drew world attention as a source of up-to-date information in the 1991 Persian Gulf War.

• 1988, saw the 1st known case of large-scale damage caused by a **computer virus** spread via the Internet—a "worm" crafted by Cornell University graduate student Robert Morris, Jr., infected thousands of computers, shutting many down and causing millions of dollars of damage.

• In 1989, the 1st commercial Internet service provider supplying dial-up access appeared, known as The World.

• In 1989-90, the **World Wide Web** was invented by Tim Berners-Lee as an environment in which scientists at the European Center for Nuclear Research in Switzerland could share information. It gradually evolved into a medium with text, graphics, audio, animation, and video.

• In 1991, commercial traffic was admitted to the NSFNET. 1991 saw release of the 1st **browser**, or software for accessing the Web. In 1993, the U.S. National Center for Supercomputing Applications released versions of Mosaic, the 1st graphical Web browser, for Microsoft Windows, Unix systems running the X Window GUI, and the Apple Macintosh.

• In 1994, **Netscape** Communications released the Netscape Navigator browser. **Microsoft** released its Internet Explorer browser the following year but initially failed to make a dent in Netscape's dominance of the browser market. But by 1998, Netscape's market share had fallen below 50%, while Internet Explorer's exceeded 25%.

• In 1996, a group of universities launched Internet2, an advanced, high-performance network for the research community. It provided a test bed for development of new capabilities that might find use in the commercial Internet.

• The release of the free **Napster** file-sharing service in 1999 enabled users to easily exchange files containing music or other content without regard to copyright restrictions. In 2001, a court ordered Napster, whose users numbered in the millions, to suspend operations because it fostered massive copyright violations; Napster users, however, switched

to other file-sharing services, such as Morpheus and KaZaA, to exchange files. (Napster was later reconstituted as a legitimate, for-pay music download service.) In Sept. 2003, the Recording Industry Association of America began filing lawsuits against individuals for allegedly violating copyright law by downloading pirated music. By mid-2004, the number of people sued by the group exceeded 3,400.

• In 2000, a federal district judge found Microsoft guilty of antitrust violations; he ordered the company split into 2 parts, but implementation of the penalty was stayed pending appeal. In 2001, the Justice Dept., Microsoft, and several states agreed on a settlement that avoided the breakup of the company but bound Microsoft to make portions of its Windows operating system code available to competitors so they could design their products to work with Windows; the accord (which was upheld by a federal appeals court in mid-2004) also included safeguards against Microsoft retaliating against computer makers that chose not to bundle Microsoft products with their machines. By mid-2002, Internet Explorer held 95% of the browser market, according to the Web analysis firm WebSideStory.

• In mid-2003, Niue, a self-governing Pacific island associated with New Zealand, became the 1st "country" to offer free nationwide **wireless access** to the Internet (using Wi-Fi technology). This technology was becoming increasingly widespread.

In late 2003, the U.S. enacted its 1st law against spam, but the so-called Can-Spam (Controlling the Assault of Non-Solicited Pornography and Marketing) Act had little effect on the rising tide of junk e-mail. By mid-2004, spam was estimated to account for upwards of $2/3$ of all e-mail. The International Telecommunication Union said the figure might be as high as 85%, with the annual cost to consumers and businesses estimated at $25 billion. A world converence of government regulators convened by the ITU in Geneva in July 2004 called for countries to adopt common antispam legislation.

In mid-2004, following discovery of major security problems in Internet Explorer that potentially exposed users to hacker attack, the U.S. Computer Emergency Response Team suggested users consider switching to a different browser. In July, WebSideStory reported that Internet Explorer's market share fell below 95% for the first time in two years; the non-Microsoft portion of the market was dominated by browsers based on the "Gecko" browsing technology (Mozilla, Mozilla Firefox, and Netscape).

How the Internet Works

The 2 most popular aspects of the Internet are electronic mail, or e-mail, and the **World Wide Web**, which may be thought of as a graphical environment that can be navigated through **hyperlinks**—from one site you click on hyperlinks to go to related sites. The Internet involves 3 basic elements: server, client, and network. A **server** is a computer program that makes data available to other programs on the same or other computers—it "serves" them. A **client** is a computer that requests data from a server. A **network** is an interconnected system in which multiple computers can communicate, via copper wire, coaxial cable, fiber-optic cable, radio waves, etc. When you use a **browser** to go to a site on the World Wide Web, you access the site's files.

Here are the steps in opening and accessing a file:

• In the browser, specify the address of the desired website—for example, www.usps.gov for the U.S. Postal Service.

• The browser sends your request to the server of your **Internet service provider** (ISP), the company that supplies your connection to the Internet.

• That server sends the request to the server at the address specified. The official address of each computer connected to the Net, the so-called Internet Protocol (IP) address, is actually numerical. If, as is commonly done, you indicated the website address using letters and words—such as www.usps.gov—then the Internet's Domain Name Service automatically converts it into the appropriate IP address (in this case, 56.0.134.24).

• The file is sent to the ISP's server, which sends it back to the browser, which displays the file.

Internet Resources

• **Domains.** A domain is the fundamental part of an address on the Internet, such as a website address or an e-mail address. Since 1998 the system of domain names has been overseen by a nonprofit corporation called the Internet Corporation for Assigned Names and Numbers (ICANN). Numerous companies offer domain registration services; examples include VeriSign, Register.com, and BulkRegister.com.

The final part of a domain name, known as the **top-level domain**, is its most basic part. For example, in *The World Almanac's* e-mail address—Walmanac@waegroup.com—com is the top-level domain. ("Walmanac" is *The World Almanac's* "username.") The top-level domains include:

Domain	What It Is
.aero	an organization in the air-transport industry
.biz	a business
.com	generally a commercial organization, business, or company
.coop	a nonprofit business cooperative, such as a rural electric coop
.edu	a 4-year higher-educational institution
.gov	a nonmilitary U.S. governmental entity, usually federal
.info	an informational site for an individual or organization, without restriction
.int	an international organization
.mil	a U.S. military organization
.museum	a museum
.name	an individual
.net	suggested for a network administration, but actually used by a wide variety of sites
.org	suggested for a nonprofit organization, but actually used by a wide variety of sites
.pro	a professional, such as an accountant, lawyer, or physician

The top-level domain .us is also available to persons, organizations, and entities in the U.S. Generally speaking, country codes are used for most top-level domains outside the U.S.—for example, jp in Japan, uk in the United Kingdom, and ru in Russia.

FAQs. Frequently Asked Questions documents contain answers to common questions. A huge collection of FAQs can be found at the site www.faqs.org/faqs.

FTP. File Transfer Protocol is a simple method of transferring files on the Internet. Using FTP, you log on to a remote site, find files, and copy them to your computer. Sites with FTP capability can be accessed with special programs and also often with browsers. The full address for such a site when accessed through a browser—the so-called Uniform Resource Locator (URL)—typically begins with ftp://.

HTTP. Hypertext Transfer Protocol is the file-exchange method underlying the World Wide Web. A website URL begins with http:// (or https:// for "secure" sites that protect the confidentiality of information you may transmit over the Web).

Newsgroups. Newsgroups, a classic institution of the Internet, are found on the part of the Internet called Usenet. In a newsgroup, messages concerning a particular topic are posted in a public forum. You can simply read the postings, or you can post something yourself.

Online Activities

Communication via e-mail, or online chat, or instant messaging is the most widely used application of the Internet. The Net can also carry telephone conversations. Use by consumers and businesses of low-cost telephone service based on the so-called Voice over Internet Protocol (VoIP) is limited but growing. The consulting firm Gartner predicted the U.S. would have 1 million VoIP subscribers by the end of 2004 and 6 million by the end of 2009. Some experts believe that a third of U.S. households could be using VoIP by 2007. How widespread the technology actually becomes, however, will depend largely on how the federal government chooses to regulate and tax it. Another form of communication practiced by many Web users is the online personal journal, or **blog**. (The name derives from "Web log.") As of mid-2004, according to a "census" by the National Institute for Technology and Liberal Education, the total number of active blogs exceeded 2 million, most of

them in English. While many blogs are of little interest to anyone not a friend of the author, others attract more attention. The 2 major U.S. political parties gave media credentials to bloggers wanting to cover their national conventions in summer 2004.

The Net is a major source of reference **information** on health and medicine, government, and a plethora of other topics. Many people rely on it for up-to-the-minute news. The job of keeping up with the latest developments is simplified in the case of sites offering RSS (which stands for Rich Site Summary or Really Simple Syndication). A program known as an RSS reader can automatically provide a Web user with a continuous "feed" of updates from sites of interest.

The Internet is an increasingly important vehicle for such activities as distributing music, broadcasting radio, gambling, and conducting business. In mid-2004, a little over a year after the establishment of Apple's iTunes online music store, the highest-profile legitimate (for-pay) music download service, iTunes saw its 100 millionth download. According to the U.S. Census Bureau, online retail sales came to $15.5 billion in the first quarter of 2004—28% more than a year earlier. A study released by Shop.org (part of the National Retail Federation) estimated that overall U.S. e-commerce sales (including travel) would reach $144 billion in 2004, a 27% increase over the preceding year. Online sales were predicted to make up 6.6% of total retail sales in 2004, up from 5.4% in 2003 and 3.6% on 2002.

Safety and Security on the Internet

Common sense dictates some basic security rules:
• Pick passwords that are difficult to guess, preferably consisting of both letters and numbers, and perhaps also other symbols (if permitted). It's a bad idea to use the same password at numerous websites.
• Do not give out your phone number, address, or other personal information, unless needed for a transaction at a site you trust.
• Be careful about giving out credit card numbers.
• If you feel someone is being threatening or dangerous, inform your Internet service provider.
• If you have a high-speed Internet connection that is always on, use protective "firewall" software to guard your system against attacks by hackers; in fact, a firewall is a wise precaution even for those who use a dial-up modem.

Users of so-called **peer-to-peer** (P2P) file-sharing networks, such as KaZaA, should open up only part of their computer system to sharing—not the entire hard drive.

Security flaws turn up from time to time in operating systems, Web browsers, and other software, and when the manufacturers provide patches to solve the problem, it is usually advisable to install these fixes. If a fix is not available for a serious security problem, you may want to consider switching to an alternative program.

Viruses. There is always a risk of acquiring a computer **virus**. In a general sense, a virus is chunk of computer code designed to produce an unexpected event. Some viruses may merely display a whimsical message on your screen. Some may wreak havoc in your system. Your system can pick up a virus from a program downloaded from the Internet or elsewhere via modem (or received on a disk); a virus can also be communicated via e-mail, as was the case with Zafi-B and Netsky-P, the most common viruses in June 2004, according to the antivirus firm Sophos. The worldwide cost of malicious software such as viruses in 2003 was put at $12.5 billion by the research firm Computer Electronics.

Some viruses propagate with the help of a carrier program. Others, such as **worms**, do not. A **worm** may or may not damage files, but reproduces itself with the help of the infected computer's resources. Zafi and Netsky are both worms. A worm may install a "back door" on the infected system, giving access to a hacker; may attempt to turn off any antivirus program on the system; and may try to log the user's keystrokes.

A **Trojan horse** is computer code concealed within harmless code or data that is capable of taking control at some point and causing damage. It can be used to mount a massive **"denial-of-service"** attack, which overwhelms targeted computers by inundating them with electronic messages. The June 2004 attack temporarily impaired the operations of Akamai Technologies, a company that operates tens of thousands of servers for major websites. The deluge of messages reportedly came from numerous computers infected with Trojan viruses. Such computers, acting under hacker control without their owners' knowledge, are referred to as **zombies**, and the network of zombie computers that carry out the attack is called a **botnet**.

You should install **antivirus software** on your computer, keep it up to date, and try to keep abreast of reports of new viruses. Be careful about opening e-mail from unknown correspondents, and if you have programs with a macro capability (macros are bits of auxiliary coding that are meant to play a helpful role but can be taken advantage of by some viruses), make sure the programs' macro virus protection (if any) is turned on. Keep macros disabled if you do not know what you might want to use them for.

Phishing. A good firewall and an up-to-date antivirus program won't help you, however, if you let down your guard and permit a hacker to trick you into disclosing your password, social security number, credit card number, or other sensitive information. A popular scam in 2003-4 was **phishing**—the use of a forged e-mail message purportedly from a respectable organization, such as a bank, to elicit such personal data. The e-mail typically contains a hyperlink that leads to a fabricated website resembling the site of the ostensible sender. A Gartner survey released in May 2004 indicated that more than 30 million Americans believed they responded to a phishing e-mail over the past year, and some 2 million revealed sensitive personal information.

A simple way to avoid falling victim to a phishing scam is to refuse to click on links in e-mails from companies where you have an account. If you want to visit such a company's website, open your browser and manually enter the site's normal address.

Spyware. Another growing concern in 2004 was spyware—software that observes your computer activity without your knowledge. Spyware programs often gain entry to your machine via a Trojan horse. They may record your keystrokes and report passwords or other personal information to a hacker or may flood your screen with ads. Antispyware programs can combat this threat, but, as with firewall and antivirus software, it is important to keep them up-to-date.

Filtering. Such browsers as Internet Explorer, Netscape Navigator, and Opera, as well as some search engines, contain features that let you filter the content that can be viewed on your computer. Special filtering software is also available, and some ISPs, such as AOL and MSN, make it possible for you to restrict the type of content seen on screen.

Parents can find more information on protecting their children while online at the websites of several U.S. government agencies, such as the FBI (www.fbi.gov/publications/ pguide/pguide.htm). Other helpful sites are www.cyber smart.org and www. safekids.com.

Spam. Junk e-mail, or **spam**, has surged in the past few years. Many sellers of goods or services love spam because it provides an extremely inexpensive form of marketing. For recipients, however, these unsolicited ads can be a time-wasting annoyance or worse—spam may hawk pornography or products dangerous to health, may seek to defraud the recipient, may carry a destructive virus, or may turn the recipient's machine into a zombie that stores illicit material, takes part in a denial-of-service attack, or distributes spam. (According to network traffic and security firm Sandvine, zombie PCs may account for up to 80% of spam.) Net administrators worry that the flood of spam may cause delays or even a breakdown in the flow of Internet traffic. Brightmail, a maker of antispam software, estimated that by June 2004 spam accounted for 65% of e-mail traffic, up from only 8% in 2001.

While filtering software can help reduce the deluge of spam—some e-mail programs include filters—it is not completely accurate, and experts also recommend that you be wary of revealing your e-mail address as you surf the Web.

In late spring 2004, the first computer virus to infect mobile phones was detected. The "Cabir" virus infected certain types of phones and would activate itself every time the phone was turned on, displaying the word "Caribe" on the menu screen. It would then use the phone's network to find other victims. The virus was essentially harmless and the problem was corrected.

Portals and Search Engines

Many people have a favorite site that they go to 1st when logging on to the World Wide Web. A convenient choice for such a site is a **portal,** a gateway site typically offering a search engine but also a variety of other features, which may include e-mail, chat, instant messaging, news services, stock updates, weather reports, real estate listings, yellow pages, people finders, maps, TV and movie listings, shopping, and tools to create and post your own Web page. Many portals permit you to customize the opening screen. Another common feature is a personal calendar to help you schedule activities.

Leading portals include:

AOL . . . . . . www.aol.com
Excite . . . . . www.excite.com
Go.com . . . www.go.com
Lycos . . . . . www.lycos.com
MSN . . . . . www.msn.com
Netscape . . www.netscape.com
Terra . . . www.terra.com (Spanish-language)
Yahoo! . . . . www.yahoo.com

By using the portal's **search engine** you can locate information and, in some cases, images on sites throughout a large part of the Internet. No search engine covers the entire Web completely, and some portals offer a list of search engines to choose from. Search engines typically allow you to find occurrences of a particular **key word or words**. Search engines use different methods for finding, indexing, and retrieving information. Some store only the title and URL of sites; others index every word of a site's content. Some give extra weight to words in titles or other key positions, or to sites for which more hyperlinks exist on the Web. Some search engines also can retrieve images or other nontext files on the Net. Many search engines work with the help of a program called a "spider," "crawler," or "bot." This visits sites across the Web and extracts information that can be used to create the search engine's index.

Some portals also offer a **subject guide**—a menu-like directory, generally compiled by humans. You drill down through the directory to find a subcategory with websites of interest. Yahoo! is a popular example.

Among other search engines and directories:

AltaVista (www.altavista.com), owned by Yahoo!, is noted for its language translation capabilities.

Ask Jeeves (www.ask.com) provides a directory but also responds to questions entered in plain English, as does its children's service, Ask Jeeves for Kids (www.ajkids.com).

Google (www.google.com) is the first choice for many Web surfers. Its search results, which rely largely on link popularity in ranking sites, are also available via certain portals. Google's many features include newsgroup, image, and product searches and the ability to retrieve an archived copy of a webpage made at the time the page was indexed (the page may since have changed its content or gone offline). Continuing to expand its offerings, Google launched an e-mail service in 2004.

LookSmart (www.looksmart.com), in addition to a directory and a search engine (WiseNut, also available at www.wisenut.com), provides access to thousands of periodicals.

Open Directory (dmoz.org) aims to cope with the vast size of the Web and produce the most comprehensive directory by using volunteer editors. Its information is used by such services as AOL, Google, Lycos, and Netscape.

Teoma (www.teoma.com), owned by Ask Jeeves, groups search results into topics and also supplies links to related resources.

A **meta-search engine** submits your request to several different search engines at the same time. However, meta-search engines typically do not exhaust each of the search engines' databases, and they may be unable to transmit complicated search requests. Among the better-known meta-search engines are **Dogpile** (www.dogpile.com); **Ixquick** (www.ixquick.com); **Queryserver** (www.queryserver.com); and **Vivísimo** (www.vivisimo.com). Also worth trying is KartOO (www.kartoo.com), noted for the attractive, and customizable, graphic presentation of its search results.

Large segments of the Web are not readily searchable by general-purpose search engines. Special search tools include those available via the Direct Search site (www.freepint.com/gary/direct.htm). Other helpful sites include Infomine (infomine.ucr.edu), Invisible web.net (www.invisible-web.net), and the Resource Discovery Network (www.rdn.ac.uk).

For more information about search engines, including links to specialized search tools, go to **Search Engine Watch,** at www.searchenginewatch.com.

The **Internet Archive** may be of help if you are looking for Web pages that existed in the past—say, previous versions of a current page or a website that has disappeared. The Archive's "Wayback Machine" (www.archive.com) holds more than 30 billion old pages.

Internet Lingo

The following abbreviations are sometimes used on the Internet documents and in e-mail.

BTW	By the way	GTG	Got to go	OTOH	On the other hand
F2F	Face to face; a personal meeting	HHOK	Ha, ha—only kidding	PLS	Please
FCOL	For crying out loud	IMHO	In my humble opinion	ROTFL	Rolling on the floor laughing
FWIW	For what it's worth	IMO	In my opinion	TAFN	That's all for now
GOK	God only knows	LOL	Laughing out loud	TTFN	Ta-ta for now

Emoticons, or **smileys,** are a series of typed characters that, when turned sideways, resemble a face and express an emotion. Here are some smileys often encountered on the Internet.

:-)	Smile	:-D	Laugh	:-(	Unhappy	:-b..	Drooling
;-)	Wink	:-*	Kiss	:-o	Shouting	{*}	A hug and a kiss

Most-Visited Websites, June 2004

Source: comScore Media Metrix, Inc.

Rank	Website*	Visitors[1]	Rank	Website*	Visitors[1]	Rank	Website*	Visitors[1]
1.	Yahoo! Sites	115,355	8.	About/Primedia	34,223	15.	Walt Disney Internet Group (WDIG)	22,706
2.	MSN-Microsoft Sites	113,871	9.	Amazon Sites	32,855	16.	Weatherbug.com Property	22,509
3.	Time Warner Network	108,852	10.	Monster Worldwide	27,803	17.	CNET Networks	21,280
4.	Google Sites	63,710	11.	Viacom Online	26,721	18.	Symantec	21,072
5.	eBay	58,311	12.	Verizon Communications Corporation	25,339	19.	Shopping.com Sites	20,180
6.	Ask Jeeves	39,275	13.	Real.com Network	23,855	20.	InfoSpace Network	19,247
7.	Terra Lycos	37,137	14.	The Weather Channel	23,534			

*In some cases, represents an aggregation of commonly owned domain names. (1) Number of visitors, in thousands, who visited website at least once in June 2004.

Internet Directory to Selected Sites

The Websites listed are but a sampling of what is available. For some others, see the following *World Almanac* features: the Where to Get Help directory (Health), the Business Directory (Consumer Information), the Sports Directory, Travel and Tourism, Associations and Societies, 100 Most Populous U.S. Cities, States of the U.S., U.S. Government, and Nations of the World. You may also find suggested websites of interest in the free monthly World Almanac E-Newsletter, available at www.worldalmanac.com. (Addresses are subject to change, and sites or products are not endorsed by *The World Almanac*.)

You must type an address exactly as written. You may be unable to connect to a site because (1) you have mistyped the address, (2) the site is busy, or (3) it has moved or no longer exists.

Online Service Providers
America Online
www.aol.com
AT&T WorldNet Service
www.att.net
CompuServe
www.compuserve.com
EarthLink
www.earthlink.net
Microsoft Network
www.msn.com
Juno
www.juno.com

Directories
Addresses.com
www.addresses.com
Bigfoot (e-mail addresses and white page listings)
www.bigfoot.com
InfoSpace, the Ultimate Directory
www.infospace.com
People Search
people.yahoo.com
Switchboard, the People and Business Directory
www.switchboard.com
WhoWhere?
www.whowhere.lycos.com

Security, Screening, and Safe Computing
Anti-Phishing Working Group
www.antiphishing.org
The National Fraud Information Center
www.fraud.org
National Cyber Security Alliance
www.staysafeonline.info
U.S. Computer Emergency Response Team (CERT)
www.cert.org
What's New on the Internet
Nerd World: Media (what's new in computer world)
www.nerdworld.com/whatsnew.html
Yahoo! What's New (listing of every new site each day; sometimes thousands)
dir.yahoo.com/new

Auctions
eBay
www.ebay.com
uBid Online Auction
www.ubid.com
Yahoo! Auctions
auctions.shopping.yahoo.com

Audio/Video
MP3.com
www.mp3.com
Real Networks
www.real.com

Bookstores
Amazon.com Inc.
www.amazon.com
AddAll Book Search
www.addall.com.com
Barnes and Noble
www.barnesandnoble.com
Powell's City of Books
www.powells.com

Chat Sites
America Online
www.aim.com
Excite
communicate.excite.com
IVILLAGE: The Women's Network
www.ivillage.com
Yahoo
chat.yahoo.com

Children's Sites
(*See also Family Resources*)
Children's Television Workshop
www.sesameworkshop.org
Judy Blume's Home Base
www.judyblume.com
The Newbery Medal
www.ala.org/alsc/newbery.html
Peace Corps Kids World
www.peacecorps.gov/kids
Rock and Roll Hall of Fame and Museum
www.rockhall.com
Seussville
www.seussville.com
SuperSite for Kids
www.bonus.com
Weekly Reader
www.weeklyreader.com
White House for Kids
www.whitehousekids.gov
World Almanac for Kids
www.worldalmanacforkids.com
Yahooligans (for homework help sites)
www.yahooligans.com

Economic Data
Bureau of Economic Analysis
www.bea.doc.gov
Bureau of Labor Statistics
www.bls.gov
Economics Statistics Briefing Room
www.whitehouse.gov/fsbr/esbr.html
Economy at a Glance
stats.bls.gov/eag/
Office of Management and Budget
www.gpoaccess.gov/usbudget
Statistical Abstract of the United States (a sampling)
www.census.gov/statab/www
STAT-USA/Internet (a subscription-based government service)
www.stat-usa.gov/stat-usa.html

Entertainment
Eonline
www.eonline.com
The Internet Movie Database
www.imdb.com
Movies.com
www.movies.go.com
The Movie Times
www.the-movie-times.com
Variety
www.variety.com

Family Resources
(*See also Children's Sites*)
Babies Online
www.babiesonline.com
BabyCenter
www.babycenter.com
FamilyFun.Com

familyfun.go.com
KidsHealth.org
www.kidshealth.org
KidSource Online
www.kidsource.com
ParenthoodWeb
www.parenthood.com
Parent Soup
www.parentsoup.com
ParentsPlace.com
www.parentsplace.com
Screen It! Entertainment Reviews for Parents
www.screenit.com
Zero to Three
www.zerotothree.org

Greeting Cards, Electronic
Blue Mountain Arts
www.bluemountain.com
Egreetings Network
www.egreetings.com
E-CARDS
www.ecards.com
1001 Postcards
www.postcards.org
123 Greetings
www.123greetings.com

Health
CenterWatch Clinical Trials Listing Service
www.centerwatch.com
drkoop.com
www.drkoop.com
Drugstore.com
www.drugstore.com
Healthfinder
www.healthfinder.gov
Mayo Clinic Health Oasis
www.mayohealth.org
Medscape
www.medscape.com
The Merck Manual
www.merck.com
National Institutes of Health
health.nih.gov
U.S. National Library of Medicine
www.nlm.nih.gov
WebMD
www.webmd.com

Job Search Sites
CareerBuilder
www.careerbuilder.com
Hotjobs
hotjobs.yahoo.com
Monster.com
www.monster.com

Money Management
Internal Revenue Service
www.irs.gov
Wall Street Journal
www.wsj.com
American Stock Exchange
www.amex.com
E*TRADE
www.etrade.com
MarketWatch
cbs.marketwatch.com
NASDAQ
www.nasdaq.com
New York Stock Exchange
www.nyse.com
Mortgage Calculator
www.mortgage-calc.com
Retirement Calculator
www.retirementcalc.com

Music
All Music Guide
www.allmusic.com
MusicMoz (open music project)
www.musicmoz.org
BBC Music
www.bbc.co.uk/music
Classical Net
www.classical.net

News
The Associated Press
www.ap.org
BBC Online
news.bbc.co.uk
Cable News Network
www.cnn.com
The Los Angeles Times
www.latimes.com
MSNBC
www.msnbc.com
The New York Times on the Web
www.nytimes.com
Reuters
www.reuters.com
USA Today
www.usatoday.com
Washington Post
www.washingtonpost.com
World Press Review Online
www.worldpress.org

Reference
About.com
www.about.com
CIA Publications and Reports
www.odci.gov/cia/publications
Explore the Internet; The Library of Congress
www.loc.gov
Great Books Online
www.bartleby.com
Libweb: Library Servers via WWW
sunsite.berkeley.edu/Libweb
Merriam-Webster Network Editions
www.m-w.com
yourDictionary.com
www.yourdictionary.com
Refdesk
www.refdesk.com
Roget's Thesaurus
www.thesaurus.com

Sports
ESPN
www.espn.go.com
Sporting News
www.sportingnews.com
Sports Illustrated
www.sportsillustrated.cnn.com
Sports Network
www.sportsnetwork.com

Weather
National Weather Service Home Page
www.nws.noaa.gov
National Center for Environmental Prediction (includes links to Storm Prediction Center and other sites)
www.ncep.noaa.gov
Weather Channel
www.weather.com

Percent of U.S. Households With Internet Access, by Selected Characteristics

Source: National Telecommunications and Information Administration, U.S. Dept. of Commerce; data as of 2001.

	TOTAL	**50.5**
Race	White, not Hispanic	55.4
	Black, not Hispanic	30.8
	Hispanic	32.0
	Asian, Pacific Islander	68.1
Household type	Married couple with children under 18	71.6
	Male householder with children under 18	44.9
	Female householder w. children under 18	40.0
	Family households without children	53.2
	Nonfamily households	35.0
Location	Urban	51.1
	Central city	45.7
	Rural	48.7
Annual income	$5,000 or less	20.5
	$5,000-9,999	14.4
	$10,000-14,999	19.4
	$15,000-19,999	23.6
	$20,000-24,999	31.8
	$25,000-34,999	42.2
	$35,000-49,999	56.4
	$50,000-74,999	71.4
	$75,000+	85.4

Percent of U.S. Households With a Computer, by Selected Characteristics

	TOTAL	**56.5**
Race	White, not Hispanic	61.1
	Black, not Hispanic	37.1
	Hispanic	40.0
	Asian, Pacific Islander	72.7
Household Type	Married couple with child under 18	78.9
	Male household with child under 18	55.1
	Female household w. child under 18	49.2
	Family households without children	58.8
	Nonfamily households	39.2
Location	Urban	56.7
	Central city	51.5
	Rural	55.6
Annual income	$5,000 or less	25.9
	$5,000-9,999	19.2
	$10,000-14,999	25.7
	$15,000-19,999	31.8
	$20,000-24,999	40.1
	$25,000-34,999	49.7
	$35,000-49,999	64.3
	$50,000-74,999	77.7
	$75,000+	89.0

Top-Selling Software, 2004

Source: NPD Techworld Data, Reston, VA
(based on unit U.S. sales, Jan.-June 2004[1])

All Software
1. TurboTax 2003 Deluxe, Intuit
2. Norton Antivirus 2004, Symantec
3. TurboTax 2003 Multi State 45, Intuit
4. Taxcut 2003 Deluxe, Block Financial
5. TurboTax 2003, Intuit
6. Norton Internet Security 2004, Symantec
7. Taxcut 2003 State, Block Financial
8. MS Office 2003 Student/Teacher Ed., Microsoft
9. MS Windows XP Home Ed. Upgrade, Microsoft
10. Taxcut 2003, Block Financial

Games
1. Battlefield Vietnam, Electronic Arts
2. Unreal Tournament 2004, Atari
3. Call Of Duty, Activision
4. City Of Heroes, NCsoft
5. The Sims Deluxe, Electronic Arts
6. Far Cry, Ubisoft
7. MS Age Of Mythology, Microsoft
8. The Sims: Makin' Magic Expansion Pack, Electronic Arts
9. MS Zoo Tycoon: Complete Collection, Microsoft
10. Drop JC, eGames

System Utilities
1. Norton Antivirus 2004, Symantec
2. Norton Internet Security 2004, Symantec
3. Norton Internet Security 2004 Upgrade, Symantec
4. Norton System Works 2004, Symantec
5. VirusScan 8.0, Network Associates
6. Norton Antivirus 2004 Pro, Symantec
7. Norton Antivirus 2004 Upgrade, Symantec
8. SpySweeper, Webroot
9. McAfee Internet Security 6.0, Network Associates
10. Norton System Works 2004/Personal Firewall 2004 Bundle, Symantec

Home Education Software
1. Instant Immersion Spanish JC, Topics Entertainment
2. Mavis Beacon Teaches Typing 15.0, Riverdeep Interactive
3. Dora The Explorer Animal Adventures, Atari
4. Adventure Workshop 1st-3rd Grade, Riverdeep Interactive

5. Snap! Typing JC, Topics Entertainment
6. Finding Nemo: Nemo's Underwater World Of Fun, THQ
7. Adventure Workshop 4th-6th Grade, Riverdeep Interactive
8. Jumpstart Advanced Preschool 2003, Vivendi Universal
9. Jumpstart Advanced Kindergarten 2003, Vivendi Universal
10. Instant Immersion Spanish Deluxe, Topics Entertainment

Personal Productivity Software
1. MS Streets & Trips 2004, Microsoft
2. DVD Ripper JC, Cosmi
3. Easy CD & DVD Creator 6.0, Roxio
4. Bible Library Deluxe JC, Valusoft (THQ)
5. Easy Media Creator 7.0, Roxio
6. DVD X Copy Platinum, 321 Studios
7. MS Works 7.0, Microsoft
8. Serene Scene Marine Aquarium 2.0, Encore
9. MS Works Suite 2004, Microsoft
10. Burn & Go CD/DVD, Valusoft (THQ)

Business Software
1. MS Office 2003 Student/Teacher Ed., Microsoft
2. Norton AntiSpam 2004, Symantec
3. MS Office XP Student & Teacher Ed. Acad., Microsoft
4. AD Guard, Valusoft (THQ)
5. MS Office 2003 Pro Upgrade, Microsoft
6. Pop-up Stopper Companion 3.0, Panicware
7. MS Office 2003, Microsoft
8. Act! 6.0, Interact Commerce
9. McAfee SpamKiller 5.0, Network Associates
10. Pop-Up AD Blocker JC, Cosmi

Finance Software
1. TurboTax 2003 Deluxe, Intuit
2. TurboTax 2003 Multi State 45, Intuit
3. Taxcut 2003 Deluxe, Block Financial
4. TurboTax 2003, Intuit
5. Taxcut 2003 State, Block Financial
6. Taxcut 2003, Block Financial
7. Quicken 2004, Intuit
8. TurboTax 2003 CA State, Intuit
9. TurboTax 2003 Home & Business, Intuit
10. TurboTax 2003 Premier, Intuit

(1) Some widely used software is often bundled with computers when sold; these are not included in sales figures above.

Glossary of Computer and Internet Terms

Source: *Microsoft Press® Computer Dictionary, Third Edition* with updates. Copyright 1997, 1998, 1999, 2000, 2001, 2002 by Microsoft Press. Reproduced by permission of Microsoft Press. All rights reserved.

Additional explanations of terms can be found in this chapter under "About Personal Computers" and "About the Internet."

Acrobat A commercial program from Adobe that converts a fully formatted document created on a Windows, Macintosh, MS-DOS, or UNIX platform into a Portable Document Format (PDF) file that can be viewed on several different platforms. Acrobat enables users to send documents that contain distinctive typefaces, color, graphics, and photographs electronically to recipients, regardless of the application used to create the originals.

application A program designed to assist in the performance of a specific task, such as word processing, accounting, or inventory management.

artificial intelligence (AI) The branch of computer science concerned with enabling computers to simulate such aspects of human intelligence as speech recognition, deduction, inference, creative response, and the ability to learn from experience.

Power line broadband (PLB) is a developing technology that, instead of using DSL, cable, or satellite, would allow people to surf the Internet over regular electrical power lines that are almost universally available. All that would be required is a special modem to be plugged into a power socket. As of mid-2004, the FCC had approved testing of this technology in Indiana, Kentucky, and Ohio.

ASCII Pronounced "askee." An acronym for American Standard Code for Information Interchange, a coding scheme using 7 or 8 bits that assigns numeric values to up to 256 characters, including letters, numerals, punctuation marks, control characters, and other symbols.

backup (noun); back up (verb) As a noun, a duplicate copy of a program, a disk, or data. As a verb, to make a duplicate copy of a program, a disk, or data.

bandwidth Data transfer capacity of a digital communications system.

baud rate Speed at which a modem can transmit data.

BBS An abbreviation for bulletin board system, a computer system equipped with one or more modems or other means of network access that serves as an information and message-passing center for remote users.

binary The binary number system has 2 as its base, so values are expressed as combinations of 2 digits, 0 and 1. These 2 digits can represent the logical values true and false as well as numerals, and they can be represented in an electronic device by the 2 states on and off, recognized as 2 voltage levels. Therefore, the binary number system is at the heart of digital computing.

bit Short for binary digit; the smallest unit of information handled by a computer. One bit expresses a 1 or a 0 in a binary numeral, or a true or a false logical condition, and is represented physically by an element such as a high or low voltage at one point in a circuit or a small spot on a disk magnetized one way or the other.

boot The process of starting or resetting a computer.

bug An error in coding or logic that causes a program to malfunction or to produce incorrect results. Also, a recurring physical problem that prevents a system or set of components from working together properly.

bulletin board system *See* **BBS.**

byte A unit of data, today almost always consisting of 8 bits. A byte can represent a single character, such as a letter, a digit, or a punctuation mark.

chat room The informal term for a data communication channel that links computers and permits users to "converse", often about a particular subject that interests them, by sending text messages to one another in real time.

chip *See* **integrated circuit.**

cookie A block of data that a Web server stores on a client system. When a user returns to the same Web site, the browser sends a copy of the cookie back to the server. Cookies are used to identify users, to instruct the server to send a customized version of the requested Web page, to submit account information for the user, and for other administrative purposes.

crash The failure of either a program or a disk drive. A program crash results in the loss of all unsaved data and can leave the operating system unstable enough to require restarting the computer.

cursor A special on-screen indicator, such as a blinking underline or rectangle, that marks the place of which keystrokes will appear when typed.

cyberspace The universe of environments, such as the Internet, in which persons interact by means of connected computers.

cyberspeak Terminology and language (often jargon, slang, and acronyms) relating to the Internet—computer-connected—environment, that is, cyberspace.

database A file composed of records, each of which contains fields, together with a set of operations for searching, sorting, recombining, and other functions.

data compression A means of reducing the space or bandwidth needed to store or transmit a block of data.

debug To detect, locate, and correct logical or syntactical errors in a program or malfunctions in hardware.

defragger A software utility for reuniting parts of a file that have become fragmented through rewriting and updating.

desktop publishing The use of a computer and specialized software to combine text and graphics to create a document that can be printed on either a laser printer or a typesetting machine.

dial-up access Connection to a data communications network through the public switched telecommunication network.

digital certificate 1. An assurance that software downloaded from the Internet comes from a reputable source. 2. A user identity card or "driver's license" for cyberspace. Issued by a certificate authority.

digital subscriber line Any of a family of high-bandwidth data communications technologies that can achieve high transmission speeds over standard twisted-pair copper wires originating from telephone companies. Envisioned as a means of enabling high-speed networking and Internet access, DSL, or xDSL, is the collective term for a number of technologies including ADSL, RADSL, IDSL, SDSL, HDSL, and VDSL.

directory service A service on a network that returns mail addresses of other users or enables a user to locate hosts and services.

disk operating system Abbreviated DOS. A generic term describing any operating system that is loaded from disk devices when the system is started or rebooted.

distance learning Broadly, any educational or learning process or system in which the teacher/instructor is separated geographically or in time from his or her students; or in which students are separated from other students or educational resources.

DOS *See* **disk operating system.**

download In communications, to transfer a copy of a file from a remote computer to the requesting computer by means of a modem or network. *See also* **upload.**

DVD *See* **digital video disc.**

dynamic HTML A technology designed to add richness, interactivity, and graphical interest to Web pages by providing those pages with the ability to change and update themselves in response to user actions, without the need for repeated downloads from a server.

encryption The process of encoding data to prevent unauthorized access, especially during transmission. The U.S. National Bureau of Standards created a complex encryption standard, DES (Data Encryption Standard), that provides almost unlimited ways to encrypt documents.

fatal exception error A Windows message signaling that an unrecoverable error, one that causes the system to halt, has occurred. Data being processed when the error occurs is usually lost, and the computer must be rebooted.

field A location in a record in which a particular type of data is stored.

file A complete, named collection of information, such as a program, a set of data used by a program, or a user-created document.

firewall A security system intended to protect an organization's network against external threats, such as hackers, from another network. *See also* **proxy server.**

flame An abusive or personally insulting e-mail message or newsgroup posting.

format In general, the structure or appearance of a unit of data. As a verb, to change the appearance of selected text or the contents of a selected cell in a spreadsheet.

forum A medium provided by an online service or BBS for users to carry on written discussions of a topic by posting messages and replying to them.

gigabyte Abbreviated GB; 1024 megabytes. *See* **megabyte.**

graphical user interface Abbreviated GUI (pronounced "gooey"). A type of environment that represents programs, files, and options by means of icons, menus, and dialog boxes on the screen. The user can select and activate these options by pointing and clicking with a mouse or, often, with the keyboard. *See also* **icon.**

hacker A computerphile—a person who is engrossed in computer technology and programming or who likes to examine the code of operating systems and other programs to see how they work. Also, a person who uses computer expertise for illicit ends, such as for gaining access to computer systems without permission and tampering with programs and data.

hard copy Printed output on paper, film, or other permanent medium.

hit Retrieval of a document, such as a home page, from a website.

home page A document intended to serve as a starting point in a hypertext system, especially the World Wide Web. Also, an entry page for a set of Web pages and other files in a website.

host The main computer in a system of computers or terminals connected by communications links.

HTML An abbreviation for HyperText Markup Language, the markup language used for documents on the World Wide Web.

hyperlink A connection between an element in a hypertext document, such as a word, phrase, symbol, or image, and a different element in the document, another hypertext document, a file, or a script. The user activates the link by clicking on the linked element, which is usually highlighted.

hypermedia The integration of any combination of text, graphics, sound, and video into a primarily associative system of information storage and retrieval in which users jump from subject to related subject.

hypertext Text linked together in a complex, nonsequential web of associations in which the user can browse through related topics.

icon A small image displayed on the screen to represent an object that can be manipulated by the user.

import To bring information from one system or program into another.

instant messaging A service that alerts users when friends or colleagues are on line and allows them to communicate with each other in real time through private online chat areas.

integrated circuit Also called a chip. A device consisting of a number of connected circuit elements, such as transistors and resistors, fabricated on a single chip of silicon crystal or other semiconductor material.

interactive Characterized by conversational exchange of input and output, as when a user enters a question or command the system immediately responds.

intranet A TCP/IP network designed for information processing within a company or organization. It usually employs Web pages for information dissemination and Internet applications, such as Web browsers.

Java A programming language, developed by Sun Microsystems, Inc., that can be run on any platform.

kilobyte Abbreviated K, KB, or Kbyte; 1,024 bytes.

LAN Rhymes with "can." Acronym for local area network, a group of computers and other devices dispersed over a limited area and connected by a link that enables any device to interact with any other on the network.

legacy system A computer, software program, network, or other computer equipment that remains in use after a business or organization installs new systems.

link *See* **hyperlink.**

local area network *See* **LAN**.

logon The process of identifying oneself to a computer after connecting to it over a communications line. Also called *login*.

lurk To receive and read articles or messages in a newsgroup or other online conference without contributing anything to the ongoing conversation.

mailing list A list of names and e-mail addresses that are grouped under a single name. When a user places the name of the mailing list in a mail client's To: field, the client automatically sends the same message to the machine where the mailing list resides, and that machine sends the message to all the addresses on the list.

mainframe computer A high-level computer designed for the most intensive computational tasks.

markup language A set of codes in a text file that instruct a printer or video display how to format, index, and link the contents of the file. Examples of markup languages are HTML (HyperText Markup Language), which is used in Web pages, and SGML (Standard Generalized Markup Language), which is used for typesetting and desktop publishing purposes and in electronic documents.

megabyte Abbreviated MB. Usually 1,048,576 bytes (2^{20}); sometimes interpreted as 1 million bytes.

menu A list of options from which a program user can make a selection in order to perform a desired action, such as choosing a command or applying a format.

microcomputer A computer built around a single-chip microprocessor.

minicomputer A mid-level computer built to perform complex computations while dealing efficiently with input and output from users connected via terminals.

modem A communications device that enables a computer to transmit information over a standard telephone line.

motherboard The main circuit board containing the primary components of a computer system.

mouse A common pointing device. It has a flat-bottomed casing designed to be gripped by one hand.

multimedia The combination of sound, graphics, animation, and video.

multitasking A mode of operation offered by an operating system in which a computer works on more than one task at a time.

Net Short for Internet.

online Activated and ready for operating; capable of communicating with or being controlled by a computer.

optical scanner An input device that uses light-sensing equipment to scan paper or another medium, translating the pattern of light and dark or color into a digital signal that can be manipulated by either optical character recognition software or graphics software.

packet A unit of information transmitted as a whole from one device to another on a network.

password A unique string of characters that a user types in as an identification code.

PDF Acronym for Portable Document Format. The Adobe specification for electronic documents that use the Adobe Acrobat family of servers and readers.

peripheral A device, such as a disk drive, printer, modem, or joystick, that is connected to a computer and is controlled by the computer's microprocessor.

pixel Short for picture element; also called *pel*. One spot in a rectilinear grid of thousands of such spots that are individually "painted" to form an image produced on the screen by a computer or on paper by a printer.

post To submit an article in a newsgroup or other online conference. *See* **thread.**

protocol A set of rules or standards designed to enable computers to communicate with one another and to exchange information with as little error as possible.

proxy server A firewall component that manages Internet traffic to and from a local area network and can provide other features, e.g., document caching and access control.

routing table In data communications, a table of information that provides network hardware (bridges and routers) with the direc-

tions needed to forward packets of data to locations on other networks.

RTF An acronym for rich text format. RTF is used for transferring formatted documents between applications, even those applications running on different platforms, such as between IBM and compatibles and Apple Macintoshes.

SGML Acronym for Standard Generalized Markup Language. An information-management standard adopted by the International Organization for Standardization (ISO) in 1986 as a means of providing platform- and application-independent documents that retain formatting, indexing, and linked information. SGML provides a grammar-like mechanism for users to define the structure of their documents, and the tags they will use to denote the structure in individual documents.

sleep mode A power management mode that shuts down all unnecessary computer operations to save energy; also known as suspend mode.

snail mail A phrase popular on the Internet for referring to mail services provided by the United States Postal Service and similar agencies in other countries.

software Computer programs; instructions that make hardware work.

spreadsheet program An application commonly used for budgets, forecasting, and other finance-related tasks that organizes data values using cells, where the relationships between cells are defined by formulas.

stream To transfer data continuously, beginning to end, in a steady flow. Many aspects of computing rely on the ability to stream data; file input and output, for example, and communications. On the Internet, streaming enables users to begin accessing and using a file before it has been transmitted in its entirety.

supercomputer A large, extremely fast, and expensive computer used for complex or sophisticated calculations.

surf To browse among collections of information on the Internet, in newsgroups, and especially the World Wide Web.

system administrator The person responsible for administering use of a multiuser computer system, communications system, or both.

TCP/IP An abbreviation for Transmission Control Protocol/Internet Protocol, a protocol developed by the Department of Defense for communications between computers. It has become the de facto standard for data transmission over networks, including the Internet.

telecommute To work in one location (often, at home) and communicate with a main office at a different location through a personal computer.

thread In electronic mail and Internet newsgroups, a series of messages and replies related to a specific topic.

upload In communications, the process of transferring a copy of a file from a local computer to a remote computer by means of a modem or network.

user interface The portion of a program with which a user interacts.

user-friendly Easy to learn and easy to use.

voice recognition The capability of a computer to understand the spoken word for the purpose of receiving commands and data input from the speaker.

WAN *See* **wide area network**.

Web *See* **World Wide Web.**

webcasting Popular term for broadcasting information via the World Wide Web, using push and pull technologies to move selected information from a server to a client.

webmaster The person or persons responsible for creating and maintaining a site on the World Wide Web.

WebTV® Trademark name for technology from Microsoft and WebTV Networks that provide consumers with the ability to access the Internet on a television by means of a set-top box equipped with a modem.

wide area network (WAN) A communications network that connects geographically separated areas.

window In applications and graphical interfaces, a portion of the screen that can contain its own document or message.

word processor A program for manipulating text-based documents; the electronic equivalent of paper, pen, typewriter, eraser, and, most likely, dictionary and thesaurus.

workstation A combination of input, output, and computing hardware used for work by an individual.

WYSIWYG Pronounced "wizzywig." An acronym for "What you see is what you get." A display method that shows documents and graphics characters on the screen as they will appear when printed.

XML Acronym for eXtensible Markup Language. A condensed form of SGML, the Standard Generalized markup Language. XML lets Web developers and designers create customized tags that offer greater flexibility in organizing and presenting information than is possible with the older HTML document coding system.

Zip drive A disk drive developed by Iomega that uses 3.5-inch removable disks (Zip disks) capable of storing 100 megabytes of data apiece. *See also* **disk drive.**

TELECOMMUNICATIONS

Worldwide Telecommunications: Market Data (1990-2003)

Source: © International Telecommunication Union

	1990	1991	1992	1993	1994	1995	1996	1997	1998	1999	2000	2001	2002[3]	2003[4]
Total market revenue (billions of U.S. $)[1]	$508	$523	$580	$605	$675	$779	$885	$946	$1,015	$1,123	$1,210	$1,232	$1,295	$1,370
Intl. phone traffic (billions of minutes)[2]	33	38	43	49	57	63	71	79	89	100	118	127	135	140
Main telephone lines (millions)	520	546	572	604	643	689	738	792	846	905	983	1,053	1,129	1,210
Mobile cellular subscriptions (millions)	11	16	23	34	56	91	145	215	318	490	740	955	1,155	1,341

(1) Revenue from installation, subscription, and local, trunk, and international call charges. (2) From 1994 including traffic between countries of the former Soviet Union. (3) Estimate. (4) Preliminary.

Worldwide Use of Cellular Telephones, Year-end 2003

Source: © International Telecommunication Union; estimated; top countries or regions ranked by subscriptions per 100 pop.

Country/Region	Subscriptions (thousands)	per 100 pop.	Country/Region	Subscriptions (thousands)	per 100 pop.	Country/Region	Subscriptions (thousands)	per 100 pop.
Taiwan	25,089.6	110.8	Germany	64,800.0	78.5	United States	158,722.0	54.3
Luxembourg	473.0	106.1	Greece	8,936.2	78.0	Jamaica	1,400.0	53.3
Hong Kong	7,241.4	105.8	Netherlands	12,500.0	76.8	Latvia	1,219.6	52.9
Italy	55,918.0	101.8	United Arab			Barbados	140.0	51.9
Iceland	279.1	96.6	Emirates	2,972.3	73.6	Antigua & Barbuda	38.2	49.0
Czech Republic	9,708.7	96.5	Malta	290.0	72.5	Poland	17,400.0	45.1
Israel	6,334.0	95.5	Australia	14,347.0	72.0	Malaysia	11,124.1	44.2
Spain	37,506.7	91.6	France	41,683.1	69.6	Chile	6,445.7	42.8
Norway	4,163.4	90.9	South Korea	33,591.8	69.4	Canada	13,221.8	41.7
Portugal	9,341.4	90.4	Slovak Republic	3,678.8	68.4	Turkey	27,887.5	40.8
Finland	4,700.0	90.1	Seychelles	54.5	68.2	Brunei	137.0	40.1
Sweden	7,949.0	88.9	Japan	86,658.6	68.0	Bahamas	121.8	39.0
Denmark	4,785.3	88.7	Hungary	6,862.8	67.6	Mauritius	462.4	37.9
Austria	7,094.5	87.9	Lithuania	2,169.9	66.6	French Polynesia	90.0	37.5
Slovenia	1,739.1	87.1	Estonia	881.0	65.0	South Africa	16,860.0	36.4
Ireland	3,400.0	84.5	New Zealand	2,599.0	64.8	Albania	1,100.0	35.8
Switzerland	6,172.0	84.3	Bahrain	443.1	63.8	New Caledonia	80.0	35.7
United Kingdom	49,677.0	84.1	Qatar	376.5	59.0	Serbia and		
Macao	364.0	81.5	Cyprus	417.9	58.4	Montenegro	3,634.6	33.8
Singapore	3,312.6	79.6	Croatia	2,553.0	58.4			
Belgium	8,135.5	78.6	Kuwait	1,420.0	57.8	**WORLD**	**1,340,667.7**	**21.9**

U.S. Cellular Telephone Subscribership, 1985–2003[1]

Source: The CTIA Semi-Annual Wireless Industry Survey. Used with permission of CTIA; in thousands of subscriptions[2]

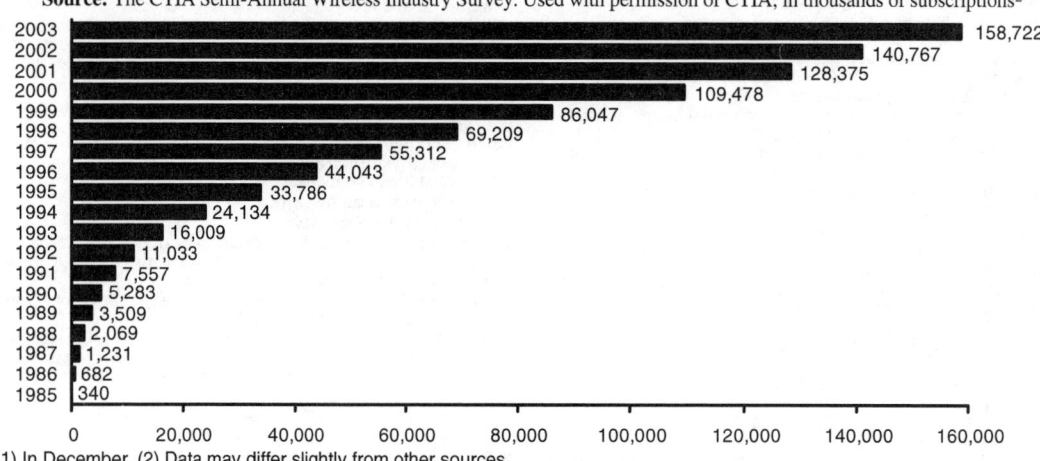

Year	Subscriptions (thousands)
2003	158,722
2002	140,767
2001	128,375
2000	109,478
1999	86,047
1998	69,209
1997	55,312
1996	44,043
1995	33,786
1994	24,134
1993	16,009
1992	11,033
1991	7,557
1990	5,283
1989	3,509
1988	2,069
1987	1,231
1986	682
1985	340

(1) In December. (2) Data may differ slightly from other sources.

U.S. Sales and Household Penetration, Selected Products[1], 1985-2003

Source: Consumer Electronics Association

	1985 Sales[2]	1985 % of all households	1990 Sales[2]	1990 % of all households	1995 Sales[2]	1995 % of all households	2000 Sales[2]	2000 % of all households	2002 Sales[2]	2002 % of all households	2003 Sales[2]	2003 % of all households
Cordless telephones	$280	11	$842	28	$1,141	55	$1,307	80	$1,261	81	$1,268	82
Pagers	—	—	118	1	300	11	750	23	810	17	729	17
Modems/fax modems	10	0	191	2.7	770	16	1,564	55	1,445	60	1,419	64
Telephone answering devices	325	7	827	35	1,077	57	984	75	1,060	78	1,210	78
Cellular phones	116	0.10	1,098	5	2,574	29	8,995	60	8,106	68	9,163	70

(1) Data may differ slightly from other sources. (2) In millions of dollars.

> ▶ **IT'S A FACT:** By the end of 2002, the number of cell phone subscriptions had surpassed the number of land lines for the first time, 1.16 billion to 1.13 billion, according to data from the International Telecommunication Union.

Cameras Everywhere

As mobile cell phones proliferate so do camera phones—cell phones with built-in digital cameras. The first camera phone was introduced in Japan in Nov. 2000 by J-Phone (now part of Vodafone). In 2004 nearly 150 million camera phones were sold worldwide, accounting for more than 25% of all cellular phone sales, according to estimates by InfoTrends Research Group. By 2008, worldwide camera phone sales are expected to reach more than 650 million.

Codes for International Direct Dial Calling From the U.S.

Basic station-to-station calls: 011 + country code (as shown) + city code (if required) + local number.
Person-to-person, operator-assisted, collect, credit card calls; calls billed to another number: 01 + country code (below) + city code (if required) + local number.

Selected city codes given below. For further information, contact your long distance company.

Country/Territory	Code	Country/Territory	Code	Country/Territory	Code	Country/Territory	Code
Afghanistan	93	Cape Verde	238	Iran	98	Poland	48
Albania	355	Cayman Islands	345*	Iraq	964	Portugal	351
Algeria	213	Central African Rep.	236	Ireland	353	Puerto Rico	787*/
American Samoa	684*	Chad Republic	235	Israel	972		939*
Andorra	376	Chile	56	Italy	39	Qatar	974
Angola	244	China	86	Jamaica	876*	Reunion Island	262
Anguilla	264*	Hong Kong	852	Japan	81	Romania	40
Antarctica	672*	Macao	853	Jordan	962	Russia	7
Antigua & Barbuda	268*	Christmas and the		Kazakhstan	7	Rwanda	250
Argentina	54	Cocos Islands	672	Kenya	254	St. Kitts & Nevis	869*
Armenia	374	Colombia	57	Kiribati	686	St. Lucia	758*
Aruba	297	Comoros	269	Korea, North	850	St. Maarten	599
Ascension Island	247	Congo, Dem. Rep.	243	Korea, South	82	St. Pierre and Miquelon	508
Australia	61	Congo Republic	242	Kuwait	965	St. Vincent &	
Austria	43	Cook Islands	682	Kyrgyzstan	996	the Grenadines	809*
Azerbaijan	994	Costa Rica	506	Laos	856	Samoa (formerly	
Bahamas	242*	Côte d'Ivoire	225	Latvia	371	Western Samoa)	685
Bahrain	973	Croatia	385	Lebanon	961	San Marino	378
Bangladesh	880	Cuba	53	Lesotho	266	São Tomé & Príncipe	239
Barbados	246*	Curacao	599	Liberia	231	Saudi Arabia	966
Belarus	375	Cyprus	357	Libya	218	Senegal	221
Belgium	32	Czech Republic	420	Liechtenstein	423	Serbia & Montenegro	381
Belize	501	Denmark	45	Lithuania	370	Seychelles	248
Benin	229	Diego Garcia	246	Luxembourg	352	Sierra Leone	232
Bermuda	441*	Djibouti	253	Macedonia	389	Singapore	65
Bhutan	975	Dominica	767*	Madagascar	261	Slovakia	421
Bolivia	591	Dominican Republic	809*	Malawi	265	Slovenia	386
Bosnia & Herzegovina	387	East Timor	670	Malaysia	60	Solomon Islands	677
Botswana	267	Ecuador	593	Maldives	960	Somalia	252
Brazil	55	Egypt	20	Mali	223	South Africa	27
Brunei	673	El Salvador	503	Malta	356	Spain	34
Bulgaria	359	Equatorial Guinea	240	Marshall Islands	692	Sri Lanka	94
Burkina Faso	226	Eritrea	291	Mauritania	222	Sudan	249
Burundi	257	Estonia	372	Mauritius	230	Suriname	597
Cambodia	855	Ethiopia	251	Mayotte Island	269	Swaziland	268
Cameroon	237	Falkland Islands	500	Mexico	52	Sweden	46
Canada	1	Faroe Islands	298	Micronesia	691	Switzerland	41
Alberta	403*	Fiji	679	Moldova	373	Syria	963
British Columbia	250*	Finland	358	Monaco	33	Taiwan	886
British Columbia		France	33	Mongolia	976	Tajikistan	992
(lower mainland)	604*	French Antilles	596	Montserrat	664*	Tanzania	255
Vancouver	604*	French Guiana	594	Morocco	212	Thailand	66
Manitoba	204*	French Polynesia	689	Mozambique	258	Togo	228
New Brunswick	506*	Gabon	241	Myanmar	95	Tonga	676
Newfoundland	709*	Gambia, The	220	Namibia	264	Trinidad & Tobago	868*
NW Territories	867*	Georgia	995	Nauru	674	Tunisia	216
Nova Scotia	902*	Germany	49	Nepal	977	Turkey	90
Nunavut	867*	Ghana	233	Netherlands	31	Turkmenistan	993
Ontario		Gibraltar	350	Netherlands Antilles	599	Turks & Caicos Isls.	649*
London	519*	Greece	30	New Caledonia	687	Tuvalu	688
Niagara Falls	289*	Greenland	299	New Zealand	64	Uganda	256
North Bay	705*	Grenada	473*	Nicaragua	505	Ukraine	380
Ottawa	613*	Guadeloupe	590	Niger	227	United Arab Emirates	971
Thunder Bay	807*	Guam	671*	Nigeria	234	United Kingdom	44
Toronto Metro	416*	Guantanamo Bay	53	Niue	683	Uruguay	598
Toronto Vicinity	905*	Guatemala	502	N. Mariana Isls.	670	Uzbekistan	998
Prince Edward Isl.	902*	Guinea	224	Norway	47	Vanuatu	678
Quebec		Guinea-Bissau	245	Oman	968	Vatican City	39
Montreal	514*	Guyana	592	Pakistan	92	Venezuela	58
Montreal N. and		Haiti	509	Palau	680	Vietnam	84
S. Shore	450*	Honduras	504	Panama	507	Virgin Islands, British	284*
Quebec City	418*	Hungary	36	Papua New Guinea	675	Virgin Islands, U.S.	340*
Sherbrooke	819*	Iceland	354	Paraguay	595	Yemen	967
Saskatchewan	306*	India	91	Peru	51	Zambia	260
Yukon Territory	867*	Indonesia	62	Philippines	63	Zimbabwe	263

* These numbers are area codes. Follow Domestic Dialing instructions: dial "1" + area code + number you are calling.

Selected city codes: Beijing, 10; Brasilia, 61; Buenos Aires, 11; Dhaka, 2; Dublin, 1; Islamabad, 51; Jakarta, 21; Jerusalem, 2; Lagos, 1; London, 20; Madrid, 91; Mexico City, 55; New Delhi, 11; Paris, 1; Rome, 06; Tokyo, 3.

Telephone Area Codes, by Number

As of Aug. 2004. For area codes listed by place, see pages 634-667.

Area Code	Location or Service	Area Code	Location or Service	Area Code	Location or Service	Area Code	Location or Service
201	New Jersey	403	Alberta	614	Ohio	811	Business Office
202	District of Columbia	404	Georgia	615	Tennessee	812	Indiana
203	Connecticut	405	Oklahoma	616	Michigan	813	Florida
204	Manitoba	406	Montana	617	Massachusetts	814	Pennsylvania
205	Alabama	407	Florida	618	Illinois	815	Illinois
206	Washington	408	California	619	California	816	Missouri
207	Maine	409	Texas	620	Kansas	817	Texas
208	Idaho	410	Maryland	623	Arizona	818	California
209	California	411	Directory Assistance	626	California	819	Quebec
210	Texas	412	Pennsylvania	630	Illinois	828	North Carolina
211	Community Info.	413	Massachusetts	631	New York	829	Dominican Republic
212	New York	414	Wisconsin	636	Missouri	830	Texas
213	California	415	California	641	Iowa	831	California
214	Texas	416	Ontario	646	New York	832	Texas
215	Pennsylvania	417	Missouri	647	Ontario	843	South Carolina
216	Ohio	418	Quebec	649	Turks & Caicos Islands	845	New York
217	Illinois	419	Ohio	650	California	847	Illinois
218	Minnesota	423	Tennessee	651	Minnesota	848	New Jersey
219	Indiana	425	Washington	660	Missouri	850	Florida
224	Illinois	430	Texas	661	California	856	New Jersey
225	Louisiana	432	Texas	662	Mississippi	857	Massachusetts
226	Ontario	434	Virginia	664	Montserrat	858	California
228	Mississippi	435	Utah	670	N. Mariana Islands	859	Kentucky
229	Georgia	438	Quebec	671	Guam	860	Connecticut
231	Michigan	440	Ohio	678	Georgia	862	New Jersey
234	Ohio	441	Bermuda	682	Texas	863	Florida
239	Florida	443	Maryland	684	American Samoa	864	South Carolina
240	Maryland	450	Quebec	700	IC Services	865	Tennessee
242	Bahamas	456	Inbound International	701	North Dakota	866	Toll-Free Service
246	Barbados	469	Texas	702	Nevada	867	Yukon, NW Terr., Nunavut
248	Michigan	473	Grenada	703	Virginia		
250	British Columbia	478	Georgia	704	North Carolina	868	Trinidad & Tobago
251	Alabama	479	Arkansas	705	Ontario	869	St. Kitts & Nevis
252	North Carolina	480	Arizona	706	Georgia	870	Arkansas
253	Washington	484	Pennyslvania	707	California	876	Jamaica
254	Texas	500	Personal Comm. Serv.	708	Illinois	877	Toll-Free Service
256	Alabama	501	Arkansas	709	Newfoundland	878	Pennsylvania
260	Indiana	502	Kentucky	710	U.S. Government	880	Toll-Free Service
262	Wisconsin	503	Oregon	711	TRS Access	881	Toll-Free Service
264	Anguilla	504	Louisiana	712	Iowa	882	Toll-Free Service
267	Pennsylvania	505	New Mexico	713	Texas	888	Toll-Free Service
268	Antigua/Barbuda	506	New Brunswick	714	California	900	Premium Service
269	Michigan	507	Minnesota	715	Wisconsin	901	Tennessee
270	Kentucky	508	Massachusetts	716	New York	902	Nova Scotia
276	Virginia	509	Washington	717	Pennsylvania	903	Texas
281	Texas	510	California	718	New York	904	Florida
284	British Virgin Islands	511	Traffic Info.	719	Colorado	905	Ontario
289	Ontario	512	Texas	720	Colorado	906	Michigan
301	Maryland	513	Ohio	724	Pennsylvania	907	Alaska
302	Delaware	514	Quebec	727	Florida	908	New Jersey
303	Colorado	515	Iowa	731	Tennessee	909	California
304	West Virginia	516	New York	732	New Jersey	910	North Carolina
305	Florida	517	Michigan	734	Michigan	911	Emergency
306	Saskatchewan	518	New York	740	Ohio	912	Georgia
307	Wyoming	519	Ontario	754	Florida	913	Kansas
308	Nebraska	520	Arizona	757	Virginia	914	New York
309	Illinois	530	California	758	St. Lucia	915	Texas
310	California	540	Virginia	760	California	916	California
311	Non-Emergency Access	541	Oregon	763	Minnesota	917	New York
312	Illinois	551	New Jersey	765	Indiana	918	Oklahoma
313	Michigan	559	California	767	Dominica	919	North Carolina
314	Missouri	561	Florida	769	Mississippi	920	Wisconsin
315	New York	562	California	770	Georgia	925	California
316	Kansas	563	Iowa	772	Florida	928	Arizona
317	Indiana	567	Ohio	773	Illinois	931	Tennessee
318	Louisiana	570	Pennsylvania	774	Massachusetts	936	Texas
319	Iowa	571	Virginia	775	Nevada	937	Ohio
320	Minnesota	573	Missouri	778	British Columbia	939	Puerto Rico
321	Florida	574	Indiana	780	Alberta	940	Texas
323	California	580	Oklahoma	781	Massachusetts	941	Florida
325	Texas	585	New York	784	St. Vincent & Gren.	947	Michigan
330	Ohio	586	Michigan	785	Kansas	949	California
334	Alabama	600	(Canadian Services)	786	Florida	951	California
336	North Carolina	601	Mississippi	787	Puerto Rico	952	Minnesota
337	Louisiana	602	Arizona	800	Toll-Free Service	954	Florida
339	Massachusetts	603	New Hampshire	801	Utah	956	Texas
340	U.S. Virgin Islands	604	British Columbia	802	Vermont	970	Colorado
345	Cayman Islands	605	South Dakota	803	South Carolina	971	Oregon
347	New York	606	Kentucky	804	Virginia	972	Texas
351	Massachusetts	607	New York	805	California	973	New Jersey
352	Florida	608	Wisconsin	806	Texas	978	Massachusetts
360	Washington	609	New Jersey	807	Ontario	979	Texas
361	Texas	610	Pennsylvania	808	Hawaii	980	North Carolina
386	Florida	611	Repair Service	809	Dominican Republic	985	Louisiana
401	Rhode Island	612	Minnesota	810	Michigan	989	Michigan
402	Nebraska	613	Ontario				

POSTAL INFORMATION
Basic U.S. Postal Service

The Postal Reorganization Act, creating a government-owned postal service under the executive branch and replacing the old Post Office Department, was signed into law by Pres. Richard Nixon, Aug. 12, 1970. The service officially came into being on July 1, 1971. The U.S. Postal Service is governed by an 11-person Board of Governors. Nine of the members are appointed by the president, with Senate approval. These 9 choose a postmaster general. The board and the postmaster general choose the 11th member, who serves as deputy postmaster general. An independent Postal Rate Commission of 5 members, appointed by the president, reviews and rules on proposed postal rate increases submitted by the Board of Governors.

U.S. Domestic Rates

(Domestic rates apply to the U.S., to its territories and possessions, and to APOs and FPOs. Many changes in domestic postal rates, fees, services, and terminology took effect June 30, 2002.)

First-Class Mail

First-Class Mail includes written matter such as letters, postal cards, and postcards (private mailing cards), plus all other matter wholly or partly in writing, whether sealed or unsealed, except book manuscripts, periodical articles and music, manuscript copy accompanying proofsheets or corrected proofsheets of the same, and the writing authorized by law on matter of other classes. Also included: matter sealed or closed against inspection, bills, and statements of accounts.

Written letters and matter sealed against inspection cost 37¢ for first ounce or fraction, 23¢ for each additional ounce or fraction up to and including 13 ounces. U.S. Postal Service cards cost 23¢ for postage, with a 2¢ fee for the card. Private postcards postage is 23¢. Presort and automation-compatible mail can qualify for lower rates if certain piece minimums, mailing permits, and other requirements are met.

Express Mail

Express Mail provides guaranteed expedited service for any mailable article (up to 70 lbs and not over 108 in. in combined length and girth). Offers next day delivery by noon to most destinations; no extra charge for Saturday, Sunday, or holiday delivery. Second-day service is available to locations not on the Next Day Delivery Network. The basic rate for Express Mail weighing up to 8 oz is $13.65. All rates include insurance up to $100, shipment receipt, and record of delivery at the destination post office. Express Mail tracking is available on the USPS Web site (www.usps.com).

Express Mail Flat Rate: $13.65, regardless of weight, if matter fits into a special Postal Service flat-rate envelope.

Scheduled pickup service is available for $12.50 per stop, regardless of the number of pieces or service used (e.g., Express Mail, Priority Mail, or Parcel Post can be picked up together).

Contact your local post office for further information.

Standard Mail

Standard Mail is limited to items less than 16 ounces such as solicitations, newsletters, advertising materials, books, cassettes, and other merchandise. A minimum volume of 200 pieces or 50 lbs of such items is necessary, and specific bulk mail preparation and sortation requirements apply.

The minimum rate per piece for pieces 3.3 ounces or less is $0.268 for basic letters and $0.344 for basic nonletters. Contact your post office for the discounts offered for auto-

mation, presorted, carrier route, destination entry, and other discounts. Separate rates are available for some nonprofit organizations.

Any mailer who uses a permit imprint is required to pay a one-time $150 fee plus an annual (calendar year) fee of $150. Additional standards apply to mailings of nonidentical-weight pieces.

Priority Mail

Due to expeditious handling and transportation, Priority Mail is delivered in 2-3 days, on average. Priority Mail may include any mailable article up to 70 lbs and not over 108 in. in length and girth combined, whether sealed or unsealed, including written and other First Class material.

Packages weighing less than 15 lbs and measuring over 84 in., but less than 108 in., in length and girth combined cost the same as a 15-lb parcel mailed to the same zone. Scheduled pickup service costs an additional $12.50 per stop, regardless of the number of pieces or service used (e.g. Express Mail, Priority Mail, or Parcel Post can be picked up together).

Priority Mail Flat Rate: $3.85, regardless of weight, if matter fits into a special Postal Service flat-rate envelope.

Priority Mail Rates

Weight not over (lbs)	ZONES 1-3	4	5	6	7	8
1	$3.85	$3.85	$3.85	$3.85	$3.85	$3.85
2	3.95	4.55	4.90	5.05	5.40	5.75
3	4.75	6.05	6.85	7.15	7.85	8.55
4	5.30	7.05	8.05	8.50	9.45	10.35
5	5.85	8.00	9.30	9.85	11.00	12.15
6	6.30	8.85	9.90	10.05	11.30	12.30
7	6.80	9.80	10.65	11.00	12.55	14.05
8	7.35	10.75	11.45	11.95	13.80	15.75
9	7.90	11.70	12.20	12.90	15.05	17.50
10	8.40	12.60	13.00	14.00	16.30	19.20
11	8.95	13.35	13.75	15.15	17.55	20.90
12	9.50	14.05	14.50	16.30	18.80	22.65
13	10.00	14.75	15.30	17.50	20.05	24.35
14	10.55	15.45	16.05	18.60	21.25	26.05
15(1)	11.05	16.20	16.85	19.75	22.50	27.80

(1) See postmaster for pieces over 15 lbs.

Periodicals

Periodicals include newspapers and magazines.

For the general public, the applicable Package Services or First-Class postage is paid for periodicals.

For publishers, rates vary according to (1) whether item is sent to same county, (2) percentage of editorial and advertising matter, (3) whether the publishing org. is nonprofit or produces educational material for use in classrooms, (4) weight, (5) distance, (6) level of presort, (7) automation compatibility.

Package Services

Package Services, formerly "Standard Mail (B)," is any mailable matter that is not included in First-Class or Periodicals (unless permitted or required by regulations). There are currently four subclasses of Package Services: Parcel Post, Bound Printed Matter, Media Mail (formerly "Special Standard Mail"), and Library Mail.

The post office determines charges for Package Services according to the weight of the package in pounds and the zone distance shipped (Media Mail and Library Mail rates are determined by weight alone). There is no minimum weight; see separate headings for maximum weight. Presort and automation-compatible mail for all Package Services can qualify for lower rates if certain piece minimums, mailing permits, and other requirements are met. Contact your

local post office for further information. Package Services is not sealed against postal inspection.

Parcel Post

Parcel Post is any Package Services not mailed as Bound Print Matter, Media Mail, or Library Mail. Any Package Services matter may be mailed at the Parcel Post rates, subject to these basic standards: not to exceed 70 lbs or 108 in. in combined length and girth (packages over 108 in., but not more than 130 in. in combined length and girth are subject to oversize rates). All fractions of a pound are counted as a full pound. Parcel Post subclass consists of two basic retail rate categories and three drop-shipped categories, the latter collectively known as Parcel Select.

> **IT'S A FACT:** The town of Nalcrest, FL, about 50 miles south of Orlando, is home to 800 people, almost all of whom are retired letter carriers and their families. Founded in 1962, the town was created by, and named after, the postal workers' union—the National Association of Letter Carriers Retirement, Education, Security and Training (NALCREST). Nalcrest features low-rent apartments on tree-lined streets, and there are no dogs allowed. There also are no home mailboxes; mail is picked up at the town's post office.

Parcel Post Basic Rate Schedule

(Inter BMC/ASF ZIP codes only, machinable[1] parcels, no discount, no surcharge)

Weight not over (lbs)	ZONES						
	1 & 2	3	4	5	6	7	8
1	$3.69	$3.75	$3.75	$3.75	$3.75	$3.75	$3.75
2	3.85	3.85	4.14	4.14	4.49	4.49	4.49
3	4.65	4.65	5.55	5.65	5.71	5.77	6.32
4	4.86	5.20	6.29	6.93	7.14	7.20	7.87
5	5.03	5.71	6.94	7.75	8.58	8.64	9.43
6	5.63	6.01	7.44	8.50	9.52	9.90	11.49
7	5.80	6.28	7.91	9.20	10.35	11.39	12.83
8	5.98	6.53	8.30	9.84	11.11	12.54	15.04
9	6.11	6.76	8.74	10.45	11.83	13.38	17.04
10	6.28	7.57	9.10	11.01	12.50	14.17	18.14
11	6.41	7.80	9.47	11.54	13.13	14.92	19.15
12	6.54	8.01	9.80	12.04	13.72	15.62	20.10
13	6.67	8.19	10.12	12.51	14.28	16.27	20.99
14	6.80	8.42	10.43	12.95	14.81	16.90	21.84
15	6.92	8.61	10.73	13.38	15.31	17.49	22.64
16	7.02	8.79	11.00	13.78	15.79	18.05	23.41
17	7.15	8.94	11.28	14.16	16.24	18.59	24.13
18	7.25	9.11	11.52	14.52	16.68	19.09	24.82
19	7.37	9.28	11.77	14.87	17.09	19.58	25.48
20[2]	7.46	9.43	11.98	15.20	17.48	20.05	26.12

(1) Machinable parcels must be: not less than 6 in. long, 3 in. high, and .25 in. thick or more than 34 in. long, 17 in. high, and 17 in. thick; at least 6 oz. but not more than 35 lbs. (2) Consult postmaster for pieces greater than 20 lbs.

Library Mail

(minimum weight: none; maximum weight: 70 lbs)

Applies to books, printed music, bound academic theses, periodicals, sound recordings, museum materials, and other library materials mailed between schools, colleges, universities, public libraries, museums, veteran and fraternal organizations, and nonprofit religious, educational, scientific, and labor organizations or associations (or to or from these organizations). Advertising restrictions apply. All packages must be marked "Library Mail," and may not exceed 108 in. in combined length and girth. Contact your local post office for further information.

Rates are calculated by weight only. Single-piece rates are: $1.35, up to 1 lb; 40¢ for each additional pound or fraction, to 7 lbs; additional pounds thereafter, 29¢ each.

Media Mail

(minimum weight: none; maximum weight: 70 lbs)

Formerly "Special Standard Mail." Applies to books of at least 8 printed pages; 16-mm or narrower-width films; printed music; printed test materials; sound recordings, playscripts, and manuscripts for books; printed educational charts; loose-leaf pages and binders consisting of medical information; computer-readable media. Advertising restrictions apply. Packages must be marked "Media Mail" and may not exceed 108 in. in combined length and girth. Contact your local post office for further information.

Rates are calculated by weight only. Single-piece rates are: $1.42, up to 1 lb; 42¢ for each additional pound or fraction, to 7 lbs; additional pounds thereafter, 30¢ each.

Bound Printed Matter

(minimum weight: none; maximum weight: 15 lbs)

Applies to advertising, promotional, directory, or editorial material that is bound by permanent fastening and consists of sheets of which at least 90% are imprinted by any process other than handwriting or typewriting. Does not include stationery (or pads of blank forms) or personal correspondence. Packages may not exceed 108 in. in combined length and girth, marked "Bound Printed Matter" or "BPM."

Bound Printed Matter Rates

(zone rate for flat single pieces; parcels pay 8¢ more)

Weight not over (lbs)	ZONES						
	1&2	3	4	5	6	7	8
1.0	$1.79	$1.84	$1.88	$1.96	$2.03	$2.12	$2.29
1.5	1.79	1.84	1.88	1.96	2.03	2.12	2.29
2.0	1.86	1.92	1.98	2.08	2.18	2.30	2.52
2.5	1.93	2.01	2.08	2.21	2.33	2.48	2.76
3.0	2.00	2.09	2.18	2.33	2.48	2.66	2.99
3.5	2.07	2.18	2.28	2.46	2.63	2.84	3.23
4.0	2.14	2.26	2.38	2.58	2.78	3.02	3.46
4.5	2.21	2.35	2.48	2.71	2.93	3.20	3.70
5.0	2.28	2.43	2.58	2.83	3.08	3.38	3.93
6.0	2.42	2.60	2.78	3.08	3.38	3.74	4.40
7.0	2.56	2.77	2.98	3.33	3.68	4.10	4.87
8.0	2.70	2.94	3.18	3.58	3.98	4.46	5.34
9.0	2.84	3.11	3.38	3.83	4.28	4.82	5.81
10.0	2.98	3.28	3.58	4.08	4.58	5.18	6.28
11.0	3.12	3.45	3.78	4.33	4.88	5.54	6.75
12.0	3.26	3.62	3.98	4.58	5.18	5.90	7.22
13.0	3.40	3.79	4.18	4.83	5.48	6.26	7.69
14.0	3.54	3.96	4.38	5.08	5.78	6.62	8.16
15.0	3.68	4.13	4.58	5.33	6.08	6.98	8.63

Domestic Mail Special Services

Insured Mail

Applicable to Standard Mail, Package Services, and First-Class or Priority Mail items eligible to be mailed as Package Services. Matter for sale addressed to prospective purchasers who have not ordered it or authorized its sending cannot be insured. Note: for Express Mail, insurance is included up to $100. Add $1.00 per $100 or fraction thereof over $100 up to $5,000.

Declared Value	Insured Mail Fee[1]
$0.01 to $50.00	$1.30
$50.01 to $100.00	2.20
$100.01 to $200.00	3.20
$200.01 to $300.00	4.20
$300.01 to $400.00	5.20
$400.01 to $500.00	6.20
$500.01 to $600.00	7.20
$600.01 to $700.00	8.20
$700.01 to $800.00	9.20
$800.01 to $900.00	10.20
$900.01 to $1,000.000	11.20
$1,000.01 to $5,000.00	11.20 plus $1.00 per $100 or fraction thereof over $1,000 in desired coverage

(1) In addition to postage. (Maximum liability is $5,000.) See postmaster for details on bulk discounts.

Special Handling

Provides preferential handling, but not preferential delivery, to the extent practicable in dispatch and transportation. Available for First-Class Mail, Priority Mail, and Package Services for the following surcharge: up to 10 lb, $5.95; over 10 lb, $8.25 Pieces must be marked "Special Handling."

Delivery Confirmation

Applies to First-Class Mail parcels, Priority Mail, Standard Mail, and Package services. Available for purchase at the time of mailing only. Provides mailer with the date and time an article was delivered and, if delivery was attempted but not successful, the date and time of the attempt. Electronic confirmation is available for barcoded matter.

Manual confirmation is available for retail purchasers on the Internet (www.usps.com) or toll-free by phone (800-222-1811).

Priority Mail fees: manual, 45¢; electronic, free. First-Class Mail parcels and Package Services fees: manual, 55¢; electronic, 13¢. Standard Mail fee: electronic, 13¢.

Registered Mail

Provides sender with mailing receipt, and a delivery record is maintained. Only matter prepaid with postage at First Class postage rates may be registered. Stamps or meter stamps must be attached. The face of the article must be at least 5″ long, 3½″ high.

Declared Value	Fee
$0.00	$7.50
$0.01 to $100.00	8.00
$100.01 to $500.00	8.85
$500.01 to $1,000.00	9.70
$1,000.01 to $2,000.00	10.55
$2,000.01 to $3,000.00	11.40
$3,000.01 to $4,000.00	12.25
$4,000.01 to $5,000.00	13.10
$5,000.01 to $6,000.00	13.95
$6,000.01 to $7,000.00	14.80
$7,000.01 to $8,000.00	15.65
$8,000.01 to $9,000.00	16.50
$9,000.01 to $10,000.00	17.35
$10,000.01 to $25,000.00	17.35 plus $0.85 for each $1,000 or fraction thereof over $10,000
$25,000.01 to $15 million	30.10 plus $0.85 handling charge for each $1,000 or fraction thereof over $25,000
Over $15 million	12,758.85 plus any additional amount determined by the Postal Service

Note: The mailer is required to declare the value of mail presented for registration.Fee for articles with declared value over $0.00 up to $25,000 includes insurance; fee is in addition to postage.

C.O.D. Unregistered: Applicable to First Class, Priority Mail, Express Mail, and Package Services. Items must be sent as bona fide orders or be in conformity with agreements between senders and addressees. Maximum amount collectible is $1,000.

C.O.D. Registered: For details, consult postmaster.

Certified mail: Available for any matter having no intrinsic value on which First Class or Priority Mail postage is paid. A receipt is furnished at the time of mailing, and evidence of delivery is obtained. Basic fee is $2.30 in addition to regular postage. Return receipt and restricted delivery available upon payment of additional fees. No indemnity.

Forwarding Addresses

To obtain a forwarding address, the mailer must write on the envelope or the cover "Address Correction Requested." The destination post office then will check for a forwarding address on file and, if available, provide it for 70¢ per manual correction, 20¢ per automated correction.

International Mail Special Services

Registration: Available to practically all countries for letter-post items only. Fee $7.50. The maximum indemnity payable—generally only in case of complete loss (of both contents and wrapper)—is $40.45. To Canada only, the fee is $8.00, providing indemnity for loss up to $100, $8.85 for loss up to $500, and $9.70 for loss up to $1,000. Contact your post office for more details.

Return Receipt: Shows to whom and when delivered; Fee: $1.75 (must be purchased at time of mailing).

Special Delivery: Not available as of June 1997.

Air Mail: Available daily to practically all countries.

Aerogrammes — Aerogrammes are letter sheets that can be folded into the form of an envelope and sealed. Intended for personal communication only and may not include enclosures. Fee: 70¢ from U.S. to all countries.

Air mail postcards (single) — 50¢ to Canada and Mexico; 70¢ to all other countries.

International Reply Coupons (IRC): Provide foreign addressees with a prepaid means of responding to communications initiated by a U.S. sender. Each IRC is equivalent to the destination country's minimum postage rate for an unregistered airmail letter. Fee: $1.75 per coupon.

Restricted Delivery: Available to many countries for registered mail; some limitations. Fee: $3.50.

Insurance: Available to many countries for loss of or damage to items paid at parcel post rate. Consult postmaster for indemnity limits for individual countries.

	Fees	
Limit of indemnity Not over	Canada[1]	All other countries[1]
$ 50	$1.30	$1.85
100	2.20	2.60
200	3.20	3.60
300	4.20	4.60
400	5.20	5.60
500	6.20	6.60
600	7.20	7.60
700	8.20	8.60
800		9.60
900		10.60
1,000[2]		11.60

(1) Not all countries insure items up to the amounts listed in the table. Canada does not insure items for more than $675.
(2) For amounts more than $1,000, add $1.00 for each $100 or fraction.

Post Office-Authorized 2-Letter State Abbreviations

The abbreviations below are approved by the U.S. Postal Service for use in addresses.

Alabama AL	Hawaii HI	Missouri MO	Pennsylvania PA
Alaska AK	Idaho ID	Montana MT	Puerto Rico PR
American Samoa AS	Illinois IL	Nebraska NE	Rhode Island RI
Arizona AZ	Indiana IN	Nevada NV	South Carolina SC
Arkansas AR	Iowa IA	New Hampshire NH	South Dakota SD
California CA	Kansas KS	New Jersey NJ	Tennessee TN
Colorado CO	Kentucky KY	New Mexico NM	Texas TX
Connecticut CT	Louisiana LA	New York NY	Utah UT
Delaware DE	Maine ME	North Carolina NC	Vermont VT
District of Columbia DC	Marshall Islands[1] MH	North Dakota ND	Virgin Islands VI
Federated States of Micronesia[1] FM	Maryland MD	Northern Mariana Is. MP	Virginia VA
Florida FL	Massachusetts MA	Ohio OH	Washington WA
Georgia GA	Michigan MI	Oklahoma OK	West Virginia WV
Guam GU	Minnesota MN	Oregon OR	Wisconsin WI
	Mississippi MS	Palau[1] PW	Wyoming WY

(1) Although an independent nation, this country is currently subject to domestic rates and fees.

Canadian Province and Territory Postal Abbreviations

Source: Canada Post

Alberta AB	Newfoundland and Labrador NF	Nunavut NU	Quebec QC[1]
British Columbia BC	Northwest Territories NT	Ontario ON	Saskatchewan SK
Manitoba MB	Nova Scotia NS	Prince Edward Island PE	Yukon Territory YT
New Brunswick NB			

(1) PQ is also acceptable.

100 MOST POPULOUS U.S. CITIES

Source: Bureau of Labor Statistics: employment; Bureau of Economic Analysis: per capita personal income; all other data from U.S. Census Bureau.

Included here are the 100 most populous U.S. cities, using 2003 Census Bureau estimates. Population rank indicated by figure in parentheses. Most data are for the city proper. Some statistics, where noted, apply to the whole Metropolitan Statistical Area (MSA). Employment figures are for 2003; per capita income figures for 2002. Mayors are as of Sept. 2004. Inc.=incorporated; est.=established. **Note:** Websites are as of Sept. 2004 and subject to change.

Akron, Ohio

Population (2003): 212,215 (86); **Pop. density:** 3,417 per. sq. mi.; **Pop. change (1990–2003):** –4.8%. **Area:** 62.1 sq. mi. **Employment (2003):** 108,965 employed; 7.9% unemployed. **Per capita income (MSA):** $30,205; increase (2001-2002): 2.4%.
Mayor: Donald L. Plusquellic, Democrat
History: settled 1825; inc. as city 1865; located on Ohio-Erie Canal and is a port of entry; polymer center of the Americas.
Transportation: 1 airport; major trucking industry; Conrail, Amtrak; metro transit system. **Communications:** 1 TV, 8 radio stations; 1 daily newspaper. **Medical facilities:** 4 hosp.; specialized children's treatment center. **Educational facilities:** 4 univ. and colleges; 68 pub. schools. **Further information:** Greater Akron Chamber, One Cascade Plaza, 17th Floor, Akron, OH 44308; www.ci.akron.oh.us; www.greaterakronchamber.org

Albuquerque, New Mexico

Population (2003): 471,856 (33); **Pop. density:** 2,613 per. sq. mi.; **Pop. change (1990–2003):** +22.6%. **Area:** 180.6 sq. mi. **Employment (2003):** 244,338 employed; 5.2% unemployed. **Per capita income (MSA):** $28,471; increase (2001-2002): 2.5%.
Mayor: Martin Chavez, Democrat
History: founded 1706 by the Spanish; inc. 1890.
Transportation: 1 intl. airport; 1 railroad; 11 bus service/charters. **Communications:** 13 TV, 32 radio stations. **Medical facilities:** 6 major hosp. **Educational facilities:** 1 univ., 25 colleges. **Further information:** Albuquerque Convention & Visitors Bureau, PO Box 26866, Albuquerque, NM 87125-6866, 1-800-733-9918; www.itsatrip.org; www.cabq.gov/a-z.org

Anaheim, California

Population (2003): 332,361 (52); **Pop. density:** 6,797 per. sq. mi.; **Pop. change (1990–2003):** +24.8%. **Area:** 48.9. **Employment (2003):** 166,499 employed; 4.4% unemployed. **Per capita income (MSA):** $32,547; increase (2001-2002): 1.5%.
Mayor: Curt Pringle, Republican
History: founded 1857; inc. 1870; now known as home of The Disneyland Resort, the Mighty Ducks of Anaheim, and the Anaheim Angels.
Transportation: Amtrak, Metrolink (2 sta.), OCTA bus service, Greyhound. **Communications:** 2 TV, 2 radio stations (MSA). **Medical facilities:** 4 hosp.; 5 medical centers. **Educational facilities:** 13 univ. and colleges; 39 elem., 11 junior high, 10 high schools (MSA). **Further information:** City Hall, 200 South Anaheim Blvd., Ste. 733, Anaheim, CA 92805; www.anaheim.net

Anchorage, Alaska

Population (2003): 270,951 (67); **Pop. density:** 160 per sq. mi; **Pop. change (1990–2003):** +19.7%. **Area:** 1,697.2 sq. mi. **Employment (2003):** 139,398 employed; 5.7% unemployed. **Per capita income (MSA):** $35,623; increase (2001-2002): 2.5%.
Mayor: Mark Begich, Democrat
History: founded 1914 as a construction camp for railroad; HQ of Alaska Defense Command, WWII; severely damaged in earthquake 1964, now rebuilt; current population center of Alaska.
Transportation: 1 intl. airport; 1 railroad; transit system, 1 port. **Communications:** 9 TV, 28 radio stations. **Medical facilities:** 4 hosp. **Educational facilities:** 3 univ., 1 college, 91 pub. schools. **Further information:** Anchorage Chamber of Commerce, 441 W. 5th Ave., Ste. 300, Anchorage, AK 99501-2309; www.ci.anchorage.ak.us; www.anchoragechamber.org

Arlington, Texas

Population (2003): 355,007 (49); **Pop. density:** 3,706 per sq. mi; **Pop. change (1990–2003):** +35.6%. **Area:** 95.8 sq. mi. **Employment (2003):** 190,024 employed; 5.7% unemployed. **Per capita income (MSA):** $33,816; decrease (2001-2002): –0.7%.
Mayor: Robert Clark, Non-Partisan
History: settled in 1840s between Dallas and Ft. Worth; inc. 1884.
Transportation: Dallas/Ft. Worth airport is 10 min. away; 11 railway lines; intercity transport system in planning stage. **Communications:** 11 TV, 44 radio stations. **Medical facilities:** 2 hosp. **Educational facilities:** 1 univ., 1 junior college; 60 pub. schools. **Further information:** Arlington Chamber of Commerce, 505 East Border, Arlington, TX 76010; www.ci.arlington.tx.us; www.arlingtontx.com

Atlanta, Georgia

Population (2003): 423,019 (41); **Pop. density:** 3,212 per sq. mi; **Pop. change (1990-2003):** +7.4%. **Area:** 131.7 sq. mi. **Employment (2003):** 221,766 employed; 7.9% unemployed. **Per capita income (MSA):** $33,257; decrease (2001-2002): –0.5%.
Mayor: Shirley Franklin, Democrat
History: founded as "Terminus" 1837; renamed Atlanta 1845; inc. 1847; played major role in Civil War; became permanent state capital 1877; birthplace of civil rights movement; host to 1996 Centennial Olympic Games.
Transportation: 1 intl. airport; 3 railroad lines; MARTA bus and rapid rail service. **Communications:** 14 TV, 56 radio stations; 29 cable TV cos. **Medical facilities:** 61 hosp.; VA hosp.; U.S. Centers for Disease Control and Prevention; American Cancer Society. **Educational facilities:** 43 colleges, univ., seminaries, junior colleges; 85 pub. schools. **Further information:** Metro Atlanta Chamber of Commerce, 235 Andrew Young Intl. Blvd. NW, Atlanta, GA 30303; www.metroatlantachamber.com; www.atlantaga.gov

Aurora, Colorado

Population (2003): 290,418 (59); **Pop. density:** 2,038 per sq. mi; **Pop. change (1990-2003):** +30.8%. **Area:** 142.5 sq. mi. **Employment (2003):** 157,114 employed; 6.6% unemployed. **Per capita income (MSA):** $38,008; decrease (2001-2002): –1.7%.
Mayor: Paul E. Tauer, Non-Partisan
History: located 5 mi east of Denver; early growth stimulated by presence of military bases; fast-growing trade, technology, and medical science center.
Transportation: adjacent to Denver Intl. Airport; bus system. **Communications:** 1 TV station. **Medical facilities:** Major pub. univ. medical center; 2 pub. hosp. **Educational facilities:** 1 univ., 4 community and junior colleges, 2 technical colleges; 68 pub. schools, 4 private schools. **Further information:** Aurora Planning Dept., 15151 E. Alameda Pkwy., Aurora, CO 80012; www.auroragov.org; www.aurorachamber.org

Austin, Texas

Population (2003): 672,011 (16); **Pop. density:** 2,672 per sq. mi; **Pop. change (1990-2003):** +44.3%. **Area:** 251.5 sq. mi. **Employment (2003):** 381,635 employed; 6.2% unemployed. **Per capita income (MSA):** $31,677; decrease (2001-2002): –3.1%.
Mayor: Will Wynn, Non-Partisan
History: first permanent settlement 1835; capital of Rep. of Texas 1839; named after Stephen Austin; inc. 1840.
Transportation: 1 intl. airport; 2 railroads. **Communications:** 8 TV, 29 radio stations. **Medical facilities:** 13 hosp. **Educational facilities:** 5 univ. and colleges. **Further information:** Greater Austin Chamber, 210 Barton Springs Rd., Ste. 400, Austin, TX 78704; www.ci.austin.tx.us; www.austinchamber.org

Bakersfield, California

Population (2003): 271,035 (66); **Pop. density:** 2,396 per sq. mi; **Pop. change (1990-2003):** +55.0%. **Area:** 113.1 sq. mi. **Employment (2003):** 95,873 employed; 9.1% unemployed. **Per capita income (MSA):** $22,635; increase (2001-2002): 3.8%.
Mayor: Harvey Hall, Non-Partisan
History: named after Col. Thomas Baker, an early settler; inc. 1898.
Transportation: 2 airports; 3 railroads; Amtrak; Greyhound buses; local bus system. **Communications:** 8 TV, 29 radio stations. **Medical facilities:** 9 major hosp.; 9 convalescent, 1 psychiatric, 3 physical rehab., 5 urgent care facilities; 3 clinics. **Educational facilities:** 9 univ., 1 community college, 14 vocational schools, 1 adult school, 15 elem. school districts, 14 high schools (Kern County). **Further information:** Greater Bakersfield Chamber of Commerce, 1725 Eye St., PO Box 1947, Bakersfield, CA 93303; www.bakersfieldchamber.org

Baltimore, Maryland

Population (2003): 628,670 (18); **Pop. density:** 7,781 per sq. mi; **Pop. change (1990-2003):** –14.6%. **Area:** 80.8 sq. mi. **Employment (2003):** 263,644 employed; 8.6% unemployed. **Per capita income (MSA):** $35,556; increase (2001-2002): 3.0%.
Mayor: Martin O'Malley, Democrat
History: founded by Maryland legislature 1729; inc. 1797; War of 1812 British bombing of Ft. McHenry (1814) inspired Francis Scott Key to write "Star-Spangled Banner"; birthplace of America's railroads 1828; rebuilt after fire 1904; site of National Aquarium 1981.
Transportation: 1 major airport; 3 railroads; bus system; subway system; light rail system; Inner Harbor water taxi system; 2 underwater tunnels. **Communications:** 6 TV, 25 radio stations. **Medical facilities:** 31 hosp.; 2 major medical centers. **Educational facilities:** over 30 univ. and colleges; 186 pub. schools. **Further information:** Greater Baltimore Committee, 111 S. Calvert St., Ste. 1700, Baltimore, MD 21202-6180; www.ci.baltimore.md.us; www.baltimore.org

Baton Rouge, Louisiana
Population (2003): 225,090 (79); **Pop. density:** 2,931 per sq. mi; **Pop. change (1990-2003):** +2.5%. **Area:** 76.8 sq. mi. **Employment (2003):** 111,765 employed; 6.6% unemployed. **Per capita income (MSA):** $25,841; increase (2001-2002): 2.9%.
Mayor: Bobby Simpson, Republican
History: claimed by Spain at time of Louisiana Purchase 1803; est. independence by rebellion 1810; inc. as town 1817; became state capital 1849; Union-held most of Civil War.
Transportation: 1 airport, 5 airlines; 1 bus line; 3 railroad trunk lines. **Communications:** 5 TV, 19 radio stations. **Medical facilities:** 5 hosp. **Educational facilities:** 107 pub., 52 nonpublic schools; 2 univ., 1 Community College, 1 Technical College. **Further information:** The Chamber of Greater Baton Rouge, PO Box 3217, Baton Rouge, LA 70821; www.brgov.com; www.brchamber.org

Birmingham, Alabama
Population (2003): 236,620 (74); **Pop. density:** 1,579 per sq. mi; **Pop. change (1990-2003):** −11.0%. **Area:** 149.9 sq. mi. **Employment (2003):** 120,264 employed; 7.2% unemployed. **Per capita income (MSA):** $30,661; increase (2001-2002): 3.2%.
Mayor: Bernard Kincaid, Democrat
History: settled 1871 at the intersection of 2 major railroads, within proximity of elements needed for iron and steel production.
Transportation: 1 intl. airport; 4 major rail freight lines, Amtrak; 1 bus line; 75 truck line terminals; 5 air cargo cos.; 7 barge lines; 5 interstate highways. **Communications:** 7 TV, 32 radio stations; 1 educational TV, 1 educational radio station. **Medical facilities:** 16, including the Univ. of Alabama at Birmingham Medical Center; VA hosp. **Educational facilities:** 1 pub., 2 private univ.; 4 private colleges, 3 private law schools. **Further information:** Birmingham Area Chamber of Commerce, 2027 First Ave. N, Birmingham, AL 35203; www.birminghamchamber.com; www.informationbirmingham.com

Boston, Massachusetts
Population (2003): 581,616 (23); **Pop. density:** 12,017 per sq. mi; **Pop. change (1990-2003):** +1.3%. **Area:** 48.4 sq. mi. **Employment (2003):** 290,842 employed; 6.0% unemployed. **Per capita income (MSA):** $42,436; decrease (2001-2002): −0.2%.
Mayor: Thomas M. Menino, Democrat
History: settled 1630 by John Winthrop; capital of Mass. Bay Colony; figured strongly in Am. Revolution, earning distinction as the "Cradle of Liberty"; inc. 1822.
Transportation: 1 major airport; 2 railroads; city rail and subway system; 3 underwater tunnels; port. **Communications:** 12 TV, 21 radio stations. **Medical facilities:** 31 hosp.; 8 major medical research centers. **Educational facilities:** 30 univ. and colleges. **Further information:** Greater Boston Convention and Visitors Bureau, 2 Copley Pl., Suite 105, Boston, MA 02116; www.bostonusa.com

Buffalo, New York
Population (2003): 285,018 (60); **Pop. density:** 7,020 per sq. mi; **Pop. change (1990-2003):** −13.1%. **Area:** 40.6 sq. mi. **Employment (2003):** 129,838 employed; 10.2% unemployed. **Per capita income (MSA):** $28,489; increase (2001-2002): 3.2%.
Mayor: Anthony M. Masiello, Democrat
History: settled 1780 by Seneca Indians; raided twice by British, War of 1812; served as western terminus for Erie Canal, became a center for trade and manufacturing; inc. 1832; last stop on the Underground Railroad; key point for Canada-U.S. political, trade, and social relations.
Transportation: 1 intl. airport; 4 Class I railroads; Amtrak metro rail system; water service to Great Lakes-St. Lawrence Seaway system and Atlantic seaboard. **Communications:** 11 TV, 12 radio stations. **Medical facilities:** 16 hosp., 40 research centers. **Educational facilities:** 15 colleges and univ.; 400 pub. and private schools. **Further information:** Buffalo Niagara Visitor Center, Market Arcade/Walden Galleria, 617 Main Street, Buffalo, NY 14203; www.ci.buffalo.ny.us; buffaloniagara.org

Chandler, Arizona
Population (2003): 211,299 (87); **Pop. density:** 3,649 per sq. mi; **Pop. change (1990-2003):** +133.4%. **Area:** 57.9 sq. mi. **Employment (2003):** 104,946 employed; 3.7% unemployed. **Per capita income (MSA):** $28,481; decrease (2001-2002): −0.1%.
Mayor: Boyd W. Dunn, Non-Partisan
History: town formed 1912; population doubled in 1990s as "the high-tech oasis of the Silicon Desert."
Transportation: 1 municipal airport; mass transit system. **Communications:** 2 TV, 3 newspapers. **Medical facilities:** 1 medical center. **Educational facilities:** 2 univ., 2 community coll.; 26 elem., 7 junior high, 4 high schools; 13 charter schools **Further information:** Chandler Chamber, 25 South Arizona Pl., Suite 201, Chandler, AZ 85225; www.chandlerchamber.com; chandleraz.gov

Charlotte, North Carolina
Population (2003): 584,658 (21); **Pop. density:** 2,413 per sq. mi; **Pop. change (1990-2003):** +47.7%. **Area:** 242.3 sq. mi. **Employment (2003):** 303,362 employed; 6.3% unemployed. **Per capita income (MSA):** $33,083; increase (2001-2002): 1.1%.
Mayor: Patrick McCrory, Republican
History: settled by Scotch-Irish immigrants 1740s; inc. 1768 and named after Queen Charlotte, George III's wife; scene of first major U.S. gold discovery 1799.
Transportation: 1 airport; 2 major railway lines; 1 bus line; 605 trucking firms. **Communications:** 12 TV, 28 radio stations. **Medical facilities:** 10 hosp., 2 medical centers. **Educational facilities:** 9 univ., 9 colleges, 89 elem. schools, 31 middle schools, 17 high schools. **Further information:** Chamber of Commerce, PO Box 32785, Charlotte, NC 28232; www.charlottechamber.com

Chesapeake, Virginia
Population (2003): 210,834 (88); **Pop. density:** 619 per sq. mi; **Pop. change (1990-2003):** +38.7%. **Area:** 340.7 sq. mi. **Employment (2003):** 108,720 employed; 3.6% unemployed. **Per capita income (MSA):** $28,365; increase (2001-2002): 2.9%.
Mayor: Dalton S. Edge, Non-Partisan
History: region settled in 1620s with first English colonies on banks of Elizabeth River; home to Great Dismal Swamp Canal, first envisioned by George Washington in 1763; Battle of Great Bridge fought here Dec. 1775; inc. as a city 1963.
Transportation: Freight rail service; bus service; 2 regional airports. **Communications:** 9 TV, 48 radio stations (serving Hampton Roads community). **Medical facilities:** 1 hosp. **Educational facilities:** 9 colleges and univ.; 49 pub. schools and educational centers. **Further information:** City of Chesapeake, Public Communications Dept., 306 Cedar Rd., Chesapeake, VA 23322; www.cityofchesapeake.net

Chicago, Illinois
Population (2003): 2,869,121 (3); **Pop. density:** 12,634 per sq. mi; **Pop. change (1990-2003):** +3.1%. **Area:** 227.1 sq. mi. **Employment (2003):** 1,192,849 employed; 8.2% unemployed. **Per capita inc. (MSA):** $35,583; increase (2001-2002): 0.4%
Mayor: Richard M. Daley, Democrat
History: site acquired from Indians 1795; significant white settlement began with opening of Erie Canal 1825; chartered as city 1837; boomed with arrival of railroads from east and canal to Mississippi R.; about one-third of city destroyed by fire 1871; major grain and livestock market.
Transportation: 2 airports; major railroad system, trucking industry. **Communications:** 9 TV, 31 radio stations. **Medical facilities:** over 123 hosp. **Educational facilities:** 95 insts. of higher learning. **Further information:** Chicagoland Chamber of Commerce, 1 IBM Plaza, Ste. 2800, Chicago, IL 60611; www.cityofchicago.org; www.chicagolandchamber.org

Chula Vista, California
Population (2003): 199,060 (95); **Pop. density:** 4,071 per sq. mi; **Pop. change (1990-2003):** +47.3%. **Area:** 48.9 sq. mi. **Employment (2003):** 74,179 employed; 4.5% unemployed. **Per capita income (MSA):** $34,872; increase (2001-2002): 2.8%.
Mayor: Stephen C. Padilla, Non-Partisan
History: visited by Spanish in 1542; became part of Spanish land grant in 1795; came into the U.S. during the Mexican War in 1847; inc. 1911. WWII brought aircraft industry and growth.
Transportation: bus system; DART. **Communications:** See San Diego, CA. **Medical facilities:** 2 hosp. **Educational facilities:** 39 elementary, 7 middle, 3 junior high, 10 senior high, 5 colleges and univ. **Further Information:** Chula Vista Chamber of Commerce, 233 Fourth Ave., Chula Vista, CA 91910. www.chulavistachamber.org

> **IT'S A FACT:** Durham, NC, a new addition to the list of 100 most populous cities, played host to the Rose Bowl game between Duke and Oregon State on Jan 1, 1942—the only Rose Bowl not held in Pasadena, CA. The game was moved to the East Coast because of security concerns after the Dec. 7 Japanese attack on Pearl Harbor.

Cincinnati, Ohio

Population (2003): 317,361 (56); **Pop. density:** 4,069 per sq. mi; **Pop. change (1990-2003):** –12.8%. **Area:** 78.0 sq. mi. **Employment (2003):** 162,226 employed; 7.3% unemployed. **Per capita income (MSA):** $31,804; increase (2001-2002): 2.3%.
Mayor: Charlie Luken, Democrat
History: founded 1788 and named after the Society of Cincinnati, an organization of Revolutionary War officers; chartered as village 1802; inc. as city 1819.
Transportation: 1 intl. airport; 3 railroads; 2 bus systems. **Communications:** 7 TV, 25 radio stations. **Medical facilities:** 28 hosp.; Cincinnati Children's Hosp. Medical Center; VA hosp. **Educational facilities:** 4 univ., 12 colleges, 8 technical & 2-year colleges. **Further information:** Chamber of Commerce, 300 Carew Tower, 441 Vine St., Cincinnati, OH 45202; www.cincinnatichamber.com; www.cincinnatiusa.org

Cleveland, Ohio

Population (2003): 461,324 (35); **Pop. density:** 5,945 per sq. mi; **Pop. change (1990-2003):** –8.8%. **Area:** 77.6 sq. mi. **Employment (2003):** 182,255 employed; 12.7% unemployed. **Per capita income (MSA):** $32,244; increase (2001-2002): 1.1%.
Mayor: Jane Campbell, Democrat
History: surveyed in 1796; given recognition as village 1815, inc. as city 1836; annexed Ohio City 1854.
Transportation: 1 intl. airport; rail service; major port; rapid transit system. **Communications:** 9 TV, 21 radio stations. **Medical facilities:** 14 hosp. **Educational facilities:** 8 univ. and colleges; 127 pub. schools. **Further information:** Greater Cleveland Growth Assn., Tower City Center, 50 Pub. Square, Suite 200, Cleveland, OH 44113-2291; www.cleveland.oh.us; www.clevelandgrowth.oh.us

Colorado Springs, Colorado

Population (2003): 370,448 (48); **Pop. density:** 1,995 per sq. mi; **Pop. change (1990-2003):** +31.8%. **Area:** 185.7 sq. mi. **Employment (2003):** 196,581 employed; 6.4% unemployed. **Per capita income (MSA):** $29,892; increase (2001-2002): 0.6%.
Mayor: Lionel Rivera, Non-Partisan
History: city founded in 1871 at the foot of Pike's Peak; inc. 1872.
Transportation: 1 municipal airport; 1 bus line. **Communications:** 9 TV, 28 radio stations. **Medical facilities:** 5 hosp. **Educational facilities:** 11 univ., 5 colleges. **Further information:** Chamber of Commerce, 2 N. Cascade, Ste. 110, Colorado Springs, CO 80901; www.springsgov.com; www.coloradospringschamber.org

Columbus, Ohio

Population (2003): 728,432 (15); **Pop. density:** 3,464 per sq. mi; **Pop. change (1990-2003):** +15.1%. **Area:** 210.3 sq. mi. **Employment (2003):** 393,542 employed; 5.7% unemployed. **Per capita income (MSA):** $32,043; increase (2001-2002): 2.2%.
Mayor: Michael B. Coleman, Democrat
History: first settlement 1797; laid out as new capital 1812 with current name; became city 1834.
Transportation: 6 airports; 2 railroads; 2 intercity bus lines. **Communications:** 8 TV, 32 radio stations. **Medical facilities:** 17 hosp. **Educational facilities:** 11 univ. and colleges; 8 technical/2-year schools; 147 pub. schools (93 elem., 26 middle, 18 high, 10 special-purpose). **Further information:** Greater Columbus Chamber of Commerce, 37 N. High St., Columbus, OH 43215. Experience Columbus, 90 N. High St., Columbus, OH 43215; www.columbus-chamber.org; www.experiencecolumbus.org

Corpus Christi, Texas

Population (2003): 279,208 (63); **Pop. density:** 1,806 per sq. mi; **Pop. change (1990-2003):** +8.5%. **Area:** 154.6 sq. mi. **Employment (2003):** 128,608 employed; 6.6% unemployed. **Per capita income (MSA):** $25,119; increase (2001-2002): 3.3%.
Mayor: Samuel Loyd Neal, Non-Partisan
History: settled 1839 and inc. 1852.
Transportation: 1 intl. airport; 2 bus lines, metro bus system; 3 freight railroads. **Communications:** 6 TV, 17 radio stations. **Medical facilities:** 14 hosp. including a children's center. **Educational facilities:** 1 univ., 1 college. **Further information:** Corpus Christi Regional Economic Development Corp., PO Box 2724, Corpus Christi, TX 78403; www.ccredc.com; www.ci.corpus christi.tx.us

Dallas, Texas

Population (2003): 1,208,318 (9); **Pop. density:** 3,528 per sq. mi; **Pop. change (1990-2003):** +20.0%. **Area:** 342.5 sq. mi. **Employment (2003):** 632,162 employed; 9.1% unemployed. **Per capita income (MSA):** $33,816; decrease (2001-2002): –0.7%.
Mayor: Laura Miller, Non-Partisan
History: first settled 1841; platted 1846; inc. 1871; developed as the financial and commercial center of Southwest; headquarters of regional Federal Reserve Bank; major center for distribution and high-tech manufacturing.
Transportation: 1 intl. airport, 1 regional airport; Amtrak; transit system. **Communications:** 17 TV, 52 radio stations. **Medical facilities:** 19 general hosp.; major medical center. **Educational facilities:** 218 pub. schools, 12 univ. and colleges, 3 community college campuses. **Further information:** Greater Dallas Chamber, Resource Center, 700 N. Pearl St., Ste. 1200, Dallas, TX 75201; www.dallaschamber.org; www.dallascityhall.com

Denver, Colorado

Population (2003): 557,478 (26); **Pop. density:** 3,634 per sq. mi; **Pop. change (1990-2003):** +19.2%. **Area:** 153.4 sq. mi. **Employment (2003):** 280,436 employed; 7.4% unemployed. **Per capita income (MSA):** $38,008; decrease (2001-2002): –1.7%.
Mayor: John W. Hickenlooper, Democrat
History: settled 1858 by gold prospectors and miners; inc. 1861; became territorial capital 1867; growth spurred by gold and silver boom; became financial, industrial, cultural center of Rocky Mt. region.
Transportation: 1 intl. airport, 3 corporate reliever airports; 5 rail freight lines, Amtrak; 1 bus line. **Communications:** 14 TV, 29 radio stations. **Medical facilities:** 20 hosp. **Educational facilities:** 15 four-yr. colleges and univ.; 8 two-yr. and community colleges. **Further information:** Denver Metro Chamber of Commerce, 1445 Market St., Denver, CO 80202-1729; www.denverchamber.org

Detroit, Michigan

Population (2003): 911,402 (10); **Pop. density:** 6,566 per sq. mi; **Pop. change (1990-2003):** –11.3%. **Area:** 138.8 sq. mi. **Employment (2003):** 333,868 employed; 14.6% unemployed. **Per capita income (MSA):** $34,129; increase (2001-2002): 0.6%.
Mayor: Kwame M. Kilpatrick, Democrat
History: founded by French 1701; controlled by British 1760; acquired by U.S. 1796; destroyed by fire 1805; inc. as city 1815; capital of state 1837-47; auto manufacturing began 1890.
Transportation: 1 intl. airport, 1 general aviation airport; 10 railroads (4 Class I); major intl. port; pub. transit system. **Communications:** 4 TV, 6 radio stations. **Medical facilities:** 13 hosp.; 3 major medical centers. **Educational facilities:** 2 univ., 3 colleges, 1 community college. **Further information:** Detroit Regional Chamber, One Woodward Ave., PO Box 33840, Detroit, MI 48232-0840; www.detroitchamber.com

Durham, North Carolina

Population (2003): 198,376 (96); **Pop. density:** 2,097 per sq. mi; **Pop. change (1990-2003):** +45.2%. **Area:** 94.6 sq. mi. **Employment (2003):** 90,330 employed; 5.9% unemployed. **Per capita income (MSA):** $31,435; increase (2001-2002): 1.0%
Mayor: William V. Bell, Non-Partisan
History: Inc. 1869; Trinity College moved to Durham in 1892, renamed Duke Univ. in 1924.
Transportation: 2 area bus systems; 1 airport; 1 train station. **Communications:** 8 radio stations; 3 TV stations. **Medical facilities:** 8 hosp. **Educational facilities:** 44 pub. schools, plus private and charter schools; 1 comm. col.; school of nursing; 2 univ. **Further information:** Durham Convention and Visitors Bureau, 101 E. Morgan St., Durham, NC 27701; www.durham-nc.com

El Paso, Texas

Population (2003): 584,113 (22); **Pop. density:** 2,345 per sq. mi; **Pop. change (1990-2003):** +13.3%. **Area:** 249.1 sq. mi. **Employment (2003):** 242,930 employed; 9.3% unemployed. **Per capita income (MSA):** $20,129; increase (2001-2002): 4.0%.
Mayor: Joe Wardy, Republican
History: first settled 1598; inc. 1873; arrival of railroad 1881 boosted city's population and industries.
Transportation: 1 intl. airport; 2 rail providers; 2 interstate highways; 4 intl. ports of entry. **Communications:** 12 TV, 21 radio stations. **Medical facilities:** 8 hosp.; 8 rehabilitation; 11 specialty centers. **Educational facilities:** 5 univ., 2 colleges; 2 grad. and doctoral programs. **Further information:** Greater El Paso Chamber of Commerce, 10 Civic Center Plaza, El Paso, TX 79901; www.elpaso.org

Fort Wayne, Indiana

Population (2003): 219,495 (80); **Pop. density:** 2,778 per sq. mi; **Pop. Change (1990-2003):** +26.8%. **Area:** 79.0 sq. mi. **Employment (2003):** 95,216 employed; 6.8% unemployed. **Per capita income (MSA):** $28,965; increase (2001-2002): 1.1%.
Mayor: Graham A. Richard, Democrat
History: French fort 1680; U.S. fort 1794; settled by 1832; inc. 1840 prior to Wabash-Erie canal completion 1843.
Transportation: 2 airports; 3 railroads; 6 bus lines. **Communications:** 6 TV, 25 radio stations, 11 newspapers. **Medical facilities:** 8 regional hosp.; VA hosp. **Educational facilities:** 5

univ., 4 colleges, 3 bus. schools; 92 pub. schools. **Further information:** Chamber of Commerce, 826 Ewing Street, Fort Wayne, IN 46802-2182; www.fwchamber.org

Fort Worth, Texas

Population (2003): 585,122 (20); **Pop. density:** 2,000 per sq. mi; **Pop. change (1990-2003):** +30.7%. **Area:** 292.5 sq. mi. **Employment (2003):** 268,772 employed; 8.5% unemployed. **Per capita income (MSA):** $33,816; decrease (2001-2002): –0.7%.
Mayor: Mike Moncrief, Non-Partisan
History: established as military post 1849; inc. 1873; oil discovered 1917.
Transportation: 2 intl. airport, 1 industrial airport; 3 major railroads, Amtrak; local bus service; 1 transcontinental, 1 intrastate bus lines. **Communications:** 18 TV, 65 local radio stations. **Medical facilities:** 10 hosp.; 1 children's hosp.; 4 government hosp.· **Educational facilities:** 5 univ. and colleges. **Further information:** Chamber of Commerce, 777 Taylor St. #900, Fort Worth, TX 76102; www.fortworthgov.org; www.fortworthchamber.com

Fremont, California

Population (2003): 204,525 (91); **Pop. density:** 2,667 per sq. mi; **Pop. change (1990-2003):** +18.0%. **Area:** 76.7 sq. mi. **Employment (2003):** 105,871 employed; 4.7% unemployed. **Per capita income (MSA):** $46,920; decrease (2001-2002): –2.1%.
Mayor: Gus Morrison, Non-Partisan
History: area first settled by Spanish 1769; inc. 1956 with consolidation of 5 communities.
Transportation: intracity bus line; Bay Area Rapid Transit System (southern terminal). **Communications:** 1 radio station. **Medical facilities:** 2 hosp.; 2 major medical facilities; 18 clinics. **Educational facilities:** 1 community college; 42 pub. schools. **Further information:** Chamber of Commerce, 39488 Stevenson Place, Suite 100, Fremont, CA 94539; www.fremontbusiness.com

Fresno, California

Population (2003): 451,455 (36); **Pop. density:** 4,324 per sq. mi; **Pop. change (1990-2003):** +27.5%. **Area:** 104.4 sq. mi. **Employment (2003):** 177,096 employed; 12.8% unemployed. **Per capita income (MSA):** $23,492; increase (2001-2002): 4.0%.
Mayor: Alan Autry, Non-Partisan
History: founded 1872; inc. as city 1885.
Transportation: 1 municipal airport; Amtrak; 1 bus line; intracity bus system. **Communications:** 15 TV, 23 radio stations. **Medical facilities:** 17 general hosp. **Educational facilities:** 9 colleges; 102 pub. schools. **Further information:** Greater Fresno Area Chamber of Commerce, PO Box 1469, Fresno, CA 93716-1469; www.fresnochamber.com; fresno-online.com

Garland, Texas

Population (2003): 218,027 (82); **Pop. density:** 3,818 per sq. mi; **Pop. change (1990-2003):** +20.7%. **Area:** 57.1 sq. mi. **Employment (2003):** 117,210 employed; 6.1% unemployed. **Per capita income (MSA):** $33,816; decrease (2001-2002): –0.7%.
Mayor: Bob Day, Democrat
History: settled 1850s; inc. 1891.
Transportation: 30 min. from Dallas/Ft. Worth Intl. Airport; 2 railroads. **Communications:** 14 local TV (Dallas/Ft. Worth), 25+ radio stations. **Medical facilities:** 2 hosp.; 348 beds. **Educational facilities:** 3 univ., 2 community colleges; 64 pub. schools. **Further information:** Chamber of Commerce, 914 S. Garland Ave., Garland, TX 75040; www.garlandchamber.com

Glendale, Arizona

Population (2003): 232,838 (76); **Pop. density:** 4,180 per sq. mi; **Pop. change (1990-2003):** +57.2%. **Area:** 55.7 sq. mi. **Employment (2003):** 120,367 employed; 4.9% unemployed. **Per capita income (MSA):** $28,481; decrease (2001-2002): –0.1%.
Mayor: Elaine M. Scruggs, Non-Partisan
History: est. 1892; inc. 1910.
Transportation: 1 local airport. **Communications:** 12 TV stations, 40 radio stations. **Medical facilities:** 3 hosp. **Educational facilities:** 12 institutes of higher education, 9 pub. school districts. **Further information:** Chamber of Commerce, PO Box 249, 7105 N. 59th Ave., Glendale, AZ 85311; www.glendaleazchamber.org

Glendale, California

Population (2003): 200,499 (92); **Pop. density:** 6,552 per sq. mi; **Pop. change (1990-2003):** +11.4%. **Area:** 30.6 sq. mi. **Employment (2003):** 92,249 employed, 6.6% unemployed. **Per capita income (MSA):** $32,547; increase (2001-2002): 1.5%.
Mayor: Bob Yousefian, Non-Partisan
History: became a town in 1887; inc. 1906.
Transportation: near Los Angeles Intl. airport; 1 local airport, commuter trains, Amtrak; bus system. **Communications:** 21 TV, 70 radio stations. **Medical facilities:** 3 hosp; other facilities. **Ed-**ucational facilities: 1 community college; 26 pub. schools. **Further information:** City of Glendale Public Information Officer, 613 E. Broadway, Glendale, CA 91206; www.ci.glendale.ca.us

Greensboro, North Carolina

Population (2003): 229,110 (77); **Pop. density:** 2,188 per sq. mi; **Pop. change (1990-2003):** +24.8%. **Area:** 104.7 sq. mi. **Employment (2003):** 116,683 employed; 6.5% unemployed. **Per capita income (MSA):** $28,508; increase (2001-2002): 1.1%.
Mayor: Keith Holliday, Non-Partisan
History: settled 1749; site of Revolutionary War conflict 1781 between Generals Nathanael Greene and Cornwallis; inc. 1807, origin of civil rights sit-in movement.
Transportation: 1 intl. airport; 2 railroads; Trailways/Greyhound bus service. **Communications:** all cable TV stations; 11 radio stations. **Medical facilities:** 4 hosp. **Educational facilities:** 2 univ., 4 colleges; 94 pub. schools. **Further information:** Chamber of Commerce, PO Box 3246, Greensboro, NC 27402; www.greensboro-nc.gov; www.greensboro.com

Henderson, Nevada

Population (2003): 214,852 (85); **Pop. density:** 2,696 per sq. mi; **Pop. change (1990-2003):** 230.8%. **Area:** 79.7 sq. mi. **Employment (2003):** 67,331 employed; 4.3% unemployed. **Per capita income (MSA):** $29,396; increase (2001-2002): 0.8%.
Mayor: James B. Gibson, Non-Partisan.
History: early growth spurred by World War II magnesium mining; inc. 1953.
Transportation: Henderson Executive Airport; Citizens Area Transit (CAT) public transportation. **Communications:** 9 TV stations; 38 radio stations. **Medical facilities:** 3 hosp.; medical center facilities. **Educational facilities:** 5 coll.; 2 vocational schools; 23 elem., 5 middle, 6 high schools. **Further information:** City of Henderson Public Information Office, 240 Water St., Henderson, NV 89015; www.cityofhenderson.gov; www.hendersonchamber.com

Hialeah, Florida

Population (2003): 226,401 (78); **Pop. density:** 11,792 per sq. mi; **Pop. change (1990-2003):** +20.4%. **Area:** 19.2 sq. mi. **Employment (2003):** 101,938 employed; 7.5% unemployed. **Per capita income (MSA):** $32,373; increase (2001-2002): 1.4%.
Mayor: Raul L. Martinez, Republican
History: founded 1917, inc. 1925; industrial and residential city NW of Miami; Hialeah Park Horse Racing Track.
Transportation: 5 mi from Miami Intl. Airport; access to Port of Miami; Amtrak; 2 rail freight lines; Metrorail, Metrobus systems. **Communications:** 5 TV, 7 radio stations. **Medical facilities:** 4 hosp. (30 more in the area). **Educational facilities:** 8 univ. and colleges, 25 pub., 39 private schools. **Further information:** Hialeah-Dade Development, Inc., 501 Palm Ave., Hialeah, FL 33010; www.ci.hialeah.fl.us; www.hddi.org

Honolulu, Hawaii

Population (2003): 380,149 (45); **Pop. density:** 4,436 per sq. mi; **Pop. change (1990-2003):** +4.1%. **Area:** 85.7 sq. mi. **Employment (MSA):** 419,541; employed, 3.9% unemployed. **Per capita income (MSA):** $31,707; increase (2001-2002): 4.0%.
Mayor: Jeremy Harris, Non-Partisan
History: harbor entered by Europeans 1778; declared capital of kingdom by King Kamehameha III 1850; Pearl Harbor naval base attacked by Japanese Dec. 7, 1941.
Transportation: 1 major airport; 3 commercial harbors. **Communications:** 16 TV, 38 radio stations. **Medical facilities:** 10 acute, 26 long-term care facilities. **Educational facilities:** 7 univ., 7 community colleges; 169 pub. schools, 88 private schools, 9 charter schools. **Further information:** Hawaii Visitors and Convention Bureau, 2270 Kalakaua Ave., 8th Fl., Honolulu, HI 96815; www.co.honolulu.hi.us; www.gohawaii.com

Houston, Texas

Population (2003): 2,009,690 (4); **Pop. density:** 3,469 per sq. mi; **Pop. change (1990-2003):** +23.3%. **Area:** 579.4 sq. mi. **Employment (2003):** 1,010,123; employed; 8.3% unemployed. **Per capita income (MSA):** $34,969; decrease (2001-2002): –0.7%.
Mayor: Bill White, Non-Partisan
History: founded 1836; inc. 1837; capital of Repub. of Texas 1837-39; developed rapidly after construction of channel to Gulf of Mexico 1914; world center of oil and natural gas technology.
Transportation: 3 commercial airports; 2 mainline railroads; major bus and rail transit system; major intl. port. **Communications:** 17 TV, 60 radio stations. **Medical facilities:** 69 hosp. (Harris Co.); major medical center. **Educational facilities:** 35 univ. and colleges (Harris Co.) **Further information:** Greater Houston Partnership, 1200 Smith St., Houston, TX 77002-4400; www. houston.org; www.cityofhouston.gov

---

WORLD ALMANAC QUICK QUIZ

Rank these states by number of cities each has (most to fewest) among the 100 most populous.
(a) Texas   (b) California   (c) Ohio   (d) Florida
For the answer look in this chapter, or on pages 626-627, or see page 1008.

IT'S A FACT: Laredo, a southern Texas city that joined the list of 100 most populous cities for the first time, was the capital of a short-lived republic that broke away from Mexico in Jan. 1840. This Republic of the Rio Grande lasted only 283 days before the Mexican army reclaimed the area. Later, the Republic of Texas, which had won independence from Mexico in 1836, tried to claim the area around Laredo, but Laredo's citizens remained loyal to Mexico. Laredo, with the rest of Texas, finally became part of the U.S. after the Mexican War under the 1848 Treaty of Guadalupe Hidalgo.

Indianapolis, Indiana

Population (2003): 783,438 (12); **Pop. density:** 2,167 per sq. mi; **Pop. change (1990-2003):** +7.1%. **Area:** 361.5 sq. mi. **Employment (2003):** 412,784 employed; 5.5% unemployed. **Per capita income (MSA):** $32,916; increase (2001-2002): 0.7%.

Mayor: Bart Peterson, Democrat

History: settled 1820; became capital 1825.

Transportation: 1 intl. airport; 5 railroads; 3 interstate bus lines. **Communications:** 10 TV, 27 radio stations. **Medical facilities:** 17 hosp.; 1 major medical and research center. **Educational facilities:** 8 univ. and colleges; major pub. library system. **Further information:** Greater Indianapolis Chamber of Commerce, 111 Monument Circle, Ste. 1950, Indianapolis, IN 46204; www.ci.indianapolis.in.us; www.indychamber.com

Jacksonville, Florida

Population (2003): 773,781 (13); **Pop. density:** 1,021 per sq. mi; **Pop. change (1990-2003):** +21.8%. **Area:** 757.7 sq. mi. **Employment (2003):** 368,294 employed; 5.8% unemployed. **Per capita income (MSA):** $30,037; increase (2001-2002): 1.7%.

Mayor: John Peyton, Republican

History: settled 1816 as Cowford; renamed after Andrew Jackson 1822; inc. 1832; rechartered 1851; scene of conflicts in Seminole and Civil wars.

Transportation: 1 intl. airport; 3 railroads; 2 interstate bus lines; 2 seaports. **Communications:** 7 TV, 34 radio stations. **Medical facilities:** 11 hosp. **Educational facilities:** 7 univ., 5 colleges, 2 community colleges; 233 pub. schools, 155 private schools. **Further information:** Chamber of Commerce, 3 Independent Drive, Jacksonville, FL 32202; www.expandinjax.com; www.myjaxchamber.com; www.coj.net

Jersey City, New Jersey

Population (2003): 239,097 (73); **Pop. density:** 16,047 per sq. mi; **Pop. change (1990-2003):** +4.6 %. **Area:** 14.9 sq. mi. **Employment (2003):** 102,676 employed; 9.9% unemployed. **Per capita income (MSA):** $40,680; increase (2001-2002): 0.0%.

Mayor: Glenn Cunningham, Democrat

History: site bought from Indians 1630; chartered as town by British 1668; scene of Revolutionary War conflict 1779; chartered under present name 1838; important station on Underground Railroad.

Transportation: Intercity bus and subway system; ferry service to Manhattan. **Communications:** see New York, NY. **Medical facilities:** 4 hosp. **Educational facilities:** 3 colleges. **Further information:** Hudson County Chamber of Commerce, 660 Newark Ave., Ste. 220, Jersey City, NJ 07306; www.jerseycityonline.com

Kansas City, Missouri

Population (2003): 442,768 (38); **Pop. density:** 1,412 per sq. mi; **Pop. change (1990-2003):** +1.8%. **Area:** 313.5 sq. mi. **Employment (2003):** 250,517 employed; 7.4% unemployed. **Per capita income (MSA):** $32,467; increase (2001-2002): 1.3%.

Mayor: Kay Barnes, Non-Partisan

History: settled by 1838 at confluence of the Missouri and Kansas rivers; inc. 1850.

Transportation: 1 intl. airport; a major rail center; more than 300 motor freight carriers; 7 barge lines. **Communications:** 9 TV, 43 radio stations. **Medical facilities:** 50 hosp.; 2 VA hosp. **Educational facilities:** 22 univ. and colleges. **Further information:** Greater Kansas City Chamber of Commerce, 911 Main St., Ste. 2600, Kansas City, MO 64105; www.kansascity.com; www.kcchamber.com

Laredo, Texas

Population (2003): 197,488 (98); **Pop. density:** 2,516 per sq. mi; **Pop. change (1990-2003):** +60.7 %. **Area:** 78.5 sq. mi. **Employment (2003):** 73,114 employed; 7.1% unemployed. **Per capita income (MSA):** $16,593; increase (2001-2002): 3.7%

Mayor: Elizabeth G. Flores, Democrat

History: founded by Spanish colonists in 1755; part of U.S. from 1848; fast growth fueled by immigration; became principal port of entry into Mexico.

Transportation: 1 intl. airport; 2 railroads; 3 interstate bus lines, 2 local bus lines. **Communications:** 3 TV, 10 radio stations; 2 newspapers. **Medical facilities:** 3 hosp. **Educational facilities:** 1 univ., 1 community college; 62 public schools, 29 private schools; 7 vocational training centers. **Further information:** Laredo Chamber of Commerce, P.O. Box 790, Laredo, TX 78042; www.laredochamber.com

Las Vegas, Nevada

Population (2003): 517,017 (30); **Pop. density:** 4,563 per sq. mi; **Pop. change (1990-2003):** +100.2%. **Area:** 113.3 sq. mi. **Employment (2003):** 272,469 employed; 5.2% unemployed. **Per capita income (MSA):** $29,396; increase (2001-2002): 0.8%.

Mayor: Oscar B. Goodman, Democrat

History: occupied by Mormons 1855-57; bought by railroad 1903; city of Las Vegas inc. 1911; gambling legalized 1931.

Transportation: 1 intl. airport; 1 railroad; monorail; bus system. **Communications:** 21 TV, 44 radio stations. **Medical facilities:** 11 hosp. **Educational facilities:** 1 univ., 2 state colleges; 277 pub. schools in area. **Further information:** Las Vegas Chamber of Commerce, 3720 Howard Hughes Parkway, Las Vegas, NV 89109-0937; www.lvchamber.com; www.lasvegasnevada.gov

Lexington, Kentucky

Population (2003): 266,798 (68); **Pop. density:** 938 per sq. mi; **Pop. change (1990-2003):** +18.4%. **Area:** 284.5 sq. mi. **Employment (2003):** 135,676 employed; 3.8% unemployed. **Per capita income (MSA):** $31,136; increase (2001-2002): 2.3%.

Mayor: Teresa Ann Isaac, Non-Partisan

History: site was founded and named in 1775 by hunters after the site of the opening battle of the Revolutionary War at Lexington, Mass.; settled 1779; chartered 1782; inc. as a city 1832.

Transportation: 6 comm. airlines; 2 railroads; city buses. **Communications:** 5 TV, 20 radio stations. **Medical facilities:** 5 general, 5 specialized hosp. **Educational facilities:** 2 univ., 4 colleges, 53 public schools: 6 high schools, 10 middle schools, 35 elementary schools, 2 technology schools. **Further information:** Greater Lexington Chamber of Commerce, 330 E. Main St., Lexington, KY 40507; www.lexchamber.com

Lincoln, Nebraska

Population (2003): 235,594 (75); **Pop. density:** 3,158 per sq. mi; **Pop. change (1990-2003):** +22.7%. **Area:** 74.6 sq. mi. **Employment (2003):** 134,159 employed; 4.2% unemployed. **Per capita income (MSA):** $30,022; increase (2001-2002): 2.6%.

Mayor: Coleen J. Seng, Non-Partisan

History: originally called Lancaster; chosen state capital 1867, renamed after Abraham Lincoln; inc. 1869.

Transportation: 1 airport; Greyhound; Amtrak, 2 railroads. **Communications:** 3 TV, 15 radio stations. **Medical facilities:** 6 hosp. including VA, rehabilitation facilities. **Educational facilities:** 3 univ., 3 voc.-tech./business colleges; 55 pub., 30 private schools, 3 focus programs. **Further information:** Chamber of Commerce, PO Box 83006, Lincoln, NE 68501-3006; www.lincoln.org; www.lcoc.com

Long Beach, California

Population (2003): 475,460 (32); **Pop. density:** 9,434 per sq. mi; **Pop. change (1990-2003):** +10.7%. **Area:** 50.4 sq. mi. **Employment (2003):** 208,743; employed; 6.5% unemployed. **Per capita income (MSA):** $32,547; increase (2001-2002): 1.5%.

Mayor: Beverly O'Neill, Non-Partisan

History: settled as early as 1784 by Spanish; by 1884 present site developed on harbor; inc. 1888; oil discovered 1921.

Transportation: 1 airport; 3 railroads; major intl. port; 4 bus co. with 40 bus lines, light rail service. **Communications:** 1 radio station, 1 CATV franchise. **Medical facilities:** 5 hosp. **Educational facilities:** 1 univ., 1 community college (2 campuses); 87 pub. schools in district. **Further information:** Long Beach City Hall, 333 W. Ocean Blvd., Long Beach, CA 90802; www.ci.longbeach.ca.us; www.lbchamber.com

Los Angeles, California

Population (2003): 3,819,951 (2); **Pop. density:** 8,143 per sq. mi; **Pop. change (1990-2003):** +9.6%. **Area:** 469.1 sq. mi. **Employment (2003):** 1,769,005 employed; 8.0% unemployed. **Per capita income (MSA):** $32,547; increase (2001-2002): 1.5%.

Mayor: James K. Hahn, Democrat

History: founded by Spanish 1781; captured by U.S. 1846; inc. 1850; grew rapidly after coming of railroads, 1876 & 1885; Hollywood a district of L.A.

Transportation: 1 intl. airport; 3 railroads; major freeway system; intracity bus and rail system. **Communications:** 21 TV, 70 radio stations. **Medical facilities:** 822 hosp. and clinics in metro. area. **Educational facilities:** 158 univ. and colleges (incl. junior, community, and other); 1,959 pub. schools; 1,470 private schools. **Further information:** Los Angeles Area Chamber of Commerce, 350 S. Bixel St., PO Box 513696, Los Angeles, CA 90051-1696; www.ci.la.ca.us; www.lachamber.org

Louisville, Kentucky

Population (2003): 248,762 (69); **Pop. density:** 4,006 per sq. mi; **Pop. change (1990-2003):** –7.5%. **Area:** 62.1 sq. mi. **Employment (2003):** 112,973 employed; 6.5% unemployed. **Per capita income (MSA):** $30,666; increase (2001-2002): 1.4%.
Mayor: Jerry Abramson, Democrat
History: settled 1778; named for Louis XVI of France; inc. 1828; base for Union forces in Civil War.
Transportation: 1 municipal airport, 2 private-craft airport; 1 terminal, 4 trunk-line railroads; metro bus line, Greyhound station; 5 barge lines. **Communications:** 6 TV, 21 radio stations, 2 educational. **Medical facilities:** 23 hosp. **Educational facilities:** 10 univ. and colleges, 32 business and vocational schools. **Further information:** Greater Louisville, Inc. Metro Chamber of Commerce, 614 W. Main St., Louisville, KY 40202; www.greaterlouisville.com

Lubbock, Texas

Population (2003): 206,481 (90); **Pop. density:** 1,799 per sq. mi; **Pop. change (1990-2003):** 10.9%. **Area:** 114.8 sq. mi. **Employment (2003):** 106,397 employed; 3.6% unemployed. **Per capita income (MSA):** $25,027; increase (2001-2002): 3.5%.
Mayor: Mark McDougal, Non-Partisan
History: settled 1879; laid out 1891; inc. 1909 through merger of two towns.
Transportation: 1 intl. airport; 2 railroads, bus line. **Communications:** 9 TV, 25 radio stations. **Medical facilities:** 7 hosp. **Educational facilities:** 3 univ., 1 junior college; 51 pub. schools. **Further information:** Chamber of Commerce, 1301 Broadway, Lubbock, TX 79401; www.ci.lubbock.tx.us; www.lubbockchamber.com

Madison, Wisconsin

Population (2003): 218,432 (81); **Pop. density:** 3,180 per sq. mi; **Pop. change (1990-2003):** +14.2%. **Area:** 68.7 sq. mi. **Employment (2003):** 135,312 employed; 2.9% unemployed. **Per capita income (MSA):** $34,650; increase (2001-2002): 3.0%.
Mayor: Dave Cieslewicz, Non-Partisan
History: first white settlement 1832; selected as site for state capital, named after James Madison, 1836; chartered 1856.
Transportation: 1 airport, 11 airlines; 1 intracity, 3 intercity bus systems; 3 freight rail lines. **Communications:** 10 TV, 26 radio stations, 3 cable providers. **Medical facilities:** 6 hosp., 92 clinics. **Educational facilities:** 7 colleges and univ., including main branch of Univ. of Wisconsin; 30 elem. schools, 11 middle schools, 5 high schools. **Further information:** Greater Madison Chamber of Commerce, PO Box 71, Madison, WI 53701-0071; www.cityofmadison.com; www.madisonchamber.com

Memphis, Tennessee

Population (2003): 645,978 (17); **Pop. density:** 2,313 per sq. mi; **Pop. change (1990-2003):** +5.8%. **Area:** 279.3 sq. mi. **Employment (2003):** 301,744 employed; 7.7% unemployed. **Per capita income (MSA):** $30,557; increase (2001-2002): 2.4%.
Mayor: Willie W. Herenton, Democrat
History: French, Spanish, and U.S. forts by 1797; settled by 1819; inc. as town 1826, as city 1840; surrendered charter to state 1879 after yellow fever epidemics; rechartered as city 1893.
Transportation: 1 intl. airport; 5 railroads; 1 bus system. **Communications:** 7 TV, 32 radio stations. **Medical facilities:** 20 hosp. **Educational facilities:** 17 univ. and colleges; 233 pub., 111 private schools. **Further information:** Memphis Regional Chamber, 22 N. Front St., Ste. 200, PO Box 224, Memphis, TN 38101-0224; www.ci.memphis.tn.us; www.memphischamber.com

Mesa, Arizona

Population (2003): 432,376 (40); **Pop. density:** 3,459 per sq. mi; **Pop. change (1990-2003):** +50.1%. **Area:** 125.0 sq. mi. **Employment (2003):** 221,619 employed; 4.2% unemployed. **Per capita income (MSA):** $28,481; decrease (2001-2002): –0.1%.
Mayor: Keno Hawker, Non-Partisan
History: founded by Mormons 1878; inc. 1883; population boomed fivefold 1960-80.
Transportation: 2 local airports; metro bus service. **Medical facilities:** 5 major hosp. **Educational facilities:** 1 univ., 3 colleges; 85 pub. schools. **Further information:** Convention and Visitor's Bureau and Mesa Chamber of Commerce, 120 N. Center, Mesa, AZ 85201; www.ci.mesa.az.us; www.mesacvb.com; www.mesachamber.org

Miami, Florida

Population (2003): 376,815 (46); **Pop. density:** 10,555 per sq. mi; **Pop. change (1990-2003):** +5.1%. **Area:** 35.7 sq. mi. **Employment (2003):** 171,997 employed; 10.4% unemployed. **Per capita income (MSA):** $32,373; increase (2001-2002): 1.4%.
Mayor: Manuel A. Diaz, Independent
History: site of fort 1836; settlement began 1870; inc. 1896; modern city developed into financial and recreation center; land speculation in 1920s added to city's growth, as did Cuban, Central and South American, and Haitian immigration since 1960.
Transportation: 1 intl. airport; seaport; Amtrak, transit rail system; 2 bus lines; 65 truck lines. **Communications:** 9 commercial, 2 educational TV stations; 48 radio stations. **Medical facilities:** 8 hosp.; VA hosp. **Educational facilities:** 6 univ. and colleges. **Further information:** Greater Miami Chamber of Commerce, Omni Intl. Complex, 1601 Biscayne Blvd., Miami, FL 33132; www.greatermiami.com; www.ci.miami.fl.us

Milwaukee, Wisconsin

Population (2003): 586,941 (19); **Pop. density:** 6,108 per sq. mi; **Pop. change (1990-2003):** –6.6%. **Area:** 96.1 sq. mi. **Employment (2003):** 249,670 employed; 9.7% unemployed. **Per capita income (MSA):** $34,308; increase (2001-2002): 1.9%.
Mayor: Tom Barrett, Democrat
History: Indian trading post by 1674; settlement began 1835; inc. as city 1848; famous beer industry.
Transportation: 1 intl. airport; 3 railroads; major port; 4 bus lines. **Communications:** 12 TV, 37 radio stations. **Medical facilities:** 8 hosp.; major medical center. **Educational facilities:** 7 univ. and colleges, 164 pub. schools. **Further information:** Greater Milwaukee Convention and Visitors' Bureau, 101 W. Wisconsin Avenue, Suite 425, Milwaukee, WI 53202; www.milwaukee.org; www.ci.mil.wi.us; www.mmac.org

Minneapolis, Minnesota

Population (2003): 373,188 (47); **Pop. density:** 6,798 per sq. mi; **Pop. change (1990-2003):** +1.3%. **Area:** 54.9 sq. mi. **Employment (2003):** 208,376 employed; 5.5% unemployed. **Per capita income (MSA):** $37,787; increase (2001-2002): 1.0%.
Mayor: R.T. Rybak, Democrat
History: site visited by Hennepin 1680; included in area of military reservations 1819; inc. 1867.
Transportation: 1 intl. airport; 5 railroads. **Communications:** 7 TV, 30 radio stations. **Medical facilities:** 7 hosp., incl. leading heart hosp. at Univ. of Minnesota. **Educational facilities:** 10 univ. and colleges; 121 pub., 28 private schools. **Further information:** City of Minneapolis Office of Pub. Affairs, 323M City Hall, 350 S. 5th Street, Minneapolis, MN 55415; www.ci.minneapolis.mn.us

Modesto, California

Population (2003): 206,872 (89); **Pop. density:** 5,779 per sq. mi; **Pop. change (1990-2003):** 25.6%. **Area:** 35.8 sq. mi. **Employment (2003):** 88,436 employed; 10.3% unemployed. **Per capita income (MSA):** $23,642; increase (2001-2002): 0.9%.
Mayor: Jim Ridenour, Republican
History: founded 1870 after the Gold Rush of 1849 brought an influx of settlers to the region; recent growth boosted by agriculture and immigration.
Transportation: 1 airport. **Communications:** 8 TV, 15 radio stations. **Medical facilities:** 2 hospitals. **Educational facilities:** 1 junior college, 5 public high schools. **Further information:** Modesto Convention & Visitor Bureau, 1150 Ninth St., Ste. C, PO Box 844, Modesto, CA 95353; www.visitmodesto.org

Montgomery, Alabama

Population (2003): 200,123 (93); **Pop. density:** 1,288 per sq. mi; **Pop. change (1990-2003):** +7.0%. **Area:** 155.4 sq. mi. **Employment:** 95,066 employed; 5.5% unemployed. **Per capita income (MSA):** $27,533; increase (2001-2002): 3.6%.
Mayor: Bobby N. Bright, Democrat
History: inc. as town 1819, as city 1837; became state capital 1846; first capital of Confederacy 1861.
Transportation: 3 airlines; 2 railroads; 2 bus lines; Alabama R. navigable to Gulf of Mexico. **Communications:** 4 TV, 2 CATV, 1 public TV, 16 radio stations. **Medical facilities:** 3 major hosp.; VA and 32 clinics. **Educational facilities:** 8 colleges and univ.; 35 pub., 35 private schools. **Further information:** Montgomery Area Chamber of Commerce, PO Box 79, Montgomery, AL 36101; www.montgomerychamber.com

Nashville, Tennessee

Population (2003): 544,765 (27); **Pop. density:** 1,151 per sq. mi; **Pop. change (1990-2003):** +11.5%. **Area:** 473.3 sq. mi. **Employment (2003):** 300,384 employed; 4.5% unemployed. **Per capita income (MSA):** $32,026; increase (2001-2002): 1.8%.
Mayor: Bill Purcell, Non-Partisan
History: settled 1779; first chartered 1806; became permanent state capital 1843; home of Grand Ole Opry.
Transportation: 1 airport; 1 railroad; bus line; transit system of buses and trolleys. **Communications:** 11 TV, 34 radio stations. **Medical facilities:** 14 hosp.; VA and speech-hearing center. **Educational facilities:** 17 universities and colleges, 129 pub. schools. **Further information:** Chamber of Commerce, 211 Commerce St., Ste 100, Nashville, TN 37201; www.nashvillechamber.com

Newark, New Jersey

Population (2003): 277,911 (64); **Pop. density:** 11,677 per sq. mi; **Pop. change (1990-2003):** 1.0%. **Area:** 23.8 sq. mi. **Employment (2003):** employed 104,408; 12.3% unemployed. **Per capita income (MSA):** $42,550; increase (2000-2001): 3.0%.
Mayor: Sharpe James, Democrat
History: settled by Puritans 1666; used as supply base by Washington 1776; inc. as town 1833, as city 1836.

Transportation: 1 intl. airport; 1 intl. seaport, 4 railroads; bus system; subways. **Communications:** 5 TV, 6 radio stations within city limits, 1 daily newspaper, 8 weekly papers. **Medical facilities:** 5 hosp. **Educational facilities:** 5 univ. and colleges; 58 pub. elementary schools, 13 junior and senior high schools, 10 special schools, 2 vocational schools, and 40 private schools. **Further information:** Newark Public Information Office, City of Newark, 920 Broad St., Newark, NJ 07102; www.ci.newark.nj.us; www.rbp.org

New Orleans, Louisiana

Population (2003): 469,032 (34); **Pop. density:** 2,597 per sq. mi; **Pop. change (1990-2003):** −5.6%. **Area:** 180.6 sq. mi. **Employment (2003):** 181,561 employed; 6.6% unemployed. **Per capita income (MSA):** $28,995; increase (2001-2002): 3.5%.

Mayor: C. Ray Nagin, Democrat

History: founded by French 1718; became major seaport on Mississippi R.; acquired by U.S. as part of Louisiana Purchase 1803; inc. as city 1805; Americans defeated British forces at the Battle of New Orleans in 1815.

Transportation: 2 airports; major railroad center; street car and bus lines. **Communications:** 8 TV, 26 radio stations. **Medical facilities:** 22 hosp.; 2 major research centers. **Educational facilities:** 10 univ. and 9 colleges. **Further information:** New Orleans Metropolitan Convention & Visitors Bureau, Inc., 1520 Sugar Bowl Dr., New Orleans, LA 70112; www.neworleanscvb.com; www.cityofno.com

New York, New York

Population (2003): 8,085,742 (1); **Pop. density:** 26,659 per sq. mi; **Pop. change (1990-2003):** +10.4%. **Area:** 303.3 sq. mi. **Employment (2003):** 3,374,898 employed; 8.4% unemployed. **Per capita income (MSA):** $40,680; increase (2001-2002): 0.0%.

Mayor: Michael Bloomberg, Republican

History: trading post established 1624; British took control from Dutch 1664 and named city New York; briefly U.S. capital; Washington inaugurated as president 1789; under new charter, 1898, city expanded to include 5 boroughs: The Bronx, Brooklyn, Queens, and Staten Island, as well as Manhattan; Sept. 11, 2001, terrorist attack destroyed World Trade Center, killed about 2,800.

Transportation: 3 intl. airports serve area; 2 rail terminals; major subway network that includes 28 routes; 244 bus routes; ferry system; 4 underwater tunnels. **Communications:** 17 TV, 67 radio stations. **Medical facilities:** 79 hosp.; 6 academic medical centers. **Educational facilities:** 100 univ. and colleges; 1,198 pub. schools. **Further information:** Convention and Visitors Bureau, 810 Seventh Ave., New York, NY 10019; www.nyc.gov; www.nycvisit.com

Norfolk, Virginia

Population (2003): 241,727 (72); **Pop. density:** 4,501 per sq. mi; **Pop. change (1990-2003):** −7.5%. **Area:** 53.7 sq. mi. **Employment (2003):** 87,576 employed, 6.5% unemployed. **Per capita income (MSA):** $28,365; increase (2001-2002): 2.9%.

Mayor: Paul D. Fraim, Non-Partisan

History: founded 1682; burned by patriots to prevent capture by British during Revolutionary War; rebuilt and inc. as town 1805, as city 1845; site of world's largest naval base; major east coast commercial port and cruise terminal.

Transportation: 1 intl. airport; 2 railroads; Amtrak; bus system; free downtown shuttle. **Communications:** 13 TV, 6 city-access TV, 27 radio stations. **Medical facilities:** 6 hosp. **Educational facilities:** 2 univ., 2 colleges, 1 medical school; 59 pub. schools. **Further information:** Norfolk Convention and Visitors Bureau, 232 E. Main St., Norfolk, VA 23510; www.norfolk.va.us; www.norfolkcvb.com

Oakland, California

Population (2003): 398,844 (43); **Pop. density:** 7,110 per sq. mi; **Pop. change (1990-2003):** +7.1%. **Area:** 56.1 sq. mi. **Employment (2003):** 178,708 employed; 10.6% unemployed. **Per capita income (MSA):** $46,920; decrease (2001-2002): −2.1%.

Mayor: Jerry Brown, Non-Partisan

History: area settled by Spanish 1820; inc. as city under present name 1854.

Transportation: 1 intl. airport; western terminus for 2 railroads; underground, 75-mi underwater subway. **Communications:** 1 TV, 3 radio stations in city. **Medical facilities:** 10 hosp. in MSA. **Educational facilities:** 12 East Bay colleges and univ.; 81 pub. schools. **Further information:** Oakland Metropolitan Chamber of Commerce, 475 14th St., Oakland, CA 94612-1903; www.oaklandchamber.com; www.oaklandnet.com

Oklahoma City, Oklahoma

Population (2003): 523,303 (29); **Pop. density:** 862 per sq. mi; **Pop. change (1990-2003):** +17.7%. **Area:** 607.0 sq. mi. **Employment (2003):** 248,778 employed; 5.6% unemployed. **Per capita income (MSA):** $27,877; increase (2001-2002): 1.4%.

Mayor: Mick Cornett, Non-Partisan

History: settled during land rush in Midwest 1889; inc. 1890; became capital 1910; oil discovered 1928. Bomb in 1995 destroyed federal office bldg., killed 168 people.

Transportation: 1 intl. airport; 1 railroad; pub. transit system; 1 major bus line. **Communications:** 6 TV, 20 radio stations. **Medical facilities:** 26 hosp. **Educational facilities:** 18 univ. and colleges; 83 pub., 36 private schools. **Further information:** Chamber of Commerce, Economic Development Division, 123 Park Ave., Oklahoma City, OK 73102; www.okcchamber.com; www.okccvb.org; www.greateroklahomacity.com.

Omaha, Nebraska

Population (2003): 404,267 (42); **Pop. density:** 3,494 per sq. mi; **Pop. change (1990-2003):** +20.4%. **Area:** 115.7 sq. mi. **Employment (2003):** 207,926 employed; 5.2% unemployed. **Per capita income (MSA):** $33,200; increase (2001-2002): 2.0%.

Mayor: Mike Fahey, Democrat

History: founded 1854; inc. 1857; large food-processing, telecommunications, information-processing center.

Transportation: 10 major airlines; 3 major railroads; intercity bus line. **Communications:** 7 TV, 18 radio stations. **Medical facilities:** 11 hosp.; institute for cancer research. **Educational facilities:** 5 univ., 6 colleges; 243 pub., 78 private schools. **Further information:** Greater Omaha Chamber of Commerce, 1301 Harney St., Omaha, NE 68102; www.ci.omaha.ne.us; www.access omaha.com

Orlando, Florida

Population (2003): 199,336 (94); **Pop. density:** 2,132 per sq. mi; **Pop. change (1990-2003):** +21.0%. **Area:** 93.5 sq. mi. **Employment (2003):** 121,820 employed; 5.3% unemployed. **Per capita income (MSA):** $27,587; increase (2001-2002): 1.6%.

Mayor: Buddy Dyer, Democrat.

History: Fort Gatlin built just south of present-day Orlando in 1838; name changed from Jernigan to Orlando, 1856; inc. 1875; Walt Disney World opened in 1971.

Transportation: 1 intl. airport; 2 bus lines. **Medical facilities:** 6 hosp. **Communications:** 7 TV, 20 radio stations. **Educational facilities:** 153 public schools; 4 tech schools; 5 colleges and univ. **Further Information:** Orlando/Orange County Convention and Visitors Bureau, 8723 International Dr., Suite 101, Orlando, FL 32819. www.orlandoinfo.com

Philadelphia, Pennsylvania

Population (2003): 1,479,339 (5); **Pop. density:** 10,950 per sq. mi; **Pop. change (1990-2003):** −6.7%. **Area:** 135.1 sq. mi. **Employment (2003):** 616,030 employed; 7.6% unemployed. **Per capita income (MSA):** $35,753; increase (2001-2002): 2.6%.

Mayor: John F. Street, Democrat

History: first settled by Swedes 1638; Swedes surrendered to Dutch 1654; settled by English and Scottish Quakers 1678; named Philadelphia 1682; chartered 1701; Continental Congresses convened 1774, 1775; Declaration of Independence signed here 1776; national capital 1790-1800; state capital 1683-1799.

Transportation: 1 major airport; 3 railroads; major freshwater port; subway, el, rail commuter, bus, and streetcar system. **Communications:** 2 major daily newspapers, 11 TV, 72 radio stations. **Medical facilities:** 40 hosp. **Educational facilities:** 27 univ. and colleges. **Further information:** Greater Philadelphia Chamber of Commerce, Business Information Center, 200 South Broad St., Suite 700, Philadelphia PA 19102; www.phila.gov; www.philachamber.com

Phoenix, Arizona

Population (2003): 1,388,416 (6); **Pop. density:** 2,924 per sq. mi; **Pop. change (1990-2003):** +41.2%. **Area:** 474.9 sq. mi. **Employment (2003):** 786,442 employed; 5.4% unemployed. **Per capita income (MSA):** $28,481; decrease (2001-2002): −0.1%.

Mayor: Phil Gordon, Democrat

History: settled 1870; inc. as city 1881; became territorial capital 1889.

Transportation: 1 intl. airport; 3 railroads; transcontinental bus line; pub. transit system. **Communications:** 12 TV, 17 radio stations. **Medical facilities:** 19 hosp., 1 medical research center. **Educational facilities:** 36 institutions of higher learning; 380 pub. schools (247 elem. and junior high schools, 35 senior high schools, 98 charter schools). **Further information:** Greater Phoenix Chamber of Commerce, 201 N. Central Ave., 27th fl., Phoenix, AZ 85073; www.phoenix.gov; www.phoenix chamber.com

Pittsburgh, Pennsylvania

Population (2003): 325,337 (54); **Pop. density:** 5,851 per sq. mi; **Pop. change (1990-2003):** −12.0%. **Area:** 55.6 sq. mi. **Employment (2003):** 149,453 employed; 5.5% unemployed. **Per capita income (MSA):** $32,381; increase (2001-2002): 2.7%.

Mayor: Tom J. Murphy, Democrat

History: settled around Ft. Pitt 1758; inc. as city 1816; has one of the largest inland ports; by Civil War, already a center for iron production.

Transportation: 1 intl. airport; 20 railroads; 2 bus lines; trolley/subway system. **Communications:** 6 TV, 26 radio stations. **Medical facilities:** 35 hosp.; VA installation. **Educational facilities:** 3 univ., 6 colleges; 93 pub. schools. **Further information:** Greater Pittsburgh Convention & Visitors Bureau, Regional Enterprise Tower, 30th Floor, 425 Sixth Ave., Pittsburgh, PA 15219; Pitts-

burgh Regional Alliance, Regional Enterprise Tower, 36th Floor, 425 Sixth Ave., Pittsburgh, PA 15219; www.visitpittsburgh.com; www.pittsburghregion.org

Plano, Texas

Population (2003): 241,991 (71); **Pop. density:** 3,380 per sq. mi; **Pop. change (1990-2003):** +88.0%. **Area:** 71.6 sq. mi. **Employment (2003):** 149,451 employed; 5.3% unemployed. **Per capita income (MSA):** $34,697; decrease (2000-2001): –1.9%.
Mayor: Pat Evans, Non-Partisan
History: settled 1846; inc. as city 1873.
Transportation: DART bus line; 2 DART (Dallas Area Rapid Transit) stations. **Communications:** 2 TV,1 radio station. **Medical facilities:** 2 full service hosp., 4 medical treatment centers. **Educational facilities:** 5 institutions of higher learning, 64 pub. schools. **Further information:** City of Plano Public Information Dept. 1520 K Ave., Suite 320, Plano, TX 75074; Plano Chamber of Commerce, PO Drawer 940287, Plano, TX 75094-0287; www. plano.gov; www.planochamber.org

Portland, Oregon

Population (2003): 538,544 (28); **Pop. density:** 4,010 per sq. mi; **Pop. change (1990-2003):** +23.1%. **Area:** 134.3 sq. mi. **Employment (2003):** 256,622 employed; 9.5% unemployed. **Per capita income (MSA):** $32,167; decrease (2001-2002): –0.5%.
Mayor: Vera Katz, Non-Partisan
History: settled by pioneers 1845; developed as trading center, aided by California Gold Rush 1849; city chartered 1851.
Transportation: 1 intl. airport; 2 major rail freight lines, Amtrak; mass transit bus, light rail, and street car system; marine port. **Com-munications:** 9 TV, 27 radio stations. **Medical facilities:** 12 hosp.; VA hosp. **Educational facilities:** 25 univ. and colleges, 1 community college. **Further information:** Portland Business Alliance, 520 SW Yamhill St., Ste. 100, Portland, OR 97204; www.portlandalliance.com

Raleigh, North Carolina

Population (2003): 316,802 (57); **Pop. density:** 2,764 per sq. mi; **Pop. change (1990-2003):** +52.3%. **Area:** 114.6 sq. mi. **Employment (2003):** 183,938 employed; 5.6% unemployed. **Per capita income (MSA):** $33,293; decrease (2001-2002): –1.9%.
Mayor: Charles Meeker, Democrat
History: named after Sir Walter Raleigh; site chosen for capital 1788; laid out 1792; inc. 1795; occupied by Gen. Sherman 1865.
Transportation: 1 intl. airport, 10 airlines, 6 commuter airlines; 3 railroads; 2 bus lines. **Communications:** 8 TV, 31 radio stations. **Medical facilities:** 3 hosp. **Educational facilities:** 6 univ. and colleges; 1 community college; 129 pub. schools (county). **Further information:** Chamber of Commerce, 800 S. Salisbury St., PO Box 2978, Raleigh, NC 27602; www.raleigh-wake.org; www.raleighchamber.org

Riverside, California

Population (2003): 281,514 (61); **Pop. density:** 3,605 per sq. mi; **Pop. change (1990-2003):** +24.3%. **Area:** 78.1 sq. mi. **Employment (2003):** 163,404 employed; 6.0% unemployed. **Per capita income (MSA):** $24,073; increase (2001-2002): 1.7%.
Mayor: Ronald O. Loveridge, Non-Partisan
History: founded 1870; inc. 1886; known for its citrus industry; home of the parent navel orange tree and the historic Mission Inn.
Transportation: municipal airport, intl. airport nearby; rail freight lines, commuter line; trolley/bus system; interstate freeways. **Communications:** 15 TV, 47 radio stations. **Medical facilities:** 3 hosp.; many clinics. **Educational facilities:** 3 univ., 1 community college. **Further information:** Chamber of Commerce, 3985 University Avenue, Riverside, CA 92501; www.ci. riverside.ca.us; www.riverside-chamber.com

Rochester, New York

Population (2003): 215,093 (84); **Pop. density:** 6,008 per sq. mi; **Pop. change (1990-2003):** –7.1%. **Area:** 35.8 sq. mi. **Employment (2003):** 105,990 employed; 9.8% unemployed. **Per capita income (MSA):** 30,499; increase (2001-2002): 1.5%.
Mayor: William A. Johnson Jr., Democrat
History: first permanent settlement 1812; inc. as village 1817, as city 1834; developed as Erie Canal town.
Transportation: 1 intl. airport; Amtrak; 2 bus lines; intracity transit service; Port of Rochester. **Communications:** 6 TV, 19 radio stations. **Medical facilities:** 8 general hosp. **Educational facilities:** 11 colleges, 3 community colleges. **Further information:** Rochester Business Alliance, 150 State St., Rochester, NY 14614; www.rochesterbusinessalliance.com; www.ci. rochester.ny.us

Sacramento, California

Population (2003): 445,335 (37); **Pop. density:** 4,582 per sq. mi; **Pop. change (1990-2003):** +20.6%. **Area:** 97.2 sq. mi. **Employment (2003):** 204,728 employed; 6.8% unemployed. **Per capita income (MSA):** $31,069; increase (2001-2002): 0.9%.
Mayor: Heather Fargo, Non-Partisan
History: settled 1839; important trading center during California Gold Rush 1840s; became state capital 1854.
Transportation: international, executive, and cargo airports; 2 mainline transcontinental rail carriers; bus and light rail system; Port of Sacramento. **Communications:** 8 TV, 34 radio stations; 3 cable TV cos. **Medical facilities:** 15 major hosp. **Educational facilities:** 7 colleges and univ., 5 community colleges, 81 pub. schools. **Further information:** Sacramento Metropolitan Chamber of Commerce, 917 Seventh St., Sacramento, CA 95814; www.metrochamber.com; www.cityofsacramento.org

St. Louis, Missouri

Population (2003): 332,223 (53); **Pop. density:** 5,367 per sq. mi; **Pop. change (1990-2003):** –16.3%. **Area:** 61.9 sq. mi. **Employment (2003):** 145,616 employed; 10.1% unemployed. **Per capita income (MSA):** $32,462; increase (2001-2002): 2.2%.
Mayor: Francis Slay, Democrat
History: founded 1764 as a fur trading post by French; acquired by U.S. 1803; chartered as city 1822; became independent city 1876; lies on Mississippi R., near confluence with Missouri R.
Transportation: 2 intl. airports; 2d largest rail center, 7 trunkline railroads; 3d largest inland port; Amtrak; Greyhound; bus & light rail; 32 barge lines, 550 motor freight carriers. **Communications:** 8 TV, 19 radio stations. **Medical facilities:** 8 hosp., incl. 2 teaching hosp.; VA hosp., 2 pediatric hosp. **Educational facilities:** 8 univ., 13 colleges and seminaries; 63 public schools; 29 parochial schools; 5 magnet/charter high schools. **Further information:** St. Louis Planning & Urban Design Agency, 1015 Locust St., Ste. 1200, St. Louis, MO 63101; stlouis.missouri.org

St. Paul, Minnesota

Population (2003): 280,404 (62); **Pop. density:** 5,311 per sq. mi; **Pop. change (1990-2003):** +3.0%. **Area:** 52.8 sq. mi. **Employment (2003):** 154,153 employed; 5.5% unemployed. **Per capita income (MSA):** $37,787; increase (2001-2002): 1.0%.
Mayor: Randy C. Kelly, Democrat
History: founded in early 1840s as "Pig's Eye Landing"; became capital of the Minnesota territory 1849 and chartered as St. Paul 1854.
Transportation: 1 intl., 1 business airport; 6 major rail lines; 2 interstate bus lines; pub. transit system. **Communications:** 9 TV, 47 radio stations. **Medical facilities:** 6 hosp. **Educational facilities:** 5 univ., 5 colleges; 1 technical, 3 law schools, 1 art and design college; 65 public, 39 private schools. **Further information:** St. Paul Area Chamber of Commerce, 401 N. Robert St., Ste. 150, St. Paul, MN 55101; www.visitsaintpaul.com; www.stpaulcvb.org

St. Petersburg, Florida

Population (2003): 247,610 (70); **Pop. density:** 4,155 per sq. mi; **Pop. change (1990-2003):** +3.8%. **Area:** 59.6 sq. mi. **Employment (2003):** 136,903 employed; 5.1% unemployed. **Per capita income (MSA):** $29,728; increase (2001-2002): 1.6%.
Mayor: Rick Baker, Non-Partisan
History: founded 1888; inc. 1903.
Transportation: 1 municipal, 2 intl. airports; Amtrak bus connection; county-wide public bus system; downtown 'Looper' bus service, largest municipal marina in Florida; 1 cruise port. **Communications:** 17 TV, 41 radio stations in area, 2 daily newspapers. **Medical facilities:** 4 major hosp.; VA hosp. **Educational facilities:** 1 univ., 1 college, 1 law school; 27 elem., 9 middle, 5 high schools; 3 alternative/vocational schools; 100 private schools. **Further information:** City of St. Petersburg , PO Box 2842, St. Petersburg, FL 33731; www.stpete.org

San Antonio, Texas

Population (2003): 1,214,725 (8); **Pop. density:** 2,980 per sq. mi; **Pop. change (1990-2003):** +29.8%. **Area:** 407.6 sq. mi. **Employment (2003):** 529,696 employed; 6.2% unemployed. **Per capita income (MSA):** $27,368; increase (2001-2002): 1.1%.
Mayor: Ed Garza, Non-Partisan
History: first Spanish garrison 1718; Battle at the Alamo in 1836; city subsequently captured by Texans; inc. 1837.
Transportation: 1 intl. airport; 2 railroads; 3 bus lines; pub. transit system. **Communications:** 14 TV, 49 radio stations. **Medical facilities:** 22 hosp.; major medical center. **Educational facilities:** 18 univ. and colleges; 16 pub. school districts. **Further information:** Chamber of Commerce, PO Box 1628, San Antonio, TX 78296; www.sachamber.org; www.sanantonio.gov

---

WORLD ALMANAC QUICK QUIZ

Can you rank these cities from largest (population, city proper) to smallest?

(a) Columbus, OH   (b) Cincinnati, OH   (c) Houston, TX   (d) Seattle, WA

For the answer look in this chapter, or see page 1008.

San Diego, California

Population (2003): 1,266,753 (7); **Pop. density:** 3,906 per sq. mi; **Pop. change (1990-2003):** +14.1%. **Area:** 324.3 sq. mi. **Employment (2003):** 650,333 employed; 4.3% unemployed. **Per capita income (MSA):** $34,872; increase (2001-2002): 2.8%.

Mayor: Dick Murphy, Republican

History: claimed by the Spanish 1542; first mission est. 1769; scene of conflict during Mexican-American War 1846; inc. 1850.

Transportation: 1 major airport; 1 railroad; major freeway system; bus system; trolley system. **Communications:** 9 TV, 25 radio stations, 2 cable providers. **Medical facilities:** 17 hosp. **Educational facilities:** 25 colleges and univ.; 177 pub. schools. **Further information:** San Diego Regional Chamber of Commerce, 402 W. Broadway, Ste. 1000, San Diego, CA 92101; www.sannet.gov; www.sdchamber.org

San Francisco, California

Population (2003): 751,682 (14); **Pop. density:** 16,096 per sq. mi; **Pop. change (1990-2003):** +3.8%. **Area:** 46.7 sq. mi. **Employment (2003):** 375,619; employed; 6.8% unemployed. **Per capita income (MSA):** $46,920; decrease (2001-2002): −2.1%.

Mayor: Gavin Newsom, Non-Partisan

History: nearby Farallon Islands sighted by Spanish 1542; city settled by 1776; claimed by U.S. 1846; became a major city during California Gold Rush 1849; inc. as city 1850; earthquake devastated city 1906.

Transportation: 1 major airport; intracity railway system; 2 railway transit systems; bus and railroad service; ferry system; 1 underwater tunnel. **Communications:** 8 TV; 8 radio stations. **Medical facilities:** 16 hosp. **Educational facilities:** 18 univ. and colleges, 116 pub. schools, 5 charter schools. **Further information:** San Francisco Convention & Visitors Bureau, 201 3rd St., Ste. 900, San Francisco, CA 94103; www.ci.sf.ca.us; www.sfchamber.com; www.sfvisitor.org

San Jose, California

Population (2003): 898,349 (11); **Pop. density:** 5,136 per sq. mi; **Pop. change (1990-2003):** +14.8%. **Area:** 174.9 sq. mi. **Employment (2003):** 415,290 employed; 9.6% unemployed. **Per capita income (MSA):** $45,925; decrease (2001-2002): −6.2%.

Mayor: Ron Gonzales, Democrat

History: founded by the Spanish 1777 between San Francisco and Monterey; state cap. 1849-51; inc. 1850.

Transportation: 1 intl. airport; 2 railroads; light rail system; bus system. **Communications:** 9 TV, 15 radio stations. **Medical facilities:** 6 hosp. **Educational facilities:** 6 univ. and colleges. **Further information:** San Jose Convention and Visitors Bureau, 100 Park Center Plaza, Ste. 560, San Jose, CA 95113; www.sanjoseca.gov; www.sanjose.org

Santa Ana, California

Population (2003): 342,510 (51); **Pop. density:** 12,639 per sq. mi; **Pop. change (1990-2003):** +16.6%. **Area:** 27.1 sq. mi. **Employment (2003):** 165,166 employed; 6.8% unemployed. **Per capita income (MSA):** $32,547; increase (2001-2002): 1.5%.

Mayor: Miguel Pulido, Non-Partisan

History: founded 1769; inc. as city 1869.

Transportation: 1 airport; 5 major freeways including main Los Angeles-San Diego artery; Amtrak. **Communications:** 14 TV, 28 radio stations. **Medical facilities:** 4 hosp. **Educational facilities:** 1 community college. **Further information:** Santa Ana Chamber of Commerce, 2020 N. Broadway, 2nd floor, Santa Ana, CA 92706; www.santaanachamber.com

Scottsdale, Arizona

Population (2003): 217,989 (83); **Pop. density:** 1,183 per sq. mi; **Pop. change (1990-2003):** +67.6%. **Area:** 184.2 sq. mi. **Employment (2003):** 114,924 employed; 3.6% unemployed. **Per capita income (MSA):** $28,481; decrease (2001-2002): −0.1%.

Mayor: Mary Manross, Democrat

History: founded 1888 by Army Chaplain Winfield Scott; inc. June 25, 1951; Frank Lloyd Wright built winter home here (Taliesin West); slogan "West's Most Western Town," by Mayor Malcolm White adopted 1951.

Transportation: 1 intl. airport in area, 1 local airport; regional bus system; local bus system; taxi system. **Communications:** 12 TV, 45 radio stations. **Medical facilities:** 2 general hospitals; Mayo Clinic. **Educational facilities:** 1 univ. nearby, 1 community college; 3 unified school districts. **Further information:** Scottsdale Convention and Visitors Bureau, 4343 N. Scottsdale Rd., Ste. 170, Scottsdale, AZ 85251; www.scottsdaleaz.gov; www.scottsdalecvb.com

Seattle, Washington

Population (2003): 569,101 (24); **Pop. density:** 6,783 per sq. mi; **Pop. change (1990-2003):** +10.2%. **Area:** 83.9 sq. mi. **Employment (2003):** 329,777 employed; 7.9% unemployed. **Per capita income (MSA):** $38,037; increase (2001-2002): 0.5%.

Mayor: Greg Nickels, Democrat

History: settled 1851; inc. 1869; suffered severe fire 1889; played prominent role during Alaska Gold Rush 1897; growth followed opening of Panama Canal 1914; center of aircraft industry WWII.

Transportation: 2 intl. airport; 2 railroads; ferries serve Puget Sound, Alaska, Canada. **Communications:** 7 TV, 39 radio stations. **Medical facilities:** 40 hosp. **Educational facilities:** 7 univ., 6 colleges, 11 community colleges. **Further information:** Greater Seattle Chamber of Commerce, 1301 5th Ave., Ste. 2500, Seattle, WA 98101-2611; www.ci.seattle.wa.us; www.seattlechamber.com

Shreveport, Louisiana

Population (2003): 198,364 (97); **Pop. density:** 1,924 per sq. mi; **Pop. change (1990-2003):** −0.1%. **Area:** 103.1 sq. mi. **Employment (2003):** 86,968 employed; 7.7% unemployed. **Per capita income (MSA):** $25,984; increase (2001-2002): 3.0%.

Mayor: Keith Hightower, Democrat

History: founded 1836 near site of a 180-mi logjam cleared by Capt. Henry Shreve; inc. 1839; oil discovered 1905.

Transportation: 2 airports, over 40 flights daily; 3 bus lines. **Communications:** 6 TV, 20 radio stations. **Medical facilities:** 16 hosp. **Educational facilities:** 2 univ., 4 colleges; approx. 100 pub. schools. **Further information:** Chamber of Commerce, PO Box 20074, 400 Edwards St., Shreveport, LA 71120; www.shreveportchamber.org

Stockton, California

Population (2003): 271,466 (65); **Pop. density:** 4,963 per sq. mi; **Pop. change (1990-2003):** +28.7%. **Area:** 54.7 sq. mi. **Employment (2003):** 101,502; employed; 11.9% unemployed. **Per capita income (MSA):** $24,119; increase (2001-2002): 0.3%.

Mayor: Ed Chavez, Non-Partisan

History: site purchased 1842; settled 1849; inc. 1850; chief distributing point for agric. products of San Joaquin Valley.

Transportation: 1 airport; deepwater inland seaport; 4 railroads; 2 bus lines, county bus system. **Communications:** 5 TV stations. **Medical facilities:** 4 hosp.; regional burn, cancer, heart centers. **Educational facilities:** 9 univ. and colleges; 58 pub. schools. **Further information:** Chamber of Commerce, 445 W. Weber Ave., Ste. 220, Stockton, CA 95203; www.stocktongov.com; www.stocktonchamber.org

Tacoma, Washington

Population (2003): 196,790 (100); **Pop. density:** 3,928 per sq. mi; **Pop. change (1990-2003):** +11.4%. **Area:** 50.1 sq. mi. **Employment (2003):** 97,470; employed, 8.9% unemployed. **Per capita income (MSA):** $38,037; increase (2001-2002): 0.5%.

Mayor: Bill Baarsma, Non-Partisan.

History: first European explorer of area was British Capt. George Vancouver 1792; colonized by Hudson's Bay Co. at Ft. Nisqually 1833; inc. 1884.

Transportation: 1 intl. airport; 3 railroads; transit and light rail systems; Port of Tacoma. **Communications:** 6 TV stations. **Medical facilities:** 7 hosp.; Army Medical Center; VA facility. **Educational facilities:** 3 univ., 4 colleges. **Further information:** Tacoma-Pierce County Chamber, PO Box 1933, Tacoma, WA 98401; www.cityoftacoma.org; www.tacomachamber.org

Tampa, Florida

Population (2003): 317,647 (55); **Pop. density:** 2,834 per sq. mi; **Pop. change (1990-2003):** +13.4%. **Area:** 112.1 sq. mi. **Employment (2003):** 188,340 employed; 5.1% unemployed. **Per capita income (MSA):** $29,728; increase (2001-2002): 1.6%.

Mayor: Pam Iorio, Non-Partisan

History: U.S. army fort on site 1824; inc. 1849; Ybor City National Historical Landmark district.

Transportation: 1 intl. airport; Port of Tampa; CSX rail, Amtrak Rail; bus system; downtown streetcar. **Communications:** 16 TV, 22 radio stations. **Medical facilities:** 21 hosp. **Educational facilities:** 6 univ. and colleges; 178 pub. schools. **Further information:** Greater Tampa Chamber of Commerce, 615 Channelside Drive, Ste. 108, P.O. Box 420, Tampa, FL 33601; www.tampachamber.com

Toledo, Ohio

Population (2003): 308,973 (58); **Pop. density:** 3,833 per sq. mi; **Pop. change (1990-2003):** −7.2%. **Area:** 80.6 sq. mi. **Employment (2003):** 148,062 employed; 9.1% unemployed. **Per capita income (MSA):** $28,612; increase (2001-2002): 2.4%.

Mayor: Jack Ford, Democrat

History: site of Ft. Industry 1794; Battles of Ft. Meigs and Ft. Timbers 1812; figured in "Toledo War" 1835-36 between Ohio and Michigan over borders; inc. 1837.

Transportation: 2 major airlines; 4 railroads; 53 motor freight lines; 16 interstate bus lines. **Communications:** 6 TV, 22 radio stations. **Medical facilities:** 5 major hosp. complexes. **Educational facilities:** 6 univ. and colleges. **Further information:** Toledo Area Chamber of Commerce, 300 Madison Ave., Ste. 200, Toledo, OH 43604; www.toledochamber.com

Tucson, Arizona

Population (2003): 507,658 (31); **Pop. density:** 2,607 per sq. mi; **Pop. change (1990-2003):** +25.2%. **Area:** 194.7 sq. mi. **Employment (2003):** 252,536 employed; 4.8% unemployed. **Per capita income (MSA):** $25,278; increase (2001-2002): 2.6%.

Mayor: Robert E. Walkup, Republican

History: settled 1775 by Spanish as a presidio; acquired by U.S. in Gadsden Purchase 1853; inc. 1877.

Transportation: 1 intl. airport; 2 railroads; 1 bus system, 1 trolley. **Communications:** 10 TV, 34 radio stations. **Medical facilities:** 12 hosp. **Educational facilities:** 2 univ., 1 community college; 216 pub. schools. **Further information:** Tucson Metropolitan Chamber of Commerce, PO Box 991, Tucson, AZ 85702; www.ci.tucson.az.us; www.tucsonchamber.org

Tulsa, Oklahoma

Population (2003): 387,807 (44); **Pop. density:** 2,124 per sq. mi; **Pop. change (1990-2003):** +5.6%. **Area:** 182.6 sq. mi. **Employment (2003):** 207,814 employed; 6.9% unemployed. **Per capita income (MSA):** $30,627; increase (2001-2002): 1.0%.

Mayor: Bill LaFortune, Republican

History: settled in 1836 by Creek Indians; modern town founded 1882 and inc. 1898; oil discovered early 20th century; emerging as telecommunications hub.

Transportation: 1 intl. airport; 5 rail lines; 5 bus lines; transit bus system. **Communications:** 130 TV, 31 radio stations. **Medical facilities:** 10 hosp. **Educational facilities:** 8 univ. and colleges; 85 pub., 39 private schools. **Further information:** Tulsa Metro Chamber, 2 West 2nd Tower II, Ste. 150, Tulsa, OK 74103; www.tulsachamber.com; www.cityoftulsa.org

Virginia Beach, Virginia

Population (2003): 439,467 (39); **Pop. density:** 1,770 per sq. mi; **Pop. change (1990-2003):** +11.8%. **Area:** 248.3 sq. mi. **Employment (2003):** 212,649 employed; 3.7% unemployed. **Per capita income (MSA):** $28,365; increase (2001-2002): 2.9%.

Mayor: Meyera E. Oberndorf, Independent

History: area founded by Capt. John Smith 1607; formed by merger with Princess Anne Co. 1963.

Transportation: 1 airport; 2 railroads; 1 bus line; pub. transit system. **Communications:** 8 TV, 44 radio stations. **Medical facilities:** 2 hosp. **Educational facilities:** 1 univ., 2 colleges; 87 pub. schools. **Further information:** Virginia Beach Dept. of Economic Development, 222 Central Park Ave., Suite 1000, Virginia Beach, VA 23462; Virginia Beach Convention and Visitors Bureau, 2100 Parks Ave., Virginia Beach, VA 23451; www.yesvirginia beach.com; www.vbfun.com

Washington, District of Columbia

Population (2003): 563,384 (25); **Pop. density:** 9,176 per sq. mi; **Pop. change (1990-2003):** −7.2%. **Area:** 61.4 sq. mi. **Employment (2003):** 281,190 employed; 7.0% unemployed. **Per capita income (MSA):** $42,773; increase (2001-2002): 1.3%.

Mayor: Anthony A. Williams, Democrat

History: U.S. capital; site at Potomac R. chosen by George Washington 1790 on land ceded from VA and MD (portion S of Potomac returned to VA 1846); Congress first met 1800; inc. 1802; sacked by British, War of 1812; one of the most important Civil War battles was fought at Ft. Stevens.

Transportation: 3 intl. airports in area; Amtrak, 6 other passenger & cargo rail lines; Metrobus/Metrorail transit system; bus line. **Communications:** 5 TV, 61 radio stations. **Medical facilities:** 16 hosp. **Educational facilities:** 10 univ. and colleges. **Further information:** DC Chamber of Commerce, 1213 K Street NW, Washington, DC 20005; www.dc.gov; www.dcchamber.org

Wichita, Kansas

Population (2003): 354,617 (50); **Pop. density:** 2,611 per sq. mi; **Pop. change (1990-2003):** +16.6%. **Area:** 135.8 sq. mi. **Employment (2003):** 167,954 employed; 7.9% unemployed. **Per capita income (MSA):** $29,587; increase (2001-2002): 1.1%.

Mayor: Carlos Mayans, Non-Partisan

History: founded 1864; inc. 1871.

Transportation: 2 airports; 3 major rail freight lines; 2 bus lines. **Communications:** 80 TV, 34 radio stations. **Medical facilities:** 7 hosp., 2 psychiatric rehab. centers. **Educational facilities:** 3 univ., 1 medical school; 96 pub. schools. **Further information:** Chamber of Commerce, 350 W. Douglas Ave., Wichita, KS 67202; www.wichitakansas.org; www.wichita.gov; www.gwedc.org

Yonkers, New York

Population (2003): 197,388 (99); **Pop. density:** 10,905 per sq. mi; **Pop. change (1990-2003):** +4.9%. **Area:** 18.1 sq. mi. **Employment (2003):** 90,079 employed; 5.4% unemployed. **Per capita income (MSA):** $40,680; increase (2001-2002): 0.0%.

Mayor: Phil Amicone, Republican

History: founded 1641 by the Dutch; inc. as town 1855; chartered as city 1872; directly north of NYC.

Transportation: intracity bus system; rail service. **Communications:** Daily newspaper; govt., public, educational access channels; also see New York, New York. **Medical facilities:** 3 hosp. **Educational facilities:** 3 colleges; 41 pub. schools. **Further information:** Chamber of Commerce, 20 S. Broadway, 12th fl., Yonkers, NY 10701; www.cityofyonkers.com; www.yonkers chamber.com; www.yonkersprogress.com

Fastest-Growing Big Cities*

City	2002 population	1990 population	% change
1. Henderson, NV	206,153	65,109	216.6
2. Chandler, AZ	202,016	90,703	122.7
3. Las Vegas, NV	508,604	259,834	95.7
4. Plano, TX.........	238,091	128,507	85.3
5. Scottsdale, AZ	215,779	130,086	65.9
6. Glendale, AZ	230,564	150,867	52.8
7. Mesa, AZ	426,841	290,212	47.1
8. Bakersfield, CA	260,969	183,959	41.9
9. Raleigh, NC	306,944	220,425	39.3
10. Phoenix, AZ	1,371,960	988,983	38.7

Fastest-Shrinking Big Cities*

City	2002 population	1990 population	% change
1. St. Louis, MO	338,353	396,685	−14.7
2. Baltimore, MD	638,614	736,014	−13.2
3. Buffalo, NY	287,698	327,931	−12.3
4. Pittsburgh, PA	327,898	370,139	−11.4
5. Cincinnati, OH.....	323,885	364,553	−11.2
6. Detroit, MI........	925,051	1,027,946	−10.01
7. Birmingham, AL ...	239,416	265,940	−9.97
8. Norfolk, VA	239,036	261,250	−8.5
9. Cleveland, OH.....	467,851	505,450	−7.4
10. Toledo, OH	309,106	332,832	−7.1

*Among those with populations of 200,000 or more, based on 2002 U.S. Census Bureau estimates.

Percent of Population by Race and Hispanic Origin, 10 Largest Cities, 2000

City	White	Black or African-Amer.	Amer. Indian, Alaska Native	Asian	Hawaiian & Other Pacific Isl.	Some other race[1]	Two or more races	Hispanic or Latino (of any race)
1. New York, NY	44.7	26.6	0.5	9.8	0.1	13.4	4.9	27.0
2. Los Angeles, CA....	46.9	11.2	0.8	10.0	0.2	25.7	5.2	46.5
3. Chicago, IL........	42.0	36.8	0.4	4.3	0.1	13.6	2.9	26.0
4. Houston, TX	49.3	25.3	0.4	5.3	0.1	16.5	3.1	37.4
5. Philadelphia, PA	45.0	43.2	0.3	4.5	0.0	4.8	2.2	8.5
6. Phoenix, AZ	71.1	5.1	2.0	2.0	0.1	16.4	3.3	34.1
7. San Diego, CA	60.2	7.9	0.6	13.6	0.5	12.4	4.8	25.4
8. Dallas, TX.........	50.8	25.9	0.5	2.7	0.0	17.2	2.7	35.6
9. San Antonio, TX	67.7	6.8	0.8	1.6	0.1	19.3	3.7	58.7
10. Detroit, MI.........	12.3	81.6	0.3	1.0	0.0	2.5	2.3	5.0

(1) Persons who, instead of checking off a race shown, filled in a designation under "some other race."

STATES AND OTHER AREAS OF THE U.S.

Sources: Population: U.S. Commerce Dept., Bureau of the Census—Census 2000: April 1, 2000, and July 2003 est. (including armed forces stationed in the state). Area: Bureau of the Census, Geography Division; forested land: Agriculture Dept., Forest Service. Lumber production: Bureau of the Census, Industry Division; mineral production: Dept. of Interior, Office of Mineral Information; commercial fishing: Commerce Dept., Natl. Marine Fisheries Service; new private housing: Bureau of the Census, Residential Construction Branch. Personal per capita income: Commerce Dept., Bureau of Economic Analysis; sales tax: CCH Inc.; unemployment: Labor Dept., Bureau of Labor Statistics. Tourism: Travel Association of America. Lottery figures (not all states have a lottery): *La Fleur's Lottery World.* Finance: Federal Deposit Insurance Corp. Federal employees: Labor Dept., Office of Personnel Management. Energy: Energy Dept., Energy Information Administration. Other information from sources in individual states. Some data on Outlying U.S. Areas & Other Islands provided by the CIA World Factbook.

NOTE: Population density is for land area only. Categories under racial distribution may not add to 100% due to rounding. "Nat. AK" (Native Alaskans) includes Eskimos and Aleuts. **Hispanic population may be any race** and is dispersed among racial categories, besides being listed separately. Nonfuel mineral values for some states exclude small amounts to avoid disclosing proprietary data. Categories under employment distribution are not all-inclusive. **Famous Persons lists may include nonnatives** associated with the state as well as persons born there. Website addresses listed may not be official state sites and are not endorsed by *The World Almanac;* all website addresses are subject to change.

Alabama
Heart of Dixie, Camellia State

People. Population (2003 est.): 4,500,752; rank: 23; **net change** (2002-2003): 0.5%. **Pop. density:** 88.7 per sq mi. **Racial distribution** (2000): 71.1% white; 26.0% black; 0.7% Asian; 0.5% Native American/Nat. AK; <0.1% Hawaiian/Pacific Islander; 0.7% other race; 2 or more races, 1.0%. **Hispanic pop.** (any race): 1.7%.

Geography. Total area: 52,419 sq mi; rank: 30. **Land area:** 50,744 sq mi; rank: 28. **Acres forested:** 23.0 mil. **Location:** East South Central state extending N-S from Tenn. to the Gulf of Mexico; E of the Mississippi River. **Climate:** long, hot summers; mild winters; generally abundant rainfall. **Topography:** coastal plains, including Prairie Black Belt, give way to hills, broken terrain; highest elevation, 2,407 ft. **Capital:** Montgomery.

Economy. Chief industries: pulp & paper, chemicals, electronics, apparel, textiles, primary metals, lumber and wood products, food processing, fabricated metals, automotive tires, oil and gas exploration. **Chief manuf. goods:** electronics, cast iron & plastic pipe, fabricated steel products, ships, paper products, chemicals, steel, mobile homes, fabrics, poultry processing, soft drinks, furniture, tires. **Chief crops:** cotton, greenhouse & nursery, peanuts, sweet potatoes, potatoes and other vegetables. **Livestock** (Jan. 2004): 1.36 mil. cattle/calves; (Jan. 2003): 165,000 hogs/pigs; (Dec. 2003): 14.4 mil. chickens (excl. broilers); 1.0 bil. broilers. **Timber/lumber** (est. 2002): 2.5 bil bd. ft.; pine, hardwoods. **Nonfuel minerals** (est. 2003): $863 mil.; cement (portland), stone (crushed), lime, sand and gravel (construction), cement (masonry). **Commercial fishing** (2002): $35.9 mil. **Chief port:** Mobile. **Principal internat. airports at:** Birmingham, Huntsville. **New private housing** (2003): 26,012 units/$2.9 bil. **Gross state product** (2001): $121.5 bil. **Employment distrib.** (May 2004): 19.2% govt.; 19.9% trade/trans./util.; 15.3% mfg.; 10% ed./health serv.; 10% prof./bus serv.; 8.4% leisure/hosp.; 5.1% finance; 5.4% constr.; 1.6% info. **Per cap. pers. income** (2003): $24,028. **Sales tax** (2004): 4.0%. **Unemployment** (2003): 5.8%. **Tourism expends.** (2002): $5.3 bil.

Finance. FDIC-insured commercial banks (2003): 151. **Deposits:** $146.3 bil. **FDIC-insured savings institutions** (2003): 11. **Assets:** $2.1 bil.

Federal govt. Fed. civ. employees (Mar. 2003): 35,223. **Avg. salary:** $58,150. **Notable fed. facilities:** Marshall Space Flight Ctr.; Maxwell/Gunter AFB; Ft. Rucker; Intern'l. Fertilizer Development Ctr.; Navy Station & U.S. Corps of Engineers; Redstone Arsenal.

Energy. Electricity production (est. 2003, kWh by source): Coal: 76.2 bil; Petroleum: 186 mil; Gas: 7.7 bil; Hydroelectric: 12.0 bil; Nuclear: 31.7 bil.

State data. Motto: We dare defend our rights. **Flower:** Camellia. **Bird:** Yellowhammer. **Tree:** Southern Longleaf pine. **Song:** Alabama. **Entered union** Dec. 14, 1819; rank, 22nd. **State fair:** Regional and county fairs held in Sept. and Oct.; no state fair.

History. Alabama was inhabited by the Creek, Cherokee, Chickasaw, Alabama, and Choctaw peoples when the Europeans arrived. The first Europeans were Spanish explorers in the early 1500s. The French made the first permanent settlement on Mobile Bay, 1702. France later gave up the entire region to England under the Treaty of Paris, 1763. Spanish forces took control of the Mobile Bay area, 1780, and it remained Spanish until U.S. troops seized the area, 1813. Most of present-day Alabama was held by the Creeks until Gen. Andrew Jackson broke their power, 1814, and they were removed to Oklahoma Territory. The state seceded, 1861, and the Confederate states were organized Feb. 4, at Montgomery, the first capital; it was readmitted, 1868.

Tourist attractions. First White House of the Confederacy, Civil Rights Memorial, Alabama Shakespeare Festival, all Montgomery; Ivy Green, Helen Keller's birthplace, Tuscumbia; Civil Rights Museum, statue of Vulcan, Birmingham; Carver Museum, Tuskegee; W. C. Handy Home & Museum, Florence; Alabama Space and Rocket Center, Huntsville; Moundville State Monument, Moundville; Pike Pioneer Museum, Troy; USS *Alabama* Memorial Park, Mobile; Russell Cave Natl. Monument, near Bridgeport: a detailed record of occupancy by humans from about 10,000 BC to AD 1650.

Famous Alabamians. Hank Aaron, Tallulah Bankhead, Hugo L. Black, Paul "Bear" Bryant, George Washington Carver, Nat King Cole, William C. Handy, Bo Jackson, Helen Keller, Coretta Scott King, Harper Lee, Joe Louis, Willie Mays, John Hunt Morgan, Jim Nabors, Jesse Owens, Condoleezza Rice, George Wallace, Booker T. Washington, Hank Williams.

Tourist information. Bureau of Tourism and Travel, 401 Adams Avenue, Suite 126, Montgomery, AL 36104; 1-800-ALABAMA out of state. **Website:** www.tourism.state.al.us

Website. www.alabama.gov

Alaska
The Last Frontier (unofficial)

People. Population (2003 est.): 648,818; rank: 47; **net change** (2002-2003): 1.1%. **Pop. density:** 1.1 per sq mi. **Racial distribution** (2000): 69.3% white; 3.5% black; 4.0% Asian; 15.6% Native American/Nat. AK; 0.5% Hawaiian/Pacific Islander; 1.6% other race; 2 or more races, 5.4%. **Hispanic pop.** (any race): 4.1%.

Geography. Total area: 663,267 sq mi; rank: 1. **Land area:** 571,951 sq mi; rank: 1. **Acres forested:** 126.9 mil. **Location:** NW corner of North America, bordered on E by Canada. **Climate:** SE, SW, and central regions, moist and mild; far north extremely dry. Extended summer days, winter nights, throughout. **Topography:** includes Pacific and Arctic mountain systems, central plateau, and Arctic slope. Mt. McKinley, 20,320 ft, is the highest point in North America. **Capital:** Juneau.

Economy. Chief industries: petroleum, tourism, fishing, mining, forestry, transportation, aerospace. **Chief manuf. goods:** fish products, lumber & pulp, furs. **Agriculture: Chief crops:** greenhouse products, barley, oats, hay, potatoes, lettuce, aquaculture. **Livestock** (Jan. 2004): 12,500 cattle/calves; (Jan. 2003): 1,500 hogs/pigs. **Timber/lumber:** (figs. undisclosed); spruce, yellow cedar, hemlock. **Nonfuel minerals** (est. 2003): $1.1 bil.; zinc, gold, lead, sand and gravel (construction), silver. **Commercial fishing** (2002): $811.5 mil. **Chief ports:** Anchorage, Dutch Harbor, Kodiak, Seward, Skagway, Juneau, Sitka, Valdez, Wrangell. **Principal internat. airports at:** Anchorage, Fairbanks, Juneau. **New private housing** (2003): 3,545 units/$562 mil. **Gross state product** (2001): $28.6 bil. **Employment distrib.** (May 2004): 27.1% govt.; 20.6% trade/trans./util.; 3.1% mfg.; 11.3% ed./health serv.; 7.7% prof./bus serv.; 10.2% leisure/hosp.; 4.8% finance; 5.8% constr.; 2.3% info. **Per cap. pers. income** (2003): $33,568. **Sales tax** (2004): none. **Unemployment** (2003): 8%. **Tourism expends.** (2002): $1.3 bil.

Finance. FDIC-insured commercial banks (2003): 5. **Deposits:** $2.6 bil. **FDIC-insured savings institutions** (2003): 2. **Assets:** $361 mil.

Federal govt. Fed. civ. employees (Mar. 2003): 12,323. **Avg. salary:** $51,391. **Notable fed. facilities:** Ft. Richardson; Ft. Wainwright; Elmendorf AFB; Eilson AFB.

Energy. Electricity production (est. 2003, kWh by source): Coal: 168 mil; Petroleum: 756 mil; Gas: 3.2 bil; Hydroelectric: 1.7 bil.

State data. Motto: North to the future. **Flower:** Forget-Me-Not. **Bird:** Willow ptarmigan. **Tree:** Sitka spruce. **Song:** Alas-

ka's Flag. **Entered union** Jan. 3, 1959; rank, 49th. **State fair** at Palmer; late Aug.-early Sept.

History. Early inhabitants were the Tlingit-Haida people and tribes of the Athabascan family. The Aleut and Inuit (Eskimo), who arrived about 4,000 years ago from Siberia, lived in the coastal areas. Vitus Bering, a Danish explorer working for Russia, was the first European to land in Alaska, 1741. The first permanent Russian settlement was established on Kodiak Island, 1784. In 1799, the Russian-American Co. controlled the region, and the first chief manager, Aleksandr Baranov, set up headquarters at Archangel, near present-day Sitka. Sec. of State William H. Seward bought Alaska from Russia for $7.2 mil in 1867, a bargain some called "Seward's Folly." In 1896, gold was discovered in the Klondike region, and the famed gold rush began. Alaska became a territory in 1912.

Tourist attractions. Inside Passage; Portage Glacier; Mendenhall Glacier; Ketchikan Totems; Glacier Bay Natl. Park and Preserve; Denali Natl. Park, one of N. America's great wildlife sanctuaries, surrounding Mt. McKinley, N. America's highest peak; Mt. Roberts Tramway, Juneau; Pribilof Islands fur seal rookeries; restored St. Michael's Russian Orthodox Cathedral, Sitka; White Pass & Yukon Route railroad; Skagway; Katmai Natl. Park & Preserve.

Famous Alaskans. Tom Bodett, Susan Butcher, Ernest Gruening, Jewel (Kilcher), Gov. Tony Knowles, Sydney Laurence, Libby Riddles, Jefferson "Soapy" Smith.

Tourist information. Alaska Travel Industry Association2600 Cordova St., Ste. 201, Juneau, AK 99503; 1-800-327-9372. **Website:** www.travelalaska.com **Website.** www.state.ak.us

Arizona
Grand Canyon State

People. Population (2003 est.): 5,580,811; rank: 18; **net change** (2002-2003): 2.6%. **Pop. density:** 49.1 per sq mi. **Racial distribution** (2000): 75.5% white; 3.1% black; 1.8% Asian; 5.0% Native American/Nat. AK; 0.1% Hawaiian/Pacific Islander; 11.6% other race; 2 or more races, 2.9%. **Hispanic pop.** (any race): 25.3%.

Geography. Total area: 113,998 sq mi; rank: 6. **Land area:** 113,635 sq mi; rank: 6. **Acres forested:** 19.4 mil. **Location:** in the southwestern U.S. **Climate:** clear and dry in the southern regions and northern plateau; high central areas have heavy winter snows. **Topography:** Colorado plateau in the N, containing the Grand Canyon; Mexican Highlands running diagonally NW to SE; Sonoran Desert in the SW. **Capital:** Phoenix.

Economy. Chief industries: manufacturing, construction, tourism, mining, agriculture. **Chief manuf. goods:** electronics, printing & publishing, foods, prim. & fabric. metals, aircraft and missiles, apparel. **Chief crops:** cotton, lettuce, cauliflower, broccoli, sorghum, barley, corn, wheat, citrus fruits. **Livestock** (Jan. 2004): 850,000 cattle/calves; 114,000 sheep/lambs; (Jan. 2003): 127,000 hogs/pigs. **Timber/lumber** (est. 2002): 62 mil bd. ft.; pine, fir, spruce. **Nonfuel minerals** (est. 2003): $2.1 bil.; copper, sand and gravel (construction), cement (portland), molybdenum concentrates, stone (crushed). **Principal internat. airports at:** Phoenix, Tucson. **New private housing** (2003): 73,070 units/$10.4 bil. **Gross state product** (2001): $160.7 bil. **Employment distrib.** (May 2004): 17.4% govt.; 19.1% trade/trans./util.; 7.3% mfg.; 11% ed./health serv.; 13.9% prof./bus serv.; 10.2% leisure/hosp.; 6.9% finance; 8.1% constr.; 2% info. **Per cap. pers. income** (2003): $26,838. **Sales tax** (2004): 5.6%. **Unemployment** (2003): 5.6%. **Tourism expends.** (2002): $9.9 bil. **Lottery** (2003): total sales: $628.06 mil; net income: $92.5 mil.

Finance. FDIC-insured commercial banks (2003): 46. **Deposits:** $19.7 bil. **FDIC-insured savings institutions** (2003): 4. **Assets:** $820 mil.

Federal govt. Fed. civ. employees (Mar. 2003): 32,076. **Avg. salary:** $49,323. **Notable fed. facilities:** Luke, Davis-Monthan AF bases; Ft. Huachuca Army Base; Yuma Proving Grounds.

Energy. Electricity production (est. 2003, kWh by source): Coal: 37.7 bil; Petroleum: 53 mil; Gas: 4.2 bil; Hydroelectric: 7.2 bil; Nuclear: 28.6 bil; Other: 42 mil.

State data. Motto: Ditat Deus (God enriches). **Flower:** Blossom of the Saguaro cactus. **Bird:** Cactus wren. **Tree:** Paloverde. **Song:** Arizona. **Entered union** Feb. 14, 1912; rank, 48th. **State fair** at Phoenix; Oct.-early Nov.

History. Anasazi, Mogollon, and Hohokam civilizations inhabited the area c 300 BC-AD 1300, later Pueblo peoples; Navajo and Apache came c 15th cent. Marcos de Niza, a Franciscan, and Estevanico, a former black slave, explored, 1539; Spanish explorer Francisco Vásquez de Coronado vis-

ited, 1540. Eusebio Francisco Kino, a Jesuit missionary, taught Indians 1692-1711, and left missions. Tubac, a Spanish fort, became the first European settlement, 1752. Spain ceded Arizona to Mexico, 1821. The U.S. took over, 1848, after the Mexican War. The area below the Gila River was obtained from Mexico in the Gadsden Purchase, 1853. Arizona became a territory, 1863. Apache wars ended with Geronimo's surrender, 1886.

Tourist attractions. The Grand Canyon; Painted Desert; Petrified Forest Natl. Park; Canyon de Chelly; Meteor Crater; London Bridge, Lake Havasu City; Biosphere 2, Oracle; Navajo Natl. Monument; Sedona.

Famous Arizonans. Bruce Babbitt, Cochise, Alice Cooper, Geronimo, Barry Goldwater, Zane Grey, Carl Hayden, George W. P. Hunt, Helen Jacobs, Bil Keane, Percival Lowell, John McCain, William H. Pickering, John J. Rhodes, Morris Udall, Stewart Udall, Frank Lloyd Wright.

Tourist information. Arizona Office of Tourism, 1110 W. Washington St., Ste. 155, Phoenix, AZ 85007; 1-866-275-5816. **Website:** www.arizonaguide.com **Website.** www.az.gov

Arkansas
The Natural State, The Razorback State

People. Population (2003 est.): 2,725,714; rank: 32; **net change** (2002-2003): 0.7%. **Pop. density:** 52.3 per sq mi. **Racial distribution** (2000): 80.0% white; 15.7% black; 0.8% Asian; 0.8% Native American/Nat. AK; 0.1% Hawaiian/Pacific Islander; 1.5% other race; 2 or more races, 1.3%. **Hispanic pop.** (any race): 3.2%.

Geography. Total area: 53,179 sq mi; rank: 29. **Land area:** 52,068 sq mi; rank: 27. **Acres forested:** 18.8 mil. **Location:** in the west south-central U.S. **Climate:** long, hot summers, mild winters; generally abundant rainfall. **Topography:** eastern delta and prairie, southern lowland forests, and the northwestern highlands, which include the Ozark Plateaus. **Capital:** Little Rock.

Economy. Chief industries: manufacturing, agriculture, tourism, forestry. **Chief manuf. goods:** food products, chemicals, lumber, paper, plastics, electric motors, furniture, auto components, airplane parts, apparel, machinery, steel. **Chief crops:** rice, soybeans, cotton, tomatoes, grapes, apples, commercial vegetables, peaches, wheat. **Livestock** (Jan. 2004): 1.9 mil. cattle/calves; (Jan. 2003): 310,000 hogs/pigs; (Dec. 2003): 23.3 mil. chickens (excl. broilers); 1.2 bil. broilers. **Timber/lumber** (est. 2002): 2.6 bil bd. ft.; oak, hickory, gum, cypress, pine. **Nonfuel minerals** (est. 2003): $445 mil.; stone (crushed), bromine, cement (portland), sand and gravel (construction), lime. **Chief ports:** Little Rock, Pine Bluff, Osceola, Helena, Fort Smith, Van Buren, Camden, Dananelle, North Little Rock, West Memphis, Crossett, McGehee, Morrilton. **New private housing** (2003): 14,177 units/$1.5 bil. **Gross state product** (2001): $67.9 bil. **Employment distrib.** (May 2004): 17.5% govt.; 20.7% trade/trans./util.; 17.7% mfg.; 12.4% ed./health serv.; 9.1% prof./bus serv.; 8% leisure/hosp.; 4.4% finance; 4.4% constr.; 1.7% info. **Per cap. pers. income** (2003): $24,289. **Sales tax** (2004): 5.1%. **Unemployment** (2003): 6.2%. **Tourism expends.** (2002): $3.9 bil.

Finance. FDIC-insured commercial banks (2003): 163. **Deposits:** $29.8 bil. **FDIC-insured savings institutions** (2003): 7. **Assets:** $1.9 bil.

Federal govt. Fed. civ. employees (Mar. 2003): 11,646. **Avg. salary:** $48,755. **Notable fed. facilities:** Nat'l. Ctr. for Toxicological Research, Jefferson; Pine Bluff Arsenal, Little Rock AFB.

Energy. Electricity production (est. 2003, kWh by source): Coal: 23.4 bil; Petroleum: 262 mil; Gas: 599 mil; Hydroelectric: 2.8 bil; Nuclear: 14.7 bil.

State data. Motto: Regnat Populus (The people rule). **Flower:** Apple blossom. **Bird:** Mockingbird. **Tree:** Pine. **Song:** Arkansas. **Entered union** June 15, 1836; rank, 25th. **State fair** at Little Rock; late Sept.-early Oct.

History. Quapaw, Caddo, Osage, Cherokee, and Choctaw peoples lived in the area at the time of European contact. The first European explorers were de Soto, 1541; Marquette and Jolliet, 1673; and La Salle, 1682. The first settlement was by the French under Henri de Tonty, 1686, at Arkansas Post. In 1762, the area was ceded by France to Spain, then given back again, 1800, and was part of the Louisiana Purchase, 1803. It was made a territory, 1819. Arkansas seceded in 1861, only after the Civil War began; more than 10,000 Arkansans fought on the Union side.

Tourist attractions. Hot Springs Natl. Park (water ranging from 95°F-147°F); Eureka Springs; Ozark Folk Center, Blanchard Caverns, both near Mountain View; Crater of Diamonds

(only U.S. diamond mine) near Murfreesboro; Toltec Mounds Archeological State Park, Little Rock; Buffalo Natl. River; Mid-America Museum, Hot Springs; Pea Ridge National Military Park, Pead Ridge; Tanyard Springs, Morrilton; Wiederkehr Wine Village, Wiederkehr Village.

Famous Arkansans. Daisy Bates, Dee Brown, Paul "Bear" Bryant, Glen Campbell, Johnny Cash, Hattie Caraway, Wesley Clark, Bill Clinton, "Dizzy" Dean, Orval Faubus, James W. Fulbright, John Grisham, John H. Johnson, Douglas MacArthur, John L. McClellan, James S. McDonnell, Scottie Pippen, Dick Powell, Brooks Robinson, Billy Bob Thornton, Winthrop Rockefeller, Mary Steenburgen, Edward Durell Stone, Sam Walton, Archibald Yell.

Tourist Information. Arkansas Dept. of Parks & Tourism, 1 Capitol Mall, Little Rock, AR 72201; 1-800-NATURAL. **Website:** www.arkansas.com

Website. www.state.ar.us

California
Golden State

People. Population (2003 est.): 35,484,453; rank: 1; **net change** (2002-2003): 1.4%. **Pop. density:** 227.5 per sq mi. **Racial distribution** (2000): 59.5%; white; 6.7% black; 10.9% Asian; 1.0% Native American/Nat. AK; 0.3% Hawaiian/Pacific Islander; 16.8% other race; 2 or more races, 4.7% **Hispanic pop.** (any race): 32.4%.

Geography. Total area: 163,696 sq mi; rank: 3. **Land area:** 155,959 sq mi; rank: 3. **Acres forested:** 40.2 mil. **Location:** on western coast of the U.S. **Climate:** moderate temperatures and rainfall along the coast; extremes in the interior. **Topography:** long mountainous coastline; central valley; Sierra Nevada on the east; desert basins of the southern interior; rugged mountains of the north. **Capital:** Sacramento.

Economy. Chief industries: agriculture, tourism, apparel, electronics, telecommunications, entertainment. **Chief manuf. goods:** electronic and electrical equip., computers, industrial machinery, transportation equip. and instruments, food. **Chief farm products:** milk and cream, grapes, cotton, flowers, oranges, rice, nursery products, hay, tomatoes, lettuce, strawberries, almonds, asparagus. **Livestock** (Jan. 2004): 5.2 mil. cattle/calves; 680,000 sheep/lambs; (Jan. 2003): 135,000 hogs/pigs; (Dec. 2003): 26.0 mil. chickens (excl. broilers). **Timber/lumber** (est. 2002): 2.9 bil bd. ft.; fir, pine, redwood, oak. **Nonfuel minerals** (est. 2003): $3.2 bil.; sand and gravel (construction), cement (portland), stone (crushed), boron minerals, soda ash. **Commercial fishing** (2002): $108.1 mil. **Chief ports:** Long Beach, Los Angeles, San Diego, Oakland, San Francisco, Sacramento, Stockton. **Principal internat. airports at:** Fresno, Los Angeles, Oakland, Ontario, Sacramento, San Diego, San Francisco, San Jose. **New private housing** (2003): 192,273 units/$32.2 bil. **Gross state product** (2001): $1,359.3 bil. **Employment distrib.** (May 2004): 16.7% govt.; 18.8% trade/trans./util.; 10.5% mfg.; 10.8% ed./health serv.; 14.8% prof./bus serv.; 9.8% leisure/hosp.; 6.2% finance; 5.6% constr.; 3.2% info. **Per cap. pers. income** (2003): $33,749. **Sales tax** (2004): 7.25%. **Unemployment** (2003): 6.7%. **Tourism expends.** (2002): $68.2 bil. **Lottery** (2003): total sales: $2.8 bil; net income: $977 mil.

Finance. FDIC-insured commercial banks (2003): 281. **Deposits:** $367.4 bil. **FDIC-insured savings institutions** (2003): 37. **Assets:** $468.3 bil.

Federal govt. Fed. civ. employees (Mar. 2003): 145,996. **Avg. salary:** $57,552. **Notable fed. facilities:** Vandenberg, Beale, Travis AF bases; San Diego Naval Sta.; Pt. Loma Naval Sub Base; USMC Camp Pendleton; Lawrence Livermore Natl. Lab; Berkeley Natl. Lab; NASA Jet Propulsion Lab; Edwards AFB (NASA Dryden Flight Test Ctr., AF Flight Rest Ctr.; San Francisco Mint.

Energy. Electricity production (est. 2003, kWh by source): Petroleum: 51 mil; Gas: 9.7 bil; Hydroelectric: 34.2 bil; Nuclear: 35.6 bil; Other: 331 mil.

State data. Motto: Eureka (I have found it). **Flower:** Golden poppy. **Bird:** California valley quail. **Tree:** California redwood. **Song:** I Love You, California. **Entered union** Sept. 9, 1850; rank, 31st. **State fair** at Sacramento; late Aug.-early Sept.

History. Early inhabitants included more than 100 different Native American tribes with multiple dialects. The first European explorers were Cabrillo, 1542, and Drake, 1579. The first settlement was the Spanish Alta California mission at San Diego, 1769, first in a string founded by Franciscan Father Junípero Serra. U.S. traders and settlers arrived in the 19th cent. and staged the Bear Flag revolt, 1846, in protest against Mexican rule; later that year U.S. forces occupied California. At the end of the Mexican War, Mexico ceded the territory to

the U.S., 1848; that same year gold was discovered, and the famed gold rush began.

Tourist attractions. The *Queen Mary*, Long Beach; Palomar Mountain; Disneyland, Anaheim; Getty Center, Los Angeles; Tournament of Roses and Rose Bowl, Pasadena; Universal Studios, Hollywood; Long Beach Aquarium of the Pacific; Golden State Museum, Sacramento; San Diego Zoo; Yosemite Valley; Lassen and Sequoia-Kings Canyon natl. parks; Lake Tahoe; Mojave and Colorado deserts; San Francisco Bay; Napa Valley; Monterey Peninsula; oldest living things on earth believed to be a stand of Bristlecone pines in the Inyo National Forest, est. 4,700 years old; world's tallest tree, 365-ft "National Geographic Society" coast redwood, in Humboldt Redwoods State Park.

Famous Californians. Edmund G. (Pat) Brown, Jerry Brown, Luther Burbank, Julia Child, Ted Danson, Cameron Diaz, Leonardo DiCaprio, Joe DiMaggio, Dianne Feinstein, John C. Fremont, Robert Frost, Tom Hanks, Bret Harte, William Randolph Hearst, Helen Hunt, Jack Kemp, Monica Lewinsky, Jack London, George Lucas, Mark McGwire, Aimee Semple McPherson, Marilyn Monroe, John Muir, Richard M. Nixon, George S. Patton Jr., Gregory Peck, Nancy Pelosi, Ronald Reagan, Sally K. Ride, William Saroyan, Father Junípero Serra, O.J. Simpson, Kevin Spacey, Leland Stanford, John Steinbeck, Arnold Schwarzenegger, Shirley Temple, Earl Warren, Ted Williams, Serena Williams, Venus Williams, Tiger Woods.

California Division of Tourism. P.O. Box 1499, Sacramento, CA 95812-1499;1-800-862-2543. **Website:** www.go calif.ca.gov

Website. www.state.ca.us

Colorado
Centennial State

People. Population (2003 est.): 4,550,688; rank: 22; **net change** (2002-2003): 1.1%. **Pop. density:** 43.9 per sq mi. **Racial distribution** (2000): 82.8% white; 3.8% black; 2.2% Asian; 1.0% Native American/Nat. AK; 0.1% Hawaiian/Pacific Islander; 7.2% other race; 2 or more races, 2.8% **Hispanic pop.** (any race): 17.1%.

Geography. Total area: 104,094 sq mi; rank: 8. **Land area:** 103,718 sq mi; rank: 8. **Acres forested:** 21.6 mil. **Location:** in W central U.S. **Climate:** low relative humidity, abundant sunshine, wide daily, seasonal temp. ranges; alpine conditions in the high mountains. **Topography:** eastern dry high plains; hilly to mountainous central plateau; western Rocky Mountains of high ranges, with broad valleys, deep, narrow canyons. **Capital:** Denver.

Economy. Chief industries: manufacturing, construction, government, tourism, agriculture, aerospace, electronics equipment. **Chief manuf. goods:** computer equip. & instruments, foods, machinery, aerospace products. **Chief crops:** corn, wheat, hay, sugar beets, barley, potatoes, apples, peaches, pears, dry edible beans, sorghum, onions, oats, sunflowers, vegetables. **Livestock:** (Jan. 2004): 2.4 mil. cattle/calves; 360,000 sheep/lambs; (Jan. 2003): 770,000 hogs/pigs; (Dec. 2003): 5.1 mil. chickens (excl. broilers). **Timber/lumber** (est. 2002): 135 mil bd. ft.; oak, ponderosa pine, Douglas fir. **Nonfuel minerals** (est. 2003): $672 mil.; sand and gravel (construction), cement (portland), molybdenum concentrates, gold, stone (crushed). **Principal internat. airport at:** Denver. **New private housing** (2003): 39,446 units/$6.3 bil. **Gross state product** (2001): $173.8 bil. **Employment distrib.** (May 2004): 16.9% govt.; 18.6% trade/trans./util.; 7.1% mfg.; 10.1% ed./health serv.; 13.7% prof./bus serv.; 11.1% leisure/hosp.; 7.1% finance; 6.7% constr.; 3.8% info. **Per cap. pers. income** (2003): $34,283. **Sales tax** (2004): 2.9%. **Unemployment** (2003): 6%. **Tourism expends.** (2002): $9.5 bil. **Lottery** (2003): total sales: $391.5 mil; net income: $104.8 mil.

Finance. FDIC-insured commercial banks (2003): 169. **Deposits:** $27.5 bil. **FDIC-insured savings institutions** (2003): 11. **Assets:** $2.7 bil.

Federal govt. Fed. civ. employees (Mar. 2003): 33,893. **Avg. salary:** $58,871. **Notable fed. facilities:** U.S. Air Force Academy; U.S. Mint; Ft. Carson; Natl. Renewable Energy Labs; U.S. Rail Transportation Test Ctr.; Cheyenne Mtn. Operations Ctr. (NORAD, U.S. Space Comm.); Denver Federal Ctr.; Natl. Ctr. for Atmospheric Research; Natl. Instit. for Standards in Technology; Natl. Wildlife Res. Ctr.; NOAA Env. Technology Lab.

Energy. Electricity production (est. 2003, kWh by source): Coal: 35.8 bil; Petroleum: 19 mil; Gas: 4.4 bil; Hydroelectric: 946 mil; Other: 58 mil.

State data. Motto: Nil Sine Numine (Nothing Without Providence). **Flower:** Rocky Mountain columbine. **Bird:** Lark bunting. **Tree:** Colorado blue spruce. **Song:** Where the Columbines Grow. **Entered union:** Aug. 1, 1876; rank 38th. **State fair** at Pueblo; mid-Aug.–early Sept.

History. Early civilization centered around the Mesa Verde c 2,000 years ago; later, Ute, Pueblo, Cheyenne, and Arapaho peoples lived in the area. The region was claimed by Spain, but passed to France. The U.S. acquired eastern Colorado in the Louisiana Purchase, 1803. Lt. Zebulon M. Pike explored the area, 1806, discovering the peak that bears his name. After the Mexican War, 1846-48, U.S. immigrants settled in the east, former Mexicans in the south. Gold was discovered in 1858, causing a population boom. Displaced Native Americans protested, resulting in the so-called Sand Creek Massacre, 1864, where more than 200 Cheyenne and Arapaho were killed. All Native Americans were later removed to Oklahoma Territory.

Tourist attractions. Rocky Mountain and Black Canyon of the Gunnison natl. parks; Aspen Ski Resort; Garden of the Gods, Colorado Springs; Great Sand Dunes, Dinosaur, and Colorado natl. monuments; Pikes Peak and Mt. Evans highways; Mesa Verde Natl. Park (ancient Anasazi Indian cliff dwellings); Grand Mesa Natl. Forest; mining towns of Central City, Silverton, Cripple Creek; Burlington's Old Town; Bent's Fort, outside La Junta; Georgetown Loop Historic Mining Railroad Park, Cumbres & Toltec Scenic Railroad; limited stakes gaming in Central City, Blackhawk, Cripple Creek, Ignacio, and Towaoe.

Famous Coloradans. Tim Allen, Frederick Bonfils, Henry Brown, Molly Brown, William N. Byers, M. Scott Carpenter, Lon Chaney, Jack Dempsey, Mamie Eisenhower, Douglas Fairbanks, Barney Ford, Scott Hamilton, John Kerry, Chief Ourey, "Baby Doe" Tabor, Lowell Thomas, Byron R. White, Paul Whiteman.

State Chamber of Commerce. 1776 Lincoln, Ste. 1200, Denver, CO 80203. Phone: 303-831-7411

Tourist information. Colorado Tourism Office, 1625 Broadway, Ste. 1700, Denver, CO 80202; 1-800-COLO-RADO. **Website:** www.colorado.com

Website. www.colorado.gov

Connecticut
Constitution State, Nutmeg State

People. Population (2003 est.): 3,483,372; rank: 29; **net change** (2002-2003): 0.7%. **Pop. density:** 719 per sq mi. **Racial distribution** (2000): 81.6% white; 9.1% black; 2.4% Asian; 0.3% Native American/Nat. AK; <0.1% Hawaiian/Pacific Islander; 4.3% other race; 2 or more races, 2.2%. **Hispanic pop.** (any race): 9.4%.

Geography. Total area: 5,543 sq mi; rank: 48. **Land area:** 4,845 sq mi; rank: 48. **Acres forested:** 1.9 mil. **Location:** New England state in NE corner of the U.S. **Climate:** moderate; winters avg. slightly below freezing; warm, humid summers. **Topography:** western upland, the Berkshires, in the NW, highest elevations; narrow central lowland N-S; hilly eastern upland drained by rivers. **Capital:** Hartford.

Economy. Chief industries: manufacturing, retail trade, government, services, finances, insurance, real estate. **Chief manuf. goods:** aircraft engines and parts, submarines, helicopters, machinery and computer equipment, electronics and electrical equipment, medical instruments, pharmaceuticals. **Chief crops:** nursery stock, Christmas trees, mushrooms, vegetables, sweet corn, tobacco, apples. **Livestock** (Jan. 2004): 54,000 cattle/calves; (Jan. 2003): 3,800 hogs/pigs; (Dec. 2003): 3.7 mil. chickens (excl. broilers). **Timber/lumber** (est. 2002): 45 mil. bd. ft.; oak, birch, beech, maple. **Nonfuel minerals** (est. 2003): $142 mil.; stone (crushed), sand and gravel (construction), stone (dimension), clays (common), gemstones. **Commercial fishing** (2002): $27.8 mil. Chief ports: New Haven, Bridgeport, New London. **Principal internat. airport at:** Windsor Locks. **New private housing** (2003): 10,758 units/$1.9 bil. **Gross state product** (2001): $166.2 bil. **Employment distrib.** (May 2004): 15.1% govt.; 18.5% trade/trans./util.; 11.8% mfg.; 16.1% ed./health serv.; 11.8% prof./bus serv.; 8% leisure/hosp.; 8.6% finance; 3.8% constr.; 2.4% info. **Per cap. pers. income** (2003): $43,173. **Sales tax** (2004): 6.0%. **Unemployment** (2003): 5.5%. **Tourism expends.** (2002): $6.6 bil. **Lottery** (2003): total sales: $865.3 mil; net income: $256.8 mil.

Finance. FDIC-insured commercial banks (2003): 24. **Deposits:** $4.4 bil. **FDIC-insured savings institutions** (2003): 39. **Assets:** $49.8 bil.

Federal govt. Fed. civ. employees (Mar. 2003): 6,994. **Avg. salary:** $57,955. **Notable fed. facilities:** U.S. Coast Guard Academy; Navy Sub Base New London.

Energy. Electricity production (est. 2002, kWh, by source): Petroleum: 8 mil; Hydroelectric: 32 mil; Other: 143 mil.

State data. Motto: Qui Transtulit Sustinet (He who transplanted still sustains). **Flower:** Mountain laurel. **Bird:** American robin. **Tree:** White oak. **Song:** Yankee Doodle. **Fifth of** the 13 original states to ratify the Constitution, Jan. 9, 1788. **State Fair:** largest fair at Durham, late Sept.; no state fair.

History. At the time of European contact, inhabitants of the area were Algonquian peoples, including the Mohegan and Pequot. Dutch explorer Adriaen Block was the first European visitor, 1614. By 1634, settlers from Plymouth Bay had started colonies along the Connecticut River; in 1637 they defeated the Pequots. The Colony of Connecticut was chartered by England, 1662, adding New Haven, 1665. In the American Revolution, Connecticut Patriots fought in most major campaigns, while Connecticut privateers captured British merchant ships.

Tourist attractions. Mark Twain House, Hartford; Yale University's Art Gallery, Peabody Museum, both in New Haven; Mystic Seaport; Mystic Marine Life Aquarium; P. T. Barnum Museum, Bridgeport; Gillette Castle, Hadlyme; U.S.S. *Nautilus* Memorial, Groton (1st nuclear-powered submarine); Mashantucket Pequot Museum & Research Center, Foxwoods Resort & Casino, both in Ledyard; Mohegan Sun, Uncasville; Lake Compounce, Bristol.

Famous "Nutmeggers." Ethan Allen, Phineas T. Barnum, Samuel Colt, Jonathan Edwards, Nathan Hale, Katharine Hepburn, Isaac Hull, Robert Mitchum, J. Pierpont Morgan, Ralph Nader, Israel Putnam, Wallace Stevens, Harriet Beecher Stowe, Mark Twain, Noah Webster, Eli Whitney.

Tourist information. Dept. of Economic and Community Development, 505 Hudson St., Hartford, CT 06106; 1-800-CTBOUND. **Website:** www.ctbound.org

Website. www.ct.gov

Delaware
First State, Diamond State

People. Population (2003 est.): 817,491; rank: 45; **net change** (2002-2003): 1.4%. **Pop. density:** 418.5 per sq mi. **Racial distribution** (2000): 74.6% white; 19.2% black; 2.1% Asian; 0.3% Native American/Nat. AK; <0.1% Hawaiian/Pacific Islander; 2.0% other race; 2 or more races, 1.7%. **Hispanic pop.** (any race): 4.8%.

Geography. Total area: 2,489 sq mi; rank: 49. **Land area:** 1,954 sq mi; rank: 49. **Acres forested:** 0.4 mil. **Location:** occupies the Delmarva Peninsula on the Atlantic coastal plain. **Climate:** moderate. **Topography:** Piedmont plateau to the N, sloping to a near sea-level plain. **Capital:** Dover.

Economy. Chief industries: chemicals, agriculture, finance, poultry, shellfish, tourism, auto assembly, food processing, transportation equipment. **Chief manuf. goods:** nylon, apparel, luggage, foods, autos, processed meats and vegetables, railroad & aircraft equipment. **Chief crops:** soybeans, potatoes, corn, mushrooms, lima beans, green peas, barley, cucumbers, wheat, corn, grain sorghum, greenhouse & nursery. **Livestock** (Jan. 2004): 25,000 cattle/calves; (Jan. 2003): 18,000 hogs/pigs; 251.2 mil. broilers. **Timber/lumber** (est. 2002): 12 mil. bd. ft.; hardwoods and softwoods (except for southern yellow pine). **Nonfuel minerals** (est. 2003): $16 mil.; sand and gravel (construction), magnesium compounds, gemstones. **Commercial fishing** (2002): $6.1 mil. **Chief ports:** Wilmington. **Principal internat. airport at:** Philadelphia/Wilmington. **New private housing** (2003): 7,786 units/$794 mil. **Gross state product** (2001): $40.5 bil. **Employment distrib.** (May 2004): 14% govt.; 18.6% trade/trans./util.; 8.6% mfg.; 12.3% ed./health serv.; 14.4% prof./bus serv.; 9.2% leisure/hosp.; 10.8% finance; 6% constr.; 1.8% info. **Per cap. pers. income** (2003): $32,810. **Sales tax** (2004): none. **Unemployment** (2003): 4.4%. **Tourism expends.** (2002): $1.1 bil. **Lottery** (2003): total sales: $628.06 mil; net income: $271.8 mil.

Finance. FDIC-insured commercial banks (2003): 27. **Deposits:** $79.2 bil. **FDIC-insured savings institutions** (2003): 7. **Assets:** $56.8 bil.

Federal govt. Fed. civ. employees (Mar. 2003): 2,563. **Avg. salary:** $51,230. **Notable fed. facilities:** Dover AFB, Federal Wildlife Refuge, Bombay Hook.

Energy. Electricity production (est. 2003, kWh by source): Petroleum: 102 mil; Gas: 13 mil.

State data. Motto: Liberty and independence. **Flower:** Peach blossom. **Bird:** Blue hen chicken. **Tree:** American holly. **Song:** Our Delaware. **First** of original 13 states to ratify the Constitution, Dec. 7, 1787. **State fair** at Harrington; end of July.

History. The Lenni Lenape (Delaware) people lived in the region at the time of European contact. Henry Hudson located the Delaware R., 1609, and in 1610, English explorer Samuel Argall entered Delaware Bay, naming the area after Virginia's governor, Lord De La Warr. The Dutch first settled near present Lewes, 1631, but the colony was destroyed by Indians. Swedes settled at Fort Christina (now Wilmington), 1638. Dutch settled anew, 1651, near New Castle and seized the Swedish settlement, 1655, only to lose all Delaware and New Netherland to the British, 1664. After 1682, Delaware became part of Pennsylvania, and in 1704 it was granted its own assembly. In 1776, it adopted a constitution as the state of Delaware. Although it remained in the Union during the Civil War, Delaware retained slavery until abolished by the 13th Amendment in 1865.

Tourist attractions. Ft. Christina Monument, site of founding of New Sweden, Holy Trinity (Old Swedes) Church, erected 1698, the oldest Protestant church in the U.S. still in use, Wilmington; Hagley Museum, Winterthur Museum and Gardens, both near Wilmington; historic district, New Castle; John Dickinson "Penman of the Revolution" home, Dover; Rehoboth Beach, "nation's summer capital," Rehoboth; Dover Downs Intl. Speedway.

Famous Delawareans. Thomas F. Bayard, Joseph Biden, Henry Seidel Canby, E. I. du Pont, John P. Marquand, Howard Pyle, Caesar Rodney.

Tourist Information. Delaware Tourism Office, 99 Kings Highway, Dover, DE 19901. 1-866-2VISITDE. **Website:** www.visitdelaware.net

Website. www.delaware.gov

Florida
Sunshine State

People. Population (2003 est.): 17,019,068; rank: 4; **net change** (2002-2003): 2.0%. **Pop. density:** 315.6 per sq mi. **Racial distribution** (2000): 78.0% white; 14.6% black; 1.7% Asian; 0.3% Native American/Nat. AK; 0.1% Hawaiian/Pacific Islander; 3.0% other race; 2 or more races, 2.4%. **Hispanic pop.** (any race): 16.8%.

Geography. Total area: 65,755 sq mi; rank: 22. **Land area:** 53,927 sq mi; rank: 26. **Acres forested:** 16.3 mil. **Location:** peninsula jutting southward 500 mi between the Atlantic and the Gulf of Mexico. **Climate:** subtropical N of Bradenton-Lake Okeechobee-Vero Beach line; tropical S of line. **Topography:** land is flat or rolling; highest point is 345 ft in the NW. **Capital:** Tallahassee.

Economy. Chief industries: tourism, agriculture, manufacturing, construction, services, international trade. **Chief manuf. goods:** electric & electronic equipment, transportation equipment, food, printing & publishing, chemicals, instruments, industrial machinery. **Chief crops:** citrus fruits, vegetables, melons, greenhouse and nursery products, potatoes, sugarcane, strawberries. **Livestock** (Jan. 2004): 1.74 mil. cattle/calves; (Jan. 2003): 30,000 hogs/pigs; (Dec. 2003): 13.3 mil. chickens (excl. broilers). 91.3 mil. broilers. **Timber/lumber** (est. 2002): 888 mil bd. ft.; pine, cypress, cedar; 751 mil bd. ft. **Nonfuel minerals** (est. 2003): $2.0 bil.; phosphate rock, stone (crushed), cement (portland), sand and gravel (construction), cement (masonry). **Commercial fishing** (2002): $178.6 mil. Chief ports: Pensacola, Tampa, Manatee, Miami, Port Everglades, Jacksonville, St. Petersburg, Canaveral. **Principal internat. airports at:** Daytona Beach, Ft. Lauderdale/Hollywood, Ft. Myers, Jacksonville, Key West, Melbourne, Miami, Orlando, Panama City, St. Petersburg/Clearwater, Sarasota/Bradenton, Tampa, West Palm Beach. **New private housing** (2003): 211,078 units/$27.7 bil. **Gross state product** (2001): $491.5 bil. **Employment distrib.** (May 2004): 14.5% govt.; 19.6% trade/trans./util.; 5.2% mgf.; 12.2% ed./health serv.; 17.6% prof./bus serv.; 11.3% leisure/hosp.; 6.6% finance; 6.2% constr.; 2.3% info. **Per cap. pers. income** (2003): $30,446. **Sales tax** (2004): 6.0%. **Unemployment** (2003): 5.1%. **Tourism expends.** (2002): $54.5 bil. **Lottery** (2003): total sales: $2.9 bil; net income: $1.0 bil.

Finance. FDIC-insured commercial banks (2003): 262. **Deposits:** $64.1 bil. **FDIC-insured savings institutions** (2003): 42. **Assets:** $31.4 bil.

Federal govt. Fed. civ. employees (Mar. 2003): 70,901. **Avg. salary:** $53,136. **Notable fed. facilities:** John F. Kennedy Space Ctr., NASA-Kennedy Space Ctr.'s Spaceport USA; Eglin AFB; MacDill AFB; Pensacola NAS; Jacksonville NAS; Mayport Naval Sta.

Energy. Electricity production (est. 2003, kWh by source): Coal: 57.2 bil; Petroleum: 35.6 mil; Gas: 58.2 bil; Hydroelectric: 263 mil; Nuclear: 31 bil; Other: 128 mil.

State data. Motto: In God we trust. **Flower:** Orange blossom. **Bird:** Mockingbird. **Tree:** Sabal palmetto palm. **Song:** Old Folks at Home. **Entered union** Mar. 3, 1845; rank, 27th. **State fair** at Tampa; early Feb.

History. The original inhabitants of Florida included the Timucua, Apalachee, and Calusa peoples. Later the Seminole migrated from Georgia to Florida, becoming dominant there in the early 18th cent. The first European to see Florida was Ponce de León, 1513. France established a colony, Fort Caroline, on the St. John River, 1564. Spain settled St. Augustine, 1565, and Spanish troops massacred most of the French. Britain's Sir Francis Drake burned St. Augustine, 1586. In 1763, Spain ceded Florida to Great Britain, which held the area briefly, 1763-83, before returning it to Spain. After Andrew Jackson led a U.S. invasion, 1818, Spain ceded Florida to the U.S., 1819. The Seminole War, 1835-42, resulted in removal of most Native Americans to Oklahoma Territory. Florida seceded from the Union, 1861, and was readmitted in 1868.

Tourist attractions. Miami Beach; St. Augustine, oldest permanent European settlement in U.S.; Castillo de San Marcos, St. Augustine; Walt Disney World's Magic Kingdom, EPCOT Center, Disney-MGM Studios, and Animal Kingdom, all near Orlando; Sea World, Universal Studios, near Orlando; Spaceport USA, Kennedy Space Center; Everglades Natl. Park; Ringling Museum of Art, Ringling Museum of Circus, both in Sarasota; Cypress Gardens, Winter Haven; Busch Gardens, Tampa; U.S. Astronaut Hall of Fame, Mariana Caverns; Church St. Station, Orlando; Silver Springs, Ocala.

Famous Floridians. Edna Buchanan, Jeb Bush, Marjory Stoneman Douglas, Henry M. Flagler, Carl Hiaasen, James Weldon Johnson, MacKinlay Kantor, John D. MacDonald, Chief Osceola, Claude Pepper, Henry B. Plant, A. Philip Randolph, Marjorie Kinnan Rawlings, Janet Reno, Joseph W. Stilwell, Charles P. Summerall, Ben Vereen.

Tourist information. Visit Florida, 661 E. Jefferson St., Tallahassee, FL 32302; 1-888-735-2872 (1-888-7FLA-USA). **Website:** www.flausa.com

Website. www.myflorida.com

Georgia
Empire State of the South, Peach State

People. Population (2003 est.): 8,684,715; rank: 9; **net change** (2002-2003): 1.6%. **Pop. density:** 150 per sq mi. **Racial distribution** (2000): 65.1% white; 28.7% black; 2.1% Asian; 0.3% Native American/Nat. AK; 0.1% Hawaiian/Pacific Islander; 2.4% other race; 2 or more races, 1.4%. **Hispanic pop.** (any race): 5.3% .

Geography. Total area: 59,425 sq mi; rank: 24. **Land area:** 57,906 sq mi; rank: 21. **Acres forested:** 24.4 mil. **Location:** South Atlantic state. **Climate:** maritime tropical air masses dominate in summer; polar air masses in winter; E central area drier. **Topography:** most southerly of the Blue Ridge Mts. cover NE and N central; central Piedmont extends to the fall line of rivers; coastal plain levels to the coast flatlands. **Capital:** Atlanta.

Economy. Chief industries: services, manufacturing, retail trade. **Chief manuf. goods:** textiles, apparel, food, and kindred products, pulp & paper products. **Chief crops:** peanuts, cotton, corn, tobacco, hay, soybeans. **Livestock** (Jan. 2004): 1.25 mil. cattle/calves; (Jan. 2003): 295,000 hogs/pigs; (Dec. 2003): 29.5 mil. chickens (excl. broilers); 1.3 bil. broilers. **Timber/lumber** (est. 2002): 3 mil bd. ft.; pine, hardwood; 3.2 bil bd. ft. **Nonfuel minerals** (est. 2003): $1.7 bil.; clays (kaolin), stone (crushed), clays (fuller's earth), cement (portland), sand and gravel (construction). **Commercial fishing** (2002): $14.5 mil. **Chief ports:** Savannah, Brunswick. **Principal internat. airports at:** Atlanta, Savannah. **New private housing** (2003): 94,773 units/$10.5 bil. **Gross state product** (2001): $299.9 bil. **Employment distrib.** (May 2004): 16.4% govt.; 21% trade/trans./util.; 11.6% mfg.; 10.1% ed./health serv.; 12.8% prof./bus serv.; 9.2% leisure/hosp.; 5.6% finance; 5.2% constr.; 3.3% info. **Per cap. pers. income** (2003): $29,442. **Sales tax** (2004): 4.0%. **Unemployment** (2003): 4.7%. **Tourism expends.** (2002): $15.3 bil. **Lottery** (2003): total sales: $2.5 bil; net income: $767.2 mil.

Finance. FDIC-insured commercial banks (2003): 323. **Deposits:** $132.4 bil. **FDIC-insured savings institutions** (2003): 22. **Assets:** $8.7 bil.

Federal govt. Fed. civ. employees (Mar. 2003): 64,931. **Avg. salary:** $54,298. **Notable fed. facilities:** Dobbins AFB; Ft. Benning; Ft. Gordon; Ft. Gillem; Ft. Stewart; King's Bay Naval Base; Moody AFB; Navy Supply Corps School; Ft. McPherson; Fed. Law Enforcement Training Ctr., Glynco, Robins AFB; Centers for Disease Control.

IT'S A FACT: About 5.8 million grandparents live with one or more of their grandchildren under the age of 18, according to U.S. Census Bureau statistics. In Hawaii, 7% of all grandparents lived with their grandchildren, the highest percentage of any state.

Energy. Electricity production (est. 2003, kWh by source): Coal: 77.9 bil.; Petroleum: 292 mil; Gas: 907 mil; Hydroelectric: 4.2 bil; Nuclear: 33.3 bil.

State data. Motto: Wisdom, justice and moderation. **Flower:** Cherokee rose. **Bird:** Brown thrasher. **Tree:** Live oak. **Song:** Georgia On My Mind. **Fourth** of the 13 original states to ratify the Constitution, Jan. 2, 1788. **State fair** at Macon, late Sept.—Oct.

History. Creek and Cherokee peoples were early inhabitants of the region. The earliest known European settlement was the Spanish mission of Santa Catalina, 1566, on Saint Catherines Island. Gen. James Oglethorpe established a colony at Savannah, 1733, for the poor and religiously persecuted. Oglethorpe defeated a Spanish army from Florida at Bloody Marsh, 1742. In the American Revolution, Georgians seized the Savannah armory, 1775, and sent the munitions to the Continental Army. They fought seesaw campaigns with Cornwallis's British troops, twice liberating Augusta and forcing final evacuation by the British from Savannah, 1782. The Cherokee were removed to Oklahoma Territory, 1832-38, and thousands died on the long march, known as the Trail of Tears. Georgia seceded from the Union, 1861, and was invaded by Union forces, 1864, under Gen. William T. Sherman, who took Atlanta, Sept. 2, and proceeded on his famous "march to the sea," ending in Dec., in Savannah. Georgia was readmitted, 1870.

Tourist attractions. State Capitol, Stone Mt. Park, Six Flags Over Georgia, Kennesaw Mt. Natl. Battlefield Park, Martin Luther King Jr. Natl. Historic Site, Underground Atlanta, Jimmy Carter Library & Museum, all Atlanta; Chickamauga and Chattanooga Natl. Military Park, near Dalton; Chattahoochee Natl. Forest; alpine village of Helen; Dahlonega, site of America's first gold rush; Brasstown Bald Mt.; Lake Lanier; Franklin D. Roosevelt's Little White House, Warm Springs; Callaway Gardens, Pine Mt.; Andersonville Natl. Historic Site; Okefenokee Swamp, near Waycross; Jekyll Island; St. Simons Island; Cumberland Island Natl. Seashore; historic riverfront district, Savannah.

Famous Georgians. Kim Basinger, Griffin Bell, James Bowie, James Brown, Erskine Caldwell, Jimmy Carter, Ray Charles, Lucius D. Clay, Ty Cobb, James Dickey, John C. Fremont, Newt Gingrich, Joel Chandler Harris, "Doc" Holliday, Holly Hunter, Alan Jackson, Martin Luther King Jr., Gladys Knight, Sidney Lanier, Little Richard, Juliette Gordon Low, Margaret Mitchell, Sam Nunn, Flannery O'Connor, Otis Redding, Burt Reynolds, Julia Roberts, Jackie Robinson, Clarence Thomas, Travis Tritt, Ted Turner, Carl Vinson, Alice Walker, Herschel Walker, Joseph Wheeler, Joanne Woodward, Trisha Yearwood, Andrew Young.

Tourist Information. Dept. of Economic Development, 75 Fifth St., NW, Ste. 1200, Atlanta, GA 30308; 1-800-VISITGA. **Website:** www.georgia.org/tourism
Website. www.georgia.gov

Kailua, Kahului. **New private housing** (2003): 7,222 units/ $1.3 bil. **Gross state product** (2001): $43.7 bil. **Employment distrib.** (May 2004): 21.3% govt.; 18.9% trade/trans./util.; 2.6% mfg.; 11.6% ed./health serv.; 12.2% prof./bus serv.; 17.5% leisure/hosp.; 5% finance; 5% constr.; 1.7% info. **Per cap. pers. income** (2003): $30,913. **Sales tax** (2004): 4.0%. **Unemployment** (2003): 4.3%. **Tourism expends.** (2002): $12.5 bil.

Finance. FDIC-insured commercial banks (2003): 6. **Deposits:** $18.2 bil. **FDIC-insured savings institutions** (2003): 2. **Assets:** $7.5 bil.

Federal govt. Fed. civ. employees (Mar. 2003): 21,241. **Avg. salary:** $49,757. **Notable fed. facilities:** Pearl Harbor Naval Shipyard; Hickam AFB; Schofield Barracks; Ft. Shafter; Marine Corps Base-Kaneohe Bay; Barbers Point NAS; Wheeler AFB; Prince Kuhio Federal Bldg.

Energy. Electricity production (est. 2003, kWh by source): Petroleum: 6.5 bil; Hydroelectric: 2 mil; Other: 2 mil.

State data. Motto: The life of the land is perpetuated in righteousness. **Flower:** Yellow hibiscus. **Bird:** Hawaiian goose. **Tree:** Kukui (Candlenut). **Song:** Hawai'i Pono'i. **Entered union** Aug. 21, 1959; rank, 50th. **State fair:** at O'ahu, late July–early Aug.

History. Polynesians from islands 2,000 mi to the south settled the Hawaiian Islands, probably between AD 300 and AD 600. The first European visitor was British captain James Cook, 1778. Between 1790 and 1810, the islands were united politically under the leadership of a native king, Kamehameha I, whose four successors—all bearing the name Kamehameha—ruled the kingdom from his death, 1819, until the end of the dynasty, 1872. Missionaries arrived, 1820, bringing Western culture. King Kamehameha III and his chiefs created the first constitution and a legislature that set up a public school system. Sugar production began, 1835, and it became the dominant industry. In 1893, Queen Liliuokalani was deposed, and a republic was instituted, 1894, headed by Sanford B. Dole. Annexation by the U.S. came in 1898. The Japanese attack on Pearl Harbor, Dec. 7, 1941, brought the U.S. into World War II.

Tourist attractions. Hawaii Volcanoes, Haleakala natl. parks; Natl. Memorial Cemetery of the Pacific, Waikiki Beach, Diamond Head, Honolulu; U.S.S. *Arizona* Memorial, Pearl Harbor; Hanauma Bay; Polynesian Cultural Center, Laie; Nu'uanu Pali; Waimea Canyon; Wailoa and Wailuku River state parks.

Famous Islanders. Bernice Pauahi Bishop, Tia Carrere, Father Damien de Veuster, Don Ho, Duke Kahanamoku, King Kamehameha, Brook Mahealani Lee, Daniel K. Inouye, Jason Scott Lee, Queen Liliuokalani, Bette Midler, Ellison Onizuka.

Tourist Information. Hawaii Visitors and Conventions Bureau, 2270 Kalakau Ave., Ste. 801, Honolulu, HI 96815; 1-800-GOHAWAII. **Website:** www.gohawaii.com
Website. www.hawaii.gov

Hawai'i
Aloha State

People. Population (2003 est.): 1,257,608; rank: 42; **net change** (2002-2003): 1.4%. **Pop. density:** 195.8 per sq mi. **Racial distribution** (2000): 24.3% white; 1.8% black; 41.6% Asian; 0.3% Native American/Nat. AK; 9.4% Hawaiian/Pacific Islander; 1.3% other race; 2 or more races, 21.4%. **Hispanic pop.** (any race): 7.2%.

Geography. Total area: 10,931 sq mi; rank: 43. **Land area:** 6,423 sq mi; rank: 47. **Acres forested:** 1.7 mil. **Location:** Hawaiian Islands lie in the North Pacific, 2,397 mi SW from San Francisco. **Climate:** subtropical, with wide variations in rainfall; Waialeale, on Kaua'i, wettest spot in U.S. (annual rainfall 460 in.) **Topography:** islands are tops of a chain of submerged volcanic mountains; active volcanoes: Mauna Loa, Kilauea. **Capital:** Honolulu.

Economy. Chief industries: tourism, defense, sugar, pineapples. **Chief manuf. goods:** processed sugar, canned pineapple, clothing, foods, printing & publishing. **Chief crops:** sugar, pineapples, macadamia nuts, fruits, coffee, vegetables, floriculture. **Livestock** (Jan. 2004): 156,000 cattle/calves; (Jan. 2003): 23,000 hogs/pigs; (Dec. 2003): 600,000 chickens (excl. broilers); 750,000. broilers. **Timber/lumber:** undisclosed. **Nonfuel minerals** (est. 2003): $74 mil.; stone (crushed), sand and gravel (construction), gemstones. **Commercial fishing** (2002): $52.1 mil. **Chief ports:** Honolulu, Hilo, Kailua. **Principal internat. airports at:** Hilo, Honolulu,

Idaho
Gem State

People. Population (2003 est.): 1,366,332; rank: 39; **net change** (2002-2003): 1.7%. **Pop. density:** 16.5 per sq mi. **Racial distribution** (2000): 91.0% white; 0.4% black; 0.9% Asian; 1.4% Native American/Nat. AK; 0.1% Hawaiian/Pacific Islander; 4.2% other race; 2 or more races, 2.0%. **Hispanic pop.** (any race): 7.9%.

Geography. Total area: 83,570 sq mi; rank: 14. **Land area:** 82,747 sq mi; rank: 11. **Acres forested:** 21.6 mil. **Location:** northwestern Mountain state bordering on British Columbia. **Climate:** tempered by Pacific westerly winds; drier, colder, continental climate in SE; altitude an important factor. **Topography:** Snake R. plains in the S; central region of mountains, canyons, gorges (Hells Canyon, 7,900 ft, deepest in N. America); subalpine northern region. **Capital:** Boise.

Economy. Chief industries: manufacturing, agriculture, tourism, lumber, mining, electronics. **Chief manuf. goods:** electronic components, computer equipment, processed foods, lumber and wood products, chemical products, primary metals, fabricated metal products, machinery. **Chief crops:** potatoes, peas, dry beans, sugar beets, alfalfa seed, lentils, wheat, hops, barley, plums and prunes, mint, onions, corn, cherries, apples, hay. **Livestock** (Jan. 2004): 2.01 mil. cattle/calves; 260,000 sheep/lambs; (Jan. 2003): 26,000 hogs/pigs; (Dec. 2003): 1.2 chickens (excl. broilers). **Timber/lumber:** 1.7 bil. bd. ft. **Nonfuel minerals** (est. 2003): $294

mil.; phosphate rock, sand and gravel (construction), molybdenum concentrates, silver, cement (portland). **Chief port:** Lewiston. **New private housing** (2003): 14,903 units/$1.9 bil. **Gross state product** (2001): $36.9 bil. **Employment distrib.** (May 2004): 20.2% govt.; 20% trade/trans./util.; 10.3% mfg.; 10.9% ed./health serv.; 12.7% prof./bus serv.; 9.3% leisure/hosp.; 4.7% finance; 6.6% constr.; 1.6% info. **Per cap. pers. income** (2003): $25,911. **Sales tax** (2004): 6.0%. **Unemployment** (2003): 5.4%. **Tourism expends.** (2002): $2.1 bil. **Lottery** (2003): total sales: $98.2 mil; net income: $18 mil.

Finance. FDIC-insured commercial banks (2003): 15. **Deposits:** $3.0 bil. **FDIC-insured savings institutions** (2003): 3. **Assets:** $1.04 bil.

Federal govt. Fed. civ. employees (Mar. 2003): 8,190. **Avg. salary:** $51,133. **Notable fed. facilities:** Idaho Natl. Engineering Lab; Mountain Home AFB.

Energy. Electricity production (est. 2003, kWh by source): Gas: 61 mil; Hydroelectric: 7.7 bil.

State data. Motto: Esto Perpetua (It is perpetual). **Flower:** Syringa. **Bird:** Mountain bluebird. **Tree:** White pine. **Song:** Here We Have Idaho. **Entered union** July 3, 1890; rank, 43rd. **State fair** at Boise, late Aug.; at Blackfoot, early Sept.

History. Early inhabitants were Shoshone, Northern Paiute, Bannock, and Nez Percé peoples. White exploration of the region began with Lewis and Clark, 1805-6. Next came fur traders, setting up posts, 1809-34, and missionaries, 1830s-50s. Mormons made their first permanent settlement at Franklin, 1860. Idaho's gold rush began the same year and brought thousands of permanent settlers. Most remarkable of the Indian wars was the 1,700-mi trek, 1877, of Chief Joseph and the Nez Percé, pursued by U.S. troops through 3 states and caught just short of the Canadian border. The Idaho territory was organized, 1863. Idaho adopted a progressive constitution and became a state, 1890.

Tourist attractions. Hells Canyon, deepest gorge in N. America; World Center for Birds of Prey; Craters of the Moon; Sun Valley, in Sawtooth Mts.; Crystal Falls Cave; Shoshone Falls; Lava Hot Springs; Lake Pend Oreille; Lake Coeur d'Alene; Sawtooth Natl. Recreation Area; River of No Return Wilderness Area; Redfish Lake.

Famous Idahoans. William E. Borah, Frank Church, Fred T. Dubois, Chief Joseph, Ezra Pound, Sacagawea, Picabo Street, Lana Turner.

Tourist information. Division of Tourism Development, 700 W. State St., Boise, ID 83720; 1-800-842-5858. **Website:** www. visitid.org

Website. www.state.id.us

Illinois
Prairie State

People. Population (2003 est.): 12,653,544; rank: 5; **net change** (2002-2003): 0.5%. **Pop. density:** 227.6 per sq mi. **Racial distribution** (2000): 73.5% white; 15.1% black; 3.4% Asian; 0.2% Native American/Nat. AK; <0.1% Hawaiian/Pacific Islander; 5.8% other race; 2 or more races, 1.9%. **Hispanic pop.** (any race): 12.3%.

Geography. Total area: 57,914 sq mi; rank: 25. **Land area:** 55,584 sq mi; rank: 24. **Acres forested:** 4.3 mil. **Location:** East North Central state; western, southern, and eastern boundaries formed by Mississippi, Ohio, and Wabash rivers, respectively. **Climate:** temperate; typically cold, snowy winters, hot summers. **Topography:** prairie and fertile plains throughout; open hills in the southern region. **Capital:** Springfield.

Economy. Chief industries: services, manufacturing, travel, wholesale and retail trade, finance, insurance, real estate, construction, health care, agriculture. **Chief manuf. goods:** machinery, electric and electronic equipment, prim. & fabric. metals, chemical products, printing & publishing, food and kindred products. **Chief crops:** corn, soybeans, wheat, sorghum, hay. **Livestock** (Jan. 2004): 1.31 mil. cattle/calves; 63,000 sheep/lambs; (Jan. 2003): 3.95 mil. hogs/pigs; (Dec. 2003): 4.2 mil. chickens (excl. broilers). **Timber/lumber** (est. 2002): 130 mil bd. ft.; oak, hickory, maple, cottonwood. **Nonfuel minerals** (est. 2003): $911 mil.; stone (crushed), cement (portland), sand and gravel (construction), sand and gravel (industrial), lime.**Chief ports:** Chicago. **Principal internat. airport at:** Chicago. **New private housing** (2003): 61,411 units/$9.0 bil. **Gross state product** (2001): $475.5 bil. **Employment distrib.** (May 2004): 14.8% govt.; 20.2% trade/trans./util.; 12.2% mfg.; 12.4% ed./health serv.; 13.1% prof./bus serv.; 8.9% leisure/hosp.; 6.9% finance; 4.8% constr.; 2.2% info. **Per cap. pers. income** (2003): $33,690. **Sales tax** (2004): 6.25%. **Unemployment** (2003): 6.7%. **Tourism ex-**

pends. (2002): $22.2 bil. **Lottery** (2003): total sales: $1.6 bil; net income: $539.8 mil.

Finance. FDIC-insured commercial banks (2003): 664. **Deposits:** $354.1 bil. **FDIC-insured savings institutions** (2003): 105. **Assets:** $36.8 bil.

Federal govt. Fed. civ. employees (Mar. 2003): 61,411. **Avg. salary:** $58,864. **Notable fed. facilities:** Fermi Natl. Accelerator Lab; Argonne Natl. Lab; Rock Island Arsenal; Great Lakes, Naval Training Station, Scott AFB.

Energy. Electricity production (est. 2003, kWh by source): Coal: 21.1 bil; Hydroelectric: 59 mil.

State data. Motto: State sovereignty—national union. **Flower:** Native violet. **Bird:** Cardinal. **Tree:** White oak. **Song:** Illinois. **Entered union** Dec. 3, 1818; rank, 21st. **State fair** at Springfield, mid-Aug.; DuQuoin, late Aug.

History. Seminomadic Algonquian peoples, including the Peoria, Illinois, Kaskaskia, and Tamaroa, lived in the region at the time of European contact. Fur traders were the first Europeans in Illinois, followed shortly by Jolliet and Marquette, 1673, and La Salle, 1680, who built a fort near present-day Peoria. The first settlements were French, at Cahokia, near present-day St. Louis, 1699, and Kaskaskia, 1703. France ceded the area to Britain, 1763, and in 1778, American Gen. George Rogers Clark took Kaskaskia from the British without a shot. Defeat of Native American tribes in the Black Hawk War, 1832, and growth of railroads brought change to the area. In 1787, it became part of the Northwest Territory. Post-Civil War Illinois became a center for the labor movement as bitter strikes, such as the Haymarket Square riot, occurred in 1885-86.

Tourist attractions. Chicago museums and parks; Lincoln shrines at Springfield, New Salem, Sangamon County; Cahokia Mounds, Collinsville; Starved Rock State Park; Crab Orchard Wildlife Refuge; Mormon settlement at Nauvoo; Fts. Kaskaskia, Chartres, Massac (parks); Shawnee Natl. Forest, Southern Illinois; Illinois State Museum, Springfield; Dickson Mounds Museum, between Havana and Lewistown.

Famous Illinoisans. Jane Addams, John Ashcroft, Saul Bellow, Jack Benny, Ray Bradbury, Gwendolyn Brooks, William Jennings Bryan, St. Frances Xavier Cabrini, Hillary Rodham Clinton, Clarence Darrow, John Deere, Stephen A. Douglas, James T. Farrell, George W. Ferris, Marshall Field, Betty Friedan, Benny Goodman, Ulysses S. Grant, Dennis Hastert, Ernest Hemingway, Charlton Heston, Wild Bill Hickok, Henry J. Hyde, Abraham Lincoln, Vachel Lindsay, Edgar Lee Masters, Oscar Mayer, Cyrus McCormick, Ronald Reagan, Donald Rumsfeld, Carl Sandburg, Adlai Stevenson, James Watson, Frank Lloyd Wright, Philip Wrigley.

Tourist information. Illinois Dept. of Commerce and Economic Opportunity, 620 E. Adams St., Springfield, IL 62701; 1-800-2-CONNECT. **Website:** www.enjoyillinois.com

Website. www.illinois.gov

Indiana
Hoosier State

People. Population (2003 est.): 6,195,643; rank: 14; **net change** (2002-2003): 0.6%. **Pop. density:** 172.7 per sq mi. **Racial distribution** (2000): 87.5% white; 8.4% black; 1.0% Asian; 0.3% Native American/Nat. AK; <0.1% Hawaiian/Pacific Islander; 1.6% other race; 2 or more races, 1.2%. **Hispanic pop.** (any race): 3.5%.

Geography. Total area: 36,418 sq mi; rank: 38. **Land area:** 35,867 sq mi; rank: 38. **Acres forested:** 4.5 mil. **Location:** East North Central state; Lake Michigan on N border. **Climate:** 4 distinct seasons with a temperate climate. **Topography:** hilly southern region; fertile rolling plains of central region; flat, heavily glaciated north; dunes along Lake Michigan shore. **Capital:** Indianapolis.

Economy. Chief industries: manufacturing, services, agriculture, government, wholesale and retail trade, transportation and public utilities. **Chief manuf. goods:** primary metals, transportation equipment, motor vehicles & equip., industrial machinery & equipment, electronic & electric equipment. **Chief crops:** corn, soybeans, wheat, nursery and greenhouse products, vegetables, popcorn, fruit, hay, tobacco, mint. **Livestock** (Jan. 2004): 830,000 cattle/calves; 45,000 sheep/lambs; (Jan. 2003): 3.1 mil. hogs/pigs; (Dec. 2003): 28.9 mil. chickens (excl. broilers). **Timber/lumber** (est. 2002): 324 mil bd. ft.; oak, tulip, beech, sycamore. **Nonfuel minerals** (est. 2003): $734 mil.; stone (crushed), cement (portland), sand and gravel (construction), lime, cement (masonry). **Chief ports:** Burns Harbor, Portage; Southwind Maritime, Mt. Vernon; Clark Maritime, Jeffersonville. **Principal internat. airports at:** Indianapolis, Ft. Wayne. **New private housing** (2003): 40,270 units/$5.5 bil. **Gross state product** (2001):

$189.9 bil. **Employment distrib.** (May 2004): 14.8% govt.; 19.5% trade/trans./util.; 19.4% mfg.; 12.5% ed./health serv.; 8.9% prof./bus serv.; 9.5% leisure/hosp.; 4.8% finance; 5.3% constr.; 1.4% info. **Per cap. pers. income** (2003): $28,783. **Sales tax** (2004): 6.0%. **Unemployment** (2003): 5.1%. **Tourism expends.** (2002): $6.7 bil. **Lottery** (2003): total sales: $664.4 mil; net income: $178.9 mil.

Finance. FDIC-insured commercial banks (2003): 399. **Deposits:** $59.6 bil. **FDIC-insured savings institutions** (2003): 58. **Assets:** $15.1 bil.

Federal govt. Fed. civ. employees (Mar. 2003): 19,093. **Avg. salary:** $53,307. **Notable fed. facilities:** Nav. Surface Warfare Ctr., Crane Div.

Energy. Electricity production (est. 2003, kWh by source): Coal: 110.9 bil; Petroleum: 408 mil; Gas: 1.7 bil; Hydroelectric: 424 mil.

State data. Motto: Crossroads of America. **Flower:** Peony. **Bird:** Cardinal. **Tree:** Tulip poplar. **Song:** On the Banks of the Wabash, Far Away. **Entered union** Dec. 11, 1816; rank, 19th. **State fair** at Indianapolis; mid-Aug.

History. When the Europeans arrived, Miami, Potawatomi, Kickapoo, Piankashaw, Wea, and Shawnee peoples inhabited the area. A French trading post was built, 1731-32, at Vincennes. La Salle visited the present South Bend area, 1679 and 1681. The first French fort was built near present-day Lafayette, 1717. France ceded the area to Britain, 1763. During the American Revolution, American Gen. George Rogers Clark captured Vincennes, 1778, and defeated British forces, 1779. At war's end, Britain ceded the area to the U.S. Miami Indians defeated U.S. troops twice, 1790, but were beaten, 1794, at Fallen Timbers by Gen. Anthony Wayne. At Tippecanoe, 1811, Gen. William H. Harrison defeated Tecumseh's Indian confederation. The Delaware, Potawatomi, and Miami were moved farther west, 1820-1850.

Tourist attractions. Lincoln Log Cabin Historic Site, near Charleston; George Rogers Clark Park, Vincennes; Wyandotte Cave; Tippecanoe Battlefield Memorial Park; Benjamin Harrison home; Indianapolis 500 raceway and museum, all Indianapolis; Indiana Dunes, near Chesterton; National College Football Hall of Fame, South Bend; Hoosier Nat'l. Forest, south-central Indiana.

Famous "Hoosiers." Larry Bird, Ambrose Burnside, Hoagy Carmichael, Jim Davis, James Dean, Eugene V. Debs, Theodore Dreiser, Paul Dresser, Jeff Gordon, Benjamin Harrison, Gil Hodges, Michael Jackson, David Letterman, Carole Lombard, John Mellencamp, Jane Pauley, Cole Porter, Gene Stratton Porter, Ernie Pyle, Dan Quayle, James Whitcomb Riley, Oscar Robertson, Red Skelton, Booth Tarkington, Kurt Vonnegut, Lew Wallace, Wendell L. Willkie, Wilbur Wright.

Tourist Information. Indiana Office of Tourism Development, 1 North Capital, Suite 700, Indianapolis, IN 46204; 1-888-ENJOYIN. **Website:** www.in.gov/enjoyindiana

Website. www.ai.org

Iowa
Hawkeye State

People. Population (2003 est.): 2,944,062; rank: 30; **net change** (2002-2003): 0.3%. **Pop. density:** 52.7 per sq mi. **Racial distribution** (2000): 93.9% white; 2.1% black; 1.3% Asian; 0.3% Native American/Nat. AK; <0.1% Hawaiian/Pacific Islander; 1.3% other race; 2 or more races, 1.1%. **Hispanic pop.** (any race): 2.8%.

Geography. Total area: 56,272 sq mi; rank: 26. **Land area:** 55,869 sq mi; rank: 23. **Acres forested:** 2.1 mil. **Location:** West North Central state bordered by Mississippi R. on the E and Missouri R. on the W. **Climate:** humid, continental. **Topography:** Watershed from NW to SE; soil especially rich and land level in the N central counties. **Capital:** Des Moines.

Economy. Chief industries: agriculture, communications, construction, finance, insurance, trade, services, manufacturing. **Chief manuf. goods:** processed food products, tires, farm machinery, electronic products, appliances, household furniture, chemicals, fertilizers, auto accessories. **Chief crops:** silage and grain corn, soybeans, oats, hay. **Livestock** (Jan. 2004): 3.45 mil. cattle/calves; 250,000 sheep/lambs; (Jan. 2003): 15.8 mil. hogs/pigs; (Dec. 2003): 50.9 mil. chickens (excl. broilers). **Timber/lumber** (est. 2002): 77 mil bd. ft.; red cedar. **Nonfuel minerals** (est. 2003): $477 mil.; cement (portland), stone (crushed), sand and gravel (construction), gypsum (crude), lime. **Principal internat. airport at:** Des Moines. **New private housing** (2003): 16,654 units/$1.7 bil. **Gross state product** (2001): $90.9 bil. **Employment distrib.** (May 2004): 17.1% govt.; 20.6% trade/trans./util.; 15% mfg.; 13.3% ed./health serv.; 7.3% prof./bus serv.; 8.8% leisure/

hosp.; 6.8% finance; 4.7% constr.; 2.3% info. **Per cap. pers. income** (2003): $29,043. **Sales tax** (2004): 5.0%. **Unemployment** (2003): 4.5%. **Tourism expends.** (2002): $4.5 bil. **Lottery** (2003): total sales: $187.8 mil; net income: $48 mil.

Finance. FDIC-insured commercial banks (2003): 399. **Deposits:** $40.0 bil. **FDIC-insured savings institutions** (2003): 23. **Assets:** $6.2 bil.

Federal govt. Fed. civ. employees (Mar. 2003): 7,475. **Avg. salary:** $49,927. **Notable fed. facilities:** Ames Lab; Natl. Animal Disease Ctr.

Energy. Electricity production (est. 2003, kWh by source): Coal: 34.3 bil; Gas: 279 mil; Hydroelectric: 776 mil; Nuclear: 4 bil; Other: 66 mil.

State data. Motto: Our liberties we prize, and our rights we will maintain. **Flower:** Wild rose. **Bird:** Eastern goldfinch. **Tree:** Oak. **Rock:** Geode. **Entered union** Dec. 28, 1846; rank, 29th. **State fair** at Des Moines; mid-Aug.

History. Early inhabitants were Mound Builders who dwelt on Iowa's fertile plains. Later, Woodland tribes including the Iowa and Yankton Sioux lived in the area. The first Europeans, Marquette and Jolliet, gave France its claim to the area, 1673. In 1762, France ceded the region to Spain, but Napoleon took it back, 1800. It became part of the U.S. through the Louisiana Purchase, 1803. Native American Sauk and Fox tribes moved into the area from states farther east but relinquished their land in defeat, after the 1832 uprising led by the Sauk chieftain Black Hawk. By mid-19th cent. they were forced to move on to Kansas. Iowa became a territory in 1838, and entered as a free state, 1846, strongly supporting the Union.

Tourist attractions. Herbert Hoover birthplace and library, West Branch; Effigy Mounds Natl. Monument, prehistoric Indian burial site, Marquette; Amana Colonies; Grant Wood's paintings and memorabilia, Davenport Municipal Art Gallery; Living History Farms, Des Moines; Adventureland, Altoona; Boone & Scenic Valley Railroad, Boone; Greyhound Parks, in Dubuque and Council Bluffs; Prairie Meadows horse racing, Altoona; riverboat cruises and casino gambling, Mississippi and Missouri Rivers; Iowa Great Lakes, Okoboji.

Famous Iowans. Tom Arnold, Johnny Carson, Marquis Childs, Buffalo Bill Cody, Mamie Dowd Eisenhower, Bob Feller, George Gallup, Susan Glaspell, James Norman Hall, Harry Hansen, Herbert Hoover, Ann Landers, Glenn Miller, Lillian Russell, Billy Sunday, James A. Van Allen, Abigail Van Buren, Carl Van Vechten, Henry Wallace, John Wayne, Meredith Willson, Grant Wood.

Tourist information. Iowa Tourism Office, Iowa Dept. of Economic Development, 200 E. Grand Ave., Des Moines, IA 50309; 1-888-472-6035. **Website:** www.traveliowa.com

Website. www.iowa.gov

Kansas
Sunflower State

People. Population (2003 est.): 2,723,507; rank: 33; **net change** (2002-2003): 0.4%. **Pop. density:** 33.3 per sq mi. **Racial distribution** (2000): 86.1% white; 5.7% black; 1.7% Asian; 0.9% Native American/Nat. AK; 0.1% Hawaiian/Pacific Islander; 3.4% other race; 2 or more races, 2.1%. **Hispanic pop.** (any race): 7.0%.

Geography. Total area: 82,277 sq mi; rank: 15. **Land area:** 81,815 sq mi; rank: 13. **Acres forested:** 1.5 mil. **Location:** West North Central state, with Missouri R. on E. **Climate:** temperate but continental, with great extremes between summer and winter. **Topography:** hilly Osage Plains in the E; central region level prairie and hills; high plains in the W. **Capital:** Topeka.

Economy. Chief industries: manufacturing, finance, insurance, real estate, services. **Chief manuf. goods:** transportation equipment, machinery & computer equipment, food and kindred products, printing & publishing. **Chief crops:** wheat, sorghum, corn, hay, soybeans, sunflowers. **Livestock** (Jan. 2004): 6.65 mil. cattle/calves; 100,000 sheep/lambs; (Jan. 2003): 1.63 mil. hogs/pigs. **Timber/lumber:** (est. 2002): 12 mil bd. ft.; oak, walnut; 14 mil bd. ft. **Nonfuel minerals** (est. 2003): $688 mil.; cement (portland), helium (Grade-A), salt, stone (crushed), helium (crude). **Chief ports:** Kansas City. **Principal internat. airport at:** Kansas City. **New private housing** (2003): 13,748 units/$1.7 bil. **Gross state product** (2001): $87.2 bil. **Employment distrib.** (May 2004): 19.6% govt.; 19.6% trade/trans./util.; 12.9% mfg.; 11.9% ed./health serv.; 9.3% prof./bus serv.; 8.5% leisure/hosp.; 5.4% finance; 4.8% constr.; 3.6% info. **Per cap. pers. income** (2003): $29,935. **Sales tax** (2004): 5.3%. **Unemployment** (2003): 5.4%. **Tourism expends.** (2002): $3.7 bil. **Lottery** (2003): total sales: $202.9 mil; net income: $62.5 mil.

Finance. FDIC-insured commercial banks (2003): 362. **Deposits:** $32.8 bil. **FDIC-insured savings institutions** (2003): 18. **Assets:** $12.1 bil.

Federal govt. Fed. civ. employees (Mar. 2003): 15,043. **Avg. salary:** $52,022. **Notable fed. facilities:** Fts. Riley, Leavenworth; Leavenworth Fed. Pen.; McConnell AFB; Colmery-O'Neal Veterans Hospital.

Energy. Electricity production (est. 2003, kWh by source): Coal: 35.1 bil; Petroleum: 952 mil; Gas: 1.3 bil; Nuclear: 8.9 bil.

State data. Motto: Ad Astra per Aspera (To the stars through difficulties). **Flower:** Native sunflower. **Bird:** Western meadowlark. **Tree:** Cottonwood. **Song:** Home on the Range. **Entered union** Jan. 29, 1861; rank, 34th. **State fair** at Hutchinson; begins Friday after Labor Day.

History. When Coronado first explored the area, Wichita, Pawnee, Kansa, and Osage peoples lived there. These Native Americans—hunters who also farmed—were joined on the Plains by the nomadic Cheyenne, Arapaho, Comanche, and Kiowa about 1800. French explorers established trading between 1682 and 1739, and the U.S. took over most of the area in the Louisiana Purchase, 1803. After 1830, thousands of eastern Native Americans were removed to Kansas. Kansas became a territory, 1854. Violent incidents between proand antislavery settlers caused the territory to be known as "Bleeding Kansas." It eventually entered the Union as a free state, 1861. Railroad construction after the war made Abilene and Dodge City terminals of large cattle drives from Texas.

Tourist attractions. Eisenhower Center, Abilene; Agricultural Hall of Fame and Natl. Center, Bonner Springs; Dodge City-Boot Hill & Frontier Town; Old Cowtown Museum, Wichita; Ft. Scott and Ft. Larned, restored 1800s cavalry forts; Kansas Cosmosphere and Space Center, Hutchinson; Woodlands Racetrack, Kansas City; U.S. Cavalry Museum, Ft. Riley; NCAA Visitors Center, Shawnee; Heartland Park Raceway, Topeka.

Famous Kansans. Kirstie Alley, Roscoe "Fatty" Arbuckle, Ed Asner, Gwendolyn Brooks, John Brown, George Washington Carver, Wilt Chamberlain, Walter P. Chrysler, Glenn Cunningham, John Stuart Curry, Robert Dole, Amelia Earhart, Wyatt Earp, Dwight D. Eisenhower, Ron Evans, Maurice Greene, Wild Bill Hickok, Cyrus Holliday, Dennis Hopper, William Inge, Don Johnson, Walter Johnson, Nancy Landon Kassebaum, Buster Keaton, Emmett Kelly, Alf Landon, Edgar Lee Masters, Hattie McDaniel, Oscar Micheaux, Carry Nation, Georgia Neese-Gray, Charlie Parker, Gordon Parks, Jim Ryun, Barry Sanders, Vivian Vance, William Allen White, Jess Willard.

Tourist information. Kansas Dept. of Commerce, Travel and Tourism Div., 1000 SW Jackson St., Ste. 100, Topeka, KS 66612; 1-800-2KANSAS. **Website:** www.travelks.com

Website. www.accesskansas.org

Kentucky
Bluegrass State

People. Population (2003 est.): 4,117,827; rank: 26; **net change** (2002-2003): 0.7%. **Pop. density:** 103.7 per sq mi. **Racial distribution** (2000): 90.1% white; 7.3% black; 0.7% Asian; 0.2% Native American/Nat. AK; <0.1% Hawaiian/Pacific Islander; 0.6% other race; 2 or more races, 1.1%. **Hispanic pop.** (any race): 1.5%.

Geography. Total area: 40,409 sq mi; rank: 37. **Land area:** 39,728 sq mi; rank: 36. **Acres forested:** 12.7 mil. **Location:** East South Central state, bordered on N by Illinois, Indiana, Ohio; on E by West Virginia and Virginia; on S by Tennessee; on W by Missouri. **Climate:** moderate, with plentiful rainfall. **Topography:** mountainous in E; rounded hills of the Knobs in the N; Bluegrass, heart of state; wooded rocky hillsides of the Pennyroyal; Western Coal Field; the fertile Purchase in the SW. **Capital:** Frankfort.

Economy. Chief industries: manufacturing, services, finance, insurance and real estate, retail trade, public utilities. **Chief manuf. goods:** transportation & industrial machinery, apparel, printing & publishing, food products, electric & electronic equipment. **Chief crops:** tobacco, corn, soybeans. **Livestock** (Jan. 2004): 2.32 mil. cattle/calves; (Jan. 2003): 380,000 hogs/pigs; (Dec. 2003): 7.2 mil. chickens (excl. broilers). 275.9 mil. broilers. **Timber/lumber** (est.2002): 691 mil bd. ft.; hardwoods, pines. **Nonfuel minerals** (est. 2003): $559 mil.; stone (crushed), lime, cement (portland), sand and gravel (construction), clays (ball). **Chief ports:** Paducah, Louisville, Covington, Owensboro, Ashland, Henderson County, Lyon County, Hickman-Fulton County. **Principal internat. airports at:** Covington/Cincinnati, Louisville. **New private housing** (2003): 20,183 units/$2.2 bil. **Gross state product** (2001):

$120.3 bil. **Employment distrib.** (May 2004): 17.4% govt.; 20.6% trade/trans./util.; 14.7% mfg.; 12.8% ed./health serv.; 8.5% prof./bus serv.; 9.2% leisure/hosp.; 4.8% finance; 4.9% constr.; 1.7% info. **Per cap. pers. income** (2003): $26,252. **Sales tax** (2004): 6.0%. **Unemployment** (2003): 6.2%. **Tourism expends.** (2002): $5.2 bil. **Lottery** (2003): total sales: $673.5 mil; net income: $180.7 mil.

Finance. FDIC-insured commercial banks (2003): 217. **Deposits:** $34.3 bil. **FDIC-insured savings institutions** (2003): 26. **Assets:** $3.0 bil.

Federal govt. Fed. civ. employees (Mar. 2003): 20,815. **Avg. salary:** $46,831. **Notable fed. facilities:** U.S. Gold Bullion Depository, Ft. Knox; Ft. Campbell; Fed. Correctional Institution, Lexington.

Energy. Electricity production (est. 2003, kWh by source): Coal: 76.4 bil; Petroleum: 138 mil; Gas: 231 mil; Hydroelectric: 3.9 bil; Other: 22 mil.

State data. Motto: United we stand, divided we fall. **Flower:** Goldenrod. **Bird:** Cardinal. **Tree:** Tulip Poplar. **Song:** My Old Kentucky Home. **Entered union** June 1, 1792; rank, 15th. **State fair** at Louisville, late Aug.

History. The area was predominantly hunting grounds for Shawnee, Wyandot, Delaware, and Cherokee peoples. Explored by Americans Thomas Walker and Christopher Gist, 1750-51, Kentucky was the first area west of the Alleghenies settled by American pioneers. The first permanent settlement was Harrodsburg, 1774. Daniel Boone blazed the Wilderness Trail through the Cumberland Gap and founded Ft. Boonesborough, 1775. Conflicts with Native Americans, spurred by the British, were unceasing until, during the American Revolution, Gen. George Rogers Clark captured British forts in Indiana and Illinois, 1778. In 1792, Virginia dropped its claims to the region, and it became the 15th state. Although officially a Union state, Kentuckians had divided loyalties during the Civil War and were forced to choose sides; its slaves were freed only after the adoption of the 13th Amendment to the U.S. Constitution, 1865.

Tourist attractions. Kentucky Derby; Louisville; Land Between the Lakes Natl. Recreation Area, Kentucky Lake and Lake Barkley; Mammoth Cave Natl. Park; Echo River, 360 ft below ground; Lake Cumberland; Lincoln's birthplace, Hodgenville; My Old Kentucky Home State Park, Bardstown; Cumberland Gap Natl. Historical Park, Middlesboro; Kentucky Horse Park, Lexington; Shaker Village, Pleasant Hill.

Famous Kentuckians. Muhammad Ali, John James Audubon, Alben W. Barkley, Daniel Boone, Louis D. Brandeis, John C. Breckinridge, Kit Carson, Albert B. "Happy" Chandler, Henry Clay, Jefferson Davis, D. W. Griffith, "Casey" Jones, Abraham Lincoln, Mary Todd Lincoln, Thomas Hunt Morgan, Carry Nation, Col. Harland Sanders, Diane Sawyer, Adlai Stevenson, Jesse Stuart, Zachary Taylor, Hunter S. Thompson, Robert Penn Warren, Whitney Young Jr.

Tourist Information. Kentucky Dept. of Tourism, 500 Mero St., Ste. 2200, Frankfort, KY 40601; 1-800-225-TRIP. **Website:** www.kentuckytourism.com

Website. www.kentucky.gov

Louisiana
Pelican State

People. Population (2003 est.): 4,496,334; rank: 24; **net change** (2002-2003): 0.4%. **Pop. density:** 103.2 per sq mi. **Racial distribution** (2000): 63.9% white; 32.5% black; 1.2% Asian; 0.6% Native American/Nat. AK; <0.1% Hawaiian/Pacific Islander; 0.7% other race; 2 or more races, 1.1%. **Hispanic pop.** (any race): 2.4%.

Geography. Total area: 51,840 sq mi; rank: 31. **Land area:** 43,562 sq mi; rank: 33. **Acres forested:** 13.8 mil. **Location:** West South Central state on the Gulf Coast. **Climate:** subtropical, affected by continental weather patterns. **Topography:** lowlands of marshes and Mississippi R. flood plain; Red R. Valley lowlands; upland hills in the Florida Parishes; average elevation, 100 ft. **Capital:** Baton Rouge.

Economy. Chief industries: wholesale and retail trade, tourism, manufacturing, construction, transportation, communication, public utilities, finance, insurance, real estate, mining. **Chief manuf. goods:** chemical products, foods, transportation equipment, electronic equipment, petroleum products, lumber, wood, and paper. **Chief crops:** soybeans, sugarcane, rice, corn, cotton, sweet potatoes, pecans, sorghum, aquaculture. **Livestock** (Jan. 2004) 850,000 cattle/calves; (Jan. 2003): 20,000 hogs/pigs. 2.6 mil. chickens (excl. broilers). **Timber/lumber** (est. 2002): 1.3 bil bd. ft.; pines, hardwoods, oak. **Nonfuel minerals** (est. 2003): $331 mil.; salt, sand and gravel (construction), stone (crushed), sand and gravel (industrial), lime. **Commercial fishing** (2002):

$305.3. **Chief ports:** New Orleans, Baton Rouge, Lake Charles, Port of S. Louisiana (La Place), Shreveport, Plaquemine, St. Bernard, Alexandria. **Principal internat. airport at:** New Orleans. **New private housing** (2003): 20,313 units/ $2.2 bil. **Gross state product** (2001): $148.7 bil. **Employment distrib.** (May 2004): 19.8% govt.; 20% trade/trans./util.; 8.1% mfg.; 13% ed./health serv.; 9.3% prof./bus serv.; 10.6% leisure/hosp.; 5.2% finance; 6.2% constr.; 1.5% info. **Per cap. pers. income** (2003): $26,100. **Sales tax** (2004): 4.0%. **Unemployment** (2003): 6.6%. **Tourism expends.** (2002): $9.3 bil. **Lottery** (2003): total sales: $311.5 mil; net income: $110.8 mil.

Finance. FDIC-insured commercial banks (2003): 139. **Deposits:** $39.1 bil. **FDIC-insured savings institutions** (2003): 31. **Assets:** $4.8 bil.

Federal govt. Fed. civ. employees (Mar. 2003): 20,540. **Avg. salary:** $50,848. **Notable federal facilities:** Strategic Petroleum Reserve, Michoud Assembly Plant, Southern Regional Research Ctr., U.S. Army Corps of Engineers, all New Orleans; Ft. Polk (Joint Readiness Training Ctr.); Barksdale AFB; New Orleans NAS.

Energy. Electricity production (est. 2003, kWh by source): Coal: 11.2 bil; Petroleum: 1.0 bil; Gas: 13.5 bil; Nuclear: 16.1 bil.

State data. Motto: Union, justice, and confidence. **Flower:** Magnolia. **Bird:** Eastern brown pelican. **Tree:** Cypress. **Song:** Give Me Louisiana. **Entered union** Apr. 30, 1812; rank, 18th. **State fair** at Shreveport; Oct.

History. Caddo, Tunica, Choctaw, Chitimacha, and Chawash peoples lived in the region at the time of European contact. Europeans Cabeza de Vaca and Panfilo de Narvaez first visited, 1530. The region was claimed for France by La Salle, 1682. The first permanent settlement was by the French at Biloxi, now in Mississippi, 1699. France ceded the region to Spain, 1762, took it back, 1800, and sold it to the U.S., 1803, in the Louisiana Purchase. During the American Revolution, Spanish Louisiana aided the Americans. Admitted as a state in 1812, Louisiana was the scene of the Battle of New Orleans, 1815.

Louisiana Creoles are descendants of early French and/or Spanish ancestry. About 4,000 Acadians, French settlers in Nova Scotia, Canada, were forcibly transported by the British to Louisiana in 1755 (an event commemorated in Longfellow's "Evangeline") and settled near Bayou Teche; their descendants became known as Cajuns. Another group, the Islenos, were descendants of Canary Islanders brought to Louisiana by a Spanish governor in 1770. Traces of Spanish and French survive in local dialects.

Tourist attractions. Mardi Gras, French Quarter, Superdome, Dixieland jazz, Aquarium of the Americas, Audubon Zoo & Gardens, all New Orleans; Battle of New Orleans site; Longfellow-Evangeline Memorial Park, St. Martinville; Kent House Museum, Alexandria; Hodges Gardens, Natchitoches, USS *Kidd* Memorial, Baton Rouge.

Famous Louisianans. Louis Armstrong, Pierre Beauregard, Judah P. Benjamin, Braxton Bragg, Kate Chopin, Harry Connick Jr., Ellen DeGeneres, Lillian Hellman, Grace King, Bob Livingston, Huey Long, Wynton Marsalis, Leonidas K. Polk, Anne Rice, Henry Miller Shreve, Britney Spears, Edward D. White Jr.

Tourist information. Louisiana Office of Tourism, PO Box 94291, Baton Rouge, LA 70804-9291; 1-800-677-4082. **Website.** www.crt.state.la/crt/tourism
Website. www.state.la.us

Maine
Pine Tree State

People. Population (2003 est.): 1,305,728; rank: 40; **net change** (2002-2003): 0.8%. **Pop. density:** 42.3 per sq mi. **Racial distribution** (2000): 96.9% white; 0.5% black; 0.7% Asian; 0.6% Native American/Nat. AK; <0.1% Hawaiian/Pacific Islander; 0.2% other race; 2 or more races, 1.0%. **Hispanic pop.** (any race): 0.7%.

Geography. Total area: 35,385 sq mi; rank: 39. **Land area:** 30,862 sq mi; rank: 39. **Acres forested:** 17.7 mil. **Location:** New England state at northeastern tip of U.S. **Climate:** Southern interior and coastal, influenced by air masses from the S and W; northern clime harsher, avg. over 100 in. snow in winter. **Topography:** Appalachian Mts. extend through state; western borders have rugged terrain; long sand beaches on southern coast; northern coast mainly rocky promontories, peninsulas, fjords. **Capital:** Augusta.

Economy. Chief industries: manufacturing, agriculture, fishing, services, trade, government, finance, insurance, real estate, construction. **Chief manuf. goods:** paper & wood

products, transportation equipment. **Chief crops:** potatoes, aquaculture products. **Livestock** (Jan. 2004) 91,000 cattle/ calves; (Jan. 2003): 6,500 hogs/pigs; (Dec. 2003): 5.5 mil. chickens (excl. broilers). **Timber/lumber** (est. 2002): 988 mil bd. ft.; pine, spruce, fir. **Nonfuel minerals** (est. 2003): $100 mil.; sand and gravel (construction), cement (portland), stone (crushed), stone (dimension), peat. **Commercial fishing** (2002): $286.4 mil. **Chief ports:** Searsport, Portland, Eastport. **Principal internat. airports at:** Bangor, Portland. **New private housing** (2003): 7,361 units/$979 mil. **Gross state product** (2001): $37.4 bil. **Employment distrib.** (May 2004): 17.5% govt.; 20% trade/trans./util.; 10% mfg.; 17.7% ed./ health serv.; 8.3% prof./bus serv.; 9.8% leisure/hosp.; 5.7% finance; 5.3% constr.; 1.8% info. **Per cap. pers. income** (2003): $28,831. **Sales tax** (2004): 5.0%. **Unemployment** (2003): 5.1%. **Tourism expends.** (2002): $1.9 bil. **Lottery** (2003): total sales: $164.6 mil; net income: $40.3 mil.

Finance. FDIC-insured commercial banks (2003): 17. **Deposits:** $21.9 bil. **FDIC-insured savings institutions** (2003): 23. **Assets:** $8.7 bil.

Federal govt. Fed. civ. employees (Mar. 2003): 9,001. **Avg. salary:** $51,053. **Notable fed. facilities:** Kittery Naval Shipyard; Brunswick NAS.

Energy. Electricity production (est. 2002, kWh, by source): Hydroelectric: 6 mil.

State data. Motto: Dirigo (I direct). **Flower:** White pine cone and tassel. **Bird:** Chickadee. **Tree:** Eastern white pine. **Song:** State of Maine Song. **Entered union** Mar. 15, 1820; rank, 23rd. **State fair:** at Bangor, late July; at Skowhegan, mid-Aug.

History. When the Europeans arrived, Maine was inhabited by Algonquian peoples including the Abnaki, Penobscot, and Passamaquoddy. Maine's rocky coast was believed to have been explored by the Cabots, 1498-99. French settlers arrived, 1604, at the St. Croix River, English, c 1607, on the Kennebec; both settlements failed. Maine was made part of Massachusetts, 1691. In the American Revolution, a Maine regiment fought at Bunker Hill. A British fleet destroyed Falmouth (now Portland), 1775, but the British ship *Margaretta* was captured near Machiasport. In 1820, Maine broke off and became a separate state.

Tourist attractions. Acadia Natl. Park, Bar Harbor, on Mt. Desert Island; Old Orchard Beach; Portland's Old Port; Kennebunkport; Common Ground Country Fair; Portland Headlight; Baxter State Pk.; Freeport/L. L. Bean.

Famous "Down Easters." Leon Leonwood (L.L.) Bean, James G. Blaine, Cyrus H. K. Curtis, Hannibal Hamlin, Sarah Jewett, Stephen King, Henry Wadsworth Longfellow, Sir Hiram and Hudson Maxim, Edna St. Vincent Millay, George Mitchell, Edmund Muskie, Judd Nelson, Edwin Arlington Robinson, Joan Benoit Samuelson, Liv Tyler, Kate Douglas Wiggin, Ben Ames Williams.

Tourist Information. Maine Office of Tourism, 59 State House Station, Augusta, ME 04333; 1-888-MAINE45 (from within the United States and Canada). **Website:** www.visitmaine.com
Website. www.state.me.us

Maryland
Old Line State, Free State

People. Population (2003 est.): 5,508,909; rank: 19; **net change** (2002-2003): 1.1%. **Pop. density:** 563.6 per sq mi. **Racial distribution** (2000): 64.0% white; 27.9% black; 4.0% Asian; 0.3% Native American/Nat. AK; <0.1% Hawaiian/Pacific Islander; 1.8% other race; 2 or more races, 2.0%. **Hispanic pop.** (any race): 4.3%.

Geography. Total area: 12,407 sq mi; rank: 42. **Land area:** 9,774 sq mi; rank: 42. **Acres forested:** 2.6 mil. **Location:** South Atlantic state stretching from the Ocean to the Allegheny Mts. **Climate:** continental in the west; humid subtropical in the east. **Topography:** Eastern Shore of coastal plain and Maryland Main of coastal plain, piedmont plateau, and the Blue Ridge, separated by the Chesapeake Bay. **Capital:** Annapolis.

Economy. Chief industries: manufacturing, biotechnology and information technology, services, tourism. **Chief manuf. goods:** electric and electronic equipment; food and kindred products, chemicals and allied products, printed materials. **Chief crops:** greenhouse and nursery products, soybeans, corn. **Livestock** (Jan. 2004) 235,000 cattle/calves; (Jan. 2003): 40,000 hogs/pigs; (Dec. 2003): 3.8 mil. chickens (excl. broilers); 292.4 mil. broilers. **Timber/lumber** (est. 2002): 268 mil bd. ft.; hardwoods. **Nonfuel minerals** (est. 2003): $382 mil.; cement (portland), stone (crushed), sand and gravel (construction), cement (masonry), stone (dimen-

sion). **Commercial fishing** (2002): $49.0 mil. **Chief port:** Baltimore. **Principal internat. airport at:** Baltimore. **New private housing** (2003): 30,125 units/$3.8 bil. **Gross state product** (2001): $195.0 bil. **Employment distrib.** (May 2004): 18.7% govt.; 18.2% trade/trans./util.; 5.7% mfg.; 13.7% ed./health serv.; 14.6% prof./bus serv.; 9.2% leisure/hosp.; 6.2% finance; 6.9% constr.; 2% info. **Per cap. pers. income** (2003): $37,331. **Sales tax** (2004): 5.0%. **Unemployment** (2003): 4.5%. **Tourism expends.** (2002): $9.0 bil. **Lottery** (2003): total sales: $1.3 bil; net income: $444.9 mil.

Finance. FDIC-insured commercial banks (2003): 70. **Deposits:** $25.1 bil. **FDIC-insured savings institutions** (2003): 52. **Assets:** $8.8 bil.

Federal govt. Fed. civ. employees (Mar. 2003): 105,702. **Avg. salary:** $68,831. **Notable fed. facilities:** U.S. Naval Academy; Natl. Agriculture Res. Ctr.; Ft. Meade, Aberdeen Proving Ground; Goddard Space Flight Ctr.; Natl. Institutes of Health; Natl. Inst. of Standards & Technology; Food & Drug Administration; Bureau of the Census; Natl. Naval Med. Ctr., Bethesda; Natl. Marine Fisheries Serv.; Natl. Oceanic and Atmospheric Admin.

Energy. Electricity production (est. 2002, kWh, by source): Petroleum: 28 mil; Gas: 3 mil.

State data. Motto: Fatti Maschii, Parole Femine (Manly deeds, womanly words). **Flower:** Black-eyed Susan. **Bird:** Baltimore oriole. **Tree:** White oak. **Song:** Maryland, My Maryland. **Seventh** of the original 13 states to ratify the U.S. Constitution, Apr. 28, 1788. **State fair** held at Timonium; late Aug.-early Sept.

History. Europeans encountered Algonquian-speaking Nanticoke and Piscataway and Iroquois-speaking Susquehannock when they first visited the area. Italian explorer Verrazano visited the Chesapeake region in the early 16th cent. English Capt. John Smith explored and mapped the area, 1608. William Claiborne set up a trading post on Kent Island in Chesapeake Bay, 1631. King Charles I granted land to Cecilius Calvert, Lord Baltimore, 1632; Calvert's brother Leonard, with about 200 settlers, founded St. Marys, 1634. The bravery of Maryland troops in the American Revolution, as at the Battle of Long Island, won the state its nickname "The Old Line State." In the War of 1812, when a British fleet tried to take Ft. McHenry, Marylander Francis Scott Key wrote "The Star-Spangled Banner," 1814. Although a slave-holding state, Maryland remained with the Union during the Civil War and was the site of the battle of Antietam, 1862, which halted Gen. Robert E. Lee's march north.

Tourist attractions. The Preakness at Pimlico track, Baltimore; The Maryland Million at Laurel Race Course; Ocean City; restored Ft. McHenry, near which Francis Scott Key wrote "The Star-Spangled Banner"; Edgar Allan Poe house, Ravens Football at Memorial Stadium, Camden Yards, Natl. Aquarium, Harborplace, all Baltimore; Antietam Battlefield, near Hagerstown; South Mountain Battlefield; U.S. Naval Academy, Annapolis; Maryland State House, Annapolis, 1772, the oldest still in legislative use in the U.S.

Famous Marylanders. John Astin, Benjamin Banneker, Tom Clancy, Jonathan Demme, Francis Scott Key, H. L. Mencken, Kweisi Mfume, Ogden Nash, Charles Willson Peale, William Pinkney, Edgar Allan Poe, Cal Ripken Jr., Babe Ruth, Upton Sinclair, Roger B. Taney, John Waters, Montel Williams.

Tourist Information. Maryland Office of Tourism Development, 217 E. Redwood St., 9th Fl., Baltimore, MD 21202; 1-800-MDISFUN. **Website:** www.mdwelcome.org
Website. www.maryland.gov

Massachusetts
Bay State, Old Colony

People. Population (2003 est.): 6,433,422; rank: 13; **net change** (2002-2003): 0.2%. **Pop. density:** 820.6 per sq mi. **Racial distribution** (2000): 84.5% white; 5.4% black; 3.8% Asian; 0.2% Native American/Nat. AK; <0.1% Hawaiian/Pacific Islander; 3.7% other race; 2 or more races, 2.3%. **Hispanic pop.** (any race): 6.8%.

Geography. Total area: 10,555 sq mi; rank: 44. **Land area:** 7,840 sq mi; rank: 45. **Acres forested:** 3.1 mil. **Location:** New England state along Atlantic seaboard. **Climate:** temperate, with colder and drier clime in western region. **Topography:** jagged indented coast from Rhode Island around Cape

Cod; flat land yields to stony upland pastures near central region and gentle hilly country in west; except in west, land is rocky, sandy, and not fertile. **Capital:** Boston.

Economy. Chief industries: services, trade, manufacturing. **Chief manuf. goods:** electric and electronic equipment, instruments, industrial machinery and equipment, printing and publishing, fabricated metal products. **Chief crops:** cranberries, greenhouse, nursery, vegetables. **Livestock** (Jan. 2004) 48,000 cattle/calves; (Jan. 2003): 14,500 hogs/pigs; (Dec. 2003): 280,000 chickens (excl. broilers). **Timber/lumber:** (figs. undisclosed); white pine, oak, other hard woods; **Nonfuel minerals** (est. 2003): $168 mil.; stone (crushed), sand and gravel (construction), lime, stone (dimension), clays (common). **Commercial fishing** (2002): $296.9 mil. **Chief ports:** Boston, Fall River, New Bedford, Salem, Gloucester, Plymouth. **Principal internat. airport at:** Boston. **New private housing** (2003): 19,273 units/$3.0 bil. **Gross state product** (2001): $287.8 bil. **Employment distrib.** (May 2004): 13.1% govt.; 17.7% trade/trans./util.; 10.1% mfg.; 18.1% ed./health serv.; 13.7% prof./bus serv.; 9.4% leisure/hosp.; 7% finance; 4.5% constr.; 2.7% info. **Per cap. pers. income** (2003): $39,815. **Sales tax** (2004): 5.0%. **Unemployment** (2003): 5.8%. **Tourism expends.** (2002): $11.3 bil. **Lottery** (2003): total sales: $4.2 bil; net income: $889.5 mil.

Finance. FDIC-insured commercial banks (2003): 38. **Deposits:** $91.5 bil. **FDIC-insured savings institutions** (2003): 171. **Assets:** $72.7 bil.

Federal govt. Fed. civ. employees (Mar. 2003): 25,304. **Avg. salary:** $58,420. **Notable fed. facilities:** Thomas P. O'Neill Jr. Fed. Bldg., J.W. McCormack Bldg., JFK Fed. Bldg., Natick Army Soldier Systems Ctr.

Energy. Electricity production (est. 2003, kWh by source): Petroleum: 282 mil; Gas: 217 mil.

State data. Motto: Ense Petit Placidam Sub Libertate Quietem (By the sword we seek peace, but peace only under liberty). **Flower:** Mayflower. **Bird:** Chickadee. **Tree:** American elm. **Song:** All Hail to Massachusetts. **Sixth** of the original 13 states to ratify Constitution, Feb. 6, 1788. **State Fair** at Springfield, mid-Sept.–early Oct.

History. Early inhabitants were the Algonquian, Nauset, Wampanoag, Massachuset, Pennacook, Nipmuc, and Pocumtuc peoples. Pilgrims settled in Plymouth, 1620, giving thanks for their survival with the first Thanksgiving Day, 1621. About 20,000 new settlers arrived, 1630-40. Native American relations with the colonists deteriorated leading to King Philip's War, 1675-76, which the colonists won, ending Native American resistance. Demonstrations against British restrictions set off the Boston Massacre, 1770, and the Boston Tea Party, 1773. The first bloodshed of American Revolution was at Lexington, 1775.

Tourist attractions. Provincetown artists' colony; Cape Cod; Plymouth Rock, Plimoth Plantation, *Mayflower II*, all Plymouth; Freedom Trail, Isabella Stewart Gardner Museum, Museum of Fine Arts, Children's Museum, Museum of Science, New England Aquarium, JFK Library, Boston Ballet, Boston Pops, Boston Symphony Orchestra, all Boston; Tanglewood, Jacob's Pillow Dance Festival, Hancock Shaker Village, Berkshire Scenic Railway Museum, Norman Rockwell Museum, Edith Wharton and Herman Melville homes, all in the Berkshires; Salem; Old Sturbridge Village; Deerfield Historic District; Walden Pond; Naismith Memorial Basketball Hall of Fame, Springfield.

Famous "Bay Staters." John Adams, John Quincy Adams, Samuel Adams, Louisa May Alcott, Horatio Alger, Susan B. Anthony, Crispus Attucks, Clara Barton, Alexander Graham Bell, Stephen Breyer, George H. W. Bush, John Cheever, E. E. Cummings, Emily Dickinson, Charles Eliot, Ralph Waldo Emerson, William Lloyd Garrison, Edward Everett Hale, John Hancock, Nathaniel Hawthorne, Oliver Wendell Holmes, Winslow Homer, Elias Howe, John F. Kennedy, John Kerry, Jack Lemmon, James Russell Lowell, Cotton Mather, Samuel F. B. Morse, Edgar Allan Poe, Paul Revere, Norman Rockwell, Dr. Seuss (Theodore Seuss Geisel), Henry David Thoreau, Barbara Walters, James McNeil Whistler, John Greenleaf Whittier.

Tourist information. Massachusetts Office of Travel & Tourism, 100 Park Plaza, Ste. 4510, Boston, MA 02116; 1-800-227-MASS. **Website:** www.massvacation.com
Website. www.mass.gov

> **IT'S A FACT:** Some 34.3 million U.S. residents claim Irish ancestry, nearly 9 times the population of Ireland (4.0 million), according to the U.S. Census Bureau. In Massachusetts, 24% of residents claimed heritage in the Emerald Isle— about double the national percentage.

Michigan
Great Lakes State, Wolverine State

People. Population (2003 est.): 10,079,985; rank: 8; **net change** (2002-2003): 0.4%. **Pop. density:** 177.5 per sq mi. **Racial distribution** (2000): 80.2% white; 14.2% black; 1.8% Asian; 0.6% Native American/Nat. AK; <0.1% Hawaiian/Pacific Islander; 1.3% other race; 2 or more races, 1.9%. **Hispanic pop.** (any race): 3.3%.

Geography. Total area: 96,716 sq mi; rank: 11. **Land area:** 56,804 sq mi; rank: 22. **Acres forested:** 19.3 mil. **Location:** East North Central state bordering on 4 of the 5 Great Lakes, divided into an Upper and Lower Peninsula by the Straits of Mackinac, which link lakes Michigan and Huron. **Climate:** well-defined seasons tempered by the Great Lakes. **Topography:** low rolling hills give way to northern tableland of hilly belts in Lower Peninsula; Upper Peninsula is level in the east, with swampy areas; western region is higher and more rugged. **Capital:** Lansing.

Economy. Chief industries: manufacturing, services, tourism, agriculture, forestry/lumber. **Chief manuf. goods:** automobiles, transportation equipment, machinery, fabricated metals, food products, plastics, office furniture. **Chief crops:** corn, wheat, soybeans, dry beans, hay, potatoes, sweet corn, apples, cherries, sugar beets, blueberries, cucumbers, Niagra grapes. **Livestock** (Jan. 2004) 1.03 mil. cattle/calves; 83,000 sheep/lambs; (Jan. 2003): 950,000 hogs/pigs; (Dec. 2003): 9.7 chickens (excl. broilers). **Timber/lumber** (est. 2002): 744 mil bd. ft.; maple, oak, aspen; 681 mil bd. ft. **Nonfuel minerals** (est. 2003): $1.4 bil.; cement (portland), sand and gravel (construction), iron ore (usable), stone (crushed), salt. **Commercial fishing** (2002): $7.4 mil. **Chief ports:** Detroit, Saginaw River, Escanaba, Muskegon, Sault Ste. Marie, Port Huron, Marine City. **Principal internat. airports at:** Detroit, Flint, Grand Rapids, Kalamazoo, Lansing, Saginaw. **New private housing** (2003): 51,486 units/$6.8 bil. **Gross state product** (2001): $320.5 bil. **Employment distrib.** (May 2004): 15.7% govt.; 18.1% trade/trans./util.; 16.1% mfg.; 12.4% ed./health serv.; 13.5% prof./bus serv.; 9.3% leisure/hosp.; 4.9% finance; 4.4% constr.; 1.6% info. **Per cap. pers. income** (2003): $30,439. **Sales tax** (2004): 6.0%. **Unemployment** (2003): 7.3%. **Tourism expends.** (2002): $12.2 bil. **Lottery** (2003): total sales: $1.7 bil; net income: $586.1 mil.

Finance. FDIC-insured commercial banks (2003): 158. **Deposits:** $126.5 bil. **FDIC-insured savings institutions** (2002): 20. **Assets:** $15.9 bil.

Federal govt. Fed. civ. employees (Mar. 2003): 23,862. **Avg. salary:** $57,177. **Notable fed. facilities:** Isle Royal, Sleeping Bear Dunes national parks.

Energy. Electricity production (est. 2003, kWh by source): Coal: 66.5 bil; Petroleum: 799 mil; Gas: 1.1 bil; Hydroelectric: 220 mil; Nuclear: 28 bil; Other: 23 mil.

State data. Motto: Si Quaeris Peninsulam Amoenam, Circumspice (If you seek a pleasant peninsula, look about you). **Flower:** Apple blossom. **Bird:** Robin. **Tree:** White pine. **Song:** Michigan, My Michigan. **Entered union** Jan. 26, 1837; rank, 26th. **State fair** at Detroit, late Aug.–early Sept.; Upper Peninsula (Escanaba), mid-Aug.

History. Early inhabitants were the Ojibwa, Ottawa, Miami, Potawatomi, and Huron. French fur traders and missionaries visited the region, 1616, set up a mission at Sault Ste. Marie, 1641, and a settlement there, 1668. French settlements were taken over, 1763, by the British, who crushed a Native American uprising led by Ottawa chieftain Pontiac that same year. Treaty of Paris ceded territory to U.S., 1783, but British remained until 1796. The British seized Ft. Mackinac and Detroit, 1812. After Oliver H. Perry's Lake Erie victory and William H. Harrison's victory near the Thames River, 1813, the British retreated to Canada. The opening of the Erie Canal, 1825, and new land laws and Native American cessions led the way for a flood of settlers.

Tourist attractions. Henry Ford Museum, Greenfield Village, both in Dearborn; Michigan Space Center, Jackson; Tahquamenon *(Hiawatha)* Falls; DeZwaan windmill and Tulip Festival, Holland; "Soo Locks," St. Mary's Falls Ship Canal, Sault Ste. Marie, Kalamazoo Aviation History Museum; Mackinac Island; Kellogg's Cereal City USA, Battle Creek; Museum of African-American History, Motown Historical Museum, both Detroit.

Famous Michiganders. Ralph Bunche, Francis Ford Coppola, Paul de Kruif, Thomas Edison, Edna Ferber, Gerald R. Ford, Henry Ford, Aretha Franklin, Edgar Guest, Lee Iacocca, Robert Ingersoll, Magic Johnson, Casey Kasem, Will Kellogg, Ring Lardner, Elmore Leonard, Charles Lindbergh, Joe Louis, Madonna, Malcolm X, Terry McMillan, Michael Moore, Pontiac, Gilda Radner, Diana Ross, Glenn Seaborg, Tom Selleck, Sinbad (David Adkins), John Smoltz, Lily Tomlin, Stewart Edward White, Serena Williams.

Tourist Information. Michigan Economic Development Corp., 300 N. Washington Square, Lansing, MI 48913. Phone: 1-888-78GREAT. **Website.** travel.michigan.org
Website. www.michigan.gov

Minnesota
North Star State, Gopher State

People. Population (2003 est.): 5,059,375; rank: 21; **net change** (2002-2003): 0.7%. **Pop. density:** 63.6 per sq mi. **Racial distribution** (2000): 89.4% white; 3.5% black; 2.9% Asian; 1.1% Native American/Nat. AK; <0.1% Hawaiian/Pacific Islander; 1.3% other race; 2 or more races, 1.7%. **Hispanic pop.** (any race): 2.9%.

Geography. Total area: 86,939 sq mi; rank: 12. **Land area:** 79,610 sq mi; rank: 14. **Acres forested:** 16.7 mil. **Location:** West North Central state bounded on the E by Wisconsin and Lake Superior, on the N by Canada, on the W by the Dakotas, and on the S by Iowa. **Climate:** northern part of state lies in the moist Great Lakes storm belt; the western border lies at the edge of the semi-arid Great Plains. **Topography:** central hill and lake region covering approx. half the state; to the NE, rocky ridges and deep lakes; to the NW, flat plain; to the S, rolling plains and deep river valleys. **Capital:** St. Paul.

Economy. Chief industries: agribusiness, forest products, mining, manufacturing, tourism. **Chief manuf. goods:** food, chemical and paper products, industrial machinery, electric and electronic equipment, computers, printing & publishing, scientific and medical instruments, fabricated metal products, forest products. **Chief crops:** corn, soybeans, wheat, sugar beets, hay, barley, potatoes, sunflowers. **Livestock** (Jan. 2004) 2.4 mil. cattle/calves; 140,000 sheep/lambs; (Jan. 2003): 6.4 mil. hogs/pigs; (Dec. 2003): 14.6 mil. chickens (excl. broilers); 44.8 mil. broilers. **Timber/lumber** (est. 2002): 272 mil bd. ft.; needle-leaves and hardwoods. **Nonfuel minerals** (est. 2003): $1.2 bil.; iron ore (usable), sand and gravel (construction), stone (crushed), sand and gravel (industrial), stone (dimension). **Commercial fishing** (2002): $179,720. **Chief ports:** Duluth, St. Paul, Minneapolis. **Principal internat. airport at:** Minneapolis-St. Paul. **New private housing** (2003): 40,086 units/$6.0 bil. **Gross state product** (2001): $188.1 bil. **Employment distrib.** (May 2004): 15.1% govt.; 19.5% trade/trans./util.; 13% mfg.; 14% ed./health serv.; 11% prof./bus serv.; 9.1% leisure/hosp.; 6.6% finance; 4.9% constr.; 2.3% info. **Per cap. pers. income** (2003): $34,443. **Sales tax** (2004): 6.5%. **Unemployment** (2003): 5%. **Tourism expends.** (2002): $8.0 bil. **Lottery** (2003): total sales: $351.7 mil; net income: $79.4 mil.

Finance. FDIC-insured commercial banks (2003): 464. **Deposits:** $74.3 bil. **FDIC-insured savings institutions** (2003): 22. **Assets:** $3.6 bil.

Federal govt. Fed. civ. employees (Mar. 2003): 14,431. **Avg. salary:** $55,327.

Energy. Electricity production (est. 2003, kWh by source): Coal: 33.2 bil; Petroleum: 840 mil; Gas: 1.1 bil; Hydroelectric: 692 mil; Nuclear: 13.4 bil; Other: 401 mil.

State data. Motto: L'Etoile du Nord (The star of the north). **Flower:** Pink and white lady's-slipper. **Bird:** Common loon. **Tree:** Red pine. **Song:** Hail! Minnesota. **Entered union** May 11, 1858; rank, 32nd. **State fair** at St. Paul/Minneapolis; late Aug.-early Sept.

History. Dakota Sioux were early inhabitants of the area, and in the 16th cent., the Ojibwa began moving in from the east. French fur traders Médard Chouart and Pierre Esprit Radisson entered the region in the mid-17th cent. In 1679, French explorer Daniel Greysolon, sieur Duluth, claimed the entire region in the name of France. Britain took the area east of the Mississippi, 1763. The U.S. took over that portion after the American Revolution and in 1803, gained the western area in the Louisiana Purchase. The U.S. built Ft. St. Anthony (now Ft. Snelling), 1819, and in 1837, bought Native American lands, spurring an influx of settlers from the east. In 1849, the Territory of Minnesota was created. Sioux Indians staged a bloody uprising, the Battle of Woods Lake, 1862, and were driven from the state.

Tourist attractions. Minneapolis Institute of Arts, Walker Art Center, Minneapolis Sculpture Garden, Minnehaha Falls (inspiration for Longfellow's *Hiawatha*), Guthrie Theater, Minneapolis; Ordway Theater, St. Paul; Voyageurs Natl. Park; Mayo Clinic, Rochester; St. Paul Winter Carnival; North Shore (of Lake Superior).

Famous Minnesotans. Warren Burger, Ethan and Joel Coen, William O. Douglas, Bob Dylan, F. Scott Fitzgerald, Al

Franken, Judy Garland, Cass Gilbert, Hubert Humphrey, Garrison Keillor, Sister Elizabeth Kenny, Jessica Lange, Sinclair Lewis, Paul Manship, Roger Maris, E. G. Marshall, William and Charles Mayo, Eugene McCarthy, Walter F. Mondale, Prince (Rodgers Nelson), Charles Schulz, Harold Stassen, Thorstein Veblen, Jesse Ventura.

Tourist Information. Explore Minnesota Tourism, 100 Metro Square, 121 7th Pl. E., St. Paul, MN 55101. Phone: 1-888-TOURISM. **Website:** www.exploreminnesota.com

Website. www.state.mn.us

Mississippi
Magnolia State

People. Population (2003 est.): 2,881,281; rank: 31; **net change** (2002-2003): 0.5%. **Pop. density:** 61.4 per sq mi. **Racial distribution** (2000): 61.4% white; 36.3% black; 0.7% Asian; 0.4% Native American/Nat. AK; <0.1% Hawaiian/Pacific Islander; 0.5% other race; 2 or more races, 0.7%. **Hispanic pop.** (any race): 1.4%.

Geography. Total area: 48,430 sq mi; rank: 32. **Land area:** 46,907 sq mi; rank: 31. **Acres forested:** 18.6 mil. **Location:** East South Central state bordered on the W by the Mississippi R. and on the S by the Gulf of Mexico. **Climate:** semi-tropical, with abundant rainfall, long growing season, and extreme temperatures unusual. **Topography:** low, fertile delta between the Yazoo and Mississippi rivers; loess bluffs stretching around delta border; sandy gulf coastal terraces followed by piney woods and prairie; rugged, high sandy hills in extreme NE followed by Black Prairie Belt, Pontotoc Ridge, and flatwoods into the north central highlands. **Capital:** Jackson.

Economy. Chief industries: warehousing & distribution, services, manufacturing, government, wholesale and retail trade. **Chief manuf. goods:** chemicals & plastics, food & kindred products, furniture, lumber & wood products, electrical machinery, transportation equipment. **Chief crops:** cotton, rice, soybeans. **Livestock** (Jan. 2004) 1.02 mil. cattle/calves; (Jan. 2003): 305,000 hogs/pigs; (Dec. 2003): 11.0 mil. chickens (excl. broilers). 790.3 mil. broilers. **Timber/lumber** (est. 2002): 2.5 bil bd. ft.; pine, oak, hardwoods. **Nonfuel minerals** (est. 2003): $174 mil.; sand and gravel (construction), clays (fuller's earth), stone (crushed), cement (portland), sand and gravel (industrial). **Commercial fishing** (2002): $47.6 mil. **Chief ports:** Pascagoula, Vicksburg, Gulfport, Natchez, Greenville. **Principal internat. airport at:** Jackson. **New private housing** (2003): 12,052 units/$1.3 bil. **Gross state product** (2001): $67.1 bil. **Employment distrib.** (May 2004): 21.8% govt.; 19.4% trade/trans./util.; 16% mfg.; 10.5% ed./health serv.; 7.2% prof./bus serv.; 11.1% leisure/hosp.; 4.2% finance; 4.5% constr.; 1.3% info. **Per cap. pers. income** (2003): $23,448. **Sales tax** (2004): 7.0%. **Unemployment** (2003): 6.3%. **Tourism expends.** (2002) $5.3 bil.

Finance. FDIC-insured commercial banks (2003): 95. **Deposits:** $30.8 bil. **FDIC-insured savings institutions** (2003): 8. **Assets:** $995 mil.

Federal govt. Fed. civ. employees (Mar. 2003): 17,021. **Avg. salary:** $50,827. **Notable fed. facilities:** Columbus AFB; Keesler AFB; Meridian NAS; NASA Stennis Space Ctr.; Army Corps of Engineers Waterways Experiment Sta.; Naval Constr. Battalion Ctr., Gulfport.

Energy. Electricity production (est. 2003, kWh by source): Coal: 17.2 bil; Petroleum: 1.6 bil; Gas: 6.4 bil; Nuclear: 10.9 bil.

State data. Motto: Virtute et Armis (By valor and arms). **Flower:** Magnolia. **Bird:** Mockingbird. **Tree:** Magnolia. **Song:** Go, Mississippi! **Entered union** Dec. 10, 1817; rank, 20th. **State fair** at Jackson; early Oct.

History. Early inhabitants of the region were Choctaw, Chickasaw, and Natchez peoples. Hernando de Soto explored the area, 1540, and sighted the Mississippi River, 1541. Robert La Salle traced the river from Illinois to its mouth and claimed the entire valley for France, 1682. The first settlement was the French Ft. Maurepas, near Ocean Springs, 1699. The area was ceded to Britain, 1763; American settlers followed. During the American Revolution, Spain seized part of the area, remaining even after the U.S. acquired title at the end of the conflict; Spain finally moved out, 1798. The Territory of Mississippi was formed, 1798. Mississippi seceded, 1861. Union forces captured Corinth and Vicksburg and destroyed Jackson and much of Meridian. Mississippi was readmitted to the Union in 1870.

Tourist attractions. Vicksburg Natl. Military Park and Cemetery, other Civil War sites; Hattiesburg; Natchez Trace; Indian mounds; Antebellum homes; pilgrimages in Natchez and some 25 other cities; The Elvis Presley Birthplace & Museum, Tupelo; Smith Robertson Museum, Mynelle Gardens, both Jackson; Mardi Gras and Shrimp Festival, both in Biloxi; Gulf Islands Natl. Seashore; Casinos on the Mississippi River; the Mississippi Coast.

Famous Mississippians. Margaret Walker Alexander, Dana Andrews, Jimmy Buffett, Hodding Carter III, Bo Diddley, William Faulkner, Brett Favre, Shelby Foote, Morgan Freeman, John Grisham, Fannie Lou Hamer, Jim Henson, Faith Hill, John Lee Hooker, Robert Johnson, James Earl Jones, B. B. King, L. Q. C. Lamar, Trent Lott, Gerald McRaney, Willie Morris, Walter Payton, Elvis Presley, Leontyne Price, Charley Pride, LeAnn Rimes, Muddy Waters, Eudora Welty, Tennessee Williams, Oprah Winfrey, Johnny Winter, Richard Wright, Tammy Wynette.

Tourist Information. Mississippi Division of Tourism. PO Box 849, Jackson, MS 39205-0849; 1-888-SEE-MISS. **Website:** www.visitmississippi.org

Website. www.ms.gov

Missouri
Show Me State

People. Population (2003 est.): 5,704,484; rank: 17; **net change** (2002-2003): 0.6%. **Pop. density:** 82.8 per sq mi. **Racial distribution** (2000): 84.9% white; 11.2% black; 1.1% Asian; 0.4% Native American/Nat. AK; 0.1% Hawaiian/Pacific Islander; 0.8% other race; 2 or more races, 1.5%. **Hispanic pop.** (any race): 2.1%.

Geography. Total area: 69,704 sq mi; rank: 21. **Land area:** 68,886 sq mi; rank: 18. **Acres forested:** 14.0 mil. **Location:** West North Central state near the geographic center of the conterminous U.S.; bordered on the E by the Mississippi R., on the NW by the Missouri R. **Climate:** continental, susceptible to cold Canadian air, moist, warm gulf air, and drier SW air. **Topography:** rolling hills, open, fertile plains, and well-watered prairie N of the Missouri R.; south of the river land is rough and hilly with deep, narrow valleys; alluvial plain in the SE; low elevation in the west. **Capital:** Jefferson City.

Economy. Chief industries: agriculture, manufacturing, aerospace, tourism. **Chief manuf. goods:** transportation equipment, food and related products, electrical and electronic equipment, chemicals. **Chief crops:** soybeans, corn, wheat, hay. **Livestock** (Jan. 2004) 4.35 mil. cattle/calves; 60,000 sheep/lambs; (Jan. 2003): 2.95 mil. hogs/pigs; (Dec. 2003): 8.3 mil. chickens (excl. broilers). **Timber/lumber** (est. 2002): 616 mil bd. ft.; oak, hickory. **Nonfuel minerals** (est. 2003): $1.3 bil.; stone (crushed), cement (portland), lead, lime, sand and gravel (construction). **Principal internat. airports at:** Kansas City, St. Louis. **New private housing** (2003): 27,307 units/$3.4 bil. **Gross state product** (2001): $181.5 bil. **Employment distrib.** (May 2004): 16.3% govt.; 19.4% trade/trans./util.; 11.6% mfg.; 13.2% ed./health serv.; 11.3% prof./bus serv.; 10.1% leisure/hosp.; 6% finance; 5% constr.; 2.4% info. **Per cap. pers. income (2003): $29,252. Sales tax** (2004): 4.2%. **Unemployment** (2003): 5.6%. **Tourism expends.** (2002): $9.5 bil. **Lottery** (2003): total sales: $708.1 mil; net income: $203.5 mil.

Finance. FDIC-insured commercial banks (2003): 345. **Deposits:** $63.7 bil. **FDIC-insured savings institutions** (2003): 32. **Assets:** $5.3 bil.

Federal govt. Fed. civ. employees (Mar. 2003): 33,310. **Avg. salary:** $50,851. **Notable fed. facilities:** Federal Reserve banks; Ft. Leonard Wood; Jefferson Barracks Natl. Cem.; Whiteman AFB.

Energy. Electricity production (est. 2003, kWh by source): Coal: 73.9 bil; Petroleum: 156 mil; Gas: 1.8 bil; Hydroelectric: 448 mil; Nuclear: 9.7 bil; Other: 122 mil.

State data. Motto: Salus Populi Suprema Lex Esto (The welfare of the people shall be the supreme law). **Flower:** Hawthorn. **Bird:** Bluebird. **Tree:** Dogwood. **Song:** Missouri Waltz. **Entered union** Aug. 10, 1821; rank, 24th. **State fair** at Sedalia; 3rd week in Aug.

History. Early inhabitants of the region were Algonquian Sauk, Fox, and Illinois & Siouan Osage, Missouri, Iowa, and Kansa peoples. Hernando de Soto visited 1541. French hunters and lead miners made the first settlement c 1735, at Ste. Genevieve. The territory was ceded to Spain by the French, 1763, then returned to France, 1800. The U.S. acquired Missouri as part of the Louisiana Purchase, 1803. The influx of white settlers drove Native American tribes to the Kansas and Oklahoma territories; most were gone by 1836. The fur trade and the Santa Fe Trail provided prosperity; St. Louis became the gateway for pioneers heading West. Missouri entered the Union as a slave state, 1821. Though it remained with the Union, pro- and anti-slavery forces battled there during the Civil War.

Tourist attractions. Silver Dollar City, Branson; Mark Twain Area, Hannibal; Pony Express Museum, St. Joseph; Harry S. Truman Library, Independence; Gateway Arch, St. Louis; Worlds of Fun, Kansas City; Lake of the Ozarks; Churchill Mem., Fulton; State Capitol, Jefferson City.

Famous Missourians. Maya Angelou, Robert Altman, Burt Bacharach, Josephine Baker, Scott Bakula, Thomas Hart Benton, Tom Berenger, Yogi Berra, Chuck Berry, George Caleb Bingham, Daniel Boone, Omar Bradley, William Burroughs, Kate Capshaw, Dale Carnegie, George Washington Carver, Bob Costas, Walter Cronkite, Walt Disney, T. S. Eliot, Richard Gephardt, John Goodman, Betty Grable, Edwin Hubble, Jesse James, Rush Limbaugh, Marianne Moore, Reinhold Niebuhr, J. C. Penney, John J. Pershing, Brad Pitt, Joseph Pulitzer, Ginger Rogers, Bess Truman, Harry S. Truman, Kathleen Turner, Tina Turner, Mark Twain, Dick Van Dyke, Tennessee Williams, Lanford Wilson, Shelley Winters, Jane Wyman.

Tourist Information. Missouri Division of Tourism. P.O. Box 1055, Jefferson City, MO 65102; 1-800-810-5500. **Website:** www.missouritourism.org
Website. www.state.mo.us

Montana
Treasure State

People. Population (2003 est.): 917,621; rank: 44; **net change** (2002-2003): 0.8%. **Pop. density:** 6.3 per sq mi. **Racial distribution** (2000): 90.6% white; 0.3% black; 0.5% Asian; 6.2% Native American/Nat. AK; 0.1% Hawaiian/Pacific Islander; 0.6% other race; 2 or more races, 1.7%. **Hispanic pop.** (any race): 2.0%.

Geography. Total area: 147,042 sq mi; rank: 4. **Land area:** 145,552 sq mi; rank: 4. **Acres forested:** 23.3 mil. **Location:** Mountain state bounded on the E by the Dakotas, on the S by Wyoming, on the SSW by Idaho, and on the N by Canada. **Climate:** colder, continental climate with low humidity. **Topography:** Rocky Mts. in western third of the state; eastern two-thirds gently rolling northern Great Plains. **Capital:** Helena.

Economy. Chief industries: agriculture, timber, mining, tourism, oil and gas. **Chief manuf. goods:** food products, wood & paper products, primary metals, printing & publishing, petroleum and coal products. **Chief crops:** wheat, barley, sugar beets, hay, oats. **Livestock** (Jan. 2004) 2.4 mil. cattle/calves; 300,000 sheep/lambs; (Jan. 2003): 170,000 hogs/pigs; (Dec. 2003): 485,000 chickens (excl. broilers). **Timber/lumber** (est. 2002): 1.2 bil bd. ft.; Douglas fir, pine, larch. **Nonfuel minerals** (est. 2003): $492 mil.; gold, palladium, platinum, sand and gravel (construction), cement (portland). **Principal internat. airports at:** Billings, Missoula. **New private housing** (2003): 3,645 units/$392 mil. **Gross state product** (2001): $22.6 bil. **Employment distrib.** (May 2004): 21.8% govt.; 20.8% trade/trans./util.; 4.6% mfg.; 13.2% ed./health serv.; 8.2% prof./bus serv.; 12.8% leisure/hosp.; 5.1% finance; 6% constr.; 1.9% info. **Per cap. pers. income** (2003): $25,920. **Sales tax** (2004): none. **Unemployment** (2003): 4.7%. **Tourism expends.** (2002): $2.0 bil. **Lottery** (2003): total sales: $34.7 mil; net income: $7.5 mil.

Finance. FDIC-insured commercial banks (2003): 77. **Deposits:** $10.4 bil. **FDIC-insured savings institutions** (2003): 3. **Assets:** $279 mil.

Federal govt. Fed. civ. employees (Mar. 2003): 9,086. **Avg. salary:** $49,446. **Notable fed. facilities:** Malmstrom AFB; Ft. Peck, Hungry Horse, Libby, Yellowtail dams; numerous missile silos.

Energy. Electricity production (est. 2003, kWh by source): Coal: 322 mil; Gas: 18 mil; Hydroelectric: 5.7 bil.

State data. Motto: Oro y Plata (Gold and silver). **Flower:** Bitterroot. **Bird:** Western meadowlark. **Tree:** Ponderosa pine. **Song:** Montana. **Entered union** Nov. 8, 1889; rank, 41st. **State fair** at Great Falls; late July-early Aug.

History. Cheyenne, Blackfoot, Crow, Assiniboin, Salish (Flatheads), Kootenai, and Kalispel peoples were early inhabitants of the area. French explorers visited the region, 1742. The U.S. acquired the area partly through the Louisiana Purchase, 1803, partly through explorations of Lewis and Clark, 1805-6. Fur traders and missionaries established posts early 19th cent. Gold was discovered, 1863, and the Montana territory was established, 1864. Indian uprisings reached their peak with the Battle of Little Bighorn, 1876. Chief Joseph and the Nez Percé tribe surrendered here, 1877, after long trek across the state. Mining activity and the coming of the Northern Pacific Railway, 1883, brought population growth. Copper wealth from the Butte pits resulted in the turn of the century

"War of Copper Kings" as factions fought for control of "the richest hill on earth."

Tourist attractions. Glacier Natl. Park; Yellowstone Natl. Park; Museum of the Rockies, Bozeman; Museum of the Plains Indian, Blackfeet Reservation, near Browning; Little Bighorn Battlefield Natl. Monument and Custer Natl. Cemetery; Flathead Lake; Helena; Lewis and Clark Caverns State Park, near Whitehall; Lewis and Clark Interpretive Center, Great Falls.

Famous Montanans. Dana Carvey, Gary Cooper, Marcus Daly, Chet Huntley, Will James, Myrna Loy, David Lynch, Mike Mansfield, Brent Musburger, Jeannette Rankin, Charles M. Russell, Lester Thurow.

Tourist Information. Travel Montana, Dept. of Commerce, PO Box 2000533, 301 S. Park, Helena, MT 59601; 1-800-VIS-ITMT. **Website:** www.visitmt.org
Website. www.state.mt.us

Nebraska
Cornhusker State

People. Population (2003 est.): 1,739,291; rank: 38; **net change** (2002-2003): 0.7%. **Pop. density:** 22.6 per sq mi. **Racial distribution** (2000): 89.6% white; 4.0% black; 1.3% Asian; 0.9% Native American/Nat. AK; 0.1% Hawaiian/Pacific Islander; 2.8% other race; 2 or more races, 1.4%. **Hispanic pop.** (any race): 5.5%.

Geography. Total area: 77,354 sq mi; rank: 16. **Land area:** 76,872 sq mi; rank: 15. **Acres forested:** 0.9 mil. **Location:** West North Central state with the Missouri R. for a NE and E border. **Climate:** continental semi-arid. **Topography:** till plains of the central lowland in the eastern third rising to the Great Plains and hill country of the north central and NW. **Capital:** Lincoln.

Economy. Chief industries: agriculture, manufacturing. **Chief manuf. goods:** processed foods, industrial machinery, printed materials, electric and electronic equipment, primary and fabricated metal products, transportation equipment. **Chief crops:** corn, sorghum, soybeans, hay, wheat, dry beans, oats, potatoes, sugar beets. **Livestock** (Jan. 2004) 6.25 mil. cattle/calves; 102,000 sheep/lambs; (Jan. 2003): 2.9 mil. hogs/pigs; (Dec. 2003): 14.2 mil. chickens (excl. broilers); 4.0 mil. broilers. **Timber/lumber** (est. 2002): 25 mil bd. ft.; oak, hickory, and elm. **Nonfuel minerals** (est. 2003): $94 mil.; cement (portland), stone (crushed), sand and gravel (construction), cement (masonry), lime. **Chief ports:** Omaha, Sioux City, Brownville, Blair, Plattsmouth, Nebraska City. **New private housing** (2003): 10,130 units/$1.2 bil. **Gross state product** (2001): $57.0 bil. **Employment distrib.** (May 2004): 18% govt.; 21.1% trade/trans./util.; 11.1% mfg.; 12.4% ed./health serv.; 10.1% prof./bus serv.; 8.9% leisure/hosp.; 6.8% finance; 5.3% constr.; 2.3% info. **Per cap. pers. income** (2003): $30,758. **Sales tax** (2004): 5.5%. **Unemployment** (2003): 4%. **Tourism expends.** (2002): $2.7 bil. **Lottery** (2003): total sales: $80.9 mil; net income: $20.2 mil.

Finance. FDIC-insured commercial banks (2003): 259. **Deposits:** $23.9 bil. **FDIC-insured savings institutions** (2003): 11. **Assets:** $15.4 bil.

Federal govt. Fed. civ. employees (Mar. 2003): 8,578. **Avg. salary:** $50,813. **Notable fed. facilities:** Offutt AFB.

Energy. Electricity production (est. 2003, kWh by source): Coal: 20.9 bil; Gas: 404 mil; Hydroelectric: 980 mil; Nuclear: 8 bil; Other: 30 mil.

State data. Motto: Equality before the law. **Flower:** Goldenrod. **Bird:** Western meadowlark. **Tree:** Cottonwood. **Song:** Beautiful Nebraska. **Entered union** Mar. 1, 1867; rank, 37th. **State fair** at Lincoln; Aug.-Sept.

History. When the Europeans first arrived, Pawnee, Ponca, Omaha, and Oto peoples lived in the region. Spanish and French explorers and fur traders visited the area prior to its acquisition in the Louisiana Purchase, 1803. Lewis and Clark passed through, 1804-6. The first permanent settlement was Bellevue, near Omaha, 1823. The region was gradually settled, despite the 1834 Indian Intercourse Act, which declared Nebraska Indian country and excluded white settlement. Conflicts with settlers eventually forced Native Americans to move to reservations. Many Civil War veterans settled under free land terms of the 1862 Homestead Act; as agriculture grew, struggles followed between homesteaders and ranchers.

Tourist attractions. State Museum (Elephant Hall), State Capitol, both Lincoln; Stuhr Museum of the Prairie Pioneer, Grand Island; Museum of the Fur Trade, Chadron; Henry Doorly Zoo, Joslyn Art Museum, both Omaha; Ashfall Fossil Beds, Strategic Air Command Museum, Ashland; Boys Town, west of Omaha; Arbor Lodge State Park, Nebraska City; Buffalo Bill Ranch State Hist. Park, North Platte; Pioneer Village,

Minden; Oregon Trail landmarks; Scotts Bluff Natl. Monument; Chimney Rock Natl. Historic Site; Ft. Robinson; Hastings Museum, Hastings.

Famous Nebraskans. Grover Cleveland Alexander, Fred Astaire, Marlon Brando, Charles W. Bryan, William Jennings Bryan, Warren Buffett, Johnny Carson, Willa Cather, Dick Cavett, Dick Cheney, William F. "Buffalo Bill" Cody, Loren Eiseley, Rev. Edward J. Flanagan, Henry Fonda, Gerald R. Ford, Bob Gibson, Rollin Kirby, Harold Lloyd, Malcolm X, J. Sterling Morton, John Neihardt, Nick Nolte, George Norris, Tom Osborne, John J. Pershing, Roscoe Pound, Chief Red Cloud, Mari Sandoz, Robert Taylor, Darryl F. Zanuck.

Tourist Infomation. Nebraska Division of Travel and Tourism, PO Box 98907, Lincoln, NE 68509-8907; 1-877-NE-BRASKA. **Website:** www.visitnebraska.org
Website. www.state.ne.us

Nevada
Sagebrush State, Battle Born State, Silver State

People. Population (2003 est.): 2,241,154; rank: 35; **net change** (2002-2003): 3.4%. **Pop. density:** 20.4 per sq mi. **Racial distribution** (2000): 75.2% white; 6.8% black; 4.5% Asian; 1.3% Native American/Nat. AK; 0.4% Hawaiian/Pacific Islander; 8.0% other race; 2 or more races, 3.8%. **Hispanic pop.** (any race): 19.7%.

Geography. Total area: 110,561 sq mi; rank: 7. **Land area:** 109,826 sq mi; rank: 7. **Acres forested:** 10.2 mil. **Location:** Mountain state bordered on N by Oregon and Idaho, on E by Utah and Arizona, on SE by Arizona, and on SW and W by California. **Climate:** semi-arid and arid. **Topography:** rugged N-S mountain ranges; highest elevation, Boundary Peak, 13,140 ft; southern area is within the Mojave Desert; lowest elevation, Colorado River at southern tip of state, 479 ft. **Capital:** Carson City.

Economy. Chief industries: gaming, tourism, mining, manufacturing, government, retailing, warehousing, trucking. **Chief manuf. goods:** food products, plastics, chemicals, aerospace products, lawn and garden irrigation equipment, seismic and machinery-monitoring devices. **Chief crops:** hay, alfalfa seed, potatoes, onions, garlic, barley, wheat. **Livestock** (Jan. 2004) 510,000 cattle/calves; 75,000 sheep/lambs; (Jan. 2003): 5,000 hogs/pigs. **Timber/lumber** (est. 2002): <.5 mil bd. ft.; piñon, juniper, other pines. **Nonfuel minerals** (est. 2003): $2.9 bil.; gold, sand and gravel (construction), lime, stone (crushed), diatomite. **Principal internat. airports at:** Las Vegas, Reno. **New private housing** (2003): 43,140 units/$4.9 bil. **Gross state product** (2001): $79.2 bil. **Employment distrib.** (May 2004): 12.5% govt.; 17.6% trade/trans./util.; 4% mfg.; 7% ed./health serv.; 11.2% prof./bus serv.; 27.5% leisure/hosp.; 5.4% finance; 9.7% constr.; 1.4% info. **Per cap. pers. income** (2003): $31,266. **Sales tax** (2004): 6.5%. **Unemployment** (2003): 5.2%. **Tourism expends.** (2002): $20.2 bil.

Finance. FDIC-insured commercial banks (2003): 34. **Deposits:** $26.8 bil. **FDIC-insured savings institutions** (2003): 3. **Assets:** $1.3 bil.

Federal govt. Fed. civ. employees (Mar. 2003): 9,441. **Avg. salary:** $52,111. **Notable fed. facilities:** Nevada Test Site; Hawthorne Army Depot; Nellis AFB and Range Complex; Fallon NAS; Natl. Wild Horse and Burro Ctr. at Palomino Valley.

Energy. Electricity production (est. 2003, kWh by source): Coal: 16.1 bil; Petroleum: 19 mil; Gas: 5.8 bil; Hydroelectric: 1.7 bil.

State data. Motto: All for our country. **Flower:** Sagebrush. **Bird:** Mountain bluebird. **Trees:** Single-leaf piñon and bristlecone pine. **Song:** Home Means Nevada. **Entered union** Oct. 31, 1864; rank, 36th. **State fair** at Reno; late Aug.

History. Shoshone, Paiute, Bannock, and Washoe peoples lived in the area at the time of European contact. Nevada was first explored by Spaniards, 1776. Hudson's Bay Co. trappers explored the north and central region, 1825; trader Jedediah Smith crossed the state, 1826-27. The area was acquired by the U.S., 1848, at the end of the Mexican War. The first settlement, Mormon Station, now Genoa, was established, 1849. Discovery of the Comstock Lode, rich in gold and silver, 1859, spurred a population boom. In the early 20th cent., Nevada adopted progressive measures such as the initiative, referendum, recall, and woman suffrage.

Tourist attractions. Legalized gambling at: Lake Tahoe, Reno, Las Vegas, Laughlin, Elko County, and elsewhere. Hoover Dam; Lake Mead; Great Basin Natl. Park; Valley of Fire State Park; Virginia City; Red Rock Canyon Natl. Conservation Area; Liberace Museum, the Las Vegas Strip, Guinness World of Records Museum, Lost City Museum, Overton,

Lamoille Canyon, Pyramid Lake, all Las Vegas. Skiing near Lake Tahoe.

Famous Nevadans. Andre Agassi, Walter Van Tilburg Clark, George Ferris, Sarah Winnemucca Hopkins, Paul Laxalt, Dat So La Lee, John William Mackay, Anne Martin, Pat McCarran, Key Pittman, William Morris Stewart.

Tourist information. Commission on Tourism, 401 N. Carson St., Carson City, NV 89701; 1-800-NEVADA8. **Website:** www.travelnevada.com
Website. www.nv.gov

New Hampshire
Granite State

People. Population (2003 est.): 1,287,687; rank: 41; **net change** (2002-2003): 1.0%. **Pop. density:** 143.6 per sq mi. **Racial distribution** (2000): 96.0% white; 0.7% black; 1.3% Asian; 0.2% Native American/Nat. AK; <0.1% Hawaiian/Pacific Islander; 0.6% other race; 2 or more races, 1.1%. **Hispanic pop.** (any race): 1.7%.

Geography. Total area: 9,350 sq mi; rank: 46. **Land area:** 8,968 sq mi; rank: 44. **Acres forested:** 4.8 mil. **Location:** New England state bounded on S by Massachusetts, on W by Vermont, on N and NW by Canada, on E by Maine and the Atlantic Ocean. **Climate:** highly varied, due to its nearness to high mountains and ocean. **Topography:** low, rolling coast followed by countless hills and mountains rising out of a central plateau. **Capital:** Concord.

Economy. Chief industries: tourism, manufacturing, agriculture, trade, mining. **Chief manuf. goods:** machinery, electrical and electronic products, plastics, fabricated metal products. **Chief crops:** dairy products, nursery & greenhouse products, hay, vegetables, fruit, maple syrup & sugar products. **Livestock:** (Jan. 2004) 39,000 cattle/calves; (Jan. 2003): 2,900 hogs/pigs; (Dec. 2003): 219,000 chickens (excl. broilers). **Timber/lumber** (est. 2002): 287 mil bd. ft.; white pine, hemlock, oak, birch. **Nonfuel minerals** (est. 2003): $64 mil.; sand and gravel (construction), stone (crushed), stone (dimension), gemstones. **Commercial fishing** (2002): $16.7 mil. **Chief ports:** Portsmouth, Hampton, Rye. **New private housing** (2003): 7,861 units/$1.1 bil. **Gross state product** (2001): $47.2 bil. **Employment distrib.** (May 2004): 15% govt.; 22.5% trade/trans./util.; 12.4% mfg.; 15.3% ed./health serv.; 8.6% prof./bus serv.; 10.2% leisure/hosp.; 6% finance; 4.8% constr.; 1.8% info. **Per cap. pers. income** (2003): $34,702. **Sales tax** (2004): none. **Unemployment** (2003): 4.3%. **Tourism expends.** (2002): $2.7 bil. **Lottery** (2003): total sales: $221.2 mil; net income: $66.6 mil.

Finance. FDIC-insured commercial banks (2003): 14. **Deposits:** $12.8 bil. **FDIC-insured savings institutions** (2003): 17. **Assets:** $12.5 bil.

Federal govt. Fed. civ. employees (Mar. 2003): 3,309. **Avg. salary:** $64,223. **Notable fed. facilities:** U.S. Army Cold Regions Res. & Engineering Lab.

Energy. Electricity production (est. 2003, kWh by source): Coal: 3.9 bil; Petroleum: 2.0 bil; Hydroelectric: 331 mil.

State data. Motto: Live free or die. **Flower:** Purple lilac. **Bird:** Purple finch. **Tree:** White birch. **Song:** Old New Hampshire. **Ninth** of the original 13 states to ratify the Constitution, June 21, 1788. **State Fair:** Many agricultural fairs statewide, July through Sept.; no State fair.

History. Algonquian-speaking peoples, including the Pennacook, lived in the region when the Europeans arrived. The first explorers to visit the area were England's Martin Pring, 1603, and France's Champlain, 1605. The first settlement was Odiorne's Point (now port of Rye), 1623. Native American conflicts were ended, 1759, by Robert Rogers' Rangers. Before the American Revolution, New Hampshire residents seized a British fort at Portsmouth, 1774, and drove the royal governor out, 1775. New Hampshire became the first colony to adopt its own constitution, 1776. Three regiments served in the Continental Army, and scores of privateers raided British shipping.

Tourist attractions. Mt. Washington, highest peak in Northeast; Lake Winnipesaukee; White Mt. National Forest; Crawford, Franconia—famous for the Old Man of the Mountain, described by Hawthorne as the Great Stone Face, Pinkham notches, all White Mt. region; the Flume, a spectacular gorge; the aerial tramway, Cannon Mt.; Strawbery Banke, Portsmouth; Shaker Village, Canterbury; Saint-Gaudens, Natl. Historic Site, Cornish; Mt. Monadnock.

Famous New Hampshirites. Salmon P. Chase, Ralph Adams Cram, Mary Baker Eddy, Daniel Chester French, Robert Frost, Horace Greeley, Sarah Buell Hale, Franklin Pierce, Au-

gustus Saint-Gaudens, Adam Sandler, Alan Shepard, David H. Souter, Daniel Webster.

Tourist information. Division of Travel & Tourism Development, PO Box 1856, Concord, NH 03302-1856; 1-800-FUNINNH, ext. 169. **Website:** www.visitnh.gov
Website. www.state.nh.us

New Jersey
Garden State

People. Population (2003 est.): 8,638,396; rank: 10; **net change** (2002-2003): 0.7%. **Pop. density:** 1,164.6 per sq mi. **Racial distribution** (2000): 72.6% white; 13.6% black; 5.7% Asian; 0.2% Native American/Nat. AK; <0.1% Hawaiian/Pacific Islander; 5.4% other race; 2 or more races, 2.5%. **Hispanic pop.** (any race): 13.3%.

Geography. Total area: 8,721 sq mi; rank: 47. **Land area:** 7,417 sq mi; rank: 46. **Acres forested:** 2.1 mil. **Location:** Middle Atlantic state bounded on N and E by New York and Atlantic Ocean, on S and W by Delaware and Pennsylvania. **Climate:** moderate, with marked difference bet. NW and SE extremities. **Topography:** Appalachian Valley in the NW also has highest elevation, High Pt., 1,801 ft; Appalachian Highlands, flat-topped NE-SW mountain ranges; Piedmont Plateau, low plains broken by high ridges (Palisades) rising 400-500 ft; Coastal Plain, covering three-fifths of state in SE, rises from sea level to gentle slopes. **Capital:** Trenton.

Economy. Chief industries: pharmaceuticals/drugs, telecommunications, biotechnology, printing & publishing. **Chief manuf. goods:** chemicals, electronic equipment, food. **Chief crops:** nursery/greenhouse, tomatoes, blueberries, peaches, peppers, cranberries, soybeans. **Livestock** (Jan. 2004) 46,000 cattle/calves; (Jan. 2003): 12,000 hogs/pigs; (Dec. 2003): 2.1 mil. chickens (excl. broilers). **Timber/lumber** (est. 2002): 20 mil bd. ft.; pine, cedar, mixed hardwoods. **Nonfuel minerals** (est. 2003): $272 mil.; stone (crushed), sand and gravel (construction), sand and gravel (industrial), greensand marl, peat. **Commercial fishing** (2002): $112.7 mil. **Chief ports:** Newark, Elizabeth, Hoboken, Camden. **Principal internat. airports at:** Atlantic City, Newark. **New private housing** (2003): 32,369 units/$3.6 bil. **Gross state product** (2001): $365.4 bil. **Employment distrib.** (May 2004): 16% govt.; 21.6% trade/trans./util.; 8.5% mfg.; 13.7% ed./health serv.; 14.5% prof./bus serv.; 8.2% leisure/hosp.; 7% finance; 4.1% constr.; 2.5% info. **Per cap. pers. income** (2003): $40,427. **Sales tax** (2004): 6.0%. **Unemployment** (2003): 5.9%. **Tourism expends.** (2002) $15.1 bil. **Lottery** (2003): total sales: $2.1 bil; net income: $765.4 mil.

Finance. FDIC-insured commercial banks (2003): 79. **Deposits:** $77.0 bil. **FDIC-insured savings institutions** (2003): 67. **Assets:** $57.9 bil.

Federal govt. Fed. civ. employees (Mar. 2003): 27,443. **Avg. Salary:** $62,458. **Notable fed. facilities:** McGuire AFB; Ft. Dix; Ft. Monmouth; Picatinny Arsenal; Lakehurst Naval Air Engineering Ctr.; FAA William J.Hughes Technical Ctr.

Energy. Electricity production (est. 2003, kWh by source): Coal: 1.7 bil; Petroleum: 209 mil; Gas: 30 mil; Hydroelectric: –120 mil.

State data. Motto: Liberty and prosperity. **Flower:** Purple violet. **Bird:** Eastern goldfinch. **Tree:** Red oak. **Third** of the original 13 states to ratify the Constitution, Dec. 18, 1787. **State fair** at Augusta; late July-early Aug.

History. The Lenni Lenape (Delaware) peoples lived in the region and had mostly peaceful relations with European colonists, who arrived after the explorers Verrazano, 1524, and Hudson, 1609. The first permanent European settlement was Dutch, at Bergen (now Jersey City), 1660. When the British took New Netherland, 1664, the area between the Delaware and Hudson Rivers was given to Lord John Berkeley and Sir George Carteret. During the American Revolution, New Jersey was the scene of nearly 100 battles, large and small, including Trenton, 1776; Princeton, 1777; Monmouth, 1778.

Tourist attractions. 127 mi of beaches; Miss America Pageant, Atlantic City; Grover Cleveland birthplace, Caldwell; Cape May Historic District; Edison Natl. Historic Site, W. Orange; Six Flags Great Adventure, Jackson; Liberty State Park, Jersey City; Meadowlands Sports Complex, E. Rutherford; Pine Barrens wilderness area; Princeton University; numerous Revolutionary War historical sites; State Aquarium, Camden.

Famous New Jerseyans. Jason Alexander, Count Basie, Judy Blume, Jon Bon Jovi, Bill Bradley, Aaron Burr, Grover Cleveland, James Fenimore Cooper, Stephen Crane, Danny DeVito, Thomas Edison, Albert Einstein, James Gandolfini, Allen Ginsberg, Alexander Hamilton, Ed Harris, Whitney Houston, Buster Keaton, Joyce Kilmer, Norman Mailer, Jack Nicholson, Thomas Paine, Dorothy Parker, Joe Pesci, Molly Pitcher, Paul Robeson, Philip Roth, Antonin Scalia, Wally Schirra, H. Norman Schwarzkopf, Frank Sinatra, Bruce Springsteen, Martha Stewart, Meryl Streep, Dave Thomas, John Travolta, Walt Whitman, William Carlos Williams, Woodrow Wilson.

Tourist Information. New Jersey Commerce and Economic Growth Commission, PO Box 820, Trenton, NJ 08625-0820; 1-800-VISITNJ. **Website:** www.visitnj.org
Website. www.state.nj.us

New Mexico
Land of Enchantment

People. Population (2003 est.): 1,874,614; rank: 36; **net change** (2002-2003): 1.2%. **Pop. density:** 15.4 per sq mi. **Racial distribution** (2000): 66.8% white; 1.9% black; 1.1% Asian; 9.5% Native American/Nat. AK; 0.1% Hawaiian/Pacific Islander; 17.0% other race; 2 or more races, 3.6%. **Hispanic pop.** (any race): 42.1%.

Geography. Total area: 121,589 sq mi; rank: 5. **Land area:** 121,356 sq mi; rank: 5. **Acres forested:** 16.7 mil. **Location:** southwestern state bounded by Colorado on the N, Oklahoma, Texas, and Mexico on the E and S, and Arizona on the W. **Climate:** dry, with temperatures rising or falling 5× F with every 1,000 ft elevation. **Topography:** eastern third, Great Plains; central third, Rocky Mts. (85% of the state is over 4,000-ft elevation); western third, high plateau. **Capital:** Santa Fe.

Economy. Chief industries: government, services, trade. **Chief manuf. goods:** foods, machinery, apparel, lumber, printing, transportation equipment, electronics, semiconductors. **Chief crops:** hay, onions, chiles, greenhouse nursery, pecans, cotton. **Livestock** (Jan. 2004) 1.51 mil. cattle/calves; 160,000 sheep/lambs; (Jan. 2003): 2,500 hogs/pigs. **Timber/lumber** (est. 2002): 111 mil bd. ft.; ponderosa pine, Douglas fir. **Nonfuel minerals** (est. 2003): $533 mil.; potash, copper, sand and gravel (construction), cement (portland), stone (crushed). **Principal internat. airport at:** Albuquerque. **New private housing** (2003): 13,400 units/$1.7 bil. **Gross state product** (2001): $55.4 bil. **Employment distrib.** (May 2004): 25.3% govt.; 17.2% trade/trans./util.; 4.5% mfg.; 13.1% ed./health serv.; 11.2% prof./bus serv.; 10.6% leisure/hosp.; 4.4% finance; 6.2% constr.; 1.9% info. **Per cap. pers. income** (2003): $25,541. **Sales tax** (2004): 5.0%. **Unemployment** (2003): 6.4%. **Tourism expends.** (2002): $4.0 bil. **Lottery** (2003): total sales: $137 mil; net income: $33.1 mil.

Finance. FDIC-insured commercial banks (2003): 51. **Deposits:** $13.5 bil. **FDIC-insured savings institutions** (2003): 9. **Assets:** $2.6 bil.

Federal govt. Fed. civ. employees (Mar. 2003): 21,848. **Avg. salary:** $52,218. **Notable fed. facilities:** Kirtland, Cannon, Holloman AF bases; Los Alamos Natl. Lab; White Sands Missile Range; Natl. Solar Observatory; Natl. Radio Astronomy Observatory, Sandia Natl. Labs.

Energy. Electricity production (est. 2003, kWh by source): Coal: 28.8 bil; Petroleum: 48 mil; Gas: 2.9 bil; Hydroelectric: 221 mil.

State data. Motto: Crescit Eundo (It grows as it goes). **Flower:** Yucca. **Bird:** Roadrunner. **Tree:** Piñon. **Song:** O, Fair New Mexico; Asi Es Nuevo Mexico. **Entered union** Jan. 6, 1912; rank, 47th. **State fair** at Albuquerque; mid-Sept.

History. Early inhabitants were peoples of the Mogollon and Anasazi civilizations, followed by the Pueblo peoples, Anasazi descendants. The nomadic Navajo and Apache tribes arrived c 15th cent. Franciscan Marcos de Niza and a former black slave, Estevanico, explored the area, 1539, seeking gold. First settlements were at San Juan Pueblo, 1598, and Santa Fe, 1610. Settlers alternately traded and fought with the Apache, Comanche, and Navajo. Trade on the Santa Fe Trail to Missouri started, 1821. The Mexican War was declared in May 1846; Gen. Stephen Kearny took Santa Fe without firing a shot, Aug. 18, 1846, declaring New Mexico part of the U.S. All Hispanic New Mexicans and Pueblo became U.S. citizens by terms of the 1848 treaty ending the war, but Congress denied the area statehood and created the territory of New Mexico, 1850. Pancho Villa raided Columbus, 1916, and U.S. troops were sent to the area. The world's first atomic bomb was exploded near Alamogordo, south of Santa Fe, 1945.

Tourist attractions. Carlsbad Caverns Natl. Park, with the largest natural underground chamber in the world; Santa Fe, oldest capital in U.S.; White Sands Natl. Monument, the largest gypsum deposit in the world; Chaco Culture National Historical Park; Acoma Pueblo, the "sky city," built atop a 357-ft mesa; Taos; Taos Art Colony; Taos Ski Valley; Ute Lake State Park; Shiprock.

> **IT'S A FACT:** New York residents had the highest state and local taxes in the U.S. in 2002, paying an average of $130.79 for every $1,000 they earned, according to the Mass. Taxpayers Foundation. Maine was close behind, at $130.16, followed by Wyoming ($121.97), Hawaii ($120.62), and Wisconsin ($117.36). Despite what many might have expected, Massachusetts itself was not near the top of this list; it ranked 40th, with residents paying $96 for every $1,000 of income. Tennessee residents paid the lowest state and local taxes, shelling out just under $84 for every $1,000.

Famous New Mexicans. Ben Abruzzo, Maxie Anderson, Jeff Bezos, Billy (the Kid) Bonney, Kit Carson, Bob Foster, Peter Hurd, Tony Hillerman, Archbishop Jean Baptiste Lamy, Nancy Lopez, Bill Mauldin, Georgia O'Keeffe, Bill Richardson, Kim Stanley, Al Unser, Bobby Unser, Lew Wallace.

Tourist information. New Mexico Dept. of Tourism, PO Box 20002, Santa Fe, NM 87503; 1-800-733-6396, ext. 0643. **Website:** www.newmexico.org

Website. www.state.nm.us

New York
Empire State

People. Population (2003 est.): 19,190,115; rank: 3; **net change** (2002-2003): 0.3%. **Pop. density:** 406.5 per sq mi. **Racial distribution** (2000): 67.9% white; 15.9% black; 5.5% Asian; 0.4% Native American/Nat. AK; 0.1% Hawaiian/Pacific Islander; 7.1% other race; 2 or more races, 3.1%. **Hispanic pop.** (any race): 15.1%.

Geography. Total area: 54,556 sq mi; rank: 27. **Land area:** 47,214 sq mi; rank: 30. **Acres forested:** 18.4 mil. **Location:** Middle Atlantic state, bordered by the New England states, Atlantic Ocean, New Jersey and Pennsylvania, Lakes Ontario and Erie, and Canada. **Climate:** variable; the SE region moderated by the ocean. **Topography:** highest and most rugged mountains in the NE Adirondack upland; St. Lawrence-Champlain lowlands extend from Lake Ontario NE along the Canadian border; Hudson-Mohawk lowland follows the flows of the rivers N and W, 10-30 mi wide; Atlantic coastal plain in the SE; Appalachian Highlands, covering half the state westward from the Hudson Valley, include the Catskill Mts., Finger Lakes; plateau of Erie-Ontario lowlands. **Capital:** Albany.

Economy. Chief industries: manufacturing, finance, communications, tourism, transportation, services. **Principal manufactured goods:** books & periodicals, clothing & apparel, pharmaceuticals, machinery, instruments, toys & sporting goods, electronic equipment, automotive & aircraft components. **Chief crops:** apples, grapes, strawberries, cherries, pears, onions, potatoes, cabbage, sweet corn, green beans, cauliflower, field corn, hay, wheat, oats, dry beans. **Products:** milk, cheese, maple syrup, wine. **Livestock** (Jan. 2004) 1.42 mil. cattle/calves; 70,000 sheep/lambs; (Jan. 2003): 73,000 hogs/pigs; (Dec. 2003): 4.7 mil. chickens (excl. broilers); 2.6 mil. broilers. **Timber/lumber** (est. 2002): 464 mil bd. ft.; birch, sugar and red maple, basswood, hemlock, pine, oak, ash. **Nonfuel minerals** (est. 2003): $978 mil.; stone (crushed), cement (portland), salt, sand and gravel (construction), wollastonite. **Commercial fishing** (2002): $51.3 mil. **Chief ports:** New York, Buffalo, Albany. **Principal internat. airports at:** Albany, Buffalo, New York, Newburgh, Rochester, Syracuse. **New private housing** (2003): 49,998 units/$6.0 bil. **Gross state product** (2001): $826.5 bil. **Employment distrib.** (May 2004): 17.7% govt.; 17.3% trade/trans./util.; 7% mfg.; 18.1% ed./health serv.; 12.4% prof./bus serv.; 7.9% leisure/hosp.; 8.2% finance; 3.8% constr.; 3.3% info. **Per cap. pers. income** (2003): $36,574. **Sales tax** (2004): 4.25%. **Unemployment** (2003): 6.3%. **Tourism expends.** (2002): $34.4 bil. **Lottery** (2003): total sales: $5.4 bil; net income: $1.8 bil.

Finance. FDIC-insured commercial banks (2003): 135. **Deposits:** $962.4 bil. **FDIC-insured savings institutions** (2003): 71. **Assets:** $138.2 bil.

Federal govt. Fed. civ. employees (Mar. 2003): 60,794. **Avg. salary:** $55,850. **Notable fed. facilities:** West Point Military Academy; Merchant Marine Academy; Ft. Drum; Rome Labs.; Watervliet Arsenal; Brookhaven Natl. Lab.

Energy. Electricity production (est. 2003, kWh by source): Coal: 1.7 bil; Petroleum: 9.7 bil; Gas: 7.7 bil; Hydroelectric: 18.5 bil; Nuclear: 3.9 bil.

State data. Motto: Excelsior (Ever upward). **Flower:** Rose. **Bird:** Bluebird. **Tree:** Sugar maple. **Song:** I Love New York. **Eleventh** of the original 13 states to ratify the Constitution, July 26, 1788. **State fair** at Syracuse; late Aug.-early Sept.

History. Algonquians including the Mahican, Wappinger, and Lenni Lenape inhabited the region, as did the Iroquoian Mohawk, Oneida, Onondaga, Cayuga, and Seneca tribes, who established the League of the Five Nations. In 1609, Henry Hudson visited the river named for him, and Champlain explored the lake named for him. The first permanent settlement was Dutch, near present-day Albany, 1624. New Amsterdam was settled, 1626, at the S tip of Manhattan Island.

A British fleet seized New Netherland, 1664. Ninety-two of the 300 or more engagements of the American Revolution were fought in New York, including the Battle of Bemis Heights-Saratoga, 1777, a turning point of the war. Completion of Erie Canal, 1825, established the state as a gateway to the West. The first women's rights convention was held in Seneca Falls, 1848.

Tourist attractions. New York City; Adirondack and Catskill Mts.; Finger Lakes; Great Lakes; Thousand Islands; Niagara Falls; Saratoga Springs; Philipsburg Manor, Sunnyside (Washington Irving's home), the Dutch Church of Sleepy Hollow, all in Tarrytown area; Corning Glass Center and Steuben factory, Corning; Fenimore House, Natl. Baseball Hall of Fame and Museum, both in Cooperstown; Ft. Ticonderoga overlooking Lakes George and Champlain; Empire State Plaza, Albany; Lake Placid; Franklin D. Roosevelt Natl. Historic Site, including the Roosevelt Library, Hyde Park; Long Island beaches; Theodore Roosevelt estate, Sagamore Hill, Oyster Bay; Turning Stone Casino.

Famous New Yorkers. Woody Allen, Susan B. Anthony, James Baldwin, Lucille Ball, L. Frank Baum, Milton Berle, Humphrey Bogart, Barbara Boxer, Mel Brooks, Benjamin Cardozo, De Witt Clinton, Peter Cooper, Aaron Copland, George Eastman, Millard Fillmore, Lou Gehrig, George and Ira Gershwin, Ruth Bader Ginsburg, Rudolph Giuliani, Jackie Gleason, Stephen Jay Gould, Julia Ward Howe, Charles Evans Hughes, Sarah Hughes, Washington Irving, Henry and William James, John Jay, Michael Jordan, Edward Koch, Fiorello LaGuardia, Herman Melville, J. Pierpont Morgan Jr., Eddie Murphy, Joyce Carol Oates, Carroll O'Connor, Rosie O'Donnell, Eugene O'Neill, George Pataki, Colin Powell, Nancy Reagan, John D. Rockefeller, Nelson Rockefeller, Ray Romano, Eleanor Roosevelt, Franklin D. Roosevelt, Theodore Roosevelt, Tim Russert, J. D. Salinger, Jerry Seinfeld, Al Sharpton, Paul Simon, Alfred E. Smith, Elizabeth Cady Stanton, Barbra Streisand, Donald Trump, William (Boss) Tweed, Martin Van Buren, Gore Vidal, Denzel Washington, Edith Wharton, Walt Whitman.

Tourist information. Empire State Development, Travel Information Center, 1 Commerce Plaza, Albany, NY 12245; 1-800-CALLNYS from U.S. states and territories and Canada; 1-518-474-4116 from other areas. **Website:** www.iloveny.com

Website. www.state.ny.us

North Carolina
Tar Heel State, Old North State

People. Population (2003 est.): 8,407,248; rank: 11; **net change** (2002-2003): 1.2%. **Pop. density:** 172.6 per sq mi. **Racial distribution** (2000): 72.10% white; 21.6% black; 1.4% Asian; 1.2% Native American/Nat. AK; 0.1% Hawaiian/Pacific Islander; 2.3% other race; 2 or more races, 1.3%. **Hispanic pop.** (any race): 4.7%.

Geography. Total area: 53,819 sq mi; rank: 28. **Land area:** 48,711 sq mi; rank: 29. **Acres forested:** 19.3 mil. **Location:** South Atlantic state bounded by Virginia, South Carolina, Georgia, Tennessee, and the Atlantic Ocean. **Climate:** sub-tropical in SE, medium-continental in mountain region; tempered by the Gulf Stream and the mountains in W. **Topography:** coastal plain and tidewater, two-fifths of state, extending to the fall line of the rivers; piedmont plateau, another two-fifths, of gentle to rugged hills; southern Appalachian Mts. contains the Blue Ridge and Great Smoky Mts. **Capital:** Raleigh.

Economy. Chief industries: manufacturing, agriculture, tourism. **Chief manuf. goods:** food products, textiles, industrial machinery and equipment, electrical and electronic equipment, furniture, tobacco products, apparel. **Chief crops:** tobacco, cotton, soybeans, corn, food grains, wheat, peanuts, sweet potatoes. **Livestock** (Jan. 2004) 880,000 cattle/calves; (Jan. 2003): 9.9 mil. hogs/pigs; (Dec. 2003): 17.5 mil. chickens (excl. broilers). 708.2 mil. broilers. **Timber/lumber** (est. 2002): 2.5 bil bd. ft.; yellow pine, oak, hickory, poplar, maple. **Principal internat. airports at:** Charlotte, Greensboro, Raleigh/Durham, Wilmington. **Nonfuel minerals** (est. 2003): $676 mil.; stone (crushed), phosphate rock, sand and gravel (construction), sand and gravel (industrial), feldspar. **Commercial fishing** (2002): $98.7 mil. **Chief ports:** Morehead

City, Wilmington. **New private housing** (2003): 77,982 units/ $10.0 bil. **Gross state product** (2001): $275.6 bil. **Employment distrib.** (May 2004): 17.3% govt.; 18.7% trade/trans./util.; 15.1% mfg/; 11.4% ed./health serv.; 11.4% prof./bus serv.; 9.1% leisure/hosp.; 5.1% finance; 5.6% constr.; 2% info. **Per cap. pers. income** (2003): $28,235. **Sales tax** (2004): 4.5%. **Unemployment** (2003): 6.5%. **Tourism expends.** (2002): $12.9 bil.

Finance. FDIC-insured commercial banks (2003): 68. **Deposits:** $742.5 bil. **FDIC-insured savings institutions** (2003): 36. **Assets:** $6.4 bil.

Federal govt. Fed. civ. employees (Mar. 2003): 32,178. **Avg. salary:** $50,271. **Notable fed. facilities:** Ft. Bragg; Camp LeJeune Marine Base; U.S. EPA R &D Labs, Cherry Point Marine Corps Air Station; Natl. Humanities Ctr.; Natl. Inst. of Environmental Health Science; Natl. Ctr. for Health Statistics Lab, Research Triangle Park.

Energy. Electricity production (est. 2003, kWh by source): Coal: 70.6 bil; Petroleum: 442 mil; Gas: 1.3 bil; Hydroelectric: 5.2 bil; Nuclear: 40.9 bil.

State data. Motto: Esse Quam Videri (To be rather than to seem). **Flower:** Dogwood. **Bird:** Cardinal. **Tree:** Pine. **Song:** The Old North State. **Twelfth** of the original 13 states to ratify the Constitution, Nov. 21, 1789. **State fair** at Raleigh; mid-Oct.

History. Algonquian, Siouan, and Iroquoian peoples lived in the region at the time of European contact. The first English colony in America was the first of 2 established by Sir Walter Raleigh on Roanoke Island, 1585 and 1587. The first group returned to England; the second, the "Lost Colony," disappeared without a trace. Permanent settlers came from Virginia, c 1660. Roused by British repression, the colonists drove out the royal governor, 1775. The province's congress was the first to vote for independence; ten regiments were furnished to the Continental Army. Cornwallis's forces were defeated at Kings Mountain, 1780, and forced out after Guilford Courthouse, 1781. The state seceded in 1861, and provided more troops to the Confederacy than any other state; readmitted in 1868.

Tourist attractions. Cape Hatteras and Cape Lookout natl. seashores; Great Smoky Mts.; Guilford Courthouse and Moore's Creek parks; 66 American Revolution battle sites; Bennett Place, near Durham, where Gen. Joseph Johnston surrendered the last Confederate army to Gen. William Sherman; Ft. Raleigh, Roanoke Island, where Virginia Dare, first child of English parents in the New World, was born Aug. 18, 1587; Wright Brothers Natl. Memorial, Kitty Hawk; Battleship *North Carolina*, Wilmington; NC Zoo, Asheboro; NC Symphony, NC Museum, Raleigh; Carl Sandburg Home, Hendersonville, Biltmore House & Gardens, Asheville.

Famous North Carolinians. David Brinkley, Robert Byrd, Shirley Caesar, John Coltrane, Rick Dees, Elizabeth Hanford Dole, John Edwards, Ava Gardner, Richard J. Gatling, Billy Graham, Andy Griffith, O. Henry, Andrew Jackson, Andrew Johnson, Michael Jordan, Wm. Rufus King, Charles Kuralt, Meadowlark Lemon, Dolley Madison, Thelonious Monk, Edward R. Murrow, Arnold Palmer, Richard Petty, James K. Polk, Charlie Rose, Carl Sandburg, Enos Slaughter, Dean Smith, James Taylor, Thomas Wolfe.

Tourist information. North Carolina Division of Tourism, Film & Sports Development, 301 N. Wilmington St., Raleigh, NC 27601; 1-800-VISITNC. **Website.** www.visitnc.com

Website. www.nc.gov

North Dakota
Peace Garden State

People. Population (2003 est.): 633,837; rank: 48; **net change** (2002-2003): 0%. **Pop. density:** 9.2 per sq mi. **Racial distribution** (2000): 92.4% white; 0.6% black; 0.6% Asian; 4.9% Native American/Nat. AK; <0.1% Hawaiian/Pacific Islander; 0.4% other race; 2 or more races, 1.2%. **Hispanic pop.** (any race): 1.2%.

Geography. Total area: 70,700 sq mi; rank: 19. **Land area:** 68,976 sq mi; rank: 17. **Acres forested:** 0.7 mil. **Location:** West North Central state, situated exactly in the middle of North America, bounded on the N by Canada, on the E by Minnesota, on the S by South Dakota, on the W by Montana. **Climate:** continental, with a wide range of temperature and moderate rainfall. **Topography:** Central Lowland in the E comprises the flat Red River Valley and the Rolling Drift Prairie; Missouri Plateau of the Great Plains on the W. **Capital:** Bismarck.

Economy. Chief industries: agriculture, mining, tourism, manufacturing, telecommunications, energy, food processing. **Chief manuf. goods:** farm equipment, processed foods, fabricated metal, high-tech. electronics. **Chief crops:** spring wheat, durum, barley, flaxseed, oats, potatoes, dry edible beans, honey, soybeans, sugar beets, sunflowers, hay. **Livestock:** (Jan. 2004) 1.75 mil. cattle/calves; 97,000 sheep/lambs; (Jan. 2003): 150,000 hogs/pigs. **Timber/lumber** (est. 2002): 1 mil bd. ft.; oak, ash, cottonwood, aspen. **Nonfuel minerals** (est. 2003): $38 mil.; sand and gravel (construction), lime, stone (crushed), clays (common), sand and gravel (industrial). **Principal internat. airport at:** Fargo. **New private housing** (2003): 3,535 units/$388 mil. **Gross state product** (2001): $19.0 bil. **Employment distrib.** (May 2004): 23.2% govt.; 21.6% trade/trans./util.; 6.9% mfg.; 14% ed./health serv.; 7% prof./bus serv.; 9% leisure/hosp.; 5.5% finance; 5% constr.; 2.3% info. **Per cap. pers. income** (2003): $29,204. **Sales tax** (2004): 5.0%. **Unemployment** (2003): 4%. **Tourism expends.** (2002): $1.2 bil.

Finance. FDIC-insured commercial banks (2003): 101. **Deposits:** $13.6 bil. **FDIC-insured savings institutions** (2003): 3. **Assets:** $982 mil.

Federal govt. Fed. civ. employees (Mar. 2003): 5,355. **Avg. salary:** $48,396. **Notable fed. facilities:** Strategic Air Command Base; Northern Prairie Wildlife Res. Ctr.; Garrison Dam; Theodore Roosevelt Natl. Park; Grand Forks Energy Res. Ctr.; Ft. Union Natl. Historic Site.

Energy. Electricity production (est. 2003, kWh by source): Coal: 29.3 bil; Petroleum: 46 mil; Hydroelectric: 1.7 bil; Other: 6 mil.

State data. Motto: Liberty and union, now and forever, one and inseparable. **Flower:** Wild prairie rose. **Bird:** Western meadowlark. **Tree:** American elm. **Song:** North Dakota Hymn. **Entered union** Nov. 2, 1889; rank, 39th. **State fair** at Minot; July.

History. At the time of European contact, the Ojibwa, Yanktonai and Teton Sioux, Mandan, Arikara, and Hidatsa peoples lived in the region. Pierre de Varennes was the first French fur trader in the area, 1738, followed later by the English. The U.S. acquired half the territory in the Louisiana Purchase, 1803. Lewis and Clark built Ft. Mandan, near present-day Stanton, 1804-5, and wintered there. In 1818, American ownership of the other half was confirmed by agreement with Britain. The first permanent settlement was at Pembina, 1812. Missouri River steamboats reached the area, 1832, the first railroad, 1873, bringing many homesteaders. The "bonanza farm" craze of the 1870s-80s attracted many settlers. The state was first to hold a national Presidential primary, 1912.

Tourist attractions. North Dakota Heritage Center, Bismarck; Bonanzaville, Fargo; Ft. Union Trading Post Natl. Historic Site; Lake Sakakawea; Intl. Peace Garden; Theodore Roosevelt Natl. Park, including Elkhorn Ranch, Badlands; Ft. Abraham Lincoln State Park and Museum, near Mandan; Dakota Dinosaur Museum, Dickinson; Knife River Indian Villages-National Historic Site.

Famous North Dakotans. Maxwell Anderson, Angie Dickinson, John Bernard Flannagan, Phil Jackson, Louis L'Amour, Peggy Lee, Eric Sevareid, Vilhjalmur Stefansson, Lawrence Welk.

Tourist Information. North Dakota Tourism Division, Century Center, 1600 E. Century Ave., Ste 2, Bismarck, ND 58503; 1-800-435-5663. **Website:** www.ndtourism.com **Website.** www.discovernd.com

Ohio
Buckeye State

People. Population (2003 est.): 11,435,798; rank: 7; **net change** (2002-2003): 0.2%. **Pop. density:** 279.3 per sq mi. **Racial distribution** (2000): 85.0% white; 11.5% black; 1.2% Asian; 0.2% Native American/Nat. AK; <0.1% Hawaiian/Pacific Islander; 0.8% other race; 2 or more races, 1.4%. **Hispanic pop.** (any race): 1.9%.

Geography. Total area: 44,825 sq mi; rank: 34. **Land area:** 40,948 sq mi; rank: 35. **Acres forested:** 7.9 mil. **Location:** East North Central state bounded on the N by Michigan and Lake Erie; on the E and S by Pennsylvania, West Virginia, and Kentucky; on the W by Indiana. **Climate:** temperate but variable; weather subject to much precipitation. **Topography:** generally rolling plain; Allegheny plateau in E; Lake Erie plains extend southward; central plains in the W. **Capital:** Columbus.

Economy. Chief industries: manufacturing, trade, services. **Chief manuf. goods:** transportation equipment, machinery, primary and fabricated metal products. **Chief crops:** corn, hay, winter wheat, oats, soybeans. **Livestock** (Jan. 2004) 1.23 mil. cattle/calves; 140,000 sheep/lambs; (Jan. 2003): 1.52 mil. hogs/pigs; (Dec. 2003): 37.7 mil. chickens

(excl. broilers); 41.0 mil. broilers. **Timber/lumber** (est. 2002): 381 mil bd. ft.; oak, ash, maple, walnut, beech. **Nonfuel minerals** (est. 2003): $968 mil.; stone (crushed), sand and gravel (construction), salt, lime, cement (portland). **Commercial fishing** (2002): $3.1 mil. **Chief ports:** Toledo, Conneaut, Cleveland, Ashtabula. **Principal internat. airports at:** Akron, Cincinnati, Cleveland, Columbus, Dayton. **New private housing** (2003): 52,419 units/$7.5 bil. **Gross state product** (2001): $373.7 bil. **Employment distrib.** (May 2004): 15.1% govt.; 19.2% trade/trans./util.; 15.3% mfg.; 13.6% ed./health serv.; 11.3% prof./bus serv.; 9.2% leisure/hosp.; 5.8% finance; 4.3% constr.; 1.8% info. **Per cap. pers. income** (2003): $29,944. **Sales tax** (2004): 6.0%. **Unemployment** (2003): 6.1%. **Tourism expends.** (2002): $12.7 bil. **Lottery** (2003): total sales: $2.1 bil; net income: $641.4 mil.

Finance. FDIC-insured commercial banks (2003): 191. **Deposits:** $356.8 bil. **FDIC-insured savings institutions** (2003): 113. **Assets:** $51.9 bil.

Federal govt. Fed. civ. employees (Mar. 2003): 42,495. **Avg. salary:** $59,553. **Notable fed. facilities:** Wright Patterson AFB; Defense Supply Ctr., Columbus; NASA John H. Glenn Res. Ctr.; Portsmouth Gaseous Diffusion Plant; Lima Army Tank Plant.

Energy. Electricity production (est. 2003, kWh by source): Coal: 129.3 bil; Petroleum: 377 mil; Gas: 312 mil; Hydroelectric: 399 mil; Nuclear: 8.5 bil; Other: 1 mil.

State data. Motto: With God, all things are possible. **Flower:** Scarlet carnation. **Bird:** Cardinal. **Tree:** Buckeye. **Song:** Beautiful Ohio. **Entered union** Mar. 1, 1803; rank, 17th. **State fair** at Columbus; Aug.

History. Wyandot, Delaware, Miami, and Shawnee peoples sparsely occupied the area when the first Europeans arrived. La Salle visited the region, 1669, and France claimed the area, 1682. Around 1730, traders from Pennsylvania and Virginia entered the area; the French and their Native American allies sought to drive them out. France ceded its claim, 1763, to Britain. During the American Revolution, George Rogers Clark seized British posts and held the region, until Britain gave up its claim, 1783, in the Treaty of Paris. The region became U.S. territory after the American Revolution. First organized settlement was at Marietta, 1788. Indian warfare ended with Anthony Wayne's victory at Fallen Timbers, 1794. In the War of 1812, Oliver Hazard Perry's victory on Lake Erie and William Henry Harrison's invasion of Canada, 1813, ended British incursions.

Tourist attractions. Mound City Group, a group of 24 prehistoric Indian burial mounds in Hopewell Culture Natl. Historical Park; Neil Armstrong Air and Space Museum, Wapakoneta; Air Force Museum, Dayton; Pro Football Hall of Fame, Canton; King's Island amusement park, Mason; Lake Erie Islands, Cedar Point amusement park, both Sandusky; birthplaces, homes of, and memorials to U.S. Pres. W. H. Harrison, Grant, Garfield, Hayes, McKinley, Harding, Taft, B. Harrison; Amish Region, Tuscarawas/Holmes counties; German Village, Columbus; Sea World, Aurora; Jack Nicklaus Sports Center, Mason; Bob Evans Farm, Rio Grande; Rock and Roll Hall of Fame and Museum, Cleveland.

Famous Ohioans. Sherwood Anderson, Neil Armstrong, George Bellows, Halle Berry, Ambrose Bierce, Erma Bombeck, Drew Carey, Hart Crane, George Custer, Clarence Darrow, Paul Laurence Dunbar, Thomas Edison, Clark Gable, John Glenn, Zane Grey, Bob Hope, William Dean Howells, Toni Morrison, Jack Nicklaus, Jesse Owens, Jack Paar, Pontiac, Eddie Rickenbacker, John D. Rockefeller Sr. and Jr., Roy Rogers, Pete Rose, Arthur Schlesinger Jr., Gen. William Sherman, Steven Spielberg, Gloria Steinem, Harriet Beecher Stowe, Charles Taft, Robert A. Taft, William H. Taft, Tecumseh, James Thurber, Ted Turner, Orville and Wilbur Wright.

Tourist Information. Division of Travel and Tourism, 77 S. High St., PO Box 1001, Columbus, OH 43216; 1-800-BUCK-EYE. **Website:** www.ohiotourism.com

Website. www.ohio.gov

Oklahoma

Sooner State

People. Population (2003 est.): 3,511,532; rank: 28; **net change** (2002-2003): 0.6%. **Pop. density:** 51.1 per sq mi. **Racial distribution** (2000): 76.2% white; 7.6% black; 1.4% Asian; 7.9% Native American/Nat. AK; 0.1% Hawaiian/Pacific Islander; 2.4% other race; 2 or more races, 4.5%. **Hispanic pop.** (any race): 5.2%.

Geography. Total area: 69,898 sq mi; rank: 20. **Land area:** 68,667 sq mi; rank: 19. **Acres forested:** 7.7 mil. **Location:** West South Central state bounded on the N by Colorado and Kansas; on the E by Missouri and Arkansas; on the S and W by Texas and New Mexico. **Climate:** temperate; southern humid belt merging with colder northern continental; humid eastern and dry western zones. **Topography:** high plains predominate in the W, hills and small mountains in the E; the east central region is dominated by the Arkansas R. Basin, and the Red R. Plains, in the S. **Capital:** Oklahoma City.

Economy. Chief industries: manufacturing, mineral and energy exploration and production, agriculture, services. **Chief manuf. goods:** nonelectrical machinery, transportation equipment, food products, fabricated metal products. **Chief crops:** wheat, cotton, hay, peanuts, grain sorghum, soybeans, corn, pecans. **Livestock** (Jan. 2004) 5.1 mil. cattle/calves; 70,000 sheep/lambs; (Jan. 2003): 2.34 mil. hogs/pigs; (Dec. 2003): 5.7 mil. chickens (excl. broilers). 223.0 mil. broilers. **Timber/lumber** (figs. undisclosed); pine, oak, hickory. **Nonfuel minerals** (est. 2003): $479 mil.; stone (crushed), cement (portland), sand and gravel (construction), sand and gravel (industrial), iodine (crude). **Chief ports:** Catoosa, Muskogee. **Principal internat. airports at:** Oklahoma City, Tulsa. **New private housing** (2003): 15,248 units/$1.8 bil. **Gross state product** (2001): $93.9 bil. **Employment distrib.** (May 2004): 20.4% govt.; 18.8% trade/trans./util.; 9.7% mfg.; 12.1% ed./health serv.; 10.9% prof./bus serv.; 8.7% leisure/hosp.; 5.8% finance; 4.4% constr.; 2.2% info. **Per cap. pers. income** (2003): $26,656. **Sales tax** (2004): 4.5%. **Unemployment** (2003): 5.7%. **Tourism expends.** (2002): $4.1 bil.

Finance. FDIC-insured commercial banks (2003): 273. **Deposits:** $35.2 bil. **FDIC-insured savings institutions** (2003): 5. **Assets** (2003): $9.4 bil.

Federal govt. Fed. civ. employees (Mar. 2003): 33,261. **Avg. salary:** $50,691. **Notable fed. facilities:** FAA Mike Monroney Aeronautical Ctr.; Altus AFB; Tinker AFB; Vance AFB; Ft. Sill; Natl. Inst. for Petroleum & Energy Res.; Natl. Severe Storms Lab.

Energy. Electricity production (est. 2003, kWh by source): Coal: 34.2 bil; Petroleum: 112 mil; Gas: 13.9 bil; Hydroelectric: 1.6 bil.

State data. Motto: Labor Omnia Vincit (Labor conquers all things). **Flower:** Mistletoe. **Bird:** Scissor-tailed flycatcher. **Tree:** Redbud. **Song:** Oklahoma! **Entered union** Nov. 16, 1907; rank, 46th. **State fair** at Oklahoma City; last 2 full weeks of Sept.

History. The region was sparsely inhabited by Native American tribes when Coronado, the first European, arrived in 1541; in the 16th and 17th cent., French traders visited. Part of the Louisiana Purchase, 1803, Oklahoma was established as Indian Territory (but not given territorial government). It became home to the "Five Civilized Tribes"—Cherokee, Choctaw, Chickasaw, Creek, and Seminole—after the forced removal of Indians from the eastern U.S., 1828-46. The land was also used by Comanche, Osage, and other Plains Indians. As white settlers pressed west, land was opened for homesteading by runs and lottery, the first run on Apr. 22, 1889. The most famous run was to the Cherokee Outlet, 1893.

Tourist attractions. Cherokee Heritage Center, Tahlequah; Oklahoma City Natl. Memorial; White Water Bay and Frontier City theme pks., both Oklahoma City; Will Rogers Memorial, Claremore; Natl. Cowboy Hall of Fame and Remington Park Race Track, both Oklahoma City; Ft. Gibson Stockade, near Muskogee; Ouachita Natl. Forest; Tulsa's art deco district; Wichita Mts. Wildlife Refuge, Lawton; Woolaroc Museum & Wildlife Preserve, Bartlesville; Sequoyah's Home Site, near Sallisaw; Philbrook Museum of Art and Gilcrease Museum, both Tulsa.

Famous Oklahomans. Troy Aikman, Carl Albert, Gene Autry, Johnny Bench, William "Hopalong Cassidy" Boyd, Garth Brooks, Lon Chaney, L. Gordon Cooper, Walter Cronkite, Jerome "Dizzy" Dean, Ralph Ellison, John Hope Franklin, James Garner, Geronimo, Woody Guthrie, Paul Harvey, Ron Howard, Gen. Patrick J. Hurley, Ben Johnson, Jeane Kirkpatrick, Louis L'Amour, Shannon Lucid, Mickey Mantle, Reba McEntire, Wiley Post, Tony Randall, Oral Roberts, Will Rogers, Sam Snead, Barry Switzer, Maria Tallchief, Jim Thorpe, J.C. Watts Jr.

Chamber of Commerce. Chamber of Commerce, 330 NE 10th, Oklahoma City, OK 73104.

Tourist Information. Travel and Tourism Division, 15 N. Robinson, Ste. 801, P.O. Box 52002, Oklahoma City, OK 73152-2002; 1-800-652-6552. **Website:** www.travelok.com

Website. www.state.ok.us

Oregon
Beaver State

People. Population (2003 est.): 3,559,596; rank: 27; **net change** (2002-2003): 1.1%. **Pop. density:** 37.1 per sq mi. **Racial distribution** (2000): 86.6% white; 1.6% black; 3.0% Asian; 1.3% Native American/Nat. AK; 0.2% Hawaiian/Pacific Islander; 4.2% other race; 2 or more races, 3.1%. **Hispanic pop.** (any race): 8.0%.

Geography. Total area: 98,381 sq mi; rank: 9. **Land area:** 95,997 sq mi; rank: 10. **Acres forested:** 29.7 mil. **Location:** Pacific state, bounded on N by Washington; on E by Idaho; on S by Nevada and California; on W by the Pacific. **Climate:** coastal mild and humid climate; continental dryness and extreme temperatures in the interior. **Topography:** Coast Range of rugged mountains; fertile Willamette R. Valley to E and S; Cascade Mt. Range of volcanic peaks E of the valley; plateau E of Cascades, remaining two-thirds of state. **Capital:** Salem.

Economy. Chief industries: manufacturing, services, trade, finance, insurance, real estate, government, construction. **Chief manuf. goods:** electronics & semiconductors, lumber & wood products, metals, transportation equipment, processed food, paper. **Chief crops:** greenhouse, hay, wheat, grass seed, potatoes, onions, Christmas trees, pears, mint. **Livestock** (Jan. 2004) 1.44 mil. cattle/calves; 215,000 sheep/lambs; (Jan. 2003): 27,000 hogs/pigs; (Dec. 2003): 3.6 mil. chickens (excl. broilers). **Timber/lumber** (est. 2002): 6.4 bil bd. ft. Douglas fir, hemlock, ponderosa pine. **Nonfuel minerals** (est. 2003): $311 mil.; sand and gravel (construction), stone (crushed), cement (portland), diatomite, lime. **Commercial fishing** (2002): $65.2 mil. **Chief ports:** Portland, Astoria, Coos Bay. **Principal internat. airports at:** Portland, Medford. **New private housing** (2003): 26,103 units/$3.8 bil. **Gross state product** (2001): $120.1 bil. **Employment distrib.** (May 2004): 17.5% govt.; 19.7% trade/trans./util.; 12.4% mfg.; 11.9% ed./health serv.; 11% prof./bus serv.; 9.8% leisure/hosp.; 6.2% finance; 5% constr.; 2.1% info. **Per cap. pers. income** (2003): $29,340. **Sales tax** (2004): none. **Unemployment** (2003): 8.2%. **Tourism expends.** (2002): $5.7 bil. **Lottery** (2003): total sales: $853.51 mil; net income: $359.4 mil.

Finance. FDIC-insured commercial banks (2003): 35. **Deposits:** $8.7 bil. **FDIC-insured savings institutions** (2003): 3. **Assets:** $2.1 bil.

Federal govt. Fed. civ. employees (Mar. 2003): 18,661. **Avg. salary:** $53,426. **Notable fed. facilities:** Bonneville Power Administration.

Energy. Electricity production (est. 2003, kWh by source): Coal: 4.3 bil; Petroleum: 44 mil; Gas: 2.0 bil; Hydroelectric: 33.1 bil.

State data. Motto: She flies with her own wings. **Flower:** Oregon grape. **Bird:** Western meadowlark. **Tree:** Douglas fir. **Song:** Oregon, My Oregon. **Entered union** Feb. 14, 1859; rank, 33rd. **State fair** at Salem; 12 days ending with Labor Day.

History. More than 100 Native American tribes inhabited the area at the time of European contact, including the Chinook, Yakima, Cayuse, Modoc, and Nez Percé. Capt. Robert Gray sighted and sailed into the Columbia River, 1792; Lewis and Clark, traveling overland, wintered at its mouth, 1805-6; John Jacob Astor established a trading post in the Columbia River region, 1811. Settlers arrived in the Williamette Valley, 1834. In 1843, the first large wave of settlers arrived via the Oregon Trail. Early in the 20th cent., the "Oregon System"—political reforms that included the initiative, referendum, recall, direct primary, and woman suffrage—was adopted.

Tourist attractions. John Day Fossil Beds Natl. Monument; Columbia River Gorge; Timberline Lodge, Mt. Hood Natl. Forest; Crater Lake Natl. Park; Oregon Dunes Natl. Recreation Area; Ft. Clatsop Natl. Memorial; Oregon Caves Natl. Monument; Oregon Museum of Science and Industry, Portland; Shakespearean Festival, Ashland; High Desert Museum, Bend; Multnomah Falls; Diamond Lake; "Spruce Goose," Evergreen Aviation Museum, McMinnville.

Famous Oregonians. Ernest Bloch, Bill Bowerman, Ernest Haycox, Chief Joseph, Ken Kesey, Phil Knight, Ursula K. Le Guin, Edwin Markham, Tom McCall, Dr. John McLoughlin, Joaquin Miller, Bob Packwood, Linus Pauling, Steve Prefontaine, John Reed, Alberto Salazar, Mary Decker Slaney, William Simon U'Ren.

Tourist information. Oregon Tourism Commission, 775 Summer St. NE, Salem, OR 97310; 1-800-547-7842. **Website:** www.traveloregon.com

Website. www.oregon.gov

Pennsylvania
Keystone State

People. Population (2003 est.): 12,365,455; rank: 6; **net change** (2002-2003): 0.3%. **Pop. density:** 275.9 per sq mi. **Racial distribution** (2000): 85.4% white; 10.0% black; 1.8% Asian; 0.1% Native American/Nat. AK; <0.1% Hawaiian/Pacific Islander; 1.5% other race; 2 or more races, 1.2%. **Hispanic pop.** (any race): 3.2%.

Geography. Total area: 46,055 sq mi; rank: 33. **Land area:** 44,817 sq mi; rank: 32. **Acres forested:** 16.9 mil. **Location:** Middle Atlantic state, bordered on the E by the Delaware R.; on the S by the Mason-Dixon Line; on the W by West Virginia and Ohio; on the N/NE by Lake Erie and New York. **Climate:** continental with wide fluctuations in seasonal temperatures. **Topography:** Allegheny Mts. run SW to NE, with Piedmont and Coast Plain in the SE triangle; Allegheny Front a diagonal spine across the state's center; N and W rugged plateau falls to Lake Erie Lowland. **Capital:** Harrisburg.

Economy. Chief industries: agribusiness, advanced manufacturing, health care, travel & tourism, depository institutions, biotechnology, printing & publishing, research & consulting, trucking & warehousing, transportation by air, engineering & management, legal services. **Chief manuf. goods:** fabricated metal products; industrial machinery & equipment, transportation equipment, rubber & plastics, electronic equipment, chemicals & pharmaceuticals, lumber & wood products, stone, clay, & glass products. **Chief crops:** corn, hay, mushrooms, apples, potatoes, winter wheat, oats, vegetables, tobacco, grapes, peaches. **Livestock** (Jan. 2004) 1.64 mil. cattle/calves; 85,000 sheep/lambs; (Jan. 2003): 1.1 mil. hogs/pigs; (Dec. 2003): 29.4 mil. chickens (excl. broilers); 129.6 mil. broilers. **Timber/lumber** (est. 2002): 1.1 bil bd. ft.; pine, oak, maple. **Nonfuel minerals** (est. 2003): $1.3 bil.; stone (crushed), cement (portland), sand and gravel (construction), lime, cement (masonry). **Commercial fishing** (2002): $37,109. **Chief ports:** Philadelphia, Pittsburgh, Erie. **Principal internat. airports at:** Allentown, Harrisburg, Philadelphia, Pittsburgh, Wilkes-Barre/Scranton. **New private housing** (2003): 42,315 units/$5.5 bil. **Gross state product** (2001): $408.4 bil. **Employment distrib.** (May 2004): 13.5% govt.; 19.7% trade/trans./util.; 12.3% mfg.; 17.5% ed./health serv.; 10.7% prof./bus serv.; 8.7% leisure/hosp.; 6% finance; 4.5% constr.; 2.2% info. **Per cap. pers. income** (2003): $31,998. **Sales tax** (2004): 6.0%. **Unemployment** (2003): 5.6%. **Tourism expends.** (2002): $15.9 bil. **Lottery** (2003): total sales: $2.1 bil; net income: $796.5 mil.

Finance. FDIC-insured commercial banks (2003): 169. **Deposits:** $131.8 bil. **FDIC-insured savings institutions** (2003): 101. **Assets:** $118 bil.

Federal govt. Fed. civ. employees (Mar. 2003): 63,138. **Avg. salary:** $52,271. **Notable fed. facilities:** Carlisle Barracks; Army War College; Naval Inventory Control Point, Phila. and Mechanicsbrg; Defense Personnel Supply Ctr., Phila.; Defense Distribution Ctr., New Cumberland; Tobyhanna Army Depot; Letterkenny Army Depot; NAS Willow Grove; 911th Air Wing, Pittsburgh; Naval Surface Warfare Ctr., Phila.; Charles E. Kelly Support Facility.

Energy. Electricity production (est. 2003, kWh by source): Coal: 15.9 bil; Petroleum: 35 mil; Hydroelectric: 1.3 bil; Nuclear: 12.6 bil.

State data. Motto: Virtue, liberty and independence. **Flower:** Mountain laurel. **Bird:** Ruffed grouse. **Tree:** Hemlock. **Song:** Pennsylvania. **Second** of the original 13 states to ratify the Constitution, Dec. 12, 1787. **State fair** at Harrisburg; 2nd week in Jan. at State Farm Show Complex.

History. At the time of European contact, Lenni Lenape (Delaware), Shawnee and Iroquoian Susquehannocks, Erie, and Seneca occupied the region. Swedish explorers established the first permanent settlement, 1643, on Tinicum Island. In 1655, the Dutch seized the settlement but lost it to the British, 1664. The region was given by Charles II to William Penn, 1681. Philadelphia ("brotherly love") was the capital of the colonies during most of the American Revolution, and of the U.S., 1790-1800. Philadelphia was taken by the British, 1777; Washington's troops encamped at Valley Forge in the bitter winter of 1777-78. The Declaration of Independence, 1776, and the Constitution, 1787, were signed in Philadelphia. The Civil War battle of Gettysburg, July 1-3, 1863, marked a turning point, favoring Union forces.

Tourist attractions. Independence Natl. Historic Park, Franklin Institute Science Museum, Philadelphia Museum of Art, all in Philadelphia; Valley Forge Natl. Historic Park; Gettysburg Natl. Military Park; Pennsylvania Dutch Country; Hershey; Duquesne Incline, Carnegie Institute, Heinz Hall, all in Pittsburgh; Pocono Mts.; Pennsylvania's Grand Canyon,

Tioga County; Allegheny Natl. Forest; Laurel Highlands; Presque Isle State Park; Fallingwater, Mill Run; Johnstown; SteamTown U.S.A.; Scranton; State Flagship Niagara, Erie; Oil Heritage Region, Northwest PA.

Famous Pennsylvanians. Marian Anderson, Maxwell Anderson, George Blanda, James Buchanan, Andrew Carnegie, Rachel Carson, Perry Como, Bill Cosby, Thomas Eakins, Stephen Foster, Benjamin Franklin, Robert Fulton, Martha Graham, Milton Hershey, Gene Kelly, Grace Kelly (Princess Grace of Monaco), Dan Marino, George C. Marshall, Chris Matthews, John J. McCloy, Margaret Mead, Andrew W. Mellon, Joe Montana, Stan Musial, Joe Namath, John O'Hara, Arnold Palmer, Robert E. Peary, Mike Piazza, Tom Ridge, Mary Roberts Rinehart, Fred Rogers, Betsy Ross, Will Smith, Jimmy Stewart, Jim Thorpe, Johnny Unitas, John Updike, Honus Wagner, Andy Warhol, Benjamin West.

Tourist Information. Department of Community and Economic Development, Office of Tourism, Film and Economic Development, 4th Fl., 400 North St., Harrisburg, PA 17120-0225; 1-800-VISITPA. **Website:** www.experiencepa.co
Website. www.state.pa.us

Rhode Island
Little Rhody, Ocean State

People. Population (2003 est.): 1,076,164; rank: 43; **net change** (2002-2003): 0.7%. **Pop. density:** 1,029.9 per sq mi. **Racial distribution** (2000): 85.0% white; 4.5% black; 2.3% Asian; 0.5% Native American/Nat. AK; 0.1% Hawaiian/Pacific Islander; 5.0% other race; 2 or more races, 2.7%. **Hispanic pop.** (any race): 8.7%.

Geography. Total area: 1,545 sq mi; rank: 50. **Land area:** 1,045 sq mi; rank: 50. **Acres forested:** 0.4 mil. **Location:** New England state. **Climate:** invigorating and changeable. **Topography:** eastern lowlands of Narragansett Basin; western uplands of flat and rolling hills. **Capital:** Providence.

Economy. Chief industries: services, manufacturing. **Chief manuf. goods:** costume jewelry, toys, machinery, textiles, electronics. **Chief crops:** nursery products, turf & vegetable production. **Livestock** (Jan. 2004) 5,500 cattle/calves; (Jan. 2003): 2,600 hogs/pigs. **Timber/lumber** (est. 2002): 10 mil bd. ft.; **Nonfuel minerals** (est. 2003): $26 mil.; sand and gravel (construction), stone (crushed), sand and gravel (industrial), gemstones. **Commercial fishing** (2002): $64.7 mil. **Chief ports:** Providence, Quonset Point, Newport. **New private housing** (2003): 2,349 units/$340 mil. **Gross state product** (2001): $36.9 bil. **Employment distrib.** (May 2004): 13.8% govt.; 16.4% trade/trans./util.; 11.9% mfg.; 18.9% ed./ health serv.; 10.1% prof./bus serv.; 10.5% leisure/hosp.; 6.8% finance; 4.6% constr.; 2.2% info. **Per cap. pers. income** (2003): $31,916. **Sales tax** (2004): 7.0%. **Unemployment** (2003): 5.3%. **Tourism expends.** (2002): $1.4 bil. **Lottery** (2003): total sales: $553.75 mil; net income: $249 mil.

Finance. FDIC-insured commercial banks (2003): 8. **Deposits:** $156.3 bil. **FDIC-insured savings institutions** (2003): 7. **Assets:** $2.4 bil.

Federal govt. Fed. civ. employees (Mar. 2003): 6,191. **Avg. salary:** $63,303. **Notable fed. facilities:** Naval War College; Naval Underwater Warfare Ctr.; Natl. Marine Fisheries Lab; EPA Environmental Res. Lab.

Energy. Electricity production (est. 2002, kWh, by source): Petroleum: 8 mil.

State data. Motto: Hope. **Flower:** Violet. **Bird:** Rhode Island red. **Tree:** Red maple. **Song:** Rhode Island. **Thirteenth** of original 13 states to ratify the Constitution, May 29, 1790. **State fair** at Richmond; mid-Aug.

History. When the Europeans arrived Narragansett, Niantic, Nipmuc, and Wampanoag peoples lived in the region. Verrazano visited the area, 1524. The first permanent settlement was founded at Providence, 1636, by Roger Williams, who was exiled from the Massachusetts Bay Colony; Anne Hutchinson, also exiled, settled Portsmouth, 1638. Quaker and Jewish immigrants seeking freedom of worship began arriving, 1650s-60s. The colonists broke the power of the Narragansett in the Great Swamp Fight, 1675, the decisive battle in King Philip's War. British trade restrictions angered colonists, and they burned the British customs vessel *Gaspee*, 1772. The colony became the first to formally renounce all allegiance to King George III, May 4, 1776. Initially opposed to joining the Union, Rhode Island was the last of the 13 colonies to ratify the Constitution, 1790.

Tourist attractions. Newport mansions; yachting races including Newport to Bermuda; Block Island; Touro Synagogue, oldest in U.S., Newport; first Baptist Church in America, Providence; Slater Mill Historic Site, Pawtucket; Gilbert Stuart birthplace, Saunderstown.

Famous Rhode Islanders. Ambrose Burnside, George M. Cohan, Nelson Eddy, Jabez Gorham, Nathanael Greene, Christopher and Oliver La Farge, John McLaughlin, Matthew C. and Oliver Hazard Perry, Gilbert Stuart.

Tourist Information. Rhode Island Tourism Division, 1 W. Exchange St., Providence, RI 02903; 1-800-556-2484. **Website:** visitrhodeisland.com
Website. www.state.ri.us

South Carolina
Palmetto State

People. Population (2003 est.): 4,147,152; rank: 25; **net change** (2002-2003): 1.1%. **Pop. density:** 137.7 per sq mi. **Racial distribution** (2000): 67.2% white; 29.5% black; 0.9% Asian; 0.3% Native American/Nat. AK; <0.1% Hawaiian/Pacific Islander; 1.0% other race; 2 or more races, 1.0%. **Hispanic pop.** (any race): 2.4%.

Geography. Total area: 32,020 sq mi; rank: 40. **Land area:** 30,109 sq mi; rank: 40. **Acres forested:** 12.5 mil. **Location:** South Atlantic state, bordered by North Carolina on the N; Georgia on the SW and W; the Atlantic Ocean on the E, SE, and S. **Climate:** humid subtropical. **Topography:** Blue Ridge province in NW has highest peaks; piedmont lies between the mountains and the fall line; coastal plain covers two-thirds of the state. **Capital:** Columbia.

Economy. Chief industries: tourism, agriculture, manufacturing. **Chief manuf. goods:** textiles, chemicals and allied products, machinery and fabricated metal products, apparel and related products. **Chief crops:** tobacco, cotton, soybeans, corn, wheat, peaches, tomatoes. **Livestock** (Jan. 2004) 425,000 cattle/calves; (Jan. 2003): 300,000 hogs/pigs; (Dec. 2003): 6.8 mil. chickens (excl. broilers); 197.4 mil. broilers. **Timber/lumber** (est. 2002): 1.4 bil bd. ft.; pine, oak. **Nonfuel minerals** (est. 2003): $484 mil.; cement (portland), stone (crushed), cement (masonry), sand and gravel (construction), clays (kaolin). **Commercial fishing** (2002): $21.3 mil. **Gross state product** (2001): $115.2 bil. **Principal internat. airports at:** Charleston, Greenville/Spartanburg, Myrtle Beach. **New private housing** (2003): 36,733 units/$4.5 bil. **Employment distrib.** (May 2004): 18.2% govt.; 19% trade/trans./util.; 14.7% mfg.; 10.1% ed./health serv.; 10.4% prof./bus serv.; 11.2% leisure/hosp.; 5.1% finance; 6.2% constr.; 1.4% info. **Per cap. pers. income** (2003): $26,132. **Sales tax** (2004): 5.0%. **Unemployment** (2003): 6.8%. **Tourism expends.** (2002): $7.5 bil. **Lottery** (2003): total sales: $724.3 mil; net income: $220.1 mil.

Finance. FDIC-insured commercial banks (2003): 75. **Deposits:** $24.7 bil. **FDIC-insured savings institutions** (2003): 22. **Assets:** $7 bil.

Federal govt. Fed. civ. employees (Mar. 2003): 16,509. **Avg. salary:** $51,183. **Notable fed. facilities:** Polaris Submarine Base; Barnwell Nuclear Power Plant; Ft. Jackson; Parris Island; Savannah River Plant.

Energy. Electricity production (est. 2003, kWh by source): Coal: 37.4 bil; Petroleum: 238 mil; Gas: 1.8 bil; Hydroelectric: 2.3 bil; Nuclear: 50.4 bil; Other: 22 mil.

State data. Motto: Dum Spiro Spero (While I breathe, I hope). **Flower:** Yellow jessamine. **Bird:** Carolina wren. **Tree:** Palmetto. **Song:** Carolina. **Eighth** of the original 13 states to ratify the Constitution, May 23, 1788. **State fair** at Columbia; mid-Oct.

History. At the time of European settlement, Cherokee, Catawba, and Muskogean peoples lived in the area. The first English colonists settled near the Ashley River, 1670, and moved to the site of Charleston, 1680. The colonists seized the government, 1775, and the royal governor fled. The British took Charleston, 1780, but were defeated at Kings Mountain that same year, and at Cowpens and Eutaw Springs, 1781. In the 1830s, South Carolinians, angered by federal protective tariffs, adopted the Nullification Doctrine, holding that a state can void an act of Congress. The state was the first to secede from the Union, 1860, and Confederate troops fired on and forced the surrender of U.S. troops at Ft. Sumter, in Charleston Harbor, launching the Civil War. South Carolina was readmitted,1868.

Tourist attractions. Historic Charleston; Ft. Sumter Natl. Monument, in Charleston Harbor; Charleston Museum, est. 1773, oldest museum in U.S.; Middleton Place, Magnolia Plantation, Cypress Gardens, Drayton Hall, all near Charleston; other gardens at Brookgreen, Edisto, Glencairn; Myrtle Beach; Hilton Head Island; Revolutionary War battle sites; Andrew Jackson State Park & Museum; South Carolina State Museum, Columbia; Riverbanks Zoo, Columbia.

Famous South Carolinians. Charles Bolden, James F. Byrnes, John C. Calhoun, Joe Fraizer, DuBose Heyward, Ernest F. Hollings, Andrew Jackson, Jesse Jackson, "Shoe-

less" Joe Jackson, James Longstreet, Francis Marion, Andie McDowell, Ronald McNair, Charles Pinckney, John Rutledge, Thomas Sumter, Strom Thurmond, John B. Watson.

Tourist information. S. Carolina Dept. of Parks, Recreation, & Tourism; 803-734-0122; 1-800-346-3634. **Website:** www.discoversouthcarolina.com

Website. www.myscgov.com

South Dakota
Coyote State, Mount Rushmore State

People. Population (2003 est.): 764,309; rank: 46; **net change** (2002-2003): 0.5%. **Pop. density:** 10.1 per sq mi. **Racial distribution** (2000): 88.7% white; 0.6% black; 0.6% Asian; 8.3% Native American/Nat. AK; <0.1% Hawaiian/Pacific Islander; 0.5% other race; 2 or more races, 1.3%. **Hispanic pop.** (any race): 1.4%.

Geography. Total area: 77,116 sq mi; rank: 17. **Land area:** 75,885 sq mi; rank: 16. **Acres forested:** 1.6 mil. **Location:** West North Central state bounded on the N by North Dakota; on the E by Minnesota and Iowa; on the S by Nebraska; on the W by Wyoming and Montana. **Climate:** characterized by extremes of temperature, persistent winds, low precipitation and humidity. **Topography:** Prairie Plains in the E; rolling hills of the Great Plains in the W; the Black Hills, rising 3,500 ft, in the SW corner. **Capital:** Pierre.

Economy. Chief industries: agriculture, services, manufacturing. **Chief manuf. goods:** food and kindred products, machinery, electric and electronic equipment. **Chief crops:** corn, soybeans, oats, wheat, sunflowers, sorghum. **Livestock** (Jan. 2004) 3.65 mil. cattle/calves; 370,000 sheep/lambs; (Jan. 2003): 1.26 mil. hogs/pigs; (Dec. 2003) 3.7 mil. chickens (excl. broilers). **Timber/lumber:** (figs. undisclosed); ponderosa pine. **Nonfuel minerals** (est. 2003): $206 mil.; cement (portland), sand and gravel (construction), stone (crushed), gold, stone (dimension). **New private housing** (2003): 4,835 units/$518 mil. **Gross state product** (2001): $24.3 bil. **Employment distrib.** (May 2004): 20% govt.; 20.3% trade/trans./util.; 9.9% mfg.; 14.5% ed./health serv.; 6.2% prof./bus serv.; 10.6% leisure/hosp.; 7.1% finance; 5.3% constr.; 1.7% info. **Per cap. pers. income** (2003): $29,234. **Sales tax** (2004): 4.0%. **Unemployment** (2003): 3.6%. **Tourism expends.** (2002): $1.5 bil. **Lottery** (2003): total sales: $240.88 mil; net income: $112.1 mil.

Finance. FDIC-insured commercial banks (2003): 90. **Deposits:** $14.7 bil. **FDIC-insured savings institutions** (2003): 4. **Assets:** $1.2 bil.

Federal govt. Fed. civ. employees (Mar. 2003): 7,158. **Avg. salary:** $47,417. **Notable fed. facilities:** Ellsworth AFB, Corp of Engineers, Nat'l Park Service.

Energy. Electricity production (est. 2003, kWh by source): Coal: 3.4 bil; Petroleum: 16 mil; Gas: 109 mil; Hydroelectric: 4.3 bil; Other: 6 mil.

State data. Motto: Under God, the people rule. **Flower:** Pasqueflower. **Bird:** Chinese ring-necked pheasant. **Tree:** Black Hills spruce. **Song:** Hail, South Dakota. **Entered union** Nov. 2, 1889; rank, 40th. **State fair** at Huron; early Sept.

History. At the time of first European contact, Mandan, Hidatsa, Arikara, and Sioux lived in the area. The French Verendrye brothers explored the region, 1742-43. The U.S. acquired the area, 1803, in the Louisiana Purchase. Lewis and Clark passed through the area, 1804-6. In 1817 a trading post was opened at Fort Pierre, which later became the site of the first European settlement in South Dakota. Gold was discovered, 1874, in the Black Hills on the great Sioux reservation; the "Great Dakota Boom" began in 1879. Conflicts with Native Americans led to the Great Sioux Agreement, 1889, which established reservations and opened up more land for white settlement. The massacre of Native American families at Wounded Knee, 1890, ended Sioux resistance.

Tourist attractions. Black Hills; Mt. Rushmore; Needles Highway; Harney Peak, tallest E. of Rockies; Deadwood, 1876 Gold Rush town; Custer State Park; Jewel Cave Natl. Monument; Badlands Natl. Park "moonscape"; "Great Lakes of S. Dakota"; Ft. Sisseton; Great Plains Zoo & Museum, Sioux Falls; Corn Palace, Mitchell; Wind Cave Natl. Park; Crazy Horse Memorial, mountain carving in progress.

Famous South Dakotans. Sparky Anderson, Black Elk, Bob Barker, Tom Brokaw, Crazy Horse, Thomas Daschle, Myron Floren, Mary Hart, Cheryl Ladd, Dr. Ernest O. Lawrence, George McGovern, Billy Mills, Allen Neuharth, Pat O'Brien, Sitting Bull.

Tourist information. Department of Tourism and State Development, Capitol Lake Plaza, 711 E. Wells Ave., c/o 500 E. Capitol Ave., Pierre, SD 57501-5070; 1-800-SDAKOTA. **Website:** www.travelsd.com

Website. www.state.sd.us

Tennessee
Volunteer State

People. Population (2003 est.): 5,841,748; rank: 16; **net change** (2002-2003): 0.9%. **Pop. density:** 141.7 per sq mi. **Racial distribution** (2000): 80.2% white; 16.4% black; 1.0% Asian; 0.3% Native American/Nat. AK; <0.1% Hawaiian/Pacific Islander; 1.0% other race; 2 or more races, 1.1%. **Hispanic pop.** (any race): 2.2%.

Geography. Total area: 42,143 sq mi; rank: 36. **Land area:** 41,217 sq mi; rank: 34. **Acres forested:** 14.4 mil. **Location:** East South Central state bounded on the N by Kentucky and Virginia; on the E by North Carolina; on the S by Georgia, Alabama, and Mississippi; on the W by Arkansas and Missouri. **Climate:** humid continental to the N; humid subtropical to the S. **Topography:** rugged country in the E; the Great Smoky Mts. of the Unakas; low ridges of the Appalachian Valley; the flat Cumberland Plateau; slightly rolling terrain and knobs of the Interior Low Plateau, the largest region; Eastern Gulf Coastal Plain to the W, laced with streams; Mississippi Alluvial Plain, a narrow strip of swamp and flood plain in the extreme W. **Capital:** Nashville.

Economy. Chief industries: manufacturing, trade, services, tourism, finance, insurance, real estate. **Chief manuf. goods:** chemicals, food, transportation equipment, industrial machinery & equipment, fabricated metal products, rubber/plastic products, paper & allied products, printing & publishing. **Chief crops:** tobacco, cotton, lint, soybeans, grain, corn. **Livestock** (Jan. 2004) 2.21 mil. cattle/calves; (Jan. 2003): 215,000 hogs/pigs; (Dec. 2003): 2.3 mil. chickens (excl. broilers); 182.3 mil. broilers. **Timber/lumber** (est. 2002): 899 mil bd. ft.; red oak, white oak, yellow poplar, hickory. **Nonfuel minerals** (est. 2003): $606 mil.; stone (crushed), cement (portland), sand and gravel (construction), zinc, clays (ball). **Chief ports:** Memphis, Nashville, Chattanooga, Knoxville. **Principal internat. airports at:** Memphis, Nashville. **New private housing** (2003): 37,427 units/$4.5 bil. **Gross state product** (2001): $182.5 bil. **Employment distrib.** (May 2004): 15.5% govt.; 21.6% trade/trans./util.; 15.3% mfg.; 11.8% ed./health serv.; 10.7% prof./bus serv.; 9.6% leisure/hosp.; 5.2% finance; 4.4% constr.; 1.9% info. **Per cap. pers. income** (2003): $28,455. **Sales tax** (2004): 7.0%. **Unemployment** (2003): 5.8%. **Tourism expends.** (2002): $10.6 bil.

Finance. FDIC-insured commercial banks (2003): 188. **Deposits:** $82.4 bil. **FDIC-insured savings institutions** (2003): 20. **Assets:** $5.7 bil.

Federal govt. Fed. civ. employees (Mar. 2003): 35,177. **Avg. salary:** $52,819. **Notable fed. facilities:** Tennessee Valley Authority; Oak Ridge Nat'l. Lab; Arnold Engineering Development Ctr.; Ft. Campbell; Naval Support Activity, Mid-South.

Energy. Electricity production (est. 2003, kWh by source): Coal: 53.4 bil; Petroleum: 297 mil; Gas: 198 mil; Hydroelectric: 10.4 bil; Nuclear: 24.2 bil; Other: 2 mil.

State data. Motto: Agriculture and commerce. **Flower:** Iris. **Bird:** Mockingbird. **Tree:** Tulip poplar. **Songs:** My Homeland, Tennessee; When It's Iris Time in Tennessee; My Tennessee; Tennessee Waltz; Rocky Top. **Entered union** June 1, 1796; rank, 16th. **State fair** at Nashville; mid-Sept.

History. When the first European explorers arrived, Creek and Yuchi peoples lived in the area; the Cherokee moved into the region in the early 18th cent. Spanish explorers first visited the area, 1541. English traders crossed the Great Smokies from the east while France's Marquette and Jolliet sailed down the Mississippi on the west, 1673. The first permanent settlement was by Virginians on the Watauga River, 1769. During the American Revolution, the colonists helped win the Battle of Kings Mountain (NC), 1780, and joined other eastern campaigns. The state seceded from the Union, 1861, and saw many Civil War engagements, but 30,000 soldiers fought for the Union. Tennessee was readmitted in 1866, the only former Confederate state not to have a postwar military government.

Tourist attractions. Reelfoot Lake; Lookout Mountain, Chattanooga; Fall Creek Falls; Great Smoky Mountains Natl. Park; Lost Sea, Sweetwater; Cherokee Natl. Forest; Cumberland Gap Natl. Park; Andrew Jackson's home, the Hermitage, near Nashville; homes of Pres. Polk and Andrew Johnson; American Museum of Science and Energy, Oak Ridge; Parthenon, Grand Old Opry, Opryland USA, all Nashville; Dollywood theme park, Pigeon Forge; Tennessee Aquarium, Chattanooga; Graceland, home of Elvis Presley, Memphis; Alex Haley Home and Museum, Henning; Casey Jones Home and Museum, Jackson.

Famous Tennesseans. Roy Acuff, Davy Crockett, David Farragut, Ernie Ford, Aretha Franklin, Morgan Freeman, Bill Frist, Al Gore Jr., Alex Haley, William C. Handy, Sam Hous-

ton, Cordell Hull, Andrew Jackson, Andrew Johnson, Casey Jones, Estes Kefauver, Grace Moore, Dolly Parton, Minnie Pearl, James Polk, Elvis Presley, Dinah Shore, Bessie Smith, Fred Thompson, Hank Williams Jr., Alvin York.

Tourist information. Dept. of Tourist Development, Wm. Snodgrass/Tennessee Tower, 312 8th Ave., 25th Fl., Nashville, TN 37243; 1-615-741-2159. **Website:** www.tennessee-anytime.org

Website. www.tn.gov

Texas
Lone Star State

People. Population (2003 est.): 22,118,509; rank: 2; **net change** (2002-2003): 1.8%. **Pop. density:** 84.5 per sq mi. **Racial distribution** (2000): 71.0% white; 11.5% black; 2.7% Asian; 0.6% Native American/Nat. AK; 0.1% Hawaiian/Pacific Islander; 11.7% other race; 2 or more races, 2.5%. **Hispanic pop.** (any race): 32.0%.

Geography. Total area: 268,581 sq mi; rank: 2. **Land area:** 261,797 sq mi; rank: 2. **Acres forested:** 17.1 mil. **Location:** Southwestern state, bounded on the SE by the Gulf of Mexico; on the SW by Mexico, separated by the Rio Grande; surrounding states are Louisiana, Arkansas, Oklahoma, New Mexico. **Climate:** extremely varied; driest region is the Trans-Pecos; wettest is the NE. **Topography:** Gulf Coast Plain in the S and SE; North Central Plains slope upward with some hills; the Great Plains extend over the Panhandle, are broken by low mountains; the Trans-Pecos is the southern extension of the Rockies. **Capital:** Austin.

Economy. Chief industries: manufacturing, trade, oil and gas extraction, services. **Chief manuf. goods:** industrial machinery and equipment, foods, electrical and electronic products, chemicals and allied products, apparel. **Chief crops:** cotton, grains (wheat), sorghum grain, vegetables, citrus and other fruits, greenhouse/nursery, pecans, peanuts. **Chief farm products:** milk, eggs **Livestock:** (Jan. 2004) 13.9 mil. cattle/calves; 1.1 mil. sheep/lambs; (Jan. 2003): 930,000 hogs/pigs; (Dec. 2003): 26.0 mil. chickens (excl. broilers); 601.5 mil. broilers. **Timber/lumber** (est. 2002): 1.6 bil bd. ft.; pine, cypress. **Nonfuel minerals** (est. 2003): $2.0 bil.; cement (portland), stone (crushed), sand and gravel (construction), lime, salt. **Commercial fishing** (2002): $173.3 mil. **Chief ports:** Houston, Galveston, Brownsville, Beaumont, Port Arthur, Corpus Christi. **Principal internat. airports at:** Amarillo, Austin, Corpus Christi, Dallas/Ft. Worth, El Paso, Harlingen, Houston, Lubbock, Odessa, San Antonio. **New private housing** (2003): 174,170 units/$19.4 bil. **Gross state product** (2001): $763.9 bil. **Employment distrib.** (May 2004): 17.7% govt.; 20.4% trade/trans./util.; 9.3% mfg.; 12.2% ed./health serv.; 11.1% prof./bus serv.; 9.4% leisure/hosp.; 6.2% finance; 5.8% constr.; 2.4% info. **Per cap. pers. income** (2003): $29,372. **Sales tax** (2004): 6.25%. **Unemployment** (2003): 6.8%. **Tourism expends.** (2002): $34.2 bil. **Lottery** (2003): total sales: $3.1 bil; net income: $949.1 mil.

Finance. FDIC-insured commercial banks (2003): 654. **Deposits:** $112.8 bil. **FDIC-insured savings institutions** (2003): 44. **Assets:** $63.7 bil.

Federal govt. Fed. civ. employees (Mar. 2003): 106,501. **Avg. salary:** $53,074. **Notable fed. facilities:** Ft. Hood, Kelly AFB; Ft. Sam Houston; NASA Johnson Space Ctr.; Naval Air Training School; Corpus Christi NAS; Kingsville NAS; Ft. Worth Western Currency Facility.

Energy. Electricity production (est. 2003, kWh by source): Coal: 92.9 bil; Petroleum: 1 bil.; Gas: 35.6 bil; Hydroelectric: 796 mil; Nuclear: 15.7 bil; Other: 2 mil.

State data. Motto: Friendship. **Flower:** Bluebonnet. **Bird:** Mockingbird. **Tree:** Pecan. **Song:** Texas, Our Texas. **Entered union** Dec. 29, 1845; rank, 28th. **State fair** at Dallas; late Sept.-mid-Oct.

History. At the time of European contact, Native American tribes in the region were numerous and diverse in culture. Coahuiltecan, Karankawa, Caddo, Jumano, and Tonkawa peoples lived in the area, and during the 19th cent., the Apache, Comanche, Cherokee, and Wichita arrived. Spanish explorer Pineda sailed along the Texas coast, 1519; Cabeza de Vaca and Coronado visited the interior, 1541. Spaniards made the first settlement at Ysleta, near El Paso, 1682. Americans moved into the land early in the 19th cent. Mexico, of which Texas was a part, won independence from Spain, 1821; Santa Anna became dictator in 1835; Texans rebelled. Santa Anna wiped out defenders of the Alamo, 1836; Sam Houston's Texans defeated Santa Anna at San Jacinto, and independence was proclaimed that same year. The Republic of Texas, with Sam Houston as its first president, functioned as a nation until 1845, when it was admitted to the Union.

Tourist attractions. Padre Island Natl. Seashore; Big Bend, Guadalupe Mts. natl. parks; The Alamo; Ft. Davis; Six Flags Amusement Park; Sea World and Fiesta Texas, both in San Antonio; San Antonio Missions Natl. Historical Park; Cowgirl Hall of Fame, Fort Worth; Lyndon B. Johnson Natl. Historical Park, marking his birthplace, boyhood home, and ranch, near Johnson City; Lyndon B. Johnson Library and Museum, Austin; Texas State Aquarium, Corpus Christi; Kimball Art Museum, Fort Worth; George Bush Library, College Station.

Famous Texans. Lance Armstrong, Stephen F. Austin, Lloyd Bentsen, James Bowie, Carol Burnett, George H. W. Bush, George W. Bush, Joan Crawford, J. Frank Dobie, Dwight D. Eisenhower, Morgan Fairchild, Farrah Fawcett, Sam Houston, Howard Hughes, Kay Bailey Hutchison, Molly Ivins, Lyndon B. Johnson, Tommy Lee Jones, Janis Joplin, Barbara Jordan, Mary Martin, Chester Nimitz, Sandra Day O'Connor, H. Ross Perot, Katherine Ann Porter, Dan Rather, Sam Rayburn, Ann Richards, Sissy Spacek, Kenneth Starr, George Strait.

Tourist Information. Travel Division, Texas Dept. of Transporation, PO Box 149249, Austin, TX 78714-9249; 1-800-8888TEX. **Website:** www.traveltex.com

Website. www.state.tx.us

Utah
Beehive State

People. Population (2003 est.): 2,351,467; rank: 34; **net change** (2002-2003): 1.4%. **Pop. density:** 28.6 per sq mi. **Racial distribution** (2000): 89.2% white; 0.8% black; 1.7% Asian; 1.3% Native American/Nat. AK; 0.7% Hawaiian/Pacific Islander; 4.2% other race; 2 or more races, 2.1%. **Hispanic pop.** (any race): 9.0%.

Geography. Total area: 84,899 sq mi; rank: 13. **Land area:** 82,144 sq mi; rank: 12. **Acres forested:** 15.7 mil. **Location:** Middle Rocky Mountain state; its southeastern corner touches Colorado, New Mexico, and Arizona, and is the only spot in the U.S. where 4 states join. **Climate:** arid; ranging from warm desert in SW to alpine in NE. **Topography:** high Colorado plateau is cut by brilliantly colored canyons of the SE; broad, flat, desert-like Great Basin of the W; the Great Salt Lake and Bonneville Salt Flats to the NW; Middle Rockies in the NE run E-W; valleys and plateaus of the Wasatch Front. **Capital:** Salt Lake City.

Economy. Chief industries: services, trade, manufacturing, government, transportation, utilities. **Chief manuf. goods:** medical instruments, electronic components, food products, fabricated metals, transportation equipment, steel and copper. **Chief crops:** hay, corn, wheat, barley, apples, potatoes, cherries, onions, peaches, pears. **Livestock** (Jan. 2004) 860,000 cattle/calves; 265,000 sheep/lambs; (Jan. 2003): 660,000 hogs/pigs; (Dec. 2003): 3.9 mil. chickens (excl. broilers). **Timber/lumber** (est. 2002): 53 mil bd. ft.; aspen, spruce, pine. **Nonfuel minerals** (est. 2003): $1.3 bil.; copper, cement (portland), salt, gold, sand and gravel (construction). **Commercial fishing** (2002): $60.2 mil. **Principal internat. airport at:** Salt Lake City. **New private housing** (2003): 22,226 units/$2.9 bil. **Gross state product** (2001): $70.4 bil. **Employment distrib.** (May 2004): 18.5% govt.; 19.9% trade/trans./util.; 10.4% mfg.; 10.9% ed./health serv.; 12.5% prof./bus serv.; 9.2% leisure/hosp.; 5.9% finance; 6.4% constr.; 2.7% info. **Per cap. pers. income** (2003): $24,977. **Sales tax** (2004): 4.75%. **Unemployment** (2003): 5.6%. **Tourism expends.** (2002): $4.1 bil.

Finance. FDIC-insured commercial banks (2003): 60. **Deposits:** $107.8 bil. **FDIC-insured savings institutions** (2003): 4. **Assets:** $1.6 bil.

Federal govt. Fed. civ. employees (Mar. 2003): 27,422. **Avg. salary:** $47,871. **Notable fed. facilities:** Hill AFB; Tooele Army Depot; Army Dugway Proving Ground.

Energy. Electricity production (est. 2003, kWh by source): Coal: 35.6 bil; Gas: 1.3 bil; Hydroelectric: 475 mil; Other: 198 mil.

State data. Motto: Industry. **Flower:** Sego lily. **Bird:** Seagull. **Tree:** Blue spruce. **Song:** Utah, We Love Thee. **Entered union** Jan. 4, 1896; rank, 45th. **State fair** at Salt Lake City; Sept.

History. Ute, Gosiute, Southern Paiute, and Navajo peoples lived in the region at the time of European contact. Spanish Franciscans visited the area, 1776; American fur traders followed. Permanent settlement began with the arrival of the Mormons, 1847; they made the arid land bloom and created a prosperous economy. The State of Deseret was organized in 1849, and asked admission to the Union. In 1850, Congress established the region as the territory of Utah, and Brigham Young was appointed governor. The Union Pacific and Central Pacific

> **IT'S A FACT:** Utah has a higher percentage of residents under 18 (30.8%) than does any other state. It is followed by Alaska (29.9%), Texas (28.0%), Idaho (27.6%), and Arizona (27.1%).

railroads met near Promontory Point, May 10, 1869, creating the first transcontinental railroad. Statehood was not achieved until 1896, after a long period of controversy over the Mormon Church's doctrine of polygamy, which it discontinued in 1890.

Tourist attractions. Temple Square, Mormon Church headquarters, Salt Lake City; Great Salt Lake; Zion, Canyonlands, Bryce Canyon, Arches, and Capitol Reef natl. parks; Dinosaur, Rainbow Bridge, Timpanogos Cave, and Natural Bridges natl. monuments; Lake Powell; Flaming Gorge Natl. Recreation Area.

Famous Utahans. Maude Adams, Ezra Taft Benson, John Moses Browning, Mariner Eccles, Philo Farnsworth, James Fletcher, David M. Kennedy, J. Willard Marriott, Merlin Olsen, Osmond family, Ivy Baker Priest, George Romney, Roseanne, Wallace Stegner, Brigham Young, Loretta Young.

Tourist information. Utah Travel Council, Council Hall, Salt Lake City, UT 84114; 1-800-200-1160 or 1-800 UTAH-FUN. **Website:** www.utah.com
Website. www.utah.gov

Vermont
Green Mountain State

People. Population (2003 est.): 619,107; rank: 49; **net change** (2002-2003): 0.4%. **Pop. density:** 66.9 per sq mi. **Racial distribution** (2000): 96.8% white; 0.5% black; 0.9% Asian; 0.4% Native American/Nat. AK; <0.1% Hawaiian/Pacific Islander; 0.2% other race; 2 or more races, 1.2%. **Hispanic pop.** (any race): 0.9%.

Geography. Total area: 9,614 sq mi; rank: 45. **Land area:** 9,250 sq mi; rank: 43. **Acres forested:** 4.6 mil. **Location:** northern New England state. **Climate:** temperate, with considerable temperature extremes; heavy snowfall in mountains. **Topography:** Green Mts. N-S backbone 20-36 mi wide; avg. altitude 1,000 ft. **Capital:** Montpelier.

Economy. Chief industries: manufacturing, tourism, agriculture, trade, finance, insurance, real estate, government. **Chief manuf. goods:** machine tools, furniture, scales, books, computer components, speciality foods. **Chief crops:** dairy products, apples, maple syrup, greenhouse/nursery, vegetables and small fruits. **Livestock** (Jan. 2004) 285,000 cattle/calves; (Jan. 2003): 2,100 hogs/pigs; (Dec. 2003): 199,000 chickens (excl. broilers). **Timber/lumber** (est. 2002): 206 mil bd. ft.; pine, spruce, fir, hemlock. **Nonfuel minerals** (est. 2003): $73 mil.; stone (dimension), stone (crushed), sand and gravel (construction), talc (crude), gemstones. **Principal internat. airport at:** Burlington. **New private housing** (2003): 2,792 units/$372 mil. **Gross state product** (2001): $19.1 bil. **Employment distrib.** (May 2004): 18% govt.; 19.2% trade/trans./util.; 12.3% mfg.; 18% ed./health serv.; 6.9% prof./bus serv.; 9.9% leisure/hosp.; 4.4% finance; 5.3% constr.; 2.2% info. **Per cap. pers. income** (2003): $30,740. **Sales tax** (2004): 6.0%. **Unemployment** (2003): 4.6%. **Tourism expends.** (2002): $1.3 bil. **Lottery** (2003): total sales: $79.4 mil; net income: $16.2 mil.

Finance. FDIC-insured commercial banks (2003): 14. **Deposits:** $5.4 bil. **FDIC-insured savings institutions** (2003): 5. **Assets:** $1.2 bil.

Federal govt. Fed. civ. employees (Mar.2003): 3,586. **Avg. salary:** $49,044.

Energy. Electricity production (est. 2003, kWh by source): Gas: 2 mil; Hydroelectric: 342 mil; Other: 234 mil.

State data. Motto: Freedom and unity. **Flower:** Red clover. **Bird:** Hermit thrush. **Tree:** Sugar maple. **Song:** These Green Mountains. **Entered union** Mar. 4, 1791; rank, 14th. **State fair** at Rutland; early Sept.

History. Before the arrival of the Europeans, Abnaki and Mahican peoples lived in the region. Champlain explored the lake that bears his name, 1609. The first American settlement was Ft. Dummer, 1724, near Brattleboro. During the American Revolution, Ethan Allen and the Green Mountain Boys captured Ft. Ticonderoga (NY), 1775; John Stark defeated part of Burgoyne's forces near Bennington, 1777. In the War of 1812, Thomas MacDonough defeated a British fleet on Lake Champlain off Plattsburgh (NY), 1814.

Tourist attractions. Shelburne Museum; Rock of Ages Quarry, Graniteville; Vermont Marble Exhibit, Proctor; Bennington Battle Monument; Pres. Calvin Coolidge homestead, Plymouth; Maple Grove Maple Museum, St. Johnsbury; Ben & Jerry's Factory, Waterbury.

Famous Vermonters. Ethan Allen, Chester A. Arthur, Calvin Coolidge, Howard Dean, John Deere, George Dewey, John Dewey, Stephen A. Douglas, Dorothy Canfield Fisher, James Fisk, James Jeffords, Rudy Vallee.

Chamber of Commerce. PO Box 37, Montpelier, VT 05601. **Tourist information.** Vermont Dept. of Tourism and Marketing, 6 Baldwin St., Drawer 33, Montpelier, VT 05633-1301; 1-800-VERMONT. **Website:** www.vermontvacation.com **Website:** www.vermont.gov

Virginia
Old Dominion

People. Population (2003 est.): 7,386,330; rank: 12; **net change** (2002-2003): 1.4%. **Pop. density:** 186.6 per sq mi. **Racial distribution** (2000): 72.3% white; 19.6% black; 3.7% Asian; 0.3% Native American/Nat. AK; 0.1% Hawaiian/Pacific Islander; 2.0% other race, 2.0%. **Hispanic pop.** (any race): 4.7%.

Geography. Total area: 42,774 sq mi; rank: 35. **Land area:** 39,594 sq mi; rank: 37. **Acres forested:** 16.1 mil. **Location:** South Atlantic state bounded by the Atlantic Ocean on the E and surrounded by North Carolina, Tennessee, Kentucky, West Virginia, and Maryland. **Climate:** mild and equable. **Topography:** mountain and valley region in the W, including the Blue Ridge Mts.; rolling piedmont plateau; tidewater, or coastal plain, including the eastern shore. **Capital:** Richmond.

Economy. Chief industries: services, trade, government, manufacturing, tourism, agriculture. **Chief manuf. goods:** food processing, transportation equipment, printing, textiles, electronic & electrical equipment, industrial machinery & equipment, lumber & wood products, chemicals, rubber & plastics, furniture. **Chief crops:** tobacco, grain corn, soybeans, winter wheat, peanuts, lint & seed cotton. **Livestock** (Jan. 2004) 1.54 mil. cattle/calves; 55,000 sheep/lambs; (Jan. 2003): 370,000 hogs/pigs; (Dec. 2003): 4.5 mil. chickens (excl. broilers); 265.1 mil. broilers. **Timber/lumber** (est. 2002): 1.5 bil bd. ft.; pine and hardwoods. **Nonfuel minerals** (est. 2003): $727 mil.; stone (crushed), cement (portland), sand and gravel (construction), lime, clays (fuller's earth). **Commercial fishing** (2002): $123.3 mil. **Chief ports:** Hampton Roads, Richmond, Alexandria. **Principal internat. airports at:** Arlington, Norfolk, Loudon, Richmond, Newport News. **New private housing** (2003): 56,951 units/$6.9 bil. **Gross state product** (2001): $273.1 bil. **Employment distrib.** (May 2004): 18.1% govt.; 18.1% trade/trans./util.; 4.3% mfg.; 10.5% ed./health serv.; 16% prof./bus serv.; 8.9% leisure/hosp.; 5.3% finance; 6.5% constr.; 2.8% info. **Per cap. pers. income** (2003): $33,671. **Sales tax** (2004): 4.5%. **Unemployment** (2003): 4.1%. **Tourism expends.** (2002): $13.7 bil. **Lottery** (2003): total sales: $1.1 bil; net income: $375.2 mil.

Finance. FDIC-insured commercial banks (2003): 125. **Deposits:** $72.5 bil. **FDIC-insured savings institutions** (2003): 16. **Assets:** $74 bil.

Federal govt. Fed. civ. employees (Mar. 2003): 116,012. **Avg. salary:** $63,623. **Notable fed. facilities:** Pentagon; Norfolk Naval Sta., Shipyard; Marine Corps Base; Langley AFB; NASA Langley Res. Ctr.; CIA George Bush Ctr. for Intelligence, Langley; Quantico USMC Base; FBI Academy (Quantico); Dahlgren Nav. Surface Warfare Ctr. & Lab; USDA Food and Nutrition Serv.; U.S. Geological Survey Natl. Ctr.

Energy. Electricity production (est. 2003, kWh by source): Coal: 29.6 bil; Petroleum: 5.0 bil; Gas: 2.3 bil; Hydroelectric: 212 mil; Nuclear: 24.8 bil.

State data. Motto: Sic Semper Tyrannis (Thus always to tyrants). **Flower:** Dogwood. **Bird:** Cardinal. **Tree:** Dogwood. **Song Emeritus:** Carry Me Back to Old Virginia. **Tenth** of the original 13 states to ratify the Constitution, June 25, 1788. **State fair** at Richmond; late Sept.-early Oct.

History. Living in the area at the time of European contact were the Cherokee and Susquehanna and the Algonquians of the Powhatan Confederacy. English settlers founded Jamestown, 1607. Virginians took over much of the government from royal governor Dunmore, 1775, forcing him to flee. Virginians under George Rogers Clark freed the Ohio-Indiana-Illinois area of British forces. Benedict Arnold burned Richmond and Petersburg for the British, 1781. That same year, Britain's Cornwallis was trapped at Yorktown and surrendered, ending the American Revolution. Virginia seceded from the Union, 1861, and Richmond became the capital of the Confederacy. Hampton Roads, off the Virginia coast, was the site of the famous naval battle of the USS *Monitor* and CSS *Virginia* (Merrimac), 1862. Virginia was readmitted, 1870.

Tourist attractions. Colonial Williamsburg; Busch Gardens, Williamsburg; Wolf Trap Farm, near Falls Church; Arlington Natl. Cemetery; Mt. Vernon, home of George Washington; Jamestown Festival Park; Yorktown; Jefferson's Monticello, Charlottesville; Robert E. Lee's birthplace, Stratford Hall, and grave, Lexington; Appomattox; Shenandoah Natl. Park; Blue Ridge Parkway; Virginia Beach; Paramount's King's Dominion, near Richmond.

Famous Virginians. Richard E. Byrd, James B. Cabell, Henry Clay, Jubal Early, Jerry Falwell, William Henry Harrison, Patrick Henry, A.P. Hill, Thomas Jefferson, Joseph E. Johnston, Robert E. Lee, Meriwether Lewis and William Clark, James Madison, John Marshall, George Mason, James Monroe, George Pickett, Pocahontas, Edgar Allan Poe, John Randolph, Walter Reed, Rev. Pat Robertson, John Smith, J.E.B. Stuart, William Styron, Zachary Taylor, John Tyler, Maggie Walker, Booker T. Washington, George Washington, L. Douglas Wilder, Woodrow Wilson.

Tourist Information. Virginia Tourism Corp., 901 Byrd St., Richmond, VA 23219; 1-800-VISITVA. **Website:** www.virginia.org

Website. www.virginia.gov

Washington
Evergreen State

People. Population (2003 est.): 6,131,445; rank: 15; **net change** (2002-2003): 1.1%. **Pop. density:** 92.1 per sq mi. **Racial distribution** (2000): 81.8% white; 3.2% black; 5.5% Asian; 1.6% Native American/Nat. AK; 0.4% Hawaiian/Pacific Islander; 3.9% other race; 2 or more races, 3.6%. **Hispanic pop.** (any race): 7.5%.

Geography. Total area: 71,300 sq mi; rank: 18. **Land area:** 66,544 sq mi; rank: 20. **Acres forested:** 21.8 mil. **Location:** Pacific state bordered by Canada on the N; Idaho on the E; Oregon on the S; and the Pacific Ocean on the W. **Climate:** mild, dominated by the Pacific Ocean and protected by the Cascades. **Topography:** Olympic Mts. on NW peninsula; open land along coast to Columbia R.; flat terrain of Puget Sound Lowland; Cascade Mts. region's high peaks to the E; Columbia Basin in central portion; highlands to the NE; mountains to the SE. **Capital:** Olympia.

Economy. Chief industries: advanced technology, aerospace, biotechnology, intl. trade, forestry, tourism, recycling, agriculture & food processing. **Chief manuf. goods:** computer software, aircraft, pulp & paper, lumber and plywood, aluminum, processed fruits and vegetables, machinery, electronics. **Chief crops:** apples, potatoes, hay, farm forest products. **Livestock** (Jan. 2004) 1.12 mil. cattle/calves; 46,000 sheep/lambs; (Jan. 2003): 24,000 hogs/pigs; (Dec. 2003): 6.2 mil. chickens (excl. broilers). **Timber/lumber** (est. 2002): 4.9 mil bd. ft.; Douglas fir, hemlock, cedar, pine. **Nonfuel minerals** (est. 2003): $430 mil.; sand and gravel (construction), cement (portland), stone (crushed), diatomite, lime. **Commercial fishing** (2002): $145.0 mil. **Chief ports:** Seattle, Tacoma, Vancouver, Kelso-Longview. **Principal internat. airports at:** Seattle/Tacoma, Spokane, Boeing Field. **New private housing** (2003): 43,580 units/$6.3 bil. **Gross state product** (2001): $223.0 bil. **Employment distrib.** (May 2004): 19.8% govt.; 19.1% trade/trans./util.; 9.6% mfg.; 11.8% ed./health serv.; 11.1% prof./bus serv.; 9.3% leisure/hosp.; 5.8% finance; 6% constr.; 3.5% info. **Per cap. pers. income** (2003): $33,332. **Sales tax** (2004): 6.5%. **Unemployment** (2003): 7.5%. **Tourism expends.** (2002): $8.4 bil. **Lottery** (2003): total sales: $460.4 mil; net income: $98.5 mil.

Finance. FDIC-insured commercial banks (2003): 78. **Deposits:** $20.6 bil. **FDIC-insured savings institutions** (2003): 22. **Assets:** $52.1 bil.

Federal govt. Fed. civ. employees (Mar. 2003): 45,767. **Avg. salary:** $55,498. **Notable fed. facilities:** Bonneville Power Admin.; Ft. Lewis; McChord AFB; Hanford Nuclear Reservation; Bremerton Naval Shipyards; Naval Sub Base, Bangor; Naval Sta., Everett; Pacific Northwest Natl. Lab.

Energy. Electricity production (est. 2003, kWh by source): Petroleum: 8 mil; Gas: 2.2 bil; Hydroelectric: 70.1 bil; Nuclear: 7.6 bil; Other: 490 mil.

State data. Motto: Alki (By and by). **Flower:** Western rhododendron. **Bird:** Willow goldfinch. **Tree:** Western hemlock. **Song:** Washington, My Home. **Entered union** Nov. 11, 1889; rank, 42nd. **State fairs:** 5 area fairs, in Aug. and Sept.; no state fair.

History. At the time of European contact, many Native American tribes lived in the area, including the Nez Percé, Spokan, Yakima, Cayuse, Okanogan, Walla Walla, and Colville peoples, who lived in the interior region, and the Nooksak, Chinook, Nisqually, Clallam, Makah, Quinault, and Puy-

allup peoples, who inhabited the coastal area. Spain's Bruno Hezeta sailed the coast, 1775. In 1792, British naval officer George Vancouver mapped Puget Sound area, and that same year, American Capt. Robert Gray sailed up the Columbia River. Canadian fur traders set up Spokane House, 1810. Americans under John Jacob Astor established a post at Ft. Okanogan, 1811, and missionary Marcus Whitman settled near Walla Walla, 1836. Final agreement on the border of Washington and Canada was made with Britain, 1846, and Washington became part of the Oregon Territory, 1848. Gold was discovered, 1855.

Tourist attractions. Seattle Waterfront, Seattle Center and Space Needle, Museum of Flight, Underground Tour, all Seattle; Mt. Rainier, Olympic, and North Cascades natl. parks; Mt. St. Helens; Puget Sound; San Juan Islands; Grand Coulee Dam; Columbia R. Gorge Natl. Scenic Area; Spokane's Riverfront Park.

Famous Washingtonians. Raymond Carver, Kurt Cobain, Bing Crosby, William O. Douglas, Bill Gates, Jimi Hendrix, Henry M. Jackson, Gary Larson, Mary McCarthy, Robert Motherwell, Edward R. Murrow, Theodore Roethke, Ann Rule, Hilary Swank, Julia Sweeney, Adam West, Marcus Whitman, Minoru Yamasaki.

Tourist information. WA State Tourism, 128 10th Ave. SW, Olympia, WA 98504; 1-800-544-1800. **Website:** www.tourism.wa.gov

Website. access.wa.gov

West Virginia
Mountain State

People. Population (2003 est.): 1,810,354; rank: 37; **net change** (2002-2003): 0.3%. **Pop. density:** 75.2 per sq mi. **Racial distribution** (2000): 95.0% white; 3.2% black; 0.5% Asian; 0.2% Native American/Nat. AK; <0.1% Hawaiian/Pacific Islander; 0.2% other race; 2 or more races, 0.9%. **Hispanic pop.** (any race): 0.7%.

Geography. Total area: 24,230 sq mi; rank: 41. **Land area:** 24,078 sq mi; rank: 41. **Acres forested:** 12.1 mil. **Location:** South Atlantic state bounded on the N by Ohio, Pennsylvania, Maryland; on the S and W by Virginia, Kentucky, Ohio; on the E by Maryland and Virginia. **Climate:** humid continental climate except for marine modification in the lower panhandle. **Topography:** ranging from hilly to mountainous; Allegheny Plateau in the W, covers two-thirds of the state; mountains here are the highest in the state, over 4,000 ft. **Capital:** Charleston.

Economy. Chief industries: manufacturing, services, mining, tourism. **Chief manuf. goods:** machinery, plastic & hardwood prods., fabricated metals, chemicals, aluminum, automotive parts, steel. **Chief crops:** apples, peaches, hay, tobacco, corn, wheat, oats. **Chief farm products:** dairy products, eggs. **Livestock** (Jan. 2004) 380,000 cattle/calves; 34,000 sheep/lambs; (Jan. 2003): 10,000 hogs/pigs; (Dec. 2003): 2.1 mil. chickens (excl. broilers); 87.2 mil. broilers. **Timber/lumber** (est. 2002): 724 mil bd. ft.; oak, yellow poplar, hickory, walnut, cherry. **Nonfuel minerals** (est. 2003): $168 mil.; stone (crushed), cement (portland), sand and gravel (industrial), lime, salt. **Chief port:** Huntington. **New private housing** (2003): 4,584 units/$580 mil. **Gross state product** (2001): $42.4 bil. **Employment distrib.** (May 2004): 19.7% govt.; 18.5% trade/trans./util.; 8.8% mfg.; 14.7% ed./health serv.; 7.7% prof./bus serv.; 9.3% leisure/hosp.; 4.2% finance; 4.6% constr.; 1.7% info. **Per cap. pers. income** (2003): $24,379. **Sales tax** (2004): 6.0%. **Unemployment** (2003): 6.1%. **Tourism expends.** (2002): $1.8 bil. **Lottery** (2003): total sales: $1.08 bil.; net income: $411 mil.

Finance. FDIC-insured commercial banks (2003): 67. **Deposits:** $13.5 bil. **FDIC-insured savings institutions** (2003): 7. **Assets:** $1.2 bil.

Federal govt. Fed. civ. employees (Mar. 2003): 12,625. **Avg. salary:** $52,931. **Notable fed. facilities:** Natl. Radio Astronomy Observatory; Bureau of Public Debt Bldg.; Harpers Ferry Natl. Park; Correctional Institution for Women; FBI Identification Ctr.

Energy. Electricity production (est. 2003, kWh by source): Coal: 63.5 bil; Petroleum: 210 mil; Gas: 4 mil; Hydroelectric: 323 mil; Other: 21 mil.

State data. Motto: Montani Semper Liberi (Mountaineers are always free). **Flower:** Big rhododendron. **Bird:** Cardinal. **Tree:** Sugar maple. **Songs:** The West Virginia Hills; This Is My West Virginia; West Virginia, My Home, Sweet Home. **Entered union** June 20, 1863; rank, 35th. **State fair** at Lewisburg (Fairlea); late Aug.

History. Sparsely inhabited at the time of European contact, the area was primarily Native American hunting grounds. British explorers Thomas Batts and Robert Fallam reached the New River, 1671. Early American explorers included George Washington, 1753, and Daniel Boone. In the fall of 1774, frontiersmen defeated an allied Indian uprising at Point Pleasant. The area was part of Virginia and often objected to rule by the eastern part of the state. When Virginia seceded in 1861, the Wheeling Convention repudiated the act and created a new state, Kanawha, later renamed West Virginia. It was admitted to the Union 1863.

Tourist attractions. Harpers Ferry Natl. Historic Park; Science and Cultural Center, Charleston; White Sulphur (in Greenbrier) and Berkeley Springs mineral water spas; New River Gorge, Fayetteville; Winter Place, Exhibition Coal Mine, both Beckley; Monongahela Natl. Forest; Fenton Glass, Williamstown; Viking Glass, New Martinsville; Blenko Glass, Milton; Sternwheel Regatta, Charleston; Mountain State Forest Festival; Snowshoe Ski Resort, Slaty Fork; Canaan State Park, Davis; Mountain State Arts & Crafts Fair, Ripley; Ogle Bay, Wheeling; White water rafting, several locations.

Famous West Virginians. Newton D. Baker, Pearl Buck, John W. Davis, Thomas "Stonewall" Jackson, Don Knotts, Dwight Whitney Morrow, Michael Owens, Mary Lou Retton, Walter Reuther, Cyrus Vance, Jerry West, Charles "Chuck" Yeager.

Tourist information. West Virginia Division of Tourism, 90 MacCorkle Ave., SW, South Charleston, WV 25303; 1-800-CALLWVA. **Website:** www.callwva.com

Website. www.wv.gov

Wisconsin
Badger State

People. Population (2003 est.): 5,472,299; rank: 20; **net change** (2002-2003): 0.6%. **Pop. density:** 100.8 per sq mi. **Racial distribution** (2000): 88.9% white; 5.7% black; 1.7% Asian; 0.9% Native American/Nat. AK; <0.1% Hawaiian/Pacific Islander; 1.6% other race; 2 or more races, 1.2%. **Hispanic pop.** (any race): 3.6%.

Geography. Total area: 65,498 sq mi; rank: 23. **Land area:** 54,310 sq mi; rank: 25. **Acres forested:** 16.0 mil. **Location:** East North Central state, bounded on the N by Lake Superior and Upper Michigan; on the E by Lake Michigan; on the S by Illinois; on the W by the St. Croix and Mississippi rivers. **Climate:** long, cold winters and short, warm summers tempered by the Great Lakes. **Topography:** narrow Lake Superior Lowland plain met by Northern Highland, which slopes gently to the sandy crescent Central Plain; Western Upland in the SW; 3 broad parallel limestone ridges running N-S are separated by wide and shallow lowlands in the SE. **Capital:** Madison.

Economy. Chief industries: services, manufacturing, trade, government, agriculture, tourism. **Chief manuf. goods:** food products, motor vehicles & equip., paper products, medical instruments and supplies, printing, plastics. **Chief crops:** corn, hay, soybeans, potatoes, cranberries, sweet corn, peas, oats, snap beans. **Chief products:** milk, butter, cheese, canned and frozen vegetables. **Livestock** (Jan. 2004) 3.35 mil. cattle/calves; 83,000 sheep/lambs; (Jan. 2003): 490,000 hogs/pigs; (Dec. 2003): 5.5 mil. chickens (excl. broilers). 34.4 mil. broilers. **Timber/lumber** (est. 2002): 583 mil bd. ft.; maple, birch, oak, evergreens. ft. **Nonfuel minerals** (est. 2003): $404 mil.; stone (crushed), sand and gravel (construction), lime, sand and gravel (industrial), stone (dimension). **Commercial fishing** (2002): $4.8 mil. **Chief ports:** Superior, Ashland, Milwaukee, Green Bay, Kewaunee, Pt. Washington, Manitowoc, Sheboygan, Marinette, Kenosha. **Principal internat. airports at:** Green Bay, Milwaukee. **New private housing** (2003): 39,212 units/$5.3 bil. **Gross state product** (2001): $177.4 bil. **Employment distrib.** (May 2004): 14.8% govt.; 19.2% trade/trans./util.; 18% mfg.; 13.2% ed./health serv.; 9.1% prof./bus serv.; 9% leisure/hosp.; 5.6% finance; 4.6% constr.; 1.7% info. **Per cap. pers. income** (2003): $30,898. **Sales tax** (2004): 5.0%. **Unemployment** (2003): 5.6%. **Tourism expends.** (2002): $7.2 bil. **Lottery** (2003): total sales: $435.1 mil; net income: $129.6 mil.

Finance. FDIC-insured commercial banks (2003): 272. **Deposits:** $66.8 bil. **FDIC-insured savings institutions** (2003): 39. **Assets:** $21.0 bil.

Federal govt. Fed. civ. employees (Mar. 2003): 11,786. **Avg. salary:** $50,717. **Notable fed. facilities:** Ft. McCoy.

Energy. Electricity production (est. 2003, kWh by source): Coal: 40.7 bil; Petroleum: 183 mil; Gas: 1.1 bil; Hydroelectric: 1.7 bil; Nuclear: 12.2 bil; Other: 326 mil.

State data. Motto: Forward. **Flower:** Wood violet. **Bird:** Robin. **Tree:** Sugar maple. **Song:** On, Wisconsin! **Entered union** May 29, 1848; rank, 30th. **State fair** at State Fair Park, West Allis; early Aug.

History. At the time of European contact, Ojibwa, Menominee, Winnebago, Kickapoo, Sauk, Fox, and Potawatomi peoples inhabited the region. Jean Nicolet was the first European to see the Wisconsin area, arriving in Green Bay, 1634; French missionaries and fur traders followed. The British took over, 1763. The U.S. won the land after the American Revolution, but the British were not ousted until after the War of 1812. Lead miners came next, then farmers. In 1816, the U.S. government built a fort at Prairie du Chien on Wisconsin's border with Iowa. Native Americans in the area rebelled against the seizure of their tribal lands in the Black Hawk War of 1832, but treaties from 1829 to 1848, transferred all land titles in Wisconsin to the U.S. government. Railroads were started in 1851, serving growing wheat harvests and iron mines. Some 96,000 soldiers served the Union cause during the Civil War.

Tourist attractions. Old Wade House and Carriage Museum, Greenbush; Villa Louis, Prairie du Chien; Circus World Museum, Baraboo; Wisconsin Dells; Old World Wisconsin, Eagle; Door County peninsula; Chequamegon and Nicolet national forests; Lake Winnebago; House on the Rock, Dodgeville; Monona Terrace, Madison.

Famous Wisconsinites. Don Ameche, Carrie Chapman Catt, Willem Dafoe, Edna Ferber, King Camp Gillette, Harry Houdini, Robert La Follette, Alfred Lunt, Pat O'Brien, Georgia O'Keeffe, William H. Rehnquist, John Ringling, Donald K. "Deke" Slayton, Spencer Tracy, Thorstein Veblen, Orson Welles, Laura Ingalls Wilder, Thornton Wilder, Frank Lloyd Wright.

Tourist information. Wisconsin Dept. of Tourism, PO Box 8690, Madison, WI 53708-8690; 1-800-432-TRIP. **Website:** www.travelwisconsin.com

Website. www.wisconsin.gov

Wyoming
Equality State, Cowboy State

People. Population (2003 est.): 501,242; rank: 51; **net change** (2002-2003): 0.5%. **Pop. density:** 5.2 per sq mi. **Racial distribution** (2000): 92.1% white; 0.8% black; 0.6% Asian; 2.3% Native American/Nat. AK; 0.1% Hawaiian/Pacific Islander; 2.5% other race; 2 or more races, 1.8%. **Hispanic pop.** (any race): 6.4%.

Geography. Total area: 97,814 sq mi; rank: 10. **Land area:** 97,100 sq mi; rank: 9. **Acres forested:** 11.0 mil. **Location:** Mountain state lying in the high western plateaus of the Great Plains. **Climate:** semi-desert conditions throughout; true desert in the Big Horn and Great Divide basins. **Topography:** the eastern Great Plains rise to the foothills of the Rocky Mts.; the Continental Divide crosses the state from the NW to the SE. **Capital:** Cheyenne.

Economy. Chief industries: mineral extraction, oil, natural gas, tourism and recreation, agriculture. **Chief manuf. goods:** refined petroleum, wood, stone, clay products, foods, electronic devices, sporting apparel, and aircraft. **Chief crops:** wheat, beans, barley, oats, sugar beets, hay. **Livestock** (Jan. 2004) 1.4 mil. cattle/calves; 430,000 sheep/lambs; (Jan. 2003): 124,000 hogs/pigs; (Dec. 2003): 17,000 mil. chickens (excl. broilers). **Timber/lumber** (est. 2002): 230 mil bd. ft.; ponderosa & lodgepole pine, Douglas fir, Engelmann spruce. **Nonfuel minerals** (est. 2003): $1.0 bil.; soda ash, clays (bentonite), helium (Grade-A), cement (portland), sand and gravel (construction). **Principal internat. airport at:** Casper. **New private housing** (2003): 2,622 units/$380 mil. **Gross state product** (2001): $20.4 bil. **Employment distrib.** (May 2004): 25.8% govt.; 19% trade/trans./util.; 3.6% mfg.; 8.5% ed./health serv.; 6.2% prof./bus serv.; 12% leisure/hosp.; 4.2% finance; 7.7% constr.; 1.6% info. **Per cap. pers. income** (2003): $32,808. **Sales tax** (2004): 4.0%. **Unemployment** (2003): 4.4%. **Tourism expends.** (2002): $1.6 bil.

Finance. FDIC-insured commercial banks (2003): 43. **Deposits:** $4.5 bil. **FDIC-insured savings institutions** (2003): 3. **Assets:** $379 mil.

Federal govt. Fed. civ. employees (Mar. 2003): 4,886. **Avg. salary:** $48,641 . **Notable fed. facilities:** Warren AFB.

Energy. Electricity production (est. 2003, kWh by source): Coal: 41.5 bil; Petroleum: 41 mil; Gas: 120 mil; Hydroelectric: 592 mil; Other: 16 mil.

State data. Motto: Equal Rights. **Flower:** Indian Paintbrush. **Bird:** Western Meadowlark. **Tree:** Plains Cottonwood. **Song:** Wyoming. **Entered union** July 10, 1890; rank, 44th. **State fair** at Douglas; late Aug.

History. Shoshone, Crow, Cheyenne, Oglala Sioux, and Arapaho peoples lived in the area at the time of European contact. France's François and Louis La Verendrye were the first Europeans to see the region, 1743. John Colter, an Amer-

ican, was first to traverse Yellowstone area, 1807-8. Trappers and fur traders followed in the 1820s. Forts Laramie and Bridger became important stops on the pioneer trails to the West Coast. Population grew after the Union Pacific crossed the state, 1868. Women won the vote, for the first time in the U.S., from the Territorial Legislature, 1869. Disputes between large land owners and small ranchers culminated in the Johnson County Cattle War, 1892; federal troops were called in to restore order.

Tourist attractions. Yellowstone Natl. Park, the first U.S. national park, est. 1872; Grand Teton Natl. Park; Natl. Elk Refuge; Devils Tower Natl. Monument; Fort Laramie Natl. Historic Site and nearby pioneer trail ruts; Buffalo Bill Historical Center, Cody; Cheyenne Frontier Days, Cheyenne.

Famous Wyomingites. James Bridger, William F. "Buffalo Bill" Cody, Curt Gowdy, Esther Hobart Morris, Nellie Tayloe Ross.

Tourist information. Wyoming Travel and Tourism, I-25 at College Dr., Cheyenne, WY 82002; 1-800-CALLWYO. **Website:** www.wyomingtourism.org

Website. www.state.wy.us

District of Columbia

People. Population (2003 est.): 563,384; rank: 50; **net change** (2002-2003): –0.1%. **Pop. density:** 9,175.6 per sq mi. **Racial distribution** (2000): 30.8% white; 60.0% black; 2.7% Asian; 0.3% Native American/Nat. AK; 0.1% Hawaiian/ Pacific Islander; 3.8% other race; 2 or more races, NA. **Hispanic pop.** (any race): 7.9%.

Geography. Total area: 68 sq mi; rank: 50. **Land area:** 61 sq mi; rank: 51. **Location:** at the confluence of the Potomac and Anacostia rivers, flanked by Maryland on the N, E, and SE and by Virginia on the SW. **Climate:** hot humid summers, mild winters. **Topography:** low hills rise toward the N away from the Potomac R. and slope to the S; highest elevation, 410 ft, lowest Potomac R., 1 ft.

Economy. Chief industries: government, service, tourism. **New private housing** (2003): 1,427 units/$96.8 mil. **Gross state product** (2001): $64.5 bil. **Employment distrib.** (May 2004): 34.3% govt.; 4.2% trade/trans./util.; 0.4% mfg.; 13.1% ed./health serv.; 21.5% prof./bus serv.; 7.8% leisure/ hosp.; 4.7% finance; 2% constr.; 3.7% info. **Per cap. pers. income** (2003): $48,342. **Sales tax** (2004): 5.75%. **Unemployment** (2003): 7%. **Tourism expends.** (2002): $5.5 bil. **Lottery** (2003): total sales: $237.9 mil; net income: $72.1 mil.

Finance. FDIC-insured commercial banks & trust companies (2003): 4. **Deposits:** $496 mil. **FDIC-insured savings institutions** (2003): 1. **Assets:** $212 mil.

Federal govt. No. of federal employees (Mar. 2003): 151,338. **Avg. salary:** $75,925.

Energy. Electricity production (2000, kWh, by source): Petroleum: 95 mil; Other: 28 mil.

District data. Motto: Justitia omnibus (Justice for all). **Flower:** American beauty rose. **Tree:** Scarlet oak. **Bird:** Wood thrush.

History. The District of Columbia, coextensive with the city of Washington, is the seat of the U.S. federal government. It lies on the west central edge of Maryland on the Potomac River, opposite Virginia. Its area was originally 100 sq mi taken from the sovereignty of Maryland and Virginia. Virginia's portion south of the Potomac was given back to that state in 1846.

The 23rd Amendment (1961) granted residents the right to vote for president and vice president for the first time since 1800 and gave them 3 members in the Electoral College. The first such votes were cast in Nov. 1964.

Congress, which has legislative authority over the District under the Constitution, established in 1874 a government of 3 commissioners appointed by the president. The Reorganization Plan of 1967 substituted a single appointive commissioner (also called mayor), assistant, and 9-member City Council. Funds were still appropriated by Congress; residents had no vote in local government, except to elect school board members. In Sept. 1970, Congress approved legislation giving the District one delegate to the House of Representatives, who can vote in committee but not on the floor. The first delegate was elected 1971.

In May 1974, voters approved a congressionally drafted charter giving them the right to elect their own mayor and a 13-member city council; the first took office Jan. 2, 1975. The district won the right to levy taxes; Congress retained power to veto council actions and approve the city budget.

Proposals for a "federal town" for the deliberations of the Continental Congress were made in 1783, 4 years before the adoption of the Constitution. Rivalry between Northern and Southern delegates over the site appeared in the First Congress, 1789. John Adams, presiding officer of the Senate, cast the deciding vote of that body for Germantown, PA. In 1790 Congress compromised by making Philadelphia the temporary capital for 10 years. The Virginia members of the House wanted a permanent capital on the eastern bank of the Potomac, while the Southerners opposed having the nation assume the war debts of the 13 original states as provided under the Assumption Bill, fathered by Alexander Hamilton. Hamilton and Jefferson arranged a compromise: the Virginia men voted for the Assumption Bill, and the Northerners conceded the capital to the Potomac. Pres. Washington chose the site in Oct. 1790 and persuaded landowners to sell their holdings to the government. The capital was named Washington.

Washington appointed Pierre Charles L'Enfant, a Frenchman, to plan the capital on an area not more than 10 mi square. The L'Enfant plan, for streets 100 to 110 ft. wide and one avenue 400 ft. wide and a mile long, seemed grandiose and foolhardy, but Washington endorsed it. When L'Enfant ordered a wealthy landowner to remove his new manor house because it obstructed a vista, and demolished it when the owner refused, Washington stepped in and dismissed the architect. Andrew Ellicott, who was working on surveying the area, finished the official map and design of the city. Ellicott was assisted by Benjamin Banneker, a distinguished black architect and astronomer.

On Sept. 18, 1793, Pres. Washington laid the cornerstone of the north wing of the Capitol. On June 3, 1800, Pres. John Adams moved to Washington, and on June 10, Philadelphia ceased to be the temporary capital. The City of Washington was incorporated in 1802; the District of Columbia was created as a municipal corporation in 1874, embracing Washington, Georgetown, and Washington County.

Tourist attractions: See Washington, DC, Capital of the U.S.

Tourist information. Washington, DC Convention and Tourism Corp., 901 12th St NW, 4th Fl., Washington, D.C., 20001-3719; 202-789-7000. **Website:** www.washington.org

Website. www.dc.gov

OUTLYING U.S. AREAS

American Samoa

People. Population (July 2004 est.): 57,902. **Population growth rate** (2003-2004 est.): 0.04%. **Pop. density** (2004): 752 per sq mi. **Major ethnic groups:** Samoan 89%, Caucasian 2%, Tongan 4%, other 5%. **Languages:** Samoan, English.

Land area: 77 sq. mi. **Total area:** 77 sq. mi. **Capital:** Pago Pago, Island of Tutuila. **Motto:** Samoa Muamua le Atua (In Samoa, God Is First). **Song:** Amerika Samoa. **Flower:** Paogo (Ula-fala). **Plant:** Ava.

Public education. Student-teacher ratio (1995): 20.

Boasting spectacular scenery and delightful South Seas climate, American Samoa is the most southerly of all lands under U.S. sovereignty. It is an unincorporated territory consisting of 7 small islands of the Samoan group: **Tutuila, Aunu'u, Manu'a Group (Ta'u, Olosega, Ofu), and Rose** and **Swains Island.** The islands are 2,300 mi SW of Honolulu.

Economy. Chief industries: tuna fishing and processing, trade, services, tourism. **Chief crops:** giant taro, taro, yams, cassava, coconuts, breadfruits, bananas. **Livestock** (2001): 103 cattle; 10,700 hogs/pigs; 37,000 chickens. **Commercial** fishing (2000): $2 mil. Gross domestic product (2000 est.): $500 mil. **Principal airport at:** Pago Pago.

Finance. FDIC-insured commercial banks (2003): 1. **Deposits** (2003): $63 mil.

Energy. Electricity production (2001): 130 mil. kWh

A tripartite agreement between Great Britain, Germany, and the U.S. in 1899 gave the U.S. sovereignty over the eastern islands of the Samoan group; these islands became American Samoa. Local chiefs ceded Tutuila and Aunu'u to the U.S. in 1900, and the Manu'a group and Rose Island in 1904; Swains Island was annexed in 1925. Samoa (Western), comprising the larger islands of the Samoan group, was a New Zealand mandate and UN Trusteeship until it became independent Jan. 1, 1962 (now called Samoa).

Tutuila and Aunu'u have an area of 53 sq mi. Ta'u has an area of 17 sq mi, and the islets of Ofu and Olosega, 5 sq mi with a population of a few thousand. Swains Island has nearly 2 sq mi and a population of about 100.

About 70% of the land is bush and mountains. Chief exports are fish products. Taro, breadfruit, yams, coconuts, pineapples, oranges, and bananas are also produced.

From 1900 to 1951, American Samoa was under the jurisdiction of the U.S. Navy. Since 1951, it has been under the Interior Dept. On Jan. 3, 1978, the first popularly elected Samoan governor and lieutenant governor were inaugurated. Previously, the governor was appointed by the Secretary of the Interior. American Samoa has a bicameral legislature and elects a delegate to the House of Representatives, with no vote except in committees.

The American Samoans are of Polynesian origin. They are nationals of the U.S.; approximately 20,000 live in Hawaii, 65,000 in California and Washington.

Website: www.amsamoa.com
Tourism website: www.asg-gov.com

Guam
Where America's Day Begins

People. Population (July 2004 est.): 166,090. **Population growth rate** (2003-2004 est.): 1.5%. **Pop. density** (2004): 783.4 per sq mi. **Major ethnic groups:** Chamorro, Filipino, Caucasian, Chinese, Japanese, Korean. (Native Guamanians, ethnically Chamorros, are basically of Indonesian stock, with a mixture of Spanish and Filipino; in addition to the official language, they speak the native Chamorro). **Languages:** English, Chamorro, Japanese. **Migration** (2000): About 48% of the population were born elsewhere; of these, 57% in Asia; 26% of the population were born in the U.S.

Geography. Total area: 212 sq mi. **Land area:** 212 sq. mi. **Location:** largest and southernmost of the Mariana Islands in the West Pacific, 3,700 mi W of Hawaii. **Climate:** tropical, with temperatures from 70° to 90° F; avg. annual rainfall, about 70 in. **Topography:** coralline limestone plateau in the N; southern chain of low volcanic mountains sloping gently to the W, more steeply to coastal cliffs on the E; general elevation, 500 ft; highest point, Mt. Lamlam, 1,334 ft. **Capital:** Hagatna.

Economy. Chief industries: tourism, U.S. military construction, banking, printing & publishing. **Chief manuf. goods:** textiles, foods. **Chief crops:** cabbages, eggplants, cucumber, long beans, tomatoes, bananas, coconuts, watermelon, yams, cantaloupe, papayas, maize, sweet potatoes. **Livestock** (2001): 100 cattle; 5,000 hogs/pigs; 20,000 chickens. **Commercial fishing** (2000): $1.3 mil. **Chief port:** Apra Harbor. **Principal internat. airport at:** Hagatna. **Construction sales** (1997): $506 mil. **Gross domestic product** (2000 est.): $3.2 bil. **Employment distrib.** (2000 est.): 26% govt.; 24% trade; 40% serv.; 10% indust. **Per capita income** (2000 est.): $21,000. **Unemployment** (2000 est.): 15%. **Tourism expends.** (1995): $4.9 bil.

Finance. FDIC-insured commercial banks (2003): 2. **Deposits:** $730 mil. **FDIC-insured savings institutions** (2003): 1. **Assets:** $86 mil.

Energy. Electricity production (2001): 830 mil. kWh
Federal govt. Federal employees (1990): 7,200. **Notable fed. facilities:** Anderson AFB; naval, air, and port bases.

Public education. Student-teacher ratio (1995): 18.3.

Misc. data. Flower: Puti Tai Nobio (Bougainvillea). **Bird:** Toto (Fruit dove). **Tree:** Ifit (Intsiabijuga). **Song:** Stand Ye Guamanians.

History. Guam was probably settled by voyagers from the Indonesian-Philippine archipelago by 3rd cent. BC. Pottery, rice cultivation, and megalithic technology show strong East Asian cultural influence. Centralized, village clan-based communities engaged in agriculture and offshore fishing. The estimated population by the early 16th cent. was 50,000-75,000. Magellan arrived in the Marianas Mar. 6, 1521. They were colonized in 1668 by Spanish missionaries, who named them the Mariana Islands in honor of Maria Anna, queen of Spain. When Spain ceded Guam to the U.S., it sold the other Marianas to Germany. Japan obtained a League of Nations mandate over the German islands in 1919; in Dec. 1941 it seized Guam, which was retaken by the U.S. in July-August 1944.

Guam is a self-governing organized unincorporated U.S. territory. The Organic Act of 1950 provided for a governor, elected to a 4-year term, and a 21-member unicameral legislature, elected biennially by the residents, who are American citizens. In 1970, the first governor was elected. In 1972, a U.S. law gave Guam one delegate to the U.S. House of Representatives who has a voice but no vote, except in committees.

Guam's quest to change its status to a U.S. Commonwealth began in the late 1970s. The Guam Commission on Self-Determination, created in 1984, developed a draft Commonwealth Act. In 1993, legislation proposing a change of status was submitted to the U.S. Congress. In 1994, the U.S. Congress passed legislation transferring 3,200 acres of land on Guam from federal to local control.

Tourist attractions. Tropical climate, oceanic marine environment; annual mid-Aug. Merizo Water Festival; Tarzan Falls; beaches; water sports; duty-free port shopping.
Website. ns.gov.gu
Tourism website. ns.gov.gu/visiting.html

Commonwealth of the Northern Mariana Islands

People. Population (July 2004 est.): 78,252. **Population growth rate** (2003-2004 est.): 2.71%. **Pop. density** (2004): 424.8 per sq mi. **Major ethnic groups:** Chamorro, Carolinians and other Micronesians, Caucasian, Japanese, Chinese, Filipino, Korean. **Languages:** English, Chamorro, Carolinian.

Total area: 184.2 sq mi. **Land area:** 184.2 sq mi. Located in the perpetually warm climes between Guam and the Tropic of Cancer, the 14 islands of the Northern Marianas form a 300-mi. long archipelago. The indigenous population is concentrated on the 3 largest of the 6 inhabited islands: **Saipan,** the seat of government and commerce, **Rota,** and **Tinian. Capital:** Saipan.

Economy. Chief industries: tourism, manufacturing, construction, apparel, handicrafts. **Chief manuf. goods:** apparel, stone, clay and glass products. **Chief crops:** coconuts, fruits, and vegetables. **Livestock:** (1998): 1,789 cattle; 831 hogs/pigs; 29,409 chickens. **Commercial fishing** (2000): $938,365. **Construction sales** (1997): $88 mil. **Chief ports:** Saipan, Tinian. **Gross domestic product** (2000 est., incl. U.S. subsidy): $900 mil. **Employment distrib.** (1999 est.): 35% manuf.; 18% managerial; 16% serv. **Unemployment** (1999): 4.3%. **Tourism expends.** (1997): $585 mil.

Education. Pupil-teacher ratio (2000): 18

The people of the Northern Marianas are predominantly of Chamorro cultural extraction, although Carolinians and immigrants from other areas of E. Asia and Micronesia have also settled in the islands. English is among the several languages commonly spoken. Pursuant to the Covenant of 1976, which established the Northern Marianas as a commonwealth in political union with the U.S., most of the indigenous population and many domiciliaries of these islands achieved U.S. citizenship on Nov. 3, 1986, when the U.S. terminated its administration of the UN trusteeship as it affected the Northern Marianas. From July 18, 1947, the U.S. had administered the Northern Marianas under a trusteeship agreement with the UN Security Council.

The Northern Mariana Islands has been self-governing since 1978, when a constitution drafted and adopted by the people became effective and a popularly elected bicameral legislature (2-year term), with offices of governor (4-year term) and lieut. governor, was inaugurated.

Website: www.gov.mp
Tourism website: www.mymarianas.com

Commonwealth of Puerto Rico
(Estado Libre Asociado de Puerto Rico)

People. Population (July 2004 est.): 3,897,960 (about mil. more Puerto Ricans reside in the mainland U.S.). **Population growth rate:** (2003-2004 est.): 0.49%. **Net change** (1999-2000): 8.1%. **Pop. density:** 1,126.9 per sq mi. . **Racial distribution** (2000): 80.5% white; 8% black; 0.2% Asian; 0.4% Native American/Nat. AK; 10.9% Other. **Hispanic pop.** (any race): 98.8%. **Languages:** Spanish and English are joint official languages.

Geography. Total area: 3,515 sq mi. **Land area:** 3,459 sq mi. **Location:** island lying between the Atlantic to the N and the Caribbean to the S; it is easternmost of the West Indies group called the Greater Antilles, of which Cuba, Hispaniola, and Jamaica are the larger islands. **Climate:** mild, with a mean temperature of 77°F. **Topography:** mountainous throughout three-fourths of its rectangular area, surrounded by a broken coastal plain; highest peak, Cerro de Punto, 4,390 ft. **Capital:** San Juan.

Economy. Chief industries: manufacturing, service, tourism. **Chief manuf. goods:** pharmaceuticals, apparel, electronics, food products. **Chief crops:** coffee, plantains, pineapples, sugarcane, bananas. **Livestock** (2001): 390,000 cattle; 118,000 hogs/pigs; 12.5 mil. chickens. **Nonfuel minerals** (1996): $31.1 mil.; mostly portland cement, crushed stone. **Commercial fishing** (2000): $6.4 mil. **Chief ports/river shipping:** San Juan, Ponce, Mayagüez. **Principal airports at:** San Juan, Ponce, Mayagüez, Aguadilla. **Construction sales** (1997): $4 bil. **Gross domestic product:** (2003 est.) $65.3 bil. **Employment distrib.** (May 2004): 30% govt.; 18.2% trade/trans./util.; 11.5% mfg.; 9.2% ed./health serv.; 9.5% prof./bus serv.; 6.8% leisure/hosp.; 4.1% finance; 6.6% con-

str.; 2.2% info. **Per capita income** (latest year available, est.): $10,950. **Unemployment** (2002): 12%. **Tourism expends.** (2002): $2.5 bil.

Finance. FDIC-insured commercial banks (2003): 11. **Deposits** (2003): $41.6 bil.

Federal govt. Fed. civ. employees (1997): 13,874. **Notable fed. facilities:** U.S. Naval Station at Roosevelt Roads; P.R. Natl. Guard Training Area at Camp Santiago, and at Ft. Allen, Juana Diaz; Sabana SECA Communications Ctr. (U.S. Navy); U.S. Army Station at Ft. Buchanan.

Energy. Electricity production (2001): 20.9 bil kWh

Public education. Student-teacher ratio (1995): 16. **Min. teachers' salary** (1997): $1,500 monthly.

Misc. data. Motto: Joannes Est Nomen Eius (John is his name). **Flower:** Maga. **Bird:** Reinita. **Tree:** Ceiba. **National anthem:** La Borinqueña.

History. Puerto Rico (or Borinquen, after the original Arawak Indian name, Boriquen) was visited by Columbus on his second voyage, Nov. 19, 1493. In 1508, the Spanish arrived. Sugarcane was introduced, 1515, and slaves were imported 3 years later. Gold mining petered out, 1570. Spaniards fought off a series of British and Dutch attacks; slavery was abolished, 1873. Under the treaty of Paris, Puerto Rico was ceded to the U.S. after the Spanish-American War, 1898. In 1952 the people voted in favor of Commonwealth status.

The Commonwealth of Puerto Rico is a self-governing part of the U.S. with a primarily Hispanic culture. The island's citizens have virtually the same control over their internal affairs as do the 50 states of the U.S. However, they do not vote in national general elections, only in national primaries.

Puerto Rico is represented in the U.S. House of Representatives by a Resident Commissioner who has a voice but no vote, except in committees.

No federal income tax is collected from residents on income earned from local sources in Puerto Rico. Nevertheless, as part of the U.S. legal system, Puerto Rico is subject to the provisions of the U.S. Constitution; most federal laws apply as they do in the 50 states.

Puerto Rico's famous "Operation Bootstrap," begun in the late 1940s, succeeded in changing the island from "The Poorhouse of the Caribbean" to an area with the highest per capita income in Latin America. This program encouraged manufacturing and development of the tourist trade by selective tax exemption, low-interest loans, and other incentives. Despite the marked success of Puerto Rico's development efforts over an extended period of time, per capita income in Puerto Rico is low in comparison to that of the 50 states.

Tourist attractions. Ponce Museum of Art; Forts El Morro and San Cristobal; Old Walled City of San Juan; Arecibo Observatory; Cordillera Central and state parks; El Yunque Rain Forest; San Juan Cathedral; Porta Coeli Chapel and Museum of Religious Art, Interamerican Univ., San Germán; Condado Convention Center; Casa Blanca, Ponce de León family home, Puerto Rican Family Museum of 16th and 17th centuries, and Fine Arts Center all in San Juan.

Cultural facilities and events. Festival Casals classical music concerts, mid-June; Puerto Rico Symphony Orchestra at Music Conservatory; Botanical Garden and Museum of Anthropology, Art, and History at the University of Puerto Rico; Institute of Puerto Rican Culture, at the Dominican Convent; and many popular festivals.

Famous Puerto Ricans. Julia de Burgos, Marta Casals Istomin, Pablo Casals, José Celso Barbosa, Orlando Cepeda, Roberto Clemente, José de Diego, José Feliciano, Doña Felisa Rincón de Gautier, Luis A. Ferré, José Ferrer, Commodore Diégo E. Hernández, Miguel Hernández Agosto, Rafael Hernández (El Jibarito), Rafael Hernández Colón, Raúl Julia, René Marqués, Ricky Martin, Concha Meléndez, Rita Moreno, Luis Muñoz Marín, Luis Palés Matos, Adm. Horacio Rivero.

Chamber of Commerce. PO Box 9024033, San Juan, PR 00902. **Websites:** www.gobierno.pr (site is in Spanish).

Tourism Website. www.gotopuertorico.com

Virgin Islands
St. John, St. Croix, St. Thomas

People. Population (July 2004 est.): 108,775. **Population growth rate** (2003-2004 est.): –0.05%. **Pop. density** (2004): 805.7 per sq mi. **Major ethnic groups:** West Indian, French, Hispanic. **Languages:** English (official), Spanish, Creole.

Geography. Total area: 136 sq mi. **Land area:** 135 sq mi. **Location:** 3 larger and 50 smaller islands and cays in the S and W of the V.I. group (British V.I. colony to the N and E), which is situated 70 mi E of Puerto Rico, located W of the Anegada Passage, a major channel connecting the Atlantic Ocean and the Caribbean Sea. **Climate:** subtropical; the sun

tempered by gentle trade winds; humidity is low; average temperature, 78° F. **Topography:** St. Thomas is mainly a ridge of hills running E and W, and has little tillable land; St. Croix rises abruptly in the N but slopes to the S to flatlands and lagoons; St. John has steep, lofty hills and valleys with little level tillable land. **Capital:** Charlotte Amalie, St. Thomas.

Economy. Chief industries: tourism, rum distilling, alumina, petroleum refining, watch assembly, textiles, electronics, printing & publishing. **Chief manuf. goods:** rum, textiles, pharmaceuticals, perfumes, stone, glass & clay products. **Chief crops:** vegetables, horticulture, fruits and nuts. **Livestock** (2001): 8,000 cattle; 2,600 hogs/pigs; 35,000 chickens. **Minerals:** sand, gravel. **Chief ports:** Cruz Bay, St. John; Frederiksted and Christiansted, St. Croix; Charlotte Amalie, St. Thomas. **Principal internat. airports on:** St. Thomas, St. Croix. **Construction sales** (1997): $185 mil. **Gross domestic product: (2001 est.) $2.4 bil. Employment distrib.** (1992): 50% trade; 43% serv. **Per capita income** (2001 est.): $19,000. **Unemployment** (2002 est.): 8.7%. **Tourism expends.** (1995): $792 mil.

Finance. FDIC-insured commercial banks (2003): 2. **Deposits:** $135 mil.

Energy. Electricity production (2001): 1 bil. kWh

Public education. Student-teacher ratio (1995): 14.

Misc. data. Flower: Yellow elder or yellow trumpet, local designation Ginger Thomas. **Bird:** Yellow breast. **Song:** Virgin Islands March.

History. The islands were visited by Columbus in 1493. Spanish forces, 1555, defeated the Caribes and claimed the territory; by 1596 the native population was annihilated. First permanent settlement in the U.S. territory, 1672, by the Danes; U.S. purchased the islands, 1917, for defense purposes.

The Virgin Islands has a republican form of government, headed by a governor and lieut. governor elected, since 1970, by popular vote for 4-year terms. There is a 15-member unicameral legislature, elected by popular vote for a 2-year term. Residents of the V.I. have been U.S. citizens since 1927. Since 1973 they have elected a delegate to the U.S. House of Representatives, who has a voice but no vote, except in committees.

Tourist attractions. Magens Bay, St. Thomas; duty-free shopping; Virgin Islands Natl. Park, beaches, Indian relics, and evidence of colonial Danes.

Tourist information. Dept. of Economic Development & Agriculture: St. Thomas, PO Box 6400, St. Thomas, VI 00801; St. Croix, PO Box 4535, Christiansted, St. Croix 00820. **Website:** www.usvitourism.vi

Website. www.usvi.net

Other Islands

Navassa lies between Jamaica and Haiti, 100 mi south of Guantanamo Bay, Cuba, in the Caribbean; it covers about 2 sq mi, is reserved by the U.S. for a lighthouse, and is uninhabited. It is administered by the U.S. Coast Guard.

Wake Atoll, and its neighboring atolls, **Wilkes** and **Peale,** lie in the Pacific Ocean on the direct route from Hawaii to Hong Kong, about 2,300 mi W of Honolulu and 1,290 mi E of Guam. The group is 4.5 mi long, 1.5 mi wide, and totals less than 3 sq mi in land area. The U.S. flag was hoisted over Wake Atoll, July 4, 1898; formal possession taken Jan. 17, 1899. Wake was administered by the U.S. Air Force, 1972-94. The population consists of about 200 persons.

Midway Atoll, acquired in 1867, consists of 2 atolls, **Sand** and **Eastern,** in N Pacific 1,150 mi. NW of Honolulu, with an area of about 2 sq mi, administered by the U.S. Navy. There is no indigenous population; total pop. is about 450. **Johnston Atoll,** 717 mi WSW of Honolulu, area 1 sq mi, is operated by the Defense Nuclear Agency, and the Fish and Wildlife Service, U.S. Dept. of the Interior; its population is about 396. **Kingman Reef,** 920 mi S of Hawaii, is under Navy control. **Howland, Jarvis,** and **Baker Islands,** 1,400-1,650 mi SW of Honolulu, uninhabited since World War II, are under the Interior Dept. **Palmyra** is an atoll about 1,000 mi S of Hawaii, area, 5 sq mi. Privately owned, it is under the Interior Dept.

WORLD ALMANAC QUICK QUIZ
Alaska is obviously the most thinly populated state in the U.S. Which state is the most densely populated?

    (a) New York   (b) New Jersey
    (c) Rhode Island   (d) Massachusetts
For the answer look in this chapter, or see page 1008.

WASHINGTON, DC, CAPITAL OF THE U.S.

Most attractions are free. All times are subject to change. For more details call the Washington, DC, Convention and Visitors Association at 1-800-422-8644, or check out the website at: www.washington.org

Bureau of Engraving and Printing

The **Bureau of Engraving and Printing** of the U.S. Treasury Dept. is the headquarters for the making of U.S. paper money. Public tour closed until further notice, dur to recent Orange threat level for financial sectors. 14th and C Sts. SW. Phone: 202-874-3019.
Website. www.moneyfactory.com

Capitol

The **United States Capitol** was originally designed by Dr. William Thornton, an amateur architect, who submitted a plan in 1793 that won him $500 and a city lot. The south, or House, wing was completed in 1807 under the direction of Benjamin H. Latrobe. The present Senate and House wings and the iron dome were designed and constructed by Thomas U. Walter, 4th architect of the Capitol, between 1851 and 1863.

The present cast iron dome at its greatest exterior measures 135 ft 5 in., and it is topped by the bronze Statue of Freedom that stands 19½ ft and weighs 14,985 lb. On its base are the words *E Pluribus Unum* (Out of Many, One).

The Capitol is open from 9 AM to 4:30 pm. The Capitol is open to the public for guided tours only. It is closed Jan. 1, Thanksgiving Day, and Dec. 25. Tours (tickets required) through the Capitol, including the House and Senate galleries, are conducted Mon.-Sat. from 9 AM to 4:30 PM.

To observe debate in the House or Senate while Congress is in session, individuals living in the U.S. may obtain tickets to the visitor's galleries from their U.S. representative or senator. Visitors from other countries may obtain passes at the Capitol. Between Constitution & Independence Ave., at Pennsylvania Ave. Phone: 202-225-6827.
Website. www.aoc.gov

Federal Bureau of Investigation

The **Federal Bureau of Investigation** offers guided one-hour tours of its headquarters, beginning with a videotape presentation. Visitors learn about the history of the FBI and see such things as the weapons confiscated from famous gangsters, photos of the most-wanted fugitives, the DNA laboratory, goods forfeited and seized in narcotics operations, and a sharpshooting demonstration.

As of late 2004, tours were suspended for building renovation; scheduled to resume in 2005. J. Edgar Hoover Bldg., Pennsylvania Ave., between 9th and 10th Sts. NW. Phone: 202-324-3000.
Website. www.fbi.gov

Folger Shakespeare Library

The **Folger Shakespeare Library,** on Capitol Hill, is a research institution holding rare books and manuscripts of the Renaissance period and the largest collection of Shakespearean materials in the world, including 79 copies of the First Folio. The library's museum and performing arts programs are presented in the Elizabethan Theatre, which resembles an innyard theater of Shakespeare's day.

Exhibit may be visited Mon.-Sat., 10 AM-4 PM, 201 E. Capitol St., SE , Phone: 202-544-4600.
Website. www.folger.edu

Holocaust Memorial Museum

The **U.S. Holocaust Memorial Museum** opened on Apr. 21, 1993. The museum documents, through permanent and temporary displays, interactive videos, and special lectures, the events of the Holocaust beginning in 1933 and continuing through World War II. The permanent exhibition is not recommended for children under the age of 11.

The museum is open daily, 10 AM-5:30 PM, except Yom Kippur and Dec. 25, and extended hours Tuesdays and Thursdays (10 AM-7:50 PM) Apr.-June. A limited number of free tickets are available on day of visit; advance tickets may be ordered for a small fee. 100 Raoul Wallenberg Pl. SW. Phone: 202-488-0400.
Website. www.ushmm.org

Jefferson Memorial

Dedicated in 1943, the **Thomas Jefferson Memorial** stands on the south shore of the Tidal Basin in West Potomac Park. It is a circular stone structure, with Vermont marble on the exterior and Georgia white marble inside, and combines architectural elements of the dome of the Pantheon in Rome and the rotunda designed by Jefferson for the Univ. of Virginia.

The memorial, on the south edge of the Tidal Basin, is open daily, 8 AM-midnight; closed Dec. 25. Has elevator and curb ramps for handicapped. Phone: 202-426-6841.
Website. www.nps.gov

John F. Kennedy Center

The **John F. Kennedy Center for the Performing Arts,** designated by Congress as the National Cultural Center and the official memorial in Washington, DC, to Pres. John F. Kennedy, opened Sept. 8, 1971. Designed by Edward Durell Stone, the center includes an opera house, a concert hall, several theaters, 2 restaurants, and a library.

Free tours are available Mon.-Fri., 10 AM-5 PM and Sat. & Sun., 10 AM-1 PM. 2700 F St. NW. Phone: 202-467-4600, or 1-800-444-1324.
Website. www.kennedy-center.org

Korean War Veterans Memorial

Dedicated on July 27, 1995, the **Korean War Veterans Memorial** honors all Americans who served in the Korean War. Situated at the west end of the Mall, across the reflecting pool from the Vietnam Memorial, the triangular-shaped stone and steel memorial features a multiservice formation of 19 troops clad in ponchos with the wind at their back, ready for combat. A granite wall, with images of the men and women who served, juts into a pool of water, the Pool of Remembrance, and is inscribed with the words *Freedom Is Not Free.*

The $18 mil memorial, which was funded by private donations, is open 8 AM-11:45 pm; closed Dec. 25. French Dr., SW across from Lincoln Memorial. Phone: 202-426-6841.
Website. www.nps.gov/kwvm

Library of Congress

Established by and for Congress in 1800, the **Library of Congress** has extended its services over the years to other government agencies and other libraries, to scholars, and to the general public, and it now serves as the national library. It contains more than 80 million items in 470 languages.

Exhibit halls are open to the public Mon.-Fri., 8:30 AM-9:30 PM; Sat., 8:30 AM-6:30 PM. The Library is closed all federal holidays. 101 Independence Ave., SE. Phone: 202-707-5000.
Website. www.loc.gov

Lincoln Memorial

Designed by Henry Bacon, the **Lincoln Memorial** in West Potomac Park, on the axis of the Capitol and the Washington Monument, is a large marble hall enclosing a heroic statue of Abraham Lincoln in meditation sitting on an armchair. The memorial was dedicated May 30, 1922. The statue was designed by Daniel Chester French and sculpted by French and the Piccirilli brothers. Murals and ornamentation on the ceiling beams are by Jules Guerin. The text of the Gettysburg Address is in the south chamber; that of Lincoln's Second Inaugural speech is in the north chamber. Each is engraved on a stone tablet.

The memorial is open daily 8 AM-midnight. An elevator for the handicapped is in service. W. Potomac Park at 23rd St. NW. Phone: 202-426-6841.
Website. www.nps.gov/linc

National Archives and Records

Original copies of the Declaration of Independence, the Constitution, and the Bill of Rights are on permanent display in the **National Archives** Exhibition Hall. The National Archives also holds other valuable U.S. government records and historic maps, photographs, and manuscripts.

Central Research and Microfilm Research Rooms are also available to the public for genealogical research.

Exhibition Hall open daily 10 AM-5:30PM (later in spring and summer). 57th & Pennsylvania Ave. NW. Phone: 202-501-5000, or 1-866-325-7208.
Website. www.archives.gov

National Gallery of Art

The **National Gallery of Art**, situated on the north side of the Mall facing Constitution Avenue, was established by Congress, Mar. 24, 1937, and opened Mar. 17, 1941. The original West building was designed by John Russell Pope. The East building, opened in 1978, was designed by I. M. Pei. The National Gallery is separate from, but maintains a relationship with, the Smithsonian Institution. Open daily, Mon.-Sat. 10 AM-5 PM, Sunday 11 AM-6 PM. Closed Jan. 1 and Dec. 25. 4th & Constitution Ave NW. Phone: 202-737-4215.
Website. www.nga.gov

Franklin Delano Roosevelt Memorial

Opened May 2, 1997, by Pres. Bill Clinton, the **FDR Memorial** features 9 bronze sculptural ensembles depicting FDR, Eleanor Roosevelt (the first First Lady to be honored in a national memorial), and events from the Great Depression and World War II. This 7.5-acre memorial is located near the Tidal Basin in a park-like setting and includes waterfalls, quiet pools, and reddish Dakota granite upon which some of Pres. Roosevelt's well-known words are carved. The monument is wheelchair accessible.

Grounds, staffed daily, 8 AM-11:45 pm, except Dec. 25. 1850 W. Basin Dr. SW. Phone: 202-426-6841.

Website. www.nps.gov/fdrm

Smithsonian Institution

The **Smithsonian Institution,** established in 1846, is the world's largest museum complex and consists of 14 museums and the National Zoo. It holds some 100 mil. artifacts and specimens in its trust. Nine museums are on the National Mall between the Washington Monument and the Capitol; 5 other museums and the zoo are elsewhere in Washington (the Cooper-Hewitt Museum and the National Museum of the American Indian, also administered by the Smithsonian, are in New York City). The **Smithsonian Information Center** is located in "the Castle" on the Mall. Also on the Mall are the **National Museum of American History**, the **National Museum of Natural History**, the **National Air and Space Museum**, the **Hirshhorn Museum and Sculpture Garden**, the **Arthur M. Sackler Gallery**, the **National Museum of African Art**, the **Freer Gallery of Art,** and the **Arts and Industries Building.** Near the Sackler Gallery is the **Enid A. Haupt Garden.** Located nearby are the **National Postal Museum**, the **National Museum of American Art**, the **National Portrait Gallery**, and the **Renwick Gallery.** Farther away, at 1901 Fort Place SE, is the **Anacostia Museum.**

Most museums are open daily, except Dec. 25, 10 AM-5:30 PM. Phone: 202-357-2700.

Website. www.si.edu

Vietnam Veterans Memorial

Originally dedicated on Nov. 13, 1982, the **Vietnam Veterans Memorial** is a recognition of the men and women who served in the armed forces in the Vietnam War. On a V-shaped black-granite wall, designed by Maya Ying Lin, are inscribed the names of the more than 58,000 Americans who lost their lives or remain missing.

Since 1982, 2 additions have been made to the Memorial. The 1st, dedicated on Nov. 11, 1984, is the Frederick Hart sculpture *Three Servicemen.* On Nov. 11, 1993, the Vietnam Women's Memorial was dedicated, honoring the more than 11,500 women who served in Vietnam. The bronze sculpture, portraying 3 women helping a wounded male soldier, was designed by Glenna Goodacre.

The memorial is open 8 AM-midnight daily. Constitution Ave. & Bacon Dr. NW. Phone: 202-426-6841.

Website. www.nps.gov/vive

Washington Monument

The **Washington Monument**, dedicated in 1885, is a tapering shaft, or obelisk, of white marble, 555 ft, 5 $^1/_8$ inches in height and 55 ft, 1½ in. square at base. Eight small windows, 2 on each side, are located at the 500-ft level, where points of interest are indicated.

Open daily (except Dec. 25), 9 AM-4:45 PM. Free timed passes are available; passes are available in advance for a small fee. 15th & Constitution Ave. NW. Phone: 202-426-6841.

Website. www.nps.gov/wash

White House

The **White House,** the President's residence, stands on 18 acres on the south side of Pennsylvania Ave., between the Treasury and the old Executive Office Building. The walls are of sandstone, quarried at Aquia Creek, VA. The exterior walls were painted, causing the building to be termed the "White House." On Aug. 24, 1814, during Madison's administration, the house was burned by the British. James Hoban rebuilt it by Oct. 1817.

The White House is normally open for free self-guided tours Tues.-Sat., 7:30 AM-12:30 pm. (Tour requests must be made at least one month in advance through your member of Congress.) Only the public rooms on the ground floor and state floor may be visited. 1600 Pennsylvania Ave. The White House Visitor Center at 1450 Pennsylvania Ave. is open daily 7:30 AM - 4 PM. Phone: 202-456-7041.

Website. www.whitehouse.gov

National World War II Memorial

The **National WWII Memorial** is dedicated to the approx. 16 mil. veterans who served and the more than 400,000 who died in the war. It rests on 7.4 acres of land at the east end of the reflecting pool between the Lincoln Memorial and Washington Monument. Built at a cost of about $172 mil., most of it raised through private contributions, the memorial opened on April 29, 2004, and was dedicated on May 29.

At the north and south entrances are 43-ft. archways, representing the Atlantic and Pacific theaters. Inside the grounds is a large, oval plaza with a wall of 4,000 gold stars; each represents 100 American deaths. Representing the states, territories, and District of Columbia are 56 pillars ringing the central area. There is also a circular garden enclosed by a stone wall (called the "Circle of Remembrance") where visitors can sit and reflect.

The memorial is wheelchair-accessible and open daily, 24 hours a day, except Dec. 25. Located on 17th St. between Constitution and Independence Aves. Phone: 202-619-7222.

Website. www.nps.gov/nwwm

Attractions Near Washington, DC

Arlington National Cemetery

Arlington National Cemetery, on the former Custis-Lee estate in Arlington, VA, is the site of the **Tomb of the Unknowns** and is the final resting place of Pres. John Fitzgerald Kennedy, who was buried there on Nov. 25, 1963. His wife, Jacqueline Bouvier Kennedy Onassis, was buried at the same site on May 23, 1994. An eternal flame burns over the grave site. In an adjacent area is the grave of Pres. Kennedy's brother Sen. Robert F. Kennedy (NY), interred on June 8, 1968. Many other famous Americans are also buried at Arlington, as well as more than 200,000 U.S. military personnel, from every major war.

North of the National Cemetery stands the **U.S. Marine Corps War Memorial**, also known as Iwo Jima. The memorial is a bronze statue of the raising of the U.S. flag on Mt. Suribachi, Feb. 23, 1945, during World War II, executed by Felix de Weldon from the photograph by Joe Rosenthal.

On the southern side of the Memorial Bridge, near the cemetery entrance, a memorial honoring the women in the military was dedicated, Oct. 18, 1997. The **Women in Military Service for America Memorial** is a half-circle granite monument, 30 ft. high and 226 ft. in diameter, with the Great Seal of the United States in the center.

Open daily, 8 AM-5 PM (8 AM-7 PM., Apr.-Sept.), Arlington, VA. Phone: 703-607-8000.

Website. www.arlingtoncemetery.org

Mount Vernon

Mount Vernon, George Washington's estate, is on the south bank of the Potomac R., 16 mi below Washington, DC, in northern Virginia. The present house is an enlargement of one apparently built on the site by Augustine Washington, who lived there 1735-38. His son Lawrence came there in 1743, and renamed the plantation Mount Vernon in honor of Admiral Vernon, under whom he had served in the West Indies. Lawrence Washington died in 1752 and was succeeded as proprietor by his half-brother, George Washington. The estate has been restored to its 18th-century appearance and includes many original furnishings. Washington and his wife, Martha, are buried on the grounds.

Open 365 days, 8 AM-5 PM, Apr.-Aug., 9 AM-5 PM, Sept., Oct., Mar.; 9 AM-4 PM, Nov.-Feb. Phone: 703-780-2000, or 1-800-429-1520. Admission: adults $11, seniors (62+) $10.50, children (6-11) $5, age 5 and under free.

Website. www.mountvernon.org

The Pentagon

The **Pentagon,** headquarters of the Department of Defense, is one of the world's largest office buildings. Situated in Arlington, VA, it has housed more than 23,000 employees in offices occupying 3,707,745 sq ft. The building was severely damaged when struck by a plane Sept. 11, 2001.

Tours available to schools, educational organizations, and other select groups by reservation only. Arlington, VA (I-395 South to Boundary Channel Drive exit). Pentagon tour office: 703-697-1776.

Website. www.defenselink.mil/pubs/pentagon

BUILDINGS, BRIDGES, AND TUNNELS

50 Tallest Buildings in the World

Source: Council on Tall Buildings and Urban Habitat, Illinois Inst. of Technology, www.ctbuh.com; Emporis.com, www.emporis.com

Structures under construction are denoted by asterisk *. Year in parentheses is date of completion or projected completion.

Building	Ht. (ft.)	Stories	Building	Ht. (ft.)	Stories
Taipei 101, Taipei, Taiwan (2004)	1,670	101	JP Morgan Chase Tower, Houston, TX, U.S. (1982)	1,002	75
Petronas Tower I, Kuala Lumpur, Malaysia (1998)	1,483	88	Baiyoke Tower II, Bangkok, Thailand (1997)	997	85
Petronas Tower II, Kuala Lumpur, Malaysia (1998)	1,483	88	Two Prudential Plaza, Chicago, IL, U.S. (1990)	995	64
Sears Tower, Chicago, IL, U.S. (1974)	1,450	110	Kingdom Centre, Riyadh, Saudi Arabia (2002)	992	41
Jin Mao Bldg., Shanghai, China (1999)	1,381	88	First Canadian Place, Toronto, Canada (1975)	978	72
Two International Finance Centre, Hong Kong, China (2003)	1,362	88	Wells Fargo Plaza, Houston, TX, U.S. (1983)	972	71
CITIC Plaza, Guangzhou, China (1996)	1,283	80	Landmark Tower, Yokohama, Japan (1993)	971	70
Shun Hing Square, Shenzhen, China (1996)	1,260	69	311 S. Wacker Drive, Chicago, IL, U.S. (1990)	961	65
Empire State Building, New York, U.S. (1931)	1,250	102	SEG Plaza, Shenzhen, China (2000)	957	71
Central Plaza, Hong Kong, China, (1992)	1,227	78	American International Bldg., New York, U.S. (1932)	952	67
Bank of China, Hong Kong, China (1989)	1,209	72	Cheung Kong Centre, Hong Kong, China (1999)	951	63
Emirates Tower One, Dubai, U.A.E. (1999)	1,165	54	Key Tower, Cleveland, OH, U.S. (1991)	947	57
The Center, Hong Kong, China (1998)	1,135	73	Plaza 66, Shanghai, China (2001)	945	66
Tuntex Sky Tower, Kaohsiung, Taiwan (1997)	1,140	85	One Liberty Place, Philadelphia, PA, U.S. (1987)	945	61
Aon Centre, Chicago, IL, U.S. (1973)	1,136	80	Sunjoy Tomorrow Square, Shanghai, China (1999)	934	55
John Hancock Center, Chicago, IL, U.S. (1969)	1,127	100	Bank of America Center, Seattle, WA, U.S. (1984)	933	76
Ryugyong Hotel, Pyongyang, North Korea (1995)	1,083	105	*Chongqing World Trade Center (2005)	929	60
Burj al Arab Hotel, Dubai, U.A.E. (1999)	1,053	60	The Trump Bldg., New York, U.S. (1930)	927	71
Chrysler Bldg., New York, U.S. (1930)	1,046	77	Bank of America Plaza, Dallas, TX, U.S. (1985)	921	72
Bank of America Plaza, Atlanta, GA, U.S. (1993)	1,023	55	Republic Plaza, Singapore (1995)	919	66
U.S. Bank Tower, Los Angeles, CA, U.S. (1990)	1,018	73	Overseas Union Bank Centre, Singapore (1986)	919	66
Menara Telekom Headquarters, Kuala Lumpur, Malaysia (1999)	1,017	55	United Overseas Bank Plaza, Singapore (1992)	919	63
			Citigroup Center, New York, U.S. (1977)	915	59
Emirates Tower Two, Dubai, U.A.E. (2000)	1,014	56	Hong Kong New World Tower, Shanghai, China (2002)	913	61
AT&T Corporate Center, Chicago, IL, U.S. (1989)	1,007	60	Scotia Plaza, Toronto, Canada (1989)	902	68
			Williams Tower, Houston, TX, U.S. (1983)	901	64

World's 10 Tallest Free-Standing Towers

Name	City	Country	Ht. (ft.)	Year	Name	City	Country	Ht. (ft.)	Year
CN Tower	Toronto	Canada	1,815	1976	Manara Kuala Lumpur	Kuala Lumpur	Malaysia	1,379	1996
Ostankino Tower	Moscow	Russia	1,772	1967	Beijing Radio & T.V. Tower	Beijing	China	1,369	1992
Oriental Pearl Television Tower	Shanghai	China	1,535	1995	Tianjin Radio & T.V. Tower	Tianjin	China	1,362	1991
Milad Tower	Tehran	Iran	1,427	2001	T.V. Tower	Kiev	Ukraine	1,246	1974
					Tashkent Tower	Tashkent	Uzbekistan	1,230	1985
					Liberation Tower	Kuwait City	Kuwait	1,220	1996

Tall Buildings in Selected North American Cities

Source: Marshall Gerometta and Rick Bronson, Emopris.com, www.emporis.com;
Council on Tall Buildings and Urban Habitat, Illinois Inst. of Technology, www.ctbuh.org

Lists include freestanding towers and other structures that do not have stories and are not technically considered "buildings." Also included are some structures still under construction as of mid-2004 (denoted by asterisk *). Year in parentheses is date of completion or projected completion. Height is generally measured from sidewalk to roof, including penthouse and tower if enclosed as integral part of structure; stories generally counted from street level. NA = not available or not applicable.

Atlanta, GA

Building	Ht. (ft.)	Stories
Bank of America Plaza (incl. spire), 600 Peachtree NE (1992)	1,023	55
SunTrust Bank Tower, 303 Peachtree NE (1992)	871	60
One Atlantic Center, 1201 W. Peachtree (1987)	820	50
191 Peachtree Tower (1991)	770	50
Westin Peachtree Plaza, 210 Peachtree NW (1976)[1]	723	73
Georgia Pacific Tower, 133 Peachtree St. NE (1981)	697	51
Promenade II, 1230 Peachtree St. NE (1989)	691	40
Bellsouth, 675 W. Peachtree (1980)	677	47
*Symphony Center Tower, 1180 Peachtree St. NE (2005)	650	41
GLG Grand/Four Seasons Hotel, 75 14th St. NE (1992)	609	53
Wachovia Bank of Georgia, 2 Peachtree St. NW (1967)	556	44
Marriott Marquis, 265 Peachtree Center Ave. NE (1985)	554	52
Park Avenue Condominiums, 750 Park Ave. NE (2000)	486	42
*Paramount at Buckhead, 3445 Stratford Rd. NE (2004)	478	40
Centennial Tower, 101 Marietta St. (1976)	459	36
Equitable Bldg., 100 Peachtree St. (1967)	453	34
*Buckhead Grand (2004)	451	38
One Park Tower, 34 Peachtree St. (1961)	439	32
*Spire, 860 Peachtree St. (2005)	429	28
1100 Peachtree St. NE (1990)	428	28
Atlanta Plaza I, 950 E. Paces Ferry Rd. (1986)	425	32
Park Place, 2660 Peachtree Rd. NW (1986)	420	40
2828 Peachtree Luxury Condominiums (2002)	420	33
Oakwood Apts., 1280 W. Peachtree St. NW (1989)	410	38
Peachtree Summit No. 1, 401 Peachtree NE (1975)	406	31
One Coca-Cola Plaza, 310 North Ave. NW (1979)	403	29
Tower Place 100, 3340 Peachtree Rd. NE (1974)	401	29

(1) 883 ft. with antenna.

Baltimore, MD

	Ht. (ft.)	Stories
Legg Mason Building, 100 Light St. (1973)	529	40
Bank of America, 10 Light St. (1924)	509	37
William Donald Schaefer Tower, 6 St. Paul Pl. (1992)	493	29
Commerce Place, 1 South St. (1992)	454	31
Marriott Baltimore Inner Harbor East, 700 Aliceanna St. (2001)	430	32
World Trade Center 401 E. Pratt St. (1977)	405	32

Bellevue, WA

Building	Ht. (ft.)	Stories
*One Lincoln Tower, 604 Bellevue Way (2005)	450	42
*Lincoln Square, 770 Bellevue Way NE (2005)	412	28

Birmingham, AL

	Ht. (ft.)	Stories
Southtrust Tower, 420 N. 20th St. (1986)	454	34
AmSouth/Harbert Plaza, 1901 6th Ave. N (1989)	437	32

Boston, MA

	Ht. (ft.)	Stories
John Hancock Tower, 200 Clarendon St. (1976)	790	62
Prudential Tower, 800 Boylston St. (1964)[1]	750	52
Federal Reserve Bldg., 600 Atlantic Ave. (1978)	604	32
Boston Company Bldg., 1 Boston Place (1970)	601	41
One International Place, 100 Oliver St. (1987)	600	46
First National Bank of Boston, 100 Federal St. (1971)	591	37
One Financial Center, 10 Dewey Sq. (1984)	590	46
111 Huntington Ave. (2002)	564	36
Two International Place (1993)	538	35
One Post Office Square (1981)	525	40
1 Federal St. (1975)	520	38
Exchange Place, 53 State St. (1984)	510	39
Sixty State St. (1977)	509	38
1 Beacon St. (1972)	507	36
1 Lincoln Place (2003)	503	36
28 State Street (1970)	500	40
Mariott's Custom House, 3 McKinley Sq. (1915)	496	32
John Hancock Bldg., 175 Berkeley St. (1949)	495	26
*33 Arch St. (2003)	489	31
State St. Bank, 225 Franklin St., (1966)	477	33
Millennium Place 1, Ritz Carlton Hotel (2001)	475	38
125 High St. (1990)	452	30
100 Summer St. (1975)	450	33
Millennium Place 2, 3 Avery St. (2001)	445	36
McCormack Bldg., 1 Ashburton Pl. (1975)	401	22
Harbor Towers I, 85 E. India (1971)	400	40
Keystone Building (1971)	400	32

(1) 836 ft. with antenna

Calgary, Alberta

	Ht. (ft.)	Stories
Petro Canada Centre West Tower, 150 6th Ave. SW (1984)	705	53
Bankers Hall East Tower, 855 2nd St. SW (1989)	645	50

Building	Ht. (ft.)	Stories
Bankers Hall West Tower, 888 3rd St. SW (2000)	645	50
Calgary Tower, 101 9th Ave. SW (1967)	626	NA
TransCanada Tower, 450 1st St. SW (2000)	608	37
Canterra Tower, 400 3rd Ave. SW (2001)	581	38
First Canadian Centre, 350 7th Ave. SW (1983)	530	43
Canada Trust, Calgary Eatons Centre, 421 7th Ave. SW (1991)	530	40
Scotia Square, 700 2nd St. SW (1975)	525	42
Western Canadian Place–N. Tower, 707 6th St. SW (1983)	507	41
Nexen Bldg., 801 7th Ave. SW (1982)	500	37
Petro-Canada Tower, E. Tower, 111 5th Ave. SW (1983)	469	33
Two Bow Valley Square, 205 5th Ave. SW (1974)	468	39
Dome Tower, 333 7th Ave. SW (1976)	463	34
5th & 5th Bldg., 605 5th Ave. SW (1980)	460	35
Shell Centre, 400 4th Ave. SW (1977)	460	34
T.D. Square North, 324 8th Ave. SW (1976)	449	33
Four Bow Valley Square, 250 6th Ave. SW (1982)	441	37
Fifth Avenue Place East Tower, 425 1st St. SW (1981)	435	35
Fifth Avenue Place West Tower, 237 4th Ave. SW (1981)	435	35
Western Canadian Place–S. Tower, 801 6th St. SW (1983)	420	32
Altius Centre, 500 4th Ave. SW (1972)	415	32
Family Life Bldg.	410	31
Encana Place, 150 9th Ave. SW (1982)	410	28
Hewlett Packard Tower, 715 5th Ave. SW (1975)	408	31
Alberta Stock Exchange, 300 5th Ave. (1979)	407	33

Charlotte, NC

Building	Ht. (ft.)	Stories
Bank of America Corporate Center, 100 N. Tryon St. (1992)	871	60
Hearst Tower, 214 N. Tryon St. (2002)	659	50
One Wachovia Center, 301 S. College St. (1988)	588	42
Bank of America Plaza, 101 S. Tryon St. (1974)	503	40
Interstate Tower, 121 W. Trade St. (1990)	462	32
IJL Financial Center, 201 N. Tryon St. (1997)	447	30
Three Wachovia Center, 401 S. Tryon St. (2000)	440	29
Two Wachovia Plaza, 301 S. Tryon St. (1971)	433	32
Wachovia Center, 400 S. Tryon St. (1974)	420	32

Chicago, IL

Building	Ht. (ft.)	Stories
Sears Tower, 233 S. Wacker Dr. (1974)[1]	1,450	108
Aon Center, 200 E. Randolph St. (1973)	1,136	83
John Hancock Center, 875 N. Michigan Ave. (1969)[2]	1,127	100
AT&T Corporate Center (incl. spire), 227 W. Monroe St. (1989)	1,007	61
Two Prudential Plaza (incl. spire), 180 N. Stetson Ave. (1990)	995	64
311 S. Wacker Drive (1990)	961	65
900 N. Michigan Ave. (1989)	871	66
Water Tower Place, 845 N. Michigan Ave. (1976)	859	74
Bank One Plaza (1969)	850	60
Park Tower, 800 N. Michigan Ave. (2000)	844	67
3 First National Plaza, 70 W. Madison St. (1981)	767	57
Chicago Title & Trust Center, 161 N. Clark St. (1992)	756	50
Olympia Centre, 737 N. Michigan Ave. (1986)	725	63
IBM Bldg., 330 N. Wabash Ave. (1973)	695	52
*Hyatt Center, 71 S. Wacker Drive (2005)	682	48
*111 S. Wacker Drive (2005)	681	51
181 W. Madison St. (1990)	680	50
One Magnificent Mile, 980 N. Michigan Ave. (1983)	673	58
R.R. Donnelley Center, 77 W. Wacker Dr. (1992)	668	49
UBS Tower, 1 N. Wacker Dr. (2001)	652	50
Daley Center, 55 W. Washington St. (1965)	648	31
55 E. Erie St. (2003)	647	56
Lake Point Tower, 505 N. Lake Shore Dr. (1968)	645	70
River East Center, 350 E. Illinois St. (2001)	644	58
Grand Plaza I, 540 N. State St. (2003)	641	57
Leo Burnett Bldg., 35 W. Wacker Dr. (1989)	635	50
*The Heritage at Millennium Park, 125 N. Wabash Ave. (2004)	631	57
NBC Tower (incl. spire), 445 N. Cityfront Plaza Dr. (1989)	627	37
*Millennium Centre, 33 W. Ontario St. (2003)	610	59
Chicago Place, 700 N. Michigan Ave. (1991)	608	49
Board of Trade (incl. statue), 141 W. Jackson Blvd. (1930)	605	44
CNA Plaza, 325 S. Wabash St. (1972)	601	45
Prudential Bldg., 130 E. Randolph St. (1955)[3]	601	41
Heller International Tower, 500 W. Monroe St. (1992)	600	45
One Madison Plaza, 200 W. Madison St. (1982)	599	45
1000 Lake Shore Plaza. (1964)	590	55
Marina City Apts. 1, 300 N. State St. (1964)	588	61
Marina City Apts. 2, 300 N. State St. (1964)	588	61
Citicorp Center, 500 W. Madison St. (1985)	588	41
Mid Continental Plaza, 55 E. Monroe St. (1972)	582	50
North Pier Apt. Tower, 474 N. Lake Shore Dr. (1990)	581	61
Bank One Center, 131 S. Dearborn St. (2003)	580	37
Smurfit-Stone Bldg., 150 N. Michigan Ave. (1983)	575	41
The Fordham, 25 E. Superior St. (2003)	574	52
190 S. LaSalle St. (1987)	573	42
*One S. Dearborn (2005)	571	39
Onterie Center, 446 E. Ontario St. (1985)	570	57
Chicago Temple, 77 W. Washington St. (1924)	568	21
Palmolive Bldg., 919 N. Michigan Ave. (incl. beacon) (1929)	565	37
Huron Plaza Apts., 30 E. Huron St. (1983)	560	56
Boeing Int'l Headquarters, 100 N. Riverside Plaza (1990)	560	36
The Parkshore, 195 N. Harbor Dr. (1991)	556	56
North Harbor Tower, 175 N. Harbor Dr. (1988)	556	55
Civic Opera Bldg., 20 N. Wacker Dr. (1929)	555	45
Newberry Plaza, 1000 N. State St. (1974)	553	53
Michigan Plaza South, 205 N. Michigan Ave. (1985)	553	44
30 N. LaSalle St. (1975)	553	43
Pittsfield Bldg., 55 E. Washington St. (1927)	551	38
Harbor Point, 155 N. Harbor Dr. (1975)	550	54
One S. Wacker Dr. (1983)	550	42
Kluczynski Federal Bldg., 230 S. Dearborn St. (1975)	545	45
Park Millennium, 222 N. Columbus Dr. (2002)	544	53
USG Building, 125 S. Franklin St. (1992)	538	35
The Pinnacle, 21 E. Huron St. (2004)	535	48
LaSalle National Bank, 135 S. LaSalle St. (1934)	535	44
Park Place Tower, 655 W. Irving Park Rd. (1973)	531	56
One N. LaSalle St. (1930)	530	49
The Elysees, 111 E. Chestnut St. (1973)	529	56
River Plaza, 405 N. Wabash St. (1977)	524	56
35 E. Wacker Dr. (1926)	523	40
Unitrin Bldg., 1 E. Wacker Dr. (1962)	522	41
Mather Tower, 75 E. Wacker Dr. (1928)	521	41
Chicago Mercantile Exchange, 10 S. Wacker Dr. (1987)	520	40
Chicago Merc. Exchange, 30 S. Wacker Dr. (1983)	520	40
191 N. Wacker Dr. (2002)	516	37
401 E. Ontario St. (1990)	515	51
One Financial Place, 440 S. LaSalle St. (1985)	515	40
Park Tower Condos, 5415 N. Sheridan Rd. (1973)	513	54
LaSalle-Wacker, 221 N. LaSalle St. (1930)[4]	512	41
321 N. Clark St. (1987)	510	35
Harris Bank III, 115 S. LaSalle St. (1977)	510	35
400 E. Ohio St. (1982)	505	50
Carbide & Carbon Bldg. , 230 N. Michigan Ave. (1929)	503	37
1 Superior Place, 1 W. Superior St. (1999)	502	52
120 N. LaSalle St. (1991)	501	41
Chase Plaza, 10 S. LaSalle St. (1986)	501	37
200 S. Wacker Dr. (1981)	500	38
Ontario Place, 10 E. Ontario St. (1983)	495	49
Xerox Centre, 55 W. Monroe St. (1980)	495	40
1 N. Franklin St. (1990)	494	34
The Bristol, 57E. Delaware Pl. (2000)	488	42
333 W. Wacker Dr. (1983)	487	36
Northern Trust Bldg., 125 S. Wacker Dr. (1974)	487	31
AT&T, 10 S. Canal St. (1971)	485	32
Plaza 440, 440 N. Wabash Ave. (1991)	480	49
33 N. LaSalle St. (1930)	479	40
Bankers Bldg., 15 W. Adams St. (1927)	476	41
Metropolitan Tower, 310 S. Michigan Ave. (1924)	475	37
Cook County Administration Bldg., 69 W. Washington St. (1965)	475	37
American Furniture Mart, 680 N. Lake Shore Dr. (1926)	474	30
Intercontinental Hotel, 505 N. Michigan Ave. (1929)	471	42
City Place, 676 N. Michigan Ave. (1990)	470	40
Columbus Plaza, 233 E. Wacker Dr. (1980)	468	49
The Sterling, 345 N. LaSalle St. (2001)	466	50
Randolph Tower, 188 W. Randolph St. (1925)	465	45
200 N. Dearborn St. (1989)	463	47
Tribune Tower, 435 N. Michigan Ave. (1925)	463	36
The New York, 3660 N. Lake Shore Dr. (1986)	461	50
Presidential Towers, 555 W. Madison St. (1985)	461	49
Presidential Towers, 575 W. Madison St. (1985)	461	49
Presidential Towers, 605 W. Madison St. (1985)	461	49
Presidential Towers, 625 W. Madison St. (1985)	461	49
Chicago Marriott, 540 N. Michigan Ave. (1978)	460	45
Swissotel, 323 E. Wacker Dr. (1989)	457	43
Equitable Bldg., 401 N. Michigan Ave. (1965)	457	35
400 N. LaSalle St. (2003)	454	45
ABN-AMRO Plaza I, 550 W. Madison St. (2003)	453	37
Roanoke Bldg., 11 S. LaSalle St. (1925)	452	37
Riverbend, 323 N. Canal St. (2002)	451	32
*The Shoreham, Lakeshore East (2005)	450	50
Eugenie Terrace on the Park, 1730 N. Clark St. (1987)	450	44
Gateway Center III, 222 S. Riverside Plaza (1972)	450	35

(1) 1,730 ft. with antenna (2) 1,499 ft. with antenna (3) 912 ft. with antenna (4) 543 ft. with antenna

Cincinnati, OH

Building	Ht. (ft.)	Stories
Carew Tower, 441 Vine St. (1931)	574	49
PNC Tower , 1 W. 4th St. (1913)	495	31
Scripps Center, 312 Walnut St. (1990)	468	36
Fifth Third Center, 511 Walnut St. (1969)	423	32
Chemed Center, 255 5th St. (1990)	410	32
Convergys Center, 600 Vine St. (1984)	402	29

Cleveland, OH

Building	Ht. (ft.)	Stories
Key Tower (incl. spire), 127 Public Square (1991)	947	57
Terminal Tower, 50 Public Square (1930)	708	52
BP America, 200 Public Square (1985)	658	46

Building	Ht. (ft.)	Stories
100 Erieview, 1801 E. 9th St. (1964)	529	40
One Cleveland Center, 1375 E. 9th St. (1983)	450	31
Bank One Center, 600 Superior Ave. (1991)	446	28
Federal Courthouse, 801 W. Superior Ave. (2002)	430	24
Justice Center, 1250 Ontario St. (1976)	420	26
Federal Building, 240 E. 9th St. (1967)	419	32
National City Center, 1900 E. 9th St. (1980)	410	35

Columbus, OH

Building	Ht. (ft.)	Stories
James A. Rhodes State Office Tower, 30 E. Broad St. (1973)	624	41
Leveque-Lincoln Tower, 50 W. Broad St. (1927)	555	47
William Green Building, 30 W. Spring St. (1990)	530	33
Huntington Center, 41 S. High St. (1983)	512	37
Vern Riffe State Office Tower, 77 S. High St. (1988)	503	33
One Nationwide Plaza (1976)	485	40
Franklin County Courthouse, 373 S. High St. (1991)	464	27
AEP Building, One Riverside Plaza (1983)	456	31
Borden Bldg., 180 E. Broad St. (1974)	438	34
Three Nationwide Plaza (1989)	408	27

Dallas, TX

Building	Ht. (ft.)	Stories
Bank of America Plaza, 901 Main St. (1985)	921	72
Renaissance Tower (incl. spire), 1201 Elm St. (1974)	886	56
Bank One Center, 1717 Main St. (1987)	787	60
Chase Texas Plaza, 2200 Ross Ave. (1987)	738	55
Fountain Place, 1445 Ross Ave. (1986)	720	58
Trammel Crow Tower, 2001 Ross Ave. (1984)	686	50
1700 Pacific Ave. (1983)	655	50
Thanksgiving Tower, 1600 Pacific Ave. (1982)	645	50
Energy Plaza, 1601 Bryan St. (1983)	629	49
Elm Place, 1401 Elm St. (1965)	625	52
Republic Center Tower I (incl. spire), 300 N. Ervay (1954)	602	36
Republic Center Tower II, 325 N. St. Paul (1964)	598	50
One Bell Plaza, 208 S. Akard St. (1984)	580	37
One Lincoln Plaza, 500 Akard St. (1984)	579	45
Cityplace Center East, 2711 N. Haskell Ave. (1989)	560	42
Reunion Tower, 300 Reunion Blvd. (1976)	560	NA
Adams Mark Hotel Center Tower, 400 Olive St. (1959)	550	42
Mercantile Bldg., 1700 Main St. (1943)	523	31
2001 Bryan St. (1973)	512	40
Harwood Center, 1999 Bryan St. (1982)	483	36
KMPG Centre, 717 N. Harwood St. (1980)	481	34
San Jacinto Tower, 2121 San Jacinto St. (1982)	456	33
Renaissance Hotel, 2222 Stemmons Fwy. (1983)	451	29
Adam's Mark Hotel North Tower (1980)	448	31
One Dallas Centre, 350 N. Paul St. (1979)	448	30
One Main Place, 1201 Main St. (1968)	445	34
1600 Pacific Bldg. (1964)	434	31
Magnolia Bldg., 108 Akard St. (1923)	430	27
Fidelity Union Tower, 1507 Pacific Ave. (1959)	400	33

Denver, CO

Building	Ht. (ft.)	Stories
Republic Plaza, 330 17th St. (1984)	714	56
1801 California St. (1982)	709	52
Wells Fargo Center, 1700 Lincoln Ave. (1983)	698	50
1999 Broadway (1985)	544	43
MCI Plaza/Marriott City Center, 707 17th St. (1981)	522	42
Qwest Tower, 555 17th St. (1978)	507	40
*Colorado Convention Center Hotel, 650 15th St. (2005)	489	38
1670 Broadway (1980)	448	36
17th St. Plaza, 1225 17th St. (1982)	438	32
First Interstate Tower North, 633 17th St. (1974)	434	32
Brooks Towers, 1020 15th St. (1968)	420	42
Denver Place South Tower, 999 18th St. (1981)	416	34
One Tabor Center, 1200 17th St. (1984)	408	32
Manville Plaza, 717 17th St. (1989)	404	29

Des Moines, IA

Building	Ht. (ft.)	Stories
801 Grand, 801 Grand Ave. (1991)	630	44
Ruan Center, 666 Grand Ave. (1974)	457	36

Detroit, MI

Building	Ht. (ft.)	Stories
Marriott Hotel, Renaissance Center I (1977)	727	73
Comerica Center, 500 Woodward Ave. (1991)	619	45
Penobscot Bldg., 633 Griswold Ave. (1928)	566	46
Renaissance Center 100 Tower (1976)	508	39
Renaissance Center 200 Tower (1976)	508	39
Renaissance Center 300 Tower (1976)	508	39
Renaissance Center 400 Tower (1976)	508	39
Guardian Bldg., 500 Griswold Ave. (1929)	489	36
Book Tower, 1249 Washington Blvd. (1925)	472	35
Madden Bldg., 150 W. Jefferson Ave. (1988)	470	29
Fisher Bldg., 3011 W. Grand Blvd. (1928)	447	28
Cadillac Tower, 65 Cadillac Sq. (1928)	437	40
David Stott Bldg., 1150 Griswold St. (1928)	436	38
ANR Bldg., 1 Woodward Ave. (1962)	430	30

Edmonton, Alberta

Building	Ht. (ft.)	Stories
Manulife Place, 10170-101 St. (1983)	480	36
Telus Plaza South, 10020-100 St. (1971)	441	34
Bell Tower, 10104-103 Ave. (1982)	426	34
Commerce Place, 10155-102 St. (1990)	404	27

Fort Worth, TX

Building	Ht. (ft.)	Stories
Burnett Plaza, 801 Cherry St. (1983)	567	40
City Center Tower II, 301 Commerce St. (1984)	547	38
Carter Burgess Plaza, 777 Main St. (1982)	525	40
Landmark Tower, 200 W. 7th St. (1957)	481	32
Chase Texas Tower, 201 Main St. (1982)	477	33
Block 82 Tower, 400 Throckmorton St. (1974)	454	36

Hartford, CT

Building	Ht. (ft.)	Stories
City Place, 185 Asylum St. (1980)	535	38
CitiGroup Building, 26 Grove St. (1919)	527	34
Goodwin Square, 225 Asylum St. (1990)	522	30
*Hartford 21 (2006)	440	36

Honolulu, HI

Building	Ht. (ft.)	Stories
First Hawaiian Bank Bldg., 999 Bishop St. (1996)	429	30
Nauru Tower, 1330 Ala Moana Blvd. (1991)	418	45
*Hokua Tower, 1288 Ala Moana Blvd. (2005)	418	41
Hawaiki Tower, 88 Pii Koi St. (1999)	400	45
One Waterfront Tower–Makai, 425 S. King St. (1990)	400	45
One Archer Lane, 801 S. King St. (1998)	400	41
Imperial Plaza, 725 Kapiolani Blvd. (1992)	400	40
One Waterfront Tower–Mauka, 415 S. King St. (1990)	400	45

Houston, TX

Building	Ht. (ft.)	Stories
JPMorgan Chase Tower, 600 Travis St. (1982)	1,002	75
Wells Fargo Plaza, 1000 Louisiana St. (1983)	972	71
Williams Tower, 2800 Post Oak Blvd. (1983)	901	64
Bank of America Center, 700 Louisiana St. (1983)	780	56
Texaco Heritage Plaza, 1111 Bagby St. (1987)	762	53
1100 Louisiana Bldg. (1980)	748	55
Reliant Energy Plaza, 1111 Louisiana St. (1974)	741	47
Continental Airlines Center, 1600 Smith St. (1984)	732	55
Chevron Tower, 1301 McKinney St. (1982)	725	52
One Shell Plaza, 900 Louisiana St. (1970)[1]	714	50
1400 Smith St. (1983)	691	50
3 Allen Center, 333 Clay St. (1980)	685	50
One Houston Center, 1221 McKinney St. (1978)	678	47
First City Tower, 1001 Fannin St. (1984)	662	47
San Felipe Plaza, 5847 San Felipe Blvd. (1984)	625	45
Exxon Bldg., 800 Bell Ave. (1962)	606	44
1500 Louisiana St. (2002)	600	40
America Tower, 2929 Allen Parkway (1983)	590	42
Two Houston Center, 909 Fannin St. (1974)	579	44
San Jacinto Column (monument) (1939)	570	NA
Marathon Oil Tower, 5555 San Felipe Blvd. (1983)	562	41
Wedge International Tower, 1415 Louisiana St. (1983)	550	44
Kellogg Tower, 601 Jefferson St. (1973)	550	40
Pennzoil Place 1, 700 Milam St. (1976)	523	36
Pennzoil Place 2, 700 Louisiana St. (1976)	523	36
Devon Energy Center, 1200 Smith St. (1978)	521	36
1000 Main Street (2003)	518	36
1201 Louisiana Bldg. (1971)	518	35
The Huntington, 2121 Kirby Dr. (1982)	503	34
El Paso Energy Bldg., 1010 Milam St. (1962)	502	33
5 Greenway Plaza (1973)	465	31
Calpine Center, 717 Texas Ave. (2003)	453	34
One Allen Center, 500 Dallas St. (1974)	452	34
Four Leafs Towers I, 5100 San Felipe Blvd. (1982)	444	40
Four Leafs Towers II, 5110 San Felipe Blvd. (1982)	444	40
9 Greenway Plaza (1978)	441	31
11 Greenway Plaza (1979)	441	31
Phoenix Tower, 3200 Southwest Fwy. (1984)	434	34
Chase Bank Bldg., 712 Main St. (1929)	428	37
The Spires, 2001 Holcomb Blvd. (1984)	426	41
Aon Tower, 4 Oaks Place, 1330 Post Oak Blvd. (1983)	420	30
One City Center, 1001 Main St. (1960)	410	32
Bob Lanier Public Works Bldg., 611 Walker Ave. (1968)	410	27
Neils Esperson Bldg., 802 Travis St. (1927)	410	31
Hyatt Regency, 1200 Lousiana St. (1972)	401	30
The Mercer West Tower, 3288 Sage Rd. (2003)	401	30

(1) 999 ft. with antenna.

Indianapolis, IN

Building	Ht. (ft.)	Stories
Bank One Tower (incl. spire), 111 Monument Circle (1990)	811	49
American United Life Ins., 1 America Sq. (1981)	533	37
One Indiana Square, 200 N. Delaware St. (1970)	504	36
Market Tower, 10 W. Market St. (1988)	421	32
300 N. Meridian Bldg. (1988)	408	28
First Indiana Plaza, 135 N. Pennsylvania St. (1988)	401	29

Jacksonville, FL

Building	Ht. (ft.)	Stories
Bank of America Tower, 50 N. Laura St. (1990)	617	42
Modis Tower, 1 Independent Dr. (1975)	535	37
BellSouth Tower 424 N. Pearl St. (1983)	435	27
Riverplace Tower, 1301 Riverplace Blvd. (1967)	433	28

Jersey City, NJ

Building	Ht. (ft.)	Stories
*30 Hudson St. (2003)	781	42
Merrill Lynch Building, 101 Hudson St. (1992)	548	42
Newport Tower, 525 Washington Blvd. (1990)	531	37
Exchange Place Centre, 10 Exchange Place (1990)	490	32
Harborside Financial Plaza 5 (2002)	480	34

Kansas City, MO

Building	Ht. (ft.)	Stories
One Kansas City Place, 1200 Main St. (1988)	632	42
Transamerica Tower, 1111 Main St. (1986)	591	38
Hyatt Regency, 2345 McGee St. (1980)	504	45
Power & Light Bldg., 1330 Baltimore Ave. (1931)	481	32
City Hall, 414 E. 12th St. (1937)	443	29
Fidelity Bank & Trust Bldg. Apts, 909 Walnut St.[1]	454	35
1201 Walnut St. (1991)	427	30
Commerce Tower, 911 Main St. (1965)	407	32
City Center Square, 1100 Main St. (1977)	404	30

(1) Renovations expected to be completed in 2006

Las Vegas, NV

Building	Ht. (ft.)	Stories
Stratosphere Tower, 2000 S. Las Vegas Blvd. (1996)	1,149	NA
*Wynn Las Vegas (2005)	614	50
Eiffel Tower, Paris Hotel and Casino, 3645 S. Las Vegas Blvd. (1998)	540	NA
New York, New York Hotel and Casino, 3790 S. Las Vegas Blvd. (1997)	529	48
Bellagio Hotel and Casino, 3600 S. Las Vegas Blvd. (1998)	508	37
Mandalay Bay Hotel, 3950 S. Las Vegas Blvd. (1999)	485	43
Turnberry Place I, 2777 Paradise Road (2001)	477	38
Turnberry Place II, 2777 Paradise Road (2002)	477	38
Turnberry Place III, 2777 Paradise Road (2004)	477	38
Venetian Resort-Hotel–Casino 1, 3355 Las Vegas Blvd. W. (1999)	475	35
Caesars Palace Tower, 3570 S. Las Vegas Blvd. (1998)	470	29
Paris Hotel and Casino, 3645 S. Las Vegas Blvd. (1999)	440	34
Rio Masquerade Tower, 3700 W. Flamingo Rd. (1997)	422	42
Palms Casino Hotel, 4321 W. Flamingo Rd. (2001)	413	42
Aladdin Hotel and Casino, 3667 S. Las Vegas Blvd. (2000)	408	39
Harrah's Carnaval Tower, 3475 S. Las Vegas Blvd. (1997)	400	35
Fitzgeralds Hotel & Casino, 301 Fremont St. (1980)	400	33

Little Rock, AR

Building	Ht. (ft.)	Stories
TCBY Tower, 425 W. Capitol Ave. (1986)	546	40
Regions Center, 400 W. Capitol Ave. (1975)	454	30

Los Angeles, CA

Building	Ht. (ft.)	Stories
US Bank Tower, 633 W. 5th St. (1990)	1,018	73
Aon Center, 707 Wilshire Blvd. (1974)	858	62
Two California Plaza, 350 S. Grand Ave. (1992)	750	52
Gas Company Tower, 555 W. 5th St. (1991)	749	52
BP Plaza, 333 South Hope St. (1975)	735	55
777 Tower, 777 S. Figueroa St. (1991)	725	53
Wells Fargo Center, 333 S. Grand Ave. (1983)	723	54
Figueroa at Wiltshire, 601 S. Figueroa St. (1989)	717	52
Paul Hastings Tower, 515 S. Flower St. (1971)	699	52
Bank of America Tower, 555 S. Flower St. (1971)	699	52
Citigroup Center, 444 S. Flower St. (1979)	625	48
611 Place, 611 W. 6th St. (1969)	620	42
One California Plaza, 300 S. Grand Ave. (1985)	578	42
Century Plaza Tower 1, 2029 Cent. Park E. (1973)	571	44
Century Plaza Tower 2, 2049 Cent. Park E. (1973)	571	44
KPMG Tower, 355 S. Grand Ave. (1984)	560	45
Ernst & Young, LLP Plaza, 725 S. Figueroa St. (1986)	534	41
SunAmerica Tower, 1999 Ave. of the Stars (1989)	533	39
TCW Tower, 865 S. Figueroa St. (1990)	517	37
Union Bank Plaza, 445 S. Figueroa St. (1968)	516	40
10 Universal City Plaza (1984)	506	36
1100 Wilshire (1987)	496	36
Fox Plaza, 2121 Ave. of the Stars (1987)	492	34
Constellation Place, 10250 Constellation Blvd. (2003)	491	34
1055 W. 7th St. (1988)	462	33
Equitable Life, 3435 Wilshire Blvd. (1969)	454	34
City Hall, 200 N. Spring St. (1927)	454	28
Transamerica Center, 1150 Olive St. (1965)	452	32
Madison Complex/Pacific Bell Switching Station, 420 S. Grand Ave. (1961)	448	17
Mutual Life Benefit Bldg., 5900 Wilshire Blvd. (1971)	435	32
550 S. Hope St. (1991)	423	28
Warner Center Plaza III, 21650 Oxnard St., Woodland Hills (1991)	415	25
MCI Plaza, 700 S. Flower St. (1973)	414	33
L.A. MTA Gateway Tower (1997)	405	26

Louisville, KY

Building	Ht. (ft.)	Stories
AEGON Center, 400 W. Market St. (1992)	549	35
National City Tower, 101 S. 5th St. (1972)	512	40
PNC Bank Bldg., 5th and Jefferson St. (1971)	420	30
Humana Center, 500 W. Main St. (1985)	417	27

Mexico City, Mexico

Building	Ht. (ft.)	Stories
Torre Mayor, Paseo de la Reforma 505 (2003)	738	55
Torre de Pemex, Marina Macional 329 Col. Huasteca (1984)	702	52
Torre Altus (1999)	640	42
Torre Latino Americana (incl. spire) (1956)	597	45
World Trade Center, Montecito 38 Col. Napoles (1972)	565	50
Los Arcos Bosques I (1997)	529	34
*Los Arcos Bosques II (2004)	529	34

Building	Ht. (ft.)	Stories
*Santa Fe Flats (2004)	492	37
Torre Las Lomas (1993)	453	36
Hotel Nikko Mexico, Campos Eliseos 24	446	38
Torre del Caballito	443	34
Torre Mural, Insurgentes Sur 1605 (1995)	440	33
Edificio Mexicana de Aviacion (1984)	433	30
Presidente Inter-Continental Hotel, Campos Eliseos 218 (1976)	427	42
Torre Dahnos I, Reforma 222 (2003)	427	31
Nonoalco Tlatelolco Tower (1962)	417	25
Torre Reforma, Andres Bello 45	410	28
JW Marriott Hotel, Andres Bello 29	400	27

Miami, FL

Building	Ht. (ft.)	Stories
Four Seasons Hotel and Tower, 1441 Brickell Ave. (2003)	789	64
Wachovia Financial Center, 200 S. Biscayne Blvd. (1983)	764	55
Bank of America Tower, 100 S. E. 2nd St. (1987)	625	47
Santa Maria, 1643 Brickell Ave. (1997)	520	51
Stephen P. Clark Center, 111 NW 1st St. (1985)	510	28
*Jade at Brickell Bay, 1295 Brickell Bay Dr. (2004)	500	48
One Biscayne Tower, 2 S. Biscayne Blvd. (1973)	492	39
*Espirito Santo Plaza, 1301 Brickell Ave. (2003)	487	36
Citicorp Tower at Miami Centre, 201 S. Biscayne Blvd. (1986)	484	35
Three Tequesta Point, 848 Brickell Key Dr. (2001)	480	46
*One Miami E. Tower, 205 S. Brickell Ave. (2005)	460	44
701 Brickell Ave. (1986)	450	33
One Miami W. Tower, 205 S. Brickell Ave. (2005)	449	45
Mellon Financial Center, 1111 Brickell Ave. (2001)	435	31
*Summit Brickell View Condominums, 1200 S. Miami Ave. (2004)	423	37
Mark on Brickell, 1155 Brickell Bay Dr. (2001)	420	36
*Brickell Bay Plaza, 1201 Brickell Ave.	411	42
Two Tequesta Point, 808 Brickell Key Dr. (1999)	410	40
Courthouse Center, 175 NW First Ave. (1986)	405	30
The Palace, 1541 Brickell Ave. (1982)	400	42

Miami Beach, FL

Building	Ht. (ft.)	Stories
Blue Diamond Tower, 4779 Collins Ave. (2000)	559	44
Green Diamond Tower, 4775 Collins Ave. (2000)	559	44
*Akoya Condominiums, 6365 Collins Ave. (2004)	492	47
PortofinoTower, 300 S. Pointe Dr. (1997)	484	44
The Continuum on South Beach, South Tower, 1 S. Pointe Dr. (2002)	474	43
Murano Grande at Portofino, 400 Alton Rd. (2003)	407	37
Murano at Portofino, 1000 S. Pointe Dr. (2001)	402	38

Milwaukee, WI

Building	Ht. (ft.)	Stories
U.S. Bank Center, 777 E. Wisconsin Ave. (1973)	601	42
100 E. Wisconsin Ave (1989)	549	37
Milwaukee Center, 111 E. Kilbourn Ave. (1987)	426	29
411 Bldg., 411 E. Wisconsin Ave. (1983)	408	30

Minneapolis, MN

Building	Ht. (ft.)	Stories
225 South Sixth (1992)	776	56
IDS Center, 80 8th St. S. (1973)[1]	774	57
Wells Fargo Center, 90 7th St. S. (1988)	774	57
33 S. 6th St. (1983)	668	52
Campbell Mithun Tower, 222 9th St. S. (1984)	579	42
Pillsbury Center I, 200 6th St. S. (1981)	561	41
Dain Rauscher Plaza, 60 6th St. S. 1992	539	40
Fifth Street Towers II, 150 5th St. S. (1988)	503	36
American Express Finance Center, 707 2nd Ave. South (2000)	498	31
Target Plaza South, 1020 Nicollet Mall (2001)	492	33
Plaza VII, 45 7th St. S. (1987)	475	36
US Bancorp Center, 800 Nicollet Mall (2000)	468	32
AT&T Tower, 901 Marquette Ave. (1991)	464	34
Accenture Tower, 333 7th St. S. (1987)	455	33
Foshay Tower, 821 Marquette Ave. (1929)	447	32
Qwest, 224 5th St. S. (1931)	416	26
Hennepin Co. Government Center, 300 6th St. S. (1977)	403	24
50 South Sixth (2001)	401	30

(1) 910 ft. with antenna.

Montreal, Quebec

Building	Ht. (ft.)	Stories
Marathon (IBM) (incl. spire), 1250 Blvd. René Lévesque (1992)	743	47
1000 Rue de la Gauchetière (1992)	673	51
Tour de la Bourse, 800 Place Victoria (1963)	624	47
1 Place Villa Marie (1962)	616	42
La Tour CIBC, 1155 Blvd. René Lévesque (1962)	604	43
Montreal Tower (1987)	574	NA
Tour McGill College, 1501 McGill College (1992)	519	38
Le Complexe Desjardins Sud (1975)	498	40
La Tour Laurier	425	36
Les Cooperants, 600 Maisonneuve (1987)	479	34
Place Montreal Trust, 1800 McGill College (1988)	440	30
Tour TELUS, 630 Blvd. René Lévesque (1962)	429	32
Le Complexe Desjardins Est (1975)	428	32
Port Royal Apts., 1455 Sherbrooke Quest (1964)	424	33
Marriott Hotel, 1 Place du Canada (1967)	420	38
Tour de la Banque Nationale, 600 Rue de la Gauchetiere (1983)	420	29

Building	Ht. (ft.)	Stories
Tour Bell, 700 Rue de la Gauchetiere (1983)	420	28
Centre Mount Royal, 1000 Sherbrooke Quest (1976).	420	28
Tour Terminal, 800 René Lévesque Blvd. Quest (1966)	400	30

Nashville, TN

Building	Ht. (ft.)	Stories
BellSouth Tower (incl. spire), 333 Commerce St. (1994)	617	33
Sun Trust Bank, 424 Church St. (1986)	490	31
William R. Snodgrass Tennessee Tower, 311 7th Avenue North (1970)	452	31
Nashville Life & Casualty Tower, 401 Church St. (1957)	409	30
City Center, 511 Union St. (1987)	402	27

Newark, NJ

Building	Ht. (ft.)	Stories
Midatlantic National Bank, 744 Broad St. (1931)	465	36
1180 Raymond Blvd. (1930)	448	34

New Orleans, LA

Building	Ht. (ft.)	Stories
One Shell Square, 701 Poydras St. (1972)	697	51
Bank One Center, 201 St. Charles Ave. (1985)	645	53
Plaza Tower, 1001 Howard Ave. (1969)	531	45
Energy Centre, 1100 Poydras St. (1984)	530	39
LL&E Tower, 901 Poydras St. (1987)	481	36
Sheraton Hotel, 500 Canal St. (1985)	478	47
Marriott Hotel, 555 Canal St. (1972)	450	42
Texaco Center, 400 Poydras St. (1983)	442	33
Canal Place One, 365 Canal St. (1979)	439	32
Bank of New Orleans, 1010 Common St. (1971)	438	31
World Trade Center, 2 Canal St. (1965)	407	33
CNG Tower, 1450 Poydras St. (1987)	406	26

New York, NY

Building	Ht. (ft.)	Stories
Empire State Bldg., 350 5th Ave. (1931)[1]	1,250	102
Chrysler Bldg. (incl. spire), 405 Lexington Ave. (1930)	1,046	77
American International Bldg., 70 Pine St. (1932)	952	67
The Trump Bldg., 40 Wall St. (1930).	927	71
Citigroup Center, 153 E. 53rd St. (1977).	915	59
Trump World Tower, 845 UN Plaza (2001).	861	72
G. E. Bldg., 30 Rockefeller Center (1933).	850	70
Cityspire, 150 W. 56th St. (1989)	814	75
One Chase Manhattan Plaza (1960).	813	60
Condé Nast Bldg., 4 Times Square (1999)[2]	809	48
MetLife Bldg., 200 Park Ave. (1963)	808	59
*Bloomberg Tower, 731 Lexington Ave. (2004)[3]	806	55
Woolworth Bldg., 233 Broadway (1913)	792	57
1 Worldwide Plaza, 935 8th Ave. (1989).	778	47
Carnegie Hall Tower, 152 W. 57th St. (1991)	757	60
Bear Stearns World Hdq., 383 Madison Ave. (2001).	755	47
AXA Center, 787 7th Ave. (1985)	752	51
One Penn Plaza, 250 W. 34th St. (1972)	750	57
Time Warner Center North Tower, 10 Columbus Circle (2004)	750	55
Time Warner Center South Tower, 10 Columbus Circle (2004)	750	55
1251 Ave. of Americas (1971).	750	54
*7 World Trade Center. (2005).	750	52
J.P. Morgan Headquarters, 60 Wall St. (1989)	745	55
1 Liberty Plaza, 165 Broadway (1973)	743	54
20 Exchange Place (1931)	741	57
American Express Tower, Three World Financial Center, 200 Vesey St. (1986)	739	51
One Astor Plaza, 1515 Broadway (1969)	730	54
Times Square Tower (2004)	726	47
Metropolitan Tower, 142 W. 57th St. (1985)	716	68
JP Morgan Chase World Headquarters, 270 Park Ave. (1960)	707	52
General Motors Bldg., 767 5th Ave. (1968).	705	50
Metropolitan Life Tower, 1 Madison Ave. (1909)	700	50
500 5th Ave. (1931).	697	60
Americas Tower, 1177 Ave. of the Amer. (1992)	692	48
Solow Bldg., 9 W. 57th St. (1974).	689	49
HSBC Bank Bldg., 140 Broadway (1967)	688	52
55 Water St. (1972).	687	53
277 Park Ave. (1963)	687	50
1585 Broadway (1989)	685	42
Random House, Park Imperial, 1739 Bway (2003).	684	52
Four Seasons Hotel, 57 E. 57th St. (1993)	682	52
Bertelsmann Bldg., 1540 Broadway (1990)	676	42
McGraw Hill Bldg., 1221 Ave. of Amer. (1972)	674	51
Lincoln Bldg., 60 E. 42nd St. (1930).	673	53
Paramount Plaza, 1633 Broadway (1970)	670	48
Trump Tower, 725 5th Ave. (1982).	664	58
Citicorp, Queens (1990)	658	50
Bank of New York Bldg., 1 Wall St. (1932).	654	50
599 Lexington Ave. (1986)	653	51
712 5th Ave. (1990).	650	53
Chanin Bldg., 122 E. 42nd St. (1929)	649	56
245 Park Ave. (1967)	648	47
Sony Bldg., 550 Madison Ave. (1983).	647	37
Merrill Lynch, Two World Financial Center, 225 Liberty St. (1986)	645	44
RCA Victor Bldg., 570 Lexington Ave. (1930).	642	50
One New York Plaza, 1 Water St. (1969).	640	50
1 Dag Hammarskjold Plaza, 885 2nd Ave. (1972)	637	48
345 Park Ave. (1968)	634	44
Mercantile Bldg., 10 E. 40th St. (1929)	632	48

Building	Ht. (ft.)	Stories
Grace Plaza, 1114 Ave. of the Amer. (1972)	630	50
Home Insurance Co., 59 Maiden Lane (1966)	630	44
Verizon Bldg., 1095 Ave. of the Amer. (1970)	630	40
101 Park Ave. (1982)	629	49
Central Park Place, 301 W. 57th St. (1988)	628	56
888 7th Ave. (1971)	628	45
Alliance Capital Bldg., 1345 Ave. of the Amer. (1969)	625	50
Waldorf-Astoria, 301 Park Ave. (1931)	625	47
Trump Palace, 200 E. 69th St. (1991)	623	55
Olympic Tower, 645 5th Ave. (1976)	620	51
425 Fifth Avenue (2003).	618	55
*125 W. 31st St. (2006)	615	58
919 Third Ave. (1970)	615	47
750 7th Ave. (incl. spire) (1989)	615	35
New York Life, 51 Madison Ave. (1928).	615	33
Tower 49, 12 E. 49th St. (1985).	614	44
Credit Lyonnais Bldg., 1301 Ave. of the Amer. (1964)	609	46
*350 W. 42nd St.	604	58
IBM Headquarters, 590 Madison Ave. (1983)	603	41
*Hearst Tower, 959 8th Avenue, (2006)	596	42
3 Lincoln Center, 160 W. 66th St. (1993).	595	60
Celanese Bldg., 1211 Ave. of the Amer. (1973).	592	45
Rihga Royal Hotel, 151 W. 54th St. (1990)	590	54
U.S. Court House, 505 Pearl St. (1927).	590	37
Millenium Hilton Hotel, 55 Church St. (1992)	588	58
Museum Tower Apts., 21 W. 53rd St. (1985).	588	52
Time-Life, 1271 Ave. of the Amer. (1959)	587	48
Jacob K. Javits Fed. Bldg., 26 Fed. Plaza (1967)	587	41
W Times Square, 1567 Broadway (2000)	584	53
Stevens Tower, 1185 Ave. of Amer. (1971).	580	42
Municipal Bldg., 1 Centre St. (1914)	580	34
Trump International Hotel & Tower, 15 Columbus Circle (1970)	579	44
520 Madison Ave. (1981).	577	43
Oppenheimer & Co., 1 World Financial Ctr., 200 Liberty St. (1985).	577	37
Merchandise Mart, 41 Madison Ave. (1973)	576	42
Park Ave. Plaza, 55 E. 52nd St. (1981)	575	44
Lehman Building, 745 7th Ave., (2001)	575	38
One Financial Square, 33 Old Slip (1987)	575	37
Marriott Marquis Times Square, 1531 Bway (1985).	574	50
Westavco Bldg., 299 Park Ave. (1967)	574	42
Ernst & Young Tower, 5 Times Sq., 590 7th Ave. (2002)	574	40
1166 Ave. of the Americas (1974)	572	44
Socony Mobil, 150 E. 42nd Street (1956)	572	42
Wang Bldg., 780 3rd Ave. (1983).	570	49
AXA Finance Center, 1290 Ave. of the Amer. (1963)	570	43
600 3rd Ave. (1971)	570	42
450 Lexington Ave. (1991).	568	38
Paramount Tower, 240 E. 39th St. (1998)	567	51
Helmsley Bldg., 230 Park Ave. (1928).	566	35
Deutsche Bank, 130 Liberty St. (1974)	565	40
New York Palace Hotel, 455 Madison Ave. (1980).	563	51
30 Broad St. (1932)	562	48
Park Ave. Tower, 65 E. 55th St. (1986)	561	36
Nelson Tower, 450 7th Ave. (1931).	560	46
Sherry-Netherland, 781 5th Ave. (1927).	560	40
Swiss Bank Tower, 10 E. 50th St. (1990)	560	36
100 UN Plaza, 327 E. 48th St. (1986)	557	52
Continental Can, 633 3rd Ave. (1962)	557	39
3 Park Ave. (1975)	556	42
Continental Corp., 180 Maiden Lane (1983)	555	41
Sperry & Hutchinson, 330 Madison Ave. (1964)	555	41
Reuters Bldg., 3 Times Square (2001)[4].	555	30
Madison Belvedere, 14 E. 29th St. (1999)	554	48
Inmont Bldg., 1133 Ave. of the Amer. (1970).	552	45
Equitable Trust Co. Bldg., 15 Broad St. (1927)	551	42
Biltmore Tower, 267 W. 47th St. (2003)	550	51
Burroughs Bldg., 605 3rd Ave. (1963)	550	44
Two Grand Central Tower, 140 E. 45th St. (1982).	550	44
Bell Atlantic, 33 Thomas St. (1974)	550	29
Bankers Trust, 33 E. 48th St. (1971)	547	41
The Corinthian, 330 E. 38th St. (1988)	546	55
Transportation Bldg., 225 Broadway (1928)	546	44
Millennium Tower, 101 W. 67th St. (1995).	545	54
Equitable, 120 Broadway (1915)	545	36
Galleria, 117 E. 57th St. (1975)	544	56
*2 Gold Street (2004)	543	51
220 Riverside Blvd. at Trump Place (2003)	542	49
17 State St. (1988)	542	41
Grand Central Plaza, 622 Third Ave. (1973)	542	38
New York Telephone, 375 Pearl St. (1976)	540	42
Paine Webber Bldg., 1285 Ave. of the Amer. (1959).	540	42
Ritz Tower, 109 E. 57th St. (1925).	540	41
Bankers Trust, 16 Wall St. (1912)	540	39
Tribeca Tower, 105 Duane St. (1990)	537	53
Lefcourt Colonial Bldg., 295 Madison Ave. (1929).	537	45
300 Madison Ave. (2003)	535	35
1700 Broadway (1969).	533	41
Westin Hotel New York, 43rd St. and 8th Ave. (2002)	532	45
515 Park. Ave. (1999)	532	43
The Metropolis, 150 E. 44th St. (2001)	528	50
North American Plywood, 800 3rd Ave. (1972)	526	41
Hotel Pierre, 2 E. 61st St. (1928)	525	44

Building	Ht. (ft.)	Stories
767 3rd Ave. (1980)	525	39
Citibank, 399 Park Ave. (1961)	524	41
High Point Condominium, 250 E. 40th St. (1988)	522	49
Random House, 825 3rd Ave. (1969)	522	51
Du Mont Bldg., 515 Madison Ave. (1931)	520	42
26 Broadway (1922)	520	31
Newsweek Bldg., 444 Madison Ave. (1931)	518	42
Downtown Athletic Club, 19 West St. (1930)	518	39
964 Third Ave. (1969)	518	39
House of Seagram, 375 Park Ave. (1958)	518	38
South Park Tower, 124 W. 60th St. (1986)	516	51
Sterling Drug Bldg., 90 Park Ave. (1964)	515	41
Consolidated Gas Bldg.,14th St. & Irving Pl. (1926)	514	34
Navarre, 512 7th Ave. (1930)	513	44
Bank of New York, 48 Wall St. (1927)	513	31
The Belaire, 524 E. 72d St. (1988)	512	50
Williamsburg Savings Bank, Brooklyn, 1 Hansen Place (1929)	512	42
1407 Broadway Realty Corp. (1950)	512	41
International, Rockefeller Center, 630 5th Ave. (1935)	512	41
ITT-American, 437 Madison Ave. (1967)	512	40
Continental Bldg, 1450 Broadway (1931)	511	42
1155 Ave. of the Americas (1984)	511	40
*10 Liberty St. (2004)	510	45
*Bloomberg Tower, 731 Lexington Ave. (2004)	506	55
810 7th Ave. (1970)	506	41
The Sheffield Apts., 325 W. 56th St. (1978)	505	50
1 UN Plaza (1975), 2 UN Plaza (1981)	505	39
United Nations Secretariat Bldg., 405 42nd St. (1950)	505	39
2 New York Plaza, 125 Broad St. (1970)	504	40
22 E. 40th St. (1931)	503	43
60 Broad St. (1962)	503	39
Lefcourt National Bldg., 521 5th Ave. (1928)	503	37
1325 Ave. of the Americas (1989)	502	35
Sheraton Centre, 811 7th Ave. (1962)	501	51
World Apparel Center, 1411 Broadway (1969)	501	39
Bristol Plaza, 200 E. 65th St. (1987)	500	50
Pennmark Towers, 315 W. 33rd St. (2001)	500	35
Dow Jones, 4 World Fin. Center, 250 Vesey (1988)	500	34

(1) 1,455 ft. with antenna (2) 1,118 ft. with antenna (3) 941 ft. with antenna (4) 659 ft. with antenna

Oklahoma City, OK

Building	Ht. (ft.)	Stories
Bank One Tower, 100 N. Broadway Ave. (1971)	500	36
First National Center, 120 N. Robinson St. (1931)	493	33
City Place, 204 N. Robinson St. (1931)	440	32
Oklahoma Tower, 210 Park Ave. (1982)	434	31

Omaha, NE

Building	Ht. (ft.)	Stories
The Tower at First National Center, 1601 Dodge St. (2002)	634	45
Woodmen Tower, 1700 Farnam St. (1969)	478	30

Orlando, FL

Building	Ht. (ft.)	Stories
SunTrust Center Tower, 200 S. Orange Ave. (1988)	441	31
Orange Co. Courthouse, 425 N. Orange Ave. (1997)	416	24
Bank of America Center, 390 N. Orange Ave. (1988)	409	28

Philadelphia, PA

Building	Ht. (ft.)	Stories
One Liberty Place (incl. spire), 1650 Market St. (1987)	945	61
Two Liberty Place, 1601 Chestnut St. (1989)	848	58
Mellon Bank Center, 1735 Market St. (1990)	792	54
Bell–Atlantic Tower, 1717 Arch St. (1991)	725	53
Blue Cross Tower, 1901 Market St. (1990)	625	45
Commerce Square #1, 2005 Market St. (1990)	572	40
Commerce Square #2, 2001 Market St. (1992)	572	40
1818 Market St. (1973)	500	40
*The St. James, 700 Walnut St. (2004)	498	45
Lowes Philadelphia Hotel , 12 S. 12th St. (1932)	492	39
PNC, 1600 Market St. (1983)	491	40
Centre Square II, 1542 Market St. (1973)	490	38
5 Penn Center (1970)	488	36
1700 Market St. (1969)	482	32
*Cira Centre, Arch St. and 30th St. (2005)	436	28
Two Logan Square, 100 N. 18th St. (1988)	435	34
2000 Market St. (1973)	435	29
11 Penn Center, 1835 Market St. (1985)	430	29
Aramark Tower, 1101 Market St. (1984)	417	31
Centre Square I, 1500 Market St. (1973)	416	32
First Union Bank, 123 S. Broad St. (1927)	405	30
Ritz-Carlton Hotel, 28 S. Broad St. (1930)	404	30
One Logan Square, 130 N. 18th St. (1982)	400	32
Philadelphia National Bank, 1 S. Broad St. (1930)	475	25
City Hall (incl. statue) (1901)	548	7
Lewis Tower, 1419 Locust St. (1929)	400	33

Phoenix, AZ

Building	Ht. (ft.)	Stories
Bank One Center, 201 N. Central (1972)	486	40
101 N. Second Ave. (1976)	407	31

Pittsburgh, PA

Building	Ht. (ft.)	Stories
USX Tower, 600 Grant St. (1970)	841	64
One Mellon Bank Center, 500 Grant St. (1983)	725	54
One PPG Place (1984)	635	40
Fifth Ave. Place, 120 5th Ave. (1987)	616	32
One Oxford Centre, 301 Grant St. (1982)	615	46

Building	Ht. (ft.)	Stories
Gulf Tower, 707 Grant St. (1932)	582	44
Univ. of Pittsburgh Cath. of Learning, 4200 5th Ave. (1936)	535	42
3 Mellon Bank Center, 525 Wm. Penn Way (1951)	520	41
Freemarket Center, 210 6th Ave. (1968)	511	40
Grant Bldg., 330 Grant St. (1928)	485	40
Koppers Bldg., 436 7th Ave. (1929)	475	34
2 PNC Plaza, 620 Liberty Ave. (1976)	445	34
Dominion Tower, 625 Liberty Ave. (1987)	430	32
One PNC Plaza, 249 5th Avenue (1972)	424	30
Regional Enterprise Tower, 425 6th Ave. (1953)	410	30

Portland, OR

Building	Ht. (ft.)	Stories
Wells Fargo Center, 1300 SW 5th Ave. (1973)	546	40
U.S. Bancorp Tower, 111 SW 5th Ave. (1983)	536	42
Koin Tower Plaza, 222 SW Columbia St. (1984)	509	31
Pacwest Center, 1211 SW 5th Ave. (1984)	418	30

Providence, RI

Building	Ht. (ft.)	Stories
Fleet Bank Bldg., 55 Exchange Pl. (1927)	428	26
FleetBoston Tower (1973)	410	28

Richmond, VA

Building	Ht. (ft.)	Stories
James Monroe Bldg., 101 N. 14th St. (1981)	449	29
SunTrust Plaza, 919 E. Main St. (1984)	400	24

Rochester, NY

Building	Ht. (ft.)	Stories
Xerox Tower, 100 Clnton Ave. S. (1967)	443	30

St. Louis, MO

Building	Ht. (ft.)	Stories
Gateway Arch (1965)	630	NA
Metropolitan Square Tower, 211 N. Broadway (1988)	593	42
One Bell Center, 900 Pine St. (1984)	588	44
Thomas F. Eagleton Fed. Courthouse, 111 S. 10th St. (2000)	557	29
U.S. Bank Plaza, 505 N. 7th St. (1976)	484	35
Laclede Gas Bldg., 720 Olive St. (1969)	400	31

St. Paul, MN

Building	Ht. (ft.)	Stories
Minnesota World Trade Center, 30 E. 7th St. (1987)	471	36
Galtier Plaza Jackson Tower, 168 E. 6th St. (1986)	453	46
First National Bank, 332 Minnesota St. (1930)	417	32

Salt Lake City, UT

Building	Ht. (ft.)	Stories
Wells Fargo Center, 299 S. Main St. (1998)	422	24
L.D.S. Church Office Bldg., 50 E. North Temple St. (1972)	420	28

San Antonio, TX

Building	Ht. (ft.)	Stories
Tower of the Americas, 600 Hemisphere Way (1968)	622	NA
Marriott Rivercenter, 101 Bowie St. (1988)	546	38
Weston Centre, 112 Pecan St. (1988)	444	32
Tower Life, 310 S. St. Mary's St. (1929)	404	30

San Diego, CA

Building	Ht. (ft.)	Stories
One American Plaza, 600 W. Broadway (1991)	500	34
Symphony Tower, 759 B St. (1989)	499	34
Manchester Grand Hyatt, One Market Pl. (1992)	497	40
*Pinnacle Museum Tower, 500 Front St. (2005)	450	36
Emerald Plaza, 400 W. Broadway (1990)	450	30
Manchester Grand Hyatt Tower 2, One Market Pl. (2003)	446	32
One and Two Harbor Drive (2 bldgs.), 100 Harbor Dr. (1992)	424	41
*The Grande North at Santa Fe Pl. (2005)	420	39
*The Grande South at Santa Fe Pl. (2004)	420	39
*Broadway 655 (2005)	412	23

Sandy Springs, GA

Building	Ht. (ft.)	Stories
Concourse Corp. Center V, 5 Concourse Pkwy. (1988)	570	34
Concourse Corp. Center VI, 6 Concourse Pkwy. (1991)	553	34

San Francisco, CA

Building	Ht. (ft.)	Stories
Sutro Tower (1972)	977	NA
Transamerica Pyramid, 600 Montgomery St. (1972)	853	48
Bank of America, 555 California St. (1969)	779	52
345 California Center (1986)	695	48
101 California St. (1986)	600	48
50 Fremont (1983)	600	43
575 Market Center (1975)	573	40
Four Embarcadero Center, 55 Clay St. (1984)	570	45
One Embarcadero Center, 355 Clay St. (1970)	569	45
Spear Tower, 1 Market St. (1976)	565	42
Wells Fargo, 44 Montgomery St. (1967)	565	43
Citicorp Center, 1 Sansome St. (1984)	550	39
Shaklee Terrace Bldg., 444 Market St. (1982)	537	38
One Post Plaza, 1 Post St. (1969)	529	38
525 Market St. (1972)	529	38
One Metro Plaza, 425 Market St. (1973)	524	38
Pacific Telesis Center, 1 Montgomery St. (1971)	500	38
333 Bush St. (1986)	495	43
Hilton Hotel, 201 Mason St. (1971)	493	46
Pacific Gas & Electric, 77 Beale St. (1971)	492	34
50 California St. (1972)	487	37
*St. Regis Museum Tower, 3rd and Mission (2004)	484	42
*The Hemisphere, 80 Natomia St. (2006)	475	51
100 Pine Center (1972)	476	27
Bechtel Bldg., 45 Fremont St. (1979)	475	34
333 Market Bldg. (1979)	474	33

Building	Ht. (ft.)	Stories
Hartford Bldg., 650 California St. (1965)	465	33
100 First Plaza (1988)	447	37
One California St. (1969)	438	32
Marriott Hotel, 777 Market St. (1989)	436	39
Russ Bldg., 235 Montgomery St. (1927)	435	32
Pacific Bell Hdqtrs., 140 Montgomery St. (1925)	435	26
JP Morgan Chase Bldg., 560 Mission St. (2002)	421	31
Paramount, 680 Mission St. (2002)	418	41
Providian Financial Bldg., 201 Mission St. (1983)	416	30
Two Embarcadero Center, 255 Clay St. (1974)	412	31
Three Embarcadero Center, 155 Clay St. (1976)	412	31
595 Market Bldg. (1977)	412	31
123 Mission Bldg. (1986)	406	29
Embarcadero Center West, 275 Battery St. (1988)	405	33
101 Montgomery St. (1983)	405	29

Seattle, WA

Building	Ht. (ft.)	Stories
Bank of America Center, 701 5th Ave. (1985)[1]	933	76
Two Union Square, 601 Union St. (1989)	740	56
Washington Mutual Tower, 1201 3rd Ave. (1988)	772	55
Seattle Municipal Tower, 700 5th Ave. (1990)	722	57
1001 Fourth Avenue Plaza (1969)	609	50
*Museum Plaza Tower, 1301 2nd Ave. (2006)	608	42
Space Needle, 203 6th Ave. (1962)	605	NA
U.S. Bank Centre, 1420 5th Ave. (1989)	580	44
Wells Fargo Center, 999 3rd Ave. (1983)	574	47
800 Fifth Avenue Plaza (1981)	543	42
Security Pacific Bank, 900 4th Ave. (1973)	536	41
Rainier Tower, 1301 5th Ave. (1977)	514	31
IDX Tower, 915 4th Ave. (2003)	512	40
1000 2nd Ave. (1986)	493	40
Henry M. Jackson Bldg., 915 2nd Ave. (1974)	487	37
Qwest Plaza, 1600 7th Ave. (1976)	466	33
Smith Tower, 506 2nd Ave. (1914)	465	38
One Union Square, 600 University Ave. (1981)	456	36
1111 3rd Ave. (1980)	454	34
Westin Hotel North Tower, 1900 5th Ave. (1982)	448	44
Westin Bldg., 2001 6th Ave. (1981)	409	34
(1) 997 ft. with antenna		

Southfield, MI

Building	Ht. (ft.)	Stories
Prudential, 3000 Town Center (1975)	448	32
1000 Town Center (1988)	405	32

Sunny Isles Beach, FL

Building	Ht. (ft.)	Stories
*Trump Palace, 18101 Collins Ave. (2005)	551	43
*Aqualina, 17875 Collins Ave. (2004)	550	51
The Pinnacle, 17555 Collins Ave. (1999)	476	40
Ocean Two Condominiums I and II (2 bldgs.), 19111 Collins Ave. (2001)	426	40
Ocean Three Condominiums, 18925 Collins Ave. (2003)	405	37

Tampa, FL

Building	Ht. (ft.)	Stories
AmSouth Bldg., 100 N. Tampa St. (1992)	579	42
Bank of America Plaza, 101 E. Kennedy Blvd. (1986)	577	42
One Tampa City Center, 201 N. Franklin St. (1981)	537	39
Suntrust Financial Center, 401 E. Jackson St. (1992)	525	36
First Financial Tower, 400 N. Tampa St. (1973)	458	36
400 N. Ashley Plaza, 400 N. Ashley Dr. (1988)	454	33

Toledo, OH

Building	Ht. (ft.)	Stories
One SeaGate (1982)	411	32
HyTower, Jefferson St. and St. Clair St. (1970)	400	30

Toronto, Ontario

Building	Ht. (ft.)	Stories
CN Tower, 310 Front St. W (1976)	1,815	NA
First Canadian Place, 100 King St. West (1975)[1]	978	72
Scotia Plaza, 40 King St. West (1989)	902	68

Building	Ht. (ft.)	Stories
BCE Place, Canada Trust Tower, 161 Bay St. (1990)	856	53
Commerce Court West, 199 Bay St. (1973)[2]	784	57
TD Centre–Toronto Dominion Bank Tower, 66 Wellington St. West (1967)	731	56
BCE Place, Bay-Wellington Tower, 181 Bay St. (1991)	679	49
TD Centre–Royal Trust Tower, 77 King St. W. (1969)	600	46
Royal Bank Plaza–South Tower, 200 Bay St. (1976)	591	41
*1 King West (2004)	578	51
Manulife Centre, 44 Charles St. West (1974)	545	51
*Residences @ College Park I, Bay St. and College St. (2005)	505	51
TD Centre–79 Wellington St. West (1985)	504	39
The 250, 250 Yonge St. (1991)	494	35
*Harbourview Estates Phase 2 (2005)	491	49
Two Bloor West (1974)	488	34
Simcoe Place, 200 Front St. (1995)	486	33
Exchange Tower, 130 King St. West (1983)	480	30
CIBC-Commerce Court North, 25 King St. West (1931)	476	34
Simpson Tower, 401 Bay St. (1968)	472	33
Cadillac-Fairview Tower, 20 Queen St. West (1982)	466	36
Pantages Tower (2002)	458	45
One Palace Pier Court, Etobicoke (1991)	455	46
Three Palace Pier Court, Etobicoke (1978)	453	46
Laurentian Bank Bldg., 130 Adelaide St. West (1980)	450	35
Sheraton Centre, 123 Queen St. West (1972)	443	43
Two Bloor East (1974)	439	35
Royal York Hotel, 200 Front Street (1929)	439	26
TD Centre–Ernst & Young Tower, 222 Bay St. (1990)	437	31
*Empire Tower, 17 Barberry Pl. (2005)	427	28
One Financial Place, 1 Adelaide St. E.(1991)	424	31
Leaside Towers (2 bldgs.), 95 Thorncliffe Park Dr. 1970)	423	44
TD Centre–Maritime Life Tower, 100 Wellington St. West (1974)	420	32
Metro Hall West, 55 John St. (1991)	420	27
Marriott Hotel/Plaza 2 Apts., 90 Bloor St. East (1973)	415	41
Sun Life Financial Centre East Tower, 150 King St. West (1981)	410	27
Young-Eglinton Centre I, 2300 Younge St. (1974)	408	30
(1) 1,116 ft. with antenna (2) 942 ft. with antenna		

Tulsa, OK

Building	Ht. (ft.)	Stories
Williams Center, 1 W. 2nd St. (1975)	667	52
Cityplex Central Tower, 2448 E. 81st St. (1981)	648	60
First National Bank, 15 E. 5th St. (1973)	516	41
Mid-Continent Tower, 401 S. Boston St. (1984)	513	36
Fourth National Bank, 15 W. 6th St. (1966)	412	33
National Bank of Tulsa, 320 S. Boston St. (1918)	400	24

Vancouver, British Columbia

Building	Ht. (ft.)	Stories
One Wall Centre, 1000 Burrard St. (2001)	491	45
*Shaw Tower, 298 Thurlow St. (2004)	489	40
200 Granville Square (1973)	466	32
Royal Bank Tower, 1055 W. Georgia St. (1973)	461	37
Park Place, 666 Burrard St. (1984)	459	35
Bentall IV Canada Trust, 1055 Dunsmir (1981)	454	36
Scotia Tower, 650 W. Georgia St. (1977)	452	36
Harbour Centre, 555 W. Hastings (1977)	426	28
TD Bank Tower, 700 W. Georgia St. (1970)	417	30
Bentall III, Bank of Montreal, 595 Burrard St. (1974)	400	31

Winnipeg, Manitoba

Building	Ht. (ft.)	Stories
Toronto Dominion Centre, 201 Portage Ave. (1990)	420	33
Richardson Bldg., 1 Lombard Place (1969)	406	34

Winston-Salem, NC

Building	Ht. (ft.)	Stories
Wachovia Center, 100 N. Main St. (1995)	460	34
301 N. Main St. (1965)	410	26

Other Tall Buildings in North American Cities

Building		Ht. (ft.)	Stories
*RSA Battlehouse Tower (2006)	Mobile, AL	750	35
Erastus Corning II Tower (1973)	Albany, NY	589	44
Washington Monument (1884)	Washington, DC	555	NA
Dataflux Tower (2000)	Monterrey, Mexico	597	43
One HSBC Center (1970)	Buffalo, NY	529	40
Vehicle Assembly Bldg. (1965)	Cape Canaveral, FL	525	40
*Frost Bank Tower (2004)	Austin, TX	516	33
Mohegan Sun Hotel (2002)	Uncasville, CT	487	34
Borgata Hotel and Casino (2003)	Atlantic City, NJ	480	40
State Capitol (1932)	Baton Rouge, LA	460	34
Tower Burbank (1988)	Burbank, CA	460	32
*Las Olas River House 1 (2004)	Ft. Lauderdale, FL	452	42
*One Lincoln Tower (2005)	Bellevue, WA	450	42
The Diplomat (2002)	Hollywood, FL	444	39
Ravinia #3 (1991)	Dunwoody, GA	444	33
One Summit Square (1981)	Fort Wayne, IN	442	27
Anadarko Tower (2002)	The Woodlands, TX	439	32
BBT/Two Hanover Square (1991)	Raleigh, NC	431	29
Union Planters Bank (1965)	Memphis, TN	430	38
Taj Mahal, 1000 Boardwalk (1990)	Atlantic City, NJ	429	43
Torre Commercial America (1994)	Monterrey, Mexico	427	35
AmSouth Bank Bldg. (1969)	Mobile, AL	424	33
Wells Fargo Center (1991)	Sacramento, CA	423	30
Century 21	Hamilton, Ont.	418	43
Hidden Bay 1 (2000)	Aventura, FL	417	40
Galaxie Apts. (3 bldgs.) (1976)	Guttenberg, NJ	415	44
Complexe G (1972)	Quebec City, Que.	415	33
AmSouth Bank Bldg. (1996)	Montgomery, AL	415	24
*Lincoln Square (2003)	Bellevue, WA	412	28
One Shoreline Plaza, South Tower (1988)	Corpus Christi, TX	411	28
Silver Legacy Hotel & Casino (1995)	Reno, NV	410	38
110 Tower (1988)	Ft. Lauderdale, FL	410	30
Lexington Financial Center (1987)	Lexington, KY	410	30
Plaza in Clayton (2002)	Clayton, MO	409	30
Kettering Tower (1970)	Dayton, OH	408	30
Ordway Bldg. (1985)	Oakland, CA	404	28
Morgan Keegan Tower	Memphis, TN	403	34
Three Lakeway Center (1987)	Metairie, LA	403	34
Clark Tower (1972)	Memphis, TN	400	34
Monarch Place (1987)	Springfield, MA	400	26
Bank of America (1990)	St. Petersburg, FL	400	26
Riverview Tower (1977)	Knoxville, TN	400	24

IT'S A FACT: The world's highest highway bridge is the Millau Viaduct, which spans the River Tarn in southwestern France. Set to open to traffic in early 2005, the bridge has a maximum height of 885 ft. above the water, and the top of its tallest tower is 1,125 ft. above the valley—higher than the Eiffel Tower. (The Royal Gorge bridge above the Arkansas River in Colorado has a higher roadway, at 1,053 ft., but its towers do not extend into the gorge and it does not carry a highway.)

Notable Bridges in North America

Source: Federal Highway Administration, Bridge Division, U.S. Dept. of Transportation; World Almanac research
Asterisk (*) designates railroad bridge. Year is date of completion. Span of a bridge is the distance between its supports.

Suspension

Year	Bridge	Location	Main span (ft.)
1964	Verrazano-Narrows	New York, NY	4,205
1937	Golden Gate	San Fran. Bay, CA	4,200
1957	Mackinac Straits	Sts. of Mackinac, MI	3,800
1931	Geo. Washington	Hudson R., NY–NJ	3,500
2003	Carquinez (Al Zampa Memorial)	Solano, CA	3,478
1940	Tacoma Narrows	Tacoma, WA	2,800
1950	Tacoma Narrows II	Tacoma, WA	2,800
1936	San. Fran.-Oakland Bay[1]	San Fran. Bay, CA	2,310
1939	Bronx-Whitestone	East R., NY	2,300
1970	Pierre Laporte	Quebec, Canada	2,190
1951	Del. Memorial	Wilmington, DE	2,150
1957	Walt Whitman	Philadelphia, PA	2,000
1929	Ambassador	Detroit, MI–Can.	1,850
1961	Throgs Neck	Long Is. Sound, NY	1,780
1926	Benjamin Franklin	Philadelphia, PA	1,750
1924	Bear Mt.	Hudson R., NY	1,632
1903	Williamsburg	East R., NY	1,600
1952	Wm. Preston La. Mem.[2]	Sandy Point, MD	1,600
1969	Newport	Narragansett Bay, RI	1,600
1883	Brooklyn	East R., NY	1,596
1939	Lion's Gate	Burrard Inlet, BC	1,550
1963	Vincent Thomas	L. A. Harbor, CA	1,500
1930	Mid-Hudson	Poughkeepsie, NY	1,495
1909	Manhattan	East R., NY	1,470
1953	MacDonald Bridge	Halifax, Nova Scotia	1,447
1970	A. Murray Mackay	Halifax, Nova Scotia	1,400
1936	Triborough Br.,QB Mainline	East R., NY	1,380
1931	St. Johns	Portland, OR	1,207
1929	Mount Hope	RI	1,200
1960	Ogdensburg-Prescott	St. Lawrence R., NY	1,150
1965	Bidwell Bar Bridge	Oroville, CA	1,108
1964	Middle Fork Feather	Butte Co., CA	1,105
1939	Deer Isle	ME	1,080
1931	Simon Kenton Memorial	Ohio R., Maysville, KY.	1,060
1936	Ile d'Orleans	St. Lawrence R., Quebec	1,059
1867	John A. Roebling	Ohio R., KY	1,057
1971	Dent	Clearwater Co., ID	1,050
1900	Miampimi	Mexico	1,030
1849	Wheeling	Ohio R., WV	1,010

Cantilever

Year	Bridge	Location	Main span (ft.)
1917	Québec Bridge	St. Lawrence R., Quebec	1,800
1988	Greater New Orleans Bridge	Mississippi R., New Orleans, LA	1,575
1936	East Bay	San Fran. Bay, CA	1,499
1995	Gramercy Bridge	Mississippi R., Gramercy, LA	1,460
1968	Baton Rouge Bridge	Mississippi R., Baton Rouge, LA.	1,235
1953	Tappan Zee	Hudson R., NY	1,212
1930	Lewis and Clark	Longview, WA–OR	1,200
1909	Queensboro	East R., NY	1,182
1927	Carquinez Strait	San Fran. Bay, CA	1,100
1958	Parallel Span	San Fran. Bay, CA	1,100
1930	Jacques Cartier	Montreal, Quebec	1,097
1968	Isaiah D. Hart	Jacksonville, FL	1,088
1956	Richmond-San Rafael[3]	San Fran. Bay, CA	1,070
1929	Grace Memorial	Charleston, SC	1,050
1980	Newburgh-Beacon	Hudson R., NY	1,000
1949	Martin Luther King	St. Louis, MO	963
1975	Caruthersville	Mississippi R., MO–TN	920
1969	Silver Memorial	Pt. Pleasant, WV–OH	900
1977	Saint Marys	Saint Marys, WV–OH	900
1981	Ravenswood	WV	900
1987	Carl Perkins	Ohio R., KY	900
1941	Mississippi R.	Natchez, MS	875
1988	Mississippi R.	Natchez, MS	875
1938	Blue Water	Pt. Huron, MI	871
1972	Mississippi R.	Vicksburg, MS	870
1972	N. Fork American R.	Auburn, CA	862
1940	*Baton Rouge	Mississippi R., LA	848
1899	*Cornwall	St. Lawrence R.	843
1940	Rte. 82	Mississippi R., AR	840
1961	Mississippi R.	Greenville, MS	840
1963	Brent Spence	KY–OH	830
1940	Mississippi R.	Vicksburg, MS	825
1963	Mississippi R.	Donaldsonville, LA.	825
1931	Mississippi R.	Vicksburg, MS	824
1929	Clark Memorial	Ohio R., KY	820

Year	Bridge	Location	Main span (ft.)
1961	Campbellton-Cross Pt.	New Brunswick, Can.	815
1932	Washington Mem.	Seattle, WA	800
1935	Rip Van Winkle	Catskill, NY	800
1938	Cairo	Ohio R., IL–KY	800
1936	McCullough	Coos Bay, OR	793
1949	Memphis	Mississippi R., TN	790
1935	Huey P. Long[4]	New Orleans, LA	790
1949	Rte. 55	Mississippi R., AR–TN	790
1910	*P&LE RR Bridge	Ohio R., PA	750
1930	Coal Grove Bridge	Ashland-Coal Grove Bridge, OH	739
1922	Ohio River, N&W RR	Ironton-Russell Bridge, OH	725
1932	Bi-State Vietnam Gold Star	Henderson, KY.	720
1979	I-275	Ohio R., Fort Thomas, KY	720
1926	Columbia R.	Cascade Locks, OR	706
1964	John F. Kennedy (I-65)	Ohio R., Louisville, KY	700
1928	Ohio River, B&O RR, HV RR	Pomeroy-Mason, OH	657
1941	*Pit River	Redding, CA	630
1941	Columbia R.	Kettle Falls, WA	600
1954	Columbia R.	Umatilla, OR	600
1965	Bi-State Vietnam Gold Star	Henderson , KY	600
1954	Columbia R.	The Dalles, OR	576
1968	W. 17th St.	Huntington, WV	562

Simple Truss

Year	Bridge	Location	Main span (ft.)
1976	Chester	Chester, WV	745
1929	Irvin S. Cobb	Ohio R., IL–KY	716
1922	*Tanana R.	Nenana, AK	700
1967	I-77, Ohio R.	Williamstown, WV.	650
1917	MacArthur[4]	St. Louis, IL–MO.	647
1992	St. Charles	Missouri R, MO.	625
1933	Atchafalaya	Morgan City, LA	608
1924	*Castleton	Hudson R., NY	598
1937	Delaware R.	Easton, PA	550
1930	Swindell Bridge	Pittsburgh, PA	545
1952	Allegheny R. Tpk.	Pittsburgh, PA	534
1951	Rankin	Pittsburgh, PA	525
1914	Old Brownsville	Brownsville, PA	520
1906	Donora-Webster	Donora-Webster, PA	515
1909	Hulton	Pittsburgh, PA	505
1967	Tanana R.	AK.	500

Steel Truss

Year	Bridge	Location	Main span (ft.)
1988	Glade Creek	Raleigh Co., WV	784
1973	Atchafalaya R.	Krotz Springs, LA	780
1972	Piscataqua R.	NH–ME.	756
1972	Atchafalaya R.	Simmesport, LA	720
1957	SR-3, Rappahannock R.	Middlesex Co., VA	648
1978	Atchafalaya R.	Morgan City, LA	607
1959	Summit	Summit, DE	600
1969	Reedy Point	Delaware City, DE	600
1937	US-22	Delaware R., NJ	550
1955	Interstate (I-5)	Columbia R., OR–WA	531
1910	McKinley, St. Louis[4]	Mississippi R., MO	517
1972	Mississippi R.	Muscatine, IA	512
1896	Newport	Ohio R., KY	511
1989	US 190, Atchafalaya R.	Krotz Springs, LA	506
1900	Norfolk Southern RR	Cincinnati, OH	500
1931	Lucy Jefferson Lewis	Cumberland R., KY	500
1958	Lake Oahe	Gettysburg, SD	500
1958	Lake Oahe	Mobridge, SD	500
1970	Lake Koocanusa	Lincoln Co., MT	500

Continuous Truss

Year	Bridge	Location	Main span (ft.)
1966	Columbia R. (Astoria)	OR–WA	1,232
1976	Francis Scott Key	Baltimore, MD.	1,200
1981	Ravenswood/Ohio R.	Ravenswood, WV.	902
1995	Central	Ohio R., KY–OH.	850
1943	Dubuque	Mississippi R., IA	845
1966	Charles Braga	Fall River, MA.	840
1956	Earl C. Clements[5]	Ohio R., IL–KY	825
1929	U.S. 31	Ohio R., IN–KY.	820
1953	John E. Mathews	Jacksonville, FL	810
1950	Maurice J. Tobin	Boston, MA.	801
1940	Gov. Nice Memorial	Potomac River, MD	800
1957	Kingston-Rhinecliff	Hudson R., NY	800
1992	Mark Clark Expy. I-526	Cooper R., Charleston, SC.	800
1986	Rochester-Monaca	Rochester-Monaca, PA	780
1940	U.S. 231	Ohio R., IN	750
1974	Carroll L. Cropper (I-275)	Ohio R., IN–KY.	750
1981	Sewickley	Sewickley, PA.	750
1984	13th St. Bridge, Ohio R.	Ashland, KY	740

Year	Bridge	Location	Main span (ft.)
1959	Monaca-E. Rochester	Monaca-E. Rochester, PA.	730
1976	Betsy Ross	Philadelphia, PA	729
1929	U.S. 421	Ohio R., IN–KY	727
1967	Matthew E. Welsh[6]	Mauckport, IN	725
1962	U.S. 41	Ohio R., IN–KY	720
1994	6th St.	Huntington, WV	720
1970	Vanport	Vanport, PA	715
1962	Champlain	Montreal, Que.	707
1962	John F. Kennedy (I-65)[7]	Ohio R., IN–KY	701
1973	Girard Point	Philadelphia, PA	700
1954	PA Tpk., Delaware R.	Philadelphia, PA	682
1938	Rainbow Br., Neches R.	Port Arthur-Orange, TX	680
1949	George Platt	Philadelphia, PA	680
1926	Cape Girardeau	Mississippi R., MO	677
1946	Chester	Mississippi R, IL	670
1994	Williamstown-Marietta	Williamstown, WV	650
1955	Jefferson City	Missouri R., MO	640
1930	Quincy Memorial Bridge	Mississippi R., IL	628
1959	US 181, over harbor	Corpus Christi, TX	620
1961	Shippingport	Shippingport, PA	620
1935	Bourne-Sagamore	Cape Cod Canal, MA	616
1965	Clarion R. (I-80)	Clarion, PA	612
1975	Donora-Monessen	Donora-Monessen, PA	608
1957	Blatnik	Duluth, MN	600
1965	Rio Grande Gorge	Taos, NM	600
1991	Hoffstadt Creek	Mt. St. Helens, WA	600
1991	Jefferson City	Missouri R., MO	596
1962	W. Branch Feather R.	Oroville, CA	576
1967	Glenwood	Pittsburgh, PA	567
1936	Mark Twain Mem.	Hannibal, MO	562
1932	Pulaski Skyway	Passaic R.-Hackensack R., NJ	550
1966	Emlenton	Emlenton, PA	540
1973	Gold Star Memorial	New London, CT	540
1936	Homestead High Level	Pittsburgh, PA	534
1962	Benicia Martinez	Benicia-Martinez, CA	528
1960	Brownsville High Level	Brownsville, PA	518
1971	Grandad	Elk River, ID	504
1945	Mansfield-Dravosburg	Pittsburgh, PA	500

Continuous Box and Plate Girder

Year	Bridge	Location	Main span (ft.)
1967	San Mateo-Hayward #2	San Fran. Bay, CA	750
1976	Intracoastal Canal	Forked Is., LA	750
1977	Intracoastal Canal	Gibbstown, LA	750
1969	San Diego-Coronado[8]	San Diego Bay, CA	660
1987	Umatilla, Columbia R.	OR–WA	660
1994	Acosta	Jacksonville, FL	630
1981	Douglas	Juneau, AK	620
1976	Wax L. Outlet	Calumet, LA	618
1963	Poplar St.	St. Louis, MO	600
1981	Glenn Jackson (I-205)	Columbia R., OR–WA	600
1976	Stanislaus River	Sonora, CA	550
1982	Illinois R.	Pekin, IL	550
1982	I-440	Arkansas R., AR	540
1980	US-64, Tennessee R.	Savannah, TN	525
1965	McDonald-Cartier	Ottawa, Ont.	520
1988	Mon City	Monongahela, PA	520
1984	Columbia R.	Richland, WA	450
1986	Veterans	Pittsburgh, PA	440
1987	SR 76, Cumberland R.	Dover, TN	440
1987	SR 20, Tennessee R.	Perryville, TN	440
1970	Willamette R., I-205	West Linn, OR	430
1974	I-430	Arkansas R., AR	430
1965	I-24, Tennessee R.	Marion Co., TN	420
1974	Dunbar-S. Charleston	S. Charleston, WV	420
1975	36th St.	Charleston, WV	420
1978	Snake R.	Clarkston, WA	420
1984	FAU 3456, TN R.	Chattanooga, TN	420

Continuous Plate

Year	Bridge	Location	Main span (ft.)
1973	Sidney Sherman Bridge, I-610	Houston, TX	630
1971	W. Atchafalaya	Henderson, LA	573
1992	State Route 76	Paris, TN	525
1997	SR 114, Clifton	Tennessee R., TN	525
1981	Illinois 23	Illinois R., IL	510
1968	IH-45 over Trinity R.	Dallas, TX	480
1978	San Joaquin R.	Antioch, CA	460
1977	Thomas Johnson Mem.	Solomons, MD	451
1967	Mississippi R.	La Crosse, WI	450
1975	I-129	Missouri R., IA–NE	450
1979	Lewis	St. Louis, MO	450
1992	Cuba Landing Bridge	Tennessee R., TN	450
1966	I-480	Missouri R., IA–NE	425
1972	Whiskey Bay Pilot	Ramah, LA	425
1972	I-80	Missouri R., IA–NE	425
1972	I-635, Kansas City	Missouri R., KS–MO	425
1983	US-36	Missouri R., KS–MO	425
1987	I-435	Missouri R., KS–MO	425
1978	I-24	Cumberland R., KY	420
1993	Bob Michel Bridge	Peoria, IL	360
1999	SR 53, Clear Fork River	Fentress/Morgan Co., TN	350

Cable-Stayed

Year	Bridge	Location	Main span (ft.)
1986	Annacis (Alex Fraser)	Vancouver, BC	1,526
1993	Quetzalapa Bridge	Quetzalapa, Mexico	1,391
1988	Dames Point	Jacksonville, FL	1,300
1995	Fred Hartlan Bridge, Houston Ship Channel	Baytown,TX	1,250
1983	Hale Boggs Memorial	Luling, LA	1,222
1987	Sunshine Skyway	Tampa Bay, FL	1,200
1988	Tampico/Panuco R.	Mexico	1,181
1988	ALRT Fraser River Bridge	Vancouver, BC	1,115
1990	Talmadge Mem.	Savannah, GA	1,100
1993	Mezcala	Mex. City/Acapulco Hwy.	1,024
1978	Pasco-Kennewick	Columbia R., WA	981
1984	Coatzacoalcos R.	Mexico	919
1985	E. Huntington	E. Huntington, WV	900
1987	Bayview Bridge	Quincy, IL	900
1970	Burton Bridge	New Brunswick, Canada	850
1990	Weirton-Steubenville	WV–OH	820
1969	Papineau-Leblanc	Montreal, Que.	790
1991	Cochrane	Mobile, AL	780
1994	Clark Bridge	Alton, IL	756
1995	Chesapeake & Delaware Canal Bridge	Dover-Wilmington, DE	750
2002	Leonard Zakim	Bunker Hill, Boston, MA	745
1966	Longs Creek	New Brunswick, Canada	713
1967	Hawkshaw	New Brunswick, Canada	713
1993	Quetzalapa Bridge	Quetzalapa, Mexico	699
1993	Burlington Bridge	Burlington, IA	660
1991	Veterans Memorial Br., Neches R.	Port Arthur-Orange,TX	640
1989	James River Bridge	Richmond, VA	630

I-Beam Girder

Year	Bridge	Location	Main span (ft.)
1980	Interstate 20	Shreveport, LA	438
2001	Moore Haven Bridge	Caloosahachee Canal, FL.	320
1988	Route 18	Weston's Mill Pond, NJ	276

Steel Arch

Year	Bridge	Location	Main span (ft.)
1977	New River Gorge	Fayetteville, WV	1,700
1931	Bayonne (Kill Van Kull)	Bayonne, NJ	1,675
1973	Fremont	Portland, OR	1,255
1964	Port Mann	Vancouver, BC	1,200
1967	Lavioleete	Three Rivers, Canada	1,100
1967	Trois-Rivieres	St. Lawrence R., Que.	1,100
1992	Roosevelt Lake	Roosevelt Lake, AZ	1,080
1917	*Hell Gate	East R., N.Y	1,038
1959	Glen Canyon	Page, AZ	1,028
1962	Lewiston-Queenston	Niagara R., Ont.	1,000
1976	Perrine	Twin Falls, ID	993
1941	Rainbow Bridge	Niagara Falls, NY	984
1977	Moundsville	Ohio R., WV	912
1992	I-255, Miss. R.	St. Louis, MO	909
1972	I-40, Miss. R.[9]	AR–TN	900
1936	Henry Hudson	Harlem R., NY	840
1967	Lincoln Trail Bridge	Ohio R., IN–KY	825
1978	I-57, Miss. R.	Cairo , IL	821
1961	Sherman-Minton Bridge, I-64	IN	800
1980	I-65, Mobile R.	Mobile, AL	800
1930	West End	Pittsburgh, PA	780
1978	I-470 Bridge, Ohio R.	Wheeling, WV	780
1996	Navajo Bridge	Glen Canyon, AZ	726
1959	Kosciusko Twin	Mohawk R., NY	600
1917	Cuyohoga River	Cleveland, OH	591
2002	Paper Mill Ridge Road	Baltimore, MD	518

Concrete Arch

Year	Bridge	Location	Main span (ft.)
1995	Natchez Trace Pkwy.	Franklin, TN	582
1993	Lake Street Bridge	St. Paul, MN	556
1971	Selah Creek (twin)	Selah, WA	549
1968	Cowlitz R.	Mossyrock, WA	520
1931	Westinghouse	Pittsburgh, PA	460
1923	Cappelen	Minneapolis, MN	435
2000	Crooked River Gorge	Madras, OR	410
1930	Jack's Run	Pittsburgh, PA	400
1931	Rogue River	Gold Beach, OR	230

Segmental Concrete

Year	Bridge	Location	Main span (ft.)
1997	Confederation Bridge	Prince Edward Isl., NB	820
1978	Shubenacadie River	S. Maitland, Nova Scotia	790
1982	Jesse H, Jones Memorial	Houston, TX	750
1992	Narragansett Bay Crossing	Jamestown, RI	674
2002	SR-895, James R. & I-95	Richmond, VA	672
1986	WB I-82 (Columbia R.)	Umatilla, OR	660
1978	Stanislaus River	Parrets Ferry. CA	640
1992	Jamestown-Verrazano	Jamestown, RI	636
1981	Gastineau Channel Br.	Juneau, AK	620
1991	Veterans Memorial Centennial Bridge	Coeur d'Alene, ID	520
2001	Smart Highway	Blacksburg, VA	472
1974	Pine Valley Creek	Pine Valley, CA	450
1988	Zilwaukee Bridge (twin)	Zilwaukee, MI	392
1985	Red River Bridge	Boyce, LA	370

Twin Concrete Trestle[10]

Year	Bridge	Location	Main span (ft.)
1979	I-55/I-10	Manchac, LA	181,157
1969	L. Pontchartrain Cswy.	Mandeville, LA	126,720
1972	Atchafalaya Flwy.	Baton Rouge, LA	93,984
1963	L. Pontchartrain	Slidell, LA	28,547
1983	*Interstate 310	Kenner, LA	25,925

Concrete Slab Dam[10]

1927	Conowingo Dam	MD	4,611
1952	SR-4, Roanoke R.	Mecklenburg Co., VA	2,785
1936	Hoover Dam	Lake Mead, NV	1,324

Miscellaneous Bridges

Year	Bridge	Type	Loc.	Main span (ft.)
1962	International	Arch Truss	Sault Ste. Marie, MI	430
1997	Second Blue Water	Continuous Tied Arch	Pt. Huron, MI	922
1982	SR 193	Seg. Box Girder	Dauphin Is., AL	400
1958	Castleton	Through Truss	Hudson R., NY	598
1939	US 43, Tenn. R.	Through Truss	Florence, AL	420
1958	SR 117, Tenn. R.	Through Truss	Stevenson, AL	500
1936	Yaquina Bay	Steel Braced and Concrete Tied Arches	Newport, OR	600
1958	Tombigbee R.	Steel Girder	Choctaw Co., AL	400
1916	C&O RR	Steel Girder	Portsmouth, OH	775
1987	Powder Point[10]	Tropical Hardwood	Duxbury, MA	2,200
2002	Croatan Sound[10]	Continuous Postension Girder	Manteo, NC	5.2 mi

Drawbridges

Vertical Lift

Year	Bridge	Location	Main span (ft.)
1959	*Arthur Kill	NY–NJ	558
1965	Pennsylvania Railroad	Kirkwood-Mt. Pleas., DE	548
1935	*Cape Cod Canal	Cape Cod, MA	544
1961	*Delair	Delaware R., NJ	542
1931	Burlington-Bristol	Delaware R., NJ–PA	540
1937	Marine Parkway	Jamaica Bay, NY	540
1908	*Willamette R.	Portland, OR	521
1968	Second Narrows	Vancouver, B.C.	493
1912	*A-S-B Fratt	Kansas City, MO	428
1945	*Harry S Truman	Kansas City, MO	427
1955	Roosevelt Island	East R., NY	418
1980	US-17, James R.	Isle of Wight, Co., VA	415

Year	Bridge	Location	Main span (ft.)
1932	*M-K-T R.R.	Missouri R., MO	414
1969	Cape Fear Mem.	Wilmington, NC	408
1930	Aerial	Duluth, MN	386
1962	Burlington	Ontario, Can.	370
1941	Main Street	Jacksonville, FL	365
1967	SR-156, James R.	Prince George Co., VA	364
1950	Red R.	Moncla, LA	360
1957	Industrial Canal	New Orleans, LA	360
1936	Triborough	Harlem R., NY	344
1939	U.S. 1&9, Passaic R.	Newark, NJ	333
1930	*Martinez	Martinez, CA.	328
1960	St. Andrews Bay	Panama City, FL	327
1929	*Penn-Lehigh	Newark Bay, PA	322
1987	Industrial Canal	New Orleans, LA	320
1920	*Chattanooga	Tennessee R., TN	310
1961	Broadway	Harlem R., NY	304
1910	Willamette R. Hawthorne	Portland, OR	244

Steel Suspension

1931	Maumee R.	Toledo, OH	785

Bascule

1917	SR-8, Tennessee R.	Chattanooga, TN	306
2003	*SW 2nd Avenue Br	Miami, FL	302
1956	Duwamish R.	Seattle, WA	300
1955	Chehalis R.	Aberdeen, WA	288
1968	Elizabeth R.	Chesapeake, VA	280
1913	Broadway	Portland, OR.	278
1936	Siuslaw River	Florence, OR	154

Swing Bridges

1927	Fort Madison[4]	Mississippi R., IA	545
1991	SW. Spokane St.	Seattle, WA	480
1930	Rigolets Pass	New Orleans, LA	400
1950	Douglass Memorial	Washington, DC	386
1945	Lord Delaware	Mattaponi R., VA	252

Swing Span

1897	*Duluth	St. Louis Bay, MN.	486
1899	*C.M.&N.R.R.	Chicago, IL	474
1913	Rt. 82, Conn-R.	E. Haddam, CT.	465
1914	*Coos Bay RR Xing	OR	458
1936	Umpqua River	Reedsport. OR	430

Floating Pontoon

1963	Evergreen Pt.	Seattle, WA	7,578
1961	Hood Canal	Pt. Gamble, WA	6,521
1993	Lacey V. Murrow[11]	Seattle, WA	6,620
1989	Third Lake Washington	Seattle, WA	5,811

(1) Swing span bridge with 2 spans of 2,310 ft. each. (2) A second bridge in parallel was completed in 1978. (3) The Richmond Bridge has twin spans 1,070 ft. each. (4) Railroad and vehicular bridge. (5) Two spans each 825 ft. (6) Two spans each 707 ft. (7) Two spans each 700 ft. (8) Two spans each 660 ft. (9) Two spans each 900 ft. (10) Length listed is total length of bridge. (11) Replaces the original Lacey V. Murrow bridge, which opened in 1940 and sank in 1990.

Oldest U.S. Bridges in Continuous Use

Built in 1697, the stone-arch Frankford Ave. Bridge crosses Pennypack Creek in Philadelphia, PA. A 3-span bridge with a total length of 75 ft., it was constructed as part of the King's Road, which eventually connected Philadelphia to New York.

The oldest covered bridge, completed in 1827, is the double-span, 278-ft. Haverhill Bath Bridge, which spans the Ammonoosuc River, between the towns of Bath and Haverhill, NH.

Some Notable International Bridges

Span of bridge is the distance between its supports. Asterisk (*) designates under construction.

Suspension

Year	Bridge	Location	Main span (ft.)
1998	Akashi Kaikyo	Japan	6,570
NA	*Izmit Bay	Turkey	5,538
1998	Storebælt (East Bridge)	Denmark	5,328
1981	Humber	England	4,626
1999	Jiangyin Yangtze	China	4,544
1997	Tsing Ma[1]	China	4,518
1997	Hoga Kusten	Sweden	3,970
1988	Minami Bisan-Seto	Japan	3,609
1988	Bosphorus II	Turkey	3,576
1973	Bosphorus I	Turkey	3,524
1999	Kurushima III	Japan	3,379
1999	Kurushima II	Japan	3,346
1966	Tagus River[2]	Portugal	3,323
1964	Forth Road	Scotland	3,300
1988	Kita Bisan-Seto	Japan	3,248
1966	Severn	England	3,241
2001	Yichang	China	3,150
1988	Shimotsui Strait	Japan	3,084

Steel Arch

1932	Sydney Harbour	Australia	1,650
1967	Zdakov	Czech Republic	1,244
1962	Thatcher	Panama Canal Zone	1,128
1961	Runcorn-Widnes	England	1,082
1935	Birchenough	Zimbabwe	1,080

Concrete Arch

1980	Krk I	Croatia	1,280
1964	Gladesville	Australia	1,000
1964	Amizade	Brazil	951

Year	Bridge	Location	Main span (ft.)
1963	Arrabida	Portugal	886
1943	Sando	Sweden	866

Cantilever

1890	Forth[3] (rail)	Scotland	1,710
1974	Nanko	Japan	1,673

Steel Plate and Box Girder

1974	President Costa e Silva	Brazil	984
1956	Sava I	Serbia & Montenegro	856
1966	Zoobrüke	Germany	850

Cable-Stayed

2005	Millau Viaduc	France	8,071
1999	Tatara	Japan	2,920
1995	Pont de Normandie	France	2,808
1996	Quingzhou Minjang	China	1,985
1993	Yangpu	China	1,975
1997	Xupu	China	1,936
1998	Meiko Chuo	Japan	1,936
1991	Skarnsundet	Norway	1,739
1999	Queshi	China	1,700
1995	Tsurumi Tsubasa	Japan	1,673
2000	Oresund	Denmark/Sweden	1,614
1991	Ikuchi	Japan	1,608
1994	Higashi Kobe	Japan	1,591
1998	Zhanjiang	China	1,559
1997	Ting Kau	China	1,558
1999	Seo Hae Grand	South Korea	1,542
1989	Yokohama Bay	Japan	1,509
1993	Second Hooghly River	India	1,499
1995	Second Severn Crossing	England/Wales	1,496

NA = not available. (1) Double-decked road and rail bridge. (2) Railroad and highway bridge. (3) Two spans of 1,710 ft. each.

World's Longest Railway Tunnels

Source: World Almanac research

Tunnel	Date	Miles	Operating railway	Country
Seikan	1988	33.5	Japan Railways	Japan
English Channel Tunnel	1994	31.3	Eurotunnel	UK-France
Iwate-ichinohe	2002	16.0	Japan Railways	Japan
Dai-shimizu	1982	13.8	Japan Railways	Japan
Simplon No. 1 and 2	1906, 1922	12.3	BLS Lötschberbahn AG	Switzerland-Italy
Vereina	1999	11.8	Rhätische Bahn	Switzerland
Kanmon	1975	11.6	Japan Railways	Japan
Apennine	1934	11.5	Italian state	Italy
Qinling No. 1 and 2	2002	11.5	Chinese state	China
Rokko	1972	10.1	Japan Railways	Japan
Furka Base Tunnel	1982	9.6	Furka Oberalp Bahn	Switzerland
Haruna	1982	9.5	Japan Railways	Japan
Severomuyskiy	2001	9.5	Baikal-Amur (state-owned)	Russia
Gorigamine	1997	9.4	Japan Railways	Japan
Monte Santomarco	1987	9.3	Italian state	Italy

Underwater Vehicular Tunnels in North America

(more than 5,000 ft. in length; year in parentheses is year of completion)

Name	Location	Waterway	Feet
Brooklyn-Battery (1950) (twin)	New York, NY	East River	9,117
Holland Tunnel (1927) (twin)	New York, NY	Hudson River	8,557
Ted Williams Tunnel (1995)	Boston, MA	Boston Harbor	8,448
Lincoln Tunnel (1937, 1945, 1957) (3 tubes)	New York, NY	Hudson River	8,216
Thimble Shoal Channel (1964)	Northampton Co., VA	Chesapeake Bay	8,187
Chesapeake Channel (1964)	Northampton Co., VA	Chesapeake Bay	7,941
Fort McHenry Tunnel (1985) (twin)	Baltimore, MD	Baltimore Harbor	7,920
Hampton Roads (1957) (twin)	Hampton, VA	Hampton Roads	7,479
Baltimore Harbor Tunnel (1957) (twin)	Baltimore, MD	Patapsco River	7,392
Queens Midtown (1940) (twin)	New York, NY	East River	6,414
Sumner Tunnel (1934)	Boston, MA	Boston Harbor	5,653
Louis-Hippolyte Lafontaine Tunnel	Montreal, Que.	St. Lawrence River	5,280
Detroit-Windsor (1930)	Detroit, MI	Detroit River	5,160
Callahan Tunnel (1961)	Boston, MA	Boston Harbor	5,070

Land Vehicular Tunnels in the U.S.

Source: Federal Highway Administration

(more than 3,000 ft. in length)

Name	Location	Feet	Name	Location	Feet
Anton Anderson Mem. Tunnel[1]	Whittier, AK	13,300	Blue Mountain (twin)	PA Turnpike	4,435
E. Johnson Memorial	I-70, CO	8,959	Lehigh (twin)	PA Turnpike	4,379
Eisenhower Memorial	I-70, CO	8,941	Wawona	Yosemite Natl. Pk., CA	4,233
Allegheny (twin)	PA Turnpike	6,072	Big Walker Mt. (twin)	Bland Co., VA	4,229
Liberty Tubes	Pittsburgh, PA	5,920	Squirrel Hill	Pittsburgh, PA	4,225
Zion Natl. Park	Rte. 9, UT	5,766	Hanging Lake (twin)	Glenwood Canyon, CO	4,000
East River Mt.	Mercer Co., WV/ Bland Co., VA	5,654	Caldecott (3 tubes)	Oakland, CA	3,616
			Fort Pitt (twin)	Pittsburgh, PA	3,560
East River Mt. (twin)	VA–WV	5,412	Mount Baker Ridge	Seattle, WA	3,456
Tuscarora (twin)	PA Turnpike	5,400	Devil's Side Tunnel	U.S. 101 CA	3,400
Tetsuo Harano (twin)	H-3, HI	5,165	Dingess Tunnel	Mingo Co., WV	3,400
Kittatinny (twin)	PA Turnpike	4,660	Mall Tunnel	Dist. of Columbia	3,400
Cumberland Gap (twin)	KY–TN	4,600	Cody No. 1	U.S. 14, 16, 20, WY	3,202

(1) Tunnel is used for vehicular and railroad traffic.

Major Dams of the World

Source: Intl. Commission on Large Dams, *World Register of Dams 2003*

World's Highest Dams

Rank order	Name	Country	Height above lowest formation (m)
1.	Rogun*	Tajikistan	335
2.	Nurek*	Tajikistan	300
3.	Xiaowan (Yunnan Gorge)*	China	292
4.	Grand Dixence	Switzerland	285
5.	Inguri	Georgia	272
6.	Vajont	Italy	262
7.	Manuel M. Torres	Mexico	261
8.	Tehri*	India	261
9.	Alvaro Obregon	Mexico	260
10.	Mauvoisin	Switzerland	250
11.	Mica	Canada	243
12.	Alberto Lleras C	Colombia	243
13.	Sayano-Shushenskskaya	Russia	242
14.	Ertan*	China	240
15.	La Esmeralda	Colombia	237
16.	Kishau*	India	236
17.	Oroville	U.S.	235
18.	El Cajón	Honduras	234
19.	Chirkey	Russia	233
20.	Shuibuya*	China	233

World's Largest-Volume Embankment Dams

Rank order	Name	Country	Volume cubic meters x 1000
1.	Tarbela	Pakistan	148,500
2.	Fort Peck Gorge	U.S.	96,050
3.	Tucurui	Brazil	85,200
4.	Ataturk	Turkey	85,000
5.	Yacyreta	Argentina	81,000
6.	Rogun*	Tajikistan	75,500
7.	Oahe	U.S.	70,339
8.	Guri	Venezuela	70,000
9.	Parambikulam	India	69,165
10.	High Island West	China	67,000
11.	Gardiner	Canada	65,000
12.	Afsluitdijk	Netherlands	63,400
13.	Mangla	Pakistan	63,379
14.	Oroville	U.S.	59,635
15.	San Luis	U.S.	59,559
16.	Nurek*	Tajikistan	58,000
17.	Tanda	Pakistan	57,250
18.	Garrison	U.S.	50,843
19.	Cochiti	U.S.	50,228
20.	Oosterschelde	Netherlands	50,000

*Under construction.

WORLD ALMANAC QUICK QUIZ

Can you rank these cities by height in feet of their tallest building (excluding antenna) highest to lowest?

(a) Seattle, WA   (b) Chicago, IL   (c) Boston, MA   (d) Los Angeles, CA

For the answer look in this chapter, or see page 1008.

> **IT'S A FACT:** When completed in 2009, the Three Gorges Dam in China will be the world's largest dam, made of 989 million cubic feet of concrete. Spanning 1.3 miles across the Yangtze (Chang) River, the dam will create a reservoir about 360 miles long, holding some 1.39 trillion cubic feet of water, so much that it will take 6 years to fill. Its 18,200-megawatt hydroelectric plant will also be the world's largest, generating as much energy as 15 nuclear power plants. To make room for the reservoir over 1 million people were being be relocated, and countless villages, burial grounds, and archaeological sites flooded.

Major U.S. Dams and Reservoirs

Source: Committee on Register of Dams, Corps of Engineers, U.S. Army, Sept. 2004

Highest U.S. Dams

Rank Order	Dam name	River	State	Type	Height Feet	Height Meters	Year completed
1.	Oroville	Feather	California	E	770	230	1968
2.	Hoover	Colorado	Nevada-Arizona	A	730	221	1936
3.	Dworshak	N. Fork Clearwater	Idaho	G	717	219	1973
4.	Glen Canyon	Colorado	Arizona	A	710	216	1964
5.	New Bullards Bar	North Yuba	California	A	645	194	1969
6.	Seven Oaks	Santa Ana	California	E	632	193	1999
7.	New Melones	Stanislaus	California	R	625	191	1979
8.	Mossyrock	Cowlitz	Washington	A	606	185	1968
9.	Shasta	Sacramento	California	G	602	183	1945
10.	Don Pedro	Tuolumne	California	G	585	178	1971

E = Embankment, Earthfill; R = Embankment, Rockfill; G = Gravity; A = Arch.

Largest U.S. Embankment Dams

Rank Order	Dam name	River	State	Type	Volume Cubic yards x 1000	Volume Cubic meters x 1000	Year completed
1.	Fort Peck	Missouri	Montana	E	125,624	96,050	1957
2.	Oahe	Missouri	South Dakota	E	91,996	70,339	1958
3.	Oroville	Feather	California	E	77,997	59,635	1968
4.	San Luis	San Luis Creek	California	E	77,897	59,559	1967
5.	Garrison	Missouri	North Dakota	E	66,498	50,843	1953
6.	Cochiti	Rio Grande	New Mexico	E	65,693	50,228	1975
7.	Fort Randall	Missouri	South Dakota	E	49,962	38,200	1952
8.	Castaic	Castaic Creek	California	E	43,998	33,640	1973
9.	Ludington P/S	Lake Michigan	Michigan	E	37,699	28,824	1973
10.	Kingsley	N. Platte	Nebraska	E	31,999	24,466	1941

E = Earthfill.

Largest U.S. Reservoirs

Rank Order	Dam name	Reservoir name	State	Reservoir capacity Acre-Feet	Reservoir capacity Cubic meters x 1000	Year completed
1.	Hoover	Lake Mead	Nevada	28,255,000	34,850,000	1936
2.	Glen Canyon	Lake Powell	Arizona	27,000,000	33,300,000	1964
3.	Oahe	Lake Oahe	South Dakota	19,300,000	27,430,000	1966
4.	Garrison	Lake Sakakawea	North Dakota	18,500,000	27,920,000	1953
5.	Fort Peck	Fort Peck Lake	Montana	15,400,000	22,120,000	1957
6.	Grand Coulee	F. D. Roosevelt Lake	Washington	9,562,000	11,790,000	1942
7.	Libby	Lake Koocanusa	Montana	5,809,000	7,170,000	1973
8.	Shasta	Lake Shasta	California	4,552,000	5,610,000	1945
9.	Toledo Bend	Toledo Bend Lake	Louisiana	4,477,000	5,520,000	1966
10.	Fort Randall	Lake Francis Case	South Dakota	3,800,000	5,700,000	1954

1 acre-foot = 1 acre of water, 1 foot deep

World's Largest-Capacity Reservoirs

Source: Intl. Commission on Large Dams, *World Register of Dams 2003*

Rank order	Name	Country	Capacity cubic meters x 1,000,000	Rank order	Name	Country	Capacity cubic meters x 1,000,000
1.	Kariba Gorges	Zimbabwe/Zambia	180,600	9.	Zeya	Russia	68,400
2.	Bratsk	Russia	169,000	10.	La Grande 2	Canada	61,715
3.	High Aswan	Egypt	162,000	11.	La Grande 3	Canada	60,020
4.	Akosombo	Ghana	147,960	12.	Ust-Ilim	Russia	59,300
5.	Daniel Johnson	Canada	141,851	13.	Boguchany	Russia	58,200
6.	Guri	Venezuela	135,000	14.	Kuibyshev	Russia	58,000
7.	W.A.C. Bennett	Canada	74,300	15.	Serra da Mesa	Brazil	54,400
8.	Krasnoyarsk	Russia	73,300				

World's Largest-Capacity Hydro Plants

Source: Intl. Commission on Large Dams, *World Register of Dams 2003*

Rank[1]	Name	Country	Rated capacity planned (MW)	Rank[1]	Name	Country	Rated capacity planned (MW)
1.	Sanxia (Three Gorges Dam)*	China	18,200	11.	Ilha Solteira	Brazil	3,230
2.	Itaipu	Brazil/Paraguay	12,600	12.	Ertan	China	3,300
3.	Guri (Raúl Leoni)	Venezuela	10,000	13.	Yacyreta	Argentina/Paraguay	3,100
4.	Tucuruí	Brazil	8,370	14.	Xingo	Brazil	3,000
5.	Sayano-Shushenskaya*	Russia	6,400	15.	Macagua II	Venzuela	2,940
6.	Krasnoyarsk	Russia	6,000	16.	Gezhouba	China	2,715
7.	Bratsk	Russia	4,500	17.	Minamiaiki	Japan	2,700
8.	Xiaowan (Yunnan)	China	4,200	18.	Volgograd	Russia	2,541
9.	Longtan (Guangxi, Tian'e)	China	4,200	19.	Chief Joseph Dam	U.S.	2,512
10.	Ust-Ilim	Russia	3,840	20.	Paulo Afonso	Brazil	2,460

(1) Ranked by rated capacity planned. *Planned or under construction.

AFGHANISTAN	ALBANIA	ALGERIA	ANDORRA	ANGOLA
ANTIGUA AND BARBUDA	ARGENTINA	ARMENIA	AUSTRALIA	AUSTRIA
AZERBAIJAN	THE BAHAMAS	BAHRAIN	BANGLADESH	BARBADOS
BELARUS	BELGIUM	BELIZE	BENIN	BHUTAN
BOLIVIA	BOSNIA AND HERZEGOVINA	BOTSWANA	BRAZIL	BRUNEI
BULGARIA	BURKINA FASO	BURUNDI	CAMBODIA	CAMEROON
CANADA	CAPE VERDE	CENTRAL AFRICAN REPUBLIC	CHAD	CHILE
CHINA	COLOMBIA	COMOROS	CONGO, DEM. REP. OF THE	CONGO REPUBLIC
COSTA RICA	CÔTE D'IVOIRE	CROATIA	CUBA	CYPRUS
CZECH REPUBLIC	DENMARK	DJIBOUTI	DOMINICA	DOMINICAN REPUBLIC
EAST TIMOR	ECUADOR	EGYPT	EL SALVADOR	EQUATORIAL GUINEA

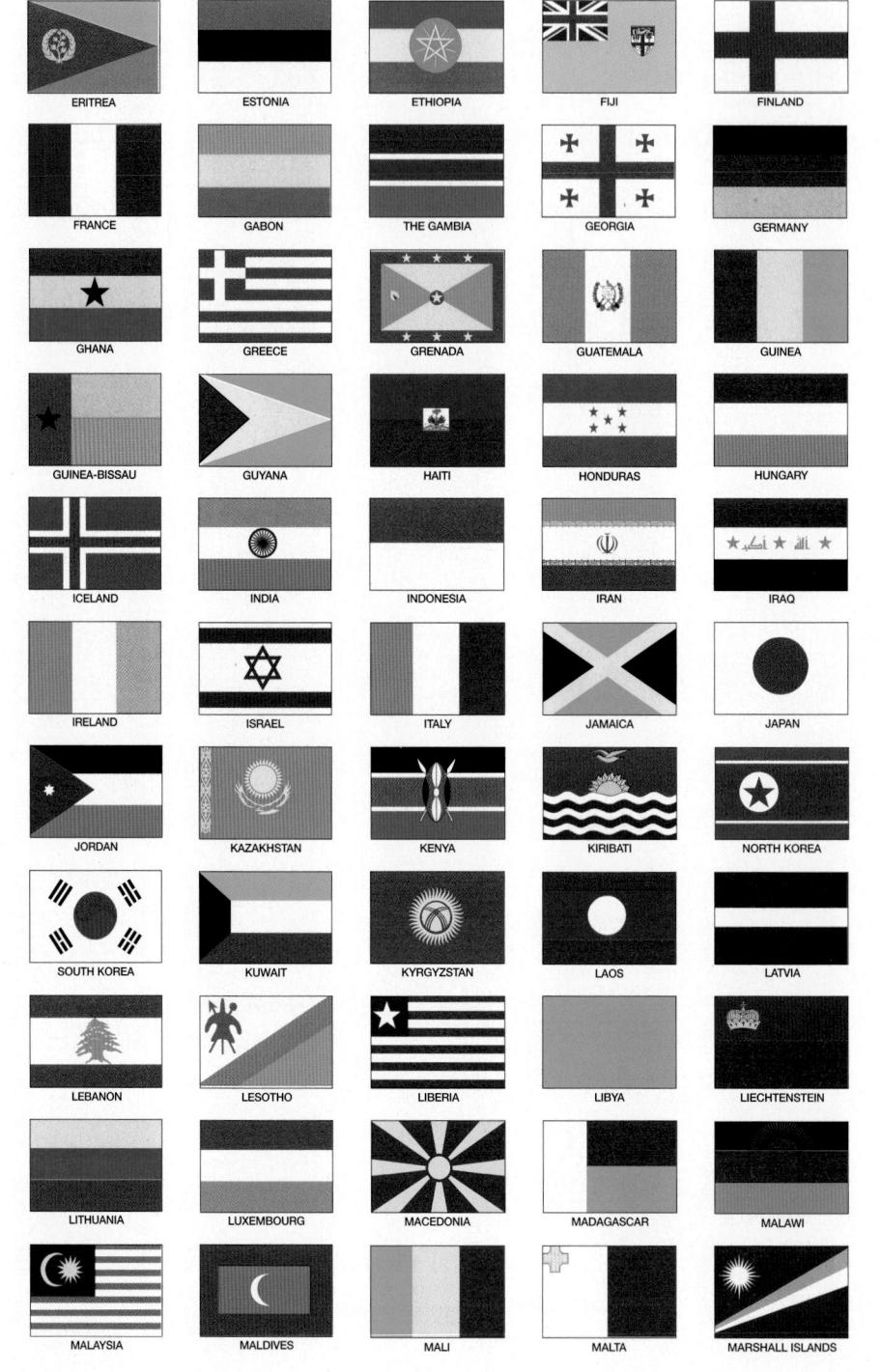

ERITREA	ESTONIA	ETHIOPIA	FIJI	FINLAND
FRANCE	GABON	THE GAMBIA	GEORGIA	GERMANY
GHANA	GREECE	GRENADA	GUATEMALA	GUINEA
GUINEA-BISSAU	GUYANA	HAITI	HONDURAS	HUNGARY
ICELAND	INDIA	INDONESIA	IRAN	IRAQ
IRELAND	ISRAEL	ITALY	JAMAICA	JAPAN
JORDAN	KAZAKHSTAN	KENYA	KIRIBATI	NORTH KOREA
SOUTH KOREA	KUWAIT	KYRGYZSTAN	LAOS	LATVIA
LEBANON	LESOTHO	LIBERIA	LIBYA	LIECHTENSTEIN
LITHUANIA	LUXEMBOURG	MACEDONIA	MADAGASCAR	MALAWI
MALAYSIA	MALDIVES	MALI	MALTA	MARSHALL ISLANDS

MAURITANIA MAURITIUS MEXICO MICRONESIA MOLDOVA

MONACO MONGOLIA MOROCCO MOZAMBIQUE MYANMAR (BURMA)

NAMIBIA NAURU NEPAL NETHERLANDS NEW ZEALAND

NICARAGUA NIGER NIGERIA NORWAY OMAN

PAKISTAN PALAU PANAMA PAPUA NEW GUINEA PARAGUAY

PERU PHILIPPINES POLAND PORTUGAL QATAR

ROMANIA RUSSIA RWANDA ST. KITTS AND NEVIS ST. LUCIA

ST. VINCENT AND THE GRENADINES SAMOA SAN MARINO SÃO TOMÉ AND PRÍNCIPE SAUDI ARABIA

SENEGAL SERBIA & MONTENEGRO SEYCHELLES SIERRA LEONE SINGAPORE

SLOVAKIA SLOVENIA SOLOMON ISLANDS SOMALIA SOUTH AFRICA

SPAIN SRI LANKA SUDAN SURINAME SWAZILAND

459

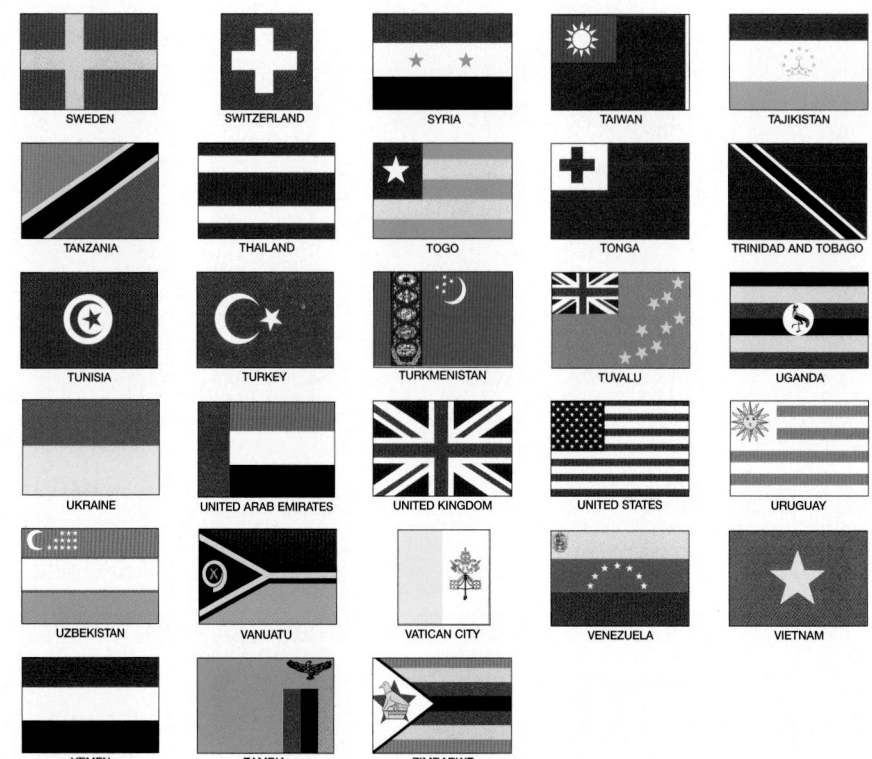

SWEDEN SWITZERLAND SYRIA TAIWAN TAJIKISTAN

TANZANIA THAILAND TOGO TONGA TRINIDAD AND TOBAGO

TUNISIA TURKEY TURKMENISTAN TUVALU UGANDA

UKRAINE UNITED ARAB EMIRATES UNITED KINGDOM UNITED STATES URUGUAY

UZBEKISTAN VANUATU VATICAN CITY VENEZUELA VIETNAM

YEMEN ZAMBIA ZIMBABWE

INTERNATIONAL TIME ZONES

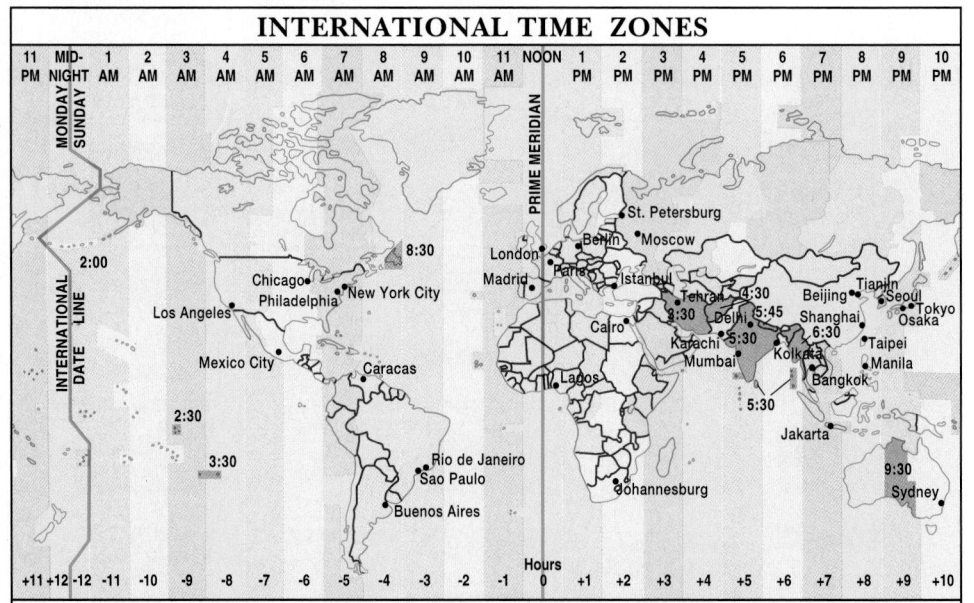

The world is divided into 24 time zones, each 15° longitude wide. The longitudinal meridian passing through Greenwich, England, is the starting point, and is called the *prime meridian.* The 12th zone is divided by the 180th meridian (International Date Line). When the line is crossed going west, the date is advanced one day; when crossed going east, the date becomes a day earlier.

© MAPQUEST

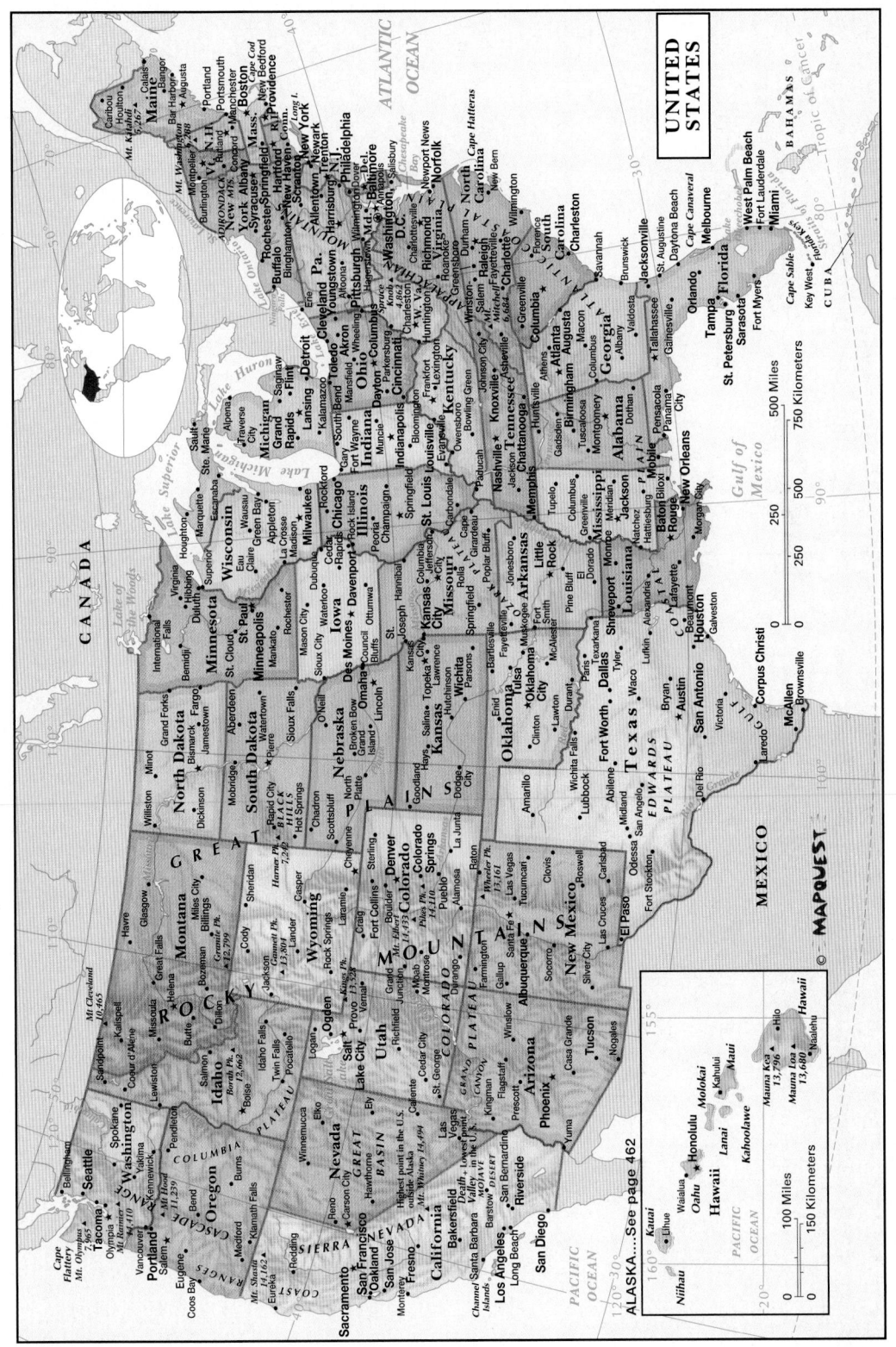

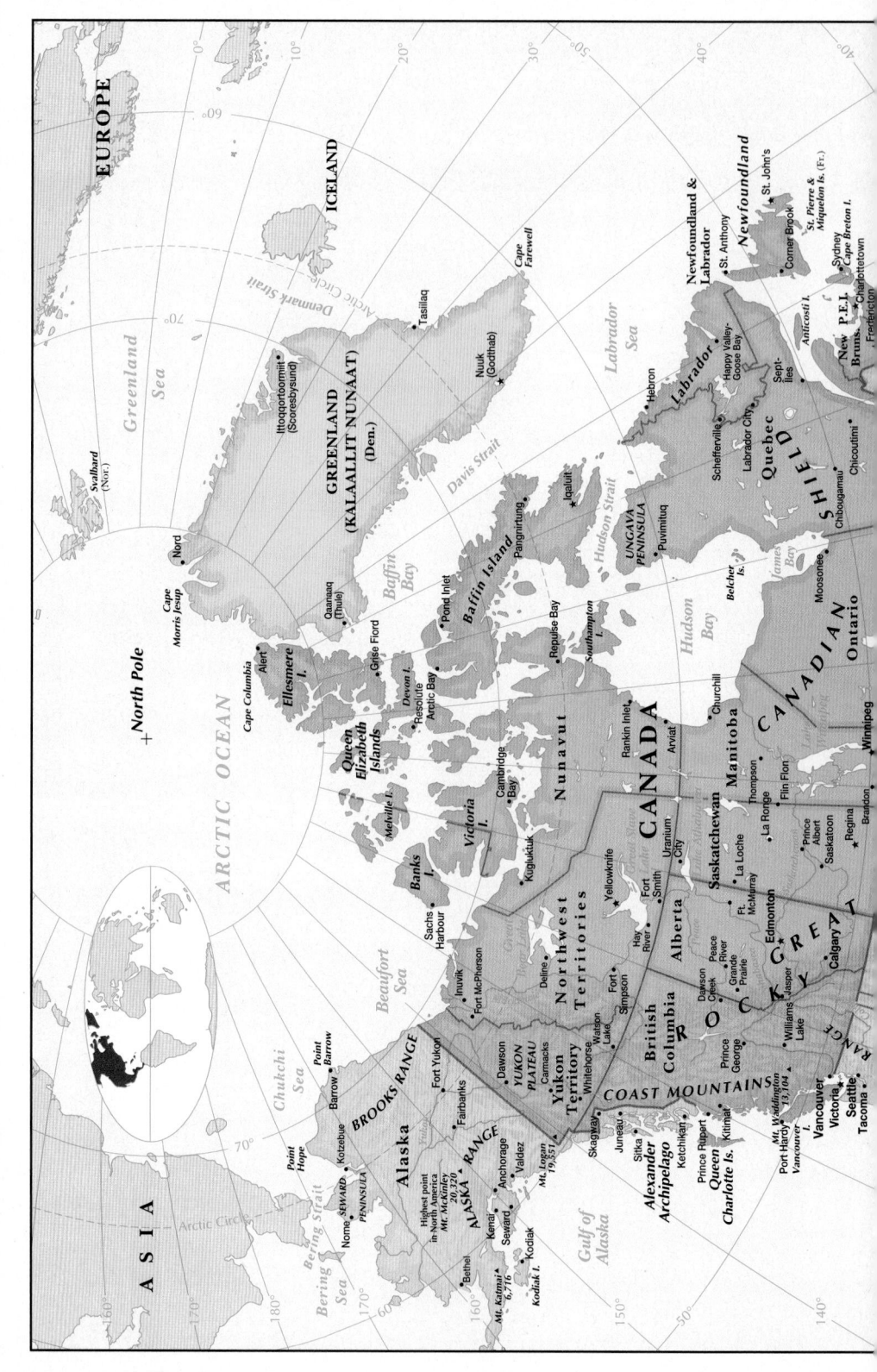

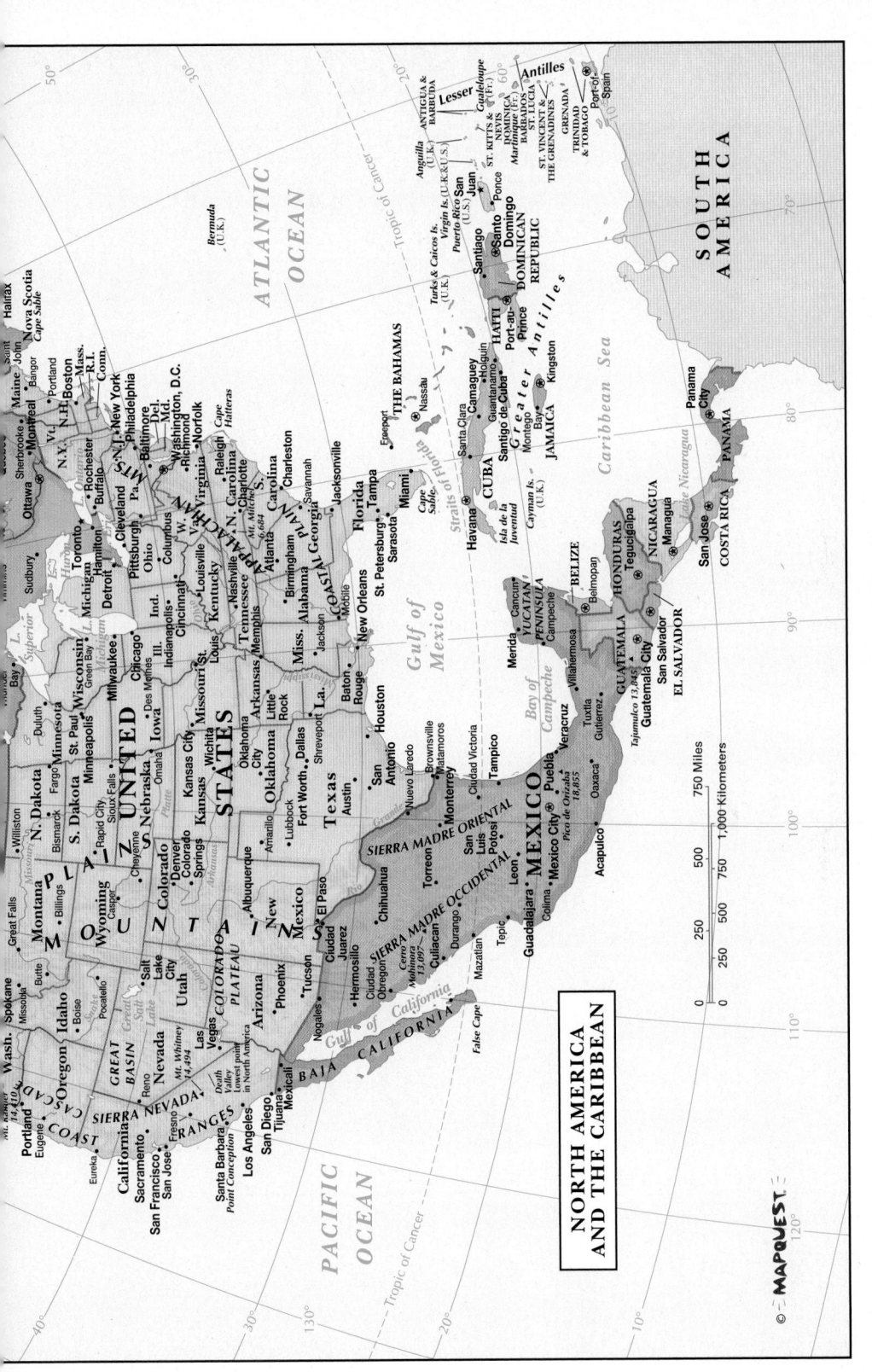

NORTH AMERICA
AND THE CARIBBEAN

© MAPQUEST

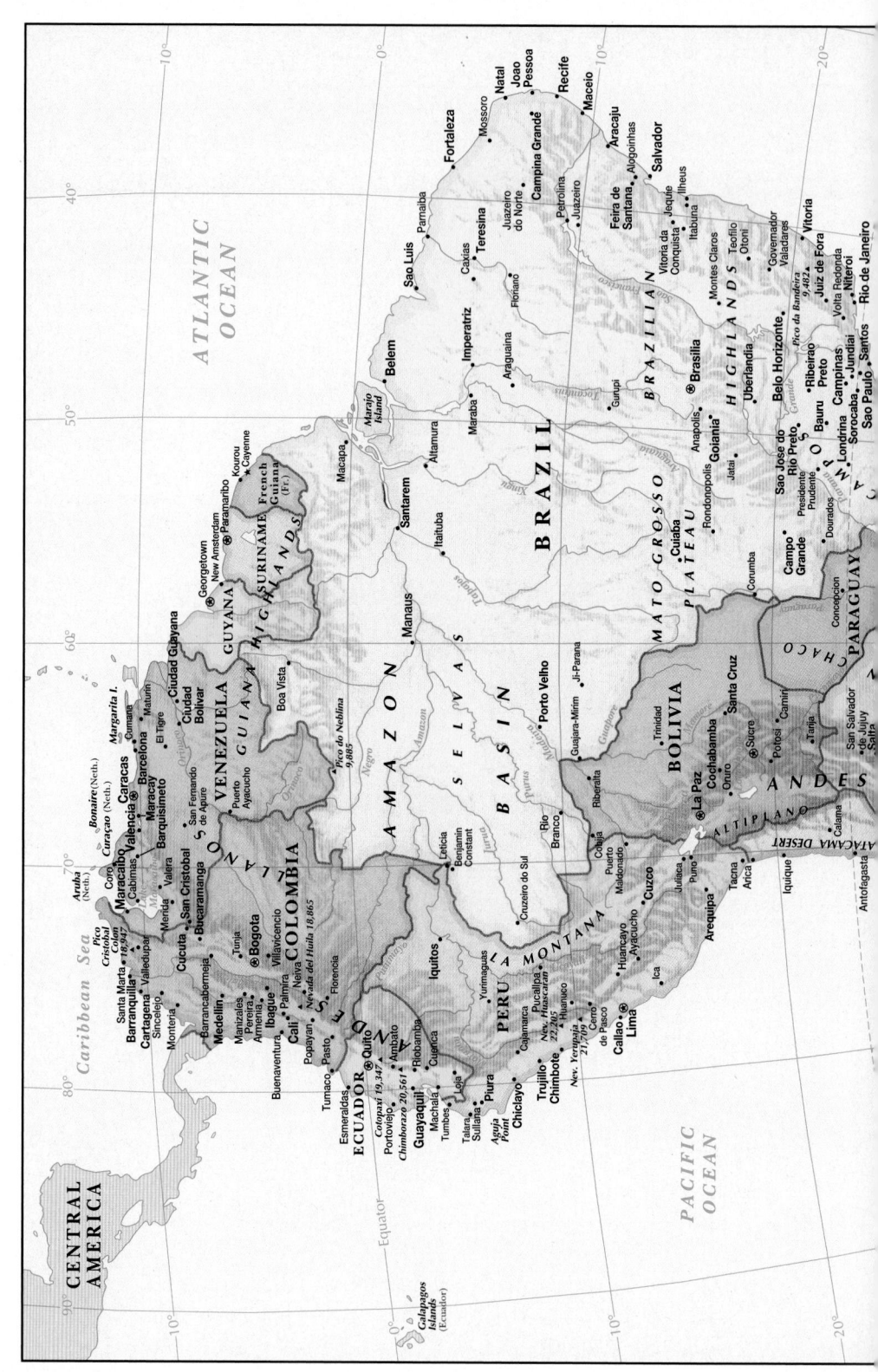

CENTRAL AMERICA

Caribbean Sea

Aruba (Neth.)
Bonaire (Neth.)
Curaçao (Neth.)
Coro
Maracaibo
Cabimas
Barranquilla
Santa Marta
Pico Cristobal Colon 18,947
Cartagena
Valledupar
Sincelejo
Monteria
Merida
Valera
San Cristobal
Cucuta
Bucaramanga
Barrancabermeja
Manizales
Pereira
Armenia
Ibague
Medellin
Palmira
Tunja
Bogota
Cali
Villavicencio
Popayan
Pasto
Nevada del Huila 18,865
Neiva
Florencia
Buenaventura

Margarita I.
Cumana
Barcelona
El Tigre
Maturin
Ciudad Guayana
Ciudad Bolivar
Maracay
Caracas
Valencia
Barquisimeto
San Fernando de Apure
Puerto Ayacucho

VENEZUELA

Georgetown
New Amsterdam
Paramaribo
Kourou
Cayenne

GUYANA
SURINAME
French Guiana (Fr.)

GUIANA HIGHLANDS

Boa Vista

Pico do Neblina 9,885

LLANOS

COLOMBIA

Tumaco
Esmeraldas
ECUADOR
Quito
Portoviejo
Ambato
Riobamba
Cotopaxi 19,347
Chimborazo 20,561
Cuenca
Guayaquil
Machala
Loja
Tumbes
Talara
Sullana
Aguja Point
Piura
Chiclayo
Trujillo
Chimbote
Nev. Huascaran 22,205
Nev. Yerupaja 21,709
Cajamarca
Cerro de Pasco
Huanuco
Pucallpa

Galapagos Islands (Ecuador)

Iquitos

Benjamin Constant
Leticia
Cruzeiro do Sul

Yurimaguas

PERU

LA MONTAÑA

ANDES

Huancayo
Huancavelica
Ayacucho
Ica
Cuzco
Callao
Lima

A M A Z O N   B A S I N

S E L V A S

Santarem
Itaituba
Manaus

Rio Branco

Guajara-Mirim
Riberalta
Cobija
Puerto Maldonado
Porto Velho
Ji-Parana

ATLANTIC OCEAN

Macapa
Marajo Island
Belem
Altamira
Maraba
Araguaina
Gurupi

BRAZIL

Sao Luis
Parnaiba
Teresina
Caxias
Floriano
Imperatriz

Natal
Joao Pessoa
Recife
Maceio
Mossoro
Campina Grande
Aracaju
Alagoinhas
Salvador
Ilheus
Jequie
Itabuna

Juazeiro do Norte
Juazeiro
Petrolina
Fortaleza

Feira de Santana
Vitoria da Conquista

BRAZILIAN HIGHLANDS

Montes Claros
Teofilo Otoni
Governador Valadares
Pico da Bandeira 9,482
Belo Horizonte
Ribeirao Preto
Uberlandia
Uberaba
Brasilia
Goiania
Anapolis
Jatai
Rondonopolis
Sao Jose do Rio Preto
Presidente Prudente
Bauru
Jundiai
Campinas
Sorocaba
Londrina
Sao Paulo
Santos
Volta Redonda
Juiz de Fora
Niteroi
Rio de Janeiro

MATO GROSSO PLATEAU

Cuiaba
Corumba

Campo Grande
Dourados
Concepcion

PARAGUAY

CHACO

BOLIVIA

Trinidad
Santa Cruz
Cochabamba
La Paz
Sucre
Oruro
Potosi
Camiri
Tarija
San Salvador de Jujuy
Salta

ALTIPLANO

ANDES

Juliaca
Puno
Tacna
Arica
Iquique
Calama
Antofagasta

ATACAMA DESERT

Arequipa

PACIFIC OCEAN

Equator

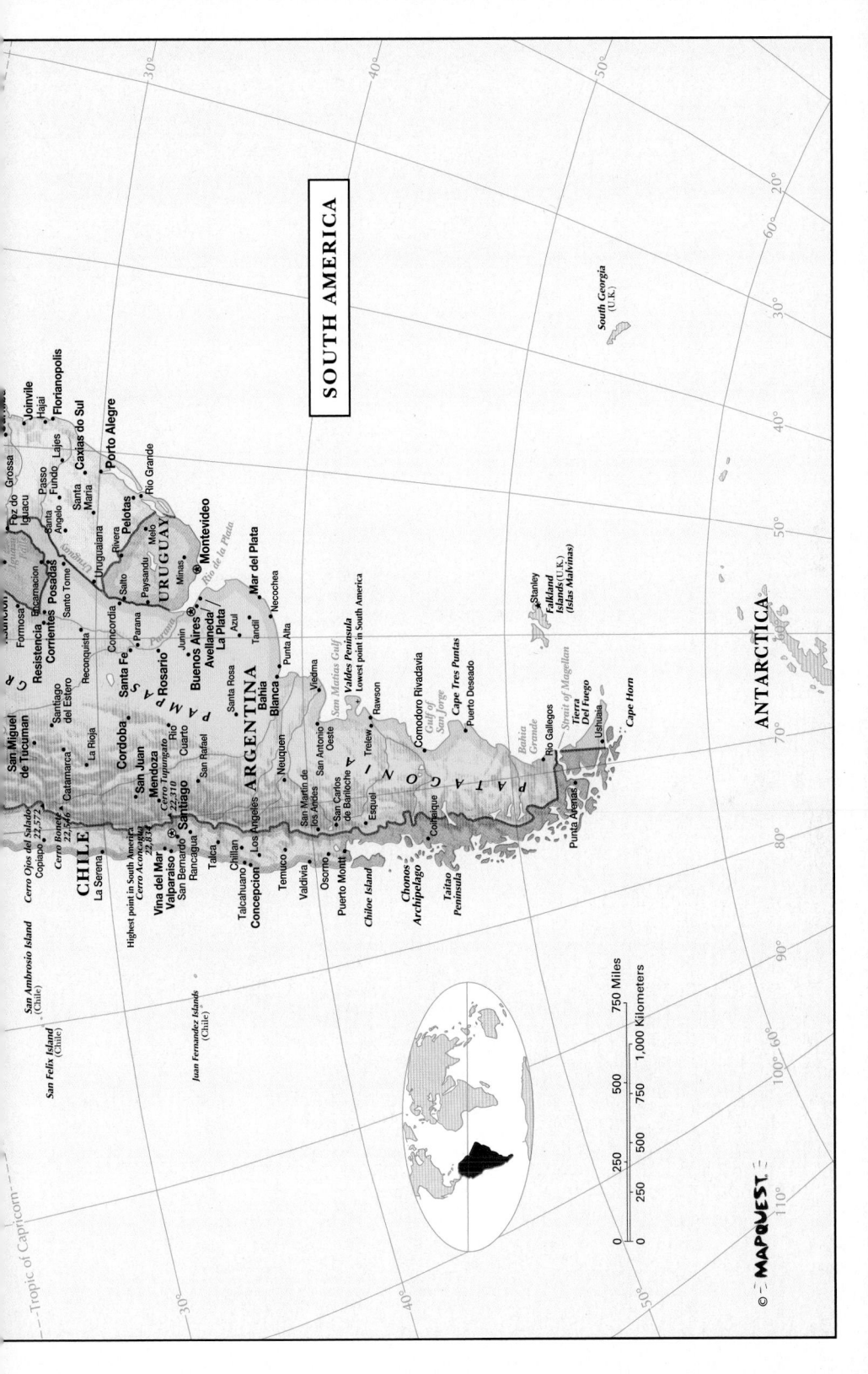

SOUTH AMERICA

Tropic of Capricorn

30°

40°

50°

20°

30°

40°

50°

60°

70°

80°

90°

100°

110°

60°

30°

40°

50°

San Ambrosio Island
(Chile)

San Felix Island
(Chile)

Juan Fernandez Islands
(Chile)

CHILE

Cerro Ojos del Salado
Copiapo 22,572

Cerro Bonete
Catamarca

La Serena

Highest point in South America
Cerro Aconcagua
22,834

La Rioja

San Miguel
de Tucuman

Santiago
del Estero

Cordoba

San Juan
Mendoza
Cerro Tupungato
22,310

Vina del Mar
Valparaiso
Rancagua
San Bernardo Santiago

Talca

Rio
Cuarto

San Rafael

Santa Rosa

Santa Fe
Parana
Rosario
Junin

Concordia

Salto
Paysandu

URUGUAY

Rivera
Melo
Minas

Mar del Plata

Resistencia
Corrientes Posadas

Reconquista

Formosa

Santa
Angelo
Santo Tome

Uruguaiana

Rio Grande

Passo
Fundo

Santa
Maria

Lajes

Caxias do Sul

Porto Alegre

Florianopolis

Hajai
Joinville

Foz do
Iguacu

Grossa

Santiago

Talcahuano
Concepcion

Chillan

Temuco

Valdivia

Osorno

Puerto Montt

Chiloe Island

Chonos
Archipelago

Taitao
Peninsula

Los Angeles

San Martin de
los Andes

San Carlos
de Bariloche

Esquel

Coihaique

Neuquen

San Antonio
Oeste

Trelew

Rawson

Viedma

Bahia
Blanca

Azul

Tandil

Punta Alta

Necochea

Buenos Aires
Avellaneda
La Plata

Montevideo

Rio de la Plata

Mar del Plata

ARGENTINA

PAMPA

PATAGONIA

Comodoro Rivadavia

Puerto Deseado

Cape Tres Puntas

Gulf of
San Jorge

Bahia
Grande

Rio Gallegos

Punta Arenas

Tierra
Del Fuego

Ushuaia

Cape Horn

Strait of Magellan

Valdes Peninsula
Lowest point in South America

San Matias Gulf

Stanley
Falkland
Islands (U.K.)
(Islas Malvinas)

South Georgia
(U.K.)

ANTARCTICA

0   250   500   750 Miles

0   250   500   750   1,000 Kilometers

© MAPQUEST

465

EUROPE

GREENLAND
(KALAALLIT NUNAAT)
(Denmark)

Isafjordhur

Keflavik •Akureyri
ICELAND
⊛ Reykjavik

•Seydhisfjordhur

Arctic Circle

Norwegian Sea

Torshavn *Faroe*
              Islands
              (Den.)

Shetland
Islands
(U.K.)

Orkney
Islands
Thurso

ATLANTIC
OCEAN

Hebrides

Scotland
Glasgow •Aberdeen
         •Dundee
Inverness

Ayr •Edinburgh

Londonderry
•Northern
Ireland   •Newcastle
Belfast

Galway   UNITED
          KINGDOM
IRELAND ⊛ Dublin
•Limerick   Liverpool Leeds
          Manchester   •Kingston upon Hull
Cork   Sheffield
Waterford Birmingham
         Wales Swansea •Coventry
         Cardiff England Norwich
         Bristol
Plymouth   London
Land's End Portsmouth Dover
                         English Channel
Channel Is.
(U.K.) Le Havre
•Brest   Caen Rouen
Rennes   Le Mans
          Paris ⊛
Nantes
          Tours   Orleans

Narvik
•Bodo

Namsos

Molde •Trondheim
Alesund

NORWAY SWEDEN

Bergen

Haugesund Oslo ⊛
Stavanger Drammen Karlstad
           Skien

Kristiansand

Alborg
Jutland Arhus Halmstad
Esbjerg   Copenhagen Helsingborg
          •Odense •Malmo
DENMARK
          Kiel
          Lubeck Rostock
Groningen Hamburg
NETHERLANDS Bremen NORTHERN
Amsterdam
The Hague Hannover Berlin
Rotterdam Bielefeld
Antwerp Essen Magdeburg GERMANY
BELGIUM Liege Bonn Leipzig
Lille Cologne Kassel Erfurt Dresden
LUXEMBOURG Wiesbaden Chemnitz Liberec
Luxembourg ⊛ Frankfurt Pilzen PRAGUE
Saarbrucken Mannheim
Nancy Nurnberg CZECH REP.
Strasbourg Stuttgart Regensburg
           Augsburg Munich Linz
Dijon Basel Salzburg Vienna
       Zurich Innsbruck AUSTRIA
Limoges Bern Klagenfurt
FRANCE Geneva SWITZERLAND
Clermont-Ferrand Lyon LIECHTENSTEIN
Saint-Etienne Grenoble Bergamo Udine SLOVENIA
Mt. Blanc Matterhorn Milan Verona Trieste Ljubljana
15,771 14,690 Toring Venice Rijeka CROATIA
Bordeaux Bologna DINARIC
Toulouse Genoa Parma
Montpellier Nice SAN MARINO
Marseille Florence Ancona
Toulon MONACO Pisa
Avignon Perugia Split

North
Sea

Borlange
Uppsala
Orebro
Stockholm
Norrkoping
Linkoping
Jonkoping
Vaxjo Olar
Goteborg

Bornholm
(Den.)

Gdansk
Szczecin
Bydgoszcz
Poznan
POLAND
Wroclaw
Walbrzyc
Ostrava
Brno
Bratislava
HU

A Coruña
Vigo
•Braga
•Porto
Coimbra

Gijon Santander Donostia-
Leon Bilbao San Sebastian
Vitoria-Gasteiz Pamplona PYRENEES
Valladolid Pico de ANDORRA
IBERIAN Anello 11,168
Salamanca Zaragoza
Madrid

PORTUGAL
Lisbon ⊛
•Setubal Badajoz Toledo
          SPAIN
Cape Valencia PENINSULA
St. Vincent Cordoba
Cadiz •Seville Murcia
Strait of Malaga Granada Alicante
Gibraltar •Gibraltar Almeria
           (U.K.)   Cartagena

Barcelona
Tarragona
Castellon de la Plana
Majorca *Minorca*
Palma de
Mallorca *Balearic*
          Is.
          (Sp.)

Corsica
(Fr.) Elba
Ajaccio
            Rome ⊛
VATICAN CITY ITALY Foggia
            Naples •Bari
Sassari *Vesuvius*
Sardinia 4,202 Taranto
(It.) Salerno
Cagliari

Reggio di
Messina Calabria
Etna Catania
11,053
Sicily
(It.)

MALTA ⊛ Valletta

Bay
of
Biscay

Adriatic
Sea

Dubrovnik
BOS. &
HERZ
Sarajevo

Tyrrhenian
Sea

Ionia
Sea

Mediterranean   Sea

AFRICA

0		250		500 Miles
0	250	500		750 Kilometers

466

Barents   Sea

North
Cape
*Hammerfest   *Vardo
*Tromso   Novaya
                                          Zemlya
*Kiruna   *Ivalo   *Murmansk   *Naryan-Mar
                                                              *Pechora
           LAPLAND   *Apatity   KOLA   ASIA
*Lulea   *Rovaniemi   PENINSULA
*Skelleftea   *Belomorsk   *Arkhangelsk   *Ukhta   RUSSIA
*Oulu   White Sea   Bereznik
-nea   *Syktyvkar   *U
FINLAND   *Perm
        *Kuopio   R   A   L
*Vaasa   Lake   *Kotlas   *Izhevsk
*Jyvaskyla   Onega   *Petrozavodsk   *Kirov   M   *Ufa
*Tampere   Lake   O
*Pori   *Lahti   Ladoga   *Yoshkar Ola   U   *Sterlitzmak
*Turku *Kotka   *Cherepovets   *Vologda   *Naberezhnye   N
*Helsinki   St.   Chelny   T   *Orsk
Aland Is.   Petersburg   *Rybinsk   *Kostroma   *Kazan   A   *Orenburg
(Fin.) Gulf of Finland   *Yaroslavl   *Nizhniy *Cheboksary   I
*Tallinn   *Ivanovo   Novgorod   N
ESTONIA *Tartu   *Velikiy   *Ulyanovsk   S
              Novgorod   *Saransk   *Tolyatti
-tland *Pskov   *Tver   *Vladimir   *Samara
we.) *Riga   *Moscow⊕   *Ryazan   *Penza   KAZAKHSTAN
*Liepaja LATVIA   *Kaluga
    *Daugavpils   *Tula   *Saratov
LITHUANIA *Vitsyebsk *Smolensk   *Astrakhan
*Kaunas *Vilnius *Orsha   *Tambov
*Kaliningrad   *Mahilyow *Bryansk *Lipetsk
(RUSSIA)⊕ *Minsk *Babruysk   *Voronezh
EUROPEAN *Hrodna   PLAIN   *Kursk   *Volgograd
*Bialystok BELARUS *Homyel *Belgorod
*Warsaw *Brest *Pinsk *Chernihiv *Sumy
-Lodz *Radom   *Kiev⊕ *Kharkiv   Caspian
*Kielce *Lublin *Zhytomyr (Kyiv) *Poltava
-atowice   *Lviv UKRAINE *Cherkasy *Luhansk
*Krakow   *Vinnytsia Dnieper *Donetsk *Horlivka   *Rostov-na-Donu   Sea
-ARPATHIAN   *Dnipropetrovsk
-OVAKIA *Chernivtsi *Zaporizhzhia
-anska *Kosice MOLDOVA *Kryvyi Rih *Mariupol
-ystrica *Miskolc *Chisinau   *Stavropol
-udapest *Iasi   *Mykolaiv Sea of
ARY *Oradea *Odesa   Azov   *Krasnodar Mt. Elbrus *Nalchik *Makhachkala
-eged *Kecskemet *Cluj-   CRIMEA   18,510 *Groznyy
*Debrecen Napoca   PENINSULA   Highest point *Vladikavkaz
ROMANIA *Brasov *Simferopol   in Europe CAUCASUS MTS.
*Timisoara *Galati *Ploiesti   40°
-Novi Sad *Bucharest *Sevastopol
*Belgrade *Craiova *Constanta
SERBIA & Danube *Ruse Black   Sea
-ONTENEGRO *Pleven *Varna
-dgorica *Nis *Stara *Burgas
*Sofia BULGARIA Zagora
-Shkoder BALKAN *Plovdiv
Durres *Skopje *Istanbul
F.Y.R. MAC. *Kavala
Tirana PENINSULA *Thessaloniki TURKEY
ALBANIA *Olympus
*Vlore 9,570   ASIA
-orfu   Dardanelles
*Larisa Aegean
*Ioannina *Volos Sea
GREECE
*Patras *Athens
-Corinth Cyclades
Peloponnese
*Kalamata *Sparta
          *Rhodes
Sea of Crete (Gr.)
    Crete
*Hania (Gr.) *Iraklion
20°   30°   40°   © MAPQUEST 50°

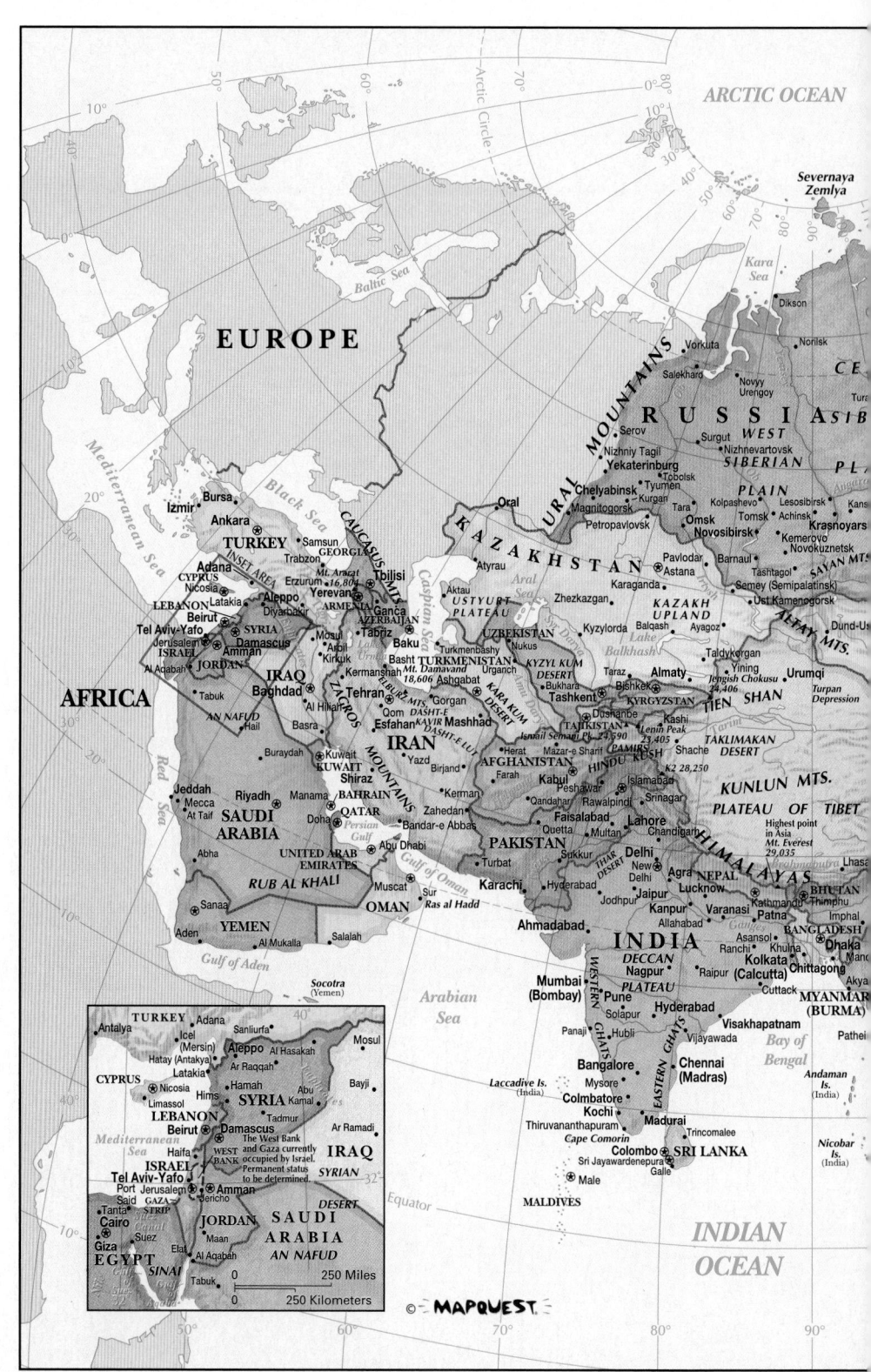

ASIA

NORTH AMERICA

Chukchi Sea

Bering Strait

Providceniya

Bering Sea

Wrangel I.

Anadyr

East Siberian Sea

Cherskiy

Laptev Sea

Nordvik

Tiksi

Zyryanka

Shiveluch 10,771
Klyuchevskaya 15,584
Karymsky 4,869

Verkhoyansk

Susuman

Magadan

Petropavlovsk-Kamchatskiy

KAMCHATKA PEN.

KOLYMA MOUNTAINS

VERKHOYANSK RA.

Vilyuysk

Yakutsk

Okhotsk

Sea of Okhotsk

Alaid 7,662

Okha

Sarycheva 4,960

Sakhalin

Kuril Is. (Russia)

Berkakit

STANOVOY RANGE

Aldan

Bodaybo

Komsomolsk-na-Amure

Yuzhno-Sakhalinsk

Tiatia 6,013

Lensk

Tynda

Svobodnyy

Khabarovsk

Hokkaido

Sapporo

Ust-Kut

Lake Baykal

YABLONOVYY RANGE

Chita

Blagoveshchensk

Hakodate

Bratsk

Hailar

Yichun

Ussuriysk
Vladivostok

Akita

Sea of Japan (East Sea)

Sendai

Tulun

kutsk

Ulan-Ude

GREATER KHINGAN RANGE

Qiqihar

Harbin

Jixi

Niigata *Honshu*

Darhan

Choybalsan

Changchun

Jilin

Chongjin

Tokyo

Moron

Ulaanbaatar

Fushun

JAPAN

Yokohama

Mt. Fuji 12,388

MONGOLIA
MONGOLIAN PLATEAU

Shenyang

Anshan

N. KOREA
Hamhung
Pyongyang

Kyoto

Nagoya

yanhongor

Dalian

Incheon

Seoul

Kobe Osaka

Hohhot

Beijing

Daegu Busan

Hiroshima

Shikoku

GOBI DESERT

Baotou

Tianjin

Shijiazhuang

S. KOREA

Kitakyushu
Fukuoka

Yumen

Yinchuan

Taiyuan

Jinan

Qingdao

Nagasaki

Kyushu

Kagoshima

Xining

Handan

Yellow Sea

Lanzhou

Luoyang

Xuzhou

Zhengzhou

Nanjing

Xian

Ryukyu Is. (Japan)

nghai Lake

Huainan

Shanghai

Hefei

Hangzhou

Okinawa

CHINA

Wuhan

Jingdezhen

East China Sea

Naha

Chengdu

Nanchang

Wenzhou

Chongqing

Changsha

Fuzhou

Zigong

Shaoyang

Ganzhou

Xiamen

Taipei

Gulyang

Guilin

TAIWAN

Kunming

Liuzhou Guangzhou

Kaohsiung

Myitkyina

Nanning

Zhanjiang

Macao

Hong Kong

Phongsali

Haiphong

Láoag

Luzon

Taunggyi

LAOS

Hanoi

Haikou

Baguio

PHILIPPINES

Philippine Sea

Louangphabang

Vinh

Hainan (China)

Quezon City

Chiang
Mai

Vientiane

Hue

Manila

Naga

Samar

Yangon (Rangoon)

THAILAND

Nakhon
Ratchasima

Da Nang

Mindoro

Tacloban

Leyte

Mawlamyine

akhon Sawan

VIETNAM

Nha Trang

Panay

Iloilo

Cebu

Dawei

Bangkok

CAMBODIA

Batdambang

Puerto
Princess

Negros

Butuan

Mindanao

Davao

Phnom Penh

Ho Chi Minh City

Palawan

Zamboanga

Kompong Som

Can Tho

Sulu Sea

Jayapura

Isthmus of Kra

Gulf of Thailand

Kota Kinabalu

Sandakan

Celebes Sea

Halmahera

New Guinea

Phuket

Hat Yai

Bandar Seri Begawan

Tarakan

Ternate

Andaman Sea

MALAYSIA

Natuna Is.

BRUNEI

Manado

Ceram

Banda Aceh

George Town

Kuching

Samainda

Gorontalo

Ambon

Arafura Sea

Medan

Kelang

Kuala Lumpur

Pontianak

Celebes

Banda Sea

Sibolga

Singapore

SINGAPORE

Borneo

Balikpapan

Palopo

Baubau

Pekanbaru

Jambi

Sampit

Banjarmasin

Parepare

Padang

Sumatra

Palembang

Makassar

Bengkulu

INDONESIA

Bandar Lampung

Jakarta

Semarang

Surabaya

Ende

EAST TIMOR

Dili

Bandung

Java

Malang *Bali*

Mataram

Sumba

Timor

Kupang

Timor Sea

AUSTRALIA

PACIFIC OCEAN

Tropic of Cancer

Equator 0°

0 500 1,000 Miles
0 500 1,000 1,500 Kilometers

469

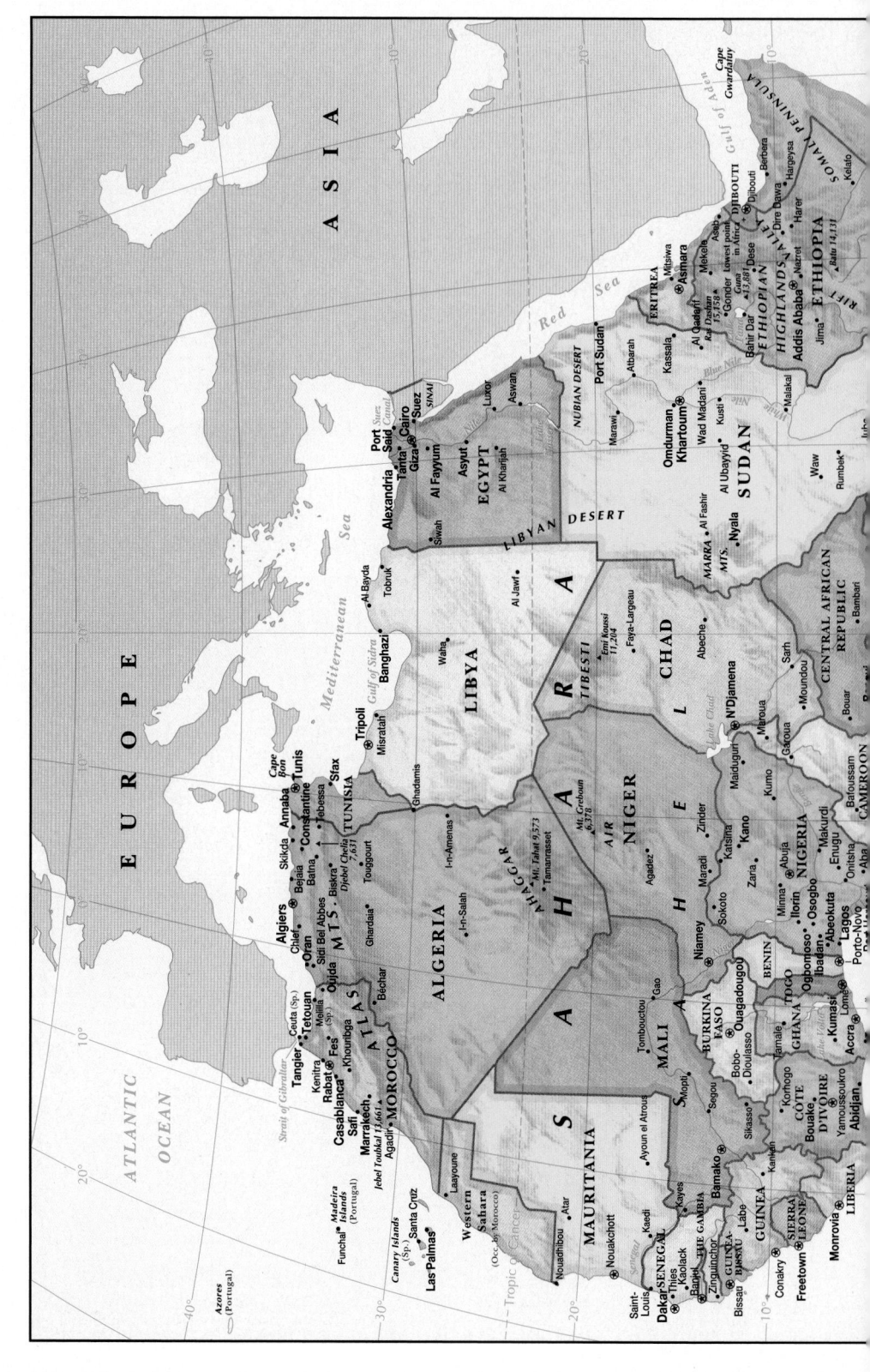

ASIA

EUROPE

ATLANTIC OCEAN

Azores
(Portugal)

Madeira Islands
(Portugal)

Funchal• *Santa Cruz*

Canary Islands
(Sp.)

Las Palmas•

Strait of Gibraltar

Ceuta (Sp.)

Melilla
(Sp.)

Tangier•
Tetouan•
Rabat⊛ •Fes
Kenitra•
Casablanca•
Safi•
•Khouribga
Marrakech•
Agadir•

Jebel Toubkal 13,661

M O R O C C O

A T L A S

M T S.

Mediterranean Sea

Cape Bon

Algiers⊛
•Chlef
•Oran •Bejaia
Sidi Bel Abbes•
Skikda •Annaba
Constantine•
•Batna •Tebessa
•Biskra
Djebel Chelia 7,631
•Touggourt
Ghardaia•

Oujda•

A L G E R I A

•Bechar

I-n-Salah•

•In-Amenas

•Ghadames

Tunis
•Stax
T U N I S I A

Tripoli•
Misratah•
Banghazi•

•Waha

Gulf of Sidra

L I B Y A

Siwah•

•Al Bayda •Tobruk

Alexandria•
Port Said•
Suez•
Tanta•Cairo
Giza• •Al Fayyum
•Asyut
•Al Kharijah

S I N A I

Suez Canal

E G Y P T

L I B Y A N   D E S E R T

•Al Jawf

Red Sea

NUBIAN DESERT

Port Sudan•

•Marawi

Omdurman•
Khartoum⊛
Wad Madani•
•Al Ubayyid
•Kusti

Attarah•

Kassala•

Blue Nile
White Nile

S U D A N

Gulf of Aden

Cape Gwardafuy•

SOMALI PENINSULA

•Berbera

•Hargeysa
•Kelafo

ERITREA

•Mitsiwa
Asmara⊛
•Mekele
•Adigrat
•Keren
•Al Qadarif

Guna 13,881

DJIBOUTI
•Djibouti
•Dire Dawa
•Harer
•Nazret

ETHIOPIAN

Ras Dashan 15,158

Gonder•
Bahir Dar•
•Dese

HIGHLANDS

Addis Ababa⊛

RIFT VALLEY

lowest point in Africa

Batu 14,131

E T H I O P I A

•Jima

•Malakal

S A H A R A

TIBESTI

Emi Koussi 11,204

AHAGGAR

Mt. Tahat 9,573

Tamanrasset•

AIR

Agadez•

•Gao

Tombouctou•

M A L I

Mopti•

Segou•
•Sikasso
Bamako⊛
Kayes•

Ayoun el Atrous•

M A U R I T A N I A

Nouadhibou•

Nouakchott⊛

Atar•

•Kaedi

Saint-Louis•
Dakar⊛ •Thies
Kaolack•

S E N E G A L

THE GAMBIA
Banjul⊛

Zinguinchor•

•Kankan
Labe•
GUINEA-BISSAU
Bissau⊛

G U I N E A

Conakry⊛
SIERRA LEONE
Freetown⊛

L I B E R I A

Monrovia⊛

Faya-Largeau•

CHAD

Abeche•

N'Djamena⊛

Lake Chad

Maiduguri•

N I G E R

Zinder•

Maradi•

•Katsina
Kano•
•Sokoto
Zaria•

Niamey⊛

B U R K I N A
F A S O
Ouagadougou⊛
•Bobo-
Dioulasso

Korhogo•
•Bouake

COTE
D'IVOIRE

Yamoussoukro⊛
Abidjan•

Tamale•

GHANA

•Kumasi
Accra⊛

Lake Volta

TOGO
Lome⊛
BENIN
Porto-Novo⊛

Minna•
Abuja⊛
Ilorin•
Ogbomoso• •Osogbo
Ibadan•
Abeokuta•
Lagos•
Enugu•
Onitsha•
•Aba

N I G E R I A

Makurdi•

CAMEROON

Bafoussam•

Mouldou•

Moundou•
Sarh•

Mbaidou•
Garoua•
Kumo•

CENTRAL AFRICAN
REPUBLIC

•Bouar

Bambari•

•Waw

•Rumbek

•Nyala

•Al Fashir

MARRA
MTS.

10°
20°
30°

20°
10°
0°
10°

Tropic of Cancer

Western
Sahara
(Occ. by Morocco)

Laayoune•

470

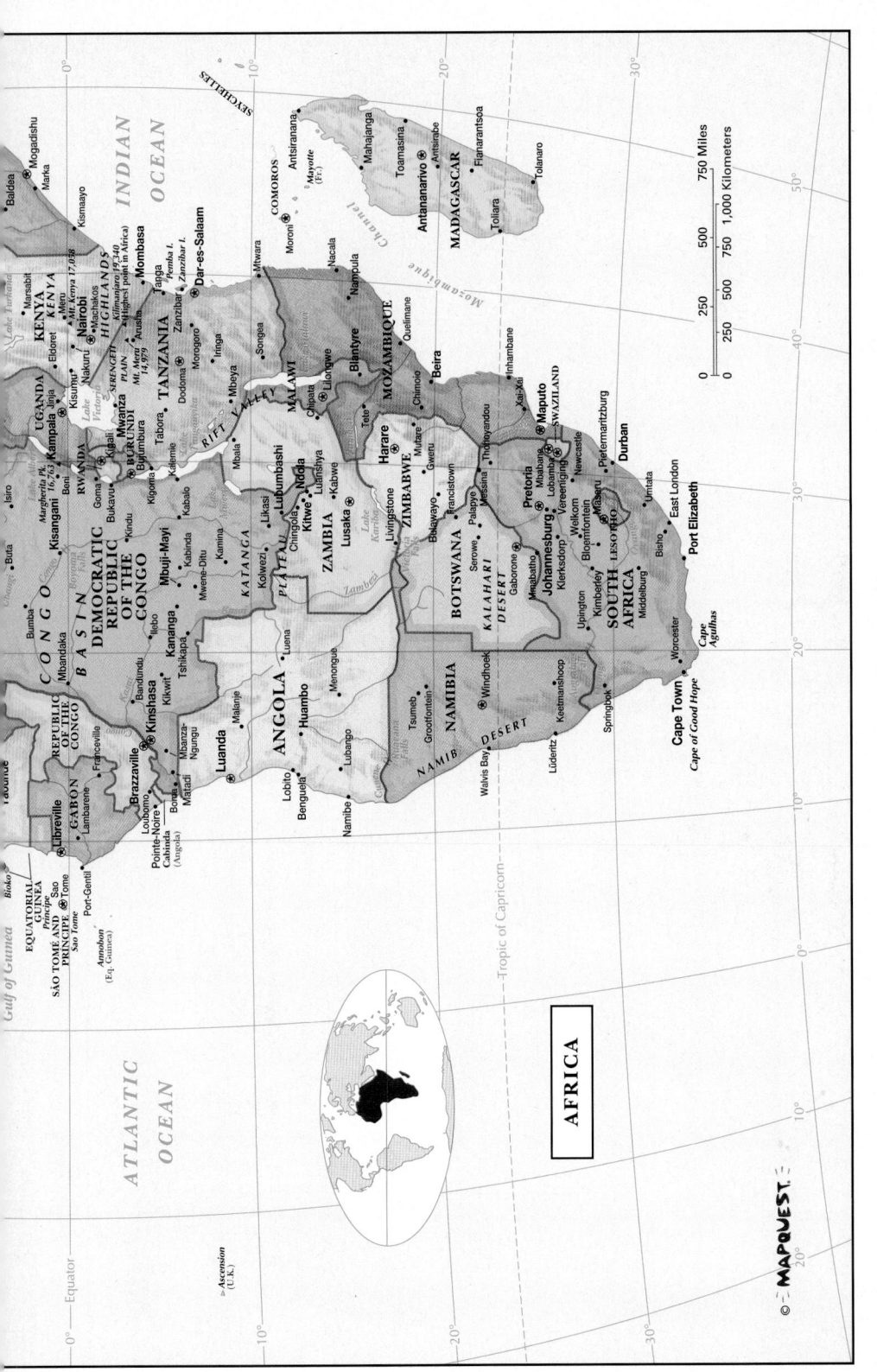

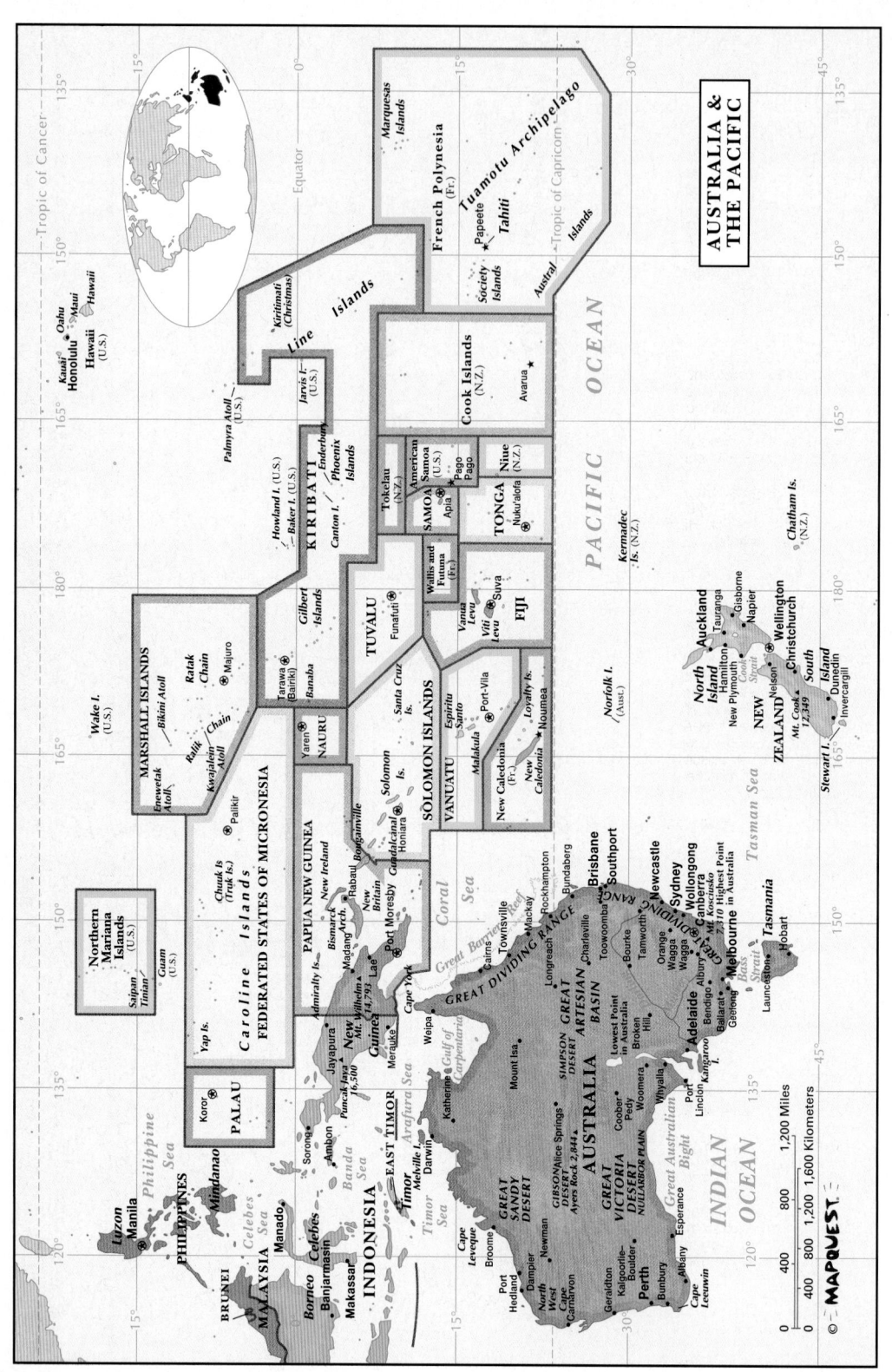

AUSTRALIA &
THE PACIFIC

472

CONSUMER INFORMATION

Business Directory

Listed below are major U.S. corporations offering products and services to consumers. Information as of Sept. 2004. Alphabetization is by first key word. Listings generally include examples of products offered.

Company Name; Address; Telephone Number; Website; Top Executive; Business, Products, or Services.

Abbott Laboratories; 100 Abbott Park Rd., Abbott Park, IL 60064; (847) 937-6100; www.abbott.com; Miles D. White; develops, manufactures, and sells broad line of health care prods., including pharmaceutical, nutritional, and hospital prods.

Aetna, Inc.; 151 Farmington Ave., Hartford, CT 06156; (860) 273-0123; www.aetna.com; John W. Rowe; health insurance, financial services.

AFLAC; 1932 Wynnton Rd., Columbus, GA 31999; (706) 323-3431; www.aflac.com; Daniel Amos; health and life insurance.

Alaska Air Group; 19300 Pacific Hwy. S., Seattle, WA 98188; (206) 431-7040; www.alaskaair.com; William Ayer; air travel (Alaska Air, Horizon Air).

Alberto-Culver; 2525 Armitage Ave., Melrose Park, IL 60160; (708) 450-3000; www.alberto.com; Leonard H. Lavin; hair care (VO5), consumer prods. (Mrs. Dash, Sugar Twin), personal care prods. (St. Ives), Sally Beauty Supply stores.

Albertson's, Inc.; 250 Parkcenter Blvd., Boise, ID 83726; (208) 395-6200; www.albertsons.com; Lawrence R. Johnston; supermarkets; largest retail food and drug co. in the U.S.

Alcoa Inc.; 201 Isabella St., Pittsburgh, PA 15212; (412) 553-4545; www.alcoa.com; Alain J.P. Belda; aluminum products; aerospace and automotive components; industrial materials/tools.

Allegheny Technologies, Inc.; 1000 Six PPG Place, Pittsburgh, PA 15222-5479; (412) 394-2800; www.allegheny-techologies.com; L. Patrick Hassey; electronics, aerospace, industrial; specialty metals.

Allied Waste Industries; 15880 N. Greenway-Hayden Loop, Suite 100, Scottsdale, AZ 85260; (480) 627-2700; www.alliedwaste.com; Thomas Van Weelden; solid waste management.

Allstate Corp.; Allstate Plaza, Northbrook, IL 60062; (847) 402-5000; www.allstate.com; Edward Liddy; property/casualty, life insurance.

Altria Group, Inc.; 120 Park Ave., NY, NY 10017; (917) 663-4000; www.altria.com; Louis C. Camilleri; cigarettes (largest U.S. tobacco company; Marlboro, Merit, Virginia Slims); beer (Miller, Molson, Red Dog); Kraft Foods products (Jell-O, Maxwell House, Kool-Aid, Oscar Mayer, Tang, Cheez Whiz and Velveeta, Post cereals, Tombstone Pizza, and Toblerone chocolate); Nabisco products (Oreo, Chips Ahoy! cookies, Ritz, Triscuit crackers, Mallomars). (Philip Morris Companies, Inc., changed its name to Altria, 1/27/03).

Amazon.com Inc.; 1200 12th Ave. S., Suite 1200 Seattle, WA 98144; (206) 266-1000; www.amazon.com; Jeff Bezos; on-line books, electronics, camera/photo, and home and garden products.

Amerada Hess Corp.; 1185 Ave. of the Americas, NY, NY 10036; (212) 997-8500; www.hess.com; J. B. Hess; integrated international oil co.

American Electric Power; 1 Riverside Plaza, Columbus, OH 43215; (614) 716-1000; www.aep.com; E. Linn Draper Jr.; utilities.

American Express Co.; 200 Vesey St., NY, NY 10285; (212) 640-2000; www.americanexpress.com; Kenneth Chenault; travel, financial, and information services.

American Greetings Corp.; 1 American Rd., Cleveland, OH 44144; (216) 252-7300; www.americangreetings.com; Zev Weiss; greeting cards, stationery, party goods, gift items.

American Home Products: *see* Wyeth.

American Intl. Group; 70 Pine St., NY, NY 10270; (212) 770-7000; www.aig.com; Maurice R. Greenberg; insurance, financial services.

American Standard; One Centennial Ave., P.O. Box 6820, Piscataway, NJ 08855; (732) 980-6000; www.americanstandard.com; Frederic M. Poses; bathroom and kitchen fixtures and fittings, air conditioning systems, vehicle control systems.

AMR Corp.;4333 Amon Carter Blvd., Ft. Worth, TX 76155; (817) 963-1234; www.aa.com; Gerard J. Arpey; Donald J. Carty; air transportation (American Airlines, American Eagle); acquired assets of Trans World Air Lines Inc. in 2001.

Anheuser-Busch Cos., Inc.; 1 Busch Pl., St. Louis, MO 63118; (314) 577-2000; www.anheuser-busch.com; August A. Busch 3rd; world's largest brewer (Budweiser, Michelob, Bud Light, Busch, O'Doul's), aluminum can manuf. and recycling, theme parks.

AOL Time Warner Inc.: *see* Time Warner, Inc.

Apple Computer, Inc.; 1 Infinite Loop, Cupertino, CA 95014-2084; (408) 996-1010; www.apple.com; Steve Jobs; manuf. of personal computers, software, peripherals.

Aramark Corp.; Aramark Tower, 1101 Market St., Philadelphia, PA 19107; (215) 238-3000; www.aramark.com; Joseph Neubauer; food and support services, uniforms and career apparel, child care and early education.

Archer Daniels Midland Co.; 4666 Faries Pkwy., Decatur, IL 62525; (217) 424-5200; www.admworld.com; G. Allen Andreas; agricultural commodities and prods.

Armstrong World Industries, Inc.; 2500 Columbia Ave., Lancaster, PA 17603; (717) 397-0611; www.armstrong.com; Michael D. Lockhart; interior furnishings, specialty prods.

Arvinmeritor Industries, Inc.; 2135 West Maple Road, Troy, MI 48084; (248) 435-1000; www.arvinmeritor.com; Charles G. McClure; auto emission and ride control systems.

Ashland Inc.; 50 E. River Center, PO Box 391, Covington, KY 41012; (859) 815-3333; www.ashland.com; James J. O' Brien; petroleum producer and refiner (Valvoline), chemicals, road construction.

AT&T Corp.; One AT&T Way, Bedminster, NJ 07921; (908) 221-2000; www.att.com; David W. Dorman; communications, global information management.

AutoNation; 110 S.E. 6th St., Ft. Lauderdale, FL 33301; (954) 769- 6000; www.autonation.com; Michael Jackson; new and used auto vehicles; auto parts, maintenance, and repair; auto protection products.

Avon Prods., Inc.; 1345 Ave. of Americas, NY, NY 10105; (212) 282-5000; www.avon.com; Andrea Jung; cosmetics, fragrances, toiletries, fashion jewelry, gift items, casual apparel, lingerie.

Bank of America Corp.; Bank of America Corporate Center, 100 N. Tryon St., Charlotte, NC 28255; (704) 386-5000; www.bankofamerica.com; Kenneth D. Lewis; major U.S. bank.

Bank One Corp.; 1 Bank One Plaza, Chicago, IL 60670; (302) 732-4000; www.bankone.com; James Dimon; banking and financial services, credit card services, investment management. Merged with JP Morgan Chase on 7/1/04.

Bausch & Lomb Inc.; One Bausch & Lomb Place, Rochester, NY 14604; (716) 338-6000; www.bausch.com; Ronald L. Zarrella; vision and health-care prods., accessories.

Baxter International Inc.; 1 Baxter Pkwy., Deerfield, IL 60015; (847) 948-2000; www.baxter.com; Robert Parkinson, Jr.; health care prods. & services.

Bear Stearns Cos. Inc.; 383 Madison Ave., NY, NY 10179; (212) 272-2000; www.bearstearns.com; James E. Cayne; investment banking, securities trading, brokerage.

Becton, Dickinson & Co.; 1 Becton Dr., Franklin Lakes, NJ 07417; (201) 847-6800; www.bd.com; E.J. Ludwig; medical, laboratory, diagnostic prods.

BellSouth Corp.; 1155 Peachtree St. NE, Atlanta, GA 30309; (404) 249-2000; www.bellsouth.com; F. Duane Ackerman; telephone service in southern U.S.

Berkshire Hathaway Inc.; 1440 Kiewit Plaza, Omaha, NE 68131; www.berkshirehathaway.com; Warren E. Buffett; subsidiaries include GEICO Direct insurance, Johns Manville building materials, Fruit of the Loom underwear, International Dairy Queen restaurants/desserts, Shaw carpets, Benjamin Moore paints.

Best Buy Co., Inc.; 7601 Penn Ave. S., Minneapolis, MN 55323; (612) 291-1000; www.bestbuy.com; Richard Schulze; retailer of software, appliances, electronics, cameras, home office equipment.

Black & Decker Corp.; 701 E. Joppa Rd., Towson, MD 21204; (410) 716-3900; www.blackanddecker.com; Nolan D. Archibald; manuf. power tools (DeWalt, Black & Decker), household prods. (Kwikset locks, Price Pfister faucets, Black & Decker small appliances).

H & R Block, Inc.; 4400 Main St., Kansas City, MO 64111; (816) 753-6900; www.hrblock.com; Mark A. Ernst; tax return preparation.

Boeing Co.; 100 N. Riverside, Chicago, IL 60606; (312) 544-2000; www.boeing.com; Harry Stonecipher; leading manufacturer of commercial, jet aircraft.

Boise Cascade Corp.; 1111 W. Jefferson St., Boise, ID 83728; (208) 384-6161; www.bc.com; George J. Harad; distributor of office products & building materials; paper, wood prods.

Borden, Inc.; 180 E. Broad St., Columbus OH 43215-3707; (614) 225-4000; E.R. Shames; snacks (Wise, Cheez Doodles), adhesives (Elmer's, Krazy Glue), pasta (Prince, Creamette, Goodman's), pasta sauce (Aunt Millie's, Classico), Wyler's bouillon, Soup Starter, Corning Consumer Prods. (Corningware, Corelle, Pyrex, Revere), chemicals, consumer adhesives (Elmer's). Owned by KKR Investments, Inc. (www.kkr.com).

Bristol-Myers Squibb Co.; 345 Park Ave., NY, NY 10154; (212) 546-4000; www.bms.com; Peter R. Dolan; drugs (Bufferin, Comtrex, Excedrin, Pravachol, TAXOL), nutritionals (Enfamil infant formula, Boost energy drink).

Brown-Forman Corp.; PO Box 1080, Louisville, KY 40201-1080; (502) 585-1100; www.brown-forman.com; Owsley Brown 2nd; distilled spirits (Jack Daniel's, Southern Comfort), wines (Bolla, Fetzer, Korbel), china and crystal (Dansk, Lenox), Gorham, Kirk Steiff silver prods., Hartmann luggage.

Brown Shoe Co., Inc.; 8300 Maryland Ave., P.O. Box 29, St. Louis, MO 63166; (314) 854-4000; www.brownshoe.com; Ronald A. Fromm; manuf. and retailer (Famous Footwear) of women's, men's, and children's shoes (Buster Brown, Naturalizer, Dr. Scholl's).

Brunswick Corp.; 1 N. Field Ct., Lake Forest, IL 60045; (847) 735-4700; www.brunswick.com; George Buckley; largest U.S. maker of leisure and recreation prods., incl. marine, camping, fitness, and fishing equip.; bowling centers and equip.

Burger King Corp.; One Whopper Way, 5505 Blue Lagoon Dr., Miami, FL 33126; (305) 378-3000; www.burgerking.com; Greg Brenneman; fast-food restaurants.

Burlington Industries; 3330 West Friendly Ave., Greensboro, NC 27410; (336) 379-2000; www.burlington.com; Joseph L. Gorga; fabrics and textile products.

Burlington Northern Santa Fe Inc.; 2650 Lou Menk Dr., Ft. Worth, TX 76131; (817) 352-1000; www.bnsf.com; Matthew Rose; one of the largest U.S. rail transportation cos.

Campbell Soup Co.; Campbell Pl., Camden, NJ 08103; (609) 342-4800; www.campbellsoup.com; Douglas R. Conant; soups, Franco-American spaghetti, V8 vegetable juice, Prego spaghetti sauce, Pepperidge Farm, Pace sauces.

Caterpillar Inc.; 100 N.E. Adams St., Peoria, IL 61629; (309) 675-1000; www.cat.com; James W. Owens; world's largest producer of earth moving equip.

Chase Manhattan Corp.; *see* JPMorgan Chase & Co. Inc.

ChevronTexaco Corp.; 6001 Bollinger Canyon Rd., San Ramon, CA 94853; (925) 842-1000; www.chevrontexaco.com; David J. O'Reilly; 2nd-largest U.S.-based oil co.

Chiquita Brands International, Inc.; 250 E. 5th St., Cincinnati, OH 45202; (513) 784-8000; www.chiquita.com; Fernando Aguirre; bananas, fruits, vegetables.

Church & Dwight Co., Inc.; 469 N. Harrison St., Princeton, NJ 08543; (609) 683-5900; www.churchdwight.com; R.A. Davies 3rd; world's largest producer of sodium bicarbonate (Arm & Hammer); household products (Brillo, Fresh'n Soft, other Arm & Hammer products); personal care products (Arrid antiperspirant, Pearl Drops, Nair, Trojan condoms, First Response pregnancy test).

CIGNA Corp.; 1 Liberty Pl., Philadelphia, PA 19103; (215) 761-1000; www.cigna.com; H. Edward Hanway; insurance holding co.

Circuit City Stores, Inc.; 9950 Mayland Dr., Richmond, VA 23233-1464; (804) 527-4000; www.circuitcity.com; Alan McCollough; retailer of electronic, audio/video equip., consumer appliances; new and used-car stores (CarMax).

Cisco Systems; 170 West Tasman Dr., San Jose, CA 95134; (408) 526-4000; www.cisco.com; John Chambers; networking and communication products.

Citigroup; 399 Park Ave., NY, NY 10043; (212) 559-1000; www.citigroup.com; Sanford I. Weill; diversified financial services.

Liz Claiborne, Inc.; 1441 Broadway, New York, NY 10018; (212) 354-4900; www.lizclaiborne.com; P. Charron; apparel, accessories.

Clorox Co.; 1221 Broadway, Oakland, CA 94612; (510) 271-7000; www.clorox.com; Gerald E. Johnston; retail consumer prods. (Clorox, Formula 409, Pine-Sol, S.O.S., Soft Scrub cleansers; Armor All, STP, Rain Dance automotive prods.; Scoop Away, Fresh Step cat litters; Kingsford charcoal briquets; Combat insecticide; Hidden Valley dressing; K.C. Masterpiece barbecue sauce; Brita water systems)

Coca-Cola Co.; 1 Coca-Cola Plaza, Atlanta, GA 30313; (404) 676-2121; www.cocacola.com; E. Neville Isdell; world's largest soft drink co. (Coca-Cola, Sprite, Nestea), world's largest dist. of juice prods. (Minute Maid, Hi-C, Fruitopia).

Colgate-Palmolive Co.; 300 Park Ave., NY, NY 10022; (212) 310-2000; www.colgate.com; Reuben Mark; soap (Palmolive, Irish Spring), detergent (Fab, Ajax), toothpaste (Colgate), Hill's pet food.

Comcast Corp.; 1500 Market St., Philadelphia, PA 19102; 215-665-1700; www.comcast.com; Brian L. Roberts; largest U.S. cable company; broadband cable, internet, and voice services. Some programming, incl. E!, Golf Channel, et al.

Compaq Computer Corp.; *see* Hewlett-Packard Co.

CompUSA Inc.; 14951 N. Dallas Pkwy., Dallas, TX 75254; (972) 982-4000; www.compusa.com; Larry Mondry; largest U.S. superstore retailer of microcomputers and peripherals.

Computer Sciences Corp.; 2100 E. Grand Ave., El Segundo, CA 90245; (310) 615-0311; www.csc.com; Van B. Honeycutt; technology services.

ConAgra; 1 ConAgra Dr., Omaha, NE 68102; (402) 595-4000; www.conagra.com; Bruce Rohde; 2nd-largest U.S. food processor (Armour, Bumble Bee, Butterball, Chef Boyardee, Healthy Choice frozen dinners, Egg Beaters, Reddi-Wip).

ConocoPhillips Co.; 600 North Dairy Ashford, P.O. Box 2197, Houston, TX 77252; (281) 293-1000; www.conocophillips.com; James J. Mulva; oil and petrochemical co. Formed by merger of Conoco and Phillips Petroleum, 8/30/02. Third-largest U.S. integrated energy company.

Continental Airlines, Inc.; 1600 Smith St. HQS11, Houston, TX 77002; (713) 324-5242; www.continental.com; Gordon M. Bethune; air transportation.

Adolph Coors Co.; 311 Tenth St., Golden, CO 80401; (303) 279-6565; www.coors.com; Peter Coors; brewer (Coors, Killian's, Zima).

Corning Inc.; 1 Riverfront Plaza, Corning, NY 14831; (607) 974-9000; www.corning.com; James R. Houghton; telecommunications, specialty materials, optical fiber and cable.

Costco Wholesale Corp.; 999 Lake Dr., Issaquah, WA 98027; (425) 313-8100; www.costco.com; James D. Sinegal; wholesale-membership warehouses.

Crane Co.; 100 First Stamford Place, Stamford, CT 06902; (203) 363-7300; www.craneco.com; Eric C. Fast; manuf. fluid control devices, vending machines, fiberglass panels, aircraft brakes.

A. T. Cross Co.; 1 Albion Rd., Lincoln, RI 02865; (401) 333-1200; www.cross.com; David Whalen; writing instruments.

Crown Cork & Seal Co.; 1 Crown Way, Philadelphia, PA 19154-4599; (215) 698-5100; www.crowncork.com; John W. Conway; world's leading supplier of packaging prods.

CSX Corp.; 500 Water St., C900, Jacksonville, FL 32202; (904) 633-1000; www.csx.com; Michael J. Ward; rail, ocean, barge freight transport.

CVS Corp.; 1 CVS Dr., Woonsocket, RI 02895; (401) 765-1500; www.CVS.com; Thomas M. Ryan; acquired Eckerd Corp. in August 2004, to become nation's largest drugstore chain.

Dana Corp.; 4500 Dorr St., Toledo, OH 43615; (419) 535-4500; www.dana.com; Michael Burns; truck and auto parts, supplies.

Darden Restaurants; 5900 Lake Ellenor Dr., Orlando, FL 32809; (407) 245-4000; www.darden.com; Joe Lee; chain restaurants (Red Lobster, Olive Garden, Bahama Breeze, Smokey Bones BBQ Sports Bar).

Dean Foods Co.; 2515 McKinney Ave., Ste. 1200, Dallas, TX 75201; 214-303-3400; www.deanfoods.com; Gregg L. Engles; milk and specialty dairy products (Land O'Lakes, Horizon Organic, Silk soymilk), salad dressings (Marie's), pickles.

Deere & Co.; One John Deere Pl., Moline, IL 61265; (309) 765-8000; www.deere.com; Robert W. Lane; world's largest manuf. of farm equip.; also makes industrial equip., and lawn and garden tractors.

Dell Computer Corp.; 1 Dell Way, Round Rock, TX 78682; (512) 338-4400; www.dell.com; Michael S. Dell; laptop and desktop computers.

Delphi Corp.; 5725 Delphi Dr., Troy, MI 48098; (248) 813-2000; www.delphi.com; J.T. Battenberg III; automotive systems, audio systems, mobile electronics.

Delta Air Lines, Inc.; P.O. Box 20706, Atlanta, GA 30320; (404) 715-2600; www.delta.com; Gerald Grinstein; air transportation.

Dial Corp.; 15501 N. Dial Blvd., Scottsdale, AZ 85260-1619; (602) 754-3425; www.dialcorp.com; Herbert Baum; consumer prods. (Dial, Coast soap, Purex detergent, Armour Star meats, Renuzit air fresheners).

Diebold, Inc; 5995 Mayfair Rd., P.O. Box 3077, North Canton, OH 44720; (330) 490-4000; www.diebold.com; Walden W. O'Dell; manuf. ATMs, security systems and prods.

Dillard's; 1600 Cantrell Rd., Little Rock, AR 72201; (501) 376-5200; www.dillards.com; William Dillard 2nd; 2nd-largest dept. store chain in U.S.

Walt Disney Co.; 500 S. Buena Vista St., Burbank, CA 91521-7320; (818) 560-1000; www.disney.com; Michael D. Eisner; motion pictures, television (ESPN, ABC, SoapNet, Disney Channel, Lifetime), radio stations, theme parks (Walt Disney World, Disneyland) and resorts, publishing, recordings, retailing (Disney Stores).

Dole Food Co., Inc.; One Dole Drive, Westlake Village, CA 91362; (818) 879-6600; www.dole.com; David H. Murdock; food prods., fresh fruits and vegetables.

R. R. Donnelley & Sons Co.; 77 W. Wacker Dr., Chicago, IL 60601-1696; (312) 326-8000; www.rrdonnelley.com; Mark A. Angelson; largest commercial printer in N. America; photo/graphics, translation; printer of *The World Almanac*.

Dow Chemical Co.; 2030 Dow Center, Midland, MI 48674; (517) 636-1000; www.dow.com; William S. Stavropoulos; chemicals, plastics (world's 2nd-largest chemical co. after merger, 2/7/01, with Union Carbide).

Dow Jones & Co., Inc.; 200 Liberty St., NY, NY 10281; (212) 416-2000; www.dowjones.com; Peter R. Kann; financial news service, publishing (*Wall Street Journal*, *Barron's*, Ottaway Newspapers).

Duke Energy Corp.; 526 S. Church St., Charlotte, NC 28202; 704-594-6200; www.duke-energy.com; Paul M. Anderson; natural gas, uilities, pipelines, fiber optics.

Dun & Bradstreet Corp.; 103 JFK Parkway, Short Hills, NJ 07078; (973) 921-5500; www.dnb.com; Allen Z. Loren.; business information, publishing ("Yellow Pages" phone books).

Duracell: *see* Gillette.

E. I. du Pont de Nemours & Co. (Dupont); 1007 Market St., Wilmington, DE 19898; (302) 774-1000; www.dupont.com; Charles Holliday; largest U.S. chemical co.; petroleum, consumer prods.

Eastman Kodak Co.; 343 State St., Rochester, NY 14650-0205; (585) 724-4000; www.kodak.com; D. Carp; world's largest producer of photographic prods.

Eaton Corp.; 1111 Superior Ave., Cleveland, OH 44114; (216) 523-5000; www.eaton.com; Alexander Cutler; manuf. of vehicle powertrain components, controls.

Eckerd Corp.: *see* CVS Corp.

Edison Intl.; 2244 Walnut Grove Ave., P.O. Box 800, Rosemead, CA 91770; (626) 302-2222; www.edisonx.com; John Bryson; electric utilities.

Electronic Data Systems; 5400 Legacy Dr., Plano, TX 75024; (972) 604-6000; www.eds.com; Michael Jordan; management consulting, e-solutions, software.

Eli Lilly and Co.; Lilly Corporate Center, Indianapolis, IN 46285; 317-276-2000; www.lilly.com; Sidney Taurel; pharmaceutical research, development, and manufacturing (Prozac, Stratera, Evista, Cialis).

El Paso Corp.; 1001 Louisiana Street, Houston, TX 77002; (713) 420-2600; www.elpaso.com; Ronald L. Kuehn Jr.; diversified energy company primarily engaged in interstate transmission of natural gas.

Emerson Electric Co.; 8000 West Florissant Avenue, St. Louis, MO 63136; (314) 553-2000; www.gotoemerson.com; David Farr; electrical, electronics prods. & systems.

Energizer Holdings Inc.; 533 Maryville Univ. Dr., St. Louis, MO 63141; (800) 742-8377; www.energizer.com; J. Patrick Mulcahy; batteries, flashlights, lanterns.

Exelon Corp.; 10 S. Dearborn St., 37th Fl., Chicago, IL 60680; www.exeloncorp.com; 312-394-7398; John W. Rowe; electricity generation and distribution; nat. gas.

Exxon Mobil Corp.; 5959 Las Colinas Blvd., Irving, TX 75039-2298; (972) 444-1000; www.exxonmobil.com; Lee Raymond; world's largest publicly owned integrated oil co.

Fannie Mae; 3900 Wisconsin Ave. NW, Washington, DC 20016; (202) 752-7000; www.fanniemae.com; Franklin Raines; largest U.S. provider of residential mortgage funds.

Fedders Corp.; 505 Martinsville Road, PO Box 813, Liberty Corner, NJ 07938; (908) 604-8686; www.fedders.com; Salvatore Giordano Jr; manuf. of room air conditioners (Fedders, Airtemp), dehumidifiers.

Federated Dept. Stores; 7 W. 7th St., Cincinnati, OH 45202; (513) 579-7000; www.Federated-fds.com; Terry J. Lundgren; full-line dept. stores (Macy's, Bloomingdale's, Burdines).

FedEx Corp.; 942 S. Shady Grove Rd., Memphis, TN 38120; (901) 369-3600; www.fedex.com; F. W. Smith; express delivery service.

First Data Corp.; 6200 S. Quebec St., Greenwood Village, CO, 30328; (303) 488-8000; www.firstdata.com; Charles Fote; info. retrieval, data processing.

FirstEnergy Corp.; 76 S. Main St., Akron, OH 44308; 800-646-0400; www.firstenergycorp.com; Anthony J. Alexander; public utility company; provides electricity and natural gas.

FleetBoston Financial Corp.; 100 Federal St., 10034F, Boston, MA 02110; (617) 434-2200; www.fleet.com; Charles Gifford; financial services company. Merged with Bank of America as of 7/1/04.

Fleetwood Enterprises, Inc.; 3125 Myers St., Riverside, CA 92503; (909) 351-3500; www.fleetwood.com; Edward B. Candill; manufactured homes, recreational vehicles.

Fleming Cos. Inc.; P.O. Box 299013, Lewisville, TX 75029; (972) 906-8000; www.fleming.com; Peter S. Willmott; one of largest U.S. wholesale food distrib.

Fluor Corp.; One Enterprise Dr., Aliso Viejo, CA 92656; (949) 349-2000; www.fluor.com; Alan L. Boeckmann; largest international engineering and construction co. in U.S.

Foot Locker, Inc.; formerly Venator Group, 112 West 34th St., NY, NY 10120; (212) 720-3700; www.footlocker-inc.com; Matthew D. Serra; operates retail stores: shoes (Kinney), apparel (Eastbay), athletic footwear (Foot Locker), athletic merchandise (Champs).

Ford Motor Co.; American Rd., Dearborn, MI 48121; (313) 322-3000; www.ford.com; William Clay Ford Jr.; 2nd-largest auto manufacturer, motor vehicle sales (Ford, Lincoln-Mercury, Volvo), rentals (Hertz).

Fortune Brands, Inc.; 300 Tower Parkway, Lincolnshire, IL 60069; (847) 484-4400; www.fortunebrands.com.index/cfm; Norman H. Wesley; spirits and wine (Jim Beam), hardware, office prods. (Swingline), golf and leisure prods. (Titleist, Cobra, FootJoy).

Freddie Mac; 8200 Jones Branch Dr., McLean, VA 22102; (703) 903-2000; www.freddiemac.com; Dick Syron; residential mortgage provider.

Fruit of the Loom, Inc.; 1 Fruit of the Loom Dr., Bowling Green, KY 42102-9015; (270) 781-6400; www.fruit.com; John B. Holland; manuf. of underwear, activewear. A subsidiary of Berkshire Hathaway, acquired 4/30/02.

Gannett Co., Inc.; 7950 Jones Branch Dr., McLean, VA 22107; (703) 854-6000; www.gannett.com; D.H. McCorkindale; newspaper publishing (*USA Today*), network and cable TV.

The Gap, Inc.; Two Folsom St., San Francisco, CA 94105; (415) 952-4400; www.gap.com; Robert Fisher; casual and activewear retailer (Gap, Banana Republic, Old Navy).

Gateway; 14303 Gateway Pl., Poway, CA 92064; (858) 848-3401; www.gateway.com; Wayne Inouye; personal computers.

General Dynamics; 2941 Fairview Park Drive, Falls Church, VA 22042; (703) 876-3000; www.generaldynamics.com; Nicholas D. Chabraja; nuclear submarines (Trident, Seawolf), armored vehicles, combat systems, computing devices, defense systems.

General Electric Co.; 3135 Easton Tpke., Fairfield, CT 06431; (203) 373-2211; www.ge.com; Jeffrey Immelt; electrical, electronic equip., radio and television broadcasting (NBC), aircraft engines, power generation, appliances.

General Mills, Inc.; Number One General Mills Blvd., PO Box 1113, Minneapolis, MN 55440; (763) 764-7600; www.generalmills.com; S. W. Sanger; foods (Total, Wheaties, Cheerios, Chex, Hamburger Helper, Betty Crocker, Bisquick).

General Motors; 100 Renaissance Center, Detroit, MI 48265; (313) 556-5000; www.gm.com; G. Richard Wagoner Jr.; world's largest auto manuf. (Chevrolet, Pontiac, Cadillac, Buick).

Genuine Parts Co.; 2999 Circle 75 Pkwy., Atlanta, GA 30339; (770) 953-1700; www.genpt.com; Larry L. Prince; distributes auto replacement parts (NAPA).

Georgia-Pacific Corp.; 133 Peachtree St. NE, Atlanta, GA 30303; (404) 652-4000; www.gp.com; A. D. Correll; manuf. of paper and wood prods.

Gillette; Prudential Tower Bldg., Boston, MA 02199; (617) 421-7000; www.gillette.com; James M. Kilts; personal care prods. (Sensor, Atra razors, Oral-B toothbrushes, Right Guard, Soft & Dri), appliances (Braun), batteries (Duracell).

Goldman Sachs Group; 85 Broad Street, NY, NY 10004; (212) 902-1000; www.gs.com; Henry M. Paulson Jr.; investment banking, asset management, securities services.

The Goodyear Tire & Rubber Co.; 1144 E. Market St., Akron, OH 44316; (330) 796-2121; www.goodyear.com; Robert Keegan; world's largest rubber manuf.; tires and other auto prods.

W. R. Grace & Co.; 7500 Grace Dr., Columbia, MD 21044; (410) 531-4000; www.grace.com; Paul J. Norris; chemicals, construction prods.

Great Atlantic & Pacific Tea Co. (A&P); 2 Paragon Dr., Montvale, NJ 07645; (201) 573-9700; www.aptea.com; Christian Haub; supermarkets (A&P, Waldbaum's, Kohl's, Dominion).

Halliburton Co.; 5 Houston Center, 1401 McKinney, Houston, TX 77010; (713) 759-2600; www.halliburton.com; Dave Lesar; energy, engineering, and construction services.

Harley-Davidson, Inc.; 3700 W. Juneau Avenue, Milwaukee, WI 53208; (414) 343-4680; www.harley-davidson.com; Jeffrey Bleustein; manuf. of motorcycles, parts, and accessories.

Harrah's Entertainment, Inc.; One Harrah's Court, Las Vegas, NV 89119; (702) 407-6000; www.harrahs.com; Philip G. Satre; casino-hotels and riverboats.

Hartford Financial Services Group, Inc.; Hartford Plaza, 690 Asylum Ave., Hartford, CT 06115; (860) 547-5000; www.thehartford.com; Ramani Ayer; insurance, financial services.

Hartmarx; 101 N. Wacker Dr., Chicago, IL 60606; (312) 372-6300; www.hartmarx.com; Hami Patel; apparel manuf. (Hart Schaffner & Marx, Hickey Freeman, Claiborne, Tommy Hilfiger, Pierre Cardin, Perry Ellis).

Hasbro, Inc.; 1027 Newport Ave., Pawtucket, RI 02862; (401) 431-8697; www.hasbro.com; Alan G. Hassenfeld; toy and game manuf. (Milton Bradley, Playskool, G. I. Joe, Parker Bros., Tiger Electronics, Play-Doh).

HCA Inc.; 1 Park Plaza, Nashville, TN 37203; (615) 344-9551; www.hcahealthcare.com; Jack O. Bovender Jr.; largest hospital mgmt. co. in the U.S.

H. J. Heinz Co.; 600 Grant St., Pittsburgh, PA 15219; (412) 456-5700; www.heinz.com; William R. Johnson; foods (StarKist, Ore-Ida, 57 Varieties), pet food (Kibbles 'n Bits, 9 Lives), Weight Watchers.

Hershey Foods Corp.; 100 Crystal A Dr., Hershey, PA 17033; (717) 534-6799; www.hersheys.com; Richard H. Lenny; largest U.S. producer of chocolate and confectionery prods. (Reese's, Kit Kat, Mounds, Almond Joy, Cadbury, Jolly Rancher, Twizzlers, Milk Duds, Good & Plenty).

Hewlett-Packard Co.; 3000 Hanover St., Palo Alto, CA 94304; (650) 857-1501; www.hp.com; Carleton Fiorina; manuf. computers, electronic prods. and systems. (On 5/3/02 Hewlett-Packard acquired Compaq Computer Co.)

Hillenbrand Industries, Inc.; 700 State Rte. 46 E, Batesville, IN 47006; (812) 934-7000; www.hillenbrand.com; Frederick Rockwood; manuf. caskets, adjustable hospital beds.

Hilton Hotels Corp.; 9336 Civic Center Dr., Beverly Hills, CA 90210; (310) 278-4321; www.hilton.com; Stephen F. Bollenbach; hotels, casinos.

Home Depot, Inc.; 2455 Paces Ferry Rd. NW, Atlanta, GA 30339; (770) 433-8211; www.homedepot.com; Robert L. Nardelli; retail building supply, home improvement warehouse stores.

Honeywell Inc.; 101 Columbia Road, Morristown, NJ 07962; (973) 455-2000; www.honeywell.com; David Cote; industrial and home control systems, aerospace guidance systems.

Hormel Foods Corp.; 1 Hormel Pl., Austin, MN 55912-3680; (507) 437-5611; www.hormel.com; Joel W. Johnson; meat processor, pork and beef prods. (SPAM, Dinty Moore, Little Sizzlers).

Houghton Mifflin Co.; 222 Berkeley St., Boston, MA 02116; (617) 351-5000; www.hmco.com; Anthony Lucki; publisher of textbooks, reference, general interest books.

Huffy Corp.; 225 Byers Rd., Miamisburg, OH 45342; (937) 866-6251; www.huffy.com; Don R. Graber; largest U.S. bicycle manuf.; sports and hardware equip.

Humana, Inc.; 500 W. Main Street, PO Box 1438, Louisville, KY 40202; (502) 580-1000; www.humana.com; David A. Jones; managed healthcare service provider, related specialty products.

Illinois Toolworks; 3600 West Lake Ave., Glenview, IL 60025; (847) 724-7500; www.itwinc.com; W. James Farrell; food equip. (Hobart), home appliances and cookware (West Bend).

Ingersoll-Rand; 200 Chestnut Ridge Road, Woodcliff Lake, NJ 07675; (201) 573-0123; www.irco.com; Herbert L. Henkel; industrial machinery.

Intel Corp.; 2200 Mission College Blvd., Santa Clara, CA 95052-8119; (408) 765-8080; www.intel.com; A. S. Grove; manuf. integrated circuits (Pentium).

International Business Machines Corp. (IBM); One New Orchard Rd., Armonk, NY 10504; (914) 499-1900; www.ibm.com; Samuel Palmisano; world's largest supplier of advanced information processing technology equip., services.

International Paper Co.; 400 Atlantic St., Stamford, CT 06921; (203) 541-8000; www.internationalpaper.com; John Faraci; world's largest paper/forest prods. co.; chemicals, packaging.

International Steel Group-Bethlehem; 3250 Interstate Dr., 2nd Fl., Richfield, OH 44286; www.bethsteel.com; Rodney B. Mott; steel & steel prods.

Interstate Bakeries Corp.; 12 E. Armour Blvd., Kansas City, MO 64111; (816) 502-4000; www.interstatebakeries corp.com; James R. Elsesser; baked goods wholesaler, distributor (Wonder, Hostess, Dolly Madison, Beefsteak, Home Pride).

J. Crew Group, Inc.; 770 Broadway, NY, NY 10003; (212) 209-2500; www.jcrew.com; Millard S. Drexler; apparel and accessories, retail and mail order.

Jet Blue Airways; 118-29 Queens Blvd., Forest Hills, NY 11375; (800) JETBLUE; www.jetblue.com; David Neeleman; air travel.

Jo-Ann Stores, Inc.; 5555 Darrow Rd., Hudson, OH 44236; (330) 656-2600; www.joann.com; Alan Rosskamm; nation's largest specialty fabric and craft stores (Jo-Ann Fabric and Crafts, Jo-Ann etc.).

Johnson & Johnson; 1 Johnson & Johnson Plaza, New Brunswick, NJ 08933; (732) 524-0400; www.jnj.com; William Weldon; surgical dressings (Band-Aid), pharmaceuticals (Tylenol), toiletries (Neutrogena).

S.C. Johnson & Son, Inc.; 1525 Howe St., Racine, WI 53403; (262) 260-2000; www.scjohnson.com; William D. Perez; cleaning and other household prods. (Johnson's Wax, Windex, pledge, Fantastik, Raid, Off!, Shout, Glade, Scrubbing Bubbles, Ziploc bags).

Johnson Controls, Inc.; 5757 N. Green Bay Avenue, Milwaukee, WI 53201; (414) 524-1200; www. johnsoncontrols.com; John Barth; fire protection services, auto seats and batteries.

Jones Apparel Group, Inc.; 250 Rittenhouse Circle, Bristol, PA 19007; 215-785-4000; www.jny.com; Peter Boneparth; apparel (Jones New York, Gloria Vanderbilt), shoes (Nine West, Anne Klein), retail and outlet stores.

Jostens Inc.; 5501 American Blvd. W., Minneapolis, MN 55437; (612) 830-3300; www.jostens.com; Michael L. Bailey; school rings, yearbooks, plaques.

JPMorgan Chase & Co. Inc; 270 Park Ave., NY, NY 10017; (212) 270-6000; www.jpmorganchase.com; William Harrison Jr.; global financial firm. (Merged with Bank One Corp., 7/1/04.)

Kellogg Co.; One Kellogg Sq., Battle Creek, MI 49016; (269) 961-2000; www.kelloggs.com; Carlos Gutierrez; world's largest mfgr. of ready-to-eat cereals, other food prods. (Frosted Flakes, Rice Krispies, Froot Loops, Pop-Tarts, Nutri-Grain, Eggo).

Kelly Services, Inc.; 999 West Big Beaver Rd., Troy, MI 48084; (248) 362-4444; www.kellyservices.com; Terence Adderley; temporary staffing services.

Kimberly-Clark Corp.; PO Box 619100, Dallas, TX 75261-9100; (972) 281-1200; www.kimberly-clark.com; Thomas Falk; personal care prods. (Kleenex, Scott, Cottonelle, Huggies, Viva, Kotex).

King World Productions, Inc.; 1700 Broadway, 33rd Floor, NY, NY 10019; (212) 315-4000; www.kingworld.com; Roger King; distributor of TV programs (*Oprah Winfrey Show, Wheel of Fortune, Jeopardy!, Inside Edition*).

Kmart Corp.; 3100 W. Big Beaver Rd., Troy, MI 48084; (248) 463-1000; www.kmart.com; Julian C. Day; discount stores.

Knight Ridder, Inc.; 50 W. San Fernando Street, San Jose, CA 95113-2413; (408) 938-7700; www.knightridder.com; P.A. Ridder; newspaper publishing.

Kraft Foods, Inc.: *see* Altria Group, Inc.

Kroger Co.; 1014 Vine St., Cincinnati, OH 45202; (513) 762-4000; www.kroger.com; David Dillon; largest U.S. retail grocery chain, convenience stores, mall jewelry stores.

(Estee) Lauder Cos.; 767 5th Ave., NY, NY 10153; (212) 572-4200; www.esteelauder.com; Leonard A. Lauder; cosmetics (Clinique), fragrance prods. (Aramis, Aveda, Tommy Hilfiger).

La-Z-Boy Inc.; 1284 N. Telegraph Rd., Monroe, MI 48162; (734) 242-1444; www.lazboy.com; Patrick H. Norton; reclining chairs, other furniture.

Leggett & Platt, Inc.; No. 1 Leggett Rd., Carthage, MO 64836; (417) 358-8131; www.leggett.com; Felix E. Wright; furniture and furniture components, industrial materials, automotive seating suspension, train and cable control systems.

Lehman Bros. Holdings, Inc.; 745 7th Ave., NY, NY 10019; (212) 526-7000; www.lehman.com; Richard S. Fuld Jr.; investment bank.

Levi Strauss & Co;; 1155 Battery St., San Francisco, CA 94111; (415) 501-6000; www.levistrauss.com; Robert D. Haas; blue jeans, casual sportswear.

Liberty Mutual Group; 175 Berkeley St., Boston, MA 02116; (617) 357-9500; www.libertymutual.com; Edmund F. Kelly; auto, home, and life insurance.

The Limited, Inc.; 3 Limited Pkwy., P.O. Box 16000, Columbus, OH 43216; (614) 479-7000; www.limited.com; Leslie H. Wexner; apparel stores (Lane Bryant, Lerner, Limited, Express, Victoria's Secret, Henri Bendel), home decor (White Barn Candle Co., Bath & Body Works).

L.L.Bean, Inc.; Casco St., Freeport, ME 04033-0001; (207) 865-4761; www.llbean.com; Leon Gorman; outdoor apparel and footwear.

Lockheed Martin Corp.; 6801 Rockledge Dr., Bethesda, MD 20817; (301) 897-6000; www.lockheedmartin.com; Vance Coffman; commercial and military aircraft, electronics, missiles.

Loews Corp.; 667 Madison Ave., NY, NY 10021; (212) 521-2000; www.loews.com; James S. Tisch; tobacco prods. (Kent, True, Newport), watches (Bulova), hotels, insurance (CNA Financial), offshore drilling (Diamond).

Longs Drug Stores, Inc.; 141 N. Civic Dr., P.O. Box 5222, Walnut Creek, CA 94596; (925) 937-1170; www.longs.com; Warren Bryant; drug store chain.

Lowe's Cos., Inc;; 1605 Curtis Bridge Rd., N. Wilkesboro, NC 28656; (336) 658-4000; www.lowes.com; Robert L. Tillman; building materials and home improvement superstores.

Luby's, Inc.; 2211 NE Loop 410, PO Box 33069, San Antonio, TX 78265; (210) 654-9000; www.lubys.com; Christopher Pappas; operates cafeterias in S and SW.

Lucent Technologies, Inc.; 600 Mountain Ave., Murray Hill, NJ 07974; (908) 582-8500; www.lucent.com; Patricia Russo; leading developer, designer, and manuf. of telecommunications systems, software, and prods.

Mandalay Resort Group; 3950 Las Vegas Boulevard South, Las Vegas, NV 89119; (702) 632-6700; www.mandalay resort-group.org; Michael Ensign; casino-resort operator (Excalibur, Luxor).

Manpower Inc.; 5301 N. Ironwood Rd., Milwaukee, WI 53217; (414) 961-1000; www.manpower.com; Jeffrey A. Joerres; 2nd-largest non-gov't. employment services co. in the world.

Marathon Oil Corp.; 555 San Felipe Rd., Houston, TX 77056; (713) 629-6600; www.marathon.com; Clarence P. Cazalot Jr.; integrated oil co. (Became independent co. 1/1/02 after being separated from USX-Marathon Group; United States Steel Corp. created as a result of a spin-off from USX.)

Marriott International, Inc.; Marriott Drive, Washington, DC 20058; (301) 380-3000; www.marriott.com; John Willard Marriott Jr; hotels, retirement communities, food service dist.

Masco Corp.; 21001 Van Born Rd., Taylor, MI 48180; (313) 274-7400; www.masco.com; Richard A. Manoogian; manuf. kitchen, bathroom prods. (Delta, Peerless faucets; Fieldstone, Merillat cabinets).

MassMutual Financial Group; 1295 State St., Springfield, MA 01111; (800) 767-1000; www.massmutual.com; Robert J. O'Connell; financial planning and investment, life insurance.

Mattel, Inc.; 333 Continental Blvd., El Segundo, CA 90245; (310) 252-2000; www.mattel.com; Robert A. Eckert; largest U.S. toymaker (Barbie, Fisher-Price, Hot Wheels, Matchbox, American Girls).

May Department Stores Co.; 611 Olive St., St. Louis, MO 63101; (314) 342-6300; www.maycompany.com; Gene S. Kahn; department stores (Hecht's, Lord & Taylor, Filene's, Foley's).

Maytag Corp.; 403 W. Fourth St. N., Newton, IA 50208; (641) 792-7000; www.maytagcorp.com; Ralph F. Hake; major appliance mfgr. (Magic Chef, Admiral, Jenn-Air), Hoover vacuum cleaners, floor care systems.

McDonald's Corp.; McDonald's Plaza, Oak Brook, IL 60523; (630) 623-3000; www.mcdonalds.com; Charlie Bell; fast-food restaurants.

McGraw-Hill Cos.; 1221 Ave. of the Americas, NY, NY 10020; (212) 512-2000; www.mcgraw-hill.com; Harold (Terry) McGraw 3rd; book, textbooks, magazine publishing (*Business Week*), information and financial services (Standard & Poor's), TV stations.

MCI, Inc.; 2201 Loudoun County Pkwy., Ashburn, VA 20147; (703) 886-5600; www.mci.com; Michael D. Capellas; long-distance telephone service.

McKesson Corp.; 1 Post St., San Francisco, CA 94104; (415) 983-8300; www.mckesson.com; John Hammergren; distributor of drugs and toiletries; provides software and services in U.S.; bottled water.

MeadWestvaco Corp.; One High Ridge Park, Stamford, CT 06905; (203) 461-7400; www.meadwestvaco.com; John A. Luke Jr.; printing and writing paper, paperboard, packaging, shipping containers.

Medco Health Solutions, Inc.; 100 Parsons Pond Rd., Parsons Lake, NJ 07417; 201-269-3400; www.medcohealth.com; David B. Snow Jr.; pharmacy benefits management.

Medtronic, Inc.; 710 Medtronic Pkwy., Minneapolis, MN 55432; (763) 514-4000; www.medtronic.com; Art Collins; world's largest manuf. of implantable biomedical devices.

Merck & Co., Inc.; PO Box 100, Whitehouse Station, NJ 08889-0100; (908) 423-1000; www.merck.com; Raymond V. Gilmartin; pharmaceuticals (Pepcid, Zocor), animal health care prods.

Meredith Corp.; 1716 Locust St., Des Moines, IA 50336; (515) 284-3000; www.meredith.com; William T. Kerr; magazine publishing (*Better Homes and Gardens, Ladies' Home Journal*), book publishing, broadcasting.

Merrill Lynch & Co., Inc.; 4 World Financial Ctr., NY, NY 10080; (212) 449-1000; www.ml.com; Stan O' Neal; securities broker, financial services.

Metropolitan Life Ins. Co.; One Madison Ave., NY, NY 10010; (212) 578-2211; www.metlife.com; Bob H. Benmosche; insurance, financial services.

MGM Mirage Resorts, Inc.; 3400 S. Las Vegas Blvd., Las Vegas, NV 89109; (702) 791-7111; www.mirage.com; J. Terrence Lanni; hotel-casino operator (Mirage, Treasure Island, Golden Nugget).

Microsoft Corp.; One Microsoft Way, Redmond, WA 98052-6399; (425) 882-8080; www.microsoft.com; William H. Gates; largest independent software maker (Windows, Word, Excel).

Mobil Corp.: *see* Exxon Mobil Corp.

MONY Group, Inc.; 1740 Broadway, NY, NY 10019; (212) 708-2000; www.mony.com; Michael Roth; life insurance, annuity, and investment products.

Motorola, Inc.; 1303 E. Algonquin Rd., Schaumburg, IL 60196; (847) 576-5000; www.motorola.com; Edward Zander; electronic equipment and components; integrated communication devices.

Morgan Stanley Dean Witter & Co.; 1585 Broadway, NY, NY 10036; (212) 761-4000; www.msdw.com; Phillip J. Purcell; diversified financial services, major U.S. credit-card issuer.

Nabisco: *see* Altria Group., Inc.

National Semiconductor Corp.; 2900 Semiconductor Dr., P.O. Box 58090; Santa Clara, CA 95052-8090; (408) 721-5000; www.national.com; Brian L. Halla; manuf. of semiconductors, integrated circuits.

Nationwide Mutual Insurance Company; One Nationwide Plaza, Columbus, OH 43215; (800) 882-2822; www.nationwide.com; W.G. Jurgensen; life insurance and financial services.

Navistar Intl. Corp.; 4201 Winfield Rd., PO Box 1488, Warrenville, IL 60555; (630) 735-2143; www.navistar.com; Daniel Ustian; manuf. heavy-duty trucks, parts, school buses.

NCR Corp.; 1700 S. Patterson Blvd., Dayton, OH 45479; (937) 445-5000; www.ncr.com; Mark Hurd; computer hardware and software, computer services and supplies.

Nestlé Purina PetCare; formerly Ralston Purina; Checkerboard Sq., St. Louis, MO 63164; (314) 982-2161; www.purina.com; W. Patrick McGinnis; world's largest producer of dog and cat food (Purina, Alpo, Fancy Feast) and some baked goods. Owned by Nestlé SA in Switzerland.

Nestlé USA, Inc.; 800 North Brand Blvd., Glendale, CA 91203; (818) 549-6000; www.nestleusa.com; Joe Weller; candy (Baby Ruth, Raisinets), beverages (Nestea, Juicy Juice), frozen foods (Stouffer's). Owned by Nestlé SA in Switzerland.

Newell Rubbermaid Inc.; Newell Center, 29 E. Stephenson St., Freeport, IL 61032; (815) 235-4171; www.newellco.com; Joseph Galli Jr.; cookware (Calphalon); hair accessories (Goody), glassware (Anchor Hocking); kitchen products (Rubbermaid); window treatments (Levolor, Kirsch); home storage; writing instruments (Eberhard Faber, Sanford, Sharpie); infant and juvenile prods. (Little Tikes, Graco).

New York Life Insurance Co.; 51 Madison Ave., New York, NY 10010; 212-576-7000; www.newyorklife.com; Seymour (Sy) Sternberg; life insurance, annuities, mutual funds.

New York Times Co.; 229 W. 43rd St., NY, NY 10036; (212) 556-1234; www.nytco.com; A. O. Sulzberger Jr.; newspapers (*Boston Globe*), radio and TV stations, magazines (*Golf Digest*).

Nextel Communications, Inc.; 2001 Edmund Halley Dr., Reston, VA 20191; 703-433-4000; www.nextel.com; Timothy M. Donahue; digital cellular, text messaging, and wireless internet services.

Nike, Inc.; 1 Bowerman Dr., Beaverton, OR 97005; (503) 671-6453; www.NikeBiz.com; Philip H. Knight; athletic and leisure footware, apparel.

Nordstrom, Inc.; 1617 6th Ave., Seattle, WA 98101; (206) 628-2111; www.nordstrom.com; Blake W. Nordstrom; upscale dept. store chain.

Norfolk Southern Corp.; Three Commercial Pl., Norfolk, VA 23510; (757) 629-2600; www.nscorp.com; David R. Goode; operates railway, freight carrier.

Northrop Grumman Corp; 1840 Century Park East, Los Angeles, CA 90067; (310) 553-6262; www.northgrum.com; Ronald D. Sugar; aircraft, electronics, data systems, information systems, missiles. (Northrop Grumman acquired TRW, 12/12/02.)

Northwest Airlines Corp.; 2700 Lone Oak Pkwy., Eagan, MN 55121; (612) 726-2111; www.nwa.com; Richard H. Anderson; air transportation.

Northwestern Mutual Life Insurance Co.; 720 E. Wisconsin Ave., Milwaukee, WI 53202; (414) 271-1444; www.north western.com; Edward J. Zore; life insurance, investment products and services, annuities.

Occidental Petroleum Corp.; 10889 Wilshire Blvd., Los Angeles, CA 90024; (310) 208-8800; www.oxy.com; Ray R. Irani; oil, natural gas, chemicals, plastics, fertilizers.

Office Depot.; 2200 Old Germantown Rd., Delray Beach, FL 33445; (561) 438-4800; www.officedepot.com; Bruce Nelson; retail office supply stores.

Omnicom Group Inc.; 437 Madison Ave., NY, NY 10022; (212) 415-3600; www.omnicomgroup.com; John Wren; advertising, market services, interactive/digital media.

Oracle Corp.; 500 Oracle Pkwy., Redwood Shores, CA 94065; www.oracle.com; Lawrence Ellison; database and file management software.

Owens Corning; 1 Owens Corning Parkway, Toledo, OH 43659; (419) 248-8000; www.owenscorning.com; David T. Brown; world leader in advanced glass, composite materials.

Owens-Illinois; 1 SeaGate, Toledo, OH 43666; (419) 247-5000; Steven McCracken; www.o-i.com; one of the world's largest producer of glass and plastic packaging.

Oxford Health Plans: *see* UnitedHealth Group.

Pacific Gas & Electric Corp. (PG&E); One Market, Spear Tower, Ste. 2400, San Francisco, CA 94105; (415) 267-7000; www.pgecorp.com; Robert D. Glynn Jr.; energy supplier.

PaineWebber Group, Inc.: *see* UBS.

Park Place Entertainment; 3930 Howard Hughes Pkwy., Las Vegas, NV 89109; (702) 699-5000; www.parkplace.com; Stephen Bollenbach; casino/hotel operators (Caesars, Paris, Bally's, Flamingo, Hilton, Grand Casino, Conrad).

J.C. Penney Co.; 6501 Legacy Dr., Plano, TX 75024; (972) 431-1000; www.jcpenney.com; Allen Questrom; dept. stores, catalog sales, drug stores (Eckerd, Fay's), insurance.

Pennzoil-Quaker State Co.(SOPUS Products); Pennzoil Pl., P.O. Box 2967, Houston, TX 77252-2967; (800) 990-9811; www.pennzoil.com; motor, gear, and transmission oils; grease; air and oil filters; cleaning and hydraulic fluids. Acquired by Royal Dutch/Shell Group (based in Neth.) 10/1/2002; U.S. affiliate is Shell Oil Co.

Pepsi Americas, Inc.; 4000 Dain Rauscher Plaza, 60 S. Sixth St., Minneapolis, MN 55402; (612) 661-4000; www.pepsiamericas.com; Robert C. Pohlad; Int'l beverage distributor, esp. Pepsi products.

PepsiCo, Inc.; 700 Anderson Hill Rd., Purchase, NY 10577; (914) 253-2000; www.pepsico.com; Steven S. Reinemund; soft drinks (Pepsi-Cola, Mountain Dew), fruit juice (Tropicana), FritoLay snacks (Ruffles, Lay's, Fritos, Doritos, Rold Gold), Quaker Oats.

Pfizer, Inc.; 235 E. 42nd St., NY, NY 10017; (212) 733-2323; www.pfizer.com; Henry McKinnell; pharmaceuticals (Celebrex, Diflucan, Viagra, Zithromax), hospital, agricultural, chemical prods., consumer prods. (Visine, Desitin, Benadryl, Listerine, Lubriderm, Schick, Sudafed, Zantac 75, BenGay). (Co. merged with Warner-Lambert 6/19/01; acquired Pharmacia Corp. 4/16/03.)

Pharmacia Corp.: *see* Pfizer, Inc.

Philip Morris Cos. Inc.: see Altria Group, Inc.

Phillips-Van Heusen Corp.; 200 Madison Ave., NY, NY 10016; (212) 381-3500; www.pvh.com; Mark Weber; designer of dress shirts, sportswear, and footwear (IZOD, Geoffrey Beene, DKNY, Kenneth Cole). (Co. acquired Calvin Klein 2/12/03.)

Pillowtex Corp.; 1 Lake Circle Dr., Kannopolis, NC 28081; (704) 939-2000; www.pillowtex.com; Mike Gannaway; household textile prods.

Pitney Bowes, Inc.; 1 Elmcroft Rd., Stamford, CT 06926; (203) 356-5000; www.pb.com; Michael J. Critelli; world's largest mfgr. of postage meters and mailing equip.

Polaroid Corp.; 1265 Main St., Bldg. W3, Waltham, MA 02451; (781) 386-2000; www.polaroid.com; Michael Pocock; photographic equip. and supplies, optical goods.

Polo Ralph Lauren Corp.; 650 Madison Ave., NY, NY 10022; (212) 318-7000; www.polo.com; Ralph Lauren; men's and women's apparel.

PPG Industries, Inc.; 1 PPG Place, Pittsburgh, PA 15272; (412) 434-3131; www.ppg.com; Raymond W. LeBoeuf; glass prods., silicas, fiberglass, chemicals; world's leading supplier of automobile/industrial coatings.

Procter & Gamble Co.; 1 Procter & Gamble Plaza, Cincinnati, OH 45202; (513) 983-1100; www.pg.com; Alan Lafley; soaps and detergents (Ivory, Cheer, Tide, Mr. Clean, Comet, Zest); toiletries (Crest, Scope, Head & Shoulders, Noxzema, Oil of Olay, Old Spice); pharmaceuticals (NyQuil, Pepto-Bismol, Vicks cough medicines); foods (Folgers coffee, Pringles); paper prods. (Charmin toilet tissues, Bounty towels, Tampax tampons, Pampers & Luvs disposable diapers); Cover Girl and Max Factor cosmetics, Clairol haircare.

Prudential Financial, Inc.; 751 Broad St., Newark, NJ 07102; (973) 802-6000; www.prudential.com; Arthur F. Ryan; insurance, financial services.

Publix Super Markets; 3300 Airport Rd., Lakeland, FL 33815; (863) 688-1188; www.publix.com; Charles Jenkins Jr.; chain of supermarkets.

Quaker Oats Co.: *see* PepsiCo, Inc.

Qwest Communications, Inc.; 1801 California St., Denver, CO 80202; (303) 992-1400; www.qwest.com; Richard Notebaert; telecommunications, wireless, and directory services for most of western and southwestern U.S.

Radio Shack, formerly Tandy Corp.; 100 Throckmorton St., Suite 1800, Fort Worth, TX 76102; (817) 415-3011; www.radioshack.com; Leonard H. Roberts; consumer electronics retailer (Computer City, Radio Shack).

Ralcorp Holdings, Inc.; 800 Market St., St. Louis, MO 63101; (314) 877-7000; www.ralcorp.com; William Stiritz; private-label breakfast cereals, snack foods, baby food (Beech-Nut).

Ralston Purina: *see* Nestlé Purina PetCare.

Raytheon Co.; 870 Winter St., Waltham, MA 02451; (781) 522-3000; www.raytheon.com; William Swanson; defense systems, electronics.

Reader's Digest Assn., Inc.; Reader's Digest Road, Pleasantville, NY 10570; (914) 238-1000; www.rd.com; Thomas Ryder; direct-mail marketer of magazines, books, music and video prods.

Reebok Intl., Ltd.; 1895 J.W. Foster Blvd., Canton, MA 02021; (781) 401-5000; www.reebok.com; Paul Fireman; athletic and leisure footwear, apparel.

Revlon, Inc.; 237 Park Ave., NY, NY 10017; (212) 527-4000; www.revlon.com; Jack Stahl; cosmetics, beauty aids, skin care.

Rite Aid Corp.; 30 Hunter Lane, Camp Hill, PA 17011-2404; (717) 761-2633; www.riteaid.com; Mary F. Sammons; discount drug stores.

Reynolds American; 401 N. Main St., Winston-Salem, NC 27102; (336) 741-5500; www.reynoldsamerican.com; Andrew J. Schindler; 2nd-largest U.S. producer of cigarettes (Winston, Salem, Camel). On 7/30/04, RJ Reynolds merged with Brown & Williamson Tobacco Corp. to form Reynolds American.

Rockwell Auto; 777 E. Wisconsin Ave., Suite 1400, Milwaukee, WI 53202; (414) 212-5200; www.rockwell.com; Don H. Davis; diversified high-tech. co. (world leader in electronic controls).

Rohm & Haas Co.; 100 Independence Mall West, Philadelphia, PA 19106; (215) 592-3000; www.rohmhaas.com; Raj Gupta; adhesives and sealants, process chemicals, automotive coatings; salt (Morton, Windsor).

Ryder System, Inc.; 3600 NW 82nd Ave., Miami, FL 33166; (305) 500-3726; www.ryder.com; Gregory T. Swienton; truck-leasing service.

Safeway Inc.; 5918 Stoneridge Mall Rd., Pleasanton, CA 94588-3229; (925) 467-3000; www.safeway.com; Steven A. Burd; supermarkets.

Sara Lee Corp.; Three First National Plaza, Chicago, IL 60602; (312) 726-2600; www.saralee.com; C. Steven McMillan; baked goods, fresh and processed meats (Ball Park, Jimmy Dean, Hillshire Farms, Kahn's), hosiery, intimate apparel, and knitwear (Hanes, L'eggs, Playtex, Champion).

SBC Communications, Inc.; 175 E. Houston, San Antonio, TX 78205; (210) 821-4105; www.sbc.com; Edward Whitacre Jr.; telephone services (Ameritech, Southwestern Bell, Pacific Bell).

Schering-Plough Corp.; 2000 Galloping Hill, Kenilworth, NJ 07033; (908) 298-4000; www.sch-plough.com; Fred Hassan;

pharmaceuticals (Claritin, Proventil), consumer prods. (Afrin, Coppertone), animal health prods.

Seagate Technology; 920 Disc Dr., Scotts Valley, CA 95066; (831) 438-6550; www.seagate.com; Stephen J. Luczo; manuf. disk drives.

Sears, Roebuck and Co.; 3333 Beverly Rd., Hoffman Estates, IL 60179; (847) 286-2500; www.sears.com; Alan J. Lacy; 2nd-largest U.S. retailer, department, specialty stores.

Shaw Industries, Inc.: *see* Berkshire Hathaway Inc.

Shell Oil Co.: *see* Pennzoil-Quaker State Co.

Sherwin-Williams Co.; 101 Prospect Ave. NW, Cleveland, OH 44115-1075; (216) 566-2000; www.sherwin.com; Christopher Connor; largest North American paint and varnish producer (Dutch Boy, Pratt & Lambert, Martha Stewart, Minwax).

Smithfield Foods, Inc.; 200 Commerce St., Smithfield, VA 23430; (757) 365-3000; www.smithfieldfoods.com; Joseph Luter III; pork and processed meat products.

J. M. Smucker Co.; One Strawberry Lane, Orrville, OH 44667; (330) 682-3000; www.smuckers.com; Timothy P. Smucker; preserves, jams, jellies (Dickinson's), toppings (Magic Shell), syrups, juices, Jif peanut butter, Crisco oil

Smurfit-Stone Container Corp.; 150 N. Michigan Ave., Chicago, IL 60601; (312) 346-6600; www.smurfit-stone.net; Patrick J. Moore; industry leader for corrugated containers, paper bags and sacks.

Southwest Airlines Co.; P.O. Box 36611, Dallas, TX 75235; (214) 792-4000; www.southwest.com; Colleen Barrett; air transportation.

Sprint Corp.; 6200 Sprint Pkwy., Overland Park, KS 66251; (913) 624-3000; www.sprint.com; Gary Forsee; long-distance and local telecommunications.

Staples, Inc; 500 Staples Dr., Framingham, MA 01702; (508) 253-5000; www.staples.com; Ron Sargent; office-supply superstores.

Starbucks Corp.; 2401 Utah Ave. S., P.O. Box 34067, Seattle, WA 98134; (206) 447-1575; www.starbucks.com; Orin Smith; coffee and tea producers, retail coffee and tea stores.

Starwood Hotels and Resorts Worldwide; 1111 Westchester Ave., White Plains, NY 10604; (914) 640-8100; www.starwood.com; Barry S. Sternlicht; hotels and leisure company (Westin, Sheraton, W Hotels).

State Farm Mutual Automobile Ins. Co.; 1 State Farm Plaza, Bloomington, IL 61701; (309) 766-2311; www.statefarm.com; Edward B. Rust Jr.; major insurance co.

Stride Rite Corp.; 191 Spring St., P.O. Box 9191, Lexington, MA 02420; (617) 824-6000; www.striderite. com; David Chamberlain; high-quality children's footwear (Keds, Sperry Top-Sider) and eyewear.

Sun Microsystems, Inc.; 4150 Network Circle, Santa Clara, CA 95054; (650) 960-1300; www.sun.com; Scott G. McNealy; supplier of network-based distributed computer systems (Java programming language).

Sunoco, Inc.; 1801 Market St., Philadelphia, PA 19103-1699; (215) 977-3000; www.sunocoinc.com; J.D. Drosdick; energy resources co., markets Sunoco gasoline.

SUPERVALU Inc.; 11840 Valley View Rd., Eden Prairie, MN 55340; (952) 828-4000; www.supervalu.com; Jeff Noddle; food wholesaler, retailer.

Sysco Corp.; 1390 Enclave Pkwy., Houston, TX 77077-2099; (281) 584-1390; www.sysco.com; Richard J. Schneiders; leading U.S. food distributor.

Target Corp.; 1000 Nicollet Mall, Minneapolis, MN 55403; (612) 370-6073; www.targetcorp.com; Robert J. Ulrich; department, specialty stores (Target, Marshall Field's, Mervyn's California).

Tenneco Automotive, Inc.; 500 N. Field Drive, Lake Forest, IL 60045; (847) 482-5000; www.tenneco-automotive.com; Mark P. Frissora; automotive parts (Monroe, Walker).

Texaco Inc.: *see* ChevronTexaco Corp.

Texas Instruments Inc.; 12500 TI Blvd., Dallas, TX 75266; (972) 995-3773; www.ti.com; T. J. Engibous; electronics, semiconductors, software.

Textron, Inc.; 40 Westminster St., Providence, RI 02903; (401) 421-2800; www.textron.com; Lewis B. Campbell; aerospace, industrial, automotive prods., financial services.

3M Company; 3M Center, St. Paul, MN 55144-1000; (612) 733-1110; www.3m.com; W. James McNerney Jr.; abrasives, adhesives, electrical, health care, cleaning (Scotch-Brite, O-Cel-O sponges), printing, consumer prods. (Scotch Tape, Post-it).

TIAA-CREF; 730 Third Ave., NY, NY 10017; (800) 842-2733; www.tiaa-cref.org; Herb Allison; financial services provider.

Timberland Company; 200 Domain Dr., Stratham, NH 03885; (603) 772-9500; www.timberland.com; Jeffrey Swartz; footwear, apparel, accessories.

Time Warner Inc.; 75 Rockefeller Plaza, New York, NY 10019; (212) 484-8000; www.timewarner.com; Richard D. Parsons; world's largest Internet online service; magazine publishing (*Time, Sports Illustrated, Fortune, Money, People,* DC Comics), TV and CATV (WB Network, HBO, Cinemax, CNN, TBS, TNT), book publishing (Little, Brown; Warner Books), motion

pictures (Warner Bros., New Line Cinema), recordings, sports teams (Atlanta Braves, Atlanta Hawks), retailing (Warner Bros. stores). (America Online and Time Warner completed the largest corporate merger in history in 2001, becoming the largest media company in the U.S. Dropped "AOL" from name, 9/18/03.)

The TJX Cos., Inc.; 770 Cochituate Rd., Framingham, MA 01701; (508) 390-1000; www.tjx.com; Edmond English; world's largest off-price apparel retailer (T.J. Maxx, Marshalls).

Tootsie Roll Industries, Inc.; 7401 S. Cicero Ave., Chicago, IL 60629; (773) 838-3400; www.tootsie.com; Ellen and Melvin Gordon; candy (Tootsie Roll, Mason Dots, Charms, Sugar Daddy, Charleston Chew, Junior Mints).

Toro Co.; 8111 Lyndale Ave. S, Bloomington, MN 55420; (952) 888-8801; www.toro.com; Kendrick B. Melrose; lawn and turf maintenance (Lawn-Boy), snow removal equipment, lighting and irrigation systems.

Toys "R" Us; 1 Geoffrey Way, Wayne, NJ 07470; (973) 617-3500; www.toysrus.com; John J. Eyler Jr.; world's largest children's specialty retailer (Toys "R" Us, Kids "R" Us, Babies "R" Us, Imaginarium).

Transamerica Corp.; 1149 Transamerica Center, Los Angeles, CA 90001; www.transamerica.com; Ron F. Wagley; insurance, financial services; wholly owned subsidiary of Netherlands-based AEGON.

Trans World Airlines, Inc.: see AMR. Corp.

Triarc Cos., Inc.; 280 Park Ave., NY, NY 10017; (212) 451-3000; www.triarc.com; Nelson Peltz; fast-food restaurants (Arby's), beverages (Royal Crown, Mystic, Nehi, Stewart's).

Tribune Co.; 435 N. Michigan Ave., Chicago, IL 60611; (312) 222-9100; www.tribune.com; Dennis J. Fitzsimmons; newspapers (*Los Angeles Times, Chicago Tribune, Newsday*), magazines (*Field & Stream, Popular Science*), broadcasting (incl. WGN-TV and 23 other stations), Chicago Cubs baseball team.

Trinity Industries, Inc.; PO Box 568887, 2525 Stemmons Freeway, Dallas, TX 75207; (214) 631-4420; www.trin.net; Timothy R. Wallace; manufactures metal prods., rail and freight prods.

TRW Inc.: see Northrop Grumman.

TWA: see AMR Corp.

Tyco Intl., Ltd.; 273 Corporate Dr., Portsmouth, NH 03801; (603) 334-3900; www.tyco.com; Edward Breen; fire protection systems, pipes, power cables, medical supplies, packaging.

Tyson Foods, Inc.; 2210 West Oaklawn Dr., Springdale, AR 72764; (501) 290-4000; www.tysonfoodsinc.com; John Tyson; fresh and processed poultry and beef, pork, and seafood prods. (Holly Farms, Weaver, Louis Kemp, IBP).

UAL Corp.; 1200 E. Algonquin Rd., Elk Grove Twp., IL 60007; (847) 700-4000; www.ual.com; Glenn Tilton; air transportation (United Airlines).

UBS; 1285 Ave. of the Americas, NY, NY 10019; (212) 713-2000; www.ubs.com; Joseph J. Grano Jr.; financial services.

Unilever US; Lever House, 390 Park Ave., New York, NY 10022; 212-888-1260; www.unilever.com; Niall Fitzgerald and Anthony Burgmans; food (Hellmann's mayonnaise, Knorr soups, Ragu pasta sauce, Wish-Bone salad dressing, Lipton Tea, Skippy Peanut Butter, Slim-Fast). Owned by Unilever NV (Neth.) and Unilever PLC (UK).

Union Carbide Corp.: see Dow Chemical Co.

Union Pacific Corp.; 1416 Dodge St., Omaha, NE, 68179; (402) 271-5000; www.up.com; Richard Davidson; largest railroad, trucking co. in U.S.; Fenix, telecommunications, software.

Unisys Corp.; Unisys Way, Blue Bell, PA 19424-0001; (215) 986-4011; www.unisys.com; Lawrence A. Weinbach; designs, manuf. computer information systems and related prods..

UnitedHealth Group Corp.; PO Box 1459, Minneapolis, MN 55440; (800) 328-5979; www.unitedhealthgroup.com; William W. McGuire; owns, manages health maintenance organizations; acquired Oxford Health Plans, July 2004.

United Parcel Service of America, Corp.; 55 Glenlake Pkwy. NE, Atlanta, GA 30328; (404) 828-6000; www.ups.com; Michael L. Eskew; courier services.

United States Steel Corp.; 600 Grant St., Pittsburgh, PA 15219-2800; (412) 433-1121; www.ussteel.com; Thomas J. Usher; steel, tin prods. (Became separate co. 1/1/02 as a result of a spin-off from USX-Marathon Group; rest of corp. became Marathon Oil Corp.)

United Technologies Corp.; One Financial Plaza, Hartford, CT 06101; (860) 728-7000; www.utc.com; George David; aerospace, industrial prods. and services (Otis Elevator, Pratt & Whitney, Sikorsky Aircraft).

Unocal Corp.; 2141 Rosecrans Ave., Ste. 4000, El Segundo, CA 90245; (310) 726-7731; www.unocal.com; Charles R. Williamson; integrated oil co.

US Airways Group, Inc.; 2345 Crystal Dr., Arlington, VA 22227; (703) 872-7000; www.usairways.com; Bruce Lakefield; air transportation.

UST Inc.; 100 W. Putnam Ave., Greenwich, CT 06830; (203) 661-1100; www.ustinc.com; Vincent A. Gierer Jr.; smokeless tobacco (Copenhagen, Skoal), pipe tobacco, wine (Chateau St. Michelle, Conn Creek, Columbia Crest).

Verizon Communications; 1095 Avenue of the Americas, New York, NY 10036; (212) 395-2121; www.verizon.com; Ivan Seidenberg; largest U.S. wireline and wireless provider; world's lgst. provider of print and on-line directory info. (co. formed from merger of Bell Atlantic and GTE, 6/30/00.)

V.F. Corp.; 105 Corporate Center Blvd., Greensboro, NC 27408; (336) 424-6000; www.vfc.com; Mackey J. McDonald; apparel (Lee, Wrangler jeans, Vanity Fair, Healthtex, Jantzen).

Viacom, Inc.; 1515 Broadway, NY, NY 10036; (212) 258-6000; www.viacom.com; Sumner Redstone; TV broadcast stations and cable systems, channels (CBS, UPN, TNN, BET, Comedy Central, Showtime, MTV, VH1, Nickelodeon); book publishing (Simon & Schuster); produces, distributes movies, TV shows (Paramount); video stores (Blockbuster), theme parks.

Visteon Corp.; 17000 Rotunda Dr., Dearborn, MI 48120; (313) 755-2800; www.visteon.com; Peter J. Pestillo; automotive parts manufacturing, architectural glass.

Wachovia Corp.; One Wachovia Center, Charlotte, NC 28288; (704) 374-6565; www.wachovia.com; G. Kennedy Thompson; financial services provider.

Walgreen Co.; 200 Wilmot Rd., Deerfield, IL 60015; (847) 940-2500; www.walgreens.com; David W. Bernauer; drugstore chain.

Wal-Mart Stores, Inc.; 702 SW 8th St., Bentonville, AR 72716; (479) 273-4000; www.walmart.com; S. Robson Walton; world's largest retailer; discount stores, wholesale clubs.

Washington Post Co.; 1150 15th St. NW, Washington, DC 20071; (202) 334-6000; www.washpostco.com; Donald E. Graham; newspapers, *Newsweek* magazine, TV and CATV stations, Stanley H. Kaplan Educational Centers.

Waste Management; 1001 Fannin, Suite 4000, Houston, TX 77002; (713) 512-6200; www.wm.com; Maurice Myers; N. America's largest solid waste collection and disposal co.

WellPoint Health Networks Inc.; 1 WellPoint Way, Thousand Oaks, CA 91362; 805-557-6655; www.wellpoint.com; Leonard D. Schaeffer; HMOs and PPOs, incl. Blue Cross Blue Shield (in CA, GA, MI, WI), HealthLink, and UNICARE. (Merger with Anthem, Inc. pending as of Sept. 1, 2004)

Wells Fargo & Co.; 420 Montgomery St., San Francisco, CA 94163; (800) 292-9932; www.wellsfargo.com; R. Kovacevich; bank holding co.

Wendy's Intl., Inc;; 4288 W. Dublin-Granville Rd., Dublin, OH 43017; (614) 764-3100; www.wendys.com; John T. Schuessler; quick-service restaurants.

Weyerhaeuser Co.; 33663 Weyerhauser Way, Federal Way, WA 98063; (253) 924-2345; www.weyerhaeuser.com; Steven R. Rogel; world's largest private owner of softwood timber, distrib. paper and wood prods.

Whirlpool Corp.; 2000 N. M-63, Benton Harbor, MI 49022; (269) 923-5000; www.whirlpoolcorp.com; David Whitwam; world's largest manuf. of major home appliances (KitchenAid, Kenmore, Roper).

Winn-Dixie Stores, Inc.; 5050 Edgewood Ct., Jacksonville, FL 32254; (904) 783-5000; www.winn-dixie.com; Frank Lazaran; supermarkets (Winn Dixie, Save RIte, Thrift Way).

Winnebago Industries, Inc.; PO Box 152, Forest City, IA 50436; (641) 585-3535; www.winnebagoind.com; Bruce D. Hertzke; manuf. and financing of motor homes, recreational vehicles.

WRC Media Inc.; 512 Seventh Ave., New York, NY 10018; (212) 768-0455; www.wrcmedia.com; Martin E. Kenney Jr.; publisher of educational and reference media; World Almanac, Facts On File News Services, Funk & Wagnalls, Gareth Stevens Publishing, CompassLearning, Weekly Reader, American Guidance.

Wm. Wrigley Jr. Co.; 410 N. Michigan Ave., Chicago, IL 60611; (312) 644-2121; www.wrigley.com; William Wrigley Jr.; world's largest mfgr. of chewing gum.

Wyeth, formerly American Home Products; 5 Giralda Farms, Madison, NJ 07940; (973) 660-5000; www.wyeth.com; Robert Essner; prescription and over-the-counter drugs (Advil, Anacin, Chap Stick, Robitussin).

Xerox Corp.; 800 Long Ridge Road, Stamford, CT 06904; (203) 968-3000; www.xerox.com; Anne Mulcahy; copiers, printers, document publishing equip.

Yahoo! Inc.; 701 First Ave. Sunnyvale, CA 94089; (408) 349-3300; www.yahoo.com; Terry Semel; global internet media company.

Yum! Brands, Inc.; 1441 Gardiner Lane, Louisville, KY 40213; (502) 874-8300; www.yum.com; David C. Novak; quick-serve restaurants (Pizza Hut, KFC, Taco Bell).

Who Owns What: Familiar Consumer Products and Services

Listed here are some consumer brands and their (U.S.) parent companies. Excluded are many brands whose parent companies have the same or a similar name (e.g., Colgate is Colgate-Palmolive Co.). For company contact information, see Business Directory on previous pages.

A&W Rootbeer: Cadbury Schweppes
ABC broadcasting: Walt Disney
Admiral appliances: Maytag
Advil: Wyeth
Ajax cleanser: Colgate-Palmolive
Almond Joy candy bar: Hershey
American Girl: Mattel
Anacin: Wyeth
Arm & Hammer: Church & Dwight
Arrid antiperspirant: Church & Dwight
Aunt Jemima Pancake mix: PepsiCo (Quaker Oats)
Aunt Millie's pasta sauce: H.J. Heinz
Banana Republic stores: The Gap
Band-Aids: Johnson & Johnson
Barbie dolls: Mattel
Ben-Gay: Pfizer
Betty Crocker prods.: General Mills
Blockbuster video stores: Viacom
Boston Market: McDonald's
Bounty paper towels: Procter & Gamble
Brillo soap pads: Church & Dwight
Brita water systems: Clorox
Budweiser beer: Anheuser-Busch
Bufferin: Bristol-Myers Squibb
Bulova watches: Loews
Business Week magazine: McGraw-Hill
Butterball: ConAgra
Cap'n Crunch cereal: PepsiCo (Quaker Oats)
Calphalon cookware: Newell Rubbermaid
Camel cigarettes: Reynolds American
CBS Broadcasting: Viacom
Charmin toilet tissue: Procter & Gamble
Cheer detergent: Procter & Gamble
Cheerios cereal: General Mills
Cheez Whiz: Altria (Kraft)
Chef Boyardee: ConAgra
Chips Ahoy!: Altria (Nabisco)
Cinemax: Time Warner
Clairol hair prods.: Procter & Gamble
Clinique: Estee Lauder
CNN: Time Warner
Combat insecticides: Clorox
Comet cleanser: Procter & Gamble
Coppertone sun care prods.: Schering-Plough
Cover Girl: Procter & Gamble
Crest toothpaste: Procter & Gamble
Crisco shortening: J.M. Smucker
DC Comics: Time Warner
Dr. Pepper: Cadbury Schweppes
Doritos chips: PepsiCo
Duracell batteries: Gillette
Dutch Boy paints: Sherwin-Williams
Efferdent dental cleanser: Pfizer
Elmer's glue: Borden
ESPN: Walt Disney
Excedrin: Bristol-Myers Squibb
Fab detergent: Colgate-Palmolive
Fantastik: S.C. Johnson
Fisher Price Toys: Mattel
Folger's coffee: Procter & Gamble
Formula 409 spray cleaner: Clorox
Fortune (magazine): Time Warner
Frito-Lays snacks: PepsiCo
Fruitopia drinks: Coca-Cola
Gatorade: PepsiCo
Glad Prods.: Clorox
Godiva chocolate: Campbell Soup
Haagen-Dazs: General Mills
Halcion: Pfizer

Halls coughdrops: Pfizer
Hamburger Helper: General Mills
Hanes hosiery: Sara Lee
HBO: Time Warner
Head and Shoulders shampoo: Procter & Gamble
Healthtex: V.F. Corp.
Hellmann's mayonnaise: Unilever Bestfoods
Hertz car rental: Ford
Hi-C fruit drinks: Coca-Cola
Hidden Valley prods.: Clorox
Hillshire Farms meats: Sara Lee
Holly Farms: Tyson Foods
Hot Wheels/Matchbox cars: Mattel
Hostess cupcakes: Interstate Bakeries
Huggies diapers: Kimberly-Clark
Irish Spring: Colgate-Palmolive
Ivory soap: Procter & Gamble
Jack Daniel's Whiskey: Brown-Forman
Jell-O: Altria (Kraft)
Jenn-Air stoves: Maytag
Jif peanut butter: J.M. Smucker
Jim Beam bourbon: Fortune Brands
Keds footwear: Stride Rite
Kent cigarettes: Loews
KFC restaurants: Yum! Brands
Kibbles 'n Bits pet foods: Del Monte
KitchenAid appliances: Whirlpool
Kit Kat candy: Hershey
Kleenex: Kimberly-Clark
Knorr soups: Unilever
Kool-Aid: Altria (Kraft)
Krazy Glue: Borden
Ladies Home Journal magazine: Meredith
Lee jeans: V.F. Corp.
L'eggs hosiery: Sara Lee
Lenox china: Brown-Forman
LifeSavers candy: Altria (Kraft)
Lipton tea: Unilever
Listerine mouthwash: Pfizer
Lord & Taylor: May Dept. Stores
Marlboro cigarettes: Altria (Philip Morris)
Max Factor beauty products: Procter & Gamble
Maxwell House coffee: Altria (Kraft)
Metamucil: Procter & Gamble
Michelob beer: Anheuser-Busch
Miller beer: South African Breweries
Milton Bradley games: Hasbro
Minute Maid juices: Coca-Cola
Monroe automotive parts: Tenneco Automotive
Mr. Clean: Procter & Gamble
MTV: Viacom
Nature Valley granola bars: General Mills
NBC broadcasting: General Electric
Neutrogena soap: Johnson & Johnson
Newport cigarettes: Loews
Newsweek magazine: Washington Post
Nickelodeon TV: Viacom
9 Lives cat food: Del Monte
Olay: Procter & Gamble
Old Navy Clothing: The Gap
Oreo cookies: Altria (Nabisco)
Oscar Mayer meats: Altria (Kraft)
Pampers: Procter & Gamble
Pantene Shampoos: Procter & Gamble
Parker Bros. games: Hasbro
People magazine: Time Warner
Pepperidge Farm prods.: Campbell Soup
Pepto-Bismol: Procter & Gamble

Philadelphia Cream Cheese: Altria (Kraft)
Pillsbury: General Mills
Pine-Sol cleaner: Clorox
Pizza Hut restaurants: Yum! Brands
Planters nuts: Altria (Kraft)
Playskool toys: Hasbro
Playtex apparel: Sara Lee
Post cereals: Altria (Kraft)
Post-it notes: 3M
Prego pasta sauce: Campbell Soup
Prozac: Eli Lilly
Ragu sauce: Unilever
Reese's candy: Hershey
Rice-A-Roni: PepsiCo (Quaker Oats)
Right Guard deodorant: Gillette
Ritz crackers: Altria (Nabisco)
Robitussin: Wyeth
Rogaine hair growth aide: Pfizer
Ruffles chips: PepsiCo
Schick razors: Energizer
Scope mouthwash: Procter & Gamble
Scotch tape: 3M
Scott tissue: Kimberly-Clark
Simon & Schuster publishing: Viacom
Skippy peanut butter: Unilever
Slimfast: Unilever
SnackWell's cookies: Altria (Nabisco)
S.O.S. cleanser: Clorox
Southern Comfort liquor: Brown-Forman
SPAM meat: Hormel Foods
Sports Illustrated magazine: Time Warner
Sprite soda: Coca-Cola
StarKist tuna: Del Monte
Sugar Twin: Alberto-Culver
Swanson broth: Campbell Soup
Swiffer: Procter & Gamble
Taco Bell restaurants: Yum! Brands
Tampax tampons: Procter & Gamble
Thomas' English muffins: Unilever
Tide detergent: Procter & Gamble
Time magazine: Time Warner
Titleist: Fortune Brands
Tombstone pizza: Altria (Kraft)
Triscuits: Altria (Nabisco)
Trojan condoms: Church & Dwight
Tropicana juice: PepsiCo
Tylenol: Johnson & Johnson
USA Today newspaper: Gannett
V8 vegetable juice: Campbell Soup
Vanity Fair apparel: V.F. Corp.
Velveeta cheese prods.: Altria (Kraft)
VH-1: Viacom
Viagra: Pfizer
Vicks cough medicines: Procter & Gamble
Victoria's Secret stores: Limited Brands
Visine eye drops: Pfizer
Wall Street Journal: Dow Jones
Weekly Reader: WRC Media
Weight Watchers: H.J. Heinz
Wheaties cereal: General Mills
Windex: S.C. Johnson
Windows software applications: Microsoft
Wise snacks: Palladium Equity
Wonderbra: Sara Lee
Wonder bread: Interstate Bakeries
The World Almanac: WRC Media
Zest soap: Procter & Gamble
Ziploc storage bags: S.C. Johnson

WORLD ALMANAC QUICK QUIZ

Which of these brands is not sold by General Mills?

    (a) Jell-O   (b) Bisquick   (c) Wheaties   (d) Rice Chex

For the answer look in this chapter, or see page 1008.

Top Brands in Selected Categories, 2002-2003[1]

Source: Information Resources, Inc., a Chicago-based marketing research company; figures for 12-month period ending 7/11/04.

Beer

	Sales	Market Share (%)
Bud Light	$79,893,984	15.7
Budweiser	55,141,852	10.8
Miller Lite	41,619,472	8.2
Coors Light	36,034,268	7.1
Natural Light	24,311,180	4.8

Ice Cream

	Sales	Market Share (%)
Private Label	$837,943,872	21.3
Breyers	525,857,856	13.4
Dreyers Edys Grand	396,139,488	10.1
Blue Bell	240,826,448	6.1
Haagen Dazs	195,961,056	5.0

Chocolate Candies

M & Ms	$81,831,312	10.6
Hersheys	79,128,624	10.3
Reeses	70,924,992	9.2
Snickers	67,013,804	8.7
Kit Kat	33,380,008	4.3

Paper Towels

Bounty	$830,155,904	39.6
Private Label	365,224,896	17.4
Brawny	233,904,960	11.2
Scott	213,858,112	10.2
Kleenex Viva	192,113,504	9.2

Ready-to-Eat Cold Cereals

Private Label	$499,301,344	8.2
General Mills Cheerios	291,624,928	4.8
Kelloggs Frosted Flakes	238,374,736	3.9
General Mills Honey Nut Cheerios	232,714,736	3.8
Post Honey Bunches Of Oats	204,353,648	3.4

Frozen Pizza

Di Giorno	$462,811,808	18.0
Tombstone	282,860,992	11.0
Red Baron	245,439,824	9.5
Freschetta	199,976,304	7.8
Private Label	176,311,264	6.8

Ground Coffee (excluding Decaf)

Folgers	$380,548,640	24.2
Maxwell House	257,130,592	16.4
Starbucks	134,402,672	8.6
Private Label	112,764,328	7.2
Maxwell House Master Blend	88,154,536	5.6

Salad Dressing

Kraft	$284,417,894	18.0
Wishbone	188,904,642	11.9
Private Label	130,438,352	8.2
Ken's Steakhouse	126,428,928	8.0
Hidden Valley Ranch	104,872,136	6.0

Cookies

Nabisco Oreo	$449,772,768	12.4
Nabisco Chips Ahoy	317,724,064	8.8
Keebler Chips Deluxe	115,821,328	3.2
Nabisco Newtons	119,715,920	3.3
Pepperidge Farm Distinctive	131,371,384	3.6

Toothpaste

Crest	$169,453,024	14.4
Colgate	119,907,288	10.2
Colgate Total	109,573,888	9.3
Sensodyne	55,052,600	4.7
Crest Whitening Expressions	49,691,380	4.3

(1) For all categories except beer, sales are for supermarkets, drugstores, and mass merchandisers, excluding Wal-Mart.

Most Visited Shopping Websites

Source: comScore Media Metrix, Inc.

Rank	Website address[1]	Visitors[2]
1.	eBay	60,824,000
2.	Amazon Sites	33,809,000
3.	Symantec	21,122,000
4.	Shopping.com Sites	20,350,000
5.	Yahoo! Shopping	17,919,000
6.	Wal-Mart	16,461,000
7.	Moviefone	13,074,000
8.	AmericanGreetings Property	12,482,000
9.	Dell	12,286,000
10.	Target Corporation	12,158,000
11.	NEXTAG.COM	11,758,000
12.	Columbia House Sites	11,123,000
13.	Adobe Sites	10,883,000
14.	Hewlett Packard	10,188,000
15.	Ticketmaster	9,943,000

(1) May include affiliated websites not shown. (2) Visited website at least once in July 2004.

The Annual Cost of Raising a Child Born in 2003

Source: Center for Nutrition Policy and Promotion, U.S. Dept. of Agriculture

Estimated annual expenditures in 2003 dollars for a child born in 2003, by income group, for each year to age 17, assuming an average inflation rate of 3.1%. Estimates are for the younger child in a 2-parent family with 2 children, for the overall U.S.

Year	Income group[1] Lowest	Middle	Highest	Year	Income group[1] Lowest	Middle	Highest
2003	$6,820	$9,510	$14,140	2013	$9,490	$13,030	$19,050
2004	7,030	9,800	14,580	2014	9,780	13,430	19,640
2005	7,250	10,110	15,030	2015	11,310	14,930	21,420
2006	7,640	10,720	15,860	2016	11,660	15,390	22,080
2007	7,880	11,050	16,350	2017	12,020	15,870	22,770
2008	8,120	11,390	16,860	2018	12,280	16,690	24,270
2009	8,460	11,690	17,100	2019	12,660	17,210	25,020
2010	8,720	12,050	17,630	2020	13,060	17,740	25,790
2011	8,990	12,420	18,180	TOTAL	$172,370	$235,670	$344,250
2012	9,200	12,640	18,480				

(1) In 2003, lowest annual income is less than $40,700 (average in this range = $25,400); middle income is $40,700-$68,400 (average = $54,100); highest income is $68,400 or more (average = $102,400).

How to Obtain Birth, Death, Marriage, Divorce Records

The pamphlet "Where to Write for Vital Records: Births, Deaths, Marriages, and Divorces" (Stock # 017-022-01539-1) is available from the U.S. Government Printing Office (GPO) at a cost of $4.25. Orders can also be placed by calling (866) 512-1800, by e-mail at orders@gpo.gov, or on the website bookstore.gpo.gov. The complete pamphlet can also be accessed online at www.cdc.gov/nchs/howto/w2w/w2welcom.htm

Median Price of Existing Single-Family Homes, by Metropolitan Area, 2002-2004

Source: National Association of REALTORS®

Median prices are based on all transactions within the time period shown.

Metropolitan Area	2002	2003	2nd Qtr 2004
Akron, OH	115,300	116,700	116,000
Albany/Schenectady/Troy, NY	126,000	141,900	158,700
Albuquerque, NM	133,800	138,400	145,400
Amarillo, TX	91,900	95,700	96,400
Orange Cnty. (Anaheim/Santa Ana MSA), CA	412,700	487,000	655,300
Appleton/Oshkosh/Neenah, WI	112,700	118,600	127,600
Atlanta, GA	146,500	152,400	156,800
Atlantic City, NJ	143,600	174,400	194,800
Aurora/Elgin, IL	193,300	208,100	225,500
Austin/San Marcos, TX	156,500	156,700	158,900
Baltimore, MD	179,600	208,900	251,700
Baton Rouge, LA	116,900	121,200	128,200
Beaumont/Port Arthur, TX	84,300	88,400	95,900
Biloxi/Gulfport, MS	100,200	107,600	113,100
Birmingham, AL	137,400	137,500	149,500
Boise City, ID	123,200	130,600	151,500
Boston, MA	NA	354,800	366,500
Bradenton, FL	150,000	172,700	213,100
Buffalo/Niagara Falls, NY	85,000	88,600	97,000
Canton, OH	109,000	114,400	115,600
Cedar Rapids, IA	118,800	122,800	131,900
Champaign/Urbana/Rantoul, IL	107,100	118,300	121,800
Charleston, SC	159,400	168,900	191,900
Charleston, WV	107,200	110,900	115,100
Charlotte/Gastonia/Rock Hill, NC/SC	149,100	151,500	NA
Chattanooga, TN/GA	112,300	116,700	131,800
Chicago, IL	220,900	238,900	263,300
Cincinnati, OH/KY/IN	134,100	138,900	147,500
Cleveland, OH	NA	NA	NA
Colorado Springs, CO	176,900	184,500	189,600
Columbia, SC	119,500	123,600	120,700
Columbus, OH	140,300	146,300	150,400
Corpus Christi, TX	94,400	102,100	111,500
Dallas, TX	135,200	138,400	141,000
Davenport/Moline/Rock Island, IA/IL	95,000	100,600	107,900
Dayton/Springfield, OH	112,600	114,600	119,700
Daytona Beach, FL	108,300	124,900	147,900
Denver, CO	228,100	238,200	241,800
Des Moines, IA	130,200	133,900	141,800
Detroit, MI	NA	NA	NA
El Paso, TX	88,900	92,900	96,000
Eugene/Springfield, OR	143,700	151,700	163,000
Fargo/Moorhead, ND/MN	107,700	115,100	124,200
Ft. Lauderdale/Hollywood/Pompano Beach, FL	197,000	227,600	277,300
Ft. Myers/Cape Coral, FL	133,600	147,600	183,800
Ft. Wayne, IN	94,900	93,200	98,600
Ft. Worth/Arlington, TX	NA	NA	NA
Gainesville, FL	130,000	145,000	167,100
Gary/Hammond, IN	114,300	119,200	124,600
Grand Rapids, MI	125,300	129,900	134,500
Green Bay, WI	130,100	NA	NA
Greensboro/Winston-Salem/High Point, NC	135,800	137,300	140,300
Greenville/Spartanburg, SC	125,300	129,600	130,900
Hartford, CT	175,900	202,300	221,500
Honolulu, HI	335,000	380,000	451,000
Houston, TX	132,800	136,400	139,200
Indianapolis, IN	116,800	121,100	125,900
Jackson, MS	NA	110,700	118,600
Jacksonville, FL	117,800	131,600	154,500
Kalamazoo, MI	117,800	123,400	127,100
Kansas City, MO/KS	137,400	144,200	152,100
Knoxville, TN	118,400	130,500	131,400
Lake County, IL	240,000	257,900	254,600
Lansing/East Lansing, MI	126,400	133,600	140,400
Las Vegas, NV	159,800	179,200	269,900
Lexington/Fayette, KY	127,100	133,400	139,400
Lincoln, NE	122,400	131,500	135,300
Little Rock-N. Little Rock, AR	95,700	104,800	109,400
Los Angeles Area, CA	290,000	354,700	438,400
Louisville, KY/IN	125,200	131,700	NA
Madison, WI	177,000	188,700	199,700
Melbourne/Titusville/Palm Bay, FL	112,700	131,300	153,900
Memphis, TNAR/MS	129,400	133,800	138,300
Miami/Hialeah, FL	189,800	226,800	271,900
Milwaukee, WI	173,800	182,100	197,300
Minneapolis/St. Paul, MN/WI	185,000	199,600	218,000
Mobile, AL	114,900	120,700	123,600
Montgomery, AL	113,600	115,700	116,900
Nashville, TN	NA	NA	NA
New Haven/Meriden, CT	192,300	225,300	246,800
New Orleans, LA	123,500	130,800	137,500
New York/N. New Jersey/Long Island,NY/NJ/CT	309,800	353,000	392,200
Bergen/Passaic, NJ	337,900	370,700	393,300
Middlesex/Somerset/Hunterdon, NJ	284,100	314,000	346,800
Monmouth/Ocean, NJ	251,700	288,300	314,300
Nassau/Suffolk, NY	312,900	364,500	414,800
Newark, NJ	300,500	331,200	370,600
Norfolk/Virginia Bch/Newport News, VA	NA	138,800	151,100
Ocala, FL	NA	NA	112,300
Oklahoma City, OK	100,100	103,000	107,000
Omaha, NE/IA	122,400	128,100	133,200
Orlando, FL	136,600	145,100	170,100
Pensacola, FL	112,200	116,400	132,700
Peoria, IL	88,000	93,100	98,400
Philadelphia, PA/NJ	146,100	168,000	189,300
Phoenix, AZ	143,800	152,500	165,600
Pittsburgh, PA	101,500	107,200	116,300
Portland, ME	180,000	199,100	231,200
Portland, OR	180,400	192,000	206,700
Providence, RI	193,200	233,400	262,000
Raleigh/Durham, NC	172,200	174,700	185,900
Reno, NV	183,200	204,900	270,500
Richland/Kennewick/Pasco, WA	140,800	145,300	147,200
Richmond/Petersburg, VA	142,300	155,100	173,000
Riverside/San Bernardino, CA	176,500	221,000	294,500
Rochester, NY	93,800	99,400	105,100
Rockford, IL	106,900	114,400	120,100
Sacramento, CA	210,200	247,600	308,600
Saginaw/Bay City/Midland, MI	NA	NA	NA
Saint Louis, MO/IL	117,000	121,200	128,800
Salt Lake City/Ogden, UT	148,800	148,000	161,500
San Antonio, TX	110,400	118,100	124,700
San Diego, CA	364,200	424,900	559,700
San Francisco Bay Area, CA	517,100	558,100	647,300
Sarasota, FL	176,200	207,900	264,800
Seattle, WA	254,000	268,800	293,200
Shreveport, LA	90,300	100,700	111,400
Sioux Falls, SD	116,700	123,200	129,700
South Bend/Mishawaka, IN	91,000	91,100	93,800
Spokane, WA	108,700	120,300	125,700
Springfield, IL	90,600	93,700	98,300
Springfield, MA	139,800	153,400	152,200
Springfield, MO	NA	NA	NA
Syracuse, NY	86,400	95,000	94,700
Tacoma, WA	170,400	178,100	195,500
Tallahassee, FL	136,900	137,100	148,800
Tampa/St. Petersburg/Clearwater, FL	133,500	138,100	158,200
Toledo, OH	109,600	111,400	116,700
Topeka, KS	89,000	97,300	103,700
Trenton, NJ	179,500	212,400	235,900
Tucson, AZ	146,400	156,300	175,800
Tulsa, OK	106,700	110,400	113,300
Washington, DC/MD/VA	250,200	286,200	352,400
Waterloo/Cedar Falls, IA	87,800	91,300	95,400
W. Palm Beach/Boca Raton/Delray Beach, FL	N/A	241,300	294,000
Wichita, KS	98,100	100,500	105,800
Wilmington, DE/NJ/MD	150,100	166,200	182,200
Worcester, MA	225,600	252,600	279,200
United States	**$158,100**	**$170,000**	**$183,800**

NA = Not available.

▶ **IT'S A FACT:** From June 2003 to June 2004, median prices for existing single-family homes in Las Vegas, NV, increased by 52.4%—the biggest such increase in any metropolitan area on record, according to the National Association of Realtors. During that time, median prices for a home in Vegas rose from $177,100 to $269,900. The fastest growing metropolitan area in the U.S., Las Vegas had a short supply of homes—only a 1.7-month supply on the market in June 2004, compared with a 4.2-month supply nationwide.

U.S. Home Ownership Rates, by Selected Characteristics, 1997, 2004[1]

Source: Bureau of the Census, U.S. Dept. of Commerce

Region	1997	2004	Age	1997	2004	Race/Ethnicity	1997	2004	Income	1997	2004
Northeast	62.4%	65.4%	Under 35	38.6%	43.6%	White, non-			Median family		
Midwest	70.3	74.2	35-44	66.3	69.4	Hispanic	72.1%	76.2%	income or more	80.8%	83.9%
South	68.1	70.9	45-54	75.6	77.0	Black	44.4	49.7	Below median		
West	59.9	64.5	55-64	80.3	82.4	Hispanic	43.3	47.4	family income	50.0	53.1
			65+	79.1	81.1	Other	52.7	58.7	**TOTAL U.S.**	**65.7%**	**69.2%**

(1) in 2004, figures are for 2nd quarter of the year. Not seasonally-adjusted.

Mortgage Loan Calculator

Source: HSH Associates, www.hsh.com

This table allows you to calculate the monthly principal and interest payment for each $1,000 of your mortgage. Divide your loan amount by 1,000 and multiply the result by the factor located at the intersection of the interest rate and term you are considering.

Example: For a 30-year mortgage at 6%, the payment factor would be 5.996. If the mortgage amount is $250,000, divide this by 1,000 to find a value of $250. That $250 times the 5.996 (payment factor) gives you a monthly principal and interest payment of $1,499 per month. Please be aware that this is approximate, as the factor you are using is only 3 decimal places (your mortgage lender will likely use a payment factor which is more precise than that). Also, this is only your P&I payment; your actual monthly payment will include property taxes, insurance, and other possible costs. **Hint:** You can calculate payments for interest rates not shown by finding the factor between 2 given interest rates. For example, the factor for 5.125% is ½ the difference between 5% and 5.25%; so subtract 5.368 from 5.522. Take the result (0.154), divide it by 2 (0.077), then add it to the 5% factor (5.368) to get 5.445, your factor for a 5.125% interest rate.

INTEREST RATE	5	10	15	20	25	30	35	40
3.75	18.304	10.006	7.272	5.929	5.141	4.631	4.279	4.025
4.00	18.417	10.125	7.397	6.060	5.278	4.774	4.428	4.179
4.25	18.530	10.244	7.523	6.192	5.417	4.919	4.579	4.336
4.50	18.643	10.364	7.650	6.326	5.558	5.067	4.733	4.496
4.75	18.757	10.485	7.778	6.462	5.701	5.216	4.889	4.658
5.00	18.871	10.607	7.908	6.600	5.846	5.368	5.047	4.822
5.25	18.986	10.729	8.039	6.738	5.992	5.522	5.207	4.989
5.50	19.101	10.853	8.171	6.879	6.141	5.678	5.370	5.158
5.75	19.217	10.977	8.304	7.021	6.291	5.836	5.535	5.329
6.00	19.333	11.102	8.439	7.164	6.443	5.996	5.702	5.502
6.25	19.449	11.228	8.574	7.309	6.597	6.157	5.871	5.677
6.50	19.566	11.355	8.711	7.456	6.752	6.321	6.042	5.855
6.75	19.683	11.482	8.849	7.604	6.909	6.486	6.214	6.034
7.00	19.801	11.611	8.988	7.753	7.068	6.653	6.389	6.214
7.25	19.919	11.740	9.129	7.904	7.228	6.822	6.565	6.397
7.50	20.038	11.870	9.270	8.056	7.390	6.992	6.742	6.581
7.75	20.157	12.001	9.413	8.209	7.553	7.164	6.922	6.766
8.00	20.276	12.133	9.557	8.364	7.718	7.338	7.103	6.953
8.25	20.396	12.265	9.701	8.521	7.885	7.513	7.285	7.141
8.50	20.517	12.399	9.847	8.678	8.052	7.689	7.469	7.331
8.75	20.637	12.533	9.994	8.837	8.221	7.867	7.654	7.522
9.00	20.758	12.668	10.143	8.997	8.392	8.046	7.840	7.714
9.25	20.880	12.803	10.292	9.159	8.564	8.227	8.027	7.907
9.50	21.002	12.940	10.442	9.321	8.737	8.409	8.216	8.101
9.75	21.124	13.077	10.594	9.485	8.911	8.592	8.406	8.296
10.00	21.247	13.215	10.746	9.650	9.087	8.776	8.597	8.491
10.25	21.370	13.354	10.900	9.816	9.264	8.961	8.789	8.688
10.50	21.494	13.493	11.054	9.984	9.442	9.147	8.981	8.886
10.75	21.618	13.634	11.209	10.152	9.621	9.335	9.175	9.084
11.00	21.742	13.775	11.366	10.322	9.801	9.523	9.370	9.283
11.25	21.867	13.917	11.523	10.493	9.982	9.713	9.565	9.483

MORTGAGE TERM IN YEARS

Housing Affordability, U.S., 1990-2004

Source: National Association of REALTORS®

Year	Median priced existing home	Average mortgage rate[1]	Monthly principal & interest payment	Payment as percentage of median monthly income
1990	$ 92,000	10.04%	$648	22.0%
1991	97,100	9.30	642	21.4
1992	99,700	8.11	591	19.3
1993	103,100	7.16	558	18.1
1994	107,200	7.47	598	18.5
1995	110,500	7.85	639	18.9
1996	115,800	7.71	661	18.8
1997	121,800	7.68	693	18.7
1998	128,400	7.10	690	17.4
1999	133,300	7.33	733	18.0
2000	139,000	8.03	818	19.3
2001	147,800	7.03	789	18.4
2002	158,100	6.55	804	18.3
2003	170,000	5.74	793	17.8
2004[2]	191,300	5.93	911	19.8

(1) All figures assume a down payment of 20% of the home price. Based on effective rate on loans closed on existing homes for the period shown. (2) Preliminary, as of July.

IT'S A FACT: The national average commitment rate for a 30-year, conventional, fixed-rate mortgage fell to 5.23% in June 2003, according to Freddie Mac. This was the lowest rate since 1971, when the company began tracking mortgage interest rates. By June 2004, the average rate was at 6.29%.

SOCIAL SECURITY

Social Security Programs

Source: Social Security Administration; World Almanac research; data as of Aug. 2004.

Old-Age, Survivors, and Disability Insurance; Medicare; Supplemental Security Income

Social Security Benefits

Social Security benefits are based on a worker's primary insurance amount (PIA), which is related by law to the average indexed monthly earnings (AIME) on which Social Security contributions have been paid. The full PIA is payable to a retired worker who becomes entitled to benefits at age 65 and to an entitled disabled worker at any age. Spouses and children of retired or disabled workers and survivors of deceased workers receive set proportions of the PIA subject to a family maximum amount. The PIA is calculated by applying varying percentages to succeeding parts of the AIME. The formula is adjusted annually to reflect changes in average annual wages.

Automatic increases in Social Security benefits are initiated for December of each year, assuming the Consumer Price Index (CPI) for the 3rd calendar quarter of the year increased relative to the base quarter, which is either the 3rd calendar quarter of the preceding year or the quarter in which an increase legislated by Congress became effective. The size of the benefit increase is determined by the percentage rise of the CPI between the quarters measured.

The average monthly benefit payable to all retired workers amounted to $922 in Dec. 2003. The average benefit for disabled workers in that month amounted to $862.

Minimum and maximum monthly retired-worker benefits payable to individuals who retired at age 65[1]

	Minimum benefit[2]		Maximum benefit[2]	
Year attaining age 65	Paid at retirement	Payable as of Dec. 2003	Payable at retirement	Payable effective Dec. 2003
1970	$64.00	$333.30	(3)	(4)
1980	133.90	333.30	$572.00	$1,397.80
1990	(5)	(5)	975.00	1,395.30
1993	(5)	(5)	1,128.80	1,414.50
1994	(5)	(5)	1,147.50	1,401.50
1995	(5)	(5)	1,199.10	1,424.70
1996	(5)	(5)	1,248.90	1,493.30
1997	(5)	(5)	1,326.60	1,422.20
1998	(5)	(5)	1,342.80	1,480.40
1999	(5)	(5)	1,373.10	1,494.40
2000	(5)	(5)	1,434.80	1,526.30
2001	(5)	(5)	1,536.70	1,576.60
2002	(5)	(5)	1,660.50	1,683.70
2003	(5)	(5)	1,741.10	1,777.60

(1) Assumes retirement at beginning of year. (2) The final benefit amount payable is rounded to next lower $1 (if not already a multiple of $1). (3) Benefits $196.40 for women and $189.80 for men. (4) Benefits $1,003.40 for women and $968.90 for men. (5) Minimum eliminated for workers who reached age 62 after 1981.

Amount of Work Required

To qualify for benefits, the worker generally must have worked a certain length of time in covered employment. Just how long depends on when the worker reaches age 62 or, if earlier, when he or she dies or becomes disabled.

A person is fully insured who has 1 quarter of coverage for every year after 1950 (or year age 21 is reached, if later) up to but not including the year the worker reaches 62, dies, or becomes disabled. In 2004, a person earns 1 quarter of coverage for each $900 of annual earnings in covered employment, up to 4 quarters per year.

To receive disability benefits, the worker, in addition to being fully insured, must generally have credit for 20 quarters of coverage out of the 40 calendar quarters before he or she became disabled. A disabled blind worker need meet only the fully insured requirement. Persons disabled before age 31 can qualify with a briefer period of coverage. Certain survivor benefits are payable if the deceased worker had 6 quarters of coverage in the 13 quarters preceding death.

Work credit for fully insured status for benefits

Born after 1929; die, become disabled, or reach age 62 in	Years needed	Born after 1929; die, become disabled, or reach age 62 in	Years needed
1983	8	1988	9¼
1984	8½	1989	9½
1985	8½	1990	9¾
1986	8¾	1991 and after	10
1987	9		

Contribution and benefit base

Calendar year	OASDI[1]	HI[2]	Calendar year	OASDI[1]	HI[2]
1990	$51,300	$51,300	1999	$72,600	no limit
1992	55,500	130,200	2000	76,200	no limit
1993	57,600	135,000	2001	80,400	no limit
1994	60,600	no limit	2002	84,900	no limit
1995	61,200	no limit	2003	87,000	no limit
1996	62,700	no limit	2004	87,900	no limit
1997	65,400	no limit	2005	89,700	no limit
1998	68,400	no limit		(est.)	

(1) Old-Age, Survivors, and Disability Ins. (2) Hospital Ins.

Tax-rate schedule
(percentage of covered earnings)

Year	Total (for employees and employers, each)	OASDI	HI
1979-80	6.13	5.08	1.05
1981	6.65	5.35	1.30
1982-83	6.70	5.40	1.30
1984	7.00	5.70	1.30
1985	7.05	5.70	1.35
1986-87	7.15	5.70	1.45
1988-89	7.51	6.06	1.45
1990 and after	7.65	6.20	1.45
	For self-employed		
1979-80	8.10	7.05	1.05
1981	9.30	8.00	1.30
1982-83	9.35	8.05	1.30
1984	14.00	11.40	2.60
1985	14.10	11.40	2.70
1986-87	14.30	11.40	2.90
1988-89	15.02	12.12	2.90
1990 and after	15.30	12.40	2.90

What Aged Workers Receive

When a person has enough work in covered employment and reaches retirement age (currently age 65 for full benefit, age 62 for reduced benefit), he or she may retire and receive monthly old-age benefits. The age when unreduced benefits become payable will increase gradually from 65 to 67 over a 21-year period beginning with workers age 62 in the year 2000 (reduced benefits will still be available as early as age 62, but with a larger reduction at that age).

Beginning with year 2000, the retirement earnings test has been eliminated beginning with the month in which the beneficiary reaches full-benefit retirement age (FRA). A person at and above FRA will not have benefits reduced because of earnings. In the calendar year in which a beneficiary reaches FRA, benefits are reduced $1 for every $3 of earnings above the limit allowed by law ($31,080 in 2004), but this reduction is only to months prior to attainment of FRA. For years before the year when the beneficiary attains FRA, the reduction in benefits is $1 for every $2 of earnings over the annual exempt amount ($11,640 for year 2004).

For workers who reached age 65 between 1982 and 1989, Social Security benefits are raised by 3% for each year for which the worker between ages 65 and 70 (72 before 1984) failed to receive benefits, whether because of earnings from work or because the worker had not applied for benefits. The delayed retirement credit is 1% per year for workers who reached age 65 before 1982. The delayed retirement credit will rise to 8% per year by 2008. The rate for workers who reached age 65 in 1998-99 is 5.5%; 2000-2001, 6.0%; 2002-2003, 6.5%; 2004-2005, 7.0%; 2006-2007, 7.5%.

For workers retiring before age 65, benefits are permanently reduced 5/9 of 1% for each month before FRA, up

to 36 months. If the number of months exceeds 36, then the benefit is further reduced 5/12 of 1% per month. For example, when FRA reaches 67, for workers who retire at exactly age 62, there are a total of 60 months of reduction. The reduction for the first 36 months is 5/9 of 36%, or 20%. The reduction for the remaining 24 months is 5/12 of 24%, or 10%. Thus, when the FRA reaches 67, the amount of reduction at age 62 will be 30%. The nearer to age 65 the worker is when he or she begins collecting a benefit, the larger the benefit will be. The nearer to the FRA the worker is when he or she begins collecting a benefit, the larger the benefit will be.

Benefits for Worker's Spouse

The spouse of a worker who is getting Social Security retirement or disability payments may become entitled to an insurance benefit of one-half of the worker's PIA when he or she reaches 65. Reduced spouse's benefits are available at age 62 and are permanently reduced 25/36 of 1% for each month before FRA, up to 36 months. If the number of months exceeds 36, then the benefit is further reduced 5/12 of 1% per month. Benefits are also payable to the aged divorced spouse of an insured worker if he or she was married to the worker for at least 10 years.

Benefits for Children of Workers

If a retired or disabled worker has a child under age 18, the child will normally get a benefit equal to half of the worker's unreduced benefit. So will the worker's spouse, even if under age 62, if he or she is caring for an entitled child of the worker who is under 16 or became disabled before age 22. However, total benefits paid on a worker's earnings record are subject to a maximum. (Total monthly benefits paid to the family of a worker who retired in Jan. 2004 at age 65 and always had the maximum earnings creditable under Social Security cannot exceed $3,194.90.)

When entitled children reach age 18, their benefits generally stop, but a child disabled before age 22 may get a benefit as long as the disability meets the definition in the law. Benefits will be paid until age 19 to a child attending elementary or secondary school full-time.

Benefits may also be paid to a grandchild or step-grandchild of a worker or of his or her spouse, in special circumstances.

OASDI	May 2004	May 2003	May 2002	May 2001
Monthly beneficiaries,				
total (in thousands)[1] ..	47,378	46,771	46,190	45,683
Aged 65 and over, total ...	33,400	33,179	32,953	32,762
Retired workers	27,014	26,680	26,352	26,055
Survivors and dependents .	6,386	6,498	6,601	6,707
Under age 65, total.......	13,978	13,592	13,236	12,921
Retired workers	2,668	2,645	2,660	2,626
Disabled workers	6,035	5,702	5,337	5,119
Survivors and dependents .	5,275	8,579	5,198	5,176
Total monthly benefits				
(in millions)	**$39,960**	**$38,244**	**$36,885**	**$35,170**

(1) Totals may not add because of rounding or incomplete enumeration.

What Disabled Workers Receive

A worker who becomes unable to work may be eligible for a monthly disability benefit. Benefits continue until it is determined that the individual is no longer disabled. When a disabled-worker beneficiary reaches age 65, the disability benefit becomes a retired-worker benefit.

Benefits generally like those for dependents of retired-worker beneficiaries may be paid to dependents of disabled beneficiaries. However, the maximum family benefit in disability cases is generally lower than in retirement cases.

Survivor Benefits

If an insured worker should die, one or more types of benefits may be payable to survivors, again subject to a maximum family benefit as described above.

1. If claiming benefits at age 65, the surviving spouse will receive a benefit equal to 100% of the deceased worker's PIA. Benefits claimed before FRA are reduced for age with a maximum reduction of 28.5 percent at age 60. However, for those whose spouses claimed their benefits before age

65, these are limited to the reduced amount the worker would be getting if alive, but not less than 82.5% of the worker's PIA. Remarriage after the worker's death ends the surviving spouse's benefit rights. However, if the widow(er) marries and the marriage is ended, he or she regains benefit rights. (A marriage after age 60, age 50 if disabled, is deemed not to have occurred for benefit purposes.) Survivor benefits may also be paid to a divorced spouse if the marriage lasted for at least 10 years.

Disabled widows and widowers may under certain circumstances qualify for benefits after attaining age 50 at the rate of 71.5% of the deceased worker's PIA. The widow or widower must have become totally disabled before or within 7 years after the spouse's death or the last month in which he or she received mother's or father's insurance benefits.

2. There is a benefit for each child until the child reaches age 18. The monthly benefit for each child of a deceased worker is ¾ of the amount the worker would have received if he or she had lived and drawn full retirement benefits. A child with a disability that began before age 22 may also receive benefits. Also, a child may receive benefits until reaching age 19 if he or she is in full-time attendance at an elementary or secondary school.

3. There is a mother's or father's benefit for the widow(er) if children of the worker under age 16 are in his or her care. The benefit is 75% of the PIA, and it continues until the youngest child reaches age 16, at which time payments stop even if the child's benefit continues. However, if the widow(er) has a disabled child beneficiary age 16 or over in care, benefits may continue.

4. Dependent parents may be eligible for benefits if they have been receiving at least half their support from the worker before his or her death, have reached age 62, and (except in certain circumstances) have not remarried since the worker's death. Each parent gets 75% of the worker's PIA; if only one parent survives, the benefit is 82%.

5. A lump sum cash payment of $255 is made when there is a spouse who was living with the worker or a spouse or child eligible for immediate monthly survivor benefits.

Self-Employed Workers

A self-employed person who has net earnings of $400 or more in a year must report such earnings for Social Security tax and credit purposes. The person reports net returns from the business. Income from real estate, savings, dividends, loans, pensions, or insurance policies are not included unless it is part of the business.

A self-employed person receives 1 quarter of coverage for each $900 (for 2004), up to a maximum of 4 quarters.

The nonfarm self-employed have the option of reporting their earnings as $2/3$ of their gross income from self-employment, but not more than $1,600 a year and not less than their actual net earnings. This option can be used only if actual net earnings from self-employment income are less than $1,600, and may be used only 5 times. Also, the self-employed person must have actual net earnings of $400 or more in 2 of the 3 taxable years immediately preceding the year in which he or she uses the option.

When a person has both taxable wages and earnings from self-employment, wages are credited for Social Security purposes first; only as much self-employment income as brings total earnings up to the current taxable maximum becomes subject to the self-employment tax.

Farm Owners and Workers

Self-employed farmers whose gross annual earnings from farming are $2,400 or less may report 2/3 of their gross earnings instead of net earnings for Social Security purposes. Farmers whose gross income is over $2,400 and whose net earnings are less than $1,600 can report $1,600. Cash or crop shares received from a tenant or share farmer count if the owner participated materially in production or management. The self-employed farmer pays contributions at the same rate as other self-employed persons.

Agricultural employees. A worker's earnings from farm work count toward benefits (1) if the employer pays the worker $150 or more in cash during the year; or (2) if the

employer spends $2,500 or more in the year for agricultural labor. Under these rules a person gets credit for 1 calendar quarter for each $900 in cash pay in 2004.

Foreign farm workers admitted to the U.S. on a temporary basis are not covered.

Household Workers

Anyone 18 or older employed as maid, cook, laundry worker, nurse, babysitter, chauffeur, gardener, or other worker in the house of another is covered by Social Security if paid $1,400 or more in cash in calendar year 2004 by any one employer. Room and board do not count, but transportation costs count if paid in cash. The job need not be regular or full-time. The employee should get a Social Security card at the Social Security office and show it to the employer.

The employer deducts the amount of the employee's Social Security tax from the worker's pay, adds an identical amount as the employer's Social Security tax, and sends the total amount to the federal government.

Medicare Coverage

The Medicare health insurance program provides acute-care coverage for Social Security and Railroad Retirement beneficiaries age 65 and over, for persons entitled for 24 months to receive Social Security or Railroad Retirement disability benefits, and for certain persons with end-stage kidney disease. What follows is a basic description and may not cover all circumstances.

The basic Medicare plan, available nationwide, is a fee-for-service arrangement, where the beneficiary may use any provider accepting Medicare; some services are not covered and there are some out-of-pocket costs.

Under "Medicare + Choice," persons eligible for Medicare may have the option of getting services through a health maintenance organization (HMO) or other managed care plan. Any such plan must provide at least the same benefits, except for hospice services, and may provide added benefits—such as lower or no deductibles and coverage for some prescription drugs—but is usually subject to restrictions in choice of health care providers. In some plans services by outside providers are still covered for an extra out-of-pocket cost. Also available as options in some areas are Medicare-approved private fee-for-service plans and Medicare medical savings accounts.

Hospital insurance (Part A). The basic hospital insurance program pays covered services for hospital and posthospital care including the following:
- All necessary inpatient hospital care for the first 60 days of each benefit period, except for a deductible ($876 in 2004). For days 61-90, Medicare pays for services over and above a coinsurance amount ($219 per day in 2004). After 90 days, the beneficiary has 60 reserve days for which Medicare helps pay. The coinsurance amount for reserve days was $438 in 2004.
- Up to 100 days' care in a skilled-nursing facility in each benefit period. Hospital insurance pays for all covered services for the first 20 days; for the 21-100th day, the beneficiary pays coinsurance ($109.50 a day in 2004).
- Part-time home health care provided by nurses or other health workers.
- Limited coverage of hospice care for individuals certified to be terminally ill.

There is a premium for this insurance in certain cases.

Medical insurance (Part B). Elderly persons can receive benefits under this supplementary program only if they sign up for them and agree to a monthly premium ($66.60 if you sign up upon being eligible in 2004). The federal government pays the rest of the cost. The medical insurance program usually pays 80% of the approved amount (after the first $100 in each calendar year) for the following services:
- Covered services received from a doctor in his or her office, in a hospital, in a skilled-nursing facility, at home, or in other locations.
- Medical and surgical services, including anesthesia.
- Diagnostic tests and procedures that are part of the patient's treatment.

- Radiology and pathology services by doctors while the individual is a hospital inpatient or outpatient.
- Other services such as X rays, services of a doctor's office nurse, drugs and biologicals that cannot be self-administered, transfusions of blood and blood components, medical supplies, physical/occupational therapy and speech pathology services.

In addition to the above, certain other tests or preventive measures are now covered without an additional premium. These include mammograms, bone mass measurement, colo-rectal cancer screening, and flu shots. Outpatient prescription drugs are generally not covered under the basic plan, nor are routine physical exams, dental care, hearing aids, or routine eye care. There is limited coverage for non-hospital treatment of mental illness.

To get medical insurance protection, persons approaching age 65 may enroll in the 7-month period that includes 3 months before the 65th birthday, the month of the birthday, and 3 months after the birthday, but if they wish coverage to begin in the month they reach age 65, they must enroll in the 3 months before their birthday. Persons not enrolling within their first enrollment period may enroll later, during the first 3 months of each year (coverage begins July 1), but their premium may be 10% higher for each 12-month period elapsed since they first could have enrolled.

The monthly premium is deducted from the cash benefit for persons receiving Social Security, Railroad Retirement, or Civil Service retirement benefits. Income from the medical premiums and the federal matching payments are put in a Supplementary Medical Insurance Trust Fund, from which benefits and administrative expenses are paid.

Further details are available on the Internet at www.medicare.gov or by calling 1-800-MEDICARE (1-800-633-4227).

Medicare card. Persons qualifying for hospital insurance under Social Security receive a health insurance card similar to cards now used by Blue Cross and other health insurers. The card indicates whether the individual has taken out medical insurance protection. It is to be shown to the hospital, skilled-nursing facility, home health agency, doctor, or whoever provides the covered services.

Payments are generally made only in the 50 states, Puerto Rico, Virgin Islands, Guam, and American Samoa.

Social Security Financing

Social Security is paid for by a tax on certain earnings (for 2004, on earnings up to $87,900) for Old Age, Survivors, and Disability Insurance and on all earnings (no upper limit) for Hospital Insurance with the Medicare Program; the taxable earnings base for OASDI has been adjusted annually to reflect increases in average wages. The employed worker and his or her employer share Social Security taxes equally.

Employers remit amounts withheld from employee wages for Social Security and income taxes to the Internal Revenue Service; employer Social Security taxes are also payable at the same time. (Self-employed workers pay Social Security taxes when filing their regular income tax forms.) The Social Security taxes (along with revenues arising from partial taxation of the Social Security benefits of certain high-income people) are transferred to the Social Security Trust Funds—the Federal Old-Age and Survivors Insurance (OASI) Trust Fund, the Federal Disability Insurance (DI) Trust Fund, and the Federal Hospital Insurance (HI) Trust Fund; they can be used only to pay benefits, the cost of rehabilitation services, and administrative expenses. Money not immediately needed for these purposes is by law invested in obligations of the federal government, which must pay interest on the money borrowed and must repay the principal when the obligations are redeemed or mature.

Supplemental Security Income

On Jan. 1, 1974, the Supplemental Security Income (SSI) program established by the 1972 Social Security Act amendments replaced the former federal grants to states for aid to the needy aged, blind, and disabled in the 50 states and the District of Columbia. The program provides both for federal payments, based on uniform national standards and eligibil-

ity requirements, and for state supplementary payments varying from state to state. The Social Security Administration administers the federal payments financed from general funds of the Treasury—and the state supplements as well, if the state elects to have its supplementary program federally administered. States may supplement the federal payment for all recipients and must supplement it for persons otherwise adversely affected by the transition from the former public assistance programs. In May 2004, the number of persons receiving federally administered payments was 6,970,366 and the payments totaled $3.2 billion.

The maximum monthly federal SSI payment for individuals with no other countable income, living in their own household, was $564 in 2004. For couples it was $846.

Social Security Statement

On Oct. 1, 1999, the Social Security Administration initiated the mailing of an annual *Social Security Statement* to all workers age 25 and older not already receiving benefits. Workers will automatically receive statements about 3 months before their birth month. The statement provides estimates of potential monthly Social Security retirement, disability, and survivor benefits as well as a record of lifetime earnings. The statement also gives workers an easy way to determine whether their earnings are accurately posted in Social Security records.

For further information contact the Social Security Administration toll-free at 1-800-772-1213 or visit its website at www.socialsecurity.gov

Examples of Monthly Benefits Available

Description of benefit or beneficiary	For low earnings ($15,776 in 2004)[1,2]	For avg. earnings ($35,057 in 2004)[2]	For max. earnings ($87,900 in 2004)
Primary insurance amount (worker retiring at 65)	$737.30	$1,216.30	$1,825.40
Maximum family benefit (worker retiring at 65)	1,106.00	2,216.30	3,194.40
Maximum family disability benefit (worker disabled at 55; in 2004)*	1,024.20	1,800.90	2,771.40
Disabled worker (worker disabled at 55)			
Worker alone	753.60	1,241.60	1,937.80
Worker, spouse, and 1 child	1,059.10	1,862.40	2,906.70
Retired worker claiming benefits at age 62:			
Worker alone[3]	571.00	941.00	1,414.00
Worker with spouse claiming benefits at—			
Age 65 or over	947.00	1,561.00	2,346.00
Age 62[3]	837.00	1,380.00	2,074.00
Widow or widower claiming benefits at—			
Age 65 or over[4]	737.00	1,216.00	1,825.00
Age 60 (spouse died at 65 without receiving reduced benefits)	527.00	869.00	1,305.00
Disabled widow or widower claiming benefits at age 50-59[5]	527.00	869.00	1,305.00
1 surviving child	552.00	912.00	1,369.00
Widow or widower age 65 or over and 1 child[6]	1,289.00	2,128.00	3,194.00
Widowed mother or father and 1 child[6]	1,104.00	1,824.00	2,738.00
Widowed mother or father and 2 children[6]	1,104.00	2,214.00	3,192.00

Effective Jan. 2004. *Assumes work beginning at age 22. (1) 45% of average. (2) Estimate. (3) Assumes maximum reduction. (4) A widow(er)'s benefit amount is limited to the amount the spouse would have been receiving if still living, but not less than 82.5% of the Primary Insurance Amount (PIA). (5) Effective Jan. 1984, disabled widow(er)s claiming a benefit at ages 50-59 receive a benefit equal to 71.5% of the PIA. (6) Based on worker dying at age 65.

Social Security Trust Funds

Old-Age and Survivors Insurance Trust Fund, 1940-2003

(in millions)

		INCOME				DISBURSEMENTS					
Fiscal year[1]	Total	Net contributions[2]	Income from taxing benefits	Payments from the Treasury fund[3]	Net interest[4]	Total	Benefit payments[5]	Administrative expenses	Transfers to Railroad Retirement program	Net increase in fund	Fund at end of period
1940	$368	$325	—	—	$43	$62	$35	$26	—	$306	$2,031
1950	2,928	2,667	—	$4	257	1,022	961	61	—	1,905	13,721
1960	11,382	10,866	—	—	516	11,198	10,677	203	$318	184	20,324
1970	32,220	30,256	—	449	1,515	29,848	28,798	471	579	2,371	32,454
1980	105,841	103,456	—	540	1,845	107,678	105,083	1,154	1,442	−1,837	22,823
1990	286,653	267,530	$4,848	−2,089	16,363	227,519	222,987	1,563	2,969	59,134	214,197
1996	363,741	321,557	6,471	7	35,706	308,217	302,861	1,802	3,554	575,096	589,121
1997	397,169	349,946	7,426	2	39,795	322,073	316,257	2,128	3,688	67,916	567,395
1998	424,848	371,207	9,149	1	44,491	332,324	326,762	1,899	3,662	92,524	681,645
1999	457,040	396,352	10,899	—	49,788	339,874	334,383	1,809	3,681	117,167	798,812
2000	484,228	418,219	12,476	—	53,532	353,396	347,868	1,990	3,538	130,832	893,003
2001	513,800	440,800	11,800	—	61,200	373,000	367,000	2,100	3,300	140,800	1,033,800
2002	529,300	448,100	13,600	—	68,100	389,500	383,900	2,100	3,500	139,700	1,173,600
2003	542,300	456,000	12,300	—	74,000	402,800	396,700	2,500	3,600	139,500	1,313,100

(1) Fiscal years 1980 and later consist of the 12 months ending on Sept. 30 of each year. Fiscal years prior to 1977 consisted of the 12 months ending on June 30 of each year. (2) Beginning in 1983, includes transfers from general fund of Treasury representing contributions that would have been paid on deemed wage credits for military service in 1957 and later, if such credits were considered covered wages. (3) Includes payments (a) in 1947-52 and in 1967 and later, for costs of noncontributory wage credits for military service performed before 1957; (b) in 1972-83, for costs of deemed wage credits for military service performed after 1956; and (c) in 1969 and later, for costs of benefits to certain uninsured persons who attained age 72 before 1968. (4) Net interest includes net profits or losses on marketable investments. Beginning in 1967, administrative expenses were charged currently to the trust fund on an estimated basis, with a final adjustment, including interest, made in the next fiscal year. The amounts of these interest adjustments are included in net interest. For years prior to 1967, the method of accounting for administrative expenses is described in the 1970 Annual Report. Beginning in Oct. 1973, the figures shown include relatively small amounts of gifts to the fund. During 1983-91, interest paid from the trust fund to the general fund on advance tax transfers is reflected. (5) Beginning in 1967, includes payments for vocational rehabilitation services furnished to disabled persons receiving benefits because of their disabilities. Beginning in 1983, amounts are reduced by amount of reimbursement for unnegotiated benefit checks.

Disability Insurance Trust Fund, 1970-2003
(in millions)

Fiscal year[1]	Total	INCOME Net contributions[2]	Income from taxation of benefits	Payments from the Treasury fund[3]	Net interest[4]	DISBURSEMENTS Total	Benefit payments[5]	Administrative expenses	Transfers to Railroad Retirement program	Net increase in fund	Fund at end of period
1970...	$4,774	$4,481	—	$16	$277	$3,259	$3,085	$164	$10	$1,514	$5,614
1980...	13,871	13,255	—	130	485	15,872	15,515	368	-12	2,001	3,629
1990...	28,791	28,539	$144	-775	883	25,616	24,829	707	80	3,174	11,079
1996...	60,710	57,325	373	—	3,012	45,351	44,189	1,160	2	15,359	52,924
1997...	60,499	56,037	470	—	3,992	47,034	45,695	1,280	59	13,465	66,389
1998...	64,357	58,966	558	—	4,832	49,931	48,207	1,567	157	14,425	80,815
1999...	69,541	63,203	661	—	5,677	53,035	51,381	1,519	135	16,507	97,321
2000...	77,023	70,001	756	-836	6,266	56,008	54,174	1,608	159	21,014	113,752
2001...	82,100	74,600	700	—	7,600	69,900	58,200	1,800	*	22,100	135,900
2002...	85,700	76,100	900	—	8,700	66,400	64,200	2,000	200	19,400	155,300
2003...	87,900	77,400	900	—	9,600	71,900	69,800	2,000	200	16,000	171,300

* Less than $50 million. (1) Fiscal years 1977 and later consist of the 12 months ending Sept. 30 of each year. Fiscal years prior to 1977 consisted of the 12 months ending June 30 of each year. (2) Beginning in 1983, includes transfers from general fund of Treasury representing contributions that would have been paid on deemed wage credits for military service in 1957 and later, if such credits were considered to be covered wages. (3) Includes payments (a) for costs of noncontributory wage credits for military service performed before 1957; and (b) in 1972-83, for costs of deemed wage credits for military service performed after 1956. (4) Net interest includes net profits or losses on marketable investments. Administrative expenses are charged currently to the trust fund on an estimated basis, with a final adjustment, including interest, made in the following fiscal year. Figures shown include relatively small amounts of gifts to the fund. During the years 1983-91, interest paid from the trust fund to the general fund on advance tax transfers is reflected. (5) Includes payments for vocational rehabilitation services. Beginning in 1983, amounts are reduced by amount of reimbursement for unnegotiated benefit checks. **NOTE:** Totals may not add because of rounding.

Supplementary Medical Insurance Trust Fund (Medicare), 1975-2003
(in millions)

Fiscal year[1]	INCOME Premium from participants	Government contributions[2]	Interest and other income[3]	Total Income	DISBURSEMENTS Benefit payments[4]	Administrative expenses	Total disbursements	Balance in fund at end of year[5]
1975....	$1,887	$2,330	$106	$4,322	$3,765	$404	$4,170	$1,424
1980....	2,928	6,932	416	10,275	10,144	593	10,737	4,532
1990....	11,494[6]	33,210	1,434[6]	46,138[6]	41,498	1,524[6]	43,022[6]	14,527[6]
1995....	19,244	36,988	1,937	58,169	63,491	1,722	65,213	13,874
1996....	18,931	61,702	1,392	82,025	67,176	1,771	68,946	26,953
1997....	19,141	59,471	2,193	80,806	71,133	1,420	72,553	35,206
1998....	19,427	59,919	2,608	81,955	74,837[7]	1,435	76,272	40,889
1999....	20,160	62,185	2,933	85,278	79,008[7]	1,510	80,518	45,649
2000....	20,515	65,561	3,164	89,239	87,212[7]	1,780	88,992	45,896
2001....	22,307	69,838	3,191	95,336	97,466[7]	1,986	99,452	41,780
2002....	24,427	78,318	2,960	105,705	106,995[7]	1,830	108,825	38,659
2003....	26,834	80,905	2,455	110,194	121,699[7]	2,356	124,055	24,799

(1) Fiscal year 1975 consists of the 12 months ending on June 30, 1975; fiscal years 1980 and later consist of the 12 months ending on Sept. 30 of each year. (2) General fund matching payments, plus certain interest-adjustment items. (3) Other income includes recoveries of amounts reimbursed from the trust fund that are not obligations of the trust fund and other miscellaneous income. (4) Includes costs of Peer Review Organizations from 1983 to 2001, and costs of Quality Improvement Organizations beginning in 2002. (5) The financial status of the program depends on both the assets and the liabilities of the program. (6) Includes the impact of the Medicare Catastrophic Coverage Act of 1988. (7) Benefit payments less monies transferred from the HI trust fund for home health agency costs, as provided for by PL 105-33. **NOTE:** Totals do not necessarily equal sums of rounded components.

Hospital Insurance Trust Fund (Medicare), 1975-2003
(in millions)

Fisc. year[1]	Payroll taxes	Income from taxation of benefits	Transfers from railroad retirement acct.	Reimbursment for uninsured persons	Premiums for voluntary enrollees	Pymts. for military wage credits	Interest on investments and other income[2]	Total income	DISBURSEMENTS Benefit pymts.[3]	Administrative expense[4]	Total disbursements	Net increase in fund	Fund at end of year
1975.	$11,291	—	$132	$481	$6	$48	$609	$12,568	$10,353	$259	$10,612	$1,956	$9,870
1980.	23,244	—	244	697	17	141	1,072	25,415	23,790	497	24,288	1,127	14,490
1990.	70,655	—	367	413	113	107	7,908	79,563	65,912	774	66,687	12,876	95,631
1995.	98,053	3,913	396	462	998	61	10,963	114,847	113,583	1,300	114,883	-36	129,520
1996.	106,934	4,069	401	419	1,107	-2,293[5]	10,496	121,135	124,088	1,229	125,317	-4,182	125,338
1997.	112,725	3,558	419	481	1,279	70	10,017	128,548	136,175	1,661	137,836	-9,287	116,050
1998.	121,913	5,067	419	34	1,320	67	9,382	138,203	135,487[6]	1,653	137,140	1,063	117,113
1999.	134,385	6,552	430	652	1,401	71	9,523	153,015	129,463[6]	1,978	131,441	21,574	138,687
2000.	137,738	8,787	465	470	1,392	2	10,827	159,681	127,934[6]	2,350	130,284	29,397	168,084
2001.	151,931	4,903	470	453	1,440	-1,175[7]	12,993	171,014	139,356[6]	2,368	141,723	29,290	197,374
2002.	151,575	10,946	425	442	1,525	0	14,850	179,762	145,566[6]	2,464	148,031	31,731	229,105
2003.	149,839	8,318	426	393	1,598	0	15,239	175,813	151,250[6]	2,541	153,792	22,021	251,127

(1) Fiscal year 1975 consists of the 12 months ending on June 30, 1975; fiscal years 1980 and later consist of the 12 months ending Sept. 30 of each year. (2) Other income includes recoveries of amounts reimbursed from the trust fund that are not obligations of the trust fund, receipts from the fraud and abuse control program, and a small amount of miscellaneous income. (3) Includes costs of Peer Review Organizations from 1983 through 2001 (beginning with the implementation of the Prospective Payment System on Oct. 1, 1983), and costs of Quality Improvement Organizations beginning in 2002. (4) Includes costs of experiments and demonstration projects. Beginning in 1997, includes fraud and abuse control expenses, as provided for by PL 104-191. (5) Includes the lump-sum general revenue adjustment of $-2,366 mil, as provided for by PL 98-21. (6) Includes monies transferred to the SMI trust fund for home health agency costs, as provided for by PL 105-33. (7) Includes the lump-sum general review adjustment of -$1,117 million, as provided for by sec. 151 of PL 98-21. **NOTE:** Totals do not necessarily equal sums of rounded components.

WORLD EXPLORATION AND GEOGRAPHY
Early Explorers of the Western Hemisphere
Reviewed by Susan Skomal, PhD, American Anthropological Assn., and Paul B. Frederic, PhD, prof. of geography, Univ. of Maine.

In the light of recent discoveries, theories about how the first people arrived in the western hemisphere are being reconsidered. It was once thought that humans came across a "land bridge" from Siberia to Alaska, spreading through the Americas 12,000 to 14,000 years ago. Whereas the preponderance of genetic, skeletal, and linguistic evidence indicate that current Native Americans are descended from peoples from N and central Asia, skeletal remains of Kennewick Man found in Washington state (dated to 9,200-9,600 BP, or before present) and "Luzia" from Brazil (11,500 BP) attest to a much earlier arrival of a people with markedly different physical characteristics and uncertain origin.

Archaeologists have confirmed evidence of habitation at least 12,900 BP at sites located on the shores of ancient lakes 2 miles high in the Atacama Desert of Monte Verde Chile. (There is also growing evidence that humans had settled the lowland jungles of Chile 2,000 years earlier.) Because a glacier covered most of N America from 20,000 to 13,000 years ago, those who settled in S America may have traveled in vessels along the west coast, sailed directly from Australia or S Asia, or spread from N to S America before the ice came. There is even recent evidence from a burial site at Santana do Riacho 1 in Brazil (8,000-11,000 BP) to suggest that some of the early immigrants who crossed to the New World via the land bridge from Siberia may have originated in Africa.

Norsemen (Norwegian Vikings sailing out of Iceland and Greenland), led by Leif Ericson, are credited with having been the first Europeans to reach America, with at least 5 voyages occurring about AD 1000 to areas they called Hellu-land, Markland, and Vinland—possibly what are known today as Labrador, Nova Scotia or Newfoundland, and New England. L'Anse aux Meadows, on the N tip of Newfoundland, is the only documented settlement.

Sustained contact between the hemispheres began with the first voyage of Christopher Columbus (born Cristoforo Colombo, c 1451, near Genoa, Italy). Columbus made trips to the New World while sailing for the Spanish.

He left Palos, Spain, Aug. 3, 1492, with 88 men and landed at San Salvador (Watling Islands, Bahamas), Oct. 12, 1492. His fleet included 3 vessels, the Niña, Pinta, and Santa María. Stops also were made on Cuba and Hispaniola. A 2nd expedition left Cadiz, Spain, Sept. 25, 1493, with 17 ships and 1,500 men, reaching the Lesser Antilles Nov. 3. His 3rd voyage brought him from Sanlucar, Spain (May 30, 1498, with 6 ships), to the N coast of S America. A 4th voyage reached the mainland of Central America, after leaving Cadiz, Spain, May 9, 1502. Columbus died in 1506 convinced he had reached Asia by sailing west.

In N America, John Cabot and Sebastian Cabot, Italian explorers sailing for the English, reached Newfoundland and possibly Nova Scotia in 1497. John's 2nd voyage (1498), seeking a new trade route to Asia, resulted in the loss of his entire fleet. During this period exploration was dominated by Spain and Portugal. In 1497 and 1499 Amerigo Vespucci (for whom the Americas are named), an Italian explorer sailing for Spain, passed along the N and E coasts of S America. He was the first to argue that the newly discovered lands were a continent other than Asia.

Year	Explorer	Nationality (sponsor, if different)	Area reached or explored
c1000	Leif Ericson	Norse	Newfoundland
1492-1502	Christopher Columbus	Italian (Spanish)	West Indies, S. and C. America
1497	John Cabot and Sebastian Cabot	Italian (English)	Atlantic Canada
1497-98	Vasco de Gama	Portuguese	Cape of Good Hope (Africa), India
1497-99	Amerigo Vespucci	Italian (Spanish)	E and N Coast of S. America
1499	Alonso de Ojeda	Spanish	N South American coast, Venezuela
1500, Feb.	Vicente Yañez Pinzon	Spanish	S. American coast, Amazon R.
1500, Apr.	Pedro Álvarez Cabral	Portuguese	Brazil
1500-02	Gaspar Corte-Real	Portuguese	Labrador
1501	Rodrigo de Bastidas	Spanish	Central America
1513	Vasco Núñez de Balboa	Spanish	Panama, Pacific Ocean
1513	Juan Ponce de León	Spanish	Florida, Yucatán Peninsula
1515	Juan de Solis	Spanish	Río de la Plata
1519	Alonso de Pineda	Spanish	Mouth of Mississippi R.
1519	Hernando Cortes	Spanish	Mexico
1519-20	Ferdinand Magellan	Portuguese (Spanish)	Straits of Magellan, Tierra del Fuego
1524	Giovanni da Verrazano	Italian (French)	Atlantic coast, incl. New York harbor
1528	Cabeza de Vaca	Spanish	Texas coast and interior
1532	Francisco Pizarro	Spanish	Peru
1534	Jacques Cartier	French	Canada, Gulf of St. Lawrence
1536	Pedro de Mendoza	Spanish	Buenos Aires
1539	Francisco de Ulloa	Spanish	California coast
1539-41	Hernando de Soto	Spanish	Mississippi R., near Memphis
1539	Marcos de Niza	Italian (Spanish)	SW United States
1540	Francisco de Coronado	Spanish	SW United States
1540	Hernando Alarcon	Spanish	Colorado R.
1540	Garcia de Lopez Cardenas	Spanish	Colorado, Grand Canyon
1541	Francisco de Orellana	Spanish	Amazon R.
1542	Juan Rodriguez Cabrillo	Portuguese (Spanish)	W Mexico, San Diego harbor
1565	Pedro Menéndez de Aviles	Spanish	St. Augustine, FL
1576	Sir Martin Frobisher	English	Frobisher Bay, Canada
1577-80	Sir Francis Drake	English	California coast
1582	Antonio de Espejo	Spanish	Southwest U.S. (New Mexico)
1584	Amadas & Barlow (for Raleigh)	English	Virginia
1585-87	Sir Walter Raleigh's men	English	Roanoke Isl., NC
1595	Sir Walter Raleigh	English	Orinoco R.
1603-09	Samuel de Champlain	French	Canadian interior, Lake Champlain
1607	Capt. John Smith	English	Atlantic coast
1609-10	Henry Hudson	English (Dutch)	Hudson R., Hudson Bay
1634	Jean Nicolet	French	Lake Michigan, Wisconsin
1673	Jacques Marquette, Louis Jolliet	French	Mississippi R., S to Arkansas
1682	Robert Cavelier, sieur de La Salle	French	Mississippi R., S to Gulf of Mexico
1727-29	Vitus Bering	Danish (Russian)	Bering Strait and Alaska
1789	Sir Alexander Mackenzie	Canadian	NW Canada
1804-06	Meriwether Lewis and William Clark	American	Missouri R., Rocky Mts., Columbia R.

Arctic Exploration

Early Explorers

1587 — John Davis (Eng.). Davis Strait to Sanderson's Hope, 72°12′N.

1596 — Willem Barents and Jacob van Heemskerck (Holland). Discovered Bear Isl., touched NW tip of Spitsbergen, 79°49′N, rounded Novaya Zemlya, wintered at Ice Haven.

1607 — Henry Hudson (Eng.). North along Greenland's E coast to Cape Hold-with-Hope, 73°30′, then N of Spitsbergen to 80°23′. Explored Hudson's Touches (Jan Mayen).

1616 — William Baffin and Robert Bylot (Eng.). Baffin Bay to Smith Sound.

1728 — Vitus Bering (Russ.). Sailed through strait (Bering) proving Asia and America are separate.

1733-40 — Great Northern Expedition (Russ.). Surveyed Siberian Arctic coast.

1741 — Vitus Bering (Russ.). Sighted Alaska, named Mount St. Elias. His lieutenant, Chirikof, explored coast.

1771 — Samuel Hearne (Hudson's Bay Co.). Overland from Prince of Wales Fort (Churchill) on Hudson Bay to mouth of Coppermine R.

1778 — James Cook (Brit.). Through Bering Strait to Icy Cape, AK, and North Cape, Siberia.

1789 — Alexander Mackenzie (North West Co., Brit.). Montreal to mouth of Mackenzie River.

1806 — William Scoresby (Brit.). N of Spitsbergen to 8°30′.

1820-23 — Ferdinand von Wrangel (Russ.). Surveyed Siberian Arctic coast. His exploration joined James Cook's at North Cape, confirming separation of the continents.

1878-79 — (Nils) Adolf Erik Nordenskjöld (Swed.). The 1st to navigate the Northeast Passage—an ocean route connecting Europe's North Sea, along the Arctic coast of Asia and through the Bering Sea, to the Pacific Ocean.

1881 — The U.S. steamer *Jeannette*, led by Lt. Cmdr. George W. DeLong, was trapped in ice and crushed, June 1881. DeLong and 11 others died; 12 survived.

1888 — Fridtjof Nansen (Nor.) crossed Greenland icecap.

1893-96 — Nansen in *Fram* drifted from New Siberian Isls. to Spitsbergen; tried polar dash in 1895, reached Franz Josef Land, 86°14′N.

1897 — Salomon A. Andrée (Sweden) and 2 others started in balloon from Spitsbergen, July 11, to drift across pole to U.S., and disappeared. Aug. 6, 1930, their bodies were found on White Isl., 82°57′N, 29°52′E.

1903-6 — Roald Amundsen (Nor.) 1st sailed the Northwest Passage—an ocean route linking the Atlantic Ocean to the Pacific via Canada's marine waterways.

North Pole Exploration

Robert E. Peary explored Greenland's coast, 1891-92; tried for North Pole, 1893. In 1900 he reached N limit of Greenland and 83°50′N; in 1902 he reached 84°17′N; in 1906 he went from Ellesmere Isl. to 87°06′N. He sailed in the *Roosevelt*, July 1908, to winter off Cape Sheridan, Grant Land. The dash for the North Pole began Mar. 1 from Cape Columbia, Ellesmere Isl. Peary reportedly reached the pole, 90°N, Apr. 6, 1909; however, later research suggests that he may have fallen short of his goal by c. 30-60 mi. Peary had several support groups carrying supplies until the last group turned back at 87°47′N. Peary, Matthew Henson, and 4 Eskimos proceeded with dog teams and sleds. They were said to have crossed the pole several times, then built an igloo there and remained 36 hours. Started south, Apr. 7 at 4 PM, for Cape Columbia.

1914 — Donald MacMillan (U.S.). Northwest, 200 mi, from Axel Heiberg Isl. to seek Peary's Crocker Land.

1915-17 — Vihjalmur Stefansson (Can.). Discovered Borden, Brock, Meighen, and Lougheed Isls.

1918-20 — Amundsen sailed the Northeast Passage.

1925 — Amundsen and Lincoln Ellsworth (U.S.) reached 87°44′N in attempt to fly to N Pole from Spitsbergen.

1926 — Richard E. Byrd and Floyd Bennett (U.S.) reputedly flew over North Pole, May 9. (Claim to have reached the pole is in dispute, however.)

1926 — Amundsen, Ellsworth, and Umberto Nobile (It.) flew from Spitsbergen over N Pole May 12, to Teller, AK, in dirigible *Norge*.

1928 — Nobile crossed N Pole in airship, May 24; crashed, May 25. Amundsen died attempting a rescue.

North Pole Exploration Records

On Aug. 3, 1958, submarine *Nautilus,* under Comdr. William R. Anderson, crossed the N Pole beneath the ice.

In Aug. 1960, the nuclear-powered U.S. submarine *Seadragon* (Comdr. George P. Steele 2nd) made the 1st E-W underwater transit through the Northwest Passage. Traveling submerged for the most part, it took 6 days to make the 850-mi trek from Baffin Bay to the Beaufort Sea.

On Aug. 16, 1977, the Soviet nuclear icebreaker *Arktika* became the 1st surface ship to reach the N Pole.

On Apr. 30, 1978, Naomi Uemura (Jap.) became the 1st person to reach the N Pole alone, traveling by dog sled in a 54-day, 600-mi trek over the frozen Arctic.

In Apr. 1982, Sir Ranulph Fiennes and Charles Burton, Brit. explorers, reached the N Pole and became the 1st to circle the earth from pole to pole. They had reached the S Pole 16 months earlier. The 52,000-mi trek took 3 years, involved 23 people, and cost an estimated $18 mil.

On May 2, 1986, 6 explorers reached the N Pole assisted only by dogs. They became the 1st to reach the pole without aerial logistics support since at least 1909. The explorers, Amer. Will Steger, Paul Schurke, Ann Bancroft, and Geoff Carroll, and Can. Brent Boddy and Richard Weber, completed the 500-mi journey in 56 days.

On June 15, 1995, Weber and Russ. Mikhail Malakhov became the 1st pair to make it to the pole and back without any mechanical assistance. The 940-mi trip, made entirely on skis, took 121 days.

On May 20, 2003, Pen Hadow (U.K.) became the 1st to reach the pole from Canada, solo and without resupply. The 377-mile journey across the ice took 64 days.

Antarctic Exploration

Antarctica has been approached since 1773-75, when Capt. James Cook (Brit.) reached 71°10′S. Many sea and landmarks bear names of early explorers. Fabian von Bellingshausen (Russ.) discovered Peter I and Alexander I Isls., 1819-21. Nathaniel Palmer (U.S.) traveled throughout Palmer Peninsula, 60°W, 1820, without realizing that this was a continent. Capt. John Davis (U.S.) made the 1st known landing on the continent on Feb. 7, 1821. Later, in 1823, James Weddell (Brit.) found Weddell Sea, 74°15′S, the southernmost point that had been reached.

First to announce existence of the continent of Antarctica was Charles Wilkes (U.S.), who followed the coast for 1,500 mi, 1840. Adelie Coast, 140°E, was found by Dumont d'Urville (Fr.), 1840. Ross Ice Shelf was found by James Clark Ross (Brit.), 1841-42.

1895 — Leonard Kristensen (Nor.) landed a party on the coast of Victoria Land. They were the 1st ashore on the main continental mass. C. E. Borchgrevink, a member of that party, returned in 1899 with a Brit. expedition, 1st to winter on Antarctica.

1902-4 — Robert Falcon Scott (Brit.) explored Edward VII Peninsula to 82°17′S, 146°33′E from McMurdo Sound.

1908-9 — Ernest Shackleton (Brit.) 1st to use Manchurian ponies in Antarctic sledging. He reached 88°23′S, discovering a route on to the plateau by way of the Beardmore Glacier and pioneering the way to the pole.

1911 — Roald Amundsen (Nor.) with 4 men and dog teams reached the S Pole, Dec. 14.

1912 — Scott reached the pole from Ross Isl., Jan. 18, with 4 companions. None of Scott's party survived. Their bodies and expedition notes were found, Nov. 12.

1928 — 1st person to use an airplane over Antarctica was Sir George Hubert Wilkins (Austral.).

1929 — Richard E. Byrd (U.S.) established Little America on Bay of Whales. On 1,600-mi airplane flight begun Nov. 28, he crossed S Pole, Nov. 29, with 3 others.

1934-35 — Byrd led 2nd expedition to Little America, explored 450,000 sq mi, wintered alone at 80°08′S.

1934-37 — John Rymill led British Graham Land expedition; discovered Palmer Penin. is part of mainland.

1935 — Lincoln Ellsworth (U.S.) flew S along E Coast of Palmer Penin., then crossed continent to Little America, making 4 landings.

1939-41 — U.S. Navy plane flights discovered about 150,000 sq mi of new land.

1940 — Byrd charted most of coast between Ross Sea and Palmer Penin.

1946-47 — U.S. Navy undertook Operation Highjump, commanded by Byrd, included 13 ships and 4,000 men. Airplanes photomapped coastline and penetrated beyond pole.

1946-48 — Ronne Antarctic Research Expedition Comdr., Finn Ronne, USNR, determined the Antarctic to be only one continent with no strait between Weddell Sea and Ross Sea; explored 250,000 sq mi of land by flights to 79°S.

1955-57 — U.S. Navy's Operation Deep Freeze led by Adm. Byrd. Supporting U.S. scientific efforts for the International Geophysical Year (IGY), the operation established 5 coastal stations fronting the Indian, Pacific, and Atlantic oceans and also 3 interior stations; explored more than 1,000,000 sq mi in Wilkes Land.

1957-58 — During the IGY, July 1957 through Dec. 1958, scientists from 12 countries conducted Antarctic research at a network of some 60 stations on Antarctica.

Dr. Vivian E. Fuchs led a 12-person Trans-Antarctic Expedition on the 1st land crossing of Antarctica. Starting from the Weddell Sea, they reached Scott Station, Mar. 2, 1958, after traveling 2,158 mi in 98 days.

1958 — A group of 5 U.S. scientists led by Edward C. Thiel, seismologist, moving by tractor from Ellsworth Station on Weddell Sea, identified a huge mountain range, 5,000 ft above the ice sheet and 9,000 ft above sea level. The range, originally seen by a Navy plane, was named the Dufek Massif, for Rear Adm. George Dufek.

1959 — Argentina, Australia, Belgium, Chile, France, Japan, New Zealand, Norway, South Africa, USSR, U.K., and U.S. signed a treaty suspending territorial claims for 30 yrs. and reserving the continent, S of 60°S, for research.

1961-62 — Scientists discovered the Bentley Trench, running from Ross Ice Shelf into Marie Byrd Land, near the end of the Ellsworth Mts., toward the Weddell Sea.

1962 — Nuclear power plant online at McMurdo Sound.

1963 — On Feb. 22, a U.S. plane made the region's longest nonstop flight] from McMurdo Station S past the pole to Shackleton Mts., SE to the "Area of Inaccessibility," and back to McMurdo Station covering 3,600 mi in 10 hrs.

1964 — New Zealanders mapped the mountain area from from Cape Adare W some 400 mi to Pennell Glacier.

1985 — Igor A. Zotikov, a Russian researcher, discovered sediments in the Ross Ice Shelf that seem to support the continental drift theory. Ocean Drilling Project finds that the ice sheets of E Antarctica are 37 million yrs. old.

1989 — Victoria Murden and Shirley Metz became both the 1st women and the 1st Americans to reach the S Pole overland when they arrived with 9 others on Jan. 17, 1989.

1991 — 24 nations approved a protocol to the 1959 Antarctica Treaty, Oct. 4. New conservation provisions, including banning oil and other mineral exploration for 50 yrs.

1994 — On Dec. 25, after 50-day trek, Liv Arnesen (Nor.) became 1st woman to ski alone and unaided to the S Pole.

1995 — On Dec. 22, a Norwegian, Borge Ousland, reached the S Pole in the fastest time on skis: 44 days.

1996-97 — Ousland became 1st person to traverse Antarctica alone; reached S Pole Dec. 19, 1996; traveled 1,675 mi in 64 days, ending Jan. 18, 1997.

2000-2001 — On Feb. 11, Ann Bancroft and Liv Arnesen (Nor.) became 1st women to ski unaided across Antarctica. The 1,717-mile journey took 94 days.

Volcanoes

Sources: *Volcanoes of the World*, Geoscience Press; Global Volcanism Network, Smithsonian Institution

Roughly 540 volcanoes are known to have erupted during historical times. Nearly 75% of these historically active volcanoes lie along the so-called Ring of Fire, running along the W coast of the Americas from the southern tip of Chile to Alaska, down the E coast of Asia from Kamchatka to Indonesia, and continuing from New Guinea to New Zealand. The Ring of Fire marks the boundary between the mobile tectonic plates underlying the Pacific Ocean and those of the surrounding continents. Other active regions occur along rift zones, where plates pull apart, as in Iceland, or where molten material moves up from the mantle over local "hot spots," as in Hawaii. The vast majority of the earth's volcanism occurs at submarine rift zones. For more information on volcanoes, see the website at www.volcano.si.edu/gvp

Notable Volcanic Eruptions

Approximately 7,000 years ago, Mazama, a 9,900-ft volcano in southern Oregon, erupted violently, ejecting large amounts of ash and pumice and voluminous pyroclastic flows. The ash spread over the entire northwestern U.S. and as far away as Saskatchewan, Can. During the eruption, the top of the mountain collapsed, leaving a caldera 6 mi across and about a half mile deep, which filled with rainwater to form what is now called Crater Lake.

In AD 79, Vesuvio, or Vesuvius, a 4,190-ft volcano overlooking Naples Bay, became active after several centuries of apparent inactivity. On Aug. 24 of that year, a heated mud and ash flow swept down the mountain, engulfing the cities of Pompeii, Herculaneum, and Stabiae with debris more than 60 ft deep. About 10% of the population of the 3 towns were killed.

In 1883, an eruption similar to the Mazama eruption occurred on the island of Krakatau. At least 2,000 people died in pyroclastic flows on Aug. 26. The next day, the 2,640-ft peak of the volcano collapsed to 1,000 ft below sea level, sinking most of the island and killing over 3,000. A tsunami (tidal wave) generated by the collapse killed more than 31,000 people in Java and Sumatra, and eventually reached England. Ash from the eruption colored sunsets around the world for 2 years. A similar, even more powerful eruption had taken place 68 years earlier at Mt. Tambora on the Indonesian island of Sumbawa.

Date	Volcano	Deaths (est.)	Date	Volcano	Deaths (est.)
Aug. 24, AD 79	Mt. Vesuvius, Italy	16,000	May 8, 1902	Mt. Pelée, Martinique	28,000
1586	Kelut, Java, Indon.	10,000	Jan. 30, 1911	Mt. Taal, Phil.	1,400
Dec. 15, 1631	Mt. Vesuvius, Italy	4,000	May 19, 1919	Mt. Kelut, Java, Indon.	5,000
Aug. 12, 1772	Mt. Papandayan, Java, Indon.	3,000	Jan. 17-21, 1951	Mt. Lamington, New Guinea	3,000
June 8, 1783	Laki, Iceland	9,350	May 18, 1980	Mt. St. Helens, U.S.	57
May 21, 1792	Mt. Unzen, Japan	14,500	Mar. 28, 1982	El Chichon, Mex.	1,880
Apr. 10-12, 1815	Mt. Tambora, Sumbawa, Indon	92,000[1]	Nov. 13, 1985	Nevado del Ruiz, Colombia	23,000
Aug. 26-28, 1883	Krakatau, Indon.	36,000	Aug. 21, 1986	Lake Nyos, Cameroon	1,700
Apr. 24, 1902	Santa María, Guatemala	1,000[2]	June 15, 1991	Mt. Pinatubo, Luzon, Phil.	800

(1) Of these, 10,000 were directly related to the eruption; an additional 82,000 were the result of starvation and disease brought on by the event. (2) An additional 3,000 deaths due to a malaria outbreak are sometimes attributed to the eruption.

IT'S A FACT: The Caribbean island of Montserrat was devastated and some 7,000 people, or about two-thirds of the population, fled abroad after the eruption of the Soufriere Hills volcano starting on July 18, 1995. Nine years later the eruption was continuing. In the U.S., where some 300 Montserratians had received temporary asylum, the government in June 2004 made moves toward revoking that asylum, on the basis that there was no end in sight.

Notable Active Volcanoes

Active volcanoes display a wide range of activity. In this table, years are given for last display of eruptive activity, as of mid-2004; the list does not include submarine volcanoes. An eruption may involve explosive ejection of new or old fragmental material, escape of liquid lava, or both. Volcanoes are listed by height, which does not reflect eruptive magnitude.

Name (latest eruption)		Height (ft)
Africa		
Mt. Cameroon (2000)	Cameroon	13,435
Nyiragongo (2004)	Congo	11,384
Nyamuragira (2002)	Congo	10,033
Mt. Oku {Lake Nyos} (1986)	Cameroon	9,878
Ol Doinyo Lengai (2004)	Tanzania	9,482
Fogo (1995)	Cape Verde Isls.	9,281
Piton de la Fournaise (2002)	Réunion Isl., Indian O.	8,632
Karthala (1991)	Comoros	7,746
Erta-Ale (2004)	Ethiopia	2,011
Antarctica		
Erebus (2004)	Ross Isl	12,447
Deception Island (1970)	S. Shetland Isl.	1,890
Asia-Oceania		
Kliuchevskoi (2003)	Kamchatka, Russia	15,863
Kerinci (2002)	Sumatra, Indon.	12,467
Fuji (1708)	Honshu, Japan	12,388
Tolbachik (1976)	Kamchatka, Russia	12,080
Semeru (2004)	Java, Indon.	12,060
Slamet (1999)	Java, Indon.	11,247
Raung (2002)	Java, Indon.	10,932
Shiveluch (2004)	Kamchatka, Russia	10,771
On-take (1980)	Honshu, Japan	10,049
Merapi (2002)	Java, Indon.	9,737
Bezymianny (2003)	Kamchatka, Russia	9,455
Peuet Sague (2000)	Sumatra, Indon.	9,190
Ruapehu (1997)	New Zealand	9,176
Heard (2001)	Indian Ocean	9,006
Baitoushan (1702)	China/Korea	9,003
Asama (2003)	Honshu, Japan	8,425
Mayon (2003)	Luzon, Phil.	8,077
Canlaon (2003)	Negros Isls., Phil.	7,989
Niigata Yake-yama (1998)	Honshu, Japan	7,874
Alaid (1996)	Kuril Isl., Russia	7,674
Ulawun (2003)	Papua New Guinea	7,657
Ngauruhoe (1977)	New Zealand	7,515
Chokai (1974)	Honshu, Japan	7,326
Galunggung (1984)	Java, Indon.	7,113
Azuma (1977)	Honshu, Japan	6,640
Sangeang Api (1988)	Lesser Sunda Isl., Indon.	6,394
Nasu (1963)	Honshu, Japan	6,283
Karkar (1979)	Papua New Guinea	6,033
Tiatia (1981)	Kuril Isl., Russia	5,968
Bandai (1888)	Honshu, Japan	5,968
Manam (2003)	Papua New Guinea	5,928
Kuju (1996)	Kyushu, Japan	5,876
Karangetang-Api Siau (2004)	Sangihe, Indon.	5,853
Soputan (2000)	Sulawesi, Indon.	5,853
Bagana (2004)	Papua New Guinea	5,741
Kelut (1990)	Java, Indon.	5,679
Adatara (1996)	Honshu, Japan	5,636
Gamalama (2003)	Halmahera, Indon.	5,627
Kirishima (1992)	Kyushu, Japan	5,577
Gamkonora (1987)	Halmahera, Indon.	5,364
Aso (2003)	Kyushu, Japan	5,223
Lokon-Empung (2003)	Sulawesi, Indon.	5,184
Bulusan (1995)	Luzon, Phil.	5,134
Karymsky (2004)	Kamchatka, Russia	5,039
Unzen (1996)	Kyushu, Japan	4,921
Akan (1998)	Hokkaido, Japan	4,918
Sarychev Peak (1989)	Kuril Isl., Russia	4,908
Pinatubo (1993)	Luzon, Phil.	4,875
Lopevi (2003)	Vanuatu.	4,636
Akita-Yake-yama (1997)	Honshu, Japan	4,482
Ambrym (2004)	Vanuatu.	4,377
Langila (2003)	Papua New Guinea	4,363
Awu (1992)	Sangihe Isl., Indon.	4,331
Dukono (2004)	Halmahera, Indonesia	3,888
Akademia Nauk (1996)	Kamchatka, Russia	3,871
Komaga-take (2000)	Hokkaido, Japan	3,740
Sakura-jima (2004)	Kyushu, Japan	3,665
Miyake-jima (2002)	Izu Isls., Japan	2,674
Krakatau (2001)	Indonesia	2,667
Suwanose-jima (2004)	Kyushu, Japan	2,621
Gaua (1982)	Vanuatu.	2,615
Oshima (1990)	Izu Isls., Japan	2,507
Usu (2001)	Hokkaido, Japan	2,418
Rabaul (2004)	Papua New Guinea	2,257
Pagan (1993)	N. Mariana Isl.	1,870
Taal (1977)	Luzon, Phil.	1,312
Yasur (2004)	Tanna Island, Vanuatu	1,184

Name (latest eruption)		Height (ft)
White Island (2001)	Bay of Plenty, New Zealand	1,053
McDonald Islands (2000)	Indian Ocn., Australia	755
Central America—Caribbean		
Tacaná (1986)	Guatemala	13,320
Acatenango (1972)	Guatemala	13,044
Santa María (2004)	Guatemala	12,375
Fuego (2004)	Guatemala	12,346
Irazú (1994)	Costa Rica	11,260
Turrialba (1866)	Costa Rica	10,958
Póas (1996)	Costa Rica	8,884
Pacaya (2002)	Guatemala	8,373
San Miguel (2002)	El Salvador	6,988
Rincón de la Vieja (1998)	Costa Rica	6,286
San Cristobal (2003)	Nicaragua	5,725
Concepción (1999)	Nicaragua	5,577
Arenal (2004)	Costa Rica	5,436
Soufrière Guadeloupe (1977)	Guadeloupe	4,813
Pelée (1932)	Martinique	4,583
Momotombo (1905)	Nicaragua	4,255
Soufrière St. Vincent (1979)	St. Vincent	4,003
Soufrière Hills (2003)	Montserrat	3,002
Masaya (2003)	Nicaragua	2,083
South America		
Llullaillaco (1877)	Argentina-Chile	22,109
Guallatiri (1960)	Chile	19,918
Tupungatito (1987)	Chile	19,685
Cotopaxi (1940)	Ecuador	19,393
El Misti (1784)	Peru	19,101
Láscar (2002)	Chile	18,346
Nevado del Ruiz (1991)	Colombia	17,457
Sangay (2004)	Ecuador	17,159
Irruputuncu (1995)	Chile	16,939
Guagua Pichincha (2004)	Ecuador	15,695
Puracé (1977)	Colombia	15,256
Tungurahua (2004)	Ecuador	14,479
Galeras (2002)	Colombia	14,029
Llaima (2003)	Chile	10,253
Villarrica (2003)	Chile	9,340
Cerro Hudson (1991)	Chile	6,250
Fernandina (1995)	Galapagos Isls., Ecuad.	4,842
Mid-Pacific		
Mauna Loa (1984)	Hawaii, HI	13,681
Kilauea (2004)	Hawaii, HI	4,009
Mid-Atlantic Ridge		
Jan Mayen (1985)	N. Atlantic Ocn., Norway	7,470
Grímsvötn (1998)	Iceland	5,659
Hekla (2000)	Iceland	4,892
Krafla (1984)	Iceland	2,133
Europe		
Etna (2003)	Italy.	10,991
Vesuvius (1944)	Italy.	4,203
Stromboli (2004)	Italy.	3,038
Santorini (1950)	Greece	1,204
North America		
Pico de Orizaba (1846)	Mexico	18,619
Popocatépetl (2004)	Mexico	17,802
Rainier (1825?)	Washington	14,409
Wrangell (1902)	Alaska	14,163
Shasta (1786)	California	14,163
Colima (2004)	Mexico	12,631
Lassen Peak (1917)	California	10,456
Redoubt (1990)	Alaska	10,197
Iliamna (1876)	Alaska	10,016
Shishaldin (1999)	Aleutian Isl., AK	9,373
St. Helens (1991)	Washington	8,363
Pavlof (1997)	Alaska	8,264
Veniaminof (2002)	Alaska	8,225
Katmai [Novarupta] (1912)	Alaska	6,716
Makushin (1995)	Aleutian Isl., AK	5,905
Great Sitkin (1974)	Aleutian Isl., AK	5,709
Cleveland (2001)	Aleutian Isl., AK	5,676
Gareloi (1989)	Aleutian Isl., AK	5,161
Korovin [Atka complex] (1998)	Aleutian Isl., AK	5,029
Akutan (1992)	Aleutian Isl., AK	4,275
Augustine (1986)	Alaska	4,108
Kiska (1990)	Aleutian Isl., AK	4,003
El Chichón (1982)	Mexico	3,773
Okmok (1997)	Aleutian Isl., AK	3,520
Seguam (1993)	Aleutian Isl., AK	3,458

> **IT'S A FACT:** In 1923 George Leigh Mallory said he wanted to climb Everest "because it's there"; a year later, he and his companion Sandy Irvine were lost on the mountain. In 1999, Mallory's preserved body was found at 27,690 feet, with no evidence that he'd reached the top. Irvine remained missing.

Mountains

Height of Mount Everest

Mt. Everest, the world's highest mountain, was considered 29,002 ft when Edmund Hillary and Tenzing Norgay became the 1st climbers to scale it, in 1953. This triangulation figure had been accepted since 1850. In 1954 the Surveyor General of the Republic of India set the height at 29,028 ft, plus or minus 10 ft because of snow; this figure was also accepted by the National Geographic Society.

In 1999, a team of climbers sponsored by Boston's Museum of Science and the National Geographic Society measured the height at the summit using sophisticated satellite-based technology. This new measurement, of 29,035 ft, was accepted by the National Geographic Society and other authorities, including the U.S. National Imagery and Mapping Agency.

By May 29, 2003, 50 years after the 1st climbers had reached the summit, some 1,300 more had followed, and about 175 had died in the attempt.

United States, Canada, Mexico

Name	Place	Height (ft)	Name	Place	Height (ft)	Name	Place	Height (ft)
McKinley	AK	20,320	Alverstone	AK-Yukon	14,565	Shavano	CO	14,229
Logan	Yukon	19,551	Browne Tower	AK	14,530	Belford	CO	14,197
Pico de Orizaba	Mexico	18,555	Whitney	CA	14,494	Princeton	CO	14,197
St. Elias	AK-Yukon	18,008	Elbert	CO	14,433	Crestone Needle	CO	14,197
Popocatépetl	Mexico	17,930	Massive	CO	14,421	Yale	CO	14,196
Foraker	AK	17,400	Harvard	CO	14,420	Bross	CO	14,172
Iztaccihuatl	Mexico	17,343	Rainier	WA	14,410	Kit Carson	CO	14,165
Lucania	Yukon	17,147	University Peak	AK	14,410	Wrangell	AK	14,163
King	Yukon	16,971	Williamson	CA	14,375	Shasta	CA	14,162
Steele	Yukon	16,644	La Plata Peak	CO	14,361	El Diente Peak	CO	14,159
Bona	AK	16,550	Blanca Peak	CO	14,345	Point Success	WA	14,158
Blackburn	AK	16,390	Uncompahgre Peak	CO	14,309	Maroon Peak	CO	14,156
Kennedy	AK	16,286	Crestone Peak	CO	14,294	Tabeguache	CO	14,155
Sanford	AK	16,237	Lincoln	CO	14,286	Oxford	CO	14,153
Vancouver	AK-Yukon	15,979	Grays Peak	CO	14,270	Sill	CA	14,153
South Buttress	AK	15,885	Antero	CO	14,269	Sneffels	CO	14,150
Wood	Yukon	15,885	Torreys Peak	CO	14,267	Democrat	CO	14,148
Churchill	AK	15,638	Castle Peak	CO	14,265	Capitol Peak	CO	14,130
Fairweather	AK-BC	15,300	Quandary Peak	CO	14,265	Liberty Cap	WA	14,112
Zinantecatl (Toluca)	Mexico	15,016	Evans	CO	14,264	Pikes Peak	CO	14,110
Hubbard	AK-Yukon	15,015	Longs Peak	CO	14,255	Snowmass	CO	14,092
Bear	AK	14,831	McArthur	Yukon	14,253	Russell	CA	14,088
Walsh	Yukon	14,780	Wilson	CO	14,246	Eolus	CO	14,083
East Buttress	AK	14,730	White Mt. Peak	CA	14,246	Windom	CO	14,082
Matlalcueyetl	Mexico	14,636	North Palisade	CA	14,242	Columbia	CO	14,073
Hunter	AK	14,573	Cameron	CO	14,238	Augusta	AK	14,070

South America

Peak, country	Height (ft)	Peak, country	Height (ft)	Peak, country	Height (ft)
Aconcagua, Argentina	22,834	Coropuna, Peru	21,083	Solo, Argentina	20,492
Ojos del Salado, Arg.-Chile	22,572	Laudo, Argentina	20,997	Polleras, Argentina	20,456
Bonete, Argentina	22,546	Ancohuma, Bolivia	20,958	Pular, Chile	20,423
Tupungato, Argentina-Chile	22,310	Ausangate, Peru	20,945	Chani, Argentina	20,341
Pissis, Argentina	22,241	Toro, Argentina-Chile	20,932	Aucanquilcha, Chile	20,295
Mercedario, Argentina	22,211	Illampu, Bolivia	20,873	Juncal, Argentina-Chile	20,276
Huascaran, Peru	22,205	Tres Cruces, Argentina-Chile	20,853	Negro, Argentina	20,184
Llullaillaco, Argentina-Chile	22,109	Huandoy, Peru	20,852	Quela, Argentina	20,128
El Libertador, Argentina	22,047	Parinacota, Bolivia-Chile	20,768	Condoriri, Bolivia	20,095
Cachi, Argentina	22,047	Tortolas, Argentina-Chile	20,745	Palermo, Argentina	20,079
Incahuasi, Argentina-Chile	21,720	Ampato, Peru	20,702	Solimana, Peru	20,068
Yerupaja, Peru	21,709	El Condor, Argentina	20,669	San Juan, Argentina-Chile	20,049
Galan, Argentina	21,654	Salcantay, Peru	20,574	Sierra Nevada, Arg.-Chile	20,023
El Muerto, Argentina-Chile	21,457	Chimborazo, Ecuador	20,561	Antofalla, Argentina	20,013
Sajama, Bolivia	21,391	Huancarhuas, Peru	20,531	Marmolejo, Argentina-Chile	20,013
Nacimiento, Argentina	21,302	Famatina, Argentina	20,505	Chachani, Peru	19,931
Illimani, Bolivia	21,201	Pumasillo, Peru	20,492		

The highest point in the West Indies is in the Dominican Republic, Pico Duarte (10,417 ft).

Africa

Peak, country	Height (ft)	Peak, country	Height (ft)	Peak, country	Height (ft)
Kilimanjaro, Tanzania	19,340	Meru, Tanzania	14,979	Guna, Ethiopia	13,881
Kenya, Kenya	17,058	Karisimbi, Congo-Rwanda	14,787	Gughe, Ethiopia	13,780
Margherita Pk., Uganda-Congo	16,763	Elgon, Kenya-Uganda	14,178	Toubkal, Morocco	13,661
Ras Dashan, Ethiopia	15,158	Batu, Ethiopia	14,131	Cameroon, Cameroon	13,435

Australia, New Zealand, SE Asian Islands

Peak, country/island	Height (ft)	Peak, country/island	Height (ft)	Peak, country/island	Height (ft)
Jaya, New Guinea	16,500	Wilhelm, New Guinea	14,793	Cook, New Zealand	12,349
Trikora, New Guinea	15,585	Kinabalu, Malaysia	13,455	Semeru, Java, Indon.	12,060
Mandala, New Guinea	15,420	Kerinci, Sumatra, Indon.	12,467	Kosciusko, Australia	7,310

Europe

Peak, country	Height (ft)	Peak, country	Height (ft)	Peak, country	Height (ft)
Alps		Dent D'Herens, Switz.	13,686	Gletscherhorn, Switz.	13,068
Mont Blanc, Fr.-It.	15,771	Breithorn, It., Switz.	13,665	Schalihorn, Switz.	13,040
Monte Rosa (highest peak		Bishorn, Switz.	13,645	Scerscen, Switz.	13,028
of group), Switz.	15,203	Jungfrau, Switz.	13,642	Eiger, Switz.	13,025
Dom, Switz.	14,911	Ecrins, Fr.	13,461	Jagerhorn, Switz.	13,024
Liskamm, It., Switz.	14,852	Monch, Switz.	13,448	Rottalhorn, Switz.	13,022
Weisshorn, Switz.	14,780	Pollux, Switz.	13,422	**Pyrenees**	
Taschhorn, Switz.	14,733	Schreckhorn, Switz.	13,379	Aneto, Sp.	11,168
Matterhorn, It., Switz.	14,690	Ober Gabelhorn, Switz.	13,330	Posets, Sp.	11,073
Dent Blanche, Switz.	14,293	Gran Paradiso, It.	13,323	Perdido, Sp.	11,007
Nadelhorn, Switz.	14,196	Bernina, It., Switz.	13,284	Vignemale, Fr.-Sp.	10,820
Grand Combin, Switz.	14,154	Fiescherhorn, Switz.	13,283	Long, Sp.	10,479
Lenzspitze, Switz.	14,088	Grunhorn, Switz.	13,266	Estats, Sp.	10,304
Finsteraarhorn, Switz.	14,022	Lauteraarhorn, Switz.	13,261	Montcalm, Sp.	10,105
Castor, Switz.	13,865	Durrenhorn, Switz.	13,238	**Caucasus (Europe-Asia)**	
Zinalrothorn, Switz.	13,849	Allalinhorn, Switz.	13,213	Elbrus, Russia	18,510
Hohberghom, Switz.	13,842	Weissmies, Switz.	13,199	Shkhara, Georgia	17,064
Alphubel, Switz.	13,799	Lagginhorn, Switz.	13,156	Dykh Tau, Russia	17,054
Rimpfischhom, Switz.	13,776	Zupo, Switz.	13,120	Kashtan Tau, Russia	16,877
Aletschorn, Switz.	13,763	Fletschhorn, Switz.	13,110	Janqi, Georgia	16,565
Strahlhorn, Switz.	13,747	Adlerhorn, Switz.	13,081	Kazbek, Georgia	16,558

Asia (Mainland)

Peak	Place	Height (ft)	Peak	Place	Height (ft)	Peak	Place	Height (ft)
Everest	Nepal-Tibet	29,035	Tirich Mir	Pakistan	25,230	Gauri Sankar	Nepal-Tibet	23,440
K2 (Godwin			Makalu II	Nepal-Tibet	25,120	Badrinath	India	23,420
Austen)	Kashmir	28,250	Minya Konka	China	24,900	Nunkun	Kashmir	23,410
Kanchenjunga	India-Nepal	28,208	Kula Gangri	Bhutan-		Lenin Peak	Tajikistan	23,405
Lhotse I (Everest)	Nepal-Tibet	27,923		Tibet	24,784	Pyramid	India-Nepal	23,400
Makalu I	Nepal-Tibet	27,824	Changtzu			Api	Nepal	23,399
Lhotse II (Everest)	Nepal-Tibet	27,560	(Everest)	Nepal-Tibet	24,780	Pauhunri	India-Tibet	23,385
Dhaulagiri	Nepal	26,810	Muz Tagh Ata	Xinjiang	24,757	Trisul	India	23,360
Manaslu I	Nepal	26,760	Skyang Kangri	Kashmir	24,750	Kangto	India-Tibet	23,260
Cho Oyu	Nepal-Tibet	26,750	Ismail Semani			Nyenchhe		
Nanga Parbat	Kashmir	26,660	Peak	Tajikistan	24,590	Thanglha	Tibet	23,255
Annapurna I	Nepal	26,504	Jongsang Peak	India-Nepal	24,472	Trisuli	India	23,210
Gasherbrum	Kashmir	26,470	Jengish Chokusu	Xinjiang-		Pumori	Nepal-Tibet	23,190
Broad	Kashmir	26,400		Kyrgyzstan	24,406	Dunagiri	India	23,184
Gosainthan	Tibet	26,287	Sia Kangri	Kashmir	24,350	Lombo Kangra	Tibet	23,165
Annapurna II	Nepal	26,041	Haramosh Peak	Pakistan	24,270	Saipal	Nepal	23,100
Gyachung Kang	Nepal-Tibet	25,910	Istoro Nal	Pakistan	24,240	Macha Pucchare	Nepal	22,958
Disteghil Sar	Kashmir	25,868	Tent Peak	India-Nepal	24,165	Numbar	Nepal	22,817
Himalchuli	Nepal	25,801	Chomo Lhari	Bhutan-		Kanjiroba	Nepal	22,580
Nuptse (Everest)	Nepal-Tibet	25,726		Tibet	24,040	Ama Dablam	Nepal	22,350
Masherbrum	Kashmir	25,660	Chamlang	Nepal	24,012	Cho Polu	Nepal	22,093
Nanda Devi	India	25,645	Kabru	India-Nepal	24,002	Lingtren	Nepal-Tibet	21,972
Rakaposhi	Kashmir	25,550	Alung Gangri	Tibet	24,000	Khumbutse	Nepal-Tibet	21,785
Kamet	India-Tibet	25,447	Baltoro Kangri	Kashmir	23,990	Hlako Gangri	Tibet	21,266
Namcha Barwa	Tibet	25,445	Mussu Shan	Xinjiang	23,890	Mt. Grosvenor	China	21,190
Gurla Mandhata	Tibet	25,355	Mana	India	23,860	Thagchhab Gangri	Tibet	20,970
Ulugh Muz Tagh	Xinjiang-		Baruntse	Nepal	23,688	Damavand	Iran	18,606
	Tibet	25,340	Nepal Peak	India-Nepal	23,500	Ararat	Turkey	16,804
Kungur	Xinjiang	25,325	Amne Machin	China	23,490			

Antarctica

Peak	Height (ft)	Peak	Height (ft)	Peak	Height (ft)
Vinson Massif	16,864	Miller	13,650	Falla	12,549
Tyree	16,290	Long Gables	13,620	Rucker	12,520
Shinn	15,750	Dickerson	13,517	Goldthwait	12,510
Gardner	15,375	Giovinetto	13,412	Morris	12,500
Epperly	15,100	Wade	13,400	Erebus	12,450
Kirkpatrick	14,855	Fisher	13,386	Campbell	12,434
Elizabeth	14,698	Fridtjof Nansen	13,350	Don Pedro Christophersen	12,355
Markham	14,290	Wexler	13,202	Lysaght	12,326
Bell	14,117	Lister	13,200	Huggins	12,247
Mackellar	14,098	Shear	13,100	Sabine	12,200
Anderson	13,957	Odishaw	13,008	Astor	12,175
Bentley	13,934	Donaldson	12,894	Mohl	12,172
Kaplan	13,878	Ray	12,808	Frankes	12,064
Andrew Jackson	13,750	Sellery	12,779	Jones	12,040
Sidley	13,720	Waterman	12,730	Gjelsvik	12,008
Ostenso	13,710	Anne	12,703	Coman	12,000
Minto	13,668	Press	12,566		

Some Notable U.S. Mountains

Name	Place	Height (ft)	Name	Place	Height (ft)	Name	Place	Height (ft)
Gannett Peak	WY	13,804	Adams	WA	12,277	Clingmans Dome	NC-TN	6,643
Grand Teton	WY	13,766	San Gorgonio	CA	11,502	Washington	NH	6,288
Kings	UT	13,528	Hood	OR	11,239	Rogers	VA	5,729
Cloud	WY	13,175	Lassen	CA	10,457	Marcy	NY	5,344
Wheeler	NM	13,161	Granite	CA	10,321	Katahdin	ME	5,268
Boundary	NV	13,140	Guadalupe	TX	8,749	Spruce Knob	WV	4,861
Granite	MT	12,799	Olympus	WA	7,965	Mansfield	VT	4,393
Borah	ID	12,662	Harney	SD	7,242	Black Mountain	KY	4,145
Humphreys	AZ	12,633	Mitchell	NC	6,684			

Important Islands and Their Areas

Reviewed by Laurel Duda, Marine Biological Laboratory/Woods Hole Oceanographic Inst. Library.

Figures are for total areas in square miles. Figure in parentheses shows rank among the world's 10 largest individual islands. Because some islands have not been surveyed accurately, some areas shown are estimates. Some "islands" listed are island groups. Only the largest islands in a group are listed individually. Only islands over 10 sq. miles in area are listed.

Antarctica

Adelaide	1,400
Alexander	16,700
Berkner	18,500
Roosevelt	2,900

Arctic Ocean

Akimiski, Nunavut	1,159
Amund Ringnes, Nun.	2,029
Axel Heiberg, Nun.	16,671
Baffin, Nun. **(5)**	195,928
Banks, Northwest Territories	27,038
Bathurst, Nun.	6,194
Bolshevik, Russia	4,368
Bolshoy Lyakhovsky, Russia	1,776
Borden, NWT., Nun.	1,079
Bylot, Nun.	4,273
Coats, Nun.	2,123
Cornwallis, Nun.	2,701
Devon, Nun.	21,331
Disko, Greenland	3,312
Ellef Ringnes, Nun.	4,361
Ellesmere, Nun. **(10)**	75,767
Faddayevskiy, Russia	1,930
Franz Josef Land, Russia	8,000
Iturup (Etorofu), Russia	2,596
King William, Nun.	5,062
Komsomolets, Russia	3,477
Mackenzie King, NWT	1,949
Mansel, Nun.	1,228
Melville, NWT, Nun.	16,274
Milne Land, Greenland	1,400
New Siberian Islands, Russia	14,500
Kotelnyy, Russia	4,504
Novaya Zemlya, Russia (2 isls.)	31,730
Oktyabrskoy, Russia	5,471
Prince Charles, NWT	3,676
Prince of Wales, Nun.	12,872
Prince Patrick, NWT	6,119
Somerset, Nun.	9,570
Southampton, Nun.	15,913
Svalbard (tot. group)	23,957
Nordaustlandet	5,410
Spitsbergen	15,060
Traill, Greenland	1,300
Victoria, NWT, Nun. **(9)**	83,897
Wrangel, Russia	2,800

Atlantic Ocean

Anticosti, Canada	3,068
Ascension, UK	34
Azores, Portugal (tot. group)	868
Faial	67
San Miguel	291
Bahama Isls., Bahama (tot. group)	5,382
Andros, Bahamas	2,300
Bermuda Islands, UK	20
Bioko Isl., Equatorial Guinea	785
Block Islands, RI, US	21
Canary Islands, Spain (tot. group)	2,807
Fuerteventura	688
Gran Canaria	592
Tenerife	795
Cape Breton, Canada	3,981
Cape Verde Islands	1,557
Caviana, Para, Brazil	1,918
Channel Islands, UK (tot. group)	75
Guernsey	24
Jersey	45
Faroe Islands, Denmark	540
Falkland Islands, UK (tot. group)	4,700
East Falkland	2,550
West Falkland	1,750
Great Britain, UK **(8)**	84,200
Greenland, Denmark **(1)**	840,000
Gurupa, Para, Brazil	1,878
Hebrides, Scotland	2,744
Iceland	39,699
Ireland (tot. group)	32,589
Irish Republic	27,137
Northern Ireland (UK)	5,452
Isle of Man, UK	227
Isle of Wight, England	147

Atlantic Ocean

Long Island, NY, US	1,320
Madeira Islands, Portugal	306
Marajo, Brazil	15,444
Martha's Vineyard, MA, US	89
Mount Desert, ME, US	104
Nantucket, MA, US	45
Newfoundland, Canada	42,031
Orkney Islands, Scotland	390
Prince Edward, Canada	2,185
St. Helena, UK	47
Shetland Islands, Scotland	587
Skye, Scotland	670
South Georgia, UK	1,450
Tierra del Fuego, Chile, Arg.	18,800
Tristan da Cunha, UK	40

Baltic Sea

Aland Islands, Finland	590
Bornholm, Denmark	227
Gotland, Sweden	1,159

Caribbean Sea

Antigua	108
Aruba, Netherlands	75
Barbados	166
Cuba	42,804
Isle of Youth	926
Cayman Islands	100
Curacao, Netherlands	171
Dominica	290
Guadeloupe, France	687
Hispaniola (Haiti and Dominican Rep)	29,389
Jamaica	4,244
Martinique, France	436
Puerto Rico, US	3,339
Tobago	116
Trinidad	1,864
Virgin Islands, UK	59
Virgin Islands, US	134

East Indies

Bali, Indonesia	2,171
Bangka, Indonesia	4,375
Borneo, Indonesia-Malaysia-Brunei **(3)**	280,100
Bougainville, Papua New Guinea	3,880
Buru, Indonesia	3,670
Celebes, Indonesia	69,000
Flores, Indonesia	5,500
Halmahera, Indonesia	6,865
Java (Jawa), Indonesia	48,900
Madura, Indonesia	2,113
Moluccas, Indonesia	32,307
New Britain, Papua New Guinea	14,093
New Guinea, Indon.-PNG **(2)**	306,000
New Ireland, PNG	3,707
Seram, Indonesia	6,621
Sumba, Indonesia	4,306
Sumbawa, Indonesia	5,965
Sumatra, Indonesia **(6)**	165,000
Timor, Indonesia	13,094
Yos Sudarsa, Indonesia	4,500

Indian Ocean

Andaman Isls., India	2,500
Kerguelen	2,247
Madagascar **(4)**	226,658
Mauritius	720
Pemba, Tanzania	380
Reunion, France	970
Seychelles	176
Sri Lanka	25,332
Zanzibar, Tanzania	640

Mediterranean Sea

Balearic Isls., Spain	1,927
Corfu, Greece	229
Corsica, France	3,369
Crete, Greece	3,189
Cyprus	3,572
Elba, Italy	86
Euboea, Greece	1,411
Malta	95
Rhodes, Greece	540
Sardinia, Italy	9,301
Sicily, Italy	9,926

Pacific Ocean

Admiralty, AK, US	1,709
Aleutian Isls., AK, US (tot. group)	6,912
Adak	275
Amchitka	116
Attu	350
Kanaga	142
Kiska	106
Tanaga	195
Umnak	686
Unalaska	1,051
Unimak	1,571
Baranof, AK, US	1,636
Chichagof, AK, US	2,062
Chiloe, Chile	3,241
Christmas, Kiribati	94
Diomede, Big, Russia	11
Easter Isl., Chile	69
Fiji (tot. group)	7,056
Vanua Levu	2,242
Viti Levu	4,109
Galapagos Isls., Ecuador	3,043
Graham Isl., British Columbia	2,456
Guadalcanal, Solomon Isls.	2,180
Guam, US	210
Hainan, China	13,000
Hawaiian Isls., HI, US (tot. group)	6,428
Hawaii	4,028
Oahu	600
Hong Kong, China	31
Hoste, Chile	1,590
Japan (tot. group)	145,850
Hokkaido	30,144
Honshu **(7)**	87,805
Kyushu	14,114
Okinawa	459
Shikoku	7,049
Kangaroo, South Australia	1,680
Kodiak, AK, US	3,485
Kupreanof, AK, US	1,084
Marquesas Isls., France	492
Marshall Isls.	70
Melville, Northern Territory, Aus.	2,240
Micronesia	271
New Caledonia, France	6,530
New Zealand (tot. group)	104,454
Chatham Isls.	372
North	44,204
South	58,384
Stewart	674
North Mariana Isls., US	179
Nunivak, AK, US	1,600
Palau	177
Philippines (tot. group)	115,860
Leyte	2,787
Luzon	40,680
Mindanao	36,775
Mindoro	3,690
Negros	4,907
Palawan	4,554
Panay	4,446
Samar	5,050
Prince of Wales, AK, US	2,770
Revillagigedo, AK, US	1,134
Riesco, Chile	1,973
St. Lawrence, AK, US	1,780
Sakhalin, Russia	29,500
Samoa Isls. (tot. group)	1,177
American Samoa, US	77
Tutuila, US	55
Savail, Samoa	659
Upolu, Samoa	432
Santa Catalina, CA, US	75
Santa Ines, Chile	1,407
Tahiti, France	402
Taiwan, China (tot. group)	13,969
Jinmen Dao (Quemoy)	56
Tasmania, Australia	26,178
Tonga Isls.	290
Vancouver Isl., Brit. Columbia	12,079
Vanuatu	4,707
Wellington, Chile	2,549

Persian Gulf

Bahrain	217

Areas and Average Depths of Oceans, Seas, and Gulfs[1]

Geographers and mapmakers recognize 4 major bodies of water: the Pacific, the Atlantic, the Indian, and the Arctic oceans. The Atlantic and Pacific oceans are considered divided at the equator into the N and S Atlantic and the N and S Pacific. The Arctic Ocean is the name for waters N of the continental landmasses in the region of the Arctic Circle.

	Area (sq mi)	Avg. depth (ft)		Area (sq mi)	Avg. depth (ft)
Pacific Ocean	64,186,300	12,925	Hudson Bay	281,900	305
Atlantic Ocean	33,420,000	11,730	East China Sea	256,600	620
Indian Ocean	28,350,500	12,598	Andaman Sea	218,100	3,667
Arctic Ocean	5,105,700	3,407	Black Sea	196,100	3,906
South China Sea	1,148,500	4,802	Red Sea	174,900	1,764
Caribbean Sea	971,400	8,448	North Sea	164,900	308
Mediterranean Sea	969,100	4,926	Baltic Sea	147,500	180
Bering Sea	873,000	4,893	Yellow Sea	113,500	121
Gulf of Mexico	582,100	5,297	Persian Gulf	88,800	328
Sea of Okhotsk	537,500	3,192	Gulf of California	59,100	2,375
Sea of Japan	391,100	5,468			

(1) The International Hydrographic Organization delimited a fifth world ocean in 2000. The Southern Ocean as defined extends from the coast of Antarctica north to 60° south latitude, covering portions of the Atlantic, Indian, and Pacific oceans, an area of 7,848,400 square miles.

Principal Ocean Depths

Source: National Imagery and Mapping Agency, U.S. Dept. of Defense

Name of area	Location (lat.)	Location (long.)	Depth (meters)	Depth (fathoms)	Depth (ft)
Pacific Ocean					
Marianas Trench	11°22′ N	142°36′ E	10,924	5,973	35,840
Tonga Trench	23°16′ S	174°44′ W	10,800	5,906	35,433
Philippine Trench	10°38′ N	126°36′ E	10,057	5,499	32,995
Kermadec Trench	31°53′ S	177°21′ W	10,047	5,494	32,963
Bonin Trench	24°30′ N	143°24′ E	9,994	5,464	32,788
Kuril Trench	44°15′ N	150°34′ E	9,750	5,331	31,988
Izu Trench	31°05′ N	142°10′ E	9,695	5,301	31,808
New Britain Trench	06°19′ S	153°45′ E	8,940	4,888	29,331
Yap Trench	08°33′ N	138°02′ E	8,527	4,663	27,976
Japan Trench	36°08′ N	142°43′ E	8,412	4,600	27,599
Peru-Chile Trench	23°18′ S	71°14′ W	8,064	4,409	26,457
Palau Trench	07°52′ N	134°56′ E	8,054	4,404	26,424
Aleutian Trench	50°51′ N	177°11′ E	7,679	4,199	25,194
New Hebrides Trench	20°36′ S	168°37′ E	7,570	4,139	24,836
North Ryukyu Trench	24°00′ N	126°48′ E	7,181	3,927	23,560
Mid. America Trench	14°02′ N	93°39′ W	6,662	3,643	21,857
Atlantic Ocean					
Puerto Rico Trench	19°55′ N	65°27′ W	8,605	4,705	28,232
S Sandwich Trench	55°42′ S	25°56′ W	8,325	4,552	27,313
Romanche Gap	0°13′ S	18°26′ W	7,728	4,226	25,354
Cayman Trench	19°12′ N	80°00′ W	7,535	4,120	24,721
Brazil Basin	09°10′ S	23°02′ W	6,119	3,346	20,076
Indian Ocean					
Java Trench	10°19′ S	109°58′ E	7,125	3,896	23,376
Ob' Trench	09°45′ S	67°18′ E	6,874	3,759	22,553
Diamantina Trench	35°50′ S	105°14′ E	6,602	3,610	21,660
Vema Trench	09°08′ S	67°15′ E	6,402	3,501	21,004
Agulhas Basin	45°20′ S	26°50′ E	6,195	3,387	20,325
Arctic Ocean					
Eurasia Basin	82°23′ N	19°31′ E	5,450	2,980	17,881
Mediterranean Sea					
Ionian Basin	36°32′ N	21°06′ E	5,150	2,816	16,896

Note: Greater depths have been reported in some areas but are not officially confirmed by research vessels.

Latitude and Longitude of World Cities

Source: National Imagery Mapping Agency, U.S. Dept. of Defense

City	Lat. ° ′	Long. ° ′	City	Lat. ° ′	Long. ° ′
Athens, Greece	37 59 N	23 44 E	Mexico City, Mexico	19 24 N	99 09 W
Bangkok, Thailand	13 45 N	100 31 E	Moscow, Russia	55 45 N	37 35 E
Beijing, China	39 56 N	116 24 E	New Delhi, India	28 36 N	77 12 E
Berlin, Germany	52 31 N	13 25 E	Panama City, Panama	08 58 N	79 32 W
Bogotá, Colombia	04 36 N	74 05 W	Paris, France	48 52 N	02 20 E
Bombay (Mumbai), India	18 58 N	72 50 E	Quito, Ecuador	00 13 S	78 30 W
Buenos Aires, Argentina	34 36 S	58 28 W	Rio de Janeiro, Brazil	22 43 S	43 13 W
Cairo, Egypt	30 03 N	31 15 E	Rome, Italy	41 53 N	12 30 E
Jakarta, Indonesia	06 10 S	106 48 E	Santiago, Chile	33 27 S	70 40 W
Jerusalem, Israel	31 46 N	35 14 E	Seoul, South Korea	37 34 N	127 00 E
Johannesburg, South Africa	26 12 S	28 05 E	Sydney, Australia	33 53 S	151 12 E
Kathmandu, Nepal	27 43 N	85 19 E	Tehran, Iran	35 40 N	51 26 E
Kiev, Ukraine	50 26 N	30 31 E	Tokyo, Japan	35 42 N	139 46 E
London, UK (Greenwich)	51 30 N	00 00	Warsaw, Poland	52 15 N	21 00 E
Manila, Philippines	14 35 N	121 00 E	Wellington, New Zealand	41 18 S	174 47 E

Latitude, Longitude, and Altitude of U.S. and Canadian Cities

Source: U.S. geographic positions, U.S. altitudes provided by Geological Survey, U.S. Dept. of the Interior. Canadian geographic positions and altitudes provided by Natural Resources Canada.

City	Lat. N °	'	"	Long. W °	'	"	Elev. (ft)
Abilene, TX	32	26	55	99	43	58	1,718
Akron, OH	41	4	53	81	31	9	1,050
Albany, NY	42	39	9	73	45	24	20
Albuquerque, NM	35	5	4	106	39	2	4,955
Alert, N.W.T.	82	30	0	62	22	0	100
Allentown, PA	40	36	30	75	29	26	350
Amarillo, TX	35	13	19	101	49	51	3,685
Anchorage, AK	61	13	5	149	54	1	101
Ann Arbor, MI	42	16	15	83	43	35	880
Asheville, NC	35	36	3	82	33	15	2,134
Ashland, KY	38	28	42	82	38	17	558
Atlanta, GA	33	44	56	84	23	17	1,050
Atlantic City, NJ	39	21	51	74	25	24	8
Augusta, GA	33	28	15	81	58	30	414
Augusta, ME	44	18	38	69	46	48	45
Austin, TX	30	16	1	97	44	34	501
Bakersfield, CA	35	22	24	119	1	4	408
Baltimore, MD	39	17	25	76	36	45	100
Bangor, ME	44	48	4	68	46	42	158
Baton Rouge, LA	30	27	2	91	9	16	53
Battle Creek, MI	42	19	16	85	10	47	820
Bay City, MI	43	35	40	83	53	20	595
Beaumont, TX	30	5	9	94	6	6	20
Belleville, Ont.	44	14	0	77	21	0	320
Bellingham, WA	48	45	35	122	29	13	100
Berkeley, CA	37	52	18	122	16	18	150
Billings, MT	45	47	0	108	30	0	3,124
Biloxi, MS	30	23	45	88	53	7	25
Binghamton, NY	42	5	55	75	55	6	865
Birmingham, AL	33	31	14	86	48	9	600
Bismarck, ND	46	48	30	100	47	0	1,700
Bloomington, IL	40	29	3	88	59	37	829
Boise, ID	43	36	49	116	12	9	2,730
Boston, MA	42	21	30	71	3	37	20
Bowling Green, KY	36	59	25	86	26	37	510
Brandon, Man.	49	54	35	99	57	03	1,343
Brantford, Ont.	43	08	0	80	16	0	815
Brattleboro, VT	42	51	3	72	33	30	240
Bridgeport, CT	41	10	1	73	12	19	10
Brockton, MA	42	5	0	71	1	8	112
Buffalo, NY	42	53	11	78	52	43	585
Burlington, Ont.	43	23	10	79	50	15	640
Burlington, VT	44	28	33	73	12	45	113
Butte, MT	46	0	14	112	32	2	5,549
Calgary, Alta.	51	03	0	114	05	0	3,557
Cambridge, MA	42	22	30	71	6	22	30
Canton, OH	40	47	56	81	22	43	1,100
Carson City, NV	39	9	50	119	45	59	4,730
Cedar Rapids, IA	42	0	30	91	38	38	730
Central Islip, NY	40	47	26	73	12	8	88
Champaign, IL	40	6	59	88	14	36	740
Charleston, SC	32	46	35	79	55	52	118
Charleston, WV	38	20	59	81	37	58	606
Charlotte, NC	35	13	37	80	50	36	850
Charlottetown, P.E.I.	46	14	25	63	08	05	160
Chattanooga, TN	35	2	44	85	18	35	685
Cheyenne, WY	41	8	24	104	49	11	6,067
Chicago, IL	41	51	0	87	39	0	596
Churchill, Man.	58	43	30	94	07	0	94
Cincinnati, OH	39	9	43	84	27	25	683
Cleveland, OH	41	29	58	81	41	44	690
Colorado Springs, CO	38	50	2	104	49	15	6,008
Columbia, MO	38	57	6	92	20	2	758
Columbia, SC	34	0	2	81	2	6	314
Columbus, GA	32	27	39	84	59	16	300
Columbus, OH	39	57	40	82	59	56	800
Concord, NH	43	12	29	71	32	17	288
Corpus Christi, TX	27	48	1	97	23	46	35
Dallas, TX	32	47	0	96	48	0	463
Dawson, Yukon	64	03	45	139	25	50	1,214
Dayton, OH	39	45	32	84	11	30	750
Daytona Beach, FL	29	12	38	81	1	23	10
Decatur, IL	39	50	25	88	57	17	670
Denver, CO	39	44	21	104	59	3	5,260
Des Moines, IA	41	36	2	93	36	32	803
Detroit, MI	42	19	53	83	2	45	585
Dodge City, KS	37	45	10	100	1	0	2,550
Dubuque, IA	42	30	2	90	39	52	620
Duluth, MN	46	47	0	92	6	23	610
Durham, NC	35	59	38	78	53	56	394
Eau Claire, WI	44	48	41	91	29	54	850
Edmonton, Alta.	53	33	0	113	28	0	2,200
Elizabeth, NJ	40	39	50	74	12	40	38
El Paso, TX	31	45	31	106	29	11	3,695
Enid, OK	36	23	44	97	52	41	1,246
Erie, PA	42	7	45	80	5	7	650
Eugene, OR	44	3	8	123	5	8	419
Eureka, CA	40	48	8	124	9	45	44
Evansville, IN	37	58	29	87	33	21	388
Fairbanks, AK	64	50	16	147	42	59	440
Fall River, MA	41	42	5	71	9	20	200
Fargo, ND	46	52	38	96	47	22	900
Flagstaff, AZ	35	11	53	111	39	2	6,900
Flint, MI	43	0	45	83	41	15	750
Ft. Smith, AR	35	23	9	94	23	54	446
Ft. Wayne, IN	41	7	50	85	7	44	781
Ft. Worth, TX	32	43	31	97	19	14	670
Fredericton, N.B.	45	56	43	66	40	0	67
Fresno, CA	36	44	52	119	46	17	296
Gadsden, AL	34	0	51	86	0	24	554
Gainesville, FL	29	39	5	82	19	30	183
Gallup, NM	35	31	41	108	44	31	6,508
Galveston, TX	29	18	4	94	47	51	10
Gary, IN	41	35	36	87	20	47	600
Grand Junction, CO	39	3	50	108	33	0	4,597
Grand Rapids, MI	42	57	48	85	40	5	610
Great Falls, MT	47	30	1	111	18	0	3,334
Green Bay, WI	44	31	9	88	1	11	594
Greensboro, NC	36	4	21	79	47	32	770
Greenville, SC	34	51	9	82	23	39	966
Guelph, Ont.	43	33	0	80	15	0	1,100
Gulfport, MS	30	22	2	89	5	34	25
Halifax, N.S.	44	52	0	63	43	0	477
Hamilton, OH	39	23	58	84	33	41	600
Hamilton, Ont.	43	14	0	79	57	0	780
Harrisburg, PA	40	16	25	76	53	5	320
Hartford, CT	41	45	49	72	41	8	40
Helena, MT	46	35	34	112	2	7	4,090
Hilo, HI	19	43	47	155	5	24	38
Honolulu, HI	21	18	25	157	51	30	18
Houston, TX	29	45	47	95	21	47	40
Huntsville, AL	34	43	49	86	35	10	641
Indianapolis, IN	39	46	6	86	9	29	717
Iowa City, IA	41	39	40	91	31	48	685
Jackson, MI	42	14	45	84	24	5	940
Jackson, MS	32	17	55	90	11	5	294
Jacksonville, FL	30	19	55	81	39	21	12
Jersey City, NJ	40	43	41	74	4	41	83
Johnstown, PA	40	19	36	78	55	20	1200
Joplin, MO	37	5	3	94	30	47	990
Juneau, AK	58	18	7	134	25	11	50
Kalamazoo, MI	42	17	30	85	35	14	755
Kansas City, KS	39	6	51	94	37	38	750
Kansas City, MO	39	5	59	94	34	42	740
Kenosha, WI	42	35	5	87	49	16	610
Key West, FL	24	33	19	81	46	58	8
Kingston, Ont.	44	18	0	76	28	0	305
Kitchener, Ont.	43	27	0	80	29	0	1,040
Knoxville, TN	35	57	38	83	55	15	889
Lafayette, IN	40	25	0	86	52	31	567
Lancaster, PA	40	2	16	76	18	21	368
Lansing, MI	42	43	57	84	33	20	830
Laredo, TX	27	30	22	99	30	26	414
Las Vegas, NV	36	10	30	115	8	11	2,000
Lawrence, MA	42	42	25	71	9	49	50
Lethbridge, Alta.	49	42	0	112	49	0	3,047
Lexington, KY	37	59	19	84	28	40	955
Lihue, HI	21	58	52	159	22	16	206
Lima, OH	40	44	33	84	6	19	875
Lincoln, NE	40	48	0	96	40	0	1,150
Little Rock, AR	34	44	47	92	17	22	350
London, Ont.	42	59	0	81	14	0	875
Los Angeles, CA	34	3	8	118	14	34	330

City	Lat. N °	'	"	Long. W °	'	"	Elev. (ft)
Louisville, KY	38	15	15	85	45	34	462
Lowell, MA	42	38	0	71	19	0	102
Lubbock, TX	33	34	40	101	51	17	3,195
Macon, GA	32	50	26	83	37	57	400
Madison, WI	43	4	23	89	24	4	863
Manchester, NH	42	59	44	71	27	19	175
Marshall, TX	32	32	41	94	22	2	410
Medicine Hat, Alta.	50	03	0	110	40	0	2,352
Memphis, TN	35	8	58	90	2	56	254
Meriden, CT	41	32	17	72	48	27	190
Miami, FL	25	46	26	80	11	38	11
Milwaukee, WI	43	2	20	87	54	23	634
Minneapolis, MN	44	58	48	93	15	49	815
Minot, ND	48	13	57	101	17	45	1,555
Mobile, AL	30	41	39	88	2	35	16
Moncton, N.B.	46	06	57	64	48	11	232
Montgomery, AL	32	22	0	86	18	0	250
Montpelier, VT	44	15	36	72	34	33	525
Montréal, Que.	45	31	0	73	39	0	221
Moose Jaw, Sask.	50	24	0	105	32	0	1,892
Muncie, IN	40	11	36	85	23	11	952
Nashville, TN	36	9	57	86	47	4	440
Natchez, MS	31	33	37	91	24	11	230
Newark, NJ	40	44	8	74	10	22	95
New Britain, CT	41	39	40	72	46	48	200
New Haven, CT	41	18	29	72	55	43	40
New Orleans, LA	29	57	16	90	4	30	11
New York, NY	40	42	51	74	0	23	55
Niagara Falls, Ont.	43	06	0	79	04	0	589
Nome, AK	64	30	4	165	24	23	25
Norfolk, VA	36	50	48	76	17	8	10
North Bay, Ont.	46	19	0	79	28	0	1,200
Oakland, CA	37	48	16	122	16	11	42
Ogden, UT	41	13	23	111	58	23	4,299
Oklahoma City, OK	35	28	3	97	30	58	1,195
Omaha, NE	41	15	31	95	56	15	1,040
Orlando, FL	28	32	17	81	22	46	106
Ottawa, Ont.	45	16	0	75	45	0	382
Paducah, KY	37	5	0	88	36	0	345
Pasadena, CA	34	8	52	118	8	37	865
Paterson, NJ	40	55	0	74	10	20	70
Pensacola, FL	30	25	16	87	13	1	32
Peoria, IL	40	41	37	89	35	20	470
Peterborough, Ont.	44	18	0	78	19	0	628
Philadelphia, PA	39	57	8	75	9	51	40
Phoenix, AZ	33	26	54	112	4	24	1,090
Pierre, SD	44	22	6	100	21	2	1,484
Pittsburgh, PA	40	26	26	79	59	46	770
Pittsfield, MA	42	27	0	73	14	45	1,039
Pocatello, ID	42	52	17	112	26	41	4,464
Pt. Arthur, TX	29	53	55	93	55	43	10
Portland, ME	43	39	41	70	15	21	25
Portland, OR	45	31	25	122	40	30	50
Portsmouth, NH	43	4	18	70	45	47	21
Portsmouth, VA	36	50	7	76	17	55	10
Prince Rupert, B.C.	54	19	0	130	19	0	116
Providence, RI	41	49	26	71	24	48	80
Provo, UT	40	14	2	111	39	28	4,549
Pueblo, CO.	38	15	16	104	36	31	4,662
Québec City, Que.	46	49	0	71	13	0	244
Racine, WI	42	43	34	87	46	58	630
Raleigh, NC	35	46	19	78	38	20	350
Rapid City, SD	44	4	50	103	13	50	3,247
Reading, PA	40	20	8	75	55	38	266
Regina, Sask.	50	27	0	104	37	0	1,894
Reno, NV	39	31	47	119	48	46	4,498
Richmond, VA	37	33	13	77	27	38	190
Roanoke, VA	37	16	15	79	56	30	940
Rochester, MN	44	1	18	92	28	11	990
Rochester, NY	43	9	17	77	36	57	515
Rockford, IL	42	16	16	89	5	38	715
Sacramento, CA	38	34	54	121	29	36	20
Saginaw, MI	43	25	10	83	57	3	595
St. Catharines, Ont.	43	10	0	79	15	0	321
St. Cloud, MN	45	33	39	94	9	44	1,040
St. John, N.B.	45	15	33	66	02	20	357
St. John's, Nfld.	47	34	0	52	44	0	461
St. Joseph, MO	39	46	7	94	50	47	850
St. Louis, MO	38	37	38	90	11	52	455

City	Lat. N °	'	"	Long. W °	'	"	Elev. (ft)
St. Paul, MN	44	56	40	93	5	35	780
St. Petersburg, FL	27	46	14	82	40	46	44
Salem, OR	44	56	35	123	2	2	154
Salina, KS	38	50	25	97	36	40	1,225
Salt Lake City, UT	40	45	39	111	53	25	4,266
San Antonio, TX	29	25	26	98	29	36	650
San Bernardino, CA	34	6	30	117	17	20	1,200
San Diego, CA.	32	42	55	117	9	23	40
San Francisco, CA	37	46	30	122	25	6	63
San Jose, CA	37	20	22	121	53	38	87
San Juan, P.R.	18	28	6	66	6	22	8
Santa Barbara, CA	34	25	15	119	41	50	50
Santa Cruz, CA	36	58	27	122	1	47	20
Santa Fe, NM	35	41	13	105	56	14	6,989
Sarasota, FL	27	20	10	82	31	51	27
Saskatoon, Sask.	52	07	0	106	38	0	1,653
Sault Ste. Marie, Ont.	46	31	0	84	20	0	630
Savannah, GA	32	5	0	81	6	0	42
Schenectady, NY	42	48	51	73	56	24	245
Seattle, WA	47	36	23	122	19	51	350
Sheboygan, WI	43	45	3	87	42	52	630
Sherbrooke, Que.	45	24	0	71	54	0	792
Sheridan, WY	44	47	50	106	57	20	3,742
Shreveport, LA	32	31	30	93	45	0	209
Sioux City, IA.	42	30	0	96	24	0	1,117
Sioux Falls, SD	43	32	48	96	43	48	1,442
South Bend, IN	41	41	0	86	15	0	725
Spartanburg, SC	34	56	58	81	55	56	816
Spokane, WA	47	39	32	117	25	30	2,000
Springfield, IL	39	48	6	89	38	37	610
Springfield, MA	42	6	5	72	35	25	70
Springfield, MO	37	12	55	93	17	53	1,300
Springfield, OH	39	55	27	83	48	32	1,000
Stamford, CT	41	3	12	73	32	21	35
Steubenville, OH	40	22	11	80	38	3	1,060
Stockton, CA	37	57	28	121	17	23	15
Sudbury, Ont.	46	31	0	80	54	0	1,140
Superior, WI	46	43	15	92	6	14	642
Sydney, N.S.	46	09	0	60	11	0	203
Syracuse, NY	43	2	53	76	8	52	400
Tacoma, WA	47	15	11	122	26	35	380
Tallahassee, FL	30	26	17	84	16	51	188
Tampa, FL	27	56	50	82	27	31	48
Terre Haute, IN	39	28	0	87	24	50	501
Texarkana, TX	33	25	30	94	2	51	324
Thunder Bay, Ont.	48	24	0	89	19	0	653
Timmins, Ont.	48	28	0	81	20	0	967
Toledo, OH	41	39	50	83	33	19	615
Topeka, KS	39	2	54	95	40	40	1,000
Toronto, Ont.	43	37	39	79	23	46	251
Trenton, NJ	40	13	1	74	44	36	54
Trois-Rivières, Que.	46	21	0	72	33	0	198
Troy, NY	42	43	42	73	41	32	35
Tucson, AZ	32	13	18	110	55	33	2,390
Tulsa, OK	36	9	14	95	59	33	804
Urbana, IL	40	6	38	88	12	26	725
Utica, NY	43	6	3	75	13	59	415
Vancouver, B.C.	49	15	0	123	07	0	14
Victoria, B.C.	48	26	0	123	22	0	63
Waco, TX.	31	32	57	97	8	47	405
Walla Walla, WA	46	3	53	118	20	31	1,000
Washington, DC	38	53	42	77	2	12	25
Waterloo, IA.	42	29	34	92	20	34	850
West Palm Beach, FL	26	42	54	80	3	13	21
Wheeling, WV	40	3	50	80	43	16	672
Whitehorse, Yukon	60	43	0	135	03	0	2,305
White Plains, NY	41	2	2	73	45	48	220
Wichita, KS	37	41	32	97	20	14	1,305
Wilkes-Barre, PA	41	14	45	75	52	54	550
Wilmington, DE	39	44	45	75	32	49	100
Wilmington, NC	34	13	32	77	56	42	50
Windsor, Ont.	42	18	0	83	01	0	622
Winnipeg, Man.	49	54	39	97	14	36	783
Winston-Salem, NC.	36	5	59	80	14	40	912
Worcester, MA.	42	15	45	71	48	10	480
Yakima, WA.	46	36	8	120	30	17	1,066
Yellowknife, N.W.T.	62	27	20	114	21	0	675
Youngstown, OH	41	5	59	80	38	59	861
Yuma, AZ	32	43	31	114	37	25	160
Zanesville, OH	39	56	25	82	0	48	710

Principal World Rivers

Reviewed by Laurel Duda, Marine Biological Laboratory, Woods Hole Oceanogr. Inst. Library. For N American rivers, see separate table.

River	Outflow	Length (mi)
Africa		
Chari	Lake Chad	500
Congo	Atlantic Ocean	2,900
Gambia	Atlantic Ocean	700
Kasai	Congo River	1,000
Limpopo	Indian Ocean	1,100
Lualaba	Congo River	1,100
Niger	Gulf of Guinea	2,590
Nile	Mediterranean	4,160
Okavango	Okavango Delta	1,000
Orange	Atlantic Ocean	1,300
Senegal	Atlantic Ocean	1,020
Ubangi	Congo River	660
Zambezi	Indian Ocean	1,700
Asia		
Amu Darya	Aral Sea	1,550
Amur	Tatar Strait	1,780
Angara	Yenisey River	1,151
Brahmaputra	Bay of Bengal	1,800
Chang	East China Sea	3,964
Euphrates	Shatt al-Arab	1,700
Ganges	Bay of Bengal	1,560
Godavari	Bay of Bengal	900
Hsi (see Xi)		
Huang	Yellow Sea	3,395
Indus	Arabian Sea	1,800
Irrawaddy	Andaman Sea	1,337
Jordan	Dead Sea	200
Kolyma	Arctic Ocean	1,323
Krishna	Bay of Bengal	800
Kura	Caspian Sea	848
Lena	Laptev Sea	2,734
Mekong	South China Sea	2,700
Narbada (see Narmada)		
Narmada	Arabian Sea	800
Ob	Gulf of Ob	2,268

River	Outflow	Length (mi)
Ob-Irtysh	Gulf of Ob	3,362
Salween	Gulf of Martaban	1,500
Songhua	Amur River	1,150
Sungari	Amur River	1,197
Sutlej	Indus River	900
Syr	Aral Sea	1,370
Tarim	Lop Nor Basin	1,261
Tigris	Shatt al-Arab	1,180
Xi	South China Sea	1,200
Yamuna	Ganges River	855
Yangtze (see Chang)		
Yellow (see Huang)		
Yenisey	Kara Sea	2,543
Australia		
Murray-Darling	Indian Ocean	2,310
Murrumbidgee	Murray River	981
Europe		
Bug, Northern	Wisla	481
Bug, Southern	Dnieper River	532
Danube	Black Sea	1,776
Don	Sea of Azov	1,224
Dnieper	Black Sea	1,420
Dniester	Black Sea	877
Drava	Danube River	447
Dvina, North	White Sea	824
Dvina, West	Gulf of Riga	634
Ebro	Mediterranean	565
Elbe	North Sea	724
Garonne	Bay of Biscay	357
Kama	Volga River	1,122
Loire	Bay of Biscay	634
Mame	Seine River	326
Meuse	North Sea	580
Oder	Baltic Sea	567
Oka	Volga River	932
Pechora	Barents Sea	1,124

River	Outflow	Length (mi)
Po	Adriatic Sea	405
Rhine	North Sea	820
Rhone	Gulf of Lions	505
Seine	English Channel	496
Shannon	Atlantic Ocean	230
Tagus	Atlantic Ocean	626
Thames	North Sea	210
Tiber	Tyrrhenian Sea	252
Tisza	Danube River	600
Ural	Caspian Sea	1,575
Volga	Caspian Sea	2,290
Weser	North Sea	454
Wisla	Gulf of Gdansk	675
South America		
Amazon	Atlantic Ocean	4,000
Araguaia	Tocantins River	1,100
Iça (see Putumayo)		
Iguaça	Parana River	808
Japura	Amazon River	1,750
Madeira	Amazon River	2,013
Magdalena	Caribbean Sea	956
Negro	Amazon River	1,400
Orinoco	Atlantic Ocean	1,600
Paraguay	Parana River	1,584
Parana	Rio de la Plata	2,485
Pilcomayo	Paraguay River	1,000
Purus	Amazon River	2,100
Putumayo	Amazon River	1,000
Rio de la Plata	Atlantic Ocean	150
Rio Roosevelt	Aripuana	400
Sao Francisco	Atlantic Ocean	1,988
Tocantins	Para River	1,677
Ucayali	Marañón River	910
Uruguay	Rio de la Plata	1,000
Xingu	Amazon River	1,300

Major Rivers in North America

Reviewed by Laurel Duda, Marine Biological Laboratory, Woods Hole Oceanographic Inst. Library.

River	Source or upper limit of length	Outflow	Length (mi)
Alabama	Gilmer County, GA	Mobile River	729
Albany	Lake St. Joseph, Ontario	James Bay	610
Allegheny	Potter County, PA.	Ohio River	325
Altamaha-Ocmulgee	Junction of Yellow and South Rivers, Newton County, GA	Atlantic Ocean	392
Apalachicola-Chattahoochee	Towns County, GA	Gulf of Mexico	524
Arkansas	Lake County, CO	Mississippi River	1,459
Assiniboine	Eastern Saskatchewan	Red River	450
Attawapiskat	Attawapiskat, Ontario	James Bay	465
Back (NWT)	Contwoyto Lake	Chantrey Inlet, Arctic Ocean	605
Big Black (MS)	Webster County, MS	Mississippi River	330
Brazos	Junction of Salt and Double Mountain Forks, Stonewall County, TX	Gulf of Mexico	950
Canadian	Las Animas County, CO	Arkansas River	906
Cedar (IA)	Dodge County, MN	Iowa River	329
Cheyenne	Junction of Antelope Creek and Dry Fork, Converse County, WY	Missouri River	290
Churchill, Lab.	Lake Ashuanipi, Labrador	Atlantic Ocean	532
Churchill, Man.	Methy Lake, Saskatchewan	Hudson Bay	1,000
Cimarron	Colfax County, NM	Arkansas River	600
Colorado (AZ)	Rocky Mountain Natl. Park, CO (90 mi in Mexico)	Gulf of California	1,450
Colorado (TX)	West Texas	Matagorda Bay	862
Columbia	Columbia Lake, British Columbia	Pacific Ocean, bet. OR and WA.	1,243
Columbia, Upper	Columbia Lake, British Columbia	To mouth of Snake River	890
Connecticut	Third Connecticut Lake, NH	Long Island Sound, CT	407
Coppermine (NWT)	Lac de Gras	Coronation Gulf, Arctic Ocean	525
Cumberland	Letcher County, KY	Ohio River	720
Delaware	Schoharie County, NY	Liston Point, Delaware Bay	390
Fraser	Near Mount Robson (on Continental Divide)	Strait of Georgia	850
Gila	Catron County, NM.	Colorado River	649
Green (UT-WY)	Junction of Wells and Trail Creeks, Sublette County, WY	Colorado River	730
Hudson	Henderson Lake, Essex County, NY	Upper NY Bay	306
Illinois	St. Joseph County, IN	Mississippi River	420
James (ND-SD)	Wells County, ND	Missouri River	710
James (VA)	Junction of Jackson and Cowpasture Rivers, Botetourt County, VA.	Hampton Roads	340
Kanawha-New	Junction of North and South Forks of New River, NC	Ohio River	352
Kentucky	Junction of North and Middle Forks, Lee County, KY	Ohio River	259
Klamath	Lake Ewauna, Klamath Falls, OR	Pacific Ocean	250
Kootenay	Kootenay Lake, British Columbia	Columbia River	485
Koyukuk	Endicott Mountains, AK	Yukon River	470
Kuskokwim	Alaska Range	Kuskokwim Bay	724

River	Source or upper limit of length	Outflow	Length (mi)
Liard	Southern Yukon, AK	Mackenzie River	693
Little Missouri	Crook County, WY	Missouri River	560
Mackenzie	Great Slave Lake, N.W.T.	Arctic Ocean	1,060
Milk	Junction of North and South Forks, Alberta	Missouri River	625
Minnesota	Big Stone Lake, MN	Mississippi River	332
Mississippi	Lake Itasca, MN	Gulf of Mexico	2,340
Mississippi-Missouri-Red Rock	Source of Red Rock, Beaverhead Co., MT	Gulf of Mexico	3,710
Missouri	Junction of Jefferson, Madison, and Gallatin Rivers, Gallatin County, MT	Mississippi River	2,315
Missouri-Red Rock	Source of Red Rock, Beaverhead Co., MT	Mississippi River	2,540
Mobile-Alabama-Coosa	Gilmer County, GA	Mobile Bay	774
Nelson (Man.)	Lake Winnipeg	Hudson Bay	410
Neosho	Morris County, KS	Arkansas River, OK	460
Niobrara	Niobrara County, WY	Missouri River, NE	431
North Canadian	Union County, NM	Canadian River, OK	800
North Platte	Junction of Grizzly and Little Grizzly Creeks, Jackson County, CO	Platte River, NE	618
Ohio	Junction of Allegheny and Monongahela Rivers, Pittsburgh, PA	Mississippi River	981
Ohio-Allegheny	Potter County, PA	Mississippi River	1,310
Osage	East-central Kansas	Missouri River	500
Ottawa	Lake Capimitchigama	St. Lawrence River	790
Ouachita	Polk County, AR	Black River	605
Peace	Stikine Mountains, B.C.	Slave River	1,210
Pearl	Neshoba County, MS	Gulf of Mexico	411
Pecos	Mora County, NM	Rio Grande	926
Pee Dee-Yadkin	Watauga County, NC	Winyah Bay	435
Pend Oreille-Clark Fork	Near Butte, MT	Columbia River	531
Platte	Junction of North and South Platte Rivers, NE	Missouri River	310
Porcupine	Ogilvie Mountains, AK	Yukon River, AK	569
Potomac	Garrett County, MD	Chesapeake Bay	383
Powder	Junction of South and Middle Forks, WY	Yellowstone River	375
Red (OK-TX-LA)	Curry County, NM	Mississippi River	1,290
Red River of the North	Junction of Otter Tail and Bois de Sioux Rivers, Wilkin County, MN.	Lake Winnipeg	545
Republican	Junction of North Fork and Arikaree River, NE	Kansas River	445
Rio Grande	San Juan County, CO	Gulf of Mexico	1,900
Roanoke	Junction of N and S Forks, Montgomery Co., VA.	Albemarle Sound	380
Rock (IL-WI)	Dodge County, WI	Mississippi River	300
Sabine	Junction of S and Caddo Forks, Hunt County, TX	Sabine Lake	380
Sacramento	Siskiyou County, CA.	Suisun Bay	377
St. Francis	Iron County, MO.	Mississippi River	425
St. John	Northwestern Maine	Bay of Fundy	418
St. Lawrence	Lake Ontario	Gulf of St. Lawrence, Atlantic Ocean	800
Saguenay	Lake St. John, Quebec	St. Lawrence River	434
Salmon (ID)	Custer County, ID	Snake River	420
San Joaquin	Junction of S and Middle Forks, Madera Co., CA	Suisun Bay	350
San Juan	Silver Lake, Archuleta County, CO.	Colorado River	360
Santee-Wateree-Catawba	McDowell County, NC	Atlantic Ocean	538
Saskatchewan, North	Rocky Mountains	Saskatchewan R.	800
Saskatchewan, South	Rocky Mountains	Saskatchewan R.	865
Savannah	Junction of Seneca and Tugaloo Rivers, Anderson County, SC	Atlantic Ocean, GA-SC	314
Severn (Ont.)	Sandy Lake	Hudson Bay	610
Smoky Hill	Cheyenne County, CO	Kansas River, KS	540
Snake	Teton County, WY	Columbia River, WA.	1,038
South Platte	Junction of S and Middle Forks, Park County, CO.	Platte River	424
Susitna	Alaska Range	Cook Inlet	313
Susquehanna	Huyden Creek, Otsego County, NY	Chesapeake Bay	447
Tallahatchie	Tippah County, MS.	Yazoo River	301
Tanana	Wrangell Mountains, AK.	Yukon River	659
Tennessee	Junction of French Broad and Holston Rivers	Ohio River	652
Tennessee-French Broad	Courthouse Creek, Transylvania County, NC	Ohio River	886
Tombigbee	Prentiss County, MS.	Mobile River	525
Trinity	North of Dallas, TX	Galveston Bay	360
Wabash	Darke County, OH	Ohio River	512
Washita	Hemphill County, TX	Red River, OK	500
White (AR-MO)	Madison County, AR	Mississippi River	722
Willamette	Douglas County, OR	Columbia River	309
Wind-Bighorn	Junction of Wind and Little Wind Rivers, Fremont Co., WY (Source of Wind R. is Togwotee Pass, Teton Co., WY)	Yellowstone River	338
Wisconsin	Lac Vieux Desert, Vilas County, WI	Mississippi River	430
Yellowstone	Park County, WY	Missouri River	682
Yukon	McNeil R., Yukon Territory	Bering Sea	1,979

Highest and Lowest Continental Altitudes

Source: National Geographic Society

Continent	Highest point	Elev. (ft)	Lowest point	ft below sea level
Asia	Mount Everest, Nepal-Tibet	29,035	Dead Sea, Israel-Jordan	1,348
South America	Mount Aconcagua, Argentina	22,834	Valdes Peninsula, Argentina	131
North America	Mount McKinley, Alaska	20,320	Death Valley, California	282
Africa	Kilimanjaro, Tanzania	19,340	Lake Assal, Djibouti	512
Europe	Mount Elbrus, Russia	18,510	Caspian Sea, Russia, Azerbaijan	92
Antarctica	Vinson Massif	16,864	Bentley Subglacial Trench	8,327[1]
Australia	Mount Kosciusko, New South Wales	7,310	Lake Eyre, South Australia	52

(1) Estimated level of the continental floor. Lower points that have yet to be discovered may exist further beneath the ice.

Major Natural Lakes of the World

Source: Geological Survey, U.S. Dept. of the Interior

A lake is generally defined as a body of water surrounded by land. By this definition some bodies of water that are called seas, such as the Caspian Sea and the Aral Sea, are really lakes. In the following table, the word *lake* is omitted when it is part of the name.

Name	Continent	Area (sq mi)	Length (mi)	Maximum depth (ft)	Elevation (ft)
Caspian Sea[1]	Asia-Europe	143,244	760	3,363	−92
Superior	North America	31,700	350	1,330	600
Victoria	Africa	26,828	250	270	3,720
Huron	North America	23,000	206	750	579
Michigan	North America	22,300	307	923	579
Aral Sea[1]	Asia	13,000[2]	260	220	125
Tanganyika	Africa	12,700	420	4,823	2,534
Baykal	Asia	12,162	395	5,315	1,493
Great Bear	North America	12,096	192	1,463	512
Nyasa (Malawi)	Africa	11,150	360	2,280	1,550
Great Slave	North America	11,031	298	2,015	513
Erie	North America	9,910	241	210	570
Winnipeg	North America	9,417	266	60	713
Ontario	North America	7,340	193	802	245
Balkhash[1]	Asia	7,115	376	85	1,115
Ladoga	Europe	6,835	124	738	13
Maracaibo	South America	5,217	133	115	sea level
Onega	Europe	3,710	145	328	108
Eyre[1]	Australia	3,600[3]	90	4	−52
Titicaca	South America	3,200	122	922	12,500
Nicaragua	North America	3,100	102	230	102
Athabasca	North America	3,064	208	407	700
Reindeer	North America	2,568	143	720	1,106
Tonle Sap	Asia	2,500[3]	...	45	...
Turkana (Rudolf)	Africa	2,473	154	240	1,230
Issyk Kul[1]	Asia	2,355	115	2,303	5,279
Torrens[1]	Australia	2,230[3]	130	...	92
Vanern	Europe	2,156	91	328	144
Nettilling	North America	2,140	67	...	95
Winnipegosis	North America	2,075	141	38	830
Albert	Africa	2,075	100	168	2,030
Nipigon	North America	1,872	72	540	1,050
Gairdner[1]	Australia	1,840[3]	90	...	112
Urmia[1]	Asia	1,815	90	49	4,180
Manitoba	North America	1,799	140	12	813
Chad	Africa	839[4]	175	24	787

(1) Salt lake. (2) Approximate figure, could be less. The diversion of feeder rivers since the 1960s has devastated the Aral—once the world's 4th-largest lake (26,000 sq. miles). By 2000, the Aral had effectively become three lakes, with the total area shown. (3) Approximate figure, subject to great seasonal variation. (4) Once 4th-largest lake in Africa (about 10,000 sq. miles in the 1960s), Chad had shrunk more than 90% by 2001 due to irrigation and long-term drought.

The Great Lakes

Source: National Ocean Service, U.S. Dept. of Commerce

The Great Lakes form the world's largest body of fresh water (in surface area), and with their connecting waterways are the largest inland water transportation unit. Draining the great North Central basin of the U.S., they enable shipping to reach the Atlantic via their outlet, the St. Lawrence R., and to reach the Gulf of Mexico via the Illinois Waterway, from Lake Michigan to the Mississippi R. A 3rd outlet connects with the Hudson R. and then the Atlantic via the New York State Barge Canal System. Traffic on the Illinois Waterway and the N.Y. State Barge Canal System is limited to recreational boating and small shipping vessels.

Only one of the lakes, Lake Michigan, is wholly in the U.S.; the others are shared with Canada. Ships move from the shores of Lake Superior to Whitefish Bay at the E end of the lake, then through the Soo (Sault Ste. Marie) locks, through the St. Mary's R. and into Lake Huron. To reach Gary and the Port of Indiana and South Chicago, IL, ships move W from Lake Huron to Lake Michigan through the Straits of Mackinac. Lake Superior is 601 ft above low water datum at Rimouski, Quebec, on the International Great Lakes Datum (1985). From Duluth, MN, to the E end of Lake Ontario is 1,156 mi.

	Superior	Michigan	Huron	Erie	Ontario
Length in mi	350	307	206	241	193
Breadth in mi	160	118	183	57	53
Deepest soundings in ft	1,333	923	750	210	802
Volume of water in cu mi	2,935	1,180	850	116	393
Area (sq mi) water surface—U.S.	20,600	22,300	9,100	4,980	3,460
Canada	11,100	.....	13,900	4,930	3,880
Area (sq mi) entire drainage basin—U.S.	16,900	45,600	16,200	18,000	15,200
Canada	32,400	.....	35,500	4,720	12,100
TOTAL AREA (sq mi) U.S. and Canada	**81,000**	**67,900**	**74,700**	**32,630**	**34,850**
Low water datum above mean water level at Rimouski, Quebec, avg. level in ft (1985)	601.10	577.50	577.50	569.20	243.30
Latitude, N	46° 25′	41° 37′	43° 00′	41° 23′	43° 11′
	49° 00′	46° 06′	46° 17′	42° 52′	44° 15′
Longitude, W	84° 22′	84° 45′	79° 43′	78° 51′	76° 03′
	92° 06′	88° 02′	84° 45′	83° 29′	79° 53′
National boundary line in mi	282.8	None	260.8	251.5	174.6
United States shoreline (mainland only) mi	863	1,400	580	431	300

Famous Waterfalls

Source: National Geographic Society

The earth has thousands of waterfalls, some of considerable magnitude. Their relative importance is determined not only by height but also by volume of flow, steadiness of flow, crest width, whether the water drops sheerly or over a sloping surface, and whether it descends in one leap or in a succession of leaps. A series of low falls flowing over a considerable distance is known as a **cascade**.

Estimated mean annual flow, in cubic feet per second, of major waterfalls are as follows: Niagara, 212,200; Paulo Afonso, 100,000; Urubupunga, 97,000; Iguazu, 61,000; Patos-Maribondo, 53,000; Victoria, 35,400; and Kaieteur, 23,400.

Height = total drop in feet in one or more leaps. #=falls of more than one leap; *= falls that diminish greatly seasonally; **= falls that reduce to a trickle or are dry for part of each year. If the river names are not shown, they are same as the falls. R. = river; (C) = cascade type.

Name and location	Height (ft)
Africa	
Angola	
Ruacana, Cuene R.	406
Ethiopia	
Fincha	508
Lesotho	
Maletsunyane*	630
Zimbabwe-Zambia	
Victoria, Zambezi R.*	343
South Africa	
Augrabies, Orange R.*	480
Tugela#	2,014
Tanzania-Zambia	
Kalambo*	726
Asia	
India	
Cauvery*	330
Jog (Gersoppa), Sharavathi R.*	830
Japan	
Kegon, Daiya R.*	330
Australia	
New South Wales	
Wentworth	614
Wollomombi	1,100
Queensland	
Tully	885
Wallaman, Stony Cr.#	1,137
New Zealand	
Helena	890
Sutherland, Arthur R.#	1,904
Europe	
Austria	
Gastein#	492
Krimml#	1,312
France	
Gavarnie*	1,385
Great Britain	
Scotland	
Glomach	370
Wales	
Rhaiadr.	240
Italy	
Frua, Toce R. (C)	470

Name and location	Height (ft)
Norway	
Mardalsfossen (Northern)	1,535
Mardalsfossen (Southern)#	2,149
Skjeggedal, Nybuai R.#**	1,378
Skykje**	984
Vetti, Morka-Koldedola R.	900
Sweden	
Handol#	427
Switzerland	
Giessbach (C)	984
Reichenbach#	656
Simmen#	459
Staubbach	984
Trummelbach#	1,312
North America	
Canada	
Alberta	
Panthver, Nigel Cr.	600
British Columbia	
Della#	1,443
Takakkaw, Daly Glacier#	1,200
Quebec	
Montmorency	274
Canada—United States	
Niagara: American	182
Horseshoe	173
United States	
California	
Feather, Fall R.*	640
Yosemite National Park	
Bridalveil*	620
Illilouette*	370
Nevada, Merced R.*	594
Ribbon**	1,612
Silver Strand, Meadow Br.**	1,170
Vernal, Merced R.*	317
Yosemite#**	2,425
Colorado	
Seven, South Cheyenne Cr.#	300
Hawaii	
Akaka, Kolekole Str.	442
Idaho	
Shoshone, Snake R.**	212
Kentucky	
Cumberland	68

Name and location	Height (ft)
Maryland	
Great, Potomac R. (C) *	71
Minnesota	
Minnehaha**	53
New Jersey	
Passaic	70
New York	
Taughannock*	215
Oregon	
Multnomah#	620
Tennessee	
Fall Creek	256
Washington	
Mt. Rainier Natl. Park	
Sluiskin, Paradise R.	300
Snoquvalmie**	268
Wisconsin	
Big Manitou, Black R. (C)*	165
Wyoming	
Yellowstone Natl. Pk. Tower	132
Yellowstone (upper)*	109
Yellowstone (lower)*	308
Mexico	
El Salo	218
South America	
Argentina-Brazil	
Iguazu	230
Brazil	
Glass	1,325
Patos-Maribondo, Grande R.	115
Paulo Afonso,	
Sao Francisco R.	275
Urubupunga, Parana R.	39
Colombia	
Catarvata de Candelas,	
Cusiana R.	984
Tequendama, Bogota R.*	427
Ecuador	
Agoyan, Pastaza R.*	200
Guyana	
Kaieteur, Potaro R.	741
Great, Kamarang R.	1,600
Marina, Ipobe R.#	500
Venezuela	
Angel#*	3,212
Cuquenan	2,000

Notable Deserts of the World

Arabian (Eastern), 70,000 sq mi in Egypt between the Nile R. and Red Sea, extending southward into Sudan

Atacama, 600-mi-long area rich in nitrate and copper deposits in N Chile

Chihuahuan, 140,000 sq mi in TX, NM, AZ, and Mexico

Dasht-e Kauir, approx. 300 mi long by approx. 100 mi wide in N central Iran

Dasht-e Lut, 20,000 sq mi in E Iran

Death Valley, 3,300 sq mi in CA and NV

Gibson, 120,000 sq mi in the interior of W Australia

Gobi, 500,000 sq mi in Mongolia and China

Great Sandy, 150,000 sq mi in W Australia

Great Victoria, 150,000 sq mi in SW Australia

Kalahari, 225,000 sq mi in S Africa

Kara Kum, 120,000 sq mi in Turkmenistan

Kyzyl Kum, 100,000 sq mi in Kazakhstan and Uzbekistan

Libyan, 450,000 sq mi in the Sahara, extending from Libya through SW Egypt into Sudan

Mojave, 15,000 sq mi in southern CA

Namib, long narrow area (varies from 30-100 mi wide) extending 800 mi along SW coast of Africa

Nubian, 100,000 sq mi in the Sahara in NE Sudan

Painted Desert, section of high plateau in northern AZ extending 150 mi

Patagonia, 300,000 sq mi in S Argentina

Rub al-Khali (Empty Quarter), 250,000 sq mi in the S Arabian Peninsula

Sahara, 3,500,000 sq mi in N Africa, extending westward to the Atlantic. Largest desert in the world

Sonoran, 70,000 sq mi in southwestern AZ and southeastern CA extending into NW Mexico

Syrian, 100,000-sq-mi arid wasteland extending over much of N Saudi Arabia, E Jordan, S Syria, and W Iraq

Taklimakan, 140,000 sq mi in Xinjiang Prov., China

Thar (Great Indian), 100,000-sq-mi arid area extending 400 mi along India-Pakistan border

▶ **IT'S A FACT:** According to the standard definition, a desert is any region that gets less than 10 inches of rain, or its equivalent, in a year. By this measure the whole continent of Antarctica is a desert. Antarctica's precipitation comes in the form of snow, anywhere from the liquid equivalent of about 8 inches a year in coastal areas down to the equivalent of about 2 inches a year in the deepest interior.

WORLD HISTORY
Chronology of World History
Prehistory: Our Ancestors Emerge
Revised by Susan Skomal, Ph.D., American Anthropological Association

Evidence of the origins of *Homo sapiens sapiens,* the species to which all humans belong, comes from a small, but increasing, number of fossils, from genetic and anatomical studies, and from interpretation of the geological record. Most scientists agree that humans evolved from apelike primate ancestors in a process that began millions of years ago. Although all humans living today are members of a single subspecies, the fossil record confirms that our ancestors co-existed with a number of similar species throughout evolution. Current theories trace the first hominid (upright walking, humanlike primate) to Africa, where several distinct species appeared 5-7 mil years ago (MYA). These species lived in a variety of environments throughout the continent including swampy forests, woodlands, and open savannas. In addition to Australopithecus—best known from "Lucy," an Ethiopian specimen found in 1974—these early hominid species include such recent discoveries as Sahelanthropus, Ardipithecus, Kenyanthropus, and Orrorin.

Our own human ancestry arose 2-3 MYA, when hominid species began to produce elaborate stone tools. The oldest tools are dated to 2.5-2.6 MYA from Ethiopia, and were made by systematically removing sharp flakes from a core. This produced tools for scraping meat and sinew, as well as a sharp chopping implement useful for obtaining marrow from long bones. Although we cannot determine whether these early hominids had the ability to speak, they were social animals, lived in semi-permanent camps, and had a food-gathering economy. A closer ancestor, *Homo erectus,* appeared in Africa 1.8 MYA and was the first to leave the continent, spreading into Asia by 1.3 MYA, and Europe by 800,000 years before the present (BP). It had a skeletal structure similar to modern humans, hunted, learned to control fire, and may have had primitive language skills.

Europe has provided a particularly rich set of fossil evidence. Human-like in many important respects, Neanderthal appeared c. 200,000 BP, had sophisticated tools and developed social culture, and was well adapted to the harsh climate of Ice Age Europe. Recent genetic evidence supports the theory that Neanderthal was a distinct species that in some places coexisted with, but probably did not interbreed with, early modern humans (also called Cro-Magnons). A similar situation may have occurred in Asia, where more primitive species of *Homo* coexisted with early modern humans 100,000-150,000 BP. Further study of *Homo antecessor,* a new species identified in Spain, may clarify the relationship between anatomically modern *Homo sapiens* and Neanderthals in Europe.

The 1st *Homo sapiens sapiens* originated in E Africa 100,000-200,000 BP. The oldest modern human fossils are dated to 160,000 BP, and were found at the Ethiopian site of Herto in 2003. Our species quickly spread. Humans were living in Israel by 100,000 BP, and in Romania by 35,000 BP. Migration from Asia to Australia via the Timor Straits took place as early as 100,000 BP. Archaeological evidence for the crossing from Asia to the Americas by land bridge dates to the end of the last Ice Age, at 14,000 BP; however, genetic data suggest that people arrived in the Americans 18,000 to 14,000 years ago, settling in both N and S America.

A variety of cultural modes—in toolmaking, diet, shelter, social arrangements, and spiritual expression—arose as humans adapted to different geographic and climatic zones and the knowledge base grew. Sites from all over the world show seasonal migration patterns and efficient exploitation of a wide range of plant and animal foods.

Fire-making probably began 1 MYA in Africa and spread to Asia and Europe. Hearths were used in N Israel by c. 750,000 BP, and by 465,000 BP in W France. Fire-hardened wooden spears, weighted and set with small stone blades, were fashioned by big-game hunters 400,000 BP in Germany. Scraping tools, dated 30,000-200,000 BP in Europe, N Africa, the Middle East, and Cent. Asia, suggest the treatment of skins for clothing. By the time Australia was settled, human ancestors had learned to navigate in boats over open water. The earliest bone tools found so far were developed 80,000 BP in the Congo basin by fishermen, who created sophisticated fishing tackle to catch giant catfish.

About 60,000 BP the earliest immigrants to Australia carved and painted designs on rocks. Painting and decoration flourished, along with stone and ivory sculpture, from 35,000 BP in Europe, where more than 200 caves show remarkable examples of naturalistic wall painting. A variety of musical instruments, including bone flutes with precisely bored holes, have been found in sites dated to 40,000-80,000 BP.

Shortly after 11,000 BC, among widely separated communities, a series of dramatic technological and social changes occurred, marking the Neolithic, or New Stone, Age. As the world climate became drier and warmer, humans learned to cultivate plants and domesticate animals. This encouraged growth of permanent settlements. Manufacture of pottery and cloth began at this time. These techniques precipitated a dramatic increase in world population and social complexity.

Sites in the Americas, SE Europe, and the Middle East show roughly contemporaneous (8000-10,000 BC) evidence of Neolithic traits. Dates near 3000-6000 BC have been given for E and S Asian, W European, and sub-Saharan African Neolithic remains. Farming spread rapidly throughout the Mediterranean, perhaps in 100-200 years. The variety of crops—field grains, rice, maize, squash, and roots—and a mix of other characteristics suggest that this adaptation occurred independently in each region.

History Begins: 4000-1000 BC

Near Eastern cradle. If history began with writing, the first chapter opened in Mesopotamia, the Tigris-Euphrates river valley. The Sumerians used clay tablets with pictographs to keep records after 4000 BC. A **cuneiform** (wedge-shaped) script evolved by 3000 BC as a full syllabic alphabet. Neighboring peoples adapted the script for their own use.

Sumerian life centered, from 4000 BC, on large cities (Eridu, Ur, Uruk, Nippur, Kish, and Lagash) organized around temples and priestly bureaucracies, with surrounding plains watered by vast irrigation works and worked with traction plows. Sailboats, wheeled vehicles, potter's wheels, and kilns were used. Copper was smelted and tempered from c 4000 BC; bronze was produced not long after. Ores, as well as precious stones and metals, were obtained through long-distance ship and caravan trade. Iron was used from c 2000 BC. Improved ironworking, developed partly by the Hittites, became widespread by 1200 BC.

Sumerian political primacy passed among cities and their kingly dynasties. Semitic-speaking peoples, with cultures derived from the Sumerian, founded a succession of dynasties that ruled in Mesopotamia and neighboring areas for most of 1,800 years; among them were the **Akkadians** (first under Sargon I, c 2350 BC), the Amorites (whose laws, codified by **Hammurabi,** c 1792-1750 BC, have biblical parallels), and the Assyrians, with interludes of rule by Hittites, Kassites, and Mitanni.

Mesopotamian learning, maintained by scribes and preserved in vast libraries, was practically oriented. Advances in mathematics related mostly to construction, commerce, and administration. Lists of astronomical phenomena, plants, animals, and stones were maintained; medical texts listed ailments and herbal cures. The Sumerians worshiped anthropomorphic gods representing natural forces. Sacrifices were made at **ziggurats**—huge stepped temples.

The Syria-Palestine area, site of some of the earliest urban remains (Jericho, 7000 BC), and of the recently uncovered **Ebla** civilization (fl 2500 BC), experienced Egyptian cultural and political influence along with Mesopotamian. The **Phoenician** coast was an active commercial center. A phonetic alphabet was invented here before 1600 BC. It became the ancestor of many other alphabets.

Major Gods & Goddesses of Ancient Egypt

Name	Relations	Sphere or Position	Emblem/Attribute
Ra (Re)/Atum/Amon	Self-created	The sun, creation	Hawk
Thoth (Djeheuty)	Son of Ra	The moon, wisdom, writing	Ibis/baboon
Ptah	Creator of Atum	Creation, craftsmen	----
Osiris	Brother of Set(h) & Isis	The underworld (dead), fertility, resurrection, vegetation	Bull
Isis	Sister/consort of Osiris	The underworld (dead)	----
Set(h)	Brother of Osiris	Evil, trickery, chaos	Boar, pig
Horus	Son of Osiris & Isis/ Ra & Hathor	The earth	Falcon
Hathor	Consort of Ra	Motherhood, love	Cow
Anubis	Son of Osiris	Embalmer & judge of the dead	Jackal/dog

Egypt. Agricultural villages along the Nile River were united by around 3300 BC into 2 kingdoms, Upper and Lower Egypt, unified (c 3100 BC) under the pharaoh Menes. A bureaucracy supervised construction of canals and monuments (**pyramids** starting 2700 BC). Control over Nubia to the S was asserted from 2600 BC. Brilliant Old Kingdom Period achievements in architecture, sculpture, and painting reached their height during the 3rd and 4th Dynasties. **Hieroglyphic writing** appeared by 3200 BC, recording a

Egyptian hieroglyphics

sophisticated literature that included religious writings, philosophy, history, and science. An ordered hierarchy of gods, including totemistic animal elements, was served by a powerful priesthood in Memphis. The pharaoh was identified with the falcon god Horus. Other trends included belief in an afterlife and short-lived quasi-monotheistic reforms introduced by the pharaoh **Akhenaton** (c 1379-1362 BC).

After a period of dominance by Semitic Hyksos from Asia (c 1700-1550 BC), the New Kingdom established an empire in Syria. Egypt became increasingly embroiled in Asiatic wars and diplomacy. Conquered by Persia in 525 BC, it eventually faded away as an independent culture.

India. An urban civilization with a so-far-undeciphered writing system stretched across the Indus Valley and along the Arabian Sea c 3000-1500 BC. Major sites are Harappa and **Mohenjo-Daro** in Pakistan, well-planned geometric cities with underground sewers and vast granaries. The entire region may have been ruled as a single state. Bronze was used, and arts and crafts were well developed. Religious life apparently took the form of fertility cults. Indus civilization was probably in decline when it was destroyed by **Aryans who arrived** from the NW, speaking an Indo-European language from which most languages of Pakistan, N India, and

Bangladesh descend. Led by a warrior aristocracy whose legendary deeds are in the **Rig Veda**, the Aryans spread E and S, bringing their sky gods, priestly (Brahman) ritual, and the beginnings of the caste system; local customs and beliefs were assimilated by the conquerors.

Europe. On Crete, the Bronze Age **Minoan civilization** emerged c 2500 BC. A prosperous economy and richly decorative art was supported by seaborne commerce. Mycenae and other cities in mainland Greece and Asia Minor (e.g., **Troy**) preserved elements of the culture until c 1200 BC. Cretan Linear A script (c 2000-1700 BC) remains undeciphered; Linear B script (c 1300-1200 BC) records an early Greek dialect. Unclear is the possible connection between Mycenaean monumental stonework and the megalithic monuments of W Europe, Iberia, and Malta (c 4000-1500 BC).

China. Proto-Chinese neolithic cultures had long covered N and SE China when the first large political state was organized in the N by the **Shang dynasty** (c 1523 BC). Shang kings called themselves Sons of Heaven, and they presided over a cgalult of human and animal sacrifice to ancestors and nature gods. The Chou dynasty, starting c 1027 BC, expanded the area of the Son of Heaven's dominion, but feudal states exercised most temporal power. A writing system with 2,000 characters was already in use under the Shang, with **pictographs** later supplemented by phonetic characters. Many of its principles and symbols, despite changes in spoken Chinese, were preserved in later writing systems. Technical advances allowed urban specialists to create fine ceramic and jade products, and bronze casting after 1500 BC was the most advanced in the world. Bronze artifacts have recently been discovered in N Thailand dating from 3600 BC, hundreds of years before similar Middle Eastern finds.

Americas. Olmecs settled (1500 BC) on the Gulf coast of Mexico and developed the first known civilization in the western hemisphere. Temple cities and huge stone sculpture date from 1200 BC. A rudimentary calendar and writing system existed. Olmec religion, centering on a jaguar god, and Olmec art forms influenced later Meso-American cultures.

Classical Era of Old World Civilizations: 1000 BC-400 BC

Greece. After a period of decline during the Dorian Greek invasions (1200-1000 BC), the Aegean area developed a

Parthenon

unique civilization. Drawing on Mycenaean traditions, Mesopotamian learning (weights and measures, lunisolar calendar, astronomy, musical scales), the Phoenician alphabet (modified for Greek), and Egyptian art, **Greek city-states** saw a rich elaboration of intellectual life. The two great epic poems attributed to Homer, the *Iliad* and the *Odyssey,* were probably composed around the 8th cent. BC. Long-range commerce was aided by metal coinage (introduced by the Lydians in Asia Minor before 700 BC); colonies were founded around the Mediterranean (Cumae in Italy in 760 BC; Massalia in France c 600 BC) and Black Sea shores.

Philosophy, starting with Ionian speculation on the nature of matter (Thales, c 634-546 BC), continued by other "Pre-

Socratics" (e.g., Heraclitus, c 535-415 BC; Parmenides, b. c 515 BC), reached a high point in Athens in the rationalist idealism of **Plato** (c 428-347 BC), a disciple of **Socrates** (c 469-399 BC; executed for alleged impiety), and in **Aristotle** (384-322 BC), a pioneer in many fields, from natural sciences to logic, ethics, and metaphysics. The **arts** were highly valued. Architecture culminated in the **Parthenon** (438 BC) by Phidias (fl 490-430 BC). Poetry (Sappho, c 610-580 BC; Pindar, c 518-438 BC) and **drama** (Aeschylus, 525-456 BC; Sophocles, c 496-406 BC; Euripides, c 484-406 BC) thrived. Male beauty and strength, a chief artistic theme, were celebrated at the national games at Olympia.

Ruled by local tyrants or **oligarchies**, the Greeks were not politically united, but managed to resist inclusion in the Persian Empire—Persian king Darius was defeated at Marathon (490 BC), his son Xerxes at Salamis (480 BC), and the Persian army at Plataea (479 BC). Local warfare was common; the **Peloponnesian Wars** (431-404 BC) ended in Sparta's victory over Athens. Greek political power subsequently waned, but Greek cultural forms spread far and wide.

The Seven Wonders of the Ancient World

These ancient works of art and architecture were considered awe-inspiring by the Greek and Roman world of the first few centuries BC. Later classical writers disagreed as to which works belonged, but the following were usually included:

The Pyramids of Egypt: The only surviving ancient Wonder, these monumental structures of masonry, located at Giza on the W bank of the Nile R above Cairo, were built from c 2700 to 2500 BC as royal tombs. Three—Khufu (Cheops), Khafra (Chephren), and Menkaura (Mycerimus)—were often grouped as the first Wonder of the World. The largest, the Great Pyramid of Khufu, is a solid mass of limestone blocks covering 13 acres. It is estimated to contain 2.3 million blocks of stone, the stones themselves averaging 2½ tons and some weighing 30 tons. Its construction reputedly took 100,000 laborers 20 years.

The Hanging Gardens of Babylon: These gardens were laid out on a brick terrace 400 ft square and 75 ft above the ground. To irrigate the plants, screws were turned to lift water from the Euphrates R. The gardens were probably built by King Nebuchadnezzar II about 600 BC. The Walls of Babylon, long, thick, and made of colorfully glazed brick, were also considered by some among the Seven Wonders.

The Pharos (Lighthouse) of Alexandria: This structure was designed about 270 BC, during the reign of Ptolemy II, by the Greek architect Sostratos. Estimates of its height range from 200 to 600 ft.

The Colossus of Rhodes: A bronze statue of the sun god Helios, the Colossus was worked on for 12 years in the third cent. BC by the sculptor Chares. It was probably 120 ft high. A symbol of the city of Rhodes at its height, the statue stood on a promontory overlooking the harbor.

The Temple of Artemis (Diana) at Ephesus: This largest and most complex temple of ancient times was built about 550 BC and was made of marble except for its tile-covered wooden roof. It was begun in honor of a non-Hellenic goddess who later became identified with the Greek goddess of the same name. Ephesus was one of the greatest of the Ionian cities.

The Mausoleum at Halicarnassus: The source of our word *mausoleum*, this marble tomb was built in what is now SE Turkey by Artemisia for her husband Mausolus, king of Caria in Asia Minor, who died in 353 BC. About 135 ft high, the tomb was adorned with the works of 4 sculptors.

The Statue of Zeus (Jupiter) at Olympia: This statue of the king of the gods showed him seated on a throne. His flesh was made of ivory, his robe and ornaments of gold. Reputedly 40 ft high, the statue was made by Phidias and was placed in the great temple of Zeus in the sacred grove of Olympia about 457 BC.

Hebrews. Nomadic Hebrew tribes entered Canaan before 1200 BC, settling among other Semitic peoples speaking the same language. They brought from the desert a **monotheistic** faith said to have been revealed to Abraham in Canaan c 1800 BC and Moses at Mt. Sinai c 1250 BC, after the Hebrews' escape from bondage in Egypt. David (r 1000-961 BC) and Solomon (r 961-922 BC) united them in a kingdom that briefly dominated the area. **Phoenicians** to the N founded Mediterranean colonies (Carthage, c 814 BC) and sailed into the Atlantic.

A temple in Jerusalem became the national religious center, with sacrifices performed by a hereditary priesthood. Polytheistic influences, especially of the fertility cult of Baal, were opposed by **prophets** (Elijah, Amos, Isaiah).

Divided into **two kingdoms** after Solomon, the Hebrews were unable to resist the revived Assyrian empire, which conquered Israel, the N kingdom, in 722 BC. Judah, the S kingdom, was conquered in 586 BC by the Babylonians under Nebuchadnezzar II. With the fixing of most of the biblical canon by the mid-4th cent. BC and the emergence of rabbis, Judaism successfully survived the loss of Hebrew autonomy. A Jewish kingdom was revived under the Hasmoneans (168-42 BC).

China. During the **Eastern Chou** dynasty (770-256 BC), Chinese culture spread E to the sea and S to the Yangtze R. Large feudal states on the periphery of the empire contended for preeminence, but continued to recognize the Son of Heaven (king), who retained a purely ritual role enriched with courtly music and dance. In the Age of Warring States (403-221 BC), when the first sections of the **Great Wall** were built, the Ch'in state in the W gained supremacy and finally united all of China.

Iron tools entered China c 500 BC, and casting techniques were advanced, aiding agriculture. Peasants owned their land and owed civil and military service to nobles. China's cities grew in number and size; barter remained the chief trade medium.

Intellectual ferment among noble scribes and officials produced the Classical Age of Chinese literature and philosophy. **Confucius** (551-479 BC) urged a restoration of a supposedly harmonious social order of the past through proper conduct in accordance with one's station and through filial and ceremonial piety. The *Analects* attributed to him are revered throughout E Asia.

Among other thinkers of this period, Mencius (d 289 BC) added the view that the Mandate of Heaven can be removed from an unjust dynasty. The Legalists sought to curb the supposed natural wickedness of people through new institutions and harsh laws; they aided the Ch'in rise to power. The Naturalists emphasized the balance of opposites—yin, yang—in the world. **Taoists** sought mystical knowledge through meditation and disengagement.

India. The political and cultural center of India shifted from the Indus to the Ganges River Valley. Buddhism, Jainism, and mystical revisions of orthodox Vedism all developed c 500-300 BC. The *Upanishads,* last part of the *Veda,* urged escape from the physical world. Vedism remained the preserve of the Brahman caste.

In contrast, **Buddhism**, founded by Siddarta Gautama (c 563-c 483 BC)—Buddha ("Enlightened One")—appealed to merchants in the urban centers and took hold at first (and most lastingly) on the geographic fringes of Indian civilization. The classic Indian epics were composed in this era: the **Ramayana** perhaps c 300 BC, the **Mahabharata** over a period starting around 400 BC.

N India was divided into a large number of monarchies and aristocratic republics, probably derived from tribal groupings, when the Magadha kingdom was formed in Bihar c 542 BC. It soon became the dominant power. The **Maurya dynasty**, founded by Chandragupta c 321 BC, expanded the kingdom, uniting most of N India in a centralized bureaucratic empire. The third Mauryan king, **Asoka** (reigned c 274-236 BC), conquered most of the subcontinent. He converted to Buddhism and inscribed its tenets on pillars throughout India. He downplayed the caste system.

Before its final decline in India, Buddhism developed into a popular worship of heavenly Bodhisattvas ("enlightened beings"), and it produced a refined architecture (the Great Stupa [shrine] at Sanchi, AD 100) and sculpture (Gandhara reliefs, AD 1-400).

Persia. Aryan peoples (Persians, Medes) dominated the area of present Iran by the beginning of the 1st millennium BC. The prophet **Zoroaster** (born c 628 BC) introduced a dualistic religion in which the forces of good (Ahura Mazda, "Lord of Wisdom") and evil (Ahriam) battle for dominance; individuals are judged by their actions and earn damnation or salvation. Zoroaster's hymns (*Gathas*) are included in the *Avesta*, the Zoroastrian scriptures. A version of this faith became the established religion of the Persian Empire.

Africa. Nubia, periodically occupied by Egypt since about 2600 BC, ruled Egypt c 750-661 BC and survived as an independent Egyptianized kingdom (**Kush**; capital Meroe) for 1,000 years. The Iron Age Nok culture flourished c 500 BC- AD 200 on the Benue Plateau of **Nigeria.**

Americas. The Chavin culture controlled N Peru c 900 BC to 200 BC. Its ceremonial centers, featuring the jaguar god, survived long after. Its architecture, ceramics, and textiles had influenced other Peruvian cultures. **Mayan civilization** began to develop in Central America as early as 1500 BC.

Mayan temple

Great Empires Unite the Civilized World: 400 BC-AD 400

Persia and Alexander the Great. Cyrus, ruler of a small kingdom in Persia from 559 BC, united the Persians and Medes within 10 years and conquered Asia Minor and Babylonia in another 10. His son Cambyses, followed by **Darius** (r 522-486 BC), added vast lands to the E and N as far as the Indus Valley and Central Asia, as well as Egypt and Thrace. The whole empire was ruled by an international bureaucracy and army, with Persians holding the chief positions. The resources and styles of all the subject civilizations were exploited to create a rich syncretic art.

The kingdom of Macedon, which under Philip II dominated the Greek world and Egypt, was passed on to his son **Alexander** in 336 BC. Within 13 years, Alexander had conquered all the Persian dominions. Imbued by his tutor Aristotle with Greek ideals, Alexander encouraged Greek colonization, and Greek-style cities were founded. After his death in 323 BC, wars of succession divided the empire into 3 parts—**Macedon,** Egypt (ruled by the **Ptolemies),** and the **Seleucid** Empire. In the ensuing 300 years (the **Hellenistic Era**), a cosmopolitan Greek-oriented culture permeated the ancient world from W Europe to the borders of India, absorbing native elites everywhere.

Hellenistic philosophy stressed the private individual's search for happiness. The Cynics followed Diogenes (c 372-287 BC), who stressed self-sufficiency and restriction of desires and expressed contempt for luxury and social convention. Zeno (c 335-c 263 BC) and the **Stoics** exalted reason, identified it with virtue, and counseled an ascetic disregard for misfortune. The **Epicureans** tried to build lives of moderate pleasure without political or emotional involvement. Hellenistic arts imitated life realistically, especially in sculpture and literature (comedies of Menander, 342-292 BC).

The sciences thrived, especially at Alexandria, where the Ptolemies financed a great library and museum. Fields of study included mathematics (**Euclid's** geometry, c 300 BC); astronomy (heliocentric theory of Aristarchus, 310-230 BC; Julian calendar, 45 BC; **Ptolemy'**s *Almagest*, c AD 150); geography (world map of Eratosthenes, 276-194 BC); hydraulics (**Archimedes,** 287-212 BC); medicine (Galen, AD 130-200); and chemistry. Inventors refined uses for siphons, valves, gears, springs, screws, levers, cams, and pulleys.

A restored Persian empire under the **Parthians** (northern Iranian tribesmen) controlled the eastern Hellenistic world from 250 BC to AD 229. The Parthians and the succeeding Sassanian dynasty (c AD 224-651) fought with Rome periodically. The **Sassanians** revived Zoroastrianism as a state religion and patronized a nationalistic artistic and scholarly renaissance.

Rome. The city of Rome was founded, according to legend, by Romulus in 753 BC. Through military expansion and colonization, and by granting citizenship to conquered tribes, the city annexed all of Italy S of the Po in the 100-year period before 268 BC. The Latin and other Italic tribes were annexed first, followed by the **Etruscans** (founders of a great civilization, N of Rome) and the Greek colonies in the S. With a large standing army and reserve forces of several hundred thousand, Rome was able to defeat **Carthage** in the 3 **Punic Wars** (264-241, 218-201, 149-146 BC), despite the invasion of Italy (218 BC) by **Hannibal,** thus gaining Sicily and territory in Spain and N Africa.

Rome exploited local disputes to conquer Greece and Asia Minor in the 2nd cent. BC, and Egypt in the 1st (after the defeat and suicide of **Antony and Cleopatra,** 30 BC). All the Mediterranean civilized world up to the disputed Parthian border was now Roman and remained so for 500 years. Less civilized regions were added to the Empire: Gaul (conquered by **Julius Caesar,** 58-51 BC), Britain (AD 43), and Dacia NE of the Danube (AD 107).

Julius Caesar

The original aristocratic republican government, with democratic features added in the 5th and 4th cent. BC, deteriorated under the pressures of empire and class conflict (**Gracchus** brothers, social reformers, murdered in 133 BC and 121 BC; slave revolts in 135 BC and 73 BC). After a series of civil wars (Marius vs. Sulla 88-82 BC, Caesar vs. **Pompey** 49-45 BC, triumvirate vs. Caesar's assassins 44-43 BC, Antony vs. Octavian 32-30 BC), the empire came under the rule of a deified monarch (first emperor, **Augustus,** 27 BC-AD 14).

Provincials (nearly all granted citizenship by Caracalla, AD 212) came to dominate the army and civil service. Traditional **Roman law,** systematized and interpreted by independent jurists, and local self-rule in provincial cities were supplanted by a vast tax-collecting bureaucracy in the 3rd and 4th cent. The legal rights of women, children, and slaves were strengthened.

Roman innovations in **civil engineering** included water mills, windmills, and rotary mills and use of cement that hardened under water. Monumental architecture (baths, theaters, temples) relied on the arch and the dome. The network of roads (some still standing) stretched 53,000 mi, passing through mountain tunnels as long as 3.5 mi. Aqueducts brought water to cities; underground sewers removed waste.

Roman art and literature were to a large extent derivative of Greek models. Innovations were made in sculpture (naturalistic busts, equestrian statues), decorative wall painting (as at Pompeii), satire (**Juvenal,** AD 60-127), history (**Tacitus,** AD 56-120), prose romance (Petronius, d AD 66). Gladiatorial contests dominated public amusements, which were supported by the state.

India. The **Gupta** monarchs reunited N India c AD 320. Their peaceful and prosperous reign saw a revival of Hindu religious thought and Brahman power. The old Vedic traditions were combined with devotion to many indigenous deities (who were seen as manifestations of Vedic gods). **Caste** lines were reinforced, and **Buddhism** gradually disappeared. The art (often erotic), architecture, and literature of

Major Gods & Goddesses of the Classical World

Greek	Roman	Relations	Sphere or Position
Aphrodite	Venus	Daughter of Zeus & Dione	Love
Apollo	——	Son of Zeus & Leto	Healing, poetry, light
Ares	Mars	Son of Zeus & Hera	War
Artemis	Diana	Daughter of Zeus & Leto	Hunting, chastity
Athena	Minerva	Daughter of Zeus & Metis	Wisdom, crafts, war
Cronus	Saturn	Father of Zeus	Titans' ruler
Demeter	Ceres	Sister of Zeus	Agriculture, fertility
Dionysus	Bacchus	Son of Zeus & Semele	Wine, fertility, ecstasy
Eros	Cupid	Son of Ares & Aphrodite	Love
Hades	Pluto	Brother of Zeus	The underworld, death
Hephaestus	Vulcan	Son of Zeus & Hera	Fire
Hera	Juno	Wife & sister of Zeus	Earth
Hermes	Mercury	Son of Zeus & Maia	Travel, commerce, gods' messenger
Hestia	Vesta	Sister of Zeus	The hearth
Pan	——	Son of Hermes & a wood nymph	Forests, flocks, shepherds
Persephone	Proserpina	Daughter of Zeus & Demeter	Grain
Poseidon	Neptune	Brother of Zeus	The sea
Rhea	Ops	Mother of Zeus	The earth
Uranus	Uranus	Father of Titans (elder gods)	The heavens
Zeus	Jupiter	Son of Cronus & Rhea	Ruler of the gods

the period, patronized by the Gupta court, are considered among India's finest achievements (Kalidasa, poet and dramatist, fl. c AD 400). Mathematical innovations included use of the zero and decimal numbers. Invasions by White Huns from the NW destroyed the empire c 550.

Rich cultures also developed in S India during this period. Emotional Tamil religious poetry contributed to the Hindu revival. The Pallava kingdom controlled much of S India c 350-880 and helped to spread Indian civilization to SE Asia.

China. The Ch'in ruler Shih Huang Ti (r 221-210 BC), known as the First Emperor, centralized political authority, standardized the written language, laws, weights, measures, and coinage, and conducted a census, but tried to destroy most philosophical texts. The **Han dynasty** (202 BC-AD 220) instituted the Mandarin bureaucracy, which lasted

2,000 years. Local officials were selected by examination in Confucian classics and trained at the imperial university and provincial schools.

The invention of **paper** facilitated this bureaucratic system. Agriculture was promoted, but peasants bore most of the tax burden. Irrigation was improved, water clocks and sundials were used, astronomy and mathematics thrived, and landscape painting was perfected.

With the expansion S and W (to nearly the present borders of today's China), trade was opened with India, SE Asia, and the Middle East, over sea and caravan routes. Indian missionaries brought Mahayana Buddhism to China by the 1st cent. AD and spawned a variety of sects. Taoism was revived and merged with popular superstitions. Taoist and Buddhist monasteries and convents multiplied in the turbulent centuries after the collapse of the Han dynasty.

Monotheism Spreads: AD 1-750

Roman Empire. Polytheism was practiced in the Roman Empire, and religions indigenous to particular Middle Eastern nations became international. Roman citizens worshiped **Isis** of Egypt, **Mithras** of Persia, **Demeter** of Greece, and the great mother **Cybele** of Phrygia. Their cults centered on mysteries (secret ceremonies) and the promise of an afterlife, symbolized by the death and rebirth of the god. The Jews of the empire preserved their monotheistic religion, Judaism, the world's oldest (c 1300 BC) continuous religion. Its teachings are contained in the Bible (the Old Testament). First-cent. Judaism embraced several sects, including the **Sadducees**, mostly drawn from the Temple priesthood, who were culturally Hellenized; the **Pharisees**, who upheld the full range of traditional customs and practices as of equal weight to literal scriptural law and elaborated synagogue worship; and the **Essenes**, an ascetic, millennarian sect. Messianic fervor led to repeated, unsuccessful rebellions against Rome (66-70, 135). As a result, the Temple in Jerusalem was destroyed and the population decimated; this event marked the beginning of the Diaspora (living in exile). To preserve the faith, a program of codification of law was begun at the academy of Yavneh. The work continued for some 500 years in Palestine and in Babylonia, ending in the final redaction (c 600) of the **Talmud**, a huge collection of legal and moral debates, rulings, liturgy, biblical exegesis, and legendary materials.

Christianity, which emerged as a distinct sect by the 2nd half of the 1st cent., is based on the teachings of **Jesus**, whom believers considered the Savior (Messiah or Christ) and son of God. Missionary activities of the Apostles and such early leaders as **Paul of Tarsus** spread the faith. Intermittent persecution, as in Rome under Nero in AD 64, on grounds of suspected disloyalty, failed to disrupt the Christian communities. Each congregation, generally urban and of plebeian character, was tightly organized under a leader (bishop), elders (presbyters or priests), and assistants (deacons). The four **Gospels** (accounts of the life and teachings of Jesus) and the Acts of the Apostles were written down in the late 1st and early 2nd cent. and circulated along with letters of Paul and other Christian leaders. An authoritative canon of these writings was not fixed until the 4th cent.

A school for priests was established at Alexandria in the 2nd cent. Its teachers (**Origen** c 182-251) helped define doctrine and promote the faith in Greek-style philosophical works. Neoplatonism underwent Christian coloration in the writings of Church Fathers such as **Augustine** (354-430). Christian hermits began to associate in monasteries, first in Egypt (St. Pachomius c 290-345), then in other eastern lands, then in the W (**St. Benedict's rule**, 529). Devotion to saints, especially Mary, mother of Jesus, spread. Under **Constantine** (r 306-37), Christianity became in effect the established religion of the Empire. Pagan temples were expropriated, state funds were used to build churches and support the hierarchy, and laws were adjusted in accordance with Christian ideas. Pagan worship was banned by the end of the 4th cent., and severe restrictions were placed on Judaism.

The newly established church was rocked by doctrinal disputes, often exacerbated by regional rivalries. Chief heresies (as defined by church councils, backed by imperial au-

thority) were **Arianism**, which denied the divinity of Jesus; **Monophysitism**, denying the human nature of Christ; **Donatism**, which regarded as invalid any sacraments administered by sinful clergy; and **Pelagianism**, which denied the necessity of unmerited divine aid (grace) for salvation.

Islam. The earliest Arab civilization emerged by the end of the 2nd millennium BC in the watered highlands of Yemen. Seaborne and caravan trade in frankincense and myrrh connected the area with the Nile and Fertile Crescent. The Minaean, Sabean (Sheba), and Himyarite states successively held sway. By Muhammad's time (7th cent. AD), the region was a province of Sassanian Persia. In the N, the Nabataean kingdom at Petra and the kingdom of Palmyra were Aramaicized, Romanized, and finally absorbed, as neighboring Judea had been, into the Roman Empire. Nomads shared the central region with a few trading towns and oases. Wars between tribes and raids on communities were common and were celebrated in a poetic tradition that by the 6th cent. helped establish a classic literary Arabic.

About 610, **Muhammad**, a 40-year-old Arab of Mecca, emerged as a prophet. He proclaimed a revelation from the one true God, calling on contemporaries to abandon idolatry and restore the faith of Abraham. He introduced his religion as "Islam," meaning "submission" to the one God, Allah, as a continuation of the biblical faith of Abraham, Moses, and Jesus, all respected as prophets in this system. His teachings, recorded in the **Koran** (al-Qur'an in Arabic), in many ways were inclusive of Abrahamic monotheistic ideas known to the Jews and Christians in Arabia. A key aspect of the Abrahamic connection was insistence on justice in society, which led to severe opposition among the aristocrats in Mecca. As conditions worsened for Muhammad and his followers, he decided in 622 to make a *hijra* (emigration) to Medina, 200 mi to the N. This event marks the beginning of the Muslim lunar calendar. Hostilities between Mecca and Medina increased, and in 629 Muhammad conquered Mecca. By the time he died in 632, nearly all the Arabian peninsula accepted his political and religious leadership.

After his death the majority of Muslims recognized the leadership of the **caliph** ("successor") Abu Bakr (632-34), followed by Umar (634-44), Uthman (644-56), and Ali (656-60). A minority, the **Shiites**, insisted instead on the leadership of Ali, Muhammad's cousin and son-in-law. By 644, **Muslim rule** over Arabia was confirmed. Muslim armies had threatened the Byzantine and Persian empires, which were weakened by wars and disaffection among subject peoples (including Coptic and Syriac Christians opposed to the Byzantine Orthodox establishment). Syria, Palestine, Egypt, Iraq, and Persia fell to Muslim armies. The new administration assimilated existing systems in the region; hence the conquered peoples participated in running of the empire. The Koran recognized the so-called Peoples of the Book, i.e., Christians, Jews, and Zoroastrians, as tolerated monotheists, and Muslim policy was relatively tolerant to minorities living as "protected" peoples. An expanded tax system, based on conquests of the Persian and Byzantine empires, provided revenue to organize campaigns against neighboring non-Muslim regions.

Major Norse Gods & Goddesses

Name	Relations	Sphere or Position	Emblem/Attribute
Odin	Father of the Aesir (gods)	War and death, poetry, wisdom, magic	Spear, mead, ring/One-eyed
Thor	Son of Odin	Thunder, lightning, rain; champion of the gods	Hammer, belt
Njord	Father of Freyja & Freyr	Wind and sea, wealth and prosperity	----
Frigg	Wife of Odin	Marriage and motherhood, home	----
Freyja (Freya)	Daughter of Njord	Fertility, birth, crops	Necklace
Freyr	Son of Njord	Agriculture, sun, rain	Magic ship, golden boar
Tyr	Son of Odin ?	Justice, war	Spear/One-handed
Heimdall	Son of nine giantesses	Watchman of the gods; keen sight & hearing	Horn
Balder (Baldur)	Son of Odin	Light, purity	----
Loki	Son of giants; father of Hel (goddess of death), Jormungand (serpent encompassing the world), Fenrir (the wolf).	Malicious trickster	----

Under the **Umayyads** (661-750) and **Abbasids** (750-1256), territorial expansion led Muslim armies across N Africa and into Spain (711). Muslim armies in the W were stopped at Tours (France) in 732 by the Frankish ruler **Charles Martel**. Asia Minor, the Indus Valley, and Transoxiana were conquered in the E. The conversion of conquered peoples to Islam was gradual. In many places the official Arabic language supplanted the local tongues. But in the eastern regions the Arab rulers and their armies adopted Persian cultures and language as part of their Muslim identity.

Disputes over succession, and pious opposition to injustices in society, led to a number of oppositional movements, which also led to the factionalization of Muslim community. The **Shiites** supported leadership candidates descended from Muhammad, believing them to be carriers of some kind of divine authority. The **Kharijites** supported an egalitarian system derived from the Koran, opposing and even engaging in battle against those who did not agree with them.

New Peoples Enter World History: 400-900

Barbarian invasions. Germanic tribes infiltrated S and E from their Baltic homeland during the 1st millennium BC, reaching S Germany by 100 BC and the Black Sea by AD 214. Organized into large federated tribes under elected kings, most resisted Roman domination and raided the empire in time of civil war (Goths took Dacia in 214, raided Thrace in 251-69). Germanic troops and commanders dominated the Roman armies by the end of the 4th cent. **Huns**, invaders from Asia, entered Europe in 372, driving more Germans into the W empire. Emperor Valens allowed Visigoths to cross the Danube in 376. Huns under Attila (d 453) raided Gaul, Italy, and the Balkans.

The W empire, weakened by overtaxation and social stagnation, was overrun in the 5th cent. Gaul was effectively lost in 406-7, Spain in 409, Britain in 410, Africa in 429-39. Rome was sacked in 410 by Visigoths under Alaric and in 455 by Vandals. The last western emperor, Romulus Augustulus, was deposed in 476 by the Germanic chief Odovacar.

Celts. Celtic cultures, which in pre-Roman times covered most of W Europe, were confined almost entirely to the British Isles after the Germanic invasions. **St. Patrick** completed (c 457-92) the conversion of Ireland. A strong monastic tradition took hold. Irish monastic missionaries in Scotland, England, and the continent (Columba c 521-97; Columban c 543-615) helped restore Christianity after the Germanic invasions. Monasteries became centers of classic and Christian learning and presided over the recording of a Christianized Celtic mythology, elaborated by secular writers and bards. An intricate decorative art style developed, especially in book illumination (Lindisfarne Gospels, c 700; Book of Kells, 8th cent.).

Successor states. The Visigothic kingdom in Spain (from 419) and much of France (to 507) saw continuation of Roman administration, language, and law (Breviary of Alaric, 506) until its destruction by the Muslims (711). The Vandal kingdom in Africa (from 429) was conquered by the Byzantines in 533. Italy was ruled successively by an Ostrogothic kingdom under Byzantine suzerainty (489-554), direct Byzantine government, and German Lombards (568-774). The Lombards divided the peninsula with the Byzantines and papacy under the dynamic reformer **Pope Gregory the Great** (590-604) and successors.

King Clovis (r 481-511) united the Franks on both sides of the Rhine and, after his conversion to Christianity, defeated the Arian heretics, Burgundians (after 500), and Visigoths (507) with the support of native clergy and the papacy. Under the **Merovingian** kings, a feudal system emerged: Power was fragmented among hierarchies of military landowners. Social stratification, which in late Roman times had acquired legal, hereditary sanction, was reinforced. The Carolingians (747-987) expanded the kingdom and restored central power. **Charlemagne** (r 768-814) conquered nearly all the Germanic lands, including Lombard Italy, and was crowned Emperor by Pope Leo III in Rome in 800. A centuries-long decline in commerce and arts was reversed under Charlemagne's patronage. He welcomed Jews to his kingdom, which became a center of Jewish learning (Rashi, 1040-1105). He sponsored the Carolingian Renaissance of learning under the Anglo-Latin scholar Alcuin (c 732-804), who reformed church liturgy.

Byzantine Empire. Under **Diocletian** (r 284-305) the empire had been divided into 2 parts to facilitate administration and defense. **Constantine** founded (330) **Constantinople** (at old Byzantium) as a fully Christian city. Commerce and taxation financed a sumptuous, orientalized court, a class of hereditary bureaucratic families, and magnificent urban construction (Hagia Sophia, 532-37). The city's fortifications and naval innovations repelled assaults by Goths, Huns, Slavs, Bulgars, Avars, Arabs, and Scandinavians. Greek replaced Latin as the official language by c 700. Byzantine art, a solemn, sacral, and stylized variation of late classical styles (mosaics at the Church of San Vitale, Ravenna, Italy 526-48), was a starting point for medieval art in E and W Europe.

Justinian (r 527-65) reconquered parts of Spain, N Africa, and Italy, codified Roman law (Codex Justinianus [529] was medieval Europe's chief legal text), closed the Platonic Academy at Athens, and ordered all pagans to convert. Lombards in Italy and Arabs in Africa retook most of his conquests. The Isaurian dynasty from Anatolia (from 717) and the Macedonian dynasty (867-1054) restored military and commercial power. The Iconoclast controversy (726-843) over the permissibility of images helped alienate the Eastern Church from the papacy.

Abbasid Empire. Baghdad (est. 762), became seat of the **Abbasid dynasty** (est. 750), while Ummayads continued to rule in Spain. A brilliant cosmopolitan civilization emerged, inaugurating a Muslim-Arab golden age. Arabic was the lingua franca of the empire; intellectual sources from Persian, Sanskrit, Greek, and Syriac were rendered into Arabic. Christians and Jews equally participated in this translation movement, which also involved interaction between Jewish legal thought and Islamic law, as much as between Christian theology and Muslim scholasticism. Persian-style court life, with art and music, flourished at the court of **Harun al-Rashid** (786-809), celebrated in the masterpiece known to English readers as *The Arabian Nights*. The sciences, medicine, and mathematics were pursued at Baghdad, Cordova, and Cairo

(est. 969). The culmination of this intellectual synthesis in Islamic civilization came with the scientific and philosophical works of **Avicenna** (Ibn Sina, 980-1037), **Averroes** (Ibn Rushd, 1126-98), and **Maimonides** (1135-1204), a Jew who wrote in Arabic. This intellectual tradition was translated into Latin and opened a new period in Christian thought.

The decentralization of the **Abbasid** empire, from 874, led to establishment of various Muslim dynasties under different ethnic groups. Persians, Berbers, and Turks ruled different regions, retaining connection with the Abbasid caliph at the religious level. The Abbasid period also saw various religious movements against the orthodox position held by governing authorities. This situation in Muslim religion led to the establishment of different legal, theological, and mystical schools of thought. The most influential mass movement was **Sufism**, which aimed at the reaching out of the average individual in quest of a spiritual path. Al-Ghazali (1058-1111) is credited with reconciling personal Sufism with orthodox Sunni tradition.

Africa. Immigrants from Saba in S Arabia helped set up the **Axum** kingdom in Ethiopia in the 1st cent. (their language, Ge'ez, is preserved by the Ethiopian Church). In the 3rd cent., when the kingdom became Christianized, it defeated Kushite Meroe and expanded its influence into Yemen. Axum was the center of a vast ivory trade and controlled the Red Sea coast until c 1100. Arab conquest in Egypt cut Axum's political and economic ties with Byzantium.

The Iron Age entered W Africa by the end of the 1st millennium BC. **Ghana**, the first known sub-Saharan state, ruled in the upper Senegal-Niger region c 400-1240, controlling the trade of gold from mines in the S to trans-Sahara caravan routes to the N. The **Bantu** peoples, probably of W African origin, began to spread S and S perhaps 2,000 years ago, displacing the Pygmies and Bushmen of central and S Africa during a 1,500-year period.

Japan. The advanced Neolithic Yayoi period, when irrigation, rice farming, and iron and bronze casting techniques were introduced from China or Korea, persisted to c AD 400. The myriad Japanese states were then united by the **Yamato** clan, under an emperor who acted as chief priest of the animistic Shinto cult. Japanese political and military intervention by the 6th cent. in Korea, then under strong Chinese influence, quickened a Chinese cultural invasion of Japan, bringing Buddhism, the Chinese language (which long remained a literary and governmental medium), Chinese ideographs, and Buddhist styles in painting, sculpture, literature, and architecture (7th cent., Horyu-ji temple at Nara). The Taika Reforms (646) tried unsuccessfully to centralize Japan according to Chinese bureaucratic and Buddhist philosophical values.

A nativist reaction against the Buddhist **Nara period** (710-94) ushered in the **Heian period** (794-1185) centered at the new capital, Kyoto. Japanese elegance and simplicity modified Chinese styles in architecture, scroll painting, and literature; the writing system was also simplified. The courtly novel *Tale of Genji* (1010-20) testifies to the enhanced role of women.

Southeast Asia. The historic peoples of SE Asia began arriving some 2,500 years ago from China and Tibet, displacing scattered aborigines. Their agriculture relied on rice and yams. Indian cultural influences were strongest; literacy and Hindu and Buddhist ideas followed the S India-China trade route. From the S tip of Indochina, the kingdom of **Funan** (1st-7th cent.) traded as far W as Persia. It was absorbed by Chenla, itself conquered by the **Khmer Empire** (600-1300). The Khmers, under Hindu god-kings (Suryavarman II, 1113-c 1150), built the monumental Angkor Wat temple center for the royal phallic cult. The **Nam-Viet** kingdom in Annam, dominated by China and Chinese culture for 1,000 years, emerged in the 10th cent., growing at the expense of the Khmers, who also lost ground in the NW to the new, highly organized **Thai** kingdom. On Sumatra, the **Srivijaya** Empire controlled vital sea lanes (7th to 10th cent.). A Buddhist dynasty, the Sailendras, ruled central **Java** (8th-9th cent.), building at Borobudur one of the largest stupas in the world.

China. The Sui dynasty (581-618) ushered in a period of commercial, artistic, and scientific achievement in China, continuing under the **Tang** dynasty (618-906). Inventions like the magnetic compass, gunpowder, the abacus, and printing were introduced or perfected. Medical innovations included cataract surgery. The state, from its cosmopolitan capital, Chang-an, supervised foreign trade, which exchanged Chinese silks, porcelains, and art for spices, ivory, etc., over Central Asian caravan routes and sea routes reaching Africa. A golden age of poetry bequeathed valuable works to later generations (Tu Fu, 712-70; Li Po, 701-62). Landscape painting flourished.

Commercial and industrial expansion continued under the **Northern Sung** dynasty (960-1126), facilitated by paper money and credit notes. But commerce never achieved respectability; government monopolies expropriated successful merchants. The population, long stable at 50 million, doubled in 200 years with the introduction of early-ripening rice and the double harvest. In art, native Chinese styles were revived.

Americas. From 300 to 600 a Native American empire stretched from the Valley of Mexico to Guatemala, centering on the huge city **Teotihuacán** (founded 100 BC). To the S, in Guatemala, a high **Mayan** civilization developed (150-900) around hundreds of rural ceremonial centers. The Mayans improved on Olmec writing and the calendar and pursued astronomy and mathematics. In South America, a widespread pre-Inca culture grew from **Tiahuanacu**, Bolivia, near Lake Titicaca (Gateway of the Sun, c 700).

Christian Europe Regroups and Expands: 900-1300

Scandinavians. Pagan Danish and Norse (Viking) adventurers, traders, and pirates raided the coasts of the British Isles (Dublin, est. c 831), France, and even the Mediterranean for over 200 years beginning in the late 8th cent. Inland settlement in the W was limited to Great Britain (King Canute, 994-1035) and Normandy, settled (911) under Rollo, as a fief of France. Vikings also reached Iceland (874), Greenland (c 986), and North America (**Leif Ericson** and others, c 1000). Norse traders (**Varangians**) developed Russian river commerce from the 8th to the 11th cent. and helped set up a state at Kiev in the late 9th cent. Conversion to Christianity occurred in the 10th cent., reaching Sweden 100 years later. In the 11th cent. Norman bands conquered S Italy and Sicily, and Duke **William of Normandy** conquered (1066) England, bringing feudalism and the French language, essential elements in later English civilization.

Central and East Europe. Slavs began to expand from about AD 150 in all directions in Europe, and by the 7th cent. they reached as far S as the Adriatic and Aegean seas. In the Balkan Peninsula they dislocated Romanized local populations or assimilated newcomers (Bulgarians, a Turkic people). The first Slavic states were Moravia (628) in Central Europe and the Bulgarian state (680) in the Balkans. Missions of St. Methodius and Cyril (whose Greek-based cyrillic alphabet is still used by some S and E Slavs) converted (863) Moravia.

The Eastern Slavs, part-civilized under the overlordship of the Turkish-Jewish **Khazar** trading empire (7th-10th cent.), gravitated toward Constantinople by the 9th cent. The **Kievan state** adopted (989) Eastern Christianity under Prince Vladimir. King Boleslav I (992-1025) began **Poland's** long history of eastern conquest. The Magyars (**Hungarians**), in present-day Hungary since 896, accepted (1001) Latin Christianity.

Germany. The German kingdom that emerged after the breakup of Charlemagne's W Empire remained a confederation of largely autonomous states. Otto I, a Saxon who was king from 936, established the **Holy Roman Empire**—a union of Germany and N Italy—in alliance with Pope John XII, who crowned (962) him emperor; he defeated (955) the Magyars. Imperial power was greatest under the **Hohenstaufens** (1138-1254), despite the growing opposition of the papacy, which ruled central Italy, and the Lombard League cities. Frederick II (1194-1250) improved administration and patronized the arts; after his death, German influence was removed from Italy.

Christian Spain. From its N mountain redoubts, Christian rule slowly migrated S through the 11th cent., when Muslim unity collapsed. After the capture (1085) of **Toledo**, the kingdoms of Portugal, Castile, and Aragon undertook repeated crusades of reconquest, finally completed in 1492. Elements of Islamic civilization persisted in recaptured areas, influencing all Western Europe.

Crusades. Pope Urban II called (1095) for a crusade to restore Asia Minor to Byzantium and to regain the Holy Land from the Turks. Some ten crusades (lasting until 1291) succeeded only in founding four temporary Frankish states in the Levant. The 4th crusade sacked (1204) Constantinople. In Rhineland (1096), England (1290), and France (1306), Jews were massacred or expelled, and wars were launched against Christian heretics (**Albigensian** crusade in France, 1229). Trade in eastern luxuries expanded, led by the Venetian naval empire.

Economy. The agricultural base of European life benefited from improvements in **plow design** (c 1000) and by draining of lowlands and clearing of forests, leading to a rural population increase. Towns grew in N Italy, Flanders, and N Germany (Hanseatic League). Improvements in **loom design** permitted factory textile production. **Guilds** dominated urban trades from the 12th cent. Banking (centered in Italy, 12th-15th cent.) facilitated long-distance trade.

The Church. The split between the Eastern and Western churches was formalized in 1054. Western and Central Europe was divided into 500 bishoprics under one united hierarchy, but conflicts between secular and church authorities were frequent (German **Investiture Controversy**, 1075-1122). Clerical power was first strengthened through the international monastic reform begun at Cluny in 910. Popular religious enthusiasm often expressed itself in heretical movements (Waldensians from 1173), but was channeled by the **Dominican** (1215) and **Franciscan** (1223) friars into the religious mainstream.

Arts. **Romanesque** architecture (11th-12th cent.) expanded on late Roman models, using the rounded arch and massed stone to support enlarged basilicas. Painting and sculpture followed Byzantine models. The literature of **chivalry** was exemplified by the epic (*Chanson de Roland*, c 1100) and by courtly love poems of the troubadours of Provence and minnesingers of Germany. **Gothic** architecture emerged in France (choir of St. Denis, c 1040) and spread along with French cultural influence. Rib vaulting and pointed arches were used to combine soaring heights with delicacy, and they freed walls for display of stained glass. Exteriors were covered with painted relief sculpture and embellished with elaborate architectural detail.

Chartres Cathedral

Learning. Law, medicine, and philosophy were advanced at independent **universities** (Bologna, late 11th cent.), originally corporations of students and masters. Twelfth-cent. translations of Greek classics, especially Aristotle, encouraged an analytic approach. Scholastic philosophy, from Anselm (1033-1109) to **Aquinas** (1225-74), attempted to understand revelation through reason.

Apogee of Central Asian Power; Islam Grows: 1250-1500

Turks. Turkic peoples, of Central Asian ancestry, were a military threat to the Byzantine and Persian Empires from the 6th cent. After several waves of invasions, during which most of the Turks adopted Islam, the **Seljuk Turks** took (1055) Baghdad. They ruled Persia, Iraq and, after 1071, Asia Minor, where massive numbers of Turks settled. The empire was divided in the 12th cent. into smaller states ruled by Seljuks, Kurds (**Saladin**, c 1137-93), and Mamluks (a military caste of former Turk, Kurd, and Circassian slaves), which governed Egypt and the Middle East until the Ottoman era (c 1290-1922).

Osman I (r c 1290-1326) and succeeding sultans united Anatolian Turkish warriors in a militaristic state that waged holy war against Byzantium and Balkan Christians. Most of the Balkans had been subdued, and Anatolia united, when Constantinople fell (1453). By the mid-16th cent., Hungary, the Middle East, and N Africa had been conquered. The Turkish advance was stopped at Vienna (1529) and at the naval battle of Lepanto (1571) by Spain, Venice, and the papacy.

The Ottoman state was governed in accordance with orthodox Muslim law. Greek, Armenian, and Jewish communities were segregated and were ruled by religious leaders responsible for taxation; they dominated trade. State offices and most army ranks were filled by slaves through a system of child conscription among Christians.

India. Mahmud of Ghazni (971-1030) led repeated Turkish raids into N India. Turkish power was consolidated in 1206 with the start of the **Sultanate at Delhi**. Centralization of state power under the early Delhi sultans went far beyond traditional Indian practice. Muslim rule of most of the subcontinent lasted until the British conquest 600 years later.

Mongols. **Genghis Khan** (c 1167-1227) first united the feuding Mongol tribes, and built their armies into an effective offensive force around a core of highly mobile cavalry. He and his immediate successors created the largest land empire in history; by 1279 it stretched from the E coast of Asia to the Danube, from the Siberian steppes to the Arabian Sea. East-West trade and contacts were facilitated (Marco Polo, c 1254-1324).

The western Mongols were Islamized by 1295; successor states soon lost their Mongol character by assimilation. They were briefly reunited under the Turk Tamerlane (1336-1405).

Kublai Khan ruled China from his new capital Beijing (est. c 1264). Naval campaigns against Japan (1274, 1281) and Java (1293) were defeated, the latter by the Hindu-Buddhist maritime kingdom of Majapahit. The **Yuan** dynasty used Mongols and other foreigners (including Europeans) in official posts and tolerated the return of Nestorian Christianity (suppressed 841-45) and the spread of Islam in the S and W. A native reaction expelled the Mongols in 1367-68.

Russia. The Kievan state in Russia, weakened by the decline of Byzantium and the rise of the Catholic Polish-Lithuanian state, was overrun (1238-40) by the Mongols. Only the northern trading republic of Novgorod remained independent. The grand dukes of Moscow emerged as leaders of a coalition of princes that eventually (by 1481) defeated the Mongols. After the fall of Constantinople in 1453, the **Tsars** (Caesars) at Moscow (from Ivan III, r 1462-1505) set up an independent Russian Orthodox Church. Commerce failed to revive. The isolated Russian state remained agrarian, with the peasant class falling into serfdom.

Persia. A revival of Persian literature, making use of the Arab alphabet and literary forms, began in the 10th cent. (epic of Firdausi, 935-1020). An art revival, influenced by Chinese styles introduced after the Mongols came to power in Iran, began in the 13th cent. Persian cultural and political forms, and often the Persian language, were used for centuries by Turkish and Mongol elites from the Balkans to India. Persian mystics from Rumi (1207-73) to Jami (1414-92) promoted **Sufism** in their poetry.

Africa. Two militant Islamic Berber dynasties emerged from the Sahara to carve out empires from the Sahel to central Spain—the **Almoravids** (c 1050-1140) and the fanatical **Almohads** (c 1125-1269). The Ghanaian empire was replaced in the upper Niger by Mali (c 1230-1340), whose Muslim rulers imported Egyptians to help make **Timbuktu** a center of commerce (in gold, leather, and slaves) and learning. The Songhay empire (to 1590) replaced Mali. To the S, forest kingdoms produced refined artworks (Ife terra cotta, **Benin** bronzes).

Other Muslim states in Nigeria (Hausas) and Chad originated in the 11th cent. and continued in some form until the 19th-cent. European conquest. Less-developed Bantu kingdoms existed across central Africa.

Some 40 Muslim Arab-Persian trading colonies and city-states were established all along the E African coast from the 10th cent. (Kilwa, Mogadishu). The interchange with Bantu peoples produced the **Swahili** language and culture. Gold, palm oil, and slaves were brought from the interior, stimulating the growth of the Monamatapa kingdom of the Zambezi (15th cent.). The Christian Ethiopian empire (from 13th cent.) continued the traditions of Axum.

Southeast Asia. Islam was introduced into Malaya and the Indonesian islands by Arab, Persian, and Indian traders. Coastal Muslim cities and states (starting before 1300) soon dominated the interior. Chief among these was the **Malacca** state (c 1400-1511), on the Malay peninsula.

Arts and Statecraft Thrive in Europe: 1350-1600

Italian Renaissance and Humanism. Distinctive Italian achievements in the arts in the late Middle Ages (**Dante**, 1265-1321; Giotto, 1276-1337) led to the vigorous new styles of the Renaissance (14th-16th cent.). Patronized by the rulers of the quarreling petty states of Italy (**Medicis** in Florence and the papacy, c 1400-1737), the plastic arts perfected realistic techniques, including **perspective** (Masaccio, 1401-28, **Leonardo**, 1452-1519). Classical motifs were used in architecture, and increased talent and expense were put into secular buildings. The Florentine dialect was refined as a national literary language (**Petrarch**, 1304-74). Greek refugees from the E strengthened the respect of humanist scholars for the classic sources. Soon an international movement aided by the spread of **printing** (Gutenberg, c 1397(?)-1468), **humanism** was optimistic about the power of human reason (Erasmus of Rotterdam, 1466-1536, **More's** *Utopia*, 1516) and valued individual effort in the arts and in politics (**Machiavelli**, 1469-1527).

France. The French monarchy, strengthened in its repeated struggles with powerful nobles (Burgundy, Flanders, Aquitaine) by alliances with the growing commercial towns, consolidated bureaucratic control under Philip IV (r 1285-1314) and extended French influence into Germany and Italy (popes at Avignon, France, 1309-1417). The **Hundred Years War** (1337-1453) ended English dynastic claims in France (battles of Crécy, 1346, and Poitiers, 1356; Joan of Arc executed, 1431). A French Renaissance, dating from royal invasions (1494, 1499) of Italy, was encouraged at the court of Francis I (r 1515-47), who centralized taxation and law. French vernacular literature consciously asserted its independence (La Pléiade, 1549).

England. The evolution of England's unique political institutions began with the **Magna Carta** (1215), by which King John guaranteed the privileges of nobles and church against the monarchy and assured jury trial. After the **Wars of the Roses** (1455-85), the **Tudor dynasty** reasserted royal prerogatives (Henry VIII, r 1509-47), but the trend toward independent departments and ministerial government also continued. English trade (wool exports from c 1340) was protected by the nation's growing maritime power (**Spanish Armada** destroyed, 1588).

English replaced French and Latin in the late 14th cent. in law and literature (**Chaucer**, c 1340-1400) and English translation of the Bible began (Wycliffe, 1380s). **Elizabeth I** (r 1558-1603) presided over a confident flowering of poetry (Spenser, 1552-99), drama (**Shakespeare**, 1564-1616), and music.

German Empire. From among a welter of minor feudal states, church lands, and independent cities, the **Habsburgs** assembled a far-flung territorial domain, based in Austria from 1276. Family members held the title of Holy Roman Emperor from 1438 to the Empire's dissolution in 1806, but failed to centralize its domains, leaving Germany disunited for centuries. Resistance to Turkish expansion brought Hungary under Austrian control from the 16th cent. The Netherlands, Luxembourg, and Burgundy were added in 1477, curbing French expansion.

The Flemish painting tradition of naturalism, technical proficiency, and bourgeois subject matter began in the 15th cent. (**Jan Van Eyck,** c 1390-1441), the earliest northern manifestation of the Renaissance. Albrecht **Dürer** (1471-1528) typified the merging of late Gothic and Italian trends in 16th-cent. German art. Imposing civic architecture flourished in the prosperous commercial cities.

Spain. Despite the unification of Castile and Aragon in 1479, the 2 countries retained separate governments, and the nobility, especially in Aragon and Catalonia, retained many privileges. Spanish lands in Italy (Naples, Sicily) and the Netherlands entangled the country in European wars through the mid-17th cent., while explorers, traders, and conquerors built up a Spanish empire in the Americas and the Philippines.

From the late 15th cent., a **golden age** of literature and art produced works of social satire (plays of Lope de Vega, 1562-1635; **Cervantes,** 1547-1616), as well as spiritual intensity (**El Greco,** 1541-1614; **Velazquez,** 1599-1660).

Black Death. The bubonic plague reached Europe from the E in 1348, killing up to half the population by 1350. Labor scarcity forced wages to rise and brought greater freedom to the peasantry, making possible **peasant uprisings** (Jacquerie in France, 1358; Wat Tyler's rebellion in England, 1381).

Explorations. Organized European maritime exploration began, seeking to evade the Venice-Ottoman monopoly of E trade and to promote Christianity. Beginning in 1418, expeditions from Portugal explored the W coast of Africa, until Vasco da Gama rounded the Cape of Good Hope in 1497 and reached India. A Portuguese trading empire was consolidated by the seizure of Goa (1510) and Malacca (1551). Japan was reached in 1542. The voyages of Christopher **Columbus** (1492-1504) uncovered a world new to Europeans, which Spain hastened to subdue. Navigation schools in Spain and Portugal, the development of large sailing ships (carracks), and the invention (c 1475) of the rifle aided European penetration.

Christopher Columbus

Mughals and Safavids. E of the Ottoman Empire, 2 Muslim dynasties ruled unchallenged in the 16th and 17th cent. The Mughal dynasty of India, founded by Persianized Turkish invaders from the NW under Babur, dates from their 1526 conquest of the Delhi Sultanate. The dynasty ruled most of India for more than 200 years, surviving nominally until 1857. **Akbar** (r 1556-1605) consolidated administration at his glorious court, where the Urdu language (Persian-influenced Hindi) developed. Trade relations with Europe increased. Under Shah Jahan (1629-58), a secularized art fusing Hindu and

Taj Mahal

Muslim elements flourished in miniature painting and in architecture (**Taj Mahal**). **Sikhism** (founded c 1519) combined elements of both faiths. Suppression of Hindus and Shi'ite Muslims in S India in the late 17th cent. weakened the empire.

Fanatical devotion to the Shi'ite sect characterized the Safavids (1502-1736) of Persia and led to hostilities with the Sunni Ottomans for more than a century. The prosperity and the strength of the empire are evidenced by the mosques at its capital city, **Isfahan**. The Safavids enhanced Iranian national consciousness.

China. The **Ming** emperors (1368-1644), the last native dynasty in China, wielded unprecedented personal power, while the Confucian bureaucracy began to suffer from inertia. European trade (Portuguese monopoly through **Macao** from 1557) was strictly controlled. Jesuit scholars and scientists (Matteo Ricci, 1552-1610) introduced some Western science; their writings familiarized the West with China. Chinese techno6logical inventiveness declined from this era, but the arts thrived, especially in the areas of painting and ceramics.

Japan. After the decline of the first hereditary shogunate (chief generalship) at **Kamakura** (1185-1333), fragmentation of power accelerated, as did the consequent social mobility. Under Kamakura and the Ashikaga shogunate (1338-1573), the daimyos (lords) and samurai (warriors) grew more powerful and promoted a martial ideology. Japanese pirates and traders plied the China coast. Popular Buddhist movements included the nationalist Nichiren sect (from c 1250) and **Zen** (brought from China, 1191), which stressed meditation and a disciplined esthetic (tea ceremony, gardening, martial arts, No drama).

Reformed Europe Expands Overseas: 1500-1700

Reformation begun. Theological debate and protests against real and perceived clerical corruption existed in the medieval Christian world, expressed by such dissenters as John **Wycliffe** (c 1320-84) and his followers, the Lollards, in England, and **Huss** (burned as a heretic, 1415) in Bohemia.

Martin **Luther** (1483-1546) preached that faith alone leads to salvation, without the mediation of clergy or good works. He attacked the authority of the pope, rejected priestly celibacy, and recommended individual study of the Bible (which he translated c 1525). His 95 Theses (1517) led to his excommunication (1521). John **Calvin** (1509-64) said that God's elect were predestined for salvation and that good conduct and success were signs of election. Calvin in Geneva and John **Knox** (1505-72) in Scotland established theocratic states.

Henry VIII asserted English national authority and secular power by breaking away (1534) from the Catholic Church. Monastic property was confiscated, and some Protestant doctrines given official sanction.

Religious wars. A century and a half of religious wars began with a S German peasant uprising (1524), repressed with Luther's support. Radical sects—democratic, pacifist, millennarian—arose (Anabaptists ruled Münster in 1534-35) and were suppressed violently. Civil war in France from 1562 between **Huguenots** (Protestant nobles and merchants) and Catholics ended with the 1598 **Edict of Nantes**, tolerating Protestants (revoked 1685). Habsburg attempts to restore Catholicism in Germany were resisted in 25 years of fighting; the 1555 Peace of Augsburg guarantee of religious independence to local princes and cities was confirmed only after the **Thirty Years War** (1618-48), when much of Germany was devastated by local and foreign armies (Sweden, France).

A Catholic Reformation, or **Counter Reformation**, met the Protestant challenge, defining an official theology at the Council of Trent (1545-63). The **Jesuit** order (Society of Jesus), founded in 1534 by Ignatius Loyola (1491-1556), helped reconvert large areas of Poland, Hungary, and S Germany and sent missionaries to the New World, India, and China, while the **Inquisition** suppressed heresy in Catholic countries. A revival of religious fervor appeared in the devotional literature (Teresa of Avila, 1515-82) and in grandiose **Baroque** art (Bernini, 1598-1680).

Scientific Revolution. The late nominalist thinkers (Ockham, c 1300-49) of Paris and Oxford challenged Aristotelian orthodoxy, allowing for a freer scientific approach. At the same time, metaphysical values, such as the Neoplatonic faith in an orderly, mathematical cosmos, still motivated and directed inquiry. Nicolaus **Copernicus** (1473-1543) promoted the heliocentric theory, which was confirmed when Johannes **Kepler** (1571-1630) discovered the mathematical laws describing the orbits of the planets. The traditional Christian-Aristotelian belief that the heavens and the earth were fundamentally different collapsed when **Galileo** (1564-1642) discovered moving sunspots, irregular moon topography, and moons around Jupiter. He and Sir Isaac **Newton** (1642-1727) developed a mechanics that unified cosmic and earthly phenomena. Newton and Gottfried von **Leibniz** (1646-1716) invented calculus. René **Descartes** (1596-1650), best known for his influential philosophy, also invented analytic geometry.

An explosion of **observational science** included the discovery of blood circulation (Harvey, 1578-1657) and microscopic life (Leeuwenhoek, 1632-1723) and advances in anatomy (Vesalius, 1514-64, dissected corpses) and chemistry (Boyle, 1627-91). Scientific research institutes were founded: Florence (1657), London (**Royal Society**, 1660), Paris (1666). Inventions proliferated (Savery's steam engine, 1696).

Arts. Mannerist trends of the High Renaissance (**Michelangelo**, 1475-1564) exploited virtuosity, grace, novelty, and exotic subjects and poses. The notion of artistic genius was promoted. Private connoisseurs entered the art market. These trends were elaborated in the 17th cent. **Baroque** era on a grander scale. Dynamic movement in painting and sculpture was emphasized by sharp lighting effects, rich materials (colored marble, gilt), and realistic details. Curved facades, broken lines, rich detail, and ceiling decoration characterized Baroque architecture. Monarchs, princes, and prelates, usually Catholic, used Baroque art to enhance and embellish their authority, as in royal portraits (Velazquez, 1599-1660; Van Dyck, 1599-1641).

National styles emerged. In France, a taste for rectilinear order and serenity (Poussin, 1594-1665), linked to the new rational philosophy, was expressed in classical forms. The influence of **classical values** in French literature (tragedies of **Racine**, 1639-99) gave rise to the "battle of the Ancients and Moderns." New forms included the essay (**Montaigne**, 1533-92) and novel (*Princesse de Cleves*, La Fayette, 1678).

Dutch painting of the 17th cent. was unique in its wide social distribution. The Flemish tradition of undemonstrative realism reached its peak in **Rembrandt** (1606-69) and Jan Vermeer (1632-75).

Economy. European economic expansion was stimulated by the new trade with the East, by New World gold and silver, and by a doubling of population (50 million in 1450, 100 million in 1600). New business and financial techniques were developed and refined, such as joint-stock companies, insurance, and letters of credit and exchange. The Bank of Amsterdam (1609) and the Bank of England (1694) broke the old monopoly of private banking families. The rise of a business mentality was typified by the spread of clock towers in cities in the 14th cent. By the mid-15th cent., portable clocks were available; the first watch was invented in 1502.

Galileo

By 1650, most governments had adopted the **mercantile system**, in which they sought to amass metallic wealth by protecting their merchants' foreign and colonial trade monopolies. The rise in prices and the new coin-based economy undermined the craft guild and feudal manorial systems. Expanding industries (clothweaving, mining) benefited from technical advances. Coal replaced disappearing wood as the chief fuel; it was used to fuel new 16th-cent. blast furnaces making cast iron.

New World. The **Aztecs** united much of the Meso-American culture area in a militarist empire by 1519, from their capital, Tenochtitlán (pop. 300,000), which was the center of a cult requiring ritual human sacrifice. Most of the civilized areas of South America were ruled by the centralized Inca Em-

Aztec ruins

pire (1476-1534), stretching 2,000 mi from Ecuador to NW Argentina. Lavish and sophisticated traditions in pottery, weaving, sculpture, and architecture were maintained in both regions.

These empires, beset by revolts, fell in 2 short campaigns to gold-seeking Spanish forces based in the Antilles and Panama. Hernan **Cortes** took Mexico (1519-21); Francisco **Pizarro,** Peru (1532-35). From these centers, land and sea expeditions claimed most of North and South America for Spain. The Indian high cultures did not survive the impact of Christian missionaries and the new upper class of whites and mestizos. In turn, New World silver and such Indian products as potatoes, tobacco, corn, peanuts, chocolate, and rubber exercised a major economic influence on Europe. Although the Spanish administration intermittently concerned itself with the welfare of Indians, the population remained impoverished at most levels. European diseases reduced the native population.

Brazil, which the Portuguese reached in 1500 and settled after 1530, and the Caribbean colonies of several European nations developed a plantation economy where sugarcane, tobacco, cotton, coffee, rice, indigo, and lumber were grown by slaves. From the early 16th to late 19th cent., 10 million Africans were transported to **slavery** in the New World.

Netherlands. The urban, Calvinist N provinces of the Netherlands rebelled (1568) against Habsburg Spain and founded an oligarchic mercantile republic. Their control of the Baltic grain market enabled them to exploit Mediterranean food shortages. Religious refugees—French and Belgian Protestants, Iberian Jews—added to the commercial talent pool. After Spain absorbed Portugal (1580), the Dutch seized Portuguese possessions and created a vast but short-lived commercial empire in Brazil, the Antilles, Africa, India, Ceylon, Malacca, Indonesia, and Taiwan. The Dutch also challenged or supplanted Portuguese traders in China and Japan. Revolution in 1640 restored Portuguese independence.

England. Anglicanism became firmly established under **Elizabeth I** after a brief Catholic interlude under "Bloody Mary" (1553-58). But religious and political conflicts led to

a rebellion (1642) by Parliament. Forces of the Roundheads (Puritans) defeated the Cavaliers (Royalists); Charles I was beheaded (1649). The new Commonwealth was ruled as a military dictatorship by Oliver **Cromwell,** who also brutally crushed (1649-51) an Irish rebellion. Conflicts within the Puritan camp (democratic Levelers defeated, 1649) aided the Stuart restoration (1660), but Parliament was strengthened and the

Elizabeth I

peaceful **"Glorious Revolution"** (1688) advanced political and religious liberties (writings of **Locke,** 1632-1704). British privateers (Drake, 1540-96) challenged Spanish control of the New World and penetrated Asian trade routes (Madras taken, 1639). North American colonies (Jamestown, 1607; Plymouth, 1620) provided an outlet for religious dissenters from Europe.

France. Emerging from the religious civil wars in 1628, France regained military and commercial great power status (under the ministries of **Richelieu**, Mazarin, and Colbert). Under **Louis XIV** (reigned 1643-1715), royal absolutism triumphed over nobles and local *parlements* (defeat of Fronde, 1648-53). Permanent colonies were founded in Canada (1608), the Caribbean (1626), and India (1674).

Sweden. Sweden seceded from the Scandinavian Union in 1523. The thinly populated agrarian state (with copper, iron, and timber exports) was united by the Vasa kings, whose conquests by the mid-17th cent. made Sweden the dominant Baltic power. The empire collapsed in the Great Northern War (1700-21).

Poland. After the union with Lithuania in 1447, Poland ruled vast territories from the Baltic to the Black Sea, resisting German and Turkish incursions. Catholic nobles failed to gain the loyalty of their Orthodox Christian subjects in the E; commerce and trades were practiced by German and Jewish immigrants. The bloody 1648-49 Cossack uprising began the kingdom's dismemberment.

China. A new dynasty, the **Manchus,** invaded from the NE, seized power in 1644, and expanded Chinese control to its greatest extent in Central and SE Asia. Trade and diplomatic contact with Europe grew, carefully controlled by China. New crops (sweet potato, maize, peanut) allowed an economic and population growth (pop. 300 million, in 1800). Traditional arts and literature were pursued with increased sophistication (*Dream of the Red Chamber*, novel, mid-18th cent.).

Japan. Tokugawa Ieyasu, shogun from 1603, finally unified and pacified feudal Japan. Hereditary daimyos and samurai monopolized government office and the professions. An urban merchant class grew, literacy spread, and a cultural renaissance occurred (**haiku,** a verse innovation of the poet Basho, 1644-94). Fear of European domination led to persecution of Christian converts from 1597 and to stringent isolation from outside contact from 1640.

Philosophy, Industry, and Revolution: 1700-1800

Science and Reason. Greater faith in reason and empirical observation, espoused since the Renaissance (Francis Bacon, 1561-1626), was bolstered by scientific discoveries despite theological opposition (Galileo's retraction, 1633). René **Descartes** (1596-1650) used a rationalistic approach modeled on geometry and introspection to discover "self-evident" truths as a foundation of knowledge. Sir Isaac **Newton** emphasized induction from experimental observation. Baruch de **Spinoza** (1632-77), who called for political and intellectual freedom, developed a systematic rationalistic philosophy in his classic work *Ethics*.

French philosophers assumed leadership of the **Enlightenment** in the 18th cent. Montesquieu (1689-1755) used British history to support his notions of limited government. **Voltaire's** (1694-1778) diaries and novels of exotic travel

illustrated the intellectual trends toward secular ethics and relativism. Jean-Jacques **Rousseau's** (1712-1778) radical concepts of the **social contract** and of the inherent goodness of the common man gave impetus to antimonarchical republicanism. The *Encyclopedia* (1751-72, edited by Diderot and d'Alembert), designed as a monument to reason, was largely devoted to practical technology.

In England, ideals of liberty were connected with empiricist philosophy and science in the followers of John **Locke.** But British empiricism, especially as developed by the skeptical David **Hume** (1711-76), radically reduced the role of reason in philosophy, as did the evolutionary approach to law and politics of Edmund Burke (1729-97) and the utilitarian ethics of Jeremy Bentham (1748-1832). Adam Smith (1723-90) and other **physiocrats** called for a rationalization

of economic activity by removing artificial barriers to a supposedly natural free exchange of goods.

German writers participated in the new philosophical trends popularized by Christian von Wolff (1679-1754). Immanuel **Kant's** (1724-1804) transcendental idealism, unifying an empirical epistemology with a priori moral and logical concepts, directed German thought away from skepticism. Italian contributions included work on electricity (Galvani, 1737-98; Volta, 1745-1827), the pioneer historiography of Vico (1668-1744), and writings on penal reform (Beccaria, 1738-94). Benjamin Franklin (1706-90) was celebrated in Europe for his varied achievements.

The growth of the **press** (*Spectator*, 1711-12) and the wide distribution of realistic but sentimental **novels** attested to the increase of a large bourgeois public.

Arts. Rococo art, characterized by extravagant decorative effects, asymmetries copied from organic models, and artificial pastoral subjects, was favored by the continental aristocracy for most of the cent. (Watteau, 1684-1721) and had musical analogies in the ornamentalized polyphony of late Baroque. The **Neoclassical** art after 1750, associated with the new scientific archaeology, was more streamlined and was infused with the supposed moral and geometric rectitude of the Roman Republic (David, 1748-1825). In England, **town planning** on a grand scale began.

Industrial Revolution in England. Agricultural improvements, such as the sowing drill (1701) and livestock breeding, were implemented on the large fields provided by enclosure of common lands by private owners. Profits from agriculture and from colonial and foreign trade (1800 volume, £54 million) were channeled through hundreds of banks and the **Stock Exchange** (est 1773) into new industrial processes.

The Newcomen steam pump (1712) aided coal mining. Coal fueled the new efficient steam engines patented by James Watt in 1769, and coke-smelting produced cheap, sturdy iron for machinery by the 1730s. The **flying shuttle** (1733) and **spinning jenny** (c 1764) were used in the large new cotton textile factories, where women and children were much of the work force. Goods were transported cheaply over **canals** (2,000 mi; built 1760-1800).

American Revolution. The British colonies in North America attracted a mass immigration of religious dissenters and poor people throughout the 17th and 18th cent., coming from the British Isles, Germany, the Netherlands, and other countries. The population reached 3 million nonnatives by the 1770s. The small native population was greatly reduced by European diseases and by wars with and between the various colonies. British attempts to control colonial trade and to tax the colonists to pay for the costs of colonial administration and defense clashed with traditions of local self-government and eventually provoked the colonies to rebellion.

Central and East Europe. The monarchs of the three states that dominated E Europe—Austria, Prussia, and Russia—accepted the advice and legitimation of philosophes in creating modern, centralized institutions in their kingdoms, which were enlarged by the division (1772-95) of Poland.

Under **Frederick II** (called the Great) (r 1740-86) Prussia, with its efficient modern army, doubled in size. State monopolies and tariff protection fostered industry, and some legal reforms were introduced. Austria's heterogeneous realms were unified under **Maria Theresa** (r 1740-80) and **Joseph II** (r 1780-90). Reforms in education, law, and religion were enacted, and the Austrian serfs were freed (1781).

With its defeat in the Seven Years' War in 1763, Austria failed to regain Silesia, which had been seized by Prussia, but it was compensated by expansion to the E and S (Hungary, Slavonia, 1699; Galicia, 1772).

Russia, whose borders continued to expand, adopted some Western bureaucratic and economic policies under **Peter I** (r 1682-1725) and **Catherine II** (r 1762-96). Trade and cultural contacts with the West multiplied from the new Baltic Sea capital, **St. Petersburg** (est 1703).

French Revolution. The growing French middle class lacked political power and resented aristocratic tax privileges, especially in light of the successful American Revolution. Peasants lacked adequate land and were burdened with feudal obligations to nobles. War with Britain led to the loss of French Canada and drained the treasury, finally forcing the king to call the **Estates-General** in 1789 (first time since 1614), in an atmosphere of food riots (poor crop in 1788).

Aristocratic resistance to absolutism was soon overshadowed by the reformist Third Estate (middle class), which proclaimed itself the **National Constituent Assembly** June 17 and took the "Tennis Court oath" on June 20 to secure a constitution. The storming of the **Bastille** on July 14, 1789, by Parisian artisans was followed by looting and seizure of aristocratic property throughout France. Assembly reforms included abolition of class and regional privileges, a Declaration of Rights, suffrage by taxpayers (75% of males), and the **Civil Constitution of the Clergy** providing for election and loyalty oaths for priests. A republic was declared Sept. 22, 1792, in spite of royalist pressure from Austria and Prussia, which had declared war in April (joined by Britain the next year). Louis XVI was beheaded Jan. 21, 1793, and Queen Marie Antoinette was beheaded Oct. 16, 1793.

Royalist uprisings in La Vendée and military reverses led to institution of a **reign of terror** in which tens of thousands of opponents of the Revolution and criminals were executed. Radical reforms in the **Convention** period (Sept. 1793-Oct. 1795) included the abolition of colonial slavery, economic measures to aid the poor, support of public education, and a short-lived de-Christianization.

Division among radicals (execution of Hebert, Danton, and Robespierre, 1794) aided the ascendancy of a moderate **Directory**, which consolidated military victories. **Napoleon Bonaparte** (1769-1821), a popular young general, exploited political divisions and participated in a coup Nov. 9, 1799, making himself first consul (dictator).

Napoleon Bonaparte

India. Sikh and Hindu rebels (Rajputs, Marathas) and Afghans destroyed the power of the Mughals during the 18th cent. After France's defeat (1763) in the Seven Years' War, Britain was the primary European trade power in India. Its control of inland **Bengal and Bihar** was recognized (1765) by the Mughal shah, who granted the **British East India Co.** (under Clive, 1725-74) the right to collect land revenue there. Despite objections from Parliament (1784 India Act), the company's involvement in local wars and politics led to repeated acquisitions of new territory. The company exported Indian textiles, sugar, and indigo.

Change Gathers Steam: 1800-40

French ideals and empire spread. Inspired by the ideals of the French Revolution, and supported by the expanding French armies, new republican regimes arose near France: the **Batavian** Republic in the Netherlands (1795-1806), the **Helvetic** Republic in Switzerland (1798-1803), the **Cisalpine** Republic in N Italy (1797-1805), the **Ligurian** Republic in Genoa (1797-1805), and the **Parthenopean** Republic in S Italy (1799). A Roman Republic existed briefly in 1798 after Pope Pius VI was arrested by French troops. In Italy and Germany, new nationalist sentiments were stimulated both in imitation of and in reaction to developments in France (anti-French and anti-Jacobin peasant uprisings in Italy, 1796-99).

From 1804, when Napoleon declared himself emperor, to 1812, a succession of military victories (Austerlitz, 1805; Jena, 1806) extended his control over most of Europe, through puppet states (**Confederation of the Rhine** united W German states for the first time and **Grand Duchy of Warsaw** revived Polish national hopes), expansion of the empire, and alliances.

Among the lasting reforms initiated under Napoleon's absolutist reign were: establishment of the Bank of France, centralization of tax collection, codification of law along Roman models (Code Napoléon), and reform and extension of secondary and university education. In an 1801 concordat, the papacy recognized the effective autonomy of the French Catholic Church.

Napoleon's continental successes were offset by British victory under Adm. Horatio Nelson in the **Battle of Trafalgar** (1805).

In all, some 400,000 French soldiers were killed in the Napoleonic Wars, along with about 600,000 foreign troops.

Last gasp of old regime. The disastrous 1812 invasion of Russia exposed Napoleon's overextension. After Napoleon's 1814 exile at Elba, his armies were defeated (1815) at **Waterloo**, by British and Prussian troops.

At the **Congress of Vienna**, the monarchs and princes of Europe redrew their boundaries, to the advantage of Prussia (in Saxony and the Ruhr), Austria (in Illyria and Venetia), and Russia (in Poland and Finland). British conquest of Dutch and French colonies (S Africa, Ceylon, Mauritius) was recognized, and France, under the restored Bourbons, retained its expanded 1792 borders. The settlement brought 50 years of international peace to Europe.

But the Congress was unable to check the advance of liberal ideals and of nationalism among the smaller European nations. The 1825 **Decembrist uprising** by liberal officers in Russia was easily suppressed. But an independence movement in **Greece**, stirred by commercial prosperity and a cultural revival, succeeded in expelling Ottoman rule by 1831, with the aid of Britain, France, and Russia.

A constitutional monarchy was secured in France by the **1830 Revolution**; Louis Philippe became king. The revolutionary contagion spread to **Belgium**, which gained its independence (1830) from the Dutch monarchy, to **Poland**, whose rebellion was defeated (1830-31) by Russia, and to Germany.

Romanticism. A new style in intellectual and artistic life began to replace Neoclassicism and Rococo after the mid-18th cent. By the early 19th cent., this style, Romanticism, had prevailed in the European world.

Rousseau had begun the reaction against rationalism; in education (*Émile*, 1762) he stressed subjective spontaneity over regularized instruction. German writers (Lessing, 1729-81; Herder, 1744-1803) favorably compared the German folk song to classical forms and began a cult of Shakespeare, whose passion and "natural" wisdom was a model for the romantic *Sturm und Drang* (Storm and Stress) move-

ment. **Goethe's** *Sorrows of Young Werther* (1774) set the model for the tragic, passionate genius.

A new interest in **Gothic architecture** in England after 1760 (Walpole, 1717-97) spread through Europe, associated with an aesthetic Christian and mystic revival (**Blake**, 1757-1827). Celtic, Norse, and German mythology and folk tales were revived or imitated (Macpherson's Ossian translation, 1762; Grimm's Fairy Tales, 1812-22). The medieval revival (Scott's *Ivanhoe*, 1819) led to a new interest in history, stressing national differences and organic growth (**Carlyle**, 1795-1881; Michelet, 1798-1874), corresponding to theories of natural evolution (Lamarck's *Philosophie Zoologique*, 1809; Lyell's *Geology*, 1830-33). A reaction against classicism characterized the English **romantic poets** (beginning with **Wordsworth**, 1770-1850). Revolution and war fed an emphasis on freedom and conflict, expressed by both poets (**Byron**, 1788-1824; **Hugo**, 1802-85) and philosophers (**Hegel**, 1770-1831).

Wild gardens replaced the formal French variety, and painters favored rural, stormy, and mountainous landscapes (**Turner**, 1775-1851; **Constable**, 1776-1837). Clothing became freer, with wigs, hoops, and ruffles discarded. Originality and genius were expected in the life as well as the work of inspired artists (Murger's *Scenes from Bohemian Life*, 1847-49). Exotic locales and themes (as in Gothic horror stories) were used in art and literature (Delacroix, 1798-1863; **Poe**, 1809-49).

Music exhibited the new dramatic style and a breakdown of classical forms (**Beethoven**, 1770-1827). The use of folk melodies and modes aided the growth of distinct national traditions (Glinka in Russia, 1804-57).

Latin America. Francois **Toussaint L'Ouverture** led a successful slave revolt in Haiti, which subsequently became the first Latin American state to achieve independence (1804). The mainland Spanish colonies won their independence (1810-24), under such leaders as Simon **Bolivar** (1783-1830). Brazil became an independent empire (1822) under the Portuguese prince regent. A new class of military officers divided power with large landholders and the church.

United States. Heavy immigration and exploitation of ample natural resources fueled rapid economic growth. The spread of the franchise, public education, and antislavery sentiment were signs of a widespread democratic ethic.

China. Failure to keep pace with Western arms technology exposed China to greater European influence and hampered efforts to bar imports of opium, which had damaged Chinese society and drained wealth overseas. In the **Opium War** (1839-42), Britain forced China to expand trade opportunities and to cede Hong Kong.

Triumph of Progress: 1840-80

Charles Darwin

Idea of Progress. As a result of the cumulative scientific, economic, and political changes of the preceding eras, the idea took hold among literate people in the West that continuing growth and improvement was the usual state of human and natural life.

Charles **Darwin's** statement of the **theory of evolution** and survival of the fittest (*Origin of Species*, 1859), defended by intellectuals and scientists against theological objections, was taken as confirmation that progress was the natural direction of life. The controversy helped define popular ideas of the dedicated scientist and of science's increasing control

over the world (Foucault's demonstration of earth's rotation, 1851; **Pasteur's** germ theory, 1861).

Liberals following Ricardo (1772-1823) in their faith that unrestrained competition would bring continuous economic expansion sought to adjust political life to the new social realities and believed that unregulated competition of ideas would yield truth (**Mill,** 1806-73). In England, successive reform bills (1832, 1867, 1884) gave representation to the new industrial towns and extended the franchise to the middle and lower classes and to Catholics, Dissenters, and Jews. On both sides of the Atlantic, reformists tried to improve conditions for the mentally ill (**Dix,** 1802-87), women (Anthony, 1820-1906), and prisoners. Slavery was barred in the British Empire (1833), the U.S. (1865), and Brazil (1888).

Socialist theories based on ideas of human perfectibility or progress were widely disseminated. Utopian socialists such as Saint-Simon (1760-1825) envisaged an orderly, just society directed by a technocratic elite. A model factory

town, New Lanark, Scotland, was set up by utopian Robert Owen (1771-1858), and communal experiments were tried in the U.S. (most notably, Brook Farm, Mass., 1841-47). Bakunin's (1814-76) anarchism represented the opposite utopian extreme of total freedom. Karl **Marx** (1818-83) posited the inevitable triumph of socialism in industrial countries through a dialectical process of class conflict.

Spread of industry. The technical processes and managerial innovations of the English industrial revolution spread to Europe (especially Germany) and the U.S., an explosion of industrial production, demand for raw materials, and competition for markets. Inventors, both trained and self-educated, provided the means for larger-scale production (Bessemer steel, 1856; sewing machine, 1846). Many inventions were shown at the 1851 London Great Exhibition at the **Crystal Palace,** the theme of which was universal prosperity.

Local specialization and long-distance trade were aided by a revolution in transportation and communication. Railroads were first introduced in the 1820s in England and the U.S. More than 150,000 mi of track had been laid worldwide by 1880, with another 100,000 mi laid in the next decade. Steamships were improved (*Savannah* crossed Atlantic, 1819). The **telegraph**, perfected by 1844 (Morse), connected the Old and New Worlds by cable in 1866 and quickened the pace of international commerce and politics. The first commercial **telephone** exchange went into operation in the U.S. in 1878.

The new class of industrial workers, uprooted from their rural homes, lacked job security and suffered from dangerous overcrowded conditions at work and at home. Many responded by organizing **trade unions** (legalized in England, 1824; France, 1884). The U.S. Knights of Labor had 700,000 members by 1886. The First International (1864-76) tried to unite workers internationally around a Marxist program. The quasi-Socialist Paris Commune uprising (1871) was violently suppressed. Factory Acts to reduce child labor and regulate conditions were passed (1833-50 in England). Social security measures were introduced by the Bismarck regime (1883-89) in Germany.

Revolutions of 1848. Among the causes of the continent-wide revolutions were an international collapse of credit and resulting unemployment, bad harvests in 1845-47, and a cholera epidemic. The new urban proletariat and expanding bourgeoisie demanded a greater political role. Republics were proclaimed in France, Rome, and Venice. Nationalist feelings reached fever pitch in the Habsburg empire, as Hungary declared independence under Kossuth, as a Slav Congress demanded equality, and as Piedmont tried to drive Austria from Lombardy. A national liberal assembly at Frankfurt called for German unification.

But riots fueled bourgeois fears of socialism (**Marx and Engels**, *Communist Manifesto*, 1848), and peasants remained conservative. The old establishment—the Papacy, the Habsburgs with the help of the Czarist Russian army — was able to rout the revolutionaries by 1849. The French Republic succumbed to a renewed monarchy by 1852 (Emperor Napoleon III).

Great nations unified. Using the "blood and iron" tactics of Bismarck from 1862, Prussia controlled N Germany by 1867 (war with Denmark, 1864; Austria, 1866). After de-

feating France in 1870 (annexation of Alsace-Lorraine), it won the allegiance of S German states. A new **German Empire** was proclaimed (1871). **Italy**, inspired by Giuseppe Mazzini (1805-72) and Giuseppe Garibaldi (1807-82), was unified by the reformed Piedmont kingdom through uprisings, plebiscites, and war.

The **U.S.**, its area expanded after the 1846-48 Mexican War, defeated (1861-65) a secession attempt by slave states. in the **Civil War.** Canadian provinces were united in an autonomous **Dominion of Canada** (1867). Control in **India** was removed from the East India Co. and centralized under British administration after the 1857-58 Sepoy rebellion, laying the groundwork for the modern Indian State. Queen Victoria was named Empress of India (1876).

Europe dominates Asia. The Ottoman Empire began to collapse in the face of Balkan nationalisms and European imperial incursions in N Africa (**Suez Canal**, 1869). The Turks had lost control of most of both regions by 1882. Russia completed its expansion S by 1884 (despite the temporary setback of the **Crimean War** with Turkey, Britain, and France, 1853-56), taking Turkestan, all the Caucasus, and Chinese areas in the E and sponsoring Balkan Slavs against the Turks. A succession of reformist and reactionary regimes presided over a slow modernization (serfs freed, 1861). Persian independence suffered as Russia and British India competed for influence.

China was forced to sign a series of unequal treaties with European powers and Japan. Overpopulation and an inefficient dynasty brought misery and caused rebellions (Taiping, Muslims) leaving tens of millions dead. **Japan** was forced by the U.S. (Commodore Perry's visits, 1853-54) and Europe to end its isolation. The Meiji restoration (1868) gave power to a Westernizing oligarchy. Intensified empire-building gave Burma to Britain (1824-85) and Indochina to France (1862-95). Christian missionary activity followed imperial and trade expansion in Asia.

Respectability. The fine arts were expected to reflect and encourage the good morals and manners among the Victorians. Prudery, exaggerated delicacy, and familial piety were heralded by **Bowdler's** expurgated edition (1818) of Shakespeare. Government-supported mass education sought to inculcate a work ethic as a means to escape poverty (**Horatio Alger,** 1832-99).

The official **Beaux Arts** school in Paris set an international style of imposing public buildings (Paris Opera, 1861-74; Vienna Opera, 1861-69) and uplifting statues (Bartholdi's Statue of Liberty, 1884). Realist painting, influenced by photography (Daguerre, 1837), appealed to a new mass audience with social or historical narrative (Wilkie, 1785-1841; Poynter, 1836-1919) or with serious religious, moral, or social messages (pre-Raphaelites, Millet's *Angelus*, 1858) often drawn from ordinary life. The Impressionists (Monet, 1840-1926; Pissarro, 1830-1903; Renoir, 1841-1919) rejected the formalism, sentimentality, and precise techniques of academic art in favor of a spontaneous, undetailed rendering of the world through careful representation of the effect of natural light on objects.

Realistic **novelists** presented the full panorama of social classes and personalities, but retained sentimentality and moral judgment (**Dickens,** 1812-70; **Eliot,** 1819-80; **Tolstoy,** 1828-1910; **Balzac,** 1799-1850).

Veneer of Stability: 1880-1900

Imperialism triumphant. The vast **African** interior, visited by European explorers (Barth, 1821-65; Livingstone, 1813-73), was conquered by the European powers in rapid, competitive thrusts from their coastal bases after 1880, mostly for domestic political and international strategic reasons. W African Muslim kingdoms (Fulani), Arab slave traders (Zanzibar), and Bantu military confederations (Zulu) were alike subdued. Only Christian Ethiopia (defeat of Italy, 1896) and Liberia resisted successfully. France (W Africa) and Britain ("Cape to Cairo," **Boer War,** 1899-1902) were the major beneficiaries. The ideology of "the white man's burden" (Kipling, *Barrack Room Ballads*, 1892) or of a "civilizing mission" (France) justified the conquests.

W European foreign capital investment soared to nearly $40 billion by 1914, but most was in E Europe (France, Germany), the Americas (Britain), and the Europeans' colonies. The foundation of the modern interdependent world economy was laid, with cartels dominating raw material trade.

An industrious world. Industrial and technological proficiency characterized the 2 new great powers—Germany and the U.S. Coal and iron deposits enabled Germany to reach 2nd or 3rd place status in iron, steel, and shipbuilding by the 1900s. German electrical and chemical industries were world leaders. The U.S. post-Civil War boom (interrupted by "panics"—1884, 1893, 1896) was shaped by massive immigration from S and E Europe from 1880, government sub-

sidy of railroads, and huge private monopolies (Standard Oil, 1870; U.S. Steel, 1901). The **Spanish-American War**, 1898 (Philippine Insurrection, 1899-1902), and the **Open Door policy** in China (1899) made the U.S. a world power.

England led in **urbanization**, with **London** the world capital of finance, insurance, and shipping. Sewer systems (Paris, 1850s), electric subways (London, 1890), parks, and bargain department stores helped improve living standards for most of the urban population of the industrial world.

Hyde Park, London

Westernization of Asia. Asian reaction to European economic, military, and religious incursions took the form of imitation of Western techniques and adoption of Western ideas of progress and freedom. The Chinese "self-strengthening" movement of the 1860s and 1870s included rail, port, and arsenal improvements and metal and textile mills. Reformers such as **K'ang Yu-wei** (1858-1927) won liberalizing reforms in 1898, right after the European and Japanese "scramble for concessions."

A universal education system in Japan and importation of foreign industrial, scientific, and military experts aided Japan's unprecedented rapid modernization after 1868, under the authoritarian Meiji regime. Japan's victory in the **Sino-Japanese War** (1894-95) put Formosa and Korea in its power.

In India, the British alliance with the remaining princely states masked reform sentiment among the Westernized urban elite; higher education had been conducted largely in English

for 50 years. The **Indian National Congress**, founded in 1885, demanded a larger government role for Indians.

***Fin-de-siècle* sophistication. Naturalist** writers pushed realism to its extreme limits, adopting a quasi-scientific attitude and writing about formerly taboo subjects such as sex, crime, extreme poverty, and corruption (Flaubert, 1821-80; Zola, 1840-1902; Hardy, 1840-1928). Unseen or repressed psychological motivations were explored in the clinical and theoretical works of Sigmund **Freud** (1856-1939) and in works of fiction (**Dostoyevsky,** 1821-81; James, 1843-1916; Schnitzler, 1862-1931; others).

A contempt for bourgeois life or a desire to shock a complacent audience was shared by the French **symbolist** poets (Verlaine, 1844-96; Rimbaud, 1854-91), by neopagan English writers (Swinburne, 1837-1909), by continental dramatists (**Ibsen,** 1828-1906), and by satirists (**Wilde,** 1854-1900). The German philosopher Friedrich **Nietzsche** (1844-1900) was influential in his elitism and pessimism.

Postimpressionist art neglected long-cherished conventions of representation (Cézanne, 1839-1906) and showed a willingness to learn from primitive and non-European art (Gauguin, 1848-1903; Japanese prints).

Racism. Gobineau (1816-82) gave a pseudobiological foundation to modern racist theories, which spread in Europe in the latter 19th cent., along with **Social Darwinism,** the belief that societies are and should be organized as a struggle for survival of the fittest. The medieval period was interpreted as an era of natural Germanic rule (Chamberlain, 1855-1927), and notions of racial superiority were associated with German national aspirations (Treitschke, 1834-96). **Anti-Semitism**, with a new racist rationale, became a significant political force in Germany (Anti-Semitic Petition, 1880), Austria (Lueger, 1844-1910), and France (**Dreyfus case**, 1894-1906).

Last Respite: 1900-9

Alliances. While the peace of Europe (and its dependencies) continued to hold (1907 **Hague Conference** extended the rules of war and international arbitration procedures), imperial rivalries, protectionist trade practices (in Germany and France), and the escalating arms race (British *Dreadnought* battleship launched; Germany widens Kiel canal, 1906) exacerbated minor disputes (German-French Moroccan "crises," 1905, 1911).

Security was sought through alliances: **Triple Alliance** (Germany, Austria-Hungary, Italy; renewed in 1902 and 1907); Anglo-Japanese Alliance (1902), Franco-Russian Alliance (1899), **Entente Cordiale** (Britain, France, 1904), Anglo-Russian Treaty (1907), German-Ottoman friendship.

Ottomans decline. The inefficient, corrupt Ottoman government was unable to resist further loss of territory. Nearly all European lands were lost in 1912 to Serbia, Greece, Montenegro, and Bulgaria. Italy took Libya and the Dodecanese islands the same year, and Britain took Kuwait (1899) and the Sinai (1906). The **Young Turk** revolution in 1908 forced the sultan to restore a constitution, and it introduced some social reform, industrialization, and secularization.

British Empire. British trade and cultural influence remained dominant in the empire, but constitutional reforms presaged its eventual dissolution: The colonies of **Australia** were united in 1901 under a self-governing commonwealth. **New Zealand** acquired dominion status in 1907. The old Boer republics joined Cape Colony and Natal in the self-governing **Union of South Africa** in 1910.

The 1909 Indian Councils Act enhanced the role of elected province legislatures in **India**. The Muslim League (founded 1906) sought separate communal representation.

East Asia. Japan exploited its growing industrial power to expand its empire. Victory in the 1904-5 war against Russia (naval battle of Tsushima, 1905) assured Japan's domination of **Korea** (annexed 1910) and Manchuria (Port Arthur taken, 1905).

In China, central authority began to crumble (empress died, 1908). Reforms (Confucian exam system ended 1905, modernization of the army, building of railroads) were inadequate, and secret societies of reformers and nationalists, in-

spired by the Westernized **Sun Yat-sen** (1866-1925) fomented periodic uprisings in the S.

Siam, whose independence had been guaranteed by Britain and France in 1896, was split into spheres of influence by those countries in 1907.

Russia. The population of the Russian Empire approached 150 million in 1900. Reforms in education, in law, and in local institutions (*zemstvos*) and an industrial boom starting in the 1880s (oil, railroads) created the beginnings of a modern state, despite the autocratic tsarist regime. Liberals (1903 Union of Liberation), Socialists (Social Democrats founded 1898, Bolsheviks split off 1903), and populists (Social Revolutionaries founded 1901) were periodically repressed, and national minorities were persecuted (anti-Jewish pogroms, 1903, 1905-6).

An industrial crisis after 1900 and harvest failures aggravated poverty among urban workers, and the 1904-5 defeat by Japan (which checked Russia's Asian expansion) sparked **the Revolution of 1905-6**. A **Duma** (parliament) was created, and an agricultural reform (under Stolypin, prime minister 1906-11) created a large class of land-owning peasants (kulaks).

1903 Wright Flyer

The world shrinks. Developments in transportation and communication and mass population movements helped create an awareness of an interdependent world. Early **automobiles** (Daimler, Benz, 1885) were experimental or were designed as luxuries. Assembly-line mass production (Ford Motor Co., 1903) made the invention practicable, and by 1910 nearly 500,000 motor vehicles were registered in the U.S. alone. **Heavier-than-air flights** began in 1903 in the U.S. (Wright brothers' *Flyer*), preceded by glider, balloon, and model plane advances in several countries. Trade was

advanced by improvements in **ship design** (gyrocompass, 1910), speed (*Lusitania* crossed Atlantic in 5 days, 1907), and reach (Panama Canal begun, 1904).

The first transatlantic **radio** telegraphic transmission occurred in 1901, 6 years after Marconi discovered radio. Radio transmission of human speech had been made in 1900. Telegraphic transmission of photos was achieved in 1904, lending immediacy to news reports. **Phonographs**, popularized by Caruso's recordings (starting 1902), made for quick international spread of musical styles (ragtime). **Motion pictures**, perfected in the 1890s (Dickson, Lumière brothers), became a popular and artistic medium after 1900; newsreels appeared in 1909.

Emigration from crowded European centers soared in the decade: 9 million migrated to the U.S., and millions more went to Siberia, Canada, Argentina, Australia, South Africa, and Algeria. Some 70 million Europeans emigrated in the cent. before 1914. Several million Chinese, Indians, and Japanese migrated to SE Asia, where their urban skills often enabled them to take a predominant economic role.

Social reform. The social and economic problems of the poor were kept in the public eye by realist fiction writers (Dreiser's *Sister Carrie*, 1900; Gorky's *Lower Depths*, 1902; Sinclair's *The Jungle*, 1906), journalists (U.S. **muckrakers**—Steffens, Tarbell), and artists (Ashcan school). Frequent labor strikes and occasional assassinations by anarchists or radicals (Empress Elizabeth of Austria, 1898; King Umberto I of Italy, 1900; U.S. Pres. McKinley, 1901; Russian Interior Minister Plehve, 1904; Portugal's King Carlos, 1908) added to social tension and fear of revolution.

But democratic reformism prevailed. In Germany, Bernstein's (1850-1932) **revisionist Marxism**, downgrading revolution, was accepted by the powerful Social Democrats and trade unions. The British Fabian Society (the Webbs, Shaw) and the Labour Party (founded 1906) worked for reforms such as Social Security and union rights (1906), while woman suffragists grew more militant. U.S. **progressives** fought big business (Pure Food and Drug Act, 1906). In France, the 10-hour work day (1904) and separation of church and state (1905) were reform victories, as was universal suffrage in Austria (1907).

Arts. An unprecedented period of experimentation, centered in France, produced several new **painting** styles: Fauvism exploited bold color areas (Matisse, *Woman With Hat*, 1905); expressionism reflected powerful inner emotions (the Brücke group, 1905); cubism combined several views of an object on one flat surface (Picasso's *Demoiselles*, 1906-7); futurism tried to depict speed and motion (Italian Futurist Manifesto, 1910). **Architects** explored new uses of steel structures, with facades either neoclassical (Adler and Sullivan in U.S.); curvilinear Art Nouveau (Gaudi's Casa Mila, 1905-10); or functionally streamlined (Wright's Robie House, 1909).

Music and dance shared the experimental spirit. Ruth St. Denis (1877-1968) and Isadora Duncan (1878-1927) pioneered modern dance, while Sergei Diaghilev in Paris revitalized classic ballet from 1909. Composers explored atonal music (Debussy, 1862-1918) and dissonance (Schoenberg, 1874-1951) or revolutionized classical forms (Stravinsky, 1882-1971), often showing jazz or folk music influences.

War and Revolution: 1910-19

War threatens. Germany under Wilhelm II sought a political and imperial role consonant with its industrial strength, challenging Britain's world supremacy and threatening France, which was still resenting the loss (1871) of Alsace-Lorraine. Austria wanted to curb an expanded Serbia (after 1912) and the threat it posed to its own Slav lands. Russia feared Austrian and German political and economic aims in the Balkans and Turkey.

An accelerated arms race resulted from these circumstances. The German standing army rose to more than 2 million men by 1914. Russia and France had more than a million each, and Austria and the British Empire nearly a million each. Dozens of enormous battleships were built by the powers after 1906.

The **assassination of Austrian Archduke Franz Ferdinand** by a Serbian, June 28, 1914, was the pretext for war. The system of alliances made the conflict Europe-wide; Germany's invasion of Belgium to outflank France forced Britain to enter the war. Patriotic fervor was nearly unanimous among all classes in most countries.

World War I. German forces were stopped in France in one month. The rival armies dug **trench networks**. Artillery and improved machine guns prevented either side from any lasting advance despite repeated assaults (600,000 dead at **Verdun**, Feb.-July 1916). Poison gas, used by Germany in 1915, proved ineffective. The entrance of more than 1 million U.S. troops tipped the balance after mid-1917, forcing Germany to sue for peace the next year. The formal armistice was signed on Nov. 11, 1918.

In the E, the Russian armies were thrown back (battle of **Tannenberg**, Aug. 20, 1914), and the war grew unpopular in Russia. An allied attempt to relieve Russia through Turkey failed (**Gallipoli**, 1915). The **Russian Revolution** (1917) abolished the monarchy. The new Bolshevik regime signed the capitulatory Brest-Litovsk peace in March 1918. Italy entered the war on the allied side in May 1915 but was pushed back by Oct. 1917. A renewed offensive with Allied aid in Oct.-Nov. 1918 forced Austria to surrender.

The British Navy successfully blockaded Germany, which responded with submarine U-boat attacks; **unrestricted submarine warfare** against neutrals after Jan. 1917 helped bring the U.S. into the war. Other battlefields included Palestine and Mesopotamia, both of which Britain wrested from the Turks in 1917, and the African and Pacific colonies of Germany, most of which fell to Britain, France, Australia, Japan, and South Africa.

Settlement. At the **Paris Peace Conference** (Jan.-June 1919), concluded by the **Treaty of Versailles**, and in subsequent negotiations and local wars (Russian-Polish War, 1920), the map of Europe was redrawn with a nod to U.S. Pres. Woodrow Wilson's principle of self-determination. Austria and Hungary were separated, and much of their land was given to Yugoslavia (formerly Serbia), Romania, Italy, and the newly independent Poland and Czechoslovakia. Germany lost territory in the W, N, and E, while Finland and the Baltic states were detached from Russia. Turkey lost nearly all its Arab lands to British-sponsored Arab states or to direct French and British rule. Belgium's sovereignty was recognized.

From 1916, the civilian populations and economies of both sides were mobilized to an unprecedented degree. Hardships intensified among fighting nations in 1917 (French mutiny crushed in May). More than 10 million soldiers died in the war.

A huge **reparations** burden and partial demilitarization were imposed on Germany. Pres. Wilson obtained approval for a League of Nations, but the U.S. Senate refused to allow the U.S. to join.

Russian revolution. Military defeats and high casualties caused a contagious lack of confidence in Tsar Nicholas, who was forced to abdicate Mar. 1917. A liberal provisional government failed to end the war, and massive desertions, riots, and fighting between factions followed. A moderate socialist government under Aleksandr Kerensky was overthrown (Nov. 1917) in a violent coup by the **Bolsheviks** in Petrograd under **Lenin,** who later disbanded the elected Constituent Assembly.

Vladimir Lenin

The Bolsheviks brutally suppressed all opposition and ended the war with Germany in Mar. 1918. **Civil war** broke out in the summer between the Red Army, including the Bolsheviks and their supporters, and monarchists, anarchists, nationalities (Ukrainians, Georgians, Poles), and oth-

ers. Small U.S., British, French, and Japanese units also opposed the Bolsheviks (1918-19; Japan in Vladivostok to 1922). The civil war, anarchy, and pogroms devastated the country until the 1920 Red Army victory. The Communist Party leadership retained absolute power.

Other European revolutions. An unpopular monarchy in **Portugal** was overthrown in 1910. The new republic took severe anticlerical measures in 1911.

After a century of Home Rule agitation, during which **Ireland** was devastated by famine (1 million dead, 1846-47) and emigration, republican militants staged an unsuccessful uprising in Dublin during **Easter 1916**. The execution of the leaders and mass arrests by the British won popular support for the rebels. The **Irish Free State,** comprising all but the 6 N counties, achieved dominion status in 1922.

In the aftermath of the world war, radical revolutions were attempted in Germany (**Spartacist** uprising, Jan. 1919), **Hungary** (Kun regime, 1919), and elsewhere. All were suppressed or failed for lack of support.

Chinese revolution. The Manchu Dynasty was overthrown and a republic proclaimed in Oct. 1911. First Pres. Sun Yat-sen resigned in favor of strongman Yuan Shih-k'ai. Sun organized the parliamentarian **Kuomintang** party.

Students launched protests on May 4, 1919, against League of Nations concessions in China to Japan. Nationalist, liberal, and socialist ideas and political groups spread. The **Communist Party** was founded in 1921. A Communist regime took power in Mongolia with Soviet support in 1921.

India restive. Indian objections to British rule erupted in nationalist riots as well as in the nonviolent tactics of Mahatma **Gandhi** (1869-1948). Nearly 400 unarmed demonstrators were shot at **Amritsar** in Apr. 1919. Britain approved limited self-rule that year.

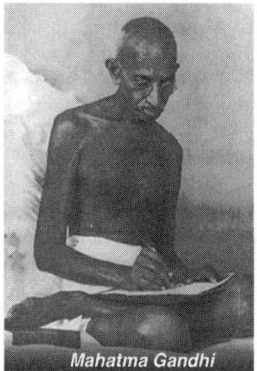
Mahatma Gandhi

Mexican revolution. Under the long Diaz dictatorship (1877-1911) the economy advanced, but Indian and mestizo lands were confiscated, and concessions to foreigners (mostly U.S.) damaged the middle class. A **revolution in 1910** led to civil wars and U.S. intervention (1914, 1916-17). Land reform and a more democratic constitution (1917) were achieved.

The Aftermath of War: 1920-29

U.S. Easy credit, technological ingenuity, and war-related industrial decline in Europe caused a long economic boom, in which ownership of the new products—**autos, phones, radios**—became democratized. Prosperity, an increase in women workers, woman suffrage (1920), and drastic change in fashion (flappers, mannish bob for women, clean-shaven men) created a wide perception of social change, despite prohibition of alcoholic beverages (1919-33). Union membership and strikes increased. Fear of radicals led to Palmer raids (1919-20) and the Sacco/Vanzetti case (1921-27).

Europe sorts itself out. Germany's liberal **Weimar constitution** (1919) could not guarantee a stable government in the face of rightist violence (Rathenau assassinated, 1922) and Communist refusal to cooperate with Socialists. Reparations and Allied occupation of the Rhineland caused staggering inflation that destroyed middle-class savings, but economic expansion resumed after mid-decade, aided by U.S. loans. A sophisticated, **innovative culture** developed in architecture and design (Bauhaus, 1919-28), film (Lang, *M*, 1931), painting (Grosz), music (Weill, *Threepenny Opera*, 1928), theater (Brecht, *A Man's a Man*, 1926), criticism (Benjamin), philosophy (Jung), and fashion. This culture was considered decadent and socially disruptive by rightists.

England elected its first Labour governments (Jan. 1924, June 1929). A 10-day general strike in support of coal miners failed in May 1926. In **Italy**, strikes, political chaos, and violence by small Fascist bands culminated in the Oct. 1922 Fascist March on Rome, which established **Mussolini's** dictatorship. Strikes were outlawed (1926), and Italian influence was pressed in the Balkans (Albania a protectorate, 1926). A conservative dictatorship was also established in **Portugal** in a 1926 military coup.

Czechoslovakia, the only stable democracy to emerge from the war in Central or East Europe, faced opposition from Germans (in the Sudetenland), Ruthenians, and some Slovaks. As the industrial heartland of the old Habsburg empire, it remained fairly prosperous. With French backing, it formed the Little Entente with Yugoslavia (1920) and **Romania** (1921) to block Austrian or Hungarian irredentism. Croats and Slovenes in **Yugoslavia** demanded a federal state until King Alexander I proclaimed (1929) a royal dictatorship. Poland faced nationality problems as well (Germans, Ukrainians, Jews); Pilsudski ruled as dictator from 1926. The Baltic states were threatened by traditionally dominant ethnic Germans and by Soviet-supported Communists.

An economic collapse and famine in **Russia** (1921-22) claimed 5 million lives. The New Economic Policy (1921) allowed land ownership by peasants and some private commerce and industry. **Stalin** was absolute ruler within 4 years of Lenin's death (1924). He inaugurated a brutal collectivization program (1929-32) and used foreign Communist parties for Soviet state advantage.

Internationalism. Revulsion against World War I led to pacifist agitation, to the Kellogg-Briand Pact renouncing aggressive war (1928), and to **naval disarmament** pacts (Washington, 1922; London, 1930). But the League of Nations was able to arbitrate only minor disputes (Greece-Bulgaria, 1925).

Middle East. Mustafa Kemal (**Ataturk**) led **Turkish** nationalists in resisting Italian, French, and Greek military advances (1919-23). The sultanate was abolished (1922), and elaborate reforms were passed, including secularization of law and adoption of the Latin alphabet. Ethnic conflict led to persecution of **Armenians** (more than 1 million dead in 1915, 1 million expelled), Greeks (forced Greek-Turk population exchange, 1923), and Kurds (1925 uprising).

With evacuation of the Turks from **Arab** lands, the puritanical Wahabi dynasty of E Arabia conquered (1919-25) what is now Saudi Arabia. British, French, and Arab dynastic and nationalist maneuvering resulted in the creation of 2 more Arab monarchies in 1921—Iraq and Transjordan (both under British control)—and 2 French mandates—Syria and Lebanon. Jewish immigration into British-mandated **Palestine**, inspired by the Zionist movement, was resisted by Arabs, at times violently (1921, 1929 massacres).

Reza Khan ruled **Persia** after his 1921 coup (shah from 1925), centralized control, and created the trappings of a modern secular state.

In 1922, English archaeologist Howard Carter discovered the **tomb** of the boy pharaoh **Tutankhamen** in the Valley of the Kings in Egypt.

China. The Kuomintang under **Chiang Kai-shek** (1887-1975) subdued the warlords by 1928. The Communists were brutally suppressed after their alliance with the Kuomintang was broken in 1927. Relative peace thereafter allowed for industrial and financial improvements, with some Russian, British, and U.S. cooperation.

Arts. Nearly all bounds of subject matter, style, and attitude were broken in the arts of the period. **Abstract** art first took inspiration from natural forms or narrative themes (Kandinsky from 1911) and then worked free of any representational aims (Malevich's suprematism, 1915-19; Mondrian's geometric style from 1917). The **Dada** movement (from 1916) mocked artistic pretension with absurd collages and constructions (Arp, Tzara, from 1916). Paradox, illusion, and psychological taboos were exploited by **surrealists** by the latter 1920s (Dali, Magritte). Architectural schools celebrated industrial values, whether vigorous abstract constructivism (Tatlin, *Monument to 3rd International*, 1919) or the ma-

chined, streamlined **Bauhaus** style, which was extended to many design fields (Helvetica typeface).

Prose writers explored revolutionary narrative modes related to dreams (Kafka's *Trial*, 1925), internal monologue (Joyce's *Ulysses*, 1922), and word play (Stein's *Making of Americans*, 1925). Poets and novelists wrote of modern alienation (Eliot's *Waste Land*, 1922) and aimlessness (Lost Generation).

Sciences. Scientific specialization prevailed by the 20th cent. Advances in knowledge and technological aptitude increased with the geometric rise in the number of practitioners. Physicists challenged common-sense views of causality, observation, and a mechanistic universe, putting science further beyond popular grasp (**Einstein's** general theory of relativity, 1916; Bohr's quantum mechanics, 1913; Heisenberg's uncertainty principle, 1927).

Rise of Totalitarians: 1930-39

Depression. A worldwide financial panic and economic depression began with the Oct. 1929 U.S. stock market crash and the May 1931 failure of the Austrian Credit-Anstalt. A credit crunch caused international bankruptcies and **unemployment**: 12 million jobless by 1932 in the U.S., 5.6 million in Germany, 2.7 million in England. Governments responded with **tariff restrictions** (Smoot-Hawley Act, 1930; Ottawa Imperial Conference, 1932), which dried up world trade. Government public works programs were vitiated by deflationary budget balancing.

Germany. Years of agitation by violent extremists were brought to a head by the Depression. Nazi leader Adolf Hitler was named chancellor in Jan. 1933 and given dictatorial power by the Reichstag in March. Opposition parties were

Mussolini & Hitler

disbanded, strikes banned, and all aspects of economic, cultural, and religious life were brought under central government and Nazi party control and manipulated by sophisticated propaganda. Severe persecution of Jews began (**Nuremberg Laws,** Sept. 1935). Many Jews, political opponents, and others were sent to concentration camps (Dachau, 1933), where thousands died or were killed. Public works, renewed conscription (1935), arms production, and a 4-year plan (1936) all but ended unemployment.

Hitler's expansionism started with reincorporation of the Saar (1935), occupation of the **Rhineland** (Mar. 1936), and annexation of Austria (Mar. 1938). At **Munich** (Sept. 1938) an indecisive Britain and France sanctioned German dismemberment of Czechoslovakia.

Russia. Urbanization and education advanced. Rapid industrialization was achieved through successive **5-year plans** starting in 1928, using severe labor discipline and mass forced labor. Industry was financed by a decline in living standards and exploitation of agriculture, which was almost totally collectivized by the early 1930s (*kolkhoz*, collective farm; *sovkhoz*, state farm, often in newly worked lands). Successive **purges** increased the role of professionals and management at the expense of workers. Millions perished in a series of manufactured disasters: extermination (1929-34) of kulaks (peasant landowners), severe famine (1932-33), party purges and show trials (Great Purge, 1936-38), suppression of nationalities, and poor conditions in labor camps.

Spain. An industrial revolution during World War I created an urban proletariat, which was attracted to socialism and anarchism; Catalan nationalists challenged central authority. The 5 years after King Alfonso left Spain in Apr. 1931 were dominated by tension between intermittent leftist and anticlerical governments and clericals, monarchists, and other rightists. Anarchist and Communist rebellions were crushed, but a July 1936 extreme right rebellion led by Gen. Francisco **Franco** and aided by Nazi Germany and Fascist

Italy succeeded, after a 3-year **civil war** (more than 1 million dead in battles and atrocities). The war polarized international public opinion.

Italy. Despite propaganda for the ideal of the Corporate State, few domestic reforms were attempted. An entente with Hungary and Austria (Mar. 1934), a pact with Germany and Japan (Nov. 1937), and intervention by 50,000-75,000 troops in Spain (1936-39) sealed Italy's identification with the fascist bloc (anti-Semitic laws after Mar. 1938). Ethiopia was conquered (1935-36), and Albania annexed (Jan. 1939) in conscious imitation of ancient Rome.

East Europe. Repressive regimes fought for power against an active opposition (liberals, socialists, Communists, peasants, Nazis). Minority groups and Jews were restricted within national boundaries that did not coincide with ethnic population patterns. In the destruction of **Czechoslovakia**, Hungary occupied S Slovakia (Nov. 1938) and Ruthenia (Mar. 1939), and a pro-Nazi regime took power in the rest of Slovakia. Other boundary disputes (e.g., Poland-Lithuania, Yugoslavia-Bulgaria, and Romania-Hungary) doomed attempts to build joint fronts against Germany or Russia. Economic depression was severe.

East Asia. After a period of liberalism in **Japan**, nativist militarists dominated the government with peasant support. Manchuria was seized (Sept. 1931-Feb. 1932), and a puppet state was set up (Manchukuo). Adjacent Jehol (Inner Mongolia) was occupied in 1933. China proper was invaded in July 1937; large areas were conquered by Oct. 1938. Hundreds of thousands of rapes, murders, and other atrocities were attributed to the Japanese.

In **China** Communist forces left Kuomintang-besieged strongholds in the S in a Long March (1934-35) to the N. The Kuomintang-Communist civil war was suspended in Jan. 1937 in the face of threatening Japan.

The democracies. The Roosevelt Administration, in office Mar. 1933, embarked on an extensive program of **New Deal** social reform and economic stimulation, including protection for labor unions (heavy industries organized), Social Security, public works, wage-and-hour laws, and assistance to farmers. Isolationist sentiment (1937 Neutrality Act) prevented U.S. intervention in Europe, but military expenditures were increased in 1939.

French political instability and polarization prevented resolution of economic and international security questions. The **Popular Front** government under Leon Blum (June 1936-Apr. 1938) passed social reforms (40-hr week) and raised arms spending. National coalition governments, which ruled Britain from Aug. 1931, brought economic recovery but failed to define a consistent international policy until Chamberlain's government (from May 1937), which practiced **appeasement** of Germany and Italy.

India. Twenty years of agitation for autonomy and then for independence (Gandhi's **salt march**, 1930) achieved some constitutional reform (extended provincial powers, 1935) despite Muslim-Hindu strife. Social issues assumed prominence with peasant uprisings (1921), strikes (1928), Gandhi's efforts for untouchables (1932 "fast unto death"), and social and agrarian reform by the provinces after 1937.

WORLD ALMANAC QUICK QUIZ

Which of the following did not take place in the 1980s?

(a) Ayatollah Khomeini came to power in Iran
(b) Leonid Brezhnev died
(c) François Mitterrand became president of France
(d) Margaret Thatcher won a 3rd term as prime minister of Great Britain

For the answer look in this chapter, or see page 1008.

War, Hot and Cold: 1940-49

Arts. The streamlined, geometric design motifs of Art Deco (from 1925) prevailed through the 1930s. **Abstract art** flourished (Moore sculptures from 1931) alongside a new **realism** related to social and political concerns (Socialist Realism, the official Soviet style from 1934; Mexican muralist Rivera, 1886-1957; and Orozco, 1883-1949), which were also expressed in fiction and poetry (Steinbeck's *Grapes of Wrath*, 1939; Sandburg's *The People, Yes*, 1936). Modern architecture (International Style, 1932) was unchallenged in its use of artificial materials (concrete, glass), lack of decoration, and monumentality (Rockefeller Center, 1929-40). U.S.-made films captured a worldwide audience with their larger-than-life fantasies *(Gone With the Wind, The Wizard of Oz,* both 1939).

War in Europe. The Nazi-Soviet nonaggression pact (Aug. 1939) freed Germany to attack Poland (Sept.). Britain and France, which had guaranteed Polish independence, declared war on Germany. Russia seized E Poland (Sept.), attacked Finland (Nov.), and took the Baltic states (July 1940). Mobile German forces staged *blitzkrieg* attacks during Apr.-June 1940, conquering neutral Denmark, Norway, and the Low Countries and defeating France; 350,000 British and French troops were evacuated at **Dunkirk** (May). The **Battle of Britain** (June-Dec. 1940) denied Germany air superiority. German-Italian campaigns won the Balkans by Apr. 1941. Three million Axis troops **invaded Russia** in June 1941, marching through Ukraine to the Caucasus, and through White Russia and the Baltic republics to Moscow and Leningrad.

Russian winter counterthrusts (1941-42 and 1942-43) stopped the German advance (**Stalingrad,** Sept. 1942-Feb. 1943). With British and U.S. Lend-Lease aid and sustaining great casualties, the Russians drove the Axis from all E Europe and the Balkans in the next 2 years. Invasions of N Africa (Nov. 1942), Italy (Sept. 1943), and **Normandy** (launched on D-Day, June 6, 1944) brought U.S., British, Free French, and allied troops to Germany by spring 1945. In Feb. 1945, the 3 Allied leaders, Winston **Churchill** (Britain), Joseph **Stalin** (USSR), and Franklin D. Roosevelt (U.S.), met in Yalta to discuss strategy and resolve political issues, including the postwar Allied occupation of Germany. Germany surrendered May 7, 1945.

Pearl Harbor

War in Asia-Pacific. Japan occupied Indochina in Sept. 1940, dominated Thailand in Dec. 1941, and attacked Hawaii (**Pearl Harbor**), the Philippines, Hong Kong, and Malaya on Dec. 7, 1941 (precipitating U.S. entrance into the war). Indonesia was attacked in Jan. 1942, and Burma was conquered in Mar. 1942. The Battle of **Midway** (June 1942) turned back the Japanese advance. "Island-hopping" battles (**Guadalcanal,** Aug. 1942-Jan. 1943; **Leyte Gulf,** Oct. 1944; **Iwo Jima,** Feb.-Mar. 1945; **Okinawa,** Apr. 1945) and massive bombing raids on Japan from June 1944 wore out Japanese defenses. U.S. atom bombs, dropped Aug. 6 and 9 on **Hiroshima** and Nagasaki, forced Japan to agree, on Aug. 14, to surrender; formal surrender was on Sept. 2, 1945.

Atrocities. The war brought 20th-cent. cruelty to its peak. The Nazi regime systematically killed an estimated 5-6 million Jews, including some 3 million who died in death camps (e.g., **Auschwitz**). Gypsies, political opponents, sick and retarded people, and others deemed undesirable were also murdered by the Nazis, as were vast numbers of Slavs, especially leaders.

Civilian deaths. German bombs killed 70,000 British civilians. More than 100,000 Chinese civilians were killed by Japanese forces in the capture and occupation of Nanking.

Severe retaliation by the Soviet army, E European partisans, Free French, and others took a heavy toll. U.S. and British bombing of Germany killed hundreds of thousands, as did U.S. bombing of Japan (80,000-200,000 at Hiroshima alone). Some 45 million people lost their lives in the war.

Settlement. The **United Nations** charter was signed in San Francisco on June 26, 1945, by 50 nations. The International Tribunal at **Nuremberg** convicted 22 German leaders for war crimes in Sept. 1946; 23 Japanese leaders were convicted in Nov. 1948. Postwar border changes included large gains in territory for the USSR, losses for Germany, a shift to the W in Polish borders, and minor losses for Italy. Communist regimes, supported by Soviet troops, took power in most of E Europe, including Soviet-occupied Germany (GDR proclaimed Oct. 1949). Japan lost all overseas lands.

Recovery. Basic political and social changes were imposed on Japan and W Germany by the western allies (Japan constitution adopted, Nov. 1946; W German basic law, May 1949). U.S. **Marshall Plan** aid ($12 billion, 1947-51) spurred W European economic recovery after a period of severe inflation and strikes in Europe and the U.S. The British Labour Party introduced a national health service and nationalized basic industries in 1946.

Cold War. Western fears of further Soviet advances (Cominform formed in Oct. 1947; Czechoslovakia coup, Feb. 1948; Berlin blockade, Apr. 1948-Sept. 1949) led to the formation of **NATO**. Civil War in Greece and Soviet pressure on Turkey led to U.S. aid under the **Truman Doctrine** (Mar. 1947). Other anti-Communist security pacts were the Organization of American States (Apr. 1948) and the SE Asia Treaty Organization (Sept. 1954). A new wave of **Soviet purges** and repression intensified in the last years of Stalin's rule, extending to E Europe (Slansky trial in Czechoslovakia, 1951). Only Yugoslavia resisted Soviet control (expelled by Cominform, June 1948; U.S. aid, June 1949).

China, Korea. Communist forces emerged from World War II strengthened by the Soviet takeover of industrial Manchuria. In 4 years of fighting, the Kuomintang was driven from the mainland; the People's Republic was proclaimed Oct. 1, 1949. Korea was divided by USSR and U.S. occupation forces. Separate republics were proclaimed in the 2 zones in Aug.-Sept. 1948.

India. India and Pakistan became independent dominions on Aug. 15, 1947. Millions of Hindu and Muslim refugees were created by the partition; riots (1946-47) took hundreds of thousands of lives; Mahatma **Gandhi** was assassinated in Jan. 1948. Burma became completely independent in Jan. 1948; Ceylon took dominion status in Feb.

Middle East. The UN approved partition of Palestine into Jewish and Arab states. **Israel** was proclaimed a state, May 14, 1948. Arabs rejected partition, but failed to defeat Israel in war (May 1948-July 1949). Immigration from Europe and the Middle East swelled Israel's Jewish population. British and French forces left Lebanon and Syria in 1946. Transjordan occupied most of Arab Palestine.

Southeast Asia. Communists and others fought against restoration of French rule in Indochina from 1946; a non-Communist government was recognized by France in Mar. 1949, but fighting continued. Both Indonesia and the Philippines became independent; the former in 1949 after 4 years of war with Netherlands, the latter in 1946. Philippine economic and military ties with the U.S. remained strong; a Communist-led peasant rising was checked in 1948.

Arts. New York became the center of the world art market; **abstract expressionism** was the chief mode (Pollock from 1943, de Kooning from 1947). Literature and philosophy explored **existentialism** (Camus's *The Stranger*, 1942; Sartre's *Being and Nothingness*, 1943). Non-Western attempts to revive or create regional styles (Senghor's Négritude, Mishima's novels) only confirmed the emergence of a universal culture. Radio and phonograph records spread American popular music (swing, bebop) around the world.

The American Decade: 1950-59

Polite decolonization. The peaceful decline of European political and military power in Asia and Africa accelerated in the 1950s. Nearly all of **N Africa** was freed by 1956, but France fought a bitter war to retain Algeria, with its large European minority, until 1962. **Ghana**, independent in 1957, led a parade of new black African nations (more than 2 dozen by 1962), which altered the political character of the UN. Ethnic disputes often exploded in the new nations after decolonization (UN troops in Cyprus, 1964; **Nigerian civil war**, 1967-70). Leaders of the new states, mostly sharing socialist ideologies, tried to create an Afro-Asian bloc (Bandung Conference, 1955), but Western economic influence and U.S. political ties remained strong (Baghdad Pact, 1955).

Trade. World trade volume soared, in an atmosphere of monetary stability assured by international accords (**Bretton Woods,** 1944). In Europe, economic integration advanced (**European Economic Community,** 1957; European Free Trade Association, 1960). Comecon (1949) coordinated the economies of Soviet-bloc countries.

U.S. Economic growth produced an abundance of consumer goods (9.3 million motor vehicles sold, 1955). Suburban housing tracts changed life patterns for middle and working classes (Levittown, 1947-51). Pres. Dwight **Eisenhower's** landslide election victories (1952, 1956) reflected consensus politics. Senate condemnation of Senator Joseph **McCarthy** (Dec. 1954) curbed the political abuse of anti-Communism. A system of alliances and military bases bolstered U.S. influence on all continents. Trade and payments surpluses were balanced by overseas investments and foreign aid ($50 billion, 1950-59).

USSR. In the "thaw" after Stalin's death in 1953, relations with the West improved (evacuation of Vienna, Geneva summit conference, both 1955). Repression of scientific and cultural life eased, and many prisoners were freed or rehabilitated culminating in **de-Stalinization** (1956). **Nikita Khrushchev's** leadership aimed at consumer sector growth, but farm production lagged, despite the virgin lands program (from 1954). Soviet crushing of the 1956 Hungarian revolution, the 1960 U-2 spy plane episode, and other incidents renewed East-West tension and domestic curbs.

East Europe. Resentment of Russian domination and Stalinist repression combined with nationalist, economic, and religious factors to produce periodic violence. E Berlin workers rioted (1953), Polish workers rioted in Poznan (June 1956), and a broad-based **revolution** broke out in **Hungary** (Oct. 1956). All were suppressed by Soviet force or threats (at least 7,000 dead in Hungary). But Poland was allowed to restore private ownership of farms, and a degree of personal and economic freedom returned to Hungary. Yugoslavia experimented with worker self-management and a market economy.

Korea. The 1945 division of Korea along the 38th parallel left industry in the N, which was organized into a militant regime and armed by the USSR. The S was politically disunited. More than 60,000 N Korean troops invaded the S on June 25, 1950. The U.S., backed by the UN Security Council, sent troops. UN troops reached the Chinese border in Nov. Some 200,000 Chinese troops crossed the Yalu R. and drove back UN forces. By spring 1951 battle lines had become stabilized near the original 38th parallel border, but heavy fighting continued. Finally, an armistice was signed on July 27, 1953. U.S. troops remained in the S, and U.S. economic and military aid continued. The war stimulated rapid economic recovery in Japan.

China. Starting in 1952, industry, agriculture, and social institutions were forcibly collectivized. In a massive purge, as many as several million people were executed as Kuomintang supporters or as class and political enemies. The **Great Leap Forward** (1958-60) unsuccessfully tried to force the pace of development by substituting labor for investment.

Indochina. Ho Chi Minh's forces, aided by the USSR and the new Chinese Communist government, fought French and pro-French Vietnamese forces to a standstill and captured the strategic **Dienbienphu** camp in May 1954. The Geneva Agreements divided Vietnam in half pending elections (never held) and recognized Laos and Cambodia as independent. The U.S. aided the anti-Communist Republic of Vietnam in the S.

Middle East. Arab revolutions placed leftist, militantly nationalist regimes in power in Egypt (1952) and Iraq (1958). But Arab unity attempts failed (United Arab Republic joined Egypt, Syria, Yemen, 1958-61). Arab refusal to recognize Israel (Arab League economic blockade began Sept. 1951) led to a permanent state of war, with repeated incidents (Gaza, 1955). Israel occupied Sinai, and Britain and France took (Oct. 1956) the Suez Canal, but were replaced by the UN Emergency Force. The Mossadegh government in Iran nationalized (May 1951) the British-owned oil industry in May, but was overthrown (Aug. 1953) in a U.S.-aided coup.

Latin America. Argentinian dictator Juan **Perón,** in office 1946, enforced land reform, some nationalization, welfare state measures, and curbs on the Roman Catholic Church, and crushed opposition. A Sept. 1955 coup deposed Perón. The 1952 revolution in Bolivia brought land reform, nationalization of tin mines, and improvement in the status of Indians, who nevertheless remained poor. The Batista regime in Cuba was overthrown (Jan. 1959) by Fidel **Castro,** who imposed a Communist dictatorship, aligned Cuba with the USSR, but improved education and health care. A U.S.-backed anti-Castro invasion (**Bay of Pigs**, Apr. 1961) was crushed. Self-government advanced in the British Caribbean.

Technology. Large outlays on research and development in the U.S. and the USSR focused on military applications (H-bomb in U.S., 1952; USSR, 1953; Britain, 1957; intercontinental missiles, late 1950s). Soviet launching of the **Sputnik** satellite (Oct. 4, 1957) spurred increases in U.S. science education funds (National Defense Education Act).

Literature and film. Alienation from social and literary conventions reached an extreme in the theater of the absurd (Beckett's *Waiting for Godot,* 1952), the "new novel" (Robbe-Grillet's *Voyeur,* 1955), and avant-garde film (Antonioni's *L'Avventura,* 1960). U.S. beatniks (Kerouac's *On the Road,* 1957) and others rejected the supposed conformism of Americans (Riesman's *The Lonely Crowd,* 1950).

Rising Expectations: 1960-69

Economic boom. The longest sustained economic boom on record spanned almost the entire decade in the capitalist world; the closely watched GNP figure doubled (1960-70) in the U.S., fueled by Vietnam War–related budget deficits. The **General Agreement on Tariffs and Trade** (1967) stimulated W European prosperity, which spread to peripheral areas (Spain, Italy, E Germany). Japan became a top economic power. Foreign investment aided the industrialization of Brazil. There were limited Soviet economic reform attempts.

Reform and radicalization. Pres. John F. **Kennedy,** inaugurated 1961, emphasized youthful idealism and vigor; his assassination Nov. 22, 1963, was a national trauma. A series of political and social reform movements took root in the U.S., later spreading to other countries. Blacks demonstrated nonviolently and with partial success against segregation and poverty (1963 March on Washington; 1964 **Civil Rights Act**), but some urban ghettos erupted in extensive riots (Watts, 1965; Detroit, 1967; **Martin Luther King** assassination, Apr. 4, 1968). New concern for the poor (Harrington's *Other America,* 1963) helped lead to Pres. Lyndon Johnson's **"Great Society"** programs (Medicare, Water Quality Act, Higher Education Act, all 1965). Concern with the **environment** surged (Carson's *Silent Spring,* 1962).

Feminism revived as a cultural and political movement (Friedan's *Feminine Mystique,* 1963; National Organization for Women founded 1966), and a movement for homosexual

rights emerged (Stonewall riot in NYC, 1969). Pope John XXIII called the **Second Vatican Council** (1962-65), which liberalized Roman Catholic liturgy and some other aspects of Catholicism.

Opposition to U.S. involvement in Vietnam, especially among university students (**Moratorium** protest, Nov. 1969), turned violent (Weatherman Chicago riots, Oct. 1969). **New Left** and Marxist theories became popular, and membership in radical groups (Students for a Democratic Society, Black Panthers) increased. Maoist groups, especially in Europe, called for total transformation of society. In France, students sparked a nationwide strike affecting 10 million workers in May-June 1968, but an electoral reaction barred revolutionary change.

China. China's revolutionary militancy under **Mao** Zedong caused disputes with the USSR under "revisionist"

Mao Zedong

Khrushchev, starting in 1960. The 2 powers exchanged fire in 1969 border disputes. China used force to capture (1962) areas disputed with India. The **"Great Proletarian Cultural Revolution"** tried to impose a utopian egalitarian program in China and spread revolution abroad; political struggle, often violent, convulsed China in 1965-68.

Indochina. Communist-led guerrillas aided by N Vietnam fought from 1960 against the S Vietnam government of Ngo Dinh Diem (killed 1963). The U.S. military role increased after the 1964 **Tonkin Gulf** incident. U.S. forces peaked at 543,400 in Apr. 1969. Massive numbers of N Vietnamese troops also fought. Laotian and Cambodian neutrality were threatened by Communist insurgencies, with N Vietnamese aid, and U.S. intrigues.

Third World. A bloc of authoritarian leftist regimes among the newly independent nations emerged in political opposition to the U.S.-led Western alliance and came to dominate the conference of nonaligned nations (Belgrade, 1961; Cairo, 1964; Lusaka, 1970). Soviet political ties and military bases were established in Cuba, Egypt, Algeria, Guinea, and other countries whose leaders were regarded as revolutionary heroes by opposition groups in pro-Western or colonial countries. Some leaders were ousted in coups by pro-Western groups—Zaire's Patrice Lumumba (killed 1961), Ghana's Kwame Nkrumah (exiled 1966), and Indo-

nesia's Sukarno (effectively ousted in 1965 after a Communist coup failed).

Middle East. Arab-Israeli tension erupted into a brief war June 1967. Israel emerged from the war as a major regional power. Military shipments before and after the war brought much of the Arab world into the Soviet political sphere. Most Arab states broke U.S. diplomatic ties, while Communist countries cut their ties to Israel. Intra-Arab disputes continued: Egypt and Saudi Arabia supported rival factions in a bloody Yemen civil war 1962-70; Lebanese troops fought Palestinian commandos 1969.

East Europe. To stop the large-scale exodus of citizens, E German authorities built (Aug. 1961) a **fortified wall across Berlin**. Soviet sway in the Balkans was weakened by Albania's support of China (USSR broke ties in Dec. 1961) and Romania's assertion (1964) of industrial and foreign policy autonomy. Liberalization (spring 1968) in Czechoslovakia was crushed with massive force by troops of 5 Warsaw Pact countries. W German treaties (1970) with the USSR and Poland facilitated the transfer of German technology and confirmed postwar boundaries.

Arts and styles. The boundary between fine and popular arts was blurred to some extent by Pop Art (Warhol) and rock musicals (*Hair*, 1968). Informality and exaggeration prevailed in fashion (beards, miniskirts). A nonpolitical "counterculture" developed, rejecting traditional bourgeois life goals and personal habits, and

Buzz Aldrin on Moon, 1969

use of marijuana and hallucinogens spread (**Woodstock** festival, Aug. 1969). Indian influence was felt in religion (Ram Dass) and fashion, and The **Beatles,** who brought unprecedented sophistication to rock music, became for many a symbol of the decade.

Science. Achievements in space (**humans on the moon,** July 1969) and electronics (lasers, integrated circuits) encouraged a faith in scientific solutions to problems in agriculture ("green revolution"), medicine (heart transplants, 1967), and other areas. Harmful technology, it was believed, could be controlled (1963 nuclear weapon test ban treaty, 1968 nonproliferation treaty).

Disillusionment: 1970-79

U.S.: Caution and neoconservatism. A relatively sluggish economy, energy shortages, and environmental problems contributed to a **"limits of growth"** philosophy. Suspicion of science and technology killed or delayed major projects (supersonic transport dropped, 1971; Seabrook nuclear power plant protests, 1977-78) and was fed by the Three Mile Island nuclear reactor accident (Mar. 1979).

There were signs of growing mistrust of big government and less support for new social policies. School busing and racial quotas were opposed (Bakke decision, June 1978); the proposed Equal Rights Amendment for women languished; civil rights legislation aimed at protecting homosexuals was opposed (Dade County referendum, June 1977).

Completion of Communist forces' takeover of **South Vietnam** (evacuation of U.S. civilians, Apr. 1975), revelations of Central Intelligence Agency misdeeds (Rockefeller Commission report, June 1975), and **Watergate** scandals (Nixon resigned in Aug. 1974) reduced faith in U.S. moral and material capacity to influence world affairs. Revelations of Soviet crimes (Solzhenitsyn's *Gulag Archipelago,* 1974) and Soviet intervention in Africa helped foster a revival of anti-Communist sentiment.

Economy sluggish. The 1960s boom faltered in the 1970s; a severe recession in the U.S. and Europe (1974-75) followed a huge oil price hike (Dec. 1973). Monetary instability (U.S. cut ties to gold in Aug. 1971), the decline of the dollar, and protectionist moves by industrial countries (1977-78) threatened trade. Business investment and spend-

ing for research declined. Severe inflation plagued many countries (25% in Britain, 1975; 18% in U.S., 1979).

China picks up pieces. After the 1976 deaths of Mao Zedong and Zhou Enlai, struggle for the leadership succession was won by pragmatists. A nationwide purge of orthodox Maoists was carried out, and the **Gang of Four,** led by Mao's widow, Chiang Ching, arrested. The new leaders freed more than 100,000 political prisoners and reduced public adulation of Mao. Political and trade ties were expanded with Japan, Europe, and the U.S. in the late 1970s, as relations worsened with the USSR, Cuba, and Vietnam (4-week invasion by China, 1979). Ideological guidelines in industry, science, education, and the armed forces, which the ruling faction said had caused chaos and decline, were reversed (bonuses to workers, Dec. 1977; exams for college entrance, Oct. 1977). Severe restrictions on cultural expression were eased.

Europe. European unity moves (EEC-EFTA trade accord, 1972) faltered as economic problems appeared (Britain floated pound, 1972; France floated franc, 1974). Germany and Switzerland curbed guest workers from southern Europe. Greece and Turkey quarreled over Cyprus and Aegean oil rights.

All non-Communist Europe was under democratic rule after free elections were held (June 1976) in **Spain** 7 months after the death of Franco. The conservative, colonialist regime in **Portugal** was overthrown in Apr. 1974. In **Greece** the 7-year-old military dictatorship yielded power in 1974. Northern Europe, though ruled mostly by Socialists (**Swed-**

ish Socialists unseated in 1976 after 44 years in power), turned more conservative. The **British** Labour government imposed (1975) wage curbs and suspended nationalization schemes. Terrorism in **Germany** (1972 Munich Olympics killings) led to laws curbing some civil liberties. **French** "new philosophers" rejected leftist ideologies, and the shaky Socialist-Communist coalition lost a 1978 election bid.

Religion and politics. The improvement in **Muslim** countries' political fortunes by the 1950s (with the exception of Central Asia under Soviet and Chinese rule) and the growth of Arab oil wealth were followed by a resurgence of traditional religious fervor. Libyan dictator Muammar al-Qaddafi mixed Islamic laws with socialism and called for Muslim return to Spain and Sicily. The illegal Muslim Brotherhood in **Egypt** was accused of violence, while extreme groups bombed (1977) theaters to protest Western and secular values.

In **Turkey**, the National Salvation Party was the first Islamic group to share (1974) power since secularization in the 1920s. In **Iran, Ayatollah Ruhollah Khomeini,** led a revolution that deposed the secular shah (Jan. 1979) and created an Islamic republic there. Religiously motivated Muslims took part in an insurrection in Saudi Arabia that briefly seized (1979) the Grand Mosque in Mecca. Muslim puritan opposition to **Pakistan** Pres. Zulfikar Ali-Bhutto helped lead to his overthrow in July 1977. Muslim solidarity, however, could not prevent Pakistan's eastern province (**Bangladesh**) from declaring (Dec. 1971) independence after a bloody civil war.

Muslim and Hindu resentment of coerced sterilization in **India** helped defeat the Gandhi government, which was replaced (Mar. 1977) by a coalition including religious Hindu parties. Muslims in the S **Philippines**, aided by Libya, rebelled against central rule from 1973.

The Buddhist Soka Gakkai movement launched (1964) the Komeito party in **Japan,** which became a major opposition party in 1972 and 1976 elections.

Evangelical Protestant groups grew in the U.S. A revival of interest in Orthodox Christianity occurred among **Russian** intellectuals (Solzhenitsyn). The secularist **Israeli** Labor party, after decades of rule, was ousted in 1977 by conservatives led by Menachem Begin; religious militants founded settlements on the disputed West Bank, part of biblically promised Israel. U.S. Reform Judaism revived many previously discarded traditional practices.

Old-fashioned religious wars raged intermittently in **Northern Ireland** (Catholic vs. Protestant, 1969-) and **Lebanon** (Christian vs. Muslim, 1975-), while religious militancy complicated the Israel-Arab dispute (1973 Israel-Arab war). Despite a 1979 **peace treaty between Egypt and Israel,** increased militancy on the West Bank impeded further progress.

Latin America. Repressive conservative regimes strengthened their hold on most of the continent, with a violent coup against the elected (Sept. 1973) Allende government in **Chile**, a 1976 military coup in **Argentina**, and coups against reformist regimes in **Bolivia** (1971, 1979) and **Peru** (1976). In Central America increasing liberal and leftist militancy led to the ouster (1979) of the Somoza regime of **Nicaragua** and to civil conflict in **El Salvador**.

Indochina. Communist victories in Vietnam, Cambodia, and Laos by May 1975 led to new turmoil. The **Pol Pot regime** ordered millions of city-dwellers to resettle in rural areas, in a program of forced labor, combined with terrorism, that cost more than 1 million lives (1975-79) and caused hundreds of thousands of ethnic Chinese and others to flee Vietnam ("boat people," 1979). The Vietnamese invasion of Cambodia swelled the refugee population and contributed to widespread starvation in that devastated country.

Russian expansion. Soviet influence, checked in some countries (troops ousted by Egypt, 1972), was projected farther afield, often with the use of Cuban troops (Angola, 1975-89; Ethiopia, 1977-88) and aided by a growing navy, a merchant fleet, and international banking ability. **Détente** with the West—1972 Berlin pact, 1972 strategic arms pact (**SALT**)—gave way to a more antagonistic relationship in the late 1970s, exacerbated by the Soviet invasion (1979) of **Afghanistan.**

Africa. The last remaining European colonies were granted independence (**Spanish Sahara**, 1976; **Djibouti,** 1977) and, after 10 years of civil war and many negotiation sessions, a black government took over (1979) in Zimbabwe (Rhodesia); white domination remained in **South Africa**. Great power involvement in local wars (Russia in **Angola, Ethiopia**; France in **Chad, Zaire, Mauritania**) and the use of tens of thousands of Cuban troops were denounced by some African leaders. Ethnic or tribal clashes made Africa a locus of sustained warfare during the late 1970s.

Arts. Traditional modes of painting, architecture, and music received increased popular and critical attention in the 1970s. These more conservative styles coexisted with modernist works in an atmosphere of increased variety and tolerance.

Revitalization of Capitalism, Demand for Democracy: 1980-89

USSR, Eastern Europe. A troublesome 1980-85 for the USSR was followed by 5 years of astonishing change: the surrender of the Communist monopoly, the remaking of the Soviet state, and the beginning of the disintegration of the Soviet empire. After the deaths of Leonid **Brezhnev** (1982) and 2 successors (Andropov in 1984 and Chernenko in 1985), the harsh treatment of dissent and restriction of emigration, and the Soviet invasion (Dec. 1979) of Afghanistan, Gen. Sec. Mikhail **Gorbachev** (in office 1985-1991) promoted *glasnost* and *perestroika*—economic, political, and social reform. Supported by the Communist Party (July 1988), he signed (Dec. 1987) the INF disarmament treaty, and he pledged (1988) to cut the military budget. Military withdrawal from Afghanistan was completed in Feb. 1989, the process of democratization went ahead unhindered in Poland and Hungary, and the Soviet people chose (Mar. 1989) part of the new Congress of People's Deputies from competing candidates. By decade's end the **Cold War** appeared to be fading away.

In **Poland, Solidarity,** the labor union founded (1980) by Lech **Walesa,** was outlawed in 1982 and then legalized in 1988, after years of unrest. Poland's first free election since the Communist takeover brought Solidarity victory (June 1989); Tadeusz Mazowiecki, a Walesa adviser, became (Aug. 1989) prime minister in a government with the Communists. In the fall of 1989 the failure of Marxist economies in **Hungary, East Germany, Czechoslovakia, Bulgaria,** and **Romania** brought the collapse of the Communist monopoly and a demand for democracy. In a historic step, the **Berlin Wall** was opened in Nov. 1989.

U.S. "The Reagan Years" (1981-88) brought the **longest economic boom** yet in U.S. history via budget and tax cuts, deregulation, "junk bond" financing, leveraged buyouts, and mergers and takeovers. However, there was a stock market crash (Oct. 1987), and federal budget deficits and the trade deficit increased. Foreign policy showed a **strong anti-Communist stance**, via increased defense spending, aid to anti-Communists in Central America, invasion of Cuba-threatened Grenada, and championing of the MX missile system and "Star Wars" missile defense program. Four Reagan-Gorbachev summits (1985-88) climaxed in the INF treaty (1987), as the Cold War began to wind down. The Iran-contra affair (North's TV testimony, July 1987) was a major political scandal. Homelessness and drug abuse (especially "crack" cocaine) were growing social problems. In 1988, Vice Pres. George Bush was elected to succeed Ronald Reagan as president.

Middle East. The Middle East remained militarily unstable, with sharp divisions along economic, political, racial, and religious lines. In **Iran,** the Islamic revolution of 1979 created a strong anti-U.S. stance (hostage crisis, Nov. 1979-Jan. 1981). In Sept. 1980, **Iraq** repudiated its border agreement with Iran and began major hostilities that led to an 8-year war in which millions were killed.

Libya's support for international terrorism induced the U.S. to close (May 1981) its diplomatic mission there and embargo (Mar. 1982) Libyan oil. The U.S. accused Libyan leader Muammar al-Qaddafi of aiding (Dec. 1985) terrorists in Rome and of Vienna airport attacks, and retaliated by bombing Libya (Apr. 1986).

Israel affirmed (July 1980) all Jerusalem as its capital, destroyed (1981) an Iraqi atomic reactor, and invaded (1982) Lebanon, forcing the PLO to agree to withdraw. A **Palestinian uprising**, including women and children hurling rocks and bottles at troops, began (Dec. 1987) in Israeli-occupied Gaza and spread to the West Bank; troops responded with force, killing 300 by the end of 1988, with 6,000 more in detention camps.

Israeli withdrawal from **Lebanon** began in Feb. 1985 and ended in June 1985, as Lebanon continued torn by military and political conflict. Artillery duels (Mar.-Apr. 1989) between Christian East Beirut and Muslim West Beirut left 200 dead and 700 wounded. At decade's end, violence still dominated.

Latin America. In **Nicaragua**, the leftist Sandinista National Liberation Front, in power after the 1979 civil war, faced problems as a result of Nicaragua's military aid to leftist guerrillas in El Salvador and U.S. backing of antigovernment contras. The U.S. CIA admitted (1984) having directed the mining of Nicaraguan ports, and the U.S. sent humanitarian (1985) and military (1986) aid. Profits from secret arms sales to Iran were found (1987) diverted to contras. Cease-fire talks between the Sandinista government and contras came in 1988, and elections were held in Nicaragua in Feb. 1990.

In **El Salvador**, a military coup (Oct. 1979) failed to halt extreme right-wing violence and left-wing terrorism. Archbishop Oscar Romero was assassinated in Mar. 1980; from Jan. to June some 4,000 civilians reportedly were killed in the civil unrest. In 1984, newly elected Pres. José Napoleon Duarte worked to stem human rights abuses, but violence continued.

In **Chile**, Gen. Augusto Pinochet yielded the presidency after a democratic election (Dec. 1989), but remained as head of the army. He had ruled the country since 1973, imposing harsh measures against leftists and dissidents; at the same time he introduced economic programs that restored prosperity to Chile.

Africa. 1980-85 marked a rapid decline in the economies of virtually all African countries, a result of accelerating desertification, the world economic recession, heavy indebtedness to overseas creditors, rapid population growth, and political instability. Some 60 million Africans faced prolonged hunger in 1981; much of Africa had one of the worst droughts ever in 1983, and by year's end **150 million faced near-famine**. "Live Aid," a marathon rock concert, was presented in July 1985, and the U.S. and Western nations sent aid in Sept. 1985. Economic hardship fueled political unrest and coups. Wars in Ethiopia and Sudan and military strife in several other nations continued. AIDS took a heavy toll.

South Africa. Anti-apartheid sentiment gathered force in South Africa as demonstrations and violent police response grew. White voters approved (Nov. 1983) the first constitution to give Coloureds and Asians a voice, while still excluding blacks (70% of the population). The U.S. imposed economic sanctions in Aug. 1985, and 11 Western nations followed in September. P. W. **Botha**, 1980s president, was succeeded by F. W. **de Klerk**, in Sept. 1989, who promised "evolutionary" change via negotiation with the black population.

China. During the 1980s the Communist government and paramount leader **Deng Xiaoping** pursued **far-reaching changes**, expanding commercial and technical ties to the industrialized world and increasing the role of market forces in stimulating urban development. Apr. 1989 brought new demands for political reforms; student demonstrators camped out in Tiananmen Square, Beijing, in a massive peaceful protest. Some 100,000 students and workers marched, and at least 20 other cities saw protests. In response, martial law was imposed; army troops crushed the demonstration in and around Tiananmen Square on June 3-4, with death toll estimates at 500-7,000, up to 10,000 dissidents arrested, 31 people tried and executed. The conciliatory Communist Party chief was ousted; the Politburo adopted (July) reforms against official corruption.

Japan. Japan's relations with other nations, especially the U.S., were dominated by **trade imbalances favoring Japan**. In 1985 the U.S. trade deficit with Japan was $49.7 billion, one-third of the total U.S. trade deficit. After Japan was found (Apr. 1986) to sell semiconductors and computer memory chips below cost, the U.S. was assured a "fair share" of the market, but charged (Mar. 1987) Japan with failing to live up to the agreement.

European Community. With the addition of Greece, Portugal, and Spain, the EC became a common market of more than **300 million people**, the West's largest trading entity. Margaret **Thatcher** became the first British prime minister in the 20th century to win a 3rd consecutive term (1987). France elected (1981) its first socialist president, François **Mitterrand**, who was reelected in 1988. Italy elected (1983) its first socialist premier, Bettino **Craxi**.

International terrorism. With the 1979 overthrow of the shah of Iran, terrorism became a prominent tactic. It increased through the 1980s, but with fewer high-profile attacks after 1985. In 1979-81, Iranian militants held 52 U.S. hostages in Iran for 444 days; in 1983 a TNT-laden suicide terrorist blew up U.S. Marine headquarters in Beirut, killing 241 Americans, and a truck bomb blew up a French paratroop barracks, killing 58. The *Achille Lauro* cruise ship was hijacked in 1986, and an American passenger killed; the U.S. subsequently intercepted the Egyptian plane flying the terrorists to safety. Incidents rose to 700 in 1985, and to 1,000 in 1988. **Assassinated leaders** included Egypt's Pres. Anwar al-**Sadat** (1981), India's Prime Min. Indira **Gandhi** (1984), and Lebanese Premier Rashid **Karami** (1987).

Post–Cold War World: 1990-99

Soviet Empire breakup. The world community witnessed the extraordinary spectacle of a superpower's disintegration when the **Soviet Union** broke apart into 15 independent states. The 1980s had already seen internal reforms and a decline of Communist power both within the Soviet Union and in Eastern Europe. The Soviet breakup began in earnest with the declarations of independence adopted by the Baltic republics of **Lithuania, Latvia,** and **Estonia** during an abortive coup against reformist leader Mikhail **Gorbachev** (Aug. 1991). The other republics soon took the same step. In Dec. 1991, **Russia, Ukraine, and Belarus** declared the Soviet Union dead; Gorbachev resigned, and the Soviet Parliament went out of existence. The Warsaw Pact and the Council for Mutual Economic Assistance (Comecon) were disbanded. Most of the former republics joined in a loose confederation called the **Commonwealth of Independent States**. **Russia** remained the predominant country after the breakup, but its people soon suffered severe economic hardship as the nation, under Pres. Boris **Yeltsin,** moved to revamp the economy and to adopt a free market system. In Oct. 1993, **anti-Yeltsin forces** occupied the Parliament building and were ousted by the army; about 140 people died in the fighting.

The Muslim republic of **Chechnya** declared independence from the rest of Russia, but this was met with an invasion by Russian troops (Dec. 1994). After almost 21 months of vicious fighting, a cease-fire took hold in 1996, and the Russians withdrew. In 1999 Russia forcibly suppressed Muslim insurgents in Dagestan and entered neighboring Chechnya, again fighting to gain control over separatist rebels there. Yeltsin resigned office Dec. 31, 1999, to be replaced by Vladimir **Putin** (elected in his own right, Mar. 2000).

Europe. Yugoslavia broke apart, and hostilities ensued among the republics along ethnic and religious lines. **Croatia, Slovenia,** and **Macedonia** declared independence (1991), followed by **Bosnia-Herzegovina** (1992). **Serbia** and **Montenegro** remained as the republic of Yugoslavia. Bitter fighting followed, especially in Bosnia, where Serbs reportedly engaged in **"ethnic cleansing"** of the Muslim population; a peace plan (Dayton accord), brokered by the United States, was signed by **Bosnia, Serbia**, and **Croatia** (Dec. 1995), with **NATO** responsible for policing its implementation. In spring 1999, NATO conducted a bombing campaign aimed at stopping Yugoslavia from its campaign to drive out ethnic Albanians from the Kosovo region; a

peace accord was reached in June under which NATO peacekeeping troops entered Kosovo.

The two **Germanys** were reunited after 45 years (Oct. 1990). The union was greeted with jubilation, but stresses became apparent when free market principles were applied to the aging East German industries, resulting in many plant closings and rising unemployment. German chancellor Helmut **Kohl**, a Christian Democrat, lost power after 16 years, in Sept. 1998 elections; Gerhard **Schroeder**, a Social Democrat, took over. Czechoslovakia broke apart peacefully (Jan. 1993), becoming the **Czech Republic** and **Slovakia**. In **Poland**, Lech **Walesa** was elected president (Dec. 1991) but was defeated in his bid for a 2nd term (Nov. 1995).

NATO approved the **Partnership for Peace** Program (Jan. 1994) coordinating the defense of **Eastern** and **Central European** countries; Russia joined the program later that year. NATO signed a pact with **Russia** (1997) providing for NATO expansion into the former Soviet-bloc countries; a similar treaty was set up with **Ukraine**. The **Czech Republic**, **Hungary**, and **Poland** became members in Jan. 1999; in that year **NATO** celebrated its 50th anniversary. Efforts toward European unity continued with adoption of a single market (Jan. 1993) and conversion of the European Community to the **European Union** as the Maestricht Treaty took effect (Nov. 1993). Agreement was reached for 11 EU members to participate in Economic and Monetary Union, adopting a common currency **(euro)** for some purposes in Jan. 1999.

An intraparty revolt forced Margaret **Thatcher** out as prime minister of **Great Britain**, to be succeeded by John **Major** (Nov. 1990); 7 years later, Major suffered an overwhelming defeat at the hands of the new Labour Party leader, Tony **Blair** (May 1997). The divorce of Prince **Charles and** Princess **Diana**, followed by the death of Diana in a car accident (Aug. 1997), made headlines around the world. Talks on **peace** in **Northern Ireland** that included participation of Sinn Fein, political arm of the IRA, led to a ground-breaking peace plan, approved in an all-Ireland vote (May 1998). In Dec. 1999, Northern Ireland was granted home rule under a power-sharing cabinet. In **Scotland** voters overwhelmingly approved establishment of a regional legislature (1997), and in **Wales** voters narrowly approved establishment of a local assembly (1997). In a historic innovation, the Church of England **ordained 32 women** as priests (Mar. 1994).

Middle East. In Aug. 1990, **Iraq's Saddam Hussein** ordered his troops to invade **Kuwait**. The UN approved military action in response (Nov. 1990), and U.S. Pres. George **Bush** put together an international military force. Allied planes bombed Iraq (Jan. 1991) and launched a land attack, crushing the invasion (Feb. 1991). After Iraq accepted a cease-fire (Apr. 1991), U.S. troops withdrew, but "no-fly" zones were set up over northern Iraq to protect the Kurds and over southern Iraq to protect Shiite Muslims. The **UN** imposed **sanctions** on Iraq for failure to abide by the cease-fire. Iraq's reported failure to cooperate with UN arms inspectors seeking to eliminate "weapons of mass destruction" led to repeated air strikes by the U.S. and Britain.

The last Western hostages were freed in **Lebanon**, June 1992. **Israel** and the **Palestine Liberation Organization** signed a peace accord (Sept. 1993) providing for Palestinian self-government in the West Bank and Gaza Strip. Prime Min. Yitzhak **Rabin** and Foreign Min. Shimon **Peres** of Israel and Yasir **Arafat** of the PLO received the Nobel Peace Prize for their efforts (1994). Six Arab nations relaxed their boycott against Israel (1994), and Israel and **Jordan** signed a peace treaty (Oct. 1994). **Rabin was assassinated** (Nov. 1995) by an Israeli opponent of the peace process. After new elections (May 1996), Benjamin Netanyahu as prime minister adopted a harder line in peace negotiations. **Arafat** was elected to the presidency of the Palestinian Authority (Jan. 1996). A long-delayed interim agreement (the Wye Memorandum) on Israel military withdrawal from part of the West Bank was reached Oct. 1998. A Labour government under Ehud **Barak** took power after May 1999 elections, but further progress in peace negotiations proved elusive.

King **Hussein** of Jordan died (Feb. 1999), to be succeeded by his son Abdullah.

Asia and the Pacific. Hong Kong was returned to **China** (July 1997) after being a British colony for 156 years. China, which emerged in the decade as a major developing economic power, had agreed to follow a policy of "one country, two systems" in Hong Kong. The territory of **Macao** reverted to Chinese sovereignty (Dec. 1999) after over 400 years of Portuguese rule; it retained its capitalist economic system. **Jiang Zemin**, general secretary of the Chinese Communist Party, assumed the additional post of president of China (Mar. 1993) and emerged as the key leader after the death of paramount leader **Deng Xiaoping** (Feb. 1997). China released from prison—and exiled—some well-known dissidents but continued to be criticized for detentions and other alleged widespread **human rights abuses**. In Nov. 1999 the U.S. and China signed a landmark pact normalizing trade relations.

After years of prosperity, **Thailand, Indonesia**, and **South Korea** in 1997 began to suffer economic reverses that had a worldwide ripple effect. These countries received billion-dollar IMF bailout packages. In **Indonesia**, protests over mismanagement led to the resignation of Pres. **Suharto** (May 1998) after 32 years of nearly autocratic rule. Abdurraham Wahid was elected (Oct. 1999) in the country's first fully democratic elections. In a referendum (Aug. 1999), **East Timor** voted overwhelmingly for independence from Indonesia; pro-Indonesian militias then rampaged through the territory, but a multinational peacekeeping force was allowed in (Sept. 1999) to help restore order. In **South Korea**, former dissident **Kim Dae Jung** was elected president (Dec. 1997). Two previous presidents, Roh Tae Woo and Chun Doo Hwan, were convicted of crimes committed in office but were given amnesty by the new president.

In **Japan** members of a religious cult, released the nerve gas sarin on 5 Tokyo subway cars, killing 12 people and injuring more than 5,500 (Mar. 1995). Tamil rebels continued their armed conflict in **Sri Lanka**. In **Afghanistan** the **Taliban**, an extreme Islamic fundamentalist group, gained control of Kabul (Sept. 1996) and, eventually, most of the country. In **North Korea**, longtime dictator **Kim Il Sung** died (July 1994), to be succeeded by his son, **Kim Jong Il**. In the same year the country signed an agreement with the U.S. setting a timetable for North Korea to eliminate its nuclear program. The country also suffered a severe drought, and widespread starvation was feared.

India was beset by riots following destruction of a mosque by Hindu militants (Dec. 1992); Indian army troops repeatedly clashed with pro-independence demonstrators in the disputed Muslim region of **Kashmir**, exacerbating relations with **Pakistan**. Uneasy relations between India and Pakistan reached a new level when both nations conducted nuclear tests in 1998. Conflict in Pakistan between government and the military led to a bloodless coup (Oct. 1999).

Africa. South Africa was transformed as the white-dominated government abandoned **apartheid** and the country made the transition to a nonracial democratic government. Pres. F. W. **de Klerk** released Nelson **Mandela** from prison (Feb. 1990), after he had been held by the government for 27 years, and lifted a ban on the African National Congress. The white government repealed its apartheid laws (1990, 1991). **Mandela** was elected **president** (Apr. 1994), and a new constitution became law (Dec. 1996). Thabo **Mbeki**, the ANC's candidate to succeed Mandela, was overwhelmingly elected president in June 1999. In **Nigeria**, Gen. Olusegun **Obasanjo** was elected president (Feb. 1999), to become the country's first civilian leader in 15 years.

The decades-long rule of **Mobutu** Sese Seko in **Zaire** came to an end (May 1997) at the hands of rebel forces led by Laurent **Kabila**; an ailing Mobutu fled the country and soon after died. Kabila changed the country's name back to **Democratic Republic of the Congo**; conditions remained unstable. After the presidents of **Burundi** and **Rwanda** were killed in an airplane crash (Apr. 1994), violence erupted in Rwanda between Hutu and Tutsi factions; tens of thousands were slain. The conflict spread to refugee camps in neighboring Zaire and Burundi. Factional fighting also erupted in **Somalia** after Pres.

Muhammad Siad Barre was ousted (Jan. 1991). The UN sent a U.S.-led **peacekeeping force**, but it was unsuccessful in restoring order. Some soldiers of the peacekeeping force were killed, including 23 Pakistanis (June 1993) and 18 U.S. Rangers (Oct. 1993). The UN ended its mission (Mar. 1995) with no durable government in place. **Liberia** endured factional fighting that lasted almost 5 years and claimed over 150,000 lives; a cease-fire was concluded in Aug. 1995. The World Health Organization reported (1995) that Africa accounted for 70% of **AIDS** cases worldwide.

A 16-year civil war appeared to end in **Angola** (May 1991) when the government signed a peace accord with the rebel UNITA faction. But despite the inauguration of a national unity government (Apr. 1997), insurgents continued to fight and gain territory. **Namibia** officially became independent in Mar. 1990. Claimed by South Africa since 1919 and placed under UN authority in 1971, it had long been a focus of colonial rivalries. In **Algeria,** the army cancelled a 2nd round of parliamentary elections (Jan. 1992) after the Islamic party won a first round. Islamic fundamentalists then began a terrorist campaign that, along with killings by progovernment squads, eventually claimed thousands of lives. A peace plan was worked out with the militants in 1999.

North America. The **North American Free Trade Agreement** (NAFTA), liberalizing trade between the United States, Canada, and Mexico, went into effect Jan. 1, 1994. In **Canada**, the Progressive Conservative Party suffered a crushing defeat in general elections (Oct. 1993), and liberal Jean **Chrétien** became prime minister. The map of Canada was altered in Apr. 1999 to create a new territory, **Nunavut,** out of an area that had been part of Northwest Territories.

In the **United States**, in the 1992 presidential election, Democrat Bill **Clinton** defeated Pres. George Bush, but in 1994 congressional elections Republicans gained control of Congress. Congress passed legislation under which federal protection for welfare recipients was ended and funds turned over to the states for their programs. Clinton reached agreement with Congress on measures to eliminate the federal budget deficit. Clinton won reelection in 1996; the new administration was plagued by scandals but remained popular amid continued economic prosperity. In Dec. 1998 **Clinton** was **impeached** by the U.S. House on charges related to the Monica Lewinsky scandal; he was **acquitted** by the Senate in Feb. 1999.

The U.S. Army and Navy were torn by sexual scandals involving abuse of women personnel. The **United States** suffered embarrassment with the discovery of espionage by CIA agents (Aldrich Ames, Harold Nicholson).

In **Mexico,** Ernesto **Zedillo** of the ruling PRI party was elected president (July 1994) after the party's first candidate was assassinated. The country soon faced a crisis affecting the value of the peso, but recovered with the help of a bailout package from the U.S. A peasant revolt spearheaded by the **Zapatista National Liberation Army** erupted in the state of Chiapas (Jan. 1994) and was suppressed.

Central America. In **Haiti,** Jean-Bertrand **Aristide** was elected president (Dec. 1990) but was ousted in a military coup after 9 months in office. The UN approved a U.S.-led invasion to restore the elected leader; shortly before troops

arrived, a delegation headed by former U.S. Pres. Jimmy Carter arranged (Sept. 1994) for the junta to step aside for Aristide. In **Nicaragua,** Violetta Chamarro defeated Daniel **Ortega** in the presidential election (Feb. 1990), thus ousting the Sandinistas. In **Panama,** U.S. troops invaded and overthrew the government of Manuel **Noriega** (Dec. 1989), who was wanted on drug charges; Noriega was captured Jan. 1990. On Dec. 31, 1999, Panama assumed full control of the **Panama Canal,** in accord with a treaty with the U.S. In **El Salvador** (1992) and **Guatemala** (1996) the governments signed agreements with rebel factions aimed at ending long-running civil conflicts.

South America. Alberto **Fujimori** was elected president of **Peru** in June 1990 and, despite his suppression of the constitution (1992), was reelected in 1995. Peru succeeded in capturing (Sept. 1992) the leader of the **Shining Path** guerrilla movement. Leftist guerrillas took hostages at an ambassador's residence in Lima (Dec. 1996); one hostage was killed during a government assault rescuing the rest (Apr. 1997). Peronist Pres. Carlos Saúl **Menem** served as **Argentina**'s president for much of the decade (elected 1989, reelected 1995), imposing stringent economic measures; he was succeeded in 1999 by Fernando de la **Rúa**.

Former Chilean Pres. Gen. Augusto **Pinochet** continued to head the army until Mar. 1998; he was arrested in London (Oct. 1998) on human rights charges but was judged medically unfit for trial and returned to Chile (Mar. 2000).

In **Brazil,** Fernando Henrique **Cardoso** was elected president (Oct. 1994) and reelected in 1998 amid a growing economic slump; the IMF announced a \$42 billion aid package (Nov. 1998). The first UN Conference on Environment and Development, or **Earth Summit,** was held (June 1992) in **Rio de Janeiro,** with delegates from 178 nations.

Terrorism and Crime. Terrorism, often linked to Mideastern sources and with the U.S. as object, continued. A terrorist bomb exploded in a garage beneath New York City's **World Trade Center,** killing 6 people (Feb. 1993). Bombings of a U.S. military training center (Nov. 1995) and a barracks holding U.S. airmen (June 1996), both in **Saudi Arabia,** killed 7 and 19, respectively. Bombs exploded outside **U.S. embassies** in Kenya and Tanzania, Aug. 1998, killing over 220 people; the U.S. retaliated with missiles fired at alleged terrorist-linked sites in Afghanistan and Sudan. The Alfred P. Murrah Federal Building in **Oklahoma City,** OK, was destroyed by a bomb that killed 168 people (Apr. 1995).

Science. The powerful **Hubble Space Telescope** was launched in Apr. 1990; flaws in its mirrors and solar panels were repaired by space-walking astronauts (Dec. 1993). U.S. space shuttle *Atlantis* docked with the orbiting Russian space station *Mir* (June 1995) in first of several joint missions in a spirit of post-Cold-War cooperation. In Nov. 1998 first component for a new **International Space Station** was launched into space from Kazakhstan. But space prospects were subsequently dimmed by disaster when U.S. space shuttle Columbia exploded on reentry (Feb. 2003), killing the 7 astronauts aboard.

Scottish scientist Ian Wilmut announced (Feb. 1997) the **cloning** of a sheep, nicknamed Dolly—the first mammal successfully cloned from a cell from an adult animal.

Opening a New Century: 2000-2003

Terrorism. In Oct. 2000, 17 American sailors were killed aboard the **USS** *Cole* in Aden, **Yemen,** when a small boat exploded alongside it in a terrorist attack. On **Sept. 11, 2001,** hijackers crashed 2 jetliners into the twin towers of the **World Trade Center** in New York City and another into the **Pentagon** outside Washington, DC; a 4th crashed in a field in **Pennsylvania**. The attacks, which destroyed both towers and damaged the Pentagon, killed about 3,000 people, including all 265 aboard the planes. Saudi exile Osama bin Laden and his **al-Qaeda terrorist network,** based in **Afghanistan** and backed by the Taliban government there, emerged as responsible for the attacks. A U.S.-led military campaign launched in Oct. 2001 **ousted the Taliban,** and a transitional government was installed (Dec. 2001), although al-Qaeda remained active in some areas of Afghanistan and elsewhere, and Bin Laden remained at large.

Among incidents elsewhere, a bomb exploded in a truck outside a synagogue in **Tunisia** (Apr. 2002), killing 17 (including the driver). A car bomb on the Indonesian island of **Bali** (Oct. 2002) killed about 200, mostly foreign tourists; Muslim extremists were arrested. Chechen guerrillas seized a **Moscow movie theater** (Oct. 2002); more than 100 hostages were killed in a subsequent raid by Russian troops. The bombing of an Israeli-owned **hotel in Kenya** (Nov. 2002) killed 13 (including the 3 bombers). Suicide attacks against Western targets in **Riyadh, Saudi Arabia** (May 2003), killed 34 people (including 9 attackers). Suicide bombings in **Istanbul,** Turkey (Nov. 2003), hit two Jewish synagogues and British targets, killing about 60 people in all.

War in Iraq. The U.S., with Great Britain, launched an **invasion of Iraq** (Mar. 2003), aimed at ousting the regime of **Saddam Hussein**. Troops took control of Baghdad and

other cities, and Pres. Bush declared major combat ended, May 1, but **insurgents** continued to mount attacks, causing continuing casualties among troops and civilians. Searches for **weapons of mass destruction**, cited as major grounds for the invasion, yielded no evidence. **Saddam Hussein** was eventually **captured** (Dec. 2003), as well as other regime leaders; they were to be put on trial by Iraqis. An interim government was installed (June 2004).

Middle East. Violence between Israelis and Palestinians escalated, with **suicide bombings** by Palestinians and retaliation by Israeli armed forces, the peace process languished. Likud leader Ariel **Sharon** was **elected** prime minister of Israel (Feb. 2001). In reponse to Palestinian suicide attacks that killed 26, Israeli forces stormed the compound of Palestinian leader Yasir Arafat (Mar. 2002), keeping him confined there until early May. The U.S., Russia, UN, and European Union formally initiated (Apr. 2003) a "**road map**" plan for Israeli-Palestinian **peace negotiations**, but little progress was made. Syrian Pres. Hafez al-**Assad died** (June 2000); succeeded by his son. Iran was censured (Dec. 2003) by the UN Internat. Atomic Energy Agency for covering up aspects of its nuclear weapons program.

Europe. In Oct. 2000, Yugoslav strongman Slobodan **Milosevic yielded** power to Vojislav Kostunica, who had declared himself president in the face of anti-Milosevic protests after a disputed election. Milosevic surrendered to Serbian authorities; in Feb. 2002 he went on trial for **war crimes** allegedly committed during 1990s ethnic conflicts in the Balkans. The first-ever **Concorde jet crash**, near Paris, killed 113 people (July 2000). The Russian nuclear sub *Kursk* **sank** in the Barents Sea (Aug. 2000) killing 118 crew members. By early 2002 the **euro** was the common currency in 12 European Union nations. Some 35,000 people across Europe, including over 11,000 in France, reportedly died in 2003 summer **heat waves**. Swedish **Foreign Minister** Anna Lindh was **murdered** (Sept. 2003) while shopping in a Stockholm department store.

Asia. South Korean Pres. Kim Dae **Jung** and **North Korean** ruler Kim **Jong Il** held a **summit** meeting and agreed to seek peace and reunification (June 2000), but tensions rose after North Korea admitted conducting a covert nuclear weapons development program (Oct. 2002). **Nepal**'s King **Birendra** and other Nepal royals were shot to death inside the palace, apparently by Crown Prince Dipendra, who then killed himself (June 2001). **Chinese** Pres. Jiang Zemin and **Russian** Pres. Vladimir Putin signed a **friendship treaty** (July 2001). With Jiang's retirement Hu Jintao was named as China's new Communist party chief (Nov. 2002) and

president (Mar. 2003). North Korea **withdrew** (Jan. 2003) from the Nuclear Nonproliferation Treaty; multi-nation talks were held in Beijing (Aug. 2003) about the status of its **nuclear program**. Pakistan and India **restored diplomatic ties** (May 2003) and declared a **cease-fire** in disputed territory (Nov. 2003). Pakistani Pres. Gen. Pervez Musharraf twice **escaped assassination** by Islamic militants (Dec. 2003).

Africa. The 13th International **AIDS Conference**, held in Durban, South Africa (July 2000), focused on ways of controlling surging AIDS rates in developing countries. **Ethiopia and Eritrea** signed a **peace treaty** (Dec. 2000). Laurent **Kabila**, president of the Democratic Republic of the **Congo**, was **shot to death** by a bodyguard (Jan. 2001). **Liberian Pres. Charles Taylor** went into voluntary exile (Aug. 2003) as part of a deal to end a 14-year-old civil war; other accords were reached aimed at **ending civil wars** in Angola (Apr. 2002) and Côte d'Ivoire (Jan. 2003). A peace agreement in the Dem. Rep. of **Congo** (Apr. 2003) did not end violence there. Civil war between the Muslim-led government and rebels from Christian areas in **Sudan** continued, with massive casualties. Zimbabwean Pres. Robert Mugabe pulled his country out of the **Commonwealth** (Dec. 2003) after the group reaffirmed suspension of **Zimbabwe** for alleged fraud in the 2002 election. **Libya** agreed (Dec. 2003) to abandon programs pursuing weapons of mass destruction.

North and South America. Vicente **Fox** of the center-right National Action Party (PAN) was elected **president of Mexico** (July 2000), in a historic defeat for the long-supreme Institutional Revolutionary Party (PRI). Peruvian Pres. Alberto **Fujimori stepped down** during his 3rd term (Nov. 2000), amid scandal, and did not seek reelection. In Jan. 2001, George W. **Bush** was inaugurated as U.S. president, after one of the tightest and most controversial elections in U.S. history. Venezuelan Pres. Hugo Chavez regained power after 48-hr. coup (Dec. 2002). Argentina's **record default** on International Monetary Fund loans resulted (Sept. 2003) in a **$12.5 billion debt-refinancing** agreement. **Haiti** was wracked by anti-govenment protests (leading to the resignation of Jean-Bertrand **Aristide** in Feb. 2004). Paul Martin succeeded Jean Chrétien as **Canadian prime minister** (Dec. 2003) after he was elected to lead the ruling Liberal Party.

Space. The U.S. space shuttle *Columbia* broke up on re-entering Earth's atmosphere Feb. 1, 2003, killing all 7 crew members.

International. Negotiators from 178 countries agreed to adopt the **Kyoto Protocol**, calling for a reduction of greenhouse gases in developed nations (July 2001).

World Population Growth

While the population of the world in ancient times can only be very roughly estimated, it is believed that there were perhaps 50 million people in the world in 1000 BC. The United Nations Population Division estimates a figure of 300 million for AD 1; this chart shows estimated population growth from that time onward as estimated by the UN. While other sources may vary, it is clear from all sources that world population began growing more rapidly in the 18th and 19th centuries, and grew much more rapidly in the 20th century. According to UN estimates, world population reached 1 billion in 1804, and went to 2 billion in 123 years, 3 billion in 33 years, 4 billion in 14 years, 5 billion in 13 years, and 6 billion in 12 years. According to UN estimates, the 6 billion figure was reached in 1999. By 2005 the total is expected to exceed 6.4 billion.

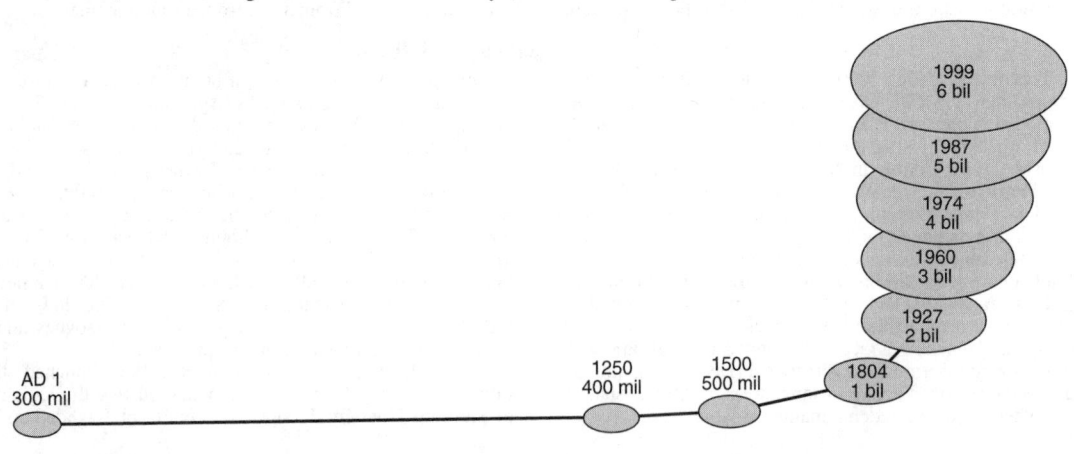

HISTORICAL FIGURES

Ancient Greeks and Romans

Greeks

Aeschines, orator, 389-314 BC
Aeschylus, dramatist, 525-456 BC
Aesop, fableist, c620-c560 BC
Alcibiades, politician, 450-404 BC
Anacreon, poet, c582-c485 BC
Anaxagoras, philosopher, c500-428 BC
Anaximander, philosopher, 611-546 BC
Anaximenes, philosopher, c570-500 BC
Antiphon, speechwriter, c480-411 BC
Apollonius, mathematician, c265-170 BC
Archimedes, math., 287-212 BC
Aristophanes, dramatist, c448-380 BC
Aristotle, philosopher, 384-322 BC
Athenaeus, scholar, fl. c200
Callicrates, architect, fl. 5th cent. BC
Callimachus, poet, c305-240 BC
Cratinus, comic dramatist, 520-421 BC
Democritus, philosopher, c460-370 BC
Demosthenes, orator, 384-322 BC
Diodorus, historian, fl. 20 BC
Diogenes, philosopher, 372-c287 BC
Dionysius, historian, d. c7 BC
Empedocles, philosopher, c490-430 BC
Epicharmus, dramatist, c530-440 BC
Epictetus, philosopher, c55-c135
Epicurus, philosopher, 341-270 BC
Eratosthenes, scientist, 276-194 BC
Euclid, mathematician, fl. c300 BC
Euripides, dramatist, c484-406 BC
Galen, physician, 130-200
Heraclitus, philosopher, c540-c475 BC
Herodotus, historian, c484-420 BC

Hesiod, poet, 8th cent. BC
Hippocrates, physician, c460-377 BC
Homer, poet, fl. c700 BC(?)
Isocrates, orator, 436-338 BC
Menander, dramatist, 342-292 BC
Parmenides, philosopher, b. c515 BC
Pericles, statesman, c495-429 BC
Phidias, sculptor, c500-435 BC
Pindar, poet, c518-c438 BC
Plato, philosopher, c428-347 BC
Plutarch, biographer, c46-120
Polybius, historian, c200-c118 BC
Praxiteles, sculptor, 400-330 BC
Pythagoras, phil., math., c580-c500 BC
Sappho, poet, c610-c580 BC
Simonides, poet, 556-c468 BC
Socrates, philosopher, 469-399 BC
Solon, statesman, 640-560 BC
Sophocles, dramatist, c496-406 BC
Strabo, geographer, c63 BC-AD 24
Thales, philosopher, c634-546 BC
Themistocles, politician, c524-c460 BC
Theocritus, poet, c310-250 BC
Theophrastus, phil., c372-c287 BC
Thucydides, historian, fl. 5th cent. BC
Timon, philosopher, c320-c230 BC
Xenophon, historian, c434-c355 BC
Zeno, philosopher, c335-c263 BC

Romans

Ammianus, historian, c330-395
Apuleius, satirist, c124-c170
Boethius, scholar, c480-524

Caesar, Julius, leader, 100-44 BC
Catiline, politician, c108-62 BC
Cato (Elder), statesman, 234-149 BC
Catullus, poet, c84-54 BC
Cicero, orator, 106-43 BC
Claudian, poet, c370-c404
Ennius, poet, 239-170 BC
Gellius, author, c130-c165
Horace, poet, 65-8 BC
Juvenal, satirist, 60-127
Livy, historian, 59 BC-AD 17
Lucan, poet, 39-65
Lucilius, poet, c180-c102 BC
Lucretius, poet, c99-c55 BC
Martial, epigrammatist, c38-c103
Nepos, historian, c100-c25 BC
Ovid, poet, 43 BC-AD 17
Persius, satirist, 34-62
Plautus, dramatist, c254-c184 BC
Pliny the Elder, scholar, 23-79
Pliny the Younger, author, 62-113
Quintilian, rhetorician, c35-c97
Sallust, historian, 86-34 BC
Seneca, philosopher, 4 BC-AD 65
Silius, poet, c25-101
Statius, poet, c45-c96
Suetonius, biographer, c69-c122
Tacitus, historian, 56-120
Terence, dramatist, 185-c159 BC
Tibullus, poet, c55-c19 BC
Vergil, poet, 70-19 BC
Vitruvius, architect, fl. 1st cent. BC

Rulers of England and Great Britain

> **IT'S A FACT:** King Henry VIII of England had six wives in succession, starting with Catherine of Aragon and ending with Catherine Parr. A common mnemonic device used to remember his wives' various fates is "divorced, beheaded, died; divorced, beheaded, survived."

ENGLAND

Name	Saxons and Danes	Reign Began	Died	Death Age	Years Reigned
Egbert	King of Wessex, won allegiance of all English	829	839	—	10
Ethelwulf	Son, King of Wessex, Sussex, Kent, Essex	839	858	—	19
Ethelbald	Son of Ethelwulf, displaced father in Wessex	858	860	—	2
Ethelbert	2nd son of Ethelwulf, united Kent and Wessex	860	866	—	6
Ethelred I	3rd son, King of Wessex, fought Danes	866	871	—	5
Alfred	The Great, 4th son, defeated Danes, fortified London	871	899	52	28
Edward	The Elder, Alfred's son, united English, claimed Scotland	899	924	55	25
Athelstan	The Glorious, Edward's son, King of Mercia, Wessex	924	940	45	16
Edmund	3rd son of Edward, King of Wessex, Mercia	940	946	25	6
Edred	4th son of Edward	946	955	32	9
Edwy	The Fair, eldest son of Edmund, King of Wessex	955	959	18	3
Edgar	The Peaceful, 2nd son of Edmund, ruled all English	959	975	32	17
Edward	The Martyr, eldest son of Edgar, murdered by stepmother	975	978	17	4
Ethelred II	The Unready, 2nd son of Edgar, married Emma of Normandy	978	1016	48	37
Edmund II	Ironside, son of Ethelred II, King of London	1016	1016	27	0
Canute	The Dane, gave Wessex to Edmund, married Emma	1016	1035	40	19
Harold I	Harefoot, natural son of Canute	1035	1040	—	5
Hardecanute	Son of Canute by Emma, Danish King	1040	1042	24	2
Edward	The Confessor, son of Ethelred II (canonized 1161)	1042	1066	62	24
Harold II	Edward's brother-in-law, last Saxon King	1066	1066	44	0

House of Normandy

Name		Reign Began	Died	Death Age	Years Reigned
William I	The Conqueror, defeated Harold at Hastings	1066	1087	60	21
William II	Rufus, 3rd son of William I, killed by arrow	1087	1100	43	13
Henry I	Beauclerc, youngest son of William I	1100	1135	67	35

House of Blois

Name		Reign Began	Died	Death Age	Years Reigned
Stephen	Son of Adela, daughter of William I, and Count of Blois	1135	1154	50	19

House of Plantagenet

Name		Reign Began	Died	Death Age	Years Reigned
Henry II	Son of Geoffrey Plantagenet (Angevin) by Matilda, daughter of Henry I	1154	1189	56	35
Richard I	Coeur de Lion, son of Henry II, crusader	1189	1199	42	10
John	Lackland, son of Henry II, approved Magna Carta, 1215	1199	1216	50	17
Henry III	Son of John, acceded at 9, under regency until 1227	1216	1272	65	56
Edward I	Son of Henry III	1272	1307	68	35
Edward II	Son of Edward I, deposed by Parliament, 1327	1307	1327	43	20
Edward III	Of Windsor, son of Edward II	1327	1377	65	50
Richard II	Grandson of Edward III, minor until 1389, deposed 1399	1377	1400	33	22

Name	House of Lancaster	Reign Began	Died	Death Age	Years Reigned
Henry IV......	Son of John of Gaunt, Duke of Lancaster, son of Edward III.................	1399	1413	47	13
Henry V	Son of Henry IV, victor of Agincourt.......................................	1413	1422	34	9
Henry VI......	Son of Henry V, deposed 1461, died in Tower........................	1422	1471	49	39
	House of York				
Edward IV	Great-great-grandson of Edward III, son of Duke of York	1461	1483	40	22
Edward V.....	Son of Edward IV, murdered in Tower of London	1483	1483	13	0
Richard III	Brother of Edward IV, fell at Bosworth Field...........................	1483	1485	32	2
	House of Tudor				
Henry VII	Son of Edmund Tudor, Earl of Richmond, whose father had married the widow of Henry V; descended from Edward III through his mother, Margaret Beaufort, via John of Gaunt. By marrying daughter of Edward IV united Lancaster and York	1485	1509	53	24
Henry VIII.....	Son of Henry VII, by Elizabeth, daughter of Edward IV................	1509	1547	56	38
Edward VI	Son of Henry VIII, by Jane Seymour, his 3rd queen. Ruled under regents. Was forced to name Lady Jane Grey his successor. Council of State proclaimed her queen July 10, 1553. Mary Tudor won Council, was proclaimed queen July 19, 1553. Mary had Lady Jane Grey beheaded for treason, Feb. 1554 ...	1547	1553	16	6
Mary I.........	Daughter of Henry VIII, by Catherine of Aragon...........................	1553	1558	43	5
Elizabeth I	Daughter of Henry VIII, by Anne Boleyn..................................	1558	1603	69	44

GREAT BRITAIN

	House of Stuart				
James I	James VI of Scotland, son of Mary, Queen of Scots. *First to call himself King of Great Britain. This became official with the Act of Union, 1707*	1603	1625	59	22
Charles I	Only surviving son of James I; beheaded Jan. 30, 1649	1625	1649	48	24
	Commonwealth, 1649–1660				
	Council of State, 1649; Protectorate, 1653[1]				
The Cromwells	Oliver Cromwell, Lord Protector...	1653	1658	59	5
	Richard Cromwell, son, Lord Protector, resigned May 25, 1659	1658	1712	86	1
	House of Stuart (Restored)				
Charles II.....	Eldest son of Charles I, died without issue.............................	1660	1685	55	25
James II.......	2nd son of Charles I. Deposed 1688. Interregnum 1688-1689	1685	1701	68	3
William III.....	Son of William, Prince of Orange, by Mary, daughter of Charles I........	1689	1702	51	13
and Mary II	Eldest daughter of James II and wife of William III.........................	1689	1694	33	6
Anne	2nd daughter of James II	1702	1714	49	12
	House of Hanover				
George I......	Son of Elector of Hanover, by Sophia, granddaughter of James I............	1714	1727	67	13
George II	Only son of George I, married Caroline of Brandenburg	1727	1760	77	33
George III.....	Grandson of George II, married Charlotte of Mecklenburg	1760	1820	81	59
George IV	Eldest son of George III, Prince Regent, from Feb. 1811.................	1820	1830	67	10
William IV	3rd son of George III, married Adelaide of Saxe-Meiningen	1830	1837	71	7
Victoria	Daughter of Edward, 4th son of George III; married (1840) Prince Albert of Saxe-Coburg and Gotha, who became Prince Consort	1837	1901	81	63
	House of Saxe-Coburg and Gotha				
Edward VII....	Eldest son of Victoria, married Alexandra, Princess of Denmark.............	1901	1910	68	9
	House of Windsor[2]				
George V	2nd son of Edward VII, married Princess Mary of Teck.....................	1910	1936	70	25
Edward VIII	Eldest son of George V; acceded Jan. 20, 1936, abdicated Dec. 11, 1936......	1936	1972	77	1
George VI	2nd son of George V; married Lady Elizabeth Bowes-Lyon..................	1936	1952	56	15
Elizabeth II	Elder daughter of George VI, acceded Feb. 6, 1952	1952			

— = age/birth date not certain. (1) The Cromwells ruled Britain following overthow of the monarchy in 1649. (2) Name adopted by proclamation of George V, July 17, 1917.

Rulers of Scotland

Kenneth I MacAlpin was the first Scot to rule both Scots and Picts, AD 846.

Duncan I was the first general ruler, 1034. Macbeth seized the kingdom 1040, was slain by Duncan's son, Malcolm III MacDuncan (Canmore), 1057.

Malcolm married Margaret, Saxon princess who had fled from the Normans. Queen Margaret introduced English language and monastic customs. She was canonized, 1250. Her son Edgar, 1097, moved the court to Edinburgh. His brothers Alexander I and David I succeeded. Malcolm IV, the Maiden, 1153, grandson of David I, was followed by his brother, William the Lion, 1165, whose son was Alexander II, 1214. The latter's son, Alexander III, 1249, defeated the Norse and regained the Hebrides. When he died, 1286, his granddaughter, Margaret, child of Eric of Norway and grandniece of Edward I of England, known as the Maid of Norway, was chosen ruler, but died 1290, aged 8.

John Baliol, 1292-1296. (Interregnum, 10 years.)

Robert Bruce (The Bruce), 1306-1329, victor at Bannockburn, 1314. David II, his only son, 1329-1371.

Robert II, 1371-1390, grandson of Robert Bruce, son of Walter, the Steward of Scotland, was called The Steward, first of the so-called Stuart line.

Robert III, son of Robert II, 1390-1406.

James I, son of Robert III, 1406-1437.

James II, son of James I, 1437-1460.

James III, eldest son of James II, 1460-1488.

James IV, eldest son of James III, 1488-1513.

James V, eldest son of James IV, 1513-1542.

Mary, daughter of James V, b. 1542, became queen at 1 week old; crowned 1543. Married, 1558, Francis, son of Henry II of France, who became king 1559, d. 1560. Mary ruled Scots 1561 until abdication, 1567. She also married Henry Stewart, Lord Darnley (1565), and James, Earl of Bothwell (1567). Imprisoned by Elizabeth I; beheaded 1587.

James VI, 1566-1625, son of Mary and Lord Darnley, became King of England on death of Elizabeth in 1603. Although the thrones were thus united, the legislative union of Scotland and England was not effected until the Act of Union, May 1, 1707.

WORLD ALMANAC QUICK QUIZ

After the March 1917 Russian Revolution, who led the Provisional Government?
  (a) Vladimir Lenin
  (b) Prince Georgi Lvov
  (c) Joseph Stalin
  (d) Leon Trotsky
For the answer look in this chapter, or see page 1008.

Prime Ministers of Great Britain

Designations in parentheses describe each government;
W=Whig; T=Tory; Cl=Coalition; P=Peelite; Li=Liberal; C=Conservative[1]; La=Labour.

Sir Robert Walpole (W)[2]	1721-1742	Benjamin Disraeli (C)	1868
Earl of Wilmington (W)	1742-1743	William E. Gladstone (Li)	1868-1874
Henry Pelham (W)	1743-1754	Benjamin Disraeli (C)	1874-1880
Duke of Newcastle (W)	1754-1756	William E. Gladstone (Li)	1880-1885
Duke of Devonshire (W)	1756-1757	Marquess of Salisbury (C)	1885-1886
Duke of Newcastle (W)	1757-1762	William E. Gladstone (Li)	1886
Earl of Bute (T)	1762-1763	Marquess of Salisbury (C)	1886-1892
George Grenville (W)	1763-1765	William E. Gladstone (Li)	1892-1894
Marquess of Rockingham (W)	1765-1766	Earl of Rosebery (Li)	1894-1895
William Pitt the Elder (Earl of Chatham) (W)	1766-1768	Marquess of Salisbury (C)	1895-1902
Duke of Grafton (W)	1768-1770	Arthur J. Balfour (C)	1902-1905
Frederick North (Lord North) (T)	1770-1782	Sir Henry Campbell Bannerman (Li)	1905-1908
Marquess of Rockingham (W)	1782	Herbert H. Asquith (Li)	1908-1915
Earl of Shelburne (W)	1782-1783	Herbert H. Asquith (Cl)	1915-1916
Duke of Portland (Cl)	1783	David Lloyd George (Cl)	1916-1922
William Pitt the Younger (T)	1783-1801	Andrew Bonar Law (C)	1922-1923
Henry Addington (T)	1801-1804	Stanley Baldwin (C)	1923-1924
William Pitt the Younger (T)	1804-1806	James Ramsay MacDonald (La)	1924
William Wyndham Grenville, Baron Grenville (W)	1806-1807	Stanley Baldwin (C)	1924-1929
Duke of Portland (T)	1807-1809	James Ramsay MacDonald (La)	1929-1931
Spencer Perceval (T)	1809-1812	James Ramsay MacDonald (Cl)	1931-1935
Earl of Liverpool (T)	1812-1827	Stanley Baldwin (Cl)	1935-1937
George Canning (T)	1827	Neville Chamberlain (Cl)	1937-1940
Viscount Goderich (T)	1827-1828	Winston Churchill (Cl)	1940-1945
Duke of Wellington (T)	1828-1830	Winston Churchill (C)	1945
Earl Grey (W)	1830-1834	Clement Attlee (La)	1945-1951
Viscount Melbourne (W)	1834	Sir Winston Churchill (C)	1951-1955
Sir Robert Peel (C)	1834-1835	Sir Anthony Eden (C)	1955-1957
Viscount Melbourne (W)	1835-1841	Harold Macmillan (C)	1957-1963
Sir Robert Peel (C)	1841-1846	Sir Alec Douglas-Home (C)	1963-1964
Lord (later Earl) John Russell (W)	1846-1852	Harold Wilson (La)	1964-1970
Earl of Derby (C)	1852	Edward Heath (C)	1970-1974
Earl of Aberdeen (P)	1852-1855	Harold Wilson (La)	1974-1976
Viscount Palmerston (Li)	1855-1858	James Callaghan (La)	1976-1979
Earl of Derby (C)	1858-1859	Margaret Thatcher (C)	1979-1990
Viscount Palmerston (Li)	1859-1865	John Major (C)	1990-1997
Earl Russell (Li)	1865-1866	Tony Blair (La)	1997-
Earl of Derby (C)	1866-1868		

(1) The Conservative Party was formed in 1834, an outgrowth of the Tory party. (2) Walpole is commonly regarded as the first prime minister of Britain, though the title was not commonly used then and did not become official until 1905.

Historical Periods of Japan

Yamato	c. 300-592	Conquest of Yamato plain c. AD 300.	Muromachi	1392-1573	Unification of Southern and Northern Courts, 1392.
Asuka	592-710	Accession of Empress Suiko, 592.	Sengoku	1467-1600	Beginning of the Onin war, 1467.
Nara	710-794	Completion of Heijo (Nara), 710; the capital moves to Nagaoka, 784.	Momoyama	1573-1603	Oda Nobunaga enters Kyoto, 1568; Nobunaga deposes last Ashikaga shogun, 1573; Tokugawa Ieyasu victor at Sekigahara, 1600.
Heian	794-1185	Completion of Heian (Kyoto), 794.			
Fujiwara	858-1160	Fujiwara-no-Yoshifusa becomes regent, 858.	Edo	1603-1867	Ieyasu becomes shogun, 1603.
Taira	1160-1185	Taira-no-Kiyomori assumes control, 1160; Minamoto-no-Yoritomo victor over Taira, 1185.	Meiji	1868-1912	Enthronement of Emperor Mutsuhito (Meiji), 1867; Meiji Restoration and Charter Oath, 1868.
Kamakura	1192-1333	Yoritomo becomes shogun, 1192.			
Namboku	1334-1392	Restoration of Emperor Godaigo, 1334; Southern Court established by Godaigo at Yoshino, 1336.	Taisho	1912-1926	Accession of Emperor Yoshihito, 1912.
			Showa	1926-1989	Accession of Emperor Hirohito, 1926.
Ashikaga	1338-1573	Ashikaga Takauji becomes shogun, 1338.	Heisei	1989-	Accession of Emperor Akihito, 1989.

Rulers of France: Kings, Queens, Presidents

Caesar to Charlemagne

Julius Caesar subdued the Gauls, native tribes of Gaul (France), 58 to 51 BC. The Romans ruled 500 years. The Franks, a Teutonic tribe, reached the Somme from the East c. AD 250. By the 5th century the Merovingian Franks ousted the Romans. In 451, with the help of Visigoths, Burgundians, and others, they defeated Attila and the Huns at Chalons-sur-Marne.

Childeric I became leader of the Merovingians 458. His son Clovis I (Chlodwig, Ludwig, Louis), crowned 481, founded the dynasty. After defeating the Alemanni (Germans) 496, he was baptized a Christian and made Paris his capital. His line ruled until Childeric III was deposed, 751.

The West Merovingians were called Neustrians, the eastern Austrasians. Pepin of Herstal (687-714), major domus,

or head of the palace, of Austrasia, took over Neustria as dux (leader) of the Franks. Pepin's son, Charles, called Martel (the Hammer), defeated the Saracens at Tours-Poitiers, 732; was succeeded by his son, Pepin the Short, 741, who deposed Childeric III and ruled as king until 768.

His son, Charlemagne, or Charles the Great (742-814), became king of the Franks, 768, with his brother Carloman, who died 771. Charlemagne ruled France, Germany, parts of Italy, Spain, and Austria, and enforced Christianity. Crowned Emperor of the Romans by Pope Leo III in St. Peter's, Rome, Dec. 25, 800. Succeeded by son, Louis I the Pious, 814. At death, 840, Louis left empire to sons, Lothair (Roman emperor); Pepin I (king of Aquitaine); Louis II (of Germany); Charles the Bald (France). They quarreled and, by the peace of Verdun, 843, divided the empire.

The date preceding each entry is year of accession.

The Carolingians

843 Charles I (the Bald); Roman Emperor, 875
877 Louis II (the Stammerer), son
879 Louis III (died 882) and Carloman, brothers
885 Charles II (the Fat); Roman Emperor, 881
888 Eudes (Odo), elected by nobles
898 Charles III (the Simple), son of Louis II, defeated by
922 Robert, brother of Eudes, killed in war
923 Rudolph (Raoul), Duke of Burgundy
936 Louis IV, son of Charles III
954 Lothair, son, aged 13, defeated by Capet
986 Louis V (the Sluggard), left no heirs

The Capets

987 Hugh Capet, son of Hugh the Great
996 Robert II (the Wise), his son
1031 Henry I, son
1060 Philip I (the Fair), son
1108 Louis VI (the Fat), son
1137 Louis VII (the Younger), son
1180 Philip II (Augustus), son, crowned at Reims
1223 Louis VIII (the Lion), son
1226 Louis IX, son, crusader; Louis IX (1214-1270) reigned 44 years, arbitrated disputes with English King Henry III; led crusades, 1248 (captured in Egypt 1250) and 1270, when he died of plague in Tunis. Canonized 1297 as St. Louis.
1270 Philip III (the Hardy), son
1285 Philip IV (the Fair), son, king at 17
1314 Louis X (the Headstrong), son. His posthumous son, John I, lived only 7 days
1316 Philip V (the Tall), brother of Louis X
1322 Charles IV (the Fair), brother of Louis X

House of Valois

1328 Philip VI (of Valois), grandson of Philip III
1350 John II (the Good), his son, retired to England
1364 Charles V (the Wise), son
1380 Charles VI (the Beloved), son
1422 Charles VII (the Victorious), son. In 1429 Joan of Arc (Jeanne d'Arc) promised Charles to oust the English, who occupied northern France. Joan won at Orleans and Patay and had Charles crowned at Reims, July 17, 1429. Joan was captured May 24, 1430, and executed May 30, 1431, at Rouen for heresy. Charles ordered her rehabilitation, effected 1455.
1461 Louis XI (the Cruel), son, civil reformer
1483 Charles VIII (the Affable), son
1498 Louis XII, great-grandson of Charles V
1515 Francis I, of Angouleme, nephew, son-in-law. Francis I (1494-1547) reigned 32 years, fought 4 big wars, was patron of the arts, aided Cellini, del Sarto, Leonardo da Vinci, Rabelais, embellished Fontainebleau.
1547 Henry II, son, killed at a joust in a tournament. He was the husband of Catherine de Medicis (1519-1589) and the lover of Diane de Poitiers (1499-1566). Catherine was born in Florence, daughter of Lorenzo de Medici. By her marriage to Henry II she became the mother of Francis II, Charles IX, Henry III, and Queen Margaret (Reine Margot), wife of Henry IV. She persuaded Charles IX to order the massacre of Huguenots on the Feast of St. Bartholomew, Aug. 24, 1572, six days after her daughter was married to Henry of Navarre.
1559 Francis II, son. In 1548, Mary, Queen of Scots since in-fancy, was betrothed when 6 to Francis, aged 4. They were married 1558. Francis died 1560, aged 16; Mary ruled Scotland, abdicated 1567.
1560 Charles IX, brother
1574 Henry III, brother, assassinated

House of Bourbon

1589 Henry IV, of Navarre, assassinated. Henry IV made enemies when he gave tolerance to Protestants by Edict of Nantes, 1598. He was grandson of Queen Margaret of Navarre, literary patron. He married Margaret of Valois, daughter of Henry II and Catherine de Medicis; was divorced; in 1600 married Marie de Medicis, who became Regent of France, 1610-1617, for her son, Louis XIII, but was exiled by Richelieu, 1631.

1610 Louis XIII (the Just), son. Louis XIII (1601-1643) married Anne of Austria. He came to be dominated by his chief minister (1622-42), Cardinal Richelieu.
1643 Louis XIV ("the Sun King"), son. Louis XIV was king 72 years. Until 1661, Anne of Austria was regent, with Cardinal Mazarin as chief minister; after that, Louis ruled absolutely. Known for his lavish court and patronage of the arts, he exhausted a prosperous country in wars for thrones and territory.
1715 Louis XV, great-grandson. Louis XV married a Polish princess; lost Canada to the English. His favorites, Mme. Pompadour and Mme. Du Barry, influenced policies. Noted for saying "After me, the deluge."
1774 Louis XVI, grandson; married Marie Antoinette, daughter of Empress Maria Therese of Austria. King and queen beheaded by Revolution, 1793. Their son, called Louis XVII, died in prison, never ruled.

First Republic

1792 National Convention of the French Revolution
1795 Directory, under Barras and others
1799 Consulate, Napoleon Bonaparte, first consul. Elected consul for life, 1802.

First Empire

1804 Napoleon I (Napoleon Bonaparte), emperor. Josephine (de Beauharnais), empress, 1804-1809; Marie Louise, empress, 1810-1814. Her son, Francois (1811-1832), titular King of Rome, later Duke de Reichstadt and "Napoleon II," never ruled. Napoleon abdicated 1814, died 1821.

Bourbons Restored

1814 Louis XVIII, king; brother of Louis XVI
1824 Charles X, brother; reactionary; deposed by the July Revolution, 1830

House of Orleans

1830 Louis-Philippe, the "citizen king"

Second Republic

1848 Louis Napoleon Bonaparte, president, nephew of Napoleon I.

Second Empire

1852 Napoleon III (Louis Napoleon Bonaparte), emperor; Eugenie (de Montijo), empress. Lost Franco-Prussian war, deposed 1870. Son, Prince Imperial (1856-1879), died in Zulu War. Eugenie died 1920.

Third Republic—Presidents

1871 Thiers, Louis Adolphe (1797-1877)
1873 MacMahon, Marshal Patrice M. de (1808-1893)
1879 Grevy, Paul J. (1807-1891)
1887 Sadi-Carnot, M. (1837-1894), assassinated
1894 Casimir-Perier, Jean P. P. (1847-1907)
1895 Faure, François Felix (1841-1899)
1899 Loubet, Emile (1838-1929)
1906 Fallieres, C. Armand (1841-1931)
1913 Poincare, Raymond (1860-1934)
1920 Deschanel, Paul (1856-1922)
1920 Millerand, Alexandre (1859-1943)
1924 Doumergue, Gaston (1863-1937)
1931 Doumer, Paul (1857-1932), assassinated
1932 Lebrun, Albert (1871-1950), resigned 1940
1940 Vichy govt. under German armistice: Henri Philippe Petain (1856-1951), Chief of State, 1940-1944.

Provisional govt. after liberation: Charles de Gaulle (1890-1970), Oct. 1944-Jan. 21, 1946; Felix Gouin (1884-1977), Jan. 23, 1946; Georges Bidault (1899-1983), June 24, 1946.

Fourth Republic—Presidents

1947 Auriol, Vincent (1884-1966)
1954 Coty, Rene (1882-1962)

Fifth Republic—Presidents

1959 De Gaulle, Charles Andre J. M. (1890-1970)
1969 Pompidou, Georges (1911-1974)
1974 Giscard d'Estaing, Valery (1926-   )
1981 Mitterrand, François (1916-1996)
1995 Chirac, Jacques (1932-   )

Rulers of Middle Europe; Rise and Fall of Dynasties; Rulers of Germany

Carolingian Dynasty

Charles the Great, or Charlemagne, ruled France, Italy, and Middle Europe; established Ostmark (later Austria); crowned Roman emperor by pope in Rome, AD 800; died 814.

Louis I (Ludwig) the Pious, son; crowned by Charlemagne 814; died 840.

Louis II, the German, son; succeeded to East Francia (Germany) 843-876.

Charles the Fat, son; inherited East Francia and West Francia (France) 876, reunited empire, crowned emperor by pope 881, deposed 887.

Arnulf, nephew, 887-899. Partition of empire.

Louis the Child, 899-911, last direct descendant of Charlemagne.

Conrad I, duke of Franconia, first elected German king, 911-918, founded House of Franconia.

Saxon Dynasty; First Reich

Henry I, the Fowler, duke of Saxony, 919-936.

Otto I, the Great, 936-973, son; crowned Holy Roman Emperor by pope, 962.

Otto II, 973-983, son; failed to oust Greeks and Arabs from Sicily.

Otto III, 983-1002, son; crowned emperor at 16.

Henry II, the Saint, duke of Bavaria, 1002-1024, great-grandson of Otto the Great.

House of Franconia

Conrad II, 1024-1039, elected king of Germany.

Henry III, the Black, 1039-1056, son; deposed 3 popes; annexed Burgundy.

Henry IV, 1056-1106, son; regency by his mother, Agnes of Poitou. Banned by Pope Gregory VII, he did penance at Canossa.

Henry V, 1106-1125, son; last of Salic House.

Lothair, duke of Saxony, 1125-1137. Crowned emperor in Rome, 1134.

House of Hohenstaufen

Conrad III, duke of Swabia, 1138-1152. In 2nd Crusade.

Frederick I, Barbarossa, 1152-1190; Conrad's nephew.

Henry VI, 1190-1196, took lower Italy from Normans. Son became king of Sicily.

Philip of Swabia, 1197-1208, brother.

Otto IV, of House of Welf, 1198-1215; deposed.

Frederick II, 1215-1250, son of Henry VI; king of Sicily; crowned king of Jerusalem in 5th Crusade.

Conrad IV, 1250-1254, son; lost lower Italy to Charles of Anjou.

Conradin, 1252-1268, son, king of Jerusalem and Sicily, beheaded. Last Hohenstaufen.

Interregnum, 1254-1273, Rise of the Electors.

Transition

Rudolph I of Hapsburg, 1273-1291, defeated King Ottocar II of Bohemia. Bequeathed duchy of Austria to eldest son, Albert.

Adolph of Nassau, 1292-1298, killed in war with Albert of Austria.

Albert I, king of Germany, 1298-1308, son of Rudolph.

Henry VII, of Luxemburg, 1308-1313, crowned emperor in Rome. Seized Bohemia, 1310.

Louis IV of Bavaria (Wittelsbach), 1314-1347. Also elected was Frederick of Austria, 1314-1330 (Hapsburg). Abolition of papal sanction for election of Holy Roman Emperor.

Charles IV, of Luxemburg, 1347-1378, grandson of Henry VII, German emperor and king of Bohemia, Lombardy, Burgundy; took Mark of Brandenburg.

Wenceslaus, 1378-1400, deposed.

Rupert, Duke of Palatine, 1400-1410.

Sigismund, 1411-1437.

Hungary

Stephen I, house of Arpad, 997-1038. Crowned king 1000; converted Magyars; canonized 1083. After several centuries of feuds Charles Robert of Anjou became Charles I, 1308-1342.

Louis I, the Great, son, 1342-1382; joint ruler of Poland with Casimir III, 1370. Defeated Turks.

Mary, daughter, 1382-1395, ruled with husband. Sigismund of Luxemburg, 1387-1437, also king of Bohemia. As brother of Wenceslaus he succeeded Rupert as Holy Roman Emperor, 1410.

Albert, 1438-1439, son-in-law of Sigismund; also Roman emperor as Albert II *(see under Hapsburg)*.

Ulaszlo I of Poland, 1440-1444.

Ladislaus V, posthumous son of Albert II, 1444-1457. John Hunyadi (Hunyadi Janos), governor (1446-1452), fought Turks, Czechs; died 1456.

Matthias I (Corvinus), son of Hunyadi, 1458-1490. Shared rule of Bohemia, captured Vienna, 1485, annexed Austria, Styria, Carinthia.

Ulaszlo II (king of Bohemia), 1490-1516.

Louis II, son, aged 10, 1516-1526. Wars with Suleiman, Turk. In 1527 Hungary split between Ferdinand I, Archduke of Austria, bro.-in-law of Louis II, and John Zapolya of Transylvania. After Turkish invasion, 1547, Hungary split between Ferdinand, Prince John Sigismund (Transylvania), and the Turks.

House of Hapsburg

Albert V of Austria, Hapsburg, crowned king of Hungary, Jan. 1438, Roman emperor, March 1438, as Albert II; died 1439.

Frederick III, cousin, 1440-1493. Fought Turks.

Maximilian I, son, 1493-1519. Assumed title of Holy Roman Emperor (German), 1493.

Charles V, grandson, 1519-1556. King of Spain with mother co-regent; crowned Roman emperor at Aix, 1520. Confronted Luther at Worms; attempted church reform and religious conciliation; abdicated 1556.

Ferdinand I, king of Bohemia, 1526, of Hungary, 1527; disputed. German king, 1531. Crowned Roman emperor on abdication of brother Charles V, 1556.

Maximilian II, son, 1564-1576.

Rudolph II, son, 1576-1612.

Matthias, brother, 1612-1619, king of Bohemia and Hungary.

Ferdinand II of Styria, king of Bohemia, 1617, of Hungary, 1618, Roman emperor, 1619. Bohemian Protestants deposed him, elected Frederick V of Palatine, starting Thirty Years War.

Ferdinand III, son, king of Hungary, 1625, Bohemia, 1627, Roman emperor, 1637. Peace of Westphalia, 1648, ended war. Leopold I, 1658-1705; Joseph I, 1705-1711; Charles VI, 1711-1740.

Maria Theresa, daughter, 1740-1780, Archduchess of Austria, queen of Hungary; ousted pretender, Charles VII, crowned 1742; in 1745 obtained election of her husband Francis I as Roman emperor and co-regent (d. 1765). Fought Seven Years' War with Frederick II of Prussia. Mother of Marie Antoinette.

Joseph II, son, 1765-1790, Roman emperor, reformer; powers restricted by Empress Maria Theresa until her death, 1780. First partition of Poland. Leopold II, 1790-1792.

Francis II, son, 1792-1835. Fought Napoleon. Proclaimed first hereditary emperor of Austria, 1804. Forced to abdicate as Roman emperor, 1806; last use of title. Ferdinand I, son, 1835-1848, abdicated during revolution.

Austro-Hungarian Monarchy

Francis Joseph I, nephew, 1848-1916, emperor of Austria, king of Hungary. Dual monarchy of Austria-Hungary formed, 1867. After assassination of heir, Archduke Francis Ferdinand, June 28, 1914, Austrian diplomacy precipitated World War I.

Charles I, grand-nephew, 1916-1918, last emperor of Austria and king of Hungary. Abdicated Nov. 11-13, 1918, died 1922.

Rulers of Prussia

Nucleus of Prussia was the Mark of Brandenburg. First margrave Albert the Bear (Albrecht), 1134-1170. First Hohenzollern margrave was Frederick, burgrave of Nuremberg, 1417-1440.

Frederick William, 1640-1688, the Great Elector. Son, Frederick III, 1688-1713, crowned King Frederick of Prussia, 1701.

Frederick William I, son, 1713-1740.

Frederick II, the Great, son, 1740-1786, annexed Silesia, part of Austria.

Frederick William II, nephew, 1786-1797.

Frederick William III, son, 1797-1840. Napoleonic wars.

Frederick William IV, son, 1840-1861. Uprising of 1848 and first parliament and constitution.

Second and Third Reich

William I, 1861-1888, brother. Annexation of Schleswig and Hanover; Franco-Prussian war, 1870-1871, proclamation of German Reich, Jan. 18, 1871, at Versailles; William, German emperor (Deutscher Kaiser), Bismarck, chancellor.

Frederick III, 1888.

William II, son, 1888-1918. Led Germany in World War I, abdicated as German emperor and king of Prussia, Nov. 9, 1918. Died in exile in Netherlands, June 4, 1941. Minor rulers of Bavaria, Saxony, Wurttemberg also abdicated.

Germany proclaimed republic at Weimar, July 1, 1919. Presidents included: Frederick Ebert, 1919-1925; Paul von Hindenburg-Beneckendorff, 1925, reelected 1932, d. Aug. 2, 1934. Adolf Hitler, chancellor, chosen successor as Leader-Chancellor (Fuehrer-Reichskanzler) of Third Reich. Annexed Austria, Mar. 1938. Precipitated World War II, 1939-1945. Suicide Apr. 30, 1945.

Germany After 1945

Following World War II, Germany was split between democratic West and Soviet-dominated East. West German chancellors: Konrad Adenauer, 1949-1963; Ludwig Erhard, 1963-1966; Kurt Georg Kiesinger, 1966-1969; Willy Brandt, 1969-1974; Helmut Schmidt, 1974-1982; Helmut Kohl, 1982-1990. East German Communist party leaders: Walter Ulbricht, 1946-1971; Erich Honecker, 1971-1989; Egon Krenz, 1989-1990.

Germany reunited Oct. 3, 1990. Post-reunification chancellors: Helmut Kohl, 1990-1998; Gerhard Schröder, 1998- .

▶ **IT'S A FACT:** The Grimaldi royal family, which currently heads the tiny European nation of Monaco, is one of the longest-ruling families in the world. The House of Grimaldi was established more than 700 years ago in 1297.

Rulers of Poland

House of Piasts

Miesko I, 962?-992; Poland Christianized 966. Expansion under 3 Boleslavs: I, 992-1025, son, crowned king 1024; II, 1058-1079, great-grandson, exiled after killing bishop Stanislav who became chief patron saint of Poland; III, 1106-1138, nephew, divided Poland among 4 sons, eldest suzerain.

1138-1306, feudal division. 1226 founding in Prussia of military order Teutonic Knights. 1226 invasion by Tartars/Mongols.

Vladislav I, 1306-1333, reunited most Polish territories, crowned king 1320. Casimir III the Great, 1333-1370, son, developed economic, cultural life, foreign policy.

House of Anjou

Louis I, 1370-1382, nephew/was also Louis I of Hungary.

Jadwiga, 1384-1399, daughter, married 1386 Jagiello, Grand Duke of Lithuania.

House of Jagiellonians

Vladislav II, 1386-1434, Christianized Lithuania, founded personal union between Poland and Lithuania. Defeated 1410 Teutonic Knights at Grunwald.

Vladislav III, 1434-1444, son, simultaneously king of Hungary. Fought Turks, killed 1444 in battle of Varna.

Casimir IV, 1446-1492, brother, competed with Hapsburgs, put son Vladislav on throne of Bohemia, later also of Hungary (Ulaszlo II).

Sigismund I, 1506-1548, son, patronized science and arts, his and son's reign "Golden Age."

Sigismund II, 1548-1572, son, established 1569 real union of Poland and Lithuania (lasted until 1795).

Elective Kings

Polish nobles in 1572 proclaimed Poland a republic headed by king to be elected by whole nobility.

Stephen Batory, 1576-1586, duke of Transylvania, married Ann, sister of Sigismund II August. Fought Russians.

Sigismund III Vasa, 1587-1632, nephew of Sigismund II. 1592-1598 also king of Sweden. His generals fought Russians, Turks.

Vladislav II Vasa, 1632-1648, son. Fought Russians.

John II Casimir Vasa, 1648-1668, brother. Fought Cossacks, Swedes, Russians, Turks, Tatars (the "Deluge"). Abdicated 1668.

John III Sobieski, 1674-1696. Won Vienna from besieging Turks, 1683.

Stanislav II, 1764-1795, last king. Encouraged reforms; 1791 1st modern Constitution in Europe. 1772, 1793, 1795 Poland partitioned among Russia, Prussia, Austria. Unsuccessful insurrection against foreign invasion 1794 under Kosciusko, American-Polish general.

1795-1918: Poland Under Foreign Rule

1807-1815 Grand Duchy of Warsaw created by Napoleon I, Frederick August of Saxony grand duke.

1815 Congress of Vienna proclaimed part of Poland "Kingdom" in personal union with Russia.

Polish uprisings: 1830 against Russia; 1846, 1848 against Austria; 1863 against Russia—all repressed.

1918-1939: Second Republic

1918-1922 Head of State Jozef Pilsudski. Presidents: Gabriel Narutowicz 1922, assassinated; Stanislav Wojciechowski 1922-1926, had to abdicate after Pilsudski's coup d'état; Ignacy Moscicki, 1926-1939, ruled (with Pilsudski until his death, 1935) as virtual dictator.

1939-1945: Poland Under Foreign Occupation

Nazi and Soviet invasion Sept. 1939. Polish government-in-exile, first in France, then in England. Vladislav Raczkiewicz president; Gen. Vladislav Sikorski, then Stanislav Mikolajczyk, prime ministers. Soviet-sponsored Polish Committee of National Liberation proclaimed at Lublin July 1944, transformed into government Jan. 1, 1945.

Poland After 1945

In the late 1940s, Poland came increasingly under Soviet control. Communist party ruled in Poland until Aug. 1989, when democratic Solidarity party, led by Lech Walesa, gained control of government. Walesa was elected president in 1990, but lost the office to former communist Aleksander Kwasniewski in 1995. The government remained democratic, and Kwasniewski was re-elected in Oct. 2000.

Rulers of Denmark, Sweden, Norway

Denmark

Earliest rulers invaded Britain; King Canute, who ruled in London 1016-1035, was most famous. The Valdemars furnished kings until the 15th century. In 1282 the Danes won the first national assembly, Danehof, from King Erik V.

Most redoubtable medieval character was Margaret, daughter of Valdemar IV, born 1353, married at 10 to King Haakon VI of Norway. In 1376 she had her first infant son Olaf made king of Denmark. After his death, 1387, she was regent of Denmark and Norway. In 1388 Sweden accepted her as sovereign. In 1389 she made her grand-nephew, Duke Erik of Pomerania, titular king of Denmark, Sweden, and Norway, with herself as regent. In 1397 she effected the Union of Kalmar of the three kingdoms and had Erik VII crowned. In 1439 the three kingdoms deposed him and elected, 1440, Christopher of Bavaria king (Christopher III). On his death, 1448, the union broke up.

Succeeding rulers were unable to enforce their claims as rulers of Sweden until 1520, when Christian II conquered Sweden. He was thrown out 1522, and in 1523 Gustavus Vasa united Sweden. Denmark continued to dominate Norway until the Napoleonic wars, when Frederick VI, 1808-1839, joined the Napoleonic cause after Britain had destroyed the Danish fleet, 1807. In 1814 he was forced to cede Norway to Sweden and Helgoland to Britain, receiving Lauenburg. Successors Christian VIII, 1839; Frederick VII, 1848; Christian IX, 1863; Frederick VIII, 1906; Christian X, 1912; Frederick IX, 1947; Margrethe II, 1972.

Sweden

Early kings ruled at Uppsala, but did not dominate the country. Sverker, c1130-c1156, united the Swedes and Goths. In 1435 Sweden obtained the Riksdag, or parliament. After the Union of Kalmar, 1397, the Danes either ruled or harried the country until Christian II of Denmark conquered it anew, 1520. This led to a rising under Gustavus Vasa, who ruled Sweden 1523-1560, and established an independent kingdom. Charles IX, 1599-1611, crowned 1604, conquered Moscow. Gustavus II Adolphus, 1611-1632, was called the Lion of the North. Later rulers: Christina, 1632; Charles X Gustavus, 1654; Charles XI, 1660; Charles XII (invader of Russia and Poland, defeated at Poltava, June 28, 1709), 1697; Ulrika Eleanora, sister, elected queen 1718; Frederick I (of Hesse), her husband, 1720; Adolphus Frederick, 1751; Gustavus III, 1771; Gustavus IV Adolphus, 1792; Charles XIII, 1809. (Union with Norway began 1814.) Charles XIV John, 1818 (he was Jean Bernadotte, Napoleon's Prince of Ponte Corvo, elected 1810 to succeed Charles XIII); he founded the present dynasty: Oscar I, 1844; Charles XV, 1859; Oscar II, 1872; Gustavus V, 1907; Gustav VI Adolf, 1950; Carl XVI Gustaf, 1973.

Norway

Overcoming many rivals, Harald Haarfager, 872-930, conquered Norway, Orkneys, and Shetlands; Olaf I, great-grandson, 995-1000, brought Christianity into Norway, Iceland, and Greenland. In 1035 Magnus the Good also became king of Denmark. Haakon V, 1299-1319, had married his daughter to Erik of Sweden. Their son, Magnus, became ruler of Norway and Sweden at 6. His son, Haakon VI, married Margaret of Denmark; their son Olaf IV became king of Norway and Denmark, followed by Margaret's regency and the Union of Kalmar, 1397.

In 1450 Norway became subservient to Denmark. Christian IV, 1588-1648, founded Christiania, now Oslo. After Napoleonic wars, when Denmark ceded Norway to Sweden, a strong nationalist movement forced recognition of Norway as an independent kingdom united with Sweden under the Swedish kings, 1814-1905. In 1905 the union was dissolved and Prince Charles of Denmark became Haakon VII. He died Sept. 21, 1957; succeeded by son, Olav V. Olav V died Jan. 17, 1991; succeeded by son, Harald V.

Rulers of the Netherlands and Belgium

The Netherlands (Holland)

William Frederick, Prince of Orange, led a revolt against French rule, 1813; crowned king, 1815. Belgium seceded Oct. 4, 1830, after a revolt. The secession was ratified by the two kingdoms by treaty, Apr. 19, 1839.

Succession: William II, son, 1840; William III, son, 1849; Wilhelmina, daughter of William III and his 2nd wife Princess Emma of Waldeck, 1890; Wilhelmina abdicated, Sept. 4, 1948, in favor of daughter, Juliana. Juliana abdicated, Apr. 30, 1980, in favor of daughter, Beatrix.

Belgium

A national congress elected Prince Leopold of Saxe-Coburg as king; he took the throne July 21, 1831, as Leopold I.

Succession: Leopold II, son, 1865; Albert I, nephew of Leopold II, 1909; Leopold III, son of Albert, 1934; Prince Charles, Regent 1944; Leopold returned 1950, yielded powers to son Baudouin, Prince Royal, Aug. 6, 1950, abdicated July 16, 1951. Baudouin I took throne July 17, 1951, died July 31, 1993; succeeded by brother, Albert II.

Roman Rulers

From Romulus to the end of the Empire in the West. Rulers in the East sat in Constantinople and, for a brief period, in Nicaea, until the capture of Constantinople by the Turks in 1453, when Byzantium was succeeded by the Ottoman Empire.

The Kingdom

BC
753 Romulus (Quirinus)
716 Numa Pompilius
673 Tullus Hostilius
640 Ancus Marcius
616 L. Tarquinius Priscus
578 Servius Tullius
534 L. Tarquinius Superbus

The Republic

509 Consulate established
509 Quaestorship instituted
498 Dictatorship introduced
494 Plebeian Tribunate created
494 Plebeian Aedileship created
444 Consular Tribunate organized
435 Censorship instituted
366 Praetorship established
366 Curule Aedileship created
362 Military Tribunate elected
326 Proconsulate introduced
311 Naval Duumvirate elected
217 Dictatorship of Fabius Maximus
133 Tribunate of Tiberius Gracchus
123 Tribunate of Gaius Gracchus
82 Dictatorship of Sulla
60 First Triumvirate formed (Caesar, Pompeius, Crassus)
46 Dictatorship of Caesar
43 Second Triumvirate formed (Octavianus, Antonius, Lepidus)

The Empire

27 Augustus (Octavian)
AD
14 Tiberius I
37 Caligula
41 Claudius I
54 Nero
68 Galba
69 Galba; Otho, Vitellius
69 Vespasianus
79 Titus

81 Domitianus
96 Nerva
98 Trajanus
117 Hadrianus
138 Antoninus Pius
161 Marcus Aurelius and Lucius Verus
169 Marcus Aurelius (alone)
180 Commodus
193 Pertinax; Julianus I
193 Septimius Severus
211 Caracalla and Geta
212 Caracalla (alone)
217 Macrinus
218 Elagabalus (Heliogabalus)
222 Alexander Severus
235 Maximinus I (the Thracian)
238 Gordianus I and Gordianus II; Pupienus and Balbinus
238 Gordianus III
244 Philippus (the Arabian)
249 Decius
251 Gallus and Volusianus
253 Aemilianus
253 Valerianus and Gallienus
258 Gallienus (alone)
268 Claudius Gothicus
270 Quintillus
270 Aurelianus
275 Tacitus
276 Florianus
276 Probus
282 Carus
283 Carinus and Numerianus
286 Diocletianus and Maximianus
305 Galerius and Constantius I
306 Galerius, Maximinus II, Severus I
307 Galerius, Maximinus II, Constantinus I, Licinius, Maxentius
311 Maximinus II, Constantinus I, Licinius, Maxentius
314 Maximinus II, Constantinus I, Licinius
314 Constantinus I and Licinius
324 Constantinus I (the Great)

337 Constantinus II, Constans I, Constantius II
340 Constantius II and Constans I
350 Constantius II
361 Julianus II (the Apostate)
363 Jovianus

West (Rome) and East (Constantinople)

364 Valentinianus I (West) and Valens (East)
367 Valentinianus I with Gratianus (West) and Valens (East)
375 Gratianus with Valentinianus II (West) and Valens (East)
378 Gratianus with Valentinianus II (West), Theodosius I (East)
383 Valentinianus II (West) and Theodosius I (East)
394 Theodosius I (the Great)
395 Honorius (West) and Arcadius (East)
408 Honorius (West) and Theodosius II (East)
423 Valentinianus III (West) and Theodosius II (East)
450 Valentinianus III (West) and Marcianus (East)
455 Maximus (West), Avitus (West); Marcianus (East)
456 Avitus (West), Marcianus (East)
457 Majorianus (West), Leo I (East)
461 Severus II (West), Leo I (East)
467 Anthemius (West), Leo I (East)
472 Olybrius (West), Leo I (East)
473 Glycerius (West), Leo I (East)
474 Julius Nepos (West), Leo II (East)
475 Romulus Augustulus (West) and Zeno (East)
476 End of Empire in West; Odovacar, King, drops title of Emperor; murdered by King Theodoric of Ostrogoths, 493

Rulers of Modern Italy

After the fall of Napoleon in 1814, the Congress of Vienna, 1815, restored Italy as a political patchwork, comprising the Kingdom of Naples and Sicily, the Papal States, and smaller units. Piedmont and Genoa were awarded to Sardinia, ruled by King Victor Emmanuel I of Savoy.

United Italy emerged under the leadership of Camillo, Count di Cavour (1810-1861), Sardinian prime minister. Agitation was led by Giuseppe Mazzini (1805-1872) and Giuseppe Garibaldi (1807-1882), soldier; Victor Emmanuel I abdicated 1821. After a brief regency for a brother, Charles Albert was king 1831-1849, abdicating when defeated by the Austrians at Novara. Succeeded by Victor Emmanuel II, 1849-1861.

In 1859 France forced Austria to cede Lombardy to Sardinia, which gave rights to Savoy and Nice to France. In 1860 Garibaldi led 1,000 volunteers in a spectacular campaign, took Sicily and expelled the King of Naples. In 1860 the House of Savoy annexed Tuscany, Parma, Modena, Romagna, the Two Sicilys, the Marches, and Umbria. Victor Emmanuel assumed the title of King of Italy at Turin Mar. 17, 1861.

In 1866, Victor Emmanuel allied with Prussia in the Austro-Prussian War, and with Prussia's victory received Venetia. On Sept. 20, 1870, his troops under Gen. Raffaele Cadorna entered Rome and took over the Papal States, ending the temporal power of the Roman Catholic Church.

Succession: Umberto I, 1878, assassinated 1900; Victor Emmanuel III, 1900, abdicated 1946, died 1947; Humbert II, 1946, ruled a month. In 1921 Benito Mussolini (1883-1945) formed the Fascist party; he became prime minister Oct. 31, 1922. He entered World War II as an ally of Hitler. He was deposed July 25, 1943.

At a plebiscite June 2, 1946, Italy voted for a republic; Premier Alcide de Gasperi became chief of state June 13, 1946. On June 28, 1946, the Constituent Assembly elected Enrico de Nicola, Liberal, provisional president. Successive presidents: Luigi Einaudi, elected May 11, 1948; Giovanni Gronchi, Apr. 29, 1955; Antonio Segni, May 6, 1962; Giuseppe Saragat, Dec. 28, 1964; Giovanni Leone, Dec. 29, 1971; Alessandro Pertini, July 9, 1978; Francesco Cossiga, July 9, 1985; Oscar Luigi Scalfaro, May 28, 1992; Carlo Azeglio Ciampi, May 18, 1999.

Rulers of Spain

From 8th to 11th centuries Spain was dominated by the Moors (Arabs and Berbers). The Christian reconquest established small kingdoms (Asturias, Aragon, Castile, Catalonia, Leon, Navarre, and Valencia). In 1474 Isabella, b. 1451, became Queen of Castile & Leon. Her husband, Ferdinand, b. 1452, inherited Aragon 1479, with Catalonia, Valencia, and the Balearic Islands, became Ferdinand V of Castile. By Isabella's request Pope Sixtus IV established the Inquisition, 1478. Last Moorish kingdom, Granada, fell 1492. Columbus opened New World of colonies, 1492. Isabella died 1504, succeeded by her daughter, Juana "the Mad," but Ferdinand ruled until his death 1516.

Charles I, b. 1500, son of Juana, grandson of Ferdinand and Isabella, and of Maximilian I of Hapsburg; succeeded later as Holy Roman Emperor, Charles V, 1520; abdicated 1556. Philip II, son, 1556-1598, inherited only Spanish throne; conquered Portugal, fought Turks, sent Armada vs. England. Married to Mary I of England, 1554-1558. Succession: Philip III, 1598-1621; Philip IV, 1621-1665; Charles II, 1665-1700, left Spain to Philip of Anjou, grandson of Louis XIV, who as Philip V, 1700-1746, founded Bourbon dynasty; Ferdinand VI, 1746-1759; Charles III, 1759-1788; Charles IV, 1788-1808, abdicated.

Napoleon now dominated politics and made his brother Joseph King of Spain 1808, but the Spanish ousted him in 1813. Ferdinand VII, 1808, 1814-1833, lost American colonies; succeeded by daughter Isabella II, aged 3, with wife Maria Christina of Naples regent until 1843. Isabella deposed by revolution 1868. Elected king by the Cortes, Amadeo of Savoy, 1870; abdicated 1873. First republic, 1873-74. Alfonso XII, son of Isabella, 1875-85. His posthumous son was Alfonso XIII, with his mother, Queen Maria Christina regent; Spanish-American war, Spain lost Cuba, gave up Puerto Rico, Philippines, Sulu Is., Marianas. Alfonso took throne 1902, aged 16, married British Princess Victoria Eugenia of Battenberg. Dictatorship of Primo de Rivera, 1923-30, precipitated revolution of 1931. Alfonso agreed to leave without formal abdication. Monarchy abolished; the second republic established, with socialist backing. Niceto Alcala Zamora was president until 1936, when Manuel Azaña was chosen.

In July 1936, the army in Morocco revolted against the government and General Francisco Franco led the troops into Spain. The revolution succeeded by Feb. 1939, when Azaña resigned. Franco became chief of state, with provisions that if he was incapacitated, the Regency Council by two-thirds vote could propose a king to the Cortes, which needed to have a two-thirds majority to elect him.

Alfonso XIII died in Rome Feb. 28, 1941, aged 54. His property and citizenship had been restored.

A law restoring the monarchy was approved in a 1947 referendum. Prince Juan Carlos, b. 1938, grandson of Alfonso XIII, was designated by Franco and the Cortes (Parliament) in 1969 as future king and chief of state. Franco died in office, Nov. 20, 1975; Juan Carlos proclaimed king, Nov. 22.

Leaders in the South American Wars of Liberation

Simon Bolivar (1783-1830), Jose Francisco de San Martin (1778-1850), and Francisco Antonio Gabriel Miranda (1750-1816) are among the heroes of the early 19th-century struggles of South American nations to free themselves from Spain. All three, and their contemporaries, operated in periods of factional strife, during which soldiers and civilians suffered.

Miranda, a Venezuelan, who had served with the French in the American Revolution and commanded parts of the French Revolutionary armies in the Netherlands, attempted to start a revolt in Venezuela in 1806 and failed. In 1810, with British and American backing, he returned and was briefly a dictator, until the British withdrew their support. In 1812 he was overcome by the royalists in Venezuela and taken prisoner, dying in a Spanish prison in 1816.

San Martin was born in Argentina and during 1789-1811 served in campaigns of the Spanish armies in Europe and Africa. He first joined the independence movement in Argentina in 1812 and in 1817 invaded Chile with 4,000 men over the mountain passes. Here he and Gen. Bernardo O'Higgins (1778-1842) defeated the Spaniards at Chacabuco, 1817; O'Higgins was named Liberator and became first director of Chile, 1817-23. In 1821 San Martin occupied Lima and Callao, Peru, and became protector of Peru.

Bolivar, the greatest leader of South American liberation from Spain, was born in Venezuela, the son of an aristocratic family. He first served under Miranda in 1812 and in 1813 captured Caracas, where he was named Liberator. Forced out next year by civil strife, he led a campaign that captured Bogota in 1814. In 1817 he was again in control of Venezuela and was named dictator. He organized Nueva Granada with the help of General Francisco de Paula Santander (1792-1840). By joining Nueva Granada, Venezuela, and the area that is now Panama and Ecuador, the republic of Colombia was formed, with Bolivar president. After numerous setbacks he decisively defeated the Spaniards in the second battle of Carabobo, Venezuela, June 24, 1821.

In May 1822, Gen. Antonio Jose de Sucre, Bolivar's lieutenant, took Quito. Bolivar went to Guayaquil to confer with San Martin, who resigned as protector of Peru and withdrew from politics. With a new army of Colombians and Peruvians Bolivar defeated the Spaniards in a battle at Junin in 1824 and cleared Peru.

De Sucre organized Charcas (Upper Peru) as Republica Bolivar (now Bolivia) and acted as president in place of Bolivar, who wrote its constitution. De Sucre defeated the Spanish faction of Peru at Ayacucho, Dec. 19, 1824.

Continued civil strife finally caused the Colombian federation to break apart. Santander turned against Bolivar, but the latter defeated him and banished him. In 1828 Bolivar gave up the presidency he had held precariously for 14 years. He became ill from tuberculosis and died Dec. 17, 1830. He is buried in the national pantheon in Caracas.

Rulers of Russia; Leaders of the USSR and Russian Federation

First ruler to consolidate Slavic tribes was Rurik, leader of the Russians who established himself at Novgorod, AD 862. He and his immediate successors had Scandinavian affiliations. They moved to Kiev after 972 and ruled as Dukes of Kiev. In 988 Vladimir was converted and adopted the Byzantine Greek Orthodox service, later modified by Slav influences. Important as organizer and lawgiver was Yaroslav, 1019-1054, whose daughters married kings of Norway, Hungary, and France. His grandson, Vladimir II (Monomakh), 1113-1125, was progenitor of several rulers, but in 1169 Andrew Bogolubski overthrew Kiev and began the line known as Grand Dukes of Vladimir.

Of the Grand Dukes of Vladimir, Alexander Nevsky, 1246-1263, had a son, Daniel, first to be called Duke of Muscovy (Moscow), who ruled 1263-1303. His successors became Grand Dukes of Muscovy. After Dmitri III Donskoi defeated the Tatars in 1380, they also became Grand Dukes of all Russia. Tatar independence and considerable territorial expansion were achieved under Ivan III, 1462-1505.

Tsars of Muscovy—Ivan III was referred to in church ritual as Tsar. He married Sofia, niece of the last Byzantine emperor. His successor, Basil III, died in 1533 when Basil's son Ivan was only 3. He became Ivan IV, "the Terrible"; crowned 1547 as Tsar of all the Russias, ruled until 1584. Under the weak rule of his son, Feodor I, 1584-1598, Boris Godunov had control. The dynasty died, and after years of tribal strife and intervention by Polish and Swedish armies, the Russians united under 17-year-old Michael Romanov, distantly related to the first wife of Ivan IV. He

ruled 1613-1645 and established the Romanov line. Fourth ruler after Michael was Peter I.

Tsars, or Emperors, of Russia (Romanovs)—Peter I, 1682-1725, known as Peter the Great, took title of Emperor in 1721. His successors and dates of accession were: Catherine, his widow, 1725; Peter II, his grandson, 1727; Anne, Duchess of Courland, 1730, daughter of Peter the Great's brother, Tsar Ivan V; Ivan VI, 1740, great-grandson of Ivan V, child, kept in prison and murdered 1764; Elizabeth, daughter of Peter I, 1741; Peter III, grandson of Peter I, 1761, deposed 1762 for his consort, Catherine II, former princess of Anhalt Zerbst (Germany) who is known as Catherine the Great; Paul I, her son, 1796, killed 1801; Alexander I, son of Paul, 1801, defeated Napoleon; Nicholas I, his brother, 1825; Alexander II, son of Nicholas, 1855, assassinated 1881 by terrorists; Alexander III, son, 1881. Nicholas II, son, 1894-1917, last Tsar of Russia, was forced to abdicate by the March 1917 Revolution that followed losses to Germany in WWI. The Tsar, Empress, Tsarevich (Crown Prince), and Tsar's 4 daughters were murdered by the Bolsheviks in Yekaterinburg, July 16, 1918.

Provisional Government—premiers, Prince Georgi Lvov, followed by Alexander Kerensky, 1917.

Union of Soviet Socialist Republics

Bolshevik Revolution, Nov. 7, 1917, removed Kerensky from power; council of People's Commissars formed, Lenin (Vladimir Ilyich Ulyanov) became premier. Lenin died Jan. 21, 1924. Aleksei Rykov (executed 1938) and V. M. Molotov held the office, but actual ruler was Joseph Stalin (Joseph Vissarionovich Djugashvili), general secretary of the Central Committee of the Communist Party. Stalin became president of the Council of Ministers (premier) May 7, 1941,

died Mar. 5, 1953. Succeeded by Georgi M. Malenkov, as head of the Council and premier, and Nikita S. Khrushchev, first secretary of the Central Committee. Malenkov resigned Feb. 8, 1955, became deputy premier, was dropped July 3, 1957. Marshal Nikolai A. Bulganin became premier Feb. 8, 1955; was demoted and Khrushchev became premier Mar. 27, 1958.

Khrushchev was ousted Oct. 14-15, 1964, replaced by Leonid I. Brezhnev as first secretary of the party and by Aleksei N. Kosygin as premier. On June 16, 1977, Brezhnev also took office as president. He died Nov. 10, 1982; 2 days later the Central Committee elected former KGB head Yuri V. Andropov president. Andropov died Feb. 9, 1984; on Feb. 13, Konstantin U. Chernenko chosen by Central Committee as its general secretary. Chernenko died Mar. 10, 1985; on Mar. 11, he was succeeded as general secretary by Mikhail Gorbachev, who replaced Andrei Gromyko as president on Oct. 1, 1988. Gorbachev resigned Dec. 25, 1991, and the Soviet Union officially disbanded the next day. Each of the 15 former Soviet constituent republics became independent.

Post-Soviet Russia

After adopting a degree of sovereignty, the Russian Republic had held elections in June 1991. Boris Yeltsin was sworn in July 10, 1991, as Russia's first elected president. With the Dec. 1991 dissolution of the Soviet Union, Russia (officially Russian Federation) became a founding member of the Commonwealth of Independent States. On Dec. 31, 1999, Yeltsin stepped down as president; he named Vladimir Putin his interim successor. Putin won a presidential election Mar. 26, 2000, and was reelected Mar. 14, 2004.

Governments of China

(Until 221 BC and frequently thereafter, China was not a unified state. Where dynastic dates overlap, the rulers or events referred to appeared in different areas of China.)

Hsia	1994 BC – c1523 BC
Shang	c1523 BC – c1028 BC
Western Chou	c1027 BC – 770 BC
Eastern Chou	770 BC – 256 BC
Warring States	403 BC – 222 BC
Ch'in (first unified empire)	221 BC – 206 BC
Han	202 BC – AD 220
Western Han (expanded Chinese state beyond the Yellow and Yangtze River valleys)	202 BC – AD 9
Hsin (Wang Mang, usurper)	AD 9 – 23
Eastern Han (expanded Chinese state into Indochina and Turkestan)	25 – 220
Three Kingdoms (Wei, Shu, Wu)	220 – 265
Chin (western)	265 – 317
(eastern)	317 – 420
Northern Dynasties (followed several short-lived governments by Turks, Mongols, etc.)	386 – 581
Southern Dynasties (capital: Nanjing)	420 – 589
Sui (reunified China)	581 – 618
Tang (a golden age of Chinese culture; capital: Xian)	618 – 906
Five Dynasties (Yellow River basin)	902 – 960
Ten Kingdoms (southern China)	907 – 979
Liao (Khitan Mongols; capital at site of Beijing)	947 – 1125
Sung	960 – 1279
Northern Sung (reunified central and southern China)	960 – 1126
Western Hsai (non-Chinese rulers in northwest)	990 – 1227
Chin (Tatars; drove Sung out of central China)	1115 – 1234
Yuan (Mongols; Kublai Khan est. capital at site of Beijing, c. 1264)	1271 – 1368
Ming (China reunified under Chinese rule; capital: Nanjing, then Beijing in 1420)	1368 – 1644
Ch'ing (Manchus, descendents of Tatars)	1644 – 1912
Republic (disunity; provincial rulers, warlords)	1912 – 1949
People's Republic of China	1949 –

Leaders of China Since 1949

Mao Zedong	Chairman, Central People's Administrative Council, Communist Party (CPC), 1949-1976
Zhou Enlai	Premier, foreign minister, 1949-1976
Deng Xiaoping	Vice Premier, 1952-1966, 1973-1976, 1977-1980; "paramount leader," 1978-1997
Liu Shaoqi	President, 1959-1969
Hua Guofeng	Premier, 1976-1980; CPC Chairman, 1976-1981
Zhao Ziyang	Premier, 1980-1988; CPC General Secretary, 1987-1989
Hu Yaobang	CPC Chairman, 1981-1982; CPC General Secretary, 1982-1987
Li Xiannian	President, 1983-1988
Yang Shangkun	President, 1988-1993
Li Peng	Premier, 1988-98
Jiang Zemin	CPC General Secretary, 1989-2002; President, 1993-2003
Zhu Rongji	Premier, 1998-2003
Hu Jintao	CPC General Secretary, 2002-; President, 2003-
Wen Jiabao	Premier, 2003-

▶ *IT'S A FACT:* The "Forbidden City" in Beijing, China, was home to the emperors of the Ming and Ch'ing dynasties from 1420 to 1912, when the last Chinese emperor, Pu Yi, abdicated. It was called the "Forbidden City" as only imperial family members and senior government officials were allowed to enter. Named a UNESCO World Heritage Site in 1987, it is the largest palace complex in the world.

UNITED STATES HISTORY

This chapter includes the following sections:

Chronology of Events

1492
Christopher Columbus and crew sighted land Oct. 12 in present-day Bahamas.

1497
John Cabot explored northeast coast to Delaware.

1513
Juan Ponce de León explored Florida coast.

1524
Giovanni da Verrazano led French expedition along coast from Carolina north to Nova Scotia; entered New York harbor.

1526
San Miguel de Guadalupe, **first European settlement** in what became U.S. territory, was established in the summer off S. Carolina coast; abandoned in Oct.

1539
Hernando de Soto landed in Florida May 28; crossed Mississippi River, **1541.**

1540
Francisco Vásquez de Coronado explored Southwest north of Rio Grande. Hernando de Alarcón reached Colorado River; Don Garcia Lopez de Cardenas reached Grand Canyon. Others explored California coast.

1562
First French colony in what became U.S. territory was founded on Parris Island off S. Carolina coast; abandoned **1564.**

1565
St. Augustine, FL, founded Sept. 8 by Pedro Menéndez. Razed by Francis Drake **1586.**

1579
Francis Drake entered San Francisco Bay and claimed region for Britain.

1585
"Lost colony" sponsored by **Sir Walter Raleigh** was founded on **Roanoke Island**, off N. Carolina coast; settlers found to have vanished, **1590.**

1587
Virginia Dare (on Roanoke Island) became first infant born in the Thirteen Colonies of English parents.

1607
Capt. John Smith and 105 cavaliers in 3 ships landed on Virginia coast, started first permanent English settlement in New World at **Jamestown** in May.

1609
Henry Hudson, English explorer of Northwest Passage, employed by Dutch, sailed into New York harbor in Sept., and up Hudson to Albany. **Samuel de Champlain** explored Lake Champlain, to the north.
Spaniards settled **Santa Fe, NM.**

1619
House of Burgesses, first representative assembly in New World, elected July 30 at Jamestown, VA.

First black laborers—indentured servants—in English N. American colonies, landed by Dutch at Jamestown in Aug. Chattel slavery legally recognized, **1650.**

1620
Pilgrims, Puritan separatists, left Plymouth, England, Sept. 16 on *Mayflower;* reached Cape Cod Nov. 19; 103 passengers landed Dec. 26 at Plymouth. **Mayflower Compact**, signed Nov. 11, was agreement to form a self-government. Half of colony died during harsh winter.

1624
Dutch colonies started in Albany and in New York area, where **New Netherland** was established in May.

1626
Peter Minuit bought **Manhattan** for Dutch West India Co. from Man-a-hat-a Indians during summer for goods valued at $24; named island **New Amsterdam.**

1630
Settlement of **Boston** established by Massachusetts colonists led by **John Winthrop**.
William Bradford began his chronicle *History of the Plymouth Plantation*; in the Mass. Bay Colony **John Winthrop** began *The History of New England.*

1634
Maryland founded as Catholic colony under charter to Lord Baltimore. Religious toleration granted **1649.**

1635
Boston Latin School, oldest U.S. public school in continuous existence, founded Apr. 23.

1636
Roger Williams founded Providence, RI, in June, as a democratically ruled colony with separation of church and state. Charter granted, **1644.**
Harvard College founded; oldest institution of higher learning in U.S.

1640
First book was printed in America, the so-called Bay Psalm Book.

1647
Liberal constitution drafted in Rhode Island.
First law in America providing for **free compulsory basic education** enacted in Massachusetts.

1660
British Parliament passed First **Navigation Act** Dec. 1, regulating colonial commerce to suit English needs.

1661
A version of the New Testament translated into Algonquian became the **first Bible** printed in the colonies.

1664
British troops **Sept. 8** seized New Netherland from Dutch. Charles II granted New Netherland and city of New Amsterdam to brother, Duke of York; both renamed **New York.** Dutch recaptured colony **1673**, but ceded it to Britain Nov. 10, **1674.**

1670
Charles Town, South Carolina, was founded by English colonists in Apr.

1673

Jacques **Marquette** and Louis **Jolliet** reached the upper **Mississippi** and traveled down it.

Regular **mail service** on horseback was instituted Jan. 1 between New York and Boston.

1674

Future **Salem witch trial** judge Samuel Sewall began a renowned diary covering events through 1729.

1676

Nathaniel Bacon led planters against autocratic British Gov. Sir William Berkeley, burned Jamestown, VA, Sept. 19. Rebellion collapsed when Bacon died; 23 followers executed.

Bloody **Indian war** in New England ended Aug. 12. **King Philip,** Wampanoag chief, and Narragansett Indians killed.

1678

A book of poetry by **Anne Bradstreet** was published posthumously in Massachusetts.

1679

A **fire** destroyed 150 houses in **Boston.**

1681

John Bunyan's The Pilgrim's Progress published in America; became a best-seller.

1682

Robert Cavelier, Sieur de La Salle, claimed lower Mississippi River country for France, called it Louisiana Apr. 9. Had French outposts built in Illinois and Texas, **1684.** Killed during mutiny Mar. 19, **1687.**

William Penn arrived in **Pennsylvania.**

Spanish colonists became the **first Europeans** to settle in **Texas**, at the site of present-day El Paso.

1683

William Penn signed treaty with Delaware Indians Apr. 23, and made payment for Pennsylvania lands. The **first German colonists** in America settled near Philadelphia.

1689

New York's English colonial governor, **Sir Edmund Andros**, resigned after an armed uprising in **Boston** on Apr. 18.

1690

The **New England Primer** came into use in elementary schools.

The **first colonial newspaper**, *Publick Occurrences*, was published by Benjamin Harris, but promptly shut down for lack of official permission.

Whaling began large-scale operations in Nantucket.

1692

Witchcraft delusion at Salem, MA; 20 alleged witches executed by special court.

1696

Capt. William Kidd arrested and sent to England; hanged for piracy **1701.**

1697

The Essays of Sir Francis Bacon, published in England in 1597, was published in America; it became a best-seller.

1699

French settlements made in Mississippi, Louisiana.

1702

Legislation was enacted making the Church of England the **established church** in Maryland.

1704

Indians attacked Deerfield, MA, Feb. 28-29; killed 40, carried off 100.

Boston News Letter, **first regular newspaper,** started by John Campbell, postmaster.

1709

British-colonial troops captured French fort, Port Royal, Nova Scotia, in **Queen Anne's War 1701-13.** France yielded Nova Scotia by treaty **1713.**

1712

Slaves revolted in New York Apr. 6; 21 were executed. Second rising, **1741;** 13 slaves hanged, 13 burned, 71 deported.

1716

First theater in colonies opened in Williamsburg, VA.

1726

Poor people **rioted** in Philadelphia.

Great Awakening religious revival began.

1731

America's **first circulating library** founded in Philadelphia by Benjamin Franklin.

1732

Benjamin Franklin published the first *Poor Richard's Almanack;* published annually to **1757.**

Last of the 13 colonies, **Georgia,** chartered.

1733

Influenza epidemic swept through New York City and Philadelphia.

1735

Editor **John Peter Zenger acquitted** Aug. 5 in New York of libeling British governor by criticizing his conduct in office.

1739

A series of **slave uprisings** put down in South Carolina.

1741

Famous sermon "Sinners in the Hands of an Angry God," delivered at Enfield, MA, July 8, by **Jonathan Edwards**, a major figure in the revivalist **Great Awakening**.

Capt. Vitus Bering reached Alaska.

1744

King George's War pitted British and colonials vs. French. Colonials captured Louisburg, Cape Breton Is., June 17, **1745**. Returned to France **1748** by Treaty of Aix-la-Chapelle.

1752

Benjamin Franklin, flying kite in thunderstorm, proved lightning is electricity June 15; invented lightning rod.

Liberty Bell, cast in England, was delivered to Pennsylvania.

1754

Delegates from 7 colonies to **Albany**, NY, **Congress**, July 19, approved a "Plan of Union" by Benjamin Franklin; but plan was rejected by the colonies.

French and Indian War began when French occupied Ft. Duquesne (Pittsburgh). British moved Acadian French from Nova Scotia to Louisiana Oct. 8, **1755**. British captured Québec Sept. 18, **1759**, in battles in which French Gen. Joseph de Montcalm and British Gen. James Wolfe were killed. Peace pact signed Feb. 10, **1763**. French lost Canada and Midwest.

1757

The first **street lights** appeared in Philadelphia.

1764

Sugar Act, Apr. 5, placed duties on lumber, foodstuffs, molasses, and rum in colonies, to pay French and Indian War debts.

1765

Stamp Act, enacted by Parliament Mar. 22, required revenue stamps to help fund royal troops. Nine colonies, at **Stamp Act Congress** in New York Oct. 7-25, adopted Declaration of Rights. Stamp Act **repealed** Mar. 17, **1766**.

Quartering Act, requiring colonists to house British troops, went into effect Mar. 24.

1767

Townshend Acts levied taxes on glass, painter's lead, paper, and tea. In **1770** all duties except on tea were repealed.

1770

British troops fired Mar. 5 into Boston mob, killed 5 including **Crispus Attucks,** a black man, reportedly leader of group; later called **Boston Massacre.**

1773

East India Co. tea ships turned back at Boston, New York, and Philadelphia in May. Cargo ship burned at Annapolis Oct. 14; cargo thrown overboard at **Boston Tea Party** Dec. 16, to protest the tea tax.

First museum in the colonies was officially established in Charleston, SC; later named the **Charleston** Museum.

1774

"Intolerable Acts" of Parliament curtailed Massachusetts self-rule; barred use of Boston harbor till tea was paid for.

First Continental Congress held in Philadelphia Sept. 5-Oct. 26; called for civil disobedience against British.

Rhode Island abolished slavery.

1775

Patrick Henry addressed Virginia convention, Mar. 23, said, "Give me liberty or give me death."

Paul Revere and William Dawes Apr. 18 rode to alert Patriots that British were on their way to Concord to destroy arms. At **Lexington,** MA, Apr. 19, Minutemen lost 8. On return from **Concord**, British took 273 casualties.

Col. Ethan Allen (joined by Col. Benedict Arnold) captured **Ft. Ticonderoga, NY,** May 10; also Crown Point. Colonials headed for **Bunker Hill,** fortified Breed's Hill, Charlestown, MA. Repulsed British under Gen. William Howe twice before retreating June 17.

Continental Congress June 15 named **George Washington** commander in chief. Established a postal system, July 26; **Benjamin Franklin** became the first postmaster general.

1776

Common Sense, famous pro-independence pamphlet by Thomas Paine, was published Jan. 10; quickly sold some 100,000 copies.

France and Spain each agreed May 2 to provide arms.

In Continental Congress June 7, Richard Henry Lee (VA) moved "that these united colonies are and of right ought to be free and independent states." Resolution adopted July 2. **Declaration of Independence** approved July 4.

Col. William Moultrie's batteries at **Charleston, SC,** repulsed British sea attack June 28. Washington lost **Battle of Long Island** Aug. 27; evacuated New York.

Nathan Hale executed as spy by British Sept. 22.

Brig. Gen. Arnold's **Lake Champlain** fleet was defeated at Valcour Oct. 11, but British returned to Canada. Howe failed to destroy Washington's army at White Plains Oct. 28. Hessians captured Ft. Washington, Manhattan, and 3,000 men Nov. 16; captured Ft. Lee, NJ, Nov. 18.

Washington, in Pennsylvania, recrossed **Delaware River** Dec. 25-26, defeated Hessians at Trenton, NJ, Dec. 26.

1777

Washington defeated Lord Cornwallis at **Princeton** Jan. 3.

Continental Congress, June 14, authorized an **American flag**, the Stars and Stripes.

Maj. Gen. John Burgoyne's force of 8,000 from Canada, captured **Ft. Ticonderoga** July 6. Americans beat back Burgoyne at Bemis Heights Oct. 7, cut off British escape route. Burgoyne surrendered 5,000 men at **Saratoga,** NY, Oct. 17.

Articles of Confederation adopted by Continental Congress Nov. 15.

1778

France signed treaty of aid with U.S. Feb. 6. Sent fleet; British evacuated Philadelphia in consequence, June 18.

1779

George Rogers Clark took Vincennes in **Feb.**

John Paul Jones on the *Bonhomme Richard* defeated *Serapis* in British North Sea waters, Sept. 23.

1780

Charleston, SC, fell to the British May 12, but a British force was defeated near **Kings Mountain, NC,** Oct. 7 by militiamen.

Benedict Arnold found to be a traitor Sept. 23. Arnold escaped, made brigadier general in British army.

1781

Articles of Confederation took effect Mar. 1.

Bank of North America incorporated May 26.

Cornwallis retired to **Yorktown, VA.** Adm. Francois Joseph de Grasse landed 3,000 French and stopped British fleet in **Hampton Roads.** Washington and Jean Baptiste de Rochambeau joined forces, arrived near Williamsburg Sept. 26. Siege of Cornwallis began Oct. 6; **Cornwallis surrendered** Oct. 19.

1782

New **British** cabinet agreed in March to **recognize U.S.** independence. Preliminary agreement signed in Paris Nov. 30.

Use of the **scarlet letter A,** sewn on clothing or branded on skin of adulterers, was **discontinued** in New England.

1783

Massachusetts Supreme Court declared **slavery** illegal in that state.

Britain, U.S. signed **Paris peace treaty** Sept. 3 recognizing American independence (Congress ratified it Jan. 14, **1784**).

Washington ordered army disbanded Nov. 3, bade farewell to his officers at **Fraunces Tavern,** New York City, Dec. 4.

First regular daily newspaper, *Pennsylvania Evening Post,* went on sale in Philadelphia, May 30.

Noah Webster published *American Spelling Book.*

1784

Thomas Jefferson's proposal to **ban slavery** in new territory after 1802 was narrowly defeated Mar. 1.

First successful daily newspaper, *Pennsylvania Packet & General Advertiser,* published Sept. 21.

1785

Regular **stagecoach routes** established between Albany, New York City, and Philadelphia.

1786

Delegates from 5 states at **Annapolis, MD,** Sept. 11-14 asked Congress to call a constitutional convention.

1787

Shays's Rebellion of debt-ridden farmers in Massachusetts failed Jan. 25.

Northwest Ordinance adopted July 13 by Continental Congress for Northwest Territory, N of Ohio River, W of New York; made rules for statehood. Guaranteed freedom of religion, support for schools, no slavery.

Constitutional convention opened at Philadelphia May 25, with Washington presiding. Constitution accepted by delegates Sept. 17; **Delaware** became 1st state to ratify it, Dec. 7; **Pennsylvania** and **New Jersey** followed. Ratification by 9th state, New Hampshire, June 21, **1788,** meant adoption; declared in effect Mar. 4, **1789.**

Federalist Papers first appeared in *NY Independent Journal.*

1788

A large fire in New Orleans, then a Spanish territory, destroyed much of the city Mar. 21.

The **Constitution was adopted** June 21 after being ratified by the requisite 9th state (New Hampshire); also ratified by **Georgia, Connecticut, Massachusetts, Maryland, S. Carolina, Virginia,** and **New York** throughout the year.

First U.S. Senators elected Sept. 30, from Pennsylvania.

Settlers founded future cities Cincinnati, OH; Dubuque, IA; and Charleston, WV.

1789

George Washington chosen president by all electors voting (73 eligible, 69 voting, 4 absent); **John Adams, vice president**, got 34 votes. **First Congress** met at Federal Hall, New York City, and declared Constitution in effect, Mar. 4; Washington **inaugurated** there Apr. 30; first inaugural ball held May 7.

Tammany Hall founded as benevolent organization, May 12.

U.S. **State Dept.** established by Congress July 27. (Thomas **Jefferson** installed as first secretary of state Feb. **1790.**)

War Dept. created, Aug. 7, with Henry **Knox** to be secretary; **Treasury Dept.** created Sept. 2, with Alexander **Hamilton** to be secretary.

Supreme Court created by Federal Judiciary Act, Sept. 24; **John Jay** confirmed by Congress as first Supreme Court **chief justice,** Sept. 26. Congress submitted **Bill of Rights** to states, Sept. 25.

1790

Congress, Mar. 1, authorized decennial **U.S. census; Naturalization Act** (2-year residency) passed Mar. 26.

John Carroll consecrated as **1st American Catholic bishop,** Aug. 15.

Congress met in **Philadelphia,** new temporary capital, Dec. 6.

1791

Bill of Rights went into effect Dec. 15.

1792

Coinage Act established **U.S. Mint** in Philadelphia Apr. 2.

Gen. **"Mad" Anthony Wayne** made commander in Ohio-Indiana area, trained "American Legion," established string of forts. Routed Indians at Fallen Timbers on Maumee River Aug. 20, **1794,** checked British at Fort Miami, OH.

White House cornerstone laid Oct. 13.

1793

Washington inaugurated for 2nd term, Mar. 4, having received 132 electoral votes; John **Adams** again became vice president, having received the 2nd highest total, 77.

Washington declared **U.S. neutrality,** Apr. 22, in war between Britain and France.

Eli Whitney invented **cotton gin,** reviving Southern slavery.

1794

Whiskey Rebellion, W Pennsylvania farmers protesting liquor tax of **1791,** suppressed by federal militia in Sept.

Jay's controversial **treaty** with Britain signed Nov. 19, ratified June 24, **1795.**

1795

U.S. bought peace from **Algerian pirates** by paying $1 mil ransom for 115 seamen Sept. 5, followed by annual tributes.

Gen. Wayne signed peace with Indians at Fort Greenville.

University of North Carolina became first operating state university.

1796

Washington's Farewell Address as president delivered Sept. 17. Warned against permanent alliances with foreign powers, big public debt, large military establishment, and devices of "small, artful, enterprising minority."

1797

U.S. **frigate** *United States* launched at Philadelphia July 10; *Constellation* at Baltimore Sept. 7; *Constitution* (Old Ironsides) at Boston Sept. 20.

John Adams inaugurated as 2nd president Mar. 4, after having received 71 electoral votes; **Thomas Jefferson** became vice president having received 68.

1798

Alien & Sedition Acts passed by Federalists June-July; intended to silence political opposition.

War with France threatened over French raids on U.S. shipping and rejection of U.S. diplomats. Navy (45 ships) and 365 privateers captured 84 French ships. USS *Constellation* took French warship *Insurgente* **1799.** Napoleon stopped French raids after becoming First Consul.

1799

Washington died at Mount Vernon Dec. 14.

1800

Federal government moved to **Washington, DC.**

1801

John Marshall named Supreme Court chief justice, Jan. 20.

Thomas Jefferson, who had received same number of electoral votes as Aaron Burr in 1800 election, won out over Burr in **House** vote reached Feb. 17; Burr named president.

Tripoli declared war June 10 against U.S., which refused added tribute to commerce-raiding Arab corsairs. Land and naval campaigns forced Tripoli to negotiate **peace** June 4, **1805.**

Oldest U.S. art institution, Pennsylvania Academy of Fine Arts, founded.

1802

Congress established the U.S. Military Academy at **West Point,** N.Y.

1803

Supreme Court, in **Marbury** *v* **Madison** case, for the first time overturned a U.S. law Feb. 24.

Napoleon sold all of **Louisiana,** stretching to Canadian border, to U.S., for $11,250,000 in bonds, plus $3,750,000 indemnities to American citizens with claims against France. U.S. took title Dec. 20. Purchase doubled U.S. area.

1804

Lewis and Clark expedition ordered by Pres. Thomas Jefferson to explore what is now northwest U.S. Started from St. Louis May 14; ended Sept. 23, **1806.**

Vice Pres. **Aaron Burr shot Alexander Hamilton** in a duel July 11 in Weehawken, NJ; Hamilton died next day.

1805

U.S. Marines aided by Arab mercenaries, Apr. 27, captured Tripolitan port of Derna, major victory in war against **Barbary pirates;** inspiration for "to the shores of Tripoli" in Marines Corps song.

1807

Robert Fulton made first practical steamboat trip; left New York City Aug. 17, reached Albany, 150 mi, in 32 hr.

Embargo Act banned all trade with foreign countries, forbidding ships to set sail for foreign ports Dec. 22.

1808

Slave importation outlawed. Some 250,000 slaves were illegally imported **1808-60.**

1810

Third U.S. Census found a population of 7,239,881. The black population was put at 1,378,110, of whom 186,746 were free citizens.

1811

William Henry Harrison, governor of Indiana, defeated Indians under the Prophet, in battle of **Tippecanoe** Nov. 7.

Cumberland Road begun at Cumberland, MD; became important route to West.

About 400 **slaves revolted** in Louisiana, killing the son of a plantation owner and marching on **New Orleans.** The insurrection was suppressed; some 75 slaves killed.

1812

War of 1812 had 3 main causes: Britain seized U.S. ships trading with France; Britain seized 4,000 naturalized U.S. sailors by **1810;** Britain armed Indians who raided western border. U.S. stopped trade with Europe **1807** and **1809.** Trade with Britain only was stopped **1810.**

Unaware that Britain had raised the blockade against France 2 days before, **Congress declared war** June 18.

USS *Essex* captured *Alert* Aug. 13; USS *Constitution* destroyed *Guerriere* Aug. 19; USS *Wasp* took *Frolic* Oct. 18; USS *United States* defeated *Macedonian* off Azores Oct. 25; USS *Constitution* beat *Java* Dec. 29. British took Detroit Aug. 16.

1813

Oliver H. Perry defeated British fleet at **Battle of Lake Erie,** Sept. 10. U.S. won Battle of the Thames, Ontario, Oct. 5, but failed in Canadian invasion attempts. York (Toronto) and Buffalo were burned.

1814

British landed in Maryland in Aug., defeated U.S. force Aug. 24, **burned Capitol and White House.** Maryland militia stopped British advance Sept. 12. Bombardment of Ft. McHenry, Baltimore, for 25 hours, Sept. 13-14, by British fleet failed; Francis Scott Key wrote words to **"The Star-Spangled Banner."**

Troops under Andrew Jackson defeated Creek Indians led by Chief Weatherford at **Battle of Horshoe Bend in Alabama,** Mar. 29, ending Creek Indian War (1813-14).

U.S. won naval **Battle of Lake Champlain** Sept. 11. Peace treaty signed at Ghent Dec. 24.

1815

Some 5,300 British, unaware of peace treaty, attacked U.S. entrenchments near **New Orleans,** Jan. 8. British had more than 2,000 casualties; Americans lost 71.

U.S. flotilla finally ended piracy by **Algiers, Tunis, Tripoli** by Aug. 6.

1816

Second **Bank of the U.S.** chartered Apr. 10.

The **American Colonization Society,** which sought to address slavery issue by transporting freed blacks to Africa, formed in Washington, DC, Dec. **1816**-Jan. **1817.**

1817

Rush-Bagot treaty signed Apr. 28-29; limited U.S., British armaments on the Great Lakes.

William Cullen Bryant's poem **"Thanatopsis"** published.

Thomas Hopkins Gallaudet established the **first free public school for the deaf** in Hartford, CT.

1818

Connecticut **expanded suffrage among white male voters.** Massachusetts followed suit in 1820, and New York in 1821, reducing or eliminating property qualifications.

1819

Spain ceded **Florida** to U.S. Feb. 22.

American steamship *Savannah* made first part-steam-powered, part-sail-powered crossing of Atlantic: Savannah, GA, to Liverpool, England, 29 days.

Washington Irving's *Sketch Book* became a best-seller.

1820

First organized **immigration of blacks to Africa** from U.S. began with 86 free blacks sailing Feb. to Sierra Leone.

Henry Clay's **Missouri Compromise** bill passed by Congress Mar. 3. Slavery was allowed in Missouri, but not elsewhere west of the Mississippi River north of 36°30´ latitude (the southern line of Missouri). Repealed **1854.**

1821

Emma Willard founded Troy Female Seminary, first U.S. women's college.

Stephen Austin established the **first American community in Texas,** San Felipe de Austin.

The Spy, a novel by James Fenimore Cooper set during the American Revolution, was published and became a best-seller.

1822

Tension between sports and academics surfaced when Yale College Pres. Timothy Dwight **banned a primitive form of football,** setting fines for violators.

1823

Monroe Doctrine, opposing European intervention in the Americas, enunciated by Pres. James Monroe Dec. 2. The **Hudson River School**, painters who focused on the beauties of nature, began to come to public attention.

1824

Pawtucket, RI, **weavers strike,** first such action by women.

Slavery abolished in the state of Illinois Aug. 2.

1825

After a deadlocked election, **John Quincy Adams** was elected president by the U.S. House, Feb. 9.

Erie Canal opened; first boat left Buffalo Oct. 26, reached New York City Nov. 4.

John Stevens, of Hoboken, NJ, built and operated first experimental **steam locomotive** in U.S.

1826

Thomas **Jefferson** and John **Adams** both died July 4.

James Fenimore Cooper's *The Last of the Mohicans* published.

1827

Massachusetts passed a law providing for **tax-supported public high schools**, the first state to do so.

1828

South Carolina Dec. 19 declared the right of state **nullification of federal laws,** opposing the "Tariff of Abominations."

Noah Webster published his *American Dictionary of the English Language.*

Baltimore & Ohio, the first U.S. passenger railroad, begun July 4.

1829

Andrew Jackson inaugurated as president, Mar. 4.

1830

Famous **debate** Jan. 27 between Sen. **Daniel Webster** (MA) and Robert Hayne (SC), on state right to nullify federal law.

Mormon church organized by Joseph Smith in Fayette, NY, Apr. 6.

Pres. Jackson, May 28, signed **Indian Removal Act** providing land and some pay to Indians agreeing to resettle in west.

1831

William Lloyd Garrison began **abolitionist newspaper** *The Liberator* Jan. 1.

Nat Turner, black slave in Virginia, led local **slave rebellion,** starting Aug. 21; 57 whites killed. Troops called in, 100 slaves killed, Turner captured, tried, hanged Nov. 11.

1832

Black Hawk War (IL-WI) Apr.-Sept. pushed Sauk and Fox Indians west across Mississippi.

South Carolina convention passed **Ordinance of Nullification** Nov. 24 against permanent tariff, threatening to withdraw from Union. Congress Feb. **1833** passed compromise tariff act, whereupon South Carolina repealed its act.

1833

American Anti-Slavery Society founded in Philadelphia, Dec. 4.

Oberlin College became first in U.S. to adopt coeducation.

1835

Liberty Bell cracked July 8, tolling death of Chief Justice **John Marshall**.

Seminole Indians in Florida under Osceola began attacks Nov. 1, protesting forced removal. The unpopular war ended Aug. 14, **1842;** most of the Indians were sent to Oklahoma.

Texas proclaimed right to secede from Mexico; Sam Houston put in command of Texas army, Nov. 2-4.

Gold discovered on **Cherokee land** in Georgia. Indians forced to cede lands, Dec. 20, and to cross Mississippi.

1836

Texans besieged at Alamo in San Antonio by Mexicans under Santa Anna, Feb. 23-Mar. 6; entire garrison killed. Texas independence declared, Mar. 2. At San Jacinto Apr. 21, Sam Houston and Texans defeated Mexicans.

Ralph Waldo Emerson published his first work, *Nature,* espousing his philosophy of **transcendentalism**.

Marcus Whitman, H. H. Spaulding, and wives reached Fort Walla Walla on Columbia River, OR. **First white women to cross plains.**

1838

Cherokee Indians made **"Trail of Tears,"** as they were removed from Georgia to Oklahoma starting Oct.

1841

First emigrant **wagon train for California,** 47 persons, left Independence, MO, May 1, reached California Nov. 4.

Edgar Allan Poe published one of the first American detective stories, *The Murders in the Rue Morgue.*
Brook Farm commune set up by New England Transcendentalist intellectuals. Lasted to **1846.**

1842

Webster-Ashburton Treaty signed Aug. 9, fixing the U.S.-Canada border in Maine and Minnesota.
First use of **anesthetic** (sulfuric ether gas).
Settlement of Oregon began via **Oregon Trail.**

1843

More than 1,000 settlers left Independence, MO, for **Oregon** May 22, arrived Oct.

1844

First message over first **telegraph line** sent May 24 by inventor Samuel F.B. Morse from Washington to Baltimore: "What hath God wrought!"

1845

Texas Congress **voted for annexation** by U.S., July 4. U.S. Congress admitted Texas to Union, Dec. 29.
Edgar Allan Poe's poem "The Raven" published.

1846

Mexican War began after Pres. James K. Polk ordered Gen. Zachary Taylor to seize disputed Texan land settled by Mexicans. After border clash, U.S. declared war May 13; Mexico May 23.
Bear flag of **Republic of California** raised by American settlers at Sonoma June 14.
About 12,000 U.S. troops took Vera Cruz Mar. 27, **1847,** and Mexico City Sept. 14, **1847.** By **treaty,** signed Feb. 2, **1848,** war was ended, and Mexico ceded claims to Texas, California, and other territory.
Treaty with Britain June 15 set **boundary in Oregon** territory at 49th parallel (extension of existing line). Expansionists had used slogan "54° 40´ or fight." The term **"manifest destiny,"** coined by a journalist in **1845,** also came into play.
Mormons, after violent clashes with settlers over polygamy, left Nauvoo, IL, for West under Brigham Young; settled July **1847** at **Salt Lake City, UT.**
Elias Howe invented **sewing machine.**

1847

First **adhesive U.S. postage stamps** on sale July 1; Benjamin Franklin 5¢, Washington 10¢.
Ralph Waldo Emerson published first book of poems; **Henry Wadsworth Longfellow** published *Evangeline.*

1848

Gold discovered Jan. 24 in California; 80,000 prospectors emigrated in **1849.**
Lucretia Mott and Elizabeth Cady Stanton led **Seneca Falls, NY, Women's Rights Convention** July 19-20.

1850

Sen. Henry Clay's **Compromise of 1850** admitted California as 31st state Sept. 9, with slavery forbidden; made Utah and New Mexico territories; made Fugitive Slave Law more harsh; ended District of Columbia slave trade.
Nathaniel Hawthorne's *The Scarlet Letter* published.

1851

Herman Melville's *Moby-Dick* published.

1852

Uncle Tom's Cabin, by **Harriet Beecher Stowe,** published as a book.

1853

Comm. Matthew C. Perry, U.S.N., received by Japan, July 14; negotiated **treaty to open Japan** to U.S. ships.
New York City hosted **first World's Fair** in the U.S., beginning July 14.
Stephen Foster published "My Old Kentucky Home."

1854

Republican Party formed at Ripon, WI, Feb. 28. Opposed Kansas-Nebraska Act (became law May 30), which left issue of slavery to vote of settlers.
Henry David Thoreau published *Walden.*

Treaty ratified with Mexico Apr. 25, providing for purchase of a strip of land **(Gadsden Purchase).**

1855

Walt Whitman published *Leaves of Grass.*
First railroad train crossed **Mississippi River** on the river's first bridge, Rock Island, IL-Davenport, IA, Apr. 21.
Castle Garden opened on island off Lower Manhattan, to process immigrants; closed **1892.**

1856

Republican Party's first nominee for president, **John C. Fremont,** defeated. Abraham Lincoln made 50 speeches for him.
Lawrence, KS, sacked May 21 by proslavery group; abolitionist **John Brown** led antislavery men against Missourians at **Osawatomie, KS,** Aug. 30.
The **first** U.S. **kindergarten** was opened, in Watertown, WI.

1857

Dred Scott decision by Supreme Court Mar. 6 held that slaves did not become free in a free state, Congress could not bar slavery from a territory, and blacks could not be citizens.
Currier & Ives issued their first print.

1858

First **Atlantic cable** completed, by Cyrus W. Field Aug. 5.
Lincoln-Douglas debates in Illinois, Aug. 21-Oct. 15.

1859

First commercially productive **oil well,** drilled near Titusville, PA, by Edwin L. Drake Aug. 27.
Abolitionist **John Brown,** with 21 men, seized U.S. Armory at **Harpers Ferry** Oct. 16. U.S. Marines captured raiders, killing several. Brown hanged for treason Dec. 2.

1860

Approximately 20,000 **New England shoe workers** went on strike Feb. 22 and won higher wages.
Abraham Lincoln, Republican, elected president Nov. 6 in 4-way race.
First **Pony Express** between Sacramento, CA, and St. Joseph, MO, started Apr. 3.

1861

Seven southern states set up **Confederate States of America** Feb. 8, with Jefferson Davis as president, captured federal arsenals and forts. **Civil War** began as Confederates fired on **Ft. Sumter** in Charleston, SC, Apr. 12, capturing it Apr. 14.
Pres. **Lincoln** called for 75,000 volunteers Apr. 15. By May, 11 states had seceded. Lincoln blockaded Southern ports Apr. 19, cutting off vital exports, aid.
Confederates repelled Union forces at first **Battle of Bull Run,** July 21.
First **transcontinental telegraph line** was put in operation.

1862

Union forces were victorious in Western campaigns, took **New Orleans** May 1. Battles in East were largely inconclusive despite heavy casualties. The Battle of **Antietam,** in western Maryland Sept. 17, was the bloodiest one-day battle of the war; each side lost over 2,000 men.
Homestead Act approved May 20; it granted free farms to settlers.
Land Grant Act approved July 7, providing for public land sale to benefit agricultural education; eventually led to establishment of state university systems.

1863

Pres. Lincoln issued **Emancipation Proclamation** Jan. 1, freeing "all slaves in areas still in rebellion."
Entire **Mississippi River** was in Union hands by July 4. Union forces won a major victory at **Gettysburg, PA,** July 1-3. Lincoln gave his **Gettysburg Address** Nov. 19.
Confederate forces under siege surrendered **Vicksburg** to Union forces under Gen. Ulysses S. Grant, July 4.
In **draft riots** in New York City about 1,000 were killed or wounded; some blacks were hanged by mobs July 13-16.
Pres. Lincoln declared **Thanksgiving** to be a national holiday.

1864
Gen. William Tecumseh **Sherman marched through Georgia,** taking Atlanta Sept. 1, Savannah Dec. 22.

Sand Creek massacre of Cheyenne and Arapaho Indians Nov. 29. Soldiers drove Indians out of village; about 150 killed.

1865
Gen. **Robert E. Lee surrendered** 27,800 Confederate troops to Gen. Grant at **Appomattox** Court House, VA, Apr. 9. J. E. Johnston surrendered 31,200 to Sherman at Durham Station, NC, Apr. 18. Last rebel troops surrendered May 26.

Pres. Lincoln was shot Apr. 14 by John Wilkes Booth in Ford's Theater, Washington, DC; died the following morning. Vice Pres. **Andrew Johnson** was sworn in as president. Booth was hunted down; fatally wounded, perhaps by his own hand, Apr. 26. Four co-conspirators hanged July 7.

13th Amendment, abolishing slavery, ratified Dec. 6.

1866
Ku Klux Klan formed secretly in South to terrorize blacks who voted. Disbanded **1869-71.** A 2nd Klan organized **1915.**

Congress took control of Southern **Reconstruction,** backed freedmen's rights in legislation vetoed by Johnson; veto overridden by Congress (for first time ever), Apr. 9.

1867
Alaska sold to U.S. by Russia for $7.2 mil Mar. 30, through efforts of Sec. of State William H. Seward.

The **Grange** was organized Dec. 4, to protect farmer interests.

Horatio Alger published first book, *Ragged Dick.*

1868
Pres. **Johnson** tried to remove Edwin M. Stanton, secretary of war; was impeached by House Feb. 24 for violation of Tenure of Office Act; acquitted by Senate Mar.-May.

14th Amendment, providing for citizenship of all persons born or naturalized in U.S., ratified July 9.

Louisa May Alcott published *Little Women.*

The World Almanac, a publication of the *New York World,* appeared for the first time.

1869
Financial **"Black Friday"** in New York Sept. 24; caused by attempt to "corner" gold.

Transcontinental railroad completed; golden spike driven at Promontory, UT, May 10, marking the junction of Central Pacific and Union Pacific.

Knights of Labor formed in Philadelphia. By **1886,** this labor union had 700,000 members nationally.

Woman suffrage law passed in Wyoming Territory Dec. 10.

1870
15th Amendment, making race no bar to voting rights, ratified Feb. 8.

First U.S. boardwalk completed, in Atlantic City, NJ.

U.S. Weather Bureau founded.

1871
Great fire destroyed **Chicago** Oct. 8-11.

National Rifle Association founded.

1872
Amnesty Act restored civil rights to citizens of the South May 22, except for 500 Confederate leaders.

Congress established first national park—**Yellowstone.**

James McNeill Whistler painted famous portrait known informally as **"Whistler's Mother."**

1873
First U.S. **postal card** issued May 1.

Jesse James and his gang robbed their first passenger train July 21.

Banks failed, panic began in Sept. Depression lasted 5 years.

"Boss" William Tweed of New York City convicted Nov. 19 of stealing public funds. He died in jail in **1878.**

New York's Bellevue Hospital started **first nursing school.**

1874
Women's Christian Temperance Union established in Cleveland.

The **first** U.S. public **zoo** was established in Philadelphia.

1875
Congress passed **Civil Rights Act** Mar. 1, giving equal rights to blacks in public accommodations and jury duty. Act invalidated in **1883** by Supreme Court.

First **Jim Crow** segregation law enacted, in Tennessee.

First **Kentucky Derby** held May 17.

1876
Samuel J. Tilden, Democrat, received majority of popular votes for president over **Rutherford B. Hayes,** Republican, but 22 electoral votes were in dispute; issue left to Congress. Congress agreed to certify Hayes as winner in Feb. **1877** after Republicans agreed to end federal Reconstruction of South.

Alexander Graham Bell patented the telephone Mar. 7

Col. **George A. Custer** and 264 soldiers of the 7th Cavalry killed June 25 in "last stand," Battle of the **Little Big Horn,** MT, in Sioux Indian War.

1877
Molly Maguires, Irish terrorist society in Scranton, PA, mining areas, was broken up by the hanging, June 21, of 11 leaders for murders of mine officials and police.

Pres. Rutherford B. Hayes sent troops in violent national **railroad strike.**

1878
First commercial **telephone** exchange opened, New Haven, CT, Jan. 28.

Thomas A. Edison founded **Edison Electric Light Co.** on Oct. 15.

1879
F. W. Woolworth opened his first five-and-ten store, in Utica, NY, Feb. 22.

Henry George published *Progress & Poverty,* advocating single tax on land.

French actress **Sarah Bernhardt** made her U.S. debut Nov. 8 at New York City's Booth Theater.

1880
Chinese Exclusion Treaty signed with China, Nov. 17, providing for restitution of Chinese naturals entering U.S.

Lew Wallace's *Ben Hur* published.

1881
Clara Barton May 21 founded the **American Red Cross.**

Pres. **James A. Garfield shot** in Washington, DC, July 2; died Sept. 19.

Famous gun battle between the Earp brothers and outlaw rustlers, Oct. 26 near the **OK Corral,** Tombstone, AZ.

Booker T. Washington founded Tuskegee Institute for blacks.

Helen Hunt Jackson published *A Century of Dishonor,* about mistreatment of Indians.

1882
Chinese Exclusion Act, barring Chinese immigration, passed by Congress May 6.

1883
Pendleton Act passed Jan. 16, reformed civil service.
Northern Pacific Railroad completed, Sept. 8.
Brooklyn Bridge opened May 24.
Buffalo Bill Cody's Wild West Show began its 30-year touring run.

1884
First **long-distance** telephone call completed, Mar. 27, between Boston and New York.
First roller coaster in the U.S. opened at Coney Island in New York City.
Mark Twain's masterpiece, *The Adventures of Huckleberry Finn*, appeared.

1885
Washington Monument dedicated Feb. 21
Postal rates lowered to 2 cents an ounce.

1886
Haymarket riot and bombing, May 4, followed bitter labor battles for 8-hour day in Chicago; 7 police and 4 workers died. Eight anarchists found guilty Aug. 20; 4 hanged Nov. 11.
Coca-Cola first sold, May 8 at Jacob's Pharmacy in Atlanta.
Geronimo, Apache Indian, surrendered Sept. 4, ending last major Indian war.
Statue of Liberty dedicated Oct. 28.
American Federation of Labor (AFL) formed Dec. 8 by 25 craft unions.

1887
Interstate Commerce Act enacted Feb. 4.
Pres. Grover Cleveland signed the **Hatch Act,** Mar. 2.
Eugene Field published poem **"Little Boy Blue."**

1888
Great blizzard struck eastern U.S. Mar. 11-14, causing about 400 deaths.
Ernest Thayer's poem **"Casey at the Bat"** was recited for the first time in public, at a New York City theater in May.

1889
U.S. opened Oklahoma to white settlement Apr. 22; within 24 hours **claims for 2 mil acres** were staked by 50,000 "sooner" settlers.
Johnstown, PA, flood May 31; 2,200 lives lost.
Electric lights installed at the White House.

1890
Battle of **Wounded Knee,** SD, Dec. 29, the last major conflict between Indians and U.S. troops. About 200 Indian men, women, and children and 29 soldiers were killed.
Sherman Antitrust Act passed July 2, began federal effort to curb monopolies.
Jacob Riis published *How the Other Half Lives,* about city slums.
Poems of **Emily Dickinson** published, 4 years after her death.

1891
Forest Reserve Act, Mar. 3, let president close public forest land to settlement for establishment of national parks.
Carnegie Hall, in New York City, opened May 5.

1892
Ellis Island, in New York Bay, opened Jan. 1 to receive immigrants.
Homestead, PA, strike at Carnegie steel mills; 7 guards and 11 strikers and spectators shot to death July 6.
Heavyweight **James J. Corbett** KO'd John L. Sullivan Sept. 7, in first title bout to use padded gloves.

1893
Columbian Exposition, blockbuster world's fair, held May-Oct. in Chicago.
Financial panic began, led to 4-year depression.
Mormon Temple dedicated in Salt Lake City, UT.

1894
Thomas A. Edison's kinetoscope, for motion pictures (invented **1887),** given first public showing Apr. 14.

Jacob S. Coxey led army of unemployed from the Midwest, reaching Washington, DC, Apr. 30. Coxey arrested May 1 for trespassing on Capitol grounds; his army disbanded.
Pullman strike began May 11 at a railroad car plant in Chicago.
Milton Hershey started **Hershey Chocolate Company**.

1895
"America the Beautiful" appeared for 1st time, in church publication, July 4.
Stephen Crane's *The Red Badge of Courage* published.

1896
William Jennings Bryan delivered "Cross of Gold" speech July 8; won Democratic Party nomination.
Supreme Court, in **Plessy *v.* Ferguson,** May 18, approved racial segregation under the "separate but equal" doctrine.
John Philip Sousa composed "Stars and Stripes Forever" on Dec. 25.

1897
Olney-Pauncefote Treaty signed with **Britain,** Jan. 11, giving wide scope to arbitration in settling disputes; never ratified by U.S.
John J. McDermott won **first Boston Marathon** Apr. 19.
First Klondike **gold** arrived in San Francisco July 14.
Coal miners **strike** settled Sept. 11, after more than 20 miners fired on and killed by lawmen.

1898
U.S. **battleship *Maine*** blown up Feb. 15 at Havana; 260 killed.
U.S. blockaded Cuba Apr. 22 in aid of independence forces. U.S. declared **war on Spain** Apr. 24; destroyed Spanish fleet in **Philippines** May 1; took **Guam** June 20.
Puerto Rico taken by U.S. July 25-Aug. 12. Spain agreed Dec. 10 to cede Philippines, Puerto Rico, and Guam, and approved independence for Cuba.
Annexation of **Hawaii** signed by Pres. William McKinley, July 7.

1899
Filipino insurgents, unable to get recognition of independence from U.S., started guerrilla war Feb. 4. Their leader, Emilio Aguinaldo, captured May 23, **1901.** Philippine Insurrection ended **1902.** 20,000 Filipino troops killed, and some 200,000 civilian deaths, mostly from disease and starvation.
Pres. McKinley signed **treaty** officially ending Spanish-America War, Feb. 10.
U.S. declared **Open Door Policy** Sept. 6, to make China an open international market.
John Dewey published *The School and Society,* advocating "progressive education."
Pianist Scott Joplin's "Maple Leaf Rag" was published, popularizing **ragtime**.

1900
Carry Nation, Kansas antisaloon agitator, began raiding with hatchet.
U.S. helped suppress **"Boxer Rebellion"** in Beijing.
International Ladies' Garment Workers Union was founded in New York City June 3.
Eastman Kodak Co. introduced the **Brownie camera,** popularizing picture-taking.

1901
Texas had first significant **oil strike,** Jan. 10.
Pres. **McKinley was shot** Sept. 6 in Buffalo, NY, by an anarchist, Leon Czolgosz; died Sept. 14. Vice Pres. Theodore **Roosevelt** sworn in as youngest-ever president, age 42 years, 11 months.
Booker T. Washington published *Up From Slavery.*

1902
Permanent Bureau of the **Census** established Mar. 6.
U.S. withdrew troops from **Cuba** May 20, and Cuba became independent.
Helen Keller autobiography appeared in serial form.

1903

Treaty between U.S. and Colombia to have U.S. dig **Panama Canal** signed Jan. 22, rejected by Colombia. Panama declared independence from Colombia with U.S. support Nov. 3; recognized by Pres. Theodore Roosevelt Nov. 6. U.S., Panama signed **canal treaty** Nov. 18.

Wisconsin set first **direct primary** voting system, May 23.

Henry Ford founded Ford Motor Co., June 16.

Boston defeated Pittsburgh, 5 games to 3, Oct. 13 in the **first modern World Series**.

First successful flight in heavier-than-air mechanically propelled airplane by **Orville Wright** Dec. 17 near Kitty Hawk, NC, 120 ft. in 12 secs. Later flight same day by **Wilbur Wright,** 852 ft. in 59 secs. Improved plane patented, **1906.**

Fire in Iroquois Theater, Chicago, killed about 600, Dec. 30

Great Train Robbery, pioneering film, produced.

1904

St. Louis hosted **first Olympics** in U.S., July 1-Nov. 23.

First section of New York **subway** system opened, Oct. 27.

Ida Tarbell published muckraking *The History of the Standard Oil Company.*

Henry James's last great novel, *The Golden Bowl,* appeared.

1905

Industrial Workers of the World (Wobblies) founded by radicals in Chicago, June 27.

First **Rotary Club** founded in Chicago.

1906

Upton Sinclair published *The Jungle.*

San Francisco earthquake and fire, Apr. 18-19, left 503 dead, $350 mil damages.

Pure Food and Drug Act and Meat Inspection Act both passed June 30.

1907

Financial panic and depression started Mar. 13.

First round-world cruise of U.S. **"Great White Fleet":** 16 battleships, 12,000 men.

1908

Springfield, IL, torn by anti-black **rioting,** Aug. 14-15.

Henry Ford introduced **Model T** car, priced at $850, Oct. 1.

1909

Adm. Robert E. Peary claimed to have reached **North Pole** Apr. 6 on 6th attempt, accompanied by Matthew Henson, a black man, and 4 Eskimos; may have fallen short.

National Conference on the Negro convened May 30, leading to founding of National Association for the Advancement of Colored People.

1910

Boy Scouts of America founded Feb. 8.

In a famous speech in Kansas, Aug. 10, former Pres. Roosevelt called for a **"new nationalism."**

1911

Supreme Court dissolved **Standard Oil** Co. May 15.

Building holding New York City's **Triangle Shirtwaist** Co. factory caught fire Mar. 25; 146 died.

First **transcontinental airplane flight** (with numerous stops) by C. P. Rodgers, New York to Pasadena, CA, Sept. 17-Nov. 5; time in air 82 hr., 4 min.

1912

American Girl Guides founded Mar. 12; name changed in **1913** to **Girl Scouts.**

U.S. sent Marines Aug. 14 to **Nicaragua,** which was in default of loans to U.S. and Europe.

1913

16th Amendment, authorizing federal income tax, ratified Feb. 3.

NY Armory Show brought modern art to U.S. Feb. 17.

17th Amendment, providing for direct popular election of U.S. senators, ratified Apr. 8.

Federal Reserve System was authorized Dec. 23, in a major reform of U.S. banking and finance.

U.S. blockaded Mexico in support of revolutionaries.

Charles Beard published his *Economic Interpretation of the Constitution.*

1914

Ford Motor Co. raised basic wage rates from $2.40 for 9-hr. day to $5 for 8-hr. day, Jan. 5.

When U.S. sailors were arrested at Tampico, Mexico, Apr. 9, Atlantic fleet was sent to **Veracruz,** occupied city.

Pres. Woodrow Wilson proclaimed **U.S. neutrality** in the European war, Aug. 4.

Panama Canal was officially opened Aug. 15.

The **Clayton Antitrust Act** was passed Oct. 15, strengthening federal antimonopoly powers.

1915

First transcontinental **telephone call,** New York to San Francisco, was completed Jan. 25, by Alexander Graham Bell and Thomas A. Watson.

British ship *Lusitania* sunk May 7 by German submarine; 128 American passengers lost (Germany had warned passengers in advance). As a result of U.S. campaign, Germany issued apology and promise of payments, Oct. 5. Pres. Wilson asked for a military fund increase, Dec. 7.

U.S. troops landed in **Haiti,** July 28. Haiti became a virtual U.S. protectorate under Sept. 16 treaty.

D.W. Griffith's film *The Birth of a Nation* released.

1916

Gen. John J. **Pershing entered Mexico** to pursue Francisco (Pancho) Villa, who had raided U.S. border areas. Forces withdrawn Feb. 5, **1917.**

Rural Credits Act passed July 17, followed by Warehouse Act Aug. 11; both provided financial aid to farmers.

Bomb exploded during **San Francisco** Preparedness Day parade July 22, killed 10. Thomas J. Mooney, labor organizer, and Warren K. Billings, shoe worker, were convicted **1917;** both later pardoned.

U.S. bought **Virgin Islands** from Denmark Aug. 4.

Jeannette Rankin (R, MT) elected as **first-ever female** member of U.S. **House.**

U.S. established military government in the **Dominican Republic** Nov. 29.

Trade and loans to **European allies** soared during the year.

1917

Germany, suffering from British blockade, declared almost unrestricted **submarine warfare** Jan. 31. U.S. cut diplomatic ties with Germany Feb. 3, and formally **declared war** Apr. 6.

Jones Act, passed Mar. 2, made **Puerto Rico U.S. territory,** its inhabitants U.S. citizens.

Conscription law was passed May 18. First U.S. troops arrived in Europe June 26.

18th Amendment to the Constitution, providing for **prohibition** of manufacture, sale, or transportation of alcoholic beverages, was submitted to the states by Congress Dec. 18.

1918

Pres. Wilson set out his **14 Points** as basis for peace, Jan. 8.

More than 1 mil **American troops** were in Europe by July. Allied counteroffensive launched at Château-Thierry July 18. War ended with signing of **armistice** Nov. 11.

Influenza epidemic killed an estimated 20 mil worldwide, 548,000 in U.S.

1919

18th **(prohibition)** Amendment, ratified Jan. 16, to take effect in 1 year.

First **transatlantic flight,** by U.S. Navy seaplane, left Rockaway, NY, May 8, stopped at Newfoundland, Azores, Lisbon May 27.

Boston police strike Sept. 9; National Guard breaks strike.

About 250 **alien radicals** were deported Dec. 22.
Sherwood Anderson published *Winesburg, Ohio.*

1920

In national **Red Scare,** some 2,700 Communists, anarchists, and other radicals were arrested Jan.-May.
League of Women Voters founded Feb. 14.
Senate refused Mar. 19 to ratify the **League of Nations Covenant.**
Radicals Nicola **Sacco** and Bartolomeo **Vanzetti** accused of killing 2 men in Massachusetts payroll holdup Apr. 15. Found guilty **1921.** A 6-year campaign for their release failed, and both were executed Aug. 23, **1927.** Verdict repudiated **1977,** by proclamation of Massachusetts Gov. Michael Dukakis.
19th Amendment ratified Aug. 18, giving women the vote.
First regular licensed **radio broadcasting** begun Aug. 20.
Wall St., New York City, **bomb** explosion killed 30, injured 100, did $2 mil damage, Sept. 16.
Sinclair Lewis's *Main Street,* **F. Scott Fitzgerald's** *This Side of Paradise,* **Edith Wharton's** *The Age of Innocence* published.

1921

Congress sharply **curbed immigration,** set national quota system May 19.
Joint congressional resolution declaring **peace with Germany, Austria,** and **Hungary** signed July 2 by Pres. Warren G. Harding; treaties were signed in Aug.
In so-called **Black Sox** scandal, 8 Chicago **White Sox players** were banned from baseball Aug. 4 for conspiring with gamblers to throw the **1919** World Series.
Limitation of Armaments Conference met in Washington, DC, Nov. 12-Feb. 6, **1922.** Major powers agreed to curtail naval construction, outlaw poison gas, restrict submarine attacks on merchant vessels, respect integrity of China.
Ku Klux Klan began revival with violence against Catholics in North, South, and Midwest.

1922

Violence during **coal-mine strike** at Herrin, IL, June 22-23 cost 36 lives, including those of 21 nonunion miners.
Reader's Digest founded.
T. S. Eliot's *The Waste Land* published in London.

1923

First **sound-on-film motion picture,** *Phonofilm,* shown at Rivoli Theater, New York City, beginning in April.
Pres. Calvin Coolidge addressed Congress, Dec. 6; **first** official **broadcast** of a presidential speech.

1924

Law approved by Congress June 15 making all **Indians citizens.**
Nellie Tayloe Ross elected governor of Wyoming Nov. 9; inaugurated as nation's first woman governor Jan. 5, **1925.**
Miriam (Ma) Ferguson elected governor of Texas Nov. 9; installed Jan. 20, **1925.**
George Gershwin wrote *Rhapsody in Blue.*

1925

John T. Scopes found guilty of having taught **evolution** in Dayton, TN, high school, fined $100 and costs, July 24.
F. Scott Fitzgerald's *The Great Gatsby* appeared.

1926

Dr. Robert H. Goddard demonstrated practicality of rockets, Mar. 16 at Auburn, MA, with first liquid-fuel rocket; rocket traveled 184 ft. in 2.5 sec.
Congress established **Army Air Corps** July 2.
Air Commerce Act passed Nov. 2, providing federal aid for airlines and airports.
Ernest Hemingway's *The Sun Also Rises* published.

1927

About 1,000 **marines landed in China** Mar. 5 to protect property in civil war.
Capt. **Charles A. Lindbergh** left Roosevelt Field, NY, May 20 alone in plane *Spirit of St. Louis* on first New York-Paris nonstop flight. Reached Le Bourget airfield May 21, 3,610 mi in 33½ hours.
The Jazz Singer, with **Al Jolson,** demonstrated part-talking pictures in New York City Oct. 6.
Show Boat opened in New York Dec. 27.
O. E. Rolvaag published *Giants in the Earth.*

1928

Amelia Earhart became first woman to fly across the Atlantic, June 17.
Herbert Hoover elected president Nov. 6, defeating New York Gov. **Alfred E. Smith,** a Catholic.

1929

"St. Valentine's Day massacre" in Chicago Feb. 14; gangsters killed 7 rivals.
Farm price stability aided by **Agricultural Marketing Act,** passed June 15.
Albert B. Fall, former secretary of the interior, was convicted of accepting bribe of $100,000 in the leasing of the **Elk Hills (Teapot Dome)** naval oil reserve; sentenced Nov. 1 to a year in prison and fined $100,000.
Stock market crash Oct. 29 marked end of past prosperity as stock prices plummeted. Stock losses for **1929-31** estimated at $50 bil; worst American depression began.
Thomas Wolfe published *Look Homeward, Angel.* **William Faulkner** published *The Sound and the Fury.*

1930

London **Naval Reduction Treaty** signed by U.S., Britain, Italy, France, and Japan Apr. 22; in effect Jan. 1, **1931;** expired Dec. 31, **1936.**
Hawley-Smoot Tariff signed; rate hikes slash world trade.
Sinclair Lewis became the first American to win a **Nobel Prize in literature**.

1931

Empire State Building opened in New York City May 1.
Al Capone was convicted of tax evasion Oct. 17.
Pearl Buck published *The Good Earth.*

1932

Reconstruction Finance Corp. established Jan. 22 to stimulate banking and business. Unemployment at 12 mil.
19-month-old **Charles Lindbergh Jr. was kidnapped** Mar. 1; found dead May 12. Bruno Hauptmann found guilty in trial Jan.-Feb. **1935;** executed Apr. 3, **1936.**
Bonus March on Washington, DC, launched May 29 by World War I veterans demanding Congress pay their bonus in full.
Franklin D. Roosevelt elected president for the first time in Democratic landslide, Nov. 8.
Chicago Bears won **first NFL title game** Dec. 18, defeating the Portsmouth (OH) Spartans, 9–0.

1933

Pres. Roosevelt named **Frances Perkins** U.S. secretary of labor; first woman in U.S. cabinet.
All **banks in the U.S. ordered closed** by Pres. Roosevelt Mar. 6.
In a "100 days" special session, Mar. 9-June 16, Congress passed **New Deal** social and economic measures, including measures to regulate banks, distribute funds to the jobless, create jobs, raise agricultural prices, and set wage and production standards for industry.
Tennessee Valley Authority created by act of Congress, May 18.
Gold standard dropped by U.S.; announced by Pres. Roosevelt Apr. 19, ratified by Congress June 5.
Prohibition ended in the U.S. as 36th state ratified 21st Amendment Dec. 5.
Pres. Roosevelt foreswore armed intervention in **western hemisphere** nations Dec. 26.

1934

Pres. Roosevelt signed law creating the **Securities and Exchange Commission**, June 6.
U.S. troops pulled out of **Haiti** Aug. 6.

1935

Boulder Dam (later renamed Hoover Dam) completed, May 29.

Works Progress Administration (**WPA**) instituted May 6. Rural Electrification Administration created May 11. National Industrial Recovery Act struck down by Supreme Court May 27.

Comedian **Will Rogers** and aviator Wiley Post killed Aug. 15 in Alaska plane crash.

Social Security Act passed by Congress Aug. 14.

Huey Long, senator from Louisiana and national political leader, **assassinated** Sept. 8.

George Gershwin's *Porgy and Bess* opened Oct. 10 in New York.

Committee for Industrial Organization (CIO; later Congress of Industrial Organizations) formed to expand industrial unionism Nov. 9.

1936

Jesse Owens won 4 gold medals a the Berlin **Olympics** in August.

Baseball Hall of Fame founded in Cooperstown, NY.

Margaret Mitchell published *Gone With the Wind.*

1937

Hindenburg exploded May 6 landing at Lakehurst, NJ.

Golden Gate Bridge opened, May 27.

Joe Louis knocked out James J. Braddock, became world heavyweight champ June 22.

Amelia Earhart, aviator, and copilot Fred Noonan lost July 2 near Howland Island, in the Pacific.

Pres. Roosevelt asked for 6 additional Supreme Court justices; **"packing" plan** defeated.

Auto, steel labor unions won first big contracts.

1938

Naval Expansion Act passed May 17.

National minimum wage enacted June 25.

Orson Welles radio dramatization of **Martian invasion,** *War of the Worlds,* Oct. 30, caused scare.

Seabiscuit beat *War Admiral* in match race of the century, at Pimlico track, MD, Nov. 1.

Artist **"Grandma Moses"** discovered.

Thornton Wilder's *Our Town* produced on Broadway.

1939

Pres. Roosevelt asked for **defense budget hike** in Jan.

New York World's Fair opened Apr. 30, closed Oct. 31; reopened May 11, **1940,** ended Oct. 21.

Lou Gehrig, seriously ill, said farewell to fans at Yankee Stadium, July 4.

Albert Einstein alerted Pres. Roosevelt to **A-bomb** possibilities in Aug. 2 letter.

U.S. declared its neutrality in European war Sept. 5.

Roosevelt proclaimed a limited national emergency Sept. 8, an unlimited emergency May 27, **1941.** Both ended by Pres. Harry Truman, Apr. 28, **1952.**

John Steinbeck published *The Grapes of Wrath.*

Pocket books appeared in U.S.

Gone With the Wind and *The Wizard of Oz* films released.

1940

U.S. okayed sale of **surplus war materiel** to Britain June 3; announced transfer of 50 overaged destroyers Sept. 3.

First **peacetime military draft** in U.S. history approved Sept. 14.

40-hour work week went into effect, Oct. 24.

Roosevelt elected Nov. 5 to 3rd term as president.

Richard Wright published *Native Son.*

1941

Four Freedoms termed essential by Pres. Roosevelt in speech to Congress Jan. 6: freedom of speech and religion, freedom from want and fear.

Lend-Lease Act signed Mar. 11 provided $7 bil in military credits for Britain. Lend-Lease for USSR approved in Nov.

The **Atlantic Charter,** 8-point declaration of principles, issued by Roosevelt and British Prime Min. Winston Churchill, Aug. 14.

U.S. occupied **Iceland** July 7.

Japan attacked **Pearl Harbor,** Hawaii, 7:55 AM Hawaiian time, Dec. 7; called by Roosevelt "a date that will live in infamy"; 19 ships sunk or damaged, 2,300 dead. U.S. declared war on Japan Dec. 8, on Germany and Italy Dec. 11.

Japanese invaded Philippines, Dec. 22; Wake Island fell Dec. 23.

1942

Japanese troops took **Bataan** peninsula Apr. 8, **Corregidor** May 6.

Federal government forcibly moved 110,000 **Japanese-Americans** from West Coast to detention camps. Exclusion lasted 3 years.

Battle of **Midway** June 4-7 was Japan's first major defeat.

Marines landed on **Guadalcanal** Aug. 7; last Japanese not expelled until Feb. 9, **1943.**

U.S., Britain invaded **North Africa** Nov. 8.

First **nuclear chain reaction** (fission of uranium isotope U-235) produced at Univ. of Chicago, under physicists Arthur Compton, Enrico Fermi, others, Dec. 2.

1943

Oklahoma! opened Mar. 31 on Broadway.

War contractors barred from **racial discrimination,** May 27.

Pres. Roosevelt signed June 10 pay-as-you-go income tax bill. Starting July 1, wage and salary earners were subject to a **paycheck withholding** tax.

Race riot in Detroit June 21; 34 dead, 700 injured. Riot in Harlem section of New York City Aug. 2; 6 killed.

U.S., Britain invaded **Sicily** July 9, Italian **mainland** Sept. 3.

Marines in Nov. recaptured the **Gilbert Islands,** captured by Japan in **1941** and **1942.**

1944

U.S., Allied forces invaded Europe at **Normandy** on "D Day," June 6, in greatest amphibious landing in history. **Battle of the Bulge,** failed Nazi counteroffensive, waged Dec. 16, 1944, to Jan. 28, 1945; 500,000 Americans fought.

GI Bill of Rights signed by Pres. Roosevelt June 22, providing benefits for veterans.

Representatives of the U.S. and other major powers met at **Dunbarton Oaks,** Washington, DC, Aug. 21-Oct. 7, to work out formation of postwar world organization that became the **United Nations.**

U.S. forces landed on **Leyte,** Philippines, Oct. 20.

Roosevelt elected to 4th term as president, Nov. 7.

Federal Highway Act passed by Congress, Nov. 29, creating national system of **interstate highways.**

1945

Yalta Conference met in the Crimea, USSR, Feb. 4-11. Roosevelt, Churchill, and Soviet leader Joseph Stalin agreed that their 3 countries, plus France, would occupy Germany and that the Soviet Union would enter war against Japan.

Marines landed on **Iwo Jima** Feb. 19, won control Mar. 16 after heavy casualties. U.S. forces invaded **Okinawa** Apr. 1, captured Okinawa June 21.

Pres. Roosevelt died in Warm Springs, GA, Apr. 12; Vice Pres. **Harry S. Truman** became president.

Germany surrendered May 7; May 8 proclaimed V-E Day.

First **atomic bomb,** produced at Los Alamos, NM, exploded at Alamogordo, NM, July 16. Bomb dropped on **Hiroshima** Aug. 6, with about 75,000 people killed; bomb dropped on **Nagasaki** Aug. 9, killing about 40,000. Japan agreed to surrender Aug. 14; formally surrendered Sept. 2.

Empire State Building struck by Army B-25 bomber, July 28, killing 13.

At **Potsdam Conference,** July 17-Aug. 2, leaders of U.S., USSR, and Britain agreed on disarmament of Germany, occupation zones, war crimes trials.

U.S. forces entered **Korea** south of 38th parallel to displace Japanese Sept. 8.

Gen. Douglas MacArthur took over supervision of Japan Sept. 9.

1946

Steel strike by 750,000 started Jan. 21, settled in 4 weeks. Strike by 400,000 **mine workers** began Apr. 1 (settled May 29); other industries followed.

At a speech at a Fulton, MO, college, Mar. 5, Winston Churchill employed the phrase **"iron curtain."**

Atomic bomb tested off Bikini Atoll in Pacific, July 1.

Philippines given independence by U.S. July 4.

Mother Frances Xavier Cabrini 1st American to be canonized, July 7.

Dr. Benjamin Spock's *Baby and Child Care* published as 1946-64 **baby boom** began.

1947

Pres. Truman asked Congress for financial and military aid for Greece and Turkey to help combat Communist subversion (**Truman Doctrine**), Mar. 12. Approved May 15.

UN Security Council voted Apr. 2 to place under **U.S. trusteeship** the Pacific islands formerly mandated to Japan.

Jackie Robinson joined the Brooklyn Dodgers Apr. 11, breaking the color barrier in major league baseball.

The **Marshall Plan,** for U.S. aid to European countries, was proposed by Sec. of State George C. Marshall June 5. Congress authorized some $12 bil in next 4 years.

Taft-Hartley Labor Act restricting labor union power was vetoed by Truman June 20; Congress overrode the veto.

Air Force Capt. **Chuck Yeager** broke the sound barrier, Oct. 14, in X-1 rocket plane.

1948

USSR halted all surface traffic into **W. Berlin,** June 23; in response, U.S. and British troops launched an **airlift.** Soviet blockade halted May 12, **1949;** airlift ended Sept. 30.

Organization of American States founded Apr. 30.

Alger Hiss indicted Dec. 15 for perjury, after denying he had passed secret documents to Whittaker Chambers to go to a **Communist spy ring.** Convicted Jan. 21, **1950.**

Pres. Truman, elected Nov. 2, defeating Gov. Thomas E. Dewey in a historic upset.

Kinsey Report on sexuality in the human male published.

1949

NATO established Aug. 24 by U.S., Canada, and 10 Western European nations, agreeing that an armed attack against one would be considered an attack against all.

Mrs. I. Toguri D'Aquino (**Tokyo Rose** of Japanese wartime broadcasts) was sentenced Oct. 7 to 10 years in prison for treason. Paroled **1956,** pardoned **1977.**

Eleven leaders of **U.S. Communist Party** convicted Oct. 14 of advocating violent overthrow of U.S. government; sentenced to prison. Supreme Court upheld convictions **1951.**

Pres. Truman Oct. 26 signed legislation raising federal **minimum wage** from 40¢ an hour to 75¢.

Arthur Miller's *Death of a Salesman* opened on Broadway.

1950

Masked bandits robbed **Brink's, Inc.,** Boston express office, Jan. 17 of $2.8 mil. Case solved **1956;** 8 sentenced to life.

Pres. Truman authorized production of the **H-bomb** Jan. 31.

North Korean forces invaded **South Korea** June 25. UN asked for troops to restore peace.

Truman ordered Air Force and Navy to Korea June 27. Truman approved ground forces, air strikes against **North Korea** June 30.

U.S. sent 35 military advisers to **South Vietnam** June 27, and agreed to aid anti-Communist government.

Army seized all railroads Aug. 27 on Truman's order to prevent a general strike; returned to owners in **1952.**

U.S. forces landed at Inchon Sept. 15; UN force took Pyongyang Oct. 20, reached China border Nov. 20; China sent troops across border Nov. 26.

Two members of **Puerto Rican nationalist** movement tried to kill Pres. Truman Nov. 1.

U.S. banned shipments Dec. 8 to Communist **China** and to Asiatic ports trading with it.

Your Show of Shows debuted on TV.

Peanuts **comic** strip appeared.

David Riesman's *The Lonely Crowd* published.

1951

Sen. Estes Kefauver led Senate probe into organized crime.

22nd Amendment, limiting **presidential term of office,** ratified Feb. 27.

Julius Rosenberg, his wife, **Ethel**, and Morton Sobell found guilty Mar. 29 of conspiracy to commit wartime **espionage.** Rosenbergs received death penalty. Sobell sentenced to 30 years; released **1969.**

Gen. Douglas MacArthur removed from Korea command Apr. 11 by Pres. Truman, for unauthorized policy statements.

Korea cease-fire talks began in July; lasted 2 years. Fighting ended July 27, **1953.**

Tariff concessions by the U.S. to the Soviet Union, China, and all Communist-dominated lands were suspended Aug. 1.

The U.S., Australia, and New Zealand signed **Anzus** mutual security pact Sept. 1.

Transcontinental TV begun Sept. 4 with Pres. Truman's address at Japanese Peace Treaty Conference in San Francisco.

Japanese peace treaty signed in San Francisco Sept. 8 by U.S., Japan, and 47 other nations.

J. D. Salinger published *Catcher in the Rye.*

1952

Seizure of nation's steel mills was ordered by Pres. Truman Apr. 8 to avert a strike. Ruled illegal by Supreme Court June 2.

Peace contract between West Germany, U.S., Great Britain, and France was signed May 26.

The last racial and ethnic barriers to naturalization removed, June 26-27, with passage of **Immigration and Naturalization Act of 1952.**

Richard Nixon, as vice-pres. candidate, gave **"Checkers" speech,** Sept. 23.

Puerto Rico proclaimed commonwealth July 25, after referendum Mar. 3.

First **hydrogen device** explosion Nov. 1 in Pacific.

1953

Federal jury in New York convicted 13 **Communist** leaders on conspiracy charges, Jan. 20.

Pres. Dwight D. Eisenhower announced May 8 that U.S. had given France $60 mil for **Indochina War.** More aid was announced in Sept.

Julius and Ethel Rosenberg executed in the Sing Sing Prison electric chair, Ossining, NY, June 19, for betraying nuclear secrets to Soviet Union.

Korean War armistice signed July 27.

California Gov. **Earl Warren** was sworn in Oct. 5 as 14th **chief justice** of U.S. Supreme Court.

1954

Nautilus, first atomic-powered submarine, was launched at Groton, CT, Jan. 21.

Five members of Congress were **wounded** in the House Mar. 1 by 4 **Puerto Rican independence supporters** who fired at random from a spectators' gallery.

At televised **Army-McCarthy hearings,** Apr. 22-June 17, before a Senate subcommittee, Army officials accused Sen. Joseph McCarthy (R, WI) of seeking preferential treatment for a draftee, and McCarthy accused the Army of hindering probe of Communist infiltration into the Army.

Racial segregation in public schools unanimously ruled unconstitutional by Supreme Court May 17, in *Brown* v. *Board of Education of Topeka.*

Southeast Asia Treaty Organization (**SEATO**) formed by defense pact signed in Manila Sept. 8 by U.S., Britain, France, Australia, New Zealand, Philippines, Pakistan, and Thailand.

Condemnation of **Sen. McCarthy** voted by Senate, 67-22, Dec. 2, for abuse of the Senate during hearings and debates.

Ernest Hemingway won Nobel Prize.

1955

U.S. agreed Feb. 12 to help train **South Vietnamese** army.

Supreme Court ordered **"all deliberate speed"** in integration of public schools May 31.

A **summit meeting** of leaders of U.S., Britain, France, and USSR took place July 18-23 in Geneva, Switzerland.

Rosa Parks refused Dec. 1 to give her seat to a white man on a **bus in Montgomery, AL.** Bus segregation ordinance declared unconstitutional by a federal court following **boycott** organized by **Rev. Martin Luther King Jr.**

America's 2 largest labor organizations merged Dec. 5, creating the **AFL-CIO.**

1956

Massive resistance to Supreme Court desegregation rulings was called for Mar. 12 by 101 Southern congressmen.

U.S. Supreme Court, Apr. 23, unanimously ruled against **racial segregation** on intrastate buses.

Federal-Aid **Highway Act** signed June 29, inaugurating interstate highway system.

First transatlantic **telephone cable** activated Sept. 25.

On Oct. 8, in Game 5, Yankee right-hander Don Larsen pitched the only **World Series perfect game.**

My Fair Lady opened on Broadway in Mar., Eugene O'Neill's *Long Day's Journey Into Night* opened in Nov.

1957

Congress approved first **civil rights bill** for blacks since Reconstruction, Apr. 29, to protect voting rights.

The U.S. surgeon general July 12 said studies showed a "direct link" between cigarette **smoking and lung cancer.**

National Guardsmen, called out by Arkansas Gov. Orval Faubus Sept. 4, barred 9 black students from entering all-white high school in **Little Rock.** Faubus complied Sept. 21 with federal court order to remove Guardsmen, but the blacks were ordered to withdraw by local authorities. Pres. Eisenhower sent troops Sept. 24 to enforce court order.

Jack Kerouac published *On the Road.*

1958

First U.S. **earth satellite** to go into orbit, **Explorer I,** launched by Army Jan. 31 at Cape Canaveral, FL; discovered Van Allen radiation belt.

U.S. Marines sent to **Lebanon** to protect elected government from threatened overthrow July-Oct.

Nuclear sub *Nautilus* made first undersea crossing of the **North Pole** Aug. 5.

Presidential aide **Sherman Adams resigned** Sept. 22 over a scandal involving alleged improper gifts.

First domestic **jet airline** passenger service in U.S. opened by National Airlines Dec. 10 between New York and Miami.

1959

Alaska admitted as 49th state Jan. 3; **Hawaii** admitted as 50th Aug. 21.

St. Lawrence Seaway opened Apr. 25.

Vice Pres. **Richard Nixon**, on tour of USSR, held so-called kitchen debate, July 24, with Soviet Prem. **Nikita Khrushchev** at U.S. exhibit in Moscow.

Prem. **Khrushchev** paid unprecedented visit to U.S. Sept. 15-27; made transcontinental tour.

Pres. Eisenhower issued an injunction Oct. 12, upheld and made effective by the Supreme Court Nov. 7, ending a record 116-day **steel strike.**

In an emerging **quiz show scandal**, Columbia Univ. Prof. Charles Van Doren admitted to a U.S. House subcommittee Nov. 2 that he had been coached before appearances on NBC-TV's *21* in 1956; he had won $129,000.

1960

Sit-ins began Feb. 1 when 4 black college students in Greensboro, NC, refused to move from a Woolworth lunch counter when denied service. By Sept. **1961** over 70,000 students, whites and blacks, had participated in sit-ins.

Congress approved a strong **voting rights act** Apr. 21.

A U.S. **U-2 reconnaissance plane** was shot down in the Soviet Union May 1; pilot Gary Powers captured. The incident led to cancellation of a Paris summit conference.

Vice Pres. Richard Nixon and Sen. John F. Kennedy faced each other Sept. 26 in the first in a series of televised **debates. Kennedy defeated Nixon** to win presidency, Nov. 8.

U.S. announced Dec. 15 it backed rightist group in **Laos,** which took power the next day.

1961

U.S. severed diplomatic and consular relations with **Cuba** Jan. 3, after disputes over nationalizations of U.S. firms, U.S. military presence at Guantanamo base.

Invasion of Cuba's **Bay of Pigs** Apr. 17 by Cuban exiles trained, armed, and directed by U.S. unsuccessfully attempted to overthrow the regime of Prem. Fidel Castro.

Peace Corps created by executive order, Mar. 1.

23rd Amendment, giving **District of Columbia** citizens the right to vote in presidential elections, ratified Mar. 29.

Commander Alan B. Shepard Jr. was rocketed from Cape Canaveral, FL, 116.5 mi above the earth in a Mercury capsule May 5, in first U.S.-crewed suborbital space flight.

"Freedom Rides" from Washington, DC, across deep South were launched May 20 to **protest segregation** in interstate transportation.

Pres. Kennedy, May 27, signed bill creating **Alliance for Progress**, for Latin America.

In *Mapp v. Ohio,* June 19, Supreme Court ruled that **illegally obtained evidence** is inadmissible in state as well as federal trials.

1962

Lt. Col. John H. Glenn Jr. became first American in orbit Feb. 20 when he circled the earth 3 times in the Mercury capsule *Friendship 7*.

Pres. John F. Kennedy said Feb. 14 that U.S. military advisers in **Vietnam** would fire if fired upon.

In *Baker v. Carr*, Mar. 26, Supreme Court backed **"one-man one-vote"** apportionment of seats in state legislatures.

James Meredith became first black student at University of Mississippi Oct. 1 after 3,000 troops put down riots.

A Soviet **offensive missile buildup in Cuba** was revealed Oct. 22 by Pres. Kennedy, who ordered a naval and air quarantine on shipment of offensive military equipment to the island. He and Soviet Prem. Khrushchev agreed Oct. 28 on formula to end the crisis. Kennedy announced Nov. 2 that Soviet missile bases in Cuba were being dismantled.

Rachel Carson's *Silent Spring* launched environmentalist movement.

1963

In *Gideon v. Wainwright,* Mar. 18, Supreme Court ruled that all **criminal defendants** must have counsel.

University of Alabama **desegregated** after Gov. **George Wallace** stepped aside when confronted by federally deployed National Guard troops June 11.

Civil rights leader **Medgar Evers** assassinated June 12.

Supreme Court ruled, 8-1, June 17 that laws requiring **recitation of the Lord's Prayer** or Bible verses in public schools were unconstitutional.

President **Kennedy**, on Europe trip, addressed huge crowd in **West Berlin**, June 23.

A limited **nuclear test-ban treaty** was agreed upon July 25 by the U.S., the Soviet Union, and Britain.

March for civil rights begun May 2 **in Birmingham, AL**, led to desegegration accord, which in turn sparked rioting and violence.

On Aug. 28, 200,000 joined in **March on Washington, DC,** in support of black demands **for equal rights** led by **Rev. Martin Luther King Jr.;** highlight was "I have a dream" speech by **King.**

16th St. Baptist Church in Birmingham, AL, bombed Sept. 15 in racial violence; 4 black girls killed.

South Vietnam Pres. **Ngo Dinh Diem assassinated** Nov. 2; U.S. had earlier withdrawn support.

Pres. Kennedy shot and fatally wounded Nov. 22 as he rode in a motorcade through downtown Dallas, TX. Vice Pres. **Lyndon B. Johnson sworn in** as president. **Lee Harvey Oswald arrested** and charged with the murder; he was shot and fatally wounded Nov. 24. **Jack Ruby,** a nightclub owner, was convicted of Oswald's murder; he died in **1967,** while awaiting retrial following reversal of his conviction.

Betty Friedan's *Feminine Mystique* was published.

1964
Panama suspended relations with U.S. Jan. 9 after riots. U.S. offered Dec. 18 to negotiate a new canal treaty.

The **Beatles** arrived in U.S. for first time, appeared Feb. 9 on CBS-TV's *Ed Sullivan Show.*

Supreme Court ordered Feb. 17 that **congressional districts** have equal populations.

U.S. reported May 27 it was sending military planes to **Laos.**

Omnibus **civil rights bill** cleared by Congress July 2, signed same day by Pres. Johnson, banning discrimination in voting, jobs, public accommodations.

Three **civil rights workers** were reported missing in Mississippi June 22; found buried Aug. 4. Twenty-one white men were arrested. On Oct. 20, **1967,** an all-white federal jury convicted 7 of conspiracy in the slayings.

Congress Aug. 7 passed the **Tonkin Gulf Resolution,** authorizing presidential action in Vietnam, after N Vietnamese boats reportedly attacked 2 U.S. destroyers Aug. 2.

Congress approved **War on Poverty** bill Aug. 11, providing for a domestic Peace Corps (**VISTA**), a **Job Corps,** and antipoverty funding.

The **Warren Commission** released Sept. 27 a report concluding that Lee Harvey Oswald was solely responsible for the Kennedy assassination.

Pres. Johnson was elected to a full term, Nov. 3, defeating Republican **Sen. Barry Goldwater** (AZ) in a landslide.

Verrazano-Narrows Bridge opened in New York City Nov. 21.

1965
In State of the Union address Jan. 4, Pres. Johnson outlined plans for his **"Great Society."**

Pres. Johnson in Feb. ordered continuous **bombing of North Vietnam** below 20th parallel.

Malcolm X assassinated Feb. 21 at New York City rally.

Some 14,000 U.S. troops sent to **Dominican Republic** during civil war Apr. 28. All troops withdrawn by next year.

March from Selma to Montgomery, AL, begun Mar. 21 by Rev. Martin Luther King Jr. to demand federal protection of **blacks' voting rights.** New **Voting Rights Act** signed Aug. 6.

Bill establishing **Medicare,** government health insurance program for elderly, signed by Pres. Johnson July 30.

Los Angeles riot by blacks living in **Watts** area resulted in 34 deaths and $200 mil in property damage Aug. 11-16.

National **immigration** quota system abolished Oct. 3.

Electric power failure blacked out most of northeastern U.S., parts of 2 Canadian provinces the night of Nov. 9-10.

1966
U.S. forces began firing into **Cambodia** May 1.

Bombing of Hanoi area of N Vietnam by U.S. planes began June 29. By Dec. 31, 385,300 U.S. troops were stationed in S Vietnam, plus 60,000 offshore and 33,000 in Thailand.

U.S. Supreme Court ruled June 13, in *Miranda v. Arizona,* that suspects must be read their rights before police questioning.

Medicare began July 1.

Charles Whitman, 25, **killed 13 students** from a tower at the **Univ. of Texas,** Austin, Aug. 1, before being shot dead by police.

U.S. **Dept. of Transportation** created, Oct. 15.

Edward Brooke (R, MA) elected Nov. 8 as first black U.S. senator in 85 years.

Robert C. Weaver named secretary of newly created Dept. of Housing and Urban Development (**HUD**), becoming **1st black cabinet member**.

1967
Green Bay Packers beat Kansas City Chiefs, 35-10, in **first Super Bowl,** Jan. 15 in Los Angeles.

Black U.S. Rep. **Adam Clayton Powell** (D, NY) was denied his seat Mar. 1 because of charges he misused government funds. Reelected in **1968,** he was seated, but fined $25,000 and stripped of his seniority.

Pres. Johnson and Soviet Prem. Aleksei Kosygin met June 23 and 25 at **Glassboro State College** in NJ; agreed not to let any crisis push them into war.

25th Amendment, providing for **presidential succession,** was ratified Feb. 10.

USS *Liberty,* an intelligence ship, was torpedoed by Israel in the Mediterranean, apparently by accident, June 8; 34 killed.

Riots by blacks in **Newark, NJ,** July 12-17 killed 26, injured 1,500; more than 1,000 arrested. In **Detroit, MI,** July 23-30, 43 died; 2,000 injured, 5,000 left homeless by rioting, looting, burning in city's black ghetto.

An **antiwar march** on Washington, Oct. 21-22, drew 50,000 participants.

Thurgood Marshall was sworn in Oct. 2 as first black U.S. Supreme Court Justice. **Carl B. Stokes** (D, Cleveland) and **Richard G. Hatcher** (D, Gary, IN) were elected first black mayors of major U.S. cities Nov. 7.

1968
USS *Pueblo* and 83-man crew seized in Sea of Japan Jan. 23 by North Koreans; 82 men released Dec. 22.

"Tet offensive": Communist troops attacked Saigon, 30 province capitals Jan. 30, suffered heavy casualties.

Pres. Johnson **curbed bombing** of North Vietnam Mar. 31. Peace talks began in Paris May 10. All bombing of North halted Oct. 31.

Martin Luther King Jr., 39, assassinated Apr. 4 in Memphis, TN. **James Earl Ray,** an escaped convict, pleaded guilty to the slaying, was sentenced to 99 years.

Students at **Columbia** Univ., Apr. 23-24, seized school buildings in protest demonstrations.

Sen. Robert F. Kennedy (D, NY), 42, **shot** June 5 in Los Angeles, after celebrating presidential primary victories. Died June 6. Sirhan Bishara Sirhan convicted of murder, **1969;** death sentence commuted to life in prison, **1972.**

Vice Pres. **Hubert Humphrey nominated** for president by Democrats **at convention in Chicago,** marked by clash between police and **antiwar protesters,** Aug. 26-29. The Republican nominee, **Richard Nixon, won** the **presidency,** defeating Hubert Humphrey in a close race Nov. 5.

Apollo 8 **orbited moon** in 5-day mission, Dec. 21-27.

1969
Expanded 4-party **Vietnam peace talks** began Jan. 18. U.S. force peaked at 543,400 in April. Withdrawal started July 8. Pres. Nixon set Vietnamization policy Nov. 3.

Earl Warren retired upon swearing in **Warren Burger,** June 23, as Supreme Court chief justice.

U.S. astronaut **Neil Armstrong,** commander of the *Apollo 11* mission, became the first person to **set foot on the moon,** July 20; followed by astronaut **Edwin "Buzz" Aldrin;** astronaut **Michael Collins** remained aboard command module.

Woodstock music festival near Bethel, NY, drew 300,000-500,000 people, Aug. 15-18.

Anti-Vietnam-War demonstrations held in cities across the U.S. marking Vietnam Mortatorium day, Oct. 15; on Nov. 15, some 250,000 marched in Washington, DC.

Massacre of hundreds of civilians by U.S. troops at **My Lai, South Vietnam,** in **1968** incident reported Nov. 16.

Sesame Street launched on public TV.

1970
United Mine Workers official **Joseph A. Yablonski,** his wife, and their daughter found shot to death Jan. 5; UMW chief W. A. (Tony) Boyle later convicted of the killing.

A federal jury Feb. 18 found the **"Chicago 7"** antiwar activists innocent of conspiring to incite riots during the 1968 **Democratic National Convention.** However, 5 were convicted of crossing state lines with intent to incite riots.

Millions of Americans participated in antipollution demonstrations Apr. 22 to mark the **first Earth Day.**

U.S. and South Vietnamese forces crossed **Cambodian** borders Apr. 30 to get at enemy bases.

Four students were killed May 4 at **Kent State** Univ. in Ohio by National Guardsmen during a protest against the war. In protest at **Jackson State** Univ. in Mississippi police fired on protesters; 2 killed.

Two **women generals,** the first in U.S. history, were named by Pres. Nixon May 15.

A **postal reform** measure was signed Aug. 12, creating an independent U.S. Postal Service.

Pres. Nixon, Dec. 31, signed **clean air bill** calling for development of a cleaner auto engine and national air quality standards for 10 major pollutants.

Doonesbury comic strip launched in 30 papers.

1971

Charles Manson and 3 of his cult followers were found guilty Jan. 25 of first-degree murder in **1969** slaying of actress Sharon Tate and 6 others.

Pres. Nixon, Apr. 14, relaxed 20-year trade embargo with **China.**

The 26th Amendment, lowering the **voting age to 18** in all elections, was ratified June 30.

A court-martial jury Mar. 29 convicted **Lt. William L. Calley Jr.** in murder of 22 South Vietnamese at **My Lai** on Mar. 16, **1968.** He was sentenced to life imprisonment Mar. 31. Sentence was reduced to 20 years Aug. 20.

Publication of classified **Pentagon papers** on U.S. involvement in Vietnam was begun June 13 by the *New York Times.* Supreme Court June 30 upheld, 6-3, the right of the *Times* and *Washington Post* to publish the documents.

Pres. Nixon, Aug. 15, instituted a 90-day **wage and price** freeze.

U.S. bombers struck massively in North Vietnam for 5 days starting Dec. 26 in retaliation for alleged violations of agreements reached prior to the 1968 bombing halt.

1972

Pres. Nixon arrived in **Beijing** Feb. 21 for an 8-day visit to China, in a "journey for peace;" a joint communiqué released Feb. 27 called for increased Sino-U.S. contracts.

By a vote of 84 to 8, the Senate, Mar. 22, approved **Equal Rights Amendment** banning **discrimination** on the basis of sex, and sent the measure to the states for ratification.

North Vietnamese forces launched the biggest attacks in 4 years across the demilitarized zone Mar. 30. The U.S. responded Apr. 15 by resumption of bombing of Hanoi and Haiphong after a 4-year lull.

Pres. Nixon announced May 8 the mining of **North Vietnam ports.** Last U.S. combat troops left Aug. 11.

Gov. George C. Wallace (AL), campaigning for president at a Laurel, MD, shopping center May 15, **was shot** and seriously wounded. Arthur Bremer **convicted** Aug. 4, sentenced to 63 years for shooting Wallace and 3 others.

In **first visit of a U.S. president to Moscow,** Pres. Nixon arrived May 22 for summit talks with Kremlin leaders that culminated in a landmark strategic arms pact **(SALT I).**

Five men were arrested June 17 for breaking into the offices of the Democratic National Committee in the **Watergate** office complex in Washington, DC.

Supreme Court in *Furman* v. *Georgia* June 29 ruled **capital punishment** as currently practiced was unconstitutional.

Mark Spitz won 7 gold medals in world record times, at the Munich Olympics in Sept.

Pres. **Nixon** was **reelected** Nov. 7 in a landslide, carrying 49 states to defeat Democratic Sen. George McGovern (SD).

The **Dow Jones** Industrial Average closed above 1,000 for the first time, Nov. 14.

Full-scale **bombing of North Vietnam** resumed after Paris peace negotiations reached an impasse Dec. 18.

1973

Five of 7 defendants in **Watergate** break-in trial pleaded guilty Jan. 11 and 15; the other 2 were convicted Jan. 30.

In **Roe v. Wade,** Supreme Court ruled, 7-2, Jan. 22, that states may not ban **abortions** during **first 3 months of preg-** nancy and may regulate, but may not ban, abortions during 2nd trimester.

Wounded Knee, SD, occupied in protest by activists in American Indian Movement, Feb. 27.

Four-party **Vietnam peace pacts** were signed in Paris Jan. 27, and North Vietnam released some 590 U.S. prisoners by Apr. 1. Last U.S. troops left Mar. 29.

End of the military **draft** announced Jan. 27.

Top **Nixon aides** H. R. Haldeman, John D. Ehrlichman, and John Dean and Attorney Gen. Richard Kleindienst **resigned** Apr. 30, amid charges of White House efforts to obstruct justice in the Watergate case.

Skylab, 1st U.S. space station, launched May 14.

Secretariat became first **Triple Crown** winner since Citation in 1948, after winning Belmont Stakes June 9 in record time.

John Dean, former Nixon counsel, told Senate hearings June 25 that Nixon, his staff and campaign aides, and the Justice Dept. had conspired to cover up **Watergate** facts.

The U.S. officially ceased bombing in **Cambodia** at midnight Aug. 14 in accord with a June congressional action.

Vice Pres. Spiro Agnew, Oct. 10, **resigned** and pleaded no contest to a charge of tax evasion on payments made to him by contractors when he was governor of Maryland. **Gerald R. Ford,** Oct. 12, became **first appointed vice president** under the 25th Amendment; sworn in Dec. 6.

A total ban on **oil exports** to the U.S. was imposed by Arab oil-producing nations Oct. 19-21 after the outbreak of an Arab-Israeli war. The ban was lifted Mar. 18, **1974.**

The **"Saturday Night Massacre"** occurred Oct. 20, when Pres. Nixon ordered **Attorney Gen. Elliot Richardson** to fire **Watergate special prosecutor Archibald Cox**, who had sought the handover of Nixon's subpoenaed White House tapes. Richardson refused to comply and resigned; **Dep. Attorney Gen. William Ruckelshaus** refused and was fired. **Solicitor Gen. Robert Bork,** as acting attorney gen., then fired Cox. **Leon Jaworski** named Nov. 1 by the Nixon administration to succeed Cox.

Congress overrode Nov. 7 Pres. Nixon's veto of the **war powers** bill, which curbed president's power to commit forces to hostilities abroad without congressional approval.

1974

On Apr. 8, **Hank Aaron** of the Atlanta Braves hit his 715th career **home run** to break **Babe Ruth's** record.

Impeachment hearings opened May 9 against Pres. Nixon by the House Judiciary Committee.

John D. Ehrlichman and 3 **White House "plumbers"** found guilty July 12 of conspiring to violate the civil rights of Pentagon Papers leaker Daniel Ellsberg's psychiatrist by breaking into his office.

Supreme Court ruled, 8-0, July 24 that Nixon had to turn over **64 tapes** of White House conversations.

House Judiciary Committee, in televised hearings July 24-30, recommended 3 **articles of impeachment** against Pres. Nixon. The first, voted 27-11, charged conspiracy to obstruct justice in the Watergate cover-up. The 2nd, voted 28-10, charged abuses of power. The 3rd, voted 21-17, charged defiance of committee subpoenas. (The House voted Aug. 20, 412-3, to accept the committee report, which included the impeachment articles.)

Pres. Nixon announced his resignation, Aug. 8, and **resigned** Aug. 9; his support in Congress had begun to collapse Aug. 5, after release of tapes appearing to implicate him in Watergate cover-up. **Vice Pres. Ford** was **sworn in** Aug. 9 as 38th U.S. president.

Ford, Aug. 20, nominated Nelson **Rockefeller** to be **vice president**; he was sworn in Dec. 10.

A **pardon** to ex-Pres. Nixon for any federal crimes he committed while president issued by Pres. Ford Sept. 8.

1975

Found guilty of Watergate cover-up charges Jan. 1 were ex-Atty. Gen. John Mitchell and ex-presidential advisers H. R. Haldeman and John Ehrlichman.

U.S. launched **evacuation** of Americans and some South Vietnamese **from Saigon** Apr. 29 as Communist forces completed takeover of South Vietnam; **South Vietnamese** government officially **surrendered** Apr. 30.

U.S. merchant ship *Mayaguez* and its crew of 39 were seized by Cambodian forces in Gulf of Siam May 12. In rescue operation, U.S. Marines attacked Tang Island, planes bombed air base; Cambodia surrendered ship and crew.

Congress voted $405 mil for **South Vietnam refugees** May 16; 140,000 were flown to the U.S.

Illegal CIA operations described by panel headed by Vice Pres. **Rockefeller** June 10.

Publishing heiress **Patricia (Patty) Hearst,** kidnapped Feb. 5, **1974,** by "Symbionese Liberation Army" militants, captured in San Francisco Sept. 18 with others. She was convicted Mar. 20, **1976,** of bank robbery.

1976

Nationwide **swine flu vaccination** program launched Mar. 24, discontinued Oct. 12 after several deaths reported.

In **"right to die"** case, NJ Supreme Court Mar. 31 allowed comatose **Karen Ann Quinlan** to be removed from respirator; she survived, dying in a nursing home in **1985.**

Supreme Court **reinstated death penalty,** July 2, subject to conditions.

U.S. celebrated **200th anniversary of independence** July 4, with festivals, parades, and New York City's Operation Sail, a gathering of tall ships from around the world.

"Legionnaire's disease" killed 29 persons who attended an American Legion convention July 21-24 in Philadelphia.

Viking II set down on **Mars'** Utopia Plains Sept. 3, following the successful landing by *Viking I* July 20.

Two U.S. officers on routine mission near DMZ slain by **North Korean soldiers,** Aug. 18; North Korea stated "regret," Aug. 21.

1977

Pres. Jimmy Carter Jan. 21 pardoned most Vietnam War **draft evaders**.

Convicted murderer **Gary Gilmore executed** by a Utah firing squad Jan. 17, in the first exercise of capital punishment in the U.S. since **1967.**

Natural gas shortage, caused by severe winter weather, led Congress Feb. 2 to approve emergency federal allocation program.

Pres. Carter signed an act Aug. 4 creating a new cabinet-level **Energy Department.**

Elvis Presley died Aug. 16.

FBI Dec. 7 released 40,000 pages of previously secret files relating to Kennedy assassination.

George Lucas's first *Star Wars* film produced.

1978

Crippling 110-day coal miners **strike** ended Mar. 25 with ratification of new contract.

Senate voted, 68-32, Apr. 18 to turn over **Panama Canal** to Panama on Dec. 31, **1999**; a Mar. 16 vote had given approval to a treaty guaranteeing the area's neutrality after the year 2000.

Californians, June 6, approved **Proposition 13,** a state constitutional amendment slashing property taxes.

Supreme Court, June 28, ruled against **racial quotas** in *Bakke* v. *University of California*.

Egyptian Pres. Anwar al-**Sadat** and Israeli Prem. Menachem **Begin** reached accord on "framework for peace," Sept. 17, after Carter-mediated talks at **Camp David**.

New York's Chemical Bank Dec. 20 led move to raise **prime interest rate** to near-record 11.75%.

1979

Former Atty. Gen. John Mitchell, last of 25 persons still jailed for crimes relating to **Watergate scandal**, released Jan. 19.

Partial meltdown released radioactive material Mar. 28, at nuclear reactor on **Three Mile Island** near Middletown, PA.

American Airlines DC-10 **jetliner crashed** May 25 after takeoff from Chicago, killing 275 persons.

In a speech July 15, Pres. Carter spoke of a national **"crisis of confidence"** and outlined a proposed 10-year $140 bil program to **reduce U.S. dependence on foreign oil.**

Federal government announced, Nov. 1, a $1.5 bil loan-guarantee plan to aid the ailing **Chrysler Corp.**

Some 90 people, including 63 Americans, **taken hostage,** Nov. 4, at **American embassy in Tehran,** Iran, by militant followers of **Ayatollah Khomeini.** He demanded return of former Shah Muhammad Reza Pahlavi, who was undergoing medical treatment in New York City.

1980

Pres. Carter announced, Jan. 4, economic sanctions against the USSR, in retaliation for Soviet invasion of Afghanistan. At Carter's request, **U.S. Olympic Committee** voted, Apr. 12, against U.S. participation in Moscow Summer Olympics.

Lake Placid, NY, hosted the **Winter Olympics** for the 2nd time. The U.S. hockey team defeated the heavily favored Russian team Feb. 22 en route to winning the gold medal.

An 11-day New York City **transit strike** ended, Apr. 11, after union leaders approved a tentative contract agreement.

Eight Americans killed and 5 wounded, Apr. 24, **in ill-fated** attempt to **rescue hostages** held by Iranian militants.

Mt. St. Helens, in Washington state, **erupted** May 18. The blast, with others May 25 and June 12, left 57 dead.

In a sweeping victory, Nov. 4, **Ronald Reagan** (R) was elected 40th president, defeating incumbent Pres. Carter. Republicans gained control of the Senate.

Former Beatle **John Lennon** was shot and **killed,** Dec. 8, in New York City.

1981

Minutes after Reagan's inauguration Jan. 20, the **52 Americans** held **hostage in Iran** for 444 days were **freed.**

Pres. Reagan was **shot and seriously wounded,** Mar. 30, in Washington, DC; also seriously wounded were a Secret Service agent, a policeman, and Press Sec. **James Brady.** John W. **Hinckley Jr.** arrested, found not guilty by reason of insanity in **1982,** committed to mental institution.

World's first reusable spacecraft, the **space shuttle *Columbia*,** was sent into space, Apr. 12.

Congress, July 29, passed Pres. Reagan's **tax-cut legislation,** expected to save taxpayers $750 bil over 5 years.

Federal air traffic controllers, Aug. 3, began an illegal **nationwide strike.** Most defied a back-to-work order and were dismissed by Pres. Reagan Aug. 5.

In a 99-0 vote, the Senate confirmed, Sept. 21, appointment of **Sandra Day O'Connor** as **first woman justice** of U.S. Supreme Court.

1982

The 13-year-old lawsuit against **AT&T** by the **Justice Dept.** was settled Jan. 8. AT&T agreed to give up the 22 Bell System companies and was allowed to expand.

The Equal Rights Amendment was **defeated** after a 10-year struggle, when the deadline for ratification expired June 30.

Centers for Disease Control, July 16, reported evidence of growing **AIDS epidemic**, responsible for 184 U.S. deaths since 1st reported in U.S. in June **1981.**

The economy showed signs of recovery from the **recession** that began in mid-**1981,** as the **Dow Jones** Industrial Average Oct. 13 hit 1016.93, its highest level in 18 months, amid falling interest rates.

The most expensive **strike** in sports history ended, Nov. 16, when **NFL** players and team owners settled.

Space shuttle *Columbia* completed its first operational flight, Nov. 16.

A retired dentist, **Dr. Barney B. Clark,** 61, became first recipient of a **permanent artificial heart,** Dec. 2; he died Mar. 23, **1983,** after 112 days.

EPA administrator Anne Gorsuch was **cited for contempt** by the House Dec. 16, after refusing to produce certain documents concerning the Superfund.

1983
Pres. Reagan, Jan. 3, declared Times Beach, MO, a federal disaster area because of toxic **dioxin** in the soil.

The Commerce Dept. Jan 19 reported that average real **GNP** in the recessionary year **1982** fell 1.8% from **1981** levels, the **worst decline** since 1946.

Harold Washington was elected Apr. 12 as the first African American **mayor of Chicago.**

On Apr. 20, **Pres. Reagan** signed a compromise bipartisan bill designed to save **Social Security** from bankruptcy.

Sally Ride became the first American **woman** to travel in **space,** June 18, when the **space shuttle** *Challenger* was launched from Cape Canaveral, FL.

On Sept. 1, **a South Korean passenger jet** infringing on Soviet air space and apparently misidentified was **shot down;** 269 people, including 61 Americans, were killed.

On Oct. 23, 241 **U.S. Marines and sailors** were killed in Lebanon when a TNT-laden suicide bomb blew up Marine headquarters at **Beirut** International Airport.

U.S. troops, with a small force from 6 **Caribbean** nations, invaded **Grenada** Oct. 25. In a few days, Grenadian militia and Cuban "construction workers" were overcome, U.S. citizens evacuated, and the **Marxist regime deposed.**

1984
Seven regional companies took over local telephone service from AT&T, Jan. 1.

The space shuttle *Challenger* was launched on its 4th trip into space, Feb. 3. On Feb. 7, Navy Capt. Bruce McCandless, followed by Army Lt. Colonel Robert Stewart, became **first humans to fly free of a spacecraft.**

On May 7, American **Vietnam war** veterans reached an out-of-court **settlement with 7 chemical companies** in a class-action suit over the herbicide **Agent Orange.**

Former Vice Pres. **Walter Mondale** won the **Democratic presidential nomination,** June 6; he chose **Rep. Geraldine Ferraro** (D, NY), as candidate for **vice president.**

Pres. Reagan signed a bill July 17 cutting federal transportation aid to states that keep their **drinking age** under 21.

Pres. **Reagan** was **reelected** Nov. 6 in a Republican **landslide,** carrying 49 states for a record 525 electoral votes.

Bernhard Goetz shot and wounded 4 allegedly menacing teen-age boys, on a NYC subway train, Dec. 22; later was acquitted of major charges but was successfully sued.

1985
Visiting Germany, Pres. Reagan, May 5, laid wreath at concentration camp site and also at a **Bitburg** cemetery, where some Nazis lay.

Philadelphia police bombed a rowhouse occupied by **MOVE anarchists,** May 13; 11 were killed, and fire damaged 2 blocks of houses.

On June 14 a **TWA jet was seized** by terrorists after takeoff from Athens; 153 passengers and crew held hostage for 17 days; 1 U.S. serviceman killed.

Reversing an earlier decision to market "new" coke, the **Coca-Cola Co.** said, July 10, it would resume marketing soda made under its original "Classic" formula.

"Live Aid," a rock concert broadcast around the world July 13, raised $70 mil for starving peoples of Africa.

On Oct. 7, **4 Palestinian hijackers seized** Italian cruise ship *Achille Lauro* in the Mediterranean and held it hostage for 2 days; one American, Leon Klinghoffer, was killed.

For first time in 6 years U.S. and Soviet leaders met at **summit in Geneva,** Nov. 19-20.

General Electric agreed Dec. 11 to buy RCA Corp. for $6.28 bil.

1986
On Jan. 20, for the first time, the U.S. officially observed **Martin Luther King Jr. Day.**

The space shuttle *Challenger* **exploded** 73 seconds after liftoff, Jan. 28, **killing 6 astronauts and Christa McAuliffe,** a New Hampshire teacher, on board.

In a 4-day extravaganza in July, the U.S. celebrated the 100th birthday of the **Statue of Liberty**.

Congress completed action Oct. 2 overriding a veto to place conomic **sanctions on South Africa**.

The Senate confirmed, Sept. 17, Reagan's nomination of **William Rehnquist** as chief justice and **Antonin Scalia** as associate justice of the Supreme Court.

Press reports in early Nov. broke first news of the **Iran-contra scandal,** involving secret U.S. sale of arms to Iran.

Ivan Boesky, accused of insider trading, agreed, Nov. 14, to plead guilty to an unspecified criminal count.

Robert Penn Warren was named by the Library of Congress as America's **first poet laureate**.

1987
Pres. Reagan produced the nation's first **trillion-dollar budget,** Jan. 5.

Dow Jones closed above 2,000 for first time, Jan. 8.

The U.S. government, Mar. 20, approved for the first time the use of a drug in the fight against AIDS (AZT).

Nearly **1.4 mil illegal aliens** met May 4 deadline for applying for **amnesty** under a new federal policy.

An **Iraqi missile killed 37 sailors** on the frigate USS *Stark* in the Persian Gulf, May 17. Iraq called it an accident.

Public hearings by Senate and House committees investigating the **Iran-contra affair** were held May-Aug. Lt. Col. **Oliver North** said he had believed all his activities were authorized by his superiors. Pres. Reagan, Aug. 12, denied knowing of a diversion of funds to the contras.

The 200th anniversary of the **U.S. Constitution** signing was observed, Sept. 17, in Philadelphia and around the U.S.

Wall Street crashed, Oct. 19, with the Dow Jones plummeting a record 508 points to 1738, ending a bull market that began in mid-**1982.**

Pres. Reagan and Soviet leader **Mikhail Gorbachev,** Dec. 8, signed a **pact to dismantle** all 1,752 U.S. and 859 Soviet **missiles** with a 300- to 3,400-mi. range.

1988
In a report issued May 16, Surgeon Gen. C. Everett Koop declared that **cigarettes** were addictive.

Congress approved, in June, the greatest expansion yet of **Medicare** benefits, to protect the **elderly and disabled** against "catastrophic" medical costs.

Much of the U.S. suffered worst **drought** in over 50 years; by late June half the nation's agricultural counties had been declared disaster areas.

A missile, fired from **U.S. Navy warship** *Vincennes,* in the Persian Gulf, mistakenly struck a commercial **Iranian airliner,** July 3, killing all 290.

George H. W. Bush was **elected** 41st U.S. **president,** Nov. 8, decisively defeating Gov. **Michael Dukakis** (MA).

Pan Am Flight 103 exploded and crashed into the town of **Lockerbie, Scotland,** Dec. 21, killing all 259 people aboard and 11 on the ground.

Drexel Burnham Lambert agreed, Dec. 21, **to plead guilty** to insider trading and other violations, and **pay penalties of $650 mil,** the largest such settlement ever.

1989
Major oil spill occurred when the *Exxon Valdez* struck Bligh Reef in Alaska's Prince William Sound, Mar. 24.

Former National Security Council staff member **Oliver North** was convicted, May 4, on charges related to **Iran-contra** scandal. Conviction thrown out on appeal in **1991** because of his immunized testimony.

A measure to **rescue the savings and loan industry** was signed into law, Aug. 9, by Pres. Bush.

Army Gen. Colin Powell was nominated Aug. 10 by Pres. Bush, as **chairman of the Joint Chiefs of Staff;** he became the first black to hold the post.

Pete Rose, a baseball legend, was **banned** from the game for life Aug. 24, for involvement with gamblers.

Hurricane Hugo swept through the Caribbean and the Carolinas Sept. 10-22, causing at least 40 deaths and $6 bil in damage in the Carolinas alone.

Just before a World Series game, Oct. 17, an **earthquake** struck the **San Francisco Bay area,** causing 62 deaths.

L. Douglas Wilder (D) elected governor of Virginia, the **first U.S. black governor** since Reconstruction.

U.S. troops invaded Panama, Dec. 20, overthrowing the government of **Manuel Noriega.** Noriega, wanted by U.S. authorities on drug charges, surrendered Jan. 3, **1990.**

1990

Junk bond financier Michael Milkin pleaded guilty to fraud related charges, Apr. 14; agreed to pay $500 mil in restitution; sentenced Nov. 21 to 10 years in prison.

Justice William Brennan announced, July 20, his resignation from the U.S. Supreme Court; his replacement, **Judge David Souter,** was confirmed Sept. 27.

Pres. Bush signed **Americans With Disabilities Act** on July 26, barring discrimination against handicapped.

Operation Desert Shield forces left for **Saudi Arabia,** Aug. 7, to defend that country following the **invasion** of its neighbor **Kuwait by Iraq,** Aug. 2.

Pres. Bush signed, Nov. 5, a bill to **reduce budget deficits** $500 bil over 5 years, by spending curbs and tax hikes.

Pres. Bush Nov. 15 signed into law a strengthened version of the 1970 **Clean Air Act.**

1991

The **U.S. and its allies defeated Iraq** in the **Persian Gulf War** and liberated Kuwait, which Iraq had overrun in Aug. **1990.** On Jan. 17, the allies launched a devastating **air attack.** In a **rapid ground war** starting Feb. 24, which lasted just 100 hours, the U.S.-led forces killed or captured thousands of Iraqi soldiers and sent the rest into retreat before Pres. Bush ordered a cease-fire Feb. 27.

An 8-month **recession** showed signs of having ended in Mar. The **Dow Jones** Industrial Average closed above **3000** for first time, Apr. 17

Justice **Thurgood Marshall,** first black to sit on U.S. Supreme Court, June 17, announced plans **to retire.**

U.S. **House bank** ordered closed Oct. 3 after revelations that House members had written 8,331 bad checks.

The **Senate approved,** Oct. 15, nomination of **Clarence Thomas** to the Supreme Court, despite allegations of sexual harassment against him by **Anita Hill,** a former aide. He became the 2nd African-American to serve on the Court, replacing retiring Justice **Thurgood Marshall,** the 1st black.

Charles Keating convicted of securities fraud Dec. 4. The prosecution asserted that as chairman of an S&L he had induced investors to buy $250 mil in uninsured bonds.

1992

Retail giant **R.H. Macy & Co.** filed for bankruptcy, Jan. 27. **Trans World Airlines,** Jan. 31, became the latest major U.S. carrier to file for bankruptcy.

Riots swept South-Central **Los Angeles** Apr. 29, after **jury acquitted 4 white policemen** on all but one count in videotaped 1991 beating of black motorist **Rodney King.** Death toll in the L.A. violence was put at 52.

The **27th Amendment**, regarding congressional pay raises, became part of the Constitution May 7 when it was ratified by the 38th state, Michigan.

Hurricane Andrew ravaged South Florida and Louisiana Aug. 24-26, killing 23 people.

White supremacist and fugitive Randall Weaver surrendered Aug. 31 after an 11-day FBI **siege** at his **Ruby Ridge,** ID, cabin, during which his wife and son and a deputy sheriff were killed in exchanges of gunfire.

Bill Clinton (D) was **elected** 42nd president, Nov. 3, defeating **Pres. Bush** (R) and independent **Ross Perot.**

A UN-sanctioned military force, led by U.S. troops, arrived in **Somalia** Dec. 9.

Presidents of U.S., Canada, and Mexico Dec. 17 signed North American Free Trade Agreement.

More than 1.1 million votes were cast in an election to choose a portrait of the late **Elvis Presley** (died 1977) for a **U.S. postage stamp**.

1993

A bomb exploded in a parking garage beneath the **World Trade Center** in New York City, Feb. 26, killing 6 people. Two Islamic militants were convicted in the bombing, Nov. 12, **1997.** Four men were found guilty, Mar. 4, **1994.**

Janet Reno became the first woman U.S. attorney general Mar. 12.

Four federal agents were killed, Feb. 28, during an unsuccessful raid on the **Branch Davidian compound near Waco, TX.** A 51-day siege by federal agents ended Apr. 19, when the compound **burned down,** leaving more than 70 cult members dead. 11 **cult** members were acquitted Feb. 26, **1994,** of charges in the deaths of the federal agents.

A federal jury, Apr. 17, found **2 Los Angeles police officers guilty** and 2 not guilty of violating the civil rights of motorist **Rodney King** in **1991** beating incident.

Defense Sec. Les Aspin, Apr. 28, removed restrictions on aerial **combat roles by women** in the armed forces.

In a May 14 **plebiscite** voters in Puerto Rico supported continuing commonwealth status with U.S.

A **"motor-voter" bill** was signed by Pres. Clinton, May 20, allowing citizens to register to vote by mail when applying for a driver's license or certain benefits.

"The Great Flood of 1993" inundated 8 mil acres in 9 Midwestern states in summer, leaving 50 dead.

Pres. Clinton July 2 approved recommendations that 33 major U.S. **military bases** be **closed.** On July 19 he announced a **"don't ask, don't tell, don't pursue"** policy for homosexuals in the U.S. military.

Vincent Foster, deputy White House counsel, found shot to death July 20 in a N Virginia park, an apparent suicide.

Judge Ruth Bader Ginsburg was sworn in, Aug. 10, as 107th justice of the Supreme Court.

Pres. Clinton, Aug. 10, signed a measure designed to **cut federal budget deficits** $496 bil over 5 years, through spending cuts and new taxes.

The **"Brady Bill,"** a major gun-control measure, was signed into law by Pres. Clinton Nov. 30.

1994

North American Free Trade Agreement took effect Jan. 1.

A predawn earthquake struck the Los Angeles area, Jan. 17, claiming 61 lives and causing widespread devastation.

Pres. Clinton Feb. 3 lifted 19-year ban on U.S. **trade with Vietnam.**

Kenneth Starr named Aug. 5 as independent counsel to probe **Whitewater affair;** congressional committees, late July, began Whitewater hearings.

Byron De La Beckwith convicted Feb. 5 of the **1963** murder of civil rights leader **Medgar Evers.**

Longtime CIA officer **Aldrich Ames** and his wife were **charged** Feb. 21 **with spying**. Under a plea bargain, he received life in prison, while she drew 63 months.

U.S. troops Mar. 25 officially ended peacekeeping and humanitarian aid mission in **Somalia** begun in **1992.**

Major league **baseball players went on strike,** following Aug. 11 games; World Series cancelled; strike ended Apr. 25, **1995.**

Senate Majority Leader George Mitchell (D, ME), Sept. 26, dropped efforts to pass Pres. Clinton's **health-care reform** package.

1995

When the 104th Congress opened, Jan. 4, **Sen. Bob Dole** (R, KS) became **Senate majority leader** and **Rep. Newt Gingrich** (R, GA) was elected **House Speaker.** A bill to end Congress's exemption from federal labor laws, first in a series of measures in Republicans' **"Contract With America,"** cleared Congress Jan. 17; signed into law Jan. 23.

Clinton invoked emergency powers, Jan. 31, to extend a **$20 bil loan** to help **Mexico** avert financial collapse.

The last UN peacekeeping troops withdrew from **Somalia** Feb. 28-Mar. 3, with the aid of U.S. Marines. In **Haiti,** peacekeeping responsibilities were transferred from U.S. to UN forces Mar. 31, with the U.S. providing 2,400 soldiers.

A truck **bomb** exploded outside **a federal office building in Oklahoma City** Apr. 19, **killing 168** people in all, in deadliest terrorist attack yet on U.S. soil; **Timothy McVeigh** was 1st and key suspect arrested, Apr. 21.

The U.S. space shuttle *Atlantis* made the first in a series of **dockings with** Russian space station *Mir,* June 29-July 4.

A U.S. **F-16 fighter jet** piloted by Air Force Capt. **Scott O'Grady** was **shot down** over Bosnia and Herzegovina June 2; O'Grady was **rescued** by U.S. Marines 6 days later.

The U.S. announced on July 11 that it was reestablishing diplomatic **relations with Vietnam.**

Former football star **O. J. Simpson** found **not guilty** Oct. 3 of the **June 1994** murders of his former wife, Nicole Brown Simpson, and her friend Ronald Goldman.

Ten Muslim militants convicted in New York, Oct. 1, in a failed plot to blow up **UN Headquarters** and other buildings and assassinate political leaders.

Shannon Faulkner won a legal fight to gain admission to the previously all-male cadet corps of **The Citadel,** Aug. 11, though she dropped out after a few days of training.

Hundreds of thousands of African-American men participated in **"Million Man March"** and rally in Washington, DC, Oct. 16, organized by Rev. Louis Farrakhan.

The federal **55-mile-per-hour speed limit** was **repealed** by a measure signed Nov. 28.

After talks outside Dayton, OH, **warring parties in Bosnia and Herzegovina reached agreement** Nov. 21 to end their conflict; treaty was signed Dec. 14, after which first of some 20,000 **U.S. peacekeeping troops** arrived in Bosnia.

Five Americans were among 7 **killed,** Nov. 13, in bombing of a U.S. military post in **Riyadh, Saudi Arabia.**

A budget impasse between Congress and Pres. Clinton led to a partial **government shutdown** beginning Nov. 14. Operations resumed Nov. 20 under continuing resolutions.

1996

Long-sought records released by White House Jan. 5 showed **Hillary Rodham Clinton** did 60 hours of work for an S&L linked to **Whitewater** scandal. Responding to a subpoena, she testified Jan. 26 before a grand jury.

Senate, Jan. 26, approved, 87-4, the Second Strategic Arms Reduction Treaty (**START II**).

On Feb. 24 **Cuban jets shot down** 2 civilian planes owned by a Cuban exile group; 4 killed. Cuba claimed its territory was violated; U.S., Feb. 26, tightened embargo.

John Salvi found guilty, Mar. 18, in the **1994 murder** of receptionists at 2 **abortion clinics** in Brookline, MA.

Congress, in Mar., approved a **"line item veto"** bill, but it was struck down by the Supreme Court, June 25, **1998**.

U.S. Commerce Sec. **Ron Brown** was killed Apr. 3 in a plane crash in Croatia.

An auction, Apr. 23-26, of items owned by former First Lady **Jacqueline Kennedy Onassis** brought in $34 mil.

James and Susan McDougal were convicted May 28 of fraud and conspiracy. Arkansas Gov. **Jim Guy Tucker** was convicted of similar charges by the same jury.

The antitax **Freemen** surrendered to federal authorities June 13 after an 81-day standoff near Jordan, MT; 4 were convicted, July 8, **1998**, of conspiring to defraud banks.

Republicans June 12 chose Sen. **Trent Lott** (MS) as new majority leader to replace Sen. **Robert Dole,** who resigned, June 11, to focus on his presidential campaign.

A **bomb** exploded at a military complex near Dhahran, **Saudi Arabia,** June 25, killing 19 American servicemen.

On July 27 a **bomb exploded** in Atlanta, GA, near the **Olympics;** one person was directly killed.

Major **welfare reform bill** was signed into law Aug. 22.

Shannon Lucid, Sept. 26, completed a space voyage of 188 days, a record for women and for U.S. astronauts.

Archer Daniels Midland Co. announced, Oct. 14, it had agreed to pay a fine of $100 mil for price fixing.

Pres. Clinton was reelected to 2nd term, Nov. 5.

1997

Bombs were detonated at **abortion clinics** in Tulsa, OK, Jan. 1, in Atlanta on Jan. 16, and again at the first site in Tulsa on Jan. 19; 6 people were injured.

Newt Gingrich (R, GA) was reelected Speaker of the U.S. House Jan. 7, but was fined and reprimanded by colleagues for alleged misuse of tax-exempt donations.

Madeleine Albright was sworn in as secretary of state Jan. 23, becoming the first woman to head State Dept.

Harold Nicholson, a former CIA official, pleaded guilty, Mar. 3, to spying for Russia.

39 members of the **Heaven's Gate religious cult** found

dead in a house in Rancho Santa Fe, CA, Mar. 26, in an apparent mass suicide.

James McDougal, former partner in Whitewater, sentenced Apr. 14 to 3 years in prison for seeking to profit from fraudulent loans. He died in prison, Mar. 8, **1998**.

Timothy McVeigh convicted of conspiracy and murder, June 2, in **1995** Oklahoma City bombing.

On **Oct. 27,** the **Dow Jones** fell 554.26 points, largest 1-day point decline yet. On Oct. 28, the Dow rebounded, surging 337.17 points, largest-yet single-day point advance.

Islamic militants **Ramzi Ahmed Yousef** and **Eyad Ismoil Yousef** convicted, Nov. 12, in the **1993** bombing of the World Trade Center in New York City.

On Nov. 19, **Bobbi McCaughey,** 29, delivered the first set of live septuplets to survive more than a month.

Terry Nichols convicted Dec. 23 on charges related to the **1995 Oklahoma City bombing**.

1998

It was reported Jan. 21 that Whitewater independent counsel Kenneth Starr had evidence of a **sexual relationship** between **Pres. Clinton** and onetime White House intern Monica Lewinsky. Clinton denied it.

Theodore Kaczynski, the "Unabomber," arrested in Montana in 1993, pleaded guilty Jan. 22 in California and New Jersey bombings that killed 3 people and injured 2.

The state of Texas, Feb. 3, executed its first female convict in 135 years—**Karla Faye Tucker.**

2 youths aged 11 and 13 were arrested, Mar. 24, in the killing of 4 schoolgirls and a teacher outside a **Jonesboro, AR,** school; later committed to a juvenile detention center.

On Apr. 25, First Lady **Hillary Rodham Clinton** provided videotaped testimony at the White House for the Little Rock, AR, grand jury in the **Whitewater** case.

Monica Lewinsky, Aug. 6, testified to having had a sexual relationship with **Pres. Clinton,** but said she was never asked to lie. In grand jury testimony and an address to the nation, Aug. 17, **Clinton** acknowledged an inappropriate relationship with Lewinsky. On Sept. 9, independent counsel **Kenneth Starr** sent the House what he called "credible information that may constitute grounds" for impeachment.

Mark McGwire, Sept. 8, hit his 62nd **home run** of the season, breaking **Roger Maris's** season record.

On Sept. 30, Pres. Clinton announced a **budget surplus** of $70 billion for fiscal year 1998, the first since 1969.

Terrorist **bombs** in **U.S. embassies** in Nairobi, Kenya, and Dar-es-Salaam, Tanzania, killed at least 257, Aug. 7. The U.S. launched **retaliatory strikes,** Aug. 20, against alleged terrorist-related targets in Afghanistan and Sudan.

The House Judiciary Committee, Oct. 5, voted 21-16 along party lines to recommend that the Clinton **impeachment** investigation proceed. The House concurred Oct. 8, voting 258-176; 31 Democrats voted yes.

Dr. Barnett Slepian, an obstetrician who performed abortions, was killed by a sniper near Buffalo, NY, Oct. 23.

John Glenn, 77, first U.S. astronaut to orbit Earth, returned to space Oct. 29-Nov. 7, aboard the shuttle *Discovery*.

Pres. Clinton, Nov. 13, settled a suit by agreeing to pay $850,000 to **Paula Corbin Jones.** She alleged that he had made an unwanted sexual advance to her in 1991.

The country's 4 largest **tobacco** companies, in a settlement, Nov. 23, with 46 states, the District of Columbia, and 4 territories, agreed to pay $206 bil over 25 years to cover public health costs related to smoking.

The U.S. House, Dec. 19, approved 2 articles of **impeachment** charging **Pres. Clinton** with grand jury perjury (228-206) and obstruction of justice (221-212) in a cover-up of his sexual relationship with **Monica Lewinsky;** 2 other impeachment articles failed.

1999

J. Dennis Hastert (IL) was elected Speaker of the House for the 106th Congress, Jan. 6.

Pres. Clinton's impeachment trial—the 2nd such trial in U.S. history—began in the GOP-controlled Senate Jan. 7. He was acquitted, Feb. 12. The perjury article failed, with 45 votes; the obstruction of justice article drew a 50-50 vote, with a two-thirds vote needed for conviction.

Dr. Jack Kevorkian, who claimed he had helped 130 people kill themselves, convicted of 2nd-degree murder Mar. 26 in one death; sentenced to 10-25 years in prison.

Two men were convicted in the **1998** beating death of **Matthew Shepard,** an openly homosexual student at the Univ. of Wyoming.

Eric Harris, 18, and Dylan Klebold, 17, killed 12 fellow students and a teacher Apr. 20 at **Columbine** High School in Littleton, CO, then shot themselves fatally.

One NYC police officer pleaded guilty to 6 charges, May 25, and another was convicted on an assault charge, June 8, in connection with the **1997** torture and sodomizing of Haitian immigrant **Abner Louima** in a police station.

John F. Kennedy Jr., son of the former president, died in a plane crash July 16 along with his wife, Carolyn Bessette **Kennedy,** and his sister-in-law, Lauren Bessette.

The **Dow Jones** Industrial Average closed the year at a **record** level of 11,497.12—25.2% above the **1998** close.

2000

Across the U.S., midnight **celebrations** marked the changeover to the **year 2000** on Jan. 1; the feared **Y2K** computer glitch caused only minor problems.

America Online Inc. announced Jan. 10 that it would buy **Time Warner Inc.,** in the largest merger to date. The FTC approved it Dec. 14.

Teams of scientists from the U.S. and Britain announced jointly, June 26, that they had determined the structure of the **human genome.**

Following a bitter legal controversy, 6-year-old Cuban **Elián González** returned to Cuba June 28, 7 months after he was rescued from a boat wreck off the coast of Florida.

The Justice Dept., July 21, cleared U.S. agents of any wrongdoing in a **1993** assault on the compound of the Branch Davidian religious sect in **Waco,** TX.

Tiger Woods, 24, became the youngest to win all 4 of golf's majors, with record score in British Open July 23.

17 U.S. sailors were killed Oct. 12 in terrorist bombing of the USS *Cole,* refueling in Aden, Yemen.

The U.S. Food and Drug Administration announced, Sept. 28, approval of **RU-486,** a pill that induces abortions.

On **election night,** Nov. 7, the winner of Florida's 25 deciding electoral votes remained uncertain. The Florida Supreme Court, Dec. 8, ordered a manual recount of all ballots that did not have a vote for president recorded by machine. On Dec. 12, the U.S. Supreme Court reversed that decision. Vice Pres. Gore conceded the presidential election to Gov. **George W. Bush** (TX) in a televised address, Dec. 13.

2001

Congress, Jan. 6, certified **George W. Bush** as president by an electoral vote of 271- 266 (1 Gore elector abstained).

AOL-Time Warner merger completed, Jan. 11.

Outgoing Pres. Clinton issued 176 pardons and commutations, Jan. 20, including that of **Marc Rich,** a fugitive commodities trader whose ex-wife was a financial backer.

George W. Bush, was sworn in as 43rd president Jan. 20.

FBI agent **Robert Hanssen** arrested Feb. 20 and charged 2 days later with spying for the Soviet Union and Russia.

A **U.S. Navy spy plane** collided with a Chinese fighter plane over the South China Sea Apr. 1, killing the fighter pilot. The 24 U.S. crew members were detained in Hainan until U.S. officials expressed apology, Apr. 12.

Sen. James Jeffords (R, VT) announced May 24 he was leaving his party, giving Democrats control of the Senate.

Congress approved, May 26, a \$1.35 trillion **tax cut** spread over 10 years.

Oklahoma City bomber **Timothy McVeigh** was executed June 11 by lethal injection in Terre Haute, IN.

Rep. **Gary Condit** (D, CA) in a TV interview Aug. 23 denied involvement in the Apr. 30 disappearance of 24-year-old intern **Chandra Levy,** with whom he had an affair. Levy's remains were found in a DC park May 22, **2002.**

Bush announced Aug. 9 he would allow federal funding of limited **stem-cell research** using human embryos.

On the morning of **Sept. 11,** 2 hijacked commercial airliners struck and destroyed the twin towers of the **World Trade Center** in New York City, in the worst-ever **terrorist attack** on American soil. A 3rd hijacked plane destroyed a portion of the **Pentagon** and a 4th crashed in **Pennsylvania.** Some 3,000 people were killed, including about 2,800 at the World Trade Center. U.S. observed a national day of mourning, Sept. 14.

Congress, Sept. 21, approved a \$15 bil bailout package for the **airline industry.**

The **U.S.** and **Britain** Oct. 7 launched a sustained air strike campaign against Afghan-based terrorist organization **al-Qaeda** and the country's ruling Taliban militia.

On Oct. 7, San Francisco Giant outfielder **Barry Bonds** hit his **73rd** home run for a single season record.

Pres. Bush created a new **Office of Homeland Security,** Oct. 8, and signed a federal **antiterrorism bill** Oct. 26.

5 people died and 14 became ill from exposure to **anthrax** traveling through the U.S. mail, Oct. 5-Nov. 21.

The **Taliban** surrendered Kabul, the Afghan capital, Nov. 13, and fled from Kandahar, their stronghold, Dec. 7.

Leading energy-trading company **Enron** became the largest firm thus far to file for bankruptcy, Dec. 2.

The U.S. government, Dec. 11, indicted **Zacarias Moussaoui** as an alleged conspirator in the Sept. 11 attacks.

Pres. Bush announced Dec. 13 that the U.S. would withdraw from the 1972 **Antiballistic Missile Treaty.**

Pres. Bush, Dec. 28, formally granted permanent normal trade status to **China,** as of Jan. 1, 2002.

Taliban member **John Walker Lindh,** a U.S. citizen, was captured Dec. 2 by U.S. forces in Afghanistan.

2002

Taliban and al-Qaeda fighters captured in Afghanistan were flown to a U.S. **naval base at Guantanamo Bay** in Cuba, with the first 20 arriving Jan. 11.

A House committee Jan. 14 released parts of an Aug. 2001 letter from Sherron Watkins, an **Enron** employee, to CEO Kenneth Lay, warning him the company could "implode" in scandal. Lay resigned Jan. 23. Committees in Congress Jan. 24 began public hearings into the **Enron** bankruptcy.

In his first State of the Union address, Jan. 29, Pres. Bush called Iran, Iraq, and North Korea part of an **"axis of evil."**

Eight U.S. troops were killed Mar. 2-4 in an assault against Taliban and al-Qaeda forces in eastern Afghanistan. By Mar. 6, 1,200 U.S. troops were involved in the mission, **Operation Anaconda,** which ended Mar. 12.

Andrea Yates, who confessed to drowning her 5 children, was convicted by a Houston, TX, jury, Mar. 12.

A final independent prosecutor's report Mar. 20 found **insufficient evidence** that Pres. Clinton or his wife had committed any crime in connection with **Whitewater.**

Pres. Bush Mar. 27 signed into law a major **campaign-finance** reform bill.

A ceremonial last girder was removed May 30 from the site of the **World Trade Center** towers in New York, signaling the end of a massive clean-up and recovery operation.

Coleen Rowley testified before a congressional committee June 6 that Washington FBI agents had stymied investigative efforts in Minneapolis.

U.S. **Roman Catholic bishops,** meeting in Dallas, TX, June 13-15, approved stringent policies dealing with priests who sexually abuse minors; revised rules formulated with Vatican approval were adopted by the bishops Nov. 13.

The **Arthur Andersen** accounting firm was convicted of obstruction of justice by a federal jury, June 15.

WorldCom announced June 25 that it had overstated its cash flow by billions; on July 21, it displaced Enron Corp. as the largest U.S. company to declare bankruptcy.

On July 4, an Egyptian-born gunman killed 2 people near an **El Al ticket counter** at the L.A. international airport; he was shot dead by an El Al guard.

A dramatic **rescue** operation July 28 saved the lives of 9 miners trapped in a Pennsylvania **coal mine.**

Pres. Bush Aug. 6 signed a **fast-track trade** bill.

US Airways filed for bankruptcy protection Aug. 11.

Ramzi bin al-Shibh, a Yemeni implicated in Sept. 11 **terrorist attacks,** was **arrested** in Pakistan Sept. 10-11 and, with 4 others, handed over to the U.S. On Sept. 13-14 the FBI arrested 5 U.S. citizens of Yemeni descent in Lack-

awanna, NY, charged with giving "material support" to terrorists. A 6th arrested in Bahrain Sept. 15 and extradited.

Pres. Bush told the **UN General Assembly** Sept. 12 that he would work with the Security Council to deal with the threat posed by **Iraqi weapons** of mass destruction.

An American soldier and a Filipino were killed Oct. 2 in the **Philippines**, when a **bomb** exploded outside a karaoke bar. A U.S. Marine was killed and a 2nd wounded Oct. 8, in an attack by 2 **gunmen** on a **Kuwaiti** island.

Richard Reid pleaded guilty Oct. 4 to all charges stemming from an incident aboard a Paris-to-Miami flight in Dec. 2001, when he tried to ignite **explosives in his shoes.**

Four men arrested in **Portland, OR,** Oct. 4, charged with plotting to join **al-Qaeda** and Taliban forces; a 5th suspect later arrested in Malaysia. On Oct. 9, the head of an Islamic charity, the Benevolence International Foundation, was charged with funneling money to al-Qaeda.

Former Pres. **Carter** was named Oct. 10 as winner of the 2002 **Nobel Peace Prize.**

After bouncing up from a low in late July, **stock** averages slid again, reaching a **5-year low** of 7286, Oct. 9.

On Oct. 10-11 the House, 296-133, and Senate, 77-23, gave Bush **backing** for using **military force** against Iraq.

The Bush administration revealed Oct. 16 that **North Korea** had acknowledged it was developing nuclear arms.

Two men were arrested Oct. 24 in connection with a series of random **sniper shootings** in the Washington, DC, area that left 10 dead.

Sen. **Paul Wellstone** (D, MN) died in a plane crash near Eveleth, MN, Oct. 25, with his wife, daughter, and 5 others.

Pres Bush, Oct. 29, signed a measure providing $3.9 bil to the states to fix shortcomings in their **election** process.

An antitrust settlement between **Microsoft** Corp. and U.S. Justice Dept. was approved Nov. 1 by a federal judge.

Republicans emerged from elections, Nov. 5, with a majority in the Senate and an increased margin in the House.

Rep. **Nancy Pelosi** (CA) was elected by House Democrats Nov. 14 to head their caucus in the new Congress, the **first woman** to lead either party in the House.

Pres. **Bush** Nov. 25 signed legislation creating a cabinet-level Dept. of **Homeland Security.**

UAL Corp., the parent of **United Airlines,** filed for bankruptcy in Chicago Dec. 9.

Cardinal Bernard Law, Dec. 13, resigned under pressure as archbishop of Boston. Sean O'Malley was installed July 30, 2003, as his successor.

On Dec. 16, Pres. Bush named former NJ Gov. Thomas Kean (R) to chair a national **commission** investigating the Sept. 11, 2001, **attacks.**

Bush Dec. 17 ordered the Pentagon to proceed with construction of a limited **missile defense shield.**

Trent Lott (R, MS), just chosen as majority leader in the new Senate, **bowed out** Dec. 20, amid furor over a comment apparently supporting segregation; Sen. **Bill Frist** (R, TN) was elected as leader Dec. 23.

A gunman linked to **Islamic Jihad** killed 3 Americans at a Baptist missionary hospital in Jibla, Yemen, Dec. 30.

2003

On Jan. 10-11, shortly before leaving office, Gov. George Ryan (R, IL) pardoned or commuted death sentences of 171 **convicts on death row.**

The Senate, Jan. 22, approved, 94-0, Pres. Bush's nomination of Tom Ridge to be **secretary of homeland security.**

The space **shuttle *Columbia*** broke apart in space Feb. 1 over southwestern U.S. during its descent toward a planned landing; all 7 crew members were killed. An official report issued Aug. 26 found the immediate cause was foam breaking off after liftoff and damaging the left wing; it also cited a "broken safety culture" at NASA.

The Senate, Mar. 6, approved, 95-0, the **Strategic Offensive Reductions Treaty** signed in 2002 by leaders of the U.S. and Russia. It required the 2 countries to reduce their deployed nuclear warheads to 1,700-2,200 by 2012.

A **U.S.-led military offensive aimed at ousting Saddam Hussein** in Iraq got underway Mar. 19, when 40 Tomahawk cruise missiles hit **targets in Baghdad**; strikes continued in succeeding nights. U.S. forces Mar. 21 seized major **oil fields near Basra**. On Apr. 1, U.S. forces announced the rescue from an Iraqi hospital of injured Army Pfc. **Jessica Lynch**, one of a group of soldiers ambushed near Nasiriyah.

On Apr. 3, **U.S. Marines** crossed the Tigris River and moved close to Baghdad. By Apr. 8, major government buildings had been occupied and **organized resistance had dropped away**. With the collapse of the regime, services in major cities were disrupted, and **looting** became widespread. Pres. Bush, speaking from the aircraft carrier *Abraham Lincoln*, declared on May 1 that **major combat operations had ended**. However, insurgents continued to mount attacks against both military and civilian targets.

Nine Democrats seeking their party's nomination for president in 2004 **debated** in Columbia, SC, May 3. Pres. Bush formally filed reelection papers May 16.

The *New York Times* May 11 published a long story documenting major deceptions and inaccuracies by reporter **Jayson Blair**, who had resigned from the paper 10 days earlier.

Pres. Bush signed a measure May 28 providing **$318 bil in tax cuts** over 10 years.

Under a settlement in a private antitrust suit brought by Netscape (a unit of AOL), **Microsoft** agreed May 29 to pay **AOL Time Warner** $750 mil.

On June 23, the Supreme Court, voting 5-4, **upheld an affirmative action program** providing preference to minorities for admission to the Univ. of Michigan law school. But the Court, 6-3, rejected an undergraduate affirmative action program at the university that employed numerical formulas.

The Labor Dept. reported July 3 that June **unemployment** had climbed to a 9-year high of 6.4%. Since Feb. 2001, the economy had lost almost 2.6 mil jobs.

U.S. soldiers killed 2 once-powerful **sons of Saddam Hussein** in a gun battle in Mosul, N Iraq, July 22.

A **power failure** spread rapidly through Ohio, Michigan, and the Northeast, as well as eastern Canada, on Aug. 14. Some 50 million people in 8 states and the province of Ontario were left without electricity for as long as 2 days.

John Geoghan, a **former priest** incarcerated for child sex abuse, was **strangled at a state prison** in Shirley, MA, Aug. 23, apparently by another inmate.

On Sept. 9, the Roman Catholic archdiocese of Boston and lawyers representing about 550 victims of **sexual abuse** by priests announced a **settlement** worth up to $85 mil.

Richard Grasso, chairman and CEO of the New York Stock Exchange, resigned under fire, Sept. 17.

In a political earthquake, California voters Oct. 7 voted to recall Gov. Gray Davis (D) from office and replace him with actor-turned-politician **Arnold Schwarzenegger**.

Forest fires in southern California in late October laid waste to over 700,000 acres and destroyed 3,000 homes.

The Senate Nov. 3 approved by voice vote the **$87.5 bil** that Pres. Bush sought **for U.S. military forces** in Iraq and for helping to rebuild the country. The House had given its approval, 298-121, on Oct. 31.

The Rev. V. Gene Robinson was consecrated Nov. 2 as Episcopal bishop of New Hampshire, becoming the **first openly gay prelate** in the Episcopal Church U.S.A.

A Virginia jury Nov. 17 found **John Muhammad** guilty in the **sniper attacks** that plagued the Washington, DC, area in 2002; he was sentenced to death. Another VA jury found **Lee Malvo** guilty of 2 counts of murder in the attacks, Dec. 18; he was sentenced to life in prison without parole.

The Massachusetts Supreme Judicial Court, in a controversial 4-3 decision Nov. 18, held that **gay couples** had a **right to marry** under the state constitution.

Saddam Hussein was captured by U.S. military forces Dec. 13, in an underground hideout southeast of Tikrit.

The Bush administration announced Dec. 23 that a Holstein in Washington State had tested positive for **mad-cow disease**; the animal, the first in the U.S. to be so identified, had been slaughtered.

Major stock indexes showed big gains for 2003. The Dow Jones Industrial Average had risen 25%, to 10,453.92; the tech-heavy NASDAQ index had advanced 50%, to 2003.37.

The Mayflower Compact

The threat of James I to "harry them out of the land" sent a band of religious dissenters from England to Holland in 1608. They were known as Separatists because they wished to cut all ties with the established church. In 1620, some of them, known now as the Pilgrims, joined with a larger group in England to set sail on the *Mayflower* for the New World. A joint stock company financed their venture.

In November, they sighted Cape Cod and decided to land an exploring party at Plymouth Harbor. A rebellious group picked up at Southampton and London troubled the Pilgrim leaders, however, and to control their actions 41 Pilgrims drew up the Mayflower Compact and signed it before going ashore. The voluntary agreement to govern themselves was America's first written constitution. It reads as follows:

In the name of God, Amen. We, whose names are underwritten, the Loyal Subjects of our dread Sovereign Lord, King *James,* by the Grace of God, of *Great Britain, France and Ireland,* King, *Defender of the Faith,* etc.

Having undertaken for the Glory of God, and Advancement of the Christian Faith, and the Honour of our King and Country, a voyage to plant the first colony in the northern Parts of Virginia; do by these Presents, solemnly and mutually in the Presence of God and one of another, covenant and combine ourselves together into a civil Body Politick, for our better Ordering and Preservation, and Furtherance of the Ends aforesaid; And by Virtue hereof to enact, constitute, and frame, such just and equal Laws, Ordinances, Acts, Constitutions and Offices, from time to time, as shall be thought most meet and convenient for the General good of the Colony; unto which we promise all due Submission and Obedience.

In Witness whereof we have hereunto subscribed our names at *Cape Cod* the eleventh of *November,* in the Reign of our Sovereign Lord, King *James* of *England, France* and *Ireland,* the eighteenth, and of *Scotland* the fifty-fourth. *Anno Domini, 1620.*

The Continental Congress: Meetings, Presidents

Meeting places	Dates of meetings	Congress presidents	Date elected
Philadelphia, PA	Sept. 5 to Oct. 26, 1774	Peyton Randolph, VA (1)	Sept. 5, 1774
"	"	Henry Middleton, SC	Oct. 22, 1774
Philadelphia, PA	May 10, 1775 to Dec. 12, 1776	Peyton Randolph, VA	May 10, 1775
"	"	John Hancock, MA	May 24, 1775
Baltimore, MD	Dec. 20, 1776 to Mar. 4, 1777	"	
Philadelphia, PA	Mar. 5 to Sept. 18, 1777	"	
Lancaster, PA	Sept. 27, 1777 (one day)		
York, PA	Sept. 30, 1777 to June 27, 1778	Henry Laurens, SC	Nov. 1, 1777 (4)
Philadelphia, PA	July 2, 1778 to June 21, 1783	John Jay, NY	Dec. 10, 1778
"	"	Samuel Huntington, CT	Sept. 28, 1779
"	"	Thomas McKean, DE	July 10, 1781
"	"	John Hanson, MD (2)	Nov. 5, 1781
"	"	Elias Boudinot, NJ	Nov. 4, 1782
Princeton, NJ	June 30 to Nov. 4, 1783	Thomas Mifflin, PA	Nov. 3, 1783
Annapolis, MD	Nov. 26, 1783 to June 3, 1784	"	
Trenton, NJ	Nov. 1 to Dec. 24, 1784	Richard Henry Lee, VA	Nov. 30, 1784
New York City, NY	Jan. 11 to Nov. 4, 1785	"	
"	Nov. 7, 1785 to Nov. 3, 1786	John Hancock, MA (3)	Nov. 23, 1785
"	"	Nathaniel Gorham, MA	June 6, 1786
"	Nov. 6, 1786 to Oct. 30, 1787	Arthur St. Clair, PA	Feb. 2, 1787
"	Nov. 5, 1787 to Oct. 21, 1788	Cyrus Griffin, VA	Jan. 22, 1788
	Nov. 3, 1788 to Mar. 2, 1789	"	

(1) Resigned Oct. 22, 1774. (2) Titled "President of the United States in Congress Assembled," John Hanson is considered by some the first U.S. president because he was the first to serve under the Articles of Confederation. He was, however, little more than presiding officer of the Congress, which retained full executive power. He could be considered the head of government, but not head of state. (3) Elected Nov. 1785, meetings held Nov. 1785-Nov. 1786; resigned May 29, 1786, without having served, because of illness. (4) Articles of Confederation agreed upon, Nov. 15, 1777; last ratification from Maryland, Mar. 1, 1781.

Patrick Henry's Speech to the Virginia Convention

The following is an excerpt from Patrick Henry's speech to the Virginia Convention on Mar. 23, 1775:

Gentlemen may cry, peace, peace—but there is no peace. The war is actually begun! The next gale that sweeps from the north will bring to our ears the clash of resounding arms! Our brethren are already in the field! Why stand we here idle? What is it that gentlemen wish? What would they have? Is life so dear, or peace so sweet, as to be purchased at the price of chains and slavery? Forbid it, Almighty God! I know not what course others may take; but as for me, give me liberty, or give me death!

How the Declaration of Independence Was Adopted

On June 7, 1776, Richard Henry Lee, who had issued the first call for a congress of the colonies, introduced in the Continental Congress at Philadelphia a resolution declaring "that these United Colonies are, and of right ought to be, free and independent states, that they are absolved from all allegiance to the British Crown, and that all political connection between them and the state of Great Britain is, and ought to be, totally dissolved."

The resolution, seconded by John Adams on behalf of the Massachusetts delegation, came up again on June 10 when a committee of 5, headed by Thomas Jefferson, was appointed to express the purpose of the resolution in a declaration of independence. The others on the committee were John Adams, Benjamin Franklin, Robert R. Livingston, and Roger Sherman.

Drafting the Declaration was assigned to Jefferson, who worked on a portable desk of his own construction in a room at Market and 7th Sts. The committee reported the result on June 28, 1776. The members of the Congress suggested a number of changes, which Jefferson called "deplorable." They didn't approve Jefferson's arraignment of the British people and King George III for encouraging and fostering the slave trade, which Jefferson called "an execrable commerce." They made 86 changes, eliminating 480 words and leaving 1,337. In the final form, capitalization was erratic. Jefferson had written that men were endowed with "inalienable" rights; in the final copy it came out as "unalienable" and has been thus ever since.

The Lee-Adams resolution of independence was adopted by 12 yeas on July 2—the actual date of the act of independence. The Declaration, which explains the act, was adopted July 4, in the evening.

After the Declaration was adopted, July 4, 1776, it was turned over to John Dunlap, printer, to be printed on broadsides. The original copy was lost and one of his broadsides was attached to a page in the journal of the Congress. It was read aloud July 8 in Philadelphia, PA, Easton, PA, and Trenton, NJ. On July 9 at 6 PM it was read by order of Gen. George Washington to the troops assembled on the Common in New York City (City Hall Park).

The Continental Congress of July 19, 1776, adopted the following resolution:

"Resolved, That the Declaration passed on the 4th, be fairly engrossed on parchment with the title and stile of 'The Unanimous Declaration of the thirteen United States of America' and that the same, when engrossed, be signed by every member of Congress."

Not all delegates who signed the engrossed Declaration were present on July 4. Robert Morris (PA), William Williams (CT), and Samuel Chase (MD) signed on Aug. 2; Oliver Wolcott (CT), George Wythe (VA), Richard Henry Lee (VA), and Elbridge Gerry (MA) signed in August and September; Matthew Thornton (NH) joined the Congress Nov. 4 and signed later. Thomas McKean (DE) rejoined Washington's army before signing and said later that he signed in 1781.

Charles Carroll of Carrollton was appointed a delegate by Maryland on July 4, 1776, presented his credentials July 18, and signed the engrossed Declaration on Aug. 2. Born Sept. 19, 1737, he was 95 years old and the last surviving signer when he died on Nov. 14, 1832.

Two Pennsylvania delegates who did not support the Declaration on July 4 were replaced.

The 4 New York delegates did not have authority from their state to vote on July 4. On July 9, the New York state convention authorized its delegates to approve the Declaration, and the Congress was so notified on July 15, 1776. The 4 signed the Declaration on Aug. 2.

The original engrossed Declaration is preserved in the National Archives Building in Washington, DC.

Declaration of Independence

The Declaration of Independence was adopted by the Continental Congress in Philadelphia on July 4, 1776. John Hancock was president of the Congress, and Charles Thomson was secretary. A copy of the Declaration, engrossed on parchment, was signed by members of Congress on and after Aug. 2, 1776. On Jan. 18, 1777, Congress ordered that "an authenticated copy, with the names of the members of Congress subscribing the same, be sent to each of the United States, and that they be desired to have the same put upon record." Authenticated copies were printed in broadside form in Baltimore, where the Continental Congress was then in session. The following text is that of the original printed by John Dunlap at Philadelphia for the Continental Congress. The original is on display at the National Archives in Washington, DC.

IN CONGRESS, July 4, 1776.
A DECLARATION
By the REPRESENTATIVES of the
UNITED STATES OF AMERICA,
In GENERAL CONGRESS assembled

When in the Course of human Events, it becomes necessary for one People to dissolve the Political Bands which have connected them with another, and to assume among the Powers of the Earth, the separate and equal Station to which the Laws of Nature and of Nature's God entitle them, a decent Respect to the Opinions of Mankind requires that they should declare the causes which impel them to the Separation.

We hold these Truths to be self-evident, that all Men are created equal, that they are endowed by their Creator with certain unalienable Rights, that among these are Life, Liberty, and the Pursuit of Happiness—That to secure these Rights, Governments are instituted among Men, deriving their just Powers from the Consent of the Governed, that whenever any Form of Government becomes destructive of these Ends, it is the Right of the People to alter or to abolish it, and to institute new Government, laying its Foundation on such Principles, and organizing its Powers in such Form, as to them shall seem most likely to effect their Safety and Happiness. Prudence, indeed, will dictate that Governments long established should not be changed for light and transient Causes; and accordingly all Experience hath shewn, that Mankind are more disposed to suffer, while Evils are sufferable, than to right themselves by abolishing the Forms to which they are accustomed. But when a long Train of Abuses and Usurpations, pursuing invariably the same Object, evinces a Design to reduce them under absolute Despotism, it is their Right, it is their Duty, to throw off such Government, and to provide new Guards for their future Security. Such has been the patient Sufferance of these Colonies; and such is now the Necessity which constrains them to alter their former Systems of Government. The History of the present King of Great-Britain is a History of repeated Injuries and Usurpations, all having in direct Object the Establishment of an absolute Tyranny over these States. To prove this, let Facts be submitted to a candid World.

He has refused his Assent to Laws, the most wholesome and necessary for the public Good.

He has forbidden his Governors to pass Laws of immediate and pressing Importance, unless suspended in their Operation till his Assent should be obtained; and when so suspended, he has utterly neglected to attend to them.

He has refused to pass other Laws for the Accommodation of large Districts of People, unless those People would relinquish the Right of Representation in the Legislature, a Right inestimable to them, and formidable to Tyrants only.

He has called together Legislative Bodies at Places unusual, uncomfortable, and distant from the Depository of their Public Records, for the sole Purpose of fatiguing them into Compliance with his Measures.

He has dissolved Representative Houses repeatedly, for opposing with manly Firmness his Invasions on the Rights of the People.

He has refused for a long Time, after such Dissolutions, to cause others to be elected; whereby the Legislative Powers, incapable of Annihilation, have returned to the People at large for their exercise; the State remaining in the mean time exposed to all the Dangers of Invasion from without, and Convulsions within.

He has endeavoured to prevent the Population of these States; for that Purpose obstructing the Laws for Naturalization of Foreigners; refusing to pass others to encourage their Migrations hither, and raising the Conditions of new Appropriations of Lands.

He has obstructed the Administration of Justice, by refusing his Assent to Laws for establishing Judiciary Powers.

He has made Judges dependent on his Will alone, for the Tenure of their Offices, and the Amount and payment of their Salaries.

He has erected a Multitude of new Offices, and sent hither Swarms of Officers to harrass our People, and eat out their Substance.

He has kept among us, in Times of Peace, Standing Armies, without the consent of our Legislatures.

He has affected to render the Military independent of, and superior to the Civil Power.

He has combined with others to subject us to a Jurisdiction foreign to our Constitution, and unacknowledged by our Laws; giving his Assent to their Acts of pretended Legislation:

For quartering large Bodies of Armed Troops among us:

For protecting them, by a mock Trial, from Punishment for any Murders which they should commit on the Inhabitants of these States:

For cutting off our Trade with all Parts of the World:

For imposing Taxes on us without our Consent:

For depriving us, in many Cases, of the Benefits of Trial by Jury:

For transporting us beyond Seas to be tried for pretended Offences:

For abolishing the free System of English Laws in a neighbouring Province, establishing therein an arbitrary Government, and enlarging its Boundaries, so as to render it at once an Example and fit Instrument for introducing the same absolute Rule into these Colonies:

For taking away our Charters, abolishing our most valuable Laws, and altering fundamentally the Forms of our Governments:

For suspending our own Legislatures, and declaring themselves invested with Power to legislate for us in all Cases whatsoever.

He has abdicated Government here, by declaring us out of his Protection and waging War against us.

He has plundered our Seas, ravaged our Coasts, burnt our towns, and destroyed the Lives of our People.

He is, at this Time, transporting large Armies of foreign Mercenaries to complete the works of Death, Desolation, and Tyranny, already begun with circumstances of Cruelty and Perfidy, scarcely paralleled in the most barbarous Ages, and totally unworthy the Head of a civilized Nation.

He has constrained our fellow Citizens taken Captive on the high Seas to bear Arms against their Country, to become the Executioners of their Friends and Brethren, or to fall themselves by their Hands.

He has excited domestic Insurrections amongst us, and has endeavoured to bring on the Inhabitants of our Frontiers, the merciless Indian Savages, whose known Rule of Warfare, is an undistinguished Destruction, of all Ages, Sexes and Conditions.

In every stage of these Oppressions we have Petitioned for Redress in the most humble Terms: Our repeated Petitions have been answered only by repeated Injury. A Prince, whose Character is thus marked by every act which may define a Tyrant, is unfit to be the Ruler of a free People.

Nor have we been wanting in Attentions to our British Brethren. We have warned them from Time to Time of Attempts by their Legislature to extend an unwarrantable Jurisdiction over us. We have reminded them of the Circumstances of our Emigration and Settlement here. We have appealed to their native Justice and Magnanimity, and we have conjured them by the Ties of our common Kindred to disavow these Usurpations, which, would inevitably interrupt our Connections and Correspondence. They too have been deaf to the Voice of Justice and of Consanguinity. We must, therefore, acquiesce in the Necessity, which denounces our Separation, and hold them, as we hold the rest of Mankind, Enemies in War, in Peace, Friends.

We, therefore, the Representatives of the UNITED STATES OF AMERICA, in General Congress, Assembled, appealing to the Supreme Judge of the World for the Rectitude of our Intentions, do, in the Name, and by Authority of the good People of these Colonies, solemnly Publish and Declare, That these United Colonies are, and of Right ought to be, Free and Independent States; that they are absolved from all Allegiance to the British Crown, and that all political Connection between them and the State of Great-Britain, is and ought to be totally dissolved; and that as Free and Independent States, they have full Power to levy War, conclude Peace, contract Alliances, establish Commerce, and to do all other Acts and Things which Independent States may of right do. And for the support of this declaration, with a firm Reliance on the Protection of Divine Providence, we mutually pledge to each other our lives, our Fortunes, and our sacred Honor.

JOHN HANCOCK, President

Attest.

CHARLES THOMSON, Secretary.

Signers of the Declaration of Independence

Delegate (state)	Occupation	Birthplace	Born	Died
Adams, John (MA)	Lawyer	Braintree (Quincy), MA	Oct. 30, 1735	July 4, 1826
Adams, Samuel (MA)	Political leader	Boston, MA	Sept. 27, 1722	Oct. 2, 1803
Bartlett, Josiah (NH)	Physician, judge	Amesbury, MA	Nov. 21, 1729	May 19, 1795
Braxton, Carter (VA)	Farmer	Newington Plantation, VA	Sept. 10, 1736	Oct. 10, 1797
Carroll, Chas. of Carrollton (MD)	Lawyer	Annapolis, MD	Sept. 19, 1737	Nov. 14, 1832
Chase, Samuel (MD)	Judge	Princess Anne, MD	Apr. 17, 1741	June 19, 1811
Clark, Abraham (NJ)	Surveyor	Roselle, NJ	Feb. 15, 1726	Sept. 15, 1794
Clymer, George (PA)	Merchant	Philadelphia, PA	Mar. 16, 1739	Jan. 23, 1813
Ellery, William (RI)	Lawyer	Newport, RI	Dec. 22, 1727	Feb. 15, 1820
Floyd, William (NY)	Soldier	Brookhaven, NY	Dec. 17, 1734	Aug. 4, 1821
Franklin, Benjamin (PA)	Printer, publisher	Boston, MA	Jan. 17, 1706	Apr. 17, 1790
Gerry, Elbridge (MA)	Merchant	Marblehead, MA	July 17, 1744	Nov. 23, 1814
Gwinnett, Button (GA)	Merchant	Down Hatherly, England	c. 1735	May 19, 1777
Hall, Lyman (GA)	Physician	Wallingford, CT	Apr. 12, 1724	Oct. 19, 1790
Hancock, John (MA)	Merchant	Braintree (Quincy), MA	Jan. 12, 1737	Oct. 8, 1793
Harrison, Benjamin (VA)	Farmer	Berkeley, VA	Apr. 5, 1726	Apr. 24, 1791
Hart, John (NJ)	Farmer	Stonington, CT	c. 1711	May 11, 1779
Hewes, Joseph (NC)	Merchant	Princeton, NJ	Jan. 23, 1730	Nov. 10, 1779
Heyward, Thos. Jr. (SC)	Lawyer, farmer	St. Luke's Parish, SC	July 28, 1746	Mar. 6, 1809
Hooper, William (NC)	Lawyer	Boston, MA	June 28, 1742	Oct. 14, 1790
Hopkins, Stephen (RI)	Judge, educator	Providence, RI	Mar. 7, 1707	July 13, 1785
Hopkinson, Francis (NJ)	Judge, author	Philadelphia, PA	Sept. 21, 1737	May 9, 1791
Huntington, Samuel (CT)	Judge	Windham County, CT	July 3, 1731	Jan. 5, 1796
Jefferson, Thomas (VA)	Lawyer	Shadwell, VA	Apr. 13, 1743	July 4, 1826
Lee, Francis Lightfoot (VA)	Farmer	Westmoreland County, VA	Oct. 14, 1734	Jan. 11, 1797
Lee, Richard Henry (VA)	Farmer	Westmoreland County, VA	Jan. 20, 1732	June 19, 1794
Lewis, Francis (NY)	Merchant	Llandaff, Wales	Mar., 1713	Dec. 31, 1802
Livingston, Philip (NY)	Merchant	Albany, NY	Jan. 15, 1716	June 12, 1778
Lynch, Thomas Jr. (SC)	Farmer	Winyah, SC	Aug. 5, 1749	(at sea) 1779
McKean, Thomas (DE)	Lawyer	New London, PA	Mar. 19, 1734	June 24, 1817
Middleton, Arthur (SC)	Farmer	Charleston, SC	June 26, 1742	Jan. 1, 1787
Morris, Lewis (NY)	Farmer	Morrisania (Bronx County), NY	Apr. 8, 1726	Jan. 22, 1798
Morris, Robert (PA)	Merchant	Liverpool, England	Jan. 20, 1734	May 9, 1806
Morton, John (PA)	Judge	Ridley, PA	1724	Apr., 1777
Nelson, Thos. Jr. (VA)	Farmer	Yorktown, VA	Dec. 26, 1738	Jan. 4, 1789
Paca, William (MD)	Judge	Abingdon, MD	Oct. 31, 1740	Oct. 23, 1799
Paine, Robert Treat (MA)	Judge	Boston, MA	Mar. 11, 1731	May 12, 1814
Penn, John (NC)	Lawyer	Near Port Royal, VA	May 17, 1741	Sept. 14, 1788
Read, George (DE)	Judge	Near North East, MD	Sept. 18, 1733	Sept. 21, 1798
Rodney, Caesar (DE)	Judge	Dover, DE	Oct. 7, 1728	June 29, 1784
Ross, George (PA)	Judge	New Castle, DE	May 10, 1730	July 14, 1779
Rush, Benjamin (PA)	Physician	Byberry, PA (Philadelphia)	Dec. 24, 1745	Apr. 19, 1813

Delegate (state)	Occupation	Birthplace	Born	Died
Rutledge, Edward (SC)	Lawyer	Charleston, SC	Nov. 23, 1749	Jan. 23, 1800
Sherman, Roger (CT)	Lawyer	Newton, MA	Apr. 19, 1721	July 23, 1793
Smith, James (PA)	Lawyer	Dublin, Ireland	c. 1719	July 11, 1806
Stockton, Richard (NJ)	Lawyer	Near Princeton, NJ	Oct. 1, 1730	Feb. 28, 1781
Stone, Thomas (MD)	Lawyer	Charles County, MD	1743	Oct. 5, 1787
Taylor, George (PA)	Ironmaster	Ireland	1716	Feb. 23, 1781
Thornton, Matthew (NH)	Physician	Ireland	1714	June 24, 1803
Walton, George (GA)	Judge	Prince Edward County, VA	1741	Feb. 2, 1804
Whipple, William (NH)	Merchant, judge	Kittery, ME	Jan. 14, 1730	Nov. 28, 1785
Williams, William (CT)	Merchant	Lebanon, CT	Apr. 23, 1731	Aug. 2, 1811
Wilson, James (PA)	Judge	Carskerdo, Scotland	Sept. 14, 1742	Aug. 28, 1798
Witherspoon, John (NJ)	Clergyman, educator	Gifford, Scotland	Feb. 5, 1723	Nov. 15, 1794
Wolcott, Oliver (CT)	Judge	Windsor, CT	Dec. 1, 1726	Dec. 1, 1797
Wythe, George (VA)	Lawyer	Elizabeth City Co. (Hampton), VA	1726	June 8, 1806

Origin of the Constitution

The War of Independence was conducted by delegates from the original 13 states, called the Congress of the United States of America and known as the Continental Congress. In 1777 the Congress submitted to the legislatures of the states the Articles of Confederation and Perpetual Union, which were ratified by New Hampshire, Massachusetts, Rhode Island, Connecticut, New York, New Jersey, Pennsylvania, Delaware, Virginia, North Carolina, South Carolina, and Georgia and finally, in 1781, by Maryland.

The first article read: "The stile of this confederacy shall be the United States of America." This did not signify a sovereign nation, because the states delegated only those powers they could not handle individually, such as to wage war, make treaties, and contract debts for general expenses (e.g. paying the army). Taxes for payment of such debts were levied by the individual states. The president signed himself "President of the United States in Congress assembled," but here the United States were considered in the plural, a cooperating group.

When the war was won, it became evident that a stronger federal union was needed. The Congress left the initiative to the legislatures. Virginia in Jan. 1786 appointed commissioners to meet with representatives of other states; delegates from Virginia, Delaware, New York, New Jersey, and Pennsylvania met at Annapolis. Alexander Hamilton prepared their call asking delegates from all states to meet in Philadelphia in May 1787 "to render the Constitution of the federal government adequate to the exigencies of the union." Congress endorsed the plan on Feb. 21, 1787. Delegates were appointed by all states except Rhode Island.

The convention met on May 14, 1787. George Washington was chosen president (presiding officer). The states certified 65 delegates, but 10 did not attend. The work was done by 55, not all of whom were present at all sessions. Of the 55 attending delegates, 16 failed to sign, and 39 actually signed Sept. 17, 1787, some with reservations. Some historians have said 74 delegates (9 more than the 65 actually certified) were named and 19 failed to attend. These 9 additional persons refused the appointment, were never delegates, and were never counted as absentees. Washington sent the Constitution to Congress, and that body, Sept. 28, 1787, ordered it sent to the legislatures, "in order to be submitted to a convention of delegates chosen in each state by the people thereof."

The Constitution was ratified by votes of state conventions as follows: Delaware, Dec. 7, 1787, unanimous; Pennsylvania, Dec. 12, 1787, 43 to 23; New Jersey, Dec. 18, 1787, unanimous; Georgia, Jan. 2, 1788, unanimous; Connecticut, Jan. 9, 1788, 128 to 40; Massachusetts, Feb. 6, 1788, 187 to 168; Maryland, Apr. 28, 1788, 63 to 11; South Carolina, May 23, 1788, 149 to 73; New Hampshire, June 21, 1788, 57 to 46; Virginia, June 25, 1788, 89 to 79; New York, July 26, 1788, 30 to 27. Nine states were needed to establish the operation of the Constitution "between the states so ratifying the same," and New Hampshire was the 9th state. The government did not declare the Constitution in effect until the first Wednesday in Mar. 1789, which was Mar. 4. After that, North Carolina ratified it on Nov. 21, 1789, 194 to 77; and Rhode Island, May 29, 1790, 34 to 32. Vermont in convention ratified it on Jan. 10, 1791, and by act of Congress approved on Feb. 18, 1791, was admitted into the Union as the 14th state, Mar. 4, 1791.

Constitution of the United States
The Original 7 Articles

The text of the Constitution given here (exception for Amendment XXVII) is taken from the pocket-size edition of the Constitution published by the U.S. Government Printing Office as a result of a U.S. House and Senate resolution to print the Constitution in its original form as amended through July 5, 1971. *Text in brackets* indicates that an item has been superseded or amended, or provides background information. **Boldface text preceding** each article, section, or amendment is a brief summary, added by *The World Almanac*.

PREAMBLE

We, the People of the United States, in Order to form a more perfect Union, establish Justice, insure domestic Tranquility, provide for the common defence, promote the general Welfare, and secure the Blessings of Liberty to ourselves and our Posterity, do ordain and establish this Constitution for the United States of America.

ARTICLE I.

Section 1—Legislative powers; in whom vested:

All legislative Powers herein granted shall be vested in a Congress of the United States, which shall consist of a Senate and House of Representatives.

Section 2—House of Representatives, how and by whom chosen. Qualifications of a Representative. Representatives and direct taxes, how apportioned. Enumeration. Vacancies to be filled. Power of choosing officers, and of impeachment.

The House of Representatives shall be composed of Members chosen every second Year by the People of the several States, and the Electors in each State shall have the Qualifications requisite for Electors of the most numerous Branch of the State Legislature.

No person shall be a Representative who shall not have attained to the Age of twenty-five Years, and been seven Years a Citizen of the United States, and who shall not, when elected, be an Inhabitant of that State in which he shall be chosen.

[Representatives and direct taxes shall be apportioned among the several States which may be included within this Union, according to their respective Numbers, which shall be determined by adding to the whole Number of free Persons, including those bound to Service for a Term of Years, and excluding Indians not taxed, three-fifths of all other persons.] *[The previous sentence was superseded by Amendment XIV, section 2.]* The actual Enumeration shall be made within three Years after the first Meeting of the Congress of the United States, and within every subsequent Term of ten Years, in such Manner as they shall by Law direct. The Number of Representatives shall not exceed one for every thirty Thousand, but each State shall have at Least one Representative; and until such enumeration shall be made, the State of New Hampshire shall be entitled to chuse three, Massachusetts eight, Rhode-Island and Providence Plantations one, Connecticut five, New-York six, New Jersey four, Pennsylvania eight, Delaware one, Maryland six, Virginia ten, North Carolina five, South Carolina five, and Georgia three.

When vacancies happen in the Representation from any State, the Executive Authority thereof shall issue Writs of Election to fill such Vacancies.

The House of Representatives shall chuse their Speaker and other Officers; and shall have the sole Power of Impeachment.

Section 3—Senators, how and by whom chosen. How classified. Qualifications of a Senator. President of the Senate, his right to vote. President pro tem., and other officers of the Senate, how chosen. Power to try impeachments. When President is tried, Chief Justice to preside. Sentence.

The Senate of the United States shall be composed of two Senators from each State, *[chosen by the Legislature thereof]* *[the preceding five words were superseded by Amendment XVII, section 1]* for six Years; and each Senator shall have one Vote.

Immediately after they shall be assembled in Consequence of the first Election, they shall be divided as equally as may be into three Classes. The Seats of the Senators of the first Class shall be vacated at the Expiration of the second Year, of the second Class at the Expiration of the fourth Year, and of the third Class at the Expiration of the Sixth year, so that one-third may be chosen every second Year; *[and if Vacancies happen by Resignation, or otherwise, during the Recess of the Legislature of any State, the Executive thereof may make temporary Appointments until the next Meeting of the Legislature, which shall then fill such Vacancies.]* *[The words in parentheses were superseded by Amendment XVII, section 2.]*

No person shall be a Senator who shall not have attained to the Age of thirty Years, and been nine Years a Citizen of the United States, and who shall not, when elected, be an Inhabitant of that State for which he shall be chosen.

The Vice President of the United States shall be President of the Senate, but shall have no Vote, unless they be equally divided.

The Senate shall chuse their other Officers, and also a President pro tempore, in the absence of the Vice President, or when he shall exercise the Office of President of the United States.

The Senate shall have the sole Power to try all Impeachments. When sitting for that Purpose, they shall be on Oath or Affirmation. When the President of the United States is tried, the Chief Justice shall preside: And no Person shall be convicted without the Concurrence of two thirds of the Members present.

Judgment in Cases of Impeachment shall not extend further than to removal from Office, and disqualification to hold and enjoy any Office of honor, Trust or Profit under the United States: but the Party convicted shall nevertheless be liable and subject to Indictment, Trial, Judgment and Punishment, according to Law.

Section 4—Times, etc., of holding elections, how prescribed. One session each year.

The Times, Places and Manner of holding Elections for Senators and Representatives, shall be prescribed in each State by the Legislature thereof; but the Congress may at any time by Law make or alter such Regulations, except as to the Place of Chusing Senators.

The Congress shall assemble at least once in every Year, and such Meeting shall *[be on the first Monday in December,]* *[The words in parentheses were superseded by Amendment XX, section 2.]* unless they shall by Law appoint a different Day.

Section 5—Membership, quorum, adjournments, rules. Power to punish or expel. Journal. Time of adjournments, how limited, etc.

Each House shall be the Judge of the Elections, Returns and Qualifications of its own Members, and a Majority of each shall constitute a Quorum to do Business; but a smaller number may adjourn from day to day, and may be authorized to compel the Attendance of absent Members, in such manner, and under such Penalties as each House may provide.

Each House may determine the Rules of its Proceedings, punish its members for disorderly Behavior, and, with the Concurrence of two thirds, expel a Member.

Each House shall keep a Journal of its Proceedings, and from time to time publish the same, excepting such Parts as may in their Judgment require Secrecy; and the Yeas and Nays of the Members of either House on any question shall, at the Desire of one fifth of those Present, be entered on the Journal.

Neither House, during the Session of Congress, shall, without the Consent of the other, adjourn for more than three days, nor to any other Place than that in which the two Houses shall be sitting.

Section 6—Compensation, privileges, disqualifications in certain cases.

The Senators and Representatives shall receive a Compensation for their Services, to be ascertained by Law, and paid out of the Treasury of the United States. They shall in all Cases, except Treason, Felony and Breach of the Peace, be privileged from Arrest during their Attendance at the Session of their respective Houses, and in going to and returning from the same; and for any Speech or Debate in either House, they shall not be questioned in any other Place.

No Senator or Representative shall, during the Time for which he was elected, be appointed to any civil Office under the Authority of the United States, which shall have been created, or the Emoluments whereof shall have been increased during such time; and no Person holding any Office under the United States, shall be a Member of either House during his Continuance in Office.

Section 7—House to originate all revenue bills. Veto. Bill may be passed by two-thirds of each House, notwithstanding, etc. Bill, not returned in ten days, to become a law. Provisions as to orders, concurrent resolutions, etc.

All bills for raising Revenue shall originate in the House of Representatives; but the Senate may propose or concur with Amendments as on other Bills.

Every Bill which shall have passed the House of Representatives and the Senate, shall, before it become a Law, be presented to the President of the United States; If he approve he shall sign it, but if not he shall return it, with his Objections to that House in which it shall have originated, who shall enter the Objections at large on their Journal, and proceed to reconsider it. If after such Reconsideration two thirds of that House shall agree to pass the Bill, it shall be sent, together with the Objections, to the other House, by which it shall likewise be reconsidered, and if approved by two thirds of that House, it shall become a Law. But in all such Cases the Votes of both Houses shall be determined by Yeas and Nays, and the Names of the Persons voting for and against the Bill shall be entered on the Journal of each House respectively. If any Bill shall not be returned by the President within ten Days (Sundays excepted) after it shall have been presented to him, the Same shall be a Law, in like Manner as if he had signed it, unless the Congress by their Adjournment prevent its Return, in which Case it shall not be a Law.

Every order, Resolution, or Vote to which the Concurrence of the Senate and House of Representatives may be necessary (except on a question of Adjournment) shall be presented to the President of the United States; and before the Same shall take Effect, shall be approved by him, or being disapproved by him, shall be repassed by two thirds of the Senate and House of Representatives, according to the Rules and Limitations prescribed in the Case of a Bill.

Section 8—Powers of Congress.

The Congress shall have Power To lay and collect Taxes, Duties, Imposts and Excises, to pay the Debts and provide for the common Defence and general Welfare of the United States; but all Duties, Imposts and Excises shall be uniform throughout the United States;

To borrow money on the credit of the United States;

To regulate Commerce with foreign Nations, and among the several States, and with the Indian Tribes;

To establish an uniform Rule of Naturalization, and uniform Laws on the subject of Bankruptcies throughout the United States;

To coin Money, regulate the Value thereof, and of foreign Coin, and fix the Standard of Weights and Measures;

To provide for the Punishment of counterfeiting the Securities and current Coin of the United States;

To establish Post Offices and post Roads;

To promote the Progress of Science and useful Arts, by securing for limited Times to Authors and Inventors the exclusive Right to their respective Writings and Discoveries;

To constitute Tribunals inferior to the supreme Court;

To define and punish Piracies and Felonies committed on the high Seas, and Offenses against the Law of Nations;

To declare War, grant Letters of Marque and Reprisal, and make Rules concerning Captures on Land and Water;

To raise and support Armies, but no Appropriation of Money to that Use shall be for a longer Term than two Years;

To provide and maintain a Navy;

To make Rules for the Government and Regulation of the land and naval Forces;

To provide for calling forth the Militia to execute the Laws of the Union, suppress Insurrections and repel Invasions;

To provide for organizing, arming, and disciplining the Militia, and for governing such Part of them as may be employed in the Service of the United States, reserving to the States respectively, the Appointment of the Officers, and the Authority of training the Militia according to the discipline prescribed by Congress;

To exercise exclusive Legislation in all Cases whatsoever, over such District (not exceeding ten Miles square) as may, by Cession of particular States, and the acceptance of Congress, become the Seat of the Government of the United States, and to exercise like Authority over all Places purchased by the Consent of the Legislature of the State in which the Same shall be, for the Erection of Forts, Magazines, Arsenals, dock-Yards, and other needful Buildings;—And

To make all Laws which shall be necessary and proper for carrying into Execution the foregoing Powers, and all other Powers vested by this Constitution in the Government of the United States, or in any Department or Officer thereof.

Section 9—Provision as to migration or importation of certain persons. Habeas corpus, bills of attainder, etc. Taxes, how apportioned. No export duty. No commercial preference. Money, how drawn from Treasury, etc. No titular nobility. Officers not to receive presents, etc.

The Migration or Importation of such Persons as any of the States now existing shall think proper to admit, shall not be prohibited by the Congress prior to the Year one thousand eight hundred and eight, but a tax or duty may be imposed on such Importation, not exceeding ten dollars for each Person.

The privilege of the Writ of Habeas Corpus shall not be suspended, unless when in Cases of Rebellion or Invasion the public Safety may require it.

No Bill of Attainder or ex post facto Law shall be passed.

No capitation, or other direct, Tax shall be laid, unless in Proportion to the Census or Enumeration herein before directed to be taken. *[Modified by Amendment XVI.]*

No Tax or Duty shall be laid on Articles exported from any State.

No Preference shall be given by any Regulation of Commerce or Revenue to the Ports of one State over those of another: nor shall Vessels bound to, or from, one State, be obliged to enter, clear, or pay Duties in another.

No Money shall be drawn from the Treasury, but in Consequence of Appropriations made by Law; and a regular Statement and Account of the Receipts and Expenditures of all public Money shall be published from time to time.

No Title of Nobility shall be granted by the United States: and no Person holding any Office of Profit or Trust under them, shall, without the Consent of the Congress, accept of any present, Emolument, Office, or Title, of any kind whatever, from any King, Prince, or foreign State.

Section 10—States prohibited from the exercise of certain powers.

No State shall enter into any Treaty, Alliance, or Confederation; grant Letters of Marque and Reprisal; coin Money; emit Bills of Credit; make any Thing but gold and silver Coin a Tender in Payment of Debts; pass any Bill of Attainder, ex post facto Law, or Law impairing the Obligation of Contracts, or grant any Title of Nobility.

No State shall, without the Consent of the Congress, lay any Imposts or Duties on Imports or Exports, except what may be absolutely necessary for executing its inspection Laws: and the net Produce of all Duties and Imposts, laid by any State on Imports or Exports, shall be for the Use of the Treasury of the United States; and all such Laws shall be subject to the Revision and Control of the Congress.

No State shall, without the Consent of Congress, lay any duty of Tonnage, keep Troops, or Ships of War in time of Peace, enter into any Agreement or Compact with another State, or with a foreign Power, or engage in War, unless actually invaded, or in such imminent Danger as will not admit of delay.

ARTICLE II.

Section 1—President: his term of office. Electors of President; number and how appointed. Electors to vote on same day. Qualification of President. On whom his duties devolve in case of his removal, death, etc. President's compensation. His oath of office.

The executive Power shall be vested in a President of the United States of America. He shall hold his Office during the Term of four Years, and, together with the Vice President, chosen for the same Term, be elected, as follows.

Each State shall appoint, in such Manner as the Legislature thereof may direct, a Number of Electors, equal to the whole Number of Senators and Representatives to which the State may be entitled in the Congress: but no Senator or Representative, or Person holding an Office of Trust or Profit under the United States, shall be appointed an Elector.

[The Electors shall meet in their respective States, and vote by Ballot for two persons, of whom one at least shall not be an Inhabitant of the same State with themselves. And they shall make a List of all the Persons voted for, and of the Number of Votes for each; which List they shall sign and certify, and transmit sealed to the Seat of the Government of the United States, directed to the President of the Senate. The President of the Senate shall, in the Presence of the Senate and House of Representatives, open all the Certificates, and the Votes shall then be counted. The Person having the greatest Number of Votes shall be the President, if such Number be a Majority of the whole Number of Electors appointed; and if there be more than one who have such Majority, and have an equal Number of Votes, then the House of Representatives shall immediately chuse by Ballot one of them for President; and if no Person have a Majority, then from the five highest on the List the said House shall in like Manner chuse the President. But in chusing the President, the Votes shall be taken by States, the Representation from each State having one Vote; a quorum for this Purpose shall consist of a Member or Members from two thirds of the States, and a Majority of all the States shall be necessary to a Choice. In every Case, after the Choice of the President, the Person having the greatest Number of Votes of the Electors shall be the Vice President. But if there should remain two or more who have equal Votes, the Senate shall chuse from them by Ballot the Vice-President.]

[This clause was superseded by Amendment XII.]

The Congress may detemine the Time of chusing the Electors, and the Day on which they shall give their Votes; which Day shall be the same throughout the United States.

No person except a natural born Citizen, or a Citizen of the United States, at the time of the Adoption of this Constitution, shall be eligible to the Office of President; neither shall any Person be eligible to that Office who shall not have attained to the Age of thirty-five Years, and been fourteen Years a Resident within the United States.

[For qualification of the Vice President, see Amendment XII.]

In Case of the Removal of the President from Office, or of his Death, Resignation, or Inability to discharge the Powers and Duties of the said Office, the same shall devolve on the Vice President, and the Congress may by Law, provide for the Case of Removal, Death, Resignation or Inability, both of the President and Vice President, declaring what Officer shall then act as President, and such Officer shall act accordingly, until the Disability be removed, or a President shall be elected.

[This clause has been modified by Amendments XX and XXV.]

The President shall, at stated Times, receive for his Services, a Compensation, which shall neither be encreased nor diminished during the Period for which he shall have been elected, and he shall not receive within that Period any other Emolument from the United States, or any of them.

Before he enter on the Execution of his Office, he shall take the following Oath or Affirmation:–"I do solemnly swear (or affirm) that I will faithfully execute the Office of President of the United States, and will to the best of my Ability, preserve, protect and defend the Constitution of the United States."

Section 2—President to be Commander-in-Chief. He may require opinions of cabinet officers, etc., may pardon. Treaty-making power. Nomination of certain officers. When President may fill vacancies.

The President shall be Commander in Chief of the Army and Navy of the United States, and of the Militia of the several States, when called into the actual Service of the United States; he may require the Opinion in writing, of the principal Officer in each of the executive Departments, upon any subject relating to the Duties of their respective Offices, and he shall have Power to Grant Reprieves and Pardons for Offenses against the United States, except in Cases of Impeachment.

He shall have Power, by and with the Advice and Consent of the Senate, to make Treaties, provided two-thirds of the Senators present concur; and he shall nominate, and by and with the Advice and Consent of the Senate, shall appoint Ambassadors, other public Ministers and Consuls, Judges of the supreme Court, and all other Officers of the United States, whose Appointments are not herein otherwise provided for,

and which shall be established by Law: but the Congress may by Law vest the Appointment of such inferior Officers, as they think proper, in the President alone, in the Courts of Law, or in the Heads of Departments.

The President shall have Power to fill up all Vacancies that may happen during the Recess of the Senate, by granting Commissions which shall expire at the End of their next Session.

Section 3—President shall communicate to Congress. He may convene and adjourn Congress, in case of disagreement, etc. Shall receive ambassadors, execute laws, and commission officers.

He shall from time to time give to the Congress Information of the State of the Union, and recommend to their Consideration such Measures as he shall judge necessary and expedient; he may, on extraordinary Occasions, convene both Houses, or either of them, and in Case of Disagreement between them, with Respect to the Time of Adjournment, he may adjourn them to such Time as he shall think proper; he shall receive Ambassadors and other public Ministers; he shall take Care that the Laws be faithfully executed, and shall Commission all the Officers of the United States.

Section 4—All civil offices forfeited for certain crimes.

The President, Vice President and all civil Officers of the United States, shall be removed from Office on Impeachment for, and Conviction of, Treason, Bribery, or other high Crimes and Misdemeanors.

ARTICLE III.
Section 1—Judicial powers, tenure. compensation.

The judicial Power of the United States, shall be vested in one supreme Court, and in such inferior Courts as the Congress may from time to time ordain and establish. The Judges, both of the supreme and inferior Courts, shall hold their Offices during good Behaviour, and shall, at stated Times, receive for their Services, a Compensation, which shall not be diminished during their Continuance in Office.

Section 2—Judicial power; to what cases it extends. Original jurisdiction of Supreme Court; appellate jurisdiction. Trial by jury, etc. Trial, where.

The judicial Power shall extend to all Cases, in Law and Equity, arising under this Constitution, the Laws of the United States, and Treaties made, or which shall be made, under their Authority;–to all Cases affecting Ambassadors, other public Ministers and Consuls;–to all Cases of admiralty and maritime Jurisdiction;–to Controversies to which the United States shall be a Party;–to Controversies between two or more States;–between a State and Citizens of another State;–between Citizens of different States;–between Citizens of the same State claiming Lands under Grants of different States, and between a State, or the Citizens thereof, and foreign States, Citizens or Subjects.

[This section is modified by Amendment XI.]

In all Cases affecting Ambassadors, other public Ministers and Consuls, and those in which a State shall be Party, the supreme Court shall have original Jurisdiction. In all the other Cases before mentioned, the supreme Court shall have appellate Jurisdiction, both as to Law and Fact, with such Exceptions, and under such Regulations as the Congress shall make.

The trial of all Crimes, except in Cases of Impeachment, shall be by Jury; and such Trial shall be held in the State where the said Crimes shall have been committed; but when not committed within any State, the Trial shall be at such Place or Places as the Congress may by Law have directed.

Section 3—Treason Defined. Proof of, Punishment of.

Treason against the United States, shall consist only in levying War against them, or in adhering to their Enemies, giving them Aid and Comfort. No Person shall be convicted of Treason unless on the Testimony of two Witnesses to the same overt Act, or on Confession in open Court.

The Congress shall have Power to declare the Punishment of Treason, but no Attainder of Treason shall work Corruption of Blood, or Forfeiture except during the Life of the Person attainted.

ARTICLE IV.
Section 1—Each State to give credit to the public acts, etc., of every other State.

Full Faith and Credit shall be given in each State to the public Acts, Records, and judicial Proceedings of every other State. And the Congress may by general Laws prescribe the Manner in which such Acts, Records and Proceedings shall be proved, and the Effect thereof.

The judicial Power of the United States, shall be vested in one supreme Court, and in such inferior Courts as the Congress may from time to time ordain and establish. The Judges, both of the supreme and inferior Courts, shall hold their Offices during good Behaviour, and shall, at stated Times, receive for their Services, a Compensation, which shall not be diminished during their Continuance in Office.

Section 2—Privileges of citizens of each State. Fugitives from justice to be delivered up. Persons held to service having escaped, to be delivered up.

The Citizens of each State shall be entitled to all Privileges and Immunities of Citizens in the several States.

A Person charged in any State with Treason, Felony, or other Crime, who shall flee from Justice, and be found in another State, shall on demand of the executive Authority of the State from which he fled, be delivered up, to be removed to the State having Jurisdiction of the Crime.

[No Person held to Service or Labour in one State, under the Laws thereof, escaping into another, shall, in Consequence of any Law or Regulation therein, be discharged from such Service or Labour, but shall be delivered up on Claim of the Party to whom such Service or Labour may be due.] [This clause was superseded by Amendment XIII.]

Section 3—Admission of new States. Power of Congress over territory and other property.

New States may be admitted by the Congress into this Union; but no new State shall be formed or erected within the Jurisdiction of any other State; nor any State be formed by the Junction of two or more States, or parts of States, without the Consent of the Legislatures of the States concerned as well as of the Congress.

The Congress shall have Power to dispose of and make all needful Rules and Regulations respecting the Territory or other Property belonging to the United States; and nothing in this Constitution shall be so construed as to Prejudice any Claims of the United States, or of any particular State.

Section 4—Republican form of government guaranteed. Each State to be protected.

The United States shall guarantee to every State in this Union a Republican Form of Government, and shall protect each of them against Invasion; and on Application of the Legislature, or of the Executive (when the Legislature cannot be convened) against domestic Violence.

ARTICLE V.
Constitution: how amended; proviso.

The Congress, whenever two-thirds of both Houses shall deem it necessary, shall propose Amendments to this Constitution, or, on the Application of the Legislatures of two-thirds of the several States, shall call a Convention for proposing Amendments, which, in either Case, shall be valid to all Intents and Purposes, as part of this Constitution, when ratified by the Legislatures of three-fourths of the several States, or by Conventions in three-fourths thereof, as the one or the other Mode of Ratification may be proposed by the Congress: Provided that no Amendment which may be made prior to the Year One thousand eight hundred and eight shall in any Manner affect the first and fourth Clauses in the Ninth Section of the first Article; and that no State, without its Consent, shall be deprived of its equal Suffrage in the Senate.

ARTICLE VI.
Certain debts, etc., declared valid. Supremacy of Constitution, treaties, and laws of the United States. Oath to support Constitution, by whom taken. No religious test.

All Debts contracted and Engagements entered into, before the Adoption of this Constitution, shall be as valid against the United States under this Constitution, as under the Confederation.

This Constitution, and the Laws of the United States which shall be made in Pursuance thereof; and all Treaties made, or which shall be made, under the Authority of the United States, shall be the supreme Law of the Land; and the Judges in every State shall be bound thereby, any Thing in the Constitution or Laws of any State to the Contrary notwithstanding.

The Senators and Representatives before mentioned, and the Members of the several State Legislatures, and all executive and judicial Officers, both of the United States and of the several States, shall be bound by Oath or Affirmation, to support this Constitution; but no religious Test shall ever be required as a Qualification to any Office or public Trust under the United States.

ARTICLE VII.
What ratification shall establish Constitution.

The Ratification of the Conventions of nine States shall be sufficient for the Establishment of this Constitution between the States so ratifying the Same.

Done in Convention by the Unanimous Consent of the States present the Seventeenth Day of September in the Year of our Lord one thousand seven hundred and Eighty seven and of the Independence of the United States of America the Twelfth.

In Witness whereof We have hereunto subscribed our Names.

Go WASHINGTON, Presidt and deputy from Virginia

New Hampshire—John Langdon, Nicholas Gilman

Massachusetts—Nathaniel Gorham, Rufus King

Connecticut—Wm. Saml. Johnson, Roger Sherman

New York—Alexander Hamilton

New Jersey—Wil: Livingston, David Brearley, Wm. Paterson, Jona: Dayton

Pennsylvania—B Franklin, Thomas Mifflin, Robt Morris, Geo. Clymer, Thos. FitzSimons, Jared Ingersoll, James Wilson, Gouv Morris

Delaware—Geo: Read, Gunning Bedford jun, John Dickinson, Richard Bassett, Jaco: Broom

Maryland—James McHenry, Dan of St Thos. Jenifer, Danl Carroll

Virginia—John Blair, James Madison Jr.

North Carolina—Wm. Blount, Rich'd Dobbs Spaight, Hu Williamson

South Carolina—J. Rutledge, Charles Cotesworth Pinckney, Charles Pinckney, Pierce Butler

Georgia—William Few, Abr Baldwin

Attest: William Jackson, Secretary.

Ten Original Amendments: The Bill of Rights
In force Dec. 15, 1791

[The First Congress, at its first session in the City of New York, Sept. 25, 1789, submitted to the states 12 amendments to clarify certain individual and state rights not named in the Constitution. They are generally called the Bill of Rights.

Influential in framing these amendments was the Declaration of Rights of Virginia, written by George Mason (1725-1792) in 1776. Mason, a Virginia delegate to the Constitutional Convention, did not sign the Constitution and opposed its ratification on the ground that it did not sufficiently oppose slavery or safeguard individual rights.

In the preamble to the resolution offering the proposed amendments, Congress said: "The conventions of a number of the States having at the time of their adopting the Constitution, expressed a desire, in order to prevent misconstruction or abuse of its powers, that further declaratory and restrictive clauses should be added, and as extending the ground of public confidence in the government will best insure the beneficent ends of its institution, be it resolved," etc.

Ten of these amendments, now commonly known as one to 10 inclusive, but originally 3 to 12 inclusive, were ratified by the states as follows: New Jersey, Nov. 20, 1789; Maryland, Dec. 19, 1789; North Carolina, Dec. 22, 1789; South Carolina, Jan. 19, 1790; New Hampshire, Jan. 25, 1790; Delaware, Jan. 28, 1790; New York, Feb. 27, 1790; Pennsylvania, Mar. 10, 1790; Rhode Island, June 7, 1790; Vermont, Nov. 3, 1791; Virginia, Dec. 15, 1791; Massachusetts, Mar. 2, 1939; Georgia, Mar. 18, 1939; Connecticut, Apr. 19, 1939. These original 10 ratified amendments follow as Amendments I to X inclusive.]

Of the two original proposed amendments that were not ratified promptly by the necessary number of states, the first related to apportionment of Representatives; the second, relating to compensation of members of Congress, was ratified in 1992 and became Amendment 27.]

AMENDMENT I.
Religious establishment prohibited. Freedom of speech, of press, right to assemble and to petition.

Congress shall make no law respecting an establishment of religion, or prohibiting the free exercise thereof; or abridging the freedom of speech, or of the press; or the right of the people peaceably to assemble, and to petition the Government for a redress of grievances.

AMENDMENT II.
Right to keep and bear arms.

A well regulated Militia, being necessary to the security of a free State, the right of the people to keep and bear Arms, shall not be infringed.

AMENDMENT III.
Conditions for quarters for soldiers.

No Soldier shall, in time of peace be quartered in any house, without the consent of the Owner, nor in time of war, but in a manner to be prescribed by law.

AMENDMENT IV.
Protection from unreasonable search and seizure.

The right of the people to be secure in their persons, houses, papers, and effects, against unreasonable searches and seizures, shall not be violated, and no Warrants shall issue, but upon probable cause, supported by Oath or affirmation, and particularly describing the place to be searched, and the persons or things to be seized.

AMENDMENT V.
Provisions concerning prosecution and due process of law. Double jeopardy restriction. Private property not to be taken without compensation.

No person shall be held to answer for a capital, or otherwise infamous crime, unless on a presentment or indictment of a Grand Jury, except in cases arising in the land or naval forces, or in the Militia, when in actual service in time of War or public danger; nor shall any person be subject for the same offence to be twice put in jeopardy of life or limb; nor shall be compelled in any criminal case to be a witness against himself, nor be deprived of life, liberty, or property, without due process of law; nor shall private property be taken for public use, without just compensation.

AMENDMENT VI.
Right to speedy trial, witnesses, etc.

In all criminal prosecutions, the accused shall enjoy the right to a speedy and public trial, by an impartial jury of the State and district wherein the crime shall have been committed, which district shall have been previously ascertained by law, and to be informed of the nature and cause of the accusation; to be confronted with the witnesses against him; to have compulsory process for obtaining witnesses in his favor, and to have the Assistance of Counsel for his defence.

AMENDMENT VII.
Right of trial by jury.

In suits at common law, where the value in controversy shall exceed twenty dollars, the right of trial by jury shall be preserved, and no fact tried by a jury, shall be otherwise reexamined in any Court of the United States, than according to the rules of the common law.

AMENDMENT VIII.
Excessive bail or fines; cruel and unusual punishment.

Excessive bail shall not be required, nor excessive fines imposed, nor cruel and unusual punishments inflicted.

AMENDMENT IX.
Rule of construction of Constitution.

The enumeration in the Constitution, of certain rights, shall not be construed to deny or disparage others retained by the people.

AMENDMENT X.
Rights of States under Constitution.

The powers not delegated to the United States by the Constitution, nor prohibited by it to the States, are reserved to the States respectively, or to the people.

Amendments Since the Bill of Rights

AMENDMENT XI.
Judicial powers construed.

The Judicial power of the United States shall not be construed to extend to any suit in law or equity, commenced or prosecuted against one of the United States by Citizens of another State, or by Citizens or Subjects of any Foreign State.

[This amendment was proposed to the Legislatures of the several States by the Third Congress on March. 4, 1794, and was declared to have been ratified in a message from the President to Congress, dated Jan. 8, 1798.

[It was on Jan. 5, 1798, that Secretary of State Pickering received from 12 of the States authenticated ratifications, and informed President John Adams of that fact.

[As a result of later research in the Department of State, it is now established that Amendment XI became part of the Constitution on Feb. 7, 1795, for on that date it had been ratified by 12 States as follows:

[1. New York, Mar. 27, 1794. 2. Rhode Island, Mar. 31, 1794. 3. Connecticut, May 8, 1794. 4. New Hampshire, June 16, 1794. 5. Massachusetts, June 26, 1794. 6. Vermont, between Oct. 9, 1794, and Nov. 9, 1794. 7. Virginia, Nov. 18, 1794. 8. Georgia, Nov. 29, 1794. 9. Kentucky, Dec. 7, 1794. 10. Maryland, Dec. 26, 1794. 11. Delaware, Jan. 23, 1795. 12. North Carolina, Feb. 7, 1795.

[On June 1, 1796, more than a year after Amendment XI had become a part of the Constitution—but before anyone was officially aware of this—Tennessee had been admitted as a State; but not until Oct. 16, 1797, was a certified copy of the resolution of Congress proposing the amendment sent to the Governor of Tennessee, John Sevier, by Secretary of State Pickering, whose office was then at Trenton, New Jersey, because of the epidemic of yellow fever at Philadelphia; it seems, however, that the Legislature of Tennessee took no action on Amendment XI, owing doubtless to the fact that public announcement of its adoption was made soon thereafter.

[Besides the necessary 12 States, one other, South Carolina, ratified Amendment XI, but this action was not taken until Dec. 4, 1797; the two remaining States, New Jersey and Pennsylvania, failed to ratify.]

AMENDMENT XII.
Manner of choosing President and Vice-President.

[Proposed by Congress Dec. 9, 1803; ratified June 15, 1804.]

The Electors shall meet in their respective states and vote by ballot for President and Vice-President, one of whom, at least, shall not be an inhabitant of the same state with themselves; they shall name in their ballots the person voted for as President, and in distinct ballots the person voted for as Vice-President, and they shall make distinct lists of all persons voted for as President, and of all persons voted for as Vice-President, and of the number of votes for each, which lists they shall sign and certify, and transmit sealed to the seat of the government of the United States, directed to the President of the Senate;–The President of the Senate shall, in presence of the Senate and House of Representatives, open all the certificates and the votes shall then be counted;—The person having the greatest number of votes for President, shall be the President, if such number be a majority of the whole number of Electors appointed; and if no person have such majority, then from the persons having the highest numbers not exceeding three on the list of those voted for as President, the House of Representatives shall choose immediately, by ballot, the President. But in choosing the President, the votes shall be taken by states, the representation from each state having one vote; a quorum for this purpose shall consist of a member or members from two-thirds of the states, and a majority of all the states shall be necessary to a choice. *[And if the House of Representatives shall not choose a President whenever the*

right of choice shall devolve upon them, before the fourth day of March next following, then the Vice-President shall act as President, as in the case of the death or other constitutional disability of the President.] [The words in parentheses were superseded by Amendment XX, section 3.] The person having the greatest number of votes as Vice-President, shall be the Vice-President, if such number be a majority of the whole number of Electors appointed, and if no person have a majority, then from the two highest numbers on the list, the Senate shall choose the Vice-President; a quorum for the purpose shall consist of two-thirds of the whole number of Senators, and a majority of the whole number shall be necessary to a choice. But no person constitutionally ineligible to the office of President shall be eligible to that of Vice-President of the United States.

THE RECONSTRUCTION AMENDMENTS

[Amendments XIII, XIV, and XV are commonly known as the Reconstruction Amendments, inasmuch as they followed the Civil War, and were drafted by Republicans who were bent on imposing their own policy of reconstruction on the South. Post-bellum legislatures there—Mississippi, South Carolina, Georgia, for example—had set up laws which, it was charged, were contrived to perpetuate Negro slavery under other names.]

AMENDMENT XIII.
Slavery abolished.

[Proposed by Congress Jan. 31, 1865; ratified Dec. 6, 1865. The amendment, when first proposed by a resolution in Congress, was passed by the Senate, 38 to 6, on Apr. 8, 1864, but was defeated in the House, 95 to 66 on June 15, 1864. On reconsideration by the House, on Jan. 31, 1865, the resolution passed, 119 to 56. It was approved by President Lincoln on Feb. 1, 1865, although the Supreme Court had decided in 1798 that the President has nothing to do with the proposing of amendments to the Constitution, or their adoption.]

1. Neither slavery nor involuntary servitude, except as a punishment for crime whereof the party shall have been duly convicted, shall exist within the United States, or any place subject to their jurisdiction.

2. Congress shall have power to enforce this article by appropriate legislation.

AMENDMENT XIV.
Citizenship rights not to be abridged.

[The following amendment was proposed to the Legislatures of the several states by the 39th Congress, June 13, 1866, ratified July 9, 1868, and declared to have been ratified in a proclamation by the Secretary of State, July 28, 1868.]

[The 14th amendment was adopted only by virtue of ratification subsequent to earlier rejections. Newly constituted legislatures in both North Carolina and South Carolina (respectively July 4 and 9, 1868), ratified the proposed amendment, although earlier legislatures had rejected the proposal. The Secretary of State issued a proclamation, which, though doubtful as to the effect of attempted withdrawals by Ohio and New Jersey, entertained no doubt as to the validity of the ratification by North and South Carolina. The following day (July 21, 1868), Congress passed a resolution which declared the 14th Amendment to be a part of the Constitution and directed the Secretary of State so to promulgate it. The Secretary waited, however, until the newly constituted Legislature of Georgia had ratified the amendment, subsequent to an earlier rejection, before the promulgation of the ratification of the new amendment.]

1. All persons born or naturalized in the United States, and subject to the jurisdiction thereof, are citizens of the United States and of the State wherein they reside. No State shall make or enforce any law which shall abridge the privileges or immunities of citizens of the United States; nor shall any State deprive any person of life, liberty, or property, without due process of law; nor deny to any person within its jurisdiction the equal protection of the laws.

2. Representatives shall be apportioned among the several States according to their respective numbers, counting the whole number of persons in each State, excluding Indians not taxed. But when the right to vote at any election for the choice of electors for President and Vice-President of the United States, Representatives in Congress, the Executive and Judicial officers of a State, or the members of the Legislature thereof, is denied to any of the male inhabitants of such State, being twenty-one years of age, and citizens of the United States, or in any way abridged, except for participation in rebellion, or other crime, the basis of representation therein shall be reduced in the proportion which the number of such male citizens shall bear to the whole number of male citizens twenty-one years of age in such State.

3. No person shall be a Senator or Representative in Congress, or elector of President and Vice-President, or hold any office, civil or military, under the United States, or under any State, who, having previously taken an oath, as a member of Congress, or as an officer of the United States, or as a member of any State legislature, or as an executive or judicial officer of any State, to support the Constitution of the United States, shall have engaged in insurrection or rebellion against the same, or given aid or comfort to the enemies thereof. But Congress may by a vote of two-thirds of each House, remove such disability.

4. The validity of the public debt of the United States, authorized by law, including debts incurred for payment of pensions and bounties for services in suppressing insurrection or rebellion, shall not be questioned. But neither the United States nor any State shall assume or pay any debt or obligation incurred in aid of insurrection or rebellion against the United States, or any claim for the loss or emancipation of any slave; but all such debts, obligations and claims shall be held illegal and void.

The Congress shall have power to enforce, by appropriate legislation, the provisions of this article.

AMENDMENT XV.
Race no bar to voting rights.

[The following amendment was proposed to the legislatures of the several States by the 40th Congress, Feb. 26, 1869, and ratified Feb. 8, 1870.]

1. The right of citizens of the United States to vote shall not be denied or abridged by the United States or by any State on account of race, color, or previous condition of servitude–

2. The Congress shall have power to enforce this article by appropriate legislation.

AMENDMENT XVI.
Income taxes authorized.

[Proposed by Congress July 12, 1909; ratified Feb. 3, 1913.]

The Congress shall have power to lay and collect taxes on incomes, from whatever source derived, without apportionment among the several States, and without regard to any census or enumeration.

AMENDMENT XVII.
United States Senators to be elected by direct popular vote.

[Proposed by Congress May 13, 1912; ratified Apr. 8, 1913.]

The Senate of the United States shall be composed of two Senators from each State, elected by the people thereof, for six years; and each Senator shall have one vote. The electors in each State shall have the qualifications requisite for electors of the most numerous branch of the State legislatures.

When vacancies happen in the representation of any State in the Senate, the executive authority of such State shall issue writs of election to fill such vacancies: *Provided,* That the legislature of any State may empower the executive thereof to make temporary appointments until the people fill the vacancies by election as the legislature may direct.

This amendment shall not be so construed as to affect the election or term of any Senator chosen before it becomes valid as part of the Constitution.

AMENDMENT XVIII.
Liquor prohibition amendment.

[Proposed by Congress Dec. 18, 1917; ratified Jan. 16, 1919. Repealed by Amendment XXI, effective Dec. 5, 1933.]

1. After one year from the ratification of this article the manufacture, sale, or transportation of intoxicating liquors within, the importation thereof into, or the exportation thereof from the United States and all territory subject to the jurisdiction thereof for beverage purposes is hereby prohibited.

2. The Congress and the several States shall have concurrent power to enforce this article by appropriate legislation.

3. This article shall be inoperative unless it shall have been ratified as an amendment to the Constitution by the legislatures of the several States as provided in the Constitution, within seven years from the date of the submission hereof to the States by the Congress.

[The total vote in the Senates of the various States was 1,310 for, 237 against—84.6% dry. In the lower houses of the States the vote was 3,782 for, 1,035 against—78.5% dry.

[The amendment ultimately was adopted by all the States except Connecticut and Rhode Island.]

AMENDMENT XIX.
Giving nationwide suffrage to women.
[Proposed by Congress June 4, 1919; ratified Aug. 18, 1920.]

The right of citizens of the United States to vote shall not be denied or abridged by the United States or by any State on account of sex.

Congress shall have power to enforce this Article by appropriate legislation.

AMENDMENT XX.
Terms of President and Vice President to begin on Jan. 20; those of Senators, Representatives, Jan. 3.
[Proposed by Congress Mar. 2, 1932; ratified Jan. 23, 1933.]

1. The terms of the President and Vice President shall end at noon on the 20th day of January, and the terms of Senators and Representatives at noon on the 3d day of January, of the years in which such terms would have ended if this article had not been ratified; and the terms of their successors shall then begin.

2. The Congress shall assemble at least once in every year, and such meeting shall begin at noon on the 3d day of January, unless they shall by law appoint a different day.

3. If, at the time fixed for the beginning of the term of the President, the President elect shall have died, the Vice President elect shall become President. If a President shall not have been chosen before the time fixed for the beginning of his term, or if the President elect shall have failed to qualify, then the Vice President elect shall act as President until a President shall have qualified; and the Congress may by law provide for the case wherein neither a President elect nor a Vice President elect shall have qualified, declaring who shall then act as President, or the manner in which one who is to act shall be selected, and such person shall act accordingly until a President or Vice President shall have qualified.

4. The Congress may by law provide for the case of the death of any of the persons from whom the House of Representatives may choose a President whenever the right of choice shall have devolved upon them, and for the case of the death of any of the persons from whom the Senate may choose a Vice President whenever the right of choice shall have devolved upon them.

5. Sections 1 and 2 shall take effect on the 15th day of October following the ratification of this article (Oct. 1933).

6. This article shall be inoperative unless it shall have been ratified as an amendment to the Constitution by the legislatures of three-fourths of the several States within seven years from the date of its submission.

AMENDMENT XXI.
Repeal of Amendment XVIII.
[Proposed by Congress Feb. 20, 1933; ratified Dec. 5, 1933.]

1. The eighteenth article of amendment to the Constitution of the United States is hereby repealed.

2. The transportation or importation into any State, Territory, or possession of the United States for delivery or use therein of intoxicating liquors, in violation of the laws thereof, is hereby prohibited.

3. This article shall be inoperative unless it shall have been ratified as an amendment to the Constitution by conventions in the several States, as provided in the Constitution, within seven years from the date of the submission hereof to the States by the Congress.

AMENDMENT XXII.
Limiting Presidential terms of office.
[Proposed by Congress Mar. 24, 1947; ratified Feb. 27, 1951.]

1. No person shall be elected to the office of the President more than twice, and no person who has held the office of President, or acted as President, for more than two years of a term to which some other person was elected President shall be elected to the office of the President more than once. But this Article shall not apply to any person holding the office of President when this Article was proposed by the Congress, and shall not prevent any person who may be holding the office of President, or acting as President, during the term within which this Article becomes operative from holding the office of President or acting as President during the remainder of such term.

2. This article shall be inoperative unless it shall have been ratified as an amendment to the Constitution by the legislatures of three-fourths of the several States within seven years from the date of its submission to the States by the Congress.

AMENDMENT XXIII.
Presidential vote for District of Columbia.
[Proposed by Congress June 16, 1960; ratified Mar. 29, 1961.]

1. The District constituting the seat of Government of the United States shall appoint in such manner as the Congress may direct:

A number of electors of President and Vice President equal to the whole number of Senators and Representatives in Congress to which the District would be entitled if it were a State, but in no event more than the least populous State; they shall be in addition to those appointed by the States, but they shall be considered, for the purposes of the election of President and Vice President, to be electors appointed by a State; and they shall meet in the District and perform such duties as provided by the twelfth article of amendment.

2. The Congress shall have power to enforce this article by appropriate legislation.

AMENDMENT XXIV.
Barring poll tax in federal elections.
[Proposed by Congress Aug. 27, 1962; ratified Jan. 23, 1964.]

1. The right of citizens of the United States to vote in any primary or other election for President or Vice President, for electors for President or Vice President, or for Senator or Representative in Congress, shall not be denied or abridged by the United States or any State by reason of failure to pay any poll tax or other tax.

2. The Congress shall have power to enforce this article by appropriate legislation.

AMENDMENT XXV.
Presidential disability and succession.
[Proposed by Congress July 6, 1965; ratified Feb. 10, 1967.]

1. In case of the removal of the President from office or of his death or resignation, the Vice President shall become President.

2. Whenever there is a vacancy in the office of the Vice President, the President shall nominate a Vice President who shall take office upon confirmation by a majority vote of both houses of Congress.

3. Whenever the President transmits to the President pro tempore of the Senate and the Speaker of the House of Representatives his written declaration that he is unable to discharge the powers and duties of his office, and until he transmits to them a written declaration to the contrary, such powers and duties shall be discharged by the Vice President as Acting President.

4. Whenever the Vice President and a majority of either the principal officers of the executive departments or of such other body as Congress may by law provide, transmit to the President pro tempore of the Senate and the Speaker of the House of Representatives their written declaration that the President is unable to discharge the powers and duties of his office, the Vice President shall immediately assume the powers and duties of the office as Acting President.

Thereafter, when the President transmits to the President pro tempore of the Senate and the Speaker of the House of Representatives his written declaration that no inability exists, he shall resume the powers and duties of his office unless the Vice President and a majority of either the principal officers of the executive department or of such other body as Congress may by law provide, transmit within four days to the President pro tempore of the Senate and the Speaker of the House of Representatives their written declaration that the President is unable to discharge the powers and duties of his office. Thereupon Congress shall decide the issue, assembling within forty-eight hours for that purpose if not in session. If the Congress,

within twenty-one days after receipt of the latter written decla-ration, or, if Congress is not in session, within twenty-one days after Congress is required to assemble, determines by two-thirds vote of both Houses that the President is unable to discharge the powers and duties of his office, the Vice President shall continue to discharge the same as Acting President; otherwise, the President shall resume the powers and duties of his office.

AMENDMENT XXVI.
Lowering voting age to 18 years.
[Proposed by Congress Mar. 23, 1971; ratified June 30, 1971.]

1. The right of citizens of the United States, who are eighteen years of age or older, to vote shall not be denied or abridged by the United States or by any State on account of age.

2. The Congress shall have the power to enforce this article by appropriate legislation.

AMENDMENT XXVII.
Congressional pay.
[Proposed by Congress Sept. 25, 1789; ratified May 7, 1992.]
No law, varying the compensation for the services of the Senators and Representatives, shall take effect, until an election of Representatives shall have intervened.

How a Bill Becomes a Law

A senator or representative introduces a bill in Congress by sending it to the clerk of the House or the Senate, who assigns it a number and title. This procedure is termed the first reading. The clerk then refers the bill to the appropriate committee of the Senate or House.

If the committee opposes the bill, it will table, or kill, it. Otherwise, the committee holds hearings to listen to opinions and facts offered by members and other interested people. The committee then debates the bill and possibly offers amendments. A vote is taken, and if favorable, the bill is sent back to the clerk of the House or Senate.

The clerk reads the bill to the house—the second reading. Members may then debate the bill and suggest amendments.

After debate and possibly amendment, the bill is given a third reading, simply of the title, and put to a voice or roll-call vote.

If passed, the bill goes to the other house, where it may be defeated or passed, with or without amendments. If defeated, the bill dies. If passed with amendments, a conference committee made up of members of both houses works out the differences and arrives at a compromise.

After passage of the final version by both houses, the bill is sent to the president. If the president signs it, the bill becomes a law. The president may, however, veto the bill by refusing to sign it and sending it back to the house where it originated, with reasons for the veto.

The president's objections are then read and debated, and a roll-call vote is taken. If the bill receives less than a two-thirds majority, it is defeated. If it receives at least two-thirds, it is sent to the other house. If that house also passes it by at least a two-thirds majority, the1 veto is overridden, and the bill becomes a law.

If the president neither signs nor vetoes the bill within 10 days—not including Sundays—it automatically becomes a law even without the president's signature. However, if Congress has adjourned within those 10 days, the bill is automatically killed; this indirect rejection is termed a pocket veto.

Note: Under "line-item veto" legislation effective Jan. 1, 1997, the president was authorized,

The Capitol

under certain circumstances, to veto a bill in part, but the legislation was found unconstitutional by the Supreme Court, June 25, 1998.

Confederate States and Secession

The American Civil War (1861-65) grew out of sectional disputes over the continued existence of slavery in the South and the contention of Southern legislators that the states retained many rights, including the right to secede.

The war was not fought by state against state but by one federal regime against another, the Confederate government in Richmond assuming control over the economic, political, and military life of the South, under protest from Georgia and South Carolina.

South Carolina voted an ordinance of secession from the Union, repealing its 1788 ratification of the U.S. Constitution on Dec. 20, 1860, to take effect on Dec. 24. Other states seceded in 1861. Their votes in conventions were: Mississippi, Jan. 9, 84-15; Florida, Jan. 10, 62-7; Alabama, Jan. 11, 61-39; Georgia, Jan. 19, 208-89; Louisiana, Jan. 26, 113-17; Texas, Feb. 1, 166-7, ratified by popular vote on Feb. 23 (for 34,794, against 11,325); Virginia, Apr. 17, 88-55, ratified by popular vote on May 23 (for 128,884; against 32,134); Arkansas, May

6, 69-1; Tennessee, May 7, ratified by popular vote on June 8 (for 104,019, against 47,238); North Carolina, May 21.

Missouri Unionists stopped secession in conventions Feb. 28 and Mar. 9. The legislature condemned secession Mar. 7. Under the protection of Confederate troops, secessionist members of the legislature adopted a resolution of secession at Neosho, Oct. 31. The Confederate Congress seated the secessionists' representatives.

Kentucky did not secede, and its government remained Unionist. In a part of the state occupied by Confederate troops, Kentuckians approved secession, and the Confederate Congress admitted their representatives.

The Maryland legislature voted against secession Apr. 27, 53-13. Delaware did not secede. Western Virginia held conventions at Wheeling, named a pro-Union governor on June 11, 1861, and was admitted to the Union as West Virginia on June 20, 1863. Its constitution provided for gradual abolition of slavery.

Confederate Government

Forty-two delegates from South Carolina, Georgia, Alabama, Mississippi, Louisiana, and Florida met in convention at Montgomery, AL, on Feb. 4, 1861. They adopted a provisional constitution of the Confederate States of America and elected Jefferson Davis (MS) as provisional president and Alexander H. Stephens (GA) as provisional vice president.

A permanent constitution was adopted Mar. 11. It abolished the African slave trade, but it did not bar interstate commerce

in slaves. On July 20 the Congress moved to Richmond, VA. Davis was elected president in October and was inaugurated on Feb. 22, 1862.

The Congress adopted a flag, consisting of a red field with a white stripe, and a blue jack with a circle of white stars. Later the more popular flag was the red field with blue diagonal crossbars that held 13 white stars, for the 11 states in the Confederacy plus Kentucky and Missouri.

> **IT'S A FACT:** One of America's founding fathers, Alexander Hamilton was not born in the orginal thirteen colonies, but on the Caribbean island of Nevis in 1757. Orphaned by age 11, he was sent by benefactors to prep school in New Jersey in 1772, and then entered King's College (now Columbia University) in New York City. By the time he was 20, he was on the personal staff of Gen. George Washington. Favoring a strong central government, he made the largest single contribution to *The Federalist Papers* and served as the first secretary of the treasury. He was killed in a duel with Vice President Aaron Burr in 1804.

Lincoln's Address at Gettysburg, 1863

Fourscore and seven years ago our fathers brought forth on this continent a new nation, conceived in liberty and dedicated to the proposition that all men are created equal.

Now we are engaged in a great civil war, testing whether that nation or any nation so conceived and so dedicated can long endure. We are met on a great battle field of that war. We have come to dedicate a portion of that field, as a final resting-place for those who here gave their lives that that nation might live. It is altogether fitting and proper that we should do this.

But, in a larger sense, we can not dedicate—we can not consecrate—we can not hallow—this ground. The brave men, living and dead, who struggled here, have consecrated it, far above our poor power to add or detract. The world will little note, nor long remember, what we say here, but it can never forget what they did here. It is for us the living, rather, to be dedicated here to the unfinished work which they who fought here have thus far so nobly advanced. It is rather for us to be here dedicated to the great task remaining before us—that from these honored dead we take increased devotion to that cause for which they gave the last full measure of devotion— that we here highly resolve that these dead shall not have died in vain—that this nation, under God, shall have a new birth of freedom—and that government of the people, by the people, for the people, shall not perish from the earth.

Selected Landmark Decisions of the U.S. Supreme Court, 1803-2003

1803: Marbury v. Madison. The Court ruled that Congress exceeded its power in the Judiciary Act of 1789; the Court thus established its power to review acts of Congress and declare invalid those it found in conflict with the Constitution.

1819: McCulloch v. Maryland. The Court ruled that Congress had the authority to charter a national bank, under the Constitution's granting of the power to enact all laws "necessary and proper" to responsibilities of government.

1819: Trustees of Dartmouth College v. Woodward. The Court ruled that a state could not arbitrarily alter the terms of a college's contract. (The Court later used a similar principle to limit the states' ability to interfere with business contracts.)

1857: Dred Scott v. Sanford. The Court declared unconstitutional the already-repealed Missouri Compromise of 1820 because it deprived a person of his or her property—a slave— without due process of law. The Court also ruled that slaves were not citizens of any state nor of the U.S. (The latter part of the decision was overturned by ratification of the 14th Amendment in 1868.)

1896: Plessy v. Ferguson. The Court ruled that a state law requiring federal railroad trains to provide separate but equal facilities for black and white passengers neither infringed upon federal authority to regulate interstate commerce nor violated the 13th and 14th Amendments. (The "separate but equal" doctrine remained effective until the 1954 **Brown v. Board of Education** decision.)

1904: Northern Securities Co. v. U.S. The Court ruled that a holding company formed solely to eliminate competition between two railroad lines was a combination in restraint of trade, violating the federal antitrust act.

1908: Muller v. Oregon. The Court upheld a state law limiting the working hours of women. (Louis D. Brandeis, counsel for the state, cited evidence from social workers, physicians, and factory inspectors that the number of hours women worked affected their health and morals.)

1911: Standard Oil Co. of New Jersey et al. v. U.S. The Court ruled that the Standard Oil Trust must be dissolved because of its unreasonable restraint of trade.

1919: Schenck v. U.S. The Court sustained the Espionage Act of 1917, maintaining that freedom of speech and press could be constrained if "the words used . . . create a clear and present danger. . ."

1925: Gitlow v. New York. The Court ruled that the First Amendment prohibition against government abridgment of the freedom of speech applied to the states as well as to the federal government. The decision was the first of a number of rulings holding that the 14th Amendment extended the guarantees of the Bill of Rights to state action.

1935: Schechter Poultry Corp. v. U.S. The Court ruled that Congress exceeded its authority to delegate legislative powers and to regulate interstate commerce when it enacted the National Industrial Recovery Act, which afforded the U.S. president too much discretionary power.

1951: Dennis et al. v. U.S. The Court upheld convictions under the Smith Act of 1940 for invoking Communist theory that advocated the forcible overthrow of the government. (In the **1957 Yates v. U.S.** decision, the Court moderated this ruling by allowing such advocacy in the abstract, if not connected to action to achieve the goal.)

1954: Brown v. Board of Education of Topeka. The Court ruled that separate public schools for black and white students were inherently unequal, so that state-sanctioned segregation in public schools violated the equal protection guarantee of the 14th Amendment. And in **Bolling v. Sharpe** the Court ruled that the congressionally mandated segregated public school system in the District of Columbia violated the 5th Amendment's due process guarantee of personal liberty. (The Brown ruling also led to abolition of state-sponsored segregation in other public facilities.)

1957: Roth v. U.S., Alberts v. California. The Court ruled obscene material was not protected by First Amendment guarantees of freedom of speech and press, defining obscene as "utterly without redeeming social value" and appealing to "prurient interests" in the view of the average person. This definition was modified in later decisions, and the "average person" standard was replaced by the "local community" standard in **Miller v. California (1973).**

1961: Mapp v. Ohio. The Court ruled that evidence obtained in violation of the 4th Amendment guarantee against unreasonable search and seizure must be excluded from use at state as well as federal trials.

1962: Engel v. Vitale. The Court held that public schools could not require pupils to recite a state-composed prayer, even if nondenominational and voluntary, because this would be an unconstitutional attempt to establish religion.

1962: Baker v. Carr. The Court held that the constitutional challenges to the unequal distribution of voters among legislative districts could be resolved by federal courts.

1963: Gideon v. Wainwright. The Court ruled that state and federal defendants charged with serious crimes must have access to an attorney, at state expense if necessary.

1964: New York Times Co. v. Sullivan. The Court ruled that the First Amendment protected the press from libel suits for defamatory reports about public officials unless an injured party could prove that a defamatory report was made out of malice or "reckless disregard" for the truth.

1965: Griswold v. Conn. The Court ruled that a state unconstitutionally interfered with personal privacy in the marriage relationship when it prohibited anyone, including married couples, from using contraceptives.

1966: Miranda v. Arizona. The Court ruled that, under the guarantee of due process, suspects in custody, before being questioned, must be informed that they have the right to remain silent, that anything they say may be used against them, and that they have the right to counsel.

1973: Roe v. Wade, Doe v. Bolton. The Court ruled that the fetus was not a "person" with constitutional rights and that a right to privacy inherent in the 14th Amendment's due process guarantee of personal liberty protected a woman's decision to have an abortion. During the first trimester of pregnancy, the Court maintained, the decision should be left entirely to a woman and her physician. Some regulation of abortion procedures was allowed in the 2nd trimester, and some restriction of abortion in the 3rd.

1974: U.S. v. Nixon. The Court ruled that neither the separation of powers nor the need to preserve the confidentiality of presidential communications could alone justify an absolute executive privilege of immunity from judicial demands for evidence to be used in a criminal trial.

1976: Gregg v. Georgia, Profitt v. Fla., Jurek v. Texas. The Court held that death, as a punishment for persons convicted of first degree murder, was not in and of itself cruel and unusual punishment in violation of the 8th Amendment. But the Court ruled that the sentencing judge and jury must consider the individual character of the offender and the circumstances of the particular crime.

1978: Regents of Univ. of Calif. v. Bakke. The Court ruled that a special admissions program for a state medical school, under which a set number of places were reserved for minorities, violated the 1964 Civil Rights Act, which forbids excluding anyone, because of race, from a federally funded program. However, the Court ruled that race could be considered as one of a complex of factors.

1986: Bowers v. Hardwick. The Court refused to extend any constitutional right of privacy to homosexual activity, upholding a Georgia antisodomy law that in effect made such activity a crime. However, the law was struck down by the state supreme court in 1998, and in **Lawrence v. Texas (2003),** the U.S. Supreme Court struck down all state antisodomy laws, as violations of liberty prohibited in the 14th Amendment's due process clause. Also, in **Romer v. Evans (1996),** the Court struck down a Colorado constitutional provision that barred legislation protecting homosexuals from discrimination.

1990: Cruzan v. Missouri. The Court ruled that a person had the right to refuse life-sustaining medical treatment. However, the Court also ruled that, before treatment could be withheld from a comatose patient, a state could require "clear and convincing evidence" that the patient would not have wanted to live. And in 2 **1997** rulings, **Washington v. Glucksberg** and **Vacco v. Quill,** the Court ruled that states could ban doctor-assisted suicide.

1995: Adarand Constructors v. Peña. The Court held that federal programs that classify people by race, unless "narrowly tailored" to accomplish a "compelling governmental interest," may violate the right to equal protection.

1995: U.S. Term Limits Inc. v. Thornton. The Court ruled that neither states nor Congress could limit terms of members of Congress, since the Constitution reserves to the people the right to choose federal lawmakers.

1997: Clinton v. Jones. Rejecting an appeal by Pres. Clinton in a sexual harassment suit, the Court ruled that a sitting president did not have temporary immunity from a lawsuit for actions outside the realm of official duties.

1997: City of Boerne v. Flores. The Court overturned a 1993 law that banned enforcement of laws that "substantially burden" religious practice unless there is a "compelling need" to do so. The Court held that the act was an unwarranted intrusion by Congress on states' prerogatives and an infringement of the judiciary's role.

1997: Reno v. ACLU. Citing the right to free expression, the Court overturned a provision making it a crime to display or distribute "indecent" or "patently offensive" material on the Internet. In **1998,** however, the Court ruled in **NEA v. Finley** that "general standards of decency" may be used as a criterion in federal arts funding.

1998: Clinton v. City of New York. The Court struck down the Line-Item Veto Act (1996), holding that it unconstitutionally gave the president "the unilateral power to change the text of duly enacted statutes."

1998: Faragher v. City of Boca Raton, Burlington Industries, Inc. v. Ellerth. The Court issued new guidelines for workplace sexual harassment suits, holding employers responsible for misconduct by supervisory employees. And in **Oncale v. Sundowner Offshore Services,** the Court ruled that the law against sexual harassment applies regardless of whether harasser and victim are the same sex.

1999: Dept. of Commerce v. U.S. House. Upholding a challenge to plans for the 2000 census, the Court required an actual head count for apportioning the U.S. House of Representatives, but allowed statistical sampling for other purposes, such as the allocation of federal funds.

1999: Alden v. Maine, Florida Prepaid v. College Savings Bank, College Savings Bank v. Florida. In a series of rulings, the Court applied the principle of "sovereign immunity" to shield states in large part from being sued under federal law.

2000: Troxel v. Granville. The justices found that a Washington state law allowing grandparents visitation rights, as broadly applied, interfered with parents' right to determine the best care for their children.

2000: Boy Scouts of America v. Dale. The Court ruled that the Boy Scouts could dismiss a troop leader after learning he was gay, holding that the right to freedom of association outweighed a New Jersey anti-discrimination statute.

2000: Stenberg v. Carhart. The Court struck down a Nebraska law that banned so-called partial-birth abortion. It argued that the law could be interpreted as banning other abortion procedures and that it should have made exception for reasons of health. (See 1973: *Roe* v. *Wade.*)

2000: Bush v. Gore. The Court ruled that manual recounts of presidential ballots in the Nov. 2000 election could not proceed because inconsistent evaluation standards in different counties violated the equal protection clause. In effect, the ruling meant existing official results leaving George W. Bush as narrow winner of the election would prevail.

2001: Easley v. Cromartie. The Court ruled that North Carolina's 12th Congressional District, whose irregular shape had been challenged as an unconstitutional racial gerrymander, was the permissible result of attempts to create a majority-Democrat district.

2001: Good News Club v. Milford Central School. The justices found that religious and secular organizations were entitled to equal access to public elementary school grounds for after-school meetings.

2002: Atkins v. Virginia. The Court ruled that the execution of mentally retarded felons violated the Eighth Amendment ban on "cruel and unusual punishment."

2002: Ring v. Arizona. The Court found that only a jury, not a judge, could decide to impose the death penalty.

2002: Zelman v. Simmons-Harris. The Court ruled that publicly funded tuition vouchers could be used at religious schools without violating the separation of church and state.

2002: Federal Maritime Commission v. South Carolina State Ports Authority. The Court ruled that the 11th Amendment gave states immunity from private lawsuits involving federal agencies.

2003: Grotter v. Bollinger, Gratz v. Bollinger. The Court upheld affirmative action in admission policies at the University of Michigan Law School. However, in a second decision, the Court ruled against a strict point system based on racial and ethnic backgrounds, as used in the university's undergraduate admissions process.

Presidential Oath of Office

The Constitution (Article II) directs that the president-elect shall take the following oath or affirmation to be inaugurated as president: "I do solemnly swear [affirm] that I will faithfully execute the office of President of the United States, and will, to the best of my ability, preserve, protect, and defend the Constitution of the United States." (Custom decrees the addition of the words "So help me God" at the end of the oath when taken by the president-elect, with the left hand on the Bible for the duration of the oath, and the right hand slightly raised.)

Law on Succession to the Presidency

If by reason of death, resignation, removal from office, inability, or failure to qualify there is neither a president nor vice president to discharge the powers and duties of the office of president, then the speaker of the House of Representatives shall upon his resignation as speaker and as representative, act as president. The same rule shall apply in the case of the death, resignation, removal from office, or inability of an individual acting as president.

If at the time when a speaker is to begin the discharge of the powers and duties of the office of president there is no speaker,

or the speaker fails to qualify as acting president, then the president pro tempore of the Senate, upon his resignation as president pro tempore and as senator, shall act as president.

An individual acting as president shall continue to act until the expiration of the then current presidential term, except that (1) if his discharge of the powers and duties of the office is founded in whole or in part in the failure of both the president-elect and the vice president-elect to qualify, then he shall act only until a president or vice president qualifies, and (2) if his discharge of the powers and duties of the office is founded in whole or in part on the inability of the president or vice president, then he shall act only until the removal of the disability of one of such individuals.

If, by reason of death, resignation, removal from office, or failure to qualify, there is no president pro tempore to act as president, then the officer of the United States who is highest on the following list, and who is not under any disability to discharge the powers and duties of president shall act as president; the secretaries of state, treasury, defense, attorney general; secretaries of interior, agriculture, commerce, labor, health and human services, housing and urban development, transportation, energy, education, veterans affairs.

(Legislation approved July 18, 1947; amended Sept. 9, 1965, Oct. 15, 1966, Aug. 4, 1977, and Sept. 27, 1979. See also Constitutional Amendment XXV.)

Origin of the United States National Motto

In God We Trust, designated as the U.S. National Motto by Congress in 1956, originated during the Civil War as an inscription for U. S. coins, although it was used by Francis Scott Key in a slightly different form when he wrote "The Star-Spangled Banner" in 1814. On Nov. 13, 1861, when Union morale had been shaken by battlefield defeats, the Rev. M. R. Watkinson, of Ridleyville, PA, wrote to Secy. of the Treasury Salmon P. Chase. "From my heart I have felt our national

shame in disowning God as not the least of our present national disasters," the minister wrote, suggesting "recognition of the Almighty God in some form on our coins." Secy. Chase ordered designs prepared with the inscription *In God We Trust* and backed coinage legislation that authorized use of this slogan. The motto first appeared on some U.S. coins in 1864, and disappeared and reappeared on various coins until 1955, when Congress ordered it placed on all paper money and all coins.

The American's Creed

William Tyler Page, Clerk of the U.S. House of Representatives, wrote "The American's Creed" in 1917. It was accepted by the House on behalf of the American people on April 3, 1918.

"I believe in the United States of America as a government of the people, by the people, for the people; whose just powers are derived from the consent of the governed; a democracy in a republic; a sovereign Nation of many sovereign States; a perfect union, one and inseparable; established upon those

principles of freedom, equality, justice, and humanity for which American patriots sacrificed their lives and fortunes.

"I therefore believe it is my duty to my country to love it, to support its Constitution, to obey its laws, to respect its flag, and to defend it against all enemies."

The Great Seal of the U.S.

On July 4, 1776, the Continental Congress appointed a committee consisting of Benjamin Franklin, John Adams, and Thomas Jefferson "to bring in a device for a seal of the United States of America." The designs submitted by this and a subsequent committee were considered unacceptable. After many delays, a third committee, appointed early in 1782, presented a design prepared by William Barton. Charles Thomson, the

secretary of Congress, suggested certain changes, and Congress finally approved the design on June 20, 1782. The obverse side of the seal shows an American bald eagle. In its mouth is a ribbon bearing the motto *e pluribus unum* (one out of many). In the eagle's talons are the arrows of war and an olive branch of peace. The reverse side shows an unfinished pyramid with an eye (the eye of Providence) above it.

The Flag of the U.S.—The Stars and Stripes

The 50-star flag of the United States was raised for the first time officially at 12:01 AM on July 4, 1960, at Fort McHenry National Monument in Baltimore, MD. The 50th star had been added for Hawaii; a year earlier the 49th, for Alaska. Before that, no star had been added since 1912, when New Mexico and Arizona were admitted to the Union.

The true history of the Stars and Stripes has become so cluttered by myth and tradition that the facts are difficult, and in some cases impossible, to establish. For example, it is not certain who designed the Stars and Stripes, who made the first such flag, or even whether it ever flew in any sea fight or land battle of the American Revolution.

All agree, however, that the Stars and Stripes originated as the result of a resolution offered by the Marine Committee of the Second Continental Congress at Philadelphia and adopted on June 14, 1777. It read:

Resolved: that the flag of the United States be thirteen stripes, alternate red and white; that the union be thirteen stars, white in a blue field, representing a new constellation.

Congress gave no hint as to the designer of the flag, no instructions as to the arrangement of the stars, and no information on its appropriate uses. Historians have been unable to find the original flag law.

The resolution establishing the flag was not even published until Sept. 2, 1777. Despite repeated requests, Washington did not get the flags until 1783, after the American Revolution was over. And there is no certainty that they were the Stars and Stripes.

Early Flags

Many historians consider the first flag of the U.S. to have been the Grand Union (sometimes called Great Union) flag, although the Continental Congress never officially adopted it. This flag was a modification of the British Meteor flag, which had the red cross of St. George and the white cross of St. Andrew combined in the blue canton. For the Grand Union flag, 6 horizontal stripes were imposed on the red field, dividing it into 13 alternating red and white stripes. On Jan. 1, 1776,

when the Continental Army came into formal existence, this flag was unfurled on Prospect Hill, Somerville, MA. Washington wrote that "we hoisted the Union Flag in compliment to the United Colonies."

One of several flags about which controversy has raged for years is at Easton, PA. Containing the devices of the national flag in reversed order, this flag has been in the public library at Easton for more than 150 years. Some contend that this flag was actually the first Stars and Stripes, first displayed on July 8, 1776. This flag has 13 red and white stripes in the canton, 13 white stars centered in a blue field.

A flag was hastily improvised from garments by the defenders of Fort Schuyler at Rome, NY, Aug. 3-22, 1777. Historians believe it was the Grand Union Flag.

The Sons of Liberty had a flag of 9 red and white stripes, to signify 9 colonies, when they met in New York in 1765 to oppose the Stamp Tax. By 1775, the flag had grown to 13 red and white stripes, with a rattlesnake on it.

At Concord, Apr. 19, 1775, the minutemen from Bedford, MA, are said to have carried a flag having a silver arm with sword on a red field. At Cambridge, MA, the Sons of Liberty used a plain red flag with a green pine tree on it.

In June 1775, Washington went from Philadelphia to Boston to take command of the army, escorted to New York by the Philadelphia Light Horse Troop. It carried a yellow flag that had an elaborate coat of arms—the shield charged with 13 knots, the motto "For These We Strive"—and a canton of 13 blue and silver stripes.

In Feb. 1776, Col. Christopher Gadsden, a member of the Continental Congress, gave the South Carolina Provincial Congress a flag "such as is to be used by the commander-in-chief of the American Navy." It had a yellow field, with a rattlesnake about to strike and the words "Don't Tread on Me."

At the Battle of Bennington, Aug. 16, 1777, patriots used a flag of 7 white and 6 red stripes with a blue canton extending down 9 stripes and showing an arch of 11 white stars over the figure 76 and a star in each of the upper corners. The stars are 7-pointed. This flag is preserved in the Historical Museum at Bennington, VT.

At the Battle of Cowpens, Jan. 17, 1781, the 3d Maryland Regiment is said to have carried a flag of 13 red and white stripes, with a blue canton containing 12 stars in a circle around one star.

Who Designed the Flag? No one knows for certain. Francis Hopkinson, designer of a naval flag, declared he also had designed the flag and in 1781 asked Congress to reimburse him for his services. Congress did not do so. Dumas Malone of Columbia University wrote: "This talented man . . . designed the American flag."

Who Called the Flag "Old Glory"? The flag is said to have been named Old Glory by William Driver, a sea captain of Salem, MA. One legend has it that when he raised the flag on his brig, the *Charles Doggett*, in 1824, he said: "I name thee Old Glory." But his daughter, who presented the flag to the Smithsonian Institution, said he named it at his 21st birthday celebration on Mar. 17, 1824, when his mother presented the homemade flag to him.

The Betsy Ross Legend. The widely publicized legend that Mrs. Betsy Ross made the first Stars and Stripes in June 1776, at the request of a committee composed of George Washington, Robert Morris, and George Ross, an uncle, was first made public in 1870, by a grandson of Mrs. Ross. Historians have been unable to find a historical record of such a meeting or committee.

Adding New Stars

The flag of 1777 was used until 1795. Then, on the admission of Vermont and Kentucky to the Union, Congress passed and Pres. Washington signed an act that after May 1, 1795, the flag should have 15 stripes, alternating red and white, and 15 white stars on a blue field.

When new states were admitted, it became evident that the flag would become burdened with stripes. Congress thereupon ordered that after July 4, 1818, the flag should have 13 stripes, symbolizing the 13 original states; that the union have 20 stars, and that whenever a new state was admitted a new star should be added on the July 4 following admission.

No law designates the permanent arrangement of the stars. However, since 1912, when a new state has been admitted, the new design has been announced by executive order. No star is specifically identified with any state.

Code of Etiquette for Display and Use of the U.S. Flag
Reviewed by National Flag Foundation

Although the Stars and Stripes originated in 1777, it was not until 146 years later that there was a serious attempt to establish a uniform code of etiquette for the U.S. flag. On Feb. 15, 1923, the War Department issued a circular on the rules of flag usage. These rules were adopted almost in their entirety June 14, 1923, by a conference of 68 patriotic organizations in Washington, D.C. Finally, on June 22, 1942, a joint resolution of Congress, amended by Public Law 94-344, July 7, 1976, codified "existing rules and customs pertaining to the display and use of the flag . . ."

When to Display the Flag—The flag should be displayed on all days, especially on legal holidays and other special occasions, on official buildings when in use, in or near polling places on election days, and in or near schools when in session. Citizens may fly the flag at any time. It is customary to display it only from sunrise to sunset on buildings and on stationary flagstaffs in the open. It may be displayed at night, however, on special occasions, preferably lighted. The flag now flies over the White House both day and night. It flies over the Senate wing of the Capitol when the Senate is in session and over the House wing when that body is in session. It flies day and night over the east and west fronts of the Capitol, without floodlights at night but receiving illumination from the Capitol Dome. It flies 24 hours a day at several other places, including the Fort McHenry National Monument in Baltimore, where it inspired Francis Scott Key to write "The Star Spangled Banner." The flag also flies 24 hours a day, properly illuminated, at U.S. Customs ports of entry.

Flying the Flag at Half-Staff—Flying the flag at half-staff, that is, halfway up the staff, is a signal of mourning. The flag should be hoisted to the top of the staff for an instant before being lowered to half-staff. It should be hoisted to the peak again before being lowered for the day or night.

As provided by presidential proclamation, the flag should fly at half-staff for 30 days from the day of death of a president or former president; for 10 days from the day of death of a vice president, chief justice or retired chief justice of the U.S., or speaker of the House of Representatives; from day of death until burial of an associate justice of the Supreme Court, cabinet member, former vice president, Senate president pro tempore, or majority or minority Senate or House leader; for a U.S. senator, representative, territorial delegate, or the resident commissioner of Puerto Rico, on day of death and the following day within the metropolitan area of the District of Columbia and from day of death until burial within the decedent's state, congressional district, territory or commonwealth; and for the death of the governor of a state, territory, or possession of the U.S., from day of death until burial.

On Memorial Day, the flag should fly at half-staff until noon and then be raised to the peak. The flag should also fly at half-staff on Korean War Veterans Armistice Day (July 27), National Pearl Harbor Remembrance Day (Dec. 7), and Peace Officers Memorial Day (May 15).

How to Fly the Flag—The flag should be hoisted briskly and lowered ceremoniously and should never be allowed to touch the ground or the floor. When the flag is hung over a sidewalk from a rope extending from a building to a pole, the union should be away from the building. When the flag is hung over the center of a street the union should be to the north in an east-west street and to the east in a north-south street. No other flag may be flown above or, if on the same level, to the right of the U.S. flag, except that at the United Nations Headquarters the UN flag may be placed above flags of all member nations and other national flags may be flown with equal prominence or honor with the flag of the U.S. At services by Navy chaplains at sea, the church pennant may be flown above the flag.

When 2 flags are placed against a wall with crossed staffs, the U.S. flag should be at right—its own right, and its staff should be in front of the staff of the other flag; when a number of flags are grouped and displayed from staffs, it should be at the center and highest point of the group.

Church and Platform Use—In an auditorium, the flag may be displayed flat, above and behind the speaker. When displayed from a staff in a church or in a public auditorium, the flag should hold the position of superior prominence, in advance of the audience, and in the position of honor at the speaker's right as she or he faces the audience. Any other flag so displayed should be placed on the left of the speaker or to the right of the audience.

When the flag is displayed horizontally or vertically against a wall, the stars should be uppermost and at the observer's left.

When used to cover a casket, the flag should be placed so that the union is at the head and over the left shoulder. It should not be lowered into the grave nor touch the ground.

How to Dispose of Worn Flags—When the flag is in such condition that it is no longer a fitting emblem for display, it should be destroyed in a dignified way, preferably by burning.

When to Salute the Flag—All persons present should face the flag, stand at attention, and salute on the following occasions: (1) when the flag is passing in a parade or in a review, (2) during the ceremony of hoisting or lowering, (3) when the national anthem is played, and (4) during the Pledge of Allegiance. Those present in uniform should render the military salute. Those not in uniform should place the right hand over the heart. A man wearing a hat should remove it with his right hand and hold it to his left shoulder during the salute.

Prohibited Uses of the Flag—The flag should not be dipped to any person or thing. (An exception—customarily, ships salute by dipping their colors.) It should never be displayed with the union down save as a distress signal. It should never be carried flat or horizontally, but always aloft and free.

It should not be displayed on a float, an automobile, or a boat except from a staff. It should never be used as a covering for a ceiling, nor have placed on it any word, design, or drawing. It should never be used as a receptacle for carrying anything. It should not be used to cover a statue or a monument.

The flag should never be used for advertising purposes, nor be embroidered on such articles as cushions or handkerchiefs, printed or otherwise impressed on boxes or anything that is designed for temporary use and discard; or used as a costume or athletic uniform. Advertising signs should not be fastened to its staff or halyard.

The flag should never be used as drapery of any sort, never festooned, drawn back, nor up, in folds, but always allowed to fall free. Bunting of blue, white, and red, always arranged with the blue above and the white in the middle, should be used for covering a speaker's desk, draping the front of a platform, and for decoration in general.

An act of Congress approved on Feb. 8, 1917, provided certain penalties for the desecration, mutilation, or improper use of the flag within the District of Columbia. A 1968 federal law provided penalties of as much as a year's imprisonment or a $1,000 fine or both for publicly burning or otherwise desecrating any U.S. flag. In addition, many states have laws against flag desecration. In 1989, the Supreme Court ruled that no laws could prohibit political protesters from burning the flag. The decision had the effect of declaring unconstitutional the flag desecration laws of 48 states, as well as a similar federal statute, in cases of peaceful political expression.

The Supreme Court, in June 1990, declared that a new federal law making it a crime to burn or deface the American flag violated the free-speech guarantee of the First Amendment. The 5-4 Court decision led to renewed calls in Congress for a constitutional amendment to make it possible to prosecute flag burners.

Pledge of Allegiance to the Flag

I pledge allegiance to the flag of the United States of America and to the republic for which it stands, one nation under God, indivisible, with liberty and justice for all.

This, the current official version of the Pledge of Allegiance, has developed from the original pledge, which was first published in the Sept. 8, 1892, issue of *Youth's Companion*, a weekly magazine then published in Boston. The original pledge contained the phrase "my flag," which was changed more than 30 years later to "flag of the United States of America." A 1954 act of Congress added the words "under God." (In June 2002 a 3-judge panel of the 9th Circuit U.S. Court of Appeals ruled, 2-1, that recitation of the pledge in public schools could not include that phrase; the decision was being appealed.)

The authorship of the pledge was in dispute for many years. The *Youth's Companion* stated in 1917 that the original draft was written by James B. Upham, an executive of the magazine who died in 1910. A leaflet circulated by the magazine later named Upham as the originator of the draft "afterwards condensed and perfected by him and his associates of the Companion force."

Francis Bellamy, a former member of *Youth's Companion* editorial staff, publicly claimed authorship of the pledge in 1923. In 1939, the United States Flag Association, acting on the advice of a committee named to study the controversy, upheld the claim of Bellamy, who had died 8 years earlier. In 1957 the Library of Congress issued a report attributing authorship to Bellamy.

The History of the National Anthem

"The Star-Spangled Banner" was ordered played by the military and naval services by Pres. Woodrow Wilson in 1916. It was designated the national anthem by Act of Congress, Mar. 3, 1931. The words were written by Francis Scott Key, of Georgetown, MD, during the bombardment of Fort McHenry, Baltimore, Sept. 13-14, 1814. Key was a lawyer, a graduate of St. John's College, Annapolis, and a volunteer in a light artillery company. When a friend, Dr. Beanes, a Maryland physician, was taken aboard Admiral Cockburn's British squadron for interfering with ground troops, Key and J. S. Skinner, carrying a note from Pres. Madison, went to the fleet under a flag of truce on a cartel ship to ask Beanes's release. Cockburn consented, but as the fleet was about to sail up the Patapsco to bombard Fort McHenry, he detained them, first on HMS *Surprise* and then on a supply ship.

Key witnessed the bombardment from his own vessel. It began at 7 AM, Sept. 13, 1814, and lasted, with intermissions, for 25 hr. The British fired more than 1,500 shells, each weighing as much as 220 lb. They were unable to approach closely because the U.S. had sunk 22 vessels. Only 4 Americans were killed and 24 wounded. A British bomb-ship was disabled.

During the event, Key wrote a stanza on the back of an envelope. Next day at Indian Queen Inn, Baltimore, he wrote out the poem and gave it to his brother-in-law, Judge J. H. Nicholson. Nicholson suggested use of the tune, "Anacreon in Heaven" (attributed to a British composer named John Stafford Smith), and had the poem printed on broadsides, of which 2 survive. On Sept. 20 it appeared in the *Baltimore American*. Later Key made 3 copies; one is in the Library of Congress, and one in the Pennsylvania Historical Society. The copy Key wrote on Sept. 14 remained in the Nicholson family for 93 years. In 1907 it was sold to Henry Walters of Baltimore. In 1934 it was bought at auction by the Walters Art Gallery, Baltimore, for $26,400. In 1953 it was sold to the Maryland Historical Society for the same price.

The flag that Key saw during the bombardment is preserved in the Smithsonian Institution, Washington, DC. It measures 30 by 42 ft and has 15 alternating red and white stripes and 15 stars, for the original 13 states plus Kentucky and Vermont. It was made by Mary Young Pickersgill. The Baltimore Flag House, a museum, occupies her premises, which were restored in 1953.

WORLD ALMANAC QUICK QUIZ

Which amendment to the U.S. Constitution repealed prohibition?

(a) 14th amendment   (b) 16th amendment
(c) 18th amendment   (d) 21st amendment

For the answer look in this chapter, or see page 1008.

The Star-Spangled Banner

I

Oh, say can you see by the dawn's early light
What so proudly we hailed at the twilight's last gleaming?
Whose broad stripes and bright stars thru the perilous fight,
O'er the ramparts we watched were so gallantly streaming?
And the rocket's red glare, the bombs bursting in air,
Gave proof through the night that our flag was still there.
Oh, say does that star-spangled banner yet wave
O'er the land of the free and the home of the brave?

II

On the shore, dimly seen through the mists of the deep,
Where the foe's haughty host in dread silence reposes,
What is that which the breeze, o'er the towering steep,
As it fitfully blows, half conceals, half discloses?
Now it catches the gleam of the morning's first beam,
In full glory reflected now shines in the stream:
'Tis the star-spangled banner! Oh long may it wave
O'er the land of the free and the home of the brave!

III

And where is that band who so vauntingly swore
That the havoc of war and the battle's confusion,
A home and a country should leave us no more!
Their blood has washed out their foul footsteps' pollution.
No refuge could save the hireling and slave
From the terror of flight, or the gloom of the grave:
And the star-spangled banner in triumph doth wave
O'er the land of the free and the home of the brave!

IV

Oh! thus be it ever, when freemen shall stand
Between their loved home and the war's desolation!
Blest with victory and peace, may the heav'n rescued land
Praise the Power that hath made and preserved us a nation.
And this be our motto: "In God is our trust."
Then conquer we must, when our cause it is just,
And the star-spangled banner in triumph shall wave,
O'er the land of the free and the home of the brave!

America (My Country 'Tis of Thee)

First sung in public on July 4, 1831, at a service in the Park Street Church, Boston, the words were written by Rev. Samuel Francis Smith, a Baptist clergyman, who set them to a melody he found in a German songbook, unaware that it was the tune for the British anthem, "God Save the King/Queen."

My country, 'tis of thee,
Sweet land of liberty,
Of thee I sing.
Land where my fathers died!
Land of the Pilgrims' pride!
From ev'ry mountainside,
Let freedom ring!

My native country, thee,
Land of the noble free,
Thy name I love.
I love thy rocks and rills,
Thy woods and templed hills;
My heart with rapture thrills
Like that above.

Let music swell the breeze,
And ring from all the trees
Sweet freedom's song.
Let mortal tongues awake;
Let all that breathe partake;
Let rocks their silence break,
The sound prolong.

Our fathers' God, to Thee,
Author of liberty,
To Thee we sing.
Long may our land be bright
With freedom's holy light;
Protect us by Thy might,
Great God, our King!

America, the Beautiful

Words composed by Katharine Lee Bates, a Massachusetts educator and author, in 1893, inspired by the view she experienced atop Pikes Peak. The final form was established in 1911, and it is set to the music of Samuel A. Ward's "Materna."

O beautiful for spacious skies.
For amber waves of grain,
For purple mountain majesties
Above the fruited plain.
America! America!
God shed His grace on thee,
And crown thy good with
  brotherhood
From sea to shining sea.

O beautiful for pilgrim feet
Whose stern impassion'd stress
A thorough-fare for freedom
  beat
Across the wilderness.
America! America!
God mend thine ev'ry flaw,
Confirm thy soul in self control,
Thy liberty in law.

O beautiful for heroes prov'd
In liberating strife,
Who more than self their
  country lov'd
And mercy more than life.
America! America!
May God thy gold refine
Till all success be nobleness,
And ev'ry gain divine.

O beautiful for patriot dream
That sees beyond the years,
Thine alabaster cities gleam,
Undimmed by human tears.
America! America!
God shed His grace on thee,
And crown thy good with
  brotherhood
From sea to shining sea.

The Liberty Bell: Its History and Significance

The Liberty Bell is housed in Independence National Historical Park, Philadelphia.

The original bell was ordered by Assembly Speaker and Chairman of the State House Superintendents Isaac Norris and was ordered from Thomas Lester, Whitechapel Foundry, London. It reached Philadelphia at the end of August 1752. It bore an inscription from Leviticus 25:10: "PROCLAIM LIBERTY THROUGHOUT ALL THE LAND UNTO ALL THE INHABITANTS THEREOF."

The bell was cracked by a stroke of its clapper in Sept. 1752 while it hung on a truss in the State House yard for testing. Pass & Stow, Philadelphia founders, recast the bell, adding 1 ½ ounces of copper to a pound of the original "Whitechapel" metal to reduce its high tone and brittleness. It was found that the bell contained too much copper, injuring its tone, so Pass & Stow recast it again, this time successfully.

In June 1753 the bell was hung in the old wooden steeple of the State House. In use while the Continental Congress was in session in the State House, it rang out in defiance of British tax and trade restrictions, and it proclaimed the Boston Tea Party and the first public reading of the Declaration of Independence.

On Sept. 18, 1777, when the British Army was about to occupy Philadelphia, the Liberty Bell was moved in a baggage train of the American Army to Allentown, PA, where it was hidden until June 27, 1778. The bell was moved back to Philadelphia after the British left the city.

In July 1781 the wooden steeple became insecure and had to be taken down. The bell was lowered into the brick section of the tower, where it remained until 1828. Between 1828 and 1844 the old State House bell continued to ring during special occasions. It rang for the last time on Feb. 23, 1846. In 1852 it was placed on exhibition in the Declaration Chamber of Independence Hall.

In 1876, when many thousands of Americans visited Philadelphia for the Centennial Exposition, the bell was placed in its old wooden support in the tower hallway. In 1877 it was hung from the ceiling of the tower by a chain of 13 links. It was returned again to the Declaration Chamber and in 1896 taken back to the tower hall, where it occupied a glass case. In 1915 the case was removed so that the public might touch it. On Jan. 1, 1976, just after midnight to mark the opening of the Bicentennial Year, the bell was moved to a new glass and steel pavilion behind Independence Hall for easier viewing.

The measurements of the bell are: circumference around the lip, 12 ft ½ in; circumference around the crown, 6 ft 11 ¼ in; lip to the crown, 3 ft; height over the crown, 2 ft 3 in; thickness at lip, 3 in; thickness at crown, 1 ¼ in; weight, 2,080 lb; length of clapper, 3 ft 2 in.

The specific source of the crack in the bell is unknown.

Statue of Liberty National Monument

Since 1886, the Statue of Liberty, formally known as "Liberty Enlightening the World," has stood as a symbol of freedom in New York harbor. It also commemorates French-American friendship, for it was given by the people of France and designed by French sculptor Frederic Auguste Bartholdi (1834-1904).

On Washington's Birthday, Feb. 22, 1877, Congress approved the use of a site on Bedloe's Island suggested by Bartholdi. This island of 12 acres had been owned in the 17th century by a Walloon named Isaac Bedloe. It was called Bedloe's until Aug. 3, 1956, when Pres. Dwight Eisenhower approved a measure changing the name to Liberty Island.

The statue was finished on May 21, 1884, and presented to the U.S. minister to France, Levi Parsons Morton, July 4, 1884, by Ferdinand de Lesseps, head of the Franco-American Union, promoter of the Panama Canal, and builder of the Suez Canal.

On Aug. 5, 1884, the Americans laid the cornerstone for the pedestal, to be built on the foundations of Fort Wood, erected by the government in 1811. The American committee had raised $125,000, but this was inadequate. Joseph Pulitzer, owner of the *New York World*, appealed on Mar. 16, 1885, for general donations. By Aug. 11, 1885, he had raised $100,000. The statue itself arrived dismantled, in 214 packing cases, from Rouen, France, in June 1885. The last rivet of the statue was driven on Oct. 28, 1886, when Pres. Grover Cleveland dedicated the monument.

The Statue of Liberty National Monument was designated as such in 1924. It is administered by the National Park Service. A $2.5 million building housing the American Museum of Immigration was opened by Pres. Richard Nixon on Sept. 26, 1972, at the base of the statue. It houses a permanent exhibition tracing the history of American immigration.

Four years of restoration work funded and led by the Statue of Liberty-Ellis Island Foundation were completed before the statue's 1986 centennial. Among other repairs, the $87 million project included replacing the 1,600 wrought iron bands that hold the statue's copper skin to its frame, replacing its torch, and installing an elevator. A 4-day "Liberty Weekend" extravaganza of concerts, tall ships, ethnic festivals, and fireworks, July 3-6, 1986, celebrated the 100th anniversary. Chief Justice Warren E. Burger swore in 5,000 new citizens on Ellis Island, while 20,000 others across the country were sworn in through a satellite telecast. Other ceremonies followed on Oct. 28, 1986, the statue's exact 100th birthday.

Following the Sept. 11 terrorist attacks, Liberty Island was closed to visitors. On Dec. 20, 2001, the Secretary of the Interior reopened the island after installing airport-type screening facilities at passenger embarkation areas at Battery Park in Manhattan and Liberty State Park in New Jersey.

To open the statue, the federal government needed to increase security throughout the park. In addition to federally funded security upgrades, significant safety improvements were made to meet building codes. The National Park Service turned to the Statue of Liberty-Ellis Island Foundation, which began a fund-raising campaign to finance safety renovations inside the statue, additional exits, improved handicapped access, and upgraded fire suppression and emergency warning systems. It was estimated that by the end of 2004, the federal investment in upgrades would come to $30 million, with the private sector contributing an additional $6.7 million.

Access to the statue was finally restored on Aug. 3, 2004. The delay in opening the statue attracted some controversy. An independent review committee commissioned by the Foundation disputed media reports that the opening had been unduly delayed, but recommended that the Foundation "reassess its mission . . . and executive compensation structure." In April 2004, the Senate Finance Committee began its own review.

Two tours are now available (they must be reserved in advance). Reservations are available by visiting www.statue reservations.com or by calling 1-866-STATUE4. A limited number of "walk up" reservations are also available at ferry embarkation areas. The "Observatory Tour" goes up the pedestal by elevator to a panoramic observation deck; also on that level is a view of the statue's interior. The "Promenade Tour" goes along the promenade above the fort on which the statue and pedestal were built. Both tours are ranger-guided and include a visit to the original torch, taken down during renovation in the 1980s, and the museum. The entire statue above the pedestal, including the crown, remains closed. (For more information, visit www.nps.gov/stli and www.statueofliberty.org)

Statue Statistics

The statue weighs 450,000 lb, or 225 tons. The copper sheeting weighs 200,000 lb. There are 167 steps from the land level to the top of the pedestal, 168 steps inside the statue to the head, and 54 rungs on the ladder leading to the arm that holds the torch.

	Ft.	In.		Ft.	In.		Ft.	In.
Height from base to torch	151	1	Size of finger nail, 13x10 in.			Right arm, max. thickness	12	0
Foundation of pedestal to torch	305	1	Head from chin to cranium	17	3	Thickness of waist	35	0
Heel to top of head	111	1	Head thickness, ear to ear	10	0	Width of mouth	3	0
Length of hand	16	5	Length of nose	4	6	Tablet, length	23	7
Index finger	8	0	Right arm, length	42	0	Table, width	13	7

Emma Lazarus's Famous Poem

Engraved on pedestal below the statue.

The New Colossus

Not like the brazen giant of Greek fame,
With conquering limbs astride from land to land;
Here at our sea-washed, sunset gates shall stand
A mighty woman with a torch, whose flame
Is the imprisoned lightning, and her name
Mother of Exiles. From her beacon-hand
Glows world-wide welcome; her mild eyes command
The air-bridged harbor that twin cities frame.
"Keep ancient lands, your storied pomp!" cries she
With silent lips. "Give me your tired, your poor,
Your huddled masses yearning to breathe free,
The wretched refuse of your teeming shore.
Send these, the homeless, tempest-tost to me,
I lift my lamp beside the golden door!"

Ellis Island

Ellis Island was the gateway to America for over 12 million immigrants between 1892 and 1924. In the late 18th century, Samuel Ellis, a New York City merchant, purchased the island and gave it his name. From Ellis, it passed to New York State, and the U.S. government bought it in 1808. On Jan. 1, 1892, the government opened the first federal immigration center in the U.S. there. The 27½-acre site eventually supported more than 35 buildings, including the Main Building with its Great Hall, in which as many as 5,000 people a day were processed.

Closed as an immigration station in 1954, Ellis Island was proclaimed part of the Statue of Liberty National Monument in 1965 by Pres. Lyndon B. Johnson. After a 6-year, $170 million restoration project funded by the Statue of Liberty-Ellis Island Foundation, Ellis Island was reopened as a museum in 1990. Artifacts, historic photographs and documents, oral histories, and ethnic music depicting 400 years of American immigration are housed in the museum. The museum also includes The American Immigrant Wall of Honor® (www.wallofhonor.com), which is inscribed with more than 600,000 names that have been placed in tribute. Registrations are still being accepted for inclusion in the memorial.

The American Family Immigration History Center® opened in April 2001. It contains an electronic database of ship passenger arrival information through the Port of New York and Ellis Island from 1892 to 1924. Data on over 25 million individuals are available, as well as an interactive database which features a Living Family Archive, multimedia presentations on various immigration groups and patterns, reproductions of original ships' passenger manifests, and pictures of over 800 immigrant ships (www.ellisisland.org).

In 1998, the Supreme Court ruled that nearly 90% of the island (the 24.2 acres which are landfill) lies in New Jersey, while the original 3.3 acres, on which the museum is located, are in New York.

PRESIDENTS OF THE UNITED STATES

U.S. Presidents

No.	Name	Politics	Born	in	Inaug.	at age	Died	at age
1.	George Washington	Fed.	1732, Feb. 22	VA	1789	57	1799, Dec. 14	67
2.	John Adams	Fed.	1735, Oct. 30	MA	1797	61	1826, July 4	90
3.	Thomas Jefferson	Dem.-Rep.	1743, Apr. 13	VA	1801	57	1826, July 4	83
4.	James Madison	Dem.-Rep.	1751, Mar. 16	VA	1809	57	1836, June 28	85
5.	James Monroe	Dem.-Rep.	1758, Apr. 28	VA	1817	58	1831, July 4	73
6.	John Quincy Adams	Dem.-Rep.	1767, July 11	MA	1825	57	1848, Feb. 23	80
7.	Andrew Jackson	Dem.	1767, Mar. 15	SC	1829	61	1845, June 8	78
8.	Martin Van Buren	Dem.	1782, Dec. 5	NY	1837	54	1862, July 24	79
9.	William Henry Harrison	Whig	1773, Feb. 9	VA	1841	68	1841, Apr. 4	68
10.	John Tyler	Whig	1790, Mar. 29	VA	1841	51	1862, Jan. 18	71
11.	James Knox Polk	Dem.	1795, Nov. 2	NC	1845	49	1849, June 15	53
12.	Zachary Taylor	Whig	1784, Nov. 24	VA	1849	64	1850, July 9	65
13.	Millard Fillmore	Whig	1800, Jan. 7	NY	1850	50	1874, Mar. 8	74
14.	Franklin Pierce	Dem.	1804, Nov. 23	NH	1853	48	1869, Oct. 8	64
15.	James Buchanan	Dem.	1791, Apr. 23	PA	1857	65	1868, June 1	77
16.	Abraham Lincoln	Rep.	1809, Feb. 12	KY	1861	52	1865, Apr. 15	56
17.	Andrew Johnson	(1)	1808, Dec. 29	NC	1865	56	1875, July 31	66
18.	Ulysses Simpson Grant	Rep.	1822, Apr. 27	OH	1869	46	1885, July 23	63
19.	Rutherford Birchard Hayes	Rep.	1822, Oct. 4	OH	1877	54	1893, Jan. 17	70
20.	James Abram Garfield	Rep.	1831, Nov. 19	OH	1881	49	1881, Sept. 19	49
21.	Chester Alan Arthur	Rep.	1829, Oct. 5	VT	1881	50	1886, Nov. 18	57
22.	Grover Cleveland	Dem.	1837, Mar. 18	NJ	1885	47	1908, June 24	71
23.	Benjamin Harrison	Rep.	1833, Aug. 20	OH	1889	55	1901, Mar. 13	67
24.	Grover Cleveland	Dem.	1837, Mar. 18	NJ	1893	55	1908, June 24	71
25.	William McKinley	Rep.	1843, Jan. 29	OH	1897	54	1901, Sept. 14	58
26.	Theodore Roosevelt	Rep.	1858, Oct. 27	NY	1901	42	1919, Jan. 6	60
27.	William Howard Taft	Rep.	1857, Sept. 15	OH	1909	51	1930, Mar. 8	72
28.	Woodrow Wilson	Dem.	1856, Dec. 28	VA	1913	56	1924, Feb. 3	67
29.	Warren Gamaliel Harding	Rep.	1865, Nov. 2	OH	1921	55	1923, Aug. 2	57
30.	Calvin Coolidge	Rep.	1872, July 4	VT	1923	51	1933, Jan. 5	60
31.	Herbert Clark Hoover	Rep.	1874, Aug. 10	IA	1929	54	1964, Oct. 20	90
32.	Franklin Delano Roosevelt	Dem.	1882, Jan. 30	NY	1933	51	1945, Apr. 12	63
33.	Harry S. Truman	Dem.	1884, May 8	MO	1945	60	1972, Dec. 26	88
34.	Dwight David Eisenhower	Rep.	1890, Oct. 14	TX	1953	62	1969, Mar. 28	78
35.	John Fitzgerald Kennedy	Dem.	1917, May 29	MA	1961	43	1963, Nov. 22	46
36.	Lyndon Baines Johnson	Dem.	1908, Aug. 27	TX	1963	55	1973, Jan. 22	64
37.	Richard Milhous Nixon (2)	Rep.	1913, Jan. 9	CA	1969	56	1994, Apr. 22	81
38.	Gerald Rudolph Ford	Rep.	1913, July 14	NE	1974	61		
39.	Jimmy (James Earl) Carter	Dem.	1924, Oct. 1	GA	1977	52		
40.	Ronald Reagan	Rep.	1911, Feb. 6	IL	1981	69	2004, June 5	93
41.	George H. W. Bush	Rep.	1924, June 12	MA	1989	64		
42.	Bill (Wm. Jefferson) Clinton	Dem.	1946, Aug. 19	AR	1993	46		
43.	George W. Bush	Rep.	1946, July 6	CT	2001	54		

(1) Andrew Johnson was a Democrat, nominated vice president by Republicans, and elected with Lincoln on National Union ticket.
(2) Resigned Aug. 9, 1974.

U.S. Presidents, Vice Presidents, Congresses

President	Service	Vice President	Congresses
1. George Washington	Apr. 30, 1789—Mar. 3, 1797	1. John Adams	1, 2, 3, 4
2. John Adams	Mar. 4, 1797—Mar. 3, 1801	2. Thomas Jefferson	5, 6
3. Thomas Jefferson	Mar. 4, 1801—Mar. 3, 1805	3. Aaron Burr	7, 8
	Mar. 4, 1805—Mar. 3, 1809	4. George Clinton	9, 10
4. James Madison	Mar. 4, 1809—Mar. 3, 1813	(1)	11, 12
	Mar. 4, 1813—Mar. 3, 1817	5. Elbridge Gerry (2)	13, 14
5. James Monroe	Mar. 4, 1817—Mar. 3, 1825	6. Daniel D. Tompkins	15, 16, 17, 18
6. John Quincy Adams	Mar. 4, 1825—Mar. 3, 1829	7. John C. Calhoun	19, 20
7. Andrew Jackson	Mar. 4, 1829—Mar. 3, 1833	(3)	21, 22
	Mar. 4, 1833—Mar. 3, 1837	8. Martin Van Buren	23, 24
8. Martin Van Buren	Mar. 4, 1837—Mar. 3, 1841	9. Richard M. Johnson	25, 26
9. William Henry Harrison (4)	Mar. 4, 1841—Apr. 4, 1841	10. John Tyler	27
10. John Tyler	Apr. 6, 1841—Mar. 3, 1845		27, 28
11. James K. Polk	Mar. 4, 1845—Mar. 3, 1849	11. George M. Dallas	29, 30
12. Zachary Taylor (4)	Mar. 5, 1849—July 9, 1850	12. Millard Fillmore	31
13. Millard Fillmore	July 10, 1850—Mar. 3, 1853		31, 32
14. Franklin Pierce	Mar. 4, 1853—Mar. 3, 1857	13. William R. King (5)	33, 34
15. James Buchanan	Mar. 4, 1857—Mar. 3, 1861	14. John C. Breckinridge	35, 36
16. Abraham Lincoln	Mar. 4, 1861—Mar. 3, 1865	15. Hannibal Hamlin	37, 38
(4)	Mar. 4, 1865—Apr. 15, 1865	16. Andrew Johnson	39
17. Andrew Johnson	Apr. 15, 1865—Mar. 3, 1869		39, 40
18. Ulysses S. Grant	Mar. 4, 1869—Mar. 3, 1873	17. Schuyler Colfax	41, 42
	Mar. 4, 1873—Mar. 3, 1877	18. Henry Wilson (6)	43, 44
19. Rutherford B. Hayes	Mar. 4, 1877—Mar. 3, 1881	19. William A. Wheeler	45, 46
20. James A. Garfield (4)	Mar. 4, 1881—Sept. 19, 1881	20. Chester A. Arthur	47
21. Chester A. Arthur	Sept. 20, 1881—Mar. 3, 1885		47, 48
22. Grover Cleveland (7)	Mar. 4, 1885—Mar. 3, 1889	21. Thomas A. Hendricks (8)	49, 50
23. Benjamin Harrison	Mar. 4, 1889—Mar. 3, 1893	22. Levi P. Morton	51, 52
24. Grover Cleveland (7)	Mar. 4, 1893—Mar. 3, 1897	23. Adlai E. Stevenson	53, 54
25. William McKinley	Mar. 4, 1897—Mar. 3, 1901	24. Garret A. Hobart (9)	55, 56
(4)	Mar. 4, 1901—Sept. 14, 1901	25. Theodore Roosevelt	57
26. Theodore Roosevelt	Sept. 14, 1901—Mar. 3, 1905		57, 58
	Mar. 4, 1905—Mar. 3, 1909	26. Charles W. Fairbanks	59, 60
27. William H. Taft	Mar. 4, 1909—Mar. 3, 1913	27. James S. Sherman (10)	61, 62

President	Service	Vice President	Congresses
28. Woodrow Wilson	Mar. 4, 1913—Mar. 3, 1921	28. Thomas R. Marshall	63, 64, 65, 66
29. Warren G. Harding (4)	Mar. 4, 1921—Aug. 2, 1923	29. Calvin Coolidge	67
30. Calvin Coolidge	Aug. 3, 1923—Mar. 3, 1925		68
	Mar. 4, 1925—Mar. 3, 1929	30. Charles G. Dawes	69, 70
31. Herbert C. Hoover	Mar. 4, 1929—Mar. 3, 1933	31. Charles Curtis	71, 72
32. Franklin D. Roosevelt (11)	Mar. 4, 1933—Jan. 20, 1941	32. John N. Garner	73, 74, 75, 76
	Jan. 20, 1941—Jan. 20, 1945	33. Henry A. Wallace	77, 78
(4)	Jan. 20, 1945—Apr. 12, 1945	34. Harry S. Truman	79
33. Harry S. Truman	Apr. 12, 1945—Jan. 20, 1949		79, 80
	Jan. 20, 1949—Jan. 20, 1953	35. Alben W. Barkley	81, 82
34. Dwight D. Eisenhower	Jan. 20, 1953—Jan. 20, 1961	36. Richard M. Nixon	83, 84, 85, 86
35. John F. Kennedy (4)	Jan. 20, 1961—Nov. 22, 1963	37. Lyndon B. Johnson	87, 88
36. Lyndon B. Johnson	Nov. 22, 1963—Jan. 20, 1965		88
	Jan. 20, 1965—Jan. 20, 1969	38. Hubert H. Humphrey	89, 90
37. Richard M. Nixon	Jan. 20, 1969—Jan. 20, 1973	39. Spiro T. Agnew (12)	91, 92, 93
(13)	Jan. 20, 1973—Aug. 9, 1974	40. Gerald R. Ford (14)	93
38. Gerald R. Ford (15)	Aug. 9, 1974—Jan. 20, 1977	41. Nelson A. Rockefeller (16)	93, 94
39. Jimmy (James Earl) Carter	Jan. 20, 1977—Jan. 20, 1981	42. Walter F. Mondale	95, 96
40. Ronald Reagan	Jan. 20, 1981—Jan. 20, 1989	43. George H. W. Bush	97, 98, 99, 100
41. George H. W. Bush	Jan. 20, 1989—Jan. 20, 1993	44. Dan Quayle	101, 102
42. Bill (Wm. Jefferson) Clinton	Jan. 20, 1993—Jan. 20, 2001	45. Al Gore	103, 104, 105, 106
43. George W. Bush	Jan. 20, 2001—	46. Richard Cheney	107, 108

(1) Died Apr. 20, 1812. (2) Died Nov. 23, 1814. (3) Resigned Dec. 28, 1832, to become U.S. senator. (4) Died in office. (5) Died Apr. 18, 1853. (6) Died Nov. 22, 1875. (7) Terms not consecutive. (8) Died Nov. 25, 1885. (9) Died Nov. 21, 1899. (10) Died Oct. 30, 1912. (11) First president to be inaugurated under 20th Amendment, Jan. 20, 1937. (12) Resigned Oct. 10, 1973. (13) Resigned Aug. 9, 1974. (14) First nonelected vice president, chosen under 25th Amendment procedure. (15) First president never elected president or vice president. (16) Second nonelected vice president, chosen under 25th Amendment.

Vice Presidents of the U.S.

The numerals given vice presidents do not coincide with those given presidents, because some presidents had none and some had more than one.

	Name	Birthplace	Year	Home	Inaug.	Politics	Place of death	Year	Age
1.	John Adams	Quincy, MA	1735	MA	1789	Fed.	Quincy, MA	1826	90
2.	Thomas Jefferson	Shadwell, VA	1743	VA	1797	Dem.-Rep.	Monticello, VA	1826	83
3.	Aaron Burr	Newark, NJ	1756	NY	1801	Dem.-Rep.	Staten Island, NY	1836	80
4.	George Clinton	Ulster Co., NY	1739	NY	1805	Dem.-Rep.	Washington, DC	1812	73
5.	Elbridge Gerry	Marblehead, MA	1744	MA	1813	Dem.-Rep.	Washington, DC	1814	70
6.	Daniel D. Tompkins	Scarsdale, NY	1774	NY	1817	Dem.-Rep.	Staten Island, NY	1825	51
7.	John C. Calhoun (1)	Abbeville, SC	1782	SC	1825	Dem.-Rep.	Washington, DC	1850	68
8.	Martin Van Buren	Kinderhook, NY	1782	NY	1833	Dem.	Kinderhook, NY	1862	79
9.	Richard M. Johnson (2)	Louisville, KY	1780	KY	1837	Dem.	Frankfort, KY	1850	70
10.	John Tyler	Greenway, VA	1790	VA	1841	Whig	Richmond, VA	1862	71
11.	George M. Dallas	Philadelphia, PA	1792	PA	1845	Dem.	Philadelphia, PA	1864	72
12.	Millard Fillmore	Summerhill, NY	1800	NY	1849	Whig	Buffalo, NY	1874	74
13.	William R. King	Sampson Co., NC	1786	AL	1853	Dem.	Dallas Co., AL	1853	67
14.	John C. Breckinridge	Lexington, KY	1821	KY	1857	Dem.	Lexington, KY	1875	54
15.	Hannibal Hamlin	Paris, ME	1809	ME	1861	Rep.	Bangor, ME	1891	81
16.	Andrew Johnson	Raleigh, NC	1808	TN	1865	(3)	Carter Co., TN	1875	66
17.	Schuyler Colfax	New York, NY	1823	IN	1869	Rep.	Mankato, MN	1885	62
18.	Henry Wilson	Farmington, NH	1812	MA	1873	Rep.	Washington, DC	1875	63
19.	William A. Wheeler	Malone, NY	1819	NY	1877	Rep.	Malone, NY	1887	68
20.	Chester A. Arthur	Fairfield, VT	1829	NY	1881	Rep.	New York, NY	1886	57
21.	Thomas A. Hendricks	Muskingum Co., OH	1819	IN	1885	Dem.	Indianapolis, IN	1885	66
22.	Levi P. Morton	Shoreham, VT	1824	NY	1889	Rep.	Rhinebeck, NY	1920	96
23.	Adlai E. Stevenson (4)	Christian Co., KY	1835	IL	1893	Dem.	Chicago, IL	1914	78
24.	Garret A. Hobart	Long Branch, NJ	1844	NJ	1897	Rep.	Paterson, NJ	1899	55
25.	Theodore Roosevelt	New York, NY	1858	NY	1901	Rep.	Oyster Bay, NY	1919	60
26.	Charles W. Fairbanks	Unionville Centre, OH	1852	IN	1905	Rep.	Indianapolis, IN	1918	66
27.	James S. Sherman	Utica, NY	1855	NY	1909	Rep.	Utica, NY	1912	57
28.	Thomas R. Marshall	N. Manchester, IN	1854	IN	1913	Dem.	Washington, DC	1925	71
29.	Calvin Coolidge	Plymouth, VT	1872	MA	1921	Rep.	Northampton, MA	1933	60
30.	Charles G. Dawes	Marietta, OH	1865	IL	1925	Rep.	Evanston, IL	1951	85
31.	Charles Curtis	Topeka, KS	1860	KS	1929	Rep.	Washington, DC	1936	76
32.	John Nance Garner	Red River Co., TX	1868	TX	1933	Dem.	Uvalde, TX	1967	98
33.	Henry Agard Wallace	Adair County, IA	1888	IA	1941	Dem.	Danbury, CT	1965	77
34.	Harry S. Truman	Lamar, MO	1884	MO	1945	Dem.	Kansas City, MO	1972	88
35.	Alben W. Barkley	Graves County, KY	1877	KY	1949	Dem.	Lexington, VA	1956	78
36.	Richard M. Nixon	Yorba Linda, CA	1913	CA	1953	Rep.	New York, NY	1994	81
37.	Lyndon B. Johnson	Johnson City, TX	1908	TX	1961	Dem.	San Antonio, TX	1973	64
38.	Hubert H. Humphrey	Wallace, SD	1911	MN	1965	Dem.	Waverly, MN	1978	66
39.	Spiro T. Agnew (5)	Baltimore, MD	1918	MD	1969	Rep.	Berlin, MD	1996	77
40.	Gerald R. Ford (6)	Omaha, NE	1913	MI	1973	Rep.			
41.	Nelson A. Rockefeller (7)	Bar Harbor, ME	1908	NY	1974	Rep.	New York, NY	1979	70
42.	Walter F. Mondale	Ceylon, MN	1928	MN	1977	Dem.			
43.	George H. W. Bush	Milton, MA	1924	TX	1981	Rep.			
44.	Dan Quayle	Indianapolis, IN	1947	IN	1989	Rep.			
45.	Al Gore	Washington, DC	1948	TN	1993	Dem.			
46.	Richard Cheney	Lincoln, NE	1941	WY	2001	Rep.			

(1) John C. Calhoun resigned Dec. 28, 1832, having been elected to the Senate to fill a vacancy. (2) Richard M. Johnson was the only vice president to be chosen by the Senate because of a tied vote in the Electoral College. (3) Andrew Johnson was a Democrat, nominated vice president by Republicans, and elected with Lincoln on the National Union Ticket. (4) Adlai E. Stevenson, 23rd vice president, was grandfather of Democratic candidate for president in 1952 and 1956. (5) Resigned Oct. 10, 1973. (6) First nonelected vice president, chosen under 25th Amendment procedure. (7) Second nonelected vice president, chosen under 25th Amendment.

Biographies of the Presidents

GEORGE WASHINGTON (1789-97), 1st president, Federalist, was born on Feb. 22, 1732, in Wakefield on Pope's Creek, Westmoreland Co., VA, the son of Augustine and Mary Ball Washington. He spent his early childhood on a farm near Fredericksburg. His father died when George was 11. He studied mathematics and surveying, and at 16, he went to live with his elder half brother, Lawrence, who built and named Mount Vernon. George surveyed the lands of Thomas Fairfax in the Shenandoah Valley, keeping a diary. He accompanied Lawrence to Barbados, West Indies, where he contracted smallpox and was deeply scarred. Lawrence died in 1752, and George inherited his property. He valued land, and when he died, he owned 70,000 acres in Virginia and 40,000 acres in what is now West Virginia. Washington's military service began in 1753, when Lt. Gov. Robert Dinwiddie of Virginia sent him on missions deep into Ohio country. He clashed with the French and had to surrender Fort Necessity on July 3, 1754. He was an aide to the British general Edward Braddock and was at his side when the army was ambushed and defeated (July 9, 1755) on a march to Fort Duquesne. He helped take Fort Duquesne from the French in 1758.

After Washington's marriage to Martha Dandridge Custis, a widow, in 1759, he managed his family estate at Mount Vernon. Although not at first for independence, he opposed the repressive measures of the British crown and took charge of the Virginia troops before war broke out. He was made commander of the newly created Continental Army by the Continental Congress on June 15, 1775.

The American victory was due largely to Washington's leadership. He was resourceful, a stern disciplinarian, and the one strong, dependable force for unity. Washington favored a federal government. He became chairman of the Constitutional Convention of 1787 and helped get the Constitution ratified. Unanimously elected president by the Electoral College, he was inaugurated Apr. 30, 1789, on the balcony of New York's Federal Hall. He was reelected in 1792. Washington made an effort to avoid partisan politics as president.

Refusing to consider a 3rd term, Washington retired to Mount Vernon in March 1797. He suffered acute laryngitis after a ride in snow and rain around his estate, was bled profusely, and died Dec. 14, 1799.

JOHN ADAMS (1797-1801), 2nd president, Federalist, was born on Oct. 30, 1735, in Braintree (now Quincy), MA, the son of John and Susanna Boylston Adams. He was a great-grandson of Henry Adams, who came from England in 1636. He graduated from Harvard in 1755 and then taught school and studied law. He married Abigail Smith in 1764. In 1765 he argued against taxation without representation before the royal governor. In 1770 he successfully defended in court the British soldiers who fired on civilians in the Boston Massacre. He was a delegate to the Continental Congress and a signer of the Declaration of Independence. In 1778, Congress sent Adams and John Jay to join Benjamin Franklin as diplomatic representatives in Europe. Because he ran second to Washington in Electoral College balloting in February 1789, Adams became the nation's first vice president, a post he characterized as highly insignificant; he was reelected in 1792.

In 1796 Adams was chosen president by the electors. His administration was marked by growing conflict with fellow Federalist Alexander Hamilton and with others in his own cabinet who supported Hamilton's strongly anti-French position. Adams avoided full-scale war with France, but became unpopular, especially after securing passage of the Alien and Sedition Acts in 1798. His foreign policy contributed significantly to the election of Thomas Jefferson in 1800.

Adams lived for a quarter century after he left office, during which time he wrote extensively. He died July 4, 1826, on the same day as his rival Thomas Jefferson (the 50th anniversary of the Declaration of Independence).

THOMAS JEFFERSON (1801-9), 3rd president, Democratic-Republican, was born on Apr. 13, 1743, in Shadwell in Goochland (now Albemarle) Co., VA, the son of Peter and Jane Randolph Jefferson. Peter died when Thomas was 14, leaving him 2,750 acres and his slaves. Jefferson attended (1760-62) the College of William and Mary, read Greek and Latin classics, and played the violin. In 1769 he was elected to the Virginia House of Burgesses. In 1770 he began building his home, Monticello, and in 1772 he married Martha Wayles Skelton, a wealthy widow. Jefferson helped establish the Virginia Committee of Correspondence. As a member of the Second Continental Congress he drafted the Declaration of Independence. He also was a member of the Virginia House of Delegates (1776-79) and was elected governor of Virginia in 1779, succeeding Patrick Henry. He was reelected in 1780 but resigned in 1781 after British troops invaded Virginia. During his term he wrote the statute on religious freedom. After his wife's death in 1782, Jefferson again became a delegate to the Congress, and in 1784 he drafted the report that was the basis for the Ordinances of 1784, 1785, and 1787. He was minister to France from 1785 to 1789, when George Washington appointed him secretary of state.

Jefferson's strong faith in the consent of the governed conflicted with the emphasis on executive control, favored by Alexander Hamilton, secretary of the Treasury, and Jefferson resigned on Dec. 31, 1793. In the 1796 election Jefferson was the Democratic-Republican candidate for president; John Adams won the election, and Jefferson became vice president. In 1800, Jefferson and Aaron Burr received equal Electoral College votes; the House of Representatives elected Jefferson president. Jefferson was a strong advocate of westward expansion; major events of his first term were the Louisiana Purchase (1803) and the Lewis and Clark Expedition. An important development during his second term was passage of the Embargo Act, barring U.S. ships from setting sail to foreign ports. Jefferson established the University of Virginia and designed its buildings. He died July 4, 1826, on the same day as John Adams (the 50th anniversary of the Declaration of Independence).

Following analysis of DNA taken from descendants of Jefferson and Sally Hemings, one of his slaves, it has been widely acknowledged that Jefferson fathered at least one, perhaps all, of her six known children.

JAMES MADISON (1809-17), 4th president Democratic-Republican, was born on Mar. 16, 1751, in Port Conway, King George Co., VA, the son of James and Eleanor Rose Conway Madison. Madison graduated from Princeton in 1771. He served in the Virginia Constitutional Convention (1776), and, in 1780, became a delegate to the Second Continental Congress. He was chief recorder at the Constitutional Convention in 1787 and supported ratification in the *Federalist Papers*, written with Alexander Hamilton and John Jay. In 1789, Madison was elected to the House of Representatives, where he helped frame the Bill of Rights and fought against passage of the Alien and Sedition Acts. In the 1790s, he helped found the Democratic-Republican Party, which ultimately became the Democratic Party. He became Jefferson's secretary of state in 1801.

Madison was elected president in 1808. His first term was marked by tensions with Great Britain, and his conduct of foreign policy was criticized by the Federalists and by his own party. Nevertheless, he was reelected in 1812, the year war was declared on Great Britain. The war that many considered a second American revolution ended with a treaty that settled none of the issues. Madison's most important action after the war was demilitarizing the U.S.-Canadian border.

► **IT'S A FACT:** Gilbert Stuart's 1797 portrait of George Washington, obtained by the White House in 1800 for $800, is the oldest possession located there. During the War of 1812, First Lady Dolley Madison saved the portrait by taking it with her while leaving the White House shortly before the British set it on fire.

In 1817, Madison retired to his estate, Montpelier, where he served as an elder statesman. He edited his famous papers on the Constitutional Convention and helped found the University of Virginia, of which he became rector in 1826. He died June 28, 1836.

JAMES MONROE (1817-25), 5th president, Democratic-Republican, was born on Apr. 28, 1758, in Westmoreland Co., VA, the son of Spence and Eliza Jones Monroe. He entered the College of William and Mary in 1774 but left to serve in the 3rd Virginia Regiment during the American Revolution. After the war, he studied law with Thomas Jefferson. In 1782 he was elected to the Virginia House of Delegates, and he served (1783-86) as a delegate to the Continental Congress. He opposed ratification of the Constitution because it lacked a bill of rights. Monroe was elected to the U.S. Senate in 1790. In 1794 President George Washington appointed Monroe minister to France. He served twice as governor of Virginia (1799-1802, 1811). President Jefferson also sent him to France as minister (1803), and from 1803 to 1807 he served as minister to Great Britain.

In 1816 Monroe was elected president; he was reelected in 1820 with all but one Electoral College vote. His administration became known as the Era of Good Feeling. He obtained Florida from Spain, settled boundary disputes with Britain over Canada, and eliminated border forts. He supported the antislavery position that led to the Missouri Compromise. His most significant contribution was the Monroe Doctrine, which opposed European intervention in the Western Hemisphere and became a cornerstone of U.S. foreign policy.

Although Monroe retired to Oak Hill, VA, financial problems forced him to sell his property and move to New York City. He died there on July 4, 1831.

JOHN QUINCY ADAMS (1825-29), 6th president, independent Federalist, later Democratic-Republican, was born on July 11, 1767, in Braintree (now Quincy), MA, the son of John and Abigail Adams. His father was the 2nd president. He studied abroad and at Harvard University, from which he graduated in 1787. In 1803, he was elected to the U.S. Senate. President Monroe chose him as his secretary of state in 1817. In this capacity he negotiated the cession of Florida from Spain, supported exclusion of slavery in the Missouri Compromise, and helped formulate the Monroe Doctrine. In 1824 Adams was elected president by the House of Representatives after he failed to win an Electoral College majority. His expansion of executive powers was strongly opposed, and in the 1828 election he lost to Andrew Jackson. In 1831 he entered the House of Representatives and served 17 years with distinction. He opposed slavery, the annexation of Texas, and the Mexican War. He helped establish the Smithsonian Institution.

Adams suffered a stroke in the House and died in the Speaker's Room on Feb. 23, 1848.

ANDREW JACKSON (1829-37), 7th president, Democratic-Republican, later a Democrat, was born on Mar. 15, 1767, in the Waxhaw district, on the border of North Carolina and South Carolina, the son of Andrew and Elizabeth Hutchinson Jackson. At the age of 13, he joined the militia to fight in the American Revolution and was captured. Orphaned at the age of 14, Jackson was brought up by a well-to-do uncle. By age 20, he was practicing law, and he later served as prosecuting attorney in Nashville, TN. In 1796 he helped draft the constitution of Tennessee, and for a year he occupied its one seat in the House of Representatives. The next year Jackson served in the U.S. Senate.

In the War of 1812, Jackson crushed (1814) the Creek Indians at Horseshoe Bend, AL, and, with an army consisting chiefly of backwoodsmen, defeated (1815) General Edward Pakenham's British troops at the Battle of New Orleans. In 1818 he briefly invaded Spanish Florida to quell Seminoles and outlaws who harassed frontier settlements. In 1824 he ran for president against John Quincy Adams. Although he won the most popular and electoral votes, he did not have a majority. The House of Representatives decided the election and chose Adams. In the 1828 election, however, Jackson defeated Adams, carrying the West and the South.

As president, Jackson introduced what became known as the spoils system—rewarding party members with government posts. Perhaps his most controversial act, however, was depositing federal funds in so-called pet banks, those directed by Democratic bankers, rather than in the Bank of the United States. "Let the people rule" was his slogan. In 1832, Jackson killed the congressional caucus for nominating presidential candidates and substituted the national convention. When South Carolina refused to collect imports under his protective tariff, he ordered army and naval forces to Charleston. After leaving office in 1837, he retired to the Hermitage, outside Nashville, where he died on June 8, 1845.

MARTIN VAN BUREN (1837-41), 8th president, Democrat, was born on Dec. 5, 1782, in Kinderhook, NY, the son of Abraham and Maria Hoes Van Buren. After attending local schools, he studied law and became a lawyer at the age of 20. A consummate politician, Van Buren began his career in the New York state senate and then served as state attorney general from 1816 to 1819. He was elected to the U.S. Senate in 1821. He helped swing eastern support to Andrew Jackson in the 1828 election and then served as Jackson's secretary of state from 1829 to 1831. In 1832 he was elected vice president. Known as the Little Magician, Van Buren was extremely influential in Jackson's administration.

In 1836, Van Buren defeated William Henry Harrison for president and took office as the financial panic of 1837 initiated a nationwide depression. Although he instituted the independent treasury system, his refusal to spend land revenues led to his defeat by William Henry Harrison in 1840. In 1844 he lost the Democratic nomination to James Knox Polk. In 1848 he again ran for president on the Free Soil ticket but lost. He died in Kinderhook on July 24, 1862.

WILLIAM HENRY HARRISON (1841), 9th president, Whig, who served only 31 days, was born on Feb. 9, 1773, in Berkeley, Charles City Co., VA, the son of Benjamin Harrison, a signer of the Declaration of Independence, and of Elizabeth Bassett Harrison. He attended Hampden-Sydney College. Harrison served as secretary of the Northwest Territory in 1798 and was its delegate to the House of Representatives in 1799. He was the first governor of the Indiana Territory and served as superintendent of Indian affairs. With 900 men he put down a Shawnee uprising at Tippecanoe, IN, on Nov. 7, 1811. A generation later, in 1840, he waged a rousing presidential campaign, using the slogan "Tippecanoe and Tyler too." The Tyler of the slogan was his running mate, John Tyler.

Although born to one of the wealthiest, most prestigious, and most influential families in Virginia, Harrison was elected president with a "log cabin and hard cider" slogan. He caught pneumonia during the inauguration and died Apr. 4, 1841, after only one month in office.

▶ **IT'S A FACT:** Early in its history, the White House was open to the public, especially after important events such as an inauguration. In 1829, after the inauguration of Andrew Jackson, the new "people's president," a rowdy crowd filled the mansion, ruining much of its furniture, carpets, and china. To escape the crowd, Jackson left through a window, and spent the night in a local hotel.

JOHN TYLER (1841-45), 10th president, independent Whig, was born on Mar. 29, 1790, in Greenway, Charles City Co., VA, the son of John and Mary Armistead Tyler. His father was governor of Virginia (1808-11). Tyler graduated from the College of William and Mary in 1807 and in 1811 was elected to the Virginia legislature. In 1816 he was chosen for the U.S. House of Representatives. He served in the Virginia legislature again from 1823 to 1825, when he was elected governor of Virginia. After a stint in the U.S. Senate (1827-36), he was elected vice president (1840).

When William Henry Harrison died only a month after taking office, Tyler succeeded him. Because he was the first person to occupy the presidency without having been elected to that office, he was referred to as "His Accidency." He gained passage of the Preemption Act of 1841, which gave squatters on government land the right to buy 160 acres at the minimum auction price. His last act as president was to sign a resolution annexing Texas. Tyler accepted renomination in 1844 from some Democrats but withdrew in favor of the official party candidate, James K. Polk. He died in Richmond, VA, on Jan. 18, 1862.

JAMES KNOX POLK (1845-49), 11th president, Democrat, was born on Nov. 2, 1795, in Mecklenburg Co., NC, the son of Samuel and Jane Knox Polk. He graduated from the University of North Carolina in 1818 and served in the Tennessee state legislature from 1823 to 1825. He served in the U.S. House of Representatives from 1825 to 1839, the last 4 years as Speaker. He was governor of Tennessee from 1839 to 1841. In 1844, after the Democratic National Convention became deadlocked, it nominated Polk, who became the first "dark horse" candidate for president. He was nominated primarily because he favored annexation of Texas.

As president, Polk reestablished the independent treasury system originated by Van Buren. He was so intent on acquiring California from Mexico that he sent troops to the Mexican border and, when Mexicans attacked, declared that a state of war existed. The Mexican War ended with the annexation of California and much of the Southwest as part of America's "manifest destiny." Polk compromised on the Oregon boundary ("54-40 or fight!") by accepting the 49th parallel and yielding Vancouver Island to the British. A few months after leaving office, Polk died in Nashville, TN, on June 15, 1849.

ZACHARY TAYLOR (1849-50), 12th president, Whig, who served only 16 months, was born on Nov. 24, 1784, in Orange Co., VA, the son of Richard and Sarah Strother Taylor. He grew up on his father's plantation near Louisville, KY, where he was educated by private tutors. In 1808 Taylor joined the regular army and was commissioned first lieutenant. He fought in the War of 1812, the Black Hawk War (1832), and the second Seminole War (beginning in 1837). He was called "Old Rough and Ready." In 1846 President Polk sent him with an army to the Rio Grande. When the Mexicans attacked him, Polk declared war. Outnumbered 4-1, Taylor defeated (1847) Santa Anna at Buena Vista.

A national hero, Taylor received the Whig nomination in 1848 and was elected president, even though he had never bothered to vote. He resumed the spoils system and, though a slaveholder, worked to admit California as a free state. He fell ill and died in office on July 9, 1850.

MILLARD FILLMORE (1850-53), 13th president, Whig, was born on Jan. 7, 1800, in Cayuga Co., NY, the son of Nathaniel and Phoebe Millard Fillmore. Although he had little schooling, he became a law clerk at the age of 22 and a year later was admitted to the bar. He was elected to the New York state assembly in 1828 and served until 1831. From 1833 until 1835 and again from 1837 to

1843, he represented his district in the U.S. House of Representatives. He opposed the entrance of Texas as a slave state and voted for a protective tariff. In 1844 he was defeated for governor of New York.

In 1848 he was elected vice president, and he succeeded as president after Taylor's death. Fillmore favored the Compromise of 1850 and signed the Fugitive Slave Law. His policies pleased neither expansionists nor slaveholders, and he was not renominated in 1852. In 1856 he was nominated by the American (Know-Nothing) Party, but despite the support of the Whigs, he was defeated by James Buchanan. He died in Buffalo, NY, on Mar. 8, 1874.

FRANKLIN PIERCE (1853-57), 14th president, Democrat, was born on Nov. 23, 1804, in Hillsboro, NH, the son of Benjamin Pierce, Revolutionary War general and governor of New Hampshire, and Anna Kendrick. He graduated from Bowdoin College in 1824 and was admitted to the bar in 1827. He was elected to the New Hampshire state legislature in 1829 and was chosen Speaker in 1831. He went to the U.S. House in 1833 and was elected a U.S. senator in 1837. He enlisted in the Mexican War and became brigadier general under Gen. Winfield Scott.

In 1852 Pierce was nominated as the Democratic presidential candidate on the 49th ballot. He decisively defeated Gen. Scott, his Whig opponent, in the election. Although against slavery, Pierce was influenced by pro-slavery Southerners. He supported the controversial Kansas-Nebraska Act, which left the question of slavery in the new territories of Kansas and Nebraska to popular vote. Pierce signed a reciprocity treaty with Canada and approved the Gadsden Purchase of a border area on a proposed railroad route, from Mexico. Denied renomination, he spent most of his remaining years in Concord, NH, where he died on Oct. 8, 1869.

JAMES BUCHANAN (1857-61), 15th president, Federalist, later Democrat, was born on Apr. 23, 1791, near Mercersburg, PA, the son of James and Elizabeth Speer Buchanan. He graduated from Dickinson College in 1809 and was admitted to the bar in 1812. He fought in the War of 1812 as a volunteer. He was twice elected to the Pennsylvania general assembly, and in 1821 he entered the U.S. House of Representatives. After briefly serving (1832-33) as minister to Russia, he was elected U.S. senator from Pennsylvania. As Polk's secretary of state (1845-49), he ended the Oregon dispute with Britain and supported the Mexican War and annexation of Texas. As minister to Great Britain, he signed the Ostend Manifesto (1854), declaring a U.S. right to take Cuba by force should efforts to purchase it fail.

Nominated by Democrats, Buchanan was elected president in 1856. On slavery he favored popular sovereignty and choice by state constitutions but did not consistently uphold this position. He denied the right of states to secede but opposed coercion and attempted to keep peace by not provoking secessionists. Buchanan left office having failed to deal decisively with the situation. He died at Wheatland, his estate, near Lancaster, PA, on June 1, 1868.

ABRAHAM LINCOLN (1861-65), 16th president, Republican, was born on Feb. 12, 1809, in a log cabin on a farm then in Hardin Co., KY, now in Larue, the son of Thomas and Nancy Hanks Lincoln. The Lincolns moved to Spencer Co., IN, near Gentryville, when Abe was 7. After Abe's mother died, his father married (1819) Mrs. Sarah Bush Johnston. In 1830 the family moved to Macon Co., IL.

Defeated in 1832 in a race for the state legislature, Lincoln was elected on the Whig ticket 2 years later and served in the lower house from 1834 to 1842. In 1837 Lincoln was admitted to the bar and became partner in a Springfield, IL, law office. He soon won recognition as an effective and resourceful

attorney. In 1846, he was elected to the House of Representatives, where he attracted attention during a single term for his opposition to the Mexican War and his position on slavery. In 1856 he campaigned for the newly founded Republican Party, and in 1858 he became its senatorial candidate against Stephen A. Douglas. Although he lost the election, Lincoln gained national recognition from his debates with Douglas.

In 1860, Lincoln was nominated for president by the Republican Party on a platform of restricting slavery. He ran against Douglas, a northern Democrat; John C. Breckinridge, a Southern proslavery Democrat; and John Bell, of the Constitutional Union Party. As a result of Lincoln's winning the election, South Carolina seceded from the Union on Dec. 20, 1860, followed in 1861 by 10 other Southern states.

The Civil War erupted when Fort Sumter, which Lincoln decided to resupply, was attacked by Confederate forces on Apr. 12, 1861. Lincoln called successfully for recruits from the North. On Sept. 22, 1862, 5 days after the Battle of Antietam, Lincoln announced that slaves in territory then in rebellion would be free Jan. 1, 1863, the date of the Emancipation Proclamation. His speeches, including his Gettysburg and Inaugural addresses, are remembered for their eloquence.

Lincoln was reelected, in 1864, over Gen. George B. McClellan, Democrat. Lee surrendered on Apr. 9, 1865. On Apr. 14, Lincoln was shot by actor John Wilkes Booth in Ford's Theater, in Washington, DC. He died the next day.

ANDREW JOHNSON (1865-69), 17th president, Democrat, was born on Dec. 29, 1808, in Raleigh, NC, the son of Jacob and Mary McDonough Johnson. He was apprenticed to a tailor as a youth, but ran away after two years and eventually settled in Greenville, TN. He became popular with the townspeople and in 1829 was elected councilman and later mayor. In 1835 he was sent to the state general assembly. In 1843 he was elected to the U.S. House of Representatives, where he served for 10 years. Johnson was governor of Tennessee from 1853 to 1857, when he was elected to the U.S. Senate. He supported John C. Breckinridge against Lincoln in the 1860 election. Although Johnson had held slaves, he opposed secession and tried to prevent Tennessee from seceding. In Mar. 1862, Lincoln appointed him military governor of occupied Tennessee.

In 1864, in order to balance Lincoln's ticket with a Southern Democrat, the Republicans nominated Johnson for vice president. He was elected vice president with Lincoln and then succeeded to the presidency upon Lincoln's death. Soon afterward, in a controversy with Congress over the president's power over the South, he proclaimed an amnesty to all Confederates, except certain leaders, if they would ratify the 13th Amendment abolishing slavery. States doing so added anti-Negro provisions that enraged Congress, which restored military control over the South. When Johnson removed Edwin M. Stanton, secretary of war, without notifying the Senate, the House, in Feb. 1868, impeached him. Charging him with thereby having violated the Tenure of Office Act, the House was actually responding to his opposition to harsh congressional Reconstruction, expressed in repeated vetoes. He was tried by the Senate, and in May, in two separate votes on different counts, was acquitted, both times by only one vote.

Johnson was denied renomination but remained politically active. He was reelected to the Senate in 1874. Johnson died July 31, 1875, at Carter Station, TN.

ULYSSES SIMPSON GRANT (1869-77), 18th president, Republican, was born on Apr. 27, 1822, in Point Pleasant, OH, the son of Jesse R. and Hannah Simpson Grant. The next year the family moved to Georgetown, OH. Grant was named Hiram Ulysses, but on entering West Point in 1839, his name was put down as Ulysses Simpson, and he adopted it. He graduated in 1843. During the Mexican War, Grant served under both Gen. Zachary Taylor and Gen. Winfield Scott. In 1854, he resigned his commission because of loneliness and

drinking problems, and in the following years he engaged in generally unsuccessful farming and business ventures. With the start of the Civil War, he was named colonel and then brigadier general of the Illinois Volunteers. He took Forts Henry and Donelson and fought at Shiloh. His brilliant campaign against Vicksburg and his victory at Chattanooga made him so prominent that Lincoln placed him in command of all Union armies. Grant accepted Lee's surrender at Appomattox Court House on Apr. 9, 1865. President Johnson appointed Grant secretary of war when he suspended Stanton, but Grant was not confirmed.

Grant was nominated for president by the Republicans in 1868 and elected over Horatio Seymour, Democrat. The 15th Amendment, the amnesty bill, and peaceful settlement of disputes with Great Britain were events of his administration. The Liberal Republicans and Democrats opposed him with Horace Greeley in the 1872 election, but Grant was reelected. His second administration was marked by scandals, including widespread corruption in the Treasury Department and the Indian Service. An attempt by the Stalwarts (Old Guard Republicans) to nominate him in 1880 failed. In 1884 the collapse of an investment firm in which he was a partner left him penniless. He wrote his personal memoirs while ill with cancer and completed them shortly before his death at Mt. McGregor, NY, on July 23, 1885.

RUTHERFORD BIRCHARD HAYES (1877-81), 19th president, Republican, was born on Oct. 4, 1822, in Delaware, OH, the son of Rutherford and Sophia Birchard Hayes. He was reared by his uncle, Sardis Birchard. Hayes graduated from Kenyon College in 1842 and from Harvard Law School in 1845. He practiced law in Lower Sandusky (now Fremont), OH, and was city solicitor of Cincinnati from 1858 to 1861. During the Civil War, he was major of the 23rd Ohio Volunteers. He was wounded several times, and by the end of the war he had risen to the rank of brevet major general. While serving (1865-67) in the U.S. House of Representatives, Hayes supported Reconstruction and Johnson's impeachment. He was twice elected governor of Ohio (1867, 1869). After losing a race for the U.S. House in 1872, he was reelected governor of Ohio in 1875.

In 1876, Hayes was nominated for president and believed he had lost the election to Samuel J. Tilden, Democrat. But a few Southern states submitted 2 sets of electoral votes, and the result was in dispute. An electoral commission, consisting of 8 Republicans and 7 Democrats, awarded all disputed votes to Hayes, allowing him to become president by one electoral vote. Hayes, keeping a promise to southerners, withdrew troops from areas still occupied in the South, ending the era of Reconstruction. He proposed civil service reforms, alienating those favoring the spoils system, and advocated repeal of the Tenure of Office Act restricting presidential power to dismiss officials. He supported sound money and specie payments.

Hayes died in Fremont, OH, on Jan. 17, 1893.

JAMES ABRAM GARFIELD (1881), 20th president, Republican, was born on Nov. 19, 1831, in Orange, Cuyahoga Co., OH, the son of Abram and Eliza Ballou Garfield. His father died in 1833, and he was reared in poverty by his mother. He worked as a canal bargeman, a farmer, and a carpenter and managed to secure a college education. He taught at Hiram College and later became principal. In 1859 he was elected to the Ohio legislature. Antislavery and antisecession, he volunteered for military service in the Civil War, becoming colonel of the 42nd Ohio Infantry and brigadier in 1862. He fought at Shiloh, was chief of staff for Gen. William Starke Rosecrans, and was made major general for gallantry at Chickamauga. He entered Congress as a radical Republican in 1863, calling for execution or exile of Confederate leaders, but he moderated his views after the Civil War. On the electoral commission in 1877 he voted for Hayes against Tilden on strict party lines.

Garfield was a senator-elect in 1880 when he became the Republican nominee for president. He was chosen as a compromise over Gen. Grant, James G. Blaine, and John Sherman, and won election despite some bitterness among Grant's supporters. Much of his brief tenure as president was concerned with a fight with New York Sen. Roscoe Conkling, who opposed two major appointments made by Garfield. On July 2, 1881, Garfield was shot and seriously wounded by a mentally disturbed office-seeker, Charles J. Guiteau, while entering a railroad station in Washington, DC. He died on Sept. 19, 1881, in Elberon, NJ.

CHESTER ALAN ARTHUR (1881-85), 21st president, Republican, was born on Oct. 5, 1829, in Fairfield, VT, to William and Malvina Stone Arthur. He graduated from Union College in 1848, taught school in Vermont, then studied law and practiced in New York City. In 1853 he argued in a fugitive slave case that slaves transported through New York state were thereby freed. In 1871, he was appointed collector of the Port of New York. President Hayes, an opponent of the spoils system, forced him to resign in 1878. This made the New York machine enemies of Hayes. Arthur and the Stalwarts (Old Guard Republicans) tried to nominate Grant for a 3rd term as president in 1880. When Garfield was nominated, Arthur was nominated for vice president in the interests of harmony.

Upon Garfield's assassination, Arthur became president. Despite his past connections, he signed major civil service reform legislation. Arthur tried to dissuade Congress from enacting the high protective tariff of 1883. He was defeated for renomination in 1884 by James G. Blaine. He died in New York City on Nov. 18, 1886.

GROVER CLEVELAND (1885-89; 1893-97) *(According to a ruling of the State Dept., Grover Cleveland should be counted as both the 22nd and the 24th president, because his 2 terms were not consecutive.)* Grover Cleveland, Democrat, was born Stephen Grover Cleveland on Mar. 18, 1837, in Caldwell, NJ, the son of Richard F. and Ann Neal Cleveland. When he was a small boy, his family moved to New York. Prevented by his father's death from attending college, he studied by himself and was admitted to the bar in Buffalo, NY, in 1859. In succession he became assistant district attorney (1863), sheriff (1871), mayor (1881), and governor of New York (1882). He was an independent, honest administrator who hated corruption. Cleveland was nominated for president over Tammany Hall opposition in 1884 and defeated Republican James G. Blaine.

As president, he enlarged the civil service and vetoed many pension raids on the Treasury. In the 1888 election he was defeated by Benjamin Harrison, although his popular vote was larger. Reelected over Harrison in 1892, he faced a money crisis brought about by a lowered gold reserve, circulation of paper, and exorbitant silver purchases under the Sherman Silver Purchase Act. He obtained a repeal of the Sherman Act, but was unable to secure effective tariff reform. A severe economic depression and labor troubles racked his administration, but he refused to interfere in business matters and rejected Jacob Coxey's demand for unemployment relief. In 1894, he broke the Pullman strike. Cleveland was not renominated in 1896. He died in Princeton, NJ, on June 24, 1908.

BENJAMIN HARRISON (1889-93), 23rd president, Republican, was born on Aug. 20, 1833, in North Bend, OH, the son of John Scott and Elizabeth Irwin Harrison. His great-grandfather, Benjamin Harrison, was a signer of the Declaration of Independence; his grandfather, William Henry Harrison, was 9th president; his father was a member of Congress. He attended school on his father's farm and graduated from Miami University in Oxford, OH, in 1852. He was admitted to the bar in 1854 and practiced in Indianapolis. During the Civil War, he rose to the rank of brevet

brigadier general and fought at Kennesaw Mountain, at Peachtree Creek, at Nashville, and in the Atlanta campaign. He lost the 1876 gubernatorial election in Indiana but succeeded in becoming a U.S. senator in 1881.

In 1888 he defeated Cleveland for president despite receiving fewer popular votes. As president, he expanded the pension list and signed the McKinley high tariff bill, the Sherman Antitrust Act, and the Sherman Silver Purchase Act. During his administration, 6 states were admitted to the Union. He was defeated for reelection in 1892. He died in Indianapolis on Mar. 13, 1901.

WILLIAM MCKINLEY (1897-1901), 25th president, Republican, was born on Jan. 29, 1843, in Niles, OH, the son of William and Nancy Allison McKinley. McKinley briefly attended Allegheny College. When the Civil War broke out in 1861, he enlisted and served for the duration. He rose to captain and in 1865 was made brevet major. After studying law in Albany, NY, he opened (1867) a law office in Canton, OH. He served twice in the U.S. House (1877-83; 1885-91) and led the fight there for the McKinley Tariff, passed in 1890; he was not reelected to the House as a result. He served two terms (1892-96) as governor of Ohio.

In 1896 he was elected president as a proponent of a protective tariff and sound money (gold standard), over William Jennings Bryan, the Democrat and a proponent of free silver. McKinley was reluctant to intervene in Cuba, but the loss of the battleship *Maine* at Havana crystallized opinion. He demanded Spain's withdrawal from Cuba; Spain made some concessions, but Congress announced a state of war as of Apr. 21, 1898. He was reelected in the 1900 campaign, defeating Bryan's anti-imperialist arguments with the promise of a "full dinner pail." McKinley was respected for his conciliatory nature and for his conservative stance on business issues. On Sept. 6, 1901, while welcoming citizens at the Pan-American Exposition, in Buffalo, NY, he was shot by Leon Czolgosz, an anarchist. He died Sept. 14.

THEODORE ROOSEVELT (1901-9), 26th president, Republican, was born on Oct. 27, 1858, in New York City, the son of Theodore and Martha Bulloch Roosevelt. He was a 5th cousin of Franklin D. Roosevelt and an uncle of Eleanor Roosevelt. Roosevelt graduated from Harvard University in 1880. He attended Columbia Law School briefly but abandoned law to enter politics. He was elected to the New York state assembly in 1881 and served until 1884. He spent the next 2 years ranching and hunting in the Dakota Territory. In 1886, he ran unsuccessfully for mayor of New York City. He was Civil Service commissioner in Washington, DC, from 1889 to 1895. From 1895 to 1897, he served as New York City's police commissioner. He was assistant secretary of the navy under McKinley. The Spanish-American War made him nationally known. He organized the 1st U.S. Volunteer Cavalry (Rough Riders) and, as lieutenant colonel, led the charge up Kettle Hill in San Juan. Elected New York governor in 1898, he fought the spoils system and achieved taxation of corporation franchises.

Nominated for vice president in 1900, he became the nation's youngest president when McKinley was assassinated. He was reelected in 1904. As president he fought corruption of politics by big business, dissolved the Northern Securities Co. and others for violating antitrust laws, intervened in the 1902 coal strike on behalf of the public, obtained the Elkins Law (1903) forbidding rebates to favored corporations, and helped pass the Hepburn Railway Rate Act of 1906 (extending jurisdiction of the Interstate Commerce Commission). He helped obtain passage of the Pure Food and Drug Act (1906), and of employers' liability laws. Roosevelt vigorously organized conservation efforts. He mediated (1905) the peace between Japan and Russia, for which he won the Nobel Peace Prize. He abetted the 1903 revolution in Panama that led to U.S. acquisition of territory for the Panama Canal.

In 1908 Roosevelt obtained the nomination of William H. Taft, who was elected. Feeling that Taft had abandoned his policies, he unsuccessfully sought the nomination in 1912. He then ran on the Progressive "Bull Moose" ticket against Taft and Woodrow Wilson, splitting the Republicans and ensuring Wilson's election. He was shot during the campaign but recovered. In 1916, after unsuccessfully seeking the presidential nomination, he supported the Republican candidate, Charles E. Hughes. A strong friend of Britain, he fought for U.S. intervention in World War I. He wrote some 40 books, of which *The Winning of the West* is perhaps best known. He died Jan. 6, 1919, at Sagamore Hill, Oyster Bay, NY.

WILLIAM HOWARD TAFT (1909-13), 27th president, Republican, and 10th chief justice of the U.S., was born on Sept. 15, 1857, in Cincinnati, OH, the son of Alphonso and Louisa Maria Torrey Taft. His father was secretary of war and attorney general in Grant's cabinet and minister to Austria and Russia under Arthur. Taft graduated from Yale in 1878 and from Cincinnati Law School in 1880. After working as a law reporter for Cincinnati newspapers, he served as assistant prosecuting attorney (1881-82), assistant county solicitor (1885), judge, superior court (1887), U.S. solicitor-general (1890), and federal circuit judge (1892). In 1900 he became head of the U.S. Philippines Commission and was the first civil governor of the Philippines (1901-4). In 1904 he served as secretary of war, and in 1906 he was sent to Cuba to help avert a threatened revolution. Taft was groomed for the presidency by Theodore Roosevelt and elected over William Jennings Bryan in 1908. Taft vigorously continued Roosevelt's trustbusting, instituted the Department of Labor, and drafted the amendments calling for direct election of senators and the income tax. His tariff and conservation policies angered progressives. Although renominated in 1912, he was opposed by Roosevelt, who ran on the Progressive Party ticket; the result was Democrat Woodrow Wilson's election.

Taft, with some reservations, supported the League of Nations. After leaving office, he was professor of constitutional law at Yale (1913-21) and chief justice of the U.S. (1921-30). Taft was the only person in U.S. history to have been both president and chief justice. He died in Washington, DC, on Mar. 8, 1930.

(THOMAS) WOODROW WILSON (1913-21), 28th president, Democrat, was born on Dec. 28, 1856, in Staunton, VA, the son of Joseph Ruggles and Janet (Jessie) Woodrow Wilson. He grew up in Georgia and South Carolina. He attended Davidson College in North Carolina before graduating from Princeton University in 1879. He studied law at the University of Virginia and political science at Johns Hopkins University, where he received his PhD in 1886. He taught at Bryn Mawr (1885-88) and then at Wesleyan (1888-90) before joining the faculty at Princeton. He was president of Princeton from 1902 until 1910, when he was elected governor of New Jersey. In 1912 he was nominated for president with the aid of William Jennings Bryan, who sought to block James "Champ" Clark and Tammany Hall. Wilson won because the Republican vote for Taft was split by the Progressives.

As president, Wilson protected American interests in revolutionary Mexico and fought for American rights on the high seas. He oversaw the creation of the Federal Reserve system, cut the tariff, and developed a reputation as a reformer. His sharp warnings to Germany led to the resignation of his secretary of state, Bryan, a pacifist. In 1916 he was reelected by a slim margin with the slogan, "He kept us out of war," although his attempts to mediate in the war failed. After several American ships had been sunk by the Germans, he secured a declaration of war against Germany on Apr. 6, 1917.

Wilson outlined his peace program on Jan. 8, 1918, in the Fourteen Points, a state paper that had worldwide influence. He enunciated a doctrine of self-determination for the settlement of territorial disputes. The Germans accepted his terms and an armistice on Nov. 11, 1918.

Wilson went to Paris to help negotiate the peace treaty, the crux of which he considered the League of Nations. The Senate demanded reservations that would not make the U.S. subordinate to the votes of other nations in case of war. Wilson refused and toured the country to get support. He suffered a stroke in Oct. 1919. An invalid, he clung to his office while his wife and doctors effectively functioned as president.

Wilson was awarded the 1919 Nobel Peace Prize, but the treaty embodying the League of Nations was ultimately rejected by the Senate in 1920. He left the White House in Mar. 1921. He died in Washington, DC, on Feb. 3, 1924.

WARREN GAMALIEL HARDING (1921-23), 29th president, Republican, was born on Nov. 2, 1865, near Corsica (now Blooming Grove), OH, the son of George Tyron and Phoebe Elizabeth Dickerson Harding. He attended Ohio Central College, studied law, and became editor and publisher of a county newspaper. He entered the political arena as state senator (1901-4) and then served as lieutenant governor (1904-6). In 1910 he ran unsuccessfully for governor of Ohio; then in 1914 he was elected to the U.S. Senate. In the Senate he voted for antistrike legislation, woman suffrage, and the Volstead Prohibition Enforcement Act over President Wilson's veto. He opposed the League of Nations. In 1920 he was nominated for president and defeated James M. Cox in the election. The Republicans capitalized on war weariness and fear that Wilson's League of Nations would curtail U.S. sovereignty.

Harding stressed a return to "normalcy" and worked for tariff revision and the repeal of excess profits law and high income taxes. His secretary of interior, Albert B. Fall, became involved in the Teapot Dome scandal. As rumors began to circulate about the corruption in his administration, Harding became ill while returning from a trip to Alaska, and he died in San Francisco on Aug. 2, 1923.

(JOHN) CALVIN COOLIDGE (1923-29), 30th president, Republican, was born on July 4, 1872, in Plymouth, VT, the son of John Calvin and Victoria J. Moor Coolidge. Coolidge graduated from Amherst College in 1895. He entered Republican state politics and served as mayor of Northampton, MA, as state senator, as lieutenant governor, and, in 1919, as governor. In Sept. 1919, Coolidge attained national prominence by calling out the state guard in the Boston police strike. He declared: "There is no right to strike against the public safety by anybody, anywhere, anytime." This brought his name before the Republican convention of 1920, where he was nominated for vice president.

Coolige succeeded to the presidency on Harding's death. As president, he opposed the League of Nations and the soldiers' bonus bill, which was passed over his veto. In 1924 he was elected to the presidency by a huge majority. He substantially reduced the national debt. He twice vetoed the McNary-Haugen farm bill, which would have provided relief to financially hard-pressed farmers.

With Republicans eager to renominate him, Coolidge simply announced, Aug. 2, 1927: "I do not choose to run for president in 1928." He died in Northampton, MA, on Jan. 5, 1933.

HERBERT CLARK HOOVER (1929-33), 31st president, Republican, was born on Aug. 10, 1874, in West Branch, IA, the son of Jesse Clark and Hulda Randall Minthorn Hoover. Hoover grew up in Indian Territory (now Oklahoma) and Oregon and graduated from Stanford University with a degree in geology in 1895. He worked briefly with the U.S. Geological Survey and then managed mines in Australia, Asia, Europe, and Africa. While chief engineer of imperial mines in China, he directed food relief for victims of the Boxer Rebellion. He gained a reputation not only as an engineer but as a humanitarian as he directed the American Relief Committee, London (1914-15) and the U.S. Commission for Relief in Belgium (1915-19). He was U.S.

Food Administrator (1917-19), American Relief Administrator (1918-23), and in charge of Russian Relief (1918-23). He served as secretary of commerce under both Harding and Coolidge. Some historians believe that he was the most effective secretary of commerce ever to hold that office.

In 1928 Hoover was elected president over Alfred E. Smith. In 1929 the stock market crashed, and the economy collapsed. During the Great Depression, Hoover inaugurated some government assistance programs, but he was opposed to administration of aid through a federal bureaucracy. As the effects of the depression continued, he was defeated in the 1932 election by Franklin D. Roosevelt. Hoover remained active after leaving office. President Truman named him coordinator of the European Food Program (1946) and chairman of the Commission on Organization of the Executive Branch (1947-49; 1953-55).

Hoover died in New York City on Oct. 20, 1964.

FRANKLIN DELANO ROOSEVELT (1933-45), 32nd president, Democrat, was born on Jan. 30, 1882, in Hyde Park, NY, the son of James and Sara Delano Roosevelt. He graduated from Harvard University in 1903. He attended Columbia University Law School without taking a degree and was admitted to the New York state bar in 1907. His political career began when he was elected to the New York state senate in 1910. In 1913 President Wilson appointed him assistant secretary of the navy, a post he held during World War I.

In 1920 Roosevelt ran for vice president with James Cox and was defeated. From 1921 to 1928 he worked in his New York law office and was also vice president of a bank. In Aug. 1921, he was stricken with poliomyelitis, which left his legs paralyzed. As a result of therapy he was able to stand, or walk a few steps, with the aid of leg braces.

Roosevelt served 2 terms as governor of New York (1929-33). In 1932, W. G. McAdoo, pledged to John N. Garner, threw his votes to Roosevelt, who was nominated for president. The Depression and the promise to repeal Prohibition ensured his election. He asked for emergency powers, proclaimed the New Deal, and put into effect a vast number of administrative changes. Foremost was the use of public funds for relief and public works, resulting in deficit financing. He greatly expanded the federal government's regulation of business and by an excess profits tax and progressive income taxes produced a redistribution of earnings on an unprecedented scale. He also promoted legislation establishing the Social Security system. He was the last president inaugurated on Mar. 4 (1933) and the first inaugurated on Jan. 20 (1937).

Roosevelt was the first president to use radio for "fireside chats." When the Supreme Court nullified some New Deal laws, he sought power to "pack" the Court with additional justices, but Congress refused to give him the authority. He was the first president to break the "no 3rd term" tradition (1940) and was elected to a 4th term in 1944, despite failing health.

Roosevelt was openly hostile to fascist governments before World War II and launched a lend-lease program on behalf of the Allies. With British Prime Min. Winston Churchill he wrote a declaration of principles to be followed after Nazi defeat (the Atlantic Charter of Aug. 14, 1941) and urged the Four Freedoms (freedom of speech, of worship, from want, from fear) Jan. 6, 1941. When Japan attacked Pearl Harbor on Dec. 7, 1941, the U.S. entered the war. Roosevelt guided the nation through the war and conferred with allied heads of state at Casablanca (Jan. 1943), Quebec (Aug. 1943), Tehran (Nov.-Dec. 1943), Cairo (Nov. and Dec. 1943), and Yalta (Feb. 1945).

Roosevelt did not, however, live to see the end of the war. He died of a cerebral hemorrhage in Warm Springs, GA, on Apr. 12, 1945.

HARRY S. TRUMAN (1945-53), 33rd president, Democrat, was born on May 8, 1884, in Lamar, MO, the son of John Anderson and Martha Ellen Young Truman. A family disagreement on whether his middle name should be Shipp or Solomon, after names of 2 grandfathers, resulted in his using only the middle initial S. After graduating from high school in Independence, MO, he worked (1901) for the *Kansas City Star,* as a railroad timekeeper, and as a clerk in Kansas City banks until about 1905. He ran his family's farm from 1906 to 1917. He served in France during World War I. After the war he opened a haberdashery shop, was a judge on the Jackson Co. Court (1922-24), and attended Kansas City School of Law (1923-25).

Truman was elected to the U.S. Senate in 1934 and re-elected in 1940. In 1944, with Roosevelt's backing, he was nominated for vice president and elected. On Roosevelt's death in 1945, Truman became president. In 1948, in a famous upset victory, he defeated Republican Thomas E. Dewey to win election to a new term.

Truman authorized the first uses of the atomic bomb (Hiroshima and Nagasaki, Aug. 6 and 9, 1945), bringing World War II to a rapid end. He was responsible for what came to be called the Truman Doctrine (to aid nations such as Greece and Turkey, threatened by Communist takeover), and his strong commitment to NATO and to the Marshall Plan helped bring them about. In 1948-49, he broke a Soviet blockade of West Berlin with a massive airlift. When Communist North Korea invaded South Korea (June 1950), he won UN approval for a "police action" and, boldly without prior congressional consent, sent in forces under Gen. Douglas MacArthur. When MacArthur opposed his policy of limited objectives, Truman removed him.

He died in Kansas City, MO, on Dec. 26, 1972.

DWIGHT DAVID EISENHOWER (1953-61), 34th president, Republican, was born on Oct. 14, 1890, in Denison, TX, the son of David Jacob and Ida Elizabeth Stover Eisenhower. He grew up on a small farm in Abilene, KS, and graduated from West Point in 1915. He was on the staff of Gen. Douglas MacArthur in the Philippines from 1935 to 1939. In 1942, he was made commander of Allied forces landing in North Africa; the next year he was made full general. He became supreme Allied commander in Europe that same year and as such led the Normandy invasion (June 6, 1944). He was given the rank of general of the army on Dec. 20, 1944, which was made permanent in 1946.

On May 7, 1945, Eisenhower received the surrender of Germany at Rheims. He returned to the U.S. to serve as chief of staff (1945-48). His war memoir, *Crusade in Europe* (1948), was a best-seller. In 1948 he became president of Columbia University; in 1950 he became Commander of NATO forces.

Eisenhower resigned from the army and was nominated for president by the Republicans in 1952. He defeated Adlai E. Stevenson in the 1952 election and again in 1956. Eisenhower called himself a moderate, favored the "free market system" vs. government price and wage controls, kept government out of labor disputes, reorganized the defense establishment, and promoted missile programs. He continued foreign aid, sped the end of the Korean War, endorsed Taiwan and SE Asia defense treaties, backed the UN in condemning the Anglo-French raid on Egypt, and advocated the "open skies" policy of mutual inspection with the USSR. He sent U.S. troops into Little Rock, AR, in Sept. 1957, during the segregation crisis.

Eisenhower died on Mar. 28, 1969, in Washington, DC.

WORLD ALMANAC QUICK QUIZ

Who was the first president born west of the Mississippi?

(a) Andrew Jackson   (b) Abraham Lincoln   (c) Theodore Roosevelt   (d) Herbert Hoover

For the answer look in this chapter, or see page 1008.

JOHN FITZGERALD KENNEDY (1961-63), 35th president, Democrat, was born on May 29, 1917, in Brookline, MA, the son of Joseph P. and Rose Fitzgerald Kennedy. He graduated from Harvard University in 1940. While serving in the navy (1941-45), he commanded a PT boat in the Solomons and won the Navy and Marine Corps Medal. In 1956, while recovering from spinal surgery, he wrote *Profiles in Courage,* which won a Pulitzer Prize in 1957. He served in the House of Representatives from 1947 to 1953 and was elected to the Senate in 1952 and 1958. In 1960, he won the Democratic nomination for president and narrowly defeated Republican Vice Pres. Richard M. Nixon. Kennedy was the youngest president ever elected to the office and the first Catholic.

Despite the image of youth and vigor he conveyed to the public, Kennedy suffered from serious medical problems, including Addison's disease and severe chronic back pain that required him to wear a back brace. The public was not aware of the extent of these problems, or of his extensive womanizing, including an affair with a young White House press aide that only became known in 2003. However, scholars have not generally claimed that these aspects of his life affected his performance in office.

In Apr. 1961, the new Kennedy administration suffered a severe setback when an invasion force of anti-Castro Cubans, trained and directed by the CIA, failed to establish a beachhead at the Bay of Pigs in Cuba. By the same token, one of Kennedy's most important acts as president was his successful demand on Oct. 22, 1962, that the Soviet Union dismantle its missile bases in Cuba. Kennedy also defied Soviet attempts to force the Allies out of Berlin. He started the Peace Corps, and he backed civil rights and expanded medical care for the aged. Space exploration was greatly developed during his administration.

On Nov. 22, 1963, President Kennedy was assassinated while riding in a motorcade in Dallas, TX. A commission chaired by Chief Justice Earl Warren concluded in Sept. 1964 that the sole assassin had been Lee Harvey Oswald, a former U.S. Marine and, at the time of the shooting, an ardent Marxist. Oswald was captured a short time after the assassination and charged with the crime, but was shot dead by nightclub owner Jack Ruby two days later while being moved to a county jail, before he could go to trial.

LYNDON BAINES JOHNSON (1963-69), 36th president, Democrat, was born on Aug. 27, 1908, near Stonewall, TX, the son of Sam Ealy and Rebekah Baines Johnson. He graduated from Southwest Texas State Teachers College in 1930 and attended Georgetown University Law School. He taught public speaking in Houston (1930-31) and then served as secretary to Rep. R. M. Kleberg (1931-35). In 1937 Johnson won an election to fill the vacancy caused by the death of a U.S. representative and in 1938 was elected to the full term, after which he returned for 4 terms. During 1941 and 1942 he also served in the Navy in the Pacific, earning a Silver Star for bravery. He was elected U.S. senator in 1948 and reelected in 1954. He became Democratic leader of the Senate in 1953. Johnson had strong support for the Democratic presidential nomination at the 1960 convention, where the nominee, John F. Kennedy, asked him to run for vice president. His campaigning helped overcome religious bias against Kennedy in the South.

Johnson became president when Kennedy was assassinated. He was elected to a full term in 1964. Johnson's domestic program was of considerable importance. He won passage of major civil rights, anti-poverty, aid to education, and health-care (Medicare, Medicaid) legislation—the "Great

Society" program. However, his escalation of the war in Vietnam came to overshadow the achievements of his administration. In the face of increasing division in the nation and in his own party over his handling of the war, Johnson declined to seek another term.

Johnson died on Jan. 22, 1973, in San Antonio, TX.

RICHARD MILHOUS NIXON (1969-74), 37th president, Republican, was born on Jan. 9, 1913, in Yorba Linda, CA, the son of Francis Anthony and Hannah Milhous Nixon. He graduated from Whittier College in 1934 and from Duke University Law School in 1937. After practicing law in Whittier and serving briefly in the Office of Price Administration in 1942, he entered the Navy and served in the South Pacific. Nixon was elected to the House of Representatives in 1946 and 1948. He achieved prominence as the House Un-American Activities Committee member who forced the showdown leading to the Alger Hiss perjury conviction. In 1950 he was elected to the Senate.

Nixon was elected vice president in the Eisenhower landslides of 1952 and 1956. He won the Republican nomination for president in 1960 but was narrowly defeated by John F. Kennedy. He ran unsuccessfully for governor of California in 1962. In 1968 he again won the GOP presidential nomination, then defeated Hubert Humphrey for the presidency.

Nixon's 2nd term was cut short by scandal, after disclosures relating to a June 1972 burglary of Democratic Party headquarters in the Watergate office complex. The courts and Congress sought tapes of Nixon's office conversations and calls for criminal proceedings against former White House aides and for a House inquiry into possible impeachment. Nixon claimed executive privilege, but the Supreme Court ruled against him. In July the House Judiciary Committee recommended adoption of 3 impeachment articles charging him with obstruction of justice, abuse of power, and contempt of Congress. On Aug. 5, he released transcripts of conversations that linked him to cover-up activities. He resigned on Aug. 9, becoming the first president ever to do so. In later years, Nixon emerged as an elder statesman.

As president, Nixon appointed 4 Supreme Court justices, including the chief justice, moving the court to the right, and as a "new federalist" sought to shift responsibility to state and local governments. He dramatically altered relations with China, which he visited in 1972—the first president to do so. With foreign affairs adviser Henry Kissinger he pursued détente with the Soviet Union. He began a gradual withdrawal from Vietnam, but U.S. troops remained there through his first term. He ordered an incursion into Cambodia (1970) and the bombing of Hanoi and mining of Haiphong Harbor (1972). Reelected by a large majority in Nov. 1972, he secured a Vietnam cease-fire in Jan. 1973.

Nixon died Apr. 22, 1994, in New York City.

GERALD RUDOLPH FORD (1974-77), 38th president, Republican, was born on July 14, 1913, in Omaha, NE, the son of Leslie and Dorothy Gardner King, and was named Leslie Jr. When he was 2, his parents were divorced, and his mother moved with the boy to Grand Rapids, MI. There she met and married Gerald R. Ford, who formally adopted him and gave him his own name. Ford graduated from the University of Michigan in 1935 and from Yale Law School in 1941. He began practicing law in Grand Rapids, but in 1942 joined the navy and served in the Pacific, leaving the service in 1946 as a lieutenant commander. He entered the House of Representatives in 1949 and spent 25 years in the House, 8 of them as Republican leader.

On Oct. 12, 1973, after Vice President Spiro T. Agnew resigned, Ford was nominated by President Nixon to replace him. It was the first use of the procedures set out in the 25th Amendment. When Nixon resigned, Aug. 9, 1974, because of the Watergate scandal, Ford became president; he was the only president who was never elected either to the presidency or to the vice presidency.

President Ford was widely credited with having contributed to rebuilding morale after the Nixon presidency. But he was also criticized by many when, in a controversial move, he pardoned Nixon for any federal crimes he might have committed as president. Ford vetoed 48 bills in his first 21 months in office, mostly in the interest of fighting high inflation; he was less successful in curbing high unemployment. In foreign policy, Ford continued to pursue détente.

Ford was narrowly defeated in the 1976 election.

JIMMY (JAMES EARL) CARTER (1977-81),

39th president, Democrat, was the first president from the Deep South since before the Civil War. He was born on Oct. 1, 1924, in Plains, GA, the son of James and Lillian Gordy Carter. Carter graduated from the U.S. Naval Academy in 1946 and in 1952 entered the navy's nuclear submarine program as an aide to Capt. (later Adm.) Hyman Rickover. He studied nuclear physics at Union College. Carter's father died in 1953, and he left the navy to take over the family peanut farming businesses. He served in the Georgia state senate (1963-67) and as governor of Georgia (1971-75). In 1976, Carter won the Democratic nomination and defeated President Gerald R. Ford.

On his first full day in office, Carter pardoned all Vietnam draft evaders. He played a major role in the negotiations leading to the 1979 peace treaty between Israel and Egypt, and he won passage of new treaties with Panama providing for U.S. control of the Panama Canal to end in 2000. However, Carter was widely criticized for the poor state of the economy and was viewed by some as weak in his handling of foreign policy. In Nov. 1979, Iranian student militants attacked the U.S. embassy in Tehran and held members of the embassy staff hostage. Efforts to obtain release of the hostages were a major preoccupation during the rest of his term. He reacted to the Soviet invasion of Afghanistan by imposing a grain embargo and boycotting the Moscow Olympic Games.

Carter was defeated by Ronald Reagan in the 1980 election. The American hostages were finally released on Inauguration Day, 1981, just after Reagan officially became president. After leaving office, Carter was active in humanitarian efforts and in seeking to mediate international disputes. In large part for his diplomatic efforts in office and subsequently, he was awarded the Nobel Peace Prize in 2002.

RONALD WILSON REAGAN (1981-89),

40th president, Republican, was born on Feb. 6, 1911, in Tampico, IL, the son of John Edward and Nellie Wilson Reagan. Reagan graduated from Eureka College in 1932, after which he worked as a sports announcer in Des Moines, IA. He began a successful career as an actor in 1937, starring in numerous movies, and later in television, until the 1960s. During World War II Reagan served in the Army Air Force, making training films. He was president of the Screen Actors Guild from 1947 to 1952 and in 1959-60. Reagan was elected governor of California in 1966 and reelected in 1970.

In 1980, Reagan gained the Republican presidential nomination and won a landslide victory over Jimmy Carter. He was easily reelected in 1984. Reagan successfully forged a bipartisan coalition in Congress, which led to enactment of his program of large-scale tax cuts, cutbacks in many government programs, and a major defense buildup. He signed a So-

cial Security reform bill designed to provide for the long-term solvency of the system. In 1986, he signed into law a major tax-reform bill. He was shot and seriously wounded in an assassination attempt in 1981.

In 1982, the U.S. joined France and Italy in maintaining a peacekeeping force in Beirut, Lebanon, and the next year Reagan sent a task force to invade the island of Grenada after 2 Marxist coups there. Reagan's opposition to international terrorism led to the U.S. bombing of Libyan military installations in 1986. He strongly supported El Salvador, the Nicaraguan contras, and other anti-communist governments and forces throughout the world. He also held 4 summit meetings with Soviet leader Mikhail Gorbachev. At the 1987 meeting in Washington, DC, a historic treaty eliminating short- and medium-range missiles from Europe was signed.

Reagan faced a crisis in 1986-87, when it was revealed that the U.S. had sold weapons through Israeli brokers to Iran in exchange for release of U.S. hostages being held in Lebanon and that subsequently some of the money was diverted to the Nicaraguan contras (Congress had barred U.S. aid to the contras). The scandal led to the resignation of leading White House aides. As Reagan left office in Jan. 1989, the nation was experiencing its 6th consecutive year of economic prosperity. Over the same period, however, the federal government recorded large budget deficits.

In 1994, in a letter to the American people, Reagan revealed that he was suffering from Alzheimer's disease. He died on June 5, 2004, in Los Angeles, CA, from complications of the disease. Well over 100,000 people filed past his coffin, which lay in repose at the Reagan Presidential Library and then in state at the U.S. Capitol rotunda.

GEORGE HERBERT WALKER BUSH (1989-93),

41st president, Republican, was born on June 12, 1924, in Milton, MA, the son of Prescott and Dorothy Walker Bush. He served as a U.S. Navy pilot in World War II. After graduating from Yale University in 1948, he settled in Texas, where, in 1953, he helped found an oil company. After losing a bid for a U.S. Senate seat in Texas in 1964, he was elected to the House of Representatives in 1966 and 1968. He lost a 2nd U.S. Senate race in 1970. Subsequently he served as U.S. ambassador to the United Nations (1971-73), headed the U.S. Liaison Office in Beijing (1974-75), and was director of central intelligence (1976-77).

Following an unsuccessful bid for the 1980 Republican presidential nomination, Bush was chosen by Ronald Reagan as his vice presidential running mate. He served as U.S. vice president from 1981 to 1989.

In 1988, Bush gained the GOP presidential nomination and defeated Michael Dukakis in the November election. Bush took office faced with U.S. budget and trade deficits as well as the rescue of insolvent U.S. savings and loan institutions. He faced a severe budget deficit annually, struggled with military cutbacks in light of reduced cold war tensions, and vetoed abortion-rights legislation. In 1990 he agreed to a budget deficit-reduction plan that included tax hikes.

Bush supported Soviet reforms, Eastern Europe democratization, and good relations with Beijing. In Dec. 1989, Bush sent troops to Panama; they overthrew the government and captured strongman Gen. Manuel Noriega.

Bush reacted to Iraq's Aug. 1990 invasion of Kuwait by sending U.S. forces to the Persian Gulf area and assembling a UN-backed coalition, including NATO and Arab League members. After a month-long air war, in Feb. 1991, Allied forces retook Kuwait in a 4-day ground assault. The quick victory, with extremely light casualties on the U.S. side, gave Bush at the time one of the highest presidential approval ratings in history. His popularity plummeted by the end of 1991, however, as the economy slipped into recession. He was defeated by Bill Clinton in the 1992 election. His son George W. Bush became the 43rd president.

BILL (WILLIAM JEFFERSON) CLINTON (1993-2001), 42nd president, Democrat, was born on Aug. 19, 1946, in Hope, AR, son of William Blythe and Virginia Cassidy Blythe, and was named William Jefferson Blythe IV. Blythe died in an automobile accident before his son was born. His widow married Roger Clinton, and at the age of 16, William Jefferson Blythe IV changed his last name to Clinton.

Clinton became interested in politics in high school and went on to Georgetown University in Washington, DC, where he graduated with high honors in 1968. He then attended Oxford University for 2 years as a Rhodes scholar. During that time he legally avoided the draft and possible service in Vietnam, according to some critics by misleading his draft board. He went on to earn a degree from Yale Law School in 1973.

Clinton worked on George McGovern's 1972 presidential campaign. He taught at the University of Arkansas from 1973 to 1976, when he was elected state attorney general. In 1978, he was elected governor, becoming the nation's youngest. Defeated for reelection in 1980, he was returned to office several times thereafter. He married Hillary Rodham in 1975.

Despite some issues raised about his character, Clinton won most of the 1992 presidential primaries, moving his party toward the center as he tried to broaden his appeal; as the party's presidential nominee he defeated Pres. George H.W. Bush and Reform Party candidate Ross Perot in the November election. In 1993, Clinton won passage of a measure to reduce the federal budget deficit and won congressional approval of the North American Free Trade Agreement. His administration's plan for major health-care reform legislation died in Congress. After 1994 midterm elections, Clinton faced Republican majorities in both houses of Congress. He followed a centrist course at home, sent troops to Bosnia to help implement a peace settlement, and cultivated relations with Russia and China.

Though accused of improprieties in his involvement in an Arkansas real estate venture (Whitewater), Clinton easily won reelection in 1996, and an independent prosecutor found insufficient evidence of any criminality by Clinton or his wife. In 1997 he reached agreement with Congress on legislation to balance the federal budget by 2002. In 1998, Clinton became the 2nd U.S. president ever to be impeached by the House of Representatives. Charged with perjury and obstruction of justice in connection with an attempted cover-up of a sexual relationship with a former White House intern, Monica Lewinsky, he was acquitted by the Senate in 1999. He retained wide popularity, aided by a strong economy.

In 1999, the United States, under Clinton, joined other NATO nations in an aerial bombing campaign that induced Serbia to withdraw troops from the Kosovo region, where they had been terrorizing ethnic Albanians. In 2000 Clinton became the 1st president since the Vietnam war to visit Vietnam.

After leaving office, Clinton remained active in political affairs and encouraged the career of his wife, who was elected in 2000 to the U.S. Senate from New York. His memoirs, *My Life*, published in 2004, immediately went to the top of the best-seller list. He had quadruple heart bypass surgery, Sept. 6, 2004.

GEORGE WALKER BUSH (2001-), 43rd president, Republican, was born on July 6, 1946, in New Haven, CT. He was the first of six children born to George Herbert Walker Bush and his wife, the former Barbara Pierce, a descendant of Pres. Franklin Pierce. (His brother Jeb won the Florida governorship in 1998.) Bush was the first son of a former president to win the White House since John Quincy Adams.

Fun-loving, athletic, and popular, the young George Bush grew up in Midland and Houston, TX. In 1961 he was sent to the Phillips Academy in Andover, MA, the same prep school his father had attended. In 1964 he entered Yale University, his father's alma mater, where he majored in history. Eligible for the draft upon graduation, he signed on with the Texas Air National Guard. After earning a master's degree from the Harvard Business School, he returned to Midland in 1975 and went into the oil business. Two years later he married Laura Welch, a schoolteacher and librarian; in 1981 she gave birth to twin daughters.

Bush, who had lost a race for Congress in 1978, returned to the oil business, but success proved elusive. Realizing that he had a drinking problem, he swore off alcohol and renewed commitment to Christian faith. After aiding in his father's successful 1988 presidential campaign, he put together a group of investors to buy the Texas Rangers baseball club and took a hands-on role as managing partner. Bush ran for governor in 1994, defeating a popular incumbent, Ann Richards. He won reelection by a landslide in 1998. As governor, he concentrated on building personal bonds with Democratic leaders and backed education reforms.

After defeating Sen. John McCain of Arizona and other rivals in the Republican party primaries, Bush chose Dick Cheney, a former U.S. representative and defense secretary, as his running mate. The Nov. 2000 presidential election was one of the closest in history. While Bush came out behind in the popular vote, by about 540,000 out of more than 100 million cast, the electoral vote total hinged on the outcome in Florida, where official totals, challenged by Democrats, gave him a razor-thin lead. In December the Supreme Court in effect ended a controversial attempt to recount the vote there, and Florida's 25 electoral votes decided the election in Bush's favor.

Among the issues Bush had campaigned on was that of lowering federal taxes, and in May 2001 he won approval from Congress for a large tax cut package.

On Sept. 11, 2001, Bush was faced with a crisis that would redefine his presidency. In a terrorist attack, 2 hijacked jetliners crashed into the twin towers of the World Trade Center in New York City, which were destroyed; another jet struck the Pentagon near Washington, DC, with a 4th crashing in rural Pennsylvania. Some 3,000 people were killed in the attack. The president vowed to punish those responsible, and in a "war against terrorism," the U.S. military attacked and deposed the Taliban regime in Afghanistan's capital, which was sheltering elements of the al-Qaeda terrorist network, held responsible for the attacks. However, Taliban and al-Qaeda continued to function in parts of Afghanistan, and al-Qaeda was blamed for continuing terrorist acts in a number of countries. In 2002 Bush won congressional approval to create a cabinet-level department for homeland security.

Bush met in May 2002 with Russian Pres. Vladimir Putin in Moscow, where they signed a pact cutting nuclear armaments in each country. In July, with corporate scandals and a slumping stock market fueling demands for tighter regulation of business, Bush signed legislation aimed at curbing financial abuses.

In March 2003, the United States, aided mainly by forces from Great Britain, launched an air and ground war against Iraq and deposed the dictatorial regime of Pres. Saddam Hussein. The regime was accused of harboring weapons of mass destruction and other violations of UN resolutions. Hussein was captured in Iraq, Dec. 13, 2003, but insurgent violence continued in 2004, and large numbers of U.S. troops remained in Iraq, sustaining further casualties. A Senate Intelligence Committee report issued in July concluded that pre-war intelligence on illicit weapons in Iraq had been seriously flawed. U.S. intelligence agencies were also criticized by a special 9-11 Commission for having failed to heed possible warnings of terrorism prior to the Sept. 11 attacks. The president continued to maintain that the removal of Saddam Hussein had been a necessity to help safeguard the U.S., as well as a benefit in itself; the administration's Iraq policy and conduct of the war and reconstruction efforts were major issues in the fall presidential campagn.

On the domestic front, the Bush administration won passage of further tax cuts, which it maintained would stimulate the lagging economy. Democrats disputed this approach and criticized rising federal budget deficits. During 2004 the economy showed signs of recovery, but job growth was disappointing. During 2004 Bush also announced new goals for the space program, imposed further sanctions on Cuba, and supported a constitutional amendment banning same-sex marriage (which was defeated in the Senate).

Wives and Children of the Presidents

Name (Born–died; married)	State	Sons/ Daughters	Name (Born–died; married)	State	Sons/ Daughters
Martha Dandridge Custis Washington (1731-1802; 1759)	VA	None	Caroline Lavinia Scott Harrison 1832-92; 1853)	OH	1/1
Abigail Smith Adams (1744-1818; 1764)	MA	3/2	Mary Scott Lord Dimmick Harrison (1858-1948; 1896)	PA	0/1
Martha Wayles Skelton Jefferson (1748-82; 1772)	VA	1/5	Ida Saxton McKinley (1847-1907; 1871)	OH	0/2
Dorothea "Dolley" Payne Todd Madison (1768-1849; 1794)	NC	None	Alice Hathaway Lee Roosevelt (1861-84; 1880)	MA	0/1
Elizabeth Kortright Monroe (1768-1830; 1786)	NY	0/2 (A)	Edith Kermit Carow Roosevelt (1861-1948; 1886)	CT	4/1
Louisa Catherine Johnson Adams (1775-1852; 1797)	MD (B)	3/1	Helen Herron Taft (1861-1943; 1886)	OH	2/1
Rachel Donelson Robards Jackson (1767-1828; 1791)	VA	None	Ellen Louise Axson Wilson (1860-1914; 1885)	GA	0/3
Hannah Hoes Van Buren (1783-1819; 1807)	NY	4/0	Edith Bolling Galt Wilson (1872-1961; 1915)	VA	None
Anna Tuthill Symmes Harrison (1775-1864; 1795)	NJ	6/4	Florence Kling De Wolfe Harding (1860-1924; 1891)	OH	None
Letitia Christian Tyler (1790-1842; 1813)	VA	3/4(A)	Grace Anna Goodhue Coolidge (1879-1957; 1905)	VT	2/0
Julia Gardiner Tyler (1820-89; 1844)	NY	5/2	Lou Henry Hoover (1875-1944; 1899)	IA	2/0
Sarah Childress Polk (1803-91; 1824)	TN	None	Anna Eleanor Roosevelt Roosevelt (1884-1962; 1905)	NY	4/1(A)
Margaret Mackall Smith Taylor (1788-1852; 1810)	MD	1/5	Elizabeth Virginia "Bess" Wallace Truman (1885-1982; 1919)	MO	0/1
Abigail Powers Fillmore (1798-1853; 1826)	NY	1/1	Mamie Geneva Doud Eisenhower (1896-1979; 1916)	IA	1/0(A)
Caroline Carmichael McIntosh Fillmore (1813-81; 1858)	NJ	None	Jacqueline Lee Bouvier Kennedy (1929-94; 1953)	NY	1/1(A)
Jane Means Appleton Pierce (1806-63; 1834)	NH	3/0	Claudia "Lady Bird" Alta Taylor Johnson (1912; 1934)	TX	0/2
Mary Todd Lincoln (1818-82; 1842)	KY	4/0	Thelma Catherine Patricia Ryan Nixon (1912-1993; 1940)	NV	0/2
Eliza McCardle Johnson (1810-76; 1827)	TN	3/2	Elizabeth Bloomer Warren Ford (1918; 1948)	IL	3/1
Julia Boggs Dent Grant (1826-1902; 1848)	MO	3/1	Rosalynn Smith Carter (1927; 1946)	GA	3/1
Lucy Ware Webb Hayes (1831-89; 1852)	OH	7/1	Anne Frances "Nancy" Robbins Davis Reagan (1921; 1952)	NY	1/1(C)
Lucretia Randolph Garfield (1832-1918; 1858)	OH	4/1	Barbara Pierce Bush (1925; 1945)	NY	4/2
Ellen Lewis Herndon Arthur (1837-80; 1859)	VA	2/1	Hillary Rodham Clinton (1947; 1975)	IL	0/1
Frances Folsom Cleveland (1864-1947; 1886)	NY	2/3	Laura Welch Bush (1946; 1977)	TX	0/2

NOTE: Pres. Buchanan was unmarried. (A) plus 1 infant, deceased. (B) Born in London, father a MD citizen. (C) Pres. Reagan married and divorced Jane Wyman; they had a daughter who died in infancy, and a son and daughter who lived past infancy.

First Lady Laura Welch Bush

Laura Welch Bush was born in Midland, TX, Nov. 4, 1946. She graduated from Southern Methodist University, earned a master's in library science at the Univ. of Texas at Austin, and became a librarian and teacher in Texas public schools. She and George W. Bush were married in 1977; in 1981, their twin daughters, Jenna and Barbara, were born.

As First Lady of Texas from 1995 to 2001, Laura Bush stressed advocacy of educational reform and literacy programs. She launched an early childhood development initiative and also worked to promote breast cancer awareness.

Laura Bush's first solo appearance as First Lady came at the launch of D.C. Teaching Fellows, a program encouraging professionals to become teachers. In Nov. 2001 she became the first First Lady to give a speech of her own in place of the president's weekly radio address. During 2004 she participated actively in reelection campaign efforts, while continuing to be involved in such interests as early childhood education, promotion of literacy and reading, breast cancer awareness, and women's rights.

Burial Places of the Presidents

President	Burial Place	President	Burial Place	President	Burial Place
Washington	Mt. Vernon, VA	Pierce	Concord, NH	Taft	Arlington Natl. Cemetery
J. Adams	Quincy, MA	Buchanan	Lancaster, PA	Wilson	Wash. Natl. Cathedral
Jefferson	Charlottesville, VA	Lincoln	Springfield, IL	Harding	Marion, OH
Madison	Montpelier Station, VA	A. Johnson	Greeneville, TN	Coolidge	Plymouth, VT
Monroe	Richmond, VA	Grant	New York, NY	Hoover	West Branch, IA
J. Q. Adams	Quincy, MA	Hayes	Fremont, OH	F. Roosevelt	Hyde Park, NY
Jackson	Nashville, TN	Garfield	Cleveland, OH	Truman	Independence, MO
Van Buren	Kinderhook, NY	Arthur	Albany, NY	Eisenhower	Abilene, KS
W. H. Harrison	North Bend, OH	Cleveland	Princeton, NJ	Kennedy	Arlington Natl. Cemetery
Tyler	Richmond, VA	B. Harrison	Indianapolis, IN	L. B. Johnson	Johnson City, TX
Polk	Nashville, TN	McKinley	Canton, OH	Nixon	Yorba Linda, CA
Taylor	Louisville, KY	T. Roosevelt	Oyster Bay, NY	Reagan	Simi Valley, CA
Fillmore	Buffalo, NY				

Presidential Facts

Tallest president: Abraham Lincoln, who was 6 feet, 4 inches
Shortest president: James Madison, who was 5 feet, 4 inches
First president to live in the White House: John Adams, who moved there in 1800
First president born in a log cabin: Andrew Jackson, in 1767
First president born a U.S. citizen: Martin Van Buren, in Kinderhook, NY; 1782
First president born outside the original colonies: Abraham Lincoln, in Kentucky, 1809
First president born west of the Mississippi River: Herbert Hoover, in 1874
First president of all 50 states: Dwight D. Eisenhower, first inaugurated in 1953
First president born from the "Baby Boom" generation: William J. Clinton, in 1946
First president to be photographed while in office: James K. Polk, in 1849
First president to have a telephone in the White House: Rutherford B. Hayes in 1879
First president to leave the continental U.S. while in office: Theodore Roosevelt, in 1906, on a visit to inspect construction work on the Panama Canal
First president to cross the Atlantic Ocean: Woodrow Wilson
First president to address the nation on radio: Warren G. Harding, in 1922
First president to appear on TV: Franklin D. Roosevelt, at opening ceremonies for the 1939 World's Fair
First president to speak from the White House on TV: Harry S. Truman, in 1947
First president to give a live, televised news conference: John F. Kennedy, in 1961
Only president elected unanimously: George Washington, by 63 electoral votes

Only presidents who lost the popular vote while winning election: John Quincy Adams, in 1824 (elected by the House after general election failed to produce a majority); Rutherford B. Hayes, in 1876; Benjamin Harrison, in 1888; George W. Bush, in 2000. Popular vote totals for elections before 1824 are unknown.
Only presidents chosen by the House of Representatives: Thomas Jefferson (1st term) and John Quincy Adams
Only presidents to graduate from West Point: Ulysses S. Grant and Dwight D. Eisenhower
Only president to graduate from Annapolis: Jimmy Carter
Only president with a Ph.D.: Woodrow Wilson; received a doctorate in political science from Johns Hopkins Univ. in 1886
Only left-handed presidents: James Garfield, Herbert Hoover, Harry Truman, Gerald Ford, Ronald Reagan, Geroge H. W. Bush, and Bill Clinton
Only president to head a labor union: Ronald Reagan was president of the Screen Actors Guild, 1947-52; 1959-60
Only bachelor presidents: James Buchanan, who never married, and Grover Cleveland, who married Frances Folsom in the White House in 1886.
Only presidents to serve in Congress after leaving office: Andrew Johnson (Senate), John Quincy Adams (House)
Only president to also serve as chief justice of the U.S.: William Howard Taft
Presidents who died on July 4: John Adams and Thomas Jefferson (both 1826) and James Monroe (1831)
Presidents who died in office: Eight presidents have died in office. Of these, 4 were assassinated: Abraham Lincoln, James Garfield, William McKinley, and John F. Kennedy. The other 4 were William Henry Harrison, Zachary Taylor, Warren G. Harding, and Franklin D. Roosevelt.
Only president buried in Washington, DC: Woodrow Wilson, who was interred at the Washington National Cathedral

IT'S A FACT: Ronald Reagan, who died on June 5, 2004, at the age of 93, lived the longest of any president in history. He was the oldest to be elected to the office, at age 69, and was the only president born in Illinois. Reagan was also the only president who had been an actor and the first president who had ever been divorced.

Presidential Libraries

The libraries listed here, except for that of Richard Nixon (which is private), are coordinated by the National Archives and Records Administration (Website: www.archives.gov/presidential_libraries/index.html). NARA also has custody of the Nixon presidential historical materials and those of Bill Clinton. The William J. Clinton Library was scheduled to open in Nov. 2004. NARA will release Clinton presidential records to the public at the Clinton Library beginning Jan. 20, 2006. Materials for presidents before Herbert Hoover are held by private institutions.

Herbert Hoover Library
210 Parkside Dr.
West Branch, IA 52358
PHONE: 319-643-5301
E-MAIL: hoover.library@nara.gov
WEBSITE: www.hoover.archives.gov

Franklin D. Roosevelt Library
4079 Albany Post Rd.
Hyde Park, NY 12538-1990
PHONE: 845-486-7770; 1-800-FDR-VISIT
E-MAIL: roosevelt.library@nara.gov
WEBSITE: www.fdrlibrary.marist.edu

Harry S. Truman Library and Museum
500 West U.S. Hwy. 24
Independence, MO 64050-2481
PHONE: 816-268-8200; 1-800-833-1225
E-MAIL: truman.library@nara.gov
WEBSITE: www.trumanlibrary.org

Dwight D. Eisenhower Library
200 S.E. 4th St.
Abilene, KS 67410-2900
PHONE: 785-263-6700; 1-877-RING-IKE
E-MAIL: eisenhower.library@nara.gov
WEBSITE: www.eisenhower.archives.gov

John Fitzgerald Kennedy Library
Columbia Pt.
Boston, MA 02125-3398
PHONE: 617-514-1600; 1-866-JFK-1960
E-MAIL: kennedy.library@nara.gov
WEBSITE: www.jfklibrary.org

Lyndon Baines Johnson Library and Museum
2313 Red River St.
Austin, TX 78705-5702
PHONE: 512-721-0200
E-MAIL: johnson.library@nara.gov
WEBSITE: www.lbjlib.utexas.edu

Richard Nixon Library & Birthplace
18001 Yorba Linda Blvd.
Yorba Linda, CA 92886
PHONE: 714-993-5075
E-MAIL: archives@nixonlibrary.org
WEBSITE: www.nixonfoundation.org

Gerald R. Ford Library
1000 Beal Ave.
Ann Arbor, MI 48109-2114
PHONE: 734-205-0555
E-MAIL: ford.library@nara.gov
WEBSITE: www.ford.utexas.edu

Jimmy Carter Library
441 Freedom Pkwy.
Atlanta, GA 30307-1498
PHONE: 404-865-7100
E-MAIL: carter.library@nara.gov
WEBSITE: www.jimmycarterlibrary.org

Ronald Reagan Library
40 Presidential Dr.
Simi Valley, CA 93065-0600
PHONE: 800-410-8354
E-MAIL: reagan.library@nara.gov
WEBSITE: www.reagan.utexas.edu

George H. W. Bush Library
1000 George Bush Dr. West
College Station, TX 77845
PHONE: 979-691-4000
E-MAIL: library.bush@nara.gov
WEBSITE: bushlibrary.tamu.edu

William J. Clinton Library
1000 La Harpe Blvd.
Little Rock, AR 72201
PHONE: 501-244-9756
E-MAIL: clinton.library@nara.gov
WEBSITE: www.clintonlibrary.gov

Impeachment in U.S. History

The U.S. Constitution provides for impeachment and removal from office of federal officials on grounds of "Treason, Bribery, or other high Crimes and Misdemeanors" (Article II, Sect. 4). Impeachment is the bringing of charges by the House of Representatives. It is followed by a Senate trial; a two-thirds Senate vote is needed for conviction and removal from office.

In 1868, Andrew Johnson became the first president impeached by the House; he was tried but not convicted by the Senate. In 1974, impeachment articles against Pres. Richard Nixon, in connection with the Watergate scandal, were voted by the House Judiciary Committee; he resigned Aug. 9, before the full House could vote on impeaching him. In 1998, Pres. Bill Clinton was impeached by the House in connection with covering up a relationship with a former White House intern; he was tried in the Senate in 1999 and acquitted.

PRESIDENTIAL ELECTIONS

The Electoral College

The president and the vice president are the only elective federal officials not chosen by direct vote of the people. They are elected by the members of the Electoral College, an institution provided for in the U.S. Constitution.

On presidential election day, the first Tuesday after the first Monday in November of every 4th year, each state chooses as many electors as it has senators and representatives in Congress. In 1964, for the first time, as provided by the 23rd Amendment to the Constitution, the District of Columbia voted for 3 electors. Thus, with 100 senators and 435 representatives, there are 538 members of the Electoral College, with a majority of 270 electoral votes needed to elect the president and vice president.

Although political parties were not part of the original plan created by the Founding Fathers, today political parties customarily nominate their lists of electors at their respective state conventions. Some states print names of the candidates for president and vice president at the top of the Nov. ballot; others list only the electors' names. In either case, the electors of the party receiving the highest vote are elected. Two states, Maine and Nebraska, allow for proportional allocation.

The electors meet on the first Monday after the 2nd Wednesday in December in their respective state capitals or in some other place prescribed by state legislatures. By long-established custom, they vote for their party nominees, although this is not required by federal law; some states do require it.

The Constitution requires electors to cast a ballot for at least one person who is not an inhabitant of that elector's home state. This ensures that presidential and vice presidential candidates from the same party will not be from the same state. (In 2000, Republican vice presidential nominee Dick Cheney changed his voter registration to Wyoming from Gov. George W. Bush's home state of Texas.) Also, an elector cannot be a member of Congress or hold federal office.

Certified and sealed lists of the votes of the electors in each state are sent to the president of the U.S. Senate, who then opens them in the presence of the members of the Senate and House of Representatives in a joint session held in early Jan., and the electoral votes of all the states are then officially counted.

If no candidate for president has a majority, the House of Representatives chooses a president from the top 3 candidates, with all representatives from each state combining to cast one vote for that state. The House decided the outcome of the 1800 and 1824 presidential elections. If no candidate for vice president has a majority, the Senate chooses from the top 2, with the senators voting as individuals. The Senate chose the vice president following the 1836 election.

Under the electoral college system, a candidate who fails to be the top vote getter in the popular vote still may win a majority of electoral votes. This happened in the elections of 1876, 1888, and 2000.

Electoral Votes for President

Electoral votes for each state, based on the 2000 Census, were in force beginning with the 2004 elections.

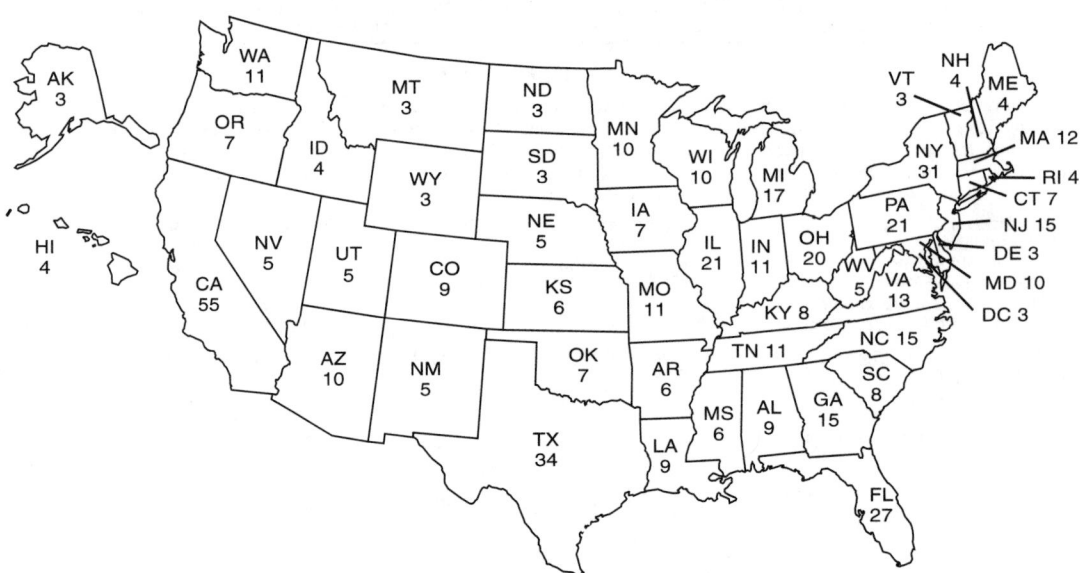

Voter Turnout in Presidential Elections, 1932-2000

Source: Federal Election Commission; Commission for Study of American Electorate; *Congressional Quarterly*

	Candidates	Voter Participation (% of voting-age population)		Candidates	Voter Participation (% of voting-age population)
1932	Roosevelt-Hoover	52.4	1968	Nixon-Humphrey	60.9
1936	Roosevelt-Landon	56.0	1972	Nixon-McGovern	55.2
1940	Roosevelt-Willkie	58.9	1976	Carter-Ford	53.5
1944	Roosevelt-Dewey	56.0	1980	Reagan-Carter	54.0
1948	Truman-Dewey	51.1	1984	Reagan-Mondale	53.1
1952	Eisenhower-Stevenson	61.6	1988	Bush-Dukakis	50.2
1956	Eisenhower-Stevenson	59.3	1992	Clinton-Bush-Perot	55.9
1960	Kennedy-Nixon	62.8	1996	Clinton-Dole-Perot	49.0
1964	Johnson-Goldwater	61.9	2000	Bush-Gore	51.3

(1) The sharp drop in 1972 followed the expansion of eligibility with the enfranchisement of 18- to 20-year-olds.

Major-Party Nominees for President and Vice President, 1856-2004

Asterisk (*) denotes winning ticket

	Democratic			Republican	
Year	President	Vice President	Year	President	Vice President
1856	James Buchanan*	John Breckinridge	1856	John Frémont	William Dayton
1860	Stephen A. Douglas (1)	Herschel V. Johnson	1860	Abraham Lincoln*	Hannibal Hamlin
1864	George McClellan	G.H. Pendleton	1864	Abraham Lincoln*	Andrew Johnson
1868	Horatio Seymour	Francis Blair	1868	Ulysses S. Grant*	Schuyler Colfax
1872	Horace Greeley	B. Gratz Brown	1872	Ulysses S. Grant*	Henry Wilson
1876	Samuel J. Tilden	Thomas Hendricks	1876	Rutherford B. Hayes*	William Wheeler
1880	Winfield Hancock	William English	1880	James A. Garfield*	Chester A. Arthur
1884	Grover Cleveland*	Thomas Hendricks	1884	James Blaine	John Logan
1888	Grover Cleveland	A.G. Thurman	1888	Benjamin Harrison*	Levi Morton
1892	Grover Cleveland*	Adlai Stevenson	1892	Benjamin Harrison	Whitelaw Reid
1896	William J. Bryan	Arthur Sewall	1896	William McKinley*	Garret Hobart
1900	William J. Bryan	Adlai Stevenson	1900	William McKinley*	Theodore Roosevelt
1904	Alton Parker	Henry Davis	1904	Theodore Roosevelt*	Charles Fairbanks
1908	William J. Bryan	John Kern	1908	William H. Taft*	James Sherman
1912	Woodrow Wilson*	Thomas Marshall	1912	William H. Taft	James Sherman (2)
1916	Woodrow Wilson*	Thomas Marshall	1916	Charles Hughes	Charles Fairbanks
1920	James M. Cox	Franklin D. Roosevelt	1920	Warren G. Harding*	Calvin Coolidge
1924	John W. Davis	Charles W. Bryan	1924	Calvin Coolidge*	Charles G. Dawes
1928	Alfred E. Smith	Joseph T. Robinson	1928	Herbert Hoover*	Charles Curtis
1932	Franklin D. Roosevelt*	John N. Garner	1932	Herbert Hoover	Charles Curtis
1936	Franklin D. Roosevelt*	John N. Garner	1936	Alfred M. Landon	Frank Knox
1940	Franklin D. Roosevelt*	Henry A. Wallace	1940	Wendell L. Willkie	Charles McNary
1944	Franklin D. Roosevelt*	Harry S. Truman	1944	Thomas E. Dewey	John W. Bricker
1948	Harry S. Truman*	Alben W. Barkley	1948	Thomas E. Dewey	Earl Warren
1952	Adlai E. Stevenson	John J. Sparkman	1952	Dwight D. Eisenhower*	Richard M. Nixon
1956	Adlai E. Stevenson	Estes Kefauver	1956	Dwight D. Eisenhower*	Richard M. Nixon
1960	John F. Kennedy*	Lyndon B. Johnson	1960	Richard M. Nixon	Henry Cabot Lodge
1964	Lyndon B. Johnson*	Hubert H. Humphrey	1964	Barry M. Goldwater	William E. Miller
1968	Hubert H. Humphrey	Edmund S. Muskie	1968	Richard M. Nixon*	Spiro T. Agnew
1972	George S. McGovern	R. Sargent Shriver Jr. (3)	1972	Richard M. Nixon*	Spiro T. Agnew
1976	Jimmy Carter*	Walter F. Mondale	1976	Gerald R. Ford	Bob Dole
1980	Jimmy Carter	Walter F. Mondale	1980	Ronald Reagan*	George H. W. Bush
1984	Walter F. Mondale	Geraldine Ferraro	1984	Ronald Reagan*	George H. W. Bush
1988	Michael S. Dukakis	Lloyd Bentsen	1988	George H.W. Bush*	Dan Quayle
1992	Bill Clinton*	Al Gore	1992	George H.W. Bush	Dan Quayle
1996	Bill Clinton*	Al Gore	1996	Bob Dole	Jack Kemp
2000	Al Gore	Joseph Lieberman	2000	George W. Bush*	Richard Cheney
2004	John Kerry	John Edwards	2004	George W. Bush	Richard Cheney

(1) Douglas and Johnson were nominated at the Baltimore convention. An earlier convention in Charleston, SC, failed to reach a consensus and resulted in a split in the party. The Southern faction of the Democrats nominated John Breckinridge for president and Joseph Lane for vice president. (2) Died Oct. 30; replaced on ballot by Nicholas Butler. (3) Chosen by Democratic National Committee after Thomas Eagleton withdrew because of controversy over past treatments for depression.

Third-Party and Independent Presidential Candidates

Although many "third party" candidates or independents have pursued the presidency, only 10 of these from 1832 to 2000 have polled more than a million votes. In most elections since 1860, fewer than one vote in 20 has been cast for a third-party candidate. Major vote getters among third-party and independent candidates include James B. Weaver (People's Party), 1892; former Pres. Theodore Roosevelt (Progressive Party), 1912; Robert M. La Follette (Progressive Party), 1924; George C. Wallace (American Independent Party), 1968; and H. Ross Perot, as an independent in 1992 and with the Reform Party in 1996. In these 5 elections non-major-party candidates pulled more than 10% of the vote.

Roosevelt outpolled the Republican candidate, William Howard Taft, in 1912, capturing 28% of the popular vote and 88 electoral votes. In 1948, Strom Thurmond was able to capture 39 electoral votes (from 5 Southern states); however, all third parties received only 5.75% of the popular vote in the election. Twenty years later, George Wallace's popularity in the same region allowed him to get 46 electoral votes and 13.5% of the popular vote.

In 1992 Perot captured 19% of the popular vote; however, he did not win a single state. In 1996, Perot won 8% of the popular vote; all third-party candidates combined won about 10%. In 2000, Ralph Nader won about 3% of the vote.

Despite the difficulty in wining the presidency, independent and third-party candidates often bring attention to their most prominent issues. They can also affect the outcome between major-party candidates.

Notable Third Party and Independent Campaigns by Year

Party	Presidential nominee	Year	Issues	Strength in . . .
Anti-Masonic	William Wirt	1832	Against secret societies and oaths	PA, VT
Liberty	James G. Birney	1844	Anti-slavery	North
Free Soil	Martin Van Buren	1848	Anti-slavery	NY, OH
American (Know-Nothing)	Millard Fillmore	1856	Anti-immigrant	Northeast, South
Greenback	Peter Cooper	1876	For "cheap money," labor rights	National
Greenback	James B. Weaver	1880	For "cheap money," labor rights	National
Prohibition	John P. St. John	1884	Anti-liquor	National
People's (Populists)	James B. Weaver	1892	For "cheap money," end of national banks	South, West
Socialist	Eugene V. Debs	1900-12; 1920	For public ownership	National
Progressive (Bull Moose)	Theodore Roosevelt	1912	Against high tariffs	Midwest, West
Progressive	Robert M. La Follette	1924	Farmer and labor rights	Midwest, West
Socialist	Norman Thomas	1928-48	Liberal reforms	National
Union	William Lemke	1936	Anti-New Deal	National
States' Rights (Dixiecrats)	Strom Thurmond	1948	For states' rights	South
Progressive	Henry A. Wallace	1948	Anti-cold war	NY, CA
American Independent	George C. Wallace	1968	For states' rights	South
American	John G. Schmitz	1972	For "law and order"	Far West, OH, LA
None (Independent)	John B. Anderson	1980	A 3rd choice	National
None (Independent)	H. Ross Perot	1992	Federal budget deficit	National
Reform	H. Ross Perot	1996	Deficit; campaign finance	National
Green	Ralph Nader	2000	Corporate power	National
Independent	Ralph Nader	2004	Corporate power; domestic priorities	National

Popular and Electoral Vote for President, 1789-2000

(D) Democrat; (DR) Democratic Republican; (F) Federalist; (LR) Liberal Republican; (NR) National Republican; (P) People's; (PR) Progressive; (R) Republican; (RF) Reform; (SR) States' Rights; (W) Whig; Asterisk (*)–See notes at bottom.

Year	President elected	Popular	Elec.	Major losing candidate(s)	Popular	Elec.
1789	George Washington (F)	Unknown	69	No opposition	—	—
1792	George Washington (F)	Unknown	132	No opposition	—	—
1796	John Adams (F)	Unknown	71	Thomas Jefferson (DR)	Unknown	68
1800*	Thomas Jefferson (DR)	Unknown	73	Aaron Burr (DR)	Unknown	73
1804	Thomas Jefferson (DR)	Unknown	162	Charles Pinckney (F)	Unknown	14
1808	James Madison (DR)	Unknown	122	Charles Pinckney (F)	Unknown	47
1812	James Madison (DR)	Unknown	128	DeWitt Clinton (F)	Unknown	89
1816	James Monroe (DR)	Unknown	183	Rufus King (F)	Unknown	34
1820	James Monroe (DR)	Unknown	231	John Quincy Adams (DR)	Unknown	1
1824*	John Quincy Adams (DR)	105,321	84	Andrew Jackson (DR)	155,872	99
				Henry Clay (DR)	46,587	37
				William H. Crawford (DR)	44,282	41
1828	Andrew Jackson (D)	647,231	178	John Quincy Adams (NR)	509,097	83
1832	Andrew Jackson (D)	687,502	219	Henry Clay (NR)	530,189	49
1836	Martin Van Buren (D)	762,678	170	William H. Harrison (W)	548,007	73
1840	William H. Harrison (W)	1,275,017	234	Martin Van Buren (D)	1,128,702	60
1844	James K. Polk (D)	1,337,243	170	Henry Clay (W)	1,299,068	105
1848	Zachary Taylor (W)	1,360,101	163	Lewis Cass (D)	1,220,544	127
				Martin Van Buren (Free Soil)	291,501	—
1852	Franklin Pierce (D)	1,601,474	254	Winfield Scott (W)	1,386,578	42
1856	James Buchanan (D)	1,927,995	174	John C. Fremont (R)	1,391,555	114
				Millard Fillmore (American)	873,053	8
1860	Abraham Lincoln (R)	1,866,352	180	Stephen A. Douglas (D)	1,375,157	12
				John C. Breckinridge (D)	845,763	72
				John Bell (Const. Union)	589,581	39
1864	Abraham Lincoln (R)	2,216,067	212	George McClellan (D)	1,808,725	21
1868	Ulysses S. Grant (R)	3,015,071	214	Horatio Seymour (D)	2,709,615	80
1872*	Ulysses S. Grant (R)	3,597,070	286	Horace Greeley (D-LR)*	2,834,079	—
1876*	Rutherford B. Hayes (R)	4,033,950	185	Samuel J. Tilden (D)	4,284,757	184
1880	James A. Garfield (R)	4,449,053	214	Winfield S. Hancock (D)	4,442,030	155
1884	Grover Cleveland (D)	4,911,017	219	James G. Blaine (R)	4,848,334	182
1888	Benjamin Harrison (R)	5,444,337	233	Grover Cleveland (D)	5,540,050	168
1892	Grover Cleveland (D)	5,554,414	277	Benjamin Harrison (R)	5,190,802	145
				James Weaver (P)	1,027,329	22
1896	William McKinley (R)	7,035,638	271	William J. Bryan (D-P)	6,467,946	176
1900	William McKinley (R)	7,219,530	292	William J. Bryan (D)	6,358,071	155
1904	Theodore Roosevelt (R)	7,628,834	336	Alton B. Parker (D)	5,084,491	140
1908	William H. Taft (R)	7,679,006	321	William J. Bryan (D)	6,409,106	162
1912	Woodrow Wilson (D)	6,286,214	435	Theodore Roosevelt (PR)	4,216,020	88
				William H. Taft (R)	3,483,922	8
1916	Woodrow Wilson (D)	9,129,606	277	Charles E. Hughes (R)	8,538,221	254
1920	Warren G. Harding (R)	16,152,200	404	James M. Cox (D)	9,147,353	127
1924	Calvin Coolidge (R)	15,725,016	382	John W. Davis (D)	8,385,586	136
				Robert M. La Follette (PR)	4,822,856	13
1928	Herbert Hoover (R)	21,392,190	444	Alfred E. Smith (D)	15,016,443	87
1932	Franklin D. Roosevelt (D)	22,821,857	472	Herbert Hoover (R)	15,761,841	59
1936	Franklin D. Roosevelt (D)	27,751,597	523	Alfred Landon (R)	16,679,583	8
1940	Franklin D. Roosevelt (D)	27,243,466	449	Wendell Willkie (R)	22,304,755	82
1944	Franklin D. Roosevelt (D)	25,602,505	432	Thomas E. Dewey (R)	22,006,278	99
1948	Harry S. Truman (D)	24,105,812	303	Thomas E. Dewey (R)	21,970,065	189
				Strom Thurmond (SR)	1,169,021	39
				Henry A. Wallace (PR)	1,157,172	—
1952	Dwight D. Eisenhower (R)	33,936,252	442	Adlai E. Stevenson (D)	27,314,992	89
1956*	Dwight D. Eisenhower (R)	35,585,316	457	Adlai E. Stevenson (D)	26,031,322	73
1960*	John F. Kennedy (D)	34,227,096	303	Richard M. Nixon (R)	34,108,546	219
1964	Lyndon B. Johnson (D)	43,126,506	486	Barry M. Goldwater (R)	27,176,799	52
1968	Richard M. Nixon (R)	31,785,480	301	Hubert H. Humphrey (D)	31,275,166	191
				George C. Wallace (3rd party)	9,906,473	46
1972*	Richard M. Nixon (R)	47,165,234	520	George S. McGovern (D)	29,170,774	17
1976*	Jimmy Carter (D)	40,828,929	297	Gerald R. Ford (R)	39,148,940	240
1980	Ronald Reagan (R)	43,899,248	489	Jimmy Carter (D)	35,481,435	49
				John B. Anderson (independent)	5,719,437	—
1984	Ronald Reagan (R)	54,281,858	525	Walter F. Mondale (D)	37,457,215	13
1988*	George H. W. Bush (R)	48,881,221	426	Michael S. Dukakis (D)	41,805,422	111
1992	Bill Clinton (D)	44,908,254	370	George H. W. Bush (R)	39,102,343	168
				H. Ross Perot (independent)	19,741,065	—
1996	Bill Clinton (D)	47,401,185	379	Bob Dole (R)	39,197,469	159
				H. Ross Perot (RF)	8,085,294	—
2000*	George W. Bush (R)	50,459,211	271	Al Gore (D)	51,003,894	266
				Ralph Nader (Green)	2,834,410	—

*1800—Elected by House of Representatives because of tied electoral vote. 1824—Elected by House of Representatives because no candidate had polled a majority. By 1824, the Democratic Republicans had become a loose coalition of competing political groups. By 1828, the supporters of Jackson were known as Democrats, and the John Q. Adams and Henry Clay supporters as National Republicans. 1872—Greeley died Nov. 29, 1872. His electoral votes were split among 4 individuals. 1876—FL, LA, OR, and SC election returns were disputed. Congress in joint session (Mar. 2, 1877) declared Hayes and Wheeler elected president and vice president. 1956—Democrats elected 74 electors, but one from Alabama refused to vote for Stevenson. 1960—Sen. Harry F. Byrd (D, VA) received 15 electoral votes. 1972—John Hospers of California received one vote from an elector of Virginia. 1976—Ronald Reagan of CA received one vote from an elector of Washington. 1988—Sen. Lloyd Bentsen (D, TX) received 1 vote from an elector of West Virginia. 2000—One Gore elector from Washington, DC, abstained. Nader was listed as "Independent" on the ballot in some states, and was not on the ballot in all states.

Popular and Electoral Vote, 1996 and 2000

Source: Voter News Service; Federal Election Commission; totals are official.

State	EV Gore	EV Bush	EV Nader	EV Buchanan	Democrat Gore	Republican Bush	Green¹ Nader	Reform² Buchanan	EV Clinton	EV Dole	EV Perot	Democrat Clinton	Republican Dole	Reform² Perot
AL	0	9	0	0	692,611	941,173	18,323	6,351	0	9	0	662,165	769,044	92,149
AK	0	3	0	0	79,004	167,398	28,747	5,192	0	3	0	80,380	122,746	26,333
AZ	0	8	0	0	685,341	781,652	45,645	12,373	8	0	0	653,288	622,073	112,072
AR	0	6	0	0	422,768	472,940	13,421	7,358	6	0	0	475,171	325,416	69,884
CA	54	0	0	0	5,861,203	4,567,429	418,707	44,987	54	0	0	5,119,835	3,828,380	697,847
CO	0	8	0	0	738,227	883,748	91,434	10,465	0	8	0	671,152	691,848	99,629
CT	8	0	0	0	816,015	561,094	64,452	4,731	8	0	0	735,740	483,109	139,523
DE	3	0	0	0	180,068	137,288	8,307	777	3	0	0	140,355	99,062	28,719
DC	2³	0	0	—	171,923	18,073	10,576	—	3	0	0	158,220	17,339	3,611
FL	0	25	0	0	2,912,253	2,912,790	97,488	17,484	25	0	0	2,545,968	2,243,324	483,776
GA	0	13	—	0	1,116,230	1,419,720	—	10,926	0	13	0	1,053,849	1,080,843	146,337
HI	4	0	0	0	205,286	137,845	21,623	1,071	4	0	0	205,012	113,943	27,358
ID	0	4	—	0	138,637	336,937	—	7,615	0	4	0	165,443	256,595	62,518
IL	22	0	0	0	2,589,026	2,019,421	103,759	16,106	22	0	0	2,341,744	1,587,021	346,408
IN	0	12	0	0	901,980	1,245,836	—	16,959	0	12	0	887,424	1,006,693	224,299
IA	7	0	0	0	638,517	634,373	29,374	5,731	7	0	0	620,258	492,644	105,159
KS	0	6	0	0	399,276	622,332	36,086	7,370	0	6	0	387,659	583,245	92,639
KY	0	8	0	0	638,923	872,520	23,118	4,152	8	0	0	636,614	623,283	120,396
LA	0	9	0	0	792,344	927,871	20,473	14,356	9	0	0	927,837	712,586	123,293
ME	4	0	0	0	319,951	286,616	37,127	4,443	4	0	0	312,788	186,378	85,970
MD	10	0	0	0	1,144,008	813,827	53,768	4,248	10	0	0	966,207	681,530	115,812
MA	12	0	0	0	1,616,487	878,502	173,564	11,149	12	0	0	1,571,509	718,058	227,206
MI	18	0	0	—	2,170,418	1,953,139	84,165	—	18	0	0	1,989,653	1,481,212	336,670
MN	10	0	0	0	1,168,266	1,109,659	126,696	22,166	10	0	0	1,120,438	766,476	257,704
MS	0	7	0	0	404,614	572,844	8,122	2,265	0	7	0	394,022	439,838	52,222
MO	0	11	0	0	1,111,138	1,189,924	38,515	9,818	11	0	0	1,025,935	890,016	217,188
MT	0	3	0	0	137,126	240,178	24,437	5,697	0	3	0	167,922	179,652	55,229
NE	0	5	0	0	231,780	433,862	24,540	3,646	0	5	0	236,761	363,467	71,278
NV	0	4	0	0	279,978	301,575	15,008	4,747	4	0	0	203,974	199,244	43,986
NH	0	4	0	0	266,348	273,559	22,198	2,615	4	0	0	246,166	196,486	48,387
NJ	15	0	0	0	1,788,850	1,284,173	94,554	6,989	15	0	0	1,652,361	1,103,099	262,134
NM	5	0	0	0	286,783	286,417	21,251	1,392	5	0	0	273,495	232,751	32,257
NY	33	0	0	0	4,112,965	2,405,570	244,360	31,554	33	0	0	3,756,177	1,933,492	503,458
NC	0	14	—	0	1,257,692	1,631,163	—	8,874	0	14	0	1,107,849	1,225,938	168,059
ND	0	3	0	0	95,284	174,852	9,486	7,288	0	3	0	106,905	125,050	32,515
OH	0	21	0	0	2,186,190	2,351,209	117,857	26,724	21	0	0	2,148,222	1,859,883	483,207
OK	0	8	—	0	474,276	744,337	—	9,014	0	8	0	488,105	582,315	130,788
OR	7	0	0	0	720,342	713,577	77,357	7,063	7	0	0	649,641	538,152	121,221
PA	23	0	0	0	2,485,967	2,281,127	103,392	16,023	23	0	0	2,215,819	1,801,169	430,984
RI	4	0	0	0	249,508	130,555	25,052	2,273	4	0	0	233,050	104,683	43,723
SC	0	8	0	0	566,039	786,892	20,279	3,309	0	8	0	506,283	573,458	64,386
SD	0	3	—	0	118,804	190,700	—	3,322	0	3	0	139,333	150,543	31,250
TN	0	11	0	0	981,720	1,061,949	19,781	4,250	11	0	0	909,146	863,530	105,918
TX	0	32	0	0	2,433,746	3,799,639	137,994	12,394	0	32	0	2,459,683	2,736,167	378,537
UT	0	5	0	0	203,053	515,096	35,850	9,319	0	5	0	221,633	361,911	66,461
VT	3	0	0	0	149,022	119,775	20,374	2,192	3	0	0	137,894	80,352	31,024
VA	0	13	0	0	1,217,290	1,437,490	59,398	5,455	0	13	0	1,091,060	1,138,350	159,861
WA	11	0	0	0	1,247,652	1,108,864	103,002	7,171	11	0	0	1,123,323	840,712	201,003
WV	0	5	0	0	295,497	336,475	10,680	3,169	5	0	0	327,812	233,946	71,639
WI	11	0	0	0	1,242,987	1,237,279	94,070	11,446	11	0	0	1,071,971	845,029	227,339
WY	0	3	—	0	60,481	147,947	—	2,724	0	3	0	77,934	105,388	25,928
Total	266³	271	0	0	51,003,894	50,459,211	2,834,410	446,743	379	159	0	47,401,185	39,197,469	8,085,294

(—) = Not listed on state's ballot. (1) Listed on the ballot in some states as party other than Green. (2) Listed on the ballot in some states as party other than Reform. (3) One Washington, DC, elector abstained.

2000 Official Presidential General Election Results

Source: Voter News Service; Federal Election Commission

Candidate (Party)	Popular Vote	Percent of Popular Vote	Candidate (Party)	Popular Vote	Percent of Popular Vote
Al Gore (Democrat)	51,003,894	48.41	Monica Moorehead (Workers World)	4,795	0.00
George W. Bush (Republican)	50,459,211	47.89	David McReynolds (Socialist)	4,194	0.00
Ralph Nader (Green)	2,834,410	2.69	Cathy Gordon Brown (Independent)	1,606	0.00
Patrick J. Buchanan (Reform)	446,743	0.42	Denny Lane (Vermont Grassroots)	1,044	0.00
Harry Browne (Libertarian)	386,041	0.37	Randall Venson (Independent)	535	0.00
Howard Phillips (Constitution)	96,919	0.09	Earl F. Dodge (Prohibition)	208	0.00
John S. Hagelin (Natural Law)	83,117	0.08	Louie G. Youngkeit (Unaffiliated)	161	0.00
James E. Harris Jr. (Socialist Workers)	7,354	0.01	Write-in	20,938	0.02
L. Neil Smith (Libertarian)	5,775	0.01	None of These Candidates (Nevada)	3,315	0.00
			Total	**105,360,260**	**100.00**

Note: Party designations may vary from one state to another

OFFICIAL PRESIDENTIAL ELECTION RESULTS, 1948-2000

Source: Voter News Service; Federal Election Commission; Alaska Division of Elections

Alabama

1948: Thurmond, States' Rights, 171,443; Dewey, Rep., 40,930; Wallace, Prog., 1,522; Watson, Proh., 1,085.
1952: Eisenhower, Rep., 149,231; Stevenson, Dem., 275,075; Hamblen, Proh., 1,814.
1956: Stevenson, Dem., 290,844; Eisenhower, Rep., 195,694; Ind. electors, 20,323.
1960: Kennedy, Dem., 324,050; Nixon, Rep., 237,981; Faubus, States' Rights, 4,367; Decker, Proh., 2,106; King, Afro-Americans, 1,485; scattering, 236.
1964: Dem. (electors unpledged), 209,848; Goldwater, Rep., 479,085; scattering, 105.
1968: Nixon, Rep., 146,923; Humphrey, Dem., 196,579; Wallace, 3rd Party, 691,425; Munn, Proh., 4,022.
1972: Nixon, Rep., 728,701; McGovern, Dem., 219,108 plus 37,815 Natl. Dem. Party of Alabama; Schmitz, Conservative, 11,918; Munn., Proh., 8,551.
1976: Carter, Dem., 659,170; Ford, Rep., 504,070; Maddox, Amer. Ind., 9,198; Bubar, Proh., 6,669; Hall, Com., 1,954; MacBride, Libertarian, 1,481.
1980: Reagan, Rep., 654,192; Carter, Dem., 636,730; Anderson, Independent, 16,481; Rarick, Amer. Ind., 15,010; Clark, Libertarian, 13,318; Bubar, Statesman, 1,743; Hall, Com., 1,629; DeBerry, Soc. Workers, 1,303; McReynolds, Socialist, 1,006; Commoner, Citizens, 517.
1984: Reagan, Rep., 872,849; Mondale, Dem., 551,899; Bergland, Libertarian, 9,504.
1988: Bush, Rep., 815,576; Dukakis, Dem., 549,506; Paul, Lib., 8,460; Fulani, Ind., 3,311.
1992: Bush, Rep., 804,283; Clinton, Dem., 690,080; Perot, Ind., 183,109; Marrou, Libertarian, 5,737; Fulani, New Alliance, 2,161.
1996: Dole, Rep., 769,044; Clinton, Dem., 662,165; Perot, Ind. (Ref.), 92,149; Browne, Libertarian, 5,290; Phillips, Ind., 2,365; Hagelin, Natural Law, 1,697; Harris, Ind., 516.
2000: Bush, Rep., 941,173; Gore, Dem., 692,611; Nader, Ind., 18,323; Buchanan, Ind., 6,351; Browne, Libertarian, 5,893; Phillips, Ind., 775 Hagelin, Ind., 447.

Alaska

1960: Kennedy, Dem., 29,809; Nixon, Rep., 30,953.
1964: Johnson, Dem., 44,329; Goldwater, Rep., 22,930.
1968: Nixon, Rep., 37,600; Humphrey, Dem., 35,411; Wallace, 3rd Party, 10,024.
1972: Nixon, Rep., 55,349; McGovern, Dem., 32,967; Schmitz, Amer., 6,903.
1976: Carter, Dem., 44,058; Ford, Rep., 71,555; MacBride, Libertarian, 6,785.
1980: Reagan, Rep., 86,112; Carter, Dem., 41,842; Clark, Libertarian, 18,479; Anderson, Ind., 11,155; write-in, 857.
1984: Reagan, Rep., 138,377; Mondale, Dem., 62,007; Bergland, Libertarian, 6,378.
1988: Bush, Rep., 119,251; Dukakis, Dem., 72,584; Paul, Lib., 5,484; Fulani, New Alliance, 1,024.
1992: Bush, Rep., 102,000; Clinton, Dem., 78,294; Perot, Ind., 73,481; Gritz, Populist/America First, 1,379; Marrou, Libertarian, 1,378.
1996: Dole, Rep., 122,746; Clinton, Dem., 80,380; Perot, Ref., 26,333; Nader, Green, 7,597; Browne, Libertarian, 2,276; Phillips, Taxpayers, 925; Hagelin, Natural Law, 729.
2000: Bush, Rep., 167,398; Gore, Dem., 79,004; Nader, Green, 28,747; Buchanan, Reform, 5,192; Browne, Libertarian, 2,636; Hagelin, Natural Law, 919; Phillips, Constitution, 596.

Arizona

1948: Truman, Dem., 95,251; Dewey, Rep., 77,597; Wallace, Prog., 3,310; Watson, Proh., 786; Teichert, Soc. Labor, 121.
1952: Eisenhower, Rep., 152,042; Stevenson, Dem., 108,528.
1956: Eisenhower, Rep., 176,990; Stevenson, Dem., 112,880; Andrews, Ind. 303.
1960: Kennedy, Dem., 176,781; Nixon, Rep., 221,241; Hass, Soc. Labor, 469.
1964: Johnson, Dem., 237,753; Goldwater, Rep., 242,535; Hass, Soc. Labor, 482.
1968: Nixon, Rep., 266,721; Humphrey, Dem., 170,514; Wallace, 3rd Party, 46,573; McCarthy, New Party, 2,751; Halstead, Soc. Workers, 85; Cleaver, Peace and Freedom, 217; Blomen, Soc. Labor, 75.
1972: Nixon, Rep., 402,812; McGovern, Dem., 198,540; Schmitz, Amer., 21,208; Soc. Workers, 30,945. Because of ballot peculiarities in 3 counties (particularly Pima), thousands of voters cast ballots for the Soc. Workers Party *and* one of the major candidates. Court ordered both votes counted as official.
1976: Carter, Dem., 295,602; Ford, Rep., 418,642; McCarthy, Ind., 19,229; MacBride, Libertarian, 7,647; Camejo, Soc. Workers, 928; Anderson, Amer., 564; Maddox, Amer. Ind., 85.
1980: Reagan, Rep., 529,688; Carter, Dem., 246,843; Anderson, Ind., 76,952; Clark, Libertarian, 18,784; De Berry, Soc. Workers, 1,100; Commoner, Citizens, 551; Hall, Com., 25; Griswold, Workers World, 2.
1984: Reagan, Rep., 681,416; Mondale, Dem., 333,854; Bergland, Libertarian, 10,585.
1988: Bush, Rep., 702,541; Dukakis, Dem., 454,029; Paul, Lib., 13,351; Fulani, New Alliance, 1,662.
1992: Bush, Rep., 572,086; Clinton, Dem., 543,050; Perot, Ind., 353,741; Gritz, Populist/America First, 8,141; Marrou, Libertarian, 6,759; Hagelin, Natural Law, 2,267.
1996: Clinton, Dem., 653,288; Dole, Rep., 622,073; Perot, Ref., 112,072; Browne, Libertarian, 14,358.
2000: Gore, Bush, Rep., 781,652; Dem., 685,341; Nader, Green, 45,645; Buchanan, Rep., 12,373; Smith, Libertarian, 5,775; Hagelin, Natural Law, 1,120.

Arkansas

1948: Truman, Dem., 149,659; Dewey, Rep., 50,959; Thurmond, States' Rights, 40,068; Thomas, Soc., 1,037; Wallace, Prog., 751; Watson, Proh., 1.
1952: Eisenhower, Rep., 177,155; Stevenson, Dem., 226,300; Hamblen, Proh., 886; MacArthur, Christian Nationalist, 458; Hass, Soc. Labor, 1.
1956: Stevenson, Dem., 213,277; Eisenhower, Rep., 186,287; Andrews, Ind., 7,008.
1960: Kennedy, Dem., 215,049; Nixon, Rep., 184,508; Natl. States' Rights, 28,952.
1964: Johnson, Dem., 314,197; Goldwater, Rep., 243,264; Kasper, Natl. States' Rights, 2,965.
1968: Nixon, Rep., 189,062; Humphrey, Dem., 184,901; Wallace, 3rd Party, 235,627.
1972: Nixon, Rep., 445,751; McGovern, Dem., 198,899; Schmitz, Amer., 3,016.
1976: Carter, Dem., 498,604; Ford, Rep., 267,903; McCarthy, Ind., 639; Anderson, Amer., 389.
1980: Reagan, Rep., 403,164; Carter, Dem., 398,041; Anderson, Ind., 22,468; Clark, Libertarian, 8,970; Commoner, Citizens, 2,345; Bubar, Statesman, 1,350; Hall, Com., 1,244.
1984: Reagan, Rep., 534,774; Mondale, Dem., 338,646; Bergland, Libertarian, 2,220.
1988: Bush, Rep., 466,578; Dukakis, Dem., 349,237; Duke, Chr. Pop., 5,146; Paul, Lib., 3,297.
1992: Clinton, Dem., 505,823; Bush, Rep., 337,324; Perot, Ind., 99,132; Phillips, U.S. Taxpayers, 1,437; Marrou, Libertarian, 1,261; Fulani, New Alliance, 1,022.
1996: Clinton, Dem., 475,171; Dole, Rep., 325,416; Perot, Ref., 69,884; Nader, Ind., 3,649; Browne, Ind., 3,076; Phillips, Ind., 2,065; Forbes, Ind., 932; Collins, Ind., 823; Masters, Ind., 749; Hagelin, Ind., 729; Moorehead, Ind., 747; Hollis, Ind., 538; Dodge, Ind., 483.
2000: Bush, Rep., 472,940; Gore, Dem., 422,768; Nader, Green, 13,421; Buchanan, Reform, 7,358; Browne, Libertarian, 2,781; Phillips, Constitution, 1,415; Hagelin, Natural Law, 1,098.

California

1948: Truman, Dem., 1,913,134; Dewey, Rep., 1,895,269; Wallace, Prog., 190,381; Watson, Proh., 16,926; Thomas, Soc., 3,459; Thurmond, States' Rights, 1,228; Teichert, Soc. Labor, 195; Dobbs, Soc. Workers, 133.
1952: Eisenhower, Rep., 2,897,310; Stevenson, Dem., 2,197,548; Hallinan, Prog., 24,106; Hamblen, Proh., 15,653; MacArthur, (Tenny Ticket), 3,326; (Kellems Ticket) 178; Hass, Soc. Labor, 273; Hoopes, Soc., 206; scattered, 3,249.
1956: Eisenhower, Rep., 3,027,668; Stevenson, Dem., 2,420,136; Holtwick, Proh., 11,119; Andrews, Constitution, 6,087; Hass, Soc. Labor, 300; Hoopes, Soc., 123; Dobbs, Soc. Workers, 96; Smith, Christian Natl., 8.

1960: Kennedy, Dem., 3,224,099; Nixon, Rep., 3,259,722; Decker, Proh., 21,706; Hass, Soc. Labor, 1,051.

1964: Johnson, Dem., 4,171,877; Goldwater, Rep., 2,879,108; Hass, Soc. Labor, 489; DeBerry, Soc. Workers, 378; Munn, Proh., 305; Hensley, Universal, 19.

1968: Nixon, Rep., 3,467,664; Humphrey, Dem., 3,244,318; Wallace, 3rd Party, 487,270; Peace and Freedom, 27,707; McCarthy, Alternative, 20,721; Gregory, write-in, 3,230; Mitchell, Com., 260; Munn, Proh., 59; Blomen, Soc. Labor, 341; Soeters, Defense, 17.

1972: Nixon, Rep., 4,602,096; McGovern, Dem., 3,475,847; Schmitz, Amer., 232,554; Spock, Peace and Freedom, 55,167; Hall, Com., 373; Hospers, Libertarian, 980; Munn, Proh., 53; Fisher, Soc. Labor, 197; Jenness, Soc. Workers, 574; Green, Universal, 21.

1976: Carter, Dem., 3,742,284; Ford, Rep., 3,882,244; MacBride, Libertarian, 56,388; Maddox, Amer. Ind., 51,098; Wright, People's, 41,731; Camejo, Soc. Workers, 17,259; Hall, Com., 12,766; write-in, McCarthy, 58,412; other write-in, 4,935.

1980: Reagan, Rep. 4,524,858; Carter, Dem., 3,083,661; Anderson, Ind., 739,833; Clark, Libertarian, 148,434; Commoner, Ind., 61,063; Smith, Peace and Freedom, 18,116; Rarick, Amer. Ind., 9,856.

1984: Reagan, Rep. 5,305,410; Mondale, Dem., 3,815,947; Bergland, Libertarian, 48,400.

1988: Bush, Rep., 5,054,917; Dukakis, Dem., 4,702,233; Paul, Lib., 70,105; Fulani, Ind., 31,181.

1992: Clinton, Dem., 5,121,325; Bush, Rep., 3,630,575; Perot, Ind., 2,296,006; Marrou, Libertarian, 48,139; Daniels, Ind., 18,597; Phillips, U.S. Taxpayers, 12,711.

1996: Clinton, Dem., 5,119,835; Dole, Rep., 3,828,380; Perot, Ref., 697,847; Nader, Green, 237,016; Browne, Libertarian, 73,600; Feinland, Peace & Freedom, 25,332; Phillips, Amer. Ind., 21,202; Hagelin, Natural Law, 15,403.

2000: Gore, Dem., 5,861,203; Bush, Rep., 4,567,429; Nader, Green, 418,707; Browne, Libertarian, 45,520; Buchanan, Reform, 44,987; Phillips, Amer. Ind., 17,042; Hagelin, Natural Law, 10,934.

Colorado

1948: Truman, Dem., 267,288; Dewey, Rep., 239,714; Wallace, Prog., 6,115; Thomas, Soc., 1,678; Dobbs, Soc. Workers, 228; Teichert, Soc. Labor, 214.

1952: Eisenhower, Rep., 379,782; Stevenson, Dem., 245,504; MacArthur, Constitution, 2,181; Hallinan, Prog., 1,919; Hoopes, Soc., 365; Hass, Soc. Labor, 352.

1956: Eisenhower, Rep., 394,479; Stevenson, Dem., 263,997; Hass, Soc. Lab., 3,308; Andrews, Ind., 759; Hoopes, Soc., 531.

1960: Kennedy, Dem., 330,629; Nixon, Rep., 402,242; Hass, Soc. Labor, 2,803; Dobbs, Soc. Workers, 572.

1964: Johnson, Dem., 476,024; Goldwater, Rep., 296,767; Hass, Soc. Labor, 302; DeBerry, Soc. Workers, 2,537; Munn, Proh., 1,356.

1968: Nixon, Rep., 409,345; Humphrey, Dem., 335,174; Wallace, 3rd Party, 60,813; Blomen, Soc. Labor, 3,016; Gregory, New-party, 1,393; Munn, Proh., 275; Halstead, Soc. Workers, 235.

1972: Nixon, Rep., 597,189; McGovern, Dem., 329,980; Fisher, Soc. Labor, 4,361; Hospers, Libertarian, 1,111; Hall, Com., 432; Jenness, Soc. Workers, 555; Munn, Proh., 467; Schmitz, Amer., 17,269; Spock, Peoples, 2,403.

1976: Carter, Dem., 460,353; Ford, Rep., 584,367; McCarthy, Ind., 26,107; MacBride, Libertarian, 5,330; Bubar, Proh., 2,882.

1980: Reagan, Rep., 652,264; Carter, Dem., 367,973; Anderson, Ind., 130,633; Clark, Libertarian, 25,744; Commoner, Citizens, 5,614; Bubar, Statesman, 1,180; Pulley, Socialist, 520; Hall, Com., 487.

1984: Reagan, Rep., 821,817; Mondale, Dem., 454,975; Bergland, Libertarian, 11,257.

1988: Bush, Rep., 728,177; Dukakis, Dem., 621,453; Paul, Lib., 15,482; Dodge, Proh., 4,604.

1992: Clinton, Dem., 629,681; Bush, Rep., 562,850; Perot, Ind., 366,010; Marrou, Libertarian, 8,669; Fulani, New Alliance, 1,608.

1996: Dole, Rep., 691,848; Clinton, Dem., 671,152; Perot, Ref., 99,629; Nader, Green, 25,070; Browne, Libertarian, 12,392; Collins, Ind., 2,809; Phillips, Amer. Constitution, 2,813; Hagelin, Natural Law, 2,547; Hollis, Soc., 669; Moorehead, Workers World, 599; Templin, Amer. 557; Dodge, Proh., 375; Harris, Soc. Workers, 244.

2000: Bush, Rep., 883,748; Gore, Dem., 738,227; Nader, Green, 91,434; Browne, Libertarian, 12,799; Buchanan, Reform, 10,465; Hagelin, Reform, 2,240; Phillips, Amer. Constitution, 1,319; McReynolds, Soc., 712; Harris, Soc. Workers, 216; Dodge, Proh., 208.

Connecticut

1948: Truman, Dem., 423,297; Dewey, Rep., 437,754; Wallace, Prog., 13,713; Thomas, Soc., 6,964; Teichert, Soc. Labor, 1,184; Dobbs, Soc. Workers, 606.

1952: Eisenhower, Rep., 611,012; Stevenson, Dem., 481,649; Hoopes, Soc., 2,244; Hallinan, Peoples, 1,466; Hass, Soc. Labor, 535; write-in, 5.

1956: Eisenhower, Rep., 711,837; Stevenson, Dem., 405,079; scattered, 205.

1960: Kennedy, Dem., 657,055; Nixon, Rep., 565,813.

1964: Johnson, Dem., 826,269; Goldwater, Rep., 390,996; scattered, 1,313.

1968: Nixon, Rep., 556,721; Humphrey, Dem., 621,561; Wallace, 3rd Party, 76,650; scattered, 1,300.

1972: Nixon, Rep., 810,763; McGovern, Dem., 555,498; Schmitz, Amer., 17,239; scattered, 777.

1976: Carter, Dem., 647,895; Ford, Rep., 719,261; Maddox, George Wallace Party, 7,101; LaRouche, U.S. Labor, 1,789.

1980: Reagan, Rep., 677,210; Carter, Dem., 541,732; Anderson, Ind., 171,807; Clark, Libertarian, 8,570; Commoner, Citizens, 6,130; scattered, 836.

1984: Reagan, Rep., 890,877; Mondale, Dem., 569,597.

1988: Bush, Rep., 750,241; Dukakis, Dem., 676,584; Paul, Lib., 14,071; Fulani, New Alliance, 2,491.

1992: Clinton, Dem., 682,318; Bush, Rep., 578,313; Perot, Ind., 348,771; Marrou, Libertarian, 5,391; Fulani, New Alliance, 1,363.

1996: Clinton, Dem., 735,740; Dole, Rep., 483,109; Perot, Ref., 139,523; Nader, Green, 24,321; Browne, Libertarian, 5,788; Phillips, Concerned Citizens, 2,425; Hagelin, Natural Law, 1,703.

2000: Gore, Dem., 816,015; Bush, Rep., 561,094; Nader, Green, 64,452; Phillips, Concerned Citizens, 9,695; Buchanan, Reform, 4,731; Browne, Libertarian, 3,484.

Delaware

1948: Truman, Dem., 67,813; Dewey, Rep., 69,688; Wallace, Prog., 1,050; Watson, Proh., 343; Thomas, Soc., 250; Teichert, Soc. Labor, 29.

1952: Eisenhower, Rep., 90,059; Stevenson, Dem., 83,315; Hass, Soc. Labor, 242; Hamblen, Proh., 234; Hallinan, Prog., 155; Hoopes, Soc., 20.

1956: Eisenhower, Rep., 98,057; Stevenson, Dem., 79,421; Oltwick, Proh., 400; Hass, Soc. Labor, 110.

1960: Kennedy, Dem., 99,590; Nixon, Rep., 96,373; Faubus, States' Rights, 354; Decker, Proh., 284; Hass, Soc. Labor, 82.

1964: Johnson, Dem., 122,704; Goldwater, Rep., 78,078; Hass, Soc. Labor, 113; Munn, Proh., 425.

1968: Nixon, Rep., 96,714; Humphrey, Dem., 89,194; Wallace, 3rd Party, 28,459.

1972: Nixon, Rep., 140,357; McGovern, Dem., 92,283; Schmitz, Amer., 2,638; Munn, Proh., 238.

1976: Carter, Dem., 122,596; Ford, Rep., 109,831; McCarthy, non-partisan, 2,437; Anderson, Amer., 645; LaRouche, U.S. Labor, 136; Bubar, Proh., 103; Levin, Soc. Labor, 86.

1980: Reagan, Rep., 111,252; Carter, Dem., 105,754; Anderson, Ind., 16,288; Clark, Libertarian, 1,974; Greaves, Amer., 400.

1984: Reagan, Rep., 152,190; Mondale, Dem., 101,656; Bergland, Libertarian, 268.

1988: Bush, Rep., 139,639; Dukakis, Dem., 108,647; Paul, Lib., 1,162; Fulani, New Alliance, 443.

1992: Clinton, Dem., 126,054; Bush, Rep., 102,313; Perot, Ind., 59,213; Fulani, New Alliance, 1,105.

1996: Clinton, Dem., 140,355; Dole, Rep., 99,062; Perot, Ind. (Ref.), 28,719; Browne, Libertarian, 2,052; Phillips, Taxpayers, 348; Hagelin, Natural Law, 274.

2000: Gore, Dem., 180,068; Bush, Rep., 137,288; Nader, Green, 8,307; Buchanan, Reform, 777; Browne, Libertarian, 774; Phillips, Constitution, 208; Hagelin, Natural Law, 107.

District of Columbia

1964: Johnson, Dem., 169,796; Goldwater, Rep., 28,801.
1968: Nixon, Rep., 31,012; Humphrey, Dem., 139, 566.

1972: Nixon, Rep., 35,226; McGovern, Dem., 127,627; Reed, Soc. Workers, 316; Hall, Com., 252.

1976: Carter, Dem., 137,818; Ford, Rep., 27,873; Camejo, Soc. Workers, 545; MacBride, Libertarian, 274; Hall, Com., 219; LaRouche, U.S. Labor, 157.

1980: Reagan, Rep., 23,313; Carter, Dem., 130,231; Anderson, Ind., 16,131; Commoner, Citizens, 1,826; Clark, Libertarian, 1,104; Hall, Com., 369; DeBerry, Soc. Workers, 173; Griswold, Workers World, 52; write-ins, 690.

1984: Mondale, Dem., 180,408; Reagan, Rep., 29,009; Bergland, Libertarian, 279.

1988: Bush, Rep., 27,590; Dukakis, Dem., 159,407; Fulani, New Alliance, 2,901; Paul, Lib., 554.

1992: Clinton, Dem., 192,619; Bush, Rep., 20,698; Perot, Ind., 9,681; Fulani, New Alliance, 1,459; Daniels, Ind., 1,186.

1996: Clinton, Dem., 158,220; Dole, Rep., 17,339; Perot, Ref., 3,611; Nader, Green, 4,780; Browne, Libertarian, 588; Hagelin, Natural Law, 283; Harris, Soc. Workers, 257.

2000: Gore, Dem., 171,923; Bush, Rep., 18,073; Nader, Green, 10,576; Browne, Libertarian, 669; Harris, Soc. Workers, 114.

Florida

1948: Truman, Dem., 281,988; Dewey, Rep., 194,280; Thurmond, States' Rights, 89,755; Wallace, Prog., 11,620.

1952: Eisenhower, Rep., 544,036; Stevenson, Dem., 444,950; scattered, 351.

1956: Eisenhower, Rep., 643,849; Stevenson, Dem., 480,371.

1960: Kennedy, Dem., 748,700; Nixon, Rep., 795,476.

1964: Johnson, Dem., 948,540; Goldwater, Rep., 905,941.

1968: Nixon, Rep., 886,804; Humphrey, Dem., 676,794; Wallace, 3rd Party, 624,207.

1972: Nixon, Rep., 1,857,759; McGovern, Dem., 718,117; scattered, 7,407.

1976: Carter, Dem., 1,636,000; Ford, Rep., 1,469,531; McCarthy, Ind., 23,643; Anderson, Amer., 21,325.

1980: Reagan, Rep., 2,046,951; Carter, Dem., 1,419,475; Anderson, Ind., 189,692; Clark, Libertarian, 30,524; write-ins, 285.

1984: Reagan, Rep., 2,728,775; Mondale, Dem., 1,448,344.

1988: Bush, Rep., 2,616,597; Dukakis, Dem., 1,655,851; Paul, Lib., 19,796, Fulani, New Alliance, 6,655.

1992: Bush, Rep., 2,171,781; Clinton, Dem., 2,071,651; Perot, Ind., 1,052,481; Marrou, Libertarian, 15,068.

1996: Clinton, Dem., 2,545,968; Dole, Rep., 2,243,324; Perot, Ref., 483,776; Browne, Libertarian, 23,312.

2000: Bush, Rep., 2,912,790; Gore, Dem., 2,912,253; Nader, Green, 97,488; Buchanan, Reform, 17,484; Browne, Libertarian, 16,415; Hagelin, Natural Law, 2,281; Moorehead, Workers World, 1,804; Phillips, Constitution, 1,371; McReynolds, Soc., 622; Harris, Soc. Workers, 562.

Georgia

1948: Truman, Dem., 254,646; Dewey, Rep., 76,691; Thurmond, States' Rights, 85,055; Wallace, Prog., 1,636; Watson, Proh., 732.

1952: Eisenhower, Rep., 198,979; Stevenson, Dem., 456,823; Liberty Party, 1.

1956: Stevenson, Dem., 444,388; Eisenhower, Rep., 222,778; Andrews, Ind., write-in, 1,754.

1960: Kennedy, Dem., 458,638; Nixon, Rep., 274,472; write-in, 239.

1964: Johnson, Dem., 522,557; Goldwater, Rep., 616,600.

1968: Nixon, Rep., 380,111; Humphrey, Dem., 334,440; Wallace, 3rd Party, 535,550; write-in, 162.

1972: Nixon, Rep., 881,496; McGovern, Dem., 289,529; scattered, 2,935; Schmitz, Amer., 812.

1976: Carter, Dem., 979,409; Ford, Rep., 483,743; write-in, 4,306.

1980: Reagan, Rep., 654,168; Carter, Dem., 890,955; Anderson, Ind., 36,055; Clark, Libertarian, 15,627.

1984: Reagan, Rep., 1,068,722; Mondale, Dem., 706,628.

1988: Bush, Rep., 1,081,331; Dukakis, Dem., 714,792; Paul, Lib., 8,435; Fulani, New Alliance, 5,099.

1992: Clinton, Dem., 1,008,966; Bush, Rep., 995,252; Perot, Ind., 309,657; Marrou, Libertarian, 7,110.

1996: Dole, Rep., 1,080,843; Clinton, Dem., 1,053,849; Perot, Ref., 146,337; Browne, Libertarian, 17,870.

2000: Bush, Rep., 1,419,720; Gore, Dem., 1,116,230; Browne, Libertarian, 36,332; Buchanan, Independent, 10,926.

Hawaii

1960: Kennedy, Dem., 92,410; Nixon, Rep., 92,295.

1964: Johnson, Dem., 163,249; Goldwater, Rep., 44,022.

1968: Nixon, Rep., 91,425; Humphrey, Dem., 141,324; Wallace, 3rd Party, 3,469.

1972: Nixon, Rep., 168,865; McGovern, Dem., 101,409.

1976: Carter, Dem., 147,375; Ford, Rep., 140,003; MacBride, Libertarian, 3,923.

1980: Reagan, Rep., 130,112; Carter, Dem., 135,879; Anderson, Ind., 32,021; Clark, Libertarian, 3,269; Commoner, Citizens, 1,548; Hall, Com., 458.

1984: Reagan, Rep., 184,934; Mondale, Dem., 147,098; Bergland, Libertarian, 2,167.

1988: Bush, Rep., 158,625; Dukakis, Dem., 192,364; Paul, Lib., 1,999; Fulani, New Alliance, 1,003.

1992: Clinton, Dem., 179,310; Bush, Rep., 136,822; Perot, Ind., 53,003; Gritz, Populist/America First, 1,452; Marrou, Libertarian, 1,119.

1996: Clinton, Dem., 205,012; Dole, Rep., 113,943; Perot, Ref., 27,358; Nader, Green, 10,386; Browne, Libertarian, 2,493; Hagelin, Natural Law, 570; Phillips, Taxpayers, 358.

2000: Gore, Dem., 205,286; Bush, Rep., 137,845; Nader, Green, 21,623; Browne, Libertarian, 1,477; Buchanan, Reform, 1,071; Phillips, Constitution, 343; Hagelin, Natural Law, 306.

Idaho

1948: Truman, Dem., 107,370; Dewey, Rep., 101,514; Wallace, Prog., 4,972; Watson, Proh., 628; Thomas, Soc., 332.

1952: Eisenhower, Rep., 180,707; Stevenson, Dem., 95,081; Hallinan, Prog., 443; write-in, 23.

1956: Eisenhower, Rep., 166,979; Stevenson, Dem., 105,868; Andrews, Ind., 126; write-in, 16.

1960: Kennedy, Dem., 138,853; Nixon, Rep., 161,597.

1964: Johnson, Dem., 148,920; Goldwater, Rep., 143,557.

1968: Nixon, Rep., 165,369; Humphrey, Dem., 89,273; Wallace, 3rd Party, 36,541.

1972: Nixon, Rep., 199,384; McGovern, Dem., 80,826; Schmitz, Amer., 28,869; Spock, Peoples, 903.

1976: Carter, Dem., 126,549; Ford, Rep., 204,151; Maddox, Amer., 5,935; MacBride, Libertarian, 3,558; LaRouche, U.S. Labor, 739.

1980: Reagan, Rep., 290,699; Carter, Dem., 110,192; Anderson, Ind., 27,058; Clark, Libertarian, 8,425; Rarick, Amer., 1,057.

1984: Reagan, Rep., 297,523; Mondale, Dem., 108,510; Bergland, Libertarian, 2,823.

1988: Bush, Rep., 253,881; Dukakis, Dem., 147,272; Paul, Lib., 5,313; Fulani, Ind., 2,502.

1992: Clinton, Dem., 137,013; Bush, Rep., 202,645; Perot, Ind., 130,395; Gritz, Populist/America First, 10,281; Marrou, Libertarian, 1,167.

1996: Dole, Rep., 256,595; Clinton, Dem., 165,443; Perot, Ref., 62,518; Browne, Libertarian, 3,325; Phillips, Taxpayers, 2,230; Hagelin, Natural Law, 1,600.

2000: Bush, Rep., 336,937; Gore, Dem., 138,637; Buchanan, Reform, 7,615; Browne, Libertarian, 3,488; Phillips, Constitution, 1,469; Hagelin, Natural Law, 1,177.

Illinois

1948: Truman, Dem., 1,994,715; Dewey, Rep., 1,961,103; Watson, Proh., 11,959; Thomas, Soc., 11,522; Teichert, Soc. Labor, 3,118.

1952: Eisenhower, Rep., 2,457,327; Stevenson, Dem., 2,013,920; Hass, Soc. Labor, 9,363; write-in, 448.

1956: Eisenhower, Rep., 2,623,327; Stevenson, Dem., 1,775,682; Hass, Soc. Labor, 8,342; write-in, 56.

1960: Kennedy, Dem., 2,377,846; Nixon, Rep., 2,368,988; Hass, Soc. Labor, 10,560; write-in, 15.

1964: Johnson, Dem., 2,796,833; Goldwater, Rep., 1,905,946; write-in, 62.

1968: Nixon, Rep., 2,174,774; Humphrey, Dem., 2,039,814; Wallace, 3rd Party, 390,958; Blomen, Soc. Labor, 13,878; write-in, 325.

1972: Nixon, Rep. 2,788,179; McGovern, Dem., 1,913,472; Fisher, Soc. Labor, 12,344; Schmitz, Amer., 2,471; Hall, Com., 4,541; others, 2,229.

1976: Carter, Dem., 2,271,295; Ford, Rep., 2,364,269; McCarthy, Ind., 55,939; Hall, Com., 9,250; MacBride, Libertarian, 8,057; Camejo, Soc. Workers, 3,615; Levin, Soc. Labor, 2,422; LaRouche, U.S. Labor, 2,018; write-in, 1,968.

1980: Reagan, Rep., 2,358,049; Carter, Dem., 1,981,413; Anderson, Ind., 346,754; Clark, Libertarian, 38,939; Commoner, Citizens, 10,692; Hall, Com., 9,711; Griswold, Workers World, 2,257; DeBerry, Soc. Workers, 1,302; write-ins, 604.

1984: Reagan, Rep., 2,707,103; Mondale, Dem., 2,086,499; Bergland, Libertarian, 10,086.

1988: Bush, Rep., 2,310,939; Dukakis, Dem., 2,215,940; Paul, Lib., 14,944; Fulani, Solid., 10,276.

1992: Clinton, Dem., 2,453,350; Bush, Rep., 1,734,096; Perot, Ind., 840,515; Marrou, Libertarian, 9,218; Fulani, New Alliance, 5,267; Gritz, Populist/America First, 3,577; Hagelin, Natural Law, 2,751; Warren, Soc. Workers, 1,361.

1996: Clinton, Dem., 2,341,744; Dole, Rep., 1,587,021; Perot, Ref., 346,408; Browne, Libertarian, 22,548; Phillips, Taxpayers, 7,606; Hagelin, Natural Law, 4,606.

2000: Gore, Dem., 2,589,026; Bush, Rep., 2,019,421; Nader, Green, 103,759; Buchanan, Ind., 16,106; Browne, Libertarian, 11,623; Hagelin, Reform, 2,127.

Indiana

1948: Truman, Dem., 807,833; Dewey, Rep., 821,079; Watson, Proh., 14,711; Wallace, Prog., 9,649; Thomas, Soc., 2,179; Teichert, Soc. Labor, 763.

1952: Eisenhower, Rep., 1,136,259; Stevenson, Dem., 801,530; Hamblen, Proh., 15,335; Hallinan, Prog., 1,222; Hass, Soc. Labor, 979.

1956: Eisenhower, Rep., 1,182,811; Stevenson, Dem., 783,908; Holtwick, Proh., 6,554; Hass, Soc. Labor, 1,334.

1960: Kennedy, Dem., 952,358; Nixon, Rep., 1,175,120; Decker, Proh., 6,746; Hass, Soc. Labor, 1,136.

1964: Johnson, Dem., 1,170,848; Goldwater, Rep., 911,118; Munn, Proh., 8,266; Hass, Soc. Labor, 1,374.

1968: Nixon, Rep., 1,067,885; Humphrey, Dem., 806,659; Wallace, 3rd Party, 243,108; Munn, Proh., 4,616; Halstead, Soc. Workers, 1,293; Gregory, write-in, 36.

1972: Nixon, Rep., 1,405,154; McGovern, Dem., 708,568; Reed, Soc. Workers, 5,575; Fisher, Soc. Labor, 1,688; Spock, Peace and Freedom, 4,544.

1976: Carter, Dem., 1,014,714; Ford, Rep., 1,185,958; Anderson, Amer., 14,048; Camejo, Soc. Workers, 5,695; LaRouche, U.S. Labor, 1,947.

1980: Reagan, Rep., 1,255,656; Carter, Dem., 844,197; Anderson, Ind., 111,639; Clark, Libertarian, 19,627; Commoner, Citizens, 4,852; Greaves, Amer., 4,750; Hall, Com., 702; DeBerry, Soc., 610.

1984: Reagan, Rep., 1,377,230; Mondale, Dem., 841,481; Bergland, Libertarian, 6,741.

1988: Bush, Rep., 1,297,763; Dukakis, Dem., 860,643; Fulani, New Alliance, 10,215.

1992: Bush, Rep., 989,375; Clinton, Dem., 848,420; Perot, Ind., 455,934; Marrou, Libertarian, 7,936; Fulani, New Alliance, 2,583.

1996: Dole, Rep., 1,006,693; Clinton, Dem., 887,424; Perot, Ref., 224,299; Browne, Libertarian, 15,632.

2000: Bush, Rep., 1,245,836; Gore, Dem., 901,980; Buchanan, Ind., 16,959; Browne, Libertarian, 15,530.

Iowa

1948: Truman, Dem., 522,380; Dewey, Rep., 494,018; Wallace, Prog., 12,125; Teichert, Soc. Labor, 4,274; Watson, Proh., 3,382; Thomas, Soc., 1,829; Dobbs, Soc. Workers, 26.

1952: Eisenhower, Rep., 808,906; Stevenson, Dem., 451,513; Hallinan, Prog., 5,085; Hamblen, Proh., 2,882; Hoopes, Soc., 219; Hass, Soc. Labor, 139; scattering, 29.

1956: Eisenhower, Rep., 729,187; Stevenson, Dem., 501,858; Andrews (A.C.P. of Iowa), 3,202; Hoopes, Soc., 192; Hass, Soc. Labor, 125.

1960: Kennedy, Dem., 550,565; Nixon, Rep., 722,381; Hass, Soc. Labor, 230; write-in, 634.

1964: Johnson, Dem., 733,030; Goldwater, Rep., 449,148; Hass, Soc. Labor, 182; DeBerry, Soc. Workers, 159; Munn, Proh., 1,902.

1968: Nixon, Rep., 619,106; Humphrey, Dem., 476,699; Wallace, 3rd Party, 66,422; Munn, Proh., 362; Halstead, Soc. Workers, 3,377; Cleaver, Peace and Freedom, 1,332; Blomen, Soc. Labor, 241.

1972: Nixon, Rep., 706,207; McGovern, Dem., 496,206; Schmitz, Amer., 22,056; Jenness, Soc. Workers, 488; Fisher, Soc. Labor, 195; Hall, Com., 272; Green, Universal, 199; scattered, 321.

1976: Carter, Dem., 619,931; Ford, Rep., 632,863; McCarthy, Ind., 20,051; Anderson, Amer., 3,040; MacBride, Libertarian, 1,452.

1980: Reagan, Rep., 676,026; Carter, Dem., 508,672; Anderson, Ind., 115,633; Clark, Libertarian, 13,123; Commoner, Citizens, 2,273; McReynolds, Socialist, 534; Hall, Com., 298; DeBerry, Soc. Workers, 244; Greaves, Amer., 189; Bubar, Statesman, 150; scattering, 519.

1984: Reagan, Rep., 703,088; Mondale, Dem., 605,620; Bergland, Libertarian, 1,844.

1988: Bush, Rep., 545,355; Dukakis, Dem., 670,557; LaRouche, Ind., 3,526; Paul, Lib., 2,494.

1992: Clinton, Dem., 586,353; Bush, Rep., 504,891; Perot, Ind., 253,468; Hagelin, Natural Law, 3,079; Gritz, Populist/America First, 1,177; Marrou, Libertarian, 1,076.

1996: Clinton, Dem., 620,258; Dole, Rep., 492,644; Perot, Ref., 105,159; Nader, Green, 6,550; Hagelin, Natural Law, 3,349; Browne, Libertarian, 2,315; Phillips, Taxpayers, 2,229; Harris, Soc. Workers, 331.

2000: Gore, Dem., 638,517; Bush, Rep., 634,373; Nader, Green, 29,374; Buchanan, Reform, 5,731; Browne, Libertarian, 3,209; Hagelin, Ind., 2,281; Phillips, Constitution, 613; Harris, Soc. Workers, 190; McReynolds, Soc., 107.

Kansas

1948: Truman, Dem., 351,902; Dewey, Rep., 423,039; Watson, Proh., 6,468; Wallace, Prog., 4,603; Thomas, Soc., 2,807.

1952: Eisenhower, Rep., 616,302; Stevenson, Dem., 273,296; Hamblen, Proh., 6,038; Hoopes, Soc., 530.

1956: Eisenhower, Rep., 566,878; Stevenson, Dem., 296,317; Holtwick, Proh., 3,048.

1960: Kennedy, Dem., 363,213; Nixon, Rep., 561,474; Decker, Proh., 4,138.

1964: Johnson, Dem., 464,028; Goldwater, Rep., 386,579; Munn, Proh., 5,393; Hass, Soc. Labor, 1,901.

1968: Nixon, Rep., 478,674; Humphrey, Dem., 302,996; Wallace, 3rd Party, 88,921; Munn, Proh., 2,192.

1972: Nixon, Rep., 619,812; McGovern, Dem., 270,287; Schmitz, Conservative, 21,808; Munn, Proh., 4,188.

1976: Carter, Dem., 430,421; Ford, Rep., 502,752; McCarthy, Ind., 13,185; Anderson, Amer., 4,724; MacBride, Libertarian, 3,242; Maddox, Conservative, 2,118; Bubar, Proh., 1,403.

1980: Reagan, Rep., 566,812; Carter, Dem., 326,150; Anderson, Ind., 68,231; Clark, Libertarian, 14,470; Shelton, Amer., 1,555; Hall, Com., 967; Bubar, Statesman, 821; Rarick, Conservative, 789.

1984: Reagan, Rep., 674,646; Mondale, Dem., 332,471; Bergland, Libertarian, 3,585.

1988: Bush, Rep., 554,049; Dukakis, Dem., 422,636; Paul, Ind.,12,553; Fulani, Ind., 3,806.

1992: Clinton, Dem., 390,434; Bush, Rep., 449,951; Perot, Ind.,312,358; Marrou, Libertarian, 4,314.

1996: Dole, Rep., 583,245; Clinton, Dem., 387,659; Perot, Ref., 92,639; Browne, Libertarian, 4,557; Phillips, Ind., 3,519; Hagelin, Ind., 1,655.

2000: Bush, Rep., 622,332; Gore, Dem., 399,276; Nader, Ind., 36,086; Buchanan, Reform, 7,370; Browne, Libertarian, 4,525; Hagelin, Ind., 1,373; Phillips, Constitution, 1,254.

Kentucky

1948: Truman, Dem., 466,756; Dewey, Rep., 341,210; Thurmond, States' Rights, 10,411; Wallace, Prog., 1,567; Thomas, Soc., 1,284; Watson, Proh., 1,245; Teichert, Soc. Labor, 185.

1952: Eisenhower, Rep., 495,029; Stevenson, Dem., 495,729; Hamblen, Proh., 1,161; Hass, Soc. Labor, 893; Hallinan, Proh., 336.

1956: Eisenhower, Rep., 572,192; Stevenson, Dem., 476,453; Byrd, States' Rights, 2,657; Holtwick, Proh., 2,145; Hass, Soc. Labor, 358.

1960: Kennedy, Dem., 521,855; Nixon, Rep., 602,607.

1964: Johnson, Dem., 669,659; Goldwater, Rep., 372,977; Kasper, Natl. States Rights, 3,469.

1968: Nixon, Rep., 462,411; Humphrey, Dem., 397,547; Wallace, 3rd Party, 193,098; Halstead, Soc. Workers, 2,843.

1972: Nixon, Rep., 676,446; McGovern, Dem., 371,159; Schmitz, Amer., 17,627; Spock, Peoples, 1,118; Jenness, Soc. Workers, 685; Hall, Com., 464.

1976: Carter, Dem., 615,717; Ford, Rep., 531,852; Anderson, Amer., 8,308; McCarthy, Ind., 6,837; Maddox, Amer. Ind., 2,328; MacBride, Libertarian, 814.

1980: Reagan, Rep., 635,274; Carter, Dem., 616,417; Anderson, Ind., 31,127; Clark, Libertarian, 5,531; McCormack, Respect For Life, 4,233; Commoner, Citizens, 1,304; Pulley, Socialist, 393; Hall, Com., 348.

1984: Reagan, Rep., 815,345; Mondale, Dem., 536,756.

1988: Bush, Rep., 734,281; Dukakis, Dem., 580,368; Duke, Pop., 4,494; Paul, Lib., 2,118.

1992: Clinton, Dem., 665,104; Bush, Rep., 617,178; Perot, Ind., 203,944; Marrou, Libertarian, 4,513.

1996: Clinton, Dem., 636,614; Dole, Rep., 623,283; Perot, Ref., 120,396; Browne, Libertarian, 4,009; Phillips, Taxpayers, 2,204; Hagelin, Natural Law, 1,493.

2000: Bush, Rep., 872,520; Gore, Dem., 638,923; Nader, Green, 23,118; Buchanan, Reform, 4,152; Browne, Libertarian, 2,885; Hagelin, Natural Law, 1,513; Phillips, Constitution, 915.

Louisiana

1948: Thurmond, States' Rights, 204,290; Truman, Dem., 136,344; Dewey, Rep., 72,657; Wallace, Prog., 3,035.

1952: Eisenhower, Rep., 306,925; Stevenson, Dem., 345,027.

1956: Eisenhower, Rep., 329,047; Stevenson, Dem., 243,977; Andrews, States' Rights, 44,520.

1960: Kennedy, Dem., 407,339; Nixon, Rep., 230,890; States' Rights (unpledged), 169,572.

1964: Johnson, Dem., 387,068; Goldwater, Rep., 509,225.

1968: Nixon, Rep., 257,535; Humphrey, Dem., 309,615; Wallace, 3rd Party, 530,300.

1972: Nixon, Rep., 686,852; McGovern, Dem., 298,142; Schmitz, Amer., 52,099; Jenness, Soc. Workers, 14,398.

1976: Carter, Dem., 661,365; Ford, Rep., 587,446; Maddox, Amer., 10,058; Hall, Com., 7,417; McCarthy, Ind., 6,588; MacBride, Libertarian, 3,325.

1980: Reagan, Rep., 792,853; Carter, Dem., 708,453; Anderson, Ind., 26,345; Rarick, Amer. Ind., 10,333; Clark, Libertarian, 8,240; Commoner, Citizens, 1,584; DeBerry, Soc. Work., 783.

1984: Reagan, Rep., 1,037,299; Mondale, Dem., 651,586; Bergland, Libertarian, 1,876.

1988: Bush, Rep., 883,702; Dukakis, Dem., 717,460; Duke, Pop., 18,612; Paul, Lib., 4,115.

1992: Clinton, Dem., 815,971; Bush, Rep., 733,386; Perot, Ind., 211,478; Gritz, Populist/America First, 18,545; Marrou, Libertarian, 3,155; Daniels, Ind., 1,663; Phillips, U.S. Taxpayers, 1,552; Fulani, New Alliance, 1,434; LaRouche, Ind., 1,136.

1996: Clinton, Dem., 927,837; Dole, Rep., 712,586; Perot, Ref., 123,293; Browne, Libertarian, 7,499; Nader, Liberty, Ecology, Community, 4,719; Phillips, Taxpayers, 3,366; Hagelin, Natural Law, 2,981; Moorehead, Workers World, 1,678.

2000: Bush, Rep., 927,871; Gore, Dem., 792,344; Nader, Green, 20,473; Buchanan, Reform, 14,356; Phillips, Constitution, 5,483; Browne, Libertarian, 2,951; Harris, Soc. Workers, 1,103; Hagelin, Natural Law, 1,075.

Maine

1948: Truman, Dem., 111,916; Dewey, Rep., 150,234; Wallace, Prog., 1,884; Thomas, Soc., 547; Teichert, Soc. Labor, 206.

1952: Eisenhower, Rep., 232,353; Stevenson, Dem., 118,806; Hallinan, Prog., 332; Hass, Soc. Labor, 156; Hoopes, Soc., 138; scattered, 1.

1956: Eisenhower, Rep., 249,238; Stevenson, Dem., 102,468.

1960: Kennedy, Dem., 181,159; Nixon, Rep., 240,608.

1964: Johnson, Dem., 262,264; Goldwater, Rep., 118,701.

1968: Nixon, Rep., 169,254; Humphrey, Dem., 217,312; Wallace, 3rd Party, 6,370.

1972: Nixon, Rep., 256,458; McGovern, Dem., 160,584; scattered, 229.

1976: Carter, Dem., 232,279; Ford, Rep., 236,320; McCarthy, Ind., 10,874; Bubar, Proh., 3,495.

1980: Reagan, Rep., 238,522; Carter, Dem., 220,974; Anderson, Ind., 53,327; Clark, Libertarian, 5,119; Commoner, Citizens, 4,394; Hall, Com., 591; write-ins, 84.

1984: Reagan, Rep., 336,500; Mondale, Dem., 214,515.

1988: Bush, Rep., 307,131; Dukakis, Dem., 243,569; Paul, Lib., 2,700; Fulani, New Alliance, 1,405.

1992: Clinton, Dem., 263,420; Perot, Ind., 206,820; Bush, Rep., 206,504; Marrou, Libertarian, 1,681.

1996: Clinton, Dem., 312,788; Dole, Rep., 186,378; Perot, Ref., 85,970; Nader, Green, 15,279; Browne, Libertarian, 2,996; Phillips, Taxpayers, 1,517; Hagelin, Natural Law, 825.

2000: Gore, Dem., 319,951; Bush, Rep., 286,616; Nader, Green, 37,127; Buchanan, Reform, 4,443; Browne, Libertarian, 3,074; Phillips, Constitution, 579.

Maryland

1948: Truman, Dem., 286,521; Dewey, Rep., 294,814; Wallace, Prog., 9,983; Thomas, Soc., 2,941; Thurmond, States' Rights, 2,476; Wright, write-in, 2,294.

1952: Eisenhower, Rep., 499,424; Stevenson, Dem., 395,337; Hallinan, Prog., 7,313.

1956: Eisenhower, Rep., 559,738; Stevenson, Dem., 372,613.

1960: Kennedy, Dem., 565,800; Nixon, Rep., 489,538.

1964: Johnson, Dem., 730,912; Goldwater, Rep., 385,495; write-in, 50.

1968: Nixon, Rep., 517,995; Humphrey, Dem., 538,310; Wallace, 3rd Party, 178,734.

1972: Nixon, Rep., 829,305; McGovern, Dem., 505,781; Schmitz, Amer., 18,726.

1976: Carter, Dem., 759,612; Ford, Rep., 672,661.

1980: Reagan, Rep., 680,606; Carter, Dem., 726,161; Anderson, Ind., 119,537; Clark, Libertarian, 14,192.

1984: Reagan, Rep., 879,918; Mondale, Dem., 787,935; Bergland, Libertarian, 5,721.

1988: Bush, Rep., 876,167; Dukakis, Dem., 826,304; Paul, Lib., 6,748; Fulani, New Alliance, 5,115.

1992: Clinton, Dem., 988,571; Bush, Rep., 707,094; Perot, Ind., 281,414; Marrou, Libertarian, 4,715; Fulani, New Alliance, 2,786.

1996: Clinton, Dem., 966,207; Dole, Rep., 681,530; Perot, Ref., 115,812; Browne, Libertarian, 8,765; Phillips, Taxpayers, 3,402; Hagelin, Natural Law, 2,517.

2000: Gore, Dem., 1,144,008; Bush, Rep., 813,827; Nader, Green, 53,768; Browne, Libertarian, 5,310; Buchanan, Reform., 4,248; Phillips, Constitution, 918.

Massachusetts

1948: Truman, Dem., 1,151,788; Dewey, Rep., 909,370; Wallace, Prog., 38,157; Teichert, Soc. Labor, 5,535; Watson, Proh., 1,663.

1952: Eisenhower, Rep., 1,292,325; Stevenson, Dem., 1,083,525; Hallinan, Prog., 4,636; Hass, Soc. Labor, 1,957; Hamblen, Proh., 886; scattered, 69; blanks, 41,150.

1956: Eisenhower, Rep., 1,393,197; Stevenson, Dem., 948,190; Hass, Soc. Labor, 5,573; Holtwick, Proh., 1,205; others, 341.

1960: Kennedy, Dem., 1,487,174; Nixon, Rep., 976,750; Hass, Soc. Labor, 3,892; Decker, Proh., 1,633; others, 31; blank and void, 26,024.

1964: Johnson, Dem., 1,786,422; Goldwater, Rep., 549,727; Hass, Soc. Labor, 4,755; Munn, Proh., 3,735; scattered, 159; blank, 48,104.

1968: Nixon, Rep., 766,844; Humphrey, Dem., 1,469,218; Wallace, 3rd Party, 87,088; Blomen, Soc. Labor, 6,180; Munn, Proh., 2,369; scattered, 53; blanks, 25,394.

1972: Nixon, Rep., 1,112,078; McGovern, Dem., 1,332,540; Jenness, Soc. Workers, 10,600; Fisher, Soc. Labor, 129; Schmitz, Amer., 2,877; Spock, Peoples, 101; Hall, Com., 46; Hospers, Libertarian, 43; scattered, 342.

1976: Carter, Dem., 1,429,475; Ford, Rep., 1,030,276; McCarthy, Ind., 65,637; Camejo, Soc. Workers, 8,138; Anderson, Amer., 7,555; La Rouche, U.S. Labor, 4,922; MacBride, Libertarian, 135.

1980: Reagan, Rep., 1,057,631; Carter, Dem., 1,053,802; Anderson, Ind., 382,539; Clark, Libertarian, 22,038; DeBerry, Soc. Workers, 3,735; Commoner, Citizens, 2,056; McReynolds, Soc., 62; Bubar, Statesman, 34; Griswold, Workers World, 19; scattered, 2,382.

1984: Reagan, Rep., 1,310,936; Mondale, Dem., 1,239,606.

1988: Bush, Rep., 1,194,635; Dukakis, Dem., 1,401,415; Paul, Lib., 24,251; Fulani, New Alliance, 9,561.

1992: Clinton, Dem., 1,318,639; Bush, Rep., 805,039; Perot, Ind., 630,731; Marrou, Libertarian, 9,021; Fulani, New Alliance, 3,172; Phillips, U.S. Taxpayers, 2,218; Hagelin, Natural Law, 1,812; LaRouche, Ind., 1,027.

1996: Clinton, Dem., 1,571,509; Dole, Rep., 718,058; Perot, Ref., 227,206; Browne, Libertarian, 20,424; Hagelin, Natural Law, 5,183; Moorehead, Workers World, 3,276.
2000: Gore, Dem., 1,616,487; Bush, Rep., 878,502; Nader, Green, 173,564; Browne, Libertarian, 16,366; Buchanan, Reform, 11,149; Hagelin, Natural Law, 2,884.

Michigan

1948: Truman, Dem., 1,003,448; Dewey, Rep., 1,038,595; Wallace, Prog., 46,515; Watson, Proh., 13,052; Thomas, Soc., 6,063; Teichert, Soc. Labor, 1,263; Dobbs, Soc. Workers, 672.
1952: Eisenhower, Rep., 1,551,529; Stevenson, Dem., 1,230,657; Hamblen, Proh., 10,331; Hallinan, Prog., 3,922; Hass, Soc. Labor, 1,495; Dobbs, Soc. Workers, 655; scattered, 3.
1956: Eisenhower, Rep., 1,713,647; Stevenson, Dem., 1,359,898; Holtwick, Proh., 6,923.
1960: Kennedy, Dem., 1,687,269; Nixon, Rep., 1,620,428; Dobbs, Soc. Workers, 4,347; Decker, Proh., 2,029; Daly, Tax Cut, 1,767; Hass, Soc. Labor, 1,718; Ind. Amer., 539.
1964: Johnson, Dem., 2,136,615; Goldwater, Rep., 1,060,152; DeBerry, Soc. Workers, 3,817; Hass, Soc. Labor, 1,704; Proh. (no candidate listed), 699; scattering, 145.
1968: Nixon, Rep., 1,370,665; Humphrey, Dem., 1,593,082; Wallace, 3rd Party, 331,968; Halstead, Soc. Workers, 4,099; Blomen, Soc. Labor, 1,762; Cleaver, New Politics, 4,585; Munn, Proh., 60; scattering, 29.
1972: Nixon, Rep., 1,961,721; McGovern, Dem., 1,459,435; Schmitz, Amer., 63,321; Fisher, Soc. Labor, 2,437; Jenness, Soc. Workers, 1,603; Hall, Com., 1,210.
1976: Carter, Dem., 1,696,714; Ford, Rep., 1,893,742; McCarthy, Ind., 47,905; MacBride, Libertarian, 5,406; Wright, People's, 3,504; Camejo, Soc. Workers, 1,804; LaRouche, U.S. Labor, 1,366; Levin, Soc. Labor, 1,148; scattering, 2,160.
1980: Reagan, Rep., 1,915,225; Carter, Dem., 1,661,532; Anderson, Ind., 275,223; Clark, Libertarian, 41,597; Commoner, Citizens, 11,930; Hall, Com., 3,262; Griswold, Workers World, 30; Greaves, Amer., 21; Bubar, Statesman, 9.
1984: Reagan, Rep., 2,251,571; Mondale, Dem., 1,529,638; Bergland, Libertarian, 10,055.
1988: Bush, Rep., 1,965,486; Dukakis, Dem., 1,675,783; Paul, Lib., 18,336; Fulani, Ind., 2,513.
1992: Clinton, Dem., 1,871,182; Bush, Rep., 1,554,940; Perot, Ind., 824,813; Marrou, Libertarian, 10,175; Phillips, U.S. Taxpayers, 8,263; Hagelin, Natural Law, 2,954.
1996: Clinton, Dem., 1,989,653; Dole, Rep., 1,481,212; Perot, Ref., 336,670; Browne, Libertarian, 27,670; Hagelin, Natural Law, 4,254; Moorehead, Workers World, 3,153; White, Soc. Equality, 1,554.
2000: Gore, Dem., 2,170,418; Bush, Rep., 1,953,139; Nader, Green, 84,165; Browne, Libertarian, 16,711; Phillips, U.S. Taxpayers, 3,791; Hagelin, Natural Law, 2,426.

Minnesota

1948: Truman, Dem., 692,966; Dewey, Rep., 483,617; Wallace, Prog., 27,866; Thomas, Soc., 4,646; Teichert, Soc. Labor, 2,525; Dobbs, Soc. Workers, 606.
1952: Eisenhower, Rep., 763,211; Stevenson, Dem., 608,458; Hallinan, Prog., 2,666; Hass, Soc. Labor, 2,383; Hamblen, Proh., 2,147; Dobbs, Soc. Workers, 618.
1956: Eisenhower, Rep., 719,302; Stevenson, Dem., 617,525; Hass, Soc. Labor (Ind. Gov.), 2,080; Dobbs, Soc. Workers, 1,098.
1960: Kennedy, Dem., 779,933; Nixon, Rep., 757,915; Dobbs, Soc. Workers, 3,077; Industrial Gov., 962.
1964: Johnson, Dem., 991,117; Goldwater, Rep., 559,624; DeBerry, Soc. Workers, 1,177; Hass, Industrial Gov., 2,544.
1968: Nixon, Rep., 658,643; Humphrey, Dem., 857,738; Wallace, 3rd Party, 68,931; scattered, 2,443; Halstead, Soc. Workers, 808; Blomen, Ind. Gov't., 285; Mitchell, Com., 415; Cleaver, Peace, 935; McCarthy, write-in, 585; scattered, 170.
1972: Nixon, Rep., 898,269; McGovern, Dem., 802,346; Schmitz, Amer., 31,407; Spock, Peoples, 2,805; Fisher, Soc. Labor, 4,261; Jenness, Soc. Workers, 940; Hall, Com., 662; scattered, 962.
1976: Carter, Dem., 1,070,440; Ford, Rep., 819,395; McCarthy, Ind., 35,490; Anderson, Amer., 13,592; Camejo, Soc. Workers, 4,149; MacBride, Libertarian, 3,529; Hall, Com., 1,092.

1980: Reagan, Rep., 873,268; Carter, Dem., 954,173; Anderson, Ind., 174,997; Clark, Libertarian, 31,593; Commoner, Citizens, 8,406; Hall, Com., 1,117; DeBerry, Soc. Workers, 711; Griswold, Workers World, 698; McReynolds, Soc., 536; write-ins, 281.
1984: Reagan, Rep., 1,032,603; Mondale, Dem., 1,036,364; Bergland, Libertarian, 2,996.
1988: Bush, Rep., 962,337; Dukakis, Dem., 1,109,471; McCarthy, Minn. Prog., 5,403; Paul, Lib., 5,109.
1992: Clinton, Dem., 1,020,997; Bush, Rep., 747,841; Perot, Ind., 562,506; Marrou, Libertarian, 3,373; Gritz, Populist/ America First, 3,363; Hagelin, Natural Law, 1,406.
1996: Clinton, Dem., 1,120,438; Dole, Rep., 766,476; Perot, Ref., 257,704; Nader, Green, 24,908; Browne, Libertarian, 8,271; Peron, Grass Roots, 4,898; Phillips, Taxpayers, 3,416; Hagelin, Natural Law, 1,808; Birrenbach, Ind. Grass Roots, 787; Harris, Soc. Workers, 684; White, Soc. Equality, 347.
2000: Gore, Dem., 1,168,266; Bush, Rep., 1,109,659; Nader, Green, 126,696; Buchanan, Reform Minnesota, 22,166; Browne, Libertarian, 5,282; Phillips, Constitution, 3,272; Hagelin, Reform, 2,294; Harris, Soc. Workers, 1,022.

Mississippi

1948: Thurmond, States' Rights, 167,538; Truman, Dem., 19,384; Dewey, Rep., 5,043; Wallace, Prog., 225.
1952: Eisenhower, Ind. vote pledged to Rep. candidate, 112,966; Stevenson, Dem., 172,566.
1956: Eisenhower, Rep., 56,372; Stevenson, Dem., 144,498; Black and Tan Grand Old Party, 4,313; total, 60,685; Byrd, Ind., 42,966.
1960: Kennedy, Dem., 108,362; Democratic unpledged electors, 116,248; Nixon, Rep., 73,561. Mississippi's victorious slate of 8 unpledged Democratic electors cast their votes for Sen. Harry F. Byrd (D, VA).
1964: Johnson, Dem., 52,618; Goldwater, Rep., 356,528.
1968: Nixon, Rep., 88,516; Humphrey, Dem., 150,644; Wallace, 3rd Party, 415,349.
1972: Nixon, Rep., 505,125; McGovern, Dem., 126,782; Schmitz, Amer., 11,598; Jenness, Soc. Workers, 2,458.
1976: Carter, Dem., 381,309; Ford, Rep., 366,846; Anderson, Amer., 6,678; McCarthy, Ind., 4,074; Maddox, Ind., 4,049; Camejo, Soc. Workers, 2,805; MacBride, Libertarian, 2,609.
1980: Reagan, Rep., 441,089; Carter, Dem., 429,281; Anderson, Ind., 12,036; Clark, Libertarian, 5,465; Griswold, Workers World, 2,402; Pulley, Soc. Workers, 2,347.
1984: Reagan, Rep., 582,377; Mondale, Dem., 352,192; Bergland, Libertarian, 2,336.
1988: Bush, Rep., 557,890; Dukakis, Dem., 363,921; Duke, Ind., 4,232; Paul, Lib., 3,329.
1992: Bush, Rep., 487,793; Clinton, Dem., 400,258; Perot, Ind., 85,626; Fulani, New Alliance, 2,625; Marrou, Libertarian, 2,154; Phillips, U.S. Taxpayers, 1,652; Hagelin, Natural Law, 1,140.
1996: Dole, Rep., 439,838; Clinton, Dem., 394,022; Perot, Ind. (Ref.), 52,222; Browne, Libertarian, 2,809; Phillips, Taxpayers, 2,314; Hagelin, Natural Law, 1,447; Collins, Ind., 1,205.
2000: Bush, Rep., 572,844; Gore, Dem., 404,614; Nader, Ind., 8,122; Phillips, Constitution, 3,267; Buchanan, Reform, 2,265; Browne, Libertarian, 2,009; Harris, Ind., 613; Hagelin, Natural Law, 450.

Missouri

1948: Truman, Dem., 917,315; Dewey, Rep., 655,039; Wallace, Prog., 3,998; Thomas, Soc., 2,222.
1952: Eisenhower, Rep., 959,429; Stevenson, Dem., 929,830; Hallinan, Prog., 987; Hamblen, Proh., 885; MacArthur, Christian Nationalist, 302; America First, 233; Hoopes, Soc., 227; Hass, Soc. Labor, 169.
1956: Stevenson, Dem., 918,273; Eisenhower, Rep., 914,299.
1960: Kennedy, Dem., 972,201; Nixon, Rep., 962,221.
1964: Johnson, Dem., 1,164,344; Goldwater, Rep., 653,535.
1968: Nixon, Rep., 811,932; Humphrey, Dem., 791,444; Wallace, 3rd Party, 206,126.
1972: Nixon, Rep., 1,154,058; McGovern, Dem., 698,531.
1976: Carter, Dem., 999,163; Ford, Rep., 928,808; McCarthy, Ind., 24,329.
1980: Reagan, Rep., 1,074,181; Carter, Dem., 931,182; Anderson, Ind., 77,920; Clark, Libertarian, 14,422; DeBerry, Soc. Workers, 1,515; Commoner, Citizens, 573; write-ins, 31.
1984: Reagan, Rep., 1,274,188; Mondale, Dem., 848,583.

1988: Bush, Rep., 1,084,953; Dukakis, Dem., 1,001,619; Fulani, New Alliance, 6,656; Paul, write-in, 434.

1992: Clinton, Dem., 1,053,873; Bush, Rep., 811,159; Perot, Ind., 518,741; Marrou, Libertarian, 7,497.

1996: Clinton, Dem., 1,025,935; Dole, Rep., 890,016; Perot, Ref., 217,188; Phillips, Taxpayers, 11,521; Browne, Libertarian, 10,522; Hagelin, Natural Law, 2,287.

2000: Bush, Rep., 1,189,924; Gore, Dem., 1,111,138; Nader, Green, 38,515; Buchanan, Reform, 9,818; Browne, Libertarian, 7,436; Phillips, Constitution, 1,957; Hagelin, Natural Law, 1,104.

Montana

1948: Truman, Dem., 119,071; Dewey, Rep., 96,770; Wallace, Prog., 7,313; Thomas, Soc., 695; Watson, Proh., 429.

1952: Eisenhower, Rep., 157,394; Stevenson, Dem., 106,213; Hallinan, Prog., 723; Hamblen, Proh., 548; Hoopes, Soc., 159.

1956: Eisenhower, Rep., 154,933; Stevenson, Dem., 116,238.

1960: Kennedy, Dem., 134,891; Nixon, Rep., 141,841; Decker, Proh., 456; Dobbs, Soc. Workers, 391.

1964: Johnson, Dem., 164,246; Goldwater, Rep., 113,032; Kasper, Natl. States' Rights, 519; Munn, Proh., 499; DeBerry, Soc. Workers, 332.

1968: Nixon, Rep., 138,835; Humphrey, Dem., 114,117; Wallace, 3rd Party, 20,015; Halstead, Soc. Workers, 457; Munn, Proh., 510; Caton, New Reform, 470.

1972: Nixon, Rep., 183,976; McGovern, Dem., 120,197; Schmitz, Amer., 13,430.

1976: Carter, Dem., 149,259; Ford, Rep., 173,703; Anderson, Amer., 5,772.

1980: Reagan, Rep., 206,814; Carter, Dem., 118,032; Anderson, Ind., 29,281; Clark, Libertarian, 9,825.

1984: Reagan, Rep., 232,450; Mondale, Dem., 146,742; Bergland, Libertarian, 5,185.

1988: Bush, Rep., 190,412; Dukakis, Dem., 168,936; Paul, Lib., 5,047; Fulani, New Alliance, 1,279.

1992: Clinton, Dem., 154,507; Bush, Rep., 144,207; Perot, Ind., 107,225; Gritz, Populist/America First, 3,658.

1996: Dole, Rep., 179,652; Clinton, Dem., 167,922; Perot, Ref., 55,229; Browne, Libertarian, 2,526; Hagelin, Natural Law, 1,754.

2000: Bush, Rep., 240,178; Gore, Dem., 137,126; Nader, Green, 24,437; Buchanan, Reform, 5,697; Browne, Libertarian, 1,718; Phillips, Constitution, 1,155; Hagelin, Natural Law, 675.

Nebraska

1948: Truman, Dem., 224,165; Dewey, Rep., 264,774.

1952: Eisenhower, Rep., 421,603; Stevenson, Dem., 188,057.

1956: Eisenhower, Rep., 378,108; Stevenson, Dem., 199,029.

1960: Kennedy, Dem., 232,542; Nixon, Rep., 380,553.

1964: Johnson, Dem., 307,307; Goldwater, Rep., 276,847.

1968: Nixon, Rep., 321,163; Humphrey, Dem., 170,784; Wallace, 3rd Party, 44,904.

1972: Nixon, Rep., 406,298; McGovern, Dem., 169,991; scattered, 817.

1976: Carter, Dem., 233,287; Ford, Rep., 359,219; McCarthy, Ind., 9,383; Maddox, Amer. Ind., 3,378; MacBride, Libertarian, 1,476.

1980: Reagan, Rep., 419,214; Carter, Dem., 166,424; Anderson, Ind., 44,854; Clark, Libertarian, 9,041.

1984: Reagan, Rep., 459,135; Mondale, Dem., 187,475; Bergland, Libertarian, 2,075.

1988: Bush, Rep., 397,956; Dukakis, Dem., 259,235; Paul, Lib., 2,534; Fulani, New Alliance, 1,740.

1992: Bush, Rep., 343,678; Clinton, Dem., 216,864; Perot, Ind., 174,104; Marrou, Libertarian, 1,340.

1996: Dole, Rep., 363,467; Clinton, Dem., 236,761; Perot, Ref., 71,278; Browne, Libertarian, 2,792; Phillips, Ind., 1,928; Hagelin, Natural Law, 1,189.

2000: Bush, Rep., 433,862; Gore, Dem., 231,780; Nader, Green, 24,540; Buchanan, Ind., 3,646; Browne, Libertarian, 2,245; Hagelin, Natural Law, 478; Phillips, Ind., 468.

Nevada

1948: Truman, Dem., 31,291; Dewey, Rep., 29,357; Wallace, Prog., 1,469.

1952: Eisenhower, Rep., 50,502; Stevenson, Dem., 31,688.

1956: Eisenhower, Rep., 56,049; Stevenson, Dem., 40,640.

1960: Kennedy, Dem., 54,880; Nixon, Rep., 52,387.

1964: Johnson, Dem., 79,339; Goldwater, Rep., 56,094.

1968: Nixon, Rep., 73,188; Humphrey, Dem., 60,598; Wallace, 3rd Party, 20,432.

1972: Nixon, Rep., 115,750; McGovern, Dem., 66,016.

1976: Carter, Dem., 92,479; Ford, Rep., 101,273; MacBride, Libertarian, 1,519; Maddox, Amer. Ind., 1,497; scattered, 5,108.

1980: Reagan, Rep., 155,017; Carter, Dem., 66,666; Anderson, Ind., 17,651; Clark, Libertarian, 4,358.

1984: Reagan, Rep., 188,770; Mondale, Dem., 91,655; Bergland, Libertarian, 2,292.

1988: Bush, Rep., 206,040; Dukakis, Dem., 132,738; Paul, Lib., 3,520; Fulani, New Alliance, 835.

1992: Clinton, Dem., 189,148; Bush, Rep., 175,828; Perot, Ind., 132,580; Gritz, Populist/America First, 2,892; Marrou, Libertarian, 1,835.

1996: Clinton, Dem., 203,974; Dole, Rep., 199,244; Perot, Ref., 43,986; "None of These Candidates," 5,608; Nader, Green, 4,730; Browne, Libertarian, 4,460; Phillips, Ind. Amer., 1,732; Hagelin, Natural Law, 545.

2000: Bush, Rep., 301,575; Gore, Dem., 279,978; Nader, Green, 15,008; Buchanan, Citizens First, 4,747; "None of these candidates," 3,315; Browne, Libertarian, 3,311; Phillips, Ind. Amer., 621; Hagelin, Natural Law, 415.

New Hampshire

1948: Truman, Dem., 107,995; Dewey, Rep., 121,299; Wallace, Prog., 1,970; Thomas, Soc., 86; Teichert, Soc. Labor, 83; Thurmond, States' Rights, 7.

1952: Eisenhower, Rep., 166,287; Stevenson, Dem., 106,663.

1956: Eisenhower, Rep., 176,519; Stevenson, Dem., 90,364; Andrews, Const., 111.

1960: Kennedy, Dem., 137,772; Nixon, Rep., 157,989.

1964: Johnson, Dem., 182,065; Goldwater, Rep., 104,029.

1968: Nixon, Rep., 154,903; Humphrey, Dem., 130,589; Wallace, 3rd Party, 11,173; New Party, 421; Halstead, Soc. Workers, 104.

1972: Nixon, Rep., 213,724; McGovern, Dem., 116,435; Schmitz, Amer., 3,386; Jenness, Soc. Workers, 368; scattered, 142.

1976: Carter, Dem., 147,645; Ford, Rep., 185,935; McCarthy, Ind., 4,095; MacBride, Libertarian, 936; Reagan, write-in, 388; La Rouche, U.S. Labor, 186; Camejo, Soc. Workers, 161; Levin, Soc. Labor, 66; scattered, 215.

1980: Reagan, Rep., 221,705; Carter, Dem., 108,864; Anderson, Ind., 49,693; Clark, Libertarian, 2,067; Commoner, Citizens, 1,325; Hall, Com., 129; Griswold, Workers World, 76; DeBerry, Soc. Workers, 72; scattered, 68.

1984: Reagan, Rep., 267,051; Mondale, Dem., 120,377; Bergland, Libertarian, 735.

1988: Bush, Rep., 281,537; Dukakis, Dem., 163,696; Paul, Lib., 4,502; Fulani, New Alliance, 790.

1992: Clinton, Dem., 209,040; Bush, Rep., 202,484; Perot, Ind., 121,337; Marrou, Libertarian, 3,548.

1996: Clinton, Dem., 246,166; Dole, Rep., 196,486; Perot, Ref., 48,387; Browne, Libertarian, 4,214; Phillips, Taxpayers, 1,344.

2000: Bush, Rep., 273,559; Gore, Dem., 266,348; Nader, Green, 22,198; Browne, Libertarian, 2,757; Buchanan, Independence, 2,615; Phillips, Constitution, 328.

New Jersey

1948: Truman, Dem., 895,455; Dewey, Rep., 981,124; Wallace, Prog., 42,683; Watson, Proh., 10,593; Thomas, Soc., 10,521; Dobbs, Soc. Workers, 5,825; Teichert, Soc. Labor, 3,354.

1952: Eisenhower, Rep., 1,373,613; Stevenson, Dem., 1,015,902; Hoopes, Soc., 8,593; Hass, Soc. Labor, 5,815; Hallinan, Prog., 5,589; Krajewski, Poor Man's, 4,203; Dobbs, Soc. Workers, 3,850; Hamblen, Proh., 989.

1956: Eisenhower, Rep., 1,606,942; Stevenson, Dem., 850,337; Holtwick, Proh., 9,147; Hass, Soc. Labor, 6,736; Andrews, Cons., 5,317; Dobbs, Soc. Workers, 4,004; Krajewski, Amer. Third Party, 1,829.

1960: Kennedy, Dem., 1,385,415; Nixon, Rep., 1,363,324; Dobbs, Soc. Workers, 11,402; Lee, Cons., 8,708; Hass, Soc. Labor, 4,262.

1964: Johnson, Dem., 1,867,671; Goldwater, Rep., 963,843; DeBerry, Soc. Workers, 8,181; Hass, Soc. Labor, 7,075.

1968: Nixon, Rep., 1,325,467; Humphrey, Dem., 1,264,206; Wallace, 3rd Party, 262,187; Halstead, Soc. Workers, 8,667; Gregory, Peace and Freedom, 8,084; Blomen, Soc. Labor, 6,784.

1972: Nixon, Rep., 1,845,502; McGovern, Dem., 1,102,211; Schmitz, Amer., 34,378; Spock, Peoples, 5,355; Fisher, Soc. Labor, 4,544; Jenness, Soc. Workers, 2,233; Mahalchik, Amer. First, 1,743; Hall, Com., 1,263.
1976: Carter, Dem., 1,444,653; Ford, Rep., 1,509,688; McCarthy, Ind., 32,717; MacBride, Libertarian, 9,449; Maddox, Amer., 7,716; Levin, Soc. Labor, 3,686; Hall, Com., 1,662; LaRouche, U.S. Labor, 1,650; Camejo, Soc. Workers, 1,184; Wright, People's, 1,044; Bubar, Proh., 554; Zeidler, Soc., 469.
1980: Reagan, Rep., 1,546,557; Carter, Dem., 1,147,364; Anderson, Ind., 234,632; Clark, Libertarian, 20,652; Commoner, Citizens, 8,203; McCormack, Right to Life, 3,927; Lynen, Middle Class, 3,694; Hall, Com., 2,555; Pulley, Soc. Workers, 2,198; McReynolds, Soc., 1,973; Gahres, Down With Lawyers, 1,718; Griswold, Workers World, 1,288; Wendelken, Ind., 923.
1984: Reagan, Rep., 1,933,630; Mondale, Dem., 1,261,323; Bergland, Libertarian, 6,416.
1988: Bush, Rep., 1,740,604; Dukakis, Dem., 1,317,541; Lewin, Peace and Freedom, 9,953; Paul, Lib., 8,421.
1992: Clinton, Dem., 1,436,206; Bush, Rep., 1,356,865; Perot, Ind., 521,829; Marrou, Libertarian, 6,822; Fulani, New Alliance, 3,513; Phillips, U.S. Taxpayers, 2,670; LaRouche, Ind., 2,095; Warren, Soc. Workers, 2,011; Daniels, Ind., 1,996; Gritz, Populist/America First, 1,867; Hagelin, Natural Law, 1,353.
1996: Clinton, Dem., 1,652,361; Dole, Rep., 1,103,099; Perot, Ref., 262,134; Nader, Green, 32,465; Browne, Libertarian, 14,763; Hagelin, Natural Law, 3,887; Phillips, Taxpayers, 3,440; Harris, Soc. Workers, 1,837; Moorehead, Workers World, 1,337; White, Soc. Equality, 537.
2000: Gore, Dem., 1,788,850; Bush, Rep., 1,284,173; Nader, Ind., 94,554; Buchanan, Ind., 6,989; Browne, Ind., 6,312; Hagelin, Ind., 2,215; McReynolds, Ind., 1,880; Phillips, Ind., 1,409; Harris, Ind., 844.

New Mexico

1948: Truman, Dem., 105,464; Dewey, Rep., 80,303; Wallace, Prog., 1,037; Watson, Proh., 127; Thomas, Soc., 83; Teichert, Soc. Labor, 49.
1952: Eisenhower, Rep., 132,170; Stevenson, Dem., 105,661; Hamblen, Proh., 297; Hallinan, Ind. Prog., 225; MacArthur, Christian National, 220; Hass, Soc. Labor, 35.
1956: Eisenhower, Rep., 146,788; Stevenson, Dem., 106,098; Holtwick, Proh., 607; Andrews, Ind., 364; Hass, Soc. Labor, 69.
1960: Kennedy, Dem., 156,027; Nixon, Rep., 153,733; Decker, Proh., 777; Hass, Soc. Labor, 570.
1964: Johnson, Dem., 194,017; Goldwater, Rep., 131,838; Hass, Soc. Labor, 1,217; Munn, Proh., 543.
1968: Nixon, Rep., 169,692; Humphrey, Dem., 130,081; Wallace, 3rd Party, 25,737; Chavez, 1,519; Halstead, Soc. Workers, 252.
1972: Nixon, Rep., 235,606; McGovern, Dem., 141,084; Schmitz, Amer., 8,767; Jenness, Soc. Workers, 474.
1976: Carter, Dem., 201,148; Ford, Rep., 211,419; Camejo, Soc. Workers, 2,462; MacBride, Libertarian, 1,110; Zeidler, Soc., 240; Bubar, Proh., 211.
1980: Reagan, Rep., 250,779; Carter, Dem., 167,826; Anderson, Ind., 29,459; Clark, Libertarian, 4,365; Commoner, Citizens, 2,202; Bubar, Statesman, 1,281; Pulley, Soc. Workers, 325.
1984: Reagan, Rep., 307,101; Mondale, Dem., 201,769; Bergland, Libertarian, 4,459.
1988: Bush, Rep., 270,341; Dukakis, Dem., 244,497; Paul, Lib., 3,268; Fulani, New Alliance, 2,237.
1992: Clinton, Dem., 261,617; Bush, Rep., 212,824; Perot, Ind., 91,895; Marrou, Libertarian, 1,615.
1996: Clinton, Dem., 273,495; Dole, Rep., 232,751; Perot, Ref., 32,257; Nader, Green, 13,218; Browne, Libertarian, 2,996; Phillips, Taxpayers, 713; Hagelin, Natural Law, 644.
2000: Gore, Dem., 286,783; Bush, Rep., 286,417; Nader, Green, 21,251; Browne, Libertarian, 2,058; Buchanan, Reform, 1,392; Hagelin, Natural Law, 361; Phillips, Constitution, 343.

New York

1948: Truman, Dem., 2,557,642; Liberal, 222,562; total, 2,780,204; Dewey, Rep., 2,841,163; Wallace, Amer. Lab., 509,559; Thomas, Soc., 40,879; Teichert, Ind. Gov't., 2,729; Dobbs, Soc. Workers, 2,675.

1952: Eisenhower, Rep., 3,952,815; Stevenson, Dem., 2,687,890; Liberal, 416,711; total, 3,104,601; Hallinan, Amer. Lab., 64,211; Hoopes, Soc., 2,664; Dobbs, Soc. Workers, 2,212; Hass, Ind. Gov't., 1,560; scattering, 178; blank and void, 87,813.
1956: Eisenhower, Rep., 4,340,340; Stevenson, Dem., 2,458,212; Liberal, 292,557; total, 2,750,769; write-in votes for Andrews, 1,027; Werdel, 492; Hass, 150; Hoopes, 82; others, 476.
1960: Kennedy, Dem., 3,423,909; Liberal, 406,176; total, 3,830,085; Nixon, Rep., 3,446,419; Dobbs, Soc. Workers, 14,319; scattering, 256; blank and void, 88,896.
1964: Johnson, Dem., 4,913,156; Goldwater, Rep., 2,243,559; Hass, Soc. Labor, 6,085; DeBerry, Soc. Workers, 3,215; scattering, 188; blank and void, 151,383.
1968: Nixon, Rep., 3,007,932; Humphrey, Dem., 3,378,470; Wallace, 3rd Party, 358,864; Blomen, Soc. Labor, 8,432; Halstead, Soc. Workers, 11,851; Gregory, Freedom and Peace, 24,517; blank, void, and scattering, 171,624.
1972: Nixon, Rep., 3,824,642; Cons., 368,136; McGovern, Dem., 2,767,956; Liberal, 183,128; Reed, Soc. Workers, 7,797; Fisher, Soc. Labor, 4,530; Hall, Com., 5,641; blank, void, or scattered, 161,641.
1976: Carter, Dem., 3,389,558; Ford, Rep., 3,100,791; MacBride, Libertarian, 12,197; Hall, Com., 10,270; Camejo, Soc. Workers, 6,996; LaRouche, U.S. Labor, 5,413; blank, void, or scattered, 143,037.
1980: Reagan, Rep., 2,893,831; Carter, Dem., 2,728,372; Anderson, Ind., 467,801; Clark, Libertarian, 52,648; McCormack, Right To Life, 24,159; Commoner, Citizens, 23,186; Hall, Com., 7,414; DeBerry, Soc. Workers, 2,068; Griswold, Workers World, 1,416; scattering, 1,064.
1984: Reagan, Rep., 3,664,763; Mondale, Dem., 3,119,609; Bergland, Libertarian, 11,949.
1988: Bush, Rep., 3,081,871; Dukakis, Dem., 3,347,882; Marra, Right to Life, 20,497; Fulani, New Alliance, 15,845.
1992: Clinton, Dem., 3,444,450; Bush, Rep., 2,346,649; Perot, Ind., 1,090,721; Warren, Soc. Workers, 15,472; Marrou, Libertarian, 13,451; Fulani, New Alliance, 11,318; Hagelin, Natural Law, 4,420.
1996: Clinton, Dem., 3,756,177; Dole, Rep., 1,933,492; Perot, Ind. (Ref.), 503,458; Nader, Green, 75,956; Phillips, Right to Life, 23,580; Browne, Libertarian, 12,220; Hagelin, Natural Law, 5,011; Harris, Soc. Workers, 2,762; Moorehead, Workers World, 3,473.
2000: Gore, Dem., 4,112,965; Bush, Rep., 2,405,570; Nader, Green, 244,360; Buchanan, Reform, 31,554; Hagelin, Independence, 24,369; Browne, Libertarian, 7,664; Harris, Soc. Workers, 1,790; Phillips, Constitution, 1,503.

North Carolina

1948: Truman, Dem., 459,070; Dewey, Rep., 258,572; Thurmond, States' Rights, 69,652; Wallace, Prog., 3,915.
1952: Eisenhower, Rep., 558,107; Stevenson, Dem., 652,803.
1956: Eisenhower, Rep., 575,062; Stevenson, Dem., 590,530.
1960: Kennedy, Dem., 713,136; Nixon, Rep., 655,420.
1964: Johnson, Dem., 800,139; Goldwater, Rep., 624,844.
1968: Nixon, Rep., 627,192; Humphrey, Dem., 464,113; Wallace, 3rd Party, 496,188.
1972: Nixon, Rep., 1,054,889; McGovern, Dem., 438,705; Schmitz, Amer., 25,018.
1976: Carter, Dem., 927,365; Ford, Rep., 741,960; Anderson, Amer., 5,607; MacBride, Libertarian, 2,219; LaRouche, U.S. Labor, 755.
1980: Reagan, Rep., 915,018; Carter, Dem., 875,635; Anderson, Ind., 52,800; Clark, Libertarian, 9,677; Commoner, Citizens, 2,287; DeBerry, Soc. Workers, 416.
1984: Reagan, Rep., 1,346,481; Mondale, Dem., 824,287; Bergland, Libertarian, 3,794.
1988: Bush, Rep., 1,237,258; Dukakis, Dem., 890,167; Fulani, New Alliance, 5,682; Paul, write-in, 1,263.
1992: Clinton, Dem., 1,114,042; Bush, Rep., 1,134,661; Perot, Ind., 357,864; Marrou, Libertarian, 5,171.
1996: Dole, Rep., 1,225,938; Clinton, Dem., 1,107,849; Perot, Ref., 168,059; Browne, Libertarian, 8,740; Hagelin, Natural Law, 2,771.
2000: Bush, Rep., 1,631,163; Gore, Dem., 1,257,692; Browne, Libertarian, 13,891; Buchanan, Reform, 8,874.

North Dakota

1948: Truman, Dem., 95,812; Dewey, Rep., 115,139; Wallace, Prog., 8,391; Thomas, Soc., 1,000; Thurmond, States' Rights, 374.
1952: Eisenhower, Rep., 191,712; Stevenson, Dem., 76,694; MacArthur, Christian Nationalist, 1,075; Hallinan, Prog., 344; Hamblen, Proh., 302.
1956: Eisenhower, Rep., 156,766; Stevenson, Dem., 96,742; Andrews, Amer., 483.
1960: Kennedy, Dem., 123,963; Nixon, Rep., 154,310; Dobbs, Soc. Workers, 158.
1964: Johnson, Dem., 149,784; Goldwater, Rep., 108,207; DeBerry, Soc. Workers, 224; Munn, Proh., 174.
1968: Nixon, Rep., 138,669; Humphrey, Dem., 94,769; Wallace, 3rd Party, 14,244; Halstead, Soc. Workers, 128; Munn, Prohibition, 38; Troxell, Ind., 34.
1972: Nixon, Rep., 174,109; McGovern, Dem., 100,384; Jenness, Soc. Workers, 288; Hall, Com., 87; Schmitz, Amer., 5,646.
1976: Carter, Dem., 136,078; Ford, Rep., 153,470; Anderson, Amer., 3,698; McCarthy, Ind., 2,952; Maddox, Amer. Ind., 269; MacBride, Libertarian, 256; scattering, 371.
1980: Reagan, Rep., 193,695; Carter, Dem., 79,189; Anderson, Ind., 23,640; Clark, Libertarian, 3,743; Commoner, Libertarian, 429; McLain, Natl. People's League, 296; Greaves, Amer., 235; Hall, Com., 93; DeBerry, Soc. Workers, 89; McReynolds, Soc., 82; Bubar, Statesman, 54.
1984: Reagan, Rep., 200,336; Mondale, Dem., 104,429; Bergland, Libertarian, 703.
1988: Bush, Rep., 166,559; Dukakis, Dem., 127,739; Paul, Lib., 1,315; LaRouche, Natl. Econ. Recovery, 905.
1992: Clinton, Dem., 99,168; Bush, Rep., 136,244; Perot, Ind., 71,084.
1996: Dole, Rep., 125,050; Clinton, Dem., 106,905; Perot, Ref., 32,515; Browne, Libertarian, 847; Phillips, Ind., 745; Hagelin, Natural Law, 349.
2000: Bush, Rep., 174,852; Gore, Dem., 95,284; Nader, Ind., 9,486; Buchanan, Reform, 7,288; Browne, Ind., 660; Phillips, Constitution, 373; Hagelin, Ind., 313.

Ohio

1948: Truman, Dem., 1,452,791; Dewey, Rep., 1,445,684; Wallace, Prog., 37,596.
1952: Eisenhower, Rep., 2,100,391; Stevenson, Dem., 1,600,367.
1956: Eisenhower, Rep., 2,262,610; Stevenson, Dem., 1,439,655.
1960: Kennedy, Dem., 1,944,248; Nixon, Rep., 2,217,611.
1964: Johnson, Dem., 2,498,331; Goldwater, Rep., 1,470,865.
1968: Nixon, Rep., 1,791,014; Humphrey, Dem., 1,700,586; Wallace, 3rd Party, 467,495; Gregory, 372; Munn, Proh., 19; Blomen, Soc. Labor, 120; Halstead, Soc. Workers, 69; Mitchell, Com., 23.
1972: Nixon, Rep., 2,441,827; McGovern, Dem., 1,558,889; Fisher, Soc. Labor, 7,107; Hall, Com., 6,437; Schmitz, Amer., 80,067; Wallace, Ind., 460.
1976: Carter, Dem., 2,011,621; Ford, Rep., 2,000,505; McCarthy, Ind., 58,258; Maddox, Amer. Ind., 15,529; MacBride, Libertarian, 8,961; Hall, Com., 7,817; Camejo, Soc. Workers, 4,717; LaRouche, U.S. Labor, 4,335; scattered, 130.
1980: Reagan, Rep., 2,206,545; Carter, Dem., 1,752,414; Anderson, Ind., 254,472; Clark, Libertarian, 49,033; Commoner, Citizens, 8,564; Hall, Com., 4,729; Congress, Ind., 4,029; Griswold, Workers World, 3,790; Bubar, Statesman, 27.
1984: Reagan, Rep., 2,678,559; Mondale, Dem., 1,825,440; Bergland, Libertarian, 5,886.
1988: Bush, Rep., 2,416,549; Dukakis, Dem., 1,939,629; Fulani, Ind., 12,017; Paul, Ind., 11,926.
1992: Clinton, Dem., 1,984,942; Bush, Rep., 1,894,310; Perot, Ind., 1,036,426; Marrou, Libertarian, 7,252; Fulani, New Alliance, 6,413; Gritz, Populist/America First, 4,699; Hagelin, Natural Law, 3,437; LaRouche, Ind., 2,446.
1996: Clinton, Dem., 2,148,222; Dole, Rep., 1,859,883; Perot, Ref., 483,207; Browne, Ind., 12,851; Moorehead, Ind., 10,813; Hagelin, Natural Law, 9,120; Phillips, Ind., 7,361.
2000: Bush, Rep., 2,351,209; Gore, Dem., 2,186,190; Nader, Ind., 117,857; Buchanan, Ind., 26,724; Browne, Libertarian, 13,475; Hagelin, Natural Law, 6,169; Phillips, Ind., 3,823.

Oklahoma

1948: Truman, Dem., 452,782; Dewey, Rep., 268,817.
1952: Eisenhower, Rep., 518,045; Stevenson, Dem., 430,939.
1956: Eisenhower, Rep., 473,769; Stevenson, Dem., 385,581.
1960: Kennedy, Dem., 370,111; Nixon, Rep., 533,039.
1964: Johnson, Dem., 519,834; Goldwater, Rep., 412,665.
1968: Nixon, Rep., 449,697; Humphrey, Dem., 301,658; Wallace, 3rd Party, 191,731.
1972: Nixon, Rep., 759,025; McGovern, Dem., 247,147; Schmitz, Amer., 23,728.
1976: Carter, Dem., 532,442; Ford, Rep., 545,708; McCarthy, Ind., 14,101.
1980: Reagan, Rep., 695,570; Carter, Dem., 402,026; Anderson, Ind., 38,284; Clark, Libertarian, 13,828.
1984: Reagan, Rep., 861,530; Mondale, Dem., 385,080; Bergland, Libertarian, 9,066.
1988: Bush, Rep., 678,367; Dukakis, Dem., 483,423; Paul, Lib., 6,261; Fulani, New Alliance, 2,985.
1992: Clinton, Dem., 473,066; Bush, Rep., 592,929; Perot, Ind., 319,878; Marrou, Libertarian, 4,486.
1996: Dole, Rep., 582,315; Clinton, Dem., 488,105; Perot, Ref., 130,788; Browne, Libertarian, 5,505.
2000: Bush, Rep., 744,337; Gore, Dem., 474,276; Buchanan, Reform, 9,014; Browne, Libertarian, 6,602.

Oregon

1948: Truman, Dem., 243,147; Dewey, Rep., 260,904; Wallace, Prog., 14,978; Thomas, Soc., 5,051.
1952: Eisenhower, Rep., 420,815; Stevenson, Dem., 270,579; Hallinan, Ind., 3,665.
1956: Eisenhower, Rep., 406,393; Stevenson, Dem., 329,204.
1960: Kennedy, Dem., 367,402; Nixon, Rep., 408,060.
1964: Johnson, Dem., 501,017; Goldwater, Rep., 282,779; write-in, 2,509.
1968: Nixon, Rep., 408,433; Humphrey, Dem., 358,866; Wallace, 3rd Party, 49,683; write-in, McCarthy, 1,496; N. Rockefeller, 69; others, 1,075.
1972: Nixon, Rep., 486,686; McGovern, Dem., 392,760; Schmitz, Amer., 46,211; write-in, 2,289.
1976: Carter, Dem., 490,407; Ford, Rep., 492,120; McCarthy, Ind., 40,207; write-in, 7,142.
1980: Reagan, Rep., 571,044; Carter, Dem., 456,890; Anderson, Ind., 112,389; Clark, Libertarian, 25,838; Commoner, Citizens, 13,642; scattered, 1,713.
1984: Reagan, Rep., 658,700; Mondale, Dem., 536,479.
1988: Bush, Rep., 560,126; Dukakis, Dem., 616,206; Paul, Lib., 14,811; Fulani, Ind., 6,487.
1992: Clinton, Dem., 621,314; Bush, Rep., 475,757; Perot, Ind., 354,091; Marrou, Libertarian, 4,277; Fulani, New Alliance, 3,030.
1996: Clinton, Dem., 649,641; Dole, Rep., 538,152; Perot, Ref., 121,221; Nader, Pacific, 49,415; Browne, Libertarian, 8,903; Phillips, Taxpayers, 3,379; Hagelin, Natural Law, 2,798; Hollis, Soc., 1,922.
2000: Gore, Dem., 720,342; Bush, Rep., 713,577; Nader, Green, 77,357; Browne, Libertarian, 7,447; Buchanan, Ind., 7,063; Hagelin, Reform, 2,574; Phillips, Constitution, 2,189.

Pennsylvania

1948: Truman, Dem., 1,752,426; Dewey, Rep., 1,902,197; Wallace, Prog., 55,161; Thomas, Soc., 11,325; Watson, Proh., 10,338; Dobbs, Militant Workers, 2,133; Teichert, Ind. Gov., 1,461.
1952: Eisenhower, Rep., 2,415,789; Stevenson, Dem., 2,146,269; Hamblen, Proh., 8,771; Hallinan, Prog., 4,200; Hoopes, Soc., 2,684; Dobbs, Militant Workers, 1,502; Hass, Ind. Gov., 1,347; scattered, 155.
1956: Eisenhower, Rep., 2,585,252; Stevenson, Dem., 1,981,769; Hass, Soc. Labor, 7,447; Dobbs, Militant Workers, 2,035.
1960: Kennedy, Dem., 2,556,282; Nixon, Rep., 2,439,956; Hass, Soc. Labor, 7,185; Dobbs, Soc. Workers, 2,678; scattering, 440.
1964: Johnson, Dem., 3,130,954; Goldwater, Rep., 1,673,657; DeBerry, Soc. Workers, 10,456; Hass, Soc. Labor, 5,092; scattering, 2,531.
1968: Nixon, Rep., 2,090,017; Humphrey, Dem., 2,259,405; Wallace, 3rd Party, 378,582; Blomen, Soc. Labor, 4,977; Halstead, Soc. Workers, 4,862; Gregory, Peace and Freedom, 7,821; others, 2,264.

1972: Nixon, Rep., 2,714,521; McGovern, Dem., 1,796,951; Schmitz, Amer., 70,593; Jenness, Soc. Workers, 4,639; Hall, Com., 2,686; others, 2,715.

1976: Carter, Dem., 2,328,677; Ford, Rep., 2,205,604; McCarthy, Ind., 50,584; Maddox, Constitution, 25,344; Camejo, Soc. Workers, 3,009; LaRouche, U.S. Labor, 2,744; Hall, Com., 1,891; others, 2,934.

1980: Reagan, Rep., 2,261,872; Carter, Dem., 1,937,540; Anderson, Ind., 292,921; Clark, Libertarian, 33,263; DeBerry, Soc. Workers, 20,291; Commoner, Consumer, 10,430; Hall, Com., 5,184.

1984: Reagan, Rep., 2,584,323; Mondale, Dem., 2,228,131; Bergland, Libertarian, 6,982.

1988: Bush, Rep., 2,300,087; Dukakis, Dem., 2,194,944; McCarthy, Consumer, 19,158; Paul, Lib., 12,051.

1992: Clinton, Dem., 2,239,164; Bush, Rep., 1,791,841; Perot, Ind., 902,667; Marrou, Libertarian, 21,477; Fulani, New Alliance, 4,661.

1996: Clinton, Dem., 2,215,819; Dole, Rep., 1,801,169; Perot, Ref., 430,984; Browne, Libertarian, 28,000; Phillips, Constitutional, 19,552; Hagelin, Natural Law, 5,783.

2000: Gore, Dem., 2,485,967; Bush, Rep., 2,281,127; Nader, Green, 103,392; Buchanan, Reform, 16,023; Phillips, Constitution, 14,428; Browne, Libertarian, 11,248.

Rhode Island

1948: Truman, Dem., 188,736; Dewey, Rep., 135,787; Wallace, Prog., 2,619; Thomas, Soc., 429; Teichert, Soc. Labor, 131.

1952: Eisenhower, Rep., 210,935; Stevenson, Dem., 203,293; Hallinan, Prog., 187; Hass, Soc. Labor, 83.

1956: Eisenhower, Rep., 225,819; Stevenson, Dem., 161,790.

1960: Kennedy, Dem., 258,032; Nixon, Rep., 147,502.

1964: Johnson, Dem., 315,463; Goldwater, Rep., 74,615.

1968: Nixon, Rep., 122,359; Humphrey, Dem., 246,518; Wallace, 3rd Party, 15,678; Halstead, Soc. Workers, 383.

1972: Nixon, Rep., 220,383; McGovern, Dem., 194,645; Jenness, Soc. Workers, 729.

1976: Carter, Dem., 227,636; Ford, Rep., 181,249; MacBride, Libertarian, 715; Camejo, Soc. Workers, 462; Hall, Com., 334; Levin, Soc. Labor, 188.

1980: Reagan, Rep., 154,793; Carter, Dem., 198,342; Anderson, Ind., 59,819; Clark, Libertarian, 2,458; Hall, Com., 218; McReynolds, Soc., 170; DeBerry, Soc. Workers, 90; Griswold, Workers World, 77.

1984: Reagan, Rep., 212,080; Mondale, Dem., 197,106; Bergland, Libertarian, 277.

1988: Bush, Rep., 177,761; Dukakis, Dem., 225,123; Paul, Lib., 825; Fulani, New Alliance, 280.

1992: Clinton, Dem., 213,299; Bush, Rep., 131,601; Perot, Ind., 105,045; Fulani, New Alliance, 1,878.

1996: Clinton, Dem., 233,050; Dole, Rep., 104,683; Perot, Ref., 43,723; Nader, Green, 6,040; Browne, Libertarian, 1,109; Phillips, Taxpayers, 1,021; Hagelin, Natural Law, 435; Moorehead, Workers World, 186.

2000: Gore, Dem., 249,508; Bush, Rep., 130,555; Nader, Ind., 25,052; Buchanan, Reform, 2,273; Browne, Ind., 742; Hagelin, Ind., 271; Moorehead, Ind., 199; Phillips, Ind., 97; McReynolds, Ind., 52; Harris, Ind., 34.

South Carolina

1948: Thurmond, States' Rights, 102,607; Truman, Dem., 34,423; Dewey, Rep., 5,386; Wallace, Prog., 154; Thomas, Soc., 1.

1952: Eisenhower ran on two tickets. Under state law votes cast for two Eisenhower slates of electors could not be combined. Eisenhower, Ind., 158,289; Nixon, R, 9,793; total, 168,082; Stevenson, Dem., 173,004; Hamblen, Proh., 1.

1956: Eisenhower, Rep., 75,700; Stevenson, Dem., 136,372; Byrd, Ind., 88,509; Andrews, Ind., 2.

1960: Kennedy, Dem., 198,129; Nixon, Rep., 188,558; write-in, 1.

1964: Johnson, Dem., 215,700; Goldwater, Rep., 309,048; write-ins: Nixon, 1, Wallace, 5; Powell, 1; Thurmond, 1.

1968: Nixon, Rep., 254,062; Humphrey, Dem., 197,486; Wallace, 3rd Party, 215,430.

1972: Nixon, Rep., 477,044; McGovern, Dem., 184,559; United Citizens, 2,265; Schmitz, Amer., 10,075; write-in, 17.

1976: Carter, Dem., 450,807; Ford, Rep., 346,149; Anderson, Amer., 2,996; Maddox, Amer. Ind., 1,950; write-in, 681.

1980: Reagan, Rep., 439,277; Carter, Dem., 428,220; Anderson, Ind., 13,868; Clark, Libertarian, 4,807; Rarick, Amer. Ind., 2,086.

1984: Reagan, Rep., 615,539; Mondale, Dem., 344,459; Bergland, Libertarian, 4,359.

1988: Bush, Rep., 606,443; Dukakis, Dem., 370,554; Paul, Lib., 4,935; Fulani, United Citizens, 4,077.

1992: Clinton, Dem., 479,514; Bush, Rep., 577,507; Perot, Ind., 138,872; Marrou, Libertarian, 2,719; Phillips, U.S. Taxpayers, 2,680; Fulani, New Alliance, 1,235.

1996: Dole, Rep., 573,458; Clinton, Dem., 506,283; Perot, Ref./Patriot, 64,386; Browne, Libertarian, 4,271; Phillips, Taxpayers, 2,043; Hagelin, Natural Law, 1,248.

2000: Bush, Rep., 786,892; Gore, Dem., 566,039; Nader, United Citizens, 20,279; Browne, Libertarian, 4,898; Buchanan, Reform, 3,309; Phillips, Constitution, 1,682; Hagelin, Natural Law, 943.

South Dakota

1948: Truman, Dem., 117,653; Dewey, Rep., 129,651; Wallace, Prog., 2,801.

1952: Eisenhower, Rep., 203,857; Stevenson, Dem., 90,426.

1956: Eisenhower, Rep., 171,569; Stevenson, Dem., 122,288.

1960: Kennedy, Dem., 128,070; Nixon, Rep., 178,417.

1964: Johnson, Dem., 163,010; Goldwater, Rep., 130,108.

1968: Nixon, Rep., 149,841; Humphrey, Dem., 118,023; Wallace, 3rd Party, 13,400.

1972: Nixon, Rep., 166,476; McGovern, Dem., 139,945; Jenness, Soc. Workers, 994.

1976: Carter, Dem., 147,068; Ford, Rep., 151,505; MacBride, Libertarian, 1,619; Hall, Com., 318; Camejo, Soc. Workers, 168.

1980: Reagan, Rep., 198,343; Carter, Dem., 103,855; Anderson, Ind., 21,431; Clark, Libertarian, 3,824; Pulley, Soc. Workers, 250.

1984: Reagan, Rep., 200,267; Mondale, Dem., 116,113.

1988: Bush, Rep., 165,415; Dukakis, Dem., 145,560; Paul, Lib., 1,060; Fulani, New Alliance, 730.

1992: Clinton, Dem., 124,888; Bush, Rep., 136,718; Perot, Ind., 73,295.

1996: Dole, Rep., 150,543; Clinton, Dem., 139,333; Perot, Ref., 31,250; Browne, Libertarian, 1,472; Phillips, Taxpayers, 912; Hagelin, Natural Law, 316.

2000: Bush, Rep., 190,700; Gore, Dem., 118,804; Buchanan, Reform, 3,322; Phillips, Ind., 1,781; Browne, Libertarian, 1,662.

Tennessee

1948: Truman, Dem., 270,402; Dewey, Rep., 202,914; Thurmond, States' Rights, 73,815; Wallace, Prog., 1,864; Thomas, Soc., 1,288.

1952: Eisenhower, Rep., 446,147; Stevenson, Dem., 443,710; Hamblen, Proh., 1,432; Hallinan, Prog., 885; MacArthur, Christian Nationalist, 379.

1956: Eisenhower, Rep., 462,288; Stevenson, Dem., 456,507; Andrews, Ind., 19,820; Holtwick, Proh., 789.

1960: Kennedy, Dem., 481,453; Nixon, Rep., 556,577; Faubus, States' Rights, 11,304; Decker, Proh., 2,458.

1964: Johnson, Dem., 635,047; Goldwater, Rep., 508,965; write-in, 34.

1968: Nixon, Rep., 472,592; Humphrey, Dem., 351,233; Wallace, 3rd Party, 424,792.

1972: Nixon, Rep., 813,147; McGovern, Dem., 357,293; Schmitz, Amer., 30,373; write-in, 369.

1976: Carter, Dem., 825,879; Ford, Rep., 633,969; Anderson, Amer., 5,769; McCarthy, Ind., 5,004; Maddox, Amer. Ind., 2,303; MacBride, Libertarian, 1,375; Hall, Com., 547; LaRouche, U.S. Labor, 512; Bubar, Proh., 442; Miller, Ind., 316; write-in, 230.

1980: Reagan, Rep., 787,761; Carter, Dem., 783,051; Anderson, Ind., 35,991; Clark, Libertarian, 7,116; Commoner, Citizens, 1,112; Bubar, Statesman, 521; McReynolds, Soc., 519; Hall, Com., 503; DeBerry, Soc. Workers, 490; Griswold, Workers World, 400; write-ins, 152.

1984: Reagan, Rep., 990,212; Mondale, Dem., 711,714; Bergland, Libertarian, 3,072.

1988: Bush, Rep., 947,233; Dukakis, Dem., 679,794; Paul, Ind., 2,041; Duke, Ind., 1,807.

1992: Clinton, Dem., 933,521; Bush, Rep., 841,300; Perot, Ind., 199,968; Marrou, Libertarian, 1,847.

1996: Clinton, Dem., 909,146; Dole, Rep., 863,530; Perot, Ind. (Ref.), 105,918; Nader, Ind., 6,427; Browne, Ind., 5,020; Phillips, Ind., 1,818; Collins, Ind., 688; Hagelin, Ind., 636; Michael, Ind., 408; Dodge, Ind., 324.
2000: Bush, Rep., 1,061,949; Gore, Dem., 981,720; Nader, Green, 19,781; Browne, Libertarian, 4,284; Buchanan, Reform, 4,250; Brown, Ind., 1,606; Phillips, Ind., 1,015; Hagelin, Reform, 613; Venson, Ind., 535.

Texas

1948: Truman, Dem., 750,700; Dewey, Rep., 282,240; Thurmond, States' Rights, 106,909; Wallace, Prog., 3,764; Watson, Proh., 2,758; Thomas, Soc., 874.
1952: Eisenhower, Rep., 1,102,878; Stevenson, Dem., 969,228; Hamblen, Proh., 1,983; MacArthur, Christian Nationalist, 833; MacArthur, Constitution, 730; Hallinan, Prog., 294.
1956: Eisenhower, Rep., 1,080,619; Stevenson, Dem., 859,958; Andrews, Ind., 14,591.
1960: Kennedy, Dem., 1,167,932; Nixon, Rep., 1,121,699; Sullivan, Constitution, 18,169; Decker, Proh., 3,870; write-in, 15.
1964: Johnson, Dem., 1,663,185; Goldwater, Rep., 958,566; Lightburn, Constitution, 5,060.
1968: Nixon, Rep., 1,227,844; Humphrey, Dem., 1,266,804; Wallace, 3rd Party, 584,269; write-in, 489.
1972: Nixon, Rep., 2,298,896; McGovern, Dem., 1,154,289; Schmitz, Amer., 6,039; Jenness, Soc. Workers, 8,664; others, 3,393.
1976: Carter, Dem., 2,082,319; Ford, Rep., 1,953,300; McCarthy, Ind., 20,118; Anderson, Amer., 11,442; Camejo, Soc. Workers, 1,723; write-in, 2,982.
1980: Reagan, Rep., 2,510,705; Carter, Dem., 1,881,147; Anderson, Ind., 111,613; Clark, Libertarian, 37,643; write-in, 528.
1984: Reagan, Rep., 3,433,428; Mondale, Dem., 1,949,276.
1988: Bush, Rep., 3,036,829; Dukakis, Dem., 2,352,748; Paul, Lib., 30,355; Fulani, New Alliance, 7,208.
1992: Clinton, Dem., 2,281,815; Bush, Rep., 2,496,071; Perot, Ind., 1,354,781; Marrou, Libertarian, 19,699.
1996: Dole, Rep., 2,736,167; Clinton, Dem., 2,459,683; Perot, Ind. (Ref.), 378,537; Browne, Libertarian, 20,256; Phillips, Taxpayers, 7,472; Hagelin, Natural Law, 4,422.
2000: Bush, Rep., 3,799,639; Gore, Dem., 2,433,746; Nader, Green, 137,994; Browne, Libertarian, 23,160; Buchanan, Ind., 12,394.

Utah

1948: Truman, Dem., 149,151; Dewey, Rep., 124,402; Wallace, Prog., 2,679; Dobbs, Soc. Workers, 73.
1952: Eisenhower, Rep., 194,190; Stevenson, Dem., 135,364.
1956: Eisenhower, Rep., 215,631; Stevenson, Dem., 118,364.
1960: Kennedy, Dem., 169,248; Nixon, Rep., 205,361; Dobbs, Soc. Workers, 100.
1964: Johnson, Dem., 219,628; Goldwater, Rep., 181,785.
1968: Nixon, Rep., 238,728; Humphrey, Dem., 156,665; Wallace, 3rd Party, 26,906; Halstead, Soc. Workers, 89; Peace and Freedom, 180.
1972: Nixon, Rep., 323,643; McGovern, Dem., 126,284; Schmitz, Amer., 28,549.
1976: Carter, Dem., 182,110; Ford, Rep., 337,908; Anderson, Amer., 13,304; McCarthy, Ind., 3,907; MacBride, Libertarian, 2,438; Maddox, Amer. Ind., 1,162; Camejo, Soc. Workers, 268; Hall, Com., 121.
1980: Reagan, Rep., 439,687; Carter, Dem., 124,266; Anderson, Ind., 30,284; Clark, Libertarian, 7,226; Commoner, Citizens, 1,009; Greaves, Amer., 965; Rarick, Amer. Ind., 522; Hall, Com., 139; DeBerry, Soc. Workers, 124.
1984: Reagan, Rep., 469,105; Mondale, Dem., 155,369; Bergland, Libertarian, 2,447.
1988: Bush, Rep., 428,442; Dukakis, Dem., 207,352; Paul, Lib., 7,473; Dennis, Amer., 2,158.
1992: Clinton, Dem., 183,429; Bush, Rep., 322,632; Perot, Ind., 203,400; Gritz, Populist/America First, 28,602; Marrou, Libertarian, 1,900; Hagelin, Natural Law, 1,319; LaRouche, Ind., 1,089.
1996: Dole, Rep., 361,911; Clinton, Dem., 221,633; Perot, Ref., 66,461; Nader, Green, 4,615; Browne, Libertarian, 4,129; Phillips, Taxpayers, 2,601; Templin, Ind. Amer., 1,290; Crane, Ind., 1,101; Hagelin, Natural Law, 1,085; Moorehead, Workers World, 298; Harris, Soc. Workers, 235; Dodge, Proh., 111.

2000: Bush, Rep., 515,096; Gore, Dem., 203,053; Nader, Green, 35,850; Buchanan, Reform, 9,319; Browne, Libertarian, 3,616; Phillips, Ind. Amer., 2,709; Hagelin, Natural Law, 763; Harris, Soc. Workers, 186; Youngkeit, Ind., 161.

Vermont

1948: Truman, Dem., 45,557; Dewey, Rep., 75,926; Wallace, Prog., 1,279; Thomas, Soc., 585.
1952: Eisenhower, Rep., 109,717; Stevenson, Dem., 43,355; Hallinan, Prog., 282; Hoopes, Soc., 185.
1956: Eisenhower, Rep., 110,390; Stevenson, Dem., 42,549; scattered, 39.
1960: Kennedy, Dem., 69,186; Nixon, Rep., 98,131.
1964: Johnson, Dem., 107,674; Goldwater, Rep., 54,868.
1968: Nixon, Rep., 85,142; Humphrey, Dem., 70,255; Wallace, 3rd Party, 5,104; Halstead, Soc. Workers, 295; Gregory, New Party, 579.
1972: Nixon, Rep., 117,149; McGovern, Dem., 68,174; Spock, Liberty Union, 1,010; Jenness, Soc. Workers, 296; scattered, 318.
1976: Carter, Dem., 77,798; Carter, Ind. Vermonter, 991; Ford, Rep., 100,387; McCarthy, Ind., 4,001; Camejo, Soc. Workers, 430; LaRouche, U.S. Labor, 196; scattered, 99.
1980: Reagan, Rep., 94,598; Carter, Dem., 81,891; Anderson, Ind., 31,760; Commoner, Citizens, 2,316; Clark, Libertarian, 1,900; McReynolds, Liberty Union, 136; Hall, Com., 118; DeBerry, Soc. Workers, 75; scattering, 413.
1984: Reagan, Rep., 135,865; Mondale, Dem., 95,730; Bergland, Libertarian, 1,002.
1988: Bush, Rep., 124,331; Dukakis, Dem., 115,775; Paul, Lib., 1,000; LaRouche, Ind., 275.
1992: Clinton, Dem., 133,590; Bush, Rep., 88,122; Perot, Ind., 65,985.
1996: Clinton, Dem., 137,894; Dole, Rep., 80,352; Perot, Ref., 31,024; Nader, Green, 5,585; Browne, Libertarian, 1,183; Hagelin, Natural Law, 498; Peron, Grass Roots, 480; Phillips, Taxpayers, 382; Hollis, Liberty Union, 292; Harris, Soc. Workers, 199.
2000: Gore, Dem., 149,022; Bush, Rep., 119,775; Nader, Green, 20,374; Buchanan, Reform, 2,192; Lane, Grass Roots, 1,044; Browne, Libertarian, 784; Hagelin, Natural Law, 219; McReynolds, Liberty Union, 161; Phillips, Constitution, 153; Harris, Soc. Workers, 70.

Virginia

1948: Truman, Dem., 200,786; Dewey, Rep., 172,070; Thurmond, States' Rights, 43,393; Wallace, Prog., 2,047; Thomas, Soc., 726; Teichert, Soc. Labor, 234.
1952: Eisenhower, Rep., 349,037; Stevenson, Dem., 268,677; Hass, Soc. Labor, 1,160; Hoopes, Soc. Dem., 504; Hallinan, Prog., 311.
1956: Eisenhower, Rep., 386,459; Stevenson, Dem., 267,760; Andrews, States' Rights, 42,964; Hoopes, Soc. Dem., 444; Hass, Soc. Labor, 351.
1960: Kennedy, Dem., 362,327; Nixon, Rep., 404,521; Coiner, Cons., 4,204; Hass, Soc. Labor, 397.
1964: Johnson, Dem., 558,038; Goldwater, Rep., 481,334; Hass, Soc. Labor, 2,895.
1968: Nixon, Rep., 590,319; Humphrey, Dem., 442,387; Wallace, 3rd Party, *320,272; Blomen, Soc. Labor, 4,671; Munn, Proh., 601; Gregory, Peace and Freedom, 1,680.
*10,561 votes for Wallace were omitted in the count.
1972: Nixon, Rep., 988,493; McGovern, Dem., 438,887; Schmitz, Amer., 19,721; Fisher, Soc. Labor, 9,918.
1976: Carter, Dem., 813,896; Ford, Rep., 836,554; Camejo, Soc. Workers, 17,802; Anderson, Amer., 16,686; LaRouche, U.S. Labor, 7,508; MacBride, Libertarian, 4,648.
1980: Reagan, Rep., 989,609; Carter, Dem., 752,174; Anderson, Ind., 95,418; Commoner, Citizens, 14,024; Clark, Libertarian, 12,821; DeBerry, Soc. Workers, 1,986.
1984: Reagan, Rep., 1,337,078; Mondale, Dem., 796,250.
1988: Bush, Rep., 1,309,162; Dukakis, Dem., 859,799; Fulani, Ind., 14,312; Paul, Lib., 8,336.
1992: Clinton, Dem., 1,038,650; Bush, Rep., 1,150,517; Perot, Ind., 348,639; LaRouche, Ind., 11,937; Marrou, Libertarian, 5,730; Fulani, New Alliance, 3,192.
1996: Dole, Rep., 1,138,350; Clinton, Dem., 1,091,060; Perot, Ref., 159,861; Phillips, Taxpayers, 13,687; Browne, Libertarian, 9,174; Hagelin, Natural Law, 4,510.

2000: Bush, Rep., 1,437,490; Gore, Dem., 1,217,290; Nader, Green, 59,398; Browne, Libertarian, 15,198; Buchanan, Reform, 5,455; Phillips, Constitution, 1,809.

Washington

1948: Truman, Dem., 476,165; Dewey, Rep., 386,315; Wallace, Prog., 31,692; Watson, Proh., 6,117; Thomas, Soc., 3,534; Teichert, Soc. Labor, 1,133; Dobbs, Soc. Workers, 103.

1952: Eisenhower, Rep., 599,107; Stevenson, Dem., 492,845; MacArthur, Christian Nationalist, 7,290; Hallinan, Prog., 2,460; Hass, Soc. Labor, 633; Hoopes, Soc., 254; Dobbs, Soc. Workers, 119.

1956: Eisenhower, Rep., 620,430; Stevenson, Dem., 523,002; Hass, Soc. Labor, 7,457.

1960: Kennedy, Dem., 599,298; Nixon, Rep., 629,273; Hass, Soc. Labor, 10,895; Curtis, Constitution, 1,401; Dobbs, Soc. Workers, 705.

1964: Johnson, Dem., 779,699; Goldwater, Rep., 470,366; Hass, Soc. Labor, 7,772; DeBerry, Freedom Soc., 537.

1968: Nixon, Rep., 588,510; Humphrey, Dem., 616,037; Wallace, 3rd Party, 96,990; Blomen, Soc. Labor, 488; Cleaver, Peace and Freedom, 1,609; Halstead, Soc. Workers, 270; Mitchell, Free Ballot, 377.

1972: Nixon, Rep., 837,135; McGovern, Dem., 568,334; Schmitz, Amer., 58,906; Spock, Ind., 2,644; Fisher, Soc. Labor, 1,102; Jenness, Soc. Workers, 623; Hall, Com., 566; Hospers, Libertarian, 1,537.

1976: Carter, Dem., 717,323; Ford, Rep., 777,732; McCarthy, Ind., 36,986; Maddox, Amer. Ind., 8,585; Anderson, Amer., 5,046; MacBride, Libertarian, 5,042; Wright, People's, 1,124; Camejo, Soc. Workers, 905; LaRouche, U.S. Labor, 903; Hall, Com., 817; Levin, Soc. Labor, 713; Zeidler, Soc., 358.

1980: Reagan, Rep., 865,244; Carter, Dem., 650,193; Anderson, Ind., 185,073; Clark, Libertarian, 29,213; Commoner, Citizens, 9,403; DeBerry, Soc. Workers, 1,137; McReynolds, Soc., 956; Hall, Com., 834; Griswold, Workers World, 341.

1984: Reagan, Rep., 1,051,670; Mondale, Dem., 798,352; Bergland, Libertarian, 8,844.

1988: Bush, Rep., 903,835; Dukakis, Dem., 933,516; Paul, Lib., 17,240; LaRouche, Ind., 4,412.

1992: Clinton, Dem., 993,037; Bush, Rep., 731,234; Perot, Ind., 541,780; Marrou, Libertarian, 7,533; Gritz, Populist/America First, 4,854; Hagelin, Natural Law, 2,456; Phillips, U.S. Taxpayers, 2,354; Fulani, New Alliance, 1,776; Daniels, Ind., 1,171.

1996: Clinton, Dem., 1,123,323; Dole, Rep., 840,712; Perot, Ref., 201,003; Nader, Ind., 60,322; Browne, Libertarian, 12,522; Hagelin, Natural Law, 6,076; Phillips, Taxpayers, 4,578; Collins, Ind., 2,374; Moorehead, Workers World, 2,189; Harris, Soc. Workers, 738.

2000: Gore, Dem., 1,247,652; Bush, Rep., 1,108,864; Nader, Green, 103,002; Browne, Libertarian, 13,135; Buchanan, Freedom, 7,171; Hagelin, Natural Law, 2,927; ; Phillips, Constitution, 1,989; Moorehead, Workers World, 1,729; McReynolds, Soc., 660; Harris, Soc. Workers, 304.

West Virginia

1948: Truman, Dem., 429,188; Dewey, Rep., 316,251; Wallace, Prog., 3,311.

1952: Eisenhower, Rep., 419,970; Stevenson, Dem., 453,578.

1956: Eisenhower, Rep., 449,297; Stevenson, Dem., 381,534.

1960: Kennedy, Dem., 441,786; Nixon, Rep., 395,995.

1964: Johnson, Dem., 538,087; Goldwater, Rep., 253,953.

1968: Nixon, Rep., 307,555; Humphrey, Dem., 374,091; Wallace, 3rd Party, 72,560.

1972: Nixon, Rep., 484,964; McGovern, Dem., 277,435.

1976: Carter, Dem., 435,864; Ford, Rep., 314,726.

1980: Reagan, Rep., 334,206; Carter, Dem., 367,462; Anderson, Ind., 31,691; Clark, Libertarian, 4,356.

1984: Reagan, Rep., 405,483; Mondale, Dem., 328,125.

1988: Bush, Rep., 310,065; Dukakis, Dem., 341,016; Fulani, New Alliance, 2,230.

1992: Clinton, Dem., 331,001; Bush, Rep., 241,974; Perot, Ind., 108,829; Marrou, Libertarian, 1,873.

1996: Clinton, Dem., 327,812; Dole, Rep., 233,946; Perot, Ref., 71,639; Browne, Libertarian, 3,062.

2000: Bush, Rep., 336,475; Gore, Dem., 295,497; Nader, Green, 10,680; Buchanan, Reform, 3,169; Browne, Libertarian, 1,912; Hagelin, Natural Law, 367.

Wisconsin

1948: Truman, Dem., 647,310; Dewey, Rep., 590,959; Wallace, Prog., 25,282; Thomas, Soc., 12,547; Teichert, Soc. Labor, 399; Dobbs, Soc. Workers, 303.

1952: Eisenhower, Rep., 979,744; Stevenson, Dem., 622,175; Hallinan, Ind., 2,174; Dobbs, Ind., 1,350; Hoopes, Ind., 1,157; Hass, Ind., 770.

1956: Eisenhower, Rep., 954,844; Stevenson, Dem., 586,768; Andrews, Ind., 6,918; Hoopes, Soc., 754; Hass, Soc. Labor, 710; Dobbs, Soc. Workers, 564.

1960: Kennedy, Dem., 830,805; Nixon, Rep., 895,175; Dobbs, Soc. Workers, 1,792; Hass, Soc. Labor, 1,310.

1964: Johnson, Dem., 1,050,424; Goldwater, Rep., 638,495; DeBerry, Soc. Workers, 1,692; Hass, Soc. Labor, 1,204.

1968: Nixon, Rep., 809,997; Humphrey, Dem., 748,804; Wallace, 3rd Party, 127,835; Blomen, Soc. Labor, 1,338; Halstead, Soc. Workers, 1,222; scattered, 2,342.

1972: Nixon, Rep., 989,430; McGovern, Dem., 810,174; Schmitz, Amer., 47,525; Spock, Ind., 2,701; Fisher, Soc. Labor, 998; Hall, Com., 663; Reed, Ind., 506; scattered, 893.

1976: Carter, Dem., 1,040,232; Ford, Rep., 1,004,987; McCarthy, Ind., 34,943; Maddox, Amer. Ind., 8,552; Zeidler, Soc., 4,298; MacBride, Libertarian, 3,814; Camejo, Soc. Workers, 1,691; Wright, People's, 943; Hall, Com., 749; LaRouche, U.S. Lab., 738; Levin, Soc. Labor, 389; scattered, 2,839.

1980: Reagan, Rep., 1,088,845; Carter, Dem., 981,584; Anderson, Ind., 160,657; Clark, Libertarian, 29,135; Commoner, Citizens, 7,767; Rarick, Constitution, 1,519; McReynolds, Soc., 808; Hall, Com., 772; Griswold, Workers World, 414; DeBerry, Soc. Workers, 383; scattering, 1,337.

1984: Reagan, Rep., 1,198,584; Mondale, Dem., 995,740; Bergland, Libertarian, 4,883.

1988: Bush, Rep., 1,047,499; Dukakis, Dem., 1,126,794; Paul, Lib., 5,157; Duke, Pop., 3,056.

1992: Clinton, Dem., 1,041,066; Bush, Rep., 930,855; Perot, Ind., 544,479; Marrou, Libertarian, 2,877; Gritz, Populist/America First, 2,311; Daniels, Ind., 1,883; Phillips, U.S. Taxpayers, 1,772; Hagelin, Natural Law, 1,070.

1996: Clinton, Dem., 1,071,971; Dole, Rep., 845,029; Perot, Ref., 227,339; Nader, Green, 28,723; Phillips, Taxpayers, 8,811; Browne, Libertarian, 7,929; Hagelin, Natural Law, 1,379; Moorehead, Workers World, 1,333; Hollis, Soc., 848; Harris, Soc. Workers, 483.

2000: Gore, Dem., 1,242,987; Bush, Rep., 1,237,279; Nader, Green, 94,070; Buchanan, Reform, 11,446; Browne, Libertarian, 6,640; Phillips, Constitution, 2,042; Moorehead, Workers World, 1,063; Hagelin, Reform, 878; Harris, Soc. Workers, 306.

Wyoming

1948: Truman, Dem., 52,354; Dewey, Rep., 47,947; Wallace, Prog., 931; Thomas, Soc., 137; Teichert, Soc. Labor, 56.

1952: Eisenhower, Rep., 81,047; Stevenson, Dem., 47,934; Hamblen, Proh., 194; Hoopes, Soc., 40; Haas, Soc. Labor, 36.

1956: Eisenhower, Rep., 74,573; Stevenson, Dem., 49,554.

1960: Kennedy, Dem., 63,331; Nixon, Rep., 77,451.

1964: Johnson, Dem., 80,718; Goldwater, Rep., 61,998.

1968: Nixon, Rep., 70,927; Humphrey, Dem., 45,173; Wallace, 3rd Party, 11,105.

1972: Nixon, Rep., 100,464; McGovern, Dem., 44,358; Schmitz, Amer., 748.

1976: Carter, Dem., 62,239; Ford, Rep., 92,717; McCarthy, Ind., 624; Reagan, Ind., 307; Anderson, Amer., 290; MacBride, Libertarian, 89; Brown, Ind., 47; Maddox, Amer. Ind., 30.

1980: Reagan, Rep., 110,700; Carter, Dem., 49,427; Anderson, Ind., 12,072; Clark, Libertarian, 4,514.

1984: Reagan, Rep., 133,241; Mondale, Dem., 53,370; Bergland, Libertarian, 2,357.

1988: Bush, Rep., 106,867; Dukakis, Dem., 67,113; Paul, Lib., 2,026; Fulani, New Alliance, 545.

1992: Clinton, Dem., 68,160; Bush, Rep., 79,347; Perot, Ind., 51,263.

1996: Dole, Rep., 105,388; Clinton, Dem., 77,934; Perot, Ind. (Ref.), 25,928; Browne, Libertarian, 1,739; Hagelin, Natural Law, 582.

2000: Bush, Rep., 147,947; Gore, Dem., 60,481; Buchanan, Reform, 2,724; Browne, Libertarian, 1,443; Phillips, Ind., 720; Hagelin, Natural Law, 411.

UNITED STATES FACTS

Superlative U.S. Statistics[1]

Source: U.S. Geological Survey, Dept. of the Interior; U.S. Bureau of the Census, Dept. of Commerce; World Almanac research

Area for 50 states and Washington, DC . **TOTAL** .... 3,794,085 sq mi[4]
Land, 3,537,440 sq mi; Water, 256,648 sq mi.

Largest state	Alaska	663,267 sq mi[1]
Smallest state	Rhode Island	1,545 sq mi
Largest county (excluding Alaska)	San Bernardino County, CA	20,105 sq mi
Smallest county	Arlington County, VA	26 sq mi
Largest incorporated city	Sitka, AK	4,812 sq mi
Northernmost city	Barrow, AK	71° 17′ N
Northernmost point	Point Barrow, AK	71° 23′ N
Southernmost city	Hilo, HI	19° 44′ N
Southernmost settlement	Naalehu, HI	19° 03′ N
Southernmost point	Ka Lae (South Cape), Island of Hawaii	18° 55′ N (155°41′ W)
Easternmost city	Eastport, ME	66° 59′05′′ W
Easternmost settlement[2]	Amchitka Isl., AK	179° 15′ E
Easternmost point[2]	Pochnoi Point, on Semisopochnoi Isl., AK	179° 46′ E
Westernmost city	Atka, AK	174° 12′ W
Westernmost settlement	Adak Station, AK	176° 39′ W
Westernmost point	Amatignak Isl., AK	179° 06′ W
Highest settlement	Climax, CO	11,360 ft
Lowest settlement	Calipatria, CA	−184 ft
Highest point on Atlantic coast	Cadillac Mountain, Mount Desert Isl., ME	1,530 ft
Oldest national park	Yellowstone National Park (1872), WY, MT, ID	2,219,791 acres
Largest national park	Wrangell-St. Elias, AK	8,323,148 acres
Highest waterfall	Yosemite Falls—Total in 3 sections	2,425 ft

(consisting of Upper Yosemite Fall, 1,430 ft; Cascades, 675 ft; Lower Yosemite Fall, 320 ft)

Longest river system	Mississippi-Missouri-Red Rock	3,710 mi
Highest mountain	Mount McKinley, AK	20,320 ft
Lowest point	Death Valley, CA	−282 ft
Deepest lake	Crater Lake, OR	1,932 ft
Rainiest spot	Mount Waialeale, HI	Annual avg rainfall 460 in
Largest gorge	Grand Canyon, Colorado River, AZ	277 mi long, 600 ft to 18 mi wide, 1 mi deep
Deepest gorge	Hells Canyon, Snake River, OR-ID	7,900 ft
Largest dam	New Cornelia Tailings, Ten Mile Wash, AZ[3]	274,026,000 cu yds material used
Tallest building	Sears Tower, Chicago, IL	1,450 ft
Largest building	Boeing Manufacturing Plant, Everett, WA	472,000,000 cu ft; covers 98 acres
Largest office building	Pentagon, Arlington, VA	77,025,000 cu ft; covers 29 acres
Tallest structure	TV tower, Blanchard, ND	2,063 ft
Longest bridge span	Verrazano-Narrows, NY	4,260 ft
Highest bridge	Royal Gorge, CO	1,053 ft above water
Deepest well	Gas well, Washita County, OK	31,441 ft

The 48 Contiguous States

Area for 48 states and Washington, DC. .... **TOTAL** .... 3,119,887 sq mi[4]
Land, 2,959,066 sq mi; Water, 160,824 sq mi

Largest state	Texas	268,581 sq mi
Northernmost city	Bellingham, WA	48°46′ N
Northernmost settlement	Angle Inlet, MN	49°21′ N
Northernmost point	Northwest Angle, MN	49°23′ N
Southernmost city	Key West, FL	24°33′ N
Southernmost mainland city	Florida City, FL	25°27′ N
Southernmost point	Key West, FL	24°33′ N
Easternmost settlement	Lubec, ME	66°58′49 W
Easternmost point	West Quoddy Head, ME	66°57′W
Westernmost town	La Push, WA	124°38′ W
Westernmost point	Cape Alava, WA	124°44′ W
Highest mountain	Mount Whitney, CA	14,494 ft

(1) All areas are total area, including water, unless otherwise noted. (2) Alaska's Aleutian Islands extend into the eastern hemisphere and thus technically contain the easternmost point and settlement in the U.S. (3) The New Cornelia Tailings Dam is a privately owned industrial dam composed of tailings, remnants of a mining process. (4) Does not add, because of rounding.

Geodetic Datum of North America

In July 1986, the National Oceanic and Atmospheric Administration's National Geodetic Survey (NGS), in cooperation with Canada and Mexico, completed readjustment and redefinition of the system of latitudes and longitudes. The resulting North American Datum of 1983 (NAD 83) replaces the North American Datum of 1927, as well as local reference systems for Hawaii and for Puerto Rico and the Virgin Islands. The change was prompted by Hawaii's increased need for accurate co-ordinate information. To facilitate use of satellite surveying and navigation systems, such as the Global Positioning System (GPS), the new datum was redefined using the Geodetic Reference System 1980 as the reference ellipsoid because this model more closely approximates the true size and shape of the earth. In addition, the origin of the coordinate system is referenced to the mass center of the earth to coincide with the orbital orientation of the GPS satellites. Positional changes resulting from the datum redefinition can reach 330 ft in the continental U.S., Canada, and Mexico. Changes that exceed 660 ft can be expected in Alaska, Puerto Rico, and the Virgin Islands. Hawaii's coordinates changed about 1,300 ft.

Additional Statistical Information About the U.S.

The annual *Statistical Abstract of the United States,* published by U.S. Dept. of Commerce, contains additional data. For information, write Supt. of Documents, Government Printing Office, PO Box 371954, Pittsburgh, PA 15250-7954, or call (202) 512-1800. For electronic products, write U.S. Dept. of Commerce, U.S. Census Bureau, PO Box 277943, Atlanta, GA 30384-7943, or call (301) 763-INFO (4636). Parts of *The Statistical Abstract* can be viewed on the Internet at www.census.gov/statab/www

▶ *IT'S A FACT:* The city of Calipatria, CA, can claim two distinctions: at 184 feet below sea level, it is the lowest settlement in the U.S.; it is also home to the world's tallest flagpole which, at 184 feet tall, flies an American flag at sea level.

Highest and Lowest Altitudes in U.S. States and Territories

Source: U.S. Geological Survey, Dept. of the Interior
(Minus sign means below sea level.)

	HIGHEST POINT			LOWEST POINT		
	Name	County	Elev. (ft)	Name	County	Elev. (ft)
Alabama	Cheaha Mountain	Cleburne	2,407	Gulf of Mexico		Sea level
Alaska	Mount McKinley	Denali	20,320	Pacific Ocean		Sea level
Arizona	Humphreys Peak	Coconino	12,633	Colorado R	Yuma	70
Arkansas	Magazine Mountain	Logan	2,753	Ouachita R	Ashley-Union	55
California	Mount Whitney	Inyo-Tulare	14,494	Death Valley	Inyo	−282
Colorado	Mount Elbert	Lake	14,433	Arikaree R	Yuma	3,315
Connecticut	S. slope of Mt. Frissell	Litchfield	2,380	Long Island Sound		Sea level
Delaware	On Ebright Road	New Castle	448	Atlantic Ocean		Sea level
Dist. of Columbia	Tenleytown	N W part	410	Potomac R		1
Florida	Britton Hill	Walton	345	Atlantic Ocean		Sea level
Georgia	Brasstown Bald	Towns-Union	4,784	Atlantic Ocean		Sea level
Guam	Mount Lamlam	Agat District	1,332	Pacific Ocean		Sea level
Hawaii	Mauna Kea	Hawaii	13,796	Pacific Ocean		Sea level
Idaho	Borah Peak	Custer	12,662	Snake R	Nez Perce	710
Illinois	Charles Mound	Jo Daviess	1,235	Mississippi R	Alexander	279
Indiana	Hoosier Hill	Wayne	1,257	Ohio R	Posey	320
Iowa	Hawkeye Point	Osceola	1,670	Mississippi R	Lee	480
Kansas	Mount Sunflower	Wallace	4,039	Verdigris R	Montgomery	679
Kentucky	Black Mountain	Harlan	4,145	Mississippi R	Fulton	257
Louisiana	Driskill Mountain	Bienville	535	New Orleans	Orleans	−8
Maine	Mount Katahdin	Piscataquis	5,268	Atlantic Ocean		Sea level
Maryland	Hoye-Crest	Garrett	3,360	Atlantic Ocean		Sea level
Massachusetts	Mount Greylock	Berkshire	3,491	Atlantic Ocean		Sea level
Michigan	Mount Arvon	Baraga	1,979	Lake Erie	Monroe	571
Minnesota	Eagle Mountain	Cook	2,301	Lake Superior		602
Mississippi	Woodall Mountain	Tishomingo	806	Gulf of Mexico		Sea level
Missouri	Taum Sauk Mt.	Iron	1,772	St. Francis R	Dunklin	230
Montana	Granite Peak	Park	12,799	Kootenai R	Lincoln	1,800
Nebraska	Panorama Point	Kimball	5,424	Missouri R	Richardson	840
Nevada	Boundary Peak	Esmeralda	13,143	Colorado R	Clark	479
New Hampshire	Mt. Washington	Coos	6,288	Atlantic Ocean		Sea level
New Jersey	High Point	Sussex	1,803	Atlantic Ocean		Sea level
New Mexico	Wheeler Peak	Taos	13,161	Red Bluff Res.	Eddy	2,842
New York	Mount Marcy	Essex	5,344	Atlantic Ocean		Sea level
North Carolina	Mount Mitchell	Yancey	6,684	Atlantic Ocean		Sea level
North Dakota	White Butte	Slope	3,506	Red R of the North	Pembina	750
Ohio	Campbell Hill	Logan	1,550	Ohio R	Hamilton	455
Oklahoma	Black Mesa	Cimarron	4,973	Little R	McCurtain	289
Oregon	Mount Hood	Clackamas-Hood R.	11,239	Pacific Ocean		Sea level
Pennsylvania	Mt. Davis	Somerset	3,213	Delaware R	Delaware	Sea level
Puerto Rico	Cerro de Punta	Ponce District	4,390	Atlantic Ocean		Sea level
Rhode Island	Jerimoth Hill	Providence	812	Atlantic Ocean		Sea level
Samoa	Lata Mountain	Tau Island	3,160	Pacific Ocean		Sea level
South Carolina	Sassafras Mountain	Pickens	3,560	Atlantic Ocean		Sea level
South Dakota	Harney Peak	Pennington	7,242	Big Stone Lake	Roberts	966
Tennessee	Clingmans Dome	Sevier	6,643	Mississippi R	Shelby	178
Texas	Guadalupe Peak	Culberson	8,749	Gulf of Mexico		Sea level
Utah	Kings Peak	Duchesne	13,528	Beaver Dam Wash	Washington	2,000
Vermont	Mount Mansfield	Lamoille	4,393	Lake Champlain		95
Virginia	Mount Rogers	Grayson-Smyth	5,729	Atlantic Ocean		Sea level
Virgin Islands	Crown Mountain	St. Thomas Island	1,556	Atlantic Ocean		Sea level
Washington	Mount Rainier	Pierce	14,411	Pacific Ocean		Sea level
West Virginia	Spruce Knob	Pendleton	4,863	Potomac R	Jefferson	240
Wisconsin	Timms Hill	Price	1,951	Lake Michigan		579
Wyoming	Gannett Peak	Fremont	13,804	Belle Fourche R	Crook	3,099

U.S. Coastline by States

Source: National Oceanic and Atmospheric Administration, U.S. Dept. of Commerce
(in statute miles)

	Coastline[1]	Shoreline[2]
ATLANTIC COAST	2,069	28,673
Connecticut	0	618
Delaware	28	381
Florida	580	3,331
Georgia	100	2,344
Maine	228	3,478
Maryland	31	3,190
Massachusetts	192	1,519
New Hampshire	13	131
New Jersey	130	1,792
New York	127	1,850
North Carolina	301	3,375
Pennsylvania	0	89
Rhode Island	40	384
South Carolina	187	2,876
Virginia	112	3,315

	Coastline[1]	Shoreline[2]
GULF COAST	1,631	17,141
Alabama	53	607
Florida	770	5,095
Louisiana	397	7,721
Mississippi	44	359
Texas	367	3,359
PACIFIC COAST	7,623	40,298
Alaska	5,580	31,383
California	840	3,427
Hawaii	750	1,052
Oregon	296	1,410
Washington	157	3,026
ARCTIC COAST	1,060	2,521
UNITED STATES	12,383	88,633

(1) Figures are lengths of general outline of seacoast. Measurements were made with a unit measure of 30 minutes of latitude on charts as near the scale of 1:1,200,000 as possible. Coastline of sounds and bays is included to a point where they narrow to width of unit measure, and includes the distance across at such point. (2) Figures obtained in 1939-40 with a recording instrument on the largest-scale charts and maps then available. Shoreline of outer coast, offshore islands, sounds, bays, rivers, and creeks is included to the head of tidewater or to a point where tidal waters narrow to a width of 100 ft.

Key Data for the 50 States

The 13 colonies that declared independence from Great Britain and fought the War of Independence (American Revolution) became the 13 original states. They were (in the order in which they ratified the Constitution): Delaware, Pennsylvania, New Jersey, Georgia, Connecticut, Massachusetts, Maryland, South Carolina, New Hampshire, Virginia, New York, North Carolina, and Rhode Island.

State	Settled[1]	Capital	Entered Union Date	Entered Union Order	Extent in miles Long (approx. mean)	Extent in miles Wide (approx. mean)	Area in sq mi Land	Area in sq mi Water	Area in sq mi Total	Rank in area[2]
AL	1702	Montgomery	Dec. 14, 1819	22	330	190	50,744	1,675	52,419	30
AK	1784	Juneau	Jan. 3, 1959	49	1,480[3]	810	571,951	91,316	663,267	1
AZ	1776	Phoenix	Feb. 14, 1912	48	400	310	113,635	364	113,998	6
AR	1686	Little Rock	June 15, 1836	25	260	240	52,068	1,110	53,179	29
CA	1769	Sacramento	Sept. 9, 1850	31	770	250	155,959	7,736	163,696	3
CO	1858	Denver	Aug. 1, 1876	38	380	280	103,718	376	104,094	8
CT	1634	Hartford	Jan. 9, 1788	5	110	70	4,845	699	5,543	48
DE	1638	Dover	Dec. 7, 1787	1	100	30	1,954	536	2,489	49
DC	NA	NA	NA	NA	...	...	61	7	68	51
FL	1565	Tallahassee	Mar. 3, 1845	27	500	160	53,927	11,828	65,755	22
GA	1733	Atlanta	Jan. 2, 1788	4	300	230	57,906	1,519	59,425	24
HI	1820	Honolulu	Aug. 21, 1959	50	...	...	6,423	4,508	10,931	43
ID	1842	Boise	July 3, 1890	43	570	300	82,747	823	83,570	14
IL	1720	Springfield	Dec. 3, 1818	21	390	210	55,584	2,331	57,914	25
IN	1733	Indianapolis	Dec. 11, 1816	19	270	140	35,867	551	36,418	38
IA	1788	Des Moines	Dec. 28, 1846	29	310	200	55,869	402	56,272	26
KS	1727	Topeka	Jan. 29, 1861	34	400	210	81,815	462	82,277	15
KY	1774	Frankfort	June 1, 1792	15	380	140	39,728	681	40,409	37
LA	1699	Baton Rouge	Apr. 30, 1812	18	380	130	43,562	8,278	51,840	31
ME	1624	Augusta	Mar. 15, 1820	23	320	190	30,862	4,523	35,385	39
MD	1634	Annapolis	Apr. 28, 1788	7	250	90	9,774	2,633	12,407	42
MA	1620	Boston	Feb. 6, 1788	6	190	50	7,840	2,715	10,555	44
MI	1668	Lansing	Jan. 26, 1837	26	490	240	56,804	39,912	96,716	11
MN	1805	St. Paul	May 11, 1858	32	400	250	79,610	7,329	86,939	12
MS	1699	Jackson	Dec. 10, 1817	20	340	170	46,907	1,523	48,430	32
MO	1735	Jefferson City	Aug. 10, 1821	24	300	240	68,886	818	69,704	21
MT	1809	Helena	Nov. 8, 1889	41	630	280	145,552	1,490	147,042	4
NE	1823	Lincoln	Mar. 1, 1867	37	430	210	76,872	481	77,354	16
NV	1849	Carson City	Oct. 31, 1864	36	490	320	109,826	735	110,561	7
NH	1623	Concord	June 21, 1788	9	190	70	8,968	382	9,350	46
NJ	1660	Trenton	Dec. 18, 1787	3	150	70	7,417	1,304	8,721	47
NM	1610	Santa Fe	Jan. 6, 1912	47	370	343	121,356	234	121,589	5
NY	1614	Albany	July 26, 1788	11	330	283	47,214	7,342	54,556	27
NC	1660	Raleigh	Nov. 21, 1789	12	500	150	48,711	5,108	53,819	28
ND	1812	Bismarck	Nov. 2, 1889	39	340	211	68,976	1,724	70,700	19
OH	1788	Columbus	Mar. 1, 1803	17	220	220	40,948	3,877	44,825	34
OK	1889	Oklahoma City	Nov. 16, 1907	46	400	220	68,667	1,231	69,898	20
OR	1811	Salem	Feb. 14, 1859	33	360	261	95,997	2,384	98,381	9
PA	1682	Harrisburg	Dec. 12, 1787	2	283	160	44,817	1,239	46,055	33
RI	1636	Providence	May 29, 1790	13	40	30	1,045	500	1,545	50
SC	1670	Columbia	May 23, 1788	8	260	200	30,109	911	32,020	40
SD	1859	Pierre	Nov. 2, 1889	40	380	210	75,885	1,232	77,116	17
TN	1769	Nashville	June 1, 1796	16	440	120	41,217	926	42,143	36
TX	1682	Austin	Dec. 29, 1845	28	790	660	261,797	6,784	268,581	2
UT	1847	Salt Lake City	Jan. 4, 1896	45	350	270	82,144	2,755	84,899	13
VT	1724	Montpelier	Mar. 4, 1791	14	160	80	9,250	365	9,614	45
VA	1607	Richmond	June 25, 1788	10	430	200	39,594	3,180	42,774	35
WA	1811	Olympia	Nov. 11, 1889	42	360	240	66,544	4,756	71,300	18
WV	1727	Charleston	June 20, 1863	35	240	130	24,078	152	24,230	41
WI	1766	Madison	May 29, 1848	30	310	260	54,310	11,188	65,498	23
WY	1834	Cheyenne	July 10, 1890	44	360	280	97,100	713	97,814	10

Note: Land and water areas may not add to totals because of rounding. NA = Not applicable. (1) First permanent settlement by Europeans. (2) Rank is based on total area as shown. (3) Aleutian Islands and Alexander Archipelago not included.

The Continental Divide of the U.S.

The Continental Divide of the U.S., also known as the Great Divide, is located at the watershed created by the mountain ranges, or tablelands, of the Rocky Mountains. This watershed separates the waters that drain easterly into the Atlantic Ocean and its marginal seas, such as the Gulf of Mexico, from those waters that drain westerly into the Pacific Ocean. The majority of easterly flowing water in the U.S. drains into the Gulf of Mexico before reaching the Atlantic Ocean. The majority of westerly flowing water, before reaching the Pacific Ocean, drains either through the Columbia River or through the Colorado River, which flows into the Gulf of California before reaching the Pacific Ocean.

The location and route of the Continental Divide across the U.S. can briefly be described as follows:

Beginning at the U.S.-Mexican boundary, near long. 108° 45′ W, the Divide, in a northerly direction, crosses New Mexico along the W edge of the Rio Grande drainage basin, entering Colorado near long. 106° 41′ W.

From there by a very irregular route north across Colorado along the W summits of the Rio Grande and of the Ar-

kansas, the South Platte, and the North Platte river basins, and across Rocky Mountain National Park, entering Wyoming near long. 106° 52′ W.

From there in a northwesterly direction, forming the W rims of the North Platte, the Big Horn, and the Yellowstone river basins, crossing the SW portion of Yellowstone National Park.

From there in a westerly and then a northerly direction forming the common boundary of Idaho and Montana, to a point on said boundary near long. 114° 00′ W.

From there northeasterly and northwesterly through Montana and the Glacier National Park, entering Canada near long. 114° 04′ W.

WORLD ALMANAC QUICK QUIZ

Which state name is NOT from an Indian language?

(a) Delaware   (b) Connecticut
(c) Michigan   (d) Missouri

For the answer look in this chapter, or see page 1008.

Chronological List of Territories, With State Admissions to Union

Source: National Archives and Records Service

Name of territory	Date of act creating territory	When act took effect	Admission as state	Yrs. terr.
Northwest Territory[1]	July 13, 1787	No fixed date	Mar. 1, 1803[2]	16
Territory southwest of River Ohio	May 26, 1790	No fixed date	June 1, 1796[3]	6
Mississippi	Apr. 7, 1798	When president acted	Dec. 10, 1817	19
Indiana	May 7, 1800	July 4, 1800	Dec. 11, 1816	16
Orleans	Mar. 26, 1804	Oct. 1, 1804	Apr. 30, 1812[4]	7
Michigan	Jan. 11, 1805	June 30, 1805	Jan. 26, 1837	31
Louisiana-Missouri[5]	Mar. 3, 1805	July 4, 1805	Aug. 10, 1821	16
Illinois	Feb. 3, 1809	Mar. 1, 1809	Dec. 3, 1818	9
Alabama	Mar. 3, 1817	When MS became a state	Dec. 14, 1819	2
Arkansas	Mar. 2, 1819	July 4, 1819	June 15, 1836	17
Florida	Mar. 30, 1822	No fixed date	Mar. 3, 1845	23
Wisconsin	Apr. 20, 1836	July 3, 1836	May 29, 1848	12
Iowa	June 12, 1838	July 3, 1838	Dec. 28, 1846	8
Oregon	Aug. 14, 1848	Date of act	Feb. 14, 1859	10
Minnesota	Mar. 3, 1849	Date of act	May 11, 1858	9
New Mexico	Sept. 9, 1850	On president's proclamation	Jan. 6, 1912	61
Utah	Sept. 9, 1850	Date of act	Jan. 4, 1896	46
Washington	Mar. 2, 1853	Date of act	Nov. 11, 1889	36
Nebraska	May 30, 1854	Date of act	Mar. 1, 1867	12
Kansas	May 30, 1854	Date of act	Jan. 29, 1861	6
Colorado	Feb. 28, 1861	Date of act	Aug. 1, 1876	15
Nevada	Mar. 2, 1861	Date of act	Oct. 31, 1864	3
Dakota	Mar. 2, 1861	Date of act	Nov. 2, 1889	28
Arizona	Feb. 24, 1863	Date of act	Feb. 14, 1912	49
Idaho	Mar. 3, 1863	Date of act	July 3, 1890	27
Montana	May 26, 1864	Date of act	Nov. 8, 1889	25
Wyoming	July 25, 1868	When officers were qualified	July 10, 1890	22
Alaska[6]	May 17, 1884	No fixed date	Jan. 3, 1959	75
Oklahoma	May 2, 1890	Date of act	Nov. 16, 1907	17
Hawaii	Apr. 30, 1900	June 14, 1900	Aug. 21, 1959	59

(1) Included what is now Ohio, Indiana, Illinois, Michigan, Wisconsin, E Minnesota. (2) Whole territory admitted as the state of Ohio. (3) Admitted as the state of Tennessee. (4) Admitted as the state of Louisiana. (5) The act creating Missouri Territory (June 4, 1812) became effective Dec. 7, 1812. (6) Although the May 17, 1884, act actually constituted Alaska as a district, it was often referred to as a territory, and administered as such. The Territory of Alaska was formally organized by an act of Aug. 24, 1912.

Geographic Centers, U.S. and Each State

Source: U.S. Geological Survey, Dept. of the Interior

There is no generally accepted definition of geographic center and no uniform method for determining it. Following the U.S. Geological Survey, the geographic center of an area is defined here as the center of gravity of the surface, or that point on which the surface would balance if it were a plane of uniform thickness. All locations in the following list are approximate.

No marked or monumented point has been officially established by any government agency as the geographic center of the 50 states, the conterminous U.S. (48 states), or the North American continent. A group of private citizens erected a monument in Lebanon, KS, marking it as geographic center of the conterminous U.S., and a cairn erected in Rugby, ND, asserts that location as the center of the North American continent.

Geographic centers as reported by the U.S. Geological Survey are indicated below:

United States, including Alaska and Hawaii—W of Castle Rock, Butte County, SD; lat. 44° 58′ N, long. 103° 46′ W
Conterminous U.S. (48 states)—Near Lebanon, Smith Co., Kansas, lat. 39° 50′ N, long. 98° 35′ W
North American continent—6 mi W of Balta, Pierce County, North Dakota; lat. 48° 10′ N, long. 100° 10′ W
Alabama—Chilton, 12 mi SW of Clanton
Alaska—lat. 63° 50′ N, long. 152° W; approx. 60 mi NW of Mt. McKinley
Arizona—Yavapai, 55 mi E-SE of Prescott
Arkansas—Pulaski, 12 mi NW of Little Rock
California—Madera, 38 mi E of Madera
Colorado—Park, 30 mi NW of Pikes Peak
Connecticut—Hartford, at East Berlin
Delaware—Kent, 11 mi S of Dover
District of Columbia—Near 4th and L Sts. NW
Florida—Hernando, 12 mi N-NW of Brooksville
Georgia—Twiggs, 18 mi SE of Macon
Hawaii—lat. 20° 15′ N, long. 156° 20′ W, off Maui Is.
Idaho—Custer, SW of Challis
Illinois—Logan, 28 mi NE of Springfield
Indiana—Boone, 14 mi N-NW of Indianapolis
Iowa—Story, 5 mi NE of Ames
Kansas—Barton, 15 mi NE of Great Bend
Kentucky—Marion, 3 mi N-NW of Lebanon
Louisiana—Avoyelles, 3 mi SE of Marksville
Maine—Piscataquis, 18 mi N of Dover
Maryland—Prince George's, 4.5 mi NW of Davidsonville
Massachusetts—Worcester, N part of city
Michigan—Wexford, 5 mi N-NW of Cadillac
Minnesota—Crow Wing, 10 mi SW of Brainerd
Mississippi—Leake, 9 mi W-NW of Carthage
Missouri—Miller, 20 mi SW of Jefferson City
Montana—Fergus, 11 mi W of Lewistown
Nebraska—Custer, 10 mi NW of Broken Bow
Nevada—Lander, 26 mi SE of Austin
New Hampshire—Belknap, 3 mi E of Ashland
New Jersey—Mercer, 5 mi SE of Trenton
New Mexico—Torrance, 12 mi S-SW of Willard
New York—Madison, 12 mi S of Oneida and 26 mi SW of Utica
North Carolina—Chatham, 10 mi NW of Sanford
North Dakota—Sheridan, 5 mi SW of McClusky
Ohio—Delaware, 25 mi N-NE of Columbus
Oklahoma—Oklahoma, 8 mi N of Oklahoma City
Oregon—Crook, 25 mi S-SE of Prineville
Pennsylvania—Centre, 2.5 mi SW of Bellefonte
Rhode Island—Kent, 1 mi S-SW of Crompton
South Carolina—Richland, 13 mi SE of Columbia
South Dakota—Hughes, 8 mi NE of Pierre
Tennessee—Rutherford, 5 mi NE of Murfreesboro
Texas—McCulloch, 15 mi NE of Brady
Utah—Sanpete, 3 mi N of Manti
Vermont—Washington, 3 mi E of Roxbury
Virginia—Buckingham, 5 mi SW of Buckingham
Washington—Chelan, 10 mi W-SW of Wenatchee
West Virginia—Braxton, 4 mi E of Sutton
Wisconsin—Wood, 9 mi SE of Marshfield
Wyoming—Fremont, 58 mi E-NE of Lander

International Boundary Lines of the U.S.

The length of the N boundary of the conterminous U.S.—the U.S.-Canadian border, excluding Alaska—is 3,987 mi according to the U.S. Geological Survey, Dept. of the Interior. The length of the Alaskan-Canadian border is 1,538 mi. The U.S.-Mexican border, from the Gulf of Mexico to the Pacific Ocean, is about 1,933 mi (1963 boundary agreement).

Origins of the Names of U.S. States

Source: State officials, Smithsonian Institution, and Topographic Division, U.S. Geological Survey, Dept. of the Interior

Alabama—Indian for tribal town, later a tribe (Alabamas or Alibamons) of the Creek confederacy.

Alaska—Russian version of Aleutian (Eskimo) word, *alakshak*, for "peninsula," "great lands," or "land that is not an island."

Arizona—Spanish version of Pima Indian word for "little spring place," or Aztec *arizuma*, meaning "silver-bearing."

Arkansas—Algonquin name for the Quapaw Indians, meaning "south wind."

California—Bestowed by the Spanish conquistadors (possibly by Cortez). It was the name of an imaginary island, an earthly paradise, in *Las Serges de Esplandian*, a Spanish romance written by Montalvo in 1510. *Baja California* (Lower California, in Mexico) was first visited by Spanish in 1533. The present U.S. state was called *Alta* (Upper) *California*.

Colorado—From Spanish for "red," first applied to Colorado River.

Connecticut—From Mohican and other Algonquin words meaning "long river place."

Delaware—Named for Lord De La Warr, early governor of Virginia; first applied to river, then to Indian tribe (Lenni-Lenape), and the state.

District of Columbia—For Christopher Columbus, 1791.

Florida—Named by Ponce de Leon *Pascua Florida*, "Flowery Easter," on Easter Sunday, 1513.

Georgia—For King George II of England, by James Oglethorpe, colonial administrator, 1732.

Hawaii—Possibly derived from native word for homeland, *Hawaiki* or *Owhyhee*.

Idaho—Said to be a coined name with an invented meaning: "gem of the mountains"; originally suggested for the Pikes Peak mining territory (Colorado), then applied to the new mining territory of the Pacific Northwest. Another theory suggests *Idaho* may be a Kiowa Apache term for the Comanche.

Illinois—French for *Illini* or "land of *Illini*," Algonquin word meaning "men" or "warriors."

Indiana—Means "land of the Indians."

Iowa—Indian word variously translated as "here I rest" or "beautiful land." Named for the Iowa R., which was named for the Iowa Indians.

Kansas—Sioux word for "south wind people."

Kentucky—Indian word that is variously translated as "dark and bloody ground," "meadowland," and "land of tomorrow."

Louisiana—Part of territory called Louisiana by Sieur de La Salle for French King Louis XIV.

Maine—From Maine, ancient French province. Also: descriptive, referring to the mainland as distinct from the many coastal islands.

Maryland—For Queen Henrietta Maria, wife of Charles I of England.

Massachusetts—From Indian tribe named after "large hill place" identified by Capt. John Smith as being near Milton, MA.

Michigan—From Chippewa words, *mici gama*, meaning "great water," after the lake of the same name.

Minnesota—From Dakota Sioux word meaning "cloudy water" or "sky-tinted water" of the Minnesota River.

Mississippi—Probably Chippewa; *mici zibi*, "great river" or "gathering-in of all the waters." Also: Algonquin word, *messipi*.

Missouri—An Algonquin Indian term meaning "river of the big canoes."

Montana—Latin or Spanish for "mountainous."

Nebraska—From Omaha or Otos Indian word meaning "broad water" or "flat river," describing the Platte River.

Nevada—Spanish, meaning "snow-clad."

New Hampshire—Named, 1629, by Capt. John Mason of Plymouth Council for his home county in England.

New Jersey—The Duke of York, 1664, gave a patent to John Berkeley and Sir George Carteret to be called Nova Caesaria, or New Jersey, after England's Isle of Jersey.

New Mexico—Spaniards in Mexico applied term to land north and west of Rio Grande in the 16th century.

New York—For Duke of York and Albany, who received patent to New Netherland from his brother Charles II and sent an expedition to capture it, 1664.

North Carolina—In 1619 Charles I gave a large patent to Sir Robert Heath to be called Province of Carolana, from *Carolus*, Latin name for Charles. A new patent was granted by Charles II to Earl of Clarendon and others. Divided into North and South Carolina, 1710.

North Dakota—*Dakota* is Sioux for "friend" or "ally."

Ohio—Iroquois word for "fine or good river."

Oklahoma—Choctaw word meaning "red man," proposed by Rev. Allen Wright, Choctaw-speaking Indian.

Oregon—Origin unknown. One theory holds that the name may have been derived from that of the Wisconsin River, shown on a 1715 French map as "Ouaricon-sint."

Pennsylvania—William Penn, the Quaker who was made full proprietor of this area by King Charles II in 1681, suggested "Sylvania," or "woodland," for his tract. The king's government owed Penn's father, Admiral William Penn, 16,000 pounds, and the land was granted as partial settlement. Charles II added the "Penn" to Sylvania, against the desires of the modest proprietor, in honor of the admiral.

Puerto Rico—Spanish for "rich port."

Rhode Island—Exact origin is unknown. One theory notes that Giovanni de Verrazano recorded an island about the size of Rhodes in the Mediterranean in 1524, but others believe the state was named *Roode Eylandt* by Adriaen Block, Dutch explorer, because of its red clay.

South Carolina—See North Carolina.

South Dakota—See North Dakota.

Tennessee—*Tanasi* was the name of Cherokee villages on the Little Tennessee River. From 1784 to 1788 this was the State of Franklin, or Frankland.

Texas—Variant of word used by Caddo and other Indians meaning "friends" or "allies," and applied to them by the Spanish in eastern Texas. Also written *Texias, Tejas, Teysas*.

Utah—From a Navajo word meaning "upper," or "higher up," as applied to a Shoshone tribe called Ute. Spanish form is *Yutta*. The English is *Uta* or *Utah*. Proposed name *Deseret*, "land of honeybees," from Book of Mormon, was rejected by Congress.

Vermont—From French words *vert* (green) and *mont* (mountain). The Green Mountains were said to have been named by Samuel de Champlain. When the state was formed, 1777, Dr. Thomas Young suggested combining *vert* and *mont* into Vermont.

Virginia—Named by Sir Walter Raleigh, who fitted out the expedition of 1584, in honor of Queen Elizabeth, the Virgin Queen of England.

Washington—Named after George Washington. When the bill creating the Territory of Columbia was introduced in the 32nd Congress, the name was changed to Washington because of the existence of the District of Columbia.

West Virginia—So named when western counties of Virginia refused to secede from the U.S. in 1863.

Wisconsin—An Indian name, spelled *Ouisconsin* and *Mesconsing* by early chroniclers. Believed to mean "grassy place" in Chippewa. Congress made it *Wisconsin*.

Wyoming—From the Algonquin words for "large prairie place," "at the big plains," or "on the great plain."

Territorial Sea of the U.S.

According to a Dec. 27, 1988, proclamation by Pres. Ronald Reagan: "The territorial sea of the United States henceforth extends to 12 nautical miles from the baselines of the United States determined in accordance with international law. In accordance with international law, as reflected in the applicable provisions of the 1982 United Nations Convention on the Law of the Sea, within the territorial sea of the United States, the ships of all countries enjoy the right of innocent passage and the ships and aircraft of all countries enjoy the right of transit passage through international straits."

Major Accessions of Territory by the U.S.

Source: U.S. Dept. of the Interior; Bureau of the Census, U.S. Dept. of Commerce

Not including territories such as Panama Canal Zone and the Philippines which are no longer under U.S. jurisdiction; area figures may differ from figures for current areas given elsewhere.

	Acquisition date	Gross area (sq mi)		Acquisition date	Gross area (sq mi)		Acquisition date	Gross area (sq mi)
Territory in 1790[1]	NA	888,685	Oregon Territory	1846	285,580	Puerto Rico[2]	1899	3,435
Louisiana Purchase ..	1803	827,192	Mexican Cession	1848	529,017	Guam[3]	1899	212
Purchase of Florida ..	1819	58,560	Gadsden			American Samoa[4] ...	1900	76
Other areas from			Purchase	1853	29,640	U.S. Virgin Islands...	1917	133
Spain	1819	13,443	Alaska	1867	586,412	Northern Mariana		
Texas	1845	390,143	Hawaii	1898	6,450	Islands[5]	1986	179

NA = Not applicable. (1) Includes that part of a drainage basin of Red River of the North, S of 49th parallel, sometimes considered part of Louisiana Purchase. (2) Ceded by Spain in 1898, ratified in 1899, and became the Commonwealth of Puerto Rico by Act of Congress on July 25, 1952. (3) Acquired in 1898; ratified 1899. (4) Acquired in 1899; ratified 1900. (5) Formerly a part of the U.S. administered Trust Territory of the Pacific Islands; became a U.S. commonwealth, Nov. 3, 1986.

Federally Owned Land, by State

Source: Office of Governmentwide Policy, General Services Administration; as of Sept. 30, 2003

State	Federal acreage[1]	Total acreage of state[2]	Percentage of federally owned acreage[1]	State	Federal acreage[1]	Total acreage of state[2]	Percentage of federally owned acreage[1]
Alabama.........	1,202,614.1	32,678,400	3.7	Montana	29,239,057.8	93,271,040	31.3
Alaska	243,847,036.6	365,481,600	66.7	Nebraska........	1,458,802.3	49,031,680	3.0
Arizona..........	36,494,843.8	72,688,000	50.2	Nevada	64,589,139.3	70,264,320	91.9
Arkansas	3,955,958.5	33,599,360	11.8	New Hampshire...	830,231.7	5,768,960	14.4
California	46,979,891.1	100,206,720	46.9	New Jersey	180,189.3	4,813,440	3.7
Colorado.........	23,174,340.1	66,485,760	34.9	New Mexico......	26,518,359.6	77,766,400	34.1
Connecticut	15,211.5	3,135,360	0.5	New York........	242,441.3	30,680,960	0.8
Delaware	29,488.4	1,265,920	2.3	North Carolina	3,602,080.4	31,402,880	11.5
District of Columbia	10,284.3	39,040	26.3	North Dakota	1,333,375.3	44,452,480	3.0
Florida	4,605,762.2	34,721,280	13.3	Ohio............	457,696.9	26,222,080	1.7
Georgia..........	2,314,385.8	37,295,360	6.2	Oklahoma	1,331,456.8	44,087,680	3.0
Hawaii	671,579.8	4,105,600	16.4	Oregon	30,638,948.7	61,598,720	49.7
Idaho	35,135,708.9	52,933,120	66.4	Pennsylvania.....	724,924.5	28,804,480	2.5
Illinois...........	651,602.9	35,795,200	1.8	Rhode Island.....	5,317.7	677,120	0.8
Indiana..........	534,126.4	23,158,400	2.3	South Carolina....	1,236,214.2	19,374,080	6.4
Iowa............	302,600.7	35,860,480	0.8	South Dakota.....	2,314,006.5	48,881,920	4.7
Kansas..........	641,561.9	52,510,720	1.2	Tennessee.......	2,016,137.5	26,727,680	7.5
Kentucky	1,706,562.3	25,512,320	6.7	Texas...........	3,171,756.5	168,217,600	1.9
Louisiana	1,501,734.6	28,867,840	5.2	Utah............	35,024,926.9	52,696,960	66.5
Maine	164,002.5	19,847,680	0.8	Vermont.........	450,016.5	5,936,640	7.6
Maryland	192,692.2	6,319,360	3.0	Virginia.........	2,617,225.9	25,496,320	10.3
Massachusetts....	105,973.4	5,034,880	2.1	Washington	13,246,559.4	42,693,760	31.0
Michigan.........	3,638,587.9	36,492,160	10.0	West Virginia	1,266,421.7	15,410,560	8.2
Minnesota........	3,534,988.6	51,205,760	6.9	Wisconsin	1,981,781.0	35,011,200	5.7
Mississippi	2,101,203.9	30,222,720	7.0	Wyoming	31,531,536.8	62,343,040	50.6
Missouri	2,237,950.8	44,248,320	5.1	**Total**	**671,759,297.7**	**2,271,343,360**	**29.6**

Note: Totals do not include inland water. (1) Excludes trust properties. (2) Bureau of the Census, U.S. Dept. of Commerce figures.

Special Recreation Areas Administered by the U.S. Forest Service, 2004

Source: U.S. Forest Service, Dept. of Agriculture

NHL=National Historic Landmark; NHS=National Historic Scenic Area; NM=National Monument; NP=National Preserve; NRA=National Recreation Area; NSA=National Scenic Area; NVM=National Volcanic Monument; SRA=Scenic Recreation Area

Area name	Location	Estab.	Acres	Area name	Location	Estab.	Acres
Admiralty Island NM.............	AK......	1980	978,881	Mount Pleasant NSA...........	VA	1994	7,580
Allegheny NRA................	PA......	1984	23,063	Mount Rogers NRA.............	VA	1966	114,520
Arapaho NRA.................	CO	1978	30,690	Mount St. Helens NVM	WA.....	1989	112,593
Beech Creek NS & Botanic Area ..	OK	1988	7,500	Newberry NVM	OR.....	1990	54,822
Cascade Head NS				North Cascades NSA	WA.....	1984	87,600
(-Research) Area	OR	1974	6,630	Opal Creek SRA	OR.....	1996	13,000
Columbia River Gorge NSA......	OR-WA..	1986	63,150	Oregon Dunes NRA	OR.....	1972	27,212
Coosa Bald NSA	GA	1991	7,100	Pine Ridge NRA	NE	1986	6,600
Ed Jenkins NRA...............	GA	1991	23,166	Rattlesnake NRA..............	MT	1980	59,119
Flaming Gorge NRA............	WY-UT..	1968	189,825	Santa Rosa and			
Giant Sequoia NM	CA......	2000	327,769	San Jacinto Mts. NM	CA	2000	272,000
Grand Island NRA	MI	1990	12,961	Sawtooth NRA................	ID	1972	729,322
Grey Towers NHL	PA......	1963	102	Smith River NRA	CA	1990	305,169
Hells Canyon NRA.............	ID-OR ...	1975	536,648	Spring Mt. NRA...............	NV	1993	316,000
Indian Nations NS & Wildlife Area .	OK	1988	40,051	Spruce Knob-Seneca Rocks NRA..	WV.....	1965	57,237
Jemez NRA	NM	1993	57,000	Valles Caldera NP	NM.....	2000	88,900
Land Between the Lakes NRA....	KY-TN...	1998	170,000	Whiskeytown-Shasta-			
Misty Fiords NM...............	AK......	1980	2,293,428	Trinity NRA	CA	1965	176,367
Mono Basin NSA	CA......	1984	115,600	White Rocks NRA	VT	1984	36,400
Mount Baker NRA	WA	1984	8,473	Winding Stair Mt. NRA	OK	1988	25,890

WORLD ALMANAC QUICK QUIZ

What was the 48th state to enter the Union?

(a) Kansas   (b) Utah   (c) Nevada   (d) Arizona

For the answer look in this chapter, or see page 1008.

► **IT'S A FACT:** Pres. Theodore Roosevelt had a large and lasting influence on the National Park Service. During his time in the White House (1901-1909) he signed legislation establishing 5 new national parks. But what had an even longer-lasting effect was enactment of the Antiquities Act of 1906. This act enabled presidents to proclaim "historic landmarks, historic and prehistoric structures, and other objects of historic or scientific interest" in federal ownership as national monuments and was the original authority for about one-quarter of the areas composing the National Park System. Roosevelt is now commemorated by 5 National Park areas—tied with Abraham Lincoln as the most for any president.

National Parks, Other Areas Administered by National Park Service

Dates when sites were authorized for initial protection by Congress or by presidential proclamation are given in parentheses. If different, the date the area got its current designation, or was transferred to the National Park Service, follows. Gross area in acres, as of Dec. 31, 2003, follows date(s). Over 84 mil acres of federal land are now administered by the National Park Service.

NATIONAL PARKS

Acadia, ME (1916/1929) 47,400. Includes Mount Desert Isl., half of Isle au Haut, Schoodic Peninsula on mainland. Highest elevation on Eastern seaboard.

American Samoa, AS (1988) 9,000. Features a paleotropical rain forest and a coral reef. No federal facilities.

Arches, UT (1929/1971) 76,519. Contains giant red sandstone arches and other products of erosion.

Badlands, SD (1929/1978) 242,756. Prairie with bison, bighorn, and antelope. Animal fossils 26-37 mil years old.

Big Bend, TX (1935) 801,163. Rio Grande, Chisos Mts.

Biscayne, FL (1968/1980) 172,924. Aquatic park encompassing chain of islands south of Miami.

Black Canyon of the Gunnison, CO (1933/1999) 30,243. Has a canyon 2,900 ft deep and 40 ft wide at its narrowest part.

Bryce Canyon, UT (1923/1928) 35,835. Spectacularly colorful and unusual display of erosion effects.

Canyonlands, UT (1964) 337,598. At junction of Colorado and Green rivers; extensive evidence of prehistoric Indians.

Capitol Reef, UT (1937/1971) 241,904. A 70-mi uplift of sandstone cliffs dissected by high-walled gorges.

Carlsbad Caverns, NM (1923/1930) 46,766. Largest known caverns; not yet fully explored.

Channel Islands, CA (1938/1980) 249,561. Sea lion breeding place, nesting sea birds, unique plants.

Congaree, SC (1976/2003) 21,744. Preserves largest intact tract of old-growth floodplain forest in North America.

Crater Lake, OR (1902) 183,224. Extraordinary blue lake in the crater of Mt. Mazama, a volcano that erupted about 7,700 years ago; deepest U.S. lake.

Cuyahoga Valley, OH (1974/2000) 32,860. Rural landscape along Ohio and Erie Canal system between Akron and Cleveland.

Death Valley, CA-NV (1933/1994) 3,372,402. Large desert area. Includes the lowest point in the Western Hemisphere; also includes Scottys Castle.

Denali, AK (1917/1980) 4,740,912. Name changed from Mt. McKinley National Park. Contains highest mountain in U.S.; wildlife.

Dry Tortugas, FL (1935/1992) 64,701. Formerly Ft. Jefferson National Monument.

Everglades, FL (1934) 1,508,538. Largest remaining subtropical wilderness in continental U.S.

Gates of the Arctic, AK (1978/1984) 7,523,898. Vast wilderness in north central region. Limited federal facilities.

Glacier, MT (1910) 1,013,572. Superb Rocky Mt. scenery, numerous glaciers and glacial lakes. Part of Waterton-Glacier Intl. Peace Park established by U.S. and Canada in 1932.

Glacier Bay, AK (1925/1986) 3,224,840. Great tidewater glaciers that move down mountainsides and break up into the sea; much wildlife.

Grand Canyon, AZ (1893/1919) 1,217,403. Most spectacular part of Colorado River's greatest canyon.

Grand Teton, WY (1929) 309,994. Most impressive part of the Teton Mts., winter feeding ground of largest American elk herd.

Great Basin, NV (1922/1986) 77,180. Includes Wheeler Pk., Lexington Arch, and Lehman Caves.

Great Smoky Mountains, NC-TN (1926/1934) 521,495. Largest Eastern mountain range, magnificent forests.

Guadalupe Mountains, TX (1966) 86,416. Extensive Permian limestone fossil reef; tremendous earth fault.

Haleakala, HI (1916/1960) 29,094. Dormant volcano on Maui with large colorful craters.

Hawaii Volcanoes, HI (1916/1961) 323,431. Contains Kilauea and Mauna Loa, active volcanoes.

Hot Springs, AR (1832/1921) 5,550. Bathhouses are furnished with thermal waters from the park's 47 hot springs; these waters are used for bathing and drinking.

Isle Royale, MI (1931) 571,790. Largest island in Lake Superior, noted for its wilderness area and wildlife.

Joshua Tree, CA (1936/1994) 789,745. Desert region includes Joshua trees, other plant and animal life.

Katmai, AK (1918/1980) 3,674,530. "Valley of Ten Thousand Smokes," scene of 1912 volcanic eruption.

Kenai Fjords, AK (1978/1980) 669,983. Abundant marine mammals, birdlife; the Harding Icefield, one of the 4 major icecaps in U.S.

Kings Canyon, CA (1890/1940) 461,901. Mountain wilderness, dominated by Kings River Canyons and High Sierra; contains giant sequoias.

Kobuk Valley, AK (1978/1980) 1,750,717. Contains geological and recreational sites. Limited federal facilities.

Lake Clark, AK (1978/1980) 2,619,733. Across Cook Inlet from Anchorage. A scenic wilderness rich in fish and wildlife. Limited federal facilities.

Lassen Volcanic, CA (1907/1916) 106,372. Contains Lassen Peak, recently active volcano, and other volcanic phenomena.

Mammoth Cave, KY (1926/1941) 52,830. 144 mi of surveyed underground passages, beautiful natural formations, river 300 ft below surface.

Mesa Verde, CO (1906) 52,122. Most notable and best preserved prehistoric cliff dwellings in the U.S.

Mount Rainier, WA (1899) 235,625. Greatest single-peak glacial system in the U.S.

North Cascades, WA (1968) 504,781. Spectacular mountainous region with many glaciers, lakes.

Olympic, WA (1909/1938) 922,651. Mountain wilderness containing finest remnant of Pacific Northwest rain forest, active glaciers, Pacific shoreline, rare elk.

Petrified Forest, AZ (1906/1962) 93,533. Extensive petrified wood and Indian artifacts. Contains part of Painted Desert.

Redwood, CA (1968) 112,513. 40 mi of Pacific coastline, groves of ancient redwoods and world's tallest trees.

Rocky Mountain, CO (1915) 265,828. On the Continental Divide; includes peaks over 14,000 ft.

Saguaro, AZ (1933/1994) 91,440. Part of the Sonoran Desert; includes the giant saguaro cacti, unique to the region.

Sequoia, CA (1890) 402,051. Groves of giant sequoias, highest mountain in conterminous U.S.—Mt. Whitney (14,494 ft). World's largest tree.

Shenandoah, VA (1926) 199,045. Portion of the Blue Ridge Mts.; overlooks Shenandoah Valley; Skyline Drive.

Theodore Roosevelt, ND (1947/1978) 70,447. Contains part of T.R.'s ranch and scenic badlands.

Virgin Islands, VI (1956) 14,689. Authorized to cover 75% of St. John Isl. and Hassel Isl.; lush growth, lovely beaches, Carib Indian petroglyphs, evidence of colonial Danes.

Voyageurs, MN (1971) 218,200. Abundant lakes, forests, wildlife, canoeing, boating.

Wind Cave, SD (1903) 28,295. Limestone caverns in Black Hills. Extensive wildlife includes a herd of bison.

Wrangell-St. Elias, AK (1978/1980) 8,323,148. Largest area in park system, most peaks over 16,000 ft, abundant wildlife; day's drive east of Anchorage. Limited federal facilities.

Yellowstone, ID-MT-WY (1872) 2,219,791. World's first national park. World's greatest geyser area has about 10,000 geysers and hot springs; spectacular falls and impressive canyons of the Yellowstone River; grizzly bear, moose, and bison.

Yosemite, CA (1890) 761,266. Yosemite Valley, the nation's highest waterfall, grove of sequoias, and mountains.

Zion, UT (1909/1919) 146,598. Unusual shapes and landscapes resulting from erosion and faulting; evidence of past volcanic activity; Zion Canyon has sheer walls ranging up to 2,640 ft.

NATIONAL HISTORICAL PARKS

Adams, MA (1946/1998) 24. Home of Pres. John Adams, John Quincy Adams, and celebrated descendants.

Appomattox Court House, VA (1930/1954) 1,774. Where Lee surrendered to Grant.

Boston, MA (1974) 43. Includes Faneuil Hall, Old North Church, Bunker Hill, Paul Revere House.

Cane River Creole (and heritage area), LA (1994) 207. Preserves the Creole culture as it developed along the Cane R.

Cedar Creek and Belle Grove, VA (2002) 3,593. Civil War battle site and an antebellum plantation in the Shenandoah Valley.

Chaco Culture, NM (1907/1980) 33,960. Ruins of pueblos built by prehistoric Indians.

Chesapeake and Ohio Canal, MD-DC-WV (1938/1971) 19,587. 184-mi historic canal; DC to Cumberland, MD.

Colonial, VA (1930/1936) 8,677. Includes most of Jamestown Isl., site of first successful English colony; Yorktown, site of Cornwallis's surrender to George Washington; and the Colonial Parkway.

Cumberland Gap, KY-TN-VA (1940) 20,507. Mountain pass of the Wilderness Road, which carried the first great migration of pioneers into America's interior.

Dayton Aviation Heritage, OH (1992) 86. Commemorates the area's aviation heritage.

George Rogers Clark, Vincennes, IN (1966) 26. Commemorates American defeat of British in West during Revolution.

Harpers Ferry, MD-VA-WV (1944/1963) 2,504. At the confluence of the Shenandoah and Potomac rivers, the site of John Brown's 1859 raid on the Army arsenal.

Hopewell Culture, OH (1923/1992) 1,170. Formerly Mound City Group National Monument.

Independence, PA (1948) 45. Contains several properties associated with the American Revolution and the founding of the U.S. Includes Independence Hall.

Jean Laffite (and preserve), LA (1907/1978) 20,005. Includes Chalmette, site of 1815 Battle of New Orleans; French Quarter.

Kalaupapa, HI (1980) 10,779. Molokai's former leper colony site and other historic areas.

Kaloko-Honokohau, HI (1978) 1,161. Preserves the native culture of Hawaii. No federal facilities.

Keweenaw, MI (1992) 1,869. Site of first significant copper mine in U.S. Federal facilities are under development.

Klondike Gold Rush, AK-WA (1976) 13,191. Alaskan Trails in 1898 Gold Rush. Museum in Seattle.

Lowell, MA (1978) 141. Textile mills, canal, 19th-cent. structures; park shows planned city of Industrial Revolution.

Lyndon B. Johnson, TX (1969/1980) 1,570. President's birthplace, boyhood home, ranch.

Marsh-Billings-Rockefeller, VT (1992) 643. Boyhood home of conservationist George Perkins Marsh. No federal facilities.

Minute Man, MA (1959) 971. Where the Minute Men battled the British, Apr. 19, 1775. Also contains Hawthorne's home.

Morristown, NJ (1933) 1,711. Sites of important military encampments during the American Revolution; Washington's headquarters, 1777, 1779-80.

Natchez, MS (1988) 105. Mansions, townhouses, and villas related to history of Natchez.

New Bedford Whaling, MA (1996) 34. Preserves structures and relics associated with the city's 19th-cent. whaling industry.

New Orleans Jazz, LA (1994) 5. Preserves, educates, and interprets jazz as it has evolved in New Orleans.

Nez Perce, ID (1965) 2,495. Illustrates the history and culture of the Nez Perce Indian country (38 separate sites).

Pecos, NM (1965/1990) 6,670. Ruins of ancient Pueblo of Pecos, archaeological sites, and 2 associated Spanish colonial missions from the 17th and 18th centuries.

Pu'uhonua o Honaunau, HI (1955/1978) 420. Until 1819, a sanctuary for Hawaiians vanquished in battle and for those guilty of crimes or breaking taboos.

Rosie the Riveter WWII Home Front, CA (2000) 145. Built on site that was a shipyard employing thousands of women in WWII; commemorates women who worked in war-time industries.

Salt River Bay (and ecological preserve), St. Croix, VI (1992) 978. The only site known where, 500 years ago, members of a Columbus party landed on what is now territory of the U.S.

San Antonio Missions, TX (1978) 826. Four of finest Spanish missions in U.S., 18th-cent. irrigation system.

San Francisco Maritime, CA (1988) 50. Artifacts, photographs, and historic vessels related to the development of the Pacific Coast.

San Juan Island, WA (1966) 1,752. Commemorates peaceful relations between the U.S., Canada, and Great Britain since the 1872 boundary disputes.

Saratoga, NY (1938) 3,392. Scene of a major 1777 battle that became a turning point in the American Revolution.

Sitka, AK (1910/1972) 113. Scene of last major resistance of the Tlingit Indians to the Russians, 1804.

Tumacacori, AZ (1908/1990) 360. Historic Spanish mission building stands near site first visited by Father Kino in 1691.

Valley Forge, PA (1976) 3,466. Continental Army campsite in 1777-78 winter.

War in the Pacific, GU (1978) 2,037. Seven distinct units illustrating the Pacific theater of WWII. Limited federal facilities.

Women's Rights, NY (1980) 7. Seneca Falls site where Lucretia Mott, Elizabeth Cady Stanton began rights movement in 1848.

NATIONAL BATTLEFIELDS

Antietam, MD (1890/1978) 3,244. Battle here ended first Confederate invasion of North, Sept. 17, 1862.

Big Hole, MT (1910/1963) 1,011. Site of major battle with Nez Perce Indians.

Cowpens, SC (1929/1972) 842. American Revolution battlefield.

Fort Donelson, TN-KY (1928/1985) 552. Site of first major Union victory.

Fort Necessity, PA (1931/1961) 903. Site of first battle of French and Indian War.

Monocacy, MD (1934/1976) 1,647. Civil War battle in defense of Washington, DC, fought here, July 9, 1864.

Moores Creek, NC (1926/1980) 88. 1776 battle between Patriots and Loyalists commemorated here.

Petersburg, VA (1926/1962) 2,659. Scene of 10-month Union campaigns, 1864-65.

Stones River, TN (1927/1960) 709. Scene of battle that began federal offensive to trisect the Confederacy.

Tupelo, MS (1929/1961) 1. Site of crucial battle over Sherman's supply line, 1865.

Wilson's Creek, MO (1960/1970) 1,750. Scene of Civil War battle for control of Missouri.

NATIONAL BATTLEFIELD PARKS

Kennesaw Mountain, GA (1917/1935) 2,884. Site of two major battles of Atlanta campaign in Civil War.

Manassas, VA (1940) 5,071. Scene of two battles in Civil War, 1861 and 1862.

Richmond, VA (1936) 2,517. Site of battles defending Confederate capital.

NATIONAL BATTLEFIELD SITE

Brices Cross Roads, MS (1929) 1. Civil War battlefield.

NATIONAL MILITARY PARKS

Chickamauga and Chattanooga, GA-TN (1890) 9,059. Site of major Confederate victory, 1863.

Fredericksburg and Spotsylvania County, VA (1927/1933) 8,352. Sites of several major Civil War battles and campaigns.

Gettysburg, PA (1895/1933) 5,990. Site of decisive Confederate defeat in North and of Gettysburg Address.

Guilford Courthouse, NC (1917/1933) 228. American Revolution battle site.

Horseshoe Bend, AL (1956) 2,040. On Tallapoosa River, where Gen. Andrew Jackson's forces broke the power of the Upper Creek Indian Confederacy.

Kings Mountain, SC (1931/1933) 3,945. Site of American Revolution battle.

Pea Ridge, AR (1956) 4,300. Scene of Civil War battle.

Shiloh, TN (1894/1933) 5,048. Major Civil War battlesite; includes some well-preserved Indian burial mounds.

Vicksburg, MS (1899/1933) 1,795. Union victory gave North control of the Mississippi and split the Confederate forces.

NATIONAL MEMORIALS

Arkansas Post, AR (1960) 758. First permanent French settlement in the lower Mississippi River valley.

Arlington House, the Robert E. Lee Memorial, VA (1925/1972) 28. Lee's home overlooking the Potomac.

Chamizal, El Paso, TX (1966/1974) 55. Commemorates 1963 settlement of 99-year border dispute with Mexico.

Coronado, AZ (1941/1952) 4,750. Commemorates first European exploration of the Southwest.

DeSoto, FL (1948) 27. Commemorates 16th-cent. Spanish explorations.

Federal Hall, NY (1939/1955) 0.45. First seat of U.S. government under the Constitution.

Fort Caroline, FL (1950) 138. On St. Johns River, overlooks site of a French Huguenot colony.

Fort Clatsop, OR (1958) 125. Lewis and Clark encampment, 1805-6.

Franklin Delano Roosevelt, DC (1982) 8. Statues of Pres. Roosevelt and Eleanor Roosevelt; waterfalls and gardens.

General Grant, NY (1958) 0.76. Tomb of Grant and wife.

Hamilton Grange, NY (1962) 1. Home of Alexander Hamilton.

Jefferson National Expansion Memorial, St. Louis, MO (1935) 91. Commemorates westward expansion.

Johnstown Flood, PA (1964) 164. Commemorates tragic flood of 1889.

Korean War Veterans, DC (1986) 2. Dedicated in 1995; honors those who served in the Korean War.

Lincoln Boyhood, IN (1962) 200. Lincoln grew up here.

Lincoln Memorial, DC (1911/1933) 107. Marble statue of the 16th U.S. president.

Lyndon B. Johnson Memorial Grove on the Potomac, DC (1973) 17. Overlooks the Potomac R.; vista of the Capitol.

Mount Rushmore, SD (1925) 1,278. World-famous sculpture of 4 presidents.

Oklahoma City, OK (1997) 6. Commemorates site of April 19, 1995, bombing which killed 168.

Perry's Victory and International Peace Memorial, Put-in-Bay, OH (1936/1972) 25. The world's most massive Doric column, constructed 1912-15, promotes pursuit of peace through arbitration and disarmament.

Roger Williams, Providence, RI (1965) 5. Memorial to founder of Rhode Island.

Thaddeus Kosciuszko, PA (1972) 0.02. Memorial to Polish hero of American Revolution.

Theodore Roosevelt Island, DC (1932/1933) 89. Statue of Roosevelt in wooded island sanctuary.

Thomas Jefferson Memorial, DC (1934) 18. Statue of Jefferson in an inscribed circular, colonnaded structure.

USS *Arizona*, HI (1980) 11. Memorializes American losses at Pearl Harbor.

Vietnam Veterans, DC (1980) 2. Black granite wall inscribed with names of those missing or killed in action in Vietnam War.

Washington Monument, DC (1848/1933) 106. Obelisk honoring the first U.S. president.

Wright Brothers, NC (1927/1953) 428. Site of first powered flight.

NATIONAL HISTORIC SITES

Abraham Lincoln Birthplace, Hodgenville, KY (1916/1959) 345. Early 17th-cent. cabin.

Allegheny Portage Railroad, PA (1964) 1,296. Linked the Pennsylvania Canal system and the West.

Andersonville, Andersonville, GA (1970) 515. Noted Civil War prisoner-of-war camp.

Andrew Johnson, Greeneville, TN (1935/1963) 17. Two homes and the tailor shop of the 17th U.S. president.

Bent's Old Fort, CO (1960) 799. Reconstruction of S Plains outpost.

Boston African-American, MA (1980) 0.59. Pre-Civil War black history structures.

Brown v. Board of Education, KS (1992) 2. Commemorates the landmark 1954 U.S. Supreme Court decision.

Carl Sandburg Home, Flat Rock, NC (1968) 264. Poet's home.

Charles Pinckney, SC (1988) 28. Statesman's farm.

Christiansted, St. Croix, VI (1952/1961) 27. Commemorates Danish colony.

Clara Barton, MD (1974) 9. Home of founder of American Red Cross.

Edgar Allan Poe, PA (1978/1980) 0.52. Writer's home.

Edison, West Orange, NJ (1955/1962) 21. Inventor's home and laboratory.

Eisenhower, Gettysburg, PA (1967) 690. Home of 34th president.

Eleanor Roosevelt, Hyde Park, NY (1977) 181. The former first lady's personal retreat.

Eugene O'Neill, Danville, CA (1976) 13. Playwright's home.

First Ladies, Canton, OH (2000) 0.33. Library devoted to America's first ladies.

Ford's Theatre, DC (1866/1970) 0.29. Includes theater, now restored, where Lincoln was assassinated, house where he died, and Lincoln Museum.

Fort Bowie, AZ (1964) 999. Focal point of operations against Geronimo and the Apaches.

Fort Davis, TX (1961) 474. Frontier outpost in West Texas.

Fort Laramie, WY (1938/1960) 833. Military post on Oregon Trail.

Fort Larned, KS (1964/1966) 718. Military post on Santa Fe Trail.

Fort Point, San Francisco, CA (1970) 29. West Coast fortification.

Fort Raleigh, NC (1941) 513. First attempted English settlement in North America.

Fort Scott, KS (1965/1978) 17. Commemorates U.S. frontier of 1840s and '50s.

Fort Smith, AR-OK (1961) 75. Active post during 1817-90.

Fort Union Trading Post, MT-ND (1966) 444. Principal fur-trading post on upper Missouri, 1829-67.

Fort Vancouver, WA (1948/1961) 209. Headquarters for Hudson's Bay Company in 1825. Early political seat.

Frederick Douglass, DC (1962/1988) 9. Home of famous black abolitionist, writer, and orator.

Frederick Law Olmsted, MA (1979) 7. Home of famous city planner.

Friendship Hill, PA (1978) 675. Home of Albert Gallatin, Jefferson's and Madison's secretary of treasury.

Golden Spike, UT (1957) 2,735. Commemorates completion of first transcontinental railroad in 1869.

Grant-Kohrs Ranch, MT (1972) 1,618. Ranch house and part of 19th-cent. ranch.

Hampton, MD (1948) 62. 18th-cent. Georgian mansion.

Harry S. Truman, MO (1983) 7. Home of Pres. Truman after 1919.

Herbert Hoover, West Branch, IA (1965) 187. Birthplace and boyhood home of 31st president.

Home of Franklin D. Roosevelt, Hyde Park, NY (1944) 800. FDR's birthplace, home, and "summer White House."

Hopewell Furnace, PA (1938/1985) 848. 19th-cent. iron-making village.

Hubbell Trading Post, AZ (1965) 160. Still active today.

James A. Garfield, Mentor, OH (1980) 8. Home of 20th president.

Jimmy Carter, GA (1987) 71. Birthplace and home of 39th president.

John Fitzgerald Kennedy, Brookline, MA (1967) 0.09. Birthplace and childhood home of 35th president.

John Muir, Martinez, CA (1964) 345. Home of early conservationist and writer.

Knife River Indian Villages, ND (1974) 1,758. Remnants of villages last occupied by Hidatsa and Mandan Indians.

Lincoln Home, Springfield, IL (1971) 12. Lincoln's residence at the time he was elected 16th president, 1860.

Little Rock Central High School, AR (1998) 27. Commemorates 1957 desegregation during which federal troops had to be called in to protect 9 black students.

Longfellow, Cambridge, MA (1972) 2. Poet's home, 1837-82; Washington's headquarters during Boston siege, 1775-76.

Maggie L. Walker, VA (1978) 1. Richmond home of black leader and bank president, daughter of an ex-slave.

Manzanar, Lone Pine, CA (1992) 814. Commemorates Manzanar War Relocation Ctr., a Japanese-American internment camp during WWII. No federal facilities.

Martin Luther King Jr., Atlanta, GA (1980) 39. Birthplace, grave, church of the civil rights leader. Limited federal facilities.

Martin Van Buren, NY (1974) 40. Lindenwald, home of 8th president, near Kinderhook.

Mary McLeod Bethune Council House, DC (1982/1991) 0.07. Commemorates Bethune's leadership in the black women's movement.

Minuteman Missile, SD (1999) 15. Missile launch facilities dating back to the Cold War era.

Nicodemus, KS (1996) 161. Only remaining western town established by African-Americans during Reconstruction.

Ninety Six, SC (1976) 1,022. Colonial trading village.

Palo Alto Battlefield, TX (1978) 3,407. Scene of first battle of the Mexican War.

Pennsylvania Avenue, DC (1965) Acreage undetermined. Also includes area next to the road between Capitol and White House, encompassing Ford's Theatre and other structures.

Puukohola Heiau, HI (1972) 86. Ruins of temple built by King Kamehameha.

Sagamore Hill, Oyster Bay, NY (1962) 83. Home of Pres. Theodore Roosevelt from 1885 until his death in 1919.

Saint-Gaudens, Cornish, NH (1964) 148. Home, studio, and gardens of American sculptor Augustus Saint-Gaudens.

Saint Paul's Church, NY, NY (1943) 6. Site associated with John Peter Zenger's "freedom of press" trial.

Salem Maritime, MA (1938) 9. Only port never seized from the patriots by the British. Major fishing and whaling port.

Sand Creek Massacre, Sand Creek, CO (2000) 12,583. Site where over 100 Cheyenne and Arapaho Indians were killed by U.S. soldiers in 1864.

San Juan, PR (1949) 75. 16th-cent. Span. fortifications.

Saugus Iron Works, MA (1974) 9. Reconstructed 17th-cent. colonial ironworks.

Springfield Armory, MA (1974) 55. Small-arms manufacturing center for nearly 200 years.

Steamtown, PA (1986) 62. Railyard, roadhouse, repair shops of former Delaware, Lackawanna & Western Railroad.

Theodore Roosevelt Birthplace, New York, NY (1962) 0.11. Reconstructed brownstone.

Theodore Roosevelt Inaugural, Buffalo, NY (1966) 1. Wilcox House where he took oath of office, 1901.

Thomas Stone, MD (1978) 328. Home of signer of Declaration of Independence, built in 1771.

Tuskegee Airmen, AL (1998) 90. Airfield where pilots of all-black air corps unit of WWII received flight training.

Tuskegee Institute, AL (1974) 58. College founded by Booker T. Washington in 1881 for blacks.

Ulysses S. Grant, St. Louis Co., MO (1989) 10. Home of Grant during pre-Civil War years.

Vanderbilt Mansion, Hyde Park, NY (1940) 212. Mansion of 19th-cent. financier.

Washita Battlefield, OK (1996) 315. Scene of Nov. 27, 1868, battle between Plains tribes and the U.S. army.

Weir Farm, Wilton, CT (1990) 74. Home and studio of American impressionist painter J. Alden Weir.

Whitman Mission, WA (1936/1963) 99. Site where Dr. and Mrs. Marcus Whitman ministered to the Indians until slain by them in 1847.

William Howard Taft, Cincinnati, OH (1969) 3. Birthplace and early home of the 27th president.

NATIONAL MONUMENTS

Name	State	Year[1]	Acreage
Agate Fossil Beds	NE	1965	3,055
Alibates Flint Quarries	TX	1965	1,371
Aniakchak[2]	AK	1978	137,176
Aztec Ruins	NM	1923	318
Bandelier	NM	1916	33,677
Booker T. Washington	VA	1956	239
Buck Island Reef	VI	1961	19,015
Cabrillo	CA	1913	160
Canyon de Chelly	AZ	1931	83,840
Cape Krusenstern[3]	AK	1978	649,085
Capulin Volcano	NM	1916	793
Casa Grande Ruins	AZ	1889	473
Castillo de San Marcos	FL	1924	20
Castle Clinton	NY	1946	1
Cedar Breaks	UT	1933	6,155
Chiricahua	AZ	1924	11,985

Name	State	Year[1]	Acreage
Colorado	CO	1911	20,534
Craters of the Moon National Monument and Preserve	ID	1924	714,727
Devils Postpile	CA	1911	798
Devils Tower	WY	1906	1,347
Dinosaur	CO-UT	1915	210,278
Effigy Mounds	IA	1949	2,526
El Malpais	NM	1987	114,277
El Morro	NM	1906	1,279
Florissant Fossil Beds	CO	1969	5,998
Fort Frederica	GA	1936	241
Fort Matanzas	FL	1924	300
Fort McHenry National Monument and Historic Shrine	MD	1925	43
Fort Pulaski	GA	1924	5,623
Fort Stanwix	NY	1935	16
Fort Sumter	SC	1948	200
Fort Union	NM	1954	721
Fossil Butte	WY	1972	8,198
George Washington Birthplace	VA	1930	662
George Washington Carver	MO	1943	210
Gila Cliff Dwellings	NM	1907	533
Governors Island	NY	2001	23
Grand Portage	MN	1951	710
Great Sand Dunes National Monument and Preserve	CO	2000	84,669
Hagerman Fossil Beds[3]	ID	1988	4,351
Hohokam Pima[4]	AZ	1972	1,690
Homestead National Monument of America	NE	1936	195
Hovenweep	CO-UT	1923	785
Jewel Cave	SD	1908	1,274
John Day Fossil Beds	OR	1974	13,944
Lava Beds	CA	1925	46,560
Little Big Horn Battlefield	MT	1879	765
Minidoka Internment [2]	ID	2001	73
Montezuma Castle	AZ	1906	858
Muir Woods	CA	1908	554
Natural Bridges	UT	1908	7,636
Navajo	AZ	1909	360
Ocmulgee	GA	1934	702
Oregon Caves	OR	1909	488
Organ Pipe Cactus	AZ	1937	330,689
Petroglyph	NM	1990	7,232
Pinnacles	CA	1908	17,855
Pipe Spring	AZ	1923	40
Pipestone	MN	1937	282
Poverty Point[2]	LA	1988	911
Rainbow Bridge[3]	UT	1910	160
Russell Cave	AL	1961	310
Salinas Pueblo Missions	NM	1909	1,071
Scotts Bluff	NE	1919	3,005
Statue of Liberty	NJ-NY	1924	58
Sunset Crater Volcano	AZ	1930	3,040
Timpanogos Cave	UT	1922	250
Tonto	AZ	1907	1,120
Tuzigoot	AZ	1939	811
Virgin Islands Coral Reef	VI	2001	13,893
Walnut Canyon	AZ	1915	3,579
White Sands	NM	1933	143,733
Wupatki	AZ	1924	35,422
Yucca House[4]	CO	1919	34

NATIONAL PRESERVES

Name	State	Year[1]	Acreage
Aniakchak	AK	1978	464,118
Bering Land Bridge	AK	1978	2,697,393
Big Cypress	FL	1974	720,567
Big Thicket	TX	1974	97,168
Denali	AK	1917	1,334,118
Gates of the Arctic	AK	1978	948,608
Glacier Bay	AK	1925	58,406
Katmai	AK	1918	418,699
Lake Clark	AK	1978	1,410,292
Little River Canyon[2]	AL	1992	13,633
Mojave	CA	1994	1,532,426
Noatak	AK	1978	6,569,904
Tallgrass Prairie	KS	1996	10,894
Timucuan Ecological & Historic Preserve[3]	FL	1988	46,287
Wrangell-St. Elias	AK	1978	4,852,753
Yukon-Charley Rivers[3]	AK	1978	2,526,512

NATIONAL SEASHORES

Name	State	Year[1]	Acreage
Assateague Island	MD-VA	1965	39,727
Canaveral	FL	1975	57,662
Cape Cod	MA	1961	43,604
Cape Hatteras	NC	1937	30,321
Cape Lookout	NC	1966	28,243
Cumberland Island	GA	1972	36,415
Fire Island	NY	1964	19,580
Gulf Islands	FL-MS	1971	137,991
Padre Island	TX	1962	130,434
Point Reyes	CA	1962	71,068

NATIONAL PARKWAYS

Name	State	Year[1]	Acreage
Blue Ridge	NC-VA	1933	92,667
George Washington Memorial	VA-MD-DC	1930	7,357
John D. Rockefeller Jr. Mem.	WY	1972	23,777
Natchez Trace	MS-AL-TN	1938	51,982

NATIONAL LAKESHORES

Name	State	Year[1]	Acreage
Apostle Islands	WI	1970	69,372
Indiana Dunes	IN	1966	15,060
Pictured Rocks	MI	1966	73,236
Sleeping Bear Dunes	MI	1970	71,199

NATIONAL RESERVES

Name	State	Year[1]	Acreage
City of Rocks[3]	ID	1988	14,107
Ebey's Landing[3]	WA	1978	19,324

NATIONAL RIVERS

Name	State	Year[1]	Acreage
Big South Fork Natl. R and Recreation Area	KY-TN	1976	125,310
Buffalo	AR	1972	94,293
Mississippi Natl. R and Recreation Area	MN	1988	53,775
New River Gorge	WV	1978	72,189
Niobrara	NE-SD	1991	5,993
Ozark	MO	1964	80,785

NATIONAL WILD AND SCENIC RIVERS

Name	State	Year[1]	Acreage
Alagnak	AK	1980	30,665
Bluestone[2]	WV	1978	4,310
Delaware	NY-NJ-PA	1978	1,973
Great Egg Harbor	NJ	1992	43,311
Missouri	NE-SD	1991	45,350
Obed	TN	1976	5,174
Rio Grande[2]	TX	1978	9,600
Saint Croix	MN-WI	1968	92,754
Upper Delaware	NY-PA	1978	75,000

NATIONAL RECREATION AREAS

Name	State	Year[1]	Acreage
Amistad	TX	1965	58,500
Bighorn Canyon	MT-WY	1966	120,296
Boston Harbor Islands	MA	1996	1,482
Chattahoochee R.	GA	1978	9,167
Chickasaw	OK	1902	9,889
Curecanti	CO	1965	41,972
Delaware Water Gap	NJ-PA	1965	66,740
Gateway	NJ-NY	1972	26,607
Gauley R.[3]	WV	1988	11,507
Glen Canyon	AZ-UT	1958	1,254,429
Golden Gate	CA	1972	74,816
Lake Chelan	WA	1968	61,946
Lake Mead	AZ-NV	1936	1,495,664
Lake Meredith	TX	1965	44,978
Lake Roosevelt[5]	WA	1946	100,390
Ross Lake	WA	1968	117,575
Santa Monica Mts.[3]	CA	1978	154,095
Whiskeytown-Shasta-Trinity	CA	1965	42,503

NATIONAL SCENIC TRAIL

Name	State	Year[1]	Acreage
Appalachian	ME to GA	1968	222,578
Natchez Trace	MS-TN	1983	10,995
Potomac Heritage	MD-DC-VA-PA	1983	NA

PARKS (no other classification)

Name	State	Year[1]	Acreage
Catoctin Mountain	MD	1954	5,810
Constitution Gardens	DC	1974	52
Fort Washington	MD	1930	341
Greenbelt	MD	1950	1,176
National Capital	DC	1933	6,629
National Mall	DC	1933	146
Piscataway	MD	1961	4,625
Prince William Forest	VA	1948	18,942
Rock Creek	DC	1890	1,755
White House	DC	1933	18
Wolf Trap Farm Park for the Performing Arts	VA	1966	130

INTERNATIONAL HISTORIC SITE

Name	State	Year[1]	Acreage
Saint Croix Island[3]	ME	1949	45

NA=Not available. (1) Year first designated. (2) No federal facilities. (3) Limited federal facilities. (4) Not open to the public. (5) Formerly Coulee Dam National Recreation Area.

20 Most-Visited Sites in the National Park System, 2003

Source: National Park Service, Dept. of the Interior

Attendance at all areas administered by the National Park Service in 2003 totaled 266,099,641 recreation visits.

Site (location)	Recreation visits	Site (location)	Recreation visits
Blue Ridge Parkway (NC-VA)	18,344,051	Cape Cod National Seashore (MA)	4,066,365
Golden Gate National Recreation Area (CA)	13,854,750	San Francisco Maritime National Historical Park (CA)	3,984,826
Great Smoky Mountains National Park (NC-TN)	9,366,845	Yosemite National Park (CA)	3,378,664
Gateway National Recreation Area (NJ-NY)	8,567,769	Colonial National Historical Park (VA)	3,329,139
Lake Mead National Recreation Area (AZ-NV)	7,915,581	Lincoln Memorial (DC)	3,272,596
George Washington Memorial Pkwy (VA-MD-DC)	6,043,508	Statue of Liberty National Monument (NJ-NY)	3,231,247
Natchez Trace Parkway (MS-AL-TN)	5,555,984	Olympic National Park (WA)	3,225,327
Delaware Water Gap National Recreation Area (NJ-PA)	5,059,410	Rocky Mountain National Park (CO)	3,067,256
Gulf Islands National Seashore (FL-MS)	4,939,771	Yellowstone National Park (ID-MT-WY)	3,019,375
Grand Canyon National Park (AZ)	4,124,900	Castle Clinton National Monument (NY)	2,941,250

U.S. States Ranked by American Indian and Alaska Native Population, 2000

Source: Bureau of the Census, U.S. Dept. of Commerce

Rank	State	One race only[1]	More than one race[2]	Rank	State	One race only[1]	More than one race[2]
1	California	333,346	294,216	27	Georgia	21,737	31,460
2	Oklahoma	273,230	118,719	28	Virginia	21,172	31,692
3	Arizona	255,879	36,673	29	New Jersey	19,492	29,612
4	New Mexico	173,483	17,992	30	Pennsylvania	18,348	34,302
5	Texas	118,362	97,237	31	Arkansas	17,808	19,194
6	North Carolina	99,551	32,185	32	Idaho	17,645	9,592
7	Alaska	98,043	21,198	33	Indiana	15,815	23,448
8	Washington	93,301	65,639	34	Maryland	15,423	24,014
9	New York	82,461	89,120	35	Tennessee	15,152	24,036
10	South Dakota	62,283	5,998	36	Massachusetts	15,015	23,035
11	Michigan	58,479	65,933	37	Nebraska	14,896	7,308
12	Montana	56,068	10,252	38	South Carolina	13,718	13,738
13	Minnesota	54,967	26,107	39	Mississippi	11,652	7,903
14	Florida	53,541	64,339	40	Wyoming	11,133	3,879
15	Wisconsin	47,228	22,158	41	Connecticut	9,639	14,849
16	Oregon	45,211	40,456	42	Iowa	8,989	9,257
17	Colorado	44,241	35,448	43	Kentucky	8,616	15,936
18	North Dakota	31,329	3,899	44	Maine	7,098	6,058
19	Illinois	31,006	42,155	45	Rhode Island	5,121	5,604
20	Utah	29,684	10,761	46	West Virginia	3,606	7,038
21	Nevada	26,420	15,802	47	Hawaii	3,535	21,347
22	Louisiana	25,477	17,401	48	New Hampshire	2,964	4,921
23	Missouri	25,076	35,023	49	Delaware	2,731	3,338
24	Kansas	24,936	22,247	50	Vermont	2,420	3,976
25	Ohio	24,486	51,589	51	Washington, DC	1,713	3,062
26	Alabama	22,430	22,019		UNITED STATES	2,475,956	1,643,345

(1) Respondents classified themselves only under the category "American Indian and Alaska Native" on Census 2000. (2) Respondents classified themselves as "American Indian and Alaska Native" in combination with one or more other races.

Largest American Indian and Alaska Native Tribes in the U.S., 2000

Source: Bureau of the Census, U.S. Dept. of Commerce

Based on self-identification in Census 2000. Some respondents reported themselves as members of two or more tribes and/or as American Indian or Alaska Native in combination with one or more other races. The last column is the sum of preceding columns.

Tribe[1]	American Indian and Alaska Native alone: One tribe reported	American Indian and Alaska Native alone: Two or more tribes reported	American Indian and Alaska Native in combination with one or more races: One tribe reported	American Indian and Alaska Native in combination with one or more races: Two or more tribes reported	American Indian and Alaska Native alone or in any combination
ALL AMERICAN INDIANS	2,416,410	59,546	1,582,860	60,485	4,119,301
Cherokee	281,069	18,793	390,902	38,769	729,533
Navajo	269,202	6,789	19,491	2,715	298,197
Canadian and Latin American	108,802	2,236	79,499	2,233	192,770
Sioux	108,272	4,794	35,179	5,115	153,360
Chippewa	105,907	2,730	38,635	2,397	149,669
Choctaw	87,349	9,552	50,123	11,750	158,774
Pueblo	59,533	3,527	9,943	1,082	74,085
Apache	57,060	7,917	24,947	6,909	96,833
Lumbee	51,913	642	4,934	379	57,868
Iroquois	45,212	2,318	29,763	3,529	80,822
Creek	40,223	5,495	21,652	3,940	71,310
Blackfeet	27,104	4,358	41,389	12,899	85,750
Yup'ik	21,212	895	1,996	134	24,237
Chickasaw	20,887	3,014	12,025	2,425	38,351
Tohono O'Odham	17,466	714	1,748	159	20,087
Inupiat Eskimo	16,047	845	2,282	191	19,365
Potawatomi	15,817	592	8,602	584	25,595
Yaqui	15,224	1,245	5,184	759	22,412
Tlingit-Haida	14,825	1,059	6,047	434	22,365
Alaskan Athabascan	14,520	815	3,218	285	18,838
Seminole	12,431	2,982	9,505	2,513	27,431
Cheyenne	11,191	1,365	4,655	993	18,204
Puget Sound Salish	11,034	226	3,212	159	14,631
Comanche	10,120	1,568	6,120	1,568	19,376
Paiute	9,705	1,163	2,315	349	13,532

(1) Ranked by totals shown in first column.

UNITED STATES POPULATION

U.S. Census Bureau Takes the Nation's Socioeconomic Pulse

by Louis Kincannon Director, U.S. Census Bureau

The U.S. Census Bureau conducts censuses and surveys of the population and businesses on a continuing basis to accurately gauge the demographic and economic state of the nation. This inventory of data is used in many ways by government and business decision-makers, as well as by researchers and the general public.

Data we have collected in the last 2 years reveal a nation that is increasingly well-educated, growing rapidly in the South and West, becoming more racially and ethnically diverse, leaving home earlier to beat traffic, and attracting more immigrants.

New Programs

The Census Bureau recently introduced 2 new programs, the American Community Survey (ACS) and the Local Employment Dynamics (LED) program. The ACS is designed to offer communities a fresh look each year at how they are changing both demographically and economically. These statistics play a critical role for states and local communities in determining their share of federal money for schools, roads, senior citizen centers, and various services. Until now, this information was gathered only once every 10 years on the decennial census long-form questionnaire. The ACS will eliminate the need for the long form in the next census, in 2010.

The Local Employment Dynamics program is a federal-state partnership to offer data on the rapidly changing job climate in states and local areas. States have had economic indicators for industries and demographic characteristics of workers before. But the LED shows how the workforce changes each quarter within a state or substate area, and what industries undergo the changes, as well as the characteristics of workers involved in the changes. These indicators give new insight into each state's economy and show how fluid employment is in local areas. Twenty-nine states are now participating in this program.

In 2004 we began releasing the first results from the 2002 Economic Census. This census of businesses, taken every 5 years, has been called "indispensable to understanding America's economy" by Federal Reserve Board Chairman Alan Greenspan. Meanwhile, we continue to present the most up-to-date information from the monthly Current Population Survey (CPS). Dating back to the 1940s, the CPS is the longest-running household survey in the country. And we compile highlights from our population estimates programs and projections, as well as information from our international database. These data sets can be quite useful to public-sector planners and private-sector marketers.

290 Million and Growing

The U.S. population has surpassed the 290 million mark—it grew an estimated 1.0% (2.8 million people) between July 1, 2002, and July 1, 2003, to 290.8 million.

This population growth was concentrated in the West and South, particularly in mountain and coastal states. Among the nation's 10 fastest-growing states over the period, 4 were in the Rocky Mountains: Nevada (ranking 1st for the 17th consecutive year, with a growth rate of 3.4%), Arizona (2nd), Idaho (5th), and Utah (8th). The remaining top 10 states were all coastal: Florida (3rd), Texas (4th), Georgia (6th), Delaware (7th), California (9th), and Hawaii (10th). States that moved into the top 10 in 2003 were Delaware, California, and Hawaii.

Five of the 10 fastest-growing counties between April 1, 2000, and July 1, 2003, are in Georgia. They are Chattahoochee (2nd), Forsyth (5th), Henry (6th), Newton (8th), and Paulding (9th)—all with growth rates above 20%. In all, the Peach State was home to 20 of the nation's 100 fastest-growing counties. However, it was a Virginia county—Loudoun, near Washington, DC—that topped the list, with a 30.7% population increase over the same 3-year, 3-month period. Douglas, CO (near Denver), ranked 3rd in growth at 27.1%. Rockwall, TX (near Dallas), was 4th at 26.8%; Flagler, FL (just north of Daytona Beach), was 7th, with 24.8%; and Kendall, IL (in the Chicago area), was 10th at 22%.

From April 1, 2000, to July 1, 2003, 8 of the top 10 fastest-growing big cities (100,000 or more population) were in the West. Gilbert, AZ, a city of 145,250 southeast of Phoenix, led the list with a growth rate of 32% (35,301 new residents). It was followed by North Las Vegas (up 25%) and Henderson (23%), both in Nevada's Clark County. Rounding out the list were 2 more in Arizona—Chandler and Peoria; 3 in southern California—Irvine, Rancho Cucamonga, and Fontana; and 2 in Florida—Port St. Lucie and Cape Coral.

A More Diverse Population

The nation's Hispanic and Asian populations continued to grow at much faster rates than the population as a whole.

Hispanics (of whatever race) reached 39.9 million on July 1, 2003, accounting for about half of the 9.4 million residents added to the nation's population since Census 2000. The growth rate of 13.0% for Hispanics was almost 4 times that of the total population (3.3%).

Among people reporting one or more races, the Asian population grew 12.5% to 13.5 million. Far behind in growth were native Hawaiians and other Pacific islanders (5.8% to 960,000), blacks (4.4% to 38.7 million), American Indians and Alaska natives (3.3% to 4.4 million), and whites (2.8% to 237.9 million). The non-Hispanic white-alone population increased only 0.9%, to 197.3 million.

According to our projections, the nation's Hispanic and Asian populations will triple over the next half century. Nearly 67 million people of Hispanic origin are expected to be added between 2000 and 2050. Their number is projected to grow to 102.6 million, which would nearly double their share of the total, from 12.6% to 24.4%. The Asian population is projected to grow to 33.4 million. Their share of the nation's population would double, to 8%. Projections for the black population put it at 61.4 million in 2050, an increase of about 26 million, or 71%. That would raise the black percentage of the U.S. population from 12.7% to 14.6%.

From 2000 to 2050, the non-Hispanic white population is projected to climb to 210.3 million, an increase of 14.6 million, or 7%. However, this group is projected to actually lose population in the 2040s; with other groups gaining ground, non-Hispanic whites will make up just 50.1% of the total population by mid-century, compared with 69.4% in 2000.

U.S. Among the Most Populous Countries

The U.S. remains one of the world's most populous nations, trailing only China and India. Even though the nation's population is not increasing at an especially rapid rate—at least in comparison to the developing world—it is still the 6th largest contributor to annual world population growth, behind only India, China, Indonesia, Nigeria, and Pakistan. One reason for this growth is that the U.S. continues to be a haven for immigrants, with more than 1 million a year moving into the country to settle.

A Nation of Immigrants

The American Community Survey shows that the nation's foreign-born population grew to more than 33.5 million in 2003, making up about 12% of the total U.S. population. The U.S. foreign-born population now exceeds the entire population of Canada!

Of this number about 53% were born in Latin America, 25% in Asia, and 14% in Europe. Thirty-seven percent of the total foreign-born came from Central America or Mexico. Forty-four percent now lived in the central city of a metropolitan area, compared with 27% of U.S. natives. The foreign-born population consists mainly of young adults, with 45% falling between the ages of 25 and 44, compared with 27% of the native-born.

The proportion of the foreign-born population that had bachelor's degrees did not vary much from the native population, at around 27% of those over age 25. However, 22% of the foreign-born had less than a 9th grade education, com-

pared with only 4% of the native-born population. Foreign-born households were larger than those of natives: 25% contained 5 or more people, compared with 13% of native-born households.

Fewer Moving, Longer Moves

Americans are moving at some of the lowest rates in more than 50 years, but long-distance moves are becoming slightly more common. About 40.1 million people moved between 2002 and 2003, making up 14% of the population. This was much lower than the 20% recorded in 1948, when the Census Bureau first began collecting information on movers. In 2003, however, 19% of all moves were to a different state, compared with 15% in 1948. Among people who changed residence, most (51%) moved for housing-related reasons, with others usually doing it for family reasons (26%) or work-related reasons (16%).

The Early, Lonely, Long Commute

A task generally considered mundane at best and stressful at worst—the journey to work—now eats up a significant portion of Americans' lives. The average daily commute takes 24 minutes, and 7% of the nation's workers have commutes of an hour or more. (Among big cities, New York has the longest average commute, 38.4 minutes, followed by Chicago and Philadelphia.)

Increasingly large numbers of commuters depart for work in the wee hours of the morning, with more than 25 million leaving home between midnight and 6:30 A.M., according to the American Community Survey. These early birds, 20% of all workers, were the fastest-growing group of commuters between the last two decennial censuses.

Most of these early risers (and later risers, too) face a solitary trip to work, as 77% of workers drive alone. Another 10% carpool, 5% use public transportation, and 2% walk. The percentage of workers using public transportation has dropped by more than half since 1960, when it stood at 12%. Of the 6.4 million Americans who use public transportation, one-third live in New York City.

Despite the relatively small proportion of commuters using public transportation, the number of privately operated urban transportation systems—local and suburban rail and passenger bus operations with regular routes in metro areas—doubled between 1997 and 2002, from 618 to 1,234. Their revenues grew from $1.5 billion to $3.6 billion.

Education on the Upswing

According to Census Bureau measurements, the U.S. is better-educated than ever before. In 2003, more than 4 out of 5 adults (85%) aged 25 or older had completed at least high school—an all-time high. More than 1 out of 4 adults (27%) had a bachelor's degree or higher, another record.

These gains cut across many different demographic groups. The proportions of both non-Hispanic whites (89%) and blacks (80%) who had a high school diploma or more education marked new highs. Blacks boosted their high school graduation rate by 10 percentage points and non-Hispanic whites by 5 percentage points from 1993 to 2003. Women made significant gains in earning college degrees. Over the past decade, the percentage of women with a bachelor's degree or higher jumped nearly 7 percentage points, from 19% to 26%. During the same time frame, men had a 4-percentage-point increase, going from 25% to 29%.

The states with the highest high school graduation rates in 2003 were New Hampshire, Minnesota, and Wyoming, all around 92%. About 46% of people 25 and older in Washington, DC, had at least a bachelor's degree, higher than any state. Among the states themselves, Massachusetts had the highest, 38%; however, this was not statistically different from those of Maryland and Colorado.

Income Stable, Poverty Up

After declining for two years, median household money income in 2003 was $43,318, virtually unchanged from 2002. Meanwhile, the nation's official poverty rate rose from 12.1% in 2002 to 12.5% in 2003; for children it rose from 16.7% to 17.6%. The number of people living in poverty in 2003 was 35.9 million—1.3 million more than in 2002. Median earnings for full-time, year-round workers decreased slightly, by 0.6% for women, while holding steady for men.

The number of people with health insurance rose by 1.0 million between 2002 and 2003, to 243.3 million, while the number of uninsured rose by 1.4 million, to 45 million (or 15.6%). The number of children not covered was unchanged at 8.4 million—11.4% of all children in the U.S.

The Census: Looking Back

The U.S. census is conducted every 10 years as mandated by the Constitution, Article I, Section 2. The primary purpose is to apportion seats in the House of Representatives and determine state legislative district boundaries. The data are also critical for a vast array of government programs at every level, and for providing demographic information to individuals and businesses.

The first U.S. census, which counted 3.9 million people, was conducted in 1790, shortly after George Washington became president. It counted the number of free white males age 16 and over, and under 16 (to measure how many men might be available for military service), the number of free white females, all other free persons (including any American Indians who paid taxes), and slaves. It took 18 months to collect the data, often on unofficial sheets of paper supplied by U.S. marshals. In contrast to today's pledge of confidentiality, the 1790 census results were publicly displayed. The 1790 census resulted in an increase of 41 seats (65 to 106) in the House of Representatives.

As the nation expanded, so did the scope of the census data. The first inquiry on manufactures was made in 1810. Questions on agriculture, mining, and fisheries were added in 1840. In 1850, the census included inquiries on social issues—taxation, churches, pauperism, and crime.

The 1880 census had so many questions that it took the full 10 years between censuses to publish all the results. Because of this delay, Congress limited the 1900 census to questions on population, manufactures, agriculture, and mortality. (Many of the dropped topics reappeared in later censuses.)

For many years, the undertaking of each census had to be authorized by a specific act of Congress. In 1954, Congress specified the laws under which the Census Bureau operates in Title 13 of the U.S. Code. This title delineates the basic scope of the census, the requirements for the public to provide information as well as for the Bureau to keep information confidential, and the penalties for violating any of these obligations.

Today, the secretary of commerce (and through that individual, the Census Bureau) is directed by law to take censuses of population, housing, agriculture, irrigation, manufactures, mineral industries, other businesses (wholesale trade, retail trade, services), construction, transportation, and governments at stated intervals, and may take surveys related to any of these subjects.

U.S. marshals supervised their assistants' enumeration of the first 9 censuses and reported to the president (1790), the secretary of state (1800-1840), or the secretary of the interior (1850-1870). There was no continuity of personnel from one census to the next. However, in 1902, Congress authorized the president to set up a permanent Census Office in the Interior Dept. In 1903, the agency was transferred to the new Dept. of Commerce and Labor, and when the department split in 1913, the Bureau of the Census was placed in the Commerce Dept.

The Census Bureau began using statistical sampling techniques in the 1940s, computers in the 1950s, and mail enumeration in the 1960s, all as part of an effort to publish more data sooner and at a lower cost, and with less burden on the public. For the 2010 Census, the Census Bureau planned to continue mailing questionnaires to most housing units in the country, but to use handheld computers, rather than paper and pencil, in doing follow-up interviews at non-responding households.

U.S. Area and Population, 1790-2000

Source: Bureau of the Census, U.S. Dept. of Commerce

| Census date | AREA | | | POPULATION | | | |
	Gross Area	Land Area	Water Area	Number	Per sq mi of land	Increase over preceding census Number	%
1790 (Aug. 2)	891,364	864,746	26,618	3,929,214	4.5	—	—
1800 (Aug. 4)	891,364	864,746	26,618	5,308,483	6.1	1,379,269	35.1
1810 (Aug. 6)	1,722,685	1,681,828	40,857	7,239,881	4.3	1,931,398	36.4
1820 (June 1)	1,792,552	1,749,462	43,090	9,638,453	5.5	2,398,572	33.1
1830 (June 1)	1,792,552	1,749,462	43,090	12,866,020[2]	7.4	3,227,567	33.5
1840 (June 1)	1,792,552	1,749,462	43,090	17,068,953[2]	9.8	4,203,433	32.7
1850 (June 1)	2,991,655	2,940,042	51,613	23,191,876	7.9	6,122,423	35.9
1860 (June 1)	3,021,295	2,969,640	51,655	31,443,321	10.6	8,251,445	35.6
1870 (June 1)	3,612,299	3,540,705	71,594	38,558,371	10.9	7,115,050	22.6
1880 (June 1)	3,612,299	3,540,705	71,594	50,189,209	14.2	11,630,838	30.2
1890 (June 1)	3,612,299	3,540,705	71,594	62,979,766	17.8	12,790,557	25.5
1900 (June 1)	3,618,770	3,547,314	71,456	76,212,168	21.5	13,232,402	21.0
1910 (Apr. 15)	3,618,770	3,547,045	71,725	92,228,496	26.0	16,016,328	21.0
1920 (Jan. 1)	3,618,770	3,546,931	71,839	106,021,537	29.9	13,793,041	15.0
1930 (Apr. 1)	3,618,770	3,551,608	67,162	123,202,624	34.7	17,181,087	16.2
1940 (Apr. 1)	3,618,770	3,554,608	64,162	132,164,569	37.2	8,961,945	7.3
1950 (Apr. 1)	3,618,770	3,552,206	66,564	151,325,798	42.6	19,161,229	14.5
1960 (Apr. 1)	3,618,770	3,540,911	77,859	179,323,175	50.6	27,997,377	18.5
1970 (Apr. 1)	3,618,770	3,536,855	81,915	203,302,031	57.5	23,978,856	13.4
1980 (Apr. 1)	3,618,770	3,539,289	79,481	226,542,203	64.0	23,240,172	11.4
1990 (Apr. 1)	3,717,796[1]	3,536,278	181,518[1]	248,709,873	70.3	22,167,670	9.8
2000 (Apr. 1)	3,794,085	3,537,440	256,648[1]	281,421,906	79.6	32,712,033	13.2

(1) Includes inland, coastal, and Great Lakes. Data before 1990 cover inland water only. (2) The U.S. total includes persons (5,318 in 1830 and 6,100 in 1840) on public ships in the service of the U.S. not credited to any region, division, or state. **NOTE:** Percent changes are computed on the basis of change in population since the preceding census date, so the period covered is not always exactly 10 years. Population density figures given for various years represent the area within the boundaries of the U.S. that was under the jurisdiction on the date in question—including, in some cases, considerable areas not organized or settled and not actually covered by the census. In 1870, for example, Alaska was not covered by the census. Population figures shown here may reflect corrections made to the initial tabulated census counts.

Congressional Apportionment

Source: Bureau of the Census, U.S. Dept. of Commerce; by census year

	2000	1990	1980	1970	1950	1900	1850		2000	1990	1980	1970	1950	1900	1850
AL.....	7	7	7	7	9	9	7	NE.....	3	3	3	3	4	6	NA
AK	1	1	1	1	NA	NA	NA	NV.....	3	2	2	1	1	1	NA
AZ.....	8	6	5	4	2	NA	NA	NH.....	2	2	2	2	2	2	3
AR	4	4	4	4	6	7	2	NJ	13	13	14	15	14	10	5
CA	53	52	45	43	30	8	2	NM.....	3	3	3	2	2	NA	NA
CO	7	6	6	5	4	3	NA	NY.....	29	31	34	39	43	37	33
CT	5	6	6	6	6	5	4	NC.....	13	12	11	11	12	10	8
DE	1	1	1	1	1	1	1	ND.....	1	1	1	1	2	2	NA
FL.....	25	23	19	15	8	3	1	OH.....	18	19	21	23	23	21	21
GA	13	11	10	10	10	11	8	OK.....	5	6	6	6	6	5	NA
HI	2	2	2	2	1	NA	NA	OR.....	5	5	5	4	4	2	1
ID	2	2	2	2	2	1	NA	PA	19	21	23	25	30	32	25
IL	19	20	22	24	25	25	9	RI......	2	2	2	2	2	2	2
IN	9	10	10	11	11	13	11	SC.....	6	6	6	6	6	7	6
IA	5	5	6	6	8	11	2	SD.....	1	1	1	2	2	2	NA
KS	4	4	5	5	6	8	NA	TN.....	9	9	9	8	9	10	10
KY....	6	6	7	7	8	11	10	TX.....	32	30	27	24	22	16	2
LA.....	7	7	8	8	8	7	4	UT.....	3	3	3	2	2	1	NA
ME	2	2	2	2	3	4	6	VT.....	1	1	1	1	1	2	3
MD	8	8	8	8	7	6	6	VA.....	11	11	10	10	10	10	13
MA	10	10	11	12	14	14	11	WA.....	9	9	8	7	7	3	NA
MI.....	15	16	18	19	18	12	4	WV.....	3	3	4	4	6	5	NA
MN	8	8	8	8	9	9	2	WI	8	9	9	9	10	11	3
MS	4	5	5	5	6	8	5	WY.....	1	1	1	1	1	1	NA
MO	9	9	9	10	11	16	7	**TOTAL**	**435**	**435**	**435**	**435**	**435**	**391**	**237**
MT	1	1	2	2	2	1	NA								

Note: NA = Not applicable.

The Constitution, in Article 1, Section 2, provided for a census of the population every 10 years to establish a basis for apportionment of representatives among the states. This apportionment largely determines the number of electoral votes allotted to each state.

The number of representatives of each state in Congress is determined by the state's population, but each state is entitled to one representative regardless of population. A congressional apportionment has been made after each decennial census except that of 1920. (The year given above is the year of the census on which apportionment for the next election year is based.) Prior to 1870, 3/5 the number of slaves were added to the total free population. Indians "not taxed" were excluded until 1940.

Under provisions of a law that became effective Nov. 15, 1941, representatives are apportioned by the method of equal proportions. In the application of this method, the apportionment is made so that the average population per representative has the least possible variation between one state and any other.

The first House of Representatives, in 1789, had 65 members, as provided by the Constitution. Of these, the largest numbers were from Virginia (19), Massachusetts (14), and Pennsylvania (13).

As the nation's population grew, the number of representatives was increased, but the total membership of the House has been fixed at 435 since the apportionment based on the 1910 census.

U.S. Population by Official

STATE	1790[1]	1800[1]	1810[1]	1820[1]	1830[1]	1840	1850	1860	1870	1880	1890	1900
AL...		1	9	128	310	590,756	771,623	964,201	996,992	1,262,505	1,513,401	1,828,697
AK..										33,426	32,052	63,592
AZ..									9,658	40,440	88,243	122,931
AR..			1	14	30	97,574	209,897	435,450	484,471	802,525	1,128,211	1,311,564
CA..							92,597	379,994	560,247	864,694	1,213,398	1,485,053
CO..								34,277	39,864	194,327	413,249	539,700
CT..	238	251	262	275	298	309,978	370,792	460,147	537,454	622,700	746,258	908,420
DE..	59	64	73	73	77	78,085	91,532	112,216	125,015	146,608	168,493	184,735
DC..		8	16	23	30	33,745	51,687	75,080	131,700	177,624	230,392	278,718
FL..					35	54,477	87,445	140,424	187,748	269,493	391,422	528,542
GA..	83	163	252	341	517	691,392	906,185	1,057,286	1,184,109	1,542,180	1,837,353	2,216,331
HI...												154,001
ID...									14,999	32,610	88,548	161,772
IL...			12	55	157	476,183	851,470	1,711,951	2,539,891	3,077,871	3,826,352	4,821,550
IN...		6	25	147	343	685,866	988,416	1,350,428	1,680,637	1,978,301	2,192,404	2,516,462
IA...						43,112	192,214	674,913	1,194,020	1,624,615	1,912,297	2,231,853
KS...								107,206	364,399	996,096	1,428,108	1,470,495
KY..	74	221	407	564	688	779,828	982,405	1,155,684	1,321,011	1,648,690	1,858,635	2,147,174
LA..			77	153	216	352,411	517,762	708,002	726,915	939,946	1,118,588	1,381,625
ME..	97	152	229	298	399	501,793	583,169	628,279	626,915	648,936	661,086	694,466
MD..	320	342	381	407	447	470,019	583,034	687,049	780,894	934,943	1,042,390	1,188,044
MA..	379	423	472	523	610	737,699	994,514	1,231,066	1,457,351	1,783,085	2,238,947	2,805,346
MI..			5	9	32	212,267	397,654	749,113	1,184,059	1,636,937	2,093,890	2,420,982
MN..							6,077	172,023	439,706	780,773	1,310,283	1,751,394
MS..		8	31	75	137	375,651	606,526	791,305	827,922	1,131,597	1,289,600	1,551,270
MO..			20	67	140	383,702	682,044	1,182,012	1,721,295	2,168,380	2,679,185	3,106,665
MT..									20,595	39,159	142,924	243,329
NE..								28,841	122,993	452,402	1,062,656	1,066,300
NV..								6,857	42,491	62,266	47,355	42,335
NH..	142	184	214	244	269	284,574	317,976	326,073	318,300	346,991	376,530	411,588
NJ...	184	211	246	278	321	373,306	489,555	672,035	906,096	1,131,116	1,444,933	1,883,669
NM..								61,547	93,516	91,874	119,565	160,282	195,310
NY..	340	589	959	1,373	1,919	2,428,921	3,097,394	3,880,735	4,382,759	5,082,871	6,003,174	7,268,894
NC..	394	478	556	639	736	753,419	869,039	992,622	1,071,361	1,399,750	1,617,949	1,893,810
ND..									2,405[2]	36,909	190,983	319,146
OH..		45	231	581	938	1,519,467	1,980,329	2,339,511	2,665,260	3,198,062	3,672,329	4,157,545
OK..											258,657	790,391
OR..							12,093	52,465	90,923	174,768	317,704	413,536
PA...	434	602	810	1,049	1,348	1,724,033	2,311,786	2,906,215	3,521,951	4,282,891	5,258,113	6,302,115
RI...	69	69	77	83	97	108,830	147,545	174,620	217,353	276,531	345,506	428,556
SC..	249	346	415	503	581	594,398	668,507	703,708	705,606	995,577	1,151,149	1,340,316
SD..								4,837[2]	11,776[2]	98,268	348,600	401,570
TN..	36	106	262	423	682	829,210	1,002,717	1,109,801	1,258,520	1,542,359	1,767,518	2,020,616
TX..							212,592	604,215	818,579	1,591,749	2,235,527	3,048,710
UT..							11,380	40,273	86,786	143,963	210,779	276,749
VT..	85	154	218	236	281	291,948	314,120	315,098	330,551	332,286	332,422	343,641
VA..	692	808	878	938	1,044	1,025,227	1,119,348	1,219,630	1,225,163	1,512,565	1,655,980	1,854,184
WA..								11,594	23,955	75,116	357,232	518,103
WV..	56	79	105	137	177	224,537	302,313	376,688	442,014	618,457	762,794	958,800
WI..						30,945	305,391	775,881	1,054,670	1,315,497	1,693,330	2,069,042
WY..									9,118	20,789	62,555	92,531
U.S. .	3,929	5,308	7,240	9,638	12,866[3]	17,068,953[3]	23,191,876	31,443,321	38,558,371	50,189,209	62,979,766	76,212,168

Note: Where possible, population shown is that of the 2000 area of the state. Members of the Armed Forces overseas or other U.S. nationals abroad are not included. Totals revised to include corrections of initial tabulated counts. (1) Totals for 1790 through 1830 are in thousands. (2) 1860 figure is for Dakota Territory; 1870 figures are for parts of Dakota Territory. (3) Includes persons (5,318 in 1830 and 6,100 in 1840) on public ships in the service of the U.S. not credited to any region, division, or state.

Estimated Population of American Colonies, 1630–1780

Source: Bureau of the Census, U.S. Dept. of Commerce; in thousands

Colony	1630	1650	1670	1690	1700	1720	1740	1750	1770	1780
TOTAL	4.6	50.4	111.9	210.4	250.9	466.2	905.6	1,170.8	2,148.1	2,780.4
Maine (counties)[1]	0.4	1.0	...	...	...	...	...	...	31.3	49.1
New Hampshire[2]	0.5	1.3	1.8	4.2	5.0	9.4	23.3	27.5	62.4	87.8
Vermont[3]	...	...	...	...	...	...	...	...	10.0	47.6
Plymouth and Massachusetts[1,2,4]	0.9	15.6	35.3	56.9	55.9	91.0	151.6	188.0	235.3	268.6
Rhode Island[2]	...	0.8	2.2	4.2	5.9	11.7	25.3	33.2	58.2	52.9
Connecticut[2]	...	4.1	12.6	21.6	26.0	58.8	89.6	111.3	183.9	206.7
New York[2]	0.4	4.1	5.8	13.9	19.1	36.9	63.7	76.7	162.9	210.5
New Jersey[2]	...	...	1.0	8.0	14.0	29.8	51.4	71.4	117.4	139.6
Pennsylvania[2]	...	...	...	11.4	18.0	31.0	85.6	119.7	240.1	327.3
Delaware[2]	...	0.2	0.7	1.5	2.5	5.4	19.9	28.7	35.5	45.4
Maryland[2]	...	4.5	13.2	24.0	29.6	66.1	116.1	141.1	202.6	245.5
Virginia[2]	2.5	18.7	35.3	53.0	58.6	87.8	180.4	231.0	447.0	538.0
North Carolina[2]	...	...	3.8	7.6	10.7	21.3	51.8	73.0	197.2	270.1
South Carolina[2]	...	...	0.2	3.9	5.7	17.0	45.0	64.0	124.2	180.0
Georgia[2]	...	...	...	...	...	...	2.0	5.2	23.4	56.1
Kentucky[5]	...	...	...	...	...	...	...	...	15.7	45.0
Tennessee[6]	...	...	...	...	...	...	...	...	1.0	10.0

(1) For 1660–1750, Maine counties are included with Massachusetts. Maine was part of Massachusetts until it became a separate state in 1820. (2) One of the original 13 states. (3) Admitted to statehood in 1791. (4) Plymouth became a part of the Province of Massachusetts in 1691. (5) Admitted to statehood in 1792. (6) Admitted to statehood in 1796.

Census, 1790–2000

1910	1920	1930	1940	1950	1960	1970	1980	1990	2000
2,138,093	2,348,174	2,646,248	2,832,961	3,061,743	3,266,740	3,444,354	3,894,025	4,040,587	4,447,100
64,356	55,036	59,278	72,524	128,643	226,167	302,583	401,851	550,043	626,932
204,354	334,162	435,573	499,261	749,587	1,302,161	1,775,399	2,716,546	3,665,228	5,130,632
1,574,449	1,752,204	1,854,482	1,949,387	1,909,511	1,786,272	1,923,322	2,286,357	2,350,725	2,673,400
2,377,549	3,426,861	5,677,251	6,907,387	10,586,223	15,717,204	19,971,069	23,667,764	29,760,021	33,871,648
799,024	939,629	1,035,791	1,123,296	1,325,089	1,753,947	2,209,596	2,889,735	3,294,394	4,301,261
1,114,756	1,380,631	1,606,903	1,709,242	2,007,280	2,535,234	3,032,217	3,107,564	3,287,116	3,405,565
202,322	223,003	238,380	266,505	318,085	446,292	548,104	594,338	666,168	783,600
331,069	437,571	486,869	663,091	802,178	763,956	756,668	638,432	606,900	572,059
752,619	968,470	1,468,211	1,897,414	2,771,305	4,951,560	6,791,418	9,746,961	12,937,926	15,982,378
2,609,121	2,895,832	2,908,506	3,123,723	3,444,578	3,943,116	4,587,930	5,462,982	6,478,216	8,186,453
191,874	255,881	368,300	422,770	499,794	632,772	769,913	964,691	1,108,229	1,211,537
325,594	431,866	445,032	524,873	588,637	667,191	713,015	944,127	1,006,749	1,293,953
5,638,591	6,485,280	7,630,654	7,897,241	8,712,176	10,081,158	11,110,285	11,427,409	11,430,602	12,419,293
2,700,876	2,930,390	3,238,503	3,427,796	3,934,224	4,662,498	5,195,392	5,490,214	5,544,159	6,080,485
2,224,771	2,404,021	2,470,939	2,538,268	2,621,073	2,757,537	2,825,368	2,913,808	2,776,755	2,926,324
1,690,949	1,769,257	1,880,999	1,801,028	1,905,299	2,178,611	2,249,071	2,364,236	2,477,574	2,688,418
2,289,905	2,416,630	2,614,589	2,845,627	2,944,806	3,038,156	3,220,711	3,660,324	3,685,296	4,041,769
1,656,388	1,798,509	2,101,593	2,363,880	2,683,516	3,257,022	3,644,637	4,206,116	4,219,973	4,468,976
742,371	768,014	797,423	847,226	913,774	969,265	993,722	1,125,043	1,227,928	1,274,923
1,295,346	1,449,661	1,631,526	1,821,244	2,343,001	3,100,689	3,923,897	4,216,933	4,781,468	5,296,486
3,366,416	3,852,356	4,249,614	4,316,721	4,690,514	5,148,578	5,689,170	5,737,093	6,016,425	6,349,097
2,810,173	3,668,412	4,842,325	5,256,106	6,371,766	7,823,194	8,881,826	9,262,044	9,295,297	9,938,444
2,075,708	2,387,125	2,563,953	2,792,300	2,982,483	3,413,864	3,806,103	4,075,970	4,375,099	4,919,479
1,797,114	1,790,618	2,009,821	2,183,796	2,178,914	2,178,141	2,216,994	2,520,770	2,573,216	2,844,658
3,293,335	3,404,055	3,629,367	3,784,664	3,954,653	4,319,813	4,677,623	4,916,766	5,117,073	5,595,211
376,053	548,889	537,606	559,456	591,024	674,767	694,409	786,690	799,065	902,195
1,192,214	1,296,372	1,377,963	1,315,834	1,325,510	1,411,330	1,485,333	1,569,825	1,578,385	1,711,263
81,875	77,407	91,058	110,247	160,083	285,278	488,738	800,508	1,201,833	1,998,257
430,572	443,083	465,293	491,524	533,242	606,921	737,681	920,610	1,109,252	1,235,786
2,537,167	3,155,900	4,041,334	4,160,165	4,835,329	6,066,782	7,171,112	7,365,011	7,730,188	8,414,350
327,301	360,350	423,317	531,818	681,187	951,023	1,017,055	1,303,302	1,515,069	1,819,046
9,113,614	10,385,227	12,588,066	13,479,142	14,830,192	16,782,304	18,241,391	17,558,165	17,990,455	18,976,457
2,206,287	2,559,123	3,170,276	3,571,623	4,061,929	4,556,155	5,084,411	5,880,095	6,628,637	8,049,313
577,056	646,872	680,845	641,935	619,636	632,446	617,792	652,717	638,800	642,200
4,767,121	5,759,394	6,646,697	6,907,612	7,946,627	9,706,397	10,657,423	10,797,603	10,847,115	11,353,140
1,657,155	2,028,283	2,396,040	2,336,434	2,233,351	2,328,284	2,559,463	3,025,487	3,145,585	3,450,654
672,765	783,389	953,786	1,089,684	1,521,341	1,768,687	2,091,533	2,633,156	2,842,321	3,421,399
7,665,111	8,720,017	9,631,350	9,900,180	10,498,012	11,319,366	11,800,766	11,864,720	11,881,643	12,281,054
542,610	604,397	687,497	713,346	791,896	859,488	949,723	947,154	1,003,464	1,048,319
1,515,400	1,683,724	1,738,765	1,899,804	2,117,027	2,382,594	2,590,713	3,120,729	3,486,703	4,012,012
583,888	636,547	692,849	642,961	652,740	680,514	666,257	690,768	696,004	754,844
2,184,789	2,337,885	2,616,556	2,915,841	3,291,718	3,567,089	3,926,018	4,591,023	4,877,185	5,689,283
3,896,542	4,663,228	5,824,715	6,414,824	7,711,194	9,579,677	11,198,655	14,225,513	16,986,510	20,851,820
373,351	449,396	507,847	550,310	688,862	890,627	1,059,273	1,461,037	1,722,850	2,233,169
355,956	352,428	359,611	359,231	377,747	389,881	444,732	511,456	562,758	608,827
2,061,612	2,309,187	2,421,851	2,677,773	3,318,680	3,966,949	4,651,448	5,346,797	6,187,358	7,078,515
1,141,990	1,356,621	1,563,396	1,736,191	2,378,963	2,853,214	3,413,244	4,132,353	4,866,692	5,894,121
1,221,119	1,463,701	1,729,205	1,901,974	2,005,552	1,860,421	1,744,237	1,950,186	1,793,477	1,808,344
2,333,860	2,632,067	2,939,006	3,137,587	3,434,575	3,951,777	4,417,821	4,705,642	4,891,769	5,363,675
145,965	194,402	225,565	250,742	290,529	330,066	332,416	469,557	453,588	493,782
92,228,496	**106,021,537**	**123,202,624**	**132,164,569**	**151,325,798**	**179,323,175**	**203,302,031**	**226,542,203**	**248,709,873**	**281,421,906**

U.S. Center of Population, 1790–2000

Source: Bureau of the Census, U.S. Dept. of Commerce

The U.S. Center of Population is considered here as the center of population gravity, or that point upon which the U.S. would balance if it were a rigid plane without weight and the population distributed thereon, with each individual assumed to have equal weight and to exert an influence on a central point proportional to his or her distance from that point. The 2000 center is 12.1 miles south and 32.5 miles west of the 1990 center of population, and is more than 1,000 miles from the 1790 center.

YEAR	N Lat °	′	″	W Long °	′	″	APPROXIMATE LOCATION
1790	39	16	30	76	11	12	23 miles east of Baltimore, MD
1800	39	16	6	76	56	30	18 miles west of Baltimore, MD
1810	39	11	30	77	37	12	40 miles northwest by west of Washington, DC (in VA)
1820	39	5	42	78	33	0	16 miles east of Moorefield, WV[1]
1830	38	57	54	79	16	54	19 miles west–southwest of Moorefield, WV[1]
1840	39	2	0	80	18	0	16 miles south of Clarksburg, WV[1]
1850	38	59	0	81	19	0	23 miles southeast of Parkersburg, WV[1]
1860	39	0	24	82	48	48	20 miles south by east of Chillicothe, OH
1870	39	12	0	83	35	42	48 miles east by north of Cincinnati, OH
1880	39	4	8	84	39	40	8 miles west by south of Cincinnati, OH (in KY)
1890	39	11	56	85	32	53	20 miles east of Columbus, IN
1900	39	9	36	85	48	54	6 miles southeast of Columbus, IN
1910	39	10	12	86	32	20	In the city of Bloomington, IN
1920	39	10	21	86	43	15	8 miles south–southeast of Spencer, Owen Co., IN
1930	39	3	45	87	8	6	3 miles northeast of Linton, Greene Co., IN
1940	38	56	54	87	22	35	2 miles southeast by east of Carlisle, Haddon township, Sullivan Co., IN
1950 (incl. Alaska & Hawaii)	38	48	15	88	22	8	3 miles northeast of Louisville, Clay Co., IL
1960	38	35	58	89	12	35	6½ miles northwest of Centralia, Clinton Co., IL
1970	38	27	47	89	42	22	5 miles east southeast of Mascoutah, St. Clair Co., IL
1980	38	8	13	90	34	26	¼ mile west of De Soto, Jefferson Co., MO
1990	37	52	20	91	12	55	9.7 miles northwest of Steelville, MO
2000	37	41	49	91	48	34	2.8 miles east of Edgar Springs, MO

(1) West Virginia was set off from Virginia on Dec. 31, 1862, and was admitted as a state on June 20, 1863.

Population, by Sex, Race, Residence, and Median Age, 1790–2003

Source: Bureau of the Census, U.S. Dept. of Commerce
(in thousands, except as indicated)

	SEX		RACE				RESIDENCE		MEDIAN AGE (years)		
				Black or Afr. Am.							
	Male	Female	White	Number	Percent	Other[5]	Urban	Rural	All races	White	Black
Conterminous U.S.[1]											
1790 (Aug. 2)	NA	NA	3,172	757	19.3	NA	202	3,728	NA	NA	NA
1810 (Aug. 6)	NA	NA	5,862	1,378	19.0	NA	525	6,714	NA	16.0	NA
1820 (Aug. 7)	4,897	4,742	7,867	1,772	18.4	NA	693	8,945	16.7	16.6	17.2
1840 (June 1)	8,689	8,381	14,196	2,874	16.8	NA	1,845	15,224	17.8	17.9	17.6
1860 (June 1)	16,085	15,358	26,923	4,442	14.1	79	6,217	25,227	19.4	19.7	17.5
1870 (June 1)	19,494	19,065	33,589	4,880	12.7	89	9,902	28,656	20.2	20.4	18.5
1880 (June 1)	25,519	24,637	43,403	6,581	13.1	172	14,130	36,026	20.9	21.4	18.0
1890 (June 1)	32,237	30,711	55,101	7,489	11.9	358	22,106	40,841	22.0	22.5	17.8
1900 (June 1)	38,816	37,178	66,809	8,834	11.6	351	30,160	45,835	22.9	23.4	19.4
1920 (Jan. 1)	53,900	51,810	94,821	10,463	9.9	427	54,158	51,553	25.3	25.5	22.3
1930 (Apr. 1)	62,137	60,638	110,287	11,891	9.7	597	68,955	53,820	26.5	26.9	23.5
1940 (Apr. 1)	66,062	65,608	118,215	12,866	9.8	589	74,424	57,246	29.0	29.5	25.3
United States											
1950 (Apr. 1)	74,833	75,864	135,150	15,045	9.9	1,131	96,467	54,230	30.2	30.7	26.2
1960 (Apr. 1)	88,331	90,992	158,832	18,872	10.5	1,620	125,269	54,054	29.5	30.3	23.5
1970 (Apr. 1)[2]	98,912	104,300	177,749	22,580	11.1	2,883	149,647	53,565	28.1	28.9	22.4
1980 (Apr. 1)[3]	110,053	116,493	194,713	26,683	11.8	5,150	167,051	59,495	30.0	30.9	24.9
1985 (July 1, est.) . . .	115,730	122,194	202,031	28,569	12.0	7,324	NA	NA	31.4	32.3	26.6
1990 (Apr. 1)	121,239	127,470	199,686	29,986	12.1	9,233	187,053	61,656	32.9	34.4	28.1
1991 (July 1, est.). . .	122,984	129,122	210,979	31,107	12.3	10,020	NA	NA	33.1	34.1	28.1
1992 (July 1, est.). . .	124,506	130,496	212,885	31,670	12.4	10,446	NA	NA	33.4	34.4	28.5
1993 (July 1, est.). . .	125,938	131,858	214,760	32,168	12.5	10,867	NA	NA	33.7	34.7	28.7
1994 (July 1, est.). . .	127,216	133,076	216,413	32,653	12.5	11,227	NA	NA	34.0	35.0	29.0
1995 (July 1, est.). . .	128,569	134,321	218,149	33,095	12.6	11,646	NA	NA	34.3	35.3	29.2
1996 (July 1, est.). . .	129,746	135,434	219,686	33,514	12.6	11,979	NA	NA	34.6	35.7	29.5
1997 (July 1, est.). . .	131,018	136,618	221,334	33,947	12.7	12,355	NA	NA	34.9	36.0	29.7
1998 (July 1, est.). . .	132,263	137,766	222,932	34,370	12.7	12,727	NA	NA	35.3	36.3	29.9
1999 (July 1, est.). . .	133,352	139,526	224,692	34,903	12.8	13,283	NA	NA	35.5	36.6	30.1
2000 (Apr. 1)[4]	138,054	143,368	228,105	35,816	12.7	13,716	222,361	59,061	35.3	36.6	30.0
2001 (July 1, est.)[4] . .	140,009	145,085	230,502	36,247	12.7	14,291	NA	NA	35.6	36.9	30.3
2002 (July 1, est.)[4] . .	141,533	146,441	232,369	36,676	12.7	14,749	NA	NA	35.7	37.0	30.5
2003 (July 1, est.)[4] . .	143,037	147,773	234,196	37,099	12.8	15,207	NA	NA	35.9	37.3	30.6

NA = Not available. **NOTE:** For 2000 "urban" includes residents of Urban Areas (densely settled areas with 50,000 or more inhabitants); or Urban Clusters (densely settled areas with at least 2,500 but fewer than 50,000). These definitions differ from previous Census years. (1) Excludes Alaska and Hawaii. (2) The revised 1970 resident population count is 203,302,031, which incorporates changes due to errors found after tabulations were completed. The race and sex data shown here reflect the official 1970 census count; the residence data come from the tabulated count. (3) The race data shown for Apr. 1, 1980, have been modified. (4) Race data for 2000–2003 are for one race alone. (5) "Other" consists of American Indians, Alaska Natives, Asians, and Pacific Islanders.

U.S. Population by Race and Latino or Hispanic Origin, 1990–2000

	2000 Census		1990 Census		% increase, 1990 – 2000	
	One race only	One race or more[3]	Number	% of total pop.	Using one race only for 2000[4]	Using one race only or in combination for 2000[4]
RACE[1]						
Total U.S. population[2]	281,421,906	281,421,906	248,709,873	100.0	13.2	13.2
White	211,460,626	216,930,975	199,686,070	80.3	5.9	8.6
Black or African American	34,658,190	36,419,434	29,986,060	12.1	15.6	21.5
American Indian and Alaska Native . . .	2,475,956	4,119,301	1,959,234	0.8	26.4	110.3
Asian	10,242,998	11,898,828	6,908,638	2.8	48.3	72.2
Native Hawaiian and other Pac. Isl.	398,835	874,414	365,024	0.1	9.3	139.5
Some other race	15,359,073	18,521,486	9,804,847	3.9	56.6	88.9
HISPANIC OR LATINO AND RACE						
Total U.S. population[2]	281,421,906	281,421,906	248,709,873	100.0	13.2	13.2
Hispanic or Latino (of any race)[2]	35,305,818	35,305,818	22,354,059	9.0	57.9	57.9
Not Hispanic or Latino[2]	246,116,088	246,116,088	226,355,814	91.0	8.7	8.7
White	195,575,485	198,177,900	188,128,296	75.6	3.4	5.3
Black or African American	34,313,007	35,383,751	29,216,293	11.7	16.2	21.1
American Indian and Alaska Native . .	2,097,440	3,444,700	1,793,773	0.7	15.3	92.0
Asian	10,356,804	11,579,494	6,642,481	2.7	52.4	74.3
Native Hawaiian and other Pac. Isl. . . .	367,104	748,149	325,878	0.1	8.5	129.6
Some other race	467,770	1,770,645	249,093	0.1	87.8	610.8

(1) Because individuals could report only one race in 1990 and could report more than one race in 2000, and because of other changes in the census questionnaire, the race data for 1990 and 2000 are not directly comparable. (2) The data for total U.S. population, Hispanic or Latino population, and total Not Hispanic or Latino population are not affected by the changes cited in (1). Hispanic or Latino persons may be of any race. (3) Alone or in combination with one or more of the other five races listed. (4) Columns 5 and 6 provide, respectively, a "minimum–maximum" range for the percent increase in population for each race between 1990 and 2000.

► **IT'S A FACT:** According to data from the 2000 Census, 42.8 million people in the U.S., or about 1 out of every 6 U.S. residents, claimed to be of German or part German ancestry, the most frequently reported ancestry. Other large groups included Irish (30.5 million), African–American (24.9 million), English (24.5 million), and Mexican (18.4 million). About 20.2 million people reported their ancestry as American.

Population by State, 2000-2003

Source: Bureau of the Census, U.S. Dept. of Commerce

Rank	State	2003 population	2000 population	Percent change 2000-2003	Rank	State	2003 population	2000 population	Percent change 2000-2003
1.	California	35,484,453	33,871,653	4.8	27.	Oregon	3,559,596	3,421,432	4.0
2.	Texas	22,118,509	20,851,790	6.1	28.	Oklahoma	3,511,532	3,450,654	1.8
3.	New York	19,190,115	18,976,821	1.1	29.	Connecticut	3,483,372	3,405,584	2.3
4.	Florida	17,019,068	15,982,820	6.5	30.	Iowa	2,944,062	2,926,382	0.6
5.	Illinois	12,653,544	12,419,570	1.9	31.	Mississippi	2,881,281	2,844,656	1.3
6.	Pennsylvania	12,365,455	12,281,054	0.7	32.	Arkansas	2,725,714	2,673,398	2.0
7.	Ohio	11,435,798	11,353,143	0.7	33.	Kansas	2,723,507	2,688,814	1.3
8.	Michigan	10,079,985	9,938,480	1.4	34.	Utah	2,351,467	2,233,198	5.3
9.	Georgia	8,684,715	8,186,517	6.1	35.	Nevada	2,241,154	1,998,257	12.2
10.	New Jersey	8,638,396	8,414,347	2.7	36.	New Mexico	1,874,614	1,819,046	3.1
11.	North Carolina	8,407,248	8,046,451	4.5	37.	West Virginia	1,810,354	1,808,350	0.1
12.	Virginia	7,386,330	7,078,483	4.3	38.	Nebraska	1,739,291	1,711,265	1.6
13.	Massachusetts	6,433,422	6,349,097	1.3	39.	Idaho	1,366,332	1,293,956	5.6
14.	Indiana	6,195,643	6,080,506	1.9	40.	Maine	1,305,728	1,274,923	2.4
15.	Washington	6,131,445	5,894,141	4.0	41.	New Hampshire	1,287,687	1,235,786	4.2
16.	Tennessee	5,841,748	5,689,262	2.7	42.	Hawaii	1,257,608	1,211,537	3.8
17.	Missouri	5,704,484	5,596,683	1.9	43.	Rhode Island	1,076,164	1,048,319	2.7
18.	Arizona	5,580,811	5,130,632	8.8	44.	Montana	917,621	902,195	1.7
19.	Maryland	5,508,909	5,296,485	4.0	45.	Delaware	817,491	783,600	4.3
20.	Wisconsin	5,472,299	5,363,704	2.0	46.	South Dakota	764,309	754,844	1.3
21.	Minnesota	5,059,375	4,919,485	2.8	47.	Alaska	648,818	626,931	3.5
22.	Colorado	4,550,688	4,301,997	5.8	48.	North Dakota	633,837	642,200	−1.3
23.	Alabama	4,500,752	4,447,100	1.2	49.	Vermont	619,107	608,827	1.7
24.	Louisiana	4,496,334	4,468,958	0.6	50.	District of Columbia	563,384	572,059	−1.5
25.	South Carolina	4,147,152	4,011,848	3.4	51.	Wyoming	501,242	493,782	1.5
26.	Kentucky	4,117,827	4,042,209	1.9	**Total Resident Pop.**		**290,809,777**	**281,423,231**	**3.3**

Density of Population by State, 1930-2000

Source: Bureau of the Census, U.S. Dept. of Commerce

(per square mile, land area only)

STATE	1930	1960	1980	1990	2000	STATE	1930	1960	1980	1990	2000
AL	51.8	64.2	76.6	79.6	87.6	MT	3.7	4.6	5.4	5.5	6.2
AK*	.1	0.4	0.7	1.0	1.1	NE	18.0	18.4	20.5	20.5	22.3
AZ	3.8	11.5	23.9	32.3	45.2	NV	.8	2.6	7.3	10.9	18.2
AR	35.2	34.2	43.9	45.1	51.3	NH	51.6	67.2	102.4	123.7	137.8
CA	36.2	100.4	151.4	190.8	217.2	NJ	537.3	805.5	986.2	1,042.0	1,134.5
CO	10.0	16.9	27.9	31.8	41.5	NM	3.5	7.8	10.7	12.5	15.0
CT	328.0	520.6	637.8	678.4	702.9	NY	262.6	350.6	370.6	381.0	401.9
DE	120.5	225.2	307.6	340.8	401.0	NC	64.5	93.2	120.4	136.1	165.2
DC	7,981.5	12,523.9	10,132.3	9,882.8	9,378.0	ND	9.7	9.1	9.4	9.3	9.3
FL	27.1	91.5	180.0	239.6	296.4	OH	161.6	236.6	263.3	264.9	277.3
GA	49.7	67.8	94.1	111.9	141.4	OK	34.6	33.8	44.1	45.8	50.3
HI*	57.5	98.5	150.1	172.5	188.6	OR	9.9	18.4	27.4	29.6	35.6
ID	5.4	8.1	11.5	12.2	15.6	PA	213.8	251.4	264.3	265.1	274.0
IL	136.4	180.4	205.3	205.6	223.4	RI	649.8	819.3	897.8	960.3	1,003.2
IN	89.4	128.8	152.8	154.6	169.5	SC	56.8	78.7	103.4	115.8	133.2
IA	44.1	49.2	52.1	49.7	52.4	SD	9.1	9.0	9.1	9.2	9.9
KS	22.9	26.6	28.9	30.3	32.9	TN	62.4	86.2	111.6	118.3	138.0
KY	65.2	76.2	92.3	92.8	101.7	TX	22.1	36.4	54.3	64.9	79.6
LA	46.5	72.2	94.5	96.9	102.6	UT	6.2	10.8	17.8	21.0	27.2
ME	25.7	31.3	36.3	39.8	41.3	VT	38.8	42.0	55.2	60.8	65.8
MD	165.0	313.5	428.7	489.2	541.9	VA	60.7	99.6	134.7	156.3	178.8
MA	537.4	657.3	733.3	767.6	809.8	WA	23.3	42.8	62.1	73.1	88.6
MI	84.9	137.7	162.6	163.6	175.0	WV	71.8	77.2	80.8	74.5	75.1
MN	32.0	43.1	51.2	55.0	61.8	WI	53.7	72.6	86.5	90.1	98.8
MS	42.4	46.0	53.4	54.9	60.6	WY	2.3	3.4	4.9	4.7	5.1
MO	52.4	62.6	71.3	74.3	81.2	**U.S.**	**41.2**	**50.6**	**64.0**	**70.3**	**79.6**

* For purposes of comparison, Alaska and Hawaii are included in above tabulation for 1930, even though not states then.

25 Largest Counties, by Population, 2000-2003

Source: Bureau of the Census, U.S. Dept of Commerce

County	2003 Population	2000 Population	Percent change	County	2003 Population	2000 Population	Percent change
Los Angeles County, CA	9,871,506	9,519,330	3.7	King County, WA	1,761,411	1,737,044	1.4
Cook County, IL	5,351,552	5,376,745	−0.5	Broward County, FL	1,731,347	1,623,018	6.7
Harris County, TX	3,596,086	3,400,578	5.7	Santa Clara County, CA	1,678,421	1,682,585	−0.2
Maricopa County, AZ	3,389,260	3,072,149	10.3	Clark County, NV	1,576,541	1,375,738	14.6
Orange County, CA	2,957,766	2,846,289	3.9	New York County, NY	1,564,798	1,537,372	1.8
San Diego County, CA	2,930,886	2,813,833	4.2	Tarrant County, TX	1,559,148	1,446,219	7.8
Kings County, NY	2,472,523	2,465,525	0.3	Philadelphia County, PA	1,479,339	1,517,550	−2.5
Miami–Dade County, FL	2,341,167	2,253,779	3.9	Middlesex County, MA	1,471,724	1,466,394	0.4
Dallas County, TX	2,284,096	2,218,774	2.9	Bexar County, TX	1,471,644	1,392,931	5.7
Queens County, NY	2,225,486	2,229,379	−0.2	Suffolk County, NY	1,468,037	1,419,369	3.4
Wayne County, MI	2,028,778	2,061,162	−1.6	Alameda County, CA	1,461,030	1,443,741	1.2
San Bernardino County, CA	1,859,678	1,709,434	8.8	Cuyahoga, OH	1,363,888	1,393,845	−2.1
Riverside County, CA	1,782,650	1,545,387	15.4				

Note on least populated counties: The following are the ten smallest counties by 2003 population: Loving County, TX (64); Kalawao County, HI (135); King County, TX (310); Arthur County, NE (395); Kenedy County, TX (411); Petroleum County, MT (488); McPherson County, NE (547); Blaine County, NE (554); San Juan County, CO (565); and Thomas County, NE (682).

> **IT'S A FACT:** Between 2002 and 2003, four U.S. cities—Orlando, FL; Chula Vista, CA; Laredo, TX; and Durham, NC—were added to the Census Bureau's list of 100 most populous cities. The four that dropped off were: Des Moines, IA; Richmond, VA; Grand Rapids, MI; and Spokane, WA.

Population of 100 Largest U.S. Cities, 1850–2003

Source: Bureau of the Census, U.S. Dept. of Commerce; ranked by estimated 2003 population

Rank	City	2003	2000	1990	1980	1970	1950	1900	1850
1.	New York, NY	8,085,742	8,008,654	7,322,564	7,071,639	7,895,563	7,891,957	3,437,202	696,115
2.	Los Angeles, CA	3,819,951	3,694,742	3,485,398	2,968,528	2,811,801	1,970,358	102,479	1,610
3.	Chicago, IL	2,869,121	2,896,047	2,783,726	3,005,072	3,369,357	3,620,962	1,698,575	29,963
4.	Houston, TX	2,009,690	1,953,633	1,630,553	1,595,138	1,233,535	596,163	44,633	2,396
5.	Philadelphia, PA	1,479,339	1,517,550	1,585,577	1,688,210	1,949,996	2,071,605	1,293,697	121,376
6.	Phoenix, AZ	1,388,416	1,321,190	983,403	789,704	584,303	106,818	5,544	...
7.	San Diego, CA	1,266,753	1,223,429	1,110,549	875,538	697,471	334,387	17,700	...
8.	San Antonio, TX	1,214,725	1,151,305	935,933	785,940	654,153	408,442	53,321	3,488
9.	Dallas, TX	1,208,318	1,188,589	1,006,877	904,599	844,401	434,462	42,638	...
10.	Detroit, MI	911,402	951,270	1,027,974	1,203,368	1,514,063	1,849,568	285,704	21,019
11.	San Jose, CA	898,349	895,193	782,248	629,400	459,913	95,280	21,500	...
12.	Indianapolis, IN[1]	783,438	781,864	741,952	700,807	736,856	427,173	169,164	8,091
13.	Jacksonville, FL[1]	773,781	735,617	635,230	540,920	504,265	204,517	28,429	1,045
14.	San Francisco, CA	751,682	776,733	723,959	678,974	715,674	775,357	342,782	34,776
15.	Columbus, OH	728,432	711,265	632,910	565,021	540,025	375,901	125,560	17,882
16.	Austin, TX	672,011	656,562	465,622	345,890	253,539	132,459	22,258	629
17.	Memphis, TN	645,978	650,100	610,337	646,174	623,988	396,000	102,320	8,841
18.	Baltimore, MD	628,670	651,154	736,014	786,741	905,787	949,708	508,957	169,054
19.	Milwaukee, WI	586,941	596,974	628,088	636,297	717,372	637,392	285,315	20,061
20.	Fort Worth, TX	585,122	541,099	447,619	385,164	393,455	278,778	26,688	...
21.	Charlotte, NC	584,658	557,834	395,934	315,474	241,420	134,042	18,091	1,065
22.	El Paso, TX	584,113	563,657	515,342	425,259	322,261	130,485	15,906	...
23.	Boston, MA	581,616	589,141	574,283	562,994	641,071	801,444	560,892	136,881
24.	Seattle, WA	569,101	563,376	516,259	493,846	530,831	467,591	80,671	...
25.	Washington, DC	563,384	572,059	606,900	638,432	756,668	802,178	278,718	40,001
26.	Denver, CO	557,478	553,693	467,610	492,686	514,678	415,786	133,859	...
27.	Nashville, TN[1]	544,765	545,535	510,784	455,651	426,029	174,307	80,865	10,165
28.	Portland, OR	538,544	529,184	437,319	368,148	379,967	373,628	90,426	...
29.	Oklahoma City, OK	523,303	506,129	444,719	404,014	368,164	243,504	10,037	...
30.	Las Vegas, NV	517,017	479,639	258,295	164,674	125,787	24,624	...	...
31.	Tucson, AZ	507,658	487,341	405,390	330,537	262,933	45,454	7,531	...
32.	Long Beach, CA	475,460	461,522	429,433	361,498	358,879	250,767	2,252	...
33.	Albuquerque, NM	471,856	448,948	384,736	332,920	244,501	96,815	6,238	...
34.	New Orleans, LA	469,032	484,674	496,938	557,927	593,471	570,445	287,104	116,375
35.	Cleveland, OH	461,324	477,472	505,616	573,822	750,879	914,808	381,768	17,034
36.	Fresno, CA	451,455	428,873	354,202	217,491	165,655	91,669	12,470	...
37.	Sacramento, CA	445,335	407,018	369,365	275,741	257,105	137,572	29,282	6,820
38.	Kansas City, MO	442,768	441,545	435,146	448,028	507,330	456,622	163,752	...
39.	Virginia Beach, VA	439,467	425,257	393,069	262,199	172,106	5,390	...	...
40.	Mesa, AZ	432,376	397,776	288,091	152,404	63,049	16,790	722	...
41.	Atlanta, GA	423,019	416,441	394,017	425,022	495,039	331,314	89,872	2,572
42.	Omaha, NE	404,267	391,019	335,795	313,939	346,929	251,117	102,555	...
43.	Oakland, CA	398,844	399,484	372,242	339,337	361,561	384,575	66,960	...
44.	Tulsa, OK	387,807	393,120	367,302	360,919	330,350	182,740	1,390	...
45.	Honolulu, HI[2]	380,149	371,657	365,272	365,048	324,871	248,034	39,306	...
46.	Miami, FL	376,815	362,437	358,548	346,681	334,859	249,276	1,681	...
47.	Minneapolis, MN	373,188	382,747	368,383	370,951	434,400	521,718	202,718	...
48.	Colorado Springs, CO	370,448	360,988	281,140	215,105	135,517	45,472	21,085	...
49.	Arlington, TX	355,007	332,969	261,721	160,113	90,229	7,692	1,079	...
50.	Wichita, KS	354,617	351,150	304,011	279,838	276,554	168,279	24,671	...
51.	Santa Ana, CA	342,510	337,977	293,742	204,023	155,710	45,533	4,933	...
52.	Anaheim, CA	332,361	328,071	266,406	219,494	166,408	14,556	1,456	...
53.	St. Louis, MO	332,223	348,189	396,685	452,801	622,236	856,796	575,238	77,860
54.	Pittsburgh, PA	325,337	334,563	369,879	423,959	520,089	676,806	321,616	46,601
55.	Tampa, FL	317,647	303,463	280,015	271,577	277,714	124,681	15,839	...
56.	Cincinnati, OH	317,361	331,285	364,040	385,409	453,514	503,998	325,902	115,435
57.	Raleigh, NC	316,802	282,956	207,951	150,255	122,830	65,679	13,643	4,518
58.	Toledo, OH	308,973	313,782	332,943	354,635	383,062	303,616	131,822	3,829
59.	Aurora, CO	290,418	275,923	222,103	158,588	74,974	11,421	202	...
60.	Buffalo, NY	285,018	292,648	328,123	357,870	462,768	580,132	352,387	42,261
61.	Riverside, CA	281,514	255,175	226,505	170,591	140,089	46,764	7,973	...
62.	St. Paul, MN	280,404	286,840	272,235	270,230	309,866	311,349	163,065	1,112
63.	Corpus Christi, TX	279,208	277,496	257,453	232,134	204,525	108,287	4,703	...
64.	Newark, NJ	277,911	272,537	275,221	329,248	381,930	438,776	246,070	38,894
65.	Stockton, CA	271,466	243,771	210,943	148,283	109,963	70,853	17,506	...
66.	Bakersfield, CA	271,035	243,082	174,820	105,611	69,515	34,784	4,836	...
67.	Anchorage, AK	270,951	260,283	226,338	174,431	48,081	11,254	...	...
68.	Lexington, KY	266,798	260,512	225,366	204,165	108,137	55,534	26,369	8,159
69.	Louisville, KY	248,762	256,207	269,063	298,694	361,706	369,129	204,731	43,194
70.	St. Petersburg, FL	247,610	248,408	238,629	238,647	216,159	96,738	1,575	...
71.	Plano, TX	241,991	222,008	128,713	72,331	17,872	2,126	1,304	...
72.	Norfolk, VA	241,727	234,403	261,229	266,979	307,951	213,513	46,624	14,326
73.	Jersey City, NJ	239,097	240,055	228,537	223,532	260,350	299,017	206,433	6,856
74.	Birmingham, AL	236,620	242,790	265,968	284,413	300,910	326,037	38,415	...

Rank City	2003	2000	1990	1980	1970	1950	1900	1850
75. Lincoln, NE	235,594	225,638	191,972	171,932	149,518	98,884	40,169	...
76. Glendale, AZ	232,838	218,831	148,134	96,988	36,228	8,179	...	...
77. Greensboro, NC	229,110	224,047	183,521	155,642	144,076	74,389	10,035	...
78. Hialeah, FL	226,401	226,419	188,004	145,254	102,452	19,676	...	...
79. Baton Rouge, LA	225,090	228,520	219,531	220,394	165,921	125,629	11,269	3,905
80. Fort Wayne, IN	219,495	220,483	173,072	172,391	178,269	133,607	45,115	4,282
81. Madison, WI	218,432	208,903	191,262	170,616	171,809	96,056	19,164	1,525
82. Garland, TX	218,027	215,794	180,650	138,857	81,437	10,571	819	...
83. Scottsdale, AZ	217,989	202,596	130,069	88,364	67,823	2,032	...	...
84. Rochester, NY	215,093	219,773	231,636	241,741	295,011	332,488	162,608	36,403
85. Henderson, NV	214,852	175,406	64,942	23,376	16,400	5,717	...	...
86. Akron, OH	212,215	217,070	223,019	237,177	275,425	274,605	42,728	3,266
87. Chandler, AZ	211,299	176,643	89,862	29,673	13,763	3,799	...	...
88. Chesapeake, VA	210,834	199,184	151,976	114,486	89,580	...	...	...
89. Modesto, CA	206,872	188,864	164,730	106,963	61,712	17,389	2,024[3]	...
90. Lubbock, TX	206,481	199,572	186,206	174,361	149,101	71,747	...	...
91. Fremont, CA	204,525	203,413	173,339	131,945	100,869	...	...	...
92. Glendale, CA	200,499	194,973	180,038	139,060	133,000	96,000	...	...
93. Montgomery, AL	200,123	201,607	187,106	177,857	133,386	106,525	30,346	8,728
94. Orlando, FL	199,336	190,914	164,693	128,394	99,006	52,367	2,481	...
95. Chula Vista, CA	199,060	173,553	135,163	83,927	67,901	31,339	...	...
96. Durham, NC	198,376	187,316	136,611	100,831	95,438	71,311	6,679	...
97. Shreveport, LA	198,364	200,172	198,525	206,989	182,064	127,206	16,013	1,728
98. Laredo, TX	197,488	177,322	122,899	91,449	69,024	51,910	13,429	...
99. Yonkers, NY	197,388	196,019	188,082	195,351	204,297	152,798	47,931	...
100. Tacoma, WA	196,790	193,556	176,664	158,501	154,407	143,673	37,714	...

(1) Indianapolis, IN; Jacksonville, FL; and Nashville, TN, are parts of consolidated city–county governments. Populations of other incorporated places in the county have been excluded from the population totals shown here. For years that predate the establishment of a consolidated city–county government, city population is shown. (2) Locations in Hawaii are called "census designated places (CDPs)." Although these areas are not incorporated, they are recognized for census purposes as large urban places. Honolulu CDP is coextensive with Honolulu Judicial District within the city and county of Honolulu. (3) Estimated.

Mobility, by Selected Characteristics, 2002–2003

Source: 2003 Annual Social and Economic Supplement to Current Population Survey, Bureau of the Census, U.S. Dept. of Commerce

(numbers in thousands)

	Total no. of movers[1]	MOVED TO: Same county	MOVED TO: Diff. county, same state	MOVED TO: Diff. state	MOVED TO: Abroad		Total no. of movers[1]	MOVED TO: Same county	MOVED TO: Diff. county, same state	MOVED TO: Diff. state	MOVED TO: Abroad
Marital status						**Income[3]**					
Married, spouse present	11,570	6,327	2,304	1,192	397	Under $5,000.........	3,247	1,799	606	351	145
Married, spouse absent	728	344	116	57	82	$5,000–$9,999	3,326	1,909	656	292	92
Widowed	924	441	214	120	33	$10,000–$19,999	6,135	3,678	1,203	555	103
Divorced..........	3,549	2,168	748	322	45	$20,000–$29,999	4,901	2,951	931	529	84
Separated..........	1,153	795	187	78	34	$30,000–$39,999	3,418	2,022	714	366	49
Never married	12,731	7,492	2,444	1,275	411	$40,000–$49,999	2,013	1,131	459	183	30
						$50,000–$59,999	1,314	748	275	121	24
Educational attainment[2]						$60,000–$74,999	1,062	527	238	147	21
Less than 9th grade	1,343	849	199	87	133	$75,000–$99,999	784	406	159	81	19
Grades 9-12, no diploma	2,070	1,351	322	162	59	$100,000 and over	875	466	159	111	17
High school grad......	6,339	3,678	1,269	718	127	**Ownership status**					
Some college or AA						Owner	14,941	8,549	3,195	1,474	301
degree	5,743	3,246	1,225	590	95	Renter	25,152	14,919	4,533	2,278	968
Bachelor's degree	4,420	2,281	901	482	235	**TOTAL[4]**	**40,093**	**23,468**	**7,728**	**3,752**	**1,269**
Prof. or graduate degree	1,905	920	357	209	112						

(1) People who moved to a new residence in the 12 months preceding the survey, made in Feb.-Apr. 2003. (2) People 25 years and older. (3) People 15 years and older. (4) People 1 year and older.

U.S. Population, by Age, Sex, and Household, 2000

Source: Bureau of the Census, U.S. Dept. of Commerce; 2000 Census

	Number	%
Total population	281,421,906	100
AGE		
Under 5 years...................	19,175,798	6.8
5 to 9 years	20,549,505	7.3
10 to 14 years	20,528,072	7.3
15 to 19 years	20,219,890	7.2
20 to 24 years	18,964,001	6.7
25 to 34 years	39,891,724	14.2
35 to 44 years	45,148,527	16.0
45 to 54 years	37,677,952	13.4
55 to 59 years	13,469,237	4.8
60 to 64 years	10,805,447	3.8
65 to 74 years	18,390,986	6.5
75 to 84 years	12,361,180	4.4
85 years and over...............	4,239,587	1.5
18 years and over...............	209,128,094	74.3
Male...........................	100,994,367	35.9
Female	108,133,727	38.4
21 years and over	196,899,193	70.0

	Number	%
62 years and over	41,256,029	14.7
65 years and over	34,991,753	12.4
SEX		
Male...........................	138,053,563	49.1
Female.........................	143,368,343	50.9
HOUSEHOLDS BY TYPES		
Total Households	105,480,101	100.0
Family households (families).......	71,787,347	68.1
Married–couple families	54,493,232	51.7
Female householder, no husband present	12,900,103	12.2
Nonfamily households	33,692,754	31.9
Householder living alone	27,230,075	25.8
Householder 65 years and over ...	9,722,857	9.2
Persons living in households.......	273,643,273	97.2
Persons per household	2.59	NA
Persons living in group quarters	7,778,633	2.8
Institutionalized persons.........	4,059,039	1.4
Other persons in group quarters ..	3,719,594	1.3

NA = Not applicable.

Metropolitan Area Populations, 1990-2000

Source: Bureau of the Census, U.S. Dept. of Commerce

(MSAs ranked by Census 2000 population counts)

Metropolitan Statistical Areas (MSAs) are defined for federal statistical use by the Office of Management and Budget (OMB), with technical assistance from the Bureau of the Census. These definitions have been revised periodically, and were last modified in 2000. The list below was released in Dec. 2003. MSAs must have at least one urbanized area of 50,000 inhabitants or more, plus an adjacent area closely integrated socially and economically with the core as measured by commuting ties. A new category, Micropolitan Statistical Areas (not listed here)—must in general have at least one urban cluster with a population of at least 10,000 but no more than 50,000. Some metropolitan areas with populations of 2.5 million or more may, under certain circumstances, be subdivided into smaller groupings of counties referred to as "metropolitan divisions."

Effective June 6, 2003, the Office of Management and Budget designated 362 MSAs in the U.S. and 8 MSAs in Puerto Rico.

Applying the 2003 OMB revisions to 2000 census figures showed that the nation in that year had 49 metropolitan areas of at least 1 mil people, including 6 that had reached that size since 1990. The 49 areas had 149.2 mil people, or 53% of the U.S. population, in 2000. In all, about 236.2 mil people resided in MSAs in 2000, 83.9% of the total U.S. population. This was an increase of 28.9 mil (13.9%) since 1990.

Rank	Metropolitan Statistical Area (MSA)	Population 2000	Population 1990	Percent Change 1990-2000
1	New York–Northern New Jersey–Long Island, NY–NJ–PA	18,323,002	16,846,046	8.8
2	Los Angeles–Long Beach–Santa Ana, CA	12,365,627	11,273,720	9.7
3	Chicago–Naperville–Joliet, IL–IN–WI	9,098,316	8,182,076	11.2
4	Philadelphia–Camden–Wilmington, PA–NJ–DE	5,687,147	5,435,468	4.6
5	Dallas–Fort Worth–Arlington, TX	5,161,544	3,989,294	29.4
6	Miami–Fort Lauderdale–Miami Beach, FL	5,007,564	4,056,100	23.5
7	Washington–Arlington–Alexandria, DC–VA–MD	4,796,183	4,122,914	16.3
8	Houston–Baytown–Sugar Land, TX	4,715,407	3,767,335	25.2
9	Detroit–Warren–Livonia, MI	4,452,557	4,248,699	4.8
10	Boston–Cambridge–Quincy, MA–NH	4,391,344	4,133,895	6.2
11	Atlanta–Sandy Springs–Marietta, GA	4,247,981	3,069,425	38.4
12	San Francisco–Oakland–Fremont, CA	4,123,740	3,686,592	11.9
13	Riverside–San Bernardino–Ontario, CA	3,254,821	2,588,793	25.7
14	Phoenix–Mesa–Scottsdale, AZ	3,251,876	2,238,480	45.3
15	Seattle–Tacoma–Bellevue, WA	3,043,878	2,559,164	18.9
16	Minneapolis–St. Paul–Bloomington, MN–WI	2,968,806	2,538,834	16.9
17	San Diego–Carlsbad–San Marcos, CA	2,813,833	2,498,016	12.6
18	St. Louis, MO–IL	2,698,687	2,580,897	4.6
19	Baltimore–Towson, MD	2,552,994	2,382,172	7.2
20	Pittsburgh, PA	2,431,087	2,468,289	-1.5
21	Tampa–St. Petersburg–Clearwater, FL	2,395,997	2,067,959	15.9
22	Denver–Aurora, CO	2,179,240	1,666,883	30.7
23	Cleveland–Elyria–Mentor, OH	2,148,143	2,102,248	2.2
24	Cincinnati–Middletown, OH–KY–IN	2,009,632	1,844,917	8.9
25	Portland–Vancouver–Beaverton, OR–WA	1,927,881	1,523,741	26.5
26	Kansas City, MO–KS	1,836,038	1,636,528	12.2
27	Sacramento–Arden–Arcade–Roseville, CA	1,796,857	1,481,102	21.3
28	San Jose–Sunnyvale–Santa Clara, CA	1,735,819	1,534,274	13.1
29	San Antonio, TX	1,711,703	1,407,745	21.6
30	Orlando, FL	1,644,561	1,224,852	34.3
31	Columbus, OH	1,612,694	1,405,168	14.8
32	Providence–New Bedford–Fall River, RI–MA	1,582,997	1,509,789	4.8
33	Virginia Beach–Norfolk–Newport News, VA–NC	1,576,370	1,449,389	8.8
34	Indianapolis, IN	1,525,104	1,294,217	17.8
35	Milwaukee–Waukesha–West Allis, WI	1,500,741	1,432,149	4.8
36	Las Vegas–Paradise, NV	1,375,765	741,459	85.5
37	Charlotte–Gastonia–Concord, NC–SC	1,330,448	1,024,643	29.8
38	New Orleans–Metairie–Kenner, LA	1,316,510	1,264,391	4.1
39	Nashville–Davidson–Murfreesboro, TN	1,311,789	1,048,216	25.1
40	Austin–Round Rock, TX	1,249,763	846,227	47.7
41	Memphis, TN–MS–AR	1,205,204	1,067,263	12.9
42	Buffalo–Niagara Falls, NY	1,170,111	1,189,288	-1.6
43	Louisville, KY–IN	1,161,975	1,055,973	10.0
44	Hartford–West Hartford–East Hartford, CT	1,148,618	1,123,678	2.2
45	Jacksonville, FL	1,122,750	925,213	21.4
46	Richmond, VA	1,096,957	949,244	15.6
47	Oklahoma City, OK	1,095,421	971,042	12.8
48	Birmingham–Hoover, AL	1,052,238	956,844	10.0
49	Rochester, NY	1,037,831	1,002,410	3.5
50	Salt Lake City, UT	968,858	768,075	26.1
51	Bridgeport–Stamford–Norwalk, CT	882,567	827,645	6.6
52	Honolulu, HI	876,156	836,231	4.8
53	Tulsa, OK	859,532	761,019	12.9
54	Dayton, OH	848,153	843,835	0.5
55	Tucson, AZ	843,746	666,880	26.5
56	Albany–Schenectady–Troy, NY	825,875	809,443	2.0
57	New Haven–Milford, CT	824,008	804,219	2.5
58	Fresno, CA	799,407	667,490	19.8
59	Raleigh–Cary, NC	797,071	541,100	47.3
60	Omaha–Council Bluffs, NE–IA	767,041	685,797	11.8
61	Oxnard–Thousand Oaks–Ventura, CA	753,197	669,016	12.6
62	Worcester, MA	750,963	709,705	5.8
63	Grand Rapids–Wyoming, MI	740,482	645,914	14.6
64	Allentown–Bethlehem–Easton, PA–NJ	740,395	686,688	7.8
65	Albuquerque, NM	729,649	599,416	21.7
66	Baton Rouge, LA	705,973	623,853	13.2
67	Akron, OH	694,960	657,575	5.7
68	Springfield, MA	680,014	672,970	1.0
69	El Paso, TX	679,622	591,610	14.9
70	Bakersfield, CA	661,645	543,477	21.7

U.S. Foreign-Born Population

Source: Bureau of the Census, U.S. Dept. of Commerce; total population based on Mar. 2002 Current Population Survey

Percentage of Population That Is Foreign-Born, 1900–2003

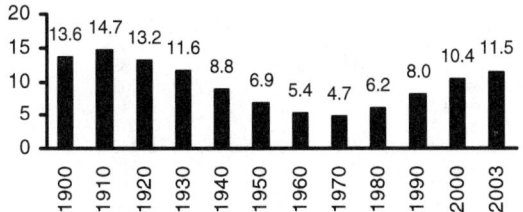

U.S. Foreign–Born Population by Regional Origin, 1995–2003

Region	2003 (thous.)	2000 (thous.)	1995 (thous.)
Europe.........	4,593	4,355	3,937
Under 18......	275	250	232
Asia...........	8,372	7,246	6,121
Under 18......	656	657	767
Latin America ...	17,840	14,477	11,777
Under 18......	1,838	1,684	1,481
Other	2,667	2,301	2,658
Under 18......	214	245	275
ALL REGIONS ..	**33,471**	**28,379**	**24,493**
Under 18	**2,984**	**2,837**	**2,726**

Foreign–Born Population: Top Countries of Origin, 1880, 1920, 1960, 1980, 2000

Source: Bureau of the Census, U.S. Dept. of Commerce

(totals in thousands; % is percent of all foreign-born)

1880 Country	No.	%	1920 Country	No.	%	1960 Country	No.	%	1980 Country	No.	%	2000 Country	No.	%
Germany .	1,967	29.4	Germany .	1,686	12.1	Italy.....	1,257	12.9	Mexico..	2,199	15.6	Mexico...	9,177	29.5
Ireland ...	1,855	27.8	Italy	1,610	11.6	Germany.	990	10.2	Germany	849	6.0	China[2] ..	1,519	4.9
Gr. Britain.	918	13.7	U.S.S.R..	1,400	10.1	Canada..	952	9.8	Canada .	843	6.0	Philippines	1,369	4.4
Canada...	717	10.7	Poland ..	1,140	8.2	Gr. Britain	765	7.9	Italy	832	5.9	India	1,023	3.3
Sweden...	194	2.9	Canada .	1,138	8.2	Poland ..	748	7.7	Gr. Britain	649	4.6	Vietnam..	988	3.2
Norway...	182	2.7	Gr. Britain	1,135	8.2	U.S.S.R..	691	7.1	Cuba ...	608	4.3	Cuba	873	2.8
France ...	107	1.6	Ireland ..	1,037	7.5	Mexico ..	576	5.9	Poland ..	418	3.0	Korea[3]...	864	2.8
China[1] ...	104	1.6	Sweden .	626	4.5	Ireland ..	339	3.5	U.S.S.R.	406	2.9	Canada ..	821	2.6
Switzerland	89	1.3	Austria ..	576	4.1	Austria ..	305	3.1	China[1]..	286	2.0	El Salvador.	817	2.6
Czech. ...	85	1.3	Mexico ..	486	3.5	Hungary .	245	2.5	Japan ..	222	1.6	Germany.	707	2.3
Total..... 6,680			**Total 13,921**			**Total.... 9,738**			**Total ... 14,080**			**Total .. 31,108**		

(1) Prior to 1980, includes Taiwan. (2) Includes Hong Kong, Taiwan, and Paracel Islands. (3) Includes N. and S. Korea.

Languages Spoken at Home by the U.S. Population[1], 2000

Source: Bureau of the Census, U.S. Dept. of Commmerce

(as of Apr. 1, in thousands; based on 2000 Census of Population and Housing)

Language	Speakers (thousands)	Language	Speakers (thousands)
Total U.S. pop. 5 years and older	**262,375**	Japanese..........................	478
Speak only English....................	215,424	Greek............................	365
Speak other language	**46,952**	Hindi	317
Spanish or Spanish Creole	28,101	Persian	312
Chinese	2,022	Urdu.............................	263
French (inc. Patois, Cajun)........	1,644	Gujarathi	236
German	1,383	Serbo-Croatian	234
Tagalog	1,224	Armenian.........................	203
Vietnamese	1,010	Hebrew	195
Italian	1,008	Mon-Khmer, Cambodian.............	182
Korean	894	Navajo	178
Russian	706	Miao, Hmong......................	168
Polish............................	667	Laotian...........................	149
Arabic...........................	615	Thai.............................	120
Portuguese or Portuguese Creole	565	Hungarian	118

(1) 5 years and older

Immigrants Admitted, by State of Intended Residence, 2002

Source: Bureau of Citizenship and Immigration Services, U.S. Dept. of Homeland Security

(fiscal year 2002)

STATE	Immigrants	STATE	Immigrants	STATE	Immigrants	STATE	Immigrants
Alabama.......	2,570	Iowa..........	5,591	New Jersey	57,721	Vermont........	1,007
Alaska........	1,564	Kansas........	4,508	New Mexico	3,399	Virginia	25,411
Arizona........	17,719	Kentucky	4,681	New York	114,827	Washington.....	25,704
Arkansas	2,535	Louisiana	3,199	North Carolina..	12,910	West Virginia....	636
California	291,216	Maine.........	1,269	North Dakota ...	776	Wisconsin	6,498
Colorado.......	12,060	Maryland	23,751	Ohio..........	13,875	Wyoming.......	281
Connecticut	11,243	Massachusetts..	31,615	Oklahoma	4,229	Guam	1,698
Delaware	1,862	Michigan	21,787	Oregon	12,125	Northern Mariana	
Dist. of Columbia	2,723	Minnesota	13,522	Pennsylvania ...	19,473	Islands......	138
Florida	90,819	Mississippi	1,155	Rhode Island ...	3,067	Puerto Rico.....	3,071
Georgia	20,555	Missouri	8,610	South Carolina..	2,966	U.S. Virgin Isls...	994
Hawaii........	5,503	Montana.......	422	South Dakota ..	902	Armed Services	
Idaho	2,236	Nebraska......	3,657	Tennessee.....	5,694	Posts........	100
Illinois.........	47,235	Nevada........	9,499	Texas.........	88,365	Other or unknown	8
Indiana	6,853	New Hampshire .	3,009	Utah..........	4,889	**Total 1,063,732**	

> ▶ **IT'S A FACT:** Based on Census 2000 data, about 1.2 million Americans claimed Arab ancestry, up by 38% from 1990. The largest Arab-American populations were in California, New York, and Michigan. Among big cities, New York had the greatest number of people claiming Arab ancestry, nearly 70,000, but they made up less than 1% of the city's total population. Dearborn, MI (total pop. 97,775), had the highest proportion of Arabs, almost 30% of its population. Among Americans reporting Arab descent, the three largest groups were from Lebanon, Egypt, and Syria.

Immigrants Admitted, by Top 50 Metropolitan Areas of Intended Residence, 2002

Source: Bureau of Citizenship and Immigration Services, U.S. Dept. of Homeland Security

(fiscal year 2002)

Metropolitan Statistical Area (MSA)	Number	Percentage	Metropolitan Statistical Area (MSA)	Number	Percentage
TOTAL immigrants admitted to U.S.	1,063,732	100.0	Sacramento, CA	8,970	0.9
Los Angeles–Long Beach, CA	100,397	9.9	Jersey City, NJ	8,204	0.8
New York, NY	86,898	8.6	Tampa–St. Petersburg–Clearwater, FL	7,947	0.8
Chicago, IL	41,616	4.1	Denver, CO	7,239	0.7
Miami, FL	39,712	3.9	West Palm Beach–Boca Raton, FL	7,183	0.7
Washington, DC–MD–VA–WV	36,371	3.6	Las Vegas, NV–AZ	7,099	0.7
Houston, TX	26,788	2.6	Baltimore, MD	6,340	0.6
San Jose, CA	25,640	2.5	Fresno, CA	5,855	0.6
Orange County, CA	24,039	2.4	Austin–San Marcos, TX	5,380	0.5
San Diego, CA	20,859	2.1	Fort Worth–Arlington, TX	5,319	0.5
Boston, MA–NH	20,769	2.0	Orlando, FL	5,317	0.5
Riverside–San Bernardino, CA	18,767	1.9	St. Louis, MO–IL	5,086	0.5
Oakland, CA	18,608	1.8	McAllen–Edinburg–Mission, TX	5,013	0.5
Dallas, TX	17,027	1.7	San Antonio, TX	4,617	0.5
Atlanta, GA	15,556	1.5	Ventura, CA	4,553	0.4
San Francisco, CA	14,685	1.4	Cleveland–Lorain–Elyria, OH	4,086	0.4
Seattle–Bellevue–Everett, WA	14,187	1.4	Honolulu, HI	3,970	0.4
Newark, NJ	13,817	1.4	El Paso, TX	3,866	0.4
Fort Lauderdale, FL	13,717	1.4	Hartford, CT	3,532	0.3
Detroit, MI	13,487	1.3	Monmouth–Ocean, NJ	3,479	0.3
Philadelphia, PA–NJ	12,925	1.3	Raleigh–Durham–Chapel Hill, NC	3,463	0.3
Nassau–Suffolk, NY	12,208	1.2	Salt Lake City–Ogden, UT	3,450	0.3
Bergen–Passaic, NJ	12,192	1.2	Columbus, OH	3,369	0.3
Middlesex–Somerset–Hunterdon, NJ	12,068	1.2	Bakersfield, CA	3,297	0.3
Phoenix–Mesa, AZ	11,738	1.2	Other MSA	180,146	17.8
Minneapolis–St. Paul, MN–WI	10,624	1.0	Unknown	62,359	6.2
Portland–Vancouver, OR–WA	9,895	1.0			

Projections of Total U.S. Population, by Age, 2010–2050

Source: Bureau of the Census, U.S. Dept. of Commerce

Age	2010 Pop.[1]	2010 % Distrib.	2020 Pop.[1]	2020 % Distrib.	2030 Pop.[1]	2030 % Distrib.	2040 Pop.[1]	2040 % Distrib.	2050 Pop.[1]	2050 % Distrib.
TOTAL	308,936	100	335,805	100	363,584	100	391,946	100	419,854	100
Under 5 years	21,426	6.9	22,932	6.8	24,272	6.7	26,299	6.7	28,080	6.7
5–14 years	40,473	13.1	44,478	13.2	47,329	13.0	50,503	12.9	54,495	13.0
15–24 years	43,012	13.9	42,229	12.6	46,639	12.8	49,721	12.7	52,869	12.6
25–34 years	41,646	13.5	45,065	13.4	44,935	12.4	49,755	12.7	52,804	12.6
35–44 years	41,121	13.3	42,816	12.8	46,676	12.8	47,008	12.0	51,796	12.3
45–54 years	44,827	14.5	40,921	12.2	42,902	11.8	46,981	12.0	47,383	11.3
55–64 years	36,186	11.7	42,732	12.7	39,378	10.8	41,629	10.6	45,721	10.9
65 years and over	40,244	13.0	54,632	16.3	71,453	19.7	80,050	20.4	86,706	20.7
85 years and over	6,123	2.0	7,269	2.2	9,603	2.6	15,409	3.9	20,861	5.0

NOTE: Estimates of U.S. population consistent with the 2000 decennial census, as enumerated. All figures shown are for July 1 of the given year, exclude Armed Forces and U.S. citizens residing overseas, and are based on middle series projections for births, deaths, and immigration. Percentage distribution may not equal 100, because of overlapping categories shown and rounding. (1) In thousands.

The Elderly U.S. Population, 1900–2030

Source: Bureau of the Census, U.S. Dept. of Commerce

Year[1]	65 AND OVER Number[2]	65 AND OVER Percent	85 AND OVER Number[2]	85 AND OVER Percent	Year[1]	65 AND OVER Number[2]	65 AND OVER Percent	85 AND OVER Number[2]	85 AND OVER Percent
1900	3,080	4.1	122	0.2	1990	31,079	12.5	3,021	1.2
1910	3,949	4.3	167	0.2	1995	33,619	12.8	3,685	1.4
1920	4,933	4.7	210	0.2	2000	34,992	12.4	4,240	1.5
1930	6,634	5.4	272	0.2	2001[3]	35,338	12.4	4,430	1.6
1940	9,019	6.8	365	0.3	2002[3]	35,608	12.4	4,570	1.6
1950	12,269	8.1	577	0.4	2003[3]	35,919	12.4	4,713	1.6
1960	16,560	9.2	929	0.5	2010[4]	40,244	13.0	6,123	2.0
1970	19,980	9.8	1,409	0.7	2020[4]	54,632	16.3	7,269	2.2
1980	25,550	11.3	2,240	1.0	2030[4]	71,453	19.6	9,603	2.6

NOTE: Figures for 1900 to 1950 exclude Alaska and Hawaii. (1) Date of Census. (2) Resident population, in thousands. (3) Estimate for July 1 of year indicated. (4) Projected.

Disability Status of the Elderly (65 and Over)[1], 2000

Source: Bureau of the Census, U.S. Dept. of Commerce

(as of Apr. 1, in thousands; based on 2000 Census of Population and Housing)

	Number	%		Number	%
Population 65 years and over	33,347	100.0	Mental disability[3]	3,593	10.8
With a disability[2]	13,978	41.9	Self-care disability[4]	3,184	9.5
Sensory disability	4,738	14.2	Go-outside-home disability[5]	6,796	20.4
Physical disability	9,546	28.6	With no disability	19,369	58.1

(1) Non-institutionalized. (2) Persons with 1 or more disabilities. (3) Learning, remembering, or concentrating. (4) Dressing, bathing, or getting around inside the home. (5) Going outside the home alone to shop or visit a doctor's office.

Young Adults Living at Home in the U.S., 1960-2002

Source: Bureau of the Census, U.S. Dept. of Commerce
(numbers in thousands)

	18–24 years old							25–34 years old					
	Male			Female				Male			Female		
YEAR	Total	At home[1]	%	Total	At home[1]	%	YEAR	Total	At home[1]	%	Total	At home[1]	%
1960....	6,842	3,583	52	7,876	2,750	35	1960	10,896	1,185	11	11,587	853	7
1970....	10,398	5,641	54	11,959	4,941	41	1970	11,929	1,129	9	12,637	829	7
1980....	14,278	7,755	54	14,844	6,336	43	1980	18,107	1,894	10	18,689	1,300	7
1985....	13,695	8,172	60	14,149	6,758	48	1985	20,184	2,685	13	20,673	1,661	8
1990....	12,450	7,232	58	12,860	6,135	48	1990	21,462	3,213	15	21,779	1,774	8
1993....	12,049	7,145	59	12,260	5,746	47	1993	20,856	3,300	16	21,007	1,844	9
1994....	12,683	7,547	60	12,792	5,924	46	1994	20,873	3,261	16	21,073	1,859	9
1995....	12,545	7,328	58	12,613	5,896	47	1995	20,589	3,166	15	20,800	1,759	8
1996....	12,402	7,327	59	12,441	5,955	48	1996	20,390	3,213	16	20,528	1,810	9
1997....	12,534	7,501	60	12,452	6,006	48	1997	20,039	2,909	15	20,217	1,745	9
1998....	12,633	7,399	59	12,568	5,974	48	1998	19,526	2,845	15	19,828	1,680	8
1999....	12,936	7,440	58	13,031	6,389	49	1999	18,924	2,636	14	19,551	1,690	9
2000....	13,291	7,593	57	13,242	6,232	47	2000	18,563	2,387	13	19,222	1,602	8
2001[2]...	13,412	7,385	55	13,361	6,068	45	2001[2]....	19,308	2,520	13	19,527	1,583	8
2002[2]...	13,696	7,575	55	13,602	6,252	46	2002[2]...19,220	19,220	2,610	14	19,428	1,618	8

(1) Includes young adults living in their parent(s)' home and unmarried college students living in a dormitory. (2) Data for 2001 and later use population controls based on Census 2000 and an expanded sample of households.

Grandchildren Living in the Home of Their Grandparents, 1970-2002

Source: Bureau of the Census, U.S. Dept. of Commerce (numbers in thousands)

		Grandchildren living with grandparents				
			WITH PARENT(S) PRESENT			
YEAR	Total children under 18	Total	Both parents present	Mother only present	Father only present	Without parent(s) present
1970	69,276	2,214	363	817	78	957
1980	63,369	2,306	310	922	86	988
1990	64,137	3,155	467	1,563	191	935
1993	66,893	3,368	475	1,647	229	1,017
1994	69,508	3,735	436	1,764	175	1,359
1995	70,254	3,965	427	1,876	195	1,466
1996	70,908	4,060	467	1,943	220	1,431
1997	70,983	3,894	554	1,785	247	1,309
1998	71,377	3,989	503	1,827	241	1,417
1999	71,703	3,919	535	1,803	250	1,331
2000	72,012	3,842	531	1,732	220	1,359
2001[1]	72,006	3,844	510	1,755	231	1,348
2002[1]	72,321	3,681	477	1,658	275	1,274

(1) Data for 2001 and 2002 are based on Census 2000 figures and an expanded sample of households.

Living Arrangements of Children, 1970-2002

Source: Bureau of the Census, U.S. Dept. of Commerce
(excludes persons under 18 years of age who maintained households or resided in group quarters)

			Percentage of children who live with—						
				MOTHER ONLY					
Race, Hispanic origin, and year	Number (1,000)	BOTH PARENTS	Total	Divorced	Married Spouse absent	Single[1]	Widowed	FATHER ONLY	NEITHER PARENT
White									
1970	58,790	90	8	3	3	Z	2	1	2
1980	52,242	83	14	7	4	1	2	2	2
1990	51,390	79	16	8	4	3	1	3	2
1998	56,118	74	18	8	4	5	1	5	3
1999	56,265	74	18	NA	NA	NA	NA	4	3
2000	56,455	75	17	NA	NA	NA	NA	4	3
2001	56,135	75	18	8	1	5	1	4	3
2002	58,276	75	18	8	1	5	1	5	3
Black									
1970	9,422	59	30	5	16	4	4	2	10
1980	9,375	42	44	11	16	13	4	2	12
1990	10,018	38	51	10	12	27	2	4	8
1998	11,407	36	51	9	9	32	1	4	9
1999	11,425	35	51	NA	NA	NA	NA	4	10
2000	11,412	38	49	NA	NA	NA	NA	4	9
2001	11,578	38	48	8	2	30	2	5	10
2002	11,646	39	48	9	2	31	1	5	8
Hispanic[2]									
1970	4,006[3]	78	NA	NA	NA	NA	NA	NA	NA
1980	5,459	75	20	6	8	4	2	2	4
1990	7,174	67	27	7	10	8	2	3	3
1998	10,857	64	27	6	8	12	1	4	5
1999	11,236	63	27	NA	NA	NA	NA	5	5
2000	11,613	65	25	NA	NA	NA	NA	4	5
2001	12,446	65	25	6	2	11	1	5	6
2002	12,817	65	25	6	2	11	1	5	5

NA = Not available. Z = Less than 0.5%. (1) Never married. (2) Hispanic persons may be of any race. (3) All persons under 18 years old.

Children by Relationship to Householder, 2000

Source: Bureau of the Census, U.S. Dept. of Commerce

(numbers in thousands)

	Total, all ages	Under 18 years					18 years and over		
		Total	Under 6	6 to 11	12 to 14	15 to 17	Total	18 to 24	25 and over
Children of householder ..	83,714	64,652	20,120	22,804	11,200	10,528	19,062	11,186	7,876
Adopted children	2,059	1,586	389	598	317	282	473	274	199
Stepchildren............	4,385	3,292	328	1,271	847	846	1,092	778	314
Biological children	77,271	59,774	19,402	20,935	10,036	9,400	17,497	10,134	7,363
Percent of age group									
Adopted children	2.5	2.5	1.9	2.6	2.8	2.7	2.5	2.4	2.5
Stepchildren............	5.2	5.1	1.6	5.6	7.6	8.0	5.7	7.0	4.0
Biological children	92.3	92.5	96.4	91.8	89.6	89.3	91.8	90.6	93.5

Block Grants for Welfare (Temporary Assistance for Needy Families), Fiscal Year 2003

Source: Office of Family Assistance, Admin. for Children and Families, U.S. Dept. of Health and Human Services

State	Total Federal and State TANF Expenditures, 2003[1]	2003 Average Monthly Expenditure per Family	2003 Average Monthly Expenditure per Recipient	2003 Average Monthly Number of Families	2003 Average Monthly Number of Recipients	2003 Average Monthly Number of Children
Alabama..........	$170,681	$754.80	$318.17	18,844	44,704	35,224
Alaska	88,140	1,376.91	483.53	5,334	15,190	10,113
Arizona...........	341,686	595.79	252.09	47,792	112,952	82,812
Arkansas	54,235	404.91	177.76	11,162	25,425	18,912
California	5,851,460	1,084.45	438.68	449,650	1,111,558	891,339
Colorado..........	236,188	1,454.26	556.14	13,534	35,391	25,833
Connecticut	449,934	1,784.23	833.87	21,014	44,964	32,097
Delaware	56,454	840.56	370.51	5,597	12,697	9,658
Dist. of Columbia	166,348	835.62	327.39	16,589	42,342	31,790
Florida	852,023	1,221.68	591.62	58,118	120,013	96,882
Georgia	500,551	745.90	311.82	55,922	133,772	103,057
Hawaii	134,070	1,142.83	434.47	9,776	25,715	18,049
Idaho	43,141	2,139.31	1,150.92	1,681	3,124	2,476
Illinois	989,412	2,175.80	840.91	37,895	98,049	80,252
Indiana	313,334	495.60	186.11	52,686	140,302	105,759
Iowa	156,099	651.44	249.35	19,969	52,170	34,905
Kansas	150,061	817.33	314.64	15,300	39,745	27,631
Kentucky	191,055	455.89	206.87	34,923	76,963	56,999
Louisiana	267,269	975.40	385.50	22,834	57,775	46,313
Maine	100,011	848.89	307.64	9,818	27,091	17,392
Maryland	365,923	1,166.82	493.51	26,134	61,789	45,966
Massachusetts......	696,664	1,175.75	532.16	49,377	109,093	76,589
Michigan..........	1,204,715	1,336.59	500.57	75,111	200,557	147,768
Minnesota.........	497,666	1,136.22	438.37	36,500	94,605	67,885
Mississippi	120,011	504.52	218.63	19,823	45,743	33,625
Missouri	298,593	609.21	244.21	40,845	101,893	73,000
Montana	55,715	752.64	268.47	6,169	17,294	11,393
Nebraska	78,906	600.77	244.67	10,945	26,876	19,354
Nevada...........	84,835	664.72	279.92	10,636	25,256	19,185
New Hampshire	72,476	993.51	426.78	6,079	14,152	9,727
New Jersey	841,684	1,653.55	683.87	42,418	102,564	77,183
New Mexico	123,013	616.11	232.55	16,638	44,081	31,241
New York	4,463,287	2,499.56	1,098.25	148,803	338,668	243,407
North Carolina	456,797	941.50	452.02	40,432	84,214	65,379
North Dakota	41,915	1,034.61	402.55	3,376	8,677	6,066
Ohio	1,006,682	995.24	447.28	84,292	187,557	139,241
Oklahoma..........	203,172	1,125.03	459.71	15,049	36,830	28,128
Oregon	225,507	1,004.50	439.87	18,708	42,722	31,500
Pennsylvania	1,108,506	1,142.49	439.04	80,855	210,405	153,753
Rhode Island	162,311	1,013.35	380.86	13,348	35,514	24,790
South Carolina	148,442	596.83	244.66	20,726	50,561	36,712
South Dakota	26,492	791.03	351.27	2,791	6,285	5,161
Tennessee	274,331	332.96	126.35	68,660	180,940	129,698
Texas	910,600	569.53	226.92	133,239	334,406	259,412
Utah	130,840	1,277.20	499.87	8,537	21,812	15,642
Vermont	66,610	1,131.32	437.03	4,907	12,701	8,132
Virginia...........	273,367	902.40	391.43	25,245	58,198	41,668
Washington	571,614	870.85	350.53	54,699	135,893	94,907
West Virginia	156,861	826.18	321.18	15,822	40,699	27,637
Wisconsin..........	489,124	1,992.18	831.53	20,460	49,019	39,209
Wyoming	NA	NA	NA	NA	NA	NA
2003 Totals	**26,339,994**	**1,092.33**	**447.99**	**2,009,468**	**4,899,677**	**3,691,479**
2002 Totals	**25,414,383**	**1,039.38**	**418.01**	**2,037,618**	**5,066,574**	**3,790,207**
2001 Totals	**25,667,381**	**1,024.57**	**400.86**	**2,087,646**	**5,335,891**	**3,968,499**
2000 Totals	**24,780,711**	**926.32**	**353.72**	**2,229,315**	**5,838,043**	**4,303,943**

NOTE: Under 1996 legislation, the Aid to Families with Dependent Children (AFDC) program was converted to this state block-grant program. (1) In thousands. FY 2003 covers period from October 2002 to September 2003. NA = Not available.

Adults Receiving TANF[1] (Welfare) Funds, by Employment Status, Fiscal Year 2002

Source: Office of Family Assistance, Admin. for Children and Families, U.S. Dept. of Health and Human Services

STATE	Adults	Employed	STATE	Adults	Employed	STATE	Adults	Employed
AL.........	9,103	26.4%	LA	12,512	27.1%	OK..........	8,714	13.7%
AK	5,623	30.1	ME..........	7,927	26.5	OR..........	10,818	12.1
AZ.........	24,556	23.6	MD..........	17,263	7.6	PA..........	54,933	19.9
AR	7,239	12.6	MA..........	32,112	13.6	Puerto Rico ...	20,388	4.5
CA.........	258,362	30.0	MI..........	52,691	31.1	RI..........	11,881	28.7
CO	8,056	20.5	MN..........	27,283	28.2	SC..........	13,141	22.9
CT	15,145	31.5	MS..........	9,922	11.6	SD..........	1,186	18.9
DE	2,945	20.6	MO..........	35,299	27.3	TN..........	45,626	15.9
DC	11,449	15.8	MT..........	5,703	24.8	TX..........	80,663	27.4
FL.........	25,604	17.2	NE..........	7,028	17.2	UT..........	5,655	25.8
GA	29,332	11.9	NV..........	6,798	5.9	VT..........	4,761	23.3
Guam	NA	NA	NH..........	4,662	27.8	Virgin Islands..	553	3.5
HI.........	9,019	36.3	NJ..........	25,125	20.4	VA..........	18,177	29.2
ID	417	21.1	NM..........	13,769	30.7	WA	42,155	30.4
IL	25,991	33.0	NY..........	121,581	23.5	WV	13,444	22.3
IN	39,922	51.8	NC..........	21,968	17.9	WI	8,537	15.4
IA	17,285	51.3	ND..........	2,384	35.6	WY	139	13.8
KS	10,417	15.1	OH..........	48,821	24.6	**U.S.........**	**1,315,029**	**25.3**
KY	20,945	19.5						

NA = Not available. (1) TANF = the state block grant program known as Temporary Assistance for Needy Families.

Marital Status of the U.S. Population, 1990-2002

Source: U.S. Bureau of the Census, Dept. of Commerce

	Total				Male				Female			
Marital status	1990	1995	2000	2002	1990	1995	2000	2002	1990	1995	2000	2002
Total..............	181.8	191.6	201.8	209.3	86.9	92.0	96.9	100.6	95.0	99.6	104.9	108.7
Never married	40.4	43.9	48.2	51.1	22.4	24.6	26.1	28.1	17.9	19.3	22.1	23.0
Married............	112.6	116.7	120.1	123.2	55.8	57.7	59.6	61.2	56.7	58.9	60.4	62.0
Widowed	13.8	13.4	13.7	14.0	2.3	2.3	2.6	2.6	11.5	11.1	11.1	11.4
Divorced...........	15.1	17.6	19.8	20.9	6.3	7.4	8.5	8.7	8.8	10.3	11.3	12.2
Percent of total												
Never married	22.2	22.9	23.9	24.4	25.8	26.8	27.0	27.9	18.9	19.4	21.1	21.2
Married............	61.9	60.9	59.5	58.9	64.3	62.7	61.5	60.9	59.7	59.2	57.6	57.1
Widowed	7.6	7.0	6.8	6.7	2.7	2.5	2.7	2.6	12.1	11.1	10.5	10.5
Divorced...........	8.3	9.2	9.8	10.0	7.2	8.0	8.8	8.6	9.3	10.3	10.8	11.3

U.S. Households Headed by Couples, 1960-2002

Source: Bureau of the Census, U.S. Dept. of Commerce

(based on 2002 Current Population Survey and earlier reports; numbers in thousands[2])

YEAR	Total U.S. households	Married-couple households	% of Total	Unmarried-couple households[1]	% of Total	YEAR	Total U.S. households	Married-couple households	% of Total	Unmarried-couple households[1]	% of Total
1960...	52,799	39,254	74	439	0.8	1991 ..	94,312	52,147	55	3,039	3.2
1970...	63,401	44,728	71	523	0.8	1992 ..	95,669	52,457	55	3,308	3.5
1980...	80,776	49,112	61	1,589	2.0	1993 ..	96,426	53,090	55	3,510	3.6
1981...	82,368	49,294	60	1,808	2.2	1994 ..	97,107	53,171	55	3,661	3.8
1982...	83,527	49,630	59	1,863	2.2	1995 ..	98,990	53,858	54	3,668	3.7
1983...	83,918	49,908	59	1,891	2.3	1996 ..	99,627	53,567	54	3,958	4.0
1984...	85,407	50,090	59	1,988	2.3	1997 ..	101,018	53,604	53	4,130	4.1
1985...	86,789	50,350	58	1,983	2.3	1998 ..	102,528	54,317	53	4,236	4.1
1986...	88,458	50,933	58	2,220	2.5	1999 ..	103,874	54,770	53	4,486	4.3
1987...	89,479	51,537	58	2,334	2.6	2000 ..	104,705	55,311	53	4,736	4.5
1988...	91,124	51,675	57	2,588	2.8	2001 ..	108,209	56,592	52	4,893	4.5
1989...	92,830	52,100	56	2,764	3.0	2002 ..	109,297	56,747	52	4,898	4.5
1990...	93,347	52,317	56	2,856	3.1						

(1) Does not include same-sex couples or families living in U.S. military barracks or emergency/homeless shelters. (2) Data may differ from Census figures.

Unmarried-Partner Households by Sex of Partners, 2000

Source: Bureau of the Census, U.S. Dept. of Commerce

(as of Apr. 1; based on 2000 Census of Population and Housing)

Household	Number	Household	Number
Total U.S. households	**105,480,101**	Female householder and female partner	293,365
Unmarried-partner households	5,475,768	Female householder and male partner	2,266,258
Male householder and male partner	301,026	All other households	100,004,333
Male householder and female partner	2,615,119		

Note: Does not include families living in U.S. military barracks or emergency/homeless shelters.

WORLD ALMANAC QUICK QUIZ

Which state had the most members in the first U.S. House of Representatives, in 1789?

(a) Virginia　　　(b) Massachusetts　　　(c) New York　　　(d) California

For the answer look in this chapter, or see page 1008.

U.S. Places of 5,000 or More Population—With ZIP and Area Codes

Source: U.S. Bureau of the Census, Dept. of Commerce; NeuStar Inc.

The following is a list of places of 5,000 or more inhabitants recognized by the Bureau of the Census, U.S. Dept. of Commerce, based on July 1, 2003, Census Bureau estimates. Also given are 1990 census populations. This list includes **places that are incorporated** under the laws of their respective states as cities, boroughs, towns, and villages, as well as boroughs in Alaska and towns in the 6 New England states, New York, and Wisconsin. Townships are not included.

When a state has more than one place with the same name, the county name is given in parentheses.

Places that the Census Bureau designates as **"census designated places"** (CDPs) are also included; these are marked (c). The Census Bureau does not calculate estimates for CDPs; for these places, the 2000 Census figure is given, in *italics*. CDP boundaries can change from one census to another.

This list also includes, in *italics*, **minor civil divisions** (MCDs), for Connecticut, Maine, Massachusetts, New Hampshire, Rhode Island, and Vermont. MCDs are not incorporated and not recognized as CDPs, but are often the primary political or administrative divisions of a county.

An **asterisk** (*) denotes that the ZIP code given is for general delivery; named streets and/or P.O. boxes within the community may differ; consult local postmaster. **Area codes** are given in parentheses. Some regions have 2 or more area codes intermixed; these are known as **overlays**. States where this occurs are noted. When 2 or more area codes are listed for one place, consult local operators for assistance. Area codes based on latest information as of Aug. 2004. For a listing in numerical order of all area codes in the U.S., Canada, and the Caribbean, see the Telecommunications chapter, page 400.

For some places listed, no area code and/or ZIP code is available. — = Not available.

Alabama

ZIP	Place	Area Code	2003	1990
35007	Alabaster	(205)	25,462	14,619
*35950	Albertville	(256)	17,891	14,507
*35010	Alexander City	(256)	14,966	14,917
36420	Andalusia	(334)	8,610	9,269
*36201	Anniston	(256)	23,750	26,638
35016	Arab	(256)	7,305	6,321
*35611	Athens	(256)	19,869	16,901
*36502	Atmore	(251)	7,497	8,046
35954	Attalla	(256)	6,394	6,859
*36830	Auburn	(334)	46,923	33,830
36507	Bay Minette	(251)	7,845	7,168
*35020	Bessemer	(205)	29,108	33,581
*35203	Birmingham	(205)	236,620	265,347
*35957	Boaz	(256)	7,628	6,928
*36426	Brewton	(251)	5,348	5,885
35243	Cahaba Heights (c)	(205)	*5,203*	4,778
*35215	Center Point (c)	(205)	*22,784*	22,658
36611	Chickasaw	(251)	6,099	6,651
35044	Childersburg	(256)	4,996	4,756
*35045	Clanton	(205)	8,096	7,669
*35055	Cullman	(256)	14,395	13,367
36526	Daphne	(251)	17,697	11,291
*36601	Decatur	(256)	54,239	49,917
36732	Demopolis	(334)	7,372	7,512
*36301	Dothan	(334)	60,036	54,131
*36330	Enterprise	(334)	21,861	20,119
*36027	Eufaula	(334)	13,651	13,220
35064	Fairfield	(205)	11,918	12,200
*36532	Fairhope	(251)	14,138	9,189
*35630	Florence	(256)	35,852	36,426
*35535	Foley	(251)	9,689	4,937
35214	Forestdale (c)	(205)	*10,509*	10,395
*35967	Fort Payne	(256)	13,279	11,838
36362	Fort Rucker (c)	(334)	*6,052*	7,593
35068	Fultondale	(205)	6,640	6,400
*35901	Gadsden	(256)	37,619	42,523
35071	Gardendale	(205)	12,106	9,251
35905	Glencoe	(256)	5,187	4,687
35235	Grayson Valley (c)	(205)	*5,447*	—
36037	Greenville	(334)	7,048	7,847
*36542	Gulf Shores	(251)	5,682	3,261
35976	Guntersville	(256)	7,533	7,038
35570	Hamilton	(205)	6,524	6,171
35640	Hartselle	(256)	12,557	11,114
35080	Helena	(205)	11,933	4,303
*35209	Homewood	(205)	24,399	23,644
*35244	Hoover	(205)	65,070	39,988
*35023	Hueytown	(205)	15,377	15,280
*35801	Huntsville	(256)	164,237	159,880
35210	Irondale	(205)	9,710	9,458
36545	Jackson	(251)	5,271	5,819
36265	Jacksonville	(256)	8,565	10,283
*35501	Jasper	(205)	13,910	13,553
35242	Lake Purdy (c)	(205)	*5,799*	1,840
36863	Lanett	(334)	7,610	8,985
35094	Leeds	(205)	10,912	10,009
*35758	Madison	(256)	34,080	14,792
35228	Midfield	(205)	5,440	5,559
36054	Millbrook	(334)	12,455	6,046
*36601	Mobile	(251)	193,464	199,973
*36460	Monroeville	(251)	6,748	6,993
*36104	Montgomery	(334)	200,123	190,350
35004	Moody	(205)	9,324	4,921
35811	Moores Mill (c)	(256)	*5,178*	3,362
*35223	Mountain Brook	(205)	19,938	19,810
*35661	Muscle Shoals	(256)	12,249	9,611
*35476	Northport	(205)	20,106	17,297
35121	Oneonta	(205)	6,034	4,844
*36801	Opelika	(334)	23,608	22,122
36467	Opp	(334)	6,426	7,011
36203	Oxford	(256)	15,470	9,537
*36360	Ozark	(334)	14,987	13,030
35124	Pelham	(205)	17,396	9,356
*35125	Pell City	(205)	10,315	7,945
*36867	Phenix City	(334)	28,444	25,311
35126	Pinson (c)	(205)	*5,033*	10,987
35127	Pleasant Grove	(205)	10,293	8,458
*36067	Prattville	(334)	26,657	19,816
36610	Prichard	(251)	27,983	34,320
35906	Rainbow City	(256)	8,760	7,667
36274	Roanoke	(334)	6,489	6,362
*35653	Russellville	(256)	8,783	7,812
36206	Saks (c)	(256)	*10,698*	11,138
36571	Saraland	(251)	12,507	11,784
36572	Satsuma	(251)	5,872	5,194
*35768	Scottsboro	(256)	14,776	13,786
*36701	Selma	(334)	19,630	23,755
35660	Sheffield	(256)	9,286	10,380
36877	Smiths (c)	(334)	*21,756*	3,456
35907	Southside	(256)	7,444	5,580
*36527	Spanish Fort	(251)	5,584	3,732
*35150	Sylacauga	(256)	12,607	12,520
*35160	Talladega	(256)	17,066	18,175
35217	Tarrant	(205)	6,775	8,046
*36582	Theodore (c)	(251)	*6,811*	6,509
36619	Tillman's Corner (c)	(251)	*15,685*	17,988
*36081	Troy	(334)	13,587	13,051
35173	Trussville	(205)	14,604	8,283
*35401	Tuscaloosa	(205)	79,294	77,866
35674	Tuscumbia	(256)	7,967	8,413
36083	Tuskegee	(334)	11,662	12,257
*36854	Valley	(334)	8,888	9,556
*35216	Vestavia Hills	(205)	30,909	19,550
*36092	Wetumpka	(334)	6,510	4,670

Alaska (907)

ZIP	Place	2003	1990
*99501	Anchorage	270,951	226,338
*99559	Bethel	5,983	4,674
99708	College (c)	*11,402*	11,249
99702	Eielson AFB (c)	*5,400*	5,251
*99701	Fairbanks	30,970	30,843
99603	Homer	5,149	3,660
*99801	Juneau	31,187	26,751
99669	Kalifornsky (c)	*5,846*	285
*99611	Kenai	7,347	6,327
*99901	Ketchikan	7,453	8,263
99654	Knik-Fairview (c)	*7,049*	272
*99615	Kodiak	6,302	6,365
99654	Lakes (c)	*6,706*	—
*99645	Palmer	5,742	2,901
*99835	Sitka	8,876	8,588
*99654	Wasilla	7,084	4,028

Arizona

ZIP	Place	Area Code	2003	1990
*85220	Apache Junction	(480)	34,027	18,092
85323	Avondale	(623)	54,710	17,595
85653	Avra Valley (c)	(520)	*5,038*	3,403
86351	Big Park (c)	(928)	*5,245*	3,024
85603	Bisbee	(520)	5,957	6,288
85326	Buckeye	(623)	8,921	4,436
*86442	Bullhead City	(928)	36,255	21,951
86322	Camp Verde	(928)	9,945	6,243
*85222	Casa Grande	(520)	29,700	19,076
85704	Casas Adobes (c)	(520)	*54,011*	—
85738	Catalina (c)	(520)	*7,025*	4,864
85718	Catalina Foothills (c)	(520)	*53,794*	—
*85225	Chandler	(480)	211,299	89,862
86503	Chinle (c)	(928)	*5,568*	5,059
86323	Chino Valley	(928)	8,816	4,837
85228	Coolidge	(520)	8,362	6,934
86326	Cottonwood	(928)	10,192	5,918
86326	Cottonwood-Verde Village (c)	(928)	*10,610*	7,037
86327	Dewey-Humboldt (c)	(928)	*6,295*	3,640
*85607	Douglas	(520)	16,556	13,908
85746	Drexel Heights (c)	(520)	*23,849*	—
85335	El Mirage	(623)	18,261	5,001

ZIP	Place	Area Code	2003	1990
85231	Eloy.	(520)	10,805	7,211
*86004	Flagstaff	(928)	55,893	45,857
85232	Florence	(520)	15,375	7,321
85705	Flowing Wells (c)	(520)	15,050	14,013
85367	Fortuna Foothills (c)	(928)	20,478	7,737
*85268	Fountain Hills	(480)	22,159	10,030
*85234	Gilbert.	(480)	145,250	29,149
*85301	Glendale.	(623)	232,838	147,070
*85501	Globe.	(928)	7,254	6,062
85219	Gold Camp (c)	(480)	6,029	—
85338	Goodyear.	(623)	31,968	6,258
*85614	Green Valley (c)	(520)	17,283	13,231
85283	Guadalupe	(480)	5,221	5,458
86025	Holbrook.	(928)	5,095	4,770
*86401	Kingman.	(928)	22,875	13,208
*86403	Lake Havasu City	(928)	49,124	24,363
85653	Marana.	(520)	20,333	2,565
*85201	Mesa.	(480)	432,376	289,199
*86440	Mohave Valley (c).	(928)	13,694	6,962
86401	New Kingman-Butler (c)	(928)	14,810	11,627
*85087	New River (c).	(623)	10,740	—
*85621	Nogales.	(520)	20,980	19,489
*85737	Oro Valley.	(520)	34,355	9,024
86040	Page.	(928)	6,923	6,598
85253	Paradise Valley.	(480)	14,169	11,903
*85541	Payson.	(928)	14,301	8,377
*85345	Peoria.	(623)	127,580	51,080
*85034	Phoenix.	(602)	1,388,416	988,015
85743	Picture Rocks (c).	(520)	8,139	4,026
*86301	Prescott.	(928)	37,576	26,592
*86314	Prescott Valley.	(928)	28,223	8,904
85242	Queen Creek	(480)	7,515	2,639
*85546	Safford.	(928)	8,956	7,359
85349	San Luis.	(928)	19,001	4,212
*85251	Scottsdale.	(480)	217,989	130,099
*86336	Sedona.	(928)	10,905	7,720
*85901	Show Low.	(928)	8,765	5,020
*85635	Sierra Vista.	(520)	39,841	32,983
85650	Sierra Vista Southeast (c).	(520)	14,348	9,237
85350	Somerton.	(928)	8,534	5,293
85713	South Tucson.	(520)	5,519	5,171
*85351	Sun City (c).	(623)	38,309	38,126
*85375	Sun City West (c).	(623)	26,344	15,997
85248	Sun Lakes (c).	(480)	11,936	6,578
*85374	Surprise.	(623)	50,585	7,122
85749	Tanque Verde (c).	(520)	16,195	—
*85282	Tempe.	(480)	158,880	141,993
85736	Three Points (c).	(520)	5,273	2,175
85353	Tolleson.	(623)	5,848	4,483
86045	Tuba City (c).	(928)	8,225	7,323
*85726	Tucson.	(520)	507,658	415,444
85735	Tucson Estates (c)	(520)	9,755	2,662
85941	Whiteriver (c).	(928)	5,220	3,775
*85390	Wickenburg.	(928)	5,345	4,515
86047	Winslow.	(928)	9,824	9,279
*85364	Yuma.	(928)	81,605	56,966

Arkansas

ZIP	Place	Area Code	2003	1990
*71923	Arkadelphia.	(870)	11,036	10,014
*72501	Batesville.	(870)	9,479	9,187
72012	Beebe.	(501)	5,407	4,809
*72714	Bella Vista (c)	(479)	16,582	9,083
*72015	Benton.	(501)	23,749	18,177
72712	Bentonville.	(479)	26,397	11,257
*72315	Blytheville.	(870)	17,092	22,523
*72022	Bryant.	(501)	12,177	5,940
72023	Cabot.	(501)	18,148	8,319
*71701	Camden.	(870)	12,520	14,701
72830	Clarksville.	(479)	8,084	5,833
*72032	Conway.	(501)	47,840	26,481
71635	Crossett.	(870)	5,919	6,282
71832	De Queen.	(870)	5,746	4,633
72065	East End (c).	(501)	5,623	—
*71730	El Dorado.	(870)	20,849	23,146
*72701	Fayetteville.	(479)	62,078	42,247
*72335	Forrest City.	(870)	14,351	13,364
*72901	Fort Smith.	(479)	81,562	72,798
72936	Greenwood.	(479)	7,493	3,984
*72601	Harrison.	(870)	12,375	9,936
*72543	Heber Springs.	(501)	6,740	5,628
72342	Helena.	(870)	5,817	7,491
*71801	Hope.	(870)	10,453	9,768
*71901	Hot Springs.	(501)	36,770	33,095
*71909	Hot Springs Village (c).	(501)	8,397	6,361
*72076	Jacksonville.	(501)	30,393	29,101
*72401	Jonesboro.	(870)	57,435	46,535
*72201	Little Rock.	(501)	184,053	175,727
72745	Lowell.	(479)	6,299	1,224
*71753	Magnolia.	(870)	10,547	11,151
*72104	Malvern.	(501)	9,011	9,236
72364	Marion.	(870)	9,108	4,405
*72113	Maumelle.	(501)	12,545	6,714
71953	Mena.	(479)	5,603	5,475
*71655	Monticello.	(870)	9,079	8,119
*72110	Morrilton.	(501)	6,532	6,551
*72653	Mountain Home.	(870)	11,405	9,027
72112	Newport.	(870)	7,386	7,459

ZIP	Place	Area Code	2003	1990
*72114	North Little Rock.	(501)	59,687	61,829
72370	Osceola.	(870)	8,335	9,165
*72450	Paragould.	(870)	22,888	18,540
*71601	Pine Bluff.	(870)	53,905	57,140
72455	Pocahontas.	(870)	6,583	6,151
*72756	Rogers.	(479)	42,795	24,692
*72801	Russellville.	(479)	24,719	21,260
*72143	Searcy.	(501)	19,714	15,180
*72120	Sherwood.	(501)	22,111	18,890
72761	Siloam Springs.	(479)	12,704	8,151
*72764	Springdale.	(479)	52,471	29,945
72160	Stuttgart.	(870)	9,398	10,420
71854	Texarkana.	(870)	28,900	22,631
72472	Trumann.	(870)	6,873	6,346
*72956	Van Buren.	(479)	20,154	14,899
71671	Warren.	(870)	6,368	6,455
72390	West Helena.	(870)	8,062	10,137
*72301	West Memphis.	(870)	28,014	28,259
72396	Wynne.	(870)	8,466	8,187

California

ZIP	Place	Area Code	2003	1990
92301	Adelanto.	(760)	20,002	6,815
*91376	Agoura Hills.	(818)	21,784	20,396
*94501	Alameda.	(510)	71,805	73,979
94507	Alamo (c)	(925)	15,626	12,277
94706	Albany.	(510)	16,400	16,327
*91802	Alhambra.	(626)	87,754	82,087
92656	Aliso Viejo.	(949)	40,450	7,612
90249	Alondra Park (c)	(310)	8,622	12,215
*91901	Alpine (San Diego Co.) (c).	(619)	13,143	9,695
*91003	Altadena (c)	(626)	42,610	42,658
95945	Alta Sierra (c)	(530)	6,522	5,709
95127	Alum Rock (c)	(408)	13,479	—
94589	American Canyon.	(707)	13,135	7,734
*92803	Anaheim.	(714)	332,361	266,406
96007	Anderson.	(530)	9,894	8,299
*94509	Antioch.	(925)	101,124	62,195
*92307	Apple Valley.	(760)	60,076	46,079
*95003	Aptos (c).	(831)	9,396	9,061
*91006	Arcadia.	(626)	55,443	48,284
*95521	Arcata.	(707)	16,891	15,211
95825	Arden-Arcade (c)	(916)	96,025	92,040
*93420	Arroyo Grande.	(805)	16,373	14,432
*90701	Artesia.	(562)	16,812	15,464
93203	Arvin.	(661)	14,009	9,286
94577	Ashland (c).	(510)	20,793	16,590
*93422	Atascadero.	(805)	27,015	23,138
94027	Atherton.	(650)	7,067	7,163
95301	Atwater.	(209)	26,515	22,282
*95603	Auburn.	(530)	12,522	10,653
95201	August (c).	(209)	7,808	6,376
93204	Avenal.	(559)	15,813	9,770
91746	Avocado Heights (c).	(626)	15,148	14,232
91702	Azusa.	(626)	46,962	41,203
*93302	Bakersfield.	(661)	271,035	176,264
91706	Baldwin Park.	(626)	78,747	69,330
92220	Banning.	(951)	27,284	20,572
*92312	Barstow.	(760)	23,073	21,472
94565	Bay Point (c).	(925)	21,534	17,453
—	Bayview-Montalvin (c).	(510)	5,004	3,988
93402	Baywood-Los Osos (c).	(805)	14,351	14,377
95903	Beale AFB (c).	(530)	5,115	6,912
92223	Beaumont.	(951)	15,083	9,685
90201	Bell.	(323)	37,694	34,365
*90706	Bellflower.	(562)	45,491	61,815
90202	Bell Gardens	(213)/(323)/(562)	74,863	42,315
94002	Belmont.	(650)	24,499	24,165
94510	Benicia.	(707)	26,941	24,437
*94704	Berkeley.	(510)	102,049	102,724
92201	Bermuda Dunes (c)	(760)	6,229	4,571
*90210	Beverly Hills	(213)/(310)/(323)	34,941	31,971
92314	Big Bear City (c).	(909)	5,779	4,920
92315	Big Bear Lake.	(909)	5,889	5,351
94526	Blackhawk-Camino Tassajara (c)	(925)	10,048	6,199
92316	Bloomington (c).	(951)	19,318	15,116
*92225	Blythe.	(760)	21,679	10,835
93637	Bonadelle Ranchos-Madera Ranchos (c).	(559)	7,300	5,705
*91902	Bonita (c).	(619)	12,401	12,542
92021	Bostonia (c).	(619)	15,169	13,670
95416	Boyes Hot Springs (c)	(707)	6,665	5,973
92227	Brawley.	(760)	22,010	18,923
*92822	Brea.	(562)/(714)	37,889	32,873
94513	Brentwood.	(925)	36,234	7,563
—	Bret Harte (c).	(209)	5,161	—
*90622	Buena Park.	(714)	78,934	68,784
*91510	Burbank (Los Angeles Co.)	(818)	103,359	93,649
—	Burbank (Santa Clara Co.) (c).	(408)	5,239	4,902
*94010	Burlingame.	(650)	27,387	26,666
*91372	Calabasas.	(818)	20,889	16,577
92231	Calexico.	(760)	32,517	18,633
*93504	California City.	(760)	11,221	5,955
92320	Calimesa.	(909)	7,633	6,654
92233	Calipatria.	(760)	7,601	2,701
94515	Calistoga.	(707)	5,254	4,468
*93010	Camarillo.	(805)	60,445	52,297
93428	Cambria (c)	(805)	6,232	5,382

ZIP	Place	Area Code	2003	1990
95682	Cameron Park (c)	(530)	14,549	11,897
*95008	Campbell	(408)	37,149	36,088
92054	Camp Pendleton North (c)	(760)	8,197	10,373
92055	Camp Pendleton South (c)	(760)	8,854	11,299
92587	Canyon Lake	(951)	10,941	9,991
95010	Capitola	(831)	9,802	10,171
*92008	Carlsbad	(760)	87,372	63,292
*95608	Carmichael (c)	(916)	49,742	48,702
*93013	Carpinteria	(805)	14,037	13,747
*90745	Carson	(310)	93,747	83,995
92077	Casa de Oro-Mt. Helix (c)	(619)	18,874	30,727
*94546	Castro Valley (c)	(510)	57,292	48,619
95012	Castroville (c)	(831)	6,724	5,272
*92235	Cathedral City	(760)	48,528	30,085
95307	Ceres	(209)	37,828	26,413
90703	Cerritos	(562)	52,800	53,244
91724	Charter Oak (c)	(626)	9,027	8,858
94541	Cherryland (c)	(510)	13,837	11,088
92223	Cherry Valley (c)	(909)	5,891	5,945
*95926	Chico	(530)	67,509	39,970
*91708	Chino	(909)	71,928	59,682
91709	Chino Hills	(909)	73,886	37,868
93610	Chowchilla	(559)	14,518	5,930
*91910	Chula Vista	(619)	199,060	135,160
91702	Citrus (c)	(626)	10,581	9,481
*95621	Citrus Heights	(916)	88,515	107,439
91711	Claremont	(909)	34,964	32,610
94517	Clayton	(925)	11,042	7,317
95422	Clearlake	(707)	14,225	11,804
95425	Cloverdale	(707)	7,480	4,924
*93612	Clovis	(559)	78,558	50,323
92236	Coachella	(760)	28,021	16,896
93210	Coalinga	(559)	16,101	8,212
92324	Colton	(909)	50,602	40,213
95932	Colusa	(530)	5,662	4,934
90022	Commerce	(323)	13,292	12,135
*90221	Compton	(310)	95,835	90,454
*94520	Concord	(925)	124,977	111,308
93212	Corcoran	(559)	21,586	13,360
96021	Corning	(530)	6,924	5,870
*91718	Corona	(951)	142,454	75,943
*92138	Coronado	(619)	23,784	26,540
*94925	Corte Madera	(415)	9,214	8,272
*92628	Costa Mesa	(714)/(949)	109,563	96,357
94931	Cotati	(707)	6,725	5,714
92679	Coto de Caza (c)	(949)	13,057	2,853
94556	Country Club (c)	(209)	9,462	9,325
*91722	Covina	(626)	48,160	43,332
95531	Crescent City	(707)	7,319	5,824
92325	Crestline (c)	(909)	10,218	8,594
90201	Cudahy	(323)	25,236	22,817
*90230	Culver City	(310)	39,788	38,793
*95014	Cupertino	(408)	50,479	39,967
90630	Cypress	(714)	47,215	42,655
*94015	Daly City	(415)/(650)	100,819	92,088
92629	Dana Point	(949)	35,745	31,896
*94526	Danville	(925)	42,547	31,306
*95616	Davis	(530)	64,348	46,322
90250	Del Aire (c)	(310)	9,012	8,040
*93215	Delano	(661)	42,801	22,762
95315	Delhi (c)	(209)	8,022	3,280
*92240	Desert Hot Springs	(760)	17,902	11,668
91765	Diamond Bar	(909)	58,160	53,672
93618	Dinuba	(559)	17,871	12,743
94514	Discovery Bay (c)	(925)	8,981	5,351
95620	Dixon	(707)	16,210	10,417
*90241	Downey	(562)	110,360	91,444
*91009	Duarte	(626)	22,196	20,716
94568	Dublin	(925)	35,581	23,229
95938	Durham (c)	(530)	5,220	4,784
93219	Earlimart (c)	(661)	6,583	5,881
90220	East Compton (c)	(310)	9,286	7,967
—	East Foothills (c)	(408)	8,133	14,898
92343	East Hemet (c)	(951)	14,823	17,611
90638	East La Mirada (c)	(562)	9,538	9,367
90022	East Los Angeles (c)	(323)	124,283	126,379
94303	East Palo Alto	(650)	31,915	23,451
91107	East Pasadena (c)	(626)	6,045	5,910
93257	East Porterville (c)	(559)	6,730	5,790
91775	East San Gabriel (c)	(626)	14,512	12,736
93524	Edwards AFB (c)	(661)	5,909	7,423
*92020	El Cajon	(619)	95,159	88,918
*92244	El Centro	(760)	37,985	31,405
94530	El Cerrito	(510)	23,339	22,869
95762	El Dorado Hills (c)	(916)	18,016	6,395
94018	El Granada (c)	(650)	5,724	4,426
*95624	Elk Grove	(916)	82,499	17,483
*91734	El Monte	(626)	121,740	106,162
*93446	El Paso de Robles	(805)	26,413	18,583
93030	El Rio (c)	(805)	6,193	6,419
90245	El Segundo	(310)	16,483	15,223
*94802	El Sobrante (c)	(510)	12,260	9,852
*94617	Emeryville	(510)	7,325	5,740
*92024	Encinitas	(760)	60,340	55,406
95320	Escalon	(209)	6,855	4,437
*92025	Escondido	(760)	136,093	108,648
*95501	Eureka	(707)	25,808	27,025
93221	Exeter	(559)	9,699	7,276
*94930	Fairfax	(415)	7,186	6,931
94533	Fairfield	(707)	102,762	78,650
95628	Fair Oaks (c)	(916)	28,008	26,867
94541	Fairview (c)	(510)	9,470	9,045
*92028	Fallbrook (c)	(760)	29,100	22,095
93223	Farmersville	(559)	9,285	6,235
*93015	Fillmore	(805)	14,949	11,992
93662	Firebaugh	(559)	6,688	4,429
90001	Florence-Graham (c)	(323)	60,197	57,147
95828	Florin (c)	(916)	27,653	24,330
*95630	Folsom	(916)	62,628	29,802
*92334	Fontana	(909)	151,903	87,535
95841	Foothill Farms (c)	(916)	17,426	17,135
92610	Foothill Ranch (c)	(949)	10,899	—
95437	Fort Bragg	(707)	6,867	6,078
95540	Fortuna	(707)	10,868	8,788
94404	Foster City	(650)	28,866	28,176
*92728	Fountain Valley	(714)	55,747	53,691
95019	Freedom (c)	(831)	6,000	8,361
*94537	Fremont	(510)	204,525	173,339
*93706	Fresno	(559)	451,455	354,091
*92834	Fullerton	(714)	131,249	114,144
95632	Galt	(209)	22,578	8,889
*90247	Gardena	(310)	59,941	51,481
95205	Garden Acres (c)	(209)	9,747	8,547
*92842	Garden Grove	(714)	167,029	142,965
*95020	Gilroy	(408)	43,817	31,487
92509	Glen Avon (c)	(951)	14,853	12,663
*91209	Glendale	(818)	200,499	180,038
*91741	Glendora	(626)	50,853	47,832
93561	Golden Hills (c)	(661)	7,434	5,423
95670	Gold River (c)	(916)	8,023	—
*93116	Goleta	(805)	28,522	—
93926	Gonzales	(831)	8,510	4,660
92324	Grand Terrace	(951)	12,205	10,946
95746	Granite Bay (c)	(916)	19,388	—
*95945	Grass Valley	(530)	11,629	9,048
93927	Greenfield	(831)	12,953	7,464
95948	Gridley	(530)	5,670	4,631
93433	Grover Beach	(805)	13,030	11,602
93434	Guadalupe	(805)	5,869	5,479
95322	Gustine	(209)	5,346	4,137
91745	Hacienda Heights (c)	(626)	53,122	52,354
94019	Half Moon Bay	(650)	12,143	8,886
*93230	Hanford	(559)	45,368	30,463
90716	Hawaiian Gardens	(562)	15,357	13,639
*90250	Hawthorne	(310)/(323)	86,173	71,349
*94544	Hayward	(510)	141,336	114,705
95448	Healdsburg	(707)	11,187	9,469
92546	Hemet	(951)	65,044	43,366
94547	Hercules	(510)	21,602	16,829
90254	Hermosa Beach	(310)	19,429	18,219
*92340	Hesperia	(760)	69,179	50,418
92346	Highland	(909)	48,516	34,439
94010	Hillsborough	(650)	10,578	10,667
*95023	Hollister	(831)	36,555	19,318
92250	Holtville	(760)	5,536	4,820
91720	Home Gardens (c)	(951)	9,461	7,780
95326	Hughson	(209)	5,498	2,918
*92647	Huntington Beach	(714)	194,248	181,519
90255	Huntington Park	(323)	63,139	56,129
93234	Huron	(559)	6,991	4,766
92251	Imperial	(760)	27,151	4,113
*91932	Imperial Beach	(619)	8,885	26,512
*92201	Indio	(760)	58,241	36,850
*90301	Inglewood	(310)/(323)	115,208	109,602
—	Interlaken (c)	(831)	7,328	6,404
95640	Ione	(209)	7,514	6,516
*92619	Irvine	(714)/(949)	170,561	110,330
93117	Isla Vista (c)	(805)	18,344	20,395
91935	Jamul (c)	(619)	5,920	2,258
94914	Kentfield (c)	(415)	6,351	6,030
93630	Kerman	(559)	9,765	5,448
93930	King City	(831)	11,323	7,634
93631	Kingsburg	(559)	10,504	7,245
*91011	La Cañada Flintridge	(818)	20,980	19,378
*91224	La Crescenta-Montrose (c)	(818)	18,532	16,968
90045	Ladera Heights (c)	(310)	6,568	6,316
94549	Lafayette	(925)	24,574	23,366
—	Laguna (c)	(916)	34,309	9,828
*92652	Laguna Beach	(949)	24,126	23,170
*92654	Laguna Hills	(949)	32,181	22,719
*92607	Laguna Niguel	(949)	64,326	44,723
—	Laguna West-Lakeside (c)		8,414	—
*92654	Laguna Woods	(949)	17,962	—
*90631	La Habra	(562)/(949)	59,703	51,263
90631	La Habra Heights	(562)	5,963	6,226
92352	Lake Arrowhead (c)	(909)	8,934	6,539
*92531	Lake Elsinore	(951)	34,914	19,733
92630	Lake Forest	(949)	76,738	56,036
92530	Lakeland Village (c)	(909)	5,626	5,159
93535	Lake Los Angeles (c)	(661)	11,523	7,977
95453	Lakeport	(707)	5,186	4,567
92040	Lakeside (c)	(619)	19,560	39,412
*90714	Lakewood	(562)	81,300	73,553
*91941	La Mesa	(619)	54,571	52,911
*90638	La Mirada	(562)/(714)	48,887	40,452
93241	Lamont (c)	(661)	13,296	11,517
*93539	Lancaster	(661)	125,896	97,300
90623	La Palma	(562)/(714)	15,903	15,392
—	La Presa (c)	(619)	32,721	—
*91747	La Puente	(626)	42,143	36,955

ZIP	Place	Area Code	2003	1990
92253	La Quinta	(760)	32,139	11,215
95401	La Riviera (c)	(916)	*10,273*	10,986
95403	Larkfield-Wikiup (c).	(707)	*7,479*	6,779
*94939	Larkspur	(415)	11,827	11,068
92688	Las Flores (c)	(949)	*5,625*	—
95330	Lathrop	(209)	12,181	6,841
91750	La Verne	(909)	33,005	30,843
*90260	Lawndale	(310)	32,490	27,331
*91945	Lemon Grove	(619)	24,935	23,984
93245	Lemoore	(559)	21,584	13,622
93245	Lemoore Station	(559)	*5,749*	0
90304	Lennox (c).	(310)	*22,950*	22,757
95648	Lincoln	(916)	23,080	7,248
95901	Linda (c)	(530)	*13,474*	13,033
93247	Lindsay	(559)	10,611	8,338
95062	Live Oak (Santa Cruz Co.) (c)	(831)	*16,628*	15,212
95953	Live Oak (Sutter Co.)	(530)	6,487	4,320
*94550	Livermore	(925)	77,744	56,741
95334	Livingston	(209)	11,484	7,317
*95240	Lodi	(209)	61,027	51,874
92354	Loma Linda	(951)	20,089	18,470
90717	Lomita	(310)	20,548	19,442
*93436	Lompoc	(805)	41,167	37,649
*90801	Long Beach	(310)/(562)	475,460	429,321
95650	Loomis	(916)	6,312	5,705
*90720	Los Alamitos	(562)/(949)	11,697	11,788
*94022	Los Altos	(650)	27,173	26,599
94022	Los Altos Hills	(650)	8,097	7,514
*90086	Los Angeles	(213)/(310)/(323)/(818)	3,819,951	3,485,557
93635	Los Banos	(209)	30,538	14,519
*95030	Los Gatos	(408)	27,976	27,357
94903	Lucas Valley-Marinwood (c)	(415)	*6,357*	5,982
90262	Lynwood	(213)/(310)/(323)	71,619	61,945
93250	Mc Farland	(661)	10,125	7,005
95521	McKinleyville (c)	(707)	*13,599*	10,749
*93638	Madera	(559)	47,952	29,283
93637	Madera Acres (c)	(559)	*7,741*	5,245
95954	Magalia (c)	(530)	*10,569*	8,987
*90265	Malibu	(310)	13,223	11,730
93546	Mammoth Lakes	(760)	7,304	4,785
*90266	Manhattan Beach	(310)	36,007	32,063
*95336	Manteca	(209)	59,500	40,773
93933	Marina	(831)	18,919	26,512
*90291	Marina del Rey (c)	(310)	*8,176*	7,431
94553	Martinez	(925)	36,595	31,800
95901	Marysville	(530)	12,498	12,324
—	Mayflower Village (c)		*5,081*	4,978
90270	Maywood	(323)	28,751	27,893
92254	Mecca	(619)	*5,402*	1,966
93640	Mendota	(559)	8,473	6,821
*94025	Menlo Park	(650)	29,811	28,403
92359	Mentone (c)	(909)	*7,803*	5,675
*95340	Merced	(209)	69,512	56,155
94030	Millbrae	(650)	20,040	20,414
*94941	Mill Valley	(415)	13,418	13,029
*95035	Milpitas	(408)	63,081	50,690
91752	Mira Loma (c)	(951)	*17,617*	15,786
93641	Mira Monte (c)	(805)	*7,177*	7,744
*92690	Mission Viejo	(949)	95,831	79,464
*95350	Modesto	(209)	206,872	164,746
*91017	Monrovia	(626)	37,996	35,733
91763	Montclair	(909)	34,776	28,434
90640	Montebello	(323)	63,747	59,564
*93940	Monterey	(831)	29,960	31,954
*91754	Monterey Park	(323)/(626)/(818)	62,213	60,738
*93021	Moorpark	(805)	35,168	25,494
*94556	Moraga	(925)	16,701	15,987
*92552	Moreno Valley	(951)	157,063	118,779
*95037	Morgan Hill	(408)	34,128	23,928
*93442	Morro Bay	(805)	10,372	9,664
*94041	Mountain View	(650)	69,366	67,365
*92564	Murrieta	(951)	66,729	18,557
92405	Muscoy (c)	(714)	*8,919*	7,541
*94558	Napa	(707)	75,560	61,865
*91950	National City	(619)	58,292	54,249
92363	Needles	(760)	5,276	5,475
94560	Newark	(510)	43,042	37,861
95360	Newman	(209)	7,874	4,158
*92658	Newport Beach	(949)	78,043	66,643
93444	Nipomo (c)	(805)	*12,626*	7,109
91760	Norco	(951)	26,265	23,302
95603	North Auburn (c)	(530)	*11,847*	10,301
94025	North Fair Oaks (c)	(650)	*15,440*	13,912
95660	North Highlands (c)	(916)	*44,187*	42,105
*90650	Norwalk	(562)	107,155	94,279
*94947	Novato	(415)	48,383	47,585
95361	Oakdale	(209)	17,440	11,978
*94617	Oakland	(510)	398,844	372,242
94561	Oakley	(925)	26,349	18,374
93445	Oceano (c)	(805)	*7,260*	6,169
*92056	Oceanside	(760)	167,082	128,090
93308	Oildale (c)	(661)	*27,885*	26,553
*93023	Ojai	(805)	8,006	7,613
95961	Olivehurst (c)	(530)	*11,061*	9,738
*91761	Ontario	(909)	167,402	133,179
95060	Opal Cliffs (c)	(831)	*6,458*	5,940
*92863	Orange	(714)	132,197	110,658
93646	Orange Cove	(559)	8,993	5,604
95662	Orangevale (c)	(916)	*26,705*	26,266
93457	Orcutt (c)	(805)	*28,830*	—
94563	Orinda	(925)	18,091	16,642
95963	Orland	(530)	6,412	5,052
93647	Orosi (c)	(559)	*7,318*	5,486
*95965	Oroville	(530)	13,137	11,885
95965	Oroville East (c)	(530)	*8,680*	8,462
*93030	Oxnard	(805)	180,872	142,560
94044	Pacifica	(650)	37,291	37,670
93950	Pacific Grove	(831)	15,444	16,117
95968	Palermo (c)	(530)	*5,720*	5,260
*93590	Palmdale	(661)	127,759	73,314
*92260	Palm Desert	(760)	45,624	23,252
*92262	Palm Springs	(760)	45,228	40,144
*94303	Palo Alto	(650)	57,233	55,900
90274	Palos Verdes Estates	(310)	13,827	13,512
*95969	Paradise	(530)	26,796	25,401
90723	Paramount	(562)	56,660	47,669
95823	Parkway-So. Sacramento (c)	(916)	*36,468*	31,903
93648	Parlier	(559)	12,358	7,938
*91109	Pasadena	(323)/(626)/(818)	141,114	131,586
	Paso Robles. See El Paso de Robles			
95363	Patterson	(209)	14,239	8,626
92509	Pedley (c)	(951)	*11,207*	8,869
*92572	Perris	(951)	41,208	21,500
*94952	Petaluma	(707)	55,175	43,166
—	Phoenix Lake-Cedar Ridge (c)		*5,123*	3,569
90660	Pico Rivera	(562)	65,317	59,177
94611	Piedmont	(510)	10,846	10,602
94564	Pinole	(510)	19,433	17,460
*93449	Pismo Beach	(805)	8,560	7,669
94565	Pittsburg	(925)	61,004	47,607
*92871	Placentia	(714)	48,210	41,259
95667	Placerville	(530)	10,123	8,286
94523	Pleasant Hill	(925)	33,859	31,583
94566	Pleasanton	(925)	65,982	50,570
*91769	Pomona	(909)	154,147	131,700
*93257	Porterville	(559)	42,484	29,521
*93041	Port Hueneme	(805)	21,837	20,322
92679	Portola Hills (c)	(949)	*6,391*	2,677
*92064	Poway	(858)	49,201	43,396
93907	Prunedale (c)	(831)	*16,432*	7,393
93551	Quartz Hill (c)	(661)	*9,890*	9,626
92065	Ramona (c)	(760)	*15,691*	13,040
*95670	Rancho Cordova (c)	(916)	*55,060*	48,731
*91729	Rancho Cucamonga	(909)	151,640	101,409
92270	Rancho Mirage	(760)	15,297	9,778
90275	Rancho Palos Verdes	(310)	42,265	41,667
91941	Rancho San Diego (c)	(619)	*20,155*	6,977
92688	Rancho Santa Margarita	(949)	49,142	11,390
96080	Red Bluff	(530)	13,690	12,363
*96049	Redding	(530)	87,579	66,176
*92373	Redlands	(909)	67,859	62,667
*90277	Redondo Beach	(310)	66,337	60,167
*94063	Redwood City	(650)	73,472	66,072
93654	Reedley	(559)	21,549	15,791
*92377	Rialto	(909)	98,091	72,395
*94802	Richmond	(510)	102,327	86,019
*93556	Ridgecrest	(760)	25,635	28,295
95003	Rio del Mar (c)	(831)	*9,198*	8,919
95673	Rio Linda (c).	(916)	*10,466*	9,481
94571	Rio Vista	(707)	6,142	3,488
95366	Ripon	(209)	12,150	7,455
95367	Riverbank	(209)	17,847	8,591
*92502	Riverside	(951)	281,514	226,546
*95677	Rocklin	(916)	46,937	18,806
94572	Rodeo (c)	(510)	*8,717*	7,589
*94928	Rohnert Park	(707)	41,871	36,326
90274	Rolling Hills Estates	(310)	7,982	7,789
93560	Rosamond (c)	(661)	*14,349*	7,430
—	Rosedale (c)	(805)	*8,445*	4,673
95401	Roseland (c)	(707)	*6,369*	8,779
91770	Rosemead	(626)	55,262	51,638
95826	Rosemont (c)	(916)	*22,904*	22,851
*95678	Roseville	(916)	98,359	44,685
90720	Rossmoor (c)	(714)	*10,298*	9,893
91748	Rowland Heights (c)	(626)	*48,553*	42,647
92519	Rubidoux (c)	(951)	*29,180*	24,367
92382	Running Springs (c)	(909)	*5,125*	4,195
*95814	Sacramento	(916)	445,335	369,365
94574	Saint Helena	(707)	6,028	4,990
95368	Salida (c)	(209)	*12,560*	4,499
*93907	Salinas	(831)	147,840	108,777
*94960	San Anselmo	(415)	12,132	11,735
*92401	San Bernardino	(909)	195,357	170,036
94066	San Bruno	(650)	39,602	38,961
*93001	San Buenaventura (Ventura)	(805)	104,140	92,557
94070	San Carlos	(650)	27,004	26,382
*92674	San Clemente	(949)	57,768	41,100
*92138	San Diego	(619)/(858)	1,266,753	1,110,623
92065	San Diego Country Estates (c).	(760)	*9,262*	6,874
91773	San Dimas	(909)	36,000	32,398
*91341	San Fernando	(818)	24,253	22,580
*94142	San Francisco	(415)	751,682	723,959
*91778	San Gabriel	(626)	40,987	37,120
93657	Sanger	(559)	20,113	16,839
*92581	San Jacinto	(951)	26,929	17,614
*95113	San Jose	(408)	898,349	782,224
*92690	San Juan Capistrano	(949)	34,796	26,183
*94577	San Leandro	(510)	80,139	68,223
94580	San Lorenzo (c)	(510)	*21,898*	19,987
*93401	San Luis Obispo	(805)	44,202	41,958

ZIP	Place	Area Code	2003	1990
*92069	San Marcos	(760)	64,242	38,974
*91109	San Marino	(626)	13,230	12,959
*94402	San Mateo	(650)	91,157	85,619
94806	San Pablo	(510)	31,041	25,158
*94915	San Rafael	(415)	55,805	48,410
94583	San Ramon	(925)	45,907	35,303
*92711	Santa Ana	(714)/(949)	342,510	293,827
*93102	Santa Barbara	(805)	88,251	85,571
*95050	Santa Clara	(408)	102,095	93,613
*91380	Santa Clarita	(661)	162,742	120,050
*95060	Santa Cruz	(831)	54,262	49,711
90670	Santa Fe Springs	(562)	17,032	15,520
*93454	Santa Maria	(805)	81,944	61,552
*90401	Santa Monica	(310)	87,162	86,905
*93060	Santa Paula	(805)	28,879	25,062
*95402	Santa Rosa	(707)	153,386	113,261
*92071	Santee	(619)	52,942	52,902
*95070	Saratoga	(408)	29,309	28,061
*94965	Sausalito	(415)	7,223	7,152
*95066	Scotts Valley	(831)	11,284	8,667
90740	Seal Beach	(562)	24,441	25,098
93955	Seaside	(831)	33,897	38,826
*95472	Sebastopol	(707)	7,732	7,008
93662	Selma	(559)	21,176	14,757
—	Shackelford (c)		5,170	
93263	Shafter	(661)	13,720	9,404
*96019	Shasta Lake	(916)	9,979	8,821
*91025	Sierra Madre	(626)	10,936	10,762
90806	Signal Hill	(562)	10,159	8,371
*93065	Simi Valley	(805)	117,115	100,218
92075	Solana Beach	(858)	12,993	12,956
93960	Soledad	(831)	25,248	13,426
*93463	Solvang	(805)	5,286	4,741
95476	Sonoma	(707)	9,521	8,168
95073	Soquel (c)	(831)	5,081	9,188
91733	South El Monte	(626)	21,776	20,850
90280	South Gate	(323)/(562)	98,966	86,284
*96151	South Lake Tahoe	(530)	23,912	21,586
95965	South Oroville (c)	(530)	7,695	7,463
*91030	South Pasadena	(213)/(323)/(626)/(818)	24,847	23,936
*94080	South San Francisco	(650)	59,415	54,312
91770	South San Gabriel (c)	(626)	7,595	7,700
91744	South San Jose Hills (c)	(626)	20,218	17,814
90605	South Whittier (c)	(562)	55,193	49,514
95991	South Yuba City (c)	(530)	12,651	8,816
*91977	Spring Valley (c)	(619)	26,663	55,331
94309	Stanford (c)	(650)	13,315	18,097
90680	Stanton	(714)	37,853	30,491
*95208	Stockton	(209)	271,466	210,943
95375	Strawberry (c)	(209)	5,302	4,377
94585	Suisun City	(707)	26,968	22,704
*92586	Sun City (c)	(951)	17,773	14,930
*94086	Sunnyvale	(408)	128,549	117,324
*96130	Susanville	(530)	17,584	12,130
93268	Taft	(661)	9,047	5,902
94941	Tamalpais-Homestead Valley (c)	(415)	10,691	9,601
94806	Tara Hills (c)	(510)	5,332	4,998
93581	Tehachapi	(661)	11,434	6,182
*92589	Temecula	(951)	76,836	27,177
91780	Temple City	(626)	36,325	31,153
95965	Thermalito (c)	(530)	6,045	5,646
*91359	Thousand Oaks	(805)	124,192	104,381
92276	Thousand Palms (c)	(760)	5,120	4,122
94920	Tiburon	(415)	8,688	7,554
*90503	Torrance	(310)	142,621	133,107
95376	Tracy	(209)	72,456	33,558
*96161	Truckee	(916)	14,930	8,848
*93274	Tulare	(559)	47,421	33,249
*95380	Turlock	(209)	63,467	42,224
*92781	Tustin	(714)/(949)	68,477	50,689
92705	Tustin Foothills (c)	(714)	24,044	24,358
*92277	Twentynine Palms	(760)	25,971	11,821
92278	Twentynine Palms Base (c)	(760)	8,413	10,606
95060	Twin Lakes (c)	(831)	5,533	5,379
95482	Ukiah	(707)	15,661	14,632
94587	Union City	(510)	69,309	53,762
*91785	Upland	(909)	72,040	63,374
*95687	Vacaville	(707)	94,121	71,476
91744	Valinda (c)	(626)	21,776	18,735
*94590	Vallejo	(707)	1119,708	109,199
92343	Valle Vista (c)	(951)	10,488	8,751
92082	Valley Center (c)	(760)	7,323	1,711
93437	Vandenberg AFB (c)	(805)	6,151	9,846
93436	Vandenberg Village (c)	(805)	5,802	5,971
	Ventura. See San Buenaventura			
*92393	Victorville	(760)	74,987	50,103
90043	View Park-Windsor Hills (c)	(310)	10,958	11,769
92861	Villa Park	(714)	6,039	6,299
—	Vincent (c)		15,097	13,713
—	Vineyard (c)		10,109	—
*93291	Visalia	(559)	100,612	75,659
*92083	Vista	(760)	91,813	71,861
—	Waldon (c)		5,133	—
*91788	Walnut	(626)	31,089	29,105
*94596	Walnut Creek	(925)	65,151	60,569
90255	Walnut Park (c)	(213)	16,180	14,722
93280	Wasco	(661)	22,476	12,412
95386	Waterford	(209)	8,038	4,771
*95076	Watsonville	(831)	46,159	31,099
90044	West Athens (c)	(310)	9,101	8,859

ZIP	Place	Area Code	2003	1990
90502	West Carson (c)	(310)	21,138	20,143
90247	West Compton (c)	(310)	5,435	5,451
*91790	West Covina	(626)	108,251	96,226
90069	West Hollywood	(310)/(323)	36,731	36,118
*91359	Westlake Village	(805)	8,575	7,455
*92685	Westminster	(714)	89,493	78,293
—	West Modesto (c)		6,096	
90047	Westmont (c)	(323)	31,623	31,044
91746	West Puente Valley (c)	(626)	22,589	20,254
*95691	West Sacramento	(916)	37,897	28,898
*90606	West Whittier-Los Nietos (c)	(562)	25,129	24,164
*90605	Whittier	(562)	85,368	77,671
92595	Wildomar (c)	(951)	14,064	10,411
95490	Willits	(707)	5,139	5,027
93060	Willowbrook (c)	(323)	34,138	32,772
95988	Willows	(530)	6,320	5,988
95492	Windsor	(707)	24,412	12,002
—	Winter Gardens (c)		19,771	—
95694	Winters	(530)	6,658	4,639
95388	Winton (c)	(209)	8,832	7,559
92502	Woodcrest (c)	(951)	8,342	7,796
93286	Woodlake	(559)	6,938	5,678
*95695	Woodland	(530)	50,988	40,230
94062	Woodside	(650)	5,256	5,034
*92885	Yorba Linda	(714)	62,358	52,422
96097	Yreka	(530)	7,204	6,948
*95991	Yuba City	(530)	48,998	27,385
92399	Yucaipa	(909)	46,171	32,819
*92286	Yucca Valley	(760)	18,301	16,539

Colorado

Area code (720) overlays area code (303). See introductory note.

ZIP	Place	Area Code	2003	1990
*80840	Air Force Academy (c)	(719)	7,526	9,062
81101	Alamosa	(719)	8,570	7,579
80401	Applewood (c)	(303)	7,123	11,069
*80004	Arvada	(303)	101,972	89,261
*81611	Aspen	(970)	5,850	5,049
*80017	Aurora	(303)	290,418	222,103
81620	Avon	(970)	6,393	1,798
—	Berkley (c)		10,743	—
80513	Berthoud	(970)	5,098	3,087
80908	Black Forest (c)	(719)	13,247	8,143
*80302	Boulder	(303)	93,051	85,127
80601	Brighton	(303)	25,459	14,203
*80020	Broomfield	(303)	42,169	24,638
80723	Brush	(970)	5,173	4,165
*81212	Canon City	(719)	15,780	12,687
81623	Carbondale	(970)	5,625	3,004
—	Castle Pines (c)	(303)	5,958	—
80104	Castle Rock	(303)	29,869	8,710
80120	Castlewood (c)	(303)	25,567	24,392
*80015	Centennial	(303)	98,586	—
80110	Cherry Hills Village	(303)	6,090	5,245
81220	Cimarron Hills (c)	(719)	15,194	11,160
81520	Clifton (c)	(970)	17,345	12,671
*80903	Colorado Springs	(719)	370,448	280,430
80120	Columbine (c)	(303)	24,095	23,969
*80022	Commerce City	(303)	26,228	16,466
81321	Cortez	(970)	8,181	7,284
*81625	Craig	(970)	9,282	8,091
81416	Delta	(970)	7,788	3,789
*80202	Denver	(303)	557,478	467,610
80022	Derby (c)	(303)	6,423	6,043
*81301	Durango	(970)	14,741	12,439
80214	Edgewater	(303)	5,356	4,613
81632	Edwards (c)	(970)	8,257	—
*80110	Englewood	(303)	32,762	29,396
80516	Erie	(303)	8,904	1,258
*80517	Estes Park	(970)	5,655	3,184
80620	Evans	(970)	15,175	5,876
*80439	Evergreen (c)	(303)	9,216	7,582
80221	Federal Heights	(303)	11,850	9,342
*80504	Firestone	(303)	5,063	1,358
*80913	Fort Carson (c)	(719)	10,566	11,309
*80525	Fort Collins	(970)	125,740	87,491
80621	Fort Lupton	(303)	7,071	5,159
80701	Fort Morgan	(970)	10,995	9,068
80817	Fountain	(719)	15,709	10,754
*80530	Frederick	(303)	5,273	988
81521	Fruita	(970)	6,751	4,045
81504	Fruitvale (c)	(303)	6,936	5,222
*81601	Glenwood Springs	(970)	8,333	6,561
*80401	Golden	(303)	17,550	13,127
*81501	Grand Junction	(970)	44,382	32,893
*80631	Greeley	(970)	83,414	60,454
*80111	Greenwood Village	(303)	12,731	7,589
80501	Gunbarrel (c)	(303)	9,435	9,388
*81230	Gunnison	(970)	5,313	4,636
80163	Highlands Ranch (c)	(303)	70,931	10,181
80534	Johnstown	(970)	5,595	1,579
80127	Ken Caryl (c)	(303)	30,887	24,391
80026	Lafayette	(303)	23,654	14,708
81050	La Junta	(719)	7,379	7,678
*80226	Lakewood	(303)	142,474	126,475
81052	Lamar	(719)	8,630	8,343
*80126	Littleton	(303)	40,599	33,711

ZIP	Place	Area Code	2003	1990
80124	Lone Tree	(303)	7,600	1,261
*80501	Longmont	(303)	79,556	51,976
80027	Louisville	(303)	18,387	12,363
*80538	Loveland	(970)	56,436	37,357
80829	Manitou Springs	(719)	5,036	4,540
*81401	Montrose	(970)	14,195	8,854
80233	Northglenn	(303)	32,943	27,195
80649	Orchard Mesa (c)	(303)	6,456	5,977
*80134	Parker	(303)	34,527	5,450
*81003	Pueblo	(719)	103,648	98,640
81007	Pueblo West (c)	(719)	16,899	4,386
81503	Redlands (c)	(970)	8,043	9,355
81650	Rifle	(970)	7,483	4,858
81201	Salida	(719)	5,494	4,737
80911	Security-Widefield (c)	(719)	29,845	23,822
80110	Sheridan	(303)	5,577	4,976
80221	Sherrelwood (c)	(303)	17,657	16,636
80122	Southglenn (c)	(303)	43,520	43,087
*80477	Steamboat Springs	(970)	9,390	6,695
80751	Sterling	(970)	12,785	10,362
—	Stonegate (c)		6,284	
80906	Stratmoor (c)	(719)	6,650	5,854
80027	Superior	(303)	10,287	255
—	The Pinery (c)	(303)	7,253	4,885
80229	Thornton	(303)	96,584	55,031
81082	Trinidad	(719)	9,152	8,580
81251	Twin Lakes (c)	(719)	6,301	—
80229	Welby (c)	(303)	12,973	10,218
80030	Westminster	(303)	103,391	74,619
*80033	Wheat Ridge	(303)	31,782	29,419
80550	Windsor	(970)	13,086	5,062
*80863	Woodland Park	(719)	6,751	4,610
80132	Woodmoor (c)	(719)	7,177	3,858

Connecticut

See introductory note.

ZIP	Place	Area Code	2003	1990
06401	Ansonia	(203)	18,818	18,403
06001	Avon	(860)	16,709	13,937
06403	Beacon Falls	(203)	5,524	5,083
06037	Berlin	(860)	19,322	16,787
06524	Bethany	(203)	5,331	—
06801	Bethel	(203)	18,566	17,541
06002	Bloomfield	(860)	19,803	19,483
06043	Bolton	(860)	5,199	—
06405	Branford	(203)	29,136	27,603
06405	Branford Center (c)	(203)	5,735	5,688
*06602	Bridgeport	(203)	139,664	141,686
*06010	Bristol	(860)	60,722	60,640
06804	Brookfield	(203)	16,037	14,113
06234	Brooklyn	(860)	7,487	6,681
06013	Burlington	(860)	8,808	7,026
06019	Canton	(860)	9,413	8,268
06040	Central Manchester (c)	(860)	30,595	30,934
06410	Cheshire	(203)	29,187	25,684
06410	Cheshire Village (c)	(203)	5,789	5,759
06413	Clinton	(860)	13,645	12,767
06415	Colchester	(860)	15,158	10,980
06237	Columbia	(860)	5,228	4,510
06340	Conning Towers-Nautilus Park (c)	(860)	10,241	10,013
06238	Coventry	(860)	12,108	10,063
06416	Cromwell	(860)	13,471	12,286
*06810	Danbury	(203)	77,353	65,585
06820	Darien	(203)	19,921	18,196
06418	Derby	(203)	12,593	12,199
06422	Durham	(860)	7,134	5,732
06423	East Haddam	(860)	8,711	6,676
06424	East Hampton	(860)	11,660	10,428
*06101	East Hartford	(860)	49,596	50,452
06512	East Haven	(203)	28,710	26,144
06333	East Lyme	(860)	18,537	15,340
06612	Easton	(203)	7,482	6,303
06088	East Windsor	(860)	10,185	10,081
06029	Ellington	(860)	13,952	11,197
*06082	Enfield	(860)	45,539	45,532
06426	Essex	(860)	6,800	5,904
*06430	Fairfield	(203)	58,407	53,418
*06032	Farmington	(860)	24,507	20,608
06033	Glastonbury	(860)	32,789	27,901
06033	Glastonbury Center (c)	(860)	7,157	7,082
06035	Granby	(860)	10,869	9,369
*06830	Greenwich	(203)	61,972	58,441
06351	Griswold	(860)	11,087	10,384
*06340	Groton	(860)	10,237	9,837
06340	Groton	(860)	40,002	45,144
06437	Guilford	(203)	22,082	19,848
06438	Haddam	(860)	7,459	6,769
*06514	Hamden	(203)	58,626	52,434
*06101	Hartford	(860)	124,387	139,739
06791	Harwinton	(860)	5,495	5,228
06248	Hebron	(860)	9,047	7,079
06037	Kensington (c)	(860)	8,541	8,306
06239	Killingly	(860)	16,940	15,889

ZIP	Place	Area Code	2003	1990
06419	Killingworth	(860)	6,373	4,814
06249	Lebanon	(860)	7,145	6,041
06339	Ledyard	(860)	15,003	14,913
06759	Litchfield	(860)	8,531	8,365
06443	Madison	(203)	18,698	15,485
*06040	Manchester	(860)	55,390	51,618
06250	Mansfield	(860)	23,324	21,103
06447	Marlborough	(860)	6,094	5,535
*06450	Meriden	(203)	58,962	59,479
06762	Middlebury	(203)	6,745	6,145
06457	Middletown	(860)	46,918	42,762
06460	Milford	(203)	52,122	48,168
06468	Monroe	(203)	19,614	16,896
06353	Montville	(860)	19,718	16,673
06770	Naugatuck	(203)	31,700	30,625
*06050	New Britain	(860)	71,572	75,491
06840	New Canaan	(203)	19,839	17,864
06812	New Fairfield	(203)	14,119	12,911
06057	New Hartford	(860)	6,548	5,769
*06511	New Haven	(203)	124,512	130,474
*06101	Newington	(860)	29,695	29,208
06320	New London	(860)	26,201	28,540
06776	New Milford	(860)	28,211	23,629
06470	Newtown	(203)	26,299	20,779
06471	North Branford	(203)	14,228	12,996
06473	North Haven	(203)	23,628	22,247
06359	North Stonington	(860)	5,165	4,907
*06856	Norwalk	(203)	84,170	78,331
06360	Norwich	(860)	36,227	37,391
06779	Oakville (c)	(860)	8,618	8,741
06371	Old Lyme	(860)	7,483	6,535
06475	Old Saybrook	(860)	10,535	9,552
06477	Orange	(203)	13,572	12,830
06478	Oxford	(203)	10,729	8,685
06379	Pawcatuck (c)	(860)	5,474	5,289
06374	Plainfield	(860)	15,174	14,363
06062	Plainville	(860)	17,461	17,392
06782	Plymouth	(860)	12,067	11,822
06480	Portland	(860)	9,264	8,418
06712	Prospect	(203)	9,161	7,775
06260	Putnam	(860)	9,079	9,031
06260	Putnam District (c)	(860)	6,746	6,835
06896	Redding	(203)	8,572	7,927
06877	Ridgefield (c)	(203)	7,212	6,363
06877	Ridgefield	(203)	24,131	20,919
06066	Rockville (c)	(860)	7,708	—
06067	Rocky Hill	(860)	18,528	16,554
06483	Seymour	(203)	16,045	14,288
06484	Shelton	(203)	39,121	35,418
06082	Sherwood Manor (c)	(860)	5,689	6,357
06070	Simsbury	(860)	23,496	22,023
06070	Simsbury Center (c)	(860)	5,603	5,577
06071	Somers	(860)	10,870	9,108
06488	Southbury	(203)	19,279	15,818
06489	Southington	(860)	41,397	38,518
06074	South Windsor	(860)	25,270	22,090
06082	Southwood Acres (c)	(860)	8,067	8,963
06075	Stafford	(860)	11,743	11,091
*06904	Stamford	(203)	120,107	108,056
06378	Stonington	(860)	18,206	16,919
06268	Storrs (c)	(860)	10,996	12,198
*06602	Stratford	(203)	50,182	49,389
06078	Suffield	(860)	14,217	11,427
06786	Terryville (c)	(860)	5,360	5,426
06787	Thomaston	(860)	7,857	6,947
06277	Thompson	(860)	9,157	8,668
06082	Thompsonville (c)	(860)	8,125	8,458
06084	Tolland	(860)	14,264	11,001
06790	Torrington	(860)	35,756	33,687
06611	Trumbull	(203)	35,013	32,016
06066	Vernon	(860)	29,206	29,841
06492	Wallingford	(203)	44,331	40,822
06492	Wallingford Center (c)	(203)	17,509	17,827
*06702	Waterbury	(203)	108,130	108,961
06385	Waterford	(860)	19,034	17,930
06795	Watertown	(860)	22,178	20,456
06498	Westbrook	(860)	6,583	5,414
*06101	West Hartford	(860)	61,424	60,110
06516	West Haven	(203)	53,004	54,021
06883	Weston	(203)	10,239	8,648
*06880	Westport	(203)	26,320	24,410
*06101	Wethersfield	(860)	26,398	25,651
06226	Willimantic (c)	(860)	15,823	14,746
06279	Willington	(860)	6,198	5,979
06897	Wilton	(203)	17,909	15,989
06094	Winchester	(860)	10,781	11,524
06280	Windham	(860)	23,014	22,039
06095	Windsor	(860)	28,565	27,817
06096	Windsor Locks	(860)	12,256	12,358
06098	Winsted	(860)	7,321	8,254
06716	Wolcott	(203)	16,024	13,700
06525	Woodbridge	(203)	9,249	7,924
06798	Woodbury	(203)	9,557	8,131
06281	Woodstock	(860)	7,685	6,008

Delaware (302)

ZIP	Place	2003	1990
19701	Bear (c)	17,593	—
19713	Brookside (c)	14,806	15,307
19703	Claymont (c)	9,220	9,800
*19901	Dover	32,808	27,630
19809	Edgemoor (c)	5,992	5,853
19805	Elsmere	5,764	5,935
19702	Glasgow (c)	12,840	—
19707	Hockessin (c)	12,902	—
19709	Middletown	6,496	3,834
19963	Milford	6,991	6,032
*19711	Newark	29,821	26,463
—	North Star (c)	8,277	—
19800	Pike Creek (c)	19,751	10,163
19973	Seaford	6,948	5,689
19977	Smyrna	6,207	5,231
*19899	Wilmington	72,051	71,529
19720	Wilmington Manor (c)	8,262	8,568

District of Columbia (202)

ZIP	Place	2003	1990
*20090	Washington	563,384	606,900

Florida

Area code (321) overlays area code (407). Area code (754) overlays (954). Area code (786) overlays (305). See introductory note.

ZIP	Place	Area Code	2003	1990
*32615	Alachua	(386)	6,759	4,667
*32714	Altamonte Springs	(407)	41,057	35,167
—	Andover (c)	(305)	8,489	6,251
33572	Apollo Beach (c)	(813)	7,444	6,025
*32712	Apopka	(407)	30,703	13,611
*34266	Arcadia	(863)	6,902	6,488
32233	Atlantic Beach	(904)	13,565	11,636
33823	Auburndale	(863)	11,956	8,846
*33160	Aventura	(305)	26,882	14,914
*33825	Avon Park	(863)	8,684	8,078
32857	Azalea Park (c)	(407)	11,073	8,926
*33830	Bartow	(863)	15,574	14,716
33154	Bay Harbor Islands	(305)	5,181	4,703
—	Bay Hill (c)	(407)	5,177	5,346
34667	Bayonet Point (c)	(727)	23,577	21,860
33505	Bayshore Gardens (c)	(941)	17,350	17,062
33589	Beacon Square (c)	(727)	7,263	6,265
34233	Bee Ridge (c)	(941)	8,744	6,406
32073	Bellair-MeadowbrookTerrace (c)	(904)	16,539	15,606
33430	Belle Glade	(561)	15,206	16,177
*32802	Belle Isle	(407)	6,242	5,272
*34420	Belleview (c)	(352)	21,201	19,386
*34465	Beverly Hills (c)	(352)	8,317	6,163
33043	Big Pine Key (c)	(305)	5,032	4,206
*33509	Bloomingdale (c)	(813)	19,839	13,912
33433	Boca Del Mar (c)	(561)	21,832	17,754
*33431	Boca Raton	(561)	78,441	61,486
*34135	Bonita Springs	(239)	36,230	13,600
33547	Boyette (c)	(813)	5,895	—
*33436	Boynton Beach	(561)	64,384	46,284
*34206	Bradenton	(941)	52,498	43,769
*33509	Brandon (c)	(813)	77,895	57,985
32503	Brent (c)	(850)	22,257	21,624
33317	Broadview Park (c)	(954)	6,798	6,109
33313	Broadview-Pompano Park (c)	(954)	5,314	5,230
*34601	Brooksville	(352)	7,436	7,589
33142	Brownsville (c)	(305)	14,393	15,607
32404	Callaway	(850)	14,639	12,253
32920	Cape Canaveral	(321)	9,509	8,014
*33902	Cape Coral	(239)	118,737	74,991
33055	Carol City (c)	(305)	59,443	53,331
*32707	Casselberry	(407)	23,707	20,736
—	Cedar Grove (c)	(850)	5,383	1,479
33401	Century Village (c)	(305)	7,616	8,363
—	Cheval (c)	(813)	7,602	—
33624	Citrus Park (c)	(813)	20,226	—
*32966	Citrus Ridge (c)	(772)	12,015	—
*33758	Clearwater	(727)	108,272	98,669
*34711	Clermont	(352)	10,577	6,910
33440	Clewiston	(863)	6,770	6,085
*32922	Cocoa	(321)	16,429	17,710
*32931	Cocoa Beach	(321)	12,432	12,123
32922	Cocoa West (c)	(321)	5,921	6,160
*33097	Coconut Creek	(954)	48,198	27,269
33064	Collier Manor-Cresthaven (c)	(954)	7,741	7,322
33801	Combee Settlement (c)	(863)	5,436	5,463
32809	Conway (c)	(407)	14,394	13,159
33328	Cooper City	(954)	28,853	21,335
*33114	Coral Gables	(305)	42,539	40,091
*33075	Coral Springs	(954)	127,005	78,864
33157	Coral Terrace (c)	(305)	24,380	23,255
33015	Country Club (c)	(305)	36,310	3,408
—	Country Walk (c)	(305)	10,653	—
*32536	Crestview	(850)	15,826	9,886
33803	Crystal Lake (c)	(863)	5,341	5,300
33157	Cutler (c)	(305)	17,390	16,201
33157	Cutler Ridge (c)	(305)	24,781	21,268
33884	Cypress Gardens (c)	(863)	8,844	9,188
33919	Cypress Lake (c)	(239)	12,072	10,491
*33525	Dade City	(352)	6,476	5,633

ZIP	Place	Area Code	2003	1990
33004	Dania Beach	(954)	28,202	—
33329	Davie	(954)	80,364	47,143
*32114	Daytona Beach	(386)	64,581	61,991
32713	De Bary	(386)	16,127	9,327
*33441	Deerfield Beach	(954)	65,694	46,997
*32433	DeFuniak Springs	(850)	5,250	5,200
*32720	De Land	(386)	21,902	16,622
*33444	Delray Beach	(561)	63,321	47,184
*32738	Deltona	(407)	76,597	49,429
*32541	Destin	(850)	11,769	8,090
32819	Doctor Phillips (c)	(407)	9,548	7,963
33178	Doral (c)	(305)	20,438	3,126
*34698	Dunedin	(727)	36,715	34,427
33610	East Lake	(813)	29,394	—
33610	East Lake-Orient Park (c)	(813)	5,703	6,171
—	East Perrine (c)	(305)	7,079	—
*32132	Edgewater	(386)	20,211	15,351
32542	Eglin AFB (c)	(850)	8,082	8,347
—	Egypt Lake-Leto (c)	(813)	32,782	—
34680	Elfers (c)	(727)	13,161	12,356
*34295	Englewood (c)	(941)	16,196	15,025
32534	Ensley (c)	(850)	18,752	16,362
33928	Estero (c)	(239)	9,503	3,177
*32726	Eustis	(352)	16,316	12,856
32804	Fairview Shores (c)	(305)	13,898	13,192
*32034	Fernandina Beach	(904)	11,059	8,765
32730	Fern Park (c)	(407)	8,318	8,294
32514	Ferry Pass (c)	(850)	27,176	26,301
32136	Flagler Beach	(386)	5,317	3,851
33034	Florida City	(305)	7,902	5,978
32960	Florida Ridge (c)	(772)	15,217	12,218
32714	Forest City (c)	(407)	12,612	10,638
*33310	Fort Lauderdale	(954)	162,917	149,238
33841	Fort Meade	(863)	5,724	5,151
*33902	Fort Myers	(239)	51,028	44,947
*33931	Fort Myers Beach	(239)	6,768	9,284
*33922	Fort Myers Shores (c)	(239)	5,793	5,460
*34981	Fort Pierce	(772)	37,841	36,830
33452	Fort Pierce North (c)	(772)	7,386	5,833
34982	Fort Pierce South (c)	(772)	5,672	5,320
*32548	Fort Walton Beach	(850)	19,936	21,407
—	Fountainbleau (c)	(305)	59,549	—
*32043	Fruit Cove (c)	(904)	16,077	5,904
34230	Fruitville (c)	(941)	12,741	9,808
33823	Fussels Corner (c)	(863)	5,313	3,840
*32602	Gainesville	(352)	109,146	91,482
33534	Gibsonton (c)	(813)	8,752	7,706
32960	Gifford (c)	(772)	7,599	6,278
33138	Gladeview (c)	(954)	14,468	15,637
33143	Glenvar Heights (c)	(305)	16,243	14,823
34116	Golden Gate (c)	(239)	20,951	14,148
33055	Golden Glades (c)	(305)	32,623	25,474
33411	Golden Lakes (c)	(561)	6,694	3,867
32733	Goldenrod (c)	(407)	12,871	12,362
32560	Gonzalez (c)	(850)	11,365	7,669
33170	Goulds (c)	(305)	7,453	7,284
—	Greater Carrollwood (c)	(813)	33,519	—
33624	Greater Northdale (c)	(813)	20,461	16,318
—	Greater Sun Center (c)	(813)	16,321	—
33454	Greenacres	(561)	31,111	18,683
32043	Green Cove Springs	(904)	5,671	4,497
*32561	Gulf Breeze	(850)	6,199	5,530
33581	Gulf Gate Estates (c)	(941)	11,647	11,622
33737	Gulfport	(727)	12,586	11,709
*33844	Haines City	(863)	13,956	11,683
*33009	Hallandale Beach	(305)/(954)	35,369	30,997
33434	Hamptons at Boca Raton (c)	(561)	11,306	11,686
34442	Hernando (c)	(352)	8,253	2,103
*33010	Hialeah	(305)	226,401	188,008
33016	Hialeah Gardens	(305)	19,867	7,727
33455	Hobe Sound (c)	(772)	11,376	11,507
*34689	Holiday (c)	(727)	21,904	19,360
32125	Holly Hill	(386)	12,586	11,141
*33022	Hollywood	(954)	143,408	121,720
34218	Holmes Beach	(941)	5,008	4,826
*33030	Homestead	(305)	34,182	26,694
34447	Homosassa Springs (c)	(352)	12,458	6,271
*34667	Hudson (c)	(727)	12,765	7,344
—	Hunters Creek (c)	(407)	9,369	—
*34142	Immokalee (c)	(239)	19,763	14,120
32937	Indian Harbour Beach	(321)	8,462	6,933
32963	Indian River Estates (c)	(772)	5,793	4,858
33785	Indian Rocks Beach	(727)	5,152	3,963
34956	Indiantown (c)	(772)	5,588	4,794
*34450	Inverness	(352)	7,184	5,797
—	Inverness Highlands South (c)	(352)	5,781	—
33880	Inwood (c)	(863)	6,925	6,824
33908	Iona (c)	(239)	11,756	9,565
33036	Islamorada, Village of Islands	(305)	6,812	1,220
33162	Ives Estates (c)	(305)	17,586	13,531
*32203	Jacksonville	(904)	773,781	635,230
*32250	Jacksonville Beach	(904)	21,339	17,839
33880	Jan Phyl Village (c)	(863)	5,633	5,308
33568	Jasmine Estates (c)	(727)	18,213	17,136
*34957	Jensen Beach (c)	(772)	11,100	9,884
*33458	Jupiter	(561)	45,100	26,753
33183	Kendale Lakes (c)	(305)	56,901	48,524
33256	Kendall (c)	(305)	75,226	87,271
—	Kendall West (c)	(305)	38,034	—

ZIP	Place	Area Code	2003	1990
33149	Key Biscayne	(305)	10,319	8,854
33037	Key Largo (c)	(305)	11,886	11,336
—	Keystone (c)	(813)	14,627	—
*33040	Key West	(305)	25,031	24,832
*33573	Kings Point (c)	(305)	12,207	12,422
*34744	Kissimmee	(407)	54,598	30,337
*32159	Lady Lake	(352)	12,740	8,071
—	Lake Butter (c)		7,062	—
*32055	Lake City	(386)	10,471	9,626
*33804	Lakeland	(863)	87,860	70,576
33801	Lakeland Highlands (c)	(863)	12,557	9,972
32569	Lake Lorraine (c)	(850)	7,106	6,779
33054	Lake Lucerne (c)	(305)	9,132	9,478
33612	Lake Magdalene (c)	(813)	28,755	15,973
*32746	Lake Mary	(407)	13,260	5,929
33403	Lake Park	(561)	9,158	6,704
—	Lakes by the Bay (c)	(305)	9,055	5,615
32073	Lakeside (c)	(904)	30,927	29,137
*33853	Lake Wales	(863)	11,194	9,670
34951	Lakewood Park (c)	(772)	10,458	7,211
*33461	Lake Worth	(561)	35,612	28,564
—	Lake Worth Corridor (c)		18,663	—
34639	Land O'Lakes (c)	(813)	20,971	7,892
33465	Lantana	(561)	9,665	8,392
*33770	Largo	(727)	71,166	65,910
33062	Lauderdale-by-the-Sea	(954)	5,895	4,014
33313	Lauderdale Lakes	(954)	31,571	27,341
33313	Lauderhill	(954)	59,096	49,015
34272	Laurel (c)	(941)	8,393	8,245
*34461	Lecanto (c)	(352)	5,161	1,243
*34748	Leesburg	(352)	17,216	14,783
*33936	Lehigh Acres (c)	(239)	33,430	13,611
33033	Leisure City (c)	(305)	22,152	19,379
33074	Lighthouse Point	(954)	11,112	10,378
*32060	Live Oak	(386)	6,670	6,332
32860	Lockhart (c)	(407)	12,944	11,636
34228	Longboat Key	(941)	7,478	5,937
*32750	Longwood	(407)	13,674	13,316
*33549	Lutz (c)	(813)	17,081	10,552
32444	Lynn Haven	(850)	14,238	9,270
33919	McGregor (c)	(239)	7,136	6,504
*32751	Maitland	(407)	11,857	8,932
33550	Mango (c)	(813)	8,842	8,700
33050	Marathon	(305)	10,143	8,857
*34145	Marco Island	(239)	15,410	—
33093	Margate	(954)	54,954	42,985
*32446	Marianna	(850)	6,112	6,292
32824	Meadow Woods (c)	(407)	11,286	4,876
33811	Medulla (c)	(863)	6,637	3,977
*32901	Melbourne	(321)	74,545	60,034
32666	Melrose Park (c)	(954)	7,114	6,477
33561	Memphis (c)	(941)	7,264	6,760
*32953	Merritt Island (c)	(321)	36,090	32,886
*33101	Miami	(305)	376,815	358,648
*33152	Miami Beach	(305)	89,312	92,639
33014	Miami Lakes	(305)	22,666	12,750
33153	Miami Shores	(305)	10,234	10,084
33266	Miami Springs	(305)	13,585	13,268
32976	Micco (c)	(772)	9,498	8,757
*32068	Middleburg (c)	(904)	10,338	6,223
*32570	Milton	(850)	7,740	7,216
32754	Mims (c)	(321)	9,147	9,412
34755	Minneola	(352)	6,151	1,515
33023	Miramar	(954)	96,646	40,663
*32757	Mount Dora	(352)	10,284	7,294
32526	Myrtle Grove (c)	(850)	17,211	17,402
*34102	Naples	(239)	21,284	19,505
34113	Naples Manor (c)	(239)	5,186	4,574
34102	Naples Park (c)	(239)	6,741	8,002
32266	Neptune Beach	(904)	7,179	6,816
*34653	New Port Richey	(727)	16,711	14,044
33552	New Port Richey East (c)	(727)	9,916	9,683
*32168	New Smyrna Beach	(386)	20,742	16,549
*32578	Niceville	(850)	12,235	10,509
33269	Norland (c)	(305)	22,995	22,109
33308	North Andrews Gardens (c)	(954)	9,656	9,002
33141	North Bay Village	(305)	6,798	5,383
33918	North Fort Myers (c)	(239)	40,214	30,027
33068	North Lauderdale	(954)	33,534	26,473
33261	North Miami	(305)	59,310	50,001
33160	North Miami Beach	(305)	40,345	35,361
33408	North Palm Beach	(561)	12,612	11,538
*34287	North Port	(941)	30,945	11,973
34234	North Sarasota (c)	(941)	6,738	6,702
33307	Oakland Park	(305)	31,462	26,326
33860	Oak Ridge (c)	(407)	22,349	15,388
*34478	Ocala	(352)	47,921	42,045
32548	Ocean City (c)	(850)	5,594	5,422
34761	Ocoee	(407)	27,133	12,778
33163	Ojus (c)	(305)	16,642	15,519
*34972	Okeechobee	(863)	5,563	4,943
34677	Oldsmar	(813)	13,609	8,361
33265	Olympia Heights (c)	(305)	13,452	37,792
*33054	Opa-Locka	(305)	14,794	15,283
33054	Opa-Locka North (c)	(305)	6,224	6,568
*32763	Orange City	(386)	6,702	5,372
*32073	Orange Park	(904)	9,210	9,488
*32802	Orlando	(407)	199,336	164,674
*32861	Orlo Vista (c)	(407)	6,047	5,990
*32174	Ormond Beach	(386)	37,617	29,721

ZIP	Place	Area Code	2003	1990
32074	Ormond By-The-Sea (c)	(386)	8,430	8,157
*32765	Oviedo	(407)	27,940	11,114
32571	Pace (c)	(850)	7,393	6,277
33476	Pahokee	(561)	6,263	6,822
*32177	Palatka	(386)	10,462	10,447
*32905	Palm Bay	(321)	85,076	62,543
33480	Palm Beach	(561)	9,759	9,814
33408	Palm Beach Gardens	(561)	41,834	24,139
*34990	Palm City (c)	(772)	20,097	3,925
*32135	Palm Coast	(386)	37,266	14,287
*34221	Palmetto	(941)	12,767	9,268
33157	Palmetto Estates (c)	(305)	13,675	12,293
*34683	Palm Harbor (c)	(727)	59,248	50,256
*33601	Palm River-Clair Mel (c)	(813)	17,589	13,691
33460	Palm Springs	(561)	13,673	9,763
33012	Palm Springs North (c)	(305)	5,460	5,300
32082	Palm Valley (c)	(904)	19,860	9,960
*32401	Panama City	(850)	37,085	34,396
32417	Panama City Beach	(850)	8,290	4,051
33060	Parkland	(954)	19,861	3,773
34108	Pelican Bay (c)		5,686	—
33021	Pembroke Park	(954)	5,651	4,933
33029	Pembroke Pines	(954)	148,927	65,566
*32502	Pensacola	(850)	54,897	59,198
*32347	Perry	(850)	6,749	7,151
32859	Pine Castle (c)	(407)	8,803	8,276
33156	Pinecrest	(305)	19,507	—
32858	Pine Hills (c)	(407)	41,764	35,322
33324	Pine Island Ridge (c)	(954)	5,199	5,244
*33781	Pinellas Park	(727)	46,449	43,571
*34465	Pine Ridge (c)	(352)	5,490	—
33168	Pinewood (c)	(305)	16,523	15,518
33318	Plantation	(954)	84,929	66,814
*33566	Plant City	(813)	31,117	22,754
*34758	Poinciana (c)	(407)	13,647	—
*33060	Pompano Beach	(954)	88,064	72,411
33064	Pompano Beach Highlands (c)	(954)	6,505	17,915
*33952	Port Charlotte (c)	(941)	46,451	41,535
32129	Port Orange	(904)	50,930	35,399
32927	Port St. John (c)	(321)	12,112	8,933
*34981	Port St. Lucie	(772)	105,507	55,761
34983	Port St. Lucie-River Park (c)	(772)	5,175	4,874
34992	Port Salerno (c)	(772)	10,141	7,786
*33032	Princeton (c)	(305)	10,090	7,073
*33950	Punta Gorda	(941)	16,720	10,637
*32351	Quincy	(850)	6,915	7,452
33156	Richmond Heights (c)	(305)	8,479	8,583
—	Richmond West (c)	(305)	28,082	—
34231	Ridge Wood Heights (c)	(941)	5,028	4,851
*33569	Riverview (c)	(813)	12,035	6,478
33419	Riviera Beach	(561)	31,733	27,646
*32955	Rockledge	(321)	22,239	16,023
33947	Rotonda (c)	(941)	6,574	3,576
33411	Royal Palm Beach	(561)	28,506	15,532
33570	Ruskin (c)	(813)	8,321	6,046
34695	Safety Harbor	(727)	17,424	15,120
*32084	Saint Augustine	(904)	11,915	11,695
32084	Saint Augustine Beach	(904)	5,413	3,830
32086	Saint Augustine South (c)	(904)	5,035	4,218
*34769	Saint Cloud	(407)	21,480	12,684
*33736	Saint Pete Beach	(727)	10,014	9,200
*33733	Saint Petersburg	(727)	247,610	240,318
33912	San Carlos Park (c)	(239)	16,317	11,785
33432	Sandalfoot Cove (c)	(305)	16,582	14,214
*32771	Sanford	(407)	43,556	32,387
33957	Sanibel	(239)	6,043	5,468
*34230	Sarasota	(941)	53,259	50,897
33577	Sarasota Springs (c)	(941)	15,875	16,088
32937	Satellite Beach	(321)	9,752	9,889
33055	Scott Lake (c)	(305)	14,401	14,588
*32958	Sebastian	(772)	17,744	10,248
*33870	Sebring	(863)	9,878	8,841
*33584	Seffner (c)	(813)	5,467	5,371
*33770	Seminole	(813)	16,628	9,251
34610	Shady Hills (c)	(727)	7,798	—
*34242	Siesta Key (c)	(941)	7,150	7,772
34472	Silver Springs Shores (c)	(352)	6,690	6,421
32809	Sky Lake (c)	(407)	5,651	6,202
32703	South Apopka (c)	(407)	5,800	6,360
33505	South Bradenton (c)	(941)	21,587	20,398
32121	South Daytona	(386)	13,799	12,488
34266	Southeast Arcadia (c)	(863)	6,064	4,145
34277	Southgate (c)	(941)	7,455	7,324
34233	South Gate Ridge (c)	(941)	5,655	5,924
—	South Highpoint (c)	(727)	8,839	—
33243	South Miami	(305)	11,355	10,404
33157	South Miami Heights (c)	(305)	33,522	30,030
33707	South Pasadena	(727)	5,740	5,644
32937	South Patrick Shores (c)	(321)	8,913	10,249
34230	South Sarasota (c)	(941)	5,314	5,298
33595	South Venice (c)	(941)	13,539	11,951
*33331	Southwest Ranches (c)	(954)	7,280	—
32401	Springfield	(850)	9,035	8,719
*34604	Spring Hill (c)	(352)	69,078	31,117
32091	Starke	(904)	5,665	5,226
*34994	Stuart	(772)	14,891	11,936
34446	Sugarmill Woods (c)	(352)	6,409	4,073
33160	Sunny Isles Beach	(305)	15,327	—
33345	Sunrise	(954)	89,136	65,683
33283	Sunset (c)	(305)	17,150	15,810

ZIP	Place	Area Code	2003	1990
33144	Sweetwater	(305)	14,137	13,909
*32301	Tallahassee	(850)	153,938	124,773
33320	Tamarac	(954)	57,967	44,822
33144	Tamiami (c)	(305)	54,788	33,845
*33601	Tampa	(813)	317,647	280,015
34689	Tarpon Springs	(727)	22,240	17,874
32778	Tavares	(352)	10,831	7,488
33687	Temple Terrace	(813)	21,860	16,444
33469	Tequesta	(561)	5,644	4,499
33186	The Crossings (c)	(305)	23,557	—
—	The Hammocks (c)	(305)	47,379	—
32159	The Villages (c)	(352)	8,333	—
33592	Thonotosassa (c)	(813)	6,091	—
—	Three Lakes (c)	(305)	6,955	—
33025	Timber Pines (c)	(352)	5,840	3,182
*32780	Titusville	(321)	41,752	39,394
32685	Town 'n' Country (c)	(813)	72,523	60,946
33706	Treasure Island	(727)	7,487	7,266
32867	Union Park (c)	(407)	10,191	6,890
33024	University (c)	(813)	30,736	—
—	University Park (c)	(305)	26,538	—
32401	Upper Grand Lagoon (c)	(850)	10,889	7,855
32580	Valparaiso	(850)	6,358	6,316
*33594	Valrico (c)	(813)	6,582	—
34231	Vamo (c)	(941)	5,285	3,325
*34285	Venice	(941)	19,351	17,052
33595	Venice Gardens (c)	(941)	7,466	7,701
*32960	Vero Beach	(772)	17,357	17,350
32960	Vero Beach South (c)	(772)	20,362	16,973
33901	Villas (c)	(239)	11,346	9,898
32507	Warrington (c)	(850)	15,207	16,040
32791	Wekiva Springs (c)	(407)	23,169	23,026
33414	Wellington	(561)	46,604	20,670
33543	Wesley Chapel (c)	(813)	5,691	—
—	West and East Lealman (c)	(727)	21,753	—
33626	Westchase (c)	(813)	11,116	—
33155	Westchester (c)	(305)	30,271	29,883
33409	Westgate-Belvedere Homes (c)	(561)	8,134	6,880
33138	West Little River (c)	(305)	32,498	33,575
32912	West Melbourne	(321)	12,334	8,398
33144	West Miami	(305)	6,009	5,727
33326	Weston	(954)	62,243	—
*33416	West Palm Beach	(561)	88,932	67,764
32505	West Pensacola (c)	(850)	21,939	22,107
33157	West Perrine (c)	(305)	8,600	—
34208	West Samoset (c)	(941)	5,507	3,819
—	West Vero Corridor (c)	(772)	7,695	—
33168	Westview (c)	(305)	9,692	9,668
33165	Westwood Lakes (c)	(305)	12,005	11,522
33496	Whisper Walk (c)	(561)	5,135	3,037
32821	Williamsburg (c)	(407)	6,736	3,093
33305	Wilton Manors	(954)	12,861	11,804
33803	Winston (c)	(813)	9,024	9,118
*34787	Winter Garden	(407)	20,307	9,863
*33880	Winter Haven	(863)	27,137	24,725
*32789	Winter Park	(407)	26,755	24,260
*32707	Winter Springs	(407)	31,808	22,151
32547	Wright (c)	(850)	21,697	18,945
34972	Yeehaw Junction (c)	(407)	21,778	—
*32097	Yulee (c)	(904)	8,392	6,915
*33540	Zephyrhills	(813)	11,554	8,220
33541	Zephyrhills West (c)	(813)	5,242	4,249

Georgia

Area code (678) overlays (770). See introductory note.

ZIP	Place	Area Code	2003	1990
*30101	Acworth	(770)	17,434	4,519
31620	Adel	(229)	5,295	5,093
*31706	Albany	(229)	76,202	78,804
*30004	Alpharetta	(770)	35,139	13,002
31709	Americus	(229)	16,886	16,516
*30603	Athens-Clarke County[1]	(706)	102,498	86,522
*30301	Atlanta	(404)	423,019	393,929
30011	Auburn	(770)	6,843	3,139
*30903	Augusta-Richmond County[2]	(706)	193,316	186,616
30168	Austell	(770)	6,430	4,173
*31717	Bainbridge	(229)	11,823	10,803
30204	Barnesville	(770)	5,890	4,747
30032	Belvedere Park (c)	(404)	18,945	18,089
31723	Blakely	(229)	5,588	5,595
30110	Bremen	(770)	5,057	4,353
*31520	Brunswick	(912)	15,984	16,433
*30518	Buford	(404)	10,820	8,771
31728	Cairo	(229)	9,342	9,035
*30701	Calhoun	(706)	12,342	7,135
31730	Camilla	(229)	5,609	5,124
30032	Candler-McAfee (c)	(404)	28,294	29,491
*30114	Canton	(770)	13,195	4,817
*30117	Carrollton	(770)	20,615	16,029
*30120	Cartersville	(770)	17,221	12,037
30125	Cedartown	(770)	9,583	7,976
31028	Centerville	(770)	5,268	3,509
30366	Chamblee	(404)	9,228	7,668
30021	Clarkston	(404)	7,122	5,385
30337	College Park	(404)	18,940	20,645
*31908	Columbus	(706)	185,702	178,683
30529	Commerce	(770)	5,333	4,108
30288	Conley (c)	(404)	6,188	5,528
*30013	Conyers	(404)	12,034	7,380
*31015	Cordele	(229)	11,500	10,833
—	Country Club Estates (c)		7,594	7,500
*30014	Covington	(770)	13,152	9,860
*30040	Cumming	(770)	5,034	2,798
*30132	Dallas	(770)	6,847	2,810
*30720	Dalton	(706)	30,341	22,218
31742	Dawson	(229)	5,035	5,295
*30030	Decatur	(404)	17,859	17,304
31520	Dock Junction (c)	(912)	6,951	7,094
30362	Doraville	(404)	10,029	7,626
*31533	Douglas	(912)	10,753	10,464
*30134	Douglasville	(404)	25,307	11,635
30333	Druid Hills (c)	(404)	12,741	12,174
*31021	Dublin	(478)	15,976	16,312
*30096	Duluth	(404)	23,697	9,821
30356	Dunwoody (c)	(404)	32,808	26,302
*31023	Eastman	(478)	5,422	5,153
30364	East Point	(404)	37,220	34,595
31024	Eatonton	(706)	6,917	6,479
30809	Evans (c)	(706)	17,727	13,713
30213	Fairburn	(770)	6,771	4,013
30060	Fair Oaks (c)	(404)	8,443	6,996
30535	Fairview (c)	(706)	6,601	6,444
*30214	Fayetteville	(404)	13,455	5,827
31750	Fitzgerald	(229)	8,752	8,901
*30297	Forest Park	(404)	21,247	16,958
31905	Fort Benning South (c)	(706)	11,737	14,617
30742	Fort Oglethorpe	(706)	7,854	5,880
*31313	Fort Stewart (c)	(912)	11,205	13,774
31030	Fort Valley	(478)	8,040	8,198
*30501	Gainesville	(770)	29,806	17,885
31418	Garden City	(912)	10,942	7,410
31754	Georgetown (c)	(912)	10,599	5,554
30316	Gresham Park (c)	(404)	9,215	9,000
*30223	Griffin	(770)	23,460	21,325
30813	Grovetown	(706)	6,675	3,596
30354	Hapeville	(404)	5,705	5,483
*31313	Hinesville	(912)	29,396	21,596
—	Irondale (c)		7,727	3,352
*31546	Jesup	(912)	9,424	8,958
*30144	Kennesaw	(404)	25,816	8,936
31548	Kingsland	(912)	11,064	6,089
30728	La Fayette	(706)	6,774	6,655
*30240	LaGrange	(706)	26,576	25,574
*30045	Lawrenceville	(404)	26,698	17,250
*30047	Lilburn	(404)	11,363	9,295
30052	Loganville	(770)	7,880	3,180
30126	Mableton (c)	(404)	29,733	25,725
30253	McDonough	(770)	11,721	2,929
*31201	Macon	(478)	95,267	107,365
*30060	Marietta	(404)	61,282	44,129
30917	Martinez (c)	(706)	27,749	33,731
—	Midway-Hardwick (c)		5,135	4,910
31061	Milledgeville	(478)	19,159	17,727
*30655	Monroe	(770)	11,892	9,759
*30260	Morrow	(770)	5,034	5,074
*31768	Moultrie	(229)	14,500	14,865
30087	Mountain Park (c)	(404)	11,753	11,025
*30263	Newnan	(770)	20,551	12,497
*30071	Norcross	(404)	9,294	5,947
30319	North Atlanta (c)	(404)	38,579	27,812
30033	North Decatur (c)	(404)	15,270	13,936
30033	North Druid Hills (c)	(404)	18,852	14,170
30032	Panthersville (c)	(404)	11,791	9,874
30269	Peachtree City	(404)	33,010	19,027
31069	Perry	(478)	10,566	9,452
31322	Pooler	(912)	8,344	4,649
30127	Powder Springs	(404)	13,760	6,862
30074	Redan (c)	(404)	33,841	24,376
31324	Richmond Hill	(912)	8,266	2,934
31326	Rincon	(912)	5,598	2,992
*30274	Riverdale	(404)	14,880	9,495
*30161	Rome	(706)	35,303	30,425
*30077	Roswell	(404)	79,229	47,986
31558	Saint Marys	(912)	15,811	8,204
31522	Saint Simons (c)	(912)	13,381	12,026
31082	Sandersville	(478)	5,981	6,290
30358	Sandy Springs (c)	(404)	85,781	67,842
*31402	Savannah	(912)	127,573	137,812
30079	Scottdale (c)	(404)	9,803	8,636
—	Skidaway Island (c)	(912)	6,914	4,495
*30080	Smyrna	(404)	45,610	32,453
*30078	Snellville	(404)	17,961	12,084
*30458	Statesboro	(912)	23,744	20,770
30281	Stockbridge	(404)	11,256	3,359
*30086	Stone Mountain	(404)	7,097	6,544
30518	Sugar Hill	(404)	13,820	4,519
30024	Suwanee	(770)	10,562	2,412
30401	Swainsboro	(478)	7,063	7,361
31791	Sylvester	(229)	5,903	6,023
30286	Thomaston	(706)	9,295	9,127
*31792	Thomasville	(229)	18,233	17,554
30824	Thomson	(706)	6,782	6,862
*31794	Tifton	(229)	15,862	14,215
*30577	Toccoa	(706)	9,324	8,720
*30084	Tucker (c)	(404)	26,532	25,781
30291	Union City	(404)	13,054	9,347
*31603	Valdosta	(229)	45,059	40,038
*30474	Vidalia	(912)	10,625	11,118

ZIP	Place	Area Code	2003	1990
30180	Villa Rica	(770)	8,087	3,916
30339	Vinings (c)	(404)	*9,677*	7,417
*31088	Warner Robins	(478)	54,264	43,861
*31501	Waycross	(912)	15,156	16,410
30830	Waynesboro	(706)	5,865	5,669
—	Whitemarsh Island (c)		*5,824*	2,824
31410	Wilmington Island (c)	(912)	*14,213*	11,230
30680	Winder	(770)	11,654	7,373
*30188	Woodstock	(770)	14,889	4,361

(1) Athens merged with Clarke County in 1991. The 2003 and 1990 populations are for all of Clarke County except Winterville and Bogart, which are part of the county but are also separate incorporated places. (2) Augusta merged with Richmond County in 1996. The 2003 and 1990 populations are for all of Richmond County except Blythe and Hephzibah, which are part of the county but are also separate incorporated places.

Hawaii (808)

ZIP	Place	2003	1990
—	Ahuimanu (c)	*8,506*	8,387
96701	Aiea (c)	*9,019*	8,906
96706	Ewa Beach(c)	*14,650*	14,315
—	Haiku-Pauwela (c)	*6,578*	4,509
—	Halawa (c)	*13,891*	13,408
96778	Hawaiian Paradise Park (c)	*7,051*	3,389
96853	Hickam Housing (c)	*5,471*	6,553
*96720	Hilo (c)	*40,759*	37,808
96725	Holualoa (c)	*6,107*	3,834
*96820	Honolulu (c)	380,149	377,059
*96732	Kahului (c)	*20,146*	16,889
96734	Kailua (Hawaii Co.) (c)	*9,870*	9,126
96863	Kailua (Honolulu Co.) (c)	*36,513*	36,818
96740	Kalaoa (c)	*6,794*	4,490
96744	Kaneohe (c)	*34,970*	35,448
—	Kaneohe Station (c)	*11,827*	11,662
96746	Kapaa (c)	*9,472*	8,149
96753	Kihei (c)	*16,749*	11,107
*96761	Lahaina (c)	*9,118*	9,073
96766	Lihue (c)	*5,674*	5,536
96792	Maili (c)	*5,943*	6,059
96792	Makaha (c)	*7,753*	7,990
96706	Makakilo (c)	*13,156*	9,828
96768	Makawao (c)	*6,327*	5,405
96789	Mililani Town (c)	*28,608*	29,359
96792	Nanakuli (c)	*10,814*	9,575
96761	Napili-Honokowai (c)	*6,788*	4,332
96782	Pearl City (c)	*30,976*	30,993
96788	Pukalani (c)	*7,380*	5,879
96786	Schofield Barracks (c)	*14,428*	19,597
—	Village Park (c)	*9,625*	7,407
96786	Wahiawa (c)	*16,151*	17,386
96792	Waianae (c)	*10,506*	8,758
—	Waihee-Waiehu (c)	*7,310*	4,004
96753	Wailea-Makena (c)	*5,671*	3,799
96793	Wailuku (c)	*12,296*	10,688
—	Waimalu (c)	*29,371*	29,967
96796	Waimea (c)	*7,028*	5,972
96797	Waipahu (c)	*33,108*	31,435
96797	Waipio (c)	*11,672*	11,812
96786	Waipio Acres (c)	*5,298*	5,304

Idaho (208)

ZIP	Place	2003	1990
83401	Ammon	8,623	5,002
83221	Blackfoot	10,646	9,646
*83707	Boise	190,117	126,685
83318	Burley	9,313	8,702
*83605	Caldwell	31,041	18,586
83202	Chubbuck	10,151	7,794
*83814	Coeur d'Alene	37,262	24,561
83616	Eagle	15,253	3,327
83617	Emmett	5,933	4,601
83714	Garden City	11,083	6,369
83333	Hailey	7,301	3,575
83835	Hayden	10,421	4,888
*83402	Idaho Falls	51,507	43,973
83338	Jerome	8,039	6,529
*83654	Kuna	8,839	1,955
83501	Lewiston	30,937	28,082
*83642	Meridian	41,127	9,596
83843	Moscow	21,707	18,398
83647	Mountain Home	11,376	7,913
83648	Mountain Home AFB (c)	*8,894*	5,936
*83653	Nampa	64,269	28,365
83661	Payette	7,298	5,672
*83201	Pocatello	51,009	46,117
*83854	Post Falls	19,984	7,349
83858	Rathdrum	5,296	2,014
83440	Rexburg	21,862	14,298
83350	Rupert	5,351	5,455
83864	Sandpoint	7,378	5,561
*83301	Twin Falls	36,742	27,634
83672	Weiser	5,386	4,571

Illinois

Area code (224) overlays area code (847). See introductory note.

ZIP	Place	Area Code	2003	1990
60101	Addison	(630)	36,767	32,053
60102	Algonquin	(847)	27,569	11,764
60803	Alsip	(708)	19,503	18,227
62002	Alton	(618)	29,841	33,060
62906	Anna	(618)	5,073	4,805
60002	Antioch	(847)	10,499	6,105
*60005	Arlington Heights	(847)	75,784	75,463
*60505	Aurora	(630)	162,184	99,672
*60010	Barrington	(847)	10,211	9,538
60103	Bartlett	(630)	37,558	19,395
61607	Bartonville	(309)	6,154	6,555
60510	Batavia	(630)	26,328	17,076
60085	Beach Park	(847)	11,126	9,492
62618	Beardstown	(217)	5,767	5,270
*62220	Belleville	(618)	41,209	42,806
60104	Bellwood	(708)	20,121	20,241
61008	Belvidere	(815)	22,927	16,059
60106	Bensenville	(630)	20,668	17,767
62812	Benton	(618)	6,817	7,216
60163	Berkeley	(708)	5,148	5,137
60402	Berwyn	(708)	52,534	45,426
62010	Bethalto	(618)	9,649	9,507
60108	Bloomingdale	(630)	21,801	16,614
*61701	Bloomington	(309)	68,507	51,889
60406	Blue Island	(708)	23,175	21,203
*60440	Bolingbrook	(630)	66,151	40,843
60538	Boulder Hill (c)	(630)	*8,169*	8,894
60914	Bourbonnais	(815)	15,840	13,929
60915	Bradley	(815)	13,386	10,954
60408	Braidwood	(815)	5,790	3,584
60455	Bridgeview	(708)	15,274	14,402
60153	Broadview	(708)	8,093	8,538
60513	Brookfield	(708)	18,933	18,876
60089	Buffalo Grove	(847)	43,237	36,417
60459	Burbank	(708)	28,049	27,600
60521	Burr Ridge	(630)	10,781	8,247
62206	Cahokia	(618)	16,043	17,550
60409	Calumet City	(708)	38,688	37,840
60643	Calumet Park	(708)	8,351	8,418
61520	Canton	(309)	14,970	13,959
*62901	Carbondale	(618)	24,952	27,033
62626	Carlinville	(217)	5,762	5,416
62821	Carmi	(618)	5,341	5,735
*60188	Carol Stream	(630)	40,114	31,759
60110	Carpentersville	(847)	34,815	23,049
60013	Cary	(847)	18,121	10,025
62801	Centralia	(618)	13,739	14,476
62206	Centreville	(618)	6,008	7,489
*61821	Champaign	(217)	71,958	63,502
60410	Channahon	(815)	10,065	4,266
61920	Charleston	(217)	20,305	20,398
62629	Chatham	(217)	9,330	6,074
62233	Chester	(618)	7,939	8,204
*60607	Chicago	(312)/(773)	2,869,121	2,783,726
*60411	Chicago Heights	(708)	32,297	32,966
60415	Chicago Ridge	(708)	13,900	13,643
61523	Chillicothe	(309)	5,778	5,959
60804	Cicero	(708)	83,029	67,436
60514	Clarendon Hills	(630)	8,235	6,994
61727	Clinton	(217)	7,336	7,437
62234	Collinsville	(618)	25,218	22,424
61241	Colona	(309)	5,217	2,237
62236	Columbia	(618)	8,545	5,524
60478	Country Club Hills	(708)	16,339	15,431
60525	Countryside	(708)	5,938	5,961
60435	Crest Hill	(815)	15,424	10,999
60445	Crestwood	(708)	11,323	10,823
60417	Crete	(708)	8,313	6,773
61610	Creve Coeur	(309)	5,306	5,938
*60014	Crystal Lake	(815)	40,021	24,692
*61832	Danville	(217)	33,106	33,828
60561	Darien	(630)	22,871	20,556
*62525	Decatur	(217)	79,285	83,900
60015	Deerfield	(847)	19,232	17,327
60115	DeKalb	(815)	41,348	35,076
*60018	Des Plaines	(847)	56,450	53,414
61021	Dixon	(815)	15,429	15,134
60419	Dolton	(708)	25,176	23,956
*60515	Downers Grove	(630)	49,222	47,464
62832	Du Quoin	(618)	6,344	6,697
62024	East Alton	(618)	6,725	7,063
61244	East Moline	(309)	21,211	20,147
61611	East Peoria	(309)	22,428	21,378
*62201	East St. Louis	(618)	30,573	40,944
62025	Edwardsville	(618)	23,600	14,582
62401	Effingham	(217)	12,498	11,927
*60120	Elgin	(847)	97,117	77,014
*60009	Elk Grove Village	(847)	34,666	33,429
60126	Elmhurst	(630)	44,054	42,029
60707	Elmwood Park	(708)	24,876	23,206
*60201	Evanston	(847)	74,360	73,233
60805	Evergreen Park	(708)	20,464	20,874
62837	Fairfield	(618)	5,327	5,439
62208	Fairview Heights	(618)	15,264	14,768
60422	Flossmoor	(708)	9,438	8,651
60130	Forest Park	(708)	15,406	14,918
60020	Fox Lake	(847)	9,937	7,539

ZIP	Place	Area Code	2003	1990	ZIP	Place	Area Code	2003	1990
60021	Fox River Grove	(847)	5,059	3,629	62863	Mount Carmel	(618)	7,772	8,287
60423	Frankfort	(815)	13,381	7,180	60056	Mount Prospect	(847)	55,784	53,168
—	Frankfort Square (c)	(815)	7,766	6,227	62864	Mount Vernon	(618)	16,486	17,082
60131	Franklin Park	(847)	19,060	18,485	60060	Mundelein	(847)	32,251	21,224
61032	Freeport	(815)	25,867	25,840	62966	Murphysboro	(618)	8,509	9,176
60030	Gages Lake (c)	(847)	10,415	8,349	*60540	Naperville	(630)	137,894	85,806
*61401	Galesburg	(309)	32,809	33,530	60451	New Lenox	(815)	21,545	9,698
61254	Geneseo	(309)	6,455	5,990	60714	Niles	(847)	29,945	28,375
60134	Geneva	(630)	22,236	12,625	61761	Normal	(309)	48,649	40,023
62034	Glen Carbon	(618)	11,135	7,774	60634	Norridge	(708)	14,362	14,459
60022	Glencoe	(847)	8,869	8,499	60542	North Aurora	(630)	13,091	6,010
60139	Glendale Heights	(630)	32,848	27,915	*60062	Northbrook	(708)	34,061	32,565
*60137	Glen Ellyn	(630)	27,210	24,919	60064	North Chicago	(847)	36,601	34,978
60025	Glenview	(847)	44,883	38,436	60093	Northfield	(847)	5,491	4,924
60425	Glenwood	(708)	8,847	9,289	60164	Northlake	(708)	11,686	12,505
62035	Godfrey	(618)	16,571	15,675	60546	North Riverside	(708)	6,568	6,180
—	Goodings Grove (c)	(815)	17,084	14,054	60521	Oak Brook	(630)	8,847	9,087
62040	Granite City	(618)	31,294	32,766	60452	Oak Forest	(708)	28,229	26,202
60030	Grayslake	(847)	21,287	7,388	*60303	Oak Lawn	(708)	55,136	56,182
62246	Greenville	(618)	7,104	5,108	*60303	Oak Park	(708)	50,824	53,648
60031	Gurnee	(847)	30,396	13,715	62269	O'Fallon	(618)	24,006	16,064
60103	Hanover Park	(630)	37,643	32,918	62450	Olney	(618)	8,575	8,873
62946	Harrisburg	(618)	9,638	9,318	60477	Orland Hills	(708)	7,144	5,510
60033	Harvard	(815)	8,600	5,975	*60462	Orland Park	(708)	54,011	35,720
60426	Harvey	(708)	29,367	29,771	60543	Oswego	(630)	18,521	3,949
60656	Harwood Heights	(708)	8,315	7,680	61350	Ottawa	(815)	18,635	17,574
60047	Hawthorn Woods	(847)	6,578	4,423	*60067	Palatine	(847)	66,848	41,554
60429	Hazel Crest	(708)	14,745	13,334	60463	Palos Heights	(708)	12,255	11,478
62948	Herrin	(618)	11,406	10,857	60465	Palos Hills	(708)	17,619	17,803
60457	Hickory Hills	(708)	13,752	13,021	62557	Pana	(217)	5,543	5,796
62249	Highland	(618)	8,739	7,546	61944	Paris	(217)	8,987	9,105
60035	Highland Park	(847)	30,897	30,575	60085	Park City	(847)	6,849	4,677
60040	Highwood	(847)	5,478	5,358	60466	Park Forest	(708)	23,560	24,656
60162	Hillside	(708)	8,005	7,672	60068	Park Ridge	(847)	37,460	37,075
*60521	Hinsdale	(630)	17,954	16,029	61554	Pekin	(309)	33,190	32,254
*60195	Hoffman Estates	(847)	50,108	46,363	*61601	Peoria	(309)	112,907	113,508
60491	Homer Glen	(708)	23,331	—	61603	Peoria Heights	(309)	6,354	6,930
60430	Homewood	(708)	19,348	19,278	61354	Peru	(815)	9,817	9,302
60942	Hoopeston	(217)	5,825	5,871	62274	Pinckneyville	(618)	5,407	3,372
60142	Huntley	(847)	11,769	2453	60544	Plainfield	(815)	20,162	4,557
60067	Inverness	(847)	6,971	6,516	60545	Plano	(630)	5,576	5,104
60042	Island Lake	(847)	8,407	4,449	61764	Pontiac	(815)	11,463	11,428
60143	Itasca	(630)	8,382	6,947	62040	Pontoon Beach	(618)	6,006	4,013
*62650	Jacksonville	(217)	19,603	19,327	61356	Princeton	(815)	7,539	7,197
62052	Jerseyville	(618)	8,051	7,382	60070	Prospect Heights	(847)	16,807	15,236
60050	Johnsburg	(815)	6,003	—	*62301	Quincy	(217)	39,922	39,682
*60436	Joliet	(815)	123,570	77,217	61866	Rantoul	(217)	13,009	17,212
60458	Justice	(708)	12,453	11,137	60471	Richton Park	(708)	12,883	10,523
60901	Kankakee	(815)	26,995	27,541	60827	Riverdale	(708)	14,752	13,671
61443	Kewanee	(309)	12,724	12,969	60305	River Forest	(708)	11,443	11,669
60525	La Grange	(708)	15,650	15,362	60171	River Grove	(708)	10,458	9,961
60526	La Grange Park	(708)	13,062	12,861	60546	Riverside	(708)	8,648	8,774
*60010	Lake Barrington	(847)	5,020	3,855	60472	Robbins	(708)	6,560	7,498
60044	Lake Bluff	(847)	6,170	5,486	62454	Robinson	(618)	6,558	6,740
60045	Lake Forest	(847)	20,762	17,836	61068	Rochelle	(815)	9,556	8,769
60102	Lake in the Hills	(847)	26,639	5,882	61071	Rock Falls	(815)	9,447	9,669
60046	Lake Villa	(847)	8,089	2,857	*61125	Rockford	(815)	151,725	142,815
60047	Lake Zurich	(847)	19,170	14,927	*61201	Rock Island	(309)	38,857	40,630
60438	Lansing	(708)	27,976	28,131	61072	Rockton	(815)	5,348	2,928
61301	La Salle	(815)	9,596	9,717	60008	Rolling Meadows	(847)	24,334	22,598
60439	Lemont	(630)	14,319	7,359	60446	Romeoville	(815)	32,481	14,101
*60048	Libertyville	(847)	21,113	19,174	61072	Roscoe	(815)	6,337	2,079
62656	Lincoln	(217)	15,039	15,418	60172	Roselle	(630)	23,237	20,803
60069	Lincolnshire	(847)	6,398	4,928	60073	Round Lake	(847)	9,333	3,550
60645	Lincolnwood	(847)	12,255	11,365	60073	Round Lake Beach	(847)	28,093	16,406
60046	Lindenhurst	(847)	14,247	8,044	60073	Round Lake Park	(847)	6,203	4,045
60532	Lisle	(630)	21,656	19,584	*60174	Saint Charles	(630)	32,010	22,636
62056	Litchfield	(217)	6,690	6,883	62881	Salem	(618)	7,747	7,470
60441	Lockport	(815)	19,217	9,401	60548	Sandwich	(815)	6,820	5,607
60148	Lombard	(630)	42,971	39,408	60411	Sauk Village	(708)	10,550	10,734
60047	Long Grove	(847)	7,494	4,747	*60194	Schaumburg	(847)	74,342	68,586
*61130	Loves Park	(815)	21,660	15,457	60176	Schiller Park	(847)	11,657	11,189
60411	Lynwood	(708)	7,599	6,535	*62269	Shiloh	(618)	9,403	2,655
60534	Lyons	(708)	10,514	9,828	60436	Shorewood	(815)	9,814	6,264
*60050	McHenry	(815)	23,119	16,343	61282	Silvis	(309)	7,341	6,926
61115	Machesney Park	(815)	21,205	19,042	*60077	Skokie	(847)	63,633	59,432
61455	Macomb	(309)	18,874	19,952	61080	South Beloit	(815)	5,435	4,072
61853	Mahomet	(217)	5,466	3,499	60177	South Elgin	(847)	20,229	7,474
60950	Manteno	(815)	6,906	3,709	60473	South Holland	(708)	22,087	22,105
60152	Marengo	(815)	6,902	4,768	*62703	Springfield	(217)	113,586	105,412
62959	Marion	(618)	16,624	14,597	61362	Spring Valley	(815)	5,362	5,246
60426	Markham	(708)	12,531	13,136	62088	Staunton	(618)	5,049	4,806
62062	Maryville	(618)	5,043	2,576	60475	Steger	(708)	10,035	9,251
62258	Mascoutah	(618)	5,687	5,511	61081	Sterling	(815)	15,272	15,142
60443	Matteson	(708)	14,278	11,378	60402	Stickney	(708)	6,040	5,678
61938	Mattoon	(217)	17,849	18,441	60165	Stone Park	(708)	5,057	4,383
60153	Maywood	(708)	26,398	27,139	60107	Streamwood	(630)	37,477	31,197
*60160	Melrose Park	(708)	23,057	20,859	61364	Streator	(815)	14,050	14,121
61342	Mendota	(815)	7,178	7,017	60554	Sugar Grove	(630)	6,619	2,123
62960	Metropolis	(618)	6,368	6,734	60501	Summit	(708)	10,467	9,971
60445	Midlothian	(708)	14,253	14,372	62221	Swansea	(618)	11,589	8,201
61264	Milan	(309)	5,309	5,753	60178	Sycamore	(815)	13,230	9,896
60448	Mokena	(708)	17,172	6,128	62568	Taylorville	(217)	11,296	11,113
*61265	Moline	(309)	43,064	43,080	60477	Tinley Park	(708)	53,792	37,115
61462	Monmouth	(309)	9,531	9,489	62294	Troy	(618)	9,069	6,194
60538	Montgomery	(630)	8,699	4,487	60466	University Park	(708)	7,658	6,204
61856	Monticello	(217)	5,184	4,775	*61801	Urbana	(217)	38,725	36,383
60450	Morris	(815)	12,352	10,274	62471	Vandalia	(618)	6,790	6,114
61550	Morton	(309)	15,365	13,799	60061	Vernon Hills	(847)	22,308	15,319
60053	Morton Grove	(847)	22,705	22,373	60181	Villa Park	(630)	22,891	22,279

ZIP	Place	Area Code	2003	1990
60555	Warrenville	(630)	13,286	11,389
61571	Washington	(309)	12,040	10,136
62204	Washington Park	(618)	5,833	7,431
62298	Waterloo	(618)	8,749	5,030
60970	Watseka	(815)	5,572	5,424
60084	Wauconda	(847)	9,991	6,294
*60085	Waukegan	(847)	91,452	69,481
60154	Westchester	(708)	16,680	17,301
*60185	West Chicago	(630)	25,262	14,808
60118	West Dundee	(847)	6,912	3,728
60558	Western Springs	(708)	12,512	11,956
62896	West Frankfort	(618)	8,215	8,526
60559	Westmont	(630)	24,639	21,402
*60187	Wheaton	(630)	55,016	51,441
60090	Wheeling	(847)	35,495	29,911
60514	Willowbrook	(630)	8,983	8,651
60480	Willow Springs	(708)	6,071	4,509
60091	Wilmette	(847)	27,266	26,694
60481	Wilmington	(815)	5,604	4,743
60190	Winfield	(630)	9,393	7,096
60093	Winnetka	(847)	12,386	12,210
60096	Winthrop Harbor	(847)	6,866	6,240
60097	Wonder Lake (c)	(815)	*7,463*	6,664
60191	Wood Dale	(630)	13,451	12,394
60517	Woodridge	(630)	33,695	26,359
62095	Wood River	(618)	11,121	11,490
60098	Woodstock	(815)	21,103	14,368
60482	Worth	(708)	10,906	11,208
60560	Yorkville	(630)	8,116	3,974
60099	Zion	(847)	23,814	19,783

Indiana

ZIP	Place	Area Code	2003	1990
46001	Alexandria	(765)	6,062	5,709
*46011	Anderson	(765)	58,394	59,518
46703	Angola	(260)	7,725	5,851
46706	Auburn	(260)	12,497	9,386
46123	Avon	(317)	7,017	—
47006	Batesville	(812)	6,306	4,720
47421	Bedford	(812)	13,469	13,817
46107	Beech Grove	(317)	14,457	13,383
*47408	Bloomington	(812)	70,642	62,735
46714	Bluffton	(260)	9,496	9,104
47601	Boonville	(812)	6,930	6,686
47834	Brazil	(812)	8,166	7,640
47025	Bright (c)	(812)	*5,405*	3,945
46112	Brownsburg	(317)	16,956	7,751
*46032	Carmel	(317)	43,083	25,380
46303	Cedar Lake	(219)	9,509	8,885
47111	Charlestown	(812)	5,927	5,889
46304	Chesterton	(219)	11,139	9,118
47129	Clarksville	(812)	21,237	19,838
46725	Columbia City	(260)	7,671	5,883
*47201	Columbus	(812)	39,058	33,948
47331	Connersville	(765)	14,844	15,550
47933	Crawfordsville	(765)	15,201	13,584
46307	Crown Point	(219)	20,980	17,728
46229	Cumberland	(317)	5,373	4,557
46122	Danville	(317)	6,941	4,345
46733	Decatur	(260)	9,459	8,642
46514	Dunlap (c)	(574)	*5,887*	5,705
46311	Dyer	(219)	14,670	10,923
46312	East Chicago	(219)	31,366	33,892
*46515	Elkhart	(574)	51,682	44,661
47429	Ellettsville	(812)	5,178	3,275
46036	Elwood	(765)	9,324	9,494
*47708	Evansville	(812)	117,881	126,272
46038	Fishers	(317)	47,790	7,189
*46802	Fort Wayne	(260)	219,495	195,680
46041	Frankfort	(765)	16,478	14,754
46131	Franklin	(317)	20,833	12,932
46738	Garrett	(260)	5,762	5,349
*46401	Gary	(219)	99,961	116,646
46933	Gas City	(765)	5,910	6,311
*46526	Goshen	(574)	29,787	23,794
46530	Granger (c)	(574)	*28,284*	20,241
46135	Greencastle	(765)	9,987	8,984
46140	Greenfield	(317)	15,721	11,657
47240	Greensburg	(812)	10,361	9,286
*46142	Greenwood	(317)	39,545	26,507
46319	Griffith	(219)	16,961	17,914
*46320	Hammond	(219)	80,547	84,236
47348	Hartford City	(765)	6,728	6,960
46322	Highland	(219)	23,444	23,696
46342	Hobart	(219)	26,972	24,440
47542	Huntingburg	(812)	5,815	5,236
46750	Huntington	(260)	17,163	16,389
*46206	Indianapolis	(317)	783,438	731,278
*47546	Jasper	(812)	13,205	10,030
*47130	Jeffersonville	(812)	28,025	24,016
46755	Kendallville	(260)	9,682	7,984
*46902	Kokomo	(765)	46,154	44,996
*47901	Lafayette	(765)	61,229	45,933
—	Lakes of the Four Seasons (c)	(219)	*7,291*	6,556
46405	Lake Station	(219)	13,818	13,899
*46350	La Porte	(219)	21,067	21,507
46226	Lawrence	(317)	40,795	26,849
46052	Lebanon	(765)	14,379	12,059

ZIP	Place	Area Code	2003	1990
47441	Linton	(812)	5,778	5,814
46947	Logansport	(574)	19,313	16,865
46356	Lowell	(219)	7,759	6,430
47250	Madison	(812)	12,249	12,006
*46952	Marion	(765)	30,609	32,607
46151	Martinsville	(765)	11,614	11,677
*46401	Merrillville	(219)	30,990	27,257
*46360	Michigan City	(219)	32,335	33,822
*46544	Mishawaka	(574)	48,396	42,635
47960	Monticello	(574)	5,548	5,237
46158	Mooresville	(317)	10,581	5,779
47620	Mount Vernon	(812)	7,318	7,217
*47302	Muncie	(765)	66,521	71,170
46321	Munster	(219)	22,135	19,949
46550	Nappanee	(574)	6,762	5,474
*47150	New Albany	(812)	36,973	36,322
47362	New Castle	(765)	18,955	17,753
46774	New Haven	(260)	13,592	11,234
*46060	Noblesville	(317)	33,046	17,655
46962	North Manchester	(260)	6,064	6,383
47265	North Vernon	(812)	6,389	5,129
47130	Oak Park (c)	(812)	*5,379*	5,630
46970	Peru	(765)	12,897	12,843
46168	Plainfield	(317)	21,386	14,953
46563	Plymouth	(574)	10,607	8,291
46368	Portage	(219)	34,915	29,062
46304	Porter	(219)	5,094	3,242
47371	Portland	(260)	6,297	6,483
47670	Princeton	(812)	8,512	8,127
47978	Rensselaer	(219)	6,167	5,045
*47374	Richmond	(765)	38,201	38,705
46975	Rochester	(574)	6,407	5,969
46173	Rushville	(765)	5,793	5,533
46373	Saint John	(219)	9,545	4,921
47167	Salem	(812)	6,325	5,619
46375	Schererville	(219)	26,142	20,155
47170	Scottsburg	(812)	5,912	5,334
47172	Sellersburg	(812)	6,140	5,936
47274	Seymour	(812)	18,500	15,605
46176	Shelbyville	(765)	17,853	15,347
*46624	South Bend	(574)	105,540	105,511
46383	South Haven (c)	(219)	*5,619*	6,112
46224	Speedway	(317)	12,793	13,092
47586	Tell City	(812)	7,684	8,088
*47808	Terre Haute	(812)	58,096	57,475
46072	Tipton	(765)	5,229	4,751
*46383	Valparaiso	(219)	28,365	24,414
47591	Vincennes	(812)	18,320	19,867
46992	Wabash	(260)	11,380	12,127
*46580	Warsaw	(574)	12,688	10,968
47501	Washington	(812)	11,292	10,864
46074	Westfield	(317)	11,182	3,304
*46580	West Lafayette	(765)	29,835	26,144
46391	Westville	(219)	5,266	5,234
46077	Zionsville	(317)	10,336	6,207

Iowa

ZIP	Place	Area Code	2003	1990
50511	Algona	(515)	5,592	6,015
50009	Altoona	(515)	11,349	7,242
*50010	Ames	(515)	53,284	47,198
52205	Anamosa	(319)	5,570	5,100
50021	Ankeny	(515)	31,144	18,482
50022	Atlantic	(712)	7,110	7,432
52722	Bettendorf	(563)	31,456	28,139
*50036	Boone	(515)	12,807	12,392
52601	Burlington	(319)	25,966	27,208
51401	Carroll	(712)	9,986	9,579
50613	Cedar Falls	(319)	36,429	34,298
*52401	Cedar Rapids	(319)	122,542	108,772
52544	Centerville	(641)	5,814	5,936
50616	Charles City	(641)	7,685	7,878
51012	Cherokee	(712)	5,158	6,026
51632	Clarinda	(712)	5,540	5,104
50428	Clear Lake	(641)	7,977	8,183
*52732	Clinton	(563)	27,437	29,201
50325	Clive	(515)	13,671	7,446
52241	Coralville	(319)	16,778	10,347
*51501	Council Bluffs	(712)	58,656	54,315
50801	Creston	(641)	7,359	7,911
*52802	Davenport	(563)	97,512	95,333
52101	Decorah	(563)	8,120	8,063
51442	Denison	(712)	7,420	6,604
*50318	Des Moines	(515)	196,093	193,189
*50274	De Witt	(563)	5,128	4,514
*52001	Dubuque	(563)	57,204	57,538
51334	Estherville	(712)	6,566	6,720
52556	Fairfield	(641)	9,486	9,955
50501	Fort Dodge	(515)	25,917	26,057
52627	Fort Madison	(319)	10,949	11,614
51534	Glenwood	(712)	5,418	4,960
50111	Grimes	(515)	5,600	2,653
50112	Grinnell	(641)	9,213	8,902
*51537	Harlan	(712)	5,165	5,148
52233	Hiawatha	(319)	6,506	5,354
50644	Independence	(319)	5,923	5,972
50125	Indianola	(515)	13,205	11,340
*52240	Iowa City	(319)	63,807	59,735

ZIP	Place	Area Code	2003	1990
50126	Iowa Falls	(641)	5,106	5,435
50131	Johnston	(515)	10,842	4,702
52632	Keokuk	(319)	10,918	12,451
50138	Knoxville	(641)	7,536	8,232
51031	Le Mars	(712)	9,241	8,454
52057	Manchester	(563)	5,139	5,137
52060	Maquoketa	(563)	6,054	6,130
52302	Marion	(319)	28,756	20,422
50158	Marshalltown	(641)	25,860	25,178
*50401	Mason City	(641)	28,274	29,040
52641	Mount Pleasant	(319)	8,518	7,959
52761	Muscatine	(563)	22,614	22,881
50201	Nevada	(515)	6,676	6,009
50208	Newton	(641)	15,794	14,799
52317	North Liberty	(319)	6,516	2,926
50211	Norwalk	(515)	7,794	5,726
50662	Oelwein	(319)	6,498	6,691
51041	Orange City	(712)	5,669	4,940
52577	Oskaloosa	(641)	11,037	10,600
52501	Ottumwa	(641)	24,697	24,488
50219	Pella	(641)	10,107	9,270
50220	Perry	(515)	8,079	6,652
*50317	Pleasant Hill	(515)	5,752	3,671
*51566	Red Oak	(712)	5,940	6,264
51601	Shenandoah	(712)	5,290	5,572
51250	Sioux Center	(712)	6,527	5,074
*51101	Sioux City	(712)	83,876	80,505
51301	Spencer	(712)	11,219	11,066
50588	Storm Lake	(712)	9,973	8,769
*50318	Urbandale	(515)	31,868	23,775
52349	Vinton	(319)	5,210	5,103
52353	Washington	(319)	7,253	7,074
*50701	Waterloo	(319)	67,054	66,467
50263	Waukee	(515)	7,287	2,512
50677	Waverly	(319)	9,075	8,539
50595	Webster City	(515)	8,106	7,894
*50265	West Des Moines	(515)	51,699	31,702

Kansas

ZIP	Place	Area Code	2003	1990
67410	Abilene	(785)	6,456	6,242
67002	Andover	(316)	8,222	4,204
67005	Arkansas City	(620)	11,788	12,762
66002	Atchison	(913)	10,111	10,656
67010	Augusta	(316)	8,486	7,848
66952	Bel Aire	(316)	6,522	3,695
66012	Bonner Springs	(913)	6,782	6,413
66720	Chanute	(620)	9,053	9,488
67337	Coffeyville	(620)	10,472	12,917
67701	Colby	(785)	5,244	5,510
66901	Concordia	(785)	5,459	6,152
67037	Derby	(316)	19,200	14,691
67801	Dodge City	(620)	25,568	21,129
67042	El Dorado	(316)	12,686	11,445
66801	Emporia	(620)	26,666	25,512
66442	Fort Riley North (c)	(785)	8,114	12,848
66701	Fort Scott	(620)	8,065	8,362
67846	Garden City	(620)	27,216	24,097
66030	Gardner	(913)	11,670	4,277
67530	Great Bend	(620)	14,927	15,427
67601	Hays	(785)	19,915	18,632
67060	Haysville	(316)	9,545	8,364
*67501	Hutchinson	(620)	40,783	39,308
67301	Independence	(620)	9,393	10,030
66749	Iola	(620)	6,033	6,351
66441	Junction City	(785)	17,667	20,642
*66102	Kansas City	(913)	145,757	151,521
66043	Lansing	(913)	10,032	7,120
*66044	Lawrence	(785)	82,120	65,608
66048	Leavenworth	(913)	35,211	38,495
66209	Leawood	(913)	28,888	19,693
66214	Lenexa	(913)	41,995	34,110
*67901	Liberal	(620)	20,067	16,573
67460	McPherson	(620)	13,731	12,422
*66502	Manhattan	(785)	44,733	43,081
66202	Merriam	(913)	10,835	11,819
66203	Mission	(913)	9,559	9,504
67110	Mulvane	(316)	5,536	4,683
67114	Newton	(316)	17,977	16,700
*66061	Olathe	(913)	105,274	63,402
66067	Ottawa	(785)	12,031	10,667
66204	Overland Park	(913)	160,368	111,790
66071	Paola	(913)	5,065	4,698
67219	Park City	(316)	6,877	5,081
67357	Parsons	(620)	11,296	11,919
66762	Pittsburg	(620)	19,276	17,789
66208	Prairie Village	(913)	21,729	23,186
67124	Pratt	(620)	6,422	6,687
66205	Roeland Park	(913)	7,075	7,706
*67401	Salina	(785)	45,833	42,299
66203	Shawnee	(913)	54,093	37,962
*66601	Topeka	(785)	122,008	119,883
67880	Ulysses	(620)	5,790	5,474
67147	Valley Center	(316)	5,167	4,272
67152	Wellington	(620)	8,299	8,517
*67202	Wichita	(316)	354,617	304,017
67156	Winfield	(620)	12,016	11,931

Kentucky

ZIP	Place	Area Code	2003	1990
41001	Alexandria	(859)	8,206	5,592
*41101	Ashland	(606)	21,491	23,622
40004	Bardstown	(502)	10,458	6,712
41073	Bellevue	(859)	6,138	6,997
40403	Berea	(859)	11,259	9,129
*42101	Bowling Green	(270)	50,663	41,688
40261	Buechel (c)	(502)	7,272	7,081
41005	Burlington (c)	(859)	10,779	6,070
*42718	Campbellsville	(270)	10,689	9,592
42330	Central City	(270)	5,787	4,979
*40701	Corbin	(606)	7,932	7,644
*41011	Covington	(859)	42,687	43,646
41031	Cynthiana	(859)	6,260	6,497
*42422	Danville	(859)	15,294	14,454
41074	Dayton	(859)	5,677	6,576
40243	Douglass Hills	(502)	5,648	5,431
41017	Edgewood	(859)	9,188	8,143
*42701	Elizabethtown	(270)	23,239	18,167
41018	Elsmere	(859)	8,059	6,847
41018	Erlanger	(859)	16,826	15,979
40118	Fairdale (c)	(502)	7,658	6,563
40291	Fern Creek (c)	(502)	17,870	16,406
41139	Flatwoods	(606)	7,593	7,799
*41042	Florence	(859)	24,689	18,586
42223	Fort Campbell North (c)	(270)	14,338	18,861
40121	Fort Knox (c)	(270)	12,377	21,495
41017	Fort Mitchell	(859)	7,822	7,438
41075	Fort Thomas	(859)	16,019	16,032
41011	Fort Wright	(859)	5,580	6,404
*40601	Frankfort	(502)	27,408	26,535
*42134	Franklin	(270)	8,009	7,607
40324	Georgetown	(502)	19,438	11,414
*42141	Glasgow	(270)	13,614	12,777
40330	Harrodsburg	(859)	8,085	7,335
*42420	Henderson	(270)	27,468	25,945
41076	Highland Heights	(859)	6,472	4,223
40228	Highview (c)	(502)	15,161	14,814
40229	Hillview	(502)	7,179	6,119
*42240	Hopkinsville	(270)	28,678	29,809
41051	Independence	(859)	17,070	10,444
40269	Jeffersontown	(502)	26,331	23,223
40031	La Grange	(502)	5,865	3,901
40342	Lawrenceburg	(502)	9,246	5,911
40033	Lebanon	(270)	5,821	5,695
*42754	Leitchfield	(270)	6,263	4,965
*40507	Lexington	(859)	266,798	225,366
40741	London	(606)	7,653	5,757
40232	Louisville	(502)	248,762	269,555
40252	Lyndon	(502)	10,293	8,037
42431	Madisonville	(270)	19,321	18,693
42066	Mayfield	(270)	10,228	9,935
41056	Maysville	(606)	8,941	8,113
40965	Middlesborough	(606)	10,266	11,328
40253	Middletown	(502)	6,005	5,016
42633	Monticello	(606)	6,053	5,357
40351	Morehead	(606)	7,627	8,357
40353	Mount Sterling	(859)	6,033	5,362
40047	Mount Washington	(502)	8,605	5,256
42071	Murray	(270)	15,311	14,442
40218	Newburg (c)	(502)	20,636	21,647
*41071	Newport	(859)	16,243	18,871
*40356	Nicholasville	(859)	22,251	13,603
—	Oakbrook (c)		7,726	4,113
42262	Oak Grove	(502)	7,564	2,863
40259	Okolona (c)	(502)	17,807	18,902
*42301	Owensboro	(270)	54,312	53,577
*42003	Paducah	(270)	25,565	27,256
*40361	Paris	(859)	9,271	8,730
*41501	Pikeville	(606)	6,286	6,324
40268	Pleasure Ridge Park (c)	(502)	25,776	25,131
42445	Princeton	(270)	6,394	6,940
*40160	Radcliff	(502)	21,894	19,778
*40475	Richmond	(859)	29,080	21,183
42276	Russellville	(270)	7,202	7,454
40216	Saint Dennis (c)	(502)	9,177	10,326
*40206	Saint Matthews	(502)	17,441	15,691
*40066	Shelbyville	(502)	10,390	6,155
40165	Shepherdsville	(502)	8,600	4,805
40256	Shively	(502)	15,343	15,535
*42501	Somerset	(606)	11,786	10,735
41015	Taylor Mill	(859)	6,866	5,530
40272	Valley Station (c)	(502)	22,946	22,840
40383	Versailles	(859)	7,487	7,269
41016	Villa Hills	(859)	7,919	7,370
40769	Williamsburg	(606)	5,033	5,493
40390	Wilmore	(859)	5,818	4,215
*40391	Winchester	(859)	16,378	15,799

Louisiana

ZIP	Place	Area Code	2003	1990
*70510	Abbeville	(337)	11,698	11,769
*71301	Alexandria	(318)	45,649	49,049
70032	Arabi (c)	(504)	8,093	8,787
70094	Avondale (c)	(504)	5,441	5,813
*70714	Baker	(225)	13,552	13,087
*71220	Bastrop	(318)	12,763	13,916
*70821	Baton Rouge	(225)	225,090	219,531

ZIP	Place	Area Code	2003	1990
70360	Bayou Cane (c)	(985)	17,046	15,876
70037	Belle Chasse (c)	(504)	9,848	8,512
*70427	Bogalusa	(985)	12,949	14,280
*71111	Bossier City	(318)	58,111	52,721
70517	Breaux Bridge	(337)	7,505	6,694
70094	Bridge City (c)	(504)	8,323	8,327
70518	Broussard	(337)	6,314	3,213
70811	Brownfields (c)	(225)	5,222	5,229
71291	Brownsville-Bawcomville (c)	(318)	7,616	7,397
70520	Carencro	(337)	6,022	5,518
*70043	Chalmette (c)	(504)	32,069	31,860
71291	Claiborne (c)	(318)	9,830	8,300
*70433	Covington	(985)	8,769	7,691
*70526	Crowley	(337)	13,940	13,983
70345	Cut Off (c)	(985)	5,635	5,325
*70726	Denham Springs	(225)	9,204	8,381
70634	De Ridder	(337)	9,758	10,475
70047	Destrehan (c)	(985)	11,260	8,031
70346	Donaldsonville	(225)	7,552	7,949
—	Eden Isle (c)		6,261	3,768
70072	Estelle (c)	(504)	15,880	14,091
70535	Eunice	(337)	11,586	11,162
71459	Fort Polk South (c)	(337)	11,000	10,911
70538	Franklin	(337)	8,059	9,004
70354	Galliano (c)	(985)	7,356	4,294
70820	Gardere (c)	(225)	8,992	7,209
*70737	Gonzales	(225)	8,339	7,208
*70053	Gretna	(504)	17,180	17,208
*70401	Hammond	(985)	17,715	15,871
70123	Harahan	(504)	9,797	9,927
*70058	Harvey (c)	(504)	22,226	21,222
*70360	Houma	(985)	32,025	30,495
70544	Jeanerette	(337)	5,955	6,205
70502	Jefferson (c)	(504)	11,843	14,521
70546	Jennings	(337)	10,712	11,305
70548	Kaplan	(337)	5,104	4,535
*70062	Kenner	(504)	70,202	72,033
70445	Lacombe (c)	(985)	7,518	6,523
*70501	Lafayette	(337)	111,667	101,865
*70601	Lake Charles	(337)	70,735	70,580
71254	Lake Providence (c)	(318)	5,104	5,380
*70068	Laplace (c)	(985)	27,684	24,194
70373	Larose (c)	(985)	7,306	5,772
*71446	Leesville	(337)	6,432	7,638
70070	Luling (c)	(985)	11,512	2,803
*70471	Mandeville	(985)	11,476	7,474
71052	Mansfield	(318)	5,486	5,389
71351	Marksville	(318)	5,695	5,526
*70072	Marrero (c)	(504)	36,165	36,671
70075	Meraux (c)	(504)	10,192	8,849
70812	Merrydale (c)	(225)	10,427	10,395
*70009	Metairie (c)	(504)	146,136	149,428
*71055	Minden	(318)	13,313	13,661
*71207	Monroe	(318)	52,163	54,909
*70380	Morgan City	(985)	12,282	14,531
70612	Moss Bluff (c)	(337)	10,535	8,039
*71457	Natchitoches	(318)	18,113	16,609
*70560	New Iberia	(337)	32,502	31,828
*70140	New Orleans	(504)	469,032	496,938
71463	Oakdale	(318)	7,992	6,837
70808	Oak Hills Place (c)	(225)	7,996	5,479
—	Old Jefferson (c)		5,631	4,531
*70570	Opelousas	(337)	22,753	19,091
70392	Patterson	(985)	5,156	5,166
*71360	Pineville	(318)	13,858	15,308
*70764	Plaquemine	(225)	6,894	7,101
*70454	Ponchatoula	(985)	5,450	5,499
70767	Port Allen	(225)	5,150	6,277
70601	Prien (c)	(337)	7,215	6,448
*70394	Raceland (c)	(985)	10,224	5,564
70578	Rayne	(337)	8,537	8,502
71037	Red Chute (c)	(318)	5,984	5,431
*70084	Reserve (c)	(985)	9,111	8,847
70123	River Ridge (c)	(504)	14,588	14,800
*71270	Ruston	(318)	20,634	20,071
70776	Saint Gabriel	(225)	5,527	3,854
70582	Saint Martinville	(337)	6,993	7,226
*70087	Saint Rose (c)	(504)	6,540	6,259
70395	Schriever (c)	(985)	5,880	4,958
70583	Scott	(337)	7,885	4,912
70817	Shenandoah (c)		17,070	13,429
*71102	Shreveport	(318)	198,364	198,518
*70458	Slidell	(985)	26,947	24,124
71075	Springhill	(318)	5,246	5,668
*70663	Sulphur	(337)	19,901	20,125
*71282	Tallulah	(318)	8,715	8,526
70056	Terrytown (c)	(504)	25,430	23,787
*70301	Thibodaux	(985)	14,463	14,125
70053	Timberlane (c)	(504)	11,405	12,614
70809	Village Saint George (c)	(225)	6,993	6,242
70586	Ville Platte	(337)	8,297	9,037
70092	Violet (c)	(504)	8,555	8,574
70094	Waggaman (c)	(504)	9,435	9,405
70785	Walker	(225)	5,317	3,846
*71291	West Monroe	(318)	13,018	14,096
*70094	Westwego	(504)	10,526	11,218
71483	Winnfield	(318)	5,484	6,138
71295	Winnsboro	(318)	5,149	5,755
—	Woodmere (c)		13,058	—
70791	Zachary	(225)	11,791	9,036

Maine (207)

See introductory note.

ZIP	Place	2003	1990
*04210	Auburn	23,313	24,309
*04330	Augusta	18,618	21,325
*04401	Bangor	31,550	33,181
04530	Bath	9,322	9,799
04915	Belfast	6,808	6,355
03901	Berwick	7,011	5,995
*04005	Biddeford	21,685	20,710
04412	Brewer	9,075	9,021
04009	Bridgton (c)	5,023	1,995
04011	Brunswick (c)	14,816	14,683
04011	Brunswick	21,529	20,906
04093	Buxton	7,913	6,494
04843	Camden	5,354	5,060
04107	Cape Elizabeth	9,013	8,854
04736	Caribou	8,308	9,415
04021	Cumberland	7,440	5,836
03903	Eliot	6,328	5,329
04605	Ellsworth	6,784	5,975
04937	Fairfield	6,600	6,718
04105	Falmouth	10,582	7,610
04938	Farmington	7,416	7,436
04032	Freeport	7,966	6,905
04345	Gardiner	6,209	6,746
04038	Gorham	15,013	11,856
04039	Gray	7,178	5,904
04444	Hampden	6,609	5,974
04079	Harpswell	5,222	5,012
04730	Houlton (c)	5,270	5,627
04730	Houlton	6,361	6,613
04043	Kennebunk	11,263	8,004
03904	Kittery	10,183	9,372
04027	Lebanon	5,334	—
*04240	Lewiston	35,922	39,757
04457	Lincoln	5,265	5,587
04250	Lisbon	9,236	9,457
04462	Millinocket	5,145	6,956
04462	Millinocket (c)	5,190	6,922
04260	New Gloucester	5,145	3,878
04963	Oakland	6,096	5,595
04064	Old Orchard Beach	9,222	7,789
04064	Old Orchard Beach (c)	8,856	7,789
04468	Old Town	8,127	8,317
04473	Orono	9,142	10,573
04473	Orono (c)	8,253	9,789
04274	Poland	5,097	4,342
*04101	Portland	63,635	64,157
04769	Presque Isle	9,449	10,550
04841	Rockland	7,613	7,972
04276	Rumford	6,449	7,078
04072	Saco	17,876	15,181
04073	Sanford (c)	10,133	10,296
04073	Sanford	21,666	20,463
*04074	Scarborough	18,459	12,518
04976	Skowhegan (c)	6,696	6,990
04976	Skowhegan	8,798	8,725
03908	South Berwick	7,197	5,877
*04101	South Portland	23,553	23,163
04084	Standish	9,712	7,678
04086	Topsham (c)	6,271	6,147
04086	Topsham	9,623	8,746
04282	Turner	5,243	4,293
04087	Waterboro	7,015	4,510
*04901	Waterville	15,758	17,173
04090	Wells	9,906	7,778
*04092	Westbrook	16,051	16,121
04062	Windham	15,448	13,020
04901	Winslow (c)	7,743	5,436
04901	Winslow	7,908	7,997
04364	Winthrop	6,394	5,968
04096	Yarmouth	8,290	7,862
03909	York	13,390	9,818

Maryland

Area code (240) overlays area code (301). Area code (443) overlays (410). See introductory note.

ZIP	Place	Area Code	2003	1990
21001	Aberdeen	(410)	14,184	13,087
20607	Accokeek (c)	(301)	7,349	4,477
20783	Adelphi (c)	(301)	14,998	13,524
20762	Andrews AFB (c)	(410)	7,925	10,228
*21401	Annapolis	(410)	36,178	33,195
21227	Arbutus (c)	(410)	20,116	19,750
21012	Arnold (c)	(410)	23,422	20,261
20916	Aspen Hill (c)	(301)	50,228	45,494
21220	Ballenger Creek (c)	(410)	13,518	5,546
*21203	Baltimore	(410)	628,670	736,014
*21014	Bel Air	(410)	9,948	8,942
21050	Bel Air North (c)	(410)	25,798	14,880
21014	Bel Air South (c)	(410)	39,711	26,421
*20705	Beltsville (c)	(301)	15,690	14,476
—	Bennsville (c)		7,325	—
*20814	Bethesda (c)	(301)	55,277	62,936
20710	Bladensburg	(301)	7,911	8,064
*20715	Bowie	(301)	53,660	37,642
21220	Bowleys Quarters (c)	(410)	6,314	5,595
21225	Brooklyn Park (c)	(410)	10,938	10,987

ZIP	Place	Area Code	2003	1990
21716	Brunswick	(301)	5,122	5,091
20866	Burtonsville (c)	(301)	7,305	5,853
20619	California (c)	(410)	9,307	7,626
20705	Calverton (c)	(301)	12,610	12,046
21613	Cambridge	(410)	10,781	11,514
20748	Camp Springs (c)	(301)	17,968	16,392
21401	Cape St. Clair (c)	(410)	8,022	7,878
21234	Carney (c)	(410)	28,264	25,578
21228	Catonsville (c)	(410)	39,820	35,233
20657	Chesapeake Ranch Estates-Drum Point (c)	(301)	11,503	5,423
20784	Cheverly	(301)	6,645	6,023
*20814	Chevy Chase (c)	(301)	9,381	8,559
20783	Chillum (c)	(301)	34,252	31,309
20735	Clinton (c)	(301)	26,064	19,987
20904	Cloverly (c)	(301)	7,835	7,904
21030	Cockeysville (c)	(410)	19,388	18,668
20914	Colesville (c)	(301)	19,810	18,819
*20740	College Park	(301)	25,329	23,714
*21045	Columbia (c)	(410)/(301)	88,254	75,883
20743	Coral Hills (c)	(410)	10,720	11,032
—	Cresaptown-Bel Air (c)		5,884	4,586
21114	Crofton (c)	(410)	20,091	12,781
*21502	Cumberland	(301)	20,833	23,712
20872	Damascus (c)	(301)	11,430	9,817
*20874	Darnestown (c)	(301)	6,378	—
*20747	District Heights	(301)	6,168	6,711
21222	Dundalk (c)	(410)	62,306	65,800
21601	Easton	(410)	12,503	9,372
20737	East Riverdale (c)	(301)	14,961	14,187
21219	Edgemere (c)	(410)	9,248	9,226
21040	Edgewood (c)	(410)	23,378	23,903
21784	Eldersburg (c)	(410)	27,741	9,720
21227	Elkridge (c)	(410)	22,042	12,953
*21921	Elkton	(410)	13,586	9,073
*21043	Ellicott City (c)	(410)	56,397	41,396
21221	Essex (c)	(410)	39,078	40,872
20904	Fairland (c)	(301)	21,738	19,828
21047	Fallston (c)	(410)	8,427	5,730
21061	Ferndale (c)	(410)	16,056	16,355
—	Forest Glen (c)		7,344	—
20747	Forestville (c)	(301)	12,707	16,731
20755	Fort Meade (c)	(301)	9,882	12,509
*20744	Fort Washington (c)	(301)	23,845	24,032
*21701	Frederick	(301)	56,128	40,186
20744	Friendly (c)	(301)	10,938	9,028
21532	Frostburg	(301)	8,107	8,069
*20877	Gaithersburg	(301)	57,365	39,676
21055	Garrison (c)	(410)	7,969	5,045
*20874	Germantown (c)	(301)	55,419	41,145
20706	Glenarden	(301)	6,559	5,025
*21061	Glen Burnie (c)	(410)	38,922	37,305
20769	Glenn Dale (c)	(301)	12,609	9,689
—	Goddard (c)		5,554	4,576
—	Greater Landover (c)		22,900	—
20772	Greater Upper Marlboro (c)		18,720	11,528
*20770	Greenbelt	(301)	22,096	20,561
21122	Green Haven (c)	(410)	17,415	14,416
21771	Green Valley (c)	(301)	12,262	9,424
*21740	Hagerstown	(301)	36,953	35,306
*21740	Halfway (c)	(301)	10,065	8,873
21074	Hampstead	(410)	5,336	2,608
21211	Hampton (c)		5,004	4,926
21078	Havre de Grace	(410)	11,398	8,952
20748	Hillcrest Heights (c)	(301)	16,359	17,136
*20780	Hyattsville	(301)	15,161	13,864
20794	Jessup (c)	(410)	7,865	6,537
21085	Joppatowne (c)	(410)	11,391	11,084
—	Kemp Mill (c)		9,956	—
20772	Kettering (c)	(301)	11,008	9,901
—	Lake Arbor (c)		8,533	—
21122	Lake Shore (c)	(410)	13,065	13,269
20787	Langley Park (c)	(301)	16,214	17,474
20706	Lanham-Seabrook (c)	(301)	18,190	16,792
21227	Lansdowne-Baltimore Highlands (c)		15,724	15,509
20646	La Plata	(301)	7,590	5,841
20772	Largo (c)	(301)	8,408	9,475
*20707	Laurel	(301)	20,653	19,086
20653	Lexington Park (c)	(410)	11,021	9,943
—	Linganore-Bartonsville (c)		12,529	4,079
21090	Linthicum (c)	(410)	7,539	7,547
21207	Lochearn (c)	(410)	25,269	25,240
21037	Londontowne (c)	(410)	7,595	6,992
*21093	Lutherville-Timonium (c)	(410)	15,814	16,442
20748	Marlow Heights (c)	(301)	6,059	5,885
20772	Marlton (c)	(301)	7,798	5,523
20707	Maryland City (c)	(301)	6,814	6,813
21093	Mays Chapel (c)	(410)	11,427	10,132
21220	Middle River (c)	(410)	23,958	24,616
21207	Milford Mill (c)	(410)	26,527	22,547
20717	Mitchellville (c)	(301)	9,611	12,593
20886	Montgomery Village (c)	(301)	38,051	32,315
21771	Mount Airy	(301)/(410)	7,904	3,730
20712	Mount Rainier	(301)	8,731	7,954
20784	New Carrollton	(301)	13,043	12,002
20815	North Bethesda (c)	(301)	38,610	29,656
20895	North Kensington (c)	(301)	8,940	8,607
20707	North Laurel (c)	(301)	20,468	15,008
20878	North Potomac (c)	(301)	23,044	18,456
*21842	Ocean City	(410)	7,142	5,146

ZIP	Place	Area Code	2003	1990
21811	Ocean Pines (c)	(410)	10,496	4,251
21113	Odenton (c)	(410)	20,534	12,833
*20832	Olney (c)	(301)	31,438	23,019
21206	Overlea (c)	(410)	12,148	12,137
21117	Owings Mills (c)	(410)	20,193	9,474
*20750	Oxon Hill-Glassmanor (c)	(301)	35,355	35,794
21234	Parkville (c)	(410)	31,118	31,617
21401	Parole (c)	(410)	14,031	10,054
*21122	Pasadena (c)	(410)	12,093	10,012
21128	Perry Hall (c)	(410)	28,705	22,723
21282	Pikesville (c)	(410)	29,123	24,815
20837	Poolesville	(301)	5,423	3,796
*20850	Potomac (c)	(301)	44,822	45,634
21227	Pumphrey (c)	(410)	5,317	5,483
21133	Randallstown (c)	(301)	30,870	26,277
—	Redland (c)	(301)	16,998	16,145
21136	Reisterstown (c)	(410)	22,438	19,314
*20737	Riverdale Park	(301)	6,564	4,843
21017	Riverside (c)		6,128	—
21122	Riviera Beach (c)	(410)	12,695	11,376
*20850	Rockville	(301)	55,213	44,830
20772	Rosaryville (c)	(301)	12,322	8,976
21237	Rosedale (c)	(410)	19,199	18,703
—	Rossmoor (c)		7,569	6,182
21221	Rossville (c)	(410)	11,515	9,492
20602	Saint Charles (c)	(301)	33,379	28,717
*21801	Salisbury	(410)	25,247	20,592
20763	Savage-Guilford (c)	(410)	12,918	9,669
20743	Seat Pleasant	(301)	5,044	5,354
21144	Severn (c)	(410)	35,076	24,499
21146	Severna Park (c)	(410)	28,507	25,879
20764	Shady Side (c)	(301)	5,559	4,107
*20907	Silver Spring (c)	(301)	76,540	76,046
21061	South Gate (c)	(410)	28,672	27,564
20895	South Kensington (c)	(301)	7,887	8,777
20707	South Laurel (c)	(301)	20,479	18,591
21666	Stevensville (c)	(410)	5,880	1,862
*20752	Suitland-Silver Hills (c)	(301)	33,515	35,111
*20913	Takoma Park	(301)	17,717	16,724
21787	Taneytown	(410)	5,335	3,695
*20748	Temple Hills (c)	(301)	7,792	6,865
21788	Thurmont	(301)	5,890	3,398
*21202	Towson (c)	(410)	51,793	49,445
—	Travilah (c)	(301)	7,442	—
*20602	Waldorf (c)	(301)	22,312	15,058
20743	Walker Mill (c)	(301)	11,104	10,920
21793	Walkersville (c)	(301)	5,517	4,145
*21157	Westminster	(410)	17,403	13,060
20902	Wheaton-Glenmont (c)	(301)	57,694	53,720
21162	White Marsh (c)	(410)	8,485	8,183
20903	White Oak (c)	(301)	20,973	18,671
21207	Woodlawn (c) (Baltimore Co.)	(410)	36,079	32,907
21284	Woodlawn (c) (Pr. George's Co.)	(410)	6,251	5,329
—	Woodmore (c)	(240)/(301)	6,077	2,874

Massachusetts

Area code (339) overlays area code (781). Area code (351) overlays (978). Area code (774) overlays (508). Area code (857) overlays (617). See introductory note.

ZIP	Place	Area Code	2003	1990
02351	Abington	(781)	16,052	13,817
01720	Acton	(978)	20,802	17,872
02743	Acushnet	(508)	10,594	9,554
01220	Adams	(413)	8,587	9,445
01220	Adams (c)	(413)	5,784	6,356
01001	Agawam (c)	(413)	28,528	27,323
01913	Amesbury	(978)	16,718	14,997
01913	Amesbury (c)	(978)	12,327	12,109
*01002	Amherst	(413)	34,567	35,228
*01002	Amherst Center (c)	(413)	17,050	17,824
01810	Andover (c)	(978)	7,900	8,242
01810	Andover	(978)	31,933	29,151
*02205	Arlington	(781)	41,903	44,630
01430	Ashburnham	(978)	5,842	5,433
01721	Ashland	(508)	15,474	12,066
01331	Athol	(978)	11,589	11,451
01331	Athol (c)	(978)	8,370	8,732
02703	Attleboro	(508)	43,502	38,383
01501	Auburn	(508)	16,424	15,005
01432	Ayer	(978)	7,258	6,871
02630	Barnstable Town	(508)	48,907	40,949
01005	Barre	(978)	5,353	1,094
01730	Bedford	(781)	12,583	12,996
01007	Belchertown	(413)	13,805	10,579
02019	Bellingham	(508)	15,705	14,877
02478	Belmont	(781)	23,859	24,720
02779	Berkley	(508)	6,273	4,237
01915	Beverly	(978)	40,255	38,195
*01821	Billerica	(978)	39,593	37,609
01504	Blackstone	(508)	9,062	8,023
—	Bliss Corner (c)	(508)	5,466	4,908
*02205	Boston	(617)	581,616	574,283
02532	Bourne	(508)	19,523	16,064
01719	Boxborough	(978)	5,012	3,343
01921	Boxford	(978)	8,214	6,266
*02205	Braintree	(781)	33,728	33,836
02631	Brewster	(508)	10,401	8,440
*02324	Bridgewater (c)	(508)	6,664	7,242

ZIP	Place	Area Code	2003	1990
02324	Bridgewater	(508)	25,142	21,249
*02303	Brockton	(508)	95,090	92,788
*02446	Brookline	(617)	56,642	54,718
01803	Burlington	(781)	22,849	23,302
*02139	Cambridge	(617)	101,587	95,802
02021	Canton	(781)	21,416	18,530
02330	Carver	(508)	11,536	10,590
01507	Charlton	(508)	12,159	9,576
02633	Chatham	(508)	6,849	6,579
01824	Chelmsford	(978)	33,957	32,383
02150	Chelsea	(617)	34,106	28,710
*01020	Chicopee	(413)	54,992	56,632
01510	Clinton	(978)	13,774	13,222
01510	Clinton (c)	(978)	7,884	7,943
01778	Cochituate (c)	(508)	6,768	6,046
02025	Cohasset	(781)	7,292	7,075
01742	Concord	(978)	16,937	17,076
*01226	Dalton	(413)	6,783	7,155
01923	Danvers	(978)	25,588	24,174
02714	Dartmouth	(508)	31,158	27,244
*02026	Dedham	(781)	23,244	23,782
02638	Dennis	(508)	16,226	13,864
02715	Dighton	(508)	6,556	5,631
01516	Douglas	(508)	7,653	5,438
02030	Dover	(508)	5,679	4,915
01826	Dracut	(978)	28,804	25,594
01571	Dudley	(508)	10,720	9,540
*02332	Duxbury	(781)	14,660	13,895
02333	East Bridgewater	(508)	13,652	11,104
02536	East Falmouth (c)	(508)	6,615	5,577
02642	Eastham	(508)	5,632	4,462
01027	Easthampton	(413)	16,340	15,537
01028	East Longmeadow	(413)	14,704	13,367
02334	Easton	(508)	22,969	19,807
02149	Everett	(617)	37,540	35,701
02719	Fairhaven	(508)	16,373	16,132
*02722	Fall River	(508)	92,760	92,703
*02540	Falmouth	(508)	33,823	27,960
01420	Fitchburg	(978)	39,948	41,194
02035	Foxborough	(508)	16,382	14,637
02035	Foxborough (c)	(508)	5,509	5,706
*01701	Framingham	(508)	66,243	64,989
02038	Franklin	(508)	30,175	22,095
02702	Freetown	(508)	8,862	8,522
01440	Gardner	(978)	21,049	20,125
01833	Georgetown	(978)	7,827	6,384
*01930	Gloucester	(978)	30,730	28,716
01519	Grafton	(508)	15,981	13,035
01033	Granby	(413)	6,361	5,565
01230	Great Barrington	(413)	7,445	7,725
01301	Greenfield	(413)	18,115	18,666
01301	Greenfield (c)	(413)	13,716	14,016
01450	Groton	(978)	10,210	7,511
01834	Groveland	(978)	6,342	5,214
02338	Halifax	(781)	7,790	6,526
01936	Hamilton	(978)	8,430	7,280
01036	Hampden	(413)	5,309	—
02339	Hanover	(781)	13,683	11,912
02341	Hanson	(781)	9,851	9,028
01451	Harvard	(978)	6,108	12,329
02645	Harwich	(508)	12,859	10,275
*01830	Haverhill	(978)	60,326	51,418
*02018	Hingham (c)	(781)	5,352	5,454
02043	Hingham	(781)	20,319	19,821
02343	Holbrook	(781)	10,871	11,041
01520	Holden	(508)	16,437	14,628
01746	Holliston	(508)	13,978	12,926
*01040	Holyoke	(413)	40,015	43,704
01747	Hopedale	(508)	6,185	5,666
01748	Hopkinton	(508)	14,018	9,191
01749	Hudson	(978)	18,348	17,233
01749	Hudson (c)	(978)	14,388	14,267
02045	Hull	(781)	11,302	10,466
02601	Hyannis (c)	(508)	11,050	14,120
01938	Ipswich	(978)	13,341	11,873
02364	Kingston (c)	(781)	5,380	4,774
02364	Kingston	(781)	12,220	9,045
02347	Lakeville	(508)	10,469	7,785
01523	Lancaster	(978)	6,618	6,661
*01842	Lawrence	(978)	72,492	70,207
01238	Lee	(413)	5,901	5,849
01524	Leicester	(508)	10,851	10,191
01240	Lenox	(413)	5,185	5,069
01453	Leominster	(978)	42,000	38,145
*02420	Lexington	(781)	30,631	28,974
01773	Lincoln	(781)	8,066	7,666
01460	Littleton	(978)	8,604	7,051
*01028	Longmeadow	(413)	15,676	15,467
*01853	Lowell	(978)	104,351	103,439
01056	Ludlow	(413)	21,842	18,820
01462	Lunenburg	(978)	9,909	9,117
*01901	Lynn	(781)	89,571	81,245
01940	Lynnfield	(781)	11,687	11,049
02148	Malden	(781)	55,816	53,884
01944	Manchester-by-the-Sea	(978)	5,363	5,286
*02048	Mansfield	(508)	23,011	16,568
02048	Mansfield Center (c)	(508)	7,320	7,170
01945	Marblehead	(781)	20,451	19,971
02738	Marion	(508)	5,282	4,496
01752	Marlborough	(508)	37,980	31,813
02050	Marshfield	(781)	24,775	21,531
02649	Mashpee	(508)	14,200	7,884
02739	Mattapoisett	(508)	6,480	5,850
01754	Maynard	(978)	10,374	10,325
02052	Medfield (c)	(508)	6,670	5,985
02052	Medfield	(508)	12,414	10,531
*02155	Medford	(781)	54,734	57,407
02053	Medway	(508)	12,900	9,931
02176	Melrose	(781)	26,784	28,150
01756	Mendon	(508)	5,691	—
01860	Merrimac	(978)	6,320	5,166
01844	Methuen	(978)	44,850	39,990
02346	Middleborough	(508)	20,909	17,867
02346	Middleborough Center (c)	(508)	6,913	6,837
01949	Middleton	(978)	8,984	4,921
01757	Milford	(508)	27,466	25,355
01757	Milford (c)	(508)	24,230	23,339
01527	Millbury	(508)	13,304	12,228
02054	Millis	(508)	8,023	7,613
02186	Milton	(617)	25,842	25,725
01057	Monson	(413)	8,625	7,776
01351	Montague	(413)	8,452	8,316
*02584	Nantucket	(508)	10,724	6,012
01760	Natick	(508)	32,321	30,510
*02205	Needham	(781)	29,137	27,557
*02740	New Bedford	(508)	94,112	99,922
01951	Newbury	(978)	6,861	5,623
01950	Newburyport	(978)	17,499	16,317
*02205	Newton	(617)	84,323	82,585
02056	Norfolk	(508)	10,450	9,259
01247	North Adams	(413)	14,334	16,797
01059	North Amherst (c)	(413)	6,019	6,239
*01060	Northampton	(413)	29,287	11,929
01845	North Andover	(978)	27,925	29,289
*02760	North Attleborough	(508)	28,102	22,792
02760	North Attleborough Center (c)	(508)	16,796	16,178
01532	Northborough (c)	(508)	6,257	5,761
01532	Northborough	(508)	14,291	13,371
01534	Northbridge	(508)	13,705	12,002
01864	North Reading	(978)	14,025	25,038
02060	North Scituate (c)	(781)	5,065	4,891
02766	Norton	(508)	19,013	14,265
02061	Norwell	(781)	10,289	9,279
02062	Norwood	(781)	28,730	28,700
02065	Ocean Bluff-Brant Rock (c)	(781)	5,100	4,541
01364	Orange	(978)	7,564	7,312
02653	Orleans	(508)	6,491	5,838
01540	Oxford (c)	(508)	5,899	5,969
01540	Oxford	(508)	13,760	12,588
01069	Palmer	(413)	12,833	12,054
*01960	Peabody	(978)	49,759	47,264
02359	Pembroke	(781)	17,675	14,544
01463	Pepperell	(978)	11,435	10,098
01866	Pinehurst (c)	(978)	6,941	6,614
*01201	Pittsfield	(413)	44,779	48,622
02762	Plainville	(508)	7,978	6,871
*02360	Plymouth (c)	(508)	7,658	7,258
*02360	Plymouth	(508)	54,109	45,608
*02205	Quincy	(617)	89,059	84,985
02368	Randolph	(781)	30,924	30,093
02767	Raynham	(508)	12,569	9,867
01867	Reading	(781)	23,585	22,539
02769	Rehoboth	(508)	10,966	8,656
02151	Revere	(781)	47,002	42,786
02770	Rochester	(508)	5,068	3,921
02370	Rockland	(781)	17,968	16,123
01966	Rockport (c)	(978)	5,606	5,448
01966	Rockport	(978)	7,810	7,482
01969	Rowley	(978)	5,610	4,452
01543	Rutland	(508)	7,036	4,936
*01970	Salem	(978)	42,067	38,091
01952	Salisbury	(978)	8,004	6,882
02563	Sandwich	(508)	20,960	15,489
01906	Saugus	(781)	26,491	25,549
02066	Scituate (c)	(781)	5,069	5,180
02066	Scituate	(781)	18,174	16,786
02771	Seekonk	(508)	13,766	13,046
02067	Sharon	(508)	17,456	15,517
02067	Sharon (c)	(781)	5,941	5,893
01464	Shirley	(978)	7,604	6,118
01545	Shrewsbury	(508)	33,091	24,146
*02722	Somerset	(508)	18,731	17,655
*02205	Somerville	(617)	76,296	76,210
01002	South Amherst (c)	(413)	5,039	5,053
01073	Southampton	(413)	5,736	4,478
01772	Southborough	(508)	9,427	6,628
01550	Southbridge	(508)	17,418	17,816
01550	Southbridge (c)	(508)	12,878	13,631
01075	South Hadley	(413)	17,414	16,685
01077	Southwick	(413)	9,305	7,667
01562	Spencer (c)	(508)	6,032	6,306
01562	Spencer	(508)	11,988	11,645
*01101	Springfield	(413)	152,157	156,983
01564	Sterling	(978)	7,693	6,481
02180	Stoneham	(781)	22,021	22,203
02072	Stoughton	(781)	27,094	26,777
01775	Stow	(978)	6,136	5,328
01566	Sturbridge	(508)	8,478	7,775
01776	Sudbury	(978)	17,246	14,358
01590	Sutton	(508)	8,865	6,824

ZIP	Place	Area Code	2003	1990
01907	Swampscott	(781)	14,452	13,650
02777	Swansea	(508)	16,292	15,411
02780	Taunton	(508)	56,781	49,832
01468	Templeton	(978)	7,254	6,438
01876	Tewksbury	(978)	29,288	27,266
01983	Topsfield	(978)	6,251	5,754
01469	Townsend	(978)	9,364	8,496
01879	Tyngsborough	(978)	11,317	8,642
01568	Upton	(508)	6,117	4,677
01569	Uxbridge	(508)	12,036	10,415
01880	Wakefield	(781)	24,781	24,825
*02081	Walpole (c)	(508)	5,867	5,495
02081	Walpole	(508)	22,521	20,223
*02205	Waltham	(781)	58,894	57,878
01082	Ware (c)	(413)	6,174	6,533
01082	Ware	(413)	9,954	9,808
02571	Wareham	(508)	21,090	19,232
*02205	Watertown	(781)	32,915	33,284
01778	Wayland	(508)	13,190	11,874
01570	Webster	(508)	16,891	16,196
01570	Webster (c)	(508)	11,600	11,849
*02205	Wellesley	(781)	26,578	26,615
01581	Westborough	(508)	18,811	14,133
01583	West Boylston	(508)	7,649	6,611
02379	West Bridgewater	(508)	6,861	6,389
01742	West Concord (c)	(978)	5,632	5,761
*01085	Westfield	(413)	40,560	38,372
01886	Westford	(978)	21,333	16,392
01473	Westminster	(978)	7,261	6,191
02493	Weston	(781)	11,645	10,200
02790	Westport	(508)	14,618	13,852
*01089	West Springfield	(413)	27,953	27,537
02090	Westwood	(781)	14,113	12,557
02673	West Yarmouth (c)	(508)	6,460	5,409
*02205	Weymouth	(781)	54,527	54,063
01588	Whitinsville (c)	(508)	6,340	5,639
02382	Whitman	(781)	14,351	13,240
01095	Wilbraham	(413)	13,866	12,635
01267	Williamstown	(413)	8,327	8,220
01887	Wilmington	(978)	21,620	17,651
01475	Winchendon	(978)	9,987	8,805
01890	Winchester	(781)	21,182	20,267
02152	Winthrop	(617)	17,981	18,127
*01801	Woburn	(781)	37,809	35,943
*01613	Worcester	(508)	175,706	169,759
02093	Wrentham	(508)	11,028	9,006
02675	Yarmouth	(508)	25,192	21,174
02675	Yarmouth Port (c)	(508)	5,395	4,271

Michigan

Area code (947) overlays area code (248). See introductory note.

ZIP	Place	Area Code	2003	1990
49221	Adrian	(517)	22,054	22,097
49224	Albion	(517)	9,130	10,066
49401	Allendale (c)	(616)	11,555	6,950
48101	Allen Park	(313)	28,762	31,092
48801	Alma	(989)	9,330	9,034
49707	Alpena	(989)	10,951	11,354
*48106	Ann Arbor	(734)	114,498	109,608
*48321	Auburn Hills	(248)	20,471	17,076
*49016	Battle Creek	(269)	53,827	53,516
*48707	Bay City	(989)	35,428	38,936
48505	Beecher (c)	(810)	12,793	14,465
48809	Belding	(616)	5,852	5,969
*49022	Benton Harbor	(269)	11,010	12,818
49022	Benton Heights (c)	(269)	5,458	5,465
48072	Berkley	(248)	15,239	16,960
48025	Beverly Hills	(248)	10,210	10,610
49307	Big Rapids	(231)	10,797	12,603
*48012	Birmingham	(248)	19,161	19,997
48301	Bloomfield (c)	(248)	43,021	42,137
48722	Bridgeport (c)	(989)	7,849	8,569
*48116	Brighton	(810)	7,029	5,686
48601	Buena Vista (c)	(989)	7,845	8,196
*48501	Burton	(810)	30,890	27,437
49601	Cadillac	(231)	10,131	10,104
*48185	Canton (c)	(734)	76,366	57,047
48724	Carrollton (c)	(989)	6,602	6,521
48015	Center Line	(586)	8,370	9,026
48813	Charlotte	(517)	8,795	8,083
49721	Cheboygan	(231)	5,290	4,997
48017	Clawson	(248)	12,447	13,874
*48046	Clinton (c)	(517)	95,648	85,866
49036	Coldwater	(517)	10,731	9,607
49321	Comstock Park (c)	(616)	10,674	6,530
49508	Cutlerville (c)	(616)	15,114	11,228
48423	Davison	(810)	5,443	5,693
*48120	Dearborn	(313)	96,670	89,286
*48127	Dearborn Heights	(313)	57,373	60,838
*48231	Detroit	(313)	911,402	1,027,974
49047	Dowagiac	(269)	5,857	6,418
49506	East Grand Rapids	(616)	10,563	10,807
*48826	East Lansing	(517)	47,245	50,677
48021	Eastpointe	(586)	33,394	35,283
49001	Eastwood (c)	(269)	6,265	6,340
48827	Eaton Rapids	(517)	5,320	4,695
48229	Ecorse	(313)	11,046	12,180
49829	Escanaba	(906)	12,778	13,659

ZIP	Place	Area Code	2003	1990
49022	Fair Plain (c)	(269)	7,828	8,051
*48333	Farmington	(248)	10,168	10,170
48333	Farmington Hills	(248)	80,874	74,614
48430	Fenton	(810)	11,832	8,434
48220	Ferndale	(248)	21,693	25,084
48134	Flat Rock	(734)	9,056	7,290
*48501	Flint	(810)	120,292	140,925
48433	Flushing	(810)	8,197	8,542
49506	Forest Hills (c)	(616)	20,942	16,690
48026	Fraser	(586)	15,120	13,899
48623	Freeland (c)	(989)	5,147	1,421
*48135	Garden City	(734)	29,547	31,846
49837	Gladstone	(906)	5,290	4,565
48439	Grand Blanc	(810)	8,018	7,760
49417	Grand Haven	(616)	10,842	11,951
48837	Grand Ledge	(517)	7,816	7,562
*49501	Grand Rapids	(616)	195,601	189,126
*49418	Grandville	(616)	16,622	15,624
48838	Greenville	(616)	8,193	8,101
48138	Grosse Ile (c)	(734)	10,894	9,781
*48231	Grosse Pointe	(313)	5,563	5,681
48230	Grosse Pointe Farms	(313)	9,557	10,092
48230	Grosse Pointe Park	(313)	12,189	12,857
48230	Grosse Pointe Woods	(313)	16,713	17,715
48212	Hamtramck	(313)	22,437	18,372
48225	Harper Woods	(313)	13,952	14,903
48625	Harrison (c)	(989)	24,461	24,685
48840	Haslett (c)	(517)	11,283	10,230
49058	Hastings	(269)	7,122	6,549
48030	Hazel Park	(248)	18,549	20,051
48203	Highland Park	(313)	16,044	20,121
49242	Hillsdale	(517)	8,070	8,175
*49423	Holland	(616)	34,666	30,745
48442	Holly	(248)	6,233	5,595
48842	Holt (c)	(517)	11,315	11,744
49931	Houghton	(906)	7,134	7,498
*48844	Howell	(517)	9,603	8,147
49426	Hudsonville	(616)	7,175	6,170
48070	Huntington Woods	(248)	6,015	6,419
48141	Inkster	(313)/(734)	29,478	30,772
48846	Ionia	(616)	12,124	10,349
49801	Iron Mountain	(906)	7,973	8,525
49938	Ironwood	(906)	5,953	6,849
49849	Ishpeming	(906)	6,535	7,200
*49204	Jackson	(517)	35,152	37,425
*49428	Jenison (c)	(616)	17,211	17,882
*49001	Kalamazoo	(269)	75,312	80,277
49518	Kentwood	(616)	46,487	37,826
49802	Kingsford	(906)	5,435	5,480
48144	Lambertville (c)	(734)	9,299	7,860
*48901	Lansing	(517)	118,379	127,321
48446	Lapeer	(810)	9,343	7,759
48146	Lincoln Park	(313)	39,131	41,832
*48150	Livonia	(734)	99,487	100,850
49431	Ludington	(231)	8,303	8,507
48071	Madison Heights	(248)	30,463	32,196
49660	Manistee	(231)	6,711	6,734
49855	Marquette	(906)	20,704	21,977
49068	Marshall	(269)	7,295	6,941
48040	Marysville	(810)	9,833	8,515
48854	Mason	(517)	7,831	6,768
48122	Melvindale	(313)	10,601	11,216
49858	Menominee	(906)	8,851	9,398
*48640	Midland	(989)	42,175	38,053
*48381	Milford	(248)	6,319	5,500
*48161	Monroe	(734)	21,630	22,902
*48046	Mount Clemens	(586)	17,111	18,405
*48804	Mount Pleasant	(989)	25,687	23,299
*49440	Muskegon	(231)	39,825	39,809
49444	Muskegon Heights	(231)	11,817	13,176
*48047	New Baltimore	(586)	9,749	5,798
49120	Niles	(269)	11,906	12,458
49505	Northview (c)	(616)	14,730	13,712
48167	Northville	(248)	6,405	6,226
49441	Norton Shores	(231)	23,193	21,755
*48376	Novi	(248)	50,786	32,998
48237	Oak Park	(248)	29,146	30,468
*48805	Okemos (c)	(517)	22,805	20,216
48867	Owosso	(989)	15,471	16,322
49770	Petoskey	(231)	6,154	6,056
48170	Plymouth	(734)	8,870	9,560
48170	Plymouth Township (c)	(734)	27,798	23,646
*48343	Pontiac	(248)	67,152	71,136
*49081	Portage	(269)	45,679	41,042
*48061	Port Huron	(810)	31,747	33,694
*48231	Redford (c)	(313)	51,622	54,387
48062	Richmond	(586)	5,371	4,028
48218	River Rouge	(313)	9,495	11,314
48192	Riverview	(734)	13,026	13,894
*48308	Rochester	(248)	11,021	7,130
48306	Rochester Hills	(248)	68,754	61,766
48174	Romulus	(313)/(734)	23,709	22,897
48066	Roseville	(586)	47,925	51,412
*48068	Royal Oak	(248)	58,650	65,410
*48605	Saginaw	(989)	59,235	69,512
48604	Saginaw Township North (c)	(989)	24,994	23,018
48603	Saginaw Township South (c)	(989)	13,801	13,987
48079	Saint Clair	(810)	5,881	5,116
*48080	Saint Clair Shores	(313)	61,896	68,107
48879	Saint Johns	(989)	7,513	7,392

ZIP	Place	Area Code	2003	1990
49085	Saint Joseph	(269)	8,656	9,214
48880	Saint Louis	(989)	5,445	3,828
48176	Saline	(734)	8,704	6,663
49783	Sault Sainte Marie	(906)	14,184	14,689
49455	Shelby (c)	(231)	65,159	48,655
48609	Shields (c)	(989)	6,590	6,634
*48037	Southfield	(248)	77,488	75,727
48195	Southgate	(734)	30,064	30,771
49090	South Haven	(269)	5,075	5,563
48178	South Lyon	(248)	10,895	6,479
48161	South Monroe (c)	(734)	6,370	5,266
49015	Springfield	(269)	5,228	5,582
*48311	Sterling Heights	(586)	59,235	117,810
48091	Sturgis	(269)	11,127	10,130
48473	Swartz Creek	(810)	5,247	4,851
48180	Taylor	(313)/(734)	65,589	70,811
49286	Tecumseh	(517)	8,751	7,462
48182	Temperance (c)	(734)	7,757	6,542
49093	Three Rivers	(269)	7,172	7,464
*49684	Traverse City	(231)	14,466	15,155
48183	Trenton	(734)	19,619	20,586
*48099	Troy	(248)	81,071	72,884
49504	Walker	(616)	23,208	17,279
*48390	Walled Lake	(248)	6,776	6,278
*48090	Warren	(586)	136,016	144,864
*48329	Waterford (c)	(248)	73,150	66,692
48917	Waverly (c)	(517)	16,194	15,614
48184	Wayne	(734)	18,934	19,899
*48323	West Bloomfield Township (c)	(248)	64,862	54,843
*48185	Westland	(313)/(734)	85,707	84,724
49019	Westwood (c)	(269)	9,122	8,957
48189	Whitmore Lake (c)	(734)	6,574	3,251
48393	Wixom	(248)	13,548	8,550
48183	Woodhaven	(734)	12,802	11,631
48192	Wyandotte	(734)	27,432	30,938
49509	Wyoming	(616)	70,205	63,891
*48197	Ypsilanti	(734)	22,492	24,846
49464	Zeeland	(616)	5,645	5,417

Minnesota

ZIP	Place	Area Code	2003	1990
56007	Albert Lea	(507)	17,886	18,310
55301	Albertville	(763)	5,236	1,252
56308	Alexandria	(320)	9,746	8,029
55304	Andover	(763)	28,938	15,216
*55303	Anoka	(612)/(763)	17,858	17,192
55124	Apple Valley	(952)	48,938	34,598
55112	Arden Hills	(651)	9,952	9,199
55912	Austin	(507)	23,466	21,926
56425	Baxter	(218)	6,733	3,695
*56601	Bemidji	(218)	12,724	11,165
55309	Big Lake	(763)	7,796	3,113
55014	Blaine	(651)/(763)	50,425	38,975
*55420	Bloomington	(952)	83,080	86,335
56401	Brainerd	(218)	13,722	12,353
55429	Brooklyn Center	(763)	28,362	28,887
55443	Brooklyn Park	(763)	67,781	56,381
55313	Buffalo	(763)	12,486	7,302
*55337	Burnsville	(651)/(952)	59,805	51,288
55008	Cambridge	(763)	6,382	5,094
55316	Champlin	(763)	23,003	16,849
55317	Chanhassen	(952)	22,124	11,736
55318	Chaska	(952)	20,654	11,339
55720	Cloquet	(218)	11,407	10,885
55421	Columbia Heights	(612)/(763)	18,428	18,910
55433	Coon Rapids	(763)	62,310	52,978
55340	Corcoran	(763)	5,733	5,199
55016	Cottage Grove	(651)	31,800	22,935
56716	Crookston	(218)	7,939	8,119
55428	Crystal	(763)	22,258	23,788
*56501	Detroit Lakes	(218)	7,652	7,141
*55806	Duluth	(218)	85,734	85,493
*55121	Eagan	(651)/(952)	64,006	47,409
55005	East Bethel	(763)	11,613	8,050
56721	East Grand Forks	(218)	7,562	8,658
*55344	Eden Prairie	(612)/(952)	59,470	39,311
55424	Edina	(952)	46,656	46,075
55330	Elk River	(763)	18,783	11,143
56031	Fairmont	(507)	10,666	11,265
55113	Falcon Heights	(651)	5,442	5,380
55021	Faribault	(507)	21,814	17,085
55024	Farmington	(651)/(952)	16,060	5,940
*56537	Fergus Falls	(218)	14,033	12,362
55025	Forest Lake	(651)	15,942	5,833
55432	Fridley	(763)	27,169	28,335
55336	Glencoe	(320)	5,534	4,648
55427	Golden Valley	(763)	20,505	20,971
*55744	Grand Rapids	(218)	7,764	7,976
*55304	Ham Lake	(763)	14,104	8,924
55033	Hastings	(651)	19,705	15,478
55810	Hermantown	(218)	8,367	6,761
*55746	Hibbing	(218)	16,851	18,046
*55343	Hopkins	(952)	17,127	16,529
55038	Hugo	(651)	8,758	4,417
55350	Hutchinson	(320)	13,451	11,459
56649	International Falls	(218)	6,454	8,325
*55076	Inver Grove Heights	(651)	31,281	22,477
55944	Kasson	(507)	5,030	3,514

ZIP	Place	Area Code	2003	1990
55947	La Crescent	(507)	5,066	4,311
55041	Lake City	(651)	5,238	4,490
55042	Lake Elmo	(651)	7,714	5,900
55044	Lakeville	(952)	47,805	24,854
55014	Lino Lakes	(651)	18,795	8,807
55355	Litchfield	(320)	6,685	6,041
55117	Little Canada	(651)	9,738	8,971
56345	Little Falls	(320)	7,848	7,371
55115	Mahtomedi	(651)	8,076	5,633
*56001	Mankato	(507)	33,925	31,459
55311	Maple Grove	(763)	57,172	38,736
55109	Maplewood	(651)	35,945	30,954
56258	Marshall	(507)	12,545	12,023
55118	Mendota Heights	(651)	11,343	9,388
*55440	Minneapolis	(612)/(763)/(952)	373,188	368,383
55345	Minnetonka	(952)	50,690	48,370
56265	Montevideo	(320)	5,383	5,499
*55362	Monticello	(763)	9,648	5,045
*56560	Moorhead	(218)	32,786	32,295
56267	Morris	(320)	5,161	5,613
55364	Mound	(952)	9,376	9,634
55112	Mounds View	(763)	12,696	12,541
55112	New Brighton	(651)	21,751	22,207
54427	New Hope	(763)	20,317	21,853
56071	New Prague	(952)	5,391	3,575
56073	New Ulm	(507)	13,401	13,132
55056	North Branch	(651)/(763)	9,457	4,267
55057	Northfield	(507)	18,187	14,684
56001	North Mankato	(507)	12,248	10,662
55109	North Saint Paul	(651)	11,839	12,376
55128	Oakdale	(651)	27,673	18,377
*55011	Oak Grove	(763)	7,353	5,488
55323	Orono	(952)	7,790	7,285
*55330	Otsego	(763)	6,837	5,219
55060	Owatonna	(507)	23,333	19,386
*55446	Plymouth	(763)	69,164	50,889
55372	Prior Lake	(952)	20,038	11,482
55303	Ramsey	(763)	19,524	12,408
55066	Red Wing	(651)	16,020	15,134
56283	Redwood Falls	(507)	5,339	4,859
55423	Richfield	(612)	34,079	35,710
55422	Robbinsdale	(763)	13,668	14,396
*55901	Rochester	(507)	92,507	70,729
55374	Rogers	(763)	5,934	722
55068	Rosemount	(651)/(952)	16,974	8,622
55113	Roseville	(651)	33,105	33,485
55418	Saint Anthony	(612)	7,830	7,727
*56301	Saint Cloud	(320)	59,458	48,812
55070	Saint Francis	(763)	6,449	2,479
*56374	Saint Joseph	(320)	5,089	3,294
55426	Saint Louis Park	(952)	44,114	43,787
*55374	Saint Michael	(763)	12,850	2,506
*55101	Saint Paul	(651)	280,404	272,235
55071	Saint Paul Park	(651)	5,028	4,965
56082	Saint Peter	(507)	10,162	9,481
56377	Sartell	(320)	11,854	5,409
56379	Sauk Rapids	(320)	11,620	7,823
55378	Savage	(952)	25,202	9,906
55379	Shakopee	(612)	26,681	11,739
55126	Shoreview	(651)	27,105	24,587
55331	Shorewood	(952)	7,522	5,913
55075	South Saint Paul	(651)	19,699	20,197
55432	Spring Lake Park	(763)	6,806	6,532
55976	Stewartville	(507)	5,522	4,520
*55082	Stillwater	(651)	16,734	13,882
56701	Thief River Falls	(218)	8,427	8,010
55127	Vadnais Heights	(651)	13,104	11,041
55386	Victoria	(952)	5,176	2,354
*55792	Virginia	(218)	8,888	9,432
55387	Waconia	(952)	7,986	3,498
56387	Waite Park	(320)	6,864	5,020
56093	Waseca	(507)	9,576	8,385
55118	West Saint Paul	(651)	19,468	19,248
*55110	White Bear Lake	(651)	24,388	24,622
56201	Willmar	(320)	18,303	17,531
55987	Winona	(507)	26,641	25,435
55125	Woodbury	(651)	49,415	20,075
56187	Worthington	(507)	11,192	9,977

Mississippi

Area code (769) overlays area code (601). See introductory note.

ZIP	Place	Area Code	2003	1990
39730	Aberdeen	(662)	6,278	6,837
38821	Amory	(662)	6,800	7,093
38606	Batesville	(662)	7,598	6,403
*39520	Bay Saint Louis	(228)	8,150	8,063
*39530	Biloxi	(228)	48,972	46,319
38829	Booneville	(662)	8,619	7,955
*39042	Brandon	(601)	18,065	11,089
*39601	Brookhaven	(601)	9,810	10,243
39272	Byram (c)	(601)	7,386	—
39046	Canton	(601)	12,856	11,723
38614	Clarksdale	(662)	19,833	21,180
*38732	Cleveland	(662)	13,184	15,384
*39056	Clinton	(601)	24,207	21,847
39429	Columbia	(601)	6,344	6,815
*39701	Columbus	(662)	24,959	23,799
*38834	Corinth	(662)	14,083	11,820

ZIP	Place	Area Code	2003	1990
39059	Crystal Springs	(601)	5,841	5,643
39525	Diamondhead (c)	(228)	5,912	2,661
39532	D'Iberville	(228)	7,539	6,566
39232	Flowood	(601)	6,260	2,770
39074	Forest	(601)	5,970	5,062
39553	Gautier	(228)	16,753	10,088
*38701	Greenville	(662)	39,521	45,226
*38930	Greenwood	(662)	17,594	18,906
*38901	Grenada	(662)	14,649	10,864
39564	Gulf Hills (c)	(228)	5,900	5,004
*39501	Gulfport	(228)	71,810	64,045
*39401	Hattiesburg	(601)	46,664	45,325
38632	Hernando	....	8,344	3,125
*38635	Holly Springs	(662)	7,924	7,261
38637	Horn Lake	(662)	15,146	9,069
38751	Indianola	(662)	11,562	11,809
*39205	Jackson	(601)	179,599	202,062
39090	Kosciusko	(662)	7,351	6,986
*39440	Laurel	(601)	18,044	18,827
38756	Leland	(662)	5,234	6,366
39560	Long Beach	(228)	16,938	15,804
39339	Louisville	(662)	6,831	7,165
*39648	McComb	(601)	13,127	11,797
*39110	Madison	(601)	15,869	7,471
*39302	Meridian	(601)	39,559	41,036
*39563	Moss Point	(228)	15,327	17,837
*39120	Natchez	(601)	17,621	19,460
38652	New Albany	(662)	7,796	6,775
*39564	Ocean Springs	(228)	17,443	15,221
38654	Olive Branch	(662)	24,938	3,567
38655	Oxford	(662)	12,761	10,026
*39567	Pascagoula	(228)	25,865	25,899
39571	Pass Christian	(228)	6,599	5,557
39288	Pearl	(601)	22,824	19,588
39465	Petal	(601)	7,687	7,883
39350	Philadelphia	(601)	7,277	6,758
39466	Picayune	(601)	10,641	10,633
38863	Pontotoc	(662)	5,636	4,570
39218	Richland	(601)	6,447	4,014
*39157	Ridgeland	(601)	21,435	11,714
38663	Ripley	(662)	5,509	5,371
39533	Saint Martin (c)	(228)	6,676	6,349
38668	Senatobia	(601)	6,667	4,772
38671	Southaven	(662)	34,760	18,705
*39759	Starkville	(662)	22,419	18,458
*38801	Tupelo	(662)	35,297	30,685
*39180	Vicksburg	(601)	26,005	26,886
39576	Waveland	(228)	6,820	5,369
39367	Waynesboro	(601)	5,133	5,143
—	West Hattiesburg (c)	(601)	6,305	5,450
39773	West Point	(662)	11,858	8,489
38967	Winona	(662)	5,086	5,965
39194	Yazoo City	(662)	12,098	12,427

Missouri

ZIP	Place	Area Code	2003	1990
63123	Affton (c)	(314)	20,535	21,106
63010	Arnold	(636)	20,070	18,828
65605	Aurora	(417)	7,121	6,459
*63011	Ballwin	(636)	31,006	27,054
63012	Barnhart (c)	(314)	6,108	4,911
63137	Bellefontaine Neighbors	(314)	10,865	10,918
64012	Belton	(816)	23,575	18,145
63134	Berkeley	(314)	9,867	12,250
63031	Black Jack	(314)	6,941	6,131
*64015	Blue Springs	(816)	49,398	40,103
65613	Bolivar	(417)	9,598	6,845
65233	Boonville	(660)	8,399	7,095
63334	Bowling Green	(573)	5,228	3,046
*65615	Branson	(417)	6,231	3,706
63144	Brentwood	(314)	7,519	8,150
63044	Bridgeton	(314)	15,515	17,732
64429	Cameron	(816)	9,908	6,782
*63701	Cape Girardeau	(573)	35,741	34,475
64834	Carl Junction	(417)	5,860	4,123
64836	Carthage	(417)	12,892	10,747
63830	Caruthersville	(573)	6,564	7,389
63834	Charleston	(573)	5,855	5,131
*63017	Chesterfield	(636)	47,067	42,325
64601	Chillicothe	(660)	8,791	8,799
63105	Clayton	(314)	15,974	13,926
64735	Clinton	(660)	9,349	8,703
*65201	Columbia	(573)	88,534	69,133
63128	Concord (c)	(314)	16,689	19,859
63126	Crestwood	(314)	11,831	11,229
63141	Creve Coeur	(314)	16,718	12,289
63366	Dardenne Prairie	(636)	5,381	1,769
*63135	Dellwood	(314)	5,144	5,245
63020	De Soto	(636)	6,501	5,993
63131	Des Peres	(636)	8,628	8,395
63841	Dexter	(573)	7,374	7,506
63011	Ellisville	(636)	9,255	7,183
63025	Eureka	(636)	8,575	4,683
64024	Excelsior Springs	(816)	11,226	10,373
63640	Farmington	(573)	14,335	11,596
63135	Ferguson	(314)	21,907	22,290
63028	Festus	(636)	9,938	8,105
*63033	Florissant	(314)	51,018	51,038
65473	Fort Leonard Wood (c)	(573)	13,666	15,863
65251	Fulton	(573)	12,315	10,033
64118	Gladstone	(816)	27,089	26,243
64254	Glasgow Village (c)	(573)	5,234	5,199
63122	Glendale	(314)	5,674	5,945
64029	Grain Valley	(816)	6,991	1,898
64030	Grandview	(816)	25,210	24,973
63401	Hannibal	(573)	17,577	18,004
64701	Harrisonville	(816)	9,418	7,696
63042	Hazelwood	(314)	25,848	15,512
*64020	Independence	(816)	112,079	112,301
63755	Jackson	(573)	12,477	9,256
*65101	Jefferson City	(573)	37,550	35,517
63136	Jennings	(314)	15,160	15,841
*64801	Joplin	(417)	46,373	41,175
*64108	Kansas City	(816)	442,768	434,829
64060	Kearney	(816)	6,573	1,790
63857	Kennett	(573)	11,072	10,941
63501	Kirksville	(660)	17,157	17,152
63122	Kirkwood	(314)	27,294	28,318
63124	Ladue (St. Louis Co.)	(314)	8,359	8,795
63367	Lake Saint Louis	(636)	12,261	7,536
65536	Lebanon	(417)	12,628	9,983
*64063	Lee's Summit	(816)	77,052	46,418
63125	Lemay (c)	(314)	17,215	18,005
*64068	Liberty	(816)	27,982	20,459
63552	Macon	(660)	5,438	5,571
63011	Manchester	(636)	19,106	6,506
63143	Maplewood	(314)	8,972	9,962
65340	Marshall	(660)	12,017	12,711
65706	Marshfield	(417)	6,291	4,374
63043	Maryland Heights	(314)	25,583	25,440
64468	Maryville	(816)	10,622	10,663
63129	Mehlville (c)	(314)	28,822	27,557
65265	Mexico	(573)	10,956	11,290
65270	Moberly	(660)	13,733	12,839
65708	Monett	(417)	7,735	6,529
63026	Murphy (c)	(636)	9,048	9,342
64850	Neosho	(417)	10,714	9,254
64772	Nevada	(417)	8,411	8,597
65714	Nixa	(417)	13,906	4,893
63121	Normandy	(314)	5,139	4,480
64075	Oak Grove	(816)	6,552	4,565
63129	Oakville (c)	(314)	35,309	31,750
63366	O'Fallon	(636)	63,677	17,427
63132	Olivette	(314)	7,508	7,573
63114	Overland	(314)	16,438	17,987
65721	Ozark	(417)	13,070	4,401
63069	Pacific	(636)	5,702	4,350
63601	Park Hills	(573)	8,322	7,866
63775	Perryville	(573)	7,777	6,933
64080	Pleasant Hill	(816)	6,176	3,827
*63901	Poplar Bluff	(573)	16,583	16,841
64083	Raymore	(816)	13,221	5,592
64133	Raytown	(816)	29,747	30,601
65738	Republic	(417)	9,680	6,290
64085	Richmond	(816)	6,078	5,738
63117	Richmond Heights	(314)	9,438	10,448
*65401	Rolla	(573)	17,266	14,090
63074	Saint Ann	(314)	13,408	14,449
*63301	Saint Charles	(636)	61,253	50,634
63114	Saint John	(314)	6,704	7,502
*64501	Saint Joseph	(816)	72,663	71,852
*63166	Saint Louis	(314)	332,223	396,685
63376	Saint Peters	(636)	53,397	40,660
63126	Sappington (c)	(314)	7,287	10,917
*65301	Sedalia	(660)	20,048	19,800
63119	Shrewsbury	(314)	6,509	6,416
63801	Sikeston	(573)	16,960	17,641
64089	Smithville	(816)	6,206	2,525
63138	Spanish Lake (c)	(314)	21,337	20,322
*65801	Springfield	(417)	150,867	140,494
63080	Sullivan	(573)	6,486	5,661
63127	Sunset Hills	(314)	8,367	4,915
63006	Town and Country	(314)	10,882	10,944
64683	Trenton	(660)	6,123	6,129
63379	Troy	(314)	8,317	3,811
63084	Union	(636)	8,421	6,196
63130	University City	(314)	37,757	40,087
63088	Valley Park	(636)	6,382	4,165
64093	Warrensburg	(660)	17,075	15,244
63383	Warrenton	(636)	6,016	3,564
63090	Washington	(636)	13,608	11,367
64870	Webb City	(417)	10,251	7,538
63119	Webster Groves	(314)	23,164	22,992
63304	Weldon Spring	(636)	5,283	1,470
63385	Wentzville	(636)	12,253	4,640
65775	West Plains	(417)	10,930	9,214
*63011	Wildwood	(314)	34,145	16,742

> **IT'S A FACT:** According to the U.S. Census Bureau, there were 19,450 incorporated places in the U.S. in 2003, and some of these were very small indeed. A few towns had only one resident, including New Amsterdam, IN; Goss, MO; Hoot Owl, OK; and Lost Springs, WY. New York, NY, was the largest, with a population of 8,085,742.

Montana (406)

ZIP	Place	2003	1990
59711	Anaconda-Deer Lodge County	8,953	10,356
59714	Belgrade	6,816	3,422
*59101	Billings	95,220	81,125
*59718	Bozeman	30,753	22,660
*59701	Butte	32,519	33,336
59901	Evergreen (c)	6,215	4,109
*59401	Great Falls	56,155	55,125
59501	Havre	9,448	10,201
*59601	Helena	26,718	24,609
—	Helena Valley Southeast (c)	7,141	4,601
—	Helena Valley West Central (c)	6,983	6,327
*59901	Kalispell	16,391	11,917
59044	Laurel	6,292	5,686
59457	Lewistown	5,923	6,097
59047	Livingston	7,073	6,701
59301	Miles City	8,242	8,461
*59801	Missoula	60,722	42,918
59801	Orchard Homes (c)	5,199	10,317
59937	Whitefish	5,784	4,368

Nebraska

ZIP	Place	Area Code	2003	1990
69301	Alliance	(308)	8,579	9,765
68310	Beatrice	(402)	12,945	12,352
*68108	Bellevue	(402)	46,734	39,240
*68008	Blair	(402)	7,798	6,860
69337	Chadron	(308)	5,598	5,588
68108	Chalco (c)	(402)	10,736	7,337
68601	Columbus	(402)	20,880	19,480
68333	Crete	(402)	6,321	4,841
68022	Elkhorn	(402)	7,869	1,398
*68025	Fremont	(402)	25,198	23,680
69341	Gering	(308)	7,832	7,946
*68802	Grand Island	(308)	43,771	39,487
*68901	Hastings	(402)	23,536	22,837
68949	Holdrege	(308)	5,521	5,671
*68847	Kearney	(308)	28,211	24,396
68128	La Vista	(402)	13,895	9,992
68850	Lexington	(308)	10,113	6,600
*68501	Lincoln	(402)	235,594	191,972
69001	McCook	(308)	7,847	8,112
68410	Nebraska City	(402)	7,113	6,547
*68701	Norfolk	(402)	24,061	21,476
*69101	North Platte	(308)	23,924	22,605
68113	Offutt AFB (c)	(402)	8,901	—
*68005	Omaha	(402)	404,267	344,463
*68046	Papillion	(402)	17,829	13,892
68048	Plattsmouth	(402)	7,031	6,415
68127	Ralston	(402)	6,241	6,236
68661	Schuyler	(402)	5,381	4,052
*69361	Scottsbluff	(308)	14,774	13,711
68434	Seward	(402)	6,752	5,641
69162	Sidney	(308)	6,443	5,959
68776	South Sioux City	(402)	12,030	9,677
68787	Wayne	(402)	5,391	5,142
68467	York	(402)	7,873	7,940

Nevada

ZIP	Place	Area Code	2003	1990
*89005	Boulder City	(702)	15,314	12,567
*89701	Carson City	(775)	55,311	40,443
89403	Dayton (c)	(775)	5,907	2,217
*89801	Elko	(775)	16,075	14,836
—	Enterprise (c)		14,676	6,412
*89406	Fallon	(775)	7,748	6,430
89408	Fernley	(775)	10,047	5,164
89410	Gardnerville Ranchos (c)	(775)	11,054	7,455
*89015	Henderson	(702)	214,852	64,948
*89450	Incline Village-Crystal Bay (c)	(775)	9,952	7,119
*89125	Las Vegas	(702)	517,017	258,877
*89028	Laughlin (c)	(702)	7,076	4,791
89506	Lemmon Valley-Golden Valley (c)	(702)	6,855	—
*89024	Mesquite	(702)	11,780	1,871
89040	Moapa Valley (c)	(775)	5,784	3,444
89191	Nellis AFB (c)	(702)	8,896	8,377
*89030	North Las Vegas	(702)	144,502	47,849
*89041	Pahrump (c)	(775)	24,631	7,424
89109	Paradise (c)	(775)	186,070	124,682
*89501	Reno	(775)	193,882	134,230
89436	Spanish Springs (c)	(775)	9,018	—
*89431	Sparks	(775)	77,295	53,367
89815	Spring Creek (c)	(702)	10,548	5,866
—	Spring Valley (c)	(702)	117,390	51,726
89110	Sunrise Manor (c)	(702)	156,120	95,362
89433	Sun Valley (c)	(775)	19,461	11,391
89101	Winchester (c)	(702)	26,958	23,365
*89445	Winnemucca	(775)	6,570	6,473

New Hampshire (603)
See introductory note.

ZIP	Place	2003	1990
03275	Allenstown	5,022	4,649
03031	Amherst	11,413	9,068
03811	Atkinson	6,626	5,188
03825	Barrington	8,066	6,164
03110	Bedford	20,181	12,563
03220	Belmont	7,219	5,796
03570	Berlin	10,122	11,824
03304	Bow	7,764	5,500
03743	Claremont	13,355	13,902
*03301	Concord	41,823	36,006
03818	Conway	9,009	7,940
03038	Derry (c)	22,661	20,446
03038	Derry	34,471	29,603
*03820	Dover	28,216	25,042
03824	Durham (c)	9,024	9,236
03824	Durham	13,080	11,818
03042	Epping	6,007	5,162
03833	Exeter (c)	9,759	9,556
03833	Exeter	14,478	12,481
03835	Farmington	6,182	5,739
03235	Franklin	8,613	8,304
03246	Gilford	7,409	5,867
03045	Goffstown	17,354	14,621
03841	Hampstead	8,524	6,732
*03842	Hampton (c)	9,126	7,989
*03842	Hampton	15,280	12,278
03755	Hanover Compact (c)	8,162	6,538
03755	Hanover	11,125	9,212
03244	Hillsborough	5,102	4,698
03049	Hollis	7,489	5,705
03106	Hooksett	12,807	9,002
03229	Hopkinton	5,579	4,806
03051	Hudson (c)	7,814	7,626
03051	Hudson	23,839	19,530
03452	Jaffrey	5,647	5,361
03431	Keene	22,780	22,430
03848	Kingston	6,139	5,591
*03246	Laconia	17,134	15,743
*03766	Lebanon	12,792	12,183
03052	Litchfield	7,975	5,516
03561	Littleton	6,086	5,827
03053	Londonderry (c)	11,417	10,114
03053	Londonderry	24,201	19,781
*03103	Manchester	108,871	99,332
03253	Meredith	6,352	4,837
03054	Merrimack	26,394	22,156
03055	Milford (c)	8,293	8,015
03055	Milford	14,235	11,795
*03060	Nashua	87,285	79,662
03857	Newmarket (c)	5,124	4,917
03857	Newmarket	8,601	7,157
03773	Newport	6,441	6,110
03076	Pelham	11,986	9,408
03275	Pembroke	7,243	6,561
03458	Peterborough	5,975	5,239
03102	Pinardville (c)	5,779	4,654
03865	Plaistow	7,855	7,316
03264	Plymouth	6,162	5,811
*03801	Portsmouth	21,002	25,925
03077	Raymond	9,990	8,713
03461	Rindge	5,826	4,941
*03867	Rochester	29,654	26,630
03870	Rye	5,271	—
03079	Salem	29,115	25,746
03873	Sandown	5,548	—
03874	Seabrook	8,428	6,503
03878	Somersworth	11,786	11,249
03106	South Hooksett (c)	5,282	3,638
03885	Stratham	6,726	4,955
03275	Suncook (c)	5,362	5,214
03446	Swanzey	7,030	6,236
03281	Weare	8,314	6,193
03087	Windham	12,205	9,000
03894	Wolfeboro	6,473	4,807

New Jersey

Area code (551) overlays area code (201). Area code (848) overlays (732). Area code (862) overlays (973). See introductory note.

ZIP	Place	Area Code	2003	1990
08201	Absecon	(609)	7,835	7,298
07401	Allendale	(201)	6,775	5,900
07712	Asbury Park	(732)	16,693	16,799
08034	Ashland (c)		8,375	—
*08401	Atlantic City	(609)	40,385	37,986
08106	Audubon	(856)	9,118	9,205
07001	Avenel (c)	(732)	17,552	15,504
—	Barclay-Kingston (c)		10,728	—
08007	Barrington	(856)	7,072	6,792
07002	Bayonne	(201)	60,905	61,464
08722	Beachwood	(732)	10,712	9,324
07109	Belleville (c)	(973)	35,928	34,213
*08031	Bellmawr	(856)	11,261	12,603
07719	Belmar	(732)	5,975	5,877
07621	Bergenfield	(201)	26,181	24,458
07922	Berkeley Heights (c)	(908)	13,407	11,980
08009	Berlin	(856)	6,819	5,672
07924	Bernardsville	(908)	7,559	6,597
07003	Bloomfield (c)	(973)	47,683	45,061
07403	Bloomingdale	(973)	7,693	7,530
07603	Bogota	(201)	8,181	7,824
07005	Boonton	(973)	8,427	8,343
08805	Bound Brook	(732)	10,151	9,487
08302	Bridgeton	(856)	22,785	18,942
08203	Brigantine	(609)	12,631	11,354
08015	Browns Mills (c)	(609)	11,257	11,429

ZIP	Place	Area Code	2003	1990
07828	Budd Lake (c)	(973)	8,100	7,272
08016	Burlington	(609)	9,809	9,835
07405	Butler	(973)	8,099	7,392
*07006	Caldwell	(973)	7,620	7,542
*08101	Camden	(856)	80,089	87,492
07072	Carlstadt	(201)	5,994	5,510
08069	Carney's Point (c)	(856)	6,914	8,443
07008	Carteret	(732)	21,653	19,025
07009	Cedar Grove (c)	(973)	12,300	12,053
07928	Chatham	(973)	8,440	8,007
08002	Cherry Hill Mall (c)	(856)	13,238	—
07066	Clark (c)	(732)/(908)	14,597	14,629
08312	Clayton	(856)	7,157	6,155
07010	Cliffside Park	(201)	22,892	20,393
*07015	Clifton	(973)	79,823	71,984
07624	Closter	(201)	8,541	8,094
08108	Collingswood	(856)	14,220	15,289
07067	Colonia (c)	(732)	17,811	18,238
07016	Cranford (c)	(908)	22,578	22,633
07626	Cresskill	(201)	7,896	7,558
08759	Crestwood Village (c)	(732)	8,392	8,030
08810	Dayton (c)	(732)	6,235	4,321
*07801	Dover	(973)	18,372	15,115
07628	Dumont	(201)	17,523	*17,187
08812	Dunellen	(732)	7,008	6,528
08816	East Brunswick (c)	(732)	46,756	43,548
*07019	East Orange	(973)	69,212	73,552
07073	East Rutherford	(201)/(973)	8,697	7,902
*07724	Eatontown	(732)	14,124	13,800
08043	Echelon (c)	(856)	10,440	—
07020	Edgewater	(201)	9,277	5,001
*08818	Edison (c)	(732)/(908)	97,687	88,680
*07207	Elizabeth	(908)	123,215	110,002
07407	Elmwood Park	(201)	18,964	17,623
07630	Emerson	(201)	7,284	6,930
07631	Englewood	(201)	26,106	24,850
07632	Englewood Cliffs	(201)	5,564	5,634
08002	Erlton-Ellisburg (c)		8,168	—
08618	Ewing (c)	(609)	35,707	34,185
07004	Fairfield (Essex Co.) (c)	(973)	7,063	7,615
07704	Fair Haven	(732)	5,949	5,270
07006	Fair Lawn	(201)/(973)	31,585	30,548
07022	Fairview (Bergen Co.)	(201)	13,379	10,733
07023	Fanwood	(908)	7,257	7,115
08518	Florence-Roebling (c)	(609)	8,200	8,564
07932	Florham Park	(973)	12,508	8,521
08863	Fords (c)	(732)	15,032	14,392
08640	Fort Dix (c)	(609)	7,464	10,205
07024	Fort Lee	(201)	37,139	31,997
07416	Franklin (Sussex Co.)	(973)	5,249	4,977
07417	Franklin Lakes	(201)	11,142	9,873
07728	Freehold	(732)	11,465	10,742
07026	Garfield	(862)/(973)	29,701	26,727
08028	Glassboro	(856)	19,094	15,614
07028	Glen Ridge	(973)	7,166	7,076
07452	Glen Rock	(201)	11,502	10,883
08030	Gloucester City	(856)	11,435	12,649
—	Greentree (c)		11,536	—
07093	Guttenberg	(201)	11,038	8,268
*07602	Hackensack	(201)	43,493	37,049
07840	Hackettstown	(908)	9,366	8,120
08033	Haddonfield	(856)	11,616	11,633
08035	Haddon Heights	(856)	7,495	7,860
*07508	Haledon	(973)	8,408	6,951
08037	Hammonton	(609)	12,994	12,208
07029	Harrison	(973)	14,262	13,425
07604	Hasbrouck Heights	(201)	11,636	11,488
*07506	Hawthorne	(973)	18,363	17,084
07422	Highland Lake (c)	(973)	5,051	4,550
08904	Highland Park	(732)	14,221	13,279
07732	Highlands	(732)	5,367	4,849
08520	Hightstown	(609)	5,311	5,126
07642	Hillsdale	(201)	10,090	9,750
07205	Hillside (c)	(908)/(973)	21,747	21,044
07030	Hoboken	(201)	39,482	33,397
08753	Holiday City-Berkeley (c)	(732)	13,884	14,293
07843	Hopatcong	(973)	16,097	15,586
07111	Irvington (c)	(973)	60,695	59,774
08830	Iselin (c)	(732)	16,698	16,141
08831	Jamesburg	(732)	6,477	5,294
*07303	Jersey City	(201)	239,097	228,517
07734	Keansburg	(732)	10,746	11,069
07032	Kearny	(201)/(973)	39,853	34,874
08824	Kendall Park (c)	(908)	9,006	7,127
07033	Kenilworth	(908)	7,736	7,574
07735	Keyport	(732)	7,504	7,586
07405	Kinnelon	(973)	9,475	8,470
07871	Lake Mohawk (c)	(973)	9,755	8,930
08701	Lakewood (c)	(732)	36,065	26,095
08879	Laurence Harbor (c)	(732)	6,227	6,361
*08733	Leisure Village West-Pine Lake Park (c)	(732)	11,085	10,139
07605	Leonia	(201)	8,888	8,365
07035	Lincoln Park	(973)	10,870	10,978
07738	Lincroft (c)	(732)	6,255	6,193
07036	Linden	(732)/(908)	39,877	36,701
08021	Lindenwold	(856)	17,377	18,734
08221	Linwood	(609)	7,370	6,866
07424	Little Falls (c)	(973)	10,855	11,294
07643	Little Ferry	(201)	10,799	9,989
07739	Little Silver	(732)	6,123	5,721
07039	Livingston (c)	(973)	27,391	26,609
07644	Lodi	(201)/(973)	24,182	22,355
07740	Long Branch	(732)	31,523	28,658
07071	Lyndhurst (c)	(201)	19,383	18,262
08641	McGuire AFB (c)	(609)	6,478	7,580
07940	Madison	(973)	15,352	15,850
08859	Madison Park (c)	(732)	6,929	7,490
08736	Manasquan	(732)	6,413	5,369
08835	Manville	(908)	10,401	10,567
07040	Maplewood (c)	(973)	23,868	21,756
08402	Margate City	(609)	8,328	8,431
08053	Marlton (c)	(856)	10,260	10,228
07747	Matawan	(732)	8,873	9,239
07607	Maywood	(201)	9,494	9,536
07945	Mendham	(973)	5,130	4,890
08619	Mercerville-Hamilton Sq. (c)	(609)	26,419	26,873
08840	Metuchen	(732)	13,293	12,804
08846	Middlesex	(732)	13,992	13,055
07432	Midland Park	(201)	6,927	7,047
07041	Millburn (c)	(973)	19,765	18,630
08850	Milltown	(732)	7,175	6,968
08332	Millville	(856)	27,119	25,992
*07042	Montclair (c)	(973)	38,977	37,729
07645	Montvale	(201)	7,289	6,946
08057	Moorestown-Lenola (c)	(856)	13,860	13,242
07751	Morganville (c)	(732)	11,255	—
07950	Morris Plains	(973)	5,513	5,219
*07960	Morristown	(973)	18,816	16,189
07092	Mountainside	(908)	6,659	6,657
07856	Mount Arlington	(973)	5,017	3,630
08087	Mystic Island (c)	(609)	8,694	7,400
07753	Neptune City	(732)	5,196	4,997
*07102	Newark	(973)	277,911	275,221
*08901	New Brunswick	(732)	49,803	41,711
07646	New Milford	(201)	16,367	15,990
07974	New Providence	(908)	11,983	11,439
*07860	Newton	(973)	8,389	7,521
07031	North Arlington	(201)	15,209	13,790
08902	North Brunswick Twp. (c)	(732)	36,287	31,287
07006	North Caldwell	(973)	7,380	6,706
08225	Northfield	(609)	7,954	7,305
07508	North Haledon	(973)	8,340	7,987
07060	North Plainfield	(908)	21,091	18,820
07648	Norwood	(201)	6,149	4,858
07110	Nutley (c)	(973)	27,362	27,099
07436	Oakland	(201)	13,616	11,997
*08050	Ocean Acres (c)	(609)	13,155	5,587
08226	Ocean City	(609)	15,558	15,512
07757	Oceanport	(732)	5,952	6,146
08857	Old Bridge (c)	(732)	22,833	22,151
07675	Old Tappan	(201)	5,798	4,254
07649	Oradell	(201)	8,025	8,024
*07051	Orange (c)	(973)	32,868	29,925
07650	Palisades Park	(201)	18,007	14,536
08065	Palmyra	(856)	7,653	7,056
*07652	Paramus	(201)	26,503	25,004
07656	Park Ridge	(201)	8,880	8,102
07055	Passaic	(973)	68,528	58,041
*07510	Paterson	(973)	150,782	140,891
08066	Paulsboro	(856)	6,116	6,577
08110	Pennsauken (c)	(856)	35,737	34,738
08070	Pennsville (c)	(856)	11,657	12,218
*08861	Perth Amboy	(732)	48,447	41,967
08865	Phillipsburg	(908)	15,177	15,757
08021	Pine Hill	(856)	11,092	9,854
08071	Pitman	(856)	9,274	9,365
*07061	Plainfield	(908)	48,025	46,577
08232	Pleasantville	(609)	19,016	16,027
08742	Point Pleasant	(732)	19,835	18,177
08742	Point Pleasant Beach	(732)	5,403	5,112
07442	Pompton Lakes	(973)	11,085	10,539
*08540	Princeton	(609)	13,577	12,016
—	Princeton Meadows (c)	(609)	13,436	—
07508	Prospect Park	(973)	5,792	5,053
07065	Rahway	(732)	26,797	25,325
08057	Ramblewood (c)	(856)	6,003	6,181
07446	Ramsey	(201)	14,490	13,228
—	Raritan (c)	(732)	5,932	—
08869	Raritan	(908)	6,357	5,798
07701	Red Bank	(732)	11,792	10,636
07657	Ridgefield	(201)	10,919	9,996
07660	Ridgefield Park	(201)	12,781	12,454
*07451	Ridgewood	(201)/(973)	24,831	24,152
07456	Ringwood	(973)	12,704	12,623
07661	River Edge	(201)	10,978	10,603
07675	River Vale (c)	(201)	9,449	9,410
07662	Rochelle Park (c)	(201)	5,528	5,587
07866	Rockaway	(973)	6,427	6,243
07068	Roseland	(973)	5,297	4,847
07203	Roselle	(908)	21,423	20,314
07204	Roselle Park	(908)	13,310	12,805
07760	Rumson	(732)	7,312	6,701
08078	Runnemede	(856)	8,541	9,042
07070	Rutherford	(201)	18,020	17,790
07663	Saddle Brook (c)	(201)/(973)	13,155	13,296
08079	Salem	(856)	5,793	6,883
*08872	Sayreville	(732)	42,064	34,998
07076	Scotch Plains (c)	(732)/(908)	22,732	21,150
*07094	Secaucus	(201)	15,735	14,061

ZIP	Place	Area Code	2003	1990
08083	Somerdale	(856)	5,185	5,440
*08873	Somerset (c)	(732)	23,040	22,070
08244	Somers Point	(609)	11,618	11,216
08876	Somerville	(908)	12,391	11,632
08879	South Amboy	(732)	8,032	7,851
07079	South Orange (c)	(973)	16,964	16,390
07080	South Plainfield	(732)/(908)	22,965	20,489
08882	South River	(732)	16,041	13,692
08884	Spotswood	(732)	8,236	7,983
—	Springdale (c)		14,409	—
07081	Springfield (c)	(908)/(973)	14,429	13,420
07762	Spring Lake Heights	(732)	5,248	5,341
08084	Stratford	(856)	7,246	7,614
07747	Strathmore (c)	(732)	6,740	7,060
07876	Succasunna-Kenvil (c)	(201)	12,569	11,781
*07901	Summit	(908)	21,262	19,757
07666	Teaneck (c)	(201)	39,260	37,825
07670	Tenafly	(201)	14,101	13,326
07724	Tinton Falls	(732)	15,975	12,361
*08753	Toms River (c)	(732)	86,327	7,524
*07512	Totowa	(973)	10,030	10,177
*08650	Trenton	(609)	85,314	88,675
08520	Twin Rivers (c)	(609)	7,422	7,715
07083	Union (Union Co.) (c)	(908)	54,405	50,024
07735	Union Beach	(732)	6,745	6,156
07087	Union City	(201)	66,573	58,012
07458	Upper Saddle River	(201)	8,237	7,198
08406	Ventnor City	(609)	12,778	11,005
07044	Verona (c)	(973)	13,533	13,597
08251	Villas (c)	(609)	9,064	8,136
*08360	Vineland	(856)	57,057	54,780
07463	Waldwick	(201)	9,628	9,757
07057	Wallington	(201)/(973)	11,522	10,828
07465	Wanaque	(201)/(973)	10,419	9,711
07882	Washington	(908)	6,829	6,474
07675	Washington Twp. (Bergen Co.) (c)	(201)	8,938	9,245
07060	Watchung	(908)	5,738	5,110
*07470	Wayne (c)	(973)	54,069	47,025
*07006	West Caldwell (c)	(973)	11,233	10,422
*07901	Westfield	(732)/(908)	29,951	28,870
07728	West Freehold (c)	(732)	12,498	11,166
07764	West Long Branch	(732)	8,216	7,690
07480	West Milford (c)	(973)	26,410	25,430
07093	West New York	(201)	46,348	38,125
07052	West Orange (c)	(973)	44,943	39,103
07424	West Paterson	(973)	11,255	10,982
07675	Westwood	(201)	11,010	10,446
07885	Wharton	(973)	6,223	5,405
08610	White Horse (c)	(609)	9,373	9,397
07886	White Meadow Lake (c)	(973)	9,052	8,002
08260	Wildwood	(609)	5,260	4,484
08094	Williamstown (c)	(856)	11,812	10,891
07095	Woodbridge (c)	(732)	18,309	17,434
08096	Woodbury	(856)	10,439	10,904
07675	Woodcliff Lake	(201)	5,846	5,303
07075	Wood-Ridge	(201)/(973)	7,622	7,506
07481	Wyckoff (c)	(201)	16,508	15,372
08620	Yardville-Groveville (c)	(609)	9,208	9,248
07726	Yorketown (c)	(609)	6,712	6,313

New Mexico (505)

ZIP	Place	2003	1990
*88310	Alamogordo	35,551	27,596
*87101	Albuquerque	471,856	384,915
88021	Anthony (c)	7,904	5,160
*88210	Artesia	10,518	10,610
87410	Aztec	6,818	5,480
87002	Belen	6,961	6,547
87004	Bernalillo	6,986	5,864
87413	Bloomfield	7,210	5,214
*88220	Carlsbad	25,303	24,952
88021	Chaparral (c)	6,117	2,962
*88101	Clovis	32,815	30,954
87048	Corrales	7,553	5,453
*88030	Deming	14,381	11,422
—	El Cerro-Monterey Park (c)	5,483	—
—	Eldorado at Santa Fe (c)	5,799	2,260
*87532	Espanola	9,762	8,389
*87401	Farmington	41,420	33,997
*87301	Gallup	19,868	19,157
87020	Grants	8,972	8,626
*88240	Hobbs	28,311	29,121
87417	Kirtland (c)	6,190	3,552
*88001	Las Cruces	76,990	62,360
87701	Las Vegas	14,194	14,753
87544	Los Alamos (c)	11,909	11,445
87002	Los Chaves (c)	5,033	3,872
87031	Los Lunas	11,265	6,013
87107	Los Ranchos de Albuquerque	5,156	5,075
88260	Lovington	9,456	9,322
87107	North Valley (c)	11,923	12,507
88130	Portales	11,078	10,690
87740	Raton	7,186	7,372
*87124	Rio Rancho	58,981	32,512
*88201	Roswell	44,228	44,260
*88345	Ruidoso	8,270	4,600
*87501	Santa Fe	66,476	56,537
87420	Shiprock c)	8,156	7,687
*88061	Silver City	10,052	10,683

ZIP	Place	2003	1990
87801	Socorro	8,708	8,159
87105	South Valley (c)	39,060	35,701
88063	Sunland Park	13,815	8,179
87571	Taos	5,008	4,065
87901	Truth or Consequences	7,116	6,221
88401	Tucumcari	5,564	6,827
87544	White Rock (c)	6,045	6,192
87327	Zuni Pueblo (c)	6,367	5,857

New York

Area code (347) overlays area code (718). Area codes (646) and (917) overlay (212). See introductory note.

ZIP	Place	Area Code	2003	1990
10901	Airmont	(845)	8,635	7,674
*12201	Albany	(518)	93,919	100,031
11507	Albertson (c)	(516)	5,200	5,166
14411	Albion	(585)	5,839	5,863
*11701	Amityville	(516)/(631)	9,551	9,286
12010	Amsterdam	(518)	17,974	20,714
12603	Arlington (c)	(845)	12,481	11,948
*13021	Auburn	(315)	28,121	31,258
11702	Babylon	(631)	12,759	12,249
11510	Baldwin (c)	(516)	23,455	22,719
11510	Baldwin Harbor (c)	(516)	8,147	7,899
13027	Baldwinsville	(315)	7,190	6,591
12020	Ballston Spa	(518)	5,565	5,194
*14020	Batavia	(585)	15,939	16,310
14810	Bath	(607)	5,574	5,801
11705	Bayport (c)	(631)	8,662	7,702
11706	Bay Shore (c)	(631)	23,852	21,279
11709	Bayville	(516)	7,139	7,193
11751	Baywood (c)	(631)	7,571	7,351
12508	Beacon	(845)	16,059	13,243
11710	Bellmore (c)	(516)	16,441	16,438
11714	Bethpage (c)	(516)	16,543	15,761
*13902	Binghamton	(607)	46,310	53,008
10913	Blauvelt (c)	(845)	5,207	4,838
11716	Bohemia (c)	(631)	9,871	9,556
11717	Brentwood (c)	(631)	53,917	45,218
10510	Briarcliff Manor	(914)	7,906	7,070
14610	Brighton (c)	(585)	35,584	34,455
14420	Brockport	(585)	8,097	8,749
10708	Bronxville	(914)	6,515	6,028
*14240	Buffalo	(716)	285,018	328,175
11933	Calverton (c)	(631)	5,704	4,759
*14424	Canandaigua	(585)	11,449	10,725
13617	Canton	(315)	5,961	6,379
11514	Carle Place (c)	(516)	5,247	5,107
10512	Carmel Hamlet (c)	(845)	5,650	4,800
11516	Cedarhurst	(516)	6,121	5,716
11720	Centereach (c)	(631)	27,285	26,720
11934	Center Moriches (c)	(631)	6,655	5,987
11721	Centerport (c)	(631)	5,446	5,333
11722	Central Islip (c)	(516)	31,950	26,028
10514	Chappaqua (c)	(914)	9,468	—
14225	Cheektowaga (c)	(716)	79,988	84,387
10977	Chestnut Ridge	(845)	7,881	7,517
12047	Cohoes	(518)	15,303	16,825
12205	Colonie	(518)	8,080	8,019
11725	Commack (c)	(631)	36,367	36,124
10920	Congers (c)	(845)	8,303	8,003
11726	Copiague (c)	(631)	21,922	20,769
11727	Coram (c)	(631)	34,923	30,111
14830	Corning	(607)	10,625	11,938
13045	Cortland	(607)	18,462	19,801
*10520	Croton-on-Hudson	(914)	7,801	7,018
11729	Deer Park (c)	(631)	28,316	28,840
12054	Delmar (c)	(518)	8,292	8,360
14043	Depew	(716)	16,194	17,673
11746	Dix Hills (c)	(631)	26,024	25,849
10522	Dobbs Ferry	(914)	11,041	9,940
14048	Dunkirk	(716)	12,715	13,989
14052	East Aurora	(585)/(716)	6,493	6,647
10709	Eastchester (c)	(914)	18,564	18,537
12302	East Glenville (c)	(518)	6,064	6,518
11576	East Hills	(516)	6,818	6,746
11730	East Islip (c)	(631)	14,078	14,325
11758	East Massapequa (c)	(516)	19,565	19,550
11554	East Meadow (c)	(516)	37,461	36,909
11731	East Northport (c)	(631)	20,845	20,411
11772	East Patchogue (c)	(631)	20,824	20,195
14445	East Rochester	(585)	6,510	6,932
11518	East Rockaway	(516)	10,341	10,152
11786	East Shoreham (c)	(631)	5,809	5,461
*14901	Elmira	(607)	30,3367	33,724
11003	Elmont (c)	(516)	32,657	28,612
11731	Elwood (c)	(631)	10,916	10,916
*13760	Endicott	(607)	12,876	13,531
13762	Endwell (c)	(607)	11,706	12,602
13219	Fairmount (c)	(315)	10,795	12,266
14450	Fairport	(585)	5,690	5,943
—	Fairview (c)	(845)	5,421	4,811
11735	Farmingdale	(516)	8,665	8,022
11738	Farmingville (c)	(631)	16,458	14,842
*11001	Floral Park	(516)	15,862	15,947
13603	Fort Drum (c)	(315)	12,123	11,578
11768	Fort Salonga (c)	(631)	9,634	9,176
11010	Franklin Square (c)	(516)	29,342	28,205
14063	Fredonia	(716)	10,569	10,436

ZIP	Place	Area Code	2003	1990
11520	Freeport	(516)	43,726	39,894
13069	Fulton	(315)	11,639	12,929
*11530	Garden City	(516)	21,787	21,675
11040	Garden City Park (c)	(516)	7,554	7,437
14624	Gates-North Gates (c)	(585)	15,138	14,995
14454	Geneseo	(585)	7,916	7,187
14456	Geneva	(315)	13,517	14,143
11542	Glen Cove	(516)	26,781	24,149
12801	Glens Falls	(518)	14,212	15,023
12801	Glens Falls North (c)	(518)	8,061	7,978
12078	Gloversville	(518)	15,227	16,656
10924	Goshen	(845)	5,370	5,255
*11021	Great Neck	(516)	9,623	8,745
11020	Great Neck Plaza	(516)	6,928	5,897
14616	Greece (c)	(585)	14,614	15,632
11740	Greenlawn (c)	(631)	13,286	13,208
*10583	Greenville (Westchester Co.) (c)	(914)	8,648	9,528
14075	Hamburg	(716)	9,841	10,442
11946	Hampton Bays (c)	(631)	12,236	7,893
10528	Harrison	(914)	25,150	23,308
10530	Hartsdale (c)	(914)	9,830	9,587
10706	Hastings-on-Hudson	(914)	7,771	8,000
*11788	Hauppauge (c)	(631)	20,100	19,750
10927	Haverstraw	(845)	10,133	9,438
10532	Hawthorne (c)	(845)	5,083	4,764
*11551	Hempstead	(516)	53,162	45,982
13350	Herkimer	(315)	7,298	7,945
11557	Hewlett (c)	(516)	7,060	6,620
*11802	Hicksville (c)	(516)	41,260	40,174
12528	Highland (c)	(845)	5,060	4,492
10977	Hillcrest (c)	(845)	7,106	6,447
14468	Hilton	(585)	5,962	5,216
11741	Holbrook (c)	(631)	27,512	25,273
11742	Holtsville (c)	(631)	17,006	14,972
14843	Hornell	(607)	8,817	9,877
*14845	Horseheads	(607)	6,363	6,802
12534	Hudson	(518)	7,296	8,034
12839	Hudson Falls	(518)	6,857	7,651
11743	Huntington (c)	(631)	18,403	18,243
11746	Huntington Station (c)	(631)	29,910	28,247
13357	Ilion	(315)	8,370	8,888
11096	Inwood (c)	(516)	9,325	7,767
14617	Irondequoit (c)	(585)	52,354	52,322
10533	Irvington	(914)	6,665	6,348
11751	Islip (c)	(631)	20,575	18,924
11752	Islip Terrace (c)	(631)	5,641	5,530
*14850	Ithaca	(607)	30,343	29,541
*14702	Jamestown	(716)	30,726	34,681
10535	Jefferson Valley-Yorktown (c)	(914)	14,891	14,118
11753	Jericho (c)	(516)	13,045	13,141
13790	Johnson City	(607)	15,230	16,578
12095	Johnstown	(518)	8,516	9,058
14217	Kenmore	(716)	15,933	17,180
11754	Kings Park (c)	(631)	16,146	17,773
11024	Kings Point	(516)	5,175	4,843
*12401	Kingston	(845)	23,294	23,095
10950	Kiryas Joel	(845)	16,442	7,437
14218	Lackawanna	(716)	18,622	20,585
10512	Lake Carmel (c)	(845)	8,663	8,489
11755	Lake Grove	(631)	10,602	9,612
10547	Lake Mohegan (c)	(914)	5,979	—
11779	Lake Ronkonkoma (c)	(631)	19,701	18,997
11552	Lakeview (c)	(516)	5,607	5,476
14086	Lancaster	(716)	11,381	11,940
10538	Larchmont	(914)	6,523	6,181
11559	Lawrence	(516)	6,546	6,513
11756	Levittown (c)	(516)	53,067	53,286
11757	Lindenhurst	(631)	28,469	26,879
13365	Little Falls	(315)	5,049	5,829
*14094	Lockport	(716)	21,600	24,426
11561	Long Beach	(516)	35,415	33,510
11563	Lynbrook	(516)	19,803	19,208
10541	Mahopac (c)	(845)	8,478	7,755
12953	Malone	(518)	5,998	6,777
11565	Malverne	(516)	8,879	9,054
10543	Mamaroneck	(914)	18,493	17,325
11030	Manhasset (c)	(516)	8,362	7,718
11050	Manorhaven	(516)	6,272	5,672
11949	Manorville (c)	(631)	11,131	6,198
11758	Massapequa (c)	(516)	22,652	22,018
11762	Massapequa Park	(516)	17,453	18,044
13662	Massena	(315)	10,982	11,716
11950	Mastic (c)	(631)	15,436	13,778
11951	Mastic Beach (c)	(631)	11,543	10,293
13211	Mattydale (c)	(315)	6,367	6,418
—	Mechanicstown (c)	(845)	6,061	—
12118	Mechanicville	(518)	5,001	5,249
11763	Medford (c)	(631)	21,985	21,274
14103	Medina	(585)/(716)	6,308	6,686
11747	Melville (c)	(631)	14,533	12,586
11566	Merrick (c)	(516)	22,764	23,042
11953	Middle Island (c)	(631)	9,702	7,848
*10940	Middletown	(845)	25,863	24,160
11764	Miller Place (c)	(631)	10,580	9,315
11501	Mineola	(516)	19,164	19,005
10950	Monroe	(845)	8,052	6,672
10952	Monsey (c)	(845)	14,504	13,986
12701	Monticello	(845)	6,493	6,597
10970	Mount Ivy (c)	(845)	6,536	6,013
10549	Mount Kisco	(914)	10,035	9,108
11766	Mount Sinai (c)	(631)	8,734	8,023
*10551	Mount Vernon	(914)	68,404	67,153
12590	Myers Corner (c)	(845)	5,546	5,599
10954	Nanuet (c)	(845)	16,707	14,065
11767	Nesconset (c)	(631)	11,992	10,712
14513	Newark	(315)	9,507	9,849
*12550	Newburgh	(845)	28,412	26,454
11590	New Cassel (c)	(516)	13,298	10,257
10956	New City (c)	(845)	34,038	33,673
*11040	New Hyde Park	(516)	9,526	9,728
12561	New Paltz	(845)	6,428	5,470
*10802	New Rochelle	(914)	72,582	67,265
10977	New Square	(845)	5,644	2,623
*12550	New Windsor (c)	(845)	9,077	8,898
*10001	New York	(212)/(718)	8,085,742	7,322,564
*14302	Niagara Falls	(716)	53,989	61,840
11701	North Amityville (c)	(631)	16,572	13,849
11703	North Babylon (c)	(631)	17,877	18,081
11706	North Bay Shore (c)	(631)	14,992	12,799
11710	North Bellmore (c)	(516)	20,079	19,707
11713	North Bellport (c)	(631)	9,007	8,182
11757	North Lindenhurst (c)	(631)	11,767	10,563
11758	North Massapequa (c)	(516)	19,152	19,365
11566	North Merrick (c)	(516)	11,844	12,113
11040	North New Hyde Park (c)	(516)	14,542	14,359
11772	North Patchogue (c)	(631)	7,825	7,374
11768	Northport	(631)	7,671	7,572
13212	North Syracuse	(315)	6,863	7,363
14120	North Tonawanda	(716)	32,359	34,989
11580	North Valley Stream (c)	(516)	15,789	14,574
11793	North Wantagh (c)	(516)	12,156	12,276
13815	Norwich	(607)	7,251	7,613
10960	Nyack	(845)	6,749	6,558
11769	Oakdale (c)	(631)	8,075	7,875
11572	Oceanside (c)	(516)	32,733	32,423
13669	Ogdensburg	(315)	11,832	13,521
11804	Old Bethpage (c)	(516)	5,400	5,610
14760	Olean	(585)/(716)	14,989	16,946
13421	Oneida	(315)	10,956	10,850
13820	Oneonta	(607)	12,799	13,954
12550	Orange Lake (c)	(845)	6,085	5,196
10562	Ossining	(914)	24,229	22,582
13126	Oswego	(315)	18,223	19,195
11771	Oyster Bay (c)	(516)	6,826	6,687
11772	Patchogue	(631)	12,016	11,060
10965	Pearl River (c)	(845)	15,553	15,314
10566	Peekskill	(914)	23,436	19,536
10803	Pelham	(914)	6,399	5,443
10803	Pelham Manor	(914)	5,450	6,413
14527	Penn Yan	(315)	5,123	5,248
11714	Plainedge (c)	(516)	9,195	8,739
11803	Plainview (c)	(516)	25,637	26,207
*12901	Plattsburgh	(518)	19,163	21,255
10570	Pleasantville	(914)	7,178	6,592
10573	Port Chester	(914)	27,955	24,728
11777	Port Jefferson	(631)	7,948	7,455
11776	Port Jefferson Station (c)	(631)	7,527	7,232
12771	Port Jervis	(845)	9,100	9,060
11050	Port Washington (c)	(516)	15,215	15,387
13676	Potsdam	(315)	9,555	10,251
*12601	Poughkeepsie	(845)	30,174	28,844
12144	Rensselaer	(518)	7,743	8,255
11961	Ridge (c)	(631)	13,380	11,734
11901	Riverhead (c)	(631)	10,513	8,814
*14692	Rochester	(585)	215,093	230,356
11571	Rockville Centre	(516)	24,397	24,727
11778	Rocky Point (c)	(631)	10,185	8,596
*13440	Rome	(315)	34,512	44,350
11779	Ronkonkoma (c)	(631)	20,029	20,391
11575	Roosevelt (c)	(516)	15,854	15,030
11577	Roslyn Heights (c)	(516)	6,295	6,405
12303	Rotterdam (c)	(518)	20,536	21,228
10580	Rye	(914)	15,066	14,936
10573	Rye Brook	(914)	9,234	7,765
11780	Saint James (c)	(631)	13,268	12,703
14779	Salamanca	(716)	5,942	6,566
13454	Salisbury (c)	(315)	12,341	12,226
12866	Saratoga Springs	(518)	27,332	25,001
11782	Sayville (c)	(631)	16,735	16,550
10583	Scarsdale	(914)	17,929	16,987
*12301	Schenectady	(518)	61,016	65,566
10940	Scotchtown (c)	(845)	8,954	8,765
12302	Scotia	(518)	7,856	7,359
11579	Sea Cliff	(516)	5,034	5,054
11783	Seaford (c)	(516)	15,791	15,597
11507	Searingtown (c)	(516)	5,034	5,020
11784	Selden (c)	(631)	21,861	20,608
13148	Seneca Falls	(315)	6,901	7,370
11733	Setauket-East Setauket (c)	(516)	15,931	13,634
11967	Shirley (c)	(631)	25,395	22,936
10591	Sleepy Hollow[1]	(914)	9,275	8,152
11787	Smithtown (c)	(631)	26,901	25,638
13209	Solvay	(315)	6,734	6,717
11789	Sound Beach (c)	(631)	9,807	9,102
11735	South Farmingdale (c)	(516)	15,061	15,377
14850	South Hill (c)	(607)	6,003	5,423
11746	South Huntington (c)	(631)	9,465	9,624
14094	South Lockport (c)	(716)	8,552	7,112
11971	Southold (c)	(631)	5,465	5,192
14904	Southport (c)	(607)	7,396	7,753

ZIP	Place	Area Code	2003	1990
11581	South Valley Stream (c)	(516)	5,638	5,328
10977	Spring Valley	(845)	25,509	21,802
*11790	Stony Brook (c)	(631)	13,727	13,726
10980	Stony Point (c)	(845)	11,744	10,587
10901	Suffern	(845)	11,014	11,055
11791	Syosset (c)	(516)	18,544	18,967
*13220	Syracuse	(315)	144,001	163,860
10983	Tappan (c)	(845)	6,757	6,867
10591	Tarrytown	(914)	11,411	10,739
11776	Terryville (c)	(631)	10,589	10,275
10594	Thornwood (c)	(914)	5,980	7,025
*14150	Tonawanda	(716)	15,700	17,284
*14150	Tonawanda (c)	(716)	61,729	65,284
*12180	Troy	(518)	48,649	54,269
10707	Tuckahoe	(914)	6,243	6,302
11553	Uniondale (c)	(516)	23,011	20,328
*13504	Utica	(315)	59,485	68,637
10595	Valhalla (c)	(914)	5,379	—
10989	Valley Cottage (c)	(845)	9,269	9,007
*11582	Valley Stream	(516)	36,214	33,946
—	Viola (c)		5,931	4,504
11792	Wading River (c)	(631)	6,668	5,317
12586	Walden	(845)	6,608	5,836
11793	Wantagh (c)	(516)	18,971	18,567
10990	Warwick	(845)	6,548	5,984
10992	Washingtonville	(845)	6,243	4,906
13165	Waterloo	(315)	5,132	5,116
*13601	Watertown	(315)	26,782	29,429
12189	Watervliet	(518)	10,052	11,061
14580	Webster	(585)	5,175	5,464
10952	Wesley Hills	(845)	5,051	4,308
*11704	West Babylon (c)	(631)	43,452	42,410
11590	Westbury	(516)	14,283	13,060
14905	West Elmira (c)	(607)	5,136	5,218
12801	West Glens Falls (c)	(518)	6,721	5,964
10993	West Haverstraw	(845)	10,331	9,183
11552	West Hempstead (c)	(516)	18,713	17,689
11743	West Hills (c)	(631)	5,607	5,849
11795	West Islip (c)	(631)	28,907	28,419
12203	Westmere (c)	(518)	7,188	6,750
*10996	West Point (c)	(845)	7,138	8,024
11796	West Sayville (c)	(631)	5,003	4,680
14224	West Seneca (c)	(716)	45,943	47,866
13219	Westvale (c)	(315)	5,166	5,952
11798	Wheatley Heights (c)	(631)	5,013	5,027
*10602	White Plains	(914)	55,900	48,718
14231	Williamsville	(716)	5,427	5,583
11596	Williston Park	(516)	7,193	7,516
11797	Woodbury (c)	(516)	9,010	8,008
11598	Woodmere (c)	(516)	16,447	15,578
11798	Wyandach (c)	(631)	10,546	8,950
11980	Yaphank (c)	(631)	5,025	4,637
*10702	Yonkers	(914)	197,388	188,082
10598	Yorktown Heights (c)	(914)	7,972	7,690

(1) North Tarrytown changed its name to Sleepy Hollow on Dec. 12, 1996.

North Carolina

Area code (980) overlays area code (704). See introductory note.

ZIP	Place	Area Code	2003	1990
*28001	Albemarle	(704)	15,408	14,940
27502	Apex	(919)	26,588	4,789
27263	Archdale	(336)	9,241	6,975
*27203	Asheboro	(336)	22,839	16,362
*28802	Asheville	(828)	69,045	63,379
28012	Belmont	(704)	8,793	8,434
28016	Bessemer City	(704)	5,100	4,698
28711	Black Mountain	(828)	7,551	7,156
28607	Boone	(828)	13,127	12,949
28712	Brevard	(828)	6,693	5,452
*27215	Burlington	(336)	46,271	39,498
27509	Butner (c)	(919)	5,792	4,679
28428	Carolina Beach	(910)	5,118	4,002
27510	Carrboro	(919)	16,747	12,134
*27511	Cary	(919)	99,824	44,394
*27514	Chapel Hill	(919)	49,301	38,719
*28204	Charlotte	(704)	584,658	419,558
28021	Cherryville	(704)	5,422	4,756
27520	Clayton	(919)	11,293	4,756
27012	Clemmons	(336)	16,118	5,982
*28328	Clinton	(910)	8,636	8,385
*28025	Concord	(704)	58,943	29,591
28613	Conover	(828)	6,772	5,311
28031	Cornelius	(704)	16,827	2,581
28036	Davidson	(704)	8,142	4,046
*28334	Dunn	(910)	9,722	9,258
*27701	Durham	(919)	198,376	138,894
*27288	Eden	(336)	15,622	15,238
*27909	Elizabeth City	(252)	17,570	16,087
27244	Elon	(336)	7,053	4,394
*28302	Fayetteville	(910)	124,372	75,850
28043	Forest City	(828)	7,373	7,475
28307	Fort Bragg (c)	(910)	29,183	34,744
27526	Fuquay-Varina	(919)	10,089	4,447
27529	Garner	(919)	20,537	14,716
*28052	Gastonia	(704)	67,781	54,725
*27530	Goldsboro	(919)	38,484	40,736
27253	Graham	(336)	13,282	10,368
*27420	Greensboro	(336)	229,110	185,125
*27834	Greenville	(252)	67,190	46,274
*28540	Half Moon (c)	(910)	6,645	6,306
28345	Hamlet	(910)	5,866	6,722
28532	Havelock	(252)	22,499	20,300
27536	Henderson	(252)	16,231	15,655
*28739	Hendersonville	(828)	11,123	7,284
*28603	Hickory	(828)	39,476	28,474
*27260	High Point	(336)	91,543	69,428
27278	Hillsborough	(919)	5,361	4,263
27540	Holly Springs	(919)	12,694	1,203
28348	Hope Mills	(910)	11,966	8,272
*28070	Huntersville	(704)	32,323	3,014
28079	Indian Trail	(704)	14,173	1,942
*28540	Jacksonville	(910)	67,386	78,031
—	James City (c)	(252)	5,420	4,279
*28081	Kannapolis	(704)	38,178	31,592
*27284	Kernersville	(336)	20,053	11,860
27948	Kill Devil Hills	(252)	6,287	4,238
27021	King	(336)	6,187	4,059
—	Kings Grant (c)		7,738	—
28086	Kings Mountain	(704)	10,537	8,768
*28502	Kinston	(252)	22,978	25,295
27545	Knightdale	(919)	6,052	1,884
*28352	Laurinburg	(910)	15,552	16,131
28645	Lenoir	(828)	17,952	16,337
27023	Lewisville	(336)	9,332	6,433
*27292	Lexington	(336)	20,385	16,583
*28092	Lincolnton	(704)	10,114	6,955
*28358	Lumberton	(910)	21,161	18,656
*28403	Masonboro (c)	(910)	11,812	7,010
*28105	Matthews	(704)	23,436	13,756
27302	Mebane	(919)	8,464	4,754
28227	Mint Hill	(704)	16,477	13,637
*28110	Monroe	(704)	28,222	18,623
*28115	Mooresville	(704)	19,606	9,563
28557	Morehead City	(252)	8,064	6,473
*28655	Morganton	(828)	17,261	15,085
27560	Morrisville	(919)	7,671	1,022
27030	Mount Airy	(336)	8,394	7,156
28120	Mount Holly	(704)	9,591	7,710
—	Murraysville (c)		7,279	—
—	Myrtle Grove (c)		7,125	4,275
*28562	New Bern	(252)	23,308	20,728
28658	Newton	(828)	12,682	11,134
*28465	Oak Island	(910)	6,965	—
—	Ogden (c)		5,481	3,228
27565	Oxford	(919)	8,495	7,965
*28374	Pinehurst	(910)	10,774	5,825
28399	Piney Green (c)	(910)	11,658	8,999
*27611	Raleigh	(919)	316,802	218,859
*27320	Reidsville	(336)	14,777	14,085
27870	Roanoke Rapids	(252)	16,512	15,722
*28379	Rockingham	(910)	9,301	9,399
*27801	Rocky Mount	(252)	55,984	53,078
27573	Roxboro	(336)	8,794	7,332
28704	Royal Pines (c)		5,334	4,418
28601	Saint Stephens (c)	(828)	9,439	8,734
*28144	Salisbury	(704)	26,548	23,626
*27330	Sanford	(919)	23,346	18,881
27576	Selma	(919)	6,333	4,600
*28150	Shelby	(704)	21,215	15,460
27344	Siler City	(919)	7,603	4,808
—	Silver Lake (c)		5,788	4,071
27577	Smithfield	(919)	11,462	10,180
*28387	Southern Pines	(910)	11,446	9,213
28052	South Gastonia (c)	(704)	5,433	5,487
28390	Spring Lake	(910)	8,163	7,552
*28677	Statesville	(704)	24,129	20,647
27358	Summerfield	(336)	7,144	2,051
27886	Tarboro	(252)	10,701	11,037
*27360	Thomasville	(336)	25,466	15,915
27370	Trinity	(336)	6,818	5,469
28110	Unionville	(704)	5,648	—
*27587	Wake Forest	(919)	16,029	5,832
27889	Washington	(252)	9,677	9,160
28786	Waynesville	(828)	9,347	7,282
28104	Weddington	(704)	7,666	3,803
28472	Whiteville	(910)	5,099	5,340
27892	Williamston	(252)	5,749	5,870
*28402	Wilmington	(910)	91,137	55,530
*27893	Wilson	(252)	45,921	38,400
*27102	Winston-Salem	(336)	190,299	162,292

North Dakota (701)

ZIP	Place	2003	1990
*58501	Bismarck	56,344	49,272
58301	Devils Lake	6,971	7,782
*58601	Dickinson	15,683	16,097
*58102	Fargo	91,484	74,084
*58201	Grand Forks	48,618	49,417
*58401	Jamestown	15,158	15,571
58554	Mandan	16,781	15,177
*58701	Minot	35,424	34,544
*58701	Minot AFB (c)	7,599	9,095
58072	Valley City	6,420	7,163
58075	Wahpeton	8,443	8,751
58078	West Fargo	16,431	12,287
*58801	Williston	12,224	13,136

Ohio

Area code (234) overlays area code (330). Area code (567) overlays (419). See introductory note.

ZIP	Place	Area Code	2003	1990
45810	Ada	(419)	5,583	5,428
*44309	Akron	(330)	212,215	223,019
44601	Alliance	(330)	22,892	23,376
44001	Amherst	(440)	11,738	10,332
44805	Ashland	(419)	21,449	20,079
*44004	Ashtabula	(440)	20,355	21,633
45701	Athens	(740)	22,220	21,265
44202	Aurora	(330)	14,270	9,192
44515	Austintown (c)	(330)	*31,627*	32,371
44011	Avon	(440)	13,877	7,337
44012	Avon Lake	(440)	19,782	15,066
44203	Barberton	(330)	27,462	27,623
44140	Bay Village	(440)	15,731	17,000
44122	Beachwood	(216)	11,906	10,644
45434	Beavercreek	(937)	39,196	33,626
—	Beckett Ridge (c)		*8,663*	4,505
44146	Bedford	(216)/(440)	13,790	14,822
44146	Bedford Heights	(216)/(440)	11,189	12,131
45305	Bellbrook	(937)	6,966	6,511
43311	Bellefontaine	(937)	12,980	12,126
44811	Bellevue	(419)	8,111	8,157
45714	Belpre	(740)	6,570	6,796
44017	Berea	(440)	18,505	19,051
43209	Bexley	(614)	12,632	13,088
43004	Blacklick Estates (c)	(614)	*9,518*	10,080
45242	Blue Ash	(513)	12,108	11,923
44513	Boardman (c)	(330)	*37,215*	38,596
43402	Bowling Green	(419)	29,382	28,303
44141	Brecksville	(440)	13,474	11,818
45211	Bridgetown North (c)	(513)	*12,569*	11,748
44147	Broadview Heights	(440)	16,721	12,219
44144	Brooklyn	(216)	11,276	11,706
44142	Brook Park	(216)/(440)	20,679	22,865
45309	Brookville	(937)	5,279	4,621
44212	Brunswick	(330)	34,788	28,218
43506	Bryan	(419)	8,241	8,348
44820	Bucyrus	(419)	12,945	13,496
43725	Cambridge	(740)	11,596	11,748
44405	Campbell	(330)	9,020	10,038
44614	Canal Fulton	(330)	5,017	4,157
43110	Canal Winchester	(614)	5,193	2,652
44406	Canfield	(330)	7,188	5,409
*44711	Canton	(330)	79,255	84,161
45005	Carlisle	(937)	5,522	4,872
45822	Celina	(419)	10,275	9,945
*45441	Centerville (Montgomery Co.)	(937)	23,133	21,082
44024	Chardon	(440)	5,270	4,446
45211	Cheviot	(513)	8,543	9,616
45601	Chillicothe	(740)	22,170	21,923
*45202	Cincinnati	(513)	317,361	364,114
43113	Circleville	(740)	13,400	11,666
45315	Clayton	(937)	13,268	713
*44101	Cleveland	(216)	461,324	505,616
44118	Cleveland Heights	(216)	49,016	54,052
43410	Clyde	(419)	6,047	6,087
44408	Columbiana	(330)	5,703	4,961
*43216	Columbus	(614)	728,432	632,945
44030	Conneaut	(440)	12,666	13,241
44410	Cortland	(330)	6,703	5,652
43812	Coshocton	(740)	11,630	12,193
45238	Covedale (c)	(513)	*6,360*	6,669
*44222	Cuyahoga Falls	(330)	50,375	48,950
*45401	Dayton	(937)	161,696	182,011
45236	Deer Park	(513)	5,800	6,181
43512	Defiance	(419)	16,163	16,787
43015	Delaware	(740)	28,358	19,966
45833	Delphos	(419)	6,872	7,093
45247	Dent (c)	(513)	*7,612*	6,416
44622	Dover	(330)	12,345	11,329
45663	Dry Run (c)	(614)	*6,553*	5,389
*43016	Dublin	(614)/(740)	33,606	16,366
44112	East Cleveland	(216)	26,255	33,096
44094	Eastlake	(440)	19,990	21,161
43920	East Liverpool	(330)	12,611	13,654
45320	Eaton	(937)	8,170	7,396
*44035	Elyria	(440)	56,096	56,746
45322	Englewood	(937)	12,460	11,402
*44117	Euclid	(216)	51,260	54,875
45324	Fairborn	(937)	32,474	31,300
*45011	Fairfield	(513)	42,544	39,709
44334	Fairlawn	(330)	7,287	5,779
44126	Fairview Park	(440)	17,087	18,028
*45839	Findlay	(419)	39,797	35,703
45224	Finneytown (c)	(513)	*13,492*	13,096
45405	Forest Park	(513)	18,738	18,621
45230	Forestville (c)	(513)	*10,978*	9,185
44830	Fostoria	(419)	13,720	14,971
45005	Franklin	(513)	12,065	11,026
43420	Fremont	(419)	17,236	17,619
43230	Gahanna	(614)	33,224	23,898
44833	Galion	(419)	11,491	11,859
44125	Garfield Heights	(216)	29,881	31,739
44041	Geneva	(440)	6,511	6,597
*45325	Germantown	(937)	5,043	4,916
44420	Girard	(330)	10,654	11,304
44044	Grafton	(440)	6,105	3,423
43212	Grandview Heights	(614)	6,452	7,010
43023	Granville	(740)	5,125	4,315
44232	Green	(330)	23,378	19,179
45331	Greenville	(937)	13,234	12,863
45253	Groesbeck (c)	(513)	*7,202*	6,684
43123	Grove City	(614)	29,165	19,661
*45011	Hamilton	(513)	60,763	61,438
45030	Harrison	(513)	7,478	7,520
43056	Heath	(740)	8,704	7,231
44134	Highland Heights	(440)	8,512	6,249
43026	Hilliard	(614)/(740)	25,808	11,794
45133	Hillsboro	(937)	6,632	6,235
44484	Howland Center (c)	(330)	*6,481*	6,732
44425	Hubbard	(330)	8,105	8,248
45424	Huber Heights	(937)	38,240	38,696
*44236	Hudson	(330)	23,053	5,159
44839	Huron	(419)	7,718	7,067
44131	Independence	(216)/(440)	7,096	6,500
45638	Ironton	(740)	11,230	12,751
45640	Jackson	(740)	6,159	6,167
*44240	Kent	(330)	28,082	28,835
43326	Kenton	(419)	8,181	8,356
43606	Kenwood (c)	(513)	*7,423*	7,469
45429	Kettering	(937)	56,494	60,569
44094	Kirtland	(440)	6,970	5,881
44107	Lakewood	(216)	54,378	59,718
43130	Lancaster	(740)	35,914	34,507
45039	Landen (c)	(513)	*12,766*	9,263
45036	Lebanon	(513)	18,766	10,461
*45802	Lima	(419)	40,549	45,553
43228	Lincoln Village (c)	(614)	*9,482*	9,958
43138	Logan	(740)	6,870	6,725
43140	London	(614)/(740)	9,087	7,807
*44052	Lorain	(440)	67,955	71,245
44641	Louisville	(330)	9,138	8,087
45140	Loveland	(513)	11,302	10,122
44124	Lyndhurst	(216)/(440)	14,875	15,982
44056	Macedonia	(330)	10,087	7,509
—	Mack South (c)		*5,837*	5,767
45243	Madeira	(513)	8,608	9,141
*44901	Mansfield	(419)	50,688	50,627
44137	Maple Heights	(216)	25,490	27,089
45750	Marietta	(740)	14,035	15,026
*43302	Marion	(740)	37,300	34,075
43935	Martins Ferry	(740)	7,021	8,003
43040	Marysville	(937)	16,245	10,362
45040	Mason	(513)	27,308	11,450
*44646	Massillon	(330)	31,542	30,969
43537	Maumee	(419)	14,705	15,561
44124	Mayfield Heights	(440)	18,922	19,847
*44256	Medina	(330)	26,487	19,231
*44060	Mentor	(440)	50,004	47,491
44060	Mentor-on-the-Lake	(216)	8,209	8,271
*45343	Miamisburg	(937)	19,857	17,834
44130	Middleburg Heights	(216)/(440)	15,680	14,702
*45042	Middletown	(513)	51,941	46,758
45150	Milford	(513)	6,404	5,660
45050	Monroe	(513)	8,821	5,380
45242	Montgomery	(513)	9,777	9,733
—	Montrose-Ghent (c)		*5,261*	4,906
45439	Moraine	(937)	6,862	5,989
45231	Mount Healthy	(513)	6,835	7,580
43050	Mount Vernon	(740)	15,826	14,550
44262	Munroe Falls	(330)	5,320	5,359
43545	Napoleon	(419)	9,279	8,884
45764	Nelsonville	(740)	5,483	4,563
43054	New Albany	(614)	5,212	1,621
*43055	Newark	(740)	46,601	44,396
45344	New Carlisle	(937)	5,655	6,049
44663	New Philadelphia	(330)	17,363	15,698
44446	Niles	(330)	20,337	21,128
45239	Northbrook (c)	(513)	*11,076*	11,471
44720	North Canton	(330)	16,722	14,904
45239	North College Hill	(513)	9,685	11,002
45251	Northgate (c)	(513)	*8,016*	7,864
44057	North Madison (c)	(440)	*8,451*	8,699
44070	North Olmsted	(440)	33,481	34,204
45502	Northridge (c) (Clark Co.)	(937)	*6,853*	5,939
45414	Northridge (c) (Montgomery Co.)	(937)	*8,487*	9,448
44039	North Ridgeville	(440)	24,294	21,564
44133	North Royalton	(440)	29,598	23,197
43619	Northwood	(419)	5,484	5,506
44203	Norton	(330)	11,648	11,477
44857	Norwalk	(419)	16,353	14,731
45212	Norwood	(513)	20,781	23,674
*45873	Oakwood	(973)	8,902	8,957
44074	Oberlin	(440)	8,139	8,191
44138	Olmsted Falls	(440)	8,445	6,741
44862	Ontario	(419)	5,271	4,026
*45054	Oregon	(419)	19,419	18,334
44667	Orrville	(330)	8,506	7,955
45056	Oxford	(513)	22,283	19,013
44077	Painesville	(440)	17,428	15,769
44129	Parma	(216)/(440)	83,861	87,876
44130	Parma Heights	(216)/(440)	21,209	21,448
43062	Pataskala	(740)	11,850	3,046
44124	Pepper Pike	(216)/(440)	5,959	6,185
44646	Perry Heights (c)	(330)	*8,900*	9,055
*43551	Perrysburg	(419)	16,840	12,551
43147	Pickerington	(614)/(740)	12,627	5,668

ZIP	Place	Area Code	2003	1990
45356	Piqua	(937)	20,728	20,612
—	Pleasant Run (c)	—	5,267	4,964
44319	Portage Lakes (c)	(330)	9,870	13,373
43452	Port Clinton	(419)	6,316	7,106
45662	Portsmouth	(740)	19,913	22,676
43065	Powell	(614)	8,179	2,154
44266	Ravenna	(330)	11,506	12,069
45215	Reading	(513)	10,747	12,038
43068	Reynoldsburg	(614)/(740)	32,878	25,748
44143	Richmond Heights	(216)/(440)	10,855	9,611
44270	Rittman	(330)	6,272	6,147
45431	Riverside	(937)	23,071	1,471
44116	Rocky River	(440)	20,188	20,410
43460	Rossford	(419)	6,357	5,861
43950	Saint Clairsville	(740)	5,025	5,136
45885	Saint Marys	(419)	8,276	8,441
44460	Salem	(330)	12,101	12,233
*44870	Sandusky	(419)	27,030	29,764
44870	Sandusky South (c)	(419)	6,599	6,336
44131	Seven Hills	(216)/(440)	12,098	12,339
44122	Shaker Heights	(216)	28,459	30,955
*45241	Sharonville	(513)	13,505	13,121
44054	Sheffield Lake	(440)	9,222	9,825
44875	Shelby	(419)	9,579	9,610
44878	Shiloh (c)	(419)	11,272	11,607
45365	Sidney	(937)	20,327	18,710
44139	Solon	(440)	22,248	18,548
44121	South Euclid	(216)	22,860	23,866
45066	Springboro	(513)	15,051	6,574
45246	Springdale	(513)	10,129	10,621
*45501	Springfield	(937)	64,483	70,487
*43952	Steubenville	(740)	19,568	22,125
44224	Stow	(330)	34,290	27,998
44241	Streetsboro	(330)	13,822	9,932
44136	Strongsville	(440)	44,560	35,308
44471	Struthers	(330)	11,334	12,284
—	Summerside (c)	—	5,523	4,573
43560	Sylvania	(419)	19,027	17,489
44278	Tallmadge	(330)	17,165	14,870
45243	The Village of Indian Hill	(513)	5,711	5,383
44883	Tiffin	(419)	17,497	18,604
45371	Tipp City	(937)	9,285	6,483
*43601	Toledo	(419)	308,973	332,943
43964	Toronto	(740)	5,537	6,127
45067	Trenton	(513)	9,953	6,189
45426	Trotwood	(937)	27,070	29,358
45373	Troy	(937)	22,169	19,478
44087	Twinsburg	(330)	17,236	9,606
44683	Uhrichsville	(740)	5,696	5,604
45322	Union	(937)	5,536	5,531
44122	University Heights	(216)	13,723	14,787
43221	Upper Arlington	(614)	32,406	34,128
43351	Upper Sandusky	(419)	6,458	5,906
43078	Urbana	(937)	11,597	11,353
45377	Vandalia	(937)	14,495	13,872
45891	Van Wert	(419)	10,599	10,922
44089	Vermilion	(440)	10,940	11,127
*44281	Wadsworth	(330)	19,462	15,718
45895	Wapakoneta	(419)	9,518	9,214
*44481	Warren	(330)	46,608	50,793
44122	Warrensville Heights	(216)	14,719	15,884
43160	Washington	(740)	13,317	13,080
43566	Waterville	(419)	5,137	4,594
43567	Wauseon	(419)	7,183	6,322
45692	Wellston	(740)	5,994	6,049
45449	West Carrollton City	(937)	13,487	14,403
*43081	Westerville	(614)	34,922	30,269
44145	Westlake	(440)	32,024	27,018
45694	Wheelersburg (c)	(740)	6,471	5,113
43213	Whitehall	(614)	18,611	20,572
45239	White Oak (c)	(513)	13,277	12,430
44092	Wickliffe	(440)	13,299	14,558
44890	Willard	(419)	6,869	6,210
*44094	Willoughby	(440)	22,488	20,510
44094	Willoughby Hills	(440)	8,476	8,427
*44095	Willowick	(440)	14,072	15,269
45177	Wilmington	(937)	12,187	11,199
45459	Woodbourne-Hyde Park (c)	(937)	7,910	7,837
44691	Wooster	(330)	25,322	22,427
43085	Worthington	(614)	13,602	14,869
45433	Wright-Patterson AFB (c)	(937)	6,656	8,579
45215	Wyoming	(513)	7,987	8,128
45385	Xenia	(937)	23,822	24,836
*44501	Youngstown	(330)	79,271	95,732
*43701	Zanesville	(740)	25,277	26,778

Oklahoma

ZIP	Place	Area Code	2003	1990
*74820	Ada	(580)	16,008	15,765
*73521	Altus	(580)	20,559	21,910
73717	Alva	(580)	5,034	5,495
73005	Anadarko	(405)	6,539	6,586
*73401	Ardmore	(580)	23,928	23,079
*74006	Bartlesville	(918)	34,748	34,256
73008	Bethany	(405)	20,009	20,075
74008	Bixby	(918)	16,611	9,502
74631	Blackwell	(580)	7,423	7,538

ZIP	Place	Area Code	2003	1990
*74012	Broken Arrow	(918)	83,607	58,082
74015	Catoosa	(918)	5,838	2,954
*73018	Chickasha	(405)	16,345	14,988
73020	Choctaw	(405)	10,156	8,545
*74017	Claremore	(918)	16,773	13,280
73601	Clinton	(580)	8,364	9,298
74429	Coweta	(918)	7,781	6,159
74023	Cushing	(918)	8,510	7,218
73115	Del City	(405)	22,171	23,928
*73533	Duncan	(580)	22,031	21,732
*74701	Durant	(580)	14,565	12,929
*73034	Edmond	(405)	71,643	52,310
*73644	Elk City	(580)	10,511	10,428
73036	El Reno	(405)	15,938	15,414
*73701	Enid	(580)	46,436	45,309
74033	Glenpool	(918)	8,407	6,688
*74344	Grove	(918)	5,574	4,020
73044	Guthrie	(405)	10,110	10,440
73942	Guymon	(580)	10,565	7,803
74437	Henryetta	(918)	6,042	5,872
74848	Holdenville	(405)	5,575	4,893
74743	Hugo	(580)	5,569	5,978
74745	Idabel	(580)	6,946	6,957
74037	Jenks	(918)	11,560	7,484
*73501	Lawton	(580)	91,730	80,561
*74501	McAlester	(918)	17,870	16,739
*74354	Miami	(918)	13,485	13,142
73140	Midwest City	(405)	54,662	52,267
73153	Moore	(405)	44,987	40,318
*74401	Muskogee	(918)	38,635	37,708
73064	Mustang	(405)	14,551	10,434
73065	Newcastle	(405)	5,814	4,214
73068	Noble	(405)	5,402	4,710
*73069	Norman	(405)	99,197	80,071
*73125	Oklahoma City	(405)	523,303	444,724
74447	Okmulgee	(918)	12,727	13,441
74055	Owasso	(918)	21,634	11,151
73075	Pauls Valley	(405)	6,179	6,150
73077	Perry	(580)	5,138	4,978
*74601	Ponca City	(580)	25,596	26,359
74953	Poteau	(918)	7,990	7,210
74361	Pryor Creek	(918)	9,098	8,327
73080	Purcell	(405)	5,627	4,784
74955	Sallisaw	(918)	8,383	7,122
74063	Sand Springs	(918)	17,695	15,339
*74066	Sapulpa	(918)	19,759	18,074
*74868	Seminole	(405)	6,756	7,071
*74801	Shawnee	(405)	29,446	26,017
74070	Skiatook	(918)	5,879	4,910
*74074	Stillwater	(405)	41,320	36,676
*74464	Tahlequah	(918)	15,405	10,586
74873	Tecumseh	(405)	6,264	5,750
73156	The Village	(405)	10,067	10,353
*74103	Tulsa	(918)	387,807	367,302
74301	Vinita	(918)	5,969	5,804
*74467	Wagoner	(918)	7,818	6,894
73123	Warr Acres	(405)	9,658	9,288
73096	Weatherford	(580)	9,510	10,124
*73801	Woodward	(580)	11,789	12,340
*73099	Yukon	(405)	21,152	20,935

Oregon

Area code (971) overlays area code (503). See introductory note.

ZIP	Place	Area Code	2003	1990
97321	Albany	(541)	43,091	33,523
*97006	Aloha (c)	(503)	41,741	34,284
97601	Altamont (c)	(541)	19,603	18,591
97520	Ashland	(541)	20,406	16,252
97103	Astoria	(503)	9,660	10,069
97814	Baker City	(541)	9,671	9,140
*97005	Beaverton	(503)	80,520	53,307
*97701	Bend	(541)	59,779	23,740
97415	Brookings	(541)	5,878	4,400
97013	Canby	(503)	14,238	8,990
97225	Cedar Hills (c)	(503)	8,949	9,294
97291	Cedar Mill (c)	(503)	12,597	9,697
97502	Central Point	(541)	14,630	7,512
97058	City of the Dalles	(541)	11,873	11,021
97015	Clackamas (c)	(503)	5,177	2,578
97420	Coos Bay	(541)	15,345	15,076
97113	Cornelius	(503)	10,165	6,148
*97333	Corvallis	(541)	50,126	44,757
97424	Cottage Grove	(541)	8,514	7,403
97338	Dallas	(503)	13,221	9,422
97524	Eagle Point	(541)	6,306	3,026
*97440	Eugene	(541)	142,185	112,733
97024	Fairview	(503)	8,749	2,588
97439	Florence	(541)	7,583	5,171
97116	Forest Grove	(503)	18,880	13,559
97301	Four Corners (c)	(503)	13,922	12,156
97223	Garden Home-Whitford (c)	(503)	6,931	6,652
97027	Gladstone	(503)	11,978	10,152
*97526	Grants Pass	(541)	25,700	17,503
97470	Green (c)	(541)	6,174	5,076
*97030	Gresham	(503)	95,816	68,285
97015	Happy Valley	(503)	6,475	1,552
97303	Hayesville (c)	(503)	18,222	14,318
97838	Hermiston	(541)	14,086	10,047
*97123	Hillsboro	(503)	77,709	37,598

ZIP	Place	Area Code	2003	1990
97031	Hood River	(541)	6,139	4,632
97351	Independence	(503)	6,974	4,425
97222	Jennings Lodge (c)	(503)	7,036	6,530
97448	Junction City	(541)	5,237	3,961
97307	Keizer	(503)	34,154	21,884
*97601	Klamath Falls	(541)	19,286	17,737
*97034	Lake Oswego	(503)	36,085	30,576
97739	La Pine (c)	(541)	5,799	—
97355	Lebanon	(541)	13,271	10,950
97367	Lincoln City	(541)	7,399	5,903
97128	McMinnville	(503)	28,514	17,894
97741	Madras	(541)	5,128	3,443
*97501	Medford	(541)	66,638	47,021
97862	Milton-Freewater	(541)	6,457	5,533
97269	Milwaukie	(503)	20,638	18,670
97038	Molalla	(503)	6,075	3,651
97361	Monmouth	(503)	8,109	6,288
97132	Newberg	(503)	19,732	13,086
97365	Newport	(541)	9,548	8,437
97459	North Bend	(541)	9,565	9,614
97268	Oak Grove (c)	(503)	12,808	12,576
—	Oak Hills (c)		9,050	6,450
—	Oatfield (c)		15,750	15,348
97914	Ontario	(541)	10,964	9,394
97045	Oregon City	(503)	28,407	14,698
97801	Pendleton	(541)	16,458	15,142
*97208	Portland	(503)	538,544	485,975
97754	Prineville	(541)	8,115	5,355
97225	Raleigh Hills (c)	(503)	5,865	6,066
97756	Redmond	(541)	16,822	7,165
—	Redwood (c)		5,844	3,702
—	Rockcreek (c)		9,404	8,282
97470	Roseburg	(541)	20,162	18,389
97470	Roseburg North (c)	(541)	5,473	6,831
97051	Saint Helens	(503)	11,209	7,535
*97309	Salem	(503)	142,914	107,793
97055	Sandy	(503)	7,186	4,154
97056	Scappoose	(503)	5,506	3,550
97138	Seaside	(503)	5,916	5,359
97378	Sheridan	(503)	5,515	3,950
97140	Sherwood	(503)	13,901	3,093
97381	Silverton	(503)	7,781	5,635
*97477	Springfield	(541)	54,773	44,664
97383	Stayton	(503)	7,060	5,011
—	Sunnyside (c)	(503)	6,791	4,423
97479	Sutherlin	(541)	7,178	5,020
97386	Sweet Home	(541)	8,238	6,850
97540	Talent	(541)	5,623	3,274
97281	Tigard	(503)	45,538	29,435
97060	Troutdale	(503)	14,851	7,852
97062	Tualatin	(503)	24,790	14,664
97882	Umatilla	(541)	5,154	3,058
97225	West Haven-Sylvan (c)	(503)	7,147	6,009
97068	West Linn	(503)	24,696	16,389
*97225	West Slope (c)	(503)	6,442	7,959
97503	White City (c)	(541)	5,466	5,891
97070	Wilsonville	(503)	15,211	7,510
97071	Woodburn	(503)	21,747	13,404

Pennsylvania

Area code (267) overlays area code (215). Area code (484) overlays (610). Area code (878) overlays (412). See introductory note.

ZIP	Place	Area Code	2003	1990
15001	Aliquippa	(724)	11,324	13,374
*18105	Allentown	(610)	105,958	105,301
*16603	Altoona	(814)	47,980	51,881
19002	Ambler	(215)	6,426	6,609
15003	Ambridge	(724)	7,460	8,133
18403	Archbald	(570)	6,213	6,291
19003	Ardmore (c)	(610)	12,616	12,646
15210	Arlington Heights (c)	(412)	5,132	4,768
15068	Arnold	(724)	5,485	6,113
19407	Audubon (c)	(610)	6,549	6,328
15202	Avalon	(412)	5,114	5,784
—	Back Mountain (c)		26,690	—
15234	Baldwin	(412)	19,420	21,923
18013	Bangor	(610)	5,275	5,383
15010	Beaver Falls	(724)	9,632	10,687
16823	Bellefonte	(814)	6,352	6,358
15202	Bellevue	(412)	8,479	9,126
18603	Berwick	(570)	10,500	10,976
15102	Bethel Park	(412)	32,915	33,823
*18016	Bethlehem	(610)	72,570	71,427
19508	Birdsboro	(610)	5,161	4,222
18447	Blakely	(570)	6,884	7,222
17815	Bloomsburg	(570)	12,652	12,439
19422	Blue Bell (c)	(215)/(610)	6,395	6,091
19061	Boothwyn (c)	(610)	5,206	5,069
16701	Bradford	(814)	8,826	9,625
15227	Brentwood	(412)	10,114	10,823
15017	Bridgeville	(412)	5,160	5,445
19007	Bristol	(215)	9,947	10,405
19015	Brookhaven	(610)	7,893	8,570
19008	Broomall (c)	(610)	11,046	10,930
*16001	Butler	(724)		15,714
15419	California	(724)	14,766	5,748
*17011	Camp Hill	(717)	5,472	7,831

ZIP	Place	Area Code	2003	1990
15317	Canonsburg	(724)	7,533	9,200
18407	Carbondale	(570)	8,716	10,664
17013	Carlisle	(717)	9,487	18,419
15106	Carnegie	(412)	18,110	9,278
15108	Carnot-Moon (c)	(412)	10,637	10,187
15234	Castle Shannon	(412)	8,521	9,135
18032	Catasauqua	(610)	6,506	6,662
17201	Chambersburg	(717)	17,864	16,647
*19013	Chester	(610)	37,017	41,856
15025	Clairton	(412)	8,204	9,656
16214	Clarion	(814)	5,953	6,457
18411	Clarks Summit	(570)	5,044	5,433
16830	Clearfield	(814)	6,413	6,633
19018	Clifton Heights	(610)	6,680	7,111
19320	Coatesville	(610)	11,221	11,038
19023	Collingdale	(610)	8,545	9,175
17109	Colonial Park (c)	(717)	13,259	13,777
17512	Columbia	(717)	10,201	10,701
15425	Connellsville	(724)	8,765	9,229
19428	Conshohocken	(610)	7,768	8,064
15108	Coraopolis	(412)	5,914	6,747
16407	Corry	(814)	6,685	7,216
15205	Crafton	(412)	6,473	7,188
19021	Croydon (c)	(215)	9,993	9,967
19023	Darby	(610)	10,136	11,140
19036	Darby Twp. (c)	(610)	9,622	10,955
19333	Devon-Berwyn (c)	(610)	5,067	5,019
18519	Dickson City	(570)	6,036	6,276
15033	Donora	(724)	5,470	5,928
15216	Dormont	(412)	8,957	9,772
19335	Downingtown	(610)	7,849	7,749
18901	Doylestown	(215)	8,185	8,575
19026	Drexel Hill (c)	(610)	29,364	29,744
15801	Du Bois	(814)	7,879	8,286
18512	Dunmore	(570)	13,715	15,403
15110	Duquesne	(412)	7,116	8,525
19401	East Norriton (c)	(610)	13,211	13,324
*18042	Easton	(610)	26,189	26,276
18301	East Stroudsburg	(570)	10,385	8,781
17402	East York (c)	(717)	8,782	8,487
15005	Economy	(724)	9,331	9,305
16412	Edinboro	(814)	7,073	7,736
17022	Elizabethtown	(717)	11,898	9,952
16117	Ellwood City	(724)	8,386	8,894
18049	Emmaus	(610)	11,243	11,157
17025	Enola (c)	(717)	5,627	5,961
17522	Ephrata	(717)	13,158	12,133
*16501	Erie	(814)	101,373	108,718
18643	Exeter	(570)	6,023	5,691
19030	Fairless Hills (c)	(215)	8,365	9,026
16121	Farrell	(724)	5,959	6,835
19053	Feasterville-Trevose (c)	(215)	6,525	6,696
16063	Fernway (c)	(724)	12,188	9,072
19032	Folcroft	(610)	6,933	7,506
19033	Folsom (c)	(610)	8,072	8,173
15221	Forest Hills	(412)	6,610	7,335
15238	Fox Chapel	(412)	5,352	5,319
16323	Franklin	(814)	6,991	7,329
15143	Franklin Park	(412)	11,596	10,109
18052	Fullerton (c)	(610)	14,268	13,127
17325	Gettysburg	(717)	7,825	7,025
19036	Glenolden	(610)	7,369	7,260
19038	Glenside (c)	(215)	7,914	8,704
15601	Greensburg	(724)	15,525	16,318
16125	Greenville	(724)	6,434	6,734
16127	Grove City	(412)	7,801	8,240
15101	Hampton Twp. (c) (Allegheny Co.)	(412)	17,526	15,568
17331	Hanover	(717)	14,835	14,399
19438	Harleysville (c)	(215)	8,795	7,405
*17105	Harrisburg	(717)	48,322	52,376
15065	Harrison Twp. (c) (Allegheny Co.)	(412)	10,934	11,763
19040	Hatboro	(215)	7,381	7,382
18201	Hazleton	(570)	22,492	24,730
18055	Hellertown	(610)	5,580	5,662
16148	Hermitage	(724)	16,521	15,260
17033	Hershey (c)	(717)	12,771	11,860
16648	Hollidaysburg	(814)	5,312	5,624
16001	Homeacre-Lyndora (c)	(724)	6,685	7,511
19044	Horsham (c)	(215)	14,779	15,051
16652	Huntingdon	(814)	6,864	6,843
15701	Indiana	(724)	14,636	15,174
15644	Jeannette	(724)	10,369	11,221
15025	Jefferson Hills	(412)	9,685	—
*15907	Johnstown	(814)	22,957	28,124
15108	Kennedy Twp. (c)	(412)	7,504	7,152
19348	Kennett Square	(610)	5,271	5,218
19406	King of Prussia (c)	(610)	18,511	18,406
18704	Kingston	(570)	13,368	14,507
19443	Kulpsville (c)	(215)	8,005	5,183
19530	Kutztown	(610)	5,067	4,704
*17604	Lancaster	(717)	55,351	55,551
19446	Lansdale	(215)	16,115	16,362
19050	Lansdowne	(610)	10,861	11,712
15650	Latrobe	(724)	8,747	9,265
17540	Leacock-Leola-Bareville (c)	(717)	6,625	5,685
*17042	Lebanon	(717)	23,894	24,800
18235	Lehighton	(610)	5,513	5,914
*19055	Levittown (c)	(215)	53,966	55,362
17837	Lewisburg	(570)	5,499	5,785
17044	Lewistown	(717)	8,752	9,341

ZIP	Place	Area Code	2003	1990
17112	Linglestown (c)	(717)	6,414	5,862
19353	Lionville-Marchwood (c)	(610)	6,298	6,468
17543	Lititz	(717)	8,957	8,280
17745	Lock Haven	(570)	8,957	9,230
17011	Lower Allen (c)	(717)	6,619	6,329
15068	Lower Burrell	(724)	12,531	12,251
15237	McCandless Twp. (c)	(412)	29,022	28,781
*15134	McKeesport	(412)	23,324	26,016
15136	McKees Rocks	(412)	6,384	7,691
19002	Maple Glen (c)	(215)	7,042	5,881
16335	Meadville	(814)	13,410	14,318
17055	Mechanicsburg	(717)	8,901	9,452
*19063	Media	(610)	5,472	5,957
17057	Middletown (Dauphin Co.)	(717)	9,105	9,254
18017	Middletown (c) (Northampton Co.)	(610)	7,378	6,866
17551	Millersville	(717)	7,573	8,099
17847	Milton	(570)	6,539	6,746
15061	Monaca	(724)	6,077	6,739
15062	Monessen	(724)	8,467	9,901
18936	Montgomeryville (c)	(215)	12,031	9,114
18507	Moosic	(570)	5,679	5,397
19067	Morrisville (Bucks Co.)	(215)	9,955	9,765
18707	Mountain Top (c)	(570)	15,269	—
17851	Mount Carmel	(570)	6,161	7,196
17552	Mount Joy	(717)	6,865	6,398
15228	Mount Lebanon (c)	(412)	33,017	34,414
15120	Munhall	(412)	11,854	13,158
15146	Municipality of Monroeville	(412)	28,707	29,169
15668	Municipality of Murrysville	(724)	19,192	17,240
18634	Nanticoke	(570)	10,533	12,267
18064	Nazareth	(610)	6,009	5,713
19086	Nether Providence Twp. (c)	(610)	13,456	12,730
15066	New Brighton	(724)	6,384	6,854
*16108	New Castle	(724)	25,338	28,334
17070	New Cumberland	(717)	7,230	7,665
17557	New Holland	(717)	5,197	4,484
15068	New Kensington	(724)	14,279	15,894
*19403	Norristown	(610)	31,069	30,754
18067	Northampton	(610)	9,599	8,717
15104	North Braddock	(412)	6,176	7,036
15137	North Versailles (c)	(412)	11,125	13,294
16421	Northwest Harborcreek (c)	(814)	8,658	7,485
19074	Norwood	(610)	5,903	6,162
15139	Oakmont	(412)	6,727	6,961
15238	O'Hara Twp. (c)	(412)	8,856	9,096
16301	Oil City	(814)	11,132	11,949
18518	Old Forge	(570)	8,603	8,834
19075	Oreland (c)	(215)	5,509	5,695
18071	Palmerton	(610)	5,248	5,394
17078	Palmyra	(717)	6,977	6,910
19301	Paoli (c)	(610)	5,425	5,277
16801	Park Forest Village (c)	(814)	8,830	6,703
17331	Parkville (c)	(717)	6,593	5,009
17112	Paxtonia (c)	(570)	5,254	4,862
15235	Penn Hills (c)	(412)	46,809	57,632
19096	Penn Wynne (c)	(610)	5,382	5,807
18944	Perkasie	(215)	8,806	7,878
*19104	Philadelphia	(215)	1,479,339	1,585,577
19460	Phoenixville	(610)	14,739	15,066
*15233	Pittsburgh	(412)	325,337	369,879
*18640	Pittston	(570)	7,807	9,389
15236	Pleasant Hills	(412)	8,178	8,884
15239	Plum	(412)	26,797	25,609
18651	Plymouth	(570)	6,250	7,134
19462	Plymouth Meeting (c)	(610)	5,593	6,241
*19464	Pottstown	(610)	21,793	21,831
17901	Pottsville	(570)	14,990	16,603
17109	Progress (c)	(717)	9,647	9,654
19076	Prospect Park	(610)	6,494	6,764
15767	Punxsutawney	(814)	6,150	6,782
18951	Quakertown	(215)	8,816	8,982
19087	Radnor Twp. (c)	(610)	30,878	27,676
*19612	Reading	(610)	80,305	78,380
17356	Red Lion	(717)	6,093	6,130
18954	Richboro (c)	(215)	6,678	5,141
19078	Ridley Park	(610)	7,103	7,592
15136	Robinson Twp. (Allegheny Co.) (c)	(412)	12,289	10,830
15237	Ross Twp. (c)	(412)	32,551	35,102
15857	Saint Marys	(814)	14,182	14,020
19464	Sanatoga (c)	(610)	7,734	3,723
18840	Sayre	(570)	5,659	5,791
17972	Schuylkill Haven	(570)	5,377	5,610
15106	Scott Twp. (c)	(412)	17,288	20,413
*18505	Scranton	(570)	74,320	81,805
17870	Selinsgrove	(570)	5,436	5,384
15116	Shaler Twp. (c)	(412)	29,757	33,694
17872	Shamokin	(570)	7,732	9,184
16146	Sharon	(724)	15,735	17,533
19079	Sharon Hill	(610)	5,386	5,771
17976	Shenandoah	(570)	5,387	6,221
19607	Shillington	(610)	5,009	5,062
17404	Shiloh (c)	(717)	10,192	5,315
17257	Shippensburg	(717)	5,620	5,331
15501	Somerset	(814)	6,617	6,454
18964	Souderton	(215)	6,768	5,957
15129	South Park Twp. (c)	(814)	14,340	14,292
17701	South Williamsport	(570)	6,240	6,496
19064	Springfield (c) (Delaware Co.)	(610)	23,677	25,326
*16804	State College	(814)	39,728	38,981
17113	Steelton	(717)	5,781	5,152
—	Stonybrook-Wilshire (c)		5,414	4,887
15136	Stowe Twp. (c)	(412)	6,706	9,202
18360	Stroudsburg	(570)	6,127	5,312
16323	Sugarcreek	(814)	5,213	5,532
17801	Sunbury	(570)	10,277	11,591
19081	Swarthmore	(610)	6,154	6,157
15218	Swissvale	(412)	9,313	10,637
18704	Swoyersville	(570)	5,002	5,630
18252	Tamaqua	(570)	6,878	7,943
18517	Taylor	(570)	6,325	6,941
16354	Titusville	(814)	5,890	6,434
19401	Trooper (c)	(610)	6,061	7,370
15145	Turtle Creek	(412)	5,868	6,556
16686	Tyrone	(814)	5,398	5,743
15401	Uniontown	(724)	12,096	12,034
19063	Upper Providence Twp. (c)	(610)	10,509	9,477
15241	Upper Saint Clair (c)	(412)	20,053	19,023
15690	Vandergrift	(724)	5,267	5,904
19013	Village Green-Green Ridge (c)	(610)	8,279	9,026
16365	Warren	(814)	9,835	11,122
15301	Washington (Washington Co.)	(724)	14,858	15,864
17268	Waynesboro	(717)	9,628	9,578
17315	Weigelstown (c)	(717)	10,117	8,665
*19380	West Chester	(610)	17,722	18,041
19380	West Goshen (c)	(610)	8,472	8,948
*15122	West Mifflin	(412)	21,892	23,644
15905	Westmont	(814)	5,330	5,789
19401	West Norriton (c)	(610)	14,901	15,209
15229	West View	(412)	7,051	7,734
15227	Whitehall (Allegheny Co.)	(412)	14,100	14,451
15131	White Oak	(412)	8,388	8,761
*18703	Wilkes-Barre	(570)	41,630	47,523
15221	Wilkinsburg	(412)	18,518	21,080
15145	Wilkins Twp. (c)	(412)	6,917	7,487
*17701	Williamsport	(570)	29,871	31,933
19090	Willow Grove (c)	(215)	16,234	16,325
17584	Willow Street (c)	(717)	7,258	5,817
15025	Wilson	(412)	7,608	7,830
19094	Woodlyn (c)	(610)	10,036	10,151
19038	Wyndmoor (c)	(215)	5,601	5,682
19610	Wyomissing	(610)	11,079	7,332
19050	Yeadon	(610)	11,587	11,980
*17405	York	(717)	40,081	42,192

Rhode Island (401)

See introductory note.

ZIP	Place	2003	1990
02806	Barrington	16,830	15,849
02809	Bristol	22,769	21,625
02830	Burrillville	16,477	16,230
02863	Central Falls	19,287	17,637
02813	Charlestown	8,225	6,478
02816	Coventry	34,910	31,083
*02904	Cranston	81,679	76,060
02864	Cumberland	33,683	29,038
02864	Cumberland Hill (c)	7,738	6,379
02818	East Greenwich	13,442	11,865
02914	East Providence	49,906	50,380
02822	Exeter	6,311	5,461
02814	Glocester	10,473	9,227
02828	Greenville (c)	8,626	8,303
02833	Hopkinton	8,121	6,873
02835	Jamestown	5,707	4,999
02919	Johnston	29,283	26,542
02881	Kingston (c)	5,446	6,504
02865	Lincoln	22,183	18,045
02842	Middletown	17,359	19,460
02882	Narragansett	16,938	15,004
02840	Newport	26,136	28,227
02843	Newport East (c)	11,463	11,080
02852	North Kingstown	27,353	23,786
02908	North Providence	33,403	32,090
02896	North Smithfield	11,008	10,497
*02860	Pawtucket	74,330	72,644
02871	Portsmouth	17,553	16,857
*02904	Providence	176,365	160,728
02812	Richmond	7,691	5,351
02857	Scituate	10,850	9,796
02917	Smithfield	21,386	19,163
02879	South Kingstown	29,069	24,612
02878	Tiverton (c)	7,282	7,259
02878	Tiverton	15,536	14,312
02864	Valley Falls (c)	11,599	11,175
*02879	Wakefield-Peacedale (c)	8,468	7,134
02885	Warren	11,390	11,385
*02886	Warwick	87,365	85,427
02891	Westerly (c)	17,682	16,477
02891	Westerly	23,758	21,605
02817	West Greenwich	5,584	—
02893	West Warwick	29,996	29,268
02895	Woonsocket	44,654	43,877

South Carolina

ZIP	Place	Area Code	2003	1990
29620	Abbeville	(864)	5,786	5,778
*29801	Aiken	(803)	26,456	20,386
*29621	Anderson	(864)	25,563	26,385
—	Batesburg-Leesville	(803)	5,536	6,107
*29902	Beaufort	(843)	12,376	9,576
29841	Belvedere (c)	(803)	5,631	6,133
29512	Bennettsville	(843)	9,296	10,095
29611	Berea (c)	(864)	14,158	13,535
29902	Burton (c)	(843)	7,180	6,917
29020	Camden	(803)	6,861	6,696
29033	Cayce	(803)	12,388	10,824
—	Centerville (c)	(573)	5,181	4,866
*29402	Charleston	(843)	101,024	88,256
29520	Cheraw	(843)	5,416	5,553
29706	Chester	(803)	6,326	7,158
*29631	Clemson	(864)	11,936	11,145
29325	Clinton	(864)	9,010	9,603
*29201	Columbia	(803)	117,357	110,734
*29526	Conway	(843)	12,538	9,819
*29532	Darlington	(843)	6,582	7,310
29204	Dentsville (c)	(803)	13,009	11,839
29536	Dillon	(843)	6,362	6,829
*29640	Easley	(864)	18,479	15,179
—	Five Forks (c)	....	8,064	—
*29501	Florence	(843)	30,267	29,913
29206	Forest Acres	(803)	10,343	7,181
*29715	Fort Mill	(803)	7,879	4,930
29644	Fountain Inn	(864)	6,440	4,388
*29341	Gaffney	(864)	12,877	13,149
29605	Gantt (c)	(864)	13,962	13,891
29576	Garden City (c)	(843)	9,357	6,305
*29442	Georgetown	(843)	8,951	9,517
29445	Goose Creek	(843)	30,574	24,692
*29602	Greenville	(864)	55,926	58,256
*29646	Greenwood	(864)	22,252	20,807
*29650	Greer	(864)	19,333	10,322
29406	Hanahan	(843)	12,971	13,176
*29550	Hartsville	(843)	7,435	8,372
*29928	Hilton Head Island	(843)	34,407	23,694
29621	Homeland Park (c)	(864)	6,337	6,569
29063	Irmo	(803)	11,170	11,284
29456	Ladson (c)	(843)	13,264	13,540
29560	Lake City	(843)	6,536	7,153
*29720	Lancaster	(803)	8,354	8,914
29902	Laurel Bay (c)	(843)	6,625	4,972
29360	Laurens	(864)	9,819	9,694
*29072	Lexington	(803)	11,746	4,046
29566	Little River (c)	(843)	7,027	3,470
29078	Lugoff (c)	(803)	6,278	3,211
29571	Marion	(843)	7,008	7,658
29662	Mauldin	(864)	17,716	11,662
29461	Moncks Corner	(843)	6,019	5,599
*29465	Mount Pleasant	(843)	54,788	30,108
29576	Murrells Inlet (c)	(843)	5,519	3,334
*29575	Myrtle Beach	(803)	24,691	24,848
29108	Newberry	(803)	10,608	10,543
*29841	North Augusta	(803)	18,413	15,684
*29410	North Charleston	(843)	81,577	70,304
*29582	North Myrtle Beach	(843)	12,442	8,731
29565	Oak Grove (c)	(803)	8,183	7,173
*29115	Orangeburg	(803)	12,758	13,772
—	Parker (c)	....	10,760	11,072
—	Powderville (c)	....	5,362	—
29072	Red Bank (c)	(803)	8,811	5,950
29020	Red Hill (c)	(843)	10,509	6,112
*29730	Rock Hill	(803)	56,114	42,112
29417	Saint Andrews (c)	(803)	21,814	25,692
29609	Sans Souci (c)	(864)	7,836	7,612
*29678	Seneca	(864)	7,674	7,726
29210	Seven Oaks (c)	(803)	15,755	15,722
*29681	Simpsonville	(864)	14,781	11,744
29577	Socastee (c)	(843)	14,295	10,426
*29306	Spartanburg	(864)	38,718	43,479
*29483	Summerville	(843)	31,734	22,519
*29150	Sumter	(803)	39,790	40,977
29687	Taylors (c)	(864)	20,125	19,619
29379	Union	(864)	8,431	9,840
29607	Wade Hampton (c)	(864)	20,458	20,014
29488	Walterboro	(843)	5,356	5,595
29611	Welcome (c)	(864)	6,390	6,560
*29169	West Columbia	(803)	12,900	10,974
29206	Woodfield (c)	(803)	9,238	8,862
29745	York	(803)	6,960	6,709

South Dakota (605)

ZIP	Place	2003	1990
*57401	Aberdeen	24,086	24,995
57005	Brandon	6,522	3,545
57006	Brookings	18,464	16,270
57350	Huron	11,377	12,448
57042	Madison	6,303	6,257
57301	Mitchell	14,677	13,798
57501	Pierre	13,939	12,906
*57701	Rapid City	60,876	54,523
57701	Rapid Valley (c)	7,043	5,968
*57101	Sioux Falls	133,834	100,836
57783	Spearfish	8,870	6,966
57785	Sturgis	6,389	5,537

ZIP	Place	2003	1990
57069	Vermillion	10,070	10,034
57201	Watertown	20,191	17,623
57078	Yankton	13,440	12,703

Tennessee

ZIP	Place	Area Code	2003	1990
37701	Alcoa	(865)	8,174	6,400
*37303	Athens	(423)	13,625	12,054
38184	Bartlett	(901)	42,245	27,038
37660	Bloomingdale (c)	(423)	10,350	10,953
38008	Bolivar	(731)	5,689	5,969
*37027	Brentwood	(615)	28,960	16,392
*37621	Bristol	(423)	25,021	23,421
38012	Brownsville	(731)	10,725	10,017
*37401	Chattanooga	(423)	154,887	152,393
37642	Church Hill	(423)	6,119	5,208
*37040	Clarksville	(931)	107,953	75,542
*37311	Cleveland	(423)	37,368	32,236
*37716	Clinton	(865)	9,328	8,960
37315	Collegedale	(423)	7,129	5,048
*38017	Collierville	(901)	35,445	14,501
37663	Colonial Heights (c)	(423)	7,067	6,716
*38401	Columbia	(931)	33,305	28,583
*38501	Cookeville	(931)	27,052	21,744
38019	Covington	(901)	9,001	7,487
*38555	Crossville	(931)	9,725	6,930
37321	Dayton	(423)	6,371	5,671
*37055	Dickson	(615)	12,688	10,487
*38024	Dyersburg	(731)	17,301	16,321
37411	East Brainerd (c)	(423)	14,132	11,594
37412	East Ridge	(423)	20,003	21,101
*37643	Elizabethton	(423)	14,015	13,087
37650	Erwin	(423)	5,764	5,318
37062	Fairview	(615)	6,548	4,210
37922	Farragut	(865)	18,669	12,802
37334	Fayetteville	(931)	6,955	7,158
*37064	Franklin	(615)	46,528	20,098
37066	Gallatin	(615)	25,107	18,794
*38138	Germantown	(901)	37,520	33,159
*37072	Goodlettsville	(615)	14,229	11,219
37073	Greenbrier	(615)	5,851	3,062
*37743	Greeneville	(423)	15,204	13,532
37215	Green Hill (c)	(615)	7,068	6,763
37748	Harriman	(865)	6,663	7,119
37341	Harrison (c)	(423)	7,630	7,191
37074	Hartsville-Trousdale	(615)	7,447	2,222
38340	Henderson	(731)	6,148	4,760
*37075	Hendersonville	(615)	43,027	32,188
38343	Humboldt	(731)	9,339	9,651
*38301	Jackson	(731)	61,110	49,145
37760	Jefferson City	(865)	7,850	5,875
*37601	Johnson City	(423)	57,394	50,354
*37662	Kingsport	(423)	44,231	40,457
37763	Kingston	(865)	5,327	4,552
*37950	Knoxville	(865)	173,278	169,761
*37766	La Follette	(423)	8,052	7,201
38002	Lakeland	(901)	7,210	1,204
37086	La Vergne	(615)	23,052	7,496
38464	Lawrenceburg	(931)	10,864	10,397
*37087	Lebanon	(615)	21,406	15,208
*37771	Lenoir City	(865)	7,271	6,147
37091	Lewisburg	(931)	10,698	9,879
38351	Lexington	(731)	7,472	5,810
37352	Lynchburg	(931)	5,911	4,721
38201	McKenzie	(731)	5,357	5,168
*37110	McMinnville	(931)	12,981	11,194
*37355	Manchester	(931)	8,929	7,709
38237	Martin	(731)	10,237	8,588
*37804	Maryville	(865)	25,062	19,208
*38101	Memphis	(901)	645,978	618,652
37343	Middle Valley (c)	(423)	11,854	12,255
38358	Milan	(731)	7,818	7,512
37072	Millersville	(615)	6,039	2,575
*38053	Millington	(901)	10,229	17,866
*37813	Morristown	(423)	25,144	22,513
37645	Mount Carmel	(423)	5,103	4,268
*37122	Mount Juliet	(615)	16,495	5,389
38058	Munford	(901)	5,249	2,944
*37130	Murfreesboro	(615)	78,074	44,922
*37202	Nashville	(615)	544,765	488,366
*37821	Newport	(423)	7,203	7,123
*37830	Oak Ridge	(865)	27,338	27,310
37363	Ooltewah (c)	(423)	5,681	4,903
38242	Paris	(731)	9,650	9,332
*37862	Pigeon Forge	(865)	5,456	3,027
37148	Portland	(615)	9,786	5,539
38478	Pulaski	(931)	7,947	7,916
37415	Red Bank	(423)	12,013	12,320
38063	Ripley	(731)	7,745	6,634
37854	Rockwood	(865)	5,389	5,348
38372	Savannah	(731)	7,135	6,547
*37862	Sevierville	(865)	14,167	7,178
37865	Seymour (c)	(865)	8,850	7,026
*37160	Shelbyville	(931)	17,538	14,042
37377	Signal Mountain	(423)	7,265	7,034
37167	Smyrna	(615)	30,172	14,720
*37379	Soddy-Daisy	(423)	11,967	8,240
37311	South Cleveland (c)	(423)	6,216	5,372
37172	Springfield	(615)	15,117	11,227

ZIP	Place	Area Code	2003	1990
37174	Spring Hill	(931)	12,205	1,464
37874	Sweetwater	(423)	5,784	5,066
37388	Tullahoma	(931)	18,434	16,761
*38261	Union City	(731)	10,769	10,513
37188	White House	(615)	8,256	2,987
37398	Winchester	(931)	7,602	6,305

Texas

Area codes (281) and (832) overlay area code (713). Area code (430) overlays (903). Area code (682) overlays (817). Area codes (972) and (469) overlay (214). See introductory note.

ZIP	Place	Area Code	2003	1990
*79604	Abilene	(325)	114,889	106,707
—	Abram-Perezville (c)		5,444	3,999
75001	Addison	(214)	13,886	8,783
78516	Alamo	(956)	15,731	8,352
78209	Alamo Heights	(210)	7,250	6,502
77039	Aldine (c)	(713)	13,979	11,133
*78332	Alice	(361)	19,310	19,788
*75002	Allen	(214)	62,400	19,315
*79830	Alpine	(432)	6,103	5,622
*78572	Alton	(956)	6,339	3,048
—	Alton North (c)		5,051	—
*77511	Alvin	(713)	21,978	19,220
*79105	Amarillo	(806)	178,612	157,571
78750	Anderson Mill (c)		8,953	9,468
79714	Andrews	(432)	9,509	10,678
*77515	Angleton	(979)	18,625	17,140
*78336	Aransas Pass	(361)	8,612	7,180
*76004	Arlington	(817)	355,007	261,717
77346	Atascocita (c)	(281)	35,757	—
75751	Athens	(903)	11,962	10,982
75551	Atlanta	(214)	5,606	6,118
*78712	Austin	(512)	672,011	472,020
*76020	Azle	(817)	10,149	8,868
77518	Bacliff (c)	(409)	6,962	5,549
75180	Balch Springs	(214)	19,455	17,406
78602	Bastrop	(512)	6,682	4,044
*77414	Bay City	(979)	18,573	18,170
*77520	Baytown	(713)	67,251	63,843
*77707	Beaumont	(409)	112,434	114,323
*76021	Bedford	(817)	48,572	43,762
*78102	Beeville	(361)	13,007	13,547
*77401	Bellaire	(713)	16,891	13,844
76715	Bellmead	(254)	9,583	8,336
76513	Belton	(254)	14,883	12,463
76126	Benbrook	(817)	21,000	19,564
*79720	Big Spring	(432)	24,556	23,093
*78006	Boerne	(830)	6,849	4,361
75418	Bonham	(903)	10,336	6,688
*79007	Borger	(806)	13,638	15,675
76230	Bowie	(940)	5,450	4,990
76825	Brady	(325)	5,331	5,946
76424	Breckenridge	(254)	5,676	5,665
*77833	Brenham	(979)	13,999	11,952
—	Briar (c)		5,350	3,899
77611	Bridge City	(409)	8,660	8,010
76426	Bridgeport	(940)	5,258	3,581
79316	Brownfield	(806)	9,237	9,560
*78520	Brownsville	(956)	156,178	107,027
*76801	Brownwood	(325)	19,320	18,387
78717	Brushy Creek (c)	(903)	15,371	5,833
*77801	Bryan	(979)	67,774	55,002
76354	Burkburnett	(940)	10,732	10,145
*76028	Burleson	(817)	25,334	16,113
78611	Burnet	(512)	5,156	3,423
76520	Cameron	(254)	5,896	5,635
—	Cameron Park (c)		5,961	3,802
79835	Canutillo (c)	(915)	5,129	4,442
79015	Canyon	(806)	12,987	11,365
78130	Canyon Lake (c)	(830)	16,870	9,975
78834	Carrizo Springs	(830)	5,635	5,745
*75006	Carrolton	(214)	116,714	82,169
75633	Carthage	(903)	6,493	6,496
*75104	Cedar Hill	(214)	39,260	19,988
*78613	Cedar Park	(512)	41,482	5,161
75935	Center	(936)	5,716	4,950
77530	Channelview (c)	(713)	29,685	25,564
79201	Childress	(940)	6,632	5,055
—	Cinco Ranch (c)	(281)	11,196	—
*76031	Cleburne	(817)	27,928	22,205
*77327	Cleveland	(713)	7,828	7,124
77015	Cloverleaf (c)	(713)	23,508	18,230
77531	Clute	(979)	10,704	9,467
*77840	College Station	(979)	73,536	52,443
76034	Colleyville	(817)	21,389	12,724
*75428	Commerce	(903)	8,782	6,825
*77301	Conroe	(936)	39,896	27,675
78109	Converse	(210)	11,967	8,887
75019	Coppell	(214)	38,938	16,881
76522	Copperas Cove	(254)	29,988	24,079
76205	Corinth	(940)	16,338	3,944
*78469	Corpus Christi	(361)	279,208	257,428
*75110	Corsicana	(903)	25,466	22,911
75835	Crockett	(936)	7,065	7,024
76036	Crowley	(817)	8,831	6,974
78839	Crystal City	(830)	7,131	8,263
77954	Cuero	(361)	6,659	6,700

ZIP	Place	Area Code	2003	1990
79022	Dalhart	(806)	7,153	6,246
*75221	Dallas	(214)	1,208,318	1,007,618
77535	Dayton	(936)	6,363	5,042
76234	Decatur	(214)	5,743	4,245
77536	Deer Park	(713)	28,844	27,424
*78840	Del Rio	(830)	35,136	30,705
*75020	Denison	(903)	23,335	21,505
*76201	Denton	(940)	93,435	66,270
*75115	De Soto	(214)	41,703	30,544
75941	Diboll	(936)	5,439	4,341
77539	Dickinson	(281)	17,847	11,692
78537	Donna	(956)	15,562	12,652
79029	Dumas	(806)	13,724	12,871
*75138	Duncanville	(214)	35,670	35,008
76135	Eagle Mountain (c)	(817)	6,599	5,847
*78852	Eagle Pass	(830)	24,462	20,651
*78539	Edinburg	(956)	55,302	31,091
77957	Edna	(361)	5,838	5,436
—	Eidson Road (c)		9,348	—
77437	El Campo	(979)	10,842	10,511
78621	Elgin	(512)	7,218	4,846
*79910	El Paso	(915)	584,113	515,342
78543	Elsa	(956)	6,174	5,242
*75119	Ennis	(214)	18,319	13,869
*76039	Euless	(817)	50,118	38,149
76140	Everman (c)	(817)	5,849	5,672
79838	Fabens (c)	(915)	8,043	5,599
*78015	Fair Oaks Ranch	(210)	5,328	1,886
78355	Falfurrias	(361)	5,100	5,788
75381	Farmers Branch	(214)	27,025	24,250
78114	Floresville	(830)	6,475	5,247
*75067	Flower Mound	(214)	60,621	15,527
76119	Forest Hill	(817)	13,265	11,482
75126	Forney	(214)	7,565	4,070
79906	Fort Bliss (c)	(915)	8,264	13,915
76544	Fort Hood (c)	(254)	33,711	35,580
79735	Fort Stockton	(432)	7,387	8,524
*76161	Fort Worth	(817)	585,122	447,619
78624	Fredericksburg	(830)	9,955	6,934
*77541	Freeport	(979)	12,715	11,389
*77546	Friendswood	(281)	32,460	22,814
*75034	Frisco	(214)	55,126	6,138
*76240	Gainesville	(940)	16,040	14,256
77547	Galena Park	(713)	10,443	10,033
*75550	Galveston	(409)	56,667	59,067
*75040	Garland	(214)	218,027	180,635
76528	Gatesville	(254)	15,373	11,492
*78626	Georgetown	(512)	34,815	14,840
78942	Giddings	(979)	5,386	4,093
*75644	Gilmer	(903)	5,025	4,822
75647	Gladewater	(903)	6,155	6,027
75115	Glenn Heights	(214)	8,100	4,564
78629	Gonzales	(830)	7,320	6,527
76450	Graham	(940)	8,651	8,986
*76048	Granbury	(817)	6,403	4,045
*75051	Grand Prairie	(214)	136,671	99,606
*76051	Grapevine	(817)	46,891	29,407
—	Greatwood (c)		6,640	—
*75401	Greenville	(903)	24,838	23,071
77619	Groves	(409)	15,333	16,744
75147	Gun Barrel City	(903)	5,570	3,526
76117	Haltom City	(817)	40,475	32,856
76548	Harker Heights	(254)	18,365	12,932
*78550	Harlingen	(956)	60,769	48,746
75032	Heath	(214)	5,787	2,128
78023	Helotes	(210)	5,239	1,556
77445	Hempstead	(979)	6,051	3,598
*75652	Henderson	(903)	11,069	11,139
79045	Hereford	(806)	14,428	14,745
76643	Hewitt	(254)	12,261	8,983
78557	Hidalgo	(956)	9,110	3,292
75205	Highland Park	(214)	8,819	8,739
77562	Highlands (c)	(713)	7,089	6,632
75067	Highland Village	(214)	14,080	7,027
76645	Hillsboro	(254)	8,705	7,072
77563	Hitchcock	(409)	7,176	5,868
—	Homestead Meadows South (c)		6,807	—
78861	Hondo	(830)	8,208	6,018
*79927	Horizon City	(915)	7,432	2,308
*77052	Houston	(281)/(713)/(832)	2,009,690	1,654,348
*77338	Humble	(713)	14,753	12,060
*77340	Huntsville	(936)	35,567	30,628
*76053	Hurst	(817)	37,141	33,574
78362	Ingleside	(361)	9,203	5,696
76367	Iowa Park	(940)	6,318	6,072
*75015	Irving	(214)	194,455	155,037
77029	Jacinto City	(713)	10,258	9,343
75766	Jacksonville	(903)	13,974	12,765
75951	Jasper	(409)	7,541	7,160
77040	Jersey Village	(713)	7,195	4,826
78729	Jollyville (c)	(512)	15,813	15,206
76058	Joshua	(817)	5,161	3,634
*77449	Katy	(713)	12,726	8,004
75142	Kaufman	(214)	7,502	5,251
76059	Keene	(817)	5,514	3,944
*76248	Keller	(817)	33,951	13,683
76060	Kennedale	(817)	6,399	4,096
79745	Kermit	(432)	5,367	6,875
*78028	Kerrville	(830)	21,343	17,384
*75662	Kilgore	(903)	11,472	11,066

ZIP	Place	Area Code	2003	1990
*76540	Killeen	(254)	96,159	63,535
*78363	Kingsville	(361)	25,270	25,276
78219	Kirby	(210)	8,712	8,326
78640	Kyle	(512)	11,248	2,225
78236	Lackland AFB (c)	(210)	7,123	9,352
76705	Lacy-Lakeview	(254)	5,805	3,617
78559	La Feria	(956)	6,436	4,360
78645	Lago Vista	(512)	5,167	2,199
—	La Homa (c)		10,433	1,403
75065	Lake Dallas	(940)	6,779	3,656
77566	Lake Jackson	(979)	26,950	22,771
78734	Lakeway	(512)	8,190	4,044
77568	La Marque	(409)	13,788	14,120
79331	Lamesa	(806)	9,462	10,809
76550	Lampasas	(512)	7,426	6,382
*75146	Lancaster	(214)	27,814	22,117
*77571	La Porte	(713)	33,263	27,923
*78041	Laredo	(956)	197,488	122,893
*77573	League City	(281)	54,775	30,159
*78641	Leander	(512)	13,846	3,354
78268	Leon Valley	(210)	9,358	9,581
*79336	Levelland	(806)	12,904	13,986
*75067	Lewisville	(214)	87,127	46,521
77575	Liberty	(936)	8,261	7,690
75068	Little Elm	(214)	12,003	1,242
79339	Littlefield	(806)	6,432	6,489
78233	Live Oak	(210)	9,786	10,023
77351	Livingston	(936)	6,317	5,019
78644	Lockhart	(512)	13,064	9,205
*75606	Longview	(903)	74,902	70,311
*79408	Lubbock	(806)	206,481	186,206
*75901	Lufkin	(936)	33,162	30,210
78648	Luling	(830)	5,291	4,661
77657	Lumberton	(409)	9,122	6,640
*78501	McAllen	(956)	116,501	84,021
*75070	McKinney	(214)	79,958	21,283
76063	Mansfield	(817)	33,123	15,615
78654	Marble Falls	(830)	5,503	4,017
76661	Marlin	(254)	6,340	6,386
*75670	Marshall	(903)	23,938	23,682
78368	Mathis	(361)	5,159	5,423
77477	Meadows Place	(281)/(713)	5,281	4,663
78570	Mercedes	(956)	14,128	12,694
*75149	Mesquite	(214)	129,270	101,484
76667	Mexia	(254)	6,710	6,933
*79701	Midland	(432)	96,573	89,343
76065	Midlothian	(214)	10,942	5,040
*76067	Mineral Wells	(940)	16,970	14,935
*78572	Mission	(956)	54,619	28,653
—	Mission Bend (c)		30,831	24,945
*77489	Missouri City	(713)	62,570	36,143
79756	Monahans	(432)	6,397	8,101
*75455	Mount Pleasant	(903)	14,266	12,291
75094	Murphy	(214)	7,991	1,603
*75961	Nacogdoches	(936)	30,441	30,872
77868	Navasota	(936)	7,235	6,296
77627	Nederland	(409)	16,928	16,192
*78130	New Braunfels	(830)	42,693	27,334
—	New Territory (c)	(281)	13,861	—
*76161	North Richland Hills	(817)	60,238	45,895
—	Nurillo (c)		5,056	—
*79761	Odessa	(432)	91,113	89,699
*77630	Orange	(409)	18,073	19,370
77465	Palacios	(361)	5,270	4,418
*75801	Palestine	(903)	17,808	18,042
—	Palmview South (c)		6,219	—
*79065	Pampa	(806)	16,897	19,959
*75460	Paris	(903)	26,523	24,799
*77501	Pasadena	(713)	144,413	119,604
*77581	Pearland	(713)	47,903	18,927
78061	Pearsall	(830)	7,132	6,924
78721	Pecan Grove (c)		13,551	9,502
79772	Pecos	(432)	8,752	12,069
79070	Perryton	(806)	7,775	7,619
*78660	Pflugerville	(512)	24,661	4,444
78577	Pharr	(956)	54,452	32,921
*79072	Plainview	(806)	21,889	21,698
*75074	Plano	(214)	241,991	127,885
78064	Pleasanton	(830)	8,999	7,678
*77640	Port Arthur	(409)	57,042	58,551
78578	Port Isabel	(956)	5,199	4,740
78374	Portland	(361)	15,489	12,224
77979	Port Lavaca	(361)	11,865	10,886
77651	Port Neches	(409)	13,269	12,908
78579	Progreso	(956)	5,043	2,808
78580	Raymondville	(956)	9,512	8,880
75154	Red Oak	(214)	5,871	3,660
76028	Rendon (c)	(817)	9,022	7,658
*75080	Richardson	(214)	99,536	74,840
76118	Richland Hills	(817)	8,184	7,978
*77469	Richmond	(713)	12,752	10,042
78043	Rio Bravo		5,674	—
78582	Rio Grande City	(956)	12,985	10,725
76219	River Oaks	(817)	7,024	6,580
76701	Robinson	(254)	8,392	7,111
78380	Robstown	(361)	12,637	12,849
76567	Rockdale	(512)	6,024	5,235
*78382	Rockport	(361)	8,469	5,619
*75087	Rockwall	(214)	24,624	10,486
78584	Roma	(956)	10,315	8,059

ZIP	Place	Area Code	2003	1990
77471	Rosenberg	(713)	27,808	20,183
*78681	Round Rock	(512)	77,946	30,923
*75088	Rowlett	(214)	51,102	23,260
75785	Rusk	(903)	5,212	4,366
75048	Sachse	(214)	14,550	5,346
76179	Saginaw	(817)	16,127	8,551
*76902	San Angelo	(325)	87,922	84,462
*78265	San Antonio	(210)	1,214,725	976,514
78586	San Benito	(956)	24,208	20,125
79849	San Elizario (c)	(915)	11,046	4,385
76266	Sanger	(940)	5,122	3,602
78589	San Juan	(956)	28,894	12,561
*78666	San Marcos	(512)	43,007	28,738
*77510	Santa Fe	(409)	10,259	8,429
78154	Schertz	(210)	23,690	10,597
77586	Seabrook	(281)	10,822	6,685
75159	Seagoville	(214)	11,019	8,969
77474	Sealy	(979)	5,771	4,541
*78155	Seguin	(830)	23,186	18,692
79360	Seminole	(432)	5,839	6,342
—	Shady Hollow (c)		5,140	—
*75090	Sherman	(903)	36,261	31,584
77656	Silsbee	(409)	6,498	6,368
78387	Sinton	(361)	5,549	5,549
79364	Slaton	(806)	6,022	6,078
*79549	Snyder	(325)	10,536	12,195
79910	Socorro	(915)	28,140	22,995
77587	South Houston	(713)	16,058	14,207
76092	Southlake	(817)	24,192	7,082
*77373	Spring (c)	(713)	36,385	33,111
*77477	Stafford	(713)	18,295	8,395
76401	Stephenville	(254)	15,216	13,502
*77478	Sugar Land	(713)	70,815	33,712
*75482	Sulphur Springs	(903)	14,787	14,062
79556	Sweetwater	(325)	10,892	11,967
76574	Taylor	(512)	14,204	11,472
*76501	Temple	(254)	54,975	46,150
*75160	Terrell	(214)	15,771	12,490
78209	Terrell Hills	(210)	5,049	4,592
*75501	Texarkana	(903)	35,199	32,294
*77590	Texas City	(409)	43,233	40,822
75056	The Colony	(214)	35,189	22,113
77387	The Woodlands (c)	(713)	55,649	29,205
—	Timberwood Park (c)	(210)	5,889	2,578
*77375	Tomball	(713)	9,784	6,370
76262	Trophy Club	(817)	7,194	3,922
*75702	Tyler	(903)	88,316	75,450
*78148	Universal City	(830)	15,428	13,057
76308	University Park	(214)	23,745	22,259
*78801	Uvalde	(830)	16,391	14,729
*76384	Vernon	(940)	10,902	12,001
*77901	Victoria	(361)	61,410	55,076
*77662	Vidor	(409)	11,283	10,935
*76702	Waco	(254)	116,887	103,590
75501	Wake Village	(903)	5,181	4,761
76148	Watauga	(817)	23,593	20,009
*75165	Waxahachie	(214)	23,915	17,984
*76086	Weatherford	(817)	21,420	14,804
77598	Webster	(281)	9,074	4,678
78728	Wells Branch (c)		11,271	7,094
*78596	Weslaco	(956)	30,416	22,739
—	West Livingston (c)		6,612	—
79764	West Odessa (c)	(432)	17,799	16,568
77005	West University Place	(713)	14,904	12,920
*77488	Wharton	(979)	9,337	9,011
75791	Whitehouse	(903)	6,582	4,018
75693	White Oak	(903)	5,858	5,136
76108	White Settlement	(817)	15,553	15,472
*76307	Wichita Falls	(940)	102,340	96,259
78239	Windcrest	(210)	5,111	5,331
—	Windemere (c)		6,868	3,207
76712	Woodway	(254)	8,747	8,695
75098	Wylie	(214)	21,720	8,716
77995	Yoakum	(361)	5,734	5,611

Utah

ZIP	Place	Area Code	2003	1990
84004	Alpine	(801)	7,937	3,492
84003	American Fork	(801)	22,876	15,722
84065	Bluffdale	(801)	5,672	2,142
*84010	Bountiful	(801)	41,401	37,544
84302	Brigham City	(435)	17,334	15,644
84109	Canyon Rim (c)	(801)	10,428	10,527
*84720	Cedar City	(435)	21,946	13,443
84062	Cedar Hills	(801)	5,160	708
84014	Centerville	(801)	14,748	11,500
*84015	Clearfield	(801)	27,146	21,435
84015	Clinton	(801)	15,281	7,945
84121	Cottonwood Heights (c)	(801)	27,569	28,766
84121	Cottonwood West (c)	(801)	18,727	17,476
84020	Draper	(801)	31,020	7,143
84043	Eagle Mountain	(801)	7,405	30
84109	East Millcreek (c)	(801)	21,385	21,184
84025	Farmington	(801)	13,407	9,049
84029	Grantsville	(435)	6,824	4,500
84032	Heber	(435)	8,605	4,782
84065	Herriman	(801)	5,632	—
84003	Highland	(801)	9,642	5,007
84117	Holladay	(801)	19,667	14,095

ZIP	Place	Area Code	2003	1990
84737	Hurricane	(435)	9,465	3,915
84319	Hyrum	(435)	6,305	4,829
84738	Ivins	(435)	6,049	1,639
84037	Kaysville	(801)	21,386	13,961
84118	Kearns (c)	(801)	33,659	28,374
*84041	Layton	(801)	60,769	41,784
84043	Lehi	(801)	23,266	8,475
84042	Lindon	(801)	8,680	3,818
—	Little Cottonwood Creek Valley (c)	(801)	7,221	5,042
*84321	Logan	(435)	43,675	32,771
84044	Magna (c)	(801)	22,770	17,829
84664	Mapleton	(801)	6,180	3,572
84047	Midvale	(801)	27,166	11,886
84109	Millcreek (c)	(801)	30,377	32,230
84117	Mount Olympus (c)	(801)	7,103	7,413
84157	Murray	(801)	43,617	31,274
84341	North Logan	(435)	6,872	3,775
84404	North Ogden	(801)	16,084	11,593
84054	North Salt Lake	(801)	9,321	6,464
*84401	Ogden	(801)	78,293	63,943
—	Oquirrh (c)	(801)	10,390	7,593
*84057	Orem	(801)	87,599	67,561
*84060	Park City	(435)	7,854	4,468
84651	Payson	(801)	14,761	9,510
84062	Pleasant Grove	(801)	23,901	13,476
84404	Pleasant View	(801)	5,965	3,597
84501	Price	(435)	8,229	8,712
84332	Providence	(435)	5,186	3,344
*84601	Provo	(801)	105,410	86,835
84701	Richfield	(435)	6,936	5,593
84403	Riverdale	(801)	7,791	6,419
84065	Riverton	(801)	29,244	11,261
84067	Roy	(801)	35,249	24,560
*84770	Saint George	(435)	56,382	28,572
*84101	Salt Lake City	(801)	179,894	159,928
*84070	Sandy	(801)	89,319	75,240
84765	Santa Clara	(435)	5,360	2,323
84655	Santaquin	(801)	5,751	2,522
84335	Smithfield	(435)	7,877	5,566
84095	South Jordan	(801)	33,589	12,215
84403	South Ogden	(801)	15,003	12,105
84165	South Salt Lake	(801)	21,719	10,129
*84403	South Weber	(801)	5,384	2,853
84660	Spanish Fork	(801)	23,000	11,272
84663	Springville	(801)	21,929	13,950
84098	Summit Park (c)		6,597	—
84015	Sunset	(801)	5,068	5,128
84075	Syracuse	(801)	14,159	4,658
84107	Taylorsville	(801)	58,701	51,550
84074	Tooele	(435)	27,052	13,887
84337	Tremonton	(435)	6,083	4,262
*84078	Vernal	(435)	7,892	6,640
84780	Washington	(435)	10,496	4,198
84403	Washington Terrace	(801)	8,455	8,189
*84084	West Jordan	(801)	84,701	42,915
84015	West Point	(801)	6,472	4,258
84170	West Valley City	(801)	111,687	86,969
84070	White City (c)	(801)	5,988	6,506
84087	Woods Cross	(801)	7,466	5,384

Vermont (802)

See introductory note.

ZIP	Place	2003	1990
05641	Barre	7,846	9,482
05641	Barre	9,166	7,411
05201	Bennington (c)	9,168	9,532
05201	Bennington	15,637	16,451
*05301	Brattleboro	11,996	12,241
*05301	Brattleboro (c)	8,289	8,612
*05401	Burlington	39,148	39,127
*05446	Colchester	17,175	14,731
05451	Essex	18,933	16,498
05047	Hartford	10,610	9,404
05465	Jericho	5,066	1,405
05849	Lyndon	5,495	5,371
05753	Middlebury (c)	6,252	6,007
*05753	Middlebury	8,190	8,034
05468	Milton	9,924	8,404
*05602	Montpelier	7,945	8,247
05661	Morristown	5,447	4,733
05855	Newport	5,092	4,434
05663	Northfield	5,804	5,610
05060	Randolph	5,011	—
05101	Rockingham	5,236	5,484
*05701	Rutland	17,103	18,230
05478	Saint Albans	7,565	7,339
05478	Saint Albans	5,718	4,606
05819	Saint Johnsbury (c)	6,319	6,424
05819	Saint Johnsbury	7,470	7,608
05482	Shelburne	6,975	5,871
*05401	South Burlington	16,285	12,809
05156	Springfield	9,012	9,579
05488	Swanton	6,379	5,636
05676	Waterbury	5,138	4,614
05495	Williston	8,156	4,887
05404	Winooski	6,387	6,649

Virginia

Area code (571) overlays area code (703). See introductory note.

ZIP	Place	Area Code	2003	1990
*24210	Abingdon	(276)	7,750	7,003
*22313	Alexandria	(703)	128,923	111,182
22003	Ananndale (c)	(703)	54,994	50,975
22554	Aquia Harbour (c)	(703)	7,856	6,308
*22210	Arlington (c)	(703)	187,873	170,897
23005	Ashland	(804)	6,876	5,864
*22041	Bailey's Crossroads (c)	(703)	23,166	19,507
24523	Bedford	(540)	6,339	6,177
22306	Belle Haven (c)	(757)	6,269	6,427
23234	Bellwood (c)	(804)	5,974	6,178
23234	Bensley (c)	(804)	5,435	5,093
24219	Big Stone Gap	(276)	5,839	4,847
*24060	Blacksburg	(540)	40,066	34,590
23235	Bon Air (c)	(804)	16,213	16,413
22812	Bridgewater	(540)	5,273	3,918
*24203	Bristol	(276)	17,206	18,426
24416	Buena Vista	(540)	6,320	6,406
—	Bull Run (c)	(703)	11,337	5,525
*22150	Burke (c)	(703)	57,737	57,734
24018	Cave Spring (c)	(540)	24,941	24,053
*20120	Centreville (c)	(703)	48,661	26,585
*20151	Chantilly (c)	(703)	41,041	29,337
*22906	Charlottesville	(434)	39,162	40,475
*23320	Chesapeake	(757)	210,834	151,982
*23831	Chester (c)	(804)	17,890	14,986
*24073	Christiansburg	(540)	17,756	15,004
24078	Collinsville (c)	(276)	7,777	7,280
23834	Colonial Heights	(804)	17,286	16,064
24426	Covington	(540)	6,284	7,198
22701	Culpeper	(540)	10,442	8,581
22193	Dale City (c)	(703)	55,971	47,170
*24541	Danville	(434)	46,988	53,056
23228	Dumbarton (c)	(804)	6,674	8,526
22027	Dunn Loring (c)	(703)	7,861	6,509
23222	East Highland Park (c)	(804)	12,488	11,850
23847	Emporia	(434)	5,656	5,479
23803	Ettrick (c)	(804)	5,627	5,290
*22030	Fairfax	(703)	22,031	19,894
*22046	Falls Church	(703)	10,485	9,522
23901	Farmville	(434)	6,959	6,505
24551	Forest (c)	(434)	8,006	5,624
22060	Fort Belvoir (c)	(703)	7,176	8,590
22308	Fort Hunt (c)	(703)	12,923	12,989
23801	Fort Lee (c)	(804)	7,269	6,895
22310	Franconia (c)	(703)	31,907	19,882
23851	Franklin	(757)	8,254	7,864
*22404	Fredericksburg	(540)	20,189	19,027
22630	Front Royal	(540)	14,160	11,880
24333	Galax	(276)	6,655	6,699
*23060	Glen Allen (c)	(804)	12,562	9,010
23062	Gloucester Point (c)	(804)	9,429	8,509
22066	Great Falls (c)	(703)	8,549	6,945
22306	Groveton (c)	(703)	21,296	19,997
*23670	Hampton	(757)	146,878	133,811
*22801	Harrisonburg	(540)	41,170	30,707
*20170	Herndon	(703)	21,721	16,139
23075	Highland Springs (c)	(804)	15,137	13,823
24019	Hollins (c)	(540)	14,309	13,305
23860	Hopewell	(804)	22,391	23,101
22303	Huntington (c)	(703)	8,325	7,489
22306	Hybla Valley (c)	(703)	16,721	15,491
22043	Idylwood (c)	(703)	16,005	14,710
22042	Jefferson (c)	(703)	27,422	25,782
22041	Lake Barcroft (c)	(703)	8,906	8,686
22963	Lake Monticello (c)	(434)	6,852	2,331
22191	Lake Ridge (c)	(540)	30,404	23,862
23228	Lakeside (c)	(804)	11,157	12,081
23060	Laurel (c)	(804)	14,875	13,011
*20175	Leesburg	(703)	33,319	16,202
24450	Lexington	(540)	7,076	6,959
22312	Lincolnia (c)	(703)	15,788	13,041
—	Linton Hall (c)		8,620	—
*22079	Lorton (c)	(703)	17,786	15,385
*24506	Lynchburg	(434)	65,113	66,049
*22101	McLean (c)	(703)	38,929	38,168
24572	Madison Heights (c)	(434)	11,584	11,700
*20110	Manassas	(703)	37,166	27,957
20113	Manassas Park	(703)	10,990	6,734
22030	Mantua (c)	(703)	7,485	6,804
24354	Marion	(276)	6,208	6,630
*24112	Martinsville	(276)	15,121	16,162
*23111	Mechanicsville (c)	(804)	30,464	22,027
*22116	Merrifield (c)	(703)	11,170	8,399
—	Montclair (c)		15,728	11,399
23231	Montrose (c)	(804)	7,018	6,405
22121	Mount Vernon (c)	(703)	28,582	27,485
22122	Newington (c)	(703)	19,784	17,965
*23607	Newport News	(757)	181,647	171,439
*23501	Norfolk	(757)	241,727	261,250
22151	North Springfield (c)	(703)	9,173	8,996
22124	Oakton (c)	(703)	29,348	24,610
*23804	Petersburg	(804)	33,091	37,027
22043	Pimmit Hills (c)	(703)	6,152	6,019
23662	Poquoson	(757)	11,844	11,005

ZIP	Place	Area Code	2003	1990
*23707	Portsmouth	(757)	99,617	103,910
24301	Pulaski	(540)	9,173	9,985
22134	Quantico Station (c)	(703)	6,571	7,425
*24141	Radford	(540)	15,006	15,940
*20190	Reston (c)	(703)	56,407	48,556
*23232	Richmond	(804)	194,729	202,798
*24022	Roanoke	(540)	92,863	96,509
24281	Rose Hill (c)	(276)	15,058	12,675
24153	Salem	(540)	24,603	23,797
22044	Seven Corners (c)	(703)	8,701	7,280
*23430	Smithfield	(757)	6,703	4,686
24592	South Boston	(434)	8,222	6,997
*22150	Springfield (c)	(703)	30,417	23,706
*24402	Staunton	(540)	23,848	24,461
24477	Stuarts Draft (c)	(540)	8,367	5,087
23162	Sudley (c)	(540)	7,719	7,321
*23434	Suffolk	(757)	73,515	52,143
24502	Timberlake (c)	(434)	10,683	10,314
22172	Triangle (c)	(703)	5,500	4,740
23229	Tuckahoe (c)	(804)	43,242	42,629
22101	Tysons Corner (c)	(703)	18,540	13,124
*22180	Vienna	(703)	14,868	14,852
24179	Vinton	(540)	7,749	7,643
*23450	Virginia Beach	(757)	439,467	393,089
*20186	Warrenton	(540)	7,840	4,882
22980	Waynesboro	(540)	20,388	18,549
22110	West Gate (c)	(703)	7,493	6,565
22152	West Springfield (c)	(703)	28,378	28,126
*23185	Williamsburg	(757)	11,605	11,409
*22601	Winchester	(540)	24,434	21,947
24592	Wolf Trap (c)	(703)	14,001	13,133
*22191	Woodbridge (c)	(703)	31,941	26,401
—	Wyndham (c)		6,176	—
24382	Wytheville (c)	(276)	7,865	8,036
22110	Yorkshire (c)	(703)	6,732	5,699

Washington

ZIP	Place	Area Code	2003	1990
98520	Aberdeen	(360)	16,207	16,565
98036	Alderwood Manor (c)	(425)	15,329	22,945
98221	Anacortes	(360)	15,474	11,451
98223	Arlington	(360)	13,911	4,037
98335	Artondale (c)	(253)	8,630	7,141
*98002	Auburn	(253)	44,655	33,650
98110	Bainbridge Island	(206)	21,701	—
98315	Bangor Trident Base (c)	(360)	7,253	3,702
98604	Battle Ground	(360)	12,731	3,758
*98009	Bellevue	(425)	112,344	95,213
*98225	Bellingham	(360)	71,289	52,179
98390	Bonney Lake	(360)	13,215	7,494
*98011	Bothell	(425)	30,568	12,575
*98337	Bremerton	(360)	39,597	38,142
98036	Brier	(425)	6,361	5,633
98178	Bryn Mawr-Skyway (c)	(206)	13,977	12,514
98166	Burien	(206)	31,116	27,507
98233	Burlington	(360)	7,710	4,349
—	Camano (c)		13,347	—
98607	Camas	(360)	14,976	6,762
98055	Cascade-Fairwood (c)	(425)	34,580	30,107
98531	Centralia	(360)	14,981	12,101
98532	Chehalis	(360)	7,105	6,527
99004	Cheney	(509)	9,743	7,723
99403	Clarkston	(509)	7,211	6,753
—	Clarkston Heights-Vineland (c)		6,117	2,832
99324	College Place	(509)	8,446	6,308
98072	Cottage Lake (c)	(206)	24,330	—
99218	Country Homes (c)	(509)	5,203	5,126
98042	Covington	(253)	15,294	—
98198	Des Moines	(206)	29,039	20,830
99213	Dishman (c)	(509)	10,031	9,671
98019	Duvall	(425)	5,568	2,640
—	East Hill-Meridian (c)		29,308	42,696
98366	East Port Orchard (c)	(360)	5,116	5,409
98056	East Renton Highlands (c)	(425)	13,264	13,218
98802	East Wenatchee	(509)	8,590	3,886
98801	East Wenatchee Bench (c)	(509)	13,658	12,539
98371	Edgewood (c)	(253)	9,526	8,702
*98020	Edmonds	(425)	39,882	30,743
98387	Elk Plain (c)		15,697	12,197
98926	Ellensburg	(509)	16,257	12,360
98022	Enumclaw	(360)	10,941	7,243
98823	Ephrata	(509)	7,069	5,349
*98201	Everett	(425)	96,643	70,937
99218	Fairwood (c)	(509)	6,764	5,807
*98002	Federal Way	(253)	81,711	67,535
98685	Felida (c)	(360)	5,683	3,109
98248	Ferndale	(360)	9,591	5,398
99336	Finley (c)	(509)	5,770	4,897
98466	Fircrest	(253)	5,993	5,270
98597	Five Corners (c)		12,207	6,776
98433	Fort Lewis (c)	(253)	19,089	22,224
98373	Frederickson (c)	(206)	5,758	3,502
*98329	Gig Harbor	(253)	6,616	3,236
98338	Graham (c)	(253)	8,739	—
98930	Grandview	(509)	8,515	7,169
99016	Green Acres (c)	(509)	5,158	4,626
98660	Hazel Dell North (c)	(360)	9,261	6,924

ZIP	Place	Area Code	2003	1990
98665	Hazel Dell South (c)	(360)	6,605	5,796
98025	Hobart (c)		6,251	—
—	Hockinson (c)	(360)	5,136	—
98550	Hoquiam	(360)	8,925	8,972
98011	Inglewood-Finn Hill (c)	(425)	22,661	29,132
*98027	Issaquah	(425)	14,662	7,786
98626	Kelso	(360)	11,744	11,767
98028	Kenmore	(425)	19,032	8,917
*99336	Kennewick	(509)	59,334	42,148
*98031	Kent	(253)/(425)	81,567	37,960
98033	Kingsgate (c)	(425)	12,222	14,259
*98033	Kirkland	(425)	45,573	40,059
98509	Lacey	(360)	32,781	19,279
98155	Lake Forest Park	(206)	12,578	4,031
98002	Lakeland North (c)	(253)	15,085	14,402
98002	Lakeland South (c)	(253)	11,436	9,027
—	Lake Morton-Berrydale (c)		9,659	—
98665	Lake Shore (c)	(360)	6,670	6,268
98258	Lake Stevens	(425)	7,015	3,435
*98498	Lakewood	(253)	58,789	55,937
—	Lea Hill (c)		10,871	6,876
98632	Longview	(360)	35,741	31,499
98264	Lynden	(360)	10,039	5,709
*98046	Lynnwood	(425)	33,704	28,637
98290	Maltby (c)	(360)	8,267	—
98038	Maple Valley	(425)	14,119	1,211
98012	Martha Lake (c)	(425)	12,633	10,155
*98270	Marysville	(360)	28,260	12,248
98040	Mercer Island	(206)	22,351	20,816
98444	Midland (c)	(253)	7,414	5,587
98082	Mill Creek	(425)	12,832	7,180
—	Mill Plain (c)	(360)	7,400	—
98354	Milton	(253)	6,028	4,995
98661	Minnehaha (c)	(360)	7,689	9,661
98272	Monroe	(360)	14,798	4,275
98837	Moses Lake	(509)	16,147	11,235
98043	Mountlake Terrace	(425)	20,606	19,320
*98273	Mount Vernon	(360)	27,935	17,647
—	Mount Vista (c)		5,770	—
98275	Mukilteo	(425)	19,169	11,575
98059	Newcastle	(425)	8,786	4,649
98166	Normandy Park	(206)	6,250	6,794
—	North Creek (c)		25,742	23,236
98270	North Marysville (c)	(425)	21,161	18,711
98277	Oak Harbor	(360)	21,071	17,176
*98501	Olympia	(360)	43,963	33,729
99214	Opportunity (c)	(509)	25,065	22,326
98662	Orchards (c)	(360)	17,852	—
*99327	Othello	(509)	6,003	4,638
99027	Otis Orchards-East Farms (c)	(360)	6,318	5,811
98047	Pacific	(253)	5,626	4,622
—	Paine Field-Lake Stickney (c)		24,383	18,670
98444	Parkland (c)	(253)	24,053	20,882
98366	Parkwood (c)	(360)	7,213	6,853
*99301	Pasco	(509)	38,233	20,337
—	Picnic Point-North Lynnwood (c)		22,953	—
*98362	Port Angeles	(360)	18,516	17,710
*98366	Port Orchard	(360)	7,903	4,984
98368	Port Townsend	(360)	8,685	7,001
98370	Poulsbo	(360)	7,336	4,848
98390	Prairie Ridge (c)		11,688	8,278
99350	Prosser	(509)	5,053	4,492
*99163	Pullman	(509)	25,237	23,478
*98371	Puyallup	(253)	35,641	23,878
98848	Quincy	(509)	5,325	3,738
*98052	Redmond	(425)	46,391	35,800
*98058	Renton	(425)	54,028	41,688
99352	Richland	(509)	42,537	32,315
98188	Riverton-Boulevard Park (c)	(206)	11,188	15,337
98686	Salmon Creek (c)	(360)	16,767	11,989
*98074	Sammamish	(425)	33,916	—
*98148	SeaTac	(206)	25,014	22,760
*98101	Seattle	(206)/(425)	569,101	516,259
—	Seattle Hill-Silver Firs (c)		35,311	—
98284	Sedro-Woolley	(360)	9,660	6,333
98942	Selah	(509)	6,573	5,113
98584	Shelton	(360)	8,789	7,241
*98133	Shoreline	(206)	52,380	46,979
*98315	Silverdale (c)	(360)	15,816	7,660
*98290	Snohomish	(360)	8,620	6,499
98373	South Hill (c)		31,623	12,963
98387	Spanaway (c)	(253)	21,588	15,001
*99210	Spokane	(509)	196,624	177,165
98388	Steilacoom	(253)	6,165	5,728
*98371	Summit (c)	(253)	8,041	6,312
98390	Sumner	(253)	9,026	7,535
98944	Sunnyside	(509)	14,080	11,238
*98402	Tacoma	(253)	196,790	176,664
98501	Tanglewilde-Thompson Place (c)	(360)	5,670	6,061
—	Terrace Heights (c)		6,447	4,223
98948	Toppenish	(509)	9,108	7,419
98138	Tukwila	(206)	17,081	14,506
98501	Tumwater	(360)	13,162	9,976
*98901	Union Gap	(509)	5,710	3,120
—	Union Hill-Novelty Hill (c)		11,265	—
98467	University Place (c)	(253)	30,638	26,724
*98661	Vancouver	(360)	151,654	62,065

ZIP	Place	Area Code	2003	1990
*98013	Vashon (c)	(206)	10,123	—
99037	Veradale (c)	(509)	9,387	7,836
99362	Walla Walla	(509)	30,134	26,482
—	Waller (c)		9,200	6,415
—	Walnut Grove (c)		7,164	3,906
98671	Washougal	(360)	9,541	4,764
*98801	Wenatchee	(509)	28,636	21,746
—	West Lake Sammamish (c)		5,937	6,087
98258	West Lake Stevens (c)	(425)	18,071	12,453
99353	West Richland	(509)	9,290	3,962
99181	West Valley (c)		10,433	6,594
98166	White Center (c)	(206)	20,975	20,531
98072	Woodinville	(425)	9,632	7,628
*98903	Yakima	(509)	80,223	58,427

West Virginia (304)

ZIP	Place	2003	1990
*25801	Beckley	16,994	18,274
24701	Bluefield	11,124	12,756
26330	Bridgeport	7,470	6,837
26201	Buckhannon	5,753	5,909
*25301	Charleston	51,394	57,287
*26507	Cheat Lake (c)	6,396	3,992
*26301	Clarksburg	16,425	17,970
25301	Cross Lanes (c)	10,353	10,878
25064	Dunbar	7,868	8,697
26241	Elkins	6,976	7,494
*26554	Fairmont	18,984	20,210
26354	Grafton	5,351	5,524
*25704	Huntington	49,533	54,844
25526	Hurricane	5,623	4,461
26726	Keyser	5,515	5,870
*25401	Martinsburg	15,309	14,073
*26505	Morgantown	27,969	25,879
26041	Moundsville	9,745	10,753
26155	New Martinsville	5,823	6,705
25143	Nitro	6,708	6,851
25901	Oak Hill	7,486	6,812
*26101	Parkersburg	32,100	33,862
—	Pea Ridge (c)	6,363	6,535
24740	Princeton	6,201	7,043
25177	Saint Albans	11,167	12,241
25303	South Charleston	12,933	13,645
25569	Teays Valley (c)	12,704	8,436
26105	Vienna	10,884	10,862
26062	Weirton	19,838	22,124
26003	Wheeling	30,096	34,882

Wisconsin

ZIP	Place	Area Code	2003	1990
54301	Allouez	(920)	15,181	14,431
54720	Altoona	(715)	6,545	5,889
54409	Antigo	(715)	8,340	8,284
*54911	Appleton	(920)	70,354	65,695
54806	Ashland	(715)	8,397	8,695
54304	Ashwaubenon	(920)	17,168	16,376
53913	Baraboo	(608)	10,768	9,203
53916	Beaver Dam	(920)	14,949	14,196
54311	Bellevue Town (c)	(920)	11,828	7,541
*53511	Beloit	(608)	35,505	35,571
54923	Berlin	(920)	5,303	5,371
*53045	Brookfield	(262)	39,637	35,184
53209	Brown Deer	(414)	12,031	12,236
53105	Burlington	(262)	10,836	8,851
53012	Cedarburg	(262)	11,159	10,086
54729	Chippewa Falls	(715)	12,708	12,749
53110	Cudahy	(414)	18,300	18,659
53532	De Forest	(608)	8,088	4,882
53018	Delafield	(262)	6,705	5,347
53115	Delavan	(262)	8,304	6,073
54115	De Pere	(920)	22,229	16,594
*54703	Eau Claire	(715)	62,496	56,806
53121	Elkhorn	(262)	8,245	5,337
53122	Elm Grove	(262)	6,290	6,261
53714	Fitchburg	(608)	21,736	15,648
*54935	Fond du Lac	(920)	42,095	37,755
53538	Fort Atkinson	(920)	11,781	10,213
53217	Fox Point	(414)	6,922	7,238
53132	Franklin	(414)	31,994	21,855
53022	Germantown	(262)	18,973	13,658
53209	Glendale	(414)	13,181	14,088
53024	Grafton	(262)	11,356	9,340
*54303	Green Bay	(920)	101,467	96,466
53129	Greendale	(414)	14,183	15,128
53220	Greenfield	(414)	36,101	33,403
53130	Hales Corners	(414)	7,688	7,623
53027	Hartford	(262)	11,852	8,188
53029	Hartland	(262)	8,558	6,906
54636	Holmen	(608)	6,976	3,220
54303	Howard	(920)	15,277	9,874
54016	Hudson	(715)	10,240	6,378
53037	Jackson	(262)	5,676	2,603
*53545	Janesville	(608)	61,145	52,210
53549	Jefferson	(920)	7,388	6,078
54130	Kaukauna	(920)	14,121	11,982
*53140	Kenosha	(262)	92,871	80,426
54136	Kimberly	(920)	6,237	5,406

ZIP	Place	Area Code	2003	1990
*54601	La Crosse	(608)	51,001	51,140
53147	Lake Geneva	(262)	7,369	5,979
54140	Little Chute	(920)	10,737	9,207
53558	McFarland	(608)	7,076	5,232
*53714	Madison	(608)	218,432	190,766
*54220	Manitowoc	(920)	34,080	32,521
54143	Marinette	(715)	11,420	11,843
54449	Marshfield	(715)	18,670	19,293
54952	Menasha	(920)	16,259	14,711
*53051	Menomonee Falls	(262)	33,727	26,840
54751	Menomonie	(715)	15,155	13,547
53097	Mequon	(262)	23,449	18,885
54452	Merrill	(715)	10,164	9,860
53562	Middleton	(608)	16,189	13,785
53563	Milton	(608)	5,335	4,574
*53201	Milwaukee	(414)	586,941	628,088
53716	Monona	(608)	7,987	8,637
53566	Monroe	(608)	10,676	10,241
53572	Mount Horeb	(608)	6,074	4,182
53149	Mukwonago	(262)	6,562	4,495
53150	Muskego	(414)	22,314	16,813
*54956	Neenah	(920)	24,629	23,219
*53186	New Berlin	(262)	38,627	33,592
54961	New London	(920)	7,063	6,658
54017	New Richmond	(715)	7,058	5,106
53154	Oak Creek	(414)	31,983	19,513
53066	Oconomowoc	(262)	13,189	10,993
54650	Onalaska	(608)	15,474	12,201
53575	Oregon	(608)	8,037	4,519
*54901	Oshkosh	(920)	63,237	55,006
53072	Pewaukee (city)	(262)	12,740	—
53072	Pewaukee (village)	(262)	8,648	5,287
53818	Platteville	(608)	9,846	9,862
53158	Pleasant Prairie	(262)	18,091	12,037
54467	Plover	(715)	11,033	8,176
53073	Plymouth	(920)	8,132	6,769
53901	Portage	(608)	9,959	8,640
53074	Port Washington	(262)	10,730	9,338
53821	Prairie du Chien	(608)	5,803	5,657
*53401	Racine	(262)	80,266	84,298
53959	Reedsburg	(608)	8,227	5,834
54501	Rhinelander	(715)	7,813	7,382
54401	Rib Mountain (c)	(715)	6,059	4,634
54868	Rice Lake	(715)	8,270	7,998
53581	Richland Center	(608)	5,173	5,018
54971	Ripon	(920)	7,274	7,241
54022	River Falls	(715)	12,967	10,610
53235	Saint Francis	(414)	8,809	9,245
54166	Shawano	(715)	8,351	7,598
*53081	Sheboygan	(920)	49,263	49,587
53085	Sheboygan Falls	(920)	6,995	5,823
53211	Shorewood	(414)	13,424	14,116
53172	South Milwaukee	(414)	21,258	20,958
54656	Sparta	(608)	8,708	7,788
54481	Stevens Point	(715)	24,412	23,002
53589	Stoughton	(608)	12,611	8,786
54235	Sturgeon Bay	(920)	9,484	9,176
53177	Sturtevant	(262)	5,225	3,803
53590	Sun Prairie	(608)	23,484	15,352
54880	Superior	(715)	27,206	27,134
53089	Sussex	(262)	9,561	5,039
54660	Tomah	(608)	8,525	7,572
53181	Twin Lakes	(262)	5,323	3,989
54241	Two Rivers	(920)	12,239	13,030
53593	Verona	(608)	9,371	5,374
*53094	Watertown	(920)	22,675	19,142
*53186	Waukesha	(262)	66,840	56,894
53597	Waunakee	(608)	9,803	5,897
54981	Waupaca	(715)	5,812	4,946
53963	Waupun	(920)	10,451	8,844
*54403	Wausau	(715)	37,430	37,060
53213	Wauwatosa	(414)	46,260	49,366
53214	West Allis	(414)	60,192	63,221
*53095	West Bend	(262)	28,932	24,470
54476	Weston	(715)	12,652	9,714
53217	Whitefish Bay	(414)	13,848	14,272
53190	Whitewater	(262)	14,120	12,636
53185	Wind Lake (c)	(262)	5,202	3,748
*54494	Wisconsin Rapids	(715)	18,041	18,245

Wyoming (307)

ZIP	Place	2003	1990
*82609	Casper	50,632	46,765
*82009	Cheyenne	54,374	50,008
82414	Cody	8,973	7,897
82633	Douglas	5,398	5,076
*82930	Evanston	11,375	10,904
*82716	Gillette	21,840	17,545
82935	Green River	11,541	12,711
*83002	Jackson	8,825	4,708
82520	Lander	6,864	7,023
*82072	Laramie	26,956	26,687
82435	Powell	5,253	5,292
82301	Rawlins	8,665	9,380
82501	Riverton	9,314	9,202
*82901	Rock Springs	18,400	19,050
82801	Sheridan	16,016	13,904
82240	Torrington	5,581	5,651

Populations and Areas of Counties and States

Source: U.S. Bureau of the Census, Dept. of Commerce; World Almanac research

Counties are the primary legal divisions of most states and generally are functioning governmental units. In **Alaska**, however, the chief units of local government are boroughs; outside the boroughs there are "census areas," delineated for statistical purposes. In **Louisiana**, the primary legal divisions are known as parishes.

State population figures are estimates for July 1, 2003. **For counties**, July 1, 2003, population estimates and Apr. 1, 1990, decennial census figures are given. **Land areas** are from 2000 census. County areas may not add to state areas because of rounding.

Alabama

(67 counties, 50,744 sq. mi. land; pop. 4,500,752)

County	County seat or courthouse	2003 Pop.	1990 Pop.	Land area sq. mi.
Autauga	Prattville	46,491	34,222	596
Baldwin	Bay Minette	151,831	98,280	1,596
Barbour	Clayton	28,816	25,417	885
Bibb	Centreville	21,206	16,598	623
Blount	Oneonta	54,136	39,248	646
Bullock	Union Springs	11,339	11,042	625
Butler	Greenville	20,693	21,892	777
Calhoun	Anniston	112,012	116,032	608
Chambers	Lafayette	35,751	36,876	597
Cherokee	Centre	24,429	19,543	553
Chilton	Clanton	40,878	32,458	694
Choctaw	Butler	15,284	16,018	914
Clarke	Grove Hill	27,487	27,240	1,238
Clay	Ashland	14,182	13,252	605
Cleburne	Heflin	14,675	12,730	553
Coffee	Elba	44,625	40,240	679
Colbert	Tuscumbia	54,531	51,666	595
Conecuh	Evergreen	13,588	14,054	851
Coosa	Rockford	11,500	11,063	652
Covington	Andalusia	36,940	36,478	1,034
Crenshaw	Luverne	13,578	13,635	610
Cullman	Cullman	78,270	67,613	738
Dale	Ozark	49,298	49,633	561
Dallas	Selma	44,977	48,130	981
De Kalb	Fort Payne	66,469	54,651	778
Elmore	Wetumpka	70,691	49,210	621
Escambia	Brewton	38,179	35,518	947
Etowah	Gadsden	103,035	99,840	535
Fayette	Fayette	18,241	17,962	628
Franklin	Russellville	30,802	27,814	636
Geneva	Geneva	25,490	23,647	576
Greene	Eutaw	9,900	10,153	646
Hale	Greensboro	18,299	15,498	644
Henry	Abbeville	16,437	15,374	562
Houston	Dothan	91,409	81,331	580
Jackson	Scottsboro	53,801	47,796	1,079
Jefferson	Birmingham	658,141	651,520	1,113
Lamar	Vernon	15,146	15,715	605
Lauderdale	Florence	86,968	79,661	669
Lawrence	Moulton	34,594	31,513	693
Lee	Opelika	119,561	87,146	609
Limestone	Athens	68,245	54,135	568
Lowndes	Hayneville	13,374	12,658	718
Macon	Tuskegee	23,449	24,928	611
Madison	Huntsville	289,662	238,912	805
Marengo	Linden	22,341	23,084	977
Marion	Hamilton	30,182	29,830	741
Marshall	Guntersville	83,698	70,832	567
Mobile	Mobile	399,747	378,643	1,233
Monroe	Monroeville	23,871	23,968	1,026
Montgomery	Montgomery	221,980	209,085	790
Morgan	Decatur	112,610	100,043	582
Perry	Marion	11,705	12,759	719
Pickens	Carrollton	20,544	20,699	881
Pike	Troy	29,276	27,595	671
Randolph	Wedowee	22,273	19,881	581
Russell	Phenix City	48,986	46,860	641
Saint Clair	Ashville & Pell City	68,659	49,811	634
Shelby	Columbiana	159,445	99,363	795
Sumter	Livingston	14,182	16,174	905
Talladega	Talladega	79,928	74,109	740
Tallapoosa	Dadeville	40,764	38,826	718
Tuscaloosa	Tuscaloosa	166,446	150,500	1,324
Walker	Jasper	70,181	67,670	794
Washington	Chatom	17,880	16,694	1,081
Wilcox	Camden	13,024	13,568	889
Winston	Double Springs	24,620	22,053	614

Alaska

(27 divisions, 571,951 sq. mi. land; pop. 648,818)

Census Division	2003 Pop.	1990 Pop.	Land area sq. mi.
Aleutians East Borough	2,656	2,464	6,988
Aleutians West Census Area	5,241	9,478	4,397
Anchorage Municipality	270,951	226,338	1,697
Bethel Census Area	16,873	13,660	40,633
Bristol Bay Borough	1,099	1,410	505
Denali Borough	1,872	1,682	12,750
Dillingham Census Area	4,933	4,010	18,675
Fairbanks North Star Borough	85,978	77,720	7,366
Haines Borough	2,296	2,117	2,344
Juneau Borough	31,187	26,752	2,717
Kenai Peninsula Borough	51,146	40,802	16,013
Ketchikan Gateway Borough	13,320	13,828	1,233
Kodiak Island Borough	13,419	13,309	6,560
Lake and Peninsula Borough	1,551	1,666	23,782
Matanuska-Susitna Borough	68,335	39,683	24,682
Nome Census Area	9,162	8,288	23,001
North Slope Borough	7,218	5,986	88,817
Northwest Arctic Borough	7,373	6,106	35,898
Prince of Wales-Outer Ketchikan Census Area	5,809	6,278	7,411
Sitka Borough	8,876	8,588	2,874
Skagway-Hoonah-Angoon Census Area	3,121	3,679	7,896
Southeast Fairbanks Census Area	5,835	5,925	24,815
Valdez-Cordova Census Area	9,933	9,920	34,319
Wade Hampton Census Area	7,314	5,789	17,194
Wrangell-Petersburg Census Area	6,296	7,042	5,835
Yakutat Borough	710	725	7,650
Yukon-Koyukuk Census Area	6,314	6,798	145,900

Arizona

(15 counties, 113,635 sq. mi. land; pop. 5,580,811)

County	County seat or courthouse	2003 Pop.	1990 Pop.	Land area sq. mi.
Apache	Saint Johns	68,129	61,591	11,205
Cochise	Bisbee	122,161	97,624	6,169
Coconino	Flagstaff	121,301	96,591	18,617
Gila	Globe	51,448	40,216	4,768
Graham	Safford	33,051	26,554	4,629
Greenlee	Clifton	7,517	8,008	1,847
La Paz	Parker	19,517	13,844	4,500
Maricopa	Phoenix	3,389,260	2,122,101	9,203
Mohave	Kingman	171,367	93,497	13,312
Navajo	Holbrook	104,280	77,674	9,953
Pima	Tucson	892,798	666,957	9,186
Pinal	Florence	204,148	116,397	5,370
Santa Cruz	Nogales	40,267	29,676	1,238
Yavapai	Prescott	184,433	107,714	8,123
Yuma	Yuma	171,134	106,895	5,514

Arkansas

(75 counties, 52,068 sq. mi. land; pop. 2,725,714)

County	County seat or courthouse	2003 Pop.	1990 Pop.	Land area sq.mi.
Arkansas	DeWitt & Stuttgart	20,158	21,653	988
Ashley	Hamburg	23,583	24,319	921
Baxter	Mountain Home	39,113	31,186	554
Benton	Bentonville	172,003	97,530	846
Boone	Harrison	34,740	28,297	591
Bradley	Warren	12,414	11,793	651
Calhoun	Hampton	5,626	5,826	628
Carroll	Berryville & Eureka Springs	26,359	18,623	630
Chicot	Lake Village	13,485	15,713	644
Clark	Arkadelphia	23,581	21,437	865
Clay	Corning & Piggott	16,912	18,107	639
Cleburne	Heber Springs	24,723	19,411	553
Cleveland	Rison	8,709	7,781	595
Columbia	Magnolia	25,034	25,691	766
Conway	Morrilton	20,485	19,151	556
Craighead	Jonesboro & Lake City	84,626	68,956	711
Crawford	Van Buren	55,647	42,493	595
Crittenden	Marion	51,155	49,939	610
Cross	Wynne	19,203	19,225	616
Dallas	Fordyce	8,708	9,614	667
Desha	Arkansas City	14,623	16,798	765
Drew	Monticello	18,468	17,369	828
Faulkner	Conway	92,060	60,006	647
Franklin	Charleston & Ozark	18,003	14,897	610
Fulton	Salem	11,632	10,037	618
Garland	Hot Springs	91,188	73,397	677
Grant	Sheridan	16,933	13,948	632
Greene	Paragould	38,353	31,804	578
Hempstead	Hope	23,429	21,621	729
Hot Spring	Malvern	30,674	26,115	615
Howard	Nashville	14,461	13,569	587
Independence	Batesville	34,426	31,192	764
Izard	Melbourne	13,202	11,364	581
Jackson	Newport	17,443	18,944	634
Jefferson	Pine Bluff	82,889	85,487	885
Johnson	Clarksville	23,592	18,221	662
Lafayette	Lewisville	8,310	9,643	527
Lawrence	Walnut Ridge	17,553	17,455	587
Lee	Marianna	11,857	13,053	602
Lincoln	Star City	14,403	13,690	561

County	County seat or courthouse	2003 Pop.	1990 Pop.	Land area sq.mi.
Little River	Ashdown	13,358	13,966	532
Logan	Booneville & Paris	22,808	20,557	710
Lonoke	Lonoke	56,718	39,268	766
Madison	Huntsville	14,354	11,618	837
Marion	Yellville	16,283	12,001	598
Miller	Texarkana	41,892	38,467	624
Mississippi	Blytheville & Osceola	49,041	57,525	898
Monroe	Clarendon	9,633	11,333	607
Montgomery	Mount Ida	9,120	7,841	781
Nevada	Prescott	9,640	10,101	620
Newton	Jasper	8,542	7,666	823
Ouachita	Camden	27,697	30,574	732
Perry	Perryville	10,461	7,969	551
Phillips	Helena	24,621	28,830	693
Pike	Murfreesboro	11,123	10,086	603
Poinsett	Harrisburg	25,415	24,664	758
Polk	Mena	20,224	17,347	859
Pope	Russellville	55,185	45,883	812
Prairie	Des Arc & De Valls Bluff	9,344	9,518	646
Pulaski	Little Rock	364,567	349,773	771
Randolph	Pocahontas	18,171	16,558	652
Saint Francis	Forrest City	28,517	28,497	634
Saline	Benton	87,554	64,183	723
Scott	Waldron	10,963	10,205	894
Searcy	Marshall	7,973	7,841	667
Sebastian	Fort Smith & Greenwood	117,252	99,590	536
Sevier	De Queen	15,858	13,637	564
Sharp	Ash Flat	17,461	14,109	604
Stone	Mountain View	11,632	9,775	607
Union	El Dorado	44,829	46,719	1,039
Van Buren	Clinton	16,348	14,008	712
Washington	Fayetteville	169,683	113,409	950
White	Searcy	69,981	54,676	1,034
Woodruff	Augusta	8,244	9,520	587
Yell	Danville & Dardanelle	21,459	17,759	928

California

(58 counties, 155,959 sq. mi. land; pop. 35,484,453)

County	County seat or courthouse	2003 Pop.	1990 Pop.	Land area sq.mi.
Alameda	Oakland	1,461,030	1,304,347	738
Alpine	Markleeville	1,209	1,113	739
Amador	Jackson	37,273	30,039	593
Butte	Oroville	211,010	182,120	1,639
Calaveras	San Andreas	44,533	31,998	1,020
Colusa	Colusa	19,678	16,275	1,151
Contra Costa	Martinez	1,001,136	803,731	720
Del Norte	Crescent City	27,913	23,460	1,008
El Dorado	Placerville	168,822	125,995	1,711
Fresno	Fresno	850,325	667,479	5,963
Glenn	Willows	27,256	24,798	1,315
Humboldt	Eureka	127,915	119,118	3,572
Imperial	El Centro	149,232	109,303	4,175
Inyo	Independence	18,326	18,281	10,203
Kern	Bakersfield	713,087	544,981	8,141
Kings	Hanford	138,564	101,469	1,391
Lake	Lakeport	63,369	50,631	1,258
Lassen	Susanville	33,926	27,598	4,557
Los Angeles	Los Angeles	9,871,506	8,863,052	4,061
Madera	Madera	133,463	88,090	2,136
Marin	San Rafael	246,073	230,096	520
Mariposa	Mariposa	17,803	14,302	1,451
Mendocino	Ukiah	88,358	80,345	3,509
Merced	Merced	231,574	178,403	1,929
Modoc	Alturas	9,417	9,678	3,944
Mono	Bridgeport	12,988	9,956	3,044
Monterey	Salinas	414,449	355,660	3,322
Napa	Napa	131,607	110,765	754
Nevada	Nevada City	96,099	78,510	958
Orange	Santa Ana	2,957,766	2,410,668	789
Placer	Auburn	292,235	172,796	1,404
Plumas	Quincy	21,148	19,739	2,554
Riverside	Riverside	1,782,650	1,170,413	7,207
Sacramento	Sacramento	1,330,711	1,066,789	966
San Benito	Hollister	56,300	36,697	1,389
San Bernardino	San Bernardino	1,859,678	1,418,380	20,053
San Diego	San Diego	2,930,886	2,498,016	4,200
San Francisco	San Francisco	751,682	723,959	47
San Joaquin	Stockton	632,760	480,628	1,399
San Luis Obispo	San Luis Obispo	253,118	217,162	3,304
San Mateo	Redwood City	697,456	649,623	449
Santa Barbara	Santa Barbara	403,134	369,608	2,737
Santa Clara	San Jose	1,678,421	1,497,577	1,291
Santa Cruz	Santa Cruz	251,584	229,734	445
Shasta	Redding	175,650	147,036	3,785
Sierra	Downieville	3,502	3,318	953
Siskiyou	Yreka	44,626	43,531	6,287
Solano	Fairfield	412,336	339,469	829
Sonoma	Santa Rosa	466,725	388,222	1,576
Stanislaus	Modesto	492,233	370,522	1,494
Sutter	Yuba City	84,703	64,409	603
Tehama	Red Bluff	58,582	49,625	2,951
Trinity	Weaverville	13,476	13,063	3,179
Tulare	Visalia	390,791	311,932	4,824
Tuolumne	Sonora	56,755	48,456	2,235
Ventura	Ventura	791,130	669,016	1,845
Yolo	Woodland	183,042	141,212	1,013
Yuba	Marysville	63,432	58,234	631

Colorado

(64 counties, 103,718 sq. mi. land; pop. 4,550,688)

County	County seat or courthouse	2003 Pop.	1990 Pop.	Land area sq. mi.
Adams[1]	Brighton	380,273	265,038	1,192
Alamosa	Alamosa	15,126	13,617	723
Arapahoe	Littleton	516,060	391,572	803
Archuleta	Pagosa Springs	11,313	5,345	1,350
Baca	Springfield	4,223	4,556	2,556
Bent	Las Animas	5,613	5,048	1,514
Boulder[1]	Boulder	278,231	225,339	742
Broomfield[2]	Broomfield	42,169	NA	27
Chaffee	Salida	16,841	12,684	1,013
Cheyenne	Cheyenne Wells	2,052	2,397	1,781
Clear Creek	Georgetown	9,538	7,619	395
Conejos	Conejos	8,403	7,453	1,287
Costilla	San Luis	3,563	3,190	1,227
Crowley	Ordway	5,449	3,946	789
Custer	Westcliffe	3,784	1,926	739
Delta	Delta	29,409	20,980	1,142
Denver	Denver	557,478	467,549	153
Dolores	Dove Creek	1,825	1,504	1,067
Douglas	Castle Rock	223,471	60,391	840
Eagle	Eagle	46,020	21,928	1,688
Elbert	Kiowa	22,254	9,646	1,851
El Paso	Colorado Springs	550,478	397,014	2,126
Fremont	Canon City	47,556	32,273	1,533
Garfield	Glenwood Springs	47,611	29,974	2,947
Gilpin	Central City	4,845	3,070	150
Grand	Hot Sulphur Springs	13,173	7,966	1,847
Gunnison	Gunnison	14,046	10,273	3,239
Hinsdale	Lake City	759	467	1,118
Huerfano	Walsenburg	7,827	6,009	1,591
Jackson	Walden	1,507	1,605	1,613
Jefferson[1]	Golden	528,563	438,430	772
Kiowa	Eads	1,444	1,688	1,771
Kit Carson	Burlington	7,911	7,140	2,161
Lake	Leadville	7,731	6,007	377
La Plata	Durango	46,229	32,284	1,692
Larimer	Fort Collins	266,610	186,136	2,601
Las Animas	Trinidad	15,499	13,765	4,772
Lincoln	Hugo	5,881	4,529	2,586
Logan	Sterling	20,928	17,567	1,839
Mesa	Grand Junction	124,676	93,145	3,328
Mineral	Creede	881	558	876
Moffat	Craig	13,527	11,357	4,742
Montezuma	Cortez	24,335	18,672	2,037
Montrose	Montrose	35,984	24,423	2,241
Morgan	Fort Morgan	27,922	21,939	1,285
Otero	La Junta	19,754	20,185	1,263
Ouray	Ouray	4,021	2,295	540
Park	Fairplay	16,465	7,174	2,201
Phillips	Holyoke	4,511	4,189	688
Pitkin	Aspen	15,002	12,661	970
Prowers	Lamar	14,164	13,347	1,640
Pueblo	Pueblo	148,751	123,051	2,389
Rio Blanco	Meeker	5,938	6,051	3,221
Rio Grande	Del Norte	12,346	10,770	912
Routt	Steamboat Springs	20,788	14,088	2,362
Saguache	Saguache	6,708	4,619	3,168
San Juan	Silverton	572	745	387
San Miguel	Telluride	7,154	3,653	1,287
Sedgwick	Julesburg	2,683	2,690	548
Summit	Breckenridge	25,143	12,881	608
Teller	Cripple Creek	21,786	12,468	557
Washington	Akron	4,813	4,812	2,521
Weld[1]	Greeley	211,272	131,821	3,992
Yuma	Wray	9,799	8,954	2,366

NA = Not available. (1) Part of this county was taken to create Broomfield county in 2001. Because the Census Bureau will not be retabulating land areas until after Census 2010, the Land area shown here is from Census 2000. (2) Created in 2001.

Connecticut

(8 counties, 4,845 sq. mi. land; pop. 3,483,372)

County	County seat or courthouse	2003 Pop.	1990 Pop.	Land area sq. mi.
Fairfield	Bridgeport	899,152	827,645	626
Hartford	Hartford	871,457	851,783	735
Litchfield	Litchfield	187,801	174,092	920
Middlesex	Middletown	161,439	143,196	369
New Haven	New Haven	841,863	804,219	606
New London	New London	263,989	254,957	666
Tolland	Rockville	145,039	128,699	410
Windham	Putnam	112,622	102,525	513

Delaware

(3 counties, 1,954 sq. mi. land; pop. 817,491)

County	County seat or courthouse	2003 Pop.	1990 Pop.	Land area sq. mi.
Kent	Dover	134,390	110,993	590
New Castle	Wilmington	515,074	441,946	426
Sussex	Georgetown	168,027	113,229	938

District of Columbia

(61 sq. mi. land; pop. 563,384)
Has no counties; coextensive with city of Washington.

Florida

(67 counties, 53,927 sq. mi. land; pop. 17,019,068)

County	County seat or courthouse	2003 Pop.	1990 Pop.	Land area sq. mi.
Alachua	Gainesville	223,578	181,596	874
Baker	Macclenny	23,424	18,486	585
Bay	Panama City	155,193	126,994	764
Bradford	Starke	26,928	22,515	293
Brevard	Titusville	505,711	398,978	1,018
Broward	Fort Lauderdale	1,731,347	1,255,531	1,205
Calhoun	Blountstown	12,921	11,011	567
Charlotte	Punta Gorda	153,392	110,975	694
Citrus	Inverness	126,458	93,513	584
Clay	Green Cove Springs	157,502	105,986	601
Collier	Naples	286,634	152,099	2,025
Columbia	Lake City	60,244	42,613	797
De Soto	Arcadia	33,879	23,865	637
Dixie	Cross City	13,982	10,585	704
Duval	Jacksonville	817,480	672,971	774
Escambia	Pensacola	295,886	262,445	662
Flagler	Bunnell	62,206	28,701	485
Franklin	Apalachicola	10,003	8,967	544
Gadsden	Quincy	45,134	41,116	516
Gilchrist	Trenton	15,633	9,667	349
Glades	Moore Haven	11,165	7,591	774
Gulf	Port Saint Joe	15,247	11,504	555
Hamilton	Jasper	13,917	10,930	515
Hardee	Wauchula	27,659	19,499	637
Hendry	La Belle	37,064	25,773	1,153
Hernando	Brooksville	143,449	101,115	478
Highlands	Sebring	91,051	68,432	1,028
Hillsborough	Tampa	1,073,407	834,054	1,051
Holmes	Bonifay	18,986	15,778	482
Indian River	Vero Beach	120,463	90,208	503
Jackson	Marianna	46,508	41,375	916
Jefferson	Monticello	14,037	11,296	598
Lafayette	Mayo	7,333	5,578	543
Lake	Tavares	245,877	152,104	953
Lee	Fort Myers	492,210	335,113	804
Leon	Tallahassee	242,577	192,493	667
Levy	Bronson	36,270	25,912	1,118
Liberty	Bristol	7,315	5,569	836
Madison	Madison	18,766	16,569	692
Manatee	Bradenton	286,804	211,707	741
Marion	Ocala	280,288	194,835	1,579
Martin	Stuart	135,122	100,900	556
Miami-Dade	Miami	2,341,167	1,937,194	1,946
Monroe	Key West	78,940	78,024	997
Nassau	Fernandina Beach	61,625	43,941	652
Okaloosa	Crestview	178,104	143,777	936
Okeechobee	Okeechobee	37,481	29,627	774
Orange	Orlando	964,865	677,491	907
Osceola	Kissimmee	205,870	107,728	1,322
Palm Beach	West Palm Beach	1,216,282	863,503	1,974
Pasco	Dade City	388,906	281,131	745
Pinellas	Clearwater	926,146	851,659	280
Polk	Bartow	510,458	405,382	1,874
Putnam	Palatka	71,841	65,070	722
Saint Johns	Saint Augustine	142,869	83,829	609
Saint Lucie	Fort Pierce	213,447	150,171	572
Santa Rosa	Milton	133,092	81,961	1,017
Sarasota	Sarasota	346,793	277,776	572
Seminole	Sanford	386,374	287,521	308
Sumter	Bushnell	58,875	31,577	546
Suwannee	Live Oak	36,695	26,780	688
Taylor	Perry	19,415	17,111	1,042
Union	Lake Butler	14,002	10,252	240
Volusia	De Land	468,663	370,737	1,103
Wakulla	Crawfordville	26,131	14,202	607
Walton	De Funiak Springs	46,373	27,759	1,058
Washington	Chipley	21,604	16,919	580

Georgia

(159 counties, 57,906 sq. mi. land; pop. 8,684,715)

County	County seat or courthouse	2003 Pop.	1990 Pop.	Land area sq. mi.
Appling	Baxley	17,797	15,744	509
Atkinson	Pearson	7,891	6,213	338
Bacon	Alma	10,135	9,566	285
Baker	Newton	4,307	3,615	343
Baldwin	Milledgeville	44,953	39,530	258
Banks	Homer	15,483	10,308	234
Barrow	Winder	53,479	29,721	162
Bartow	Cartersville	84,730	55,915	459
Ben Hill	Fitzgerald	17,235	16,245	252
Berrien	Nashville	16,484	14,153	452
Bibb	Macon	154,287	150,137	250
Bleckley	Cochran	11,842	10,430	217
Brantley	Nahunta	15,279	11,077	444
Brooks	Quitman	16,242	15,398	494
Bryan	Pembroke	26,340	15,438	442
Bulloch	Statesboro	58,360	43,125	682
Burke	Waynesboro	22,949	20,579	830
Butts	Jackson	22,099	15,326	187
Calhoun	Morgan	6,122	5,013	280
Camden	Woodbine	45,470	30,167	630
Candler	Metter	10,023	7,744	247
Carroll	Carrollton	98,525	71,422	499
Catoosa	Ringgold	58,085	42,464	162
Charlton	Folkston	10,707	8,496	781
Chatham	Savannah	235,270	216,774	438
Chattahoochee	Cusseta	19,333	16,934	249
Chattooga	Summerville	26,422	22,236	313
Cherokee	Canton	166,639	90,204	424
Clarke	Athens	103,691	87,594	121
Clay	Fort Gaines	3,358	3,364	195
Clayton	Jonesboro	259,736	181,436	143
Clinch	Homerville	6,967	6,160	809
Cobb	Marietta	651,027	447,745	340
Coffee	Douglas	38,994	29,592	599
Colquitt	Moultrie	43,203	36,645	552
Columbia	Appling	97,505	66,031	290
Cook	Adel	15,951	13,456	229
Coweta	Newnan	101,395	53,853	443
Crawford	Knoxville	12,553	8,991	325
Crisp	Cordele	21,994	20,011	274
Dade	Trenton	15,910	13,183	174
Dawson	Dawsonville	18,575	9,429	211
Decatur	Bainbridge	28,212	25,517	597
DeKalb	Decatur	674,334	546,174	268
Dodge	Eastman	19,374	17,607	500
Dooly	Vienna	11,552	9,901	393
Dougherty	Albany	95,684	96,321	330
Douglas	Douglasville	102,015	71,120	199
Early	Blakely	12,224	11,854	511
Echols	Statenville	3,999	2,334	404
Effingham	Springfield	42,715	25,687	479
Elbert	Elberton	20,636	18,949	369
Emanuel	Swainsboro	21,885	20,546	686
Evans	Claxton	11,365	8,724	185
Fannin	Blue Ridge	21,234	15,992	386
Fayette	Fayetteville	98,914	62,415	197
Floyd	Rome	93,368	81,251	513
Forsyth	Cumming	123,811	44,083	226
Franklin	Carnesville	21,164	16,650	263
Fulton	Atlanta	818,322	648,776	529
Gilmer	Ellijay	25,973	13,368	427
Glascock	Gibson	2,636	2,357	144
Glynn	Brunswick	70,131	62,496	422
Gordon	Calhoun	47,777	35,067	356
Grady	Cairo	24,185	20,279	458
Greene	Greensboro	15,263	11,793	388
Gwinnett	Lawrenceville	673,345	352,910	433
Habersham	Clarkesville	38,446	27,622	278
Hall	Gainesville	156,101	95,434	394
Hancock	Sparta	9,977	8,908	473
Haralson	Buchanan	27,460	21,966	282
Harris	Hamilton	25,891	17,788	464
Hart	Hartwell	23,432	19,712	232
Heard	Franklin	11,152	8,628	296
Henry	McDonough	150,003	58,741	323
Houston	Perry	120,434	89,208	377
Irwin	Ocilla	10,060	8,649	357
Jackson	Jefferson	46,998	30,005	342
Jasper	Monticello	12,547	8,453	370
Jeff Davis	Hazlehurst	12,888	12,032	333
Jefferson	Louisville	17,001	17,408	528
Jenkins	Millen	8,765	8,247	350
Johnson	Wrightsville	9,421	8,329	304
Jones	Gray	25,472	20,739	394
Lamar	Barnesville	16,234	13,038	185
Lanier	Lakeland	7,361	5,531	187
Laurens	Dublin	46,108	39,988	812
Lee	Leesburg	28,410	16,250	356
Liberty	Hinesville	58,925	52,745	519
Lincoln	Lincolnton	8,536	7,442	211
Long	Ludowici	10,780	6,202	401
Lowndes	Valdosta	94,579	75,981	504
Lumpkin	Dahlonega	23,185	14,573	284
McDuffie	Thomson	21,445	20,119	260
McIntosh	Darien	10,885	8,634	433
Macon	Oglethorpe	14,025	13,114	403
Madison	Danielsville	27,075	21,050	284
Marion	Buena Vista	7,170	5,590	367
Meriwether	Greenville	22,786	22,411	503
Miller	Colquitt	6,328	6,280	283
Mitchell	Camilla	23,832	20,275	512
Monroe	Forsyth	23,244	17,113	396
Montgomery	Mount Vernon	8,691	7,379	245
Morgan	Madison	16,775	12,883	350

County	County seat or courthouse	2003 Pop.	1990 Pop.	Land area sq. mi.
Murray	Chatsworth	39,446	26,147	344
Muscogee	Columbus	185,702	179,280	216
Newton	Covington	76,144	41,808	276
Oconee	Watkinsville	28,087	17,618	186
Oglethorpe	Lexington	13,379	9,763	441
Paulding	Dallas	100,071	41,611	313
Peach	Fort Valley	24,320	21,189	151
Pickens	Jasper	26,905	14,432	232
Pierce	Blackshear	16,327	13,328	343
Pike	Zebulon	14,979	10,224	218
Polk	Cedartown	39,800	33,815	311
Pulaski	Hawkinsville	9,724	8,108	247
Putnam	Eatonton	19,575	14,137	345
Quitman	Georgetown	2,480	2,210	152
Rabun	Clayton	15,757	11,648	371
Randolph	Cuthbert	7,465	8,023	429
Richmond	Augusta	198,149	189,719	324
Rockdale	Conyers	74,941	54,091	131
Schley	Ellaville	3,935	3,590	168
Screven	Sylvania	15,407	13,842	648
Seminole	Donalsonville	9,270	9,010	238
Spalding	Griffin	60,483	54,457	198
Stephens	Toccoa	25,264	23,436	179
Stewart	Lumpkin	5,001	5,654	459
Sumter	Americus	33,217	30,232	485
Talbot	Talbotton	6,562	6,524	393
Taliaferro	Crawfordville	1,957	1,915	195
Tattnall	Reidsville	22,385	17,722	484
Taylor	Butler	8,901	7,642	377
Telfair	McRae	11,523	11,000	441
Terrell	Dawson	10,854	10,653	335
Thomas	Thomasville	43,667	38,943	548
Tift	Tifton	39,523	34,998	265
Toombs	Lyons	26,469	24,072	367
Towns	Hiawassee	9,901	6,754	167
Treutlen	Soperton	6,952	5,994	201
Troup	La Grange	60,218	55,532	414
Turner	Ashburn	9,570	8,703	286
Twiggs	Jeffersonville	10,466	9,806	360
Union	Blairsville	19,119	11,993	323
Upson	Thomaston	27,978	26,300	325
Walker	La Fayette	62,584	58,310	447
Walton	Monroe	69,381	38,586	329
Ware	Waycross	35,503	35,471	902
Warren	Warrenton	6,129	6,078	286
Washington	Sandersville	20,780	19,112	680
Wayne	Jesup	27,509	22,356	645
Webster	Preston	2,295	2,263	210
Wheeler	Alamo	6,593	4,903	298
White	Cleveland	22,815	13,006	242
Whitfield	Dalton	87,833	72,462	290
Wilcox	Abbeville	8,764	7,008	380
Wilkes	Washington	10,653	10,597	471
Wilkinson	Irwinton	10,267	10,228	447
Worth	Sylvester	21,849	19,744	570

Hawaii

(5 counties, 6,423 sq. mi. land; pop. 1,257,608)

County	County seat or courthouse	2003 Pop.	1990 Pop.	Land area sq. mi.
Hawaii	Hilo	158,423	120,317	4,028
Honolulu	Honolulu	902,704	836,231	600
Kalawao[1]		129	130	13
Kauai	Lihue	60,747	51,177	622
Maui	Wailuku	135,605	100,374	1,159

(1) Administered by state government.

Idaho

(44 counties, 82,747 sq. mi. land; pop. 1,366,332)

County	County seat or courthouse	2003 Pop.	1990 Pop.	Land area sq. mi.
Ada	Boise	325,151	205,775	1,055
Adams	Council	3,515	3,254	1,365
Bannock	Pocatello	75,630	66,026	1,113
Bear Lake	Paris	6,306	6,084	971
Benewah	Saint Maries	9,029	7,937	776
Bingham	Blackfoot	42,926	37,583	2,095
Blaine	Hailey	20,791	13,552	2,645
Boise	Idaho City	7,236	3,509	1,902
Bonner	Sandpoint	39,162	26,622	1,738
Bonneville	Idaho Falls	87,007	72,207	1,868
Boundary	Bonners Ferry	10,173	8,332	1,269
Butte	Arco	2,873	2,918	2,233
Camas	Fairfield	1,049	727	1,075
Canyon	Caldwell	151,508	90,076	590
Caribou	Soda Springs	7,152	6,963	1,766
Cassia	Burley	21,610	19,532	2,566
Clark	Dubois	904	762	1,765
Clearwater	Orofino	8,401	8,505	2,461
Custer	Challis	4,090	4,133	4,925
Elmore	Mountain Home	28,872	21,205	3,078
Franklin	Preston	11,874	9,232	665
Fremont	Saint Anthony	12,107	10,937	1,867
Gem	Emmett	15,795	11,844	563
Gooding	Gooding	14,329	11,633	731
Idaho	Grangeville	15,413	13,768	8,485
Jefferson	Rigby	20,194	16,543	1,095
Jerome	Jerome	18,913	15,138	600
Kootenai	Coeur d'Alene	117,481	69,795	1,245
Latah	Moscow	35,087	30,617	1,077
Lemhi	Salmon	7,731	6,899	4,564
Lewis	Nez Perce	3,748	3,516	479
Lincoln	Shoshone	4,321	3,308	1,206
Madison	Rexberg	29,878	23,674	472
Minidoka	Rupert	19,349	19,361	760
Nez Perce	Lewiston	37,699	33,754	849
Oneida	Malad City	4,132	3,492	1,200
Owyhee	Murphy	11,186	8,392	7,678
Payette	Payette	21,466	16,434	408
Power	American Falls	7,373	7,086	1,406
Shoshone	Wallace	12,993	13,931	2,634
Teton	Driggs	7,058	3,439	450
Twin Falls	Twin Falls	67,082	53,580	1,925
Valley	Cascade	7,743	6,109	3,678
Washington	Weiser	9,995	8,550	1,456

Illinois

(102 counties, 55,584 sq. mi. land; pop. 12,653,544)

County	County seat or courthouse	2003 Pop.	1990 Pop.	Land area sq. mi.
Adams	Quincy	67,582	66,090	857
Alexander	Cairo	9,327	10,626	236
Bond	Greenville	17,941	14,991	380
Boone	Belvidere	46,477	30,806	281
Brown	Mount Sterling	6,879	5,836	306
Bureau	Princeton	35,221	35,688	869
Calhoun	Hardin	5,069	5,322	254
Carroll	Mount Carroll	16,242	16,805	444
Cass	Virginia	13,841	13,437	376
Champaign	Urbana	186,800	173,025	997
Christian	Taylorville	35,127	34,418	709
Clark	Marshall	16,998	15,921	502
Clay	Louisville	14,316	14,460	469
Clinton	Carlyle	36,135	33,944	474
Coles	Charleston	51,880	51,644	508
Cook	Chicago	5,351,552	5,105,044	946
Crawford	Robinson	19,899	19,464	444
Cumberland	Toledo	11,063	10,670	346
DeKalb	Sycamore	94,041	77,932	634
De Witt	Clinton	16,679	16,516	398
Douglas	Tuscola	19,923	19,464	417
DuPage	Wheaton	925,188	781,689	334
Edgar	Paris	19,396	19,595	624
Edwards	Albion	6,850	7,440	222
Effingham	Effingham	34,529	31,704	479
Fayette	Vandalia	21,539	20,893	716
Ford	Paxton	14,094	14,275	486
Franklin	Benton	39,117	40,319	412
Fulton	Lewiston	37,658	38,080	866
Gallatin	Shawneetown	6,220	6,909	324
Greene	Carrollton	14,708	15,317	543
Grundy	Morris	39,528	32,337	420
Hamilton	McLeansboro	8,334	8,499	435
Hancock	Carthage	19,393	21,373	795
Hardin	Elizabethtown	4,711	5,189	178
Henderson	Oquawka	8,073	8,096	379
Henry	Cambridge	50,644	51,159	823
Iroquois	Watseka	30,684	30,787	1,116
Jackson	Murphysboro	58,976	61,067	588
Jasper	Newton	9,955	10,609	494
Jefferson	Mount Vernon	40,334	37,020	571
Jersey	Jerseyville	22,188	20,539	369
Jo Daviess	Galena	22,526	21,821	601
Johnson	Vienna	12,951	11,347	345
Kane	Geneva	457,122	317,471	520
Kankakee	Kankakee	105,625	96,255	677
Kendall	Yorkville	66,565	39,413	321
Knox	Galesburg	54,491	56,393	716
Lake	Waukegan	685,019	516,418	448
La Salle	Ottawa	112,037	106,913	1,135
Lawrence	Lawrenceville	15,287	15,972	372
Lee	Dixon	35,537	34,392	725
Livingston	Pontiac	39,208	39,301	1,044
Logan	Lincoln	30,716	30,798	618
McDonough	Macomb	32,852	35,244	589
McHenry	Woodstock	286,091	183,241	604
McLean	Bloomington	156,879	129,180	1,184
Macon	Decatur	111,175	117,206	581
Macoupin	Carlinville	49,055	47,679	864
Madison	Edwardsville	261,689	249,238	725
Marion	Salem	40,751	41,561	572
Marshall	Lacon	13,039	12,846	386
Mason	Havana	15,884	16,269	539
Massac	Metropolis	15,138	14,752	239
Menard	Petersburg	12,593	11,164	314
Mercer	Aledo	17,003	17,290	561
Monroe	Waterloo	29,723	22,422	388
Montgomery	Hillsboro	30,352	30,728	704
Morgan	Jacksonville	35,990	36,397	569
Moultrie	Sullivan	14,469	13,930	336

County	County seat or courthouse	2003 Pop.	1990 Pop.	Land area sq. mi.
Ogle	Oregon	52,858	45,957	759
Peoria	Peoria	182,335	182,827	620
Perry	Pinckneyville	22,684	21,412	441
Piatt	Monticello	16,426	15,548	440
Pike	Pittsfield	16,927	17,577	830
Pope	Golconda	4,261	4,373	371
Pulaski	Mound City	7,077	7,523	201
Putnam	Hennepin	6,119	5,730	160
Randolph	Chester	33,244	34,583	578
Richland	Olney	15,997	16,545	360
Rock Island	Rock Island	147,912	148,723	427
Saint Clair	Belleville	258,606	262,852	664
Saline	Harrisburg	26,158	26,551	383
Sangamon	Springfield	191,875	178,386	868
Schuyler	Rushville	7,021	7,498	437
Scott	Winchester	5,505	5,644	251
Shelby	Shelbyville	22,407	22,261	759
Stark	Toulon	6,198	6,534	288
Stephenson	Freeport	48,151	48,052	564
Tazewell	Pekin	128,056	123,692	649
Union	Jonesboro	18,170	17,619	416
Vermilion	Danville	82,804	88,257	899
Wabash	Mount Carmel	12,680	13,111	223
Warren	Monmouth	18,246	19,181	543
Washington	Nashville	15,179	14,965	563
Wayne	Fairfield	16,944	17,241	714
White	Carmi	15,106	16,522	495
Whiteside	Morrison	59,886	60,186	685
Will	Joliet	586,706	357,313	837
Williamson	Marion	62,448	57,733	423
Winnebago	Rockford	284,313	252,913	514
Woodford	Eureka	36,367	32,653	528

Indiana

(92 counties, 35,867 sq. mi. land; pop. 6,195,643)

County	County seat or courthouse	2003 Pop.	1990 Pop.	Land area sq. mi.
Adams	Decatur	33,592	31,095	339
Allen	Fort Wayne	340,153	300,836	657
Bartholomew	Columbus	72,341	63,657	407
Benton	Fowler	9,189	9,441	406
Blackford	Hartford City	13,876	14,067	165
Boone	Lebanon	49,370	38,147	423
Brown	Nashville	15,313	14,080	312
Carroll	Delphi	20,499	18,809	372
Cass	Logansport	40,415	38,413	413
Clark	Jeffersonville	99,482	87,774	375
Clay	Brazil	26,772	24,705	358
Clinton	Frankfort	33,947	30,974	405
Crawford	English	11,146	9,914	306
Daviess	Washington	30,047	27,533	431
Dearborn	Lawrenceburg	47,849	38,835	305
Decatur	Greensburg	24,747	23,645	373
De Kalb	Auburn	41,129	35,324	363
Delaware	Muncie	117,488	119,659	393
Dubois	Jasper	40,200	36,616	430
Elkhart	Goshen	188,779	156,198	464
Fayette	Connersville	24,999	26,015	215
Floyd	New Albany	71,148	64,404	148
Fountain	Covington	17,750	17,808	396
Franklin	Brookville	22,773	19,580	386
Fulton	Rochester	20,508	18,840	369
Gibson	Princeton	32,991	31,913	489
Grant	Marion	71,552	74,169	414
Greene	Bloomfield	33,244	30,410	542
Hamilton	Noblesville	216,826	108,936	398
Hancock	Greenfield	59,446	45,527	306
Harrison	Corydon	35,706	29,890	485
Hendricks	Danville	118,850	75,717	408
Henry	New Castle	47,699	48,139	393
Howard	Kokomo	84,880	80,827	293
Huntington	Huntington	38,143	35,427	383
Jackson	Brownstown	41,639	37,730	509
Jasper	Rensselaer	31,078	24,823	560
Jay	Portland	21,732	21,512	384
Jefferson	Madison	32,250	29,797	361
Jennings	Vernon	28,111	23,661	377
Johnson	Franklin	123,256	88,109	320
Knox	Vincennes	38,745	39,884	516
Kosciusko	Warsaw	75,301	65,294	538
Lagrange	Lagrange	36,026	29,477	380
Lake	Crown Point	487,476	475,594	497
La Porte	La Porte	109,878	107,066	598
Lawrence	Bedford	46,201	42,836	449
Madison	Anderson	131,121	130,669	452
Marion	Indianapolis	863,251	797,159	396
Marshall	Plymouth	46,352	42,182	444
Martin	Shoals	10,347	10,369	336
Miami	Peru	36,177	36,897	376
Monroe	Bloomington	122,903	108,978	394
Montgomery	Crawfordsville	37,911	34,436	505
Morgan	Martinsville	68,656	55,920	406
Newton	Kentland	14,403	13,551	402
Noble	Albion	47,039	37,877	411
Ohio	Rising Sun	5,732	5,315	87
Orange	Paoli	19,616	18,409	400
Owen	Spencer	22,827	17,281	385
Parke	Rockville	17,329	15,410	445
Perry	Tell City	18,717	19,107	381
Pike	Petersburg	12,931	12,509	336
Porter	Valparaiso	152,533	128,932	418
Posey	Mount Vernon	26,876	25,968	409
Pulaski	Winamac	13,835	12,780	434
Putnam	Greencastle	36,692	30,315	480
Randolph	Winchester	26,833	27,148	453
Ripley	Versailles	27,316	24,616	446
Rush	Rushville	18,016	18,129	408
Saint Joseph	South Bend	266,348	247,052	457
Scott	Scottsburg	23,556	20,991	190
Shelby	Shelbyville	43,717	40,307	413
Spencer	Rockport	20,343	19,490	399
Starke	Knox	23,139	22,747	309
Steuben	Angola	33,706	27,446	309
Sullivan	Sullivan	21,861	18,993	447
Switzerland	Vevay	9,435	7,738	221
Tippecanoe	Lafayette	154,848	130,598	500
Tipton	Tipton	16,422	16,119	260
Union	Liberty	7,238	6,976	162
Vanderburgh	Evansville	171,889	165,058	235
Vermillion	Newport	16,572	16,773	257
Vigo	Terre Haute	104,540	106,107	403
Wabash	Wabash	34,339	35,069	413
Warren	Williamsport	8,703	8,176	365
Warrick	Boonville	54,744	44,920	384
Washington	Salem	27,618	23,717	514
Wayne	Richmond	70,235	71,951	404
Wells	Bluffton	27,912	25,948	370
White	Monticello	24,852	23,265	505
Whitley	Columbia City	31,651	27,651	336

Iowa

(99 counties, 55,869 sq. mi. land; pop. 2,944,062)

County	County seat or courthouse	2003 Pop.	1990 Pop.	Land area sq. mi.
Adair	Greenfield	7,922	8,409	569
Adams	Corning	4,371	4,866	424
Allamakee	Waukon	14,551	13,855	640
Appanoose	Centerville	13,590	13,743	496
Audubon	Audubon	6,479	7,334	443
Benton	Vinton	26,243	22,429	716
Black Hawk	Waterloo	126,418	123,798	567
Boone	Boone	26,247	25,186	571
Bremer	Waverly	23,368	22,813	438
Buchanan	Independence	20,903	20,844	571
Buena Vista	Storm Lake	20,205	19,965	575
Butler	Allison	14,968	15,731	580
Calhoun	Rockwell City	10,653	11,508	570
Carroll	Carroll	21,086	21,423	569
Cass	Atlantic	14,314	15,128	564
Cedar	Tipton	18,264	17,444	580
Cerro Gordo	Mason City	45,118	46,733	568
Cherokee	Cherokee	12,541	14,098	577
Chickasaw	New Hampton	12,702	13,295	505
Clarke	Osceola	9,242	8,287	431
Clay	Spencer	17,073	17,585	569
Clayton	Elkader	18,454	19,054	779
Clinton	Clinton	49,804	51,040	695
Crawford	Denison	16,930	16,775	714
Dallas	Adel	46,148	29,755	586
Davis	Bloomfield	8,557	8,312	503
Decatur	Leon	8,706	8,338	532
Delaware	Manchester	18,140	18,035	578
Des Moines	Burlington	41,247	42,614	416
Dickinson	Spirit Lake	16,399	14,909	381
Dubuque	Dubuque	90,049	86,403	608
Emmet	Estherville	10,805	11,569	396
Fayette	West Union	21,408	21,843	731
Floyd	Charles City	16,608	17,058	501
Franklin	Hampton	10,693	11,364	582
Fremont	Sidney	7,862	8,226	511
Greene	Jefferson	10,047	10,045	568
Grundy	Grundy Center	12,341	12,029	503
Guthrie	Guthrie Center	11,500	10,935	591
Hamilton	Webster City	16,316	16,071	577
Hancock	Garner	11,945	12,638	571
Hardin	Eldora	18,297	19,094	569
Harrison	Logan	15,667	14,730	697
Henry	Mount Pleasant	20,023	19,226	434
Howard	Cresco	9,784	9,809	473
Humboldt	Dakota City	10,090	10,756	434
Ida	Ida Grove	7,512	8,365	432
Iowa	Marengo	15,920	14,630	586
Jackson	Maquoketa	20,221	19,950	636
Jasper	Newton	37,708	34,795	730
Jefferson	Fairfield	16,022	16,310	435
Johnson	Iowa City	115,548	96,119	614
Jones	Anamosa	20,299	19,444	575
Keokuk	Sigourney	11,352	11,624	579
Kossuth	Algona	16,443	18,591	973
Lee	Fort Madison & Keokuk	36,714	38,687	517
Linn	Cedar Rapids	196,202	168,767	717

County	County seat or courthouse	2003 Pop.	1990 Pop.	Land area sq. mi.
Louisa	Wapello	12,201	11,592	402
Lucas	Chariton	9,501	9,070	431
Lyon	Rock Rapids	11,746	11,952	588
Madison	Winterset	14,510	12,483	561
Mahaska	Oskaloosa	22,303	21,532	571
Marion	Knoxville	32,425	30,001	554
Marshall	Marshalltown	39,103	38,276	572
Mills	Glenwood	14,909	13,202	437
Mitchell	Osage	10,946	10,928	469
Monona	Onawa	9,746	10,034	693
Monroe	Albia	7,796	8,114	433
Montgomery	Red Oak	11,289	12,076	424
Muscatine	Muscatine	42,093	39,907	439
O'Brien	Primghar	14,627	15,444	573
Osceola	Sibley	6,819	7,267	399
Page	Clarinda	16,346	16,870	535
Palo Alto	Emmetsburg	9,705	10,669	564
Plymouth	Le Mars	24,719	23,388	864
Pocahontas	Pocahontas	8,251	9,525	578
Polk	Des Moines	388,606	327,140	569
Pottawattamie	Council Bluffs	88,477	82,628	954
Poweshiek	Montezuma	19,033	19,033	585
Ringgold	Mount Ayr	5,421	5,420	538
Sac	Sac City	10,872	12,324	576
Scott	Davenport	159,414	150,973	458
Shelby	Harlan	12,717	13,230	591
Sioux	Orange City	32,104	29,903	768
Story	Nevada	83,021	74,252	573
Tama	Toledo	17,876	17,419	721
Taylor	Bedford	6,793	7,114	534
Union	Creston	11,932	12,750	424
Van Buren	Keosauqua	7,777	7,676	485
Wapello	Ottumwa	35,885	35,696	432
Warren	Indianola	41,997	36,033	572
Washington	Washington	21,314	19,612	569
Wayne	Corydon	6,669	7,067	526
Webster	Fort Dodge	39,590	40,342	715
Winnebago	Forest City	11,445	12,122	400
Winneshiek	Decorah	21,307	20,847	690
Woodbury	Sioux City	103,220	98,276	873
Worth	Northwood	7,773	7,991	400
Wright	Clarion	13,765	14,269	581

Kansas

(105 counties, 81,815 sq. mi. land; pop. 2,723,507)

County	County seat or courthouse	2003 Pop.	1990 Pop.	Land area sq. mi.
Allen	Iola	13,907	14,638	503
Anderson	Garnett	8,208	7,803	583
Atchison	Atchison	16,741	16,932	432
Barber	Medicine Lodge	5,034	5,874	1,134
Barton	Great Bend	27,467	29,382	894
Bourbon	Fort Scott	15,086	14,966	637
Brown	Hiawatha	10,442	11,128	571
Butler	El Dorado	61,127	50,580	1,428
Chase	Cottonwood Falls	3,107	3,021	776
Chautauqua	Sedan	4,185	4,407	642
Cherokee	Columbus	21,815	21,374	587
Cheyenne	Saint Francis	2,955	3,243	1,020
Clark	Ashland	2,333	2,418	975
Clay	Clay Center	8,573	9,158	644
Cloud	Concordia	9,859	11,023	716
Coffey	Burlington	8,815	8,404	630
Comanche	Coldwater	1,915	2,313	788
Cowley	Winfield	35,860	36,915	1,126
Crawford	Girard	38,398	35,582	593
Decatur	Oberlin	3,295	4,021	894
Dickinson	Abilene	19,255	18,958	848
Doniphan	Troy	8,149	8,134	392
Douglas	Lawrence	102,983	81,798	457
Edwards	Kinsley	3,275	3,787	622
Elk	Howard	3,167	3,327	647
Ellis	Hays	27,212	26,004	900
Ellsworth	Ellsworth	6,347	6,586	716
Finney	Garden City	39,176	33,070	1,302
Ford	Dodge City	33,012	27,463	1,099
Franklin	Ottawa	25,540	21,994	574
Geary	Junction City	26,313	30,453	385
Gove	Gove	2,910	3,231	1,071
Graham	Hill City	2,808	3,543	898
Grant	Ulysses	7,745	7,159	575
Gray	Cimarron	6,063	5,396	869
Greeley	Tribune	1,420	1,774	778
Greenwood	Eureka	7,485	7,847	1,140
Hamilton	Syracuse	2,666	2,388	996
Harper	Anthony	6,206	7,124	801
Harvey	Newton	33,502	31,028	539
Haskell	Sublette	4,246	3,886	577
Hodgeman	Jetmore	2,151	2,177	860
Jackson	Holton	13,017	11,525	656
Jefferson	Oskaloosa	18,798	15,905	536
Jewell	Mankato	3,433	4,251	909
Johnson	Olathe	486,515	355,021	477
Kearny	Lakin	4,591	4,027	871
Kingman	Kingman	8,382	8,292	863
Kiowa	Greensburg	3,152	3,660	722

County	County seat or courthouse	2003 Pop.	1990 Pop.	Land area sq. mi.
Labette	Oswego	22,259	23,693	649
Lane	Dighton	1,946	2,375	717
Leavenworth	Leavenworth	71,546	64,371	463
Lincoln	Lincoln	3,498	3,653	719
Linn	Mound City	9,722	8,254	599
Logan	Oakley	2,855	3,081	1,073
Lyon	Emporia	35,805	34,732	851
McPherson	McPherson	29,346	27,268	900
Marion	Marion	13,299	12,888	943
Marshall	Marysville	10,589	11,705	903
Meade	Meade	4,662	4,247	978
Miami	Paola	29,187	23,466	577
Mitchell	Beloit	6,707	7,203	700
Montgomery	Independence	34,934	38,816	645
Morris	Council Grove	5,995	6,198	697
Morton	Elkhart	3,317	3,480	730
Nemaha	Seneca	10,500	10,446	718
Neosho	Erie	16,580	17,035	572
Ness	Ness City	3,158	4,033	1,075
Norton	Norton	5,796	5,947	878
Osage	Lyndon	16,784	15,248	704
Osborne	Osborne	4,179	4,867	892
Ottawa	Minneapolis	6,177	5,634	721
Pawnee	Larned	6,796	7,555	754
Phillips	Phillipsburg	5,657	6,590	886
Pottawatomie	Westmoreland	18,714	16,128	844
Pratt	Pratt	9,437	9,702	735
Rawlins	Atwood	2,843	3,404	1,070
Reno	Hutchinson	63,832	62,389	1,254
Republic	Belleville	5,307	6,482	716
Rice	Lyons	10,412	10,610	727
Riley	Manhattan	62,291	67,139	610
Rooks	Stockton	5,417	6,039	888
Rush	LaCrosse	3,418	3,842	718
Russell	Russell	6,907	7,835	885
Saline	Salina	53,737	49,301	720
Scott	Scott City	4,806	5,289	718
Sedgwick	Wichita	462,896	403,662	999
Seward	Liberal	23,091	18,743	640
Shawnee	Topeka	170,902	160,976	550
Sheridan	Hoxie	2,662	3,043	895
Sherman	Goodland	6,277	6,926	1,056
Smith	Smith Center	4,181	5,078	895
Stafford	Saint John	4,589	5,365	792
Stanton	Johnson	2,404	2,333	680
Stevens	Hugoton	5,389	5,048	728
Sumner	Wellington	25,256	25,841	1,182
Thomas	Colby	7,933	8,258	1,075
Trego	WaKeeney	3,103	3,694	888
Wabaunsee	Alma	6,767	6,603	797
Wallace	Sharon Springs	1,621	1,821	914
Washington	Washington	6,131	7,073	898
Wichita	Leoti	2,447	2,758	719
Wilson	Fredonia	10,080	10,289	574
Woodson	Yates Center	3,631	4,116	501
Wyandotte	Kansas City	157,091	162,026	151

Kentucky

(120 counties, 39,728 sq. mi. land; pop. 4,117,827)

County	County seat or courthouse	2003 Pop.	1990 Pop.	Land area sq. mi.
Adair	Columbia	17,458	15,360	407
Allen	Scottsville	18,262	14,628	346
Anderson	Lawrenceburg	19,812	14,571	203
Ballard	Wickliffe	8,193	7,902	251
Barren	Glasgow	39,133	34,001	491
Bath	Owingsville	11,413	9,692	279
Bell	Pineville	29,953	31,506	361
Boone	Burlington	97,139	57,589	246
Bourbon	Paris	19,598	19,236	291
Boyd	Catlettsburg	49,554	51,096	160
Boyle	Danville	27,837	25,590	182
Bracken	Brooksville	8,487	7,766	203
Breathitt	Jackson	15,850	15,703	495
Breckinridge	Hardinsburg	19,011	16,312	572
Bullitt	Shepherdsville	64,900	47,567	299
Butler	Morgantown	13,199	11,245	428
Caldwell	Princeton	12,824	13,232	347
Calloway	Murray	34,671	30,735	386
Campbell	Newport	87,970	83,866	152
Carlisle	Bardwell	5,384	5,238	192
Carroll	Carrollton	10,230	9,292	130
Carter	Grayson	27,144	24,340	411
Casey	Liberty	15,977	14,211	446
Christian	Hopkinsville	69,912	68,941	721
Clark	Winchester	33,958	29,496	254
Clay	Manchester	24,346	21,746	471
Clinton	Albany	9,605	9,135	197
Crittenden	Marion	9,092	9,196	362
Cumberland	Burkesville	7,159	6,784	306
Daviess	Owensboro	92,540	87,189	462
Edmonson	Brownsville	11,869	10,357	303
Elliott	Sandy Hook	6,935	6,455	234
Estill	Irvine	15,192	14,614	254
Fayette	Lexington	266,798	225,366	285
Fleming	Flemingsburg	14,379	12,292	351

County	County seat or courthouse	2003 Pop.	1990 Pop.	Land area sq. mi.
Floyd	Prestonsburg	42,272	43,586	394
Franklin	Frankfort	48,051	44,143	210
Fulton	Hickman	7,419	8,271	209
Gallatin	Warsaw	7,995	5,393	99
Garrard	Lancaster	15,850	11,579	231
Grant	Williamstown	23,983	15,737	260
Graves	Mayfield	37,252	33,550	556
Grayson	Leitchfield	24,600	21,050	504
Green	Greensburg	11,787	10,371	289
Greenup	Greenup	36,952	36,796	346
Hancock	Hawesville	8,433	7,864	189
Hardin	Elizabethtown	96,052	89,240	628
Harlan	Harlan	32,095	36,574	467
Harrison	Cynthiana	18,227	16,248	310
Hart	Munfordville	17,879	14,890	416
Henderson	Henderson	45,129	43,044	440
Henry	New Castle	15,543	12,823	289
Hickman	Clinton	5,165	5,566	244
Hopkins	Madisonville	46,839	46,126	551
Jackson	McKee	13,595	11,955	346
Jefferson	Louisville	699,017	665,123	385
Jessamine	Nicholasville	41,508	30,508	173
Johnson	Paintsville	23,647	23,248	262
Kenton	Covington	152,287	142,005	162
Knott	Hindman	17,614	17,906	352
Knox	Barbourville	31,708	29,676	388
Larue	Hodgenville	13,437	11,679	263
Laurel	London	55,488	43,438	436
Lawrence	Louisa	15,895	13,998	419
Lee	Beattyville	7,900	7,422	210
Leslie	Hyden	12,203	13,642	404
Letcher	Whitesburg	24,843	27,000	339
Lewis	Vanceburg	13,796	13,029	484
Lincoln	Stanford	24,535	20,096	336
Livingston	Smithland	9,726	9,062	316
Logan	Russellville	26,841	24,416	556
Lyon	Eddyville	8,078	6,624	216
McCracken	Paducah	64,768	62,879	251
McCreary	Whitley City	17,190	15,603	428
McLean	Calhoun	9,872	9,628	254
Madison	Richmond	74,814	57,508	441
Magoffin	Salyersville	13,334	13,077	309
Marion	Lebanon	18,533	16,499	346
Marshall	Benton	30,559	27,205	305
Martin	Inez	12,521	12,526	231
Mason	Maysville	16,815	16,666	241
Meade	Brandenburg	27,619	24,170	309
Menifee	Frenchburg	6,618	5,092	204
Mercer	Harrodsburg	21,410	19,148	251
Metcalfe	Edmonton	10,042	8,963	291
Monroe	Tompkinsville	11,740	11,401	331
Montgomery	Mount Sterling	23,535	19,561	199
Morgan	West Liberty	14,278	11,648	381
Muhlenberg	Greenville	31,691	31,318	475
Nelson	Bardstown	39,635	29,710	423
Nicholas	Carlisle	6,937	6,725	197
Ohio	Hartford	23,165	21,105	594
Oldham	La Grange	50,517	33,263	189
Owen	Owenton	11,092	9,035	352
Owsley	Booneville	4,755	5,036	198
Pendleton	Falmouth	15,090	12,062	281
Perry	Hazard	29,492	30,283	342
Pike	Pikeville	67,495	72,584	788
Powell	Stanton	13,347	11,686	180
Pulaski	Somerset	58,013	49,489	662
Robertson	Mount Olivet	2,320	2,124	100
Rockcastle	Mount Vernon	16,644	14,803	318
Rowan	Morehead	22,397	20,353	281
Russell	Jamestown	16,586	14,716	254
Scott	Georgetown	36,726	23,867	285
Shelby	Shelbyville	35,900	24,824	384
Simpson	Franklin	16,664	15,145	236
Spencer	Taylorsville	14,301	6,801	186
Taylor	Campbellsville	23,347	21,146	270
Todd	Elkton	12,019	10,940	376
Trigg	Cadiz	12,877	10,361	443
Trimble	Bedford	8,759	6,090	149
Union	Morganfield	15,751	16,557	345
Warren	Bowling Green	95,778	77,720	545
Washington	Springfield	11,260	10,441	301
Wayne	Monticello	20,277	17,468	459
Webster	Dixon	14,051	13,955	335
Whitley	Williamsburg	37,261	33,326	440
Wolfe	Campton	6,939	6,503	223
Woodford	Versailles	23,659	19,955	191

Louisiana

(64 parishes, 43,562 sq. mi. land; pop. 4,496,334)

Parish	Parish seat or courthouse	2003 Pop.	1990 Pop.	Land area sq. mi.
Acadia	Crowley	59,246	55,882	655
Allen	Oberlin	25,268	21,226	765
Ascension	Donaldsonville	84,424	58,214	292
Assumption	Napoleonville	23,269	22,753	339
Avoyelles	Marksville	41,791	39,159	832
Beauregard	De Ridder	33,514	30,083	1,160
Bienville	Arcadia	15,320	16,232	811
Bossier	Benton	101,999	86,088	839
Caddo	Shreveport	250,342	248,253	882
Calcasieu	Lake Charles	183,889	168,134	1,071
Caldwell	Columbia	10,599	9,806	529
Cameron	Cameron	9,708	9,260	1,313
Catahoula	Harrisonburg	10,615	11,065	704
Claiborne	Homer	16,534	17,405	755
Concordia	Vidalia	19,730	20,828	696
De Soto	Mansfield	25,990	25,668	877
East Baton Rouge	Baton Rouge	412,447	380,105	455
East Carroll	Lake Providence	8,997	9,709	421
East Feliciana	Clinton	21,095	19,211	453
Evangeline	Ville Platte	35,149	33,274	664
Franklin	Winnsboro	20,860	22,387	624
Grant	Colfax	18,887	17,526	645
Iberia	New Iberia	74,146	68,297	575
Iberville	Plaquemine	32,811	31,049	619
Jackson	Jonesboro	15,259	15,859	570
Jefferson	Gretna	452,459	448,306	307
Jefferson Davis	Jennings	31,113	30,722	652
Lafayette	Lafayette	194,239	164,762	270
Lafourche	Thibodaux	91,281	85,860	1,085
La Salle	Jena	14,179	13,662	624
Lincoln	Ruston	42,413	41,745	471
Livingston	Livingston	102,046	70,523	648
Madison	Tallulah	13,079	12,463	624
Morehouse	Bastrop	30,671	31,938	794
Natchitoches	Natchitoches	39,002	37,254	1,255
Orleans	New Orleans	469,032	496,938	181
Ouachita	Monroe	147,898	142,191	611
Plaquemines	Pointe a la Hache	28,025	25,575	845
Pointe Coupee	New Roads	22,564	22,540	557
Rapides	Alexandria	127,394	131,556	1,323
Red River	Coushatta	9,524	9,526	389
Richland	Rayville	20,623	20,629	558
Sabine	Many	23,406	22,646	865
Saint Bernard	Chalmette	66,113	66,631	465
Saint Charles	Hahnville	49,353	42,437	284
Saint Helena	Greensburg	10,307	9,874	408
Saint James	Convent	21,118	20,879	246
Saint John the Baptist	Edgard	44,816	39,996	219
Saint Landry	Opelousas	89,041	80,312	929
Saint Martin	Saint Martinville	49,911	44,097	740
Saint Mary	Franklin	52,357	58,086	613
Saint Tammany	Covington	207,743	144,500	854
Tangipahoa	Amite	103,591	85,709	790
Tensas	Saint Joseph	6,247	7,103	602
Terrebonne	Houma	106,107	96,982	1,255
Union	Farmerville	22,966	20,796	878
Vermilion	Abbeville	54,222	50,055	1,174
Vernon	Leesville	50,669	61,961	1,328
Washington	Franklinton	43,947	43,185	670
Webster	Minden	41,404	41,989	595
West Baton Rouge	Port Allen	21,717	19,419	191
West Carroll	Oak Grove	12,236	12,093	359
West Feliciana	Saint Francisville	15,235	12,915	406
Winn	Winnfield	16,397	16,498	950

Maine

(16 counties, 30,862 sq. mi. land; pop. 1,305,728)

County	County seat or courthouse	2003 Pop.	1990 Pop.	Land area sq. mi.
Androscoggin	Auburn	106,115	105,259	470
Aroostook	Houlton	73,428	86,936	6,672
Cumberland	Portland	270,923	243,135	836
Franklin	Farmington	29,763	29,008	1,698
Hancock	Ellsworth	52,792	46,948	1,588
Kennebec	Augusta	119,683	115,904	868
Knox	Rockland	40,406	36,310	366
Lincoln	Wiscasset	34,729	30,357	456
Oxford	South Paris	56,151	52,602	2,078
Penobscot	Bangor	146,982	146,601	3,396
Piscataquis	Dover-Foxcroft	17,394	18,653	3,966
Sagadahoc	Bath	36,455	33,535	254
Somerset	Skowhegan	51,154	49,767	3,927
Waldo	Belfast	38,248	33,018	730
Washington	Machias	33,479	35,308	2,568
York	Alfred	198,026	164,587	991

Maryland

(23 counties, 1 ind. city, 9,774 sq. mi. land; pop. 5,508,909)

County	County seat or courthouse	2003 Pop.	1990 Pop.	Land area sq. mi.
Allegany	Cumberland	73,668	74,946	425
Anne Arundel	Annapolis	506,620	427,239	416
Baltimore	Towson	777,184	692,134	599
Calvert	Prince Frederick	84,110	51,372	215
Caroline	Denton	30,861	27,035	320
Carroll	Westminster	163,207	123,372	449
Cecil	Elkton	92,746	71,347	348
Charles	La Plata	133,049	101,154	461
Dorchester	Cambridge	30,612	30,236	558

County	County seat or courthouse	2003 Pop.	1990 Pop.	Land area sq. mi.
Frederick	Frederick	213,662	150,208	663
Garrett	Oakland	30,049	28,138	648
Harford	Bel Air	232,175	182,132	440
Howard	Ellicott City	264,265	187,328	252
Kent	Chestertown	19,680	17,842	279
Montgomery	Rockville	918,881	762,875	496
Prince George's	Upper Marlboro	838,716	722,705	485
Queen Anne's	Centreville	44,108	33,953	372
Saint Mary's	Leonardtown	92,754	75,974	361
Somerset	Princess Anne	25,447	23,440	327
Talbot	Easton	34,670	30,549	269
Washington	Hagerstown	136,796	121,393	458
Wicomico	Salisbury	87,375	74,339	377
Worcester	Snow Hill	49,604	35,028	473
Independent City				
Baltimore		628,670	736,014	81

Massachusetts

(14 counties, 7,840 sq. mi. land; pop. 6,433,422)

County	County seat or courthouse	2003 Pop.	1990 Pop.	Land area sq. mi.
Barnstable	Barnstable	229,545	186,605	396
Berkshire	Pittsfield	133,310	139,352	931
Bristol	Taunton	547,008	506,325	556
Dukes	Edgartown	15,601	11,639	104
Essex	Salem	737,848	670,080	501
Franklin	Greenfield	72,204	70,086	702
Hampden	Springfield	461,190	456,310	618
Hampshire	Northampton	155,101	146,568	529
Middlesex	East Cambridge	1,471,724	1,398,468	823
Nantucket	Nantucket	10,724	6,012	48
Norfolk	Dedham	654,331	616,087	400
Plymouth	Plymouth	487,521	435,276	661
Suffolk	Boston	680,705	663,906	59
Worcester	Worcester	776,610	709,711	1,513

Michigan

(83 counties, 56,804 sq. mi. land; pop. 10,079,985)

County	County seat or courthouse	2003 Pop.	1990 Pop.	Land area sq. mi.
Alcona	Harrisville	11,572	10,145	674
Alger	Munising	9,767	8,972	918
Allegan	Allegan	110,331	90,509	827
Alpena	Alpena	30,781	30,605	574
Antrim	Bellaire	24,094	18,185	477
Arenac	Standish	17,309	14,906	367
Baraga	L'Anse	8,782	7,954	904
Barry	Hastings	58,774	50,057	556
Bay	Bay City	109,452	111,723	444
Benzie	Beulah	17,078	12,200	321
Berrien	Saint Joseph	162,766	161,378	571
Branch	Coldwater	46,414	41,502	507
Calhoun	Marshall	138,854	135,982	709
Cass	Cassopolis	51,385	49,477	492
Charlevoix	Charlevoix	26,712	21,468	417
Cheboygan	Cheboygan	27,405	21,398	716
Chippewa	Sault Sainte Marie	38,822	34,604	1,561
Clare	Harrison	31,589	24,952	567
Clinton	Saint Johns	67,609	57,893	571
Crawford	Grayling	14,808	12,260	558
Delta	Escanaba	38,317	37,780	1,170
Dickinson	Iron Mountain	27,186	26,831	766
Eaton	Charlotte	106,197	92,879	576
Emmet	Petoskey	32,741	25,040	468
Genesee	Flint	442,250	430,459	640
Gladwin	Gladwin	26,939	21,896	507
Gogebic	Bessemer	17,329	18,052	1,102
Grand Traverse	Traverse City	82,011	64,273	465
Gratiot	Ithaca	42,501	38,982	570
Hillsdale	Hillsdale	47,230	43,431	599
Houghton	Houghton	36,249	35,446	1,012
Huron	Bad Axe	35,216	34,951	837
Ingham	Mason	282,030	281,912	559
Ionia	Ionia	63,573	57,024	573
Iosco	Tawas City	26,888	30,209	549
Iron	Crystal Falls	12,787	13,175	1,166
Isabella	Mount Pleasant	64,663	54,624	574
Jackson	Jackson	162,321	149,756	707
Kalamazoo	Kalamazoo	242,110	223,411	562
Kalkaska	Kalkaska	17,177	13,497	561
Kent	Grand Rapids	590,417	500,631	856
Keweenaw	Eagle River	2,227	1,701	541
Lake	Baldwin	11,795	8,583	567
Lapeer	Lapeer	91,314	74,768	654
Leelanau	Leland	21,860	16,527	348
Lenawee	Adrian	100,786	91,476	751
Livingston	Howell	172,881	115,645	568
Luce	Newberry	6,919	5,763	903
Mackinac	Saint Ignace	11,470	10,674	1,022
Macomb	Mount Clemens	813,948	717,400	480
Manistee	Manistee	25,317	21,265	544
Marquette	Marquette	64,616	70,887	1,821
Mason	Ludington	28,685	25,537	495
Mecosta	Big Rapids	41,728	37,308	556

County	County seat or courthouse	2003 Pop.	1990 Pop.	Land area sq. mi.
Menominee	Menominee	25,084	24,920	1,044
Midland	Midland	84,492	75,651	521
Missaukee	Lake City	15,189	12,147	567
Monroe	Monroe	150,863	133,600	551
Montcalm	Stanton	62,926	53,059	708
Montmorency	Atlanta	10,492	8,936	548
Muskegon	Muskegon	173,090	158,983	509
Newaygo	White Cloud	49,271	38,206	842
Oakland	Pontiac	1,207,869	1,083,592	873
Oceana	Hart	28,074	22,455	540
Ogemaw	West Branch	21,792	18,681	564
Ontonagon	Ontonagon	7,571	8,854	1,312
Osceola	Reed City	23,509	20,146	566
Oscoda	Mio	9,461	7,842	565
Otsego	Gaylord	24,268	17,957	515
Ottawa	Grand Haven	249,391	187,768	566
Presque Isle	Rogers City	14,286	13,743	660
Roscommon	Roscommon	26,230	19,776	521
Saginaw	Saginaw	209,327	211,946	809
Saint Clair	Port Huron	169,063	145,607	724
Saint Joseph	Centreville	62,864	58,913	504
Sanilac	Sandusky	44,583	39,928	964
Schoolcraft	Manistique	8,772	8,302	1,178
Shiawassee	Corunna	72,543	69,770	539
Tuscola	Caro	58,382	55,498	812
Van Buren	Paw Paw	78,210	70,060	611
Washtenaw	Ann Arbor	338,562	282,937	710
Wayne	Detroit	2,028,778	2,111,687	614
Wexford	Cadillac	31,251	26,360	565

Minnesota

(87 counties, 79,610 sq. mi. land; pop. 5,059,375)

County	County seat or courthouse	2003 Pop.	1990 Pop.	Land area sq. mi.
Aitkin	Aitkin	15,782	12,425	1,819
Anoka	Anoka	314,074	243,641	424
Becker	Detroit Lakes	31,174	27,881	1,310
Beltrami	Bemidji	41,797	34,384	2,505
Benton	Foley	36,925	30,185	408
Big Stone	Ortonville	5,653	6,285	497
Blue Earth	Mankato	57,306	54,044	752
Brown	New Ulm	26,505	26,984	611
Carlton	Carlton	33,044	29,259	860
Carver	Chaska	78,960	47,915	357
Cass	Walker	28,205	21,791	2,018
Chippewa	Montevideo	12,808	13,228	583
Chisago	Center City	46,165	30,521	418
Clay	Moorhead	51,983	50,422	1,045
Clearwater	Bagley	8,424	8,309	995
Cook	Grand Marais	5,282	3,868	1,451
Cottonwood	Windom	12,019	12,694	640
Crow Wing	Brainerd	58,430	44,249	997
Dakota	Hastings	373,311	275,210	570
Dodge	Mantorville	18,931	15,731	440
Douglas	Alexandria	34,117	28,674	634
Faribault	Blue Earth	15,737	16,937	714
Fillmore	Preston	21,314	20,777	861
Freeborn	Albert Lea	31,961	33,060	708
Goodhue	Red Wing	45,167	40,690	758
Grant	Elbow Lake	6,243	6,246	546
Hennepin	Minneapolis	1,121,035	1,032,431	557
Houston	Caledonia	19,980	18,497	558
Hubbard	Park Rapids	18,635	14,939	922
Isanti	Cambridge	35,372	25,921	439
Itasca	Grand Rapids	44,265	40,863	2,665
Jackson	Jackson	11,170	11,677	702
Kanabec	Mora	15,867	12,802	525
Kandiyohi	Willmar	41,148	38,761	796
Kittson	Hallock	4,968	5,767	1,097
Koochiching	International Falls	14,018	16,299	3,102
Lac qui Parle	Madison	7,867	8,924	765
Lake	Two Harbors	11,160	10,415	2,099
Lake of the Woods	Baudette	4,384	4,076	1,297
Le Sueur	Le Center	26,763	23,239	449
Lincoln	Ivanhoe	6,159	6,890	537
Lyon	Marshall	24,819	24,789	714
McLeod	Glencoe	35,864	32,030	492
Mahnomen	Mahnomen	5,113	5,044	556
Marshall	Warren	9,997	10,993	1,772
Martin	Fairmont	21,221	22,914	709
Meeker	Litchfield	23,205	20,846	609
Mille Lacs	Milaca	24,317	18,670	574
Morrison	Little Falls	32,589	29,604	1,125
Mower	Austin	38,823	37,385	712
Murray	Slayton	8,981	9,660	704
Nicollet	Saint Peter	30,733	28,076	452
Nobles	Worthington	20,621	20,098	715
Norman	Ada	7,191	7,975	876
Olmsted	Rochester	131,384	106,470	653
Otter Tail	Fergus Falls	58,847	50,714	1,980
Pennington	Thief River Falls	13,636	13,306	617
Pine	Pine City	27,746	21,264	1,411
Pipestone	Pipestone	9,681	10,491	466
Polk	Crookston	30,905	32,589	1,970
Pope	Glenwood	11,252	10,745	670
Ramsey	Saint Paul	506,355	485,760	156

County	County seat or courthouse	2003 Pop.	1990 Pop.	Land area sq. mi.
Red Lake	Red Lake Falls	4,319	4,525	432
Redwood	Redwood Falls	16,231	17,254	880
Renville	Olivia	16,851	17,673	983
Rice	Faribault	59,667	49,183	498
Rock	Luverne	9,614	9,806	483
Roseau	Roseau	16,318	15,026	1,663
Saint Louis	Duluth	198,799	198,232	6,225
Scott	Shakopee	108,578	57,846	357
Sherburne	Elk River	74,667	41,945	436
Sibley	Gaylord	15,277	14,366	589
Stearns	Saint Cloud	137,149	119,324	1,345
Steele	Owatonna	34,753	30,729	430
Stevens	Morris	9,888	10,634	562
Swift	Benson	11,656	10,724	744
Todd	Long Prairie	24,309	23,363	942
Traverse	Wheaton	3,911	4,463	574
Wabasha	Wabasha	22,144	19,744	525
Wadena	Wadena	13,603	13,154	535
Waseca	Waseca	19,435	18,079	423
Washington	Stillwater	213,564	145,860	392
Watonwan	Saint James	11,621	11,682	435
Wilkin	Breckenridge	6,945	7,516	751
Winona	Winona	49,482	47,828	626
Wright	Buffalo	102,529	68,710	661
Yellow Medicine	Granite Falls	10,677	11,684	758

County	County seat or courthouse	2003 Pop.	1990 Pop.	Land area sq. mi.
Scott	Forest	28,450	24,137	609
Sharkey	Rolling Fork	6,224	7,066	428
Simpson	Mendenhall	27,592	23,953	589
Smith	Raleigh	15,834	14,798	636
Stone	Wiggins	14,206	10,750	445
Sunflower	Indianola	33,374	35,129	694
Tallahatchie	Charleston & Sumner	14,394	15,210	644
Tate	Senatobia	25,794	21,432	404
Tippah	Ripley	20,920	19,523	458
Tishomingo	Iuka	18,966	17,683	424
Tunica	Tunica	9,917	8,164	455
Union	New Albany	26,113	22,085	415
Walthall	Tylertown	15,191	14,352	404
Warren	Vicksburg	48,993	47,880	587
Washington	Greenville	60,345	67,935	724
Wayne	Waynesboro	21,149	19,517	810
Webster	Walthall	10,159	10,222	422
Wilkinson	Woodville	10,241	9,678	677
Winston	Louisville	19,911	19,433	607
Yalobusha	Coffeeville & Water Valley	13,347	12,033	467
Yazoo	Yazoo City	28,272	25,506	919

Mississippi

(82 counties, 46,907 sq. mi. land; pop. 2,881,281)

County	County seat or courthouse	2003 Pop.	1990 Pop.	Land area sq. mi.
Adams	Natchez	33,233	35,356	460
Alcorn	Corinth	34,930	31,722	400
Amite	Liberty	13,594	13,328	730
Attala	Kosciusko	19,673	18,481	735
Benton	Ashland	7,774	8,046	407
Bolivar	Cleveland & Rosedale	39,235	41,875	876
Calhoun	Pittsboro	14,827	14,908	587
Carroll	Carrollton & Vaiden	10,462	9,237	628
Chickasaw	Houston & Okolona	19,204	18,085	502
Choctaw	Ackerman	9,661	9,071	419
Claiborne	Port Gibson	11,502	11,370	487
Clarke	Quitman	17,746	17,313	691
Clay	West Point	21,625	21,120	409
Coahoma	Clarksdale	29,546	31,665	554
Copiah	Hazlehurst	28,928	27,592	777
Covington	Collins	20,177	16,527	414
De Soto	Hernando	124,378	67,910	478
Forrest	Hattiesburg	74,386	68,314	467
Franklin	Meadville	8,340	8,377	565
George	Lucedale	20,407	16,673	478
Greene	Leakesville	13,169	10,220	713
Grenada	Grenada	22,809	21,555	422
Hancock	Bay Saint Louis	45,145	31,760	477
Harrison	Gulfport	189,614	165,365	581
Hinds	Jackson & Raymond	249,087	254,441	869
Holmes	Lexington	21,347	21,604	756
Humphreys	Belzoni	10,722	12,134	418
Issaquena	Mayersville	2,016	1,909	413
Itawamba	Fulton	22,964	20,017	532
Jackson	Pascagoula	133,928	115,243	727
Jasper	Bay Springs & Paulding	18,280	17,114	676
Jefferson	Fayette	9,533	8,653	519
Jefferson Davis	Prentiss	13,399	14,051	408
Jones	Ellisville & Laurel	65,168	62,031	694
Kemper	De Kalb	10,435	10,356	766
Lafayette	Oxford	40,188	31,826	631
Lamar	Purvis	41,957	30,424	497
Lauderdale	Meridian	77,706	75,555	704
Lawrence	Monticello	13,520	12,458	431
Leake	Carthage	21,820	18,436	583
Lee	Tupelo	77,690	65,579	450
Leflore	Greenwood	36,470	37,341	592
Lincoln	Brookhaven	33,549	30,278	586
Lowndes	Columbus	60,658	59,308	502
Madison	Canton	79,758	53,794	717
Marion	Columbia	25,090	25,544	542
Marshall	Holly Springs	35,442	30,361	706
Monroe	Aberdeen	37,842	36,582	764
Montgomery	Winona	11,935	12,387	407
Neshoba	Philadelphia	29,134	24,800	570
Newton	Decatur	22,044	20,291	578
Noxubee	Macon	12,318	12,604	695
Oktibbeha	Starkville	42,573	38,375	458
Panola	Batesville & Sardis	35,243	29,996	684
Pearl River	Poplarville	50,894	38,714	811
Perry	New Augusta	12,288	10,865	647
Pike	Magnolia	38,935	36,882	409
Pontotoc	Pontotoc	27,575	22,237	497
Prentiss	Booneville	25,581	23,278	415
Quitman	Marks	9,740	10,490	405
Rankin	Brandon	124,695	87,161	775

Missouri

(114 counties, 1 ind. city, 68,886 sq. mi. land; pop. 5,704,484)

County	County seat or courthouse	2003 Pop.	1990 Pop.	Land area sq. mi.
Adair	Kirksville	24,790	24,577	567
Andrew	Savannah	16,813	14,632	435
Atchison	Rockport	6,286	7,457	545
Audrain	Mexico	25,716	23,599	693
Barry	Cassville	34,629	27,547	779
Barton	Lamar	12,999	11,312	594
Bates	Butler	16,937	15,025	848
Benton	Warsaw	18,076	13,859	706
Bollinger	Marble Hill	12,318	10,619	621
Boone	Columbia	141,122	112,379	685
Buchanan	Saint Joseph	84,909	83,083	410
Butler	Poplar Buff	40,854	38,765	698
Caldwell	Kingston	9,159	8,380	429
Callaway	Fulton	42,225	32,809	839
Camden	Camdenton	38,302	27,495	655
Cape Girardeau	Jackson	69,876	61,633	579
Carroll	Carrollton	10,149	10,748	695
Carter	Van Buren	5,974	5,515	508
Cass	Harrisonville	88,834	63,808	699
Cedar	Stockton	13,838	12,093	476
Chariton	Keytesville	8,251	9,202	756
Christian	Ozark	61,571	32,644	563
Clark	Kahoka	7,420	7,547	507
Clay	Liberty	194,247	153,411	396
Clinton	Plattsburg	20,140	16,595	419
Cole	Jefferson City	72,454	63,579	391
Cooper	Boonville	17,009	14,835	565
Crawford	Steelville	23,513	19,173	743
Dade	Greenfield	7,845	7,449	490
Dallas	Buffalo	16,113	12,646	542
Daviess	Gallatin	8,004	7,865	567
De Kalb	Maysville	13,063	9,967	424
Dent	Salem	14,921	13,702	754
Douglas	Ava	13,363	11,876	815
Dunklin	Kennett	32,654	33,112	546
Franklin	Union	96,905	80,603	923
Gasconade	Hermann	15,542	14,006	521
Gentry	Albany	6,566	6,854	492
Greene	Springfield	245,765	207,949	675
Grundy	Trenton	10,311	10,536	436
Harrison	Bethany	8,828	8,469	725
Henry	Clinton	22,419	20,044	702
Hickory	Hermitage	9,005	7,335	399
Holt	Oregon	5,145	6,034	462
Howard	Fayette	10,007	9,631	466
Howell	West Plains	37,499	31,447	928
Iron	Ironton	10,306	10,726	551
Jackson	Independence	659,723	633,234	605
Jasper	Carthage	108,112	90,465	640
Jefferson	Hillsboro	206,786	171,380	657
Johnson	Warrensburg	50,262	42,514	830
Knox	Edina	4,311	4,482	506
Laclede	Lebanon	33,326	27,158	766
Lafayette	Lexington	32,951	31,107	629
Lawrence	Mount Vernon	36,426	30,236	613
Lewis	Monticello	10,226	10,233	505
Lincoln	Troy	44,207	28,892	630
Linn	Linneus	13,460	13,885	620
Livingston	Chillicothe	14,387	14,592	535
McDonald	Pineville	21,973	16,938	540
Macon	Macon	15,577	15,345	804
Madison	Fredericktown	11,804	11,127	497
Maries	Vienna	8,841	7,976	528
Marion	Palmyra	28,289	27,682	438
Mercer	Princeton	3,596	3,723	454
Miller	Tuscumbia	24,255	20,700	592
Mississippi	Charleston	14,386	14,442	413
Moniteau	California	14,965	12,298	417

County	County seat or courthouse	2003 Pop.	1990 Pop.	Land area sq. mi.
Monroe	Paris	9,396	9,104	646
Montgomery	Montgomery City	12,068	11,355	537
Morgan	Versailles	20,000	15,574	597
New Madrid	New Madrid	19,187	20,928	678
Newton	Neosho	54,033	44,445	626
Nodaway	Maryville	21,743	21,709	877
Oregon	Alton	10,301	9,470	791
Osage	Linn	13,134	12,018	606
Ozark	Gainesville	9,498	8,598	742
Pemiscot	Caruthersville	19,729	21,921	493
Perry	Perryville	18,225	16,648	475
Pettis	Sedalia	39,344	35,437	685
Phelps	Rolla	41,668	35,248	673
Pike	Bowling Green	18,519	15,969	673
Platte	Platte City	79,390	57,867	420
Polk	Bolivar	28,081	21,826	637
Pulaski	Waynesville	45,254	41,307	547
Putnam	Unionville	5,148	5,079	518
Ralls	New London	9,653	8,476	471
Randolph	Huntsville	25,045	24,370	482
Ray	Richmond	23,926	21,968	569
Reynolds	Centerville	6,581	6,661	811
Ripley	Doniphan	13,781	12,303	629
Saint Charles	Saint Charles	311,531	212,751	560
Saint Clair	Osceola	9,679	8,457	677
Sainte Genevieve	Sainte Genevieve	18,094	16,037	502
Saint Francois	Farmington	57,929	48,904	449
Saint Louis	Clayton	1,013,123	993,508	508
Saline	Marshall	22,887	23,523	756
Schuyler	Lancaster	4,209	4,236	308
Scotland	Memphis	4,905	4,822	438
Scott	Benton	40,779	39,376	421
Shannon	Eminence	8,293	7,613	1,004
Shelby	Shelbyville	6,702	6,942	501
Stoddard	Bloomfield	29,626	28,895	827
Stone	Galena	29,941	19,078	463
Sullivan	Milan	7,080	6,326	651
Taney	Forsyth	41,403	25,561	632
Texas	Houston	24,142	21,476	1,179
Vernon	Nevada	20,283	19,041	834
Warren	Warrenton	26,862	19,534	431
Washington	Potosi	23,884	20,380	760
Wayne	Greenville	13,090	11,543	761
Webster	Marshfield	33,124	23,753	593
Worth	Grant City	2,270	2,440	267
Wright	Hartville	18,186	16,758	682
Independent City				
Saint Louis		332,223	396,685	62

Montana
(56 counties, 145,552 sq. mi. land; pop. 917,621)

County	County seat or courthouse	2003 Pop.	1990 Pop.	Land area sq. mi.
Beaverhead	Dillon	8,919	8,424	5,542
Big Horn	Hardin	12,894	11,337	4,995
Blaine	Chinook	6,729	6,728	4,226
Broadwater	Townsend	4,430	3,318	1,191
Carbon	Red Lodge	9,770	8,080	2,048
Carter	Ekalaka	1,333	1,503	3,340
Cascade	Great Falls	79,561	77,691	2,698
Chouteau	Fort Benton	5,576	5,452	3,973
Custer	Miles City	11,369	11,697	3,783
Daniels	Scobey	1,940	2,266	1,426
Dawson	Glendive	8,776	9,505	2,373
Deer Lodge	Anaconda	8,953	10,356	737
Fallon	Baker	2,752	3,103	1,620
Fergus	Lewistown	11,695	12,083	4,339
Flathead	Kalispell	79,485	59,218	5,098
Gallatin	Bozeman	73,243	50,484	2,606
Garfield	Jordan	1,233	1,589	4,668
Glacier	Cut Bank	13,250	12,121	2,995
Golden Valley	Ryegate	1,047	912	1,175
Granite	Philipsburg	2,894	2,548	1,727
Hill	Havre	16,350	17,654	2,896
Jefferson	Boulder	10,499	7,939	1,657
Judith Basin	Stanford	2,192	2,282	1,870
Lake	Polson	27,197	21,041	1,494
Lewis & Clark	Helena	57,137	47,495	3,461
Liberty	Chester	2,055	2,295	1,430
Lincoln	Libby	18,835	17,481	3,613
McCone	Circle	1,818	2,276	2,643
Madison	Virginia City	6,967	5,989	3,587
Meagher	White Sulphur Springs	1,967	1,819	2,392
Mineral	Superior	3,884	3,315	1,220
Missoula	Missoula	98,616	78,687	2,598
Musselshell	Roundup	4,464	4,106	1,867
Park	Livingston	15,840	14,515	2,802
Petroleum	Winnett	491	519	1,654
Phillips	Malta	4,271	5,163	5,140
Pondera	Conrad	6,166	6,433	1,625
Powder River	Broadus	1,834	2,090	3,297
Powell	Deer Lodge	7,006	6,620	2,326
Prairie	Terry	1,154	1,383	1,737
Ravalli	Hamilton	38,662	25,010	2,394
Richland	Sidney	9,155	10,716	2,084
Roosevelt	Wolf Point	10,451	10,999	2,356

County	County seat or courthouse	2003 Pop.	1990 Pop.	Land area sq. mi.
Rosebud	Forsyth	9,303	10,505	5,012
Sanders	Thompson Falls	10,455	8,669	2,762
Sheridan	Plentywood	3,668	4,732	1,677
Silver Bow	Butte	33,208	33,941	718
Stillwater	Columbus	8,459	6,536	1,795
Sweet Grass	Big Timber	3,604	3,154	1,855
Teton	Choteau	6,369	6,271	2,273
Toole	Shelby	5,337	5,046	1,911
Treasure	Hysham	735	874	979
Valley	Glasgow	7,349	8,239	4,921
Wheatland	Harlowton	2,106	2,246	1,423
Wibaux	Wibaux	977	1,191	889
Yellowstone	Billings	133,191	113,419	2,635

Nebraska
(93 counties, 76,872 sq. mi. land; pop. 1,739,291)

County	County seat or courthouse	2003 Pop.	1990 Pop.	Land area sq. mi.
Adams	Hastings	30,890	29,625	563
Antelope	Neligh	7,211	7,965	857
Arthur	Arthur	398	462	715
Banner	Harrisburg	774	852	746
Blaine	Brewster	533	675	711
Boone	Albion	5,923	6,667	687
Box Butte	Alliance	11,669	13,130	1,075
Boyd	Butte	2,330	2,835	540
Brown	Ainsworth	3,490	3,657	1,221
Buffalo	Kearney	43,043	37,447	968
Burt	Tekamah	7,562	7,868	493
Butler	David City	8,899	8,601	584
Cass	Plattsmouth	25,242	21,318	559
Cedar	Hartington	9,242	10,131	740
Chase	Imperial	4,041	4,381	895
Cherry	Valentine	6,053	6,307	5,961
Cheyenne	Sidney	9,940	9,494	1,196
Clay	Clay Center	6,896	7,123	573
Colfax	Schuyler	10,497	9,139	413
Cuming	West Point	9,863	10,117	572
Custer	Broken Bow	11,542	12,270	2,576
Dakota	Dakota City	20,492	16,742	264
Dawes	Chadron	8,985	9,021	1,396
Dawson	Lexington	24,598	19,940	1,013
Deuel	Chappell	2,053	2,237	440
Dixon	Ponca	6,121	6,143	476
Dodge	Fremont	35,961	34,500	534
Douglas	Omaha	476,703	416,444	331
Dundy	Benkelman	2,225	2,582	920
Fillmore	Geneva	6,425	7,103	576
Franklin	Franklin	3,442	3,938	575
Frontier	Stockville	2,904	3,101	975
Furnas	Beaver City	5,196	5,553	718
Gage	Beatrice	23,363	22,794	855
Garden	Oshkosh	2,193	2,460	1,704
Garfield	Burwell	1,841	2,141	570
Gosper	Elwood	2,089	1,928	458
Grant	Hyannis	695	769	776
Greeley	Greeley	2,603	3,006	569
Hall	Grand Island	54,293	48,925	546
Hamilton	Aurora	9,478	8,862	544
Harlan	Alma	3,664	3,810	553
Hayes	Hayes Center	1,104	1,222	713
Hitchcock	Trenton	3,031	3,750	710
Holt	O'Neill	11,078	12,599	2,413
Hooker	Mullen	737	793	721
Howard	Saint Paul	6,632	6,057	569
Jefferson	Fairbury	8,082	8,759	573
Johnson	Tecumseh	4,429	4,673	376
Kearney	Minden	6,862	6,629	516
Keith	Ogallala	8,472	8,584	1,061
Keya Paha	Springview	953	1,029	773
Kimball	Kimball	3,853	4,108	952
Knox	Center	9,054	9,564	1,108
Lancaster	Lincoln	260,995	213,641	839
Lincoln	North Platte	34,802	32,508	2,564
Logan	Stapleton	710	878	571
Loup	Taylor	744	683	570
McPherson	Tryon	542	546	859
Madison	Madison	35,777	32,655	573
Merrick	Central City	8,134	8,062	485
Morrill	Bridgeport	5,284	5,423	1,424
Nance	Fullerton	3,741	4,275	441
Nemaha	Auburn	7,136	7,980	409
Nuckolls	Nelson	4,841	5,786	575
Otoe	Nebraska City	15,504	14,252	616
Pawnee	Pawnee City	2,918	3,317	432
Perkins	Grant	3,057	3,367	883
Phelps	Holdrege	9,630	9,715	540
Pierce	Pierce	7,713	7,827	574
Platte	Columbus	31,197	29,820	678
Polk	Osceola	5,478	5,655	439
Red Willow	McCook	11,252	11,705	717
Richardson	Falls City	9,008	9,937	553
Rock	Bassett	1,613	2,019	1,008
Saline	Wilber	14,189	12,715	575
Sarpy	Papillion	132,476	102,583	241
Saunders	Wahoo	20,008	18,285	754

County	County seat or courthouse	2003 Pop.	1990 Pop.	Land area sq. mi.
Scotts Bluff	Gering	36,954	36,025	739
Seward	Seward	16,671	15,450	575
Sheridan	Rushville	5,808	6,750	2,441
Sherman	Loup City	3,127	3,718	566
Sioux	Harrison	1,491	1,549	2,067
Stanton	Stanton	6,582	6,244	430
Thayer	Hebron	5,662	6,635	575
Thomas	Thedford	669	851	713
Thurston	Pender	7,142	6,936	394
Valley	Ord	4,572	5,169	568
Washington	Blair	19,690	16,607	390
Wayne	Wayne	9,474	9,364	443
Webster	Red Cloud	3,867	4,279	575
Wheeler	Bartlett	821	948	575
York	York	14,363	14,428	576

Nevada

(16 counties, 1 ind. city, 109,826 sq. mi. land; pop. 2,241,154)

County	County seat or courthouse	2003 Pop.	1990 Pop.	Land area sq. mi.
Churchill	Fallon	24,773	17,938	4,929
Clark	Las Vegas	1,576,541	741,368	7,910
Douglas	Minden	44,110	27,637	710
Elko	Elko	44,094	33,463	17,179
Esmeralda	Goldfield	858	1,344	3,589
Eureka	Eureka	1,513	1,547	4,176
Humboldt	Winnemucca	14,709	12,844	9,648
Lander	Battle Mountain	5,049	6,266	5,494
Lincoln	Pioche	4,264	3,775	10,634
Lyon	Yerington	40,126	20,001	1,994
Mineral	Hawthorne	4,791	6,475	3,756
Nye	Tonopah	35,717	17,781	18,147
Pershing	Lovelock	6,444	4,336	6,037
Storey	Virginia City	3,511	2,526	263
Washoe	Reno	370,853	254,667	6,342
White Pine	Ely	8,490	9,264	8,876
Independent City				
Carson City		55,311	40,443	143

New Hampshire

(10 counties, 8,968 sq. mi. land; pop. 1,287,687)

County	County seat or courthouse	2003 Pop.	1990 Pop.	Land area sq. mi.
Belknap	Laconia	60,356	49,216	401
Carroll	Ossipee	46,134	35,410	934
Cheshire	Keene	75,965	70,121	707
Coos	Lancaster	33,019	34,828	1,800
Grafton	Woodsville	84,038	74,929	1,713
Hillsborough	Nashua	394,663	335,838	876
Merrimack	Concord	143,622	120,240	934
Rockingham	Brentwood	290,102	245,845	695
Strafford	Dover	117,740	104,233	369
Sullivan	Newport	42,048	38,592	537

New Jersey

(21 counties, 7,417 sq. mi. land; pop. 8,638,396)

County	County seat or courthouse	2003 Pop.	1990 Pop.	Land area sq. mi.
Atlantic	Mays Landing	263,410	224,327	561
Bergen	Hackensack	897,569	825,380	234
Burlington	Mount Holly	444,381	395,066	805
Camden	Camden	513,909	502,824	222
Cape May	Cape May Court House	101,845	95,089	255
Cumberland	Bridgeton	149,306	138,053	489
Essex	Newark	796,313	777,964	126
Gloucester	Woodbury	266,962	230,082	325
Hudson	Jersey City	607,419	553,099	47
Hunterdon	Flemington	128,265	107,852	430
Mercer	Trenton	361,981	325,759	226
Middlesex	New Brunswick	780,995	671,712	310
Monmouth	Freehold	632,274	553,192	472
Morris	Morristown	483,150	421,330	469
Ocean	Toms River	546,081	433,203	636
Passaic	Paterson	498,357	470,872	185
Salem	Salem	64,854	65,294	338
Somerset	Somerville	311,600	240,222	305
Sussex	Newton	151,146	130,936	521
Union	Elizabeth	529,360	493,819	103
Warren	Belvidere	109,219	91,675	358

New Mexico

(33 counties, 121,356 sq. mi. land; pop. 1,874,614)

County	County seat or courthouse	2003 Pop.	1990 Pop.	Land area sq. mi.
Bernalillo	Albuquerque	581,442	480,577	1,166
Catron	Reserve	3,415	2,563	6,928
Chaves	Roswell	60,591	57,849	6,071
Cibola	Grants	26,453	23,794	4,539
Colfax	Raton	14,051	12,925	3,757
Curry	Clovis	45,440	42,207	1,406
DeBaca	Fort Sumner	2,091	2,252	2,325
Dona Ana	Las Cruces	182,165	135,510	3,807
Eddy	Carlsbad	51,470	48,605	4,182
Grant	Silver City	29,818	27,676	3,966
Guadalupe	Santa Rosa	4,574	4,156	3,030
Harding	Mosquero	747	987	2,125
Hidalgo	Lordsburg	5,234	5,958	3,446
Lea	Lovington	55,504	55,765	4,393
Lincoln	Carrizozo	20,322	12,219	4,831
Los Alamos	Los Alamos	18,802	18,115	109
Luna	Deming	25,732	18,110	2,965
McKinley	Gallup	72,555	60,686	5,449
Mora	Mora	5,216	4,264	1,931
Otero	Alamogordo	62,371	51,928	6,627
Quay	Tucumcari	9,605	10,823	2,875
Rio Arriba	Tierra Amarilla	40,731	34,365	5,858
Roosevelt	Portales	18,107	16,702	2,449
Sandoval	Bernalillo	98,786	63,319	3,709
San Juan	Aztec	122,272	91,605	5,514
San Miguel	Las Vegas	29,670	25,743	4,717
Santa Fe	Santa Fe	136,423	98,928	1,909
Sierra	Truth or Consequences	13,125	9,912	4,180
Socorro	Socorro	18,178	14,764	6,646
Taos	Taos	31,269	23,118	2,203
Torrance	Estancia	16,802	10,285	3,345
Union	Clayton	3,814	4,124	3,830
Valencia	Los Lunas	67,839	45,235	1,068

New York

(62 counties, 47,214 sq. mi. land; pop. 19,190,115)

County	County seat or courthouse	2003 Pop.	1990 Pop.	Land area sq. mi.
Albany	Albany	297,845	292,812	523
Allegany	Belmont	50,562	50,470	1,030
Bronx[1]	Bronx	1,363,198	1,203,789	42
Broome	Binghamton	199,360	212,160	707
Cattaraugus	Little Valley	83,354	84,234	1,310
Cayuga	Auburn	81,726	82,313	693
Chautauqua	Mayville	137,645	141,895	1,062
Chemung	Elmira	90,413	95,195	408
Chenango	Norwich	51,659	51,768	894
Clinton	Plattsburgh	81,366	85,969	1,039
Columbia	Hudson	63,405	62,982	636
Cortland	Cortland	48,691	48,963	500
Delaware	Delhi	47,226	47,352	1,446
Dutchess	Poughkeepsie	290,885	259,462	802
Erie	Buffalo	941,293	968,584	1,044
Essex	Elizabethtown	38,992	37,152	1,797
Franklin	Malone	51,056	46,540	1,631
Fulton	Johnstown	55,206	54,191	496
Genesee	Batavia	60,020	60,060	494
Greene	Catskill	48,865	44,739	648
Hamilton	Lake Pleasant	5,278	5,279	1,720
Herkimer	Herkimer	63,704	65,809	1,411
Jefferson	Watertown	114,651	110,943	1,272
Kings[1]	Brooklyn	2,472,523	2,300,664	71
Lewis	Lowville	26,636	26,796	1,275
Livingston	Geneseo	64,658	62,372	632
Madison	Wampsville	70,182	69,166	656
Monroe	Rochester	736,738	713,968	659
Montgomery	Fonda	49,371	51,981	405
Nassau	Mineola	1,339,463	1,287,873	287
New York[1]	New York	1,564,798	1,487,536	23
Niagara	Lockport	218,150	220,756	523
Oneida	Utica	234,373	250,836	1,213
Onondaga	Syracuse	460,517	468,973	780
Ontario	Canandaigua	102,445	95,101	644
Orange	Goshen	363,153	307,571	816
Orleans	Albion	43,629	41,846	391
Oswego	Oswego	123,495	121,785	953
Otsego	Cooperstown	62,196	60,390	1,003
Putnam	Carmel	99,550	83,941	231
Queens[1]	Jamaica	2,225,486	1,951,598	109
Rensselaer	Troy	154,007	154,429	654
Richmond[1]	Saint George	459,737	378,977	58
Rockland	New City	292,989	265,475	174
Saint Lawrence	Canton	111,655	111,974	2,686
Saratoga	Ballston Spa	209,818	181,276	812
Schenectady	Schenectady	147,289	149,285	206
Schoharie	Schoharie	31,685	31,840	622
Schuyler	Watkins Glen	19,455	18,662	329
Seneca	Waterloo	35,183	33,683	325
Steuben	Bath	99,012	99,088	1,393
Suffolk	Riverhead	1,468,037	1,321,339	912
Sullivan	Monticello	74,948	69,277	970
Tioga	Owego	51,746	52,337	519
Tompkins	Ithaca	101,411	94,097	476
Ulster	Kingston	181,111	165,380	1,126
Warren	Lake George	64,715	59,209	869
Washington	Hudson Falls	61,872	59,330	835
Wayne	Lyons	93,728	89,123	604
Westchester	White Plains	940,302	874,866	433
Wyoming	Warsaw	42,932	42,507	593
Yates	Penn Yan	24,720	22,810	338

(1) New York City comprises 5 counties: Bronx, Kings (Brooklyn), New York (Manhattan), Queens, and Richmond (Staten Island).

North Carolina

(100 counties, 48,711 sq. mi. land; pop. 8,407,248)

County	County seat or courthouse	2003 Pop.	1990 Pop.	Land area sq. mi.
Alamance	Graham	136,773	108,213	430
Alexander	Taylorsville	34,784	27,544	260
Alleghany	Sparta	10,874	9,590	235
Anson	Wadesboro	25,168	23,474	532
Ashe	Jefferson	25,071	22,209	426
Avery	Newland	17,700	14,867	247
Beaufort	Washington	45,407	42,283	828
Bertie	Windsor	19,544	20,388	699
Bladen	Elizabethtown	32,723	28,663	875
Brunswick	Bolivia	81,592	50,985	855
Buncombe	Asheville	212,672	174,357	656
Burke	Morganton	89,657	75,740	507
Cabarrus	Concord	142,740	98,935	364
Caldwell	Lenoir	78,728	70,709	472
Camden	Camden	7,863	5,904	241
Carteret	Beaufort	60,865	52,407	520
Caswell	Yanceyville	23,632	20,662	425
Catawba	Newton	146,971	118,412	400
Chatham	Pittsboro	55,238	38,979	683
Cherokee	Murphy	25,048	20,170	455
Chowan	Edenton	14,433	13,506	173
Clay	Hayesville	9,288	7,155	215
Cleveland	Shelby	98,249	84,958	465
Columbus	Whiteville	54,518	49,587	935
Craven	New Bern	91,754	81,812	708
Cumberland	Fayetteville	303,953	274,713	653
Currituck	Currituck	20,834	13,736	262
Dare	Manteo	33,116	22,746	384
Davidson	Lexington	152,178	126,688	552
Davie	Mocksville	37,151	27,859	265
Duplin	Kenansville	51,181	39,995	818
Durham	Durham	236,781	181,844	290
Edgecombe	Tarboro	54,895	56,692	505
Forsyth	Winston-Salem	317,810	265,855	410
Franklin	Louisburg	52,006	36,414	492
Gaston	Gastonia	193,097	174,769	356
Gates	Gatesville	10,754	9,305	341
Graham	Robbinsville	7,994	7,196	292
Granville	Oxford	51,852	38,341	531
Greene	Snow Hill	19,990	15,384	265
Guilford	Greensboro	433,789	347,431	649
Halifax	Halifax	56,491	55,516	725
Harnett	Lillington	99,407	67,833	595
Haywood	Waynesville	55,442	46,948	554
Henderson	Hendersonville	93,871	69,747	374
Hertford	Winton	22,310	22,317	353
Hoke	Raeford	37,643	22,856	391
Hyde	Swan Quarter	5,567	5,411	613
Iredell	Statesville	133,387	93,205	576
Jackson	Sylva	34,304	26,835	491
Johnston	Smithfield	136,802	81,306	792
Jones	Trenton	10,197	9,361	472
Lee	Sanford	49,138	41,370	257
Lenoir	Kinston	58,549	57,274	400
Lincoln	Lincolnton	67,275	50,319	299
McDowell	Marion	42,867	35,681	442
Macon	Franklin	31,175	23,504	516
Madison	Marshall	19,858	16,953	449
Martin	Williamston	25,070	25,078	461
Mecklenburg	Charlotte	752,366	511,211	526
Mitchell	Bakersville	15,831	14,433	221
Montgomery	Troy	27,306	23,359	492
Moore	Carthage	79,267	59,000	698
Nash	Nashville	89,732	76,677	540
New Hanover	Wilmington	168,088	120,284	199
Northampton	Jackson	21,782	21,004	536
Onslow	Jacksonville	147,524	149,838	767
Orange	Hillsborough	118,183	93,662	400
Pamlico	Bayboro	12,783	11,368	337
Pasquotank	Elizabeth City	36,071	31,298	227
Pender	Burgaw	43,527	28,855	871
Perquimans	Hertford	11,644	10,447	247
Person	Roxboro	36,864	30,180	392
Pitt	Greenville	138,690	108,480	652
Polk	Columbus	18,824	14,458	238
Randolph	Asheboro	135,151	106,546	787
Richmond	Rockingham	46,643	44,511	474
Robeson	Lumberton	125,756	105,170	949
Rockingham	Wentworth	92,590	86,064	566
Rowan	Salisbury	133,931	110,605	511
Rutherford	Rutherfordton	63,540	56,956	564
Sampson	Clinton	62,037	47,297	945
Scotland	Laurinburg	35,757	33,763	319
Stanly	Albemarle	58,846	51,765	395
Stokes	Danbury	45,168	37,224	452
Surry	Dobson	72,278	61,704	537
Swain	Bryson City	13,126	11,268	528
Transylvania	Brevard	29,406	25,520	378
Tyrrell	Columbia	4,156	3,856	390
Union	Monroe	145,986	84,210	637
Vance	Henderson	43,736	38,892	254
Wake	Raleigh	695,681	426,311	832
Warren	Warrenton	19,812	17,265	429
Washington	Plymouth	13,399	13,997	348
Watauga	Boone	42,808	36,952	313
Wayne	Goldsboro	113,104	104,666	553
Wilkes	Wilkesboro	67,055	59,393	757
Wilson	Wilson	75,338	66,061	371
Yadkin	Yadkinville	37,421	30,488	336
Yancey	Burnsville	18,069	15,419	312

North Dakota

(53 counties, 68,976 sq. mi. land; pop. 633,837)

County	County seat or courthouse	2003 Pop.	1990 Pop.	Land area sq. mi.
Adams	Hettinger	2,505	3,174	988
Barnes	Valley City	11,083	12,545	1,492
Benson	Minnewaukan	6,881	7,198	1,381
Billings	Medora	850	1,108	1,151
Bottineau	Bottineau	6,820	8,011	1,669
Bowman	Bowman	3,045	3,596	1,162
Burke	Bowbells	2,098	3,002	1,104
Burleigh	Bismarck	71,693	60,131	1,633
Cass	Fargo	127,138	102,874	1,765
Cavalier	Langdon	4,484	6,064	1,488
Dickey	Ellendale	5,492	6,107	1,131
Divide	Crosby	2,247	2,899	1,260
Dunn	Manning	3,539	4,005	2,010
Eddy	New Rockford	2,598	2,951	630
Emmons	Linton	4,005	4,830	1,510
Foster	Carrington	3,495	3,983	635
Golden Valley	Beach	1,828	2,108	1,002
Grand Forks	Grand Forks	64,736	70,683	1,438
Grant	Carson	2,665	3,549	1,659
Griggs	Cooperstown	2,578	3,303	709
Hettinger	Mott	2,548	3,445	1,132
Kidder	Steele	2,577	3,332	1,351
La Moure	La Moure	4,512	5,383	1,147
Logan	Napoleon	2,157	2,847	993
McHenry	Towner	5,722	6,528	1,874
McIntosh	Ashley	3,178	4,021	975
McKenzie	Watford City	5,615	6,383	2,742
McLean	Washburn	8,935	10,457	2,110
Mercer	Stanton	8,449	9,808	1,045
Morton	Mandan	25,135	23,700	1,926
Mountrail	Stanley	6,480	7,021	1,824
Nelson	Lakota	3,454	4,410	982
Oliver	Center	1,905	2,381	724
Pembina	Cavalier	8,201	9,238	1,119
Pierce	Rugby	4,480	5,052	1,018
Ramsey	Devils Lake	11,616	12,681	1,185
Ransom	Lisbon	5,838	5,921	863
Renville	Mohall	2,473	3,160	875
Richland	Wahpeton	17,598	18,148	1,437
Rolette	Rolla	13,732	12,772	902
Sargent	Forman	4,225	4,549	859
Sheridan	McClusky	1,540	2,148	972
Sioux	Fort Yates	4,070	3,761	1,094
Slope	Amidon	746	907	1,218
Stark	Dickinson	22,131	22,832	1,338
Steele	Finley	2,081	2,420	712
Stutsman	Jamestown	21,255	22,241	2,221
Towner	Cando	2,667	3,627	1,025
Traill	Hillsboro	8,278	8,752	862
Walsh	Grafton	11,720	13,840	1,282
Ward	Minot	56,721	57,921	2,013
Wells	Fessenden	4,702	5,864	1,271
Williams	Williston	19,316	21,129	2,070

Ohio

(88 counties, 40,048 sq. mi. land; pop. 11,435,798)

County	County seat or courthouse	2003 Pop.	1990 Pop.	Land area sq. mi.
Adams	West Union	28,026	25,371	584
Allen	Lima	108,241	109,755	404
Ashland	Ashland	53,749	47,507	424
Ashtabula	Jefferson	103,120	99,880	702
Athens	Athens	64,380	59,549	507
Auglaize	Wapakoneta	46,740	44,585	401
Belmont	Saint Clairsville	69,636	71,074	537
Brown	Georgetown	43,807	34,966	492
Butler	Hamilton	343,207	291,479	467
Carroll	Carrollton	29,599	26,521	395
Champaign	Urbana	39,544	36,019	429
Clark	Springfield	143,351	147,538	400
Clermont	Batavia	185,799	150,094	452
Clinton	Wilmington	41,756	35,444	411
Columbiana	Lisbon	111,523	108,276	532
Coshocton	Coshocton	37,132	35,427	564
Crawford	Bucyrus	46,091	47,870	402

County	County seat or courthouse	2003 Pop.	1990 Pop.	Land area sq. mi.
Cuyahoga	Cleveland	1,363,888	1,412,140	458
Darke	Greenville	52,960	53,617	600
Defiance	Defiance	39,054	39,350	411
Delaware	Delaware	132,797	66,929	442
Erie	Sandusky	78,709	76,781	255
Fairfield	Lancaster	132,549	103,468	505
Fayette	Washington Court House	28,158	27,466	407
Franklin	Columbus	1,088,944	961,437	540
Fulton	Wauseon	42,446	38,498	407
Gallia	Gallipolis	31,398	30,954	469
Geauga	Chardon	93,941	81,087	404
Greene	Xenia	151,257	136,731	415
Guernsey	Cambridge	41,362	39,024	522
Hamilton	Cincinnati	823,472	866,228	407
Hancock	Findlay	73,133	65,536	531
Hardin	Kenton	31,608	31,111	470
Harrison	Cadiz	15,967	16,085	404
Henry	Napoleon	29,318	29,108	417
Highland	Hillsboro	41,963	35,728	553
Hocking	Logan	28,644	25,533	423
Holmes	Millersburg	40,681	32,849	423
Huron	Norwalk	60,231	56,238	493
Jackson	Jackson	33,074	30,230	420
Jefferson	Steubenville	71,888	80,298	410
Knox	Mount Vernon	56,930	47,473	527
Lake	Painesville	228,878	215,500	228
Lawrence	Ironton	62,550	61,834	455
Licking	Newark	150,634	128,300	687
Logan	Bellefontaine	46,411	42,310	458
Lorain	Elyria	291,164	271,126	493
Lucas	Toledo	454,216	462,361	340
Madison	London	40,624	37,078	465
Mahoning	Youngstown	251,660	264,806	415
Marion	Marion	66,396	64,274	404
Medina	Medina	161,641	122,354	422
Meigs	Pomeroy	23,242	22,987	429
Mercer	Celina	40,933	39,443	463
Miami	Troy	100,230	93,184	407
Monroe	Woodsfield	14,927	15,497	456
Montgomery	Dayton	552,187	573,809	462
Morgan	McConnelsville	14,843	14,194	418
Morrow	Mount Gilead	33,568	27,749	406
Muskingum	Zanesville	85,423	82,068	665
Noble	Caldwell	14,054	11,336	399
Ottawa	Port Clinton	41,192	40,029	255
Paulding	Paulding	19,665	20,488	416
Perry	New Lexington	35,074	31,557	410
Pickaway	Circleville	51,723	48,248	502
Pike	Waverly	28,194	24,249	441
Portage	Ravenna	154,870	142,585	492
Preble	Eaton	42,417	40,113	425
Putnam	Ottawa	34,754	33,819	484
Richland	Mansfield	128,267	126,137	497
Ross	Chillicothe	74,424	69,330	688
Sandusky	Fremont	61,753	61,963	409
Scioto	Portsmouth	77,453	80,327	612
Seneca	Tiffin	57,734	59,733	551
Shelby	Sidney	48,566	44,915	409
Stark	Canton	377,519	367,585	576
Summit	Akron	546,773	514,990	413
Trumbull	Warren	221,785	227,795	616
Tuscarawas	New Philadelphia	91,706	84,090	568
Union	Marysville	43,750	31,969	437
Van Wert	Van Wert	29,277	30,464	410
Vinton	McArthur	13,231	11,098	414
Warren	Lebanon	181,743	113,973	400
Washington	Marietta	62,505	62,254	635
Wayne	Wooster	113,121	101,461	555
Williams	Bryan	38,802	36,956	422
Wood	Bowling Green	123,020	113,269	617
Wyandot	Upper Sandusky	22,826	22,254	406

Oklahoma

(77 counties, 68,667 sq. mi. land; pop. 3,511,532)

County	County seat or courthouse	2003 Pop.	1990 Pop.	Land area sq. mi.
Adair	Stillwell	21,614	18,421	576
Alfalfa	Cherokee	5,910	6,416	867
Atoka	Atoka	14,142	12,778	978
Beaver	Beaver	5,582	6,023	1,814
Beckham	Sayre	19,894	18,812	902
Blaine	Watonga	11,678	11,470	928
Bryan	Durant	37,306	32,089	909
Caddo	Anadarko	30,070	29,550	1,278
Canadian	El Reno	92,904	74,409	900
Carter	Ardmore	46,396	42,919	824
Cherokee	Tahlequah	43,783	34,049	751
Choctaw	Hugo	15,431	15,302	774
Cimarron	Boise City	2,961	3,301	1,835
Cleveland	Norman	219,966	174,253	536
Coal	Coalgate	5,946	5,780	518
Comanche	Lawton	113,890	111,486	1,069
Cotton	Walters	6,582	6,651	637
Craig	Vinita	14,880	14,104	761
Creek	Sapulpa	68,794	60,915	956
Custer	Arapaho	24,962	26,897	987
Delaware	Jay	38,709	28,070	741
Dewey	Taloga	4,549	5,551	1,000
Ellis	Arnett	3,996	4,497	1,229
Garfield	Enid	57,105	56,735	1,058
Garvin	Pauls Valley	27,218	26,605	807
Grady	Chickasha	47,439	41,747	1,101
Grant	Medford	4,973	5,689	1,001
Greer	Mangum	5,888	6,559	639
Harmon	Hollis	3,053	3,793	538
Harper	Buffalo	3,398	4,063	1,039
Haskell	Stigler	12,044	10,940	577
Hughes	Holdenville	13,898	13,014	807
Jackson	Altus	27,338	28,764	803
Jefferson	Waurika	6,535	7,010	759
Johnston	Tishomingo	10,522	10,032	645
Kay	Newkirk	47,260	48,056	919
Kingfisher	Kingfisher	14,072	13,212	903
Kiowa	Hobart	9,977	11,347	1,015
Latimer	Wilburton	10,575	10,333	722
Le Flore	Poteau	48,896	43,270	1,586
Lincoln	Chandler	32,262	29,216	958
Logan	Guthrie	35,420	29,011	744
Love	Marietta	8,905	7,788	515
McClain	Purcell	28,595	22,795	570
McCurtain	Idabel	34,006	33,433	1,852
McIntosh	Eufaula	19,735	16,779	620
Major	Fairview	7,422	8,055	957
Marshall	Madill	13,652	10,829	371
Mayes	Pryor	38,870	33,366	656
Murray	Sulphur	12,718	12,042	418
Muskogee	Muskogee	70,255	68,078	814
Noble	Perry	11,251	11,045	732
Nowata	Nowata	10,836	9,992	565
Okfuskee	Okemah	11,679	11,551	625
Oklahoma	Oklahoma City	676,066	599,611	709
Okmulgee	Okmulgee	39,681	36,490	697
Osage	Pawhuska	45,249	41,645	2,251
Ottawa	Miami	32,761	30,561	471
Pawnee	Pawnee	16,789	15,575	569
Payne	Stillwater	71,059	61,507	686
Pittsburg	McAlester	44,168	40,950	1,306
Pontotoc	Ada	35,174	34,119	720
Pottawatomie	Shawnee	67,348	58,760	788
Pushmataha	Antlers	11,750	10,997	1,397
Roger Mills	Cheyenne	3,201	4,147	1,142
Rogers	Claremore	77,193	55,170	675
Seminole	Wewoka	24,489	25,412	633
Sequoyah	Sallisaw	39,979	33,828	674
Stephens	Duncan	42,474	42,299	874
Texas	Guymon	19,935	16,419	2,037
Tillman	Frederick	8,835	10,384	872
Tulsa	Tulsa	570,313	503,341	570
Wagoner	Wagoner	61,827	47,883	563
Washington	Bartlesville	49,121	48,066	417
Washita	Cordell	11,247	11,441	1,003
Woods	Alva	8,670	9,103	1,287
Woodward	Woodward	18,461	18,976	1,242

Oregon

(36 counties, 95,997 sq. mi. land; pop. 3,559,596)

County	County seat or courthouse	2003 Pop.	1990 Pop.	Land area sq. mi.
Baker	Baker City	16,375	15,317	3,068
Benton	Corvallis	79,335	70,811	676
Clackamas	Oregon City	357,435	278,850	1,868
Clatsop	Astoria	35,820	33,301	827
Columbia	Saint Helens	46,261	37,557	657
Coos	Coquille	63,019	60,273	1,600
Crook	Prineville	20,600	14,111	2,979
Curry	Gold Beach	21,813	19,327	1,627
Deschutes	Bend	129,492	74,976	3,018
Douglas	Roseburg	102,332	94,649	5,037
Gilliam	Condon	1,778	1,717	1,204
Grant	Canyon City	7,454	7,853	4,529
Harney	Burns	7,184	7,060	10,134
Hood River	Hood River	20,760	16,903	522
Jackson	Medford	190,077	146,387	2,785
Jefferson	Madras	19,667	13,676	1,781
Josephine	Grants Pass	79,030	62,649	1,640
Klamath	Klamath Falls	64,769	57,702	5,944
Lake	Lakeview	7,440	7,186	8,136
Lane	Eugene	330,527	282,912	4,554
Lincoln	Newport	44,667	38,889	980
Linn	Albany	106,121	91,227	2,292
Malheur	Vale	31,239	26,038	9,887
Marion	Salem	296,995	228,483	1,184
Morrow	Heppner	11,627	7,625	2,032
Multnomah	Portland	677,813	583,887	435
Polk	Dallas	65,995	49,541	741

County	County seat or courthouse	2003 Pop.	1990 Pop.	Land area sq. mi.
Sherman	Moro	1,754	1,918	823
Tillamook	Tillamook	24,590	21,570	1,102
Umatilla	Pendleton	72,008	59,249	3,215
Union	La Grande	24,561	23,598	2,037
Wallowa	Enterprise	7,082	6,911	3,145
Wasco	The Dalles	23,591	21,683	2,381
Washington	Hillsboro	479,496	311,554	724
Wheeler	Fossil	1,505	1,396	1,715
Yamhill	McMinnville	89,384	65,551	716

Pennsylvania

(67 counties, 44,817 sq. mi. land; pop. 12,365,455)

County	County seat or courthouse	2003 Pop.	1990 Pop.	Land area sq. mi.
Adams	Gettysburg	96,456	78,274	520
Allegheny	Pittsburgh	1,261,303	1,336,449	730
Armstrong	Kittanning	71,659	73,478	654
Beaver	Beaver	178,697	186,093	434
Bedford	Bedford	49,941	47,919	1,015
Berks	Reading	385,307	336,523	859
Blair	Hollidaysburg	127,175	130,542	526
Bradford	Towanda	62,643	60,967	1,151
Bucks	Doylestown	613,110	541,174	607
Butler	Butler	180,040	152,013	789
Cambria	Ebensburg	149,453	163,062	688
Cameron	Emporium	5,777	5,913	397
Carbon	Jim Thorpe	60,131	56,803	381
Centre	Bellefonte	141,636	124,812	1,108
Chester	West Chester	457,393	376,389	756
Clarion	Clarion	41,208	41,699	602
Clearfield	Clearfield	82,874	78,097	1,147
Clinton	Lock Haven	37,435	37,182	891
Columbia	Bloomsburg	64,605	63,202	486
Crawford	Meadville	89,846	86,166	1,013
Cumberland	Carlisle	219,892	195,257	550
Dauphin	Harrisburg	253,388	237,813	525
Delaware	Media	554,432	547,658	184
Elk	Ridgway	34,310	34,878	829
Erie	Erie	279,966	275,575	802
Fayette	Uniontown	146,121	145,351	790
Forest	Tionesta	4,989	4,802	428
Franklin	Chambersburg	133,155	121,082	772
Fulton	McConnellsburg	14,534	13,837	438
Greene	Waynesburg	40,398	39,550	576
Huntingdon	Huntingdon	45,865	44,164	874
Indiana	Indiana	89,054	89,994	829
Jefferson	Brookville	45,945	46,083	655
Juniata	Mifflintown	23,065	20,625	392
Lackawanna	Scranton	210,458	219,097	459
Lancaster	Lancaster	482,775	422,822	949
Lawrence	New Castle	93,408	96,246	360
Lebanon	Lebanon	122,652	113,744	362
Lehigh	Allentown	320,517	291,130	347
Luzerne	Wilkes-Barre	313,528	328,149	891
Lycoming	Williamsport	118,438	118,710	1,235
McKean	Smethport	45,236	47,131	982
Mercer	Mercer	119,895	121,003	672
Mifflin	Lewistown	46,335	46,197	412
Monroe	Stroudsburg	154,495	95,681	609
Montgomery	Norristown	770,747	678,193	483
Montour	Danville	18,083	17,735	131
Northampton	Easton	278,169	247,110	374
Northumberland	Sunbury	93,323	96,771	460
Perry	New Bloomfield	44,188	41,172	554
Philadelphia	Philadelphia	1,479,339	1,585,577	135
Pike	Milford	52,163	28,032	547
Potter	Coudersport	18,141	16,717	1,081
Schuylkill	Pottsville	147,944	152,585	778
Snyder	Middleburg	38,015	36,680	331
Somerset	Somerset	79,365	78,218	1,075
Sullivan	Laporte	6,427	6,104	450
Susquehanna	Montrose	41,812	40,380	823
Tioga	Wellsboro	41,557	41,126	1,134
Union	Lewisburg	42,552	36,176	317
Venango	Franklin	56,600	59,381	675
Warren	Warren	42,820	45,050	883
Washington	Washington	204,286	204,584	857
Wayne	Honesdale	49,092	39,944	729
Westmoreland	Greensburg	368,224	370,321	1,025
Wyoming	Tunkhannock	28,153	28,076	397
York	York	394,915	339,574	904

Rhode Island

(5 counties, 1,045 sq. mi. land; pop. 1,076,164)

County	County seat or courthouse	2003 Pop.	1990 Pop.	Land area sq. mi.
Bristol	Bristol	50,989	48,859	25
Kent	East Greenwich	171,297	161,143	170
Newport	Newport	85,934	87,194	104
Providence	Providence	639,442	596,270	413
Washington	West Kingston	128,502	109,998	333

South Carolina

(46 counties, 30,110 sq. mi. land; pop. 4,147,152)

County	County seat or courthouse	2003 Pop.	1990 Pop.	Land area sq. mi.
Abbeville	Abbeville	26,381	23,862	508
Aiken	Aiken	146,736	120,991	1,073
Allendale	Allendale	10,934	11,727	408
Anderson	Anderson	171,510	145,177	718
Bamberg	Bamberg	16,040	16,902	393
Barnwell	Barnwell	23,369	20,293	548
Beaufort	Beaufort	132,889	86,425	587
Berkeley	Moncks Corner	146,449	128,658	1,098
Calhoun	Saint Matthews	15,367	12,753	380
Charleston	Charleston	321,014	295,159	919
Cherokee	Gaffney	53,555	44,506	393
Chester	Chester	33,906	32,170	581
Chesterfield	Chesterfield	43,251	38,575	799
Clarendon	Manning	32,871	28,450	607
Colleton	Walterboro	39,173	34,377	1,056
Darlington	Darlington	67,956	61,851	561
Dillon	Dillon	31,027	29,114	405
Dorchester	Saint George	104,168	83,060	575
Edgefield	Edgefield	24,703	18,360	502
Fairfield	Winnsboro	23,840	22,295	687
Florence	Florence	128,335	114,344	800
Georgetown	Georgetown	58,924	46,302	815
Greenville	Greenville	395,357	320,127	790
Greenwood	Greenwood	67,503	59,567	456
Hampton	Hampton	21,391	18,186	560
Horry	Conway	210,757	144,053	1,134
Jasper	Ridgeland	20,998	15,487	656
Kershaw	Camden	54,481	43,599	726
Lancaster	Lancaster	62,520	54,516	549
Laurens	Laurens	70,269	58,132	715
Lee	Bishopville	20,331	18,437	410
Lexington	Lexington	226,528	167,526	699
McCormick	McCormick	10,233	8,868	360
Marion	Marion	35,113	33,899	489
Marlboro	Bennettsville	28,411	29,716	480
Newberry	Newberry	36,840	33,172	631
Oconee	Walhalla	68,523	57,494	625
Orangeburg	Orangeburg	91,028	84,804	1,106
Pickens	Pickens	112,859	93,896	497
Richland	Columbia	332,104	286,321	756
Saluda	Saluda	19,087	16,441	452
Spartanburg	Spartanburg	261,281	226,793	811
Sumter	Sumter	105,957	101,276	665
Union	Union	29,105	30,337	514
Williamsburg	Kingstree	36,008	36,815	934
York	York	178,070	131,497	682

South Dakota

(66 counties, 75,885 sq. mi. land; pop. 764,309)

County	County seat or courthouse	2003 Pop.	1990 Pop.	Land area sq. mi.
Aurora	Plankinton	2,926	3,135	708
Beadle	Huron	16,269	18,253	1,259
Bennett	Martin	3,530	3,206	1,185
Bon Homme	Tyndall	7,104	7,089	563
Brookings	Brookings	28,265	25,207	794
Brown	Aberdeen	34,666	35,580	1,713
Brule	Chamberlain	5,205	5,485	819
Buffalo	Gannvalley	1,994	1,759	471
Butte	Belle Fourche	9,212	7,914	2,249
Campbell	Mound City	1,679	1,965	736
Charles Mix	Lake Andes	9,178	9,131	1,098
Clark	Clark	3,915	4,403	958
Clay	Vermillion	13,191	13,186	412
Codington	Watertown	25,929	22,698	688
Corson	McIntosh	4,288	4,195	2,473
Custer	Custer	7,585	6,179	1,558
Davison	Mitchell	18,744	17,503	435
Day	Webster	5,891	6,978	1,029
Deuel	Clear Lake	4,364	4,522	624
Dewey	Timber Lake	6,133	5,523	2,303
Douglas	Armour	3,310	3,746	434
Edmunds	Ipswich	4,221	4,356	1,146
Fall River	Hot Springs	7,305	7,353	1,740
Faulk	Faulkton	2,469	2,744	1,000
Grant	Milbank	7,625	8,372	683
Gregory	Burke	4,500	5,359	1,016
Haakon	Philip	2,007	2,624	1,813
Hamlin	Hayti	5,615	4,974	507
Hand	Miller	3,520	4,272	1,437
Hanson	Alexandria	3,510	2,994	435
Harding	Buffalo	1,288	1,669	2,671
Hughes	Pierre	16,684	14,817	741
Hutchinson	Olivet	7,731	8,262	813
Hyde	Highmore	1,573	1,696	861
Jackson	Kadoka	2,853	2,811	1,869
Jerauld	Wessington Springs	2,180	2,425	530
Jones	Murdo	1,087	1,324	971
Kingsbury	De Smet	5,555	5,925	838
Lake	Madison	11,040	10,550	563
Lawrence	Deadwood	21,880	20,655	800
Lincoln	Canton	29,302	15,427	578
Lyman	Kennebec	3,916	3,638	1,640

County	County seat or courthouse	2003 Pop.	1990 Pop.	Land area sq. mi.
McCook	Salem	5,864	5,688	575
McPherson	Leola	2,723	3,228	1,137
Marshall	Britton	4,272	4,844	838
Meade	Sturgis	24,715	21,878	3,471
Mellette	White River	2,118	2,137	1,306
Miner	Howard	2,717	3,272	570
Minnehaha	Sioux Falls	154,617	123,809	810
Moody	Flandreau	6,511	6,507	520
Pennington	Rapid City	91,881	81,343	2,776
Perkins	Bison	3,187	3,932	2,872
Potter	Gettysburg	2,508	3,190	866
Roberts	Sisseton	10,128	9,914	1,101
Sanborn	Woonsocket	2,612	2,833	569
Shannon	(Attached to Fall River)	13,209	9,902	2,094
Spink	Redfield	6,972	7,981	1,504
Stanley	Fort Pierre	2,752	2,453	1,443
Sully	Onida	1,456	1,589	1,007
Todd	(Attached to Tripp)	9,468	8,352	1,388
Tripp	Winner	6,177	6,924	1,614
Turner	Parker	8,594	8,576	617
Union	Elk Point	13,024	10,189	460
Walworth	Selby	5,562	6,087	708
Yankton	Yankton	21,452	19,252	522
Ziebach	Dupree	2,551	2,220	1,962

Tennessee

(95 counties, 41,217 sq. mi. land; pop. 5,841,748)

County	County seat or courthouse	2003 Pop.	1990 Pop.	Land area sq. mi.
Anderson	Clinton	71,904	68,250	338
Bedford	Shelbyville	40,253	30,411	474
Benton	Camden	16,500	14,524	395
Bledsoe	Pikeville	12,556	9,669	406
Blount	Maryville	111,510	85,962	559
Bradley	Cleveland	90,264	73,712	329
Campbell	Jacksboro	40,125	35,079	480
Cannon	Woodbury	13,204	10,467	266
Carroll	Huntingdon	29,342	27,514	599
Carter	Elizabethton	58,394	51,505	341
Cheatham	Ashland City	37,364	27,140	303
Chester	Henderson	15,842	12,819	289
Claiborne	Tazewell	30,415	26,137	434
Clay	Celina	7,947	7,238	236
Cocke	Newport	34,329	29,141	434
Coffee	Manchester	49,643	40,343	429
Crockett	Alamo	14,491	13,378	265
Cumberland	Crossville	49,391	34,736	682
Davidson	Nashville	569,842	510,786	502
Decatur	Decaturville	11,610	10,472	334
De Kalb	Smithville	18,037	14,360	305
Dickson	Charlotte	44,935	35,061	490
Dyer	Dyersburg	37,308	34,854	511
Fayette	Somerville	32,289	25,559	705
Fentress	Jamestown	16,935	14,669	499
Franklin	Winchester	40,512	34,923	555
Gibson	Trenton	47,922	46,315	603
Giles	Pulaski	29,390	25,741	611
Grainger	Rutledge	21,445	17,095	280
Greene	Greeneville	63,991	55,832	622
Grundy	Altamont	14,389	13,362	361
Hamblen	Morristown	58,851	50,480	161
Hamilton	Chattanooga	309,510	285,536	542
Hancock	Sneedville	6,702	6,739	222
Hardeman	Bolivar	28,174	23,377	668
Hardin	Savannah	25,927	22,633	578
Hawkins	Rogersville	55,037	44,565	487
Haywood	Brownsville	19,626	19,437	533
Henderson	Lexington	25,900	21,844	520
Henry	Paris	31,185	27,888	562
Hickman	Centerville	23,352	16,754	613
Houston	Erin	8,085	7,018	200
Humphreys	Waverly	18,123	15,813	532
Jackson	Gainesboro	11,208	9,297	309
Jefferson	Dandridge	46,919	33,016	274
Johnson	Mountain City	17,948	13,766	298
Knox	Knoxville	392,995	335,749	508
Lake	Tiptonville	7,824	7,129	163
Lauderdale	Ripley	27,077	23,491	470
Lawrence	Lawrenceburg	40,704	35,303	617
Lewis	Hohenwald	11,438	9,247	282
Lincoln	Fayetteville	31,773	28,157	570
Loudon	Loudon	41,624	31,255	229
McMinn	Athens	50,632	42,383	430
McNairy	Selmer	24,938	22,422	560
Macon	Lafayette	21,023	15,906	307
Madison	Jackson	93,873	77,982	557
Marion	Jasper	27,880	24,683	498
Marshall	Lewisburg	27,537	21,539	375
Maury	Columbia	73,198	54,812	613
Meigs	Decatur	11,430	8,033	195
Monroe	Madisonville	41,051	30,541	635
Montgomery	Clarksville	141,064	100,498	539
Moore	Lynchburg	5,911	4,696	129
Morgan	Wartburg	20,080	17,300	522
Obion	Union City	32,386	31,717	545
Overton	Livingston	20,151	17,636	433
Perry	Linden	7,627	6,612	415
Pickett	Byrdstown	5,006	4,548	163
Polk	Benton	16,171	13,643	435
Putnam	Cookeville	64,973	51,373	401
Rhea	Dayton	29,286	24,344	316
Roane	Kingston	52,424	47,227	361
Robertson	Springfield	58,181	41,492	476
Rutherford	Murfreesboro	202,310	118,570	619
Scott	Huntsville	21,675	18,358	532
Sequatchie	Dunlap	11,958	8,863	266
Sevier	Sevierville	75,503	51,050	592
Shelby	Memphis	906,178	826,330	755
Smith	Carthage	18,225	14,143	314
Stewart	Dover	12,847	9,479	458
Sullivan	Blountville	153,050	143,596	413
Sumner	Gallatin	138,752	103,281	529
Tipton	Covington	54,184	37,568	459
Trousdale	Hartsville	7,447	5,920	114
Unicoi	Erwin	17,709	16,549	186
Union	Maynardville	18,830	13,694	224
Van Buren	Spencer	5,478	4,846	273
Warren	McMinnville	39,129	32,992	433
Washington	Jonesborough	110,078	92,336	326
Wayne	Waynesboro	16,947	13,935	734
Weakley	Dresden	34,314	31,972	580
White	Sparta	23,584	20,090	377
Williamson	Franklin	141,301	81,021	583
Wilson	Lebanon	95,366	67,675	571

Texas

(254 counties, 261,797 sq. mi. land; pop. 22,118,509)

County	County seat or courthouse	2003 Pop.	1990 Pop.	Land area sq. mi.
Anderson	Palestine	54,790	48,024	1,071
Andrews	Andrews	12,868	14,338	1,501
Angelina	Lufkin	80,935	69,884	802
Aransas	Rockport	23,574	17,892	252
Archer	Archer City	9,189	7,973	910
Armstrong	Claude	2,056	2,021	914
Atascosa	Jourdanton	41,867	30,533	1,232
Austin	Bellville	25,057	19,832	653
Bailey	Muleshoe	6,660	7,064	827
Bandera	Bandera	19,347	10,562	792
Bastrop	Bastrop	67,077	38,263	888
Baylor	Seymour	3,909	4,385	871
Bee	Beeville	32,431	25,135	880
Bell	Belton	248,727	191,073	1,060
Bexar	San Antonio	1,471,644	1,185,394	1,247
Blanco	Johnson City	8,809	5,972	711
Borden	Gail	682	799	899
Bosque	Meridian	17,696	15,125	989
Bowie	Boston	89,699	81,665	888
Brazoria	Angleton	263,149	191,707	1,386
Brazos	Bryan	159,830	121,862	586
Brewster	Alpine	9,247	8,653	6,193
Briscoe	Silverton	1,663	1,971	900
Brooks	Falfurrias	7,720	8,204	943
Brown	Brownwood	38,103	34,371	944
Burleson	Caldwell	16,941	13,625	666
Burnet	Burnet	38,809	22,677	996
Caldwell	Lockhart	35,572	26,392	546
Calhoun	Port Lavaca	20,454	19,053	512
Callahan	Baird	13,110	11,859	899
Cameron	Brownsville	363,092	260,120	906
Camp	Pittsburg	11,756	9,904	198
Carson	Panhandle	6,507	6,576	923
Cass	Linden	29,995	29,982	937
Castro	Dimmitt	7,900	9,070	898
Chambers	Anahuac	27,581	20,088	599
Cherokee	Rusk	47,568	41,049	1,052
Childress	Childress	7,563	5,953	710
Clay	Henrietta	11,207	10,024	1,098
Cochran	Morton	3,486	4,377	775
Coke	Robert Lee	3,725	3,424	899
Coleman	Coleman	8,777	9,710	1,260
Collin	McKinney	597,147	264,036	848
Collingsworth	Wellington	3,023	3,573	919
Colorado	Columbus	20,643	18,383	963
Comal	New Braunfels	87,785	51,832	561
Comanche	Comanche	13,541	13,381	938
Concho	Paint Rock	3,774	3,044	991
Cooke	Gainesville	37,996	30,777	874
Coryell	Gatesville	75,195	64,226	1,052
Cottle	Paducah	1,752	2,247	901
Crane	Crane	3,885	4,652	786
Crockett	Ozona	3,934	4,078	2,807
Crosby	Crosbyton	6,742	7,304	900
Culberson	Van Horn	2,760	3,407	3,812
Dallam	Dalhart	6,100	5,461	1,505
Dallas	Dallas	2,284,096	1,852,691	880
Dawson	Lamesa	14,411	14,349	902
Deaf Smith	Hereford	18,415	19,153	1,497
Delta	Cooper	5,451	4,857	277
Denton	Denton	510,795	273,644	889
DeWitt	Cuero	20,100	18,840	909

County	County seat or courthouse	2003 Pop.	1990 Pop.	Land area sq. mi.	County	County seat or courthouse	2003 Pop.	1990 Pop.	Land area sq. mi.
Dickens	Dickens	2,705	2,571	904	Martin	Stanton	4,600	4,956	915
Dimmit	Carrizo Springs	10,341	10,433	1,331	Mason	Mason	3,777	3,423	932
Donley	Clarendon	3,877	3,696	930	Matagorda	Bay City	38,290	36,928	1,114
Duval	San Diego	12,616	12,918	1,793	Maverick	Eagle Pass	50,178	36,378	1,280
Eastland	Eastland	18,300	18,488	926	Medina	Hondo	41,553	27,312	1,328
Ector	Odessa	122,692	118,934	901	Menard	Menard	2,354	2,252	902
Edwards	Rocksprings	2,031	2,266	2,120	Midland	Midland	118,624	106,611	900
Ellis	Waxahachie	124,411	85,167	940	Milam	Cameron	25,103	22,946	1,017
El Paso	El Paso	705,436	591,610	1,013	Mills	Goldthwaite	5,038	4,531	748
Erath	Stephenville	33,370	27,991	1,086	Mitchell	Colorado City	9,316	8,016	910
Falls	Marlin	17,860	17,712	769	Montague	Montague	19,416	17,274	931
Fannin	Bonham	32,276	24,804	891	Montgomery	Conroe	344,700	182,201	1,044
Fayette	La Grange	22,370	20,095	950	Moore	Dumas	20,234	17,865	900
Fisher	Roby	4,142	4,842	901	Morris	Daingerfield	13,167	13,200	255
Floyd	Floydada	7,446	8,497	992	Motley	Matador	1,304	1,532	989
Foard	Crowell	1,541	1,794	707	Nacogdoches	Nacogdoches	59,584	54,753	947
Fort Bend	Richmond	419,772	225,421	875	Navarro	Corsicana	47,331	39,926	1,008
Franklin	Mount Vernon	9,906	7,802	286	Newton	Newton	14,869	13,569	933
Freestone	Fairfield	18,605	15,818	877	Nolan	Sweetwater	15,110	16,594	912
Frio	Pearsall	16,345	13,472	1,133	Nueces	Corpus Christi	315,206	291,145	836
Gaines	Seminole	14,438	14,123	1,502	Ochiltree	Perryton	8,986	9,128	918
Galveston	Galveston	266,775	217,396	398	Oldham	Vega	2,159	2,278	1,501
Garza	Post	5,011	5,143	896	Orange	Orange	84,390	80,509	356
Gillespie	Fredericksburg	22,226	17,204	1,061	Palo Pinto	Palo Pinto	27,325	25,055	953
Glasscock	Garden City	1,355	1,447	901	Panola	Carthage	22,606	22,035	801
Goliad	Goliad	7,116	5,980	854	Parker	Weatherford	97,480	64,785	904
Gonzales	Gonzales	19,057	17,205	1,068	Parmer	Farwell	9,896	9,863	882
Gray	Pampa	21,496	23,967	928	Pecos	Fort Stockton	16,039	14,675	4,764
Grayson	Sherman	115,153	95,019	934	Polk	Livingston	45,323	30,687	1,057
Gregg	Longview	113,941	104,948	274	Potter	Amarillo	117,335	97,841	909
Grimes	Anderson	24,963	18,843	794	Presidio	Marfa	7,591	6,637	3,856
Guadalupe	Seguin	97,101	64,873	711	Rains	Emory	10,857	6,715	232
Hale	Plainview	35,874	34,671	1,005	Randall	Canyon	107,333	89,673	914
Hall	Memphis	3,833	3,905	903	Reagan	Big Lake	3,054	4,514	1,175
Hamilton	Hamilton	8,118	7,733	836	Real	Leakey	3,020	2,412	700
Hansford	Spearman	5,210	5,848	920	Red River	Clarksville	13,812	14,317	1,050
Hardeman	Quanah	4,440	5,283	695	Reeves	Pecos	12,238	15,852	2,636
Hardin	Kountze	49,634	41,320	894	Refugio	Refugio	7,625	7,976	770
Harris	Houston	3,596,086	2,818,101	1,729	Roberts	Miami	820	1,025	924
Harrison	Marshall	62,708	57,483	899	Robertson	Franklin	15,832	15,511	855
Hartley	Channing	5,223	3,634	1,462	Rockwall	Rockwall	54,630	25,604	129
Haskell	Haskell	5,739	6,820	903	Runnels	Ballinger	10,911	11,294	1,051
Hays	San Marcos	114,193	65,614	678	Rusk	Henderson	47,255	43,735	924
Hemphill	Canadian	3,333	3,720	910	Sabine	Hemphill	10,379	9,586	490
Henderson	Athens	77,277	58,543	874	San Augustine	San Augustine	8,913	7,999	528
Hidalgo	Edinburg	635,540	383,545	1,570	San Jacinto	Coldspring	23,917	16,372	571
Hill	Hillsboro	34,444	27,146	962	San Patricio	Sinton	68,050	58,749	692
Hockley	Levelland	22,807	24,199	908	San Saba	San Saba	6,053	5,401	1,134
Hood	Granbury	45,046	28,981	422	Schleicher	Eldorado	2,816	2,990	1,311
Hopkins	Sulphur Springs	32,681	28,833	782	Scurry	Snyder	16,081	18,634	903
Houston	Crockett	23,109	21,375	1,231	Shackelford	Albany	3,305	3,316	914
Howard	Big Spring	32,849	32,343	903	Shelby	Center	25,882	22,034	794
Hudspeth	Sierra Blanca	3,193	2,915	4,571	Sherman	Stratford	3,158	2,858	923
Hunt	Greenville	81,024	64,343	841	Smith	Tyler	184,015	151,309	928
Hutchinson	Stinnett	22,959	25,689	887	Somervell	Glen Rose	7,331	5,360	187
Irion	Mertzon	1,742	1,629	1,051	Starr	Rio Grande City	57,678	40,518	1,223
Jack	Jacksboro	8,949	6,981	917	Stephens	Breckenridge	9,449	9,010	895
Jackson	Edna	14,247	13,039	829	Sterling	Sterling City	1,342	1,438	923
Jasper	Jasper	35,509	31,102	937	Stonewall	Aspermont	1,448	2,013	919
Jeff Davis	Fort Davis	2,236	1,946	2,264	Sutton	Sonora	4,110	4,135	1,454
Jefferson	Beaumont	248,605	239,389	904	Swisher	Tulia	8,015	8,133	900
Jim Hogg	Hebbronville	5,024	5,109	1,136	Tarrant	Fort Worth	1,559,148	1,170,103	863
Jim Wells	Alice	40,469	37,679	865	Taylor	Abilene	125,339	119,655	916
Johnson	Cleburne	139,068	97,165	729	Terrell	Sanderson	1,034	1,410	2,358
Jones	Anson	20,039	16,490	931	Terry	Brownfield	12,453	13,218	890
Karnes	Karnes City	15,276	12,455	750	Throckmorton	Throckmorton	1,697	1,880	912
Kaufman	Kaufman	81,955	52,220	786	Titus	Mount Pleasant	28,603	24,009	411
Kendall	Boerne	26,178	14,589	662	Tom Green	San Angelo	103,528	98,458	1,522
Kenedy	Sarita	408	460	1,457	Travis	Austin	857,204	576,407	989
Kent	Jayton	770	1,010	902	Trinity	Groveton	14,151	11,445	693
Kerr	Kerrville	45,311	36,304	1,106	Tyler	Woodville	20,651	16,646	923
Kimble	Junction	4,535	4,122	1,251	Upshur	Gilmer	36,959	31,370	588
King	Guthrie	319	354	912	Upton	Rankin	3,153	4,447	1,242
Kinney	Brackettville	3,311	3,119	1,363	Uvalde	Uvalde	26,787	23,340	1,557
Kleberg	Kingsville	31,308	30,274	871	Val Verde	Del Rio	46,569	38,721	3,170
Knox	Benjamin	3,928	4,837	849	Van Zandt	Canton	50,664	37,944	849
Lamar	Paris	49,464	43,949	917	Victoria	Victoria	85,395	74,361	883
Lamb	Littlefield	14,637	15,072	1,016	Walker	Huntsville	62,038	50,917	787
Lampasas	Lampasas	19,407	13,521	712	Waller	Hempstead	34,579	23,374	514
La Salle	Cotulla	5,822	5,254	1,489	Ward	Monahans	10,293	13,115	835
Lavaca	Hallettsville	19,063	18,690	970	Washington	Brenham	30,950	26,154	609
Lee	Giddings	16,530	12,854	629	Webb	Laredo	213,615	133,239	3,357
Leon	Centerville	16,017	12,665	1,072	Wharton	Wharton	41,144	39,955	1,090
Liberty	Liberty	74,117	52,726	1,160	Wheeler	Wheeler	4,809	5,879	914
Limestone	Groesbeck	22,621	20,946	909	Wichita	Wichita Falls	129,257	122,378	628
Lipscomb	Lipscomb	3,092	3,143	932	Wilbarger	Vernon	13,858	15,121	971
Live Oak	George West	11,902	9,556	1,036	Willacy	Raymondville	20,094	17,705	597
Llano	Llano	18,034	11,631	935	Williamson	Georgetown	303,587	139,551	1,123
Loving	Mentone	62	107	673	Wilson	Floresville	35,244	22,650	807
Lubbock	Lubbock	250,446	222,636	899	Winkler	Kermit	6,780	8,626	841
Lynn	Tahoka	6,182	6,758	892	Wise	Decatur	54,465	34,679	905
McCulloch	Brady	7,896	8,778	1,069	Wood	Quitman	39,286	29,380	650
McLennan	Waco	219,807	189,123	1,042	Yoakum	Plains	7,249	8,786	800
McMullen	Tilden	868	817	1,113	Young	Graham	17,901	18,126	922
Madison	Madisonville	12,821	10,931	470	Zapata	Zapata	12,905	9,279	997
Marion	Jefferson	11,028	9,984	381	Zavala	Crystal City	11,593	12,162	1,298

▶ **IT'S A FACT:** From 2000 to 2003, Loudoun County, VA, grew by 52,147 people or 30.7%, to 221,746, making it the fastest-growing U.S. county during that period. Since its formation in 1757, the county had been primarily agricultural, with a relatively constant population of about 20,000 for about two centuries. Then with the 1962 opening of Dulles International Airport in the southeastern part of the county (about 25 miles from Washington, DC), new businesses began to move in. At the same time, Washington was going through a period of rapid growth. With road improvements making the commute from Loudoun County to Washington easier, the population of Loudoun began to surge.

Utah
(29 counties, 82,144 sq. mi. land; pop. 2,351,467)

County	County seat or courthouse	2003 Pop.	1990 Pop.	Land area sq. mi.
Beaver	Beaver	6,105	4,765	2,590
Box Elder	Brigham City	44,504	36,485	5,723
Cache	Logan	95,664	70,183	1,165
Carbon	Price	19,764	20,228	1,478
Daggett	Manila	889	690	698
Davis	Farmington	255,597	187,941	304
Duchesne	Duchesne	14,846	12,645	3,238
Emery	Castle Dale	10,651	10,332	4,452
Garfield	Panguitch	4,542	3,980	5,174
Grand	Moab	8,759	6,620	3,682
Iron	Parowan	35,741	20,789	3,298
Juab	Nephi	8,792	5,817	3,392
Kane	Kanab	6,039	5,169	3,992
Millard	Fillmore	12,455	11,333	6,589
Morgan	Morgan	7,518	5,528	609
Piute	Junction	1,380	1,277	758
Rich	Randolph	2,019	1,725	1,029
Salt Lake	Salt Lake City	924,247	725,956	737
San Juan	Monticello	13,901	12,621	7,820
Sanpete	Manti	23,689	16,259	1,588
Sevier	Richfield	19,103	15,431	1,910
Summit	Coalville	33,020	15,518	1,871
Tooele	Tooele	47,965	26,601	6,930
Uintah	Vernal	26,296	22,211	4,477
Utah	Provo	398,059	263,590	1,998
Wasatch	Heber City	17,509	10,089	1,177
Washington	Saint George	104,132	48,560	2,427
Wayne	Loa	2,454	2,177	2,460
Weber	Ogden	205,827	158,330	576

Vermont
(14 counties, 9,250 sq. mi. land; pop. 619,107)

County	County seat or courthouse	2003 Pop.	1990 Pop.	Land area sq. mi.
Addison	Middlebury	36,835	32,953	770
Bennington	Bennington	37,178	35,845	676
Caledonia	Saint Johnsbury	29,940	27,846	651
Chittenden	Burlington	148,990	131,761	539
Essex	Guildhall	6,569	6,405	665
Franklin	Saint Albans	47,023	39,980	637
Grand Isle	North Hero	7,490	5,318	83
Lamoille	Hyde Park	24,284	19,735	461
Orange	Chelsea	29,081	26,149	689
Orleans	Newport	27,103	24,053	698
Rutland	Rutland	63,504	62,142	933
Washington	Montpelier	58,836	54,928	689
Windham	Newfane	44,379	41,588	789
Windsor	Woodstock	57,895	54,055	971

Virginia
(95 counties, 39 ind. cities, 39,594 sq. mi. land; pop. 7,386,330)

County	County seat or courthouse	2003 Pop.	1990 Pop.	Land area sq. mi.
Accomack	Accomac	39,025	31,703	455
Albemarle	Charlottesville	87,670	68,177	723
Alleghany[1]	Covington	16,816	12,815	445
Amelia	Amelia Court House	11,742	8,787	357
Amherst	Amherst	31,891	28,578	475
Appomattox	Appomattox	13,710	12,300	334
Arlington	Arlington	187,873	170,895	26
Augusta	Staunton	67,427	54,557	970
Bath	Warm Springs	5,013	4,799	532
Bedford	Bedford	62,661	45,553	755
Bland	Bland	6,965	6,514	359
Botetourt	Fincastle	31,448	24,992	543
Brunswick	Lawrenceville	18,199	15,987	566
Buchanan	Grundy	25,598	31,333	504
Buckingham	Buckingham	15,839	12,873	581
Campbell	Rustburg	51,322	47,499	504
Caroline	Bowling Green	23,190	19,217	533
Carroll	Hillsville	29,336	26,519	476
Charles City	Charles City	7,118	6,282	183
Charlotte	Charlotte Court House	12,452	11,688	475
Chesterfield	Chesterfield	276,840	209,599	426
Clarke	Berryville	13,364	12,101	177
Craig	New Castle	5,159	4,372	331
Culpeper	Culpeper	38,555	27,791	381
Cumberland	Cumberland	9,189	7,825	298
Dickenson	Clintwood	16,119	17,620	332
Dinwiddie	Dinwiddie	24,853	22,279	504
Essex	Tappahannock	10,260	8,689	258
Fairfax	Fairfax	1,000,405	818,310	395

County	County seat or courthouse	2003 Pop.	1990 Pop.	Land area sq. mi.
Fauquier	Warrenton	61,137	48,700	650
Floyd	Floyd	14,350	11,965	381
Fluvanna	Palmyra	23,078	12,429	287
Franklin	Rocky Mount	49,095	39,549	692
Frederick	Winchester	64,565	45,723	415
Giles	Pearisburg	16,956	16,366	357
Gloucester	Gloucester	36,698	30,131	217
Goochland	Goochland	18,138	14,163	284
Grayson	Independence	16,557	16,278	443
Greene	Stanardsville	16,779	10,297	157
Greensville	Emporia	11,581	8,553	295
Halifax	Halifax	36,632	36,030	819
Hanover	Hanover	94,081	63,306	473
Henrico	Richmond	271,083	217,878	238
Henry	Collinsville	57,090	56,942	382
Highland	Monterey	2,504	2,635	416
Isle of Wight	Isle of Wight	31,925	25,053	316
James City	Williamsburg	53,487	34,779	143
King and Queen	King and Queen Court House	6,588	6,289	316
King George	King George	18,213	13,527	180
King William	King William	14,131	10,913	275
Lancaster	Lancaster	12,074	10,896	133
Lee	Jonesville	23,734	24,496	437
Loudoun	Leesburg	221,746	86,185	520
Louisa	Louisa	28,031	20,325	497
Lunenburg	Lunenburg	13,167	11,419	432
Madison	Madison	13,036	11,949	321
Mathews	Mathews	9,216	8,348	86
Mecklenburg	Boydton	32,551	29,241	624
Middlesex	Saluda	10,211	8,653	130
Montgomery	Christiansburg	85,614	73,913	388
Nelson	Lovingston	14,942	12,778	472
New Kent	New Kent	14,843	10,466	210
Northampton	Eastville	13,285	13,061	207
Northumberland	Heathsville	12,742	10,524	192
Nottoway	Nottoway	15,603	14,993	315
Orange	Orange	28,018	21,421	342
Page	Luray	23,589	21,690	311
Patrick	Stuart	19,182	17,473	483
Pittsylvania	Chatham	61,640	55,672	971
Powhatan	Powhatan	24,649	15,328	261
Prince Edward	Farmville	20,180	17,320	353
Prince George	Prince George	34,305	27,390	266
Prince William	Manassas	325,324	214,954	338
Pulaski	Pulaski	35,030	34,496	321
Rappahannock	Washington	7,110	6,622	267
Richmond	Warsaw	9,006	7,273	191
Roanoke	Salem	87,329	79,278	251
Rockbridge	Lexington	20,973	18,350	600
Rockingham	Harrisonburg	69,365	57,482	851
Russell	Lebanon	28,861	28,667	475
Scott	Gate City	23,005	23,204	537
Shenandoah	Woodstock	37,199	31,636	512
Smyth	Marion	32,700	32,370	452
Southampton	Courtland	17,453	17,022	600
Spotsylvania	Spotsylvania	107,838	57,397	401
Stafford	Stafford	111,021	62,255	270
Surry	Surry	7,009	6,145	279
Sussex	Sussex	11,956	10,248	491
Tazewell	Tazewell	44,362	45,960	520
Warren	Front Royal	33,871	26,142	214
Washington	Abingdon	51,405	45,887	563
Westmoreland	Montross	16,946	15,480	229
Wise	Wise	41,803	39,573	404
Wythe	Wytheville	27,941	25,471	463
York	Yorktown	60,948	42,434	106

Independent Cities

City	2003 Pop.	1990 Pop.	Land area sq. mi.
Alexandria	128,923	111,183	15
Bedford	6,339	6,176	7
Bristol	17,206	18,426	13
Buena Vista	6,320	6,406	7
Charlottesville	39,162	40,470	10
Chesapeake	210,834	151,982	341
Colonial Heights	17,286	16,064	7
Covington	6,284	7,352	6
Danville	46,988	53,056	43
Emporia	5,656	5,556	7
Fairfax	22,031	19,945	6
Falls Church	10,485	9,464	2
Franklin	8,254	8,392	8
Fredericksburg	20,189	19,033	11
Galax	6,655	6,745	8
Hampton	146,878	133,773	52
Harrisonburg	41,170	30,707	18
Hopewell	22,391	23,101	10
Lexington	7,076	6,959	2
Lynchburg	65,113	66,120	49
Manassas	37,166	27,757	10

Independent Cities	2003 Pop.	1990 Pop.	Land area sq. mi.
Manassas Park	10,990	6,798	2
Martinsville	15,121	16,162	11
Newport News	181,647	171,477	68
Norfolk	241,727	261,250	54
Norton	3,909	4,247	8
Petersburg	33,091	37,071	23
Poquoson	11,844	11,005	16
Portsmouth	99,617	103,910	33
Radford	15,006	15,940	10
Richmond	194,729	202,713	60
Roanoke	92,863	96,487	43
Salem	24,603	23,835	15
Staunton	23,848	24,581	20
Suffolk	73,515	52,143	400
Virginia Beach	439,467	393,089	248
Waynesboro	20,388	18,549	15
Williamsburg	11,605	11,600	9
Winchester	24,434	21,947	9
Manassas Park	10,990	6,798	2
Martinsville	15,121	16,162	11
Newport News	181,647	171,477	68

(1) The independent city of Clifton Forge became part of Alleghany County in 2001.

Washington
(39 counties, 66,544 sq. mi. land; pop. 6,131,445)

County	County seat or courthouse	2003 Pop.	1990 Pop.	Land area sq. mi.
Adams	Ritzville	16,602	13,603	1,925
Asotin	Asotin	20,625	17,605	635
Benton	Prosser	153,660	112,560	1,703
Chelan	Wenatchee	67,973	52,250	2,921
Clallam	Port Angeles	66,892	56,210	1,739
Clark	Vancouver	379,577	238,053	628
Columbia	Dayton	4,093	4,024	869
Cowlitz	Kelso	95,146	82,119	1,139
Douglas	Waterville	33,753	26,205	1,821
Ferry	Republic	7,417	6,295	2,204
Franklin	Pasco	56,126	37,473	1,242
Garfield	Pomeroy	2,371	2,248	711
Grant	Ephrata	78,691	54,798	2,681
Grays Harbor	Montesano	69,406	64,175	1,917
Island	Coupeville	76,384	60,195	208
Jefferson	Port Townsend	27,716	20,406	1,814
King	Seattle	1,761,411	1,507,305	2,126
Kitsap	Port Orchard	240,719	189,731	396
Kittitas	Ellensburg	35,206	26,725	2,297
Klickitat	Goldendale	19,547	16,616	1,872
Lewis	Chehalis	70,404	59,358	2,408
Lincoln	Davenport	10,201	8,864	2,311
Mason	Shelton	52,129	38,341	961
Okanogan	Okanogan	39,134	33,350	5,268
Pacific	South Bend	21,103	18,882	933
Pend Oreille	Newport	12,254	8,915	1,400
Pierce	Tacoma	740,957	586,203	1,679
San Juan	Friday Harbor	14,761	10,035	175
Skagit	Mount Vernon	109,234	79,545	1,735
Skamania	Stevenson	10,292	8,289	1,656
Snohomish	Everett	639,409	465,628	2,089
Spokane	Spokane	431,027	361,333	1,764
Stevens	Colville	40,776	30,948	2,478
Thurston	Olympia	221,950	161,238	727
Wahkiakum	Cathlamet	3,748	3,327	264
Walla Walla	Walla Walla	56,751	48,439	1,271
Whatcom	Bellingham	176,571	127,780	2,120
Whitman	Colfax	40,702	38,775	2,159
Yakima	Yakima	226,727	188,823	4,296

West Virginia
(55 counties, 24,078 sq. mi. land; pop. 1,810,354)

County	County seat or courthouse	2003 Pop.	1990 Pop.	Land area sq. mi.
Barbour	Philippi	15,653	15,699	341
Berkeley	Martinsburg	85,272	59,253	321
Boone	Madison	25,785	25,870	503
Braxton	Sutton	14,771	12,998	513
Brooke	Wellsburg	24,939	26,992	89
Cabell	Huntington	95,043	96,827	282
Calhoun	Grantsville	7,294	7,885	281
Clay	Clay	10,352	9,983	342
Doddridge	West Union	7,491	6,994	320
Fayette	Fayetteville	47,207	47,952	664
Gilmer	Glenville	7,037	7,669	340
Grant	Petersburg	11,434	10,428	477
Greenbrier	Lewisburg	34,656	34,693	1,021
Hampshire	Romney	21,247	16,498	642
Hancock	New Cumberland	31,742	35,233	83
Hardy	Moorefield	12,990	10,977	583
Harrison	Clarksburg	68,032	69,371	416
Jackson	Ripley	28,285	25,938	466
Jefferson	Charles Town	46,270	35,926	210
Kanawha	Charleston	195,413	207,619	903
Lewis	Weston	17,148	17,223	382
Lincoln	Hamlin	22,251	21,382	437
Logan	Logan	36,745	43,032	454
McDowell	Welch	25,348	35,233	535

County	County seat or courthouse	2003 Pop.	1990 Pop.	Land area sq. mi.
Marion	Fairmont	56,484	57,249	310
Marshall	Moundsville	34,897	37,356	307
Mason	Point Pleasant	26,079	25,178	432
Mercer	Princeton	62,113	64,980	420
Mineral	Keyser	27,147	26,697	328
Mingo	Williamson	27,585	33,739	423
Monongalia	Morgantown	84,370	75,509	361
Monroe	Union	13,503	12,406	473
Morgan	Berkeley Springs	15,514	12,128	229
Nicholas	Summersville	26,243	26,775	649
Ohio	Wheeling	45,828	50,871	106
Pendleton	Franklin	7,896	8,054	698
Pleasants	St. Marys	7,521	7,546	131
Pocahontas	Marlinton	8,944	9,008	940
Preston	Kingwood	29,705	29,037	648
Putnam	Winfield	53,035	42,835	346
Raleigh	Beckley	79,254	76,819	607
Randolph	Elkins	28,254	27,803	1,040
Ritchie	Harrisville	10,515	10,233	454
Roane	Spencer	15,362	15,120	484
Summers	Hinton	13,917	14,204	361
Taylor	Grafton	16,127	15,144	173
Tucker	Parsons	7,162	7,728	419
Tyler	Middlebourne	9,439	9,796	258
Upshur	Buckhannon	23,668	22,867	355
Wayne	Wayne	42,418	41,636	506
Webster	Webster Springs	9,790	10,729	556
Wetzel	New Martinsville	17,160	19,258	359
Wirt	Elizabeth	5,790	5,192	233
Wood	Parkersburg	87,336	86,915	367
Wyoming	Pineville	24,830	28,990	501

Wisconsin
(72 counties, 54,310 sq. mi. land; pop. 5,472,299)

County	County seat or courthouse	2003 Pop.	1990 Pop.	Land area sq. mi.
Adams	Friendship	20,567	15,682	648
Ashland	Ashland	16,651	16,307	1,044
Barron	Barron	45,514	40,750	863
Bayfield	Washburn	15,114	14,008	1,476
Brown	Green Bay	233,888	194,594	529
Buffalo	Alma	13,814	13,584	684
Burnett	Siren	16,242	13,084	822
Calumet	Chilton	43,383	34,291	320
Chippewa	Chippewa Falls	56,773	52,360	1,010
Clark	Neillsville	33,969	31,647	1,216
Columbia	Portage	54,076	45,088	774
Crawford	Prairie du Chien	16,949	15,940	573
Dane	Madison	449,378	367,085	1,202
Dodge	Juneau	87,115	76,559	882
Door	Sturgeon Bay	28,402	25,690	483
Douglas	Superior	44,093	41,758	1,309
Dunn	Menomonie	41,114	35,909	852
Eau Claire	Eau Claire	94,186	85,183	638
Florence	Florence	5,081	4,590	488
Fond du Lac	Fond du Lac	97,833	90,083	723
Forest	Crandon	9,938	8,776	1,014
Grant	Lancaster	49,368	49,266	1,148
Green	Monroe	34,280	30,339	584
Green Lake	Green Lake	19,204	18,651	354
Iowa	Dodgeville	23,288	20,150	763
Iron	Hurley	6,727	6,153	757
Jackson	Black River Falls	19,538	16,588	987
Jefferson	Jefferson	77,421	67,783	557
Juneau	Mauston	25,029	21,650	768
Kenosha	Kenosha	156,209	128,181	273
Kewaunee	Kewaunee	20,455	18,878	343
La Crosse	La Crosse	108,612	97,904	453
Lafayette	Darlington	16,341	16,074	634
Langlade	Antigo	20,788	19,505	873
Lincoln	Merrill	30,076	26,993	883
Manitowoc	Manitowoc	82,065	80,421	592
Marathon	Wausau	127,168	115,400	1,545
Marinette	Marinette	43,237	40,548	1,402
Marquette	Montello	14,853	12,321	455
Menominee	Keshena	4,623	4,075	358
Milwaukee	Milwaukee	933,221	959,212	242
Monroe	Sparta	41,796	36,633	901
Oconto	Oconto	36,904	30,226	998
Oneida	Rhinelander	37,187	31,679	1,125
Outagamie	Appleton	167,411	140,510	640
Ozaukee	Port Washington	84,772	72,894	232
Pepin	Durand	7,383	7,107	232
Pierce	Ellsworth	37,872	32,765	576
Polk	Balsam Lake	43,270	34,773	917
Portage	Stevens Point	67,386	61,405	806
Price	Phillips	15,401	15,600	1,253
Racine	Racine	192,284	175,034	333
Richland	Richland Center	18,193	17,521	586
Rock	Janesville	154,794	139,510	720
Rusk	Ladysmith	15,268	15,079	913
Saint Croix	Hudson	71,155	50,251	722
Sauk	Baraboo	56,432	46,975	838
Sawyer	Hayward	16,713	14,181	1,256
Shawano	Shawano	41,050	37,157	893
Sheboygan	Sheboygan	113,376	103,877	514
Taylor	Medford	19,539	18,901	975

County	County seat or courthouse	2003 Pop.	1990 Pop.	Land area sq. mi.		County	County seat or courthouse	2003 Pop.	1990 Pop.	Land area sq. mi.
Trempealeau	Whitehall	27,306	25,263	734		Carbon	Rawlins	15,302	16,659	7,896
Vernon	Viroqua	28,496	25,617	795		Converse	Douglas	12,330	11,128	4,255
Vilas	Eagle River	22,041	17,707	874		Crook	Sundance	5,928	5,294	2,859
Walworth	Elkhorn	96,812	75,000	555		Fremont	Lander	35,914	33,662	9,182
Washburn	Shell Lake	16,466	13,772	810		Goshen	Torrington	12,219	12,373	2,225
Washington	West Bend	122,241	95,328	431		Hot Springs	Thermopolis	4,665	4,809	2,004
Waukesha	Waukesha	374,079	304,715	556		Johnson	Buffalo	7,543	6,145	4,166
Waupaca	Waupaca	52,564	46,104	751		Laramie	Cheyenne	84,083	73,142	2,686
Waushara	Wautoma	23,623	19,385	626		Lincoln	Kemmerer	15,208	12,625	4,069
Winnebago	Oshkosh	158,500	140,320	439		Natrona	Casper	68,211	61,226	5,340
Wood	Wisconsin Rapids	75,402	73,605	793		Niobrara	Lusk	2,237	2,499	2,626
						Park	Cody	26,284	23,178	6,942

Wyoming

(23 counties, 97,100 sq. mi. land; pop. 501,242)

County	County seat or courthouse	2003 Pop.	1990 Pop.	Land area sq. mi.		County	County seat or courthouse	2003 Pop.	1990 Pop.	Land area sq. mi.
						Platte	Wheatland	8,628	8,145	2,085
						Sheridan	Sheridan	27,111	23,562	2,523
						Sublette	Pinedale	6,368	4,843	4,883
Albany	Laramie	31,887	30,797	4,273		Sweetwater	Green River	37,018	38,823	10,425
Big Horn	Basin	11,199	10,525	3,137		Teton	Jackson	18,625	11,173	4,008
Campbell	Gillette	36,240	29,370	4,797		Unita	Evanston	19,700	18,705	2,082
						Washakie	Worland	7,883	8,388	2,240
						Weston	Newcastle	6,659	6,518	2,398

Population of Outlying Areas

Source: Bureau of the Census, U.S. Dept. of Commerce; World Almanac research

Population estimates for July 1, 2003, are given for Puerto Rican municipios (a municipio is the governmental unit that is the primary legal subdivision of Puerto Rico; the Census Bureau treats the municipio as the statistical equivalent of a county). All other population counts and all land area figures are from the 2000 census. Because only selected areas are shown, the population and land area figures may not equal the total reported.

ZIP codes with an asterisk (*) are general delivery ZIP codes. Consult the local postmaster for more specific delivery information. Wake Atoll, Johnston Atoll, and Midway Atoll receive mail through APO and FPO addresses.

Commonwealth of Puerto Rico

ZIP code	Municipio	2003 Pop.	Land area sq. mi.		ZIP code	Municipio	2003 Pop.	Land area sq. mi.		ZIP code	Municipio	2003 Pop.	Land area sq. mi.
*00601	Adjuntas	19,014	67		00650	Florida	13,403	15		00720	Orocovis	24,502	63
*00602	Aguada	43,579	31		00653	Guánica	22,347	37		00723	Patillas	20,272	47
*00605	Aguadilla	65,970	37		*00785	Guayama	44,943	65		00624	Peñuelas	27,782	44
00703	Aguas Buenas	29,923	31		00656	Guayanilla	23,426	42		*00732	Ponce	185,930	115
00705	Aibonito	26,853	31		*00970	Guaynabo	101,762	27		00678	Quebradillas	26,468	23
00610	Añasco	29,110	39		00778	Gurabo	38,859	28		00677	Rincón	15,420	14
*00613	Arecibo	101,735	126		00659	Hatillo	40,501	42		00745	Río Grande	54,025	61
00714	Arroyo	19,164	15		00660	Hormigueros	16,951	11		00637	Sabana Grande	26,696	36
00617	Barceloneta	22,648	19		*00791	Humacao	59,945	45		00751	Salinas	31,783	69
00794	Barranquitas	29,720	34		00662	Isabela	45,748	55		00683	San Germán	37,611	55
*00958	Bayamón	224,915	44		00664	Jayuya	17,754	45		*00936	San Juan	433,733	48
00623	Cabo Rojo	49,065	70		00795	Juana Díaz	51,832	60		00754	San Lorenzo	42,456	53
*00726	Caguas	142,161	59		00777	Juncos	37,931	27		00685	San Sebastián	45,537	70
00627	Camuy	36,869	46		00667	Lajas	26,994	60		00757	Santa Isabel	22,238	34
00729	Canóvanas	44,975	33		00669	Lares	35,780	61		*00954	Toa Alta	69,574	27
*00984	Carolina	187,337	45		00670	Las Marías	11,505	46		*00950	Toa Baja	95,173	23
*00963	Cataño	28,341	5		00771	Las Piedras	36,192	34		*00976	Trujillo Alto	79,518	21
*00737	Cayey	47,520	52		00772	Loíza	33,321	19		00641	Utuado	35,418	113
00735	Ceiba	18,206	29		00773	Luquillo	20,230	26		00692	Vega Alta	38,718	28
00638	Ciales	20,227	67		00674	Manatí	47,096	45		*00694	Vega Baja	63,366	46
00739	Cidra	44,614	36		00606	Maricao	6,506	37		00765	Vieques	9,225	51
00769	Coamo	38,511	78		00707	Maunabo	12,833	21		00766	Villalba	29,013	35
00782	Comerío	19,892	28		*00681	Mayagüez	97,627	78		00767	Yabucoa	39,904	55
00783	Corozal	37,785	43		00676	Moca	41,425	50		00698	Yauco	47,430	68
00775	Culebra	1,951	12		00687	Morovis	31,146	39					
00646	Dorado	34,806	23		00718	Naguabo	24,019	52		**TOTAL**		**3,878,532**	**3,425**
00738	Fajardo	41,639	30		00719	Naranjito	30,134	27					

Commonwealth of the Northern Mariana Islands

ZIP code	Municipality	2000 Pop.	Land area sq. mi.		ZIP code	Municipality	2000 Pop.	Land area sq. mi.		ZIP code	Municipality	2000 Pop.	Land area sq. mi.
96950	Northern Islands	6	60		96950	Saipan	62,392	45					
96951	Rota	3,283	33		96952	Tinian	3,540	42		**TOTAL**		**69,221**	**179**

Other U.S. External Territories

ZIP code	Location	2000 Pop.	Land area sq. mi.		ZIP code	Location	2000 Pop.	Land area sq. mi.		ZIP code	Location	2000 Pop.	Land area sq. mi.
American Samoa					*96910	Hagåtña	1,100	1		96929	Yigo	19,474	35
96799	American Samoa	57,291	77		96915	Inarajan	3,052	19		96915	Yona	6,484	20
Guam					96913	Mangilao	13,313	10		**TOTAL**		**154,805**	**210**
*96910	Agaña Hts	3,940	1		96915	Merizo	2,163	6		**Virgin Islands**			
96928	Agat	5,656	10		*96910	Mongmong-Toto-Maite	5,845	2		00820	Saint Croix	53,234	83
*96910	Asan	2,090	6		96915	Piti	1,666	7		*00820	Christiansted	2,637	
*96913	Barrigada	8,652	8		96915	Santa Rita	7,500	16		*00841	Frederiksted	732	
96924	Chalan Pago-Ordot	5,923	6		96910	Sinajana	2,853	1		*00830	Saint John	4,197	20
96929	Dededo	42,980	31		96915	Talofofo	3,215	18		*00804	Saint Thomas	51,181	31
					*96913	Tamuning	18,012	6		*00802	Charlotte Amalie	11,004	
					96915	Umatac	887	6		**TOTAL**		**108,612**	**134**

ASSOCIATIONS AND SOCIETIES

Source: World Almanac questionnaire; World Almanac research

Selected list, by first distinctive key word in each title. (Listed by acronym when that is the official name.) Founding year in parentheses; figure after ZIP code = membership as reported. Information, especially website addresses, subject to change. For other organizations, see Directory of Sports Organizations; Where to Get Help directory in Health chapter; Labor Union Directory in Employment chapter; Membership of Religious Groups in Religion chapter; Major International Organizations in Nations chapter.

Abortion Federation, National (1977), 1755 Massachusetts Ave. NW, Ste. 600, Washington, DC 20036; 440 institutions; www.prochoice.org

Academies, Natl. (1863), 500 Fifth St. NW, Washington, DC 20001; approx. 6,000; www.nationalacademies.org

Accountants, American Institute of Certified Public (1887), 1211 Ave. of the Americas, New York, NY 10036; 328,000+; www.aicpa.org

Acoustical Society of America (1929), 2 Huntington Quad., Ste. 1NO1, Melville, NY 11747; 7,000; asa.aip.org

Actuaries, Society of (1949), 475 N. Martingale Rd., Ste. 600, Schaumburg, IL 60173; 17,000; www.soa.org

Administrative Professionals, Intl. Assn. of (1942), 10502 NW Ambassador Dr., Kansas City, MO 64195-0404; 40,000; www.iaap-hq.org

Advance Collegiate Schools of Business, Assn. to (AACSB) (1916), 600 Emerson Rd., Ste. 300, St. Louis, MO 63141; 941 institutions; www.aacsb.edu

Advancement and Support of Education, Council for (1974); 1307 New York Ave. NW, Ste. 1000, Washington, DC 20005; 3,000 schools; www.case.org

Aeronautic Assn., Natl. (1922), 1815 N. Fort Myer Dr., Ste. 500, Arlington, VA 22209; 3,000; www.naa-usa.org

Aerospace Industries Assn. of America Inc. (1919), 1000 Wilson Blvd., Ste. 1700, Arlington, VA 22209; 89 cos.; www.aia-aerospace.org

Aerospace Medical Assn. (1929), 320 S. Henry St., Alexandria, VA 22314; 3,300; www.asma.org

AFCEA (Armed Forces Communications and Electronics Assn.) (1946), 4400 Fair Lakes Ct., Fairfax, VA 22033; 20,000 indiv., 10,000 corp.; www.afcea.org

African-American Life and History, Assn. for the Study of (1915), CB Powell Building, 525 Bryant St. NW, Ste. C142, Washington, DC 20059; 3500; www.asalh.org

African Violet Soc. of America Inc. (1946), 2375 North St., Beaumont, TX 77702; 9,000; www.avsa.org

AFS Intercultural Programs USA (1947), 198 Madison Ave., 8th Fl., New York, NY 10016; www.afs.org/usa

Agricultural Economics Assn., American (1910), 415 S. Duff Ave., Ste. C, Ames, IA 50010; 3,000; www.aaea.org

Agricultural Engineers, American Soc. of (ASAE) (1907), 2950 Niles Road, St. Joseph, MI 49085; 9,000; www.asae.org

Air & Waste Management Assn. (1907), One Gateway Center, 3rd Fl., 420 Fort Duquesne Blvd., Pittsburgh, PA 15222; 8,000+; www.awma.org

Aircraft Owners and Pilots Assn. (1939), 421 Aviation Way, Frederick, MD 21701; 390,000+; www.aopa.org

Air Force Assn. (1946), 1501 Lee Hwy., Arlington, VA 22209; 142,000+; www.afa.org

Al-Anon Family Group Headquarters, Inc. (1951), 1600 Corporate Landing Pkwy., Virginia Beach, VA 23454; 350,000+ worldwide; www.al-anon.alateen.org

Alcoholics Anonymous (1935), Box 459, Grand Central Station, New York, NY 10163; 2,000,000; www.aa.org

Alcoholism and Drug Dependence, Inc., Natl. Council on (1944), 20 Exchange Pl., Ste. 2902, New York, NY 10005; 100 affil.; www.ncadd.org

Alexander Graham Bell Assn. for the Deaf & Hard of Hearing (1890), 3417 Volta Pl. NW, Washington, DC 20007; 5,000; www.agbell.org

Allergy, Asthma, and Immunology, American Academy of (1943), 611 E. Wells St., Ste. 1100, Milwaukee, WI 53202; 6,000+; www.aaaai.org

Alpha Delta Kappa Sorority Inc. (1947), 1615 W. 92nd St., Kansas City, MO 64114; 47,550; www.alphadeltakappa.org

Alpha Lambda Delta, Natl. (1924), P.O. Box 4403, Macon, GA 31208-4403; 700,000; www.mercer.edu/ald

Alpine Club, American (1902), 710 Tenth St., Ste. 100, Golden, CO 80401; 7,500; www.americanalpineclub.org

Alzheimer's Assn. (1980), 225 N. Michigan Ave., 17th Fl., Chicago, IL 60611; 81 chapt.; www.alz.org

Amateur Chamber Music Players, Inc. (1969), 1123 Broadway, Rm. 304, New York, NY 10010-2007; 5,400; www.acmp.net

AMBUCS, Inc., Natl. (1922), 3315 N Main St., High Point, NC 27262; 5,400; www.ambucs.com

American Indians, Natl. Congress of (1944), 1301 Connecticut Ave. NW, Ste. 200, Washington, DC 20036; 250+ member tribes; www.ncai.org

American-Islamic Relations, Council on, 453 New Jersey Ave. SE, Washington, DC 20003; www.cair-net.org

American Legion (1919), P.O. Box 1055, 700 N. Pennsylvania St., Indianapolis, IN 46206; 3 mil.+; www.legion.org

American Legion Auxiliary (1919), 777 N. Meridian St., 3rd Floor, Indianapolis, IN 46204; 910,000+; www.legion-aux.org

AmeriCares Foundation (1982), 161 Cherry St., New Canaan, CT 06840; www.americares.org

AMIDEAST (formerly American Mideast Educational & Training Services) (1951), 1730 M St. NW, Ste. 1100, Washington, DC 20036; www.amideast.org

Amnesty Intl. USA (1961), 322 8th Ave., New York, NY 10001; 320,000+; www.amnestyusa.org

Amputation Foundation, Inc., Natl. (1919), 40 Church St., Malverne, NY 11565; 700; www.nationalamputation.org

AMVETS (American Veterans) (1943); **AMVETS Natl. Auxiliary** (1946), 4647 Forbes Blvd., Lanham, MD 20706; 250,000; www.amvets.org

Amusement Parks and Attractions, Intl. Assn. of (IAAPA) (1918), 1448 Duke St., Alexandria, VA 22316; 4,500; www.iaapa.org

Animals, American Society for Prevention of Cruelty to (ASPCA) (1866), 424 E. 92nd St., New York, NY 10128-6804; 750,000; www.aspca.org

Animal Protection Institute (1968), 1122 S St., Sacramento, CA 95814; 85,000; www.api4animals.org

Animal Welfare Institute (1951), P.O. Box 3650, Washington, DC 20027; 20,000; www.awionline.org

Anthropological Assn., American (1902), 2200 Wilson Blvd., Ste. 600, Arlington, VA 22201; 11,500; www.aaanet.org

Antiquarian Society, American (1812), 185 Salisbury St., Worcester, MA 01609; 675; www.americanantiquarian.org

Anti-Vivisection Society, American (AAVS), (1883), 801 Old York Road, #204, Jenkintown, PA 19046; 12,000; www.aavs.org

APICS (Educational Society for Resource Mgmt.) (1957), 5301 Shawnee Rd., Alexandria, VA 22312- 2317; 60,000; www.apics.org

Appalachian Mountain Club (1876), 5 Joy St., Boston, MA 02108; 90,000+; www.outdoors.org

Appalachian Trail Conference (1925), 799 Washington St., P.O. Box 807, Harpers Ferry, WV 25425; 125,000; www.appalachiantrail.org

Arbitration Assn., American (1926), 335 Madison Ave., 10th Fl., New York, NY 10017; 7,000; www.adr.org

Arc of the United States, The (1950), 1010 Wayne Avenue, Ste. 650, Silver Spring, MD 20910; 140,000; www.thearc.org

Archaeological Institute of America (1879), 656 Beacon St., 4th Fl., Boston, MA 02215; 9,000; www.archaeological.org

Archery Assn. of the United States, Natl. (1879), One Olympic Plaza, Colorado Springs, CO 80909; 6,000; www.USArchery.org

Architects, American Institute of (1857), 1735 New York Ave. NW, Washington, DC 20006; 63,000; www.aia.org

ARMA Intl. (formerly Assn. of Records Managers & Administrators) (1955), 13725 W. 109th St., Lenexa, KS 66218; 10,000; www.arma.org

Army, Assn. of the United States (1950), 2425 Wilson Blvd., Arlington, VA 22201; 128 chapt.; www.ausa.org

Arthritis Foundation (1948), 1330 W. Peachtree St., Ste. 100, Atlanta, GA 30309; www.arthritis.org

Arts, Americans for the (1996), 1000 Vermont Ave. NW, 6th Fl., Washington, DC 20005; 1,500; www.artsusa.org

Arts and Sciences, American Academy of (1780), Norton's Woods, 136 Irving St., Cambridge, MA 02138; 4,300 fellows; www.amacad.org

ASPRS, The Imaging and Geospatial Information Society (1934), 5410 Grosvenor Ln., Ste. 210, Bethesda, MD 20814; 7,000; www.asprs.org

Associated Press (1848), 50 Rockefeller Plaza, New York, NY 10020; 1,500+ newspapers, 5,000+ U.S. broadcast stations; www.ap.org

Astrologers, Inc., American Federation of (AFA, Inc.) (1938), 6535 South Rural Road, Tempe, AZ 85283; 4,000; www.astrologers.com

▶ IT'S A FACT: The American Federation of Astrologers' website (www.astrologers.com) features an "Astro Economic Stock Watch" newsletter that analyzes certain stocks and market trends using astrological charts and predictions.

Astronautical Society, American (1954), 6352 Rolling Mill Pl., #102, Springfield, VA 22152; 1,400; www.astronautical.org

Astronomical Society, American (1899), 2000 Florida Ave. NW, Ste. 400, Washington, DC 20009; 7,000; www.aas.org

Ataxia Foundation, Natl. (1957), 2600 Fernbrook Ln., Ste. 119, Minneapolis, MN 55447-4752; 10,000; www.ataxia.org

Atheists, American (1963), P.O. Box 5733, Parsippany, NJ 07054; 2,300; www.atheists.org

Audubon Soc., Natl. (1905), 700 Broadway, New York, NY 10003; 600,000; www.audubon.org

Authors Guild, The (1912), 31 E. 28th St., New York, NY 10016; 8,200; www.authorsguild.org

Authors Registry, The (1995), 31 E. 28th St., New York, NY 10016; 30,000; www.authorsregistry.org

Autism Soc. of America (1965), 7910 Woodmont Ave., Ste. 300, Bethesda, MD 20814; 24,000; www.autism-society.org

Autograph Collectors Club, Universal (1965), P.O. Box 6181, Washington, DC 20044-6181; 1,500; www.uacc.org

Automobile Club of America, Antique (1935), 501 W. Governor Road, P.O. Box 417, Hershey, PA 17033; 60,000; www.aaca.org

Automobile License Plate Collectors Assn. (1953), 7365 Main. St., #214, Stratford, CT 06614; 3,200; www.alpca.org

Automotive Hall of Fame (1939), 21400 Oakwood Blvd., Dearborn, MI 48124; 200; www.automotivehalloffame.org

Badminton Assn., USA (1938), One Olympic Plaza, Colorado Springs, CO 80909; 3,000; www.usabadminton.org

Bald-Headed Men of America (1973), 102 Bald Dr., Morehead City, NC 28557; approx. 22,000; members.aol.com/baldusa

Bar Assn., American (1878), 321 N. Clark St., Chicago, IL 60610; 400,000+; www.abanet.org

Bar Assn., Federal (1920), 2215 M Street NW, Washington, DC 20037; 16,000; www.fedbar.org

Barbershop Harmony Society (1938), 7930 Sheridan Rd., Kenosha, WI 53143; 31,000; www.spebsqsa.org

Baseball Congress, American Amateur (1935), 118-119 Redfield Plaza, P.O. Box 467, Marshall, MI 49068; 14,500 teams; www.aabc.us

Baseball Congress, Natl. (1935), 300 S. Sycamore, P.O. Box 1420, Wichita, KS 67201; 35,000; www.nbcbaseball.com

Baseball Research, Inc., Society for American (1971), 812 Huron Road E #719, Cleveland, OH 44115; 6,800; www.sabr.org

Battleship Assn., American (1964), P.O. Box 711247, San Diego, CA 92171; 1,025

Beer Can Collectors of America (1970), 747 Merus Ct., Fenton, MO 63026; 4,000; www.bcca.com

Beta Gamma Sigma Honor Society (1913), 125 Weldon Parkway, Maryland Heights, MO 63043; 475,000; www.betagamasigma.org

Beta Sigma Phi (1931), 1800 W. 91st Pl., Kansas City, MO 64114; 200,000; www.betasigmaphi.org

Better Business Bureaus, Council of (1970), 4200 Wilson Blvd., Suite 800, Arlington, VA 22203; 150 bureaus; www.bbb.org

Bible Society, American (1816), 1865 Broadway, New York, NY 10023; 650,000; www.americanbible.org

Biblical Literature, Society of (1880), 825 Houston Mill Rd., Ste. 350, Atlanta, GA 30329; 6,000; www.sbl-site.org

Bibliographical Society of America (1904), P.O. Box 1537, Lenox Hill Station, New York, NY 10021; 1,200; www.bibsocamer.org

Big Brothers/Big Sisters of America (1904), 230 N. 13th St., Philadelphia, PA 19107; 470 agencies; bbbsa.org

Biochemistry and Molecular Biology, American Society for (1906), 9650 Rockville Pike, Bethesda, MD 20814; 11,900; www.asbmb.org

Biological Sciences, American Institute of (1947), 1444 I St. NW, Ste. 200, Washington, DC 20005; 240,000; www.aibs.org

Blind, American Council of the (1961), 1155 15th St. NW, Ste. 1004, Washington, DC 20005; 15,000; www.acb.org

Blind, Natl. Federation of the (1940), 1800 Johnson St., Baltimore, MD 21230; 50,000; www.nfb.org

Blinded Veterans Assn. (1958), 477 H St. NW, Washington, DC 20001; 10,035; www.bva.org

Blindness America, Prevent (1908), 500 E. Remington Rd., Ste. 200, Schaumburg, IL 60173; 50,000; www.preventblindness.org

B'nai B'rith Intl. (1843), 2020 K St. NW, 7th Fl., Washington, DC 20006; 250,000; www.bnaibrith.org

Boat Owners Assn. of the U.S. (1966), 880 S. Pickett St., Alexandria, VA 22304; 540,000; www.boatUS.com

Bookplate Collectors and Designers, American Soc. of (1922), P.O. Box 380340, Cambridge, MA 02238-0340; 200; www.bookplate.org

Boy Scouts of America (1910), P.O. Box 152079, Irving, TX 75015; 4 mil+; www.scouting.org

Boys & Girls Clubs of America (1906), 1230 W. Peachtree St. NW, Atlanta, GA 30309; 4 mil; www.bgca.org

Bread for the World (1974), 50 F St. NW, Ste. 500, Washington, DC 20001; 47,000; www.bread.org

Brewing Chemists, American Society of (1934), 3340 Pilot Knob Road, St. Paul, MN 55121; 700; www.asbcnet.org

Broadcasters, Natl. Assn. of (1923), 1771 N St. NW, Washington, DC 20036; www.nab.org

Burroughs Bibliophiles, The (1960), 454 Elaine Dr., Pittsburgh, PA 15236-2417; 823

Business Communicators, Intl. Assn. of (1970), 1 Hallidie Plaza, Ste. 600, San Francisco, CA 94102; 13,700; www.iabc.com

Business Women's Assn., American (1949), 9100 Ward Pkwy., P.O. Box 8728, Kansas City, MO 64114; 55,000; www.abwa.org

Button Society, Natl. (1938), 2733 Juno Pl., Akron, OH 44333-4137; 4,000

Camp Fire USA (formerly Camp Fire Boys & Girls) (1910), 4601 Madison Ave., Kansas City, MO 64112; 735,000; www.campfireusa.org

Camping Assn., American (1910), 5000 State Rd. 67 N., Martinsville, IN 46151; 6,700; www.acacamps.org

Cancer Society, American (1913), 1599 Clifton Rd. NE, Atlanta, GA 30329; 3,400 local offices; www.cancer.org

Cartoonists Society, Natl. (1948), 1133 West Morse Blvd., Ste. 201, Winter Park, FL 32789; 600; www.reuben.org

Cat Fanciers' Assn., The (1906), 1805 Atlantic Ave., P.O. Box 1005, Manasquan, NJ 08736-0805; www.cfainc.org

Catholic Bishops, United States Conference of (1966), 3211 4th St. NE, Washington, DC 20017; 402 members, 350 staff; www.nccbuscc.org

Catholic Church Extension Society of the USA (1905), 150 S. Wacker Dr., 20th Fl., Chicago, IL 60606; www.catholic-extension.org

Catholic Daughters of the Americas (1903), 10 West 71st Street, New York, NY 10023; 96,000; www.catholicdaughters.org

Catholic Educational Assn., Natl. (1904), 1077 30th St. NW, Ste. 100, Washington, DC 20007; 200,000; www.ncea.org

Catholic Historical Soc., American (1884), 263 S. Fourth St., Philadelphia, PA 19106-3819; 475; www.AMCHS.org

Catholic Library Association (1921), 100 North St., Ste. 224, Pittsfield, MA 01201-5109; 1,000; www.cathla.org

Catholic War Veterans, USA Inc. (1935), 441 N. Lee St., Alexandria, VA 22314-2301; 20,000; cwv.org

Cemetery and Funeral Assn., Intl. (1887), 1895 Preston White Dr., #220, Reston, VA 22091; 6,000; www.icfa.org

Ceramic Society, The American (1899), 735 Ceramic Pl., Westerville, OH 43081; 8,000; www.ceramics.org

Cereal Chemists, American Assn. of (1915), 3340 Pilot Knob Road, St. Paul, MN 55121; 3,000; www.aaccnet.org

Cerebral Palsy Assns., Inc., United (1949), 1660 L St. NW, Ste. 700, Washington, DC 20036; 150; www.ucpa.org

Certification of Computing Professionals, Institute for (1973), 2350 E. Devon Ave., Ste. 115, Des Plaines, IL 60018-4610; 55,000; www.iccp.org

Chamber of Commerce of the U.S.A. (1912), 1615 H St. NW, Washington, DC 20062; 215,000; www.uschamber.com

Chamber Music Players, Inc., Amateur (1969), 1123 Broadway, Rm. 304, New York, NY 10010; 5,200; www.acmp.net

Checker Federation, American (1949), 5304 Barton Vale Ct., Nashville, TN 37211; 500; www.acfcheckers.com

Chemical Society, American (1876), 1155 16th St. NW, Washington, DC 20036; 163,000; www.chemistry.org

Chemistry Council, American (1872), 1300 Wilson Blvd., Arlington, VA 22209; 170; www.americanchemistry.com

Chess Federation, U.S. (1939), 3054 US Rt. 9W, New Windsor, NY 12553; 90,000+; www.uschess.org

Chiefs of Police, Intl. Assn. of (1893), 515 N. Washington St., Alexandria, VA 22314; 19,000; www.theiacp.org

Childhood Education Intl., Assn. for (1892), 17904 Georgia Ave., Ste. 215, Olney, MD 20832; 10,000; www.acei.org

Children's Aid Society (1912), 181 West Valley Ave., Ste. 300, Homewood, AL 35209; www.childrensaid.org

Children's Book Council, The (1945), 12 W. 37th St., 2nd Fl., New York, NY 10018; 78 publishers; www.cbcbooks.org

Child Welfare League of America (1920), 440 First St. NW, Third Fl., Washington, DC 20001; 1,100 agencies; www.cwla.org

Chiropractic Assn., American (1963), 1701 Clarendon Blvd., Arlington, VA 22209; 19,000; www.amerchiro.org

Chris-Craft Antique Boat Club (1973), 217 S. Adams St., Tallahassee, FL 32301-1734; 3,000; www.chris-craft.org

Christian Children's Fund (1938), 2821 Emerywood Pkwy., Richmond, VA 23294; 161; www.christianchildrensfund.org

Cities, Natl. League of (1924), 1301 Pennsylvania Ave. NW, Ste. 550, Washington, DC 20004; 1,780; www.nlc.org

Citizen Information Center, Federal (1970), Pueblo, CO 81009; www.pueblo.gsa.gov

Civil Air Patrol (1941), 105 S. Hansell St., Bldg. 714, Maxwell AFB, AL 36112; 60,000; www.capnhq.gov

Civil Engineers, American Society of (1852), 1801 Alexander Bell Dr., Reston, VA 20191; 123,000+; www.asce.org

Civil Liberties Union, American (ACLU) (1920), 125 Broad St., 18th Fl., New York, NY 10004; 380,000; www.aclu.org

Coaster Enthusiasts, American (1978), ACE, EB 110, P.O. Box 1691, Minneapolis, MN 55480; 8,420; www.aceonline.org

Coast Guard Combat Veterans Assn. (1985), 295 Shalimar Dr., Shalimar, FL 32579; 1,800; www.aug.edu/~libwrw/cgcva/cgcva.htm

Collectors, Natl. Assn. of (1996), 18222 Flower Hill Way, #299, Gaithersburg, MD 20879; 30,000; collectors.org

Collecting Clubs, Assn. of (2002), 18222 Flower Hill Way, #299, Gaithersburg, MD 20879; 96 clubs; collectors.org

Co-dependents Anonymous (1986), PO Box 33577, Phoenix, AZ 85067; www.codependents.org

College Admission Counseling, Natl. Assn. for (1937), 1631 Prince Street, Alexandria, VA 22314; 8,000; www.nacac.com

College Board, The (1900), 45 Columbus Ave., New York, NY 10023; 500; www.collegeboard.org

College Music Society, The (1958), 312 East Pine St., Missoula, MT 59802; 9,000; www.music.org

Colleges and Employers, Natl. Assn. of (1956), 62 Highland Ave., Bethlehem, PA 18017; 3,082; www.naceweb.org

Colleges and Universities, Assn. of American (1915), 1818 R St. NW, Washington, DC 20009; 850+ institutions; www.aacu.org

Colonial Dames XVII Century, Natl. Soc. (1915), 1300 New Hampshire Ave. NW, Washington, DC 20036; 13,240; www.colonialdames17c.net

Commercial Collectors, Inc., Int'l. Assn. of (1970), 4040 W. 70th Street, Minneapolis, MN 55435; 382; www.commercialcollector.com

Commercial Law League of America (1895), 150 N. Michigan Ave., # 600, Chicago, IL 60601; 3,400; www.clla.org

Common Cause (1970), 1250 Connecticut Ave. NW, Ste. 600, Washington, DC 20036; 200,000+; www.commoncause.org

Communication Assn., Natl. (1914), 1765 N St. NW, Washington, DC, 20036; 5,600; www.natcom.org

Community and Justice, National Conference for (1927), 475 Park Ave. S.; New York, NY 10016; 3,500; www.nccj.org

Community Colleges, American Assn. of (1920), One Dupont Circle NW, Ste. 410, Washington, DC 20036; 1,113 inst; www.aacc.nche.edu

Composers, Authors & Publishers, American Soc. of (ASCAP) (1914), One Lincoln Plaza, New York, NY 11217; 180,000; www.ascap.org

Composers/USA, Natl. Assn. of (1933), P.O. Box 49256, Barrington Station, Los Angeles, CA 90049; 600; www.music-usa.org/nacusa

Computing Machinery, Assn. for (1947), 1515 Broadway, 17th Fl., New York, NY 10036; 75,000+; www.acm.org

Concerned Women for America (1979), 1015 Fifteenth St. NW, Ste. 1100, Washington, DC 20005; 500,000; www.cwfa.org

Congress of Racial Equality (CORE) (1942), 817 Broadway, 3rd Floor, New York, NY 10003; 100,000; www.core-online.org

Conscientious Objectors, Central Committee for (1948), 405 14th St., #205, Oakland, CA 94612; 5,000-6,000; www.objector.org

Construction Inspectors, Assn. of (1974), 1224 N. Nokomis NE, Alexandria, MN 56308; 1,000; www.iami.org/aci

Construction Specifications Institute (1948); 99 Canal Center Plaza, Ste. 300, Alexandria, VA 22301; 17,500; www.csinet.org

Consumer Federation of America (1968), 1424 16th St. NW, Ste. 604, Washington, DC 20036; 300 member organizations; www.consumerfed.org

Consumer Interests, American Council on (ACCI) (1953), 415 S. Duff Ave. Ste. C, Ames, IA 50010-6600; 750; www.consumerinterests.org

Consumers Union of the U.S. (1936), 101 Truman Ave., Yonkers, NY 10703; 405,990; www.consumersunion.org

Contract Bridge League, American (1937), 2990 Airways Blvd., Memphis, TN 38116; 170,000; www.acbl.org

Co-op America (1982), 1612 K St. NW, Ste. 600, Washington, DC 20006; 50,000 individuals, 2,000 businesses; www.coopamerica.org

Correctional Assn., American (1870), 4380 Forbes Blvd., Lanham, MD 20706; 20,000; www.aca.org

Cosmetology Assn., Natl. (1921); 401 N. Michigan Ave., Chicago, IL 60611; 30,000; www.salonprofessionals.org

Counseling Assn., American (1952), 5999 Stevenson Ave., Alexandria, VA 22304; 55,000; www.counseling.org

Country Music Assn. (1958), One Music Circle S., Nashville, TN 37203; 6,700; www.CMAworld.com

Crafts & Creative Industries, Assn. of (ACCI) (1976), 1100-H Brandywine Blvd., P.O. Box 3388, Zanesville, OH 43702; 6,327; www.accicrafts.org

Crime and Delinquency, Natl. Council on (1907), 1970 Broadway, Ste. 500, Oakland, CA 94612; 300+; www.nccdcrc.org

Croplife America (1933), 1156 15th St. NW, Ste. 400, Washington, DC 20005; 80 cos.; www.croplifeamerica.org

Cryogenic Soc. of America, Inc. (1964), 1033 South Blvd., Ste. 13, Oak Park, IL 60302; 600; www.cryogenicsociety.org

Customs Brokers and Forwarders Assn. of America, Inc., Natl. (1897), 1200 18th St. NW, Ste. 901, Washington, DC 20036; 800; www.ncbfaa.org

Cystic Fibrosis Foundation (1955), 6931 Arlington Rd., Bethesda, MD 20814; 30,000; www.cff.org

Dark-Sky Association, Intl. (1988), 3225 N. First Ave., Tucson, AZ 85719-2103; 10,600; www.darksky.org

Daughters of the American Revolution Natl. Society (1890), 1776 D Street NW, Washington, DC 20006; 170,000; www.dar.org

Daughters of the Confederacy, United (1894), 328 North Blvd., Richmond, VA 23220; 25,000; www.hqudc.org

Deaf, Natl. Assn. of the (1880), 814 Thayer Ave., Ste. 250, Silver Spring, MD 20910; 16,500; www.nad.org

Defenders of Wildlife (1947), 1130 17th St. NW, Washington, DC 20030; 430,000; www.defenders.org

Delta Kappa Gamma Society Intl. (1929), P.O. Box 1589., Austin, TX 78767; 136,000; www.deltakappagamma.org

Delta Mu Delta Honor Soc. (1913), 2 Salt Creek Ln., Ste. 6, Hinsdale, IL 60521; 125,000; www.deltamudelta.org

Democratic Natl. Committee (1848), 430 S. Capitol Street SE, Washington, DC 20003; 440 elected members; www.democrats.org

DeMolay International (1919), 10200 NW Ambassador Dr., Kansas City, MO 64153; 30,000; www.demolay.org

Dental Assn., American (1859), 211 E. Chicago Ave., Chicago, IL 60611; 149,000; www.ada.org

Diabetes Assn., American (1940), 1701 North Beauregard St., Alexandria, VA 22311; 416,967; www.diabetes.org

Dialect Society, American (1889), c/o Allan Metcalf, English Dept., MacMurray College, 447 E. College Ave., Jacksonville, IL 62650; 500; www.americandialect.org

Directors Guild of America (1936), 7920 Sunset Blvd., Los Angeles, CA 90046; 12,700+; dga.org

Disabled American Veterans (1932), P.O. Box 14301, Cincinnati, OH 45250-0301; 1,000,000; www.dav.org

Disabled Sports USA (1967), 451 Hungerford Dr., Ste. 100, Rockville, MD 20850; 60,000+; www.dsusa.org

Doctors Without Borders/Médecins Sans Frontières (1971), 333 Seventh Ave., 2nd Fl., New York, NY 10001; 2,500+; www.doctorswithoutborders.org

Dogs on Stamps Study Unit (1979), 202A Newport Rd., Monroe Twp., NJ 08831-3920; 300; www.dossu.org

Down Syndrome Society, Natl. (1979), 666 Broadway, 8th Fl., New York, NY 10012; 50,000; www.ndss.org

Dozenal Society of America (1944), Six Brancatelli, West Islip, NY 11795; 144; www.dozens.org

Ducks Unlimited (1937), One Waterfowl Way, Memphis, TN 38120; 620,000; www.ducks.org

Eagles, Fraternal Order of (1898), 1623 Gateway Circle South, Grove City, OH 43123; 1.1 mil; www.foe.com

Easter Seals (1919), 230 W. Monroe St., Ste. 1800, Chicago, IL 60606; www.easter-seals.org

Eastern Star, General Grand Chapter, Order of the (1876), 1618 New Hampshire Ave. NW, Washington, DC 20009; 1 mil.+; www.easternstar.org

Edsel Club (1967), 19296 Tuckaway Ct., N. Fort Myers, FL 33903; 300; www.edselworld.com

Education, American Council on (1918), One Dupont Circle NW, Ste. 800, Washington, DC 20036; 1,700 org.; www.acenet.edu

Education, Council for Advancement & Support of (1974), 1307 New York Ave. NW, Ste 1000, Washington, DC 20005; 3,000+ schools; www.case.org

Education of Young Children, Natl. Assn. for the (1926), 1509 16th St. NW, Washington, DC 20036; 103,000; www.naeyc.org

Educators for World Peace, Intl. Assn. of (1969), P.O. Box 3282, Mastin Lake Station, Huntsville, AL 35810; 55,000; www.earthportals.com/portal_messenger/mercieca.html

Egalitarian Communities, Federation of (1978), HC-3 Box 3370-BF, Tecumseh, MO, 65760; 250; www.thefec.org

88th Infantry Division Assn. (1946), 11 Lovett Ave., Brockton, MA 02301-1750; 4,200; www.88infdiv.org

84th Infantry Div. Railsplitter Soc., (1945), P.O. Box 827, Sioux Falls, SD 57101-0827; 2,115

82nd Airborne Division Assn., Inc. (1946), P.O. Box 9308, Fayetteville, NC 28311; 27,000+; www.82ndassociation.org

Electrical and Electronics Engineers, Institute of (1963), 445 Hoes Lane, Piscataway, NJ 08854; 380,000; www.ieee.org

Electrical Manufacturers Assn., Natl. (1926), 1300 N. 17th St., Ste. 1847, Rosslyn, VA 22209; 560 cos.; www.nema.org

Electrochemical Society, Inc., The (ECS, Inc.) (1902), 65 South Main St., Bldg. D, Pennington, NJ 08534-2839; 8,000+; www.electrochem.org

Electronics Service Dealers Assciation, Natl. (NESDA) (1963), 3608 Pershing Ave., Ft. Worth, TX 76107; 734; www.nesda.com

Electronics Technicians, Intl. Society of Certified (1980), 3608 Pershing Ave., Ft. Worth, TX 76107-4527; 2,812; www.iscet.org

Elks of the U.S.A., Benevolent and Protective Order of (1868), 2750 N. Lakeview Ave., Chicago, IL 60614; 1.1 mil+; www.elks.org

Energy Engineers, Assn. of (1977), 4025 Pleasantdale Rd., Ste. 420, Atlanta, GA 30340; 9,000; www.aeecenter.org

Engineers, Natl. Society of Professional (1934), 1420 King St., Alexandria, VA 22314; 54,000; www.nspe.org

English Inc., U.S. (1983), 1747 Pennsylvania Ave. NW, Washington, DC 20006; 1 mil+; www.usenglish.org

English-Speaking Union of the US (1920), 144 E. 39th St., New York, NY 10036; 18,000; www.english-speakingunion.org

Entomological Society of America (1953), 10001 Derekwood Ln., Ste 100, Lanham, MD 20706-4876; 5,500; www.entsoc.org

Environmental Assessment Association (1972), 1224 North Nokomis NE, Alexandria, MN 56308; 3,000; www.iami.org/eaa

Environmental Health Assn., Natl. (1937), 720 S. Colorado Blvd., Ste. 970-S, Denver, CO 80246; approx. 5,000; www.neha.org

Environmental Medicine, American Academy of (1965), 7701 E. Kellogg, Ste. 625, Wichita, KS 67207; 397; www.aaem.com

Equipment Manufacturers, Assn. of (1894), 111 E. Wisconsin Ave., Milwaukee, WI 53202; 700+ cos.; www.aem.org

Esperanto League for North America Inc. (1952), P.O. Box 1129, El Cerrito, CA 94530; 700; www.esperanto-usa.org

Evangelism Crusades, Inc., Intl. (1959) 14617 Victory Blvd., Van Nuys, CA 91411; 300

Experimental Aircraft Assn. (1953), P.O. Box 3086, Oshkosh, WI 54903; 170,000+; www.eaa.org

Ex-Prisoners of War, American (1942), 3201 E. Pioneer Pkwy., #40, Arlington, TX 76010; 30,000; www.axpow.org

Fairs & Expositions, Intl. Assn. of (1885), P.O. Box 985, Springfield, MO 65809; 2,900; www.fairsandexpos.com

Family, Career and Community Leaders of America (1945), 1910 Association Dr., Reston, VA 20791; 227,000; www.fcclainc.org

Family Physicians, American Academy of (1947), PO Box 11210, Leawood, KS 66211; 94,300; www.aafp.org

Family Relations, Natl. Council on (1938), 3989 Central Avenue NE, Suite 550, Minneapolis, MN 55421; 4,000; www.ncfr.org

Farm Bureau, American (1919), 600 Maryland Ave. SW, Ste. 800, Washington, DC 20024; 5 mil+ families; www.fb.com

Farmers of America Org., Natl. Future (1929), P.O. Box 68960, 6060 FFA Drive, Indianapolis, IN 46268-0960; 1 mil.; www.ffa.org

Farmers Union, Natl. (1902), 11900 E. Cornell Ave., Aurora, CO 80014; 300,000; www.nfu.org

Fat Acceptance, Inc., Natl. Assn. to Advance (NAAFA) (1969), P.O. Box 188620, Sacramento, CA 95818; 2,500; www.naafa.org

Fellowship of Reconciliation, The (1915), 521 N. Broadway, Nyack, NY 10960; 30,000; www.forusa.org

Feminists for Life of America (1972), 733 15th St. NW, Ste. 1100, Wash., DC 20005; c. 5,000; www.feministsforlife.org

Financial Professionals, Assn. for (formerly Treasury Management Assn.) (1979), 7315 Wisconsin Ave., Ste. 600W, Bethesda, MD 20814; 14,000; www.AFPonline.org

Financial Service Professionals, Soc. of (formerly American Society of CLU & ChFC) (1928), 270 S. Bryn Mawr Ave., Bryn Mawr, PA 19010; 25,000; www.financialpro.org

Financial Women Intl. (1921 as Natl. Assoc. of Bank Women), 200 N. Glebe Rd., Ste. 820, Arlington, VA 22203; 2,000+; www.fwi.org

Fire Chiefs, Intl. Assn. of (1873), 4025 Fair Ridge Dr., Ste. 300, Fairfax, VA 22033; 12,000; www.iafc.org

Fire Protection Assn., Natl. (NFPA) (1896), 1 Batterymarch Park, Quincy, MA 02169; 75,000; www.nfpa.org

Fire Protection Engineers, Soc. of (1950), 7315 Wisconsin Avenue, Ste. 1225W, Bethesda, MD 20814; 3,500; www.sfpe.org

Fisheries Soc., American (1870), 5410 Grosvenor Ln., Ste. 110, Bethesda, MD 20814; 9,000; www.fisheries.org

Fleet Reserve Association (1924), 125 N. West St., Alexandria, VA 22314-2754; 135,000; www.fra.org

Food Industry Suppliers, Intl. Assn. of (1911), 1451 Dolley Madison Blvd., McLean, VA 22101; 700 cos.; www.iafis.org

Food Technologists, Institute of (1939), 525 W. Van Buren, Ste. 1000, Chicago, IL 60607; 28,000; www.ift.org

Foreign Study, American Institute for, The (1964), River Plaza, 9 W. Broad St., Stamford, CT 06902; 1 mil+; www.aifs.com

Foreign Trade Council, Inc., Natl. (1914), 1625 K St. NW, Washington, DC 20006; 300 companies.; www.nftc.org

Forensic Sciences, American Academy of (1948), P.O. Box 669, Colorado Springs, CO 80901-0669; 6,000; www.aafs.org

Foresters, Society of American (1900), 5400 Grosvenor La., Bethesda, MD 20814; 17,500; www.safnet.org

Forest History Society (1946), 701 Wm. Vickers Ave., Durham, NC 27701-3162; 1,000; www.foresthistory.org

Forests, American (1875), P.O. 2000, Washington, DC 20013; 12,000; www.americanforests.org

4-H Clubs (1914), CSREES/USDA, 1400 Independence Ave. SW, Washington, DC 20250; 6.8 mil; www.4h-usa.org

Frederick A. Cook Society, (1940), P.O. Box 11421, Pittsburgh, PA 15238; 274; www.cookpolar.org

Freedom From Religion Foundation (1978), P.O. Box 750, Madison, WI 53701; 5,000; www.ffrf.org

Freedom of Information Center (1958), Missouri School of Journalism, 133 Neff Annex, Columbia, MO 65211-0012; foi.missouri.edu

Freemasonry, Scottish Rite of, Supreme Council Ancient and Accepted Scottish Rite of, Northern Masonic Jurisdiction (1872), P.O. Box 519, Lexington, MA 02420; 270,000; www.supremecouncil.org

Freemasonry, Scottish Rite of, Supreme Council Ancient and Accepted Scottish Rite of, Southern Jurisdiction (1801), 1733 16th St. NW, Washington, DC 20009-3103; 350,000; www.srmason-sj.org

Free Men, Natl. Coalition of (1977), P.O. Box 582023, Minneapollis, MN 55458; 2,000; www.ncfm.org

Free Press Readership Council, American (2001), 1433 Pennsylvania Ave., S.E., Washington, DC 20003; 4,500; www.americanfreepress.net

French Institute/Alliance Française (1971), 22 E. 60th St., New York, NY 10022; 6,500; www.fiaf.org

Frozen Food Institute, American (1942), 2000 Corporate Ridge, Suite 1000, McLean, VA 22102; 505; www.affi.com

Funeral Consumers Alliance (FAMSA) (1963), 33 Patchen Rd., South Burlington, VT 05403; 280,000; www.funerals.org/famsa

Future Business Leaders of America/Phi Beta Lambda, Inc. (1942), 1912 Association Dr. Reston, VA 20191; 240,000; www.fbla-pbl.org

Gamblers Anonymous (1957), P.O. Box 17173, Los Angeles, CA 90017; approx. 30,000; www.gamblersanonymous.org

Garden Club of America (1913), 14 E. 60th St., New York, NY 10022; 18,000; www.gcamerica.org

Garden Clubs, Inc., National Council of State (1929), 4401 Magnolia Ave., St. Louis, MO 63110; 235,316; www.gardenclub.org

Gay and Lesbian Task Force, Natl. (1973), 1325 Massachusetts Ave. NW, Ste. 600, Washington, DC 20005; 30,000; www.thetaskforce.org

Genealogical Society, Natl. (1903), 4527 17th St. N, Arlington, VA 22207; 17,000; www.ngsgenealogy.org

General Contractors of America, The Associated (1918), 333 John Carlyle St., Ste. 200, Alexandria, VA 22314; 33,000+ cos.; www.agc.org

Genetic Association, American (1903), P.O. Box 257, Buckeystown, MD 21717; www.theaga.org

Geographers, Assn. of American (1904), 1710 16th St. NW, Washington, DC 20009; 7,500+; www.aag.org

Geographic Education, Natl. Council for (1915), 206-A Martin Hall, Jacksonville State University, 700 Pelham Rd. N, Jacksonville, AL 36265; 2,550; www.ncge.org

Geographic Society, Natl. (1888), 1145 17th St. NW, Washington, DC 20036; 10 mil.; www.nationalgeographic.com

Geographical Society, The American (1851), 120 Wall St., Ste. 100, New York, NY 10005; 1,000; www.amergeog.org

Geological Society of America (1888), 3300 Penrose Pl., P.O. Box 9140, Boulder, CO 80301; 17,500; www.geosociety.org

George S. Patton, Jr. Society (1970), 3116 Thorn St., San Diego, CA 92104; 350; www.pattonhq.com

Geriatrics Society, American (1942), 350 5th Ave., Ste. 801, New York, NY 10118; 6,739; www.americangeriatrics.org

Gideons Intl. (1899), P.O. Box 140800, Nashville, TN 37214; 249,250; www.gideons.org

Gifted Children, Natl. Assn. for (1954), 1707 L Street NW, Suite 550, Washington, DC 20036; 8,000; www.nagc.org

Girl Scouts of the U.S.A. (1912), 420 5th Ave., New York, NY 10018; 3.7 mil; www.girlscouts.org

Golden Key Intl. Honor Society (1977), 621 North Ave., Ste. C-100, Atlanta, GA 30308; 335 chapters; www.goldenkey.org

Gold Star Mothers of America, Inc. (1928), 2128 Leroy Place NW, Washington, DC 20008; 1,200; www.goldstarmoms.com.

Golf Assn., U.S. (1894), Golf House, P.O. Box 708, Far Hills, NJ 07931; 800,000; www.usga.org

Gospel Music Assn. (1964), 1205 Division St., Nashville, TN 37203; 5,000+; www.gospelmusic.org

Governors' Assn., Natl. (1908), Hall of the States, 444 N. Capitol, Ste. 267, Washington, DC 20001; 55 govs.; www.nga.org

Grange Patrons of Husbandry, Natl. (1867), 1616 H Street NW, Washington, DC 20006; 300,000; www.nationalgrange.org

Graphic Arts, American Institute of (1914), 164 5th Ave., New York, NY 10010; 17,000; www.aiga.org

Gray Panthers (1970), 733 15th St. NW, Ste 437, Washington, DC 20005; approx. 17,000; www.graypanthers.org

Green Mountain Club, The (1910), 4711 Waterbury-Stowe Rd., Waterbury Ctr., VT 05677; 7,500+; www.greenmountainclub.org

Green Party (1984), P.O. Box 1406, Chicago, IL 60690; www.greenparty.org

Greenpeace, Inc. (1971), 702 H St. NW, Suite 300, Washington, DC 20001; 250,000; www.greenpeaceusa.org.

Ground Water Assn., Natl. (1948), 601 Dempsey Rd., Westerville, OH 43081; 16,500; www.ngwa.org

Group Against Smokers' Pollution, Inc. (GASP) (1971), P.O. Box 632, College Park, MD 20741; 10,000+

Guide Dog Foundation for the Blind, Inc. (1946), 371 E. Jericho Turnpike, Smithtown, NY 11787; 162,500; www.guidedog.org

Hadassah, the Women's Zionist Organization of America (1912), 50 W. 58th St., New York, NY 10019; 300,000+; www.hadassah.org

Handball Assn., U.S. (1951), 2333 N. Tucson Blvd., Tucson, AZ 85716; 8,000; www.ushandball.org

Health Council, Natl. (1920), 1730 M St. NW, Ste. 500, Washington, DC 20036; 115 org.; www.nationalhealthcouncil.org

Hearing Society, Intl. (1951), 16880 Middlebelt Rd., Ste. 4, Livonia, MI 48154; 3,000; www.ihsinfo.org

Heart Assn., American (1924), 7272 Greenville Ave., Dallas, TX 75231; 22.5 mil.; www.americanheart.org

Heating, Refrigerating & Air-Conditioning Engineers, Inc., American Soc. of (1894), 1791 Tullie Cir. NE, Atlanta, GA 30329; 55,000; www.ashrae.org

Hebrew Immigrant Aid Society (HIAS) (1881), 333 Seventh Ave., 17th Fl., New York, NY 10001; 20,000; www.hias.org

Helicopter Society, American (1944), 271 N. Washington St., Alexandria, VA 22314, 6,140; www.vtol.org

Hemispheric Affairs, Council on (1975), 1730 M St., Ste. 1010, NW, Washington, DC 20036; 1,875; www.coha.org

Hibernians in America, Ancient Order of (1836), 1301 S.W. 26th Avenue, Ft. Lauderdale, FL 33312; 200,000; www.aoh.com

Highpointers Club (1986), P.O. Box 1496, Golden, CO 80402; 2,600; www.highpointers.org

High School Band Directors Hall of Fame, Natl. (1985), 4166 Will Rhoades Dr., Columbus, GA 31909; 29; www.hsbanddirectorhalloffame.com

Hiking Society, American (1976), 1422 Fenwick Lane, Silver Spring, MD 20910; 5,000; www.americanhiking.org

Historic Preservation, Natl. Trust for (1949), 1785 Massachusetts Avenue NW, Washington, DC 20036; 200,000; www.nationaltrust.org

Historical Assn., American (1884), 400 A St. SE, Washington, DC 20003; 14,756; www.historians.org

Historical Society Doll Collection, United States (1971), 1st and Main Sts., Richmond, VA 23219; 250,000; www.ushsdolls.com

Hockey, U.S.A. (1936), 1775 Bob Johnson Dr., Colorado Springs, CO 80906; 585,000; www.usahockey.com.

Home Builders, Natl. Assn. of (1942), 1201 15th St. NW, Washington, DC 20005; 203,000; www.nahb.org

Homeless, Natl. Coalition for the (1984), 1012 14th St., Ste. 600, Washington, DC 20005; 10,000; www.nationalhomeless.org

Honor Society, Natl. (1921), 1904 Association Dr., Reston, VA 20191; 15,000 chapters; www.nhs.us

Horatio Alger Soc. (1961), P.O. Box 70361, Richmond, VA 23255; 185; www.ihot.com/~has

Horse Council, American (1969), 1616 H St., NW, 7th Fl., Washington, DC 20006; 175 org.,1,800 ind.; www.horsecouncil.org

Hospital Assn., American (1898), 1 N. Franklin, Chicago, IL 60606; 5,000 hospitals, 37,000 individual members; www.aha.org

Hostelling Intl. USA (1934), 8401 Colesville Rd, Ste. 600, Silver Spring, MD 20910; 120,000; www.hiayh.org

Hotel & Motel Assn., American (1910), 1201 New York Ave. NW, #600, Washington, DC 20005; 11,000+; www.ahma.com

Hot Rod Assn., Natl. (1951), 2035 Financial Way, Glendora, CA 91741; 80,000; www.nhra.com

Housing Inspection Foundation (1979), 1224 N. Nokomis NE, Alexandria, MN 56308; 1,800; www.iami.org/hif

Huguenot Society, Natl. (1951), 3 Free Ferry Heights, Fort Smith, AR 72903; 3,800; www.huguenot.netnation.com

Humane Society of the U.S. (1954), 2100 L St. NW, Washington, DC 20037; 650,000; www.hsus.org

Human Resource Management, Society for (SHRM) (1948), 1800 Duke St., Alexandria, VA 22314; 175,000; www.shrm.org

Hydrogen Energy, Intl. Assn. for (1975), P.O. Box 248266, Coral Gables, FL 33124; 2,500; www.iahe.org

Illustrators, Inc., Society of (1901), 128 E. 63rd St., New York, NY 10021-7303; 1,000; www.societyillustrators.org

Independent Community Bankers of America (1930), One Thomas Circle NW, Ste. 400, Washington, DC 20005; 5,000; www.icba.org

Industrial and Applied Mathematics, Society for (1952), 3600 Univ. City Science Ctr., Philadelphia, PA 19104; 9,000; www.siam.org

Industrial Designers Society of America (1965), 45195 Business Ct., Ste. 250, Dulles, VA 20166; 3,200; www.idsa.org

Industrial Security, American Soc. for (1955), 1625 Prince St., Alexandria, VA 22314; 33,000; www.asisonline.org

Insurance Assn., American (1866), 1130 Connecticut Avenue NW, Suite 1000, Washington, DC 20036; 450 companies; www.aiadc.org

Intellectual Property Owners Assoc. (1972), 1255 23rd St. NW, Ste. 200, Washington, DC 20037; 350; www.ipo.org

Intelligence Officers, Assoc. of Former (1975), 6723 Whittier Ave., Ste. 303A, McLean, VA 22101-4533; 4,000; www.afio.com

Intercollegiate Athletics, Natl. Assn. of (1937), 23500 W. 105th St., P.O. Box 1325, Olathe, KS 66051-1325; 360 member colleges/universities; www.naia.org

Interfaith Alliance, The (1994), 1331 H St., 11th Floor, Washington, DC 20005-4706; 150,000; www.interfaithalliance.org

Interior Designers, American Society of (1975), 608 Massachusetts Avenue NE, Washington, DC 20002; 35,500; www.asid.org

Intl. Education, Institute of (1919), 89 United Nations Plaza, New York, NY 10017; 800 colleges and universities; www.iie.org

Intl. Educational Exchange, Council on (1947), 7 Custom House St., 3rd Fl., Portland, ME 04101; 240 organizations; www.ciee.org

Intl. Educators, Assn. of (NAFSA) (1948), 1307 New York Ave. NW, 8th Fl., Washington, DC 20005; 7,500; www.nafsa.org

Intl. Law, American Society of (1906), 2223 Massachusetts Ave. NW, Washington, DC 20008; 4,000; www.asil.org

Inventors, American Soc. of (1953), P.O. Box 58426, Philadelphia, PA 19102; 150; www.asoi.org

Investigative Pathology, American Soc. for (1900), 9650 Rockville Pike, Bethesda, MD 20814; 1,718; www.asip.org

Investment Management and Research, Assn. for (AIMR) (1990), 560 Ray C. Hunt Dr., Charlottesville, VA 22903-0668; 65,000; www.aimr.org

Investors Corp., Natl. Assn. of (1951), P.O. Box 220, Royal Oak, MI 48068; 400,000; www.better-investing.org

Irish American Cultural Inst. (1962), 1 Lackawanna Pl., Morristown, NJ 07960; 4,500; www.irishaci.org

Irish Historical Society, American (1897), 991 5th Ave., New York, NY 10028; about 600; www.aihs.org

Jail Assn., American (1981), 1135 Professional Ct., Hagerstown, MD 21740; 4,500; www.corrections.com/aja

Japanese-American Citizens League (1929), 1765 Sutter St., San Francisco, CA 94115; 21,000; www.jacl.org

Jewish Committee, American (1906), 165 E. 65th St., New York, NY 10022; 125,000; www.ajc.org

Jewish Community Centers Assn. of North America (1917), 15 E. 26th St., New York, NY 10010; 1,000,000+; www.jcca.org

Jewish Congress, American (1918), 15 E. 84th St., New York, NY 10028; 50,000; www.ajcongress.org

Jewish Historical Society, American (1892), 15 West 16th St. New York, NY 10011; 9,000; www.ajhs.org

Jewish War Veterans of the U.S.A. (1896), 1811 R St. NW, Washington, DC 20009; 37,000; jwv.org

Jewish Women, Natl. Council of (1893), 53 W. 23rd St., 6th Fl., New York, NY 10010; 90,000; www.ncjw.org

John Birch Society (1958), P.O. Box 8040, Appleton, WI 54912; www.jbs.org

Joint Action in Community Service (JACS) (1967), 5225 Wisconsin Ave. NW, Ste. 404, Washington, DC 20015; www.jacsinc.org

Joseph Diseases Foundation, Inc., Intl. (1977), P.O. Box 994268, Redding CA 96099; 1,550; www.ijdf.net

Journalists, Society of Professional (1909), 3909 N. Meridian St., Indianapolis, IN 46208; 9,000; spj.org

Journalists and Authors, American Society of (1948), 1501 Broadway, Ste. 302, New York, NY 10036; 1,000+; www.asja.org

Judicature Society, American (1913), 2700 University Ave., Des Moines, IA 50311; 6,000; www.ajs.org

Jugglers Assn., Intl. (1947), P.O. Box 112550, Carrollton, TX, 75011; 2,500; www.juggle.org

Junior Achievement, Inc. (1919), One Education Way, Colorado Springs, CO 80906; www.ja.org

Junior Auxiliaries, Natl. Assn. of (1941), 845 South Main St., Greenville, MS 38701; 12,876; www.najanet.org

Junior Chamber of Commerce, U.S. (1920), P.O. Box 7, Tulsa, OK 74102; 200,000; www.usjaycees.org

Junior College Athletic Assn., Natl. (1937), P.O. Box 7305, Colorado Springs, CO 80933; 520; www.njcaa.org

Junior Honor Society, Natl. (1929), 1904 Association Dr., Reston, VA 20191; 6,000 chapt.; www.njhs.us

Junior Leagues, Assn. of (1901), 132 West 31st St., New York, NY 10016; 193,000; www.ajli.org

Kidney Fund, The American (1971), 6110 Executive Blvd., Ste. 1010, Rockville, MD 20852; www.akfinc.org

Kiwanis International (1915), 3636 Woodview Trace, Indianapolis, IN 46268; 500,000+; www.kiwanis.org

Knights of Columbus (1882), One Columbus Plaza, New Haven, CT 06510-4000; 1,660,197; www.kofc.org

Knights of Pythias, (1864), 59 Coddington Street, Quincy, MA 02169; approx. 70,000; www.pythias.org

Krishna Consciousness, Intl. Soc. for (ISKON, Inc.) (1966), 3764 Watseka Ave., Los Angeles, CA 90034; approx. 250,000; www.krishna.com

La Leche League Intl. (1957), P.O. Box 4079, Schaumburg, IL 60168; 26,000; www.lalecheleague.org

Lady Bird Johnson Wildflower Center (1982), 4801 La Crosse Avenue, Austin, TX 78739; 22,000; www.wildflower.org

Landscape Architects, American Society of (1899), 636 I St. NW, Washington, DC 20001-3736; 12,500; www.asla.org

Law Libraries, American Assn. of (1906), 53 W. Jackson Blvd., #940, Chicago, IL 60604; 5,150; www.aallnet.org

Learned Societies, American Council of (1919), 633 Third Ave., New York, NY 10017; 64 societies; www.acls.org

Legal Administrators, Assn. of (1971), 75 Tri-State Intl., Ste. 222, Lincolnshire, IL 60069-4435; 9,200; www.alanet.org

Legal Secretaries, Natl. Assn. of (NALS) (1929), 314 E 3rd St., Ste. 210, Tulsa, OK 74120; 8,500; www.nals.org

Legion of Valor Museum. (1991), 2425 Fresno St., Fresno, CA 93721; 900; www.legionofvalormuseum.org

Leprosy Missions, Inc., American (1906), One Alm Way, Greenville, SC 29601; www.leprosy.org

Leukemia and Lymphoma Society (1949), 1311 Mamaroneck Ave., White Plains, NY 10605; www.lls.org

Lewis and Clark Trail Heritage Foundation. (1969), P.O. Box 3434, Great Falls, MT 59403; 3,600; www.lewisandclark.org

Libertarian Party (1971), 2600 Virginia Ave. NW, Ste. 100, Washington, DC 20037; 224,000; www.lp.org

Libraries Assn., Special (1909), 1700 18th St. NW, Washington, DC 20009; 12,000; www.sla.org

Library Assn., American (1876), 50 E. Huron St., Chicago, IL 60611; 64,000+; www.ala.org

Lifesaving Assn., U.S. (1964), PO Box 366, Huntington Beach, CA 92648; 11,000; www.usla.org

Lighter-Than-Air Society (1952), 526 S. Main St., Akron, OH 44306; 850; www.blimpinfo.com.

Linguistic Society of America (1924), 1325 18th St. NW, Ste. 211, Washington, DC 20036-6501; 4,200 indiv.; www.lsadc.org

Lions Clubs, Intl., Assn. of (1917), 300 W. 22nd St., Oak Brook, IL 60523; 1,400,000; www.lionsclubs.org

Little League Baseball, Inc. (1939), P.O. Box 3489, S. Williamsport, PA 17701; 4 mil, www.littleleague.org

Little People of America, Inc. (1961), Box 65030, Lubbock, TX 79464; 8,000+; www.lpaonline.org

Logistics, International Society of (SOLE) (1966), 8100 Professional Place, Ste. 111, Hyattsville, MD 20785; 3,500; www.sole.org

London Club (1975), Route One, Lecompton, KS 66050; 100+.

Lung Assn., American (1904), 61 Broadway, 6th Fl., New York, NY 10006; www.lungusa.org

Magazine Publishers of America (1919), 919 Third Ave., 22nd Fl., New York, NY 10022; 1,200 titles; www.magazine.org

Magicians, Intl. Brotherhood of (1922), 11155 S. Towne Sq., Ste. B, St. Louis, MO 63123-7813; 13,253; www.magician.org

Management Accountants, Institute of (1919), 10 Paragon Dr., Montvale, NJ 07645; 75,000; www.imanet.org

Management Assn., American (1923), 1601 Broadway, New York, NY 10019; 70,000+; www.amanet.org

Manufacturing Engineers, Soc. of (1932), One SME Dr., Dearborn, MI 48121-0930; 40,000; www.sme.org

Manufacturers, Natl. Assn. of (1895), 1331 Pennsylvania Ave. NW, Washington, DC 20004; 14,000 cos.; www.nam.org

March of Dimes Birth Defects Foundation (1938), 1275 Mamaroneck Avenue, White Plains, NY 10605; 3 mil; www.modimes.org

Marine Corps League (1923), P.O. Box 3070, Merrifield, VA 22116; 56,000; www.mcleague.org

Marketing Assn., Am. (1915), 311 S. Wacker Dr., Ste. 5800, Chicago, IL 60606; 38,000; www.marketingpower.com

Master Brewers Association of the Americas (1887), 3340 Pilot Knob Rd., St. Paul, MN 55121; 3,500; www.mbaa.com

Materials and Process Engineering, Soc. for the Advancement of (1944), P.O Box 2459, Covina, CA 91722; 5,000; www.sampe.org

Mathematical Society, American (1888), 201 Charles St., Providence, RI 02904; 30,000; www.ams.org

Mayflower Descendants, General Society of (1897), 4 Winslow St., Plymouth, MA 02361; 26,000; www.mayflower.org

Mayors, U.S. Conference of (1932), 1620 Eye St. NW, Washington, DC 20006; 1,183; www.usmayors.org

Mechanical Engineers, American Soc. of (1880), 3 Park Ave., New York, NY 10016; 125,000; www.asme.org

Medical Assn., American (1847), 515 N. State St., Chicago, IL 60610; 300,000; www.ama-assn.org

Medical Library Assn. (1898), 65 E. Wacker Pl., Ste. 1900, Chicago, IL 60602; 5,000; www.mlanet.org

Medieval Academy of America (1925), 104 Mt. Auburn St., Cambridge, MA 02138; 4,250; www.medievalacademy.org

Meeting Planners, Intl. Society of (1981) 1224 N. Nokomis NE, Alexandria, MN 56308; 500; www.iami.org/ismp

MENC: The Natl. Assn. for Music Education (formerly Music Educators Natl. Conference) (1907), 1806 Robert Fulton Dr., Reston, VA 20191; 120,000; www.menc.org

Mended Hearts, Inc. (1950), 7272 Greenville Ave., Dallas, TX 75231; 24,000; www.mendedhearts.org

Mensa, Ltd., American (1960), 1229 Corporate Dr. W, Arlington, TX 76006; 50,000; www.us.mensa.org

Mental Health Assn., Natl. (1909), 2001 N. Beauregard St., 12th Fl., Alexandria, VA 22311; 340 affiliates; www.nmha.org

Mentally Ill, Natl. Alliance for the (1979), Colonial Place Three, 2107 Wilson Blvd. Ste. 300, Arlington, VA 22201; 220,000; www.nami.org

Merrill's Marauders Assn. (1947), 11244 N. 33rd St., Phoenix, AZ 85028-2723; 1,698; www.marauder.org

Meteorological Society, American (1919), 45 Beacon St., Boston, MA 02108; 11,000+; www.ametsoc.org

Metric Assn., Inc., U.S. (1916), 10245 Andasol Ave., Northridge, CA 91325-1504; 1,200; www.metric.org

Microbiology, American Society for (1899), 1752 N. St. NW, Washington, DC 20036; 42,000; www.asmusa.org

Military Officers Assn. (1940), 201 N. Washington St., Alexandria, VA 22314; 391,000; www.moaa.org

Military Order of the Purple Heart of the USA (1958), 5413-B Backlick Road, Springfield, VA 22151; 36,765; www.purpleheart.org

Military Order of the World Wars (1919), 435 N. Lee St., Alexandria, VA 22314; 11,250; www.militaryorder.net

Military Surgeons of the U.S., Assn. of (1898), 9320 Old Georgetown Road, Bethesda, MD 20814; 10,000+; www.amsus.org

Missing and Exploited Children, Natl. Center for (1984), The Charles B. Wang International Children's Building, 699 Prince St., Alexandria, VA 22314; www.missingkids.com

Model A Ford Club of America, Inc. (1955), 250 S. Cypress St., La Habra, CA 90631; 15,500; www.mafca.com

Model Railroad Assn., Natl. (1935), 4121 Cromwell Rd., Chattanooga, TN 37421-2119; 20,500; www.nmra.org

Modern Language Assn. of America (1883), 26 Broadway, 3rd Fl., New York, NY 10004; 30,000+; www.mla.org

Molecular Plant-Microbe Interactions, Intl. Soc. for (1990), 3340 Pilot Knob Rd., St. Paul, MN 55121-2097; 450; www.ismpinet.org

Moose Intl., Inc. (1888), 155 S. International Dr., Mooseheart, IL 60539; 1.5 mil; www.mooseintl.org

Mothers, Inc.®, American (1938), 15 DuPont Circle N.W., Washington, DC 20036; 3,700; www.americanmothers.org

Mothers of Twins Clubs, Natl. Organization of (1963), P.O. Box 438, Thompson Station, TN 37179-0438; 24,000; www.nomotc.org

Motion Picture Arts & Sciences, Academy of (1927), 8949 Wilshire Blvd., Beverly Hills, CA 90211; 6,300; www.oscars.org

Motion Picture & Television Engineers, Soc. of (1916), 595 W. Hartsdale Ave., White Plains, NY 10607; 10,000; www.smpte.org

Motorcyclist Assn., American (1924), 13515 Yarmouth Dr., Pickerington, OH 43147; 250,000+; www.amadirectlink.com

Motorists Association, Natl. (1982), 402 W. 2nd St., Waunakee, WI 53597; 7,000; www.motorists.org

Multiple Sclerosis Society, Natl. (1946), 733 Third Ave. 6th Fl., New York, NY 10017; 616,305; www.nationalmssociety.org

Muscular Dystrophy Assn., Inc. (1950), 3300 E. Sunrise Dr., Tucson, AZ 85718; 2 mil. volunteers; www.mdausa.org

Museums, American Assn. of (1906), 1575 Eye St. NW, Ste. 400, Washington, DC 20005; 18,000, 3,000 institutions; www.aam-us.org

Music Center, American (1939), 30 W. 26th St., #1001, New York, NY 10010; 2,500; www.amc.net

Music Teachers Natl. Assn. (1876), 441 Vine St., Ste. 505, Cincinnati, OH 45202; 24,000; www.mtna.org

Musicological Society, American (1934), 201 S. 34th St., Philadelphia, PA 19104-6313; 3,300; www.ams-net.org

Muzzle Loading Rifle Assn., Natl. (1933), P.O. Box 67-SR 62, Friendship, IN 47021; 18,000; www.nmlra.org

Myasthenia Gravis Foundation of America (1952), 1821 University Ave. W., Ste S256, St. Paul, MN 55104; www.myasthenia.org

Mystery Writers of America, Inc. (1945), 17 E. 47th St., 6th Fl., New York, NY 10017; 2,235; www.mysterywriters.org

NA'AMAT USA (1921), 350 Fifth Ave., Ste. 4700, New York, NY 10118; 50,000 U.S.; 900,000 worldwide; www.naamat.org

Name Society, American (1951), c/o Michael McGoff, Vice Provost, Provost's Office, SUNY Binghamton, Binghamton, NY 13902; 700; www.wtsn.binghamton.edu/ANS

Narcotics Anonymous World Services (1953), P.O Box 9999, Van Nuys, CA 94109; 250,000; www.na.org

Natl. Assn. for the Advancement of Colored People (NAACP) (1909), 4805 Mt. Hope Dr., Baltimore, MD 21215; www.naacp.org

National Guard Assn. of the U.S. (1878), One Massachusetts Ave. NW, Washington, DC 20001; 56,000; www.ngaus.org

National Press Club (1908), 529 14th St., 13th Fl., NW, Washington, DC 20045; 4,000; www.press.org

Nature Conservancy, The (1951), 4245 N. Fairfax Drive, Ste. 100, Arlington, VA 22203; 1 mil+; nature.org

Naturist Society LLC (1980), P.O. Box 132, Oshkosh, WI 54903; 25,000; www.naturistsociety.com

Naval Institute, U.S. (1873), 291 Wood Rd., Annapolis, MD 21402; 70,000; www.usni.org

Naval Reserve Assn. (1954), 1619 King St., Alexandria, VA 22314; 23,000; www.navy-reserve.org

Navy League of the United States (1902), 2300 Wilson Blvd., Arlington, VA 22201-3308; 75,000; www.navyleague.org

Negro College Fund, United (1944), 8260 Willow Oaks Corporate Dr., Fairfax, VA 22031; 39 institutions; www.uncf.org

Neurofibromatosis Foundation, Natl. (1978), 95 Pine St., 16th Fl., New York, NY 10005; 30,000; www.nf.org

Newspaper Assn. of America (NAA) (1992), 1921 Gallows Rd., Ste. 600, Vienna, VA 22182-3900; 2,000+; www.naa.org

Ninety-Nines (Intl. Organization of Women Pilots) (1929), 4300 Amelia Earhart Rd., Oklahoma City, OK 73159; 6,000; www.ninety-nines.org

Non-Commissioned Officers Assn. (1960), 10635 IH 35 N., San Antonio, TX 78233; 160,000; www.ncoausa.org

Northern Cross Society (1983), Route One, Lecompton, KS 66050; 80

NOT-SAFE: Nat'l Organization Taunting Safety and Fairness Everywhere (1984), P.O. Box 5743-WA, Montecito, CA 93150; 9,110; www.notsafe.org

Notaries, American Society of (1965), P.O. Box 5707, Tallahassee, FL 32314; approx. 20,000; www.notaries.org

Nuclear Society, American (1954), 555 N. Kensington Ave., La Grange Park, IL 60526; 11,000; www.ans.org

Nude Recreation Inc., American Assn. for (1931), 1703 N. Main St., Ste. E, Kissimmee, FL 34744; 44,712; www.aanr.com

Numismatic Assn., American (1891), 818 N. Cascade Ave., Colorado Springs, CO 80903; 28,000; www.money.org

Numismatic Society, The American (1858), 96 Fulton St., New York, NY 10038; 2,028; www.amnumsoc.org

Nursing, Natl. League fo (1952), 61 Broadway, New York, NY 10006; 5,000; www.nln.org

Nutritional Sciences, American Society for (1928), 9650 Rockville Pike, Ste. 4500, Bethesda, MD 20814; 3,500+; www.asns.org

Ocean Conservancy (1972), 1725 DeSales St. NW, #600, Wash.,DC 20036; 500,000; www.oceanconservancy.org

Odd Fellows, Independent Order of (1819), 422 Trade St., Winston-Salem, NC 27101; 250,000; www.ioof.org

Optimist Intl. (1919), 4494 Lindell Blvd., St. Louis, MO 63108; 114,000; www.optimist.org

Optometric Assn., American (1918), 243 N. Lindbergh Blvd., St. Louis, MO 63141; 32,904; www.aoa.org

Organ Sharing, United Network for (1984), P.O. Box 2484, Richmond, VA 23218; 434; www.unos.org

Organists, American Guild of (1896), 475 Riverside Dr., Ste. 1260, New York, NY 10115; 20,000; www.agohq.org

Oriental Society, American (1842), Univ. of Michigan, Hatcher Graduate Library, 110D, Ann Arbor, MI 48109; 1,350; www.umich.edu/~aos

ORT Inc., American (Org. for Rehabilitation Through Training) (1922), 817 Broadway, 10th Fl., New York, NY 10003; 10,000; www.aort.org.

Ornithologists' Union, American (1883), 10th St. and Constitution, Washington, DC 20001; 4,200; www.aou.org

Outlaw and Lawman History, Inc., Natl. Assn. for (NOLA) (1974), 1917 Sutton Place Trail., Harker Heights, TX 76548-6043; 480; www.outlawlawman.com

Overeaters Anonymous (1960) P.O. Box 44020, Rio Rancho, NM 87124-4020; www.oa.org

Oxfam America (1970) 26 West St., Boston, MA 02111; 100,000; www.oxfamamerica.org

Paralyzed Veterans of America (1946), 801 18th St. NW, Washington, DC 20006; 18,000; www.pva.org

Parapsychology Institute of America (1971), P.O. Box 5442, Babylon, NY, 11707; 400

Parents Without Partners, Inc. (1957), 1650 South Dixie Highway, Suite 510, Boca Raton, FL 33432; 20,000; www.parentswithoutpartners.org

Parkinson's Disease Foundation, Inc. (1957), 710 W. 168th St., New York, NY 10032; 100,000; www.pdf.org

Parliamentarians, Natl. Assn. of (1930), 213 S. Main St., Independence, MO 64050; 4,000; www.parliamentarians.org

PBY Catalina International Association (1987), 1510 Kabel Dr., New Orleans, LA 70131; 700; www.pbycia.org

Peace Corps (1961), 1111 20th St., NW, Washington, DC 20526; 6,700; www.peacecorps.gov

Pearl Harbor History Associates, Inc. (1985), P.O. Box 1007, Stratford, CT 06615; 275; www.pearlharborhistory.org

PEN American Center, Inc. (1921), 568 Broadway, 4th Fl., New York, NY 10012; 2,700; www.pen.org

Pen Friends, Intl. (1967), 500 University Ave., #2415, Honolulu, HI 96826; 300,000; www.pen-pals.net

Pension Plan, Committee For a National (1979) P.O. Box 27851, Las Vegas, NV 89126; 375

Pen Women, Natl. League of American (1897), 1300 17th St. NW, Washington, DC 20036-1973; 3,569: www.americanpenwomen.org

People for the Ethical Treatment of Animals (PETA) (1980), 501 Front St., Norfolk, VA 23510; 800,000; www.peta.org

Performance Improvement, Intl. Society for (1962), 1400 Spring St., Ste. 260, Silver Spring, MD 20910; 6,000; www.ispi.org

Petroleum Institute, American (1919), 1220 L St. NW, Washington, DC 20005; 400 companies; www.api.org

Pharmaceutical Assn., American (1852), 2215 Constitution Ave. NW, Washington, DC 20037; 50,000; www.aphanet.org

Phi Beta Kappa Society (1776), 1606 New Hampshire Ave. NW, Washington, DC 20009; approx. 500,000; www.pbk.org

Phi Delta Kappa Intl., Inc. (1906), 408 N. Union St., P.O. Box 789, Bloomington, IN 47402; 95,223; www.pdkintl.org

Phi Kappa Phi, Honor Society of (1897), P.O. Box 16000, LSU Baton Rouge, Baton Rouge, LA 70893; 1,500,000+; www.phikappaphi.org

Phi Theta Kappa Int'l. Honor Society (1918), 1625 Eastover Drive, Jackson, MS 39211; 800,000; www.ptk.org

Philatelic Society, American (1886), 100 Oakwood Ave., State College, PA 16803; 48,327; www.stamps.org

Philological Association, American (1869), Univ. of Penn., 292 Logan Hall, 249 S. 36th St., Philadelphia, PA, 19104-6304; 3,100; www.apaclassics.org

Philosophical Assn., American (1900), 31 Amstel Ave., Univ. of Delaware, Newark, DE 19716; 11,097; www.apa.udel.edu/apa

Photographers of America, Inc., Professional (1880) 229 Peachtree St. NE, Ste. 2200, Atlanta, GA 30303; 14,000; www.ppa.com

Physical Therapy Assn., American (1921), 1111 N. Fairfax St., Alexandria, VA 22314; 75,000; www.apta.org

Physically Handicapped, Inc., Natl. Assn. of the (1958), Scarlet Oaks, 440 Lafayette Ave., #GA4, Cincinnati, OH 45220-1022; approx. 400; www.naph.net

Physics, American Inst. of (1931), One Physics Ellipse, College Park, MD 20740; 123,500; www.aip.org

Physiological Society, American (1887), 9650 Rockville Pike, Bethesda, MD 20814-3991; 10,500; www.the-aps.org

Phytopathological Society, American (1908), 3340 Pilot Knob Rd., St. Paul, MN 55121; 5,000; www.apsnet.org

Pilgrims Natl. Soc., Sons and Daughters of (1909), 3917 Heritage Dr., #104, Bloomington, MN 55437-2633; 2,000; www.nssdp.org

Pilot Intl. & Pilot Intl. Foundation (1921), P.O. Box 4844, Macon, GA 31208; 14,557; www.pilotinternational.org

Planetary Society (1979), 65 N. Catalina Ave., Pasadena, CA 91106; approx. 70,000; www.planetary.org

Planned Parenthood Federation of America, Inc. (1916), 434 West 33rd Street, New York, NY 10001; www.plannedparenthood.org

Plastics Engineers, Society of (1942), 14 Fairfield Dr., P.O. Box 403, Brookfield, CT 06804; 25,000+; www.4spe.org

Poetry Society of America (1910), 15 Gramercy Park, New York, NY 10003; approx. 3,000; www.poetrysociety.org

Poets, The Academy of American (1934), 588 Broadway, Ste. 604, New York, NY 10012; 8,000; www.poets.org

Police Assn., Intl. (1950 in UK, 1962 in U.S.), 100 Chase Ave., Yonkers, NY 10703; 291,000+; www.ipa-usa.org

Political Items Collectors, American (1945), P.O. Box 5632, Derwood, MD 20855; 2,500; apic.us

Political Science Assn., American (1903), 1527 New Hampshire Ave. NW, Washington, DC 20036; 15,000; www.apsanet.org

Political Science Assn., Southern (1928), PO Box 8101, Georgia Southern Univ., Statesboro, GA 30460; www2.gasou.edu/spsa

Political Science, Academy of (1880), 475 Riverside Drive, Ste. 1274, New York, NY 10115; 6,000; www.psqonline.org

Political & Social Science, American Academy of (1889), 3814 Walnut St., Univ. of Penn., Philadelphia, PA 19104; 400; www.aapss.org

Polo Assn., U.S. (1890), 771 Corporate Dr., Ste. 505, Lexington, KY 40503; 3,737; www.uspolo.org

Population Assn. of America (1931), 8630 Fenton St., Ste. 722, Silver Spring, MD 20910; 3,000; www.popassoc.org

Population Connection (formerly Zero Population Growth) (1968), 1400 16th St. NW, Ste 320, Washington, DC 20036; www.populationconnection.org

Postal Stationery Society, United (1945) P.O. Box 1792, Norfolk, VA 23501-1792; 1,100; www.upss.org

Postcard Dealers, Inc., International Federation of (1979), P.O. Box 1765, Manassas, VA 20109; 248; www.playle.com/IFPD

Postmasters of the U.S., Natl. League of (1887), 1023 N. Royal St., Alexandria, VA 22314; 27,000; www.postmasters.org

Postmasters of the U.S., Natl. Assn. of (1898), 8 Herbert St., Arlington, VA 22305; 43,000, www.napus.org

Power Boat Assn., American (1903), 17640 Nine Mile Rd., Eastpointe, MI 48021; 6,000; www.apba-racing.com

Printing Industries of America, Inc. (1887), 100 Daingerfield Rd., Alexandria, VA 22314; 14,000; www.gain.net

Procrastinators Club of America (1956), P.O. Box 712, Bryn Athyn, PA 19009; 14,100; www.geocities.com/procrastinators_club_of_america

Professional Ball Players of America, Assn. of (1924), 1820 W. Orangewood Ave., Ste. 206, Orange, CA 92868; 11,000; www.apbpa.org

ProLiteracy Worldwide (2002), 1320 Jamesville Ave., Syracuse, NY 13210; 1400 affiliates; www.proliteracy.org

Protection of Old Fishes, Soc. for the (1967), NOAA HAZMAT, 7600 Sand Point Way, N.E., Seattle, WA 98115; 150.

Psoriasis Foundation, Natl. (1968), 6600 SW 92nd Ave., Ste. 300, Portland, OR 97223; 33,000; www.psoriasis.org

Psychiatric Assn., American (1844), 1000 Wilson Blvd., Suite 1825, Arlington, VA 22209-3901; 37,000; www.psych.org

Psychical Research, American Society for (1885), 5 W. 73rd St., New York, NY 10023; www.aspr.com

Psychoanalytic Assn., American (1911), 309 E. 49th St., New York, NY 10017; 3,500; apsa.org

Psychological Assn., American (1892), 750 1st St. NE, Washington, DC 20002; 150,000; www.apa.org

PTA, Natl. (1897), 330 N. Wabash Ave., Ste. 2100, Chicago, IL 60611; approx. 6 mil; www.pta.org

Public Administration, American Soc. for (1939), 1120 G St. NW, Washington, DC 20005; 9,000+; www.aspanet.org

Public Health Assn., American (1872), 800 I St. NW, Washington, DC 20001; 50,000+; www.apha.org

Publishers, Assn. of American (1970), 71 5th Ave., New York, NY 10003; 300; www.publishers.org

Quill and Scroll Society (1926), School of Journalism, The University of Iowa, Iowa City, IA 52242; www.uiowa.edu/~quill-sc

Quota International, Inc. (1919), 1420 21st St. NW, Washington, DC 20036; 11,000+; www.quota.org

Rabbis, Central Conference of American (1889), 355 Lexington Ave., New York, NY 10017; 1,800; ccarnet.org

Racquetball Assn., U.S. (1968), 1685 W. Uintah, Colorado Springs, CO 80904; 20,000; www.usra.org

Radio Relay League, American (1914), 225 Main St., Newington, CT 06111; 160,000; www.arrl.org

Radio and Television Society Foundation, Intl. (1939), 420 Lexington Ave., Ste. 1601, New York, NY 10170; 1,787; www.irts.org

Railway Historical Society, Natl. (1935), P.O. Box 58547, Philadelphia, PA 19102; app. 17,840; www.nrhs.com

Range Management, Society for (1948), 445 Union Blvd., Ste. 230, Lakewood, CO 80228; 3,700; www.rangelands.org/srm.shtml

Reading Assn., Intl. (1956), 800 Barksdale Rd., P.O. Box 8139, Newark, DE 19714; 300,000; www.reading.org

Real Estate Institute, Intl. (1975), 1224 N. Nokomis, Alexandria, MN 56308; 700; www.iami.org/irei

Real Estate Appraisers, Natl. Assn. of (1966) 1224 N. Nokomis NE, Alexandria, MN 56308; 3,000; www.iami.org/narea

Recreation and Park Assn., Natl. (1965), 22377 Belmont Ridge Rd., Ashburn, VA 20148; 21,000; www.nrpa.org

Recycling Coalition, Natl. (1978), 1325 G St., NW, Washington, DC, 20005; 3,500; www.nrc-recycle.org

Red Cross, American Natl. (1881), 2025 E St. NW, Washington, DC 20006; 1.3 mil volunteers; www.redcross.org

Reform Party of the U.S.A. (1996), 420 1/2 S. 22nd Ave., Hattiesburg, MS 39401; 500,000; www.reformparty.org

Refugee Committee, American (1978), 430 Oak Grove St., Ste. 204, Minneapolis, MN 55403; www.archq.org

Rehabilitation Assn., Natl. (1925), 633 S. Washington St., Alexandria, VA 22310-4109; approx. 11,000; www.nationalrehab.org

Religion, American Academy of (1909), 825 Houston Mill Rd., Suite 300, Atlanta, GA 30329; 9,000; www.aarweb.org

Renaissance Society of America (1954), (CUNY) 365 5th. Ave., Rm. 5400, New York, NY 10016; 3,000; www.rsa.org

Republican National Committee (1856), 310 1st St. SE, Washington, DC 20003; www.rnc.org

Reserve Officers Assn. of the U.S. (1922), One Constitution Ave. NE, Washington, DC 20002; 75,000; www.roa.org

Retail Federation, Natl. (1908), 325 7th St. NW, Ste. 1100, Washington, DC 20004; 50,000; www.nrf.com

Retired Persons, American Assn. of (1958), 601 E St. NW, Washington, DC 20049; 35 mil+; www.aarp.org

Reye's Syndrome Foundation, Natl. (1974), 426 N. Lewis St., Bryan, OH 43506-0829; 6,723; www.reyessyndrome.org

Richard III Society, Inc. (1961),P.O. Box 13786, New Orleans, LA 70185; 750; www.r3.org

Rifle Assn., Natl. (1871), 11250 Waples Mill Rd., Fairfax, VA 22030; approx 3 mil; www.nra.org

Road & Transportation Builders Assn., American (1902), The ARTBA Building, 1010 Massachusetts Ave. NW, Washington, DC 20001; 5,000+; www.artba.org

Roller Sports, U.S.A. (1937), 4730 South St., Lincoln, NE 68506; 30,000; www.usarollersports.org

Rose Society, American (1892), P.O. Box 30,000, Shreveport, LA 71130; 24,000; www.ars.org

Rotary Intl. (1905), One Rotary Center, 1560 Sherman Ave., Evanston, IL 60201; 1,220,543; www.rotary.org

Running Assn., American (1968), 4405 East West Highway, Ste. 405, Bethesda, MD 20814; 15,000; www.americanrunning.org

Ruritan Natl., Inc. (1928), P.O. Box 487, Dublin, VA 24084; 33,447; www.ruritan.org

Safety Council, Natl. (1913), 1121 Spring Lake Dr., Itasca, IL 60143; 45,000 member facilities; www.nsc.org

Safety Engineers, American Soc. of (1911), 1800 E. Oakton St., Des Plaines, IL 60018; 32,000; www.asse.org

Salt Institute (1914), 700 N. Fairfax St., Ste. 600, Alexandria, VA, 22314; 36 cos.; www.saltinstitute.org

Save-the-Redwoods League (1918), 114 Sansome St., Ste. 1200, San Francisco, CA 94104; 40,000; www.savetheredwoods.org

School Administrators, American Assn. of (1865), 801 N. Quincy St., Ste 700, Arlington, VA 22203; 14,000+; www.aasa.org

Science, American Assn. for the Advancement of (1848), 1200 New York Ave. NW, Washington, DC 20005; approx. 10 mil.; www.aaas.org

Science Fiction Society, World (1939), P.O. Box 426159, Kendall Square Station, Cambridge, MA 02142; 10,000; www.wsfs.org

> **IT'S A FACT:** Members of the National Scrabble® Association receive special word lists that include among others, U-less Q words (such as qat, qaid, and tranqs), short J, X, and Z words (haj, xu, adz), and vowel "dumps" (aalii, ourie, zoeae).

Sciences, Natl. Academy of (1863), 500 5th St. NW, Washington, DC 20001; 2,000+; www.nas.edu

Science Teachers Assn., Natl. (1944), 1840 Wilson Blvd., Arlington, VA 22201; 55,000; www.nsta.org

Science Writers, Natl. Assn. of (1934), P.O. Box 890, Hedgeville, WV 25427; 2,350; www.nasw.org

Scrabble® Assn., Natl. (1980), P.O. Box 700, 403 Front St., Greenport, NY 11944; 10,000+; www.scrabble-assoc.com

Screen Actors Guild (1933), 5757 Wilshire Blvd., Los Angeles, CA 90036; 90,000; www.sag.com

Screenprinting & Graphic Imaging Assn., Intl. (1958), 10015 Main St., Fairfax, VA 22031; 4,000 ; www.sgia.org

2nd Air Division Assn. of the 8th Air Force (1950), P.O. Box 484, Elkhorn, WI 53121-0484; 4,500.

Secular Humanism, Council for (1980), P.O. Box 664, Amherst, NY 14226; 24,000; www.secularhumanism.org

Separation of Church & State, Americans United for (1947), 518 C St. NE, Washington, DC 20002; 75,000; www.au.org

Sertoma International (1912), 1912 E. Meyer Blvd., Kansas City, MO 64132; 20,000; www.sertoma.org

Sharkhunters Intl. (1983), P.O. Box 1539, Hernando, FL 34442; 6,900; www.sharkhunters.com

Shipbuilders Council of America (1920), 1455 F St., NW, Ste. 225, Washington, DC 20005; 37 member cos; www.shipbuilders.org

Ships in Bottles Assn. of America (1982), P.O. Box 180550, Coronado, CA 92178; 250; www.shipsinbottles.org

Shriners of North America, The (1872), 2900 N. Rocky Point Dr., Tampa, FL 33607; approx 500,000+; shrinershq.org

Sierra Club (1892), 85 2nd St., 2nd Fl., San Francisco, CA 94105; 700,000+; www.sierraclub.org

Sigma Beta Delta (1994) P.O. Box 210570, St. Louis, MO 63121-0570; 20,000; www.sigmabetadelta.org

Skeet Shooting Assn., Natl. (1946), 5931 Roft Rd., San Antonio, TX 78253; 30,000; www.mynsca.com

Small Business United, Natl. (1937), 1156 15th St. NW, Ste. 1100, Washington, DC 20005; 65,000+; www.nsba.biz

Social Work Education, Council on (1952), 1725 Duke St., Ste. 500, Alexandria, VA 22314; 2,501; www.cswe.org

Sociological Assn., American (1905), 1307 New York Avenue NW, Suite 700, Washington, DC 20005; 13,000; www.asanet.org

Softball Assn., Amateur (1933), 2801 NE 50th St., Oklahoma City, OK 73111; 250,000+ teams; www.softball.org

Software and Information Industry Assn. (formerly Information Industry Assn.) (1999), 1090 Vermont Ave. NW, 6th Fl., Wash. DC 20005; 1,200 companies; www.siia.net

Soldiers', Sailors', Marines' and Airmen's Club (1919), 283 Lexington Ave., New York, NY 10016; 190; www.ssmaclub.org

Songwriters Guild of America (1931), 1222 16th Ave S., Ste. 25, Nashville, TN 37212; 5,000+; www.songwriters.org

Sons of the American Colonists, Natl. Society of (1970) 5611 N. 15th St., Arlington, VA 22205-0482; 250

Sons of the American Legion (1932), Box 1055, Indianapolis, IN 46206; 281,500; www.sal.legion.org

Sons of the American Revolution, Natl. Society of (1889), 1000 S. Fourth St., Louisville, KY 40203; 26,000; www.sar.org

Sons of Confederate Veterans (1896), P.O. Box 59, Columbia, TN 38402; 35,000; www.scv.org

Sons of the Desert Laurel & Hardy Appreciation Society (1965), Way Out West Tent, P.O. Box 1918, Burbank, CA 91507; 3,000; www.wayoutwest.org.

Sons of Italy in America, Order (1905), 219 E St. NE, Washington, DC 20002; 72,500; www.osia.org

Sons of Norway (1895), 1455 W. Lake St., Minneapolis, MN 55408; 65,000; www.sofn.com

Soroptimist Intl. of the Americas (1921), Two Penn Center Plaza, Ste. 1000, Philadelphia, PA 19102; 45,000; www.soroptimist.org

Southern Christian Leadership Conference (1957), P.O. Box 89128, Atlanta, GA 30312; 1 mil.; www.sclcnational.org

Space Society, Natl. (1974), 600 Pennsylvania Ave SE, Ste. 201, Washington, DC 20003; 22,000+; www.nss.org

Speech-Language-Hearing Assn., American (1925), 10801 Rockville Pike, Rockville, MD 20852; 110,000; www.asha.org

Speedskating, U.S. (1966), P.O. Box 450639, Westlake, OH 44145; 1,800; www.usspeedskating.org

Speleological Society, Natl. (1941), 2813 Cave Ave., Huntsville, AL 35810; 12,000; www.caves.org

Sports Car Club of America (1944), P.O. Box 19400, Topeka, KS 66619; 50,000+; www.scca.org

Sportscasters Assn., The American (1980), 225 Broadway, New York, NY 10007; 500+; americansportscastersonline.com

State & Local History, American Assn. for (1940), 1717 Church St., Nashville, TN 37203; 6,100; www.aaslh.org

State Governments, Council of (1933), 2760 Research Park Drive, P.O. Box 11910, Lexington, KY 40578; 50 states, 4 territories; www.csg.org

Statistical Assn., American (1839), 1429 Duke St., Alexandria, VA 22314; 16,000; www.amstat.org

Steamship Historical Society of America, Inc. (1935), P.O. Box 2394, Providence, RI 02906; 3,000; www.sshsa.org

Stock Exchange, American (1911), 86 Trinity Pl., New York, NY 10006; www.amex.com

Stock Exchange, New York (1792), 11 Wall St., New York, NY 10005; www.nyse.com

Stock Exchange, Philadelphia (1790), 1900 Market St., Philadelphia, PA 19103; www.phlx.com

Student Councils, Natl. Assn. of (1931) 1904 Association Dr., Reston, VA 20191; 17,000 councils; www.nasc.us

Stuttering Project, Natl. (1977), 4071 E. LaPalma Ave., Ste. A, Anaheim Hills, CA 92807; 2,800; www.nsastutter.org

Sudden Infant Death Syndrome Alliance (1987), 1314 Bedford Avenue, Suite 210, Baltimore, MD 21208; www.sidsalliance.org

Supreme Council, 33°, Scottish Rite of Freemasonry, Southern Jurisdiction (1801), 1733 16th St. NW, Washington, DC 20009-3103; 413,793; www.srmason-sj.org

Supreme Court Historical Society (1974), Opperman House, 224 East Capitol St. NE, Washington, DC 20003; 5,000; www.supremecourthistory.org

Surgeons, American College of (1913), 633 N. Saint Clair St., Chicago, IL 60611; 65,000; www.facs.org

Symphony Orchestra League, American (1942), 33 W. 60th St., 5th Fl., New York, NY 10023; 850; www.symphony.org

Table Tennis Assn., U.S. (1933), One Olympic Plaza, Colorado Springs, CO 80903; 8,000; www.usatt.org

Tailhook Assn. (1956), 9696 Businesspark Ave., San Diego, CA 92131; 10,850; www.tailhook.org

Tall Buildings and Urban Habitat, Council on (1969), Illinois Inst. of Tech., 3360 S. State St., Chicago, IL 60616; 1,200; www.ctbuh.org

Tau Beta Pi Association (1885), 508 Daugherty, Engineering Hall, Univ of Tenn., Knoxville, TN 37901-2697; 400,000; www.tbp.org

Tax Administrators, Federation of (1932), 444 N. Capitol St. NW, Ste. 348, Washington, DC 20001; www.taxadmin.org

Tax Foundation (1937), 1900 M St. NW, Ste. 550, Washington, DC 20036; 50 U.S. states; www.taxfoundation.org

Taxpayers Union, Natl. (1969), 108 N. Alfred St., Alexandria, VA 22314; 335,000; www.ntu.org

Tea Assn. of the U.S.A., Inc. (1899), 420 Lexington Ave., New York, NY 10170; 300 corps; www.teausa.com

Teachers of English, Natl. Council of (1911), 1111 W. Kenyon Rd., Urbana, IL 61801; 50,000; www.ncte.org

Teachers of English to Speakers of Other Languages (1966), 700 S. Washington St., Ste. 200, Alexandria, VA 22314; 16,000; www.tesol.edu

Teachers of French, American Assn. of (1927), Southern Illinois University, Mailcode 4510, Carbondale, IL 62901-4510; 9,500; www.frenchteachers.org

Teachers of German, Inc., American Assn. of (AATG) (1926), 112 Haddontowne Ct. #104, Cherry Hill, NJ 08034-3668; 6,000; www.aatg.org

Teachers of Mathematics, Natl. Council of (1920), 1906 Association Drive, Reston, VA 20191-1502; 100,000; www.nctm.org

Teachers of Singing, Natl. Assn. of (1944), 4745 Sutton Park Ct. Ste. 201, Jacksonville, FL 32224; 6,000; www.nats.org

Teachers of Spanish & Portuguese, American Assn. of (1917), 423 Exton Commons, Exton, PA, 19341-2451; 11,522; www.aatsp.org

TeachKind (2001), 501 Front St., Norfolk, VA 23510; 7,500; www.teachkind.org

TelecomPioneers (1911), P.O. Box 13888, Denver, CO 80201; 750,000; www.telecom-pioneers.org

Television Arts & Sciences, Natl. Academy of (1957), 111 W. 57th St., Ste. 600, New York, NY 10019; 11,000; www.emmyonline.org

Theodore Roosevelt Assn. (1919), P.O. Box 719, Oyster Bay, NY 11771; 2,239; www.theodoreroosevelt.org

Theological Library Assn., American (1946), 250 S. Wacker Dr., Ste. 1600, Chicago, IL 60606; 800+; www.atla.com

Theological Schools in the U.S. and Canada, The Assn. of (1918), 10 Summit Park Dr., Pittsburgh, PA 15275-1103; 243; www.ats.edu

Theosophical Society in America (1875), P.O. Box 270, Wheaton, IL 60189; 5,000; www.theosophical.org

Therapy Dogs Intl., Inc (1976), 88 Bartley Rd., Flanders, NJ 07836; 12,000; www.tdi-dog.org

Thoreau Society (1941), 44 Baker Farm, Lincoln, MA 01773; 1,700+; www.walden.org

Thoroughbred Racing Assns. (1942), 420 Fair Hill Dr., Ste. 1, Elkton, MD 21921; 43 racing assoc.; www.tra-online.com

318th Service Group Assn. 9th AF (1991), 2114 West 29th St., Erie, PA 16508-1066; 112

Tin Can Sailors (1976), P.O. Box 100, Somerset, MA 02726; 24,000; www.destroyers.org

Titanic Historical Society, Inc. & Museum (1963), 208 Main St., Indian Orchard, MA 01151-0053; 4,328; www.titanic historicalsociety.org

Toastmasters Intl. (1924), P.O. Box 57, Mission Viejo, CA 92690; 180,000+; www.toastmasters.org

Topical Assn., American (1949), P.O. Box 57, Arlington, TX, 76004-0057; 3,400; americantopicalassn.org

Tortilla Industry Assn. (1990), 3340 Pilot Knob Rd., St. Paul, MN 55121; 150 companies; www.tortilla-info.com

Toy Industry Assn., Inc. (1916), 1115 Broadway, Suite 400, New York, NY 10010; 300+ cos; www.toy-tma.com

Transportation Alternatives (1973), 115 W. 30th St., #1207, New York, NY 10001; 5,000; www.transalt.org

Transportation Engineers, Inst. of (1930), 1099 14th St. NW, Suite 300 West, Washington, DC 20005-3438; 15,000; www.ite.org

Trapshooting Assn. of America, Amateur (1923), 601 W. National Road, Vandalia, OH 45377; 54,000; www.shoot ata.com

Travel Agents, American Soc. of (1931), 1101 King St., Ste. 200, Alexandria, VA 22314; 20,000+; www.astanet.com

Travelers Protective Assn. of America (1890), 3755 Lindell Blvd., St. Louis, MO 63108; 91,008; www.tpahq.org

Trilateral Commission (1973), 1156 15th St., NW, Ste. 505, Washington, DC 20005; 350; www.trilateral.org

Truck Historical Soc., American (1971), 10380 N. Ambassador Dr., Kansas City, MO 64153; 22,679; www.aths.org

Tuberous Sclerosis Alliance (1974), 801 Roeder Rd., Ste. 750, Silver Spring, MD 20910; aprox. 2,000; www.tsalliance.org

UFOs, Natl. Investigations Committee on (1967) 14617 Victory Blvd., Ste. 4, Van Nuys, CA 91411; 250; www.nicufo.com

Underwriters (CPCU), Soc. of Chartered Property and Casualty (1944), 720 Providence Rd., P.O. Box 3009, Malvern, PA 19355; 28,500; www.cpcusociety.org

UNICEF, U.S. Fund for (1947), 333 E. 38th St., New York, NY 10016; www.unicefusa.org

Uniformed Services, Natl. Assn. for (1968), 5535 Hempstead Way, Springfield, VA 22151; 160,000+; www.naus.org

United Nations Assn. of the U.S.A. (1943), 801 2nd Ave., 2nd Fl., New York, NY 10017; 20,000+; www.unausa.org

United Order True Sisters, Inc. (1846), 100 State St., Ste. 1020, Albany, NY 12207; approx. 2,000; uots.org

United Press Intl. (1907), 1510 H St. NW, Washington, DC 20005; www.upi.com

United Service Organizations (USO) (1941), Washington Navy Yard, 1008 Eberle Place SE, Ste. 301, Washington, DC 20374; 12,000+; www.uso.org

United Way of America (1918), 701 N. Fairfax St., Alexandria, VA 22314; approx. 1,400 org.; national.unitedway.org

Universities, Assn. of American (1900), 1200 New York Ave., NW, Ste. 550, Washington, DC 20005; 61 institutions; www.aau.edu

University Women, American Assn. of (1881), 1111 16th St. NW, Washington, DC 20036; 100,000+; www.aauw.org

Urban League, Natl. (1910), 120 Wall St., New York, NY 10005; 50,000; www.nul.org

U.S. Term Limits (1992), 10 G St.; Ste. 410, Washington, DC 20002; www.termlimits.org

USO World Headquarters (1941), 2111 Wilson Blvd., Ste. 1200, Arlington, VA 22124; www.uso.org

USS *Forrestal* CVA/CV/AVT-59 Assn., Inc. (1991), 300 Cassady Avenue, Virginia Beach, VA 23452; 2,458; www.uss forrestal.com

USS *Idaho* Assn. (1957), P.O. Box 711247, San Diego, CA 92171; 248

USS *Los Angeles CA-135* Assn. (1978), c/o George Bell, 5937 Eureka, CA 95503; 365; www.uss-la-ca135.org

USS *Missouri* (BB-63) Assn., Inc. (1974), 24 Clark St., Plainview, NY 11803-5114; 1,500; www.ussmissouri.org

Ventriloquists, North American Assn. of (1944), P.O. Box 420, Littleton, CO 80160; 1,450; www.maherstudios.com/naav.htm

Veterans of Foreign Wars of the U.S. (1899), 406 W. 34th St., Kansas City, MO 64111; 1.8 mil+.; www.vfw.org

Veterans of Foreign Wars of the U.S., Ladies Auxiliary to the (1914), 406 W. 34th St., Kansas City, MO 64111; 671,501; www.ladiesauxvfw.com

Veterans of the Vietnam War, Inc. (1980), 805 S. Township Blvd., Pittston, PA 18640-3327; 15,000; www.vvnw.org

Veterinary Medical Assn., American (1863), 1931 N. Meacham Rd., Ste. 100, Schaumburg, IL 60173; 64,000; www.avma.org

Victorian Society in America (1966), 205 S Camac St., Philadelphia, PA 19107; 3,000; www.victoriansociety.org

Volleyball, USA (1928), 715 S. Circle Dr., Colorado Springs, CO 80910; 175,039; www.usavolleyball.org

Volunteers of America (1896), 1660 Duke St., Alexandria, VA 22314-3421; 11,000 staff; www.voa.org

War Mothers, American (1917), 5415 Connecticut Ave., NW, Ste. L-30, Washington, DC 20015; 500

Watch & Clock Collectors, Inc., Natl. Assn. of (NAWCC) (1943), 514 Poplar St., Columbia, PA 17512; 28,645; www.nawcc.org

Watercolor Society, American (1866), 47 5th Ave., New York, NY 10003; 480; www.americanwatercolorsociety.com

Water Environment Federation (1928), 601 Wythe St., Alexandria, VA 22314; 73 assns.; www.wef.org

Water Works Assn., American (1881), 6666 W. Quincy Ave., Denver, CO 80235; 57,000; www.awwa.org

Wheelchair Sports, USA (1956), 1668 320th Way, Earlham, IA 50072; 4,000; www.wsusa.org

Wildlife Federation, Natl. (1936),11100 Wildlife Center Dr., Reston, VA, 20190; 4 mil.; www.nwf.org

Wildlife Management Institute (1911), 1146 19th St. NW, Ste. 700, Washington, DC 20036; 300; www.wildlifemanagement institute.org

Wizard of Oz Club, Intl. (1957), P.O. Box 26249, San Francisco, CA 94126-6249; app.1,300; www.ozclub.org

Women and Families, Natl. Partnership for (1971), 1875 Connecticut Ave. NW, Ste. 650, Washington, DC 20009; 2,000; www.nationalpartnership.org

Women Artists, Inc., Natl. Assn. of (1889), 80 5th Ave., Ste. 1405, New York, NY 10001; 802; www.nawanet.org

Women in Communications, The Association for (1909 as Theta Sigma Phi), 780 Ritchie Hwy., Ste. 28, Severna Park, MD 21146; 7,500; www.womcom.org

Women in Radio and Television Inc., Amer. (1951), 8405 Greensboro Dr., Ste. 800, McLean, VA 22102; www.awrt.org

Women Engineers, Society of (1950), 230 E. Ohio St., Ste. 400, Chicago, IL 60611; 17,000; www.swe.org

Women, Natl. Organization for (NOW) (1966), 1100 H St. NW, 3rd Fl., Washington, DC 20005; 500,000; www.now.org

Women Voters of the U.S., League of (1920), 1730 M St. NW, Ste. 1000, Washington, DC 20036; 130,000; www.lwv.org

Women's Army Corps Veterans Assn. (1984), P.O. Box 5577, Ft. McClellan, AL 36205; 2,630; www.armywomen.org

Women's Christian Temperance Union, Natl. (1874), 1730 Chicago Ave., Evanston, IL 60201-4585; www.wctu.org

Women's Clubs, General Federation of (1890), 1734 N St. NW, Washington, DC, 20036; 180,000 U.S.; www.gfwc.org

Woodmen of America, Modern (1883), 1701 1st Ave., P.O. Box 2005, Rock Island, IL 61204; 750,000; www.modern-woodmen.org

Workmen's Circle (1900), 45 E. 33rd St., New York, NY 10016; 35,000; www.circle.org

World Council of Churches, U.S. Office (1948), 475 Riverside Drive, Rm. 1371, New York, NY 10115; 330+ denominations, www.wcc-usa.org.

World Federalist Assn. (1947), 418 7th St. SE, Washington, DC 20003; 11,000; www.wfa.org

World Future Society (1966), 7910 Woodmont Ave., Ste. 450, Bethesda, MD 20814; 25,000; www.wfs.org

World Learning (1932), Kipling Rd., P.O. Box 676, Brattleboro, VT 05302-0676; 100,000; www.worldlearning.org

World Wildlife Fund (1961), 1250 24th St. NW, P.O. Box 97180, Washington, DC 20037; 1 mil+; www.worldwildlife.org

World's Fair Collectors Soc., Inc. (1968), P.O. Box 20806, Sarasota, FL 34276-3806; 350; members.aol.com/bbqprod/wfcs.html

Writers Guild of America, West (1933), 7000 W. Third St., Los Angeles, CA 90048; 10,500; www.wga.org

YMCA (Young Men's Christian Assns.) of the U.S.A. (1851) 101 N. Wacker Dr., Chicago, IL 60606; 18.9 mil.; www.ymca.net

YWCA (Young Women's Christian Assn.) of the U.S.A. (1907), 1015 18th St. NW, Ste. 1100, Washington, DC 20036; approx. 2 mil.; www.ywca.org

Zionist Organization of America (1897), 4 E. 34th St., New York, NY 10016; 55,000; www.zoa.org

Zoo and Aquarium Assn., American (1924), 8403 Colesville Road, Suite 710, Silver Spring, MD 20910; 212 institutions, 5,500 individuals; www.aza.org

EDUCATION

U.S. Public Schools: Students, Staff, Spending, 1899-2002

Source: National Center for Education Statistics, U.S. Dept. of Education

	1899-1900	1919-20	1939-40	1959-60	1969-70	1979-80	1989-90	1999-2000	2001-02
Population statistics (thousands)									
Total U.S. population[1]	75,995	104,514	131,028	177,830	201,385	224,567	246,819	279,040	285,318
Population 5-17 years of age	21,573	27,571	30,151	43,881	52,386	48,041	44,947	52,811	53,253
Percentage 5-17 years of age	28.4	26.4	23.0	24.7	26.0	21.4	18.2	18.9	18.7
Enrollment (thousands)									
Elementary and secondary[2]	15,503	21,578	25,434	36,087	45,550	41,651	40,543	46,857	47,665
Kindergarten & grades 1-8	14,984	19,378	18,833	27,602	32,513	28,034	29,152	33,488	33,933
Grades 9-12	519	2,200	6,601	8,485	13,037	13,616	11,390	13,369	13,732
Percentage pop. 5-17 enrolled	71.9	78.3	84.4	82.2	87.0	86.7	90.2	88.7	89.5
Percentage in high schools	3.3	10.2	26.0	23.5	28.6	32.7	28.1	28.5	28.8
High school graduates (thousands)	62	231	1,143	1,627	2,589	2,748	2,320	2,554	2,635
School term; staff									
Average school term (in days)	144.3	161.9	175.0	178.0	178.9	178.5	*	*	*
Total instructional staff (thousands)	*	678	912	1,457	2,286	2,406	2,986	3,820	3,989
Teachers, librarians, and other non-supervisory instructional staff (thousands)	423	657	875	1,393	2,195	2,300	2,860	3,683	3,829
Revenue and expenditures (millions)									
Total revenue	$220	$970	$2,261	$14,747	$40,267	$96,881	$208,548	$372,944	$419,767
Total expenditures	215	1,036	2,344	15,613	40,683	95,962	212,770	381,838	435,439
Current expenditures[3]	180	861	1,942	12,329[5]	34,218[5]	86,984[5]	188,229[5]	323,889[5]	368,499[5]
Capital outlay	35	154	258	2,662	4,659	6,506	17,781	43,357	49,915
Interest on school debt	*	18	131	490	1,171	1,874	3,776	9,135	10,495
Others	*	3	13	133	636	598	2,983	5,457	6,529
Salaries and pupil cost									
Avg. annual salary of instruct. staff[4]	$325	$871	$1,441	$3,010	$8,626	$15,970	$31,367	$41,827	$44,683
Expenditure per capita total pop.	2.83	9.91	17.89	88	202	427	862	1,368	1,526
Current expenditure per pupil ADA[6]	16.67	53.32	88.09	375	816	2,272	4,980	7,394	8,261

NOTE: Because of rounding, details may not add to totals. * = Data not collected. Prior to 1959-60, data do not include Alaska and Hawaii. (1) Population data for 1899-1900 are based on total population from the decennial census. From 1919-20 to 1959-60, population data are total population, including armed forces overseas, as of July 1 preceding the school year. Data for later years are for resident population that excludes armed forces overseas. (2) Data for 1899 through 1960 are school year enrollment; data for later years are fall enrollment. (3) In 1899-1900, includes interest on school debt. (4) Data prior to 1959-60 includes supervisors, principals, teachers, and nonsupervisory instructional staff. (5) Because of changes in the definition of "current expenditures," data for 1959-60 and later years are not entirely comparable with prior years. (6) ADA means average daily attendance.

Programs for the Disabled, 1992-2003

Source: Office of Special Education Programs, U.S. Dept. of Education

(Number of children from 6 to 21 years old served annually in educational programs for the disabled; in thousands)

Type of Disability	1992-93	1993-94	1994-95	1995-96	1996-97	1997-98	1998-99	1999-2000	2000-01	2001-02	2002-03
Learning disabilities	2,366	2,428	2,510	2,602	2,674	2,754	2,817	2,834	2,848	2,846	2,834
Speech impairments	998	1,018	1,020	1,027	1,049	1,064	1,075	1,081	1,085	1,084	1,102
Mental retardation	532	554	571	586	594	603	611	600	599	592	580
Emotional disturbance	402	415	428	439	446	454	463	469	472	476	480
Multiple disabilities	103	110	90	95	99	107	108	111	121	127	130
Hearing impairments	61	65	65	68	69	70	71	71	70	70	71
Orthopedic impairments	53	57	60	63	66	67	69	71	73	73	74
Other health impairments	66	83	107	134	161	191	221	253	290	337	390
Visual impairments	24	25	25	25	26	26	26	65	25	25	25
Autism	16	19	23	29	34	43	54	65	78	97	118
Deaf-blindness	1	1	1	1	1	1	2	2	1	2	2
Traumatic brain injury	4	5	7	10	10	12	13	14	15	21	21
Developmental delay*	—	—	—	—	—	—	—	—	—	45	58
ALL DISABILITIES	4,626	4,779	4,908	5,079	5,231	4,397	5,541	5,614	5,705	5,795	5,885

NOTE: Counts based on reports from states and District of Columbia. Details may not add to totals because of rounding and/or incomplete enumeration. — = not available or reliable data. * Applicable only to ages 3-9.

Technology in U.S. Public Schools, 2004

Source: Quality Education Data, Inc., Denver, CO

(Number and percentage of schools in each category that have the technology indicated.)

	Total		Elementary[1]		Middle/ Jr. High[2]		Senior High[3]		K-12[4]		Special Ed./ Adult Ed.	
TOTAL SCHOOLS	92,117	100%	55,964	100%	14,330	100%	19,479	100%	2,472	100%	2,330	100%
Schools with computers	81,646	89	50,945	91	12,715	89	16,485	85	1,875	76	1,590	68
By number of computers:												
1-10	3,703	4	2,545	5	246	2	587	3	55	2	416	18
11-20	5,219	6	3,714	7	440	3	790	4	138	6	274	12
21-50	16,353	18	11,691	21	1,804	13	2,437	13	450	18	420	18
51-100	22,099	24	15,756	28	3,139	22	2,952	15	550	22	252	11
100+	34,272	37	17,239	31	7,086	49	9,719	50	682	28	228	10
Schools with LANs[5]	61,104	66	36,791	66	10,652	74	14,030	72	1,614	65	707	30
By enrollment:												
100-299	13,607	15	8,610	15	1,212	8	3,309	17	774	31	476	20
300-499	18,256	20	13,802	25	2,098	15	2,294	12	403	16	62	3
500+	29,241	32	14,379	26	7,342	51	8,427	43	437	18	169	7
Schools with WANs[6]	45,933	50	27,549	49	8,011	56	9,932	51	996	40	441	19
By enrollment:												
100-299	8,816	10	5,701	10	769	5	2,032	10	434	18	314	13
300-499	14,574	16	11,100	20	1,735	12	1,707	9	289	12	32	1
500+	22,543	24	10,748	19	5,507	38	6,193	32	273	11	95	4

(1) Includes preschool and schools with grade spans of Preschool-3, K-6, K-8, and K-12. (2) Includes schools with grade spans of 4-8, 7-8, and 7-9. (3) Includes vocational, technical, and alternative high schools and schools with grade spans of 7-12, 9-12, and 10-12. (4) K-12 also included under Elementary schools. (5) LAN=Local area computer network. (6) WAN=Wide area computer network.

Students Per Computer in U.S. Public Schools, 1983-2003

Source: Quality Education Data, Inc., Denver, CO

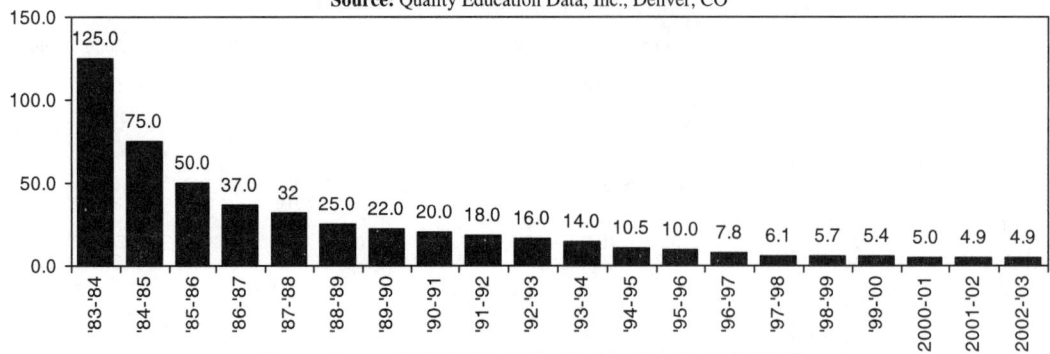

Overview of U.S. Public Schools, Fall 2002*

Source: National Center for Education Statistics, U.S. Dept. of Education; National Education Association

	Local school districts	Elementary schools[1]	Secondary schools[2]	Classroom teachers	Total enrollment	Pupils per teacher	Teacher's avg. pay[3]	Expend. per pupil[4]
Alabama	128	925	400	47,104	739,678	15.7	$38,246	$6,029
Alaska	53	194	89	8,080	134,364	16.6	49,685	9,564
Arizona	319	1,201	498	47,101	937,755	19.9	40,894	5,964
Arkansas	311	714	421	30,330	450,985	14.9	37,753	6,276
California	986	6,518	2,147	307,672	6,356,348	20.7	56,283	7,405
Colorado	178	1,200	407	45,401	751,862	16.6	41,275	6,941
Connecticut	166	863	236	42,296	570,023	13.5	54,362	10,577
Delaware	19	137	43	7,698	116,342	15.1	50,772	9,288
Dist. of Columbia	1	136	46	5,005	75,392	15.1	50,763	13,330
Florida	67	2,311	482	138,226	2,539,929	18.4	39,465	6,213
Georgia	180	1,610	354	96,044	1,496,012	15.6	45,533	7,380
Hawaii	1	207	57	10,973	183,829	16.8	44,464	7,306
Idaho	114	419	229	13,896	248,515	17.9	40,148	6,011
Illinois	893	3,199	998	131,046	2,084,187	15.9	51,289	7,956
Indiana	294	1,412	450	59,968	1,003,875	16.7	45,097	7,734
Iowa	371	1,034	426	34,573	482,210	13.9	38,921	7,338
Kansas	303	995	432	32,643	470,957	14.4	38,123	7,339
Kentucky	176	1,014	349	40,662	660,782	16.3	38,981	6,523
Louisiana	66	1,037	317	50,062	730,464	14.6	36,878	6,567
Maine	282	526	159	16,837	204,337	12.1	38,121	8,818
Maryland	24	1,082	267	55,382	866,743	15.7	49,677	8,692
Massachusetts	350	1,496	336	74,214	982,989	13.2	52,043	10,232
Michigan	553	2,722	830	89,595	1,785,160	19.9	54,071	8,653
Minnesota	417	1,298	807	52,808	846,891	16.0	42,833	7,736
Mississippi	152	594	318	31,598	492,645	15.6	34,555	5,354
Missouri	524	1,571	642	66,717	924,445	13.9	38,826	7,135
Montana	442	504	362	10,362	149,995	14.5	35,754	7,062
Nebraska	536	895	339	21,043	285,402	13.6	37,896	7,741
Nevada	17	396	127	20,038	369,498	18.4	41,795	6,079
New Hampshire	178	377	96	14,977	207,671	13.9	40,519	7,935
New Jersey	598	1,894	462	107,004	1,367,438	12.8	54,166	11,793
New Mexico	89	571	208	21,172	320,234	15.1	36,687	6,882
New York	701	3,172	964	210,926	2,888,233	13.7	52,600	11,218
North Carolina	117	1,765	388	87,677	1,335,954	15.2	43,076	6,501
North Dakota	221	331	203	8,078	104,225	12.9	33,210	6,709
Ohio	613	2,776	1,008	125,372	1,838,285	14.7	45,452	8,069
Oklahoma	541	1,212	590	40,638	624,548	15.4	34,854	6,229
Oregon	198	932	281	27,126	554,071	20.4	47,600	7,642
Pennsylvania	501	2,383	798	118,256	1,816,747	15.4	51,800	8,537
Rhode Island	36	266	65	11,196	159,205	14.2	51,076	9,703
South Carolina	89	848	282	46,577	694,584	14.9	41,279	7,017
South Dakota	174	455	273	9,257	128,039	13.8	32,416	6,424
Tennessee	138	1,243	344	58,652	928,000	15.8	39,677	5,959
Texas	1,039	5,175	1,820	288,655	4,259,823	14.8	40,001	6,771
Utah	40	523	261	22,415	489,072	21.8	38,413	4,899
Vermont	298	275	69	8,542	99,978	11.7	41,603	9,806
Virginia	135	1,470	389	99,919	1,177,229	11.8	43,152	7,496
Washington	296	1,415	630	52,953	1,014,798	19.2	44,949	7,039
West Virginia	55	592	193	20,119	282,455	14.0	38,508	7,844
Wisconsin	437	1,570	597	60,385	881,231	14.6	42,871	8,634
Wyoming	48	263	110	6,795	88,116	13.0	37,876	8,645
TOTAL U.S.	**14,465**	**65,718**	**22,599**	**3,034,065**	**48,201,550**	**15.9**	**$45,822**	**$7,731**

*Full-time elementary and secondary day schools only. (1) Includes schools below grade 9. (2) Includes schools with no grade lower than 7. (3) National Education Association estimate, Fall 2002. (4) Fall 2001, per total number of pupils.

WORLD ALMANAC QUICK QUIZ

Measured in U.S. dollars and adjusted for purchasing power, in which of these four nations did high school teachers receive the highest average starting salary ($48,704) in 2002, and in which did they receive the lowest ($25,403)?

   (a) United States   (b) Spain   (c) England   (d) Switzerland

For the answer look in this chapter, or see page 1008.

IT'S A FACT: An estimated 1.1 million students age 5-17 were homeschooled in the U.S. in 2003, up from 850,000 in 1999, according to a National Center for Education Statistics survey. Of the major reasons given for homeschooling, 31% of parents claimed concern about school environment, 30% cited a need for religious or moral instruction, and 16% were dissatisfied with academic instruction in schools.

Mathematics, Reading, and Science Achievement of U.S. Students

Source: National Assessment of Educational Progress, National Center for Education Statistics, U.S. Dept. of Education

Percent of students who scored at or above basic level in national tests.[1]

State	Grade 4 Math 2000	Grade 4 Math 2003	Grade 4 Reading 1998	Grade 4 Reading 2003	Grade 8 Math 2000	Grade 8 Math 2003	Grade 8 Reading 1998	Grade 8 Reading 2003	Grade 8 Science 1996	Grade 8 Science 2000
AL	57	65	56	53	52	53	67	65	47	51
AK	NA	76	NA	58	NA	70	NA	67	65	NA
AZ	58	70	51	54	62	62	72	66	55	57
AR	56	71	54	60	52	57	68	70	55	54
CA	52	67	48	49	52	55	63	61	47	40
CO	NA	77	69	70	NA	74	76	78	68	NA
CT	77	82	76	74	72	73	81	77	68	65
DE	NA	81	53	71	NA	68	64	77	51	NA
DC	24	36	27	32	23	29	44	47	19	NA
FL	NA	76	53	63	NA	61	67	67	51	NA
GA	58	71	54	58	55	59	68	70	49	52
HI	55	69	45	53	52	55	59	61	42	40
ID	71	79	NA	64	71	72	NA	76	NA	73
IL	66	73	NA	61	68	66	NA	76	NA	62
IN	78	82	NA	66	76	73	NA	77	65	68
IA	78	83	67	71	NA	76	NA	80	71	NA
KS	76	86	70	66	77	76	81	77	NA	NA
KY	60	72	62	65	63	66	74	78	58	62
LA	57	68	44	49	48	57	63	64	40	45
ME	74	83	72	71	76	74	83	79	78	75
MD	61	72	58	62	65	67	70	71	55	59
MA	79	84	70	73	76	76	79	81	69	74
MI	72	78	62	64	70	68	NA	76	65	69
MN	78	84	69	69	80	82	81	78	72	73
MS	45	62	47	48	41	47	62	66	39	42
MO	72	79	61	68	67	71	75	80	64	68
MT	73	81	72	69	80	79	83	82	77	80
NE	67	79	NA	66	74	74	NA	77	71	70
NV	60	69	51	52	58	60	70	63	NA	54
NH	NA	88	75	75	NA	79	NA	81	NA	NA
NJ	NA	81	NA	70	NA	71	NA	78	NA	NA
NM	51	63	51	48	50	52	71	62	49	48
NY	67	79	62	67	68	71	76	75	57	61
NC	76	85	58	65	70	71	74	72	56	56
ND	75	83	NA	69	77	81	NA	82	78	74
OH	73	81	NA	68	75	73	NA	78	NA	73
OK	69	73	66	60	64	64	80	74	NA	62
OR	65	79	58	64	71	70	78	74	68	67
PA	NA	78	NA	65	NA	69	NA	76	NA	NA
RI	67	71	64	63	64	63	76	71	59	61
SC	60	79	53	59	55	67	66	69	45	50
SD	NA	82	NA	68	NA	78	NA	82	NA	NA
TN	60	69	57	57	53	59	71	69	53	57
TX	77	82	59	60	68	69	74	71	55	53
UT	70	79	62	66	68	72	77	76	70	68
VT	73	84	NA	74	75	77	NA	82	70	74
VA	73	83	62	69	67	72	78	78	59	63
WA	NA	81	64	67	NA	72	76	76	61	NA
WV	68	75	60	65	62	63	75	72	56	61
WI	NA	79	72	68	NA	75	79	78	73	NA
WY	73	87	64	68	70	76	76	79	71	71
U.S.[2]	67	77	58	62	65	66	71	72	60	59

NA = Not administered. (1) Basic level denotes a partial mastery of prerequisite knowledge and skills fundamental for proficient work at each grade. (2) Includes public schools only.

Revenues[1] for Public Elementary and Secondary Schools, by State, 2003-2004

Source: National Education Association; in thousands

STATE	Total	Federal Amount	Federal %	State Amount	State %	Local and intermediate Amount	Local %
Alabama	$5,897,873*	$692,499*	11.7*	$3,386,393*	57.4*	$1,818,980*	30.8*
Alaska	1,285,435*	161,096*	12.5*	816,753*	63.5*	307,586*	23.9*
Arizona	7,282,664*	732,267*	10.1*	3,642,178*	50.0*	2,908,220*	39.9*
Arkansas	2,956,560*	253,484*	8.6*	1,819,584*	61.5*	883,492*	29.9*
California	58,475,826*	6,720,692*	11.5*	33,418,991*	57.2*	18,336,143*	31.4*
Colorado	6,546,455*	405,030*	6.2*	2,700,464*	41.3*	3,440,962*	52.6*
Connecticut	7,406,864	384,959	5.2	2,932,516	39.6	4,089,389	55.2
Delaware	1,370,945*	112,962*	8.2*	932,320*	68.0*	325,663*	23.8*
District of Columbia	826,929	115,039	13.9	0	0.0	711,890	86.1
Florida	19,933,161	2,268,611	11.4	8,520,788	42.7	9,143,762	45.9
Georgia	14,363,970*	1,140,516*	7.9*	6,821,586*	47.5*	6,401,868*	44.6*
Hawaii	1,918,991	174,127	9.1	1,711,656	89.2	33,208	1.7
Idaho	1,650,000	150,000	9.1	1,000,000	60.6	500,000	30.3
Illinois	20,311,924*	1,744,732*	8.6*	6,579,070*	32.4*	11,988,123*	59.0*
Indiana	10,154,471*	583,175*	5.7*	5,338,246*	52.6*	4,233,050*	41.7*
Iowa	4,073,080	240,066	5.9	2,019,795	49.6	1,813,219	44.5
Kansas	4,132,642	352,642	8.5	2,382,000	57.6	1,398,000	33.8
Kentucky	5,136,717	513,482	10.0	3,085,142	60.1	1,538,093	29.9
Louisiana	5,643,847	747,373	13.2	2,763,778	49.0	2,132,696	37.8
Maine	2,056,314	132,834	6.5	885,499	43.1	1,037,981	50.5
Maryland	8,572,963*	512,121*	6.0*	2,995,107*	34.9*	5,065,735*	59.1*
Massachusetts	10,692,829	709,402	6.6	3,864,414	36.1	6,119,013	57.2
Michigan	16,502,438*	819,743*	5.0*	11,444,628*	69.4*	4,238,067*	25.7*
Minnesota	8,563,266	499,918	5.8	6,185,550	72.2	1,877,798	21.9
Mississippi	3,437,851*	524,927*	15.3*	1,866,087*	54.3*	1,046,837*	30.5*
Missouri	7,972,335	697,498*	8.7	2,577,150	32.3	4,697,687*	58.9
Montana	1,262,395*	146,436*	11.6*	615,567*	48.8*	500,392*	39.6*
Nebraska	2,200,316	156,587	7.1	888,893	40.4	1,154,836	52.5
Nevada	3,225,269*	195,342*	6.1*	887,986*	27.5*	2,141,941*	66.4*
New Hampshire	2,065,830*	103,789*	5.0*	1,545,110*	74.8*	416,931*	20.2*
New Jersey	18,142,852	520,192	2.9	6,892,105	38.0	10,730,555	59.1
New Mexico	2,797,345	388,939	13.9	1,927,881	68.9	480,525	17.2
New York	38,621,058*	1,617,179*	4.2*	19,011,653*	49.2*	17,992,226*	46.6*
North Carolina	10,542,718*	813,820*	7.7*	7,649,967*	72.6*	2,078,931*	19.7*
North Dakota	847,385	110,649	13.1	307,290	36.3	429,446	50.7
Ohio	19,267,792*	1,241,298*	6.4*	8,856,675*	46.0*	9,169,819*	47.6*
Oklahoma	4,408,252*	564,550*	12.8*	2,354,253*	53.4*	1,489,449*	33.8*
Oregon	4,530,082*	475,631*	10.5*	2,393,726*	52.8*	1,660,725*	36.7*
Pennsylvania	18,595,068*	934,638*	5.0*	7,428,464*	39.9*	10,231,966*	55.0*
Rhode Island	1,495,660*	54,762*	3.7*	553,057*	37.0*	887,841*	59.4*
South Carolina	5,952,739	546,478	9.2	2,900,000	48.7	2,506,261	42.1

STATE	Total	Federal Amount	%	State Amount	%	Local and intermediate Amount	%
South Dakota	984,699*	151,926*	15.4*	357,140*	36.3*	475,633*	48.3*
Tennessee	5,807,694*	662,315*	11.4*	2,692,390*	46.4*	2,452,989*	42.2*
Texas	35,771,063	3,962,010	11.1	14,099,134	39.4	17,709,919	49.5
Utah	3,021,976	278,734	9.2	1,756,043	58.1	987,199	32.7
Vermont	1,182,553	75,966	6.4	843,280	71.3	263,307	22.3
Virginia	12,089,354*	704,569*	5.8*	5,534,902*	45.8*	5,849,882*	48.4*
Washington	8,827,609	941,048	10.7	5,440,456	61.6	2,446,105	27.7
West Virginia	2,725,053	287,794	10.6	1,634,063	60.0	803,196	29.5
Wisconsin	9,413,140	522,492	5.6	5,052,379	53.7	3,838,269	40.8
Wyoming	964,000	84,000	8.7	490,000	50.8	390,000	40.5
50 States and DC	$451,908,251	$36,930,338	8.2	$221,802,107	49.1	$193,175,805	42.7

*Indicates NEA estimate. (1) Included as revenue receipts are all appropriations from general funds of federal, state, county, and local governments; receipts from taxes levied for school purposes; income from permanent school funds and endowments; and income from leases of school lands and miscellaneous sources (interest on bank deposits, tuition, gifts, school lunch charges, etc.).

Enrollment in U.S. Public and Private Schools, 1899-2013*

Source: National Center for Education Statistics, U.S. Dept. of Education

School year[1]	Public school[2]	Private school[2]	% Private	School year[1]	Public school[2]	Private school[2]	% Private
1899-1900	15,503	1,352	8.7	1979-80	41,651	5,000[3]	12.0
1909-10	17,814	1,558	8.7	1989-90	40,543	5,198	11.4
1919-20	21,578	1,699	7.9	1999-2000	46,857	6,018	11.4
1929-30	25,678	2,651	10.3	2000-2001	47,688	6,202	11.5
1939-40	25,434	2,611	10.3	2004-2005[4] ...	48,304	6,311	11.5
1949-50	25,111	3,380	13.5	2005-2006[4] ...	48,524	6,383	11.6
1959-60	35,182	5,675	16.1	2012-2013[4] ...	49,737	6,627	11.8
1969-70	45,550	5,500[3]	12.1				

*Private includes all nonpublic schools, including religious schools. (1) Fall enrollment. (2) In thousands. (3) Estimated. (4) Projected.

U.S. Public High School Graduation Rates, 2001-2002

Source: National Center for Education Statistics, U.S. Dept. of Education

	Rate (%)[1]	Rank		Rate (%)[1]	Rank		Rate (%)[1]	Rank
Alabama...........	57.2	47	Louisiana	59.2	45	Ohio..............	72.3	24
Alaska	60.7	43	Maine..............	75.7	13	Oklahoma	73.2	22
Arizona............	69.9	32	Maryland	74.1	18	Oregon	68.8	34
Arkansas	74.2	17	Massachusetts......	74.0	19	Pennsylvania.......	77.1	12
California..........	69.6	33	Michigan	71.5	27	Rhode Island.......	72.0	26
Colorado...........	70.0	31	Minnesota	82.3	5	South Carolina	49.2	51
Connecticut	74.9	16	Mississippi.........	59.1	46	South Dakota	77.8	9
Delaware	62.0	41	Missouri...........	73.6	21	Tennessee	56.7	48
District of Columbia ..	70.4	29	Montana...........	77.3	10	Texas	64.2	39
Florida	55.7	49	Nebraska..........	80.0	6	Utah..............	82.5	4
Georgia	53.6	50	Nevada	70.2	30	Vermont...........	78.6	8
Hawaii	64.8	38	New Hampshire.....	75.2	15	Virginia	73.7	20
Idaho	77.2	11	New Jersey	89.8	1	Washington........	68.5	36
Illinois.............	72.2	25	New Mexico........	61.5	42	West Virginia.......	71.2	28
Indiana............	68.6	35	New York..........	62.1	40	Wisconsin.........	79.0	7
Iowa..............	82.9	3	North Carolina	60.6	44	Wyoming...........	72.7	23
Kansas	75.2	14	North Dakota	83.7	2	TOTAL U.S.	68.5	
Kentucky	64.9	37						

NOTE: Data exclude ungraded pupils and have not been adjusted for interstate migration. (1) Graduates as percentage of fall 1998 9th-grade enrollment.

Teachers' Salaries in Upper Secondary Education, Selected Countries, 2002

Source: Organization for Economic Cooperation and Development

Annual statutory teachers' salaries in public institutions in upper secondary (senior high school) education, general programs, in equivalent U.S. dollars converted using PPPs[1]; ranked by starting salaries.

	Starting salary	Salary with 15 years' experience	Salary at top of scale		Starting salary	Salary with 15 years' experience	Salary at top of scale
Switzerland.....	$48,704	$63,200	$74,689	Tunisia	$19,878	$20,065	$26,167
Germany	41,441	50,805	53,085	Portugal.......	19,445	31,876	51,829
Spain	32,679	38,067	47,323	India[2].........	18,247	26,831	26,831
Finland	32,136	40,482	42,652	New Zealand ...	18,109	35,034	35,034
Belgium (Fl.)....	31,924	46,076	55,383	Czech Republic .	15,476	18,898	23,452
Belgium (Fr.) ...	30,793	44,854	54,100	Paraguay[2, 3] ...	15,269	15,269	15,269
Denmark.......	30,384	43,063	46,096	Brazil[2]	13,853	16,397	NA
United States ..	29,641	42,918	51,308	Malaysia[2]......	13,647	23,315	23,315
Netherlands	29,326	51,444	58,913	Argentina[2]	12,076	17,007	17,007
Scotland	27,789	40,619	40,619	Chile	11,033	13,454	13,926
Australia.......	27,394	40,479	40,479	Jamaica.......	10,955	12,686	12,686
Korea	26,852	46,269	74,541	Turkey	10,272	11,759	13,342
Norway.......	26,637	30,533	32,695	Philippines.....	9,857	10,880	10,880
France	25,563	33,394	48,070	Hungary.......	8,790	12,851	16,797
England	25,403	39,350	39,350	Jordan........	7,976	10,414	868
Austria	24,846	34,444	52,294	Uruguay[2, 3]	5,873	6,944	NA
Italy............	24,710	31,073	38,604	Thailand.......	5,862	14,406	14,406
Sweden	24,544	29,315	31,711	Slovak Republic.	5,134	6,611	9,786
Ireland	23,767	38,066	43,137	Peru[2, 3]	4,577	4,577	5,273
Japan	23,493	44,372	58,286	Sri Lanka......	3,574	4,596	3,319
Iceland	22,017	27,941	30,551	Indonesia......	1,014	1,858	1,990
Greece	20,906	25,563	31,013				

NA = Not available. (1) Purchasing power parities (PPPs) are the rates of currency conversion that equalize the purchasing power of different currencies by eliminating the differences in price levels between countries. (2) Year of reference 2001. (3) Salaries for a position of 20 hours per week. Most teachers hold two positions.

Percent of Population with Upper Secondary Education, Selected Countries, 2002
Source: Organization for Economic Cooperation and Development

Percentage of the population ages 25-64 that received at least some upper secondary (senior high school) education

Czech Republic .88	Switzerland.... 82	Hungary 71	Ireland........ 60	Peru[1]......... 44	Brazil[1] 27
United States ..87	Sweden 82	Korea 71	Iceland 59	Philippines... 43	Turkey 25
Norway........86	Denmark...... 80	Netherlands .. 66	Luxembourg ... 57	Argentina[1] ... 42	Indonesia...... 22
Slovak Republic .86	Israel........ 80	France 65	Greece 50	Malaysia[1] 41	Paraguay[1] 22
Japan 84	Austria 78	United Kingdom 64	Chile 47	Spain......... 41	Portugal....... 20
Canada........83	New Zealand .. 76	Australia 61	Poland........ 47	Jordan........ 39	Thailand 19
Germany 83	Finland 75	Belgium....... 61	Italy 44	Uruguay[1]...... 33	Mexico........ 13

(1) Year of reference 2001.

Government Expenditure Per Student, Selected Countries, 2001
Source: Organization for Economic Cooperation and Development

Expenditure per student in U.S. dollars, converted using PPPs[1], on public and private institutions, by level of education, based on full-time equivalents

	Primary[2]	Secondary[3]		Primary[2]	Secondary[3]		Primary[2]	Secondary[3]
Argentina	1,655	2,306	Indonesia......	108	322	Philippines*	492	465
Australia......	5,052	7,239	Ireland	3,743	5,245	Poland*........	2,322	NA
Austria	6,571	8,562	Israel	4,650	5,617	Portugal.......	4,181	5,976
Belgium.......	5,321	7,912	Italy*	6,783	8,258	Slovak Republic .	1,252	1,874
Brazil*[4]........	832	864	Jamaica.......	646	922	Russian		
Canada[4]	(5)	5,947	Japan..........	5,771	6534	Federation[4] ...	(5)	954
Chile[6]	2,110	2,085	Jordan*	811	840	Spain..........	4,168	5,442
Czech Republic .	1,871	3,448	Korea.........	3,714	5,159	Sweden........	6,295	6,482
Denmark.......	7,572	8,113	Luxembourg....	7,873	11,091	Switzerland*....	6,889	10,916
Finland	4,708	6,537	Malaysia*	1,562	2,600	Thailand	1,045	1,081
France	4,777	8,107	Mexico........	1,357	1,915	Tunisia*	(5)	2,473
Germany	4,237	6,620	Netherlands	4,862	6,403	United Kingdom..	4,415	5,933
Greece	3,299	3,768	Norway	7,404	9,040	**United States ...**	**7,560**	**8,779**
Hungary*	2,592	2,633	Paraguay......	802	1,373	Uruguay*	1,202	1,046
Iceland........	6,373	7,265	Peru..........	431	534	Zimbabwe[6]	878	1,368
India	405	650						

NA = Not available. * Public institutions only. (1) Purchasing power parities (PPPs) are the rates of currency conversion that equalize the purchasing power of different currencies by eliminating the differences in price levels between countries. (2) Elementary school age. (3) Junior high and upper secondary (senior high school) combined. (4) Data for 2000. (5) Data for primary and secondary combined. (6) Data for 2002.

Charges at U.S. Institutions of Higher Education, 1969 to 2003
Source: National Center for Education Statistics, U.S. Dept. of Education

Figures for 1969-70 are average charges for full-time resident degree-credit students; figures for later years are average charges per full-time equivalent student. Room and board are based on full-time students. These figures are enrollment-weighted, according to the number of full-time-equivalent undergraduates, and thus may vary from averages given elsewhere.

	TUITION AND FEES			BOARD RATES			DORMITORY CHARGES		
	All institutions	2-yr	4-yr	All institutions	2-yr	4-yr	All institutions	2-yr	4-yr
PUBLIC (in-state)									
1969-70	$323	$178	$427	$511	$465	$540	$369	$308	$395
1979-80	583	355	840	867	894	898	715	572	749
1989-90	1,356	756	2,035	1,635	1,581	1,728	1,513	962	1,561
1990-91	1,454	824	2,159	1,691	1,594	1,767	1,612	1,050	1,658
1991-92	1,624	937	2,410	1,780	1,612	1,852	1,731	1,074	1,789
1992-93	1,782	1,025	2,349	1,841	1,668	1,854	1,756	1,106	1,816
1993-94	1,942	1,125	2,537	1,880	1,681	1,895	1,873	1,190	1,934
1994-95	2,057	1,192	2,681	1,949	1,712	1,967	1,959	1,232	2,023
1995-96	2,179	1,239	2,848	2,020	1,681	2,045	2,057	1,297	2,121
1996-97	2,271	1,276	2,987	2,111	1,789	2,133	2,148	1,339	2,214
1997-98	2,360	1,314	3,110	2,228	1,795	2,263	2,225	1,401	2,301
1998-99	2,430	1,327	3,229	2,347	1,828	2,389	2,330	1,450	2,409
1999-2000	2,506	1,338	3,349	2,364	1,834	2,406	2,440	1,549	2,519
2000-2001	2,562	1,333	3,501	2,455	1,906	2,499	2,569	1,600	2,654
2001-2002	2,700	1,380	3,735	2,598	2,036	2,645	2,723	1,722	2,816
2002-2003[1]	2,928	1,479	4,059	2,702	2,174	2,747	2,925	1,943	3,022
PRIVATE									
1969-70	1,533	1,034	1,809	561	546	608	436	413	503
1979-80	3,130	2,062	3,811	955	924	1,078	827	769	999
1989-90	8,147	5,196	10,348	1,948	1,811	2,339	1,923	1,663	2,411
1990-91	8,772	5,570	11,379	2,074	1,989	2,470	2,063	1,744	2,654
1991-92	9,434	5,752	12,192	2,252	2,090	2,727	2,221	1,789	2,860
1992-93	9,942	6,059	10,294	2,344	1,875	2,354	2,348	1,970	2,362
1993-94	10,572	6,370	10,952	2,434	1,970	2,445	2,490	2,067	2,506
1994-95	11,111	6,914	11,481	2,509	2,023	2,520	2,587	2,233	2,601
1995-96	11,864	7,094	12,243	2,606	2,098	2,617	2,738	2,371	2,751
1996-97	12,498	7,236	12,881	2,663	2,181	2,672	2,878	2,537	2,889
1997-98	12,801	7,464	13,344	2,762	2,785	2,761	2,954	2,672	2,964
1998-99	13,428	7,854	13,973	2,865	2,884	2,865	3,075	2,581	3,091
1999-2000	14,081	8,235	14,588	2,882	2,922	2,881	3,224	2,808	3,237
2000-2001	15,000	9,067	15,470	2,993	3,000	2,993	3,374	2,722	3,392
2001-2002	15,742	10,076	16,211	3,104	2,633	3,109	3,567	3,116	3,576
2002-2003[1]	16,517	10,755	16,948	3,236	3,821	3,229	3,750	3,184	3,762

(1) Preliminary.

> **IT'S A FACT:** Women received 57% of all bachelor's degrees in 2002, up from 43% in 1970, according to the Dept. of Education. Women earned 86% of the bachelor's degrees in health professions and related sciences, and 78% of those in psychology. Men dominated the engineering and computer science degrees, earning 79% and 72% respectively.

Top 20 Colleges and Universities in Endowment Assets, 2003[1]

Source: *2003 NACUBO Endowment Study*, National Association of College and University Business Officers (NACUBO)

College/University	Endowment assets[2]	College/University	Endowment assets[2]
1. Harvard University...................	$18,849,491	11. University of Pennsylvania..............	$3,547,473
2. Yale University	11,034,600	12. University of Michigan	3,464,515
3. Princeton University	8,730,100	13. Washington University	3,454,704
4. University of Texas System.............	8,708,818	14. University of Chicago	3,221,833
5. Stanford University	8,614,000	15. Northwestern University	3,051,167
6. Massachusetts Institute of Technology.....	5,133,613	16. Duke University	3,017,261
7. University of California	4,368,911	17. Rice University	2,937,649
8. Columbia University	4,350,000	18. Cornell University	2,854,771
9. Emory University.....................	4,019,766	19. University of Notre Dame	2,573,346
10. The Texas A&M University System and Foundations.......................	3,802,712	20. Dartmouth College	2,121,183

NOTE: Market value of endowment assets, excluding pledges and working capital. (1) As of June 30, 2003. (2) In thousands.

U.S. Higher Education Trends: Bachelor's Degrees Conferred

Source: National Center for Education Statistics, U.S. Dept. of Education

Figures for 2003-2004 and 2009-2010 are projected.

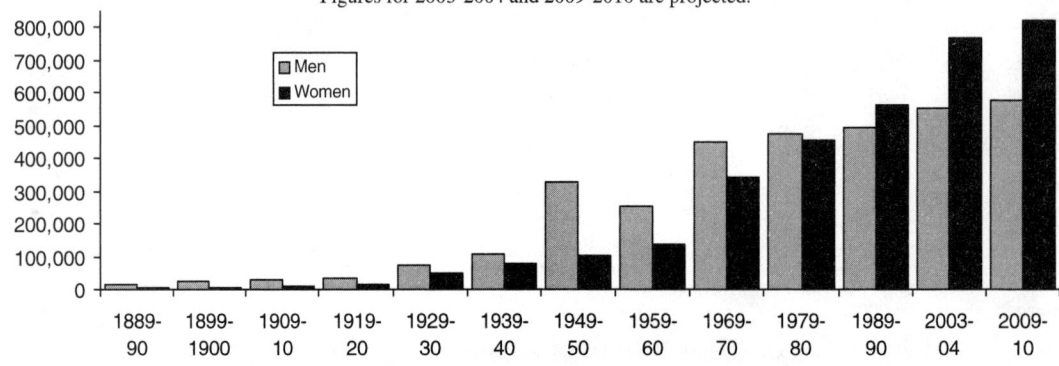

Financial Aid for College and Other Postsecondary Education

Reviewed by National Assoc. of Student Financial Aid Administrators

The cost of postsecondary education in the U.S. has increased in recent years, but financial aid, which may be in the form of grants (no repayment needed), loans, and/or work-study programs, is widely available to help families meet these expenses. Most aid is limited to family financial need as determined by standard formulas. Students interested in receiving aid are advised to apply, without making prior assumptions. Financial aid personnel at each school can provide information about programs available to students, steps to apply for them, and deadlines, all of which may vary.

All applicants for federal aid must file a Free Application for Federal Student Aid (FAFSA), generally as soon as possible after Jan. 1 for the academic year starting the following September. Figures provided should agree with federal income tax forms filed for the previous year. Other possible sources of aid include state governments, employers and unions, civic organizations, and the institutions themselves. There are also special federal programs that pay for postsecondary education in return for service: AmeriCorps (phone: 1-800-942-2677) and ROTC (phone: 1-800-USA-ROTC). Additional forms and certain fees may be required if a student is to be considered for institutional aid. Aid must be re-applied for annually.

A federal formula, based on information provided on the FAFSA, takes into account such factors as family after-tax income in the preceding calendar year, parental and student assets (excluding the parents' home) and length of time to parents' retirement, and unusual expenses (such as very high medical expenses).

The resulting Expected Family Contribution, or EFC (which is divided among the family members—excluding parents—in college), is subtracted from the total cost of attendance for each person (including room and board or allowance for living costs, books and supplies, transportation to and from school, and other miscellaneous costs) to determine financial need. (Some institutions use a separate formula for need-based institutional aid.) Some schools guarantee to meet the full financial need of each admitted student; others try to do so but may fall short, depending on the availability of funds. Outside scholarships (even if non-need-based) are taken into account in determining the amount of aid eligibility for federal, institutional, and state financial aid programs.

The aid package offered by each school may include one or more of the following resources: Federal Pell Grants, for those with greatest financial need; Federal Supplemental Educational Opportunity Grants, for those with great financial need who are also eligible for Pell Grants; grants from the school; Federal Work-Study or other work programs; low-interest Perkins loans; and subsidized and unsubsidized Stafford loans. Parents of undergraduate students may also apply for a Federal PLUS loan. For unsubsidized Stafford loans and all PLUS loans, financial need is not a requirement. Loans have varying interest rates and other requirements. Repayment of Perkins and Stafford loans does not begin until after graduation; deferments are available under certain circumstances. For PLUS loans, parents must pass a credit check and begin repayment of both principal and interest while the student is still in school.

Certain federal income tax credits—dollar for dollar reductions of the amount of tax due—are available to families who meet income and other requirements; see the chapter on Taxes.

Rules for financial aid are complex and changeable. *The Student Guide*, a comprehensive resource on financial aid from the U.S. Dept. of Education, can be found at the website www.studentaid.ed.gov/students/publications/student_ guide/ index.html

Further information and FAFSA forms are available from the school or from the Federal Student Aid Information Center, PO Box 84, Washington, DC 20044; phone: 1-800-4-FED-AID, Mon.-Fri., 8 AM - 12 midnight Eastern Time. The Information Center also has a free booklet called *The EFC Formula Book*. FAFSA forms can be obtained online at www.fafsa.ed.gov

Average Salaries of U.S. College Professors, 2003-2004

Source: American Association of University Professors

TEACHING LEVEL		MEN Type of institution			WOMEN Type of institution		
		Public	Private/ Independent	Church-related	Public	Private/ Independent	Church-related
Doctoral level	Professor.........	$96,238	$124,099	$105,673	$87,214	$113,283	$95,329
	Associate	67,906	80,759	74,146	63,233	75,254	69,014
	Assistant.........	58,478	71,169	62,068	53,350	63,613	57,734
Master's level	Professor.........	75,524	82,991	77,859	73,067	77,502	71,441
	Associate	60,370	64,483	60,714	57,856	60,658	57,191
	Assistant.........	50,804	52,828	49,775	48,684	51,000	47,191
General 4-year	Professor.........	69,925	83,436	63,449	66,590	79,642	60,235
	Associate	56,956	61,033	51,792	54,243	59,166	49,982
	Assistant.........	47,324	50,171	43,575	45,373	48,692	42,813
2-year	Professor.........	66,030	54,879	NA	62,357	54,040	NA
	Associate	53,018	43,015	NA	50,695	46,510	NA
	Assistant.........	46,104	37,346	NA	44,448	39,165	NA

NA = Not available.

ACT (formerly American College Testing) Mean Scores and Characteristics of College-Bound Students, 1991-2004

Source: ACT, Inc.

(for school year ending in year shown)

SCORES[1]	Unit[1]	1991	1992	1993	1994	1995	1996	1997	1998	1999	2000	2001	2002	2003	2004
Composite Scores	Points	20.6	20.6	20.7	20.8	20.8	20.9	21.0	21.0	21.0	21.0	21.0	20.8	20.8	20.9
Male...........	Points	20.9	20.9	21.0	20.9	21.0	21.0	21.1	21.2	21.1	21.2	21.1	20.9	21.0	21.0
Female.........	Points	20.4	20.5	20.5	20.7	20.7	20.8	20.8	20.9	20.9	20.9	20.9	20.7	20.8	20.9
English Score	Points	20.3	20.2	20.3	20.3	20.2	20.3	20.3	20.4	20.5	20.5	20.5	20.2	20.3	20.4
Male...........	Points	19.8	19.8	19.8	19.8	19.8	19.8	19.9	19.9	20.0	20.0	20.0	19.7	19.8	19.9
Female.........	Points	20.7	20.6	20.6	20.7	20.6	20.7	20.7	20.8	20.9	20.9	20.8	20.6	20.7	20.8
Math Score	Points	20.0	20.0	20.1	20.2	20.2	20.2	20.6	20.8	20.7	20.7	20.7	20.6	20.6	20.7
Male...........	Points	20.6	20.7	20.8	20.8	20.9	20.9	21.3	21.5	21.4	21.4	21.4	21.2	21.2	21.3
Female.........	Points	19.4	19.5	19.6	19.6	19.7	19.7	20.1	20.2	20.2	20.2	20.2	20.1	20.1	20.2
PARTICIPANTS															
Total Number	(1000s)	796	832	875	892	945	925	959	995	1,019	1,065	1,070	1,116	1,175	1,171
Male...........	Percent	45	45	45	45	44	44	44	43	43	43	43	44	44	43
White...........	Percent	79	79	79	79	80	79	74	76	72	72	71	69	68	67
Black	Percent	9	9	9	9	9	9	10	11	10	10	11	11	11	11
Hispanic........	Percent	4	5	5	5	5	5	5	5	5	5	6	6	6	7
Composite Scores															
27 or above	Percent	11	12	12	13	13	13	14	14	14	14	14	13	14	14
18 or below	Percent	35	35	35	34	34	34	33	33	33	32	33	35	35	34

(1) Minimum point score, 1; maximum score, 36. Test scores and characteristics of college-bound students are based on the performance of all ACT-tested students who graduated in the spring of a given school year and took the ACT Assessment during junior or senior year of high school.

ACT Average Composite Scores by State, 2003-2004

Source: ACT, Inc.

STATE	Avg. Comp. Score	% Grads Taking ACT[1]	STATE	Avg. Comp. Score	% Grads Taking ACT[1]	STATE	Avg. Comp. Score	% Grads Taking ACT[1]
Alabama............	20.2	76	Louisiana	19.8	87	Oklahoma	20.6	69
Alaska	21.3	29	Maine..............	22.6	9	Oregon	22.5	12
Arizona............	21.5	20	Maryland...........	20.8	12	Pennsylvania........	21.8	9
Arkansas..........	20.4	73	Masschusetts.......	22.4	12	Rhode Island........	21.9	7
California	21.6	14	Michigan	21.4	68	South Carolina	19.3	36
Colorado..........	20.3	100	Minnesota	22.2	66	South Dakota	21.5	75
Connecticut	22.5	9	Mississippi..........	18.8	91	Tennessee	20.5	87
Delaware	21.5	5	Missouri............	21.5	70	Texas	20.2	29
District of Columbia ...	17.8	29	Montana............	21.7	56	Utah................	21.5	67
Florida	20.5	44	Nebraska...........	21.7	77	Vermont.............	22.7	12
Georgia	20.0	26	Nevada	21.2	33	Virginia	20.9	13
Hawaii	21.7	18	New Hampshire......	22.5	9	Washington..........	22.5	15
Idaho	21.3	59	New Jersey	21.2	6	West Virginia........	20.5	65
Illinois	20.3	99	New Mexico.........	20.1	61	Wisconsin	22.2	68
Indiana............	21.6	20	New York...........	22.3	16	Wyoming............	21.4	70
Iowa..............	22.0	67	North Carolina	20.3	15			
Kansas	21.6	75	North Dakota	21.2	81			
Kentucky	20.3	75	Ohio...............	21.4	66	**U.S. AVG.**	**20.9**	**40**

(1) Based on number of high school graduates in 2004, as projected by the Western Interstate Commission for Higher Education, and number of students in the class of 2004 who took the ACT.

SAT Mean Verbal and Math Scores of College-Bound Seniors, 1975-2004

Source: The College Board

(recentered scale; for school year ending in year shown)

	1975	1980	1985	1990	1995	1997	1998	1999	2000	2001	2002	2003	2004
Verbal Scores	512	502	509	500	504	505	505	505	505	506	504	507	508
Male.............	515	506	514	505	505	507	509	509	507	509	507	512	512
Female...........	509	498	503	496	502	503	502	502	504	502	502	503	504
Math Scores	498	492	500	501	506	511	512	511	514	514	516	519	518
Male.............	518	515	522	521	525	530	531	531	533	533	534	537	537
Female...........	479	473	480	483	490	494	496	495	498	498	500	503	501

NOTE: In 1995, the College Board recentered the scoring scale for the SAT by reestablishing the original mean score of 500 on the 200-800 scale. Earlier scores have been adjusted to account for this recentering.

SAT Mean Scores by State, 1990 and 1999-2004

Source: The College Board

(recentered scale; for school year ending in year shown)

STATE	1990 V	1990 M	1999 V	1999 M	2000 V	2000 M	2001 V	2001 M	2002 V	2002 M	2003 V	2003 M	2004 V	2004 M	% Grads Taking SAT[1]
Alabama	545	534	561	555	559	555	559	554	560	559	559	552	560	553	10
Alaska	514	501	516	514	519	515	514	510	516	519	518	518	518	514	53
Arizona	521	520	524	525	521	523	523	525	520	523	524	525	523	524	32
Arkansas	545	532	563	556	563	554	562	550	560	556	564	554	569	555	6
California	494	508	497	514	497	518	498	517	496	517	499	519	501	519	49
Colorado	533	534	536	540	534	537	539	542	543	548	551	553	554	553	27
Connecticut	506	496	510	509	508	509	509	510	509	509	512	514	515	515	85
Delaware	510	496	503	497	502	496	501	499	502	500	501	501	500	499	73
District of Columbia	483	467	494	478	494	486	482	474	480	473	484	474	489	476	77
Florida	495	493	499	498	498	500	498	499	496	499	498	498	499	499	67
Georgia	478	473	487	482	488	486	491	489	489	491	493	491	494	493	73
Hawaii	480	505	482	513	488	519	486	515	488	520	486	516	487	514	60
Idaho	542	524	542	540	540	541	543	542	539	541	540	540	540	539	20
Illinois	542	547	569	585	568	586	576	589	578	596	583	596	585	597	10
Indiana	486	486	496	498	498	501	499	501	498	503	500	504	501	506	64
Iowa	584	588	594	598	589	600	593	603	591	602	586	597	593	602	5
Kansas	566	563	578	576	574	580	577	580	578	580	578	582	584	585	9
Kentucky	548	541	547	547	548	550	550	550	550	552	554	552	559	557	12
Louisiana	551	537	561	558	562	558	564	562	561	559	563	559	564	561	8
Maine	501	490	507	503	504	500	506	500	503	502	503	501	505	501	76
Maryland	506	502	507	507	507	509	508	510	507	513	509	515	511	515	68
Massachusetts	503	498	511	511	511	513	511	515	512	516	516	522	518	523	85
Michigan	529	534	557	565	557	569	561	572	558	572	564	576	563	573	11
Minnesota	552	558	586	598	581	594	580	589	581	591	582	591	587	593	10
Mississippi	552	538	563	548	562	549	566	551	559	547	565	551	562	547	5
Missouri	548	541	572	572	572	577	577	577	574	580	582	583	587	585	8
Montana	540	542	545	546	543	546	539	539	541	547	538	543	537	539	29
Nebraska	559	562	568	571	560	571	562	568	561	570	573	578	569	576	8
Nevada	511	511	512	517	510	517	509	515	509	518	510	517	507	514	40
New Hampshire	518	510	520	518	520	519	520	516	519	519	522	521	522	521	80
New Jersey	495	498	498	510	498	513	499	513	498	513	501	515	501	514	83
New Mexico	554	546	549	542	549	543	551	542	551	543	548	540	554	543	14
New York	489	496	495	502	494	506	495	505	494	506	496	510	497	510	87
North Carolina	478	470	493	493	492	496	493	499	493	505	495	506	499	507	70
North Dakota	579	578	594	605	588	609	592	599	597	610	602	613	582	601	5
Ohio	526	522	534	568	533	539	534	539	533	540	536	541	538	542	28
Oklahoma	553	542	567	560	563	560	567	561	565	562	569	562	569	566	7
Oregon	515	509	525	525	527	527	526	526	524	528	526	527	527	528	56
Pennsylvania	497	490	498	495	498	497	500	499	498	500	500	502	501	502	74
Rhode Island	498	488	504	499	505	500	501	499	504	503	502	504	503	502	72
South Carolina	475	467	479	475	484	482	486	488	488	493	493	496	491	495	62
South Dakota	580	570	585	588	587	588	577	582	576	586	588	588	594	597	5
Tennessee	558	544	559	553	563	553	562	553	562	555	568	560	567	557	16
Texas	490	489	494	499	493	500	493	499	491	500	500	491	493	499	52
Utah	566	555	570	568	570	569	575	570	563	559	566	559	565	556	7
Vermont	507	493	514	506	513	508	511	506	512	510	515	512	516	512	66
Virginia	501	496	508	499	509	500	510	501	510	506	514	510	515	509	71
Washington	513	511	525	526	526	528	527	527	525	529	530	532	528	531	52
West Virginia	520	514	527	512	526	511	527	512	525	515	522	510	524	514	19
Wisconsin	552	559	584	595	584	597	584	596	583	599	585	594	587	596	7
Wyoming	534	538	546	551	545	545	547	545	531	537	548	549	551	546	12
NATIONAL AVG.	**500**	**501**	**505**	**511**	**505**	**514**	**506**	**514**	**504**	**516**	**507**	**519**	**508**	**518**	**48**

NOTE: In 1995, the College Board recentered the scoring scale for the SAT by reestablishing the original mean score of 500 on the 200-800 scale. The College Board states that comparing states or ranking them on the basis of SAT scores alone is invalid, and the College Board discourages doing so. (1) Based on number of high school graduates in 2004, as projected by the Western Interstate Commission for Higher Education, and number of students in the class of 2004 who took the SAT.

Average SAT Scores by Parental Education, 2004

Source: The College Board

(Deviation in points from mean score shown by highest level of educational attainment of test taker's parent. Mean 2004 verbal score was 508. Mean 2004 math score was 518.)

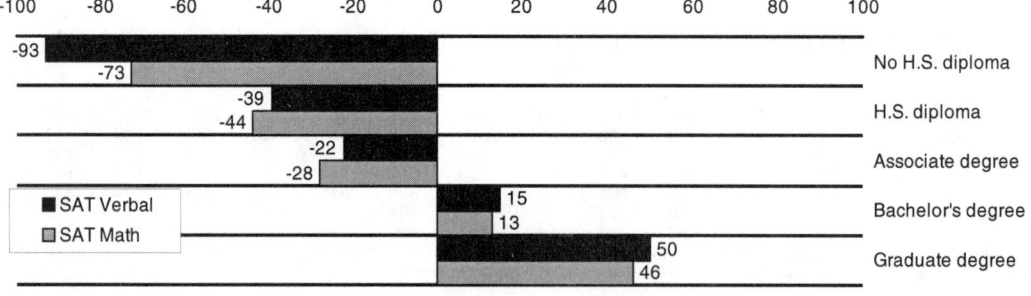

Top 50 Public Libraries in the U.S. and Canada, 2004

Source: Public Library Data Service, Statistical Report 2004, Public Library Association

Ranked at end of the 2003 fical year by population served.

Population served	Library name and location	No. of branches	No. of holdings	Circulation	Annual acquisition expenditures
3,864,400	Los Angeles Public Library (CA)	67	5,554,904	14,845,774	$9,629,561
3,550,000	Los Angeles Public Library, County of (CA)	84	9,185,321	15,912,865	5,944,738
3,313,573	New York Public Library (NY)	84	6,777,587	14,399,959	9,635,546
2,896,016	Chicago Public Library (IL)	78	10,745,608	7,011,409	11,500,000
2,481,494	Toronto Public Library (ON)	98	7,597,581	28,667,470	11,221,060
2,465,326	Brooklyn Public Library (NY)	59	5,845,212	10,278,195	7,587,094
2,229,379	Queens Borough Public Library (NY)	62	9,691,126	16,910,527	9,540,254
2,000,759	Houston Public Library (TX)	37	4,339,128	5,825,318	6,303,710
1,939,755	Miami-Dade Public Library System (FL)	36	3,998,192	5,146,278	6,086,772
1,698,425	Broward County Libraries Division (FL)	37	2,825,077	8,575,661	6,628,282
1,530,900	San Antonio Public Library (TX)	19	1,852,221	5,066,201	3,384,234
1,517,550	Philadelphia, The Free Library of (PA)	54	6,388,077	7,056,608	8,410,015
1,456,600	Orange County Public Library (CA)	32	2,794,942	6,612,447	3,186,912
1,397,500	Phoenix Public Library (AZ)	12	1,999,752	11,726,840	4,774,452,
1,336,449	Carnegie Library of Pittsburgh (PA)	19	2,315,602	2,981,163	2,904,795
1,275,000	San Diego Public Library (CA)	34	3,169,565	7,516,898	4,296,108
1,255,364	Las Vegas-Clark County Library District (NV)	24	2,172,259	8,827,511	8,009,541
1,245,800	Sacramento Public Library (CA)	25	2,017,341	5,303,277	4,345,097
1,240,663	Hawaii State Public Library System (HI)	50	3,281,117	6,722,783	2,369,146
1,200,817	Harris County Public Library (TX)	25	2,233,464	8,755,334	2,946,105
1,188,580	Dallas Public Library (TX)	22	5,916,549	5,703,875	3,489,621
1,139,915	King County Library System (WA)	42	4,213,810	15,925,593	8,732,313
1,136,900	San Bernadino County Library (CA)	29	1,227,984	2,902,322	1,137,370
1,079,587	Tampa-Hillsborough County Public Library (FL)	21	2,068,219	5,234,321	4,109,487
1,048,319	Providence Public Library (RI)	9	794,823	819,982	794,233
1,029,800	Fairfax County Public Library (VA)	21	2,712,212	11,566,681	6,134,933
951,270	Detroit Public Library (MI)	24	7,265,306	1,026,971	1,982,400
950,265	Buffalo & Erie County Public Library (NY)	51	3,539,038	8,875,762	5,090,601
924,950	San Jose Public Library (CA)	17	1,923,031	13,491,212	3,925,092
922,417	San Diego County Library (CA)	32	1,494,666	4,843,981	3,012,561
922,315	Calgary Public Library (AB)	15	2,000,042	12,289,356	4,300,590
921,359	Orange County Library System (FL)	13	2,282,093	5,952,236	5,337,391
905,678	Memphis/Shelby County Pub. Lib. & Info Ctr. (TN)	22	1,944,830	3,479,606	1,738,818
903,000	Montgomery County Dept. of Public Libraries (MD)	22	2,959,184	11,634,801	5,039,660
893,500	Contra Costa County Library (CA)	22	1,218,781	4,253,135	2,099,848
890,356	Tucson-Pima Public Library (AZ)	21	1,338,000	6,063,771	2,954,304
873,490	Saint Louis County Library District (MO)	19	2,781,301	9,088,803	4,713,702
845,807	Atlanta-Fulton Public Library (GA)	33	2,000,000	3,060,452	3,491,239
835,362	Cincinnati and Hamilton County, The P.L. of (OH)	41	9,885,359	14,861,011	9,131,725
832,693	Indianapolis-Marion County Public Library (IN)	22	2,304,196	13,476,589	5,072,128
816,791	Prince George's County Memorial Lib. Sys. (MD)	18	2,170,308	3,964,314	4,236,800
807,685	Columbus Metropolitan Library (OH)	20	2,955,569	15,350,134	7,925,749
793,898	Jacksonville Public Library (FL)	14	2,138,547	5,212,422	3,401,330
793,600	San Francisco Public Library (CA)	26	2,240,873	6,793,335	5,462,907
790,000	Ottawa Public Library (ON)	32	2,381,656	8,870,826	3,418,144
789,370	Palm Beach County Library System (FL)	14	1,232,518	5,757,262	4,621,034
773,299	Charlotte & Mecklenburg County, Pub. Lib. of (NC)	22	1,377,720	6,824,777	3,392,655
764,600	Baltimore County Public Library (MD)	16	1,702,356	9,603,033	5,924,952
748,180	Hennepin County Library (MN)	26	1,820,000	11,622,800	4,494,909
735,343	Rochester Public Library (NY)	10	1,262,242	1,685,450	1,452,766

Number of Public Libraries and Operating Income, by State, 2002

Source: Public Libraries Survey, National Center for Education Statistics, U.S. Dept. of Education

(data for fiscal year 2002; operating income in thousands)

STATE	No. of libraries[1]	Operating income[2]	STATE	No. of libraries[1]	Operating income[2]	STATE	No. of libraries[1]	Operating income[2]
Alabama	282	$71,059	Kentucky	189	$87,316	Ohio	717	$645,383
Alaska	102	24,139	Louisiana	329	122,029	Oklahoma	205	66,313
Arizona	176	122,036	Maine	281	29,586	Oregon	209	120,079
Arkansas	210	40,042	Maryland	176	192,316	Pennsylvania	628	292,397
California	1,074	959,701	Massachusetts	489	238,952	Rhode Island	72	39,904
Colorado	243	181,292	Michigan	659	335,297	South Carolina	184	79,675
Connecticut	242	151,858	Minnesota	359	161,240	South Dakota	144	17,194
Delaware	33	17,553	Mississippi	240	37,985	Tennessee	287	81,765
District of Columbia	27	28,413	Missouri	365	159,964	Texas	848	337,926
Florida	478	422,470	Montana	108	18,831	Utah	108	62,314
Georgia	366	155,492	Nebraska	291	39,232	Vermont	192	13,702
Hawaii	50	25,414	Nevada	86	62,644	Virginia	341	203,157
Idaho	142	27,048	New Hampshire	237	37,743	Washington	325	241,379
Illinois	788	581,222	New Jersey	457	335,803	West Virginia	176	27,259
Indiana	432	258,505	New Mexico	113	29,070	Wisconsin	455	176,262
Iowa	562	77,008	New York	1,088	884,665	Wyoming	74	17,279
Kansas	376	83,344	North Carolina	381	155,205	**U.S. TOTAL**	**16,486**	**8,585,738**
			North Dakota	90	9,173			

(1) Includes central libraries and branches. (2) Some totals may be underestimated because of nonresponse.

Four-Year Colleges and Universities

General Information for the 2003-2004 Academic Year

Source: © Thomson Peterson's, a part of The Thomson Corporation. All Rights Reserved.

These listings **include only accredited degree-granting institutions** in the U.S. and the U.S. territories **with a total enrollment of 1,000 or more**. Only **four-year** colleges and universities (which award a bachelor's degree as their highest undergraduate degree) are included. Data reported **only for institutions that provided updated information** on Peterson's Annual Survey of Undergraduate Institutions for the 2003-2004 academic year.

All institutions are coeducational except those where the ZIP code is followed directly by a number in parentheses. (1) = men only, (2) = primarily men, (3) = women only, (4) = primarily women.

The **Tuition & Fees** column shows the annual tuition and required fees for full-time students, or, where indicated, the tuition and standard fees per unit for part-time students. Where tuition varies according to residence, the figure is given for the most local resident and is coded: (A) = area residents, (S) = state residents; all other figures apply to all students regardless of residence. Where annual expenses are expressed as a lump sum (including full-time tuition, mandatory fees, and room and board), the figure is coded: (C) = comprehensive fee. **Rm. & Board** is the average cost for one academic year. * indicates fee only.

Control: 1 = independent (nonprofit), 2 = independent-religious, 3 = proprietary (profit-making), 4 = federal, 5 = state, 6 = commonwealth (Puerto Rico), 7 = territory (U.S. territories), 8 = county, 9 = district, 10 = city, 11 = state and local, 12 = state-related, 13 = private (unspecified). **Degree** means the highest degree offered (B = bachelor's, M = master's, F = first professional, D = doctorate).

Enrollment is the total number of matriculated undergraduate and (if applicable) graduate students.

Faculty is the total number of faculty members teaching undergraduate courses and (if available) graduate courses.

NA or a **dash** indicates category is inapplicable or data not available. **NR** indicates data not reported.

Name, address	Year Founded	Tuition & Fees	Rm. & Board	Control, Degree	Enrollment	Faculty
Abilene Christian Univ, Abilene, TX 79699-9100	1906	$13,290	$5,080	2-D	4,648	330
Acad of Art Univ, San Francisco, CA 94105-3410	1929	$13,200	$12,000	3-M	6,702	725
Adams State Coll, Alamosa, CO 81102	1921	$2,492 (S)	$5,730	5-M	8,370	198
Adelphi Univ, Garden City, NY 11530	1896	$17,800	$8,500	1-D	7,355	698
Adrian Coll, Adrian, MI 49221-2575	1859	$16,570	$5,760	2-B	1,028	107
Alabama Agr & Mech Univ, Huntsville, AL 35811	1875	$3,872 (S)	$4,500	5-D	6,588	374
Alabama State Univ, Montgomery, AL 36101-0271	1867	$3,600 (S)	$3,700	5-M	6,024	408
Albany State Univ, Albany, GA 31705-2717	1903	$2,774 (S)	$3,760	5-M	3,681	220
Albertus Magnus Coll, New Haven, CT 06511-1189	1925	$16,808	$7,330	2-M	2,216	NA
Albion Coll, Albion, MI 49224-1831	1835	$21,948	$6,262	2-B	1,732	157
Albright Coll, Reading, PA 19612-5234	1856	$24,580	$7,510	2-M	2,127	150
Alcorn State Univ, Alcorn State, MS 39096-7500	1871	$4,440 (S)	$3,821	5-M	3,309	224
Alfred Univ, Alfred, NY 14802-1205	1836	$19,278	$9,012	1-D	2,367	214
Allegheny Coll, Meadville, PA 16335	1815	$24,400	$5,880	1-B	1,849	147
Alliant Intl Univ, San Diego, CA 92131-1799	1952	$19,360	$7,430	1-D	3,508	589
Alma Coll, Alma, MI 48801-1599	1886	$18,854	$6,712	2-B	1,291	135
Alvernia Coll, Reading, PA 19607-1799	1958	$16,362	$6,950	2-M	2,380	133
Alverno Coll, Milwaukee, WI 53234-3922 (3)	1887	$13,638	$5,260	2-M	2,160	205
Amberton Univ, Garland, TX 75041-5595	1971	$6,000	NA	2-M	1,648	39
Amer Coll of Comp & Info Sci, Birmingham, AL 35205 (2)	1988	NA	NA	3-M	11,291	43
Amer InterContinental Univ, Los Angeles, CA 90066	1982	$15,210	NA	3-M	1,405	133
Amer InterContinental Univ, Atlanta, GA 30328	1970	$22,400	NA	3-M	1,248	119
Amer InterContinental Univ, Atlanta, GA 30326-1016	1977	$14,805	$4,500	3-M	1,277	115
Amer Intl Coll, Springfield, MA 01109-3189	1885	$17,800	$8,500	1-D	1,595	158
Amer Publ Univ System, Charles Town, WV 25414	1991	$9,000	NA	3-M	6,826	342
Amer Univ, Washington, DC 20016-8001	1893	$26,307	$10,260	2-D	10,977	965
Amer Univ of Puerto Rico, BayamÚn, PR 00960-2037	1963	$3,800	NA	1-B	4,060	221
Amherst Coll, Amherst, MA 01002-5000	1821	$29,730	$7,740	1-B	1,623	219
Anderson Coll, Anderson, SC 29621-4035	1911	$14,225	$5,765	2-B	1,664	122
Anderson Univ, Anderson, IN 46012-3495	1917	$17,050	$5,560	2-D	2,506	233
Andrews Univ, Berrien Springs, MI 49104	1874	$15,446	$5,120	2-D	2,995	234
Angelo State Univ, San Angelo, TX 76909	1928	$2,930 (S)	$4,646	5-M	6,043	314
Anna Maria Coll, Paxton, MA 01612	1946	$19,145	$6,995	2-M	1,147	163
Appalachian State Univ, Boone, NC 28608	1899	$2,927 (S)	$4,435	5-D	14,343	934
Aquinas Coll, Grand Rapids, MI 49506-1799	1886	$16,400	$5,494	2-M	2,338	218
Arcadia Univ, Glenside, PA 19038-3295	1853	$22,720	$8,960	2-D	3,417	332
Argosy Univ/Chicago Northwest, Rolling Meadows, IL 60008	1979	NA	NA	3-D	NA	NA
Argosy Univ/Twin Cities, Eagan, MN 55121	1961	$11,232	NA	3-D	1,334	140
Arizona State Univ, Tempe, AZ 85287	1885	$3,595 (S)	$6,453	5-D	48,901	1,844
Arizona State Univ East, Mesa, AZ 85212	1995	$3,544 (S)	$4,770	5-M	3,551	99
Arizona State Univ West, Phoenix, AZ 85069-7100	1984	$3,595 (S)	$4,101	5-M	7,105	335
Arkansas State Univ, State University, AR 72467	1909	$4,810 (S)	$3,640	5-D	10,573	614
Arkansas Tech Univ, Russellville, AR 72801	1909	$3,820 (S)	$3,725	5-M	6,249	351
Armstrong Atlantic State Univ, Savannah, GA 31419-1997	1935	$2,602 (S)	$4,500	5-M	6,653	408
Art Ctr Coll of Design, Pasadena, CA 91103-1999	1930	$23,450	NA	1-M	1,533	407
The Art Inst of Atlanta, Atlanta, GA 30328	1949	$16,560	$6,645	3-B	2,699	169
The Art Inst of California-Orange Cty, Santa Ana, CA 92704-9888	2000	$17,949	$9,020	3-B	1,415	88
The Art Inst of California-San Diego, San Diego, CA 92121	1981	$18,067	$8,580	3-B	1,329	91
The Art Inst of Colorado, Denver, CO 80203	1952	$18,752	$5,760	3-B	2,226	135
The Art Inst of Fort Lauderdale, Fort Lauderdale, FL 33316-3000	1968	$16,425	$4,785	3-B	3,500	110
The Art Inst of Phoenix, Phoenix, AZ 85021-2859	1995	$16,320	NA	3-B	1,216	80
The Art Inst of Portland, Portland, OR 97209	1963	$15,750	$7,695	3-B	1,327	118
Asbury Coll, Wilmore, KY 40390-1198	1890	$17,808	$4,498	2-M	1,258	143
Ashland Univ, Ashland, OH 44805-3702	1878	$18,858	$6,964	2-D	6,835	553
Assumption Coll, Worcester, MA 01609-1296	1904	$21,165	$5,090	2-M	2,412	180
Athens State Univ, Athens, AL 35611-1902	1822	$3,570 (S)	$900	5-B	2,537	194
Auburn Univ, Auburn University, AL 36849	1856	$4,426 (S)	$5,970	5-D	23,152	1,314
Auburn Univ Montgomery, Montgomery, AL 36124-4023	1967	$4,130 (S)	$4,890	5-D	5,298	311
Augsburg Coll, Minneapolis, MN 55454-1351	1869	$19,398	$5,900	2-M	3,172	289
Augustana Coll, Rock Island, IL 61201-2296	1860	$20,829	$5,781	2-B	2,309	223
Augustana Coll, Sioux Falls, SD 57197	1860	$16,972	$5,026	2-M	1,848	166
Augusta State Univ, Augusta, GA 30904-2200	1925	$2,592 (S)	NA	5-M	6,116	312
Aurora Univ, Aurora, IL 60506-4892	1893	$14,750	$6,614	1-D	3,450	216
Austin Coll, Sherman, TX 75090-4400	1849	$19,165	$7,089	2-M	1,332	122
Austin Peay State Univ, Clarksville, TN 37044-0001	1927	$4,004 (S)	$4,096	5-M	7,623	453
Averett Univ, Danville, VA 24541-3692	1859	$17,600	$6,020	2-M	2,849	252

Name, address	Year Founded	Tuition & Fees	Rm. & Board	Control, Degree	Enroll-ment	Faculty
Avila Univ, Kansas City, MO 64145-1698	1916	$15,870	$5,400	2-M	1,683	202
Azusa Pacific Univ, Azusa, CA 91702-7000	1899	$19,024	$5,696	2-D	8,191	920
Babson Coll, Babson Park, MA 02457-0310	1919	$27,248	$9,978	1-M	3,342	223
Baker Coll of Auburn Hills, Auburn Hills, MI 48326-1586	1911	$5,940	NA	1-B	3,177	115
Baker Coll of Cadillac, Cadillac, MI 49601	1986	$5,940	NA	1-B	1,386	73
Baker Coll of Clinton Township, Clinton Township, MI 48035-4701	1990	$5,940	NA	1-B	4,510	147
Baker Coll of Flint, Flint, MI 48507-5508	1911	$5,940	$2,600	1-B	5,639	173
Baker Coll of Jackson, Jackson, MI 49202	1994	$5,940	NA	1-B	1,593	90
Baker Coll of Muskegon, Muskegon, MI 49442-3497	1888	$5,940	$2,400	1-B	4,076	145
Baker Coll of Owosso, Owosso, MI 48867-4400	1984	$5,940	$2,175	1-B	2,538	103
Baker Coll of Port Huron, Port Huron, MI 48060-2597	1990	$5,940	NA	1-B	1,477	95
Baker Univ, Baldwin City, KS 66006-0065	1858	$14,560	$5,300	2-M	1,015	101
Baldwin-Wallace Coll, Berea, OH 44017-2088	1845	$18,478	$5,402	2-M	4,692	389
Ball State Univ, Muncie, IN 47306-1099	1918	$5,930 (S)	$5,880	5-D	20,533	1,162
Bard Coll, Annandale-on-Hudson, NY 12504	1860	$29,038	$8,544	1-D	1,605	224
Barnard Coll, New York, NY 10027-6598 (3)	1889	$26,528	$10,462	1-B	2,281	293
Barry Univ, Miami Shores, FL 33161-6695	1940	$21,350	$7,400	2-D	9,042	871
Barton Coll, Wilson, NC 27893-7000	1902	$14,278	$5,036	2-B	1,188	104
Bastyr Univ, Kenmore, WA 98028-4966	1978	$12,518	$4,420	1-F	1,005	130
Bates Coll, Lewiston, ME 04240-6028	1855	$37,500 (C)	NA	1-B	1,746	183
BayamÚn Central Univ, BayamÚn, PR 00960-1725	1970	$3,740	NA	2-M	3,334	218
Baylor Univ, Waco, TX 76798	1845	$18,430	$5,434	2-D	13,937	921
Bay Path Coll, Longmeadow, MA 01106-2292 (3)	1897	$16,890	$8,020	1-M	1,314	127
Becker Coll, Worcester, MA 01609	1784	$17,670	$8,000	1-B	1,467	104
Belhaven Coll, Jackson, MS 39202-1789	1883	$13,440	$5,240	2-M	2,353	211
Bellarmine Univ, Louisville, KY 40205-0671	1950	$19,950	$5,780	2-D	3,134	251
Bellevue Univ, Bellevue, NE 68005-3098	1965	$4,740	NA	1-M	5,110	264
Belmont Univ, Nashville, TN 37212-3757	1951	$15,954	$6,032	2-D	3,629	421
Beloit Coll, Beloit, WI 53511-5596	1846	$24,386	$5,478	1-B	1,332	126
Bemidji State Univ, Bemidji, MN 56601-2699	1919	$5,048 (S)	$4,597	5-M	5,024	401
Benedict Coll, Columbia, SC 29204	1870	$11,586	$5,434	2-B	3,005	168
Benedictine Coll, Atchison, KS 66002-1499	1859	$14,613	$5,920	2-M	1,330	96
Benedictine Univ, Lisle, IL 60532-0900	1887	$17,470	$6,370	2-D	2,968	313
Bentley Coll, Waltham, MA 02452-4705	1917	$24,324	$9,580	1-M	5,673	456
Berea Coll, Berea, KY 40404	1855	$507*	$4,523	1-B	1,560	161
Berklee Coll of Mus, Boston, MA 02215-3693	1945	$23,530	$10,900	1-B	3,799	473
Bernard M. Baruch Coll of the City Univ of New York, New York, NY 10010-5585	1919	$4,300 (S)	NA	11-D	15,126	995
Berry Coll, Mount Berry, GA 30149-0159	1902	$15,220	$6,190	2-M	2,045	175
Bethel Coll, Mishawaka, IN 46545-5591	1947	$14,530	$4,680	2-M	1,847	149
Bethel Coll, McKenzie, TN 38201	1842	$9,630	$5,080	2-F	1,283	45
Bethel Univ, St. Paul, MN 55112-6999	1871	$19,990	$6,570	2-M	3,303	255
Bethune-Cookman Coll, Daytona Beach, FL 32114-3099	1904	$10,106	$6,374	2-B	2,794	192
Biola Univ, La Mirada, CA 90639-0001	1908	$19,564	$5,967	2-D	4,666	404
Birmingham-Southern Coll, Birmingham, AL 35254	1856	$18,930	$6,104	2-M	1,388	121
Black Hills State Univ, Spearfish, SD 57799	1883	$5,504 (S)	$3,196	5-M	3,873	194
Bloomfield Coll, Bloomfield, NJ 07003-9981	1868	$13,900	$6,750	2-B	2,083	228
Bloomsburg Univ of Pennsylvania, Bloomsburg, PA 17815-1301	1839	$5,844 (S)	$5,000	5-M	8,282	384
Bluefield State Coll, Bluefield, WV 24701-2198	1895	$2,806 (S)	NA	5-B	3,511	296
Bluffton Coll, Bluffton, OH 45817-1196	1899	$18,350	$6,270	2-M	1,121	117
Boise State Univ, Boise, ID 83725-0399	1932	$3,251 (S)	$4,426	5-D	18,332	1,015
Boricua Coll, New York, NY 10032-1560	1974	$7,350	NA	1-M	1,520	116
Boston Coll, Chestnut Hill, MA 02467-3800	1863	$27,542	$9,300	2-D	13,611	1,207
Boston Univ, Boston, MA 02215	1839	$28,906	$9,288	1-D	29,048	3,492
Bowdoin Coll, Brunswick, ME 04011	1794	$30,120	$7,670	1-B	1,647	179
Bowie State Univ, Bowie, MD 20715-9465	1865	$4,722 (S)	$6,020	5-D	5,454	306
Bowling Green State Univ, Bowling Green, OH 43403	1910	$7,144 (S)	$5,892	5-D	18,534	1,026
Bradley Univ, Peoria, IL 61625-0002	1897	$16,930	$5,980	1-M	6,137	528
Brandeis Univ, Waltham, MA 02454-9110	1948	$29,875	$8,323	1-D	4,985	441
Brewton-Parker Coll, Mt. Vernon, GA 30445-0197	1904	$11,070	$4,450	2-B	1,109	155
Briarcliffe Coll, Bethpage, NY 11714	1966	$14,120	NA	3-B	2,911	203
Briar Cliff Univ, Sioux City, IA 51104-0100	1930	$16,350	$5,310	2-M	1,063	53
Bridgewater Coll, Bridgewater, VA 22812-1599	1880	$17,990	$8,480	2-B	1,403	121
Bridgewater State Coll, Bridgewater, MA 02325-0001	1840	$4,560 (S)	$5,922	5-M	9,626	494
Brigham Young Univ-Hawaii, Laie, HI 96762-1294	1955	$2,580	$4,660	2-B	2,703	208
Brigham Young Univ, Provo, UT 84602-1001	1875	$3,150	$5,354	2-D	33,008	1,741
Brooklyn Coll of the City Univ of New York, Brooklyn, NY 11210-2889	1930	$4,353 (S)	NA	11-M	15,513	953
Brooks Inst of Photog, Santa Barbara, CA 93108-2399	1945	$20,250	NA	3-M	1,507	39
Brown Univ, Providence, RI 02912	1764	$29,846	$8,096	1-D	7,882	789
Bryant Coll, Smithfield, RI 02917-1284	1863	$23,580	$8,974	1-M	3,459	228
Bryn Mawr Coll, Bryn Mawr, PA 19010-2899 (3)	1885	$27,520	$9,370	1-D	1,781	198
Bucknell Univ, Lewisburg, PA 17837	1846	$28,960	$6,302	1-M	3,678	310
Buena Vista Univ, Storm Lake, IA 50588	1891	$19,862	$5,544	2-M	1,364	114
Buffalo State Coll, State Univ of New York, Buffalo, NY 14222-1095	1867	$5,059 (S)	$5,866	5-M	11,157	698
Butler Univ, Indianapolis, IN 46208-3485	1855	$21,210	$7,040	1-F	4,424	425
Cabrini Coll, Radnor, PA 19087-3698	1957	$20,420	$8,550	2-M	2,203	222
Caldwell Coll, Caldwell, NJ 07006-6195	1939	$17,060	$7,000	2-M	2,219	184
California Baptist Univ, Riverside, CA 92504-3206	1950	$15,940	$6,310	2-M	2,359	162
California Coll for Health Sci, National City, CA 91950-6605	1978	$13,975	NA	3-M	5,458	19
California Coll of the Arts, San Francisco, CA 94107	1907	$23,250	$8,030	1-M	1,492	337
California Inst of Tech, Pasadena, CA 91125-0001	1891	$25,551	$8,013	1-D	2,172	324
California Inst of the Arts, Valencia, CA 91355-2340	1961	$24,685	$7,120	1-M	1,222	270
California Lutheran Univ, Thousand Oaks, CA 91360-2787	1959	$20,400	$7,200	2-D	2,920	249
California Polytechnic State Univ, San Luis Obispo, San Luis Obispo, CA 93407	1901	$3,459 (S)	$7,479	5-M	18,303	1,268
California State Polytechnic Univ, Pomona, Pomona, CA 91768-2557	1938	$2,046 (A)	$6,747	5-M	19,804	1,224
California State Univ, Bakersfield, Bakersfield, CA 93311-1099	1970	$2,427 (S)	$4,900	5-M	7,924	515
California State Univ, Chico, Chico, CA 95929-0722	1887	$2,796 (S)	$7,245	5-M	15,516	883
California State Univ, Dominguez Hills, Carson, CA 90747-0001	1960	$2,478 (S)	$5,022	5-M	13,248	762
California State Univ, Fresno, Fresno, CA 93740-8027	1911	$2,414 (S)	$7,073	5-D	22,348	1,234
California State Univ, Fullerton, Fullerton, CA 92834-9480	1957	$2,516 (S)	$4,127	5-M	32,592	1,940
California State Univ, Hayward, Hayward, CA 94542-3000	1957	$2,418 (S)	$3,705	5-M	13,455	741
California State Univ, Long Beach, Long Beach, CA 90840	1949	$2,362 (S)	$5,800	5-M	34,715	2,080

Name, address	Year Founded	Tuition & Fees	Rm. & Board	Control, Degree	Enroll- ment	Faculty
California State Univ, Los Angeles, Los Angeles, CA 90032-8530........	1947	$2,440 (S)	$3,338	5-D	20,637	1,062
California State Univ, Monterey Bay, Seaside, CA 93955-8001..........	1994	$2,474 (S)	$6,190	5-M	3,020	280
California State Univ, Northridge, Northridge, CA 91330	1958	$2,444 (S)	$6,400	5-M	31,448	1,746
California State Univ, Sacramento, Sacramento, CA 95819-6048........	1947	$2,513 (S)	$6,523	5-D	28,375	1,587
California State Univ, San Bernardino, San Bernardino, CA 92407-2397 ..	1965	$1,932 (S)	$5,383	5-M	16,927	981
California State Univ, San Marcos, San Marcos, CA 92096-0001	1990	$2,414 (S)	$7,470	5-M	7,723	408
California State Univ, Stanislaus, Turlock, CA 95382.................	1957	$2,503 (S)	$7,242	5-M	8,072	495
California Univ of Pennsylvania, California, PA 15419-1394............	1852	$6,008 (S)	$5,378	5-M	6,428	357
Calumet Coll of St Joseph, Whiting, IN 46394-2195..................	1951	$9,000	NA	2-M	1,332	123
Calvin Coll, Grand Rapids, MI 49546-4388.........................	1876	$16,775	$5,840	2-M	4,323	382
Cambridge Coll, Cambridge, MA 02138-5304	1971	$9,150	NA	1-M	2,700	150
Cameron Univ, Lawton, OK 73505-6377	1908	$2,943 (S)	$2,854	5-M	5,632	267
Campbellsville Univ, Campbellsville, KY 42718-2799.................	1906	$12,824	$4,976	2-M	2,006	183
Campbell Univ, Buies Creek, NC 27506...........................	1887	$13,512	$4,756	2-D	3,975	316
Canisius Coll, Buffalo, NY 14208-1098............................	1870	$20,193	$7,970	2-M	5,095	468
Capella Univ, Minneapolis, MN 55402	1993	$12,000	NA	3-D	8,406	372
Capital Univ, Columbus, OH 43209-2394..........................	1830	$20,500	$6,050	2-F	3,959	445
Cardinal Stritch Univ, Milwaukee, WI 53217-3985	1937	$14,540	$5,160	2-D	6,785	880
Caribbean Univ, Bayamón, PR 00960-0493........................	1969	NA	NA	1-M	3,352	158
Carleton Coll, Northfield, MN 55057-4001	1866	$28,527	$5,868	1-B	1,943	220
Carlow Coll, Pittsburgh, PA 15213-3165 (4)........................	1929	$15,264	$6,110	2-M	2,200	229
Carnegie Mellon Univ, Pittsburgh, PA 15213-3891..................	1900	$29,410	$8,155	1-D	9,756	956
Carroll Coll, Helena, MT 59625-0002	1909	$14,666	$5,810	2-B	1,411	126
Carroll Coll, Waukesha, WI 53186-5593...........................	1846	$18,170	$5,600	2-M	2,953	243
Carson-Newman Coll, Jefferson City, TN 37760	1851	$14,420	$4,930	2-M	2,115	199
Carthage Coll, Kenosha, WI 53140-1994	1847	$21,250	$6,250	2-M	2,632	170
Case Western Reserve Univ, Cleveland, OH 44106	1826	$24,342	$7,660	1-D	9,186	600
Castleton State Coll, Castleton, VT 05735	1787	$6,146 (S)	$6,454	5-M	1,879	182
Catawba Coll, Salisbury, NC 28144-2488..........................	1851	$16,400	$5,600	2-M	1,471	126
The Catholic Univ of America, Washington, DC 20064	1887	$24,750	$9,498	2-D	5,740	676
Cedar Crest Coll, Allentown, PA 18104-6196 (3)	1867	$21,900	$7,595	2-M	1,777	82
Cedarville Univ, Cedarville, OH 45314-0601	1887	$14,944	$5,010	2-M	2,997	271
Centenary Coll, Hackettstown, NJ 07840-2100	1867	$17,700	$7,150	2-M	2,182	121
Central Coll, Pella, IA 50219-1999	1853	$17,753	$6,145	2-B	1,698	153
Central Connecticut State Univ, New Britain, CT 06050-4010	1849	$5,384 (S)	$6,706	5-D	12,131	856
Central Michigan Univ, Mount Pleasant, MI 48859	1892	$5,218 (S)	$5,924	5-D	27,758	1,118
Central Missouri State Univ, Warrensburg, MO 64093................	1871	$5,340 (S)	$4,796	5-M	10,351	551
Central State Univ, Wilberforce, OH 45384	1887	$4,287 (S)	$6,069	5-M	1,621	143
Central Washington Univ, Ellensburg, WA 98926...................	1891	$4,023 (S)	$5,745	5-M	9,903	494
Centre Coll, Danville, KY 40422-1394	1819	$20,400	$6,900	2-B	1,062	100
Chadron State Coll, Chadron, NE 69337	1911	$3,241 (S)	$3,862	5-M	2,711	118
Chaminade Univ of Honolulu, Honolulu, HI 96816-1578	1955	$13,500	$7,930	2-M	1,742	182
Champlain Coll, Burlington, VT 05402-0670........................	1878	$13,075	$8,955	1-M	2,584	215
Chapman Univ, Orange, CA 92866	1861	$26,150	$9,082	2-F	5,138	518
Charleston Southern Univ, Charleston, SC 29423-8087	1964	$14,456	$5,544	2-M	2,990	176
Charter Oak State Coll, New Britain, CT 06053-2142.................	1973	$890 (S)	NA	5-B	1,578	71
Chatham Coll, Pittsburgh, PA 15232-2826 (3)	1869	$20,552	$6,714	1-D	1,256	75
Chestnut Hill Coll, Philadelphia, PA 19118-2693 (4).................	1924	$20,345	$7,500	2-D	1,555	241
Cheyney Univ of Pennsylvania, Cheyney, PA 19319-0200	1837	$5,353 (S)	$5,383	5-M	1,536	111
Chicago State Univ, Chicago, IL 60628	1867	$6,143 (S)	$6,032	5-M	7,040	364
Christian Brothers Univ, Memphis, TN 38104-5581	1871	$17,190	$5,100	2-M	1,929	243
Christopher Newport Univ, Newport News, VA 23606-2998............	1960	$4,600 (S)	$6,700	5-M	4,812	311
The Citadel, The Military Coll of South Carolina, Charleston, SC 29409 (2)............................	1842	$5,897 (S)	$4,778	5-M	3,695	221
City Coll of the City Univ of New York, New York, NY 10031-9198	1847	$4,339 (S)	NA	11-F	12,400	966
City Univ, Bellevue, WA 98005..................................	1973	$8,060	NA	1-M	7,124	1,095
Claflin Univ, Orangeburg, SC 29115.............................	1869	$9,654	$5,184	2-B	1,546	120
Claremont McKenna Coll, Claremont, CA 91711.....................	1946	$27,700	$9,180	1-B	1,050	159
Clarion Univ of Pennsylvania, Clarion, PA 16214....................	1867	$5,998 (S)	$4,560	5-M	6,497	327
Clark Atlanta Univ, Atlanta, GA 30314	1865	$12,862	$6,438	2-D	4,915	291
Clarke Coll, Dubuque, IA 52001-3198	1843	$17,090	$6,075	2-M	1,126	92
Clarkson Univ, Potsdam, NY 13699	1896	$24,140	$9,068	1-D	3,105	199
Clark Univ, Worcester, MA 01610-1477	1887	$26,965	$5,150	1-D	3,084	275
Clayton Coll & State Univ, Morrow, GA 30260-0285	1969	$2,702 (S)	NA	5-B	5,661	364
Clemson Univ, Clemson, SC 29634	1889	$6,934 (S)	$5,038	5-D	17,016	1,107
Cleveland State Univ, Cleveland, OH 44115	1964	$6,072 (S)	$7,805	5-D	16,014	920
Coastal Carolina Univ, Conway, SC 29528-6054	1954	$5,270 (S)	$5,770	5-M	6,780	398
Coe Coll, Cedar Rapids, IA 52402-5092...........................	1851	$21,605	$5,780	2-M	1,317	127
Colby Coll, Waterville, ME 04901-8840	1813	$37,570 (C)	NA	1-B	1,768	202
Colgate Univ, Hamilton, NY 13346-1386	1819	$29,940	$7,155	1-M	2,800	290
Coll for Creative Stds, Detroit, MI 48202-4034	1926	$21,376	$3,500	1-B	1,218	217
Coll for Lifelong Learning, Concord, NH 03301	1972	$4,563 (S)	NA	11-B	1,827	223
Coll Misericordia, Dallas, PA 18612-1098.........................	1924	$17,970	$7,500	2-M	2,360	184
Coll of Aeronautics, Flushing, NY 11369-1037 (2)	1932	$9,650	NA	1-B	1,316	60
Coll of Biblical Stds-Houston, Houston, TX 77036	1979	$4,050	NA	2-B	1,472	46
Coll of Charleston, Charleston, SC 29424-0001....................	1770	$5,770 (S)	$6,117	5-M	11,536	853
Coll of Mount St Joseph, Cincinnati, OH 45233-1670................	1920	$18,440	$5,845	2-M	2,110	193
Coll of Mount St Vincent, Riverdale, NY 10471-1093.................	1911	$19,050	$7,800	1-M	1,626	158
The Coll of New Jersey, Ewing, NJ 08628	1855	$8,206 (S)	$7,744	5-M	6,912	664
The Coll of New Rochelle, New Rochelle, NY 10805-2308 (4)..........	1904	$19,350	$7,400	1-M	2,450	162
Coll of Notre Dame of Maryland, Baltimore, MD 21210-2476 (3)	1873	$20,300	$7,800	2-M	3,030	86
Coll of St Benedict, Saint Joseph, MN 56374-2091 (4)...............	1887	$20,685	$5,987	2-B	2,054	174
Coll of St Catherine-Minneapolis, Minneapolis, MN 55454-1494 (4)	1964	$14,270	$5,808	2	4,807	519
Coll of St Catherine, St. Paul, MN 55105-1789 (3)..................	1905	$19,770	$5,460	2-D	4,807	528
Coll of St Elizabeth, Morristown, NJ 07960-6989 (3)	1899	$17,450	$8,130	2-M	1,848	176
The Coll of St Rose, Albany, NY 12203-1419.......................	1920	$15,638	$7,226	1-M	4,666	425
The Coll of St Scholastica, Duluth, MN 55811-4199.................	1912	$19,302	$5,668	2-M	2,838	209
Coll of Santa Fe, Santa Fe, NM 87505-7634	1947	$19,505	$5,788	1-M	1,761	251
Coll of Staten Island of the City Univ of New York, Staten Island, NY 10314-6600	1955	$4,308 (S)	NA	11-M	12,422	770
Coll of the Holy Cross, Worcester, MA 01610-2395.................	1843	$28,011*	$8,440	2-B	2,773	287
Coll of the Ozarks, Point Lookout, MO 65726......................	1906	$250*	$3,550	2-B	1,348	119
The Coll of William & Mary, Williamsburg, VA 23187-8795	1693	$6,430 (S)	$5,794	5-D	7,749	729

Name, address	Year Founded	Tuition & Fees	Rm. & Board	Control, Degree	Enroll- ment	Faculty
The Coll of Wooster, Wooster, OH 44691-2363	1866	$25,040	$6,260	2-B	1,871	179
Colorado Christian Univ, Lakewood, CO 80226-7499	1914	$15,140	$6,042	2-M	1,583	334
The Colorado Coll, Colorado Springs, CO 80903-3294	1874	$27,635	$6,840	1-M	1,968	211
Colorado Sch of Mines, Golden, CO 80401-1887	1874	$6,433 (S)	$6,100	5-D	3,398	282
Colorado State Univ, Fort Collins, CO 80523-0015	1870	$3,744 (S)	$6,045	5-D	26,870	901
Colorado State Univ-Pueblo, Pueblo, CO 81001-4901	1933	$2,930 (S)	$5,742	5-M	6,299	293
Colorado Tech Univ, Colorado Springs, CO 80907-3896	1965	$9,438	NA	3-D	1,684	137
Colorado Tech Univ Sioux Falls Cmps, Sioux Falls, SD 57108	1965	$9,963	NA	3-M	1,036	61
Columbia Coll, Columbia, MO 65216-0002	1851	$11,589	$4,913	2-M	1,068	88
Columbia Coll, New York, NY 10027	1754	$29,788	$8,802	1-B	4,181	NA
Columbia Coll, Columbia, SC 29203-5998 (3)	1854	$17,280	$5,245	2-M	1,515	146
Columbia Coll Chicago, Chicago, IL 60605-1996	1890	$15,270	$8,874	1-M	9,915	1,662
Columbia Southern Univ, Orange Beach, AL 36561	NR	$3,750	NA	3-M	2,200	45
Columbia Union Coll, Takoma Park, MD 20912-7796	1904	$15,248	$5,295	2-M	1,183	56
Columbia Univ, Sch of Genl Stds, New York, NY 10027-6939	1754	$30,398	$6,240	1-B	1,517	632
Columbia Univ, The Fu Foundation Sch of Engr & Appl Sci, New York, NY 10027	1864	$29,788	$8,802	1-D	2,782	NA
Columbus Coll of Art & Design, Columbus, OH 43215-1758	1879	$18,420	$6,300	1-B	1,634	187
Columbus State Univ, Columbus, GA 31907-5645	1958	$2,676 (S)	$5,270	5-M	6,937	373
Concord Coll, Athens, WV 24712-1000	1872	$3,198 (S)	$4,938	5-M	3,026	189
Concordia Coll, Moorhead, MN 56562	1891	$16,560	$4,540	2-B	2,856	268
Concordia Univ, Irvine, CA 92612-3299	1972	$18,800	$6,670	2-M	1,747	168
Concordia Univ, River Forest, IL 60305-1499	1864	$18,200	$5,400	2-D	1,706	NA
Concordia Univ, Seward, NE 68434-1599	1894	$16,000	$4,480	2-M	1,317	120
Concordia Univ, Portland, OR 97211-6099	1905	$17,490	$5,050	2-M	1,274	103
Concordia Univ at Austin, Austin, TX 78705-2799	1926	$14,410	$6,150	2-M	1,155	85
Concordia Univ, St Paul, St. Paul, MN 55104-5494	1893	$19,928	$6,156	2-M	2,051	382
Concordia Univ Wisconsin, Mequon, WI 53097-2402	1881	$15,575	$5,790	2-D	5,152	191
Connecticut Coll, New London, CT 06320-4196	1911	$37,900 (C)	NA	1-M	1,849	223
Converse Coll, Spartanburg, SC 29302-0006 (3)	1889	$18,915	$5,795	1-M	1,124	87
Coppin State Univ, Baltimore, MD 21216-3698	1900	$4,384 (S)	$5,952	5-M	4,003	202
Cornell Coll, Mount Vernon, IA 52314-1098	1853	$21,790	$6,035	2-B	1,117	101
Cornell Univ, Ithaca, NY 14853-0001	1865	$28,754	$9,580	1-D	19,620	1,796
Cornerstone Univ, Grand Rapids, MI 49525-5897	1941	$14,420	$5,426	2-F	2,353	143
Covenant Coll, Lookout Mountain, GA 30750	1955	$18,230	$5,600	2-M	1,266	61
Creighton Univ, Omaha, NE 68178-0001	1878	$19,922	$6,826	2-D	6,537	860
Crichton Coll, Memphis, TN 38111	1941	$11,615	$3,600	1-B	1,032	118
Crown Coll, St. Bonifacius, MN 55375-9001	1916	$13,168	$5,552	2-M	1,031	69
The Culinary Inst of America, Hyde Park, NY 12538-1499	1946	$17,815	$6,270	1-B	2,404	190
Cumberland Coll, Williamsburg, KY 40769-1372	1889	$11,858	$5,126	2-M	1,727	96
Cumberland Univ, Lebanon, TN 37087-3408	1842	$12,230	$4,480	1-M	1,420	123
Curry Coll, Milton, MA 02186-9984	1879	$22,340	$8,180	1-M	2,599	399
Daemen Coll, Amherst, NY 14226-3592	1947	$15,120	$7,000	1-F	2,205	199
Dakota State Univ, Madison, SD 57042-1799	1881	$4,378 (S)	$3,089	5-M	2,291	98
Dallas Baptist Univ, Dallas, TX 75211-9299	1965	$11,010	$4,290	2-M	4,538	379
Dalton State Coll, Dalton, GA 30720-3797	1963	$1,522 (S)	NA	5-B	4,201	153
Daniel Webster Coll, Nashua, NH 03063-1300	1965	$21,630	$8,170	1-B	1,109	61
Dartmouth Coll, Hanover, NH 03755	1769	$29,256	$8,739	1-D	5,683	590
Davenport Univ, Dearborn, MI 48126-3799	1985	$10,270	$3,400	1-M	2,512	170
Davenport Univ, Warren, MI 48092-5209	1985	$10,270	$3,400	1-M	1,407	86
Davenport Univ, Grand Rapids, MI 49503	1866	$10,270	$3,400	1-M	1,868	104
David N. Myers Univ, Cleveland, OH 44115-1096	1848	$11,160	NA	1-M	1,177	165
Davidson Coll, Davidson, NC 28035	1837	$25,903	$7,371	2-B	1,712	170
Defiance Coll, Defiance, OH 43512-1610	1850	$17,365	$5,250	2-M	1,036	93
Delaware State Univ, Dover, DE 19901-2277	1891	$4,296 (S)	$6,344	5-D	3,178	264
Delaware Valley Coll, Doylestown, PA 18901-2697	1896	$19,304	$7,372	1-M	2,037	176
Delta State Univ, Cleveland, MS 38733-0001	1924	$3,772 (S)	$3,270	5-D	3,785	277
Denison Univ, Granville, OH 43023	1831	$25,760	$7,290	1-B	2,232	191
DePaul Univ, Chicago, IL 60604-2287	1898	$18,790	$8,790	2-D	23,610	1,516
DePauw Univ, Greencastle, IN 46135-0037	1837	$24,450	$7,050	2-B	2,365	249
DeSales Univ, Center Valley, PA 18034-9568	1964	$18,390	$7,080	2-M	2,914	136
DeVry Univ, Phoenix, AZ 85021-2995	1967	$10,155	NA	3-M	2,282	101
Dickinson Coll, Carlisle, PA 17013-2896	1773	$30,300	$7,600	1-B	2,276	202
Dickinson State Univ, Dickinson, ND 58601-4896	1918	$3,139 (S)	$3,350	5-B	2,461	146
Dillard Univ, New Orleans, LA 70122-3097	1869	$10,865	$6,440	2-B	2,312	182
Doane Coll, Crete, NE 68333-2430	1872	$15,970	$4,720	2-M	2,273	127
Dominican Coll, Orangeburg, NY 10962-1210	1952	$16,650	$8,160	1-M	1,428	165
Dominican Univ, River Forest, IL 60305-1099	1901	$19,000	$5,890	2-M	2,900	251
Dominican Univ of California, San Rafael, CA 94901-2298	1890	$22,650	$9,420	2-M	1,742	228
Dordt Coll, Sioux Center, IA 51250-1697	1955	$15,770	$4,400	2-M	1,359	116
Dowling Coll, Oakdale, NY 11769-1999	1955	$15,330	$5,300	1-D	6,247	502
Drake Univ, Des Moines, IA 50311-4516	1881	$19,420	$5,700	1-D	5,164	362
Drew Univ, Madison, NJ 07940-1493	1867	$27,906	$7,644	2-D	2,521	166
Drexel Univ, Philadelphia, PA 19104-2875	1891	$21,305	$9,600	1-D	17,000	1,308
Drury Univ, Springfield, MO 65802-3791	1873	$13,904	$5,128	1-B	1,933	179
Duke Univ, Durham, NC 27708-0586	1838	$29,345	$8,210	2-D	12,398	NA
Duquesne Univ, Pittsburgh, PA 15282-0001	1878	$19,425	$7,482	2-D	9,701	902
D'Youville Coll, Buffalo, NY 14201-1084	1908	$14,160	$6,960	1-D	2,476	196
Earlham Coll, Richmond, IN 47374-4095	1847	$24,560	$5,416	2-F	1,262	111
East Carolina Univ, Greenville, NC 27858-4353	1907	$3,131 (S)	$5,540	5-D	21,756	1,225
East Central Univ, Ada, OK 74820-6899	1909	$3,458 (S)	$2,774	5-M	4,442	265
Eastern Connecticut State Univ, Willimantic, CT 06226-2295	1889	$6,122 (S)	$7,266	5-M	5,095	361
Eastern Illinois Univ, Charleston, IL 61920-3099	1895	$4,982 (S)	$6,210	5-M	11,522	682
Eastern Kentucky Univ, Richmond, KY 40475-3102	1906	$3,298 (S)	$5,450	5-M	15,951	987
Eastern Mennonite Univ, Harrisonburg, VA 22802-2462	1917	$17,350	$5,640	2-F	1,245	154
Eastern Michigan Univ, Ypsilanti, MI 48197	1849	$5,627 (S)	$5,850	5-D	24,129	1,223
Eastern Nazarene Coll, Quincy, MA 02170-2999	1918	$16,608	$5,638	2-M	1,212	48
Eastern New Mexico Univ, Portales, NM 88130	1934	$2,472 (S)	$4,290	5-M	3,706	199
Eastern Oregon Univ, La Grande, OR 97850-2899	1929	$5,517 (S)	$6,100	5-M	3,287	114
Eastern Univ, St. Davids, PA 19087-3696	1952	$17,700	$7,600	2-M	3,253	343
Eastern Washington Univ, Cheney, WA 99004-2431	1882	$3,812 (S)	$5,200	5-D	10,337	505
East Stroudsburg Univ of Pennsylvania, East Stroudsburg, PA 18301-2999	1893	$5,979 (S)	$4,464	5-M	6,162	322

Name, address	Year Founded	Tuition & Fees	Rm. & Board	Control, Degree	Enroll-ment	Faculty
East Tennessee State Univ, Johnson City, TN 37614	1911	$3,839 (S)	$4,658	5-D	11,624	728
East Texas Baptist Univ, Marshall, TX 75670-1498	1912	$10,290	$3,624	2-B	1,354	107
East-West Univ, Chicago, IL 60605-2103	1978	$10,395	NA	1-B	1,113	79
Eckerd Coll, St. Petersburg, FL 33711	1958	$22,774	$5,970	2-B	1,631	147
Edgewood Coll, Madison, WI 53711-1997	1927	$15,100	$5,350	2-M	2,422	235
Edinboro Univ of Pennsylvania, Edinboro, PA 16444	1857	$5,764 (S)	$5,086	5-M	8,045	401
Edward Waters Coll, Jacksonville, FL 32209-6199	1866	$7,567	$5,469	2-B	1,320	49
Elizabeth City State Univ, Elizabeth City, NC 27909-7806	1891	$2,643 (S)	$4,608	5-M	2,308	201
Elizabethtown Coll, Elizabethtown, PA 17022-2298	1899	$22,500	$6,300	2-M	1,988	215
Elmhurst Coll, Elmhurst, IL 60126-3296	1871	$18,600	$6,030	2-M	2,593	278
Elmira Coll, Elmira, NY 14901	1855	$27,030	$8,330	1-B	1,805	97
Elon Univ, Elon, NC 27244-2010	1889	$16,570	$5,670	2-D	4,584	324
Embry-Riddle Aeron Univ, Prescott, AZ 86301-3720 (2)	1978	$22,180	$6,206	1-M	1,669	113
Embry-Riddle Aeron Univ, Daytona Beach, FL 32114-3900 (2)	1926	$22,190	$6,630	1-M	4,926	274
Embry-Riddle Aeron Univ, Extended Cmps, Daytona Beach, FL 32114-3900 (2)	1970	$21,330	$6,370	1-M	10,416	3,499
Emerson Coll, Boston, MA 02116-4624	1880	$22,693	$9,828	1-D	4,385	345
Emmanuel Coll, Boston, MA 02115	1919	$20,500	$9,000	2-M	1,871	109
Emory Univ, Atlanta, GA 30322-1100	1836	$27,952	$8,920	2-D	11,362	2,938
Emporia State Univ, Emporia, KS 66801-5087	1863	$2,776 (S)	$4,222	5-D	6,278	273
Endicott Coll, Beverly, MA 01915-2096	1939	$17,408	$8,858	1-M	2,678	133
Evangel Univ, Springfield, MO 65802-2191	1955	$11,945	$4,360	2-M	1,852	147
The Evergreen State Coll, Olympia, WA 98505	1967	$3,804 (S)	$5,772	5-M	4,380	219
Excelsior Coll, Albany, NY 12203-5159	1970	NA	NA	1-M	26,273	NA
Fairfield Univ, Fairfield, CT 06824-5195	1942	$26,585	$8,920	2-M	5,053	426
Fairleigh Dickinson Univ, Coll at Florham, Madison, NJ 07940-1099	1942	$21,880	$8,250	1-M	3,743	340
Fairleigh Dickinson Univ, Metropolitan Cmps, Teaneck, NJ 07666-1914	1942	$20,334	$8,250	1-D	7,118	604
Fairmont State Univ, Fairmont, WV 26554	1865	$3,130 (S)	$5,080	5-M	6,813	517
Farmingdale State Univ of New York, Farmingdale, NY 11735	1912	$5,211 (S)	$7,680	5-B	5,949	416
Fashion Inst of Tech, New York, NY 10001-5992 (4)	1944	$4,620 (S)	$6,549	11-M	10,765	967
Faulkner Univ, Montgomery, AL 36109-3398	1942	$10,200	$5,000	2-F	2,585	118
Fayetteville State Univ, Fayetteville, NC 28301-4298	1867	$2,354 (S)	$4,120	5-D	5,329	255
Felician Coll, Lodi, NJ 07644-2117	1942	$17,125	$7,500	2-M	1,526	162
Ferris State Univ, Big Rapids, MI 49307	1884	$6,186 (S)	$6,326	5-F	11,821	1,023
Fitchburg State Coll, Fitchburg, MA 01420-2697	1894	$4,200 (S)	$5,506	5-M	4,948	226
Five Towns Coll, Dix Hills, NY 11746-6055	1972	$13,800	$9,000	1-D	1,145	110
Flagler Coll, St. Augustine, FL 32085-1027	1968	$8,000	$4,750	1-B	2,033	155
Florida Agr & Mech Univ, Tallahassee, FL 32307-3200	1887	$2,951 (S)	$5,238	5-D	13,013	592
Florida Atlantic Univ, Boca Raton, FL 33431-0991	1961	$2,943 (S)	$5,600	5-D	25,018	1,304
Florida Gulf Coast Univ, Fort Myers, FL 33965-6565	1991	$2,921 (S)	$8,000	5-M	5,972	402
Florida Inst of Tech, Melbourne, FL 32901-6975	1958	$22,600	$6,140	1-D	4,689	283
Florida Intl Univ, Miami, FL 33199	1965	$2,889 (S)	$8,822	5-D	33,228	1,119
Florida Memorial Coll, Miami-Dade, FL 33054	1879	$10,433	$4,547	2-B	1,771	NA
Florida Metropolitan Univ-Brandon Cmps, Tampa, FL 33619	1890	$8,980	NA	3-M	1,384	68
Florida Metropolitan Univ-Fort Lauderdale Cmps, Pompano Beach, FL 33062	1940	$9,150	NA	3-M	1,612	70
Florida Metropolitan Univ-North Orlando Cmps, Orlando, FL 32810-5674	1953	$8,640	NA	3-M	1,444	89
Florida Metropolitan Univ-Pinellas Cmps, Clearwater, FL 33759	1890	$8,640	NA	3-M	1,201	44
Florida Metropolitan Univ-South Orlando Cmps, Orlando, FL 32819	NR	$8,640	NA	3-M	1,964	77
Florida Metropolitan Univ-Tampa Cmps, Tampa, FL 33614-5899	1890	$8,640	NA	3-M	1,218	93
Florida Southern Coll, Lakeland, FL 33801-5698	1885	$17,492	$6,050	2-M	1,880	172
Florida State Univ, Tallahassee, FL 32306	1851	$2,860 (S)	$6,168	5-D	36,884	1,403
Fontbonne Univ, St. Louis, MO 63105-3098	1917	$15,420	$6,988	2-M	2,538	294
Fordham Univ, New York, NY 10458	1841	$24,720	$9,700	2-D	14,731	1,132
Fort Hays State Univ, Hays, KS 67601-4099	1902	$2,539 (S)	$4,843	5-M	7,373	291
Fort Lewis Coll, Durango, CO 81301-3999	1911	$2,788 (S)	$5,564	5-B	4,182	243
Fort Valley State Univ, Fort Valley, GA 31030-4313	1895	$2,782 (S)	$4,178	5-D	2,537	114
Framingham State Coll, Framingham, MA 01701-9101	1839	$4,324 (S)	$5,058	5-M	6,156	286
Franciscan Univ of Steubenville, Steubenville, OH 43952-1763	1946	$15,050	$5,250	2-M	2,281	172
Francis Marion Univ, Florence, SC 29501-0547	1970	$5,082 (S)	$4,282	5-M	3,590	214
Franklin & Marshall Coll, Lancaster, PA 17604-3003	1787	$28,860	$7,070	1-B	1,923	195
Franklin Coll, Franklin, IN 46131-2598	1834	$16,925	$5,270	2-B	1,038	111
Franklin Pierce Coll, Rindge, NH 03461-0060	1962	$22,510	$7,655	1-M	1,591	142
Franklin Univ, Columbus, OH 43215-5399	1902	$6,720	NA	1-M	6,286	429
Freed-Hardeman Univ, Henderson, TN 38340-2399	1869	$11,046	$5,320	2-M	1,966	117
Fresno Pacific Univ, Fresno, CA 93702-4709	1944	$17,592	$4,870	2-M	2,243	92
Friends Univ, Wichita, KS 67213	1898	$13,790	$6,464	1-M	3,190	225
Frostburg State Univ, Frostburg, MD 21532-1099	1898	$5,830 (S)	$5,772	5-M	5,469	339
Furman Univ, Greenville, SC 29613	1826	$22,712	$5,968	1-M	3,320	253
Gallaudet Univ, Washington, DC 20002-3625	1864	$9,660	$8,030	1-D	1,573	218
Gannon Univ, Erie, PA 16541-0001	1925	$17,500	$7,070	2-D	3,459	285
Gardner-Webb Univ, Boiling Springs, NC 28017	1905	$14,340	$5,140	2-D	3,964	131
Geneva Coll, Beaver Falls, PA 15010-3599	1848	$16,590	$6,600	2-M	2,121	153
George Fox Univ, Newberg, OR 97132-2697	1891	$19,810	$6,300	2-D	3,022	361
George Mason Univ, Fairfax, VA 22030	1957	$5,112 (S)	$6,040	5-D	28,246	1,855
Georgetown Coll, Georgetown, KY 40324-1696	1829	$16,370	$5,190	2-M	1,708	144
Georgetown Univ, Washington, DC 20057	1789	$28,209	$10,033	2-D	13,164	1,036
The George Washington Univ, Washington, DC 20052	1821	$30,820	$10,210	1-D	23,417	1,922
Georgia Coll & State Univ, Milledgeville, GA 31061	1889	$3,596 (S)	$6,282	5-M	5,695	420
Georgia Inst of Tech, Atlanta, GA 30332-0001	1885	$4,076 (S)	$6,264	5-D	16,643	818
Georgian Court Univ, Lakewood, NJ 08701-2697 (3)	1908	$17,924	$7,200	2-M	2,976	261
Georgia Southern Univ, Statesboro, GA 30460	1906	$2,912 (S)	$5,628	5-D	15,704	702
Georgia Southwestern State Univ, Americus, GA 31709-4693	1906	$2,782 (S)	$4,204	5-M	2,410	141
Georgia State Univ, Atlanta, GA 30303-3083	1913	$4,312 (S)	$7,118	5-D	28,042	1,363
Gettysburg Coll, Gettysburg, PA 17325-1483	1832	$28,674	$6,972	2-B	2,597	259
Glenville State Coll, Glenville, WV 26351-1200	1872	$2,952 (S)	$4,860	5-B	1,377	96
Global Univ of the Assemblies of God, Springfield, MO 65804	1948	$2,160	NA	2-M	6,748	498
Golden Gate Univ, San Francisco, CA 94105-2968	1853	$9,984	NA	1-D	4,299	662
Goldey-Beacom Coll, Wilmington, DE 19808-1999	1886	$11,349	$3,937	1-M	1,324	49
Gonzaga Univ, Spokane, WA 99258	1887	$20,735	$5,960	2-D	5,778	532
Gordon Coll, Wenham, MA 01984-1899	1889	$20,234	$5,748	2-M	1,683	146
Goucher Coll, Baltimore, MD 21204-2794	1885	$24,450	$8,350	1-M	2,311	NA

Name, address	Year Founded	Tuition & Fees	Rm. & Board	Control, Degree	Enroll- ment	Faculty
Governors State Univ, University Park, IL 60466-0975	1969	$3,192 (S)	NA	5-M	5,317	204
Grace Coll, Winona Lake, IN 46590-1294	1948	$14,070	$5,755	2-M	1,208	91
Graceland Univ, Lamoni, IA 50140	1895	$14,800	$4,750	2-M	2,359	118
Grambling State Univ, Grambling, LA 71245	1901	$3,182 (S)	$3,356	5-D	4,673	268
Grand Canyon Univ, Phoenix, AZ 85017-1097	1949	$14,500	$7,130	2-M	4,113	274
Grand Valley State Univ, Allendale, MI 49401-9403	1960	$5,648 (S)	$5,768	5-M	21,429	1,259
Grand View Coll, Des Moines, IA 50316-1599	1896	$14,740	$5,232	2-B	1,630	163
Grantham Univ, Slidell, LA 70460-6815 (2)	1951	$3,489	NA	3-M	4,500	NA
Greensboro Coll, Greensboro, NC 27401-1875	1838	$15,720	$6,030	2-M	1,248	123
Greenville Coll, Greenville, IL 62246-0159	1892	$15,776	$5,566	2-M	1,342	133
Grinnell Coll, Grinnell, IA 50112-1690	1846	$24,490	$6,570	1-B	1,524	142
Grove City Coll, Grove City, PA 16127-2104	1876	$9,526	$4,852	2-B	2,314	179
Guilford Coll, Greensboro, NC 27410-4173	1837	NA	NA	2-B	2,101	165
Gustavus Adolphus Coll, St. Peter, MN 56082-1498	1862	$21,660	$5,460	2-B	2,574	247
Gwynedd-Mercy Coll, Gwynedd Valley, PA 19437-0901	1948	$16,700	$7,300	2-M	2,615	265
Hamilton Coll, Clinton, NY 13323-1296	1812	$30,200	$7,360	1-B	1,797	209
Hamline Univ, St. Paul, MN 55104-1284	1854	$20,832	$6,220	2-D	4,469	344
Hampden-Sydney Coll, Hampden-Sydney, VA 23943 (1)	1776	$21,387	$7,020	2-B	1,039	106
Hampshire Coll, Amherst, MA 01002	1965	$29,392	$7,689	1-B	1,332	141
Hampton Univ, Hampton, VA 23668	1868	$12,864	$6,118	1-D	5,790	400
Hannibal-LaGrange Coll, Hannibal, MO 63401-1999	1858	$10,160	$3,780	2-B	1,133	92
Harding Univ, Searcy, AR 72149-0001	1924	$10,120	$4,770	2-M	5,110	295
Hardin-Simmons Univ, Abilene, TX 79698-0001	1891	$13,376	$3,922	2-D	2,361	183
Harrington Coll of Design, Chicago, IL 60606 (4)	1931	$12,800	$4,800	3-B	1,364	123
Harris-Stowe State Coll, St. Louis, MO 63103-2136	1857	$3,280 (S)	NA	5-B	1,911	145
Hartwick Coll, Oneonta, NY 13820-4020	1797	$26,560	$7,280	1-B	1,466	144
Harvard Univ, Cambridge, MA 02138	1636	$29,060	$8,868	1-D	20,130	760
Haskell Indian Nations Univ, Lawrence, KS 66046-4800	1884	$210*	$70	4-B	1,028	48
Hastings Coll, Hastings, NE 68901-7696	1882	$15,398	$4,530	2-M	1,113	117
Haverford Coll, Haverford, PA 19041-1392	1833	$28,880	$9,020	1-B	1,163	113
Hawai`i Pacific Univ, Honolulu, HI 96813-2785	1965	$10,368	$8,770	1-M	7,900	582
Heidelberg Coll, Tiffin, OH 44883-2462	1850	$14,900	$6,710	2-M	1,243	118
Henderson State Univ, Arkadelphia, AR 71999-0001	1890	$3,635 (S)	$3,984	5-M	3,479	217
Hendrix Coll, Conway, AR 72032-3080	1876	$15,630	$5,340	2-M	1,059	100
Heritage Coll, Toppenish, WA 98948-9599	1982	$6,760	NA	1-M	1,127	130
High Point Univ, High Point, NC 27262-3598	1924	$15,700	$6,780	2-M	2,918	210
Hilbert Coll, Hamburg, NY 14075-1597	1957	$14,000	$5,670	1-B	1,055	95
Hillsdale Coll, Hillsdale, MI 49242-1298	1844	$16,050	$6,400	1-B	1,230	130
Hiram Coll, Hiram, OH 44234-0067	1850	$21,134	$7,100	2-B	1,110	121
Hobart & William Smith Colls, Geneva, NY 14456-3397	1822	$28,948	$7,588	1-B	1,873	189
Hofstra Univ, Hempstead, NY 11549	1935	$18,412	$8,700	1-D	13,221	1,294
Hollins Univ, Roanoke, VA 24020-1603 (3)	1842	$20,675	$7,290	1-M	1,091	107
Holy Family Univ, Philadelphia, PA 19114-2094	1954	$15,490	NA	2-M	2,670	258
Hood Coll, Frederick, MD 21701-8575	1893	$20,275	$7,520	1-M	1,325	175
Hope Coll, Holland, MI 49422-9000	1866	$19,322	$6,018	2-B	3,068	293
Hope Intl Univ, Fullerton, CA 92831-3138	1928	$15,200	$5,874	2-M	1,204	62
Houghton Coll, Houghton, NY 14744	1883	$17,984	$6,000	2-M	1,467	103
Houston Baptist Univ, Houston, TX 77074-3298	1960	$12,180	$4,680	2-M	2,340	189
Howard Payne Univ, Brownwood, TX 76801-2715	1889	$11,150	$4,026	2-B	1,385	125
Howard Univ, Washington, DC 20059-0002	1867	$10,935	$5,570	1-D	10,658	1,598
Humboldt State Univ, Arcata, CA 95521-8299	1913	$2,539 (S)	$6,861	5-M	7,725	489
Hunter Coll of the City Univ of New York, New York, NY 10021-5085	1870	$4,165 (S)	NA	11-M	20,797	1,365
Husson Coll, Bangor, ME 04401-2999	1898	$10,700	$5,680	1-M	2,038	110
Idaho State Univ, Pocatello, ID 83209	1901	$3,448 (S)	$4,680	5-D	13,621	615
Illinois Coll, Jacksonville, IL 62650-2299	1829	$13,300	$5,800	2-B	1,016	93
The Illinois Inst of Art, Chicago, IL 60654	1916	$16,948	NA	3-B	1,950	110
The Illinois Inst of Art-Schaumburg, Schaumburg, IL 60173	NR	$16,200	NA	3-B	1,107	55
Illinois Inst of Tech, Chicago, IL 60616-3793	1890	$21,342	$6,946	1-D	6,167	524
Illinois State Univ, Normal, IL 61790-2200	1857	$5,530 (S)	$5,414	5-D	20,860	1,084
Illinois Wesleyan Univ, Bloomington, IL 61702-2900	1850	$26,130	$6,140	1-B	2,106	208
Immaculata Univ, Immaculata, PA 19345	1920	$17,200	$8,000	2-D	3,381	277
Indiana Inst of Tech, Fort Wayne, IN 46803-1297	1930	$16,680	$6,272	1-M	3,390	272
Indiana State Univ, Terre Haute, IN 47809-1401	1865	$5,422 (S)	$5,297	5-D	11,360	715
Indiana Univ-Purdue Univ Fort Wayne, Fort Wayne, IN 46805-1499	1917	$5,108 (S)	NA	5-M	11,806	690
Indiana Univ-Purdue Univ Indianapolis, Indianapolis, IN 46202-2896	1969	$5,703 (S)	$2,554	5-D	29,860	2,919
Indiana Univ Bloomington, Bloomington, IN 47405	1820	$6,517 (S)	$5,872	5-D	38,589	2,071
Indiana Univ East, Richmond, IN 47374-1289	1971	$4,433 (S)	NA	5-B	2,568	204
Indiana Univ Kokomo, Kokomo, IN 46904-9003	1945	$4,463 (S)	NA	5-M	2,954	177
Indiana Univ Northwest, Gary, IN 46408-1197	1959	$4,538 (S)	NA	5-M	5,097	380
Indiana Univ of Pennsylvania, Indiana, PA 15705-1087	1875	$5,785 (S)	$4,704	5-D	13,868	694
Indiana Univ South Bend, South Bend, IN 46634-7111	1922	$4,571 (S)	NA	5-M	7,280	541
Indiana Univ Southeast, New Albany, IN 47150-6405	1941	$4,504 (S)	NA	5-M	6,408	446
Indiana Wesleyan Univ, Marion, IN 46953-4974	1920	$14,420	$5,480	2-M	8,765	167
Inter Amer Univ of Puerto Rico, Aguadilla Cmps, Aguadilla, PR 00605	1957	$3,604	NA	1-B	4,197	254
Inter Amer Univ of Puerto Rico, Arecibo Cmps, Arecibo, PR 00614-4050	1957	$3,544	NA	1-M	3,926	234
Inter Amer Univ of Puerto Rico, Barranquitas Cmps, Barranquitas, PR 00794	1957	$4,000	NA	1-B	2,271	105
Inter Amer Univ of Puerto Rico, Bayamón Cmps, Bayamón, PR 00957	1912	$3,522	NA	1-M	5,264	283
Inter Amer Univ of Puerto Rico, Fajardo Cmps, Fajardo, PR 00738-7003	1965	$3,296	NA	1-B	1,710	118
Inter Amer Univ of Puerto Rico, Guayama Cmps, Guayama, PR 00785	1958	$1,682	NA	1-B	1,246	139
Inter Amer Univ of Puerto Rico, Metropolitan Cmps, San Juan, PR 00919-1293	1960	$3,536	NA	1-D	10,675	599
Inter Amer Univ of Puerto Rico, Ponce Cmps, Mercedita, PR 00715-1602	1962	$4,262	NA	1-M	5,134	242
Inter Amer Univ of Puerto Rico, San Germán Cmps, San Germán, PR 00683-5008	1912	$4,466	$2,400	1-D	6,210	311
Intl Acad of Design & Tech, Tampa, FL 33634-7350	1984	$16,620	NA	3-B	2,043	151
Intl Acad of Design & Tech, Chicago, IL 60602-9736	1977	$18,700	NA	3-B	2,769	183
Intl Coll, Naples, FL 34119	1990	$8,540	NA	1-M	1,500	107
Iona Coll, New Rochelle, NY 10801-1890	1940	$18,290	$9,698	2-M	4,388	381
Iowa State Univ of Sci & Tech, Ames, IA 50011	1858	$5,426 (S)	$6,121	5-D	27,380	1,659
Ithaca Coll, Ithaca, NY 14850-7020	1892	$22,264	$9,466	1-M	6,496	633
Jackson State Univ, Jackson, MS 39217	1877	$3,612 (S)	$4,770	5-D	7,815	448

Name, address	Year Founded	Tuition & Fees	Rm. & Board	Control, Degree	Enroll-ment	Faculty
Jacksonville State Univ, Jacksonville, AL 36265-1602	1883	$3,540 (S)	$3,288	5-M	9,031	433
Jacksonville Univ, Jacksonville, FL 32211-3394	1934	$17,940	$6,100	1-M	2,632	264
James Madison Univ, Harrisonburg, VA 22807	1908	$5,058 (S)	$5,966	5-D	16,203	996
Jamestown Coll, Jamestown, ND 58405	1883	$9,400	$3,970	2-B	1,152	70
John Brown Univ, Siloam Springs, AR 72761-2121	1919	$14,356	$5,040	2-M	1,834	122
John Carroll Univ, University Heights, OH 44118-4581	1886	$20,766	$6,892	2-M	4,242	411
John F. Kennedy Univ, Pleasant Hill, CA 94523-4817	1964	$13,947	NA	1-D	1,606	715
John Jay Coll of Criminal Justice of the City Univ of New York, New York, NY 10019-1093	1964	$4,259 (S)	NA	11-D	12,984	585
The Johns Hopkins Univ, Baltimore, MD 21218-2699	1876	$29,230	$9,142	1-D	6,229	478
Johnson & Wales Univ, Denver, CO 80220	1993	$19,992	$8,115	1-B	1,328	70
Johnson & Wales Univ, North Miami, FL 33181	1992	$19,992	$7,185	1-B	2,379	80
Johnson & Wales Univ, Providence, RI 02903-3703	1914	$17,460	$7,185	1-D	9,868	644
Johnson C. Smith Univ, Charlotte, NC 28216-5398	1867	$13,062	$5,046	1-B	1,474	115
Johnson State Coll, Johnson, VT 05656-9405	1828	$5,876 (S)	$6,013	5-M	1,759	203
Jones Intl Univ, Englewood, CO 80112	1995	$8,160	$1,360	3-M	1,053	93
Judson Coll, Elgin, IL 60123-1498	1963	$16,050	$6,000	2-M	1,166	114
Juniata Coll, Huntingdon, PA 16652-2119	1876	$24,270	$6,770	2-B	1,396	128
Kalamazoo Coll, Kalamazoo, MI 49006-3295	1833	$22,908	$6,480	2-B	1,280	117
Kansas State Univ, Manhattan, KS 66506	1863	$4,059 (S)	$5,080	5-D	23,050	976
Kean Univ, Union, NJ 07083	1855	$6,724 (S)	$7,755	5-M	12,978	1,000
Keene State Coll, Keene, NH 03435	1909	$6,530 (S)	$5,682	5-M	4,920	410
Kennesaw State Univ, Kennesaw, GA 30144-5591	1963	$3,344 (S)	$3,897	5-M	17,477	805
Kent State Univ, Kent, OH 44242-0001	1910	$6,882 (S)	$7,920	5-D	23,536	1,335
Kentucky State Univ, Frankfort, KY 40601	1886	$3,370 (S)	$5,394	12-M	2,306	155
Kenyon Coll, Gambier, OH 43022-9623	1824	$30,330	$5,040	1-B	1,612	168
Kettering Univ, Flint, MI 48504-4898	1919	$21,554	$4,924	1-M	3,126	153
Keuka Coll, Keuka Park, NY 14478-0098	1890	$16,660	$7,800	2-M	1,148	88
King's Coll, Wilkes-Barre, PA 18711-0801	1946	$19,060	$7,930	2-M	2,204	183
Knox Coll, Galesburg, IL 61401	1837	$25,236	$6,102	1-B	1,127	116
Kutztown Univ of Pennsylvania, Kutztown, PA 19530-0730	1866	$5,776 (S)	$4,812	5-M	9,008	416
Lafayette Coll, Easton, PA 18042-1798	1826	$27,328	$8,418	2-B	2,285	224
LaGrange Coll, LaGrange, GA 30240-2999	1831	$14,482	$6,018	2-M	1,020	103
Lake Forest Coll, Lake Forest, IL 60045-2399	1857	$24,406	$5,764	1-M	1,348	151
Lakeland Coll, Sheboygan, WI 53082-0359	1862	$14,900	$5,655	2-M	3,829	65
Lake Superior State Univ, Sault Sainte Marie, MI 49783-1626	1946	$5,454 (S)	$5,993	5-B	3,258	232
Lamar Univ, Beaumont, TX 77710	1923	$3,260 (S)	$5,760	5-D	10,379	491
Lander Univ, Greenwood, SC 29649-2099	1872	$5,550 (S)	$4,946	5-M	2,950	208
Langston Univ, Langston, OK 73050-0907	1897	$2,787 (S)	$4,380	5-M	3,008	NA
La Roche Coll, Pittsburgh, PA 15237-5898	1963	$16,582	$6,862	2-M	1,771	204
La Salle Univ, Philadelphia, PA 19141-1199	1863	$22,960	$8,770	2-D	5,949	NA
Lasell Coll, Newton, MA 02466-2709	1851	$17,500	$8,500	1-M	1,099	130
La Sierra Univ, Riverside, CA 92515-8247	1922	$16,740	$4,560	2-D	1,758	95
Lawrence Tech Univ, Southfield, MI 48075-1058	1932	$14,362	$6,125	1-M	4,241	424
Lawrence Univ, Appleton, WI 54912-0599	1847	$25,089	$5,652	1-B	1,407	166
Lebanon Valley Coll, Annville, PA 17003-1400	1866	$22,510	$6,360	2-D	1,906	181
Lee Univ, Cleveland, TN 37320-3450	1918	$9,075	$4,560	2-M	3,806	297
Lehigh Univ, Bethlehem, PA 18015-3094	1865	$29,340	$8,230	1-D	6,732	547
Lehman Coll of the City Univ of New York, Bronx, NY 10468-1589	1931	$4,270 (S)	NA	11-M	9,712	709
Le Moyne Coll, Syracuse, NY 13214-1399	1946	$18,950	$7,450	2-M	3,403	287
Lenoir-Rhyne Coll, Hickory, NC 28603	1891	$17,850	$6,300	2-M	1,550	154
Lesley Univ, Cambridge, MA 02138-2790 (4)	1909	$21,275	$9,370	1-D	6,333	66
LeTourneau Univ, Longview, TX 75607-7001	1946	$15,030	$6,050	2-M	3,597	260
Lewis & Clark Coll, Portland, OR 97219-7899	1867	$24,670	$7,030	1-F	3,071	331
Lewis-Clark State Coll, Lewiston, ID 83501-2698	1893	$3,126 (S)	$4,336	5-B	3,471	186
Lewis Univ, Romeoville, IL 60446	1932	$16,906	$7,200	2-M	4,468	157
Liberty Univ, Lynchburg, VA 24502	1971	$13,150	$5,400	2-D	9,050	339
Life Univ, Marietta, GA 30060-2903	1974	$5,040 (S)	NA	1-F	1,182	30
Lincoln Memorial Univ, Harrogate, TN 37752-1901	1897	$12,600	$4,910	1-M	2,442	152
Lincoln Univ, Jefferson City, MO 65102	1866	$4,562 (S)	$3,790	5-M	3,128	224
Lincoln University, PA 19352	1854	$6,952 (S)	$6,368	12-M	1,938	172
Lindenwood Univ, St. Charles, MO 63301-1695	1827	$11,650	$5,400	2-M	7,838	426
Lindsey Wilson Coll, Columbia, KY 42728-1298	1903	$12,602	$5,484	2-M	1,680	123
Linfield Coll, McMinnville, OR 97128-6894	1849	$20,970	$6,120	2-B	1,659	164
Lipscomb Univ, Nashville, TN 37204-3951	1891	$13,447	$5,590	2-F	2,661	215
Livingstone Coll, Salisbury, NC 28144-5298	1879	$12,298	$5,803	2-B	1,005	67
Lock Haven Univ of Pennsylvania, Lock Haven, PA 17745-2390	1870	$5,874 (S)	$5,224	5-M	4,908	244
Logan Univ-Coll of Chiropractic, Chesterfield, MO 63006-1065	1935	$3,310	NA	1-F	1,118	90
Loma Linda Univ, Loma Linda, CA 92350	1905	$21,805	$2,780	2-D	3,574	202
Long Island Univ, Brooklyn Cmps, Brooklyn, NY 11201-8423	1926	$17,122	$6,480	1-D	8,008	965
Long Island Univ, C.W. Post Cmps, Brookville, NY 11548-1300	1954	$20,490	$7,730	1-D	8,425	1,186
Long Island Univ, Southampton Cmps, Southampton, NY 11968-4198	1963	$20,560	$8,810	1-M	1,453	240
Longwood Univ, Farmville, VA 23909-1800	1839	$5,877 (S)	$5,298	5-M	4,252	228
Loras Coll, Dubuque, IA 52004-0178	1839	$18,338	$5,895	2-M	1,764	173
Louisiana Coll, Pineville, LA 71359-0001	1906	$9,650	$3,610	2-B	1,135	100
Louisiana State Univ & Agr & Mech Coll, Baton Rouge, LA 70803	1860	$3,910 (S)	$5,216	5-D	31,934	1,548
Louisiana State Univ in Shreveport, Shreveport, LA 71115-2399	1965	$2,884 (S)	$2,196	5-M	4,377	254
Louisiana Tech Univ, Ruston, LA 71272	1894	$3,270 (S)	$3,885	5-D	11,960	496
Lourdes Coll, Sylvania, OH 43560-2898	1958	$15,100	NA	2-M	1,249	125
Loyola Coll in Maryland, Baltimore, MD 21210-2699	1852	$26,610	$8,630	2-D	6,033	514
Loyola Marymount Univ, Los Angeles, CA 90045-2659	1911	$23,934	$8,260	2-F	8,880	865
Loyola Univ Chicago, Chicago, IL 60611-2196	1870	$22,340	$8,824	2-D	13,362	975
Loyola Univ New Orleans, New Orleans, LA 70118-6195	1912	$23,618	$7,994	2-F	5,518	469
Lubbock Christian Univ, Lubbock, TX 79407-2099	1957	$11,452	$4,380	2-M	1,933	134
Luther Coll, Decorah, IA 52101-1045	1861	$23,070	$4,170	2-B	2,565	235
Luther Rice Bible Coll & Sem, Lithonia, GA 30038-2454	1962	$3,580	NA	2-D	1,600	33
Lycoming Coll, Williamsport, PA 17701-5192	1812	$21,723	$5,866	2-B	1,417	103
Lynchburg Coll, Lynchburg, VA 24501-3199	1903	$21,515	$4,800	2-M	2,013	170
Lyndon State Coll, Lyndonville, VT 05851-0919	1911	$5,806 (S)	$6,014	5-M	1,444	141
Lynn Univ, Boca Raton, FL 33431-5598	1962	$22,750	$8,000	1-D	1,891	247
Macalester Coll, St. Paul, MN 55105-1899	1874	$26,806	$7,350	2-B	1,884	215
Macon State Coll, Macon, GA 31206-5144	1968	$1,764 (S)	NA	5-B	5,400	262
Madonna Univ, Livonia, MI 48150-1173	1947	$9,800	$5,612	2-M	4,276	324

Name, address	Year Founded	Tuition & Fees	Rm. & Board	Control, Degree	Enroll- ment	Faculty
Malone Coll, Canton, OH 44709-3897	1892	$14,995	$6,000	2-M	2,206	199
Manchester Coll, North Manchester, IN 46962-1225	1889	$18,060	$6,650	2-M	1,170	92
Manhattan Coll, Riverdale, NY 10471	1853	$19,300	$8,100	2-M	3,233	282
Manhattanville Coll, Purchase, NY 10577-2132	1841	$24,570	$10,130	1-M	2,571	196
Mansfield Univ of Pennsylvania, Mansfield, PA 16933	1857	$5,972 (S)	$5,248	5-M	3,520	198
Marian Coll, Indianapolis, IN 46222-1997	1851	$17,460	$5,800	2-M	1,561	132
Marian Coll of Fond du Lac, Fond du Lac, WI 54935-4699	1936	$15,025	$4,600	2-M	2,777	151
Marietta Coll, Marietta, OH 45750-4000	1835	$20,892	$5,946	1-M	1,341	116
Marist Coll, Poughkeepsie, NY 12601-1387	1929	$18,962	$8,634	1-M	5,616	601
Marquette Univ, Milwaukee, WI 53201-1881	1881	$20,710	$7,000	2-D	11,355	1,018
Marshall Univ, Huntington, WV 25755	1837	$3,260 (S)	$5,856	5-D	13,960	721
Mars Hill Coll, Mars Hill, NC 28754	1856	$15,458	$6,760	2-B	1,351	150
Martin Luther Coll, New Ulm, MN 56073	1995	$8,500	$3,300	2-B	1,020	88
Mary Baldwin Coll, Staunton, VA 24401-3610	1842	$19,414	$5,525	1-M	1,731	133
Marygrove Coll, Detroit, MI 48221-2599 (4)	1905	$11,750	$5,800	2-M	5,584	74
Maryland Inst Coll of Art, Baltimore, MD 21217-4191	1826	$23,710	$7,180	1-M	1,476	217
Marylhurst Univ, Marylhurst, OR 97036-0261	1893	$13,455	NA	2-M	1,212	184
Marymount Coll of Fordham Univ, Tarrytown, NY 10591-3796 (3)	1907	$18,426	$9,260	1-B	1,083	167
Marymount Manhattan Coll, New York, NY 10021-4597	1936	$17,352	$12,366	1-B	2,183	309
Marymount Univ, Arlington, VA 22207-4299	1950	$16,438	$7,230	2-M	3,740	378
Maryville Coll, Maryville, TN 37804-5907	1819	$21,065	$6,500	2-B	1,052	103
Maryville Univ of St Louis, St. Louis, MO 63141-7299	1872	$16,300	$7,000	1-M	3,301	342
Mary Washington Coll, Fredericksburg, VA 22401-5358	1908	$4,424 (S)	$5,478	5-M	4,792	331
Marywood Univ, Scranton, PA 18509-1598	1915	$19,475	$8,134	2-D	3,136	311
Massachusetts Coll of Art, Boston, MA 02115-5882	1873	$4,968 (S)	$9,800	5-M	2,096	185
Massachusetts Coll of Lib Arts, North Adams, MA 01247-4100	1894	$5,397 (S)	$5,620	5-M	1,811	122
Massachusetts Coll of Pharm & Health Sci, Boston, MA 02115-5896	1823	$19,400	$10,170	1-D	2,513	146
Massachusetts Inst of Tech, Cambridge, MA 02139-4307	1861	$29,600	$8,710	1-D	10,340	2,182
The Master's Coll & Sem, Santa Clarita, CA 91321-1200	1927	$17,200	$6,050	2-D	1,426	140
McDaniel Coll, Westminster, MD 21157-4390	1867	$23,160	$5,280	1-M	3,294	180
McKendree Coll, Lebanon, IL 62254-1299	1828	$15,200	$5,920	2-M	2,115	204
McMurry Univ, Abilene, TX 79697	1923	$12,980	$5,046	2-B	1,376	119
McNeese State Univ, Lake Charles, LA 70609	1939	$2,772 (S)	$3,788	5-M	8,447	393
Medaille Coll, Buffalo, NY 14214-2695	1875	$13,660	$6,400	1-M	2,000	279
Medgar Evers Coll of the City Univ of New York, Brooklyn, NY 11225-2298	1969	$4,230 (S)	NA	11-B	4,722	401
Med Coll of Georgia, Augusta, GA 30912	1828	$3,794 (S)	$2,835	5-D	2,078	741
Med Univ of South Carolina, Charleston, SC 29425-0002	1824	$8,282 (S)	NA	5-D	2,306	1,264
Mercer Univ, Macon, GA 31207-0003	1833	$22,050	$7,060	2-D	7,200	547
Mercy Coll, Dobbs Ferry, NY 10522-1189	1951	$10,844	$8,180	1-M	10,395	989
Mercyhurst Coll, Erie, PA 16546	1926	$16,980	$6,414	2-M	3,795	247
Meredith Coll, Raleigh, NC 27607-5298 (3)	1891	$19,000	$5,350	1-M	2,152	278
Merrimack Coll, North Andover, MA 01845-5800	1947	$20,875	$8,750	2-M	2,404	240
Mesa State Coll, Grand Junction, CO 81501-3122	1925	$2,516 (S)	$6,266	5-M	5,560	333
Messiah Coll, Grantham, PA 17027	1909	$19,550	$6,340	2-B	2,952	295
Methodist Coll, Fayetteville, NC 28311-1498	1956	$16,760	$6,370	2-M	2,255	171
Metropolitan Coll of New York, New York, NY 10013-1919 (4)	1964	$16,635	NA	1-M	1,592	273
Metropolitan State Coll of Denver, Denver, CO 80217-3362	1963	$2,668 (S)	NA	5-B	20,261	1,000
Metropolitan State Univ, St. Paul, MN 55106-5000	1971	$3,852 (S)	NA	5-M	6,447	439
Miami Intl Univ of Art & Design, Miami, FL 33132-1418	1965	$17,570	$4,600	3-M	1,207	91
Miami Univ, Oxford, OH 45056	1809	$8,353 (S)	$6,680	12-D	16,795	1,137
Michigan State Univ, East Lansing, MI 48824	1855	$6,703 (S)	$5,230	5-D	44,542	2,653
Michigan Tech Univ, Houghton, MI 49931-1295	1885	$7,440 (S)	$5,795	5-D	6,565	394
MidAmerica Nazarene Univ, Olathe, KS 66062-1899	1966	$12,910	$5,828	2-M	1,952	163
Middlebury Coll, Middlebury, VT 05753-6002	1800	$38,100 (C)	NA	1-D	2,424	237
Middle Tennessee State Univ, Murfreesboro, TN 37132	1911	$3,910 (S)	$4,624	5-D	21,744	1,007
Midway Coll, Midway, KY 40347-1120 (3)	1847	$11,850	$5,800	2-B	1,154	131
Midwestern State Univ, Wichita Falls, TX 76308	1922	$3,650 (S)	$4,630	5-M	6,483	307
Miles Coll, Birmingham, AL 35208	1905	$5,470	$4,338	2-B	1,660	134
Millersville Univ of Pennsylvania, Millersville, PA 17551-0302	1855	$5,819 (S)	$5,450	5-M	7,861	431
Millikin Univ, Decatur, IL 62522-2084	1901	$19,234	$6,123	2-M	2,633	NA
Millsaps Coll, Jackson, MS 39210-0001	1890	$18,414	$6,768	2-M	1,200	97
Mills Coll, Oakland, CA 94613-1000 (3)	1852	$24,441	$8,930	1-D	1,210	159
Milwaukee Sch of Engr, Milwaukee, WI 53202-3109 (2)	1903	$23,034	$5,445	1-M	2,383	294
Minnesota State Univ Mankato, Mankato, MN 56001	1868	$4,506 (S)	$4,297	5-M	14,065	633
Minnesota State Univ Moorhead, Moorhead, MN 56563-0002	1885	$4,254 (S)	$4,340	5-M	7,695	315
Minot State Univ, Minot, ND 58707-0002	1913	$3,228 (S)	$3,274	5-M	3,825	221
Mississippi Coll, Clinton, MS 39058	1826	$11,529	$5,396	2-F	3,406	263
Mississippi State Univ, Mississippi State, MS 39762	1878	$3,874 (S)	$5,265	5-D	16,173	979
Mississippi Univ for Women, Columbus, MS 39701-9998 (4)	1884	$3,298 (S)	$3,230	5-M	2,328	214
Mississippi Valley State Univ, Itta Bena, MS 38941-1400	1946	$3,411 (S)	$3,544	5-M	4,009	155
Missouri Baptist Univ, St. Louis, MO 63141-8660	1964	$12,280	$5,800	2-M	3,656	157
Missouri Southern State Univ, Joplin, MO 64801-1595	1937	$3,976 (S)	$4,770	5-B	5,410	286
Missouri Valley Coll, Marshall, MO 65340-3197	1889	$13,500	$5,200	2-B	1,623	113
Missouri Western State Coll, St. Joseph, MO 64507-2294	1915	$4,464 (S)	$4,058	5-B	4,928	318
Molloy Coll, Rockville Centre, NY 11571-5002	1955	$15,130	NA	1-M	3,007	357
Monmouth Coll, Monmouth, IL 61462-1998	1853	$19,350	$5,450	2-B	1,162	111
Monmouth Univ, West Long Branch, NJ 07764-1898	1933	$18,766	$7,568	1-M	6,212	517
Montana State Univ-Billings, Billings, MT 59101-0298	1927	$4,180 (S)	$4,430	5-M	4,670	244
Montana State Univ-Bozeman, Bozeman, MT 59717	1893	$4,145 (S)	$5,370	5-D	12,135	808
Montana State Univ-Northern, Havre, MT 59501-7751	1929	$4,100 (S)	$5,600	5-M	1,589	103
Montana Tech of The Univ of Montana, Butte, MT 59701-8997	1895	$4,350 (S)	$4,980	5-M	2,232	156
Montclair State Univ, Upper Montclair, NJ 07043-1624	1908	$6,410 (S)	$7,902	5-D	15,204	997
Montreat Coll, Montreat, NC 28757-1267	1916	$15,108	$4,862	2-M	1,035	120
Moody Bible Inst, Chicago, IL 60610-3284	1886	$1,401	$6,340	2-F	1,732	100
Moravian Coll, Bethlehem, PA 18018-6650	1742	$23,574	$7,310	2-F	2,107	201
Morehead State Univ, Morehead, KY 40351	1922	$3,364 (S)	$4,100	5-M	9,509	475
Morehouse Coll, Atlanta, GA 30314 (1)	1867	$14,310	$8,418	1-B	2,859	205
Morgan State Univ, Baltimore, MD 21251	1867	$5,718 (S)	$6,780	5-D	6,621	458
Morningside Coll, Sioux City, IA 51106-1751	1894	$16,350	$5,260	2-M	1,176	111
Morris Coll, Sumter, SC 29150-3599	1908	$7,410	$3,564	2-B	1,007	63
Mountain State Univ, Beckley, WV 25802-9003	1933	$6,300	$5,172	1-M	3,973	236
Mount Aloysius Coll, Cresson, PA 16630-1999	1939	$16,040	$5,960	2-M	1,473	142

Name, address	Year Founded	Tuition & Fees	Rm. & Board	Control, Degree	Enroll- ment	Faculty
Mount Holyoke Coll, South Hadley, MA 01075 (3)	1837	$29,338	$8,580	1-M	2,152	254
Mount Ida Coll, Newton Center, MA 02459-3310	1899	$17,075	$9,400	1-B	1,076	97
Mount Marty Coll, Yankton, SD 57078-3724	1936	$14,186	$4,670	2-M	1,185	107
Mount Mary Coll, Milwaukee, WI 53222-4597 (3)	1913	$15,270	$5,100	2-M	1,600	192
Mount Mercy Coll, Cedar Rapids, IA 52402-4797	1928	$16,070	$5,330	2-B	1,473	135
Mount Olive Coll, Mount Olive, NC 28365	1951	$11,220	$4,600	2-B	2,289	185
Mount St Mary Coll, Newburgh, NY 12550-3494	1960	$14,290	$6,980	1-M	2,606	200
Mount St Mary's Coll, Los Angeles, CA 90049-1599 (4)	1925	$20,756	$8,224	2-M	2,127	268
Mount St Mary's Univ, Emmitsburg, MD 21727-7799	1808	$21,000	$7,400	2-F	2,088	149
Mt. Sierra Coll, Monrovia, CA 91016	1990	$16,200	NA	3-B	1,100	50
Mount Union Coll, Alliance, OH 44601-3993	1846	$18,810	$5,630	2-B	2,425	211
Mount Vernon Nazarene Univ, Mount Vernon, OH 43050-9500	1964	$14,976	$4,734	2-M	2,392	214
Muhlenberg Coll, Allentown, PA 18104-5586	1848	$25,160	$6,540	2-B	2,452	273
Murray State Univ, Murray, KY 42071-0009	1922	$3,436 (S)	$4,380	5-M	10,093	540
Muskingum Coll, New Concord, OH 43762	1837	$15,630	$6,200	2-M	2,142	129
Naropa Univ, Boulder, CO 80302-6697	1974	$15,764	$6,308	1-F	1,234	288
Natl-Louis Univ, Chicago, IL 60603	1886	$17,136	$5,913	1-D	7,665	284
Natl Univ, La Jolla, CA 92037-1011	1971	$8,550	NA	1-M	17,064	2,357
Nazareth Coll of Rochester, Rochester, NY 14618-3790	1924	$18,574	$7,700	1-M	3,062	230
Nebraska Wesleyan Univ, Lincoln, NE 68504-2796	1887	$16,430	$4,530	2-M	1,840	168
Neumann Coll, Aston, PA 19014-1298	1965	$17,190	$7,740	2-M	2,589	224
Newbury Coll, Brookline, MA 02445	1962	$16,125	$7,575	1-B	1,167	89
New Coll of California, San Francisco, CA 94102-5206	1971	$12,223	NA	1-M	1,133	90
New England Coll, Henniker, NH 03242-3293	1946	$21,120	$7,740	1-M	1,136	96
The New England Inst of Art, Brookline, MA 02445	NR	$17,197	$9,600	3-B	1,045	89
New Jersey City Univ, Jersey City, NJ 07305-1597	1927	$6,051 (S)	$6,586	5-M	9,361	582
New Jersey Inst of Tech, Newark, NJ 07102	1881	$8,500 (S)	$8,076	5-D	8,770	634
Newman Univ, Wichita, KS 67213-2097	1933	$13,348	$4,820	2-M	2,063	192
New Mexico Highlands Univ, Las Vegas, NM 87701	1893	$2,229 (S)	$4,085	5-M	3,960	241
New Mexico Inst of Mining & Tech, Socorro, NM 87801	1889	$3,080 (S)	$4,200	5-D	1,798	148
New Mexico State Univ, Las Cruces, NM 88003-8001	1888	$3,372 (S)	$4,560	5-D	16,174	977
New Orleans Baptist Theol Sem, New Orleans, LA 70126-4858 (2)	1917	$3,770	NA	2-D	2,712	84
New Sch Bach of Arts, New Sch Univ, New York, NY 10011-8603	1919	$16,254	$10,810	1-D	1,809	515
New York Inst of Tech, Old Westbury, NY 11568-8000	1955	$17,226	$7,780	1-D	9,387	866
New York Univ, New York, NY 10012-1019	1831	$28,496	$10,910	1-D	38,188	4,302
Niagara Univ, Niagara University, NY 14109	1856	$17,380	$7,670	2-M	3,548	307
Nicholls State Univ, Thibodaux, LA 70310	1948	$2,993 (S)	$3,402	5-M	7,247	285
Nichols Coll, Dudley, MA 01571-5000	1815	$19,723	$7,810	1-M	1,672	61
Norfolk State Univ, Norfolk, VA 23504	1935	$3,840 (S)	$5,882	5-D	6,846	446
North Carolina Agr & Tech State Univ, Greensboro, NC 27411	1891	$2,722 (S)	$4,968	5-D	8,319	458
North Carolina Central Univ, Durham, NC 27707-3129	1910	$3,218 (S)	$4,311	5-F	7,191	349
North Carolina State Univ, Raleigh, NC 27695	1887	$4,344 (S)	$6,496	5-D	29,854	1,823
North Carolina Wesleyan Coll, Rocky Mount, NC 27804-8677	1956	$12,279	$6,555	2-B	1,695	194
North Central Coll, Naperville, IL 60566-7063	1861	$19,281	$6,375	2-M	2,458	217
Northcentral Univ, Prescott, AZ 86301-1747	NR	NA	NA	3-D	1,101	103
North Central Univ, Minneapolis, MN 55404-1322	1930	$10,594	$4,680	2-B	1,227	97
North Dakota State Univ, Fargo, ND 58105	1890	$3,964 (A)	$4,471	5-D	11,623	596
Northeastern Illinois Univ, Chicago, IL 60625-4699	1961	$4,235 (S)	NA	5-M	11,825	627
Northeastern State Univ, Tahlequah, OK 74464-2399	1846	$2,700 (S)	$3,080	5-F	9,297	446
Northeastern Univ, Boston, MA 02115-5096	1898	$25,840	$9,810	1-D	18,760	1,146
Northern Arizona Univ, Flagstaff, AZ 86011	1899	$3,628 (S)	$5,374	5-D	18,824	1,142
Northern Illinois Univ, De Kalb, IL 60115-2854	1895	$5,164 (S)	$5,360	5-D	25,260	1,146
Northern Kentucky Univ, Highland Heights, KY 41099	1968	$3,744 (S)	$5,066	5-F	13,910	839
Northern Michigan Univ, Marquette, MI 49855-5301	1899	$5,370 (S)	$5,724	5-M	9,326	428
Northern State Univ, Aberdeen, SD 57401-7198	1901	$4,208 (S)	$3,306	5-M	3,083	111
North Georgia Coll & State Univ, Dahlonega, GA 30597-1001	1873	$2,824 (S)	$4,160	5-M	4,517	287
North Greenville Coll, Tigerville, SC 29688-1892	1892	$9,300	$5,280	2-B	1,615	131
North Park Univ, Chicago, IL 60625-4895	1891	$20,350	$6,510	2-D	2,181	121
Northwest Coll, Kirkland, WA 98083-0579	1934	$14,760	$6,450	2-M	1,161	80
Northwestern Coll, Orange City, IA 51041-1996	1882	$15,290	$4,350	2-B	1,285	121
Northwestern Coll, St. Paul, MN 55113-1598	1902	$18,370	$6,020	2-B	2,592	156
Northwestern Oklahoma State Univ, Alva, OK 73717-2799	1897	$2,728 (S)	$2,720	5-M	2,126	142
Northwestern State Univ of Louisiana, Natchitoches, LA 71497	1884	$3,006 (S)	$3,326	5-D	10,505	511
Northwestern Univ, Evanston, IL 60208	1851	$30,085	$9,393	1-D	16,266	1,078
Northwest Missouri State Univ, Maryville, MO 64468-6001	1905	$5,025 (S)	$5,042	5-M	6,514	247
Northwest Nazarene Univ, Nampa, ID 83686-5897	1913	$16,570	$4,630	2-M	1,565	98
Northwood Univ, Midland, MI 48640-2398	1959	$13,995	$6,270	1-M	3,770	75
Northwood Univ, Texas Cmps, Cedar Hill, TX 75104-1204	1966	$13,995	$5,910	1-B	1,117	33
Norwich Univ, Northfield, VT 05663	1819	$18,210	$6,722	1-M	2,707	272
Notre Dame de Namur Univ, Belmont, CA 94002-1908	1851	$21,500	$9,650	2-M	1,798	189
Nova Southeastern Univ, Fort Lauderdale, FL 33314-7796	1964	$15,220	$8,126	1-D	23,522	1,509
Nyack Coll, Nyack, NY 10960-3698	1882	$14,790	$7,250	2-F	2,814	233
Oakland City Univ, Oakland City, IN 47660-1099	1885	$12,920	$4,800	2-D	1,753	168
Oakland Univ, Rochester, MI 48309-4401	1957	$5,260 (S)	$5,540	5-D	16,575	786
Oakwood Coll, Huntsville, AL 35896	1896	$9,798	$4,620	2-B	1,778	161
Oberlin Coll, Oberlin, OH 44074	1833	$29,688	$7,250	1-M	2,898	292
Occidental Coll, Los Angeles, CA 90041-3314	1887	$28,306	$7,820	1-M	1,858	206
Oglethorpe Univ, Atlanta, GA 30319-2797	1835	$20,307	$6,550	1-M	1,029	80
Ohio Dominican Univ, Columbus, OH 43219-2099	1911	$18,000	$5,900	2-M	2,566	160
Ohio Northern Univ, Ada, OH 45810-1599	1871	$24,645	$6,030	2-F	3,451	275
The Ohio State Univ-Mansfield Cmps, Mansfield, OH 44906-1599	1958	$4,443 (S)	NA	5-M	1,640	82
The Ohio State Univ-Newark Cmps, Newark, OH 43055-1797	1957	$4,443 (S)	NA	5-M	2,148	124
The Ohio State Univ, Columbus, OH 43210	1870	$6,651 (S)	$6,429	5-D	50,731	3,657
The Ohio State Univ at Lima, Lima, OH 45804-3576	1960	$4,443 (S)	NA	5-M	1,338	83
The Ohio State Univ at Marion, Marion, OH 43302-5695	1958	$4,443 (S)	NA	5-M	1,567	106
Ohio Univ-Chillicothe, Chillicothe, OH 45601-0629	1946	$4,008 (S)	NA	5-M	2,000	106
Ohio Univ-Eastern, St. Clairsville, OH 43950-9724	1957	$4,008 (S)	NA	5-B	1,118	114
Ohio Univ-Lancaster, Lancaster, OH 43130-1097	1968	$4,008 (S)	NA	5-M	1,744	104
Ohio Univ-Southern Cmps, Ironton, OH 45638-2214	1956	$3,693 (S)	NA	5-M	1,746	155
Ohio Univ-Zanesville, Zanesville, OH 43701-2695	1946	$4,008 (S)	NA	5-M	1,826	130
Ohio Univ, Athens, OH 45701-2979	1804	$7,128 (S)	$7,320	5-D	20,394	1,163
Ohio Wesleyan Univ, Delaware, OH 43015	1842	$25,440	$7,110	2-B	1,929	188
Oklahoma Baptist Univ, Shawnee, OK 74804	1910	$11,580	$3,640	2-M	1,883	119

Name, address	Year Founded	Tuition & Fees	Rm. & Board	Control, Degree	Enroll- ment	Faculty
Oklahoma Christian Univ, Oklahoma City, OK 73136-1100	1950	$13,160	$4,820	2-M	1,684	153
Oklahoma City Univ, Oklahoma City, OK 73106-1402	1904	$14,030	$5,550	2-F	3,668	270
Oklahoma Panhandle State Univ, Goodwell, OK 73939-0430	1909	$2,970 (S)	$2,810	5-B	1,226	65
Oklahoma State Univ, Stillwater, OK 74078	1890	$3,665 (S)	$5,468	5-D	23,577	1,060
Old Dominion Univ, Norfolk, VA 23529	1930	$4,928 (S)	$5,513	5-D	20,802	896
Olivet Coll, Olivet, MI 49076-9701	1844	$15,941	$5,330	2-M	1,070	79
Olivet Nazarene Univ, Bourbonnais, IL 60914-2271	1907	$15,740	$5,800	2-M	4,314	123
Oral Roberts Univ, Tulsa, OK 74171-0001	1963	$13,970	$5,900	2-D	4,117	282
Oregon Health & Sci Univ, Portland, OR 97239-3098	1974	$7,071 (S)	NA	12-D	1,849	836
Oregon Inst of Tech, Klamath Falls, OR 97601-8801	1947	$4,443 (S)	$6,135	5-B	3,236	130
Oregon State Univ, Corvallis, OR 97331	1868	$4,869 (S)	$6,336	5-D	18,979	789
Otis Coll of Art & Design, Los Angeles, CA 90045-9785	1918	$23,420	NA	1-M	1,066	214
Otterbein Coll, Westerville, OH 43081	1847	$20,133	$5,952	2-M	3,031	249
Ouachita Baptist Univ, Arkadelphia, AR 71998-0001	1886	$15,170	$4,800	2-B	1,530	153
Our Lady of Holy Cross Coll, New Orleans, LA 70131-7399	1916	$5,890	NA	2-M	1,432	123
Our Lady of the Lake Coll, Baton Rouge, LA 70808 (4)	1990	$6,810	NA	2-B	1,807	134
Our Lady of the Lake Univ of San Antonio, San Antonio, TX 78207-4689	1895	$16,358	$5,230	2-D	3,245	310
Pace Univ, New York, NY 10038	1906	$21,104	$7,650	1-D	13,962	1,138
Pacific Lutheran Univ, Tacoma, WA 98447	1890	$19,610	$6,105	2-M	3,462	304
Pacific Union Coll, Angwin, CA 94508-9707	1882	$17,355	$4,902	2-M	1,502	104
Pacific Univ, Forest Grove, OR 97116-1797	1849	$19,890	$5,540	1-D	2,420	140
Palm Beach Atlantic Univ, West Palm Beach, FL 33416-4708	1968	$14,890	$5,800	2-F	2,996	223
Palmer Coll of Chiropractic, Davenport, IA 52803-5287	1897	$5,325	NA	1-F	1,859	112
Park Univ, Parkville, MO 64152-3795	1875	$5,600	$5,180	1-M	11,868	805
Parsons Sch of Design, New Sch Univ, New York, NY 10011-8878	1896	$25,925	$10,810	1-M	2,958	759
Peirce Coll, Philadelphia, PA 19102-4699	1865	$11,800	NA	1-B	1,765	162
The Pennsylvania State Univ Abington Coll, Abington, PA 19001-3918	1950	$9,018 (S)	NA	12-B	3,202	217
The Pennsylvania State Univ Altoona Coll, Altoona, PA 16601-3760	1939	$9,304 (S)	$5,940	12-B	3,774	284
The Pennsylvania State Univ at Erie, The Behrend Coll, Erie, PA 16563-0001	1948	$9,304 (S)	$5,940	12-M	3,683	273
The Pennsylvania State Univ Berks Cmps of the Berks- Lehigh Valley Coll, Reading, PA 19610-6009	1924	$9,304 (S)	$6,490	12-B	2,428	180
The Pennsylvania State Univ Harrisburg Cmps of the Capital Coll, Middletown, PA 17057-4898	1966	$9,284 (S)	$7,290	12-D	3,441	258
The Pennsylvania State Univ Schuylkill Cmps of the Capital Coll, Schuylkill Haven, PA 17972-2208	1934	$9,008 (S)	$3,882	12-B	1,028	87
The Pennsylvania State Univ Univ Park Cmps, University Park, PA 16802-1503	1855	$9,706 (S)	$5,940	12-D	41,795	2,516
Pepperdine Univ, Malibu, CA 90263	1937	$28,720	$8,640	2-D	8,021	332
Peru State Coll, Peru, NE 68421	1867	$3,284 (S)	$4,911	5-M	1,671	123
Pfeiffer Univ, Misenheimer, NC 28109-0960	1885	$14,570	$5,830	2-M	2,027	134
Philadelphia Biblical Univ, Langhorne, PA 19047-2990	1913	$13,495	$5,855	2-F	1,397	144
Philadelphia Univ, Philadelphia, PA 19144-5497	1884	$20,022	$7,370	1-M	3,093	406
Piedmont Coll, Demorest, GA 30535-0010	1897	$13,500	$4,700	2-M	2,159	195
Pikeville Coll, Pikeville, KY 41501	1889	$9,900	$5,000	2-F	1,013	72
Pittsburg State Univ, Pittsburg, KS 66762	1903	$2,962 (S)	$4,166	5-M	6,731	NA
Plymouth State Univ, Plymouth, NH 03264-1595	1871	$6,240 (S)	$6,058	5-M	4,910	340
Point Loma Nazarene Univ, San Diego, CA 92106-2899	1902	$18,500	$6,380	2-M	3,170	272
Point Park Univ, Pittsburgh, PA 15222-1984	1960	$15,180	$6,660	1-M	3,226	343
Polytechnic Univ, Brooklyn Cmps, Brooklyn, NY 11201-2990	1854	$25,772	$8,000	1-D	2,846	292
Polytechnic Univ of Puerto Rico, Hato Rey, PR 00919	1966	$5,370	NA	1-M	5,702	404
Pomona Coll, Claremont, CA 91711	1887	$27,150	$9,980	1-B	1,555	212
Pontifical Catholic Univ of Puerto Rico, Ponce, PR 00717-0777	1948	$4,618	$2,840	2-D	7,468	234
Portland State Univ, Portland, OR 97207-0751	1946	$4,278 (S)	$8,175	5-D	23,117	1,138
Prairie View A&M Univ, Prairie View, TX 77446-0519	1878	$3,592 (S)	$5,826	5-D	7,808	387
Pratt Inst, Brooklyn, NY 11205-3899	1887	$25,680	$8,320	1-F	4,444	802
Presbyterian Coll, Clinton, SC 29325	1880	$20,110	$5,811	2-B	1,175	111
Princeton Univ, Princeton, NJ 08544-1019	1746	$29,910	$8,387	1-D	6,849	1,015
Providence Coll, Providence, RI 02918	1917	$22,104	$8,500	2-M	5,258	337
Purchase Coll, State Univ of New York, Purchase, NY 10577-1400	1967	$5,536 (S)	$7,122	5-M	4,063	332
Purdue Univ, West Lafayette, IN 47907	1869	$5,860 (S)	$6,700	5-D	38,847	1,977
Purdue Univ Calumet, Hammond, IN 46323-2094	1951	$4,826 (S)	NA	5-M	9,128	295
Purdue Univ North Central, Westville, IN 46391-9542	1967	$4,712 (S)	NA	5-M	3,467	244
Queens Coll of the City Univ of New York, Flushing, NY 11367-1597	1937	$4,361 (S)	NA	11-M	16,993	1,190
Queens Univ of Charlotte, Charlotte, NC 28274-0002	1857	$17,008	$6,190	2-M	1,964	113
Quincy Univ, Quincy, IL 62301-2699	1860	$16,850	$6,735	2-M	1,269	115
Quinnipiac Univ, Hamden, CT 06518-1940	1929	$22,500	$9,900	1-F	7,121	731
Radford Univ, Radford, VA 24142	1910	$4,140 (S)	$5,660	5-M	9,219	522
Ramapo Coll of New Jersey, Mahwah, NJ 07430-1680	1969	$7,411 (S)	$7,792	5-M	5,631	386
Randolph-Macon Coll, Ashland, VA 23005-5505	1830	$21,160	$6,030	2-B	1,118	134
Reed Coll, Portland, OR 97202-8199	1908	$29,200	$7,750	1-M	1,340	133
Regis Coll, Weston, MA 02493 (3)	1927	$19,910	$9,090	2-M	1,083	126
Regis Univ, Denver, CO 80221-1099	1877	$20,900	$7,600	2-M	1,268	1,225
Reinhardt Coll, Waleska, GA 30183-2981	1883	$12,200	$5,762	2-B	1,308	115
Rensselaer Polytechnic Inst, Troy, NY 12180-3590	1824	$28,496	$9,083	1-D	8,265	479
Rhode Island Coll, Providence, RI 02908-1991	1854	$4,270 (S)	$6,650	5-D	8,923	628
Rhode Island Sch of Design, Providence, RI 02903-2784	1877	$26,665	$7,370	1-F	2,294	502
Rhodes Coll, Memphis, TN 38112-1690	1848	$24,278	$6,638	2-M	1,560	173
Rice Univ, Houston, TX 77251-1892	1912	$19,670	$7,880	1-D	4,959	802
The Richard Stockton Coll of New Jersey, Pomona, NJ 08240-0195	1969	$6,224 (S)	$6,748	5-M	6,881	458
Rider Univ, Lawrenceville, NJ 08648-3001	1865	$21,050	$8,060	1-M	5,509	490
Rivier Coll, Nashua, NH 03060-5086	1933	$18,450	$7,092	2-M	2,317	171
Roanoke Coll, Salem, VA 24153-3794	1842	$20,865	$6,528	2-B	1,899	166
Robert Morris Coll, Chicago, IL 60605	1913	$14,250	NA	1-B	5,139	365
Robert Morris Univ, Moon Township, PA 15108-1189	1921	$13,484	$6,954	1-D	4,816	342
Roberts Wesleyan Coll, Rochester, NY 14624-1997	1866	$16,752	$6,200	2-M	1,843	196
Rochester Coll, Rochester Hills, MI 48307-2764	1959	$11,094	$5,624	2-B	1,001	106
Rochester Inst of Tech, Rochester, NY 14623-5603	1829	$21,384	$7,833	1-D	14,685	1,145
Rockford Coll, Rockford, IL 61108-2393	1847	$21,200	NA	1-M	1,280	162
Rockhurst Univ, Kansas City, MO 64110-2561	1910	$17,410	$5,750	2-M	2,764	208
Rogers State Univ, Claremore, OK 74017-3252	1909	$2,170 (S)	$5,481	5-B	3,300	151
Roger Williams Univ, Bristol, RI 02809	1956	$20,840	$9,456	1-F	4,918	435

Name, address	Year Founded	Tuition & Fees	Rm. & Board	Control, Degree	Enroll-ment	Faculty
Rollins Coll, Winter Park, FL 32789-4499	1885	$26,250	$8,050	1-M	2,565	NA
Roosevelt Univ, Chicago, IL 60605-1394	1945	$15,430	$7,150	1-D	7,524	662
Rose-Hulman Inst of Tech, Terre Haute, IN 47803-3999 (2)	1874	$24,705	$6,720	1-M	1,864	145
Rosemont Coll, Rosemont, PA 19010-1699 (3)	1921	$19,470	$8,400	2-M	1,069	157
Rowan Univ, Glassboro, NJ 08028-1701	1923	$7,222 (S)	$7,394	5-D	9,667	780
Rush Univ, Chicago, IL 60612-3832	1969	$15,600	$11,970	1-D	1,252	796
Rutgers, The State Univ of New Jersey, Camden, Camden, NJ 08102-1401	1927	$7,756 (S)	$7,552	5-F	5,485	378
Rutgers, The State Univ of New Jersey, Newark, Newark, NJ 07102	1892	$7,580 (S)	$8,140	5-D	10,465	605
Rutgers, The State Univ of New Jersey, New Brunswick/ Piscataway, New Brunswick, NJ 08901-1281	1766	$7,927 (S)	$7,711	5-D	35,318	2,164
Sacred Heart Univ, Fairfield, CT 06825-1000	1963	$20,268	$8,910	2-M	5,781	457
Saginaw Valley State Univ, University Center, MI 48710	1963	$5,410 (S)	$5,645	5-M	9,168	243
St Ambrose Univ, Davenport, IA 52803-2898	1882	$17,565	$6,635	2-D	3,447	293
St Anselm Coll, Manchester, NH 03102-1310	1889	$23,710	$8,580	2-B	2,008	170
St Augustine Coll, Chicago, IL 60640-3501	1980	$7,128	NA	1-B	1,710	159
St Augustine's Coll, Raleigh, NC 27604-2298	1867	$9,530	$4,960	2-B	1,635	121
St Bonaventure Univ, St. Bonaventure, NY 14778-2284	1858	$17,925	$6,530	2-M	2,806	229
St Cloud State Univ, St. Cloud, MN 56301-4498	1869	$4,550 (S)	$3,812	5-M	15,925	793
St Edward's Univ, Austin, TX 78704-6489	1885	$14,710	$6,018	2-M	4,443	389
St Francis Coll, Brooklyn Heights, NY 11201-4398	1884	$10,880	NA	2-B	2,468	220
St Francis Univ, Loretto, PA 15940-0600	1847	$19,342	$7,346	2-M	1,945	117
St John Fisher Coll, Rochester, NY 14618-3597	1948	$17,450	$7,420	2-M	3,152	295
St John's Univ, Collegeville, MN 56321 (2)	1857	$20,685	$5,788	2-F	2,067	167
St John's Univ, Jamaica, NY 11439	1870	$20,080	$10,100	2-D	19,777	1,304
St Joseph Coll, West Hartford, CT 06117-2700 (3)	1932	$20,900	$8,785	2-M	1,836	86
St Joseph's Coll, New York, NY 11205-3688	1916	$11,297	NA	1-M	1,226	134
St Joseph's Coll, Suffolk Cmps, Patchogue, NY 11772-2399	1916	$11,297	NA	1-M	3,831	298
St Joseph's Univ, Philadelphia, PA 19131-1395	1851	$24,230	$9,400	2-D	7,565	514
St Lawrence Univ, Canton, NY 13617-1455	1856	$28,190	$7,755	1-M	2,277	203
St Leo Univ, Saint Leo, FL 33574-6665	1889	$13,570	$7,030	2-M	1,518	108
St Louis Univ, St. Louis, MO 63103-2097	1818	$22,218	$7,740	2-D	11,217	933
St Martin's Coll, Lacey, WA 98503-1297	1895	$18,950	$5,720	2-M	1,489	72
St Mary-of-the-Woods Coll, Saint Mary-of-the-Woods, IN 47876 (3)	1840	$17,030	$6,250	2-M	1,687	67
St Mary's Coll, Notre Dame, IN 46556 (3)	1844	$21,974	$7,289	2-B	1,475	186
St Mary's Coll of California, Moraga, CA 94575	1863	$23,775	$9,075	2-D	4,486	524
St Mary's Coll of Maryland, St. Mary's City, MD 20686-3001	1840	$9,680 (S)	$7,400	5-B	1,922	197
St Mary's Univ of Minnesota, Winona, MN 55987-1399	1912	$17,925	$5,450	2-D	4,996	553
St Mary's Univ of San Antonio, San Antonio, TX 78228-8507	1852	$17,756	$6,498	2-D	4,118	328
St Michael's Coll, Colchester, VT 05439	1904	$22,420	$7,680	2-M	2,473	200
St Norbert Coll, De Pere, WI 54115-2099	1898	$21,510	$5,980	2-M	2,155	164
St Olaf Coll, Northfield, MN 55057-1098	1874	$25,150	$5,800	2-B	2,994	334
St Peter's Coll, Jersey City, NJ 07306-5997	1872	$18,592	$7,800	2-M	3,300	NA
St Thomas Aquinas Coll, Sparkill, NY 10976	1952	$15,700	$8,590	1-M	2,394	132
St Thomas Univ, Miami Gardens, FL 33054-6459	1961	$16,200	$10,200	2-F	2,520	214
St Vincent Coll, Latrobe, PA 15650-2690	1846	$19,470	$6,060	2-M	1,508	138
St Xavier Univ, Chicago, IL 60655-3105	1847	$16,680	$6,464	2-M	5,566	339
Salem Coll, Winston-Salem, NC 27108-0548 (3)	1772	$15,715	$8,870	2-M	1,091	95
Salem State Coll, Salem, MA 01970-5353	1854	$5,038 (S)	$5,940	5-M	9,120	562
Salisbury Univ, Salisbury, MD 21801-6837	1925	$6,994 (S)	$6,900	5-M	6,816	498
Salve Regina Univ, Newport, RI 02840-4192	1934	$20,510	$8,700	2-D	2,357	277
Samford Univ, Birmingham, AL 35229-0002	1841	$13,154	$5,244	2-D	4,440	419
Sam Houston State Univ, Huntsville, TX 77341	1879	$3,652 (S)	$4,160	5-D	13,460	541
San Diego State Univ, San Diego, CA 92182	1897	$2,488 (S)	$8,787	5-D	33,676	1,684
San Francisco State Univ, San Francisco, CA 94132-1722	1899	$2,498 (S)	$8,090	5-D	29,686	1,646
San Jose State Univ, San Jose, CA 95192-0001	1857	$2,562 (S)	$8,465	5-M	28,932	1,685
Santa Clara Univ, Santa Clara, CA 95053	1851	$25,365	$9,336	2-D	7,794	695
Sarah Lawrence Coll, Bronxville, NY 10708-5999	1926	$30,824	$10,394	1-M	1,606	236
Savannah Coll of Art & Design, Savannah, GA 31402-3146	1978	$20,250	$8,330	1-M	6,207	331
Savannah State Univ, Savannah, GA 31404	1890	$2,830 (S)	$4,498	5-M	2,752	175
Sch of the Art Inst of Chicago, Chicago, IL 60603-3103	1866	$24,000	$7,300	1-M	2,728	468
Sch of Visual Arts, New York, NY 10010-3994	1947	$18,700	$10,000	3-M	3,365	848
Seattle Pacific Univ, Seattle, WA 98119-1997	1891	$19,158	$7,017	2-D	3,728	283
Seattle Univ, Seattle, WA 98122	1891	$20,070	$6,858	2-D	6,659	522
Seton Hall Univ, South Orange, NJ 07079-2697	1856	$21,580	$9,546	2-D	9,746	860
Seton Hill Univ, Greensburg, PA 15601	1883	$18,930	$6,000	2-M	1,679	140
Shawnee State Univ, Portsmouth, OH 45662-4344	1986	$4,734 (S)	$6,297	5-B	3,693	276
Shaw Univ, Raleigh, NC 27601-2399	1865	$9,178	$5,654	2-F	2,616	238
Shenandoah Univ, Winchester, VA 22601-5195	1875	$18,390	$6,800	2-D	2,851	320
Shepherd Univ, Shepherdstown, WV 25443-3210	1871	$3,270 (S)	$5,338	5-M	4,831	NA
Shippensburg Univ of Pennsylvania, Shippensburg, PA 17257-2299	1871	$5,746 (S)	$5,080	5-M	7,607	365
Siena Coll, Loudonville, NY 12211-1462	1937	$19,130	$7,575	2-B	3,379	324
Siena Heights Univ, Adrian, MI 49221-1796	1919	$15,520	$5,455	2-M	2,153	NA
Silver Lake Coll, Manitowoc, WI 54220-9319	1869	$14,350	$4,100	2-M	1,104	162
Simmons Coll, Boston, MA 02115 (3)	1899	$24,490	$9,820	1-D	4,121	456
Simpson Coll, Indianola, IA 50125-1297	1860	$18,097	$6,062	2-B	1,937	140
Simpson Coll & Grad Sch, Redding, CA 96003-8606	1921	$14,760	$5,740	2-M	1,175	80
Skidmore Coll, Saratoga Springs, NY 12866-1632	1903	$29,630	$8,300	1-M	2,584	201
Slippery Rock Univ of Pennsylvania, Slippery Rock, PA 16057-1383	1889	$5,801 (S)	$4,542	5-D	7,789	388
Smith Coll, Northampton, MA 01063 (3)	1871	$27,544	$9,490	1-D	3,159	305
Sojourner-Douglass Coll, Baltimore, MD 21205-1814 (4)	1980	$5,590	NA	1-M	1,124	136
Sonoma State Univ, Rohnert Park, CA 94928-3609	1960	$3,010 (S)	$7,411	5-M	8,371	590
South Carolina State Univ, Orangeburg, SC 29117-0001	1896	$5,755 (S)	$4,672	5-D	4,466	220
South Dakota Sch of Mines & Tech, Rapid City, SD 57701-3995	1885	$4,293 (S)	$3,561	5-D	2,454	133
South Dakota State Univ, Brookings, SD 57007	1881	$4,536 (S)	$3,586	5-D	10,642	638
Southeastern Coll of the Assemblies of God, Lakeland, FL 33801-6099	1935	$9,120	$5,329	2-B	1,675	97
Southeastern Louisiana Univ, Hammond, LA 70402	1925	$2,951 (S)	$3,840	5-M	15,662	715
Southeastern Oklahoma State Univ, Durant, OK 74701-0609	1909	$2,947 (S)	$3,200	5-M	4,203	223
Southeast Missouri State Univ, Cape Girardeau, MO 63701-4799	1873	$4,575 (S)	$5,450	5-M	9,570	524
Southern Adventist Univ, Collegedale, TN 37315-0370	1892	$13,410	$4,390	2-M	2,377	193
Southern Arkansas Univ-Magnolia, Magnolia, AR 71753	1909	$3,496 (S)	$3,460	5-M	3,008	199
Southern Connecticut State Univ, New Haven, CT 06515-1355	1893	$5,622 (S)	$7,019	5-D	12,143	726
Southern Illinois Univ Carbondale, Carbondale, IL 62901-4701	1869	$5,981 (S)	$5,200	5-D	21,387	1,116

Name, address	Year Founded	Tuition & Fees	Rm. & Board	Control, Degree	Enrollment	Faculty
Southern Illinois Univ Edwardsville, Edwardsville, IL 62026-0001	1957	$4,183 (S)	$5,364	5-F	13,295	763
Southern Methodist Univ, Dallas, TX 75275	1911	$25,358	$8,852	2-D	11,161	887
Southern Nazarene Univ, Bethany, OK 73008	1899	$12,834	$5,110	2-M	2,199	204
Southern New Hampshire Univ, Manchester, NH 03106-1045.	1932	$19,314	$7,866	1-D	5,584	265
Southern Oregon Univ, Ashland, OR 97520	1926	$4,153 (S)	$6,039	5-M	5,506	337
Southern Polytechnic State Univ, Marietta, GA 30060-2896	1948	$2,754 (S)	$4,866	5-M	3,768	228
Southern Univ & Agr & Mech Coll, Baton Rouge, LA 70813.	1880	$3,066 (S)	$4,306	5-D	8,884	551
Southern Univ at New Orleans, New Orleans, LA 70126-1009	1959	$2,828 (S)	NA	5-M	5,000	NA
Southern Utah Univ, Cedar City, UT 84720-2498.	1897	$2,794 (S)	$5,400	5-M	6,048	252
Southern Wesleyan Univ, Central, SC 29630-1020	1906	$14,100	$4,935	2-M	2,430	236
Southwest Baptist Univ, Bolivar, MO 65613-2597	1878	$12,332	$3,888	2-M	3,563	295
Southwestern Adventist Univ, Keene, TX 76059	1894	$11,156	$5,270	2-M	1,191	92
Southwestern Assemblies of God Univ, Waxahachie, TX 75165-2397	1927	$8,430	$4,470	2-M	1,676	95
Southwestern Coll, Winfield, KS 67156-2499	1885	$15,349	$5,098	2-M	1,405	173
Southwestern Oklahoma State Univ, Weatherford, OK 73096-3098	1901	$2,758 (S)	$2,910	5-F	4,741	229
Southwestern Univ, Georgetown, TX 78626	1840	$18,870	$6,540	2-B	1,265	165
Southwest Minnesota State Univ, Marshall, MN 56258-1598.	1963	$4,615 (S)	$4,491	5-M	5,636	159
Southwest Missouri State Univ, Springfield, MO 65804-0094	1905	$4,636 (S)	$4,282	5-M	18,930	1,000
Spalding Univ, Louisville, KY 40203-2188	1814	$13,990	$5,334	2-D	1,702	213
Spelman Coll, Atlanta, GA 30314-4399 (3).	1881	$14,125	$7,625	1-B	2,063	227
Spring Arbor Univ, Spring Arbor, MI 49283-9799	1873	$14,916	$5,290	2-M	3,531	118
Springfield Coll, Springfield, MA 01109-3797	1885	$19,610	$7,520	1-D	3,119	346
Spring Hill Coll, Mobile, AL 36608-1791	1830	$19,000	$6,868	2-M	1,479	138
Stanford Univ, Stanford, CA 94305-9991	1891	$29,847	$9,500	1-D	17,823	1,749
State Univ of New York at Binghamton, Binghamton, NY 13902-6000	1946	$5,687 (S)	$7,100	5-D	13,385	704
State Univ of New York at New Paltz, New Paltz, NY 12561	1828	$5,145 (S)	$6,420	5-M	7,908	689
State Univ of New York at Oswego, Oswego, NY 13126	1861	$5,176 (S)	$7,540	5-M	8,465	528
State Univ of New York at Plattsburgh, Plattsburgh, NY 12901-2681	1889	$5,200 (S)	$6,448	5-M	6,047	434
State Univ of New York Coll at Brockport, Brockport, NY 14420-2997	1867	$5,221 (S)	$6,890	5-M	8,742	555
State Univ of New York Coll at Cortland, Cortland, NY 13045	1868	$5,235 (S)	$6,860	5-M	7,337	512
State Univ of New York Coll at Fredonia, Fredonia, NY 14063-1136	1826	$5,362 (S)	$6,120	5-M	5,260	432
State Univ of New York Coll at Geneseo, Geneseo, NY 14454-1401	1871	$5,390 (S)	$6,750	5-M	5,550	349
State Univ of New York Coll at Old Westbury, Old Westbury, NY 11568-0210.	1965	$5,041 (S)	$7,749	5-B	3,227	214
State Univ of New York Coll at Oneonta, Oneonta, NY 13820-4015	1889	$5,256 (S)	$6,458	5-M	5,724	426
State Univ of New York Coll at Potsdam, Potsdam, NY 13676	1816	$5,190 (S)	$6,970	5-M	4,307	362
State Univ of New York Coll of Agr & Tech at Cobleskill, Cobleskill, NY 12043	1916	$5,261 (S)	$6,880	5-B	2,443	163
State Univ of New York Coll of Envir Sci & For, Syracuse, NY 13210-2779	1911	$4,991 (S)	$9,790	5-D	2,016	147
State Univ of New York Empire State Coll, Saratoga Springs, NY 12866-4391	1971	$4,714 (S)	NA	5-M	10,252	487
State Univ of New York Inst of Tech, Utica, NY 13504-3050	1966	$5,154 (S)	$6,800	5-M	2,682	170
State Univ of New York Maritime Coll, Throggs Neck, NY 10465-4198 (2).	1874	$5,850 (S)	$7,046	5-M	1,128	82
State Univ of New York Upstate Med Univ, Syracuse, NY 13210-2334	1950	$4,850 (S)	$7,785	5-D	1,177	695
State Univ of West Georgia, Carrollton, GA 30118.	1933	$2,774 (S)	$4,406	5-D	10,255	477
Stephen F. Austin State Univ, Nacogdoches, TX 75962	1923	$2,639 (S)	$4,766	5-D	11,408	582
Stetson Univ, DeLand, FL 32723	1883	$22,380	$6,855	1-F	3,439	251
Stevens Inst of Tech, Hoboken, NJ 07030	1870	$26,960	$8,500	1-D	4,548	300
Stillman Coll, Tuscaloosa, AL 35403-9990	1876	$8,718	$4,200	2-B	1,458	86
Stonehill Coll, Easton, MA 02357-5510	1948	$21,302	$9,450	2-M	2,582	239
Stony Brook Univ, State Univ of New York, Stony Brook, NY 11794	1957	$5,316 (S)	$7,458	5-D	22,344	1,339
Strayer Univ, Washington, DC 20005-2603	1892	$9,841	NA	3-M	20,138	881
Suffolk Univ, Boston, MA 02108-2770	1906	$17,690	$10,290	1-D	7,804	632
Sullivan Univ, Louisville, KY 40205.	1864	$12,655	$3,690	3-M	4,928	136
Sul Ross State Univ, Alpine, TX 79832.	1920	$3,402 (S)	$3,850	5-M	1,954	133
Susquehanna Univ, Selinsgrove, PA 17870	1858	$23,480	$6,510	2-B	2,009	186
Swarthmore Coll, Swarthmore, PA 19081-1397	1864	$28,802	$8,914	1-B	1,500	203
Syracuse Univ, Syracuse, NY 13244-0003.	1870	$24,830	$9,590	1-D	15,598	1,362
Tarleton State Univ, Stephenville, TX 76402	1899	$3,505 (S)	$4,804	5-D	8,845	471
Taylor Univ, Upland, IN 46989-1001.	1846	$18,528	$5,292	2-M	1,843	162
Teikyo Post Univ, Waterbury, CT 06723-2540	1890	$17,500	$7,375	1-B	1,325	85
Temple Univ, Philadelphia, PA 19122-6096	1884	$8,594 (S)	$7,276	12-D	32,877	2,361
Tennessee State Univ, Nashville, TN 37209-1561	1912	$3,818 (S)	$4,270	5-D	9,024	578
Tennessee Tech Univ, Cookeville, TN 38505.	1915	$3,778 (S)	$5,092	5-D	9,107	509
Texas A&M Intl Univ, Laredo, TX 78041-1900	1969	$3,833 (S)	$5,240	5-D	4,078	252
Texas A&M Univ-Comm, Commerce, TX 75429-3011	1889	$4,578 (S)	$5,004	5-D	8,359	488
Texas A&M Univ-Corpus Christi, Corpus Christi, TX 78412-5503	1947	$3,833 (S)	$7,688	5-D	7,860	386
Texas A&M Univ-Kingsville, Kingsville, TX 78363	1925	$3,846 (S)	$3,966	5-D	6,840	412
Texas A&M Univ-Texarkana, Texarkana, TX 75505-5518	1971	$2,100 (S)	NA	5-M	1,480	98
Texas A&M Univ, College Station, TX 77843	1876	$5,051 (S)	$6,030	5-D	44,813	2,276
Texas A&M Univ at Galveston, Galveston, TX 77553-1675	1962	$3,698 (S)	$4,870	5-M	1,620	154
Texas Christian Univ, Fort Worth, TX 76129-0002	1873	$17,630	$5,780	2-D	8,275	703
Texas Lutheran Univ, Seguin, TX 78155-5999.	1891	$15,590	$4,780	2-B	1,410	118
Texas Southern Univ, Houston, TX 77004-4584	1947	$3,096 (S)	$5,824	5-D	10,891	511
Texas State Univ-San Marcos, San Marcos, TX 78666	1899	$4,010 (S)	$5,310	5-D	26,306	1,098
Texas Tech Univ, Lubbock, TX 79409	1923	$4,745 (S)	$6,023	5-D	28,549	1,070
Texas Wesleyan Univ, Fort Worth, TX 76105-1536	1890	$11,960	$5,242	2-F	2,734	266
Texas Woman's Univ, Denton, TX 76201 (4)	1901	$2,964 (S)	$4,780	5-D	9,709	592
Thiel Coll, Greenville, PA 16125-2181	1866	$14,386	$6,584	2-B	1,261	114
Thomas Edison State Coll, Trenton, NJ 08608-1176	1972	$3,325 (S)	NA	5-M	10,233	NA
Thomas Jefferson Univ, Philadelphia, PA 19107	1824	$20,979	$6,669	1-M	2,332	221
Thomas More Coll, Crestview Hills, KY 41017-3495	1921	$16,000	$5,400	2-M	1,526	123
Tiffin Univ, Tiffin, OH 44883-2161.	1888	$14,290	$6,075	1-M	1,407	147
Touro Coll, New York, NY 10010	1971	$10,400	$5,000	1-D	11,447	999
Touro Univ Intl, Cypress, CA 90630	NR	$7,200	NA	1-D	1,748	89
Towson Univ, Towson, MD 21252-0001.	1866	$6,672 (S)	$6,468	5-D	17,188	1,282
Transylvania Univ, Lexington, KY 40508-1797.	1780	$17,660	$6,120	2-B	1,134	91
Trevecca Nazarene Univ, Nashville, TN 37210-2877.	1901	$12,792	$5,868	2-D	1,911	184
Trinity Christian Coll, Palos Heights, IL 60463-0929.	1959	$15,490	$6,000	2-B	1,263	124
Trinity Coll, Hartford, CT 06106-3100	1823	$30,230	$7,810	1-M	2,371	237
Trinity Coll, Washington, DC 20017-1094 (3)	1897	$16,860	$7,290	2-M	1,637	164

Name, address	Year Founded	Tuition & Fees	Rm. & Board	Control, Degree	Enroll-ment	Faculty
Trinity Intl Univ, Deerfield, IL 60015-1284	1897	$17,150	$5,830	2-D	2,863	155
Trinity Univ, San Antonio, TX 78212-7200	1869	$19,176	$7,290	2-M	2,633	295
Tri-State Univ, Angola, IN 46703-1764	1884	$18,000	$5,600	1-M	1,192	98
Troy State Univ, Troy, AL 36082	1887	$3,842 (S)	$4,580	5-M	8,031	498
Troy State Univ Dothan, Dothan, AL 36303	1961	$3,842 (S)	NA	5-M	1,899	121
Troy State Univ Montgomery, Montgomery, AL 36103-4419	1965	$3,600 (S)	NA	5-M	3,758	198
Truman State Univ, Kirksville, MO 63501-4221	1867	$4,656 (S)	$5,072	5-M	5,833	377
Tufts Univ, Medford, MA 02155	1852	$29,593	$8,640	1-D	9,509	889
Tulane Univ, New Orleans, LA 70118-5669	1834	$32,120	$7,641	1-D	12,443	1,095
Tusculum Coll, Greeneville, TN 37743-9997	1794	$14,410	$5,880	2-M	2,132	207
Tuskegee Univ, Tuskegee, AL 36088	1881	$11,310	$5,940	1-D	3,176	250
Union Coll, Barbourville, KY 40906-1499	1879	$13,200	$4,400	2-M	1,016	76
Union Coll, Schenectady, NY 12308-2311	1795	$28,928	$7,077	1-B	2,174	218
Union Inst & Univ, Cincinnati, OH 45206-1925	1969	$7,848	NA	1-D	2,910	240
Union Univ, Jackson, TN 38305-3697	1823	$15,350	$4,970	2-D	2,774	227
United States Air Force Acad, USAF Academy, CO 80840-5025 (2)	1954	$0 (C)	$0	4-B	4,157	531
United States Coast Guard Acad, New London, CT 06320-8100	1876	$0 (C)	$0	4-B	1,016	NA
United States Military Acad, West Point, NY 10996 (2)	1802	$0 (C)	$0	4-B	4,242	598
United States Naval Acad, Annapolis, MD 21402-5000 (2)	1845	$0 (C)	$0	4-B	4,335	598
Universidad del Este, Carolina, PR 00984-2010	1949	$4,498	NA	1-B	7,077	439
Universidad del Turabo, Turabo, PR 00778-3030	1972	$4,498	NA	1-M	8,065	410
Universidad Metropolitana, Río Piedras, PR 00928-1150	1980	$4,498	NA	1-M	5,857	358
Univ at Albany, State Univ of New York, Albany, NY 12222-0001	1844	$5,770 (S)	$7,181	5-D	16,998	937
Univ at Buffalo, The State Univ of New York, Buffalo, NY 14260	1846	$5,851 (S)	$6,816	5-D	27,255	1,711
The Univ of Akron, Akron, OH 44325-0001	1870	$7,510 (S)	$6,660	5-D	24,335	1,721
The Univ of Alabama, Tuscaloosa, AL 35487	1831	$4,134 (S)	$4,906	5-D	20,291	1,084
The Univ of Alabama at Birmingham, Birmingham, AL 35294	1969	$4,274 (S)	$2,588	5-D	16,357	881
The Univ of Alabama in Huntsville, Huntsville, AL 35899	1950	$4,126 (S)	$5,000	5-D	7,051	447
Univ of Alaska Anchorage, Anchorage, AK 99508-8060	1954	$2,656 (S)	$6,830	5-M	16,607	1,318
Univ of Alaska Fairbanks, Fairbanks, AK 99775-7520	1917	$4,165 (S)	$5,130	5-D	8,724	311
Univ of Alaska Southeast, Juneau, AK 99801	1972	$3,783 (S)	$5,320	5-M	3,268	240
The Univ of Arizona, Tucson, AZ 85721	1885	$3,603 (S)	$6,810	5-D	37,083	1,362
Univ of Arkansas, Fayetteville, AR 72701-1201	1871	$4,768 (S)	$5,087	5-D	16,405	839
Univ of Arkansas at Fort Smith, Fort Smith, AR 72913-3649	1928	$1,920 (A)	NA	11-B	6,395	332
Univ of Arkansas at Little Rock, Little Rock, AR 72204-1099	1927	$4,598 (S)	$2,700	5-D	11,757	749
Univ of Arkansas at Monticello, Monticello, AR 71656	1909	$3,385 (S)	$3,150	5-M	2,875	247
Univ of Arkansas at Pine Bluff, Pine Bluff, AR 71601-2799	1873	$3,687 (S)	$5,180	5-M	3,251	223
Univ of Arkansas for Med Sci, Little Rock, AR 72205-7199	1879	$3,288 (S)	$1,530	5-D	2,016	NA
Univ of Baltimore, Baltimore, MD 21201-5779	1925	$5,913 (S)	NA	5-D	4,937	306
Univ of Bridgeport, Bridgeport, CT 06601	1927	$17,924	$8,000	1-D	3,165	341
Univ of California, Berkeley, Berkeley, CA 94720-1500	1868	$5,250 (S)	$11,212	5-D	33,076	1,889
Univ of California, Davis, Davis, CA 95616	1905	$5,853 (S)	$9,143	5-D	30,229	1,950
Univ of California, Irvine, Irvine, CA 92697	1965	$6,165 (S)	$8,055	5-D	24,874	1,194
Univ of California, Los Angeles, Los Angeles, CA 90095	1919	$5,820 (S)	$10,452	5-D	38,598	2,462
Univ of California, Riverside, Riverside, CA 92521-0102	1954	$5,950 (S)	$9,350	5-D	17,302	816
Univ of California, San Diego, La Jolla, CA 92093	1959	$5,507 (S)	$8,620	5-D	24,707	1,092
Univ of California, Santa Barbara, Santa Barbara, CA 93106	1909	$5,639 (S)	$9,236	5-D	20,847	1,036
Univ of California, Santa Cruz, Santa Cruz, CA 95064	1965	$4,629 (S)	$10,314	5-D	14,997	717
Univ of Central Arkansas, Conway, AR 72035-0001	1907	$4,505 (S)	$3,786	5-D	9,516	542
Univ of Central Florida, Orlando, FL 32816	1963	$3,013 (S)	$7,026	5-D	41,102	1,628
Univ of Central Oklahoma, Edmond, OK 73034-5209	1890	$2,649 (S)	$3,670	5-M	15,246	773
Univ of Charleston, Charleston, WV 25304-1099	1888	$19,400	$7,200	1-M	1,018	99
Univ of Chicago, Chicago, IL 60637-1513	1891	$29,238	$9,315	1-D	13,887	1,934
Univ of Cincinnati, Cincinnati, OH 45221	1819	$7,623 (S)	$7,113	5-D	26,817	1,173
Univ of Colorado at Boulder, Boulder, CO 80309	1876	$4,020 (S)	$6,754	5-D	32,041	1,737
Univ of Colorado at Colorado Springs, Colorado Springs, CO 80918	1965	$5,156 (S)	$6,729	5-D	7,620	423
Univ of Colorado at Denver, Denver, CO 80217-3364	1912	$3,551 (S)	NA	5-D	15,596	916
Univ of Colorado Health Sci Ctr, Denver, CO 80262	1883	$6,110 (S)	NA	5-D	2,567	2,573
Univ of Connecticut, Storrs, CT 06269	1881	$7,308 (S)	$7,300	5-D	22,053	1,098
Univ of Dallas, Irving, TX 75062-4736	1955	$19,162	$6,736	2-D	3,157	215
Univ of Dayton, Dayton, OH 45469-1300	1850	$20,630	$6,300	2-D	10,284	822
Univ of Delaware, Newark, DE 19716	1743	$6,498 (S)	$6,118	12-D	20,501	1,371
Univ of Denver, Denver, CO 80208	1864	$26,610	$8,363	1-D	9,521	972
Univ of Detroit Mercy, Detroit, MI 48219-0900	1877	$20,970	$7,040	2-D	5,571	655
Univ of Dubuque, Dubuque, IA 52001-5099	1852	$16,260	$5,420	2-D	1,253	148
Univ of Evansville, Evansville, IN 47722-0002	1854	$19,230	$5,510	2-M	2,650	232
The Univ of Findlay, Findlay, OH 45840-3653	1882	$19,952	$7,062	2-M	4,712	336
Univ of Florida, Gainesville, FL 32611	1853	$2,780 (S)	$5,800	5-D	47,858	1,720
Univ of Georgia, Athens, GA 30602	1785	$4,078 (S)	$5,756	5-D	33,878	2,024
Univ of Guam, Mangilao, GU 96923	1952	NA	NA	7-M	3,748	230
Univ of Hartford, West Hartford, CT 06117-1599	1877	$22,470	$8,610	1-D	7,245	719
Univ of Hawaii at Hilo, Hilo, HI 96720-4091	1970	$2,538 (S)	$5,081	5-M	3,300	264
Univ of Hawaii at Manoa, Honolulu, HI 96822	1907	$3,561 (S)	$5,675	5-D	19,863	1,215
Univ of Houston-Clear Lake, Houston, TX 77058-1098	1971	$2,639 (S)	NA	5-M	7,776	444
Univ of Houston-Downtown, Houston, TX 77002-1001	1974	$3,164 (S)	NA	5-M	10,528	528
Univ of Houston-Victoria, Victoria, TX 77901-4450	1973	$3,060 (S)	NA	5-M	2,411	115
Univ of Houston, Houston, TX 77204	1927	$3,948 (S)	$5,870	5-D	35,066	1,513
Univ of Idaho, Moscow, ID 83844-2282	1889	$3,348 (S)	$4,868	5-D	12,894	585
Univ of Illinois at Chicago, Chicago, IL 60607-7128	1946	$7,860 (S)	$6,884	5-D	25,763	1,456
Univ of Illinois at Springfield, Springfield, IL 62703-5407	1969	$4,310 (S)	$7,000	5-D	4,569	300
Univ of Illinois at Urbana-Champaign, Champaign, IL 61820	1867	$9,384 (S)	$6,848	5-D	40,458	2,537
Univ of Indianapolis, Indianapolis, IN 46227-3697	1902	$17,200	$6,150	2-D	3,986	358
The Univ of Iowa, Iowa City, IA 52242-1316	1847	$5,396 (S)	$6,350	5-D	29,744	1,705
Univ of Kansas, Lawrence, KS 66045	1866	$4,101 (S)	$4,822	5-D	28,580	1,332
Univ of Kentucky, Lexington, KY 40506-0032	1865	$4,547 (S)	$4,285	5-D	25,397	1,725
Univ of La Verne, La Verne, CA 91750-4443	1891	$21,500	$8,510	1-D	3,604	263
Univ of Louisiana at Lafayette, Lafayette, LA 70504	1898	$2,700 (S)	$3,126	5-D	16,208	698
Univ of Louisiana at Monroe, Monroe, LA 71209-0001	1931	$2,910 (S)	$1,645	5-D	8,571	466
Univ of Louisville, Louisville, KY 40292-0001	1798	$4,344 (S)	$4,312	5-D	20,825	1,253
Univ of Maine, Orono, ME 04469	1865	$5,914 (S)	$6,166	5-D	11,222	726
The Univ of Maine at Augusta, Augusta, ME 04330-9410	1965	$4,395 (S)	NA	5-B	5,942	305
Univ of Maine at Farmington, Farmington, ME 04938-1990	1863	$4,872 (S)	$5,318	5-B	2,420	157
Univ of Maine at Machias, Machias, ME 04654-1321	1909	$4,121 (S)	$5,150	5-B	1,313	83

Name, address	Year Founded	Tuition & Fees	Rm. & Board	Control, Degree	Enroll- ment	Faculty
Univ of Maine at Presque Isle, Presque Isle, ME 04769-2888	1903	$4,190 (S)	$4,965	5-B	1,546	123
Univ of Mary, Bismarck, ND 58504-9652	1959	$10,290	$4,080	2-M	2,619	218
Univ of Mary Hardin-Baylor, Belton, TX 76513	1845	$11,540	$4,000	2-M	2,631	201
Univ of Maryland, Baltimore Cty, Baltimore, MD 21250	1963	$7,388 (S)	$7,007	5-D	11,872	702
Univ of Maryland, Coll Park, College Park, MD 20742	1856	$6,758 (S)	$7,608	5-D	35,262	2,097
Univ of Maryland Eastern Shore, Princess Anne, MD 21853-1299	1886	$5,105 (S)	$5,630	5-D	3,762	234
Univ of Maryland Univ Coll, Adelphi, MD 20783	1947	$5,328 (S)	NA	5-D	25,857	1,023
Univ of Massachusetts Amherst, Amherst, MA 01003	1863	$8,410 (S)	$5,748	5-D	24,310	1,277
Univ of Massachusetts Boston, Boston, MA 02125-3393	1964	$6,977 (S)	NA	5-D	12,394	831
Univ of Massachusetts Dartmouth, North Dartmouth, MA 02747-2300	1895	$6,129 (S)	$7,099	5-D	8,284	512
Univ of Massachusetts Lowell, Lowell, MA 01854-2881	1894	$6,213 (S)	$5,724	5-D	11,706	NA
The Univ of Memphis, Memphis, TN 38152	1912	$4,234 (S)	$4,690	5-D	19,911	1,435
Univ of Miami, Coral Gables, FL 33124	1925	$26,722	$8,323	1-D	15,235	1,194
Univ of Michigan-Dearborn, Dearborn, MI 48128-1491	1959	$5,946 (S)	NA	5-M	9,021	502
Univ of Michigan-Flint, Flint, MI 48502-1950	1956	$5,548 (S)	NA	5-F	6,152	367
Univ of Michigan, Ann Arbor, MI 48109	1817	$7,975 (S)	$6,704	5-D	39,031	2,835
Univ of Minnesota, Crookston, Crookston, MN 56716-5001	1966	$6,780 (S)	$4,684	5-B	2,320	100
Univ of Minnesota, Duluth, Duluth, MN 55812-2496	1947	$7,370 (S)	$5,100	5-F	10,114	467
Univ of Minnesota, Morris, Morris, MN 56267-2134	1959	$8,096 (S)	$4,800	5-B	1,861	132
Univ of Minnesota, Twin Cities Cmps, Minneapolis, MN 55455-0213	1851	$7,116 (S)	$6,044	5-D	49,474	3,079
Univ of Mississippi, University, MS 38677	1844	$3,916 (S)	$5,300	5-D	13,804	NA
Univ of Mississippi Med Ctr, Jackson, MS 39216-4505	1955	$3,078 (S)	$2,080	5-D	1,773	2,301
Univ of Missouri-Columbia, Columbia, MO 65211	1839	$6,558 (S)	$5,770	5-D	26,805	1,545
Univ of Missouri-Kansas City, Kansas City, MO 64110-2499	1929	$6,146 (S)	$7,270	5-D	14,226	910
Univ of Missouri-Rolla, Rolla, MO 65409-0910	1870	$6,839 (S)	$5,453	5-D	5,459	392
Univ of Missouri-St Louis, St. Louis, MO 63121-4499	1963	$6,866 (S)	$5,600	5-D	15,605	679
Univ of Mobile, Mobile, AL 36663-0220	1961	$9,520	$5,440	2-M	1,854	153
The Univ of Montana-Missoula, Missoula, MT 59812-0002	1893	$4,377 (S)	$5,432	5-D	13,352	658
The Univ of Montana-Western, Dillon, MT 59725-3598	1893	$3,780 (S)	$4,600	5-B	1,160	69
Univ of Montevallo, Montevallo, AL 35115	1896	$4,784 (S)	$3,638	5-M	3,121	188
Univ of Nebraska-Lincoln, Lincoln, NE 68588	1869	$4,711 (S)	$5,204	5-D	22,559	1,022
Univ of Nebraska at Kearney, Kearney, NE 68849-0001	1903	$3,885 (S)	$4,436	5-M	6,395	374
Univ of Nebraska at Omaha, Omaha, NE 68182	1908	$4,082 (S)	$3,998	5-D	13,997	781
Univ of Nebraska Med Ctr, Omaha, NE 68198	1869	$5,228 (S)	NA	5-D	2,865	883
Univ of Nevada, Las Vegas, Las Vegas, NV 89154-9900	1957	$3,006 (S)	$8,258	5-D	25,749	1,435
Univ of Nevada, Reno, Reno, NV 89557	1874	$91/credit (S)	NA	5-D	15,534	1,134
Univ of New England, Biddeford, ME 04005-9526	1831	$19,640	$7,560	1-F	3,192	217
Univ of New Hampshire, Durham, NH 03824	1866	$8,664 (S)	$6,234	5-D	14,431	694
Univ of New Hampshire at Manchester, Manchester, NH 03101-1113	1967	$6,047 (S)	NA	5-M	1,349	88
Univ of New Haven, West Haven, CT 06516-1916	1920	$20,735	$8,500	1-M	4,386	413
Univ of New Mexico, Albuquerque, NM 87131-2039	1889	$3,313 (S)	$5,910	5-D	25,686	1,372
Univ of New Orleans, New Orleans, LA 70148	1958	$3,234 (S)	$4,122	5-D	17,360	598
Univ of North Alabama, Florence, AL 35632-0001	1830	$3,458 (S)	$4,272	5-M	5,630	276
The Univ of North Carolina at Asheville, Asheville, NC 28804-3299	1927	$3,101 (S)	$4,978	5-M	3,446	309
The Univ of North Carolina at Chapel Hill, Chapel Hill, NC 27599	1789	$4,072 (S)	$6,045	5-D	26,359	1,408
The Univ of North Carolina at Charlotte, Charlotte, NC 28223-0001	1946	$3,105 (S)	$5,076	5-D	19,605	1,074
The Univ of North Carolina at Greensboro, Greensboro, NC 27412-5001	1891	$3,038 (S)	$4,760	5-D	14,328	947
The Univ of North Carolina at Pembroke, Pembroke, NC 28372-1510	1887	$2,565 (S)	$4,364	5-M	4,722	294
The Univ of North Carolina at Wilmington, Wilmington, NC 28403-3297	1947	$3,362 (S)	$5,578	5-D	10,929	650
Univ of North Dakota, Grand Forks, ND 58202	1883	$4,156 (S)	$4,234	5-D	13,034	897
Univ of Northern Colorado, Greeley, CO 80639	1890	$3,205 (S)	$5,782	5-D	13,204	547
Univ of Northern Iowa, Cedar Falls, IA 50614	1876	$4,916 (S)	$4,918	5-D	13,666	799
Univ of North Florida, Jacksonville, FL 32224-2645	1965	$2,913 (S)	$5,856	5-D	13,966	646
Univ of North Texas, Denton, TX 76203	1890	$3,782 (S)	$4,885	5-D	31,065	1,573
Univ of Notre Dame, Notre Dame, IN 46556	1842	$27,612	$6,930	2-D	11,415	NA
Univ of Oklahoma, Norman, OK 73019-0390	1890	$3,741 (S)	$5,485	5-D	24,483	1,191
Univ of Oklahoma Health Sci Ctr, Oklahoma City, OK 73190	1890	$3,057 (S)	NA	5-D	3,129	361
Univ of Oregon, Eugene, OR 97403	1872	$4,914 (S)	$6,981	5-D	19,992	1,131
Univ of Pennsylvania, Philadelphia, PA 19104	1740	$29,318	$8,642	1-D	19,428	1,879
Univ of Phoenix-Atlanta Cmps, Atlanta, GA 30350-4153	NR	$9,420	NA	3-D	1,096	41
Univ of Phoenix-Colorado Cmps, Lone Tree, CO 80124-5453	NR	$8,610	NA	3-D	2,905	827
Univ of Phoenix-Dallas Cmps, Dallas, TX 75251	2001	$9,360	NA	3-D	1,711	70
Univ of Phoenix-Fort Lauderdale Cmps, Fort Lauderdale, FL 33324-1393	NR	$8,850	NA	3-D	1,941	171
Univ of Phoenix-Hawaii Cmps, Honolulu, HI 96813-4317	NR	$11,070	NA	3-D	1,273	292
Univ of Phoenix-Houston Cmps, Houston, TX 77079-2004	2001	$9,360	NA	3-D	2,565	141
Univ of Phoenix-Jacksonville Cmps, Jacksonville, FL 32216-0959	1976	$8,850	NA	3-D	1,589	184
Univ of Phoenix-Louisiana Cmps, Metairie, LA 70001-2082	1976	$8,160	NA	3-D	1,855	239
Univ of Phoenix-Maryland Cmps, Columbia, MD 21045-5424	NR	$10,200	NA	3-D	1,704	153
Univ of Phoenix-Metro Detroit Cmps, Troy, MI 48098-2623	NR	$10,110	NA	3-D	3,102	653
Univ of Phoenix-Nevada Cmps, Las Vegas, NV 89106-3797	1994	$8,910	NA	3-D	3,170	495
Univ of Phoenix-New Mexico Cmps, Albuquerque, NM 87109-4645	NR	$8,550	NA	3-D	3,584	507
Univ of Phoenix-Northern California Cmps, Pleasanton, CA 94588-3677	NR	$12,150	NA	3-D	4,765	1,424
Univ of Phoenix-Oregon Cmps, Portland, OR 97223-8368	1976	$9,540	NA	3-D	1,514	355
Univ of Phoenix-Orlando Cmps, Maitland, FL 32751-7057	1996	$8,850	NA	3-D	1,225	243
Univ of Phoenix-Philadelphia Cmps, Wayne, PA 19087-2121	1999	$11,400	NA	3-D	1,002	80
Univ of Phoenix-Phoenix Cmps, Phoenix, AZ 85040-1958	1976	$8,760	NA	3-D	4,766	2,256
Univ of Phoenix-Puerto Rico Cmps, Guaynabo, PR 00970-3800	1995	$5,160	NA	3-D	1,427	115
Univ of Phoenix-Sacramento Cmps, Sacramento, CA 95833-3632	1993	$12,540	NA	3-D	2,192	608
Univ of Phoenix-St Louis Cmps, St. Louis, MO 63043-4828	2000	$10,500	NA	3-D	1,711	43
Univ of Phoenix-San Diego Cmps, San Diego, CA 92130-2092	1988	$11,760	NA	3-D	2,453	956
Univ of Phoenix-Southern Arizona Cmps, Tucson, AZ 85712-2732	1979	$8,490	NA	3-D	1,683	650
Univ of Phoenix-Southern California Cmps, Fountain Valley, CA 92708-6027	1980	$12,660	NA	3-D	7,757	2,890
Univ of Phoenix-Tampa Cmps, Tampa, FL 33637-1920	NR	$8,850	NA	3-D	1,434	209
Univ of Phoenix-Utah Cmps, Salt Lake City, UT 84123-4617	1984	$9,120	NA	3-D	2,001	629
Univ of Phoenix-Washington Cmps, Seattle, WA 98188-7500	1997	$9,900	NA	3-D	1,401	232
Univ of Phoenix Online Cmps, Phoenix, AZ 85034-7209	1989	$12,660	NA	3-D	45,827	4,363
Univ of Pittsburgh, Pittsburgh, PA 15260	1787	$9,274 (S)	$6,800	12-D	26,795	1,914
Univ of Pittsburgh at Bradford, Bradford, PA 16701-2812	1963	$9,264 (S)	$6,030	12-B	1,417	121
Univ of Pittsburgh at Greensburg, Greensburg, PA 15601-5860	1963	$9,214 (S)	$6,770	12-B	1,918	131
Univ of Pittsburgh at Johnstown, Johnstown, PA 15904-2990	1927	$9,256 (S)	$5,760	12-B	3,146	NA
Univ of Portland, Portland, OR 97203-5798	1901	$22,140	$6,670	2-M	3,263	275

Name, address	Year Founded	Tuition & Fees	Rm. & Board	Control, Degree	Enroll- ment	Faculty
Univ of Puerto Rico at Arecibo, Arecibo, PR 00614-4010	1967	$1,245 (A)	$5,240	6-B	4,617	274
Univ of Puerto Rico at Humacao, Humacao, PR 00791	1962	$1,090 (S)	NA	6-B	4,507	284
Univ of Puerto Rico at Ponce, Ponce, PR 00732-7186	1970	NA	NA	6-B	3,837	201
Univ of Puerto Rico at Utuado, Utuado, PR 00641-2500	1979	$1,315 (S)	NA	6-B	1,766	106
Univ of Puerto Rico, Cayey Univ Coll, Cayey, PR 00736	1967	$1,245 (A)	NA	6-B	3,987	219
Univ of Puerto Rico, Mayagüez Cmps, Mayagüez, PR 00681-9000	1911	NA	NA	6-D	12,414	761
Univ of Puerto Rico, Med Sci Cmps, San Juan, PR 00936-5067 (4)	1950	$1,620 (A)	NA	6-D	2,457	693
Univ of Puerto Rico, Río Piedras, San Juan, PR 00931	1903	$1,383 (S)	$4,940	6-D	21,666	1,793
Univ of Puget Sound, Tacoma, WA 98416	1888	$25,360	$6,400	1-F	2,760	259
Univ of Redlands, Redlands, CA 92373-0999	1907	$24,096	$8,478	1-M	2,311	275
Univ of Rhode Island, Kingston, RI 02881	1892	$6,202 (S)	$7,518	5-D	14,791	693
Univ of Richmond, University of Richmond, VA 23173	1830	$24,940	$5,160	1-F	3,626	366
Univ of Rio Grande, Rio Grande, OH 45674	1876	$10,034 (A)	$5,768	1-M	2,076	146
Univ of Rochester, Rochester, NY 14627-0250	1850	$27,573	$8,770	1-D	8,543	532
Univ of St Francis, Joliet, IL 60435-6169	1920	$16,840	$6,030	2-M	1,988	189
Univ of St Francis, Fort Wayne, IN 46808-3994	1890	$15,514	$5,450	2-M	1,834	211
Univ of St Thomas, St. Paul, MN 55105-1096	1885	$19,343	$6,484	2-D	11,037	800
Univ of St Thomas, Houston, TX 77006-4696	1947	$15,112	$6,840	2-D	4,875	271
Univ of San Diego, San Diego, CA 92110-2492	1949	$23,518	$9,630	2-D	7,262	683
Univ of San Francisco, San Francisco, CA 94117-1080	1855	$24,920	$9,780	2-D	8,159	767
Univ of Sci & Arts of Oklahoma, Chickasha, OK 73018	1908	$2,891 (S)	$3,530	5-B	1,449	91
The Univ of Scranton, Scranton, PA 18510	1888	$21,408	$9,335	2-D	4,679	396
Univ of Sioux Falls, Sioux Falls, SD 57105-1699	1883	$14,900	$4,200	2-D	1,485	128
Univ of South Alabama, Mobile, AL 36688-0002	1963	$3,770 (S)	$3,990	5-D	13,096	721
Univ of South Carolina, Columbia, SC 29208	1801	$5,748 (S)	$5,327	5-D	25,288	1,461
Univ of South Carolina Aiken, Aiken, SC 29801-6309	1961	$5,084 (S)	$4,400	5-M	3,350	232
Univ of South Carolina Beaufort, Beaufort, SC 29902-4601	1959	$4,208 (S)	NA	5	1,203	64
Univ of South Carolina Spartanburg, Spartanburg, SC 29303-4999	1967	$5,586 (S)	$4,310	5-M	4,507	340
The Univ of South Dakota, Vermillion, SD 57069-2390	1862	$4,205 (S)	$3,504	5-D	8,093	297
Univ of Southern California, Los Angeles, CA 90089	1880	$28,692	$8,632	1-D	31,606	2,341
Univ of Southern Indiana, Evansville, IN 47712-3590	1965	$3,885 (S)	$5,140	5-M	9,899	573
Univ of Southern Maine, Portland, ME 04104-9300	1878	$5,198 (S)	$6,014	5-D	11,007	611
Univ of Southern Mississippi, Hattiesburg, MS 39406-0001	1910	$3,874 (S)	$4,785	5-D	14,894	848
Univ of South Florida, Tampa, FL 33620-9951	1956	$2,983 (S)	$6,508	5-D	40,945	2,295
The Univ of Tampa, Tampa, FL 33606-1490	1931	$17,572	$6,410	1-M	4,661	364
The Univ of Tennessee, Knoxville, TN 37996	1794	$4,950 (S)	$5,110	5-D	27,281	1,534
The Univ of Tennessee at Chattanooga, Chattanooga, TN 37403-2598	1886	$3,852 (S)	$3,000	5-F	8,528	607
The Univ of Tennessee at Martin, Martin, TN 38238-1000	1900	$3,846 (S)	$3,800	5-M	5,810	402
The Univ of Texas-Pan Amer, Edinburg, TX 78541-2999	1927	$4,075 (S)	$3,488	5-D	15,914	713
The Univ of Texas at Arlington, Arlington, TX 76019	1895	$4,423 (S)	$4,829	5-D	24,979	1,034
The Univ of Texas at Austin, Austin, TX 78712-1111	1883	$4,548 (S)	$6,082	5-D	51,426	2,646
The Univ of Texas at Brownsville, Brownsville, TX 78520-4991	1973	$2,433 (S)	$6,276	5-M	7,018	553
The Univ of Texas at Dallas, Richardson, TX 75083-0688	1969	$5,493 (S)	$6,122	5-D	13,718	626
The Univ of Texas at El Paso, El Paso, TX 79968-0001	1913	$3,948 (S)	$2,835	5-D	18,542	883
The Univ of Texas at San Antonio, San Antonio, TX 78249-0617	1969	$4,319 (S)	$7,898	5-D	24,665	1,089
The Univ of Texas at Tyler, Tyler, TX 75799-0001	1971	$2,944 (S)	$3,240	5-M	4,764	265
The Univ of Texas Health Sci Ctr at San Antonio, San Antonio, TX 78229-3900	1976	$3,107 (S)	NA	5-D	2,754	1,372
The Univ of Texas of the Permian Basin, Odessa, TX 79762-0001	1969	$3,900 (S)	$4,176	5-M	2,695	158
The Univ of Texas Southwestern Med Ctr at Dallas, Dallas, TX 75390	1943	$2,820 (S)	NA	5-D	1,780	111
The Univ of the Arts, Philadelphia, PA 19102-4944	1870	$22,910	$5,800	1-M	2,142	434
Univ of the District of Columbia, Washington, DC 20008-1175	1976	$2,070 (S)	NA	9-M	5,241	360
Univ of the Incarnate Word, San Antonio, TX 78209-6397	1881	$16,082	$5,690	2-D	4,434	379
Univ of the Pacific, Stockton, CA 95211-0197	1851	$23,600	$7,490	1-D	6,121	627
Univ of the Sacred Heart, San Juan, PR 00914-0383	1935	$4,790	$1,900	2-M	5,210	338
Univ of the Sci in Philadelphia, Philadelphia, PA 19104-4495	1821	$20,958	$8,352	1-D	2,687	241
Univ of the South, Sewanee, TN 37383-1000	1857	$24,135	$6,720	2-D	1,485	172
Univ of the Virgin Islands, Charlotte Amalie, VI 00802-9990	1962	$2,986 (S)	$2,000	7-M	2,788	264
Univ of Toledo, Toledo, OH 43606-3390	1872	$6,414 (S)	$6,834	5-D	20,594	1,180
Univ of Tulsa, Tulsa, OK 74104-3189	1894	$15,736	$5,610	2-D	4,072	412
Univ of Utah, Salt Lake City, UT 84112-1107	1850	$3,647 (S)	$5,036	5-D	28,437	1,246
Univ of Vermont, Burlington, VT 05405	1791	$9,636 (S)	$6,680	5-D	10,967	678
Univ of Virginia, Charlottesville, VA 22903	1819	$6,149 (S)	$5,591	5-D	23,077	1,292
The Univ of Virginia's Coll at Wise, Wise, VA 24293	1954	$4,531 (S)	$5,586	5-B	1,703	124
Univ of Washington, Seattle, WA 98195	1861	$4,968 (S)	$6,726	5-D	39,246	3,383
The Univ of West Alabama, Livingston, AL 35470	1835	$3,710 (S)	$2,986	5-M	2,372	88
Univ of West Florida, Pensacola, FL 32514-5750	1963	$2,855 (S)	$6,000	5-D	9,452	479
Univ of Wisconsin-Eau Claire, Eau Claire, WI 54702-4004	1916	$4,313 (S)	$4,150	5-M	10,594	479
Univ of Wisconsin-Green Bay, Green Bay, WI 54311-7001	1968	$4,654 (S)	$4,500	5-M	5,420	274
Univ of Wisconsin-La Crosse, La Crosse, WI 54601-3742	1909	$4,741 (S)	$4,050	5-M	8,746	410
Univ of Wisconsin-Madison, Madison, WI 53706-1380	1848	$5,140 (S)	$6,130	5-D	41,588	2,225
Univ of Wisconsin-Milwaukee, Milwaukee, WI 53201-0413	1956	$5,107 (S)	$4,320	5-D	25,440	NA
Univ of Wisconsin-Oshkosh, Oshkosh, WI 54901	1871	$4,044 (S)	$4,100	5-M	11,155	575
Univ of Wisconsin-Parkside, Kenosha, WI 53141-2000	1968	$3,532 (S)	$5,056	5-M	5,072	282
Univ of Wisconsin-Platteville, Platteville, WI 53818-3099	1866	$4,254 (S)	$4,196	5-M	6,077	306
Univ of Wisconsin-River Falls, River Falls, WI 54022-5001	1874	$4,450 (S)	$3,968	5-M	5,893	337
Univ of Wisconsin-Stevens Point, Stevens Point, WI 54481-3897	1894	$4,148 (S)	$3,964	5-M	9,029	424
Univ of Wisconsin-Stout, Menomonie, WI 54751	1891	$5,680 (S)	$4,038	5-M	7,708	389
Univ of Wisconsin-Superior, Superior, WI 54880-4500	1893	$4,276 (S)	$4,246	5-F	2,874	198
Univ of Wisconsin-Whitewater, Whitewater, WI 53190-1790	1868	$4,934 (S)	$3,742	5-M	10,811	506
Univ of Wyoming, Laramie, WY 82070	1886	$3,090 (S)	$5,546	5-D	13,130	655
Urbana Univ, Urbana, OH 43078-2091	1850	$14,220	$5,680	1-M	1,527	115
Ursinus Coll, Collegeville, PA 19426-1000	1869	$27,500	$6,900	1-B	1,485	158
Ursuline Coll, Pepper Pike, OH 44124-4398 (3)	1871	$17,270	$5,458	2-M	1,409	185
Utah State Univ, Logan, UT 84322	1888	$3,141 (S)	$3,930	5-D	16,460	737
Utica Coll, Utica, NY 13502-4892	1946	$20,270	$8,070	1-M	2,465	223
Valdosta State Univ, Valdosta, GA 31698	1906	$2,860 (S)	$5,002	5-D	10,547	557
Valparaiso Univ, Valparaiso, IN 46383-6493	1859	$20,632	$5,480	2-F	3,850	344
Vanderbilt Univ, Nashville, TN 37240-1001	1873	$28,440	$9,457	1-D	11,092	NA
Vanguard Univ of Southern California, Costa Mesa, CA 92626-9601	1920	$16,358	$5,510	2-M	1,673	164
Vassar Coll, Poughkeepsie, NY 12604	1861	$29,540	$7,490	1-M	2,444	293
Vermont Tech Coll, Randolph Center, VT 05061-0500	1866	$6,844 (S)	$6,014	5-B	1,218	106
Villa Julie Coll, Stevenson, MD 21153	1952	$13,693	$4,700	1-M	2,710	272

Name, address	Year Founded	Tuition & Fees	Rm. & Board	Control, Degree	Enroll-ment	Faculty
Villanova Univ, Villanova, PA 19085-1699	1842	$26,223	$8,827	2-D	10,619	973
Virginia Coll at Birmingham, Birmingham, AL 35209	1989	$8,820	NA	3-B	2,407	201
Virginia Commonwealth Univ, Richmond, VA 23284-9005	1838	$5,138 (S)	$6,920	5-D	26,770	1,991
Virginia Intermont Coll, Bristol, VA 24201-4298	1884	$14,400	$5,400	2-B	1,147	152
Virginia Military Inst, Lexington, VA 24450 (2)	1839	$6,181 (S)	$5,266	5-B	1,333	148
Virginia Polytechnic Inst & State Univ, Blacksburg, VA 24061	1872	$5,095 (S)	$4,146	5-D	21,343	1,463
Virginia State Univ, Petersburg, VA 23806-0001	1882	$4,530 (S)	$6,008	5-D	4,933	285
Virginia Union Univ, Richmond, VA 23220-1170	1865	$12,205	$5,420	2-D	1,648	140
Virginia Wesleyan Coll, Norfolk, VA 23502-5599	1961	$19,200	$6,150	2-B	1,429	123
Viterbo Univ, La Crosse, WI 54601-4797	1890	$15,990	$5,220	2-M	2,549	169
Wagner Coll, Staten Island, NY 10301-4495	1883	$23,900	$7,500	1-M	2,218	188
Wake Forest Univ, Winston-Salem, NC 27109	1834	$28,310	$8,000	1-D	6,451	552
Walden Univ, Minneapolis, MN 55401	1970	NA	NA	3	NA	NA
Walla Walla Coll, College Place, WA 99324-1198	1892	$17,025	$3,855	2-M	1,917	201
Walsh Coll of Accountancy & Bus Admin, Troy, MI 48007-7006	1922	$7,400	NA	1-M	3,111	128
Walsh Univ, North Canton, OH 44720-3396	1958	$15,610	$7,700	2-M	1,801	196
Warner Southern Coll, Lake Wales, FL 33859	1968	$11,380	$5,271	2-M	1,198	120
Wartburg Coll, Waverly, IA 50677-0903	1852	$18,550	$5,180	2-B	1,775	162
Washburn Univ, Topeka, KS 66621	1865	NA	$4,860	10-F	7,002	497
Washington & Jefferson Coll, Washington, PA 15301-4801	1781	$23,260	$6,310	1-B	1,233	119
Washington & Lee Univ, Lexington, VA 24450-0303	1749	$23,295	$6,368	1-F	2,137	203
Washington Coll, Chestertown, MD 21620-1197	1782	$24,300	$5,740	1-M	1,481	143
Washington State Univ, Pullman, WA 99164	1890	$5,210 (S)	$6,054	5-D	22,712	1,289
Washington Univ in St Louis, St. Louis, MO 63130-4899	1853	$30,546	$9,640	1-D	13,020	1,100
Wayland Baptist Univ, Plainview, TX 79072-6998	1908	$8,500	$3,354	2-M	1,034	77
Waynesburg Coll, Waynesburg, PA 15370-1222	1849	$13,850	$5,520	2-M	1,887	122
Wayne State Coll, Wayne, NE 68787	1910	$3,432 (S)	$3,920	5-M	3,317	191
Wayne State Univ, Detroit, MI 48202	1868	$5,190 (S)	$6,500	5-D	33,091	1,805
Weber State Univ, Ogden, UT 84408-1001	1889	$3,134 (S)	$5,313	5-M	18,821	802
Webster Univ, St. Louis, MO 63119-3194	1915	$15,480	$6,368	1-D	7,250	842
Wellesley Coll, Wellesley, MA 02481 (3)	1870	$27,724	$8,612	1-B	2,312	320
Wentworth Inst of Tech, Boston, MA 02115-5998	1904	$15,000	$8,200	1-B	3,273	239
Wesleyan Univ, Middletown, CT 06459-0260	1831	$29,998	$8,226	1-D	3,221	362
Wesley Coll, Dover, DE 19901-3875	1873	$14,364	$6,480	2-M	2,167	101
West Chester Univ of Pennsylvania, West Chester, PA 19383	1871	$4,598 (S)	$5,642	5-M	12,695	762
Western Carolina Univ, Cullowhee, NC 28723	1889	$2,806 (S)	$3,826	5-D	7,561	537
Western Connecticut State Univ, Danbury, CT 06810-6885	1903	$5,044 (S)	$6,580	5-M	6,079	443
Western Illinois Univ, Macomb, IL 61455-1390	1899	$5,402 (S)	$5,366	5-M	13,469	685
Western Intl Univ, Phoenix, AZ 85021-2718	1978	$9,180	NA	3-M	3,751	243
Western Kentucky Univ, Bowling Green, KY 42101-3576	1906	$169/cr. hr. (S)	NA	5-M	18,380	1,159
Western Michigan Univ, Kalamazoo, MI 49008-5202	1903	$5,536 (S)	$6,496	5-D	29,178	1,189
Western New England Coll, Springfield, MA 01119-2654	1919	$20,824	$8,100	1-F	4,448	339
Western New Mexico Univ, Silver City, NM 88062-0680	1893	$2,451 (S)	$4,280	5-M	3,074	145
Western Oregon Univ, Monmouth, OR 97361-1394	1856	$4,305 (S)	$5,976	5-M	5,032	323
Western State Coll of Colorado, Gunnison, CO 81231	1901	$2,564 (S)	$5,680	5-B	2,385	120
Western Washington Univ, Bellingham, WA 98225-5996	1893	$4,182 (S)	$5,945	5-M	13,845	618
Westfield State Coll, Westfield, MA 01086	1838	$4,557 (S)	$5,290	5-M	4,938	280
West Liberty State Coll, West Liberty, WV 26074	1837	$3,138 (S)	$4,730	5-B	2,511	158
Westminster Coll, New Wilmington, PA 16172-0001	1852	$21,470	$6,360	2-M	1,577	147
Westminster Coll, Salt Lake City, UT 84105-3697	1875	$16,994	$5,300	1-M	2,498	253
Westmont Coll, Santa Barbara, CA 93108-1099	1937	$24,890	$8,390	2-B	1,343	139
West Texas A&M Univ, Canyon, TX 79016-0001	1909	$3,227 (S)	$4,342	5-D	7,023	294
West Virginia State Coll, Institute, WV 25112-1000	1891	$2,814 (S)	$4,400	5-M	4,992	282
West Virginia Univ, Morgantown, WV 26506	1867	$3,548 (S)	$5,822	5-D	24,260	1,061
West Virginia Univ Inst of Tech, Montgomery, WV 25136	1895	$3,488 (S)	$4,832	5-M	2,468	176
West Virginia Wesleyan Coll, Buckhannon, WV 26201	1890	$20,450	$5,200	2-M	1,621	150
Wheaton Coll, Wheaton, IL 60187-5593	1860	$20,000	$6,466	2-D	2,944	279
Wheaton Coll, Norton, MA 02766	1834	$28,900	$7,430	1-B	1,565	162
Wheeling Jesuit Univ, Wheeling, WV 26003-6295	1954	$20,340	$6,305	2-D	1,650	86
Whitman Coll, Walla Walla, WA 99362-2083	1859	$25,626	$6,900	1-B	1,454	185
Whittier Coll, Whittier, CA 90608-0634	1887	$23,492	$7,588	1-F	2,170	133
Whitworth Coll, Spokane, WA 99251-0001	1890	$20,078	$6,350	2-M	2,298	NA
Wichita State Univ, Wichita, KS 67260	1895	$3,506 (S)	$4,620	5-D	14,896	540
Widener Univ, Chester, PA 19013-5792	1821	$21,500	$8,795	1-D	5,821	398
Wilberforce Univ, Wilberforce, OH 45384	1856	$10,770	$5,320	2-B	1,180	74
Wilkes Univ, Wilkes-Barre, PA 18766-0002	1933	$19,630	$8,430	1-F	4,390	NA
Willamette Univ, Salem, OR 97301-3931	1842	$25,462	$6,600	2-F	2,590	269
William Carey Coll, Hattiesburg, MS 39401-5499	1906	$7,815	$3,390	2-M	2,586	193
William Jewell Coll, Liberty, MO 64068-1843	1849	$16,500	$4,820	2-B	1,274	134
William Paterson Univ of New Jersey, Wayne, NJ 07470-8420	1855	$7,120 (S)	$7,630	5-M	11,210	972
William Penn Univ, Oskaloosa, IA 52577-1799	1873	$14,604	$4,746	2-B	1,499	52
Williams Coll, Williamstown, MA 01267	1793	$28,090	$7,660	1-M	2,102	278
William Woods Univ, Fulton, MO 65251-1098	1870	$14,420	$5,700	2-M	2,670	92
Wilmington Coll, New Castle, DE 19720-6491	1967	$6,980	NA	1-D	6,954	473
Wilmington Coll, Wilmington, OH 45177	1870	$17,682	$6,490	2-M	1,262	131
Wingate Univ, Wingate, NC 28174-0159	1896	$16,000	$6,200	2-F	1,495	122
Winona State Univ, Winona, MN 55987-5838	1858	$4,800 (S)	$4,640	5-M	8,236	357
Winston-Salem State Univ, Winston-Salem, NC 27110-0003	1892	$2,394 (S)	$5,306	5-M	4,102	333
Winthrop Univ, Rock Hill, SC 29733	1886	$6,672 (S)	$4,630	5-M	6,558	486
Wittenberg Univ, Springfield, OH 45501-0720	1845	$26,196	$6,686	2-M	2,189	200
Wofford Coll, Spartanburg, SC 29303-3663	1854	$20,610	$6,100	2-B	1,132	110
Woodbury Univ, Burbank, CA 91504-1099	1884	$20,310	$7,183	1-M	1,404	206
Worcester Polytechnic Inst, Worcester, MA 01609-2280	1865	$28,620	$8,984	1-D	3,789	338
Worcester State Coll, Worcester, MA 01602-2597	1874	$4,123 (S)	$5,500	5-M	5,470	369
Wright State Univ, Dayton, OH 45435	1964	$5,892 (S)	$6,019	5-D	15,694	864
Xavier Univ, Cincinnati, OH 45207	1831	$19,150	$8,000	2-D	6,626	591
Xavier Univ of Louisiana, New Orleans, LA 70125-1098	1925	$11,400	$6,200	2-F	3,913	284
Yale Univ, New Haven, CT 06520	1701	$28,400	$8,600	1-D	11,471	1,389
Yeshiva Univ, New York, NY 10033-3201	1886	$22,240	$6,980	1-D	5,998	NA
York Coll of Pennsylvania, York, PA 17405-7199	1787	$8,550	$5,950	1-M	5,515	404
York Coll of the City Univ of New York, Jamaica, NY 11451-0001	1967	$4,242 (S)	NA	11-B	5,672	400
Youngstown State Univ, Youngstown, OH 44555-0001	1908	$5,478 (S)	$5,700	5-D	12,850	951

LANGUAGE

New Words in English

The following words and definitions were provided by Merriam-Webster Inc., publishers of *Merriam-Webster's Collegiate Dictionary, Eleventh Edition,* released in 2003. The words or meanings are among those that the Merriam-Webster editors decided had achieved enough currency in English to be added to this latest revision of the dictionary. (See also the glossary in the Science and Technology and Computers and the Internet chapters for some other new words.)

assisted living a system of housing and limited care that is designed for senior citizens who need some assistance with daily activities but do not require care in a nursing home

barista a person who makes and serves coffee (as espresso) to the public

bioinformatics the collection, classification, storage, and analysis of biochemical and biological information using computers, especially as applied to molecular genetics and genomics

body wrap a body treatment involving the application of usually oils or gels followed by a wrapping of the body with a sheet

bruschetta thick slices of bread grilled, rubbed with garlic, drizzled with olive oil, often topped with tomatoes and herbs, and usually served as an appetizer

chin music 1: idle talk **2**: a usually high inside pitch intended to intimidate the batter

clafouti a dessert consisting of a layer of fruit (as cherries) topped with batter and baked

digital subscriber line (DSL) a high-speed communications connection used for accessing the Internet and carrying short-range transmissions over ordinary telephone lines

information technology the technology involving the development, maintenance, and use of computer systems, software, and networks for the processing and distribution of data

intifada uprising, rebellion; *specifically*: an armed uprising of Palestinians against Israeli occupation of the West Bank and Gaza Strip

jones *slang*: to have a strong desire or craving for something

lookism prejudice or discrimination based on physical appearance and especially physical appearance believed to fall short of societal notions of beauty

mai tai a cocktail made with rum, curaçao, orgeat, lime, and fruit juices

megaplex a large multiplex typically housing 16 or more movie theaters

menudo a tripe stew seasoned with chili peppers

metacognition awareness or analysis of one's own learning or thinking processes

MPEG 1: any of a group of computer file formats for the compression and storage of digital video and audio data **2**: a computer file (as of a movie) in an MPEG format

MP3 1: a computer file format for the compression and storage of digital audio data **2**: a computer file (as of a song) in the MP3 format

neo-pagan a person who practices a contemporary form of paganism (as Wicca)

peloton the main body of riders in a bicycle race

pleather a plastic fabric made to look like leather

posole or **pozole** a thick soup chiefly of Mexico and the United States Southwest made with pork, hominy, garlic, and chili

postconsumer 1: discarded by an end consumer **2**: having been used and recycled for reuse in another consumer product

props 1 *slang*: something due or owed **2** *slang*: respect **3** *slang*: recognition, acknowledgment

scrunchie (or **scrunchy**) a fabric-covered elastic used for holding back hair (as in a ponytail)

sildenafil a drug used in the form of its citrate to treat erectile dysfunction

sleep apnea apnea that recurs during sleep and is caused especially by obstruction of the airway or a disturbance in the brain's respiratory center

streaming relating to or being the transfer of data (as audio or video material) in a continuous stream especially for immediate processing or playback

teensploitation the exploitation of teenagers by producers of teen-oriented films

trans-fatty acid an unsaturated fatty acid that is formed especially during the hydrogenation of vegetable oils and has been linked to an increase in blood cholesterol

vermiculture the cultivation of annelid worms (as earthworms or bloodworms) especially for use as bait or in composting

world music popular music originating from or influenced by non-Western musical traditions and often having a danceable rhythm

Words About Words

allegory: extended use of symbols, in the form of characters, animals, or events, that represent ideas or themes. Ex: John Bunyan, *Pilgrim's Progress*

alliteration: repetition of same, initial consonant sounds of two or more words in sequence or in short intervals. Ex: "I have *st*ood *st*ill and *st*opped the *s*ound of feet." — Robert Frost

anagram: a word or phrase made by rearranging letters from another word or phrase. Ex: Clint Eastwood = Old West Action.

antithesis: an expression in which contrasting ideas are intentionally juxtaposed, usually in parallel structure. Ex: "The world will little note, nor long remember, what we say here, but it can never forget what they did here." — Abraham Lincoln, "Gettysburg Address"

assonance: repetition of same or similar vowel sounds in words located near each other. Ex: "Gr*ee*n as a dr*ea*m, and d*ee*p as death." — Rupert Brooke

cliché: a saying or expression that has been used so often it has lost its effect. Ex: work like a dog

eponym: a word derived from the name of a person. Ex: sandwich, from the Earl of Sandwich.

euphemism: a mild, indirect expression used instead of a plainer one that might be harsh or offensive. Ex: restroom, pass away.

hyperbole: exaggeration for emphasis or effect. Ex: "And fired the shot heard round the world." — Ralph Waldo Emerson, "Concord Hymn"

irony: an expression in which the intended meaning is contrary to its literal meaning; the words say one thing but mean another. Ex: "Yet Brutus says he was ambitious;/ And Brutus is an honorable man." — Shakespeare, *Julius Caesar*

litotes: intentional understatement made by negating the opposite of what is meant. Ex: This was no small matter.

metaphor: implied comparison of two dissimilar things, without using "as" or "like." Ex: "Dawn's rosy fingers" — Homer

metonymy: substitution of one word for another which it suggests. Ex: The pen is mightier than the sword.

onomatopoeia: words that imitate the sounds they describe. Ex: buzz, murmur.

oxymoron: juxtaposition of contradictory words. Ex: deafening silence.

palindrome: a type of anagram in which a word, phrase, or sentence reads the same backward and forward. Ex: Ma is a nun as I am.

paradox: a statement that is seemingly contradictory, odd, or opposed to common sense or expectation and yet is presented as true. Ex: "What a pity that youth must be wasted on the young." — George Bernard Shaw

personification: treating ideas or objects as though they were persons. Ex: "Because I could not stop for Death—/He kindly stopped for me." — Emily Dickinson

portmanteau: two words combined to form one word. Ex: smog (smoke + fog).

simile: a comparison between two dissimilar things using "like" or "as." Ex: "My love is like a red, red rose" — Robert Burns

synecdoche: (a form of metonymy) the use of a part for the whole, or the whole for the part. Ex: All hands on deck!

tautology: unnecessary repetition of an idea in different words, phrases, or sentences. Ex: close proximity.

National Spelling Bee

The Scripps Howard National Spelling Bee, conducted by Scripps Howard Newspapers and other leading newspapers since 1939, was instituted by the Louisville (KY) *Courier-Journal* in 1925. Children under 16 years old and not beyond 8th grade are eligible to compete for cash prizes at the finals, held annually in Washington, DC. (*Spellbound*, a film chronicling the experiences of 8 contestants in the 1999 spelling bee, was released in late 2002.) The 2004 winners were: 1st place, David Tidmarsh, South Bend, IN; 2nd place, Akshay Buddiga, Colorado Springs, CO.

Here are the last words given, and spelled correctly, in each of the years 1980-2004 at the national spelling bee.

1980	elucubrate	1985	milieu	1990	fibranne	1995	xanthosis	2000	demarche
1981	sarcophagus	1986	odontalgia	1991	antipyretic	1996	vivisepulture	2001	succedaneum
1982	psoriasis	1987	staphylococci	1992	lyceum	1997	euonym	2002	prospicience
1983	purim	1988	elegiacal	1993	kamikaze	1998	chiaroscurist	2003	pococurante
1984	luge	1989	spoliator	1994	antediluvian	1999	logorrhea	2004	autochthonous

Names of the Days

ENGLISH	RUSSIAN	HEBREW	FRENCH	ITALIAN	SPANISH	GERMAN	JAPANESE
Sunday	voskresenye	yom rishon	dimanche	domenica	domingo	Sonntag	nichiyoubi
Monday	ponedelnik	yom sheni	lundi	lunedì	lunes	Montag	getsuyoubi
Tuesday	vtornik	yom shlishi	mardi	martedì	martes	Dienstag	kayoubi
Wednesday	sreda	yom ravii	mercredi	mercoledì	miércoles	Mittwoch	suiyoubi
Thursday	chetverg	yom hamishi	jeudi	giovedì	jueves	Donnerstag	mokuyoubi
Friday	pyatnitsa	yom shishi	vendredi	venerdì	viernes	Freitag	kinyoubi
Saturday	subbota	shabbat	samedi	sabato	sábado	Samstag	doyoubi

Foreign Words and Phrases

(F=French; Ger=German; Gk=Greek; I=Italian; L=Latin; S=Spanish; Y=Yiddish)

ad absurdum (L; ad ahb-SUR-dum): to the point of absurdity

ad hoc (L; ad HOK): for the end or purpose at hand; impromptu.

ad hominem (L; ad HOH-mee-nem): emotional rather than intellectual; in a dispute, using slander to obscure issues.

adios (S; ah-di-OHS): goodbye

antebellum (L; AHN-teh-BEL-lum): pre-war

apercu(s) (F; ah-per-SOO): first perception or insight; outline

auf Wiedersehen (Ger; owf-VEE-duh-zehn): Good-bye

belles lettres (F; bel-LET-truh): writing valued for artistic merit

bête noire (F; BET NWAHR): a thing or person viewed with particular dislike or fear

Bildungsroman (Ger; BIL-doongs-roh-mahn): novel with coming-of-age story

bourgeois (F; boo-ZHWAH): middle-class; conventional; materialistic

carte blanche (F; kahrt BLANSH): full discretionary power

cause célèbre (F; kawz suh-LEB-ruh): a notorious incident

cognoscenti (I; koh-nyoh-SHEN-tee): experts; connoisseurs

contretemps (F; kon-truh-tahm): awkward situation

coup de grâce (F; kooh duh GRAHS): the final blow

cum laude/magna cum laude/summa cum laude (L; kuhm LOUD-ay; MAGN-a ...; SOO-ma ...): with praise or honor/with great praise or honor/with the highest praise or honor

de facto (L; day FAK-toh): in fact, if not by law

de jure (L; dee JOOR-ee, day YOOR-ay): in accordance with right or law; officially

deo gratias (L; DAY-oh GRAH-tsee-ahs): thanks be to God

de rigueur (F; duh ree-GUR): necessary according to convention or etiquette

détente (F; day-TAHNT): an easing of strained relations

deus ex machina (L; DAY-us eks MAH-keh-nah): a person/event that provides a solution unexpectedly or suddenly, espec. (in literature) a contrived solution to a plot

double entendre (F; DOO-blahn-TAHN-druh): expression with with double meaning, one meaning of which is often risqué

éminence grise (F; ay-meh-nahns-GREEZ): one who wields power behind the scenes

enfant terrible (F; ahn-FAHN te-REE-bluh): one who is noteworthy for embarrassing or unconventional behavior

ennui (F; ah-NOOEE): boredom; world-weariness; annoyance

e pluribus unum (L; eh-PLOO-ree-boos-OO-noom): out of many, one (U.S. motto)

ersatz (Ger; EHR-zats): artificial, inferior

esprit de corps (F; es-PREE duh KAWR): group spirit; feeling of camaraderie

eureka (Gk; yoor-EE-kuh): I have found it!; hurrah!

ex post facto (L; eks pohst FAK-toh): retroactive(ly)

fait accompli (F; fayt uh-kom-PLEE): an accomplished fact

faux pas (F; foh PAH): as false step; a social blunder or breach of etiquette

habeas corpus (L; HAY-bee-ahs KOR-pus): an order for an accused person to be brought to court

hasta la vista (S; asta-la-VIS-ta): goodbye

hoi polloi (Gk; hoy puh-LOY): the masses

in loco parentis (L; in LOH-koh puh-REN-tis): in place of parent

in omnibus (L; in OHM-nee-bus): in all things; in all ways

je ne sais quoi (F; zhuh nuh say KWAH): I don't know what; the little something that eludes description

joie de vivre (F; zhwah duh VEEV-ruh): zest for life

mano a mano (S; MAH-noh ah MAH-noh): hand to hand; in direct combat

mea culpa (L; MAY-uh CUL-puh): through my fault

mensch (Y; mentsh): an upright, noble, admirable person

modus operandi (L; MOH-duhs op-uh-RAN-dee): method of operation

noblesse oblige (F; noh-BLES oh-BLEEZH): the obligation of nobility to help the less fortunate

nolo contendere (L; NOH-loh-kohn-TEN-deh-reh): "I will not contest," a plea of no defense, equivalent to a plea of guilty.

non compos mentis (L; non KOM-puhs MEN-tis): not of sound mind

non sequitur (L; non SEH-kwi-tour): a conclusion that does not logically follow from what preceded it

nouveau riche (F; noo-voh REESH): a person newly rich, perhaps one who spends money conspicuously

par excellence (F; par ek-seh-LANS): best of all; incomparable.

parvenu (F; par-vuh-NOO): upstart

persona non grata (L; per-SOH-nah non GRAH-tah): unwelcome person

pièce de résistance (F; pee-es duh ray-ZEES-tonz): the outstanding item in a series or group

pro bono (L; proh BOH-noh): (legal work) donated for the public good

qué será será (S; keh sair-AH sair-AH): what will be will be

quid pro quo (L; kwid proh KWOH): something given or received for something else

raison d'être (F; RAY-zohnn DET-ruh): reason for being

sans souci (F; SAHNN sooh-SEE): without worry

savoir faire (F; sav-wahr-FAIR): dexterity in social affairs

Schadenfreude (Ger; SHAH-d'n-froy-deh): joy at another's misfortune

schlemiel (Y; shleh-MEEL): an unlucky, bungling person

schlepp (Y; shlep): move slowly, tediously, drag oneself along

semper fidelis (L; SEM-puhr fee-DAY-lis): always faithful

sobriquet (F; soh-bree-KAY): nickname

terra firma (L; TER-uh FUR-muh): solid ground

tour de force (F; TOOR duh FAWRS): feat accomplished through great skill

vis-à-vis (F; vee-zuh-VEE): compared with; with regard to

zeitgeist (Ger; ZITE-gyste): the general intellectual, moral, and cultural climate of an era

Names for Animal Young

bunny: rabbit
calf: cattle, elephant, antelope, rhino, hippo, whale, others
cheeper: grouse, partridge, quail
chick, chicken: fowl
cockerel: rooster
codling, sprag: codfish
colt: horse (male)
cub: lion, bear, shark, fox, others
cygnet: swan

duckling: duck
eaglet: eagle
elver: eel
eyas: hawk, others
fawn: deer
filly: horse (female)
fingerling: fish generally
flapper: wild fowl
fledgling: birds generally
foal: horse, zebra, others
fry: fish generally
gosling: goose
heifer: cow

joey: kangaroo, others
kid: goat
kit: fox, beaver, rabbit, cat
kitten, kitty, catling: cats, other small mammals
lamb, lambkin, cosset, hog: sheep
leveret: hare
nestling: birds generally
owlet: owl
parr, smolt, grilse: salmon
piglet, shoat, farrow, suckling: pig

polliwog, tadpole: frog
poult: turkey
pullet: hen
pup: dog, seal, sea lion, fox
puss, pussy: cat
spike, blinker, tinker: mackerel
squab: pigeon
squeaker: pigeon, others
whelp: dog, tiger, beasts of prey
yearling: cattle, sheep, horse, others

Names for Animal Collectives

alligators: congregation
ants: army or colony
apes: shrewdness
badgers: cete
bats: colony
bears: sleuth
bees: grist or swarm
birds: flight or volery
boars/swine: sounder
butterflies: flutter
buzzards: wake
camels: train or caravan
cats: clowder or clutter
cattle: drove
chicks: brood or clutch
clams/oysters: bed
cockroaches: intrusion
cormorants: gulp

cranes: sedge or siege
crocodiles: bask
crows: murder
doves: dule or pitying
ducks: brace or team
eagles: convocation
elephants: herd
elks: gang
finches: charm
fish: school or shoal
flamingos: stand
foxes: skulk
frogs: army
geese: flock, gaggle, or skein
gnats: cloud or horde
goats: tribe or trip
gorillas: band
grasshoppers: cloud

hares: down or husk
hawks: cast
horses: pair or team
hounds: cry, mute, or pack
jellyfish: smack
kangaroos: mob or troop
kittens: kindle or kendle
larks: exaltation
leopards: leap
lions: pride
monkeys: troop
mules: span
nightingales: watch
oxen: yoke
partridge/quail: covey
peacocks: muster
pheasants: nest or nide
pigs: litter

ravens: unkindness
rhinoceroses: crash
seals: pod
sharks: shiver
sheep: flock, drove
snakes: nest
squirrels: dray or scurry
swans: bevy
swine: drift
tigers: streak
toads: knot
turkeys: gang or rafter
turtles: bale
vultures: committee
whales: gam
wolves: pack
woodchuck: fall
woodpeckers: descent

Some Common Abbreviations and Acronyms

Acronyms are pronounceable words formed from first letters (or syllables) of other words. Some **abbreviations** below (e.g., AIDS, NATO) are thus acronyms. Some acronyms are words coined as abbreviations and written in lower case (e.g., "radar," "yuppie"). Acronyms do not have periods; usage for other abbreviations varies, but periods have become less common. Capitalization usage may vary from what is shown here. Italicized words preceding parenthetical definitions below are Latin unless otherwise noted. See also other chapters, including Computers and the Internet; Weights and Measures.

AA=Alcoholics Anonymous; Associate in Arts; administrative assistant
AAA=American Automobile Association
AARP=American Association of Retired Persons
ABA=American Bar Association
AC=alternating current
AD=*anno Domini* (in the year of the Lord)
AFL-CIO=American Federation of Labor and Congress of Industrial Organizations
AI=artificial intelligence
AIDS=acquired immune deficiency syndrome
AM=*ante meridiem* (before noon)
AMA=American Medical Association
anon=anonymous
APO=army post office
APR=annual percentage rate
ASCAP=American Society of Composers, Authors, and Publishers
ASPCA=American Society for Prevention of Cruelty to Animals
ATM=automated teller machine
AWOL=absent without leave
BA=Bachelor of Arts
bbl=barrel(s)
BC=before Christ
BCE=before Common Era
bpd=barrels per day
BS=Bachelor of Science
Btu=British thermal unit(s)
bu=bushel(s)
byob=bring your own bottle
C= Celsius, centigrade

c=*circa* (about), copyright
CAT=computerized axial tomography
CDC=Centers for Disease Control and Prevention
CE=Common Era
CEO=chief executive officer
cf.=*confer* (compare)
CFO=chief financial officer
CIA=Central Intelligence Agency
CIF=cost, insurance, and freight
CIO=chief information officer
COD=cash (or collect) on delivery
Col.=Colonel
COLA=cost of living adjustment
COO=chief operating officer
CPA=certified public accountant
CPI=Consumer Price Index
Cpl.=Corporal
CPR=cardiopulmonary resuscitation
CPU=central processing unit
CST=Central Standard Time
DA=district attorney
DC=direct current
DD=Doctor of Divinity
DDS=Doctor of Dental Science (or Surgery)
DMD=Doctor of Dental Medicine
DMZ=demilitarized zone
DNA=deoxyribonucleic acid
DNR=do not resuscitate
DOA=dead on arrival
DOB=date of birth
dpi=dots per inch
DPT=diphtheria, pertussis, tetanus

DUI=driving under the influence
DVD=digital video disc
DVM=Doctor of Veterinary Medicine
DWI=driving while intoxicated
ed.=edited, edition, editor
EEG=electroencephalogram
e.g.=*exempli gratia* (for example)
EKG=electrocardiogram
EOE=equal opportunity employer
EPA=Environmental Protection Agency
ERA=Equal Rights Amendment; earned run average
ESL=English as a second language
ESP=extrasensory perception
EST=Eastern standard time
et al.=*et alii* (and others)
etc.=*et cetera* (and so forth)
EU=European Union
EVA=extravehicular activity
F=Fahrenheit
FBI=Federal Bureau of Investigation
FDA=Food and Drug Administration
FDIC=Federal Deposit Insurance Corp.
FEMA=Federal Emergency Management Agency
ff.=and those following
FICA=Federal Insurance Contributions Act (Social Security)
fl.=*floruit* (flourished), used for historical figures when dates of birth and death uncertain
FOB=free on board
fte=full-time equivalent
FY=fiscal year
FYI=for your information

GATT=General Agreement on Tariffs and Trade
GB=gigabyte(s)
GDP=gross domestic product
GED=general equivalency diploma (for high school)
GMT=Greenwich mean time
GNP=gross national product
GOP=Grand Old Party (Republican Party)
Hazmat=hazardous material
HMS=His/Her Majesty's Ship (UK)
Hon.=the Honorable
HOV=high-occupancy vehicle
HRH=her (his) royal highness
HVAC=heating, ventilating, and air-conditioning
Hz=hertz
ibid=*ibidem* (in the same place)
i.e.=*id est* (that is)
IMF=International Monetary Fund
IOC=International Olympic Committee
IQ=intelligence quotient
IRA=individual retirement account; Irish Republican Army
IRS=Internal Revenue Service
ISBN=International Standard Book Number
JCS=Joint Chiefs of Staff
JD=*Juris Doctor* (doctor of laws)
K=Kelvin
k=karat
KCB=Knight Commander of the Bath (UK)
K of C=Knights of Columbus
kWh=kilowatt-hour(s)
laser=Light Amplification by Stimulated Emission of Radiation
Lieut. or Lt.=Lieutenant
LLB=*Legum Baccalaurens* (Bachelor of Laws)
LLP=limited licensed partners
loc. cit.=*loco citato* (in the place cited)

MA=Master of Arts
MBA=Master of Business Administration
MV=megabyte(s)
MD=*Medicinae Doctor* (doctor of medicine)
MFN=most favored nation
MIA=missing in action
modem=MOdulator-DEModulator
MP=Member of Parliament (UK)
mph=miles per hour
MRI=magnetic resonance imaging
MS=Master of Science; manuscript; multiple sclerosis
MSG=monosodium glutamate
MST=Mountain standard time
MVP=most valuable player
NA=not applicable; not available
NAACP=National Association for the Advancement of Colored People
NAFTA=North American Free Trade Agreement
NASA=National Aeronautics and Space Administration
NATO=North Atlantic Treaty Org.
NB=*nota bene* (note carefully)
NCAA=National Collegiate Athletic Assn.
NIH=National Institutes of Health
NOW=National Organization for Women
NRA=National Rifle Association
OE=Old English
op=*opus* (work)
OPEC=Organization of Petroleum Exporting Countries
OTC=over the counter
p, pp=page(s)
PAC=political action committee
Ph.D.=*Philosophiae Doctor* (doctor of philosophy)
PIN=Personal Identification Number
PM=*post meridiem* (afternoon)
PS=*post scriptum* (postscript)
PST=Pacific Standard Time
pt=part(s), pint(s), point(s)
Pvt.=Private

q.v.=*quod vide* (which see)
radar=radio detecting and ranging
REM=rapid eye movement
Rev.=Reverend
rev.=revised
RFD=rural free delivery
RIP=*requiescat in pace* (May he/she rest in peace)
RN=registered nurse
RNA=ribonucleic acid
ROTC=Reserve Officers' Training Corps
rpm=revolutions per minute
RSVP=*répondez s'il vous plaît* (Fr.) (Please reply)
SARS=severe acute respiratory syndrome
SASE=self-addressed stamped envelope
Sgt.=Sergeant
SIDS=suddent infant death syndrome
S.J.=Society of Jesus (Jesuits)
sonar=sound navigation and ranging
SRO=standing room only
SSI=Supplementary Security Income
SUV=sport utility vehicle
TBA=to be announced
TBD=to be determined
TGIF=thank God it's Friday
UFO=unidentified flying object
UPC=Universal Product Code
USS=United States ship
UTC=coordinated univeral time
v (or vs)=*versus* (against)
VCR=videocassette recorder
W=watt(s)
WHO=World Health Organization
WMD=weapons of mass destruction
WPM=words per minute
YTD=year to date
yuppie=young urban professional
ZIP=zone improvement plan (U.S. Postal Service)

PALINDROMES

DID HANNAH SAY AS HANNAH DID? is a palindrome. A palindrome, from Greek words for "run back again," reads the same backward as forward. Famous palindromes range from Adam's possible introduction to his wife ("Madam, I'm Adam.") to a slogan that could have applied to Theodore Roosevelt ("A man, a plan, a canal, Panama!"). Some are one word only (e.g., "deified," "kayak," "radar") or simple phrases (e.g. "senile felines," "war, sir, is raw"). Some are more involved (e.g., "Deer flee freedom in Oregon? No, Geronimo, deer feel freed.")

Eponyms
(words named for people)

Bloody Mary—a vodka and tomato juice drink; after the nickname of Mary I, Queen of England (1553-58), notorious for persecution of Protestants

bloomers—full, loose trousers that are gathered at the knee; after Amelia Bloomer, an American social reformer who advocated (1851) such clothing

bobbies—in Great Britain, police officers; after Sir Robert Peel, who organized the London police force in 1850

bowdlerize—to delete written matter considered indelicate; after Thomas Bowdler, English editor of an expurgated Shakespeare (1825)

boycott—to avoid trade or dealings with, as a protest; after Charles C. Boycott, an English land agent in County Mayo, Ireland, ostracized in 1880 for refusing to reduce rents

Braille—a system of writing for the blind; after Louis Braille, the French teacher of the blind who invented it (1853)

Casanova—a man who is a promiscuous and unscrupulous lover; after Giovanni Giacomo Casanova (1725-98), an Italian adventurer

chauvinist—excessively patriotic; after Nicolas Chauvin, a character in a 19th-cent. play who is devoted to Napoleon

derby—a stiff felt hat with a dome-shaped crown and rather narrow rolled brim; after Edward Stanley, 12th earl of Derby, who in 1780 founded the Derby horse race, to which these hats are worn

diesel—a type of internal combustion engine; after Rudolf Diesel (1858-1913), who built the first successful diesel engine

gerrymander—to draw an election district in such a way as to favor a political party; after Elbridge Gerry, who created (1812) just such an election district (shaped like a salamander) during his governorship of Massachusetts

guillotine—a machine for beheading; after Joseph Guillotin, a French physician who proposed its use in 1789 as more humane than hanging

leotard—a close-fitting garment, worn by dancers, acrobats, and the like; after Julius Leotard, a 19th-cent. French aerial gymnast

sandwich—2 or more slices of bread with a filling in between; after John Montagu, 4th earl of Sandwich (1718-92), who supposedly ate these at the gaming table

silhouette—an outline image; from Étienne de Silhouette (1709-67), a close-fisted French finance minister

WORLD ALMANAC QUICK QUIZ

Which language is spoken as a first language in the most countries?

(a) Mandarin Chinese   (b) English   (c) Hindi   (d) Spanish

For the answer look in this chapter, or see page 1008.

Top 10 First Names of Americans by Decade of Birth

Source: Compiled by Dr. Cleveland Kent Evans, Bellevue University, Bellevue, NE; based on Social Security Administration records

BOYS:

1880-1889 . . . . .John, William, Charles, George, James, Frank, Joseph, Harry, Henry, Edward
1890-1899 . . . . .John, William, George, James, Charles, Joseph, Frank, Robert, Harry, Henry
1900-1909 . . . . .John, William, James, George, Joseph, Charles, Robert, Frank, Edward, Henry
1910-1919 . . . . .John, William, James, Robert, Joseph, Charles, George, Edward, Frank, Walter
1920-1929 . . . . .John, Robert, James, William, Charles, George, Joseph, Richard, Edward, Donald
1930-1939 . . . . .Robert, James, John, William, Richard, Charles, Donald, George, Thomas, Joseph
1940-1949 . . . . .James, Robert, John, William, Richard, David, Charles, Thomas, Michael, Ronald
1950-1959 . . . . .Michael, James, Robert, John, David, William, Steven, Richard, Thomas, Mark
1960-1969 . . . . .Michael, John, David, James, Robert, Mark, Steven, William, Jeffrey, Richard
1970-1979 . . . . .Michael, Christopher, Jason, David, James, John, Brian, Robert, Steven, William
1980-1989 . . . . .Michael, Christopher, Matthew, Joshua, David, Daniel, James, John, Robert, Brian
1990-1999 . . . . .Michael, Christopher, Matthew, Joshua, Nicholas, Jacob, Andrew, Daniel, Brandon, Tyler

GIRLS:

1880-1889 . . . . .Mary, Anna, Elizabeth, Catherine, Margaret, Emma, Bertha, Minnie, Florence, Clara
1890-1899 . . . . .Mary, Anna, Margaret, Helen, Catherine, Elizabeth, Florence, Ruth, Rose, Ethel
1900-1909 . . . . .Mary, Helen, Margaret, Anna, Ruth, Catherine, Elizabeth, Dorothy, Marie, Mildred
1910-1919 . . . . .Mary, Helen, Dorothy, Margaret, Ruth, Catherine, Mildred, Anna, Elizabeth, Frances
1920-1929 . . . . .Mary, Dorothy, Betty, Helen, Margaret, Ruth, Virginia, Catherine, Doris, Frances
1930-1939 . . . . .Mary, Betty, Barbara, Shirley, Patricia, Dorothy, Joan, Margaret, Carol, Nancy
1940-1949 . . . . .Mary, Linda, Barbara, Patricia, Carol, Sandra, Nancy, Sharon, Judith, Susan
1950-1959 . . . . .Deborah, Mary, Linda, Patricia, Susan, Barbara, Karen, Nancy, Donna, Catherine
1960-1969 . . . . .Lisa, Deborah, Mary, Karen, Michelle, Susan, Kimberly, Lori, Teresa, Linda
1970-1979 . . . . .Jennifer, Michelle, Amy, Melissa, Kimberly, Lisa, Angela, Heather, Kelly, Sarah
1980-1989 . . . . .Jessica, Jennifer, Ashley, Sarah, Amanda, Stephanie, Nicole, Melissa, Katherine, Megan
1990-1999 . . . . .Ashley, Jessica, Sarah, Brittany, Emily, Kaitlyn, Samantha, Megan, Brianna, Katherine

Origins of Popular American Given Names

Source: Dr. Cleveland Kent Evans, Bellevue University, Bellevue, NE

Boys

Andrew: Gr. *andreios*, "man, manly"
Brandon: Eng. place name, "gorse-covered hill"
Brian: Irish, perhaps Celtic *Brigonos*, "high, noble"
Charles: Ger. *ceorl*, "free man"
Christopher: Gr. *Khristophoros*, "bearing Christ [in one's heart]"
Daniel: Heb. "God is my judge"
David: Heb. *Dodavehu*, perhaps "darling"
Donald: Scots Gaelic *Domhnall*, "world rule"
Edward: Old Eng. *Eadweard*, "wealth-guard"
Ethan: Heb. "solid," "firm"

Frank: Ger. "Frenchman"
George: Gr. *georgos*, "soil tiller, farmer"
Harry: Middle Eng. form of Henry
Henry: Ger. *Haimric*, "home-power"
Jacob: Heb. *Yaakov*, "God protects" or "supplanter"
James: Late Lat. *Iacomus*, form of Jacob
Jason: Gr. *Iason*, "healer"
Jeffrey: Norman Fr. , from Ger. *Gaufrid*, "land-peace," or *Gisfrid*, "pledge-peace"
John: Heb. *Yohanan*, "God is gracious"
Joseph: Heb. *Yosef*, "[God] shall add"
Joshua: Heb. *Yoshua*, "God saves"
Mark: Lat. *Marcus*, perhaps "of Mars, the war god"

Matthew: Heb. *Mattathia*, "gift of God"
Michael: Heb. "Who could ever be like God?"
Nicholas: Gr. *Nikolaos*, "victory-people"
Patrick: Lat. *Patricius*, "belonging to the noble class"
Richard: Ger. "power-hardy"
Robert: Ger. *Hrodberht*, "fame-bright"
Sean: Gaelic form of John
Steven: Gr. *stephanos*, "crown, garland"
Theodore: Gr. *Theodoros*, "gift of God"
Thomas: Aramaic "twin"
Tyler: Old Eng. *tigeler*, "tile layer"
Walter: Ger. *Waldheri*, "rule-army"
William: Ger. *Wilhelm*, "will-helmet"

Girls

Abigail: Heb. "My father is joy"
Alexis: Gr. "helper" or "defender"
Amanda: 17th-cent. invention from Lat., "lovable"
Amy: Old Fr. *Amee*, "beloved"
Angela: Gr. *angelos*, "messenger [of God]"
Ann (Eng. form), **Anne** (Eng., Fr., Ger. form) of Hannah
Anna: Lat. and Gr. form of Hannah
Ashley: Eng. place name, "ash grove"
Barbara: Gr. *barbarus*, "foreign"
Bertha: Ger. *behrt*, "bright"
Betty: 18th-cent. pet form of Elizabeth
Brianna: modern fem. form of Brian
Brittany: place name, Fr. province settled by Britons
Carol: form of Charles
Clara: Lat. *clarus*, "famous"
Deborah: Heb. "bee"
Donna: Ital. "lady"
Doris: Gr. "woman of the Dorian tribe," name of a sea nymph
Dorothy: Gr. *Dorothea*, "gift of God"
Elizabeth: Heb. *Elisheba*, perhaps "God is my oath" or "God is good fortune"
Emily: Roman *Aemilia*, possibly from Lat. *aemulus*, "rival"
Emma: Ger. *ermen*, "whole, entire"
Ethel: Old Eng. *aethel*, "noble"
Florence: Lat. *florens*, "flourishing"
Frances: fem. form of Francis, "a Frenchman"

Haley: Eng. place name, "hay clearing"
Hannah: Heb. "He has favored me"
Heather: Middle Eng. *hathir*, "heather"
Helen: Gr. *Helene*, possibly "sunbeam"
Jennifer: Cornish form of Welsh *Gwenhwyfar*, "fair-smooth"
Jessica: Shakespearean invention, probably fem. form of Jesse, Heb. "God exists"
Joan: Middle Eng. fem. form of John
Judith: Hebrew "Jewish woman"
Kaitlyn: American spelling of Caitlin, the Irish form of Katherine
Karen: Danish form of Katherine
Katherine: from *Aikaterine*, Egyptian name later modified to resemble Gr. *katharos*, "pure"
Kelly: Irish Gaelic *Ceallagh*, perhaps "churchgoer" or "bright-headed"
Kimberly: Eng. place name, "Cyneburgh's clearing"
Linda: Sp. "pretty" or Ger. "tender"
Lisa: pet form of Elizabeth
Lori: pet form of either Lorraine (French "land of Lothar's people") or Laura (Latin "laurel")
Madison: Middle Eng. surname, "son of Madeline or Maud"
Margaret: Gr. *margaron*, "pearl"
Maria: Lat. form of Mary
Marie: Fr. form of Mary

Mary: Eng. form of Heb. *Maryam*, perhaps "seeress" or "wished-for child"
Megan: Welsh form of Margaret
Melissa: Gr. "bee"
Michelle: Fr. fem. form of Michael
Mildred: Old Eng. *Mildthryth*, "mild-strength"
Minnie: Pet form of Wilhelminia, fem. form of William
Nancy: medieval Eng. pet form of Agnes, Gr. *hagnos*, "holy"; later also used as pet form for Ann
Nicole: Fr. fem. form of Nicholas
Patricia: Lat. fem. form of Patrick
Rose: Ger. *hros*, "horse," or Lat. *rosa*, "rose"
Ruth: Heb., perhaps "companion"
Samantha: colonial American invention, probably combining Sam from Samuel [Heb. "name of God"] with -antha from Gr. *anthos*, "flower"
Sandra: short form of Alessandra, Ital. fem. of Alexander, Gr. "defend-man"
Sarah: Heb., "princess"
Sharon: Biblical place name, Hebrew "plain"
Shirley: Eng. place name, "bright clearing" or "shire meadow"
Stephanie: Fr. fem. form of Steven
Susan: Eng. form of Heb. *Shoshana*, "lily"
Teresa: Spanish, perhaps "woman from Therasia"
Virginia: Lat., "virgin-like"

> **IT'S A FACT:** The top ten baby names in 2003, according to the Social Security Administration, were: **boys,** Jacob, Michael, Joshua, Matthew, Andrew, Joseph, Ethan, Daniel, Christopher, Anthony; **girls,** Emily, Emma, Madison, Hannah, Olivia, Abigail, Alexis, Ashley, Elizabeth, Samantha.

30 Most Common Last Names in the U.S. Population

Source: U.S. Census Bureau, based on 1990 Census data

Rank	Name	Frequency[1] (%)	Rank	Name	Frequency[1] (%)	Rank	Name	Frequency[1] (%)	Rank	Name	Frequency[1] (%)
1.	Smith	1.006	9.	Moore	0.312	17.	Thompson	0.269	24.	Lee	0.220
2.	Johnson	0.810	10.	Taylor	0.311	18.	Garcia	0.254	25.	Walker	0.219
3.	Williams	0.699	11.	Anderson	0.311	19.	Martinez	0.234	26.	Hall	0.200
4.	Jones	0.621	12.	Thomas	0.311	20.	Robinson	0.233	27.	Allen	0.199
5.	Brown	0.621	13.	Jackson	0.310	21.	Clark	0.231	28.	Young	0.193
6.	Davis	0.480	14.	White	0.279	22.	Rodriguez	0.229	29.	Hernandez	0.192
7.	Miller	0.424	15.	Harris	0.275	23.	Lewis	0.226	30.	King	0.190
8.	Wilson	0.339	16.	Martin	0.273						

(1) Percent of people in the population sample with the name shown.

Pen Names

Shalom Aleichem . . . . Solomon J. Rabinowitz
Woody Allen . . . . Allen Stewart Konigsberg
John le Carré . . . . David John Moore Cornwell
Lewis Carroll . . . . Charles Lutwidge Dodgson
Colette .Sidonie Gabrielle Colette
Amanda Cross . . . . Carolyn Heilbrun
Isak Dinesen . . . . Karen Blixen
Elia . . . . Charles Lamb
George Eliot . . . . Mary Ann or Marian Evans
Maksim Gorky . . . . Aleksey Maksimovich Peshkov
O. Henry .William Sydney Porter
James Herriot . . . . .James Alfred Wight
P. D. James . . . . .Phyllis Dorothy James White
[John] Ross Macdonald . . . . Kenneth Millar
André Maurois . . . . .Émile Herzog
Molière . . . . Jean Baptiste Poquelin
Toni Morrison . . . . Chloe Anthony Wofford
Frank O'Connor . . . . Michael Donovan
George Orwell . . . . Eric Arthur Blair
Mary Renault . . . . Mary Challans
Ellery Queen . . . . Frederic Dannay and Manfred B. Lee
Françoise Sagan . . . . Françoise Quoirez
Saki . . . . Hector Hugh Munro
George Sand . . . . Amandine Lucie Aurore Dupin
Dr. Seuss . . . . Theodor Seuss Geisel
Stendhal . . . . Marie Henri Beyle
Mark Twain . . . . Samuel Clemens
Voltaire . . . . François Marie Arouet

Forms of Address

	Address	Salutation
GOVERNMENT		
President of the U.S.	The President, The White House, Washington, DC 20500; also, The President and Mrs. ____ or The President and Mr. ____	Dear Sir or Madam; Mr. President or Madam President; Dear Mr. President or Dear Madam President
U.S. Vice President	The Vice President, The White House, Washington, DC 20500; also, The Vice President and Mrs. ____ or The Vice President and Mr. ____	Dear Sir or Madam; Mr. Vice President or Madam Vice President; Dear Mr. Vice President or Dear Madam Vice President
Chief Justice	The Hon. *Firstname Surname*, Chief Justice of the U.S., The Supreme Court, Washington, DC 20543	Dear Sir or Madam; Dear Mr. or Madam Chief Justice
Associate Justice	The Hon. Justice *Firstname Surname,* The Supreme Court, Washington, DC 20543	Dear Sir or Madam; Dear Justice *Surname*
Judge	The Hon. *Firstname Surname*, Associate Judge, U.S. District Court	Dear Judge *Surname*
Attorney General	The Hon. *Firstname Surname*, Attorney General, Dept. of Justice, Constitution Ave. & 10th St. NW, Washington, DC 20530	Dear Sir or Madam; Dear Mr. or Ms. Attorney General
Cabinet Officer	The Hon. *Firstname Surname*, Secretary of ____	Dear Mr. or Madam Secretary; or Dear Mr. or Ms. *Surname*
Senator	The Hon. or Sen. *Firstname Surname*, U.S. Senate, Washington, DC 20510	Dear Mr. or Madam Senator, or Dear Mr. or Ms. *Surname*
Representative	The Hon. or Rep. *Firstname Surname*, House of Representatives, Washington, DC 20515	Dear Mr. or Madam *Surname*
Speaker of the House	The Hon. Speaker of the House of Representatives, House of Representatives, Washington, DC 20515	Dear Mr. or Madam Speaker
Ambassador, U.S.	The Hon. *Firstname Surname*, American Ambassador[1]	Sir or Madam; Dear Mr. or Madam Ambassador
Ambassador, Foreign	His or Her Excellency[2] *Firstname Surname*, Ambassador of _____	Excellency[2] ; Dear Mr. or Madam Ambassador
Governor	The Hon. *Firstname Surname*, Governor of *State*; or in some states, His or Her Excellency, the Governor of *State*	Sir or Madam; Dear Governor *Surname*
Mayor	The Hon. *Firstname Surname*, Mayor of *City*	Sir or Madam; Dear Mayor *Surname*
MILITARY PERSONNEL		
All Titles	Full or abbreviated rank + full name + comma + abbreviation for branch of service. *Example*: Adm. John Smith, USN	Dear *Rank Surname*
RELIGIOUS		
Clergy, Protestant	The Reverend *Firstname Surname*[3]	Dear Ms. or Mr. *Surname*
Pope	His Holiness Pope *Name* or His Holiness the Pope	Your Holiness or Most Holy Father
Priest	The Reverend *Firstname Surname* or The Reverend Father *Surname*	Reverend Father, Dear Father *Surname*, or Dear Father
Rabbi	Rabbi *Firstname Surname*	Dear Rabbi *Surname*
ROYALTY AND NOBILITY		
King/Queen	His or Her Majesty, King or Queen of *Country*	Sir or Madam, or May it please Your Majesty

(1) If in Canada or Latin America, The Ambassador of the United States of America. (2) An American ambassador is not properly addressed as His or Her Excellency. (3) A member of the Protestant clergy who has a doctorate may be so addressed; for example, The Reverend Firstname Surname, DD, and Dear Dr. Surname.

Commonly Misspelled English Words

accidentally	Cincinnati	existence	irresistible	mysterious	receive
accommodate	collectible	fascinating	judgment	necessary	restaurant
acknowledgment	commitment	feasible	laboratory	noticeable	rhythm
acquainted	committee	February	leisure	occasionally	ridiculous
acquire	connoisseur	fluorine	library	occurrence	separate
across	conscientious	foreign	license	opportunity	seize
all right	conscious	forty	lieutenant	optimistic	sincerely
already	convenience	gauge	lightning	parallel	stubbornness
amateur	deceive	government	liquefy	performance	supersede
appearance	defendant	grammar	maintenance	permanent	tangible
appropriate	definitely	grateful	marriage	permissible	temperament
bureau	desirable	harass	medieval	perseverance	temperature
business	despair	humorous	millennium	personnel	transferred
calendar	desperate	hurrying	miniature	possess	truly
Caribbean	eligible	incidentally	miscellaneous	privilege	twelfth
cemetery	eliminate	independent	Mississippi	propaganda	Wednesday
changeable	embarrass	indispensable	misspelled	questionnaire	weird
chrysanthemum	environment	inoculate	mnemonic	receipt	wholly

WORLD ALMANAC EDITORS' PICKS
Most Commonly Misspelled Words

The editors of *The World Almanac* have ranked the following as most commonly misspelled words. Editors considered both how commonly the word is used and how frequently it is misspelled. The editors did not include words that are misspelled because they are confused with other words, such as *affect/effect* or *principal/principle* or *their/there/they're*.

1. separate	3. privilege	5. conscious	7. necessary	9. definitely
2. embarrass	4. occurrence	6. accommodate	8. calendar	10. receive

---

Commonly Confused English Words

adverse: unfavorable
averse: opposed

affect: to influence
effect: to bring about

allusion: an indirect reference
illusion: an unreal impression

appraise: to set a value on
apprise: to inform

biannual: occurring twice a year
biennial: occurring every two years

capital: the seat of government
capitol: building where a legislature meets

complement: to make complete; something that completes
compliment: to praise; praise

counselor: one who gives advice or counsel
councilor: a member of a council

denote: to mean
connote: to suggest beyond the explicit meaning

discreet: prudent
discrete: separate, distinct

disinterested: impartial
uninterested: without interest

elicit: to draw or bring out
illicit: illegal

emigrate: to leave for another place
immigrate: to come to another place

ensure: to make certain
insure: to protect against
assure: to inform postively or confidently

exalt: to glorify
exult: to rejoice

farther: at a greater distance
further: to a greater extent or degree

fewer: a smaller *number* (of things)
less: a smaller *amount* (of something)

grisly: inspiring horror or great fear
grizzly: sprinkled or streaked with gray

historic: important in history
historical: relating to history

hoard: a supply stored up and often hidden
horde: a teeming croud or throng

I: nominative case
me: objective case

immanent: inherent; residing within
imminent: ready to take place
eminent: standing out

imply: to suggest but not explicitly
infer: to assume or understand information not relayed explicitly

include: used when the items following are part of a whole
comprise: used when the items following are all of a whole

ingenious: clever
ingenuous: innocent

it's: it is
its: a possessive adjective

lay: to put or place
lie: (intransitive) to recline or rest

oral: spoken, as opposed to written
verbal: relating to language

principal: n., business owner, head of school; adj., most important
principle: a basic law or truth; a moral or ethical standard

their: belonging to them
there: in that place
they're: they are

who: nominative case
whom: objective case

your: belonging to you
you're: you are

American Manual Alphabet

In the American Manual Alphabet, each letter of the alphabet is represented by a position of the fingers. This system was originally developed in France by Abbe Charles Michel De I'Epee in the late 1700s. It was brought to the United States by Laurent Clerce (1785-1869), a Frenchman who taught deaf or hearing-impaired people.

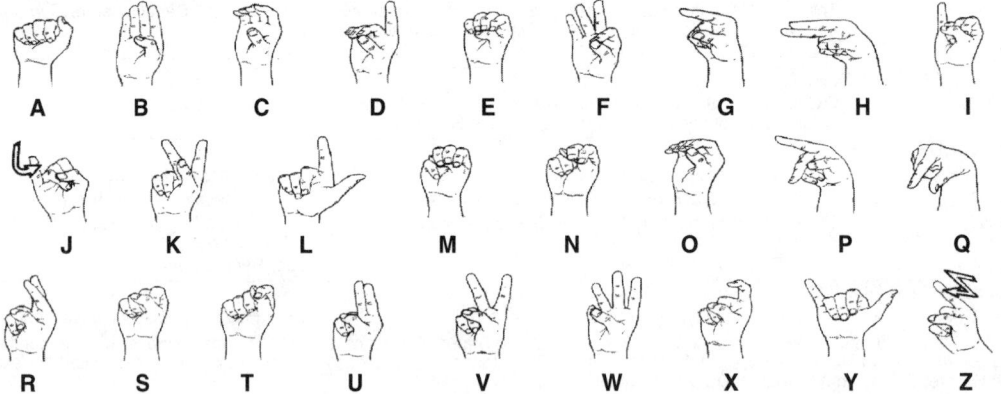

IT'S A FACT: Esperanto is an artificial language devised by a Polish eye doctor, L. L. Zamenhof, and introduced in 1887. The name comes from his pen name, Dr. Esperanto, which in the language means "one who hopes." Based on Indo-European roots, with a simple grammar, it was intended to be an international second language that people from different countries could learn easily and use to communicate. Thousands of books have been published in Esperanto, and there are 100,000 or more Esperanto speakers according to some estimates. *Esperantistoj esperas ke pliaj homoj lernos paroli esperanton.* That is, if you need a translation, Esperantists hope that more people will learn to speak Esperanto.

The Principal Languages of the World

Source: Database of *Ethnologue: Languages of the World,* 15th Edition, www.ethnologue.com. Raymond G. Gordon, Editor. Copyright © 2004, SIL International. Used by permission.

The following tables count only "first language" speakers. All figures are estimates, as of Aug. 2004.

Languages Spoken by the Most People

Speakers	(millions)	Speakers	(millions)	Speakers	(millions)
Chinese, Mandarin	873	Bengali	171	Javanese	75
Spanish	322	Russian	145	Telugu	69
English	309	Japanese	122	Marathi	68
Hindi	180	German, standard	95	Vietnamese	67
Portuguese	177	Chinese, Wu	77	Korean	67

Languages Spoken by at Least 2 Million People

A "Hub" country is the country of origin, not necessarily the country where the most speakers reside (e.g., Portugal is the "hub" country of Portuguese, although more Portuguese speakers live in Brazil).

Language	Hub	Countries	Speakers (millions)	Language	Hub	Countries	Speakers (millions)
Chinese, Mandarin	China	16	873	Arabic, Moroccan spoken	Morocco	8	19
Spanish	Spain	43	322	Yoruba	Nigeria	5	19
English	United Kingdom	107	309	Arabic, Sudanese spoken	Sudan	5	18
Hindi	India	17	180	Arabic, Sa'idi spoken	Egypt	1	18
Portuguese	Portugal	33	177	Uzbek, Northern	Uzbekistan	12	18
Bengali	Bangladesh	9	171	Igbo	Nigeria	1	18
Russian	Russia	31	145	Malay	Malaysia	8	17
Japanese	Japan	25	122	Amharic	Ethiopia	4	17
German, standard	Germany	41	95	Dutch	Netherlands	8	17
Chinese, Wu	China	1	77	Nepali	Nepal	4	17
Javanese	Indonesia	4	75	Tagalog	Philippines	7	15
Telugu	India	7	69	Assamese	India	3	15
Marathi	India	3	68	Arabic, Mesopotamian spoken	Iraq	5	15
Vietnamese	Vietnam	20	67	Thai, Northeastern	Thailand	1	15
Korean	Korea, South	31	67	Arabic, North Levantine spoken	Syria	15	14
Tamil	India	15	66	Chittagonian	Bangladesh	2	14
French	France	56	64	Seraiki	Pakistan	3	13
Italian	Italy	30	61	Madura	Indonesia	2	13
Panjabi, Western	Pakistan	7	60	Hungarian	Hungary	11	13
Urdu	Pakistan	21	60	Sinhala	Sri Lanka	6	13
Chinese, Yue	China	20	54	Marwari	India	3	13
Turkish	Turkey	35	50	Haryanvi	India	1	13
Arabic, Egyptian spoken	Egypt	9	46	Magahi	India	1	13
Chinese, Min Nan	China	9	46	Somali	Somalia	12	12
Gujarati	India	17	46	Greek	Greece	35	12
Chinese, Jinyu	China	1	45	Chhattisgarhi	India	1	11
Polish	Poland	21	42	Czech	Czech Republic	10	11
Ukrainian	Ukraine	25	39	Serbian	Serbia and Montenegro	16	11
Chinese, Xiang	China	1	36	Deccan	India	1	10
Malayalam	India	9	35	Shona	Zimbabwe	4	10
Kannada	India	1	35	Sylheti	Bangladesh	10	10
Burmese	Myanmar	5	32	Chinese, Min Bei	China	2	10
Oriya	India	2	31	Belarusan	Belarus	16	10
Chinese, Hakka	China	16	29	Zhuang, Northern	China	1	10
Panjabi, Eastern	India	11	27	Arabic, Najdi spoken	Saudi Arabia	7	9
Sunda	Indonesia	1	27	Pashto, Northern	Pakistan	5	9
Bhojpuri	India	3	26	Zulu	South Africa	6	9
Maithili	India	2	24	Arabic, Tunisian spoken	Tunisia	4	9
Azerbaijani, South	Iran	8	24	Lombard	Italy	3	9
Farsi, Western	Iran	26	24	Kurdish, Northern	Turkey	31	9
Hausa	Nigeria	13	24	Chinese, Min Dong	China	6	9
Romanian	Romania	17	23	Dhundari	India	1	9
Indonesian	Indonesia	6	23	Bulgarian	Bulgaria	11	8
Arabic, Algerian spoken	Algeria	5	21	Oromo, West Central	Ethiopia	2	8
Chinese, Gan	China	1	20	Swedish	Sweden	7	8
Awadhi	India	2	20	Akan	Ghana	1	8
Thai	Thailand	4	20	Kazakh	Kazakhstan	13	8
Cebuano	Philippines	2	20				
Sindhi	Pakistan	7	19				

Language	Hub	Countries	Speakers (millions)
Ilocano	Philippines	2	8
Pashto, Central	Pakistan	1	7
Uyghur	China	16	7
Farsi, Eastern	Afghanistan	3	7
Arabic, Sanaani spoken	Yemen	1	7
Bavarian	Austria	5	7
Haitian Creole French	Haiti	9	7
Rwanda	Rwanda	4	7
Xhosa	South Africa	3	7
Khmer, Central	Cambodia	7	7
Azerbaijani, North	Azerbaijan	9	7
Napoletano-Calabrese	Italy	1	7
Hiligaynon	Philippines	2	7
Arabic, Ta'izzi-Adeni spoken	Yemen	5	6
Catalan-Valencian-Balear	Spain	18	6
Armenian	Armenia	30	6
Minangkabau	Indonesia	1	6
Turkmen	Turkmenistan	13	6
Luba-Kasai	Democratic Republic of Congo	1	6
Arabic, North Mesopotamian spoken	Iraq	4	6
Croatian	Croatia	8	6
Santali	India	4	6
Arabic, South Levantine spoken	Jordan	8	6
Schwyzerdütsch	Switzerland	5	6
Thai, Northern	Thailand	2	6
Kanauji	India	1	6
Arabic, Hijazi spoken	Saudi Arabia	2	6
Afrikaans	South Africa	10	5
Malagasy, Plateau	Madagascar	3	5
Kurdish, Southern	Iran	2	5
Nyanja	Malawi	5	5
Gikuyu	Kenya	1	5
Danish	Denmark	8	5
Finnish	Finland	7	5
Tigrigna	Ethiopia	4	5
Hebrew	Israel	8	5
Mòoré	Burkina Faso	6	5
Slovak	Slovakia	8	5
Mewati	India	1	5
Sukuma	Tanzania	1	5
Thai, Southern	Thailand	1	5
Rundi	Burundi	4	4
Guaraní, Paraguayan	Paraguay	2	4
Sicilian	Italy	1	4
Kashmiri	India	3	4
Sotho, Southern	Lesotho	3	4
Oromo, Eastern	Ethiopia	1	4
Arabic, Libyan spoken	Libya	3	4
Tswana	Botswana	4	4
Tajiki	Tajikistan	8	4
Kituba	Democratic Republic of Congo	1	4
Georgian	Georgia	13	4
Umbundu	Angola	2	4
Bosnian	Bosnia and Herzegovina	1	4
Zhuang, Southern	China	1	4
Konkani	India	1	4
Oromo, Borana-Arsi-Guji	Ethiopia	3	3
Bali	Indonesia	1	3
Kurdish, Central	Iraq	2	3
Sotho, Northern	South Africa	2	3
Luyia	Kenya	2	3
Quechua, South Bolivian	Bolivia	2	3
Konkani, Goanese	India	3	3
Wolof	Senegal	6	3

Language	Hub	Countries	Speakers (millions)
Bugis	Indonesia	2	3
Kanuri, Central	Nigeria	6	3
Luo	Kenya	2	3
Balochi, Southern	Pakistan	4	3
Mongolian, Peripheral	China	2	3
Tsonga	South Africa	4	3
Gilaki	Iran	1	3
Mazanderani	Iran	1	3
Pulaar	Senegal	6	3
Lao	Laos	7	3
Galician	Spain	2	3
Jamaican Creole English	Jamaica	7	3
Malay, Balinese	Indonesia	1	3
Tamazight, Central Atlas	Morocco	3	3
Yiddish, Eastern	Israel	21	3
Kirghiz	Kyrgyzstan	7	3
Lithuanian	Lithuania	19	3
Kabyle	Algeria	3	3
Éwé	Ghana	2	3
Piemontese	Italy	3	3
Malay, Pattani	Thailand	1	3
Ganda	Uganda	1	3
Mbundu	Angola	1	3
Shekhawati	India	1	3
Aceh	Indonesia	1	3
Banjar	Indonesia	2	3
Tachelhit	Morocco	3	3
Rajbanshi	India	3	2
Albanian, Tosk	Albania	9	2
Shan	Myanmar	3	2
Garhwali	India	1	2
Pular	Guinea	6	2
Lambadi	India	1	2
Hassaniyya	Mauritania	6	2
Bamanankan	Mali	7	2
Albanian, Gheg	Serbia and Montenegro	7	2
Betawi	Indonesia	1	2
Ndau	Mozambique	2	2
Pashto, Southern	Pakistan	6	2
Chinese, Pu-Xian	China	3	2
Makhuwa	Mozambique	1	2
Bicolano, Central	Philippines	1	2
Kalenjin	Kenya	1	2
Kamba	Kenya	1	2
Waray-Waray	Philippines	1	2
Kumauni	India	2	2
Arabic, Gulf spoken	Iraq	9	2
Mongolian, Halh	Mongolia	4	2
Bemba	Zambia	4	2
Aymara, Central	Bolivia	4	2
Tiv	Nigeria	2	2
Brahui	Pakistan	4	2
Hazaragi	Afghanistan	4	2
Zarma	Niger	4	2
Venetian	Italy	3	2
Sadri	India	2	2
Lingala	Democratic Republic of Congo	3	2
Baoulé	Côte d'Ivoire	1	2
Dogri	India	1	2
Sasak	Indonesia	1	2
Bagri	India	2	2
Arakanese	Myanmar	3	2
Mundari	India	3	2
Kurux	India	2	2
Bouyei	China	4	2
Emiliano-Romagnolo	Italy	2	2
Maninkakan, Eastern	Guinea	3	2
Beti	Cameroon	1	2
Saxon, Upper	Germany	1	2
Batak Toba	Indonesia	1	2

> **IT'S A FACT:** Mandarin Chinese is a tonal language; it uses four different tones to convey different meanings. Depending on whether the tone is: flat, rising, falling then rising, or falling, the word *da* may mean "echo," "distressed," "strike," or "big."

RELIGION
Membership of Religious Groups in the U.S.

Sources: *2004 Yearbook of American & Canadian Churches*, © National Council of the Churches of Christ in the USA; World Christian Database; *World Almanac* research

These membership figures are the latest available and generally are based on reports made by officials of each group, and not on any religious census. Figures from other sources may vary. Many groups keep careful records; others only estimate. Not all groups report annually. Church membership figures reported in this table are generally inclusive and do not refer simply to full communicants or confirmed members. Specific definitions of "member" vary from one denomination to another.

The number of houses of worship appears in parentheses. * Indicates that the group declines to make membership figures public. Groups reporting fewer than 5,000 members are not included; where membership numbers are not available, only those groups with 50 or more houses of worship are listed.

Religious Group	Members
Adventist churches:	
Advent Christian Ch. (303)	25,277
Seventh-day Adventist Ch. (4,619)	918,882
American Catholic Church (100).	**25,000**
Apostolic Christian Churches of America (86)	**12,930**
Apostolic Episcopal Church (250)	**18,000**
Bahá'í Faith (1,127 assemblies)	**151,771**
Baptist churches:	
American Baptist Assn. (1,760)	275,000
American Baptist Chs. in the U.S.A. (5,836)	1,484,291
Baptist Bible Fellowship Intl. (4,500)	1,200,000
Baptist General Conference (902)	145,148
Baptist Missionary Assn. of America (1,334)	234,732
Conservative Baptist Assn. of America (1,200)	200,000
Free Will Baptists, Natl. Assn. of (2,470)	197,919
General Assn. of General Baptists (713)	85,346
General Assn. of Regular Baptist Chs. (1,415)	129,407
Natl. Baptist Convention, U.S.A., Inc. (9,000)	5,000,000
Natl. Missionary Baptist Convention of America	2,500,000
North American Baptist Conference (270)	47,692
Progressive National Baptist Convention (2,000)	2,500,000
Separate Baptists in Christ (100)	8,000
Southern Baptist Convention (42,775)	16,247,736
Brethren in Christ (232)	**20,739**
Brethren (German Baptists):	
Brethren Ch. (Ashland, OH) (117)	10,287
Church of the Brethren (1,069)	134,844
Grace Brethren Chs., Fellowship of (260)	30,371
Old German Baptist Brethren (55)	6,205
Buddhists	**2,900,000**
Christian Brethren (Plymouth Brethren) (1,165)	**85,050**
Christian Church (Disciples of Christ) (3,691)	**786,334**
Christian Ch. of N. America, Gen. Council (96)	**7,200**
Christian Congregation, Inc. (1,439)	**119,391**
Christian and Missionary Alliance (1,963)	**389,232**
Christian Union (111)	6,153
Christian Union, Churches of Christ in (233).	**10,104**
Church of Christ (Holiness) U.S.A. (159)	**10,321**
Church of Christ, Scientist (2,000)	**880,000[1]**
Chs. of God, General Conference (Oregon, IL and Morrow, GA) (89)	**5,018**
Church of the United Brethren in Christ (217).	**22,740**
Churches of Christ (15,000).	**1,500,000**
Churches of God:	
Chs. of God, General Conference (337)	32,654
Ch. of God (Anderson, IN) (2,290)	247,007
Ch. of God (Seventh Day), Denver, CO (200).	11,000
Ch. of God by Faith, Inc. (148)	30,000
Ch. of God, Mountain Assembly, Inc.(118)	6,140
Church of the Nazarene (4,983).	**643,649**
Community Churches, Intl. Council of (192)	**115,812**
Congreg. Christian Chs., Nat'l Assoc. of (432)	**65,392**
Conservative Congregational Christian Conference (259)	**40,041**
Eastern Catholic Churches:	
Armenian Catholic Church (U.S. and Canada) (9)	36,000
Chaldean Catholic Church (14)	90,000
Maronite Catholic Church (65)	56,133
Melkite Greek Catholic Church (35)	28,026
Romanian Greek Catholic Church (15)	5,000
Ruthenian Byzantine Catholic Church (205)	100,688
Syrian Catholic Church (11)	12,390
Syro-Malabar Catholic Church (5)	112,000
Ukrainian Greek Catholic Church (202)	105,074
Eastern Orthodox churches:	
American Carpatho-Russian Orthodox Greek Catholic Ch. (80)	13,425
Antiochian Orthodox Christian Archdiocese of N.A. (225)	360,000
Apostolic Catholic Assyrian Ch. of the East, N.A. Dioceses (22)	120,000
Armenian Apostolic Ch. of America (34)	360,000
Armenian Apostolic Church, Dioceses of America (72)	414,000
Coptic Orthodox Ch. (100)	300,000
Greek Orthodox Archdiocese of America (510)	1,500,000

Religious Group	Members
Mar Thoma Syrian Church of India (68)	32,000
Orthodox Ch. in America (725)	900,000
Patriarchal Parishes of the Russian Orthodox Ch. in the USA (31)	7,000
Russian Orthodox Church Outside of Russia (177)	*
Serbian Orthodox Ch. of the U.S. and Can. (68)	67,000
Syrian Orthodox Ch. of Antioch (25)	32,500
Ukrainian Orthodox Ch. of the USA (115)	13,000
Episcopal Church (7,344)	**2,333,628**
Evangelical Church (133)	**12,475**
Evangelical Congregational Church (150)	**21,208**
Evangelical Covenant Church (718)	**103,549**
Evangelical Free Church of America (1,224)	**242,619**
Friends:	
Evangelical Friends Intl.-N.A. Region (278)	27,057
Friends General Conference (650)	34,000
Friends United Meeting (427)	42,680
Religious Society of Friends (Conservative) (1,200)	104,000
Full Gospel Fellowship of Churches and Ministers Intl. (902)	**326,900**
General Church of the New Jerusalem (35)	**6,444**
Grace Gospel Fellowship (128)	**60,000**
Hindus	**c. 1,130,000[1]**
Independent Fundamental Churches of America Int'l., Inc. (IFCA) (659)	**61,655**
Jehovah's Witnesses (11,876)	**1,022,397**
Jews	**6,150,000[2]**
Jewish organizations:[3]	
Union for Reform Judaism (900+)	1,500,000
Union of Orthodox Jewish Congregations of America (1,000)	*
United Synagogue of Conservative Judaism, The (760)	1,500,000+
Jewish Reconstructionist Federation (103)	180,000
Latter-day Saints:	
Ch. of Jesus Christ of Latter-day Saints (Mormon) (11,879)	5,410,544
Reorganized Ch. of Jesus Christ of Latter-day Saints (Community of Christ) (951)	142,106
Liberal Catholic Church—Province of the U.S.A. (24)	**6,500**
Lutheran churches:	
Apostolic Lutheran Ch. of America (58)	*
Ch. of the Lutheran Brethren of America (108)	13,702
Ch. of the Lutheran Confession (77)	8,492
Evangelical Lutheran Ch. in America (10,721)	5,038,006
Evangelical Lutheran Synod (138)	21,442
Free Lutheran Congregations, Assn. of (252)	36,431
Latvian Evangelical Lutheran Church in America (68)	13,584
Lutheran Ch.—Missouri Synod (6,142)	2,512,714
Lutheran Chs., American Assn. of (101)	18,252
Wisconsin Evangelical Lutheran Synod (1,250)	403,345
Mennonite churches:	
Beachy Amish Mennonite Chs. (153)	9,205
Church of God in Christ (Mennonite) (115)	12,984
Hutterian Brethren (444)	43,000
Mennonite Brethren Chs., Gen. Conf. (368)	82,130
Mennonite Church USA (964)	112,688
Old Order Amish Ch. (898)	80,820
Methodist churches:	
African Methodist Episcopal Ch.	2,500,000
African Methodist Episcopal Zion Ch. (3,226)	1,430,795
Evangelical Methodist Ch. (123)	8,615
Free Methodist Ch. of North America (978)	69,342
Southern Methodist Ch. (108)	6,493
United Methodist Ch. (35,102)	8,251,042
The Wesleyan Church (1,628)	123,160
Messianic Jews	**c. 75,000**
Metropolitan Community Churches, Universal Fellowship of (300)	**44,000**
Missionary Church (386).	**35,287**
Moravian Ch. in America, Northern Province (93)	**25,140**
Muslims	**4,600,000[1]**
Natl. Organization of the New Apostolic Ch. of North America (340)	**37,382**

Religious Group	Members
Pentecostal churches:	
Apostolic Faith Mission Ch. of God (23)	10,426
Assemblies of God (12,133)	2,687,366
Bible Church of Christ, Inc. (6)	6,850
Bible Fellowship Church (57)	7,308
Church of God (Cleveland, TN) (6,623)	944,857
Church of God in Christ (15,300)	5,499,875
Church of God of Prophecy (1,841)	110,000
Elim Fellowship (100)	*
Intl. Ch. of the Foursquare Gospel (1,847)	305,852
Intl. Pentecostal Church of Christ (67)	4,961
Intl. Pentecostal Holiness Church (1,905).	213,348
Open Bible Standard Chs. (314)	38,000
Pentecostal Assemblies of the World Inc. (1,750).	1,500,000
Pentecostal Church of God (1,197).	104,000
Pentecostal Free Will Baptist Ch. (150)	28,000
United Pentecostal Ch. Intl. (4,100)	*
Presbyterian churches:	
Associate Reformed Presbyterian Ch. (General	
Synod) (264).	40,905
Cumberland Presbyterian Ch. (780)	84,417
Cumberland Presbyterian Ch. in America (152) . .	15,142

Religious Group	Members
Evangelical Presbyterian Ch. (190)	69,351
Genl. Assembly of the Korean Presbyterian	
Church in America (305)	55,100
Orthodox Presbyterian Ch. (237)	26,448
Presbyterian Ch. in America (1,499)	310,750
Presbyterian Ch. (U.S.A.) (11,097).	3,407,329
Reformed Presbyterian Ch. of N. America (86) . .	6,105
Reformed churches:	
Christian Reformed Ch. in N. America (762)	197,339
Hungarian Reformed Ch. in America (27)	6,000
Netherlands Reformed Congregations (27)	9,500
Protestant Reformed Churches in	
America (27)	6,915
Reformed Ch. in America (901)	281,475
United Church of Christ (5,850)	1,330,985
Reformed Episcopal Church (137).	**10,665**
Roman Catholic Church (19,484).	**66,407,105**
Salvation Army (1,369)	**454,982**
Sikhs.	**251,000[1]**
Unitarian Universalist Assn. of	
Congregations (1,010).	**214,738**

(1) Source: World Christian Database. (2) From American Jewish Committee. (3) As reported by organizations.

Headquarters of Selected Religious Groups in the U.S.

Sources: *2004 Yearbook of American & Canadian Churches*, © National Council of the Churches of Christ in the USA; *World Almanac* research

(Year organized in parentheses)

African Methodist Episcopal Church (1787), 3801 Market St., Suite 300, Philadelphia, PA 29204; Senior Bishop, Bishop John Hurst Adams

African Methodist Episcopal Zion Church (1796), 3225 West Sugar Creek Rd., Charlotte, NC 28269; Pres. Keith Thompson (Note: Presidency rotates every 6 mos. according to seniority.)

American Baptist Churches in the U.S.A. (1907), PO Box 851, Valley Forge, PA 19482; www.abc-usa.org; Pres., Margaret Johnson

American Rescue Workers (1890), 25 Ross St., Williamsport, PA 17701; www.arwus.com; Commander-in-Chief & Pres., Gen. Claude S. Astin Jr., Rev.

Antiochian Orthodox Christian Archdiocese of North America (1895), 358 Mountain Rd., Englewood, NJ 07631; www.antiochian.org; Primate, Metropolitan Philip Saliba

Armenian Apostolic Church of America (1887), **Eastern Prelacy**: 138 E. 39th St., New York, NY 10016; www.armprelacy.org; Prelate, Archbishop Oshagan Choloyan; **Western Prelacy**: 6252 Honolulu Ave., La Crecsenta, CA 91214; Prelate, Bishop Moushegh Mardirossian

Assemblies of God (1914), 1445 N. Boonville Ave., Springfield, MO 65802; www.ag.org; Gen. Supt., Thomas E. Trask

Bahá'í Faith, National Spiritual Assembly of the Bahá'í's of the U.S., 1233 Central St., Evanston, IL 60201; www.us.bahai. org; Secy. Gen., Dr. Robert C. Henderson

Baptist Bible Fellowship Intl. (1950), Baptist Bible Fellowship Missions Bldg., 720 E. Kearney St., Springfield, MO 65803; www.bbfi.org; Pres., Rev. Bill Monroe

Baptist Convention, Southern (1845), 901 Commerce St., Nashville, TN 37203; www.sbc.net; Pres., Jack Graham

Baptist Convention, U.S.A., Inc., National (1895), 1700 Baptist World Center Dr., Nashville, TN 37207; www.nationalbaptist.com; Pres., Dr. William J. Shaw

Baptist Convention of America, Inc., National (1880), 777 S. R.L. Thornton Freeway, Ste. 205, Dallas, TX 75203; Pres., Dr. E. Edward Jones

Baptist Convention of America, Natl. Missionary (1988), 1404 E. Firestone, Los Angeles, CA 90001; www.nmbca.com; Pres., Dr. W. T. Snead Sr.

Baptist General Conference (1852), 2002 S. Arlington Heights Rd., Arlington Heights, IL 60005; www.bgcworld.org; Pres. and CEO, Dr. Gerald Sheveland

Brethren in Christ Church (1778), PO Box A, Grantham, PA 17027; www.bic-church.org/index.htm; Moderator, Dr. Warren L. Hoffman

Buddhist Churches of America (1899), 1710 Octavia St., San Francisco, CA 94109; www.buddhistchurchesofamerica. com; Presiding Bishop, Hakubun Watanabe

Christian and Missionary Alliance (1897), PO Box 35000, Colorado Springs, CO 80935; www.cmalliance.org; Pres., Rev. Peter N. Nanfelt, D.D.

Christian Church (Disciples of Christ) (1832), Disciples Center, 130 E. Washington St., PO Box 1986, Indianapolis, IN 46206; www.disciples.org; Gen. Minister and Pres., William Chris Hobgood

Christian Churches and Churches of Christ, 4210 Bridgetown Rd., Box 11326, Cincinnati, OH 45211; www.cwv.net/christ'n

Christian Congregation, Inc., The (1787), 812 W. Hemlock St., LaFollette, TN 37766; www.netministries.org/see/churches. exe/ch10619; Gen. Supt., Rev. Ora W. Eads, D.D.

Christian Methodist Episcopal Church (1870), 4466 Elvis Presley Blvd., Memphis, TN 38116; Executive Secretary, Attorney Juanita Bryant

Christian Reformed Church in North America (1857), 2850 Kalamazoo Ave. SE, Grand Rapids, MI 49560; www.crcna.org; Gen. Secy., Dr. David H. Engelhard

Church of the Brethren (1708), General Offices, 1451 Dundee Ave., Elgin, IL 60120; www.brethren.org; Moderator, Christopher D. Bowman

Church of Christ (1830), Temple Lot, 200 S. River St., PO Box 472, Independence, MO 64051; http://church-of-christ.com; Council of Apostles, Secy., Apostle Smith N. Brickhouse

Church of Christ, Scientist, *see* First Church of Christ, Scientist.

Church of God (Anderson, IN) (1881), Box 2420, Anderson, IN 46018; www.chog.org; Gen. Dir., Pres. Ronald V. Duncan

Church of God (Cleveland, TN) (1886), 2490 Keith St. NW, Cleveland, TN 37320; www.churchofgod.cc/default_nav40.asp; Gen. Overseer, R. Lamar Vest

Church of God in Christ (1907), Mason Temple, 938 Mason St., Memphis, TN 38126; www.netministries.org/see/churches/ ch00833; Presiding Bishop, Bishop Chandler D. Owens

Church of Jesus Christ (Bickertonites) (1862), 6th & Lincoln Sts., Monongahela, PA 15063; Pres., Dominic Thomas

Church of Jesus Christ of Latter-day Saints (Mormon), The (1830), 47 E. South Temple St., Salt Lake City, UT 84150; www.lds.org; Pres., Gordon B. Hinckley

Church of the Nazarene (1907), 6401 The Paseo, Kansas City, MO 64131; www.nazarene.org; Gen. Secy., Dr. Jack Stone

Community of Christ (Reorganized Church of Jesus Christ of Latter-Day Saints) (1830), Int'l. Headquarters, 1001 W. Walnut, Independence, MO 54050; www.CofChrist.org; Pres. W. Grant McMurray

Community Churches, International Council of (1950), 21116 Washington Pkwy., Frankfort, IL 60423; Pres., Grace O'Neal

Conservative Judaism, United Synagogue of, 155 5th Ave., New York, NY 10010; www.uscj.org; Pres., Judy Yudof

Coptic Orthodox Church, 5 Woodstone Dr., Cedar Grove, NJ 07009; www.coptic.org; Fr. Isaac Boulos Azmy

Cumberland Presbyterian Church (1810), 1978 Union Ave., Memphis, TN 38104; www.cumberland.org; Moderator, Rev. Dr. Charles McCaskey

Episcopal Church (1789), 815 Second Ave., New York, NY 10017; www.ecusa.anglican.org; Presiding Bishop and Primate, Most Rev. Frank Tracy Griswold

Evangelical Free Church of America (1884), 901 E. 78th St., Minneapolis, MN 55420; www.efca.org; Acting Pres., Rev. William Hamel

Evangelical Lutheran Church in America (1987), 8765 W. Higgins Rd., Chicago, IL 60631; www.elca.org; Presiding Bishop, Rev. Mark S. Hanson

Fellowship of Grace Brethren Churches (1882), PO Box 386, Winona Lake, IN 46590; www.fgbc.org; Moderator, Dr. Galen Wiley

First Church of Christ, Scientist, The (1879), Christian Science Plaza, 175 Huntington Ave., Boston, MA 02115; www. spirituality.com; Pres., Hans-Joachim Trapp

Free Methodist Church of North America (1860), World Ministries Center, 770 N. High School Rd., Indianapolis, IN 46214; www.freemethodistchurch.org

Friends General Conference (1900), 1216 Arch St., 2B, Philadelphia, PA 19107; www.fgcquaker.org; Gen. Secy., Bruce Birchard

Full Gospel Fellowship of Churches and Ministers Int'l. (1962), 1000 N. Belt Line Rd., Irving, TX 75061; www.fgfcmi.org Pres., Dr. Don Arnold

Greek Orthodox Archdiocese of America (1922), 8-10 E. 79th St., New York, NY 10021; www.goarch.org; Primate, Archbishop Demetrios

International Church of the Foursquare Gospel (1927), 1910 W. Sunset Blvd., Ste. 200, PO Box 26902, Los Angeles, CA 90026; www.foursquare.org; Pres., Dr. Paul C. Risser

Islamic Society of North America, P.O. Box 38, Plainfield, IN 46168; www.isna.net; Genl. Secy., Dr. Sayyid M. Syeed

Jehovah's Witnesses (1884), 25 Columbia Heights, Brooklyn, NY 11201; www.watchtower.org; Pres., Don Adams

Jewish Reconstructionist Federation (1935), Beit Devora, 7804 Montgomery Ave., Suite 9, Elkins Park, PA 19027; www.jrf.org; Dir., Chayim Herzig-Moss

Lutheran Church—Missouri Synod (1847), 1333 S. Kirkwood Rd., St. Louis, MO 63122; www.lcms.org; Pres., Dr. Gerald B. Kieschnick

Mennonite Brethren Churches, General Conference of (1860), 4812 E. Butler Ave., Fresno CA 93727; Moderator, Ed Boschman

Mennonite Church USA (2001), 722 Main St., PO Box 347, Newton, KS 67114. www.MennoniteChurchUSA.org; Moderator, Duane Oswald

Moravian Church in America (1735), **Northern Prov.:** 1021 Center St., PO Box 1245, Bethlehem, PA 18016; www.moravian.org; Pres., David L. Wickmann; **Southern Prov.:** 459 S. Church St., Winston-Salem, NC 27101; Pres., Rev. Dr. Robert E. Sawyer; **Alaska Prov.:** PO Box 545, 361 3rd Ave., Bethel, AK 99559; Pres., Rev. Isaac Amik

North American Shi'a Muslim Communities Organization (NASIMCO), P.O. Box 29691, Minneapolis, MN 55429; www.nasimco.org; Pres., Hussein Walji

Orthodox Church in America (1794), PO Box 675, Syosset, NY 11791; www.oca.org; Primate, Most Blessed Herman

Orthodox Jewish Congregations in America, Union of (1898), 11 Broadway, New York, NY 10004; www.ou.org; Pres., Harvey Blitz

Pentecostal Assemblies of the World, Inc., 3939 Meadows Dr., Indianapolis, IN 46205; Presiding Bishop, Norman L. Wagner

Presbyterian Church (U.S.A.), (1983), 100 Witherspoon St., Louisville, KY 40202; www.pcusa.org; Moderator, Susan Andrews

Presbyterian Church in America (1973), 1700 N. Brown Rd., Lawrenceville, GA 30043 www.pcanet.org; Moderator, Dr. Skip Ryan

Progressive National Baptist Convention, Inc. (1961), 601 50th St., NE, Washington, DC 20019; www.pribc.org; Pres., Dr. Bennett W. Smith Sr.

Reformed Church in America (1628), 475 Riverside Dr., New York, NY 10115; www.rca.org; Pres., Rev. David Schutt

Reform Judaism, Union for, 633 3rd Ave., New York, NY 10017; www.urj.org; Pres., Rabbi Eric Yoffie

Roman Catholic Church (1634), U.S. Conference of Catholic Bishops, 3211 Fourth St. NE, Washington, DC 20017; www.usccb.org; Pres., Bishop Wilton D. Gregory

Romanian Orthodox Episcopate of America (1929), 2525 Grey Tower Rd., Jackson, MI 49201; www.roea.org; Ruling Bishop, Most Rev. Archbishop Nathaniel Popp

Salvation Army (1865), 615 Slaters Lane, Alexandria, VA 22313; www.salvationarmy.org; National Comdr., Commissioner W. Todd Bassett

Seventh-day Adventist Church (1863), 12501 Old Columbia Pike, Silver Spring, MD 20904; Pres., Jan Paulsen

Swedenborgian Church (1792), 11 Highland Ave., Newtonville, MA 02460; www.swedenborg.org; Pres., Rev. Ronald P. Brugler

Unitarian Universalist Association of Congregations (1961), 25 Beacon St., Boston, MA 02108; www.uua.org; Pres., The Rev. William Sinkford

United Church of Christ (1957), 700 Prospect Ave., Cleveland, OH 44115; www.ucc.org; Pres., Rev. John H. Thomas

United Methodist Church (1968), www.umc.org; Pres. Council of Bishops, Bishop Sharon Brown Christopher

United Pentecostal Church Intl. (1925), 8855 Dunn Rd., Hazelwood, MO 63042; www.upci.org; Gen. Supt., Rev. Kenneth F. Haney

Volunteers of America (1896), 1660 Duke St., Alexandria, VA 22314; www.voa.org; Chairperson, Frances Hesselbein

Wesleyan Church (1968), PO Box 50434, Indianapolis, IN 46250; www.wesleyan.org; Gen. Supts., Dr. Earle L. Wilson, Dr. David H. Holdren, Dr. Thomas E. Armiger

Membership of Religious Groups in Canada

Sources: *2004 Yearbook of American & Canadian Churches,* © National Council of the Churches of Christ in the USA; Statistics Canada

Figures are generally based on reports by officials of each group. The numbers are generally inclusive and not restricted to full communicants or the like. Specific definitions of "member" may vary, however. Some groups keep careful records; others only estimate. Not all groups report annually. The number of houses of worship appears in parentheses. *Indicates membership figures were not reported. Groups reporting fewer than 5,000 members are not included. Where membership numbers are not available, only groups with 50 or more houses of worship are listed.

Religious Group	Members
Anglican Church of Canada (2,836)	686,362
Antiochian Orthodox Christian Archdiocese of North America (15)	100,000
Apostolic Church of Pentecost of Canada, Inc. (144)	24,000
Armenian Holy Apostolic Church (Canadian Diocese) (15)	85,000
Associated Gospel Churches (139)	10,516
Bahá'í Faith (1,480)	18,020
Baptist Conference, North American (124)	16,873
Baptist Convention of Ontario and Quebec (373)	57,263
Baptist General Conf. of Canada (92)	7,045
Baptist Ministries, Canadian (1,133)	129,055
Baptist Union of Western Canada (155)	20,427
Buddhists	300,345[1]
Canadian Yearly Meeting of the Religious Society of Friends (24)	17,333
Christian Brethren (also known as Plymouth Brethren) (585)	47,745
Christian and Missionary Alliance in Canada (419)	117,397
Christian Reformed Church in North America (243)	81,469
Church of God (Cleveland, TN) (135)	11,993
Church of Jesus Christ of Latter-day Saints in Canada (467)	163,666
Church of the Nazarene Canada (166)	12,673
Churches of Christ in Canada (151)	6,857
Community of Christ (75)	11,264
Congreg. Christian Chs. in Canada (95)	7,500
The Coptic Orthodox Ch. in Canada (24)	45,000
Estonian Evangelical Lutheran Church (11)	5,536
Evangelical Baptist Churches in Canada, Fellowship of (493)	71,073
Evangelical Free Church of Canada (139)	7,980
Evangelical Lutheran Church in Canada (623)	199,236
Evangelical Mennonite Conference (50)	7,000
Evangelical Missionary Church of Canada (145)	12,217
Free Methodist Church in Canada (140)	7,502

Religious Group	Members
Greek Orthodox Metropolis of Toronto (Canada) (76)	350,000[1]
Hindus	297,200[1]
Independent Assemblies of God Intl. (Canada) (340)	*
Jehovah's Witnesses (1,383)	184,787
Jews (270+)	329,995[1]
Lutheran Church–Canada (328)	79,178
Maronite Catholic Church (12)	80,000
Melkite Greek Catholic Church (3)	43,000
Mennonite Brethren Churches, Canadian Conference of (232)	34,864
Mennonite Church (Canada) (233)	34,478
Muslims	579,640[1]
North American Baptist Conference (124)	16,873
Open Bible Faith Fellowship of Canada (87)	10,500
Orthodox Church in America (Canada Section) (606)	1,000,000
Pentecostal Assemblies of Canada (1,108)	232,000
Pentecostal Assemblies of Newfoundland (126)	25,431
Presbyterian Church in Canada (968)	198,693
Reformed Church in Canada (42)	5,832
Reformed Churches, Canadian and American (50)	15,620
Reorganized Church of Jesus Christ of Latter Day Saints (75)	11,264
Roman Catholic Church in Canada (5,496)	12,936,905[1]
Salvation Army in Canada (356)	75,732
Serbian Orthodox Church in the U.S.A. and Canada, Diocese of Canada (23)	230,000
Seventh-Day Adventist Church in Canada (330)	51,804
Sikhs	278,410[1]
Southern Baptists, Canadian Convention of (196)	10,622
Ukrainian Greek Catholic Church (393)	117,450
Ukrainian Orthodox Church of Canada (258)	120,000
United Baptist Convention of the Atlantic Provinces (556)	63,236
United Church of Canada (3,640)	1,518,000
United Pentecostal Church in Canada (199)	*
The Wesleyan Church of Canada (89)	6,481

(1) According to 2001 Canadian census

Headquarters of Selected Religious Groups in Canada

Sources: *2004 Yearbook of American & Canadian Churches,* © National Council of the Churches of Christ in the USA; *World Almanac* research
(Year organized in parentheses)

Anglican Church of Canada (1700), Church House, 80 Hayden St., Toronto, ON M4Y 3G2; www.anglican.ca; Primate, Most Rev. Andrew Hutchinson

Bahá'í National Centre of Canada (1898), 7200 Leslie St., Thornhill, ON L3T 6L8; Gen'l.-Secy., Judy Filson

Baptist Convention of Ontario and Quebec (1888), 195 The West Mall, Ste. 414, Etobicoke, ON M9C 5K1; Pres., Brenda Mann

Baptist Ministries, Canadian, 7185 Millcreek Dr., Mississauga, ON L5N 5R4; www.cbmin.org; Pres., Doug Coomas

Christian and Missionary Alliance in Canada (1887), 30 Carrier Dr., Suite 100, Toronto, ON M9W 5T7; www.cmacan.org; Pres., Dr. Franklin Pyles

Church of Jesus Christ of Latter-day Saints (Mormon), The (1830), 50 E. North Temple St., Salt Lake City, UT 84150; www.lds.org; Pres., Gordon B. Hinckley

Church of the Nazarene in Canada (1902), 20 Regan Rd. Unit 9, Brampton, ON L7A 1C3; www.nazarene.ca; Natl. Dir., Dr. William E. Stewart

Conference of Mennonite Brethren Churches, Canadian (1945), 3-169 Riverton Ave., Winnipeg, MB R2L 2E5; Mod., Jascha Boge

Evangelical Baptist Churches in Canada, Fellowship of (1953), 679 Southgate Dr., Guelph, ON N1G 4S2; Pres., Rev. Terry D. Cuthbert

Evangelical Lutheran Church in Canada (1985), 302-393 Portage Ave., Winnipeg, MB R3B 3H6; www.elcic.ca; Bishop, Rev. Raymond L. Schultz

Evangelical Missionary Church of Canada (1993), 4031 Brentwood Rd., NW, Calgary, AB T2L 1L1; Pres., Rev. David Crouse

Greek Orthodox Metropolis of Toronto, 86 Overlea Blvd., Toronto, ON M4H 1C6; www.gocanada.org; His Eminence Metropolitan Archbishop Sotirios

Islamic Society of North America Canada, 2200 S. Sheridan Way, Mississauga, ON, L5J 2M4; www.isnacanada.com; Secy. Gen., Mohammed Ashraf

Jehovah's Witnesses (1879), Canadian office: Box 4100, Halton Hills, ON L7G 4Y4; Pres., Don Adams

Jewish Congress, Canadian (1919), 100 Sparks St., Ste. 650, Ottawa, Ont. K1P 5B7; www.cjc.ca; Pres., Prof. Ed Morgan (Nonreligious umbrella organization of Jewish groups)

Lutheran Church—Canada (1959), 3074 Portage Ave., Winnipeg, MB R3K OY2; www.lutheranchurch-canada.ca; Pres., Rev. Ralph Mayan

Mennonite Church Canada (1902), 600 Shaftesbury Blvd., Winnipeg, MB R3P 0M4; www.mennonitechurch.ca; Chairperson, Henry Krause

North American Shi'a Muslim Communities Organization (NASIMCO), 300 John St., PO Box 87629, Thornhill, ON L3T 7R3; www.nasimco.org; Pres. Hussein Walji

Orthodox Church in America (Canada Archdiocese) (1916), P.O. Box 179 Spencerville, ON K0E 1X0

Pentecostal Assemblies of Canada (1919), 2450 Milltower Ct., Mississauga, ON L5N 5Z6; www.paoc.org; Gen. Supt., Rev. William D. Morrow

Presbyterian Church in Canada (1925), 50 Wynford Dr., Toronto, ON M3C 1J7; www.presbyterian.ca; Principal Clerk: Rev. Stephen Kendall

Roman Catholic Church (1618), Canadian Conference of Catholic Bishops, 2500 Don Reid Dr., Ottawa, ON K1H 2J2; www.cccb.ca; Gen. Secy., Msgr. Peter Schonenbach

Salvation Army (1909), 2 Overlea Blvd., Toronto, ON M4H 1P4; www.salvationarmy.ca; Territorial Cmdr., Commissioner Bill Luttrell

Seventh-Day Adventist Church (1901), 1148 King St. E., Oshawa, ON L1H 1H8; Pres., Daniel R. Jackson

Ukrainian Orthodox Church (1918), Office of the Consistory, 9 St. John's Ave., Winnipeg, MB R2W 1G8; www.uocc.ca; Primate, Most Rev. Metropolitan Wasyly Fedak

United Brethren Church (1767) 302 Lake St., Huntington, IN 46750; Pres., Rev. Brian Magnus

United Church of Canada (1925), The United Church House, 3250 Bloor St. W., Ste. 300, Etobicoke, ON M8X 2Y4; www.uccan.org; Mod., Marion Pardy

Wesleyan Church (1968), The Wesleyan Church Intl. Center, PO Box 50434, Indianapolis, IN 46250; Dist. Supt., Rev. Donald E. Hodgins

Adherents of All Religions by Six Continental Areas[1], Mid-2003

Source: *2004 Encyclopædia Britannica Book of the Year; figures rounded*

	Africa	Asia	Europe	Latin America	Northern America	Oceania	World
Baha'is	1,937,000	3,632,000	146,000	822,000	844,000	122,000	7,503,000
Buddhists	152,000	366,790,000	1,594,000	698,000	3,086,000	654,000	372,974,000
Chinese Universists	34,900	396,720,000	271,000	200,000	695,000	185,000	398,106,300
Christians	394,640,000	325,034,000	554,234,000	501,319,000	269,399,000	25,257,000	2,069,883,000
Roman Catholics	138,970,000	117,710,000	276,490,000	473,000,000	78,310,000	8,373,000	1,092,853,000
Protestants	105,710,000	54,684,000	74,015,000	51,306,000	70,795,000	8,020,000	364,530,000
Orthodox	36,953,000	13,985,000	158,450,000	477,000	6,426,000	739,000	217,030,000
Anglicans	43,809,000	726,000	26,053,000	950,000	3,121,000	5,329,000	79,988,000
Independents	86,395,000	169,070,000	24,675,000	41,776,000	82,533,000	1,625,000	406,074,000
Confucianists	300	6,330,000	17,000	500	0	77,500	6,425,000
Ethnic religionists	100,420,000	132,590,000	1,247,000	2,531,000	1,010,000	298,000	238,096,000
Hindus	2,547,000	830,530,000	1,504,000	801,000	1,410,000	470,000	837,262,000
Jains	73,000	4,332,000	0	0	7,500	1,200	4,414,000
Jews	220,000	4,465,000	2,427,000	1,152,000	6,182,000	105,000	14,551,000
Muslims	344,920,000	869,880,000	32,117,000	1,752,000	4,828,000	725,000	1,254,222,000
New-Religionists	37,000	103,230,000	191,000	660,000	900,000	88,000	105,106,000
Shintoists	0	2,615,000	0	7,000	58,000	0	2,680,000
Sikhs	59,000	23,410,000	243,000	0	551,000	33,000	24,295,000
Spiritists	3,000	2,000	137,000	12,426,000	157,000	7,500	12,733,000
Taoists	0	2,684,000	0	0	12,000	0	2,696,000
Zoroastrians	1,000	2,553,000	91,000	0	83,000	6,000	2,734,000
Other religionists	70,000	65,000	250,000	103,000	620,000	10,000	1,118,000
Nonreligious	5,863,000	620,290,000	107,210,000	16,693,000	30,923,000	3,290,000	784,269,000
Atheists	579,000	120,950,000	22,111,000	2,707,000	1,944,000	369,000	148,660,000

(1) **Continental Areas.** Following current UN demographic terminology, which divides the world into the 6 major areas shown above. Note that "Asia" includes the former Soviet Central Asian states and "Europe" includes all of Russia extending eastward to Vladivostok, the East Sea/Sea of Japan, and the Bering Strait.
Adherents. As defined in the 1948 Universal Declaration of Human Rights, a person's religion is what he or she says it is. Totals are enumerated following the methodology of the *World Christian Encyclopedia*, 2nd ed. (2001) and *World Christian Trends* (2001), using recent censuses, polls, literature, and other data. As a result of the varieties of sources used, totals may differ from standard estimates for total populations.
Buddhists. 56% Mahayana, 38% Theravada (Hinayana), 6% Tantrayana (Lamaism). **Chinese Universists (folk religionists).** Followers of traditional Chinese religion (local deities, ancestor veneration, Confucian ethics, universism, divination, some Buddhist elements). **Christians.** Total Christians include those affiliated with churches not shown, plus other persons professing in censuses or

polls to be Christians but not affiliated with any church. Figures for the subgroups of Christians do not add up to the totals because all subgroups are not shown and some Christians adhere to more than one denomination. **Confucianists.** Non-Chinese followers of Confucius and Confucianism, mostly Koreans in Korea. **Ethnic religionists.** Followers of local, tribal, animistic, or shamanistic religions, with members restricted to one ethnic group. **Hindus.** 70% Vaishnavites, 25% Shaivites, 2% neo-Hindus and reform Hindus. **Independents.** Members of churches and networks that regard themselves as postdenominationalist and neo-apostolic and thus independent of historic, organized, institutionalized denominationalist Christianity. **Jews.** Adherents of Judaism. **Muslims.** 83% Sunni Muslims, 16% Shia Muslims (Shi'ites), 1% other schools. **New-Religionists.** Followers of Asian 20th-cent. New Religions, New Religious movements, radical new crisis religions, and non-Christian syncretistic mass religions, all founded since 1800 and most since 1945. **Other religionists.** Including a handful of religions, quasi-religions, pseudoreligions, parareligions, religious or mystic systems, and religious and semireligious brotherhoods of numerous varieties. **Nonreligious.** Persons professing no religion, nonbelievers, agnostics, freethinkers, uninterested, dereligionized secularists indifferent to all religion. **Atheists.** Persons professing atheism, skepticism, disbelief, or irreligion, including antireligious (opposed to all religion).

Episcopal Church Liturgical Colors and Calendar

Source: The Rt. Reverend Barry E. Yingling, Editor, the *Churchman's Ordo Kalendar*

The most common liturgical colors in the Episcopal Church are: **White**—Christmas Day through First Sunday after Epiphany; Maundy Thursday (as an alternative to crimson at the Eucharist); from the Vigil of Easter to the Day of Pentecost (Whitsunday); Trinity Sunday; Feasts of the Lord (except Holy Cross Day); the Confession of St. Peter; the Conversion of St. Paul; St. Joseph; St. Mary Magdalene; St. Mary the Virgin; St. Michael and All Angels; All Saints' Day; St. John the Evangelist; memorials of other saints who were not martyred; Independence Day and Thanksgiving Day; weddings and funerals. **Red**—the Day of Pentecost; Holy Cross Day; feasts of apostles and evangelists (except those listed above); feasts and memorials of martyrs (including Holy Innocents' Day). **Violet**—Advent and Lent. **Crimson** or oxblood (dark red)—Holy Week. **Green**—the seasons after Epiphany and after Pentecost. **Black**—optional alternative for funerals and Good Friday.

The days of fasting are Ash Wednesday and Good Friday. Other days of special devotion (penitence) include the 40 days of Lent. Ember Days are days of prayer for the church's ministry. They fall on the Wednesday, Friday, and Saturday after the first Sunday in Lent, the Day of Pentecost, Holy Cross Day, and December 13. Rogation Days, the 3 days before Ascension Day, are days of prayer for God's blessing on the crops, on commerce and industry, and for conservation of the earth's resources.

Days, etc.	2004	2005	2006	2007	2008
Golden Number	10	11	12	13	14
Sunday Letter	D & C	B	A	G	F
Sundays after Epiphany	7	5	8	7	4
Ash Wednesday	Feb. 25	Feb. 9	Mar. 1	Feb. 21	Feb. 6
First Sunday in Lent	Feb. 29	Feb. 13	Mar. 5	Feb. 25	Feb. 10
Passion/Palm Sunday	Apr. 4	Mar. 20	Apr. 9	Apr. 1	Mar. 16
Good Friday	Apr. 9	Mar. 25	Apr. 14	Apr. 6	Mar. 21
Easter Day	Apr. 11	Mar. 27	Apr. 16	Apr. 8	Mar. 23
Ascension Day	May 20	May 5	May 25	May 17	May 1
The Day of Pentecost	May 30	May 15	June 4	May 27	May 11
Trinity Sunday	June 6	May 22	June 11	June 3	May 18
Numbered Proper of 2 Pentecost	#6	#4	#6	#5	#3
First Sunday of Advent	Nov. 28	Nov. 27	Dec. 3	Dec. 2	Nov. 30

Greek Orthodox Movable Ecclesiastical Dates, 2004-2008

This 5-year chart has the dates of feast days and fasting days, which are determined annually on the basis of the date of Holy Pascha (Easter). This ecclesiastical cycle begins with the first day of the Triodion and ends with the Sunday of All Saints, a total of 18 weeks.

	2004	2005	2006	2007	2008
Triodion begins	Feb. 1	Feb. 20	Feb. 12	Jan. 28	Feb. 17
1st Sat. of Souls	Feb. 14	Mar. 5	Feb. 25	Feb. 10	Mar. 1
Meat Fare	Feb. 15	Mar. 6	Feb. 26	Feb. 11	Mar. 2
2nd Sat. of Souls	Feb. 21	Mar. 12	Mar. 4	Feb. 17	Mar. 8
Lent Begins	Feb. 23	Mar. 14	Mar. 6	Feb. 19	Mar. 10
St. Theodore—3rd Sat. of Souls	Feb. 28	Mar. 19	Mar. 11	Feb. 24	Mar. 15
Sunday of Orthodoxy	Feb. 29	Mar. 20	Mar. 12	Feb. 25	Mar. 16
Sat. of Lazarus	Apr. 3	Apr. 23	Apr. 15	Mar. 31	Apr. 19
Palm Sunday	Apr. 4	Apr. 24	Apr. 16	Apr. 1	Apr. 20
Holy (Good) Friday	Apr. 9	Apr. 29	Apr. 21	Apr. 6	Apr. 25
Western Easter	Apr. 11	Mar. 27	Apr. 16	Apr. 8	Mar. 23
Orthodox Easter	Apr. 11	May 1	Apr. 23	Apr. 8	Apr. 27
Ascension	May 20	June 9	June 1	May 17	June 5
Sat. of Souls	May 29	June 18	June 10	May 26	June 14
Pentecost	May 30	June 19	June 11	May 27	June 15
All Saints	June 6	June 26	June 18	June 3	June 22
Fast of Holy Apostles (First day)	June 7	June 27	June 19	June 4	June 23

Important Islamic Dates, 1425-1429 AH (2004-2008)

Source: Imad-ad-Dean, Inc., Bethesda, MD 20814

The Islamic calendar is a strict lunar calendar reckoned from the year of the Hijra (Anno Hegirae, or AH)—Muhammad's flight from Mecca to Medina in 622 CE. Each year consists of 12 lunar months of 29 or 30 days beginning and ending with each new moon's visible crescent. Common years have 354 days; leap years have 355 days. Some Muslim countries employ a conventionalized calendar with the leap day added to the last month, Dhûl Hijah, but for religious purposes the leap date is taken into account by tracking each new moon sighting. The dates given below are based on the convention that the first new moon must be seen before the following dawn on the East Coast of the Americas. Actual (local) Western Hemisphere sightings may occur a day later, but never a day earlier, than these dates reflect. Holy days begin at sunset on the previous day.

	(1425) 2004-05	(1426) 2005-06	(1427) 2006	(1428) 2007	(1429) 2008
New Year's Day (Muharram 1)	Feb. 21, 2004	Feb. 10, 2005	Jan. 30, 2006	Jan. 20, 2007	Jan. 9, 2008
Ashura (Muharram 10)	Mar. 1, 2004	Feb. 19, 2005	Feb. 8, 2006	Jan. 29, 2007	Jan. 18, 2008
Mawlid (Rabi'I 12)	May 1, 2004	April 21, 2005	Apr. 10, 2006	Mar. 31, 2007	Mar. 20, 2008
Ramadan 1	Oct. 15, 2004	Oct. 4, 2005	Sept. 23, 2006	Sept. 12, 2007	Sept. 1, 2008
Eid al-Fitr (Shawwal 1)	Nov. 13, 2004	Nov. 3, 2005	Oct. 23, 2006	Oct. 12, 2007	Sept. 30, 2008
Eid al-Adha (Dhûl-Hijjah 10)	Jan. 20, 2005	Jan. 10, 2006	Dec. 30, 2006	Dec. 20, 2007	Dec. 8, 2008

Jewish Holy Days, Festivals, and Fasts, 5765-5769 (2004-2009)

The Jewish Calendar consists of 12 lunar months, alternating between 29 and 30 days. It is lunisolar, and adjusts for the solar cycle by adding an extra month (Adar II) in the 3rd, 6th, 8th, 11th, 14th, 17th, and 19th years of a 19-year cycle. The calendar started on the day of Creation, reckoned in the 2nd-3rd cent. BC as Tishrei 1, 3,761 years before the common era.

The religious calendar begins with the month Nisan, from which all other months are counted, and the civil calendar with Tishrei. The months are 1) Nisan; 2) Iyar; 3) Sivan; 4) Tammuz; 5) Av (also Abh); 6) Elul; 7) Tishrei; 8) Cheshvan (also Marcheshvan); 9) Kislev; 10) Tevet (also Tebeth); 11) Shevat (also Shebhat); 12) Adar; 12a) Adar Sheni (II), added in leap years. The names are Aramaic versions of the Babylonian months, adopted during the Jews' exile in Babylon in the 4th century bc. Rosh Hashanah, the New Year, begins on Tishrei 1 (Sept.-Oct.). Yom Kippur is the holiest day of the year. All holidays listed below begin at sunset on the previous day, except where noted.

Holiday	Date on Jewish Cal.	(5765) 2004-05		(5766) 2005-06		(5767) 2006-07		(5768) 2007-08		(5769) 2008-09	
Rosh Hashanah (New Year)	Tishrei 1-2	Sept. 16	Thu.	Oct. 4	Tue.	Sept. 23	Sat.	Sept. 13	Thu.	Sept. 30	Tue.
		Sept. 17	Fri.	Oct. 5	Wed.	Sept. 24	Sun	Sept. 14	Fri.	Oct. 1	Wed.
Fast of Gedalya[1]	Tishrei 3	Sept. 19	Sun.*	Oct. 6	Thu.	Sept. 25	Mon.	Sept. 16	Sun.*	Oct. 2	Thu.
Yom Kippur (Day of Atonement) .	Tishrei 10	Sept. 25	Sat.	Oct. 13	Thu.	Oct. 2	Mon.	Sept. 22	Sat.	Oct. 9	Thu.
Sukkot	Tishrei 15-21	Sept. 30	Thu.	Oct. 18	Tue.	Oct. 7	Sat.	Sept. 27	Thu.	Oct. 14	Tue.
		Oct. 6	Wed.	Oct. 24	Mon.	Oct. 13	Fri.	Oct. 3	Wed.	Oct. 20	Mon.
Shemini Atzeret	Tishrei 22	Oct. 7	Thu.	Oct. 25	Tue.	Oct. 14	Sat.	Oct. 4	Thu.	Oct. 21	Tue.
Simchat Torah	Tishrei 23	Oct. 8	Fri.	Oct. 26	Wed.	Oct. 15	Sun.	Oct. 5	Fri.	Oct. 22	Wed.
Hanukkah..................	Kislev 25- Tevet 3	Dec. 8	Wed.	Dec. 26	Mon.	Dec. 16	Sat.	Dec. 5	Wed.	Dec. 22	Mon.
		Dec. 15	Wed.	Jan. 2, 2006	Mon.	Dec. 23	Sat.	Dec. 12	Wed.	Dec. 29	Mon.
Fast of the 10th of Tevet[1]	Tevet 10	Dec. 22	Wed.	Jan. 10	Tue.	Dec. 31	Sun.	Dec. 19	Wed.	Jan. 6, 2009	Tue.
Tu B'Shevat	Shevat 15	Jan. 25, 2005	Tue.	Feb. 13, 2006	Mon.	Feb. 3, 2007	Sat.	Jan. 22, 2008	Tue.	Feb. 9	Mon.
Ta'anis Esther (Fast of Esther)[1] . .	Adar 13	Mar. 24	Thu.	Mar. 13	Mon.	Mar. 1	Thu.*	Mar. 20	Thu.	Mar. 9	Mon.
Purim	Adar 14	Mar. 25	Fri.	Mar. 14	Tue.	Mar. 4	Sun.	Mar. 21	Fri.	Mar. 10	Tue.
Pesach (Passover)...........	Nisan 15-22	Apr. 24	Sun.	Apr. 13	Thu.	Apr. 3	Tue.	Apr. 20	Sun.	Apr. 9	Thu.
		May 1	Sun.	Apr. 20	Thu.	Apr. 10	Tue.	Apr. 27	Sun.	Apr. 16	Thu.
Lag B'Omer	Iyar 18	May 27	Fri.	May 16	Tue.	May 6	Sun.	May 23	Fri.	May 12	Tue.
Shavuot (Pentecost)..........	Sivan 6-7	June 13	Mon.	June 2	Fri.	May 23	Wed.	June 9	Mon.	May 29	Fri.
		June 14	Tue.	June 3	Sat.	May 24	Thu.	June 10	Tue.	May 30	Sat.
Fast of the 17th Day of Tammuz[1] .	Tammuz 17	July 24	Sun.	July 13	Thu.	July 3	Tue.	July 20	Sun.	July 9	Thu.
Fast of the 9th Day of Av	Av 9	Aug. 14	Sun.	Aug. 3	Thu.	July 24	Tue.	Aug.10	Sun.	July 30	Thu.

*Date changed to avoid Sabbath. (1) "Minor fasts" begin at sunrise.

Ash Wednesday and Easter Sunday (Western churches), 1901-2100

Year	Ash Wed.	Easter Sunday	Year	Ash Wed.	Easter Sunday	Year	Ash Wed.	Easter Sunday	Year	Ash Wed.	Easter Sunday	Year	Ash Wed.	Easter Sunday	Year	Ash Wed.	Easter Sunday
1901	Feb. 20	Apr. 7	1941	Feb. 26	Apr. 13	1981	Mar. 4	Apr. 19	2021	Feb. 17	Apr. 4	2061	Feb. 23	Apr. 10
1902	Feb. 12	Mar. 30	1942	Feb. 18	Apr. 5	1982	Feb. 24	Apr. 11	2022	Mar. 2	Apr. 17	2062	Feb. 8	Mar. 26
1903	Feb. 25	Apr. 12	1943	Mar. 10	Apr. 25	1983	Feb. 16	Apr. 3	2023	Feb. 22	Apr. 9	2063	Feb. 28	Apr. 15
1904	Feb. 17	Apr. 3	1944	Feb. 23	Apr. 9	1984	Mar. 7	Apr. 22	2024	Feb. 14	Mar. 31	2064	Feb. 20	Apr. 6
1905	Mar. 8	Apr. 23	1945	Feb. 14	Apr. 1	1985	Feb. 20	Apr. 7	2025	Mar. 5	Apr. 20	2065	Feb. 11	Mar. 29
1906	Feb. 28	Apr. 15	1946	Mar. 6	Apr. 21	1986	Feb. 12	Mar. 30	2026	Feb. 18	Apr. 5	2066	Feb. 24	Apr. 11
1907	Feb. 13	Mar. 31	1947	Feb. 19	Apr. 6	1987	Mar. 4	Apr. 19	2027	Feb. 10	Mar. 28	2067	Feb. 16	Apr. 3
1908	Mar. 4	Apr. 19	1948	Feb. 11	Mar. 28	1988	Feb. 17	Apr. 3	2028	Mar. 1	Apr. 16	2068	Mar. 7	Apr. 22
1909	Feb. 24	Apr. 11	1949	Mar. 2	Apr. 17	1989	Feb. 8	Mar. 26	2029	Feb. 14	Apr. 1	2069	Feb. 27	Apr. 14
1910	Feb. 9	Mar. 27	1950	Feb. 22	Apr. 9	1990	Feb. 28	Apr. 15	2030	Mar. 6	Apr. 21	2070	Feb. 12	Mar. 30
1911	Mar. 1	Apr. 16	1951	Feb. 7	Mar. 25	1991	Feb. 13	Mar. 31	2031	Feb. 26	Apr. 13	2071	Mar. 4	Apr. 19
1912	Feb. 21	Apr. 7	1952	Feb. 27	Apr. 13	1992	Mar. 4	Apr. 19	2032	Feb. 11	Mar. 28	2072	Feb. 24	Apr. 10
1913	Feb. 5	Mar. 23	1953	Feb. 18	Apr. 5	1993	Feb. 24	Apr. 11	2033	Mar. 2	Apr. 17	2073	Feb. 8	Mar. 26
1914	Feb. 25	Apr. 12	1954	Mar. 3	Apr. 18	1994	Feb. 16	Apr. 3	2034	Feb. 22	Apr. 9	2074	Feb. 28	Apr. 15
1915	Feb. 17	Apr. 4	1955	Feb. 23	Apr. 10	1995	Mar. 1	Apr. 16	2035	Feb. 7	Mar. 25	2075	Feb. 20	Apr. 7
1916	Mar. 8	Apr. 23	1956	Feb. 15	Apr. 1	1996	Feb. 21	Apr. 7	2036	Feb. 27	Apr. 13	2076	Mar. 4	Apr. 19
1917	Feb. 21	Apr. 8	1957	Mar. 6	Apr. 21	1997	Feb. 12	Mar. 30	2037	Feb. 18	Apr. 5	2077	Feb. 24	Apr. 11
1918	Feb. 13	Mar. 31	1958	Feb. 19	Apr. 6	1998	Feb. 25	Apr. 12	2038	Mar. 10	Apr. 25	2078	Feb. 16	Apr. 3
1919	Mar. 5	Apr. 20	1959	Feb. 11	Mar. 29	1999	Feb. 17	Apr. 4	2039	Feb. 23	Apr. 10	2079	Mar. 8	Apr. 23
1920	Feb. 18	Apr. 4	1960	Mar. 2	Apr. 17	2000	Mar. 8	Apr. 23	2040	Feb. 15	Apr. 1	2080	Feb. 21	Apr. 7
1921	Feb. 9	Mar. 27	1961	Feb. 15	Apr. 2	2001	Feb. 28	Apr. 15	2041	Mar. 6	Apr. 21	2081	Feb. 12	Mar. 30
1922	Mar. 1	Apr. 16	1962	Mar. 7	Apr. 22	2002	Feb. 13	Mar. 31	2042	Feb. 19	Apr. 6	2082	Mar. 4	Apr. 19
1923	Feb. 14	Apr. 1	1963	Feb. 27	Apr. 14	2003	Mar. 5	Apr. 20	2043	Feb. 11	Mar. 29	2083	Feb. 17	Apr. 4
1924	Mar. 5	Apr. 20	1964	Feb. 12	Mar. 29	2004	Feb. 25	Apr. 11	2044	Mar. 2	Apr. 17	2084	Feb. 9	Mar. 26
1925	Feb. 25	Apr. 12	1965	Mar. 3	Apr. 18	2005	Feb. 9	Mar. 27	2045	Feb. 22	Apr. 9	2085	Feb. 28	Apr. 15
1926	Feb. 17	Apr. 4	1966	Feb. 23	Apr. 10	2006	Mar. 1	Apr. 16	2046	Feb. 7	Apr. 25	2086	Feb. 13	Mar. 31
1927	Mar. 2	Apr. 17	1967	Feb. 8	Mar. 26	2007	Feb. 21	Apr. 8	2047	Feb. 27	Apr. 14	2087	Mar. 5	Apr. 20
1928	Feb. 22	Apr. 8	1968	Feb. 28	Apr. 14	2008	Feb. 6	Mar. 23	2048	Feb. 19	Apr. 5	2088	Feb. 25	Apr. 11
1929	Feb. 13	Mar. 31	1969	Feb. 19	Apr. 6	2009	Feb. 25	Apr. 12	2049	Mar. 3	Apr. 18	2089	Feb. 16	Apr. 3
1930	Mar. 5	Apr. 20	1970	Feb. 11	Mar. 29	2010	Feb. 17	Apr. 4	2050	Feb. 23	Apr. 10	2090	Mar. 1	Apr. 16
1931	Feb. 18	Apr. 5	1971	Feb. 24	Apr. 11	2011	Mar. 9	Apr. 24	2051	Feb. 15	Apr. 2	2091	Feb. 21	Apr. 8
1932	Feb. 10	Mar. 27	1972	Feb. 16	Apr. 2	2012	Feb. 22	Apr. 8	2052	Mar. 6	Apr. 21	2092	Feb. 13	Mar. 30
1933	Mar. 1	Apr. 16	1973	Mar. 7	Apr. 22	2013	Feb. 13	Mar. 31	2053	Feb. 19	Apr. 6	2093	Feb. 25	Apr. 12
1934	Feb. 14	Apr. 1	1974	Feb. 27	Apr. 14	2014	Mar. 5	Apr. 20	2054	Feb. 11	Mar. 29	2094	Feb. 17	Apr. 4
1935	Mar. 6	Apr. 21	1975	Feb. 12	Mar. 30	2015	Feb. 18	Apr. 5	2055	Mar. 3	Apr. 18	2095	Mar. 9	Apr. 24
1936	Feb. 26	Apr. 12	1976	Mar. 3	Apr. 18	2016	Feb. 10	Mar. 27	2056	Feb. 16	Apr. 2	2096	Feb. 29	Apr. 15
1937	Feb. 10	Mar. 28	1977	Feb. 23	Apr. 10	2017	Mar. 1	Apr. 16	2057	Mar. 7	Apr. 22	2097	Feb. 13	Mar. 31
1938	Mar. 2	Apr. 17	1978	Feb. 8	Mar. 26	2018	Feb. 14	Apr. 1	2058	Feb. 27	Apr. 14	2098	Mar. 5	Apr. 20
1939	Feb. 22	Apr. 9	1979	Feb. 28	Apr. 15	2019	Mar. 6	Apr. 21	2059	Feb. 12	Mar. 30	2099	Feb. 25	Apr. 12
1940	Feb. 7	Mar. 24	1980	Feb. 20	Apr. 6	2020	Feb. 26	Apr. 12	2060	Mar. 3	Apr. 18	2100	Feb. 10	Mar. 28

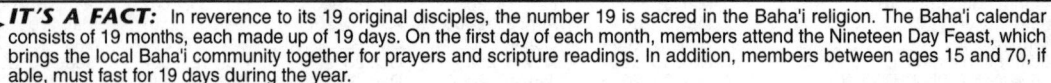

IT'S A FACT: In reverence to its 19 original disciples, the number 19 is sacred in the Baha'i religion. The Baha'i calendar consists of 19 months, each made up of 19 days. On the first day of each month, members attend the Nineteen Day Feast, which brings the local Baha'i community together for prayers and scripture readings. In addition, members between ages 15 and 70, if able, must fast for 19 days during the year.

The Ten Commandments

In the Hebrew Bible (Old Testament) the Ten Commandments (also called the Decalogue, from the Greek meaning "ten words") were revealed by God to Moses on Mt. Sinai. They form the covenant between God and the Israelites and the moral code that is the basis for the Jewish and Christian religions. The Ten Commandments appear in 2 places in the Old Testament—Exodus 20:1-17 and Deuteronomy 5:6-21.

Most Protestant, Anglican, and Orthodox Christians follow Jewish tradition, as here, which considers the introduction ("I am the Lord . . .") the first commandment and makes the prohibition against idolatry the second. Roman Catholic and Lutheran traditions combine I and II and split the last commandment into 2 that separately prohibit coveting of a neighbor's wife and a neighbor's goods. This arrangement alters the numbering of the other commandments by one.

Following is the text of the Ten Commandments as it appears in Exodus 20:1-17, in the King James version of the Bible [Roman numerals added]:

And God spake all these words, saying,

I. I *am* the LORD thy God, which have brought thee out of the land of Egypt, out of the house of bondage. Thou shalt have no other gods before me.

II. Thou shalt not make unto thee any graven image, or any likeness of *any thing* that *is* in heaven above, or that *is* in the earth beneath, or that *is* in the water under the earth. Thou shalt not bow down thyself to them, nor serve them: for I the LORD thy God *am* a jealous God, visiting the iniquity of the fathers upon the children unto the third and fourth *generation* of them that hate me; and shewing mercy unto thousands of them that love me, and keep my commandments.

III. Thou shalt not take the name of the LORD thy God in vain: for the LORD will not hold him guiltless that taketh his name in vain.

IV. Remember the sabbath day, to keep it holy. Six days shalt thou labour, and do all thy work: but the seventh day *is* the sabbath of the LORD thy God: *in it* thou shalt not do any work, thou, nor thy son, nor thy daughter, thy manservant, nor thy maidservant, nor thy cattle, nor thy stranger that *is* within thy gates: for *in* six days the LORD made heaven and earth, the sea, and all that in them *is*, and rested the seventh day: wherefore the LORD blessed the sabbath day, and hallowed it.

V. Honour thy father and thy mother: that thy days may be long upon the land which the LORD thy God giveth thee.

VI. Thou shalt not kill.

VII. Thou shalt not commit adultery.

VIII. Thou shalt not steal.

IX. Thou shalt not bear false witness against thy neighbour.

X. Thou shalt not covet thy neighbour's house, thou shalt not covet thy neighbour's wife, nor his manservant, nor his maidservant, nor his ox, nor his ass, nor any thing that *is* thy neighbour's.

Books of the Bible

Old Testament—Standard Protestant List

Genesis	I Kings	Ecclesiastes	Obadiah
Exodus	II Kings	Song of Solomon	Jonah
Leviticus	I Chronicles	Isaiah	Micah
Numbers	II Chronicles	Jeremiah	Nahum
Deuteronomy	Ezra	Lamentations	Habakkuk
Joshua	Nehemiah	Ezekiel	Zephaniah
Judges	Esther	Daniel	Haggai
Ruth	Job	Hosea	Zechariah
I Samuel	Psalms	Joel	Malachi
II Samuel	Proverbs	Amos	

New Testament List

Matthew	Ephesians	Hebrews
Mark	Phillippians	James
Luke	Colossians	I Peter
John	I Thessalonians	II Peter
Acts	II Thessalonians	I John
Romans	I Timothy	II John
I Corinthians	II Timothy	III John
II Corinthians	Titus	Jude
Galatians	Philemon	Revelation

The standard Protestant Old Testament consists of the same 39 books as in the Bible of Judaism, but the latter is organized differently. The Old Testament used by Roman Catholics has 7 additional "deuterocanonical" books, plus some additional parts of books. The 7 are: **Tobit, Judith, Wisdom, Sirach (Ecclesiasticus), Baruch, I Maccabees,** and **II Maccabees**. Both Catholic and Protestant versions of the New Testament have 27 books, with the same names.

Roman Catholic Hierarchy

Sources: U.S. Catholic Conference; Holy See Press Office

Supreme Pontiff

At the head of the Roman Catholic Church is the supreme pontiff, Pope John Paul II, Karol Wojtyla, born at Wadowice (Kraków), Poland, May 18, 1920; ordained priest Nov. 1, 1946; appointed bishop July 4, 1958; named archbishop of Kraków Jan. 13, 1964; proclaimed cardinal June 26, 1967; elected pope Oct. 16, 1978; installed Oct. 22, 1978.

Chronological List of Popes

Source: Annuario Pontificio. Table lists year of accession of each pope.

The Roman Catholic Church named the Apostle Peter as founder of the church in Rome and the first pope. He arrived there c 42, was martyred there c 67, and was ultimately canonized as a saint. **The pope's temporal title is:** Sovereign of the State of Vatican City. **The pope's spiritual titles are:** Bishop of Rome, Vicar of Jesus Christ, Successor of St. Peter, Prince of the Apostles, Supreme Pontiff of the Universal Church, Patriarch of the West, Primate of Italy, Archbishop and Metropolitan of the Roman Province.

The names of antipopes are *in italics* and followed by an *. Antipopes were illegitimate claimants to the papal throne.

Year	Pope	Year	Pope	Year	Pope	Year	Pope	Year	Pope
	St. Peter	222	St. Urban I	336	St. Marcus	492	St. Gelasius I	590	St. Gregory I
67	St. Linus	230	St. Pontian	337	St. Julius I	496	Anastasius II	604	Sabinian
76	St. Anacletus	235	St. Anterus	352	Liberius	498	St. Symmachus	607	Boniface III
	or Cletus	236	St. Fabian	355	*Felix II**	498	*Lawrence** (501-	608	St. Boniface IV
88	St. Clement I	251	St. Cornelius	366	St. Damasus I		505)	615	St. Deusdedit or
97	St. Evaristus	251	*Novatian**	366	*Ursinus**	514	St. Hormisdas		Adeodatus
105	St. Alexander I	253	St. Lucius I	384	St. Siricius	523	St. John I, Martyr	619	Boniface V
115	St. Sixtus I	254	St. Stephen I	399	St. Anastasius I	526	St. Felix IV (III)	625	Honorius I
125	St. Telesphorus	257	St. Sixtus II	401	St. Innocent I	530	Boniface II	640	Severinus
136	St. Hyginus	259	St. Dionysius	417	St. Zosimus	530	*Dioscorus**	640	John IV
140	St. Pius I	269	St. Felix I	418	St. Boniface I	533	John II	642	Theodore I
155	St. Anicetus	275	St. Eutychian	418	*Eulalius**	535	St. Agapitus I	649	St. Martin I, Martyr
166	St. Soter	283	St. Caius	422	St. Celestine I	536	St. Silverius, Martyr	654	St. Eugene I
175	St. Eleutherius	296	St. Marcellinus	432	St. Sixtus III	537	Vigilius	657	St. Vitalian
189	St. Victor I	308	St. Marcellus I	440	St. Leo I	556	Pelagius I	672	Adeodatus II
199	St. Zephyrinus	309	St. Eusebius	461	St. Hilary	561	John III	676	Donus
217	St. Callistus I	311	St. Melchiades	468	St. Simplicius	575	Benedict I	678	St. Agatho
217	*St. Hippolytus**	314	St. Sylvester I	483	St. Felix III (II)	579	Pelagius II	682	St. Leo II

Year	Pope	Year	Pope	Year	Pope	Year	Pope	Year	Pope
684	St. Benedict II	903	Leo V	1061	Alexander II	1276	Adrian V	1555	Paul IV
685	John V	903	*Christopher**	1061	*Honorius II**	1276	John XXI	1559	Pius IV
686	Conon	904	Sergius III	1073	St. Gregory VII	1277	Nicholas III	1566	St. Pius V
687	*Theodore**	911	Anastasius III	1080	*Clement III**	1281	Martin IV	1572	Gregory XIII
687	*Paschal**	913	Landus	1086	Bl. Victor III	1285	Honorius IV	1585	Sixtus V
687	St. Sergius I	914	John X	1088	Bl. Urban II	1288	Nicholas IV	1590	Urban VII
701	John VI	928	Leo VI	1099	Paschal II	1294	St. Celestine V	1590	Gregory XIV
705	John VII	928	Stephen VII(VIII)	1100	*Theodoric**	1294	Boniface VIII	1591	Innocent IX
708	Sisinnius	931	John XI	1102	*Albert**	1303	Bl. Benedict XI	1592	Clement VIII
708	Constantine	936	Leo VII	1105	*Sylvester IV**	1305	Clement V	1605	Leo XI
715	St. Gregory II	939	Stephen VIII(IX)	1118	Gelasius II	1316	John XXII	1605	Paul V
731	St. Gregory III	942	Marinus II	1118	*Gregory VIII**	1328	*Nicholas V**	1621	Gregory XV
741	St. Zachary	946	Agapitus II	1119	Callistus II	1334	Benedict XII	1623	Urban VIII
752	Stephen II (III)[1]	955	John XII	1124	Honorius II	1342	Clement VI	1644	Innocent X
757	St. Paul I	963	Leo VIII	1124	*Celestine II**	1352	Innocent VI	1655	Alexander VII
767	*Constantine**	964	Benedict V	1130	Innocent II	1362	Bl. Urban V	1667	Clement IX
768	*Philip**	965	John XIII	1130	*Anacletus II**	1370	Gregory XI	1670	Clement X
768	Stephen III (IV)	973	Benedict VI	1138	*Victor IV**	1378	Urban VI	1676	Bl. Innocent XI
772	Adrian I	974	*Boniface VII**	1143	Celestine II	1378	*Clement VII**	1689	Alexander VIII
795	St. Leo III	974	Benedict VII	1144	Lucius II	1389	Boniface IX	1691	Innocent XII
816	Stephen IV (V)	983	John XIV	1145	Bl. Eugene III	1394	*Benedict XIII**	1700	Clement XI
817	St. Paschal I	985	John XV	1153	Anastasius IV	1404	Innocent VII	1721	Innocent XIII
824	Eugene II	996	Gregory V	1154	Adrian IV	1406	Gregory XII	1724	Benedict XIII
827	Valentine	997	*John XVI**	1159	Alexander III	1409	*Alexander V**	1730	Clement XII
827	Gregory IV	999	Sylvester II	1159	*Victor IV**	1410	*John XXIII**	1740	Benedict XIV
844	*John**	1003	John XVII	1164	*Paschal III**	1417	Martin V	1758	Clement XIII
844	Sergius II	1004	John XVIII	1168	*Callistus III**	1431	Eugene IV	1769	Clement XIV
847	St. Leo IV	1009	Sergius IV	1179	*Innocent III**	1439	*Felix V**	1775	Pius VI
855	Benedict III	1012	Benedict VIII	1181	Lucius III	1447	Nicholas V	1800	Pius VII
855	*Anastasius**	1012	*Gregory**	1185	Urban III	1455	Callistus III	1823	Leo XII
858	St. Nicholas I	1024	John XIX	1187	Clement III	1458	Pius II	1829	Pius VIII
867	Adrian II	1032	Benedict IX	1187	Gregory VIII	1464	Paul II	1831	Gregory XVI
872	John VIII	1045	Sylvester III	1191	Celestine III	1471	Sixtus IV	1846	Pius IX
882	Marinus I	1045	Benedict IX	1198	Innocent III	1484	Innocent VIII	1878	Leo XIII
884	St. Adrian III	1045	Gregory VI	1216	Honorius III	1492	Alexander VI	1903	St. Pius X
885	Stephen V (VI)	1046	Clement II	1227	Gregory IX	1503	Pius III	1914	Benedict XV
891	Formosus	1047	Benedict IX	1241	Celestine IV	1503	Julius II	1922	Pius XI
896	Boniface VI	1048	Damasus II	1243	Innocent IV	1513	Leo X	1939	Pius XII
896	Stephen VI (VII)	1049	St. Leo IX	1254	Alexander IV	1522	Adrian VI	1958	John XXIII
897	Romanus	1055	Victor II	1261	Urban IV	1523	Clement VII	1963	Paul VI
897	Theodore II	1057	Stephen IX (X)	1265	Clement IV	1534	Paul III	1978	John Paul I
898	John IX	1058	*Benedict X**	1271	Bl. Gregory X	1550	Julius III	1978	John Paul II
900	Benedict IV	1059	Nicholas II	1276	Bl. Innocent V	1555	Marcellus II		

(1) After St. Zachary, a Roman priest named Stephen was elected, but died before assuming the papacy. Another Stephen was then elected to succeed Zachary as Stephen II. He is sometimes listed as Stephen III.

College of Cardinals

Members of the Sacred College of Cardinals are chosen by the pope to be his chief assistants and advisers in the administration of the church. Among their duties is the election of the pope when the Holy See becomes vacant.

In its present form, the College of Cardinals dates from the 12th century. The first cardinals, from about the 6th century, were deacons and priests of the leading churches of Rome and were bishops of neighboring dioceses. The title of cardinal was limited to members of the college in 1567. The number of cardinals was set at 70 in 1586 by Pope Sixtus V. From 1959 Pope John XXIII began to increase the number; however, the number eligible to participate in papal elections was limited to 120. Previous limitations were set aside by Pope John Paul II in 1998, and again in 2001 when he created 44 new cardinals. As of Aug. 2004, there were 190 members of the College, of whom 123 remained eligible to vote. In 1918 the Code of Canon Law specified that all cardinals must be priests. Pope John XXIII in 1962 established that all cardinals must be bishops, but this can be dispensed with, as in the case of Cardinal Avery Dulles. In 1971, Pope Paul VI decreed that at age 80 cardinals must retire from curial departments and offices and from participation in papal elections.

North American Cardinals

Name	Office	Born	Named Cardinal
Aloysius M. Ambrozic	Archbishop of Toronto	1930	1998
William W. Baum	Archbishop emeritus of Washington, DC	1926	1976
Anthony J. Bevilacqua[1]	Archbishop emeritus of Philadelphia	1923	1991
Ernesto Corripio Ahumada[1]	Archbishop emeritus of Mexico	1919	1979
Avery Robert Dulles[1]	Professor, Fordham University, NYC	1918	2001
Edward M. Egan	Archbishop of New York	1932	2001
Edouard Gagnon[1]	Pres. Emeritus of the Commission of Intl. Eucharistic Congresses	1918	1985
Francis E. George	Archbishop of Chicago	1937	1998
James A. Hickey[1]	Archbishop emeritus of Washington, DC	1920	1988
William Henry Keeler	Archbishop of Baltimore	1931	1994
Bernard F. Law	Archbishop emeritus of Boston	1931	1985
Roger Mahony	Archbishop of Los Angeles	1936	1991
Adam Joseph Maida	Archbishop of Detroit	1930	1994
Luis Aponte Martinez[1]	Archibishop emeritus of San Juan	1922	1973
Theodore E. McCarrick	Archbishop of Washington, DC	1930	2001
Marc Ouellet	Archbishop of Quebec	1944	2003
Norberto Rivera Carrera	Archbishop of Mexico City	1942	1998
Juan Sandoval Iniguez	Archbishop of Guadalajara	1933	1994
James F. Stafford	President of the Pontifical Council for the Laity	1932	1998
Adolfo Antonio Suarez Rivera	Archbishop of Monterrey	1927	1994
Edmund C. Szoka	Pres. of Prefecture of Economic Affairs of Holy See, the Vatican	1927	1988
Jean-Claude Turcotte	Archbishop of Montreal	1936	1994
Louis-Albert Vachon[1]	Archbishop emeritus of Quebec	1912	1985

(1) Ineligible to take part in papal elections (as of Sept. 2004).

Major Non-Christian World Religions

Sources: Reviewed by Anthony Padovano, PhD, STD, prof. of literature & relig. studies, Ramapo College, NJ, adj. prof. of theol., Fordham U., NYC; Islam reviewed by Abdulaziz Sachedina, PhD, prof. of Islamic studies, Univ. of Virginia

Buddhism

Founded: About 525 BC, reportedly near Benares, India.

Founder: Gautama Siddhartha (c 563-483 BC), the Buddha, who achieved enlightenment through intense meditation.

Sacred Texts: The *Tripitaka*, a collection of the Buddha's teachings, rules of monastic life, and philosophical commentaries on the teachings; also a vast body of Buddhist teachings and commentaries, many of which are called *sutras.*

Organization: The basic institution is the *sangha*, or monastic order, through which the traditions are passed from generation to generation. Monastic life tends to be democratic and anti-authoritarian. Large lay organizations have developed in some sects.

Practice: Varies widely according to the sect, and ranges from austere meditation to magical chanting and elaborate temple rites. Many practices, such as exorcism of devils, reflect pre-Buddhist beliefs.

Divisions: A variety of sects grouped into 3 primary branches: Theravada (sole survivor of the ancient Hinayana schools), which emphasizes the importance of pure thought and deed; Mahayana (includes Zen and Soka-gakkai), which ranges from philosophical schools to belief in the saving grace of higher beings or ritual practices and to practical meditative disciplines; and Tantrism, a combination of belief in ritual magic and sophisticated philosophy.

Location: Throughout Asia, from Sri Lanka to Japan. Zen and Soka-gakkai have some 15,000 adherents in the U.S.

Beliefs: Life is misery and decay, and there is no ultimate reality in it or behind it. The cycle of endless birth and rebirth continues because of desire and attachment to the unreal "self." Right meditation and deeds will end the cycle and achieve Nirvana, the Void, nothingness.

Hinduism

Founded: About 1500 BC by Aryans who migrated to India, where their Vedic religion intermixed with the practices and beliefs of the natives.

Sacred texts: The *Veda,* including the *Upanishads,* a collection of rituals and mythological and philosophical commentaries; a vast number of epic stories about gods, heroes, and saints, including the *Bhagavadgita,* a part of the *Mahabharata,* and the *Ramayana;* and a great variety of other literature.

Organization: None, strictly speaking. Generally, rituals should be performed or assisted by Brahmins, the priestly caste, but in practice, simpler rituals can be performed by anyone. Brahmins are the final judges of ritual purity, the vital element in Hindu life. Temples and religious organizations are usually presided over by Brahmins.

Practice: A variety of private rituals, primarily passage rites (e.g., initiation, marriage, death, etc.) and daily devotions, and a similar variety of public rites in temples. Of the public rites, the *puja,* a ceremonial dinner for a god, is the most common.

Divisions: There is no concept of orthodoxy in Hinduism, which presents a variety of sects, most of them devoted to the worship of one of the many gods. The 3 major living traditions are those devoted to the gods Vishnu and Shiva and to the goddess Shakti; each is divided into further subsects. Numerous folk beliefs and practices, often in amalgamation with the above groups, exist side by side with sophisticated philosophical schools and exotic cults.

Location: Mainly India, Nepal, Malaysia, Guyana, Suriname, and Sri Lanka.

Beliefs: There is only one divine principle; the many gods are only aspects of that unity. Life in all its forms is an aspect of the divine, but it appears as a separation from the divine, a meaningless cycle of birth and rebirth (*samsara*) determined by the purity or impurity of past deeds (*karma*). To improve one's *karma* or escape *samsara* by pure acts, thought, and/or devotion is the aim of every Hindu.

Islam

Founded: About AD 622 in Mecca, Arabian Peninsula.

Founder: Muhammad (c 570-632), the Prophet.

Sacred texts: The *Koran* (al-Qur'an), the Word of God; *Sunna*, collections of *Hadith*, describing what Muhammad said or did.

Organization: Since the founder was both a prophet and a statesman, Muslim leadership has combined the civil and moral function of a state. Within the larger community, there are cultural and national groups, held together by a common religious law, the *Shari'a*, enforced uniformly in matters of religion only. In social transactions the community has often departed from traditional formulations. Although Islam is basically egalitarian and suspicious of authoritarianism, Muslim culture tends to be dominated by the conservative spirit of its religious establishment, the *ulema.*

Practice: Besides the general moral guidance that determines everyday life, there are "Five Pillars of Islam": profession of faith (oneness of God and prophethood of Muhammad); prayer 5 times a day; alms *(zakat)* from one's savings and estate; dawn-to-dusk fasting in the month of Ramadan; and once in a lifetime, pilgrimage to Mecca, if possible.

Divisions: There are 2 major groups: the majority known as Sunni and the minority Shiites. Shiites believe in Twelve Imams (perfect teachers) after the Prophet, of whom the last Imam has lived an invisible existence since 874, continuing to guide his community. Sunni Muslims believe in God's overpowering will over their affairs and tend to be predestinarian; Shiites believe in free will and give a substantial role to human reason in daily life. Sufism (mystical dimension of Islam) is prevalent among both Sunni and Shiites. Sufis emphasize personal relation to God and obedience informed by love of God.

Location: W Africa to Philippines, across band including E Africa, Central Asia and W China, India, Malaysia, Indonesia. Islam has several million adherents in North America.

Beliefs: Strictly monotheistic. God is creator of the universe, omnipotent, omniscient, just, forgiving, and merciful. The human is God's highest creation, but weak and egocentric, prone to forget the goal of life, constantly tempted by the Satan, an evil being. God revealed the Koran to Muhammad to guide humanity to truth and justice. Those who repent and sincerely "submit" (literal meaning of "islam") to God attain salvation. The forgiven enter the Paradise, and the wicked burn in Hell.

Judaism

Founded: About 2000 BC.

Founder: Abraham is regarded as the founding patriarch, but the Torah of Moses is the basic source of the teachings.

Sacred Texts: The 5 books of Moses constitute the written Torah. Special sanctity is also assigned other writings of the Hebrew Bible—the teachings of oral Torah are recorded in the Talmud, in the Midrash, and in various commentaries.

Organization: Originally theocratic, Judaism has evolved a congregational polity. The basic institution is the local synagogue, operated by the congregation and led by a rabbi of their choice. Chief rabbis in France and Great Britain have authority only over those who accept it; in Israel, the 2 chief rabbis have civil authority in family law.

Practice: Among traditional practicioners, almost all areas of life are governed by strict religious discipline. Sabbath and holidays are marked by special observances, and attendance at public worship is considered especially important then. Chief annual observances are Passover, celebrating liberation of the Israelites from Egypt and marked by the Seder meal in homes, and the 10 days from Rosh Hashanah (New Year) to Yom Kippur (Day of Atonement), a period of fasting and penitence.

Divisions: Judaism is an unbroken spectrum from ultra-conservative to ultraliberal, largely reflecting different points of view regarding the binding character of the prohibitions and duties—particularly the dietary and Sabbath observations—traditionally prescribed for the daily life of the Jew.

Location: Almost worldwide, with concentrations in Israel and the U.S.

Beliefs: Strictly monotheistic. God is the creator and absolute ruler of the universe. God established a particular relationship with the Hebrew people: by obeying a divine law God gave them, they would be a special witness to God's mercy and justice. Judaism stresses ethical behavior and, among the traditional, careful ritual obedience) as true worship of God.

Major Christian Denominations:

Brackets indicate some features that tend to

Denom-ination	Origins	Organization	Authority	Special rites
Baptists	In radical Reformation, objections to infant baptism, demands for church and state separation; John Smyth, English Separatist, in 1609; Roger Williams, 1638, Providence, RI.	Congregational; each local church is autonomous.	Scripture; some Baptists, particularly in the South, interpret the Bible literally.	*[Baptism, usually early teen years and after, by total immersion;]* Lord's Supper.
Church of Christ (Disciples)	Among evangelical Presbyterians in KY (1804) and PA (1809), in distress over Protestant factionalism and decline of fervor; organized in 1832.	Congregational.	*["Where the Scriptures speak, we speak; where the Scriptures are silent, we are silent."]*	Adult baptism; Lord's Supper (weekly).
Episcopalians	Henry VIII separated English Catholic Church from Rome, 1534, for political reasons; Protestant Episcopal Church in U.S. founded in 1789.	*[Diocesan bishops, in apostolic succession, are elected by parish representatives; the national Church is headed by General Convention and Presiding Bishop; part of the Anglican Communion.]*	Scripture as interpreted by tradition, especially 39 Articles (1563); tri-annual convention of bishops, priests, and lay people.	Infant baptism, Eucharist, and other sacraments; sacrament taken to be symbolic, but as having real spiritual effect.
Jehovah's Witnesses	Founded in 1870 in PA by Charles Taze Russell; incorporated as Watch Tower Bible and Tract Society of PA, 1884; name Jehovah's Witnesses adopted in 1931.	A governing body located in NY coordinates worldwide activities; each congregation cared for by a body of elders; each Witness considered a minister.	The Bible.	Baptism by immersion; annual Lord's Meal ceremony.
Latter-day Saints (Mormons)	In a vision of the Father and the Son reported by Joseph Smith (1820s) in NY. Smith also reported receiving new scripture on golden tablets: The Book of Mormon.	Theocratic; 1st Presidency (church president, 2 counselors), 12 Apostles preside over international church. Local congregations headed by lay priesthood leaders.	Revelation to living prophet (church president). The Bible, Book of Mormon, and other revelations to Smith and his successors.	Baptism, at age 8; laying on of hands (which confers the gift of the Holy Ghost); Lord's Supper; temple rites: baptism for the dead, marriage for eternity, others.
Lutherans	Begun by Martin Luther in Wittenberg, Germany, in 1517; objection to Catholic doctrine of salvation and sale of indulgences; break complete, 1519.	Varies from congregational to episcopal; in U.S., a combination of regional synods and congregational polities is most common.	Scripture alone. *The Book of Concord* (1580), which includes the three Ecumenical Creeds, is subscribed to as a correct exposition of Scripture.	Infant baptism; Lord's Supper; Christ's true body and blood present "in, with, and under the bread and wine."
Methodists	Rev. John Wesley began movement in 1738, within Church of England; first U.S. denomination, Baltimore (1784).	Conference and superintendent system; *[in United Methodist Church, general superintendents are bishops—not a priestly order, only an office—who are elected for life.]*	Scripture as interpreted by tradition, reason, and experience.	Baptism of infants or adults; Lord's Supper commanded; other rites: marriage, ordination, solemnization of personal commitments.
Orthodox	Developed in original Christian proselytizing; broke with Rome in 1054, after centuries of doctrinal disputes and diverging traditions.	Synods of bishops in autonomous, usually national, churches elect a patriarch, archbishop, or metropolitan; these men, as a group, are the heads of the church.	Scripture, tradition, and the first 7 church councils up to Nicaea II in 787; bishops in council have authority in doctrine and policy.	Seven sacraments: infant baptism and anointing, Eucharist, ordination, penance, marriage, and anointing of the sick.
Pentecostal	In Topeka, KS (1901) and Los Angeles (1906), in reaction to perceived loss of evangelical fervor among Methodists and others.	Originally a movement, not a formal organization, Pentecostalism now has a variety of organized forms and continues also as a movement.	Scripture; individual charismatic leaders, the teachings of the Holy Spirit.	*[Spirit baptism, especially as shown in "speaking in tongues"; healing and sometimes exorcism;]* adult baptism; Lord's Supper.
Presbyterians	In 16th-cent. Calvinist reformation; differed with Lutherans over sacraments, church government; John Knox founded Scotch Presbyerian church about 1560.	*[Highly structured representational system of ministers and lay persons (presbyters) in local, regional, and national bodies (synods).]*	Scripture.	Infant baptism; Lord's Supper; bread and wine symbolize Christ's spiritual presence.
Roman Catholics	Traditionally, founded by Jesus who named St. Peter the 1st vicar; developed in early Christian proselytizing, especially after the conversion of imperial Rome in the 4th cent.	*[Hierarchy with supreme power vested in pope elected by cardinals;]* councils of bishops advise on matters of doctrine and policy.	*[The pope, when speaking for the whole church in matters of faith and morals; and tradition (which is expressed in church councils and in part contained in Scripture).]*	Mass; 7 sacraments: baptism, reconciliation, Eucharist, confirmation, marriage, ordination, and anointing of the sick (unction).
United Church of Christ	*[By ecumenical union, in 1957, of Congregationalists and Evangelical & Reformed, representing both Calvinist and Lutheran traditions.]*	Congregational; a General Synod, representative of all congregations, sets general policy.	Scripture.	Infant baptism; Lord's Supper.

How Do They Differ?

distinguish a denomination sharply from others.

Practice	Ethics	Doctrine	Other	Denomination
Worship style varies from staid to evangelistic; extensive missionary activity.	Usually opposed to alcohol and tobacco; some tendency toward a perfectionist ethical standard.	*[No creed; true church is of believers only, who are all equal.]*	Believing no authority can stand between the believer and God, the Baptists are strong supporters of church and state separation.	**Baptists**
Tries to avoid any rite not considered part of the 1st-century church; some congregations may reject instrumental music.	Some tendency toward perfectionism; increasing interest in social action programs.	Simple New Testament faith; avoids any elaboration not firmly based on Scripture.	Highly tolerant in doctrinal and religious matters; strongly supportive of scholarly education.	**Church of Christ (Disciples)**
Formal, based on "Book of Common Prayer," updated 1979; services range from austerely simple to highly liturgical.	Tolerant, sometimes permissive; some social action programs.	Scripture; the "historic creeds," which include the Apostles', Nicene, and Athanasian, and the "Book of Common Prayer"; ranges from Anglo-Catholic to low church, with Calvinist influences.	Strongly ecumenical, holding talks with many branches of Christendom.	**Episcopalians**
Meetings are held in Kingdom Halls and members' homes for study and worship; *[extensive door-to-door visitations.]*	High moral code; stress on marital fidelity and family values; avoidance of tobacco and blood transfusions.	*[God, by his first creation, Christ, will soon destroy all wickedness; 144,000 faithful ones will rule in heaven with Christ over others on a paradise earth.]*	Total allegiance proclaimed only to God's kingdom or heavenly government by Christ; main periodical, *The Watchtower,* is printed in 115 languages.	**Jehovah's Witnesses**
Simple service with prayers, hymns, sermon; private temple ceremonies may be more elaborate.	Temperance; strict moral code; *[tithing];* a strong work ethic with communal self-reliance; *[strong missionary activity];* family emphasis.	Jesus Christ is the Son of God, the Eternal Father. Jesus' atonement saves all humans; those who are obedient to God's laws may become joint-heirs with Christ in God's kingdom.	Mormons believe theirs is the true church of Jesus Christ, restored by God through Joseph Smith. Official name: The Church of Jesus Christ of Latter-day Saints.	**Latter-day Saints (Mormons)**
Relatively simple, formal liturgy with emphasis on the sermon.	Generally conservative in personal and social ethics; doctrine of "2 kingdoms" (worldly and holy) supports conservatism in secular affairs.	Salvation by grace alone through faith; Lutheranism has made major contributions to Protestant theology.	Though still somewhat divided along ethnic lines (German, Swedish, etc.), main divisions are between fundamentalists and liberals.	**Lutherans**
Worship style varies widely by denomination, local church, geography.	Originally pietist and perfectionist; always strong social activist elements.	No distinctive theological development; 25 Articles abridged from Church of England's 39, not binding.	In 1968, The United Methodist Church was formed by the union of The Methodist Church and The Evangelical United Brethren Church.	**Methodists**
[Elaborate liturgy, usually in the vernacular, though extremely traditional; the liturgy is the essence of Orthodoxy; veneration of icons.]	Tolerant; little stress on social action; divorce, remarriage permitted in some cases; bishops are celibate; priests need not be.	Emphasis on Christ's resurrection, rather than crucifixion; the Holy Spirit proceeds from God the Father only.	Orthodox Church in America originally under Patriarch of Moscow, was granted autonomy in 1970; Greek Orthodox do not recognize this autonomy.	**Orthodox**
Loosely structured service with rousing hymns and sermons, culminating in spirit baptism.	Usually, emphasis on perfectionism, with varying degrees of tolerance.	Simple traditional beliefs, usually Protestant, with emphasis on the immediate presence of God in the Holy Spirit.	Once confined to lower-class "holy rollers," Pentecostalism now appears in mainline churches and has established middle-class congregations.	**Pentecostal**
A simple, sober service in which the sermon is central.	Traditionally, a tendency toward strictness, with firm church- and self-discipline; otherwise tolerant.	Emphasizes the sovereignty and justice of God; no longer dogmatic.	Although traces of belief in predestination (that God has foreordained salvation for the "elect") remain, this idea is no longer a central element in Presbyterianism.	**Presbyterians**
Relatively elaborate ritual centered on the Mass; also rosary recitation, novenas, etc.	Traditionally strict, but increasingly tolerant in practice; divorce and remarriage not accepted, but annulments sometimes granted; celibate clergy, except in Eastern rite.	Highly elaborated; salvation by merit gained through grace; dogmatic; special veneration of Mary, the mother of Jesus.	Relatively rapid change followed Vatican Council II; Mass now in vernacular; more stress on social action, tolerance, ecumenism.	**Roman Catholics**
Usually simple services with emphasis on the sermon.	Tolerant; some social action emphasis.	Standard Protestant; "Statement of Faith" (1959) is not binding.	The 2 main churches in the 1957 union represented earlier unions with small groups of almost every Protestant denomination.	**United Church of Christ**

TRAVEL AND TOURISM

Tourism Trends

After increasing by 2.7% in 2002, world tourist arrivals fell slightly, by 1.2% in 2003, according to the World Tourism Organization based in Madrid, Spain. Worldwide, there were 694 million international tourist arrivals in 2003, 8.6 million fewer than in 2002. However, worldwide tourism receipts as measured in U.S. dollars rose by 8.4%, from $474 billion in 2002 to $514 billion in 2003, but this was largely because of the depreciation of the U.S. dollar. Europe commanded the largest share of international arrivals, about 57.8% of the world total, with 401.5 million international tourist arrivals, a slight increase of 0.4%. Despite a 9.3% decrease, Asia and the Pacific still had the second-largest share at 17.2%, with about 119.1 million arrivals in 2003. Africa saw 30.5 million arrivals, up by 4.9%. The Middle East had 30.4 million arrivals, a 10.3% increase from 2002. With about 112.4 million arrivals, the Americas experienced an overall decline in tourism for a second year, down by about 2.1% from 2002. Within this region, only North America's tourism declined, while South America, Central America, and the Caribbean all had increases.

Tourism began to rebound in the first half of 2004, most significantly in Asia, which had a strong recovery from the 2003 SARS outbreak. Travel in Africa and the Middle East continued to climb, while tourism in Europe and North America rose slightly. The International Air Transport Assoc., which measures air passenger traffic in revenue passenger kilometers, reported a 20.4% increase in passenger traffic in Jan.-June 2004, compared with the same period in 2003. The Asia-Pacific and Middle East regions had the largest increases, at 35.0% and 44.3%, respectively. According to the Air Transport Assoc. of America, air passenger traffic in the U.S. (measured in revenue passenger miles) rose by 2.3% in 2003, and was up by 11.7% in the first half of 2004 compared with same period in 2003. The Travel Industry Assoc. of America reported that average airfares in the U.S. were 2.4% lower in June 2004 than in June 2003.

World Tourism Receipts, 1990-2003

Source: World Tourism Organization

(in billions; figures rounded)

1990.... $264	1992 ....$317	1994.... $356	1996... $439	1998 ....$445	2000.... $473	2002 ....$474
1991.... 278	1993 323	1995.... 405	1997... 443	1999 455	2001.... 459	2003 514

Top Countries in Tourism Earnings, 2003

Source: World Tourism Organization

International tourism receipts (excluding transportation); in billions of dollars

Rank	Country	Receipts 2002	2003	% change	Rank	Country	Receipts 2002	2003	% change
1.	United States......	$66.5	$65.1	−2.2	9.	Turkey..........	$11.9	$13.2	10.9
2.	Spain..........	33.6	41.7	24.1	10.	Greece..........	9.7	10.6	9.5
3.	France..........	32.3	36.3	12.4	11.	Mexico	8.9	9.5	6.8
4.	Italy	26.9	31.3	16.2	12.	Canada..........	9.7	9.3	−4.1
5.	Germany........	19.2	22.8	19.2	13.	Netherlands	7.7	9.2	19.8
6.	United Kingdom....	17.6	19.5	10.9	14.	Japan[2]	3.5	8.8	152.8
7.	China[1]	20.4	17.4	−14.6	15.	Belgium..........	6.9	8.3	20.3
8.	Austria..........	11.4	13.6	19.0					

(1) Excluding Hong Kong. (2) Tabulation method modified by Japanese govt. in Jan. 2003.

Average Number of Vacation Days per Year, Selected Countries

Source: World Tourism Organization

Country	Days	Country	Days	Country	Days
Italy...............	42	Brazil...............	34	Korea	25
France	37	United Kingdom.......	28	Japan	25
Germany	35	Canada	26	United States	13

World's Top 10 Tourist Destinations, 2003

Source: World Tourism Organization

(number of arrivals in millions; excluding same-day visitors)

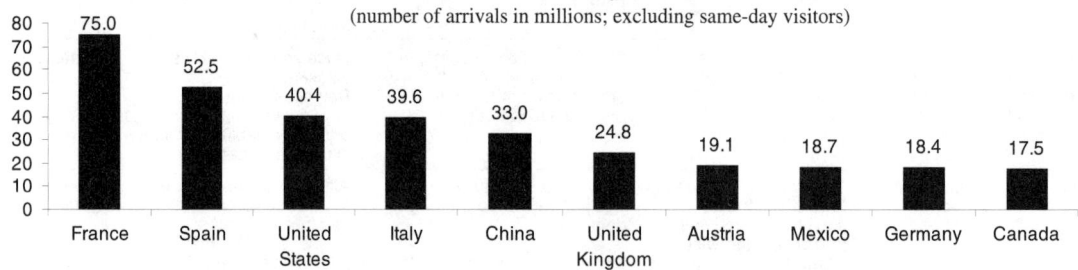

France 75.0, Spain 52.5, United States 40.4, Italy 39.6, China 33.0, United Kingdom 24.8, Austria 19.1, Mexico 18.7, Germany 18.4, Canada 17.5

International Travel to the U.S., 1986-2003

Source: Tourism Industries, International Trade Administration, Dept. of Commerce

(Visitors each year are in millions; some figures are revised and may differ from other sources.)

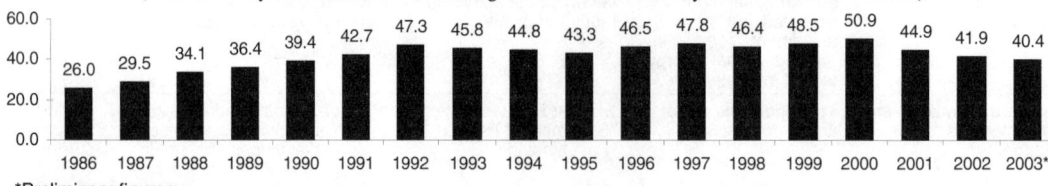

1986 26.0, 1987 29.5, 1988 34.1, 1989 36.4, 1990 39.4, 1991 42.7, 1992 47.3, 1993 45.8, 1994 44.8, 1995 43.3, 1996 46.5, 1997 47.8, 1998 46.4, 1999 48.5, 2000 50.9, 2001 44.9, 2002 41.9, 2003* 40.4

*Preliminary figures

International Visitors to the U.S., 2002[1]

Source: Tourism Industries, International Trade Administration, Dept. of Commerce

Country of origin	Visitors (thousands)	Expenditures (millions)[2]	Expenditures per visitor	Country of origin	Visitors (thousands)	Expenditures (millions)[2]	Expenditures per visitor
Canada[3]	12,968	$6,268	$483	South Korea	639	$2,175	$3,405
Mexico[3]	9,807	5,507	562	Australia	407	1,473	3,618
United Kingdom	3,817	8,177	2,142	Italy	406	1,107	2,726
Japan	3,627	8,492	2,341	Brazil	405	1,373	3,389
Germany	1,190	2,934	2,466	All countries	41,892	$66.55 bil[3]	$1,589
France	734	1,974	2,688				

(1) Excludes cruise travel. (2) Excludes international passenger fare payments. (3) Does not include international traveler spending on U.S. carriers for transactions made outside the U.S.

Traveler Spending in the U.S., 1987-2003

Source: Tourism Industries, International Trade Administration, Dept. of Commerce

(in billions)

	Domestic Travelers	International Travelers		Domestic Travelers	International Travelers		Domestic Travelers	International Travelers
1987	$235	$31	1993	$323	$58	1999	$458	$75
1988	258	38	1994	340	58	2000	488	82
1989	273	47	1995	360	63	2001	479	72
1990	291	43	1996	385	70	2002	474	67
1991	296	48	1997	406	73	2003	490*	66
1992	306	55	1998	425	71			

*Preliminary figure.

U.S. Domestic Leisure Travel Volume, 1994-2003[1]

Source: Travel Industry Assn. of America, TravelScope

(in millions of person-trips of 50 mi or more, one-way)

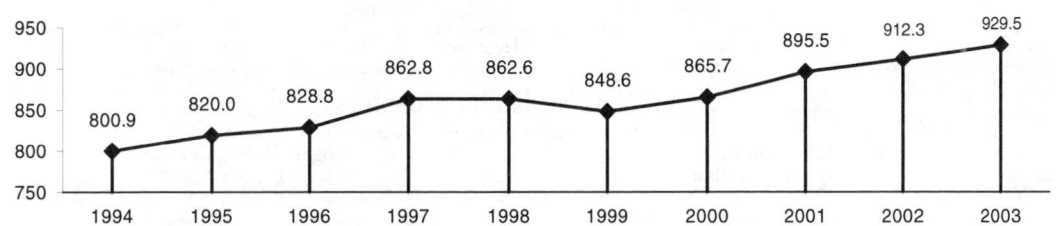

1994: 800.9; 1995: 820.0; 1996: 828.8; 1997: 862.8; 1998: 862.6; 1999: 848.6; 2000: 865.7; 2001: 895.5; 2002: 912.3; 2003: 929.5

(1) 2003 survey based on revised methods to collect more traveling data; earlier years re-estimated to maintain comparability.

Top U.S. States by Domestic Traveler Spending

Source: Travel Industry Assn. of America

(billions of dollars; in 2001)

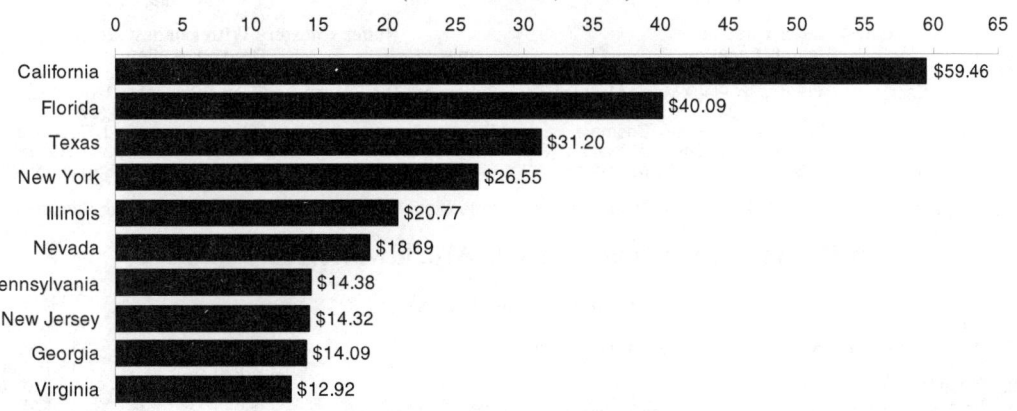

State	Spending
California	$59.46
Florida	$40.09
Texas	$31.20
New York	$26.55
Illinois	$20.77
Nevada	$18.69
Pennsylvania	$14.38
New Jersey	$14.32
Georgia	$14.09
Virginia	$12.92

Top 15 Travel Websites

Source: comScore Media Metrix

Rank	Visitors[1]	Rank	Visitors[1]	Rank	Visitors[1]
1. Expedia Travel	22,154,000	7. AOL Travel	7,798,000	12. American Airlines	4,717,000
2. Trip Network Inc.	16,058,000	8. SOUTHWEST.COM	7,186,000	13. Delta Airlines	4,605,000
3. ORBITZ.COM	15,219,000	9. Yahoo! Travel	7,125,000	14. United Airlines	4,005,000
4. Travelocity	12,843,000	10. TRIPADVISOR.COM	6,730,000	15. InterContinental Hotels Group	3,596,000
5. Hotels.com sites	12,088,000	11. HOTWIRE.COM	6,653,000		
6. PRICELINE.COM	11,177,000				

(1) Number of users who visited at least once in July 2004.

▶ **IT'S A FACT:** According to a survey by the Travel Industry Assoc. of America, the top activities for domestic travelers in the U.S. in 2003 were shopping (30%), attending a social/family event (27%), and outdoor activities (11%).

Travel Websites

The following websites are among those that may be of use in planning trips and making arrangements. Websites listed under "Maps" enable the user to plot a route to a destination. Inclusion here does not represent endorsement by *The World Almanac*.

AIRLINES
American Airlines
www.aa.com
America West Airlines
www.americawest.com
Continental Airlines
www.continental.com
Delta Air Lines
www.delta.com
Northwest Airlines
www.nwa.com
Southwest Airlines
www.southwest.com
United Airlines
www.ual.com
USAirways
www.usair.com

BUSES
Gray Line Worldwide
www.grayline.com
Greyhound Lines
www.greyhound.com
Peter Pan Bus Lines
www.peterpanbus.com

TRAINS
Amtrak
www.amtrak.com
BC Rail (Canada)
www.bcrail.com
Rail Europe
www.raileurope.com

CAR RENTALS
Alamo Rent A Car
www.goalamo.com
Avis Rent-A-Car
www.avis.com
Budget Rent A Car
www.budget.com
Dollar Rent A Car
www.dollar.com
Enterprise Rent-A-Car
www.enterprise.com
Hertz
www.hertz.com
National Car Rental
www.nationalcar.com
Rent-A-Wreck
www.rentawreck.com
Thrifty Rent-A-Car
www.thrifty.com

CRUISE LINES
Carnival Cruise Lines
www.carnival.com
Celebrity Cruises
www.celebrity.com
Costa Cruise Lines
www.costacruises.com
Cunard Line
www.cunardline.com
Holland America Line
www.hollandamerica.com
Norwegian Cruise Line
www.ncl.com

Princess Cruises
www.princess.com
Royal Caribbean Int'l.
www.royalcaribbean.com
Windjammer Barefoot Cruises
www.windjammer.com

HOTELS/RESORTS
Best Western Int'l.
www.bestwestern.com
Choice Hotels Int'l.,
  Clarion Hotels & Resorts,
  Comfort Inns,
  Econo Lodges,
  MainStay Suites,
  Quality Inns,
  Rodeway Inns,
  Sleep Inns
www.hotelchoice.com
Days Inn of America
www.daysinn.com
Doubletree Hotels
www.doubletree.com
Embassy Suites
www.embassysuites.com
Four Seasons Hotels
www.fourseasons.com
Hilton Hotels
www.hilton.com
Holiday Inn Worldwide
www.holidayinn.com
Hyatt Hotels and Resorts
www.hyatt.com

Hotels.com
www.hotels.com
Inter-Continental Hotels
www.interconti.com
Loews Hotels
www.loewshotels.com
Marriott Int'l.
www.marriott.com
Radisson Hotels Int'l.
www.radisson.com
Sheraton Hotels & Resorts
www.starwood.com/sheraton
Westin Hotels & Resorts
www.starwood.com/westin
Wyndham Hotels & Resorts
www.wyndham.com

TRAVEL PLANNING
www.travelocity.com
www.priceline.com
www.expedia.com
www.itn.net (American Express)
www.lowestfare.com
www.cheaptickets.com
www.bestfares.com
www.frommers.com
www.fodors.com
www.libertytravel.com
www.orbitz.com

MAPS
www.freetrip.com
www.mapquest.com
www.mapsonus.com

Some Notable Roller Coasters

Source: American Coasters Network; as of Sept. 2004

Fastest Roller Coasters

Name	Speed	Location
Top Thrill Dragster	120 mph	Cedar Point; Sandusky, OH
Dodonpa.	107 mph	Fujikyu Highland; Yamanashi, Japan
Tower of Terror	100 mph	Dreamworld; Coomera, Queensland, Australia
Superman: The Escape .	100 mph	Six Flags Magic Mountain; Valencia, CA
Steel Dragon 2000	95 mph	Nagashima Spaland; Mie, Japan

Longest Roller Coasters

Name	Length	Location
Steel Dragon 2000	8,133 ft	Nagashima Spaland; Mie, Japan
Daidarasaurus.	7,677 ft	Expoland; Osaka, Japan
The Ultimate	7,442 ft	Lightwater Valley; Yorkshire, UK
Beast	7,400 ft	Paramount's Kings Island; Kings Mills, OH
Son of Beast	7,032 ft	Paramount's Kings Island; Kings Mills, OH

Tallest Roller Coasters

Name	Height	Location
Top Thrill Dragster	420 ft	Cedar Point; Sandusky, OH
Superman The Escape .	415 ft	Six Flags Magic Mountain; Valencia, CA
Tower of Terror	377 ft	Dreamworld; Coomera, Queensland, Australia
Steel Dragon 2000	318 ft	Nagashima Spaland; Mie, Japan
Millennium Force	310 ft	Cedar Point; Sandusky, OH

Roller Coasters With Longest Drop

Name	Drop	Location
Top Thrill Dragster.	400 ft	Cedar Point; Sandusky, OH
Superman: The Escape.	328 ft	Six Flags Magic Mountain; Valencia, CA
Tower of Terror	328 ft	Dreamworld; Coomera, Queensland, Australia
Steel Dragon 2000	307 ft	Nagashima Spaland; Mie, Japan
Millennium Force	300 ft	Cedar Point; Sandusky, OH

Top 50 Amusement/Theme Parks Worldwide, Year-end 2003

(ranked by attendance)

Source: Amusement Business

Rank	Park and Location	Country	Attendance
1.	Magic Kingdom at Walt Disney World, Lake Buena Vista, FL	United States	14,044,000*
2.	Tokyo Disneyland	Japan	13,188,000*
3.	Disneyland, Anaheim, CA	United States	12,720,000*
4.	Tokyo Disneysea	Japan	12,174,000*
5.	Disneyland Paris, Marne-La-Vallee	France	10,230,000*
6.	Universal Studios Japan, Osaka	Japan	8,811,000*
7.	Everland, Kyonggi-Do	South Korea	8,800,000
8.	Epcot at Walt Disney World, Lake Buena Vista, FL	United States	8,620,768*
9.	Lotte World, Seoul	South Korea	8,500,000*
10.	Disney-MGM Studios at Walt Disney World, Lake Buena Vista, FL	United States	7,870,733*
11.	Disney's Animal Kingdom at Walt Disney World, Lake Buena Vista, FL	United States	7,305,600*
12.	Universal Studios at Universal Orlando, Orlando, FL	United States	6,850,000*
13.	Blackpool Pleasure Beach, Blackpool, England	United Kingdom	6,200,000*
14.	Islands of Adventure at Universal Orlando, Orlando, FL	United States	6,072,000*
15.	Disney's California Adventure, Anaheim, CA	United States	5,311,000*
16.	Yokohama Hakkeijima Sea Paradise	Japan	5,300,000*
17.	Seaworld Florida, Orlando, FL	United States	5,200,000*
18.	Universal Studios Hollywood, Universal City, CA	United States	4,576,000*
19.	Busch Gardens, Tampa Bay, FL	United States	4,300,000*
	Adventuredome at Circus Circus, Las Vegas, NV	United States	4,300,000*

Rank	Park and Location	Country	Attendance
21.	Seaworld California, San Diego, CA	United States	4,000,000*
22.	Knott's Berry Farm, Buena Park, CA	United States	3,479,895*
23.	Europa-Park, Rust	Germany	3,300,000*
24.	Cedar Point, Sandusky, OH	United States	3,300,000*
25.	Paramount's Kings Island, Kings Island, OH	United States	3,277,975*
26.	Tivoli Gardens, Copenhagen	Denmark	3,266,000
27.	Morey's Piers, Wildwood, NJ	United States	3,230,000*
28.	Efteling, Kaatsheuvel	The Netherlands	3,200,000
29.	Six Flags Great Adventure, Jackson, NJ	United States	3,150,000*
30.	Six Flags Magic Mountain, Valencia, CA	United States	3,050,000*
31.	Universal's Mediterrania, Salou	Spain	3,040,000*
32.	Santa Cruz Beach Boardwalk, Santa Cruz, CA	United States	3,000,000*
	Ocean Park, Hong Kong	China	3,000,000*
34.	Gardaland, Castelnuovo Del Garda	Italy	2,950,000
35.	Huis Ten Bosch, Seasebo City	Japan	2,840,000*
36.	Seoul Land, Kyonggi-Do	South Korea	2,802,500*
37.	La Feria De Chapultapec, Mexico City	Mexico	2,800,000
38.	Liseburg, Gothenburg	Sweden	2,749,000*
39.	Suzuka Circuit	Japan	2,705,000*
40.	Bakken, Klampenborg	Denmark	2,700,000*
41.	Paramount Canada's Wonderland, Maple, Ontario	Canada	2,628,413*
42.	Six Flags Over Texas, Arlington, TX	United States	2,600,000*
43.	Six Flags Great America, Gurnee, IL	United States	2,575,000*
44.	HersheyPark, Hershey, PA	United States	2,551,000
45.	Busch Gardens, Williamsburg, VA	United States	2,500,000*
46.	Alton Towers, Staffordshire, England	United Kingdom	2,500,000
47.	Camp Snoopy at Mall of America, Bloomington, MN	United States	2,469,000*
48.	Six Flags Mexico, Mexico City	Mexico	2,450,000*
49.	Nagashima Spa Land, Kuwana	Japan	2,375,000*
50.	Walt Disney Studios Park, Marne-La-Valee	France	2,200,000*

*Estimated attendance.

Passports, Health Regulations, and Travel Warnings for Foreign Travel

Source: Bureau of Consular Affairs, U.S. Dept. of State; www.travel.state.gov

Passports are issued by the U.S. Department of State to citizens and nationals of the U.S. to provide documentation for foreign travel. For U.S. citizens traveling on business or as tourists, especially in Europe, a U.S. passport is often sufficient to gain admission for a limited stay. For many countries, however, a **visa** must also be obtained before entering. It is the responsibility of the traveler to check in advance and obtain any required visas from the appropriate embassies or nearest consulates.

Each country has its own specific guidelines concerning length and purpose of visit, etc. Some may require visitors to display proof that they have (1) sufficient funds to stay for the intended time period, (2) onward/return tickets, and/or (3) at least 6-months remaining validity on their U.S. passports.

Some countries, including **Canada, Mexico,** and some **Caribbean** islands, do not require a passport or a visa for limited stays. However, they do require proof of U.S. citizenship, and may have other requirements. Apart from governmental requirements, some airlines and cruiselines to these locations require passengers to have passports in order to board. For further information, check with the embassy or nearest consulate of the country you plan to visit and the airline or cruiseline you plan to use.

How to Obtain a Passport

Those who have never been issued a passport in their own name, and those who do not meet all the requirements for application by mail, must apply in person at one of 6,000 designated passport acceptance facilities across the U.S. An appointment may be needed. Those leaving the country or in need of a passport for a foreign visa within 14 days must appear by appointment at one of 13 Regional Passport Agencies. If abroad, application at a U.S. embassy or consulate is required.

A DS-11 *Application for Passport* is the form to use when applying in person. All persons, including infants, are now required to obtain passports in their own name. For children under 14, there are special additional requirements: (1) Both parents/guardians must have identification and sign the application in person, and (2) birth/citizenship evidence must include proof of parental relationship to the child, such as parents' names on the child's certified birth certificate. Minors 14-17 years old must apply in person and may require parental consent. Visit www.travel.state.gov or call the NPIC if you have questions.

Persons who (1) possess their most recent, undamaged passport, which (2) was issued within the last 15 years and; (3) after their 16th birthday; and (4) whose name has not changed or who have proper documentation for their name change, may be eligible to apply for a new passport by mail. The form DS-82, *Application for Passport by Mail,* must be mailed, together with the previous passport, 2 recent identical photographs (see below), and a fee of $55.

Proof of citizenship—A valid passport previously issued to the applicant, or one in which he or she was included (prior to the individual passport requirement), may be accepted as proof of U.S. citizenship. If the applicant has no prior passport and was born in the U.S., a certified copy of the birth certificate generally must be presented. It must generally show the given name and surname, the date and place of birth, and that the birth record was filed shortly after birth. A delayed birth certificate (filed more than 1 year after date of birth) is acceptable if it shows that acceptable secondary evidence was used for creating this record.

If a birth certificate is not obtainable, a notice from a state registrar must be submitted stating that no birth record exists. It must be accompanied by the best obtainable secondary evidence, such as a baptismal certificate or hospital birth record.

A **naturalized citizen** with no previous passport must present a Certificate of Naturalization issued by the Bureau of Citizenship and Immigration (BCIS) in the Dept. of Homeland Security (formerly the Immigration and Naturalization Service). **A person born abroad** claiming U.S. citizenship through either a native-born or a naturalized citizen parent must normally submit a Certificate of Citizenship issued by the BCIS or a Consular Report of Birth or Certification of Birth Abroad issued by the Dept. of State. Also, the applicant must submit proof of U.S. citizenship of the parent(s) through whom citizenship is claimed, along with the parents' marriage certificate if citizenship is claimed through both. In addition, the applicant must present an affidavit from parent(s) showing periods and places of residence or presence in the U.S. and abroad before the applicant's birth. (See website for further details.) If citizenship is derived through naturalization of parents, evidence of admission to the U.S. for permanent residence also is required.

> ▶ **IT'S A FACT:** According to Cruise Lines International Assoc., 8.2 million people from North America took cruise vacations in 2003, up from 7.6 million in 2002. The number of cruise passengers from North America increased by an average of 8.1% a year from 1980 to 2003.

It is important to apply for a passport as far in advance as possible. Passport acceptance facilities and agencies are busiest between March and August. It can take several weeks to receive a passport.Visit travel.state.gov or call the NPIC for information about expedited service.

Photographs—Applicants must submit 2 identical photos taken in the last 6 months that are a good current likeness. They should be 2 x 2 in. in size. The image size, from bottom of chin to top of head (including hair), should not be less than 1 in. or more than 1-3/8 in. Photos should be portrait-type prints. They must be clear, front view, full face, with plain white or off-white background.

Identity—Applicants must establish their identity to the satisfaction of the accepting agent. Generally, acceptable documents of identity include a previous U.S. passport, a Certificate of Naturalization, a Certificate of Citizenship, a valid driver's license, or a government or military identification card. Applicants may not use a Social Security card, learner's or temporary driver's license, credit card, or expired ID card. Extremely old documents cannot be used by themselves.

Applicants unable to establish identity must present some documentation in their own name and be accompanied by a person who has known them at least 2 years and is a U.S. citizen or legal U.S. permanent resident alien. That person must sign an affidavit before the individual who executes the application, and must establish his or her own identity.

Fees—For persons under 16 years of age, the basic fee is $40, for a 5-year passport. For persons 16 and older, the basic fee is $55 for a 10-year passport. For all first-time passports there is an additional $30 execution fee. To receive a passport within 14 days or less, an additional $60 is required; plus two-way overnight delivery is strongly recommended. Fees are nonrefundable. There is no execution fee when using form DS-82, *Application for Passport by Mail*. **Forms are available on-line** at travel.state.gov

Passport loss—The loss or theft of a valid passport should be reported immediately. In the U.S., call 1-202-955-0430. Voice mail is available after business hours. If abroad, contact the nearest U.S. embassy or consulate. The DS-64, *Statement Regarding Lost or Stolen Passport*, is available on-line at travel.state.gov

General Information—For up-to-date passport and international travel information, visit the Consular Affairs website (www.travel.state.gov), or call the National Passport Information Center at 1-877-487-2778 (TDD/TYY: 1-888-874-7793). Customer service representatives are available from 8 A.M. to 8 P.M., Eastern Time, Mon.-Fri., excluding Federal Holidays.

Health Regulations

Under World Health Organization regulations, a country may require International Certificates of Vaccination against yellow fever. Cholera immunization may be required for travelers from infected areas. Check with health care providers or your records to see that other immunizations (e.g., for tetanus and polio) are up-to-date.

Other preventative measures, including prophylactic medication for malaria, are advisable for travel to some countries. No immunizations are needed to return to the U.S. Many countries have regulations regarding AIDS testing, particularly for longtime visitors. Detailed information and recommendations are included in *Health Information for International Travel*, the "Yellow Book" published every 2 years by the Centers for Disease Control (CDC). It can be ordered from the Public Health Foundation for $29 by going to bookstore.phf.org/cat24.htm, or by calling 1-877-252-1200. Updates to the book are available online at www.cdc.gov/travel/yb/index.htm. Information may also be obtained from your local health department or physician, or by calling the Centers for Disease Control and Prevention at 1-877-FYI-TRIP (1-877-394-8747). The more technical *International Travel and Health* is available from the World Health Organization for $22.50, with portions of the book accessible online, at www.who.int/ith

Travel Warnings

The State Dept. issues travel warnings when it decides, based on relevant information, to recommend that Americans avoid travel to certain countries; these are subject to change. As of Sept. 1, 2004, travel warnings were in effect for: Afghanistan, Algeria, Bosnia and Herzegovina, Burundi, Central African Rep., Colombia, Côte d'Ivoire, Dem. Rep. of the Congo, Haiti, Indonesia, Iran, Iraq, Israel (incl. West Bank and Gaza), Kenya, Lebanon, Liberia, Libya, Nepal, Nigeria, Pakistan, Saudi Arabia, Somalia, Sudan, Yemen, and Zimbabwe. For the most current information, visit www.travel.state.gov

Customs Exemptions for Travelers

Source: U.S. Customs and Border Protection, Department of Homeland Security

U.S. residents returning after a stay abroad of at least 48 hours are usually granted customs exemptions of **$800 each** (this and all exemptions figured according to fair retail value). The duty-free articles must accompany the traveler at the time of return, be for personal or household use, have been acquired as an incident of the trip, and be properly declared to Customs. No more than 1 liter of alcoholic beverages or more than 100 cigars and 200 cigarettes (1 carton) may be included in the $800 exemption. The exemption for alcoholic beverages holds only if the returning resident is at least 21 years old at the time of arrival. Cuban cigars may be included only if purchased in Cuba while on authorized travel.

If a U.S. resident arrives directly or indirectly from a U.S. island possession—American Samoa, Guam, or U.S. Virgin Islands—a customs exemption of **$1,200 is allowed**. Up to 1,000 cigarettes may be included, but only 200 of them may have been purchased elsewhere. If a U.S. resident returns from any one of the following places, **the exemption is $600**: Antigua and Barbuda, Aruba, Bahamas, Barbados, Belize, British Virgin Islands, Costa Rica, Dominica, Dominican Republic, El Salvador, Grenada, Guatemala, Guyana, Haiti, Honduras, Jamaica, Montserrat, Netherlands Antilles, Nicaragua, Panama, St. Kitts and Nevis, St. Lucia, St. Vincent and the Grenadines, Trinidad and Tobago.

The $800, $1,200, or $600 exemption can be granted only if the exemption has not been used in whole or part within the preceding 30-day period and only if the stay abroad was for at least 48 hours. The 48-hr absence requirement does not apply to travelers returning from Mexico or U.S. Virgin Islands. Travelers who cannot claim the $800, $600, or $1,200 exemption because of the 30-day or 48-hr provisions may bring in free of duty and tax articles acquired abroad for personal or household use up to a value of **$200**.

There are also allowances for goods when shipped. Goods shipped for personal use may be imported free of duty and tax if the total value is no more than $200. This exemption does not apply to perfume containing alcohol if it is valued at more than $5 retail, to alcoholic beverages, or to cigars and cigarettes. The $200 mail exemption does not apply to merchandise subject to absolute or tariff-rate quotas unless the item is for personal use. Tailor-made suits ordered from Hong Kong, however, are subject to quota/visa requirements even if imported for personal use.

Bona fide gifts of not more than $100 in value, when shipped, can be received in the U.S. free of duty and tax, provided that the same person does not receive more than $100 in gift shipments in one day. The limit is increased to $200 for bona fide gift items shipped from U.S. Virgin Islands, American Samoa, or Guam. (Shipping of alcoholic beverages, including wine and beer, by mail is prohibited by U.S. postal laws.) These gifts are not declared by the traveler upon return to the U.S.

The U.S. Customs and Border Protection booklet "Know Before You Go" answers frequently asked customs questions and is available free by writing U.S. Customs and Border Protection, KBYG, PO Box 7407, Washington, DC 20044, or by visiting the agency's website at www.cbp.gov

NATIONS OF THE WORLD

As of mid-2004, there were **193 nations** in the world. This number includes 2 nations that are not members of the United Nations—Taiwan and Vatican City (the Holy See). The 193 nations are profiled below, in alphabetical order. Certain regions and territories that are not independent nations can be found under the entry for the governing nation. Following the nation profiles you will find comparative statistics, population projections, information on the UN and other international organizations, and other information about nations.

Sources: U.S. Census Bureau: Intl. Data Base; U.S. Central Intelligence Agency: *The World Factbook;* U.S. Dept. of Energy; U.S. Dept. of State. UN Education, Scientific, and Cultural Org. (UNESCO); UN Food and Agriculture Org.: FAO Statistical Database and Yearbook of Fishery Statistics; Intl. Monetary Fund; Intl. Telecommunication Union (for telephone and internet data); UN Population Division: *World Population Prospects and World Urbanization Prospects;* UN Statistics Division: *Statistical Yearbook*; World Tourism Organization; Intl. Institute for Strategic Studies: *The Military Balance.*

Note: Because of rounding or incomplete enumeration, some percentages may not add to 100%. **FY = fiscal year.** **National population and health** figures are mid-2004 estimates, unless otherwise noted. **Percentage of urban population** is for mid-2003. **City** populations, except capitals, are 2000 estimates for **urban agglomerations,** i.e., whole metropolitan areas. All **capital** populations are estimates for urban agglomerations in 2003. Where indicated, the latest available population of the city proper is also given. **GDP** estimates are based on purchasing power parity calculations, which involve use of intl. dollar price weights applied to quantities of goods and services produced. **Tourism** figures represent receipts from international tourism. **Budget** figures are for expenditures, unless otherwise noted. **Motor vehicle** and **civil aviation** statistics are latest available; comm. (commercial) vehicles include trucks and buses. Airport figures include total number with paved runways in 2002. **TV, radio,** and **daily newspapers** figures are latest available. **Telephone and Internet** data are for 2003, unless otherwise noted. **Life expectancy** is at birth for persons born in 2004. **AIDS rate** is the est. number of adults, aged 15-49, living with HIV at year-end 2003, divided by the total 2003 population aged 15-49. **Education** figures are for the 2001-2002 school year. **Literacy rates** given generally measure the percent of population able to read and write on a lower elementary school level, not the (smaller) percent able to read instructions necessary for a job or license. Figures for **gold reserves, international reserves less gold,** and change in **consumer prices** are for 2003, except where noted. **Embassy addresses** are for Wash., DC, area code (202), unless otherwise noted.

For further details and later information on developments around the world, see the front-of-the-book Feature section and the Chronology of the Year's Events. See pages 457-472 for full-color maps and flags of all nations.

Afghanistan
Transitional Islamic State of Afghanistan

People: Population: 28,513,677. **Age distrib.** (%): <15: 42; 65+: 2.8. **Pop. density:** 114 per sq km, 44 per sq km. **Urban:** 23.3%. **Ethnic groups:** Pashtun 44%, Tajik 25%, Hazara 10%, Uzbek 8%. **Principal languages:** Dari (Afghan Persian), Pashtu (both official); Turkic (incl. Uzbek, Turkmen); Balochi, Pashai, many others. **Chief religion:** Muslim (official; Sunni 85%, Shi'a 15%).
Geography: Total area: 250,001 sq mi, 647,500 sq km; **Land area:** 250,001 sq mi, 647,500 sq km. **Location:** In SW Asia, NW of the Indian subcontinent. **Neighbors:** Pakistan on E, S; Iran on W; Turkmenistan, Tajikistan, Uzbekistan on N. The NE tip touches China. **Topography:** The country is landlocked and mountainous, much of it over 4,000 ft. above sea level. The Hindu Kush Mts. tower 16,000 ft. above Kabul and reach a height of 25,000 ft. to the E. Trade with Pakistan flows through the 35-mile-long Khyber Pass. The climate is dry, with extreme temperatures, and there are large desert regions, though mountain rivers produce intermittent fertile valleys. **Capital:** Kabul, 2,956,000.
Government: Type: Transitional administration. **Head of state and gov.:** Pres. Hamid Karzai; b Dec. 24, 1957; in office: June 19, 2002. **Local divisions:** 32 provinces. **Defense budget** (2002): $250 mil. **Active troops:** 60,000–70,000.
Economy: Industries: textiles, soap, furniture, shoes. **Chief crops:** wheat, fruits, nuts, wool. **Natural resources:** nat. gas, oil, coal, copper, chromite, talc, barite, sulfur, lead, zinc, iron ore, salt, gems. **Arable land:** 12%. **Livestock** (2002): chickens: 6.50 mil.; goats: 5 mil.; sheep: 11 mil. **Fish catch** (2002 est): 900 metric tons. **Electricity prod.** (2002): 0.54 bil. kWh. **Labor force** (1990 est.): agriculture 80%, industry 10%, services 10%.
Finance: Monetary unit: Afghani (AFA) (Sept. 2004: 43.83 = $1 U.S.). **GDP** (2003 est.): $20.0 bil.; **per capita GDP:** $700; **GDP growth:** 29.0%. **Imports** (2002 est.): $1.0 bil.; partners (2002): Pakistan 24.3%, South Korea 14%, Japan 9.1%, U.S. 8.7%, Germany 5.7%, Kenya 5.6%. **Exports** (2002 est.): $98.0 mil.; partners (2002): Pakistan 28.6%, India 27.6%, Finland 6.1%, Belgium 5.1%, Germany 5.1%, Russia 4.1%, U.S. 4.1%. **Tourism** (1998): $1 mil. **Budget** (2003 est.): $550.0 mil.
Transport: Railroad: Length: 15 mi. **Motor vehicles** (2000): 6,200 pass. cars, 7,000 comm. vehicles. **Civil aviation:** 62.8 mil pass.-mi.; 10 airports.
Communications: TV sets: 14 per 1,000 pop. **Radios:** 132 per 1,000 pop. **Telephone lines:** 29,000 main lines. **Daily newspaper circ.:** 5.6 per 1,000 pop.
Health: Life expect.: 42.3 male; 42.7 female. **Births** (per 1,000 pop.): 47.3. **Deaths** (per 1,000 pop.): 21.1. **Natural inc.:** 2.62%. **Infant mortality** (per 1,000 live births): 166.0.
Education: Compulsory: ages 7-12. **Literacy** (1999 est.): 36%.
Major Intl. Organizations: UN (FAO, IBRD, ILO, IMF, WHO). **Embassy:** 2341 Wyoming Ave. NW 20008; 234-3770.
Website: www.embassyofafghanistan.org

Afghanistan, occupying a favored invasion route since antiquity, has been variously known as Ariana or Bactria (in ancient times) and Khorasan (in the Middle Ages). Foreign empires alternated rule with local emirs and kings until the 18th century, when a unified kingdom was established. In 1973, a military coup ushered in a republic.

Pro-Soviet leftists took power in a bloody 1978 coup and concluded an economic and military treaty with the USSR. In Dec. 1979 the USSR began a massive airlift into Kabul and backed a new coup, leading to installation of a more pro-Soviet leader. Soviet troops fanned out over Afghanistan and waged a protracted guerrilla war with Muslim rebels, in which some 15,000 Soviet troops reportedly died.

A UN-mediated agreement was signed Apr. 14, 1988, providing for withdrawal of Soviet troops, a neutral Afghan state, and repatriation of refugees. Afghan rebels rejected the pact, vowing to continue fighting while "Soviets and their puppets" remained in Afghanistan. The Soviets completed their troop withdrawal Feb. 15, 1989; fighting between Afghan rebels and government forces ensued.

Communist Pres. Najibullah resigned Apr. 16, 1992, as competing guerrilla forces advanced on Kabul. The rebels achieved power Apr. 28, ending 14 years of Soviet-backed regimes. More than 2 million Afghans had been killed and 6 million had left the country since 1979.

Following the rebel victory there were clashes between moderates and Islamic fundamentalist forces. Burhanuddin Rabbani, a guerrilla leader, became president June 28, 1992, but fierce fighting continued around Kabul and elsewhere. The Taliban, an insurgent Islamic radical faction, gained increasing control and in Sept. 1996 captured Kabul and set up a government. The Taliban executed former President Najibullah and empowered Islamic religious police to enforce codes of dress and behavior that were especially restrictive to women. Rabbani and other ousted leaders fled to the north.

Victories in the northern cities of Mazar-e Sharif, Aug. 8, 1998, and Taloqan, Aug. 8-11, 1998, gave the Taliban control over more than 90% of the country; the killing of several Iranian diplomats during the Mazar-e Sharif takeover further heightened tensions with Iran. On Aug. 20, 1998, U.S. cruise missiles struck SE of Kabul, hitting facilities the U.S. said were terrorist training camps run by a wealthy Saudi, Osama bin Laden. The UN imposed sanctions Nov. 14, 1999, when Afghanistan refused to turn over bin Laden to the U.S. for prosecution; a UN ban on all military aid to the Taliban took effect Jan. 19, 2001. By March, aid agencies reported that drought and continued warfare had put more than 1 million people at risk of famine. Meanwhile, the Taliban launched a campaign to destroy non-Islamic antiquities.

Ahmed Shah Massoud, leader of the anti-Taliban resistance, died in Sept. 2001 of wounds sustained in a suicide bombing by assassins posing as journalists. After the Sept. 11 attacks on the World Trade Center and Pentagon, the U.S., blaming bin Laden, demanded that the Taliban surrender him and shut down his al-Qaeda terrorist network. When the Taliban refused, the U.S., with British assistance, began bombing Afghanistan Oct. 7. Supported by the U.S., the opposition Northern Alliance recaptured Mazar-e Sharif Nov. 9 and took Kabul 4 days later; the Taliban forces abandoned Kandahar, their last stronghold, to S tribesmen Dec. 7. A power-sharing agreement signed in Bonn, Germany, Dec. 5 by 4 anti-Taliban factions, including the Northern Alliance, provided for an interim government headed by Hamid Karzai, a Pashtun tribal leader; the UN authorized Dec. 20 a multinational security force. Meanwhile, U.S. and allied forces continued to hunt for bin Laden and other top al-Qaeda and Taliban officials.

At a conference in Tokyo, Jan. 21-22, 2002, donor countries and agencies pledged more than $4.5 bil in aid to Afghanistan over 5 years. In March 2002, the U.S. launched Operation Anaconda to hunt down Taliban in the mountains of the SE. Meeting June 13 in Kabul, a traditional council (loya jirga) chose Karzai to head a new

transitional government. An errant U.S. air strike on the night of June 30-July 1 apparently killed 48 people celebrating a wedding at Kakarak, N of Kandahar. Gunmen July 6 assassinated Vice Pres. Haji Abdul Qadir, a Pashtun. A car bomb in Kabul killed 26 people Sept. 5; in Kandahar that same day, Karzai, guarded by U.S. troops, survived an assassination attempt. Continued lawlessness allowed for a dramatic increase in opium production by the end of 2002.

The U.S. announced the end of major combat operations in Afghanistan, May 1, 2003, but resistance continued. Attacks against aid workers forced the UN to suspend humanitarian operations Aug. 10 in many southern regions. NATO officially assumed control of peacekeeping forces (ISAF) Aug. 11.

A new constitution took effect Jan. 26, 2004. The aid group Doctors Without Borders suspended Afghan operations after 5 relief workers were killed in a Taliban ambush, June 2. In Kunduz, June 10, gunmen killed 11 Chinese road construction workers and an Afghan guard. At midyear, about 20,000 U.S. troops and a NATO security force of 6,500 remained in the country, but limited delivery of foreign aid hampered reconstruction efforts. Security concerns forced postponement of presidential elections to be rescheduled for Oct. 9, 2004. During the campaign, insurgents attempted to kill Pres. Karzai, Sept. 16, and Vice Pres. Nematullah Shahrani, Sept. 20.

Albania
Republic of Albania

People: Population: 3,544,808. **Age distrib.** (%): <15: 28.8; 65+: 7.2. **Pop. density:** 335 per sq mi, 129 per sq km. **Urban:** 23.3%. **Ethnic groups:** Albanian 95%, Greek 3%. **Principal languages:** Albanian (Tosk is the official dialect), Greek. **Chief religions:** Muslim 70%, Albanian Orthodox 20%, Roman Catholic 10%.

Geography: Total area: 11,100 sq mi, 28,748 sq km; **Land area:** 10,578 sq mi, 27,398 sq km. **Location:** SE Europe, on SE coast of Adriatic Sea. **Neighbors:** Greece on S, Yugoslavia on N, Macedonia on E. **Topography:** Apart from a narrow coastal plain, Albania consists of hills and mountains covered with scrub forest, cut by small E-W rivers. **Capital:** Tirana, 367,000.

Government: Type: Republic. **Head of state:** Pres. Alfred Moisiu; b Dec. 1, 1929; in office: July 24, 2002. **Head of gov.:** Prime Min. Fatos Nano; b 1952; in office: July 31, 2002. **Local divisions:** 12 counties divided into 36 districts. **Defense budget** (2003): $65 mil. **Active troops:** 22,000.

Economy: Industries: food proc., textiles, clothing, lumber. **Chief crops:** wheat, corn, potatoes, sugar beets, grapes. **Natural resources:** oil, nat. gas, coal, chromium, copper, timber, nickel, hydropower. **Crude oil reserves** (2003): 165.0 mil. bbls. **Arable land:** 21%. **Livestock** (2003): cattle: 700,000; chickens: 4.3 mil.; goats: 1.03 mil.; pigs: 109,000; sheep: 1.8 mil. **Fish catch** (2002): 4,815 metric tons. **Electricity prod.:** 3.88 bil. kWh. **Labor force** (2003 est.): agriculture 57%, non-agricultural private sector 20%, public sector 23%.

Finance: Monetary unit: Lek (ALL) (Sept. 2004: 102.10=$1 U.S.). **GDP** (2003 est.): $16.1 bil.; **per capita GDP:** $4,500; **GDP growth:** 7.0%. **Imports** (2003 est.): $1.8 bil.; partners (2002): Italy 34.6%, Greece 21.7%, Turkey 6.1%, Germany 5.6%. **Exports** (2003 est.): $425.0 mil.; partners (2002): Italy 71.5%, Greece 12.7%, Germany 5.5%. **Tourism** (2002): $487 mil. **Budget** (2004 est.): $2.0 bil. **Intl. reserves less gold:** $679 mil. **Gold:** 70,000 oz t. **Consumer prices:** 0.5%.

Transport: Railroad: Length: 278 mi. **Motor vehicles** (2001): 133,500 pass. cars, 73,000 comm. vehicles. **Civil aviation:** 62.8 mil. pass.-mi; 4 airports. **Chief ports:** Durres, Sarande, Vlore.

Communications: TV sets: 146 per 1,000 pop. **Radios:** 259 per 1,000 pop. **Telephone lines:** 255,000. **Daily newspaper circ.:** 36 per 1,000 pop. **Internet:** 30,000 users.

Health: Life expect.: 74.4 male; 80.0 female. **Births** (per 1,000 pop.): 15.1. **Deaths** (per 1,000 pop.): 5.0. **Natural inc.:** 1.01%. **Infant mortality** (per 1,000 live births): 22.3.

Major Intl. Organizations: UN (IBRD, ILO, IMF, IMO, WHO), OSCE.

Education: Compulsory: ages 6-13. **Literacy:** 86.5%.
Embassy: 2100 S St. NW 20008; 223-4942.
Websites: www.keshilliministrave.al; www.president.al

Ancient Illyria was conquered by Romans, Slavs, and Turks (15th century); the latter Islamized the population. Independent Albania was proclaimed in 1912, republic was formed in 1920. King Zog I ruled 1925-39, until Italy invaded.

Communist partisans took over in 1944, allied Albania with USSR, then broke with USSR in 1960 over de-Stalinization. Strong political alliance with China followed, leading to several billion dollars in aid, which was curtailed after 1974. China cut off aid in 1978 when Albania attacked its policies after the death of Chinese ruler Mao Zedong. Large-scale purges of officials occurred during the 1970s.

Enver Hoxha, the nation's ruler for 4 decades, died Apr. 11, 1985. Eventually the new regime introduced some liberalization, including measures in 1990 providing for freedom to travel abroad. Efforts were begun to improve ties with the outside world. Mar. 1991 elections left the former Communists in power, but a general strike and urban opposition led to the formation of a coalition cabinet including non-Communists.

Albania's former Communists were routed in elections Mar. 1992, amid economic collapse and social unrest. Sali Berisha was elected as the first non-Communist president since World War II. Berisha's party claimed a landslide victory in disputed parliamentary elections, May 26 and June 2, 1996. Public protests over the collapse of fraudulent investment schemes in Jan. 1997 led to armed rebellion and anarchy. The UN Security Council, Mar. 28, authorized a 7,000-member force to restore order. Socialists and their allies won parliamentary elections, June 29 and July 6, and international peacekeepers completed their pullout by Aug. 11, 1997. During NATO's air war against Yugoslavia, Mar.-June 1999, Albania hosted some 465,000 Kosovar refugees.

Algeria
People's Democratic Republic of Algeria

People: Population: 32,129,324. **Age distrib.** (%): <15: 33.5; 65+: 4.1. **Pop. density:** 35 per sq mi, 13 per sq km. **Urban:** 58.8%. **Ethnic groups:** Arab-Berber 99%. **Principal languages:** Arabic (official), French, Berber dialects. **Chief religion:** Sunni Muslim (official) 99%.

Geography: Total area: 919,595 sq mi, 2,381,740 sq km; **Land area:** 919,595 sq mi, 2,381,740 sq km. **Location:** In NW Africa, from Mediterranean Sea into Sahara Desert. **Neighbors:** Morocco on W; Mauritania, Mali, Niger on S; Libya, Tunisia on E. **Topography:** The Tell, located on the coast, comprises fertile plains 50-100 miles wide, with a moderate climate and adequate rain. Two major chains of the Atlas Mts., running roughly E-W and reaching 7,000 ft., enclose a dry plateau region. Below lies the Sahara, mostly desert with major mineral resources. **Capital:** Algiers (El Djazair), 3,060,000.

Government: Type: Republic. **Head of state:** Pres. Abdelaziz Bouteflika; b Mar. 2, 1937; in office: Apr. 27, 1999. **Head of gov.:** Prime Min. Ahmed Ouyahia; b July 2, 1952; in office: May 5, 2003. **Local divisions:** 48 provinces. **Defense budget** (2003): $2.2 bil. **Active troops:** 127,500.

Economy: Industries: oil, nat. gas, light industries, mining, petrochemical, food proc. **Chief crops:** wheat, barley, oats, grapes, olives, citrus. **Natural resources:** oil, nat. gas, iron ore, phosphates, uranium, lead, zinc. **Crude oil reserves** (2003): 9.2 bil. bbls **Arable land:** 3%. **Livestock** (2003): cattle: 1.54 mil.; chickens: 115.0 mil.; goats: 3.2 mil.; pigs: 5,700; sheep: 17.3 mil. **Fish catch** (2002): 134,796 metric tons. **Electricity prod.** (2002): 25.76 bil. kWh. **Labor force:** (2002 est.): government 32%, agriculture 14%, construction and public works 10%, industry 13.4%, trade 16%, other 14.6%.

Finance: Monetary unit: Dinar (DZD) (Sept. 2004: 72.12 = $1 U.S.). **GDP** (2003 est.): $194.3 bil.; **per capita GDP:** $5,900; **GDP growth:** 7.3%. **Imports** (2003 est.): $12.4 bil.; partners (2002): France 22.7%, U.S. 9.8%, Italy 9.6%, Germany 7.2%, Spain 5.3%. **Exports** (2003 est.): $25.0 bil.; partners (2002): Italy 20.1%, U.S. 14.2%, France 13.6%, Spain 12.1%, Netherlands 9%, Turkey 5.1%, Canada 5%, Brazil 4.8%. **Tourism:** $161 mil. **Budget** (2003 est.): $22.3 bil. **Intl. reserves less gold:** $22.29 bil. **Gold:** 5.58 mil. oz t. **Consumer prices:** 2.6%.

Transport: Railroad: Length: 2,469 mi. **Motor vehicles** (2000): 1.72 mil. pass. cars, 1.01 mil. comm. vehicles. **Civil aviation:** 1.5 bil. pass.-mi; 54 airports. **Chief ports:** Algiers, Annaba, Oran.

Communications: TV sets: 107 per 1,000 pop. **Radios:** 242 per 1,000 pop. **Telephone lines:** 2.2 mil. **Daily newspaper circ.:** 27.2 per 1,000 pop. **Internet** (2002): 500,000 users.

Health: Life expect.: 71.2 male; 74.3 female. **Births** (per 1,000 pop.): 17.8. **Deaths** (per 1,000 pop.): 4.6. **Natural inc.:** 1.31%. **Infant mortality** (per 1,000 live births): 32.2. **AIDS rate:** 0.1%.

Education: Compulsory: ages 6-14. **Literacy:** 70%.
Major Intl. Organizations: UN (FAO, IBRD, ILO, IMF, IMO, WHO), AL, AU, OPEC.
Embassy: 2118 Kalorama Rd. NW 20008; 265-2800.
Website: www.algeria-us.org

Earliest known inhabitants were ancestors of Berbers, followed by Phoenicians, Romans, Vandals, and, finally, Arabs. Turkey ruled 1518 to 1830, when France took control.

Large-scale European immigration and French cultural inroads did not prevent an Arab nationalist movement from launching guerrilla war. Peace, and French withdrawal, was negotiated with French Pres. Charles de Gaulle. One million Europeans left. Independence came July 5, 1962. Ahmed Ben Bella was the victor of infighting and ruled until 1965, when an army coup installed Col. Houari Boumedienne as leader; Boumedienne led until his death from a blood disease, 1978.

In 1967, Algeria declared war on Israel, broke ties with U.S., and moved toward eventual military and political ties with the USSR. Some 500 died in riots protesting economic hardship in 1988. In 1989, voters approved a new constitution, which cleared the way for a multiparty system.

The government canceled the Jan. 1992 elections that Islamic fundamentalists were expected to win, and banned all nonreligious activities at Algeria's 10,000 mosques. Pres. Mohammed Boudiaf was assassinated June 29, 1992. There were repeated attacks on high-ranking officials, security forces, foreigners, and others by militant Muslim fundamentalists over the next 7 years; pro-government death squads also were active.

Liamine Zeroual won the presidential election of Nov. 16, 1995. A new constitution banning Islamic political parties and increasing the president's powers passed in a referendum on Nov. 28, 1996. Abdelaziz Bouteflika, who became president after a flawed elec-

tion on Apr. 15, 1999, made peace with rebels and won approval for an amnesty plan in a referendum on Sept. 16; by then, about 100,000 people had died in the civil war. Some 100 people died and thousands were injured in violent protests Apr.-June 2001, chiefly by Algeria's Berber minority. Floods in Nov. killed over 700 people. An earthquake in N Algeria, May 21, 2003, claimed over 2,200 lives and left about 200,000 people homeless. Pres. Bouteflika won reelection, Apr. 8, 2004, with an 83.5% majority. The army launched a campaign against the militant Islamic group GSPC after its members killed 12 soldiers in early June. GSPC leader Nabil Sahraoui was killed by Algerian forces, June 20.

Andorra
Principality of Andorra

People: Population: 69,865. **Age distrib.** (%): <15: 15.2; 65+: 12.9. **Pop. density:** 387 per sq mi, 149 per sq km. **Urban:** 91.7%. **Ethnic groups:** Spanish 43%, Andorran 33%, Portuguese 11%, French 7%. **Principal languages:** Catalan (official), Castilian Spanish, French. **Chief religion:** Predominantly Roman Catholic.

Geography: Total area: 181 sq mi, 468 sq km; **Land area:** 181 sq mi, 468 sq km. **Location:** SW Europe, in Pyrenees Mts. **Neighbors:** Spain on S, France on N. **Topography:** High mountains and narrow valleys cover the country. **Capital:** Andorra la Vella, 21,000.

Government: Type: Parliamentary co-principality. **Heads of state:** President of France & Bishop of Urgel (Spain), as co-princes. **Head of gov.:** Marc Forné Molné; b Dec. 30, 1946; in office: Dec. 21, 1994. **Local divisions:** 7 parishes. **Defense budget:** Responsibility of France and Spain.

Economy: Industries: tourism, cattle raising, timber, tobacco, banking. **Chief crops:** tobacco, rye, wheat, barley, oats. **Natural resources:** hydropower, mineral water, timber, iron ore, lead. **Arable land:** 2%. **Labor force:** (2000 est.): agriculture 1%, industry 21%, services 78%.

Finance: Monetary unit: Euro (EUR) (Sept. 2004: 0.82 = $1 U.S.). **GDP** (2000 est.): $1.3 bil.; **per capita GDP:** $19,000; **GDP growth:** 3.8%. **Imports** (1998): $1.1 bil.; partners (2000): Spain 48%, France 35%, U.S. 2.3%. **Exports** (1998): $58.0 mil.; partners (2000): Spain 58%, France 34%. **Budget** (1997): $342.0 mil.

Transport: Motor vehicles: 35,358 pass. cars, 4,238 comm. vehicles.

Communications: TV sets: 440 per 1,000 pop. **Radios:** 229 per 1,000 pop. **Telephone lines:** 35,000. **Daily newspaper circ.:** 60 per 1,000 pop. **Internet** (2002): 7,000 users.

Health: Life expect.: 80.6 male; 86.6 female. **Births** (per 1,000 pop.): 9.3. **Deaths** (per 1,000 pop.): 5.9. **Natural inc.:** 0.34%. **Infant mortality** (per 1,000 live births): 4.1.

Education: Compulsory: ages 6-15. **Literacy:** 100%.

Major Intl. Organizations: UN.

Embassy: 2 UN Plaza, 25th floor, New York, NY 10017; 750-8064.

Website: www.andorra.ad

Andorra was a co-principality, with joint sovereignty by France and the bishop of Urgel, from 1278 to 1993.

Tourism, especially skiing, is the economic mainstay. A free port, allowing for an active trading center, draws some 13 million tourists annually. Andorran voters chose to end a feudal system that had been in place for 715 years and adopt a parliamentary system of government Mar. 14, 1993.

Angola
Republic of Angola

People: Population: 10,978,552. **Age distrib.** (%): <15: 43.3; 65+: 2.8. **Pop. density:** 23 per sq mi, 9 per sq km. **Urban:** 35.7%. **Ethnic groups:** Ovimbundu 37%, Kimbundu 25%, Bakongo 13%. **Principal languages:** Portuguese (official), Bantu and other African languages. **Chief religions:** Indigenous beliefs 47%, Roman Catholic 38%, Protestant 15%.

Geography: Total area: 481,353 sq mi, 1,246,700 sq km; **Land area:** 481,353 sq mi, 1,246,700 sq km. **Location:** In SW Africa on Atlantic coast. **Neighbors:** Namibia on S, Zambia on E, Congo-Kinshasa (formerly Zaire) on N; Cabinda, an enclave separated from rest of country by short Atlantic coast of Congo-Kinshasa, borders Congo-Brazzaville. **Topography:** Most of Angola consists of a plateau elevated 3,000 to 5,000 feet above sea level, rising from a narrow coastal strip. There is also a temperate highland area in the west-central region, a desert in the S, and a tropical rains forest covering Cabinda. **Capital:** Luanda, 2,623,000.

Government: Type: Republic. **Head of state:** Pres. José Eduardo dos Santos; b Aug. 28, 1942; in office: Sept. 20, 1979. **Head of gov.:** Prime Min. Fernando da Piedade Dias dos Santos; b Mar. 5, 1952; in office: Dec. 6, 2002. **Local divisions:** 18 provinces. **Defense budget** (2003): $386 mil. **Active troops:** 129,000-131,000.

Economy: Industries: oil, mining, cement, metals, fish & food proc. **Chief crops:** bananas, sugarcane, coffee, sisal. **Natural resources:** oil, diamonds, iron ore, phosphates, copper, feldspar, gold, bauxite, uranium. **Livestock** (2003): cattle: 4.15 mil.; chickens: 6.8 mil.; goats: 2.05 mil.; pigs: 780,000; sheep: 340,000. **Crude oil reserves** (2003): 5.4 bil. bbls. **Arable land:** 2%. **Fish catch** (2002): 260,797 metric tons. **Electricity prod.** (2002): 1.71 bil. kWh. **Labor force** (2003 est.): agriculture 85%, industry and services 15%.

Finance: Monetary unit: New Kwanza (AON) (Sept. 2004: 85.30 = $1 U.S.). **GDP** (2003 est.): $20.6 bil.; **per capita GDP:** $1,900; **GDP growth:** 7.1%. **Imports** (2003 est.): $4.1 bil.; partners (2002): Portugal 19.2%, South Africa 14.7%, U.S. 13.2%, Brazil 7.1%, France 6.4%, Belgium 5%. **Exports** (2003 est.): $9.7 bil.; partners (2002): U.S. 41%, China 13.6%, France 7.9%, Taiwan 7.5%, Belgium 6.2%, Japan 4.9%, Spain 4.3%. **Tourism:** $71 mil. **Budget** (1992 est.): $2.5 bil. **Intl. reserves less gold:** $427 mil. **Consumer prices** (change in 2003): 98.2%.

Transport: Railroad: Length: 1,716 mi. **Motor vehicles** (1999): 107,100 pass. cars, 110,500 comm. vehicles. **Civil aviation:** 351.1 mil. pass.-mi; 32 airports. **Chief ports:** Cabinda, Lobito, Luanda.

Communications: TV sets: 15 per 1,000 pop. **Radios:** 67 per 1,000 pop. **Telephone lines:** 96,300. **Daily newspaper circ.:** 11 per 1,000 pop. **Internet** (2002): 41,000 users.

Health: Life expect.: 36.1 male; 37.6 female. **Births** (per 1,000 pop.): 45.1. **Deaths** (per 1,000 pop.): 25.9. **Natural inc.:** 1.93%. **Infant mortality** (per 1,000 live births): 192.5. **AIDS rate:** 3.9%.

Education: Compulsory: ages 6-9. **Literacy** (1998 est.): 42%.

Major Intl. Organizations: UN (FAO, IBRD, ILO, IMF, IMO, WHO, WTrO), AU.

Embassy: 2100-2108 16th St. NW 20009; 785-1156.

Website: www.angola.org

From the early centuries AD to 1500, Bantu tribes penetrated most of the region. Portuguese came in 1583, allied with the Bakongo kingdom in the north, and developed the slave trade. Large-scale colonization did not begin until the 20th century, when 400,000 Portuguese immigrated.

A guerrilla war begun in 1961 lasted until 1975, when Portugal granted independence. Fighting then erupted between three rival rebel groups—the National Front, based in Zaire (now Congo), the Soviet-backed Popular Movement for the Liberation of Angola (MPLA), and the National Union for the Total Independence of Angola (UNITA), aided by the U.S. and South Africa.

Cuban troops and Soviet aid helped the MPLA win control of most of the country by 1976, although fighting continued through the 1980s. A peace accord between the MPLA government and UNITA was signed May 1, 1991.

Elections were held in Sept. 1992, but fighting again broke out, as UNITA rejected the results. UNITA signed a new peace treaty with the government, Nov. 20, 1994, but the rebels were slow to demobilize. The UN Security Council voted, Aug. 28, 1997, to impose sanctions on UNITA. In Aug. 1998, Angola sent thousands of troops into Congo-Kinshasa (formerly Zaire) to support Laurent Kabila's regime. The UN ended its mission in Angola in Mar. 1999, as the civil war continued.

As of 2001, the UN estimated that the war with UNITA had claimed some 1 million lives and left another 2.5 million people homeless. More than 250 died when UNITA rebels ambushed a train Aug. 10. Rebel leader Jonas Savimbi was killed by government troops Feb. 22, 2002. UNITA agreed to a truce Apr. 4 of that year, ending the 27-year-long civil war. Fighting continued, however, between government forces and separatist guerrillas in oil-rich Cabinda.

Mismanagement and corruption led to the diversion of up to $4.2 bil in oil revenues during 1997-2002, according to a Human Rights Watch report. In Apr. 2004, the govt. arrested nearly 3,000 illegal diamond diggers, many of them foreigners. More than 11,000 people were expelled since Dec. 2003, for "exploiting resources."

Antigua and Barbuda

People: Population: 68,320. **Age distrib.** (%): <15: 28; 65+: 4.7. **Pop. density:** 399 per sq mi, 154 per sq km. **Urban:** 37.7%. **Ethnic groups:** Black, British, Portuguese, Lebanese, Syrian. **Principal languages:** English (official), local dialects. **Chief religions:** Predominantly Protestant; some Roman Catholic.

Geography: Total area: 171 sq mi, 443 sq km; **Land area:** 171 sq mi, 443 sq km. **Location:** Eastern Caribbean. **Neighbors:** St. Kitts & Nevis to W, Guadeloupe (Fr.) to S. Topography: These are mostly low-lying and limestone coral islands. Antigua is mostly hilly with an indented coast; Barbuda is a flat island with a large lagoon on the W. **Capital:** Saint John's, (2001) 28,000.

Government: Type: Constitutional monarchy with British-style parliament. **Head of state:** Queen Elizabeth II; represented by Gov.-Gen. James Carlisle; b Aug. 5, 1937; in office: June 10, 1993. **Head of gov.:** Prime Min. Baldwin Spencer; b Oct. 8, 1948; in office: Mar. 24, 2004. **Local divisions:** 6 parishes, 2 dependencies. **Defense budget** (2003): $4 mil. **Active troops:** 170.

Economy: Industries: tourism, constr., light mfg. **Chief crops:** cotton, fruits, vegetables. **Arable land:** 18%. **Livestock** (2003): cattle: 14,000; chickens: 100,000; goats: 35,500; pigs: 5,500; sheep: 18,600. **Fish catch** (2002): 2,374 metric tons. **Electricity prod.** (2002): 0.11 bil. kWh. **Labor force** (1983): commerce and services 82%, agriculture 11%, industry 7%.

Finance: Monetary unit: East Caribbean Dollar (XCD) (Sept. 2004: 2.67 = $1 U.S.). **GDP** (2002 est.): $750.0 mil.; **per capita GDP:** $11,000; **GDP growth:** 3.0%. **Imports** (2002 est.): $692.0 mil.; partners (2002): France 23%, Germany 14.9%, U.S. 13%, South Korea 8.1%, Singapore 4.9%, Poland 4.6%, UK 4.3%. **Exports** (2002): $689.0 mil.; partners (2002): France 68.7%, Germany 26.6%, Italy 1.2%. **Tourism:** $301 mil. **Budget** (2000 est.): $145.9 mil. **Intl. reserves less gold:** $77 mil.

Transport: Railroad: Length: 48 mi. **Motor vehicles** (1998): 24,000 pass. cars. **Civil aviation:** 185.2 mil. pass.-mi; 2 airports.
Communications: TV sets: 493 per 1,000 pop. **Radios:** 545 per 1,000 pop. **Telephone lines** (2002): 38,000. **Daily newspaper circ.:** 91 per 1,000 pop. **Internet** (2002): 10,000 users.
Health: Life expect.: 69.3 male; 74.1 female. **Births** (per 1,000 pop.): 17.7. **Deaths** (per 1,000 pop.): 5.5. **Natural inc.:** 1.22%. **Infant mortality** (per 1,000 live births): 20.2.
Education: Compulsory: ages 5-16. **Literacy** (1992): 90%.
Major Intl. Organizations: UN (FAO, IBRD, ILO, IMF, IMO, WHO, WTrO), Caricom, the Commonwealth, OAS, OECS.
Embassy: 3216 New Mexico Ave. NW 20016; 362-5211.
Website: www.antiguagov.com
Columbus landed on Antigua in 1493. The British colonized it in 1632.
The British associated state of Antigua achieved independence as Antigua and Barbuda on Nov. 1, 1981. The government maintains close relations with the U.S., United Kingdom, and Venezuela. The country was hit hard by Hurricane Luis, Sept. 1995. About 3,000 refugees from the nearby island of Montserrat settled in Antigua following volcanic eruptions there in 1995-97.

Argentina
Argentine Republic

People: Population: 39,144,753. **Age distrib.** (%): <15: 26.3; 65+: 10.5. **Pop. density:** 37 per sq mi, 14 per sq km. **Urban:** 90.1%. **Ethnic groups:** European 97%, Amerindian 3%. **Principal languages:** Spanish (official), English, Italian, German, French. **Chief religion:** Roman Catholic 92% (official).
Geography: Total area: 1,068,302 sq mi, 2,766,890 sq km; **Land area:** 1,056,641 sq mi, 2,736,690 sq km. **Location:** Occupies most of southern South America. **Neighbors:** Chile on W; Bolivia, Paraguay on N; Brazil, Uruguay on NE. **Topography:** Mountains in the W are: the Andean, Central, Misiones, and Southern ranges. Aconcagua is the highest peak in the western hemisphere, alt. 22,834 ft. E of the Andes are heavily wooded plains, called the Gran Chaco in the N, and the fertile, treeless Pampas in the central region. Patagonia, in the S, is bleak and arid. Rio de la Plata, an estuary in the NE, 170 by 140 mi., is mostly fresh water, from 2,485-mi Parana and 1,000-mi Uruguay rivers. **Capital:** Buenos Aires, 13,047,000 (the Senate has approved moving the capital to the Patagonia Region). **Cities (urban aggr.):** Cordoba, 1,444,000; Rosario, 1,231,000.
Government: Type: Republic. **Head of state and gov.:** Pres. Néstor Kirchner; b Feb. 25, 1950; in office: May 25, 2003. **Local divisions:** 23 provinces, 1 federal district. **Defense budget** (2003): $1.6 bil. **Active troops:** 71,400.
Economy: Industries: food proc., vehicles, consumer durables, textiles, chemicals. **Chief crops:** sunflower seeds, lemons, soybeans, grapes, corn. **Natural resources:** lead, zinc, tin, copper, iron ore, mang., oil, uranium. **Crude oil reserves** (2003): 2.9 bil. bbls. **Arable land:** 9%. **Livestock** (2003): cattle: 50.87 mil.; chickens: 110.7 mil.; goats: 4.2 mil.; pigs: 4.3 mil.; sheep: 12.45 mil. **Fish catch** (2002): 945,803 metric tons. **Electricity prod.** (2002): 81.39 bil. kWh.
Finance: Monetary unit: Peso (ARS) (Sept. 2004: 2.99 = $1 U.S.). **GDP** (2003 est.): $432.7 bil.; **per capita GDP:** $11,200; **GDP growth:** 8.0%. **Imports** (2003 est.): $13.3 bil.; partners (2002): Brazil 28.1%, U.S. 20.1%, Germany 6.2%. **Exports** (2003 est.): $29.6 bil.; partners (2002): Brazil 18.8%, Chile 11.5%, U.S. 11.5%, Spain 4.5%, China 4.2%, Netherlands 4.1%. **Tourism:** $2.0 bil. **Budget** (2000 est.): $48.0 bil. **Intl. reserves less gold:** $9.5 bil. **Gold:** 10,000 oz t. **Consumer prices:** 13.4%.
Transport: Railroad: Length: 21,183 mi. **Motor vehicles** (2000): 5.39 mil pass. cars, 1.0 mil comm. vehicles. **Civil aviation:** 5.8 bil. pass.-mi; 145 airports. **Chief ports:** Buenos Aires, Bahia Blanca, La Plata.
Communications: TV sets: 293 per 1,000 pop. **Radios:** 681 per 1,000 pop. **Telephone lines** (2002): 8.0 mil. **Daily newspaper circ.:** 37.3 per 1,000 pop. **Internet** (2002): 4.1 mil. users.
Health: Life expect.: 72.0 male; 79.7 female. **Births** (per 1,000 pop.): 17.2. **Deaths** (per 1,000 pop.): 7.6. **Natural inc.:** 0.96%. **Infant mortality** (per 1,000 live births): 15.7. **AIDS rate:** 0.7%.
Education: Compulsory: ages 5-15. **Literacy:** 97.1%.
Major Intl. Organizations: UN (FAO, IBRD, ILO, IMF, IMO, WHO, WTrO), OAS.
Embassy: 1600 New Hampshire Ave. NW 20009; 238-6400.
Website: www.embajadaargentinaeeuu.org/english/home
Nomadic Indians roamed the Pampas when Spaniards arrived, 1515-16, led by Juan Diaz de Solis. Nearly all the Indians were killed by the late 19th century. The colonists won independence, 1816, and a long period of disorder ended in a strong centralized government.
Large-scale Italian, German, and Spanish immigration in the decades after 1880 spurred modernization. Social reforms were enacted in the 1920s, but military coups prevailed 1930-46, until the election of Gen. Juan Perón as president.
Perón, with his wife, Eva Duarte (d 1952), effected labor reforms, but also suppressed speech and press freedoms, closed religious schools, and ran the country into debt. A 1955 coup exiled Perón, who was followed by a series of military and civilian re-

gimes. Perón returned in 1973, and was once more elected president. He died 10 months later, succeeded by his wife Isabel, who had been elected vice president, and who became the first woman head of state in the western hemisphere.
A military junta ousted Mrs. Perón in 1976 amid charges of corruption. Under a continuing state of siege, the army conducted a "dirty war" against guerrillas and leftists in which an estimated 30,000 people "disappeared." On Dec. 9, 1985, after a trial of 5 months and nearly 1,000 witnesses, 5 former junta members were found guilty of murder and human rights abuses.
Argentine troops seized control of the British-held Falkland Islands on Apr. 2, 1982. Both countries had claimed sovereignty over the islands, located 250 miles off the Argentine coast, since 1833. The British dispatched a task force and declared a total air and sea blockade around the Falklands. Fighting began May 1; several hundred lost their lives as the result of the destruction of a British destroyer and the sinking of an Argentine cruiser.
British troops landed on East Falkland Island May 21 and eventually surrounded Stanley, the capital city and Argentine stronghold. The Argentine troops surrendered, June 14; Argentine Pres. Leopoldo Galtieri resigned June 17.
Democratic rule returned in 1983 as Raul Alfonsín's Radical Civic Union party gained an absolute majority in the presidential electoral college and Congress. By 1989 the nation was plagued by severe financial and political problems, as hyperinflation sparked looting and rioting in several cities. The government of Perónist Pres. Carlos Saúl Menem, installed 1989, introduced harsh economic measures to curtail inflation, control government spending, and restructure the foreign debt.
About 100 people were killed in the terrorist bombing of a Jewish cultural center in Buenos Aires, July 18, 1994. Following passage of a new constitution in Aug. 1994, Menem was reelected president on May 14, 1995. A pact restoring commercial air links between Argentina and the Falklands was signed July 14, 1999.
Buenos Aires Mayor Fernando de la Rúa won the presidential election Oct. 24, 1999. A prolonged recession and a debt of more than $130 billion left Argentina facing an economic crisis in 2001, which austerity measures and IMF aid failed to remedy. After widespread rioting and looting Dec. 19, de la Rúa resigned.
A 2-week period of protests and political upheavals abated when Congress, Jan. 1, 2002, chose a Peronist, Eduardo Alberto Duhalde, to finish de la Rúa's term. Duhalde devalued the peso by cutting its ties with the U.S. dollar. Further economic decline and renewed protests led Duhalde July 2 to schedule an early presidential election for Mar. 2003; another Peronist, Néstor Kirchner, took office May 25, 2003, after Menem pulled out of a runoff election. Kirchner moved to end corruption and human rights abuses among the military and police. A new IMF aid deal, approved Sept. 10, 2003, rescued Argentina from default.

Armenia
Republic of Armenia

People: Population: 2,991,360. **Age distrib.** (%): <15: 22.2; 65+: 10.1. **Pop. density:** 273 per sq mi, 105 per sq km. **Urban:** 64.4%. **Ethnic groups:** Armenian 93%, Russian 2%. **Principal languages:** Armenian (official), Russian. **Chief religions:** Armenian Apostolic 94%, other Christian 4%, Yezidi 2%.
Geography: Total area: 11,506 sq mi, 29,800 sq km; **Land area:** 10,965 sq mi, 28,400 sq km. **Location:** SW Asia. **Neighbors:** Georgia on N, Azerbaijan on E, Iran on S, Turkey on W. **Topography:** Mountainous with many peaks above 10,000 ft. **Capital:** Yerevan, 1,079,000.
Government: Type: Republic. **Head of state:** Pres. Robert Kocharian; b Aug. 31, 1954; in office: Apr. 9, 1998. **Head of gov.:** Prime Min. Andranik Markarian; b June 12, 1951; in office: May 12, 2000. **Local divisions:** 10 provinces, 1 city. **Defense budget** (2003): $66 mil. **Active troops:** 44,660.
Economy: Industries: machine tools & machines, electric motors, tires, knitted wear. **Chief crops:** grapes, vegetables. **Natural resources:** gold, copper, molybd., zinc, alumina. **Arable land:** 17%. **Livestock** (2003): cattle: 514,200; chickens: 3.31 mil.; goats: 50,022; pigs: 111,031; sheep: 552,538. **Fish catch** (2002): 1,485 metric tons. **Electricity prod.** (2002): 6.49 bil. kWh. **Labor force** (2002 est.): agriculture 45%, services 30%, industry 25%.
Finance: Monetary unit: Dram (AMD) (Sept. 2004: 516.54 = $1 U.S.). **GDP** (2003 est.): $11.8 bil.; **per capita GDP:** $3,900; **GDP growth:** 9.9%. **Imports** (2003 est.): $1.2 bil.; partners (2002): U.S. 14.1%, Russia 11.9%, Belgium 11.3%, Israel 10%, Iran 9.5%, UAE 5.7%, Germany 5.1%, Italy 4.5%, Ukraine 4.2%. **Exports** (2003 est.): $735.0 mil.; partners (2002): Belgium 21.9%, Israel 16.4%, Russia 14.7%, Iran 11.2%, U.S. 8.4%, Germany 6.6%. **Tourism:** $206 mil. **Budget** (2003 est.): $482.0 mil. **Intl. reserves less gold:** $343 mil. **Gold:** 40,000 oz t. **Consumer prices:** 4.8%.
Transport: Railroad: Length: 525 mi. **Civil aviation:** 355.4 mil. pass.-mi; 8 airports.
Communications: TV sets: 241 per 1,000 pop. **Radios:** 239 per 1,000 pop. **Telephone lines:** 562,600. **Daily newspaper circ.:** 5.0 per 1,000 pop. **Internet:** 150,000 users.
Health: Life expect.: 67.7 male; 75.4 female. **Births** (per 1,000 pop.): 11.4. **Deaths** (per 1,000 pop.): 8.1. **Natural inc.:** 0.33%. **Infant mortality** (per 1,000 live births): 24.2. **AIDS rate:** 0.1%.
Education: Compulsory: ages 7-17. **Literacy:** 98.6%.

Major Intl. Organizations: UN (FAO, IBRD, ILO, IMF, WHO, WTrO), CIS, OSCE. **Embassy:** 2225 R St. NW 20008; 319-1976. **Website:** www.armeniaemb.org

Ancient Armenia extended into parts of what are now Turkey and Iran. Present-day Armenia was set up as a Soviet republic Apr. 2, 1921. It joined Georgian and Azerbaijan SSRs Mar. 12, 1922, to form the Transcaucasian SFSR, which became part of the USSR Dec. 30, 1922. Armenia became a constituent republic of the USSR Dec. 5, 1936. An earthquake struck Armenia Dec. 7, 1988; approximately 55,000 were killed and several cities and towns were left in ruins.

Armenia declared independence Sept. 23, 1991, and became an independent state when the USSR disbanded Dec. 26, 1991.

Fighting between mostly Christian Armenia and mostly Muslim Azerbaijan escalated in 1992 and continued through 1993. Each country claimed Nagorno-Karabakh, an enclave in Azerbaijan that has a majority population of ethnic Armenians. A temporary cease-fire was announced in May 1994, with Armenian forces in control of the enclave. Voters approved, July 5, 1995, a new constitution increasing presidential powers. Pres. Levon Ter-Petrosian won reelection on Sept. 22, 1996, amid claims of fraud; he resigned Feb. 3, 1998, in a conflict over Nagorno-Karabakh. Robert Kocharian, a nationalist born in the disputed region, won the presidency on Mar. 30, 1998. Gunmen stormed Parliament Oct. 27, 1999, killing Prime Min. Vazgen Sarkissian and 7 others. Kocharian won a 2nd term Mar. 5, 2003, in a runoff vote viewed as flawed by opposition groups and Western observers.

Australia
Commonwealth of Australia

People: Population: 19,913,144. **Age distrib.** (%): <15: 20.4; 65+: 12.6. **Pop. density:** 7 per sq mi, 3 per sq km. **Urban:** 92.0%. **Ethnic groups:** White 92%, Asian 7%, Aborigine and other 1%. **Principal languages:** English (official), Aboriginal languages. **Chief religions:** Anglican 26%, Roman Catholic 26%, other Christian 24%.

Geography: Total area: 2,967,908 sq mi, 7,686,850 sq km; **Land area:** 2,941,298 sq mi, 7,617,930 sq km. **Location:** SE of Asia, Indian O. is W and S, Pacific O. (Coral, Tasman seas) is E; they meet N of Australia in Timor and Arafura seas. Tasmania lies 150 mi. S of Victoria state, across Bass Strait. **Neighbors:** Nearest are Indonesia, Papua New Guinea on N; Solomons, Fiji, and New Zealand on E. **Topography:** An island continent. The Great Dividing Range along the E coast has Mt. Kosciusko, 7,310 ft. The W plateau rises to 2,000 ft., with arid areas in the Great Sandy and Great Victoria deserts. The NW part of Western Australia and Northern Terr. are arid and hot. The NE has heavy rainfall and Cape York Peninsula has jungles. **Capital:** Canberra, 373,000. **Cities (urban aggr.):** Sydney, 4,099,000; Melbourne, 3,447,000; Brisbane, 1,626,000; Perth, 1,376,000; Adelaide, 1,104,000.

Government: Type: Democratic, federal state system. **Head of state:** Queen Elizabeth II, represented by Gov.-Gen. Michael Jeffery; b 1937; in office; Aug. 11, 2003. **Head of gov.:** Prime Min. John Howard; b July 26, 1939; in office: Mar. 11, 1996. **Local divisions:** 6 states, 2 territories. **Defense budget** (2003): $9.9 bil. **Active troops:** 53,650.

Economy: Industries: mining, industrial & transp. equip., food proc., chemicals, steel. **Chief crops:** wheat, barley, sugarcane, fruits. **Natural resources:** bauxite, coal, iron ore, copper, tin, silver, uranium, nickel, tungsten, mineral sands, lead, zinc, diamonds, nat. gas, oil. **Crude oil reserves** (2003): 3.5 bil. bbls. **Other resources:** Wool (world's leading producer), beef. **Arable land:** 6%. **Livestock** (2003): cattle: 27.22 mil.; chickens: 94.0 mil.; goats: 420,000; pigs: 2.96 mil.; sheep: 98.2 mil. **Fish catch** (2002): 233,018 metric tons. **Electricity prod.** (2002): 210.32 bil. kWh. **Labor force** (1997 est.): services 73%, industry 22%, agriculture 5%.

Finance: Monetary unit: Australian Dollar (AUD) (Sept. 2004: 1.44 = $1 U.S.). **GDP** (2003 est.): $570.3 bil.; **per capita GDP:** $28,900; **GDP growth:** 2.8%. **Imports** (2003 est.): $82.9 bil.; partners (2002): U.S. 18.3%, Japan 12.3%, China 10.1%, Germany 5.7%, UK 4.6%. **Exports** (2003 est.): $68.7 bil.; partners (2002): Japan 18.5%, U.S. 9.6%, South Korea 8.3%, China 6.9%, New Zealand 6.5%, UK 4.7%, Singapore 4.1%, Taiwan 4%. **Tourism:** $7.1 bil. **Budget** (FY00/01 est.): $84.1 bil. **Intl. reserves less gold:** $21.67 bil. **Gold:** 2.56 mil oz t. **Consumer prices:** 2.8%.

Transport: Railroad: Length: 27,350 mi. **Motor vehicles** (2001): 9.84 mil pass. cars, 2.24 mil comm. vehicles. **Civil aviation:** 32.9 bil. pass.-mi; 294 airports. **Chief ports:** Sydney, Melbourne, Brisbane, Adelaide, Fremantle, Geelong.

Communications: TV sets: 716 per 1,000 pop. **Radios:** 1,391 per 1,000 pop. **Telephone lines:** 10.8 mil. **Daily newspaper circ.:** 293 per 1,000 pop. **Internet** (2002): 9.5 mil. users.

Health: Life expect.: 77.4 male; 83.3 female. **Births** (per 1,000 pop.): 12.4. **Deaths** (per 1,000 pop.): 7.4. **Natural inc.:** 0.50%. **Infant mortality** (per 1,000 live births): 4.8. **AIDS rate:** 0.1%.

Education: Compulsory: ages 5-15. **Literacy** (1996 est.): 100%.

Major Intl. Organizations: UN and all of its specialized agencies, APEC, the Commonwealth, OECD.

Embassy: 1601 Massachusetts Ave. NW 20036; 797-3000. **Website:** www.austemb.org

Australia harbors many plant and animal species not found elsewhere, including kangaroos, koalas, platypuses, dingos (wild dogs), Tasmanian devils (raccoon-like marsupials), wombats (bear-like marsupials), and barking and frilled lizards.

Capt. James Cook explored the E coast in 1770, when the continent was inhabited by a variety of different tribes. The first settlers, beginning in 1788, were mostly convicts, soldiers, and government officials. By 1830, Britain had claimed the entire continent, and the immigration of free settlers began to accelerate. The Commonwealth was proclaimed Jan. 1, 1901. Northern Terr. was granted limited self-rule July 1, 1978.

State/Territory, Capital	Area (sq. mi.)	Population (2002 est.)
New South Wales, Sydney	309,500	6,257,351
Victoria, Melbourne	87,900	4,888,234
Queensland, Brisbane	666,990	3,729,028
Western Australia, Perth	975,100	1,934,494
South Australia, Adelaide	379,900	1,522,456
Tasmania, Hobart	26,200	473,365
Australian Capital Terr., Canberra	900	322,234
Northern Terr., Darwin	519,800	197,724

Racially discriminatory immigration policies were abandoned in 1973, after 3 million Europeans (half British) had entered since 1945. The 50,000 aborigines and 150,000 part-aborigines are mostly detribalized, but there are several preserves in the Northern Territory. They remain economically disadvantaged.

Australia's agricultural success makes the country among the top exporters of beef, lamb, wool, and wheat. Major mineral deposits have been developed, largely for export. Industrialization has been completed. The nation endured a deep recession 1990-93 but has rebounded strongly.

The Labor Party won a majority in Feb. 1983 general elections and was reelected in 1984, 1987, 1990, and 1993. After an election that focused mainly on economic issues, conservatives swept into power in elections Mar. 2, 1996.

Incumbent Prime Min. John Howard retained power, but with a reduced majority, in parliamentary elections Oct. 3, 1998. Australia led an international peacekeeping force into East Timor in Sept. 1999. In a referendum Nov. 6, voters rejected a proposal that would have made Australia a republic. Sydney hosted the Summer Olympics Sept. 15-Oct. 1, 2000. Howard won a 3rd term in the elections of Nov. 10, 2001.

Australian troops fought in U.S.-led military operations in Afghanistan (2001) and Iraq (2003). Some 2,000 Australian peacekeepers began arriving in the Solomon Is., July 24, 2003; about 450 remained in mid-2004. Howard, seeking a 4th term, set new elections for Oct. 9, 2004.

Australian External Territories

Norfolk Isl., area 13 sq. mi., pop. (2004 est.) 1,841, was taken over, 1914. The soil is very fertile, suitable for citrus, bananas, and coffee. Many of the inhabitants are descendants of the *Bounty* mutineers, moved to Norfolk 1856 from Pitcairn Isl. Australia offered the island limited home rule in 1978.

Coral Sea Isls. Territory, area 1 sq. mi., is administered from Norfolk Isl.

Territory of Ashmore and Cartier Isls., area 2 sq. mi., in the Indian O., came under Australian authority 1934 and are administered as part of Northern Territory. **Heard Isl. and McDonald Isls.,** area 159 sq. mi., are administered by the Dept. of Science.

Cocos (Keeling) Isls., 27 small coral islands in the Indian O. 1,750 mi. NW of Australia. Pop. (2004 est.) 629; area 5 sq. mi. The residents voted to become part of Australia, Apr. 1984.

Christmas Isl., area 52 sq. mi. (2004 est.) 396; 230 mi. S of Java, was transferred by Britain in 1958. It has phosphate deposits.

Australian Antarctic Territory was claimed by Australia in 1933, including 2,362,000 sq. mi. of territory S of 60th parallel S Lat. and between 160th-45th meridians E Long. It does not include Adelie Coast.

Austria
Republic of Austria

People: Population: 8,174,762. **Age distrib.** (%): <15: 16.4; 65+: 15.4. **Pop. density:** 257 per sq mi, 97 per sq km. **Urban:** 65.8%. **Ethnic groups:** German 88%. **Principal languages:** German (official), Serbo-Croatian, Slovenian. **Chief religions:** Roman Catholic 78%, Protestant 5%.

Geography: Total area: 32,382 sq mi, 83,870 sq km; **Land area:** 31,832 sq mi, 82,444 sq km. **Location:** In S Central Europe. **Neighbors:** Switzerland, Liechtenstein on W; Germany, Czech Rep. on N; Slovakia, Hungary on E; Slovenia, Italy on S. **Topography:** Austria is primarily mountainous, with the Alps and foothills covering the western and southern provinces. The eastern provinces and Vienna are located in the Danube River Basin. **Capital:** Vienna, 2,179,000.

Government: Type: Federal republic. **Head of state:** Pres. Heinz Fischer; b Oct. 9, 1938; in office: July 8, 2004. **Head of gov.:** Chancellor Wolfgang Schüssel; b June 7, 1945; in office: Feb. 4, 2000. **Local divisions:** 9 bundeslaender (states). **Defense budget** (2003): $2.5 bil. **Active troops:** 34,600.

Economy: Industries: constr., machinery, vehicles & parts, food, chemicals. **Chief crops:** grains, potatoes, sugar beets,

grapes. **Natural resources:** iron ore, oil, timber, magnesite, lead, coal, lignite, copper, hydropower. **Crude oil reserves** (2003): 85.7 mil. bbls. **Arable land:** 17%. **Livestock** (2003): cattle: 2.07 mil.; chickens: 11.0 mil.; goats: 57,842; pigs: 3.30 mil.; sheep: 304,364. **Fish catch** (2002): 2,683 metric tons. **Electricity prod.** (2002): 58.49 bil. kWh. **Labor force** (2001 est.): services 67%, industry and crafts 29%, agriculture and forestry 4%.

Finance: Monetary unit: Euro (EUR) (Sept. 2004: 0.82 = $1 U.S.). **GDP** (2003 est.): $245.5 bil.; **per capita GDP:** $30,000; **GDP growth:** 0.8%. **Imports** (2003 est.): $81.6 bil.; partners (2002): Germany 42.6%, Italy 6.6%, Hungary 5.1%, Switzerland 4.8%, Netherlands 4.4%. **Exports** (2003 est.): $83.5 bil.; partners (2002): Germany 31.5%, Italy 9.3%, Switzerland 5.4%, U.S. 4.9%, UK 4.9%, France 4.7%, Hungary 4.3%. **Tourism:** $13.6 bil **Budget** (2004 est.): $70.0 bil. **Intl. reserves less gold:** $5.7 bil. **Gold:** 10.21 mil oz t. **Consumer prices:** 1.4%.

Transport: Railroad: Length: 3,741 mi. **Motor vehicles** (2001): 4.2 mil pass. cars, 787,900 comm. vehicles. **Civil aviation:** 8.8 bil. pass.-mi; 24 airports. **Chief ports:** Linz, Vienna, Enns, Krems.

Communications: TV sets: 526 per 1,000 pop. **Radios:** 751 per 1,000 pop. **Telephone lines:** 3.9 mil. **Daily newspaper circ.:** 296 per 1,000 pop. **Internet:** 3.7 mil. users.

Health: Life expect.: 76.0 male; 81.9 female. **Births** (per 1,000 pop.): 8.9. **Deaths** (per 1,000 pop.): 9.6. **Natural inc.:** –0.07%. **Infant mortality** (per 1,000 live births): 4.7. **AIDS rate:** 0.3%.

Education: Compulsory: ages 6-14. **Literacy:** 98%.

Major Intl. Organizations: UN and all of its specialized agencies, EU, OECD, OSCE.

Embassy: 3524 International Ct. NW 20008; 895-6700.

Website: www.austria.gv.at

Rome conquered Austrian lands from Celtic tribes around 15 BC. In 788 the territory was incorporated into Charlemagne's empire. By 1300, the House of Hapsburg had gained control; they added vast territories in all parts of Europe to their realm in the next few hundred years.

Austrian dominance of Germany was undermined in the 18th century and ended by Prussia by 1866. But the Congress of Vienna, 1815, confirmed Austrian control of a large empire in southeast Europe consisting of Germans, Hungarians, Slavs, Italians, and others. The dual Austro-Hungarian monarchy was established in 1867, giving autonomy to Hungary and almost 50 years of peace.

World War I, started after the June 28, 1914, assassination of Archduke Franz Ferdinand, the Hapsburg heir, by a Serbian nationalist, destroyed the empire. By 1918 Austria was reduced to a small republic, with the borders it has today.

Nazi Germany invaded Austria Mar. 13, 1938. The republic was reestablished in 1945, under Allied occupation. Full independence and neutrality were restored in 1955. Austria joined the European Union Jan. 1, 1995.

The rise of the right-wing, anti-immigrant Austrian Freedom Party challenged the dominance of the Austrian Social Democratic Party in the late 1990s. When Freedom Party members joined the cabinet, Feb. 4, 2000, the EU imposed political sanctions on Austria, Feb. 4-Sept. 12, 2000. Party support plummeted in elections Nov. 24, 2002. Pres. Thomas Klestil died July 6, 2004, 2 days before his term expired; he was succeeded by recently elected Heinz Fischer, a Social Democrat.

Azerbaijan
Republic of Azerbaijan

People: Population: 7,868,385. **Age distrib.** (%): <15: 28.3; 65+: 7.4. **Pop. density:** 237 per sq mi, 91 per sq km. **Urban:** 50.0%. **Ethnic groups:** Azeri 90%, Dagestani 3%, Russian 3%, Armenian 2%. **Principal languages:** Azeri (official), Russian, Armenian. **Chief religions:** Muslim 93%, Russian Orthodox 3%, Armenian Orthodox 2%.

Geography: Total area: 33,436 sq mi, 86,600 sq km; **Land area:** 33,243 sq mi, 86,100 sq km. **Location:** SW Asia. **Neighbors:** Russia, Georgia on N; Iran on S; Armenia on W; Caspian Sea on E. **Topography:** The Great Caucasus Mts. in N, Karabakh Upland in W border the Kur-Abas lowland; climate is arid except in the subtropical SE. **Capital:** Baku, 1,816,000.

Government: Type: Republic. **Head of state:** Pres. Ilham Aliyev; b Dec. 24, 1961; in office: Oct. 31, 2003. **Head of gov.:** Prime Min. Artur Rasizade; b Feb. 26, 1935; in office: Nov. 4, 2003. **Local division:** 59 rayons, 11 cities, 1 autonomous republic. **Defense budget** (2003): $138 mil. **Active troops:** 66,490.

Economy: Industries: oil products, oil field equip., steel, iron ore, cement. **Chief crops:** cotton, grain, rice, grapes. **Natural resources:** oil, nat. gas, iron ore, nonferrous metals, alumina. **Crude oil reserves** (2003): 7.0 bil. bbls. **Arable land:** 18%. **Livestock** (2003): cattle: 2.18 mil.; chickens: 16.7 mil.; goats: 593,979; pigs: 19,809; sheep: 6.39 mil. **Fish catch** (2002): 11,502 metric tons. **Electricity prod.** (2002): 17.55 bil. kWh. **Labor force** (2001): agriculture and forestry 41%, industry 7%, services 52%.

Finance: Monetary unit: Manat (AZM) (Sept. 2004: 4,911.63 = $1 U.S.). **GDP** (2003 est.): $26.3 bil.; **per capita GDP:** $3,400; **GDP growth:** 9.9%. **Imports** (2003 est.): $2.5 bil.; partners (2002): Russia 16.8%, Turkey 13.5%, Germany 7.4%, Kazakhstan 6.8%, France 6.5%, Ukraine 6.3%, China 5.7%, UK 5.1%, U.S.

4.2%. **Exports** (2003 est.): $2.6 bil.; partners (2002): Italy 30.1%, Germany 15.5%, Czech Republic 10.8%, France 8.8%, Georgia 7%, Russia 4.9%. **Tourism** (2002): $51 mil. **Budget** (2001): $807.0 mil. **Intl. reserves less gold:** $552 mil. **Consumer prices** (change in 2002): 2.8%.

Transport: Railroad: Length: 1,837 mi. **Motor vehicles** (2001): 343,000 pass. cars; 127,600 comm. vehicles. **Civil aviation:** 169.0 mil. pass.-mi; 27 airports. **Chief port:** Baku.

Communications: TV sets: 257 per 1,000 pop. **Radios:** 23 per 1,000 pop. **Telephone lines** (2002): 923,800. **Daily newspaper circ.:** 27 per 1,000 pop. **Internet (2002):** 300,000 users.

Health: Life expect.: 59.1 male; 67.6 female. **Births** (per 1,000 pop.): 19.8. **Deaths** (per 1,000 pop.): 9.8. **Natural inc.:** 1.00%. **Infant mortality** (per 1,000 live births): 82.1. **AIDS rate:** <0.1%.

Education: Compulsory: ages 6-16. **Literacy** (2002): 100%.

Major Intl. Organizations: UN (FAO, IBRD, ILO, IMF, IMO, WHO), CIS, OSCE.

Embassy: 927 15th St. NW, Suite 700, 20035; 337-3500.

Website: www.azembassy.com

Azerbaijan was the home of Scythian tribes and part of the Roman Empire. Overrun by Turks in the 11th century and conquered by Russia in 1806 and 1813, it joined the USSR Dec. 30, 1922, and became a constituent republic in 1936. Azerbaijan declared independence Aug. 30, 1991, and became an independent state when the Soviet Union disbanded Dec. 26, 1991.

Fighting between mostly Muslim Azerbaijan and mostly Christian Armenia escalated in 1992 and continued in 1993 and 1994. Each country claimed Nagorno-Karabakh, an enclave in Azerbaijan with a majority population of ethnic Armenians. A temporary cease-fire was announced in May 1994, with Armenian forces in control of the enclave.

A National Council ousted Communist Pres. Mutaibov and took power May 19, 1992. Abulfez Elchibey became the nation's first democratically elected president June 7, but was ousted from office by Surat Huseynov, commander of a private militia, June 30, 1993. Huseynov became prime minister, and Haydar Aliyev, a pro-Russian former Communist, became president. Huseynov fled the country after his supporters staged an unsuccessful coup attempt Oct. 1994. Voters approved a new constitution expanding presidential powers, Nov. 12, 1995. Pres. Aliyev was reelected Oct. 11, 1998, but international monitors called the election seriously flawed. In Dec. 2001, a presidential decree made Latin script obligatory for the Azerbaijaini language, replacing the Cyrillic alphabet used during Soviet rule.

The dying Pres. Aliyev named his son Ilham prime minister Aug. 4, 2003. The younger Aliyev won the presidential election of Oct. 15, in a vote considered fraudulent by international observers; he responded to violent protests Oct. 16 by arresting hundreds of opposition leaders and their supporters.

The Bahamas
Commonwealth of The Bahamas

People: Population: 299,697. **Age distrib.** (%): <15: 29; 65+: 6.3. **Pop. density:** 77 per sq mi, 30 per sq km. **Urban:** 89.5%. **Ethnic groups:** Black 85%, White 12%. **Principal languages:** English, Creole (among Haitian immigrants). **Chief religions:** Baptist 32%, Anglican 20%, Roman Catholic 19%, other Christian 24%.

Geography: Total area: 5,382 sq mi, 13,940 sq km; **Land area:** 3,888 sq mi, 10,070 sq km. **Location:** In Atlantic O., E of Florida. **Neighbors:** Nearest are U.S. on W, Cuba on S. **Topography:** Nearly 700 islands (29 inhabited) and over 2,000 islets in the W Atlantic O. extend 760 mi. NW to SE. **Capital:** Nassau, 222,000. **Cities (urban aggr.):** (2001 est.) Grand Bahama, 40,898.

Government: Type: Independent commonwealth. **Head of state:** Queen Elizabeth II, represented by Gov.-Gen. Dame Ivy Dumont; b Oct. 2, 1930; in office: Nov. 13, 2001. **Head of gov.:** Prime Min. Perry Christie; b Aug. 21,1943; in office: May 3, 2002. **Local divisions:** 21 districts. **Defense budget** (2003): $29 mil. **Active troops:** 860.

Economy: Industries: tourism, banking, cement, oil refining & shipment, salt, rum. **Chief crops:** citrus, vegetables. **Natural resources:** salt, aragonite, timber. **Arable land:** 1%. **Livestock** (2003): cattle: 700; chickens: 2.98 mil.; goats: 14,000; pigs: 4,950; sheep: 6,450. **Fish catch** (2002 est): 9,313 metric tons. **Electricity prod.:** 1.72 bil. kWh. **Labor force** (1999 est.): tourism 50%, other services 40%, industry 5%, agriculture 5%.

Finance: Monetary unit: Bahamian Dollar (BSD) (Sept. 2004: 1.00 = $1 U.S.). **GDP** (2003 est.): $5.1 bil.; **per capita GDP:** $16,800; **GDP growth:** 1.0%. **Imports** (2002 est.): $1.6 bil.; partners (2002): U.S. 18.4%, South Korea 18.3%, Germany 10.5%, Norway 9.2%, Japan 9.1%, Italy 6.6%, Venezuela 4.1%. **Exports** (2002 est.): $617.0 mil.; partners (2002): U.S. 37.8%, Germany 11.8%, Spain 10.4%, Peru 8.6%, France 7.1%, Mexico 4.2%. **Tourism:** $1.8 bil. **Budget** (FY99/00): $956.5 mil. **Intl. reserves less gold:** $330 mil. **Consumer prices:** 3.0%.

Transport: Motor vehicles (1998): 67,400 pass. cars, 16,800 comm. vehicles. **Civil aviation:** 174.0 mil. pass.-mi; 30 airports. **Chief ports:** Nassau, Freeport.

Communications: TV sets: 243 per 1,000 pop. **Radios:** 739 per 1,000 pop. **Telephone lines:** 131,700.**Daily newspaper circ.:** 125 per 1,000 pop. **Internet:** 84,000 users.

Health: Life expect.: 62.2 male; 69.1 female. **Births** (per 1,000 pop.): 18.2. **Deaths** (per 1,000 pop.): 8.8. **Natural inc.:** 0.94%. **Infant mortality** (per 1,000 live births): 25.7. **AIDS rate:** 3%.

Education: Compulsory: ages 5-16. **Literacy:** 95.6%.

Major Intl. Organizations: UN (FAO, IBRD, ILO, IMF, IMO, WHO), Caricom, the Commonwealth, OAS.

Embassy: 2220 Massachusetts Ave. NW 20008; 319-2660.

Websites: www.bahamas.gov.bs; www.bahamas.com

Christopher Columbus first set foot in the New World on San Salvador (Watling Isl.) in 1492, when Arawak Indians inhabited the islands. British settlement began in 1647; the islands became a British colony in 1783. Internal self-government was granted in 1964; full independence within the Commonwealth was attained July 10, 1973. International banking and investment management have become major industries alongside tourism.

Bahrain
Kingdom of Bahrain

People: Population: 677,886. **Age distrib.** (%): <15: 29.2; 65+: 3.1. **Pop. density:** 2,640 per sq mi, 1,019 per sq km. **Urban:** 90.0%. **Ethnic groups:** Arab 73%, Asian 19%, Iranian 8%. **Principal languages:** Arabic (official), English, Farsi, Urdu. **Chief religion:** Muslim (official; Shi'a 70%, Sunni 30%).

Geography: Total area: 257 sq mi, 665 sq km; **Land area:** 257 sq mi, 665 sq km. **Location:** SW Asia, in Persian Gulf. **Neighbors:** Nearest are Saudi Arabia on W, Qatar on E. **Topography:** Bahrain Island, and several adjacent, smaller islands, are flat, hot, and humid, with little rain. **Capital:** Manama, 139,000.

Government: Type: Constitutional monarchy. **Head of state:** King Hamad bin Isa al-Khalifa; b Jan. 28, 1950; in office: as emir Mar. 6, 1999; as king Feb. 14, 2002. **Head of gov.:** Prime Min. Khalifa bin Sulman al-Khalifa; b 1936; in office: Jan. 19, 1970. **Local divisions:** 12 municipalities. **Defense budget** (2003): $329 mil. **Active troops:** 11,200.

Economy: Industries: oil proc. & refining, aluminum smelting, offshore banking, ship repair. **Chief crops:** fruit, vegetables. **Natural resources:** oil, nat. gas, fish, pearls. **Crude oil reserves** (2003): 124.6 mil. bbls.. **Arable land:** 1%. **Livestock** (2003): cattle: 13,000; chickens: 470,000; goats: 16,000; sheep: 17,500. **Fish catch** (2002): 11,207 metric tons. **Electricity prod.** (2002): 6.86 bil. kWh. **Labor force:** (1997 est.): industry, commerce, and service 79%, government 20%, agriculture 1%.

Finance: Monetary unit: Dinar (BHD) (Sept. 2004: 0.38 = $1 U.S.). **GDP** (2003 est.): $11.4 bil.; **per capita GDP:** $17,100; **GDP growth:** 3.6%. **Imports** (2003 est.): $5.1 bil.; partners (2002): Saudi Arabia 29.5%, U.S. 11.4%, Japan 7%, Germany 6.4%, UK 5.5%. **Exports** (2003 est.): $6.5 bil.; partners (2002): U.S. 4.5%, India 3.2%, Saudi Arabia 2.1%. **Tourism** (2002): $741 mil. **Budget** (2002 est.): $2.2 bil. **Intl. reserves less gold:** $1.2 bil. **Gold:** 150,000 oz t. **Consumer prices** (change in 2002): 1.2%

Transport: Motor vehicles (1999): 169,600 pass. cars, 35,700 comm. vehicles. **Civil aviation:** 2.0 bil. pass.-mi; 3 airports. **Chief ports:** Manama, Sitrah.

Communications: TV sets: 446 per 1,000 pop. **Radios:** 64 per 1,000 pop. **Telephone lines:** 185,800. **Daily newspaper circ.:** 117 per 1,000 pop. **Internet:** 195,700 users.

Health: Life expect.: 71.5 male; 76.5 female. **Births** (per 1,000 pop.): 18.5. **Deaths** (per 1,000 pop.): 4.0. **Natural inc.:** 1.45%. **Infant mortality** (per 1,000 live births): 17.9. **AIDS rate:** 0.2%.

Education: Free, compulsory: ages 6-17. **Literacy:** 89.1%.

Major Intl. Organizations: UN (FAO, IBRD, ILO, IMF, IMO, WHO, WTrO), AL.

Embassy: 3502 International Dr. NW 20008; 342-0741.

Website: www.bahrainemb.org

Long ruled by the Khalifa family, Bahrain was a British protectorate from 1861 to Aug. 15, 1971, when it regained independence.

Pearls, shrimp, fruits, and vegetables were the mainstays of the economy until oil was discovered in 1932. By the 1970s, oil reserves were depleted; international banking thrived.

Bahrain took part in the 1973-74 Arab oil embargo against the U.S. and other nations. The government bought controlling interest in the oil industry in 1975. Shiite dissidents have clashed with the Sunni-led government since 1996.

Emir Hamad bin Isa al-Khalifa proclaimed himself king Feb. 14, 2002. Local elections in May marked the 1st time Bahraini women were allowed to vote and run for office.

Bangladesh
People's Republic of Bangladesh

People: Population: 141,340,476. **Age distrib.** (%): <15: 33.8; 65+: 3.4. **Pop. density:** 2,734 per sq mi, 1,055 per sq km. **Urban:** 24.2%. **Ethnic groups:** Bengali 98%. **Principal languages:** Bangla (official, also known as Bengali), English. **Chief religions:** Muslim 83% (official), Hindu 16%.

Geography: Total area: 55,599 sq mi, 144,000 sq km; **Land area:** 51,703 sq mi, 133,910 sq km. **Location:** In S Asia, on N bend of Bay of Bengal. **Neighbors:** India nearly surrounds country on W, N, E; Myanmar on SE. **Topography:** The country is mostly a low plain cut by the Ganges and Brahmaputra rivers and their delta. The land is alluvial and marshy along the coast, with hills only in the extreme SE and NE. A tropical monsoon climate pre-

vails, among the rainiest in the world. **Capital:** Dhaka, 11,560,000. **Cities (urban aggr.):** Chittagong, 3,271,000; Khulna, 1,264,000.

Government: Type: Parliamentary democracy. **Head of state:** Pres. Iajuddin Ahmed; b Feb. 1,1931; in office: Sept. 6, 2002. **Head of gov.:** Prime Min. Khaleda Zia; b Aug. 15,1945; in office: Oct. 10, 2001. **Local divisions:** 6 divisions. **Defense budget** (2003): $609 mil. **Active troops:** 125,500.

Economy: Industries: cotton textiles, jute, garments, tea processing, newsprint, cement, chemical fertilizer, light engineering, sugar. **Chief crops:** rice, jute, tea, wheat, sugarcane, potatoes, tobacco. **Natural resources:** nat. gas, timber, coal. **Crude oil reserves** (2003): 56.9 mil. bbls. **Arable land:** 73%. **Livestock** (2003): cattle: 24.5 mil.; chickens: 140.0 mil.; goats: 34.5 mil.; sheep: 1.26 mil. **Fish catch** (2002): 1,890,459 metric tons. **Electricity prod.** (2002): 16.45 bil. kWh. **Labor force:** (FY95/96): agriculture 63%, services 26%, industry 11%.

Finance: Monetary unit: Taka (BDT) (Sept. 2004: 59.29 = $1 U.S.). **GDP** (2003 est.): $258.8 bil.; **per capita GDP:** $1,900; **GDP growth:** 5.3%. **Imports** (2003 est.): $9.5 bil.; partners (2002): India 14.6%, China 11.6%, Singapore 11.5%, Japan 7.6%, Hong Kong 5.4%, South Korea 4.3%. **Exports** (2003 est.): $6.7 bil.; partners (2002): U.S. 27.6%, Germany 10.4%, UK 9.8%, France 5.7%, Italy 4%. **Tourism** (2002): $57 mil. **Budget** (FY99/00 est.): $6.8 bil. **Intl. reserves less gold:** $1.7 bil. **Gold:** 110,000 oz t. **Consumer prices:** 5.7%.

Transport: Railroad: Length: 1,681 mi. **Motor vehicles** (1998): 65,000 pass. cars, 145,900 comm. vehicles. **Civil aviation:** 2.4 bil. pass.-mi; 15 airports. **Chief ports:** Chittagong, Dhaka, Mongla Port.

Communications: TV sets: 7 per 1,000 pop. **Radios:** 50 per 1,000 pop. **Telephone lines:** 740,000. **Daily newspaper circ.:** 53.4 per 1,000 pop. **Internet:** 243,000 users.

Health: Life expect.: 61.8 male; 61.6 female. **Births** (per 1,000 pop.): 30.0. **Deaths** (per 1,000 pop.): 8.5. **Natural inc.:** 2.15%. **Infant mortality** (per 1,000 live births): 64.3.

Education: Compulsory: ages 6-10. **Literacy:** 43.1%.

Major Intl. Organizations: UN (FAO, IBRD, ILO, IMF, IMO, WHO, WTrO), the Commonwealth.

Embassy: 3510 International Dr. NW 20007; 202-244-2745.

Website: www.bangladoot.org

Muslim invaders conquered the formerly Hindu area in the 12th century. British rule lasted from the 18th century to 1947, when East Bengal became part of Pakistan.

Charging West Pakistani domination, the Awami League, based in the East, won National Assembly control in 1971. Assembly sessions were postponed; riots broke out. Pakistani troops attacked Mar. 25; Bangladesh independence was proclaimed the next day. In the ensuing civil war, one million died and 10 million fled to India.

War between India and Pakistan broke out Dec. 3, 1971. Pakistan surrendered in the East on Dec. 16. Mujibur Rahman, known as Sheikh Mujib, became prime minister; he was killed in a coup Aug. 15, 1975. During the 1970s the country moved into the Indian and Soviet orbits in response to U.S. support of Pakistan, and much of the economy was nationalized.

On May 30, 1981, Pres. Ziaur Rahman was killed in an unsuccessful coup attempt by army rivals. Vice Pres. Abdus Sattar assumed the presidency but was ousted in a coup led by army chief of staff Gen. H. M. Ershad, Mar. 1982. Ershad declared Bangladesh an Islamic Republic in 1988; a parliamentary system of government was adopted in 1991.

Bangladesh is subject to devastating storms and floods that kill thousands. A cyclone struck Apr. 1991, killing over 131,000 people and causing $2.7 billion in damages. Chronic destitution in the densely crowded population has been worsened by the decline of jute as a world commodity. Pollution of surface water and naturally occurring contamination of groundwater by arsenic have caused widespread health problems.

Political turmoil led to the resignation, Mar. 30, 1996, of Prime Min. Khaleda Zia, the widow of Ziaur Rahman. Sheikh Mujib's daughter, Hasina Wazed (known as Sheikh Hasina), led the country after the June 12, 1996 election. Bangladesh and India signed a treaty, Dec. 12, resolving their long-standing dispute over the use of water from the Ganges River. A cyclone in May 1997 left an estimated 800,000 people homeless. Floods in July-Sept. 1998 inundated most of the country, killed over 1,400 people (many through disease), and stranded at least 30 million.

An interim government was installed July 2001 pending national elections. Khaleda Zia returned to power following the parliamentary elections of Oct. 1, 2001. Floods July-Aug. 2004 caused at least 950 deaths and $7 billion in property damage.

Barbados

People: Population: 278,289. **Age distrib.** (%): <15: 21.4; 65+: 8.8. **Pop. density:** 1,672 per sq mi, 646 per sq km. **Urban:** 51.7%. **Ethnic groups:** Black 90%, White 4%. **Principal languages:** English. **Chief religions:** Protestant 67%, Roman Catholic 4%.

Geography: Total area: 166 sq mi, 431 sq km; **Land area:** 166 sq mi, 431 sq km. **Location:** In Atlantic O., farthest E of West Indies. **Neighbors:** Nearest are St. Lucia and St. Vincent & the Grenadines to the W. **Topography:** The island lies alone in the Atlantic almost completely surrounded by coral reefs. Highest point is Mt. Hillaby, 1,115 ft. **Capital:** Bridgetown, 140,000.

Government: Type: Parliamentary democracy. **Head of state:** Queen Elizabeth II, represented by Gov.-Gen. Sir Clifford Husbands; b Aug. 5, 1926; in office: June 1, 1996. **Head of gov.:** Prime Min. Owen Arthur; b Oct. 17, 1949; in office: Sept. 7, 1994. **Local divisions:** 11 parishes and Bridgetown. **Defense budget** (2003): $13 mil. **Active troops:** 610.

Economy: Industries: tourism, sugar, light mfg., component assembly. **Chief crops:** sugarcane, vegetables, cotton. **Natural resources:** oil, fish, nat. gas. **Crude oil reserves** (2003): 2.5 mil. bbls. **Other resources:** Fish. **Arable land:** 37%. **Livestock** (2003): cattle: 13,500; chickens: 3.45 mil.; goats: 5,000; pigs: 16,550; sheep: 27,000. **Fish catch** (2002): 2,500 metric tons. **Electricity prod.** (2002): 0.8 bil. kWh. **Labor force** (1996 est.): services 75%, industry 15%, agriculture 10%.

Finance: Monetary unit: Barbados Dollar (BBD) (Sept. 2004: 2.02 = $1 U.S.). **GDP** (2003 est.): $4.5 bil.; **per capita GDP:** $16,200; **GDP growth:** –0.6%. **Imports** (2002) $1.0 bil.; partners (2002): U.S. 41.1%, Trinidad and Tobago 17%, UK 7.4%, Japan 4.2%. **Exports** (2002): $206.0 mil.; partners (2002): U.S. 14.9%, Trinidad and Tobago 12%, UK 10.8%, Jamaica 6.2%, Saint Lucia 4.6%. **Tourism** (2002): $648 mil. **Budget** (2003 est.): $886.0 mil. **Intl. reserves less gold:** $497 mil. **Consumer prices:** 1.6%.

Transport: Motor vehicles (1999).: 62,100 pass. cars; 9,400 comm. vehicles. **Civil aviation:** 204.9 mil pass.-mi.; 1 airport. **Chief port:** Bridgetown.

Communications: TV sets: 290 per 1,000 pop. **Radios:** 651 per 1,000 pop. **Telephone lines:** 134,000. **Daily newspaper circ.:** 155 per 1,000 pop. **Internet:** 100,000 users.

Health: Life expect.: 69.5 male; 73.8 female. **Births** (per 1,000 pop.): 13.0. **Deaths** (per 1,000 pop.): 9.1. **Natural inc.:** 0.39%. **Infant mortality** (per 1,000 live births): 12.6. **AIDS rate:** 1.5%.

Education: Compulsory: ages 5-15. **Literacy** (2002): 97%.

Major Intl. Organizations: UN (FAO, IBRD, ILO, IMF, IMO, WHO, WTrO), Caricom, the Commonwealth, OAS.

Embassy: 2144 Wyoming Ave. NW 20008; 939-9200.

Website: www.barbados.gov.bb

Barbados was probably named by Portuguese sailors in reference to bearded fig trees. An English ship visited in 1605, and British settlers arrived on the uninhabited island in 1627. Slaves worked the sugar plantations until slavery was abolished in 1834. Self-rule came gradually, with full independence proclaimed Nov. 30, 1966. British traditions have remained.

Belarus
Republic of Belarus

People: Population: 10,310,520. **Age distrib.** (%): <15: 17.3; 65+: 14.1. **Pop. density:** 129 per sq mi, 50 per sq km. **Urban:** 70.9%. **Ethnic groups:** Belarusian 81%, Russian 11%. **Principal languages:** Belarusian, Russian. **Chief religions:** Eastern Orthodox 80%, other 20%.

Geography: Total area: 80,155 sq mi, 207,600 sq km; **Land area:** 80,155 sq mi, 207,600 sq km. **Location:** E Europe. **Neighbors:** Poland on W; Latvia, Lithuania on N; Russia on E; Ukraine on S. **Topography:** Belarus is a landlocked country consisting mostly of hilly lowland with significant marsh areas in S. **Capital:** Minsk, 1,705,000.

Government: Type: Republic. **Head of state:** Pres. Aleksandr Lukashenko; b Aug. 30, 1954; in office: July 20,1994. **Head of gov.:** Prime Min. Syarhey Sidorski; b Mar. 13, 1954; in office: Dec. 19, 2003 (acting from July 10, 2003). **Local divisions:** 6 oblasts and 1 municipality. **Defense budget** (2003): $100 mil. **Active troops:** 72,940.

Economy: Industries: machine tools, tractors, trucks, earthmovers, motorcycles. **Chief crops:** grain, potatoes, vegetables, sugar beets, flax. **Natural resources:** timber, peat, oil, nat. gas, granite, dolomitic limestone, marl, chalk, sand, gravel, clay. **Crude oil reserves** (2003): 198.0 mil. bbls. **Arable land:** 29%. **Livestock** (2003): cattle: 4.01 mil.; chickens: 30.0 mil.; goats: 78,000; pigs: 3.33 mil.; sheep: 72,700. **Fish catch** (2002): 12,400 metric tons. **Electricity prod.** (2002): 24.82 bil. kWh. **Labor force:** 41% services; 40% ind. & const.; 19% agric. & forestry.

Finance: Monetary unit: Ruble (BYR) (Sept. 2004: 2,185.31 = $1 U.S.). **GDP** (2003 est.): $61.9 bil.; **per capita GDP:** $6,000; **GDP growth:** 6.1%. **Imports** (2003 est.): $11.1 bil.; partners (2002): Russia 68%, Germany 9.6%, Poland 3%. **Exports** (2003 est.): $9.4 bil.; partners (2002): Russia 59.8%, Germany 4.9%, Ukraine 3.9%. **Tourism** (2002): $193 mil. **Budget** (1997 est.): $4.1 bil. **Intl. reserves less gold:** $400 mil. **Consumer prices:** 28.4%.

Transport: Railroad: Length: 3,432 mi. **Motor vehicles** (2001): 1.47 mil pass. cars, 10,000 comm. vehicles. **Civil aviation:** 197.0 mil. pass.-mi; 28 airports. **Chief port:** Mazyr.

Communications: TV sets: 331 per 1,000 pop. **Radios:** 292 per 1,000 pop. **Telephone lines:** 3.1 mil. **Daily newspaper circ.:** 151.9 per 1,000 pop. **Internet:** 1.4 mil. users.

Health: Life expect.: 62.8 male; 74.7 female. **Births** (per 1,000 pop.): 10.5. **Deaths** (per 1,000 pop.): 14.1. **Natural inc.:** –0.36%. **Infant mortality** (per 1,000 live births): 13.6.

Education: Compulsory: ages 6-14. **Literacy:** 99.6%.

Major Intl. Organizations: UN (IBRD, ILO, IMF, WHO), CIS, OSCE.

Embassy: 1619 New Hampshire Ave. NW 20009; 986-1604.

Website: www.belarusembassy.org

The region was subject to Lithuanians and Poles in medieval times, and was a prize of war between Russia and Poland beginning in 1503. It became part of the USSR in 1922, although the western part of the region was controlled by Poland. Belarus was overrun by German armies in 1941; recovered by Soviet troops in 1944. Following World War II, Belarus increased in area through Soviet annexation of part of NE Poland. Belarus declared independence Aug. 25, 1991. It became an independent state when the Soviet Union disbanded Dec. 26, 1991.

A new constitution was adopted, Mar. 15, 1994, and a new president was chosen in elections concluding July 1. Russia and Belarus signed a pact Apr. 2, 1996, linking their political and economic systems. An authoritarian constitution enacted in Nov. gave Pres. Aleksandr Lukashenko vast new powers. Lukashenko's insistence on tightening ties with Russia resulted in the signing of new accords in 1997 and 1998. Opponents charged harassment and fraud in the presidential election of Sept. 9, 2001, won by Lukashenko.

Belgium
Kingdom of Belgium

People: Population: 10,348,276. **Age distrib.** (%): <15: 17.3; 65+: 17.1. **Pop. density:** 885 per sq mi, 342 per sq km. **Urban:** 97.2%. **Ethnic groups:** Fleming 58%, Walloon 31%. **Principal languages:** Dutch, French, German (all official); Flemish, Luxembourgish. **Chief religions:** Roman Catholic 75%, Protestant, other 25%.

Geography: Total area: 11,786 sq mi, 30,528 sq km; **Land area:** 11,690 sq mi, 30,278 sq km. **Location:** In W Europe, on North Sea. **Neighbors:** France on W and S, Luxembourg on SE, Germany on E, Netherlands on N. **Topography:** Mostly flat, the country is trisected by the Scheldt and Meuse, major commercial rivers. The land becomes hilly and forested in the SE (Ardennes) region. **Capital:** Brussels, 998,000.

Government: Type: Parliamentary democracy under a constitutional monarch. **Head of state:** King Albert II; b June 6, 1934; in office: Aug. 9, 1993. **Head of gov.:** Premier Guy Verhofstadt; b Apr. 11, 1953; in office: July 12, 1999. **Local divisions:** 10 provinces and Brussels. **Defense budget** (2003): $3.0 bil. **Active troops:** 40,800.

Economy: Industries: engineering & metal products, motor vehicle assembly, proc. food & beverages, chemicals, textiles, glass, oil, coal. **Chief crops:** sugar beets, vegetables, fruits, grain, tobacco. **Natural resources:** coal, nat. gas. **Arable land:** 24%. **Livestock** (2003): cattle: 2.78 mil.; chickens: 32.0 mil.; goats: 26,237; pigs: 6.54 mil.; sheep: 146,030. **Fish catch** (2002): 30,628 metric tons. **Electricity prod.** (2002): 76.58 bil. kWh. **Labor force** (1999 est.): services 73%, industry 25%, agriculture 2%.

Finance: Monetary unit: Euro (EUR) (Sept. 2004: 0.82 = $1 U.S.). **GDP** (2003 est.): $298.2 bil.; **per capita GDP:** $29,000; **GDP growth:** 0.8%. **Imports** (2003 est.): $173.0 bil.; partners (2002): Germany 17.2%, Netherlands 15.6%, France 12.8%, UK 7.3%, Ireland 7%, U.S. 6.4%, Italy 4%. **Exports** (2003 est.): $182.9 bil.; partners (2002): Germany 18.6%, France 16.3%, Netherlands 11.6%, UK 9.6%, U.S. 7.9%, Italy 5.4%. **Tourism** (2000): $106.0 bil. **Intl. reserves less gold:** $7.4bil. **Gold:** 8.29 mil oz t. **Consumer prices:** 1.6%.

Transport: Railroad: Length: 2,186 mi. **Motor vehicles** (2001): 4.74 mil pass. cars, 587,300 comm. vehicles. **Civil aviation:** 12.0 bil. pass.-mi; 25 airports. **Chief ports:** Antwerp (one of the world's busiest), Zeebrugge, Ghent.

Communications: TV sets: 532 per 1,000 pop. **Radios:** 797 per 1,000 pop. **Telephone lines** (2002): 5.1 mil. **Daily newspaper circ.:** 160 per 1,000 pop. **Internet** (2002): 3.4 mil. users.

Health: Life expect.: 75.3 male; 81.8 female. **Births** (per 1,000 pop.): 10.6. **Deaths** (per 1,000 pop.): 10.2. **Natural inc.:** 0.04%. **Infant mortality** (per 1,000 live births): 4.8. **AIDS rate:** 0.2%.

Education: Compulsory: ages 6-18. **Literacy:** 98%.

Major Intl. Organizations: UN and all of its specialized agencies, EU, NATO, OECD, OSCE.

Embassy: 3330 Garfield St. NW 20008; 333-6900.

Website: www.diplobel.us

Belgium derives its name from the Belgae, the first recorded inhabitants, probably Celts. The land was conquered by Julius Caesar, and was ruled for 1800 years by conquerors, including Rome, the Franks, Burgundy, Spain, Austria, and France. After 1815, Belgium was made a part of the Netherlands, but it became an independent constitutional monarchy in 1830.

Belgian neutrality was violated by Germany in both world wars. King Leopold III surrendered to Germany, May 28, 1940. After the war, he was forced by political pressure to abdicate in favor of his son, King Baudouin. Baudouin was succeeded by his brother, Albert II, Aug. 9, 1993.

The Flemings of northern Belgium speak Dutch, while French is the language of the Walloons in the south. The language difference has been a perennial source of controversy and led to antagonism between the 2 groups. Parliament has passed measures aimed at transferring power from the central government to 3 regions—Wallonia, Flanders, and Brussels. Constitutional changes in 1993 made Belgium a federal state. Sabena, the national airline, went bankrupt Nov. 6, 2001.

Belize

People: Population: 272,945. **Age distrib.** (%): <15: 41.6; 65+: 3.5. **Pop. density:** 31 per sq mi, 12 per sq km. **Urban:** 48.3%. **Ethnic groups:** Mestizo 49%, Creole 25%, Maya 11%, Garifuna 6%. **Principal languages:** English (official), Spanish, Mayan, Garifuna (Carib), Creole. **Chief religions:** Roman Catholic 50%, Protestant 27%.

Geography: Total area: 8,867 sq mi, 22,966 sq km; **Land area:** 8,805 sq mi, 22,806 sq km. **Location:** Eastern coast of Central America. **Neighbors:** Mexico on N, Guatemala on W and S. Topography: Belize has swampy lowlands in N, Maya Mts. in S, coral reefs and cays near coast. Climate is tropical. **Capital:** Belmopan, 9,000.

Government: Type: Parliamentary democracy. **Head of state:** Queen Elizabeth II, represented by Gov.-Gen. Sir Colville Young; b Nov. 20, 1932; in office: Nov. 17, 1993. **Head of gov.:** Prime Min. Said Musa; b Mar. 19, 1944; in office: Aug. 28, 1998. **Local divisions:** 6 districts. **Defense budget** (2003): $19 mil. **Active troops:** 1,050.

Economy: Industries: clothing, food proc., tourism, constr. **Chief crops:** bananas, coca, citrus, sugarcane. **Natural resources:** timber, fish, hydropower. **Arable land:** 2%. **Livestock** (2003): cattle: 58,380; chickens: 1.45 mil.; goats: 141; pigs: 21,224; sheep: 4,927. **Fish catch** (2002): 29,153 metric tons. **Electricity prod.** (2002): 0.12 bil. kWh. **Labor force:** (2001 est.): agriculture 27%, industry 18%, services 55%.

Finance: Monetary unit: Belize Dollar (BZD) (Sept. 2004: 1.98 = $1 U.S.). **GDP** (2002 est.): $1.3 bil.; **per capita GDP:** $4,900; **GDP growth:** 3.7%. **Imports** (2003 est.): $500.6 mil.; partners (2002): Mexico 69%, U.S. 12%, Netherlands Antilles 2.3%. **Exports** (2003 est.): $207.8 mil.; partners (2002): Mexico 68.3%, U.S. 12.6%, UK 7.1%. **Tourism:** $156 mil. **Budget** (2002 est.) $209.0 mil. **Intl. reserves less gold:** $57 mil. **Consumer prices:** 2.6%.

Transport: Motor vehicles (2000): 21,500 pass. cars, 3,900 comm. vehicles. **Civil aviation:** 4 airports. **Chief ports:** Belize City, Big Creek.

Communications: TV sets: 183 per 1,000 pop. **Radios:** 594 per 1,000 pop. **Telephone lines:** 33,300. **Internet** (2002): 30,000 users.

Health: Life expect.: 65.1 male; 69.9 female. **Births** (per 1,000 pop.): 29.9. **Deaths** (per 1,000 pop.): 6.0. **Natural inc.:** 2.38%. **Infant mortality** (per 1,000 live births): 26.4. **AIDS rate:** 2.4%.

Education: Compulsory: ages 5-14. **Literacy:** 94.1%.

Major Intl. Organizations: UN (FAO, IBRD, ILO, IMF, IMO, WHO, WTrO), Caricom, the Commonwealth, OAS.

Embassy: 2535 Massachusetts Ave. NW 20008; 332-9636.

Website: www.embassyofbelize.org

Belize (formerly British Honduras) was Britain's last colony on the American mainland; independence was achieved Sept. 21, 1981. Relations with neighboring Guatemala, initially tense, have improved in recent years. Belize has become a center for drug trafficking between Colombia and the U.S.

Benin
Republic of Benin

People: Population: 7,250,033. **Age distrib.** (%): <15: 47.2; 65+: 2.3. **Pop. density:** 170 per sq mi, 66 per sq km. **Urban:** 44.6%. **Ethnic groups:** 42 groups, incl. Fon, Adja, Yoruba, and Bariba. **Principal languages:** French (official), Fon, Yoruba, various tribal languages. **Chief religions:** Indigenous beliefs 50%, Christian 30%, Muslim 20%.

Geography: Total area: 43,483 sq mi, 112,620 sq km; **Land area:** 42,711 sq mi, 110,620 sq km. **Location:** In W Africa on Gulf of Guinea. **Neighbors:** Togo on W; Burkina Faso, Niger on N; Nigeria on E. **Topography:** Most of Benin is flat and covered with dense vegetation. The coast is hot, humid, and rainy. **Capitals:** Porto-Novo (constitutional), 238,000; Cotonou (administrative), 828,000.

Government: Type: Republic. **Head of state and gov.:** Pres. Mathieu Kerekou; b Sept. 2, 1933; in office: Apr. 4, 1996. **Local divisions:** 12 departments. **Defense budget** (2003): $61 mil. **Active troops:** 4,550.

Economy: Industries: textiles, food proc., chemical prod., constr. materials. **Chief crops:** cotton, corn, cassava, yams, beans. **Natural resources:** oil, limestone, marble, timber. **Crude oil reserves** (2003): 8.2 mil. bbls. **Arable land:** 13%. **Livestock** (2003): cattle: 1.6 mil.; chickens: 10.0 mil.; goats: 1.3 mil.; pigs: 550,000; sheep: 670,000. **Fish catch** (2002): 40,670 metric tons. **Electricity prod.** (2002): 0.29 bil. kWh.

Finance: Monetary unit: CFA Franc BCEAO (XOF) (Sept. 2004: 539.40 = $1 U.S.). **GDP** (2003 est.): $7.7 bil.; **per capita GDP:** $1,100; **GDP growth:** 5.5%. **Imports** (2003 est.): $726.0 mil.; partners (2002): China 30%, France 15.3%, UK 4.7%, Italy 4.1%. **Exports** (2003 est.): $485.0 mil.; partners (2002): India 27.3%, Italy 12.1%, Indonesia 8.1%, China 7.6%, Thailand 7.1%, UK 5.1%, Niger 4.5%. **Tourism** (2002): $60 mil. **Budget** (2001): $561.8 mil. **Intl. reserves less gold:** $343 mil. **Consumer prices:** 1.5%.

Transport: Railroad: Length: 359 mi. **Motor vehicles** (1998): 7,300 pass. cars, 6,200 comm. vehicles. **Civil aviation:** 134.2 mil. pass.-mi; 1 airport. **Chief port:** Cotonou.

Communications: TV sets: 44 per 1,000 pop. **Radios:** 448 per 1,000 pop. **Telephone lines:** 66,500. **Daily newspaper circ.:** 5.3 per 1,000 pop. **Internet:** 70,000 users.

Health: Life expect.: 50.3 male; 51.4 female. **Births** (per 1,000 pop.): 42.6. **Deaths** (per 1,000 pop.): 13.7. **Natural inc.:** 2.89%. **Infant mortality** (per 1,000 live births): 85.9. **AIDS rate:** 1.9%.

Education: Compulsory: ages 6-11. **Literacy** (2002): 37%.

Major Intl. Organizations: UN (FAO, IBRD, ILO, IMF, IMO, WHO, WTrO), AU.

Embassy: 2124 Kalorama Rd. NW 20008; 232-6656.

Websites: www.gouv.bj; www.benintourism.com

The Kingdom of Abomey, rising to power in wars with neighboring kingdoms in the 17th century, came under French domination in the late 19th century and was incorporated into French West Africa by 1904.

Under the name Dahomey, the country gained independence Aug. 1, 1960; it became Benin in 1975. In the fifth coup since independence Col. Ahmed Kerekou took power in 1972; two years later he declared a socialist state with a "Marxist-Leninist" philosophy. In Dec. 1989, Kerekou announced Marxism-Leninism would no longer be the state ideology.

In Mar. 1991, Kerekou lost to Nicéphore Soglo in Benin's first free presidential election in 30 years. Kerekou defeated Soglo in Mar. 1996 to reclaim the presidency. He won reelection in a runoff Mar. 22, 2001. A plane bound for Beirut, Lebanon, crashed on takeoff from Cotonou, Dec. 25, 2003, killing 140 people.

Bhutan
Kingdom of Bhutan

People: Population: 2,185,569. **Age distrib.** (%): <15: 39.8; 65+: 4. **Pop. density:** 120 per sq mi, 47 per sq km. **Urban:** 8.5%. **Ethnic groups:** Bhote 50%, Nepalese 35%, indigenous tribes 15%. **Principal languages:** Dzongkha (official); Tibetan, Nepalese dialects. **Chief religions:** Lamaistic Buddhist 75% (official), Hindu 25%.

Geography: Total area: 18,147 sq mi, 47,000 sq km; **Land area:** 18,147 sq mi, 47,000 sq km. **Location:** S Asia, in eastern Himalayan Mts. **Neighbors:** India on W (Sikkim) and S, China on N. **Topography:** Bhutan is comprised of very high mountains in the N, fertile valleys in the center, and thick forests in the Duar Plain in the S. **Capital:** Thimphu, 35,000.

Government: Type: Monarchy. **Head of state:** King Jigme Singye Wangchuk; b Nov. 11, 1955; in office: July 21, 1972. **Head of gov.:** Prime Min. Lyonpo Yeshey Zimba; b Oct. 10, 1952; in office: Aug. 20, 2004. **Local divisions:** 18 districts. **Defense budget** (2002): $19 mil. **Active troops:** NA.

Economy: Industries: cement, wood products, proc. fruits, alcoholic beverages, calcium carbide. **Chief crops:** rice, corn, root crops, citrus, grains. **Natural resources:** timber, hydropower, gypsum, calcium carbide. **Livestock** (2003): cattle: 340,000; chickens: 220,000; goats: 30,000; pigs: 41,000; sheep: 21,000.. **Fish catch** (2002 est): 300 metric tons. **Arable land:** 2%. **Electricity prod.** (2002): 2.0 bil. kWh. **Labor force:** agriculture 93%, services 5%, industry and commerce 2%.

Finance: Monetary unit: Ngultrum (BTN) (Sept. 2004: 45.80 = $1 U.S.). **GDP** (2002 est.): $2.7 bil.; **per capita GDP:** $1,300; **GDP growth:** 7.7%. **Imports** (2000 est.): $196.0 mil.; partners (2002): India 62.8%, Japan 16.3%, Germany 4.3%. **Exports** (2000 est.): $154.0 mil.; partners (2002): India 88.5%, U.S. 2.7%, UK 2.7%. **Tourism:** $8 mil. **Budget (FY 95/96 est.):** $152.0 mil. **Intl. reserves less gold:** $247 mil. **Consumer prices** (change in 2002): 2.5%

Transport: Civil aviation: 29.2 mil. pass.-mi; 1 airport.

Communications: TV sets: 6 per 1,000 pop. **Radios:** 19 per 1,000 pop. **Telephone lines:** 25,200. **Internet:** 15,000 users.

Health: Life expect.: 54.3 male; 53.7 female. **Births** (per 1,000 pop.): 34.4. **Deaths** (per 1,000 pop.): 13.2. **Natural inc.:** 2.12%. **Infant mortality** (per 1,000 live births): 102.6.

Education: Compulsory: ages 6-16. **Literacy** (2002): 42.2%.

Major Intl. Organizations: UN (FAO, IBRD, IMF, WHO).

Embassy: (Consulate-General): 2 UN Plaza, 27th Fl., New York, NY 10017; 212-826-1919

Website: www.kingdomofbhutan.com

The region came under Tibetan rule in the 16th century. British influence grew in the 19th century. A Buddhist monarchy was set up in 1907. According to a 1910 treaty, Britain guided Bhutan's external affairs, while the country remained internally self-governing. Upon independence, India assumed Britain's role in a 1949 revision of the treaty. Isolated for much of its history, Bhutan took tentative steps toward modernization in the 1990s.

Bolivia
Republic of Bolivia

People: Population: 8,724,156. **Age distrib.** (%): <15: 37.8; 65+: 4.5. **Pop. density:** 21 per sq mi, 8 per sq km. **Urban:** 63.4%. **Ethnic groups:** Quechua 30%, Mestizo 30%, Aymara 25%, white 15%. **Principal languages:** Spanish, Quechua, Aymara (all official) **Chief religion:** Roman Catholic 95% (official).

Geography: Total area: 424,164 sq mi, 1,098,580 sq km; **Land area:** 418,685 sq mi, 1,084,390 sq km. **Location:** In W central South America, in the Andes Mts. (one of 2 landlocked countries in South America). **Neighbors:** Peru and Chile on W, and Paraguay on S, on E and N. **Topography:** The great central plateau, at an altitude of 12,000 ft., over 500 mi. long, lies between two great cordilleras having 3 of the highest peaks in South America. Lake Titicaca, on Peruvian border, is highest lake in world on

which steamboats ply (12,506 ft.). The E central region has semi-tropical forests; the llanos, or Amazon-Chaco lowlands are in E. **Capitals:** La Paz (administrative), 1,477,000; Sucre (judicial), 212,000. **Cities (urban aggr.):** Santa Cruz, 1,061,000.

Government: Type: Republic. **Head of state and gov.:** Pres. Carlos D. Mesa Gisbert; b Aug. 12, 1953: in office: Oct. 17, 2003. **Local divisions:** 9 departments. **Defense budget** (2003): $118 mil. **Active troops:** 31,500.

Economy: Industries: mining, smelting, oil, food & beverages, tobacco, handicrafts, clothing. **Chief crops:** soybeans, coffee, coca, cotton, corn, sugarcane, rice, potatoes, timber. **Natural resources:** tin, nat. gas, oil, zinc, tungsten, antimony, silver, iron, lead, gold, timber, hydropower. **Crude oil reserves** (2003): 440.5 mil. bbls. **Other resources:** Timber. **Arable land:** 2%. **Livestock** (2003): cattle: 6.68 mil.; chickens: 75.0 mil.; goats: 1.50 mil.; pigs: 2.92 mil.; sheep: 8.60 mil. **Fish catch** (2002 est): 6,218 metric tons. **Electricity prod.** (2002): 4.13 bil. kWh.

Finance: Monetary unit: Boliviano (BOB) (Sept. 2004: 7.97 = $1 U.S.). **GDP** (2003 est.): $20.9 bil.; **per capita GDP:** $2,400; **GDP growth:** 2.1%. **Imports** (2003 est.): $1.5 bil.; partners (2002): Brazil 22%, Argentina 17.4%, U.S. 15.6%, Chile 6.9%, Japan 5.5%, Peru 5.4%, China 4.8%. **Exports** (2003 est.): $1.5 bil.; partners (2002): Brazil 24.3%, Switzerland 15.7%, U.S. 14.1%, Venezuela 12.8%, Colombia 10.2%, Peru 5.4%. **Tourism:** $172 mil. **Budget** (2002 est.): $4.0 bil. **Intl. reserves less gold:** $482 mil. **Gold:** 910,000 oz t. **Consumer prices:** 3.3%.

Transport: Railroad: Length: 2,187 mi. **Motor vehicles** (2001): 316,300 pass. cars, 155,500 comm. vehicles. **Civil aviation:** 871.8 mil. pass.-mi; 12 airports.

Communications: TV sets: 118 per 1,000 pop. **Radios:** 675 per 1,000 pop. **Telephone lines:** 600,100. **Daily newspaper circ.:** 55 per 1,000 pop. **Internet** (2002): 270,000 users.

Health: Life expect.: 62.5 male; 67.9 female. **Births** (per 1,000 pop.): 24.6. **Deaths** (per 1,000 pop.): 7.8. **Natural inc.:** 1.69%. **Infant mortality** (per 1,000 live births): 54.6. **AIDS rate:** 0.1%.

Education: Compulsory: ages 6-13. **Literacy:** 87.2%.

Major Intl. Organizations: UN (FAO, IBRD, ILO, IMF, IMO, WHO, WTrO), OAS.

Embassy: 3014 Massachusetts Ave. NW 20008; 483-4410.

The Incas conquered the region from earlier Indian inhabitants in the 13th century. Spanish rule began in the 1530s and lasted until Aug. 6, 1825. The country is named after Simon Bolivar, independence fighter.

Websites: www.bolivia.gov.bo; www.bolivia-usa.org

In a series of wars, Bolivia lost its Pacific coast to Chile, the oil-bearing Chaco to Paraguay, and rubber-growing areas to Brazil, 1879-1935.

Economic unrest, especially among militant mine workers, has contributed to continuing political instability. A reformist government under Victor Paz Estenssoro, 1951-64, nationalized tin mines and attempted to improve conditions for Indian majority but was overthrown by a military junta. A long series of coups and countercoups continued until constitutional government was restored in 1982.

U.S. pressure on the government to reduce the country's coca output, the raw material for cocaine, has led to clashes between police and coca growers and increased anti-U.S. feeling among Bolivians. Gen. Hugo Banzer Suárez, who ruled as a dictator, 1971-78, became president in Aug. 1997. 105 people died in earthquakes near Aiquile May 22, 1998. Stricken with cancer, Banzer resigned and was succeeded Aug. 7, 2001, by Vice-Pres. Jorge Quiroga Ramírez.

After an inconclusive presidential election June 30, 2002, Congress Aug. 4 chose Gonzalo Sánchez de Lozada, a U.S.-educated mining executive, as head of state. He quit Oct. 17, 2003, after a month of antigovernment protests, led by Bolivian Indians, in which over 70 people died. His successor, Vice-Pres. Carlos D. Mesa Gisbert, a former historian and TV reporter, won a referendum July 18, 2004, on his plan to boost exports of Bolivia's huge natural gas reserves.

Bosnia and Herzegovina

People: Population: 4,007,608. **Age distrib.** (%): <15: 19.8; 65+: 9.6. **Pop. density:** 203 per sq mi, 78 per sq km. **Urban:** 44.3%. **Ethnic groups:** Bosniak 48%, Serbian 37%, Croatian 14%. **Principal languages:** Bosnian (official), Croatian, Serbian. **Chief religions:** Muslim 40%, Orthodox 31%, Roman Catholic 15%, Protestant 4%.

Geography: Total area: 19,741 sq mi, 51,129 sq km; **Land area:** 19,741 sq mi, 51,129 sq km. **Location:** On Balkan Peninsula in SE Europe. **Neighbors:** Yugoslavia on E and SE, Croatia on N and W. **Topography:** Hilly with some mountains. About 36% of the land is forested. **Capital:** Sarajevo, 579,000.

Government: Type: Federal republic. **Heads of state:** Collective presidency with rotating leadership. **Head of gov.:** Chrm. of Council Ministers Adnan Terzic; b 1960; in office: Dec. 23, 2002. **Local divisions:** Muslim-Croat Federation, divided into 10 cantons; Serbian-led region (Republika Srpska); internationally supervised Brcko district. **Defense budget** (2003): $154 mil. **Active troops:** 19,800 (13,200 Muslim-Croat; 6,600 Serbian).

Economy: Industries: steel, mining, vehicle assembly, textiles, tobacco products, wooden furniture, tank & aircraft assem-

bly, domestic appliances. **Chief crops:** wheat, corn, fruits, vegetables. **Natural resources:** coal, iron, bauxite, mang., timber, copper, chromium, lead, zinc, hydropower. **Arable land:** 14%. **Livestock** (2003): cattle: 440,000; chickens: 4.7 mil.; pigs: 300,000; sheep: 670,000. **Fish catch** (2002 est): 7,185 metric tons. **Electricity prod.** (2002): 10.04 bil. kWh.

Finance: Monetary unit: Converted Marka (BAM) (Sept. 2004: 1.61 = $1 U.S.). **GDP** (2003 est.): $24.4 bil.; **per capita GDP:** $6,100; **GDP growth:** 3.8%. **Imports** (2003 est.): $4.7 bil.; partners (2002): Croatia 22.8%, Slovenia 15.3%, Germany 13.7%, Italy 12.6%, Hungary 7.6%, Austria 7.4%. **Exports** (2003 est.): $1.3 bil.; partners (2002): Italy 31.4%, Croatia 17.8%, Germany 13%, Austria 10%, Slovenia 7.1%, Greece 4.2%. **Tourism:** $234 mil. **Budget** (1999 est.): $2.2 bil. **Intl. reserves less gold:** $1.2 bil.

Transport: Railroad: Length: 634 mi. **Chief port:** Bosanski Brod. **Civil aviation:** 29.8 mil. pass.-mi; 14 airports.

Communications: TV sets: 112 per 1,000 pop. **Radios:** 245 per 1,000 pop. **Telephone lines:** 938,000. **Daily newspaper circ.:** 152 per 1,000 pop. **Internet** (2002): 100,000 users.

Health: Life expect.: 69.8 male; 75.5 female. **Births** (per 1,000 pop.): 12.6. **Deaths** (per 1,000 pop.): 8.3. **Natural inc.:** 0.42%. **Infant mortality** (per 1,000 live births): 21.9. **AIDS rate:** <0.1%.

Education: Free, compulsory: ages 7-15. **Literacy:** (1991): 86%.

Major Intl. Organizations: UN (FAO, IBRD, ILO, IMF, IMO, WHO), OSCE.

Embassy: 2109 E St. NW, 20037; 337-1500.

Website: www.bosnianembassy.org

Bosnia was ruled by Croatian kings c. AD 958, and by Hungary 1000-1200. It became organized c. 1200 and later took control of Herzegovina. The kingdom disintegrated from 1391, with the southern part becoming the independent duchy Herzegovina. It was conquered by Turks in 1463 and made a Turkish province. The area was placed under control of Austria-Hungary in 1878, and made part of the province of **Bosnia and Herzegovina,** which was formally annexed to Austria-Hungary 1908; Bosnia became a province of Yugoslavia in 1918. It was reunited with Herzegovina as a federated republic in the 1946 Yugoslavian constitution.

Bosnia and Herzegovina declared sovereignty Oct. 15, 1991. A referendum for independence was passed Feb. 29, 1992. Ethnic Serbs' opposition to the referendum spurred violent clashes and bombings. The U.S. and EU recognized the republic Apr. 7. Fierce three-way fighting continued between Bosnia's Serbs, Muslims, and Croats. Serb forces massacred thousands of Bosnian Muslims and engaged in "ethnic cleansing" (the expulsion of Muslims and other non-Serbs from areas under Bosnian Serb control). The capital, Sarajevo, was surrounded and besieged by Bosnian Serb forces. Muslims and Croats in Bosnia reached a cease fire Feb. 23, 1994, and signed an accord, Mar. 18, to create a Muslim-Croat confederation in Bosnia. However, by mid-1994, Bosnian Serbs controlled over 70% of the country.

As fighting continued in 1995, the balance of power began to shift toward the Muslim-Croat alliance. Massive NATO air strikes at Bosnian Serb targets beginning Aug. 30 triggered a new round of peace talks, and the siege of Sarajevo was lifted Sept. 15. The new talks produced an agreement in principle to create autonomous regions within Bosnia, with the Serb region (Republika Srpska) constituting 49% of the country. A Croat-Muslim offensive in Sept. recaptured significant territory, leaving Bosnian Serbs in control of approximately half that percentage.

A peace agreement initialed in Dayton, Ohio, Nov. 21, 1995, was signed in Paris, Dec. 14, by leaders of Bosnia, Croatia, and Serbia. Some 60,000 NATO troops (about 20,000 from the U.S.) moved in to police the accord. Meanwhile, a UN tribunal began bringing charges against suspected war criminals. Elections were held Sept. 14, 1996, for a 3-person collective presidency, for seats in a federal parliament, and for regional offices. In Dec. a revamped NATO "stabilization force" (SFOR) of over 30,000 members (more than 8,000 from the U.S.) received an 18-month mandate, which was later extended.

In a landmark verdict Aug. 2, 2001, the UN tribunal found Radislav Krstic, a Bosnian Serb general, guilty in connection with the genocide of thousands of Muslims at Srebrenica in 1995. By mid-2004, SFOR troop strength in Bosnia had been cut to 7,000.

Botswana
Republic of Botswana

People: Population: 1,561,973. **Age distrib.** (%): <15: 40; 65+: 4.2. **Pop. density:** 7 per sq mi, 3 per sq km. **Urban:** 51.6%. **Ethnic groups:** Tswana 79%, Kalanga 11%, Basarwa 3%. **Principal languages:** English (official), Setswana. **Chief religions:** Indigenous beliefs 85%, Christian 15%.

Geography: Total area: 231,804 sq mi, 600,370 sq km; **Land area:** 226,013 sq mi, 585,370 sq km. **Location:** In southern Africa. **Neighbors:** Namibia on N and W, South Africa on S, Zimbabwe on NE; Botswana claims border with Zambia on N. **Topography:** The Kalahari Desert, supporting nomadic Bushmen and wildlife, spreads over SW; there are swamplands and farming areas in N, and rolling plains in E where livestock are grazed. **Capital:** Gaborone, 199,000.

Government: Type: Parliamentary republic. **Head of state and gov.:** Pres. Festus Mogae; b Aug. 21, 1939; in office: Apr. 1, 1998. **Local divisions:** 10 districts, 4 town councils. **Defense budget** (2003): $414 mil. **Active troops:** 9,000.

Economy: Industries: diamonds, copper, nickel, salt, soda ash, potash, proc., textiles. **Chief crops:** sorghum, maize, millet, beans, sunflowers. **Natural resources:** diamonds, copper, nickel, salt, soda ash, potash, coal, iron ore, silver. **Arable land:** 1%. **Livestock** (2003): cattle: 1.7 mil.; chickens: 4.0 mil.; goats: 2.25 mil.; pigs: 8,000; sheep: 400,000. **Fish catch** (2002): 139 metric tons. **Electricity prod.** (2002): 0.93 bil. kWh.

Finance: Monetary unit: Pula (BWP) (Sept. 2004: 4.77 = $1 U.S.). **GDP** (2003 est.): $13.9 bil.; **per capita GDP:** $8,800; **GDP growth:** 7.6%. **Imports** (2003 est.): $1.8 bil.; partners (2000): Southern African Customs Union (SACU) 74%, European Free Trade Association (EFTA) 17%, Zimbabwe 4%. **Exports** (2003 est.): $2.5 bil.; partners (2000): EFTA 87%, SACU 7%, Zimbabwe 4%. **Tourism** (2002): $309 mil. **Budget** (FY01/02): $2.4 bil. **Intl. reserves less gold:** $3.59 bil. **Consumer prices:** 9.2%.

Transport: Railroad: Length: 552 mi. **Motor vehicles** (1999): 44,500 pass. cars, 67,900 comm. vehicles. **Civil aviation:** 32.9 mil. pass.-mi; 10 airports.

Communications: TV sets: 21 per 1,000 pop. **Radios:** 154 per 1,000 pop. **Telephone lines** (2002): 142,400. **Daily newspaper circ.:** 27 per 1,000 pop. **Internet** (2002): 60,000 users.

Health: Life expect.: 31.0 male; 30.5 female. **Births** (per 1,000 pop.): 24.7. **Deaths** (per 1,000 pop.): 33.6. **Natural inc.:** −0.89%. **Infant mortality** (per 1,000 live births): 70.0. **AIDS rate:** 37.3%.

Education: Compulsory: ages 6-15. **Literacy:** 79.8%.

Major Intl. Organizations: UN (FAO, IBRD, ILO, IMF, WHO, WTrO), the Commonwealth, AU.

Embassy: 1531-3 New Hampshire Ave. NW 20036; 244-4990.

Website: www.botswanaembassy.org

First inhabited by bushmen, then Bantus, the region became the British protectorate of Bechuanaland in 1886, halting encroachment by Boers and Germans from the south and southwest. The country became fully independent Sept. 30, 1966, as Botswana. Cattle raising and mining (diamonds, copper, nickel) have contributed to economic growth; economy is closely tied to South Africa. According to UN estimates, more than one-third of the adult population has HIV/AIDS.

Brazil
Federative Republic of Brazil

People: Population: 184,101,109. **Age distrib.** (%): <15: 28; 65+: 5.6. **Pop. density:** 56 per sq mi, 22 per sq km. **Urban:** 83.1%. **Ethnic groups:** European 55%, Creole 38%, African 6%. **Principal languages:** Portuguese (official), Spanish, English, French. **Chief religion:** Roman Catholic (nominal) 80%.

Geography: Total area: 3,286,487 sq mi, 8,511,965 sq km; **Land area:** 3,265,075 sq mi, 8,456,510 sq km. **Location:** Occupies E half of South America. **Neighbors:** French Guiana, Suriname, Guyana, Venezuela on N; Colombia, Peru, Bolivia, Paraguay, on W; Uruguay on S. **Topography:** Brazil's Atlantic coastline stretches 4,603 miles. In N is the heavily wooded Amazon basin covering half the country. Its network of rivers is navigable for 15,814 mi. The Amazon itself flows 2,093 miles in Brazil, all navigable. The NE region is semiarid scrubland, heavily settled and poor. The S central region, favored by climate and resources, has almost half of the population, produces 75% of farm goods and 80% of industrial output. The narrow coastal belt includes most of the major cities. Almost the entire country has a tropical or semitropical climate. **Capital:** Brasília, 3,099,000. **Cities (urban aggr.):** São Paulo, 17,099,000, (2001 city est.: 10.4 mil.); Rio de Janeiro, 10,803,000; Belo Horizonte, 4,659,000.

Government: Type: Federal republic. **Head of state and gov.:** Luiz Inacio Lula da Silva; b. Oct. 27, 1945; in office: Jan. 1, 2003. **Local divisions:** 26 states, 1 federal district (Brasília). **Defense budget** (2003): $9.7 bil. **Active troops:** 287,600.

Economy: Industries: textiles, shoes, chemicals, cement, lumber, iron ore, steel, aircraft, motor vehicles & parts. **Chief crops:** coffee, soybeans, wheat, rice, corn, sugarcane, cocoa, citrus. **Natural resources:** bauxite, gold, iron ore, mang., nickel, phosphates, platinum, tin, uranium, oil, hydropower, timber. **Crude oil reserves** (2003): 8.3 bil. bbls. **Arable land:** 5%. **Livestock** (2003): cattle: 189.5 mil.; chickens: 1.1 bil.; goats: 9.09 mil.; pigs: 32.6 mil.; sheep: 14.2 mil. **Fish catch** (2002): 1,068,342 metric tons. **Electricity prod.** (2002): 339.05 bil. kWh. **Labor force:** services 53%, agriculture 23%, industry 24%.

Finance: Monetary unit: Real (BRL) (Sept. 2004: 2.91 = $1 U.S.). **GDP** (2003 est.): $1.379 tril.; **per capita GDP:** $7,600; **GDP growth:** 0.1%. **Imports** (2003 est.): $48.3 bil.; partners (2002): U.S. 22.1%, Argentina 10.1%, Germany 9.3%, Japan 5%. **Exports** (2003 est.): $73.3 bil.; partners (2002): U.S. 25.8%, Netherlands 5.3%, Germany 4.2%. **Tourism** (2002): $3.1 bil. **Budget** (2000): $91.6 bil. **Intl. reserves less gold:** $33.05 bil. **Gold:** 450,000 oz t. **Consumer prices:** 14.7%.

Transport: Railroad: Length: 18,276 mi. **Motor vehicles** (1999): 11.63 mil pass. cars, 2.63 mil comm. vehicles. **Civil aviation:** 14.2 bil. pass.-mi; 665 airports. **Chief ports:** Santos, Rio de Janeiro, Vitoria, Salvador, Rio Grande, Recife.

Communications: TV sets: 333 per 1,000 pop. **Radios:** 434 per 1,000 pop. **Telephone lines** (2002): 38.8 mil. **Daily newspaper circ.:** 43.1 per 1,000 pop. **Internet** (2002): 14.3 mil. users.

Health: Life expect.: 67.5 male; 75.6 female. **Births** (per 1,000 pop.): 17.2. **Deaths** (per 1,000 pop.): 6.1. **Natural inc.:** 1.11%. **Infant mortality** (per 1,000 live births): 30.7. **AIDS rate:** 0.7%.

Education: Compulsory: ages 7-14. **Literacy:** 86.4%.

Major Intl. Organizations: UN and most of its specialized agencies, OAS.

Embassy: 3006 Massachusetts Ave. NW 20008; 238-2700.

Website: www.brasilemb.org

Pedro Alvares Cabral, a Portuguese navigator, is generally credited as the first European to reach Brazil, in 1500. The country was thinly settled by various Indian tribes. Only a few have survived to the present, mostly in the Amazon basin.

In the next centuries, Portuguese colonists gradually pushed inland, bringing along large numbers of African slaves. (Slavery was not abolished until 1888.) The King of Portugal, fleeing before Napoleon's army, moved the seat of government to Brazil in 1808. Brazil thereupon became a kingdom under Dom Joao VI. After his return to Portugal, his son Pedro proclaimed the independence of Brazil, Sept. 7, 1822, and was crowned emperor. The second emperor, Dom Pedro II, was deposed in 1889, and a republic proclaimed, called the United States of Brazil. In 1967 the country was renamed the Federative Republic of Brazil.

A military junta took control in 1930; dictatorial power was assumed by Getulio Vargas, until finally forced out by the military in 1945. A democratic regime prevailed 1945-64, during which time the capital was moved from Rio de Janeiro to Brasília. In 1964, Pres. Joao Belchoir Marques Goulart instituted economic policies that aggravated Brazil's inflation; he was overthrown by an army revolt. The next 5 presidents were all military leaders. Censorship was imposed, and much of the opposition was suppressed amid charges of torture.

Since 1930, successive governments have pursued industrial and agricultural growth and interior area development. Exploiting vast natural resources and a huge labor force, Brazil became the leading industrial power of Latin America by the 1970s, while agricultural output soared. By the 1990s, Brazil had one of the world's largest economies; income was poorly distributed, however, and more than one out of four Brazilians continued to survive on less than $1 a day. Despite protective environmental legislation, development has destroyed much of the Amazon ecosystem. Brazil hosted delegates from 178 countries at the Earth Summit, June 3-14, 1992.

Democratic presidential elections were held in 1985 as the nation returned to civilian rule. Fernando Collor de Mello was elected president in Dec. 1989. In Sept. 1992, Collor was impeached for corruption. He resigned on Dec. 29 as his trial was beginning, and Itamar Franco, who had been acting president, was sworn in as president. In elections held on Oct. 3, 1994, Fernando Henrique Cardoso was elected president. Reelected Oct. 4, 1998, he guided Brazil through a series of financial crises. New presidential elections were set for Oct. 2002.

A new civil code guaranteeing legal equality for women was enacted Aug. 15, 2001. The IMF approved a $30 bil. loan to Brazil Aug. 7, 2002; by then, Brazil's debt already exceeded $260 bil. Luiz Inacio Lula da Silva, a union leader and reformer, won a presidential runoff Oct. 27 with 61% of the vote. Brazil's space program suffered a setback when a rocket exploded on its launchpad Aug. 22, 2003, killing 21 people. Prison riots Apr. 18-22 and May 29-31, 2004, left more than 50 inmates dead.

Brunei
State of Brunei Darussalam

People: Population: 365,251. **Age distrib.** (%): <15: 30.2; 65+: 2.8. **Pop. density:** 180 per sq mi, 69 per sq km. **Urban:** 76.2%. **Ethnic groups:** Malay 67%, Chinese 15%, indigenous 6%. **Principal languages:** Malay (official), English, Chinese. **Chief religions:** Muslim (official) 67%, Buddhist 13%, Christian 10%; indigenous beliefs, other 10%.

Geography: Total area: 2,228 sq mi, 5,770 sq km; **Land area:** 2,035 sq mi, 5,270 sq km. **Location:** In SE Asia, on the N coast of the island of Borneo; it is surrounded on its landward side by the Malaysian state of Sarawak. **Topography:** Brunei has a narrow coastal plain, with mountains in E, hilly lowlands in W. There are swamps in W and NE. Climate is tropical. **Capital:** Bandar Seri Begawan, 61,000.

Government: Type: Independent sultanate. **Head of state and gov.:** Sultan Sir Muda Hassanal Bolkiah Mu'izzadin Waddaulah; b July 15, 1946; in office: Jan. 1, 1984 (sultan since Oct. 5, 1967). **Local divisions:** 4 districts. **Defense budget** (2003): $258 mil. **Active troops:** 7,000.

Economy: Industries: oil, oil refining, nat. gas liquefaction, constr. **Chief crops:** rice, vegetables, fruits. **Natural resources:** oil, nat. gas, timber. **Crude oil reserves** (2003): **1.4 bil. bbls.** **Arable land:** 1%. **Livestock** (2003): cattle: 2,200; chickens: 11.0 mil.; goats: 3,000; pigs: 1,000; sheep: 4,000. **Fish catch** (2002): 2,215 metric tons. **Electricity prod.** (2002): 2.46 bil. kWh. **Labor force:** (1999 est.): government 48%, production of oil, natural gas, services, and construction 42%, agriculture, forestry, and fishing 10%.

Finance: Monetary unit: Dollar (BND) (Sept. 2004: 1.69 = $1 U.S.). **GDP** (2002 est.): $6.5 bil.; **per capita GDP:** $18,600; **GDP**

growth: 3.0%. **Imports** (2002 est.): $1.6 bil.; partners (2002): Singapore 30.7%, Japan 21.5%, Malaysia 17.4%, UK 6.1%. **Exports** (2002 est.): $3.4 bil.; partners (2002): Japan 40%, South Korea 12.2%, Thailand 12%, Australia 9.1%, U.S. 8.1%, China 6.4%, Singapore 5.6%. **Tourism** (1998): $37 mil. **Budget** (1997 est.): $2.6 bil.

Transport: Railroad: Length: 8 mi. **Motor vehicles** (1999): 176,000 pass. cars, 19,400 comm. vehicles. **Civil aviation:** 1.9 bil. pass.-mi; 1 airport.

Communications: TV sets: 637 per 1,000 pop. **Radios:** 302 per 1,000 pop. **Telephone lines** (2002): 90,000. **Daily newspaper circ.:** 69 per 1,000 pop. **Internet** (2001): 35,000 users.

Health: Life expect.: 72.1 male; 77.1 female. **Births** (per 1,000 pop.): 19.3. **Deaths** (per 1,000 pop.): 3.4. **Natural inc.:** 1.59%. **Infant mortality** (per 1,000 live births): 13.1. **AIDS rate:** <0.1%.

Education: Compulsory: ages 5-16. **Literacy:** 91.8%.

Major Intl. Organizations: UN and some of its specialized agencies, APEC, ASEAN, the Commonwealth.

Embassy: 3520 International Court NW 20008; 237-1838.

Websites: www.bruneiembassy.org; www.gov.bn

The Sultanate of Brunei was a powerful state in the early 16th century, with authority over all of the island of Borneo as well as parts of the Sulu Islands and the Philippines. In 1888, a treaty placed the state under the protection of Great Britain.

Brunei became a fully sovereign and independent state on Jan. 1, 1984. Much of the country's oil wealth has been squandered in recent years by members of the royal family.

Bulgaria
Republic of Bulgaria

People: Population: 7,517,973. **Age distrib.** (%): <15: 14.6; 65+: 16.9. **Pop. density:** 176 per sq mi, 68 per sq km. **Urban:** 69.8%. **Ethnic groups:** Bulgarian 84%, Turk 10%, Roma 5%. **Principal languages:** Bulgarian (official), Turkish. **Chief religions:** Bulgarian Orthodox 84%, Muslim 12%.

Geography: Total area: 42,823 sq mi, 110,910 sq km; **Land area:** 42,684 sq mi, 110,550 sq km. **Location:** SE Europe, in E Balkan Peninsula on Black Sea. **Neighbors:** Romania on N; Yugoslavia, Macedonia on W; Greece, Turkey on S. **Topography:** The Stara Planina (Balkan) Mts. stretch E-W across the center of the country, with the Danubian plain on N, the Rhodope Mts. on SW, and Thracian Plain on SE. **Capital:** Sofia, 1,076,000.

Government: Type: Republic. **Head of state:** Pres. Georgi Parvanov; b June 28, 1957; in office: Jan. 22, 2002. **Head of gov.:** Prime Min. Simeon Sakskoburggotski (Simeon II); b June 16, 1937; in office: July 24, 2001. **Local divisions:** 28 provinces. **Defense budget** (2003): $527 mil. **Active troops:** 51,000.

Economy: Industries: utilities, food, beverages, tobacco, machinery, metals, chemicals. **Chief crops:** vegetables, fruits, tobacco, wine, wheat, barley, sunflowers, sugar beets. **Natural resources:** bauxite, copper, lead, zinc, coal, timber. **Crude oil reserves** (2003): 15.0 mil. bbls. **Arable land:** 37%. **Livestock** (2003): cattle: 691,226; chickens: 18.0 mil.; goats: 900,000; pigs: 1.0 mil.; sheep: 1.73 mil. **Fish catch** (2002): 17,315 metric tons. **Electricity prod.** (2002): 43.07 bil. kWh. **Labor force** (1998 est.): agriculture 26%, industry 31%, services 43%.

Finance: Monetary unit: Lev (BGL) (Sept. 2004: 1.60 = $1 U.S.). **GDP** (2003 est.): $57.1 bil.; **per capita GDP:** $7,600; **GDP growth:** 4.4%. **Imports** (2003 est.): $9.7 bil.; partners (2002): Russia 14.6%, Germany 14.4%, Italy 11.4%, France 6.1%, France 5.7%, Turkey 5%. **Exports** (2003 est.): $7.3 bil.; partners (2002): Italy 15.5%, Germany 9.6%, Turkey 9.4%, Greece 9.2%, France 5.3%, U.S. 4.8%. **Tourism:** $1.6 bil. **Budget** (2002 est.): $6.7 bil. **Intl. reserves less gold:** $4.23 bil. **Gold:** 1.28 mil oz t. **Consumer prices:** 2.2%.

Transport: Railroad: Length: 2,668 mi. **Motor vehicles** (2001): 2.09 mil pass. cars, 312,500 comm. vehicles. **Civil aviation:** 499.6 mil. pass.-mi; 128 airports. **Chief ports:** Burgas, Varna.

Communications: TV sets: 429 per 1,000 pop. **Radios:** 537 per 1,000 pop. **Telephone lines** (2002): 2.9 mil. **Daily newspaper circ.:** 116.4 per 1,000 pop. **Internet** (2002): 630,000 users.

Health: Life expect.: 68.1 male; 75.6 female. **Births** (per 1,000 pop.): 9.7. **Deaths** (per 1,000 pop.): 14.2. **Natural inc.:** −0.46%. **Infant mortality** (per 1,000 live births): 21.3. **AIDS rate:** <0.1%.

Education: Compulsory: ages 7-14. **Literacy:** 98.6%.

Major Intl. Organizations: UN (FAO, IBRD, ILO, IMF, IMO, WHO, WTrO), OSCE.

Embassy: 1621 22d St. NW 20008; 387-0174.

Websites: www.bulgaria-embassy.org; www.government.bg/English

Bulgaria was settled by Slavs in the 6th century. Turkic Bulgars arrived in the 7th century, merged with the Slavs, became Christians by the 9th century, and set up powerful empires in the 10th and 12th centuries. The Ottomans prevailed in 1396 and remained for 500 years.

An 1876 revolt led to an independent kingdom in 1908. Bulgaria expanded after the first Balkan War but lost its Aegean coastline in World War I, when it sided with Germany. Bulgaria joined the Axis in World War II but withdrew in 1944. Communists took power with Soviet aid; monarchy was abolished Sept. 8, 1946.

On Nov. 10, 1989, Communist Party leader and head of state Todor Zhivkov, who had held power for 35 years, resigned. Zhivkov was imprisoned, Jan. 1990, and convicted, Sept. 1992, of corruption and abuse of power. In Jan. 1990, Parliament voted to revoke the constitutionally guaranteed dominant role of the Communist Party. A new constitution took effect July 13, 1991. An economic austerity program was launched in May 1996. Former Prime Min. Andrei Lukanov, a longtime Communist leader, was assassinated Oct. 2 in Sofia. Petar Stoyanov won a presidential runoff election Nov. 3.

Bulgaria's deteriorating economy provoked nationwide strikes and demonstrations in Jan. 1997. The Union of Democratic Forces, an anti-Communist group, won national elections on Apr. 19, 1997. The UDF lost the elections of June 17, 2001, to a party headed by the former king, Simeon II. Socialist opposition leader Georgi Parvanov won a presidential runoff vote Nov. 18.

Bulgaria became a full member of NATO, Apr. 2, 2004, and was expected to enter the European Union by 2007.

Burkina Faso

People: Population: 13,574,820. **Age distrib.** (%): <15: 47.3; 65+: 2.9. **Pop. density:** 128 per sq mi, 50 per sq km. **Urban:** 17.8%. **Ethnic groups:** Mossi (approx. 40%), Gurunsi, Senufo, Lobi, Bobo, Mande, Fulani. **Principal languages:** French (official), Sudanic languages. **Chief religions:** Muslim 50%, indigenous beliefs 40%, Christian (mainly Roman Catholic) 10%.

Geography: Total area: 105,869 sq mi, 274,200 sq km; **Land area:** 105,715 sq mi, 273,800 sq km. **Location:** In W Africa, S of the Sahara. **Neighbors:** Mali on NW; Niger on NE; Benin, Togo, Ghana, Côte d'Ivoire on S. **Topography:** Landlocked Burkina Faso is in the savanna region of W Africa. The N is arid, hot, and thinly populated. **Capital:** Ouagadougou, 821,000.

Government: Type: Republic. **Head of state:** Pres. Blaise Compaoré; b Feb. 3, 1951; in office: Oct. 15, 1987. **Head of gov.:** Prime Min. Paramanga Ernest Yonli; b 1956; in office: Nov. 7, 2000. **Local divisions:** 45 provinces. **Defense budget** (2003): $56 mil. **Active troops:** 10,800.

Economy: Industries: cotton, beverages, agric. proc., soap, cigarettes, textiles, gold. **Chief crops:** peanuts, shea nuts, sesame, cotton, sorghum, millet. **Natural resources:** mang., limestone, marble, gold, antimony, copper, nickel, bauxite, lead, phosphates, zinc, silver. **Arable land:** 13%. **Livestock** (2003): cattle: 5.0 mil.; chickens: 24.0 mil.; goats: 8.8 mil.; pigs: 640,000; sheep: 6.9 mil. **Fish catch** (2002 est): 8,505 metric tons. **Electricity prod.** (2002): 0.36 bil. kWh. **Labor force** (2003 est.): agriculture 90%.

Finance: Monetary unit: CFA Franc BCEAO (XOF) (Sept. 2004: 539.40 = $1 U.S.). **GDP** (2003 est.): $14.3 bil.; **per capita GDP:** $1,100; **GDP growth:** 4.6%. **Imports** (2003 est.): $633.6 mil.; partners (2002): France 27.4%, Côte d'Ivoire 22.6%, Togo 4.2%. **Exports** (2003 est.): $293.0 mil.; partners (2002): Singapore 15.2%, Italy 11.7%, Colombia 8.8%, France 7.6%, India 7%, Ghana 6.4%, Japan 4.7%, Thailand 4.1%. **Tourism** (2002): $39 mil. **Budget** (1995 est.): $492 mil. **Intl. reserves less gold:** $293 mil. **Consumer prices:** 2.0%.

Transport: Railroad: Length: 386 mi. **Motor vehicles** (1999): 26,300 pass. cars, 19,600 comm. vehicles. **Civil aviation:** 153.5 mil. pass.-mi; 2 airports.

Communications: TV sets: 11 per 1,000 pop. **Radios:** 34 per 1,000 pop. **Telephone lines:** 65,400. **Daily newspaper circ.:** 1.3 per 1,000 pop. **Internet:** 48,000 users.

Health: Life expect.: 42.6 male; 45.8 female. **Births** (per 1,000 pop.): 44.5. **Deaths** (per 1,000 pop.): 18.8. **Natural inc.:** 2.57%. **Infant mortality** (per 1,000 live births): 98.7. **AIDS rate:** 4.2%.

Education: Compulsory: ages 6-16. **Literacy:** 26.6%.

Major Intl. Organizations: UN and many of its specialized agencies, AU.

Embassy: 2340 Massachusetts Ave. NW 20008; 332-5577.

Website: www.burkinaembassy-usa.org

The Mossi tribe entered the area in the 11th to 13th centuries. Their kingdoms ruled until they were defeated by the Mali and Songhai empires.

French control came by 1896, but Upper Volta (renamed Burkina Faso on Aug. 4, 1984) was not established as a separate territory until 1947. Full independence came Aug. 5, 1960, and a pro-French government was elected. The military seized power in 1980. A 1987 coup established the current regime, which instituted a multiparty democracy in the early 1990s.

Several hundred thousand farm workers migrate each year to Côte d'Ivoire and Ghana. Burkina Faso is heavily dependent on foreign aid.

Burma
(See Myanmar)

Burundi
Republic of Burundi

People: Population: 6,231,221. **Age distrib.** (%): <15: 46.5; 65+: 2.8. **Pop. density:** 629 per sq mi, 243 per sq km. **Urban:** 9.9%. **Ethnic groups:** Hutu 85%, Tutsi 14%, Twa (Pygmy) 1%. **Principal languages:** Kirundi, French (both official); Swahili. **Chief religions:** Roman Catholic 62%, indigenous beliefs 23%, Muslim 10%, Protestant 5%.

Geography: Total area: 10,745 sq mi, 27,830 sq km; **Land area:** 9,904 sq mi, 25,650 sq km. **Location:** In central Africa. **Neighbors:** Rwanda on N, Dem. Rep. of the Congo (formerly Zaire) on W, Tanzania on E and S. **Topography:** Much of the country is grassy highland, with mountains reaching 8,900 ft. The southernmost source of the White Nile is located in Burundi. Lake Tanganyika is the second deepest lake in the world. **Capital:** Bujumbura, 378,000.

Government: Type: In transition. **Head of state and gov.:** Pres. Domitien Ndayizeye; b May 2, 1953; in office: Apr. 30, 2003. **Local divisions:** 16 provinces. **Defense budget** (2003): $39 mil. **Active troops:** 50,500.

Economy: Industries: light consumer goods, component assembly, constr., food proc. **Chief crops:** coffee, cotton, tea, corn, sorghum, sweet potatoes, bananas. **Natural resources:** nickel, uranium, rare earth oxides, peat, cobalt, copper, platinum, vanadium, hydropower. **Arable land:** 44%. **Livestock** (2003): cattle: 325,000; chickens: 4.3 mil.; goats: 750,000; pigs: 70,000; sheep: 230,000. **Fish catch** (2002 est): 9,100 metric tons. **Electricity prod.** (2002): 0.13 bil. kWh. **Labor force** (2002 est.): agriculture 93.6%, industry 2.3%, services 4.1%.

Finance: Monetary unit: Franc (BIF) (Sept. 2004: 1,075.80 = $1 U.S.). **GDP** (2003 est.): $3.8 bil.; **per capita GDP:** $600; **GDP growth:** 0.0%. **Imports** (2003 est.): $128.0 mil.; partners (2002): Belgium 12%, Saudi Arabia 12%, France 7.5%, Kenya 7.5%, Tanzania 6%, Algeria 5.3%, India 4.5%. **Exports** (2003 est.): $40.0 mil.; partners (2002): Germany 25%, Belgium 14.3%, Kenya 10.7%, Netherlands 7.1%, Rwanda 7.1%. **Tourism** (2002): $1 mil. **Budget** (2000 est.): $176.0 mil. **Intl. reserves less gold:** $45 mil. **Gold** (2000): 20,000 oz t. **Consumer prices:** 16.0%.

Transport: Motor vehicles (1999): 6,900 pass. cars, 9,300 comm. vehicles. **Civil aviation:** 5.0 mil. pass.-mi; 1 airport. **Chief port:** Bujumbura.

Communications: TV sets: 15 per 1,000 pop. **Radios:** 152 per 1,000 pop. **Telephone lines:** 23,900. **Daily newspaper circ.:** 2.4 per 1,000 pop. **Internet** (2002): 14,000 users.

Health: Life expect.: 42.7 male; 44.0 female. **Births** (per 1,000 pop.): 39.7. **Deaths** (per 1,000 pop.): 17.6. **Natural inc.:** 2.21%. **Infant mortality** (per 1,000 live births): 70.4. **AIDS rate:** 6.0%.

Education: Compulsory: ages 7-12. **Literacy:** 51.6%.

Major Intl. Organizations: UN (FAO, IBRD, ILO, IMF, WHO, WTrO), AU.

Embassy: 2233 Wisconsin Ave. NW , Suite 212, 20007; 342-2574.

Website: travel.state.gov/travel/burundi.html

The pygmy Twa were the first inhabitants, followed by Bantu Hutus, who were conquered in the 16th century by the Tutsi (Watusi), probably from Ethiopia. Under German control in 1899, the area fell to Belgium in 1916, which exercised successively a League of Nations mandate and UN trusteeship over Ruanda-Urundi (now the two countries of Rwanda and Burundi). Burundi became independent July 1, 1962.

An unsuccessful Hutu rebellion in 1972-73 left 10,000 Tutsi and 150,000 Hutu dead. Over 100,000 Hutu fled to Tanzania and Zaire (now Congo). In the 1980s, Burundi's Tutsi-dominated regime pledged itself to ethnic reconciliation and democratic reform. In the nation's first democratic presidential election, in June 1993, a Hutu, Melchior Ndadaye, was elected. He was killed in an attempted coup, Oct. 21, 1993. At least 150,000 Burundians died as a result of ethnic conflict during the next three years. Pres. Cyprien Ntaryamira, elected Jan. 1994, was killed with the president of Rwanda in a mysterious plane crash, Apr. 6. The incident sparked massive carnage in Rwanda; violence in Burundi, initially far more limited, intensified in 1995. Ethnic strife continued after a military coup, July 25, 1996. Former South African Pres. Nelson Mandela mediated peace talks from Dec. 1999; most warring groups signed a draft peace treaty in Arusha, Tanzania, Aug. 28, 2000. Coup attempts were suppressed Apr. 18 and July 23, 2001. A power-sharing government headed by Buyoya was sworn in Nov. 1, but clashes with rebels continued.

Domitien Ndayizeye, a Hutu, became president Apr. 30, 2003. The UN Security Council authorized, May 21, 2004, a 5,650-member peacekeeping force for Burundi. Hutu rebels Aug. 13 attacked a UN camp for Congolese Tutsi refugees in W Burundi, killing more than 160 people, many of them women and children.

Cambodia
Kingdom of Cambodia

People: Population: 13,363,421. **Age distrib.** (%): <15: 40.7; 65+: 3.5. **Pop. density:** 196 per sq mi, 76 per sq km. **Urban:** 18.6%. **Ethnic groups:** Khmer 90%, Vietnamese 5%, Chinese 1%. **Principal languages:** Khmer (official), French, English. **Chief religion:** Theravada Buddhist 95% (official).

Geography: Total area: 69,900 sq mi, 181,040 sq km; **Land area:** 68,155 sq mi, 176,520 sq km. **Location:** SE Asia, on Indochina Peninsula. **Neighbors:** Thailand on W and N, Laos on NE, Vietnam on E. **Topography:** The central area, formed by the Mekong R. basin and Tonle Sap lake, is level. Hills and mountains are in SE, a long escarpment separates the country from Thailand on NW. 76% of the area is forested. **Capital:** Phnom Penh, 1,157,000.

Government: Type: Constitutional monarchy. **Head of state:** King Norodom Sihanouk; b Oct. 31, 1922; in office: Sept. 24, 1993. **Head of gov.:** Prime Min. Samdech Hun Sen; b Aug. 5, 1952; in office: Nov. 30, 1998. **Local divisions:** 20 provinces and 4 municipalities. **Defense budget** (2003): $78 mil. **Active troops:** 125,000.

Economy: Industries: tourism, garments, rice milling, fishing, wood & wood products, rubber, cement, gem mining, textiles. **Chief crops:** rice, rubber, corn, vegetables. **Natural resources:** timber, gems, iron ore, mang., phosphates. **Arable land:** 13%. **Livestock** (2003): cattle: 2.95 mil.; chickens: 17.0 mil.; pigs: 2.15 mil. **Fish catch** (2002): 420,782 metric tons. **Electricity prod.** (2002): 0.11 bil. kWh. **Labor force** (2003 est.): agriculture 75%.

Finance: Monetary unit: Riel (KHR) (Sept. 2004: 3,850.00 = $1 U.S.). **GDP** (2003 est.): $22.8 bil.; **per capita GDP:** $1,700; **GDP growth:** 5.5%. **Imports** (2003 est.): $2.1 bil.; partners (2002): Thailand 22.9%, Singapore 15.7%, Hong Kong 15.1%, China 11.2%, Taiwan 8.5%, South Korea 5.1%, Vietnam 4.8%. **Exports** (2003 est.): $1.6 bil.; partners (2002): U.S. 59.8%, Germany 9.2%, UK 7%, Singapore 4.4%. **Tourism** (2002): $379 mil. **Budget** (2002 est.): $630.0 mil. **Intl. reserves less gold:** $549 mil. **Gold:** 400,000 oz t. **Consumer prices:** 1.2%.

Transport: Railroad: Length: 374 mi. **Motor vehicles** (2000): 8,300 pass. cars, 3,100 comm. vehicles. **Civil aviation:** 5 airports. **Chief port:** Kampong Saom (Sihanoukville).

Communications: TV sets: 9 per 1,000 pop. **Radios:** 128 per 1,000 pop. **Telephone lines** (2002): 35,400. **Daily newspaper circ.:** 1.7 per 1,000 pop. **Internet** (2002): 30,000 users.

Health: Life expect.: 55.7 male; 61.2 female. **Births** (per 1,000 pop.): 27.1. **Deaths** (per 1,000 pop.): 9.1. **Natural inc.:** 1.80%. **Infant mortality** (per 1,000 live births): 73.7. **AIDS rate:** 2.6%.

Education: Compulsory: ages 6-12. **Literacy:** 69.9%.

Major Intl. Organizations: UN (FAO, IBRD, ILO, IMF, IMO, WHO, WTrO), ASEAN.

Embassy: 4530 16th St. NW 20011; 726-7742.

Website: www.embassy.org/cambodia

Early kingdoms dating from that of Funan in the 1st century AD culminated in the great Khmer empire that flourished from the 9th century to the 13th, encompassing present-day Thailand, Cambodia, Laos, and southern Vietnam. The peripheral areas were lost to invading Siamese and Vietnamese, and France established a protectorate in 1863. Independence came in 1953.

Prince Norodom Sihanouk, king 1941-1955 and head of state from 1960, tried to maintain neutrality. Relations with the U.S. were broken in 1965, after South Vietnam planes attacked Vietcong forces within Cambodia. Relations were restored in 1969, after Sihanouk charged Viet Communists with arming Cambodian insurgents.

In 1970, pro-U.S. Prem. Lon Nol seized power, demanding removal of 40,000 North Viet troops; the monarchy was abolished. Sihanouk formed a government-in-exile in Beijing, and open war began between the government and Communist Khmer Rouge guerrillas. The U.S. provided heavy military and economic aid.

Khmer Rouge forces captured Phnom Penh Apr. 17, 1975. The new government evacuated all cities and towns, and shuffled the rural population, sending virtually the entire population to clear jungle, forest, and scrub. Over one million people were killed in executions and enforced hardships.

Severe border fighting broke out with Vietnam in 1978 and developed into a full-fledged Vietnamese invasion. Formation of a Vietnamese-backed government was announced, Jan. 8, 1979, one day after the Vietnamese capture of Phnom Penh. Thousands of refugees flowed into Thailand, and widespread starvation was reported.

On Jan. 10, 1983, Vietnam launched an offensive against rebel forces in the west. They overran a refugee camp, Jan. 31, driving 30,000 residents into Thailand. In March, Vietnam launched a major offensive against camps on the Cambodian-Thailand border, engaged Khmer Rouge guerrillas, and crossed the border, instigating clashes with Thai troops. Vietnam withdrew nearly all its troops by Sept. 1989.

Following UN-sponsored elections in Cambodia that ended May 28, 1993, the 2 leading parties agreed to share power in an interim government until a new constitution was adopted. On Sept. 21, a constitution reestablishing a monarchy was adopted by the National Assembly. It took effect Sept. 24, with Sihanouk as king. The Khmer Rouge, which had boycotted the elections, opposed the new government, and armed violence continued in the mid-1990s. Ieng Sary, a Khmer Rouge leader, broke with the guerrillas, formed a rival group, and announced his support for the monarchy in Aug. 1996, as Khmer Rouge strength rapidly diminished.

Co-Prime Min. Hun Sen staged a coup July 5, 1997, ousting his rival, Prince Norodom Ranariddh. Pol Pot, the Khmer Rouge leader who held power during the late 1970s, was denounced by his former comrades at a show trial, July 25, and sentenced to house arrest; he died Apr. 15, 1998. Hun Sen's party won parliamentary elections on July 26. He retained power in elections July 27, 2003, but without a parliamentary majority.

Cambodia was formally admitted to ASEAN on Apr. 30, 1999.

Cameroon
Republic of Cameroon

People: Population: 16,063,678. **Age distrib.** (%): <15: 42.1; 65+: 3.4. **Pop. density:** 89 per sq mi, 34 per sq km. **Urban:** 51.4%. **Ethnic groups:** Highlanders 31%, Equatorial Bantu 19%, Kirdi 11%, Fulani 10%, NW Bantu 8%, E Nigritic 7%. **Principal languages:** English, French (both official); 24 African language groups. **Chief religions:** Indigenous beliefs 40%, Christian 40%, Muslim 20%. **Geography: Total area:** 183,568 sq mi, 475,440 sq km; **Land area:** 181,252 sq mi, 469,440 sq km. **Location:** Between W and central Africa. **Neighbors:** Nigeria on NW; Chad, Central African Republic on E; Congo, Gabon, Equatorial Guinea on S. **Topography:** A low coastal plain with rain forests is in S; plateaus in center lead to forested mountains in W, including Mt. Cameroon, 13,435 ft.; grasslands in N lead to marshes around Lake Chad. **Capital:** Yaoundé, 1,616,000. **Cities** (urban ag.): Douala, 1,663,000.

Government: Type: Republic. **Head of state:** Pres. Paul Biya; b Feb. 13, 1933; in office: Nov. 6, 1982. **Head of gov.:** Prime Min. Peter Mafani Musonge; b Dec. 3, 1942; in office: Sept. 19, 1996. **Local divisions:** 10 provinces. **Defense budget** (2003): $166 mil. **Active troops:** 23,100.

Economy: Industries: oil prod. & refining, food proc., light consumer goods, textiles, lumber. **Chief crops:** coffee, cocoa, cotton, rubber, bananas, oilseed, grains. **Natural resources:** oil, bauxite, iron ore, timber, hydropower. **Crude oil reserves (2003): 400.0 mil. bbls. Arable land:** 13%. **Livestock** (2003): cattle: 5.9 mil.; chickens: 31.0 mil.; goats: 4.4 mil.; pigs: 1.35 mil.; sheep: 3.8 mil. **Fish catch** (2002): 120,465 metric tons. **Electricity prod.** (2002): 3.57 bil. kWh. **Labor force:** agriculture 70%, industry and commerce 13%, other 17%.

Finance: Monetary unit: CFA Franc BEAC (XAF) (Sept. 2004: 539.54 = $1 U.S.). **GDP** (2003 est.): $27.6 bil.; **per capita GDP:** $1,800; **GDP growth:** 3.6%. **Imports** (2003 est.): $2.0 bil.; partners (2002): France 28%, Nigeria 12.7%, U.S. 7.9%, Belgium 5.7%, Germany 4.8%, Italy 4.3%. **Exports** (2003 est.): $1.9 bil.; partners (2002): Italy 17.4%, Spain 16.8%, France 13.4%, U.S. 8.7%, Netherlands 8.6%, China 5.4%, UK 4.7%, Germany 4.1%. **Tourism** (2000): $39 mil. **Budget** (FY00/01 est.): $2.1 bil. **Intl. reserves less gold:** $430 mil. **Gold:** 30,000 oz t. **Consumer prices** (2002): 2.8%.

Transport: Railroad: Length: 626 mi. **Motor vehicles:** 115,900 pass. cars, 47,400 comm. vehicles. **Civil aviation:** 360.4 mil. pass.-mi; 11 airports. **Chief ports:** Douala, Kribi.

Communications: TV sets: 34 per 1,000 pop. **Radios:** 163 per 1,000 pop. **Telephone lines** (2002): 110,900. **Daily newspaper circ.:** 6.7 per 1,000 pop. **Internet** (2002): 60,000 users.

Health: Life expect.: 47.1 male; 48.8 female. **Births** (per 1,000 pop.): 35.1. **Deaths** (per 1,000 pop.): 15.3. **Natural inc.:** 1.97%. **Infant mortality** (per 1,000 live births): 69.2. **AIDS rate:** 6.9%.

Education: Compulsory: ages 6-11. **Literacy:** 79%.

Major Intl. Organizations: UN (FAO, IBRD, ILO, IMF, IMO, WHO, WTrO), the Commonwealth, AU.

Embassy: 2349 Massachusetts Ave. NW 20008; 265-8790.

Websites: www.prc.cm; www.spm.gov.cm; www.camnet.cm/mintour/tourisme

Portuguese sailors were the first Europeans to reach Cameroon, in the 15th century. The European and American slave trade was very active in the area. German control lasted from 1884 to 1916, when France and Britain divided the territory, later receiving League of Nations mandates and UN trusteeships. French Cameroon became independent Jan. 1, 1960; one part of British Cameroon joined Nigeria in 1961, the other part joined Cameroon. Stability has allowed for development of roads, railways, agriculture, and petroleum production.

Pres. Paul Biya has retained power in a series of elections that were boycotted by opposition parties or disputed as fraudulent.

Canada

People: Population: 32,507,874. **Age distrib.** (%): <15: 18.7; 65+: 12.9. **Pop. density:** 9 per sq mi, 4 per sq km. **Urban:** 80.4%. **Ethnic groups:** British 28%, French 23%, other European 15%, Amerindian 2%. **Principal languages:** English, French (both official). **Chief religions:** Roman Catholic 46%, Protestant 36%, other 18%.

Geography: Total area: 3,855,101 sq mi, 9,984,670 sq km; **Land area:** 3,511,021 sq mi, 9,093,507 sq km., the largest country in land size in the western hemisphere. **Topography:** Canada stretches 3,426 miles from east to west and extends southward from the North Pole to the U.S. border. Its seacoast includes 36,356 miles of mainland and 115,133 miles of islands, including the Arctic islands almost from Greenland to near the Alaskan border. **Climate:** While generally temperate, varies from freezing winter cold to blistering summer heat. **Capital:** Ottawa, 1,093,000. **Cities** (urban ag.): Toronto, 4.6 mil; Montreal, 3.4 mil; Vancouver, 2.0 mil; Edmonton, 924,000; Calgary, 927,000.

Government: Type: Confederation with parliamentary democracy. **Head of state:** Queen Elizabeth II, represented by Gov.-Gen. Adrienne Clarkson; b Feb. 10, 1939; in office: Oct. 7, 1999. **Head of gov.:** Prime Min. Paul Martin; b Aug. 28, 1938; in office: Dec. 12, 2003. **Local divisions:** 10 provinces, 3 territories. **Defense budget** (2003): $9.1 bil. **Active troops:** 52,300.

Economy: Industries: transp. equip., chemicals, minerals, food & fish products, wood & paper products, oil & nat. gas. **Chief crops:** wheat, barley, oilseed, tobacco, fruits, vegetables. **Natural resources:** iron ore, nickel, zinc, copper, gold, lead, molybd., potash, silver, fish, timber, wildlife, coal, oil, nat. gas, hydropower. **Crude oil reserves** (2003): 180.0 bil. bbls. **Arable land:** 5%. **Livestock** (2003): cattle: 13.45 mil.; chickens: 160.0 mil.; goats: 30,000; pigs: 14.67 mil.; sheep: 975,600. **Fish catch** (2002): 1,186,333 metric tons. **Electricity prod.** (2002): 548.86 bil. kWh. **Labor force** (2000): services 74%, manufacturing 15%, construction 5%, agriculture 3%, other 3%.

Finance: Monetary unit: Dollar (CAD) (Sept. 2004: 1.30 = $1 U.S.). **GDP** (2003 est.): $957.7 bil.; **per capita GDP:** $29,700; **GDP growth:** 1.6%. **Imports** (2003 est.): $240.4 bil.; partners (2002): U.S. 62.6%, China 4.6%, Japan 4.4%. **Exports** (2003 est.): $279.3 bil.; partners (2002): U.S. 87.7%, Japan 2%, UK 1.1%. **Tourism:** $9.3 bil. **Budget** (FY00/01 est.): $161.4 bil. **Intl. reserves less gold:** $24.4 bil. **Gold:** 110,000 oz t. **Consumer prices:** 2.8%.

Transport: Railroad: Length: 45,547 mi. **Motor vehicles:** 16.86 mil pass. cars, 668,000 comm. vehicles. **Civil aviation:** 29.5 bil. pass.-mi; 507 airports. **Chief ports:** Halifax, Montreal, Quebec, Saint John, Toronto, Vancouver.

Communications: TV sets: 709 per 1,000 pop. **Radios:** 1,038 per 1,000 pop. **Telephone lines:** 20.0 mil. **Daily newspaper circ.:** 159 per 1,000 pop. **Internet** (2002): 16.1 mil. users.

Health: Life expect.: 76.6 male; 83.5 female. **Births** (per 1,000 pop.): 10.9. **Deaths** (per 1,000 pop.): 7.7. **Natural inc.:** 0.32%. **Infant mortality** (per 1,000 live births): 4.8. **AIDS rate:** 0.3%.

Education: Compulsory: ages 6-16. **Literacy** (1994): 97%.

Major Intl. Organizations: UN and all of its specialized agencies, APEC, the Commonwealth, NATO, OAS, OECD, OSCE.

Embassy: 501 Pennsylvania Ave. NW 20001; 682-1740.

Website: www.canadianembassy.org

French explorer Jacques Cartier, who reached the Gulf of St. Lawrence in 1534, is generally regarded as Canada's founder. But English seaman John Cabot sighted Newfoundland in 1497, and Vikings are believed to have reached the Atlantic coast centuries before either explorer.

Canadian settlement was pioneered by the French who established Quebec City (1608) and Montreal (1642) and declared New France a colony in 1663.

Britain acquired Acadia (later Nova Scotia) in 1717 and, through military victory over French forces in Canada, captured Quebec (1759) and obtained control of the rest of New France in 1763. The French, through the Quebec Act of 1774, retained the rights to their own language, religion, and civil law. The British presence in Canada increased during the American Revolution when many colonials, proudly calling themselves United Empire Loyalists, moved north to Canada. Fur traders and explorers led Canadians westward across the continent. Sir Alexander Mackenzie reached the Pacific in 1793 and scrawled on a rock by the ocean, "from Canada by land."

Canada's Provinces and Territories							
Provinces/Territories	Joined Confed.	Area (sq. mi.)	Population (2004 est.)*	Capital	Premier	Party	In office
Alberta................	1905	255,287	3,172,121	Edmonton	Ralph Klein	Prog. Cons.	1992
British Columbia.........	1871	365,948	4,168,123	Victoria	Gordon Campbell	Liberal	2001
Manitoba.............	1870	250,947	1,165,944	Winnipeg	Gary Doer	New Democratic	1999
New Brunswick.........	1867	28,355	750,096	Fredericton	Bernard Lord	Prog. Cons.	1999
Newfoundland & Labrador .	1949	156,649	519,897	St. John's	Danny Williams	Prog. Cons.	2003
Nova Scotia............	1867	21,425	936,892	Halifax	Dr. John Hamm	Prog. Cons.	1999
Ontario..............	1867	412,581	12,293,669	Toronto	Dalton McGuinty	Liberal	2003
Prince Edward Island.....	1873	2,185	138,102	Charlottetown	Pat Binns	Prog. Cons.	1996
Quebec...............	1867	594,860	7,509,928	Québec	Jean Charest	Liberal	2003
Saskatchewan..........	1905	251,866	994,845	Regina	Lorne Calvert	New Democratic	2001
Northwest Territories[1].....	1871	503,951	42,321	Yellowknife	Joe Handley	non-partisan	2003
Nunavut[1].............	(2)	818,959	29,496	Iqaluit	Paul Okalik	non-partisan	1999
Yukon Territory[1]........	1898	186,661	31,408	Whitehorse	Dennis Fentie	Yukon	2002

*Excludes incompletely enumerated Indian reserves or settlements. (1) Territories also have federally appointed commissioners to represent federal interests. (2) Territory created in 1999 from eastern portion of Northwest Territories.

In Upper and Lower Canada (later called Ontario and Quebec) and in the Maritimes, legislative assemblies appeared in the 18th century and reformers called for responsible government. But the War of 1812 intervened. The war, a conflict between Great Britain and the United States fought mainly in Upper Canada, ended in a stalemate in 1814.

In 1837 political agitation for more democratic government culminated in rebellions in Upper and Lower Canada. Britain sent Lord Durham to investigate; in a famous report (1839), he recommended union of the 2 parts into one colony called Canada. The union lasted until Confederation, July 1, 1867, when proclamation of the British North America (BNA) Act (now known as the Constitution Act, 1867) launched the Dominion of Canada, consisting of Ontario, Quebec, and the former colonies of Nova Scotia and New Brunswick.

Since 1840 the Canadian colonies had held the right to internal self-government. The BNA Act, which was the basis for the country's written constitution, established a federal system of government on the model of a British parliament and cabinet structure under the crown. Canada was proclaimed a self-governing Dominion within the British Empire in 1931. With the ratification of the Constitution Act, 1982, Canada severed its last formal legislative link with Britain by obtaining the right to amend its constitution.

The so-called Meech Lake Agreement was signed (subject to provincial ratification) June 3, 1987. The accord would have assured constitutional protection for Quebec's efforts to preserve its French language and culture. Critics charged it did not make any provision for other minority groups and it gave Quebec too much power, which might enable Quebec to override the nation's 1982 Charter of Rights and Freedoms (an integral part of the constitution). The accord died June 22, 1990.

Its failure sparked a separatist revival in Quebec, which culminated in Aug. 1992 in the Charlottetown agreement. This called for changes to the constitution, such as recognition of Quebec as a "distinct society" within the Canadian confederation. It was defeated in a national referendum Oct. 26, 1992.

Canada became the first nation to ratify the North American Free Trade Agreement between Canada, Mexico, and the U.S. June 23, 1993. It went into effect Jan. 1, 1994.

On Feb. 24, 1993, Brian Mulroney resigned as prime minister after more than 8 years in office; he was succeeded by Kim Campbell. In elections Oct. 25, 1993, the ruling Conservatives were defeated in a landslide that left them only 2 of the 295 seats in the House of Commons. Jean Chrétien became prime minister. In a Quebec referendum held Oct. 30, 1995, proponents of secession lost by a razor-thin margin. The elections of June 2, 1997, left the Liberals with a slim majority.

On Jan. 7, 1998, the government apologized to native peoples for 150 years of mistreatment and pledged to set up a "healing fund." Canada's highest court ruled, Aug. 20, that Quebec cannot secede unilaterally, even if a majority of the province approves. Nunavut ("Our Land"), carved from Northwest Territories as a homeland for the Inuit, was established Apr. 1, 1999. Victory by the Liberals in national elections Nov. 27, 2000, made Chrétien the 1st Canadian prime minister in over 50 years to head a 3rd successive majority government.

Canada sent 5 warships in Oct. 2001, and 850 troops in Feb. 2002, to join U.S. counterterrorism operations in Afghanistan. Four Canadian soldiers conducting a training exercise near Kandahar were accidentally killed Apr. 17 by U.S. forces, Canada's first war casualties since its participation in the Korean War. The Canadian government contributed $100 mil. for humanitarian and reconstruction efforts in Afghanistan in Jan. 2002, and in Mar. 2003 pledged $250 mil more. Relations between Canada and the U.S. cooled after Prime Min. Chrétien refused to contribute troops to the U.S.-led invasion of Iraq in Mar. 2003.

A SARS outbreak killed more than 40 people in the Toronto area in 2003, and cost the city and national economy millions of dollars in lost revenues. The Ontario Court of Appeal ruled June 10 that provincial governments must extend full marriage rights to same-sex couples. A massive power blackout in the Northeast, Aug. 14, cut power to parts of Ontario and Manitoba, including Ottawa and Toronto.

Chrétien retired Dec. 12, 2003, and Paul Martin became prime minister. Weakened by a scandal involving improper payments to Quebec firms for advertising and sponsorship of cultural and sporting events, the Liberals won only 135 of 308 seats in parliamentary elections June 28, 2004; the Conservatives finished 2nd with 99. Martin stayed in office as head of a minority government.

Prime Ministers of Canada

Canada is a constitutional monarchy with a parliamentary system of government. It is also a federal state. Canada's official head of state, Queen Elizabeth II, is represented by a resident Governor-General. However, in practice the nation is governed by the Prime Minister, leader of the party that commands the support of a majority of the House of Commons, dominant chamber of Canada's bicameral Parliament.

Name	Party	Term
Sir John A. Macdonald	Conservative	1867-1873
Alexander Mackenzie	Liberal	1873-1878
Sir John A. Macdonald	Conservative	1878-1891

Name	Party	Term
Sir John J. C. Abbott	Conservative	1891-1892
Sir John S. D. Thompson	Conservative	1892-1894
Sir Mackenzie Bowell.	Conservative	1894-1896
Sir Charles Tupper.	Conservative	1896[1]
Sir Wilfrid Laurier.	Liberal	1896-1911
Sir Robert Laird Borden.	Cons./Union.[2]	1911-1920
Arthur Meighen	Unionist	1920-1921
W. L. Mackenzie King	Liberal	1921-1926
Arthur Meighen	Conservative	1926[3]
W. L. Mackenzie King	Liberal	1926-1930
Richard Bedford Bennett	Conservative	1930-1935
W. L. Mackenzie King	Liberal	1935-1948
Louis St. Laurent	Liberal	1948-1957
John G. Diefenbaker	Prog. Cons.	1957-1963
Lester Bowles Pearson	Liberal	1963-1968
Pierre Elliott Trudeau.	Liberal	1968-1979
Joe Clark	Prog. Cons.	1979-1980
Pierre Elliott Trudeau.	Liberal	1980-1984
John Napier Turner	Liberal	1984[4]
Brian Mulroney.	Prog. Cons.	1984-1993
Kim Campbell	Prog. Cons.	1993[5]
Jean Chrétien	Liberal	1993-2003
Paul Martin.	Liberal	2003-

(1) May-July. (2) Conservative 1911-1917, Unionist 1917-1920. (3) June-Sept. (4) June-Sept. (5) June-Oct.

Cape Verde
Republic of Cape Verde

People: Population: 415,294. **Age distrib. (%):** <15: 41.9; 65+: 6.6. **Pop. density:** 267 per sq mi, 103 per sq km. **Urban:** 55.9%. **Ethnic groups:** Creole 71%, African 28%, European 1%. **Principal languages:** Portuguese (official), Crioulo. **Chief religions:** Roman Catholic (infused with indigenous beliefs); Protestant (mostly Church of the Nazarene).

Geography: Total area: 1,557 sq mi, 4,033 sq km; **Land area:** 1,557 sq mi, 4,033 sq km. **Location:** In Atlantic O., off W tip of Africa. **Neighbors:** Nearest are Mauritania, Senegal to E. **Topography:** Cape Verde Islands are 15 in number, volcanic in origin (active crater on Fogo). The landscape is eroded and stark, with vegetation mostly in interior valleys. **Capital:** Praia, 107,000.

Government: Type: Republic. **Head of state:** Pres. Pedro Pires; b Apr. 29, 1934; in office: Mar. 22, 2001. **Head of gov.:** Prime Min. José Maria Neves; b Mar. 28, 1960; in office: Feb. 1, 2001. **Local divisions:** 17 districts. **Defense budget** (2003): $10.2 mil. **Active troops:** 1,200.

Economy: Industries: food & beverages, fish proc., shoes & garments, salt mining, ship repair. **Chief crops:** bananas, corn, beans, sweet potatoes, sugarcane, coffee, peanuts. **Natural resources:** salt, basalt rock, limestone, kaolin, fish. **Arable land:** 11%. **Livestock** (2003): cattle: 21,823; chickens: 417,000; goats: 112,337; pigs: 200,000; sheep: 9,216. **Fish catch** (2002 est): 8,000 metric tons. **Electricity prod.** (2002): 0.04 bil. kWh.

Finance: Monetary unit: Escudo (CVE) (Sept. 2004: 91.07 = $1 U.S.). **GDP** (2002 est.): $600.0 mil.; **per capita GDP:** $1,400; **GDP growth:** 4.0%. **Imports** (2003 est.): $315.5 mil.; partners (2002): Portugal 47.7%, Netherlands 7.1%, Germany 5.6%. **Exports** (2003 est.): $50.7 mil.; partners (2002): Portugal 38.1%, France 23.8%, UK 23.8%, U.S. 9.5%. **Tourism** (2002): $66 mil. **Budget** (2000): $198.0 mil. **Intl. reserves less gold:** $63 mil. **Consumer prices** (changes in 2002): 1.9%.

Transport: Motor vehicles (1999): 13,500 pass. cars, 3,100 comm. vehicles. **Civil aviation:** 190.8 mil. pass.-mi; 6 airports. **Chief ports:** Mindelo, Praia.

Communications: TV sets: 5 per 1,000 pop. **Radios:** 183 per 1,000 pop. **Telephone lines:** 71,700. **Internet:** 20,400 users.

Health: Life expect.: 66.8 male; 73.5 female. **Births** (per 1,000 pop.): 26.1. **Deaths** (per 1,000 pop.): 6.7. **Natural inc.:** 1.94%. **Infant mortality** (per 1,000 live births): 49.1.

Education: Compulsory: ages 6-11. **Literacy:** 76.6%.

Major Intl. Organizations: UN (FAO, IBRD, ILO, IMF, IMO, WHO), AU.

Embassy: 3415 Massachusetts Ave. NW 20007; 965-6820.

Websites: www.governo.cv; www.capeverdeusa.org

The uninhabited Cape Verdes were discovered by the Portuguese in 1456 or 1460. The first Portuguese colonists landed in 1462; African slaves were brought soon after, and most Cape Verdeans descend from both groups. Cape Verde independence came July 5, 1975. Antonio Mascarenhas Monteiro won the nation's first free presidential election Feb. 17, 1991; he was reelected without opposition five years later. Pedro Pires won a presidential runoff election Feb. 25, 2001.

Central African Republic

People: Population: 3,742,482. **Age distrib. (%):** <15: 43; 65+: 3.8. **Pop. density:** 16 per sq mi, 6 per sq km. **Urban:** 42.7%. **Ethnic groups:** Baya 33%, Banda 27%, Mandjia 13%, Sara 10%, Mboum 7%, M'Baka 4%, Yakoma 4%. **Principal languages:** French (official), Sangho (national), tribal languages. **Chief religions:** Indigenous beliefs 35%, Protestant 25%, Roman Catholic 25%, Muslim 15%.

Geography: Total area: 240,535 sq mi, 622,984 sq km; **Land area:** 240,535 sq mi, 622,984 sq km. **Location:** In central Africa. **Neighbors:** Chad on N, Cameroon on W, Congo-Brazzaville and Congo-Kinshasa (formerly Zaire) on S, Sudan on E. **Topography:** Mostly rolling plateau, average altitude 2,000 ft., with rivers draining S to the Congo and N to Lake Chad. Open, well-watered savanna covers most of the area, with an arid area in NE, and tropical rain forest in SW. **Capital:** Bangui, 698,000.

Government: Type: In transition. **Head of state:** Pres. François Bozizé; b Oct. 14, 1946; in office: Mar. 15, 2003. **Head of gov.:** Prime Min. Célestin Gaombalet; in office: Dec. 12, 2003. **Local divisions:** 14 prefectures, 2 economic prefectures, 1 commune. **Defense budget** (2003): $30 mil. **Active troops:** 2,550.

Economy: Industries: diamond mining, sawmills, breweries, textiles, footwear, bicycle & motorcycle assembly. **Chief crops:** cotton, coffee, tobacco, cassava, yams, millet, corn, bananas. **Natural resources:** diamonds, uranium, timber, gold, oil, hydropower. **Arable land:** 3%. **Livestock** (2003): cattle: 3.35 mil.; chickens: 4.58 mil.; goats: 2.92 mil.; pigs: 771,000; sheep: 246,000. **Fish catch** (2002 est): 15,000 metric tons. **Electricity prod.** (2002): 0.11 bil. kWh.

Finance: Monetary unit: CFA Franc BEAC (XAF) (Sept. 2004: 539.54 = $1 U.S.). **GDP** (2003 est.): $4.6 bil.; **per capita GDP:** $1,200; **GDP growth:** 1.0%. **Imports** (2002 est.): $136.0 mil.; partners (2002): France 30.9%, U.S. 5.1%, Cameroon 4.4%. **Exports** (2002 est.): $172.0 mil.; partners (2002): Belgium 70.3%, Spain 7%, Italy 4.1%. **Tourism** (2002): $3 mil. **Intl. reserves less gold:** $89 mil. **Gold:** 10,000 oz t. **Consumer prices:** 3.1%.

Transport: Motor vehicles (1999): 4,900 pass. cars, 5,800 comm. vehicles. **Civil aviation:** 134.2 mil. pass.-mi; 3 airport. **Chief port:** Bangui.

Communications: TV sets: 6 per 1,000 pop. **Radios:** 83 per 1,000 pop. **Telephone lines** (2002): 9,000. **Daily newspaper circ.:** 1.8 per 1,000 pop. **Internet** (2002): 5,000 users.

Health: Life expect.: 39.7 male; 43.1 female. **Births** (per 1,000 pop.): 35.5. **Deaths** (per 1,000 pop.): 20.0. **Natural inc.:** 1.56%. **Infant mortality** (per 1,000 live births): 92.2. **AIDS rate:** 13.5%.

Education: Compulsory: ages 6-14. **Literacy:** 51%. **Major Intl. Organizations:** UN (FAO, IBRD, ILO, IMF, WHO, WTrO), AU. **Embassy:** 1618 22d St. NW 20008; 483-7800. **Websites:** www.rca-gouv.net; www.embassy.org/embassies/cf.html

Various Bantu tribes migrated through the region for centuries before French control was asserted in the late 19th century, when the region was named Ubangi-Shari. Complete independence was attained Aug. 13, 1960.

All political parties were dissolved in 1960, and the country became a center for Chinese political influence in Africa. Relations with China were severed after 1965. Pres. Jean-Bedel Bokassa, who seized power in a 1965 military coup, proclaimed himself constitutional emperor of the renamed Central African Empire Dec. 1976.

Bokassa's rule was characterized by ruthless authoritarianism and human rights violations. He was ousted in a bloodless coup aided by the French government, Sept. 20, 1979. In 1981, Gen. André Kolingba became head of state in another bloodless coup. Multiparty legislative and presidential elections were held in Oct. 1992 but were canceled by the government when Kolingba was losing. New elections, held in Aug. and Sept. 1993, led to the replacement of Kolingba with a civilian government under Pres. Ange-Félix Patassé.

France sent in troops to suppress army mutinies in 1996 and 1997. Patassé loyalists won a narrow majority in legislative elections on Nov. 22 and Dec. 13, 1998, and he was reelected to a 2nd 6-year term on Sept. 19, 1999. After thwarting several coup attempts, Patassé was ousted Mar. 15, 2003, by rebels under former army chief François Bozizé.

Chad
Republic of Chad

People: Population: 9,538,544. **Age distrib.** (%): <15: 47.8; 65+: 2.8. **Pop. density:** 20 per sq mi, 8 per sq km. **Urban:** 24.9%.. **Ethnic groups:** About 200 groups; largest are Arabs in N and Sara in S. **Principal languages:** French, Arabic (both official), Sara, more than 120 different languages and dialects. **Chief religions:** Muslim 51%, Christian 35%, animist 7%, other 7%.

Geography: Total area: 495,755 sq mi, 1,284,000 sq km; **Land area:** 486,180 sq mi, 1,259,200 sq km. **Location:** In central N Africa. **Neighbors:** Libya on N; Niger, Nigeria, Cameroon on W; Central African Republic on S; Sudan on E. **Topography:** Wooded savanna, steppe, and desert in the S; part of the Sahara in the N. Southern rivers flow N to Lake Chad, surrounded by marshland. **Capital:** N'Djamena, 797,000.

Government: Type: Republic. **Head of state:** Pres. Idriss Déby; b 1952; in office: Dec. 4, 1990. **Head of gov.:** Prime Min. Moussa Faki; in office: June 24, 2003. **Local divisions:** 14 prefectures. **Defense budget** (2003): $19 mil. **Active troops:** 30,350.

Economy: Industries: cotton textiles, meatpacking, beer brewing, sodium carbonate, soap, cigarettes, constr. materials. **Chief crops:** cotton, sorghum, millet, peanuts, rice, potatoes, cassava. **Natural resources:** oil, uranium, natron, kaolin, fish. **Arable land:** 3%. **Livestock** (2003): cattle: 6.27 mil.; chickens: 5.0 mil.; goats: 5.59

mil.; pigs: 24,000; sheep: 2.51 mil. **Fish catch** (2002 est): 84,000 metric tons. **Electricity prod.** (2002): 0.1 bil. kWh. **Labor force:** agriculture more than 80% (subsistence farming, herding, and fishing).

Finance: Monetary unit: CFA Franc BEAC (XAF) (Sept. 2004: 539.54 = $1 U.S.). **GDP** (2003 est.): $10.9 bil.; **per capita GDP:** $1,200; **GDP growth:** 15.0%. **Imports** (2003 est.): $760.0 mil.; partners (2002): France 31.5%, U.S. 31.3%, Germany 5.6%, Nigeria 4.7%. **Exports** (2003 est.): $365.0 mil.; partners (2002): Portugal 30.3%, Germany 15.2%, U.S. 9.1%, France 6.1%, Nigeria 6.1%, Spain 6.1%, Morocco 4.5%, Poland 4.5%. **Tourism** (2001): $23 mil. **Budget** (1998 est.): $218.0 mil. **Intl. reserves less gold:** $126 mil. **Gold:** 10,000 oz t. **Consumer prices:** -1.9%.

Transport: Motor vehicles (1995): 8,700 pass. cars, 12,400 comm. vehicles. **Civil aviation:** 134.2 mil. pass.-mi; 7 airports.

Communications: TV sets: 1 per 1,000 pop. **Radios:** 236 per 1,000 pop. **Telephone lines** (2002): 11,800. **Daily newspaper circ.:** .2 per 1,000 pop. **Internet** (2002): 15,000 users.

Health: Life expect.: 46.9 male; 49.6 female. **Births** (per 1,000 pop.): 46.5. **Deaths** (per 1,000 pop.): 16.4. **Natural inc.:** 3.01%. **Infant mortality** (per 1,000 live births): 94.8. **AIDS rate:** 4.8%.

Education: Compulsory: ages 6-11. **Literacy:** 47.5%. **Major Intl. Organizations:** UN (FAO, IBRD, ILO, IMF, WHO, WTrO), AU.

Embassy: 2002 R St. NW 20009; 462-4009. **Website:** www.chadembassy.org

Chad was the site of paleolithic and neolithic cultures before the Sahara Desert formed. A succession of kingdoms and Arab slave traders dominated Chad until France took control around 1900. Independence came Aug. 11, 1960.

Northern Muslim rebels have fought animist and Christian southern government and French troops from 1966, despite numerous cease-fires and peace pacts.

Libyan troops entered the country at the request of a pro-Libyan Chad government, Dec. 1980. The troops were withdrawn from Chad in Nov. 1981. Rebel forces, led by Hissène Habré, captured the capital and forced Pres. Goukouni Oueddei to flee the country in June 1982.

In 1983, France sent some 3,000 troops to Chad to assist Pres. Habré in opposing Libyan-backed rebels. France and Libya agreed to a simultaneous withdrawal of troops from Chad in Sept. 1984, but Libyan forces remained in the north until Mar. 1987, when Chad forces drove them from their last major stronghold. In Dec. 1990, Habré was overthrown by a Libyan-supported insurgent group, the Patriotic Salvation Movement.

On Feb. 3, 1994, the World Court dismissed a long-standing territorial claim by Libya to the mineral-rich Aozou Strip, on the Libyan border. Libyan troops reportedly withdrew at the end of May. Following approval of a new constitution in March 1996, Chad's first multiparty presidential election was held in June and July. The U.S. Peace Corps withdrew from Chad in Apr. 1998 because of continuing clashes between rebels and Chad government forces.

Pres. Idriss Déby won reelection May 20, 2001, to another 5-year term. Oil began flowing July 15, 2003, through a 665-mi pipeline that allows landlocked Chad to export via Cameroon.

Chile
Republic of Chile

People: Population: 15,823,957. **Age distrib.** (%): <15: 26.9; 65+: 7.5. **Pop. density:** 55 per sq mi, 21 per sq km. **Urban:** 87.0%. **Ethnic groups:** European and Mestizo 95%, Amerindian 3%. **Principal languages:** Spanish (official), Araucanian. **Chief religions:** Roman Catholic 89%, Protestant 11%.

Geography: Total area: 292,260 sq mi, 756,950 sq km; **Land area:** 289,113 sq mi, 748,800 sq km. **Location:** Occupies western coast of S South America. **Neighbors:** Peru on N, Bolivia on NE, on E. **Topography:** Andes Mts. on E border incl. some of the world's highest peaks; on W is 2,650-mile Pacific coast. Width varies between 100 and 250 miles. In N is Atacama Desert, in center are agricultural regions, in S, forests and grazing lands. **Capital:** Santiago, 5,478,000.

Government: Type: Republic. **Head of state and gov.:** Pres. Ricardo Lagos Escobar; b Mar. 2, 1938; in office: Mar. 11, 2000. **Local divisions:** 13 regions. **Defense budget** (2003): $1.1 bil. **Active troops:** 77,300.

Economy: Industries: copper, other minerals, foodstuffs, fish proc., iron, steel, wood & wood products, transp. equip., cement, textiles. **Chief crops:** wheat, corn, grapes, beans, sugar beets, potatoes, fruit. **Natural resources:** copper, timber, iron ore, nitrates, prec. metals, molybd., hydropower. **Crude oil reserves** (2003): 150.0 mil. bbls. **Arable land:** 5%. **Livestock** (2003): cattle: 3.93 mil.; chickens: 80.0 mil.; goats: 990,000; pigs: 3.20 mil.; sheep: 4.10 mil. **Fish catch** (2002): 4,817,130 metric tons. **Electricity prod.** (2002): 42.98 bil. kWh. **Labor force** (2003 est.): agriculture 13.6%, industry 23.4%, services 63%.

Finance: Monetary unit: Peso (CLP) (Sept. 2004: 615.37 = $1 U.S.). **GDP** (2003 est.): $154.6 bil.; **per capita GDP:** $9,900; **GDP growth:** 3.2%. **Imports** (2003 est.): $17.4 bil.; partners (2002): Argentina 18%, U.S. 14.9%, Brazil 9.5%, China 6.5%, Germany 4.3%. **Exports** (2003 est.): $20.4 bil.; partners (2002): U.S. 19.1%, Japan 10.5%, China 6.7%, Mexico 5%, Italy 4.7%, U.K. 4.4%. **Tourism** $860 mil. **Budget** (2003 est.): $15.6 bil. **Intl. reserves less gold:** $10.66 bil. **Gold:** 10,000 oz. t. **Consumer prices:** 2.8%.

Transport: Railroad: Length: 4,092 mi. **Motor vehicles:** 1.32 mil. pass. cars, 701,300 comm. vehicles. **Civil aviation:** 4.8 bil. pass.-mi; 71 airports. **Chief ports:** Valparaiso, Arica, Antofagasta.

Communications: TV sets: 240 per 1,000 pop. **Radios:** 354 per 1,000 pop. **Telephone lines** (2002): 3.5 mil. **Daily newspaper circ.:** 98 per 1,000 pop. **Internet** (2002): 3.6 mil. users.

Health: Life expect.: 73.1 male; 79.8 female. **Births** (per 1,000 pop.): 15.8. **Deaths** (per 1,000 pop.): 5.7. **Natural inc.:** 1.01%. **Infant mortality** (per 1,000 live births): 9.1. **AIDS rate:** 0.3%.

Education: Compulsory: ages 6-13. **Literacy:** 96.2%.

Major Intl. Organizations: UN and all of its specialized agencies, APEC, OAS.

Embassy: 1732 Massachusetts Ave. NW 20036; 785-1746.

Website: www.chile-usa.org

Northern Chile was under Inca rule before the Spanish conquest, 1536-40. The southern Araucanian Indians resisted until the late 19th century. Independence was gained 1810-18, under José de San Martin and Bernardo O'Higgins; the latter, as supreme director 1817-23, sought social and economic reforms until deposed. Chile defeated Peru and Bolivia in 1836-39 and 1879-84, gaining mineral-rich northern land.

In 1970, Salvador Allende Gossens, a Marxist, became president with a third of the national vote. His government improved conditions for the poor, but illegal and violent actions by extremist supporters of the government, the regime's failure to attain majority support, and poorly planned socialist economic programs led to political and financial chaos.

A military junta seized power Sept. 11, 1973, and said Allende had killed himself. The junta, headed by Gen. Augusto Pinochet Ugarte, named a mostly military cabinet and announced plans to "exterminate Marxism." Repression continued during the 1980s with little sign of any political liberalization.

In a plebiscite held Oct. 5, 1988, voters rejected the incumbent president, Pinochet. He agreed to presidential elections. In Dec. 1989 voters elected a civilian president, although Pinochet continued to head the army until Mar. 10, 1998. In Mar. 1994 a Chilean human rights group estimated that human rights violations had claimed more than 3,100 lives during Pinochet's rule. Initial attempts to prosecute him failed when he was declared mentally unfit to stand trial by courts in Britain and Chile. Ricardo Lagos Escobar, Chile's 1st Socialist president since the 1973 coup, took office Mar. 11, 2000. Chile and the U.S. signed a free trade accord June 6, 2003.

In Aug. 2004, Chile's Supreme Court voted to strip Pinochet of immunity from prosecution, allowing for the possibility of a future trial.

Tierra del Fuego is the largest (18,800 sq. mi.) island in the archipelago of the same name at the southern tip of South America, an area of majestic mountains, tortuous channels, and high winds. It was visited 1520 by Magellan and named Land of Fire because of its many Indian bonfires. Part of the island is in Chile, part in Argentina. Punta Arenas, on a mainland peninsula, is a center of sheep raising and the world's southernmost city (pop. about 70,000); Puerto Williams is the southernmost settlement.

China
People's Republic of China
(Statistical data do not include Hong Kong or Macao.)

People: Population: 1,298,847,624. **Age distrib.** (%): <15: 24.3; 65+: 7.3. **Pop. density:** 361 per sq mi, 139 per sq km. **Urban:** 38.6%. **Ethnic groups:** 56 groups; Han 92%. Also Zhuang, Manchu, Hui, Miao, Uygur, Yi, Tujia, Tong, Tibetan, Mongol, et al. **Principal languages:** Mandarin (official), Yue (Cantonese), Wu (Shanghaiese), Minbei (Fuzhou), Minnan (Hokkien-Taiwanese), Xiang, Gan, Hakka, minority languages. **Chief religions:** Officially atheist; Buddhism, Taoism, some Muslims, Christians.

Geography: Total area: 3,705,405 sq mi, 9,596,960 sq km; **Land area:** 3,600,946 sq mi, 9,326,410 sq km. **Location:** Occupies most of the habitable mainland of E Asia. **Neighbors:** Mongolia on N; Russia on NE and NW; Afghanistan, Pakistan, Tajikistan, Kyrgystan, Kazakhstan on W; India, Nepal, Bhutan, Myanmar, Laos, Vietnam on S; North Korea on NE. **Topography:** Two-thirds of the vast territory is mountainous or desert; only one-tenth is cultivated. Rolling topography rises to high elevations in the N in the Daxinganlingshanmai separating Manchuria and Mongolia; the Tien Shan in Xinjiang; the Himalayan and Kunlunshanmai in the SW and in Tibet. Length is 1,860 mi. from N to S, width E to W is more than 2,000 mi. The eastern half of China is one of the world's best-watered lands. Three great river systems, the Chang (Yangtze), Huang (Yellow), and Xi, provide water for vast farmlands. **Capital:** Beijing,10,848,000. **Cities (urban aggr.):** Shanghai,12,887,000; Tianjin, 9,156,000; Chongqing, 4,635,000; Shenyang, 4,828,000; Guangzhou, 3,893,000.

Government: Type: Communist Party-led state. **Head of state:** Pres. Hu Jintao; b Dec. 1942; in office: Mar. 15, 2003 (also gen. secy of Communist Party since Nov. 15, 2002). **Head of gov.:** Premier Wen Jiabao; b. Sept. 1942; in office: Mar. 16, 2003. **Local divisions:** 22 provinces (not including Taiwan), 5 autonomous regions, and 4 municipalities, plus the special administrative regions of Hong Kong (as of July 1, 1997) and Macao (as of Dec. 20, 1999). **Defense budget** (2003): $22.4 bil. **Active troops:** 2,250,000.

Economy: Industries: iron, steel, coal, machine building, armaments, textiles & apparel, oil, cement, chemical fertilizers.

Chief crops: rice, wheat, potatoes, sorghum, peanuts, tea. **Natural resources:** coal, iron ore, oil, nat. gas, mercury, tin, tungsten, antimony, mang., molybd., vanadium, magnetite, aluminum, lead, zinc, uranium, hydropower. **Crude oil reserves** (2003): 18.3 bil. bbls. **Arable land:** 10%. **Livestock** (2003): cattle: 103.47 mil.; chickens: 398.05 bil.; goats: 172.92 mil.; pigs: 469.80 mil.; sheep: 143.79 mil. **Fish catch** (2002): 44,320,395 metric tons. **Electricity prod.** (2002): 1,575.13 bil. kWh. **Labor force** (2001 est.): agriculture 50%, industry 22%, services 28%.

Finance: Monetary unit: Yuan Renminbi (CNY) (Sept. 2004: 8.28 = $1 U.S.). **GDP** (2003 est.): $6.449 tril.; **per capita GDP:** $5,000; **GDP growth:** 9.1%. **Imports** (2003 est.): $397.4 bil.; partners (2002): Japan 18.1%, Taiwan 12.8%, South Korea 9.7%, U.S. 9.2%, Germany 5.6%. **Exports** (2003 est.): $436.1 bil.; partners (2002): U.S. 21.5%, Hong Kong 18%, Japan 14.9%, South Korea 4.8%. **Tourism:** $17.4 bil. **Budget** (2002 est.): $267.1 bil. **Intl. reserves less gold:** $274.7 bil. **Gold:** 19.3 mil oz t. **Consumer prices:** 1.2%.

Transport: Railroad: Length: 43,532 mi. **Motor vehicles** (1998): 6.5 mil. pass. cars, 6.25 mil. comm. vehicles. **Civil aviation:** 13.8 bil. pass.-mi; 351 airports. **Chief ports:** Shanghai, Qinhuangdao, Dalian, Guangzhou (Canton).

Communications: TV sets: 291 per 1,000 pop. **Radios:** 342 per 1,000 pop. **Telephone lines:** 263.0 mil. **Daily newspaper circ.:** 376.5 per 1,000 pop. **Internet:** 79.5 mil. users.

Health: Life expect.: 70.4 male; 73.7 female. **Births** (per 1,000 pop.): 13.0. **Deaths** (per 1,000 pop.): 6.9. **Natural inc.:** 0.61%. **Infant mortality** (per 1,000 live births): 25.3. **AIDS rate:** 0.1%.

Education: Compulsory: ages 6-14. **Literacy:** 86%.

Major Intl. Organizations: UN (FAO, IBRD, ILO, IMF, IMO, WHO, WTrO), APEC.

Embassy: 2300 Conn. Ave. NW 20008; 328-2500.

Website: www.china-embassy.org/eng

Remains of various humanlike creatures who lived as early as several hundred thousand years ago have been found in many parts of China. Neolithic agricultural settlements dotted the Huang (Yellow) R. basin from about 5000 BC. Their language, religion, and art were the sources of later Chinese civilization.

Bronze metallurgy reached a peak and Chinese pictographic writing, similar to today's, was in use in the more developed culture of the Shang Dynasty (c. 1500 BC-c. 1000 BC), which ruled much of North China.

A succession of dynasties and interdynastic warring kingdoms ruled China for the next 3,000 years. They expanded Chinese political and cultural domination to the south and west, and developed a brilliant technologically and a culturally advanced society. Rule by foreigners (Mongols in the Yuan Dynasty, 1271-1368, and Manchus in the Ch'ing Dynasty, 1644-1911) did not alter the underlying culture.

A period of relative stagnation left China vulnerable to internal and external pressures in the 19th century. Rebellions left tens of millions dead, and Russia, Japan, Britain, and other powers exercised political and economic control in large parts of the country. China became a republic Jan. 1, 1912, following the Wuchang Uprising inspired by Dr. Sun Yat-sen, founder of the Kuomintang (Nationalist) party. By 1928, the Kuomintang, led by Chiang Kai-shek, succeeded in nominal reunification of China. About the same time, a bloody purge of Communists from the ranks of the Kuomintang fomented hostilities between the two groups that would continue for decades.

For over 50 years, 1894-1945, China was involved in conflicts with Japan. In 1895, China ceded Korea, Taiwan, and other areas. On Sept. 18, 1931, Japan seized the Northeastern Provinces (Manchuria) and set up a puppet state called Manchukuo. The border province of Jehol was cut off as a buffer state in 1933. Taking advantage of Chinese dissension, Japan invaded China proper July 7, 1937. On Nov. 20 the retreating Nationalist government moved its capital to Chongqing (Chungking) from Nanking (Nanjing), which Japanese troops then ravaged Dec. 13.

From 1939 the Sino-Japanese War (1937-45) became part of the broader world conflict. After its defeat in World War II, Japan gave up all seized land, and internal conflicts involving the Kuomintang, Communists, and other factions resumed. China came under the domination of Communist armies, 1945-1950. The Kuomintang government moved to Taiwan, Dec. 8, 1949.

The Chinese People's Political Consultative Conference convened Sept. 21, 1949; The People's Republic of China was proclaimed in Beijing (Peking) Oct. 1, 1949, under Mao Zedong. China and the USSR signed a 30-year treaty of "friendship, alliance and mutual assistance," Feb. 15, 1950. The U.S. refused recognition of the new regime. On Nov. 26, 1950, the People's Republic sent armies into Korea against U.S. troops and forced a stalemate in the Korean War.

After an initial period of consolidation, 1949-52, industry, agriculture, and social and economic institutions were forcibly molded according to Maoist ideals. However, frequent drastic changes in policy and violent factionalism interfered with economic development. In 1957, Mao admitted an estimated 800,000 people had been executed 1949-54; opponents claimed much higher figures.

The Great Leap Forward, 1958-60, tried to force the pace of economic development through intensive labor on huge new rural communes, and through emphasis on ideological purity. The program caused resistance and was largely abandoned.

By the 1960s, relations with the USSR deteriorated, with disagreements on borders, ideology, and leadership of world Communism. The USSR canceled aid accords, and China, with Albania, launched anti-Soviet propaganda drives.

The Great Proletarian Cultural Revolution, 1965, was an attempt to oppose pragmatism and bureaucratic power and instruct a new generation in revolutionary principles. Massive purges took place. A program of forcibly relocating millions of urban teenagers into the countryside was launched. By 1968 the movement had run its course; many purged officials returned to office in subsequent years, and reforms that had placed ideology above expertise were gradually weakened.

On Oct. 25, 1971, the UN General Assembly ousted the Taiwan government from the UN and seated the People's Republic in its place. The U.S. had supported the mainland's admission but opposed Taiwan's expulsion.

U.S. Pres. Richard Nixon visited China Feb. 21-28, 1972, on invitation from Premier Zhou Enlai, ending years of antipathy between the 2 nations. China and the U.S. opened liaison offices in each other's capitals, May-June 1973. The U.S., Dec. 15, 1978, formally recognized the People's Republic of China as the sole legal government of China; diplomatic relations between the 2 nations were established, Jan. 1, 1979.

Mao died Sept. 9, 1976. By 1978, Vice Premier Deng Xiaoping had consolidated his power, succeeding Mao as "paramount leader" of China. The new ruling group modified Maoist policies in education, culture, and industry, and sought better ties with non-Communist countries. During this "reassessment" of Mao's policies his widow, Jiang Qing, and other "Gang of Four" leftists were convicted of "committing crimes during the 'Cultural Revolution,' " Jan. 25, 1981.

By the mid-1980s, China had enacted far-reaching economic reforms, deemphasizing centralized planning and incorporating market-oriented incentives. Some 100,000 students and workers staged a march in Beijing to demand political reforms, May 4, 1989. The demonstrations continued during a visit to Beijing by Soviet leader Mikhail Gorbachev May 15-18; it was the first Sino-Soviet summit since 1959. As the unrest spread, martial law was imposed, May 20. Troops entered Beijing, June 3-4, and crushed the pro-democracy protests, as tanks and armored personnel carriers rolled through Tiananmen Square. It is estimated that 5,000 died, 10,000 were injured, and hundreds of students and workers were arrested.

Deng Xiaoping died Feb. 19, 1997, leaving Jiang Zemin in control as president; he was re-elected in 1998. NATO bombs hit the Chinese embassy in Belgrade, Yugoslavia, on May 7, 1999, killing 3 people and wounding 27, for which the U.S. paid compensation. The government banned a popular religious sect, the Falun Gong, July 22, after it staged the largest unauthorized demonstrations in Beijing since 1989. The U.S. and China signed a major trade agreement Nov. 15. Portugal returned Macao to China Dec. 20, 1999.

Beijing was chosen, July 13, 2001, to host the 2008 Summer Olympics. Admission to the WTrO Dec. 11 marked an economic milestone, though protested by many human rights and labor organizations. Hu Jintao was named Communist Party general secretary at the 16th party congress, Nov. 15, 2002, and elected president by the 10th National People's Congress, Mar. 15, 2003. The leadership transition was completed Sept. 25, 2004, when he took over the top military post upon Jiang's resigning it.

A SARS epidemic beginning in late 2002 killed 349 people in mainland China by mid-2003.

In Aug. 2003, China assumed an unprecedented diplomatic role when it hosted talks between North and South Korea, the U.S., Russia, and Japan regarding N. Korea's nuclear weapons program. With the successful launch and recovery, Oct. 15-16, of the *Shenzhou 5* spacecraft, China became the 3rd nation (after the U.S. and U.S.S.R.) to send a man into space. A gas well explosion at Chongqing, Dec. 23, 2003, killed 233 people. Floods in summer 2004 killed more than 1,000 people and caused $8 billion in damage.

More than 1 million adults have HIV/AIDS, a rapidly growing problem in China.

Manchuria. Home of the Manchus, rulers of China 1644-1911, Manchuria has accommodated millions of Chinese settlers in the 20th century. Under Japanese rule 1931-45, the area became industrialized. The region is divided into the 3 NE provinces of Heilongjiang, Jilin, and Liaoning.

Autonomous Regions

Guangxi Zhuang is in SE China, bounded on N by Guizhou and Hunan provinces, E and S by Guangdong, on SW by Vietnam, and on W by Yunnan. It produces rice in the river valleys and has valuable forest products. Pop. (2000): 44.89 mil

Inner Mongolia was organized by the People's Republic in 1947. Its boundaries have undergone frequent changes, reaching its greatest extent in 1956 (and restored in 1979), with an area of 454,600 sq. mi., allegedly in order to dilute the minority Mongol

population. Chinese settlers outnumber the Mongols more than 10 to 1. Pop. (2000): 23.76 mil. Capital: Hohhot.

Ningxia Hui, in N central China, is about 60,000 sq. mi., pop. (2000): 5.62 mil. Capital: Yinchuan. Situated mainly of the semi-arid Inner Mongolian plateau region with desert areas in the N. The Huang He (Yellow R.) flows across the N furnishes water for irrigation. Coal is mined in the E. Modern industry is relatively undeveloped and only one railroad crosses the region. The majority of the population is Han, and the Hui (Chinese Muslims) constitute about one-third of the population. The region experienced a significant population boom from 1950-80, which has now stabilized.

Xinjiang Uygur, in Central Asia, is 635,900 sq. mi., pop. (2000): 19.25 mil (75% Uygurs, a Turkic Muslim group, with a heavy Chinese increase in recent years). Capital: Urumqi. It is China's richest region in strategic minerals. China has moved to crack down on Uygur separatists, whom Beijing regards as terrorists.

Tibet, 471,700 sq. mi., is a thinly populated region of high plateaus and massive mountains, the Himalayas on the S, the Kunluns on the N. High passes connect with India and Nepal; roads lead into China proper. Capital: Lhasa. Average altitude is 15,000 ft. Jiachan, 15,870 ft., is believed to be the highest inhabited town on earth. Agriculture is primitive. Pop. (2000): 2.62 mil (of whom about 500,000 are Chinese). Another 4 million Tibetans form the majority of the population of vast adjacent areas that have long been incorporated into China.

China ruled all of Tibet from the 18th century, but independence came in 1911. China reasserted control in 1951, and a Communist government was installed in 1953, revising the theocratic Lamaist Buddhist rule. Serfdom was abolished, but all land remained collectivized.

A Tibetan uprising within China in 1956 spread to Tibet in 1959. The rebellion was crushed with Chinese troops, and Buddhism was almost totally suppressed. The Dalai Lama and 100,000 Tibetans fled to India.

Hong Kong

Hong Kong (Xianggang), located at the mouth of the Zhu Jiang (Pearl R.) in SE China, 90 mi. S of Canton (Guangzhou), was a British dependency from 1842 until July 1, 1997, when it became a Special Administrative Region of China. Its nucleus is Hong Kong Isl., 31 sq. mi., occupied by the British in 1841 and formally ceded to them in 1842, on which is located the seat of government. Opposite is Kowloon Peninsula, 3 sq. mi., and Stonecutters Isl., added to the territory in 1860. An additional 355 sq. mi. known as the New Territories, a mainland area and islands, were leased from China, 1898, for 99 years. Area 604,249 sq. mi. (total); 600,543 sq. mi. (land); pop. (2004 est.) 6,855,125, including fewer than 20,000 British.

Hong Kong is a major center for trade and banking. Per capita GDP, $25,400 (2000 est.), is among the highest in the world. Principal industries are textiles and apparel; also tourism ($7.21 bil expenditures in 1999), electronics, shipbuilding, iron and steel, fishing, cement, and small manufactures. Hong Kong's spinning mills are among the best in the world.

Hong Kong harbor was long an important British naval station and one of the world's great transshipment ports. The colony was often a place of refuge for exiles from mainland China. It was occupied by Japan during World War II.

From 1949 to 1962 Hong Kong absorbed more than a million refugees fleeing Communist China. Starting in the 1950s, cheap labor led to a boom in light manufacturing, while liberal tax policies attracted foreign investment; Hong Kong became one of the wealthiest, most productive areas in the Far East. Poor living and working conditions and low wages for many led to political unrest in the 1960s, but legislation and public works programs raised the standard of living by the 1970s.

With the end of the 99-year lease on the New Territories drawing near, Britain and China signed an agreement, Dec. 19, 1984, under which all of Hong Kong was to be returned to China in 1997; under this agreement Hong Kong was to be allowed to keep its capitalist system for 50 years. In Dec. 1996, an electoral college appointed by China chose a shipping magnate, Tung Chee-hwa, to be Hong Kong's chief executive when it reverted to Chinese control.

Following the transfer of government on July 1, Hong Kong retained its street names and its currency, the Hong Kong dollar (HK$7.80 = $1 U.S.), but without the queen's picture. Official languages remained Chinese (Cantonese dialect) and English. Pro-democracy candidates did well in May 24, 1998, elections, despite having been excluded from the provisional gov't. in 1997. A SARS outbreak in 2003 claimed almost 300 lives and damaged the economy.

Hundreds of thousands of Hong Kong residents turned out July 1, 2003, to protest a proposed anti-subversion law; the bill was withdrawn Sept. 5. Another mass march, July 1, 2004, protested Beijing's refusal to allow greater freedom. Pro-democracy candidates won a majority of the popular vote in elections, Sept. 12, but failed to gain control of the Legislative Council.

> ➤ **IT'S A FACT:** Which is bigger, Canada or China? The answer is either one, depending on what kind of area you are talking about. The total area of Canada is 3,885,101 sq. mi., compared to 3,709,405 sq. mi. for China. But if you count land area only, Canada has an area of 3,511,021 sq. mi., somewhat less than China's 3,600,946 sq. mi.

Macao

Macao, area of 10 sq. mi., is an enclave, a peninsula and 2 small islands, at the mouth of the Xi (Pearl) R. in China. It was established as a Portuguese trading colony in 1557. In 1849, Portugal claimed sovereignty over the territory; this claim was accepted by China in an 1887 treaty. Portugal granted broad autonomy in 1976. Under a 1987 agreement, Macao reverted to China Dec. 20, 1999. As in the case of Hong Kong, the Chinese government guaranteed Macao it would not interfere in its way of life and capitalist system for a period of 50 years. Pop. (2004 est.): 445,286.

Colombia
Republic of Colombia

People: Population: 42,310,775. **Age distrib.** (%): <15: 31.6; 65+: 4.8. **Pop. density:** 106 per sq mi, 41 per sq km. **Urban:** 76.5%. **Ethnic groups:** Mestizo 58%, European 20%, Creole 14%, Black 4%, Black-Amerindian 1%, Amerindian 3%. **Principal languages:** Spanish (official). **Chief religion:** Roman Catholic 90%.

Geography: Total area: 439,735 sq mi, 1,138,910 sq km; **Land area:** 401,044 sq mi, 1,038,700 sq km. **Location:** At the NW corner of South America. **Neighbors:** Panama on NW, Ecuador and Peru on S, Brazil and Venezuela on E. **Topography:** Three ranges of Andes—Western, Central, and Eastern Cordilleras—run through the country from N to S. The eastern range consists mostly of high tablelands, densely populated. The Magdalena R. rises in the Andes, flows N to Caribbean, through a rich alluvial plain. Sparsely settled plains in E are drained by Orinoco and Amazon systems. **Capital:** Bogotá (Full name: Santa Fe de Bogotá.), 7,290,000. **Cities (urban aggr.):** Medellin, 2,866,000; Cali, 2,233,000; Barranquilla, 1,683,000.

Government: Type: Republic. **Head of state and gov.:** Pres. Álvaro Uribe Vélez; b July 4, 1952; in office: Aug. 7, 2002. **Local divisions:** 32 departments, capital district of Bogota. **Defense budget** (2003): $1.9 bil. **Active troops:** 200,000.

Economy: Industries: textiles, food proc., oil, clothing & footwear, beverages, chemicals, cement, mining. **Chief crops:** coffee, cut flowers, bananas, rice, tobacco, corn, sugarcane, cocoa. **Natural resources:** oil, nat. gas, coal, iron ore, nickel, gold, copper, emeralds, hydropower. **Crude oil reserves** (2003): 1.8 bil. bbls. **Arable land:** 4%. **Livestock** (2003): cattle: 25.0 mil.; chickens: 118.0 mil.; goats: 1.15 mil.; pigs: 2.3 mil.; sheep: 2.1 mil. **Fish catch** (2002 est): 200,000 metric tons. **Electricity prod.** (2002): 44.87 bil. kWh. **Labor force** (1990): services 46%, agriculture 30%, industry 24%.

Finance: Monetary unit: Peso (COP) (Sept. 2004: 2,537.50 = $1 U.S.) **GDP** (2003 est.): $262.5 bil.; **per capita GDP:** $6,300; **GDP growth:** 3.4%. **Imports** (2003 est.): $13.1 bil.; partners (2002): U.S. 32.7%, Venezuela 6.7%, Brazil 5.8%, Japan 5.3%, Mexico 5.1%, Germany 4.2%. **Exports** (2003 est.): $13.0 bil.; partners (2002): U.S. 44.8%, Venezuela 9.4%, Ecuador 6.8%. **Tourism** (2002): $962 mil. **Budget** (2001 est.): $25.6 bil. **Intl. reserves less gold:** $7.26 bil. **Gold:** 330,000 oz t. **Consumer prices:** 7.1%.

Transport: Railroad: Length: 2,053 mi. **Motor vehicles** (1999): 762,000 pass. cars, 542,000 comm. vehicles. **Civil aviation:** 3.3 bil. pass.-mi; 96 airports. **Chief ports:** Buenaventura, Barranquilla, Cartagena.

Communications: TV sets: 279 per 1,000 pop. **Radios:** 539 per 1,000 pop. **Telephone lines:** 8.8 mil. **Daily newspaper circ.:** 46 per 1,000 pop. **Internet:** 2.7 mil. users.

Health: Life expect.: 67.6 male; 75.4 female. **Births** (per 1,000 pop.): 21.2. **Deaths** (per 1,000 pop.): 5.6. **Natural inc.:** 1.56%. **Infant mortality** (per 1,000 live births): 21.7. **AIDS rate:** 0.7%.

Education: Compulsory: ages 5-14. **Literacy:** 92.5%.

Major Intl. Organizations: UN (FAO, IBRD, ILO, IMF, IMO, WHO, WTrO), OAS.

Embassy: 2118 Leroy Pl. NW 20008; 387-8338.

Websites: www.colombiaemb.org; www.turismocolumbia.com

Spain subdued the local Indian kingdoms (Funza, Tunja) by the 1530s and ruled Colombia and neighboring areas as New Granada for 300 years. Independence was won by 1819. Venezuela and Ecuador broke away in 1829-30, and Panama withdrew in 1903.

Colombia is plagued by rural and urban violence. "La Violencia" of 1948-58 claimed 200,000 lives; since 1989, political violence has killed an average of 3,500 people a year, most of them civilians. Attempts at land and social reform and progress in industrialization have not reduced massive social problems.

The government's increased activity against local drug traffickers sparked a series of retaliation killings. On Aug. 18, 1989, Luis Carlos Galán, the ruling party's presidential hopeful for the 1990 election, was assassinated. In 1990, 2 other presidential candidates were assassinated, as drug traffickers carried on a campaign of intimidation.

Right-wing paramilitaries launched a campaign Dec. 22, 2000, against suspected left-wing guerrillas. Legislation expanding the powers of the military was signed Aug. 13, 2001. The collapse of talks with the rebels in Feb. 2002 brought an upsurge of fighting. A hardliner, Álvaro Uribe Vélez, whose father had been killed by leftist rebels in 1983, won a presidential election May 26. A wave of guerrilla violence as he took office led Uribe to declare a "state of unrest" Aug. 12. Police powers were increased Sept. 10 as part of a new government offensive.

Colombia produces an estimated 90% of the cocaine reaching the U.S. Since 2000 the U.S. has provided $3.3 billion to Colombia, much of it to combat narco-terrorism.

Comoros
Union of Comoros

People: Population: 651,901. **Age distrib.** (%): <15: 42.9; 65+: 2.9. **Pop. density:** 778 per sq mi, 300 per sq km. **Urban:** 35.0%. **Ethnic groups:** Antalote, Cafre, Makoa, Oimatsaha, Sakalava (all are mostly an African-Arab mix). **Principal languages:** Arabic, French (both official), Shikomoro (a blend of Swahili and Arabic). **Chief religion:** Muslim 98% (official).

Geography: Total area: 838 sq mi, 2,170 sq km; **Land area:** 838 sq mi, 2,170 sq km. **Location:** 3 islands—Grande Comore (Njazidja), Anjouan (Nzwani), and Moheli (Mwali)—in the Mozambique Channel between NW Madagascar and SE Africa. **Neighbors:** Nearest are Mozambique on W, Madagascar on E. **Topography:** The islands are of volcanic origin, with an active volcano on Grande Comore. **Capital:** Moroni, 53,000.

Government: Type: In transition. **Head of state and gov.:** Pres. Azali Assoumani; b Jan. 1,1959; in office: May 26, 2002. **Local divisions:** 3 main islands with 4 municipalities.

Economy: Industries: tourism, perfume distillation. **Chief crops:** vanilla, cloves, perfume essences, copra, coconuts, bananas, cassava. **Arable land:** 35%. **Livestock** (2003): cattle: 52,000; chickens: 490,000; goats: 115,000; sheep: 21,000. **Fish catch** (2002 est): 12,200 metric tons. **Electricity prod.** (2002): 0.02 bil. kWh. **Labor force:** agriculture 80%.

Finance: Monetary unit: Franc (KMF) (Sept. 2004: 404.79 = $1 U.S.). **GDP** (2002 est.): $441.0 mil.; **per capita GDP:** $700; **GDP growth:** 2.0%. **Imports** (2002 est.): $88.0 mil.; partners (2002): France 34.1%, South Africa 11.4%, Japan 5.7%, Kenya 5.7%, UAE 5.7%, Mauritius 4.5%, Thailand 4.5%. **Exports** (2002 est.): $28.0 mil.; partners (2002): France 31%, Germany 17.2%, U.S. 17.2%, Singapore 10.3%, Netherlands 6.9%. **Tourism** (2002): $11 mil. **Budget** (1997): $53 mil. **Intl. reserves less gold:** $63 mil.

Transport: Civil aviation (1996): 11 mil pass.-mi.; 4 airports. **Chief ports:** Fomboni, Moroni, Moutsamoudou.

Communications: TV sets: 4 per 1,000 pop. **Radios:** 141 per 1,000 pop. **Telephone lines:** 13,200. **Internet:** 5,000 users.

Health: Life expect.: 59.3 male; 63.9 female. **Births** (per 1,000 pop.): 38.0. **Deaths** (per 1,000 pop.): 8.6. **Natural inc.:** 2.94%. **Infant mortality** (per 1,000 live births): 77.2.

Education: Compulsory: ages 6-13. **Literacy:** 56.5%.

Major Intl. Organizations: UN (FAO, IBRD, ILO, IMF, WHO), AL, AU.

Embassy: 420 E. 50th St., New York, NY 10022; 212-750-1637.

Website: www.presidence-rfic.com

The islands were controlled by Muslim sultans until the French acquired them 1841-1909. They became a French overseas territory in 1947. A 1974 referendum favored independence, with only the Christian island of Mayotte preferring association with France. The French National Assembly decided to allow each of the islands to decide its own fate. The Comore Chamber of Deputies declared independence July 6, 1975, with Ahmed Abdallah as president. In a referendum in 1976, Mayotte voted to remain French.

A leftist regime that seized power from Abdallah in 1975 was deposed in a pro-French 1978 coup in which he regained the presidency. In Nov. 1989, Pres. Abdallah was assassinated; soon after, a multiparty system was instituted. A Sept. 1995 military coup, assisted by French mercenaries, ousted Pres. Said Mohamed Djohar. French troops invaded, Oct. 4, and forced coup leaders to surrender. Djohar returned from exile in Jan. 1996, and in Mar. a new presidential election was held. A hijacked Ethiopian Airlines Boeing 767 crashed offshore on Nov. 23, killing 123 of the 175 people on board.

Attempts to work out a new constitutional relationship between Grande Comore, Anjouan, and Moheli have been ongoing since Anjouan and Moheli seceded from the Comoros in 1997. Unrest on Grande Comore culminated in a military coup, Apr. 30, 1999. Anjouans endorsed secession in a disputed vote Jan. 23, 2000. Irregularities marred the presidential runoff election of Apr. 14, 2002, won by Azali Assoumani, who led the 1999 coup; each of the 3 islands also elected its own president in 2002. Elections for national and island assemblies took place Mar.-Apr. 2004.

Congo (formerly Zaire)
Democratic Republic of the Congo

(Congo, officially Democratic Republic of the Congo, is also known as Congo-Kinshasa. It should not be confused with Republic of the Congo, commonly called Congo Republic, and also known as Congo-Brazzaville.)

People: Population: 58,317,930. **Age distrib.** (%): <15: 48.2; 65+: 2.5. **Pop. density:** 67 per sq mi, 26 per sq km. **Urban:** 53.5%. **Ethnic groups:** Over 200 groups. Four largest, the Mongo, Luba, Kongo (all Bantu), and Mangbetu-Azande (Hamitic), make up 45% of pop. **Principal languages:** French (official), Lingala, Kingswana (a swahili dialect), Tshiluba. **Chief religions:** Roman Catholic 50%, Protestant 20%, Kimbanguist 10%, Muslim 10%.

Geography: Total area: 905,567 sq mi, 2,345,410 sq km; **Land area:** 875,525 sq mi, 2,267,600 sq km. **Location:** In central Africa. **Neighbors:** Congo-Brazzaville on W; Central African Re-

public, Sudan on N; Uganda, Rwanda, Burundi, Tanzania on E; Zambia, Angola on S. **Topography:** Congo includes the bulk of the Congo R. basin. The vast central region is a low-lying plateau covered by rain forest. Mountainous terraces in the W, savannas in the S and SE, grasslands toward the N, and the high Ruwenzori Mts. on the E surround the central region. A short strip of territory borders the Atlantic O. **Capital:** Kinshasa, 5,277,000. **Cities (urban aggr.):** Lubumbashi, 906,000.

Government: Type: In transition. **Head of state and gov.:** Pres. Joseph Kabila; b June 24, 1971; in office: Jan. 26, 2001. **Local divisions:** 10 provinces, 1 city. **Defense budget** (2002): $400 mil. **Active troops:** 97,800.

Economy: Industries: mining, mineral proc., textiles, footwear, cigarettes, proc. foods & beverages, cement. **Chief crops:** coffee, sugar, rubber, tea, quinine, cassava, bananas, root crops, corn, fruits, wood products. **Natural resources:** cobalt, copper, cadmium, oil, diamonds, gold, silver, zinc, mang., tin, germanium, uranium, radium, bauxite, iron ore, coal, hydropower, timber. **Crude oil reserves** (2003): 187.0 mil. bbls. **Arable land:** 3%. **Livestock** (2003): cattle: 761,270; chickens: 19.6 mil.; goats: 4.00 mil.; pigs: 953,100; sheep: 896,900. **Fish catch** (2002 est): 222,965 metric tons. **Electricity prod.** (2002): 6.09 bil. kWh. **Labor force:** 65% agriculture, 16% industry, 19% service.

Finance: Monetary unit: franc (CDF) (Sept. 2004: 396.51 = $1 U.S.). **GDP** (2003 est.): $35.6 bil.; **per capita GDP:** $600; **GDP growth:** 6.0%. **Imports** (2002 est.): $933.0 mil.; partners (2002): South Africa 15.9%, Belgium 14.1%, Nigeria 10.1%, France 9.2%, Germany 7.4%, Netherlands 5.1%, Kenya 5%. **Exports** (2002 est.): $1.4 bil.; partners (2002): Belgium 64.3%, U.S. 13.4%, Zimbabwe 6.7%, Finland 4.9%. **Tourism** (1998): $2 mil. **Budget** (1996 est.): $244.0 mil. **Consumer prices** (changes in 2002): 32%.

Transport: Railroad: Length: 2,965 mi. **Motor vehicles** (1999): 172,600 pass. cars, 34,600 comm. vehicles. **Civil aviation:** 137.9 mil. pass.-mi; 24 airports. **Chief ports:** Matadi, Boma, Kinshasa.

Communications: TV Sets: 2 per 1,000 pop. **Radios:** 376 per 1,000 pop. **Telephone lines (2002):** 10,000. **Daily newspaper circ.:** 2.7 per 1,000 pop. **Internet** (2002): 50,000 users.

Health: Life expect.: 47.1 male; 51.3 female. **Births** (per 1,000 pop.): 44.7. **Deaths** (per 1,000 pop.): 14.6. **Natural inc.:** 3.01%. **Infant mortality** (per 1,000 live births): 94.7. **AIDS rate:** 4.2%.

Education: Compulsory: ages 6-13. **Literacy:** 83.8%.

Major Intl. Organizations: UN and most of its specialized agencies, AU.

Embassy: 1800 New Hampshire Ave. NW 20009; 234-7690.

Website: www.embassy.org/embassies/zr.htm l

The earliest inhabitants of Congo may have been the pygmies, followed by Bantus from the E and Nilotic tribes from the N. The large Bantu Bakongo kingdom ruled much of Congo and Angola when Portuguese explorers visited in the 15th century.

Leopold II, king of the Belgians, formed an international group to exploit the Congo region in 1876. In 1877 Henry M. Stanley explored the Congo, and in 1878 the king's agent sent him back to organize the region and win over the native chiefs. The Conference of Berlin, 1884-85, organized the Congo Free State with Leopold as king and chief owner. Exploitation of native laborers on the rubber plantations caused international criticism and led to granting of a colonial charter, 1908; the colony became known as the Belgian Congo. Millions of Congolese are believed to have died between 1880 and 1920 as a result of slave labor and other causes under European rule.

Belgian and Congolese leaders agreed Jan. 27, 1960, the Congo would become independent in June. In the first general elections, May 31, the National Congolese movement of Patrice Lumumba won a plurality in the National Assembly. He was appointed premier June 21, and formed a coalition cabinet. The Republic of the Congo was proclaimed June 30.

Widespread violence caused Europeans and others to flee. The UN Security Council, Aug. 9, 1960, called on Belgium to withdraw its troops and sent a UN contingent. Pres. Joseph Kasavubu removed Lumumba as premier in Sept.; Lumumba was murdered Jan. 17, 1961.

The last UN troops left the Congo June 30, 1964, and Moise Tshombe became president.

On Sept. 7, 1964, leftist rebels set up a "People's Republic" in Stanleyville (now Kisangani). Tshombe hired foreign mercenaries and sought to rebuild the Congolese Army. In Nov. and Dec. 1964 rebels killed scores of white hostages and thousands of Congolese; Belgian paratroopers, dropped from U.S. transport planes, rescued hundreds. By July 1965 the rebels had lost their effectiveness.

In late 1965 Gen. Joseph D. Mobutu was named president. He later changed his name to Mobutu Sese Seko and ruled as a dictator. The country became the Democratic Republic of the Congo (1966) and the Republic of Zaire (1971).

Economic decline and government corruption plagued Zaire in the 1980s and worsened in the 1990s. In 1990, Pres. Mobutu announced an end to a 20-year ban on multiparty politics. He sought to retain power despite mounting international pressure and internal opposition.

During 1994, Zaire was inundated with refugees from the massive ethnic bloodshed in Rwanda. Ethnic violence spread to E Zaire in 1996. In Oct. militant Hutus, who dominated in the refugee camps, fought against rebels (mostly Tutsis) in Zaire, precipitating intervention by government troops. As a result of the fighting, Rwan-

dan refugees abandoned the camps; hundreds of thousands returned to Rwanda, while hundreds of thousands more were dispersed throughout E Zaire. The rebels, led by Gen. Laurent Kabila—a former Marxist and longtime opponent of Mobutu—gained momentum and began to move W across Zaire. As turmoil engulfed his nation, Mobutu stayed in W Europe during the latter part of 1996.

With Mobutu out of the country, the Zairean army put up little resistance; rebels were aided by several of Mobutu's enemies, notably Rwanda and Uganda. Mobutu returned to Zaire in March 1997, but attempts to negotiate with Kabila were ineffectual. On May 17, Kabila's troops entered Kinshasa and Mobutu went into exile. The country again assumed the name Democratic Republic of the Congo. Mobutu died Sept. 7 in Rabat, Morocco.

Kabila, who ruled by decree, alienated UN officials, international aid donors, and former allies. Rebels assisted by Rwanda and Uganda threatened Kinshasa in Aug. 1998, but the assault was turned back with help from Angola, Namibia, and Zimbabwe. Rebel groups agreed to a cease-fire on Aug. 31, 1999, but the truce was widely violated. Kabila was assassinated Jan. 16, 2001, apparently by one of his bodyguards, and was succeeded by his son Joseph.

A volcanic eruption in E Congo near Goma, Jan. 17, 2002, engulfed much of the city in lava and left thousands homeless.

The overall death toll from the civil war and related causes was estimated at 3.3 million through Nov. 2002. By then the war had apparently begun to wind down, with agreements by Rwanda and Uganda to pull out their remaining troops. A power-sharing accord signed Apr. 2, 2003, led to the installation of a new Congolese government in July. An apparent coup attempt by presidential guard members was crushed June 11, 2004. A UN peacekeeping force (MONUC), established in 1999, had more than 10,000 troops in the Congo as of mid-2004.

Congo Republic
Republic of the Congo

(Congo Republic, officially Republic of the Congo, is also known as Congo-Brazzaville. It should not be confused with Democratic Republic of the Congo [formerly Zaire], now commonly called Congo, and also known as Congo-Kinshasa.)

People: Population: 2,998,040. **Age distrib.** (%): <15: 42.4; 65+: 3.3. **Pop. density:** 23 per sq mi, 9 per sq km. **Urban:** 31.6%. **Ethnic groups:** Kongo 48%, Sangha 20%, M'Bochi 12%, Teke 17%. **Principal languages:** French (official), Lingala, Monokutuba, Kikongo, many local languages and dialects. **Chief religions:** Christian 50%, animist 48%, Muslim 2%.

Geography: Total area: 132,047 sq mi, 342,000 sq km; **Land area:** 131,854 sq mi, 341,500 sq km. **Location:** In W central Africa. **Neighbors:** Gabon and Cameroon on W, Central African Republic on N, Congo-Kinshasa (formerly Zaire) on E, Angola on SW. **Topography:** Much of the country is covered by thick forests. A coastal plain leads to the fertile Niari Valley. The center is a plateau; the Congo R. basin consists of flood plains in the lower and savanna in the upper portion. **Capital:** Brazzaville, 1,080,000.

Government: Type: Republic. **Head of state and gov.:** Pres. Denis Sassou-Nguesso; b 1943; in office: Oct. 25, 1997. **Local divisions:** 10 regions, 6 communes. **Defense budget** (2003): $114 mil. **Active troops:** 10,000.

Economy: Industries: oil, cement, lumber, brewing, sugar, palm oil. **Chief crops:** cassava, sugar, rice, corn, peanuts, vegetables, coffee, cocoa. **Natural resources:** oil, timber, potash, lead, zinc, uranium, copper, phosphates, nat. gas, hydropower. **Crude oil reserves** (2003): 1.5 bil. bbls. **Livestock** (2003): cattle: 122,370; chickens: 2.0 mil.; goats: 294,000; pigs: 46,300; sheep: 97,000. **Fish catch** (2002 est): 43,000 metric tons. **Electricity prod.** (2002): 0.35 bil. kWh.

Finance: Monetary unit: CFA Franc BEAC (XAF) (Sept. 2004: 539.54 = $1 U.S.). **GDP** (2003 est.): $2.2 bil.; **per capita GDP:** $700; **GDP growth:** 2.0%. **Imports** (2003 est.): $666.9 mil.; partners (2002): France 21.9%, Italy 8.5%, Belgium 6%, U.S. 5.2%, India 4.1%. **Exports** (2003 est.): $2.3 bil.; partners (2002): South Korea 24.1%, Taiwan 16.3%, China 11%, U.S. 10%, Germany 6.9%, France 6.1%. **Tourism** (2002): $25 mil. **Budget** (1997 est.): $970.0 mil. **Intl. reserves less gold:** $23 mil. **Gold:** 10,000 oz t. **Consumer prices:** −0.85%.

Transport: Railroad: Length: 556 mi. **Motor vehicles** (1999): 26,200 pass. cars, 20,400 comm. vehicles. **Civil aviation:** 4 airports. **Chief ports:** Pointe-Noire, Brazzaville.

Communications: TV sets: 13 per 1,000 pop. **Radios:** 126 per 1,000 pop. **Telephone lines:** 7,000. **Daily newspaper circ.:** 8 per 1,000 pop. **Internet:** 15,000 users.

Health: Life expect.: 48.5 male; 50.6 female. **Births** (per 1,000 pop.): 28.7. **Deaths** (per 1,000 pop.): 14.5. **Natural inc.:** 1.42%. **Infant mortality** (per 1,000 live births): 93.9. **AIDS rate:** 4.9%.

Education: Compulsory: ages 6-13. **Literacy:** 65.5%.

Major Intl. Organizations: UN (FAO, IBRD, ILO, IMF, IMO, WHO), AU.

Embassy: 4891 Colorado Ave. NW 20011; 726-5500.

Website: travel.state.gov/travel/congo.html

The Loango Kingdom flourished in the 15th century, as did the Anzico Kingdom of the Batekes; by the late 17th century they had become weakened. By 1885, France established control of the region, then called the Middle Congo. Republic of the Congo gained independence Aug. 15, 1960.

After a 1963 coup sparked by trade unions, the country adopted a Marxist-Leninist stance, with the USSR and China vying for influence. France remained a dominant trade partner and source of technical assistance, however, and French-owned private enterprise retained a major economic role. In 1970, the country was renamed People's Republic of the Congo.

In 1990, Marxism was renounced and opposition parties were legalized. In 1991 the country's name was changed back to Republic of the Congo, and a new constitution was approved. A democratically elected government came into office in 1992. Factional fighting broke out in Brazzaville, June 5, 1997, and intensified during the summer, devastating the capital. Troops loyal to former Marxist dictator Denis Sassou-Nguesso took control of the city Oct. 15. He claimed a lopsided victory in the presidential election of Mar. 10, 2002. The government and "Ninja" rebels in the Pool Region agreed to a cease-fire Mar. 17, 2003.

Costa Rica
Republic of Costa Rica

People: Population: 3,956,507. **Age distrib.** (%): <15: 30.8; 65+: 5.3. **Pop. density:** 202 per sq mi, 78 per sq km. **Urban:** 60.6%. **Ethnic groups:** European and Mestizo 94%, black 3%, Amerindian 1%, Chinese 1%. **Principal languages:** Spanish (official), English spoken around Puerto Limon. **Chief religions:** Roman Catholic 76% (official), Protestant 14%.

Geography: Total area: 19,730 sq mi, 51,100 sq km; **Land area:** 19,560 sq mi, 50,660 sq km. **Location:** In Central America. **Neighbors:** Nicaragua on N, Panama on S. **Topography:** Lowlands by the Caribbean are tropical. The interior plateau, with an altitude of about 4,000 ft., is temperate. **Capital:** San José, 1,085,000.

Government: Type: Republic. **Head of state and gov.:** Pres. Abel Pacheco; b Dec. 22, 1933; in office: May 8, 2002. **Local divisions:** 7 provinces. **Defense budget** (2003): $100 mil. **Active troops:** N/A.

Economy: Industries: microprocessors, food proc., textiles and clothing, constr. materials, fertilizer, plastics. **Chief crops:** coffee, pineapples, bananas, sugar, corn, rice, beans, potatoes, timber. **Natural resources:** hydropower. **Arable land:** 6%. **Livestock** (2003): cattle: 1.2 mil.; chickens: 18.5 mil.; goats: 3,600; pigs: 500,000; sheep: 2,700. **Fish catch** (2002): 50,830 metric tons. **Electricity prod.** (2002): 6.61 bil. kWh. **Labor force** (1999 est.): agriculture 20%, industry 22%, services 58%.

Finance: Monetary unit: Colon (CRC) (Sept. 2004: 445.96 = $1 U.S.). **GDP** (2003 est.): $35.2 bil.; **per capita GDP:** $9,000; **GDP growth:** 5.2%. **Imports** (2003 est.): $7.1 bil.; partners (2002): U.S. 35.4%, Japan 4.3%, Mexico 3.9%. **Exports** (2003 est.): $6.2 bil.; partners (2002): U.S. 29.1%, Netherlands 8.2%, UK 4.2%, Mexico 4%. **Tourism** (2002): $1.1 bil. **Budget** (2002 est.): $2.8 bil. **Intl. reserves less gold:** $1.24 bil. **Consumer prices:** 9.4%.

Transport: Railroad: Length: 590 mi. **Motor vehicles** (2000): 342,000 pass. cars, 177,900 comm. vehicles. **Civil aviation:** 1.5 bil. pass.-mi; 30 airports. **Chief ports:** Limon, Puntarenas, Golfito. **Communications: TV sets:** 229 per 1,000 pop. **Radios:** 774 per 1,000 pop. **Telephone lines** (2002): 1.0 mil. **Daily newspaper circ.:** 94 per 1,000 pop. **Internet** (2002): 800,000 users.

Health: Life expect.: 74.1 male; 79.3 female. **Births** (per 1,000 pop.): 19.0. **Deaths** (per 1,000 pop.): 4.3. **Natural inc.:** 1.47%. **Infant mortality** (per 1,000 live births): 10.3. **AIDS rate:** 0.6%. **Education:** Compulsory: ages 5-15. **Literacy:** 96%.

Major Intl. Organizations: UN (FAO, IBRD, ILO, IMF, IMO, WHO, WTrO), OAS.

Embassy: 2114 S St. NW 20008; 234-2945.

Websites: www.costarica-embassy.org; www.visitcostarica.com

Guaymi Indians inhabited the area when Spaniards arrived, 1502. Independence came in 1821. Costa Rica seceded from the Central American Federation in 1838. Since the civil war of 1948-49, there has been little violent social conflict, and free political institutions have been preserved. During 1993 there was an unusual wave of kidnappings and hostage-taking, some of it related to the international cocaine trade.

Costa Rica, though still a largely agricultural country, has achieved a relatively high standard of living, and land ownership is widespread. Tourism is growing rapidly.

Côte d'Ivoire
Republic of Côte d'Ivoire

People: Population: 17,327,724. **Age distrib.** (%): <15: 46; 65+: 2.2. **Pop. density:** 141 per sq mi, 54 per sq km. **Urban:** 44.9%. **Ethnic groups:** Akan 42%, Voltaiques (Gur) 18%, N Mandes 17%, Krous 11%, S Mandes 10%. **Principal languages:** French (official), Dioula, many native dialects. **Chief religions:** Muslim 35-40%, Christian 20-30%, indigenous beliefs 25-40%.

Geography: Total area: 124,502 sq mi, 322,460 sq km; **Land area:** 122,780 sq mi, 318,000 sq km. **Location:** On S coast of W Africa. **Neighbors:** Liberia, Guinea on W; Mali, Burkina Faso on N; Ghana on E. **Topography:** Forests cover the W half of the country, and range from a coastal belt to halfway to the N on the E. A sparse inland plain leads to low mountains in NW. **Capital:** Yamoussoukro (official), 416,000; Abidjan (de facto), 3,337,000.

Government: Type: In transition. **Head of state:** Pres. Laurent Gbagbo; b May 31, 1945; in office: Oct. 26, 2000. **Head of gov.:** Prime Min. Seydou Diarra; b Nov. 23, 1933; in office: Feb. 10, 2003. **Local divisions:** 58 departments. **Defense budget** (2003): $175 mil. **Active troops:** 17,050.

Economy: Industries: foodstuffs, beverages, wood products, oil refining, truck & bus assembly, textiles, fertilizer, building materials, electricity. **Chief crops:** coffee, cocoa beans, bananas, palm kernels. **Natural resources:** oil, nat. gas, diamonds, mang., iron ore, cobalt, bauxite, copper, hydropower. **Crude oil reserves** (2003): 100.0 mil. bbls. **Arable land:** 8%. **Livestock** (2003): cattle: 1.48 mil.; chickens: 33.0 mil.; goats: 1.19 mil.; pigs: 336,000; sheep: 1.52 mil. **Fish catch** (2002 est): 80,549 metric tons. **Electricity prod.** (2002): 4.76 bil. kWh. **Labor force:** 51% agric.; 12% manuf. & mining.

Finance: Monetary unit: CFA Franc BCEAO (XOF) (Sept. 2004: 539.40 = $1 U.S.). **GDP** (2003 est.): $24.5 bil.; **per capita GDP:** $1,400; **GDP growth:** -1.9%. **Imports** (2003 est.): $2.8 bil.; partners (2002): France 22.4%, Nigeria 16.3%, China 7.8%, Italy 4.1%. **Exports** (2003 est.): $5.3 bil.; partners (2002): France 13.7%, Netherlands 12.2%, U.S. 7.2%, Germany 5.3%, Mali 4.4%, Belgium 4.2%, Spain 4.1%. **Tourism** (2002): $50 mil. **Budget** (2001 est.): $2.4 bil. **Intl. reserves less gold:** $1.50 bil. **Consumer prices:** 3.4%.

Transport: Railroad: Length: 410 mi. **Motor vehicles** (1999): 109,600 pass. cars, 54,100 comm. vehicles. **Civil aviation:** 149.1 mil. pass.-mi; 7 airports. **Chief ports:** Abidjan, Dabou, San-Pédro. **Communications: TV sets:** 65 per 1,000 pop. **Radios:** 161 per 1,000 pop. **Telephone lines:** 328,000. **Daily newspaper circ.:** 17 per 1,000 pop. **Internet** (2002): 90,000 users.

Health: Life expect.: 40.3 male; 44.8 female. **Births** (per 1,000 pop.): 39.6. **Deaths** (per 1,000 pop.): 18.5. **Natural inc.:** 2.12%. **Infant mortality** (per 1,000 live births): 97.1. **AIDS rate:** 7.0%. **Education:** Compulsory: ages 6-15. **Literacy:** 50.9%.

Major Intl. Organizations: UN and all of its specialized agencies, AU.

Embassy: 2424 Massachusetts Ave. NW 20008; 797-0300. **Website:** www.embassy.org/embassies/ci.html

A French protectorate from 1842, Côte d'Ivoire became independent in 1960. It is the most prosperous of all the tropical African nations, as a result of diversification of agriculture for export, close ties to France, and encouragement of foreign investment. About 20% of the population are workers from neighboring countries. Côte d'Ivoire officially changed its name from Ivory Coast in Oct. 1985.

Students and workers protested, Feb. 1990, demanding the ouster of longtime Pres. Félix Houphouët-Boigny. Côte d'Ivoire held its first multiparty presidential election Oct. 1990, and Houphouët-Boigny retained his office. He died Dec. 7, 1993. The National Assembly named a successor, Henri Konan Bédié, who was reelected Oct. 22, 1995; he was ousted in a military coup Dec. 24, 1999. The coup leader, Robert Guéi, apparently lost a presidential vote Oct. 22, 2000, but claimed victory anyway. After mass protests, he fled, and Laurent Gbagbo became president.

Guéi was killed in Abidjan Sept. 19, 2002, after a mutiny broke out there and in Bouaké and Korhogo. French troops Sept. 25 rescued 160 students (100 from the U.S.) trapped in Bouaké. Fueled by the conflict in neighboring Liberia, fighting in Côte d'Ivoire continued for months, despite the presence of 3,000 French peacekeepers. Agreement on power sharing was reached in Mar. 2003, and Gbagbo and former rebel leaders held a ceremony July 5, declaring that the war was over. The country remained divided, however, with rebels holding the north and government forces controlling the south. In Feb. 2004, the UN Security Council approved a peacekeeping force (UNOCI) of about 6,240 troops for the nation.

Croatia
Republic of Croatia

People: Population: 4,496,869. **Age distrib.** (%): <15: 18.3; 65+: 15.4. **Pop. density:** 206 per sq mi, 80 per sq km. **Urban:** 59.0%. **Ethnic groups:** Croat 78%, Serb 12%, Bosniak 1%. **Principal languages:** Croatian (official), Serbian. **Chief religions:** Roman Catholic 88%, Orthodox 5%.

Geography: Total area: 21,831 sq mi, 56,542 sq km; **Land area:** 21,782 sq mi, 56,414 sq km. **Location:** SE Europe, on the Balkan Peninsula. **Neighbors:** Slovenia, Hungary on N; Bosnia and Herzegovina, Yugoslavia on E. **Topography:** Flat plains in NE; highlands, low mtns. along Adriatic coast. **Capital:** Zagreb, 688,000.

Government: Type: Parliamentary democracy. **Head of state:** Pres. Stipe Mesic; b Dec. 24, 1934; in office: Feb. 18, 2000. **Head of gov.:** Prime Min. Ivo Sanader; b June 8, 1953; in office: Dec. 23, 2003. **Local divisions:** 20 counties and Zagreb. **Defense budget** (2003): $627 mil. **Active troops:** 20,800.

Economy: Industries: chemicals, plastics, machine tools, fabricated metal, electronics. **Chief crops:** wheat, corn, sugar beets, sunflower seeds, barley. **Natural resources:** oil, coal, bauxite, iron ore, calcium, natural asphalt, silica, mica, clays, salt, hydropower. **Crude oil reserves** (2003): 92.2 mil. bbls. **Arable land:** 21%. **Livestock** (2003): cattle: 444,320; chickens: 11.78 mil.; goats: 86,087; pigs: 1.35 mil.; sheep: 586,641. **Fish catch** (2002): 29,646 metric tons. **Electricity prod.** (2002): 12.51 bil. kWh. **Labor force** (2002): agriculture 13.2%, industry 25.4%, services 46.4%.

Finance: Monetary unit: Kuna (HRK) (Sept. 2004: 6.07 = $1 U.S.). **GDP** (2003 est.): $47.1 bil.; **per capita GDP:** $10,700; **GDP growth:** 4.5%. **Imports** (2003 est.): $12.9 bil.; partners (2002): Italy 16.8%, Germany 16.4%, Slovenia 7.8%, Russia 6.8%, Austria

6.7%, France 5.2%. **Exports** (2003 est.): $6.4 bil.; partners (2002): Italy 22.4%, Bosnia and Herzegovina 14.4%, Germany 12.6%, Slovenia 8%, Austria 7.3%. **Tourism:** $6.4 bil. **Budget** (2001 est.): $9.0 bil. **Intl. reserves less gold:** $5.51 bil. **Consumer prices:** 0.1%.

Transport: Railroad: Length: 1,427 mi. **Motor vehicles** (2001): 1.2 mil. pass. cars, 134,300 comm. vehicles. **Civil aviation:** 334.3 mil. pass.-mi; 16 airports. **Chief ports:** Rijeka, Split, Dubrovnik.

Communications: TV sets: 286 per 1,000 pop. **Radios:** 337 per 1,000 pop. **Telephone lines** (2002): 1.8 mil. **Daily newspaper circ.:** 115 per 1,000 pop. **Internet** : 1.0 mil. users.

Health: Life expect.: 70.2 male; 78.3 female. **Births** (per 1,000 pop.): 9.5. **Deaths** (per 1,000 pop.): 11.3. **Natural inc.:** –0.18%. **Infant mortality** (per 1,000 live births): 7.0. **AIDS rate:** <0.1%.

Education: Compulsory: ages 7-14. **Literacy:** 98.5%.

Major Intl. Organizations: UN (FAO, IBRD, ILO, IMF, IMO, WHO), OSCE.

Embassy: 2343 Massachusetts Ave. NW 20008; 588-5899.

Website: www.croatiaemb.org

From the 7th century the area was inhabited by Croats, a south Slavic people. It was formed into a kingdom under Tomislav in 924, and joined with Hungary in 1102. The Croats became westernized and separated from Slavs under Austro-Hungarian influence. The Croats retained autonomy under the Hungarian crown. Slavonia was taken by Turks in the 16th century; the northern part was restored by the Treaty of Karlowitz in 1699. Croatia helped Austria put down the Hungarian revolution 1848-49 and as a result was set up with Slavonia as the separate Austrian crownland of Croatia and Slavonia, which was reunited to Hungary as part of Ausgleich in 1867. It united with other Yugoslav areas to proclaim the Kingdom of Serbs, Croats, and Slovenes in 1918. At the reorganization of Yugoslavia in 1929, Croatia and Slavonia became Savska county, which in 1939 was united with Primorje county to form the county of Croatia. A nominally independent state between 1941 and 1945, it became a constituent republic in the 1946 constitution.

On June 25, 1991, Croatia declared independence from Yugoslavia. Fighting began between ethnic Serbs and Croats, with the former gaining control of about 30% of Croatian territory. A cease-fire was declared in Jan. 1992, but new hostilities broke out in 1993. A cease-fire with Serb rebels forming a self-declared republic of Krajina was agreed to Mar. 30, 1994. Croatian government troops recaptured most of the Serb-held territory Aug. 1995. Pres. Franjo Tudjman signed a peace accord with leaders of Bosnia and Serbia in Paris, Dec. 14. Tudjman won reelection June 15, 1997; international monitors called the vote "free but not fair." The last Serb-held enclave, E Slavonia, returned to Croatian control Jan. 15, 1998.

Tudjman died Dec. 10, 1999. Stipe Mesic, a moderate, won a presidential runoff election Feb. 7, 2000. EU leaders pledged June 18, 2004, to begin membership talks with Croatia in 2005.

Cuba
Republic of Cuba

People: Population: 11,308,764. **Age distrib.** (%): <15: 20.6; 65+: 10.1. **Pop. density:** 264 per sq mi, 102 per sq km. **Urban:** 75.6%. **Ethnic groups:** Creole 51%, White 37%, Black 11%, Chinese 1%. **Principal language:** Spanish (official). **Chief religions:** Roman Catholic, Santeria.

Geography: Total area: 42,803 sq mi, 110,860 sq km; **Land area:** 42,803 sq mi, 110,860 sq km. **Location:** In the Caribbean, westernmost of West Indies. **Neighbors:** Bahamas and U.S. to N, Mexico to W, Jamaica to S, Haiti to E. **Topography:** The coastline is about 2,500 miles. The N coast is steep and rocky, the S coast low and marshy. Low hills and fertile valleys cover more than half the country. Sierra Maestra, in the E, is the highest of 3 mountain ranges. **Capital:** Havana, 2,189,000.

Government: Type: Communist state. **Head of state and gov.:** Pres. Fidel Castro Ruz; b Aug. 13, 1926; in office: Dec. 3, 1976 (formerly prime min. since Feb. 16, 1959). **Local divisions:** 14 provinces, 1 special municipality. **Defense budget** (2001): $37.7 mil. **Active troops:** 46,000.

Economy: Industries: sugar, oil, tobacco, chemicals, constr., services. **Chief crops:** sugar, tobacco, citrus, coffee, rice. **Natural resources:** cobalt, nickel, iron ore, copper, mang., salt, timber, silica, oil. **Crude oil reserves** (2003): 750.0 mil. bbls. **Arable land:** 24%. **Livestock** (2003): cattle: 4.0 mil.; chickens: 23.21 mil.; goats: 410,000; pigs: 1.68; sheep: 3.12 mil. **Fish catch** (2002): 59,571 metric tons. **Electricity prod.** (2002): 14.41 bil. kWh. **Labor force:** (1999): agriculture 24%, industry 25%, services 51%.

Finance: Monetary unit: Peso (CUP) (Sept. 2004: 21.00 = $1 U.S.). **GDP** (2003 est.): $31.6 bil.; **per capita GDP:** $2,800; **GDP growth:** 1.3%. **Imports** (2003 est.): $4.5 bil.; partners (2002): Spain 16.3%, China 11.3%, Venezuela 11.1%, Italy 8.6%, France 7.2%, Canada 5.9%, U.S. 5.3%, Mexico 4.7%. **Exports** (2003 est.): $1.5 bil.; partners (2002): Netherlands 18.5%, Russia 17.5%, Canada 13.8%, Spain 9.2%, China 7%. **Tourism** (2002): $1.6 bil. **Budget** (2000 est.): $15.6 bil.

Transport: Railroad: Length: 2,139 mi. **Motor vehicles:** 16,500 pass. cars, 30,000 comm. vehicles. **Civil aviation:** 1.7 bil. pass.-mi; 70 airports. **Chief ports:** Havana, Matanzas, Cienfuegos, Santiago de Cuba.

Communications: TV sets: 248 per 1,000 pop. **Radios:** 352 per 1,000 pop. **Telephone lines** (2001): 574,400. **Daily newspaper circ.:** 118 per 1,000 pop. **Internet** (2001): 120,000 users.

Health: Life expect.: 74.8 male; 79.4 female. **Births** (per 1,000 pop.): 12.2. **Deaths** (per 1,000 pop.): 7.2. **Natural inc.:** 0.50%. **Infant mortality** (per 1,000 live births): 6.5. **AIDS rate:** 0.1%.

Education: Compulsory: ages 6-14. **Literacy:** 97%.

Major Intl. Organizations: UN (FAO, ILO, IMO, WHO, WTrO).

Cuba Interests Section: 2630 and 2639 16th St. NW 20009; 797-8518.

Websites: www.cubagob.gov.cu/ingles/; travel.state.gov/travel/cuba.html

Some 50,000 Indians lived in Cuba when it was reached by Columbus in 1492. Its name derives from the Indian Cubanacan. Except for British occupation of Havana, 1762-63, Cuba remained Spanish until 1898. A slave-based sugar plantation economy developed from the 18th century, aided by early mechanization of milling. Sugar remains the chief product and chief export despite government attempts to diversify.

A ten-year uprising ended in 1878 with guarantees of rights by Spain, which Spain failed to carry out. A full-scale movement under Jose Marti began Feb. 24, 1895.

The U.S. declared war on Spain in Apr. 1898, after the sinking of the USS *Maine* in Havana harbor, and defeated it in the Spanish-American War. Spain gave up all claims to Cuba. U.S. troops withdrew in 1902, but under 1903 and 1934 agreements, the U.S. leases a site at Guantánamo Bay in the SE as a naval base. U.S. and other foreign investments acquired a dominant role in the economy. In 1952, former Pres. Fulgencio Batista seized control and established a dictatorship, which grew increasingly harsh and corrupt. Fidel Castro assembled a rebel band in 1956; guerrilla fighting intensified in 1958. Batista fled Jan. 1, 1959, and in the resulting political vacuum Castro took power, becoming premier Feb. 16.

The government began a program of sweeping economic and social changes, without restoring promised liberties. Opponents were imprisoned, and some were executed. Some 700,000 Cubans emigrated in the first years after the Castro takeover, mostly to the U.S.

Cattle and tobacco lands were nationalized, while a system of cooperatives was instituted. By 1960 all banks and industrial companies had been nationalized, including over $1 billion worth of U.S.-owned properties, mostly without compensation.

Poor sugar crops resulted in farm collectivization, tight labor controls, and rationing, despite continued aid from the USSR and other Communist nations. A U.S.-imposed export embargo in 1962 severely damaged the economy.

In 1961, some 1,400 Cubans, trained and backed by the U.S. Central Intelligence Agency, unsuccessfully tried to invade and overthrow the regime. In the fall of 1962, the U.S. learned the USSR had brought nuclear missiles to Cuba. After an Oct. 22 warning from Pres. John F. Kennedy, the missiles were removed.

In 1977, Cuba and the U.S. signed agreements to exchange diplomats, without restoring full ties, and to regulate offshore fishing. In 1978 and 1980, the U.S. agreed to accept political prisoners released by Cuba, some of whom were criminals and mental patients. A 1987 agreement provided for 20,000 Cubans to emigrate to the U.S. each year; Cuba agreed to take back some 2,500 jailed in the U.S. since 1980.

In 1975-78, Cuba sent troops to aid one faction in the Angola civil war; the last Cuban troops were withdrawn by May 1991. Cuba's involvement in Central America, Africa, and the Caribbean contributed to poor relations with the U.S.

Cuba's economy, dependent on aid from other Communist countries, was severely shaken by the collapse of the Communist bloc in the late 1980s. Stiffer trade sanctions enacted by the U.S. in 1992 made things worse. Antigovernment demonstrations in Aug. 1994 prompted Castro to loosen emigration restrictions. A new U.S.-Cuba accord in Sept. ended the exodus of "boat people" after more than 30,000 had left Cuba. In another policy shift, the U.S. announced May 2, 1995, it would admit 20,000 Cuban refugees held at the Guantánamo base but would send further boat people back to Cuba.

The U.S. imposed additional sanctions after Cuba, Feb. 24, 1996, shot down 2 aircraft operated by an anti-Castro exile group based in Miami. Cuba blamed exile groups for bombings at Havana tourist hotels, July-Sept. 1997. Pope John Paul II visited Cuba, Jan. 21-25, 1998; he called for an end to U.S. trade sanctions, while pressing Castro to release political prisoners and allow political and religious freedom. U.S. restrictions on contact with Cuba were eased in 1999. On June 28, 2000, Elián González was returned to Cuba to live with his father, ending a 7-month legal battle that began when the boy was rescued off Florida from a shipwreck in which his mother was killed; the boy's Miami relatives had sought to keep him in the U.S.

The U.S., Jan. 11, 2002, began using its naval base at Guantánamo Bay to detain prisoners captured in Afghanistan.

Visiting Havana May 12-17, 2002, former U.S. Pres. Jimmy Carter called for democratic reforms and for lifting the U.S. trade embargo. In one of its largest crackdowns in recent years, Cuba arrested about 78 dissidents in Mar. 2003. On Apr. 11, the government executed 3 men who had hijacked a ferry in Havana bay in a failed attempt to escape to the U.S. Both the crackdown and executions were denounced worldwide. New U.S. sanctions in May 2004 restricted Cuban exiles in the U.S. to one visit to the island every 3 years instead of one trip annually, and limited money sent by exiles to immediate family only (who were not Communist Party officials). The measures also approved U.S. govt. TV and radio broadcasts via airplane and set aside $36 million to support Cuban dissidents.

Cyprus
Republic of Cyprus

(Figures below marked with a # do not include Turkish-held area—Turkish Republic of Northern Cyprus.)

People: Population: 775,927. **Age distrib.** (%): <15: 22.4; 65+: 11. **Pop. density:** 217 per sq mi, 84 per sq km. **Urban:** 69.2%. **Ethnic groups:** Greek 85%, Turkish 12%. **Principal languages:** Greek, Turkish (both official), English. **Chief religions:** Greek Orthodox 78%, Muslim 18%.

Geography: Total area: 3,571 sq mi, 9,250 sq km; **Land area:** 3,568 sq mi, 9,240 sq km. **Location:** In eastern Mediterranean Sea, off Turkish coast. **Neighbors:** Nearest are Turkey on N, Syria and Lebanon on E. **Topography:** Two mountain ranges run E-W, separated by a wide, fertile plain. **Capital:** Nicosia, 205,000.

Government: Type: Republic. **Head of state and gov.:** Pres. Tassos Papadopoulos; b Jan. 7, 1934; in office: Feb. 28, 2003. **Local divisions:** 6 districts. **Defense budget** (2003): $380 mil. **Active troops:** 10,000.

Economy: Industries: food, beverages, textiles, chemicals, metal products, tourism. **Chief crops:** potatoes, citrus, vegetables, barley, grapes, olives. **Natural resources:** copper, pyrites, asbestos, gypsum, timber, salt, marble, clay earth pigment. **Arable land:** 12%. **Livestock** (2003): cattle: 54,000; chickens: 3.5 mil.; goats: 450,000; pigs: 451,000; sheep: 300,000. **Fish catch** (2002 est): 3,840 metric tons. **Electricity prod.** (2002): 3.56 bil. kWh. **Labor force** (2003): Greek area: services 75.6%, industry 19.4%, agriculture 4.9% ; Turkish area: services 68.9%, industry 20.5%, agriculture 10.6%.

Finance: Monetary unit: Pound (CYP) (Sept. 2004: 0.47 = $1 U.S.). **GDP** (2003 est.): Greek area: $8.9 bil.; Turkish area: $1.2 bil; **per capita GDP:** Greek area: $16,000, Turkish area: $5,600; **GDP growth:** Greek area: 1.6%; Turkish area: 2.6%. **Imports** (2003 est.): Greek area: $4.6 bil., Turkish area: $301 mil., partners (2002): Russia 17.1%, Greece 7.1%, Germany 6.6%, France 6.4%, UK 6.3%, Italy 6.3%, South Korea 5.4%, Japan 5.1%. **Exports** (2003 est.): Greek area: $1.1 bil.; Turkish area: $46 mil.; partners (2002): UK 26.7%, Greece 6.6%, France 4.9%, Poland 4.3%. **Tourism:** $2.0 bil. **Budget** (2003 est.): Greek area —$539 mil., Turkish area—$432.8 mil. **Intl. reserves less gold:** $2.19 bil. **Gold:** 470,000 mil. oz t. **Consumer prices:** 4.1%.

Transport: Motor vehicles (2001): 280,100 pass. cars, 123,200 comm. vehicles. **Civil aviation:** 1.7 bil. pass.-mi; 13 airports. **Chief ports:** Famagusta, Limassol.

Communications: Television sets: 154 per 1000 pop. **Radios:** 406 per 1,000 pop. **Telephone lines** (2002): 492,000. **Daily newspaper circ.:** 111 per 1,000 pop. **Internet** (2002): 210,000 users.

Health: Life expect.: 75.1 male; 79.9 female. **Births** (per 1,000 pop.): 12.7. **Deaths** (per 1,000 pop.): 7.6. **Natural inc.:** 0.50%. **Infant mortality** (per 1,000 live births): 7.4.

Education: Compulsory: ages 6-14. **Literacy:** 97.6%.

Major Intl. Organizations: UN (FAO, IBRD, ILO, IMF, IMO, WHO, WTrO), the Commonwealth, EU, OSCE.

Embassy: 2211 R St. NW 20008; 462-5772.

Websites: www.cyprusembassy.net

Agitation for enosis (union) with Greece increased after World War I, with the Turkish minority opposed, and broke into violence in 1955-56. In 1959, Britain, Greece, Turkey, and Cypriot leaders approved a plan for an independent republic, with constitutional guarantees for the Turkish minority and permanent division of offices on an ethnic basis. Greek and Turkish Communal Chambers dealt with religion, education, and other matters.

Archbishop Makarios III, formerly the leader of the enosis movement, was elected president, and full independence became final Aug. 16, 1960. Further communal strife led the United Nations to send a peacekeeping force in 1964; its mandate has been repeatedly renewed.

The Cypriot National Guard, led by officers from the army of Greece, seized the government July 15, 1974. On July 20, Turkey invaded the island; Greece mobilized its forces but did not intervene. A cease-fire was arranged but collapsed. By Aug. 16, Turkish forces had occupied the NE 40% of the island, despite the presence of UN peacekeeping forces.

Face-to-face talks between the Greek and Turkish Cypriot leaders resumed Dec. 4, 2001, for the 1st time in 4 years. Turkish Cyprus opened its border with Greek Cyprus Apr. 23, 2003, for the 1st time since partition. In separate referendums Apr. 24, 2004, 65% of Turkish Cypriot voters accepted a UN-sponsored reunification plan, but 76% of Greek Cypriots rejected it. Still divided, Cyprus became a full member of the EU on May 1.

Turkish Republic of Northern Cyprus

A declaration of independence was announced by Turkish-Cypriot leader Rauf Denktash, Nov. 15, 1983. The state is not internationally recognized, although it does have trade relations with some countries. Area of TRNC: 1,295 sq mi.; pop. (2001 est.): 208,886, 99% Turkish. Capital: Lefkosa (Nicosia).

Czech Republic

People: Population: 10,246,178. **Age distrib.** (%): <15: 15.7; 65+: 14. **Pop. density:** 343 per sq mi, 133 per sq km. **Urban:** 74.3%. **Ethnic groups:** Czech 81%, Moravian 13%, Slovak 3%. **Principal languages:** Czech (official), German, Polish, Romani.

Chief religions: Atheist 40%, Roman Catholic 39%, Protestant 5%, Orthodox 3%.

Geography: Total area: 30,450 sq mi, 78,866 sq km; **Land area:** 29,836 sq mi, 77,276 sq km. **Location:** In E central Europe. **Neighbors:** Poland on N, Germany on N and W, Austria on S, Slovakia on E and SE. **Topography:** Bohemia, in W, is a plateau surrounded by mountains; Moravia is hilly. **Capital:** Prague, 1,170,000.

Government: Type: Republic. **Head of state:** Vaclav Klaus; b June 19, 1941; in office: Mar. 7, 2003. **Head of gov.:** Prime Min. Stanislav Gross; b Oct. 30, 1969; in office: July 26, 2004. **Local divisions:** 13 regions and Prague. **Defense budget** (2003): $1.9 bil. **Active troops:** 57,050.

Economy: Industries: metallurgy, machinery, motor vehicles, glass, armaments. **Chief crops:** wheat, potatoes, sugar beets, hops, fruit. **Natural resources:** coal, kaolin, clay, graphite, timber. **Arable land:** 41%. **Crude oil reserves** (2003): 15.0 mil. bbls. **Livestock** (2003): cattle: 1.47 mil.; chickens: 12.4 mil.; goats: 12,779; pigs: 3.36 mil.; sheep: 103,129. **Fish catch** (2002): 24,193 metric tons. **Electricity prod.** (2002): 71.75 bil. kWh. **Labor force** (2001 est.): agriculture 5%, industry 35%, services 60%.

Finance: Monetary unit: Koruna (CZK) (Sept. 2004: 25.91 = $1 U.S.). **GDP** (2003 est.): $160.5 bil.; **per capita GDP:** $15,700; **GDP growth:** 2.5%. **Imports** (2003 est.): $50.4 bil.; partners (2002): Germany 32.9%, Italy 5.5%, Slovakia 5.3%, France 4.9%, China 4.7%, Russia 4.6%, Austria 4.4%, Poland 4.1%. **Exports** (2003 est.): $46.8 bil.; partners (2002): Germany 36.6%, Slovakia 7.7%, UK 5.8%, Austria 5.6%, Poland 4.7%, France 4.7%, Italy 4.1%. **Tourism:** $3.6 bil. **Budget** (2001 est.): $18.0 bil. **Intl. reserves less gold:** $18.01 bil. **Gold:** 440,000 oz t. **Consumer prices:** 0.1%.

Transport: Railroad: Length: 5,879 mi. **Motor vehicles** (2001): 3.53 mil pass. cars, 364,100 comm. vehicles. **Civil aviation:** 2.1 bil. pass.-mi; 44 airports. **Chief ports:** Decin, Prague, Ustinad Labem.

Communications: TV sets: 487 per 1,000 pop. **Radios:** 803 per 1,000 pop. **Telephone lines:** 3.6 mil. **Daily newspaper circ.:** 254 per 1,000 pop. **Internet:** 2.7 mil. users.

Health: Life expect.: 72.5 male; 79.2 female. **Births** (per 1,000 pop.): 9.1. **Deaths** (per 1,000 pop.): 10.5. **Natural inc.:** −0.14%. **Infant mortality** (per 1,000 live births): 4.0. **AIDS rate:** 0.1%.

Education: Compulsory: ages 6-15. **Literacy** (1999 est.): 99.9%.

Major Intl. Organizations: UN (FAO, IBRD, ILO, IMF, IMO, WHO, WTrO), NATO, OECD, OSCE.

Embassy: 3900 Spring of Freedom St. NW 20008; 274-9100.

Website: www.czech.cz; www.mzv.cz/washington

Bohemia and Moravia were part of the Great Moravian Empire in the 9th century and later became part of the Holy Roman Empire. Under the kings of Bohemia, Prague in the 14th century was the cultural center of Central Europe. Bohemia and Hungary became part of Austria-Hungary.

In 1914-18 Thomas G. Masaryk and Eduard Benes formed a provisional government with the support of Slovak leaders including Milan Stefanik. They proclaimed the Republic of Czechoslovakia Oct. 28, 1918.

Czechoslovakia

By 1938 Nazi Germany had worked up disaffection among German-speaking citizens in Sudetenland and demanded its cession. British Prime Min. Neville Chamberlain, with the acquiescence of France, signed with Hitler at Munich, Sept. 30, 1938, an agreement to the cession, with a guarantee of peace by Hitler and Mussolini. Germany occupied Sudetenland Oct. 1-2.

Hitler on Mar. 15, 1939, dissolved Czechoslovakia, made protectorates of Bohemia and Moravia, and supported the autonomy of Slovakia, proclaimed independent Mar. 14, 1939.

Soviet troops with some Czechoslovak contingents entered eastern Czechoslovakia in 1944 and reached Prague in May 1945; Benes returned as president. In May 1946 elections, the Communist Party won 38% of the votes, and Benes accepted Klement Gottwald, a Communist, as prime minister.

In Feb. 1948, the Communists seized power in advance of scheduled elections. In May 1948 a new constitution was approved. Benes refused to sign it. On May 30 the voters were offered a one-slate ballot and the Communists won full control. Benes resigned June 7 and Gottwald became president. The country was renamed the Czechoslovak Socialist Republic. A harsh Stalinist period followed, with complete and violent suppression of all opposition.

In Jan. 1968 a liberalization movement spread through Czechoslovakia. Antonin Novotny, long the Stalinist ruler, was deposed as party leader and succeeded by Alexander Dubcek, a Slovak, who supported democratic reforms. On Mar. 22 Novotny resigned as president and was succeeded by Gen. Ludvik Svoboda. On Apr. 6, Prem. Joseph Lenart resigned and was succeeded by Oldrich Cernik, a reformer.

In July 1968 the USSR and 4 Warsaw Pact nations demanded an end to liberalization. On Aug. 20, the Soviet, Polish, East German, Hungarian, and Bulgarian armies invaded Czechoslovakia. Despite demonstrations and riots by students and workers, press censorship was imposed, liberal leaders were ousted from office and promises of loyalty to Soviet policies were made by some old-line Communist Party leaders.

On Apr. 17, 1969, Dubcek resigned as leader of the Communist Party and was succeeded by Gustav Husak. In Jan. 1970, Cernik was ousted. Censorship was tightened, and the Communist Party

expelled a third of its members. In 1973, amnesty was offered to some of the 40,000 who fled the country after the 1968 invasion, but repressive policies continued.

More than 700 leading Czechoslovak intellectuals and former party leaders signed a human rights manifesto in 1977, called Charter 77, prompting a renewed crackdown by the regime.

The police crushed the largest antigovernment protests since 1968, when tens of thousands of demonstrators took to the streets of Prague, Nov. 17, 1989. As protesters demanded free elections, the Communist Party leadership resigned Nov. 24; millions went on strike Nov. 27.

On Dec. 10, 1989, the first cabinet in 41 years without a Communist majority took power; Vaclav Havel, playwright and human rights campaigner, was chosen president, Dec. 29. In Mar. 1990 the country was officially renamed the Czech and Slovak Federal Republic. Havel failed to win reelection July 3, 1992; his bid was blocked by a Slovak-led coalition.

Slovakia declared sovereignty, July 17. Czech and Slovak leaders agreed, July 23, on a basic plan for a peaceful division of Czechoslovakia into 2 independent states.

Czech Republic

Czechoslovakia split into 2 separate states—the Czech Republic and Slovakia—on Jan. 1, 1993. Havel was elected president of the Czech Republic on Jan. 26. Record floods in July 1997 caused more than $1.7 billion in damage. The country became a full member of NATO on Mar. 12, 1999. Floods Aug. 2002 damaged cultural treasures in Prague.

Vaclav Klaus was chosen Feb. 28, 2003, to replace the retiring Havel. After Czech voters June 13-14, 2003, endorsed joining the EU, the nation became a full EU member May 1, 2004. When his Social Democratic Party fared poorly in EU elections June 11-12, Prime Min. Vladimir Spidla resigned; his successor, 34-year-old Stanislav Gross, was Europe's youngest head of government.

Denmark
Kingdom of Denmark

People: Population: 5,413,392. **Age distrib.** (%): <15: 18.7; 65+: 14.9. **Pop. density:** 331 per sq mi, 128 per sq km. **Urban:** 85.3%. **Ethnic groups:** Mainly Danish; German minority in S. **Principal languages:** Danish (official), Faroese, Greenlandic (an Inuit dialect), German. **Chief religion: Chief religions:** Evangelical Lutheran 95% (official), other Christian 3%, Muslim 2%.

Geography: Total area: 16,639 sq mi, 43,094 sq km; **Land area:** 16,368 sq mi, 42,394 sq km. **Location:** In N Europe, separating the North and Baltic seas. **Neighbors:** Germany on S, Norway on NW, Sweden on NE. **Topography:** Denmark consists of the Jutland Peninsula and about 500 islands, 100 inhabited. The land is flat or gently rolling and is almost all in productive use. **Capital:** Copenhagen, 1,066,000.

Government: Type: Constitutional monarchy. **Head of state:** Queen Margrethe II; b Apr. 16, 1940; in office: Jan. 14, 1972. **Head of gov.:** Prime Min. Anders Fogh Rasmussen; b Jan. 26, 1953; in office: Nov. 27, 2001. **Local divisions:** 14 counties, 2 kommunes. **Defense budget** (2003): $2.6 bil. **Active troops:** 22,880.

Economy: Industries: food proc., machinery, textiles & clothing, chemicals, electronics, constr., furniture. **Chief crops:** barley, wheat, potatoes, sugar beets. **Natural resources:** oil, nat. gas, fish, salt, limestone, stone, gravel, sand. **Crude oil reserves** (2003): 1.3 bil. bbls. **Arable land:** 60%. **Livestock** (2003): cattle: 1.72 mil.; chickens: 19.7 mil.; pigs: 12.95 mil.; sheep: 143,699. **Fish catch** (2002): 1,474,094 metric tons. **Electricity prod.** (2002): 36.38 bil. kWh. **Labor force** (2002 est.): services 79%, industry 17%, agriculture 4%.

Finance: Monetary unit: Krone (DKK) (Sept. 2004: 6.12 = $1 U.S.). **GDP** (2003 est.): $167.7 bil.; **per capita GDP:** $31,200; **GDP growth:** 0.3%. **Imports** (2003 est.): $54.5 bil.; partners (2002): Germany 22.3%, Sweden 12.1%, UK 8.9%, Netherlands 6.8%, France 6%, Norway 4.7%, Italy 4.3%. **Exports** (2003 est.): $64.2 bil.; partners (2002): Germany 19.4%, Sweden 11.8%, UK 9.8%, U.S. 6.4%, Norway 6%, France 4.7%, Netherlands 4.5%. **Tourism** (2002): $5.8 bil. **Budget** (2001 est.): $51.3 bil. **Intl. reserves less gold:** $24.97 bil. **Gold:** 2.14 mil oz t. **Consumer prices:** 2.1%.

Transport: Railroad: Length: 1,966 mi. **Motor vehicles** (1999): 1.85 mil pass. cars, 375,600 comm. vehicles. **Civil aviation:** 3.4 bil. pass.-mi; 28 airports. **Chief ports:** Copenhagen, Alborg, Arhus, Odense.

Communications: TV sets: 776 per 1,000 pop. **Radios:** 1,325 per 1,000 pop. **Telephone lines:** 3.6 mil. **Daily newspaper circ.:** 283.3 per 1,000 pop. **Internet** (2002): 2.8 mil. users.

Health: Life expect.: 75.2 male; 79.8 female. **Births** (per 1,000 pop.): 11.6. **Deaths** (per 1,000 pop.): 10.5. **Natural inc.:** 0.11%. **Infant mortality** (per 1,000 live births): 4.6. **AIDS rate:** 0.2%.

Education: Compulsory: ages 7-16. **Literacy:** 100%.

Major Intl. Organizations: UN and all of its specialized agencies, EU, NATO, OECD, OSCE.

Embassy: 3200 Whitehaven St. NW 20008; 234-4300.

Website: www.denmarkemb.org; www.denmark.dk

The origin of Copenhagen dates back to ancient times, when the fishing and trading place named Havn (port) grew up on a cluster of islets, but Bishop Absalon (1128-1201) is regarded as the actual founder of the city.

Danes formed a large component of the Viking raiders in the early Middle Ages. The Danish kingdom was a major power until the 17th century, when it lost its land in southern Sweden. Norway was separated in 1815, and Schleswig-Holstein in 1864. Northern Schleswig was returned in 1920.

Voters ratified the Maastricht Treaty, the basic document of the European Union, in May 1993, after rejecting it in 1992. On Sept. 28, 2000, Danes voted not to join the euro currency zone.

The **Faroe Islands** in the North Atlantic, about 300 mi. NW of the Shetlands, and 850 mi. from Denmark proper, 18 inhabited, have an area of 540 sq. mi. and pop. (2004 est.) of 46,662. They are an administrative division of Denmark, self-governing in most matters. Torshavn is the capital. Fish is a primary export (571,255 metric tons in 2002).

Greenland (Kalaallit Nunaat)

Greenland, a huge island between the North Atlantic and the Polar Sea, is separated from the North American continent by Davis Strait and Baffin Bay. Its total area is 836,330 sq. mi., 84% of which is ice-capped. Most of the island is a lofty plateau 9,000 to 10,000 ft. in altitude. The average thickness of the cap is 1,000 ft. The population (2004 est.) is 56,384. Under the 1953 Danish constitution the colony became an integral part of the realm with representatives in the Folketing (Danish legislature). The Danish parliament, 1978, approved home rule for Greenland, effective May 1, 1979. With home rule, Greenlandic place names came into official use. The technically correct name for Greenland is now Kalaallit Nunaat; the official name for its capital is Nuuk, rather than Godthab. Fish is the principal export (158,485 metric tons in 2001).

Djibouti
Republic of Djibouti

People: Population: 466,900. **Age distrib.** (%): <15: 42.6; 65+: 2.9. **Pop. density:** 53 per sq mi, 20 per sq km. **Urban:** 83.7%. **Ethnic groups:** Somali 60%, Afar 35%. **Principal languages:** French, Arabic (both official); Somali, Afar. **Chief religions:** Muslim 94%, Christian 6%.

Geography: Total area: 8,880 sq mi, 23,000 sq km; **Land area:** 8,873 sq mi, 22,980 sq km. **Location:** On E coast of Africa, separated from Arabian Peninsula by the strategically vital strait of Bab el-Mandeb. **Neighbors:** Ethiopia on W and SW, Eritrea on NW, Somalia on SE. **Topography:** The territory, divided into a low coastal plain, mountains behind, and an interior plateau, is arid, sandy, and desolate. The climate is generally hot and dry. **Capital:** Djibouti, 502,000.

Government: Type: Republic. **Head of state:** Pres. Ismail Omar Guelleh; b Nov. 27, 1947; in office: May 8, 1999. **Head of gov.:** Prime Min. Dileita Mohamed Dileita; b Mar. 12, 1958; in office: Mar. 7, 2001. **Local divisions:** 5 districts. **Defense budget** (2003): $25 mil. **Active troops:** 9,850.

Economy: Industries: constr., agricult. proc. **Chief crops:** fruits, vegetables. **Natural resources:** geothermal areas. **Livestock** (2003): cattle: 297,000; goats: 512,000. sheep: 466,000. **Fish catch** (2002 est): 350 metric tons. **Electricity prod.** (2002): 0.18 bil. kWh. **Labor force:** agri. 75%, ind. 11%, services 14%.

Finance: Monetary unit: Franc (DJF) (Sept. 2004: 169.75 = $1 U.S.). **GDP** (2002 est.): $619.0 mil.; **per capita GDP:** $1,300; **GDP growth:** 3.5%. **Imports** (2002 est.): $665.0 mil.; partners (2002): Saudi Arabia 18.2%, Ethiopia 10.5%, U.S. 9.3%, France 8.6%, China 8.3%, Netherlands 4.2%. **Exports** (2002 est.): $155.0 mil.; partners (2002): Somalia 61.9%, Yemen 21.9%, Pakistan 5.2%, Ethiopia 4.5%. **Tourism** (1998): $4 mil. **Budget** (1999 est.): $182.0 mil. **Intl. reserves less gold:** $67 mil.

Transport: Railroad: Length: 62 mi. **Motor vehicles** (1994): 13,500 pass. cars, 3,000 comm. vehicles. **Civil aviation:** 4.3 mil. pass.-mi; 3 airports. **Chief port:** Djibouti.

Communications: TV sets: 48 per 1,000 pop. **Radios:** 86 per 1,000 pop. **Telephone lines:** 9,500. **Daily newspaper circ.:** 8 per 1,000 pop. **Internet:** 6,500 users.

Health: Life expect.: 41.8 male; 44.4 female. **Births** (per 1,000 pop.): 40.4. **Deaths** (per 1,000 pop.): 19.4. **Natural inc.:** 2.10%. **Infant mortality** (per 1,000 live births): 105.5. **AIDS rate:** 2.9%.

Education: Compulsory: ages 6-15. **Literacy:** 67.9%.

Major Intl. Organizations: UN (FAO, IBRD, ILO, IMF, IMO, WHO, WTrO), AL, AU.

Embassy: 1156 15th St. NW, Ste. 515, 20005; 331-0270.

Website: www.office-tourisme.dj

France gained control of the territory in stages between 1862 and 1900. As French Somaliland it became an overseas territory of France in 1945; in 1967 it was renamed the French Territory of the Afars and the Issas.

Ethiopia and Somalia have renounced their claims to the area, but each has accused the other of trying to gain control. There were clashes between Afars (ethnically related to Ethiopians) and Issas (related to Somalis) in 1976. Immigrants from both countries continued to enter the country up to independence, which came June 27, 1977.

French aid is the mainstay of the economy, as well as assistance from Arab countries. A peace accord Dec. 1994 ended a 3-year-long uprising by Afar rebels. As of mid-2004 some 2,800 French and 1,500 U.S. troops were based in Djibouti.

Dominica
Commonwealth of Dominica

People: Population: 69,278. **Age distrib.** (%): <15: 28.3; 65+: 7.9. **Pop. density:** 238 per sq mi, 92 per sq km. **Urban:** 72.0%. **Ethnic groups:** Black, Creole, White, Carib Amerindian. **Principal languages:** English (official), French patois. **Chief religions:** Roman Catholic 77%, Protestant 15%.

Geography: Total area: 291 sq mi, 754 sq km; **Land area:** 291 sq mi, 754 sq km. **Location:** In Eastern Caribbean, most northerly Windward Isl. **Neighbors:** Guadeloupe to N, Martinique to S. **Topography:** Mountainous, a central ridge running from N to S, terminating in cliffs; volcanic in origin, with numerous thermal springs; rich deep topsoil on leeward side, red tropical clay on windward coast. **Capital:** Roseau, 27,000.

Government: Type: Parliamentary democracy. **Head of state:** Pres. Nicholas Liverpool; b 1934; in office: Oct. 2, 2003. **Head of gov.:** Prime Min. Roosevelt Skerrit; b June 8, 1972; in office: Jan. 8, 2004. **Local divisions:** 10 parishes.

Economy: Industries: soap, coconut oil, tourism, copra, furniture, cement blocks, shoes. **Chief crops:** bananas, citrus, mangoes, coconuts, cocoa. **Natural resources:** timber, hydropower. **Arable land:** 9%. **Livestock** (2003): cattle: 13,400; chickens: 190,000; goats: 9,700; pigs: 5,000; sheep: 7,600. **Fish catch** (2002): 1,220 metric tons. **Electricity prod.** (2002): 0.07 bil. kWh. **Labor force:** agriculture 40%, industry and commerce 32%, services 28%.

Finance: Monetary unit: East Caribbean Dollar (XCD) (Sept. 2004: 2.70 = $1 U.S.). **GDP** (2002 est.): $380.0 mil.; **per capita GDP:** $5,400; **GDP growth:** -1.0%. **Imports** (2003 est.): $98.2 mil.; **partners** (2002): China 23.8%, U.S. 23.8%, Trinidad and Tobago 11.9%, South Korea 7.6%, UK 7.1%, Japan 4.3%. **Exports** (2003 est.): $39.0 mil.; **partners** (2002): UK 36.1%, Jamaica 16.4%, U.S. 8.2%, Antigua and Barbuda 6.6%, Guyana 4.9%, Trinidad and Tobago 4.9%. **Tourism:** $51 mil. **Budget** (2001): $84.4 mil. **Intl. reserves less gold:** $32 mil. **Consumer prices:** 1.6%.

Transport: Motor vehicles (1998): 8,700 pass. cars, 3,400 comm. vehicles. **Civil aviation:** 2 airports. **Chief port:** Roseau.

Communications: TV sets: 232 per 1,000 pop. **Radios:** 648 per 1,000 pop. **Telephone lines** (2002): 23,700. **Internet** (2002): 12,500 users.

Health: Life expect.: 71.5 male; 77.4 female. **Births** (per 1,000 pop.): 16.2. **Deaths** (per 1,000 pop.): 6.9. **Natural inc.:** 0.94%. **Infant mortality** (per 1,000 live births): 14.8.

Education: Compulsory: ages 5-17. **Literacy:** 94%.

Major Intl. Organizations: UN (FAO, IBRD, ILO, IMF, IMO, WHO, WTrO), Caricom, the Commonwealth, OAS, OECS.

Embassy: 3216 New Mexico Ave. NW 20016; 364-6781.

Website: www.ndcdominica.dm

A British colony since 1805, Dominica was granted self-government in 1967. Independence was achieved Nov. 3, 1978.

Hurricane David struck, Aug. 30, 1979, devastating the island and destroying the banana plantations, Dominica's economic mainstay. Coups were attempted in 1980 and 1981.

Dominica participated in the 1983 U.S.-led invasion of nearby Grenada. Prime Min. Pierre Charles, 49, died of a heart attack Jan. 6, 2004, and was succeeded by Roosevelt Skerrit.

Dominican Republic

People: Population: 8,833,634. **Age distrib.** (%): <15: 33.7; 65+: 5. **Pop. density:** 473 per sq mi, 183 per sq km. **Urban:** 59.3%. **Ethnic groups:** Creole 73%, White 16%, Black 11%. **Principal languages:** Spanish (official). **Chief religion:** Roman Catholic 95%.

Geography: Total area: 18,815 sq mi, 48,730 sq km; **Land area:** 18,680 sq mi, 48,380 sq km. **Location:** In West Indies, sharing isl. of Hispaniola with Haiti. **Neighbors:** Haiti on W, Puerto Rico (U.S.) to E. **Topography:** The Cordillera Central range crosses the center of the country, rising to over 10,000 ft., highest in the Caribbean. The Cibao Valley to the N is major agricultural area. **Capital:** Santo Domingo, 1,865,000. **Cities (urban aggr.):** Santiago de los Caballeros, 804,000.

Government: Type: Republic. **Head of state and gov.:** Pres. Leonel Fernández Reyna; b Dec. 26, 1953; in office: Aug. 16, 2004. **Local divisions:** 29 provinces and national district. **Defense budget** (2002): $125 mil. **Active troops:** 24,500.

Economy: Industries: tourism, sugar proc., mining, textiles, cement, tobacco. **Chief crops:** sugarcane, coffee, cotton, cocoa, tobacco, rice, beans. **Natural resources:** nickel, bauxite, gold, silver. **Arable land:** 21%. **Livestock** (2003): cattle: 2.16 mil.; chickens: 46.5 mil.; goats: 188,500; pigs: 577,500; sheep: 122,000. **Fish catch** (2002): 21,893 metric tons. **Electricity prod.** (2002): 9.58 bil. kWh. **Labor force** (1998 est.): services and government 58.7%, industry 24.3%, agriculture 17%.

Finance: Monetary unit: Peso (DOP) (Sept. 2004: 36.25 = $1 U.S.). **GDP** (2003 est.): $52.2 bil.; **per capita GDP:** $6,000; **GDP growth:** -1.8%. **Imports** (2003 est.): $7.9 bil.; **partners** (2002): U.S. 51.1%, Venezuela 9.1%, Mexico 4.8%. **Exports** (2003 est.): $5.5 bil.; **partners** (2002): U.S. 85.3%, Canada 1.6%, UK 1.6%. **Tourism:** $2.92 bil. **Budget** (2001 est.): $3.2 bil. **Intl. reserves less gold:** $170 mil. **Gold:** 20,000 oz t. **Consumer prices:** 27.4%.

Transport: Railroad: Length: 934 mi. **Motor vehicles** (2001): 561,300 pass. cars, 284,700 comm. vehicles. **Civil aviation:** 3.1 mil. pass.-mi; 13 airports. **Chief ports:** Santo Domingo, San Pedro de Macoris, Puerto Plata.

Communications: TV sets: 96 per 1,000 pop. **Radios:** 178 per 1,000 pop. **Telephone lines:** 901,800. **Daily newspaper circ.:** 27.5 per 1,000 pop. **Internet:** 500,000 users.

Health: Life expect.: 66.0 male; 69.4 female. **Births** (per 1,000 pop.): 23.6. **Deaths** (per 1,000 pop.): 7.1. **Natural inc.:** 1.65%. **Infant mortality** (per 1,000 live births): 33.3. **AIDS rate:** 1.7%.

Education: Compulsory: ages 5-13. **Literacy:** 84.7%.

Major Intl. Organizations: UN (FAO, IBRD, ILO, IMF, IMO, WHO, WTrO), OAS.

Embassy: 1715 22d St. NW 20008; 332-6280.

Websites: www.domrep.org; www.presidencia.gov.do/ingles

Carib and Arawak Indians inhabited the island of Hispaniola when Columbus landed in 1492. The city of Santo Domingo, founded 1496, is the oldest settlement by Europeans in the hemisphere and has the supposed ashes of Columbus in an elaborate tomb in its ancient cathedral.

The western third of the island was ceded to France in 1697. Santo Domingo itself was ceded to France in 1795. Haitian leader Toussaint L'Ouverture seized it, 1801. Spain returned intermittently 1803-21, as several native republics came and went. Haiti ruled again, 1822-44; Spanish occupation occurred 1861-63.

The country was occupied by U.S. Marines from 1916 to 1924, when a constitutionally elected government was installed.

In 1930, Gen. Rafael Leonidas Trujillo Molina was elected president. Trujillo ruled brutally until his assassination in 1961. Pres. Joaquín Balaguer, appointed by Trujillo in 1960, resigned under pressure in 1962.

Juan Bosch, elected president in the first free elections in 38 years, was overthrown in 1963. On Apr. 24, 1965, a revolt was launched by followers of Bosch and others, including a few Communists. Four days later U.S. Marines intervened against pro-Bosch forces. Token units were later sent by 5 South American countries as a peacekeeping force. A provisional government supervised a June 1966 election, in which Balaguer defeated Bosch. Balaguer remained in office for most of the next 28 years, but his May 1994 reelection was widely denounced as fraudulent. He cut short his term and on June 30, 1996, Leonel Fernández Reyna was elected.

Hurricane Georges struck Sept. 22, 1998, causing extensive property damage and claiming more than 200 lives. The leftist candidate, Hipólito Mejía, won a presidential vote May 16, 2000. With the nation reeling from a banking scandal and soaring inflation, Fernández defeated Mejía in the election of May 16, 2004. Floods and mudslides in late May killed about 395 people.

East Timor
Democratic Republic of Timor-Leste

People: Population: 1,019,252. **Age distrib.** (%): NA. **Pop. density:** 176 per sq mi, 68 per sq km. **Urban:** 7.6%. **Ethnic groups:** Austronesian, Papuan. **Principal languages:** Tetum, Portuguese (both official); Indonesian, English, other native languages. **Chief religions:** Roman Catholic 90%, Muslim 4%, Protestant 3%.

Geography: Total area: 5,794 sq mi, 15,007 sq km. **Location:** E half of Timor Is. in the SW Pacific O. **Neighbors:** Indonesia (West Timor) on W. **Topography:** Terrain is rugged, rising to 9,721 ft at Mt. Ramelau. **Capital:** Dili, 49,000.

Government: Type: Republic. **Head of state:** Pres. Xanana Gusmão; b June 20, 1946; in office: May 20, 2002. **Head of gov.:** Prime Min. Mari Alkatiri; b Nov. 26, 1949; in office: May 20, 2002. **Local divisions:** 13 districts. **Active troops:** 650.

Economy: Industries: printing, soap, handicrafts, clothing. **Chief crops:** coffee, rice, maize, cassava, sweet potatoes. **Natural resources:** gold, oil, nat. gas, mang., marble. **Livestock** (2003): cattle: 170,000; chickens: 1.30 mil.; goats: 80,000; pigs: 345,000; sheep: 25,000.

Finance: Monetary unit: U.S. dollar and Indonesian Rupiah (Sept. 2002: 9,113 = $1 U.S.). **GDP** (2001 est.): $440.0 mil.; **per capita GDP:** $500; **GDP growth:** -3.0%. **Imports** (2001 est.): $237.0 mil.; **Exports** (2001 est.): $8.0 mil.; **Budget** (2003 est.): $97.0 mil.

Transport: Civil aviation: 3 airports. **Chief port:** Dili.

Health: Life expect.: 63.3 male; 67.9 female. **Births** (per 1,000 pop.): 27.5. **Deaths** (per 1,000 pop.): 6.4. **Natural inc.:** 2.11%. **Infant mortality** (per 1,000 live births): 48.9.

Education: Compulsory: ages 7-15. Literacy (2001): 48%.

Major Intl. Organizations: UN.

Website: www.gov.east-timor.org

The collapse of Portuguese rule in East Timor led to an outbreak of factional fighting in Aug. 1975 and an invasion by Indonesia in Dec. Indonesia annexed East Timor as a 27th province in 1976, despite international condemnation. In over 2 decades some 200,000 Timorese died as a result of civil war, famine, and persecution by Indonesian authorities. In a referendum held Aug. 30, 1999, under UN auspices, Timorese voted overwhelmingly for independence. Pro-Indonesian militias then went on a rampage, terrorizing the population. Under pressure, the government allowed entrance of an international peacekeeping force, which began arriving in Sept.; a UN interim administration formally took command Oct. 26, 1999.

Pro-independence forces won elections for a constituent assembly Aug. 30, 2001. Xanana Gusmão, a former guerrilla leader, won the presidential election Apr. 14, 2002. East Timor became independent May 20 and entered the UN Sept. 27. A sovereignty dispute with Australia over the oil-rich Timor Sea was resolved in Aug. 2004.

Ecuador
Republic of Ecuador

People: Population: 13,212,742. **Age distrib.** (%): <15: 35.4; 65+: 4.4. **Pop. density:** 124 per sq mi, 48 per sq km. **Urban:** 61.8%. **Ethnic groups:** Mestizo 65%, Amerindian 25%, Black 3%. **Principal languages:** Spanish (official), Amerindian languages (especially Quechua). **Chief religion:** Roman Catholic 95%.

Geography: Total area: 109,483 sq mi, 283,560 sq km; **Land area:** 106,888 sq mi, 276,840 sq km. **Location:** In NW South America, on Pacific coast, astride the Equator. **Neighbors:** Colombia on N, Peru on E and S. **Topography:** Two ranges of Andes run N and S, splitting the country into 3 zones: hot, humid lowlands on the coast; temperate highlands between the ranges; and rainy, tropical lowlands to the E. **Capital:** Quito, 1,451,000. **Cities (urban aggr.):** Guayaquil, 2,077,000.

Government: Type: Republic. **Head of state and gov.:** Pres. Lucio Gutiérrez Borbúa; b Mar. 23, 1957; in office: Jan. 15, 2003. **Local divisions:** 22 provinces. **Defense budget** (2003): $841 mil. **Active troops:** 59,500.

Economy: Industries: oil, food proc., textiles, metal work, paper & wood products. **Chief crops:** bananas, coffee, cocoa, rice, potatoes, cassava, plantains, sugarcane. **Natural resources:** oil, fish, timber, hydropower. **Crude oil reserves** (2003): 4.6 bil. bbls. **Arable land:** 6%. **Livestock** (2003): cattle: 4.98 mil.; chickens: 142.0 mil.; goats: 279,000; pigs: 3.01 mil.; sheep: 2.65 mil. **Fish catch** (2002 est) 388,721 metric tons. **Electricity prod.** (2002): 11.54 bil. kWh. **Labor force** (2001 est.): agriculture 30%, industry 25%, services 45%.

Finance: Monetary unit: U.S. dollar. **GDP** (2003 est.): $45.5 bil.; **per capita GDP:** $3,300; **GDP growth:** 2.6%. **Imports** (2003 est.): $6.2 bil.; partners (2002): U.S. 26.8%, Colombia 13.6%, Brazil 6.5%, Venezuela 5.7%, Japan 5.7%, Chile 4.2%. **Exports** (2003 est.): $6.1 bil.; partners (2002): U.S. 40.3%, Colombia 5.8%, Germany 5.4%, South Korea 5.3%, Italy 4.6%. **Tourism:** $406 mil. **Budget** (2002): $5.3 bil. **Intl. reserves less gold:** $547 mil. **Gold:** 850,000 oz t. **Consumer prices:** 7.9%.

Transport: Railroad: Length: 600 mi. **Motor vehicles** (1999): 322,300 pass. cars, 272,000 comm. vehicles. **Civil aviation:** 338.0 mil. pass.-mi; 61 airports. **Chief ports:** Guayaquil, Manta, Esmeraldas, Puerto Bolivar.

Communications: TV sets: 213 per 1,000 pop. **Radios:** 406 per 1,000 pop. **Telephone lines:** 1.5 mil. **Daily newspaper circ.:** 96.5 per 1,000 pop. **Internet:** 569,700 users.

Health: Life expect.: 73.2 male; 79.0 female. **Births** (per 1,000 pop.): 23.2. **Deaths** (per 1,000 pop.): 4.3. **Natural inc.:** 1.89%. **Infant mortality** (per 1,000 live births): 24.5. **AIDS rate:** 0.3%.

Education: Compulsory: ages 5-14. **Literacy:** 92.5%.

Major Intl. Organizations: UN (FAO, IBRD, ILO, IMF, IMO, WHO, WTrO), OAS.

Embassy: 2535 15th St. NW 20009; 234-7200.

Website: www.ecuador.org

The region, which was the northern Inca empire, was conquered by Spain in 1533. Liberation forces defeated the Spanish May 24, 1822, near Quito. Ecuador became part of the Great Colombia Republic but seceded, May 13, 1830.

Since 1972, the economy has revolved around petroleum exports; oil revenues have declined since 1982, causing severe economic problems. Ecuador suspended interest payments for 1987 on its estimated $8.2 billion foreign debt following a Mar. 5-6 earthquake that left 20,000 homeless and destroyed a stretch of the country's main oil pipeline.

Ecuadoran Indians staged protests in the 1990s to demand greater rights. A border war with Peru flared from Jan. 26, 1995, until a truce took effect Mar. 1. Vice-Pres. Alberto Dahik resigned and fled Ecuador, Oct. 11, 1995, to avoid arrest on corruption charges. Elected president in a runoff, July 7, 1996, Abdalá Bucaram—a populist known as El Loco, or "The Crazy One"—imposed stiff price increases and other austerity measures. His rising unpopularity and erratic behavior led the National Congress, Feb. 6, 1997, to dismiss him for "mental incapacity." Bucaram went into exile, and Congress, on Feb. 11, confirmed its leader, Fabian Alarcón, as president for 18 months. Voters endorsed the actions in a referendum May 25.

Jamil Mahuad Witt, mayor of Quito, won a presidential runoff election July 12, 1998. In Sept. 1998 and Mar. 1999 he imposed emergency measures to cope with a continuing economic crisis. Opposed by Indian groups and military leaders, he was ousted Jan. 21, 2000, and succeeded by Vice-Pres. Gustavo Noboa Bejarano. Noboa went ahead with a plan introduced by Mahuad to replace the sucre with the U.S. dollar as Ecuador's currency. Lucio Gutiérrez Borbúa, a leader in the 2000 coup, won a presidential runoff Nov. 24, 2002. Noboa, under investigation for financial mismanagement, went into exile Aug. 23, 2003.

The **Galápagos Islands,** pop. (2001 est.) 16,000, about 600 mi. to the W, are the home of huge tortoises and other unusual animals. The oil tanker *Jessica* ran aground Jan. 16, 2001, off San Cristóbal Is., spilling some 185,000 gallons of fuel.

Egypt
Arab Republic of Egypt

People: Population: 76,117,421. **Age distrib.** (%): <15: 33.96; 65+: 3.86. **Pop. density:** 198 per sq mi, 76 per sq km. **Urban:** 42.1%. **Ethnic groups:** Egyptian Arab 99%. **Principal languages:** Arabic (official); English, French. **Chief religions:** Muslim (official; mostly Sunni) 94%, Coptic Christian and other 6%.

Geography: Total area: 386,662 sq mi, 1,001,450 sq km; **Land area:** 384,345 sq mi, 995,450 sq km. **Location:** Northeast corner of Africa. **Neighbors:** Libya on W, Sudan on S, Israel and Gaza Strip on E. **Topography:** Almost entirely desolate and barren, with hills and mountains in E and along Nile. The Nile Valley, where most of the people live, stretches 550 miles. **Capital:** Cairo, 10,834,000. **Cities (urban aggr.):** Alexandria, 3,506,000.

Government: Type: Republic. **Head of state:** Pres. Hosni Mubarak; b May 4, 1928; in office: Oct. 14, 1981. **Head of gov.:** Prime Min. Ahmed Nazif; b 1952; in office: July 14, 2004. **Local divisions:** 26 governorates. **Defense budget** (2002): $1.7 bil. **Active troops:** 450,000.

Economy: Industries: textiles, food proc., tourism, chemicals, hydrocarbons, constr., cement, metals. **Chief crops:** cotton, rice, corn, wheat, beans, fruits, vegetables. **Natural resources:** oil, nat. gas, iron ore, phosphates, mang., limestone, gypsum, talc, asbestos, lead, zinc. **Crude oil reserves** (2003): 3.7 bil. bbls. **Arable land:** 2%. **Livestock** (2003): cattle: 3.81 mil.; chickens: 92.0 mil.; goats: 3.47 mil.; pigs: 30,000; sheep: 4.67 mil. **Fish catch** (2002): 801,466 metric tons. **Electricity prod.** (2002): 81.27 bil. kWh. **Labor force** (2001 est.): agriculture 32%, industry 17%, services 51%.

Finance: Monetary unit: Pound (EGP) (Sept. 2004: 6.23 = $1 U.S.). **GDP** (2003 est.): $294.3 bil.; **per capita GDP:** $3,900; **GDP growth:** 2.8%. **Imports** (2003 est.): $14.8 bil.; partners (2002): U.S. 16.1%, Germany 7.5%, Italy 6.4%, France 6.2%, China 4.8%. **Exports** (2003 est.): $8.8 bil.; partners (2002): U.S. 18.5%, Italy 13.8%, UK 8.5%, France 4%. **Tourism:** $4.6 bil. **Budget** (2003 est.): $18.1 bil. **Intl. reserves less gold:** $9.15 bil. **Gold:** 2.43 mil oz t. **Consumer prices:** 4.2%.

Transport: Railroad: Length: 3,172 mi. **Motor vehicles** (1999): 1.7 mil pass. cars, 600,000 comm. vehicles. **Civil aviation:** 5.0 bil. pass.-mi; 71 airports. **Chief ports:** Alexandria, Port Said, Suez, Damietta.

Communications: TV sets: 170 per 1,000 pop. **Radios:** 317 per 1,000 pop. **Telephone lines:** 8.7 mil. **Daily newspaper circ.:** 31.2 per 1,000 pop. **Internet:** 2.7 mil. users.

Health: Life expect.: 68.2 male; 73.3 female. **Births** (per 1,000 pop.): 23.8. **Deaths** (per 1,000 pop.): 5.3. **Natural inc.:** 1.85%. **Infant mortality** (per 1,000 live births): 33.9. **AIDS rate:** <0.1%.

Education: Compulsory: ages 6-13. **Literacy:** 57.7%.

Major Intl. Organizations: UN (FAO, IBRD, ILO, IMF, IMO, WHO, WTrO), AL, AU.

Embassy: 3521 International Ct. NW 20008; 895-5400.

Website: www.egyptembassy.us; www.sis.gov.eg

Archaeological records of ancient Egyptian civilization date back to 4000 BC. A unified kingdom arose around 3200 BC and extended its way south into Nubia and as far north as Syria. A high culture of rulers and priests was built on an economic base of serfdom, fertile soil, and annual flooding of the Nile.

Imperial decline facilitated conquest by Asian invaders (Hyksos, Assyrians). The last native dynasty fell in 341 BC to the Persians, who were in turn replaced by Greeks (Alexander and the Ptolemies), Romans, Byzantines, and Arabs, who introduced Islam and the Arabic language. The ancient Egyptian language is preserved only in Coptic Christian liturgy.

Egypt was ruled as part of larger Islamic empires for many centuries. Britain intervened in Egypt in 1882 and ruled the country as a protectorate, 1914-22. A 1936 treaty strengthened Egyptian autonomy, but Britain retained bases in Egypt and a condominium over the Sudan. When the state of Israel was proclaimed in 1948, Egypt joined other Arab nations invading Israel and was defeated. In 1951 Egypt abrogated the 1936 treaty; the Sudan became independent in 1956.

An uprising on July 23, 1952 was led by the Society of Free Officers, who named Maj. Gen. Mohammed Naguib commander in chief and forced King Farouk to abdicate. When the republic was proclaimed June 18, 1953, Naguib became its first president and premier. Lt. Col. Gamal Abdel Nasser removed Naguib and became premier in 1954 and president In 1956. Nasser emerged as the most influential leader in the Arab world at the time; within Egypt, he pushed construction of the Aswan High Dam, completed in 1970.

After guerrilla raids across its border, Israel invaded Egypt's Sinai Peninsula, Oct. 29, 1956. Egypt rejected a cease-fire demand by Britain and France; on Oct. 31 the 2 nations dropped bombs and on Nov. 5-6 landed forces. Egypt and Israel accepted a UN cease-fire; fighting ended Nov. 7. Subsequently, a UN Emergency Force guarded the border. Full-scale war with Israel broke out again, June 5, 1967; before it ended under a UN cease-fire June 10, Israel had captured Gaza and the Sinai Peninsula and taken control of the E bank of the Suez Canal.

Nasser died Sept. 28,1970, and was replaced by Vice Pres. Anwar Sadat. In a surprise attack Oct. 6, 1973, Egyptian forces crossed the Suez Canal into the Sinai. (At the same time, Syrian forces attacked Israelis on the Golan Heights.) Egypt was supplied by a USSR military airlift; the U.S. responded with an airlift to Israel. Israel counterattacked, crossed the canal, and surrounded Suez City. A UN cease-fire took effect Oct. 24. Under an agreement signed Jan. 18, 1974, Israeli forces withdrew from the canal's W bank; limited numbers of Egyptian forces occupied a strip along the E bank. A second accord was signed in 1975, with Israel yielding Sinai oil fields.

Pres. Sadat's surprise visit to Jerusalem, Nov. 1977, opened the prospect of peace with Israel. On Mar. 26, 1979, Egypt and Israel signed a formal peace treaty, ending 30 years of war, and establishing diplomatic relations. Israel returned control of the Sinai to Egypt in Apr. 1982. However, tension between Muslim fundamentalists and Christians had caused street riots leading to a nationwide security crackdown in Sept. 1981, and on Oct. 6, 1981, Pres. Sadat was assassinated by Muslim extremists within the army; he was succeeded by Hosni Mubarak.

Egypt saw a rising tide of Islamic fundamentalist violence in the 1990s. U.S. aid to Egypt, totaling more than $50 billion since 1975, helped to keep Mubarak in power. Egypt supported the U.S.-led coalition against Iraq in the Persian Gulf War, 1991. Egyptian security forces conducted raids against Islamic militants, some of whom were executed for terrorism. Naguib Mahfouz, winner of the 1988 Nobel Prize for literature, was stabbed by Islamic militants Oct. 14, 1994. Pres. Mubarak escaped assassination in Ethiopia, June 26, 1995; Egypt blamed Sudan for the attack. On Nov. 17, 1997, near Luxor, Muslim extremists killed 58 foreign tourists and 4 Egyptians.

Mubarak, who was grazed by a knife-wielding assailant Sept. 6, 1999, was confirmed by popular vote Sept. 26 for a 4th presidential term. An EgyptAir jetliner bound from New York to Cairo plunged into the Atlantic near Nantucket Is., Oct. 31, 1999, killing all 217 people on board. Fire on a train bound from Cairo to Luxor, Feb. 20, 2002, left more than 360 people dead. An Egyptian charter plane plunged into the Red Sea shortly after takeoff Jan. 3, 2004, killing 148 people, including 133 French tourists.

The **Suez Canal**, 103 mi. long, links the Mediterranean and Red seas. It was built by a French corporation 1859-69, but Britain obtained controlling interest in 1875. The last British troops were removed June 13, 1956. On July 26, Egypt nationalized the canal.

El Salvador
Republic of El Salvador

People: Population: 6,587,541. **Age distrib.** (%): <15: 37.4; 65+: 5.1. **Pop. density:** 823 per sq mi, 318 per sq km. **Urban:** 59.6%. **Ethnic groups:** Mestizo 90%, White 9%, Amerindian 1%. **Principal languages:** Spanish (official), Nahua. **Chief religions:** Roman Catholic 83%, many Protestant groups.

Geography: Total area: 8,124 sq mi, 21,040 sq km; **Land area:** 8,000 sq mi, 20,720 sq km. **Location:** In Central America. **Neighbors:** Guatemala on W, Honduras on N. **Topography:** A hot Pacific coastal plain in the south rises to a cooler plateau and valley region, densely populated. The N is mountainous, including many volcanoes. **Capital:** San Salvador, 1,424,000.

Government: Type: Republic. **Head of state and gov.:** Pres. Antonio Elías Saca González; b Mar. 9, 1965; in office: June 1, 2004. **Local divisions:** 14 departments. **Defense budget** (2003): $106 mil. **Active troops:** 15,500.

Economy: Industries: food proc., beverages, oil, chemicals, fertilizer, textiles, furniture, light metals. **Chief crops:** coffee, sugar, corn, rice, beans, oilseed, cotton, sorghum. **Natural resources:** hydropower, geothermal power, oil. **Arable land:** 27%. **Livestock** (2003): cattle: 1.0 mil.; chickens: 8.1 mil.; goats: 10,750; pigs: 153,480; sheep: 5,100. **Fish catch** (2002): 35,236 metric tons. **Electricity prod.** (2002): 4.29 bil. kWh. **Labor force** (1999 est.): agriculture 30%, industry 15%, services 55%.

Finance: Monetary unit: Colon (SVC) (Sept. 2004: 8.75 = $1 U.S.). **GDP** (2003 est.): $31.0 bil.; **per capita GDP:** $4,800; **GDP growth:** 1.4%. **Imports** (2003 est.): $5.5 bil.; partners (2002): U.S. 38.2%, Guatemala 9.9%, Mexico 6.1%. **Exports** (2003 est.): $3.2 bil.; partners (2002): U.S. 62.9%, Guatemala 11.9%, Honduras 6.8%, Nicaragua 4.4%. **Tourism** (2002): $342 mil. **Budget** (2001 est.): $2.5 bil. **Intl. reserves less gold:** $1.31 bil. **Gold:** 470,000 oz t. **Consumer prices:** 2.1%.

Transport: Railroad: Length: 176 mi. **Motor vehicles** (2000): 148,000 pass. cars, 250,800 comm. vehicles. **Civil aviation:** 1.8 bil. pass.-mi; 4 airports. **Chief ports:** La Union, Acajutla, La Libertad.

Communications: TV sets: 191 per 1,000 pop. **Radios:** 478 per 1,000 pop. **Telephone lines:** 752,600. **Daily newspaper circ.:** 28.3 per 1,000 pop. **Internet** (2002): 550,000 users.

Health: Life expect.: 67.3 male; 74.7 female. **Births** (per 1,000 pop.): 27.5. **Deaths** (per 1,000 pop.): 5.9. **Natural inc.:** 2.15%. **Infant mortality** (per 1,000 live births): 25.9. **AIDS rate:** 0.7%.

Education: Compulsory: ages 7-15. **Literacy:** 80.2%.

Major Intl. Organizations: UN (FAO, IBRD, ILO, IMF, IMO, WHO, WTrO), OAS.

Embassy: 2308 California St. NW 20008; 265-9671.

Website: www.elsalvador.org (Spanish & English)

El Salvador became independent of Spain in 1821, and of the Central American Federation in 1839.

A fight with Honduras in 1969 over the presence of 300,000 Salvadoran workers left 2,000 dead.

A military coup overthrew the government of Pres. Carlos Humberto Romero in 1979, but the ruling military-civilian junta failed to quell a rebellion by leftist insurgents, armed by Cuba and Nicaragua. Extreme right-wing death squads organized to eliminate suspected leftists were blamed for thousands of deaths in the 1980s. The Reagan administration staunchly supported the government with military aid. The 12-year civil war ended Jan. 16, 1992, as the government and leftist rebels signed a formal peace treaty. The civil war had taken the lives of some 75,000 people. The treaty provided for military and political reforms.

Nine soldiers, including 3 officers, were indicted Jan. 1990 in the Nov. 1989 slaying of 6 Jesuit priests in San Salvador. Two of the officers received maximum 30-year jail sentences. They were released Mar. 20, 1993, when the National Assembly passed a sweeping amnesty.

Francisco Flores, candidate of the right-wing ARENA party, won the presidential election of Mar. 7, 1999. Another ARENA nominee, Antonio Saca, a businessman and former sportscaster, won the presidential election of Mar. 21, 2004.

Equatorial Guinea
Republic of Equatorial Guinea

People: Population: 523,051. **Age distrib.** (%): <15: 42.4; 65+: 3.8. **Pop. density:** 48 per sq mi, 19 per sq km. **Urban:** 48.1%. **Ethnic groups:** Fang 83%, Bubi 10%. **Principal languages:** Spanish, French (both official), Fang, Bubi, pidgin English, Portuguese Creole, Ibo. **Chief religions:** nominally Christian and predominantly Roman Catholic, pagan practices.

Geography: Total area: 10,831 sq mi, 28,051 sq km; **Land area:** 10,831 sq mi, 28,051 sq km. **Location:** Bioko Isl. off W Africa coast in Gulf of Guinea, and Rio Muni, mainland enclave. **Neighbors:** Gabon on S, Cameroon on E and N. **Topography:** Bioko Isl. consists of 2 volcanic mountains and a connecting valley. Rio Muni, with over 90% of the area, has a coastal plain and low hills beyond. **Capital:** Malabo, 95,000.

Government: Type: Republic. **Head of state:** Pres. Teodoro Obiang Nguema Mbasogo; b June 5, 1942; in office: Oct. 10, 1979. **Head of gov.:** Prime Min. Miguel Abia Biteo Borico; b 1961; in office: June 14, 2004. **Local divisions:** 7 provinces. **Defense budget** (2003): $6.0 mil. **Active troops:** 1,320.

Economy: Industries: oil, fishing, sawmilling, nat. gas. **Chief crops:** coffee, cocoa, rice, yams, cassava, bananas. **Natural resources:** oil, timber, gold, mang., uranium. **Crude oil reserves** (2003): 12.0 mil. bbls. **Arable land:** 5%. **Livestock** (2003): cattle: 5,050; chickens: 320,000; goats: 9,000; pigs: 6,100; sheep: 37,600. **Fish catch** (2002 est): 3,500 metric tons. **Electricity prod.** (2002): 0.03 bil. kWh.

Finance: Monetary unit: CFA Franc BEAC (XAF) (Sept. 2004: 539.54 = $1 U.S.). **GDP** (2002 est.): $1.3 bil.; **per capita GDP:** $2,700; **GDP growth:** 20.0%. **Imports** (2003 est.): $1.4 bil.; partners (2002): U.S. 27.8%, Spain 15.1%, UK 14.2%, Norway 10.7%, France 10%, Netherlands 4.6%, Italy 4.4%. **Exports** (2003 est.): $2.1 bil.; partners (2002): U.S. 28.3%, Spain 25.3%, China 17.5%, Canada 10.6%, France 5%. **Tourism** (2001): $14 mil. **Budget** (2001 est.): $158.0 mil. **Intl. reserves less gold:** $160 mil.

Transport: Motor vehicles: 4,000 pass. cars, 3,600 comm. vehicles. **Civil aviation:** 621,371 pass.-mi; 2 airport. **Chief ports:** Malabo, Bata.

Communications: TV sets: 116 per 1,000 pop. **Radios:** 429 per 1,000 pop. **Telephone lines:** 9,600. **Daily newspaper circ.:** 4.9 per 1,000 pop. **Internet** (2002): 1,800 users.

Health: Life expect.: 53.0 male; 57.4 female. **Births** (per 1,000 pop.): 36.6. **Deaths** (per 1,000 pop.): 12.3. **Natural inc.:** 2.43%. **Infant mortality** (per 1,000 live births): 87.1.

Education: Compulsory: ages 7-11. **Literacy:** 85.7%.

Major Intl. Organizations: UN (FAO, IBRD, ILO, IMF, IMO, WHO), AU.

Embassy: 2020 16th St. NW 20009; 202-518-5700.

Website: www.embassy.org/embassies/gq.html

Fernando Po (now Bioko) Island was reached by Portugal in the late 15th century and ceded to Spain in 1778. Independence came Oct. 12, 1968. Riots occurred in 1969 over disputes between the island and the more backward Rio Muni province on the mainland. Masie Nguema Biyogo, a mainlander, became pres. for life in 1972.

Masie's reign was one of the most brutal in Africa, resulting in a bankrupted nation; most of the nation's 7,000 Europeans emigrated. He was ousted in a military coup, Aug. 1979. Teodoro Obiang Nguema Mbasogo, leader of the coup, became president and installed his family members in key government posts. His regime eventually agreed to elections, held Nov. 21, 1993. These were nominally won by the ruling party, but boycotted by opposition parties that maintained the rules were rigged. Elections for president, Feb. 25, 1996, and Dec. 15, 2002, were similarly condemned.

Oil sales, especially to the U.S., have boomed in recent years. Authorities in Zimbabwe and Equatorial Guinea arrested 85 people in Mar. 2004 on charges of plotting to overthrow the Obiang regime. Mark Thatcher, son of the former British prime min., was arrested in South Africa Aug. 25 for alleged involvement.

Eritrea
State of Eritrea
People: Population: 4,447,307. **Age distrib.** (%): <15: 42.9; 65+: 3.2. **Pop. density:** 95 per sq mi, 37 per sq km. **Urban:** 19.9%. **Ethnic groups:** Tigrinya 50%, Tigre and Kunama 40%, Afar 4%, Saho 3%. **Principal languages:** Arabic, Tigrinya (both official); Afar, Amharic, Tigre, Kunama, other Cushitic languages. **Chief religions:** Muslim, Coptic Christian, Roman Catholic, Protestant.
Geography: Total area: 46,842 sq mi, 121,320 sq km; **Land area:** 46,842 sq mi, 121,320 sq km. **Location:** In E Africa, on SW coast of Red Sea. **Neighbors:** Ethiopia on S, Djibouti on SE, Sudan on W. **Topography:** Includes many islands of the Dahlak Archipelago, low coastal plains in S, mountain range with peaks to 9,000 ft. in N. **Capital:** Asmara, 556,000.
Government: Type: in transition. **Head of state and gov.:** Isaias Afwerki; b Feb. 2, 1946; in office: May 24, 1993. **Local divisions:** 8 provinces. **Defense budget** (2003): $116 mil. **Active troops:** 202,200.
Economy: Industries: food proc., beverages, clothing, textiles. **Chief crops:** sorghum, lentils, vegetables, corn, cotton, tobacco, coffee, sisal. **Natural resources:** gold, potash, zinc, copper, salt, fish. **Arable land:** 12%. **Livestock** (2003): cattle: 1.93 mil.; chickens: 1.37 mil.; goats: 1.7 mil.; sheep: 2.10 mil. **Fish catch** (2002): 7,832 metric tons. **Electricity prod.** (2002): 0.25 bil. kWh. **Labor force:** agriculture 80%, industry and services 20%.
Finance: Monetary unit: Nakfa (ERN) (Sept. 2004: 13.50 = $1 U.S.). **GDP** (2002 est.): $3.3 bil.; **per capita GDP:** $700; **GDP growth:** 2.0%. **Imports** (2003 est.): $600.0 mil.; partners (2002): Italy 25.7%, U.S. 14.9%, Germany 6.9%, Ukraine 5.5%, Turkey 5.2%, France 4.3%. **Exports** (2003 est.): $56.0 mil.; partners (2002): Malaysia 30.8%, Italy 25.2%, Germany 11.4%, France 7%. **Tourism** (2002): $73 mil. **Budget** (2000 est.): $615.7 mil. **Intl. reserves less gold:** $17 mil. **Gold** (2001): 40,000 oz t.
Transport: Railroad: Length: 190 mi. **Civil aviation:** 4 airports. **Chief ports:** Mitsiwa, Aseb.
Communications: TV sets: 16 per 1,000 pop. **Radios:** 484 per 1,000 pop. **Telephone lines:** 38,100. **Internet:** 9,500 users.
Health: Life expect.: 51.3 male; 54.1 female. **Births** (per 1,000 pop.): 39.0. **Deaths** (per 1,000 pop.): 13.4. **Natural inc.:** 2.57%. **Infant mortality** (per 1,000 live births): 75.6. **AIDS rate:** 2.7%.
Education: Compulsory: ages 7-13. **Literacy:** 58.6%.
Major Intl. Organizations: UN (FAO, IBRD, ILO, IMF, IMO, WHO), AU.
Embassy: 1708 New Hampshire Ave. NW 20009; 319-1991.
Website: www.embassy.org/embassies/er.html
Eritrea was part of the Ethiopian kingdom of Aksum. It was an Italian colony from 1890 to 1941, when it was captured by the British. Following a period of British and UN supervision, Eritrea was awarded to Ethiopia as part of a federation in 1952. Ethiopia annexed Eritrea as a province in 1962. This led to a 31-year struggle for independence, which ended when Eritrea formally declared itself an independent nation May 24, 1993. A constitution was ratified in 1997 but not implemented. A border war with Ethiopia which erupted in June 1998 intensified in May 2000, as Ethiopian troops plunged into W Eritrea; a cease-fire signed June 18 provided for UN peacekeepers to patrol a buffer zone on Eritrean territory. A peace treaty was signed Dec. 12, 2000. An international tribunal adjudicated the boundary dispute in Apr. 2002, but the ruling was rejected by Ethiopia in Sept. 2003.

Estonia
Republic of Estonia
People: Population: 1,341,664. **Age distrib.** (%): <15: 16.4; 65+: 15.1. **Pop. density:** 80 per sq mi, 31 per sq km. **Urban:** 69.4%. **Ethnic groups:** Estonian 65%, Russian 28%. **Principal languages:** Estonian (official), Russian, Ukrainian, Finnish. **Chief religions:** Evangelical Lutheran, Russian Orthodox, Estonian Orthodox.
Geography: Total area: 17,462 sq mi, 45,226 sq km; **Land area:** 16,684 sq mi, 43,211 sq km. **Location:** E Europe, bordering the Baltic Sea and Gulf of Finland. **Neighbors:** Russia on E, Latvia on S. **Topography:** Estonia is a marshy lowland with numerous lakes and swamps; about 40% forested. Elongated hills show evidence of former glaciation. More than 800 islands on Baltic coast. **Capital:** Tallinn, 391,000.
Government: Type: Republic. **Head of state:** Pres. Arnold Rüütel; b May 10, 1928; in office: Oct. 8, 2001. **Head of gov.:** Prime Min. Juhan Parts; b Aug. 27, 1966; in office: Apr. 10, 2003. **Local divisions:** 15 counties. **Defense budget** (2003): $158 mil. **Active troops:** 5,510.
Economy: Industries: engineering, electronics, timber, wood products, textiles, telecom. **Chief crops:** potatoes, vegetables. **Natural resources:** oil shale, peat, phosphorite, clay, limestone, sand, dolomite, sea mud. **Arable land:** 25%. **Livestock** (2003): cattle: 253,900; chickens: 2.10 mil.; goats: 3,900; pigs: 340,800; sheep: 29,900. **Fish catch** (2002): 101,709 metric tons. **Electricity prod.** (2002): 8.3 bil. kWh. **Labor force** (1999 est.): industry 20%, agriculture 11%, services 69%.
Finance: Monetary unit: Kroon (EEK) (Sept. 2004: 12.90 = $1 U.S.). **GDP** (2003 est.): $17.4 bil.; **per capita GDP:** $12,300; **GDP growth:** 4.8%. **Imports** (2003 est.): $5.5 bil.; partners (2002): Finland 15.6%, Russia 12%, Germany 11.1%, Sweden 8.4%, China

4.6%, Italy 4.1%. **Exports** (2003 est.): $4.1 bil.; partners (2002): Finland 20.4%, Sweden 12.4%, Russia 10%, Germany 8.3%, Latvia 7.7%, UK 4.2%, Lithuania 4.1%. **Tourism:** $682 mil. **Budget** (2003 est.): $3.0 bil. **Intl. reserves less gold:** $924 mil. **Gold:** 10,000 oz t. **Consumer prices:** 1.3%.
Transport: Railroad: Length: 601 mi. **Motor vehicles** (2001): 407,300 pass. cars, 80,500 comm. vehicles. **Civil aviation:** 146.0 mil. pass.-mi; 14 airports. **Chief port:** Tallinn.
Communications: TV sets: 567 per 1,000 pop. **Radios:** 992 per 1,000 pop. **Telephone lines** (2002): 475,000. **Daily newspaper circ.:** 174 per 1,000 pop. **Internet** (2002): 444,000 users.
Health: Life expect.: 65.8 male; 77.3 female. **Births** (per 1,000 pop.): 9.8. **Deaths** (per 1,000 pop.): 13.3. **Natural inc.:** –0.35%. **Infant mortality** (per 1,000 live births): 8.1. **AIDS rate:** 1.1%.
Education: Compulsory: ages 7-15. **Literacy:** 99.8%.
Major Intl. Organizations: UN (FAO, IBRD, ILO, IMF, IMO, WHO), EU, NATO, OSCE.
Embassy: 1730 M Street NW, Suite 503, 20036; 588-0101.
Website: www.estemb.org
Estonia was a province of imperial Russia before World War I, and was independent between World Wars I and II. It was conquered by the USSR in 1940 and incorporated as the Estonian SSR. Estonia declared itself an "occupied territory," and proclaimed itself a free nation Mar. 1990. During an abortive Soviet coup, Estonia declared immediate full independence, Aug. 20, 1991; the Soviet Union recognized its independence in Sept. 1991. The first free elections in over 50 years were held Sept. 20, 1992. The last occupying Russian troops were withdrawn by Aug. 31, 1994. Estonia became a full member of the EU and NATO in 2004.

Ethiopia
Federal Democratic Republic of Ethiopia
People: Population: 67,851,281. **Age distrib.** (%): <15: 47.2; 65+: 2.8. **Pop. density:** 157 per sq mi, 61 per sq km. **Urban:** 15.6%. **Ethnic groups:** Oromo 40%, Amhara and Tigre 32%, Sidamo 9%, Shankella 6%, Somali 6%, Afar 4%, Gurage 2%. **Principal languages:** Amharic, Tigrinya, Oromigna, Guaragigna, Somali, Arabic, over 200 other languages. **Chief religions:** Muslim 45%-50%, Ethiopian Orthodox 35%-40%, animist 12%.
Geography: Total area: 435,186 sq mi, 1,127,127 sq km; **Land area:** 432,312 sq mi, 1,119,683 sq km. **Location:** In East Africa. **Neighbors:** Sudan on W, Kenya on S, Somalia and Djibouti on E, Eritrea on N. **Topography:** A high central plateau, between 6,000 and 10,000 ft. high, rises to higher mountains near the Great Rift Valley, cutting in from the SW. The Blue Nile and other rivers cross the plateau, which descends to plains on both W and SE. **Capital:** Addis Ababa, 2,723,000.
Government: Type: Federal republic. **Head of state:** Pres. Girma Wolde Giorgis; b Dec. 1924; in office: Oct. 8, 2001. **Head of gov.:** Prime Min. Meles Zenawi; b May 8, 1955; in office: Aug. 23, 1995. **Local divisions:** 9 states, 2 charted cities. **Defense budget** (2003): $408 mil. **Active troops:** 162,500.
Economy: Industries: food proc., beverages, textiles, chemicals, metals proc., cement. **Chief crops:** cereals, coffee, oilseed, sugarcane, potatoes. **Natural resources:** gold, platinum, copper, potash, nat. gas, hydropower. **Arable land:** 12%. **Crude oil reserves** (2003): 0.4 mil. bbls. **Livestock** (2003): cattle: 35.5 mil.; chickens: 39.0 mil.; goats: 9.62 mil.; pigs: 26,000; sheep: 11.45 mil. **Fish catch** (2002): 12,300 metric tons. **Electricity prod.** (2002): 2.15 bil. kWh. **Labor force** (1985): agriculture and animal husbandry 80%, government and services 12%, industry and construction 8%.
Finance: Monetary unit: Birr (ETB) (Sept. 2004: 8.69 = $1 U.S.). **GDP** (2003 est.): $48.5 bil.; **per capita GDP:** $700; **GDP growth:** -2.0%. **Imports** (2003 est.): $2.0 bil.; partners (2002): Saudi Arabia 27.9%, Switzerland 6.3%, China 5.9%, Italy 5.7%, India 4.6%, Germany 4%. **Exports** (2003 est.): $537.0 mil.; partners (2002): UK 16.5%, Djibouti 11.1%, Germany 7.5%, Italy 7.3%, Japan 6.8%, Saudi Arabia 6.6%, U.S. 4.5%. **Tourism** (2002): $77 mil. **Budget** (FY02/03 est.): $643 mil. **Intl. reserves less gold:** $643 mil. **Gold** (2002): 250,000 oz t. **Consumer prices:** 17.8%.
Transport: Railroad: Length: 423 mi. **Motor vehicles** (1999): 71,000 pass. cars, 34,600 comm. vehicles. **Civil aviation:** 1.6 bil. pass.-mi; 14 airports.
Communications: TV sets: 5 per 1,000 pop. **Radios:** 185 per 1,000 pop. **Telephone lines:** 435,000. **Daily newspaper circ.:** .4 per 1,000 pop. **Internet:** 75,000 users.
Health: Life expect.: 40.0 male; 41.8 female. **Births** (per 1,000 pop.): 39.2. **Deaths** (per 1,000 pop.): 20.4. **Natural inc.:** 1.89%. **Infant mortality** (per 1,000 live births): 102.1. **AIDS rate:** 4.4%.
Education: Compulsory: ages 7-12. **Literacy:** 42.7%.
Major Intl. Organizations: UN (FAO, IBRD, ILO, IMF, IMO, WHO), AU.
Embassy: 3506 International Dr. NW 20008; 364-1200.
Websites: www.ethiopianembassy.org
Ethiopian culture was influenced by Egypt and Greece. The ancient monarchy was invaded by Italy in 1880 but maintained its independence until another Italian invasion in 1936. British forces freed the country in 1941.
The last emperor, Haile Selassie I, established a parliament and judiciary system in 1931 but barred all political parties.
A series of droughts in the 1970s killed hundreds of thousands. An army mutiny, strikes, and student demonstrations led to the de-

thronement of Selassie in 1974; he died Aug. 1975, while being held by the ruling junta. The junta pledged to form a one-party socialist state and instituted a successful land reform; opposition was violently suppressed. The influence of the Coptic Church, embraced in AD 330, was curbed, and the monarchy was abolished in 1975.

The regime, torn by bloody coups, faced uprisings by tribal and political groups in part aided by Sudan and Somalia. Ties with the U.S., once a major ally, deteriorated, while cooperation accords were signed with the USSR in 1977. In 1978, Soviet advisers and Cuban troops helped defeat Somalian forces. Ethiopia and Somalia signed a peace agreement in 1988.

A worldwide relief effort began in 1984, as an extended drought threatened the country with famine; up to a million people may have died as a result of starvation and disease.

The Ethiopian People's Revolutionary Democratic Front (EPRDF), an umbrella group of 6 rebel armies, launched a major push against government forces, Feb. 1991. In May, Pres. Mengistu Haile Mariam resigned and left the country. The EPRDF took over and set up a transitional government. Ethiopia's first multiparty general elections were held in 1995.

Eritrea, a province on the Red Sea, declared its independence May 24, 1993. Fighting along the border with Eritrea, which erupted in June 1998, intensified in May 2000, as Ethiopian forces plunged into Eritrean territory; a cease-fire was signed June 18 and a peace treaty Dec. 12. The war displaced 350,000 Ethiopians and is estimated to have cost the country nearly $3 billion. A collapse of crop prices in 2001, followed by drought in 2002-03, led to severe food shortages. Ethnic clashes Dec. 2003-Jan. 2004 in the state of Gambella, W Ethiopia, left more than 250 people dead; thousands fled to Sudan.

Fiji
Republic of the Fiji Islands

People: Population: 880,874. **Age distrib.** (%): <15: 32.5; 65+: 3.7. **Pop. density:** 125 per sq mi, 48 per sq km. **Urban:** 51.7%. **Ethnic groups:** Fijian 51%, Indian 44%. **Principal languages:** English (official), Fijian, Hindustani. **Chief religions:** Christian 52%, Hindu 38%, Muslim 8%.

Geography: Total area: 7,054 sq mi, 18,270 sq km; **Land area:** 7,054 sq mi, 18,270 sq km. **Location:** In western South Pacific O. **Neighbors:** Nearest are Vanuatu to W, Tonga to E. **Topography:** 322 islands (106 inhabited), many mountainous, with tropical forests and large fertile areas. Viti Levu, the largest island, has over half the total land area. **Capital:** Suva, 210,000.

Government: Type: Republic. **Head of state:** Pres. Ratu Josefa Iloilo; b Dec. 29, 1920; in office: July 18, 2000. **Head of gov.:** Prime Min. Laisenia Qarase; b Feb. 4, 1941; in office: Mar. 16, 2001. **Local divisions:** 4 divisions comprising 14 provinces and 1 dependency. **Defense budget** (2003): $33 mil. **Active troops:** 3,500.

Economy: Industries: tourism, sugar, clothing, copra, gold & silver prod. **Chief crops:** sugarcane, coconuts, cassava, rice, sweet potatoes, bananas. **Natural resources:** timber, fish, gold, copper, oil, hydropower. **Arable land:** 10%. **Livestock** (2003): cattle: 320,000; chickens: 3.8 mil.; goats: 248,000; pigs: 1.37 mil.; sheep: 6,000. **Fish catch** (2002 est): 44,517 metric tons. **Electricity prod.** (2002): 0.75 bil. kWh. **Labor force** (2001 est.): agriculture (including subsistence agriculture) 70%.

Finance: Monetary unit: Fiji Dollar (FJD) (Sept. 2004: 1.76 = $1 U.S.). **GDP** (2003 est.): $5.0 bil.; **per capita GDP:** $5,800; **GDP growth:** 4.8%. **Imports** (2002): $835.0 mil.; partners (2002): Australia 37.5%, New Zealand 17.2%, Singapore 16%, Japan 4.2%, China 4.1%. **Exports** (2002): $609.0 mil.; partners (2002): U.S. 25.5%, Australia 19.7%, UK 10.7%, Japan 6.4%, Samoa 5.6%. **Tourism:** $349 mil. **Budget** (2000 est.): $531.4 mil. **Intl. reserves less gold:** $285 mil. **Consumer prices:** 4.2%.

Transport: Railroad: Length: 371 mi. **Motor vehicles:** (1998): 51,700 pass. cars, 48,600 comm. vehicles. **Civil aviation:** 1.5 bil. pass.-mi; 3 airports. **Chief ports:** Suva, Lautoka.

Communications: TV sets: 110 per 1,000 pop. **Radios:** 677 per 1,000 pop. **Telephone lines:** 102,000. **Daily newspaper circ.:** 46 per 1,000 pop. **Internet:** 55,000 users.

Health: Life expect.: 66.7 male; 71.8 female. **Births** (per 1,000 pop.): 22.9. **Deaths** (per 1,000 pop.): 5.7. **Natural inc.:** 1.72%. **Infant mortality** (per 1,000 live births): 13.0. **AIDS rate:** 0.1%.

Education: Compulsory: ages 6-15. **Literacy:** 93.7%.

Major Intl. Organizations: UN (FAO, IBRD, ILO, IMF, IMO, WHO, WTrO), the Commonwealth.

Embassy: 2233 Wisconsin Ave. NW, Suite 240, 20007; 337-8320.

Website: www.fiji.gov.fj

A British colony since 1874, Fiji became an independent parliamentary democracy Oct. 10, 1970. Cultural differences between the Indian community (descendants of contract laborers brought to the islands in the 19th century) and indigenous Fijians have led to political polarization.

In 1987, a military coup ousted the government; order was restored May 21 under a compromise granting Lt. Col. Sitiveni Rabuka, the coup's leader, increased power. Rabuka staged a second coup Sept. 25 and declared Fiji a republic. Civilian government was restored in Dec. A new constitution favoring indigenous Fijians was issued July 25, 1990; amendments enacted in July 1997 made the constitution more equitable.

Fiji's 1st Indian prime minister, Mahendra Chaudhry, took office May 19, 1999. He and other government officials were taken captive May 19, 2000, by indigenous Fijian gunmen led by George Speight. The hostage crisis led to a military takeover, May 29. Release of the last remaining hostages in July 2000 coincided with the installation of an interim military-backed government. Speight was charged with treason (sentenced to life in prison Feb. 18, 2002). The government was reconstituted in Mar. 2001 after an appellate court ruled it illegal. Voting ending Sept. 1, 2001, returned caretaker Prime Min. Laisenia Qarase to office. Fiji's High Court, Aug. 5, 2004, convicted Vice Pres. Jope Seniloli of aiding the 2000 coup plot; he received a 4-year jail sentence.

Finland
Republic of Finland

People: Population: 5,214,512. **Age distrib.** (%): <15: 17.9; 65+: 15.2. **Pop. density:** 44 per sq mi, 17 per sq km. **Urban:** 60.9%. **Ethnic groups:** Finnish 93%, Swedish 6%. **Principal languages:** Finnish, Swedish (both official); Russian, Sami. **Chief religion:** Evangelical Lutheran 89%.

Geography: Total area: 130,128 sq mi, 337,030 sq km; **Land area:** 117,943 sq mi, 305,470 sq km. **Location:** In northern Europe. **Neighbors:** Norway on N, Sweden on W, Russia on E. **Topography:** South and central Finland are generally flat areas with low hills and many lakes. The N has mountainous areas, 3,000-4,000 ft. above sea level. **Capital:** Helsinki, 1,075,000.

Government: Type: Constitutional republic. **Head of state:** Pres. Tarja Halonen; b Dec. 24, 1943; in office: Mar. 1, 2000. **Head of gov.:** Prim Min. Matti Vanhanen, b Nov. 4, 1955; in office: June 24, 2003. **Local divisions:** 6 laanit (provinces). **Defense budget** (2003): $2.3 bil. **Active troops:** 27,000.

Economy: Industries: metal products, electronics, shipbuilding, paper, copper refining, foodstuffs, chemicals, textiles, clothing. **Chief crops:** barley, wheat, sugar beets, potatoes. **Natural resources:** timber, copper, zinc, iron ore, silver. **Arable land:** 8%. **Livestock** (2003): cattle: 1 mil.; chickens: 6.0 mil.; goats: 4,800; pigs: 1.37 mil.; sheep: 67,400. **Fish catch** (2002): 159,940 metric tons. **Electricity prod.** (2002): 71.59 bil. kWh. **Labor force:** public services 32%, industry 22%, commerce 14%, finance, insurance, and business services 10%, agriculture and forestry 8%, transport and communications 8%, construction 6%.

Finance: Monetary unit: Euro (EUR) (Sept. 2004: 0.82 = $1 U.S.). **GDP** (2003 est.): $141.7 bil.; **per capita GDP:** $27,300; **GDP growth:** 1.5%. **Imports** (2003 est.): $37.4 bil.; partners (2002): Germany 14.5%, Sweden 10.9%, Russia 9.9%, UK 5.7%, France 4.3%, Denmark 4.2%. **Exports** (2003 est.): $54.3 bil.; partners (2002): Germany 11.8%, UK 9.6%, U.S. 9%, Sweden 8.5%, Russia 6.6%, Netherlands 4.6%, France 4.5%. **Tourism:** $1.9 bil. **Budget** (2000 est.): $31.0 bil. **Intl. reserves less gold:** $7.08 bil. **Gold:** 1.58 mil oz t. **Consumer prices:** 0.9%.

Transport: Railroad: Length: 3,635 mi. **Motor vehicles:** 2.13 mil pass. cars, 314,200 comm. vehicles. **Civil aviation:** 3.9 bil. pass.-mi; 74 airports. **Chief ports:** Helsinki, Turku, Rauma, Kotka.

Communications: TV sets: 643 per 1,000 pop. **Radios:** 1,564 per 1,000 pop. **Telephone lines:** 2.5 mil. **Daily newspaper circ.:** 445.5 per 1,000 pop. **Internet** (2002): 2.7 mil. users.

Health: Life expect.: 74.7 male; 81.9 female. **Births** (per 1,000 pop.): 10.6. **Deaths** (per 1,000 pop.): 9.7. **Natural inc.:** 0.09%. **Infant mortality** (per 1,000 live births): 3.6. **AIDS rate:** 0.1%.

Education: Compulsory: ages 7-16. **Literacy** (1997): 100%.

Major Intl. Organizations: UN (FAO, IBRD, ILO, IMF, IMO, WHO, WTrO), EU, OECD, OSCE.

Embassy: 3301 Massachusetts Ave. NW 20008; 298-5800.

Websites: www.finland.org; www.finland.fi

The early Finns probably migrated from the Ural area at about the beginning of the Christian era. Swedish settlers brought the country into Sweden, 1154 to 1809, when Finland became an autonomous grand duchy of the Russian Empire. Russian exactions created a strong national spirit; on Dec. 6, 1917, Finland declared its independence and in 1919 became a republic.

On Nov. 30, 1939, the Soviet Union invaded, and the Finns were forced to cede 16,173 sq. mi. of territory. After World War II, further cessions were exacted. In 1948, Finland signed a treaty of mutual assistance with the USSR; Finland and Russia nullified this treaty with a new pact in Jan. 1992.

Following approval by Finnish voters in an advisory referendum Oct. 16, 1994, Finland joined the European Union effective Jan. 1, 1995.

Aland or **Ahvenanmaa,** constituting an autonomous province, is a group of small islands, 590 sq. mi., in the Gulf of Bothnia, 25 mi. from Sweden, 15 mi. from Finland. Mariehamn is the chief port.

WORLD ALMANAC QUICK QUIZ

Which of these countries have joined the UN since the beginning of 2000?

(a) Switzerland   (b) Tajikistan
(c) Tuvalu   (d) East Timor

For the answer look in this chapter, or see page 1008.

France
French Republic

People: Population: 60,424,213. **Age distrib.** (%): <15: 18.5; 65+: 16.3. **Pop. density:** 287 per sq mi, 111 per sq km. **Urban:** 76.3%. **Ethnic groups:** French, with Slavic, N African, Indochinese, Basque minorities. **Principal languages:** French (official), Italian, Breton, Alsatian (German), Corsican, Gascon, Portuguese, Provençal, Dutch, Flemish, Catalan, Basque, Romani. **Chief religions:** Roman Catholic 83%-88%, Muslim 5%-10%.

Geography: Total area: 211,209 sq mi, 547,030 sq km; **Land area:** 210,669 sq mi, 545,630 sq km. **Location:** In western Europe, between Atlantic O. and Mediterranean Sea. **Neighbors:** Spain on S; Italy, Switzerland, Germany on E; Luxembourg, Belgium on N. **Topography:** A wide plain covers more than half of the country, in N and W, drained to W by Seine, Loire, Garonne rivers. The Massif Central is a mountainous plateau in center. In E are Alps (Mt. Blanc is tallest in W Europe, 15,771 ft.), the lower Jura range, and the forested Vosges. The Rhone flows from Lake Geneva to Mediterranean. Pyrenees are in SW, on border with Spain. **Capital:** Paris, 9,794,000. **Cities (urban aggr.):** Lyon, 1,362,000; Marseilles, 1,357,000; Lille, 1,007,000.

Government: Type: Republic. **Head of state:** Pres. Jacques Chirac; b Nov. 29, 1932; in office: May 17, 1995. **Head of gov.:** Prime Min. Jean-Pierre Raffarin; b Aug. 3, 1948; in office: May 6, 2002. **Local divisions:** 22 administrative regions containing 96 departments. **Defense budget** (2003): $34.9 bil. **Active troops:** 259,050.

Economy: Industries: machinery, chemicals, automobiles, metallurgy, aircraft, electronics, textiles, food proc. tourism. **Chief crops:** wheat, cereals, sugar beets, potatoes, wine grapes. **Natural resources:** coal, iron ore, bauxite, zinc, potash, timber, fish. **Crude oil reserves** (2003): 148.5 mil. bbls. **Other resources:** Timber, dairy. **Arable land:** 33%. **Livestock** (2003): cattle: 19.52 mil.; chickens: 220.0 mil.; goats: 1.21 mil.; pigs: 15.06 mil.; sheep: 9.20 mil. **Fish catch** (2002): 869,777 metric tons. **Electricity prod.** (2002): 528.6 bil. kWh. **Labor force** (1999): services 71.5%, industry 24.4%, agriculture 4.1%.

Finance: Monetary unit: Euro (EUR) (Sept. 2004: 0.82 = $1 U.S.). **GDP** (2003 est.): $1.654 tril.; **per capita GDP:** $27,500; **GDP growth:** 0.1%. **Imports** (2003 est.): $339.9 bil.; partners (2002): Germany 19.4%, Belgium 9.2%, Italy 8.8%, UK 7.3%, Netherlands 7%, U.S. 6.8%, Spain 6.7%. **Exports** (2003 est.): $346.5 bil.; partners (2002): Germany 15%, UK 9.8%, Spain 9%, Italy 9%, U.S. 7.8%, Belgium 6.9%. **Tourism:** $36.3 bil. **Budget** (2003 est.): $274.0 bil. **Intl. reserves less gold:** $20.31 bil. **Gold:** 97.25 mil oz t. **Consumer prices:** 2.1%.

Transport: Railroad: Length: 20,308 mi. **Motor vehicles:** 28.1 mil pass. cars, 5.93 mil comm. vehicles. **Civil aviation:** 46.8 bil. pass.-mi; 273 airports. **Chief ports:** Marseille, Le Havre, Bordeaux, Rouen.

Communications: TV sets: 620 per 1,000 pop. **Radios:** 946 per 1,000 pop. **Telephone lines:** 33.9 mil. **Daily newspaper circ.:** 218 per 1,000 pop. **Internet:** 21.9 mil. users.

Health: Life expect.: 75.8 male; 83.3 female. **Births** (per 1,000 pop.): 12.3. **Deaths** (per 1,000 pop.): 9.1. **Natural inc.:** 0.33%. **Infant mortality** (per 1,000 live births): 4.3. **AIDS rate:** 0.4%.

Education: Compulsory: ages 6-16. **Literacy** (1994): 99%.

Major Intl. Organizations: UN and most of its specialized agencies, EU, NATO, OECD, OSCE.

Embassy: 4101 Reservoir Rd. NW 20007; 944-6000. **Website:** www.info-france-usa.org

Celtic Gaul was conquered by Julius Caesar 58-51 BC; Romans ruled for 500 years. Under Charlemagne, Frankish rule extended over much of Europe. After his death France emerged as one of the successor kingdoms.

The monarchy was overthrown by the French Revolution (1789-93) and succeeded by the First Republic; followed by the First Empire under Napoleon (1804-15), a monarchy (1814-48), the Second Republic (1848-52), the Second Empire (1852-70), the Third Republic (1871-1946), the Fourth Republic (1946-58), and the Fifth Republic (1958 to present).

France suffered severe losses in manpower and wealth in the First World War, when it was invaded by Germany. By the Treaty of Versailles, France exacted return of Alsace and Lorraine, provinces seized by Germany in 1871. Germany invaded France again in May 1940, and signed an armistice with a government based in Vichy. After France was liberated by the Allies in Sept. 1944, Gen. Charles de Gaulle became head of the provisional government, serving until 1946.

De Gaulle again became premier in 1958, during a crisis over Algeria, and obtained voter approval for a new constitution, ushering in the Fifth Republic. He became president Jan. 1959. Using strong executive powers, he promoted French economic and technological advances in the context of the European Economic Community and guarded French foreign policy independence.

France had withdrawn from Indochina in 1954, and from Morocco and Tunisia in 1956. Most of its remaining African territories, including Algeria, were freed 1958-62. In 1966, France withdrew all its troops from the integrated military command of NATO, though 60,000 remained stationed in Germany.

In May 1968 rebellious students in Paris and other centers rioted, battled police, and were joined by workers who launched nationwide strikes. The government awarded pay increases to the strikers May 26. De Gaulle resigned from office in Apr. 1969, after losing a nationwide referendum on constitutional reform. Georges Pompidou, who was elected to succeed him, continued De Gaulle's emphasis on French independence from the U.S. and Soviet Union. After Pompidou's death, in 1974, Valery Giscard d'Estaing was elected president; he continued the basically conservative policies of his predecessors.

On May 10, 1981, France elected François Mitterrand, a Socialist, president. Under Mitterrand the government nationalized 5 major industries and most private banks. After 1986, however, when rightists won a narrow victory in the National Assembly, Mitterrand chose conservative Jacques Chirac as premier. A 2-year period of "cohabitation" ensued, and France began to pursue a privatization program in which many state-owned companies were sold. After Mitterrand was elected to a 2nd 7-year term in 1988, he appointed a Socialist as premier. The center-right won a large majority in 1993 legislative elections, ushering in another period of "cohabitation" with a conservative premier.

In 1993, France set tighter rules for entry into the country and made it easier for the government to expel foreigners. In 1994, France sent troops to Rwanda in an effort to help protect civilians there from ongoing massacres. The international terrorist known as Carlos the Jackal (Ilich Ramirez Sánchez) was arrested in Sudan in Aug. 1994 and extradited to France, where he had been sentenced in absentia to life imprisonment.

Former conservative Prime Min. Jacques Chirac won the presidency in a runoff May 7, 1995. A series of terrorist bombings and bombing attempts began in summer 1995; Islamic extremists, opposed to France's support of the Algerian government and its struggle with Islamic fundamentalists, were believed responsible. In Sept. 1995, France stirred widespread protests by resuming nuclear tests in the South Pacific, after a 3-year moratorium; the tests ended Jan. 1996.

Chirac cut government spending to help the French economy meet the budgetary goals set for the introduction of a common European currency. With unemployment at nearly 13%, legislative elections completed June 1, 1997, produced a decisive victory for the leftist parties. The result was a new period of "cohabitation," this time between a conservative president and a Socialist prime minister, Lionel Jospin. France contributed 7,000 troops to the NATO-led security force (KFOR) that entered Kosovo in June 1999.

French voters, disaffected by government scandals, shocked the political establishment in the 1st round of presidential voting Apr. 21, 2002, by giving far-right leader Jean-Marie Le Pen, leader of the far-right National Front, a 2nd place finish with 16.9% of the vote; Chirac won only 19.9%, and Jospin was 3rd, with 16.2%. Chirac easily won the May 5 runoff, with 82%, and his center-right allies won parliamentary elections June 9 and 16.

In Mar. 2003, Parliament approved constitutional amendments granting certain powers to regional governments. Parliament gave final approval Mar. 3, 2004, to a law barring the wearing of Islamic head scarves and other religious symbols in public schools. Despite threats from Isamic extremists who abducted 2 French journalists in Iraq, it went into effect Sept. 20.

Displeased with sluggish economic growth and budget cuts in entitlement programs, voters boosted left-wing parties in elections for regional offices, Mar. 21 and 28, 2004, and for the European Parliament, June 13. A roof collapsed, May 23, in a new terminal at De Gaulle airport outside Paris, leaving 4 dead.

On June 6, 2004, world leaders and thousands of WWII veterans gathered in Normandy to mark the 60th anniversary of D-Day.

The island of **Corsica**, in the Mediterranean W of Italy and N of Sardinia, is a territorial collectivity and region of France comprising 2 departments. It elects a total of 2 senators and 3 deputies to the French Parliament. Area: 3,369 sq. mi.; pop. (2001 census): 260,149. The capital is Ajaccio, birthplace of Napoleon I. Violence by Corsican separatist groups has hurt tourism, a leading industry on the island. Corsicans rejected, 51-49%, a limited autonomy plan in a referendum July 6, 2003.

Overseas Departments

French Guiana is on the NE coast of South America with Suriname on the W and Brazil on the E and S. Its area is 35,135 sq. mi. (total); 34,421 sq. mi. (land).; pop. (2004 est.) 191,309. Guiana sends one senator and 2 deputies to the French Parliament. Guiana is administered by a prefect and has a Council General of 16 elected members; capital is Cayenne.

The famous penal colony, Devil's Island, was phased out between 1938 and 1951. The European Space Agency maintains a satellite-launching center (established by France in 1964) in the city of Kourou.

Immense forests of rich timber cover 88% of the land. Fishing (especially shrimp), forestry, and gold mining are the most important industries.

Guadeloupe, in the West Indies' Leeward Islands, consists of 2 large islands, Basse-Terre and Grande-Terre, separated by the Salt River, plus Marie Galante and the Saintes group to the S and, to the N, Desirade, St. Barthelemy, and over half of St. Martin (the Netherlands' portion is called St. Maarten). A French possession

since 1635, the department is represented in the French Parliament by 2 senators and 4 deputies; administration consists of a prefect (governor) as well as an elected general and regional councils.

Area of the islands is 687 sq. mi. (total); 659 sq. mi. (land); pop. (2004 est.) 444,515, mainly descendants of slaves; capital is Basse-Terre on Basse-Terre Island. The land is fertile; sugar, rum, and bananas are exported. Tourism is an important industry.

Martinique, the northernmost of the Windward Islands, in the West Indies, has been a possession since 1635, and a department since Mar. 1946. It is represented in the French Parliament by 2 senators and 4 deputies. The island was the birthplace of Napoleon's Empress Josephine.

It has an area of 425 sq. mi. (total); 409 sq. mi. (land); pop. (2004 est.) 429,510, mostly descendants of slaves. The capital is Fort-de-France (pop. 1991: 101,000). It is a popular tourist stop. The chief exports are rum, bananas, and petroleum products.

Réunion is a volcanic island in the Indian O. about 420 mi. E of Madagascar, and has belonged to France since 1665. Area, 972 sq. mi. (total); 968 sq. mi. (land); pop. (2004 est.) 766,153, 30% of French extraction. Capital: Saint-Denis. The chief export is sugar. It elects 5 deputies, 3 senators to the French Parliament.

Overseas Territorial Collectivities

Mayotte, claimed by Comoros and administered by France, voted in 1976 to become a territorial collectivity of France. An island NW of Madagascar, area is 144 sq. mi., pop. (2004 est.) 186,026. The capital is Mamoutzou.

St. Pierre and Miquelon, formerly an overseas territory (1816-1976) and department (1976-85), made the transition to territorial collectivity in 1985. It consists of 2 groups of rocky islands near the SW coast of Newfoundland, inhabited by fishermen. The exports are chiefly fish products. The St. Pierre group has an area of 10 sq. mi.; Miquelon, 83 sq. mi. Total pop. (2004 est.) 6,995. The capital is St. Pierre.

Both Mayotte and St. Pierre and Miquelon elect a deputy and a senator to the French Parliament.

Overseas Territories

Territory of **French Polynesia** comprises 130 islands widely scattered among 5 archipelagos in the South Pacific; administered by a Council of Ministers (headed by a president). Territorial Assembly and the Council have headquarters at Papeete, on Tahiti, one of the **Society Islands** (which include the **Windward** and **Leeward** islands). Two deputies and a senator are elected to the French Parliament.

Other groups are the **Marquesas Islands,** the **Tuamotu Archipelago,** including the **Gambier Islands,** and the **Austral Islands.**

Total area of the islands administered from Tahiti is 1,609 sq. mi. (total), 1,413 sq. mi. (land); pop. (2004 est.) 266,339, more than half on Tahiti. Tahiti is picturesque and mountainous with a productive coastline bearing coconuts, citrus, pineapples, and vanilla. Cultured pearls are also produced.

Tahiti was visited by Capt. James Cook in 1769 and by Capt. Bligh in the *Bounty*, 1788-89. Its beauty impressed Herman Melville, Paul Gauguin, and Charles Darwin. A coalition favoring independence for French Polynesia within 20 years gained control of the territorial assembly after elections May 23, 2004.

Territory of the **French Southern and Antarctic Lands** comprises **Adelie Land,** on Antarctica, and 4 island groups in the Indian O. **Area:** 3,023 sq. mi. (total); 3,023 sq. mi. (land).

Adelie, reached 1,840, has a research station, a coastline of 185 mi., and tapers 1,240 mi. inland to the South Pole. The U.S. does not recognize national claims in Antarctica. There are 2 huge glaciers, Ninnis, 22 mi. wide, 99 mi. long, and Mentz, 11 mi. wide, 140 mi. long. The Indian O. groups are:

Kerguelen Archipelago, visited 1772, consists of one large and 300 small islands. The chief is 87 mi. long, 74 mi. wide, and has Mt. Ross, 6,429 ft. tall. Principal research station is Port-aux-Français. Seals often weigh 2 tons; there are blue whales, coal, peat, semiprecious stones. **Crozet Archipelago,** reached 1772, covers 195 sq. mi. Eastern Island rises to 6,560 ft. **Saint Paul,** in southern Indian O., has warm springs with earth at places heating to 120° to 390° F. **Amsterdam** is nearby; both produce cod and rock lobster.

Territory of **New Caledonia** and Dependencies is a group of islands in the Pacific O. about 1,115 mi. E of Australia and approx. the same distance NW of New Zealand. Dependencies are the **Loyalty Islands, Isle of Pines, Belep Archipelago,** and **Huon Islands.**

The largest island, New Caledonia, is 6,530 sq. mi. Total area of the territory is 7,359 sq. mi. (total); 7,172 sq. mi. (land); pop. (2004 est.) 213,679. The group was acquired by France in 1853.

The territory is administered by a High Commissioner. There is a popularly elected Territorial Congress. Two deputies and a senator are elected to the French Parliament. Capital: Noumea.

Mining is the chief industry. New Caledonia is one of the world's largest nickel producers. Other minerals found are chrome, iron, cobalt, manganese, silver, gold, lead, and copper. Agricultural products include yams, sweet potatoes, potatoes, manioc (cassava), corn, and coconuts.

In 1987, New Caledonian voters chose by referendum to remain within the French Republic. There were clashes between French and Melanesians (Kanaks) in 1988. An agreement Apr. 21, 1998, between France and rival New Caledonian factions specified a 15-to 20-year period of "shared sovereignty." The French constitution was amended, July 6, to allow the territory a gradual increase in autonomy, and New Caledonian voters approved the plan Nov. 8, 1998, by a 72% majority.

Territory of the **Wallis and Futuna Islands** comprises 2 island groups in the SW Pacific S of Tuvalu, N of Fiji, and W of Western Samoa; became an overseas territory July 29, 1961. The islands have a total area of 106 sq. mi. and population (2004 est.) of 15,880. **Alofi,** attached to Futuna, is uninhabited. Capital: Mata-Utu. Chief products are copra, yams, taro roots, bananas, and coconuts. A senator and a deputy are elected to the French Parliament.

Gabon
Gabonese Republic

People: Population: 1,355,246. **Age distrib.** (%): <15: 33.3; 65+: 6.1. **Pop. density:** 14 per sq mi, 5 per sq km. **Urban:** 83.8%. **Ethnic groups:** Fang, Bapounou, Nzebi, Obamba, European. **Principal languages:** French (official), Fang, Myene, Nzebi, Bapounou/Eschira, Bandjabi. **Chief religion:** Christian 55%-75%.

Geography: Total area: 103,347 sq mi, 267,667 sq km; **Land area:** 99,486 sq mi, 257,667 sq km. **Location:** On Atlantic coast of W central Africa. **Neighbors:** Equatorial Guinea and Cameroon on N, Congo on E and S. **Topography:** Heavily forested, the country consists of coastal lowlands; plateaus in N, E, and S; mountains in N, SE, and center. The Ogooue R. system covers most of Gabon. **Capital:** Libreville, 611,000.

Government: Type: Republic. **Head of state:** Pres. Omar Bongo; b Dec. 30, 1935; in office: Dec. 2, 1967. **Head of gov.:** Prime Min. Jean-François Ntoutoume-Emane; b Oct. 6, 1939; in office: Jan. 23, 1999. **Local divisions:** 9 provinces. **Defense budget** (2003): $105 mil. **Active troops:** 4,700.

Economy: Industries: food & beverages, textiles, lumber, cement, oil, mining, chemicals, ship repair. **Chief crops:** cocoa, coffee, sugar, palm oil, rubber. **Natural resources:** oil, mang., uranium, gold, timber, iron, hydropower. **Crude oil reserves** (2003): 2.5 bil. bbls. **Arable land:** 1%. **Livestock** (2003): cattle: 35,000; chickens: 3.1 mil.; goats: 90,000; pigs: 212,000; sheep: 195,000. **Fish catch** (2002): 40,958 metric tons. **Electricity prod.** (2002): 1.16 bil. kWh. **Labor force:** agriculture 60%, services 25%, industry 15%.

Finance: Monetary unit: CFA Franc BEAC (XAF) (Sept. 2004: 539.54 = $1 U.S.). **GDP** (2003 est.): $7.3 bil.; **per capita GDP:** $5,500; **GDP growth:** 1.2%. **Imports** (2003 est.): $1.1 bil.; partners (2002): France 51%, U.S. 6.3%, Netherlands 3.7%. **Exports** (2003 est.): $2.9 bil.; partners (2002): U.S. 50.9%, France 12.7%, China 7.1%. **Tourism** (2001): $17 mil. **Budget** (2002 est.): $1.8 bil. **Intl. reserves less gold:** $132 mil. **Gold:** 10,000 oz t. **Consumer prices** (change in 2000): 0.5%.

Transport: Railroad: Length: 506 mi. **Motor vehicles** (1998): 23,000 pass. cars, 10,00 comm. vehicles. **Civil aviation:** 480.9 mil. pass.-mi; 10 airports. **Chief ports:** Port-Gentil, Owendo, Libreville.

Communications: TV sets: 251 per 1,000 pop. **Radios:** 501 per 1,000 pop. **Telephone lines:** 38,400.**Daily newspaper circ.:** 29 per 1,000 pop. **Internet:** 35,000 users.

Health: Life expect.: 54.9 male; 58.1 female. **Births** (per 1,000 pop.): 36.4. **Deaths** (per 1,000 pop.): 11.4. **Natural inc.:** 2.50%. **Infant mortality** (per 1,000 live births): 54.3. **AIDS rate:** 8.1%.

Education: Compulsory: ages 6-16. **Literacy** (2002): 63%.

Major Intl. Organizations: UN (FAO, IBRD, ILO, IMF, IMO, WHO, WTrO), AU.

Embassy: 2034 20th St. NW, Ste. 200, 20009; 797-1000. **Website:** www.embassy.org/embassies/ga.html

France established control over the region in the second half of the 19th century. Gabon became independent Aug. 17, 1960. A multiparty political system was introduced in 1990, and a new constitution was enacted Mar. 14, 1991. However, the reelection of longtime Pres. Omar Bongo, on Dec. 5, 1993, prompted rioting and charges of vote fraud; another Bongo victory on Dec. 6, 1998, was likewise allegedly marred by irregularities.

Gabon is one of the most prosperous black African countries, thanks to abundant natural resources, foreign private investment, and government development programs.

The Gambia
Republic of The Gambia

People: Population: 1,546,848. **Age distrib.** (%): <15: 45.1; 65+: 2.6. **Pop. density:** 401 per sq mi, 155 per sq km. **Urban:** 26.1%. **Ethnic groups:** Mandinka 42%, Fula 18%, Wolof 16%, Jola 10%, Serahuli 9%. **Principal languages:** English (official), Mandinka, Wolof, Fula, other native dialects. **Chief religions:** Muslim 90%, Christian 9%.

Geography: Total area: 4,363 sq mi, 11,300 sq km; **Land area:** 3,861 sq mi, 10,000 sq km. **Location:** On Atlantic coast near W tip of Africa. **Neighbors:** Surrounded on 3 sides by Senegal. **Topography:** A narrow strip of land on each side of the lower Gambia R. **Capital:** Banjul, 372,000.

Government: Type: Republic. **Head of state and gov.:** Yahya Jammeh; b May 25, 1965; in office: July 23, 1994. **Local divisions:** 5 divisions, 1 city. **Defense budget** (2003): $2.7 mil. **Active troops:** 800.

Economy: Industries: peanuts, fish, hides, tourism, beverages, agric. machinery, woodworking, metalworking, clothing. **Chief crops:** peanuts, millet, sorghum, rice, corn, sesame, cassava, palm kernels. **Natural resources:** fish. **Livestock** (2003): cattle: 327,000; chickens: 600,000; goats: 262,000; pigs: 17,500; sheep: 146,000. **Fish catch** (2002): 45,769 metric tons. **Electricity prod.** (2002): 0.09 bil. kWh. **Labor force:** agriculture 75%, industry, commerce, and services 19%, government 6%.

Finance: Monetary unit: Dalasi (GMD) (Sept. 2004: 29.25 = $1 U.S.). **GDP** (2003 est.): $2.6 bil.; **per capita GDP:** $1,700; **GDP growth:** 0.5%. **Imports** (2003 est.): $271.0 mil.; partners (2002): China 22.3%, Senegal 9.2%, UK 6.7%, Brazil 5.9%, Netherlands 5.4%, India 5%, Belgium 4.7%, Germany 4%. **Exports** (2003 est.): $156.0 mil.; partners (2002): France 22.2%, UK 18.5%, Italy 11.1%, Malaysia 11.1%, Belgium 7.4%, Germany 7.4%. **Tourism** (1998): $49 mil. **Budget** (2001 est.): $80.9 mil. **Intl. reserves less gold** (2002): $79 mil. **Consumer prices** (change in 2002): 4.9%.

Transport: Motor vehicles (1998): 6,400 pass. cars, 3,500 comm. vehicles. **Civil aviation:** 31.1 mil pass.-mi.; 1 airport. **Chief port:** Banjul.

Communications: TV Sets: 3 per 1,000 pop. Radios: 394 per 1,000 pop. **Telephone lines** (2002): 38,400. **Daily newspaper circ.:** 1.7 per 1,000 pop. **Internet** (2002): 25,000 users.

Health: Life expect.: 52.8 male; 56.9 female. **Births** (per 1,000 pop.): 40.3. **Deaths** (per 1,000 pop.): 12.1. **Natural inc.:** 2.82%. **Infant mortality** (per 1,000 live births): 73.5. **AIDS rate:** 1.2%.

Education: Free: ages 7-13. **Literacy:** 40.1%.

Major Intl. Organizations: UN (FAO, IBRD, ILO, IMF, IMO, WHO, WTrO), the Commonwealth, AU.

Embassy: 1155 15th St., NW, Ste. 1000, 20005S; 785-1399. **Websites:** www.statehouse.gm; www.visitthegambia.gm

The tribes of Gambia were at one time associated with the West African empires of Ghana, Mali, and Songhay. The area became Britain's first African possession in 1588.

Independence came Feb. 18, 1965; republic status within the Commonwealth was achieved in 1970. The country suffered from severe famine in the 1970s. After a coup attempt in 1981, The Gambia formed the confederation of Senegambia with Senegal that lasted until 1989.

On July 23, 1994, after 24 years in power, Pres. Dawda K. Jawara was deposed in a bloodless coup by a military officer, Yahya Jammeh. Jammeh barred political activity, detained potential opponents, and governed by decree. A new constitution was approved by referendum, Aug. 8, 1996. On Sept. 27 Jammeh won the presidential election. Parliamentary balloting on Jan. 2, 1997, completed the nominal return to civilian rule, but Jammeh retained a firm grip on power. He followed his reelection win on Oct. 18, 2001, with a new crackdown on dissidents.

Georgia

People: Population: 4,693,892. **Age distrib.** (%): <15: 19; 65+: 12.8. **Pop. density:** 174 per sq mi, 67 per sq km. **Urban:** 51.9%. **Ethnic groups:** Georgian 70%, Armenian 8%, Russian 6%, Azeri 6%. **Principal languages:** Georgian (official), Russian, Armenian, Azeri, Abkhaz (official in Abkhazia). **Chief religions:** Georgian Orthodox 65%, Muslim 11%, Russian Orthodox 10%, Armenian Apostolic 8%.

Geography: Total area: 26,911 sq mi, 69,700 sq km; **Land area:** 26,911 sq mi, 69,700 sq km. **Location:** SW Asia, on E coast of Black Sea. **Neighbors:** Russia on N and NE, Turkey and Armenia on S, Azerbaijan on SE. **Topography:** Separated from Russia on NE by main range of the Caucasus Mts. **Capital:** Tbilisi, 1,064,000.

Government: Type: Republic. **Head of state:** Pres. Mikhail Saakashvili; b Dec. 21, 1967; in office: Jan. 25, 2004. **Head of gov.:** Zurab Zhvania; b Dec. 9, 1963; in office: Feb. 17, 2004. **Local divisions:** 53 rayons, 9 cities, and 2 autonomous republics. **Defense budget** (2003): $24 mil. **Active troops:** 17,500.

Economy: Industries: steel, aircraft, machine tools, appliances, mining, chemicals. **Chief crops:** citrus, grapes, tea, vegetables, potatoes. **Natural resources:** timber, hydropower, mang., iron ore, copper, coal, oil. **Crude oil reserves** (2003): 35.0 mil. bbls. **Arable land:** 9%. **Livestock** (2003): cattle: 1.22 mil.; chickens: 9.95 mil.; goats: 88,300; pigs: 446,134; sheep: 611,200. **Fish catch** (2002): 2,589 metric tons. **Electricity prod.** (2002): 6.73 bil. kWh. **Labor force** (1999 est.): industry 20%, agriculture 40%, services 40%.

Finance: Monetary unit: Lari (GEL) (Sept. 2004: 1.92 = $1 U.S.). **GDP** (2003 est.): $12.2 bil.; **per capita GDP:** $2,500; **GDP growth:** 5.5%. **Imports** (2003 est.): $1.3 bil.; partners (2002): Azerbaijan 11.7%, Turkey 10.6%, U.S. 10.4%, Russia 9.5%, Germany 7.4%, Ukraine 6%, Italy 5.3%, Bulgaria 5.1%, France 4.4%. **Exports** (2003 est.): $615.0 mil.; partners (2002): Turkey 21.7%, Italy 11.4%, Russia 10.7%, Greece 8.1%, Netherlands 7.1%, Spain 5.5%, Turkmenistan 4.5%. **Tourism** (2002): $472 mil. **Budget** (2001 est.): $554.0 mil. **Intl. reserves less gold:** $128 mil. **Consumer prices** (change in 2002): 5.6%.

Transport: Railroad: Length: 1,002 mi. **Motor vehicles:** 244,900 pass. cars, 66,800 comm. vehicles. **Civil aviation:** 142.9 mil. pass.-mi; 22 airports. **Chief ports:** Batumi, Sukhumi.

Communications: TV sets: 516 per 1,000 pop. **Radios:** 590 per 1,000 pop. **Telephone lines:** 650,500. **Daily newspaper circ.:** 4.9 per 1,000 pop. **Internet:** 150,500 users.

Health: Life expect.: 72.4 male; 79.4 female. **Births** (per 1,000 pop.): 10.1. **Deaths** (per 1,000 pop.): 9.0. **Natural inc.:** 0.11%. **Infant mortality** (per 1,000 live births): 19.3. **AIDS rate:** 0.1%.

Education: Compulsory: ages 6-14. **Literacy** (1999 est.): 99%.

Major Intl. Organizations: UN (FAO, IBRD, ILO, IMF, IMO, WHO), CIS, OSCE.

Embassy: 1615 New Hampshire Ave. NW, Ste. 300, 20009; 393-5959.

Website: www.georgiaemb.org

The region, which contained the ancient kingdoms of Colchis and Iberia, was Christianized in the 4th century and conquered by Arabs in the 8th century. Annexed by Russia in 1801, Georgia was forcibly incorporated into the USSR in 1922.

Georgia declared independence Apr. 9, 1991. It became an independent state when the Soviet Union disbanded Dec. 26, 1991. There was fighting during 1991 between rebel forces and loyalists of Pres. Zviad Gamsakhurdia, who fled the capital Jan. 6, 1992. The ruling Military Council picked former Soviet Foreign Minister Eduard A. Shevardnadze to chair a newly created State Council. An attempted coup by forces loyal to Gamsakhurdia was crushed June 24, 1992. Shevardnadze was later elected president. Gamsakhurdia died Jan. 1994, reportedly by suicide.

On Feb. 3, 1994, Georgia signed agreements with Russia for economic and military cooperation. On Mar. 1, Georgia's Supreme Council ratified membership by Georgia in the Commonwealth of Independent States.

Shevardnadze was wounded by a car bomb Aug. 29, 1995, while on his way to Parliament to sign a new constitution. He was reelected president Nov. 5. Shevardnadze escaped another assassination attempt, Feb. 9, 1998, when gunmen ambushed his motorcade. A mutiny by more than 200 soldiers was crushed Oct. 19.

Shevardnadze won another 5-year presidential term Apr. 9, 2000. But parliamentary elections Nov. 2, 2003, denounced as fraudulent by opposition groups and international observers, sparked massive antigovernment protests, causing him to resign Nov. 23. Opposition leader Mikhail Saakashvili won the presidential election of Jan. 4, 2004.

Since the country gained independence, rebel movements have challenged the Tbilisi government. In Abkhazia, an autonomous republic within Georgia, ethnic Abkhazis, reportedly aided by Russia, launched a bloody military campaign and, by late 1993, had gained control of much of the region. A cease-fire providing for Russian peacekeepers was signed in Moscow May 14, 1994, but intermittent clashes continued. Georgian government troops also fought South Ossetia secessionists. Chechen rebels based in Pankisi Gorge, NE of Tbilisi, launched attacks against Russian troops in Chechnya, heightening tensions with Russia.

Germany
Federal Republic of Germany

People: Population: 82,424,609. **Age distrib.** (%): <15: 15.4; 65+: 17. **Pop. density:** 611 per sq mi, 236 per sq km. **Urban:** 88.1%. **Ethnic groups:** German 92%, Turkish 2%. **Principal languages:** German (official), Turkish, Italian, Greek, English, Danish, Dutch, Slavic languages. **Chief religions:** Protestant 34%, Roman Catholic 34%, Muslim 4%.

Geography: Total area: 137,847 sq mi, 357,021 sq km; **Land area:** 134,836 sq mi, 349,223 sq km. **Location:** In central Europe. **Neighbors:** Denmark on N; Netherlands, Belgium, Luxembourg, France on W; Switzerland, Austria on S; Czech Rep., Poland on E. **Topography:** Germany is flat in N, hilly in center and W, and mountainous in Bavaria in the S. Chief rivers are Elbe, Weser, Ems, Rhine, and Main, all flowing toward North Sea, and Danube, flowing toward Black Sea. **Capital:** Berlin, 3,327,000. **Cities (urban aggr.):** Rhein-Ruhr North (including Essen), 6.54 mil.; Rhein Main (Frankfurt am Mein), 3.68 mil.; Rhein-Ruhr Middle (Dusseldorf), 3.24 mil.; Rhein-Ruhr South (Cologne), 3.06 mil.; Stuttgart, 2.68 mil; **Cities (proper):** Hamburg, 2.67 mil.; Munich, 2.3 mil.; Cologne, 963,200; Frankfurt am Main, 644,700.

Government: Type: Federal republic. **Head of state:** Pres. Horst Köhler; b Feb. 22, 1943; in office: July 1, 2004. **Head of gov.:** Chan. Gerhard Schröder; b Apr. 7, 1944; in office: Oct. 27, 1998. **Local divisions:** 16 laender (states). **Defense budget** (2003): $27.4 bil. **Active troops:** 284,500.

Economy: Industries: iron, steel, coal, cement, chemicals, machinery, vehicles, machine tools, electronics, food & beverages, shipbuilding. **Chief crops:** potatoes, wheat, barley, sugar beets, fruit, cabbages. **Natural resources:** iron ore, coal, potash, timber, lignite, uranium, copper, nat. gas, salt, nickel. **Crude oil reserves** (2003): 342.3 mil. bbls. **Arable land:** 33%. **Livestock** (2003): cattle: 13.7 mil.; chickens: 110.0 mil.; goats: 165,000; pigs: 26.3 mil. sheep: 2.66 mil. **Fish catch** (2002): 274,303 metric tons. **Electricity prod.** (2002): 548.29 bil. kWh. **Labor force** (1999): industry 33.4%, agriculture 2.8%, services 63.8%.

Finance: Monetary unit: Euro (EUR) (Sept. 2004: 0.82 = $1 U.S.). **GDP** (2003 est.): $2.271 tril.; **per capita GDP:** $27,600; **GDP growth:** –0.1%. **Imports** (2003 est.): $585.0 bil.; partners (2002): France 9.4%, Netherlands 8.2%, U.S. 7.7%, Italy 6.4%, UK 6.4%, Belgium 5.1%, Austria 4.1%, China 4.1%. **Exports** (2003 est.): $696.9 bil.; partners (2002): France 10.7%, U.S. 10.3%, UK 8.4%, Italy 7.3%, Netherlands 6.1%, Austria 5.1%, Belgium 4.8%, Spain 4.6%, Switzerland 4.2%. **Tourism:** $22.8 bil.

Budget (2001 est.): $825.0 bil. **Intl. reserves less gold:** $34.12 bil. **Gold:** 110.58 mil oz t. **Consumer prices:** 1.0%.

Transport: Railroad: Length: 28,281 mi. **Motor vehicles** (2001): 43.77 mil pass. cars, 3.38 mil comm. vehicles. **Civil aviation:** 65.6 bil. pass.-mi; 328 airports. **Chief ports:** Hamburg, Bremen, Bremerhaven, Lubeck, Rostock.

Communications: TV sets: 581 per 1,000 pop. **Radios:** 948 per 1,000 pop. **Telephone lines:** 54.4 mil. **Daily newspaper circ.:** 304.8 per 1,000 pop. **Internet :** 39.0 mil. users.

Health: Life expect.: 75.6 male; 81.7 female. **Births** (per 1,000 pop.): 8.4. **Deaths** (per 1,000 pop.): 10.4. **Natural inc.:** −0.20%. **Infant mortality** (per 1,000 live births): 4.2. **AIDS rate:** 0.1%.

Education: Compulsory: ages 6-18. **Literacy** (1993): 100%.

Major Intl. Organizations: UN and all of its specialized agencies, EU, NATO, OECD, OSCE.

Embassy: 4645 Reservoir Rd. NW 20007; 298-4000.

Website: www.germany-info.org

Germany is a central European nation originally composed of numerous states, with a common language and traditions, that were united in one country in 1871; Germany was split into 2 countries from the end of World War II until 1990, when it was reunified.

History and government. Germanic tribes were defeated by Julius Caesar, 55 and 53 BC, but Roman expansion N of the Rhine was stopped in AD 9. Charlemagne, ruler of the Franks, consolidated Saxon, Bavarian, Rhenish, Frankish, and other lands; after him the eastern part became the German Empire. The Thirty Years' War, 1618-1648, split Germany into small principalities and kingdoms. After Napoleon, Austria contended with Prussia for dominance, but lost the Seven Weeks' War to Prussia, 1866. Otto von Bismarck, Prussian chancellor, formed the North German Confederation, 1867.

In 1870 Bismarck maneuvered Napoleon III into declaring war. After the quick defeat of France, Bismarck formed the **German Empire** and on Jan. 18, 1871, in Versailles, proclaimed King Wilhelm I of Prussia German emperor (Deutscher kaiser).

The German Empire reached its peak before World War I in 1914, with 208,780 sq. mi., plus a colonial empire. After that war Germany ceded Alsace-Lorraine to France; West Prussia and Posen (Poznan) province to Poland; part of Schleswig to Denmark; lost all colonies and ports of Memel and Danzig.

Republic of Germany, 1919-1933, adopted the Weimar constitution; met reparation payments and elected Friedrich Ebert and Gen. Paul von Hindenburg presidents.

Third Reich, 1933-1945, Adolf Hitler led the National Socialist German Workers' (Nazi) party after World War I. In 1923 he attempted to unseat the Bavarian government and was imprisoned. Pres. von Hindenburg named Hitler chancellor Jan. 30, 1933; on Aug. 3, 1934, the day after Hindenburg's death, the cabinet joined the offices of president and chancellor and made Hitler fuehrer (leader). Hitler abolished freedom of speech and assembly, and began a long series of persecutions climaxed by the murder of millions of Jews and others.

He repudiated the Versailles treaty and reparations agreements, remilitarized the Rhineland (1936), and annexed Austria (Anschluss, 1938). At Munich he made an agreement with Neville Chamberlain, British prime minister, which permitted Germany to annex part of Czechoslovakia. He signed a nonaggression treaty with the USSR, 1939 and declared war on Poland Sept. 1, 1939, precipitating World War II. With total defeat near, Hitler committed suicide in Berlin Apr. 1945. The victorious Allies voided all acts and annexations of Hitler's Reich.

Division of Germany. Germany was sectioned into 4 zones of occupation, administered by the Allied Powers (U.S., USSR, U.K., and France). The USSR took control of many E German states. The territory E of the so-called Oder-Neisse line was assigned to, and later annexed by, Poland. Northern East Prussia (now Kaliningrad) was annexed by the USSR. Greater Berlin, within but not part of the Soviet zone, was administered by the 4 occupying powers under the Allied Command. In 1948 the USSR withdrew, established its single command in East Berlin, and cut off supplies. The Western Allies utilized a gigantic airlift to bring food to West Berlin, 1948-49.

In 1949, 2 separate German states were established; in May the zones administered by the Western Allies became West Germany; in Oct. the Soviet sector became East Germany. West Berlin was considered an enclave of West Germany, although its status was disputed by the Soviet bloc.

East Germany. The German Democratic Republic (East Germany) was proclaimed in the Soviet sector of Berlin Oct. 7, 1949. It was declared fully sovereign in 1954, but Soviet troops remained on grounds of security and the 4-power Potsdam agreement.

Coincident with the entrance of West Germany into the European defense community in 1952, the East German government decreed a prohibited zone 3 miles deep along its 600-mile border with West Germany and cut Berlin's telephone system in two. Berlin was further divided by erection of a fortified wall in 1961, after over 3 million East Germans had fled to the West.

East Germany suffered severe economic problems at least until the mid-1960s. Then a "new economic system" was introduced, easing central planning controls and allowing factories to make profits provided they were reinvested in operations or redistributed to workers as bonuses. By the early 1970s, the economy of East Germany was highly industrialized, and the nation was credited

with the highest standard of living among Warsaw Pact countries. But growth slowed in the late 1970s, because of shortages of natural resources and labor, and a huge debt to lenders in the West. Comparison with the lifestyle in the West caused many young people to emigrate.

The government firmly resisted following the USSR's policy of *glasnost,* but by Oct. 1989, was faced with nationwide demonstrations demanding reform. Pres. Erich Honecker, in office since 1976, was forced to resign, Oct. 18. On Nov. 4, the border with Czechoslovakia was opened and permission granted for refugees to travel to the West. On Nov. 9, the East German government announced its decision to open the border with the West, signaling the end of the "Berlin Wall," which was the supreme emblem of the cold war. On Aug. 23, 1990, the East German parliament agreed to formal unification with West Germany; this occurred Oct. 3.

West Germany. The Federal Republic of Germany (West Germany) was proclaimed May 23, 1949, in Bonn, after a constitution had been drawn up by a consultative assembly formed by representatives of the 11 laender (states) in the French, British, and American zones. Later reorganized into 9 units, the laender numbered 10 with the addition of the Saar, 1957. Berlin also was granted land (state) status, but the 1945 occupation agreements placed restrictions on it.

The occupying powers, the U.S., Britain, and France, restored civil status, Sept. 21, 1949. The Western Allies ended the state of war with Germany in 1951 (the U.S. resumed diplomatic relations July 2), while the USSR did so in 1955. The powers lifted controls and the republic became fully independent May 5, 1955.

Dr. Konrad Adenauer, Christian Democrat, was made chancellor Sept. 15, 1949, reelected 1953, 1957, 1961. Willy Brandt, heading a coalition of Social Democrats and Free Democrats, became chancellor Oct. 21, 1969. Brandt resigned May 1974 because of a spy scandal.

In 1970 Brandt signed friendship treaties with the USSR and Poland. In 1971, the U.S., Britain, France, and the USSR signed an agreement on Western access to West Berlin. In 1972 East and West Germany signed their first formal treaty, implementing the agreement easing access to West Berlin. In 1973 a West Germany-Czechoslovakia pact normalized relations and nullified the 1938 "Munich Agreement."

West Germany experienced strong economic growth from the 1950s through the 1980s. The country led Europe in provisions for worker participation in the management of industry.

In 1989 the changes in the East German government and opening of the Berlin Wall sparked talk of reunification of the 2 Germanys. In 1990, under Chancellor Helmut Kohl's leadership, West Germany moved rapidly to reunite with East Germany.

A New Era. As Communism was being rejected in East Germany, talks began concerning German reunification. At a meeting in Ottawa, Feb. 1990, the foreign ministers of the World War II "Big Four" Allied nations and East Germany and West Germany reached agreement on a format for high-level talks on German reunification.

In May 1990, NATO ministers adopted a package of proposals on reunification, including the inclusion of the united Germany as a full member of NATO and the barring of the new Germany from having its own nuclear, chemical, or biological weapons. In July, the USSR agreed to conditions that would allow Germany to become a member of NATO.

The 2 nations agreed to monetary unification under the West German mark beginning in July. The merger of the 2 Germanys took place Oct. 3, and the first all-German elections since 1932 were held Dec. 2. Eastern Germany received over $1 trillion in public and private funds from western Germany between 1990 and 1995. In 1991, Berlin again became the capital of Germany; the legislature, most administrative offices, and most foreign embassies had shifted from Bonn to Berlin by late 1999.

Germany's highest court ruled, July 12, 1994, that German troops could participate in international military missions abroad, when approved by Parliament. Ceremonies were held marking the final withdrawal of Russian troops from Germany, Aug. 31. Ceremonies were held the following week marking the final withdrawal of American, British, and French troops from Berlin. General elections Oct. 16 left Chancellor Helmut Kohl's governing coalition with a slim parliamentary majority. On Oct. 31, 1996, after more than 14 years in office, Kohl surpassed Adenauer as Germany's longest-serving chancellor in the 20th century.

Unemployment hit a postwar high of 12.6% in Jan. 1998. The Kohl era ended with the defeat of the Christian Democrats in parliamentary elections Sept. 27; Gerhard Schröder, of the Social Democratic Party, became chancellor. Germany contributed 8,500 troops to the NATO-led security force (KFOR) that entered Kosovo in June 1999. Kohl resigned as honorary party chairman Jan. 18, 2000, amid allegations of illegal fund-raising. Kohl reached an agreement with prosecutors Feb. 8, 2001, in which he acknowledged committing a "breach of trust" and agreed to pay a fine, but did not plead guilty to any criminal charges.

Despite a stagnant economy, Schröder's coalition of Social Democrats and Greens retained a slim majority in the elections of Sept. 22, 2002; the chancellor was apparently aided by his government's response to devastating summer floods and by his criticism of U.S. policy toward Iraq. In early 2003, Germany worked with

France and Russia to block the UN Security Council from endorsing the U.S.-led invasion of Iraq. However, polls showed Schröder's support sharply falling; in Feb. 2004 he resigned as party chairman saying he needed to focus more on economic reform as chancellor. Schröder's coalition did poorly in elections for the European Parliament, June 13, 2004. As of mid-2004, about 1,900 German troops were serving in Afghanistan as part of a NATO peacekeeping force.

Helgoland, an island of 130 acres in the North Sea, was taken from Denmark by a British Naval Force in 1807 and later ceded to Germany to become part of Schleswig-Holstein province in return for rights in East Africa. The heavily fortified island was surrendered to UK, May 23, 1945, demilitarized in 1947, and returned to West Germany, Mar. 1, 1952. It is a free port.

Ghana
Republic of Ghana

People: Population: 20,757,032. **Age distrib.** (%): <15: 40.4; 65+: 3.5. **Pop. density:** 233 per sq mi, 90 per sq km. **Urban:** 45.4%. **Ethnic groups:** Akan 44%, Moshi-Dagomba 16%, Ewe 13%, Ga 8%, Gurma 3%, Yoruba 1%. **Principal languages:** English (official); about 75 African languages incl. Akan, Moshi-Dagomba, Ewe, and Ga. **Chief religions:** Christian 63%, indigenous beliefs 21%, Muslim 16%.

Geography: Total area: 92,456 sq mi, 239,460 sq km; **Land area:** 89,166 sq mi, 230,940 sq km. **Location:** On southern coast of W Africa. **Neighbors:** Côte d'Ivoire on W, Burkina Faso on N, Togo on E. **Topography:** Most of Ghana consists of low fertile plains and scrubland, cut by rivers and by the artificial Lake Volta. **Capital:** Accra, 1,847,000.

Government: Type: Republic. **Head of state and gov.:** Pres. John Agyekum Kufuor; b Dec. 8, 1938; in office: Jan. 7, 2001. **Local divisions:** 10 regions. **Defense budget** (2003): $29 mil. **Active troops:** 7,000.

Economy: Industries: mining, lumbering, light mfg., aluminum smelting, food proc. **Chief crops:** cocoa, rice, coffee, cassava, peanuts, corn, shea nuts, bananas. **Natural resources:** gold, timber, diamonds, bauxite, mang., fish, rubber, hydropower. **Crude oil reserves** (2003): 17 mil. bbls. **Arable land:** 12%. **Livestock** (2003): cattle: 1.35 mil.; chickens: 26.7 mil.; goats: 3.26 mil.; pigs: 308,000; sheep: 3.10 mil. **Fish catch** (2002 est): 377,178 metric tons. **Electricity prod.** (2002): 6.92 bil. kWh. **Labor force** (1999 est.): agriculture 60%, industry 15%, services 25%.

Finance: Monetary unit: Cedi (GHC) (Sept. 2004: 9,097.00 = $1 U.S.). **GDP** (2003 est.): $44.5 bil.; **per capita GDP:** $2,200; **GDP growth:** 4.8%. **Imports** (2003 est.): $3.2 bil.; partners (2002): Nigeria 20.8%, UK 7%, U.S. 6.4%, China 6%, Italy 6%, Cote d'Ivoire 6%, Germany 4.6%. **Exports** (2003 est.): $2.6 bil.; partners (2002): Netherlands 14.6%, UK 9.7%, U.S. 6.9%, Germany 6.4%, France 5.7%, Nigeria 4.7%, Belgium 4.4%, Italy 4.1%. **Tourism** (2002): $358 mil. **Budget** (2001 est.): $2.0 bil. **Intl. reserves less gold:** $910 mil. **Gold:** 280,000 oz t. **Consumer prices:** 26.7%.

Transport: Railroad: Length: 592 mi. **Motor vehicles** (1999): 90,400 pass. cars, 119,900 comm. vehicles. **Civil aviation:** 748.1 mil. pass.-mi; 7 airports. **Chief ports:** Tema, Takoradi.

Communications: TV sets: 115 per 1,000 pop. **Radios:** 680 per 1,000 pop. **Telephone lines:** 302,300. **Daily newspaper circ.:** 14 per 1,000 pop. **Internet** (2002): 170,000 users.

Health: Life expect.: 55.4 male; 57.2 female. **Births** (per 1,000 pop.): 24.9. **Deaths** (per 1,000 pop.): 10.7. **Natural inc.:** 1.42%. **Infant mortality** (per 1,000 live births): 52.2. **AIDS rate:** 3.1%.

Education: Compulsory: ages 6-13. **Literacy:** 74.8%.

Major Intl. Organizations: UN and all of its specialized agencies, the Commonwealth, AU.

Embassy: 3512 International Dr. NW 20008; 686-4520.

Website: www.ghana-embassy.org; www.ghana.gov.gh

Named for an African empire along the Niger River, AD 400-1240, Ghana was ruled by Britain for 113 years as the Gold Coast. The UN in 1956 approved merger with the British Togoland trust territory. Independence came Mar. 6, 1957, and republic status within the Commonwealth in 1960.

Pres. Kwame Nkrumah built hospitals and schools, promoted development projects like the Volta R. hydroelectric and aluminum plants but ran the country into debt, jailed opponents, and was accused of corruption. A 1964 referendum gave Nkrumah dictatorial powers and set up a one-party socialist state. Nkrumah was overthrown in 1966 by a police-army coup, which expelled Chinese and East German teachers and technicians. Elections were held in 1969, but 4 further coups occurred in 1972, 1978, 1979, and 1981. The 1979 and 1981 coups, led by Flight Lieut. Jerry Rawlings, were followed by suspension of the constitution and banning of political parties. A new constitution, allowing multiparty politics, was approved in April 1992.

In Feb. 1993 more than 1,000 people were killed in ethnic clashes in northern Ghana. Rawlings won the presidential election of Dec. 7, 1996. Kofi Annan, a career UN diplomat from Ghana, became UN secretary general on Jan. 1, 1997. Opposition leader John Agyekum Kufuor won a runoff vote Dec. 28, 2000, and was sworn in Jan. 7, 2001, marking Ghana's 1st peaceful transfer of power from one elected president to another.

Greece
Hellenic Republic

People: Population: 10,647,529. **Age distrib.** (%): <15: 14.8; 65+: 18.1. **Pop. density:** 211 per sq mi, 81 per sq km. **Urban:** 60.8%.. **Ethnic groups:** Greek 98%. **Principal languages:** Greek (official), English, French. **Chief religions:** Greek Orthodox 98% (official), Muslim 1%.

Geography: Total area: 50,942 sq mi, 131,940 sq km; **Land area:** 50,502 sq mi, 130,800 sq km. **Location:** Occupies southern end of Balkan Peninsula in SE Europe. **Neighbors:** Albania, Macedonia, Bulgaria on N; Turkey on E. **Topography:** About three-quarters of Greece is nonarable, with mountains in all areas. Pindus Mts. run through the country N to S. The heavily indented coastline is 9,385 mi. long. Of over 2,000 islands, only 169 are inhabited, among them Crete, Rhodes, Milos, Kerkira (Corfu), Chios, Lesbos, Samos, Euboea, Delos, Mykonos. **Capital:** Athens, 3,215,000 (1999 city proper: 748,110).

Government: Type: Parliamentary republic. **Head of state:** Pres. Konstantinos Stephanopoulos; b Aug. 15, 1926; in office: Mar. 8, 1995. **Head of gov.:** Prime Min. Konstantinos (Costas) Karamanlis; b Sept. 14, 1956; in office: Mar. 10, 2004. **Local divisions:** 13 regions comprising 51 prefectures. **Defense budget** (2003): $4.0 bil. **Active troops:** 177,600.

Economy: Industries: tourism, food & tobacco proc., textiles, chemicals, metal products, mining, oil. **Chief crops:** wheat, corn, barley, sugar beets, olives, tomatoes, grapes. **Natural resources:** bauxite, lignite, magnesite, oil, marble, hydropower potential. **Crude oil reserves** (2003): 9.0 mil. bbls. **Arable land:** 19%. **Livestock** (2003): cattle: 585,000; chickens: 28.0 mil.; goats: 5.0 mil.; pigs: 903,000; sheep: 9.1 mil. **Fish catch** (2002 est): 176,911 metric tons. **Electricity prod.** (2002): 47.22 bil. kWh. **Labor force** (2000 est.): industry 20%, agriculture 20%, services 59%.

Finance: Monetary unit: Euro (EUR) (Sept. 2004: 0.82 = $1 U.S.). **GDP** (2003 est.): $212.2 bil.; **per capita GDP:** $19,900; **GDP growth:** 4.0%. **Imports** (2003 est.): $33.3 bil.; partners (2002): Germany 12.2%, Italy 11.5%, Russia 7.4%, South Korea 6%, France 5.7%, Netherlands 5.6%, U.S. 4.7%, Belgium 4.3%, UK 4.1%. **Exports** (2003 est.): $5.9 bil.; partners (2002): Germany 10.4%, Italy 8.5%, UK 6.3%, Bulgaria 5.4%, U.S. 5.3%, Cyprus 4.7%. **Tourism:** $10.6 bil. **Budget** (1998 est.): $47.6 bil. **Intl. reserves less gold:** $2.94 bil. **Gold:** 3.45 mil oz t. **Consumer prices:** 3.6%.

Transport: Railroad: Length: 1,598 mi. **Motor vehicles** (2001): 3.42 mil pass. cars, 1.11 mil. comm. vehicles. **Civil aviation:** 5.3 bil. pass.-mi;; 66 airports. **Chief ports:** Piraeus, Thessaloníki, Patrai.

Communications: TV sets: 480 per 1,000 pop. **Radios:** 475 per 1,000 pop. **Telephone lines:** 2 mil. **Daily newspaper circ.:** 22.4 per 1,000 pop. **Internet:** 1.7 mil. users.

Health: Life expect.: 76.4 male; 81.6 female. **Births** (per 1,000 pop.): 9.7. **Deaths** (per 1,000 pop.): 10.1. **Natural inc.:** −0.04%. **Infant mortality** (per 1,000 live births): 5.6. **AIDS rate:** 0.2%.

Education: Compulsory: ages 6-14. **Literacy:** 97.5%.

Major Intl. Organizations: UN (FAO, IBRD, ILO, IMF, IMO, WHO, WTrO), EU, NATO, OECD, OSCE.

Embassy: 2221 Massachusetts Ave. NW 20008; 939-5800.

Website: www.greekembassy.org

The achievements of ancient Greece in art, architecture, science, mathematics, philosophy, drama, literature, and democracy became legacies for succeeding ages. Greece reached the height of its glory and power, particularly in the Athenian city-state, in the 5th century BC. Greece fell under Roman rule in the 2d and 1st centuries BC. In the 4th century AD it became part of the Byzantine Empire, and, after the fall of Constantinople to the Turks in 1453, part of the Ottoman Empire.

Greece won its war of independence from Turkey 1821-1829, and became a kingdom. A republic was established 1924; the monarchy was restored, 1935, and George II, King of the Hellenes, resumed the throne. In Oct. 1940, Greece rejected an ultimatum from Italy. Nazi support resulted in its defeat and occupation by Germans, Italians, and Bulgarians. By the end of 1944 the invaders withdrew. Communist resistance forces were defeated by Royalist and British troops. A plebiscite again restored the monarchy.

Communists waged guerrilla war 1947-49 against the government but were defeated with the aid of the U.S. A period of reconstruction and rapid development followed, mainly with conservative governments under Premier Constantine Karamanlis. The Center Union, led by George Papandreou, won elections in 1963 and 1964, but King Constantine, who acceded in 1964, forced Papandreou to resign. A period of political maneuvers ended in the military takeover of April 21, 1967, by Col. George Papadopoulos. King Constantine tried to reverse the consolidation of the harsh dictatorship Dec. 13, 1967, but failed and fled to Italy. Papadopoulos was ousted Nov. 25, 1973.

Greek army officers serving in the National Guard of Cyprus staged a coup on the island July 15, 1974. Turkey invaded Cyprus a week later, precipitating the collapse of the Greek junta, which was implicated in the Cyprus coup. Democratic government returned (and in 1975 the monarchy was abolished).

The 1981 electoral victory of the Panhellenic Socialist Movement (Pasok) of Andreas Papandreou brought substantial changes in Greece's internal and external policies. A scandal centered on George Kostokas, a banker and publisher, led to the arrest or

investigation of leading Socialists, implicated Papandreou, and contributed to the defeat of the Socialists at the polls in 1989. However, Papandreou, who was narrowly acquitted Jan. 1992 of corruption charges, led the Socialists to a comeback victory in general elections Oct. 10, 1993.

Tensions between Greece and the Former Yugoslav Republic of Macedonia eased when the 2 countries agreed to normalize relations Sept. 13, 1995. The ailing Papandreou was replaced as prime minister by Costas Simitis, Jan. 18, 1996. Simitis led the Socialists to victory in the election of Sept. 22.

An earthquake that shook Athens Sept. 7, 1999, killed at least 143 people and left over 60,000 homeless. The Socialists retained power by a narrow margin in the elections of Apr. 9, 2000. Police in 2002 cracked down on the November 17 terrorist movement, blamed for 23 killings since the mid-1970s.

The conservative New Democracy Party won parliamentary elections, Mar. 7, 2004, and Konstantinos (Costas) Karamanlis became prime minister. Athens hosted the Olympic Summer Games, Aug. 13-29.

Grenada

People: Population: 89,357. **Age distrib.** (%): <15: 35.9; 65+: 3.8. **Pop. density:** 673 per sq mi, 260 per sq km. **Urban:** 40.7%. **Ethnic groups:** Black 82%, Creole 13%. **Principal languages:** English (official), French patois. **Chief religions:** Roman Catholic 53%, Anglican 14%, other Protestant 33%.

Geography: Total area: 133 sq mi, 344 sq km; **Land area:** 133 sq mi, 344 sq km. **Location:** In Caribbean, 90 mi. N of Venezuela. **Neighbors:** Venezuela, Trinidid & Tobago to S; St. Vincent & the Grenadines to N. **Topography:** Main island is mountainous; country includes Carriacou and Petit Martinique islands. **Capital:** Saint George's, 33,000.

Government: Type: Parliamentary democracy. **Head of state:** Queen Elizabeth II, represented by Gov.-Gen. Daniel Williams; b Nov. 4, 1935; in office: Aug. 8, 1996. **Head of gov.:** Prime Min. Keith Mitchell; b Nov. 12, 1946; in office: June 22, 1995. **Local divisions:** 6 parishes, 1 dependency.

Economy: Industries: food, beverages, textiles, light assembly operations, tourism, constr. **Chief crops:** bananas, cocoa, nutmeg, mace, citrus, avocados. **Natural resources:** timber. **Arable land:** 15%. **Livestock** (2003): cattle: 4,450; chickens: 268,000; goats: 7,200; pigs: 5,850; sheep: 13,200. **Fish catch** (2002): 2,171 metric tons. **Electricity prod.** (2002): 0.15 bil. kWh. **Labor force** (1999 est.): services 62%, agriculture 24%, industry 14%.

Finance: Monetary unit: East Caribbean Dollar (XCD) (Sept. 2004: 2.67 = $1 U.S.). **GDP** (2002 est.): $440.0 mil.; **per capita GDP:** $5,000; **GDP growth:** 2.5%. **Imports** (2002 est.): $208.0 mil.; partners (2002): U.S. 29.8%, Trinidad and Tobago 26.9%, UK 4.3%. **Exports** (2002 est.): $46.0 mil.; partners (2002): U.S. 15.2%, Germany 13%, Bangladesh 10.9%, Netherlands 8.7%, Saint Lucia 6.5%, Antigua and Barbuda 4.3%, Dominica 4.3%, France 4.3%, Saint Kitts and Nevis 4.3%, Trinidad and Tobago 4.3%, UK 4.3%. **Tourism:** $104 mil. **Budget** (1997): $102.1 mil. **Intl. reserves less gold:** $56 mil. **Consumer prices** (change in 2002): 1.1%.

Transport: Motor vehicles (2001): 15,800 pass. cars, 4,200 comm. vehicles. **Civil aviation:** 3 airports. **Chief ports:** Saint George's, Grenville.

Communications: TV sets: 376 per 1,000 pop. **Radios:** 613 per 1,000 pop. **Telephone lines** (2002): 33,500. **Internet** (2002): 15,000 users.

Health: Life expect.: 62.7 male; 66.3 female. **Births** (per 1,000 pop.): 22.6. **Deaths** (per 1,000 pop.): 7.3. **Natural inc.:** 1.53%. **Infant mortality** (per 1,000 live births): 14.6.

Education: Compulsory: ages 5-16. **Literacy** (1994): 85%.

Major Intl. Organizations: UN (FAO, IBRD, ILO, IMF, WHO, WTrO), Caricom, the Commonwealth, OAS, OECS.

Embassy: 1701 New Hampshire Ave. NW 20009; 265-2561.

Website: www.grenadagrenadines.com

Columbus sighted Grenada in 1498. First European settlers were French, 1650. The island was held alternately by France and England until final British occupation, 1784. Grenada became fully independent Feb. 7, 1974, during a general strike. It is the smallest independent nation in the western hemisphere.

On Oct. 14, 1983, a military coup ousted Prime Minister Maurice Bishop, who was put under house arrest, later freed by supporters, rearrested, and, finally, on Oct. 19, executed. U.S. forces, with a token force from 6 area nations, invaded Grenada, Oct. 25. Resistance from the Grenadian army and Cuban advisors was quickly overcome as most people welcomed the invading forces. U.S. troops left Grenada in June 1985. Hurricane Ivan slammed into Grenada, Sept. 7, 2004, killing 39 people and damaging an estimated 90% of the buildings on the island.

Guatemala
Republic of Guatemala

People: Population: 14,280,596. **Age distrib.** (%): <15: 41.8; 65+: 3.7. **Pop. density:** 341 per sq mi, 132 per sq km. **Urban:** 46.3%. **Ethnic groups:** Mestizo 55%, Amerindian 43%. **Principal languages:** Spanish (official); more than 20 Amerindian languages, incl. Quiche, Cakchiquel, Kekchi, Mam, Garifuna, and Xinca. **Chief religions:** Mostly Roman Catholic; some Protestant, indigenous Mayan beliefs.

Geography: Total area: 42,043 sq mi, 108,890 sq km; **Land area:** 41,865 sq mi, 108,430 sq km. **Location:** In Central America. **Neighbors:** Mexico on N and W, El Salvador on S, Honduras and Belize on E. **Topography:** The central highland and mountain areas are bordered by the narrow Pacific coast and the lowlands and fertile river valleys on the Caribbean. There are numerous volcanoes in S, more than half a dozen over 11,000 ft. **Capital:** Guatemala City, 951,000.

Government: Type: Republic. **Head of state and gov.:** Pres. Oscar Berger Perdomo; b Aug. 11, 1946; in office: Jan. 14, 2004. **Local divisions:** 22 departments. **Defense budget** (2003): $151 mil. **Active troops:** 31,400.

Economy: Industries: sugar, textiles, clothing, furniture, chemicals, oil, metals, rubber, tourism. **Chief crops:** sugarcane, corn, bananas, coffee, beans, cardamom. **Natural resources:** oil, nickel, rare woods, fish, chicle, hydropower. **Crude oil reserves** (2003): 526.0 mil. bbls. **Arable land:** 12%. **Livestock** (2003): cattle: 2.54 mil.; chickens: 27.0 mil.; goats: 112,000; pigs: 780,000; sheep: 260,000. **Fish catch** (2002 est): 32,142 metric tons. **Electricity prod.** (2002): 6.61 bil. kWh. **Labor force** (1999 est.): agriculture 50%, industry 15%, services 35%.

Finance: Monetary unit: Quetzal (GTQ) (Sept. 2004: 7.89 = $1 U.S.). **GDP** (2003 est.): $56.5 bil.; **per capita GDP:** $4,100; **GDP growth:** 2.2%. **Imports** (2003 est.): $5.7 bil.; partners (2002): U.S. 34.3%, Mexico 8.6%, South Korea 8.4%, El Salvador 5.9%, China 4.1%. **Exports** (2003 est.): $2.8 bil.; partners (2002): U.S. 59%, El Salvador 9.4%, Nicaragua 3.2%. **Tourism:** $599 mil. **Budget** (2002 est.): $2.7 bil. **Intl. reserves less gold:** $1.91 bil. **Gold:** 220,000 oz t. **Consumer prices:** 5.5%.

Transport: Railroad: Length: 551 mi. **Motor vehicles** (1998): 646,500 pass. cars, 21,200 comm. vehicles. **Civil aviation:** 205.7 mil. pass.-mi; 11 airports. **Chief ports:** Puerto Barrios, San Jose.

Communications: TV sets: 61 per 1,000 pop. **Radios:** 79 per 1,000 pop. **Telephone lines** (2002): 846,000. **Daily newspaper circ.:** 33 per 1,000 pop. **Internet** (2002): 400,000 users.

Health: Life expect.: 64.3 male; 66.1 female. **Births** (per 1,000 pop.): 34.6. **Deaths** (per 1,000 pop.): 6.8. **Natural inc.:** 2.78%. **Infant mortality** (per 1,000 live births): 36.9. **AIDS rate:** 1.1%.

Education: Compulsory: ages 5-15. **Literacy:** 70.6%.

Major Intl. Organizations: UN (FAO, IBRD, ILO, IMF, IMO, WHO, WTrO), OAS.

Embassy: 2220 R St. NW 20008; 745-4952.

Website: www.guatemala-embassy.org

The old Mayan Indian empire flourished in what is today Guatemala for over 1,000 years before the Spanish.

Guatemala was a Spanish colony 1524-1821; briefly a part of Mexico and then of the U.S. of Central America, the republic was established in 1839.

Since 1945 when a liberal government was elected to replace the long-term dictatorship of Jorge Ubico, the country has seen a variety of military and civilian governments and periods of civil war. Dissident army officers seized power Mar. 23, 1982, denouncing a presidential election as fraudulent and pledging to restore "authentic democracy" to the nation. Political violence caused large numbers of Guatemalans to seek refuge in Mexico. Another military coup occurred Oct. 8, 1983. The nation returned to civilian rule in 1986.

The crisis-ridden government of Pres. Jorge Serrano Elías was ousted by the military June 1, 1993. Ramiro de León Carpio was elected president by Congress June 6. A conservative businessman, Alvaro Arzú Irigoyen, won the presidency, Jan. 7, 1996. On Sept. 19 the Guatemalan government and leftist rebels approved a peace accord; the final agreement was signed Dec. 29. During more than 35 years of armed conflict, some 200,000 people were killed or "disappeared" (and are presumed dead); most of these casualties were attributed to the government and its paramilitary allies.

Violent episodes in 1998 included the daylight ambush of a busload of U.S. college students, Jan. 16, resulting in the rape of five young women, and the murder of Bishop Juan José Gerardi, a human rights activist, Apr. 26. U.S. Pres. Bill Clinton, on a visit to Guatemala Mar. 10, 1999, apologized for aid the U.S. had given to forces which he said "engaged in violence and widespread repression." Candidates of the right-wing populist Guatemalan Republican Front won control of Congress, Nov. 7, 1999, and the presidency, Dec. 26.

Drought and weak export prices during 2001-02 worsened the plight of Guatemala's poor, who make up 80% of the population. Oscar Berger Perdomo, the conservative former mayor of Guatemala City, won a presidential runoff election Dec. 28, 2003.

Guinea
Republic of Guinea

People: Population: 9,246,462. **Age distrib.** (%): <15: 42.8; 65+: 2.7. **Pop. density:** 97 per sq mi, 38 per sq km. **Urban:** 34.9%. **Ethnic groups:** Peuhl 40%, Malinke 30%, Soussou 20%. **Principal languages:** French (official); many African languages. **Chief religions:** Muslim 85%, Christian 8%, indigenous beliefs 7%.

Geography: Total area: 94,926 sq mi, 245,857 sq km; **Land area:** 94,926 sq mi, 245,857 sq km. **Location:** On Atlantic coast of W Africa. **Neighbors:** Guinea-Bissau, Senegal, Mali on N; Côte d'Ivoire on E; Liberia on S. **Topography:** A narrow coastal belt leads to the mountainous middle region, the source of the Gambia, Senegal, and Niger rivers. Upper Guinea, farther inland, is a cooler upland. The SE is forested. **Capital:** Conakry, 1,366,000.

Government: Type: Republic. **Head of state:** Pres. Gen. Lansana Conté; b 1934; in office: Apr. 5, 1984. **Head of gov.:** Vacant. **Local divisions:** 33 prefectures, 1 special zone. **Defense budget** (2003): $71 mil. **Active troops:** 9,700.

Economy: Industries: bauxite, gold, diamonds, aluminum refining, light mfg., agric. proc. **Chief crops:** rice, coffee, pineapples, palm kernels, cassava, bananas, sweet potatoes. **Natural resources:** bauxite, iron ore, diamonds, gold, uranium, hydropower, fish. **Arable land:** 2%. **Livestock** (2003): cattle: 3.29 mil.; chickens: 13.5 mil.; goats: 1.20 mil.; pigs: 65,000; sheep: 1.01 mil. **Fish catch** (2002 est): 104,000 metric tons. **Electricity prod.** (2002): 0.86 bil. kWh. **Labor force** (2000 est.): agriculture 80%, industry and services 20%.

Finance: Monetary unit: Franc (GNF) (Sept. 2004: 2,592.90 = $1 U.S.). **GDP** (2003 est.): $18.9 bil.; **per capita GDP:** $2,100; **GDP growth:** 2.2%. **Imports** (2003 est.): $646.0 mil.; partners (2002): France 17.9%, Cote d'Ivoire 10.6%, Italy 8.5%, U.S. 7.8%, Belgium 7.2%, China 5.4%, UK 5%. **Exports** (2003 est.): $726.0 mil.; partners (2002): South Korea 17%, Spain 9.7%, Cameroon 9.3%, Belgium 9.2%, U.S. 8.9%, Ireland 8.2%, France 6.8%, Russia 6.4%, Ukraine 6.3%, Germany 4.8%. **Tourism** (2002): $43 mil. **Budget** (2000 est.): $472.4 mil. **Intl. reserves less gold** (change in 2002): $126 mil.

Transport: Railroad: Length: 693 mi. **Motor vehicles** (1995): 23,200 pass. cars, 13,000 comm. vehicles. **Civil aviation:** 58.4 mil. pass.-mi; 5 airports. **Chief port:** Conakry.

Communications: TV sets: 47 per 1,000 pop. **Radios:** 52 per 1,000 pop. **Telephone lines:** 26,200. **Internet:** 40,000 users.

Health: Life expect.: 48.5 male; 51.0 female. **Births** (per 1,000 pop.): 42.3. **Deaths** (per 1,000 pop.): 15.5. **Natural inc.:** 2.67%. **Infant mortality** (per 1,000 live births): 91.8. **AIDS rate:** 3.2%.

Education: Compulsory: ages 7-16. **Literacy** (2002): 36%.

Major Intl. Organizations: UN and most of its specialized agencies, AU.

Embassy: 2112 Leroy Pl. NW 20008; 483-9420.

Website: www.embassy.org/gn.html

Sékou Touré, Guinea's 1st president (1958-84), turned to Communist nations for support and set up a one-party state. Thousands of opponents were jailed in the 1970s, after an unsuccessful Portuguese invasion. Many were tortured and killed.

The military took control in a bloodless coup after the March 1984 death of Touré. A new constitution was approved in 1991, but movement toward democracy was slow. When presidential elections were finally held, in Dec. 1993, the incumbent, Gen. Lansana Conté, was the official winner; outside monitors called the elections flawed. Parliamentary elections June 11, 1995, raised similar complaints. Conté suppressed an army mutiny in Conakry, Feb. 2-3, 1996, and won reelection in Dec. 1998.

Fighting in early 2001 along the border with Liberia and Sierra Leone created a refugee crisis; as of mid-2004 more than 130,000 refugees, mostly Liberians, remained in Guinea. Major opposition parties boycotted the presidential election Dec. 21, 2003, in which the ailing Conté won 95.6% of the vote. After 2 months in office, Prime Min. François Fall resigned, Apr. 30, 2004, charging Conté with thwarting reform efforts.

Guinea-Bissau
Republic of Guinea-Bissau

People: Population: 1,388,363. **Age distrib.** (%): <15: 41.9; 65+: 2.9. **Pop. density:** 128 per sq mi, 50 per sq km. **Urban:** 34.0%. **Ethnic groups:** Balanta 30%, Fula 20%, Manjaca 14%, Mandinga 13%, Papel 7%. **Principal languages:** Portuguese (official), Crioulo, African languages. **Chief religions:** Indigenous beliefs 50%, Muslim 45%, Christian 5%.

Geography: Total area: 13,946 sq mi, 36,120 sq km; **Land area:** 10,811 sq mi, 28,000 sq km. **Location:** On Atlantic coast of W Africa. **Neighbors:** Senegal on N, Guinea on E and S. **Topography:** A swampy coastal plain covers most of the country; to the east is a low savanna region. **Capital:** Bissau, 336,000.

Government: Type: In transition. **Head of state:** Pres. Henrique Rosa; b. 1946; in office: Sept. 28, 2003 (interim). **Head of gov.:** Carlos Gomes Júnior; b 1949; in office: May 10, 2004. **Local divisions:** 9 regions. **Defense budget** (2002): $4 mil. **Active troops:** 9,250.

Economy: Industries: agric. proc., beer, soft drinks. **Chief crops:** rice, corn, beans, cassava, cashew nuts, peanuts, palm kernels, cotton. **Natural resources:** fish, timber, phosphates, bauxite, oil. **Arable land:** 11%. **Livestock** (2003): cattle: 520,000; chickens: 1.5 mil.; goats: 330,000; pigs: 360,000; sheep: 290,000. **Fish catch** (2002 est): 5,000 metric tons. **Electricity prod.** (2002): 0.06 bil. kWh. **Labor force** (2000 est.): agriculture 82%.

Finance: Monetary unit: CFA Franc BCEAO (XOF) (Sept. 2004: 539.40 = $1 U.S.) **GDP** (2003 est.): $1.2 bil.; **per capita GDP:** $900; **GDP growth:** 1.8%. **Imports** (2002 est.): $104.0 mil.; partners (2002): Senegal 19.6%, Portugal 18.8%, India 15.2%. **Exports** (2002 est.): $54.0 mil.; partners (2002): India 50%, Thailand 19.2%, Uruguay 19.2%. **Tourism** (2002): $12 mil. **Intl. reserves less gold:** $111 mil. **Consumer prices:** -3.52%.

Transport: Motor vehicles: 3,500 pass. cars, 2,500 comm. vehicles. **Civil aviation:** 3.7 mil. pass.-mi; 3 airports. **Chief port:** Bissau.

Communications: Radios: 43 per 1,000 pop. **Telephone lines:** 10,600. **Daily newspaper circ.:** 5.4 per 1,000 pop. **Internet:** 19,000 users.

Health: Life expect.: 45.1 male; 48.9 female. **Births** (per 1,000 pop.): 38.0. **Deaths** (per 1,000 pop.): 16.6. **Natural inc.:** 2.15%. **Infant mortality** (per 1,000 live births): 108.7.

Education: Compulsory: ages 7-12. **Literacy** (2002): 55%.

Major Intl. Organizations: UN (FAO, IBRD, ILO, IMF, IMO, WHO, WTrO), AU.

Embassy: 15929 Yukon Lane, Rockville, MD 20855; 301-947-3958.

Website: embassy.org/embassies/gw.html

Portuguese mariners explored the area in the mid-15th century; the slave trade flourished in the 17th and 18th centuries, and colonization began in the 19th.

Beginning in the 1960s, an independence movement waged a guerrilla war and formed a government in the interior that had international support. Independence came Sept. 10, 1974, after the Portuguese regime was overthrown.

The November 1980 coup gave Vieira absolute power. Vieira eventually initiated political liberalization; multiparty elections were held July 3, 1994. An army uprising June 7, 1998, triggered a civil war, with Senegal and Guinea aiding the Vieira regime. After a peace accord signed on Nov. 2 broke down, rebel troops ousted Vieira on May 7, 1999. Elections Nov. 28-29, 1999, and Jan. 16, 2000, brought a return of civilian rule. Top military officers staged an apparently bloodless coup Sept. 14, 2003. A caretaker government was established Sept. 28, and legislative elections were held Mar. 2004.

Guyana
Co-operative Republic of Guyana

People: Population: 705,803. **Age distrib.** (%): <15: 27.6; 65+: 5. **Pop. density:** 9 per sq mi, 4 per sq km. **Urban:** 37.6%. **Ethnic groups:** East Indian 50%, black 36%, Amerindian 7%. **Principal languages:** English (official), Amerindian dialects, Creole, Hindi, Urdu. **Chief religions:** Christian 50%, Hindu 35%, Muslim 10%.

Geography: Total area: 83,000 sq mi, 214,970 sq km; **Land area:** 76,004 sq mi, 196,850 sq km. **Location:** On N coast of South America. **Neighbors:** Venezuela on W, Brazil on S, Suriname on E. **Topography:** Dense tropical forests cover much of the land, although a flat coastal area up to 40 mi. wide, where 90% of the population lives, provides rich alluvial soil for agriculture. A grassy savanna divides the 2 zones. **Capital:** Georgetown, 231,000.

Government: Type: Republic. **Head of state:** Pres. Bharrat Jagdeo; b Jan. 23, 1964; in office: Aug. 11, 1999. **Head of gov.:** Prime Min. Samuel Hinds; b Dec. 27, 1943; in office: Dec. 22, 1997. **Local divisions:** 10 regions. **Defense budget** (2003): $5.8 mil. **Active troops:** 1,600.

Economy: Industries: bauxite, sugar, rice milling, timber, textiles, gold mining. **Chief crops:** sugar, rice, wheat, vegetable oils. **Natural resources:** bauxite, gold, diamonds, hardwood timber, shrimp, fish. **Arable land:** 2%. **Livestock** (2003): cattle: 110,000; chickens: 21.3 mil.; goats: 79,000; pigs: 20,000; sheep: 130,000. **Fish catch** (2002): 48,625 metric tons. **Electricity prod.** (2002): 0.81 bil. kWh. **Labor force:** 39% agriculture, forestry, fishing; 24% mining, manufacturing, construction

Finance: Monetary unit: Dollar (GYD) (Sept. 2004: 178.50 = $1 U.S.). **GDP** (2003 est.): $2.8 bil.; **per capita GDP:** $4,000; **GDP growth:** 0.3%. **Imports** (2003 est.): $612.0 mil.; partners (2002): U.S. 25.1%, Trinidad and Tobago 16%, Netherlands Antilles 13.7%, Italy 6.6%, UK 5.5%, Cuba 4.4%. **Exports** (2003 est.): $512.0 mil.; partners (2002): Canada 26.3%, U.S. 22.3%, UK 13%, Jamaica 5.1%, Portugal 5.1%, Belgium 4.2%. **Tourism** (2002): $49 mil. **Budget** (2000): $235.2 mil. **Intl. reserves less gold:** $186 mil. **Consumer prices** (change in 2002): 5.3%.

Transport: Railroad: Length: 116 mi. **Motor vehicles** (1998): 9,500 pass. cars, 3,200 comm. vehicles. **Civil aviation:** 185.8 mil. pass.-mi; 8 airports. **Chief port:** Georgetown.

Communications: TV sets: 70 per 1,000 pop. **Radios:** 468 per 1,000 pop. **Telephone lines** (2002): 80,400. **Daily newspaper circ.:** 74.6 per 1,000 pop. **Internet** (2002): 125,000 users.

Health: Life expect.: 60.1 male; 64.8 female. **Births** (per 1,000 pop.): 17.9. **Deaths** (per 1,000 pop.): 9.7. **Natural inc.:** 0.81%. **Infant mortality** (per 1,000 live births): 37.2. **AIDS rate:** 2.5%.

Education: Compulsory: ages 6-15. **Literacy:** 98.8%.

Major Intl. Organizations: UN (FAO, IBRD, ILO, IMF, IMO, WHO, WTrO), Caricom, the Commonwealth, OAS.

Embassy: 2490 Tracy Place NW 20008; 265-6900.

Website: www.guyana.org

Guyana became a Dutch possession in the 17th century, but sovereignty passed to Britain in 1815. Indentured servants from India soon outnumbered African slaves. Ethnic tension has affected political life.

Guyana became independent May 26, 1966. A Venezuelan claim to the western half of Guyana was suspended in 1970 but renewed in 1982; an agreement was reached in 1989. The Suriname border is disputed. The government has nationalized most of the economy, which has remained severely depressed.

The Port Kaituma ambush of U.S. Rep. Leo J. Ryan and others investigating mistreatment of American followers of the Rev. Jim Jones's People's Temple cult triggered a mass suicide-execution of 911 cultists at Jonestown in the jungle, Nov. 18, 1978.

The People's National Congress, the party in power since Guyana became independent, was voted out of office with the election of Cheddi Jagan in Oct. 1992. When Pres. Jagan died Mar. 6, 1997, Prime Min. Samuel Hinds succeeded him; his widow, Janet Jagan, became prime min. Mar. 17. She won the presidency in a disputed election Dec. 15. She resigned because of ill health Aug. 11, 1999, and was succeeded by Bharrat Jagdeo, then 35, who became the youngest head of state in the Americas. He was re-elected Mar. 19, 2001.

Haiti
Republic of Haiti

People: Population: 7,656,166. **Age distrib.** (%): <15: 39.5; 65+: 4.2. **Pop. density:** 719 per sq mi, 278 per sq km. **Urban:** 37.5%. **Ethnic groups:** Black 95%, Creole and other 5%. **Principal languages:** French, Creole (both official). **Chief religions:** Roman Catholic 80%, Protestant 16%; Voodoo widely practiced.

Geography: Total area: 10,714 sq mi, 27,750 sq km; **Land area:** 10,641 sq mi, 27,560 sq km. **Location:** In Caribbean, occupies western third of Isl. of Hispaniola. **Neighbors:** Dominican Republic on E, Cuba to W. **Topography:** About two-thirds of Haiti is mountainous. Much of the rest is semiarid. Coastal areas are warm and moist. **Capital:** Port-au-Prince, 1,961,000.

Government: Type: In transition. **Head of state:** Pres. Boniface Alexandre; b July 31, 1936; in office Feb. 29, 2004 (interim). **Head of gov.:** Gérard Latortue; b June 19, 1934; in office: Mar. 12, 2004. **Local divisions:** 9 departments. **Defense budget:** NA. **Active troops:** NA.

Economy: Industries: sugar refining, flour milling, textiles, cement, light assembly. **Chief crops:** coffee, mangoes, sugarcane, rice, corn, sorghum. **Natural resources:** bauxite, copper, calcium carbonate, gold, marble, hydropower. **Arable land:** 20%. **Livestock** (2003): cattle: 1.46 mil.; chickens: 5.65 mil.; goats: 1.94 mil.; pigs: 1 mil.; sheep: 153,500. **Fish catch** (2002 est): 5,000 metric tons. **Electricity prod.** (2002): 0.62 bil. kWh. **Labor force:** agriculture 66%, services 25%, industry 9%.

Finance: Monetary unit: Gourde (HTG) (Sept. 2004: 35.00 = $1 U.S.). **GDP** (2003 est.): $12.2 bil.; **per capita GDP:** $1,600; **GDP growth:** -1.0%. **Imports** (2003 est.): $1.0 bil.; partners (2002): U.S. 52.5%, Dominican Republic 5.2%, Colombia 3.4%. **Exports** (2003 est.): $321.0 mil.; partners (2002): U.S. 84.5%, Dominican Republic 6.7%, Canada 2.5%. **Tourism** (2001): $54 mil. **Budget** (FY00/01 est.): $361.0 mil. **Intl. reserves less gold:** $42 mil. **Consumer prices:** 39.3%.

Transport: Railroad: Length: 25 mi. **Motor vehicles** (1999): 93,000 pass. cars, 61,600 comm. vehicles. **Civil aviation:** 2 airports. **Chief ports:** Port-au-Prince, Les Cayes, Cap-Haitien.

Communications: TV sets: 5 per 1,000 pop. **Radios:** 53 per 1,000 pop. **Telephone lines** (2002): 130,000. **Daily newspaper circ.:** 2.5 per 1,000 pop. **Internet** (2002): 80,000 users.

Health: Life expect.: 50.5 male; 53.1 female. **Births** (per 1,000 pop.): 33.8. **Deaths** (per 1,000 pop.): 13.2. **Natural inc.:** 2.06%. **Infant mortality** (per 1,000 live births): 74.4. **AIDS rate:** 5.6%.

Education: Compulsory: ages 6-11. **Literacy:** 52.9%.

Major Intl. Organizations: UN and most of its specialized agencies, OAS.

Embassy: 2311 Massachusetts Ave. NW 20008; 332-4090.

Website: www.haiti.org

Haiti, visited by Columbus, 1492, and a French colony from 1697, attained its independence, 1804, following the rebellion led by former slave Toussaint L'Ouverture. After a period of political violence, the U.S. occupied the country 1915-34.

François Duvalier, known as Papa Doc, was elected president in Sept. 1957; in 1964 he was named president for life. Upon his death in 1971, he was succeeded by his son, Jean Claude Duvalier, known as Baby Doc. Following several weeks of unrest, Jean Claude fled Haiti aboard a U.S. Air Force jet Feb. 7, 1986, ending the 28-year dictatorship by the Duvalier family.

Father Jean-Bertrand Aristide was elected president Dec. 1990, but in Sept. 1991, he was arrested by the military and expelled from the country. Some 35,000 Haitian refugees were intercepted by the U.S. Coast Guard as they tried to enter the U.S., 1991-92. Most were returned to Haiti. There was a new upsurge of refugees starting in late 1993.

The UN Security Council authorized, July 31, 1994, an invasion of Haiti by a multinational force. With U.S. troops already en route, a full-scale invasion was averted, Sept. 18, when military leaders agreed to step down. Aristide returned to Haiti and was restored in office Oct. 15. A UN peacekeeping force exercised responsibility in Haiti from Mar. 31, 1995 to Nov. 30, 1997. Aristide transferred power to his elected successor, René Préval, on Feb. 7, 1996.

At least 140 people died and more than 160,000 became homeless when Hurricane Georges struck Haiti Sept. 22, 1998. Aristide won the presidency Nov. 26, 2000, in an election boycotted by opposition groups. An armed uprising in early 2004 and pressure from France and the U.S. toppled Aristide, who went into exile Feb. 29.

Poverty, political violence, and government corruption have plagued Haiti for decades. Health officials estimate that at least 30,000 Haitians die each year of AIDS-related illness. Flooding in late May killed more than 1,000 people, and another 2,400 were missing or dead after Tropical Storm Jeanne in Sept.

Honduras
Republic of Honduras

People: Population: 6,823,568. **Age distrib.** (%): <15: 41.8; 65+: 3.6. **Pop. density:** 158 per sq mi, 61 per sq km. **Urban:** 45.6%. **Ethnic groups:** Mestizo 90%, Amerindian 7%, Black 2%, White 1%. **Principal languages:** Spanish (official), Garífuna, Amerindian dialects. **Chief religion:** Roman Catholic 97%.

Geography: Total area: 43,278 sq mi, 112,090 sq km; **Land area:** 43,201 sq mi, 111,890 sq km. **Location:** In Central America. **Neighbors:** Guatemala on W, El Salvador and Nicaragua on S. **Topography:** The Caribbean coast is 500 mi. long. Pacific coast, on Gulf of Fonseca, is 40 mi. long. Honduras is mountainous, with wide fertile valleys and rich forests. **Capital:** Tegucigalpa, 1,007,000.

Government: Type: Republic. **Head of state:** Pres. Ricardo Maduro; b Apr. 20, 1946; in office: Jan. 27, 2002. **Local divisions:** 18 departments. **Defense budget** (2003): $53 mil. **Active troops:** 12,000.

Economy: Industries: sugar, coffee, textiles, clothing, wood products. **Chief crops:** bananas, coffee, citrus. **Natural resources:** timber, gold, silver, copper, lead, zinc, iron ore, antimony, coal, fish, hydropower. **Arable land:** 15%. **Livestock** (2003): cattle: 2.40 mil.; chickens: 18.7 mil.; goats: 32,200; pigs: 478,000 mil.; sheep: 12,500. **Fish catch** (2002): 26,833 metric tons. **Electricity prod.** (2002): 3.63 bil. kWh. **Labor force** (2001 est.): agriculture 34%, industry 21%, services 45%.

Finance: Monetary unit: Lempira (HNL) (Sept. 2004: 18.40 = $1 U.S.). **GDP** (2003 est.): $17.5 bil.; **per capita GDP:** $2,600; **GDP growth:** 2.5%. **Imports** (2003 est.): $3.1 bil.; partners (2002): U.S. 53.3%, Mexico 4.3%, El Salvador 4.2%. **Exports** (2003 est.): $1.4 bil.; partners (2002): U.S. 69%, El Salvador 3%, Guatemala 2%. **Tourism** (2003): $342 mil. **Budget** (1999 est.): $411.9 mil. **Intl. reserves less gold:** $962 mil. **Gold:** 20,000 oz t. **Consumer prices:** 7.7%.

Transport: Railroad: Length: 434 mi. **Motor vehicles:** (1998): 17,200 pass. cars, 53,900 comm. vehicles. **Civil aviation:** 189.5 mil pass.-mi.; 12 airports. **Chief ports:** Puerto Cortes, La Ceiba.

Communications: TV sets: 95 per 1,000 pop. **Radios:** 410 per 1,000 pop. **Telephone lines** (2002): 322,500. **Daily newspaper circ.:** 55 per 1,000 pop. **Internet** (2002): 168,600 users.

Health: Life expect.: 65.0 male; 67.4 female. **Births** (per 1,000 pop.): 31.0. **Deaths** (per 1,000 pop.): 6.6. **Natural inc.:** 2.44%. **Infant mortality** (per 1,000 live births): 29.6. **AIDS rate:** 1.8%.

Education: Free, compulsory: ages 7-13. **Literacy:** 76.2%.

Major Intl. Organizations: UN, (FAO, IBRD, ILO, IMF, IMO, WHO, WTrO), OAS.

Embassy: 3007 Tilden St. NW, Suite 4M, 20008; 966-7702.

Website: www.hondurasemb.org

Mayan civilization flourished in Honduras in the 1st millennium AD. Columbus arrived in 1502. Honduras became independent after freeing itself from Spain, 1821, and from the Fed. of Central America, 1838.

Gen. Oswaldo Lopez Arellano, president for most of the period 1963-75 by virtue of one election and 2 coups, was ousted by the army in 1975 over charges of pervasive bribery by United Brands Co. of the U.S. An elected civilian government took power in 1982. Some 3,200 U.S. troops were sent to Honduras after the Honduran border was violated by Nicaraguan forces, Mar. 1988.

Already one of the poorest countries in the western hemisphere, Honduras was devastated in late Oct. 1998 by Hurricane Mitch, which killed at least 5,600 people and caused more than $850 million in damage to crops and livestock.

Ricardo Maduro, a businessman who pledged to crack down on crime, won the presidency Nov. 25, 2001. A fire May 17, 2004, killed 104 inmates at an overcrowded prison in San Pedro Sula.

Hungary
Republic of Hungary

People: Population: 10,032,375. **Age distrib.** (%): <15: 16.4; 65+: 14.8. **Pop. density:** 281 per sq mi, 108 per sq km. **Urban:** 65.1%. **Ethnic groups:** Hungarian 90%, Roma 4%, German 3%, Serb 2%. **Principal languages:** Hungarian (official), Romani, German, Slavic languages, Romanian. **Chief religions:** Roman Catholic 68%, Protestant 25%.

Geography: Total area: 35,919 sq mi, 93,030 sq km; **Land area:** 35,653 sq mi, 92,340 sq km. **Location:** In E central Europe. **Neighbors:** Slovakia, Ukraine on N; Austria on W; Slovenia, Yugoslavia, Croatia on S; Romania on E. **Topography:** The Danube R. forms the Slovak border in the NW, then swings S to bisect the country. The eastern half of Hungary is mainly a great fertile plain, the Alfold; the W and N are hilly. **Capital:** Budapest, 1,708,000.

Government: Type: Parliamentary democracy. **Head of state:** Pres. Ferenc Mádl; b Jan. 29, 1931; in office: Aug. 4, 2000. **Head of gov.:** Prime Min. Ferenc Gyurcsány; b June 4, 1961; in office: Sept. 29, 2004. **Local divisions:** 19 counties, 20 urban counties, 1 capital. **Defense budget** (2002): $1.08 bil. **Active troops:** 33,400.

Economy: Industries: mining, metallurgy, constr. materials, proc. foods, textiles, pharm., auto. **Chief crops:** wheat, corn, sunflower seed, potatoes, sugar beets. **Natural resources:** bauxite, coal, nat. gas, fertile soils. **Crude oil reserves** (2003): 102.5 mil.

bbls. **Arable land:** 51%. **Livestock** (2003): cattle: 770,000; chickens: 32.21 mil.; goats: 140,000; pigs: 5.08 mil.; sheep: 1.10 mil. **Fish catch** (2002): 18,324 metric tons. **Electricity prod.** (2002): 34.07 bil. kWh. **Labor force** (1996): services 65%, industry 27%, agriculture 8%.

Finance: Monetary unit: Forint (HUF) (Sept. 2004: 203.56 = $1 U.S.). **GDP** (2003 est.): $139.7 bil.; **per capita GDP:** $13,900; **GDP growth:** 2.8%. **Imports** (2003 est.): $46.2 bil.; partners (2002): Germany 24.2%, Italy 7.5%, Austria 6.9%, Russia 6.1%, China 5.6%, France 4.8%, Japan 4.2%. **Exports** (2003 est.): $42.0 bil.; partners (2002): Germany 35.5%, Austria 7.1%, Italy 5.8%, France 5.7%, UK 4.7%, Sweden 4.3%, Netherlands 4.2%. **Tourism** (2002): $3.3 bil. **Budget** (2000 est.): $14.4 bil. **Intl. reserves less gold:** $8.6 bil. **Gold:** 100,000 oz t. **Consumer prices:** 4.6%.

Transport: Railroad: Length: 4,893 mi. **Motor vehicles** (2001): 2.48 mil pass. cars, 398,300 comm. vehicles. **Civil aviation:** 2.2 bil. pass.-mi; 17 airport.

Communications: TV sets: 447 per 1,000 pop. **Radios:** 690 per 1,000 pop. **Telephone lines** (2002): 3.7 mil. **Daily newspaper circ.:** 465.5 per 1,000 pop. **Internet** (2002): 1.6 mil. users.

Health: Life expect.: 68.1 male; 76.7 female. **Births** (per 1,000 pop.): 9.8. **Deaths** (per 1,000 pop.): 13.2. **Natural inc.:** −0.34%. **Infant mortality** (per 1,000 live births): 8.7. **AIDS rate:** 0.1%.

Education: Compulsory: ages 7-16. **Literacy:** 99.4%.

Major Intl. Organizations: UN (FAO, IBRD, ILO, IMF, IMO, WHO, WTrO), EU, NATO, OECD, OSCE.

Embassy: 3910 Shoemaker St. NW 20008; 362-6730.

Website: www.huembwas.org

Earliest settlers, chiefly Slav and Germanic, were overrun by Magyars from the E. Stephen I (997-1038) was made king by Pope Sylvester II in AD 1000. The country suffered repeated Turkish invasions in the 15th-17th centuries. After the defeats of the Turks, 1686-1697, Austria dominated, but Hungary obtained concessions until it regained internal independence in 1867, with the emperor of Austria as king of Hungary in a dual monarchy with a single diplomatic service. Defeated with the Central Powers in 1918, Hungary lost Transylvania to Romania, Croatia and Bacska to Yugoslavia, Slovakia and Carpatho-Ruthenia to Czechoslovakia, all of which had large Hungarian minorities. A republic under Michael Karolyi and a bolshevist revolt under Bela Kun were followed by a vote for a monarchy in 1920 with Admiral Nicholas Horthy as regent.

Hungary joined Germany in World War II, and was allowed to annex most of its lost territories. Russian troops captured the country, 1944-1945. By terms of an armistice with the Allied powers Hungary agreed to give up territory acquired by the 1938 dismemberment of Czechoslovakia and to return to its borders of 1937.

A republic was declared Feb. 1, 1946; Zoltan Tildy was elected president. In 1947 the Communists forced Tildy out. Premier Imre Nagy, who had been in office since mid-1953, was ousted for his moderate policy of favoring agriculture and consumer production, April 18, 1955.

In 1956, popular demands to oust Erno Gero, Communist Party secretary, and for formation of a government by Nagy, resulted in the latter's appointment Oct. 23; demonstrations against Communist rule developed into open revolt. On Nov. 4 Soviet forces launched a massive attack against Budapest with 200,000 troops, 2,500 tanks and armored cars.

About 200,000 persons fled the country. Thousands were arrested and executed, including Nagy in June 1958. In spring 1963 the regime freed many captives from the 1956 revolt.

Hungarian troops participated in the 1968 Warsaw Pact invasion of Czechoslovakia. Major economic reforms were launched early in 1968, switching from a central planning system to one based on market forces and profit.

In 1989 Parliament legalized freedom of assembly and association as Hungary shifted away from Communism. In Oct. the Communist Party was formally dissolved. The last Soviet troops left Hungary June 19, 1991. Hungary became a full member of NATO Mar. 12, 1999, and of the European Union May 1, 2004.

Iceland
Republic of Iceland

People: Population: 293,966. **Age distrib.** (%): <15: 23; 65+: 11.9. **Pop. density:** 8 per sq mi, 3 per sq km. **Urban:** 92.8%. **Ethnic groups:** Icelandic 94%. **Principal languages:** Icelandic (official) **Chief religion:** Evangelical Lutheran 93% (official).

Geography: Total area: 39,769 sq mi, 103,000 sq km; **Land area:** 38,707 sq mi, 100,250 sq km. **Location:** Isl. at N end of Atlantic O. **Neighbors:** Nearest is Greenland (Den.), to W. **Topography:** Recent volcanic origin. Three-quarters of the surface is wasteland: glaciers, lakes, a lava desert. There are geysers and hot springs, and the climate is moderated by the Gulf Stream. **Capital:** Reykjavík, 184,000.

Government: Type: Constitutional republic. **Head of state:** Pres. Olafur Ragnar Grímsson; b May 14, 1943; in office: Aug. 1, 1996. **Head of gov.:** Prime Min. Halldór Ásgrímsson; b Sept. 8, 1947; in office: Sept. 15, 2004. **Local divisions:** 23 counties, 14 independent towns. **Defense budget:** Icelandic Defense Force provided by the U.S.

Economy: Industries: fish proc., aluminum smelting, ferrosilicon prod., tourism. **Chief crops:** potatoes, turnips. **Natural re-**

sources: fish, hydropower, geothermal power, diatomite. **Livestock** (2003): cattle: 67,000; chickens: 220,000; goats: 361; pigs: 44,000; sheep: 470,000. **Fish catch** (2002): 2,133,240 metric tons. **Electricity prod.** (2002): 8.27 bil. kWh. **Labor force** (1999): agriculture 5.1%, fishing and fish processing 11.8%, manufacturing 12.9%, construction 10.7%, other services 59.5%.

Finance: Monetary unit: Krona (ISK) (Sept. 2004: 71.98 = $1 U.S.). **GDP** (2003 est.): $8.7 bil.; **per capita GDP:** $30,900; **GDP growth:** 2.6%. **Imports** (2003 est.): $2.6 bil.; partners (2002): U.S. 10.9%, Germany 10.7%, Denmark 8.5%, Norway 8%, UK 7.5%, Netherlands 6.1%, Sweden 5.9%. **Exports** (2003 est.): $2.4 bil.; partners (2002): Germany 18.5%, UK 17.5%, Netherlands 11.4%, U.S. 10.9%, Spain 5.2%, Denmark 4.6%, Portugal 4.3%, Norway 4.2%. **Tourism** (2002): $319 mil. **Budget** (1999): $3.3 bil. **Intl. reserves less gold:** $533 mil. **Gold:** 60,000 oz t. **Consumer prices:** 2.1%.

Transport: Motor vehicles (2000): 158,900 pass. cars, 21,100 comm. vehicles. **Civil aviation:** 2.4 bil. pass.-mi; 13 airports.

Communications: TV sets: 505 per 1,000 pop. **Radios:** 1,075 per 1,000 pop. **Telephone lines:** 190,700. **Daily newspaper circ.:** 335.7per 1,000 pop. **Internet:** 195,000 users.

Health: Life expect.: 78.2 male; 82.3 female. **Births** (per 1,000 pop.): 13.8. **Deaths** (per 1,000 pop.): 6.6. **Natural inc.:** 0.73%. **Infant mortality** (per 1,000 live births): 3.3. **AIDS rate:** 0.2%.

Education: Compulsory: ages 6-16. **Literacy** (1997 est.): 99.9%.

Major Intl. Organizations: UN (FAO, IBRD, ILO, IMF, IMO, WHO, WTrO), EFTA, NATO, OECD, OSCE.

Embassy: 1156 15th St. NW, Ste. 1200, 20005; 265-6653.

Website: www.iceland.org

Iceland was an independent republic from 930 to 1262, when it joined with Norway. Its language has maintained its purity for 1,000 years. Danish rule lasted from 1380-1918; the last ties with the Danish crown were severed in 1941. The Althing, or assembly, is the world's oldest surviving parliament.

India
Republic of India

People: Population: 1,065,070,607. **Age distrib.** (%): <15: 32.7; 65+: 4.7. **Pop. density:** 943 per sq mi, 323 per sq km. **Urban:** 28.3%. **Ethnic groups:** Indo-Aryan 72%, Dravidian 25%. **Principal languages:** Hindi, English, Bengali, Telugu, Marathi, Tamil, Urdu, Gujarati, Malayalam, Kannada, Oriya, Punjabi, Assamese, Kashmiri, Sindhi, and Sanskrit (all official); Hindustani, a mix of Hindi and Urdu spoken in the north, is popular but not official. **Chief religions:** Hindu 82%, Muslim 12%, Christian 2%, Sikh 2%.

Geography: Total area: 1,269,345 sq mi, 3,287,590 sq km; **Land area:** 1,147,955 sq mi, 2,973,190 sq km. **Location:** Occupies most of the Indian subcontinent in S Asia. **Neighbors:** Pakistan on W; China, Nepal, Bhutan on N; Myanmar, Bangladesh on E. **Topography:** The Himalaya Mts., highest in world, stretch across India's northern borders. Below, the Ganges Plain is wide, fertile, and among the most densely populated regions of the world. The area below includes the Deccan Peninsula. Close to one quarter of the area is forested. The climate varies from tropical heat in S to near-Arctic cold in N. Rajasthan Desert is in NW; NE Assam Hills get 400 in. of rain a year. **Capital:** New Delhi (2001 city est.), 300,000. **Cities (urban aggr.):** Mumbai (Bombay), 16,086,000; Kolkata (Calcutta), 13,058,000 Delhi 12,441,000; Hyderabad, 5,445,000; Chennai (Madras), 6,353,000; Bangalore, 5,567,000.

Government: Type: Federal republic. **Head of state:** Pres. A. P. J. Abdul Kalam; b Oct. 15, 1931; in office: July 25, 2002. **Head of gov.:** Prime Min. Manmohan Singh; b Sept. 26, 1932; in office May 22, 2004. **Local divisions:** 28 states, 6 union territories, 1 national capital territory. **Defense budget** (2003): $16.2 bil. **Active troops:** 1,325,000.

Economy: Industries: textiles, chemicals, food proc., steel, transp. equip., cement, mining, oil, machinery, software. **Chief crops:** rice, wheat, oilseed, cotton, jute, tea, sugarcane, potatoes. **Natural resources:** coal, iron ore, mang., mica, bauxite, titanium ore, chromite, nat. gas, diamonds, oil, limestone. **Crude oil reserves** (2003): 5.4 bil. bbls. **Arable land:** 56%. **Livestock** (2003): cattle: 226.1 mil.; chickens: 842.0 mil.; goats: 124.5 mil.; pigs: 18.5 mil.; sheep: 59.0 mil. **Fish catch** (2002): 5,962,616 metric tons. **Electricity prod.** (2002): 547.21 bil. kWh. **Labor force** (1999): agriculture 60%, services 23%, industry 17%.

Finance: Monetary unit: Rupee (INR) (Sept. 2004: 45.80 = $1 U.S.). **GDP** (2003 est.): $3.022 tril.; **per capita GDP:** $2,900; **GDP growth:** 7.6%. **Imports** (2003 est.): $74.2 bil.; partners (2002): U.S. 6.9%, Belgium 6.4%, China 4.5%, Singapore 4.4%, UK 4.4%. **Exports** (2003 est.): $57.2 bil.; partners (2002): U.S. 22.4%, UK 5.1%, Hong Kong 4.5%, Germany 4.3%, China 4.1%. **Tourism** (2002): $2.9 bil. **Budget** (FY01/02 est.): $78.2 bil. **Intl. reserves less gold:** $66.58 bil. **Gold:** 11.50 mil oz t. **Consumer prices:** 3.8%.

Transport: Railroad: Length: 39,468 mi. **Motor vehicles** (1998): 5.06 mil pass. cars, 7.54 mil comm. vehicles. **Civil aviation:** 8.6 bil. pass.-mi;232 airports. **Chief ports:** Kolkata (Calcutta), Mumbai (Bombay), Chennai (Madras), Vishakhapatnam, Kandla.

Communications: TV sets: 75 per 1,000 pop. **Radios:** 120 per 1,000 pop. **Telephone lines:** 48.9 mil. **Daily newspaper circ.:** 60.5 per 1,000 pop. **Internet:** 18.5 mil. users.

Health: Life expect.: 63.3 male; 64.8 female. **Births** (per 1,000 pop.): 22.8. **Deaths** (per 1,000 pop.): 8.4. **Natural inc.:** 1.44%. **Infant mortality** (per 1,000 live births): 57.9. **AIDS rate:** 0.9%.

Education: Compulsory: ages 6-14. **Literacy:** 59.5%.

Major Intl. Organizations: UN (FAO, IBRD, ILO, IMF, IMO, WHO, WTrO), the Commonwealth.

Embassy: 2107 Massachusetts Ave. NW 20008; 939-7000.

Websites: www.indianembassy.org

India has one of the oldest civilizations in the world. Excavations trace the Indus Valley civilization back for at least 5,000 years. Paintings in the mountain caves of Ajanta, richly carved temples, the Taj Mahal in Agra, and the Kutab Minar in Delhi are among relics of the past.

Aryan tribes, speaking Sanskrit, invaded from the NW around 1500 BC. Asoka ruled most of the Indian subcontinent in the 3d century BC, and established Buddhism. But Hinduism revived and eventually predominated. Under the Guptas, 4th-6th century AD, science, literature, and the arts enjoyed a "golden age."

Arab invaders established a Muslim foothold in the W in the 8th century, and Turkish Muslims gained control of North India by 1200. The Mogul emperors ruled 1526-1857.

Vasco da Gama established Portuguese trading posts 1498-1503. The Dutch followed. The British East India Co. sent Capt. William Hawkins, 1609, to get concessions from the Mogul emperor for spices and textiles. Operating as the East India Co. the British gained control of most of India. The British parliament assumed political direction; under Lord Bentinck, 1828-35, rule by rajahs was curbed. After the Sepoy troops mutinied, 1857-58, the British supported the native rulers.

Nationalism grew rapidly after World War I. The Indian National Congress and the Muslim League demanded constitutional reform. A leader emerged in Mohandas K. Gandhi (called Mahatma, or Great Soul), born Oct. 2, 1869, assassinated Jan. 30, 1948. He advocated self-rule, nonviolence, and removal of the caste system of untouchability. In 1930 he launched a program of civil disobedience, including a boycott of British goods and rejection of taxes without representation.

In 1935 Britain gave India a constitution providing a bicameral federal congress. Muhammad Ali Jinnah, head of the Muslim League, sought creation of a Muslim nation, Pakistan.

The British government partitioned British India into the dominions of India and Pakistan. India became a member of the UN in 1945, a self-governing member of the Commonwealth in 1947, and a democratic republic, Jan. 26, 1950. More than 12 million Hindu and Muslim refugees crossed the India-Pakistan borders in a mass transferal of some of the 2 peoples during 1947; about 200,000 were killed in communal fighting.

After Pakistan troops began attacks on Bengali separatists in East Pakistan, Mar. 25, 1971, some 10 million refugees fled into India. India and Pakistan went to war Dec. 3, 1971, on both the East and West fronts. Pakistan troops in the east surrendered Dec. 16; Pakistan agreed to a cease-fire in the west Dec. 17.

Indira Gandhi, India's prime minister since Jan. 1966, invoked emergency powers in June 1975. Thousands of opponents were arrested and press censorship imposed. These and other actions, including enforcement of coercive birth control measures in some areas, were widely resented. Opposition parties, united in the Janata coalition, turned Gandhi's New Congress Party from power in federal and state parliamentary elections in 1977.

Gandhi became prime minister for the second time, Jan. 14, 1980. She was assassinated by 2 of her Sikh bodyguards Oct. 31, 1984, in response to the government suppression of a Sikh uprising in Punjab in June 1984, which included an assault on the Golden Temple at Amritsar, the holiest Sikh shrine. Widespread rioting followed the assassination; thousands of Sikhs were killed and some 50,000 left homeless. Rajiv, Indira Gandhi's son, replaced her as prime minister. He was swept from office in 1989 amid charges of incompetence and corruption, and assassinated May 21, 1991, while campaigning to regain power.

A gas leak at a Union Carbide chemical plant in Bhopal, in Dec. 1984, eventually killed an estimated 14,000 people. A lawsuit settled in 1989 provided $470 mil. in compensation to victims; in 2002 an Indian High Court upheld a culpable homicide conviction against former UC chairman Warren Anderson.

Many died in religious, ethnic, and political conflicts during the 1980s and '90s. To suppress the Sikh insurgency in Punjab, Indian government troops attacked the the Golden Temple again in 1988. Nationwide riots followed the destruction of a 16th-century mosque by Hindu militants in Dec. 1992. Ethnic clashes in Assam in NW India, killed thousands in Feb. 1993. In the biggest wave of criminal violence in Indian history, a series of bombs jolted Bombay and Calcutta, Mar. 12-19, 1993, killing over 300.

Mother Teresa of Calcutta, renowned for her work among the poor, died Sept. 5, 1997. India's 1st lowest-caste president, K. R. Narayanan, took office July 25. The Hindu nationalist Bharatiya Janata Party (BJP) won enough seats in parliamentary elections, Feb. 1998, to form a government. Atal Bihari Vajpayee was sworn in as prime minister Mar. 19. India conducted a series of nuclear tests in mid-May, drawing wide condemnation and raising tensions with Pakistan.

An alliance led by Vajpayee won a majority in legislative elections, Sept. 5-Oct. 3, 1999. A cyclone that hit the state of Orissa,

E India, on Oct. 29, 1999, left some 10,000 people dead. A powerful earthquake in Gujarat state on Jan. 26, 2001, claimed more than 20,000 lives. India blamed Pakistani-sponsored terrorist groups for an Oct. 1 suicide attack on the state legislature in Jammu and Kashmir (see below), in which at least 40 people died, and a Dec. 13 assault on the Indian parliament in New Delhi Dec. 13, which left 13 people dead. Hindu-Muslim clashes in Gujarat Feb. 27-Mar. 11, 2002, claimed more than 700 lives. A. P. J. Abdul Kalam, a Muslim scientist who spearheaded India's nuclear weapons program, became president July 25.

Two bombs in Mumbai, Aug. 25, 2003, killed more than 50 people; Indian authorities blamed Muslim militants. Led by Rajiv Gandhi's Italian-born widow, Sonia, the Congress Party won the most seats in parliamentary elections Apr.-May 2004. When Hindu nationalists objected to her candidacy, she chose not to become prime minister, and Manmohan Singh, a Sikh economist, took office instead. Monsoon floods July-Aug. in Assam and Bihar states left more than 930 people dead.

Despite robust economic growth since the 1990s, especially in high-technology industries, nearly 80% of India's population still earns less than $2 per day. According to UN estimates, about 5.1 million Indians have HIV/AIDS.

Sikkim, bordered by Tibet, Bhutan, and Nepal, formerly British protected, became a protectorate of India in 1950. Area, 2,740 sq. mi; pop. (2001 census) 540,493; capital: Gangtok. In Sept. 1974, India's parliament voted to make Sikkim an associate Indian state, absorbing it into India.

Kashmir is a predominantly Muslim region in the NW that borders India, Pakistan, Afghanistan, and China. Originally a Hindu kingdom, Muslim rule began in 1341; after almost 200 years under the Moguls, the area was incorporated into British India in 1846. Fighting broke out in the region between India and Pakistan in 1947 following independence from Britain. A cease-fire was negotiated by the UN Jan. 1, 1949; it gave Pakistan control of one-third of the area as Azad Kashmir, in the west and northwest, and India the remaining two-thirds, as the Indian state of Jammu and Kashmir. It is India's only Muslim-majority state. Area: 39,146 sq. mi.; pop. 10,000,000, 2001 cens.; capitals: Srinagar (summer) and Jammu (winter). Fighting returned to the area during the 1965 and 1971 wars with Pakistan. China occupied about 14,000 sq. miles in the Ladakh district after a war with India in 1962.

In the 1990s there were repeated clashes between Indian army troops and separatist fighters triggered by India's decision to impose central government rule. The clashes strained relations between India and Pakistan, which India charged was aiding the separatists; fighting was especially heavy in May-June 1999. As 2002 began, some 1 million Indian and Pakistani troops faced each other across the "line of control" that divides Kashmir. Tensions escalated when Muslin gunmen May 14 killed 34 people, many of them women and children, at an army base near Jammu, and Pakistan conducted missile tests May 25-28. U.S. mediation in June helped ease the crisis. Legislative elections were held Sept.-Oct. 2002.

A cease-fire between Indian and Pakistani troops along the line of control took effect Nov. 25, 2003, but clashes between Indian forces and Islamic militants continued. Estimates of conflict-related deaths since 1989 range from 40,000 to over 80,000.

France, 1952-54, peacefully yielded to India its 5 colonies, former French India, comprising Pondicherry, Karikal, Mahe, Yanaon (which became **Pondicherry Union Territory,** area 190 sq. mi; pop. (2001 census) 973,829 and Chandernagor (which was incorporated into the state of **West Bengal).**

Indonesia

Republic of Indonesia

People: Population: 238,452,952. **Age distrib.** (%): <15: NA; 65+: NA. **Pop. density:** 338 per sq mi, 131 per sq km. **Urban:** 45.6%. **Ethnic groups:** Javanese 45%, Sundanese 14%, Madurese 8%, Malay 8%. **Principal languages:** Bahasa Indonesia (official, modified form of Malay), English, Dutch, Javanese, other dialects. **Chief religions:** Muslim 88%, Protestant 5%, Roman Catholic 3%, Hindu 2%, Buddhist 1%.

Geography: Total area: 741,100 sq mi, 1,919,440 sq km; **Land area:** 705,192 sq mi, 1,826,440 sq km. **Location:** Archipelago SE of Asian mainland along the Equator. **Neighbors:** Malaysia on N, Papua New Guinea on E. **Topography:** Indonesia comprises over 13,500 islands (6,000 inhabited), including Java (one of the most densely populated areas in the world with over 2,000 persons per sq. mi.), Sumatra, Kalimantan (most of Borneo), Sulawesi (Celebes), and West Irian (Irian Jaya, the W half of New Guinea). Also: Bangka, Billiton, Madura, Bali, Timor. The mountains and plateaus on the major islands have a cooler climate than the tropical lowlands. **Capital:** Jakarta, 12,296,000. **Cities (urban aggr.):** Bandung, 3,409,000; Surabaja, 2,461,000.

Government: Type: Republic. **Head of state and gov.:** Megawati Sukarnoputri; b Jan. 23, 1947; in office: July 23, 2001. **Local divisions:** 30 provinces, 2 special regions, 1 capital district. **Defense budget** (2002): $1.8 bil. **Active troops:** 302,000.

Economy: Industries: oil & nat. gas, textiles, apparel & footwear, mining, cement, fertilizers, plywood, rubber. **Chief crops:** rice, cassava, peanuts, rubber, cocoa, coffee, palm oil, copra. **Natural resources:** oil, tin, nat. gas, nickel, timber, bauxite, copper, coal, gold, silver. **Crude oil reserves** (2003): 5.0 bil. bbls. **Arable**

land: 10%. **Livestock** (2003): cattle: 11.40 mil.; chickens: 1,290.1 mil.; goats: 13.3 mil.; pigs: 6.34 mil.; sheep: 8.13 mil. **Fish catch** (2002): 5,419,540 metric tons. **Electricity prod.** (2002): 99.34 bil. kWh. **Labor force** (1999 est.): agriculture 45%, industry 16%, services 39%.

Finance: Monetary unit: Rupiah (IDR) (Sept. 2004: 9,113.54 = $1 U.S.). **GDP** (2003 est.): $758.1 bil.; **per capita GDP:** $3,200; **GDP growth:** 4.0%. **Imports** (2003 est.): $40.2 bil.; partners (2002): Japan 14.1%, Singapore 13.1%, U.S. 8.5%, China 7.8%, South Korea 5.3%, Australia 5.1%. **Exports** (2003 est.): $63.9 bil.; partners (2002): Japan 21.1%, U.S. 13.2%, Singapore 9.4%, South Korea 7.2%, China 5.1%. **Tourism** (2002): $4.3 bil. **Budget** (2003 est.): $43.0 bil. **Intl. reserves less gold:** $23.5 bil. **Gold:** 3.10 mil oz t. **Consumer prices:** 2.4%.

Transport: Railroad: Length: 4,013 mi. **Motor vehicles** (2001): 3.24 mil pass. cars, 2.48 mil comm. vehicles. **Civil aviation:** 6.7 bil. pass.-mi; 153 airports. **Chief ports:** Jakarta, Surabaya, Palembang, Semarang, Ujungpandang.

Communications: TV sets: 143 per 1,000 pop. **Radios:** 155 per 1,000 pop. **Telephone lines** (2002): 7.8 mil. **Daily newspaper circ.:** 22.8 per 1,000 pop. **Internet** (2002): 8.0 mil. users.

Health: Life expect.: 66.8 male; 71.8 female. **Births** (per 1,000 pop.): 21.1. **Deaths** (per 1,000 pop.): 6.3. **Natural inc.:** 1.49%. **Infant mortality** (per 1,000 live births): 36.8. **AIDS rate:** 0.1%.

Education: Compulsory: ages 7-15. **Literacy:** 88.5%.

Major Intl. Organizations: UN and all of its specialized agencies, APEC, ASEAN, OPEC.

Embassy: 2020 Massachusetts Ave. NW 20036; 775-5200.

Websites: www.dfa-deplu.go.id; www.embassyofindonesia.org

Hindu and Buddhist civilization from India reached Indonesia nearly 2,000 years ago, taking root especially in Java. Islam spread along the maritime trade routes in the 15th century, and became predominant by the 16th century. The Dutch replaced the Portuguese as the area's most important European trade power in the 17th century, securing territorial control over Java by 1750. The outer islands were not finally subdued until the early 20th century, when the full area of present-day Indonesia was united under one rule for the first time.

Following Japanese occupation, 1942-45, nationalists led by Sukarno and Hatta declared independence. The Netherlands ceded sovereignty Dec. 27, 1949, after 4 years of fighting. A republic was declared, Aug. 17, 1950, with Sukarno as president. West Irian, on New Guinea, remained under Dutch control. After the Dutch in 1957 rejected proposals for new negotiations over West Irian, Indonesia stepped up the seizure of Dutch property. In 1963 the UN turned the area (later renamed Irian Jaya and now known as Papua) over to Indonesia, which promised a plebiscite. In 1969, voting by tribal chiefs favored staying with Indonesia, despite an uprising and widespread opposition.

Sukarno suspended Parliament in 1960, and was named president for life in 1963. He made close alliances with Communist governments. In Sept. 1965 an attempted coup in which several military officers were murdered was successfully put down, but Sukarno was forced to cede power to the army, led by Gen. Suharto, who became acting president in 1967 and ruled Indonesia for the next 31 years. The regime blamed the coup on the Communist Party; more than 300,000 alleged Communists were killed in army-initiated massacres.

Parliament reelected Suharto to a 7th consecutive 5-year term Mar. 10, 1998, as a severe economic downturn focused public anger on nepotism, cronyism, and corruption in the Suharto regime. Price increases in May sparked mass protests and then mob violence in Jakarta and other cities, claiming some 500 lives. Suharto resigned May 21 and was succeeded by his vice-president, Bacharuddin Jusuf Habibie. Abdurrahman Wahid, leader of Indonesia's largest Muslim organization, was elected president Oct. 20, 1999. In Aug. 2000, under pressure from the legislature, he agreed to share power with Vice-Pres. Megawati Sukarnoputri, daughter of the late Pres. Sukarno. Charging Wahid with incompetence and corruption, the legislature ousted him July 23, 2001, and Megawati became Indonesia's 1st woman president.

Clashes between Muslims and Christians in the Maluku (Molucca) Is. have claimed more than 2,500 lives since Jan. 1999; in addition, some 550 people, many refugees from the fighting, died when their ferry sank June 29, 2000. Ethnic violence in Kalimantan, Borneo, killed more than 400 in Feb. 2001. Separatists in Aceh, NW Sumatra, fought repeatedly against government troops during the 1980s and 90s; when peace talks broke down in May 2003, the Indonesian military launched a new offensive to put down the independence movement there. East Timor, a former Portuguese colony that Indonesia invaded in Dec. 1975 and controlled until Oct. 1999, became a fully independent country May 20, 2002.

Investigators blamed Islamic terrorists affiliated with al-Qaeda for bombings that killed 202 people, mostly foreign tourists, at nightclubs in Bali, Oct. 12, 2002, and 12 people at a Marriott hotel in Jakarta, Aug. 5, 2003. Radical Islamic cleric Abu Bakar Bashir, sentenced to 4 years in jail for terrorism and treason, Sept. 2003, was cleared of these charges in Mar. 2004. As of Sept. 2004, he was still in custody awaiting further terrorism charges.

A car bomb attack outside the Australian embassy in Jakarta, Sept. 9, 2004, killed 9 people and injured more than 180.

Susilo Bambang Yudhoyono, a retired general, defeated Megawati Sept. 20 in a direct presidential runoff vote; he was scheduled to take office Oct. 20.

Iran
Islamic Republic of Iran

People: Population: 67,503,205. **Age distrib.** (%): <15: 31.6; 65+: 4.7. **Pop. density:** 106 per sq mi, 41 per sq km. **Urban:** 66.7%. **Ethnic groups:** Persian 51%, Azeri 24%, Gilaki/Mazandarani 8%, Kurd 7%, Arab 3%, Lur 2%, Balochi 2%, Turkmen 2%. **Principal languages:** Farsi/Persian (official), Kurdish, Pashto, Luri, Balochi, Gilaki, Mazandarami; Azeri and Turkic languages; Arabic, Turkish. **Chief religion:** Muslim (official; Shi'a 89%, Sunni 10%).

Geography: Total area: 636,296 sq mi, 1,648,000 sq km; **Land area:** 631,663 sq mi, 1,636,000 sq km. **Location:** Between the Middle East and S Asia. **Neighbors:** Turkey, Iraq on W; Armenia, Azerbaijan, Turkmenistan on N; Afghanistan, Pakistan on E. **Topography:** Interior highlands and plains surrounded by high mountains, up to 18,000 ft. Large salt deserts cover much of area, but there are many oases and forest areas. Most of the population inhabits the N and NW. **Capital:** Tehran, 7,190,000. **Cities** (urban aggr.): Esfahan, 1,381,000; Mashhad, 1,990,000.

Government: Type: Islamic republic. **Religious head:** Ayatollah Sayyed Ali Khamenei; b 1939; in office: June 4, 1989. **Head of state and gov.:** Pres. Mohammad Khatami; b 1943; in office: Aug. 3, 1997. **Local divisions:** 28 provinces. **Defense budget** (2003): $4.2 bil. **Active troops:** 540,000.

Economy: Industries: oil, petrochems., textiles, constr. materials, food proc., metal fabricating, armaments. **Chief crops:** wheat, rice, other grains, sugar beets, fruits, nuts, cotton. **Natural resources:** oil, nat. gas, coal, chromium, copper, iron ore, lead, mang., zinc, sulfur. **Crude oil reserves** (2003): 89.7 bil. bbls. **Arable land:** 10%. **Livestock** (2003): cattle: 9.0 mil.; chickens: 280.0 mil.; goats: 26.0 mil.; sheep: 53.9 mil. **Fish catch** (2002): 401,670 metric tons. **Electricity prod.** (2002): 128.96 bil. kWh. **Labor force** (2001 est.): agriculture 30%, industry 25%, services 45%.

Finance: Monetary unit: Rial (IRR) (Sept. 2004: 8,762.01 = $1 U.S.). **GDP** (2003 est.): $477.8 bil.; **per capita GDP:** $7,000; **GDP growth:** 6.0%. **Imports** (2003 est.): $25.3 bil.; partners (2002): Germany 17.1%, Switzerland 9.3%, UAE 9.1%, France 5.9%, Italy 5.8%, South Korea 4.8%, China 4.7%, Russia 4.3%. **Exports** (2003 est.): $29.9 bil.; partners (2002): Japan 20.1%, China 9.9%, Italy 7.6%, South Korea 5.7%. **Tourism** (2002): $1.2 bil. **Budget** (2003 est.): $43.4 bil. **Consumer prices:** 16.5%.

Transport: Railroad: Length: 4,474 mi. **Motor vehicles** (2000): 935,900 pass. cars, 384,900 comm. vehicles. **Civil aviation:** 2.0 bil. pass.-mi; 122 airports. **Chief port:** Bandar-e Abbas.

Communications: TV sets: 154 per 1,000 pop. **Radios:** 265 per 1,000 pop. **Telephone lines:** 14.6 mil. **Daily newspaper circ.:** 28 per 1,000 pop. **Internet** (2002): 4.3 mil. users.

Health: Life expect.: 68.3 male; 71.1 female. **Births** (per 1,000 pop.): 17.1. **Deaths** (per 1,000 pop.): 5.6. **Natural inc.:** 1.15%. **Infant mortality** (per 1,000 live births): 42.9. **AIDS rate:** 0.1%.

Education: Compulsory: ages 6-10. **Literacy:** 79.4%.

Major Intl. Organizations: UN (FAO, IBRD, ILO, IMF, IMO, WHO), OPEC.

Iranian Interests Section: 2209 Wisconsin Ave. NW, 20007; 965-4990.

Websites: www.daftar.org/eng; www.un.int/iran

Iran was once called Persia. The Iranians, who supplanted an earlier agricultural civilization, came from the E during the 2d millennium BC; they were an Indo-European group related to the Aryans of India.

In 549 BC Cyrus the Great united the Medes and Persians in the Persian Empire, conquered Babylonia in 538 BC, and restored Jerusalem to the Jews. Alexander the Great conquered Persia in 333 BC, but Persians regained independence in the next century under the Parthians, themselves succeeded by Sassanian Persians in AD 226. Arabs brought Islam to Persia in the 7th century, replacing the indigenous Zoroastrian faith. After Persian political and cultural autonomy was reasserted in the 9th century, arts and sciences flourished.

Turks and Mongols ruled Persia in turn from the 11th century to 1502, when Ismael I established the Iranian Safavid dynasty, and made Shiite Islam the offical religion. The dynasty lasted until 1722. The British and Russian empires vied for influence in the 19th century; Afghanistan was severed from Iran by Britain in 1857.

Reza Khan, a miltary officer, became prime min., 1923, and shah in 1925. He began modernization, curbed foreign influence, and officially changed the country's name from Persia to Iran in 1935. Fearing the shah's Axis sympathies, British and Soviet troops forced him to abdicate, 1941; succeeded by his son, Mohammad Reza Pahlavi. With U.S. backing, he brought economic and social change to Iran, (the "White Revolution"), but repression, often severe, of conservative Islamic opposition intensified. Violent protests in 1978 eventually forced the shah to depart, Jan. 16, 1979. He appointed Prime Min. Shahpur Bakhtiar to head a regency council in his absence. Shiite leader Ayatollah Ruhollah Khomeini, exiled by the shah in 1963, returned to Tehran, Feb. 1, and by Feb. 11 pro-Khomeini foces had defeated gov. troops. Khomeini then established an Islamic theocracy.

Iranian militants seized the U.S. embassy, Nov. 4, 1979, and took hostages including 62 Americans. Despite international condemnations and U.S. efforts, including an abortive Apr. 1980 rescue attempt, the crisis continued. The U.S. broke diplomatic relations with Iran, Apr. 7. The shah died in Egypt, July 27. The hostage drama ended Jan. 20, 1981, when an accord, involving the release of frozen Iranian assets, was reached.

A dispute over the Shatt al-Arab waterway situated between Iran and Iraq led to a long and costly war between the 2 countries, beginning Sept. 22, 1980. Iraqi troops occupied Iranian territory, including the port city of Khorramshahr in October. Iranian troops recaptured the city and drove Iraqi troops back across the border, May 1982. In Nov. 1986 it became known that the U.S., which had generally sided with Iraq during the war, had secretly shipped arms to Iran to gain that country's help in obtaining the release of U.S. hostages held by terrorists in Lebanon. The revelation sparked a major scandal in the Reagan administration.

A U.S. Navy warship shot down an Iranian commercial airliner, July 3, 1988, after mistaking it for an F-14 fighter jet; all 290 aboard the plane died. In Aug. 1988, Iran agreed to accept a UN resolution calling for a cease-fire with Iraq.

An earthquake struck northern Iran June 21, 1990, killing more than 45,000, injuring 100,000, and leaving 400,000 homeless. Some one million Kurdish refugees fled from Iraq to Iran following the Persian Gulf War. To curb Iran's alleged support for international terrorism, the U.S. in 1996 authorized sanctions on foreign companies that invest there.

Mohammad Khatami, a moderate Shiite Muslim cleric, was elected president on May 23, 1997, winning nearly 70% of the vote. During the next 3 years, hardline Islamists clashed repeatedly and sometimes violently with reformers, who won a majority in parliamentary elections Feb. 18 and May 5, 2000. Inviting rapprochement with Iran, the U.S. eased some sanctions Mar. 18. Khatami was reelected June 8, 2001, with a 77% majority but continued to face resistance from religious conservatives.

The U.S.-led war in Iraq, beginning Mar. 2003, contributed to a new period of instability in Iran, which the U.S. suspected was developing nuclear weapons and harboring members of al-Qaeda. In June, armed Islamist vigilantes harassed students who were holding pro-democracy protests in Tehran and other cities. An earthquake Dec. 26 in Bam, SE Iran, killed about 26,000 people. After the Guardian Council, dominated by religious conservatives, disqualified some 2,400 reformist candidates, hardliners won control of parliament in elections Feb. 20, 2004.

The International Atomic Energy Agency, June 1, criticized Iran for concealing information about an ongoing nuclear program, which Iran claimed was for peaceful purposes.

Iraq
Republic of Iraq

People: Population: 25,374,691 **Age distrib.** (%): <15: 41.1; 65+: 3. **Pop. density:** 152 per sq mi, 59 per sq km. **Urban:** 67.2%. **Ethnic groups:** Arab 75%-80%, Kurdish 15%-20%. **Principal languages:** Arabic (official), Kurdish (official in Kurdish regions), Assyrian, Armenian. **Chief religion:** Muslim (official; Shi'a 60%-65%, Sunni 32%-37%)

Geography: Total area: 168,754 sq mi, 437,072 sq km; **Land area:** 166,859 sq mi, 432,162 sq km.. **Location:** In the Middle East, occupying most of historic Mesopotamia. **Neighbors:** Jordan and Syria on W, Turkey on N, Iran on E, Kuwait and Saudi Arabia on S. **Topography:** Mostly an alluvial plain, including the Tigris and Euphrates rivers, descending from mountains in N to desert in SW. Persian Gulf region is marshland. **Capital:** Baghdad, 5,620,000. **Cities (urban aggr.):** Arbil, 2,369,000; Basra (city est.), 1,076,000; Mosul, 1,056,000.

Government: Type: In transition. **Head of state:** Pres. Ghazi al-Yawer; b 1958; in office: June 28, 2004. **Head of gov.:** Prime Min. Iyad Allawi; b 1945; in office: June 28, 2004 (acting from June 1). **Local divisions:** 18 governorates (3 in Kurdish Autonomous Region). **Defense budget** (2003): NA. **Active troops:** NA.

Economy: Industries: oil, chemicals, textiles, constr. materials, food proc. **Chief crops:** wheat, barley, rice, vegetables, dates, cotton. **Natural resources:** oil, nat. gas, phosphates, sulfur. **Arable land:** 12%. **Crude oil reserves** (2003): 112.5 bil. bbls. **Livestock** (2002): cattle: 1.35 mil.; chickens: 23 mil.; goats: 1.60 mil.; sheep: 6.78 mil. **Fish catch** (2002 est): 14,500 metric tons. **Electricity prod.** (2002): 33.99 bil. kWh.

Finance: Monetary unit: Dinar (IQD) (Sept. 2004: 1,462.45 = $1 U.S.). **GDP** (2003 est.): $38.8 bil.; **per capita GDP:** $1,600; **GDP growth:** -20.0%. **Imports** (2003 est.): $6.5 bil.; partners (2002): Jordan 10.4%, France 8.4%, China 7.9%, Vietnam 7.9%, Germany 7.2%, Russia 6.9%, Australia 6.8%, Italy 6.1%, Japan 5.3%. **Exports** (2003 est.): $7.5 bil.; partners (2002): U.S. 37.4%, Taiwan 7.7%, Canada 7.5%, France 7.5%, Jordan 6.9%, Netherlands 5.8%, Italy 4.9%, Morocco 4.3%, Spain 4.1%. **Tourism** (1998): 13 mil. **Budget** (2004 budget): $13.4 bil. **Tourism** (1998): $13 mil.

Transport: Railroad: Length: 1,220 mi. **Motor vehicles** (1995): 680,100 pass. cars, 319,900 comm. vehicles. **Civil aviation:** 12.4 mil pass.-mi.; 77 airports. **Chief port:** Basra.

Communications: TV sets: 82 per 1,000 pop. **Radios:** 229 per 1,000 pop. **Telephone lines:** 1,860,000. **Daily newspaper circ.:** 19 per 1,000 pop.

Health: Life expect.: 67.1 male; 69.5 female. **Births** (per 1,000 pop.): 33.1. **Deaths** (per 1,000 pop.): 5.7. **Natural inc.:** 2.74%. **Infant mortality** (per 1,000 live births): 52.7. **AIDS rate:** <0.1%. **Education:** Compulsory: ages 6-11. **Literacy:** 40.4%. **Major Intl. Organizations:** UN (FAO, IBRD, ILO, IMF, IMO, WHO), AL, OPEC.

Iraqi Interests Section: 1801 P St., NW, 20036; 483-7500. **Website:** www.cpa-iraq.org

The Tigris-Euphrates valley, formerly called Mesopotamia, was the site of one of the earliest civilizations in the world. Mesopotamia ceased to be a separate entity after the Persian, Greek, and Arab conquests. The Arabs founded Baghdad, from where the caliph ruled a vast Islamic empire in the 8th and 9th centuries. Mongol and Turkish conquests led to a decline in the region's population, economy, cultural life, and irrigation system.

Britain secured a League of Nations mandate over Iraq after World War I. Independence under a king came in 1932. Rebellious army officers killed King Faisal II, July 14, 1958, and established a leftist, pan-Arab republic, which pursued close ties with the USSR. Successive regimes were increasingly dominated by the Baath Arab Socialist Party. In the 1973 Arab-Israeli war Iraq sent forces to aid Syria.

A Baath leader, Saddam Hussein, became president of Iraq, July 16, 1979. After purging his enemies, he ruled as a dictator for more than 2 decades, repressing Iraq's Kurds and Shiites and launching disastrous wars against 2 neighboring nations, Iran and Kuwait. Hussein was believed to be seeking to develop weapons of mass destruction; Israeli planes destroyed a nuclear reactor near Baghdad June 7, 1981, claiming it could be used to produce nuclear weapons.

After skirmishing intermittently for 10 months over the sovereignty of the disputed Shatt al-Arab waterway that divides the two countries, Iraq and Iran entered into open warfare on Sept. 22, 1980. Iran repulsed early Iraqi advances, producing a long and costly stalemate; hundreds of thousands of Iraqis lost their lives during the 8-year conflict. Hussein used poison gas against the Iraqi Kurdish minority in 1988, killing up to 5,000 people in Halabja, in the 1st mass use of poison gas since the Holocaust.

Iraq attacked and overran Kuwait Aug. 2, 1990, sparking an international crisis. Backed by the UN, a U.S.-led coalition launched air and missile attacks on Iraq, Jan. 16, 1991. The coalition began a ground attack to retake Kuwait Feb. 23. Iraqi forces showed little resistance and were soundly defeated in 4 days. Some 175,000 Iraqis were taken prisoner, and Iraqi casualties were estimated at over 85,000. As part of the cease-fire agreement, Iraq agreed to scrap all poison gas and germ weapons and allow UN observers to inspect the sites. UN trade sanctions would remain in effect until Iraq complied with all terms.

In Feb. 1991, Iraqi troops drove Kurdish insurgents and civilians to the borders of Iran and Turkey, causing a refugee crisis. The U.S. and allies established havens inside Iraq for the Kurds. The U.S. launched a missile attack aimed at Iraq's intelligence headquarters in Baghdad June 26, 1993, citing evidence that Iraq had sponsored a plot to kill former Pres. George Bush. Iraqi cooperation with UN weapons inspection teams was intermittent throughout the 1990s. On Dec. 9, 1996, the UN began a program that allowed Baghdad to begin selling limited amounts of oil for food and medicine. (The UN, Apr. 2004, launched an investigation of the program amid charges that the administration of the program was corrupt and that the Hussein regime skimmed billions of dollars from the fund.)

Iraqi resistance to UN access to suspected weapons sites touched off diplomatic crises during 1997-98, culminating in intensive U.S. and British aerial bombardment of Iraqi military targets, Dec. 16-19, 1998. After 2 years of sporadic activity, U.S. and British warplanes struck harder at sites near Baghdad on Feb. 16, 2001.

In a speech before the UN, Sept. 12, 2002, Pres. George W. Bush accused Iraq of repeatedly violating UN resolutions to eliminate weapons of mass destruction, refrain from supporting terrorism, and end repression. Under Security Council Resolution 1441, approved Nov. 8, Iraq allowed UN inspectors to search for banned weapons, while the U.S. and Britain built up troops in the Persian Gulf. Despite opposition from some countries, including France, Germany, and Russia, a U.S.-led coalition launched an invasion of Iraq on the evening of Mar. 19 (EST), 2003. By Apr. 6 the British controlled Basra and other areas in the S, and the U.S. entered Baghdad Apr. 7. Hussein had disappeared, the Iraqi government had collapsed, and most of Iraq's armed forces had dissolved into the civilian population. On May 1, Pres. Bush declared that major combat there was over. Continuing searches failed to uncover evidence of stockpiled chemical, biological, or nuclear weapons.

The U.S. initially governed Iraq through a Coalition Provisional Authority, headed by L. Paul Bremer. A 25-member Iraqi Governing Council was appointed and named a cabinet Sept. 1, 2003. Reconstruction efforts continued but were hampered by guerrilla attacks from Baath remnants, Islamic extremists, and others. Iraqi resistance activities widened with the bombings of the Jordanian embassy, Aug. 7, the UN headquarters in Baghdad, Aug. 19, killing UN special envoy Sergio Vieira de Mello and 21 others, and a blast in Najaf Aug. 29 that killed at least 83 people, including Ayatollah Mohammad Bakir al-Hakim, a Shiite leader. After a 2nd bombing at its Baghdad headquarters Sept. 22, the UN scaled back its presence in Iraq.

Coalition forces succeeded in neutralizing many leaders of the former regime. Two of Hussein's sons, Uday and Qusay, were killed July 22, 2003 by U.S. troops in Mosul. Saddam Hussein was captured in an underground hideout Dec. 13; he appeared before an Iraqi tribunal July 1, 2004, and was charged with crimes against humanity. The insurgency continued to mount attacks that killed large numbers of Iraqi civilians as well as many foreign troops and civilians participating in reconstruction, under leaders such as radical Shiite cleric Moqtada al-Sadr and Jordanian militant Abu Musab al-Zarqawi; the U.S. believed Zarqawi was behind a series of kidnappings, beheadings, and suicide bombings. Fallujah remained a center of Sunni Muslim resistance. Among other atroocities, gunmen ambushed and killed 4 security contractors in Fallujah in March, and a mob dragged their bodies through the streets. Attacks on pipelines and other facilities cut Iraq's oil production.

Photographs released in Apr. 2004 graphically showed instances of physical abuse and sexual humiliation of Iraqi inmates by U.S. military personnel at Baghdad's Abu Ghraib prison in fall 2003. The images sparked widespread outrage.

On June 28, 2004, the U.S. authorities officially transferred sovereignty to a transitional Iraqi government led by Prime Min. Iyad Allawi. About 140,000 U.S. troops remained, along with 25,000 allied forces and thousands of foreign civilian advisers and contractors. A 3-week confrontation at Najaf, with U.S. and Iraqi forces battling Sadr's Mahdi Army guerrillas, was defused Aug. 27 by Iraq's most influential Shiite leader, the Grand Ayatollah Ali al-Sistani.

By Sept. 2004, over 1,000 U.S. service members had been killed and at least 6,500 wounded during the war and occupation. Attacks against coalition troops remained near their highest levels since the war officially ended. British troop losses were put at over 60; Italy, Spain, Poland, and other countries had smaller losses. Many thousands of Iraqi troops and civilians were killed in the continuing violence.

Ireland

People: Population: 3,969,558. **Age distrib.** (%): <15: 21.3; 65+: 11.4. **Pop. density:** 149 per sq mi, 58 per sq km. **Urban:** 59.9%. **Ethnic groups:** Celtic; English minority. **Principal languages:** English, Irish Gaelic (both official); Irish Gaelic spoken by small number in western areas. **Chief religions:** Roman Catholic 92%, Anglican 3%.

Geography: Total area: 27,135 sq mi, 70,280 sq km; **Land area:** 26,599 sq mi, 68,890 sq km. **Location:** In the Atlantic O. just W of Great Britain. **Neighbors:** United Kingdom (Northern Ireland) on E. **Topography:** Ireland consists of a central plateau surrounded by isolated groups of hills and mountains. The coastline is heavily indented by the Atlantic O. **Capital:** Dublin, 1,015,000.

Government: Type: Parliamentary republic. **Head of state:** Pres. Mary McAleese; b June 27, 1951; in office: Nov. 11, 1997. **Head of gov.:** Prime Min. Bertie Ahern; b Sept. 12, 1951; in office: June 26, 1997. **Local divisions:** 26 counties. **Defense budget** (2003): $794 mil. **Active troops:** 10,460.

Economy: Industries: food products, brewing, textiles, clothing, pharm., chemicals. **Chief crops:** turnips, barley, potatoes, sugar beets; wheat. **Natural resources:** zinc, lead, nat. gas, barite, copper, gypsum, limestone, dolomite, peat, silver. **Arable land:** 13%. **Livestock** (2003): cattle: 6.92 mil.; chickens: 11.34 mil.; goats: 7,700; pigs: 1.78 mil.; sheep: 4.83 mil. **Fish catch** (2002): 344,899 metric tons. **Electricity prod.** (2002): 22.88 bil. kWh. **Labor force** (2002 est.): agriculture 8%, industry 29%, services 64%.

Finance: Monetary unit: Euro (EUR) (Sept. 2004: 0.82 = $1 U.S.). **GDP** (2003 est.): $117.0 bil.; **per capita GDP:** $29,800; **GDP growth:** 2.1%. **Imports** (2003 est.): $57.5 bil.; partners (2002): UK 41.1%, U.S. 15.3%, Germany 6.8%. **Exports** (2003 est.): $98.3 bil.; partners (2002): UK 23.3%, U.S. 16.7%, Belgium 14.6%, Germany 7.3%, France 5%. **Tourism** (2002): $3.8 bil. **Budget** (2002): $30.5 bil. **Intl. reserves less gold:** $2.75 bil. **Gold:** 180,000 oz t. **Consumer prices:** 3.5%.

Transport: Railroad: Length: 2,058 mi. **Motor vehicles** (1999): 1.28 mil pass. cars, 193,100 comm. vehicles. **Civil aviation:** 8.4 bil. pass.-mi; 16 airports. **Chief ports:** Dublin, Cork.

Communications: TV sets: 406 per 1,000 pop. **Radios:** 697 per 1,000 pop. **Telephone lines:** 2.0 mil. **Daily newspaper circ.:** 335.7 per 1,000 pop. **Internet:** 1.3 mil. users.

Health: Life expect.: 74.7 male; 80.2 female. **Births** (per 1,000 pop.): 14.5. **Deaths** (per 1,000 pop.): 7.9. **Natural inc.:** 0.66%. **Infant mortality** (per 1,000 live births): 5.5. **AIDS rate:** 0.1%.

Education: Compulsory: ages 6-15. **Literacy** (1993): 100%.

Major Intl. Organizations: UN (FAO, IBRD, ILO, IMF, IMO, WHO, WTrO), EU, OECD, OSCE.

Embassy: 2234 Massachusetts Ave. NW 20008; 462-3939.

Websites: www.irlgov.ie/; www.irelandemb.org

Celtic tribes invaded the islands about the 4th century BC; their Gaelic culture and literature flourished and spread to Scotland and elsewhere in the 5th century AD, the same century in which St. Patrick converted the Irish to Christianity. Invasions by Norsemen began in the 8th century, ended with defeat of the Danes by the Irish King Brian Boru in 1014. English invasions started in the 12th century; for over 700 years the Anglo-Irish struggle continued with bitter rebellions and savage repressions.

The Easter Monday Rebellion in 1916 failed but was followed by guerrilla warfare and harsh reprisals by British troops called the "Black and Tans." The Dail Eireann (Irish parliament) reaffirmed independence in Jan. 1919. The British offered dominion status to Ulster (6 counties) and southern Ireland (26 counties) Dec. 1921. The constitution of the Irish Free State, a British dominion, was adopted Dec. 11, 1922. Northern Ireland remained part of the United Kingdom.

A new constitution adopted by plebiscite came into operation Dec. 29, 1937. It declared the name of the state Eire in the Irish language (Ireland in the English) and declared it a sovereign democratic state. On Dec. 21, 1948, an Irish law declared the country a republic rather than a dominion and withdrew it from the Commonwealth. The British Parliament recognized both actions, 1949, but reasserted its claim to incorporate the 6 northeastern counties in the U.K. This claim has not been recognized by Ireland *(see United Kingdom—Northern Ireland).*

Irish governments have favored peaceful unification of all Ireland and cooperated with Britain against terrorist groups. On Dec. 15, 1993, Irish and British governments agreed on outlines of a peace plan to resolve the Northern Ireland issue. On Aug. 31, 1994, the Irish Republican Army announced a cease-fire; when peace talks lagged, however, the IRA returned to its terror campaign on Feb. 9, 1996. The IRA proclaimed a new cease-fire as of July 20, 1997, and peace talks resumed Sept. 15.

Ireland's first woman president, Mary Robinson, resigned Sept. 12 to become UN high commissioner for human rights. She was succeeded by Mary McAleese, a law professor from Northern Ireland and the first northerner to hold the office. After negotiators in Northern Ireland approved a peace settlement on Good Friday, April 10, 1998, voters in the Irish Republic endorsed the accord on May 22. Irish voters rejected, June 7, 2001, then reversed themselves and approved, Oct. 19, 2002, a plan calling for EU expansion.

A referendum June 11 ended the automatic right of citizenship for children born in the country.

Israel
State of Israel

People: Population: 6,199,008. **Age distrib.** (%): <15: 27.1; 65+: 9.9. **Pop. density:** 790 per sq mi, 305 per sq km. **Urban:** 51.8%. **Ethnic groups:** Jewish 80%, Arab and other 20%. **Principal languages:** Hebrew, Arabic (both official), English. **Chief religions:** Jewish 80%, Muslim (mostly Sunni) 15%, Christian 2%.

Geography: Total area: 8,019 sq mi, 20,770 sq km; **Land area:** 7,849 sq mi, 20,330 sq km. **Location:** Middle East, on E end of Mediterranean Sea. **Neighbors:** Lebanon on N; Syria, West Bank, and Jordan on E; Gaza Strip and Egypt on W. **Topography:** The Mediterranean coastal plain is fertile and well-watered. In the center is the Judean Plateau. A triangular-shaped semi-desert region, the Negev, extends from south of Beersheba to an apex at the head of the Gulf of Aqaba. The E border drops sharply into the Jordan Rift Valley, including Lake Tiberias (Sea of Galilee) and the Dead Sea, which is c.1,300 ft. below sea level, lowest point on the earth's surface. **Capital:** Jerusalem (most countries maintain their embassies in Tel Aviv), 686,000. **Cities (urban aggr.):** Tel Aviv-Yafo, 2,752,000; Haifa, 865,000.

Government: Type: Republic. **Head of state:** Pres. Moshe Katsav; b 1945; in office: Aug. 1, 2000. **Head of gov.:** Prime Min. Ariel Sharon; b 1928; in office: Mar. 7, 2001. **Local divisions:** 6 districts. **Defense budget** (2003): $7.4 bil. **Active troops:** 167,600.

Economy: Industries: high-tech products, wood & paper products, potash & phosphates, food, beverages, tobacco. **Chief crops:** citrus, vegetables, cotton. **Natural resources:** timber, potash, copper ore, nat. gas, phosphate rock, magnesium bromide, clays, sand. **Crude oil reserves** (2003): 3.8 mil. bbls. **Arable land:** 17%. **Livestock** (2003): cattle: 390,000; chickens: 30.0 mil.; goats: 63,000; pigs: 190,000; sheep: 395,000. **Fish catch** (2002): 27,141 metric tons. **Electricity prod.** (2002): 42.67 bil. kWh. **Labor force** (1996): public services 31.2%, manufacturing 20.2%, finance and business 13.1%, commerce 12.8%, construction 7.5%, personal and other services 6.4%, transport, storage, and communications 6.2%, agriculture, forestry, and fishing 2.6%.

Finance: Monetary unit: New Shekel (ILS) (Sept. 2004: 4.48 = $1 U.S.). **GDP** (2003 est.): $120.6 bil.; **per capita GDP:** $19,700; **GDP growth:** 1.0%. **Imports** (2003 est.): $32.3 bil.; partners (2002): U.S. 18.5%, Belgium 9.1%, Germany 7.1%, UK 6.7%, Switzerland 6.3%, Italy 4.6%. **Exports** (2003 est.): $29.3 bil.; partners (2002): U.S. 40.3%, Belgium 6.3%, Hong Kong 4.7%, UK 4%. **Tourism** (2002): $1.2 bil. **Budget** (2002 est.): $45.1 bil. **Intl. reserves less gold:** $17.71 bil. **Consumer prices:** 0.7%.

Transport: Railroad: Length: 398 mi. **Motor vehicles** (2001): 1.47 mil pass. cars, 350,200 comm. vehicles. **Civil aviation:** 8.8 bil. pass.-mi; 28 airports. **Chief ports:** Haifa, Ashdod, Elat.

Communications: TV sets: 328 per 1,000 pop. **Radios:** 524 per 1,000 pop. **Telephone lines** (2002): 3.0 mil. **Daily newspaper circ.:** 290 per 1,000 pop. **Internet** (2002): 2.0 mil. users.

Health: Life expect.: 77.1 male; 81.4 female. **Births** (per 1,000 pop.): 18.4. **Deaths** (per 1,000 pop.): 6.2. **Natural inc.:** 1.23%. **Infant mortality** (per 1,000 live births): 7.2. **AIDS rate:** 0.1%.

Education: Free, compulsory: ages 5-15. **Literacy:** 95.4%.
Major Intl. Organizations: UN (FAO, IBRD, ILO, IMF, IMO, WHO, WTrO).
Embassy: 3514 International Dr. NW 20008; 364-5500.
Websites: www.mfa.gov.il/mfa; www.israelemb.org

Occupying the SW corner of the ancient Fertile Crescent, Israel contains some of the oldest known evidence of agriculture and of primitive town life. The Hebrews probably arrived early in the 2d millennium BC. Under King David and his successors (c.1000 BC-597 BC), Judaism was developed and secured. After conquest by Babylonians, Persians, and Greeks, an independent Jewish kingdom was revived, 168 BC, but Rome took effective control in the next century, suppressed Jewish revolts in AD 70 and AD 135, and renamed Judea Palestine, after the earlier coastal inhabitants, the Philistines.

Arab invaders conquered Palestine in 636. The Arabic language and Islam prevailed within a few centuries, but a Jewish minority remained. The land was ruled from the 11th century as a part of non-Arab empires by Seljuks, Mamluks, and Ottomans (with a crusader interval, 1098-1291).

After 4 centuries of Ottoman rule, the land was taken in 1917 by Britain, which pledged in the Balfour Declaration to support a Jewish national homeland there. In 1920 a British Palestine Mandate was recognized; in 1922 the land east of the Jordan was detached.

Jewish immigration, begun in the late 19th century, swelled in the 1930s with refugees from the Nazis; heavy Arab immigration from Syria and Lebanon also occurred. Arab opposition to Jewish immigration turned violent in 1920, 1921, 1929, and 1936. The UN General Assembly voted in 1947 to partition Palestine into an Arab and a Jewish state. Britain withdrew in May 1948.

Israel was declared an independent state May 14, 1948; the Arabs rejected partition. Egypt, Jordan, Syria, Lebanon, Iraq, and Saudi Arabia invaded, but failed to destroy the Jewish state, which gained territory. Separate armistices with the Arab nations were signed in 1949; Jordan occupied the West Bank, Egypt occupied Gaza; neither granted Palestinian autonomy.

After persistent terrorist raids, Israel invaded Egypt's Sinai, Oct. 29, 1956, aided briefly by British and French forces. A UN cease-fire was arranged Nov. 6.

An uneasy truce between Israel and the Arab countries lasted until 1967, when Egypt reoccupied the Gaza Strip and closed the Gulf of Aqaba to Israeli shipping. In a 6-day war that started June 5, the Israelis took the Gaza Strip, occupied the Sinai Peninsula to the Suez Canal, and captured East Jerusalem, Syria's Golan Heights, and Jordan's West Bank.

Egypt and Syria attacked Israel, Oct. 6, 1973 (on Yom Kippur, the most solemn day on the Jewish calendar). Israel counter-attacked, driving the Syrians back, and crossed the Suez Canal. A cease-fire took effect Oct. 24 and a UN peacekeeping force went to the area. Under a disengagement agreement signed Jan. 18, 1974, Israel withdrew from the canal's west bank.Israeli forces raided Entebbe, Uganda, July 3, 1976, and rescued 103 hostages who had been seized by Arab and German terrorists.

Israel's prime ministers, including David Ben-Gurion, Golda Meir, and Yitzhak Rabin, pursued a moderate socialist program, 1948-77. In 1977, the conservative opposition, led by Menachem Begin, was voted into office for the first time. Egypt's Pres. Anwar al-Sadat visited Jerusalem Nov. 1977, and on Mar. 26, 1979, Egypt and Israel signed a formal peace treaty, ending 30 years of war. Israel returned the Sinai to Egypt in 1982.

On June 7, 1981, Israeli jets destroyed an Iraqi atomic reactor near Baghdad that, Israel claimed, would have enabled Iraq to manufacture nuclear weapons. Israeli forces invaded Lebanon, June 6, 1982, to destroy PLO strongholds there. After massive Israeli bombing of West Beirut, the PLO agreed to evacuate the city. Israeli troops entered West Beirut after newly elected Lebanese Pres. Bashir Gemayel was assassinated on Sept. 14. Israel drew widespread condemnation when Lebanese Christian forces, Sept. 16, entered two West Beirut refugee camps and slaughtered hundreds of Palestinian refugees.

In 1989, violence escalated over the Israeli military occupation of the West Bank and Gaza Strip. In a series of uprisings known as the 1st intifada, Palestinian protesters defied Israeli troops, who forcibly retaliated. During the Persian Gulf War, 1991, Iraq fired Scud missiles at Israel. The Labor Party of Yitzhak Rabin won parliamentary elections, June 23, 1992.

Ongoing peace talks led to historic agreements between Israel and the PLO, Sept. 1993. The PLO recognized Israel's right to exist; Israel recognized the PLO as the Palestinians' representative; the two sides then signed, Sept. 13, an agreement for limited Palestinian self-rule and the West Bank and Gaza. Israel and Jordan signed, July 25, 1994, in Washington, DC, a declaration ending their 46-year state of war.

Arab and Jewish extremists repeatedly challenged the peace process. A Jewish gunman opened fire on Arab worshippers at a mosque in Hebron, Feb. 25, 1994, killing at least 29 before he himself was killed. On Nov. 4, 1995, an Orthodox Jewish Israeli assassinated Rabin as he left a peace rally in Tel Aviv. Support for Rabin's successor, Shimon Peres, was shaken by a series of suicide bombings and rocket attacks against Israel by Islamic militants. Emphasizing security issues, the candidate of the conservative Likud bloc, Benjamin Netanyahu, was elected prime minister on May 29.

Under an interim accord brokered by Pres. Bill Clinton and signed by Netanyahu and PLO leader Yasir Arafat at the White House, Oct. 23, 1998, Israel yielded more West Bank territory to the Palestinians, in exchange for new security guarantees. Negotiations bogged down, however, and full implementation did not begin until Sept. 1999. In the interim, Netanyahu lost by a landslide to the Labor party candidate, Ehud Barak, in the general election of May 17.

Israel pulled virtually all its troops out of S Lebanon by May 24, 2000. Marathon summit talks in the U.S. between Barak and Arafat, July 11-25, failed. A 2nd intifada began in late Sept. in Israel and the Palestinian territories. Barak called new elections for prime minister but lost Feb. 6, 2001, to Ariel Sharon, a hardliner. The bloodshed intensified during the summer, as Palestinian suicide bombers launched attacks on Israeli civilians and Israel struck at against Palestinian-controlled territory and carried out an assassination campaign against suspected terrorists.

Israel launched a major West Bank offensive Mar. 29, 2002, 2 days after a suicide bomber killed 26 Israeli Jews at a Passover celebration in Netanya. Fighting was particularly fierce at the Jenin refugee camp, where 23 Israeli troops and at least 50 Palestinians were killed. Israel withdrew in early May but, after another wave of suicide bombings, reoccupied much of the West Bank June 21-27. In June 2002 the Israeli government began building a controversial security barrier in the West Bank to restrict Palestinian access to Israel; in a nonbinding ruling, July 9, 2004, the World Court said the barrier violated international law.

A U.S.-sponsored "road map" to Middle East in Gaza city peace, unveiled Apr. 30, 2003, made little headway. Israel Sept. 1 vowed "all-out war" against Hamas terrorists. Israeli missile strikes in Gaza City killed Hamas founder and leader Sheikh Ahmed Yassin Mar. 22, 2004, and his successor, Abdel Aziz al-Rantisi, Apr. 17. Hamas suicide bombers Aug. 31 blew up 2 buses in Beersheba, killing 16 people. A Sharon plan to create a more broad-based government, including Labor, and to pull Israeli soldiers and settlers out of Gaza faced stiff opposition from within his own Likud party.

Since Sept. 2000, the conflict has claimed the lives of more than 900 Israelis and at least 3,200 Palestinians.

Gaza Strip

The Gaza Strip, also known as Gaza, extends NE from the Sinai Peninsula for 40 km (25 mi), with the Mediterranean Sea to the W and Israel to the E. The Palestinian Authority is responsible for civil government, but Israel retains control over security. Nearly all the inhabitants are Palestinian Arabs, more than 35% of whom live in refugee camps. Population (2004 est) 1,324,991. Area: 139 sq. mi.

Israel captured Gaza from Egypt in the 1967 war. It remained under Israeli occupation until May 1994, when the Israel Defense Forces withdrew. Agreements between Israel and the PLO in 1993 and 1994 provided for interim self-rule in Gaza, pending the completion of final status negotiations.

West Bank

Located W of the Jordan R. and Dead Sea, the West Bank is bounded by Jordan on the E and by Israel on the N, W, and S. The Palestinian Authority administers several major cities, but Israel retains control over much land, including Jewish settlements. Population (2004 est) 2,311,204. Area: 2,263 sq. mi.

Israel captured the West Bank from Jordan in the 1967 war. A 1974 Arab summit conference designated the PLO as sole representative of West Bank Arabs. In 1988 Jordan cut legal and administrative ties with the territory. Jericho was returned to Palestinian control in May 1994. An accord between Israel and the PLO expanding Palestinian self-rule in the West Bank was signed Sept. 28, 1995. Later agreements gave Palestinians full or shared control of 40% of West Bank territory.

Italy
Italian Republic

People: Population: 58,057,477. **Age distrib. (%):** <15: 14.1; 65+: 18.6. **Pop. density:** 511 per sq mi, 197 per sq km. **Urban:** 91.6%. **Ethnic groups:** Mostly Italian; small minorities of German, Slovene, Albanian. **Principal languages:** Italian (official), German, French, Slovenian, Albanian. **Chief religion:** Predominately Roman Catholic.

Geography: Total area: 116,306 sq mi, 301,230 sq km; **Land area:** 113,522 sq mi, 294,020 sq km. **Location:** In S Europe, jutting into Mediterranean Sea. **Neighbors:** France on W, Switzerland and Austria on N, Slovenia on E. **Topography:** Occupies a long boot-shaped peninsula, extending SE from the Alps into the Mediterranean, with the islands of Sicily and Sardinia offshore. The alluvial Po Valley drains most of N. The rest of the country is rugged and mountainous, except for intermittent coastal plains, like the Campania, S of Rome. Apennine Mts. run down through center of peninsula. **Capital:** Rome, 2,665,000. **Cities (urban agr.):** Milan, 4,183,000; Naples, 2,995,000; Turin, 1,247,000.

Government: Type: Republic. **Head of state:** Pres. Carlo Azeglio Ciampi; b Dec. 9, 1920; in office: May 18, 1999. **Head of gov.:** Prime Min. Silvio Berlusconi; b Sept. 29, 1936; in office: June 11, 2001. **Local divisions:** 20 regions divided into 103 provinces. **Defense budget** (2003): $22.3 bil. **Active troops:** 200,000.

Economy: Industries: tourism, machinery, iron & steel, chemicals, food proc., textiles, autos. **Chief crops:** fruits, vegetables,

grapes, potatoes, sugar beets, soybeans, grain, olives. **Natural resources:** mercury, potash, marble, sulfur, nat. gas, oil, fish, coal. **Crude oil reserves** (2003): 621.7 mil. bbls. **Arable land:** 31%. **Livestock** (2003): cattle: 6.43 mil.; chickens: 100.0 mil.; goats: 1.33 mil.; pigs: 9.1 mil.; sheep: 10.95 mil. **Fish catch** (2002): 453,808 metric tons. **Electricity prod.** (2002): 261.61 bil. kWh. **Labor force** (2001): services 63%, industry 32%, agriculture 5%.

Finance: Monetary unit: Euro (EUR) (Sept. 2004: 0.82 = $1 U.S.). **GDP** (2003 est.): $1.552 tril.; **per capita GDP:** $26,800; **GDP growth:** 0.5%. **Imports** (2003 est.): $271.1 bil.; partners (2002): Germany 17.8%, France 11.3%, Netherlands 5.9%, UK 5%, U.S. 4.9%, Spain 4.6%, Belgium 4.4%. **Exports** (2003 est.): $278.1 bil.; partners (2002): Germany 13.7%, France 12.2%, U.S. 9.8%, UK 6.9%, Spain 6.4%. **Tourism:** $31.3 bil. **Budget** (2001 est.): $517.0 bil. **Intl. reserves less gold:** $20.44 bil. **Gold:** 78.83 mil oz t. **Consumer prices:** 2.7%.

Transport: Railroad: Length: 12,112 mi. **Motor vehicles** (2001): 32.58 mil pass. cars, 3.37 mil comm. vehicles. **Civil aviation:** 21.3 bil. pass.-mi; 96 airports. **Chief ports:** Genoa, Venice, Trieste, Palermo, Naples, La Spezia.

Communications: TV sets: 492 per 1,000 pop. **Radios:** 880 per 1,000 pop. **Telephone lines:** 26.6 mil. **Daily newspaper circ.:** 104 per 1,000 pop. **Internet:** 18.5 mil. users.

Health: Life expect.: 76.6 male; 82.7 female. **Births** (per 1,000 pop.): 9.1. **Deaths** (per 1,000 pop.): 10.2. **Natural inc.:** −0.12%. **Infant mortality** (per 1,000 live births): 6.1. **AIDS rate:** 0.5%.

Education: Compulsory: ages 6-14. **Literacy:** 98.6%.

Major Intl. Organizations: UN and all of its specialized agencies, EU, NATO, OECD, OSCE.

Embassy: 3000 Whitehaven St. NW 20008; 612-4400.

Websites: www.italyemb.org; www.travel.it

Rome emerged as the major power in Italy after 500 BC, dominating the Etruscans to the N and Greeks to the S. Under the Empire, which lasted until the 5th century AD, Rome ruled most of Western Europe, the Balkans, the Middle East, and N Africa.

After the Germanic invasions, lasting several centuries, a high civilization arose in the city-states of the N, culminating in the Renaissance. But German, French, Spanish, and Austrian intervention prevented the unification of the country. In 1859 Lombardy came under the crown of King Victor Emmanuel II of Sardinia. By plebiscite in 1860, Parma, Modena, Romagna, and Tuscany joined, followed by Sicily and Naples, and by the Marches and Umbria. The first Italian Parliament declared Victor Emmanuel king of Italy Mar. 17, 1861. Mantua and Venetia were added in 1866 as an outcome of the Austro-Prussian war. The Papal States were taken by Italian troops Sept. 20, 1870, on the withdrawal of the French garrison. The states were annexed to the kingdom by plebiscite. Italy recognized Vatican City as independent Feb. 11, 1929.

Fascism appeared in Italy Mar. 23, 1919, led by Benito Mussolini, who took over the government at the invitation of the king Oct. 28, 1922. Mussolini acquired dictatorial powers. He made war on Ethiopia and proclaimed Victor Emmanuel III emperor, defied the sanctions of the League of Nations, sent troops to fight for Franco against the Republic of Spain, and joined Germany in World War II.

After Fascism was overthrown in 1943, Italy declared war on Germany and Japan and contributed to the Allied victory. It surrendered conquered lands and lost its colonies. Mussolini was killed by partisans Apr. 28, 1945. Victor Emmanuel III abdicated May 9, 1946; his son Humbert II was king until June 10, when Italy became a republic after a referendum, June 2-3.

Since World War II, Italy has enjoyed growth in industrial output and living standards, in part a result of membership in the European Community (now European Union). Political stability has not kept pace with economic prosperity, and organized crime and corruption have been persistent problems.

Christian Democratic leader and former Prime Min. Aldo Moro was abducted and murdered in 1978 by Red Brigade terrorists. The wave of left-wing political violence, including other kidnappings and assassinations, continued into the 1980s.

In the early 1990s, scandals implicated some of Italy's most prominent politicians. In Mar. 1994 voting, under reformed election rules, right-wing parties won a majority, dislodging Italy's long-powerful Christian Democratic Party. After a series of short-lived governments, a coalition of center-left parties won the election of Apr. 21, 1996. Italy led a 7,000-member international peacekeeping force in Albania, Apr.-Aug. 1997, and contributed 2,000 troops to the NATO-led security force (KFOR) that entered Kosovo in June 1999.

Supporters of Silvio Berlusconi, a multibillionaire media magnate, won the parliamentary elections of May 13, 2001. An earthquake Oct. 31, 2002, in San Giuliano di Puglia, killed 26 schoolchildren. Berlusconi backed the U.S.-led war in Iraq, and Italian troops served in the coalition. On trial for bribing judges in the 1980s, he was helped when Parliament passed a bill in June immunizing top government leaders from prosecution while they held office. Over 4,100 elderly Italians died because of a severe summer heat wave.

Turin has been chosen to host the Winter Olympics in 2006.

Sicily, 9,926 sq. mi., pop. (2001 est.) 4,866,200 is an island 180 by 120 mi., seat of a region that embraces the island of **Pantelleria,** 32 sq. mi., and the **Lipari** group, 44 sq. mi., including 2 active volcanoes: **Vulcano,** 1,637 ft., and **Stromboli,** 3,038 ft. From prehistoric times Sicily has been settled by various peoples; a Greek

state had its capital at Syracuse. Rome took Sicily from Carthage 215 BC. **Mt. Etna,** an 11,053-ft. active volcano, is its tallest peak.

Sardinia, 9,301 sq. mi., pop. (2001 est.) 1,599,500, lies in the Mediterranean, 115 mi. W of Italy and 7$^1/_2$ mi. S of Corsica. It is 160 mi. long, 68 mi. wide, and mountainous, with mining of coal, zinc, lead, copper. In 1720 Sardinia was added to the possessions of the Dukes of Savoy in Piedmont and Savoy to form the Kingdom of Sardinia. Giuseppe Garibaldi is buried on the nearby isle of Caprera. **Elba,** 86 sq. mi., lies 6 mi. W of Tuscany. Napoleon I lived in exile on Elba 1814-1815.

Jamaica

People: Population: 2,713,130. **Age distrib.** (%): <15: 29.1; 65+: 6.8. **Pop. density:** 649 per sq mi, 250 per sq km. **Urban:** 67.4%. **Ethnic groups:** Black 91%, mixed 7%, East Indian and other 2%. **Principal languages:** English, patois English. **Chief religions:** Protestant 61%, Roman Catholic 4%, spiritual cults and other 35%.

Geography: Total area: 4,244 sq mi, 10,991 sq km; **Land area:** 4,182 sq mi, 10,831 sq km. **Location:** In West Indies. **Neighbors:** Nearest are Cuba to N, Haiti to E. **Topography:** Four-fifths of Jamaica is covered by mountains. **Capital:** Kingston, 575,000.

Government: Type: Parliamentary democracy. **Head of state:** Queen Elizabeth II, represented by Gov.-Gen. Sir Howard Cooke; b Nov. 13, 1915; in office: Aug. 1, 1991. **Head of gov.:** Prime Min. Percival J. Patterson; b Apr. 10, 1935; in office: Mar. 30, 1992. **Local divisions:** 14 parishes. **Defense budget** (2003): $51 mil. **Active troops:** 2,830.

Economy: Industries: tourism, bauxite, textiles, food proc., light manufactures, rum, cement, metal, paper, chemical products. **Chief crops:** sugarcane, bananas, coffee, citrus, potatoes. **Natural resources:** bauxite, gypsum, limestone. **Arable land:** 14%. **Livestock** (2003): cattle: 430,000; chickens: 11.0 mil.; goats: 440,000; pigs: 180,000; sheep: 1,400. **Fish catch** (2002 est): 11,800 metric tons. **Electricity prod.** (2002): 6.29 bil. kWh. **Labor force** (1998): services 60%, agriculture 21%, industry 19%.

Finance: Monetary unit: Jamaican Dollar (JMD) (Sept. 2004: 61.91 = $1 U.S.). **GDP** (2003 est.): $10.2 bil.; **per capita GDP:** $3,800; **GDP growth:** 1.9%. **Imports** (2003 est.): $3.3 bil.; partners (2002): U.S. 44%, Trinidad and Tobago 9.1%, Japan 5.9%, Venezuela 4%. **Exports** (2003 est.): $1.4 bil.; partners (2002): U.S. 28.3%, Canada 14.1%, Netherlands 12.2%, UK 12.1%, Norway 8.4%. **Tourism:** $1.3 bil. **Budget** (FY99/00 est.): $2.6 bil. **Intl. reserves less gold:** $804 mil. **Consumer prices:** 10.3%.

Transport: Railroad: Length: 169 mi. **Motor vehicles** (1999): 140,400 pass. cars, 56,600 comm. vehicles. **Civil aviation:** 2.5 bil. pass.-mi; 11 airports. **Chief ports:** Kingston, Montego Bay.

Communications: TV sets: 191 per 1,000 pop. **Radios:** 796 per 1,000 pop. **Telephone lines** (2002): 444,400. **Daily newspaper circ.:** 62 per 1,000 pop. **Internet** (2002): 600,000 users.

Health: Life expect.: 74.0 male; 78.2 female. **Births** (per 1,000 pop.): 16.9. **Deaths** (per 1,000 pop.): 5.4. **Natural inc.:** 1.15%. **Infant mortality** (per 1,000 live births): 12.8. **AIDS rate:** 1.2%.

Education: Compulsory: ages 6-11. **Literacy:** 87.9%.

Major Intl. Organizations: UN (FAO, IBRD, ILO, IMF, IMO, WHO, WTrO), Caricom, the Commonwealth, OAS.

Embassy: 1520 New Hampshire Ave. NW 20036; 452-0660.

Websites: www.cabinet.gov.jm; www.emjamusa.org

Jamaica was visited by Columbus, and ruled by Spain (under whom Arawak Indians died out) until seized by Britain, 1655. Jamaica won independence Aug. 6, 1962.

In 1974 Jamaica sought an increase in taxes paid by U.S. and Canadian bauxite mines. The socialist government acquired 50% ownership of the companies' Jamaican interests in 1976, and was reelected that year. Rudimentary welfare state measures were passed. Relations with the U.S. improved in the 1980s when Jamaican politics entered a more conservative phase. Violence between government forces and West Kingston slum residents claimed at least 20 lives July 7-10, 2001. At least 17 died when Hurricane Ivan hit S Jamaica Sept. 10-11, 2004.

Japan

People: Population: 127,333,002. **Age distrib.** (%): <15: 14.5; 65+: 18. **Pop. density:** 880 per sq mi, 340 per sq km. **Urban:** 52.1%. **Ethnic groups:** Japanese 99%; Korean, Chinese, and other 1%. **Principal languages:** Japanese (official), Ainu, Korean. Chief religions: Shinto and Buddhist, observed together by 84%.

Geography: Total area: 145,883 sq mi, 377,835 sq km; **Land area:** 144,689 sq mi, 374,744 sq km. **Location:** Archipelago off E coast of Asia. **Neighbors:** Russia to N, South Korea to W. **Topography:** Japan consists of 4 main islands: Honshu ("mainland"), 87,805 sq. mi.; Hokkaido, 30,144 sq. mi.; Kyushu, 14,114 sq. mi.; and Shikoku, 7,049 sq. mi. The coast, deeply indented, measures 16,654 mi. The northern islands are a continuation of the Sakhalin Mts. The Kunlun range of China continues into southern islands, the ranges meeting in the Japanese Alps. In a vast transverse fissure crossing Honshu E-W rises a group of volcanoes, mostly extinct or inactive, including 12,388 ft. Mt. Fuji (Fujiyama) near Tokyo. **Capital:** Tokyo, 34,997,000. **Cities (urban aggr.):** Osaka, 11,165,000, (1998 city proper: 2,599,642); Nagoya, 3,122,000; Sapporo, 1,756,000; Kyoto, 1,806,000.

Government: Type: Parliamentary democracy. **Head of state:** Emp. Akihito; b Dec. 23, 1933; in office: Jan. 7, 1989. **Head of**

gov.: Prime Min. Junichiro Koizumi; b Jan. 8, 1942; in office: Apr. 26, 2001. **Local divisions:** 47 prefectures. **Defense budget** (2003): $41.4 bil. **Active troops:** 239,900.

Economy: Industries: motor vehicles, electronic equip., machine tools, steel & nonferrous metals, ships, chemicals, textiles, proc. foods. **Chief crops:** rice, sugar beets, vegetables, fruit. **Natural resources:** fish. **Crude oil reserves** (2003): 58.5 mil. bbls. **Arable land:** 11%. **Livestock** (2003): cattle: 4.52 mil.; chickens: 283.9 mil.; goats: 34,000; pigs: 9.73 mil.; sheep: 11,000. **Fish catch** (2002 est): 5,271,433 metric tons. **Electricity prod.** (2002): 1,044.04 bil. kWh. **Labor force** (2002 est.): services 70%, industry 25%, agriculture 5%.

Finance: Monetary unit: Yen (JPY) (Sept. 2004: 110.34 = $1 U.S.). **GDP** (2003 est.): $3.567 tril.; **per capita GDP:** $28,000; **GDP growth:** 2.3%. **Imports** (2003 est.): $346.6 bil.; partners (2002): China 18.3%, U.S. 17.4%, South Korea 4.6%, Indonesia 4.2%, Australia 4.1%. **Exports** (2003 est.): $447.1 bil.; partners (2002): U.S. 28.8%, China 9.6%, South Korea 6.9%, Taiwan 6.3%, Hong Kong 6.1%. **Tourism:** $8.8 bil. **Budget** (FY03/04 est.): $746.0 bil. **Intl. reserves less gold:** $446.37 bil. **Gold:** 24.6 mil oz t. **Consumer prices:** −0.3%.

Transport: Railroad: Length: 14,395 mi. **Motor vehicles** (2001): 53.54 mil pass. cars, 18.1 mil comm. vehicles. **Civil aviation:** 63.8 bil. pass.-mi; 141 airports. **Chief ports:** Tokyo, Kobe, Osaka, Nagoya, Chiba, Kawasaki, Hakodate.

Communications: TV sets: 719 per 1,000 pop. **Radios:** 956 per 1,000 pop. **Telephone lines** (2002): 71.1 mil. **Daily newspaper circ.:** 578 per 1,000 pop. **Internet** (2002): 57.2 mil. users.

Health: Life expect.: 77.7 male; 84.5 female. **Births** (per 1,000 pop.): 9.6. **Deaths** (per 1,000 pop.): 8.8. **Natural inc.:** 0.08%. **Infant mortality** (per 1,000 live births): 3.3. **AIDS rate:** <0.1%.

Education: Compulsory: ages 6-15. **Literacy** (2002): 100%.

Major Intl. Organizations: UN and all its specialized agencies, APEC, OECD.

Embassy: 2520 Massachusetts Ave. NW 20008; 238-6700.

Websites: www.us.emb-japan.go.jp; www.jnto.go.jp

According to Japanese legend, the empire was founded by Emperor Jimmu, 660 BC, but earliest records of a unified Japan date from 1,000 years later. Chinese influence was strong in the formation of Japanese civilization. Buddhism was introduced before the 6th century AD.

A feudal system, with locally powerful noble families and their samurai warrior retainers, dominated from 1192. Central power was held by successive families of shoguns (military dictators), 1192-1867, until recovered by Emperor Meiji, 1868. The Portuguese and Dutch had minor trade with Japan in the 16th and 17th centuries; U.S. Commodore Matthew C. Perry opened the country to U.S. trade in a treaty ratified 1854. Industrialization was begun in the late 19th century. Japan fought China, 1894-95, gaining Taiwan. After war with Russia, 1904-5, Russia ceded S half of Sakhalin and gave concessions in China. Japan annexed Korea 1910.

In World War I Japan ousted Germany from Shandong in China and took over German Pacific islands. Japan took Manchuria in 1931 and launched full-scale war in China in 1937. Japan launched war against the U.S. by attacking Pearl Harbor Dec. 7, 1941. The U.S. dropped atomic bombs on Hiroshima, Aug. 6, and Nagasaki, Aug. 9, 1945. Japan surrendered Aug. 14, 1945.

In a new constitution adopted May 3, 1947, Japan renounced the right to wage war; the emperor gave up claims to divinity; the Diet became the sole law-making authority. The U.S. and 48 other non-Communist nations signed a peace treaty and the U.S. a bilateral defense agreement with Japan, in San Francisco Sept. 8, 1951, restoring Japan's sovereignty as of April 28, 1952.

Rebuilding after World War II, Japan emerged as one of the most powerful economies in the world, and as a leader in technology.The U.S. and Western Europe criticized Japan for its restrictive policy on imports, which eventually allowed Japan to accumulate huge trade surpluses.

On June 26, 1968, the U.S. returned to Japanese control the Bonin Isls., Volcano Isls. (including Iwo Jima), and Marcus Isls. On May 15, 1972, Okinawa, the other Ryukyu Isls., and the Daito Isls. were returned by the U.S.; it was agreed the U.S. would continue to maintain military bases on Okinawa.

The Recruit scandal, the nation's worst political scandal since World War II, which involved illegal political donations and stock trading, led to the resignation of Premier Noboru Takeshita in May 1989. Following new political and economic scandals, the ruling Liberal Democratic Party (LDP) was denied a majority in general elections July 18, 1993. On June 29, 1994, Tomiichi Murayama became Japan's first Socialist premier since 1947-48.

An earthquake in the Kobe area in Jan. 1995 claimed more than 5,000 lives, injured nearly 35,000, and caused over $90 billion in property damage. On Mar. 20, a nerve gas attack in the Tokyo subway (blamed on a religious cult) killed 12 and injured thousands. Public anger at the rape of a 12-year-old Okinawa schoolgirl by 3 U.S. servicemen, Sept. 4, led the U.S. to begin reducing its military presence there.

Murayama resigned as prime minister, Jan. 5, 1996, and was replaced by Ryutaro Hashimoto of the LDP. Hashimoto signed a joint security declaration with U.S. Pres. Bill Clinton in Tokyo, Apr. 17, 1996. Nagano hosted the Winter Olympics, Feb. 7-22, 1998.

With Japan mired in a lengthy recession, the LDP suffered a sharp rebuke in elections for parliament's upper house, July 12,

1998. Hashimoto resigned, and on July 24, the LDP chose Keizo Obuchi as prime minister. After Obuchi had a stroke Apr. 3, 2000, an LDP stalwart, Yoshiro Mori, succeeded him on Apr. 5. Obuchi died May 14. Parliamentary elections June 25 left the LDP and its allies with a reduced majority in the lower house.

The unpopular Mori was replaced as LDP leader and prime minister in Apr. 2001 by Junichiro Koizumi, a populist reformer. In Sept. 2002, Koizumi became the first Japanese leader to visit N. Korea; during the meeting N. Korean Prem. Kim Jong-Il apologized for abducting Japanese citizens. Five of these abductees returned to Japan in Oct. 2002.

Koizumi's parliamentary coalition retained power in the elections of Nov. 9, 2003. The cabinet Dec. 9 approved deploying more than 500 noncombat troops to aid Iraq reconstruction, the first time since WWII that Japanese troops were sent to a combat zone. A steam leak (non-radioactive) at a nuclear power plant at Mihama, Aug. 9, 2004, killed 5 workers.

Jordan
Hashemite Kingdom of Jordan

People: Population: 5,611,202. **Age distrib.** (%): <15: 36.6; 65+: 3.4. **Pop. density:** 158 per sq mi, 61 per sq km. **Urban:** 79.0%. **Ethnic groups:** Arab 98%, Armenian 1%, Circassian 1%. **Principal languages:** Arabic (official), English. **Chief religions:** Muslim (official; mostly Sunni) 92%, Christian 6%.

Geography: Total area: 35,637 sq mi, 92,300 sq km; **Land area:** 35,510 sq mi, 91,971 sq km. **Location:** In Middle East. **Neighbors:** Israel and West Bank on W, Saudi Arabia on S, Iraq on E, Syria on N. **Topography:** About 88% of Jordan is arid. Fertile areas are in W. Only port is on short Aqaba Gulf coast. Country shares Dead Sea (about 1,300 ft. below sea level) with Israel. **Capital:** Amman, 1,237,000.

Government: Type: Constitutional monarchy. **Head of state:** King Abdullah II; b Jan. 30, 1962; in office: Feb. 7, 1999. **Head of gov.:** Prime Min. Faisal Akef al-Fayez; b Apr. 22, 1952; in office: Oct. 25, 2003. **Local divisions:** 12 governorates. **Defense budget** (2003): $928 mil. **Active troops:** 100,500.

Economy: Industries: phosphates, oil refining, cement, potash, light mfg. **Chief crops:** wheat, barley, citrus, tomatoes, melons, olives. **Natural resources:** phosphates, potash, shale oil. **Crude oil reserves** (2003): 0.9 mil. bbls. **Arable land:** 4%. **Livestock** (2003): cattle: 66,560; chickens: 24.0 mil.; goats: 547,490; sheep: 1.48 mil. **Fish catch** (2002): 1,041 metric tons. **Electricity prod.** (2002): 7.31 bil. kWh. **Labor force** (2001 est.): services 82.5%, industry 12.5%, agriculture 5%.

Finance: Monetary unit: Dinar (JOD) (Sept. 2004: 0.71 = $1 U.S.). **GDP** (2003 est.): $23.6 bil.; **per capita GDP:** $4,300; **GDP growth:** 3.1%. **Imports** (2003 est.): $4.9 bil.; partners (2002): Iraq 13.3%, Germany 8.7%, U.S. 7.9%, China 6%, France 4.2%, UK 4.1%, Italy 4%. **Exports** (2003 est.): $2.9 bil.; partners (2002): Iraq 20.6%, U.S. 14.9%, India 8.3%, Saudi Arabia 5.5%, UAE 4%. **Tourism:** $815 mil. **Budget** (2003 est.): $3.7 bil. **Intl. reserves less gold:** $3.50 bil. **Gold:** 410,000 oz t. **Consumer prices:** 2.3%.

Transport: Railroad: Length: 314 mi. **Motor vehicles** (2001): 322,400 pass. cars, 138,600 comm. vehicles. **Civil aviation:** 2.6 bil. pass.-mi; 15 airports. **Chief port:** Al Aqabah.

Communications: TV sets: 83 per 1,000 pop. **Radios:** 271 per 1,000 pop. **Telephone lines:** 622,600. **Daily newspaper circ.:** 75.4 per 1,000 pop. **Internet:** 457,000 users.

Health: Life expect.: 75.6 male; 80.7 female. **Births** (per 1,000 pop.): 22.7. **Deaths** (per 1,000 pop.): 2.6. **Natural inc.:** 2.01%. **Infant mortality** (per 1,000 live births): 18.1. **AIDS rate:** <0.1%.

Education: Compulsory: ages 6-15. **Literacy:** 91.3%.

Major Intl. Organizations: UN (FAO, IBRD, ILO, IMF, IMO, WHO), AL.

Embassy: 3504 International Dr. NW 20008; 966-2664.

Websites: www.nic.gov.jo; www.jordanembassyus.org

From ancient times to 1922 the lands to the E of the Jordan River were culturally and politically united with the lands to the W. Arabs conquered the area in the 7th century; the Ottomans took control in the 16th. Britain's 1920 Palestine Mandate covered both sides of the Jordan. In 1921, Abdullah, son of the ruler of Hejaz in Arabia, was installed by Britain as emir of an autonomous Transjordan, covering two-thirds of Palestine. An independent kingdom was proclaimed, 1946.

During the 1948 Arab-Israeli war the West Bank and East Jerusalem were added to the kingdom, which changed its name to Jordan. All these territories were lost to Israel in the 1967 war, which swelled the number of Arab refugees on the East Bank.

Some 700,000 refugees entered Jordan following Iraq's invasion of Kuwait, Aug. 1990. Jordan was viewed as supporting Iraq during the 1990-1991 Persian Gulf crisis.

Jordan and Israel officially agreed, July 25, 1994, to end their state of war; a formal peace treaty was signed Oct. 26. Following a prolonged bout with cancer, King Hussein died Feb. 7, 1999; his eldest son and designated successor immediately assumed the throne as Abdullah II.

Jordanian authorities Apr. 2004 said they had foiled a possible chemical attack against the U.S. embassy and other Amman targets; the plot was traced to Abu Musab al-Zarqawi, a high-ranking Jordanian member of al-Qaeda whom the U.S. accused of leading guerrilla activities in Iraq.

Kazakhstan
Republic of Kazakhstan

People: Population: 15,143,704. **Age distrib.** (%): <15: 26; 65+: 7.5. **Pop. density:** 15 per sq mi, 6 per sq km. **Urban:** 55.8%. **Ethnic groups:** Kazakh 53%, Russian 30%, Ukrainian 4%, Uzbek 3%, German 2%, Uighur 1%. **Principal languages:** Kazakh, Russian (both official); Ukrainian, German, Uzbek. **Chief religions:** Muslim 47%, Russian Orthodox 44%.

Geography: Total area: 1,049,155 sq mi, 2,717,300 sq km; **Land area:** 1,030,815 sq mi, 2,669,800 sq km. **Location:** In Central Asia. **Neighbors:** Russia on N; China on E; Kyrgyzstan, Uzbekistan, Turkmenistan on S; Caspian Sea on W. **Topography:** Extends from the lower reaches of Volga in Europe to the Altay Mts. on the Chinese border. **Capital:** Astana, 332,000. **Cities (urban aggr.):** Alma-Ata, 1,130,000.

Government: Type: Republic. **Head of state:** Pres. Nursultan A. Nazarbayev; b July 6, 1940; in office: Apr. 1990. **Head of gov.:** Prime Min. Daniyal Akhmetov; b June 15, 1954; in office: June 13, 2003. **Local divisions:** 14 oblystar, 3 cities. **Defense budget** (2003): $274 mil. **Active troops:** 65,800.

Economy: Industries: mining and oil producer, agric. machinery, electric motors, constr. materials. **Chief crops:** wheat, cotton, wool. **Natural resources:** oil, nat. gas, coal, iron ore, mang., chrome ore, nickel, cobalt, copper, molybd., lead, zinc, bauxite, gold, uranium. **Crude oil reserves** (2003): 9.0 bil. bbls. **Arable land:** 12%. **Livestock** (2003): cattle: 4.56 mil.; chickens: 23.6 mil.; goats: 1.35 mil.; pigs: 1.23 mil.; sheep: 9.92 mil. **Fish catch** (2002): 25,688 metric tons. **Electricity prod.** (2002): 55.41 bil. kWh. **Labor force** (2002 est.): industry 30%, agriculture 20%, services 50%.

Finance: Monetary unit: Tenge (KZT) (Sept. 2004: 135.25 = $1 U.S.). **GDP** (2003 est.): $105.3 bil.; **per capita GDP:** $7,000; **GDP growth:** 9.0%. **Imports** (2003 est.): $8.6 bil.; partners (2002): Russia 38.7%, Germany 8.9%, U.S. 7%, China 4.8%. **Exports** (2003 est.): $12.7 bil.; partners (2002): Bermuda 20.8%, Russia 15.5%, China 10.6%, Italy 9.3%, Switzerland 8.2%, UAE 4.9%. **Tourism:** $564 mil. **Budget** (2001 est.): $5.1 bil. **Intl. reserves less gold:** $2.85 bil. **Gold:** 1.74 mil oz t. **Consumer prices:** 6.4%.

Transport: Railroad: Length: 8,451 mi. **Motor vehicles** (2000): 1.0 mil pass. cars, 256,600 comm. vehicles. **Civil aviation:** 569.2 mil. pass.-mi; 60 airports. **Chief ports:** Aqtau, Atyrau.

Communications: TV sets: 240 per 1,000 pop. **Radios:** 395 per 1,000 pop. **Telephone lines** (2002): 2.1 mil. **Internet** (2002): 250,000 users.

Health: Life expect.: 60.7 male; 71.7 female. **Births** (per 1,000 pop.): 15.5. **Deaths** (per 1,000 pop.): 9.6. **Natural inc.:** 0.59%. **Infant mortality** (per 1,000 live births): 30.5. **AIDS rate:** 0.2%.

Education: Compulsory: ages 7-17. **Literacy** (2002): 98%. **Major Intl. Organizations:** UN (IBRD, ILO, IMF, IMO, WHO), CIS, OSCE.

Embassy: 1401 16th St. NW 20036; 232-5488.

Websites: www.kazakhembus.com; www.president.kz

The region came under the Mongols' rule in the 13th century and gradually came under Russian rule, 1730-1853. It was admitted to the USSR as a constituent republic 1936. Kazakhstan declared independence Dec. 16, 1991. It became an independent state when the Soviet Union dissolved Dec. 26, 1991. The party chief, Nursultan Nazarbayev, was elected president unopposed. In legislative elections Mar. 7, 1994, criticized by international monitors, his party won a sweeping victory. Kazakhstan agreed, Feb. 14, to dismantle nuclear missiles and adhere to the 1968 Nuclear Nonproliferation Treaty; the U.S. pledged increased aid. Private land ownership was legalized Dec. 26, 1995.

Astana (formerly Akmola) was dedicated as the nation's new capital on June 9, 1998.

Pres. Nazarbayev won reelection to a 7-year term Jan. 10, 1999, after his leading opponent, former Prime Min. Akezhan Kazhegeldin, was barred on a technicality.

Kenya
Republic of Kenya

People: Population: 32,021,856. **Age distrib.** (%): <15: 41.1; 65+: 2.8. **Pop. density:** 146 per sq mi, 56 per sq km. **Urban:** 39.4%. **Ethnic groups:** Kikuyu 22%, Luhya 14%, Luo 13%, Kalenjin 12%, Kamba 11%, Kisii 6%, Meru 6%. **Principal languages:** English, Swahili (both official); numerous indigenous languages. **Chief religions:** Protestant 45%, Roman Catholic 33%, indigenous beliefs 10%, Muslim 10%.

Geography: Total area: 224,962 sq mi, 582,650 sq km; **Land area:** 219,789 sq mi, 569,250 sq km. **Location:** E Africa, on coast of Indian O. **Neighbors:** Uganda on W, Tanzania on S, Somalia on E, Ethiopia on N, Sudan on NW. **Topography:** The northern three-fifths of Kenya is arid. To the S, a low coastal area and a plateau varying from 3,000 to 10,000 ft. The Great Rift Valley enters the country N-S, flanked by high mountains. **Capital:** Nairobi, 2,575,000. **Cities (urban aggr.):** Mombasa (1991 est.), 600,000.

Government: Type: Republic. **Head of state and gov.:** Pres. Mwai Kibaki; b Nov. 15, 1931; in office: Dec. 30, 2002. **Local divisions:** 7 provinces and Nairobi area. **Defense budget** (2003): $310 mil. **Active troops:** 24,120.

Economy: Industries: light consumer goods, agric. proc., oil refining, cement, tourism. **Chief crops:** coffee, tea, corn, wheat, sugarcane, fruit. **Natural resources:** gold, limestone, soda ash, salt barites, rubies, fluorspar, garnets, wildlife, hydropower. **Arable land:** 7%. **Livestock** (2003): cattle: 11.5 mil.; chickens: 28.0 mil.; goats: 11.0 mil.; pigs: 332,000; sheep: 7.7 mil. **Fish catch** (2002): 145,310 metric tons. **Electricity prod.** (2002): 4.47 bil. kWh. **Labor force** (2003 est.): agriculture 75%.

Finance: Monetary unit: Shilling (KES) (Sept. 2004: 80.51 = $1 U.S.). **GDP** (2003 est.): $33.1 bil.; **per capita GDP:** $1,000; **GDP growth:** 1.7%. **Imports** (2003 est.): $3.7 bil.; partners (2002): UAE 12%, Saudi Arabia 8.7%, South Africa 8.1%, U.S. 8.1%, UK 7.1%, France 5.8%, China 5.5%, Japan 5%, India 4.8%. **Exports** (2003 est.): $2.5 bil.; partners (2002): Uganda 18.5%, UK 13%, U.S. 8.1%, Netherlands 7.6%, Pakistan 5%, Egypt 4.1%. **Tourism** (2002): $297 mil. **Budget** (2000 est.): $3.0 bil. **Intl. reserves less gold:** $997 mil. **Consumer prices:** 9.8%.

Transport: Railroad: Length: 1,726 mi. **Motor vehicles** (2001): 255,400 pass. cars, 263,700 comm. vehicles. **Civil aviation:** 1.9 bil. pass.-mi; 19 airports. **Chief ports:** Mombasa, Kisumu, Lamu.

Communications: TV sets: 22 per 1,000 pop. **Radios:** 216 per 1,000 pop. **Telephone lines:** 328,400. **Daily newspaper circ.:** 9.4 per 1,000 pop. **Internet** (2002): 400,000 users.

Health: Life expect.: 44.8 male; 45.1 female. **Births** (per 1,000 pop.): 27.8. **Deaths** (per 1,000 pop.): 16.3. **Natural inc.:** 1.15%. **Infant mortality** (per 1,000 live births): 62.6. **AIDS rate:** 6.7%.

Education: Compulsory: ages 6-13. **Literacy:** 85.1%. **Major Intl. Organizations:** UN and all of its specialized agencies, the Commonwealth, AU.

Embassy: 2249 R St. NW 20008; 387-6101.

Website: www.kenyaembassy.com

Arab colonies exported spices and slaves from the Kenya coast as early as the 8th century. Britain obtained control in the 19th century. Kenya won independence Dec. 12, 1963, 4 years after the end of the violent Mau Mau uprising.

Kenya had steady growth in industry and agriculture under a modified private enterprise system, and enjoyed a relatively free political life. But stability was shaken in 1974-75, with opposition charges of corruption and oppression. Jomo Kenyatta, the country's leader since independence, died Aug. 22, 1978. He was succeeded by his vice president, Daniel arap Moi.

During the first half of the 1990s, Kenya suffered widespread unemployment and high inflation. Tribal clashes in the western provinces claimed thousands of lives and left tens of thousands homeless. Pres. Moi won a third term in Dec. 1992 elections, which were marred by violence and fraud. Clashes in the Mombasa region, Aug. 1997, left more than 40 people dead. Pres. Moi was reelected Dec. 29, in an election again plagued by irregularities.

A truck bomb explosion at the U.S. embassy in Nairobi, Aug. 7, 1998, killed more than 200 people and injured about 5,000. The U.S. blamed the attack and a near-simultaneous embassy bombing in Tanzania on al-Qaeda. After a trial in New York City, 4 conspirators were convicted May 29, 2001. In Mombasa, Nov. 28, 2002, terrorists linked with al-Qaeda killed 12 Kenyans and 3 Israeli tourists at an Israeli-owned hotel and narrowly missed shooting down an Israeli-bound jet.

Constitutionally barred from seeking another term, Moi was succeeded Dec. 30, 2002, by Mwai Kibaki, the presidential candidate of the opposition Democratic Party.

Kiribati
Republic of Kiribati

People: Population: 100,798. **Age distrib.** (%): <15: 40.2; 65+: 3.2. **Pop. density:** 322 per sq mi, 124 per sq km. **Urban:** 47.3%. **Ethnic groups:** Micronesian. **Principal languages:** English (official), I-Kiribati. **Chief religions:** Roman Catholic 52%, Protestant 40%.

Geography: Total area: 313 sq mi, 811 sq km; **Land area:** 313 sq mi, 811 sq km. **Location:** 33 Micronesian islands (the Gilbert, Line, and Phoenix groups) in the mid-Pacific scattered in a 2-mil sq. mi. chain around the point where the International Date Line formerly cut the Equator. In 1997 the Date Line was moved to follow Kiribati's E border. **Neighbors:** Nearest are Nauru to SW, Tuvalu and Tokelau Isls. to S. **Topography:** Except Banaba (Ocean) Isl., all are low-lying, with soil of coral sand and rock fragments, subject to erratic rainfall. **Capital:** South Tarawa, 42,000.

Government: Type: Republic. **Head of state and gov.:** Pres. Anote Tong; b June 11, 1952; in office: July 10, 2003. **Local divisions:** 3 units, 6 districts.

Economy: Industries: fishing, handicrafts. **Chief crops:** copra, taro, breadfruit, sweet potatoes. **Natural resources:** phosphates. **Livestock** (2003): chickens: 450,000; pigs: 12,000. **Fish catch** (2002): 31,015 metric tons. **Electricity prod.** (2002): 0.01 bil. kWh.

Finance: Monetary unit: Australian Dollar (Sept. 2004: 1.44 = $1 U.S.). **GDP** (2001 est.): $79.0 mil.; **per capita GDP:** $800; **GDP growth:** 1.5%. **Imports** (2002): $83.0 mil.; partners (2002): France 30.1%, Australia 27.7%, Fiji 13.3%, Japan 9.6%, U.S. 4.8%. **Exports** (2002): $35.0 mil.; partners (2002): Japan 54.3%, South Korea 17.1%, Thailand 17.1%. **Tourism** (2001): $3 mil. **Budget** (2000 est.): $37.2 mil.

Transport: Civil aviation: 4.3 mil pass.-mi.; 4 airports. **Chief port:** Tarawa.

Communications: TV sets: 23 per 1,000 pop. **Radios:** 341 per 1,000 pop. **Telephone lines:** 3,600. **Internet:** 2,000 users.

Health: Life expect.: 58.3 male; 64.4 female. **Births** (per 1,000 pop.): 31.0. **Deaths** (per 1,000 pop.): 8.5. **Natural inc.:** 2.25%. **Infant mortality** (per 1,000 live births): 49.9.

Education: Compulsory: ages 6-15. **Literacy** (2002): 90%

Major Intl. Organizations: UN (IBRD, IMF, WHO), the Commonwealth.

Website: www.state.gov/p/eap/ci/kr

A British protectorate since 1892, the Gilbert and Ellice Islands colony was completed with the inclusion of the Phoenix Islands, 1937. Tarawa Atoll was the scene of some of the bloodiest fighting in the Pacific during World War II.

Self-rule was granted 1971; the Ellice Islands separated from the colony 1975 and became independent Tuvalu, 1978. Kiribati (pronounced *Kiribass)* independence was attained July 12, 1979. Under a treaty of friendship the U.S. relinquished its claims to several Line and Phoenix islands, including Christmas (Kiritimati), Canton, and Enderbury. Kiribati was admitted to the UN Sept. 14, 1999.

Korea, North
Democratic People's Republic of Korea

People: Population: 22,697,553. **Age distrib.** (%): <15: 25.4; 65+: 7.2. **Pop. density:** 488 per sq mi, 189 per sq km. **Urban:** 61.1%. **Ethnic group:** Korean. **Principal languages:** Korean (official). **Chief religions:** Activities almost non-existent; traditionally Buddhist, Confucianist, Chondogyo.

Geography: Total area: 46,541 sq mi, 120,540 sq km; **Land area:** 46,491 sq mi, 120,410 sq km. **Location:** In northern E Asia. **Neighbors:** China and Russia on N, South Korea on S. **Topography:** Mountains and hills cover nearly all the country, with narrow valleys and small plains in between. The N and the E coasts are the most rugged areas. **Capital:** Pyongyang, 3,228,000. **Cities (urban aggr.):** Nampo, 1,022,000.

Government: Type: Communist state. **Leader:** Kim Jong Il; b Feb. 16, 1942; officially assumed post Oct. 8, 1997. **Local divisions:** 9 provinces, 4 special cities. **Defense budget** (2002): $1.6 bil. **Active troops:** 1,082,000.

Economy: Industries: armaments, machine building, electric power, chemicals, mining, metallurgy, textiles. **Chief crops:** rice, corn, potatoes, soybeans. **Natural resources:** coal, lead, tungsten, zinc, graphite, magnesite, iron ore, copper, gold, pyrites, salt, fluorspar, hydropower. **Arable land:** 14%. **Livestock** (2003): cattle: 576,000; chickens: 19.96 mil.; goats: 2.72 mil.; pigs: 3.18 mil.; sheep: 171,000. **Fish catch** (2002 est): 268,700 metric tons. **Electricity prod.** (2002): 33.62 bil. kWh. **Labor force:** agricultural 36%, nonagricultural 64%.

Finance: Monetary unit: Won (KPW) (Sept. 2004: 2.20 = $1 U.S.). **GDP** (2003 est.): $22.9 bil.; **per capita GDP:** $1,000; **GDP growth:** 1.0%. **Imports** (2002 est.): $2.0 bil.; partners (2002): China 39.7%, Thailand 14.6%, Japan 11.2%, Germany 7.6%, South Korea 6.2%. **Exports** (2002 est.): $1.0 bil.; partners (2002): South Korea 28.5%, China 28.4%, Japan 24.7%.

Transport: Railroad: Length: 3,240 mi. **Civil Aviation:** 23.0 mil. pass.-mi; 34 airports. **Chief ports:** Chongjin, Hamhung, Nampo.

Communications: TV sets: 55 per 1,000 pop. **Radios:** 146 per 1,000 pop. **Telephone lines** (1998): 23,257,000. **Daily newspaper circ.:** 199 per 1,000 pop.

Health: Life expect.: 68.4 male; 73.9 female. **Births** (per 1,000 pop.): 16.8. **Deaths** (per 1,000 pop.): 7.0. **Natural inc.:** 0.98%. **Infant mortality** (per 1,000 live births): 24.8.

Labor force: agri. 36%, other 64%.

Education: Compulsory: ages 6-15. **Literacy:** 99%

Major Intl. Organizations: UN (FAO, IMO, WHO).

Permanent UN Representative: 820 Second Ave., 13th Floor, New York, NY 10017; (212) 972-3105.

Website: www.korea-dpr.com

The Democratic People's Republic of Korea was founded May 1, 1948, in the zone occupied by Russian troops after World War II. Its armies tried to conquer the south, 1950. After 3 years of fighting, with Chinese and U.S. intervention, a cease-fire was proclaimed. For the next four decades, a hardline Communist regime headed by Kim Il Sung kept tight control over the nation's political, economic, and cultural life. The nation used its abundant mineral and hydroelectric resources to develop its military strength and heavy industry. By the early 1990s, North Korea was widely believed to be developing nuclear weapons. The U.S. and North Korea signed an agreement, Oct. 21, 1994, providing for phased dismantling of North Korea's nuclear development program in return for U.S. energy aid and improved ties with the U.S.

Kim Il Sung died July 8, 1994. He was succeeded by his son, Kim Jong Il. North Korea suffered from defections by high officials, a deteriorating economy, and severe food shortages in the late 1990s.

On Sept. 17, 1999, the U.S. eased travel and trade restrictions on North Korea after Pyongyang agreed to suspend long-range missile testing. A first-ever summit conference in Pyongyang between North and South Korean leaders, June 13-15, 2000, marked an unexpected improvement in relations between the 2 Koreas, and brought an end to many U.S. sanctions. In Sept.

2002, Japanese Prime Min. Junichiro Koizumi became the 1st Japanese prime minister to visit North Korea; there, in a landmark summit, North Korea agreed to begin normalizing relations and admitted for the 1st time that its agents had helped to kidnap 11 Japanese in the late 1970s.

Pres. George Bush, in a speech Jan. 31, 2002, included North Korea with Iraq and Iran as part of an "axis of evil." In Oct. 2002, N. Korea admitted to pursuing a secret nuclear weapons program, in violation of past agreements, and, in Jan. 2003, withdrew from the Nuclear Non-Proliferation Treaty. The U.S. insisted that North Korea dismantle its nuclear weapons program, while North Korea demanded a nonaggression treaty and economic aid from the U.S. Six-nation talks sponsored by China in Aug. 2003 and in Feb. and June 2004 failed to result in an agreement.

A huge explosion in the Ryongchon railway station Apr. 22, 2004, killed 161 people, injured more than 1,300, and destroyed at least 8,100 homes.

Korea, South
Republic of Korea

People: Population: 48,598,175. **Age distrib.** (%): <15: 21.4; 65+: 7.6. **Pop. density:** 1,282 per sq mi, 495 per sq km. **Urban:** 80.3%. **Ethnic group:** Korean. **Principal languages:** Korean (official). **Chief religions:** Christian 49%, Buddhist 47%, Confucianist 3%.

Geography: Total area: 38,023 sq mi, 98,480 sq km; **Land area:** 37,911 sq mi, 98,190 sq km. **Location:** In northern E Asia. **Neighbors:** North Korea on N. **Topography:** The country is mountainous, with a rugged east coast. The western and southern coasts are deeply indented, with many islands and harbors. **Capital:** Seoul, 9,714,000. **Cities (urban aggr.):** Pusan, 3,673,000; Inch'on, 2,464,000: Taegu, 2,478,000.

Government: Type: Republic. **Head of state:** Pres. Roh Moo Hyun; b Aug. 6, 1946; in office: Feb. 25, 2003. **Head of gov.:** Prime Min. Lee Hai Chan; b 1952; in office: June 30, 2004 **Local divisions:** 9 provinces, 7 special cities. **Defense budget** (2003): $14.8 bil. **Active troops:** 686,000.

Economy: Industries: electronics, autos, chemicals, shipbuilding, steel, textiles, clothing, footwear, food proc. **Chief crops:** rice, root crops, barley, vegetables, fruit. **Natural resources:** coal, tungsten, graphite, molybd., lead, hydropower potential. **Arable land:** 19%. **Livestock** (2003): cattle: 1.94 mil.; chickens: 98.0 mil.; goats: 435,000; pigs: 8.91 mil.; sheep: 700. **Fish catch** (2002): 1,965,762 metric tons. **Electricity prod.** (2002): 287.57 bil. kWh. **Labor force** (2001): services 69%, industry 21.5%, agriculture 9.5%.

Finance: Monetary unit: Won (KRW) (Sept. 2004: 1,147.30 = $1 U.S.). **GDP** (2003 est.): $855.3 bil.; **per capita GDP:** $17,700; **GDP growth:** 2.8%. **Imports** (2003 est.): $175.6 bil.; partners (2002): Japan 19.6%, U.S. 15.2%, China 11.4%, Saudi Arabia 5%. **Exports** (2003 est.): $201.3 bil.; partners (2002): U.S. 20.4%, China 14.7%, Japan 9.4%, Hong Kong 6.3%, Taiwan 4.1%. **Tourism:** $5.2 bil. **Budget** (2002): $108.0 bil. **Intl. reserves less gold:** $104.5 bil. **Gold:** 450,000 oz t. **Consumer prices:** 3.6%.

Transport: Railroad: Length: 1,942 mi. **Motor vehicles** (1999): 7.84 mil pass. cars, 3.29 mil comm. vehicles. **Civil aviation:** 34.1 bil. pass.-mi; 69 airports. **Chief ports:** Pusan, Inchon.

Communications: TV sets: 364 per 1,000 pop. **Radios:** 1,039 per 1,000 pop. **Telephone lines:** 22.9 mil. **Daily newspaper circ.:** 393 per 1,000 pop. **Internet:** 29.2 mil. users.

Health: Life expect.: 72.0 male; 79.5 female. **Births** (per 1,000 pop.): 12.3. **Deaths** (per 1,000 pop.): 6.1. **Natural inc.:** 0.62%. **Infant mortality** (per 1,000 live births): 7.2. **AIDS rate:** <0.1%.

Education: Free, compulsory: ages 6-14. **Literacy:** 98%.

Major Intl. Organizations: UN (FAO, IBRD, ILO, IMF, IMO, WHO, WTrO), APEC, OECD.

Embassy: 2450 Massachusetts Ave. NW 20008; 939-5600.

Websites: www.koreaembassyusa.org; www.korea.net

Korea, once called the Hermit Kingdom, has a recorded history since the 1st century BC. It was united in a kingdom under the Silla Dynasty, AD 668. It was at times associated with the Chinese empire; the treaty that concluded the Sino-Japanese war of 1894-95 recognized Korea's complete independence. In 1910 Japan forcibly annexed Korea as Chosun.

At the Potsdam conference, July 1945, the 38th parallel was designated as the line dividing the Soviet and the American occupation. Russian troops entered Korea Aug. 10, 1945; U.S. troops entered Sept. 8, 1945.

The South Koreans formed the Republic of Korea in May 1948 with Seoul as the capital. Dr. Syngman Rhee was chosen president. A separate, Communist regime was formed in the N; its army attacked the S in June 1950, initiating the Korean War. UN troops, under U.S. command, supported the S in the war, which ended in an armistice (July 1953) leaving Korea divided by a "no-man's land" along the 38th parallel.

Rhee's authoritarian rule became increasingly unpopular, and a movement spearheaded by college students forced his resignation Apr. 26, 1960. In an army coup May 16, 1961, Gen. Park Chung Hee became chairman of a ruling junta. He was elected president, 1963; a 1972 referendum allowed him to be reelected for an unlimited series of 6-year terms. Park was assassinated by the chief of the Korean CIA, Oct. 26, 1979.

In May 1980, Gen. Chun Doo Hwan, head of military intelligence, ordered the brutal suppression of pro-democracy demonstrations in Kwangju. On July 1, 1987, following weeks of antigovernment protests, some of them violent, Chun, agreed to permit election of the next president by direct popular vote and other democratic reforms. In Dec., Roh Tae Woo was elected president. In 1990, the nation's 3 largest political parties merged; some 100,000 students protested the merger as undemocratic.

Pres. Kim Young Sam took office in 1993. Convicted of mutiny, treason, and corruption, Chun was sentenced to death by a Seoul court, Aug. 26, 1996, for his role in the 1979 coup and 1980 Kwangju massacre; Roh received a 22-1/2 year prison sentence. On Dec. 16, Chun's term was reduced to life in prison, and Roh's to 17 years.

The collapse in Jan. 1997 of the Hanbo steel firm triggered a series of corruption scandals. With currency and stock values plummeting, the nation averted default by agreeing, Dec. 4, on a $57 billion bailout from the IMF. Kim Dae Jung, a longtime dissident, won the presidential election Dec. 18. Chun and Roh were released and pardoned Dec. 22, 1997.

At an unprecedented summit meeting in Pyongyang, June 13-15, 2000, Pres. Kim Dae Jung and North Korean leader Kim Jong Il agreed to work for reconciliation and eventual reunification of their 2 countries. On Oct. 13, 2000, Kim Dae Jung was named the winner of the 2000 Nobel Peace Prize. Roh Moo Hyun won a presidential election Dec. 19.

A subway fire in Taegu, Feb. 18, 2003, killed 198 people; the arsonist was given a life term, and 8 subway officials charged with negligence also received prison sentences. Typhoon Maemi battered Pusan and other areas Sept. 12-13, 2003, leaving about 130 people dead and causing at least $4.1 billion in damage.

The National Assembly, Mar. 12, 2004, impeached Pres. Roh Moo Hyun for violating political neutrality and urging voters to support the Uri Party in upcoming legislative elections; voters backed Roh Apr. 15 by electing a Uri majority, and the Constitutional Court May 14 restored Roh to office. In Aug., South Korea began deploying 3,000 troops to N Iraq.

The International Atomic Energy Commission Sept. 2 said South Korea had acknowledged having secretly processed a small amount of uranium to near weapons-grade level in 2000, in violation of the Nuclear Non-Proliferation Treaty and a bilateral agreement with North Korea.

Kuwait
State of Kuwait

People: Population: 2,257,549. **Age distrib.** (%): <15: 28.3; 65+: 2.5. **Pop. density:** 328 per sq mi, 127 per sq km. **Urban:** 96.3%. **Ethnic groups:** Arab 80%, South Asian 9%, Iranian 4%. **Principal languages:** Arabic (official), English. **Chief religion:** Muslim 85% (official; Sunni 70%, Shi'a 30%).

Geography: Total area: 6,880 sq mi, 17,820 sq km; **Land area:** 6,880 sq mi, 17,820 sq km. **Location:** In Middle East, at N end of Persian Gulf. **Neighbors:** Iraq on N, Saudi Arabia on S. **Topography:** The country is flat, very dry, and extremely hot. **Capital:** Kuwait City, 1,222,000.

Government: Type: Constitutional monarchy. **Head of state:** Emir Sheikh Jabir al-Ahmad al-Jabir as-Sabah; b 1928; in office: Dec. 31, 1977. **Head of gov.:** Prime Min. Sheikh Sabah al-Ahmad as-Sabah; b 1929; in office: July 13, 2003. **Local divisions:** 5 governorates. **Defense budget** (2003): $3.5 bil. **Active troops:** 15,500.

Economy: Industries: oil, petrochems., desalination, food proc., constr. materials. **Natural resources:** oil, fish, shrimp, nat. gas. **Crude oil reserves** (2003): 96.5 bil. bbls. **Livestock** (2003): cattle: 20,000; chickens: 32.5 mil.; goats: 130,000; sheep: 850,000. **Fish catch** (2002 est): 6,095 metric tons. **Electricity prod.** (2002): 32.43 bil. kWh. **Labor force:** 50% gov't. and social services; 40% services; 10% industry and agric.

Finance: Monetary unit: Dinar (KWD) (Sept. 2004: 0.29 = $1 U.S.). **GDP** (2003 est.): $39.5 bil.; **per capita GDP:** $18,100; **GDP growth:** 4.4%. **Imports** (2003 est.): $9.6 bil.; partners (2002): U.S. 12.8%, Japan 10.9%, Germany 9.7%, Saudi Arabia 6.4%, UK 5.9%, Italy 5.3%, France 5.1%. **Exports** (2003 est.): $22.3 bil.; partners (2002): Japan 24.1%, South Korea 12.8%, U.S. 11.8%, Singapore 10%, Taiwan 7.4%, Netherlands 4.3%, Pakistan 4.3%. **Tourism** (2002): $119 mil. **Budget** (FY03/04): $19.5 bil. **Intl. reserves less gold:** $5.01 bil. **Gold:** 2.54 mil oz t. **Consumer prices:** 1.2%.

Transport: Motor vehicles (1999): 624,000 pass. cars, 130,000 comm. vehicles. **Civil aviation:** 3.8 bil. pass.-mi; 3 airports. **Chief port:** Mina al-Ahmadi.

Communications: TV sets: 480 per 1,000 pop. **Radios:** 633 per 1,000 pop. **Telephone lines:** 486,900. **Daily newspaper circ.:** 374 per 1,000 pop. **Internet** (2002): 567,000 users.

Health: Life expect.: 75.9 male; 77.9 female. **Births** (per 1,000 pop.): 21.9. **Deaths** (per 1,000 pop.): 2.4. **Natural inc.:** 1.94%. **Infant mortality** (per 1,000 live births): 10.3.

Education: Compulsory: ages 6-13. **Literacy:** 83.5%.

Major Intl. Organizations: UN (FAO, IBRD, ILO, IMF, IMO, WHO, WTrO), AL, OPEC.

Embassy: 2940 Tilden St. NW 20008; 966-0702.

Website: www.kuwait-info.org

Kuwait is ruled by the Sabah dynasty, founded 1759. Britain ran foreign relations and defense from 1899 until independence in 1961. The majority of the population is non-Kuwaiti, with many Palestinians, and cannot vote.

Oil is the fiscal mainstay, providing most of Kuwait's income. Oil pays for free medical care, education, and social security. There are no taxes, except customs duties.

Kuwait was attacked and overrun by Iraqi forces Aug. 2, 1990. The emir and senior members of the ruling family fled to Saudi Arabia to establish a government in exile. On Aug. 28, Iraq announced that Kuwait was its 19th province. Following several weeks of aerial attacks on Iraq and Iraqi forces in Kuwait, a U.S.-led coalition began a ground attack Feb. 23, 1991. By Feb. 27, Iraqi forces were routed and Kuwait liberated.

Former U.S. Pres. George Bush visited Kuwait, Apr. 14-16, 1993. Kuwaiti authorities arrested 14 Iraqis and Kuwaitis for allegedly plotting to assassinate him during his visit; 13 were convicted and sentenced to prison or death, June 4, 1994. The UN Security Council ruled, Sept. 27, 2000, that Iraq had to pay the Kuwait Petroleum Corp. $15.9 billion for damage to Kuwaiti oil fields during the Persian Gulf War. Iraq recognized Kuwait's territorial integrity Mar. 28, 2002. N Kuwait was used by U.S. and British troops as a staging area prior to the Mar. 2003 invasion of Iraq.

Kyrgyzstan
Kyrgyz Republic

People: Population: 5,081,429. **Age distrib.** (%): <15: 34.4; 65+: 6.2. **Pop. density:** 69 per sq mi, 27 per sq km. **Urban:** 33.9%. **Ethnic groups:** Kyrgyz 52%, Russian 18%, Uzbek 13%, Ukrainian 3%, German 2%. **Principal languages:** Kyrgyz, Russian (both official); Uzbek. **Chief religions:** Muslim 75%, Russian Orthodox 20%.

Geography: Total area: 76,641 sq mi, 198,500 sq km; **Land area:** 73,861 sq mi, 191,300 sq km. **Location:** In Central Asia. **Neighbors:** Kazakhstan on N, China on E, Uzbekistan on W, Tajikistan on S. **Topography:** Kyrgystan is an landlocked country nearly covered by Tien Shan and Pamir Mts.; avg. elevation 9,020 ft. A large lake, Issyk-Kul, in NE is 1 mi. above sea level. **Capital:** Bishkek, 806,000.

Government: Type: Republic. **Head of state:** Pres. Askar Akayev; b Nov. 10, 1944; in office: Oct. 28, 1990. **Head of gov.:** Prime Min. Nikolay Tanayev; b Nov. 5, 1945; in office: May 30, 2002. **Local divisions:** 7 oblasts and Bishkek. **Defense budget** (2003): $24.0 mil. **Active troops:** 10,900.

Economy: Industries: small machinery, textiles, food proc., cement, shoes, timber, refrigerators, furniture, electric motors. **Chief crops:** tobacco, cotton, potatoes, vegetables, grapes, fruits & berries. **Natural resources:** hydropower, gold, rare earth metals, coal, oil, nat. gas, nepheline, mercury, bismuth, lead, zinc. **Crude oil reserves** (2003): 40.0 mil. bbls. **Arable land:** 7%. **Livestock** (2003): cattle: 988,016; chickens: 3.65 mil.; goats: 661,304; pigs: 87,159; sheep: 3.10 mil. **Fish catch** (2002): 142 metric tons. **Electricity prod.** (2002): 11.72 bil. kWh. **Labor force** (2000 est.): agriculture 55%, industry 15%, services 30%.

Finance: Monetary unit: Som (KGS) (Sept. 2004: 42.22 = $1 U.S.). **GDP** (2003 est.): $7.7 bil.; **per capita GDP:** $1,600; **GDP growth:** 6.0%. **Imports** (2003 est.): $601.0 mil.; partners (2002): Kazakhstan 21.1%, Russia 19.9%, Uzbekistan 10.2%, China 10.1%, U.S. 8%, Germany 5.3%. **Exports** (2003 est.): $548.0 mil.; partners (2002): Switzerland 19.8%, Russia 16.5%, UAE 14.2%, China 8.4%, Kazakhstan 7.6%, U.S. 7.4%, Uzbekistan 5.8%. **Tourism** (2002): $36 mil. **Budget** (1999 est.): $238.7 mil. **Intl. reserves less gold:** $245 mil. **Gold:** 80,000 oz t. **Consumer prices:** 3.5%.

Transport: Railroad: Length: 261 mi. **Motor vehicles** (2001): 191,600 pass. cars. **Civil aviation:** 231.8 mil. pass.-mi; 18 airports. **Chief port:** Ysyk-Kol.

Communications: TV sets: 49 per 1,000 pop. **Radios:** 113 per 1,000 pop. **Telephone lines** (2002): 394,800. **Daily newspaper circ.:** 11 per 1,000 pop. **Internet** (2002): 152,000 users.

Health: Life expect.: 63.8 male; 72.1 female. **Births** (per 1,000 pop.): 22.1. **Deaths** (per 1,000 pop.): 7.2. **Natural inc.:** 1.49%. **Infant mortality** (per 1,000 live births): 36.8. **AIDS rate:** 0.1%.

Education: Compulsory: ages 7-16. **Literacy** (1993): 97%.

Major Intl. Organizations: UN (FAO, IBRD, ILO, IMF, WHO), CIS, OSCE.

Embassy: 1732 Wisconsin Ave. NW, 20007; 338-5141.

Website: www.kyrgyzstan.org

The region was inhabited around the 13th century by the Kyrgyz. It was annexed to Russia 1864. After 1917, it was nominally a Kara-Kyrgyz autonomous area, which was reorganized 1926, and made a constituent republic of the USSR in 1936. Kyrgyzstan declared independence Aug. 31, 1991. It became an independent state when the USSR disbanded Dec. 26, 1991. A constitution was adopted May 5, 1993.

Reelected Dec. 24, 1995, Pres. Askar Akayev gained approval by referendum of a constitutional amendment expanding his presidential powers, Feb. 10, 1996. Amendments restricting the powers of parliament and allowing private ownership of land were ratified by referendum Oct. 17, 1998. Akayev won a 3d 5-year term in the Oct. 29, 2000, election. The U.S. military presence in Kyrgyzstan has been expanding since Dec. 2001.

Laos
Lao People's Democratic Republic

People: Population: 6,068,117. **Age distrib.** (%): <15: 42.5; 65+: 3.3. **Pop. density:** 68 per sq mi, 26 per sq km. **Urban:** 20.7%. **Ethnic groups:** Lao Loum 68%, Lao Theung 22%, Lao Soung (incl. Hmong and Yao) 9%. **Principal languages:** Lao (official), French, English, and various ethnic languages. **Chief religions:** Buddhist 60%, animist and other 40%.

Geography: Total area: 91,429 sq mi, 236,800 sq km; **Land area:** 89,112 sq mi, 230,800 sq km. **Location:** In Indochina Peninsula in SE Asia. **Neighbors:** Myanmar and China on N, Vietnam on E, Cambodia on S, Thailand on W. **Topography:** Landlocked, dominated by jungle. High mountains along eastern border are the source of the E-W rivers slicing across the country to the Mekong R., which defines most of the western border. **Capital:** Vientiane, 716,000.

Government: Type: Communist. **Head of state:** Pres. Khamtai Siphandon; b Feb. 8, 1924; in office: Feb. 24, 1998. **Head of gov.:** Prime Min. Boungnang Vorachith; b Aug. 15, 1937; in office: Mar. 27, 2001. **Local divisions:** 16 provinces, 1 municipality, 1 special zone. **Defense budget** (2003): $15 mil. **Active troops:** 29,100.

Economy: Industries: mining, timber, electric power, agric. proc., constr., garments, tourism. **Chief crops:** sweet potatoes, vegetables, corn, coffee, sugarcane. **Natural resources:** timber, hydropower, gypsum, tin, gold, gemstones. **Arable land:** 3%. **Livestock** (2003): cattle: 1.2 mil.; chickens: 20.0 mil.; goats: 128,000; pigs: 1.65 mil. **Fish catch** (2002): 93,156 metric tons. **Electricity prod.** (2002): 3.56 bil. kWh. **Labor force** (1997 est.): agriculture 80%.

Finance: Monetary unit: Kip (LAK) (Sept. 2004: 10,552.00 = $1 U.S.). **GDP** (2003 est.): $10.3 bil.; **per capita GDP:** $1,700; **GDP growth:** 5.7%. **Imports** (2003 est.): $492.0 mil.; partners (2002): Thailand 60.7%, Vietnam 10.5%, China 8.2%, Singapore 4%. **Exports** (2003 est.): $332.0 mil.; partners (2002): Thailand 21.5%, Vietnam 16.9%, France 8.6%, Germany 5.6%. **Tourism** (2002): $113 mil. **Budget** (FY98/99 est.): $462.0 mil. **Intl. reserves less gold:** $140 mil. **Gold** (2002): 17,100 oz t. **Consumer prices:** 15.5%.

Transport: Motor vehicles: 9,000 pass. cars, 9,000 comm. vehicles. **Civil aviation:** 23.6 mil. pass.-mi; 9 airports.

Communications: TV sets: 10 per 1,000 pop. **Radios:** 145 per 1,000 pop. **Telephone lines** (2002): 61,900. **Daily newspaper circ.:** 3.7 per 1,000 pop. **Internet** (2002): 15,000 users.

Health: Life expect.: 52.7 male; 56.8 female. **Births** (per 1,000 pop.): 36.5. **Deaths** (per 1,000 pop.): 12.1. **Natural inc.:** 2.44%. **Infant mortality** (per 1,000 live births): 87.1. **AIDS rate:** 0.1%.

Education: Compulsory: ages 6-10. **Literacy:** 52.8%.

Major Intl. Organizations: UN (FAO, IBRD, ILO, IMF, WHO), ASEAN.

Embassy: 2222 S St. NW 20008; 332-6416.

Website: www.laoembassy.com

Laos became a French protectorate in 1893, but regained independence as a constitutional monarchy July 19, 1949.

Conflicts among neutralist, Communist, and conservative factions created a chaotic political situation. Armed conflict increased after 1960.

The 3 factions formed a coalition government in June 1962, with neutralist Prince Souvanna Phouma as premier. A 14-nation conference in Geneva signed agreements, 1962, guaranteeing neutrality and independence. By 1964 the Pathet Lao had withdrawn from the coalition, and, with aid from North Vietnamese troops, renewed sporadic attacks. U.S. planes bombed the Ho Chi Minh trail, supply line from North Vietnam to Communist forces in Laos and South Vietnam.

In 1970 the U.S. stepped up air support and military aid. After Pathet Lao military gains, Souvanna Phouma in May 1975 ordered government troops to cease fighting; the Pathet Lao took control. The Lao People's Democratic Republic was proclaimed Dec. 3, 1975.

From the mid-1970s through the 1980s, the Laotian government relied on Vietnam for military and financial aid. Since easing its foreign investment laws in 1988, Laos has attracted more than $5 billion from Thailand, the U.S., and other nations. Laos was admitted to ASEAN on July 23, 1997.

Latvia
Republic of Latvia

People: Population: 2,306,306. **Age distrib.** (%): <15: 15.8; 65+: 15.6. **Pop. density:** 94 per sq mi, 36 per sq km. **Urban:** 66.2%. **Ethnic groups:** Latvian 58%, Russian 30%, Belarusian 4%, Ukrainian 3%, Polish 2%, Lithuanian 1%. **Principal languages:** Latvian (official), Russian, Belorusian, Ukrainian, Polish. **Chief religions:** Lutheran, Roman Catholic, Russian Orthodox.

Geography: Total area: 24,938 sq mi, 64,589 sq km; **Land area:** 24,552 sq mi, 63,589 sq km. **Location:** E Europe, on the Baltic Sea. **Neighbors:** Estonia on N, Lithuania and Belarus on S, Russia on E. **Topography:** Latvia is a lowland with numerous lakes, marshes and peat bogs. Principal river, W. Dvina (Daugava), rises in Russia. There are glacial hills in E. **Capital:** Riga, 733,000.

Government: Type: Republic. **Head of state:** Pres. Vaira Vike-Freiberga; b Dec. 1, 1937; in office: July 8, 1999. **Head of gov.:** Prime Min. Indulis Emsis; Jan. 2, 1952; in office: Mar. 9, 2004. **Lo-**

cal divisions: 26 counties, 7 municipalities. **Defense budget** (2003): $198 mil. **Active troops:** 4,880.

Economy: Industries: vehicles, railroad cars, synthetics, agric. machinery, fertilizers, washing machines. **Chief crops:** grain, sugar beets, potatoes, other vegetables. **Natural resources:** peat, limestone, dolomite, hydropower, wood, amber. **Arable land:** 27%. **Livestock** (2003): cattle: 388,100; chickens: 3.88 mil.; goats: 13,200; pigs: 453,200; sheep: 31,500. **Fish catch** (2002): 114,107 metric tons. **Electricity prod.** (2002): 4.55 bil. kWh. **Labor force** (2000 est.): agriculture 15%, industry 25%, services 60%.

Finance: Monetary unit: Lats (LVL) (Sept. 2004: 0.54 = $1 U.S.). **GDP** (2003 est.): $23.8 bil.; **per capita GDP:** $10,100; **GDP growth:** 6.8%. **Imports** (2003 est.): $4.9 bil.; partners (2002): Germany 17.2%, Lithuania 9.8%, Russia 8.8%, Finland 8%, Sweden 6.4%, Estonia 6.2%, Poland 5%, Italy 4.2%. **Exports** (2003 est.): $3.0 bil.; partners (2002): Germany 15.3%, UK 14.4%, Sweden 10.4%, Lithuania 8.2%, Estonia 5.9%, Russia 5.8%, Denmark 5.6%, U.S. 4.3%. **Tourism:** $222 mil. **Budget** (2002 est.): $2.6 bil. **Intl. reserves less gold:** $964 mil. **Gold:** 250,000 mil. oz t. **Consumer prices:** 2.9%.

Transport: Railroad: Length: 1,458 mi. **Motor vehicles:** (2001): 586,200 pass. cars, 111,000 comm. vehicles. **Civil aviation:** 146.6 mil. pass.-mi; 22 airports. **Chief port:** Riga.

Communications: TV sets: 757 per 1,000 pop. **Radios:** 701 per 1,000 pop. **Telephone lines:** 653,900. **Daily newspaper circ.:** 135.1 per 1,000 pop. **Internet** (2002): 936,000 users.

Health: Life expect.: 65.9 male; 76.1 female. **Births** (per 1,000 pop.): 8.9. **Deaths** (per 1,000 pop.): 13.7. **Natural inc.:** −0.49%. **Infant mortality** (per 1,000 live births): 9.7. **AIDS rate:** 0.6%.

Education: Compulsory: ages 7-15. **Literacy:** 99.8%.

Major Intl. Organizations: UN (FAO, IBRD, ILO, IMF, IMO, WHO), EU, NATO, OSCE.

Embassy: 4325 17th St. NW 20011; 726-8213.

Website: www.latvia-usa.org

Prior to 1918, Latvia was occupied by the Russians and Germans. It was an independent republic, 1918-39. The Aug. 1939 Soviet-German agreement assigned Latvia to the Soviet sphere of influence. It was officially accepted as part of the USSR on Aug. 5, 1940. It was overrun by the German army in 1941, but retaken in 1945.

During an abortive Soviet coup, Latvia declared independence, Aug. 21, 1991. The Soviet Union recognized Latvia's independence in Sept. 1991. The last Russian troops in Latvia withdrew by Aug. 31, 1994. Responding to international pressure, Latvian voters on Oct. 3, 1998, eased citizenship laws that had discriminated against some 500,000 ethnic Russians. On June 17, 1999, the legislature elected Vaira Vike-Freiberga as Latvia's 1st woman president. Latvia joined the EU and NATO in 2004. Indulis Emsis, a Green, became prime minister Mar. 9.

Lebanon
Lebanese Republic

People: Population: 3,777,218. **Age distrib.** (%): <15: 27.3; 65+: 6.8. **Pop. density:** 956 per sq mi, 369 per sq km. **Urban:** 87.5%. **Ethnic groups:** Arab 95%, Armenian 4%. **Principal languages:** Arabic (official), French, English, Armenian. **Chief religions:** Muslim 70%, Christian 30%.

Geography: Total area: 4,015 sq mi, 10,400 sq km; **Land area:** 3,950 sq mi, 10,230 sq km. **Location:** In Middle East, on E end of Mediterranean Sea. **Neighbors:** Syria on E, Israel on S. **Topography:** There is a narrow coastal strip, and 2 mountain ranges running N-S enclosing the fertile Beqaa Valley. The Litani R. runs S through the valley, turning W to empty into the Mediterranean. **Capital:** Beirut, 1,792,000.

Government: Type: Republic. **Head of state:** Pres. Emile Lahoud; Jan. 12, 1936; in office: Nov. 24, 1998. **Head of gov.:** Prime Min. Rafiq al-Hariri; b Nov. 1944; in office: Oct. 23, 2000. **Local divisions:** 6 governorates. **Defense budget** (2003): $498 mil. **Active troops:** 72,100.

Economy: Industries: banking, food proc., jewelry, cement, textiles, mineral & chemical products. **Chief crops:** citrus, grapes, tomatoes, apples, vegetables, potatoes, olives, tobacco. **Natural resources:** limestone, iron ore, salt, water. **Arable land:** 21%. **Livestock** (2003): cattle: 90,000; chickens: 35.0 mil.; goats: 382,000; pigs: 20,000; sheep: 350,000. **Fish catch** (2002): 4,760 metric tons. **Electricity prod.** (2002): 8.07 bil. kWh. **Labor force:** 62% services; 31% industry; 7% agriculture.

Finance: Monetary unit: Pound (LBP) (Sept. 2004: 1,514.00 = $1 U.S.). **GDP** (2003 est.): $17.8 bil.; **per capita GDP:** $4,800; **GDP growth:** 3.0%. **Imports** (2003 est.): $6.1 bil.; partners (2002): Italy 11.3%, France 10.7%, Germany 8.3%, U.S. 5.6%, Syria 5.4%, China 4.8%, Belgium 4.5%, UK 4.2%. **Exports** (2003 est.): $1.4 bil.; partners (2002): UAE 11%, Switzerland 9.1%, Saudi Arabia 8.2%, U.S. 6.2%, Jordan 4.2%. **Tourism** (2002): $956 mil. **Budget** (2003 est.): $7.1 bil. **Intl. reserves less gold:** $8.43 bil. **Gold:** 9.22 mil oz t.

Transport: Railroad: Length: 249 mi. **Motor vehicles** (1998): 1.34 mil pass. cars, 95,400 comm. vehicles. **Civil aviation:** 922.1 mil. pass.-mi; 5 airports. **Chief ports:** Beirut, Tripoli, Sidon.

Communications: TV sets: 355 per 1,000 pop. **Radios:** 907 per 1,000 pop. **Telephone lines** (2002): 678,800. **Newspaper circ.:** 107 per 1,000 pop. **Internet** (2002): 400,000 users.

796

Health: Life expect.: 69.9 male; 74.9 female. **Births** (per 1,000 pop.): 19.3. **Deaths** (per 1,000 pop.): 6.3. **Natural inc.:** 1.30%. **Infant mortality** (per 1,000 live births): 25.5. **AIDS rate:** 0.1%.
Education: Compulsory: ages 6-14. **Literacy:** 87.4%.
Major Intl. Organizations: UN (FAO, IBRD, ILO, IMF, IMO, WHO), AL.
Embassy: 2560 28th St. NW 20008; 939-6300.
Website: www.lebanonembassyus.org

Formed from 5 former Turkish Empire districts, Lebanon became an independent state Sept. 1, 1920, administered under French mandate 1920-41. French troops withdrew in 1946.

Under the 1943 National Covenant, all public positions were divided among the various religious communities, with Christians in the majority. By the 1970s, Muslims became the majority and demanded a larger political and economic role.

U.S. Marines intervened, May-Oct. 1958, during a Syrian-aided revolt. Continued raids against Israeli civilians, 1970-75, brought Israeli attacks against guerrilla camps and villages. Israeli troops occupied S Lebanon, Mar. 1978, and again in Apr. 1980.

An estimated 60,000 were killed and billions of dollars in damage inflicted in a 1975-76 civil war. Palestinian units and leftist Muslims fought against the Maronite militia, the Phalange, and other Christians. Several Arab countries provided political and arms support to the various factions, while Israel aided Christian forces. Up to 15,000 Syrian troops intervened in 1976 to fight Palestinian groups. A cease-fire was mainly policed by Syria.

New clashes between Syrian troops and Christian forces erupted, Apr. 1, 1981. By Apr. 22, fighting had also broken out between two Muslim factions. In July, Israeli air raids on Beirut killed or wounded some 800 persons.

Israeli forces invaded Lebanon June 6, 1982, in a coordinated land, sea, and air attack aimed at crushing strongholds of the Palestine Liberation Organization (PLO). Israeli and Syrian forces engaged in the Bekaa Valley. By June 14, Israeli troops had encircled Beirut. On Aug. 21, the PLO evacuated west Beirut after massive Israeli bombings there. Israeli troops entered west Beirut following the Sept. 14 assassination of newly elected Lebanese Pres. Bashir Gemayel. On Sept. 16, Lebanese Christian troops entered 2 refugee camps and massacred hundreds of Palestinian refugees. An agreement May 17, 1983, between Lebanon, Israel, and the U.S. (but not Syria) provided for the withdrawal of Israeli troops; at least 30,000 Syrian troops remained in Lebanon, and Israeli forces continued to occupy a "security zone" in the south.

In 1983, terrorist bombings became a way of life in Beirut as some 50 people were killed in an explosion at the U.S. Embassy, Apr. 18; 241 U.S. servicemen and 58 French soldiers died in separate Muslim suicide attacks, Oct. 23.

Kidnapping of foreign nationals by Islamic militants became common in the 1980s. U.S., British, French, and Soviet citizens were victims. All were released by 1992.

A treaty signed May 22, 1991, between Lebanon and Syria recognized Lebanon as a separate state for the first time since the 2 countries gained independence in 1943.

Israeli forces conducted air raids and artillery strikes against guerrilla bases and villages in S Lebanon, causing over 200,000 to flee their homes July 25-29, 1993. Some 500,000 civilians fled their homes in Apr. 1996 when Israel again struck suspected guerrilla bases in the south. Pope John Paul II visited Lebanon May 10-11, 1997. During May-June 1998 the nation held its 1st municipal elections in 35 years. With Syria's approval, the legislature unanimously elected Lebanese armed forces chief Emile Lahoud as president Oct. 15.

Israel withdrew virtually all its troops from S Lebanon by May 24, 2000, leaving Hezbollah, an Iranian-backed guerrilla group, in control of much of the region. As of Sept. 2004, Syria still had an estimated 20,000 troops in Lebanon. Bowing to Syrian pressure, Lebanon's parliament amended the constitution to allow Pres. Lahoud to serve 3 more years.

Lesotho
Kingdom of Lesotho

People: Population: 1,865,040. **Age distrib.** (%): <15: 39; 65+: 4.7. **Pop. density:** 159 per sq mi, 61 per sq km. **Urban:** 17.9%. **Ethnic groups:** Sotho 99%. **Principal languages:** Sesotho, English (both official), Zulu, Xhosa. **Chief religions:** Christian 80%, indigenous beliefs 20%.
Geography: Total area: 11,720 sq mi, 30,355 sq km; **Land area:** 11,720 sq mi, 30,355 sq km. **Location:** In southern Africa. **Neighbors:** Completely surrounded by Republic of South Africa. **Topography:** Landlocked and mountainous, altitudes from 5,000 to 11,000 ft. **Capital:** Maseru, 170,000.
Government: Type: Modified constitutional monarchy. **Head of state:** King Letsie III; b July 17, 1963; in office: Feb. 7, 1996. **Head of gov.:** Pakalitha Mosisili; b Mar. 14, 1945; in office: May 29, 1998. **Local divisions:** 10 districts. **Defense budget** (2003): $34 mil. **Active troops:** 2,000.
Economy: Industries: food, beverages, textiles, apparel, handicrafts. **Chief crops:** corn, wheat, sorghum, barley. **Natural resources:** water, diamonds, other minerals. **Arable land:** 11%. **Livestock** (2003): cattle: 540,000; chickens: 1.8 mil.; goats: 650,000; pigs: 65,000; sheep: 850,000. **Fish catch** (2002 est): 32 metric tons. **Electricity prod.** (2002): 0.31 bil. kWh. **Labor force:**

86% of resident population engaged in subsistence agriculture; roughly 35% of the active male wage earners work in South Africa.
Finance: Monetary unit: Loti (LSL) (Sept. 2004: 6.58 = $1 U.S.). **GDP** (2003 est.): $5.6 bil.; **per capita GDP:** $3,000; **GDP growth:** 4.2%. **Imports** (2003 est.): $661.0 mil.; partners (2002): Hong Kong 48.3%, China 23.2%, Singapore 3.7%. **Exports** (2003 est.): $450.0 mil.; partners (2002): U.S. 97.1%, Canada 0.9%, France 0.6%. **Tourism** (2002): $20 mil. **Budget** (FY99/00 est.): $80.0 mil. **Intl. reserves less gold:** $310 mil. **Consumer prices:** 6.7%.
Transport: Railroad: Length: 2 mi. **Motor vehicles:** 5,000 pass. cars, 18,000 comm. vehicles. **Civil aviation:** 4 airports.
Communications: TV sets: 16 per 1,000 pop. **Radios:** 52 per 1,000 pop. **Telephone lines** (2002): 28,600. **Daily newspaper circ.:** 7.6 per 1,000 pop. **Internet** (2002): 21,000 users.
Health: Life expect.: 36.8 male; 36.8 female. **Births** (per 1,000 pop.): 26.9. **Deaths** (per 1,000 pop.): 24.8. **Natural inc.:** 0.21%. **Infant mortality** (per 1,000 live births): 85.2. **AIDS rate:** 28.9%.
Education: Compulsory: ages 6-12. **Literacy:** 84.8%.
Major Intl. Organizations: UN (FOA, IBRD, ILO, IMF, WHO, WTrO), the Commonwealth, AU.
Embassy: 2511 Massachusetts Ave. NW 20008; 797-5533.
Website: www.lesotho.gov.ls

Lesotho (once called Basutoland) became a British protectorate in 1868 when Chief Moshesh sought protection against the Boers. Independence came Oct. 4, 1966. Elections were suspended in 1970. Most of Lesotho's GNP is provided by citizens working in South Africa. Livestock raising is the chief industry; diamonds are the chief export.

South Africa imposed a blockade, Jan. 1, 1986, because Lesotho had given sanctuary to anti-apartheid groups. The blockade sparked a Jan. 20 military coup, and was lifted, Jan. 25, when the new leaders agreed to expel the rebels.

In Mar. 1990, King Moshoeshoe was exiled by the military government. Letsie III became king Nov. 12. In Mar. 1993, Ntsu Mokhehle, a civilian, was elected prime minister, ending 23 years of military rule. After a series of violent disturbances, the king dismissed the Mokhele government Aug. 17, 1994; constitutional rule was restored Sept. 14. Letsie abdicated and Moshoeshoe was reinstated Jan. 25, 1995.

Moshoeshoe died in an automobile accident, Jan. 15, 1996. Letsie was reinstated Feb. 7; his formal coronation was Oct. 31, 1997. South Africa and Botswana sent troops Sept. 22, 1998, to help suppress violent antigovernment protests.

According to UN estimates, about 30% of the adult population has HIV/AIDS.

Liberia
Republic of Liberia

People: Population: 3,390,635. **Age distrib.** (%): <15: 43.3; 65+: 3.5. **Pop. density:** 91 per sq mi, 35 per sq km. **Urban:** 46.7%. **Ethnic groups:** Kpelle, Bassa, Dey, and other tribes 95%; Americo-Liberians 2.5%, Caribbean 2.5%. **Principal languages:** English (official); Mande, West Atlantic, and Kwa languages. **Chief religions:** Indigenous beliefs 40%, Christian 40%, Muslim 20%.
Geography: Total area: 43,000 sq mi, 111,370 sq km; **Land area:** 37,189 sq mi, 96,320 sq km. **Location:** On SW coast of W Africa. **Neighbors:** Sierra Leone on W, Guinea on N, Côte d'Ivoire on E. **Topography:** Marshy Atlantic coastline rises to low mountains and plateaus in the forested interior; 6 major rivers flow in parallel courses to the ocean. **Capital:** Monrovia, 572,000.
Government: Type: In transition. **Head of state and gov.:** Chmn. Charles Gyude Bryant; b Jan. 17, 1949; in office: Oct. 14, 2003 (interim). **Local divisions:** 15 counties. **Defense budget:** NA. **Active troops:** 11,000-15,000.
Economy: Industries: rubber & palm oil proc., timber, diamonds. **Chief crops:** rubber, coffee, cocoa, rice, cassava, palm oil, sugarcane, bananas. **Natural resources:** iron ore, timber, diamonds, gold, hydropower. **Arable land:** 1%. **Livestock** (2003): cattle: 36,000; chickens: 6.0 mil.; goats: 220,000; pigs: 130,000; sheep: 210,000. **Fish catch** (2002 est): 11,514 metric tons. **Electricity prod.** (2002): 0.49 bil. kWh. **Labor force:** (2000 est.): agriculture 70%, industry 8%, services 22%.
Finance: Monetary unit: Liberian Dollar (LRD) (Sept. 2004: 45.00 = $1 U.S.). **GDP** (2003 est.): $3.3 bil.; **per capita GDP:** $1,000; **GDP growth:** 3.0%. **Imports** (2002 est.): $5.1 bil.; partners (2002): South Korea 31.1%, Japan 19.5%, Germany 16%, France 9.3%, Singapore 8.1%. **Exports** (2002 est.): $1.1 bil.; partners (2002): Germany 52.7%, France 8.2%, Poland 6.8%, Denmark 5.3%, China 4.7%, Italy 4.4%, U.S. 4%. **Budget** (2000 est.): $90.5 mil. **Intl. reserves less gold:** $5 mil.
Transport: Railroad: Length: 304 mi. **Motor vehicles:** 16,000 pass. cars, 12,500 comm. vehicles. **Civil aviation:** 4.3 mil pass.-mi; 2 airports. **Chief ports:** Monrovia, Buchanan, Greenville, Harper.
Communications: TV sets: 26 per 1,000 pop. **Radios:** 329 per 1,000 pop. **Telephone lines:** 6,700 main lines. **Daily newspaper circ.:** 17 per 1,000 pop.
Health: Life expect.: 46.9 male; 49.0 female. **Births** (per 1,000 pop.): 44.8. **Deaths** (per 1,000 pop.): 17.9. **Natural inc.:** 2.69%. **Infant mortality** (per 1,000 live births): 130.5. **AIDS rate:** 5.9%.
Education: Compulsory: ages 6-15. **Literacy:** 57.5%.
Major Intl. Organizations: UN and most of its specialized agencies, AU.
Embassy: 5201 16th St. NW 20011; 723-0437.

Website: www.liberian-connection.com

Liberia was founded in 1822 by U.S. black freedmen who settled at Monrovia with the aid of colonization societies. It became a republic July 26, 1847, with a constitution modeled on that of the U.S. Descendants of freedmen dominated politics.

Under Pres. William V. S. Tubman, Liberia was a founding member of the UN in 1945. Tubman died in 1971 and succeeded by his vice-president, William R. Tolbert, Jr. Charging rampant corruption, an Army Redemption Council of enlisted men staged a bloody predawn coup, April 12, 1980, which Pres. Tolbert was killed and replaced as head of state by Sgt. Samuel Doe. Doe was chosen pres. in a disputed election, and survived a subsequent coup, in 1985.

A civil war began Dec. 1989. In Sept. 1990, Pres. Doe was captured and put to death. Despite the introduction of peacekeeping forces from several countries, factional fighting intensified, and a series of cease-fires failed. Factional fighting devastated Monrovia in Apr. 1996.

On Sept. 3, 1996, Ruth Perry became modern Africa's first female head of state, leading another transitional government. By then, the civil war had claimed more than 150,000 lives and uprooted over half the population.

Former rebel leader Charles Taylor was elected president July 19, 1997, in Liberia's 1st national election in 12 years. The UN imposed sanctions May 4, 2001, to punish Liberia for aiding the Revolutionary United Front (RUF) insurgency in Sierra Leone. Taylor declared a state of emergency Feb. 8, 2002, after Liberian rebels launched raids near Monrovia.

A U.N.-sponsored war crimes tribunal indicted Taylor June 4, 2003, for his role in Sierra Leone. With rebels again threatening Monrovia, Taylor resigned Aug. 11 and went into exile. The UN authorized a 15,000-member peacekeeping force (UNMIL) Sept. 19 to help stabilize the nation. A businessman, Charles Gyude Bryant, was sworn in Oct. 14 to head a power-sharing interim government.

Libya
Great Socialist People's Libyan Arab Jamahiriya

People: Population: 5,631,585. **Age distrib.** (%): <15: 35; 65+: 4. **Pop. density:** 8 per sq mi, 3 per sq km. **Urban:** 86.3%. **Ethnic groups:** Arab-Berber 97%. **Principal languages:** Arabic (official), Italian, English. **Chief religion:** Muslim (official; mostly Sunni) 97%.

Geography: Total area: 679,362 sq mi, 1,759,540 sq km; **Land area:** 679,362 sq mi, 1,759,540 sq km. **Location:** On Mediterranean coast of N Africa. **Neighbors:** Tunisia, Algeria on W; Niger, Chad on S; Sudan, Egypt on E. **Topography:** Desert and semidesert regions cover 92% of the land, with low mountains in N, higher mountains in S, and a narrow coastal zone. **Capital**, Tripoli, 2,006,000. **Cities (urban aggr.):** Benghazi, 912,000.

Government: Type: Islamic Arabic Socialist "Mass-State." **Head of state and gov.:** Col. Muammar al-Qaddafi; b Sept. 1942; in power: Sept. 1969. **Local divisions:** 25 municipalities. **Defense budget:** NA. **Active troops:** 76,000.

Economy: Industries: oil, food proc., textiles, handicrafts, cement. **Chief crops:** wheat, barley, olives, dates, citrus, vegetables, peanuts, soybeans. **Natural resources:** oil, nat. gas, gypsum. **Crude oil reserves** (2003): 29.5 bil. bbls. **Arable land:** 1%. **Livestock** (2003): cattle: 130,000; chickens: 25.0 mil.; goats: 1.27 mil.; sheep: 4.13 mil. **Fish catch** (2002 est): 33,666 metric tons. **Electricity prod.** (2002): 20.89 bil. kWh. **Labor force** (1997 est.): services 54%, industry 29%, agriculture 17%.

Finance: Monetary unit: Dinar (LYD) (Sept. 2004: 1.32 = $1 U.S.). **GDP** (2003 est.): $35.0 bil.; **per capita GDP:** $6,400; **GDP growth:** 3.2%. **Imports** (2003 est.): $6.3 bil.; partners (2002): Italy 25.4%, Germany 9.9%, South Korea 6.5%, UK 6.5%, Tunisia 6.4%, Japan 6.3%, France 5.7%. **Exports** (2003 est.): $14.3 bil.; partners (2002): Italy 42.8%, Germany 14.1%, Spain 13.6%, Turkey 6.9%. **Tourism** $79 mil. **Budget** (2003 est.): $7.8 bil. **Intl. reserves less gold:** $13.18 bil. **Gold:** 4.62 mil oz t.

Transport: Motor vehicles (1997): 859,000 pass. cars, 362,400 comm. vehicles. **Civil aviation:** 254.1 mil. pass.-mi; 58 airports. **Chief ports:** Tripoli, Banghazi.

Communications: TV sets: 139 per 1,000 pop. **Radios:** 259 per 1,000 pop. **Telephone lines:** 750,000. **Daily newspaper circ.:** 14 per 1,000 pop. **Internet:** 160,000 users.

Health: Life expect.: 74.1 male; 78.6 female. **Births** (per 1,000 pop.): 27.2. **Deaths** (per 1,000 pop.): 3.5. **Natural inc.:** 2.37%. **Infant mortality** (per 1,000 live births): 25.7. **AIDS rate:** 0.3%.

Education: Compulsory: ages 6-14. **Literacy:** 82.6%.

Major Intl. Organizations: UN (FAO, IBRD, ILO, IMF, IMO, WHO), AL, AU, OPEC.

Permanent UN Representative: 309-315 E. 48th St., New York, NY 10017; (212) 752-5775.

Website: www.libya-un.org

First settled by Berbers, Libya was ruled in succession by Carthage, Rome, the Vandals, and the Ottomans. Italy ruled from 1912, and Britain and France after WW II. Libya became an independent constitutional monarchy Jan. 2, 1952. In 1969 a junta led by Col. Muammar al-Qaddafi seized power.

Libya and Egypt fought several air and land battles along their border in July 1977. Chad charged Libya with military occupation of its uranium-rich northern region in 1977. Libyan troops were driven from their last major stronghold by Chad forces in 1987, leaving over $1 billion in military equipment behind.

Libya reportedly helped arm violent revolutionary groups in Egypt and Sudan and aided terrorists of various nationalities, and was blamed for aiding the attacks on the Rome and Vienna airports in Dec. 1985. The U.S. and Libya clashed, Jan.-Mar. 1986, over access to the Gulf of Sidra, which Libya claimed as territorial waters. The U.S. accused Qaddafi of ordering the Apr. 5, bombing of a West Berlin discotheque, which killed 3, including a U.S. serviceman. In response, the U.S. sent warplanes to attack terrorist-related targets in Tripoli and Banghazi, Libya, Apr. 14.

Libyan agents were accused of planting bombs that blew up Pan Am Flight 103 over Lockerbie, Scotland, killing 270 people Dec. 21, 1988; and UTA Flight 772 over Niger, killing 170 people Sept. 19, 1989. The UN imposed sanctions, Apr. 15, 1992, for Libya's failure to cooperate in the Lockerbie and UTA cases.

After prolonged negotiations, Libya agreed in 2003 to renounce terrorism and settle compensation cases for the families of the Lockerbie and UTA bombing victims. The UN lifted sanctions, Sept. 12, 2003. Nine months of secret talks with the U.S. and UK led to Libya's announcement Dec. 19 that it would stop developing nuclear, chemical, and biological weapons and long-range missiles. The U.S. ended most economic sanctions Apr. 23, 2004, and formally restored diplomatic relations with Libya June 28, but Libya remained on the State Dept. list of nations sponsoring terrorism. Libya pledged Aug. 10 to compensate non-U.S. victims of the 1986 Berlin disco bombing.

Liechtenstein
Principality of Liechtenstein

People: Population: 33,436. **Age distrib.** (%): <15: 18.3; 65+: 11.2. **Pop. density:** 541 per sq mi, 209 per sq km. **Urban:** 21.6%. **Ethnic groups:** Alemannic 86%; Italian, Turkish, and other 14%. **Principal languages:** German (official), Alemannic dialect. **Chief religions:** Roman Catholic 80%, Protestant 7%.

Geography: Total area: 62 sq mi, 160 sq km; **Land area:** 62 sq mi, 160 sq km. **Location:** Central Europe, in the Alps. **Neighbors:** Switzerland on W, Austria on E. **Topography:** The Rhine Valley occupies one-third of the country, the Alps cover the rest. **Capital:** Vaduz, 5,000.

Government: Type: Hereditary constitutional monarchy. **Head of state:** Prince Hans-Adam II; b Feb. 14, 1945; in office: Nov. 13, 1989. **Head of gov.:** Otmar Hasler; b Sept. 28, 1953; in office: Apr. 5, 2001. **Local divisions:** 11 communes.

Economy: Industries: electronics, metallurgy, textiles, ceramics, pharm., food products, precision instruments, tourism. **Chief crops:** wheat, barley, corn, potatoes. **Natural resources:** hydropower. **Arable land:** 24%. **Livestock** (2003): cattle: 6,000; pigs: 3,000; sheep: 2,900. **Labor force:** industry 47.4%, services 51.3%, agriculture 1.3% (31 December 2001 est.).

Finance: Monetary unit: Swiss Franc (CHF) (Sept. 2004: 1.27 = $1 U.S.). **GDP** (1999 est.): $825.0 mil.; **per capita GDP:** $25,000; **GDP growth:** 11.0%. **Imports** (1996): $917.3 mil.; partners EU, Switzerland. **Exports** (1996): $2.5 bil.; partners EU 62.6% (Germany 24.3%, Austria 9.5%, France 8.9%, Italy 6.6%, UK 4.6%), U.S. 18.9%, Switzerland 15.7%). **Budget** (1998 est.): $414.1 mil.

Transport: Railroad: Length: 11 mi.

Communications: TV sets: 469 per 1,000 pop. **Radios:** 656 per 1,000 pop. **Daily newspaper circ.:** 602 per 1,000 pop.

Health: Life expect.: 75.8 male; 83.0 female. **Births** (per 1,000 pop.): 10.7. **Deaths** (per 1,000 pop.): 6.9. **Natural inc.:** 0.37%. **Infant mortality** (per 1,000 live births): 4.8.

Education: Compulsory: ages 7-16. **Literacy** (1997): 100%.

Major Intl. Organizations: UN (WTrO), EFTA, OSCE.

Permanent UN Representative: 633 Third Ave., 27th Fl., New York, NY 10017; (212) 599-0220.

Websites: www.news.li; www.fuerstenhaus.li

Liechtenstein became sovereign in 1806. Austria administered Liechtenstein's ports up to 1920; Switzerland has administered its postal services since 1921. Liechtenstein is united with Switzerland by a customs and monetary union. Taxes are low; many international corporations have headquarters there. Foreign workers comprise 2/3 of the labor force. On Aug. 15, 2004, Prince Hans-Adam II assigned day-to-day responsibilities for running the tiny country to his son, Crown Prince Alois.

Lithuania
Republic of Lithuania

People: Population: 3,607,899. **Age distrib.** (%): <15: 18.2; 65+: 13.8. **Pop. density:** 143 per sq mi, 55 per sq km. **Urban:** 66.7%. **Ethnic groups:** Lithuanian 81%, Russian 9%, Polish 7%, Belarusian 2%. **Principal languages:** Lithuanian (official), Belorusian, Russian, Polish. **Chief religion:** Predominantly Roman Catholic.

Geography: Total area: 25,174 sq mi, 65,200 sq km. **Location:** In E Europe, on SE coast of Baltic. **Neighbors:** Latvia on N, Belarus on E, S, Poland and Russia on W. **Topography:** Lithuania is a lowland with hills in W and S; fertile soil; many small lakes and rivers, with marshes espec. in N and W. **Capital:** Vilnius, 549,000. **Cities (urban aggr.):** Kaunas, 412,639.

Government: Type: Republic. **Head of state:** Pres. Valdas Adamkus; b Nov. 3, 1926; in office: July 12, 2004. **Head of gov.:** Prime Min. Algirdas Brazauskas; b Sept. 22, 1932; in office: July 3, 2001. **Local divisions:** 10 provinces. **Defense budget** (2003): $359 mil. **Active troops:** 12,700.

Economy: Industries: machine tools, electric motors, large appliances, oil refining, shipbuilding. **Chief crops:** grain, potatoes, sugar beets, flax, vegetables. **Natural resources:** peat. **Crude oil reserves** (2003): 12.0 mil. bbls. **Arable land:** 35%. **Livestock** (2003): cattle: 779,100; chickens: 6.85 mil.; goats: 22,000; pigs: 1.06 mil.; sheep: 13,600. **Fish catch** (2002): 151,896 metric tons. **Electricity prod.** (2002): 17.93 bil. kWh. **Labor force** (1997 est.): industry 30%, agriculture 20%, services 50%.

Finance: Monetary unit: Litas (LTL) (Sept. 2004: 2.85 = $1 U.S.). **GDP** (2003 est.): $40.2 bil.; **per capita GDP:** $11,200; **GDP growth:** 7.1%. **Imports** (2003 est.): $9.2 bil.; partners (2002): Russia 22.2%, Germany 17.8%, Italy 5.1%, Poland 5%. **Exports** (2003 est.): $7.9 bil.; partners (2002): UK 13.4%, Russia 12.1%, Germany 10.4%, Latvia 9.7%, Denmark 5.1%, Sweden 4.2%, France 4.1%. **Tourism:** $568 mil. **Budget** (2001 est.): $1.8 bil. **Intl. reserves less gold:** $2.27 bil. **Gold:** 190,000 oz t. **Consumer prices:** –1.2%.

Transport: Railroad: Length: 1,241 mi. **Motor vehicles** (2001): 1.13 mil. pass. cars, 115,600 comm. vehicles. **Civil aviation:** 200.1 mil. pass.-mi; 22 airports. **Chief port:** Klaipeda.

Communications: TV sets: 422 per 1,000 pop. **Radios:** 502 per 1,000 pop. **Telephone lines:** 824,200. **Daily newspaper circ.:** 29.3 per 1,000 pop. **Internet** 695,700 users.

Health: Life expect.: 68.2 male; 79.0 female. **Births** (per 1,000 pop.): 8.5. **Deaths** (per 1,000 pop.): 11.0. **Natural inc.:** –0.25%. **Infant mortality** (per 1,000 live births): 7.1. **AIDS rate:** 0.1%.

Education: Compulsory: ages 7-15. **Literacy:** 99.6%.

Major Intl. Organizations: UN (FAO, IBRD, ILO, IMF, IMO, WHO), EU, NATO, OSCE.

Embassy: 2622 16th St. NW 20009; 234-5860.

Websites: www.ltembassyus.org

Lithuania was occupied by the German army, 1914-18. It was annexed by the Soviet Russian army, but the Soviets were overthrown, 1919. Lithuania was a democratic republic until 1926, when the regime was ousted by a coup. In 1939 the Soviet-German treaty assigned most of Lithuania to the Soviet sphere of influence. Lithuania was annexed by the USSR Aug. 3, 1940.

Lithuania formally declared its independence from the Soviet Union Mar. 11, 1990. During an abortive Soviet coup in Aug., the Western nations recognized Lithuania's independence, which was ratified by the Soviet Union in Sept. 1991.

The last Russian troops withdrew on Aug. 31, 1993. The conservative Homeland Union defeated the former Communists in parliamentary elections Oct. 20 and Nov. 10, 1996. A Lithuanian-American, Valdas Adamkus, won the presidency in a runoff election Jan. 4, 1998. Adamkus lost to Rolandas Paksas in a runoff election, Jan. 5, 2003. After the legislature impeached and removed Paksas from office, Apr. 6, 2004, Adamkus regained the presidency in a runoff vote June 27. Lithuania joined the EU and NATO in 2004.

Luxembourg
Grand Duchy of Luxembourg

People: Population: 462,690. **Age distrib.** (%): <15: 18.9; 65+: 14.1. **Pop. density:** 463 per sq mi, 179 per sq km. **Urban:** 91.9%. **Ethnic groups:** Mixture of French and German. **Principal languages:** Luxembourgish (national); German, French (official). **Chief religion:** Majority is Roman Catholic; 1979 law forbids collection of such statistics.

Geography: Total area: 998 sq mi, 2,586 sq km; **Land area:** 998 sq mi, 2,586 sq km. **Location:** In W Europe. **Neighbors:** Belgium on W, France on S, Germany on E. **Topography:** Heavy forests (Ardennes) cover N, S is a low, open plateau. **Capital:** Luxembourg-Ville, 77,000.

Government: Type: Constitutional monarchy. **Head of state:** Grand Duke Henri; b Apr. 16, 1955; in office: Oct. 7, 2000. **Head of gov.:** Prime Min. Jean-Claude Juncker; b Dec. 9, 1954; in office: Jan. 19, 1995. **Local divisions:** 3 districts. **Defense budget** (2003): $229 mil. **Active troops:** 900.

Economy: Industries: banking, iron & steel, food proc., chemicals, metal products, engineering, tires, glass, aluminum. **Chief crops:** barley, oats, potatoes, wheat, fruits, grapes. **Natural resources:** iron ore. **Arable land:** 24%. **Livestock** (2003): cattle: 189,674; chickens: 79.28 mil.; goats:1,878; pigs: 84,140; sheep: 9,446. **Electricity prod.** (2003): 2.51 bil. kWh. **Labor force** (1999 est.): services 90.1%, industry 8%, agriculture 1.9%.

Finance: Monetary unit: Euro (EUR) (Sept. 2004: 0.82 = $1 U.S.). **GDP** (2003 est.): $25.0 bil.; **per capita GDP:** $55,100; **GDP growth:** 1.2%. **Imports** (2002): $11.6 bil.; partners (2002): Belgium 29.7%, Germany 23%, France 13.2%, Taiwan 7.3%, Netherlands 4.6%. **Exports** (2002): $8.6 bil.; partners (2002): Germany 23.9%, France 20.1%, Belgium 10.5%, UK 8.7%, Italy 6.1%, Spain 4.5%, Netherlands 4.4%. **Tourism:** $2.8 bil. **Budget** (2002 est.): $5.5 bil. **Intl. reserves less gold:** $188 mil. **Gold:** 80,000 oz t. **Consumer prices:** 2.0%.

Transport: Railroad: Length: 170 mi. **Motor vehicles** (2001): 280,700 pass. cars, 48,700 comm. vehicles. **Civil aviation:** 346.1 mil. pass.-mi; 1 airport. **Chief port:** Mertert.

Communications: TV sets: 599 per 1,000 pop. **Radios:** 683 per 1,000 pop. **Telephone lines** (2002): 355,400. **Daily newspaper circ.:** 332 per 1,000 pop. **Internet** (2002): 165,000 users.

Health: Life expect.: 75.3 male; 82.1 female. **Births** (per 1,000 pop.): 12.2. **Deaths** (per 1,000 pop.): 8.4. **Natural inc.:** 0.38%. **Infant mortality** (per 1,000 live births): 4.9. **AIDS rate:** 0.2%.

Education: Compulsory: ages 6-15. **Literacy** (2000 est.): 100%.

Major Intl. Organizations: UN (FAO, IBRD, ILO, IMF, IMO, WHO, WTrO), EU, NATO, OECD, OSCE.

Embassy: 2200 Massachusetts Ave. NW 20008; 265-4171.

Websites: www.luxembourg-usa.org

Luxembourg, founded about 963, was ruled by Burgundy, Spain, Austria, and France from 1448 to 1815. It left the Germanic Confederation in 1866. Overrun by Germany in 2 world wars, Luxembourg ended its neutrality in 1948, when a customs union with Belgium and Netherlands was adopted.

Macedonia
Former Yugoslav Republic of Macedonia

People: Population: 2,071,210. **Age distrib.** (%): <15: 22.4; 65+: 10.4. **Pop. density:** 216 per sq mi, 83 per sq km. **Urban:** 59.5%. **Ethnic groups:** Macedonian 67%, Albanian 23%, Turkish 4%, Roma 2%, Serb 2%. **Principal languages:** Macedonian (official), Albanian, Turkish, Romani, Serbo-Croatian. **Chief religions:** Macedonian Orthodox 67%, Muslim 30%.

Geography: Total area: 9,781 sq mi, 25,333 sq km; **Land area:** 9,597 sq mi, 24,856 sq km. **Location:** In SE Europe. **Neighbors:** Bulgaria on E, Greece on S, Albania on W, Serbia on N. **Topography:** Macedonia is a landlocked, mostly mountainous country, with deep river valleys, 3 large lakes; country is bisected by Vardar R. **Capital:** Skopje, 447,000.

Government: Type: Republic. **Head of state:** Pres. Branko Crvenkovski; b Oct. 12, 1962; in office: May 12, 2004. **Head of gov.:** Prime Min. Hari Kostov; b Nov. 13, 1959; in office: June 2, 2004. **Local divisions:** 123 municipalities. **Defense budget** (2003): $138 mil. **Active troops:** 12,850.

Economy: Industries: mining, textiles, wood products, tobacco, food proc., buses. **Chief crops:** rice, tobacco, wheat, corn, millet, cotton, sesame. **Natural resources:** chromium, lead, zinc, mang., tungsten, nickel, iron ore, asbestos, sulfur, timber. **Arable land:** 24%. **Livestock** (2003): cattle: 265,000; chickens: 3.35 mil.; pigs: 200,000; sheep: 1.2 mil. **Fish catch** (2002): 1,363 metric tons. **Electricity prod.** (2002): 6.31 bil. kWh.

Finance: Monetary unit: (MKD) Denar (Sept. 2004: 50.12 = $1 U.S.). **GDP** (2003 est.): $13.8 bil.; **per capita GDP:** $6,700; **GDP growth:** 2.8%. **Imports** (2003 est.): $2.2 bil.; partners (2002): Greece 18.2%, Germany 13.6%, Yugoslavia 8.6%, Slovenia 8.4%, Bulgaria 7%, Italy 6.4%, Turkey 5.6%. **Exports** (2003 est.): $1.3 bil.; partners (2002): Germany 27.4%, Italy 13.2%, U.S. 9.5%, Croatia 7.9%, Greece 6.6%, Netherlands 5.6%. **Tourism:** $57 mil. **Budget** (2003 est.): $1.1 bil. **Intl. reserves less gold:** $604 mil. **Gold:** 90,000 oz t. **Consumer prices:** 0.1%.

Transport: Railroad: Length: 434 mi. **Motor vehicles** (2000): 300,000 pass. cars, 23,300 comm. vehicles. **Civil aviation:** 460 mil. pass.-mi; 10 airports.

Communications: TV sets: 273 per 1,000 pop. **Radios:** 550 per 1,000 pop. **Telephone lines** (2002): 560,000. **Daily newspaper circ.:** 53.3 per 1,000 pop. **Internet** (2002): 100,000 users.

Health: Life expect.: 72.5 male; 77.2 female. **Births** (per 1,000 pop.): 13.1. **Deaths** (per 1,000 pop.): 7.8. **Natural inc.:** 0.53%. **Infant mortality** (per 1,000 live births): 11.7. **AIDS rate:** <0.1%.

Education: Free, compulsory: ages 7-14. **Literacy:** NA.

Major Intl. Organizations: UN (FAO, IBRD, ILO, IMF, IMO, WHO, WTrO).

Embassy: 1101 30th St., NW, Ste., 302, 20007; 337-3063.

Website: www.macedonianembassy.org

Macedonia, as part of a larger region also called Macedonia, was ruled by Muslim Turks from 1389 to 1912, when native Greeks, Bulgarians, and Slavs won independence. Serbia received the largest part of the territory, the rest going to Greece and Bulgaria. In 1913, the area was incorporated into Serbia, which in 1918 became part of the Kingdom of Serbs, Croats, and Slovenes (later Yugoslavia). In 1946, Macedonia became a constituent republic of Yugoslavia.

Macedonia declared its independence Sept. 8, 1991, and was admitted to the UN under a provisional name in 1993. A UN force, which included several hundred U.S. troops, was deployed there to deter the warring factions in Bosnia from carrying their dispute into other areas of the Balkans.

In Feb. 1994 both Russia and the U.S. recognized Macedonia. Greece, which objected to Macedonia's use of what it considered a Hellenic name and symbols, imposed a trade blockade on the landlocked nation; the 2 countries agreed to normalize relations Sept. 13, 1995. A car bombing, Oct. 3, seriously injured Pres. Kiro Gligorov. Macedonia and Yugoslavia signed a treaty normalizing relations Apr. 8, 1996.

By the end of NATO's air war against Yugoslavia, Mar.-June 1999, Macedonia had a Kosovar refugee population of more than 250,000; over 90% had been repatriated by Sept. 1. Boris Trajkovski, candidate of the ruling center-right coalition, won a presidential runoff vote Nov. 14.

Ethnic Albanian guerrillas launched an offensive Mar. 2001 in NW Macedonia. An accord signed Aug. 13 paved the way for the introduction of a NATO peacekeeping force. A law broadening the rights of ethnic Albanians was enacted Jan. 24, 2002. A 320-member EU force replaced the NATO peacekeepers Mar. 31, 2003. After Trajkovski died in a plane crash Feb. 26, 2004, Prime Min. Branko Crvenkovski won a presidential runoff vote Apr. 28.

Madagascar
Republic of Madagascar

People: Population: 17,501,871. **Age distrib.** (%): <15: 45; 65+: 3.2. **Pop. density:** 78 per sq mi, 30 per sq km. **Urban:** 26.5%. **Ethnic groups:** Mainly Malagasy (Indonesian-African); also Cotiers, French, Indian, Chinese. **Principal languages:** Malagasy, French (both official). **Chief religions:** Indigenous beliefs 52%, Christian 41%, Muslim 7%.

Geography: Total area: 226,657 sq mi, 587,040 sq km; **Land area:** 224,534 sq mi, 581,540 sq km. **Location:** In the Indian O., off the SE coast of Africa. **Neighbors:** Comoro Isls. to NW, Mozambique to W. **Topography:** Humid coastal strip in the E, fertile valleys in the mountainous center plateau region, and a wider coastal strip on the W. **Capital:** Antananarivo, 1,678,000.

Government: Type: Republic. **Head of state:** Pres. Marc Ravalomanana; b Dec. 12, 1949; in office: Feb. 22, 2002. **Head of gov.:** Prime Min. Jacques Sylla; b 1946; in office: Feb. 26, 2002 (de facto). **Local divisions:** 6 provinces. **Defense budget** (2003): $53 mil. **Active troops:** 13,500.

Economy: Industries: meat proc., soap, brewing, hides, sugar, textiles, glassware, cement, autos. **Chief crops:** coffee, vanilla, sugarcane, cloves, cocoa, rice, cassava, beans, bananas, peanuts. **Natural resources:** graphite, chromite, coal, bauxite, salt, quartz, tar sands, gemstones, mica, fish, hydropower. **Arable land:** 4%. **Livestock** (2003): cattle: 10.5 mil.; chickens: 24.0 mil.; goats: 1.2 mil.; pigs: 1.60 mil.; sheep: 650,000. **Fish catch** (2002): 149,250 metric tons. **Electricity prod.** (2002): 0.84 bil. kWh.

Finance: Monetary unit: Malagsy Franc (MGF) (Sept. 2004: 2,021.00 = $1 U.S.). **GDP** (2003 est.): $13.0 bil.; **per capita GDP:** $800; **GDP growth:** 6.0%. **Imports** (2003 est.): $920.0 mil.; partners (2002): France 37.9%, U.S. 19.1%, Germany 5.3%, Japan 4.7%, Singapore 4.1%. **Exports** (2003 est.): $700.0 mil.; partners (2002): France 39.2%, U.S. 19.8%, Germany 5.5%, Japan 4.8%, Singapore 4.2%. **Tourism** (2002): $36 mil. **Budget** (2001): $798.9 mil. **Intl. reserves less gold:** $279 mil. **Consumer prices:** –1.2%.

Transport: Railroad: Length: 455 mi. **Motor vehicles** (1998): 64,000 pass. cars, 9,100 comm. vehicles. **Civil aviation:** 563.6 mil. pass.-mi; 29 airports. **Chief ports:** Toamasina, Antsiranana, Mahajanga, Toliara, Antsohimbondrona.

Communications: TV sets: 23 per 1,000 pop. **Radios:** 209 per 1,000 pop. **Telephone lines:** 59,600. **Daily newspaper circ.:** 4.6 per 1,000 pop. **Internet:** 70,500 users.

Health: Life expect.: 54.2 male; 59.0 female. **Births** (per 1,000 pop.): 41.9. **Deaths** (per 1,000 pop.): 11.6. **Natural inc.:** 3.03%. **Infant mortality** (per 1,000 live births): 78.5. **AIDS rate:** 1.7%.

Education: Compulsory: ages 6-14. **Literacy:** 68.9%.

Major Intl. Organizations: UN (FAO, IBRD, ILO, IMF, IMO, WHO, WTrO), AU.

Embassy: 2374 Massachusetts Ave. NW 20008; 265-5525.

Website: www.embassy.org/madagascar

Madagascar was settled 2,000 years ago by Malayan-Indonesian people, whose descendants still predominate. A unified kingdom ruled the 18th and 19th centuries. The island became a French protectorate, 1885, and a colony 1896. Independence came June 26, 1960.

Discontent with inflation and French domination led to a coup in 1972. The new regime nationalized French-owned financial interests, closed French bases and a U.S. space-tracking station, and obtained Chinese aid. The government conducted a program of arrests, expulsion of foreigners, and repression of strikes, 1979.

In 1990, Madagascar ended a ban on multiparty politics that had been in place since 1975. Albert Zafy was elected president in 1993, ending the 17-year rule of Adm. Didier Ratsiraka. After Zafy was impeached by the legislature, Madagascar's constitutional court removed him from office, Sept. 5, 1996. Prime Min. Norbert Ratsirahonana then became interim president pending national elections, Nov. 3 and Dec. 29, in which Ratsiraka edged Zafy. A cholera epidemic, exacerbated by cyclones in Feb. and Apr. 2000, claimed at least 1,600 lives.

Marc Ravalomanana won a power struggle with Ratsiraka that followed a disputed presidential election Dec. 16, 2001.

Malawi
Republic of Malawi

People: Population: 11,906,855. **Age distrib.** (%): <15: 44; 65+: 2.8. **Pop. density:** 328 per sq mi, 127 per sq km. **Urban:** 16.3%. **Ethnic groups:** Chewa, Nyanja, Tumbuka, Yao, Lomwe, Sena, Tonga, Ngoni, Ngonde. **Principal languages:** Chichewa, English (both official), several African languages. **Chief religions:** Protestant 55%, Roman Catholic 20%, Muslim 20%.

Geography: Total area: 45,745 sq mi, 118,480 sq km; **Land area:** 36,324 sq mi, 94,080 sq km. **Location:** In SE Africa. **Neighbors:** Zambia on W, Mozambique on S and E, Tanzania on N. **Topography:** Malawi stretches 560 mi. N-S along Lake Malawi (Lake Nyasa), most of which belongs to Malawi. High plateaus and mountains line the Rift Valley the length of the nation. **Capital:** Lilongwe, 587,000. **Cities (urban aggr., 1998 est.):** Blantyre, 2,000,000.

Government: Type: Republic. **Head of state and gov.:** Pres. Bingu wa Mutharika; b Feb. 24, 1934; in office: May 24, 2004. **Lo-**cal divisions: 3 regions, 26 districts. **Defense budget** (2003): $12 mil. **Active troops:** 5,300.

Economy: Industries: tobacco, tea, sugar, wood products, cement, consumer goods. **Chief crops:** tobacco, sugarcane, cotton, tea, corn, potatoes, cassava, sorghum. **Natural resources:** limestone, hydropower, uranium, coal, bauxite. **Arable land:** 18%. **Livestock** (2003): cattle: 750,000; chickens: 15.2 mil.; goats: 1.7 mil.; pigs: 456,300; sheep: 115,000. **Fish catch** (2002): 41,971 metric tons. **Electricity prod.** (2002): 1.09 bil. kWh. **Labor force** (2003 est.): agriculture 90%.

Finance: Monetary unit: Kwacha (MWK) (Sept. 2004: 108.05 = $1 U.S.). **GDP** (2003 est.): $6.8 bil.; **per capita GDP:** $600; **GDP growth:** 1.7%. **Imports** (2003 est.): $505.0 mil.; partners (2002): South Africa 45.1%, Zambia 12.3%, U.S. 5.4%, India 4.1%. **Exports** (2003 est.): $455.0 mil.; partners (2002): South Africa 22%, U.S. 14.7%, Germany 12.2%, Egypt 5.3%, Japan 5.1%, Netherlands 4.7%, Russia 4.1%. **Tourism:** $72 mil. **Budget** (FY99/00 est.): $523.0 mil. **Intl. reserves less gold:** $85 mil. **Gold:** 10,000 oz t. **Consumer prices:** 9.6%.

Transport: Railroad: Length: 495 mi. **Motor vehicles** (1999): 12,600 pass. cars, 22,700 comm. vehicles. **Civil aviation:** 84.5 mil. pass.-mi; 6 airports.

Communications: TV sets: 3 per 1,000 pop. **Radios:** 476 per 1,000 pop. **Telephone lines:** 85,000. **Daily newspaper circ.:** 3 per 1,000 pop. **Internet:** 36,000 users.

Health: Life expect.: 37.1 male; 37.9 female. **Births** (per 1,000 pop.): 44.4. **Deaths** (per 1,000 pop.): 23.0. **Natural inc.:** 2.13%. **Infant mortality** (per 1,000 live births): 104.2. **AIDS rate:** 14.2%.

Education: Compulsory: ages 6-13. **Literacy:** 62.7%.

Major Intl. Organizations: UN (FAO, IBRD, ILO, IMF, IMO, WHO, WTrO), the Commonwealth, AU.

Embassy: 2408 Massachusetts Ave. NW 20008; 797-1007.

Website: www.malawi.gov.mw

Bantus came to the land in the 16th century, Arab slavers in the 19th. The area became the British protectorate Nyasaland in 1891. It became independent July 6, 1964, and a republic in 1966. After 3 decades as a one-party state under Pres. Hastings Kamuzu Banda, Malawi adopted a new constitution and, in multiparty elections held May 17, 1994, chose a new leader, Bakili Muluzi. Banda was acquitted, Dec. 23, 1995, of complicity in the deaths of 4 political opponents in 1983; he died Nov. 25, 1997. Bingu wa Mutharika, candidate of the ruling United Democratic Front, won a disputed presidential election May 20, 2004.

Malaysia

People: Population: 23,522,482. **Age distrib.** (%): <15: 34.1; 65+: 4.3. **Pop. density:** 185 per sq mi, 72 per sq km. **Urban:** 63.9%. **Ethnic groups:** Malay and other indigenous 58%, Chinese 24%, Indian 8%. **Principal languages:** Malay (official), English, Chinese dialects, Tamil, Telugu, Malayalam, Panjabi, Thai, Iban, and Kadazan in East. **Chief religions:** Muslim (official) 60%, Buddhist 19%, Christian 9%, Hindu 6%, Confucianist/Taoist 3%.

Geography: Total area: 127,317 sq mi, 329,750 sq km; **Land area:** 126,854 sq mi, 328,550 sq km. **Location:** On the SE tip of Asia, plus the N coast of the island of Borneo. **Neighbors:** Thailand on N, Indonesia on S. **Topography:** Most of W Malaysia is covered by tropical jungle, including the central mountain range that runs N-S through the peninsula. The western coast is marshy, the eastern, sandy. E Malaysia has a wide, swampy coastal plain, with interior jungles and mountains. **Capital:** Kuala Lumpur, 1,352,000.

Government: Type: Constitutional monarchy. **Head of state:** Paramount Ruler Syed Sirajuddin Syed Putra Jamalullail; b May 16, 1943; in office: Dec. 13, 2001. **Head of gov.:** Prime Min. Datuk Seri Abdullah Ahmad Badawi; b Nov. 26, 1939; in office: Oct. 31, 2003. **Local divisions:** 13 states, 3 federal territories. **Defense budget** (2003): $2.0 bil. **Active troops:** 104,000.

Economy: Industries: rubber & palm oil proc., light mfg., electronics, tin, mining, timber, oil. **Chief crops:** rubber, palm oil, cocoa, rice, coconuts, pepper. **Natural resources:** tin, oil, timber, copper, iron ore, nat. gas, bauxite. **Crude oil reserves** (2003): 3.0 bil. bbls. **Arable land:** 3%. **Livestock** (2003): cattle: 750,000; chickens: 170.0 mil.; goats: 245,000; pigs: 1.70 mil.; sheep: 110,000. **Fish catch** (2002): 1,440,674 metric tons. **Electricity prod.** (2002): 66.87 bil. kWh. **Labor force** (2000 est.): agriculture 14.5%, industry 36%, services 49.5%.

Finance: Monetary unit: Ringgit (MYR) (Sept. 2004: 3.80 = $1 U.S.). **GDP** (2003 est.): $207.2 bil.; **per capita GDP:** $9,000; **GDP growth:** 4.9%. **Imports** (2003 est.): $74.4 bil.; partners (2002): Japan 17.8%, U.S. 16.5%, Singapore 12%, China 7.7%, Taiwan 5.6%, South Korea 5.3%, Thailand 4%. **Exports** (2003 est.): $98.4 bil.; partners (2002): U.S. 20.2%, Singapore 17.1%, Japan 11.3%, Hong Kong 5.7%, China 5.6%, Thailand 4.3%. **Tourism** (2002): $6.8 bil. **Budget** (2004 est.): $28.9 bil. **Intl. reserves less gold:** $29.96 bil. **Gold:** 1.17 mil. oz t. **Consumer prices:** 1.1%.

Transport: Railroad: Length: 1,502 mi. **Motor vehicles** (2001): 400,400 pass. cars, 40,100 comm. vehicles. **Civil aviation:** 20.4 bil. pass.-mi; 35 airports. **Chief ports:** Kuantan, Kelang, Kota Kinabalu, Kuching.

Communications: TV sets: 174 per 1,000 pop. **Radios:** 434 per 1,000 pop. **Telephone lines:** 4.6 mil. **Daily newspaper circ.:** 158 per 1,000 pop. **Internet:** 8.7 mil. users.

Health: Life expect.: 69.3 male; 74.8 female. **Births** (per 1,000 pop.): 23.4. **Deaths** (per 1,000 pop.): 5.1. **Natural inc.:** 1.83%. **Infant mortality** (per 1,000 live births): 18.4. **AIDS rate:** 0.4%.

Education: Compulsory: ages 6-16. **Literacy:** 88.9%.

Major Intl. Organizations: UN (FAO, IBRD, ILO, IMF, IMO, WHO, WTrO), APEC, ASEAN, the Commonwealth.

Embassy: 3516 International Court NW 20008; 572-9700.

Websites: www.gov.my; www.tourism.gov.my

European traders appeared in the 16th century; Britain established control in 1867. Malaysia was created Sept. 16, 1963. It included Malaya (which had become independent in 1957 after the suppression of Communist rebels), plus the formerly British Singapore, Sabah (N Borneo), and Sarawak (NW Borneo). Singapore was separated in 1965, in order to end tensions between Chinese, the majority in Singapore, and Malays in control of the Malaysian government.

A monarch is elected by a council of hereditary rulers of the Malayan states every 5 years.

Abundant natural resources have bolstered prosperity, and foreign investment has aided industrialization. Work on a new federal capital at Putrajaya, south of Kuala Lumpur, began in 1995. However, sagging stock and currency prices forced the postponement of major development projects in Sept. 1997.

Mahathir bin Mohamad dominated Malaysian politics as prime minister, 1981-2003. His successor, Abdullah Ahmad Badawi, took office Oct. 31, 2003, and led his National Front coalition to a resounding win in parliamentary elections Mar. 21, 2004.

Maldives
Republic of Maldives

People: Population: 339,330. **Age distrib.** (%): <15: 45.3; 65+: 3. **Pop. density:** 2,930 per sq mi, 1,131 per sq km. **Urban:** 28.8%. **Ethnic groups:** Dravidian, Sinhalese, Arab. **Principal languages:** Divehi (Sinhala dialect, Arabic script; official), English. **Chief religion:** Muslim (official; mostly Sunni).

Geography: Total area: 116 sq mi, 300 sq km; **Land area:** 116 sq mi, 300 sq km. **Location:** In the Indian O., SW of India. **Neighbors:** Nearest is India on N. **Topography:** 19 atolls with 1,190 islands, 198 inhabited. None of the islands are over 5 sq. mi. in area, and all are nearly flat. **Capital:** Male, 83,000.

Government: Type: Republic. **Head of state and gov.:** Pres. Maumoon Abdul Gayoom; b Dec. 29, 1937; in office: Nov. 11, 1978. **Local divisions:** 19 atolls and Male capital atoll. **Defense budget:** $36 mil. **Active troops:** NA.

Economy: Industries: fish proc., tourism, shipping, boat building, coconut proc., garments. **Chief crops:** coconuts, corn, sweet potatoes. **Natural resources:** fish. **Arable land:** 10%. **Fish catch** (2002): 160,981 metric tons. **Electricity prod.** (2002): 0.12 bil. kWh. **Labor force** (1995): agriculture 22%, industry 18%, services 60%.

Finance: Monetary unit: Rufiyaa (MVR) (Sept. 2004: 11.77 = $1 U.S.). **GDP** (2002 est.): $1.3 bil.; **per capita GDP:** $3,900; **GDP growth:** 2.3%. **Imports** (2002 est.): $392.0 mil.; partners (2002): Singapore 26.6%, UAE 15%, Sri Lanka 13.2%, India 7%, Malaysia 5.7%, Thailand 4.1%. **Exports** (2002 est.): $90.0 mil.; partners (2002): U.S. 52.6%, Sri Lanka 13.3%, Thailand 9.5%, Japan 7.6%, UK 4.7%. **Tourism:** $388 mil. **Budget** (2002 est.): $282.0 mil. **Intl. reserves less gold:** $107 mil. **Consumer prices:** -2.9%.

Transport: Motor vehicles (2001): 100 pass. cars, 100 comm. vehicles. **Civil aviation:** 239.2 mil. pass.-mi; 2 airports. **Chief ports:** Male, Gan.

Communications: TV sets: 38 per 1,000 pop. **Radios:** 129 per 1,000 pop. **Telephone lines** (2002): 28,700. **Daily newspaper circ.:** 12 per 1,000 pop. **Internet** (2002): 15,000 users.

Health: Life expect.: 62.4 male; 65.0 female. **Births** (per 1,000 pop.): 36.1. **Deaths** (per 1,000 pop.): 7.4. **Natural inc.:** 2.86%. **Infant mortality** (per 1,000 live births): 58.3.

Education: Compulsory: ages 6-12. **Literacy:** 97.2%.

Major Intl. Organizations: UN (FAO, IBRD, IMF, IMO, WHO, WTrO), the Commonwealth.

Permanent UN Representative: 111 E. 69th St., New York, NY 10021; (212) 737-4150.

Website: www.themaldives.com

The islands had been a British protectorate since 1887. The country became independent July 26, 1965. Long a sultanate, the Maldives became a republic in 1968. Natural resources and tourism are being developed; however, the Maldives remains one of the world's poorest countries. Tourism and fishing are the most important sectors of the economy. Pres. Gayoom has held power since 1978; political parties are suppressed.

Mali
Republic of Mali

People: Population: 11,956,788. **Age distrib.** (%): <15: 47.2; 65+: 3. **Pop. density:** 25 per sq mi, 10 per sq km. **Urban:** 32.3%. **Ethnic groups:** Mande 50% (Bambara, Malinke, Soninke), Peul 17%, Voltaic 12%, Tuareg and Moor 10%, Songhai 6%. **Principal languages:** French (official); Bambara and other African languages. **Chief religions:** Muslim 90%, indigenous beliefs 9%.

Geography: Total area: 478,766 sq mi, 1,240,000 sq km; **Land area:** 471,044 sq mi, 1,220,000 sq km. **Location:** In the interior of W Africa. **Neighbors:** Mauritania, Senegal on W; Guinea, Côte d'Ivoire, Burkina Faso on S; Niger on E; Algeria on N. **Topography:** A landlocked grassy plain in the upper basins of the Senegal and Niger rivers, extending N into the Sahara. **Capital:** Bamako, 1,264,000.

Government: Type: Republic. **Head of state:** Pres. Amadou Toumani Touré; b Nov. 4, 1948; in office: June 8, 2002. **Head of gov.:** Prime Min. Ousmane Issoufi Maïga; b 1946; in office: Apr. 30, 2004. **Local divisions:** 8 regions, 1 capital district. **Defense budget** (2003): $91 mil. **Active troops:** 7,350.

Economy: Industries: food proc., constr., phosphates, gold. **Chief crops:** cotton, millet, rice, corn, vegetables, peanuts. **Natural resources:** gold, phosphates, kaolin, salt, limestone, uranium, hydropower. **Arable land:** 2%. **Livestock** (2003): cattle: 7.31 mil.; chickens: 29.0 mil.; goats: 11.5 mil.; pigs: 67,600; sheep: 7.97 mil. **Fish catch** (2002 est): 101,008 metric tons. **Electricity prod.** (2002): 0.7 bil. kWh. **Labor force** (2001 est.): agriculture and fishing 80%.

Finance: Monetary unit: CFA Franc BCEAO (XOF) (Sept. 2004: 539.40 = $1 U.S.). **GDP** (2003 est.): $10.5 bil.; **per capita GDP:** $900; **GDP growth:** 0.5%. **Imports** (2002 est.): $927.0 mil.; partners (2002): Cote d'Ivoire 16.9%, France 13.4%, Senegal 6.4%. **Exports** (2002 est.): $915.0 mil.; partners (2002): Thailand 14.4%, Italy 10.2%, India 7.8%, Germany 4.8%, Spain 4.8%, Mauritius 4.2%, Portugal 4.2%. **Tourism:** $71 mil. **Budget** (2002 est.): $828.0 mil. **Intl. reserves less gold:** $611 mil. **Consumer prices:** -1.35%.

Transport: Railroad: Length: 453 mi. **Motor vehicles:** (1999): 17,600 pass. cars, 28,100 comm. vehicles. **Civil aviation:** 134.2 mil. pass.-mi; 7 airports. **Chief port:** Koulikoro.

Communications: TV sets: 13 per 1,000 pop. **Radios:** 55 per 1,000 pop. **Telephone lines** (2002): 56,600. **Daily newspaper circ.:** 1.2 per 1,000 pop. **Internet** (2002): 25,000 users.

Health: Life expect.: 44.7 male; 45.9 female. **Births** (per 1,000 pop.): 47.3. **Deaths** (per 1,000 pop.): 19.1. **Natural inc.:** 2.82%. **Infant mortality** (per 1,000 live births): 118.0. **AIDS rate:** 1.9%.

Education: Compulsory: ages 7-15. **Literacy:** 46.4%.

Major Intl. Organizations: UN and most of its specialized agencies, AU.

Embassy: 2130 R St. NW 20008; 332-2249.

Website: www.maliembassy-usa.org

Until the 15th century the area was part of the great Mali Empire. Timbuktu (Tombouctou) was a center of Islamic study. French rule was secured, 1898. The Sudanese Rep. and Senegal became independent as the Mali Federation June 20, 1960, but Senegal withdrew, and the Sudanese Rep. was renamed Mali.

Mali signed economic agreements with France and, in 1963, with Senegal. In 1968, a coup ended the socialist regime. Famine struck in 1973-74, killing as many as 100,000 people. Drought conditions returned in the 1980s.

The military, Mar. 26, 1991, overthrew the government of Pres. Moussa Traoré, who had been in power since 1968. Oumar Konare, a coup leader, was elected president, Apr. 26, 1992. A peace accord between the government and a Tuareg rebel group was signed in June 1994. Konare and his party won a series of flawed elections, Apr.-Aug. 1997. Twice condemned to death for crimes committed in office, Traoré had his sentences commuted to life imprisonment in Dec. 1997 and Sept. 1999.

Amadou Toumani Touré, who led the 1991 coup, won a presidential runoff election May 12, 2002.

Malta
Republic of Malta

People: Population: 396,851 **Age distrib.** (%): <15: 19.7; 65+: 12.8. **Pop. density:** 3,253 per sq mi, 1,256 per sq km. **Urban:** 91.7%. **Ethnic group:** Maltese, other Mediterranean. **Principal languages:** Maltese (a Semitic dialect), English (both official). **Chief religion:** Roman Catholic 91% (official).

Geography: Total area: 122 sq mi, 316 sq km; **Land area:** 122 sq mi, 316 sq km. **Location:** In center of Mediterranean Sea. **Neighbors:** Nearest is Italy on N. **Topography:** Island of Malta is 95 sq. mi.; other islands in the group: Gozo, 26 sq. mi.; Comino, 1 sq. mi. The coastline is heavily indented. Low hills cover the interior. **Capital:** Valletta, 83,000.

Government: Type: Parliamentary democracy. **Head of state:** Pres. Edward (Eddie) Fenech-Adami; b Feb. 7, 1934; in office: Apr. 4, 2004. **Head of gov.:** Prime Min. Lawrence Gonzi; b July 1, 1953; in office: Mar. 23, 2004. **Local divisions:** 3 regions comprising 67 local councils. **Defense budget** (2003): $31 mil. **Active troops:** 2,140.

Economy: Industries: tourism, electronics, shipbuilding, food & beverages, textiles. **Chief crops:** potatoes, cauliflower, grapes, wheat, barley, tomatoes, citrus. **Natural resources:** limestone, salt. **Arable land:** 38%. **Livestock** (2003): cattle: 17,940; chickens: 958,000; goats: 5,374; pigs: 73,067; sheep: 14,861. **Fish catch** (2002): 2,120 metric tons. **Electricity prod.** (2002): 2.15 bil. kWh. **Labor force** (1999 est.): industry 24%, services 71%, agriculture 5%.

Finance: Monetary unit: Lira (MTL) (Sept. 2004: 0.35 = $1 U.S.). **GDP** (2003 est.): $7.1 bil.; **per capita GDP:** $17,700; **GDP growth:** 0.8%. **Imports** (2003 est.): $2.8 bil.; partners (2002): Italy 18.2%, France 12%, South Korea 11.3%, UK 7.5%, Germany 5.3%, Singapore 5.3%, Japan 4.9%, U.S. 4.6%, Spain 4.2%. **Exports** (2003 est.): $2.2 bil.; partners (2002): Singapore 17.3%, U.S. 11.4%, UK 9.4%, Germany 9.2%, France 7.3%, China 6.5%, Italy 5.9%. **Tourism** (2002): $568 mil. **Budget** (2000): $1.6 bil. **Intl. reserves less gold** (2002): $1.63 bil. **Gold** (2001): 10,000 oz t. **Consumer prices:** 0.5%.

Transport: Motor vehicles (2001): 219,000 pass. cars, 52,600 comm. vehicles. **Civil aviation:** 1.5 bil. pass.-mi; 1 airport. **Chief ports:** Valletta, Marsaxlokk.

Communications: TV sets: 549 per 1,000 pop. **Radios:** 669 per 1,000 pop. **Telephone lines:** 208,300. **Daily newspaper circ.:** 133 per 1,000 pop. **Internet** (2002): 120,000 users.

Health: Life expect.: 76.5 male; 81.0 female. **Births** (per 1,000 pop.): 10.1. **Deaths** (per 1,000 pop.): 7.9. **Natural inc.:** 0.22%. **Infant mortality** (per 1,000 live births): 3.9. **AIDS rate:** 0.2%.

Education: Compulsory: ages 5-15. **Literacy:** 92.8%.

Major Intl. Organizations: UN (FAO, IBRD, ILO, IMF, IMO, WHO, WTrO), the Commonwealth, EU,OSCE.

Embassy: 2017 Connecticut Ave. NW 20008; 462-3611.

Websites: www.gov.mt;
www.foreign.gov.mt/ORG/ministry/missions/washington2.htm

Malta was ruled by Phoenicians, Romans, Arabs, Normans, the Knights of Malta, France, and Britain (since 1814). It became independent Sept. 21, 1964. Malta became a republic in 1974. The withdrawal of the last British sailors, Apr. 1, 1979, ended 179 years of British military presence on the island.

From 1971 to 1987 and again from 1996 to 1998, Malta was governed by the socialist Labour Party; the Nationalist Party, which pressed for Malta's entry into the EU, held office 1987-96 and won the elections of Sept. 5, 1998, and Apr. 12, 2003. Malta became a full member of the EU May 1, 2004.

Marshall Islands
Republic of the Marshall Islands

People: Population: 57,738 **Age distrib.** (%): <15: 49.1; 65+: 2. **Pop. density:** 825 per sq mi, 318 per sq km. **Urban:** 66.3%. **Ethnic groups:** Micronesian. **Principal languages:** English, Marshallese (both official); Malay-Polynesian dialects, Japanese. **Chief religion:** Mostly Protestant.

Geography: Total area: 70 sq mi, 181.3 sq km; **Land area:** 70 sq mi, 181.3 sq km. **Location:** In N Pacific Ocean; composed of two 800-mi-long parallel chains of coral atolls. **Neighbors:** Nearest are Micronesia to W, Nauru and Kiribati to S. **Topography:** Marshall Islands are low coral limestone and sand islands. **Capital:** Majuro, 25,000.

Government: Type: Republic. **Head of state and gov.:** Pres. Kessai Note; b 1950; in office: Jan. 10, 2000. **Local divisions:** 33 municipalities.

Economy: Industries: copra, fish, tourism, handicrafts, wood, pearls. **Chief crops:** coconuts, tomatoes, melons, taro, breadfruit, fruits. **Natural resources:** fish, minerals. **Fish catch** (2002): 38,742 metric tons. **Labor force:** agriculture 21.4%, industry 20.9%, services 57.7%.

Finance: Monetary unit: U.S. Dollar. **GDP** (2001 est.): $115.0 mil.; **per capita GDP:** $1,600; **GDP growth:** 1.0%. **Imports** (2000): $54.0 mil.; partners (2000): U.S., Japan, Australia, NZ, Singapore, Fiji, China, Philippines. **Exports** (2000): $9.0 mil.; partners (2000): U.S., Japan, Australia, China. **Tourism** (2002): $4 mil. **Budget** (1999): $40.0 mil.

Transport: Civil aviation: 1.2 mil. pass.-mi; 4 airports. **Chief port:** Majuro.

Communications: Telephone lines: 4,500. **Internet:** 1,400 users.

Health: Life expect.: 67.8 male; 71.7 female. **Births** (per 1,000 pop.): 33.9. **Deaths** (per 1,000 pop.): 4.9. **Natural inc.:** 2.89%. **Infant mortality** (per 1,000 live births): 30.5.

Education: Compulsory: ages 6-14. **Literacy** (1999): 93.7%.

Major Intl. Organizations: UN (IBRD, IMF, WHO).

Embassy: 2433 Massachusetts Ave. NW 20008; 234-5414.

Website: www.rmiembassyus.org

The Marshall Islands were a German possession until World War I and were administered by Japan between the World Wars. After WW II, they were administered as part of the UN Trust Territory of the Pacific Islands by the U.S. From 1946-1958, Bikini and Enewetak atolls were used as test sites for the U.S. nuclear weapons program, including the Hydrogen bomb.

The Compact of Free Association, ratified by the U.S. on Oct. 21, 1986, gave the islands their independence. In the compact, the U.S. agreed to provide financial aid to the islands, maintain their defense, and compensate victims of nuclear testing; it was renewed Dec. 2003. The Marshall Islands joined the UN Sept. 17, 1991. Amata Kabua, the islands' first and only president since 1979, died Dec. 19, 1996. His cousin Imata Kabua, elected president Jan. 13, 1997, was succeeded by Kessai Note on Jan. 10, 2000; he began a 2nd term Jan. 5, 2004.

Mauritania
Islamic Republic of Mauritania

People: Population: 2,998,563. **Age distrib.** (%): <15: 46.1; 65+: 2.2. **Pop. density:** 8 per sq mi, 3 per sq km. **Urban:** 61.8%. **Ethnic groups:** Mixed Maur/Black 40%, Maur 30%, Black 30%. **Principal languages:** Hassaniya Arabic, Wolof (both official); Fulani, Pulaar, Soninke (all national); French. **Chief religion:** Predominantly Muslim (official).

Geography: Total area: 397,955 sq mi, 1,030,700 sq km; **Land area:** 397,840 sq mi, 1,030,400 sq km. **Location:** In NW Africa. **Neighbors:** Morocco on N, Algeria and Mali on E, Senegal

on S. **Topography:** The fertile Senegal R. valley in the S gives way to a wide central region of sandy plains and scrub trees. The N is arid and extends into the Sahara. **Capital:** Nouakchott, 600,000.

Government: Type: Islamic republic. **Head of state:** Pres. Maaouya Ould Sidi Ahmed Taya; b 1941; in office: Apr. 18, 1992. **Head of gov.:** Prime Min. Sghair Ould M'Bareck; b 1954; in office: July 6, 2003. **Local divisions:** 12 regions, 1 capital district. **Defense budget** (2003): $18.7 mil. **Active troops:** 15,750.

Economy: Industries: fish proc., iron ore, gypsum. **Chief crops:** dates, millet, sorghum, rice, corn. **Natural resources:** iron ore, gypsum, copper, phosphate, diamonds, gold, oil, fish. **Livestock** (2003): cattle: 1.5 mil.; chickens: 4.2 mil.; goats: 5.5 mil.; sheep: 8.7 mil. **Fish catch** (2002 est): 78,902 metric tons. **Electricity Prod.** (2002): 0.19 bil. kWh. **Labor force** (2001 est.): agriculture 50%, services 40%, industry 10%.

Finance: Monetary unit: Ouguiya (MRO) (Sept. 2004: 253.52=1 U.S.). **GDP** (2003 est.): $5.2 bil.; **per capita GDP:** $1,800; **GDP growth:** 4.5%. **Imports** (2002): $860.0 mil.; partners (2002): France 17.6%, Belgium 7.4%, China 6.6%, Spain 5.7%, Germany 5%. **Exports** (2002): $541.0 mil.; partners (2002): Italy 14.2%, France 13.9%, Spain 11.6%, Germany 10.7%, Belgium 9.8%, Japan 7%. **Tourism** (1999): $28 mil. **Budget** (2002 est.): $378.0 mil. **Intl. reserves less gold:** $280 mil. **Gold:** 10,000 oz t. **Consumer prices:** 5.2%.

Transport: Railroad: Length: 446 mi. **Motor vehicles** (1999): 9,900 pass. cars, 17,300 comm. vehicles. **Civil aviation:** 147.9 mil. pass.-mi; 10 airports. **Chief ports:** Nouakchott, Nouadhibou.

Communications: TV sets: 95 per 1,000 pop. **Radios:** 146 per 1,000 pop. **Telephone lines** (2002): 31,500. **Daily newspaper circ.:** .5 per 1,000 pop. **Internet** (2002): 10,000 users.

Health: Life expect.: 50.2 male; 54.6 female. **Births** (per 1,000 pop.): 41.8. **Deaths** (per 1,000 pop.): 12.7. **Natural inc.:** 2.90%. **Infant mortality** (per 1,000 live births): 72.4. **AIDS rate:** 0.6%.

Education: Compulsory: ages 6-14. **Literacy:** 41.7%.

Major Intl. Organizations: UN (FAO, IBRD, ILO, IMF, IMO, WHO, WTrO), AL, AU.

Embassy: 2129 Leroy Pl. NW 20008; 232-5700.

Websites: www.ambarim-dc.org; www.mauritania.mr

Mauritania was a French protectorate from 1903. It became independent Nov. 28, 1960 and annexed the south of former Spanish Sahara (now Western Sahara) in 1976. Saharan guerrillas of the Polisario Front stepped up attacks in 1977; 8,000 Moroccan troops and French bomber raids aided the government. Mauritania signed a peace treaty with the Polisario Front, 1979, and renounced sovereignty over its share of Western Sahara.

Maaouiya Ould Sid Ahmed Taya took power in a military coup in 1984. Opposition parties were legalized and a new constitution approved in 1991. Pres. Taya was reelected with 67% of the vote, Nov. 7, 2003; opposition leaders were allegedly harassed.

Although slavery has been repeatedly abolished, most recently in 1980, thousands of Mauritanians continued to live under conditions of servitude.

Mauritius
Republic of Mauritius

People: Population: 1,220,481. **Age distrib.** (%): <15: 25.4; 65+: 6.3. **Pop. density:** 1,557 per sq mi, 601 per sq km. **Urban:** 43.3%. **Ethnic groups:** Indo-Mauritian 68%, Creole 27%, Sino-Mauritian 3%, Franco-Mauritian 2%. **Principal languages:** English (official), Creole, French, Hindi, Urdu, Hakka, Bhojpuri. **Chief religions:** Hindu 52%, Christian 28%, Muslim 17%.

Geography: Total area: 788 sq mi, 2,040 sq km; **Land area:** 784 sq mi, 2,030 sq km. **Location:** In the Indian O., 500 mi. E of Madagascar. **Neighbors:** Nearest is Madagascar to W. **Topography:** A volcanic island nearly surrounded by coral reefs. A central plateau is encircled by mountain peaks. **Capital:** Port Louis, 143,000.

Government: Type: Republic. **Head of state:** Pres. Karl Auguste Offmann; b Nov. 25, 1940; in office: Feb. 25, 2002. **Head of state:** Pres. Aneerood Jugnauth; b Mar. 29, 1930; in office: Oct. 7, 2003. **Head of gov.:** Prime Min. Paul Berenger; b Mar. 26, 1945; in office: Sept. 30, 2003. **Local divisions:** 9 districts, 3 dependencies. **Defense budget** (2003): $8.9 mil. **Active troops:** Nil

Economy: Industries: sugar & food proc., textiles, clothing, chemicals. **Chief crops:** sugarcane, tea, corn, potatoes, bananas. **Natural resources:** fish. **Arable land:** 49%. **Livestock** (2003): cattle: 28,000; chickens: 9.8 mil.; goats: 93,000; pigs: 12,925; sheep: 11,500. **Fish catch** (2002): 10,762 metric tons. **Electricity prod.** (2002): 1.84 bil. kWh. **Labor force** (1995): construction and industry 36%, services 24%, agriculture and fishing 14%, trade, restaurants, hotels 16%, transportation and communication 7%, finance 3%.

Finance: Monetary unit: Rupee (MUR) (Sept. 2004: 28.50=1 U.S.). **GDP** (2003 est.): $13.9 bil.; **per capita GDP:** $11,400; **GDP growth:** 4.1%. **Imports** (2003 est.): $2.1 bil.; partners (2002): South Africa 12.6%, France 11%, China 8.5%, India 7.3%, Australia 4%. **Exports** (2003 est.): $2.0 bil.; partners (2002): UK 30.5%, France 20.3%, U.S. 20.2%, Madagascar 4%. **Tourism:** $695 mil. **Budget** (1999 est.): $1.2 bil. **Intl. reserves less gold:** $1.06 bil. **Gold:** 60,000 oz t. **Consumer prices:** 4.2%.

Transport: Motor vehicles (2001): 92,700 pass. cars, 36,500 comm. vehicles. **Civil aviation:** 3.0 bil. pass.-mi; 2 airports. **Chief port:** Port Louis.

Communications: TV sets: 248 per 1,000 pop. **Radios:** 371 per 1,000 pop. **Telephone lines:** 348,200. **Daily newspaper circ.:** 118.8 per 1,000 pop. **Internet:** 150,000 users.

Health: Life expect.: 68.1 male; 76.1 female. **Births** (per 1,000 pop.): 15.8. **Deaths** (per 1,000 pop.): 6.8. **Natural inc.:** 0.90%. **Infant mortality** (per 1,000 live births): 15.6.

Education: Compulsory: ages 6-11. **Literacy:** 85.6%.

Major Intl. Organizations: UN and all of its specialized agencies, the Commonwealth, AU.

Embassy: 4301 Connecticut Ave. NW, Suite 441, 20008; 244-1491.

Website: www.gov.mu; www.maurinet.com/embasydc.html

Mauritius was uninhabited when settled in 1638 by the Dutch, who introduced sugarcane. France took over in 1721, bringing African slaves. Britain ruled from 1810 to Mar. 12, 1968, bringing Indian workers for the sugar plantations.

Mauritius formally severed its association with the British crown Mar. 12, 1992.

Mexico
United Mexican States

People: Population: 104,959,594. **Age distrib.** (%): <15: 32.8; 65+: 4.5. **Pop. density:** 141 per sq mi, 55 per sq km. **Urban:** 75.5%. **Ethnic groups:** Mestizo 60%, Amerindian 30%, White 9%. **Principal languages:** Spanish (official), Náhuatl, Maya, Zapotec, Otomi, Mixtec, other indigenous. **Chief religions:** Roman Catholic 89%, Protestant 6%.

Geography: Total area: 761,606 sq mi, 1,972,550 sq km; **Land area:** 742,490 sq mi, 1,923,040 sq km. **Location:** In southern North America. **Neighbors:** U.S. on N, Guatemala and Belize on S. **Topography:** The Sierra Madre Occidental Mts. run NW-SE near the west coast; the Sierra Madre Oriental Mts. run near the Gulf of Mexico. They join S of Mexico City. Between the 2 ranges lies the dry central plateau, 5,000 to 8,000 ft. alt., rising toward the S, with temperate vegetation. Coastal lowlands are tropical. About 45% of land is arid. **Capital:** Mexico City, 18,660,000. **Cities (urban aggr.):** Guadalajara, 3,697,000; Monterrey, 3,267,000; Puebla, 1,888,000.

Government: Type: Federal republic. **Head of state and gov.:** Pres. Vicente Fox Quesada; b July 2, 1942; in office: Dec. 1, 2000. **Local divisions:** 31 states, 1 federal district. **Defense budget** (2003): $3.1 bil. **Active troops:** 192,770.

Economy: Industries: food & beverages, tobacco, chemicals, iron & steel, oil, mining, textiles, clothing, autos, consumer durables, tourism. **Chief crops:** corn, wheat, soybeans, rice, beans, cotton, coffee, fruit, tomatoes. **Natural resources:** oil, silver, copper, gold, lead, zinc, nat. gas, timber. **Crude oil reserves** (2003): 12.6 bil. bbls. **Arable land:** 12%. **Livestock** (2003): cattle: 30.8 mil.; chickens: 540 mil.; goats: 9.5 mil.; pigs: 18.1 mil.; sheep: 6.56 mil. **Fish catch** (2002): 1,524,329 metric tons. **Electricity prod.** (2002): 203.65 bil. kWh. **Labor force** (2003): agriculture 18%, industry 24%, services 58%.

Finance: Monetary unit: Peso (MXN) (Sept. 2004: 11.53=1 U.S.). **GDP** (2003 est.): $942.2 bil.; **per capita GDP:** $9,000; **GDP growth:** 1.2%. **Imports** (2003 est.): $168.9 bil.; partners (2002): U.S. 63.2%, Japan 5.5%, China 3.7%. **Exports** (2003 est.): $164.8 bil.; partners (2002): U.S. 89%, Canada 1.7%, Spain 0.9%. **Tourism:** $9.5 bil. **Budget** (2004 est.): $176.0 bil. **Intl. reserves less gold:** $39.68 bil. **Gold:** 170,000 oz t. **Consumer prices:** 4.5%.

Transport: Railroad: Length: 12,123 mi. **Motor vehicles** (2001): 11 mil pass. cars, 4.89 mil comm. vehicles. **Civil aviation:** 9.4 bil. pass.-mi; 231 airports. **Chief ports:** Coatzacoalcos, Mazatlan, Tampico, Veracruz.

Communications: TV sets: 272 per 1,000 pop. **Radios:** 329 per 1,000 pop. **Telephone lines** (2002): 14.9 mil. **Daily newspaper circ.:** 93.6 per 1,000 pop. **Internet** (2002): 10.0 mil. users.

Health: Life expect.: 72.2 male; 77.8 female. **Births** (per 1,000 pop.): 21.4. **Deaths** (per 1,000 pop.): 4.7. **Natural inc.:** 1.67%. **Infant mortality** (per 1,000 live births): 21.7. **AIDS rate:** 0.3%.

Education: Compulsory: ages 6-15. **Literacy:** 92.2%.

Major Intl. Organizations: UN (FAO, IBRD, ILO, IMF, IMO, WHO, WTrO), APEC, OAS, OECD.

Embassy: 1911 Pennsylvania Ave. NW 20006; 728-1600.

Website: portal.sre.gob.mx/usa

Mexico was the site of advanced Indian civilizations. The Mayas, an agricultural people, moved up from Yucatan, built immense stone pyramids, invented a calendar. The Toltecs were overcome by the Aztecs, who founded Tenochtitlan AD 1325, now Mexico City. Hernando Cortes, Spanish conquistador, destroyed the Aztec empire, 1519-21.

After 3 centuries of Spanish rule the people rose, under Fr. Miguel Hidalgo y Costilla, 1810, Fr. Morelos y Payon, 1812, and Gen. Agustin Iturbide, who made himself emperor as Agustin I, 1821. A republic was declared in 1823.

Mexican territory extended into the present American Southwest and California until Texas revolted and established a republic

in 1836; the Mexican legislature refused recognition but was unable to enforce its authority there. After numerous clashes, the U.S.-Mexican War, 1846-48, resulted in the loss by Mexico of the lands north of the Rio Grande.

French arms supported an Austrian archduke on the throne of Mexico as Maximilian I, 1864-67, but pressure from the U.S. forced France to withdraw. Dictatorial rule by Porfirio Diaz, president 1877-80, 1884-1911, led to a period of rebellion and factional fighting. A new constitution, Feb. 5, 1917, brought social reform.

The Institutional Revolutionary Party (PRI) dominated politics from 1929 until the late 1990s. Radical opposition, including some guerrilla activity, was contained by strong measures. Some gains in agriculture, industry, and social services were achieved, but much of the work force remained jobless or underemployed. Although prospects brightened with the discovery of vast oil reserves, inflation and a drop in world oil prices aggravated Mexico's economic problems in the 1980s.

Mexico reached agreement with the U.S. and Canada on the North American Free Trade Agreement (NAFTA) Aug. 12, 1992; it took effect Jan. 1, 1994.

Guerrillas of the Zapatista National Liberation Army (EZLN) launched an uprising, Jan. 1, 1994, in southern Mexico. A tentative peace accord was reached Mar. 2. The presidential candidate of the governing PRI, Luis Donaldo Colosio Murrieta, was assassinated at a political rally in Tijuana, Mar. 23. The new PRI candidate, Ernesto Zedillo Ponce de León, won election Aug. 21 and was inaugurated Dec. 1, 1994.

An austerity plan and pledges of aid from the U.S. saved Mexico's currency from collapse in early 1995. Popular Revolutionary Army guerrillas launched coordinated attacks on government targets in Aug. 1996. In elections July 6, 1997, the PRI failed to win a congressional majority for the first time since 1929. An armed gang massacred 45 peasants in Chiapas on Dec. 22, 1997.

In the presidential election of July 2, 2000, the PRI lost for the 1st time in over 7 decades; the winner, opposition candidate Vicente Fox Quesada, took office Dec. 1, 2000. Fox's National Action Party suffered a setback in midterm elections, July 6, 2003.

Micronesia
Federated States of Micronesia

People: Population: 108,155. **Age distrib.** (%): <15: NA; 65+: NA. **Pop. density:** 399 per sq mi, 154 per sq km. **Urban:** 29.3%. **Ethnic groups:** Nine distinct Micronesian and Polynesian groups. **Principal languages:** English (official), Trukese, Pohnpeian, Yapese, Kosrean, Ulithian, Woleaian, Nukuoro, Kapingamaran. **Chief religions:** Roman Catholic 50%, Protestant 47%.

Geography: Total area: 271 sq mi, 702 sq km; **Land area:** 271 sq mi, 702 sq km. **Location:** Consists of 607 islands in the W Pacific Ocean. **Topography:** The country includes both high mountainous islands and low coral atolls; volcanic outcroppings on Pohnpei, Kosrae, and Truk. Climate is tropical. **Capital:** Palikir, on Pohnpei, 7,000 (1994 island pop.) 33,372.

Government: Type: Republic. **Head of state and gov.:** Pres. Joseph J. Urusemal; b Mar. 19, 1952; in office: May 11, 2003. **Local divisions:** 4 states.

Economy: Industries: tourism, constr., fish proc., handicrafts. **Chief crops:** black pepper, fruits & vegetables, coconuts, cassava, sweet potatoes. **Natural resources:** timber, fish, minerals. **Livestock** (2003): cattle: 13,900; chickens: 185,000; goats: 4,000; pigs: 32,000. **Fish catch** (2002 est): 20,387 metric tons. **Electricity prod.:** NA. **Labor force:** two-thirds are government employees.

Finance: Monetary unit: U.S. Dollar. **GDP** (2002 est.): $277.0 mil.; **per capita GDP:** $2,000; **GDP growth:** 1.0%. **Imports** (FY99/00 est.): $149.0 mil.; partners (2000): U.S., Australia, Japan. **Exports** (FY99/00 est.): $22.0 mil.; partners (2000): Japan, U.S., Guam. **Tourism** (2001): $13 mil. **Budget** (1998 est.): $160.0 mil. **Intl. reserves less gold:** $60 mil.

Transport: 6 airports. **Chief ports:** Colonia (Yap), Kolonia (Pohnpei), Lele, Moen.

Communications: TV sets: 20 per 1,000 pop. **Radios:** 70 per 1,000 pop. **Telephone lines:** 10,100. **Internet:** 5,000 users.

Health: Life expect.: 67.7 male; 71.3 female. **Births** (per 1,000 pop.): 25.8. **Deaths** (per 1,000 pop.): 5.0. **Natural inc.:** 2.08%. **Infant mortality** (per 1,000 live births): 31.3.

Education: Compulsory: ages 6-13. **Literacy** (1991): 90%.

Major Intl. Organizations: UN (IBRD, IMF, WHO).

Embassy: 1725 N St. NW 20036; 223-4383.

Websites: www.fsmgov.org; www.visit-fsm.org

The Federated States of Micronesia, formerly known as the Caroline Islands, was ruled successively by Spain, Germany, Japan, and the U.S. The nation gained independence under a compact of free association with the U.S., Nov. 1986 and was admitted to the UN, Sept. 17, 1991. Tropical Storm Chata'an July 1-2, 2002, left 47 people dead and over 1,000 homeless in Chuuk. Typhoon Sudal battered Yap Apr. 9, 2004, leaving at least 1,500 homeless.

Moldova
Republic of Moldova

People: Population: 4,446,455. **Age distrib.** (%): <15: 21.7; 65+: 10.1. **Pop. density:** 345 per sq mi, 133 per sq km. **Urban:** 46.0%. **Ethnic groups:** Moldovan/Romanian 65%, Ukrainian 14%, Russian 13%. **Principal languages:** Moldovan (official,), Russian, Gagauz (a Turkish dialect). **Chief religion:** Eastern Orthodox 99%.

Geography: Total area: 13,067 sq mi, 33,843 sq km; **Land area:** 12,885 sq mi, 33,371 sq km. **Location:** In E Europe. **Neighbors:** Romania on W; Ukraine on N, E, and S. Topography: The country is landlocked; mainly hilly plains, with steppelands in S near the Black Sea. **Capital:** Chisinau, 662,000.

Government: Type: Republic. **Head of state:** Pres. Vladimir Voronin; b May 25, 1941; in office: Apr. 7, 2001. **Head of gov.:** Prime Min. Vasile Tarlev; b Oct. 9, 1963; in office: Apr. 19, 2001. **Local divisions:** 9 counties, 1 municipality, 1 autonomous territory. **Defense budget** (2003): $7.2 mil. **Active troops:** 6,910.

Economy: Industries: food proc., agric. machinery, foundry equip. **Chief crops:** vegetables, grapes, grain, sunflower seed, tobacco. **Natural resources:** lignite, phosphorite, gypsum, limestone. **Arable land:** 53%. **Livestock** (2003): cattle: 409,639; chickens: 14.9 mil.; goats: 126,336; pigs: 508,345; sheep: 829,725. **Fish catch** (2002): 2,330 metric tons. **Electricity prod.** (2002): 3.88 bil. kWh. **Labor force** (1998): agriculture 40%, industry 14%, services 46%.

Finance: Monetary unit: Leu (MDL) (Sept. 2004: 11.99=1 U.S.). **GDP** (2003 est.): $7.8 bil.; **per capita GDP:** $1,800; **GDP growth:** 6.3%. **Imports** (2003 est.): $1.3 bil.; partners (2002): Ukraine 22.6%, Russia 20.2%, Germany 10.7%, Romania 8.3%, Italy 7%. **Exports** (2003 est.): $790.0 mil.; partners (2002): Russia 34.6%, Italy 11.5%, Germany 9.1%, Ukraine 6.9%, Romania 6.2%, U.S. 5.2%, Belarus 4.5%, Spain 4.1%. **Tourism** (2002): $4 mil. **Budget** (1998 est.): $594.0 mil. **Intl. reserves less gold:** $203 mil. **Consumer prices:** 11.7%.

Transport: Railroad: Length: 808 mi. **Motor vehicles** (2001): 256,500 pass. cars, 6,300 comm. vehicles. **Civil aviation:** 77.7 mil. pass.-mi; 8 airport.

Communications: TV sets: 297 per 1,000 pop. **Radios:** 742 per 1,000 pop. **Telephone lines** (2002): 706,900. **Daily newspaper circ.:** 153 per 1,000 pop. **Internet** (2002): 150,000 users.

Health: Life expect.: 60.9 male; 69.4 female. **Births** (per 1,000 pop.): 14.8. **Deaths** (per 1,000 pop.): 12.8. **Natural inc.:** 0.20%. **Infant mortality** (per 1,000 live births): 41.0. **AIDS rate:** 0.2%.

Education: Compulsory: ages 6-16. **Literacy:** 99.1%.

Major Intl. Organizations: UN (FAO, IBRD, ILO, IMF, WHO, WTrO), CIS, OSCE.

Embassy: 2101 S St. NW 20008; 667-1130.

Website: www.moldova.org

In 1918, Romania annexed all of Bessarabia that Russia had acquired from Turkey in 1812 by the Treaty of Bucharest. In 1924, the Soviet Union established the Moldavian Autonomous Soviet Socialist Republic on the eastern bank of the Dniester. It was merged with the Romanian-speaking districts of Bessarabia in 1940 to form the Moldavian SSR.

During World War II, Romania, allied with Germany, occupied the area. It was recaptured by the USSR in 1944. Moldova declared independence Aug. 27, 1991. It became an independent state when the USSR disbanded Dec. 26, 1991.

Fighting erupted Mar. 1992 in the Dnestr (Dniester) region between Moldovan security forces and Slavic separatists—ethnic Russians and ethnic Ukrainians—who feared Moldova would merge with neighboring Romania. In a plebiscite on Mar. 6, 1994, voters in Moldova supported independence, without unification with Romania.

Defying the Moldovan government, voters in the breakaway Dnestr region held legislative elections and approved a separatist constitution Dec. 24, 1995. Petru Lucinschi, a former Communist, won a presidential runoff election Dec. 1, 1996. A peace accord with Dnestr separatists was signed in Moscow May 8, 1997. The Communists won the most seats in parliamentary elections Mar. 22, 1998, but a coalition of three center-right parties formed the government. New elections Feb. 25, 2001, brought a decisive Communist victory.

Monaco
Principality of Monaco

People: Population: 32,270. **Age distrib.** (%): <15: 15.5; 65+: 22.4. **Pop. density:** 42,861 per sq mi, 16,549 per sq km. **Urban:** 100.0%. **Ethnic groups:** French 47%, Monegasque 16%, Italian 16%. **Principal languages:** French (official), English, Italian, Monegasque. **Chief religion:** Roman Catholic 90% (official).

Geography: Total area: <1 sq mi, 1.95 sq km; **Land area:** <1 sq mi, 1.95 sq km. **Location:** On the NW Mediterranean coast. **Neighbors:** France to W, N, E. **Topography:** Monaco-Ville sits atop a high promontory, the rest of the principality rises from the port up the hillside. **Capital:** Monaco-ville, 34,000.

Government: Type: Constitutional monarchy. **Head of state:** Prince Rainier III; b May 31, 1923; in office: May 9, 1949. **Head of gov.:** Min. of State Patrick Leclercq; b 1938; in office: Jan. 5, 2000. **Local divisions:** 4 quarters.

Economy: Industries: tourism, constr., light industrial products. **Chief crops:** none. **Natural resources:** none. **Fish catch** (2002 est): 3 metric tons.

Finance: Monetary unit: Euro (EUR) (Sept. 2004: 0.82=1 U.S.). **GDP** (1999 est.): $870.0 mil.; **per capita GDP:** $27,000. **Budget** (1995): $531.0 mil.

Transport: Railroad: Length: 1 mi. **Motor vehicles:** 17,000 pass. cars, 4,000 comm. vehicles. **Civil aviation:** 1.2 mil. pass.-mi. **Chief port:** Monaco.

Communications: TV sets: 758 per 1,000 pop. **Radios:** 1,030 per 1,000 pop. **Daily newspaper circ.:** 251 per 1,000 pop.

Health: Life expect.: 75.5 male; 83.5 female. **Births** (per 1,000 pop.): 9.4. **Deaths** (per 1,000 pop.): 12.7. **Natural inc.:** −0.34%. **Infant mortality** (per 1,000 live births): 5.5.

Education: Compulsory: ages 6-15. **Literacy:** 99%.

Major Intl. Organizations: UN (IMO, WHO), OSCE.

Consulate General: 565 Fifth Ave., 23rd Fl. New York, NY 10017; (212) 286-0500.

Websites: www.monaco-consulate.com; www.gouv.mc/PortGb

An independent principality for over 300 years, Monaco has belonged to the House of Grimaldi since 1297, except during the French Revolution. It was placed under the protectorate of Sardinia in 1815, and under France, 1861. The Prince of Monaco was an absolute ruler until the 1911 constitution. Monaco was admitted to the UN on May 28, 1993.

Monaco's fame as a tourist resort is widespread. It is noted for its mild climate, magnificent scenery, and elegant casinos.

Mongolia

People: Population: 2,751,314. **Age distrib.** (%): <15: 32; 65+: 3.9. **Pop. density:** 5 per sq mi, 2 per sq km. **Urban:** 56.7%. **Ethnic groups:** Mongol 85%, Turkic 7%, Tungusic 5%. **Principal languages:** Khalkha Mongol, Turkic, Russian. **Chief religion:** Tibetan Buddhist Lamaism 96%.

Geography: Total area: 604,250 sq mi, 1,565,000 sq km; **Land area:** 600,543 sq mi, 1,555,400 sq km. **Location:** In E Central Asia. **Neighbors:** Russia on N, China on E, W, and S. **Topography:** Mostly a high plateau with mountains, salt lakes, and vast grasslands. Arid lands in the S are part of the Gobi Desert. **Capital:** Ulaanbaatar, 812,000.

Government: Type: Republic. **Head of state:** Pres. Natsagiyn Bagabandi; b Apr. 22, 1950; in office: June 20, 1997. **Head of gov.:** Prime. Min. Tsakhiagiyn Elbegdorj; b 1963; in office: Aug. 20, 2004. **Local divisions:** 18 provinces, 3 municipalities. **Defense budget** (2003): $26.6 mil. **Active troops:** 8,600.

Economy: Industries: constr. materials, mining, oil, food, beverages. **Chief crops:** wheat, barley, potatoes, forage crops. **Natural resources:** oil, coal, copper, molybd., tungsten, phosphates, tin, nickel, zinc, fluorspar, gold, silver, iron. **Arable land:** 1%. **Livestock** (2003): cattle: 2.05 mil.; chickens: 75,000; goats: 8.86 mil.; pigs: 15,000; sheep: 11.80 mil. **Fish catch** (2002): 129 metric tons. **Electricity prod.** (2002): 2.91 bil. kWh. **Labor force** (2001): herding/agriculture 46%, manufacturing 6%, trade 10.3%, public sector 4.7%, other/unemployed 33%.

Finance: Monetary unit: Tugrik (MNT) (Sept. 2004: 1,199.00=1 U.S.). **GDP** (2003 est.): $4.9 bil.; **per capita GDP:** $1,800; **GDP growth:** 5.0%. **Imports** (2002 est.): $691.0 mil.; partners (2002): Russia 34.4%, China 20.1%, South Korea 12.4%, Japan 6.2%, Germany 4.3%, Hong Kong 4.1%. **Exports** (2002 est.): $524.0 mil.; partners (2002): China 41.4%, U.S. 31.7%, Russia 9.2%, South Korea 4.2%. **Tourism:** $149 mil. **Budget** (2001 est.): $428.0 mil. **Intl. reserves less gold:** $159 mil. **Gold:** 20,000 oz t. **Consumer prices** (change in 2001): 8.0%.

Transport: Railroad: Length: 1,128 mi. **Motor vehicles:** 21,000 pass. cars, 27,000 comm. vehicles. **Civil aviation:** 249.2 mil. pass.-mi; 10 airports.

Communications: TV sets: 58 per 1,000 pop. **Radios:** 142 per 1,000 pop. **Telephone lines** (2002): 128,000. **Daily newspaper circ.:** 27 per 1,000 pop. **Internet** (2002): 50,000 users.

Health: Life expect.: 62.0 male; 66.5 female. **Births** (per 1,000 pop.): 21.4. **Deaths** (per 1,000 pop.): 7.1. **Natural inc.:** 1.43%. **Infant mortality** (per 1,000 live births): 55.5. **AIDS rate:** <0.1%.

Education: Compulsory: ages 8-15. **Literacy:** 99%.

Major Intl. Organizations: UN (FAO, IBRD, ILO, IMF, IMO, WHO, WTrO).

Embassy: 2833 M St. NW 20007; 333-7117.

Websites: www.mongolianembassy.us; www.mongoliatourism.gov.mn

One of the world's oldest countries, Mongolia reached the zenith of its power in the 13th century when Genghis Khan and his successors conquered all of China and extended their influence as far west as Hungary and Poland. In later centuries, the empire dissolved and Mongolia became a province of China.

With the advent of the 1911 Chinese revolution, Mongolia, with Russian backing, declared its independence. A Communist regime was established July 11, 1921.

In 1990, the Mongolian Communist Party yielded its monopoly on power but won election in July. A new constitution took effect Feb. 12, 1992. A democratic alliance won legislative elections, June 30, 1996. Natsagiyn Bagabandi, a former Communist, won the presidential election of May 18, 1997. A protracted political crisis took a violent turn Oct. 2, 1998, with the murder of Sanjaasuregiyn Zorig, a popular cabinet member seeking to become prime minister. The former Communists won 72 of 76 seats in parliamentary elections, July 2, 2000. Pres. Bagabandi was reelected May 20, 2001.

Morocco
Kingdom of Morocco

People: Population: 32,209,101. **Age distrib.** (%): <15: 33.8; 65+: 4.7. **Pop. density:** 187 per sq mi, 72 per sq km. **Urban:** 57.5%. **Ethnic groups:** Arab-Berber 99%. **Principal languages:** Arabic (official), Berber dialects, French, Spanish, English. **Chief religion:** Muslim 99% (official).

Geography: Total area: 172,414 sq mi, 446,550 sq km; **Land area:** 172,317 sq mi, 446,300 sq km. **Location:** On NW coast of Africa. **Neighbors:** Western Sahara on S, Algeria on E. **Topography:** Consists of 5 natural regions: mountain ranges (Riff in the N, Middle Atlas, Upper Atlas, and Anti-Atlas); rich plains in the W; al-iuvial plains in SW; well-cultivated plateaus in the center; a pre-Sahara arid zone extending from SE. **Capital:** Rabat, 1,759,000. **Cities (urban aggr.):** Casablanca, 3,344,000; Fes, 904,000.

Government: Type: Constitutional monarchy. **Head of state:** King Mohammed VI; b Aug. 21, 1963; in office: July 23, 1999. **Head of gov.:** Prime Min. Driss Jettou; b May 24, 1945; in office: Oct. 9, 2002. **Local divisions:** 16 regions. **Defense budget** (2003): $1.6 bil. **Active troops:** 196,300.

Economy: Industries: mining, food proc., leather goods, textiles, constr., tourism. **Chief crops:** barley, wheat, citrus, grapes, vegetables, olives. **Natural resources:** phosphates, iron ore, mang., lead, zinc, fish, salt. **Crude oil reserves** (2003): 1.6 mil. bbls. **Arable land:** 21%. **Livestock** (2003): cattle: 2.69 mil.; chickens: 137.0 mil.; goats: 5.2 mil.; pigs: 8,000; sheep: 16.7 mil. **Fish catch** (2002): 896,627 metric tons. **Electricity prod.** (2002): 13.91 bil. kWh. **Labor force** (2003 est.): agriculture 40%, services 45%, industry 15%.

Finance: Monetary unit: Dirham (MAD) (Sept. 2004: 9.05=1 U.S.). **GDP** (2003 est.): $128.3 bil.; **per capita GDP:** $4,000; **GDP growth:** 6.0%. **Imports** (2003 est.): $12.8 bil.; partners (2002): France 21.1%, Spain 12.7%, Italy 6.4%, Germany 5.6%, U.S. 4.6%, UK 4.1%, Saudi Arabia 4.1%. **Exports** (2003 est.): $8.5 bil.; partners (2002): France 25.9%, Spain 14%, UK 7.8%, Germany 5.7%, Italy 5.5%, U.S. 4.7%. **Tourism:** $2.8 bil. **Budget** (2004 est.): $14.0 bil. **Intl. reserves less gold:** $9.32 bil. **Gold:** 710,000 oz t. **Consumer prices:** 1.2%.

Transport: Railroad: Length: 1,185 mi. **Motor vehicles** (2000): 1.21 mil pass. cars, 415,700 comm. vehicles. **Civil aviation:** 4.3 bil. pass.-mi; 26 airports. **Chief ports:** Tangier, Casablanca, Kenitra.

Communications: TV sets: 165 per 1,000 pop. **Radios:** 247 per 1,000 pop. **Telephone lines:** 1.2 mil. **Daily newspaper circ.:** 28.3 per 1,000 pop. **Internet:** 800,000 users.

Health: Life expect.: 68.1 male; 72.7 female. **Births** (per 1,000 pop.): 22.8. **Deaths** (per 1,000 pop.): 5.7. **Natural inc.:** 1.71%. **Infant mortality** (per 1,000 live births): 43.3. **AIDS rate:** 0.1%.

Education: Compulsory: ages 6-14. **Literacy:** 51.7%.

Major Intl. Organizations: UN (FAO, IBRD, ILO, IMF, IMO, WHO, WTrO), AL.

Embassy: 1601 21st St. NW 20009; 462-7979.

Website:www.mincom.gov.ma

Berbers were the original inhabitants, followed by Carthaginians and Romans. Arabs conquered in 683. In the 11th and 12th centuries, a Berber empire ruled all NW Africa and most of Spain from Morocco.

Part of Morocco came under Spanish rule in the 19th century; France controlled the rest in the early 20th. Tribal uprisings lasted from 1911 to 1933. The country became independent Mar. 2, 1956. Tangier, an internationalized seaport, was turned over to Morocco, 1956. Ifni, a Spanish enclave, was ceded in 1969. Morocco annexed the disputed territory of Western Sahara during the second half of the 1970s.

King Hassan II assumed the throne in 1961, reigning until his death on July 23, 1999; he was immediately succeeded by his eldest son. Political reforms in the 1990s included the establishment of a bicameral legislature in 1997.

Five terrorist attacks in Casablanca May 16, 2003, left about 40 people dead, including 10 suicide bombers; the government blamed Salafia Jihadia, an extremist group connected with al-Qaeda. An earthquake Feb. 24, 2004, killed at least 629 people in the vicinity of al-Hoceima, N coastal Morocco.

Western Sahara

Western Sahara, formerly the protectorate of Spanish Sahara, is bounded the in N by Morocco, the NE by Algeria, the E and S by Mauritania, and on the W by the Atlantic Ocean. Phosphates are the major resource. Population (2004 est.): 267,405; capital: Laayoune (El Aaiun). Area: 102,600 sq mi.

Spain withdrew from its protectorate in Feb. 1976. On Apr. 14, 1976, Morocco annexed over 70,000 sq. mi, with the remainder annexed by Mauritania. A guerrilla movement, the Polisario Front, which had proclaimed the region independent Feb. 27, launched attacks with Algerian support. After Mauritania signed a treaty with Polisario on Aug. 5, 1979, Morocco occupied Mauritania's portion of Western Sahara.

After years of bitter fighting, Morocco controlled the main urban areas, but Polisario guerrillas moved freely in the vast, sparsely populated deserts. The 2 sides implemented a cease-fire in 1991, when a UN peacekeeping force was deployed. Former U.S. Sec. of State James A. Baker III served as UN envoy, 1997-2004, but was unable to resolve the dispute.

Mozambique
Republic of Mozambique

People: Population: 18,811,731. **Age distrib.** (%): <15: 42.5; 65+: 2.8. **Pop. density:** 62 per sq mi, 24 per sq km. **Urban:** 35.6%. **Ethnic groups:** Shangaan, Chokwe, Manyika, Sena, Makua. **Principal languages:** Portuguese (official) and dialects, English. **Chief religions:** Indigenous beliefs 50%, Christian 30%, Muslim 20%.

Geography: Total area: 309,496 sq mi, 801,590 sq km; **Land area:** 302,739 sq mi, 784,090 sq km. **Location:** On SE coast of Africa. **Neighbors:** Tanzania on N; Malawi, Zambia, Zimbabwe on W; South Africa, Swaziland on S. **Topography:** Coastal lowlands comprise nearly half the country with plateaus rising in steps to the mountains along the western border. **Capital:** Maputo, 1,221,000.

Government: Type: Republic. **Head of state:** Pres. Joaquim Chissano; b Oct. 22, 1939; in office: Oct. 19, 1986. **Head of gov.:** Prime Min. Luisa Diogo; b Apr. 11, 1958; in office: Feb. 17, 2004. **Local divisions:** 10 provinces and Maputo municipality. **Defense budget** (2003): $86 mil. **Active troops:** 8,200.

Economy: Industries: food, beverages, chemicals, oil products, textiles, cement. **Chief crops:** cotton, cashews, sugarcane, tea, cassava, corn, coconuts, sisal, trop. fruits. **Natural resources:** coal, titanium, nat. gas, hydropower, tantalum, graphite. **Arable land:** 4%. **Livestock** (2003): cattle: 1.32 mil.; chickens: 28.0 mil.; goats: 392,000; pigs: 180,000; sheep: 125,000. **Fish catch** (2002): 37,139 metric tons. **Electricity prod.** (2002): 8.86 bil. kWh. **Labor force** (1997 est.): agriculture 81%, industry 6%, services 13%.

Finance: Monetary unit: Metical (MZM) (Sept. 2004: 21,845.00=1 U.S.). **GDP** (2003 est.): $21.2 bil.; **per capita GDP:** $1,200; **GDP growth:** 7.0%. **Imports** (2003 est.): $1.1 bil.; partners (2002): South Africa 30.4%, Portugal 6.1%, U.S. 5.2%, India 4.2%, Australia 4.1%. **Exports** (2003 est.): $795.0 mil.; partners (2002): Belgium 42.4%, South Africa 17.6%, Zimbabwe 5.7%, Spain 5.4%, Portugal 4.4%. **Tourism** (2002): $144 mil. **Budget** (2001 est.): $1.0 bil. **Intl. reserves less gold:** $672 mil. **Consumer prices:** 13.4%.

Transport: Railroad: Length: 1,941 mi. **Motor vehicles** (1999): 78,600 pass. cars, 46,900 comm. vehicles. **Civil aviation:** 128.6 mil. pass.-mi; 22 airports. **Chief ports:** Maputo, Beira, Nacala, Inhambane.

Communications: TV sets: 5 per 1,000 pop. **Radios:** 40 per 1,000 pop. **Telephone lines** (2002): 83,700. **Daily newspaper circ.:** 2.5 per 1,000 pop. **Internet** (2002): 50,000 users.

Health: Life expect.: 37.8 male; 36.3 female. **Births** (per 1,000 pop.): 36.1. **Deaths** (per 1,000 pop.): 23.9. **Natural inc.:** 1.22%. **Infant mortality** (per 1,000 live births): 137.1. **AIDS rate:** 12.2%.

Education: Compulsory: ages 6-12. **Literacy:** 47.8%.

Major Intl. Organizations: UN (FAO, IBRD, ILO, IMF, IMO, WHO, WTrO), the Commonwealth, AU.

Embassy: 1990 M St. NW, Suite 570, 20036; 293-7146.

Website: www.embamoc-usa.org

The first Portuguese post on the Mozambique coast was established in 1505, on the trade route to the East. Mozambique became independent June 25, 1975, after a ten-year war against Portuguese colonial domination. The 1974 revolution in Portugal had paved the way for the orderly transfer of power to Frelimo (Front for the Liberation of Mozambique). Frelimo took over local administration Sept. 20, 1974, although opposed, in part violently, by some blacks and whites.

The new government, led by Maoist Pres. Samora Machel, provided for a gradual transition to a Communist system. Economic problems included the emigration of most of the country's whites, a politically untenable economic dependence on white-ruled South Africa, and a large external debt.

In the 1980s, severe drought and civil war caused famine and heavy loss of life. Pres. Machel was killed in a plane crash just inside the South African border, Oct. 19, 1986.

The ruling party formally abandoned Marxist-Leninism in 1989, and a new constitution, effective Nov. 30, 1990, provided for multiparty elections and a free-market economy.

On Oct. 4, 1992, a peace agreement was signed aimed at ending hostilities between the government and the rebel Mozambique National Resistance (MNR). Repatriation of 1.7 million Mozambican refugees officially ended June 1995. In Mar. 1999 the heaviest floods in 4 decades left nearly 200,000 people stranded. Even worse flooding in Feb.-Mar. 2000 claimed more than 600 lives, displaced over 1 million people, and devastated the economy. A train crash May 25, 2002, in S Mozambique killed 196 people.

Myanmar (*formerly* Burma)
Union of Myanmar

People: Population: 42,720,196. **Age distrib.** (%): <15: 28.6; 65+: 4.8. **Pop. density:** 168 per sq mi, 65 per sq km. **Urban:** 29.4%. **Ethnic groups:** Burman 68%, Shan 9%, Karen 7%, Rakhine 4%, Chinese 3%, Indian 2%, Mon 2%. **Principal languages:** Burmese (official); many ethnic minority languages. Chief religions: Buddhist 89%, Christian 4%, Muslim 4%, Animist 1%.

Geography: Total area: 261,970 sq mi, 678,500 sq km; **Land area:** 253,955 sq mi, 657,740 sq km. **Location:** Between S and SE Asia, on Bay of Bengal. **Neighbors:** Bangladesh, India on W; China, Laos, Thailand on E. **Topography:** Mountains surround Myanmar on W, N, and E, and dense forests cover much of the nation. N-S rivers provide habitable valleys and communications, es-

pecially the Irrawaddy, navigable for 900 miles. The country has a tropical monsoon climate. **Capital:** Yangon (Rangoon), 3,874,000. **Cities (urban aggr.):** Mandalay, 807,000.

Government: Type: Military. **Head of State:** Gen. Than Shwe; b Feb. 2, 1933; in office: Apr. 24, 1992. **Head of gov.:** Khin Nyunt; b Oct. 11, 1939; in office: Aug. 25, 2003. **Local divisions:** 7 states, 7 divisions. **Defense budget** (2003): $1.5 bil. **Active troops:** 488,000.

Economy: Industries: agric. proc., apparel, wood & wood products, mining, constr. materials. **Chief crops:** rice, beans, sesame, peanuts, sugarcane. **Natural resources:** oil, timber, tin, antimony, zinc, copper, tungsten, lead, coal, marble, limestone, gemstones, nat. gas, hydropower. **Crude oil reserves** (2003): 50.0 mil. bbls. **Arable land:** 15%. **Livestock** (2003): cattle: 11.7 mil.; chickens: 60.0 mil.; goats: 1.72 mil.; pigs: 4.8 mil; sheep: 482,000. **Fish catch** (2002): 1,433,908 metric tons. **Electricity prod.** (2002): 6.06 bil. kWh. **Labor force** (2001 est.): agriculture 70%, industry 7%, services 23%.

Finance: Monetary unit: Kyat (MMK) (Sept. 2004: 6.02=1 U.S.). **GDP** (2003 est.): $78.8 bil.; **per capita GDP:** $1,900; **GDP growth:** 5.2%. **Imports** (2003 est.): $2.1 bil.; partners (2002): China 27%, Singapore 19.6%, Thailand 12.1%, Malaysia 8.9%, South Korea 5.4%, Taiwan 4.9%, Japan 4.3%. **Exports** (2003 est.): $2.4 bil.; partners (2002): Thailand 31.6%, U.S. 13.1%, India 7.4%, China 4.7%. **Tourism** (2001): $45 mil. **Budget** (FY96/97): $12.2 mil. **Intl. reserves less gold:** $370 mil. **Gold:** 230,000 oz t. **Consumer prices:** 36.6%.

Transport: Railroad: Length: 2,458 mi. **Motor vehicles** (2001): 175,400 pass. cars, 98,900 comm. vehicles. **Civil aviation:** 94.4 mil. pass.-mi; 8 airports. **Chief ports:** Bassein, Moulmein.

Communications: TV sets: 7 per 1,000 pop. **Radios:** 72 per 1,000 pop. **Telephone lines:** 357,300. **Daily newspaper circ.:** 8.6 per 1,000 pop. **Internet:** 28,000 users.

Health: Life expect.: 54.2 male; 57.9 female. **Births** (per 1,000 pop.): 18.6. **Deaths** (per 1,000 pop.): 12.2. **Natural inc.:** 0.65%. **Infant mortality** (per 1,000 live births): 68.8. **AIDS rate:** 1.2%.

Education: Compulsory: ages 5-9. **Literacy** (1995 est.): 83.1%. **Major Intl. Organizations:** UN (FAO, IBRD, ILO, IMF, IMO, WHO, WTrO), ASEAN.

Embassy: 2300 S St. NW 20008; 332-9044.

Websites: www.mewashingtondc.com; www.myanmar-tourism.com

The Burmese arrived from Tibet before the 9th century, displacing earlier cultures, and a Buddhist monarchy was established by the 11th. Burma was conquered by the Mongol dynasty of China in 1272, then ruled by Shans as a Chinese tributary, until the 16th century.

Britain subjugated Burma in 3 wars, 1824-84, and ruled the country as part of India until 1937, when it became self-governing. Independence outside the Commonwealth was achieved Jan. 4, 1948.

Gen. Ne Win dominated politics from 1962 to 1988, first as military ruler then as constitutional president. His regime drove Indians from the civil service and Chinese from commerce. Economic socialization was advanced, isolation from foreign countries enforced. In 1987 Burma, once the richest nation in SE Asia, was granted less-developed status by the UN.

Ne Win resigned July 1988, following waves of antigovernment riots. Rioting and street violence continued, and in Sept. the military seized power, under Gen. Saw Maung. In 1989 the country's name was changed to Myanmar.

The first free multiparty elections in 30 years took place May 27, 1990, with the main opposition party winning a decisive victory, but the military refused to hand over power. A key opposition leader, Aung San Suu Kyi, awarded the Nobel Peace Prize in 1991, was held under house arrest from July 20, 1989, to July 10, 1995; after her release, the military government continued to restrict her activities and to harass and imprison her supporters. New U.S. economic sanctions took effect on May 21, 1997. Myanmar was admitted to ASEAN July 23, 1997.

Confined again in Sept. 2000, Aung San Suu Kyi was freed May 6, 2002. She was rearrested May 30, 2003, as part of a broader government crackdown on dissidents. The regime has been accused of committing many human rights abuses in its attempt to stay in power.

Namibia
Republic of Namibia

People: Population: 1,954,033. **Age distrib.** (%): <15: 42.6; 65+: 3.7. **Pop. density:** 6 per sq mi, 2 per sq km. **Urban:** 32.4%. **Ethnic groups:** Ovambo 50%, Kavangos 9%, Herero 7%, Damara 7% White 6%, mixed 7%. **Principal languages:** English (official), Afrikaans, German, Oshivambo, Herero, Nama. **Chief religions:** Lutheran 50%, other Christian 30%, indigenous beliefs 10-20%.

Geography: Total area: 318,696 sq mi, 825,418 sq km; **Land area:** 318,696 sq mi, 825,418 sq km. **Location:** In S Africa on the coast of the Atlantic Ocean. **Neighbors:** Angola on N, Botswana on E, South Africa on S. **Topography:** Three distinct regions incl. Namib desert along the Atlantic coast, a mountainous central plateau with woodland savanna, and Kalahari desert in E. True forests are found in NE. There are 4 rivers, but little other surface water. **Capital:** Windhoek, 237,000.

Government: Type: Republic. **Head of state:** Pres. Sam Nujoma; b May 12, 1929; in office: Mar. 21, 1990. **Head of gov.:** Prime Min. Theo-Ben Gurirab; b Jan. 23, 1939; in office: Aug. 28, 2002.

Local divisions: 13 regions. **Defense budget** (2003): $131 mil. **Active troops:** 9,000.

Economy: meatpacking, fish proc., dairy products, mining. **Chief crops:** millet, sorghum, peanuts. **Natural resources:** diamonds, copper, uranium, gold, lead, tin, lithium, cadmium, zinc, salt, vanadium, nat. gas, hydropower, fish. **Arable land:** 1%. **Livestock** (2003): cattle: 2.51 mil.; chickens: 2.6 mil.; goats: 1.78 mil.; pigs: 22,000; sheep: 2.37 mil. **Fish catch** (2002): 624,941 metric tons. **Electricity prod.** (2002): 1.17 bil. kWh. **Labor force** (1999 est.): agriculture 47%, industry 20%, services 33%.

Finance: Monetary unit: Namibia Dollar (NAD) (Sept. 2004: 6.57=1 U.S.). **GDP** (2003 est.): $13.7 bil.; **per capita GDP:** $7,100; **GDP growth:** 3.3%. **Imports** (2003 est.): $1.4 bil.; partners (2001): U.S. 50%, EU 31%. **Exports** (2003 est.): $1.1 bil.; partners (2001): EU 79%, U.S. 4%. **Tourism** (2002): $219 mil. **Budget** (1998): $950.0 mil. **Intl. reserves less gold:** $219 mil. **Consumer prices:** 7.2%.

Transport: Railroad: Length: 1,480 mi. **Motor vehicles:** 62,500 pass. cars, 66,500 comm. vehicles. **Civil aviation:** 447.4 mil. pass.-mi; 21 airports. **Chief ports:** Luderitz, Walvis Bay.

Communications: TV sets: 38 per 1,000 pop. **Radios:** 143 per 1,000 pop. **Telephone lines:** 127,400. **Daily newspaper circ.:** 19 per 1,000 pop. **Internet:** 65,000 users.

Health: Life expect.: 42.4 male; 38.6 female. **Births** (per 1,000 pop.): 33.5. **Deaths** (per 1,000 pop.): 21.0. **Natural inc.:** 1.25%. **Infant mortality** (per 1,000 live births): 69.6. **AIDS rate:** 21.3%.

Education: Compulsory: ages 6-15. **Literacy:** 84%. **Major Intl. Organizations:** UN (FAO, IBRD, ILO, IMF, IMO, WHO, WTrO), the Commonwealth, AU.

Embassy: 1605 New Hampshire Ave. NW 20009; 986-0540.

Websites: www.namibianembassyusa.org; www.met.gov.na

Namibia was declared a German protectorate in 1890 and officially called South-West Africa. South Africa seized the territory from Germany in 1915 during World War I; the League of Nations gave South Africa a mandate over the territory in 1920. In 1966, the Marxist South-West Africa People's Organization (SWAPO) launched a guerrilla war for independence. The UN General Assembly named the area Namibia in 1968.

After many years of guerrilla warfare and failed diplomatic efforts, South Africa, Angola, and Cuba signed a U.S.-mediated agreement Dec. 22, 1988, to end South African administration of Namibia and provide for a cease-fire and transition to independence, in accordance with a 1978 UN plan. A separate accord between Cuba and Angola provided for a phased withdrawal of Cuban troops from Namibia. A constitution providing for multiparty government was adopted Feb. 9, 1990, and Namibia gained independence Mar. 21.

Walvis Bay, the principal deepwater port, had been turned over to South African administration in 1922. It remained in South African hands after independence, but South Africa turned control of the port back to Namibia, as of Mar. 1, 1994. Separatist violence flared in the Caprivi Strip in the late 1990s.

The UN estimates that over 20% of adults have HIV/AIDS.

Nauru
Republic of Nauru

People: Population: 12,809. **Age distrib.** (%): <15: 39.6; 65+: 1.7. **Pop. density:** 1,580 per sq mi, 610 per sq km. **Urban:** 100.0%. **Ethnic groups:** Nauruan 58%, other Pacific Islander 26%, Chinese 8%, European 8%. **Principal languages:** Nauruan (official), English. **Chief religions:** Protestant 66%, Roman Catholic 33%.

Geography: Total area: 8 sq mi, 21 sq km; **Land area:** 8 sq mi, 21 sq km. **Location:** In W Pacific O. just S of the Equator. **Neighbors:** Nearest is Kiribati to E. **Topography:** Mostly a plateau bearing high-grade phosphate deposits, surrounded by a sandy shore and coral reef in concentric rings. **Capital:** Nauru, 13,000.

Government: Type: Republic. **Head of state and gov.:** Pres. Ludwig Scotty; in office June 22, 2004. **Local divisions:** 14 districts.

Economy: Industries: phosphate mining, offshore banking, coconut products. **Chief crops:** coconuts. **Natural resources:** phosphates, fish. **Livestock** (2003): chickens: 5,000; pigs: 2,800. **Fish catch** (2002): 21 metric tons. **Electricity prod.** (2002): 0.03 bil. kWh. **Labor force:** employed in mining phosphates, public administration, education, and transportation.

Finance: Monetary unit: Australian Dollar (AUD) (Sept. 2004: 1.44=1 U.S.). **GDP** (2001 est.): $60.0 mil.; **per capita GDP:** $5,000. **Imports** (2002): $31.0 mil.; partners (2002): Australia 61.3%, U.S. 9.7%, Ireland 6.5%, Malaysia 6.5%. **Exports** (2002): $18.0 mil.; partners (2002): India 44.4%, South Korea 16.7%, Australia 11.1%, Netherlands 5.6%, New Zealand 5.6%, U.S. 5.6%. **Budget** (FY95/96): $64.8 mil.

Transport: Railroad: Length: 3 mi. **Civil aviation:** 178.3 mil. pass.-mi; 1 airport. **Chief port:** Nauru.

Communications: TV sets: 1 per 1,000 pop. **Radios:** 45 per 1,000 pop.

Health: Life expect.: 58.8 male; 66.1 female. **Births** (per 1,000 pop.): 25.6. **Deaths** (per 1,000 pop.): 7.0. **Natural inc.:** 1.87%. **Infant mortality** (per 1,000 live births): 10.1.

Education: Compulsory: ages 6-16. **Major Intl. Organizations:** UN (WHO), the Commonwealth. **Permanent UN Representative:** 800 Second Avenue, Ste. 400D New York, NY 10017; (212) 937-0074.

Website: www.un.int/nauru

The island was discovered in 1798 by the British but was formally annexed to the German Empire in 1886. After World War I, Nauru became a League of Nations mandate administered by Australia. During World War II the Japanese occupied the island. In 1947 Nauru was made a UN trust territory, administered by Australia. It became an independent republic Jan. 31, 1968, and was admitted to the UN Sept. 14, 1999.

Phosphate exports provided Nauru with per capita revenues that were among the highest in the Third World. Phosphate reserves, however, are nearly depleted, and environmental damage from strip-mining has been severe. Lax banking practices have made Nauru a haven for money laundering; the country has also raised funds by selling passports to noncitizens, possibly to some with terrorist connections. Nauru defaulted on a loan payment for its real estate holdings in Australia and was virtually bankrupt in 2004.

Nepal
Kingdom of Nepal

People: Population: 27,070,666. **Age distrib.** (%): <15: 40; 65+: 3.6. **Pop. density:** 513 per sq mi, 198 per sq km. **Urban:** 15.0%. **Ethnic groups:** Newar, Indian, Gurung, Magar, Tamang, Rai, Limbu, Sherpa, Tharu. **Principal languages:** Nepali (official); about 30 dialects and 12 other languages. **Chief religions:** Hinduism 86% (official), Buddhism 8%, Muslim 4%.

Geography: Total area: 54,363 sq mi, 140,800 sq km; **Land area:** 52,819 sq mi, 136,800 sq km. **Location:** Astride the Himalaya Mts. **Neighbors:** China on N, India on S. **Topography:** The Himalayas stretch across the N, the hill country with its fertile valleys extends across the center, while the S border region is part of the flat, subtropical Ganges Plain. **Capital:** Kathmandu, 741,000. **Cities (urban aggr.):** (1995 metro. est.) Lalitpur, 190,000; Biratnagar, 132,000.

Government: Type: Constitutional monarchy. **Head of state:** King Gyanendra Bir Bikram Shah Dev; b July 7, 1947; in office: June 4, 2001. **Head of gov.:** Prime Min. Sher Bahadur Deuba; b June 13, 1946; in office: June 3, 2004. **Local divisions: Local divisions:** 5 regions subdivided into 14 zones. **Defense budget** (2003): $96 mil. **Active troops:** 63,000.

Economy: Industries: tourism, carpets, textiles, rice, jute, sugar, oilseed. **Chief crops:** rice, corn, wheat, sugarcane. **Natural resources:** quartz, water, timber, hydropower, lignite, copper, cobalt, iron ore. **Arable land:** 17%. **Livestock** (2003): cattle: 7.0 mil.; chickens: 21.5 mil.; goats: 6.65 mil.; pigs: 950,000; sheep: 850,000. **Fish catch** (2002): 35,000 metric tons. **Electricity prod.** (2002): 2.05 bil. kWh. **Labor force:** agriculture 81%, services 16%, industry 3%.

Finance: Monetary unit: Rupee (NPR) (Sept. 2004: 75.13=1 U.S.). **GDP** (2003 est.): $38.1 bil.; **per capita GDP:** $1,400; **GDP growth:** 2.4%. **Imports** (2002 est.): $1.4 bil.; partners (2002): India 21.5%, China 13.3%, UAE 11.3%, Singapore 8.7%, Saudi Arabia 4.9%, Hong Kong 4.6%, Kuwait 4.2%. **Exports** $568.0 mil.; partners (2002): India 47.9%, U.S. 27.8%, Germany 7.6%. **Tourism** (2002): $107 mil. **Budget** (FY99/00 est.): $1.1 bil. **Intl. reserves less gold:** $823 mil. **Gold:** 150,000 oz t. **Consumer prices:** 5.7%.

Transport: Railroad: Length: 37 mi. **Motor vehicles** (1999): 49,400 pass. cars, 185,800 comm. vehicles. **Civil aviation:** 705.3 mil. pass.-mi; 9 airports.

Communications: TV sets: 6 per 1,000 pop. **Radios:** 38 per 1,000 pop. **Telephone lines:** 371,800. **Daily newspaper circ.:** 11 per 1,000 pop. **Internet** (2002): 80,000 users.

Health: Life expect.: 59.7 male; 59.1 female. **Births** (per 1,000 pop.): 32.0. **Deaths** (per 1,000 pop.): 9.7. **Natural inc.:** 2.23%. **Infant mortality** (per 1,000 live births): 68.8. **AIDS rate:** 0.5%.

Education: Compulsory: ages 6-10. **Literacy:** 45.2%.

Major Intl. Organizations: UN (FAO, IBRD, ILO, IMF, IMO, WHO, WTrO).

Embassy: 2131 Leroy Pl. NW 20008; 667-4550.

Website: www.nepalembassyusa.org

Nepal was originally a group of petty principalities, the inhabitants of one of which, the Gurkhas, became dominant about 1769. In 1951 King Tribhubana Bir Bikram, member of the Shah family, ended the system of rule by hereditary premiers of the Ranas family, who had kept the kings virtual prisoners, and established a cabinet system of government.

Virtually closed to the outside world for centuries, Nepal is now linked to India and Pakistan by roads and air service and to Tibet by road. Polygamy, child marriage, and the caste system were officially abolished in 1963.

The government announced the legalization of political parties in 1990. Elections on Nov. 15, 1994, led to the installation of Nepal's first Communist government, which held power until a no-confidence vote Sept. 10, 1995.

Nine members of Nepal's royal family, including King Birendra and Queen Aishwarya, died as the result of a massacre on the night of June 1, 2001. An official inquiry blamed the carnage on a 10th family member, Crown Prince Dipendra, who reportedly shot himself that night and died 3 days later, allowing Birendra's brother Gyanendra to assume the throne. A Maoist insurgency has claimed more than 10,000 lives since 1996. A seven-month truce collapsed in Aug. 2003 and violence continued. In Aug. 2004, Islamic radicals kidnapped and killed 12 Nepalese contract workers en route from Jordan to jobs in Iraq.

Netherlands
Kingdom of the Netherlands

People: Population: 16,318,199. **Age distrib.** (%): <15: 18.3; 65+: 13.8. **Pop. density:** 1,247 per sq mi, 482 per sq km. **Urban:** 65.8%. **Ethnic groups:** Dutch 83%. **Principal languages:** Dutch (official), Frisian, Flemish. **Chief religions:** Roman Catholic 31%, Protestant 21%, Muslim 4%.

Geography: Total area: 16,033 sq mi, 41,526 sq km; **Land area:** 13,082 sq mi, 33,883 sq km. **Location:** In NW Europe on North Sea. **Neighbors:** Germany on E, Belgium on S. **Topography:** The land is flat, an average alt. of 37 ft. above sea level, with much land below sea level reclaimed and protected by some 1,500 miles of dikes. Since 1920 the government has been draining the IJsselmeer, formerly the Zuider Zee. **Capital:** Amsterdam (official), 1,145,000, The Hague (administrative), 705,000. **Cities (urban aggr.):** Rotterdam, 1,094,000.

Government: Type: Parliamentary democracy under a constitutional monarch. **Head of state:** Queen Beatrix; b Jan. 31, 1938; in office: Apr. 30, 1980. **Head of gov.:** Prime Min. Jan Peter Balkenende; b May 7, 1956; in office: July 22, 2002. **Seat of govt.:** The Hague. **Local divisions:** 12 provinces. **Defense budget** (2003): $7.2 bil. **Active troops:** 53,130.

Economy: Industries: agro industries, metal & engineering products, electrical machinery & equip., chemicals, oil, constr., microelectronics, fishing. **Chief crops:** grains, potatoes, sugar beets, fruits, vegetables. **Natural resources:** nat. gas, oil. **Crude oil reserves** (2003): 106.0 mil. bbls. **Livestock** (2003): cattle: 3.78 mil.; chickens: 98.0 mil.; goats: 265,000; pigs: 11.2 mil.; sheep: 1.3 mil. **Fish catch** (2002): 518,477 metric tons. **Electricity prod.** (2002): 90.61 bil. kWh. **Labor force** (1998 est.): services 73%, industry 23%, agriculture 4%.

Finance: Monetary unit: Euro (EUR) (Sept. 2004: 0.82=1 U.S.). **GDP** (2003 est.): $461.4 bil.; **per capita GDP:** $28,600; **GDP growth:** –0.7%. **Imports** (2003 est.): $217.7 bil.; partners (2002): Germany 17.9%, Belgium 9.7%, U.S. 9.1%, UK 6.9%, France 5.5%, China 5.1%, Japan 4%. **Exports** (2003 est.): $253.2 bil.; partners (2002): Germany 25.1%, Belgium 12.7%, UK 10.7%, France 10.2%, Italy 6%, U.S. 4.6%. **Tourism:** $9.2 bil. **Budget** (2001 est.): $134.0 bil. **Intl. reserves less gold:** $7.4 bil. **Gold:** 25 mil oz t. **Consumer prices:** 2.1%.

Transport: Railroad: Length: 1,745 mi. **Motor vehicles** (1999): 6.12 mil pass. cars, 806,000 comm. vehicles. **Civil aviation:** 45.4 bil. pass.-mi; 21 airports. **Chief ports:** Rotterdam, Amsterdam, Ijmuiden.

Communications: TV sets: 540 per 1,000 pop. **Radios:** 980 per 1,000 pop. **Telephone lines:** 10.0 mil. **Daily newspaper circ.:** 306 per 1,000 pop. **Internet:** 8.5 mil. users.

Health: Life expect.: 76.2 male; 81.3 female. **Births** (per 1,000 pop.): 11.4. **Deaths** (per 1,000 pop.): 8.7. **Natural inc.:** 0.27%. **Infant mortality** (per 1,000 live births): 5.1. **AIDS rate:** 0.2%.

Education: Compulsory: ages 6-18. **Literacy** (2000 est.): 99%.

Major Intl. Organizations: UN and all of its specialized agencies, EU, NATO, OECD, OSCE.

Embassy: 4200 Linnean Ave. NW 20008; 244-5300.

Website: www.netherlands-embassy.org

Julius Caesar conquered the region in 55 BC, when it was inhabited by Celtic and Germanic tribes. After the empire of Charlemagne fell apart, the Netherlands (Holland, Belgium, Flanders) split among counts, dukes, and bishops, passed to Burgundy and thence to Spain. William the Silent, prince of Orange, led a confederation of the northern provinces, called Estates, in the Union of Utrecht, 1579; in 1581 they repudiated allegiance to Spain. The rise of the Dutch republic to naval, economic, and artistic eminence came in the 17th century.

The United Dutch Republic ended 1795 when the French formed the Batavian Republic. Napoleon made his brother Louis king of Holland, 1806; Louis abdicated 1810 when Napoleon annexed Holland. In 1813 the French were expelled. In 1815 the Congress of Vienna formed a kingdom of the Netherlands, including Belgium, under William I. In 1830, the Belgians seceded and formed a separate kingdom.

The constitution, promulgated 1814, and subsequently revised, provides for a hereditary constitutional monarchy.

The Netherlands maintained its neutrality in World War I, but was invaded and brutally occupied by Germany, 1940-45. In 1949, after several years of fighting, the Netherlands granted independence to Indonesia. Immigration from former Dutch colonies has been substantial.

The murder May 6, 2002, of right-wing populist leader Pim Fortuyn, 9 days before legislative elections, marked the 1st political assassination in modern Dutch history. Queen Juliana, who reigned 1948-80, died Mar. 20, 2004.

Netherlands Dependencies

The **Netherlands Antilles,** constitutionally on a level of equality with the Netherlands homeland within the kingdom, consist of 2 groups of islands in the West Indies. **Curaçao** and **Bonaire** are near the coast of Venezuela; **St. Eustatius, Saba,** and the southern part of **St. Maarten** are SE of Puerto Rico. The northern two-thirds of St. Maarten belongs to French Guadeloupe; the French call the island St. Martin. Total area of the 2 groups is 370.7 sq. mi., includ-

ing Bonaire (111), Curaçao (171), St. Eustatius (8), St. Maarten (Dutch part) (13). St. Maarten suffered extensive damage from Hurricane Luis, Sept. 1995. Total pop. of the Netherlands Antilles (2004 est.) was 218,126. Willemstad, on Curaçao, is the capital. The principal industry is the refining of crude oil from Venezuela. Tourism is also an important industry, as is shipbuilding.

Aruba, about 26 mi. W of Curaçao, was separated from the Netherlands Antilles on Jan. 1, 1986; it is an autonomous member of the Netherlands, the same status as the Netherland Antilles. Area 74.5 sq. mi.; pop. (2004 est.) 71,218; capital Oranjestad. Chief industries are oil refining and tourism.

New Zealand

People: Population: 3,993,817. **Age distrib.** (%): <15: 22.2; 65+: 11.5. **Pop. density:** 39 per sq mi, 15 per sq km. **Urban:** 85.9%. **Ethnic groups:** New Zealand European 75%, Maori 10%, other European 5%, Pacific Islander 4%. **Principal languages:** English, Maori (both official). **Chief religions:** Protestant 52%, Roman Catholic 15%.

Geography: Total area: 103,738 sq mi, 268,680 sq km. **Location:** In SW Pacific O. **Neighbors:** Nearest are Australia on W, Fiji and Tonga on N. **Topography:** Each of the 2 main islands (North and South Isls.) is mainly hilly and mountainous. The east coasts consist of fertile plains, especially the broad Canterbury Plains on South Isl. A volcanic plateau is in center of North Isl. South Isl. has glaciers and 15 peaks over 10,000 ft. **Capital:** Wellington, 343,000. **Cities (urban aggr.):** Auckland, 1,063,000; Christchurch, 331,443.

Government: Type: Parliamentary democracy. **Head of state:** Queen Elizabeth II, represented by Gov.-Gen. Dame Silvia Cartwright; b Nov. 7, 1943; in office: Apr. 4, 2001. **Head of gov.:** Prime Min. Helen Clark; b Feb. 26, 1950; in office: Dec. 10, 1999. **Local divisions:** 16 regions. **Defense budget** (2003): $824 mil. **Active troops:** 8,610.

Economy: Industries: food proc., wood & paper products, textiles, machinery, transp. equip., banking & insurance, tourism, mining. **Chief crops:** wheat, barley, potatoes, fruits, vegetables. **Natural resources:** nat. gas, iron ore, sand, coal, timber, hydropower, gold, limestone. **Crude oil reserves** (2003): 189.7 mil. bbls. **Arable land:** 9%. **Livestock** (2003): cattle: 9.66 mil.; chickens: 18.0 mil.; goats: 154,500; pigs: 380,000; sheep: 39.3 mil. **Fish catch** (2002): 645,872 metric tons. **Electricity prod.** (2002): 38.39 bil. kWh. **Labor force** (1995): services 65%, industry 25%, agriculture 10%.

Finance: Monetary unit: New Zealand Dollar (NZD) (Sept. 2004: 1.52=1 U.S.). **GDP** (2003 est.): $85.3 bil.; **per capita GDP:** $21,600; **GDP growth:** 3.4%. **Imports** (2003 est.): $16.1 bil.; partners (2002): Australia 22.1%, U.S. 13.7%, Japan 12%, China 8%, Germany 5.2%. **Exports** (2003 est.): $15.9 bil.; partners (2002): Australia 20.3%, U.S. 15.6%, Japan 11.5%, UK 4.8%, China 4.6%, South Korea 4.4%. **Tourism:** $3.8 bil. **Budget** (2002): $31.2 bil. **Intl. reserves less gold:** $3.3 bil. **Consumer prices:** 1.8%.

Transport: Railroad: Length: 2,422 mi. **Motor vehicles:** 1.94 mil pass. cars, 436,300 comm. vehicles. **Civil aviation:** 12.6 bil. pass.-mi; 46 airports. **Chief ports:** Auckland, Christchurch, Wellington, Dunedin, Tauranga.

Communications: TV sets: 516 per 1,000 pop. **Radios:** 997 per 1,000 pop. **Telephone lines** (2002): 1.8 mil. **Daily newspaper circ.:** 207 per 1,000 pop. **Internet** (2002): 2.1 mil. users.

Health: Life expect.: 75.5 male; 81.6 female. **Births** (per 1,000 pop.): 14.0. **Deaths** (per 1,000 pop.): 7.5. **Natural inc.:** 0.65%. **Infant mortality** (per 1,000 live births): 6.0. **AIDS rate:** 0.1%.

Education: Compulsory: ages 5-16. **Literacy** (1997): 100%.

Major Intl. Organizations: UN (FAO, IBRD, ILO, IMF, IMO, WHO, WTrO), APEC, the Commonwealth, OECD.

Embassy: 37 Observatory Cir. NW 20008; 328-4800.

Websites: www.nzembassy.com; www.govt.nz

The Maoris, a Polynesian group from the eastern Pacific, reached New Zealand before and during the 14th century. The first European to sight New Zealand was Dutch navigator Abel Janszoon Tasman, but Maoris refused to allow him to land. British Capt. James Cook explored the coasts, 1769-1770.

British sovereignty was proclaimed and Maori land rights were recognized in the Treaty of Waitangi, 1840, with organized settlement beginning in the same year. Representative institutions were granted in 1853. Maori Wars ended in 1870 with British victory. The colony became a dominion in 1907 and gained full independence in 1947. It is a member of the Commonwealth.

A progressive tradition in politics dates back to the 19th century, when New Zealand was internationally known for social experimentation; much of the nation's economy has been deregulated in recent years. Jenny Shipley of the National Party became the nation's first female prime minister, Dec. 8, 1997. The Labour Party, led by Helen Clark, won the general elections of Nov. 27, 1999, and July 27, 2002.

The legislature legalized prostitution June 2003. In July, New Zealand contributed troops to the Aus.-led force in the Solomon Islands. A measure establishing a Supreme Court and ending appeals to the UK Privy Council passed Oct. 14.

The native Maoris number nearly 15% of the population. Six of 120 members of the House of Representatives are elected directly by the Maori people. Prime Min. Clark, May 4, 2004, survived a no-confidence vote on a plan to nationalize New Zealand's coastline. The coastline plan was opposed by some Maoris, who claimed it infringed their land rights under the Waitangi Treaty.

New Zealand comprises **North Island,** 44,702 sq. mi.; **South Island,** 58,384 sq. mi.; **Stewart Island,** 674 sq. mi.; **Chatham Islands,** 372 sq. mi.; and several groups of smaller islands.

In 1965, the **Cook Islands** (pop.,2004 est., 21,200; area 92.7 sq. mi.), halfway between New Zealand and Hawaii, became self-governing; New Zealand retains responsibility for defense and foreign affairs. **Niue** attained the same status in 1974; it lies 400 mi. to W. (pop., 2004 est., 2,156; area 100 sq. mi.) Cyclone Heta devastated Niue Jan. 6, 2004. **Tokelau** (pop., 2004 est., 1,405; area 4 sq. mi sq. mi.) comprises 3 atolls 300 mi. N of Samoa.

Ross Dependency, administered by New Zealand since 1923, comprises 160,000 sq. mi. of Antarctic territory.

Nicaragua
Republic of Nicaragua

People: Population: 5,359,759. **Age distrib.** (%): <15: 38.3; 65+: 3. **Pop. density:** 115 per sq mi, 45 per sq km. **Urban:** 57.3%. **Ethnic groups:** Mestizo 69%, White 17%, Black 9%, Amerindian 5%. **Principal languages:** Spanish (official); indigenous languages, English on Atlantic coast. **Chief religion:** Roman Catholic 85%.

Geography: Total area: 49,998 sq mi, 129,494 sq km; **Land area:** 46,430 sq mi, 120,254 sq km. **Location:** In Central America. **Neighbors:** Honduras on N, Costa Rica on S. **Topography:** Both Caribbean and Pacific coasts are over 200 mi. long. The Cordillera Mts., with many volcanic peaks, run NW-SE through the middle of the country. Between this and a volcanic range to the E lie Lakes Managua and Nicaragua. **Capital:** Managua, 1,098,000.

Government: Type: Republic. **Head of state and gov.:** Pres. Enrique Bolaños Geyer; b May 13, 1928; in office Jan. 10, 2002. **Local divisions:** 15 departments, 2 autonomous regions. **Defense budget** (2003): $33 mil. **Active troops:** 14,000.

Economy: Industries: food proc., chemicals, machinery & metal products, textiles, clothing, oil refining & distribution, beverages, footwear, wood. **Chief crops:** coffee, bananas, sugarcane, cotton, rice, corn, tobacco, sesame, soya. **Natural resources:** gold, silver, copper, tungsten, lead, zinc, timber, fish. **Arable land:** 9%. **Livestock** (2003): cattle: 3.5 mil.; chickens: 16.2 mil.; goats: 6,800; pigs: 440,000; sheep: 4,350. **Fish catch** (2002): 29,821 metric tons. **Electricity prod.** (2002): 2.48 bil. kWh. **Labor force** (1999 est.): services 43%, agriculture 42%, industry 15%.

Finance: Monetary unit: Gold Cordoba (NIO) (Sept. 2004: 15.96=1 U.S.). **GDP** (2003 est.): $11.5 bil.; **per capita GDP:** $2,200; **GDP growth:** 1.4%. **Imports** (2003 est.): $1.7 bil.; partners (2002): U.S. 23.6%, Costa Rica 10.2%, Guatemala 7.8%, Venezuela 7.1%, El Salvador 6%, Mexico 4.9%, South Korea 4.6%. **Exports** (2003 est.): $632.0 mil.; partners (2002): U.S. 59.4%, El Salvador 7.5%, Honduras 4.8%. **Tourism:** $152 mil. **Budget** (2000 est.): $908.0 mil. **Intl. reserves less gold:** $338 mil. **Gold** (2002): 20,000 oz t. **Consumer prices:** 5.1%.

Transport: Railroad: Length: 4 mi. **Motor vehicles** (2001): 82,200 pass. cars, 107,7000 comm. vehicles. **Civil aviation:** 44.7 mil. pass.-mi; 11 airports. **Chief ports:** Corinto, Puerto Sandino, San Juan del Sur.

Communications: TV sets: 69 per 1,000 pop. **Radios:** 270 per 1,000 pop. **Telephone lines** (2002): 171,600. **Daily newspaper circ.:** 30 per 1,000 pop. **Internet** (2002): 90,000 users.

Health: Life expect.: 68.0 male; 72.2 female. **Births** (per 1,000 pop.): 25.5. **Deaths** (per 1,000 pop.): 4.5. **Natural inc.:** 2.10%. **Infant mortality** (per 1,000 live births): 30.2. **AIDS rate:** 0.2%.

Education: Compulsory: ages 7-12. **Literacy:** 67.5%.

Major Intl. Organizations: UN and most of its specialized agencies, OAS.

Embassy: 1627 New Hampshire Ave. NW 20009; 939-6570.

Website: www.consuladodenicaragua.com

Nicaragua, inhabited by various Indian tribes, was conquered by Spain in 1552. After gaining independence from Spain, 1821, Nicaragua was united for a short period with Mexico, then with the United Provinces of Central America, finally becoming an independent republic, 1838.

U.S. Marines occupied the country at times in the early 20th century, the last time from 1926 to 1933.

Gen. Anastasio Somoza Debayle was elected president in 1967. He resigned in 1972, but was re-elected president in 1974. Martial law was imposed in Dec. 1974, after officials were kidnapped by the Marxist Sandinista guerrillas. Violent opposition spread to nearly all classes in 1978; nationwide strikes called against the government touched off a civil war, which ended when Somoza fled Nicaragua and the Sandinistas took control of Managua in July 1979. Somoza was assassinated in Paraguay, Sept. 17, 1980.

Relations with the U.S. were strained as a result of Nicaragua's aid to leftist guerrillas in El Salvador and U.S. backing of anti-Sandinista contra guerrilla groups. In 1983 the contras launched a major offensive; the Sandinistas imposed rule by decree. In 1985 the U.S. House rejected Pres. Reagan's request for military aid to the contras. The subsequent diversion of funds to the contras from the proceeds of a secret arms sale to Iran caused a major scandal in the U.S.

In a stunning upset, Violeta Barrios de Chamorro defeated Sandinista leader Daniel Ortega Saavedra in national elections, Feb. 25, 1990. Arnoldo Alemán Lacayo, a conservative former mayor of Managua, defeated Ortega in the presidential election of Oct. 20, 1996. Up to 2,000 people died in W Nicaragua Oct. 30, 1998, in a

mudslide caused by rains from Hurricane Mitch. Drought and a drop in coffee prices plunged Nicaragua into an economic crisis in 2001. Enrique Bolaños Geyer, a conservative businessman, defeated Ortega in a presidential election Nov. 4. The corruption trial of former Pres. Alemán ended with a guilty verdict, Dec. 7, 2003; he was fined $10 million and sentenced to 20 years in prison. After a medical review, Alemán was allowed to serve the sentence under house arrest.

Niger
Republic of Niger

People: Population: 11,360,538. **Age distrib.** (%): <15: 47.9; 65+: 2.3. **Pop. density:** 23 per sq mi, 9 per sq km. **Urban:** 22.2%. **Ethnic groups:** Hausa 56%, Djerma 22%, Fula 9%, Tuareg 8%, Beri Beri (Kanouri) 4%. **Principal languages:** French (official); Hausa, Djerma, Fulani (all national). **Chief religion:** Muslim 80%.

Geography: Total area: 489,191 sq mi, 1,267,000 sq km; **Land area:** 489,075 sq mi, 1,266,700 sq km. **Location:** In the interior of N Africa. **Neighbors:** Libya, Algeria on N; Mali, Burkina Faso on W; Benin, Nigeria on S; Chad on E. **Topography:** Mostly arid desert and mountains. A narrow savanna in the S and the Niger R. basin in the SW contain most of the population. **Capital:** Niamey, 890,000.

Government: Type: Republic. **Head of state:** Pres. Tandja Mamadou; b 1938; in office: Dec. 22, 1999. **Head of gov.:** Prime Min. Hama Amadou; b 1950; in office: Jan. 3, 2000. **Local divisions:** 7 departments, 1 capital district. **Defense budget** (2003): $45 mil. **Active troops:** 5,300.

Economy: Industries: uranium mining, cement, brick, textiles, food proc., chemicals. **Chief crops:** cowpeas, cotton, peanuts, millet, sorghum, cassava, rice. **Natural resources:** uranium, coal, iron ore, tin, phosphates, gold, oil. **Arable land:** 3%. **Livestock** (2003): cattle: 2.26 mil.; chickens: 25.0 mil.; goats: 6.9 mil.; pigs: 39,500; sheep: 4.5 mil. **Fish catch** (2002): 23,560 metric tons. **Electricity prod.** (2002): 0.27 bil. kWh. **Labor force:** agriculture 90%, industry and commerce 6%, government 4%.

Finance: Monetary unit: CFA Franc BCEAO (XOF) (Sept. 2004: 539.40=1 U.S.). **GDP** (2003 est.): $9.1 bil.; **per capita GDP:** $800; **GDP growth:** 3.8%. **Imports** (2002 est.): $400.0 mil.; partners (2002): France 17%, Cote d'Ivoire 14.9%, China 9.9%, Nigeria 7.3%, U.S. 5.3%, Japan 4.6%, India 4.3%. **Exports** (2002 est.): $280.0 mil.; partners (2002): France 39.1%, Nigeria 33.3%, Japan 17.3%. **Tourism** (2002): $28 mil. **Budget** (2002 est.): $320.0 mil. **Intl. reserves less gold:** $77 mil. **Consumer prices:** −1.61%.

Transport: Motor vehicles (1999): 26,000 pass. cars, 35,600 comm. vehicles. **Civil aviation:** 134.2 mil. pass.-mi; 9 airports.

Communications: TV sets: 15 per 1,000 pop. **Radios:** 36 per 1,000 pop. **Telephone lines** (2002): 22,400. **Daily newspaper circ.:** .2 per 1,000 pop. **Internet** (2002): 15,000 users.

Health: Life expect.: 42.4 male; 42.0 female. **Births** (per 1,000 pop.): 48.9. **Deaths** (per 1,000 pop.): 21.5. **Natural inc.:** 2.74%. **Infant mortality** (per 1,000 live births): 122.7. **AIDS rate:** 1.2%.

Education: Compulsory: ages 7-12. **Literacy:** 17.6%.

Major Intl. Organizations: UN (FAO, IBRD, ILO, IMF, WHO, WTrO), AU.

Embassy: 2204 R St. NW 20008; 483-4224.

Website: www.nigerembassyusa.org

Niger was part of ancient and medieval African empires. European explorers reached the area in the late 18th century. The French colony of Niger was established 1900-22, after the defeat of Tuareg fighters, who had invaded the area from the N a century before. The country became independent Aug. 3, 1960. The next year it signed a bilateral agreement with France.

In 1993, Niger held its first free and open elections since independence; an opposition leader, Mahamane Ousmane, won the presidency. A peace accord Apr. 24, 1995, ended a Tuareg rebellion that began in 1990. A coup, Jan. 27, 1996, followed by a disputed presidential election in July, left the military in control of Niger. On Apr. 9, 1999, Gen. Ibrahim Bare Mainassara, Niger's president since 1996, was assassinated, apparently by members of his security team. Elections were held Oct. 17 and Nov. 24, 1999, under a new constitution, approved by referendum July 18, that provided for a return to civilian rule.

Nigeria
Federal Republic of Nigeria

People: Population: 137,253,133. **Age distrib.** (%): <15: 43.6; 65+: 2.8. **Pop. density:** 390 per sq mi, 151 per sq km. **Urban:** 46.7%. **Ethnic groups:** More than 250; Hausa and Fulani 29%, Yoruba 21%, Igbo (Ibo) 18%, Ijaw 10%. **Principal languages:** English (official), Hausa, Yoruba, Igbo (Ibo), Fulani. **Chief religions:** Muslim 50%, Christian 40%, indigenous beliefs 10%.

Geography: Total area: 356,669 sq mi, 923,768 sq km; **Land area:** 351,649 sq mi, 910,768 sq km. **Location:** On the S coast of W Africa. **Neighbors:** Benin on W, Niger on N, Chad and Cameroon on E. **Topography:** 4 E-W regions divide Nigeria: a coastal mangrove swamp 10-60 mi. wide, a tropical rain forest 50-100 mi. wide, a plateau of savanna and open woodland, and semidesert in the N. **Capital:** Abuja, 452,000. **Cities (urban aggr.):** Lagos, 8,665,000; Ibadan, 2,160,000; Ogbomosho, 829,000.

Government: Type: Republic. **Head of state and gov.:** Pres. Olusegun Obasanjo; b Mar. 5, 1937; in office: May 29, 1999. **Local divisions:** 36 states, 1 capital territory. **Defense budget** (2003): $426 mil. **Active troops:** 78,500.

Economy: Industries: crude oil, mining, palm oil, peanuts, cotton, rubber. **Chief crops:** cocoa, peanuts, palm oil, corn, rice, sorghum, millet, cassava, yams, rubber. **Natural resources:** nat. gas, oil, tin, columbite, iron ore, coal, limestone, lead, zinc. **Crude oil reserves** (2003): 24.0 bil. bbls. **Arable land:** 33%. **Livestock** (2003): cattle: 15.2 mil.; chickens: 137.7 mil.; goats: 27.0 mil.; pigs: 6.36 mil.; sheep: 22.5 mil. **Fish catch** (2002): 511,719 metric tons. **Electricity prod.** (2002): 19.85 bil. kWh. **Labor force** (1999 est.): agriculture 70%, industry 10%, services 20%.

Finance: Monetary unit: Naira (NGN) (Sept. 2004: 133.45=1 U.S.). **GDP** (2003 est.): $110.8 bil.; **per capita GDP:** $800; **GDP growth:** 3.4%. **Imports** (2003 est.): $14.5 bil.; partners (2002): UK 9.5%, U.S. 9.4%, China 9.3%, France 8.7%, Germany 6.5%, South Korea 6.1%, Netherlands 5.2%, Italy 4.7%, Brazil 4.5%. **Exports** (2003 est.): $21.8 bil.; partners (2002): U.S. 33.2%, Spain 7.4%, Brazil 6.4%, Indonesia 6%, France 5.7%, India 4.8%, Japan 4%. **Tourism** (2002): $263 mil. **Budget** (2000 est.): $3.6 bil. **Intl. reserves less gold:** $4.80 bil. **Gold:** 690,000 oz t. **Consumer prices:** 14.0%.

Transport: Railroad: Length: 2,210 mi. **Motor vehicles** (1997): 52,300 pass. cars, 13,500 comm. vehicles. **Civil aviation:** 39.1 mil. pass.-mi; 36 airports. **Chief ports:** Port Harcourt, Lagos, Warri, Calabar.

Communications: TV sets: 69 per 1,000 pop. **Radios:** 226 per 1,000 pop. **Telephone lines:** 853,100. **Daily newspaper circ.:** 24 per 1,000 pop. **Internet:** 750,000 users.

Health: Life expect.: 50.4 male; 50.6 female. **Births** (per 1,000 pop.): 38.2. **Deaths** (per 1,000 pop.): 14.0. **Natural inc.:** 2.42%. **Infant mortality** (per 1,000 live births): 70.5. **AIDS rate:** 5.4%.

Education: Compulsory: ages 6-11. **Literacy:** 68%.

Major Intl. Organizations: UN (FAO, IBRD, ILO, IMF, IMO, WHO, WTrO), the Commonwealth, AU, OPEC.

Embassy: 1333 16th St. NW 20036; 986-8400.

Website: www.nigeriaembassyusa.org

Early cultures in Nigeria date back to at least 700 BC. From the 12th to the 14th centuries, more advanced cultures developed in the Yoruba area, at Ife, and in the north, where Muslim influence prevailed. Portuguese and British slavers appeared from the 15th-16th centuries. Britain seized Lagos, 1861, and gradually extended control inland until 1900. Nigeria became independent Oct. 1, 1960, and a republic Oct. 1, 1963.

On May 30, 1967, the Eastern Region seceded, proclaiming itself the Republic of Biafra, plunging the country into civil war. Casualties in the war were estimated at over 1 million, including many "Biafrans" (mostly Ibos) who died of starvation despite international efforts to provide relief. The secessionists, after steadily losing ground, capitulated Jan. 12, 1970.

Nigeria emerged as one of the world's leading oil exporters in the 1970s, but much of the revenue has been squandered through corruption and mismanagement.

After 13 years of military rule, the nation made a peaceful return to civilian government, Oct. 1979. Military rule resumed, Dec. 31, 1983; a second coup came in 1985.

Headed by Gen. Ibrahim Babangida, the military regime held elections June 12, 1993, but annulled the vote June 23 when it appeared that Moshood Abiola would win. Riots followed and many were killed. Babangida resigned and appointed a civilian to head an interim government, Aug. 26, but that government was ousted Nov. 17 in a coup led by Gen. Sani Abacha. On June 11, 1994, Abiola declared himself president; he was jailed June 23.

Abacha's brutal rule ended June 8, 1998, when he died of an apparent heart attack. Abiola died in prison July 7, as Abacha's successor, Gen. Abdulsalam Abubakar, was reportedly preparing to free him. Abiola's death sparked riots in Lagos and other cities; on July 20, Abubakar promised early elections and a return to civilian rule. Olusegun Obasanjo (a former military ruler) won the presidential vote Feb. 27, 1999, Nigeria's 1st civilian government in 15 years.

An oil fire that exploded from a ruptured pipeline in S. Nigeria, Oct. 17, 1998, killed at least 700 people who were scavenging for fuel. The imposition of strict Islamic law in northern states led to clashes, Jan.-Mar. 2000, in which at least 800 people died. U.S. Pres. Bill Clinton visited Nigeria Aug. 26-27, 2000, the 1st visit there by a U.S. head of state in 22 years. Clashes between Muslims and Christians Sept. 7-12 and Oct. 13-14 claimed an estimated 600 lives; another 200 people died when soldiers went on a rampage in SE Nigeria Oct. 22-24.

At least 1,000 people were killed Jan. 27, 2002, when an army weapons depot in Lagos exploded; many of the victims drowned in a drainage canal while fleeing the blasts.

By 2002, the strict Islamic legal code of sharia had been adopted by about one-third of Nigeria's 36 states. Controversy over Nigeria's plans to host a Miss World pageant sparked sectarian riots in Kaduna, Nov. 20-24, leaving more than 200 people dead and 1,100 injured. Obasanjo won reelection Apr. 19, 2003.

Christian militia members massacred about 630 Muslims at Yelwa, central Nigeria, May 2, 2004. Although the World Court awarded the oil-rich Bakassi peninsula to Cameroon in 2002, Nigeria delayed the handover in Sept. 2004.

PAUL HYNDMAN

◀ **TRANSIT OF VENUS**
Venus appears as a dark disk
passing between the Earth
and the Sun, June 8, in this
filtered telescopic picture of
a rare event.

SATURN'S RINGS ▶
On June 21, still 4 million miles from
Saturn, the *Cassini* spacecraft
captured this natural-color image of
the planet's rings as it approached its
scheduled orbit. The rings are
primarily water ice believed to be
colored by rock or carbon
compounds.

NASA/JPL/SPACE SCIENCE INST.

RED HILLS OF MARS ▼
The panoramic camera of the Mars
Exploration Rover *Spirit* shows the
"Columbia Hills," named in honor of
the 7 astronauts who died Feb. 1, 2003,
in the Space Shuttle *Columbia* disaster.

NASA/JPL/CORNELL

World Scene

AP/WIDE WORLD PHOTOS

AP/WIDE WORLD PHOTOS

▲ **TERRORISM IN SPAIN**
Rescue workers cover bodies in Madrid, March 11, after bombs exploded on 3 morning commuter trains, killing nearly 200 people, 3 days before Spain's general elections. Prosecutors said suspects arrested in the case had links to the al-Qaeda terrorist network led by Saudi multi-millionaire Osama bin Laden (above, right).

SUDAN REFUGEES ▶
Women at a refugee camp in the Darfur region of Sudan are visited by UN Sec. Gen. Kofi Annan in July. By then an estimated 50,000 black Africans in Sudan had been killed and a million displaced since early 2003 as a result of raids on villages by marauding Arab militias.

AP/WIDE WORLD PHOTOS

◀ **NEW OLD BRIDGE**
Destroyed by bombs in 1993 during the war in Bosnia, the 16th-century Old Bridge connecting the two sides of Mostar reopened July 23. It was rebuilt with international aid, using traditional construction techniques and pieces pulled out of the Neretva River below.

AP/WIDE WORLD PHOTOS

◄ HORROR IN BESLAN

A man carries his daughter to safety, Sept. 3, at a school in Beslan, Russia. A 3-day standoff between Russian special forces and Chechen terrorists holding hostages had ended after explosions in the school led to a lengthy gun battle. More than 300 people, half of them schoolchildren, died; hundreds of others were hospitalized.

SERGEI DOLZHENKO/EPA/LANDOV

▼ REMEMBERING D-DAY

Below right: U.S. Army troops wade through the surf toward Omaha Beach on the Normandy coast of France, June 6, 1944. At left, on June 6, 2004, the 60th anniversary of the D-Day landings, a Canadian veteran sits with his memories on Juno Beach.

AP/WIDE WORLD PHOTOS

U.S. COAST GUARD COLLECTION IN NATIONAL ARCHIVES

AP/WIDE WORLD PHOTOS

◄ EU EXPANDS

A Guard of Honor from the Polish army joins in ceremonies at midnight May 1 in Warsaw marking the entry of Poland into the European Union. Nine other countries (Lithuania, Estonia, Latvia, Hungary, Czech Republic, Slovenia, Slovakia, Malta, and Cyprus) also joined the EU at this time.

MUCH DEBATED MEGA-HIT ▶
Actor Jim Caviezel as Jesus in Mel Gibson's film *The Passion of the Christ*. Many criticized the film for being excessively graphic, but others found it moving, and it grossed a stunning $370 million during its U.S. release.

PHILIPPE ANTONELLO/EPA/LANDOV

◀ TONY STREET
Avenue Q, an irreverent low-budget musical featuring puppets, live actors, and four-letter words, won 3 Tony Awards, including Best Musical, in ceremonies June 6 at New York's Radio City Music Hall.

◀ LORD OF THE OSCARS
Ian McKellen, as the wizard Gandalf in *The Return of the King*. The blockbuster hit that concluded the Lord of the Rings™ trilogy won a record-tying 11 Oscars Feb. 29, including Best Picture and Best Director for Peter Jackson.

OSCAR-WINNING LINE-UP ▼
Posing together happily at the 76th Academy Awards Feb. 29 were (left to right) winners Renée Zellweger (supporting actress, *Cold Mountain*), Sean Penn (best actor, *Mystic River*), Tim Robbins (supporting actor, *Mystic River*), and Charlize Theron (best actress, *Monster*).

AP/WIDE WORLD PHOTOS

FAREWELL, FRIENDS ▶

NBC aired the final episode of its 10-season hit show *Friends* on May 6. Shown at a taping in January are (left to right) *Friends* stars Jennifer Aniston, Matt LeBlanc, David Schwimmer, Lisa Kudrow, Matthew Perry, and Courteney Cox Arquette.

"WARDROBE MALFUNCTION" ▶

Singer Janet Jackson covers her breast after Justin Timberlake pulled off part of her corset during their duet at the halftime show for Super Bowl XXXVIII, Feb. 1 in Houston. The performers later apologized for the incident, described as an unintentional "wardrobe malfunction."

◀ **GRAMMY GATHERER**

Beyoncé, shown here performing at the 2004 NBA All-Star Game, won 5 Grammys Feb. 8, including Best Contemporary R&B Album for *Dangerously in Love*, her first solo CD. She tied the record for wins by a female artist in single year with Lauryn Hill, Alicia Keys, and Norah Jones.

WHO IS KEN JENNINGS? ▶

That would be the correct answer on TV's *Jeopardy* if you were asked to identify the Salt Lake City software developer (right) whose record winnings topped $1 million. The popular quiz show, hosted by Alex Trebek (left), had previously lifted its 5-game limit for winning contestants.

$1,004,960

AP/WIDE WORLD PHOTOS

◀ HISTORIC DOUBLE

At the 2004 Summer Games in Athens, Morocco's Hicham el Guerrouj (foreground) beat out Kenya's Bernard Lagat (left) in the 1,500m, Aug. 24, and later became the first man in 80 years to win both the 1,500m and 5,000m races in a single Olympics.

ALL-AROUND CONTROVERSY ▼

American Paul Hamm (center) received the gold for men's individual all-around gymnastics, Aug. 18. A scoring error apparently cost S. Korean bronze medalist Yang Tae-young (right) the win. Kim Dae-eun of S. Korea (left) won the silver.

FITTING FINALE ▼

The U.S. women's soccer team won Olympic gold Aug. 26, beating Brazil 2-1 in overtime. These veterans of the 1991 women's world soccer team (left to right, Julie Foudy, Joy Fawcett, Mia Hamm, Kristine Lilly, and Brandi Chastain) were credited with having brought U.S. women's soccer to the forefront both at home and abroad.

AP/WIDE WORLD PHOTOS

WOLFGANG RATTAY/REUTERS/LANDOV

◀ WE DID IT!

American Michael Phelps (left) celebrates his team's victory in the men's 4x200 freestyle relay with teammate Ryan Lochte (2nd from left), Aug. 17. Phelps ended up winning 8 medals in all, tying the record for a single Olympics set in 1980 by Soviet gymnast Aleksandr Dityatin. Among the 8 were 6 golds.

JERRY LAMPEN/REUTERS/LANDOV

TIGER TAMER ▼

Vijay Singh raised his arm in victory after winning the 86th PGA Championship golf tournament Aug. 15, in a 3-hole, 3-way playoff. Singh went on to dethrone Tiger Woods in September as the #1-ranked golfer in the world, ending Woods's 264-week run at the top.

300 AND COUNTING ▼

Four-time Cy Young winner Greg Maddux became the first NL pitcher in over 20 years to win 300 games, leading the Chicago Cubs to an 8-4 victory over the Giants in San Francisco Aug. 7. Maddux, who won 194 games with Atlanta, was the 22nd major league pitcher to win 300.

UCONN DOUBLE ▼

Diana Taurasi, a two-time Final Four Most Outstanding Player, led the UConn women to their third straight national title in 2004. With the men's win over Georgia Tech, Connecticut became the first school to win both men's and women's NCAA championships in the same year.

◀ V FOR VINATIERI

At Super Bowl XXXVIII in Houston Feb. 1, kicker Adam Vinatieri hit a 41-yard field goal to give the New England Patriots a 32-29 win over the Carolina Panthers. For the second time in three years his last-second kick gave the Pats an NFL title.

815

DETROIT DOMINATES ▶

All-Star Laker guard Kobe Bryant is smothered by Detroit's Mehmet Okur (13) and Tayshaun Prince in Game 5 of the NBA Finals, June 15 in Auburn Hills, MI. The Pistons upset the heavily favored Lakers, winning the game 100-87 and the series 4-1.

◀ **ARMSTRONG TRIUMPHANT**

American Lance Armstrong (center), shown here at the Arc de Triomphe in Paris with U.S. Postal teammates Pavel Padrnos of the Czech Republic (left) and José Luis Rubiera of Spain, rode into the record books July 25 with his sixth consecutive Tour de France win.

LIGHTNING STRIKES ▶

Tampa Bay captain Dave Andreychuk holds the Stanley Cup aloft for the first time in his 22-year career, after the Lightning defeated the Calgary Flames, 2-1, in Game 7 to take the series, June 7 in Tampa. It was the first-ever NHL title for the Lightning.

Norway
Kingdom of Norway

People: Population: 4,574,560. **Age distrib.** (%): <15: 20; 65+: 15. **Pop. density:** 38 per sq mi, 15 per sq km. **Urban:** 78.6%. **Ethnic groups:** Norwegian, Sami. **Principal languages:** Norwegian (official), Sami, Finnish. Chief religion: Evangelical Lutheran 86% (official).

Geography: Total area: 125,182 sq mi, 324,220 sq km; **Land area:** 118,865 sq mi, 307,860 sq km. **Location:** W part of Scandinavian peninsula in NW Europe (extends farther north than any European land). **Neighbors:** Sweden, Finland, Russia on E. **Topography:** A highly indented coast is lined with tens of thousands of islands. Mountains and plateaus cover most of the country, which is only 25% forested. **Capital:** Oslo, 795,000. **Cities (urban aggr.):** Bergen (1996 est.), 223,773.

Government: Type: Hereditary constitutional monarchy. **Head of state:** King Harald V; b Feb. 21, 1937; in office: Jan. 17, 1991. **Head of gov.:** Prime Min. Kjell Magne Bondevik; b Sept. 3, 1947; in office: Oct. 19, 2001. **Local divisions:** 19 provinces. **Defense budget** (2003): $4.2 bil. **Active troops:** 26,600.

Economy: Industries: oil & gas, food proc., shipbuilding, pulp & paper products, metals, chemicals, timber, mining, textiles, fishing. **Chief crops:** barley, wheat, potatoes. **Natural resources:** oil, copper, nat. gas, pyrites, nickel, iron ore, zinc, lead, fish, timber, hydropower. **Crude oil reserves** (2003): 10.3 bil. bbls. **Arable land:** 3%. **Livestock** (2003): cattle: 922,500; chickens: 3.3 mil.; goats: 64,875; pigs: 459,700; sheep: 1.08 mil. **Fish catch** (2002): 3,297,117 metric tons. **Electricity prod.** (2002): 125.94 bil. kWh. **Labor force** (1995): services 74%, industry 22%, agriculture, forestry, and fishing 4%.

Finance: Monetary unit: Kroner (NOK) (Sept. 2004: 6.92=1 U.S.). **GDP** (2003 est.): $171.6 bil.; **per capita GDP:** $37,700; **GDP growth:** 0.5%. **Imports** (2003 est.): $40.2 bil.; partners (2002): Sweden 15.7%, Germany 13.4%, Denmark 8.1%, UK 7.4%, U.S. 6.2%, France 4.8%, Netherlands 4.8%. **Exports** (2003 est.): $67.3 bil.; partners (2002): UK 19.4%, Germany 12.4%, France 11.5%, Netherlands 9.3%, U.S. 8.6%, Sweden 7.3%. **Tourism:** $2.5 bil. **Budget** (2000 est.): $57.6 bil. **Intl. reserves less gold:** $15.48 bil. **Gold:** 1.18 mil oz t. **Consumer prices:** 2.5%.

Transport: Railroad: Length: 2,596 mi. **Motor vehicles** (2001): 1.87 mil pass. cars, 463,700 comm. vehicles. **Civil aviation:** 3.6 bil. pass.-mi; 66 airports. **Chief ports:** Bergen, Stavanger, Oslo, Kristiansand.

Communications: TV sets: 653 per 1,000 pop. **Radios:** 917 per 1,000 pop. **Telephone lines** (2002): 3.3 mil. **Daily newspaper circ.:** 569.5 per 1,000 pop. **Internet** (2002): 2.3 mil. users.

Health: Life expect.: 76.6 male; 82.0 female. **Births** (per 1,000 pop.): 11.9. **Deaths** (per 1,000 pop.): 9.5. **Natural inc.:** 0.24%. **Infant mortality** (per 1,000 live births): 3.7. **AIDS rate:** 0.1%.

Education: Compulsory: ages 6-16. **Literacy:** 100%.

Major Intl. Organizations: UN and all of its specialized agencies, EFTA, NATO, OECD, OSCE.

Embassy: 2720 34th St. NW 20008; 333-6000.

Website: www.norway.org

The first ruler of Norway was Harald the Fairhaired, who came to power in AD 872. Between 800 and 1000, Norway's Vikings raided and occupied widely dispersed parts of Europe.

The country was united with Denmark 1381-1814, and with Sweden, 1814-1905. In 1905, the country became independent with Prince Charles of Denmark as king.

Norway remained neutral during World War I. Germany attacked Norway Apr. 9, 1940, and held it until liberation May 8, 1945. The country abandoned its neutrality after the war, and joined NATO. In a referendum Nov. 28, 1994, Norwegian voters rejected European Union membership.

Abundant hydroelectric resources provided the base for industrialization, giving Norway one of the highest living standards in the world. The country is a leading producer and exporter of crude oil, with extensive reserves in the North Sea. Norway's merchant marine is one of the world's largest.

Svalbard is a group of mountainous islands in the Arctic O., area 23,957.2 sq mi, pop. (2004 est.) 2,756. The largest, Spitsbergen (formerly called West Spitsbergen), 15,060 sq mi, seat of the governor, is about 370 mi. N of Norway. By a treaty signed in Paris, 1920, major European powers recognized the sovereignty of Norway, which incorporated it in 1925.

Jan Mayen, area 144 sq mi, is a volcanic island located about 565 mi WNW of Norway; it was annexed in 1929.

Oman
Sultanate of Oman

People: Population: 2,903,165. **Age distrib.** (%): <15: 41.9; 65+: 2.4. **Pop. density:** 35 per sq mi, 14 per sq km. **Urban:** 77.6%. **Ethnic groups:** Arab, Baluchi, South Asian, African. **Principal languages:** Arabic (official), English, Baluchi, Urdu, Indian dialects. **Chief religion:** Muslim 75% (official; mostly Ibadhi).

Geography: Total area: 82,031 sq mi, 212,460 sq km; **Land area:** 82,031 sq mi, 212,460 sq km. **Location:** On SE coast of Arabian peninsula. **Neighbors:** United Arab Emirates, Saudi Arabia, Yemen on W. **Topography:** Oman has a narrow coastal plain up to 10 mi. wide, a range of barren mountains reaching 9,900 ft., and a wide, stony, mostly waterless plateau, avg. alt. 1,000 ft. Al-so, an enclave at the tip of the Musandam peninsula controls access to the Persian Gulf. **Capital:** Muscat, 638,000.

Government: Type: Absolute monarchy. **Head of state and gov.:** Sultan Qabus bin Said; b Nov. 18, 1940; in office: July 23, 1970 (also prime min. since Jan. 2, 1972). **Local divisions:** 6 regions and 2 governorates. **Defense budget** (2003): $2.5 bil. **Active troops:** 41,700.

Economy: Industries: oil, gas, constr., cement, copper. **Chief crops:** dates, limes, bananas, alfalfa, vegetables. **Natural resources:** oil, copper, asbestos, marble, limestone, chromium, gypsum, nat. gas. **Crude oil reserves** (2003): 5.5 bil. bbls. **Livestock** (2003): cattle: 315,000; chickens: 3.4 mil.; goats: 1.0 mil.; sheep: 355,000. **Fish catch** (2002): 142,670 metric tons. **Electricity prod.** (2002): 9.78 bil. kWh.

Finance: Monetary unit: Rial (OMR) (Sept. 2004: 0.38=1 U.S.). **GDP** (2003 est.): $37.5 bil.; **per capita GDP:** $13,400; **GDP growth:** 3.3%. **Imports** (2003 est.): $5.7 bil.; partners (2002): UAE 27.6%, Japan 16.7%, UK 7.4%, U.S. 6.9%, Germany 5%. **Exports** (2003 est.): $11.7 bil.; partners (2002): Japan 22.1%, South Korea 19.9%, China 15.2%, Thailand 12.6%, Taiwan 5.5%, Singapore 4.7%, U.S. 4.4%. **Tourism** (2002): $208 mil. **Budget** (2000 est.): $6.9 bil. **Intl. reserves less gold:** $2.42 bil. **Gold** (2001): 290,000 oz t. **Consumer prices:** –0.4%.

Transport: Motor vehicles (2001): 359,200 pass. cars, 132,900 comm. vehicles. **Civil aviation:** 2.5 bil. pass.-mi; 6 airports. **Chief ports:** Matrah, Mina' al Fahl.

Communications: TV sets: 575 per 1,000 pop. **Radios:** 607 per 1,000 pop. **Telephone lines** (2002): 233,900. **Daily newspaper circ.:** 29 per 1,000 pop. **Internet** (2002): 180,000 users.

Health: Life expect.: 70.7 male; 75.2 female. **Births** (per 1,000 pop.): 37.1. **Deaths** (per 1,000 pop.): 3.9. **Natural inc.:** 3.32%. **Infant mortality** (per 1,000 live births): 20.3. **AIDS rate:** 0.1%.

Education: Literacy: 75.8%.

Major Intl. Organizations: UN (FAO, IBRD, ILO, IMF, IMO, WHO), AL.

Embassy: 2535 Belmont Rd. NW 20008; 387-1980.

Website: www.omanet.om

Oman was originally called Muscat and Oman. A long history of rule by other lands, including Portugal in the 16th century, ended with the ouster of the Persians in 1744. By the early 19th century, Muscat and Oman was one of the most important countries in the region, controlling much of the Persian and Pakistan coasts, and also ruling far-away Zanzibar, which was separated in 1861 under British mediation.

British influence was confirmed in a 1951 treaty, and Britain helped suppress an uprising by traditionally rebellious interior tribes against control by Muscat in the 1950s.

On July 23, 1970, Sultan Said bin Taimur was overthrown by his son, who changed the nation's name to Sultanate of Oman.

Oil is the major source of income.

Oman opened its air bases to Western forces following the Iraqi invasion of Kuwait on Aug. 2, 1990. Oman served as a base for U.S. aircraft in the Afghanistan war, 2001.

Pakistan
Islamic Republic of Pakistan

People: Population: 159,196,336. **Age distrib.** (%): <15: 39.9; 65+: 4.1. **Pop. density:** 529 per sq mi, 204 per sq km. **Urban:** 34.1%. **Ethnic groups:** Punjabi, Sindhi, Pashtun, Balochi. **Principal languages:** English, Urdu (both official); Punjabi, Sindhi, Siraiki, Pashtu, Balochi, Hindko, Brahui, Burushaski. **Chief religions:** Muslim 97% (official; Sunni 77%, Shi'a 20%).

Geography: Total area: 310,403 sq mi, 803,940 sq km; **Land area:** 300,665 sq mi, 778,720 sq km. **Location:** In W part of South Asia. **Neighbors:** Iran on W, Afghanistan and China on N, India on E. **Topography:** The Indus R. rises in the Hindu Kush and Himalaya Mts. in the N (highest is K2, or Godwin Austen, 28,250 ft., 2nd highest in world), then flows over 1,000 mi. through fertile valley and empties into Arabian Sea. Thar Desert, Eastern Plains flank Indus Valley. **Capital:** Islamabad, 698,000. **Cities (urban aggr.):** Karachi, 10,032,000; Lahore, 5,452,000; Faisalabad, 2,142,000.

Government: Type: Republic with strong military influence. **Head of state:** Pres. Pervez Musharraf; b Aug. 11,1943; in office: Oct. 5, 1999 (as pres. from June 20, 2001). **Head of gov.:** Shaukat Aziz; b Mar. 6, 1949; in office: Aug. 28, 2004. **Local divisions:** 4 provinces and 1 capital territory, plus federally administered tribal areas. **Defense budget** (2003): $2.8 bil. **Active troops:** 620,000.

Economy: Industries: textiles, food proc., beverages, constr. materials, clothing, paper products. **Chief crops:** cotton, wheat, rice, sugarcane, fruits. **Natural resources:** nat. gas, oil, coal, iron ore, copper, salt, limestone. **Crude oil reserves** (2003): 310.4 mil. bbls. **Arable land:** 27%. **Livestock** (2003): cattle: 23.3 mil.; chickens: 155.0 mil.; goats: 52.8 mil.; sheep: 24.6 mil. **Fish catch** (2002): 611,544 metric tons. **Electricity prod.** (2002): 67.7 bil. kWh. **Labor force:** (1999 est.): agriculture 44%, industry 17%, services 39%.

Finance: Monetary unit: Rupee (PKR) (Sept. 2004: 58.89=1 U.S.). **GDP** (2003 est.): $317.7 bil.; **per capita GDP:** $2,100; **GDP growth:** 5.4%. **Imports** (2003 est.): $12.5 bil.; partners (2002): Saudi Arabia 11.8%, UAE 11.1%, Kuwait 6.8%, U.S. 6.5%, China 6.3%, Japan 6%, Malaysia 4.6%, Germany 4.4%. **Exports** (2003 est.): $11.7 bil.; partners (2002): U.S. 24.5%, UAE 8.4%, UK 7.2%,

Germany 4.9%, Hong Kong 4.8%. **Tourism**: $136 mil. **Budget** (FY02/03 est.): $12.3 bil. **Intl. reserves less gold**: $7.36 bil. **Gold**: 2.10 mil oz t. **Consumer prices**: 2.9%.

Transport: Railroad: Length: 5,072 mi. **Motor vehicles** (2001):1.13 mil. pass. cars, 463,000 comm. vehicles. **Civil aviation**: 6.3 bil. pass.-mi; 87 airports. **Chief port**: Karachi.

Communications: TV sets: 105 per 1,000 pop. **Radios**: 94 per 1,000 pop. **Telephone lines**: 4.0 mil. **Daily newspaper circ.**: 40.4 per 1,000 pop. **Internet** (2002): 1.5 mil. users.

Health: Life expect.: 61.7 male; 63.6 female. **Births** (per 1,000 pop.): 31.2. **Deaths** (per 1,000 pop.): 8.7. **Natural inc.**: 2.25%. **Infant mortality** (per 1,000 live births): 74.4. **AIDS rate**: 0.1%.

Education: Compulsory: ages 5-9. **Literacy**: 45.7%.

Major Intl. Organizations: UN (FAO, IBRD, ILO, IMF, IMO, WHO, WTrO), the commonwealth.

Embassy: 3517 International Ct., NW Washington DC 20008; 243-6500.

Website: www.embassyofpakistan.org

Pakistan shares the 5,000-year history of the India-Pakistan subcontinent. At present-day Harappa and Mohenjo Daro, the Indus Valley Civilization, with large cities and elaborate irrigation systems, flourished c. 4,000-2,500 BC. Aryan invaders from the NW conquered the region around 1,500 BC, forging the Vedic civilization that dominated the region for over a thousand years. Other invaders from the W followed. The first Arab invasion, AD 712, introduced Islam. Present-day Pakistan and India were part of the Mogul empire from 1526 to 1857. Muslim power faded by the end of the 19th cent. as the British gained control of the N and NW areas of the subcontinent.

After World War I, the Muslims of British India began agitation for minority rights in elections. Muhammad Ali Jinnah (1876-1948) was the principal architect of Pakistan. When the British withdrew Aug. 14, 1947, the Islamic majority areas of India acquired self-government and became Pakistan, with dominion status in the Commonwealth. Pakistan was divided into 2 sections, West Pakistan and East Pakistan. The 2 areas were nearly 1,000 mi. apart on opposite sides of India.

The Awami League, which had sought regional autonomy for East Pakistan for several years, won a majority in Dec. 1970 elections to a constituent assembly. In Mar. 1971, Pakistan's military-dominated government postponed the assembly. Rioting and strikes broke out in the East. On Mar. 25, 1971, government troops launched attacks in the East. The Easterners, aided by India, proclaimed the independent nation of Bangladesh. In months of widespread fighting, countless thousands were killed. Some 10 million Easterners fled into India. Full-scale war between India and Pakistan had spread to both the East and West fronts by Dec. 3. Pakistan troops in the East surrendered Dec. 16; Pakistan agreed to a cease-fire in the West Dec. 17. On July 3, 1972, Pakistan and India signed a pact agreeing to withdraw troops from their borders and seek peaceful solutions to all problems.

Zulfikar Ali Bhutto, leader of the Pakistan People's Party, which had won the most West Pakistan votes in Dec. 1970 elections, became president Dec. 20, 1971. Bhutto was overthrown in a military coup July 1977. Convicted of complicity in a 1974 political murder, he was executed Apr. 4, 1979. Over 3 million Afghan refugees flooded into Pakistan after the USSR invaded Afghanistan Dec. 1979; by 2004, 2 million refugees had been repatriated, but more than a million remained.

Pres. Mohammad Zia ul-Haq was killed when his plane exploded in Aug. 1988. Following Nov. elections, Benazir Bhutto, daughter of Zulfikar Ali Bhutto, was named prime minister, becoming the first woman leader of a Muslim nation. She was accused of corruption and dismissed by the president, Aug. 1990; her party was soundly defeated in the Oct. 1990 election. Bhutto returned to power Oct. 1993, but was dismissed again, Nov. 1996, amid further corruption charges.

Responding to nuclear weapons tests by India, Pakistan conducted its own tests, May 28-30, 1998; the U.S. imposed economic sanctions on both countries.

In mid-1999, Muslim infiltrators, apparently including Pakistani troops, seized Indian-held positions in the disputed territory of Kashmir, which witnessed its heaviest fighting in over 2 decades (see India). After meeting with Pres. Bill Clinton on July 4, Prime Min. Nawaz Sharif agreed to a Pakistani pullback. Growing conflict between Sharif and the military climaxed in his firing on Oct. 12 of army chief Gen. Pervez Musharraf, whose supporters staged a bloodless coup. Musharraf assumed the presidency June 20, 2001.

Following the Sept. 11, 2001, terrorist attack on the U.S., Pres. Musharraf, Sept. 19, pledged cooperation with the U.S. in fighting Taliban and al-Qaeda militants within its own tribal areas and in neighboring Afghanistan. In return, the U.S. waived its 1998 sanctions and offered Pakistan financial aid and debt relief. To defuse mounting tensions with India, Musharraf in late Dec. 2001 ordered the arrest of members of Islamic militant groups that India blamed for a Dec. 13 attack on the parliament in New Delhi. Guerrilla violence in Kashmir and Pakistani missile tests May 25-28, 2002, heightened fears of war with India, but the crisis was eased in June with U.S. mediation. A referendum Apr. 30, 2002, extended Musharraf's rule for another 5 years; many observers called the vote rigged.

During 2002-04 there was evidence of growing al-Qaeda and Taliban activity within Pakistan. Militants kidnapped *Wall Street*

Journal reporter Daniel Pearl Jan. 23, 2002, and eventually killed him; 4 Islamic extremists were convicted July 15. Several alleged al-Qaeda operatives, including Ramzi bin al-Shibh, believed to have been a close associate of Sept. 11 ringleader Mohamed Atta, were captured in a shootout in Karachi, Sept. 11, 2002. The alleged mastermind of the Sept. 11 attack, Khalid Sheikh Mohammed, was apprehended in Rawalpindi, Mar. 1, 2003. Islamic extremists carried out bombings in Rawalpindi Dec. 14 and 25, in unsuccessful attempts to assassinate Musharraf. A top al-Qaeda figure implicated in those attempts, Amjad Hussain Farooqi, was killed by security forces in late Sept. 2004.

Accused of selling atomic secrets to Iran, Libya, and North Korea, Pakistan's top nuclear scientist, Abdul Qadeer Khan, made a televised apology, Feb. 4, 2004, and said his actions were unauthorized; he received a pardon from Musharraf Feb. 5. A joint U.S.-Pakistani raid July 25 broke up an al-Qaeda cell in Gujrat, revealing possible evidence of planned attacks against U.S. financial institutions.

On Oct. 1, more than 20 worshippers were killed in the bombing of a Shiite mosque in Sialkot. Earlier bombings and other attacks on Shiite religious targets in Karachi and Quetta had killed more than 100.

Shaukat Aziz, who survived a suicide bomb attack July 30, was elected prime min. Aug. 27.

Palau
Republic of Palau

People: Population: 20,016. **Age distrib.** (%): <15: 26.8; 65+: 4.6. **Pop. density**: 113 per sq mi, 44 per sq km. **Urban**: 68.6%. **Ethnic groups**: Palauan (Micronesian/Malayan/Melanesian mix) 70%, Asian 28%, White 2%. **Principal languages**: English (official); Palauan, Sonsorolese, Tobi, Angaur, Japanese (all official in certain states). **Chief religions**: Roman Catholic 49%, Modekngei 30%.

Geography: Total area: 177 sq mi, 458 sq km; **Land area**: 177 sq mi, 458 sq km. **Location**: Archipelago (26 islands, more than 300 islets) in the W Pacific Ocean, about 530 mi SE of the Philippines. **Neighbors**: Micronesia to E, Indonesia to S. **Topography**: Palau is comprised of a mountainous main island and low coral atolls, usually fringed with large barrier reefs. **Capital**: Koror, 14,000. (Note: a new capital is being built in Babelthuap.)

Government: Type: Republic. **Head of state and gov.**: Pres. Tommy Esang Remengesau, Jr.; b Feb. 28, 1956; in office: Jan. 19, 2001. **Local divisions**: 16 states.

Economy: Industries: tourism, handicrafts, constr., garment making. **Chief crops**: coconuts, copra, cassava, sweet potatoes. **Natural resources**: timber, gold & other minerals, fish. **Fish catch** (2002 est): 1,010 metric tons. **Labor force** (1990): agriculture 20%.

Finance: Monetary unit: U.S. Dollar. **GDP**: $174.0 mil.; **per capita GDP**: $9,000; **GDP growth**: 1.0%. **Imports** (2001 est.): $99.0 mil.; partners (2000) U.S., Guam, Japan, Singapore, Korea. **Exports** (2001 est.): $18.0 mil.; partners (2000): U.S., Japan, Singapore. **Tourism** (2002): $59 mil. **Budget** (FY98/99 est.): $80.8 mil.

Transport: 1 airport.

Communications: TV sets: 98 per 1,000 pop. **Radios**: 550 per 1,000 pop.

Health: Life expect.: 66.7 male; 73.2 female. **Births** (per 1,000 pop.): 18.7. **Deaths** (per 1,000 pop.): 6.9. **Natural inc.**: 1.18%. **Infant mortality** (per 1,000 live births): 15.3.

Education: Compulsory: ages 6-14. **Literacy** (1990): 98%.

Major Intl. Organizations: UN (WHO).

Embassy: 1800 K St. NW, # 714, 20006; 452-6814.

Spain acquired the Palau Islands in 1886 and sold them to Germany in 1899. Japan seized them in 1914. American forces occupied the islands in 1944; in 1947, they became part of the U.S.-administered UN Trust Territory of the Pacific Islands. In 1981 Palau became an autonomous republic; in 1993 the republic ratified a compact of free association with the U.S., which provides financial aid in return for U.S. use of Palauan military facilities over 15 years. Palau became an independent nation on Oct. 1, 1994. Vice-Pres. Tommy Remengesau won the presidential election held Nov. 7, 2000.

Website: www.palauembassy.com

Panama
Republic of Panama

People: Population: 3,000,463. **Age distrib.** (%): <15: 29.6; 65+: 6.1. **Pop. density**: 102 per sq mi, 39 per sq km. **Urban**: 57.1%. **Ethnic groups**: Mestizo 70%, Amerindian-West Indian 14%, White 10%, Amerindian 6%. **Principal languages**: Spanish (official), English. **Chief religions**: Roman Catholic 85%, Protestant 15%.

Geography: Total area: 30,193 sq mi, 78,200 sq km; **Land area**: 29,340 sq mi, 75,990 sq km. **Location**: In Central America. **Neighbors**: Costa Rica on W, Colombia on E. **Topography**: 2 mountain ranges run the length of the isthmus. Tropical rain forests cover the Caribbean coast and eastern Panama. **Capital**: Panama City, 930,000.

Government: Type: Republic. **Head of state and gov.**: Pres. Martin Torrijos Espino; b July 18, 1963; in office: Sept. 1, 2004. **Local divisions**: 9 provinces, 5 territories. **Defense budget**: NA. **Active troops**: Nil. (11,800 paramilitary).

Economy: Industries: constr., oil refining, brewing, constr. materials, sugar milling. **Chief crops**: bananas, rice, corn, coffee, sugarcane. **Natural resources**: copper, mahogany, shrimp, hydropower.

Arable land: 7%. **Livestock** (2003): cattle: 1.55 mil.; chickens: 14.0 mil.; goats: 6,200; pigs: 305,000; **Fish catch** (2002 est): 309,400 metric tons. **Electricity prod.** (2002): 4.87 bil. kWh. **Labor force:** (1995 est.): agriculture 20.8%, industry 18%, services 61.2%.

Finance: Monetary unit: Balboa (PAB) (Sept. 2004: 1.00=1 U.S.). **GDP** (2003 est.): $18.6 bil.; **per capita GDP:** $6,300; **GDP growth:** 3.2%. **Imports** (2003 est.): $6.6 bil.; partners (2002): U.S. 34.4%, Colombia 5.9%, Japan 5.4%, Costa Rica 4.2%, Venezuela 4.2%. **Exports** (2003 est.): $5.2 bil.; partners (2002): U.S. 47.8%, Sweden 5.8%, Costa Rica 4.8%, Honduras 4.5%. **Tourism** (2002): $805 mil. **Budget** (2000 est.): $2.0 bil. **Intl. reserves less gold:** $680 mil. **Consumer prices:** 1.4%.

Transport: Railroad: Length: 221 mi. **Motor vehicles** (2000): 223,100 pass. cars, 74,400 comm. vehicles. **Civil aviation:** 1.6 bil. pass.-mi; 41 airports. **Chief ports:** Balboa, Cristobal.

Communications: TV sets: 192 per 1,000 pop. **Radios:** 299 per 1,000 pop. **Telephone lines** (2002): 386,900. **Daily newspaper circ.:** 62 per 1,000 pop. **Internet** (2001): 120,000 users.

Health: Life expect.: 69.8 male; 74.6 female. **Births** (per 1,000 pop.): 20.4. **Deaths** (per 1,000 pop.): 6.4. **Natural inc.:** 1.40%. **Infant mortality** (per 1,000 live births): 21.0. **AIDS rate:** 0.9%.

Education: Compulsory: ages 6-11. **Literacy:** 92.6%.

Major Intl. Organizations: UN (FAO, IBRD, ILO, IMF, IMO, WHO), the Commonwealth.

Embassy: 2862 McGill Terrace NW 20008; 483-1407.

Websites: www.presidencia.gob.pa
www.consuladogeneraldepanama.com

The coast of Panama was sighted by Rodrigo de Bastidas, sailing with Columbus for Spain in 1501, and was visited by Columbus in 1502. Vasco Nunez de Balboa crossed the isthmus and "discovered" the Pacific Ocean, Sept. 13, 1513. Spanish colonies were ravaged by Francis Drake, 1572-95, and Henry Morgan, 1668-71. Morgan destroyed the old city of Panama which had been founded in 1519. Freed from Spain, Panama joined Colombia in 1821.

Panama declared its independence from Colombia Nov. 3, 1903, with U.S. recognition. In support of Panama, U.S. naval forces deterred action by Colombia. Panama granted use, occupation, and control of the Canal Zone to the U.S. by treaty, ratified Feb. 26, 1904. In 1978, a new treaty provided for a gradual takeover by Panama of the canal, and withdrawal of U.S. troops, to be completed before the end of the century. U.S. payments were substantially increased in the interim.

President Delvalle was ousted by the National Assembly, Feb. 26, 1988, after he tried to fire the head of the Panama Defense Forces, Gen. Manuel Antonio Noriega, who was under U.S. federal indictment on drug charges. U.S. troops invaded Panama Dec. 20, 1989, and Noriega surrendered Jan. 3, 1990.

Mireya Moscoso, widow of former Pres. Arnulfo Arias, was elected president May 2, 1999, becoming Panama's first female head of state. The U.S. handed over control of the Panama Canal to Panama Dec. 31, 1999. Martin Torrijos Espino, son of Brig. Gen. Omar Torrijos Herrera (dictator of Panama, 1968-81), won the presidential election of May 2, 2004.

Papua New Guinea
Independent State of Papua New Guinea

People: Population: 5,420,280. **Age distrib.** (%): <15: 38.6; 65+: 3.7. **Pop. density:** 31 per sq mi, 12 per sq km. **Urban:** 13.2%. **Ethnic groups:** Melanesian, Papuan, Negrito, Micronesian, Polynesian. **Principal languages:** English (official), pidgin English, Motu; 715 indigenous languages. **Chief religions:** Indigenous beliefs 34%, Roman Catholic 22%, Protestant 44%.

Geography: Total area: 178,703 sq mi, 462,840 sq km; **Land area:** 174,850 sq mi, 452,860 sq km. **Location:** SE Asia, occupying E half of island of New Guinea and about 600 nearby islands. **Neighbors:** Indonesia (West Irian) on W, Australia on S. **Topography:** Thickly forested mts. cover much of the center of the country, with lowlands along the coasts. Included are some islands of Bismarck and Solomon groups, such as the Admiralty Isls., New Ireland, New Britain, and Bougainville. **Capital:** Port Moresby, 275,000.

Government: Type: Parliamentary democracy. **Head of state:** Queen Elizabeth II, represented by Gov-Gen. Sir Paulias Matane; b 1931; in office: June 29, 2004. **Head of gov.:** Prime Min. Sir Michael Somare; b Apr. 9, 1936; in office: Aug. 5, 2002. **Local divisions:** 20 provinces. **Defense budget** (2003): $19 mil. **Active troops:** 3,100.

Economy: Industries: copra & palm oil proc., wood products, mining. **Chief crops:** coffee, cocoa, coconuts, palm kernels, tea, rubber, sweet potatoes. **Natural resources:** gold, copper, silver, nat. gas, timber, oil, fish. **Crude oil reserves** (2003): 240.0 mil. bbls. **Livestock** (2003): cattle: 90,000; chickens: 3.9 mil.; goats: 2,500; pigs: 1.8 mil.; sheep: 7,000. **Fish catch** (2002 est): 148,715 metric tons. **Electricity prod.** (2002): 1.68 bil. kWh. **Labor force:** agriculture 85%.

Finance: Monetary unit: Kina (PGK) (Sept. 2004: 3.03=1 U.S.). **GDP** (2003 est.): $11.4 bil.; **per capita GDP:** $2,200; **GDP growth:** 0.7%. **Imports** (2003 est.): $967.0 mil.; partners (2002): Australia 49.2%, Singapore 18.8%, New Zealand 4.4%, Japan 4.3%. **Exports** (2003 est.): $1.9 bil.; partners (2002): Australia 24.2%, Japan 9.4%, China 5.4%. **Tourism** (2001): $101 mil. **Bud-**

get (2000 est.): $1.1 bil. **Intl. reserves less gold:** $333 mil. **Gold:** 60,000 oz t. **Consumer prices:** 14.7%.

Transport: Motor vehicles (1998): 21,700 pass. cars, 89,700 comm. vehicles. **Civil aviation:** 390.2 mil. pass.-mi; 21 airports. **Chief ports:** Port Moresby, Lae.

Communications: TV sets: 13 per 1,000 pop. **Radios:** 91 per 1,000 pop. **Telephone lines** (2002): 62,000. **Daily newspaper circ.:** 15 per 1,000 pop. **Internet** (2002): 75,000 users.

Health: Life expect.: 62.4 male; 66.8 female. **Births** (per 1,000 pop.): 30.5. **Deaths** (per 1,000 pop.): 7.5. **Natural inc.:** 2.30%. **Infant mortality** (per 1,000 live births): 53.2. **AIDS rate:** 0.6%.

Education: Compulsory: ages 6-14. **Literacy:** 66%.

Major Intl. Organizations: UN (FAO, IBRD, ILO, IMF, IMO, WHO, WTrO), the Commonwealth, APEC.

Embassy: 1779 Massachusetts Ave NW, 20036; 745-3680.

Websites: www.pngonline.gov.pg; www.pngembassy.org

Human remains have been found in the interior of New Guinea dating back at least 10,000 years and possibly much earlier. Successive waves of peoples probably entered the country from Asia through Indonesia. The indigenous population consists of a huge number of tribes, many living in almost complete isolation with mutually unintelligible languages.

Europeans visited in the 15th century, but actual land claims did not begin until the 19th century, when the Dutch took control of the island's western half. The southern half of eastern New Guinea was first claimed by Britain in 1884, and transferred to Australia in 1905. The northern half was claimed by Germany in 1884, but captured in World War I by Australia, which was first granted a League of Nations mandate and then a UN trusteeship over the area. The 2 territories were administered jointly after 1949, given self-government Dec. 1, 1973, and became independent Sept. 16, 1975.

Secessionist rebels clashed with government forces on Bougainville beginning in 1988; a truce signed Oct. 10, 1997, brought a halt to the fighting, which had claimed an estimated 20,000 lives. The country suffered from a severe drought in 1997. A tsunami killed at least 3,000 people July 17, 1998. A Bougainville autonomy agreement was signed Aug. 30, 2001. Army mutinies were suppressed in Mar. 2001 and Mar. 2002.

Paraguay
Republic of Paraguay

People: Population: 6,191,368. **Age distrib.** (%): <15: 38.7; 65+: 4.7. **Pop. density:** 40 per sq mi, 16 per sq km. **Urban:** 57.2%. **Ethnic groups:** Mestizo 95%. **Principal languages:** Spanish, Guaraní (both official). **Chief religions:** Roman Catholic 90%.

Geography: Total area: 157,047 sq mi, 406,750 sq km; **Land area:** 153,398 sq mi, 397,300 sq km. **Location:** Landlocked country in central South America. **Neighbors:** Bolivia on N, Argentina on S, Brazil on E. **Topography:** Paraguay R. bisects the country. To E are fertile plains, wooded slopes, grasslands. To W is the Gran Chaco plain, with marshes and scrub trees. Extreme W is arid. **Capital:** Asunción, 1,639,000.

Government: Type: Republic. **Head of state and gov.:** Pres. Nicanor Duarte Frutos; b Oct. 11, 1956; in office: Aug. 15, 2003. **Local divisions:** 17 departments and capital city. **Defense budget** (2003): $41 mil. **Active troops:** 18,600.

Economy: Industries: sugar, cement, textiles, beverages, wood products. **Chief crops:** cotton, sugarcane, soybeans, corn, wheat, tobacco, cassava. **Natural resources:** hydropower, timber, iron ore, mang., limestone. **Arable land:** 6%. **Livestock** (2003): cattle: 8.8 mil.; chickens: 15.55 mil.; goats: 108,100; pigs: 3.3 mil.; sheep: 361,900. **Fish catch** (2002 est): 25,000 metric tons. **Electricity prod.** (2002): 48.36 bil. kWh. **Labor force:** agriculture 45%.

Finance: Monetary unit: Guarani (PYG) (Sept. 2004: 5,914.75=1 U.S.). **GDP** (2003 est.): $28.0 bil.; **per capita GDP:** $4,600; **GDP growth:** 1.3%. **Imports** (2003 est.): $2.8 bil.; partners (2002): Brazil 28.9%, U.S. 22.5%, Argentina 17.7%, Uruguay 4.7%, Hong Kong 4.3%, China 4.1%. **Exports** (2003 est.): $2.7 bil.; partners (2002): Brazil 29.8%, Argentina 18%, Chile 5.5%, Bermuda 4%. **Tourism** (2002): $62 mil. **Budget** (1999 est.): $2.0 bil. **Intl. reserves less gold:** $652 mil. **Gold:** 30,000 oz t. **Consumer prices:** 14.2%.

Transport: Railroad: Length: 274 mi. **Motor vehicles** (1993): 250,700 pass. cars, 37,700 comm. vehicles. **Civil aviation:** 165.3 mil. pass.-mi; 11 airports. **Chief port:** Asunción.

Communications: TV sets: 205 per 1,000 pop. **Radios:** 182 per 1,000 pop. **Telephone lines:** 273,200. **Daily newspaper circ.:** 43 per 1,000 pop. **Internet** (2002): 120,000 users.

Health: Life expect.: 72.1 male; 77.3 female. **Births** (per 1,000 pop.): 29.8. **Deaths** (per 1,000 pop.): 4.6. **Natural inc.:** 2.52%. **Infant mortality** (per 1,000 live births): 26.7. **AIDS rate:** 0.5%.

Education: Compulsory: ages 6-14. **Literacy:** 94%.

Major Intl. Organizations: UN (FAO, IBRD, ILO, IMF, IMO, WHO, WTrO), OAS.

Embassy: 2400 Massachusetts Ave. NW, 20008; 483-6960.

Website: www.paraguay.com

The Guarani Indians were settled farmers speaking a common language before the arrival of Europeans. Visited by Sebastian Cabot in 1527 and settled as a Spanish possession in 1535, Paraguay gained its independence from Spain in 1811. It lost much of its territory to Brazil, Uruguay, and Argentina in the War of the Triple Alliance, 1865-1870. Large areas were won from Bolivia in the Chaco War, 1932-35.

Gen. Alfredo Stroessner, who had ruled since 1954, was ousted in a military coup led by Gen. Andrés Rodríguez on Feb. 3, 1989. Rodríguez was elected president May 1. Juan Carlos Wasmosy was elected president May 9, 1993, becoming the nation's first civilian head of state in many years.

A prolonged power struggle involving a popular military leader, Gen. Lino César Oviedo, who was accused of insubordination, culminated in his surrender Dec. 12, 1997. He was freed Aug. 18, 1998, following the inauguration of Pres. Raúl Cubas Grau, Oviedo's successor as Colorado Party nominee.

The assassination of Vice Pres. Luis María Argaña, Mar. 23, 1999, by an unidentified gunman, was widely attributed to Cubas and triggered protests and an impeachment vote; Cubas resigned Mar. 28 and was succeeded by Senate leader Luis Angel González Macchi. An attempted military coup was suppressed May 18, 2000.

Mass protests over the depressed economy led to the proclamation of a state of emergency July 15, 2002. Nicanor Duarte Frutos won the presidency, Apr. 27, 2003, maintaining 55 years of uninterrupted Colorado Party rule. A supermarket fire in Asunción Aug. 1, 2004, killed more than 400 people.

Peru
Republic of Peru

People: Population: 27,544,305. **Age distrib.** (%): <15: 34; 65+: 4.9. **Pop. density:** 56 per sq mi, 22 per sq km. **Urban:** 73.9%. **Ethnic groups:** Amerindian 45%, Mestizo 37%, White 15%. **Principal languages:** Spanish, Quechua (both official); Aymara. **Chief religions:** Roman Catholic 90% (official).

Geography: Total area: 496,226 sq mi, 1,285,220 sq km; **Land area:** 494,211 sq mi, 1,280,000 sq km. **Location:** On the Pacific coast of South America. **Neighbors:** Ecuador, Colombia on N; Brazil, Bolivia on E; Chile on S. **Topography:** An arid coastal strip, 10 to 100 mi. wide, supports much of the population thanks to widespread irrigation. The Andes cover 27% of land area. The uplands are well-watered, as are the eastern slopes reaching the Amazon basin, which covers half the country with its forests and jungles. **Capital:** Lima, 7,899,000. **Cities (urban aggr.):** Arequipa, 710,103; Callao, 424,294.

Government: Type: Republic. **Head of state:** Pres. Alejandro Toledo; b Mar. 28, 1946; in office: July 28, 2001. **Head of gov.:** Prime Min. Carlos Ferrero Costa; b Feb. 7, 1941; in office: Dec. 15, 2003. **Local divisions:** 12 regions, 24 departments, 1 constitutional province. **Defense budget** (2003): $900 mil. **Active troops:** 100,000.

Economy: Industries: mining, oil, fishing, textiles, clothing, food proc. **Chief crops:** coffee, cotton, sugarcane, rice, wheat, potatoes, corn, plantains, coca. **Natural resources:** copper, silver, gold, oil, timber, fish, iron ore, coal, phosphate, potash, hydropower, nat. gas. **Crude oil reserves** (2003): 323.4 mil. bbls. **Arable land:** 3%. **Livestock** (2003): cattle: 5.0 mil.; chickens: 95.0 mil.; goats: 2.86 mil.; pigs: 12.22 mil.; sheep: 14.1 mil. **Fish catch** (2002): 8,775,431 metric tons. **Electricity prod.** (2002): 21.74 bil. kWh. **Labor force:** agriculture, mining and quarrying, manufacturing, construction, transport, services.

Finance: Monetary unit: Nuevo Sol (PEN) (Sept. 2004: 3.35=1 U.S.). **GDP** (2003 est.): $146.9 bil.; **per capita GDP:** $5,200; **GDP growth:** 4.0%. **Imports** (2003 est.): $8.2 bil.; partners (2002): U.S. 27.5%, Spain 8.3%, Chile 7.9%, Brazil 4.7%, Colombia 4.6%. **Exports** (2003 est.): $9.0 bil.; partners (2002): U.S. 26.1%, UK 11.6%, China 7.9%, Switzerland 7.5%, Japan 4.9%. **Tourism:** $832 mil. **Budget** (2002 est.): $10.4 bil. **Intl. reserves less gold:** $6.58 bil. **Gold:** 1.11 mil oz t. **Consumer prices:** 2.3%.

Transport: Railroad: Length: 1,136 mi. **Motor vehicles** (2000): 731,300 pass. cars, 459,600 comm. vehicles. **Civil aviation:** 340.5 mil. pass.-mi; 49 airports. **Chief ports:** Callao, Chimbote, Matarani, Salaverry.

Communications: TV sets: 147 per 1,000 pop. **Radios:** 273 per 1,000 pop. **Telephone lines:** 1.8 mil. **Daily newspaper circ.:** 85 per 1,000 pop. **Internet:** 2.9 mil. users.

Health: Life expect.: 67.5 male; 71.0 female. **Births** (per 1,000 pop.): 21.3. **Deaths** (per 1,000 pop.): 6.3. **Natural inc.:** 1.50%. **Infant mortality** (per 1,000 live births): 33.0. **AIDS rate:** 0.5%.

Education: Compulsory: ages 6-16. **Literacy:** 90.9%.

Major Intl. Organizations: UN and all of its specialized agencies, APEC, OAS.

Embassy: 1700 Massachusetts Ave. NW 20036; 833-9860.

Website: www.peruvianembassy.us; www.peru.org.pe

The powerful Inca empire had its seat at Cuzco in the Andes and covered most of Peru, Bolivia, and Ecuador, as well as parts of Colombia, Chile, and Argentina. Building on the achievements of 800 years of Andean civilization, the Incas had a high level of skill in architecture, engineering, textiles, and social organization.

A civil war had weakened the empire when Francisco Pizarro, Spanish conquistador, began raiding Peru for its wealth, 1532. In 1533 he seized the ruling Inca, Atahualpa, filled a room with gold as a ransom, then executed him and enslaved the natives.

Lima was the seat of Spanish viceroys until the Argentine liberator, José de San Martin, captured it in 1821; Spanish forces were ultimately routed by Simón Bolívar, 1824.

On Oct. 3, 1968, a military coup ousted Pres. Fernando Belaunde Terry. In 1968-74, the military government started socialist pro-

grams. Food shortages, escalating foreign debt, and strikes led to another coup, Aug. 29, 1976.

After 12 years of military rule, Peru returned to democratic leadership in 1980 but was plagued by economic problems and by leftist Shining Path (Sendero Luminoso) guerrillas. Conflict between guerrillas and government troops, 1980-2000, killed more than 69,000 people, mostly Andean Indians.

Elected president in June 1990, Alberto Fujimori, the son of Japanese immigrants, dissolved the National Congress, suspended parts of the constitution, and initiated press censorship, Apr. 5, 1992. The leader of Shining Path was captured Sept. 12.

With the economy booming and signs of significant progress in curtailing guerrilla activity, Fujimori won reelection Apr. 9, 1995. Repressive antiterrorism tactics, however, drew international criticism. On Dec. 17, 1996, leftist Tupac Amaru guerrillas infiltrated a reception at the Japanese ambassador's residence in Lima and took hundreds of hostages, most of whom were later released. Peruvian soldiers stormed the embassy Apr. 22, 1997, rescuing 71 of the remaining hostages; 1 hostage, 2 soldiers, and all 14 guerrillas were killed. Fujimori's path to a 3rd term was cleared when his lone remaining challenger withdrew, charging electoral fraud, 6 days before a runoff vote on May 28, 2000. Scandals involving his top aide and intelligence chief, Vladimiro Montesinos, led Fujimori to resign his office Nov. 20, while on a visit to Japan; instead of accepting his resignation, Congress ousted him as "morally unfit."

Alejandro Toledo won a presidential runoff election June 3, 2001. Montesinos was captured in Venezuela June 23 and extradited to Peru and sentenced on abuse of power charges July 1, 2002. Charges were filed Sept. 5 against the exiled Fujimori, alleging his complicity in the killings by a paramilitary death squad of at least 25 people during 1991-92.

Fireworks explosions killed 291 people in a crowded Lima commercial district Dec. 29, 2001. A sagging economy, resurgent rebel activity, and a series of scandals eroded Toledo's popularity during 2003-04.

Philippines
Republic of the Philippines

People: Population: 86,241,697. **Age distrib.** (%): <15: 36.6; 65+: 3.7. **Pop. density:** 749 per sq mi, 289 per sq km. **Urban:** 61.0%. **Ethnic groups:** Christian Malay 91.5%, Muslim Malay 4%, Chinese 1.5%. **Principal languages:** Filipino, English (both official); many dialects. **Chief religions:** Roman Catholic 83%, Protestant 9%, Muslim 5%.

Geography: Total area: 115,831 sq mi, 300,000 sq km; **Land area:** 115,124 sq mi, 298,170 sq km. **Location:** An archipelago off the SE coast of Asia. **Neighbors:** Nearest are Malaysia and Indonesia on S, Taiwan on N. **Topography:** The country consists of some 7,100 islands stretching 1,100 mi. N-S. About 95% of area and population are on 11 largest islands, which are mountainous, except for the heavily indented coastlines and for the central plain on Luzon. **Capital:** Manila, 10,352,000. **Cities (urban aggr.):** Quezon City, 2,160,000; Davao, 1,152,000.

Government: Type: Republic. **Head of state and gov.:** Pres. Gloria Macapagal Arroyo; b Apr. 5, 1947; in office: Jan. 20, 2001. **Local divisions:** 79 provinces. **Defense budget** (2003): $808 mil. **Active troops:** 106,000.

Economy: Industries: textiles, pharm., chemicals, wood products, food proc., electronics. **Chief crops:** rice, coconuts, corn, sugarcane, bananas, pineapples. **Natural resources:** timber, oil, nickel, cobalt, silver, gold, salt, copper. **Crude oil reserves** (2003): 152.0 mil. bbls. **Arable land:** 19%. **Livestock** (2003): cattle: 2.56 mil.; chickens: 128.2 mil.; goats: 6.3 mil.; pigs: 12.4 mil.; sheep: 30,000. **Fish catch** (2002): 2,473,861 metric tons. **Electricity prod.** (2002): 45.57 bil. kWh. **Labor force** (2003 est.): agriculture 45%, industry 15%, services 40%.

Finance: Monetary unit: Peso (PHP) (Sept. 2004: 56.13=1 U.S.). **GDP** (2003 est.): $390.7 bil.; **per capita GDP:** $4,600; **GDP growth:** 4.5%. **Imports** (2003 est.): $36.0 bil.; partners (2002): U.S. 20.6%, Japan 20.4%, South Korea 7.8%, Singapore 6.5%, Taiwan 5%, Hong Kong 4.5%. **Exports** (2003 est.): $34.6 bil.; partners (2002): U.S. 24.7%, Japan 15%, Netherlands 8.7%, Taiwan 7.1%, Singapore 7%, Hong Kong 6.7%, Malaysia 4.7%. **Tourism:** $1.5 bil. **Budget** (2002): $15.1 bil. **Intl. reserves less gold:** $9.06 bil. **Gold:** 8.22 mil oz t. **Consumer prices:** 3.0%.

Transport: Railroad: Length: 557 mi. **Motor vehicles** (2001): 2.22 mil. pass. cars, 285,300 comm. vehicles. **Civil aviation:** 6.8 bil. pass.-mi; 82 airports. **Chief ports:** Cebu, Manila, Iloilo, Davao.

Communications: TV sets: 110 per 1,000 pop. **Radios:** 161 per 1,000 pop. **Telephone lines** (2002): 3.3 mil. **Daily newspaper circ.:** 79 per 1,000 pop. **Internet** (2002): 3.5 mil. users.

Health: Life expect.: 66.7 male; 72.6 female. **Births** (per 1,000 pop.): 25.8. **Deaths** (per 1,000 pop.): 5.5. **Natural inc.:** 2.03%. **Infant mortality** (per 1,000 live births): 24.2. **AIDS rate:** <0.1%.

Education: Compulsory: ages 6-12. **Literacy:** 95.9%.

Major Intl. Organizations: UN (FAO, IBRD, ILO, IMF, IMO, WHO, WTrO), ASEAN.

Embassy: 1600 Massachusetts Ave. NW 20036; 467-9300.

Websites: www.philippineembassy-usa.org; www.gov.ph

Originally inhabited by Malay peoples, the archipelago was visited by Magellan, 1521. The Spanish founded Manila, 1571. The

islands, named for King Philip II of Spain, were ceded by Spain to the U.S. for $20 million, 1898, following the Spanish-American War. U.S. troops suppressed a guerrilla uprising in a brutal 6-year war, 1899-1905.

Japan attacked the Philippines Dec. 8, 1941, and occupied the islands during WW II. On July 4, 1946, independence was proclaimed in accordance with an act passed by the U.S. Congress in 1934. A republic was established.

The repressive and corrupt regime of Pres. Ferdinand Marcos and his wife, Imelda, ruled the Philippines 1965-86. The assassination of prominent opposition leader Benigno S. Aquino Jr., Aug. 21, 1983, sparked demonstrations calling for Marcos's resignation. After a bitter presidential campaign, amid allegations of widespread election fraud, Marcos was declared the victor Feb. 16, 1986, over Corazon Aquino, widow of the slain opposition leader. With his support collapsing, Marcos fled the country Feb. 25, and Corazon Aquino became president.

Her government was plagued by a weak economy, widespread poverty, Communist and Muslim insurgencies, and lukewarm military support. Rebel troops seized military bases and TV stations and bombed the presidential palace, Dec. 1, 1989. Government forces, with U.S. air support, defeated the attempted coup. Aquino endorsed Fidel Ramos in the May 1992 presidential election, which he won. The U.S. vacated the Subic Bay Naval Station in late 1992, ending its long military presence in the Philippines. The government signed a cease-fire agreement, Jan. 30, 1994, with Muslim separatist guerrillas, but some rebels refused to abide by the accord. A new treaty providing for expansion and development of an autonomous Muslim region on Mindanao was signed Sept. 2, 1996, formally ending a rebellion that had claimed more than 120,000 lives since 1972.

Running as a populist, Joseph (Erap) Estrada, a former movie actor, won the presidential election of May 11, 1998. Charged with bribery and corruption, he was impeached Nov. 13, 2000. When the Supreme Court ruled the presidency vacant Jan. 20, 2001, Vice-Pres. Gloria Macapagal Arroyo became president.

As part of the war on terrorism, the U.S. assisted Filipino troops in combating Abu Sayyaf, an Islamic guerrilla group; the leader of the extremists, Abu Sabaya, was killed June 21, 2002. A resurgence of terrorism on Mindanao in 2003 included bombings at Davao's airport, Mar. 4, and ferry terminal, Apr. 2. A mutiny by some 300 troops in Manila, July 27, was suppressed.

Pres. Arroyo won reelection May 10, 2004. Arroyo, who sent a small contingent of Filipino troops to support the U.S. in Iraq, removed them July 19, ahead of schedule, in order to win the freedom of a Filipino truck driver held hostage by Iraqi insurgents.

Poland
Republic of Poland

People: Population: 38,626,349. **Age distrib.** (%): <15: 17.9; 65+: 12.6. **Pop. density:** 329 per sq mi, 127 per sq km. **Urban:** 61.9%. **Ethnic groups:** Polish 98%, German 1%. **Principal languages:** Polish (official), Ukrainian, German. **Chief religion:** Roman Catholic 95%.

Geography: Total area: 120,728 sq mi, 312,685 sq km; **Land area:** 117,555 sq mi, 304,465 sq km. **Location:** On the Baltic Sea in E central Europe. **Neighbors:** Germany on W; Czech Rep., Slovakia on S; Lithuania, Belarus, Ukraine on E; Russia on N. **Topography:** Mostly lowlands forming part of the Northern European Plain. The Carpathian Mts. along the S border rise to 8,200 ft. **Capital:** Warsaw, 2,200,000. **Cities:** Katowice, 3,069,000; Lodz, 974,000; Krakow, 859,000.

Government: Type: Republic. **Head of state:** Pres. Aleksander Kwasniewski; b Nov. 15, 1954; in office: Dec. 23, 1995. **Head of gov.:** Prime Min. Marek Belka; b Jan. 9, 1952; in office: May 2, 2004. **Local divisions:** 16 provinces. **Defense budget** (2003): $3.9 bil. **Active troops:** 163,000.

Economy: Industries: machinery, iron & steel, coal, chemicals, shipbuilding, food proc., glass, beverages, textiles. **Chief crops:** potatoes, fruits, vegetables, wheat. **Natural resources:** coal, sulfur, copper, nat. gas, silver, lead, salt. **Crude oil reserves** (2003): 96.4 mil. bbls. **Arable land:** 47%. **Livestock** (2003): cattle: 5.49 mil.; chickens: 48.4 mil.; pigs: 18.6 mil.; sheep: 337,792. **Fish catch** (2002): 255,150 metric tons. **Electricity prod.** (2002): 133.78 bil. kWh. **Labor force** (1999): industry 22.1%, agriculture 27.5%, services 50.4%.

Finance: Monetary unit: Zloty (PLN) (Sept. 2004: 3.58=1 U.S.). **GDP** (2003 est.): $426.7 bil.; **per capita GDP:** $11,000; **GDP growth:** 3.6%. **Imports** (2003 est.): $63.7 bil.; partners (2002): Germany 24.3%, Italy 8.4%, Russia 8%, France 7%. **Exports** (2003 est.): $57.6 bil.; partners (2002): Germany 32.3%, France 6%, Italy 5.5%, UK 5.2%, Netherlands 4.5%, Czech Republic 4%. **Tourism:** $4.1 bil. **Budget** (1999): $52.3 bil. **Intl. reserves less gold:** $21.92 bil. **Gold:** 3.31 mil oz t. **Consumer prices:** 0.7%.

Transport: Railroad: Length: 14,553 mi. **Motor vehicles** (2001): 10.5 mil pass. cars, 2.06 mil comm. vehicles. **Civil aviation:** 2.9 bil. pass.-mi; 88 airports. **Chief ports:** Gdansk, Gdynia, Ustka, Szczecin.

Communications: TV sets: 387 per 1,000 pop. **Radios:** 522 per 1,000 pop. **Telephone lines:** 12.3 mil. **Daily newspaper circ.:** 101.7 per 1,000 pop. **Internet:** 9.0 mil. users.

Health: Life expect.: 70.0 male; 78.5 female. **Births** (per 1,000 pop.): 10.6. **Deaths** (per 1,000 pop.): 10.0. **Natural inc.:** 0.07%. **Infant mortality** (per 1,000 live births): 8.7. **AIDS rate:** 0.1%.

Education: Compulsory: ages 7-15. **Literacy:** 99.8%.

Major Intl. Organizations: UN (FAO, IBRD, ILO, IMF, IMO, WHO, WTrO), EU, NATO, OECD, OSCE.

Embassy: 2640 16th St. NW 20009; 234-3800.

Websites: www.polandembassy.org; www.poland.pl

Slavic tribes in the area were converted to Latin Christianity in the 10th century. Poland was a great power from the 14th to the 17th centuries. In 3 partitions (1772, 1793, 1795) it was apportioned among Prussia, Russia, and Austria. Overrun by the Austro-German armies in World War I, it declared its independence on Nov. 11, 1918, and was recognized as independent by the Treaty of Versailles, June 28, 1919. Large territories to the east were taken in a war with Russia, 1921.

Germany and the USSR invaded Poland Sept. 1-27, 1939, and divided the country. During the war, some 6 million Polish citizens, half of them Jews, were killed by the Nazis. With Germany's defeat, a Polish government-in-exile in London was recognized by the U.S., but the USSR pressed the claims of a rival group. The election of 1947 was completely dominated by the Communists.

In compensation for 69,860 sq. mi. ceded to the USSR, in 1945 Poland received approx. 40,000 sq. mi. of German territory E of the Oder-Neisse line comprising Silesia, Pomerania, West Prussia, and part of East Prussia.

In 12 years of rule by Stalinists, large estates were abolished, industries nationalized, schools secularized, and Roman Catholic prelates jailed. Farm production fell off. Harsh working conditions caused a riot in Poznan, June 28-29, 1956. A new Politburo, committed to a more independent Polish Communism, was named Oct. 1956, with Wladyslaw Gomulka as first secretary of the party. Collectivization of farms was ended. Gomulka agreed to permit religious liberty and religious publications, provided the church kept out of politics.

In Dec. 1970 workers in port cities rioted because of price rises and new incentive wage rules. On Dec. 20 Gomulka resigned as party leader; he was succeeded by Edward Gierek. The rules were dropped and price rises revoked.

After 2 months of labor turmoil had crippled the country, the Polish government, Aug. 30, 1980, met the demands of striking workers at the Lenin Shipyard, Gdansk. Government concessions included the right to form independent trade unions and the right to strike. By 1981, 9.5 mil workers had joined the independent trade union (Solidarity). As Solidarity's demands grew bolder, the government, spurred by fear of Soviet intervention, imposed martial law Dec. 13. Lech Walesa and other Solidarity leaders were arrested.

On Apr. 5, 1989, an accord was reached between the government and opposition factions on political and economic reforms, including free elections. Candidates endorsed by Solidarity swept the parliamentary elections, June 4. Lech Walesa became president Dec. 22, 1990.

A radical economic program designed to transform the economy into a free-market system led to inflation and unemployment. In Sept. 1993, former Communists and other leftists won a majority in the lower house of Parliament. Walesa lost to a former Communist, Aleksander Kwasniewski, in a presidential runoff election, Nov. 19, 1995.

A new constitution was approved by referendum May 25, 1997. Flooding in July caused more than $1 billion in property damage. Solidarity won parliamentary elections held Sept. 21. Poland became a full member of NATO on Mar. 12, 1999. Pres. Kwasniewski was reelected Oct. 8, 2000. The former Communists won a plurality in parliamentary voting Sept. 23, 2001.

Poland, a close U.S. ally, assumed command Sept. 3, 2003, of a 9,000-member multinational force in south-central Iraq. Poland entered the European Union May 1, 2004.

Portugal
Portuguese Republic

People: Population: 10,524,145. **Age distrib.** (%): <15: 16.9; 65+: 15.8. **Pop. density:** 296 per sq mi, 114 per sq km. **Urban:** 54.6%. **Ethnic groups:** Mainly Portuguese. **Principal languages:** Portuguese (official). **Chief religion:** Roman Catholic 94%.

Geography: Total area: 35,672 sq mi, 92,391 sq km; **Land area:** 35,502 sq mi, 91,951 sq km. **Location:** At SW extreme of Europe. **Neighbors:** Spain on N, E. **Topography:** Portugal N of Tajus R., which bisects the country NE-SW, is mountainous, cool and rainy. To the S there are drier, rolling plains, and a warm climate. **Capital:** Lisbon, 1,962,000. **Cities (urban agg.):** Porto, 1,254,000.

Government: Type: Republic. **Head of state:** Pres. Jorge Sampaio; b Sept. 18, 1939; in office: Mar. 9, 1996. **Head of gov.:** Prime Min. Pedro Santana Lopes; b June 29, 1956; in office: July 17, 2004. **Local divisions:** 18 districts, 2 autonomous regions. **Defense budget** (2003): $1.9 bil. **Active troops:** 44,900.

Economy: Industries: textiles, footwear, wood and paper products, metalworking, oil refining, chemicals, fish proc, wine, tourism. **Chief crops:** grain, potatoes, olives, grapes. **Natural resources:** fish, cork, tungsten, iron ore, uranium ore, marble, hydropower. **Arable land:** 26%. **Livestock** (2003): cattle: 1.40 mil.; chickens: 35.0 mil.; goats: 550,000; pigs: 2.34 mil.; sheep: 5.5 mil.

Fish catch (2002): 208,474 metric tons. **Electricity prod.** (2002): 43.28 bil. kWh. **Labor force** (1999 est.): services 60%, industry 30%, agriculture 10%.

Finance: Monetary unit: Euro (EUR) (Sept. 2004: 0.82=1 U.S.). **GDP** (2003 est.): $182.3 bil.; **per capita GDP:** $18,000; **GDP growth:** -1.0%. **Imports** (2003 est.): $43.7 bil.; partners (2002): Spain 28.1%, Germany 15%, France 10.2%, Italy 6.5%, UK 5.2%, Netherlands 4.5%. **Exports** (2003 est.): $31.1 bil.; partners (2002): Spain 20.3%, Germany 18.4%, France 12.6%, UK 10.5%, U.S. 5.8%, Italy 4.8%, Belgium 4.5%. **Tourism:** $6.9 bil. **Budget** (2001 est.): $48.0 bil. **Intl. reserves less gold:** $3.96 bil. **Gold:** 16.63 mil oz t. **Consumer prices:** 3.3%.

Transport: Railroad: Length: 1,771 mi. **Motor vehicles** (2001): 5.26 mil pass. cars, 1.73 mil. comm. vehicles. **Civil aviation:** 6.0 bil. pass.-mi; 40 airports. **Chief ports:** Lisbon, Setubal, Leixoes.

Communications: TV sets: 567 per 1,000 pop. **Radios:** 306 per 1,000 pop. **Telephone lines:** 4.3 mil. **Daily newspaper circ.:** 32 per 1,000 pop. **Internet** (2002): 2.0 mil. users.

Health: Life expect.: 74.1 male; 80.9 female. **Births** (per 1,000 pop.): 10.9. **Deaths** (per 1,000 pop.): 10.4. **Natural inc.:** 0.05%. **Infant mortality** (per 1,000 live births): 5.1. **AIDS rate:** 0.4%.

Education: Compulsory: ages 6-14. **Literacy:** 93.3%.

Major Intl. Organizations: UN (FAO, IBRD, ILO, IMF, IMO, WHO, WTrO), EU, NATO, OECD, OSCE.

Embassy: 2125 Kalorama Rd. NW 20008; 328-8610.

Website: www.portugal.org

Portugal, an independent state since the 12th century, was a kingdom until a revolution in 1910 drove out King Manoel II and a republic was proclaimed.

From 1932 a strong, repressive government was headed by Premier Antonio de Oliveira Salazar. Illness forced his retirement in Sept. 1968.

On Apr. 25, 1974, the government was seized by a military junta led by Gen. Antonio de Spinola, who became president. The new government reached agreements providing independence for Guinea-Bissau, Mozambique, Cape Verde Islands, Angola, and São Tomé and Príncipe. Banks, insurance companies, and other industries were nationalized.

Parliament approved, June 1, 1989, a package of reforms that did away with the socialist economy and created a "democratic" economy, denationalizing industries. Portugal returned Macao to China on Dec. 20, 1999.

Azores Islands, in the Atlantic, 740 mi W of Portugal, have an area of 868 sq mi and a pop. (1993 est.) of 238,000. A 1951 agreement gave the U.S. the rights to use defense facilities in the Azores. The **Madeira Islands,** 350 mi off the NW coast of Africa, have an area of 306 sq mi and a pop. (1993 est.) of 437,312. Both groups were offered partial autonomy in 1976.

Qatar
State of Qatar

People: Population: 840,290. **Age distrib.** (%): <15: 25.2; 65+: 2.7. **Pop. density:** 190 per sq mi, 73 per sq km. **Urban:** 92.0%. **Ethnic groups:** Arab 40%, Pakistani 18%, Indian 18%, Iranian 10%. **Principal languages:** Arabic (official), English. **Chief religion:** Muslim 95% (official).

Geography: Total area: 4,416 sq mi, 11,437 sq km; **Land area:** 4,416 sq mi, 11,437 sq km. **Location:** Middle East, occupying peninsula on W coast of Persian Gulf. **Neighbors:** Saudi Arabia on S. **Topography:** Mostly a flat desert, with some limestone ridges; vegetation of any kind is scarce. **Capital:** Doha, 286,000.

Government: Type: Traditional monarchy. **Head of state:** Emir Hamad bin Khalifa ath-Thani; b 1952; in office: June 27, 1995. **Head of gov.:** Prime Min. Abdullah bin Khalifa ath-Thani; b Dec. 25, 1959; in office: Oct. 29, 1996. **Local divisions:** 9 municipalities. **Defense budget** (2003): $1.9 bil. **Active troops:** 12,400.

Economy: Industries: oil prod. & refining, fertilizers, petrochems., constr. materials. **Chief crops:** fruits, vegetables. **Natural resources:** oil, nat. gas, fish. **Crude oil reserves** (2003): 15.2 bil. bbls. **Livestock** (2003): cattle: 15,000; chickens: 4.0 mil.; goats: 180,000; sheep: 200,000. **Fish catch** (2002): 6,880 metric tons. **Electricity prod.** (2002): 9.73 bil. kWh. **Arable land:** 10%.

Finance: Monetary unit: Rial (QAR) (Sept. 2004: 3.64=1 U.S.). **GDP** (2003 est.): $17.5 bil.; **per capita GDP:** $21,500; **GDP growth:** 8.5%. **Imports** (2003 est.): $5.7 bil.; partners (2002): France 17.8%, Japan 10.1%, U.S. 8.5%, UK 8.3%, Germany 8.2%, Italy 6.7%, UAE 5.1%, Saudi Arabia 4.2%, South Korea 4%. **Exports** (2003 est.): $12.4 bil.; partners (2002): Japan 41.2%, South Korea 17.1%, Singapore 8.4%, U.S. 4.2%. **Tourism:** $5.17 bil. **Budget** (FY02/03 est.): $5.5 bil. **Intl. reserves less gold:** $1.98 bil. **Gold:** 20,000 oz t. **Consumer prices:** 2.3%.

Transport: Motor vehicles (2000): 199,600 pass. cars, 92,900 comm. vehicles. **Civil aviation:** 3.8 bil. pass.-mi; 2 airports. **Chief ports:** Doha, Umm Sáid.

Communications: TV sets: 866 per 1,000 pop. **Radios:** 450 per 1,000 pop. **Telephone lines:** 184,500. **Daily newspaper circ.:** 146 per 1,000 pop. **Internet:** 126,000 users.

Health: Life expect.: 70.9 male; 76.0 female. **Births** (per 1,000 pop.): 15.6. **Deaths** (per 1,000 pop.): 7.8. **Natural inc.:** 1.11%. **Infant mortality** (per 1,000 live births): 19.3.

Education: Compulsory: ages 6-17. **Literacy:** 82.5%.

Major Intl. Organizations: UN (FAO, IBRD, ILO, IMF, IMO, WHO, WTrO), AL, OPEC.

Embassy: 4200 Wisconsin Ave. NW, Suite 200, 20016; 274-1600.

Websites: www.qatarembassy.net; www.qatar-info.com

Qatar was under Bahrain's control until the Ottoman Turks took power, 1872 to 1915. In a treaty signed 1916, Qatar gave Great Britain responsibility for its defense and foreign relations. After Britain announced it would remove its military forces from the Persian Gulf area by the end of 1971, Qatar sought a federation with other British-protected states in the area; this failed and Qatar declared itself independent, Sept. 1, 1971. Crown Prince Hamad bin Khalifa ath-Thani ousted his father, Emir Khalifa bin Hamad ath-Thani, June 27, 1995. In municipal elections held Mar. 8, 1999, women participated for the 1st time as candidates and voters.

Oil and natural gas revenues give Qatar a per capita income among the world's highest. Military ties with the U.S. have been expanding; Camp As-Sayliyah, a base near Doha, served as a command center for the U.S.-led invasion of Iraq, Mar. 2003. The influential Arab news network Al-Jazeera is based in Qatar.

Romania

People: Population: 22,355,551. **Age distrib.** (%): <15: 17.4; 65+: 13.8. **Pop. density:** 251 per sq mi, 97 per sq km. **Urban:** 54.5%. **Ethnic groups:** Romanian 90%, Hungarian, Roma, and others 10%. **Principal languages:** Romanian (official), Hungarian, German, Romani. **Chief religions:** Romanian Orthodox 70%, Roman Catholic 6%, Protestant 6%.

Geography: Total area: 91,699 sq mi, 237,500 sq km; **Land area:** 88,935 sq mi, 230,340 sq km. **Location:** SE Europe, on the Black Sea. **Neighbors:** Moldova on E, Ukraine on N, Hungary and Serbia and Montenegro on W, Bulgaria on S. **Topography:** The Carpathian Mts. encase the north-central Transylvanian plateau. There are wide plains S and E of the mountains, through which flow the lower reaches of the rivers of the Danube system. **Capital:** Bucharest ,1,853,000.

Government: Type: Republic. **Head of state:** Pres. Ion Iliescu; b Mar. 3, 1930; in office: Dec. 20, 2000. **Head of gov.:** Prime Min. Adrian Nastase; b June 22, 1950; in office: Dec. 28, 2000. **Local divisions:** 41 counties and Bucharest. **Defense budget** (2002): $1.4 bil. **Active troops:** 97,200.

Economy: Industries: textiles & footwear, light machinery, auto assembly, mining, timber. **Chief crops:** wheat, corn, sugar beets, sunflower seed, potatoes, grapes. **Natural resources:** oil, timber, nat. gas, coal, iron ore, salt, hydropower. **Crude oil reserves** (2003): 956 mil. bbls. **Arable land:** 41%. **Livestock** (2003): cattle: 2.90 mil.; chickens: 76.62 mil.; goats: 678,000; pigs: 5.15 mil.; sheep: 7.45 mil. **Fish catch** (2002): 16,237 metric tons. **Electricity prod.** (2002): 53.62 bil. kWh. **Labor force** (2000): agriculture 41.4%, industry 27.3%, services 31.3%.

Finance: Monetary unit: Lei (ROL) (Sept. 2004: 33,533.55=1 U.S.). **GDP** (2003 est.): $154.4 bil.; **per capita GDP:** $6,900; **GDP growth:** 4.5%. **Imports** (2003 est.): $22.2 bil.; partners (2002): Italy 20.8%, Germany 14.9%, Russia 7.2%, France 6.4%. **Exports** (2003 est.): $17.6 bil.; partners (2002): Italy 25.2%, Germany 15.6%, France 7.6%, UK 5.8%, U.S. 4.3%, Turkey 4.1%. **Tourism** (2002): $612 mil. **Budget** (2002 est.): $9.6 bil. **Intl. reserves less gold:** $6.06 bil. **Gold:** 3.38 mil oz t. **Consumer prices:** 15.3%.

Transport: Railroad: Length: 7,074 mi **Motor vehicles** (2001): 3.23 mil pass. cars; 504,000 comm. vehicles. **Civil aviation:** 1.3 bil. pass.-mi; 26 airports. **Chief ports:** Constanta, Braila.

Communications: TV sets: 312 per 1,000 pop. **Radios:** 335 per 1,000 pop. **Telephone lines:** 4.3 mil. **Daily newspaper circ.:** 300 per 1,000 pop. **Internet:** 4.0 mil. users.

Health: Life expect.: 67.6 male; 74.8 female. **Births** (per 1,000 pop.): 10.7. **Deaths** (per 1,000 pop.): 11.7. **Natural inc.:** −0.10%. **Infant mortality** (per 1,000 live births): 27.2. **AIDS rate:** <0.1%.

Education: Compulsory: ages 7-14. **Literacy:** 98.4%.

Major Intl. Organizations: UN (FAO, IBRD, ILO, IMF, IMO, WHO, WTrO), NATO, OSCE.

Embassy: 1607 23rd St. NW 20008; 332-4846.

Website: www.roembus.org

Romania's earliest known people merged with invading Proto-Thracians, preceding by centuries the Dacians. The Dacian kingdom was occupied by Rome, AD 106-271; people and language were Romanized. The principalities of Wallachia and Moldavia, dominated by Turkey, were united in 1859, became Romania in 1861, and gained recognition as an independent kingdom, 1881.

After World War I, Romania acquired Bessarabia, Bukovina, Transylvania, and Banat. In 1940 it ceded Bessarabia and Northern Bukovina to the USSR, part of southern Dobrudja to Bulgaria, and northern Transylvania to Hungary. In 1941, Prem. Marshal Ion Antonescu led Romania in support of Germany against the USSR. In 1944 he was overthrown, and Romania joined the Allies. After occupation by Soviet troops, a People's Republic was proclaimed, Dec. 30, 1947.

On Aug. 22, 1965, a new constitution proclaimed Romania a Socialist Republic. Pres. Nicolae Ceausescu maintained an independent course in foreign affairs, but his domestic policies were repressive. All industry was state-owned, and state farms and cooperatives owned almost all arable land. Ceausescu's security forces fired on antigovernment demonstrators in Dec. 1989, killing hun-

dreds, but when the army sided with the protesters, his regime fell. Ceausescu and his wife were captured and, following a trial in which they were found guilty of genocide, were executed Dec. 25, 1989.

Former Communists dominated the government in succeeding years. A new constitution providing for a multiparty system took effect Dec. 8, 1991. Many of Romania's state-owned companies were privatized in 1996. The former Communists lost in elections Nov. 3 and 17, 1996, but made a comeback in balloting Nov. 26 and Dec. 10, 2000. Romania became a full NATO member in 2004 and is expected to enter the EU in 2007.

Russia
Russian Federation

People: Population: 143,782,338. **Age distrib.** (%): <15: 16.7; 65+: 13.1. **Pop. density:** 22 per sq mi, 8 per sq km. **Urban:** 73.3%. **Ethnic groups:** Russian 82%, Tatar 4%, Ukrainian 3%, Chuvash 1%, Bashkir 1%, Belarusian 1%, Moldavian 1%. **Principal languages:** Russian (official), many others. **Chief religions:** Russian Orthodox, Muslim.

Geography: Total area: 6,592,769 sq mi, 17,075,200 sq km; **Land area:** 6,562,112 sq mi, 16,995,800 sq km., more than 76% of total area of the former USSR and the largest country in the world. **Location:** Stretches from E Europe across N Asia to the Pacific O. **Neighbors:** Finland, Norway, Estonia, Latvia, Belarus, Ukraine on W; Georgia, Azerbaijan, Kazakhstan, China, Mongolia, North Korea on S; Kaliningrad exclave bordered by Poland on the S, Lithuania on the N and E. **Topography:** Russia contains every type of climate except the distinctly tropical, and has a varied topography. The European portion is a low plain, grassy in S, wooded in N, with Ural Mts. on the E, and Caucasus Mts. on the S. Urals stretch N-S for 2,500 mi The Asiatic portion is also a vast plain, with mountains on the S and in the E; tundra covers extreme N, with forest belt below; plains, marshes are in W, desert in SW. **Capital:** Moscow, 10,469,000. **Cities (urban aggr.):** St. Petersburg, 5,214,000; Nizhniy Novgorod, 1,331,000; Novosibirsk, 1,426,000.

Government: Type: Federal republic. **Head of state:** Vladimir Putin; b Oct. 7, 1952; in office: May 7, 2000. **Head of gov.:** Prime Min. Mikhail Fradkov; b Sep. 1, 1950; in office: Mar. 5, 2004. **Local divisions:** 7 federal districts incl. 49 provinces, 21 autonomous republics, 6 territories, 1 autonomous region, 10 autonomous districts, 2 federal cities. **Defense budget** (2003): $10.5 bil. **Active troops:** 960,600.

Economy: Industries: coal, oil, gas, chemicals, metals; light machinery, shipbuilding; transp., communic. equip., agric. machinery, constr. equip., electric power equip., medical & scientific instruments, consumer durables, textiles. **Chief crops:** grain, sugar beets, sunflower seed, vegetables, fruits. **Natural resources:** oil, nat. gas, coal, minerals, timber. **Crude oil reserves** (2003): 60.0 bil. bbls. **Arable land:** 8%. **Livestock** (2003): cattle: 26.52 mil.; chickens: 337.03 mil.; goats: 2.32 mil.; pigs: 17.34 mil.; sheep: 13.73 mil. **Fish catch** (2002): 3,333,635 metric tons. **Electricity prod.** (2002): 850.61 bil. kWh. **Labor force** (2002 est.): agriculture 12.3%, industry 22.7%, services 65%.

Finance: Monetary unit: Rouble (RUB) (Sept. 2004: 29.22=1 U.S. NOTE: On Jan 1, 1998, Russia eliminated 3 digits from the ruble.) **GDP:** $1.287 trillion tril.; **per capita GDP:** $8,900; **GDP growth:** 7.3%. **Imports** (2003 est.): $74.8 bil.; partners (2002): Germany 14.3%, Belarus 8.9%, Ukraine 7.1%, U.S. 6.4%, China 5.2%, Italy 4.8%, Kazakhstan 4.3%, France 4.1%. **Exports** (2003 est.): $134.4 bil.; partners (2002): Germany 7.5%, Italy 6.9%, Netherlands 6.7%, China 6.3%, U.S. 6.1%, Ukraine 5.5%, Belarus 5.4%, Switzerland 5%. **Tourism:** $4.5 bil. **Budget** (2002 est.): $62.0 bil. **Intl. reserves less gold:** $49.24 bil. **Gold:** 12.55 mil oz t. **Consumer prices:** 13.7%.

Transport: Railroad: Length: 54,157 mi **Motor vehicles:** (2001): 21.23 mil pass. cars, 3.33 mil comm. vehicles. **Civil aviation:** 10.9 bil. pass.-mi; 471 airports. **Chief ports:** St. Petersburg, Murmansk, Arkhangelsk.

Communications: TV sets: 421 per 1,000 pop. **Radios:** 417 per 1,000 pop. **Telephone lines** (2002): 35.5 mil. **Daily newspaper circ.:** 105 per 1,000 pop. **Internet** (2002): 6.0 mil. users.

Health: Life expect.: 59.9 male; 73.3 female. **Births** (per 1,000 pop.): 9.6. **Deaths** (per 1,000 pop.): 15.2. **Natural inc.:** −0.55%. **Infant mortality** (per 1,000 live births): 17.0. **AIDS rate:** 1.1%.

Education: Compulsory: ages 6-15. **Literacy:** 99.6%.

Major Intl. Organizations: UN (IBRD, ILO, IMF, IMO, WHO), APEC, CIS, OSCE.

Embassy: 2650 Wisconsin Ave. NW 20007; 298-5700.

Website: www.russianembassy.org

History. Slavic tribes began migrating into Russia from the W in the 5th century AD. The first Russian state, founded by Scandinavian chieftains, was established in the 9th century, centering in Novgorod and Kiev. In the 13th century the Mongols overran the country. It recovered under the grand dukes and princes of Muscovy, or Moscow, and by 1480 freed itself from the Mongols. Ivan the Terrible was the first to be formally proclaimed Tsar (1547). Peter the Great (1682-1725) extended the domain and, in 1721, founded the Russian Empire.

Western ideas and the beginnings of modernization spread through the huge Russian empire in the 19th and early 20th centuries. But political evolution failed to keep pace.

Military reverses in the 1905 war with Japan and in World War I led to the breakdown of the Tsarist regime. The 1917 Revolution began in March with a series of sporadic strikes for higher wages by factory workers. A provisional democratic government under Prince Georgi Lvov was established but was quickly followed in May by the second provisional government, led by Alexander Kerensky. The Kerensky government and the freely-elected Constituent Assembly were overthrown in a Communist coup led by Vladimir Ilyich Lenin Nov. 7.

Soviet Union

Lenin's death Jan. 21, 1924, resulted in an internal power struggle from which Joseph Stalin eventually emerged on top. Stalin secured his position at first by exiling opponents, but from the 1930s to 1953, he resorted to a series of "purge" trials, mass executions, and mass exiles to work camps. These measures resulted in millions of deaths, according to most estimates.

Germany and the Soviet Union signed a non-aggression pact Aug. 1939; Germany launched a massive invasion of the Soviet Union, June 1941. A notable heroic episode was the "900 days" siege of Leningrad (now St. Petersburg), lasting to Jan. 1944, and causing a million deaths; the city was never taken. Russian winter counterthrusts, 1941-42 and 1942-43, stopped the German advance. Turning point was the failure of German troops to take and hold Stalingrad (now Volgograd), Sept. 1942 to Feb. 1943. With British and U.S. Lend-Lease aid and sustaining great casualties, the Russians drove the German forces from eastern Europe and the Balkans in the next 2 years.

After Stalin died, Mar. 5, 1953, Nikita Khrushchev was elected first secretary of the Central Committee. In 1956 he condemned Stalin and "de-Stalinization" began.

Under Khrushchev the open antagonism of Poles and Hungarians toward domination by Moscow was brutally suppressed in 1956. He advocated peaceful co-existence with the capitalist countries, but continued arming the Soviet Union with nuclear weapons. He aided the Cuban revolution under Fidel Castro but withdrew Soviet missiles from Cuba during confrontation by U.S. Pres. Kennedy, Sept.-Oct. 1962. Khrushchev was suddenly deposed, Oct. 1964, and replaced by Leonid I. Brezhnev.

In Aug. 1968 Russian, Polish, East German, Hungarian, and Bulgarian military forces invaded Czechoslovakia to put a curb on liberalization policies of the Czech government.

Massive Soviet military aid to North Vietnam in the late 1960s and early 1970s helped assure Communist victories throughout Indo-China. Soviet arms aid and advisers were sent to several African countries in the 1970s.

In Dec. 1979, Soviet forces entered Afghanistan to support that government against rebels. In Apr. 1988, the Soviets agreed to withdraw their troops, ending a futile 8-year war.

Mikhail Gorbachev was chosen gen. secy. of the Communist Party, Mar. 1985. He held 4 summit meetings with U.S. Pres. Ronald Reagan.In 1987 he initiated a program of political and economic reforms, through openness (*glasnost*) and restructuring (*perestroika*). Gorbachev faced economic problems as well as ethnic and nationalist unrest in the republics. An apparent coup by Communist hardliners, Aug. 1991, was foiled with help from the pres. of the Russian Republic, Boris Yeltsin. On Aug. 24, Gorbachev resigned as leader of the Communist Party. Several republics declared their independence, including Russia, Ukraine, and Kazakhstan. On Aug. 29, the Soviet Parliament voted to suspend all activities of the Communist Party.

The Soviet Union officially broke up Dec. 26, 1991. The Soviet hammer and sickle flying over the Kremlin was lowered and replaced with the flag of Russia, ending the domination of the Communist Party over all areas of national life since 1917.

Russian Federation

Led by Pres. Yeltsin, Russia took steps toward privatization; immediate effects were inflation and a severe economic downturn. In June 1992, Yeltsin and U.S. Pres. George H.W. Bush agreed to massive arms reductions. A power struggle between Yeltsin and the Congress of People's Deputies, which was dominated by conservatives and former Communists, reached a climax Oct. 3, 1993, when anti-Yeltsin forces attacked some facilities in Moscow and broke into the Parliament building. Yeltsin ordered the army to seize the building; about 140 people were killed in the fighting.

Yeltsin remained in power, and in a referendum Dec. 12, 1993, a new constitution was approved. In Dec. 1994 the Russian government sent troops into the breakaway republic of Chechnya. Grozny, the Chechen capital, fell in Feb. 1995 after heavy fighting, but Chechen rebels continued to resist.

Despite poor health, Yeltsin won a presidential runoff election over a Communist opponent, July 3, 1996. On Aug. 14, after rebels embarrassed the Russian military by retaking Grozny, Yeltsin gave his security chief, Alexander Lebed, broad powers to negotiate an end to the Chechnya war. Lebed and Chechen leaders signed a peace accord Aug. 31. On Oct. 17, Yeltsin dismissed Lebed for insubordination. Russian troops remaining in Chechnya were pulled out Jan. 1997. On May 27, Yeltsin signed a "founding act" increasing cooperation with NATO and paving the way for NATO to admit Eastern European nations.

Russia's economic crisis deepened in the late 1990s, heightening tensions between Yeltsin and parliament. Russia moved forcibly in Aug. 1999 to suppress Islamic rebels in Dagestan; the conflict soon spread to neighboring Chechnya, where Russia launched a full-scale assault. A series of 5 bombings in Moscow and Dagestan, which the Russian government attributed to Chechen rebels, killed over 300 people.

Yeltsin unexpectedly resigned Dec. 31, 1999, naming Prime Min. Vladimir Putin as his interim successor. Russian troops took control of Grozny in early Feb. 2000. Putin defeated 10 opponents in a presidential election Mar. 26. The Russian parliament ratified 2 nuclear weapons treaties, the START II arms-reduction accord Apr. 14 and the Comprehensive Test Ban Treaty Apr. 21. A reorganization plan announced May 17 sought to reassert Moscow's control over Russia's regional governments. The Russian nuclear submarine *Kursk* sank in the Barents Sea Aug. 12, killing 118 sailors.

Russia and China signed a 20-year friendship and cooperation treaty July 16, 2001. Putin and U.S. Pres. George W. Bush signed May 24, 2002, an agreement calling for a $2/_3$ reduction in nuclear weapons stockpiles. However, Russia pulled out of the START II treaty Jun. 14 after the U.S. withdrew from the 1972 ABM Treaty June 13 to develop a missile defense program. Russia joined a new partnership agreement with NATO May 28.

As Russian forces continued their campaign against Islamic separatists in Chechnya, some 50 Chechen guerrillas seized more than 800 hostages in a Moscow theater, Oct. 23, 2002; 129 hostages and nearly all the guerrillas were killed Oct. 26 when Russian special forces used knockout gas in retaking the theater. Russia, which supported the U.S.-led war in Afghanistan in 2001, sided with France and Germany in blocking UN Security Council endorsement of the U.S.-led invasion of Iraq, Mar. 2003.

Putin's allies won legislative elections, Dec. 7, 2003, and the president was reelected Mar. 14, 2004, with 71% of the vote; international election monitors cited flaws on both occasions. Putin blamed Chechen terrorists for a blast on a Moscow subway car, Feb. 6, that killed at least 39 people. A bomb in Grozny, May 9, killed Chechnya's pro-Moscow president, Akhmad Kadyrov, and at least 6 others. Putin's choice for the Chechen presidency, Maj. Gen. Alu Alkhanov, was elected Aug. 29.

The Chechnya conflict unleashed a wave of terrorism elsewhere during Aug.-Sept. 2004. After taking off the night of Aug. 24 from Moscow's Domodedovo airport, 2 passenger planes exploded in midair, killing 90 people. A suicide bombing in a Moscow subway station Aug. 31 left 11 dead. Chechen rebels Sept. 1 seized control of a school in Beslan, N Ossetia, taking more than 1,100 hostages; Russian troops stormed the school Sept. 3; in the end more than 330 people died, about half of them children. Putin cited the terrorist threat Sept. 13 in proposing a government overhaul that would tighten his control over parliament and regional officeholders.

Health: Life expect.: 38.4 male; 40.0 female. **Births** (per 1,000 pop.): 40.0. **Deaths** (per 1,000 pop.): 21.9. **Natural inc.:** 1.81%. **Infant mortality** (per 1,000 live births): 101.7. **AIDS rate:** 5.1%.
Education: Compulsory: ages 7-12. **Literacy:** 70.4%.
Major Intl. Organizations: UN (FAO, IBRD, ILO, IMF, WHO, WTrO), AU.
Embassy: 1714 New Hampshire Ave. NW 20009; 232-2882.
Websites: www.rwandemb.org; www.rwanda1.com

For centuries, the Tutsi (an extremely tall people) dominated the Hutu (90% of the population). A civil war broke out in 1959 and Tutsi power was ended. Many Tutsi went into exile. A referendum in 1961 abolished the monarchic system. Rwanda, which had been part of the Belgian UN trusteeship of Rwanda-Urundi, became independent July 1, 1962.

In 1963 Tutsi exiles invaded in an unsuccessful coup; a large-scale massacre of Tutsi followed. Rivalries among Hutu led to a bloodless coup July 1973 in which Juvénal Habyarimana took power. After an invasion and coup attempt by Tutsi exiles in 1990, a multiparty democracy was established.

Renewed ethnic strife led to an Aug. 1993 peace accord between the government and rebels of the Tutsi-led Rwandan Patriotic Front (RPF). But after Habyarimana and the president of Burundi were killed Apr. 6, 1994, in a suspicious plane crash, massive violence broke out. More than 1 million may have died in massacres, mostly of Tutsi by Hutu militias, and in civil warfare as the RPF sought power. About 2 million Tutsi and Hutu fled to camps in Zaire (now Congo) and other countries, where many died of cholera and other natural causes. French troops under a UN mandate moved into SW Rwanda June 23 to establish a so-called safe zone. The RPF claimed victory, installing a government in July led by a moderate Hutu president. French troops pulled out Aug. 22. A UN peacekeeping mission ended Mar. 8, 1996, but the Rwandan government and a UN-sponsored tribunal in Tanzania continued to gather evidence against those responsible for genocide. More than 1 million refugees (mostly Hutu) flooded back to Rwanda from Tanzania and Zaire in Nov. and Dec. 1996.

Firing squads in Rwanda on Apr. 24, 1998, executed 22 people convicted of genocide. Former Prime Min. Jean Kambanda pleaded guilty May 1 before the UN tribunal and received a life sentence Sept. 4, 1998. Maj. Gen. Paul Kagame, leader of the RPF, was sworn in as Rwanda's 1st Tutsi president Apr. 22, 2000. A Belgian court June 8, 2001, convicted 2 Roman Catholic nuns and 2 other Rwandans for their role in the 1994 genocide.

Rwanda and the Congo signed an accord July 30, 2002, in which Rwanda agreed to withdraw troops from the Congo and the Congo agreed to stop harboring Hutu guerrillas. Rwandans in 2003 approved a new constitution, May 26, reelected Pres. Kagame, Aug. 25, and chose a new parliament, Sept. 29-30. Former Pres. Bizimungu was sentenced to 15 yrs. for embezzlement, June 2004.

Rwanda
Republic of Rwanda

People: Population: 7,954,013. **Age distrib.** (%): <15: 41.7; 65+: 2.9. **Pop. density:** 826 per sq mi, 319 per sq km. **Urban:** 18.3%. **Ethnic groups:** Hutu 84%, Tutsi 15%, Twa (Pygmy) 1%. **Principal languages:** Kinyarwanda, French, English (all official); Swahili. **Chief religions:** Roman Catholic 57%, Protestant 26%, Adventist 11%, Muslim 5%.
Geography: Total area: 10,169 sq mi, 26,338 sq km; **Land area:** 9,632 sq mi, 24,948 sq km. **Location:** In E central Africa. **Neighbors:** Uganda on N, Congo (formerly Zaire) on W, Burundi on S, Tanzania on E. **Topography:** Grassy uplands and hills cover most of the country, with a chain of volcanoes in the NW. The source of the Nile R. has been located in the headwaters of the Kagera (Akagera) R., SW of Kigali. **Capital:** Kigali, 656,000.
Government: Type: Republic. **Head of state:** Pres. Paul Kagame; b Oct. 1957; in office: Apr. 22, 2000 (de facto from Mar. 24). **Head of gov.:** Prime Min. Bernard Makuza; b 1961; in office: Mar. 8, 2000. **Local divisions:** 12 prefectures subdivided into 155 communes. **Defense budget** (2003): $72 mil. **Active troops:** 51,000.
Economy: Industries: cement, agric. products. **Chief crops:** coffee, tea, pyrethrum (insecticide made from chrysanthemums), bananas. **Natural resources:** gold, tin, tungsten, methane, hydropower. **Crude oil reserves** (2002): 48.6 bil. bbls. **Arable land:** 35%. **Livestock** (2003): cattle: 815,000; chickens: 1.2 mil.; goats: 760,000; pigs: 180,000; sheep: 260,000. **Fish catch** (2002 est): 7,612 metric tons. **Electricity prod.** (2002): 0.17 bil. kWh. **Labor force:** agriculture 90%.
Finance: Monetary unit: Franc (RWF) (Sept. 2004: 561.78=1 U.S.). **GDP** (2003 est.): $10.1 bil.; **per capita GDP:** $1,300; **GDP growth:** 3.5%. **Imports** (2003 est.): $245.8 mil.; partners (2002): Kenya 23.2%, Belgium 8.3%, Germany 6.6%. **Exports** (2003 est.): $73.3 mil.; partners (2002): Indonesia 37.5%, Hong Kong 6.9%, China 3.5%. **Tourism** (2002): $31 mil. **Budget** (2001 est.): $445.0 mil. **Intl. reserves less gold:** $144 mil. **Consumer prices:** 6.9%.
Transport: Motor vehicles (2000): 10,700 pass. cars, 16,300 comm. vehicles. **Civil aviation:** 1.2 mil pass.-mi; 4 airports. **Chief ports:** Gisenyi, Cyangugu.
Communications: TV sets: .09 per 1,000 pop. **Radios:** 101 per 1,000 pop. **Telephone lines** (2002): 23,200. **Daily newspaper circ.:** 0.1 per 1,000 pop. **Internet** (2002): 25,000 users.

Saint Kitts and Nevis
Federation of Saint Kitts and Nevis

People: Population: 38,836. **Age distrib.** (%): <15: 29.4; 65+: 8.7. **Pop. density:** 385 per sq mi, 149 per sq km. **Urban:** 32.2%. **Ethnic group:** Black, British, Portuguese, Lebanese. **Principal languages:** English (official). **Chief religions:** Anglican, other Protestant, Roman Catholic.
Geography: Total area: 101 sq mi, 261 sq km; **Land area:** 101 sq mi, 261 sq km. **Location:** In the N part of the Leeward group of the Lesser Antilles in the E Caribbean Sea. **Neighbors:** Antigua and Barbuda to E. **Topography:** St. Kitts has forested volcanic slopes; Nevis rises from beaches to central peak. Climate is tropical moderated by sea breezes. **Capital:** Basseterre, 13,000.
Government: Type: Constitutional monarchy. **Head of state:** Queen Elizabeth II, represented by Gov.-Gen. Sir Cuthbert M. Sebastian; b Oct. 22, 1921; in office: Jan. 1, 1996. **Head of gov.:** Prime Min. Denzil Llewellyn Douglas; b Jan. 14, 1953; in office: July 7, 1995. **Local divisions:** 14 parishes.
Economy: Industries: sugar proc., tourism, cotton, salt, copra, clothing, footwear, beverages. **Chief crops:** sugarcane, rice, yams, vegetables, bananas. **Arable land:** 22%. **Livestock** (2003): cattle: 4,300; chickens: 60,000; goats: 14,400; pigs: 4,000; sheep:14,000. **Fish catch** (2002): 355 metric tons. **Electricity prod.** (2002): 0.11 bil. kWh.
Finance: Monetary unit: East Caribbean Dollar (XCD) (Sept. 2004: 2.67=1 U.S.). **GDP** (2002 est.): $339.0 mil.; **per capita GDP:** $8,800; **GDP growth:** -1.9%. **Imports** (2002 est.): $195.0 mil.; partners (2002): U.S. 39%, Trinidad and Tobago 15.4%, Canada 9.2%, UK 6.7%, Denmark 6.2%. **Exports** (2002 est.): $70.0 mil.; partners (2002): U.S. 65.7%, Canada 7.1%, UK 7.1%, Portugal 5.7%. **Tourism:** $61 mil. **Budget** (2003 est.): $128.2 mil. **Intl. reserves less gold:** $44 mil. **Consumer prices** (change in 1999): 3.9%.
Transport: Railroad: Length: 31 mi **Motor vehicles** (1999): 7,700 pass. cars, 3,900 comm. vehicles. Civil aviation: 2 airports. **Chief ports:** Basseterre, Charlestown.
Communications: TV sets: 256 per 1,000 pop. **Radios:** 718 per 1,000 pop. **Telephone lines** (2002): 23,500. **Internet** (2002): 10,000 users.
Health: Life expect.: 69.0 male; 74.9 female. **Births** (per 1,000 pop.): 18.3. **Deaths** (per 1,000 pop.): 8.7. **Natural inc.:** 0.96%. **Infant mortality** (per 1,000 live births): 14.9.

Education: Compulsory, ages 5-17. **Literacy** (1992): 90%.

Major Intl. Organizations: UN (FAO, IBRD, ILO, IMF, WHO, WTrO), Caricom, the Commonwealth, OAS, OECS.

Embassy: 3216 New Mexico Ave., NW 20016; 686-2636.

Websites: www.stkittsnevis.org; www.stkittsnevis.net

St. Kitts (formerly St. Christopher; known by the natives as Lia-muiga) and Nevis were reached (and named) by Columbus in 1493. They were settled by Britain in 1623, but ownership was disputed with France until 1713. They were part of the Leeward Islands Federation, 1871-1956, and the Federation of the West Indies, 1958-62. The colony achieved self-government as an Associated State of the UK in 1967, and became fully independent Sept. 19, 1983. A secession referendum on Nevis, Aug. 10, 1998, fell short of the two-thirds majority required.

Saint Lucia

People: Population: 164,213. **Age distrib.** (%): <15: 31.6; 65+: 5.3. **Pop. density:** 702 per sq mi, 271 per sq km. **Urban:** 30.5%. **Ethnic groups:** Black 90%, mixed 6%, East Indian 3%, White 1%. **Principal languages:** English (official), French patois. **Chief religions:** Roman Catholic 90%, Protestant 10%.

Geography: Total area: 238 sq mi, 616 sq km; **Land area:** 234 sq mi, 606 sq km. **Location:** In E Caribbean, 2d largest of the Windward Isls. **Neighbors:** Martinique to N, St. Vincent to S. **Topography:** Mountainous, volcanic in origin; Soufriere, a volcanic crater, in the S. Wooded mountains run N-S to Mt. Gimie, 3,145 ft., with streams through fertile valleys. **Capital:** Castries, 14,000.

Government: Type: Parliamentary democracy. **Head of state:** Queen Elizabeth II, represented by Gov.-Gen. Dame Calliopa Pearlette Louisy; b June 8, 1946; in office: Sept. 17, 1997. **Head of gov.:** Prime Min. Kenny Anthony; b Jan. 8, 1951; in office: May 24, 1997. **Local divisions:** 11 quarters.

Economy: Industries: clothing, electronic components, beverages, cardboard, tourism, lime & coconut proc. **Chief crops:** bananas, coconuts, vegetables, citrus, root crops, cocoa. **Natural resources:** timber, pumice, mineral springs, geothermal areas. **Arable land:** 8%. **Livestock** (2003): cattle: 12,400; chickens: 240,000; goats: 9,800; pigs: 14,950; sheep: 12,500. **Fish catch** (2002): 1,639 metric tons. **Electricity prod.** (2002): 0.27 bil. kWh. **Labor force** (2002 est.): agriculture 21.7%, services 53.6%, industry, commerce, and manufacturing 24.7%.

Finance: Monetary unit: East Caribbean Dollar (XCD) (Sept. 2004: 2.67=1 U.S.). **GDP** (2002 est.): $866.0 mil.; **per capita GDP:** $5,400; **GDP growth:** 3.3%. **Imports** (2002 est.): $267.0 mil.; partners (2002): Brazil 46.1%, U.S. 18.6%, Trinidad and Tobago 10.3%. **Exports** (2002 est.): $66.0 mil.; partners (2002): UK 48.5%, U.S. 27.3%, Barbados 7.6%. **Tourism:** $282 mil. **Budget** (2000 est.): $146.7 mil. **Intl. reserves less gold:** $73 mil. **Consumer prices:** 0.9%.

Transport: Motor vehicles (1996): 13,500 pass. cars, 10,800 comm. vehicles. **Civil aviation:** 2 airports. **Chief ports:** Castries, Vieux Fort.

Communications: TV sets: 368 per 1,000 pop. **Radios:** 750 per 1,000 pop. **Telephone lines** (2002): 51,100. **Internet** (2001): 13,000 users.

Health: Life expect.: 69.8 male; 77.2 female. **Births** (per 1,000 pop.): 20.5. **Deaths** (per 1,000 pop.): 5.2. **Natural inc.:** 1.53%. **Infant mortality** (per 1,000 live births): 14.0.

Education: Compulsory: ages 5-16. **Literacy** (1993): 80%.

Major Intl. Organizations: UN (FAO, IBRD, ILO, IMF, IMO, WHO, WTrO), Caricom, the Commonwealth, OAS, OECS.

Embassy: 3216 New Mexico Ave. NW 20016; 364-6792.

Website: www.stlucia.gov.lc

St. Lucia was ceded to Britain by France at the Treaty of Paris, 1814. Self-government was granted with the West Indies Act, 1967. Independence was attained Feb. 22, 1979.

Saint Vincent and the Grenadines

People: Population: 117,193. **Age distrib.** (%): <15: 28.9; 65+: 6.3. **Pop. density:** 780 per sq mi, 301 per sq km. **Urban:** 58.3%. **Ethnic groups:** Black 66%, mixed 19%, East Indian 6%, Carib Amerindian 2%. **Principal languages:** English (official), French patois. **Chief religions:** Anglican 47%, Methodist 28%, Roman Catholic 13%.

Geography: Total area: 150 sq mi, 389 sq km; **Land area:** 150 sq mi, 389 sq km. **Location:** In the E Caribbean, St. Vincent (133 sq mi) and the northern islets of the Grenadines form a part of the Windward chain. **Neighbors:** St. Lucia to N, Barbados to E, Grenada to S. **Topography:** St. Vincent is volcanic, with a ridge of thickly wooded mountains running its length. **Capital:** Kingstown, 29,000.

Government: Constitutional monarchy. **Head of State:** Queen Elizabeth II, represented by Sir Frederick Ballantyne; in office: Sept. 2, 2002. **Head of gov.:** Prime Min. Ralph Gonsalves; b Aug. 8, 1946; in office: Mar. 29, 2001. **Local divisions:** 6 parishes.

Economy: Industries: food proc., cement, furniture, clothing, starch. **Chief crops:** bananas, coconuts, sweet potatoes, spices. **Natural resources:** hydropower. **Arable land:** 10%. **Livestock** (2003): cattle: 5,000; chickens: 125,000; goats: 7,000; pigs: 9,150; sheep: 12,700. **Fish catch** (2002): 43,879 metric tons. **Electricity prod.** (2002): 0.09 bil. kWh. **Labor force** (1980 est.): agriculture 26%, industry 17%, services 57%.

Finance: Monetary unit: East Caribbean Dollar (Sept. 2004: 2.67=1 U.S.). **GDP** (2002 est.): $339.0 mil.; **per capita GDP:** $2,900; **GDP growth:** −0.5%. **Imports** (2002 est.): $174.0 mil.; partners (2002): France 32.6%, U.S. 11.2%, Trinidad and Tobago 10.4%, Singapore 10.2%, Spain 7.9%, Greece 4.3%. **Exports** (2002 est.): $38.0 mil.; partners (2002): France 25.2%, Greece 19.2%, Spain 16.4%, UK 9.3%, U.S. 7%. **Tourism:** $85 mil. **Budget** (2000 est.): $85.8 mil. **Intl. reserves less gold:** $34 mil. **Consumer prices:** 0.3%.

Transport: Motor vehicles (2001): 9,900 pass. cars, 4,000 comm. vehicles. **Civil aviation:** 5 airports. **Chief port:** Kingstown.

Communications: TV sets: 230 per 1,000 pop. **Radios:** 688 per 1,000 pop. **Telephone lines** (2002): 27,300. **Daily newspaper circ.:** 9 per 1,000 pop. **Internet** (2002): 7,000 users.

Health: Life expect.: 71.5 male; 75.2 female. **Births** (per 1,000 pop.): 16.8. **Deaths** (per 1,000 pop.): 6.0. **Natural inc.:** 1.07%. **Infant mortality** (per 1,000 live births): 15.2.

Education: Compulsory: ages 5-15. **Literacy** (1994): 82%.

Major Intl. Organizations: UN (FAO, IBRD, ILO, IMF, IMO, WHO, WTrO), Caricom, the Commonwealth, OAS, OECS.

Embassy: 3216 New Mexico Ave. NW 20016; 364-6730.

Website: www.embsvg.com

Columbus landed on St. Vincent on Jan. 22, 1498 (St. Vincent's Day). Britain and France both laid claim to the island in the 17th and 18th centuries; the Treaty of Versailles, 1783, finally ceded it to Britain. Associated State status was granted 1969; independence was attained Oct. 27, 1979.

Samoa (*formerly* Western Samoa)
Independent State of Samoa

People: Population: 177,714. **Age distrib.** (%): <15: 30.6; 65+: 5.9. **Pop. density:** 157 per sq mi, 61 per sq km. **Urban:** 22.3%. **Urban:** 22%. **Ethnic groups:** Samoan 92.5%, Euronesians 7%. **Principal languages:** Samoan, English (both official). **Chief religion:** Christian 99.7%.

Geography: Total area: 1,137 sq mi, 2,944 sq km; **Land area:** 1,133 sq mi, 2,934 sq km. **Location:** In the S Pacific O. **Neighbors:** Nearest are Fiji to SW, Tonga to S. **Topography:** Main islands, Savaii (659 sq mi) and Upolu (432 sq mi), both ruggedly mountainous, and small islands Manono and Apolima. **Capital:** Apia, 40,000.

Government: Type: Constitutional monarchy. **Head of state:** Malietoa Tanumafili II; b Jan. 4, 1913; in office: Jan. 1, 1962. **Head of gov.:** Prime Min. Tuilaepa Sailele Malielegaoi; b Apr. 14, 1945; in office: Nov. 23, 1998. **Local divisions:** 11 districts.

Economy: Industries: food proc., building materials, auto parts. **Chief crops:** coconuts, bananas, taro, yams. **Natural resources:** timber, fish, hydropower. **Arable land:** 19%. **Livestock** (2003): cattle: 29,000; chickens: 450,000; pigs: 201,000. **Fish catch** (2002 est): 12,392 metric tons. **Electricity Prod.** (2002): 0.12 bil. kWh. **Labor force:** agriculture 65%, services 30%, industry 5%.

Finance: Monetary unit: Tala (WST) (Sept. 2004: 2.86=1 U.S.). **GDP** (2002 est.): $1.0 bil.; **per capita GDP:** $5,600; **GDP growth:** 5.0%. **Imports** (2002): $113.0 mil.; partners (2002): New Zealand 23.7%, Fiji 20.9%, Australia 16.4%, Japan 13.6%, U.S. 4.5%. **Exports** (2002): $14.0 mil.; partners (2002): Australia 61%, Hong Kong 10.4%, U.S. 9.1%. **Tourism:** $53 mil. **Budget** (2001/2002): $119.0 mil. **Intl. reserves less gold:** $56 mil. **Consumer prices:** 0.1%.

Transport: Motor vehicles (1997): 1,200 pass. cars, 1,400 comm. vehicles. **Civil aviation:** 174 mil pass.-mi; 3 airports. **Chief ports:** Apia, Asau.

Communications: TV sets: 56 per 1,000 pop. **Radios:** 1,035 per 1,000 pop. **Telephone lines** (2002): 11,800. **Internet** (2002): 4,000 users.

Health: Life expect.: 67.6 male; 73.3 female. **Births** (per 1,000 pop.): 15.7. **Deaths** (per 1,000 pop.): 6.5. **Natural inc.:** 0.92%. **Infant mortality** (per 1,000 live births): 28.7.

Education: Compulsory: ages 5-14. **Literacy** (1994): 99.7%.

Major Intl. Organizations: UN (FAO, IBRD, IMF, IMO, WHO), the Commonwealth.

Embassy: 800 Second Avenue, Ste. 400D, New York, NY 10017; (212) 599-6196.

Website: www.visitsamoa.ws

Samoa (formerly known as Western Samoa to distinguish it from American Samoa, a small U.S. territory) was a German colony, 1899 to 1914, when New Zealand landed troops and took over. It became a New Zealand mandate under the League of Nations and, in 1945, a New Zealand UN Trusteeship.

An elected local government took office in Oct. 1959, and the country became fully independent Jan. 1, 1962.

San Marino
Republic of San Marino

People: Population: 28,503. **Age distrib.** (%): <15: 16.1; 65+: 16.4. **Pop. density:** 1,206 per sq mi, 466 per sq km. **Urban:** 88.7%. **Ethnic groups:** Sammarinese, Italian **Principal language:** Italian (official). **Chief religion:** Predominantly Roman Catholic.

Geography: Total area: 24 sq mi, 61 sq km; **Land area:** 24 sq mi, 61 sq km. **Location:** In N central Italy near Adriatic coast. **Neighbors:** Completely surrounded by Italy. **Topography:** The country lies on the slopes of Mt. Titano. **Capital:** San Marino, 5,000.

Government: Type: Republic. **Heads of state and gov.:** Two co-regents appt. every 6 months. **Local divisions:** 9 castelli.

Economy: Industries: tourism, banking, textiles, electronics, ceramics, cement, wine. **Chief crops:** wheat, grapes, corn, olives. **Natural resources:** building stone. **Arable land:** 17%. **Labor force** (2000 est.): services 57%, industry 42%, agriculture 1%.

Finance: Monetary unit: Euro (EUR) (Sept. 2004: 0.82=1 U.S.). **GDP** (2001 est.): $940.0 mil.; **per capita GDP:** $34,600; **GDP growth:** 7.5%. **Budget** (2000 est.): $400.0 mil.

Transport: Motor vehicles (1997): 24,825 pass. cars, 4,149 comm. vehicles.

Communications: TV sets: 875 per 1,000 pop. **Radios:** 1,346 per 1,000 pop. **Daily newspaper circ.:** 70.4 per 1,000 pop.

Health: Life expect.: 78.0 male; 85.3 female. **Births** (per 1,000 pop.): 10.3. **Deaths** (per 1,000 pop.): 8.0. **Natural inc.:** 0.23%. **Infant mortality** (per 1,000 live births): 5.9.

Education: Compulsory: ages 6-14. **Literacy** (1997): 99%.

Major Intl. Organizations: UN (ILO, IMF, WHO), OSCE.

Website: www.sanmarinosite.com

San Marino claims to be the oldest state in Europe and to have been founded in the 4th century. A Communist-led coalition ruled 1947-57; a similar coalition ruled 1978-86. It has had a treaty of friendship with Italy since 1862.

São Tomé and Príncipe
Democratic Republic of São Tomé and Príncipe

People: Population: 181,565. **Age distrib.** (%): <15: 47.7; 65+: 4. **Pop. density:** 470 per sq mi, 181 per sq km. **Urban:** 37.8%. **Ethnic groups:** Mestizo, Black, Portuguese. **Principal languages:** Portuguese (official), Creole, Fang. **Chief religions:** Predominantly Roman Catholic.

Geography: Total area: 386 sq mi, 1,001 sq km; **Land area:** 386 sq mi, 1,001 sq km. **Location:** In the Gulf of Guinea about 125 miles off W central Africa. **Neighbors:** Gabon, Equatorial Guinea to E. **Topography:** São Tomé and Príncipe islands, part of an extinct volcano chain, are both covered by lush forests and croplands. **Capital:** São Tomé, 54,000.

Government: Type: Republic. **Head of state:** Pres. Fradique Melo de Menezes; b Mar. 21, 1942; in office: Sept. 3, 2001. **Head of gov.:** Prime Min. Damião Vaz d'Almeida; b 1951; in office: Sept. 18, 2004. **Local divisions:** 2 provinces.

Economy: Industries: light constr., textiles, soap, beer; fish proc. **Chief crops:** cocoa, coconuts, palm kernels, cinnamon, pepper, coffee. **Natural resources:** fish, hydropower. **Arable land:** 2%. **Livestock** (2003): cattle, 4,300; chickens: 350,000; goats: 4,850; pigs: 2,200; sheep: 2,600. **Fish catch** (2002 est): 3,500 metric tons. **Electricity prod.** (2002): 0.02 bil. kWh. **Labor force:** population mainly engaged in subsistence agriculture and fishing.

Finance: Monetary unit: Dobra (STD) (Sept. 2003): 8,856.65=1 U.S.). **GDP** (2002 est.): $200.0 mil.; **per capita GDP:** $1,200; **GDP growth:** 4.0%. **Imports** (2003 est.): $30.0 mil.; partners (2002): Portugal 50.8%, Germany 10.2%, UK 8.5%, Belgium 6.8%. **Exports** (2003 est.): $6.5 mil.; partners (2002): Netherlands 37.5%, Belgium 12.5%, Canada 12.5%, Germany 12.5%, Spain 12.5%. **Tourism** (2002): $10 mil. **Budget** (1993 est.): $114.0 mil. **Intl. reserves less gold:** $17 mil.

Transport: Civil aviation: 4.3 mil. pass.-mi; 2 airports. **Chief ports:** São Tomé, Santo Antonio.

Communications: TV sets: 229 per 1,000 pop. **Radios:** 319 per 1,000 pop. **Telephone lines:** 7,000. **Internet:** 15,000 users.

Health: Life expect.: 65.1 male; 68.2 female. **Births** (per 1,000 pop.): 41.4. **Deaths** (per 1,000 pop.): 6.9. **Natural inc.:** 3.45%. **Infant mortality** (per 1,000 live births): 44.6.

Education: Compulsory: ages 7-12. **Literacy** (1991 est.): 79.3%.

Major Intl. Organizations: UN (FAO, IBRD, ILO, IMF, IMO, WHO), AU.

Permanent UN Representative: 400 Park Ave., 7th Floor, New York, NY 10022; (212) 317-0580.

Websites: www.stome.com; www.saotome.st

The islands were discovered in 1471 by the Portuguese, who brought the first settlers—convicts and exiled Jews. Sugar planting was replaced by the slave trade as the chief economic activity until coffee and cocoa were introduced in the 19th century.

Portugal agreed, 1974, to turn the colony over to the Gabon-based Movement for the Liberation of São Tomé and Príncipe, which proclaimed as first president its East German-trained leader, Manuel Pinto da Costa. Independence came July 12, 1975. Democratic reforms were instituted in 1987. In 1991 Miguel Trovoada won the first free presidential election following da Costa's withdrawal. A military coup that ousted Trovoada Aug. 15, 1995, was reversed a week later after Angolan mediation. Trovoada defeated da Costa in a presidential runoff election, July 21, 1996.

Fradique de Menezes, a wealthy cocoa exporter, easily beat da Costa in the presidential election of July 29, 2001. The government was ousted in a military coup July 16, 2003, but restored to power July 23. The country, long one of the world's poorest, is expected to reap billions of dollars from oil development in the Gulf of Guinea.

Saudi Arabia
Kingdom of Saudi Arabia

People: Population: 25,795,938. **Age distrib.** (%): <15: 42.4; 65+: 2.8. **Pop. density:** 34 per sq mi, 13 per sq km. **Urban:** 87.7%. **Ethnic groups:** Arab 90%, Afro-Asian 10% **Principal languages:** Arabic (official). **Chief religion:** Muslim (official).

Geography: Total area: 756,985 sq mi, 1,960,582 sq km; **Land area:** 756,985 sq mi, 1,960,582 sq km. **Location:** Occupies most of Arabian Peninsula in Mid-East. **Neighbors:** Kuwait, Iraq, Jordan on N; Yemen, Oman on S; United Arab Emirates, Qatar on E. **Topography:** Bordered by Red Sea on the W. The highlands on W, up to 9,000 ft., slope as an arid, barren desert to the Persian Gulf on the E. **Capital:** Riyadh, 5,126,000. **Cities (urban aggr.):** Jeddah, 3,171,000; Mecca, 1,326,000.

Government: Type: Monarchy with council of ministers. **Head of state and gov.:** King Fahd ibn Abdul Aziz; b 1923; in office: June 13, 1982 (prime min. since 1982). **Local divisions:** 13 provinces. **Defense budget** (2003): $18.4 bil. **Active troops:** 124,500.

Economy: Industries: oil prod. & refining, petrochems., cement, construction, fertilizers, plastics. **Chief crops:** wheat, barley, tomatoes, melons, dates, citrus. **Natural resources:** oil, nat. gas, iron ore, gold, copper. **Crude oil reserves** (2003): 261.8 bil. bbls. **Arable land:** 2%. **Livestock** (2003): cattle: 340,000; chickens: 135.0 mil.; goats: 2.7 mil.; sheep: 8.29 mil. **Fish catch** (2002): 62,074 metric tons. **Electricity prod.** (2002): 138.18 bil. kWh. **Labor force:** (1999 est.): agriculture 12%, industry 25%, services 63%.

Finance: Monetary unit: Riyal (SAR) (Sept. 2004: 3.75=1 U.S.). **GDP** (2003 est.): $286.2 bil.; **per capita GDP:** $11,800; **GDP growth:** 4.7%. **Imports** (2003 est.): $30.4 bil.; partners (2002): U.S. 11.1%, Japan 8.7%, Germany 7.5%, UK 4.9%, France 4.8%, Italy 4%. **Exports** (2003 est.): $86.5 bil.; partners (2002): U.S. 18.9%, Japan 15.9%, South Korea 10.3%, Singapore 5.2%, China 4.7%. **Tourism** (2002): $3.4 bil. **Budget** (2003 est.): $66.7 bil. **Intl. reserves less gold:** $15.22 bil. **Gold:** 4.60 mil oz t. **Consumer prices:** 0.6%.

Transport: Railroad: Length: 865 mi. **Motor vehicles** (1998): 7.05 mil pass. cars. **Civil aviation:** 8.6 bil. pass.-mi; 71 airports. **Chief ports:** Jiddah, Ad Dammam.

Communications: TV sets: 263 per 1,000 pop. **Radios:** 321 per 1,000 pop. **Telephone lines:** 3.5 mil. **Daily newspaper circ.:** 318.1 per 1,000 pop. **Internet:** 1.5 mil. users.

Health: Life expect.: 73.3 male; 77.3 female. **Births** (per 1,000 pop.): 29.7. **Deaths** (per 1,000 pop.): 2.7. **Natural inc.:** 2.71%. **Infant mortality** (per 1,000 live births): 13.7.

Education: Compulsory: ages 6-11. **Literacy:** 78.8%.

Major Intl. Organizations: UN (FAO, IBRD, ILO, IMF, IMO, WHO), AL, OPEC.

Embassy: 601 New Hampshire Ave. NW 20037; 337-4076.

Website: www.saudiembassy.net

Before Muhammad, Arabia was divided among numerous warring tribes and small kingdoms. It was united for the first time by Muhammad, in the early 7th century AD. His successors conquered the entire Near East and North Africa, bringing Islam and the Arabic language. But Arabia itself soon returned to its former status.

Nejd, in central Arabia, long an independent state and center of the Wahhabi sect, fell under Turkish rule in the 18th century. In 1913 Ibn Saud, founder of the Saudi dynasty, overthrew the Turks and captured the Turkish province of Hasa in E Arabia; he took the Hejaz region in W Arabia in 1925 and most of Asir, in SW Arabia, by 1926. The discovery of oil in the 1930s transformed the new country.

Ibn Saud reigned until his death, Nov. 1953. Subsequent kings have been sons of Ibn Saud. The king exercises authority together with a Council of Ministers. The Islamic religious code is the law of the land. Alcohol and public entertainments are restricted, and women have an inferior legal status. There is no constitution and no parliament, although a Consultative Council was established by the king in 1993.

Saudi Arabia has often allied itself with the U.S. and other Western nations, and billions of dollars of advanced arms have been purchased from Britain, France, and the U.S.; however, Western support for Israel has often strained relations. Saudi units fought against Israel in the 1948 and 1973 Arab-Israeli wars. Beginning with the 1967 Arab-Israeli war, Saudi Arabia provided large annual financial gifts to Egypt; aid was later extended to Syria, Jordan, and Palestinian groups, as well as to other Islamic countries.

King Faisal played a leading role in the 1973-74 Arab oil embargo against the U.S. and other nations. Crown Prince Khalid was proclaimed king on Mar. 25, 1975, after the assassination of Faisal. Fahd became king on June 13, 1982, following Khalid's death.

The Hejaz contains the holy cities of Islam—Medina, where the Mosque of the Prophet enshrines the tomb of Muhammad, and Mecca, his birthplace. More than 2 million Muslims make pilgrimage to Mecca annually. In 1987, Iranians making a pilgrimage to Mecca clashed with anti-Iranian pilgrims and Saudi police; more than 400 were killed. Some 1,426 Muslim pilgrims died July 2, 1990, in a stampede in a pedestrian tunnel leading to Mecca. Nearly 300 pilgrims were killed in a stampede in Mecca, May 26, 1994. More than 340 pilgrims died in a tent fire near Mecca, Apr. 15, 1997. A stampede at Mina killed more than 250, Feb. 1, 2004.

Following Iraq's attack on Kuwait, Aug. 2, 1990, Saudi Arabia accepted the Kuwait royal family and more than 400,000 Kuwaiti refugees. King Fahd invited Western and Arab troops to deploy on

its soil in support of Saudi defense forces. During the Persian Gulf War, 28 U.S. soldiers were killed when an Iraqi missile hit their barracks in Dhahran, Feb. 25, 1991. Islamic extremists were blamed for truck bombs that killed 7 (5 from the U.S.) at a military training center in Riyadh, Nov. 13, 1995, and 19 Americans at a base in Dhahran, June 25, 1996.

The presence of 15 Saudis among the 19 al-Qaeda hijackers who took part in the Sept. 11, 2001, attacks on the U.S. raised new tensions between the U.S. and Saudi governments, and some blamed the Saudi government for allowing Muslim extremism to flourish in Saudi Arabia. Policy differences over Iraq and the Israeli-Palestinian dispute were further irritants. The U.S. completed a pull-out of its combat forces in Sept. 2003. Alarmed at guerrilla attacks that killed more than 100 people, mostly foreigners, in Saudi Arabia during 2003-04, the Saudi government stepped up antiterrorist activities in cooperation with the U.S.

With King Fahd ailing, his half-brother, Crown Prince Abdullah, has taken a leading role in recent years. In Sept. 2004, the govt. announced that its first elections ever, mainly for municipal councils, would be held in early 2005.

Senegal
Republic of Senegal

People: Population: 10,852,147. **Age distrib.** (%): <15: 43.5; 65+: 3.1. **Pop. density:** 146 per sq mi, 57 per sq km. **Urban:** 49.6%. **Ethnic groups:** Wolof 43%, Pular 24%, Serer 15%, Jola 4%, Mandinka 3%, Soninke 1%. **Principal languages:** French (official), Wolof, Pulaar, Jola, Mandinka. **Chief religions:** Muslim 94%, Christian 5%.

Geography: Total area: 75,749 sq mi, 196,190 sq km; **Land area:** 74,132 sq mi, 192,000 sq km. **Location:** At W extreme of Africa. **Neighbors:** Mauritania on N, Mali on E, Guinea and Guinea-Bissau on S; surrounds Gambia on three sides. **Topography:** Low rolling plains cover most of Senegal, rising somewhat in the SE. Swamp and jungles are in SW. **Capital:** Dakar, 2,167,000.

Government: Type: Republic. **Head of state:** Pres. Abdoulaye Wade; b May 29, 1926; in office: Apr. 1, 2000. **Head of gov.:** Prime Min. Macky Sall; b Dec. 11, 1961; in office: Apr. 21, 2004. **Local divisions:** 11 regions. **Defense budget** (2003): $88 mil. **Active troops:** 13,620.

Economy: Industries: food & fish proc., phosphate mining, fertilizer. **Chief crops:** peanuts, millet, corn, sorghum, rice, cotton. **Natural resources:** fish, phosphates, iron ore. **Arable land:** 12%. **Livestock:** (2003): cattle: 3.02 mil.; chickens: 45.0 mil.; goats: 3.97 mil.; pigs: 303,368; sheep: 4.61 mil. **Fish catch** (2002): 375,933 metric tons. **Electricity Prod.** (2002): 1.74 bil. kWh. **Labor force:** agriculture 70%.

Finance: Monetary unit: CFA Franc BCEAO (XOF) (Sept. 2004: 539.40=1 U.S.). **GDP** (2003 est.): $16.9 bil.; **per capita GDP:** $1,600; **GDP growth:** 4.5%. **Imports** (2003 est.): $1.8 bil.; partners (2002): France 25.6%, Nigeria 8.7%, Thailand 7.2%, U.S. 5.4%, Germany 5.4%, Italy 4.5%. **Exports** (2003 est.): $1.2 bil.; partners (2002): India 20.8%, France 13%, Mali 8.9%, Greece 7.7%, Italy 4.4%. **Tourism** (2002): $184 mil. **Budget** (2002 est.): $1.4 bil. **Intl. reserves less gold:** $535 mil. **Consumer prices:** −0.03%.

Transport: Railroad: Length: 563 mi. **Motor vehicles** (1995): 106,000 pass. cars, 48,00 comm. vehicles. **Civil aviation:** 134.2 mil. pass.-mi; 9 airports. **Chief ports:** Dakar, Saint-Louis.

Communications: TV sets: 41 per 1,000 pop. **Radios:** 141 per 1,000 pop. **Telephone lines:** 228,800. **Daily newspaper circ.:** 5.3 per 1,000 pop. **Internet:** 225,000 users.

Health: Life expect.: 54.9 male; 58.2 female. **Births** (per 1,000 pop.): 35.7. **Deaths** (per 1,000 pop.): 10.7. **Natural inc.:** 2.50%. **Infant mortality** (per 1,000 live births): 56.5. **AIDS rate:** 0.8%.

Education: Compulsory: ages 7-12. **Literacy:** 40.2%.

Major Intl. Organizations: UN and all of its specialized agencies, AU.

Embassy: 2112 Wyoming Ave. NW 20008; 234-0540.

Websites: www.senegal-tourism.com; www.gouv.sn

Portuguese settlers arrived in the 15th century, but French control grew from the 17th century. The last independent Muslim state was subdued in 1893. Senegal became an independent republic Aug. 20, 1960, but French political and economic influence remained strong. Senegambia, a loose confederation of Senegal and The Gambia, was established in 1982 but dissolved 7 years later.

Separatists in Casamance Province of S Senegal have clashed with government forces since 1982. Senegal sent troops in June 1998 to help the Guinea-Bissau government suppress an army uprising. Forty years of Socialist Party rule ended when Abdoulaye Wade, leader of the Senegalese Democratic Party, won a presidential runoff election Mar. 19, 2000. A Senegalese ferry capsized off the coast of The Gambia Sept. 26, 2002, killing at least 1,863 people.

Serbia and Montenegro
(*formerly* Yugoslavia)

People: Population: 10,825,900. **Age distrib.** (%): <15: 19.6; 65+: 15.1. **Pop. density:** 275 per sq mi, 106 per sq km. **Urban:** 52.0%. **Ethnic groups:** Serb 63%, Albanian 17%, Montenegrin 5%, Hungarian 3%. **Principal languages:** Serbian (official), Albanian. **Chief religions:** Orthodox 65%, Muslim 19%, Roman Catholic 4%.

Geography: Total area: 39,518 sq mi, 102,350 sq km; **Land area:** 39,435 sq mi, 102,136 sq km. **Location:** On the Balkan Peninsula in SE Europe. **Neighbors:** Croatia, Bosnia and Herzegovina on W; Hungary on N; Romania, Bulgaria on E; Albania, on S. **Topography:** Terrain varies widely, with fertile plains drained by the Danube and other rivers in N, limestone basins in E, ancient mountains and hills in SE, and very high coastline in Montenegro along SW. **Capital:** Belgrade, 1,118,000.

Government: Type: Federal republic. **Head of state and gov.:** Pres. Svetozar Marovic; b Mar. 31, 1955; in office: Mar. 7, 2003. **Local divisions:** 2 republics, 2 autonomous provinces. **Defense budget** (2003): $641 mil. **Active troops:** 74,200.

Economy: Industries: aircraft, vehicle, & other machine building; metallurgy, mining, consumer goods, electronics, oil products, chemicals. **Chief crops:** cereals, fruits, vegetables, tobacco, olives. **Natural resources:** oil, gas, coal, antimony, copper, lead, zinc, nickel, gold, pyrite, chrome, hydropower. **Crude oil reserves** (2003): 77.5 mil. bbls. **Livestock** (2003): cattle: 1.34 mil.; chickens: 21.1 mil.; goats: 200,000; pigs: 3.66 mil.; sheep: 1.76 mil. **Fish catch** (2002): 3,839 metric tons. **Electricity prod.** (2002): 31.64 bil. kWh.

Finance: Monetary unit: Dinar (YUN) (Sept. 2004: 60.94=1 U.S.). **GDP** (2003 est.): $24.0 bil.; **per capita GDP:** $2,300; **GDP growth:** 2.0%. **Imports** (2003 est.): $7.1 bil.; partners (2002): Germany 18.9%, Italy 17.1%, Austria 8%, Slovenia 7.6%, Hungary 5.2%, Greece 4.1%, France 4.1%, Bulgaria 4%. **Exports** (2003 est.): $2.7 bil.; partners (2002): Italy 31.3%, Germany 19.7%, Greece 6.9%, Austria 5.9%, France 4.5%, Hungary 4.3%. **Tourism** (2002): $77 mil. **Budget** (2001 est.): $4.3 bil.

Transport: Railroad: Length: 2,522 mi. **Motor vehicles:** 1.00 mil pass. cars, 331,000 comm. vehicles. **Civil aviation:** 93 mil pass.-mi; 19 airports. **Chief ports:** Bar, Novi Sad.

Communications: TV sets: 277 per 1,000 pop. **Radios:** 296 per 1,000 pop. **Telephone lines:** 2.6 mil. **Daily newspaper circ.:** 107 per 1,000 pop. **Internet:** 847,000 users.

Health: Life expect.: 71.9 male; 77.1 female. **Births** (per 1,000 pop.): 12.1. **Deaths** (per 1,000 pop.): 10.5. **Natural inc.:** 0.16%. **Infant mortality** (per 1,000 live births): 13.4. **AIDS rate:** 0.2%.

Education: Compulsory: ages 7-14. **Literacy** (2002): 98%.

Major Intl. Organizations: Currently suspended from UN and its agencies.

Embassy: 2134 Kalorama Rd. NW 20008; 332-0333.

Website: www.gov.yu

Serbia, which had since 1389 been a vassal principality of Turkey, was established as an independent kingdom by the Treaty of Berlin, 1878. Montenegro, independent since 1389, also obtained international recognition in 1878. After the Balkan wars, Serbia's boundaries were enlarged by the annexation of Old Serbia and Macedonia, 1913.

When the Austro-Hungarian empire collapsed after World War I, the Kingdom of Serbs, Croats, and Slovenes was formed from the former provinces of Croatia, Dalmatia, Bosnia, Herzegovina, Slovenia, Vojvodina, and the independent state of Montenegro. The name became Yugoslavia in 1929.

Nazi Germany invaded in 1941. Many Yugoslav partisan troops continued to operate. Among these were the Chetniks led by Draja Mikhailovich, who fought other partisans led by Josip Broz, known as Marshal Tito. Tito, backed by the USSR and Britain from 1943, was in control by the time the Germans had been driven from Yugoslavia in 1945. Mikhailovich was executed July 17, 1946, by the Tito regime.

A constituent assembly proclaimed Yugoslavia a republic Nov. 29, 1945. It became a federal republic Jan. 31, 1946, with Tito, a Communist, heading the government. Tito rejected Stalin's policy of dictating to all Communist nations, and he accepted economic and military aid from the West.

Pres. Tito died May 4, 1980. After his death, Yugoslavia was governed by a collective presidency, with a rotating succession. On Jan. 22, 1990, the Communist Party renounced its leading role in society.

Croatia and Slovenia formally declared independence June 25, 1991. In Croatia, fighting began between Croats and ethnic Serbs. Serbia sent arms and medical supplies to the Serb rebels in Croatia. Croatian forces clashed with Yugoslav army units and their Serb supporters.

The republics of Serbia and Montenegro proclaimed a new "Federal Republic of Yugoslavia" Apr. 17, 1992. Serbia, under Pres. Slobodan Milosevic, was the main arms supplier to ethnic Serb fighters in Bosnia and Herzegovina. The UN imposed sanctions May 30 on the newly reconstituted Yugoslavia as a means of ending the bloodshed in Bosnia.

A peace agreement initialed in Dayton, Ohio, Nov. 21, 1995, was signed in Paris, Dec. 14, by Milosevic and leaders of Bosnia and Croatia. In May 1996, a UN tribunal in the Netherlands began trying suspected war criminals from the former Yugoslavia. The UN lifted sanctions against Yugoslavia Oct. 1, 1996, after elections were held in Bosnia. Mass protests erupted when Milosevic refused to accept opposition victories in local elections Nov. 17; non-Communist governments took office in Belgrade and other cities in Feb. 1997. Barred from running for a 3rd term as Serbian president, Milosevic had himself inaugurated as president of Yugoslavia on July 23, 1997.

Defeated in a presidential election Sept. 24, 2000, by opposition leader Vojislav Kostunica, Milosevic initially refused to accept the

result. A rising tide of mass demonstrations forced him to resign Oct. 6, and Kostunica was sworn in the next day. Charged with corruption and abuse of power, Milosevic surrendered to Serbian authorities Apr. 1, 2001. He was extradited June 28, 2001, to The Hague, where a UN tribunal had indicted him for war crimes. A pact to reconstitute Yugoslavia as a new union of Serbia and Montenegro was signed Mar. 14, 2002, and took effect Feb. 4, 2003. Zoran Djindjic, premier of the Republic of Serbia, was assassinated in Belgrade, Mar. 12; the murder triggered a roundup of more than 4,500 people associated with organized crime or the Milosevic regime.

Kosovo: A nominally autonomous province in southern Serbia (4,203 sq. mi.), with a population of about 2,000,000, mostly Albanians. The capital is Pristina. Revoking provincial autonomy, Serbia began ruling Kosovo by force in 1989. Albanian secessionists proclaimed an independent Republic of Kosovo in July 1990. Guerrilla attacks by the Kosovo Liberation Army in 1997 brought a ferocious counteroffensive by Serbian authorities.

Fearful that the Serbs were employing "ethnic cleansing" tactics, as they had in Bosnia, the U.S. and its NATO allies sought to pressure the Yugoslav government. When Milosevic refused to comply, NATO launched an air war against Yugoslavia, Mar.-June 1999; the Serbs retaliated by terrorizing the Kosovars and forcing hundreds of thousands to flee, mostly to Albania and Macedonia. A 50,000-member multinational force (KFOR) entered Kosovo in June, and most of the Kosovar refugees had returned by Sept. 1. In the worst fighting there since 1999, Albanians and Serbs clashed in Mar. 2004, killing about 30 people, and injuring 500+, incl. UN/NATO troops. As of 2004, Kosovo was under UN administration, with a NATO-led security force of more than 17,500.

Vojvodina: A nominally autonomous province in northern Serbia (8,304 sq. mi.), with a population of about 2,000,000, mostly Serbian. The capital is Novi Sad.

Seychelles
Republic of Seychelles

People: Population: 80,832 **Age distrib.** (%): <15: 27.8; 65+: 6.2. **Pop. density:** 460 per sq mi, 178 per sq km. **Urban:** 49.9%. **Ethnic groups:** Mainly Seychellois (mix of French, African, and Asian). **Principal languages:** English, French, Creole (all official). **Chief religions:** Roman Catholic 87%, Anglican 7%.

Geography: Total area: 176 sq mi, 455 sq km; **Land area:** 176 sq mi, 455 sq km. **Location:** In the Indian O. 700 miles NE of Madagascar. **Neighbors:** Nearest are Madagascar on SW, Somalia on NW. **Topography:** A group of 86 islands, about half of them composed of coral, the other half granite, the latter predominantly mountainous. **Capital:** Victoria, 25,000.

Government: Type: Republic. **Head of state and gov.:** Pres. James Michel, b. Aug. 18, 1944; in office: Apr. 14, 2004. **Local divisions:** 23 districts. **Defense budget** (2003): $11 mil. **Active troops:** 450.

Economy: Industries: fishing, tourism, coconut & vanilla proc., rope, boats. **Chief crops:** coconuts, cinnamon, vanilla, sweet potatoes, cassava, bananas. **Natural resources:** fish, copra, cinnamon. **Arable land:** 2%. **Livestock** (2003): cattle: 1,400; chickens: 520,000; goats: 5,150; pigs: 18.500. **Fish catch** (2002): 63,443 metric tons. **Electricity prod.** (2002): 0.22 bil. kWh. **Labor force** (1989): industry 19%, services 71%, agriculture 10%.

Finance: Monetary unit: Rupee (SCR) (Sept. 2004: 5.42=1 U.S.). **GDP** (2002 est.): $626.0 mil.; **per capita GDP:** $7,800; **GDP growth:** 1.5%. **Imports** (2003 est.): $383.7 mil.; partners (2002): Saudi Arabia 14.8%, France 12.2%, South Africa 10.9%, Spain 9.4%, Italy 9.1%, Singapore 6.8%, UK 5.7%. **Exports** (2003 est.): $250.0 mil.; partners (2002): UK 24.6%, France 17.1%, Mauritius 8.7%, Italy 7.5%, U.S. 7.2%, Germany 6.7%, Japan 5.8%, Netherlands 5.8%, Spain 5.8%, Thailand 5.5%. **Tourism:** $126 mil. **Budget** (1998 est.): $262.0 mil. **Intl. reserves less gold:** $45 mil. **Consumer prices:** 3.3%.

Transport: Motor vehicles (1999): 6,400 pass. cars, 2,200 comm. vehicles. **Civil aviation:** 494.0 mil. pass.-mi 7 airports. **Chief port:** Victoria.

Communications: TV sets: 214 per 1,000 pop. **Radios:** 560 per 1,000 pop. **Telephone lines** (2002): 21,700. **Daily newspaper circ.:** 45 per 1,000 pop. **Internet** (2002): 11,700 users.

Health: Life expect.: 66.1 male; 77.1 female. **Births** (per 1,000 pop.): 16.6. **Deaths** (per 1,000 pop.): 6.4. **Natural inc.:** 1.01%. **Infant mortality** (per 1,000 live births): 16.0.

Education: Compulsory: ages 6-15. **Literacy** (2002): 84%.

Major Intl. Organizations: UN (FAO, IBRD, ILO, IMF, IMO, WHO), the Commonwealth, AU.

Embassy: 800 2d Ave., Suite 400, New York, NY 10017; 212-687-9766.

Websites: www.seychelles-online.com.sc/seychelles.html
www.seychelles.com

The islands were occupied by France in 1768, and seized by Britain in 1794. Ruled as part of Mauritius from 1814, the Seychelles became a separate colony in 1903. Independence was declared June 29, 1976. The first president was ousted in a coup a year later by a socialist leader, France Albert René. A new constitution, approved June 1993, provided for a multiparty state. After nearly 27 years in power, Pres. René resigned Apr. 14, 2004, and was succeeded by Vice Pres. James Michel.

Sierra Leone
Republic of Sierra Leone

People: Population: 5,883,889. **Age distrib.** (%): <15: 44.7; 65+: 3.2. **Pop. density:** 213 per sq mi, 82 per sq km. **Urban:** 38.8%. **Ethnic groups:** Temne 30%, Mende 30%, other tribes 30%; Creole 10%. **Principal languages:** English (official), Mende in S, Temne in N, Krio (English Creole). **Chief religions:** Muslim 60%, indigenous beliefs 30%, Christian 10%.

Geography: Total area: 27,699 sq mi, 71,740 sq km; **Land area:** 27,653 sq mi, 71,620 sq km. **Location:** On W coast of W Africa. **Neighbors:** Guinea on N and E, Liberia on S. **Topography:** The heavily-indented, 210-mi. coastline has mangrove swamps. Behind are wooded hills, rising to a plateau and mountains in the E. **Capital:** Freetown, 921,000.

Government: Type: Republic. **Head of state and gov.:** Ahmad Tejan Kabbah; b Feb. 16, 1932; in office: Mar. 10, 1998. **Local divisions:** 3 provinces, 1 area. **Defense budget** (2003): $18 mil. **Active troops:** 13,000-14,000.

Economy: Industries: diamonds, light mfg., oil refining. **Chief crops:** rice, coffee, cocoa, palm kernels & oil, peanuts. **Natural resources:** diamonds, titanium ore, bauxite, iron ore, gold, chromite. **Arable land:** 7%. **Livestock** (2003): cattle: 400,000; chickens: 7.5 mil.; goats: 220,000; pigs: 52,000; sheep: 375,000. **Fish catch** (2002): 82,990 metric tons. **Electricity Prod.** (2002): 0.26 bil. kWh.

Finance: Monetary unit: Leone (SLL) (Sept. 2004: 2,450.00=1 U.S.). **GDP** (2003 est.): $3.1 bil.; **per capita GDP:** $500; **GDP growth:** 6.5%. **Imports** (2002 est.): $264.0 mil.; partners (2002): Germany 26.1%, UK 10.7%, Netherlands 7.5%, U.S. 5.7%, Cote d'Ivoire 4.9%, Italy 4.3%. **Exports** (2002 est.): $49.0 mil.; partners (2002): Belgium 41.6%, Germany 31.7%, UK 4%, U.S. 4%. **Tourism:** $52 mil. **Budget** (2000 est.): $351.0 mil. **Intl. reserves less gold:** $45 mil. **Consumer prices:** 7.6%.

Transport: Railroad: Length: 52 mi. **Motor vehicles** (1999): 19,200 pass. cars, 14,800 comm. vehicles. **Civil aviation:** 57.8 mil. pass.-mi; 1 airport. **Chief ports:** Freetown, Bonthe.

Communications: TV sets: 13 per 1,000 pop. **Radios:** 274 per 1,000 pop. **Telephone lines** (2002): 24,000. **Daily newspaper circ.:** 4.7 per 1,000 pop. **Internet** (2002): 8,000 users.

Health: Life expect.: 40.2 male; 45.2 female. **Births** (per 1,000 pop.): 43.3. **Deaths** (per 1,000 pop.): 20.6. **Natural inc.:** 2.27%. **Infant mortality** (per 1,000 live births): 145.2.

Education: Literacy (2002): 31%.

Major Intl. Organizations: UN (FAO, IBRD, ILO, IMF, IMO, WHO, WTrO), the Commonwealth, AU.

Embassy: 1701 19th St. NW 20009; 939-9261.

Websites: www.Sierra-Leone.org; www.slhc-uk.org.uk

Freetown was founded in 1787 by the British government as a haven for freed slaves. Their descendants, known as Creoles, number more than 60,000.

Successive steps toward independence followed the 1951 constitution. Ten years later, full independence arrived Apr. 27, 1961. Sierra Leone declared itself a republic Apr. 19, 1971. A one-party state approved by referendum in 1978 brought political stability, but mismanagement and corruption plagued the economy.

Mutinous soldiers ousted Pres. Joseph Momoh Apr. 30, 1992. Another coup, Jan. 16, 1996, paved the way for multiparty elections and a return to civilian rule. A peace accord, signed Nov. 30 with the Revolutionary United Front (RUF), brought a temporary halt to a civil war that had claimed over 10,000 lives in 5 years.

A coup on May 25, 1997, was met with widespread international opposition. Armed intervention by Nigeria restored Pres. Ahmad Tejan Kabbah to power on Mar. 10, 1998, but RUF rebels mounted a guerrilla counteroffensive, reportedly killing thousands of civilians and mutilating thousands more. The Kabbah government signed a power-sharing agreement with the RUF on July 7, 1999. A UN mission (UNAMSIL) was established in Oct. to help maintain the agreement. The accord collapsed in early May 2000, as RUF guerrillas took more than 500 UN peacekeepers hostage. Rebel leader Foday Sankoh was captured in Freetown May 17. The hostages were freed by the end of May, and 233 more UN personnel behind rebel lines were rescued July 15.

A UN-sponsored disarmament program in 2001 reduced the level of violence. On Jan. 16, 2002, the govt. and the UN signed an agreement creating the Sierra Leone Special Court to try war crimes that had occurred from Nov. 1996 onwards. Government and rebel leaders declared an official end to the war Jan. 18. Kabbah won the May 14 presidential election. Sankoh, an indicted war criminal, died in UN custody July 29, 2003. The Special Court opened trials against 3 former leaders of a pro-govt. militia in June 2004. A UN helicopter crashed June 29, 2004, in E Sierra Leone, killing all 24 people on board.

Singapore
Republic of Singapore

People: Population: 4,353,893. **Age distrib.** (%): <15: 17.6; 65+: 7.1. **Pop. density:** 16,518 per sq mi, 6,377 per sq km. **Urban:** 100.0%. **Ethnic groups:** Chinese 77%, Malay 14%, Indian 8%. **Principal languages:** Chinese, Malay, Tamil, English (all official). **Chief religions:** Buddhist, Muslim, Christian, Taoist, Hindu.

Geography: Total area: 267 sq mi, 693 sq km; **Land area:** 264 sq mi, 693 sq km. **Location:** Off tip of Malayan Peninsula in SE

Asia. **Neighbors:** Nearest are Malaysia on N, Indonesia on S. **Topography:** Singapore is a flat, formerly swampy island. The nation includes 40 nearby islets. **Capital:** Singapore, 4,253,000.

Government: Type: Republic. **Head of state:** Pres. S. R. Nathan; b July 3, 1924; in office: Sept. 1, 1999. **Head of gov.:** Prime Min. Lee Hsien Loong; b Feb. 10, 1952; in office: Aug. 12, 2004. **Defense budget** (2003): $4.7 bill. **Active troops:** 72,500.

Economy: Industries: electronics, chemicals, financial services, oil drilling equip., oil refining, rubber proc. **Chief crops:** rubber, copra, fruit, orchids, vegetables. **Natural resources:** fish. **Arable land:** 2%. **Livestock** (2003): cattle: 200; chickens: 2.0 mil.; goats: 300; pigs: 250,000. **Fish catch** (2002): 7,796 metric tons. **Electricity prod.** (2002): 32.18 bil. kWh. **Labor force** (2003): financial, business, and other services 49%, manufacturing 18%, construction 6%, transportation and communication 11%, other 16%.

Finance: Monetary unit: Singapore Dollar (SGD) (Sept. 2004: 1.69=1 U.S.). **GDP** (2003 est.): $109.1 bil.; **per capita GDP:** $23,700; **GDP growth:** 0.8%. **Imports** (2003 est.): $121.6 bil.; partners (2002): Malaysia 18.2%, U.S. 14.3%, Japan 12.5%, China 7.6%, Thailand 4.6%, Taiwan 4.6%. **Exports** (2003 est.): $142.4 bil.; partners (2002): Malaysia 17.4%, U.S. 15.3%, Hong Kong 9.2%, Japan 7.1%, China 5.5%, Taiwan 4.9%, Thailand 4.6%, South Korea 4.2%. **Tourism** (2002): $4.4 bil. **Budget** (FY03/04 est.): $17.6 bil. **Intl. reserves less gold:** $64.43 bil. **Consumer prices:** 0.5%.

Transport: Railroad: Length: 24 mi. **Motor vehicles** (2001): 426,400 pass. cars, 139,900 comm. vehicles. **Civil aviation:** 44.6 bil. pass.-mi; 9 airports. **Chief port:** Singapore.

Communications: TV sets: 341 per 1,000 pop. **Radios:** 744 per 1,000 pop. **Telephone lines** (2002): 1.9 mil. **Daily newspaper circ.:** 324 per 1,000 pop. **Internet** (2002): 2.1 mil. users.

Health: Life expect.: 79.0 male; 84.3 female. **Births** (per 1,000 pop.): 9.6. **Deaths** (per 1,000 pop.): 4.0. **Natural inc.:** 0.56%. **Infant mortality** (per 1,000 live births): 2.3. **AIDS rate:** 0.2%.

Education: Compulsory: ages 6-16: 93.2%.

Major Intl. Organizations: UN (IBRD, ILO, IMF, IMO, WHO, WTrO), the Commonwealth, APEC, ASEAN.

Embassy: 3501 International Pl. NW 20008; 537-3100.

Website: www.gov.sg

Founded in 1819 by Sir Thomas Stamford Raffles, Singapore was a British colony until 1959, when it became autonomous within the Commonwealth. On Sept. 16, 1963, it joined with Malaya, Sarawak, and Sabah to form the Federation of Malaysia. Tensions between Malayans, dominant in the federation, and ethnic Chinese, dominant in Singapore, led to an accord under which Singapore became a separate nation, Aug. 9, 1965.

Singapore is one of the world's largest ports and a major center of manufacturing, banking, and commerce. Standards in health, education, and housing are generally high. The government, dominated by a single party, has taken strong actions to keep order and suppress dissent.

In Dec. 2001, the government thwarted an alleged plot to blow up the U.S. Embassy; in Sept. 2002, authorities reported arrests of 21 militants identified as members of Jemaah Islamiah, a radical Muslim group active in Southeast Asia.

Singapore has had only 3 prime ministers: Lee Kuan Yew, who dominated national politics, 1959-90; Goh Chok Tong, 1990-2004; and Lee Kuan Yew's son, Lee Hsien Loong, who took office Aug. 12, 2004.

Slovakia
Slovak Republic

People: Population: 5,423,567. **Age distrib.** (%): <15: 18.3; 65+: 11.6. **Pop. density:** 288 per sq mi, 111 per sq km. **Urban:** 57.4%. **Ethnic groups:** Slovak 86%, Hungarian 11%, Roma 2%. **Principal languages:** Slovak (official), Hungarian. **Chief religions:** Roman Catholic 60%, Protestant 8%, Orthodox 4%.

Geography: Total area: 18,859 sq mi, 48,845 sq km; **Land area:** 18,842 sq mi, 48,800 sq km. **Location:** In E central Europe. **Neighbors:** Poland on N, Hungary on S, Austria and Czech Rep. on W, Ukraine on E. **Topography:** Mountains (Carpathians) in N, fertile Danube plane in S. **Capital:** Bratislava, 425,000. **Cities (urban aggr.):** Kosice, 242,000.

Government: Type: Republic. **Head of state:** Ivan Gasparovic; b Mar. 27, 1941; in office: June 15, 2004. **Head of gov.:** Prime Min. Mikuláš Dzurinda; b Feb. 4, 1955; in office: Oct. 30, 1998. **Local divisions:** 8 departments. **Defense budget** (2002): $624 mil. **Active troops:** 22,000.

Economy: Industries: metals; food & beverages; electricity, gas, coke, oil, nuclear fuels. **Chief crops:** grains, potatoes, sugar beets, hops, fruit. **Natural resources:** coal, lignite, iron ore, copper, mang., salt. **Crude oil reserves** (2003): 9.0 mil. bbls. **Arable land:** 31%. **Livestock** (2003): cattle: 593,182; chickens: 5.6 mil.; goats: 39,225; pigs: 1.44 mil.; sheep: 325,521. **Fish catch** (2002): 2,575 metric tons. **Electricity prod.** (2002): 30.48 bil. kWh. **Labor force** (1994): industry 29.3%, agriculture 8.9%, construction 8%, transport and communication 8.2%, services 45.6%.

Finance: Monetary unit: Koruna (SKK) (Sept. 2004: 32.89=1 U.S.). **GDP** (2003 est.): $72.3 bil.; **per capita GDP:** $13,300; **GDP growth:** 3.9%. **Imports** (2003 est.): $21.9 bil.; partners (2002): Germany 22.6%, Czech Republic 15.1%, Russia 12.5%, Italy 6.9%, France 4.4%, Austria 4.2%. **Exports** (2003 est.): $21.3 bil.;

partners (2002): Germany 26%, Czech Republic 15.2%, Italy 10.8%, Austria 7.7%, Hungary 5.5%, Poland 5.3%, France 4.2%. **Tourism:** $863 mil. **Budget** (1999): $5.6 bil. **Intl. reserves less gold:** $7.86 bil. **Gold:** 1.13 mil. oz t. **Consumer prices:** 8.6%.

Transport: Railroad: Length: 2,279 mi. **Motor vehicles** (2001): 1.29 mil. pass. cars, 161,500 comm. vehicles. **Civil aviation:** 64.0 mil. pass.-mi; 20 airports. **Chief ports:** Bratislava, Komarno.

Communications: TV sets: 418 per 1,000 pop. **Radios:** 967 per 1,000 pop. **Telephone lines:** 1.3 mil. **Daily newspaper circ.:** 130.6 per 1,000 pop. **Internet:** 1.4 mil. users.

Health: Life expect.: 70.2 male; 78.4 female. **Births** (per 1,000 pop.): 10.6. **Deaths** (per 1,000 pop.): 9.5. **Natural inc.:** 0.11%. **Infant mortality** (per 1,000 live births): 7.6. **AIDS rate:** <0.1%.

Education: Compulsory: ages 6-15. **Literacy** (1994): 100%.

Major Intl. Organizations: UN (FAO, IBRD, ILO, IMF, IMO, WHO, WTrO), EU, NATO, OSCE.

Embassy: 3523 International Ct. NW 20008; 237-1054.

Websites: www.slovakembassy-us.org
www.vlada.gov.sk/english

Slovakia was originally settled by Illyrian, Celtic, and Germanic tribes and was incorporated into Great Moravia in the 9th century. It became part of Hungary in the 11th century. Overrun by Czech Hussites in the 15th century, it was restored to Hungarian rule in 1526. The Slovaks disassociated themselves from Hungary after World War I and joined the Czechs of Bohemia to form the Republic of Czechoslovakia, Oct. 28, 1918.

Germany invaded Czechoslovakia, 1939, and declared Slovakia independent. Slovakia rejoined Czechoslovakia in 1945.

Czechoslovakia split into 2 separate states—the Czech Republic and Slovakia—on Jan. 1, 1993. A prolonged parliamentary standoff left the country without a president for much of 1998.

Prime Min. Vladimir Meciar, a nationalist, suffered a setback in legislative elections Sept. 25-26, 1998, and was defeated in a presidential runoff vote by Rudolf Schuster, May 29, 1999. A center-right coalition governed Slovakia after parliamentary elections Sept. 20-21, 2002. Meciar lost another bid for the presidency to his former ally, Ivan Gasparovic, Apr. 17, 2004. Slovakia became a full member of the EU and NATO in 2004.

Slovenia
Republic of Slovenia

People: Population: 2,011,473. **Age distrib.** (%): <15: 15.7; 65+: 14.5. **Pop. density:** 259 per sq mi, 100 per sq km. **Urban:** 50.8%. **Ethnic groups:** Slovene 88%, Croat 3%, Serb 2%, Bosniak 1%. **Principal languages:** Slovenian (official), Serbo-Croatian. **Chief religion:** Roman Catholic 71%.

Geography: Total area: 7,827 sq mi, 20,273 sq km; **Land area:** 7,780 sq mi, 20,151 sq km. **Location:** In SE Europe. **Neighbors:** Italy on W, Austria on N, Hungary on NE, Croatia on SE, S. **Topography:** Mostly hilly; 42% of the land is forested. **Capital:** Ljubljana, 256,000.

Government: Type: Republic. **Head of state:** Pres. Janez Drnovsek; b May 17, 1950; in office: Dec. 22, 2002. **Head of gov.:** Prime Min. Anton Rop; Dec. 27, 1960; in office: Dec. 11, 2002. **Local divisions:** 183 municipalities, 11 urban municipalities. **Defense budget** (2003): $387 mil. **Active troops:** 6,550.

Economy: Industries: metallurgy, electronics, trucks, electric power equip., wood products, textiles, chemicals, machine tools. **Chief crops:** potatoes, hops, wheat, sugar beets, corn, grapes. **Natural resources:** lignite, lead, zinc, mercury, uranium, silver, hydropower, timber. **Livestock** (2003): cattle: 473,242; chickens: 4.98 mil.; goats: 21,977; pigs: 655,665; sheep: 107,400. **Fish catch** (2002): 2,976 metric tons. **Electricity prod.** (2002): 13.86 bil. kWh.

Finance: Monetary unit: Tolar (SIT) (Sept. 2004: 196.07=1 U.S.). **GDP** (2003 est.): $36.9 bil.; **per capita GDP:** $18,300; **GDP growth:** 2.5%. **Imports** (2003 est.): $12.6 bil.; partners (2002): Germany 19.2%, Italy 17.9%, France 10.2%, Austria 8.3%. **Exports** (2003 est.): $12.0 bil.; partners (2002): Germany 24.7%, Italy 12.1%, Croatia 8.7%, Austria 7.1%, France 6.7%, Bosnia and Herzegovina 4.5%. **Tourism:** $1.3 bil. **Budget** (2003 est.): $10.5 bil. **Intl. reserves less gold:** $5.72 bil. **Gold:** 240,000 oz t. **Consumer prices:** 5.6%.

Transport: Railroad: Length: 746 mi. **Motor vehicles** (2001): 884,200 pass. cars, 58,600 comm. vehicles. **Civil aviation:** 349.8 mil. pass.-mi; 6 airports. **Chief ports:** Izola, Koper, Piran.

Communications: TV sets: 362 per 1,000 pop. **Radios:** 404 per 1,000 pop. **Telephone lines:** 812,300. **Daily newspaper circ.:** 168.5 per 1,000 pop. **Internet** (2002): 750,000 users.

Health: Life expect.: 72.2 male; 79.9 female. **Births** (per 1,000 pop.): 8.9. **Deaths** (per 1,000 pop.): 10.2. **Natural inc.:** –0.12%. **Infant mortality** (per 1,000 live births): 4.5. **AIDS rate:** <0.1%.

Education: Compulsory: ages 7-14. **Literacy:** 99.7%.

Major Intl. Organizations: UN (FAO, IBRD, ILO, IMF, IMO, WHO, WTrO), EU, NATO, OSCE.

Embassy: 1525 New Hampshire Ave. NW 20036; 667-5363.

Websites: www.embassy.org/slovenia; www.sigov.si

The Slovenes settled in their current territory during the period from the 6th to the 8th century. They fell under German domination as early as the 9th century. Modern Slovenian political history began after 1848 when the Slovenes, who were divided among several Austrian provinces, began their struggle for political and national

unification. In 1918 a majority of Slovenes became part of the Kingdom of Serbs, Croats, and Slovenes, later renamed Yugoslavia.

Slovenia declared independence June 25, 1991, and joined the UN May 22, 1992. The country attained full membership in the EU and NATO in 2004.

Solomon Islands

People: Population: 523,617. **Age distrib.** (%): <15: 43.4; 65+: 3.1. **Pop. density:** 49 per sq mi, 19 per sq km. **Urban:** 16.5%. **Ethnic groups:** Melanesian 93%, Polynesian 4%, Micronesian, European, and others 3%. **Principal languages:** English (official), Melanesian pidgin, and 120 indigenous languages. **Chief religions:** Anglican 45%, Roman Catholic 18%, other Christian 35%.

Geography: Total area: 10,985 sq mi, 28,450 sq km; **Land area:** 10,633 sq mi, 27,540 sq km. **Location:** Melanesian Archipelago in the W Pacific O. **Neighbors:** Nearest is Papua New Guinea to W. **Topography:** 10 large volcanic and rugged islands and 4 groups of smaller ones. **Capital:** Honiara, 56,000.

Government: Type: In transition. **Head of state:** Queen Elizabeth II, represented by Gov.-Gen. Nathaniel Waena; in office: July 7, 2004. **Head of gov.:** Prime Min. Sir Allan Kemakeza; b 1951; in office: Dec. 17, 2001. **Local divisions:** 9 provinces and Honiara.

Economy: Industries: tuna, mining, timber. **Chief crops:** cocoa, beans, coconuts, palm kernels, rice, potatoes. **Natural resources:** fish, timber, gold, bauxite, phosphates, lead, zinc, nickel. **Arable land:** 1%. **Livestock** (2003): cattle: 13,000; chickens: 220,000; pigs: 68,000. **Electricity prod.** (2002): 0.03 bil. kWh. **Fish catch** (2002 est): 31,003 metric tons. **Labor force** (2000 est.): agriculture 75%, industry 5%, services 20%.

Finance: Monetary unit: Dollar (SBD) (Sept. 2004: 7.48=1 U.S.). **GDP** (2001 est.): $800.0 mil.; **per capita GDP:** $1,700; **GDP growth:** −10.0%. **Imports** (2002 est.): $100.0 mil.; partners (2002): Australia 32.3%, Singapore 20.2%, Fiji 5.1%, New Zealand 5.1%, Papua New Guinea 4%. **Exports** (2002 est.): $90.0 mil.; partners (2002): Japan 21.1%, China 18.9%, South Korea 15.6%, Philippines 10%, Thailand 7.8%, Singapore 4.4%. **Tourism** (2002): $1 mil. **Budget** (1997 est.): $168 mil. **Intl. reserves less gold:** $25 mil. **Consumer prices:** 10.0%.

Transport: Civil aviation: 23.0 mil. pass.-mi; 2 airports. **Chief port:** Honiara.

Communications: TV sets: 16 per 1,000 pop. **Radios:** 141 per 1,000 pop. **Telephone lines** (2002): 6,600. **Internet** (2002): 2,200 users.

Health: Life expect.: 69.9 male; 75.0 female. **Births** (per 1,000 pop.): 31.6. **Deaths** (per 1,000 pop.): 4.0. **Natural inc.:** 2.76%. **Infant mortality** (per 1,000 live births): 22.1.

Education: Literacy (1994): 54%

Major Intl. Organizations: UN (FAO, IBRD, ILO, IMF, IMO, WHO, WTrO), the Commonwealth.

Embassy: 800 Second Ave., Suite 400L, New York, NY 10017; (212) 599-6193.

Website: www.commerce.gov.sb

The Solomon Islands were sighted in 1568 by an expedition from Peru. Britain established a protectorate in the 1890s over most of the group, inhabited by Melanesians. The islands saw major World War II battles. Self-government came Jan. 2, 1976, and independence was formally attained July 7, 1978.

A coup attempt June 5, 2000, sparked factional fighting in Honiara. During the next 3 years, violence, lawlessness, and corruption became widespread. To restore order, a 2,225-member intervention force, led by Australia and authorized by the Pacific Islands Forum, began arriving in Honiara July 24, 2003; about 100 foreign troops remained by the end of Aug. 2004.

Somalia

People: Population: 8,304,601. **Age distrib.** (%): <15: 44.7; 65+: 2.7. **Pop. density:** 34 per sq mi, 13 per sq km. **Urban:** 34.8%. **Ethnic groups:** Somali 85%, Bantu and other 15%. **Principal languages:** Somali, Arabic (both official); Italian, English. **Chief religion:** Sunni Muslim (official).

Geography: Total area: 246,201 sq mi, 637,657 sq km; **Land area:** 242,216 sq mi, 627,337 sq km. **Location:** Occupies the eastern horn of Africa. **Neighbors:** Djibouti, Ethiopia, Kenya on W. **Topography:** The coastline extends for 1,700 mi. Hills cover the N; the center and S are flat. **Capital:** Mogadishu, 1,175,000.

Government: Type: In transition. **Head of state:** Abdiqassim Salad Hassan; b 1941; in office: Aug. 27, 2000. **Head of gov.:** Prime Min. Prime Min. Muhammad Abdi Yusuf; in office: Dec. 8, 2003. **Local divisions:** 18 regions. **Defense budget:** NA. **Active troops:** Nil.

Economy: Industries: a few light industries, incl. sugar refining, textiles, wireless communication. **Chief crops:** bananas, sorghum, corn, coconuts, rice. **Natural resources:** uranium, iron ore, tin, gypsum, bauxite, copper, salt, nat. gas, oil. **Arable land:** 2%. **Livestock** (2002): cattle: 5.30 mil.; chickens: 3.30 mil.; goats: 12.50 mil.; pigs: 4,000; sheep: 13.20 mil. **Fish catch** (2002 est): 18,000 metric tons. **Electricity prod.** (2002): 0.24 bil. kWh. **Labor force:** agriculture (mostly pastoral nomadism) 71%, industry and services 29%.

Finance: Monetary unit: Shilling (SOS) (Sept. 2004: 2,764.95=1 U.S.). **GDP** (2003 est.): $4.4 bil.; **per capita GDP:** $500; **GDP growth:** 2.1%. **Imports** (2002 est.): $344.0 mil.; partners (2002): Djibouti 30.2%, Kenya 14%, Brazil 8.7%, Thailand

4.9%, UK 4.7%, UAE 4.4%. **Exports** (2002 est.): $79.0 mil.; partners (2002): UAE 41.8%, Yemen 22.8%, Oman 11.4%.

Transport: Motor vehicles (1995): 12,000 pass. cars, 12,000 comm. vehicles. **Civil aviation:** 86.9 mil pass.-mi; 6 airports. **Chief ports:** Mogadishu, Berbera.

Communications: TV sets: 14 per 1,000 pop. **Radios:** 53 per 1,000 pop. **Telephone lines:** 15,000 main lines. **Daily newspaper circ.:** 1.2 per 1,000 pop.

Health: Life expect.: 46.0 male; 49.5 female. **Births** (per 1,000 pop.): 46.0. **Deaths** (per 1,000 pop.): 17.3. **Natural inc.:** 2.87%. **Infant mortality** (per 1,000 live births): 118.5.

Education: Compulsory: ages 6-13. **Literacy** (2001 est.): 37.8%.

Major Intl. Organizations: UN (FAO, IBRD, ILO, IMF, IMO, WHO), AL, AU.

Website: travel.state.gov/travel/somalia.html

British Somaliland (present-day N Somalia) was formed in the 19th century, as was Italian Somaliland (now central and S Somalia). Italy lost its African colonies in World War II. British Somaliland gained independence, June 26, 1960, and by prearrangement, merged July 1 with the UN Trust Territory of Somalia to create the independent Somali Republic.

On Oct. 16, 1969, Pres. Abdi Rashid Ali Shirmarke was assassinated. On Oct. 21, a military group led by Maj. Gen. Muhammad Siad Barre seized power. In 1970, Barre declared the country a socialist state—the Somali Democratic Republic.

Somalia has laid claim to Ogaden, the huge eastern region of Ethiopia, peopled mostly by Somalis. Ethiopia battled Somali rebels in 1977. Some 11,000 Cuban troops with Soviet arms defeated Somali army troops and ethnic Somali rebels in Ethiopia, 1978. As many as 1.5 million refugees entered Somalia. Guerrilla fighting in Ogaden continued until 1988, when a peace agreement was reached with Ethiopia.

The civil war intensified again and Barre was forced to flee the capital, Jan. 1991. Fighting between rival factions caused 40,000 casualties in 1991 and 1992, and by mid-1992 the civil war, drought, and banditry combined to produce a famine that threatened some 1.5 million people with starvation.

In Dec. 1992 the UN accepted a U.S. offer of troops to safeguard food delivery to the starving. The UN took control of the multinational relief effort from the U.S. May 4, 1993. While the operation helped alleviate the famine, there were significant U.S. and other casualties; a failed mission Oct. 3-4 left 18 U.S. troops and more than 500 Somalis dead. The U.S. withdrew its peacekeeping forces Mar. 25, 1994.

When the last UN troops pulled out Mar. 3, 1995, Mogadishu had no functioning central government, and armed factions controlled different regions. By 1999 a joint police force was operating in the capital, but much of the country, especially in S Somalia, faced continued violence and food shortages. After political and factional leaders signed a peace deal Jan. 29, 2004, a transitional parliament, Somalia's 1st legislature in 13 yrs, was inaugurated Aug. 22.

South Africa
Republic of South Africa

People: Population: 42,718,530. **Age distrib.** (%): <15: 31.6; 65+: 5. **Pop. density:** 91 per sq mi, 35 per sq km. **Urban:** 56.9%. **Ethnic groups:** Black 75%, White 14%, mixed 8%, Indian 3%. **Principal languages:** Afrikaans, English, Ndebele, Pedi, Sotho, Swazi, Tsonga, Tswana, Venda, Xhosa, Zulu (all official). **Chief religions:** Christian 68%, indigenous beliefs and animist 29%.

Geography: Total area: 471,010 sq mi, 1,219,912 sq km; **Land area:** 471,010 sq mi, 1,219,912 sq km. **Location:** At the southern extreme of Africa. **Neighbors:** Namibia, Botswana, Zimbabwe on N; Mozambique, Swaziland on E; surrounds Lesotho. **Topography:** The large interior plateau reaches close to the country's 2,700-mi. coastline. There are few major rivers or lakes; rainfall is sparse in W, more plentiful in E. **Capitals:** Cape Town (legislative), 2,967,000, Pretoria (administrative), 1,209,000, and Bloemfontein (judicial), 381,000. **Cities (urban aggr.):** Durban, 2,370,000; Johannesburg, 2,732,000.

Government: Type: Republic. **Head of state and gov.:** Pres. Thabo Mvuyelwa Mbeki; b: June 18, 1942; in office: June 16, 1999. **Local divisions:** 9 provinces. **Defense budget** (2003): $2.5 bil. **Active troops:** 55,750.

Economy: Industries: mining (espec. platinum, gold, chromium), auto assembly, metalworking, machinery, textiles, chemicals, fertilizer, foodstuffs. **Chief crops:** corn, wheat, sugarcane, fruits, vegetables. **Natural resources:** gold, chromium, antimony, coal, iron ore, mang., nickel, phosphates, tin, uranium, diamonds, platinum, copper, vanadium, salt, nat. gas. **Crude oil reserves** (2003): 15.7 mil. bbls. **Arable land:** 10%. **Livestock** (2003): cattle: 13.60 mil.; chickens: 120.0 mil.; goats: 6.85 mil.; pigs: 1.62 mil.; sheep: 29.1 mil. **Fish catch** (2002 est): 770,461 metric tons. **Electricity Prod.** (2002): 202.62 bil. kWh. **Labor force** (1999 est.): agriculture 30%, industry 25%, services 45%.

Finance: Monetary unit: Rand (ZAR) (Sept. 2004: 6.57=1 U.S.). **GDP** (2003 est.): $456.7 bil.; **per capita GDP:** $10,700; **GDP growth:** 1.9%. **Imports** (2003 est.): $33.9 bil.; partners (2002): Germany 15.5%, U.S. 9.5%, UK 9.1%, Japan 5.8%, Saudi Arabia 5.3%, France 5%, China 4.9%. **Exports** (2003 est.): $36.8 bil.; partners (2002): UK 12.8%, U.S. 12.7%, Germany 9.3%, Japan 8.9%, Italy 5.8%. **Tourism** (2002): $2.7 bil. **Budget** (FY02/

03): $24.7 bil. **Intl. reserves less gold:** $4.37 bil. **Gold:** 3.98 mil oz t. **Consumer prices:** 5.9%.

Transport: Railroad: Length: 13,855 mi. **Motor vehicles** (1999): 3.97 mil pass. cars, 2.25 mil comm. vehicles. **Civil aviation:** 9.9 bil. pass.-mi; 143 airports. **Chief ports:** Durban, Cape Town, East London, Port Elizabeth.

Communications: TV sets: 138 per 1,000 pop. **Radios:** 355 per 1,000 pop. **Telephone lines** (2002): 4.8 mil. **Daily newspaper circ.:** 32 per 1,000 pop. **Internet** (2002): 3.1 mil. users.

Health: Life expect.: 44.4 male; 44.0 female. **Births** (per 1,000 pop.): 18.4. **Deaths** (per 1,000 pop.): 20.5. **Natural inc.:** −0.22%. **Infant mortality** (per 1,000 live births): 62.2. **AIDS rate:** 21.5%.

Education: Compulsory: ages 7-15. **Literacy:** 86.4%.

Major Intl. Organizations: UN (FAO, IBRD, ILO, IMF, IMO, WHO, WTrO), the Commonwealth, AU.

Embassy: 3051 Massachusetts Ave. NW 20008; 232-4400.

Websites: www.saembassy.org; www.gov.za

Bushmen and Hottentots were the original inhabitants. Bantus, including Zulu, Xhosa, Swazi, and Sotho, had occupied the area from NE to S South Africa before the 17th century.

The Cape of Good Hope area was settled by Dutch, beginning in the 17th century. Britain seized the Cape in 1806. Many Dutch trekked north and founded 2 republics, Transvaal and Orange Free State. Diamonds were discovered, 1867, and gold, 1886. The Dutch (Boers) resented encroachments by the British and others; the Anglo-Boer War followed, 1899-1902. Britain won and, effective May 31, 1910, created the Union of South Africa, incorporating 2 British colonies (Cape and Natal) with Transvaal and Orange Free State. After a referendum, the Union became the Republic of South Africa, May 31, 1961, and withdrew from the Commonwealth.

With the election victory of Daniel Malan's National Party in 1948, the policy of separate development of the races, or apartheid, already existing unofficially, became official. Under apartheid, blacks were severely restricted to certain occupations, and paid far lower wages than whites for similar work. Only whites could vote or run for public office. Persons of Asian Indian ancestry and those of mixed race (Coloureds) had limited political rights. In 1959 the government passed acts providing for the eventual creation of several Bantu nations, or Bantustans.

Protests against apartheid were brutally suppressed. At Sharpeville on Mar. 21, 1960, 69 black protesters were killed by government troops. At least 600 persons, mostly Bantus, were killed in 1976 riots protesting apartheid. In 1981, South Africa launched military operations in Angola and Mozambique to combat guerrilla groups.

A new constitution was approved by referendum, Nov. 1983, extending the parliamentary franchise to the Coloured and Asian minorities. Laws banning interracial sex and marriage were repealed in 1985.

In 1986, Nobel Peace Prize winner Bishop Desmond Tutu called for Western nations to apply sanctions against South Africa to force an end to apartheid. Pres. P. W. Botha announced in Apr. the end to the nation's system of racial pass laws and offered blacks an advisory role in government. On May 19, South Africa attacked 3 neighboring countries—Zimbabwe, Botswana, Zambia—to strike at guerrilla strongholds of the black nationalist African National Congress (ANC). A nationwide state of emergency was declared June 12, giving almost unlimited power to the security forces.

Some 2 million South African black workers staged a massive strike, June 6-8, 1988. Pres. Botha, head of the government since 1978, resigned Aug. 14, 1989, and was replaced by F. W. de Klerk. In 1990 the government lifted its ban on the ANC. Black nationalist leader Nelson Mandela was freed Feb. 11 after more than 27 years in prison. In Feb. 1991, Pres. de Klerk announced plans to end all apartheid laws.

In 1993 negotiators agreed on basic principles for a new democratic constitution. South Africa's partially self-governing black territories, or "homelands," were dissolved and incorporated into a national system of 9 provinces. In elections Apr. 26-29, 1994, the ANC won 62.7% of the vote, making Mandela president. The National Party won 20.4%. The Inkatha Freedom Party won 10.5% and control of the legislature in a mainly Zulu province. By then, fighting between the ANC and Inkatha (aided, during the apartheid era, by South African defense forces) had killed more than 14,000 people in the Zulu region since the mid-1980s.

In 1995, Mandela appointed a truth commission, led by Desmond Tutu, to document human rights abuses under apartheid. A post-apartheid constitution, modified to meet the objections of the Constitutional Court, became law Dec. 10, 1996, with provisions to take effect over a 3-year period.

The ANC won a landslide victory in elections held June 2, 1999. ANC leader Thabo Mbeki, Mandela's deputy president, thus became South Africa's 2nd popularly elected president.

The UN recently estimated that more than 5 million South Africans, including 21.5% of all adults, have HIV/AIDS. South Africa was the site, in July 2000, of an international AIDS conference. Pharmaceutical firms, Apr. 19, 2001, dropped their challenge to a 1997 law that allowed cheaper, generic versions of patented AIDS drugs imported.

Led by Mbeki, the ANC won almost 70% of the vote in national elections Apr. 14, 2004. Reversing previous policy, the govt approved a plan in Nov. 2003 to distribute AIDS drugs free of charge. In a farewell address before parliament, Nelson Mandela, 85, retired from public life, May 10, 2004.

Spain
Kingdom of Spain

People: Population: 40,280,780. **Age distrib.** (%): <15: 14.5; 65+: 17.4. **Pop. density:** 209 per sq mi, 81 per sq km. **Urban:** 76.5%. **Ethnic groups:** Castilian, Catalan, Basque, Galician. **Principal languages:** Castilian Spanish (official), Catalan, Galician, Basque. **Chief religion:** Roman Catholic 94%.

Geography: Total area: 194,897 sq mi, 504,782 sq km; **Land area:** 192,874 sq mi, 499,542 sq km. **Location:** In SW Europe. **Neighbors:** Portugal on W, France on N. **Topography:** The interior is a high, arid plateau broken by mountain ranges and river valleys. The NW is heavily watered, the S has lowlands and a Mediterranean climate. **Capital:** Madrid, 5,103,000. **Cities (urban agg.):** Barcelona, 4,378,000; Valencia, 754,000.

Government: Type: Constitutional monarchy. **Head of state:** King Juan Carlos I de Borbon y Borbon; b Jan. 5, 1938; in office: Nov. 22, 1975. **Head of gov.:** Prime Min. José Luis Rodríguez Zapatero; b Aug. 4, 1960; in office: Apr. 17, 2004. **Local divisions:** 17 autonomous communities and two autonomous cities. **Defense budget** (2003): $8.5 bil. **Active troops:** 150,700.

Economy: Industries: textiles & apparel, food & beverages, metals, chemicals, shipbuilding, autos, machine tools, tourism. **Chief crops:** grain, vegetables, olives, grapes, sugar beets, citrus. **Natural resources:** coal, lignite, iron ore, uranium, mercury, pyrites, fluorspar, gypsum, zinc, lead, tungsten, copper, kaolin, potash, hydropower. **Crude oil reserves** (2003): 157.6 mil. bbls. **Arable land:** 30%. **Livestock** (2003): cattle: 6.48 mil.; chickens: 128.0 mil.; goats: 3.05 mil.; pigs: 23.52 mil.; sheep: 23.81 mil. **Fish catch** (2002): 1,146,395 metric tons. **Electricity prod.** (2002): 229.0 bil. kWh. **Labor force** (2001 est.): services 64%, manufacturing, mining, and construction 29%, agriculture 7%.

Finance: Monetary unit: (EUR) (Sept. 2004: 0.82=1 U.S.) **GDP** (2003 est.): $885.5 bil.; **per capita GDP:** $22,000; **GDP growth:** 2.4%. **Imports** (2003 est.): $197.1 bil.; partners (2002): France 17%, Germany 16.5%, Italy 8.6%, UK 6.4%, Netherlands 4.8%. **Exports** (2003 est.): $159.4 bil.; partners (2002): France 19%, Germany 11.4%, UK 9.6%, Portugal 9.5%, Italy 9.3%, U.S. 4.6%. **Tourism:** $41.7 bil. **Budget** (2003 est.): $109.0 bil. **Intl. reserves less gold:** $13.32 bil. **Gold:** 16.83 mil oz t. **Consumer prices:** 3.0%.

Transport: Railroad: Length: 8,817 mi. **Motor vehicles** (2001): 18.15 mil pass. cars, 4.16 mil comm. vehicles. **Civil aviation:** 21.7 bil. pass.-mi; 93 airports. **Chief ports:** Barcelona, Bilbao, Valencia, Cartagena.

Communications: TV sets: 555 per 1,000 pop. **Radios:** 331 per 1,000 pop. **Telephone lines:** 17.6 mil. **Daily newspaper circ.:** 100.3 per 1,000 pop. **Internet:** 9.8 mil. users.

Health: Life expect.: 76.0 male; 82.9 female. **Births** (per 1,000 pop.): 10.1. **Deaths** (per 1,000 pop.): 9.6. **Natural inc.:** 0.06%. **Infant mortality** (per 1,000 live births): 4.5. **AIDS rate:** 0.7%.

Education: Compulsory: ages 6-16. **Literacy:** 97.9%.

Major Intl. Organizations: UN and all of its specialized agencies, EU, NATO, OECD, OSCE.

Embassy: 2375 Pennsylvania Ave. NW 20037; 452-0100.

Website: www.spainemb.org/ingles/indexing.htm

Initially settled by Iberians, Basques, and Celts, Spain was successively ruled (wholly or in part) by Carthage, Rome, and the Visigoths. Muslims invaded Iberia from North Africa in 711. Reconquest of the peninsula by Christians from the N laid the foundations of modern Spain. In 1469 the kingdoms of Aragon and Castile were united by the marriage of Ferdinand II and Isabella I. Moorish rule ended with the fall of the kingdom of Granada, 1492. Spain's large Jewish community was expelled the same year.

Spain obtained a colonial empire with the "discovery" of America by Columbus, 1492, the conquest of Mexico by Cortes, and Peru by Pizarro. It also controlled the Netherlands and parts of Italy and Germany. Spain lost its American colonies in the early 19th century. It lost Cuba, the Philippines, and Puerto Rico during the Spanish-American War, 1898.

Primo de Rivera became dictator in 1923. King Alfonso XIII revoked the dictatorship, 1930, but was forced to leave the country in 1931. A republic was proclaimed, which disestablished the church, curtailed its privileges, and secularized education. During 1936-39 a Popular Front composed of socialists, Communists, republicans, and anarchists governed Spain.

Army officers under Francisco Franco revolted against the government, 1936. In a destructive 3-year war, in which some one million died, Franco received massive help and troops from Italy and Germany, while the USSR, France, and Mexico supported the republic. The war ended Mar. 28, 1939. Franco was named caudillo, leader of the nation. Spain was officially neutral in World War II, but its cordial relations with fascist countries caused its exclusion from the UN until 1955.

In July 1969, Franco and the Cortes (Parliament) designated Prince Juan Carlos as the future king and chief of state. After Franco's death, Nov. 20, 1975, Juan Carlos was sworn in as king. In free elections June 1977, moderates and democratic socialists emerged as the largest parties.

In 1981 a coup attempt by right-wing military officers was thwarted by the king. The Socialist Workers' Party, under Felipe

González Márquez, won 4 consecutive general elections, from 1982 to 1993, but lost to a coalition of conservative and regional parties in the election of Mar. 3, 1996.

Catalonia and the Basque country were granted autonomy, Jan. 1980, following overwhelming approval in home-rule referendums. Basque extremists, however, have pushed for independence. The militant Basque separatist group ETA proclaimed a cease-fire as of Sept. 18, 1998, but announced an end to the truce Nov. 28, 1999.

The Popular Party of conservative Prime Min. José María Aznar won a majority in the parliamentary election of Mar. 12, 2000. Aznar, going against Spanish public opinion, openly supported the U.S.-led invasion of Iraq, Mar. 2003.

Four commuter trains were bombed in central Madrid, Mar. 11, 2004, killing 191 people. Aznar's govt initially blamed the attacks on the Basque separatist group, ETA, but evidence pointed to Islamic extremists angered by Spain's role in Iraq. The opposition Socialist Workers Party won elections 3 days later, and Socialist leader José Luis Rodríguez Zapatero, who became prime min. Apr. 17, fulfilled a campaign pledge to remove the 1,300 Spanish troops stationed in Iraq. Spanish authorities arrested several suspects in the bombing, mainly from Morocco. In April, 4 other suspects, incl. the leader of the terrorist cell, blew themselves up in their Madrid apt.

The **Balearic Islands** in the W Mediterranean, 1,927 sq. mi., are a province of Spain; they include **Majorca** (Mallorca; capital Palma de Mallorca), **Minorca, Cabrera, Ibiza,** and **Formentera.** The **Canary Islands,** 2,807 sq. mi., in the Atlantic W of Morocco, form 2 provinces, and include the islands of **Tenerife, Palma, Gomera, Hierro, Grand Canary, Fuerteventura,** and **Lanzarote; Las Palmas** and Santa Cruz are thriving ports. **Ceuta** and **Melilla,** small Spanish enclaves on Morocco's Mediterranean coast, gained limited autonomy in Sept. 1994.

Spain has sought the return of Gibraltar, in British hands since 1704.

Sri Lanka
Democratic Socialist Republic of Sri Lanka

People: Population: 19,905,165. **Age distrib.** (%): <15: 25.6; 65+: 6.7. **Pop. density:** 796 per sq mi, 307 per sq km. **Urban:** 21.0%. **Ethnic groups:** Sinhalese 74%, Tamil 18%, Moor 7%. **Principal languages:** Sinhala, Tamil (both official); English. **Chief religions:** Buddhist 70%, Hindu 15%, Christian 8%, Muslim 7%.

Geography: Total area: 25,332 sq mi, 65,610 sq km; **Land area:** 24,996 sq mi, 64,740 sq km. **Location:** In Indian O. off SE coast of India. **Neighbors:** India on NW. **Topography:** The coastal area and the northern half are flat; the S-central area is hilly and mountainous. **Capital:** Colombo, 648,000; Kotte (seat of Parliament), 117,000.

Government: Type: Republic. **Head of state:** Pres. Chandrika Bandaranaike Kumaratunga; b June 29, 1945; in office: Nov. 12, 1994. **Head of gov.:** Prime Min. Mahinda Rajapakse; b Nov. 18, 1945; in office: Apr. 6, 2004. **Local divisions:** 9 provinces with 25 districts. **Defense budget** (2003): $366 mil. **Active troops:** 152,300.

Economy: Industries: rubber proc., tea & coconut prod., clothing, cement, oil refining, textiles, tobacco. **Chief crops:** rice, sugarcane, grains, oilseed, spices, tea, rubber. **Natural resources:** limestone, graphite, mineral sands, gems, phosphates, clay, hydropower. **Arable land:** 14%. **Livestock** (2003): cattle: 1.14 mil.; chickens: 9.78 mil.; goats: 490,000; pigs: 67,000 sheep: 11,800. **Fish catch** (2002): 306,572 metric tons. **Electricity prod.** (2002): 6.7 bil. kWh. **Labor force** (1998 est.): services 45%, agriculture 38%, industry 17%.

Finance: Monetary unit: Rupee (LKR) (Sept. 2004: 103.51=1 U.S.). **GDP** (2003 est.): $73.5 bil.; **per capita GDP:** $3,700; **GDP growth:** 5.2%. **Imports** (2003 est.): $6.6 bil.; partners (2002): India 13.8%, Hong Kong 8.1%, Singapore 7.2%, Japan 5.9%, South Korea 5%, Taiwan 4.8%, UAE 4.5%, UK 4.3%, China 4.3%. **Exports** (2003 est.): $5.3 bil.; partners (2002): U.S. 37.7%, UK 12.6%, Germany 4.3%. **Tourism:** $340 mil. **Budget** (2001 est.): $4.1 bil. **Intl. reserves less gold** (2002): $1.2 bil. **Gold** (2002): 60,000 oz t. **Consumer prices:** 6.3%.

Transport: Railroad: Length: 937 mi. **Motor vehicles** (2000): 335,000 pass. cars, 236,900 comm. vehicles. **Civil aviation:** 4.3 bil. pass.-mi; 14 airports. **Chief ports:** Colombo, Trincomalee, Galle.

Communications: TV sets: 102 per 1,000 pop. **Radios:** 211 per 1,000 pop. **Telephone lines** (2002): 881,400. **Daily newspaper circ.:** 29 per 1,000 pop. **Internet** (2002): 200,000 users.

Health: Life expect.: 70.3 male; 75.6 female. **Births** (per 1,000 pop.): 15.9. **Deaths** (per 1,000 pop.): 6.5. **Natural inc.:** 0.94%. **Infant mortality** (per 1,000 live births): 14.8. **AIDS rate:** <0.1%.

Education: Compulsory: ages 5-13. **Literacy:** 92.3%.

Major Intl. Organizations: UN (FAO, IBRD, ILO, IMF, IMO, WHO, WTrO), the Commonwealth.

Embassy: 2148 Wyoming Ave. NW 20008; 483-4025.

Websites: www.priu.gov.lk; www.slembassyusa.org

The island was known to the ancient world as Taprobane (Greek for copper-colored) and later as Serendip (from Arabic). Colonists from N India subdued the indigenous Veddahs about 543 BC; their descendants, the Buddhist Sinhalese, still form most of the population. Hindu descendants of Tamil immigrants from S India account for about one-fifth of the population.

Parts were occupied by the Portuguese in 1505 and the Dutch in 1658. The British seized the island in 1796. As Ceylon it became an independent member of the Commonwealth in 1948, and the Republic of Sri Lanka May 22, 1972.

Prime Min. W. R. D. Bandaranaike was assassinated Sept. 25, 1959. In new elections, the Freedom Party was victorious under Mrs. Sirimavo Bandaranaike, widow of the former prime minister. After May 1970 elections, Mrs. Bandaranaike became prime minister again. In 1971 the nation suffered economic problems and terrorist activities by ultra-leftists, thousands of whom were executed. Massive land reform and nationalization of foreign-owned plantations were undertaken in the mid-1970s. Mrs. Bandaranaike was ousted in 1977 elections. Presidential powers were increased in 1978 in an effort to restore stability.

Tensions between Sinhalese and Tamil separatists erupted into violence in the early 1980s. More than 64,000 died in the civil war, which continued through the late 1990s; another 20,000, mostly young Tamils, "disappeared" after they were taken into custody by government security forces.

Pres. Ranasinghe Premadasa was assassinated May 1, 1993, by a Tamil rebel. Mrs. Bandaranaike's daughter, Chandrika Bandaranaike Kumaratunga, became prime minister after the Aug. 16, 1994, general elections. Elected president Nov. 9, Kumaratunga appointed her mother prime minister. Kumaratunga, who was injured in a suicide bomb attack at a campaign rally Dec. 18, 1999, won a 2nd 6-year term 3 days later. In failing health, Mrs. Bandaranaike resigned Aug. 10 and died Oct. 10, 2000.

Facing a possible no-confidence motion, Pres. Kumaratunga suspended parliament July 10, 2001. Elections Dec. 5 resulted in a victory for the United National Party, headed by Ranil Wickremesinghe. A truce accord intended to bring an end to the 18-year-long civil war was signed Feb. 22, 2002. Severe monsoon flooding in the S and SW, May 2003, killed at least 265 people. A dispute with Wickremesinghe over how to negotiate with rebel Tamils led Kumaratunga again to suspend parliament, Nov. 4, 2003. Her United People's Freedom Alliance won a plurality in legislative elections Apr. 2, 2004, and formed a coalition govt. Rebel infighting and a suicide bombing in July in Colombo threatened peace initiatives.

Sudan
Republic of the Sudan

People: Population: 39,148,162. **Age distrib.** (%): <15: 44.2; 65+: 2.2. **Pop. density:** 43 per sq mi, 16 per sq km. **Urban:** 38.9%. **Ethnic groups:** Black 52%, Arab 39%, Beja 6%. **Principal languages:** Arabic (official), Nubian, Ta Bedawie; Nilotic, Sudanic dialects; English. **Chief religions:** Sunni Muslim 70%, indigenous beliefs 25%, Christian 5%.

Geography: Total area: 967,498 sq mi, 2,505,810 sq km; **Land area:** 917,378 sq mi, 2,376,000 sq km. **Location:** At the E end of Sahara desert zone. **Neighbors:** Egypt on N; Libya, Chad, Central African Republic on W; Congo (formerly Zaire), Uganda, Kenya on S; Ethiopia, Eritrea on E. **Topography:** The N consists of the Libyan Desert in the W, and the mountainous Nubia Desert in E, with narrow Nile valley between. The center contains large, fertile, rainy areas with fields, pasture, and forest. The S has rich soil, heavy rain. **Capital:** Khartoum, 4,286,000. **Cities (urban agr.):** Omdurman (1993), 1,271,403.

Government: Type: Republic with strong military influence. **Head of state and gov.:** Pres. Gen. Omar Hassan Ahmad Al-Bashir; b Jan. 1, 1944; in office: June 30, 1989. **Local divisions:** 26 states. **Defense budget** (2003): $480 mil. **Active troops:** 104,500.

Economy: Industries: oil, cotton ginning, textiles, cement, edible oils, sugar. **Chief crops:** cotton, peanuts, sorghum, millet, wheat, gum arabic, sugarcane. **Natural resources:** oil, iron ore, copper, chromium ore, zinc, tungsten, mica, silver, gold, hydropower. **Crude oil reserves** (2003): 563.0 mil. bbls. **Arable land:** 5%. **Livestock** (2003): cattle: 38.33 mil.; chickens: 38.5 mil.; goats: 40.0 mil.; sheep: 47.0 mil. **Fish catch** (2002): 59,600 metric tons. **Electricity prod.** (2002): 2.58 bil. kWh. **Labor force** (1998 est.): agriculture 80%, industry and commerce 7%, government 13%.

Finance: Monetary unit: Dinar (SDD) (Sept. 2004: 259.54=1 U.S.). **GDP** (2003 est.): $70.8 bil.; **per capita GDP:** $1,900; **GDP growth:** 6.1%. **Imports** (2003 est.): $2.4 bil.; partners (2002): China 20.1%, Saudi Arabia 7.5%, India 5.6%, UK 5.4%, Germany 5.4%, Indonesia 4.7%, Australia 4%. **Exports** (2003 est.): $2.5 bil.; partners (2002): China 53.3%, Japan 13.4%, South Africa 4.9%, Saudi Arabia 4.7%. **Tourism** (2002): $62 mil. **Budget** (2001 est.): $1.6 bil. **Intl. reserves less gold:** $570 mil. **Consumer prices** (change in 2001): 5.8%.

Transport: Railroad: Length: 3,715 mi. **Motor vehicles** (1999): 40,600 pass. cars, 53,900 comm. vehicles. **Civil aviation:** 397.1 mil. pass.-mi 12 airports. **Chief port:** Port Sudan.

Communications: TV sets: 173 per 1,000 pop. **Radios:** 480 per 1,000 pop. **Telephone lines:** 900,000. **Daily newspaper circ.:** 27 per 1,000 pop. **Internet:** 300,000 users.

Health: Life expect.: 57.0 male; 59.4 female. **Births** (per 1,000 pop.): 35.8. **Deaths** (per 1,000 pop.): 9.4. **Natural inc.:** 2.64%. **Infant mortality** (per 1,000 live births): 64.1. **AIDS rate:** 2.3%.

Education: Compulsory: ages 6-13. **Literacy:** 61.1%.

Major Intl. Organizations: UN (FAO, IBRD, ILO, IMF, IMO, WHO), AL, AU.

Embassy: 2210 Massachusetts Ave. NW 20008; 338-8565.
Website: www.sudanembassy.org

Northern Sudan, ancient Nubia, was settled by Egyptians in antiquity. The population was converted to Coptic Christianity in the 6th century. Arab conquests brought Islam to the area in the 15th century.

In the 1820s Egypt took over Sudan, defeating the last of earlier empires, including the Fung. In the 1880s a revolution was led by Muhammad Ahmad, who called himself the Mahdi (leader of the faithful), and his followers, the dervishes.

In 1898 an Anglo-Egyptian force crushed the Mahdi's successors. In 1951 the Egyptian Parliament abrogated its 1899 and 1936 treaties with Great Britain and amended its constitution to provide for a separate Sudanese constitution. Sudan voted for complete independence effective Jan. 1, 1956.

In 1969, a Revolutionary Council took power, but a civilian premier and cabinet were appointed; the government announced it would create a socialist state

Economic problems plagued the nation in the 1980s and 1990s, aggravated by civil war and influxes of refugees from neighboring countries. After 16 years in power, Pres. Jaafar al-Nimeiry was overthrown in a bloodless coup, Apr. 6, 1985. Sudan held its first democratic parliamentary elections in 18 years in 1986, but the elected government was overthrown in a bloodless coup June 30, 1989.

In the mid-1980s, rebels in the south (populated largely by black Christians and followers of tribal religions) took up arms against government domination by northern Sudan, mostly Arab-Muslim. War and related famine cost an estimated 2 million lives and displaced millions of southerners. In 1993, Amnesty International accused the Sudanese government of "ethnic cleansing."

A new constitution based on Islamic law took effect June 30, 1998. On Aug. 20, in retaliation for bombings in Kenya and Tanzania, U.S. missiles destroyed a Khartoum pharmaceutical plant the U.S. alleged was associated with terrorist activities; independent inquiries later cast some doubt on the U.S. claim.

During 2002-04, as the conflict subsided in the south, a new crisis developed in the Darfur region of W Sudan, where marauding Arab militias, known as the *janjaweed*, attacked black African villagers, looting and burning homes and killing inhabitants, reportedly in collusion with Sudanese government troops. The UN Security Council passed resolutions calling on Sudan to disarm the militias. The African Union sponsored peace talks Aug. 23, which failed to solve the crisis, and was set to send about 2,000 AU peacekeeping troops. The U.S. govt declared the conflict genocide and was seeking more int'l. pressure. By Aug. 2004, an estimated 50,000 civilians had been killed and more than 1 million had fled their homes.

Suriname
Republic of Suriname

People: Population: 436,935. **Age distrib.** (%): <15: 31.1; 65+: 5.8. **Pop. density:** 7 per sq mi, 3 per sq km. **Urban:** 76.1%. **Ethnic groups:** East Indians 37%, Creole 31%, Javanese 15%, Maroons 10%, Amerindian 2%, Chinese 2%, White 1%. **Principal languages:** Dutch (official), English, Sranang Tongo (an English Creole), Hindustani, Javanese. **Chief religions:** Hindu 27%, Protestant 25%, Roman Catholic 23%, Muslim 20%.

Geography: Total area: 63,039 sq mi, 163,270 sq km; **Land area:** 62,344 sq mi, 161,470 sq km. **Location:** On N shore of South America. **Neighbors:** Guyana on W, Brazil on S, French Guiana on E. **Topography:** A flat Atlantic coast, where dikes permit agriculture. Inland is a forest belt; to the S, largely unexplored hills cover 75% of the country. **Capital:** Paramaribo, 253,000.

Government: Type: Republic. **Head of state and gov.:** Pres. Runaldo Ronald Venetiaan; b June 18, 1936; in office: Aug. 12, 2000. **Local divisions:** 10 districts. **Defense budget:** NA. **Active troops:** 1,840.

Economy: Industries: mining, oil, lumber, food proc., fishing. **Chief crops:** rice, bananas, palm kernels, coconuts, plantains, peanuts. **Natural resources:** timber, hydropower, fish, kaolin, shrimp, bauxite, gold, nickel, copper, platinum, iron ore. **Crude oil reserves** (2003): 170.0 mil. bbls. **Livestock** (2003): cattle: 137,000; chickens: 3.8 mil.; goats: 7,100; pigs: 24,500; sheep: 7,700. **Fish catch** (2002 est): 19,122 metric tons. **Electricity prod.** (2002): 1.98 bil. kWh.

Finance: Monetary unit: Guilder (SRG) (Sept. 2004: 2.73=1 U.S.). **GDP** (2003 est.): $1.5 bil.; **per capita GDP:** $3,500; **GDP growth:** 1.5%. **Imports** (2002): $604.0 mil.; partners (2002): U.S. 22.7%, Netherlands 16.1%, China 12.3%, Trinidad and Tobago 11.4%, France 7.6%, Japan 6%, Netherlands Antilles 4.5%. **Exports** (2002): $495.0 mil.; partners (2002): U.S. 25.7%, Norway 20.4%, France 8.3%, Trinidad and Tobago 6.5%, Canada 6.1%, Iceland 6.1%, Netherlands 5.7%. **Tourism** (2002): $3 mil. **Budget** (1997 est.): $403.0 mil. **Intl. reserves less gold:** $71 mil. **Gold:** 20,000 mil. oz t. **Consumer prices:** 23.0%.

Transport: Railroad: Length: 103 mi. **Motor vehicles** (2000): 61,400 pass. cars, 23,500 comm. vehicles. **Civil aviation:** 714.0 mil. pass.-mi; 5 airports. **Chief ports:** Paramaribo, New Nickerie, Albina.

Communications: TV sets: 241 per 1,000 pop. **Radios:** 728 per 1,000 pop. **Telephone lines:** 79,800. **Daily newspaper circ.:** 67.7 per 1,000 pop. **Internet** (2002): 20,000 users.

Health: Life expect.: 66.8 male; 71.6 female. **Births** (per 1,000 pop.): 18.9. **Deaths** (per 1,000 pop.): 7.0. **Natural inc.:** 1.19%. **Infant mortality** (per 1,000 live births): 24.2. **AIDS rate:** 1.7%.
Education: Compulsory: ages 7-12. **Literacy** (2002): 93%.
Major Intl. Organizations: UN (FAO, IBRD, ILO, IMF, IMO, WHO, WTrO), Caricom, OAS.
Embassy: 4301 Connecticut Ave., Suite 460, NW 20008; 244-7488.
Website: www.surinameembassy.org

The Netherlands acquired Suriname in 1667 from Britain, in exchange for New Netherlands (New York). The 1954 Dutch constitution raised the colony to a level of equality with the Netherlands and the Netherlands Antilles. Independence was granted Nov. 25, 1975, despite objections from East Indians. Some 40% of the population (mostly East Indians) immigrated to the Netherlands in the months before independence.

The National Military Council took control of the government, Feb. 1982. Civilian rule was restored in 1987, but political turmoil continued until 1992, disrupting the nation's economy.

Swaziland
Kingdom of Swaziland

People: Population: 1,169,241. **Age distrib.** (%): <15: 45.5; 65+: 2.6. **Pop. density:** 176 per sq mi, 68 per sq km. **Urban:** 23.5%. **Ethnic groups:** African 97%, European 3% **Principal languages:** English, siSwati (both official). **Chief religions:** Christian 60%, Muslim 10%, indigenous and other 30%.

Geography: Total area: 6,704 sq mi, 17,363 sq km; **Land area:** 6,642 sq mi, 17,203 sq km. **Location:** In southern Africa, near Indian O. coast. **Neighbors:** South Africa on N, W, S; Mozambique on E. **Topography:** The country descends from W-E in broad belts, becoming more arid in the low veld region, then rising to a plateau in the E. **Capitals:** Mbabane (administrative), 70,000; Lobamba (legislative).

Government: Type: Constitutional monarchy. **Head of state:** King Mswati III; b Apr. 19, 1968; in office: Apr. 25, 1986. **Head of gov.:** Prime Min. Absalom Themba Dlamini; in office: Nov. 26, 2003. **Local divisions:** 4 districts.

Economy: Industries: coal mining, pulp, sugar, soft drinks, textiles, apparel. **Chief crops:** sugarcane, cotton, corn, tobacco, rice, citrus. **Natural resources:** asbestos, coal, clay, cassiterite, hydropower, timber, gold, diamonds, quarry stone, talc. **Arable land:** 11%. **Livestock** (2003): cattle: 580,000; chickens: 3.2 mil.; goats: 422,000; pigs: 30,000; sheep: 27,000. **Fish catch** (2002 est): 70 metric tons. **Electricity prod.** (2002): 0.4 bil. kWh. **Labor force:** private sector: 70%, public sector: 30%.

Finance: Monetary unit: Lilangeni (SZL) (Sept. 2004: 6.58=1 U.S.). **GDP** (2003 est.): $5.7 bil.; **per capita GDP:** $4,900; **GDP growth:** 2.2%. **Imports** (2003 est.): $1.1 bil.; partners (1999): South Africa 88.8%, EU 5.6%, Japan 0.6%, Singapore 0.4%. **Exports** (2003 est.): $905.6 mil.; partners (1999): South Africa 72%, EU 14.2%, Mozambique 3.7%, U.S. 3.5%. **Tourism** (2002): $26 mil. **Budget** (FY01/02): $506.9 mil. **Intl. reserves less gold:** $187 mil. **Consumer prices:** 7.3%.

Transport: Railroad: Length: 187 mi. **Motor vehicles** (1999): 108,700 pass. cars, 49,500 comm. vehicles. **Civil aviation:** 42.3 mil. pass.-mi; 1 airport.

Communications: TV sets: 112 per 1,000 pop. **Radios:** 168 per 1,000 pop. **Telephone lines:** 46,200. **Daily newspaper circ.:** 17 per 1,000 pop. **Internet:** 27,000 users.

Health: Life expect.: 39.1 male; 35.9 female. **Births** (per 1,000 pop.): 28.6. **Deaths** (per 1,000 pop.): 23.1. **Natural inc.:** 0.55%. **Infant mortality** (per 1,000 live births): 68.4. **AIDS rate:** 38.8%.
Education: Compulsory: ages 6-12. **Literacy:** 81.6%.
Major Intl. Organizations: UN (FAO, IBRD, ILO, IMF, WHO, WTrO), the Commonwealth, AU.
Embassy: 3400 International Dr. NW 20008; 362-6683.
Website: www.gov.sz

The royal house of Swaziland traces back 400 years, and is one of Africa's last ruling dynasties. The Swazis, a Bantu people, were driven to Swaziland from lands to the N by the Zulus in 1820. Their autonomy was later guaranteed by Britain and Transvaal (later part of South Africa), with Britain assuming control after 1903. Independence came Sept. 6, 1968. In 1973 the king repealed the constitution and assumed full powers.

A new constitution banning political parties took effect Oct. 13, 1978. A shrinking economy and the AIDS crisis have fueled student and labor unrest in recent years. The UN has estimated that nearly 40% of the adult population has HIV/AIDS.

Sweden
Kingdom of Sweden

People: Population: 8,986,400. **Age distrib.** (%): <15: 18; 65+: 17.3. **Pop. density:** 57 per sq mi, 22 per sq km. **Urban:** 83.4%. **Ethnic groups:** Swedish 89%, Finnish 2%; Sami and others 9%. **Principal languages:** Swedish (official), Sami, Finnish. **Chief religion:** Lutheran 87%.

Geography: Total area: 173,732 sq mi, 449,964 sq km; **Land area:** 158,662 sq mi, 410,934 sq km. **Location:** On Scandinavian Peninsula in N Europe. **Neighbors:** Norway on W, Denmark on S (across Kattegat), Finland on E. **Topography:** Mountains along NW

border cover 25% of Sweden, flat or rolling terrain covers the central and southern areas, which include several large lakes. **Capital:** Stockholm,1,697,000. **Cities (urban aggr.):** Göteborg, 792,000.

Government: Type: Constitutional monarchy. **Head of state:** King Carl XVI Gustaf; b Apr. 30, 1946; in office: Sept. 19, 1973. **Head of gov.:** Prime Min. Goran Persson; b June 20, 1949; in office: Mar. 21, 1996. **Local divisions:** 21 counties. **Defense budget** (2003): $5.2 bil. **Active troops:** 27,600.

Economy: Industries: iron & steel, precision equip., wood & paper products, proc. foods, autos. **Chief crops:** barley, wheat, sugar beets. **Natural resources:** zinc, iron ore, lead, copper, silver, timber, uranium, hydropower. **Arable land:** 7%. **Livestock** (2003): cattle: 1.61 mil.; chickens: 5.75 mil.; pigs: 1.90 mil.; sheep: 451,000. **Fish catch** (2002): 300,581 metric tons. **Electricity prod.** (2002): 142.77 bil. kWh. **Labor force** (2000 est.): agriculture 2%, industry 24%, services 74%.

Finance: Monetary unit: Krona (SEK) (Sept. 2004: 7.52=1 U.S.). **GDP** (2003 est.): $238.1 bil.; **per capita GDP:** $26,800; **GDP growth:** 1.6%. **Imports** (2003 est.): $83.3 bil.; partners (2002): Germany 18.5%, Denmark 8.8%, UK 8.6%, Norway 8.2%, Netherlands 6.7%, France 5.4%, Finland 5.2%, U.S. 5%. **Exports** (2003 est.): $102.8 bil.; partners (2002): U.S. 11.6%, Germany 10.1%, Norway 9%, UK 8.2%, Denmark 5.9%, Finland 5.5%, Netherlands 5.3%, France 5.1%, Belgium 4.7%. **Tourism:** $5.3 bil. **Budget** (2001 est.): $110.0 bil. **Intl. reserves less gold:** $13.25 bil. **Gold:** 5.96 mil oz t. **Consumer prices:** 1.9%.

Transport: Railroad: Length: 7,134 mi. **Motor vehicles** (2001): 4.02 mil pass. cars, 409,900 comm. vehicles. **Civil aviation:** 4.8 bil. pass.-mi; 145 airports. **Chief ports:** Göteborg, Stockholm, Malmö.

Communications: TV sets: 551 per 1,000 pop. **Radios:** 932 per 1,000 pop. **Telephone lines** (2002): 6.6 mil. **Daily newspaper circ.:** 410.2 per 1,000 pop. **Internet** (2002): 5.1 mil. users.

Health: Life expect.: 78.1 male; 82.6 female. **Births** (per 1,000 pop.): 10.5. **Deaths** (per 1,000 pop.): 10.4. **Natural inc.:** 0.01%. **Infant mortality** (per 1,000 live births): 2.8. **AIDS rate:** 0.1%.

Education: Compulsory: ages 7-16. **Literacy (2002):** 100%.

Major Intl. Organizations: UN and all of its specialized agencies, EU, OECD, OSCE.

Embassy: 1501 M St. NW 20005; 467-2600.

Websites: www.swedish-embassy.org; www.sweden.se

The Swedes have lived in present-day Sweden for at least 5,000 years, longer than nearly any other European people. Gothic tribes from Sweden played a major role in the disintegration of the Roman Empire. Other Swedes helped create the first Russian state in the 9th century.

The Swedes were Christianized from the 11th century, and a strong centralized monarchy developed. A parliament, the Riksdag, was first called in 1435, the earliest parliament on the European continent, with all classes of society represented.

Swedish independence from rule by Danish kings (dating from 1397) was secured by Gustavus I in a revolt, 1521-23; he built up the government and military and established the Lutheran Church. In the 17th century Sweden was a major European power, gaining most of the Baltic seacoast, but its international position subsequently declined.

The Napoleonic wars, 1799-1815, in which Sweden acquired Norway (it became independent 1905), were the last in which Sweden participated. Armed neutrality was maintained in both world wars.

More than 4 decades of Social Democratic rule ended in the 1976 parliamentary elections; the party returned to power in the 1982 elections. After Prime Min. Olof Palme was shot to death in Stockholm, Feb. 28, 1986, Ingvar Carlsson took office. Carl Bildt, a non-Socialist, became prime minister Oct. 1991, with a mandate to restore Sweden's economic competitiveness. The Social Democrats returned to power following 1994 elections.

Swedish voters approved membership in the European Union Nov. 13, 1994, and Sweden entered the EU as of Jan. 1, 1995. Carlsson retired and was succeeded by Goran Persson in Mar. 1996. Persson and his Social Democrats led coalition governments after the elections of Sept. 20, 1998, and Sept. 15, 2002. Foreign Min. Anna Lindh died Sept. 11, 2003, after being stabbed in a Stockholm department store. Her killer, Mijailo Mijailovic, was sentenced to life in prison Mar. 2004; an appeals court later deemed him mentally ill and sent him to a psychiatric ward.

Swedish voters Sept. 14, 2003, rejected adoption of the euro currency.

Switzerland
Swiss Confederation

People: Population: 7,450,867. **Age distrib.** (%): <15: 16.8; 65+: 15.5. **Pop. density:** 485 per sq mi, 187 per sq km. **Urban:** 67.5%. **Ethnic groups:** German 65%, French 18%, Italian 10%, Romansch 1%. **Principal languages:** German, French, Italian (all official); Romansch (semi-official). **Chief religions:** Roman Catholic 46%, Protestant 40%.

Geography: Total area: 15,942 sq mi, 41,290 sq km; **Land area:** 15,355 sq mi, 39,770 sq km. **Location:** In the Alps Mts. in central Europe. **Neighbors:** France on W, Italy on S, Austria on E, Germany on N. **Topography:** The Alps cover 60% of the land area; the Jura, near France, 10%. Running between, from NE to SW,

are midlands, 30%. **Capitals:** Bern (administrative), 320,000; Lausanne (judicial). **Cities (urban aggr.):** Zurich, 939,000; Basel, 166,700; Geneva, 398,910.

Government: Type: Federal republic. **Head of state and gov.:** The president is elected by the Federal Assembly to a nonrenewable 1-year term. **Local divisions:** 20 full cantons, 6 half cantons. **Defense budget** (2003): $3.5 bil. **Active troops:** 3,300.

Economy: Industries: machinery, chemicals, watches, textiles, precision instruments. **Chief crops:** grains, fruits, vegetables. **Natural resources:** hydropower, timber, salt. **Arable land:** 10%. **Livestock** (2003): cattle: 1.56 mil.; chickens: 7.44 mil.; goats: 67,600; pigs: 1.52 mil.; sheep: 441,000. **Fish catch** (2002): 2,679 metric tons. **Electricity prod.** (2002): 63.47 bil. kWh. **Labor force** (1998): services 69.1%, industry 26.3%, agriculture 4.6%.

Finance: Monetary unit: Franc (CHF) (Sept. 2004: 1.27=1 U.S.). **GDP** (2003 est.): $239.8 bil.; **per capita GDP:** $32,800; **GDP growth:** –0.3%. **Imports** (2003 est.): $102.2 bil.; partners (2002): Germany 31.4%, Italy 10.3%, France 10%, U.S. 6.6%, Netherlands 5.1%, UK 4.9%, Austria 4.1%. **Exports** (2003 est.): $110.0 bil.; partners (2002): Germany 20.4%, U.S. 11.9%, France 9.1%, Italy 8.2%, UK 5.1%. **Tourism** (2002): $7.6 bil. **Budget** (2001 est.): $30.0 bil. **Intl. reserves less gold:** $32.07 bil. **Gold:** 52.51 mil oz t. **Consumer prices:** 0.6%.

Transport: Railroad: Length: 2,803 mi. **Motor vehicles** (2000): 3.55 mil pass. cars, 318,800 comm. vehicles. **Civil aviation:** 22.6 bil. pass.-mi; 41 airports. **Chief port:** Basel.

Communications: TV sets: 457 per 1,000 pop. **Radios:** 979 per 1,000 pop. **Telephone lines** (2002): 5.4 mil. **Daily newspaper circ.:** 373.2 per 1,000 pop. **Internet** (2002): 2.6 mil. users.

Health: Life expect.: 77.5 male; 83.3 female. **Births** (per 1,000 pop.): 9.8. **Deaths** (per 1,000 pop.): 8.4. **Natural inc.:** 0.14%. **Infant mortality** (per 1,000 live births): 4.4. **AIDS rate:** 0.4%.

Education: Compulsory: ages 7-15. **Literacy** (1994): 100%.

Major Intl. Organizations: UN and most of its specialized agencies, EFTA, OECD, OSCE.

Embassy: 2900 Cathedral Ave. NW 20008; 745-7900.

Websites: www.swissemb.org; usa.myswitzerland.com

Switzerland, the former Roman province of Helvetia, traces its modern history to 1291, when 3 cantons created a defensive league. Other cantons were subsequently admitted to the Swiss Confederation, which obtained its independence from the Holy Roman Empire through the Peace of Westphalia (1648). The cantons were joined under a federal constitution in 1848, with large powers of local control retained by each.

Switzerland has maintained an armed neutrality since 1815, and has not been involved in a foreign war since 1515. It is the seat of many UN and other international agencies but did not become a full member of the UN until Sept. 10, 2002.

Switzerland is a world banking center. Stung by charges that assets seized by the Nazis and deposited in Swiss banks in World War II had not been properly returned, the government announced, March 5, 1997, a $4.7 billion fund to compensate victims of the Holocaust and other catastrophies. Swiss banks agreed Aug. 12, 1998, to pay $1.25 billion in reparations. Abortion was decriminalized by a June 2, 2002 referendum. The rightist Swiss People's Party topped Oct. 2003 parlimentary voting and entered a coalition government.

Syria
Syrian Arab Republic

People: Population: 18,016,874. **Age distrib.** (%): <15: 39.3; 65+: 3.2. **Pop. density:** 254 per sq mi, 98 per sq km. **Urban:** 50.1%. **Ethnic groups:** Arab 90%, Kurds, Armenians, and other 10%. **Principal languages:** Arabic (official); Kurdish, Armenian. **Chief religions:** Sunni Muslim 74%, other Muslims 16%, Christian 10%.

Geography: Total area: 71,498 sq mi, 185,180 sq km; **Land area:** 71,062 sq mi, 184,050 sq km. **Location:** Middle East, at E end of Mediterranean Sea. **Neighbors:** Lebanon and Israel on W, Jordan on S, Iraq on E, Turkey on N. **Topography:** Syria has a short Mediterranean coastline, then stretches E and S with fertile lowlands and plains, alternating with mountains and large desert areas. **Capital:** Damascus, 2,228,000. **Cities (urban aggr.):** Aleppo, 2,188,000; Homs, 797,000.

Government: Type: Republic (under military regime). **Head of state:** Pres. Bashar al-Assad; b Sept. 11, 1965; in office: July 17, 2000. **Head of gov.:** Prime Min. Muhammad Naji al-Otari; b 1944; in office: Sept. 10, 2003. **Local divisions:** 14 provinces. **Defense budget** (2003): $1.4 bil. **Active troops:** 319,000.

Economy: Industries: oil, textiles, food proc., beverages, tobacco, phosphate mining. **Chief crops:** wheat, barley, cotton, lentils, chickpeas, olives, sugar beets. **Natural resources:** oil, phosphates, chrome, mang., asphalt, iron ore, salt, marble, gypsum, hydropower. **Crude oil reserves** (2003): 2.5 bil. bbls. **Arable land:** 28%. **Livestock** (2003): cattle: 880,000; chickens: 30.0 mil.; goats: 1.0 mil.; sheep: 13.5 mil. **Fish catch** (2002): 15,166 metric tons. **Electricity prod.** (2002): 26.15 bil. kWh. **Labor force:** agriculture 40%, industry 20%, services 40%.

Finance: Monetary unit: Pound (SYP) (Sept. 2004: 51.60=1 U.S.). **GDP** (2003 est.): $58.0 bil.; **per capita GDP:** $3,300; **GDP growth:** 0.9%. **Imports** (2003 est.): $4.8 bil.; partners (2002): Italy 8.1%, Germany 7.4%, China 5.6%, South Korea 4.6%, France 4.4%, U.S. 4.3%, Turkey 4%. **Exports** (2003 est.): $5.1 bil.; part-

ners (2002): Germany 17.5%, Italy 15.9%, Turkey 7.1%, France 6.8%, UAE 6.6%, Lebanon 4.8%. **Tourism:** $1.4 bil. **Budget** (2004 est.): $8.6 bil. **Gold:** 830,000 oz t. **Consumer prices** (change in 2002): 1.0%.

Transport: Railroad: Length: 1,704 mi. **Motor vehicles** (2000): 181,700 pass. cars, 345,600 comm. vehicles. **Civil aviation:** 858.1 mil. pass.-mi; 24 airports. **Chief ports:** Latakia, Tartus.

Communications: TV sets: 68 per 1,000 pop. **Radios:** 278 per 1,000 pop. **Telephone lines** (2002): 2.1 mil. **Daily newspaper circ.:** 20 per 1,000 pop. **Internet** (2002): 220,000 users.

Health: Life expect.: 68.5 male; 71.0 female. **Births** (per 1,000 pop.): 28.9. **Deaths** (per 1,000 pop.): 5.0. **Natural inc.:** 2.40%. **Infant mortality** (per 1,000 live births): 30.6. **AIDS rate:** <0.1%.

Education: Compulsory: ages 6-11. **Literacy:** 76.9%.

Major Intl. Organizations: UN (FAO, IBRD, ILO, IMF, IMO, WHO), AL.

Embassy: 2215 Wyoming Ave. NW 20008; 232-6313.

Website: www.moi-syria.com/e_index.html

Syria was the center of the Seleucid empire, but later became absorbed in the Roman and Arab empires. Ottoman rule prevailed for 4 centuries, until the end of World War I.

The state of Syria was formed from former Turkish districts, separated by the Treaty of Sevres, 1920, and divided into the states of Syria and Greater Lebanon. Both were administered under a French League of Nations mandate 1920-1941.

Syria was proclaimed a republic by the occupying French Sept. 16, 1941, and exercised full independence Apr. 17, 1946. Syria joined the Arab invasion of Israel in 1948.

Syria joined Egypt Feb. 1958 in the United Arab Republic but seceded Sept. 1961. The Socialist Baath party and military leaders seized power Mar. 1963. The Baath, a pan-Arab organization, became the only legal party. The government has been dominated by the Alawite minority.

In the Arab-Israeli war of June 1967, Israel seized and occupied the Golan Heights, from which Syria had shelled Israeli settlements. On Oct. 6, 1973, Syria joined Egypt in an attack on Israel. Syrian troops entered Lebanon in 1976, during the Lebanese civil war and remained a strong presence in the country. They fought Palestinian guerrillas and, later, Christian militiamen. Syria sided with Iran during the Iran-Iraq war, 1980-88.

Following Israel's invasion of Lebanon, June 6, 1982, Israeli planes destroyed 17 Syrian antiaircraft missile batteries in the Bekaa Valley, June 9. Some 25 Syrian planes were downed during the engagement. Israel and Syria agreed to a cease-fire June 11. Syria's role in promoting international terrorism led to strained relations with the U.S. and Great Britain.

Syria condemned the Aug. 1990 Iraqi invasion of Kuwait and sent troops to help Allied forces in the Gulf War. In 1991, Syria accepted U.S. proposals for the terms of an Arab-Israeli peace conference. Syria subsequently participated in negotiations with Israel, but progress toward peace was slow.

Former Prime Min. Mahmoud Al-Zoubi killed himself May 21, 2000, after being charged with corruption. Hafez al-Assad, president of Syria since 1971, died June 10, 2000, and was succeeded by his son Bashar al-Assad.

Following the invasion of Iraq, Mar. 2003, the U.S. pressured Syria to rein in extremist groups and deny safe haven to fugitive Iraqi leaders. Israeli planes attacked an alleged terrorist camp near Damascus Oct. 4, 2003. Stating that the gov't. continued to support terrorists and was allowing militants to enter Iraq from its territory, the U.S. imposed limited sanctions on Syria, May 11, 2004. About 20,000 Syrian troops remain in Lebanon.

Taiwan
Republic of China

People: Population: 22,749,838. **Age distrib.** (%): <15: 21; 65+: 9. **Pop. density:** 1,826 per sq mi, 705 per sq km. **Ethnic groups:** Taiwanese 84%, mainland Chinese 14%, Aborigine 2%. **Principal languages:** Mandarin Chinese (official), Taiwanese (Min), Hakka dialects. **Chief religions:** Buddhist, Confucian, and Taoist 93%; Christian 5%.

Geography: Total area: 13,892 sq mi, 35,980 sq km; **Land area:** 12,456 sq mi, 32,260 sq km. **Location:** Off SE coast of China, between East and South China seas. **Neighbors:** Nearest is China. **Topography:** A mountain range forms the backbone of the island; the eastern half is very steep and craggy, the western slope is flat, fertile, and well cultivated. **Capital:** Taipei, 2,550,000. **Cities:** Kaohsiung, 1,463,000; Taichung, 950,000.

Government: Type: Democracy. **Head of state:** Pres. Chen Shui-bian; b 1950; in office: May 20, 2000. **Head of gov't.:** Prime Min. Yu Shyi-kun; b Apr. 25, 1948; in office: Feb. 1, 2002. **Local divisions:** 16 counties, 5 municipalities, 2 special municipalities (Taipei, Kaohsiung). **Defense budget** (2003): 6.6 bil. **Active troops:** 290,000.

Economy: Industries: electronics, oil refining, chemicals, textiles, iron & steel, machinery, cement, food proc. **Chief crops:** rice, corn, vegetables, fruit, tea. **Natural resources:** coal, nat. gas, limestone, marble, asbestos. **Crude oil reserves** (2003): 4.0 mil. bbls. **Arable land:** 24%. **Fish catch** (2002): 1,372,922 metric tons. **Electricity prod.** (2002): 158.54 bil. kWh. **Labor force** (2001 est.): services 57%, industry 35%, agriculture 8%.

Finance: Monetary unit: Dollar (TWD) (Sept. 2004: 33.85=1 U.S.). **GDP** (2003 est.): $528.6 bil.; **per capita GDP:** $23,400; **GDP growth:** 3.2%. **Imports** (2003 est.): $119.6 bil.; partners (2002): Japan 24.2%, U.S. 16.1%, China 7.1%, South Korea 6.9%. **Exports** (2003 est.): $143.0 bil.; partners (2002): China 25.3%, U.S. 20.5%, Japan 9.2%. **Tourism:** $3.0 bil. **Budget** (2002 est.): $63.0 bil.

Transport: Railroad: Length: 688 mi. **Motor vehicles** (1997): 4.40 mil pass. cars, 833,545 comm. vehicles. **Civil aviation:** 22.8 bil pass.-mi; 37 airports. **Chief ports:** Kaohsiung, Chilung (Keelung), Hualien, Taichung.

Communications: TV sets: 327 per 1,000 pop. **Radios:** 402 per 1,000 pop. **Telephone lines:** 13.4 mil. **Daily newspaper circ.:** 20.2 per 1,000 pop. **Internet:** 8.8 mil. users.

Health: Life expect.: 74.3 male; 80.1 female. **Births** (per 1,000 pop.): 12.7. **Deaths** (per 1,000 pop.): 6.3. **Natural inc.:** 0.64%. **Infant mortality** (per 1,000 live births): 6.5.

Education: Free, compulsory: ages 6-15. **Literacy** (1998): 94%.

Major Intl. Organizations: APEC.

Embassy: 4201 Wisconsin Ave. NW, 20016; 895-1800.

Website: www.roc-taiwan.org

Large-scale Chinese immigration began in the 17th century. The island came under mainland control after an interval of Dutch rule, 1620-62. Taiwan (also called Formosa) was ruled by Japan 1895-1945. The Kuomintang (Chinese nationalist govt) fled to Taiwan in 1949 and established the Republic of China under Chang Kai-shek, who ruled for over 20 years with increasingly broad power. The U.S. provided military aid deterring a Communist invasion. In 1971, the UN expelled Taiwan from its seat and recognized the mainland govt. The U.S. officially recognized the People's Republic, Dec. 15, 1978, and severed ties with Taiwan. However, the U.S. and Taiwan have continued a strong trading relationship, and maintain contact via quasi-official agencies.

Land reform, government planning, U.S. aid and investment, and free universal education brought huge advances in industry, agriculture, and living standards. In 1987 martial law was lifted after 38 years, and in 1991 the 43-year period of emergency rule ended. Taiwan held its first direct presidential election Mar. 23, 1996. An earthquake on Sept. 21, 1999, killed more than 2,300 people and injured thousands more. Five decades of Nationalist Party rule ended with the presidential election of Mar. 18, 2000, won by Chen Shui-bian, leader of the pro-independence Democratic Progressive Party. Chen was wounded in an apparent assassination attempt Mar. 19, 2004, one day before he narrowly won a 2nd term as president.

Since 1949, the People's Republic has considered Taiwan a rebel province of the mainland, while, until 1991, Taiwan claimed to be the sole gov't. of both. Beijing and Taipei increased economic cooperation in the 1990s. In 1999, relations between the 2 soured, when Taiwan redefined its relationship with mainland China as "state to state." Since 2000, Taipei has hinted at a referendum on officially stating independence, to which mainland China has threatened military action. Taiwan has official diplomatic relations with only 26 nations.

Taiwan has one of the world's strongest economies and is among the 10 leading capital exporters.

The **Penghu Isls.** (Pescadores), 49 sq mi, pop. (1996 est.) 90,142, lie between Taiwan and the mainland. **Quemoy** and **Matsu,** pop. (1996 est.) 53,286, lie just off the mainland.

Tajikistan
Republic of Tajikistan

People: Population: 7,011,556. **Age distrib.** (%): <15: 40.4; 65+: 4.7. **Pop. density:** 127 per sq mi, 49 per sq km. **Urban:** 24.7%. **Ethnic groups:** Tajik 65%, Uzbek 25%, Russian 4%. **Principal languages:** Tajik (official), Russian. **Chief religions:** Sunni Muslim 85%, Shi'a Muslim 5%.

Geography: Total area: 55,251 sq mi, 143,100 sq km; **Land area:** 55,097 sq mi, 142,700 sq km. **Location:** Central Asia. **Neighbors:** Uzbekistan on N and W, Kyrgyzstan on N, China on E, Afghanistan on S. **Topography:** Mountainous region that contains the Pamirs, Trans-Alai mountain system. **Capital:** Dushanbe, 554,000.

Government: Type: Republic. **Head of state:** Pres. Imomali Rakhmonov; b Oct. 5, 1952; in office: Nov. 6, 1994. **Head of gov't.:** Akil Akilov; b 1944; in office: Dec. 20, 1999. **Local divisions:** 2 viloyats, 1 autonomous viloyat. **Defense budget** (2003): $16.2 mil. **Active troops:** 6,000.

Economy: Industries: metals, chemicals & fertilizers, cement, vegetable oil, machine tools. **Chief crops:** cotton, grain, fruits, grapes, vegetables. **Natural resources:** hydropower, oil, uranium, mercury, lignite, lead, zinc, antimony, tungsten, silver, gold. **Crude oil reserves** (2003): 12.0 mil. bbls. **Arable land:** 6%. **Livestock** (2003): cattle: 1.14 mil.; chickens: 1.54 mil.; goats: 841,900; pigs: 500; sheep: 1.59 mil. **Fish catch** (2002): 324 metric tons. **Electricity prod.** (2002): 15.08 bil. kWh. **Labor force** (2000 est.): agriculture 67.2%, industry 7.5%, services 25.3%.

Finance: Monetary unit: Somoni (TJS) (Sept. 2004: 2.79=1 U.S.). **GDP** (2003 est.): $7.0 bil.; **per capita GDP:** $1,000; **GDP growth:** 9.9%. **Imports** (2003 est.): $890.0 mil.; partners (2002): Russia 23.1%, Uzbekistan 18.6%, Ukraine 11.4%, Kazakhstan 10.1%, Turkmenistan 6.6%, Azerbaijan 5.8%, India 4.5%. **Exports** (2003 est.): $750.0 mil.; partners (2002): Netherlands 29.4%, Turkey

16.1%, Russia 11.9%, Uzbekistan 9.9%, Switzerland 9.4%, Hungary 5.4%, Latvia 4.2%. **Tourism** (2002): $2 mil. **Budget** (2002 est.): $520.0 mil. **Intl. reserves less gold:** $75 mil. **Gold:** 10,000 oz t.

Transport: Railroad: Length: 300 mi. **Motor vehicles** (2000): 117,100 pass. cars, 16,800 comm. vehicles. **Civil aviation:** 159.7 mil. pass.-mi; 13 airport.

Communications: TV sets: 328 per 1,000 pop. **Radios:** 143 per 1,000 pop. **Telephone lines:** 242,100. **Daily newspaper circ.:** 20 per 1,000 pop. **Internet:** 4,100 users.

Health: Life expect.: 61.5 male; 67.6 female. **Births** (per 1,000 pop.): 32.6. **Deaths** (per 1,000 pop.): 8.4. **Natural inc.:** 2.42%. **Infant mortality** (per 1,000 live births): 112.1. **AIDS rate:** <0.1%.

Education: Compulsory: ages 7-15. **Literacy:** 99.4%.

Major International Organizations: UN (FAO, IBRD, ILO, IMF, WHO), CIS, OSCE.

Embassy: 1725 K St. NW, Ste. 409, 20006; 223-6090.

Website: www.tajikistan.tajnet.com

There were settled societies in the region from about 3000 BC. Throughout history, it has undergone invasions by Iranians (Arabs who converted the population to Islam), Mongols, Uzbeks, Afghans, and Russians. The USSR gained control of the region 1918-25. In 1924, the Tajik ASSR was created within the Uzbek SSR. The Tajik SSR was proclaimed in 1929.

Tajikistan declared independence Sept. 9, 1991. Factional fighting led to the installation of a pro-Communist regime, Jan. 1993. A new constitution establishing a presidential system was approved by referendum Nov. 6, 1994.

Clashes between Muslim rebels, reportedly armed by Afghanistan, and troops loyal to the government and supported by Russia, claimed an estimated 55,000 lives by mid-1997, despite a series of peace accords. Constitutional changes including legalization of Islamic political parties were approved by referendum Sept. 26, 1999. Pres. Imomali Rakhmonov won a Nov. 6 election called "a farce" by human-rights observers. Voters approved, June 22, 2003, constitutional changes giving Rakhmonov the right to serve as president until 2020.

Tanzania
United Republic of Tanzania

People: Population: 36,588,225. **Age distrib.** (%): <15: 44.6; 65+: 2.9. **Pop. density:** 107 per sq mi, 41 per sq km. **Urban:** 35.4%. **Ethnic groups:** Mainland: Bantu 95%; Zanzibar: Arab, African, mixed. **Principal languages:** Swahili, English (both official); Arabic, many local languages. **Chief religions:** Christian 30%, Muslim 35%, indigenous beliefs 35%; Zanzibar is 99% Muslim.

Geography: Total area: 364,900 sq mi, 945,087 sq km. **Land area:** 342,101 sq mi, 886,037 sq km. **Location:** On coast of E Africa. **Neighbors:** Kenya, Uganda on N; Rwanda, Burundi, Congo (formerly Zaire) on W; Zambia, Malawi, Mozambique on S. **Topography:** Hot, arid central plateau, surrounded by the lake region in the W, temperate highlands in N and S, the coastal plains. Mt. Kilimanjaro, 19,340 ft., is highest in Africa. **Capital:** Dodoma, 155,000. **Cities (urban aggr.):** Dar-es-Salaam, 2,347,000.

Government: Type: Republic. **Head of state:** Pres. Benjamin William Mkapa; b Nov. 12, 1938; in office: Nov. 23, 1995. **Head of gov.:** Prime Min. Frederick Tluway Sumaye; b May 29, 1950; in office: Nov. 28, 1995. **Local divisions:** 25 regions. **Defense budget** (2003): $131 mil. **Active troops:** 27,000.

Economy: Industries: agric. proc., diamond & gold mining, oil refining, shoes. **Chief crops:** coffee, sisal, tea, cotton, pyrethrum (insecticide from chrysanthemums), cashews. **Natural resources:** hydropower, tin, phosphates, iron ore, coal, diamonds, gemstones, gold, nat. gas, nickel. **Arable land:** 3%. **Livestock** (2003): cattle: 17.7 mil.; chickens: 30.0 mil.; goats: 12.6 mil.; pigs: 455,000; sheep: 3.52 mil. **Fish catch** (2002): 324,160 metric tons. **Electricity prod.** (2002): 2.73 bil. kWh. **Labor force** (2002 est.): agriculture 80%, industry and services 20%.

Finance: Monetary unit: Shilling (TZS) (Sept. 2004: 1,069.95=1 U.S.). **GDP** (2003 est.): $21.6 bil.; **per capita GDP:** $600; **GDP growth:** 5.2%. **Imports** (2003 est.): $1.7 bil.; partners (2002): South Africa 10.8%, Japan 7.9%, India 6.1%, UAE 5.5%, Kenya 5.4%, UK 5.4%, U.S. 5.2%, China 4.5%, Australia 4.1%, Bahrain 4%. **Exports** (2003 est.): $978.0 mil.; partners (2002): UK 17.1%, France 16.2%, Japan 10.1%, India 6.7%, Netherlands 5.7%. **Tourism:** $731 mil. **Budget** (FY02/03 est.): $2.0 bil. **Intl. reserves less gold:** $1.37 bil. **Consumer prices:** 4.4%.

Transport: Railroad: Length: 2,293 mi. **Motor vehicles** (1999): 33,900 pass. cars; 98,800 comm. vehicles. **Civil aviation:** 90.7 mil. pass.-mi; 11 airports. **Chief ports:** Dar-es-Salaam, Mtwara, Tanga.

Communications: TV sets: 21 per 1,000 pop. **Radios:** 280 per 1,000 pop. **Telephone lines:** 149,100. **Daily newspaper circ.:** 3.9 per 1,000 pop. **Internet:** 250,000 users.

Health: Life expect.: 43.2 male; 45.6 female. **Births** (per 1,000 pop.): 39.0. **Deaths** (per 1,000 pop.): 17.4. **Natural inc.:** 2.15%. **Infant mortality** (per 1,000 live births): 102.1. **AIDS rate:** 8.8%.

Education: Compulsory: ages 7-13. **Literacy:** 78.2%.

Major Intl. Organizations: UN and all of its specialized agencies, the Commonwealth, AU.

Embassy: 2139 R St. NW 20008; 939-6125.

Websites: www.tanzaniaembassy-us.org; www.tanzania.go.tz

The Republic of Tanganyika in E Africa and the island Republic of Zanzibar, off the coast of Tanganyika, both of which had recently gained independence, joined into a single nation, the United Republic of Tanzania, Apr. 26, 1964. Zanzibar retains internal self-government.

Until resigning as president in 1985, Julius K. Nyerere, a former Tanganyikan independence leader, dominated Tanzania's politics, which emphasized government planning and control of the economy, with single-party rule. In 1992 the constitution was amended to establish a multiparty system. Privatization of the economy was undertaken in the 1990s.

At least 500 people died when an overcrowded Tanzanian ferry sank in Lake Victoria, May 21, 1996. About 460,000 Rwandan refugees, mostly Hutu, returned from Tanzania to Rwanda in Dec. 1996. A bomb at the U.S. embassy in Dar-es-Salaam, Aug. 7, 1998, killed 11 people and injured at least 70 others. The U.S. blamed the attack and a near-simultaneous embassy bombing in Kenya on Islamic terrorists associated with Osama bin Laden. After a trial in New York City, 4 conspirators were convicted May 29, 2001.

Former Pres. Nyerere died in London Oct. 14, 1999. President since 1995, Benjamin Mkapa was reelected Oct. 29, 2000. Over 280 people died in a train wreck June 24, 2002, SE of Dodoma.

Tanganyika. Arab colonization and slaving began in the 8th century AD; Portuguese sailors explored the coast by about 1500. Other Europeans followed.

In 1885 Germany established German East Africa of which Tanganyika formed the bulk. It became a League of Nations mandate and, after 1946, a UN trust territory, both under Britain. It became independent Dec. 9, 1961, and a republic within the Commonwealth a year later.

Zanzibar, the Isle of Cloves, lies 23 mi off mainland Tanzania; area 640 sq mi and pop. (2002) 622,459. The island of **Pemba,** 25 mi to the NE, area 380 sq mi and pop. (2002) 362,166 is included in the administration.

Chief industry is cloves and clove oil production, of which Zanzibar and Pemba produce most of the world's supply.

Zanzibar was for centuries the center for Arab slave traders. Portugal ruled the region for 2 centuries until ousted by Arabs around 1700. Zanzibar became a British Protectorate in 1890; independence came Dec. 10, 1963. Revolutionary forces overthrew the Sultan Jan. 12, 1964. The new government ousted Western diplomats and newsmen, slaughtered thousands of Arabs, and nationalized farms. Union with Tanganyika followed.

Thailand
Kingdom of Thailand

People: Population: 64,865,523. **Age distrib.** (%): <15: 23.3; 65+: 6.8. **Pop. density:** 328 per sq mi, 127 per sq km. **Urban:** 31.9%. **Ethnic groups:** Thai 75%, Chinese 14%. **Principal languages:** Thai, Chinese, Malay, Khmer. **Chief religions:** Buddhism 95% (official), Muslim 4%.

Geography: Total area: 198,456 sq mi, 514,000 sq km. **Land area:** 197,595 sq mi, 511,770 sq km. **Location:** On Indochinese and Malayan peninsulas in SE Asia. **Neighbors:** Myanmar on W and N, Laos on N, Cambodia on E, Malaysia on S. **Topography:** A plateau dominates the NE third of Thailand, dropping to the fertile alluvial valley of the Chao Phraya R. in the center. Forested mountains are in the N, with narrow fertile valleys. The S peninsula region is covered by rain forests. **Capital:** Bangkok, 6,486,000.

Government: Type: Constitutional monarchy. **Head of state:** King Bhumibol Adulyadej; b Dec. 5, 1927; in office: June 9, 1946. **Head of gov.:** Prime Min. Thaksin Shinawatra; b July 26, 1949; in office: Feb. 18, 2001. **Local divisions:** 76 provinces. **Defense budget** (2003): $1.9 bil. **Active troops:** 314,200.

Economy: Industries: tourism; textiles & garments, agric. proc., beverages, tobacco, cement, light mfg.; electric appliances & components, computers & parts. **Chief crops:** rice, cassava, rubber, corn, sugarcane, coconuts, soybeans. **Natural resources:** tin, rubber, nat. gas, tungsten, tantalum, timber, lead, fish, gypsum, lignite, fluorite. **Crude oil reserves** (2003): 583.4 mil. bbls. **Arable land:** 34%. **Livestock** (2003): cattle: 5.05 mil.; chickens: 177.1 mil.; goats: 178,000; pigs: 7.06 mil.; sheep: 42,000. **Fish catch** (2002 est): 3,566,106 metric tons. **Electricity prod.** (2002): 102.38 bil. kWh. **Labor force** (2000 est.): agriculture 49%, industry 14%, services 37%.

Finance: Monetary unit: Baht (THB) (Sept. 2004: 41.25=1 U.S.). **GDP** (2003 est.): $475.7 bil.; **per capita GDP:** $7,400; **GDP growth:** 6.3%. **Imports** (2003 est.): $65.3 bil.; partners (2002): Japan 23%, U.S. 9.6%, China 7.6%, Malaysia 5.6%, Singapore 4.5%, Taiwan 4.4%. **Exports** (2003 est.): $76.0 bil.; partners (2002): U.S. 19.6%, Japan 14.5%, Singapore 8.1%, Hong Kong 5.4%, China 5.2%, Malaysia 4.1%. **Tourism:** $7.8 bil. **Budget** (2000 est.): $22.0 bil. **Intl. reserves less gold:** $27.64 bil. **Gold:** 2.6 mil oz t. **Consumer prices:** 1.8%.

Transport: Railroad: Length: 2,530 mi. **Motor vehicles** (2000): 2.67 mil pass. cars, 4.22 mil comm. vehicles. **Civil aviation:** 24.0 bil. pass.-mi; 62 airports. **Chief ports:** Bangkok, Sattahip.

Communication: TV sets: 274 per 1,000 pop. **Radios:** 234 per 1,000 pop. **Telephone lines:** 6.6 mil pop. **Daily newspaper circ.:** 63 per 1,000 pop. **Internet** (2002): 6.0 mil. users.

Health: Life expect.: 69.2 male; 73.7 female. **Births** (per 1,000 pop.): 16.0. **Deaths** (per 1,000 pop.): 6.9. **Natural inc.:** 0.91%. **Infant mortality** (per 1,000 live births): 21.1. **AIDS rate:** 1.5%.

Education: Compulsory: ages 6-14. **Literacy:** 96%.

Major Intl. Organizations: UN (FAO, IBRD, ILO, IMF, IMO, WHO, WTrO), ASEAN, APEC.

Embassy: 1024 Wisconsin Ave., Suite 401, NW 20007; 944-3600.

Websites: www.thaiembdc.org; www.thaigov.go.th

Thais began migrating from southern China during the 11th century. A unified Thai kingdom was established in 1350. Known as Siam until 1939, Thailand is the only country in SE Asia never taken over by a European power, thanks to King Mongkut and his son King Chulalongkorn. Ruling successively from 1851 to 1910, they modernized the country and signed trade treaties with Britain and France. A bloodless revolution in 1932 limited the monarchy. Thailand was an ally of Japan during World War II and of the U.S. during the postwar period. For decades, the military had a dominant role in governing the country.

A steep downturn in the economy forced Thailand to seek more than $15 billion in emergency international loans in Aug. 1997. A new constitution won legislative approval Sept. 27. As the economic crisis deepened, Chuan Leekpai became prime minister Nov. 9, 1997, and implemented financial reforms. By the end of the 1990s, according to UN estimates, more than 750,000 people in Thailand had HIV/AIDS; a nationwide prevention campaign has reduced the number of new infections.

Following elections in Jan. 2001, Thaksin Shinawatra, a wealthy former telecommunications executive, became prime minister. Thailand's Constitutional Court acquitted him Aug. 3 of corruption while he was deputy prime minister in 1997. On Feb. 1, 2003, Thaksin launched a nationwide crackdown on methamphetamines; human rights observers criticized police tactics in the drug war, which killed more than 2,200 people by Apr. 30.

The government launched a campaign against suspected Muslim insurgents Jan. 2004.

Togo
Togolese Republic

People: Population: 5,556,812. **Age distrib.** (%): <15: 45.1; 65+: 2.5. **Pop. density:** 265 per sq mi, 102 per sq km. **Urban:** 35.1%. **Ethnic groups:** 37 African tribes; largest are Ewe, Mina, and Kabre. **Principal languages:** French (official); Ewe, Mina in S; Kabye, Dagomba in N. **Chief religions:** Indigenous beliefs 51%, Christian 29%, Muslim 20%.

Geography: Total area: 21,925 sq mi, 56,785 sq km; **Land area:** 20,998 sq mi, 54,385 sq km. **Location:** On S coast of W Africa. **Neighbors:** Ghana on W, Burkina Faso on N, Benin on E. **Topography:** A range of hills running SW-NE splits Togo into 2 savanna plains regions. **Capital:** Lomé, 799,000.

Government: Type: Republic. **Head of state:** Pres. Gnassingbé Eyadéma; b Dec. 26, 1937; in office: Apr. 14, 1967. **Head of gov.:** Prime Min. Koffi Sama; b 1944; in office: June 29, 2002. **Local divisions:** 5 regions. **Defense budget** (2003): $32 mil. **Active troops:** 8,550.

Economy: Industries: phosphates mining, agric. proc., cement, handicrafts. **Chief crops:** coffee, cocoa, cotton, yams, cassava, corn. **Natural resources:** phosphates, limestone, marble. **Arable land:** 38%. **Livestock** (2003): cattle: 279,000; chickens: 8.5 mil.; goats: 1.47 mil.; pigs: 310,000; sheep: 1.8 mil. **Fish catch** (2002): 21,971 metric tons. **Electricity prod.** (2002): 0.11 bil. kWh. **Labor force** (1998 est.): agriculture 65%, industry 5%, services 30%.

Finance: Monetary unit: CFA Franc BCEAO (XOF) (Sept. 2004: 539.40=1 U.S.). **GDP** (2003 est.): $8.2 bil.; **per capita GDP:** $1,500; **GDP growth:** 3.2%. **Imports** (2003 est.): $501.3 mil.; partners (2002): France 20.3%, China 16.2%, Netherlands 6.2%, Hong Kong 5.3%, Germany 4.9%, UK 4.6%, Italy 4.3%. **Exports** (2003 est.): $398.1 mil.; partners (2002): Ghana 17.7%, Benin 13.1%, Burkina Faso 8.2%. **Tourism** (2002): $9 mil. **Budget** (1997 est.): $252.0 mil. **Intl. reserves less gold:** $123 mil. **Consumer prices:** –0.96%.

Transport: Railroad: Length: 326 mi. **Motor vehicles** (1999): 36,000 pass. cars, 17,600 comm. vehicles. **Civil aviation:** 134.2 mil. pass.-mi; 2 airports. **Chief port:** Lomé.

Communications: TV sets: 22 per 1,000 pop. **Radios:** 244 per 1,000 pop. **Telephone lines:** 60,600. **Daily newspaper circ.:** 2.2 per 1,000 pop. **Internet:** 210,000 users.

Health: Life expect.: 51.1 male; 55.1 female. **Births** (per 1,000 pop.): 34.4. **Deaths** (per 1,000 pop.): 11.6. **Natural inc.:** 2.27%. **Infant mortality** (per 1,000 live births): 67.7. **AIDS rate:** 4.1%.

Education: Compulsory: ages 6-15. **Literacy:** 60.9%.

Major Intl. Organizations: UN (FAO, IBRD, ILO, IMF, IMO, WHO, WTrO), AU.

Embassy: 2208 Massachusetts Ave. NW, 20008; 234-4212.

Website: www.republicoftogo.com

In Jan. 1993 police fired on protesters, killing at least 22. Some 25,000 people fled to Ghana and Benin as a result of civil unrest. In Jan. 1994 at least 40 people were killed when gunmen reportedly attacked an army base. Further violence marred Togo's 1st multiparty legislative elections, held Feb. 1994.

In office since 1967, Pres. Gnassingbé Eyadéma is Africa's longest-serving head of state. He was reelected June 1, 2003, in a vote that, like previous elections, was viewed as undemocratic.

Tonga
Kingdom of Tonga

People: Population: 110,237. **Age distrib.** (%): <15: 39.5; 65+: 4.1. **Pop. density:** 398 per sq mi, 154 per sq km. **Urban:** 33.4%. **Ethnic groups:** Polynesian. **Principal languages:** Tongan, English (both official). **Chief religions:** Wesleyan 41%, Roman Catholic 16%, Mormon 14%.

Geography: Total area: 289 sq mi, 748 sq km; **Land area:** 277 sq mi, 718 sq km. **Location:** In western South Pacific O. **Neighbors:** Nearest are Fiji to W, Samoa to NE. **Topography:** Tonga comprises 170 volcanic and coral islands, 36 inhabited. **Capital:** Nuku'alofa, 35,000.

Government: Type: Constitutional monarchy. **Head of state:** King Taufa'ahau Tupou IV; b July 4, 1918; in office: Dec. 16, 1965. **Head of gov.:** Prime Min. Prince Ulukalala Lavaka Ata; b July 12, 1959; in office: Jan. 3, 2000. **Local divisions:** 3 island groups.

Economy: Industries: tourism, fishing. **Chief crops:** squash, coconuts, copra, bananas, vanilla, cocoa. **Natural resources:** fish. **Arable land:** 24%. **Livestock** (2003): cattle: 11,250; chickens: 300,000; goats: 12,500; pigs: 81,000. **Fish catch** (2002): 4,818 metric tons. **Electricity prod.** (2002): 0.02 bil. kWh. **Labor force** (1997 est.): agriculture 65%.

Finance: Monetary unit: Pa'anga (TOP) (Sept. 2004: 2.01=1 U.S.). **GDP** (2001 est.): $236.0 mil.; **per capita GDP:** $2,200; **GDP growth:** 3.0%. **Imports** (2002 est.): $86.0 mil.; partners (2002): New Zealand 31.4%, Fiji 20.9%, U.S. 14%, Australia 12.8%, China 5.8%. **Exports** (2002 est.): $27.0 mil.; partners (2002): Japan 40.7%, U.S. 37%, Germany 3.7%. **Tourism** (2002): $9 mil. **Budget** (FY99/00 est.): $52.4 mil. **Intl. reserves less gold:** $29 mil. **Consumer prices:** 11.6%.

Transport: Motor vehicles (1999): 10,800 pass. cars, 10,400 comm. vehicles. **Civil aviation:** 6.8 mil. pass.-mi; 1 airport. **Chief port:** Nuku'alofa.

Communications: TV sets: 61 per 1,000 pop. **Radios:** 663 per 1,000 pop. **Telephone lines** (2002): 11,200. **Daily newspaper circ.:** 72 per 1,000 pop. **Internet** (2002): 2,900 users.

Health: Life expect.: 66.7 male; 71.8 female. **Births** (per 1,000 pop.): 24.9. **Deaths** (per 1,000 pop.): 5.5. **Natural inc.:** 1.94%. **Infant mortality** (per 1,000 live births): 13.0.

Education: Compulsory: ages 6-14. **Literacy** (1996 est.): 98.5%.

Major Intl. Organizations: UN (FAO, IBRD, IMF, WHO), the Commonwealth.

Embassy: 250 E. 51st St. New York, NY 10022; (917) 369-1025.

Website: www.pmo.gov.to

The islands were first visited by the Dutch in the early 17th century. A series of civil wars ended in 1845 with establishment of the Tupou dynasty. In 1900 Tonga became a British protectorate. On June 4, 1970, Tonga became independent and a member of the Commonwealth. It joined the UN on Sept. 14, 1999.

Trinidad and Tobago
Republic of Trinidad and Tobago

People: Population: 1,096,585. **Age distrib.** (%): <15: 23; 65+: 6.8. **Pop. density:** 554 per sq mi, 214 per sq km. **Urban:** 75.4%. **Ethnic groups:** Black 40%, East Indian 40%, mixed 18%. **Principal languages:** English (official), Hindi, French, Spanish, Chinese. **Chief religions:** Roman Catholic 29%, Hindu 24%, Protestant 14%, Muslim 6%.

Geography: Total area: 1,980 sq mi, 5,128 sq km; **Land area:** 1,980 sq mi, 5,128 sq km. **Location:** In Caribbean, off E coast of Venezuela. **Neighbors:** Nearest is Venezuela to SW. **Topography:** Three low mountain ranges cross Trinidad E-W, with a well-watered plain between N and central ranges. Parts of E and W coasts are swamps. Tobago, 116 sq. mi., lies 20 mi. NE. **Capital:** Port-of-Spain, 55,000.

Government: Type: Parliamentary democracy. **Head of state:** Pres. George Maxwell Richards; b 1931; in office: Mar. 17, 2003. **Head of gov.:** Prime Min. Patrick Augustus Mervyn Manning; b Aug. 17, 1946; in office: Dec. 24, 2001. **Local divisions:** 8 counties, 3 municipalities, 1 ward. **Defense budget** (2003): $70 mil. **Active troops:** 2,700.

Economy: Industries: oil, chemicals, tourism, food proc. **Chief crops:** cocoa, sugarcane, rice, citrus, coffee, vegetables. **Natural resources:** oil, nat. gas, asphalt. **Crude oil reserves** (2003): 716.0 mil. bbls. **Arable land:** 15%. **Livestock** (2003): cattle: 28,980; chickens: 27,500; goats: 23,000; pigs: 75,686; sheep: 7,050. **Fish catch** (2002 est): 12,546 metric tons. **Electricity prod.** (2002): 5.74 bil. kWh. **Labor force** (1997 est.): construction and utilities 12.4%, manufacturing, mining, and quarrying 14%, agriculture 9.5%, services 64.1%.

Finance: Monetary unit: Tobago Dollar (TTD) (Sept. 2004: 6.29=1 U.S.). **GDP** (2003 est.): $10.6 bil.; **per capita GDP:** $9,600; **GDP growth:** 4.5%. **Imports** (2003 est.): $3.9 bil.; partners (2002): U.S. 35.8%, Venezuela 12.7%, Brazil 5.1%, Cote d'Ivoire 4.7%, UK 4.3%. **Exports** (2003 est.): $4.9 bil.; partners (2002): U.S. 54.4%, Jamaica 6.7%, France 4.2%. **Tourism** (2002): $224 mil. **Budget** (1998): $1.6 bil. **Intl. reserves less gold:** $1.65 bil. **Gold:** 60,000 mil. oz t. **Consumer prices:** 3.8%.

Transport: Motor vehicles (1999): 229,400 pass. cars, 53,900 comm. vehicles. **Civil aviation:** 1.7 bil. pass.-mi; 3 airports. **Chief ports:** Port-of-Spain, Scarborough.

Communications: TV sets: 337 per 1,000 pop. **Radios:** 532 per 1,000 pop. **Telephone lines** (2002): 325,100. **Daily newspaper circ.:** 123 per 1,000 pop. **Internet** (2002): 138,000 users.

Health: Life expect.: 66.9 male; 71.8 female. **Births** (per 1,000 pop.): 12.8. **Deaths** (per 1,000 pop.): 9.0. **Natural inc.:** 0.37%. **Infant mortality** (per 1,000 live births): 24.6. **AIDS rate:** 3.2%.

Education: Compulsory: ages 5-11. **Literacy:** 98.6%.

Major Intl. Organizations: UN (FAO, IBRD, ILO, IMF, IMO, WHO, WTrO), Caricom, the Commonwealth, OAS.

Embassy: 1708 Massachusetts Ave. NW 20036; 467-6490.

Websites: ttembassy.cjb.net; www.gov.tt

Columbus sighted Trinidad in 1498. A British possession since 1802, Trinidad and Tobago won independence Aug. 31, 1962. It became a republic in 1976.

The nation is one of the most prosperous in the Caribbean. Oil production has increased with offshore finds. Middle Eastern oil is refined and exported, mostly to the U.S.

In July 1990, some 120 Muslim extremists captured the Parliament building and TV station and took about 50 hostages, including Prime Min. Arthur N. R. Robinson, who was beaten, shot in the legs, and tied to explosives. After a 6-day siege, the rebels surrendered.

Basdeo Panday, the country's first prime minister of East Indian ancestry, took office Nov. 9, 1995. Robinson became president on Mar. 19, 1997. Patrick Manning of the People's National Movement became prime minister after elections Dec. 10, 2001. George Maxwell Richards, a former university dean, succeeded Robinson as president, Mar. 17, 2003.

Tunisia
Tunisian Republic

People: Population: 9,974,722. **Age distrib.** (%): <15: 27.8; 65+: 6.3. **Pop. density:** 166 per sq mi, 64 per sq km. **Urban:** 63.7%. **Ethnic groups:** Arab 98%, European 1%, Jewish and other 1%. **Principal languages:** Arabic (official), French prevalent. **Chief religion:** Muslim 98% (official; mostly Sunni).

Geography: Total area: 63,170 sq mi, 163,610 sq km; **Land area:** 59,985 sq mi, 155,360 sq km. **Location:** On N coast of Africa. **Neighbors:** Algeria on W, Libya on E. **Topography:** The N is wooded and fertile. The central coastal plains are given to grazing and orchards. The S is arid, approaching Sahara Desert. **Capital:** Tunis, 1,996,000.

Government: Type: Republic. **Head of state:** Pres. Gen. Zine al-Abidine Ben Ali; b Sept. 3, 1936; in office: Nov. 7, 1987. **Head of gov.:** Prime Min. Mohamed Ghannouchi; b Aug. 18, 1941; in office: Nov. 17, 1999. **Local divisions:** 24 governorates. **Defense budget** (2003): $472 mil. **Active troops:** 35,000.

Economy: Industries: oil, mining, tourism, textiles, footwear, agribusiness. **Chief crops:** olives, grain, tomatoes, citrus, sugar beets, dates, almonds. **Natural resources:** oil, phosphates, iron ore, lead, zinc, salt. **Crude oil reserves** (2003): 307.6 mil. bbls. **Arable land:** 19%. **Livestock** (2003): cattle: 760,000; chickens: 72.0 mil.; goats: 1.4 mil.; pigs: 6,000; sheep: 6.85 mil. **Fish catch** (2002): 98,660 metric tons. **Electricity prod.** (2002): 10.72 bil. kWh. **Labor force** (1995 est.): services 55%, industry 23%, agriculture 22%.

Finance: Monetary unit: Dinar (TND) (Sept. 2004: 1.27=1 U.S.). **GDP** (2003 est.): $68.8 bil.; **per capita GDP:** $6,900; **GDP growth:** 6.0%. **Imports** (2003 est.): $10.3 bil.; partners (2002): France 25.6%, Italy 19.5%, Germany 8.9%, Spain 5%. **Exports** (2003 est.): $8.0 bil.; partners (2002): France 31.3%, Italy 21.6%, Germany 11.5%, Spain 4.8%, Libya 4.7%, Belgium 4.3%. **Tourism:** $1.5 bil. **Budget** (2002 est.): $5.7 bil. **Intl. reserves less gold:** $1.98 bil. **Gold:** 220,000 oz t. **Consumer prices:** 2.7%.

Transport: Railroad: Length: 1,337 mi. **Motor vehicles** (2001): 552,900 pass. cars, 281,500 comm. vehicles. **Civil aviation:** 1.7 bil. pass.-mi; 14 airports. **Chief ports:** Tunis, Sfax, Bizerte.

Communications: TV sets: 190 per 1,000 pop. **Radios:** 158 per 1,000 pop. **Telephone lines:** 1.2 mil. **Daily newspaper circ.:** 19 per 1,000 pop. **Internet:** 630,000 users.

Health: Life expect.: 73.0 male; 76.4 female. **Births** (per 1,000 pop.): 15.7. **Deaths** (per 1,000 pop.): 5.0. **Natural inc.:** 1.07%. **Infant mortality** (per 1,000 live births): 25.8. **AIDS rate:** <0.1%.

Education: Compulsory: ages 6-16. **Literacy:** 74.2%.

Major Intl. Organizations: UN (FAO, IBRD, ILO, IMF, IMO, WHO, WTrO), AL, AU.

Embassy: 1515 Massachusetts Ave. NW 20005; 862-1850.

Websites: www.ministeres.tn; www.tourismtunisia.com

Site of ancient Carthage and a former Barbary state under the suzerainty of Turkey, Tunisia became a protectorate of France under a treaty signed May 12, 1881. The nation became independent Mar. 20, 1956, and ended the monarchy the following year. Habib Bourguiba, an independence leader, served as president until 1987, when he was deposed by his prime minister, Zine al-Abidine Ben Ali.

Tunisia has actively repressed Islamic fundamentalism. A synagogue blast on Djerba Is., Apr. 11, 2002, apparently set off by al-Qaeda, killed 17 people, including 12 German tourists.

Turkey
Republic of Turkey

People: Population: 68,893,918. **Age distrib.** (%): <15: 27.8; 65+: 6.3. **Pop. density:** 232 per sq mi, 89 per sq km. **Urban:** 66.3%. **Ethnic groups:** Turkish 80%, Kurdish 20%. **Principal languages:** Turkish (official), Kurdish, Arabic, Armenian, Greek. **Chief religion:** Muslim 99.8% (mostly Sunni).

Geography: Total area: 301,383 sq mi, 780,580 sq km; **Land area:** 297,592 sq mi, 770,760 sq km. **Location:** Occupies Asia Minor, stretches into continental Europe; borders on Mediterranean and Black seas. **Neighbors:** Bulgaria, Greece on W; Georgia, Armenia on N; Iran on E; Iraq, Syria on S. **Topography:** Central Turkey has wide plateaus, with hot, dry summers and cold winters. High mountains ring the interior on all but W, with more than 20 peaks over 10,000 ft. Rolling plains are in W; mild, fertile coastal plains are in S, W. **Capital:** Ankara, 3,428,000. **Cities (urban agr.):** Istanbul, 8,744,000; Izmir, 2,216,000.

Government: Type: Republic. **Head of state:** Pres. Ahmet Necdet Sezer; b Sept. 13, 1941; in office: May 16, 2000. **Head of gov.:** Prime Min. Recep Tayyip Erdogan; b Feb. 26, 1954; in office: Mar. 14, 2003. **Local divisions:** 81 provinces. **Defense budget** (2003): $7.8 bil. **Active troops:** 514,850.

Economy: Industries: textiles, food proc., autos, mining, steel, oil, constr. **Chief crops:** tobacco, cotton, grain, olives, sugar beets, citrus. **Natural resources:** antimony, coal, chromium, mercury, copper, borate, sulfur, iron ore, hydropower. **Crude oil reserves** (2003): 300.0 mil. bbls. **Arable land:** 32%. **Livestock** (2003): cattle: 10.4 mil.; chickens: 217.0 mil.; goats: 7.0 mil.; pigs: 2,700; sheep: 27.0 mil. **Fish catch** (2002): 627,847 metric tons. **Electricity prod.** (2002): 123.32 bil. kWh. **Labor force** (3rd quarter, 2001): agriculture 39.7%, services 37.9%, industry 22.4%.

Finance: Monetary unit: Lira (TRL) (Sept. 2004: 1,497,751.13=1 U.S.). **GDP** (2003 est.): $455.3 bil.; **per capita GDP:** $6,700; **GDP growth:** 5.0%. **Imports** (2003 est.): $62.4 bil.; partners (2002): Germany 13.7%, Italy 8%, Russia 7.5%, U.S. 6%, France 6%, UK 4.7%, Switzerland 4.2%. **Exports** (2003 est.): $49.1 bil.; partners (2002): Germany 16.6%, U.S. 9.2%, UK 8.5%, Italy 6.4%, France 6%. **Tourism:** $13.2 bil. **Budget** (2001): $69.1 bil. **Intl. reserves less gold:** $22.88 bil. **Gold:** 3.73 mil oz t. **Consumer prices:** 25.3%.

Transport: Railroad: Length: 5,348 mi. **Motor vehicles** (2001): 4.53 mil pass. cars, 1.63 mil comm. vehicles. **Civil aviation:** 8.0 bil. pass.-mi; 86 airports. **Chief ports:** Istanbul, Izmir, Mersin.

Communications: TV sets: 328 per 1,000 pop. **Radios:** 510 per 1,000 pop. **Telephone lines:** 18.9 mil. **Daily newspaper circ.:** 111 per 1,000 pop. **Internet:** 5.5 mil. users.

Health: Life expect.: 69.7 male; 74.6 female. **Births** (per 1,000 pop.): 17.2. **Deaths** (per 1,000 pop.): 6.0. **Natural inc.:** 1.13%. **Infant mortality** (per 1,000 live births): 42.6.

Education: Compulsory: ages 6-14. **Literacy:** 86.5%.

Major Intl. Organizations: UN (FAO, IBRD, ILO, IMF, IMO, WHO, WTrO), NATO, OECD, OSCE.

Embassy: 2525 Massachusetts Ave. NW 20008; 612-6700.

Website: www.turkey.org

Ancient inhabitants of Turkey were among the world's first agriculturalists. Such civilizations as the Hittite, Phrygian, and Lydian flourished in Asiatic Turkey (Asia Minor), as did much of Greek civilization. After the fall of Rome in the 5th century, Constantinople (now Istanbul) was the capital of the Byzantine Empire for 1,000 years. It fell in 1453 to Ottoman Turks, who ruled a vast empire for over 400 years.

Just before World War I, Turkey, or the Ottoman Empire, ruled what is now Syria, Lebanon, Iraq, Jordan, Israel, Saudi Arabia, Yemen, and islands in the Aegean Sea. Turkey joined Germany and Austria in World War I, and its defeat resulted in the loss of much territory and the fall of the sultanate. A republic was declared Oct. 29, 1923, with Mustafa Kemal (later Kemal Ataturk) as its first president. Ataturk led Turkey until his death in 1938.

Turkey kept neutral during most of World War II. The country became a full member of NATO in 1952 and remained a Western ally despite domestic political instability. Military coups overthrew civilian governments in 1960 and 1980. Turkey invaded nearby Cyprus July 20, 1974, to prevent that country from being united with Greece; since then, Cyprus has been divided into Greek and Turkish zones.

In recent decades, Turkish governments have contended with Kurdish separatism and the rise of militant Islam. Turkey was a member of the U.S.-led force that ousted Iraq from Kuwait, 1991. In the aftermath of the war, millions of Kurdish refugees fled to Turkey's border to escape Iraqi forces. Turkish offensives against the Kurds caused heavy casualties among guerrillas and civilians. Kurdish militants raided Turkish diplomatic missions in some 25 Western European cities June 24, 1993.

Tansu Ciller officially became Turkey's first woman prime minister July 5, 1993. The Welfare Party, an Islamic group, gained strength in the 1990s but was unable to form a government until June 1996, when it came to power in coalition with Ciller's True Path Party. The pro-Islamic government resigned June 18, 1997, under pressure from the military, which stepped up its campaign against Islamic fundamentalism in 1998.

Kurdish rebel leader Abdullah Öcalan was captured Feb. 15, 1999; convicted of terrorism June 29, he was sentenced to death by a Turkish security court. His organization, the Kurdistan Workers' Party, announced Aug. 5, 1999, that it would abandon its 14-year-old armed insurgency. A major earthquake Aug. 17, 1999, in NW Turkey killed over 17,000 people and injured thousands more. Another quake in the same region Nov. 12 claimed at least 675 lives.

The IMF announced $7.5 billion in emergency loans Dec. 6, 2000, to help Turkey cope with a severe financial crisis. The death penalty was abolished Aug. 3, 2002, and Öcalan's sentence was commuted to life in prison Oct. 3. The Justice and Development Party, an Islamic group headed by Recep Tayyip Erdogan, won a plurality in parliamentary elections Nov. 3.

During the U.S.-led invasion of Iraq, Mar.-Apr. 2003, Turkey, a NATO ally, refused to allow coalition forces to launch attacks on N Iraq from Turkish soil. Suicide bombings by Islamic extremists Nov. 15-20, 2003, killed 58 people and wounded about 750 at 2 synagogues, the British consulate, and the offices of a London-based bank, all in Istanbul.

Turkey has long sought to become a full member of the European Union, but the EU has deferred talks on accession until Turkey has made more human rights reforms.

Turkmenistan

People: Population: 4,863,169 **Age distrib.** (%): <15: 37.3; 65+: 4.1. **Pop. density:** 26 per sq mi, 10 per sq km. **Urban:** 45.3%. **Ethnic groups:** Turkmen 77%, Uzbek 9%, Russian 7%, Kazakh 2%. **Principal languages:** Turkmen, Russian, Uzbek. **Chief religions:** Muslim 89%, Eastern Orthodox 9%.

Geography: Total area: 188,456 sq mi, 488,100 sq km; **Land area:** 188,456 sq mi, 488,100 sq km. **Neighbors:** Kazakhstan on N, Uzbekistan on N and E, Afghanistan and Iran on S. **Topography:** The Kara Kum Desert occupies 80% of the area. Bordered on W by Caspian Sea. **Capital:** Ashgabat, 574,000.

Government: Type: Republic with authoritarian rule. **Head of state and gov.:** Pres. Saparmurad Niyazov; b Feb. 18, 1940; in office: Oct. 27, 1990. **Local divisions:** 5 regions. **Defense budget** (2003): $173 mil. **Active troops:** 29,000.

Economy: Industries: nat. gas, oil, oil products, textiles, food proc. **Chief crops:** cotton, grain. **Natural resources:** oil, nat. gas, coal, sulfur, salt. **Crude oil reserves** (2003): 546.0 mil. bbls. **Arable land:** 3%. **Livestock** (2003): cattle: 860,000; chickens: 4.8 mil.; goats: 370,000; pigs: 45,000; sheep: 6.0 mil. **Fish catch** (2002): 12,850 metric tons. **Electricity prod.** (2002): 11.19 bil. kWh. **Labor force** (1998 est.): agriculture 48%, industry 15%, services 37%.

Finance: Monetary unit: Manat (TMM) (Sept. 2004: 5,200.00= 1 U.S.). **GDP** (2003 est.): $27.1 bil.; **per capita GDP:** $5,700; **GDP growth:** 20.0%. **Imports** (2003 est.): $2.5 bil.; partners (2002): Russia 19.8%, Turkey 12.9%, Ukraine 11.7%, UAE 10%, U.S. 7.5%, China 6%, Germany 5.7%, Iran 4.5%. **Exports** (2003 est.): $3.4 bil.; partners (2002): Ukraine 49.7%, Italy 18%, Iran 13.1%, Turkey 6.2%. **Tourism** (1998): $192 mil. **Budget** (1999 est.): $658.2 mil.

Transport: Railroad: Length: 1,516 mi. **Civil aviation:** 625.7 mil. pass.-mi; 13 airports. **Chief port:** Turkmenbashi.

Communications: TV sets: 198 per 1,000 pop. **Radios:** 289 per 1,000 pop. **Telephone lines** (2002): 374,000. **Daily newspaper circ.:** 6.7 per 1,000 pop. **Internet** (2001): 8,000 users.

Health: Life expect.: 57.9 male; 64.9 female. **Births** (per 1,000 pop.): 27.8. **Deaths** (per 1,000 pop.): 8.8. **Natural inc.:** 1.90%. **Infant mortality** (per 1,000 live births): 73.1. **AIDS rate:** <0.1%.

Education: Compulsory: ages 7-15. **Literacy** (2002): 100%.

Major Intl. Organizations: UN (FAO, IBRD, ILO, IMF, IMO, WHO), CIS, OSCE.

Embassy: 2207 Massachusetts Ave., NW 20008; 588-1500.

Website: www.turkmenistanembassy.org

The region has been inhabited by Turkic tribes since the 10th century. It became part of Russian Turkestan in 1881, and a constituent republic of the USSR in 1925. Turkmenistan declared independence Oct. 27, 1991, and became an independent state when the USSR disbanded Dec. 26, 1991.

Extensive oil and gas reserves place Turkmenistan in a more favorable economic position than other former Soviet republics. A new rail line linking Iran and Turkmenistan was inaugurated May 13, 1996. Political power centered around the former Communist Party apparatus, and Pres. Saparmurad Niyazov became the object of a personality cult. An alleged coup plot Nov. 25, 2002, triggered a crackdown on Niyazov's political opponents.

Tuvalu

People: Population: 11,468. **Age distrib.** (%): <15: 32.6; 65+: 5.1. **Pop. density:** 1,142 per sq mi, 441 per sq km. **Urban:** 55.2%. **Ethnic group:** Polynesian 96%, Micronesian 4%. **Principal languages:** Tuvaluan, English, Samoan, Kiribati (on the island of Nui). **Chief religions:** Church of Tuvalu (Congregationalist) 97%.

Geography: Total area: 10 sq mi, 26 sq km; **Land area:** 10 sq mi, 26 sq km. **Location:** 9 islands forming a NW-SE chain 360 mi. long in the SW Pacific O. **Neighbors:** Nearest are Kiribati to N, Fiji to S. **Topography:** The islands are all low-lying atolls, nowhere

rising more than 15 ft. above sea level, composed of coral reefs. **Capital:** Funafuti, 6,000.

Government: Type: Parliamentary democracy. **Head of state:** Queen Elizabeth II, represented by Gov.-Gen. Faimalaga Luka; in office: Sept. 9, 2003. **Head of gov.:** Prime Min. Maatia Toafa; in office: Aug. 27, 2004 (acting).

Economy: Industries: fishing, tourism, copra. **Chief crops:** coconuts. **Natural resources:** fish. **Livestock:** (2003): chickens: 40,000; pigs: 13,200. **Fish catch** (2002 est): 500 metric tons. **Labor force:** people make a living mainly through exploitation of the sea, reefs, and atolls and from wages sent home by those abroad (mostly workers in the phosphate industry and sailors).

Finance: Monetary unit: Australian Dollar (AUD) (Sept. 2004: 1.43=1 U.S.). **per capita GDP:** $1,100; **GDP growth:** 3.0%. **Imports** (2002): $79.0 mil.; partners (2002): Japan 54.2%, Fiji 18%, Australia 13.6%, New Zealand 5.2%, Germany 4.3%. **Exports** (2002): $1.0 mil.; partners (2002): UK 49.4%, Italy 16.7%, France 9.6%, Fiji 8.3%, Sudan 5.1%. **Budget** (2000 est.): $11.2 mil.

Transport: Civil aviation: 1 airport. **Chief port:** Funafuti.

Communications: TV sets: 9 per 1,000 pop. **Radios:** 364 per 1,000 pop.

Health: Life expect.: 65.5 male; 70.0 female. **Births** (per 1,000 pop.): 21.6. **Deaths** (per 1,000 pop.): 7.2. **Natural inc.:** 1.44%. **Infant mortality** (per 1,000 live births): 20.7.

Education: Compulsory: ages 7-14. **Literacy** (1996): 55%.

Major Intl. Organizations: UN, WHO, the Commonwealth.

UN Mission: 800 Second Ave., Ste. 400D, New York, NY 10017; (212) 490-0534.

Website: www.tuvaluislands.com

The Ellice Islands separated from the British Gilbert and Ellice Islands Colony in 1975 and became Tuvalu; independence came Oct. 1, 1978. In 2000, Tuvalu joined the United Nations.

Uganda
Republic of Uganda

People: Population: 26,404,543. **Age distrib.** (%): <15: 50.9; 65+: 2.1. **Pop. density:** 342 per sq mi, 132 per sq km. **Urban:** 12.2%. **Ethnic groups:** Baganda 17%, Ankole 8%, Basoga 8%, Iteso 8%, Bakiga 7%; many other groups. **Principal languages:** English (official), Swahili, Ganda, many Bantu and Nilotic languages, Arabic. **Chief religions:** Roman Catholic 33%, Protestant 33%, Muslim 16%, indigenous beliefs 18%.

Geography: Total area: 91,136 sq mi, 236,040 sq km; **Land area:** 77,108 sq mi, 199,710 sq km. **Location:** In E Central Africa. **Neighbors:** Sudan on N, Congo (formerly Zaire) on W, Rwanda and Tanzania on S, Kenya on E. **Topography:** Most of Uganda is a high plateau 3,000-6,000 ft. high, with high Ruwenzori range in W (Mt. Margherita 16,763 ft.), volcanoes in SW; NE is arid, W and SW rainy. Lakes Victoria, Edward, Albert form much of borders. **Capital:** Kampala, 1,246,000.

Government: Type: Republic. **Head of state:** Pres. Yoweri Kaguta Museveni; Aug. 15, 1944; in office: Jan. 29, 1986. **Head of gov.:** Prime Min. Apollo Nsibambi; b Nov. 27, 1938; in office: Apr. 5, 1999. **Local divisions:** 56 districts. **Defense budget** (2003): $153 mil. **Active troops:** 60,000.

Economy: Industries: sugar, brewing, tobacco, cotton textiles, cement. **Chief crops:** coffee, tea, cotton, cassava, potatoes. **Natural resources:** copper, cobalt, hydropower, limestone, salt. **Arable land:** 25%. **Livestock** (2003): cattle:6.1 mil.; chickens: 33,000; goats: 6.85 mil.; pigs: 1.71 mil.; sheep: 1.15 mil. **Fish catch** (2002): 226,813 metric tons. **Electricity prod.** (2002): 1.78 bil. kWh. **Labor force** (1999 est.): agriculture 82%, industry 5%, services 13%.

Finance: Monetary unit: Shilling (UGS) (Sept. 2004: 1,715.50=1 U.S.). **GDP** (2003 est.): $36.1 bil.; **per capita GDP:** $1,400; **GDP growth:** 4.4%. **Imports** (2003 est.): $1.2 bil.; partners (2002): Kenya 46.4%, South Africa 6.9%, India 5.7%, UK 5.6%. **Exports** (2003 est.): $495.0 mil.; partners (2002): Belgium 16.8%, Netherlands 14.3%, Germany 7.9%, Spain 5.8%, U.S. 4.9%, Italy 4.3%, Portugal 4.3%, UK 4.3%, Japan 4%. **Tourism** (2002): $185 mil. **Budget** (FY98/99 est.): $1.0 bil. **Intl. reserves less gold:** $727 mil. **Consumer prices:** 7.8%.

Transport: Railroad: Length: 771 mi. **Motor vehicles** (2001): 53,100 pass. cars, 79,900 comm. vehicles. **Civil aviation:** 133.6 mil. pass.-mi;4 airports. **Chief ports:** Entebbe, Jinja.

Communications: TV sets: 28 per 1,000 pop. **Radios:** 130 per 1,000 pop. **Telephone lines:** 61,000. **Daily newspaper circ.:** 2.1 per 1,000 pop. **Internet:** 125,000 users.

Health: Life expect.: 43.8 male; 46.8 female. **Births** (per 1,000 pop.): 46.3. **Deaths** (per 1,000 pop.): 16.6. **Natural inc.:** 2.97%. **Infant mortality** (per 1,000 live births): 86.2. **AIDS rate:** 4.1%.

Education: Literacy: 69.9%.

Major Intl. Organizations: UN (FAO, IBRD, ILO, IMF, WHO, WTrO), the Commonwealth, AU.

Embassy: 5911 16th St. NW 20011; 726-7100.

Websites: www.ugandaembassy.com; www.government.go.ug

Britain obtained a protectorate over Uganda in 1894. The country became independent Oct. 9, 1962, and a republic within the Commonwealth a year later. In 1967, the traditional kingdoms, including the powerful Buganda state, were abolished.

Gen. Idi Amin seized power from Prime Min. Milton Obote in 1971. During his 8 years of dictatorial rule, he was responsible for the deaths of up to 300,000 of his opponents. In 1972 he expelled nearly all of Uganda's 45,000 Asians. Tanzanian troops and Ugandan exiles and rebels ousted Amin, Apr. 11, 1979.

Obote held the presidency from Dec. 1980 until his ouster in a military coup July 27, 1985. Guerrilla war and rampant human rights abuses plagued Uganda under Obote's regime.

Conditions improved after Yoweri Museveni took power in Jan. 1986. In 1993 the government authorized restoration of the Buganda and other monarchies, but only for ceremonial purposes. Under a constitution ratified Oct. 1995, nonparty presidential and legislative elections were held in 1996. Uganda helped Laurent Kabila seize power in the Congo (formerly Zaire) in 1997 but sent troops in 1998 to aid insurgents seeking his ouster. A withdrawal accord was signed Sept. 6, 2002.

At least 330 members of the Movement for the Restoration of the Ten Commandments of God died in a church fire in Kanungu, Mar. 17, 2000; in all, over 900 deaths were associated with the cult.

Pres. Museveni won reelection Mar. 12, 2001. An ongoing insurgency against Museveni in N Uganda has forced some 1.2 million people to flee their homes. The Lord's Resistance Army, a rebel group that has fought the govt since 1986 and has abducted some 30,000 children over the last decade to serve as soldiers and sex slaves, massacred an estimated 200 civilians at a refugee camp near Lira, Feb. 21, 2004.

Ukraine

People: Population: 47,732,079. **Age distrib.** (%): <15: 16.8; 65+: 14.5. **Pop. density:** 205 per sq mi, 79 per sq km. **Urban:** 67.2%. **Ethnic groups:** Ukrainian 78%, Russian 17%. **Principal languages:** Ukrainian (official), Russian, Romanian, Polish, Hungarian. **Chief religions:** Ukrainian Orthodox (Kiev patriarchate and Russian patriarchate), Autocephalous Orthodox, Ukrainian Greek Catholic.

Geography: Total area: 233,090 sq mi, 603,700 sq km; **Land area:** 233,090 sq mi, 603,700 sq km. **Location:** In E Europe. **Neighbors:** Belarus on N; Russia on NE and E; Moldova and Romania on SW; Hungary, Slovakia, and Poland on W. **Topography:** Part of the E European plain. Mountainous areas include the Carpathians in the SW and Crimean chain in the S. Arable black soil constitutes a large part of the country. **Capital:** Kiev, 2,618,000. **Cities (urban aggr.):** Kharkov, 1,484,000 Dnepropetrovsk, 1,077,000.

Government: Type: Republic. **Head of state:** Pres. Leonid Danylovich Kuchma; b Aug. 9, 1938; in office: July 19, 1994. **Head of gov.:** Prime Min. Viktor Yanukovych; b July 9, 1950; in office: Nov. 21, 2002. **Local divisions:** 24 oblasts, 2 municipalities, 1 autonomous republic. **Defense budget** (2003): $843 mil. **Active troops:** 295,500.

Economy: Industries: coal, electric power, metals, machinery & transp. equip., chemicals, sugar. **Chief crops:** grain, sugar beets, sunflower seeds, vegetables. **Natural resources:** iron ore, coal, mang., nat. gas, oil, salt, sulfur, graphite, titanium, magnesium, kaolin, nickel, mercury, timber. **Crude oil reserves** (2003): 395.0 mil. bbls. **Arable land:** 58%. **Livestock** (2003): cattle: 9.11 mil.; chickens: 147.7 mil.; goats:1.03 mil.; pigs: 9.20 mil.; sheep: 950,000. **Fish catch** (2002): 296,418 metric tons. **Electricity Prod.** (2002): 167.26 bil. kWh. **Labor force** (1996): industry 32%, agriculture 24%, services 44%.

Finance: Monetary unit: Hryvnia (UAH) (Sept. 2004: 5.31=1 U.S.). **GDP** (2003 est.): $256.5 bil.; **per capita GDP:** $5,300; **GDP growth:** 8.2%. **Imports** (2003 est.): $23.6 bil.; partners (2002): Russia 37.6%, Turkmenistan 11.2%, Germany 9.9%. **Exports** (2003 est.): $23.6 bil.; partners (2002): Russia 17.8%, Turkey 6.9%, Italy 4.7%, Germany 4.2%. **Tourism** (2002): $3.0 bil. **Budget** (2002 est.): $11.1 bil. **Intl. reserves less gold:** $4.53 bil. **Gold:** 500,000 oz t. **Consumer prices:** 5.2%.

Transport: Railroad: Length: 13,964 mi. **Motor vehicles:** (2001): 5.31 mil pass. cars. **Civil aviation:** 770.5 mil. pass.-mi; 182 airports. **Chief ports:** Odesa, Kiev, Berdiansk.

Communications: TV sets: 433 per 1,000 pop. **Radios:** 882 per 1,000 pop. **Telephone lines** (2002): 10.8 mil. **Daily newspaper circ.:** 175.2 per 1,000 pop. **Internet** (2002): 900,000 users.

Health: Life expect.: 61.4 male; 72.3 female. **Births** (per 1,000 pop.): 10.2. **Deaths** (per 1,000 pop.): 16.4. **Natural inc.:** −0.62%. **Infant mortality** (per 1,000 live births): 20.6. **AIDS rate:** 1.4%.

Education: Compulsory: ages 7-15. **Literacy:** 99.7%.

Major Intl. Organizations: UN (IBRD, ILO, IMF, IMO, WHO), CIS, OSCE.

Embassy: 3350 M St. NW 20007; 333-0606.

Websites: www.ukraineinfo.us; www.kmu.gov.ua

Ukrainians' Slavic ancestors inhabited modern Ukrainian territory well before the first century AD. In the 9th century, the princes of Kiev established a strong state called Kievan Rus, which included much of present-day Ukraine. At the crossroads of European trade routes, Kievan Rus reached its zenith under Yaroslav the Wise (1019-1054). Internal conflicts led to the disintegration of the Ukrainian state by the 13th century. Mongol rule was supplanted by Poland and Lithuania in the 14th and 15th centuries. The N Black Sea coast and Crimea came under the control of the Turks in 1478. Ukrainian Cossacks, starting in the late 16th century, rebelled against the occupiers of Ukraine: Russia, Poland, and Turkey.

An independent Ukrainian National Republic was proclaimed on Jan. 22, 1918. But in 1921, Ukraine's neighbors occupied and divided Ukrainian territory. In 1922, Ukraine became a constituent republic of the USSR as the Ukrainian SSR. In 1932-33, the Soviet government engineered a famine in eastern Ukraine, resulting in the deaths of 7-10 million Ukrainians. During World War II the Ukrainian nationalist underground fought both Nazi and Soviet forces. Over 5 million Ukrainians died in the war. With the reoccupation of Ukraine by Soviet troops in 1944 came a renewed wave of mass arrests, executions, and deportations.

The world's worst nuclear power plant disaster occurred in Chernobyl, Ukraine, in April 1986; many thousands were killed or disabled as a result of the radiation leak. The plant was finally shut down Dec. 15, 2000.

Ukrainian independence was restored in Dec. 1991 with the dissolution of the Soviet Union. In the post-Soviet period Ukraine was burdened with a deteriorating economy. Following a 1994 accord with Russia and the U.S., Ukraine's large nuclear arsenal was transferred to Russia for destruction. A new constitution legalizing private property and establishing Ukrainian as the sole official language was approved by parliament June 29, 1996. In May 1997, Russia and Ukraine resolved disputes over the Black Sea fleet and the future of Sevastopol and signed a long-delayed treaty of friendship.

President since 1994, Leonid Kuchma won a 2nd 5-year term in a runoff vote Nov. 14, 1999; a referendum expanding his powers passed Apr. 16, 2000. Kuchma has faced corruption allegations and increasing opposition. A border dispute with Russia over the latter's new highway off the Crimean shore was settled in Dec. 2003. Former Pres. Lazerenko was convicted in the U.S. of money laundering and fraud, June 2004.

Ukraine has about 1,300 troops in Iraq under Polish leadership.

United Arab Emirates

People: Population: 2,523,915. **Age distrib.** (%): <15: 27.7; 65+: 2.6. **Pop. density:** 79 per sq mi, 30 per sq km. **Urban:** 85.1%. **Ethnic groups:** Arab and Iranian 42%, Indian 50%. **Principal languages:** Arabic (official), Persian, English, Hindi, Urdu. **Chief religion:** Muslim 96% (official; Shi'a 16%).

Geography: Total area: 32,000 sq mi, 82,880 sq km; **Land area:** 32,000 sq mi, 82,880 sq km. **Location:** Middle East, on the S shore of the Persian Gulf. **Neighbors:** Saudi Arabia on W and S, Oman on E. **Topography:** A barren, flat coastal plain gives way to uninhabited sand dunes on the S. Hajar Mts. are on E. **Capital:** Abu Dhabi, 475,000.

Government: Type: Federation of emirates. **Head of state:** Pres. Zaid ibn Sultan an-Nahayan; b 1918; in office: Dec. 2, 1971. **Head of gov.:** Prime Min. Sheik Maktum ibn Rashid al-Maktum; b 1946; in office: Nov. 20, 1990. **Local divisions:** 7 autonomous emirates: Abu Dhabi, Ajman, Dubai, Fujaira, Ras al-Khaimah, Sharjah, Umm al-Qaiwain. **Defense budget** (2003): $1.6 bil. **Active troops:** 50,500.

Economy: Industries: oil, fishing, petrochems., constr. materials, boat building, handicrafts, pearling. **Chief crops:** dates, vegetables, watermelons. **Natural resources:** oil, nat. gas. **Crude oil reserves** (2003): 97.8 bil. bbls. **Livestock** (2003): cattle: 110,000; chickens: 12.7 mil.; goats: 1.45 mil.; sheep: 560,000. **Fish catch** (2002): 97,574 metric tons. **Electricity Prod.** (2002): 39.26 bil. kWh. **Labor force:** (2000 est.): services 78%, industry 15%, agriculture 7%.

Finance: Monetary unit: Dirham (AED) (Sept. 2004: 3.67=1 U.S.). **GDP** (2003 est.): $57.7 bil.; **per capita GDP:** $23,200; **GDP growth:** 5.2%. **Imports** (2003 est.): $37.2 bil.; partners (2002): Japan 8.7%, China 8.2%, U.S. 7.7%, UK 7.4%, Germany 7.1%, India 6.7%, France 6.6%, South Korea 5.3%, Italy 5.1%. **Exports** (2003 est.): $56.7 bil.; partners (2002): Japan 27.3%, South Korea 9.9%, Iran 4.3%. **Tourism:** $1.5 bil. **Budget** (2002 est.): $23.5 bil. **Intl. reserves less gold:** $10.1 bil. **Gold** (2002): 40,000 oz t.

Transport: Motor vehicles (1999): 346,300 pass. cars, 89,300 comm. vehicles. **Civil aviation:** 14.1 mil. pass.-mi; 22 airports. **Chief ports:** Ajman, Das Island.

Communications: TV sets: 309 per 1,000 pop. **Radios:** 355 per 1,000 pop. **Telephone lines:** 1.1 mil. **Daily newspaper circ.:** 156 per 1,000 pop. **Internet:** 1.1 mil. users.

Health: Life expect.: 72.5 male; 77.6 female. **Births** (per 1,000 pop.): 18.6. **Deaths** (per 1,000 pop.): 4.1. **Natural inc.:** 1.45%. **Infant mortality** (per 1,000 live births): 15.1.

Education: Compulsory: ages 6-11. **Literacy:** 77.9%.

Major Intl. Organizations: UN (FAO, IBRD, ILO, IMF, IMO, WHO, WTrO), AL, OPEC.

Embassy: 3522 International Ct. NW, Suite 400, 20008; 243-2400.

Websites: www.uae.gov.ae; www.uaeinteract.com

The 7 "Trucial Sheikdoms" gave Britain control of defense and foreign relations in the 19th century. They merged to become an independent state Dec. 2, 1971.

The Abu Dhabi Petroleum Co. was fully nationalized in 1975. Oil revenues have given the UAE one of the highest per capita GDPs in the world. International banking has grown in recent years.

United Kingdom
United Kingdom of Great Britain and Northern Ireland

People: Population: 60,270,708. **Age distrib.** (%): <15: 18.7; 65+: 15.8. **Pop. density:** 646 per sq mi, 249 per sq km. **Urban:** 89.1%. **Ethnic groups:** English 81.5%, Scottish 9.6%, Irish 2.4%, Welsh 1.9%, Ulster 1.9%, West Indian, Indo-Pakistani, and other 2.8%. **Principal languages:** English (official), Welsh and Scottish Gaelic. **Chief religions:** Christian 72%, Muslim 3%, many others.

Geography: Total area: 94,525 sq mi, 244,820 sq km; **Land area:** 93,278 sq mi, 241,590 sq km. **Location:** Off the NW coast of Europe, across English Channel, Strait of Dover, and North Sea. **Neighbors:** Ireland to W, France to SE. **Topography:** England is mostly rolling land, rising to Uplands of southern Scotland; Lowlands are in center of Scotland, granite Highlands are in N. Coast is heavily indented, especially on W. British Isles have milder climate than N Europe due to the Gulf Stream and ample rainfall. Severn, 220 mi., and Thames, 215 mi., are longest rivers. **Capital:** London, 7,619,000. **Cities (urban aggr.):** Birmingham, 2,243,000; Manchester, 2,223,000; Leeds, 1,417,000; Liverpool 924,000.

Government: Type: Constitutional monarchy. **Head of state:** Queen Elizabeth II; b Apr. 21, 1926; in office: Feb. 6, 1952. **Head of gov.:** Prime Min. Tony Blair; b May 6, 1953; in office: May 2, 1997. **Local divisions:** 467 local authorities, including England: 387; Wales: 22; Scotland: 32; Northern Ireland: 26. **Defense budget** (2003): $41.3 bil. **Active troops:** 212,660.

Economy: Industries: machine tools, electric power equip., automation equip., railroad equip., shipbuilding, aircraft, vehicles, electronics & comm. equip., metals, chemicals, coal, oil. **Chief crops:** cereals, oilseed, potatoes, vegetables. **Natural resources:** coal, oil, nat. gas, tin, limestone, iron ore, salt, clay, chalk, gypsum, lead, silica. **Crude oil reserves** (2003): 4.7 bil. bbls. **Arable land:** 25%. **Livestock** (2003): cattle: 10.46 mil.; chickens: 167.1 mil.; pigs: 5.05 mil.; sheep: 35.7 mil. **Fish catch** (2002 est): 868,955 metric tons. **Electricity Prod.** (2002): 360.8 bil. kWh. **Labor force** (1999): agriculture 1%, industry 25%, services 74%.

Finance: Monetary unit: Pound (GBP) (Sept. 2004: 0.56 = $1 U.S.). **GDP** (2003 est.): $1.664 tril.; **per capita GDP:** $27,700; **GDP growth:** 2.1%. **Imports** (2003 est.): $363.6 bil.; partners (2002): Germany 12.9%, U.S. 11.9%, France 7.8%, Netherlands 6.3%, Belgium 5%, Italy 4.4%. **Exports** (2003 est.): $304.5 bil.; partners (2002): U.S. 15.5%, Germany 11.2%, France 9.4%, Ireland 8%, Netherlands 7.1%, Belgium 5.2%, Italy 4.4%, Spain 4.3%. **Tourism:** $19.5 bil. **Budget** (FY01): $540.0 bil. **Intl. reserves less gold:** $28.16 bil. **Gold:** 10.07 mil oz t. **Consumer prices:** 2.9%.

Transport: Railroad: Length: 10,497 mi. **Motor vehicles** (1999): 24.59 mil pass. cars, 3.33 mil comm. vehicles. **Civil aviation:** 101.2 bil. pass.-mi; 334 airports. **Chief ports:** London, Liverpool, Cardiff, Belfast.

Communications: TV sets: 661 per 1,000 pop. **Radios:** 1,437 per 1,000 pop. **Telephone lines** (2002): 34.9 mil. **Daily newspaper circ.:** 329 per 1,000 pop. **Internet** (2002): 25.0 mil. users.

Health: Life expect.: 75.8 male; 80.8 female. **Births** (per 1,000 pop.): 10.9. **Deaths** (per 1,000 pop.): 10.2. **Natural inc.:** 0.07%. **Infant mortality** (per 1,000 live births): 5.2. **AIDS rate:** 0.2%.

Education: Compulsory: ages 5-16. **Literacy** (2000 est.): 99%.

Major Intl. Organizations: UN and all of its specialized agencies, the Commonwealth, EU, NATO, OECD, OSCE.

Embassy: 3100 Massachusetts Ave. NW 20008; 588-6500.

Website: www.britainusa.com

The United Kingdom of Great Britain and Northern Ireland comprises England, Wales, Scotland, and Northern Ireland.

Queen and Royal Family. The ruling sovereign is Elizabeth II of the House of Windsor, b Apr. 21, 1926, elder daughter of King George VI. She succeeded to the throne Feb. 6, 1952, and was crowned June 2, 1953. She was married Nov. 20, 1947, to Lt. Philip Mountbatten, b June 10, 1921, former Prince of Greece. He was created Duke of Edinburgh, and given the title H.R.H., Nov. 19, 1947; he was named Prince of the United Kingdom and Northern Ireland Feb. 22, 1957. Prince Charles Philip Arthur George, b Nov. 14, 1948, is the Prince of Wales and heir apparent. His 1st son, William Philip Arthur Louis, b June 21, 1982, is second in line to the throne.

Parliament is the legislative body for the UK, with certain powers over dependent units. It consists of 2 houses: The **House of Commons** has 659 members, elected by direct ballot and divided as follows: England 529; Wales 40; Scotland 72; Northern Ireland 18. Following a drastic reduction in the number of hereditary peerages, the **House of Lords** (July 2004) comprised 91 hereditary peers, 586 life peers, and 2 archbishops and 24 bishops of the Church of England, for a total of 703.

Resources and Industries. Great Britain's major occupations are manufacturing and trade. Metals and metal-using industries contribute more than 50% of exports. Of about 60 million acres of land in England, Wales, and Scotland, 46 million are farmed, of which 17 million are arable, the rest pastures.

Large oil and gas fields have been found in the North Sea. Commercial oil production began in 1975. There are large deposits of coal.

Britain imports all of its cotton, rubber, sulphur, about 80% of its wool, half of its food and iron ore, also certain amounts of paper, tobacco, chemicals. Manufactured goods made from these basic materials have been exported since the industrial age began. Main exports are machinery, chemicals, textiles, clothing, autos and trucks, iron and steel, locomotives, ships, jet aircraft, farm machinery, drugs, radio, TV, radar and navigation equipment, scientific instruments, arms, whisky.

Religion and Education. The Church of England is Protestant Episcopal. The queen is its temporal head, with rights of appointments to archbishoprics, bishoprics, and other offices. There are 2 provinces, Canterbury and York, each headed by an archbishop. The most famous church is Westminster Abbey (1050-1760), site of coronations, tombs of Elizabeth I, Mary, Queen of Scots, kings, poets, and of the Unknown Warrior.

The most celebrated British universities are Oxford and Cambridge, each dating to the 13th century. There are about 70 other universities.

History. Britain was part of the continent of Europe until about 6,000 BC, but migration across the English Channel continued long afterward. Celts arrived 2,500 to 3,000 years ago. Their language survives in Welsh, and Gaelic enclaves.

England was added to the Roman Empire in AD 43. After the withdrawal of Roman legions in 410, waves of Jutes, Angles, and Saxons arrived from German lands. They contended with Danish raiders for control from the 8th through 11th centuries. The last successful invasion was by French speaking Normans in 1066, who united the country with their dominions in France.

Opposition by nobles to royal authority forced King John to sign the Magna Carta in 1215, a guarantee of rights and the rule of law. In the ensuing decades, the foundations of the parliamentary system were laid.

English dynastic claims to large parts of France led to the Hundred Years War, 1338-1453, and the defeat of England. A long civil war, the War of the Roses, lasted 1455-85, and ended with the establishment of the powerful Tudor monarchy. A distinct English civilization flourished. The economy prospered over long periods of domestic peace unmatched in continental Europe. Religious independence was secured when the Church of England was separated from the authority of the pope in 1534.

Under Queen Elizabeth I, England became a major naval power, leading to the founding of colonies in the new world and the expansion of trade with Europe and the Orient. Scotland was united with England when James VI of Scotland was crowned James I of England in 1603.

A struggle between Parliament and the Stuart kings led to a bloody civil war, 1642-49, and the establishment of a republic under the Puritan Oliver Cromwell. The monarchy was restored in 1660, but the "Glorious Revolution" of 1688 confirmed the sovereignty of Parliament: a Bill of Rights was granted 1689.

In the 18th century, parliamentary rule was strengthened. Technological and entrepreneurial innovations led to the Industrial Revolution. The 13 North American colonies were lost, but replaced by growing empires in Canada and India. Britain's role in the defeat of Napoleon, 1815, strengthened its position as the leading world power.

The extension of the franchise in 1832 and 1867, the formation of trade unions, and the development of universal public education were among the drastic social changes that accompanied the spread of industrialization and urbanization in the 19th century. Large parts of Africa and Asia were added to the empire during the reign of Queen Victoria, 1837-1901.

Though victorious in World War I, Britain suffered huge casualties and economic dislocation. Ireland became independent in 1921, and independence movements became active in India and other colonies. The country suffered major bombing damage in World War II, but held out against Germany single-handedly for a year after France fell in 1940.

Industrial growth continued in the postwar period, but Britain lost its leadership position to other powers. Labor governments passed socialist programs nationalizing some basic industries and expanding social security. Prime Min. Margaret Thatcher's Conservative government, however, tried to increase the role of private enterprise. In 1987, Thatcher became the first British leader in 160 years to be elected to a 3rd consecutive term as prime minister. Falling on unpopular times, she resigned as prime minister in Nov. 1990. Her successor, John Major, led Conservatives to an upset victory at the polls, Apr. 9, 1992.

The UK supported the UN resolutions against Iraq and sent military forces to the Persian Gulf War. The Channel Tunnel linking Britain to the Continent was inaugurated May 6, 1994. Britain's relations with the European Union, and France especially, were frayed in 1996 when the EU banned British beef because of the threat of "mad cow" disease.

On May 1, 1997, the Labour Party swept into power in a landslide victory, the largest of any party since 1935. Labour Party leader Tony Blair, 43, became Britain's youngest prime minister since 1812. Diana, Princess of Wales, died in a car crash in Paris, Aug. 31. Britain played a leading role in the NATO air war against Yugoslavia, Mar.-June 1999, and contributed 12,000 troops to the multinational security force in Kosovo (KFOR).

Blair led Labour to another landslide election victory June 7, 2001. After the Sept. 11 attack on the U.S., Britain took an important role in the U.S.-led war against terrorism. The U.K. participated in the bombing of Afghanistan that began Oct. 7.

Overcoming dissent within his own cabinet, Blair committed British troops to the U.S.-led invasion of Iraq, Mar.-Apr. 2003. Forces from the U.K. then remained to occupy S Iraq. Blair's credibility was challenged after the death of arms expert David Kelly fueled controversy over whether a prewar dossier about Iraq's weapons capabilities had been modified to provide a rationale for war. Parliamentary and judicial panels probed the affair; an inquiry headed by Lord Butler concluded, July 14, 2004, that prewar intelligence was faulty but that the available evidence had not been deliberately distorted.

Wales

The Principality of Wales in western Britain has an area of 8,019 sq. mi. and a population (2003 est.) of 2,938,200. Cardiff is the capital, pop. (2001 est.; city proper) 305,000.

Less than 20% of Wales residents speak English and Welsh; about 32,000 speak Welsh solely. A 1979 referendum rejected, 4-1, the creation of an elected Welsh assembly; a similar proposal passed by a thin margin on Sept. 18, 1997. Elections for the 60-seat assembly were held May 6, 1999, and May 1, 2003.

Early Anglo-Saxon invaders drove Celtic peoples into the mountains of Wales, terming them Waelise (Welsh, or foreign). There they developed a distinct nationality. Members of the ruling house of Gwynedd in the 13th century fought England but were crushed, 1283. Edward of Caernarvon, son of Edward I of England, was created Prince of Wales, 1301.

Scotland

Scotland, a kingdom now united with England and Wales in Great Britain, occupies the northern 37% of the main British island, and the Hebrides, Orkney, Shetland, and smaller islands. Length 275 mi., breadth approx. 150 mi., area 30,418 sq. mi., population (2003 est) 5,057,400.

The Lowlands, a belt of land approximately 60 mi. wide from the Firth of Clyde to the Firth of Forth, divide the farming region of the Southern Uplands from the granite Highlands of the North; they contain 75% of the population and most of the industry. The Highlands, famous for hunting and fishing, have been opened to industry by many hydroelectric power stations.

Edinburgh, pop. (2001 est., city proper) 449,000, is the capital. Glasgow, pop. (2001 est.; city proper) 579,000, is Britain's greatest industrial center. It is a shipbuilding complex on the Clyde and an ocean port. Aberdeen, pop. (1996 est.) 227,430, NE of Edinburgh, is a major port, center of granite industry, fish-processing, and North Sea oil exploration. Dundee, pop. (1996 est.) 150,250, NE of Edinburgh, is an industrial and fish-processing center. About 90,000 persons speak Gaelic as well as English.

History. Scotland was called Caledonia by the Romans who battled early Celtic tribes and occupied southern areas from the 1st to the 4th centuries. Missionaries from Britain introduced Christianity in the 4th century; St. Columba, an Irish monk, converted most of Scotland in the 6th century.

The Kingdom of Scotland was founded in 1018. William Wallace and Robert Bruce both defeated English armies 1297 and 1314, respectively.

In 1603 James VI of Scotland, son of Mary, Queen of Scots, succeeded to the throne of England as James I, and effected the Union of the Crowns. In 1707 Scotland received representation in the British Parliament, resulting from the union of former separate Parliaments. Its executive in the British cabinet is the Secretary of State for Scotland. The growing Scottish National Party urges independence. A 1979 referendum on the creation of an elected Scottish assembly was defeated, but a proposal to create a regional legislature with limited taxing authority passed by a landslide Sept. 11, 1997. Elections for the 129-seat parliament were held May 6, 1999, and May 1, 2003.

Memorials of Robert Burns, Sir Walter Scott, John Knox, and Mary, Queen of Scots, draw many tourists, as do the beauties of the Trossachs, Loch Katrine, Loch Lomond, and abbey ruins.

Industries. Engineering products are the most important industry, with growing emphasis on office machinery, autos, electronics, and other consumer goods. Oil has been discovered offshore in the North Sea, stimulating on-shore support industries.

Scotland produces fine woolens, worsteds, tweeds, silks, fine linens, and jute. It is known for its special breeds of cattle and sheep. Fisheries have large hauls of herring, cod, whiting. Whisky is the biggest export.

The Hebrides are a group of c. 500 islands, 100 inhabited, off the W coast. The Inner Hebrides include **Skye, Mull,** and **Iona,** the last famous for the arrival of St. Columba, AD 563. The Outer Hebrides include **Lewis** and **Harris.** Industries include sheep raising and weaving. The **Orkney Islands,** c. 90, are to the NE. The capital is Kirkwall, on Pomona Isl. Fish curing, sheep raising, and weaving are occupations. NE of the Orkneys are the 200 **Shetland Islands,** 24 inhabited, home of Shetland pony. The Orkneys and Shetlands are centers for the North Sea oil industry.

Northern Ireland

Northern Ireland was constituted in 1920 from 6 of the 9 counties of Ulster, the NE corner of Ireland. Area 5,452 sq. mi., pop. (2003 est) 1,702,600. Capital and chief industrial center, Belfast, pop. (2001 est.; city proper) 277,000.

Industries. Shipbuilding, including large tankers, has long been an important industry, centered in Belfast, the largest port. Linen manufacture is also important, along with apparel, rope, and twine. Growing diversification has added engineering products, synthetic fibers, and electronics. There are large numbers of cattle, hogs, and sheep. Potatoes, poultry, and dairy foods are also produced.

Government. An act of the British Parliament, 1920, divided Northern from Southern Ireland, each with a parliament and government. When Ireland became a dominion, 1921, and later a republic, Northern Ireland chose to remain a part of the United Kingdom. It elects 18 members to the House of Commons.

During 1968-69, large demonstrations were conducted by Roman Catholics who charged they were discriminated against in voting rights, housing, and employment. The Catholics, a minority comprising about a third of the population, demanded abolition of property qualifications for voting in local elections. Violence and terrorism intensified, involving branches of the Irish Republican Army (outlawed in the Irish Republic), Protestant groups, police, and British troops.

A succession of Northern Ireland prime ministers pressed reform programs but failed to satisfy extremists on both sides. Between 1969 and 1994 more than 3,000 were killed in sectarian violence, many in England itself. Britain suspended the Northern Ireland parliament Mar. 30, 1972, and imposed direct British rule. A coalition government was formed in 1973 when moderates won election to a new one-house Assembly. But a Protestant general strike overthrew the government in 1974 and direct rule was resumed.

The agony of Northern Ireland was dramatized in 1981 by the deaths of 10 Irish nationalist hunger strikers in Maze Prison near Belfast. In 1985 the Hillsborough agreement gave the Rep. of Ireland a voice in the governing of Northern Ireland; the accord was strongly opposed by Ulster loyalists. On Dec. 12, 1993, Britain and Ireland announced a declaration of principles to resolve the Northern Ireland conflict.

On Aug. 31, 1994, the IRA announced a cease-fire, saying it would rely on political means to achieve its objectives; the IRA resumed its terrorist tactics on Feb. 9, 1996. Reinstatement of the IRA cease-fire as of July 20, 1997, led to the resumption of peace talks Sept. 15.

A settlement reached on Good Friday, April 10, 1998, provided for restoration of home rule and election of a 108-member assembly with safeguards for minority rights. Both Ireland and Great Britain agreed to give up their constitutional claims on Northern Ireland. The accord was approved May 22 by voters in Northern Ireland and the Irish Republic, and elections to the assembly were held June 25. IRA dissidents seeking to derail the agreement were responsible for a bomb at Omagh Aug. 15 that killed 29 people and injured over 330.

London transferred authority to a Northern Ireland power-sharing government Dec. 2, 1999. Delays in IRA disarmament led to several suspensions of self-government, most recently from Oct. 15, 2002.

Education and Religion. Northern Ireland is about 58% Protestant, 42% Roman Catholic. Education is compulsory between the ages of 5 and 16 years.

Channel Islands

The Channel Islands, area 75 sq. mi., pop. (2003 est.) 145,000, off the NW coast of France, the only parts of the one-time Dukedom of Normandy belonging to England, are Jersey, Guernsey and the dependencies of Guernsey—Alderney, Brechou, Great Sark, Little Sark, Herm, Jethou and Lihou. Jersey, pop. (2004 est.) 90,502, and Guernsey, pop. (2004 est.) 65,031, have separate legal existences and lieutenant governors named by the Crown. The islands were the only British soil occupied by German troops in World War II.

Isle of Man

The Isle of Man, area 220.9 sq. mi., pop. (2004 est.) 74,655, is in the Irish Sea, 20 mi. from Scotland, 30 mi. from Cumberland. It is rich in lead and iron. The island has its own laws and a lieutenant governor appointed by the Crown. The Tynwald (legislature) consists of the Legislative Council, partly elected, and House of Keys, elected. Capital: Douglas. Farming, tourism, and fishing (kippers, scallops) are chief occupations. Man is famous for the Manx tailless cat.

Gibraltar

Gibraltar, a dependency on the southern coast of Spain, guards the entrance to the Mediterranean. The Rock of Gibraltar has been in British possession since 1704. The Rock is 2.5 mi. long, 3/4 of a mi. wide and 1,396 ft. in height; a narrow isthmus connects it with the mainland. Pop. (2004 est.) 27,833.

Gibraltar has historically been an object of contention between Britain and Spain. Residents voted with near unanimity to remain under British rule, in a 1967 referendum held in pursuance of a UN resolution on decolonization. A new constitution, May 30, 1969, increased Gibraltarian control of domestic affairs (the UK continues to handle defense and internal security matters). Following a 1984 agreement between Britain and Spain, the border, closed by Spain in 1969, was fully reopened in Feb. 1985. A UN General Assembly resolution requested Britain to end Gibraltar's colonial status by Oct. 1, 1996. A plan for the U.K. and Spain to share sovereignty was rejected by Gibraltar voters, Nov. 7, 2002.

British West Indies

Swinging in a vast arc from the coast of Venezuela NE, then N and NW toward Puerto Rico are the Leeward Islands, forming a coral and volcanic barrier sheltering the Caribbean from the open Atlantic. Many of the islands are self-governing British possessions. Universal suffrage was instituted 1951-54; ministerial systems were set up 1956-1960.

The **Leeward Islands** still associated with the UK are **Montserrat**, area 39.4 sq. mi., pop. (2004 est.) 9,245, capital Plymouth; the **British Virgin Islands**, 59.1 sq. mi., pop. (2004 est.) 22,187, capital Road Town; and **Anguilla**, the most northerly of the Leeward Islands, 39.4 sq. mi., pop. (2004 est.) 13,008, capital The Valley. Montserrat has been devastated by the Soufrière Hills volcano, which began erupting July 18, 1995.

The three **Cayman Islands**, a dependency, lie S of Cuba, NW of Jamaica. Pop. (2004 est.) 43,103, most of it on Grand Cayman. It is a free port; in the 1970s Grand Cayman became a tax-free refuge for foreign funds and branches of many Western banks were opened there. Total area 101.2 sq. mi., capital Georgetown.

The **Turks and Caicos Islands** are a dependency at the SE end of the Bahama Islands. Of about 30 islands, only 6 are inhabited; area 166 sq. mi., pop. (2004 est.) 19,956; capital Grand Turk. Salt, shellfish, and conch shells are the main exports.

Bermuda

Bermuda is a British dependency governed by a royal governor and an assembly, dating from 1620, the oldest legislative body among British dependencies. Capital is Hamilton.

It is a group of about 150 small islands of coral formation, 20 inhabited, comprising 20.6 sq. mi. in the western Atlantic, 580 mi. E of North Carolina. Pop. (2004 est.) 64,935 (about 61% of African descent). Pop. density is high.

The U.S. maintains a NASA tracking facility; a U.S. naval air base was closed in 1995.

Tourism is the major industry; Bermuda boasts many resort hotels. The government raises most revenue from import duties. Exports: petroleum products, medicine. In a referendum Aug. 15, 1995, voters rejected independence by nearly a 3-to-1 majority.

Hurricane Fabian, the most potent storm to reach Bermuda in 50 years, struck Sept. 5, 2003; 4 people were missing and presumed dead, and damage was estimated at over $300 million.

South Atlantic

The **Falkland Islands**, a dependency, lie 300 mi. E of the Strait of Magellan at the southern end of South America.

The Falklands or Islas Malvinas include 2 large islands and about 200 smaller ones, area 4,700 sq. mi., pop. (2004 est.) 2,967, capital Stanley. The licensing of foreign fishing vessels has become the major source of revenue. Sheep-grazing is a main industry; wool is the principal export. There are indications of large oil and gas deposits. The islands are also claimed by Argentina, though 97% of inhabitants are of British origin. Argentina invaded the islands Apr. 2, 1982. The British responded by sending a task force to the area, landing their main force on the Falklands, May 21, and forcing an Argentine surrender at Port Stanley, June 14. A pact resuming commercial air service with Argentina was signed July 14, 1999.

British Antarctic Territory, south of 60° S lat., formerly a dependency of the Falkland Isls., was made a separate colony in 1962 and includes the **South Shetland Islands,** the **South Orkneys,** and the Antarctic Peninsula. A chain of meteorological stations is maintained.

South Georgia and the South Sandwich Islands, formerly administered by the Falklands Isls., became a separate dependency in 1985. South Georgia, 1507 sq mi, with no permanent population, is about 800 mi SE of the Falklands; the South Sandwich Isls., 130 sq mi, are uninhabited, about 470 mi SE of South Georgia.

St. Helena, an island 1,200 mi. off the W. coast of Africa and 1,800 mi. E of South America, 158 sq. mi. and pop. (2004 est.) 7,415. Flax, lace, and rope-making are the chief industries. After Napoleon Bonaparte was defeated at Waterloo the Allies exiled him to St. Helena, where he lived from Oct. 16, 1815, to his death, May 5, 1821. Capital is Jamestown.

Tristan da Cunha is the principal of a group of islands of volcanic origin, total area 40 sq. mi., halfway between the Cape of Good Hope and South America. A volcanic peak 6,760 ft. high erupted in 1961. The 262 inhabitants were removed to England, but most returned in 1963. The islands are dependencies of St. Helena. Pop. (2002) 284.

Ascension is an island of volcanic origin, 34 sq mi in area, 700 mi. NW of St. Helena, through which it is administered. It is a communications relay center for Britain, and has a U.S. satellite tracking center. Pop. (2002) was 1,050, half of them communications workers. The island is noted for sea turtles.

Hong Kong
(See China/Hong Kong*)*

British Indian Ocean Territory

Formed Nov. 1965, embracing islands formerly dependencies of Mauritius or Seychelles: the Chagos Archipelago (including Diego Garcia), Aldabra, Farquhar, and Des Roches. The latter 3 were transferred to Seychelles, which became independent in 1976. Area 23 sq. mi. No permanent civilian population remains; the U.K. and the U.S. maintain a military presence.

Pacific Ocean

Pitcairn Island is in the Pacific, halfway between South America and Australia. The island was discovered in 1767 by Philip Carteret but was not inhabited until 23 years later when the mutineers of the *Bounty* landed there. The area is 18 sq. mi. and 2004 pop. was 46. It is a British dependency and is administered by a British High Commissioner in New Zealand and a local Council. The uninhabited islands of **Henderson, Ducie,** and **Oeno** are in the Pitcairn group.

United States
United States of America

People: Population: 293,027,571. (incl. 50 states & Dist. of Columbia). (Note: U.S. pop. figures may differ elsewhere in *The World Almanac.*) **Age distrib.** (%): <15: 21; 65+: 12.6. **Pop. density:** 83 per sq mi, 32 per sq km. **Urban:** 80.1%. **Ethnic groups:** White 75.1%, Black 12.3%, Asian 3.6%, Amerindian and Alaska native 0.9%. (Hispanics of any race or group 12.5%.) **Principal languages:** English, Spanish. **Chief religions:** Protestant 56%, Roman Catholic 28%, Jewish 2%

Geography: Total area: 3,718,709 sq mi, 9,631,418 sq km; **Land area:** 3,537,437 sq mi, 9,161,923 sq km. **Topography:** Vast central plain, mountains in west, hills and low mountains in east. **Capital:** Washington, D.C., 4,098,000

Government: Federal republic, strong democratic tradition. **Head of state and gov.:** Pres. George W. Bush; b July 6, 1946; in office: Jan. 20, 2001. **Local divisions:** 50 states and Dist. of Columbia. **Defense budget** (2003): $382.7 bil. **Active troops:** 1,427,000.

Economy: Industries: oil, steel, motor vehicles, aerospace, telecom., chemicals, electronics, food proc., consumer goods, lumber, mining. **Chief crops:** wheat, corn, fruits, vegetables, cotton. **Natural resources:** coal, copper, lead, molybd., phosphates, uranium, bauxite, gold, iron, mercury, nickel, potash, silver, tungsten, zinc, oil, nat. gas, timber. **Crude oil reserves** (2003): 22.7 bil. bbls. **Arable land:** 19%. **Livestock** (2003): cattle: 96.1 mil.; chickens: 1.95 mil.; goats: 1.2 mil.; pigs: 59.5 mil.; sheep: 6.30 mil. **Fish catch** (2002): 5,434,651 metric tons. **Electricity prod.** (2002): 3,838.55 bil. kWh. **Labor force** (2001): managerial, professional, and technical 31%, sales and office 28.9%, services 13.6%, manufacturing, extraction, transportation, and crafts 24.1%, farming, forestry, and fishing 2.4%.

Finance: GDP (2003 est.): $10.98 tril.; **per capita GDP:** $37,800; **GDP growth:** 3.1%. **Imports** (2003 est.): $1.3 trillion; partners (2002): Canada 17.8%, Mexico 11.3%, China 11.1%, Japan 10.4%, Germany 5.3%. **Exports** (2003 est.): $714.5 bil.; partners (2002): Canada 23.2%, Mexico 14.1%, Japan 7.4%, UK 4.8%. **Tourism:** $65.1 bil. **Budget** (2002): $2.1 tril. **Intl. reserves less gold:** $50.40 bil. **Gold:** 262 mil oz t. **Consumer prices:** 2.3%.

Transport: Railroad: Length: 121,000 mi. **Motor vehicles** (2001): 221.82 mil pass. cars, 8.6 mil comm. vehicles. **Civil aviation:** 190.1 bil. pass.-mi; 5,131 airports.

Communications: TV sets: 844 per 1,000 pop. **Radios:** 2,116 per 1,000 pop. **Telephone lines:** 181.6 mil. **Daily newspaper circ.:** 212 per 1,000 pop. **Internet** (2002): 159.0 mil. users.

Health: Life expect.: 74.6 male; 80.4 female. **Births** (per 1,000 pop.): 14.1. **Deaths** (per 1,000 pop.): 8.3. **Natural inc.:** 0.58%. **Infant mortality** (per 1,000 live births): 6.6. **AIDS rate:** 0.6%.

Education: Free, compulsory: ages 6-17. **Literacy** (1994): 97%.

Major Intl. Organizations: UN (FAO, IBRD, ILO, IMF, IMO, WHO, WTrO), APEC, NATO, OAS, OECD, OSCE.

Websites: www.census.gov; www.whitehouse.gov
www.firstgov.gov

See also **United States History chapter.**

Uruguay
Oriental Republic of Uruguay

People: Population: 3,399,237. **Age distrib.** (%): <15: 24.4; 65+: 13. **Pop. density:** 51 per sq mi, 20 per sq km. **Urban:** 92.6%. **Ethnic groups:** White 88%, Mestizo 8%, Black 4%. **Principal languages:** Spanish (official), Portunol/Brazilero (Portuguese-Spanish). **Chief religion:** Roman Catholic 66%.

Geography: Total area: 68,039 sq mi, 176,220 sq km; **Land area:** 67,035 sq mi, 173,620 sq km. **Location:** In southern South America, on the Atlantic O. **Neighbors:** Argentina on W, Brazil on N. **Topography:** Uruguay is composed of rolling, grassy plains and hills, well watered by rivers flowing W to Uruguay R. **Capital:** Montevideo, 1,341,000.

Government: Type: Republic. **Head of state and gov.:** Pres. Jorge Batlle Ibáñez; b Oct. 25, 1927; in office: Mar. 1, 2000. **Local divisions:** 19 departments. **Defense budget** (2003): $170 mil. **Active troops:** 24,000.

Economy: Industries: food proc., electrical machinery, transp. equip., oil products, textiles. **Chief crops:** rice, wheat, corn, barley. **Natural resources:** hydropower, minor minerals, fisheries. **Arable land:** 7%. **Livestock** (2003): cattle: 11.69 mil.; chickens: 13.3 mil.; goats: 16,000; pigs: 240,000; sheep: 9.78 mil. **Fish catch** (2002): 108,782 metric tons. **Electricity prod.** (2002): 9.08 bil. kWh. **Labor force:** agriculture 14%, industry 16%, services 70%.

Finance: Monetary unit: Peso (UYP) (Sept. 2004: 27.73=1 U.S.). **GDP** (2003 est.): $42.9 bil.; **per capita GDP:** $12,600; **GDP growth:** 0.3%. **Imports** (2003 est.): $2.0 bil.; partners (2002): Ar-

gentina 23.1%, Brazil 17.5%, U.S. 8.9%, Mexico 4.7%, China 4%. **Exports** (2003 est.): $2.2 bil.; partners (2002): Brazil 22.1%, U.S. 8.4%, Germany 5.4%, Argentina 5.1%, Mexico 4.2%, Italy 4.1%, Paraguay 4.1%, Spain 4%. **Tourism:** $318 mil. **Budget** (2002): $3.4 bil. **Intl. reserves less gold:** $1.4 bil. **Gold:** 10,000 oz t. **Consumer prices:** 19.4%.

Transport: Railroad: Length: 1,288 mi. **Motor vehicles** (2000): 652,300 pass. cars, 56,100 comm. vehicles. **Civil aviation:** 464.2 mil. pass.-mi; 15 airports. **Chief port:** Montevideo.

Communications: TV sets: 531 per 1,000 pop. **Radios:** 603 per 1,000 pop. **Telephone lines** (2002): 946,500. **Daily newspaper circ.:** 293 per 1,000 pop. **Internet** (2001): 400,000 users.

Health: Life expect.: 72.7 male; 79.2 female. **Births** (per 1,000 pop.): 14.4. **Deaths** (per 1,000 pop.): 9.1. **Natural inc.:** 0.54%. **Infant mortality** (per 1,000 live births): 12.3. **AIDS rate:** 0.3%.

Education: Compulsory: ages 6-15. **Literacy:** 98%.

Major Intl. Organizations: UN (FAO, IBRD, ILO, IMF, IMO, WHO, WTrO), OAS.

Embassy: 1913 I St. NW, 20006; 331-1313.

Website: www.uruwashi.org

Spanish settlers began to supplant the indigenous Charrua Indians in 1624. Portuguese from Brazil arrived later, but Uruguay was attached to the Spanish Viceroyalty of Rio de la Plata in the 18th century. Rebels fought against Spain beginning in 1810. An independent republic was declared Aug. 25, 1825.

Terrorist activities led Pres. Juan María Bordaberry to agree to military control of his administration Feb. 1973. In June he abolished Congress and set up a Council of State in its place. Bordaberry was removed by the military in a 1976 coup. Civilian government was restored in 1985.

Socialist measures were adopted in the early 1900s. The state retains a dominant role in the power, telephone, railroad, cement, oil-refining, and other industries, although some privatization began in the early 2000s. Uruguay's standard of living remains one of the highest in South America, and political and labor conditions among the freest.

Uzbekistan
Republic of Uzbekistan

People: Population: 26,410,416. **Age distrib.** (%): <15: 35.5; 65+: 4.7. **Pop. density:** 161 per sq mi, 62 per sq km. **Urban:** 36.6%. **Ethnic groups:** Uzbek 80%, Russian 6%, Tajik 5%, Kazakh 3%, Karakalpak 3%, Tatar 2%. **Principal languages:** Uzbek (official), Russian, Tajik. **Chief religions:** Muslim 88% (mostly Sunni), Eastern Orthodox 9%.

Geography: Total area: 172,742 sq mi, 447,400 sq km; **Land area:** 164,248 sq mi, 425,400 sq km. **Location:** Central Asia. **Neighbors:** Kazakhstan on N and W, Kyrgyzstan and Tajikistan on E, Afghanistan and Turkmenistan on S. **Topography:** Mostly plains and desert. **Capital:** Tashkent, 2,155,000.

Government: Type: Republic. **Head of state:** Pres. Islam A. Karimov; b Jan. 30, 1938; in office: Mar. 24, 1990. **Head of gov.:** Prime Min. Shavkat Mirziyaev; b 1957; in office: Dec. 11, 2003. **Local divisions:** 12 regions, 1 autonomous republic, 1 city. **Defense budget** (2003): $46 mil. **Active troops:** 50,000–55,000.

Economy: Industries: textiles, food proc., machine building, metallurgy, nat. gas, chemicals. **Chief crops:** cotton, vegetables, fruits, grain. **Natural resources:** nat. gas, oil, coal, gold, uranium, silver, copper, lead, zinc, tungsten, molybd. **Crude oil reserves** (2003): 594.0 mil. bbls. **Arable land:** 11%. **Livestock** (2003): cattle: 5.4 mil.; chickens: 14.5 mil.; goats: 820,000; pigs: 90,000; sheep: 8.2 mil. **Fish catch** (2002): 7,121 metric tons. **Electricity prod.** (2002): 47.7 bil. kWh. **Labor force** (1995): agriculture 44%, industry 20%, services 36%.

Finance: Monetary unit: Som (UZS) (Sept. 2004: 1,031.95=1 U.S.). **GDP** (2003 est.): $44.1 bil.; **per capita GDP:** $1,700; **GDP growth:** 3.4%. **Imports** (2003 est.): $2.3 bil.; partners (2002): Russia 24%, Germany 10.8%, South Korea 10%, U.S. 7.3%, China 5.5%, Kazakhstan 5.3%, Turkey 4.9%. **Exports** (2003 est.): $2.8 bil.; partners (2002): Russia 19.9%, Italy 8.6%, Tajikistan 7.7%, South Korea 5.6%, Kazakhstan 5.1%, U.S. 4.7%, Turkey 4.4%, Japan 4.3%. **Tourism:** $48 mil. **Budget** (2003 est.): $2.5 bil.

Transport: Railroad: Length: 2,454 mi. **Motor vehicles:** 865,000 pass. cars, 14,500 comm. vehicles. **Civil aviation:** 2.1 bil. pass.-mi; 27 airports. **Chief port:** Termiz.

Communications: TV sets: 280 per 1,000 pop. **Radios:** 465 per 1,000 pop. **Telephone lines:** 1.7 mil. **Daily newspaper circ.:** 3.3 per 1,000 pop. **Internet:** 492,000 users.

Health: Life expect.: 60.7 male; 67.7 female. **Births** (per 1,000 pop.): 26.1. **Deaths** (per 1,000 pop.): 8.0. **Natural inc.:** 1.82%. **Infant mortality** (per 1,000 live births): 71.3. **AIDS rate:** 0.1%.

Education: Compulsory: ages 7-15. **Literacy:** 99.3%.

Major Intl. Organizations: UN (IBRD, ILO, IMF, WHO), CIS, OSCE.

Embassy: 1746 Massachusetts Ave. NW 20036; 887-5300.

The region was overrun by the Mongols under Genghis Khan in 1220. In the 14th century, Uzbekistan became the center of a native empire—that of the Timurids. In later centuries Muslim feudal states emerged. Russian military conquest began in the 19th century.

Websites: www.uzbekistan.org
    travel.state.gov/travel/uzbekistan.html

The Uzbek SSR became a Soviet Union republic in 1925. Uzbekistan declared independence Aug. 29, 1991. It became an independent republic when the Soviet Union disbanded Dec. 26, 1991. Since then, the authoritarian government of Uzbekistan has been led by a former Communist. U.S. forces used Uzbek bases during the Afghanistan war, 2001. A pact tightening military and economic ties with the U.S. was signed Mar. 12, 2002.

Attacks by Islamic militants, Mar.-July 2004, killed more than 50 people. Citing lack of progress on human rights, the U.S., July 13, cut $18 million in aid to Uzbekistan. In June 2004, Russia's 2nd largest oil producer, OAO Lukoil, signed a $1 billion agreement with the govt to develop its natural gas fields. Militants bombed the U.S. and Israeli embassies in Tashkent, July 31.

Vanuatu
Republic of Vanuatu

People: Population: 202,609. **Age distrib.** (%): <15: 35.6; 65+: 3.3. **Pop. density:** 43 per sq mi, 17 per sq km. **Urban:** 22.8%. **Ethnic groups:** Melanesian 98%, French, Vietnamese, Chinese, other Pacific Islanders. **Principal languages:** Bislama, English, French (all official); more than 100 local languages. **Chief religions:** Presbyterian 37%, Anglican 15%, Roman Catholic 15%, indigenous beliefs 8%, other Christian 10%.

Geography: Total area: 4,710 sq mi, 12,200 sq km; **Land area:** 4,710 sq mi, 12,200 sq km. **Location:** SW Pacific, 1,200 mi. NE of Brisbane, Australia. **Neighbors:** Fiji to E, Solomon Isls. to NW. **Topography:** Dense forest with narrow coastal strips of cultivated land. **Capital:** Port-Vila, 34,000.

Government: Type: Republic. **Head of state:** Pres. Kalkot Mataskelekele; in office: Aug. 16, 2004. **Head of gov.:** Prime Min. Serge Vohor; b 1955; in office: July 29, 2004. **Local divisions:** 6 provinces

Economy: Industries: food & fish freezing, wood proc., meat canning. **Chief crops:** copra, coconuts, cocoa, coffee, taro, yams. **Natural resources:** mang., timber, fish. **Arable land:** 2%. **Livestock** (2003): cattle: 130,000; chickens: 340,000; goats: 12,000; pigs: 62,000. **Fish catch** (2002 est): 17,139 metric tons. **Electricity prod.** (2002): 0.05 bil. kWh. **Labor force:** (2000 est.): agriculture 65%, services 30%, industry 5%.

Finance: Monetary unit: Vatu (VUV) (Sept. 2004: 115.05=1 U.S.). **GDP** (2002 est.): $563.0 mil.; **per capita GDP:** $2,900; **GDP growth:** –0.3%. **Imports** (2002): $138.0 mil.; partners (2002): Australia 21%, Japan 18.8%, New Zealand 9.4%, Singapore 8%, Fiji 6.5%, India 5.1%. **Exports** (2002): $79.0 mil.; partners (2002): India 32.9%, Thailand 22.8%, South Korea 10.1%, Indonesia 6.3%, Japan 5.1%. **Tourism** (2001): $46 mil. **Budget** (1996 est.): $99.8 mil. **Intl. reserves less gold:** $29 mil. **Consumer prices** (change in 2002): 2.0%.

Transport: Motor vehicles: (1999): 2,600 pass. cars, 4,100 comm. vehicles. **Civil aviation:** 137.3 mil. pass.-mi; 3 airports. **Chief ports:** Forai, Port-Vila.

Communications: TV sets: 12 per 1,000 pop. **Radios:** 350 per 1,000 pop. **Telephone lines:** 6,500. **Internet:** 7,500 users.

Health: Life expect.: 60.6 male; 63.6 female. **Births** (per 1,000 pop.): 23.7. **Deaths** (per 1,000 pop.): 8.0. **Natural inc.:** 1.56%. **Infant mortality** (per 1,000 live births): 56.6.

Education: Compulsory: ages 6-12. **Literacy** (1997): 53%.

Major Intl. Organizations: UN (FAO, IBRD, IMF, IMO, WHO), the Commonwealth.

Website: www.vanuatugovernment.gov.vu

The Anglo-French condominium of the New Hebrides, administered jointly by France and Great Britain since 1906, became the independent Republic of Vanuatu on July 30, 1980.

Vatican City (The Holy See)

People: Population: 921. **Urban:** 100%. **Ethnic groups:** Italian, Swiss, other. **Principal languages:** Latin (official), Italian, French, Monastic Sign Language, various others. **Chief religion:** Roman Catholic.

Geography: Area: (total): 108.7 acres. **Location:** In Rome, Italy. **Neighbors:** Completely surrounded by Italy. Note: dignitaries, priests, nuns, guards, and 3,000 lay workers live outside the Vatican.

Finance: Euros (EUR) (Sept. 2004: 0.82=1 U.S.).

Transport: Railroad: Length: 1 mi.

Labor force: essentially services with a small amount of industry.

Apostolic Nunciature in U.S.: 3339 Massachusetts Ave. NW 20008; 333-7121.

Website: www.vatican.va

The popes for many centuries, with brief interruptions, held temporal sovereignty over mid-Italy (the so-called Papal States), comprising an area of some 16,000 sq. mi., with a population in the 19th century of more than 3 million. This territory was incorporated in the new Kingdom of Italy (1861), the sovereignty of the pope being confined to the palaces of the Vatican and the Lateran in Rome and the villa of Castel Gandolfo, by an Italian law, May 13, 1871. This law also guaranteed to the pope and his successors a yearly indemnity of over $620,000. The allowance, however, remained unclaimed.

A Treaty of Conciliation, a concordat, and a financial convention were signed Feb. 11, 1929, by Cardinal Gasparri and Premier Mussolini. The documents established the independent state of Vatican City and gave the Roman Catholic church special status in Italy. The treaty (Lateran Agreement) was made part of the Constitution of Italy (Article 7) in 1947. Italy and the Vatican signed an agreement in 1984 on revisions of the concordat; the accord eliminated Roman Catholicism as the state religion and ended required religious education in Italian schools.

Vatican City includes the Basilica of Saint Peter, the Vatican Palace and Museum covering over 13 acres, the Vatican gardens, and neighboring buildings between Viale Vaticano and the church. Thirteen buildings in Rome, outside the boundaries, enjoy extraterritorial rights; these buildings house congregations or officers necessary for the administration of the Holy See.

The legal system is based on the code of canon law, the apostolic constitutions, and laws especially promulgated for the Vatican City by the pope. The Secretariat of State represents the Holy See in its diplomatic relations. By the Treaty of Conciliation the pope is pledged to a perpetual neutrality unless his mediation is specifically requested. This, however, does not prevent the defense of the Church whenever it is persecuted.

The present sovereign of the State of Vatican City is the Supreme Pontiff John Paul II, born Karol Wojtyla in Wadowice, Poland, May 18, 1920, elected Oct. 16, 1978 (the first non-Italian to be elected pope in 456 years).

The U.S. restored formal relations in 1984 after the U.S. Congress repealed an 1867 ban on diplomatic relations with the Vatican. The Vatican and Israel agreed to establish formal relations Dec. 30, 1993.

Venezuela
Bolivarian Republic of Venezuela

People: Population: 25,017,387. **Age distrib.** (%): <15: 31.6; 65+: 4.8. **Pop. density:** 73 per sq mi, 28 per sq km. **Urban:** 87.7%. **Ethnic groups:** Spanish, Italian, Portuguese, Arab, German, Black, indigenous. **Principal languages:** Spanish (official), numerous indigenous dialects. **Chief religion:** Roman Catholic 96%.

Geography: Total area: 352,144 sq mi, 912,050 sq km; **Land area:** 340,561 sq mi, 882,050 sq km. **Location:** On Caribbean coast of South America. **Neighbors:** Colombia on W, Brazil on S, Guyana on E. **Topography:** Flat coastal plain and Orinoco Delta are bordered by Andes Mts. and hills. Plains, called llanos, extend between mountains and Orinoco. Guiana Highlands and plains are S of Orinoco, which stretches 1,600 mi. and drains 80% of Venezuela. **Capital:** Caracas, 3,226,000. **Cities (urban aggr.):** Maracaibo, 1,901,000; Valencia, 1,893,000.

Government: Type: Federal republic. **Head of state and gov.:** Pres. Hugo Rafael Chávez Frías; b July 28, 1954; in office: Feb. 2, 1999. **Local divisions:** 23 states, 1 federal district (Caracas), 1 federal dependency (72 islands). **Defense budget** (2003): $1.1 bil. **Active troops:** 82,300.

Economy: Industries: oil, iron, constr. materials, food proc., textiles, steel, aluminum, auto assembly. **Chief crops:** corn, sorghum, sugarcane, rice, bananas, vegetables, coffee. **Natural resources:** oil, nat. gas, iron ore, gold, bauxite, other minerals, hydropower, diamonds. **Crude oil reserves** (2003): 77.8 bil. bbls. **Arable land:** 4%. **Livestock** (2003): cattle: 16.1 mil.; chickens: 110.0 mil.; goats: 2.70 mil.; pigs: 2.92 mil.; sheep: 820,000. **Fish catch** (2002): 533,244 metric tons. **Electricity prod.** (2002): 87.02 bil. kWh. **Labor force** (1997 est.): services 64%, industry 23%, agriculture 13%.

Finance: Monetary unit: Bolivar (VEB) (Sept. 2004: 1,917.60=1 U.S.). **GDP** (2003 est.): $117.9 bil.; **per capita GDP:** $4,800; **GDP growth:** -9.2%. **Imports** (2003 est.): $10.7 bil.; partners (2002): U.S. 32.1%, Colombia 8%, Brazil 6.2%, Germany 4.6%, Mexico 4.4%, Italy 4.1%. **Exports** (2003 est.): $25.9 bil.; partners (2002): U.S. 45.1%, Netherlands Antilles 12.8%, Dominican Republic 2.8%. **Tourism:** $314 mil. **Budget** (2002): $23.3 bil. **Intl. reserves less gold:** $10.79 bil. **Gold:** 11.47 mil oz t. **Consumer prices:** 31.1%.

Transport: Railroad: Length: 424 mi. **Motor vehicles** (1999): 1.42 mil pass. cars, 846,000 comm. vehicles. **Civil aviation:** 1.1 bil. pass.-mi; 127 airports. **Chief ports:** Maracaibo, La Guaira, Puerto Cabello.

Communications: TV sets: 185 per 1,000 pop. **Radios:** 296 per 1,000 pop. **Telephone lines** (2002): 2.8 mil. **Daily newspaper circ.:** 206 per 1,000 pop. **Internet** (2002): 1.3 mil. users.

Health: Life expect.: 71.0 male; 77.3 female. **Births** (per 1,000 pop.): 19.3. **Deaths** (per 1,000 pop.): 4.9. **Natural inc.:** 1.44%. **Infant mortality** (per 1,000 live births): 23.0. **AIDS rate:** 0.7%.

Education: Free, compulsory: ages 6-15. **Literacy:** 93.4%.

Major Intl. Organizations: UN (FAO, IBRD, ILO, IMF, IMO, WHO, WTrO), OAS, OPEC.

Embassy: 1099 30th St. NW 20007; 342-2214.

Website: www.embavenez-us.org

Columbus first set foot on the South American continent on the peninsula of Paria, Aug. 1498. Alonso de Ojeda, 1499, was the first European to see Lake Maracaibo. He called the land Venezuela, or Little Venice, because the Indians had houses on stilts. Spanish colonialists dominated Venezuela until Simón Bolívar's victory near Carabobo in June 1821. The republic was formed after secession from the Colombian Federation in 1830. Military strongmen ruled Venezuela for much of its history. Since 1959, the country has had democratically elected governments.

Oil accounts for more than 75% of export earnings and about half of government revenues. Venezuela helped found the Organization of Petroleum Exporting Countries (OPEC) in 1960. The government, Jan. 1, 1976, nationalized the oil industry with compensation. The economy suffered a cash crisis in the 1980s and 1990s as a result of depressed oil revenues. Government attempts to reduce dependence on oil have met with limited success.

An attempted coup by midlevel military officers was thwarted by loyalist troops Feb. 4, 1992. A 2nd coup attempt was thwarted in Nov. Pres. Carlos Andrés Pérez was removed from office on corruption charges, May 1993; he was convicted, May 1996, of mismanaging a $17 million secret government fund. A 1992 coup leader, Hugo Chávez, who ran as a populist, was elected president Dec. 6, 1998. Voters on Dec. 15 approved a new constitution greatly increasing his powers. Floods and mudslides in Dec. 1999 killed, by official estimates, at least 30,000.

Popular among the poor, Chávez alienated some middle- and upper-class Venezuelans with his program of economic and political reform, and his foreign policy antagonized the U.S. Gunfire erupted at a mass protest Apr. 11, 2002, in Caracas, killing at least 17 people. Chávez was forced to relinquish power, but when an interim government issued decrees suspending democratic institutions, Chávez loyalists rebelled; the coup fell apart, and the president reclaimed his office Apr. 14. Opponents of Chávez mounted a crippling general strike, Dec. 2002-Feb. 2003, which ended after mediation by the OAS and former U.S. Pres. Jimmy Carter. Several dissidents were killed later that month. The Colombian and Spanish embassies in Caracas were bombed Feb. 25. Chávez and opposition groups pledged, May 29, 2003, to halt political violence.

Opponents presented petitions with over 3 mil. signatures Aug. 20, 2003, demanding a vote to recall Chávez. After prolonged legal wrangling, the recall election was set for Aug. 15, 2004. The referendum was monitored by Carter and the OAS, and Chávez won with 59% of the vote.

Vietnam
Socialist Republic of Vietnam

People: Population: 82,689,518. **Age distrib.** (%): <15: 31.6; 65+: 5.5. **Pop. density:** 658 per sq mi, 254 per sq km. **Urban:** 25.7%. **Ethnic groups:** Vietnamese 85%-90%, Chinese, Hmong, Thai, Khmer, Cham. **Principal languages:** Vietnamese (official), French, Chinese, English. **Chief religions:** Buddhist, Taoist, Roman Catholic, indigenous beliefs.

Geography: Total area: 127,244 sq mi, 329,560 sq km; **Land area:** 125,622 sq mi, 325,360 sq km. **Location:** SE Asia, on the E coast of the Indochinese Peninsula. **Neighbors:** China on N, Laos and Cambodia on W. **Topography:** Vietnam is long and narrow, with a 1,400-mi. coast. About 22% of country is readily arable, including the densely settled Red R. valley in the N, narrow coastal plains in center, and the wide, often marshy Mekong R. Delta in the S. The rest consists of semi-arid plateaus and barren mountains, with some stretches of tropical rain forest. **Capital:** Hanoi, 3,977,000. **Cities (urban aggr.):** Ho Chi Minh City, 4,619,000; Hai Phong, 1,676,000.

Government: Type: Communist. **Head of state:** Pres. Tran Duc Luong; b May 1937; in office: Sept. 24, 1997. **Head of gov.:** Prime Min. Phan Van Khai; b Dec. 1933; in office: Sept. 25, 1997. **Local divisions:** 58 provinces, 3 cities, 1 capital region. **Defense budget** (2003): $2.3 bil. **Active troops:** 484,000.

Economy: Industries: food proc., garments, shoes, machinery, mining. **Chief crops:** rice, corn, potatoes, rubber, soybeans, coffee, tea. **Natural resources:** phosphates, coal, mang., bauxite, chromate, oil, nat. gas, timber, hydropower. **Crude oil reserves** (2003): 600.0 mil. bbls. **Arable land:** 17%. **Livestock** (2003): cattle: 4.39 mil.; chickens: 185.2 mil.; goats: 780,354; pigs: 24.9 mil. **Fish catch** (2002 est.): 2,026,500 metric tons. **Electricity prod.** (2002): 34.48 bil. kWh. **Labor force** (2000 est.): agriculture 63%, industry and services 37%.

Finance: Monetary unit: Dong (VND) (Sept. 2004: 15,744.00=1 U.S.). **GDP** (2003 est.): $203.9 bil.; **per capita GDP:** $2,500; **GDP growth:** 7.3%. **Imports** (2003 est.): $22.5 bil.; partners (2002): Taiwan 12.6%, South Korea 12.3%, China 11.7%, Japan 11.7%, Singapore 11.4%, Thailand 5.2%, Hong Kong 4.2%. **Exports** (2003 est.): $19.9 bil.; partners (2002): U.S. 15%, Japan 14.6%, Australia 7.5%, China 6.4%, Germany 6.4%, Singapore 5.4%, UK 4.2%. **Tourism** (1998): $86 mil. **Budget** (1999 est.): $5.6 bil. **Intl. reserves less gold:** $4.19 bil. **Consumer prices:** 3.1%.

Transport: Railroad: Length: 1,952 mi. **Motor vehicles** (2000): 69,900 comm. vehicles. **Civil aviation:** 1.9 bil. pass.-mi; 24 airports. **Chief ports:** Ho Chi Minh City, Haiphong, Da Nang.

Communications: TV sets: 184 per 1,000 pop. **Radios:** 107 per 1,000 pop. **Telephone lines:** 4.4 mil. **Daily newspaper circ.:** 4 per 1,000 pop. **Internet:** 3.5 mil. users.

Health: Life expect.: 67.9 male; 73.0 female. **Births** (per 1,000 pop.): 19.6. **Deaths** (per 1,000 pop.): 6.1. **Natural inc.:** 1.34%. **Infant mortality** (per 1,000 live births): 29.9. **AIDS rate:** 0.4%.

Education: Compulsory: ages 6-14. **Literacy:** 94%.

Major Intl. Organizations: UN (FAO, IBRD, ILO, IMF, IMO, WHO), APEC, ASEAN.

Embassy: 1233 20th St. NW, Ste. 400, 20037; 861-0737.

Website: www.vietnamembassy-usa.org

Vietnam's recorded history began in Tonkin before the Christian era. Settled by Viets from central China, Vietnam was held by China, 111 BC-AD 939, and was a vassal state during subsequent periods. Vietnam defeated the armies of Kublai Khan, 1288. Conquest by France began in 1858 and ended in 1884 with the protectorates of Tonkin and Annam in the N and the colony of Cochin-China in the S.

Japan occupied Vietnam in 1940; nationalist aims gathered force. A number of groups formed the Vietminh (Independence) League, headed by Ho Chi Minh, Communist guerrilla leader. In Aug. 1945 the Vietminh forced out Bao Dai, former emperor of Annam, head of a Japan-sponsored regime. France, seeking to reestablish colonial control, battled Communist and nationalist forces, 1946-54, and was defeated at Dienbienphu, May 8, 1954. Meanwhile, on July 1, 1949, Bao Dai had formed a State of Vietnam, with himself as chief of state, with French approval. China backed Ho Chi Minh.

A cease-fire signed in Geneva July 21, 1954, provided for a buffer zone, withdrawal of French troops from the North, and elections to determine the country's future. Under the agreement the Communists gained control of territory north of the 17th parallel, with its capital at Hanoi and Ho Chi Minh as president. South Vietnam came to comprise the 39 southern provinces. Some 900,000 North Vietnamese fled to South Vietnam. On Oct. 26, 1955, Ngo Dinh Diem proclaimed the Republic of Vietnam and became its president.

Communists in the North sought to take over South Vietnam beginning in 1954. The North provided aid to Vietcong guerrillas in the South; the Soviet Union and China supplied weapons for the Communist cause. The U.S. began sending military advisers to help the anti-Communist South. Northern aid to Vietcong guerrillas was intensified in 1959, and large-scale troop infiltration began in 1964, with Soviet and Chinese arms assistance. Large Northern forces were stationed in border areas of Laos and Cambodia.

During 1963, Buddhists in the South denounced the Diem government's authoritarianism and brutality. This paved the way for a military coup Nov. 1-2, 1963, which overthrew Diem. Several other military coups followed.

In 1964, the U.S. launched air strikes against North Vietnam. Beginning in 1965, the raids were stepped up and U.S. troops became combatants. U.S. troop strength in Vietnam reached a high of 543,400 in Apr. 1969, but the North Vietnamese and Vietcong continued to mount new offensives. In response to a growing anti-war movement in the U.S., Pres. Nixon gradually withdrew U.S. ground troops. U.S. warplanes conducted massive bombing raids on the Northern cities of Hanoi and Haiphong in Dec. 1972.

A cease-fire agreement was signed in Paris Jan. 27, 1973 by the U.S., North and South Vietnam, and the Vietcong. It was never implemented. North Vietnamese forces attacked remaining government outposts in the Central Highlands in the first months of 1975. Government retreats turned into a rout, and the Saigon regime surrendered April 30. North Vietnam assumed control, and began transforming society along Communist lines. The country was officially reunited July 2, 1976. The war's toll included—Combat deaths: U.S. 47,369; South Vietnam more than 200,000; other allied forces 5,225. Total U.S. fatalities numbered more than 58,000. Vietnamese civilian casualties were more than a million. Displaced war refugees in South Vietnam totaled more than 6.5 million.

Conditions in the region remained unstable after the Vietnam War ended. Heavy fighting with Cambodia took place, 1977-80. Relations with China soured as 140,000 ethnic Chinese left Vietnam charging discrimination; China cut off economic aid. Reacting to Vietnam's invasion of Cambodia, China attacked 4 Vietnamese border provinces, Feb. 1979. Vietnam launched an offensive against Cambodian refugee strongholds along the Thai-Cambodian border in 1985; they also engaged Thai troops.

Vietnam announced reforms aimed at reducing central control of the economy in 1987, as many of the old revolutionary followers of Ho Chi Minh were removed from office.

Citing Vietnamese cooperation in returning remains of U.S. soldiers killed in the Vietnam War, the U.S. announced an end, Feb. 3, 1994, to a 19-year-old U.S. embargo on trade with Vietnam. The U.S. extended full diplomatic recognition to Vietnam July 11, 1995. The Communist Party replaced the country's ill and aging leadership in Sept. 1997.

Floods in central Vietnam, Oct.-Nov. 1999, killed some 550 people and left over 600,000 families homeless. The U.S. and Vietnam signed a comprehensive trade deal July 13, 2000. U.S. Pres. Bill Clinton made a historic visit to Vietnam Nov. 17-19, 2000. Nong Duc Manh, a moderate, was named to head the Communist Party Apr. 22, 2001.

Western Samoa
See **Samoa**

Yemen
Republic of Yemen

People: Population: 20,024,867. **Age distrib.** (%): <15: 47; 65+: 2.9. **Pop. density:** 98 per sq mi, 38 per sq km. **Urban:** 25.6%. **Ethnic groups:** Mainly Arab; Afro-Arab, South Asian, European. **Principal languages:** Arabic (official). **Chief religion:** Muslim (official; Sunni 60% and Shi'a 40%).

Geography: Total area: 203,850 sq mi, 527,970 sq km; **Land area:** 203,850 sq mi, 527,970 sq km. **Location:** Middle East, on the S coast of the Arabian Peninsula. **Neighbors:** Saudi Arabia on N, Oman on the E. **Topography:** A sandy coastal strip leads to well-watered fertile mountains in interior. **Capital:** Sana'a, 1,469,000. **Cities (urban aggr.):** Aden (1995 est.), 562,000.

Government: Type: Republic. **Head of state:** Pres. Ali Abdullah Saleh; b. 1942; in office: July 17, 1978. **Head of gov.:** Prime Min. Abd-al-Qadir Bajamal; b 1946; in office: Apr. 4, 2001. **Local divisions:** 19 governorates and capital region. **Defense budget** (2003): $561 mil. **Active troops:** 66,700

Economy: Industries: oil prod. & refining, cotton textiles, leather goods, food proc. **Chief crops:** grain, fruits, vegetables, pulses, coffee, cotton. **Natural resources:** oil, fish, salt, marble, coal, gold, lead, nickel, copper. **Crude oil reserves** (2003): 4.0 bil. bbls. **Arable land:** 3%. **Livestock** (2003): cattle: 1.4 mil.; chickens: 34.8 mil.; goats: 7.25 mil.; sheep: 6.5 mil. **Fish catch** (2002): 159,262 metric tons. **Electricity prod.** (2002): 3.04 bil. kWh. **Labor force:** most people are employed in agriculture and herding; services, construction, industry, and commerce account for less than one-fourth of the labor force.

Finance: Monetary unit: Rial (YER) (Sept. 2004: 184.20=1 U.S.). **GDP** (2003 est.): $15.2 bil.; **per capita GDP:** $800; **GDP growth:** 3.1%. **Imports** (2003 est.): $3.0 bil.; partners (2002): UAE 16%, Saudi Arabia 12.7%, China 6.2%, Kuwait 5.5%, U.S. 4.7%. **Exports** (2003 est.): $3.9 bil.; partners (2002): Thailand 19%, India 16.7%, China 15.3%, South Korea 12.4%, Malaysia 6.1%, U.S. 5.4%. **Tourism** (2002): $38 mil. **Budget** (2004 est.): $4.1 bil. **Intl. reserves less gold:** $3.36 bil. **Gold:** 50,000 oz t. **Consumer prices:** 10.8%.

Transport: Motor vehicles (1998): 380,600 pass. cars, 422,100 comm. vehicles. **Civil aviation:** 930.8 mil. pass.-mi; 16 airports. **Chief ports:** Al Hudaydah, Al Mukalla, Aden.

Communications: TV sets: 286 per 1,000 pop. **Radios:** 64 per 1,000 pop. **Telephone lines** (2002): 542,200. **Daily newspaper circ.:** 15 per 1,000 pop. **Internet** (2002): 100,000 users.

Health: Life expect.: 59.5 male; 63.3 female. **Births** (per 1,000 pop.): 43.2. **Deaths** (per 1,000 pop.): 8.8. **Natural inc.:** 3.44%. **Infant mortality** (per 1,000 live births): 63.3. **AIDS rate:** 0.1%.

Education: Compulsory: ages 6-14. **Literacy** (1994): 50.2%.

Major Intl. Organizations: UN (FAO, IBRD, ILO, IMF, IMO, WHO), AL.

Embassy: 2319 Wyoming Ave. NW 20008; 965-4760.

Website: www.yemenembassy.org

Yemen's territory once was part of the ancient biblical Kingdom of Sheba, or Saba, a prosperous link in trade between Africa and India. Yemen became independent in 1918, after centuries of Ottoman Turkish rule, but remained politically and economically backward.

Imam Ahmed ruled 1948-1962. Army officers headed by Brig. Gen. Abdullah al-Salal declared the country to be the Yemen Arab Republic, Sept. 1962. Ahmed's heir, the Imam Mohamad al-Badr, fled to the mountains where tribesmen joined royalist forces, aided by the Saudi monarchy. Fighting between royalists and republicans killed about 150,000 people until hostilities ended in 1970.

Meanwhile, South Yemen, formed from the British colony of Aden and the British protectorate of South Arabia, became independent Nov. 1967. A Marxist state and a Soviet ally, it took the name People's Democratic Republic of Yemen in 1970. More than 300,000 Yemenis fled from the South to the North after independence, contributing to 2 decades of hostility between the 2 states that flared into warfare twice in the 1970s.

The 2 countries were formally united May 21, 1990, but regional clan-based rivalries led to full-scale civil war in 1994. Secessionists declared a breakaway state in S Yemen, May 21, 1994, but northern troops captured the former southern capital of Aden in July. A new constitution was approved Sept. 28.

Yemen, the ancestral home of Osama bin Laden, has been caught in a crossfire between the U.S. and Islamic extremists. While on a refueling stop in Aden, Oct. 12, 2000, the destroyer U.S.S. *Cole* was bombed, leaving 17 Americans dead and more than 3 dozen injured; the U.S. government blamed the attack on terrorists associated with bin Laden. The U.S. sent troops in 2002 to help track down members of al-Qaeda. Six alleged al-Qaeda operatives were convicted of the

A missile fired Nov. 3, 2002, from an unmanned CIA surveillance aircraft killed 6 suspected al-Qaeda members, including an American. Three U.S. missionaries were slain at a Baptist hospital in Jibla, Dec. 30; the gunman, an Islamic militant, received a death sentence May 10, 2003. Clashes beginning in June 2004

between Yemeni government forces and rebels led by an anti-U.S. cleric, Hussein al-Houthi, left more than 200 people dead. The government announced Sept. 10 that Yemeni troops had killed al-Houthi and crushed the rebellion.

Yugoslavia
See **Serbia and Montenegro**

Zaire
See **Congo**

Zambia
Republic of Zambia

People: Population: 10,462,436. **Age distrib.** (%): <15: 47.1; 65+: 2.5. **Pop. density:** 37 per sq mi, 14 per sq km. **Urban:** 35.7%. **Ethnic groups:** More than 70 groups; largest are Bemba, Tonga, Ngoni, and Lozi. **Principal languages:** English (official), Bemba, Kaonda, Lozi, Lunda, Luvale, Nyanja, Tonga, 70 others. **Chief religions:** Christian 50%-75%, Muslim and Hindu 24%-49%.

Geography: Total area: 290,586 sq mi, 752,614 sq km; **Land area:** 285,995 sq mi, 740,724 sq km. **Location:** In S central Africa. **Neighbors:** Congo (formerly Zaire) on N; Tanzania, Malawi, Mozambique on E; Zimbabwe, Namibia on S; Angola on W. **Topography:** Zambia is mostly high plateau country covered with thick forests, and drained by several important rivers, including the Zambezi. **Capital:** Lusaka 1,394,000.

Government: Type: Republic. **Head of state and gov.:** Pres. Levy Patrick Mwanawasa; b Sept. 3, 1948; in office: Jan. 2, 2002. **Local divisions:** 9 provinces. **Defense budget** (2003): $27 mil. **Active troops:** 18,100.

Economy: Industries: copper mining & proc., constr., foodstuffs. **Chief crops:** corn, sorghum, rice, peanuts, sunflower seeds. **Natural resources:** copper, cobalt, zinc, lead, coal, emeralds, gold, silver, uranium, hydropower. **Arable land:** 7%. **Livestock** (2003): cattle: 2.6 mil.; chickens: 30.0 mil.; goats: 1.27 mil.; pigs: 340,000; sheep: 150,000. **Fish catch** (2002 est): 69,200 metric tons. **Electricity prod.** (2002): 8.17 bil. kWh. **Labor force:** agriculture 85%, industry 6%, services 9%.

Finance: Monetary unit: Kwacha (ZMK) (Sept. 2004: 4,787.50=1 U.S.). **GDP** (2003 est.): $8.6 bil.; **per capita GDP:** $800; **GDP growth:** 4.0%. **Imports** (2003 est.): $1.1 bil.; partners (2002): South Africa 69.4%, U.S. 3.3%, China 3.2%. **Exports** (2003 est.): $1.0 bil.; partners (2002): South Africa 27.8%, Malawi 8.5%, Thailand 7.6%, Japan 7.5%, Saint Pierre and Miquelon 7.5%, China 5.2%, Egypt 5.2%, Netherlands 4.6%. **Tourism:** $149 mil. **Budget** (2001 est.): $1.3 bil. **Intl. reserves less gold:** $167 mil. **Consumer prices** (change in 2002): 22.2%.

Transport: Railroad: Length: 1,350 mi. **Motor vehicles** (1996): 3,700 pass. cars, 3,900 comm. vehicles. **Civil aviation:** 23.6 mil. pass.-mi; 11 airports. **Chief port:** Mpulungu.

Communications: TV sets: 145 per 1,000 pop. **Radios:** 160 per 1,000 pop. **Telephone lines:** 88,400. **Daily newspaper circ.:** 12 per 1,000 pop. **Internet:** 68,200 users.

Health: Life expect.: 35.2 male; 35.2 female. **Births** (per 1,000 pop.): 39.0. **Deaths** (per 1,000 pop.): 24.4. **Natural inc.:** 1.46%. **Infant mortality** (per 1,000 live births): 98.4. **AIDS rate:** 16.5%.

Education: Compulsory: ages 7-13. **Literacy:** 80.6%.

Major Intl. Organizations: UN (FAO, IBRD, ILO, IMF, WHO, WTrO), the Commonwealth, AU.

Embassy: 2419 Massachusetts Ave. NW 20008; 265-9717.

Websites: www.zambiatourism.com
www.travel.state.gov/travel/zambia.html

As Northern Rhodesia, the country was under the administration of the South Africa Company, 1889 until 1924, when the office of governor was established, and, subsequently, a legislature. The country became an independent republic within the Commonwealth Oct. 24, 1964.

As part of a program of government participation in major industries, a government corporation in 1970 took over 51% of the ownership of 2 foreign-owned copper-mining companies. Privately-held land and other enterprises were nationalized in 1975. In the 1980s and 1990s lowered copper prices hurt the economy and severe drought caused famine.

Food riots erupted in June 1990, as the nation suffered its worst violence since independence. Elections held Oct. 1991 brought an end to one-party rule. The new government sought to sell state enterprises, including the copper industry. Pres. Frederick Chiluba won reelection Nov. 18, 1996, but international observers cited harassment of opposition parties. A coup attempt was suppressed Oct. 28, 1997.

Thwarted in his effort to change the constitution to allow himself to run for a 3rd term, Chiluba endorsed Levy Patrick Mwanawasa, who won a disputed election Dec. 27, 2001. Chiluba was arrested Feb. 24, 2003, on charges that he stole government funds while he was president; his trial began Dec. 9 but was slowed by prosecution delays.

Food shortages threatened more than 2 million Zambians in 2002; the government refused to distribute shipments of U.S. grain because it was genetically modified. According to UN estimates, about one-sixth of the adult population has HIV/AIDS.

Zimbabwe
Republic of Zimbabwe

People: Population: 12,671,860. **Age distrib.** (%): <15: 37.9; 65+: 3.7. **Pop. density:** 85 per sq mi, 33 per sq km. **Urban:** 34.9%. **Ethnic groups:** Shona 82%, Ndebele 14%. **Principal languages:** English (official), Shona, Sindebele, numerous dialects. **Chief religions:** Syncretic (Christian-indigenous mix) 50%, Christian 25%, indigenous beliefs 24%.

Geography: Total area: 150,804 sq mi, 390,580 sq km; **Land area:** 149,294 sq mi, 386,670 sq km. **Location:** In southern Africa. **Neighbors:** Zambia on N, Botswana on W, South Africa on S, Mozambique on E. **Topography:** Zimbabwe is high plateau country, rising to mountains on eastern border, sloping down on the other borders. **Capital:** Harare, 1,469,000. **Cities (urban aggr.):** Bulawayo, 824,000.

Government: Type: Republic. **Head of state and gov.:** Pres. Robert Mugabe; b Feb. 21, 1924; in office: Dec. 31, 1987. **Local divisions:** 8 provinces, 2 cities. **Defense budget** (2003): $93 mil. **Active troops:** 29,000

Economy: Industries: mining, steel, wood products, cement, chemicals. **Chief crops:** corn, cotton, tobacco, wheat, coffee. **Natural resources:** coal, chromium ore, asbestos, gold, nickel, copper, iron ore, vanadium, lithium, tin, platinum. **Arable land:** 7%. **Livestock** (2003): cattle: 5.75 mil.; chickens: 22.0 mil.; goats: 2.97 mil.; pigs: 605,000; sheep: 610,000. **Fish catch** (2002 est): 15,213 metric tons. **Electricity prod.** (2002): 8.84 bil. kWh. **Labor force** (1996): agriculture 66%, services 24%, industry 10%.

Finance: Monetary unit: Zimbabwe Dollar (ZWD) (Sept. 2004: 5,549.80=1 U.S.). **GDP** (2003 est.): $24.0 bil.; **per capita GDP:** $1,900; **GDP growth:** -13.6%. **Imports** (2003 est.): $1.7 bil.; partners (2002): South Africa 50%, Congo, Democratic Republic of the 5.9%, UK 3.2%. **Exports** (2003 est.): $1.3 bil.; partners (2002): China 6%, South Africa 5.7%, Germany 5.4%, UK 4.8%, Japan 4.7%, Netherlands 4.4%, U.S. 4.1%. **Tourism:** $44 mil. **Budget** (2003): $2.0 bil. **Intl. reserves less gold** (2002): $61 mil. **Gold** (2002): 140,000 oz t. **Consumer prices** (change in 2002): 140.1%.

Transport: Railroad: Length: 1,912 mi. **Motor vehicles** (2000): 544,500 pass. cars, 67,700 comm. vehicles. **Civil aviation:** 405.8 mil. pass.-mi; 17 airports. **Chief ports:** Binga, Kariba.

Communications: TV sets: 35 per 1,000 pop. **Radios:** 389 per 1,000 pop. **Telephone lines:** 300,900. **Daily newspaper circ.:** 19 per 1,000 pop. **Internet** (2002): 500,000 users.

Health: Life expect.: 38.6 male; 37.0 female. **Births** (per 1,000 pop.): 30.1. **Deaths** (per 1,000 pop.): 23.3. **Natural inc.:** 0.68%. **Infant mortality** (per 1,000 live births): 67.1. **AIDS rate:** 24.6%.

Education: Compulsory: ages 6-12. **Literacy:** 90.7%.

Major Intl. Organizations: UN (FAO, IBRD, ILO, IMF, WHO, WTrO), AU.

Embassy: 1608 New Hampshire Ave. NW 20009; 332-7100.

Websites: www.zimbabwetourism.co.zw; www.zim.gov.zw

Britain took over the area as Southern Rhodesia in 1923 from the British South Africa Co. (which, under Cecil Rhodes, had conquered it by 1897) and granted internal self-government. Under a 1961 constitution, voting was restricted to keep whites in power. On Nov. 11, 1965, Prime Min. Ian D. Smith announced his country's unilateral declaration of independence.

Britain termed the act illegal and demanded that the country (known as Rhodesia until 1980) broaden voting rights to provide for eventual rule by the black African majority. The UN imposed sanctions and, in May 1968, a trade embargo. Intermittent negotiations between the government and various black nationalist groups failed to prevent increasing guerrilla warfare.

In the country's first universal-franchise election, Apr. 21, 1979, Bishop Abel Muzorewa's United African National Council gained a bare majority of the black-dominated Parliament. A cease-fire was accepted by all parties, Dec. 5. Independence as Zimbabwe was finally achieved Apr. 18, 1980.

On Mar. 6, 1992, Pres. Robert Mugabe declared a national disaster because of drought and appealed to foreign donors for food, money, and medicine. An economic adjustment program caused widespread hardship. Mugabe was reelected Mar. 1996 after opposition candidates withdrew. A land redistribution campaign launched by Mugabe triggered violent attacks in Apr. 2000 against some white farmers; whites made up less than 1% of the population but held 70% of the land. Mugabe's opponents gained in legislative elections June 24-25, 2000.

International observers criticized Mugabe for relying on fraud and intimidation to win the presidential election of Mar. 9-11, 2002. The EU, the U.S., and the Commonwealth imposed sanctions on the Mugabe regime. Zimbabwe withdrew from the Commonwealth as of Dec. 7, 2003. The UN recently estimated that about 25% of the adult population has HIV/AIDS.

WORLD ALMANAC QUICK QUIZ

Which of these countries is the world's second smallest in land area, after Vatican City?

(a) Monaco (b) Tuvalu (c) San Marino (d) Liechtenstein

For the answer look in this chapter, or see page 1008.

National Rankings by Population, Area, Population Density, 2004

Source: International Programs Center, Bureau of the Census, U.S. Dept. of Commerce

As of mid-2004, according to U.S. Census Bureau projections, the world had an estimated population of 6,377,641,642. China was the most populous nation, with $\frac{1}{5}$ of the world total. India, the 2nd-largest, passed the 1-billion mark in 1999. Russia is the largest country in land area.

	Largest Populations			Largest Populations			Smallest Populations	
Rank	Country	Population	Rank	Country	Population	Rank	Country	Population
1.	China[1]	1,298,847,624	11.	Mexico	104,959,594	1.	Vatican City	921
2.	India	1,065,070,607	12.	Philippines	86,241,697	2.	Tuvalu	11,468
3.	United States	293,027,571	13.	Vietnam	82,689,518	3.	Nauru	12,809
4.	Indonesia	238,452,952	14.	Germany	82,424,609	4.	Palau	20,016
5.	Brazil	184,101,109	15.	Egypt	76,117,421	5.	San Marino	28,503
6.	Pakistan	159,196,336	16.	Turkey	68,893,918	6.	Monaco	32,270
7.	Russia	143,782,338	17.	Ethiopia	67,851,281	7.	Liechtenstein	33,436
8.	Bangladesh	141,340,476	18.	Iran	67,503,205	8.	Saint Kitts and Nevis	38,836
9.	Nigeria	137,253,133	19.	Thailand	64,865,523	9.	Marshall Islands	57,738
10.	Japan	127,333,002	20.	France	60,424,213	10.	Antigua and Barbuda	68,230

(1) Excluding Hong Kong, pop. 6,855,125, and Macao, population 445,286.

	Largest Land Areas[1]				Smallest Land Areas[1]		
Rank	Country	Area (sq km)	Area (sq mi)	Rank	Country	Area (sq km)	Area (sq mi)
1.	Russia	16,995,800	6,562,112	1.	Vatican City	0.4	0.15
2.	China	9,326,410	3,600,946	2.	Monaco	1.95	.75
3.	Canada	9,093,507	3,511,021	3.	Nauru	21	8
4.	United States	9,161,923	3,537,437	4.	Tuvalu	26	10
5.	Brazil	8,456,510	3,265,075	5.	San Marino	61	24
6.	Australia	7,617,930	2,941,298	6.	Liechtenstein	160	62
7.	India	2,973,190	1,147,955	7.	Marshall Islands	181	70
8.	Argentina	2,736,690	1,056,641	8.	Saint Kitts and Nevis	261	101
9.	Kazakhstan	2,669,800	1,030,815	9.	Maldives	300	116
10.	Algeria	2,381,740	919,595	10.	Malta	316	122

	Most Densely Populated				Most Sparsely Populated		
Rank	Country	Persons per sq km[2]	Persons per sq mi[2]	Rank	Country	Persons per sq km[2]	Persons per sq mi[2]
1.	Monaco	16,548.7	42,861.0	1.	Mongolia	1.8	4.6
2.	Singapore	6,377.5	16,517.6	2.	Namibia	2.4	6.1
3.	Vatican City	2,302.5	6,140.0	3.	Australia	2.6	6.8
4.	Malta	1,255.9	3,252.7	4.	Botswana	2.7	6.9
5.	Maldives	1,131.1	2,929.5	5.	Suriname	2.7	7.0
6.	Bangladesh	1,055.5	2,733.7	6.	Mauritania	2.9	7.5
7.	Bahrain	1,019.4	2,640.2	7.	Iceland	3.2	8.0
8.	Taiwan	705.2	1,826.5	8.	Libya	3.2	8.3
9.	Nauru	610.0	1,579.8	9.	Canada	3.5	9.1
10.	Mauritius	601.2	1,557.2	10.	Guyana	3.6	9.3

(1) Note: Land area of a country does not include inland water. Rankings by total area, including inland water, may differ from these. For total area figures, see pages 747–808 and 817–847. (2) Density is calculated here according to land area.

Current Population and Projections for All Countries: 2004, 2025, and 2050

Source: International Programs Center, Bureau of the Census, U.S. Dept. of Commerce
(midyear figures, in thousands)

Country	2004	2025	2050	Country	2004	2025	2050
Afghanistan	28,514	50,252	81,933	Chad	9,539	16,659	29,171
Albania	3,545	3,944	4,017	Chile	15,824	18,521	19,245
Algeria	32,129	40,255	43,984	China[1]	1,298,848	1,453,124	1,424,162
Andorra	70	78	69	Colombia	42,311	55,065	64,534
Angola	10,979	15,656	21,688	Comoros	652	1,127	1,835
Antigua and Barbuda	68	75	69	Congo, Rep. of	2,998	3,567	4,189
Argentina	39,145	45,757	48,740	Congo, Dem. Rep. of	58,318	104,863	181,260
Armenia	2,991	3,044	2,943	Costa Rica	3,957	5,074	5,697
Australia	19,913	23,023	24,176	Cote d'Ivoire	17,328	24,584	34,066
Austria	8,175	8,190	7,521	Croatia	4,497	4,374	3,864
Azerbaijan	7,868	9,453	10,665	Cuba	11,309	11,669	10,478
Bahamas, The	300	327	324	Cyprus	776	852	841
Bahrain	678	866	973	Czech Republic	10,246	9,844	8,540
Bangladesh	141,340	204,539	279,955	Denmark	5,413	5,698	5,575
Barbados	278	289	271	Djibouti	467	681	993
Belarus	10,311	10,135	9,067	Dominica	69	78	82
Belgium	10,348	10,453	9,883	Dominican Republic	8,834	11,148	13,425
Belize	273	411	558	East Timor	1,019	1,494	1,943
Benin	7,250	11,781	17,991	Ecuador	13,213	17,099	20,332
Bhutan	2,186	3,295	4,653	Egypt	76,117	103,353	126,921
Bolivia	8,724	11,370	13,773	El Salvador	6,588	9,108	12,039
Bosnia and Herzegovina	4,008	4,180	3,897	Equatorial Guinea	523	835	1,240
Botswana	1,562	1,043	890	Eritrea	4,447	6,954	10,535
Brazil	184,101	217,825	228,427	Estonia	1,342	1,149	862
Brunei	365	506	601	Ethiopia	67,851	91,205	121,164
Bulgaria	7,518	6,258	4,651	Fiji	881	1,153	1,448
Burkina Faso	13,575	22,459	39,484	Finland	5,215	5,251	4,820
Burundi	6,231	10,090	15,371	France	60,424	63,085	61,017
Cambodia	13,363	19,325	25,492	Gabon	1,355	2,197	3,877
Cameroon	16,064	22,440	30,873	Gambia, The	1,547	2,654	4,165
Canada	32,508	38,165	41,430	Georgia	4,694	4,341	3,785
Cape Verde	415	451	381	Germany	82,425	80,637	73,607
Central African Republic	3,742	4,782	6,178	Ghana	20,757	25,365	29,846

Country	2004	2025	2050
Greece	10,648	10,671	10,036
Grenada	89	96	87
Guatemala	14,281	22,985	34,257
Guinea	9,246	16,165	30,567
Guinea-Bissau	1,388	2,047	2,947
Guyana	706	763	787
Haiti	7,656	11,083	15,083
Honduras	6,824	9,495	12,325
Hungary	10,032	9,438	8,375
Iceland	294	338	351
India	1,065,071	1,361,625	1,601,005
Indonesia	238,453	300,277	336,247
Iran	67,503	83,187	89,691
Iraq	25,375	40,418	56,361
Ireland	3,970	4,842	5,396
Israel	6,199	7,612	8,517
Italy	58,057	56,234	50,390
Jamaica	2,713	3,250	3,505
Japan	127,333	120,001	99,887
Jordan	5,611	8,652	11,773
Kazakhstan	15,144	16,041	15,100
Kenya	32,022	35,271	40,156
Kiribati	101	158	235
Korea, North	22,698	25,755	26,364
Korea, South	48,598	51,801	47,840
Kuwait	2,258	4,175	6,375
Kyrgyzstan	5,081	6,679	8,238
Laos	6,068	9,450	13,176
Latvia	2,306	1,993	1,544
Lebanon	3,777	4,565	4,941
Lesotho	1,865	1,788	1,951
Liberia	3,391	5,453	8,780
Libya	5,632	8,323	10,817
Liechtenstein	33	38	36
Lithuania	3,608	3,356	2,788
Luxembourg	463	586	721
Macedonia, The Former Yugo. Rep. of .	2,071	2,185	2,108
Madagascar	17,502	32,966	65,460
Malawi	11,907	17,729	28,977
Malaysia	23,522	33,065	43,122
Maldives	339	564	815
Mali	11,957	20,002	32,465
Malta	397	421	396
Marshall Islands	58	83	103
Mauritania	2,999	5,292	8,636
Mauritius	1,220	1,407	1,451
Mexico	104,960	130,199	147,908
Micronesia, Fed. States of	108	99	74
Moldova	4,446	4,780	4,796
Monaco	32	35	33
Mongolia	2,751	3,576	4,086
Morocco	32,209	42,553	50,872
Mozambique	18,812	21,010	25,399
Myanmar	42,720	45,169	44,463
Namibia	1,954	2,116	2,636
Nauru	13	18	23
Nepal	27,071	39,918	53,294
Netherlands	16,318	17,540	17,334
New Zealand	3,994	4,673	4,842
Nicaragua	5,360	7,510	9,438
Niger	11,361	18,386	27,750
Nigeria	137,253	206,398	307,420
Norway	4,575	4,917	4,966
Oman	2,903	5,294	8,338

Country	2004	2025	2050
Pakistan	159,196	228,822	294,995
Palau	20	24	26
Panama	3,000	3,676	4,112
Papua New Guinea	5,420	8,001	10,670
Paraguay	6,191	9,880	14,636
Peru	27,544	34,476	38,300
Philippines	86,242	118,686	147,631
Poland	38,626	38,011	33,780
Portugal	10,524	10,806	9,933
Qatar	840	1,154	1,239
Romania	22,356	21,260	18,678
Russia	143,782	132,586	115,113
Rwanda	7,954	11,000	16,220
Saint Kitts and Nevis	39	46	52
Saint Lucia	164	209	235
Saint Vincent and the Grenadines	117	118	92
Samoa	178	177	171
San Marino	29	35	35
Sao Tome and Principe	182	329	502
Saudi Arabia	25,796	35,669	49,707
Senegal	10,852	17,054	24,578
Serbia and Montenegro	10,826	10,642	9,782
Seychelles	81	88	90
Sierra Leone	5,884	8,995	13,810
Singapore	4,354	5,101	4,635
Slovakia	5,424	5,459	4,944
Slovenia	2,011	1,908	1,597
Solomon Islands	524	816	1,111
Somalia	8,305	14,862	25,500
South Africa	42,719	34,045	30,955
Spain	40,281	39,578	35,564
Sri Lanka	19,905	22,594	23,086
Sudan	39,148	61,339	84,192
Suriname	437	435	358
Swaziland	1,169	1,089	1,143
Sweden	8,986	9,316	9,085
Switzerland	7,451	7,774	7,296
Syria	18,017	26,548	34,437
Taiwan	22,750	24,636	23,204
Tajikistan	7,012	11,042	16,630
Tanzania	36,588	52,813	74,990
Thailand	64,866	73,260	73,951
Togo	5,557	7,605	9,687
Tonga	110	151	188
Trinidad and Tobago	1,097	873	615
Tunisia	9,975	11,931	12,463
Turkey	68,894	82,205	86,474
Turkmenistan	4,863	7,053	9,626
Tuvalu	11	16	20
Uganda	26,405	48,040	83,662
Ukraine	47,732	43,293	37,726
United Arab Emirates	2,524	3,270	3,697
United Kingdom	60,271	63,819	63,977
United States	293,028	349,666	420,081
Uruguay	3,399	3,675	3,728
Uzbekistan	26,410	36,947	48,597
Vanuatu	203	263	310
Vatican City[2]	921		
Venezuela	25,017	32,061	37,106
Vietnam	82,690	104,436	116,813
Yemen	20,025	39,644	71,119
Zambia	10,462	12,840	16,526
Zimbabwe	12,672	12,773	14,581

(1) Excludes Hong Kong, population 6,855,125, and Macau, population 445,286. (2) 2025, 2050 not available.

Area and Population of the Continents

Source: International Programs Center, Bureau of the Census, U.S. Dept. of Commerce

Continent or Region	AREA[1] (sq km)	AREA[1] (sq mi)	% of Earth	% World Total, 2004	POPULATION (est., midyear)				
					2004	1950	1975	2000	2025
Asia	31,027,230	11,979,676	21.4	60.6	3,866,437,804	1,436,893,576	2,415,569,909	3,686,061,532	4,754,323,464
Africa	29,805,048	11,507,789	20.6	13.7	873,742,214	227,332,997	410,827,151	803,234,623	1,246,442,723
Europe	22,825,905	8,813,128	15.7	11.4	729,389,373	546,415,793	677,127,418	729,934,730	715,456,241
N. America . .	21,393,762	8,260,174	14.8	8.0	508,915,797	220,857,588	346,832,644	487,223,694	621,390,935
S. America . .	17,522,371	6,765,422	12.1	5.8	366,803,836	111,384,890	215,773,399	348,279,541	447,188,122
Oceania, incl. Australia. . .	8,428,702	3,254,339	5.8	0.5	32,352,618	12,476,128	21,220,574	30,744,658	39,685,917
Antarctica[2] . .	14,000,000	5,405,428	9.7	—	—	—	—	—	—
WORLD	145,003,018	55,985,955			6,377,641,642	2,555,360,972	4,087,351,095	6,085,478,778	7,824,487,402

Note: Areas are as defined by the U.S. Bureau of the Census. Area for Europe includes all of Russia. Figures may not add to totals because of rounding. (1) Projected. (2) Antarctica has no indigenous inhabitants; researchers stay for various periods of time.

Population of the World's Largest Cities

Source: United Nations, Dept. for Economic and Social Information and Policy Analysis

Population figures are 2003 revised UN estimates and projections for "urban agglomerations"—i.e., contiguous densely populated urban areas, not demarcated by administrative boundaries. Data may differ from figures elsewhere in *The World Almanac*.

Rank[1] City, Country	Pop. (thousands) 2000	Pop. (thousands, projected) 2015	Annual growth rate (percent) 1995-2000	Pop. (thousands) 1975	Total Growth (percent) 1975-2000	Total Growth (percent) 2000-2015[2]	Pop. of city as percentage of nation's 2000 pop.
1. Tokyo, Japan	34,450	36,214	0.51	26,615	29.4	5.1	27.1
2. Mexico City, Mexico	18,066	20,647	1.47	10,690	69.0	14.3	18.3
3. New York City, U.S.	17,846	19,717	1.04	15,880	12.4	10.5	6.3
4. São Paulo, Brazil	17,099	19,963	1.39	9,614	77.9	16.7	10.0
5. Mumbai (Bombay), India	16,086	22,645	2.62	7,347	118.9	40.8	1.6
6. Kolkata (Calcutta), India	13,058	16,798	1.82	7,888	65.5	28.6	1.3
7. Shanghai, China	12,887	12,666	−0.35	11,443	12.6	−1.7	1.0
8. Buenos Aires, Argentina	12,583	14,563	1.18	9,143	37.6	15.7	33.9
9. Delhi, India	12,441	20,946	4.18	4,426	181.1	68.4	1.2
10. Los Angeles, U.S.	11,814	12,904	0.82	8,926	32.4	9.2	4.1
11. Osaka, Japan	11,165	11,359	0.20	9,844	13.4	1.7	8.8
12. Jakarta, Indonesia	11,018	17,498	3.69	4,813	128.9	58.8	5.2
13. Beijing, China	10,839	11,060	0.02	8,545	26.8	2.0	0.8
14. Rio de Janeiro, Brazil	10,803	12,364	1.20	7,557	43.0	14.4	6.3
15. Cairo, Egypt	10,398	13,123	1.38	6,437	61.5	26.2	15.3

(1) Ranked by 2000 population. (2) Projected.

The World's Refugees, 2003

Source: *World Refugee Survey 2004*, U.S. Committee for Refugees, a nonprofit corp.

These estimates are conservative and have been rounded. Totals include individuals granted asylum and those who had pending asylum claims as of year-end 2003. Figures generally do not include those who have achieved permanent resettlement.

(as of Dec. 31, 2003; only countries estimated to host 50,000 or more refugees are listed)

Place of asylum	Origin of Most Refugees	Number
AFRICA		3,245,500
Algeria	Western Sahara, Palestinians	170,000*
Central African Rep.	Sudan, Dem. Rep. of Congo	51,000
Chad	Sudan, Central African Republic	156,000
Dem. Rep. of the Congo	Angola, Sudan, Burundi, Uganda	241,000*
Rep. of the Congo	Dem. Rep. of Congo, Rwanda	91,000
Côte d'Ivoire	Liberia	74,000*
Egypt	Palestinians, Sudan, Somalia	69,000*
Ethiopia	Sudan, Somalia, Eritrea	112,000*
Guinea	Liberia, Sierra Leone, Côte d'Ivoire	223,000*
Kenya	Somalia, Sudan, Ethiopia	219,000*
Liberia	Côte d'Ivoire, Sierra Leone	60,000*
Sierra Leone	Liberia	70,000*
South Africa	Dem. Rep. of the Congo, Somalia, Angola	104,000
Sudan	Eritrea, Uganda, Ethiopia	280,000*
Tanzania	Burundi, Dem. Rep. of the Congo, Somalia	480,000*
Uganda	Sudan, Rwanda, Dem. Rep. of the Congo	231,500*
Zambia	Angola, Dem. Rep. of the Congo, Rwanda	239,000*
EUROPE		884,500
Germany	Serbia and Montenegro (Kosovo), Bosnia and Herzegovina, Afghanistan	90,800

Place of asylum	Origin of Most Refugees	Number
Serbia and Montenegro	Croatia, Bosnia and Herzegovina	291,100
Russia	Afghanistan, Georgia	161,300*
United Kingdom	Somalia, Zimbabwe, Turkey	55,700**
AMERICAS AND THE CARIBBEAN		543,500
Canada	Colombia, Pakistan, Mexico	70,200
United States	Cuba, Haiti, Liberia, Colombia	244,200**
EAST ASIA AND THE PACIFIC		953,400
China	Vietnam, North Korea	396,000*
Malaysia	Philippines, Myanmar, Indonesia	75,700
Thailand	Myanmar, Laos	421,500
MIDDLE EAST		4,353,100
Gaza Strip	Palestinians	923,000
Iran	Afghanistan, Iraq	1,335,000*
Iraq	Palestinians, Iran, Turkey, Syria	131,500*
Jordan	Palestinians, Iraq	163,700*
Kuwait	Palestinians, Iraq	65,000
Lebanon	Palestinians, Iraq	256,000*
Saudi Arabia	Palestinians, Iraq	240,900
Syria	Palestinians, Iraq	497,000*
West Bank	Palestinians	665,000
Yemen	Somalia, Ethiopia	75,000*
SOUTH AND CENTRAL ASIA		1,872,900
Bangladesh	Myanmar	119,900*
India	Sri Lanka, China (Tibet), Myanmar, Afghanistan, Bhutan	316,900
Nepal	Bhutan, China (Tibet)	134,600
Pakistan	Afghanistan, India	1,219,000*
TOTAL		11,852,900

* Estimates vary widely in number reported. **Approximate number of refugees based on cases reported.

Principal Sources of Refugees, 2003

Sources: *World Refugee Survey 2004*, U.S. Committee for Refugees (as of Dec. 31, 2003)

Former Palestine	3,000,000*	Bosnia and Herzegovina	142,200	Cuba	28,200*
Afghanistan	2,500,000*	Bhutan	128,700	Uganda	28,000
Sudan	600,000	Sri Lanka	105,700	Haiti	25,800
Myanmar	586,000*	North Korea	101,700*	Georgia	25,000
Dem. Rep. of the Congo	440,000	Serbia and Montenegro	70,100	Indonesia	23,600
Liberia	384,000	Sierra Leone	68,000	Mauritania	23,000
Burundi	355,000	Tajikistan	59,800	Pakistan	21,000
Angola	323,000*	Philippines	58,500	Mexico	20,700
Vietnam	307,200	Côte d'Ivoire	55,000	Rep. of the Congo	20,000
Iraq	280,600*	Russia	49,000	Ethiopia	19,000
Eritrea	280,000*	Rwanda	46,000*	Cambodia	16,100
Somalia	277,000	Central African Republic	41,000	Laos	15,000
Colombia	233,600	Turkey	40,000	Senegal	13,000
Croatia	209,100	Nigeria	39,000	Ghana	12,000
Western Sahara	190,000*	India	35,800	Guatemala	11,600
China	157,500	Iran	35,000	Ukraine	11,200

*Estimates from different sources may vary significantly.

> **IT'S A FACT:** By Sept. 2004, there were more than 1 million Sudanese refugees in camps in Sudan and Chad who fled their homes because of continuing raids on black African towns and villages by marauding Arab militias.

IT'S A FACT: The world's urban population reached 1 billion in 1960, 3 billion in 2003, and was projected to reach 5 billion by 2030. In 1960, 33% of all people lived in urban areas, rising to 48% in 2003. The urban population is growing faster than the world population, and is expected to surpass 50% of the world total by 2007.

Estimated HIV Infection and Reported AIDS Cases, Year-end 2003

Source: UNAIDS, Joint United Nations Program on HIV/AIDS

The spread of AIDS (acquired immune deficiency syndrome) has had a major impact on life expectancies in sub-Saharan Africa and parts of Asia. In some parts of Africa, for instance, life expectancy at birth has dropped to less than 33 years, primarily as a result of AIDS.

According to UN estimates for year-end 2003, the number of people living with HIV/AIDS worldwide continued to climb, with about 37.8 million people infected with the virus, up from 34.9 million in 2001. The largest number of AIDS victims were in sub-Saharan Africa, which had more than 60% of total cases. Asia had its largest increase in infections in 2003, and the number of cases in India rose to 5.1 million. The world total also includes about 2.1 million children (under 15 years old); most children with AIDS are believed to have acquired HIV (human immuno-deficiency virus) from their mother before or at birth, or through breast feeding. UNAIDS estimates that 4.8 million new HIV infections occurred in 2003 and that almost 3 million people died of AIDS that year, including about 500,000 children.

The 15th International AIDS Conference took place July 11-16, 2004, in Bangkok, Thailand. The major theme addressed was the need for increasing access to education, information, and medication for the millions infected with HIV, as well as increasing cooperation among scientists, community workers, and political leaders in battling the epidemic. In Dec. 2003, UN-AIDS and the World Health Organization announced the "3 by 5" plan to treat 3 million people with antiretroviral drugs by 2005.

Studies, primarily in industrialized nations, have indicated that about 60% of adults infected by HIV develop AIDS within 12-13 years of becoming infected; development of the disease may be more rapid in Third World countries.

Since the start of the global epidemic in the late 1970s, more than 60 million people have been infected with HIV, and over 20 million people have died of the disease. By the end of 2003, some 14 million children had been orphaned as a result of AIDS.

Current, New HIV/AIDS Cases and Deaths by Region, Year-end 2003

Region	Current cases[1]	Percent[2]	New Cases 2003	Est. Deaths 2003
Sub-Saharan Africa	25,000,000	66.1	3,000,000	2,200,000
South/Southeast Asia	6,500,000	17.2	850,000	460,000
Latin America	1,600,000	4.2	200,000	84,000
East Asia/Pacific	900,000	2.4	200,000	44,000
Eastern Europe/Central Asia	1,300,000	3.4	360,000	49,000
North America	1,000,000	2.6	44,000	16,000
Western Europe	580,000	1.5	20,000	6,000
North Africa/Middle East	480,000	1.3	75,000	24,000
Caribbean	430,000	1.1	52,000	35,000
Oceania	32,000	—	5,000	700
WORLD[3]	**37,800,000**	**100.0**	**4,800,000**	**2,900,000**

(1) Adults and children living with HIV/AIDS. (2) Percentage of total number of people worldwide living with HIV. (3) Details do not add to total because of rounding. (—) Dash means less than 1%.

Major Foreign Development Aid Donors, 2001-2002

Source: Organization for Economic Cooperation and Development; ranked by percent of GNI (Gross National Income) in 2002.

In 2002, the U.S. gave the highest total amount of development aid but ranked 22nd by percent of GNI.

Country	ODA[1], as % of GNI 2001	ODA[1], as % of GNI 2002	ODA[1] in U.S. dollars (millions) 2001	ODA[1] in U.S. dollars (millions) 2002	Country	ODA[1], as % of GNI 2001	ODA[1], as % of GNI 2002	ODA[1] in U.S. dollars (millions) 2001	ODA[1] in U.S. dollars (millions) 2002
1. Denmark	1.03	0.96	$1,634	$1,632	12. Canada	0.22	0.28	$1,533	$2,013
2. Norway	0.80	0.91	1,346	1,746	13. Germany	0.27	0.27	4,990	5,359
3. Netherlands	0.82	0.82	3,172	3,377	14. Spain	0.30	0.25	1,737	1,608
4. Luxembourg	0.82	0.78	1,41	1,43	16. Australia	0.25	0.25	873	962
5. Sweden	0.77	0.74	1,666	1,754	Portugal	0.25	0.24	268	282
6. Belgium	0.37	0.42	867	1,061	17 Austria	0.29	0.23	533	475
7. Ireland	0.33	0.41	287	397	New Zealand	0.25	0.23	112	124
8. France	0.32	0.36	4,198	5,182	Japan	0.23	0.23	9,847	9,220
9. Finland	0.32	0.35	389	466	20. Greece	0.17	0.22	202	295
10. Switzerland	0.34	0.32	908	933	21. Italy	0.15	0.20	1,627	2,313
11. United Kingdom	0.32	0.30	4,579	4,749	22. United States	0.11	0.12	11,429	12,900

(1) ODA = official development assistance.

Top 10 Recipients of U.S. Development Aid, 2001-2002

Source: Organization for Economic Cooperation and Development

Country	Millions of U.S. $ (avg. 2001-2002)	Country	Millions of U.S. $ (avg. 2001-2002)	Country	Millions of U.S. $ (avg. 2001-2002)
1. Egypt	$919	5. Serbia and Montenegro	$353	8. Jordan	$225
2. Russia	813	6. Colombia	330	9. Peru	188
3. Israel	529	7. Ukraine	257	10. Afghanistan	188
4. Pakistan	494				

Nuclear Powers of the World

As of Sept. 2004, 7 countries were acknowledged nuclear powers: **Britain**, **France**, **China**, **India**, **Pakistan**, **Russia**, and the **United States**. In addition, **Israel** was thought to have a nuclear arsenal of 98 to 172 warheads, and **Iran** and **North Korea** were suspected of developing nuclear weapons, despite strong international pressure for them to desist. More than 40 nations have the knowledge or technology needed to produce nuclear weapons. All have signed the Nuclear Non-Proliferation Treaty (NPT) except for Israel, India, and Pakistan. North Korea withdrew in Jan. 2003

Several countries have abandoned their nuclear ambitions. **South Africa** announced in 1993 that it had built 7 fission weapons, but had dismantled all of them. In the 1980s **Argentina** and **Brazil** had active nuclear weapons programs, but they abandoned them by mutual treaty and signed the NPT. After the Soviet Union dissolved in 1993, **Belarus**, **Kazakhstan**, and **Ukraine** joined the NPT and allowed Russia to remove its nuclear weapons located there.

Estimate Numbers of Nuclear Weapons by Country, 1945-2002

Source: Natural Resources Defense Council; Carnegie Endowment for Int. Peace

End Year	United States	U.S.S.R. Russia	United Kingdom	France	China[3]	India	Pakistan
1945	6	—	—	—	—	—	—
1950	369	5	—	—	—	—	—
1960	20,434	1,605	30	—	—	—	—
1970	26,119	11,643	280	36	75	—	—
1980	23,764	30,062	350	250	280	—	—
1990	21,211	33,417	300	505	430	—	—
1995	10,953	14,978	300	500	400	—	—
2000	10,615	10,201	185	450	400	—	—
2002	10,640[1]	8,600[2]	200	350	400	50-90[4]	50[4]

(1) Number excludes weapons marked for dismantlement. (2) Excludes weapons marked for dismantlement or in reserve status; in 2002 there were an estimated 18,000 intact warheads. (3) Based on estimates of number of tactical warheads that may be up to 50% inaccurate. (4) Estimated number of weapons the nation has enough weapons-grade material to produce; number of assembled weapons is unknown.

Major International Organizations

African Union (AU), inaugurated July 9, 2002, in Durban, South Africa, following disbanding of the Organization of African Unity, and consisting of the same 53 members; i.e., all countries of Africa except Morocco, including the territory of Western Sahara. The new organization was intended to focus achieving greater socio-economic integration, peace, and unity among its member states. The founders provided for a peer review committee to oversee member states' adherence to standards of good government, respect for human rights, and financial transparency. The AU's founding document authorized the organization to intervene to stop genocide, war crimes, or human rights abuses within individual member nations. **Headquarters:** Ethiopia. **Website:** www.africa-union.org

Asia-Pacific Economic Cooperation (APEC), founded Nov. 1989 as a forum to further cooperation on trade and investment between nations of the region and the rest of the world. Members in 2004 were Australia, Brunei, Canada, Chile, China, Hong Kong, Indonesia, Japan, Malaysia, Mexico, New Zealand, Papua New Guinea, Peru, Philippines, Russia, Singapore, South Korea, Taiwan, Thailand, U.S., and Vietnam. **Headquarters:** Singapore. **Website:** www.apecsec.org.sg

Association of Southeast Asian Nations (ASEAN), formed Aug. 8, 1967, to promote economic, social, and cultural cooperation and development among states of the Southeast Asian region. Members in 2004 were Brunei, Cambodia, Indonesia, Laos, Malaysia, Myanmar, Philippines, Singapore, Thailand, and Vietnam. **Headquarters:** Jakarta. **Website:** www.aseansec.org

Caribbean Community and Common Market (CARICOM), established Aug. 1, 1973. Its aim is to increase cooperation in economics, health, education, culture, science and technology, and tax administration, as well as the coordination of foreign policy. Members in 2004 were Antigua and Barbuda, Bahamas (Community only), Barbados, Belize, Dominica, Grenada, Guyana, Haiti, Jamaica, Montserrat, Saint Kitts and Nevis, Saint Lucia, Saint Vincent and the Grenadines, Suriname, and Trinidad and Tobago. Associate members in 2004 were Anguilla, Bermuda, Virgin Islands, Cayman Islands, Turks and Caicos. **Headquarters:** Georgetown, Guyana. **Website:** www.caricom.org

The Commonwealth, originally called the British Commonwealth of Nations, then the Commonwealth of Nations; an association of nations and dependencies that were once parts of the former British Empire. The British monarch is the symbolic head of the Commonwealth.

There are 53 independent nations in the Commonwealth. As of 2004, regular members included the United Kingdom and 15 other nations recognizing the British monarch, represented by a governor-general, as their head of state: Antigua and Barbuda, Australia, Bahamas, Barbados, Belize, Canada, Grenada, Jamaica, New Zealand, Papua New Guinea, Saint Kitts and Nevis, Saint Lucia, Saint Vincent and the Grenadines, the Solomon Islands, and Tuvalu. Also members in good standing were 37 countries with their own heads of state: Bangladesh, Botswana, Brunei, Cameroon, Cyprus, Dominica, Fiji, The Gambia, Ghana, Guyana, India, Kenya, Kiribati, Lesotho, Malawi, Malaysia, Maldives, Malta, Mauritius, Mozambique (the only member never part of the British Empire), Namibia, Nauru, Nigeria, Pakistan, Samoa, Seychelles, Sierra Leone, Singapore, South Africa, Sri Lanka, Swaziland, Tanzania, Tonga, Trinidad and Tobago, Uganda, Vanuatu, and Zambia.

Pakistan was suspended from the councils of the Commonwealth in Oct. 1999, following a military coup, but regained its member status Mar. 22, 2004. Zimbabwe was suspended in Mar. 2002, following election and land redistribution controversies; Zimbabwe withdrew from the Commonwealth, Dec. 7, 2003. The Commonwealth facilitates consultation among members through meetings of ministers and through a permanent Secretariat. **Headquarters:** London. **Website:** www.thecommonwealth.org

Commonwealth of Independent States (CIS), an alliance established in Dec. 1991, made up of former Soviet constituent republics. Members in 2004 were: Armenia, Azerbaijan, Belarus, Georgia, Kazakhstan, Kyrgyzstan, Moldova, Russia, Tajikistan, Turkmenistan, Ukraine, and Uzbekistan. Policy is set through coordinating bodies such as a Council of Heads of State and Council of Heads of Government. **Headquarters** of the commonwealth: Minsk, Belarus. **Website:** www.cis.minsk.by

European Free Trade Association (EFTA), created May 3, 1960, to promote expansion of free trade. By Dec. 31, 1966, tariffs and quotas between member nations had been eliminated. Members entered into free trade agreements with the EU in 1972 and 1973. In 1992, EFTA and EU agreed to create a single market—with free flow of goods, services, capital, and labor—among nations of the 2 organizations. Members in 2004 were Iceland, Liechtenstein, Norway, and Switzerland. Many former EFTA members are now EU members. **Headquarters:** Geneva. **Website:** www.efta.int

European Union (EU)—known as the European Community (EC) until 1994; the name covers 3 organizations with

common membership: the European Economic Community (Common Market), European Coal and Steel Community, and European Atomic Energy Community (Euratom). A merger of the 3 communities' executives went into effect July 1, 1967. As of Sept. 2004, there were 25 EU members. These included 12 original members (France, Germany, Greece, Ireland, Italy, Luxembourg, Netherlands, Portugal, Spain, and UK), 3 states that entered Jan. 1, 1995 (Austria, Finland, and Sweden), and 10 members that joined on May 1, 2004 (Cyprus, Czech Republic, Estonia, Hungary, Latvia, Lithuania, Malta, Poland, Slovakia, and Slovenia.). Some 70 nations in Africa, the Caribbean, and the Pacific are affiliated under the Lomé Convention. **Headquarters:** Brussels, Belgium. **Website:** europa.eu.int

The EU aims to integrate the economies, coordinate social developments, and bring about political union of the member states. The Council of the Union, European Commission, European Parliament, and European Courts of Justice and of Auditors comprise the permanent structure. Effective Dec. 31, 1992, there are no restrictions on the movement of goods, services, capital, workers, and tourists within the EU. There are also common agricultural, fisheries, and nuclear research policies.

Leaders of member nations (12 at the time), meeting Dec. 9-11, 1991, in Maastricht, the Netherlands, committed the organization to launching a common currency (the euro) by 1999; sought to establish common foreign policies; laid the groundwork for a common defense policy; gave the organization a leading role in social policy (Britain was not included in this plan); pledged increased aid for poorer member nations; and slightly increased the powers of the 567-member European Parliament. The treaties went into effect Nov. 1, 1993, following ratification by all 12 members.

In June 1998 the European Central Bank was established. In Jan. 1999, 11 of the then-15 EU countries began using the euro for some purposes: Austria, Belgium, Finland, France, Germany, Ireland, Italy, Luxembourg, Netherlands, Portugal, and Spain. By Feb. 2002, national currencies in these 11 countries and Greece were removed from circulation and replaced with the euro as the only currency of legal tender. EU peacekeeping forces replaced NATO troops in Macedonia, Mar. 31, 2003, the first such mission for the organization.

Group of Eight (G-8), established Sept. 22, 1985; organization of 7 major industrial democracies (Canada, France, Germany, Italy, Japan, UK, and U.S.) and (later) Russia, meeting periodically to discuss economic and other issues. At its annual economic summit in May 1998, the name was changed to G-8 from G-7. The 7 were still free to meet without Russia on some issues, especially those relating to global finance. The annual G-8 summit was hosted in the U.S. at Sea Island, GA, June 8-10, 2004. The 2005 summit was scheduled to be held July 6-8 in Perthshire, Scotland.

International Criminal Police Organization (Interpol), created June 13, 1956, to promote mutual assistance among all police authorities within the limits of the law existing in the different countries. There were 181 members (independent nations), plus 14 subbureaus (dependencies) in 2004. **Website:** www.interpol.com

League of Arab States (Arab League), created Mar. 22, 1945. The League promotes economic, social, political, and military cooperation, mediates disputes, and represents Arab states in certain international negotiations. Members in 2004 were Algeria, Bahrain, Comoros, Djibouti, Egypt, Iraq, Jordan, Kuwait, Lebanon, Mauritania, Morocco, Oman, Palestine (considered an independent state by the League), Qatar, Saudi Arabia, Somalia, Sudan, Syria, Tunisia, United Arab Emirates, and Yemen. Libya withdrew its membership Oct. 2002. **Headquarters:** Cairo. **Website:** www.arableagueonline.org

North Atlantic Treaty Organization (NATO), created by treaty (signed Apr. 4, 1949; in effect Aug. 24, 1949). Members in 2004 included Belgium, Bulgaria, Canada, Czech Republic, Denmark, Estonia, France, Germany, Greece, Hungary, Iceland, Italy, Latvia, Lithuania, Luxembourg, Netherlands, Norway, Poland, Portugal, Romania, Slovakia, Slovenia, Spain, Turkey, U.K, and U.S. In addition, on March 29, 2004, 7 new states—Bulgaria, Estonia,

Latvia, Lithuania, Romania, Slovakia, and Slovenia—joined the alliance. All are former Warsaw Pact nations from Eastern Europe. This marked the fifth time NATO increased its membership, and was the largest expansion at one time.

Members have agreed to settle disputes by peaceful means, to develop their capacity to resist armed attack, to regard an attack on one as an attack on all, and to take necessary action to repel an attack under Article 51 of the UN Charter. **Headquarters:** Brussels. **Website:** www.nato.int

The NATO structure consists of the North Atlantic Council (NAC), the Defense Planning Committee, the Military Committee (realigned in June 2003 and consisting of 2 commands: Allied Command Operations, and Allied Command Transformation), the Nuclear Planning Group, and the Canada-U.S. Regional Planning Group. France detached itself from the military command structure in 1966.

With the end of the cold war in the early 1990s, members put greater stress on political action and on creating a rapid deployment force to react to local crises. By the mid-1990s, 27 nations, including Russia and other former Soviet republics, had joined with NATO in the so-called Partnership for Peace (PfP; drafted Dec. 1993), which provided for limited joint military exercises, peace-keeping missions, and information exchange. NATO has proceeded gradually toward extending full membership to former Eastern bloc nations. On Mar. 12, 1999, 3 former Warsaw Pact members, Hungary, Poland, and the Czech Republic, formally became members. NATO and Russia signed a cooperation pact May 28, 2002, forming NATO-Russia Council, and NATO invited 7 former eastern-bloc nations to join the alliance, Nov. 21.

In Dec. 1995, a NATO-led multinational force (SFOR) was deployed to help keep the peace in Bosnia and Herzegovina; in 1999, another force (KFOR) was deployed in Kosovo.

Following the terrorist attacks on the U.S., the NATO Council agreed, Sept. 12, 2001, to invoke for the first time Article 5 of the treaty, which stipulates mutual defense of alliance members. NATO assumed control of the International Security Assistance Force in Afghanistan (ISAF), Aug. 2003, marking the first time NATO led a mission outside Europe. As of Sept. 2004, the ISAF numbered about 6,500.

Organization of African Unity (OAU), formed May 25, 1963, by 32 African countries. Disbanded July, 2002, and re-formed as the African Union (AU).

Organization of American States (OAS), formed in Bogotá, Colombia, Apr. 30, 1948. It has a Permanent Council, Inter-American Council for Integral Development, Juridical Committee, and Commission on Human Rights. The Permanent Council can call meetings of foreign ministers to deal with urgent security matters. A General Assembly meets annually.

Members in 2004 were Antigua and Barbuda, Argentina, Bahamas, Barbados, Belize, Bolivia, Brazil, Canada, Chile, Colombia, Costa Rica, Cuba, Dominica, Dominican Republic, Ecuador, El Salvador, Grenada, Guatemala, Guyana, Haiti, Honduras, Jamaica, Mexico, Nicaragua, Panama, Paraguay, Peru, Saint Kitts and Nevis, Saint Lucia, Saint Vincent and the Grenadines, Suriname, Trinidad and Tobago, U.S., Uruguay, and Venezuela. In 1962, the OAS suspended Cuba from participation in activities but not from membership. **Headquarters:** Washington, DC. **Website:** www.oas.org

Organization for Economic Cooperation and Development (OECD), established Dec. 14, 1960, to promote the economic and social welfare of all its member countries and to stimulate efforts on behalf of developing nations. The OECD also collects and disseminates economic and environmental information. Members in 2004 were Australia, Austria, Belgium, Canada, Czech Republic, Denmark, Finland, France, Germany, Greece, Hungary, Iceland, Ireland, Italy, Japan, Luxembourg, Mexico, Netherlands, New Zealand, Norway, Poland, Portugal, Slovakia, South Korea, Spain, Sweden, Switzerland, Turkey, United Kingdom, and the United States. **Headquarters:** Paris. **Website:** www.oecd.org

Organization of Petroleum Exporting Countries (OPEC), created Sept. 14, 1960. This group made up of most—but not all—major petroleum exporting nations, seeks to stabilize the oil market and set world oil prices by controlling production. Members in 2004 were Algeria, In-

donesia, Iran, Iraq, Kuwait, Libya, Nigeria, Qatar, Saudi Arabia, United Arab Emirates, and Venezuela. **Headquarters:** Vienna. **Website:** www.opec.org

Organization for Security and Cooperation in Europe (OSCE), established in 1972 as the Conference on Security and Cooperation in Europe; name adopted Jan. 1, 1995. The group, formed by NATO and Warsaw Pact members, seeks improved East-West relations through a commitment to nonaggression and human rights as well as cooperation in economics, science and technology, cultural exchange, and environmental protection. There were 55 member states in 2004. **Headquarters:** Vienna. **Website:** www.osce.org

United Nations

The 59th regular session of United Nations General Assembly opened Sept. 14, 2004, attended by world leaders and other delegates from 191 nations.

UN headquarters is in New York, NY, between First Ave. and Roosevelt Drive and E. 42d St. and E. 48th St.

The 6 main organs of the UN are the General Assembly, Security Council, Economic and Social Council, Trusteeship Council, International Court of Justice, and Secretariat. The UN family is much larger, encompassing 15 agencies and several programs and bodies.

The UN Dept. of Public Information maintains its own news service, which can be accessed at www.un.org/news. It also publishes the *UN Chronicle*, available at www.un.org/pubs/chronicle. The UN has a post office originating its own stamps.

Proposals to establish an organization of nations for maintenance of world peace led to convening of the United Nations Conference on International Organization at San Francisco, Apr. 25-June 26, 1945, where the UN charter was drawn up. It was signed June 26 by 50 nations, and by Poland, one of the original 51 members, on Oct. 15, 1945. It came into effect Oct. 24, 1945, upon ratification by the permanent members of the Security Council and a majority of other signatories.

Purposes: To maintain international peace and security; to develop friendly relations among nations; to achieve international cooperation in solving economic, social, cultural, and humanitarian problems and in promoting respect for human rights and basic freedoms; to be a center for harmonizing the actions of nations in attaining these common ends.

Visitors to the UN: Headquarters is open to the public every day except Thanksgiving, Christmas, New Year's Day, Eid al-Adha (Jan. 21, 2005), and Eid al Fitr (Nov. 4, 2005). Guided tours are given approximately every half hour from 9:30 AM to 4:45 PM weekdays; 10 AM to 4:30 PM weekends. The UN is closed weekends in Jan. and Feb.

Groups of 12 or more should write to the Group Programmes Unit, Room GA-56, United Nations, New York, NY 10017, e-mail unitg@un.org, or telephone (212) 963-TOUR. Children under 5 not permitted on tours.

Organization of the United Nations

The United Nations consists of 6 principal organs, 15 agencies, and many programs and other bodies. The 6 principal organs are the General Assembly, the Security Council, the Secretariat, the Economic and Social Council, the Trusteeship Council, and the Intl. Court for Justice.

General Assembly. The General Assembly is composed of representatives of all the member nations. Each nation is entitled to one vote. The General Assembly meets in regular annual sessions and in special session when convoked at the request of the Security Council or a majority of UN members. On important questions a two-thirds majority of members present and voting is required; on other questions a simple majority is sufficient.

The General Assembly must approve the UN budget and apportion expenses among members. A member in arrears can lose its vote if the amount of arrears equals or exceeds the amount of the contributions due for the preceding 2 full years. **Website:** www.un.org/ga

Security Council. The Security Council consists of 15 members, 5 with permanent seats. The remaining 10 are elected for 2-year terms by the General Assembly. **Website:** www.un.org/docs/sc

Permanent members of the Council are: China, France, Russia, United Kingdom, and the United States. Nonpermanent members are (with terms expiring Dec. 31, 2004): Angola, Chile, Germany, Pakistan, Spain; (with terms expiring Dec. 31, 2005): Algeria, Benin, Brazil, Philippines, and Romania.

The Security Council has the primary responsibility within the UN for maintaining international peace and security. The Council may investigate any dispute that threatens international peace and security.

Any member of the UN at UN headquarters may, if invited by the Council, participate in its discussions, and a nation not a member of the UN may appear if it is a party to a dispute. Decisions on procedural questions are made by an affirmative vote of 9 members. On all other matters the affirmative vote of 9 members must include the concurring votes of all permanent members (giving them veto power). A party to a dispute must refrain from voting.

The Security Council directs the various peacekeeping forces deployed throughout the world.

Secretariat. The Secretariat is an international staff of about 8,900 that carries out the day-to-day operations of the UN and is headed by the secretary general. The secretary general is the chief administrative officer of the UN, and is appointed by the General Assembly, on the recommendation of the Security Council, for a five-year, renewable term. The Secretary General reports to the General Assembly and may bring to the attention of the Security Council any matter that threatens international peace.

Economic and Social Council. The Economic and Social Council consists of 54 members elected by the General Assembly for 3-year terms. The council is responsible for carrying out UN functions with regard to international economic, social, cultural, educational, health, and related matters. It meets once a year. **Website:** www.un.org/esa

Trusteeship Council. The administration of trust territories was under UN supervision; however, all 11 Trust Territories have attained their right to self-determination. The work of the Council was suspended May 1994.

Budget: The General Assembly approved a total budget for the biennium 2004-2005 of $3.16 billion.

International Court of Justice (World Court). The International Court of Justice is the principal judicial organ of the UN. All members are ipso facto parties to the statute of the Court. The Court has jurisdiction over cases the parties submit to it and matters especially provided for in the charter or in treaties. It gives advisory opinions and renders judgments. In disputes between nations, the Court's decisions are binding only between parties concerned and in respect to a particular dispute. If any party to a case fails to heed a judgment, the other party may have recourse to the Security Council.

The 15 judges are elected for 9-year terms by the General Assembly and the Security Council. Retiring judges are eligible for reelection. The Court remains permanently in session, except during vacations. All questions are decided by majority. The International Court of Justice sits in The Hague, Netherlands. **Website:** www.icj-cij.org

The text of the **UN Charter** may be obtained from the Public Inquiries Unit, Department of Public Information, United Nations, New York, NY 10017. (212) 963-4475. **Website:** www.un.org/aboutUN/charter/index.html

---

IT'S A FACT: World population is expected to rise by nearly 50% by 2050, according to recent projections from the Population Reference Bureau, an independent educational organization. However, populations of industrialized nations are expected to increase by only 4%, while those of developing countries are projected to rise by 55%. The populations of some industrialized nations are expected to decline. By 2050, Japan's population is projected to drop by 20%, Russia's by 17%, and Germany's by 9%.

Roster of the United Nations

The 191 members of the United Nations, with the years in which they became members; as of Oct. 2003.

Member	Year	Member	Year	Member	Year	Member	Year
Afghanistan	1946	Dominica	1978	Liberia	1945	Saint Vincent and the	1980
Albania	1955	Dominican Republic	1945	Libya	1955	Grenadines	
Algeria	1962	East Timor	2002	Liechtenstein	1990	Samoa (formerly	1976
Andorra	1993	Ecuador	1945	Lithuania	1991	Western Samoa)	
Angola	1976	Egypt[3]	1945	Luxembourg	1945	San Marino	1992
Antigua and Barbuda	1981	El Salvador	1945	Macedonia[5]	1993	São Tomé and Príncipe	1975
Argentina	1945	Equatorial Guinea	1968	Madagascar	1960	Saudi Arabia	1945
Armenia	1992	Eritrea	1993	Malawi	1964	Senegal	1960
Australia	1945	Estonia	1991	Malaysia[6]	1957	Serbia and Montenegro[8]	1945
Austria	1955	Ethiopia	1945	Maldives	1965	Seychelles	1976
Azerbaijan	1992	Fiji	1970	Mali	1960	Sierra Leone	1961
Bahamas	1973	Finland	1955	Malta	1964	Singapore[6]	1965
Bahrain	1971	France	1945	Marshall Islands	1991	Slovakia[2]	1993
Bangladesh	1974	Gabon	1960	Mauritania	1961	Slovenia	1992
Barbados	1966	Gambia, The	1965	Mauritius	1968	Solomon Islands	1978
Belarus	1945	Georgia	1992	Mexico	1945	Somalia	1960
Belgium	1945	Germany	1973	Micronesia	1991	South Africa[9]	1945
Belize	1981	Ghana	1957	Moldova	1992	Spain	1955
Benin	1960	Greece	1945	Monaco	1993	Sri Lanka	1955
Bhutan	1971	Grenada	1974	Mongolia	1961	Sudan	1956
Bolivia	1945	Guatemala	1945	Morocco	1956	Suriname	1975
Bosnia & Herzegovina	1992	Guinea	1958	Mozambique	1975	Swaziland	1968
Botswana	1966	Guinea-Bissau	1974	Myanmar (Burma)	1948	Sweden	1946
Brazil	1945	Guyana	1966	Namibia	1990	Switzerland	2002
Brunei	1984	Haiti	1945	Nauru	1999	Syria[3]	1945
Bulgaria	1955	Honduras	1945	Nepal	1955	Tajikistan	1992
Burkina Faso	1960	Hungary	1955	Netherlands	1945	Tanzania[10]	1961
Burundi	1962	Iceland	1946	New Zealand	1945	Thailand	1946
Cambodia	1955	India	1945	Nicaragua	1945	Togo	1960
Cameroon	1960	Indonesia[4]	1950	Niger	1960	Tonga	1999
Canada	1945	Iran	1945	Nigeria	1960	Trinidad and Tobago	1962
Cape Verde	1975	Iraq	1945	Norway	1945	Tunisia	1956
Central African Rep.	1960	Ireland	1955	Oman	1971	Turkey	1945
Chad	1960	Israel	1949	Pakistan	1947	Turkmenistan	1992
Chile	1945	Italy	1955	Palau	1994	Tuvalu	2000
China[1]	1945	Jamaica	1962	Panama	1945	Uganda	1962
Colombia	1945	Japan	1956	Papua New Guinea	1975	Ukraine	1945
Comoros	1975	Jordan	1955	Paraguay	1945	United Arab Emirates	1971
Congo, Democratic	1960	Kazakhstan	1992	Peru	1945	United Kingdom	1945
Rep. of the (Zaire)		Kenya	1963	Philippines	1945	United States	1945
Congo, Republic of the.	1960	Kiribati	1999	Poland	1945	Uruguay	1945
Costa Rica	1945	Korea, North	1991	Portugal	1955	Uzbekistan	1992
Côte d'Ivoire	1960	Korea, South	1991	Qatar	1971	Vanuatu	1981
Croatia	1992	Kuwait	1963	Romania	1955	Venezuela	1945
Cuba	1945	Kyrgyzstan	1992	Russia[7]	1945	Vietnam	1977
Cyprus	1960	Laos	1955	Rwanda	1962	Yemen[11]	1947
Czech Republic[2]	1993	Latvia	1991	Saint Kitts and Nevis	1983	Zambia	1964
Denmark	1945	Lebanon	1945	Saint Lucia	1979	Zimbabwe	1980
Djibouti	1977	Lesotho	1966				

(1) The General Assembly voted in 1971 to expel the Chinese government on Taiwan and admit the Beijing government. (2) Czechoslovakia, which split into Czech Republic and Slovakia on Jan. 1, 1993, was a UN member from 1945 to 1992. (3) Egypt and Syria were original members. In 1958, the United Arab Republic was established by a union of Egypt and Syria and continued as one single member of the UN. In 1961, Syria resumed its separate membership. (4) Indonesia withdrew from the UN in 1965 and rejoined in 1966. (5) Admitted under the provisional name of The Former Yugoslav Republic of Macedonia. (6) Malaya joined the UN in 1957. In 1963, its name was changed to Malaysia following the accession of Singapore, Sabah, and Sarawak. Singapore became an independent UN member in 1965. (7) The USSR was an original member from 1945. After the USSR's dissolution in 1991, Russia informed the UN it would be continuing the USSR's membership in the Security Council and all other UN organs with the support of the Commonwealth of Independent States (comprising most of the former Soviet republics). (8) The Socialist Federal Republic of Yugoslavia became a member in 1945. After 4 of its 6 republics (Bosnia and Herzegovina, Croatia, Macedonia, and Slovenia) declared independence in 1991-92, the 2 remaining republics, Montenegro and Serbia, reconstituted themselves as the Federal Republic of Yugoslavia, which assumed Yugoslavia's UN seat Apr. 8, 1992. In Sept. 1992, the General Assembly decided the Federal Republic of Yugoslavia could not automatically take the seat of the former Yugoslavia. Membership was granted in Nov. 2000 by a vote of the General Assembly. In Feb. 2003, Yugoslavia changed its name to Serbia and Montenegro. (9) In 1994, the General Assembly admitted the South African delegation, which had been rejected for 24 years because of apartheid. (10) Tanganyika was a member from 1961 and Zanzibar from 1963. Following the ratification in 1964 of Articles of Union between Tanganyika and Zanzibar, the United Republic of Tanganyika and Zanzibar continued as a single member of the UN, later changing its name to United Republic of Tanzania. (11) The Yemen Arab Republic was admitted in 1947; the People's Republic of Yemen, in 1967. The 2 nations merged in 1990. **NOTE:** China (Taiwan) and Vatican City are not members. Vatican City is a permanent observer.

United Nations Secretaries General

Took Office	Secretary, Nation	Took Office	Secretary, Nation	Took Office	Secretary, Nation
1946	Trygve Lie, Norway	1972	Kurt Waldheim, Austria	1992	Boutros Boutros-Ghali, Egypt
1953	Dag Hammarskjold, Sweden	1982	Javier Perez de Cuellar, Peru	1997	Kofi Annan, Ghana
1961	U Thant, Burma				

U.S. Representatives to the United Nations

The U.S. Representative to the United Nations is the chief of the U.S. Mission to the United Nations in New York and holds the rank and status of Ambassador Extraordinary and Plenipotentiary (A.E.P.). Year given is the year each took office.

Year	Representative	Year	Representative	Year	Representative	Year	Representative
1946	Edward R. Stettinius, Jr.	1968	George W. Ball	1976	William W. Scranton	1992	Edward J. Perkins
1946	Herschel V. Johnson (act.)	1968	James Russell Wiggins	1977	Andrew Young	1993	Madeleine K. Albright
1947	Warren R. Austin	1969	Charles W. Yost	1979	Donald McHenry	1997	Bill Richardson
1953	Henry Cabot Lodge, Jr.	1971	George H. W. Bush	1981	Jeane J. Kirkpatrick	1999	Richard C. Holbrooke
1960	James J. Wadsworth	1973	John A. Scali	1985	Vernon A. Walters	2001	John D. Negroponte
1961	Adlai E. Stevenson	1975	Daniel P. Moynihan	1989	Thomas R. Pickering	2004	John C. Danforth
1965	Arthur J. Goldberg						

Selected Specialized and Related Agencies

These specialized and related agencies are autonomous, with their own memberships and organs, and at the same time have a functional relationship or working agreement with the UN (headquarters), except for UNICEF and UNHCR, which report directly to the Economic and Social Council and to the General Assembly.

Food and Agriculture Organization (FAO) aims to increase production from farms, forests, and fisheries; improve food distribution and marketing, nutrition, and the living conditions of rural people. (Viale delle Terme di Caracalla, 00100 Rome, Italy.) **Website:** www.fao.org

International Atomic Energy Agency (IAEA) aims to promote the safe, peaceful uses of atomic energy. (Vienna International Centre, P.O. Box 100, Wagramer Strasse 5, A-1400, Vienna, Austria.) **Website:** www.iaea.org

International Civil Aviation Org. (ICAO) promotes international civil aviation standards and regulations. (999 University St., Montreal, Quebec, Canada H3C 5H7.) **Website:** www.icao.org

International Fund for Agricultural Development (IFAD) aims to mobilize funds for agricultural and rural projects in developing countries. (Via del Seratico 107, 00142 Rome, Italy.) **Website:** www.ifad.org

Industrial Development Org. (UNIDO) helps developing nations and those in transition pursue sustainable industrial development while promoting economic, environmental, and labor practices. (Vienna Intl. Centre, P.O. Box 300, 5 Wagramer Strasse, 1400-A Vienna, Austria). **Website:** www.unido.org

International Labor Org. (ILO) aims to promote employment; improve labor conditions and living standards. (4 route des Morillons, CH-1211 Geneva 22, Switzerland.) **Website:** www.ilo.org

International Maritime Org. (IMO) aims to promote cooperation on technical matters affecting international shipping. (4 Albert Embankment, London SE1 7SR, U.K.) **Website:** www.imo.org

International Monetary Fund (IMF) aims to promote international monetary cooperation and currency stabilization and expansion of international trade. (700 19th St. NW, Washington, DC 20431.) **Website:** www.imf.org

International Telecommunication Union (ITU) establishes regulations for radio, telegraph, telephone, and space radio-communications, and allocates radio frequencies. (Place des Nations, 1211 Geneva 20, Switzerland.) **Website:** www.itu.int

Office of the High Commissioner for Human Rights (OHCHR) seeks to uphold human rights standards by monitoring areas of concern, investigating abuses, and working with gov. institutions to improve conditions. (Palais des Nations, CH-1211 Geneva 10, Switzerland.) **Website:** www.ohchr.org/english

United Nations Children's Fund (UNICEF) provides financial aid and development assistance to programs for children and mothers in developing countries. (333 E. 38th St., GC-6, New York, NY 10016.) **Website:** www.unicef.org

United Nations Educational, Scientific, and Cultural Org. (UNESCO) aims to promote collaboration among nations through education, science, and culture. After a 19-year boycott, the United States rejoined the organization on Sept. 29, 2003. (7 Place de Fontenoy, 75352 Paris 07 SP, France.) **Website:** www.unesco.org

United Nations High Commissioner for Refugees (UNHCR) provides essential assistance for refugees. (UN High Comm. for Refugees, 2500 CH-1211, Geneva 2, Switzerland.) **Website:** www.unhcr.org

Universal Postal Union (UPU) aims to perfect postal services and promote international collaboration. (Case Postale 13, 3000 Berne 15, Switzerland.) **Website:** www.upu.int

World Bank Group encompasses 5 development institutions focused on worldwide poverty reduction. **The International Bank for Reconstruction and Development (IBRD)** provides loans and technical assistance for projects in developing member countries; encourages cofinancing for projects from other public and private sources. The **International Development Association (IDA)** provides funds for development projects on concessionary terms to the poorer developing member countries. The **International Finance Corporation (IFC)** promotes the growth of the private sector in developing member countries; encourages the development of local capital markets; stimulates the international flow of private capital. The **Multilateral Investment Guarantee Agency (MIGA)** promotes investment in developing countries; guarantees investments to protect investors from noncommercial risks, such as nationalization; advises governments on attracting private investment. The **International Center for Settlement of Investment Disputes (ICSID)** provides conciliation and arbitration services for disputes between foreign investors and host governments which arise out of an investment. (1818 H St., NW Washington, DC 20433.) **Website:** www.worldbank.org

World Health Org. (WHO) aims to aid the attainment of the highest possible level of health. (Avenue Appia 20, CH-1211 Geneva 27, Switzerland.) **Website:** www.who.int

World Intellectual Property Org. (WIPO) seeks to protect, through international cooperation, literary, industrial, scientific, and artistic works. (34, Chemin des Columbettes, 1211 Geneva, Switzerland.) **Website:** www.wipo.org

World Meteorological Org. (WMO) aims to coordinate and improve world meteorological work. (7 bis avenue de la Paix, CP 2300, 1211 Geneva 2, Switzerland.) **Website:** www.wmo.ch

World Tourism Org. (WTO) promotes development of responsible, sustainable, and universally accessible tourism, and provides incentives for environmental and cultural protection. (Capitán Haya 42, 28020 Madrid, Spain.) **Website:** www.world-tourism.org

World Trade Org. (WTrO) replacing the General Agreement on Tariffs and Trade (GATT), administers trade agreements and treaties, examines the trade regimes of members, keeps track of various trade measures and statistics, and attempts to settle trade disputes. (Centre William Rappard, Rue de Lausanne 154, CH-1211 Geneva 21, Switzerland.) **Website:** www.wto.org

Ongoing UN Peacekeeping Missions, 2004

Source: United Nations Cartographic Section, Map No. 4000(E) Rev. 25

(Year given is the year each mission began operation)

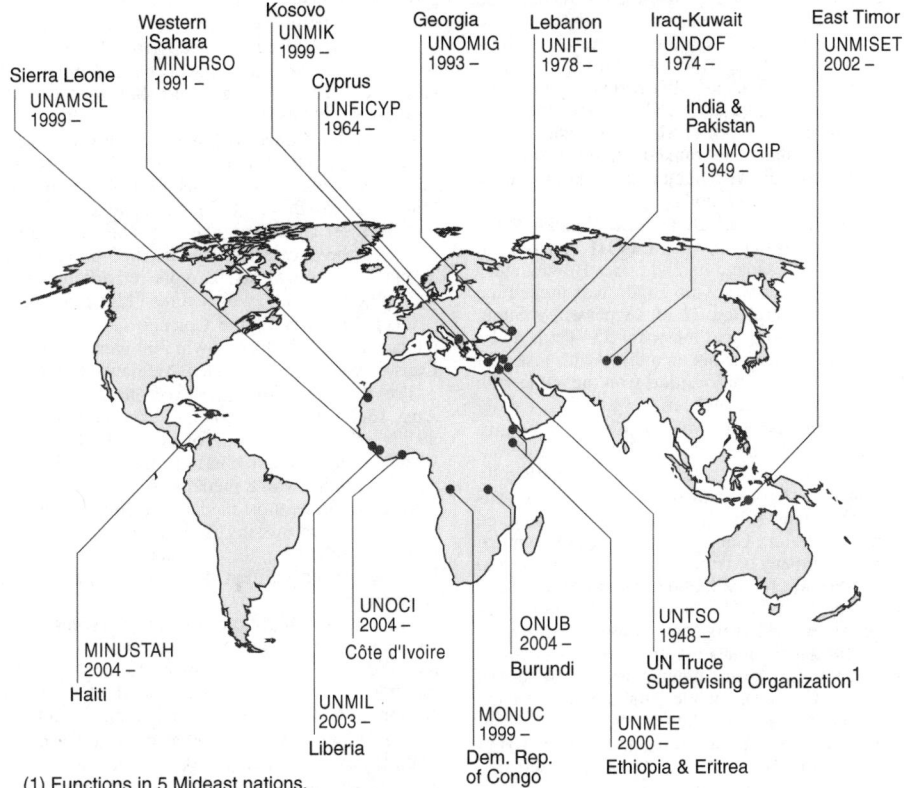

(1) Functions in 5 Mideast nations.

Peacekeeping personnel
As of July 31, 2004

Military personnel and civilian police serving in peacekeeping operations	58,741
Countries contributing military personnel and civilian police	100
International civilian personnel	3,704
Local civilian personnel	6,913
Total number of fatalities in peacekeeping operations since 1948	1,837

International Criminal Court (ICC)

The International Criminal Court was created when 120 nations signed the Rome Statute on July 17, 1998. Its mission is to try individuals accused of genocide, war crimes, or other crimes against humanity, as has been undertaken in the past by temporary tribunals. The statute came into force July 1, 2002, 60 days after the 60th nation ratified it. As of Sept. 2004, 96 nations were members of the ICC, although China, Japan, Russia, and the U.S. had not joined. The U.S. expressed opposition to some provisions of the ICC, mainly regarding liability of its military in peace-keeping situations.

The ICC, unlike the World Court, is not an organ of the UN, but an independent international agency with its own budget and administration. It consists of 18 judges elected by member nations. A president and 1st and 2nd vice presidents are elected for 3-year, renewable terms by an absolute majority of the judges. A Registry handles the nonjudicial aspects of administration. The Office of the Prosecutor will review, investigate, and, when necessary, prosecute cases referred to it by a state or by the UN Security Council.

Jurisdiction is limited to member nations, and only when their courts are deemed either inoperable or unfit for fair trial. The court, which as of Sept. 2004 was not yet operational, will hear cases in The Hague, Netherlands. **Website:** www.icc-cpi.int

Geneva Conventions

The Geneva Conventions are 4 international treaties governing the protection of civilians in time of war, the treatment of prisoners of war, and the care of the wounded and sick in the armed forces. The first convention, covering the sick and wounded, was concluded in Geneva, Switzerland, in 1864; it was amended and expanded in 1906. A third convention, in 1929, covered prisoners of war. Outrage at the treatment of prisoners and civilians during World War II by some belligerents, notably Germany and Japan, prompted the conclusion, in Aug. 1949, of 4 new conventions. Three of these restated and strengthened the previous conventions, and the fourth codified general principles of international law governing the treatment of civilians in wartime.

The 1949 convention for civilians provided for special safeguards for wounded persons, children under 15 years of age, pregnant women, and the elderly. Discrimination on racial, religious, national, or political grounds was forbidden. Torture, collective punishment, reprisals, unwarranted destruction of property, and forced use of civilians for an occupier's armed forces were also prohibited. Also included was a pledge to treat prisoners humanely, feed them adequately, and deliver relief supplies to them. They were not to be forced to disclose more than minimal information. Two additional protocols were adopted in June 1977 dealing with the protection of war victims, especially civilians, and protection for non-international conflicts.

Most countries have formally accepted all or most of the humanitarian conventions as binding. However, there is no permanent machinery in place to apprehend, try, or punish violators.

SPORTS

Sports Highlights of 2004

Louisiana State and the University of Southern California split the **NCAA football national title Jan. 5**. LSU defeated Oklahoma, 21-14, in New Orleans, LA, Jan. 4 to win the Sugar Bowl. USC, which had been ranked atop both final 2003 regular-season polls—the Associated Press poll of media members and the USA Today/ESPN coaches' poll—beat Michigan, 28-14, Jan. 1 in Pasadena, CA, to win the Rose Bowl. With its Sugar Bowl win, LSU, which had a final record of 13-1, was automatically ranked number 1 in the final coaches' poll under Bowl Championship Series rules. USC (12-1) topped the final AP poll.

The New England Patriots defeated the Carolina Panthers, 32-29, **Feb. 1** to win **Super Bowl XXXVIII** in Houston, TX. The win gave New England its 2nd Super Bowl victory in 3 years. Patriots quarterback Tom Brady was named the game's MVP. Brady completed 32 of 48 passes, a Super Bowl record for completions, and threw for 354 yards and 3 touchdowns. Brady led the Patriots on a drive with just over 1 minute remaining, and Adam Vinatieri won the game with a 41-yard field goal with 9 seconds left.

Attorney Gen. John Ashcroft on **Feb. 12** announced indictments handed down by a federal grand jury in San Francisco, CA, against 4 men for crimes including **illegally distributing** anabolic steroids and other **performance-enhancing drugs** to dozens of top athletes. The case centered on the Bay Area Laboratory Cooperative (**BALCO**), a nutritional supplement company of which many top athletes from track and field, baseball, football, and other sports were clients. As a result of the case, U.S. sprinter Kelli White was banned from the sport for 2 years May 19 after admitting to having taken performance-enhancing drugs since December 2000. Several top track stars were banned prior to the start of the 2004 Summer Olympics, while others linked to the BALCO case failed to qualify for the Games.

Two-time defending champion Connecticut defeated Tennessee, 70-61, in New Orleans, LA, **April 6** to win the **women's NCAA basketball championship**. Connecticut's men's team beat Georgia Tech, 82-73, in San Antonio, TX, **April 5** to win the **men's tournament**. The double victory by Connecticut was the first time a Division I school's men's and women's teams won the NCAA titles in the same year. Connecticut's Diana Taurasi was named most outstanding player of Final Four for the 2nd straight year. Huskie Emeka Okafor earned the men's honor.

The Tampa Bay Lightning defeated the Calgary Flames, 2-1, in Tampa, FL, **June 7**, to win the **Stanley Cup** in Game 7 of the series. It was the 1st NHL title for Tampa Bay, which had begun play as an expansion team in 1992. However, because of a labor dispute, the **NHL locked out its players Sept. 16**, after the collective bargaining agreement expired.

The Detroit Pistons won the **NBA championship**, defeating the Los Angeles Lakers, 100-87, **June 15** to win the finals, 4 games to 1. The Pistons, coached by Larry Brown, used tough defense to pull off one of the biggest upsets in NBA finals history. Pistons guard Chauncey Billups, who averaged 21 points per game, was named MVP of the series.

On **July 4**, Greece defeated Portugal, 1-0, in Lisbon, Portugal, to win the final of **soccer's European Championships**. Greece, a 100-1 long shot to win prior to the tournament, claimed its 1st major soccer title.

U.S. cyclist **Lance Armstrong won the Tour de France** for the record 6th straight year **July 25**. Armstrong, 32, had been tied with France's Jacques Anquetil and Bernard Hinault, Belgium's Eddy Merckx, and Spain's Miguel Indurain for most victories in the race's history, with 5. Indurain had been the only other rider to win 5 times in a row. Armstrong's record was all the more remarkable in view of his triumph over cancer, which almost killed him in 1996.

Greg Maddux of the Chicago Cubs became the 22nd pitcher in MLB history to win **300** games **Aug. 7**, when the Cubs defeated the San Francisco Giants, 8-4, on the road.

The **Summer Olympics** were held in Athens, Greece, **Aug. 13-29**. The U.S. won the most medals, with 35 golds, 39 silvers, and 29 bronzes for a total of 103. Russia was 2nd, with 92 medals, and China was 3rd, with 63. U.S. swimmer Michael Phelps won 8 medals—6 gold and 2 bronze—to tie the record for the most medals in a single Olympics. Several track stars were missing from the Games because of a performance-enhancing drug scandal. A record number of athletes were disqualified for drug violations during the competition.

Fiji's **Vijay Singh** knocked **Tiger Woods** out of the top spot in the world golf rankings **Sept. 6**, ending Woods's record 264-week run at number 1. Singh clinched the top ranking by winning the Deutsche Bank Championship, in Norton, MA, beating Woods and Adam Scott by 3 strokes.

Switzerland's **Roger Federer** captured his 3rd Grand Slam tennis tournament of 2004 when he won the U.S. Open **Sept. 12**, defeating Australia's Lleyton Hewitt, 6-0, 7-6, 6-0. Federer, the top-ranked men's player, also won Wimbledon July 4 and the Australian Open Feb. 1.

Giants left fielder **Barry Bonds** hit his 700th career home run **Sept. 17** off pitcher Jake Peavy during the Giants' 4-1 win over the San Diego Padres in San Francisco. Bonds, 40, became the 3rd player to reach 700 home runs, and trailed only all-time leader Hank Aaron (755) and Babe Ruth (714). Bonds also shattered his previous season records with a .609 on-base pct., 232 walks, and 120 intentional walks.

Europe beat the U.S., 18½-9½, to win the **Ryder Cup** in Bloomfield Township, MI, **Sept. 19**, winning the 3-day match-play competition under German captain Bernhard Langer by a record margin for a European team.

Seattle Mariners right fielder **Ichiro Suzuki** got his 258th hit of 2004 on **Oct. 1**, breaking George Sisler's 84-year-old MLB record for **most hits in a season**. The Japanese-born Suzuki ended the season with 262 hits.

Miscellaneous Sports Facts

Bronx Bummer. On Aug. 31, 2004, the New York Yankees suffered their worst loss in franchise history, a 22-0 drubbing by the Cleveland Indians at Yankee Stadium in the Bronx.

Gunners' Record Streak. With a 3-0 win over Blackburn Aug. 25, English soccer club Arsenal set a new record for consecutive games unbeaten—43—in England's top league. The Gunners, as the London-based team is known, had gone the entire 2003-2004 season without losing, becoming the 1st to accomplish that feat in England's top league since 1889.

Extreme Golf. Andre Tolme, a civil engineer from New Hampshire, completed a 1,234-mile golf round across Mongolia July 10. Tolme, 35, divided the harsh Mongolian countryside into 18 holes, and estimated par at 11,880. Using only a 3-iron, he took 180 days to complete the round, which he finished at 290 over par.

Centenarian Feats. Australian Frank Moody, 101, became the world's first centenarian skydiver June 16, when he jumped in tandem from an airplane from 9,900 feet. And 100-year-old South African Philip Rabinowitz, nicknamed "Flying Phil," set a new record for centenarian sprinting when he ran the 100 meters in 30.86 seconds on July 10.

It's a Start. The U.S. national cricket team took part in its 1st international tournament, the Champions Trophy in London. The American side lost to New Zealand Sept. 10 by 210 runs—the largest winning margin ever for the "Black Caps." The U.S. then fell to world champion Australia Sept. 13, losing by 9 wickets.

Driving on Water. British entrepreneur Sir Richard Branson drove across the English Channel in his amphibious car, the Gibbs Aquada, on June 14. He set a new record for such crossings on the 22-mile trip from Dover, Britain, to Calais, France, finishing in 1 hour, 40 minutes, 6 seconds.

OLYMPICS

The 2004 Summer Olympic Games

Athens, Greece, Aug. 13-29, 2004

The Olympic Games were born in ancient Greece and the first modern Games were held in Athens in 1896. In 2004, 10,500 athletes representing 202 nations gathered in Athens to compete in 301 events in 28 sports at the 28th Olympiad. Women competed for the first time in freestyle wrestling and the sabre event in fencing. The U.S. topped the medal standings, with 103, and won the most gold medals, with 35. Russia was 2nd in total medals, with 92, and China was 3rd, with 63.

American swimmer Michael Phelps captured 8 medals—6 gold and 2 bronze—in individual and relay events, tying a record for the number of medals won in a single Olympics. American gymnasts Paul Hamm and Carly Patterson claimed gold medals in the individual all-around gymnastics competitions. However, a controversy erupted when it emerged that judges had erred in scoring Yang Tae Young, who won the men's bronze medal, on his parallel bar routine. South Korea filed a protest, pointing out that Yang would have won gold if his routine had been scored correctly by the judges. The International Gymnastics Federation admitted that the gold medal had been awarded to Hamm in error, but allowed the results to stand. The U.S. also fared well in women's team sports, with the soccer, softball, and basketball teams all capturing golds. Argentina won the gold medal in men's soccer and basketball; the favored U.S. men's basketball team won the bronze. Windsurfer Gal Fridman became the first Israeli to win an Olympic gold medal when he captured the men's Mistral event. Many track and field stars were absent, because of doping scandals or failure to qualify. As a result, new faces emerged, with the U.S.'s Justin Gatlin winning the men's 100 meters and Yuliya Nesterenko of Belarus taking the women's 100. Morocco's Hicham el-Guerrouj, a longtime middle-distance star, won his first Olympic gold medals, capturing both the 1,500 and 5,000 meters.

A record 24 athletes were expelled for drug violations as of the closing ceremony. Medals in 7 events, including 3 golds, were taken away for doping violations. The Games also featured unprecedented spending on security, with Greece expending an estimated $1.5 billion of an overall cost estimate at $7 billion to protect the first Summer Games since the Sept. 11, 2001, terrorist attacks on the U.S.

Final Medal Standings

	G	S	B	T		G	S	B	T		G	S	B	T
United States	35	39	29	103	Kazakhstan	1	4	3	8	Morocco	2	1	0	3
Russia	27	27	38	92	Czech Republic	1	3	4	8	Chile	2	0	1	3
China	32	17	14	63	Sweden	4	1	2	7	Lithuania	1	2	0	3
Australia	17	16	16	49	Austria	2	4	1	7	Zimbabwe	1	1	1	3
Germany	14	16	18	48	Ethiopia	2	3	2	7	Belgium	1	0	2	3
Japan	16	9	12	37	Kenya	1	4	2	7	Portugal	0	2	1	3
France	11	9	13	33	Norway	5	0	1	6	Estonia	0	1	2	3
Italy	10	11	11	32	Iran	2	2	2	6	Bahamas	1	0	1	2
South Korea	9	12	9	30	Slovakia	2	2	2	6	Israel	1	0	1	2
Great Britain	9	9	12	30	Argentina	2	0	4	6	Finland	0	2	0	2
Cuba	9	7	11	27	South Africa	1	3	2	6	Serbia/Montenegro	0	2	0	2
Ukraine	9	5	9	23	New Zealand	3	2	0	5	Nigeria	0	0	2	2
Netherlands	4	9	9	22	Chinese Taipei	2	2	1	5	Venezuela	0	0	2	2
Romania	8	5	6	19	Jamaica	2	1	2	5	Cameroon	1	0	0	1
Spain	3	11	5	19	Uzbekistan	2	1	2	5	Dominican Rep	1	0	0	1
Hungary	8	6	3	17	Croatia	1	2	2	5	Ireland	1	0	0	1
Greece	6	6	4	16	Egypt	1	1	3	5	U.A.E.	1	0	0	1
Belarus	2	6	7	15	Switzerland	1	1	3	5	Hong Kong	0	1	0	1
Canada	3	6	3	12	Azerbaijan	1	0	4	5	India	0	1	0	1
Bulgaria	2	1	9	12	North Korea	0	4	1	5	Paraguay	0	1	0	1
Brazil	4	3	3	10	Georgia	2	2	0	4	Colombia	0	0	1	1
Turkey	3	3	4	10	Indonesia	1	1	2	4	Eritrea	0	0	1	1
Poland	3	2	5	10	Latvia	0	4	0	4	Mongolia	0	0	1	1
Thailand	3	1	4	8	Mexico	0	3	1	4	Syria	0	0	1	1
Denmark	2	0	6	8	Slovenia	0	1	3	4	Trinidad/Tobago	0	0	1	1

WORLD ALMANAC EDITORS' PICKS
GREATEST SINGLE-COMPETITION SPORTS FEATS OF THE PAST 50 YEARS

The editors of *The World Almanac* have ranked the following as the ten greatest feats achieved in a single competition in the past 50 years

1. New York Yankee Don Larsen pitches a 2-0 perfect game win over the Dodgers in Game 5 of the 1956 World Series on Oct. 8 in Yankee Stadium. (He threw a total of 97 pitches.)

2. Bob Beamon leaps to a long-jump world record of 29 feet, 2.5 inches (8.9 meters) in the 1968 Olympics in Mexico City on Oct. 18, breaking the previous record of 27 feet, 4.75 inches.

3. Philadelphia Warrior Wilt Chamberlain scores an NBA-record 100 points in a single game against the New York Knicks in Hershey, PA, on March 2, 1962.

4. In a clinching Game 6 of the 1977 World Series on Oct. 18 in Yankee Stadium, New York Yankee Reggie Jackson hits 3 homers on 3 consecutive pitches to him off 3 Dodgers pitchers (Burt Hooton, Elias Sosa, Charlie Hough).

5. Tiger Woods, 21, wins the 1997 Masters, setting a 72-hole tournament record of 18-under-par and winning by a record 12 strokes, April 13 in Augusta, GA.

6. Romania's Nadia Comaneci scores the first-ever perfect 10 in Olympic gymnastics on the uneven bars on July 18, the first of 7 perfect marks she would receive at the 1976 Summer Olympic Games in Montreal.

7. The racehorse Secretariat, with Ron Turcotte aboard, wins the Belmont Stakes in Elmont, NY, June 9, 1973, by a record 31 lengths, on the way to claiming the Triple Crown.

8. The U.S. ice hockey team defeats the overwhelmingly favored Russians, 4-3, in the Feb. 22 semifinal game of the 1980 Winter Olympics in Lake Placid, NY.

9. Quarterback Frank Reich, in for an injured Jim Kelly, leads the Buffalo Bills back from a 32-point halftime deficit (35-3) to a 41-38 win at home over the Houston Oilers in the AFC Wild Card Game on Jan. 3, 1993. It is the greatest comeback in NFL history.

10. Diego Maradona dribbles through nearly the whole English team on a 50-yard run to score in Argentina's 2-1 quarterfinal win, June 22 in the 1986 World Cup in Mexico.

2004 Summer Olympics Medal Winners

Archery

Men's Individual—G-Marco Galiazzo, Italy; S-Hiroshi Yamamoto, Japan; B-Tim Cuddihy, Australia

Men's Team—G-South Korea; S-Taiwan; B-Ukraine

Women's Individual—G-Park Sung Hyun, South Korea; S-Lee Sung Jin, South Korea; B-Alison Williamson, Britain

Women's Team—G-South Korea; S-China; B-Taiwan

Badminton

Men's Singles—G-Taufik Hidayat, Indonesia; S-Shon Seung Mo, South Korea; B-Soni Dwi Kuncoro, Indonesia

Men's Doubles—G-Ha Tae Kwon and Kim Dong Moon, South Korea; S-Lee Dong Soo and Yoo Yong Sung, South Korea; B-Eng Hian and Flandy Limpele, Indonesia

Women's Singles—G-Zhang Ning, China; S-Mia Audina, Netherlans; B-Zhou Mi, China

Women's Doubles—G-Yang Wei and Zhang Jiewen, China; S-Gao Ling and Huang Sui, China; B-Lee Kyung Won and Ra Kyung Min, South Korea

Mixed Doubles—G-Gao Ling and Zhang Jun, China; S-Nathan Robertson and Gail Emms, Britain; B-Jens Eriksen and Mette Schjoldager, Denmark

Baseball

G-Cuba; S-Australia; B-Japan

Basketball

Men—G-Argentina; S-Italy; B-U.S.

Women—G-U.S.; S-Australia; B-Australia

Beach Volleyball

Men—G-Ricardo Alex Santos and Emanuel Rego, Brazil; S-Javier Bosma and Pablo Herrera, Spain; B-Stefan Kobel and Patrick Heuscher, Switzerland

Women—G-Kerri Walsh and Misty May, U.S.; S-Adriana Behar and Shelda Bede, Brazil; B-Holly McPeak and Elaine Youngs, U.S.

Boxing

Lt. Flyweight 48 kg (106 lbs)—G-Yan Bhartelemy Varela, Cuba; S-Atagun Yalcinkaya, Turkey; B-Sergey Kazakov, Russia; B-Zou Shiming, China

Flyweight 51 kg (112 lbs)—G-Yuriorkis Gamboa Toledano, Cuba; S-Jerome Thomas, France; B-Fuad Aslanov, Azerbaijun; B-Ruhamhodza Rahimov, Germany

Bantamweight 54 kg (119 lbs)—G-Guillermo Rigondeaux Ortiz, Cuba; S-Worapoj Petchkoom, Thailand; B-Ahgasi Mammadov, Azerbaijan; B-Bahodirjon Sooltonov, Uzbekistan

Featherweight 57 kg (125 lbs)—G-Alexei Tichtchenko, Russia; S-Kim Song Guk, North Korea; B-Jo Seok Hwan, South Korea; B-Vitali Tajbert, Germany

Lightweight 60 kg (132 lbs)—G-Mario Kindelan Mesa, Cuba; S-Amir Khan, Great Britain; B-Murat Khrachev, Russia; B-Serik Yeleuov, Kazakhstan

Lt. Welterweight 63.5 kg (139 lbs)—G-Manus Boonjumnong, Thailand; S-Yudel Johnson Cedeno, Cuba; B-Boris Georgiev, Bulgaria; B-Ionut Gheorghe, Romania

Welterweight 67 kg (147 lbs)—G-Artayev Bakhtiyar, Kazakhstan; S-Lorenzo Aragon Armenteros, Cuba; B-Kim Jung Joo, South Korea; B-Oleg Saitov, Russia

Middleweight 75 kg (165 lbs)—G-Gaydarbek Gaydarbekov, Russia; S-Gennadiy Golovkin, Kazakhstan; B-Andre Dirrell, U.S.; B-Suriya Prasathinphimai, Thailand

Lt. Heavyweight 81 kg (178 lbs)—G-Andre Ward, U.S.; S-Magomed Aripgadjiev, Belarus; B-Utkirbek Haydarov, Uzbekistan; B-Ahmed Ismail, Egypt

Heavyweight 91 kg (201 lbs)—G-Odlanier Solis Fonte, Cuba; S-Viktar Zuyev, Belarus; B-Naser Al Shami, Syria; B-Mohamed Elsayed, Egypt

Super Heavyweight 91+ kg (201+ lbs)—G-Alexander Povetkin, Russia; S-Mohamed Aly, Egypt; B-Roberto Cammarelle, Italy; B-Michel Lopez Nuñez, Cuba

Canoe/Kayak

Men

Kayak Slalom—G-Benoit Peschier, France; S-Campbell Walsh, Great Britain; B-Fabien Lefevre, France

Kayak 500M Singles—G-Adam van Koeverden, Canada; S-Nathan Baggaley, Australia; B-Ian Wynne, Great Britain

Kayak 500M Doubles—G-Germany; S-Australia; B-Belarus

Kayak 1,000M Singles—G-Eirik Veraas Larsen, Norway; S-Ben Fouhy, New Zealand; B-Adam van Koeverden, Canada

Kayak 1,000M Doubles—G-Sweden; S-Italy; B-Norway

Kayak 1,000M Fours—G-Hungary; S-Germany; B-Slovakia

Canoe Slalom Singles—G-Tony Estanguet, France; S-Michal Martikan, Slovakia; B-Stefan Pfannmoeller, Germany

Canoe Slalom Doubles—G-Slovakia; S-Germany; B-Czech Republic

Canoe 500M Singles—G-Andreas Dittmer, Germany; S-David Cal, Spain; B-Maxim Opalev, Russia

Canoe 500M Doubles—G-China; S-Cuba; B-Russia

Canoe 1,000M Singles—G-David Cal, Spain; S-Andreas Dittmer, Germany; B-Attila Vajda, Hungary

Canoe 1,000M Doubles—G-Germany; S-Russia; B-Hungary

Women

Kayak Slalom—G-Elena Kaliska, Slovakia; S-Rebecca Giddens, U.S.; B-Helen Reeves, Great Britain

Kayak 500M Singles—G-Natasa Janics, Hungary; S-Josefa Idem, Italy; B-Caroline Brunet, Canada

Kayak 500M Doubles—G-Hungary; S-Germany; B-Poland

Kayak 500M Fours—G-Germany; S-Hungary; B-Ukraine

Cycling

Men

Mountain Bike—G-Julien Absalon, France; S-Jose Antonio Hermida, Spain; B-Bart Brentjens, Netherlands

Individual Road Race—G-Paolo Bettini, Italy; S-Sergio Paulinho, Portugal; B-Alex Merckx, Belgium

Individual Time Trial—G-Tyler Hamilton, U.S.; S-Viatcheslav Ekimov, Russia; B-Bobby Julich, U.S.

Individual Pursuit—G-Bradley Wiggins, Great Britain; S-Brad McGee, Australia; B-Sergi Escobar, Spain

Team Pursuit—G-Australia; S-Great Britain; B-Spain

Keirin—G-Ryan Bayley, Australia; S-Jose Escuredo, Spain; B-Shane Kelly, Australia

Madison—G-Australia; S-Switzerland; B-Great Britain

Team Sprint—G-Germany; S-Japan; B-France

Sprint—G-Ryan Bayley, Australia; S-Theo Bos, Netherlands; B-Rene Wolff, Germany

Individual Points Race—G-Mikhail Ignatyev, Russia; S-Joan Llaneras, Spain; B-Guido Fulst, Germany

1KM Time Trial—G-Chris Hoy, Great Britain; S-Arnaud Tournant, France; B-Stefan Nimke, Germany

Women

Mountain Bike—G-Gunn-Rita Dahle, Norway; S-Marie-Helene Premont, Canada; B-Sabine Spitz, Germany

Individual Road Race—G-Sara Carrigan, Australia; S-Judith Arndt, Germany; B-Olga Slyusareva, Russia

Individual Time Trial—G-Leontien Zijlaard-van Moorsel, Netherlands; S-Dierdre Demet-Barry, U.S.; B-Karin Thuerig, Switzerland

Individual Pursuit—G- Sarah Ulmer, New Zealand; S-Katie Maciter, Australia; B-Leontien Zijlaard-van Moorsel, Netherlands

Sprint—G-Lori-Ann Muenzer, Canada; S-Tamilla Abassova, Russia; B-Anna Meares, Australia

Individual Points Race—G-Olga Slyusareva, Russia; S-Belem Guerrero Mendez, Mexico; B-Erin Mirabella, U.S.

500M Time Trial—G-Anna Meares, Australia; S-Jiang Yonghua, China; B-Natallia Tsylinksaya, Belarus

Diving

Men

Platform—G-Hu Jia, China; S-Mathew Helm, Australia; B-Tian Liang, China

Springboard—G-Peng Bo, China; S-Alexandre Despatie, Canada; B-Dmitri Sautin, Russia

Synchronized Platform—G-Tian Liang and Yang Jinghui, China; S-Peter Waterfield and Leon Taylor, Great Britain; B-Mathew Helm and Robert Newbery, Australia

Synchronized Springboard—G-Nikolaos Siranidis and Thomas Bimis, Greece; S-Andreas Wels and Tobias Schellenberg, Germany; B-Robert Newbery and Steven Barnett, Australia

Women

Platform—G-Chantelle Newbery, Australia; S-Lao Lishi, China; B-Loudy Tourky, Australia

Springboard—G-Guo Jingjing, China; S-Wu Minxia, China; B-Yulia Pakhalina, Russia

Synchronized Platform—G-Lao Lishi and Li Ting, China; S-Natalia Goncharova and Yulia Koltunova, Russia; B-Blythe Hartley and Emilie Heymans, Canada

Synchronized Springboard—G-Lao Lishi and Li Ting, China; S-Natalia Goncharova and Yulia Koltunova, Russia; B-Blythe Hartley and Emilie Heymans, Canada

Equestrian

Individual Dressage—G-Anky van Grunsven, Netherlands; S-Ulla Salzgeber, Germany; B-Beatriz Ferrer-Salat, Spain

Team Dressage—G-Germany; S-Spain; B-U.S.

Individual Jumping—G-Cian O'Connor, Ireland; S-Rodrigo Pessoa, Brazil; B-Chris Kappler, U.S.

Team Jumping—G-Germany; S-U.S.; B-Sweden

Individual Three-Day Event—G-Leslie Law, Great Britain; S-Kimberly Severson, U.S.; B-Philippa Funnell, Great Britain

Team Three-Day Event—G-France; S-Great Britain; B-U.S.

Fencing

Men

Individual Foil—G-Brice Guyart, France; S-Salvatore Sanzo, Italy; B-Andrea Cassara, Italy

Individual Épée—G-Marcel Fischer, Switzerland; S-Wang Lei, China; B-Pavel Kolobkov, Russia

Team Épée—G-France; S-Hungary; B-Germany
Team Foil—G- Italy; S-China; B-Russia
Individual Saber—G-Aldo Montano, Italy; S-Zsolt Nemcsik, Hungary; B-VladislaveTretiak, Ukraine
Team Saber—G-France; S-Italy; B-Russia

Women

Individual Épée—G-Timea Nagy, Hungary; S-Laura Flessel-Colovic, France; B-Maureen Nisima, France
Team Épée—G-Russia; S-Switzerland; B-China
Individual Foil—G-Valentina Vezzali, Italy; S-Giovanna Trillini, Italy; B-Sylwia Gruchala, Poland
Team Foil—G-Italy; S-Poland; B-Germany
Individual Sabre—G-Mariel Zagunis, U.S.; S-Tan Xue, China; B-Sada Jacobson, U.S.
Team Épée—G-Russia; S-Germany; B-France

Field Hockey

Men—G-Australia; S-Netherlands; B-Germany
Women—G-Germany; S-Netherlands; B-Argentina

Gymnastics
Men

Team—G-Japan; S-U.S.; B-Romania
Individual All-Around—G-Paul Hamm, U.S.; S-Kim Dae Eun, South Korea, China; B-Yang Tae Young, South Korea
Floor Exercise—G-Kyle Shewfelt, Canada; S-Marian Dragulescu, Romania; B-Jordan Jovtchev, Bulgaria
Vault—G-Gervasio Deferr, Spain; S-Evgeni Sapronenko, Latvia; B-Marian Dragulescu, Romania
Parallel Bars—G-Valeri Goncharov, Ukraine; S-Hioyuki Tomita, Japan; B-Li Xiaopeng, China
Horizontal Bar—G-Igor Cassina, Italy; S-Paul Hamm, U.S.; B-Isao Yoneda, Japan
Pommel Horse—G-Teng Haibin, China; S-Marius Urzica, Romania; B-Takehiro Kashima, Japan
Rings—G-Dimosthenis Tampakos, Greece; S-Jordan Jovtchev, Bulgaria; B-Yuri Chechi, Italy
Trampoline—G-Yuri Nikitin, Ukraine; S-Aleksandr Moskalenko, Russia; B-Henrik Stehlik, Germany

Women

Team—G-Romania; S-U.S.; B-Russia
Individual All-Around—G-Carly Patterson, U.S.; S-Svetlana Khorkina, Russia; B-Zhang Nan, China
Floor Exercise—G-Catalina Ponor, Romania; S-Nicoleta Daniela Sofronie, Romania; B-Patricia Moreno, Spain
Vault—G-Monica Rosu, Romania; S-Annia Hatch, U.S.; B-Anna Pavlova, Russia
Uneven Bars—G-Emilie Lepennec, France; S-Terin Humphrey, U.S.; B-Courtney Kupets, U.S.
Balance Beam—G-Catalina Ponor, Romania; S-Carly Patterson, U.S.; B-Alexandra Georgiana Eremia, Romania
Trampoline—G-Anna Dogonadze, Germany; S-Karen Cockburn, Canada; B-Huang Shanshan, China

Rhythmic Gymnastics

Individual All-Around—G-Alina Kabaeva, Russia; S-Irina Tchachina, Russia; B-Anna Bessonova, Ukraine
Team—G- Russia; S-Italy; B-Bulgaria

Handball

Men—G-Croatia; S-Germany; B-Russia
Women—G-Denmark; S-South Korea; B-Ukraine

Judo
Men

Extra Lightweight 60 kg (132 lbs)—G-Tadahiro Nomura, Japan; S-Nestor Khergiani, Georgia; B-Tsagaanbaatar Khashbataar, Mongolia; B-Choi Min Ho, South Korea
Half lightweight 66 kg (145 lbs)—G-Masato Uchishiba, Japan; S-Jozef Krnac, Slovakia; B-Georgi Georgiev, Bulgaria; B-Yordanis Arencibia Verdecia, Cuba
Lightweight 73 kg (161 lbs)—G-Lee Won Hee, South Korea; S-Vitaliy Makarov, Russia; B-Lenadro Guilheiro, Brazil; B-Jimmy Pedro, U.S.
Half middleweight 81 kg (178 lbs)—G-Ilias Iliadis, Greece; S-Roman Gontyuk, Ukraine; B-Dmitri Nossov, Russia; B-Flavio Canto, Brazil
Middleweight 90 kg (198 lbs)—G-Zurab Zviadauri, Georgia; S-Hiroshi Izumi, Japan; B-Khasanbi Taov, Russia; B-Mark Huizinga, Netherlands
Half heavyweight 100 kg (220 lbs)—G-Ihar Makarau, Belarus; S-Jang Sung Ho, South Korea; B-Michael Jurack, Germany; B-Ariel Zeevi, Israel
Heavyweight 100+ kg (220+ lbs)—G-Keiji Suzuki, Japan; S-Tamerlan Tmenov, Russia; B-Dennis van der Geest, Netherlands; B-Indrek Pertelson, Estonia

Women

Extra lightweight 48 kg (106 lbs)—G-Ryoko Tani, Japan; S-Frederique Jossinet, France; B-Julia Matijass, Germany; B-Gao Feng, China

Half lightweight 52 kg (114 lbs)—G-Xian Dongmei, China; S-Yuki Yokosawa, Japan; B-Amarilys Savon, Cuba; B-Ilse Heylen, Belgium
Lightweight 57 kg (125 lbs)—G-Yvonne Boenisch, Germany; S-Kye Sun Hui, North Korea; B-Deborah Gravenstijn, Netherlands; B-Yurisleidy Lupetey, Cuba
Half middleweight 63 kg (139 lbs)—G-Ayumi Tanimoto, Japan; S-Claudia Heill, Austria; B-Urska Zolnir, Slovenia; B-Driulys Gonzalez, Cuba
Middleweight 70 kg (154 lbs)—G-Masae Ueno, Japan; S-Edith Bosch, Netherlands; B-Qin Dongya, China; B-Annett Boehm, Germany
Half heavyweight 78 kg (172 lbs)—G-Noriko Anno, Japan; S-Liu Xia, China; B-Lucia Morico, Italy; B-Yurisel Laborde, Cuba
Heavyweight 78+ kg (172+ lbs)—G-Maki Tsukada, Japan; S-Dayma Mayelis Beltran, Cuba; B-Tea Donguzashvili, Russia; B-Sun Fuming, China

Modern Pentathlon

Men—G-Andrey Moiseev, Russia; S-Andrejus Zadneprovskis, Lithuania; B-Libor Capalini, Czech Republic
Women—G-Zsuzsanna Voros, Hungary; S-Jelena Rublevska, Latvia; B-Georgina Harland, Great Britain

Rowing
Men

Single Sculls—G-Olaf Tufte, Norway; S-Jueri Jaanson, Estonia; B-Ivo Yanakiev, Bulgaria
Double Sculls—G-France; S-Slovenia; B-Italy
Lightweight Double Sculls—G-Poland; S-France; B-Greece
Quadruple Sculls—G-Russia; S-Czech Republic; B-Ukraine
Coxless Pairs—G-Australia; S-Croatia; B-South Africa
Coxless Fours—G-Great Britain; S-Canada; B-Canada
Lightweight Coxless Fours—G-Denmark; S-Australia; B-Italy
Coxed Eights—G-U.S.; S-Netherlands; B-Australia

Women

Single Sculls—G-Katrin Rutschow-Stomporowski, Germany; S-Ekaterina Karsten-Khodotovitch, Belarus; B-Rumyana Neykova, Bulgaria
Double Sculls—G-New Zealand; S-Germany; B-Great Britain
Lightweight Double Sculls—G-Romania; S-Germany; B-Netherlands
Quadruple Sculls—G-Germany; S-Great Britain; B-Australia
Coxless Pairs—G-Romania; S-Great Britain; B-Belarus
Coxed Eights—G-Romania; S-U.S.; B-Netherlands

Sailing
Men

Mistral—G-Gal Fridman, Israel; S-Nikolaos Kaklamanakis, Greece; B-Nick Dempsey, Great Britain
Finn—G-Ben Ainslie, Great Britain; S-Rafael Trujillo, Spain; B-Mateusz Kusznierewicz, Poland
470—G-U.S.; S-Great Britain; B-Japan

Women

Mistral—G-Faustine Merret, France; S-Yin Jian, China; B-Alessandra Sensini, Italy
Europe—G-Siren Sundby, Norway; S-Lenka Smidova, Czech Republic; B-Signe Livbjerg, Denmark
470—G-Greece; S-Spain; B-Sweden

Open

Laser—G-Robert Scheidt, Brazil; S-Andreas Geritzer, Austria; B-Vasilij Zbogar, Slovenia
Tornado—G-Austria; S-U.S.; B-Argentina
Star—G-Brazil; S-Canada; B-France
49er—G-Spain; S-Ukraine; B-Great Britain
Yngling—G-Great Britain; S-Ukraine; B-Denmark

Shooting
Men

Air Pistol—G-Wang Yifu, China; S-Mikhail Nestruev, Russia; B-Vladimir Isakov, Russia
Rapid Fire Pistol—G-Ralf Schumann, Germany; S-Sergei Poliakov, Russia; B-Sergei Alifirenko, Russia
Free Pistol—G-Mikhail Nestruev, Russia; S-Jin Jong Oh, South Korea; B-Kim Jong Su, North Korea
Air Rifle—G-Zhu Qinan, China; S-Li Jie, Chi; B-Jozef Gonci, Slovakia
Three-Position Rifle—G-Jia Zhanbo, China; S-Michael Anti, U.S.; B-Christian Planer, Austria
Rifle Prone—G-Matthew Emmons, U.S.; S-Christian Lusch, Germany; B-Sergei Martynov, Belarus
Trap—G-Aleksei Alipov, Russia; S-Giovanni Pellielo, Italy; B-Adam Vella, Australia
Double Trap—G-Ahmed Almaktoum, United Arab Emirates; S-Rajyavardhan Rathore, India; B-Wang Zheng, China
Skeet—G-Andrea Benelli, Italy; S-Marko Kemppainen, Finland; B-Juan Miguel Rodriguez, Cuba
Running Game Target—G-Manfred Kurzer, Germany; S-Alexander Blinov, Russia; B-Dimitri Lykin, Russia

Women

Air Pistol—G-Olena Kostevych, Ukraine; S-Jasna Sekaric, Serbia-Montenegro; B-Maria Grozdeva, Bulgaria

Sport Pistol—G-Maria Grozdeva, Bulgaria; S-Lenka Hykova, Czech Republic; B-Irada Ashumova, Azerbaijan

Air Rifle—G-Du Li, China; S-Lioubov Galkina, Russia; B-Katerina Kurkova, Czech Republic

Three-Position Rifle—G-Lioubov Galkina, Russia; S-Valentina Turisini, Italy; B-Wang Chengyi, China

Trap—G-Suzanne Balogh, Australia; S-Maria Quintanal, Spain; B-Lee Bo Na, South Korea

Double Trap—G-Kimberly Rhode, U.S.; S-Lee Bo Na, South Korea; B-Gao E, China

Skeet—G-Diana Igaly, Hungary; S-Wei Ning, China; B-Zemfira Meftakhetdinova, Azerbaijan

Soccer

Men—G-Argentina; S-Paraguay; B-Italy
Women—G-U.S.; S-Brazil; B-Germany

Softball

G-U.S.; S-Australia; B-Japan

Swimming
Men

50M Freestyle—G-Gary Hall Jr., U.S.; S-Duje Draganja, Croatia; B-Roland Mark Schoeman, South Africa

100M Freestyle—G-Pieter van den Hoogenband, Netherlands; S-Roland Mark Schoeman, South Africa; B-Ian Thorpe, Australia.

200M Freestyle—G-Ian Thorpe, Australia; S-Pieter van den Hoogenband, Netherlands; B-Michael Phelps, U.S.

400M Freestyle—G-Ian Thorpe, Australia; S-Grant Hackett, Australia; B-Klete Keller, U.S.

1,500M Freestyle—G-Grant Hackett, Australia; S-Larsen Jensen, U.S.; B-David Davies, Great Britain.

100M Backstroke—G-Aaron Peirsol U.S.; S-Markus Rogan, Austria; B-Tomomi Morita, Japan

200M Backstroke—G-Aaron Peirsol U.S.; S-Markus Rogan, Austria; B-Razvan Florea, Romania

100M Breaststroke—G-Kosuke Kitajima, Japan; S-Brendan Hansen, U.S.; B-Hugues Duboscq, France

200M Breaststroke—G-Kosuke Kitajima, Japan; S-Daniel Gyurta, Netherlands; B-Brendan Hansen, U.S.

100M Butterfly—G-Michael Phelps, U.S.; S-Ian Crocker, U.S.; B-Andriy Serdinov, Ukraine

200M Butterfly—G-Michael Phelps, U.S.; S-Takashi Yamamoto, Japan; B-Stephen Parry, Great Britain

200M Individual Medley—G-Michael Phelps, U.S.; S-Ryan Lochte, U.S.; B-George Bovell, Trinidad

400M Individual Medley—G-Michael Phelps, U.S.; S-Erik Vendt, U.S.; B-Laszlo Cseh, Hungary

400M Freestyle Relay—G-South Africa; S-Netherlands; B-U.S.

800M Freestyle Relay—G-U.S.; S-Australia; B-Italy

400M Medley Relay—G-U.S.; S-Germany; B-Japan

Women

50M Freestyle—G-Inge de Bruijn, Netherlands; S-Malia Metella, France; B-Lisbeth Lenton, Australia

100M Freestyle—G-Jodie Henry, Australia; S-Inge de Bruijn, Netherlands; B-Natalie Coughlin, U.S.

200M Freestyle—G-Camelia Potec, Romania; S-Federica Pellegrini, Italy; B-Solenne Figues, France

400M Freestyle—G-Laure Manaudou, France; S-Otylia Jedrzejczak, Poland; B-Kaitlin Sandeno, U.S.

800M Freestyle—G-Ai Shibata, Japan; S-Laure Manaudou, France; B-Diana Munz, U.S.

100M Backstroke—G-Natalie Coughlin, U.S.; S-Kirsty Coventry, Zimbabwe; B-Laure Manaudou, France

200M Backstroke—G-Kirsty Coventry, Zimbabwe; S-Stanislava Komarova, Russia; B-Reiko Nakamura, Japan

100M Breaststroke—G-Luo Xuejuan, China; S-Brooke Hanson, Australia; B-Leisel Jones, Australia

200M Breaststroke—G-Amanda Beard, U.S.; S-Leisel Jones, Australia; B-Anne Poleska, German

100M Butterfly—G-Petria Thomas, Australia; S-Otylia Jedrzejczak, Poland; B-Inge de Bruijn, Netherlands

200M Butterfly—G-Otylia Jedrzejczak, Poland; S-Petria Thomas, Australia; B-Yuko Nakanishi, Japan

200M Individual Medley—G-Yana Klochkova, Ukraine; S-Amanda Beard, U.S.; B-Kirsty Coventry, Zimbabwe

400M Individual Medley—G-Yana Klochkova, Ukraine; S-Kaitlin Sandeno, U.S.; B-Georgina Bardach, Argentina

400M Freestyle Relay—G-Australia; S-U.S.; B-Netherlands

800M Freestyle Relay—G-U.S.; S-China; B-Germany

400M Medley Relay—G-Australia; S-U.S.; B-Germany

Synchronized Swimming

Duet—G-Anastasia Davidova and Anastasia Ermakova, Russia; S-Miho Takeda and Miya Tachibana, Japan; B-Alison Bartosik and Anna Kozlova, U.S.

Team—G-Russia; S-Japan; B-U.S.

Table Tennis

Men's Singles—G-Ryu Seung Min, South Korea; S-Wang Hao, China; B- Wang Liqin, China

Men's Doubles—G-Chen Qi and Ma Lin, China; S-Ko Lai Chak and Li Ching, Hong Kong; B-Michael Maze and Finn Tugwell, Denmark

Women's Singles—G-Zhang Yining, China; S-Kim Hyang Mi, North Korea; B-Kim Kyung Ah, South Korea

Women's Doubles—G-Zhang Yining and Wang Nan, China; S-Lee Eun Sil and Seok Eun Mi, South Korea; B-Guo Yue and Niu Jianfeng, China

Taekwondo
Men

Up to 58 kg (127¾ lbs)—G-Mu Yen Chu, Taiwan; S-Oscar Francisco Salazar Blanco, Mexico; B-Tamer Bayoumi, Egypt

Up to 68 kg (150 lbs)—G-Hadi Saei Bonehkohal, Iran; S-Chih Hsiung Huang, Taiwan; B-Myeong Seob Song, South Korea

Up to 80 kg (176¼ lbs)—G-Steven Lopez, U.S.; S-Bahri Tanrikulu, Turkey; B-Yossef Karami, Iran

Over 80 kg (176¼ lbs)—G-Dae Sung Moon, South Korea; S-Alexandros Nikolaidis, Greece; B-Pascal Gentil, France

Women

Up to 49 kg (108 lbs)—G-Shih Hsin Chen (Taiwan); S-Yanelis Yuliet Labrada Diaz, Cuba; B-Yaowapa Boorapolchai, Thailand

Up to 57 kg (125½ lbs)—G-Jang Ji Won, South Korea; S-Niah Abdallah, U.S.; B-Iridia Salazar Blanco, Mexico

Up to 67 kg (147¾ lbs)—G-Luo Wei, China; S-Elisavet Mystakidou, Greece; B-Hwang Kyung Sun, South Korea

Over 67 kg (147¾ lbs)—G-Chen Zhong, China; S-Myriam Baverel, France; B-Adriana Carmona, Venezuela

Tennis

Men's Singles—G-Nicolas Massu, Chile; S-Mardy Fish, U.S.; B-Fernando Gonzalez, Chile

Men's Doubles—G-Nicolas Massu and Fernando Gonzalez, Chile; S-Nicolas Kiefer and Rainer Schuettler, Germany; B-Mario Ancic and Ivan Ljubicic, Croatia

Women's Singles—G-Justine Henin-Hardenne, Belgium; S-Amelie Mauresmo, France; B-Alicia Molik, Australia

Women's Doubles—G-Li Ting and Sun Tian Tian, China; S-Conchita Martinez and Virgina Ruano Pascual, Spain; B-Paola Suarez and Patricia Tarabini, Argentina

Track and Field
Men

100M—G-Justin Gatlin, U.S.; S-Francis Obikwelu, Portugal; B-Maurice Greene, U.S.

200M—G-Shawn Crawford, U.S.; S-Bernard Williams, U.S.; B-Justin Gatlin, U.S.

400M—G-Jeremy Wariner, U.S.; S-Otis Harris, U.S.; B-Derrick Brew, U.S.

800M—G-Yuriy Borzakovskiy, Russia; S-Mbulaeni Tongai Mulaudzi, South Africa; B-Wilson Kipketer, Denmark

1,500M—G-Hicham el-Guerrouj, Morocco; S-Bernard Lagat, Kenya; B-Rui Silva, Portugal

5,000M—G-Hicham el-Guerrouj, Morocco; S-Kenenisa Bekele, Ethiopia; B-Eliud Kipchoge, Kenya

10,000M—G-Kenenisa Bekele, Ethiopia; S-Sileshi Sihine, Ethiopia; B-Zersenay Tadesse, Eritrea

3,000M Steeplechase—G-Ezekiel Kemboi, Kenya; S-Brimin Kipruto, Kenya; B-Paul Kipsiele Koech, Kenya

110M Hurdles—G-Liu Xiang, China; S-Terrence Trammell, U.S.; B-Anier Garcia, Cuba

400M Hurdles—G-Felix Sanchez, Dominican Republic; S-Danny Mcfarlane, Jamaica; B-Naman Keita, France

400M Relay—G-Great Britain; S-U.S.; B-Nigeria

1,600M Relay—G-U.S.; S-Australia; B-Nigeria

20KM Walk—G-Ivano Brugnetti, Italy; S-Francisco Fernandez, Spain; B-Nathan Deakes, Australia

50KM Walk—G-Robert Korzeniowski, Poland; S-Denis Nizhegorodov, Russia; B-Aleksey Voyevodin, Russia

Marathon—G-Stefano Baldino, Italy; S-Meb Keflezighi, U.S.; B-Vanderlei de Lima, Brazil

High Jump—G-Stefen Holm, Sweden; S-Matt Hemingway, U.S.; B-Jaroslav Baba, Czech Republic

Long Jump—G-Dwight Phillips, U.S.; S-John Moffitt, U.S.; B-Joan Lino Martinez, Spain

Triple Jump—G-Christian Olsson, Sweden; S-Marian Oprea, Romania; B-Danila Burkenya, Russia

Discus Throw—G-Virgilijus Alekna, Lithuania; S-Zoltan Kovago, Hungary; B-Aleksander Tammert, Estonia

Hammer Throw—G-Koji Murofushi, Japan; S-Ivan Tikhon, Belarus; B-Esref Apak, Turkey

Javelin Throw—G-Andreas Thorkildsen, Norway; S-Vadims Vasilevskis, Latvia; B-Sergey Makarov, Russia

Pole Vault—G-Timothy Mack, U.S.; S-Toby Stevenson, U.S.; B-Giuseppe Gibilisco, Italy

Shot Put—G-Yuriy Bilonog, Ukraine; S-Adam Nelson, U.S.; B-Joachim Olsen, Denmark

Decathlon—G-Roman Sebrle, Czech Republic; S-Bryan Clay, U.S.; B-Dmitriy Karpov, Kazakhstan

Women

100M—G-Yuliya Nesterenko, Belarus; S-Lauryn Williams, U.S.; B-Veronica Campbell, Jamaica

200M—G- Veronica Campbell, Jamaica; S-Allyson Felix, U.S.; B-Debbie Ferguson, Bahamas

400M—G-Tonique Williams-Darling, Bahamas; S-Ana Guevara, Mexico; B-Natalya Antyukh, Russia

800M—G-Kelly Holmes, Great Britain; S-Hasna Benhassi, Morocco; B-Jolanda Ceplak, Slovenia

1,500M—G-Kelly Holmes, Great Britain; S-Tatyana Tomashova, Russia; B-Maria Cioncan, Romania

5,000M—G-Meseret Defar, Ethiopa; S-Isabella Ochichi, Kenya; B-Tirunesh Dibaba, Ethiopia

10,000M—G-Xing Huina, China; S-Ejegayehu Dibaba, Ethiopia; B-Derartu Tulu, Ethiopia

100M Hurdles—G-Joanna Hayes, U.S.; S-Olena Krasovska, Ukraine; B-Melissa Morrison, U.S.

400M Hurdles—G-Fani Halkia, Greece; S-Ionela Tirlea-Manolache, Romania; B-Tetiana Tereshchuk-Antipova, Ukraine

400M Relay—G-Jamaica; S-Russia; B-France

1,600M Relay—G-U.S.; S-Russia; B-Jamaica

20KM Walk—G-Athanasia Tsoumeleka, Greece; S-Olimpiada Ivanova, Russia; B-Jane Saville, Australia

Marathon—G-Mizuki Noguchi, Japan; S-Catherine Ndereba, Kenya; B-Deena Kastor, U.S.

High Jump—G-Yelena Slesarenko, Russia; S-Hestrie Cloete, South Africa; B-Viktoriya Styopina, Ukraine

Long Jump—G-Tatyana Lebedeva, Russia S-Irina Simagina, Russia; B-Tatyana Kotova, Russia

Triple Jump—G-Francoise Mbango Etone, Cameroon; S-Hrysopiyi Devetzi, Greece; B-Trecia Smith, Jamaica

Discus Throw—G-Natalya Sadova; S-Anastasia Kelesidou, Greece; B-Irina Yatchenko, Belarus

Hammer Throw—G-Olga Kuzenkova, Russia; S-Yipsi Moreno, Cuba; B-Yunaika Crawford, Cuba

Javelin Throw—G-Osleidys Menendez; S-Steffi Nerius, Germany; B-Mirela Manjani, Greece

Pole Vault—G-Yelena Isinbayeva, Russia; S-Svetlana Feofanova, Russia; B-Anna Rogowska, Poland

Shot Put—G-Yumileidi Cumba Jay, Cuba; S-Nadine Kleinert, Germany; B-Svetlana Krivelyova, Russia

Heptathlon—G-Carolina Kluft, Sweden; S-Austra Skujyte, Lithuania; B-Kelly Sotherton, Great Britain

Triathlon

Men—G-Hamish Carter, New Zealand; S-Bevan Docherty, New Zealand; B-Sven Riederer, Switzerland

Women—G-Kate Allen, Austria; S-Loretta Harrop, Australia; B-Susan Williams, U.S.

Volleyball

Men—G-Brazil; S-Italy; B-Russia

Women—G-China; S-Russia; B-Cuba

Water Polo

Men—G-Hungary; S-Serbia and Montenegro; B-Russia

Women—G-Italy; S-Greece; B.-U.S.

Weight Lifting

Men

Up to 56 kg (123½ lbs)—G-Halil Mutlu, Turkey; S-Wu Meijin, China; B-Sedat Artuc, Turkey

Up to 62 kg (136¾ lbs)—G-Shi Zhiyong, China; S-Le Maosheng, China; B-Jose Rubio Israel, Venezuela

Up to 69 kg (152 lbs)—G-Zhang Guozhang, China; S-Lee Bae Young, South Korea; B-Nikolay Pechalov, Croatia

Up to 77 kg (169¾ lbs)—G-Taner Sagir, Turkey; S-Sergey Filiimonov, Kazakhstan; B-Oleg Perepetchenov, Russia

Up to 85 kg (187¼ lbs)—G-George Asanidze, Georgia; S-Andrei Rybakou, Belarus; B-Pyrros Dimas, Greece

Up to 94 kg (207¼ lbs)—G-Milen Dobrev, Bulgaria; S-Khadjumourad Akkaev, Russia; B-Eduard Tjukin, Russia

Up to 105 kg (231½ lbs)—G-Dmitry Berestov, Russia; S-Igor Razoronov, Ukraine; B-Gleb Pisarevskiy, Russia

Over 105 kg (231½ lbs)—G-Hossein Reza Zadeh, Iran; S-Viktors Scerbatihs, Latvia; B-Velichko Cholakov, Bulgaria

Women

Up to 48 kg (105¾ lbs)—G-Nurcan Taylan, Turkey; S-Li Zhuo, China; B-Aree Wiratthaworn, Thailand

Up to 53 kg (116¾ lbs)—G-Udomporn Polsak, Thailand; S-Raema Lisa Rumbewas, Indonesia; B-Mabel Mosquera, Colombia

Up to 58 kg (128 lbs)—G-Chen Yanqing, China; S-Ri Song Hui, North Korea; B-Wandee Kameaim, Thailand

Up to 63 kg (139 lbs)—G-Nataliya Skakun, Ukraine; S-Hanna Batsiushka, Belarus; B-Tatsiana Stukalava, Belarus

Up to 69 kg (152¼ lbs)—G-Liu Chunhung, China; S-Eszter Krutzler, Hungary; B-Zarema Kasaeva, Russia

Up to 75 kg (165¼ lbs)—G-Pawina Thongsuk, Thailand; S-Natalia Zalobotnaia, Russia; B-Valentina Popova, Russia

Over 75 kg (165¼ lbs)—G-Tang Gonghong, China; S-Jang Mi Ran, South Korea; B-Agata Wrobel, Poland.

Wrestling

Men's Freestyle

55 kg (121¼ lbs)—G-Mavlet Batirov, Russia; S-Stephen Abas, U.S.; B-Chikara Tanabe, Japan

60 kg (132 1/3)—G-Yandro Miguel Quintana, Cuba; S-Masuod Jokar, Iran; B-Kenji Inoue, Japan

66 kg (145½ lbs)—G-Elbrus Tedeyev, Ukraine; S-Jamill Kelly, U.S.; B-Makhach Murtazaliev, Russia

74 kg (163 lbs)—G-Buvaysa Saytiev, Russia; S-Gennadiy Laliyev, Kazakhstan; B-Ivan Fundora, Cuba

84 kg (185 lbs)—G-Cael Sanderson, U.S.; S-Moon Eui Jae, South Korea; B-Sazhid Sazhidov, Russia

96 kg (211¾ lbs)—G-Khadjimourat Gatsalov, Russia; S-Magomed Ibragimov, Uzbekistan; B-Alireza Heidari, Iran

120 kg (264¾ lbs)—G-Artur Taymazov, Uzbekistan; S-Alireza Rezaei, Iran; B-Aydin Polatci, Turkey

Men's Greco-Roman

55 kg (121¼ lbs)—G-Istvan Majoros, Hungary; S-Gueidar Mamedaliev, Russia; B-Artiom Kiouregkian, Greece

60 kg (132 1/3)—G-Jung Ji Hyun, South Korea; S-Roberto Monzon, Cuba; B-Armen Nazarian, Bulgaria

66 kg (145½ lbs)—G-Farid Mansurov, Azerbaijan; S-Seref Eroglu, Turkey; B-Mkkhitar Manukyan, Kazakhstan

74 kg (163 lbs)—G-Alexandr Dokturishivili, Uzbekistan; S-Marko Yli-Hannuksela, Finland; B-Varteres Samourgachev, Russia

84 kg (185 lbs)—G-Alexei Michine, Russia; S-Ara Abrahamian, Sweden; B-Viachaslau Makaranka, Bulgaria

96 kg (211¾ lbs)—G-Karam Ibrahim, Egypt; S-Ramaz Nozadze, Georgia; B-Mehmet Ozal, Turkey

120 kg (264¾ lbs)—G-Khasan Baroev, Russia; S-Georgiy Tsurtsumia, Kazakhstan; B-Rulon Gardner, U.S.

Women's Freestyle

48 kg (105¾ lbs)—G-Irini Merleni, Ukraine; S-Chiharu Icho, Japan; B-Patricia Miranda, U.S.

55 kg (121¼ lbs)—G-Saori Yoshida, Japan; S-Tonya Verbeek, Canada; B-Anna Gomis, France

63 kg (139 kg)—G-Kaori Icho, Japan; S-Sara McMann, U.S.; B-Lise Legrand, France

72 kg (158¾ lbs)—G-Wang Xu, China; S-Gouzel Maniourova, Russia; B-Kyoko Hamaguchi, Japan

Summer Olympic Games Champions, 1896-2004

(*indicates Olympic record; w indicates wind-aided)

The 1980 games were boycotted by 62 nations, including the U.S. The 1984 games were boycotted by the USSR and most Eastern bloc nations. E and W Germany competed separately, 1968-88. The 1992 Unified Team consisted of 12 former Soviet republics. The 1992 Independent Olympic Participants (I.O.P.) were from Serbia, Montenegro, and Macedonia.

Track and Field—Men

100-Meter Run

1896	Thomas Burke, United States	12.0s
1900	Francis W. Jarvis, United States	11.0s
1904	Archie Hahn, United States	11.0s
1908	Reginald Walker, South Africa	10.8s
1912	Ralph Craig, United States	10.8s
1920	Charles Paddock, United States	10.8s
1924	Harold Abrahams, Great Britain	10.6s
1928	Percy Williams, Canada	10.8s
1932	Eddie Tolan, United States	10.3s
1936	Jesse Owens, United States	10.3s
1948	Harrison Dillard, United States	10.3s
1952	Lindy Remigino, United States	10.4s

100-Meter Run

1956	Bobby Morrow, United States	10.5s
1960	Armin Hary, Germany	10.2s
1964	Bob Hayes, United States	10.0s
1968	Jim Hines, United States	9.95s
1972	Valery Borzov, USSR	10.14s
1976	Hasely Crawford, Trinidad	10.06s
1980	Allan Wells, Great Britain	10.25s
1984	Carl Lewis, United States	9.99s
1988	Carl Lewis, United States	9.92s
1992	Linford Christie, Great Britain	9.96s
1996	Donovan Bailey, Canada	9.84s*
2000	Maurice Greene, United States	9.87s
2004	Justin Gatlin, United States	9.85s

200-Meter Run

1900	Walter Tewksbury, United States	22.2s
1904	Archie Hahn, United States	21.6s
1908	Robert Kerr, Canada	22.6s
1912	Ralph Craig, United States	21.7s
1920	Allan Woodring, United States	22.0s
1924	Jackson Scholz, United States	21.6s
1928	Percy Williams, Canada	21.8s
1932	Eddie Tolan, United States	21.2s
1936	Jesse Owens, United States	20.7s
1948	Mel Patton, United States	21.1s
1952	Andrew Stanfield, United States	20.7s
1956	Bobby Morrow, United States	20.6s
1960	Livio Berruti, Italy	20.5s
1964	Henry Carr, United States	20.3s
1968	Tommie Smith, United States	19.83s
1972	Valeri Borzov, USSR	20.00s
1976	Donald Quarrie, Jamaica	20.23s
1980	Pietro Mennea, Italy	20.19s
1984	Carl Lewis, United States	19.80s
1988	Joe DeLoach, United States	19.75s
1992	Mike Marsh, United States	20.01s
1996	Michael Johnson, United States	19.32s*
2000	Konstantinos Kenteris, Greece	20.09s
2004	Shawn Crawford, United States	19.79s

400-Meter Run

1896	Thomas Burke, United States	54.2s
1900	Maxey Long, United States	49.4s
1904	Harry Hillman, United States	49.2s
1908	Wyndham Halswelle, Great Brit., walkover	50.0s
1912	Charles Reidpath, United States	48.2s
1920	Bevil Rudd, South Africa	49.6s
1924	Eric Liddell, Great Britain	47.6s
1928	Ray Barbuti, United States	47.8s
1932	William Carr, United States	46.2s
1936	Archie Williams, United States	46.5s
1948	Arthur Wint, Jamaica	46.2s
1952	George Rhoden, Jamaica	45.9s
1956	Charles Jenkins, United States	46.7s
1960	Otis Davis, United States	44.9s
1964	Michael Larrabee, United States	45.1s
1968	Lee Evans, United States	43.86s
1972	Vincent Matthews, United States	44.66s
1976	Alberto Juantorena, Cuba	44.26s
1980	Viktor Markin, USSR	44.60s
1984	Alonzo Babers, United States	44.27s
1988	Steven Lewis, United States	43.87s
1992	Quincy Watts, United States	43.50s
1996	Michael Johnson, United States	43.49s*
2000	Michael Johnson, United States	43.84s
2004	Jeremy Wariner, United States	44.00s

800-Meter Run

1896	Edwin Flack, Australia	2m. 11s
1900	Alfred Tysoe, Great Britain	2m. 1.2s
1904	James Lightbody, United States	1m. 56s
1908	Mel Sheppard, United States	1m. 52.8s
1912	James Meredith, United States	1m. 51.9s
1920	Albert Hill, Great Britain	1m. 53.4s
1924	Douglas Lowe, Great Britain	1m. 52.4s
1928	Douglas Lowe, Great Britain	1m. 51.8s
1932	Thomas Hampson, Great Britain	1m. 49.8s
1936	John Woodruff, United States	1m. 52.9s
1948	Mal Whitfield, United States	1m. 49.2s
1952	Mal Whitfield, United States	1m. 49.2s
1956	Thomas Courtney, United States	1m. 47.7s
1960	Peter Snell, New Zealand	1m. 46.3s
1964	Peter Snell, New Zealand	1m. 45.1s
1968	Ralph Doubell, Australia	1m. 44.3s
1972	Dave Wottle, United States	1m. 45.9s
1976	Alberto Juantorena, Cuba	1m. 43.50s
1980	Steve Ovett, Great Britain	1m. 45.40s
1984	Joaquim Cruz, Brazil	1m. 43.00s
1988	Paul Ereng, Kenya	1m. 43.45s
1992	William Tanui, Kenya	1m. 43.66s
1996	Vebjoern Rodal, Norway	1m. 42.58s*
2000	Nils Schumann, Germany	1m. 45.08s
2004	Yuriy Borzakovskiy, Russia	1m: 44.45s

1,500-Meter Run

1896	Edwin Flack, Australia	4m. 33.2s
1900	Charles Bennett, Great Britain	4m. 6.2s
1904	James Lightbody, United States	4m. 5.4s
1908	Mel Sheppard, United States	4m. 3.4s
1912	Arnold Jackson, Great Britain	3m. 56.8s
1920	Albert Hill, Great Britain	4m. 1.8s
1924	Paavo Nurmi, Finland	3m. 53.6s
1928	Harry Larva, Finland	3m. 53.2s
1932	Luigi Beccali, Italy	3m. 51.2s
1936	Jack Lovelock, New Zealand	3m. 47.8s
1948	Henri Eriksson, Sweden	3m. 49.8s

1,500-Meter Run

1952	Joseph Barthel, Luxembourg	3m. 45.2s
1956	Ron Delany, Ireland	3m. 41.2s
1960	Herb Elliott, Australia	3m. 35.6s
1964	Peter Snell, New Zealand	3m. 38.1s
1968	Kipchoge Keino, Kenya	3m. 34.9s
1972	Pekka Vasala, Finland	3m. 36.3s
1976	John Walker, New Zealand	3m. 39.17s
1980	Sebastian Coe, Great Britain	3m. 38.4s
1984	Sebastian Coe, Great Britain	3m. 32.53s
1988	Peter Rono, Kenya	3m. 35.96s
1992	Fermin Cacho Ruiz, Spain	3m. 40.12s
1996	Noureddine Morceli, Algeria	3m. 35.78s
2000	Noah Ngeny, Kenya	3m. 32.07s*
2004	Hicham el-Guerrouj, Morocco	3m. 34.18s

5,000-Meter Run

1912	Hannes Kolehmainen, Finland	14m. 36.6s
1920	Joseph Guillemot, France	14m. 55.6s
1924	Paavo Nurmi, Finlands	14m. 31.2
1928	Willie Ritola, Finland	14m. 38s
1932	Lauri Lehtinen, Finland	14m. 30s
1936	Gunnar Hockert, Finland	14m. 22.2s
1948	Gaston Reiff, Belgium	14m. 17.6s
1952	Emil Zatopek, Czechoslovakia	14m. 6.6s
1956	Vladimir Kuts, USSR	13m. 39.6s
1960	Murray Halberg, New Zealand	13m. 43.4s
1964	Bob Schul, United States	13m. 48.8s
1968	Mohamed Gammoudi, Tunisia	14m. 05.0s
1972	Lasse Viren, Finland	13m. 26.4s
1976	Lasse Viren, Finland	13m. 24.76s
1980	Miruts Yifter, Ethiopia	13m. 21.0s
1984	Said Aouita, Morocco	13m. 05.59s*
1988	John Ngugi, Kenya	13m. 11.70s
1992	Dieter Baumann, Germany	13m. 12.52s
1996	Venuste Niyongabo, Burundi	13m. 07.96s
2000	Millon Wolde, Ethiopia	13m. 35.49s
2004	Hicham el-Guerrouj, Morocco	13m. 14.39s

10,000-Meter Run

1912	Hannes Kolehmainen, Finland	31m. 20.8s
1920	Paavo Nurmi, Finland	31m. 45.8s
1924	Willie Ritola, Finland	30m. 23.2s
1928	Paavo Nurmi, Finland	30m. 18.8s
1932	Janusz Kusocinski, Poland	30m. 11.4s
1936	Ilmari Salminen, Finland	30m. 15.4s
1948	Emil Zatopek, Czechoslovakia	29m. 59.6s
1952	Emil Zatopek, Czechoslovakia	29m. 17.0s
1956	Vladimir Kuts, USSR	28m. 45.6s
1960	Pyotr Bolotnikov, USSR	28m. 32.2s
1964	Billy Mills, United States	28m. 24.4s
1968	Naftali Temu, Kenya	29m. 27.4s
1972	Lasse Viren, Finland	27m. 38.4s
1976	Lasse Viren, Finland	27m. 40.4s
1980	Miruts Yifter, Ethiopia	27m. 42.7s
1984	Alberto Cova, Italy	27m. 47.54s
1988	Brahim Boutaib, Morocco	27m. 21.46s
1992	Khalid Skah, Morocco	27m. 46.70s
1996	Haile Gebrselassie, Ethiopia	27m. 07.34s
2000	Haile Gebrselassie, Ethiopia	27m. 18.20s
2004	Kenenisa Bekele, Ethiopia	27m. 05.10s*

110-Meter Hurdles

1896	Thomas Curtis, United States	17.6s
1900	Alvin Kraenzlein, United States	15.4s
1904	Frederick Schule, United States	16.0s
1908	Forrest Smithson, United States	15.0s
1912	Frederick Kelly, United States	15.1s
1920	Earl Thomson, Canada	14.8s
1924	Daniel Kinsey, United States	15.0s
1928	Sydney Atkinson, South Africa	14.8s
1932	George Saling, United States	14.6s
1936	Forrest Towns, United States	14.2s
1948	William Porter, United States	13.9s
1952	Harrison Dillard, United States	13.7s
1956	Lee Calhoun, United States	13.5s
1960	Lee Calhoun, United States	13.8s
1964	Hayes Jones, United States	13.6s
1968	Willie Davenport, United States	13.33s
1972	Rod Milburn, United States	13.24s
1976	Guy Drut, France	13.30s
1980	Thomas Munkelt, E. Germany	13.39s
1984	Roger Kingdom, United States	13.20s
1988	Roger Kingdom, United States	12.98s
1992	Mark McCoy, Canada	13.12s
1996	Allen Johnson, United States	12.95s
2000	Anier Garcia, Cuba	13.00s
2004	Liu Xiang, China	12.91s*

400-Meter Hurdles

1900	J.W.B. Tewksbury, United States	57.6s
1904	Harry Hillman, United States	53.0s
1908	Charles Bacon, United States	55.0s

400-Meter Hurdles

1920	Frank Loomis, United States	54.0s
1924	F. Morgan Taylor, United States	52.6s
1928	Lord Burghley, Great Britain	53.4s
1932	Robert Tisdall, Ireland	51.7s
1936	Glenn Hardin, United States	52.4s
1948	Roy Cochran, United States	51.1s
1952	Charles Moore, United States	50.8s
1956	Glenn Davis, United States	50.1s
1960	Glenn Davis, United States	49.3s
1964	Rex Cawley, United States	49.6s
1968	Dave Hemery, Great Britain	48.12s
1972	John Akii-Bua, Uganda	47.82s
1976	Edwin Moses, United States	47.64s
1980	Volker Beck, E. Germany	48.70s
1984	Edwin Moses, United States	47.75s
1988	Andre Phillips, United States	47.19s
1992	Kevin Young, United States	46.78s*
1996	Derrick Adkins, United States	47.54s
2000	Angelo Taylor, United States	47.50s
2004	Felix Sanchez, Dominican Republic	47.63s

400-Meter Relay

1912	Great Britain	42.4s
1920	United States	42.2s
1924	United States	41.0s
1928	United States	41.0s
1932	United States	40.0s
1936	United States	39.8s
1948	United States	40.6s
1952	United States	40.1s
1956	United States	39.5s
1960	Germany (U.S. disqualified)	39.5s
1964	United States	39.0s
1968	United States	38.24s
1972	United States	38.19s
1976	United States	38.33s
1980	USSR	38.26s
1984	United States	37.83s
1988	USSR (U.S. disqualified)	38.19s
1992	United States	37.40s*
1996	Canada	37.69s
2000	United States	37.61s
2004	Great Britain	38.07s

1,600-Meter Relay

1908	United States	3m. 29.4s
1912	United States	3m. 16.6s
1920	Great Britain	3m. 22.2s
1924	United States	3m. 16s
1928	United States	3m. 14.2s
1932	United States	3m. 8.2s
1936	Great Britain	3m. 9s
1948	United States	3m. 10.4s
1952	Jamaica	3m. 03.9s
1956	United States	3m. 04.8s
1960	United States	3m. 02.2s
1964	United States	3m. 00.7s
1968	United States	2m. 56.16s
1972	Kenya	2m. 59.8s
1976	United States	2m. 58.65s
1980	USSR	3m. 01.1s
1984	United States	2m. 57.91s
1988	United States	2m. 56.16s
1992	United States	2m. 55.74s*
1996	United States	2m. 55.99s
2000	United States	2m. 56.35s
2004	United States	2m. 55.91s

3,000-Meter Steeplechase

1920	Percy Hodge, Great Britain	10m. 0.4s
1924	Willie Ritola, Finland	9m. 33.6s
1928	Toivo Loukola, Finland	9m. 21.8s
1932	Volmari Iso-Hollo, Finland	10m. 33.4s
	(About 3,450 m; extra lap by error.)	
1936	Volmari Iso-Hollo, Finland	9m. 3.8s
1948	Thore Sjoestrand, Sweden	9m. 4.6s
1952	Horace Ashenfelter, United States	8m. 45.4s
1956	Chris Brasher, Great Britain	8m. 41.2s
1960	Zdzislaw Krzyszkowiak, Poland	8m. 34.2s
1964	Gaston Roelants, Belgium	8m. 30.8s
1968	Amos Biwott, Kenya	8m. 51s
1972	Kipchoge Keino, Kenya	8m. 23.6s
1976	Anders Garderud, Sweden	8m. 08.2s
1980	Bronislaw Malinowski, Poland	8m. 09.7s
1984	Julius Korir, Kenya	8m. 11.8s
1988	Julius Kariuki, Kenya	8m. 05.51s*
1992	Matthew Birir, Kenya	8m. 08.84s
1996	Joseph Keter, Kenya	8m. 07.12s
2000	Reuben Kosgei, Kenya	8m. 21.43s
2004	Ezekiel Kemboi, Kenya	8m. 05.81s

20-Kilometer Walk

1956	Leonid Spirin, USSR	1h. 31m. 27.4s
1960	Vladimir Golubnichy, USSR	1h. 33m. 7.2s
1964	Kenneth Mathews, Great Britain	1h. 29m. 34.0s
1968	Vladimir Golubnichy, USSR	1h. 33m. 58.4s
1972	Peter Frenkel, E. Germany	1h. 26m. 42.4s
1976	Daniel Bautista, Mexico	1h. 24m. 40.6s
1980	Maurizio Damilano, Italy	1h. 23m. 35.5s
1984	Ernesto Canto, Mexico	1h. 23m. 13.0s
1988	Josef Pribilinec, Czechoslovakia	1h. 19m. 57.0s
1992	Daniel Plaza Montero, Spain	1h. 21m. 45.0s
1996	Jefferson Perez, Ecuador	1h. 20m.7s
2000	Robert Korzeniowski, Poland	1h. 18m. 59.0s*
2004	Ivano Brugnetti, Italy	1h. 19m. 40s

50-Kilometer Walk

1932	Thomas W. Green, Great Britain	4h. 50m. 10s
1936	Harold Whitlock, Great Britain	4h. 30m. 41.4s
1948	John Ljunggren, Sweden	4h. 41m. 52s
1952	Giuseppe Dordoni, Italy	4h. 28m. 07.8s
1956	Norman Read, New Zealand	4h. 30m. 42.8s
1960	Donald Thompson, Great Britain	4h. 25m. 30s
1964	Abdon Pamich, Italy	4h. 11m. 12.4s
1968	Christoph Hohne, E. Germany	4h. 20m. 13.6s
1972	Bern Kannenberg, W. Germany	3h. 56m. 11.6s
1980	Hartwig Gauter, E. Germany	3h. 49m. 24.0s
1984	Raul Gonzalez, Mexico	3h. 47m. 26.0s
1988	Vyacheslav Ivanenko, USSR	3h. 38m. 29.0s*
1992	Andrei Perlov, Unified Team	3h. 50m. 13.0s
1996	Robert Korzeniowski, Poland	3h. 43m. 30s
2000	Robert Korzeniowski, Poland	3h. 42m. 22s
2004	Robert Korzeniowski, Poland	3h. 38m. 46s

Marathon

1896	Spiridon Loues, Greece	2h. 58m. 50s
1900	Michel Theato, France	2h. 59m. 45s
1904	Thomas Hicks, United States	3h. 28m. 63s
1908	John J. Hayes, United States	2h. 55m. 18.4s
1912	Kenneth McArthur, South Africa	2h. 36m. 54.8s
1920	Hannes Kolehmainen, Finland	2h. 32m. 35.8s
1924	Albin Stenroos, Finland	2h. 41m. 22.6s
1928	A.B. El Ouafi, France	2h. 32m. 57s
1932	Juan Zabala, Argentina	2h. 31m. 36s
1936	Kijung Son, Japan (Korean)	2h. 29m. 19.2s
1948	Delfo Cabrera, Argentina	2h. 34m. 51.6s
1952	Emil Zatopek, Czechoslovakia	2h. 23m. 03.2s
1956	Alain Mimoun, France	2h. 25m.
1960	Abebe Bikila, Ethiopia	2h. 15m. 16.2s
1964	Abebe Bikila, Ethiopia	2h. 12m. 11.2s
1968	Mamo Wolde, Ethiopia	2h. 20m. 26.4s
1972	Frank Shorter, United States	2h. 12m. 19.8s
1976	Waldemar Cierpinski, E. Germany	2h. 09m. 55s
1980	Waldemar Cierpinski, E. Germany	2h. 11m. 03s
1984	Carlos Lopes, Portugal	2h. 09m. 21s*
1988	Gelindo Bordin, Italy	2h. 10m. 32s
1992	Hwang Young-Cho, S. Korea	2h. 13m. 23s
1996	Josia Thugwane, South Africa	2h. 12m. 36s
2000	Gezahgne Abera, Ethiopia	2h. 10m. 11s
2004	Stefano Baldino, Italy	2h. 10m. 55s

High Jump

1896	Ellery Clark, United States	1.81m. (5'11¼")
1900	Irving Baxter, United States	1.90m. (6' 2¾")
1904	Samuel Jones, United States	1.80m. (5' 11")
1908	Harry Porter, United States	1.90m. (6' 2¾ ")
1912	Alma Richards, United States	1.93m. (6' 4")
1920	Richmond Landon, United States	1.93m. (6' 4")
1924	Harold Osborn, United States	1.98m. (6' 6")
1928	Robert W. King, United States	1.94m. (6' 4¼")
1932	Duncan McNaughton, Canada	1.97m. (6' 5½")
1936	Cornelius Johnson, United States	2.03m. (6' 8")
1948	John L. Winter, Australia	1.98m. (6' 6")
1952	Walter Davis, United States	2.04m. (6' 8¼")
1956	Charles Dumas, United States	2.12m. (6' 11½")
1960	Robert Shavlakadze, USSR	2.16m. (7' 1")
1964	Valery Brumel, USSR	2.18m. (7' 1¾")
1968	Dick Fosbury, United States	2.24m. (7' 4¼")
1972	Jüri Tarmak, USSR	2.23m. (7' 3¾")
1976	Jacek Wszola, Poland	2.25m. (7' 4½")
1980	Gerd Wessig, E. Germany	2.36m. (7' 8¾")
1984	Dietmar Mögenburg, W. Germany	2.35m. (7' 8½")
1988	Hennady Avdeyenko, USSR	2.38m. (7' 9¾")
1992	Javier Sotomayor Sanabria, Cuba	2.34m. (7' 8")
1996	Charles Austin, United States	2.39m. (7' 10")*
2000	Sergey Kliugin, Russia	2.35m. (7' 8½")
2004	Stefen Holm, Sweden	2.63m. (7' 8¾")

Long Jump

1896	Ellery Clark, United States	6.35m. (20' 10")
1900	Alvin Kraenzlein, United States	7.18m. (23' 6¾")
1904	Meyer Prinstein, United States	7.34m. (24' 1")
1908	Frank Irons, United States	7.48m. (24' 6½")
1912	Albert Gutterson, United States	7.60m. (24' 11¼")

Long Jump

1920	William Petterssen, Sweden	7.15m.	(23' 5½")
1924	William DeHart Hubbard, United States	7.44m.	(24' 5")
1928	Edward B. Hamm, United States	7.73m.	(25' 4½")
1932	Edward Gordon, United States	7.64m.	(25' ¾")
1936	Jesse Owens, United States	8.06m.	(26' 5½")
1948	Willie Steele, United States	7.82m.	(25' 8")
1952	Jerome Biffle, United States	7.57m.	(24' 10")
1956	Gregory Bell, United States	7.83m.	(25' 8¼")
1960	Ralph Boston, United States	8.12m.	(26' 7¾")
1964	Lynn Davies, Great Britain	8.07m.	(26' 5¾")
1968	Bob Beamon, United States	8.90m.	(29' 2½")*
1972	Randy Williams, United States	8.24m.	(27' ½")
1976	Arnie Robinson, United States	8.35m.	(27' 4¾")
1980	Lutz Dombrowski, E. Germany	8.54m.	(28' ¼")
1984	Carl Lewis, United States	8.54m.	(28' ¼")
1988	Carl Lewis, United States	8.72m.	(28' 7½")
1992	Carl Lewis, United States	8.67m.	(28' 5½")
1996	Carl Lewis, United States	8.50m.	(27' 10¾")
2000	Ivan Pedroso, Cuba	8.55m.	(28' ¾")
2004	Dwight Phillips, United States	8.59m.	(28' 2¼")

Triple Jump

1896	James Connolly, United States	13.71m.	(44' 11¾")
1900	Meyer Prinstein, United States	14.47m.	(47' 5¾")
1904	Meyer Prinstein, United States	14.35m.	(47' 1")
1908	Timothy Ahearne, G.B.-Ireland	14.92m.	(48' 11½")
1912	Gustaf Lindblom, Sweden	14.76m.	(48' 5")
1920	Vilho Tuulos, Finland	14.50m.	(47' 7")
1924	Anthony Winter, Australia	15.52m.	(50' 11")
1928	Mikio Oda, Japan	15.21m.	(49' 11")
1932	Chuhei Nambu, Japan	15.72m.	(51' 7")
1936	Naoto Tajima, Japan	16.00m.	(52' 6")
1948	Arne Ahman, Sweden	15.40m.	(50' 6¼")
1952	Adhemar Ferreira da Silva, Brazil	16.22m.	(53' 2¾")
1956	Adhemar Ferreira da Silva, Brazil	16.35m.	(53' 7¾")
1960	Jozef Schmidt, Poland	16.81m.	(55' 1½")
1964	Jozef Schmidt, Poland	16.85m.	(55' 3½")
1968	Viktor Saneyev, USSR	17.39m.	(57' ¾")
1972	Viktor Saneyev, USSR	17.35m.	(56' 11¼")
1976	Viktor Saneyev, USSR	17.29m.	(56' 8¾")
1980	Jaak Uudmae, USSR	17.35m.	(56' 11")
1984	Al Joyner, United States	17.26m.	(56' 7½")
1988	Khristo Markov, Bulgaria	17.61m.	(57' 9½")
1992	Mike Conley, United States	18.17m.	(59' 7½")w
1996	Kenny Harrison, United States	18.09m.	(59' 4¼")*
2000	Jonathan Edwards, Britain	17.71m.	(58' 1¼")
2004	Christian Olsson, Sweden	17.79m.	(58' 4 ½")

Discus Throw

1896	Robert Garrett, United States	29.15m.	(95' 7")
1900	Rudolf Bauer, Hungary	36.04m.	(118' 3")
1904	Martin Sheridan, United States	39.28m.	(128' 10")
1908	Martin Sheridan, United States	40.89m.	(134' 1")
1912	Armas Taipale, Finland	45.21m.	(148' 3")
1920	Elmer Niklander, Finland	44.68m.	(146' 7")
1924	Clarence Houser, United States	46.15m.	(151' 4")
1928	Clarence Houser, United States	47.32m.	(155' 3")
1932	John Anderson, United States	49.49m.	(162' 4")
1936	Ken Carpenter, United States	50.48m.	(165' 7")
1948	Adolfo Consolini, Italy	52.78m.	(173' 2")
1952	Sim Iness, United States	55.03m.	(180' 6")
1956	Al Oerter, United States	56.36m.	(184' 11")
1960	Al Oerter, United States	59.18m.	(194' 2")
1964	Al Oerter, United States	61.00m.	(200' 1")
1968	Al Oerter, United States	64.78m.	(212' 6")
1972	Ludvik Danek, Czechoslovakia	64.40m.	(211' 3")
1976	Mac Wilkins, United States	67.50m.	(221' 5")
1980	Viktor Rashchupkin, USSR	66.64m.	(218' 8")
1984	Rolf Dannenberg, W. Germany	66.60m.	(218' 6")
1988	Jurgen Schult, E. Germany	68.82m.	(225' 9")
1992	Romas Ubartas, Lithuania	65.12m.	(213' 8")
1996	Lars Riedel, Germany	69.40m.	(227' 8")
2000	Virgilijus Alekna, Lithuania	69.30m.	(227' 4")
2004	Virgilijus Alekna, Lithuania	69.89m.	(228' 9¾")*

Hammer Throw

1900	John Flanagan, United States	49.73m.	(163' 1")
1904	John Flanagan, United States	51.22m.	(168' 0")
1908	John Flanagan, United States	51.92m.	(170' 4")
1912	Matt McGrath, United States	54.74m.	(179' 7")
1920	Pat Ryan, United States	52.86m.	(173' 5")
1924	Fred Tootell, United States	53.28m.	(174' 10")
1928	Patrick O'Callaghan, Ireland	51.38m.	(168' 7")
1932	Patrick O'Callaghan, Ireland	53.92m.	(176' 11")
1936	Karl Hein, Germany	56.48m.	(185' 4")
1948	Imre Németh, Hungary	56.06m.	(183' 11")
1952	József Csérmák, Hungary	60.34m.	(197' 11")
1956	Harold Connolly, United States	63.18m.	(207' 3")
1960	Vasily Rudenkov, USSR	67.10m.	(202' 0")
1964	Romuald Klim, USSR	69.74m.	(228' 10")

Hammer Throw

1968	Gyula Zsivótsky, Hungary	73.36m.	(240' 8")
1972	Anatoly Bondarchuk, USSR	75.50m.	(247' 8")
1976	Yuri Syedykh, USSR	77.52m.	(254' 4")
1980	Yuri Syedykh, USSR	81.80m.	(268' 4")
1984	Juha Tiainen, Finland	78.08m.	(256' 2")
1988	Sergei Litvinov, USSR	84.80m.	(278' 2")*
1992	Andrey Abduvaliyev, Unified Team.	82.54m.	(270' 9")
1996	Balázs Kiss, Hungary	81.24m.	(266' 6")
2000	Szymon Ziolkowski, Poland	80.02m.	(262' 6")
2004	Koji Murofushi, Japan	82.91m.	(272')

Javelin Throw

1908	Erik Lemming, Sweden	54.82m.	(179' 10")
1912	Erik Lemming, Sweden	60.64m.	(198' 11")
1920	Jonni Myyrä, Finland	64.78m.	(215' 10")
1924	Jonni Myyrä, Finland	62.96m.	(206' 7")
1928	Eric Lundkvist, Sweden	66.60m.	(218' 6")
1932	Matti Järvinen, Finland	72.70m.	(238' 6")
1936	Gerhard Stöck, Germany	71.84m.	(235' 8")
1948	Kai Tapio Rautavaara, Finland	69.76m.	(228' 11")
1952	Cy Young, United States	73.78m.	(242' 1")
1956	Egil Danielsen, Norway	85.70m.	(281' 2")
1960	Viktor Tsibulenko, USSR	84.64m.	(277' 8")
1964	Pauli Nevala, Finland	82.66m.	(271' 2")
1968	Janis Lusis, USSR	90.10m.	(295' 7")
1972	Klaus Wolfermann, W. Germany	90.48m.	(296' 10")
1976	Miklós Németh, Hungary	94.58m.	(310' 4")
1980	Dainis Kula, USSR	91.20m.	(299' 2")
1984	Arto Härkönen, Finland	86.76m.	(284' 8")
1988	Tapio Korjus, Finland	84.28m.	(276' 6")
1992	Jan Zelezny, Czechoslovakia (a)	89.66m.	(294' 2")
1996	Jan Zelezny, Czech Republic	88.16m.	(289' 3")
2000	Jan Zelezny, Czech Republic	90.17m.	(295' 9½")*
2004	Andreas Thorkildsen, Norway	86.50m.	(283' 10")

(a) New records were kept after javelin was modified in 1986.

Pole Vault

1896	William Welles Hoyt, United States	3.30m.	(10' 10")
1900	Irving Baxter, United States	3.30m.	(10' 10")
1904	Charles Dvorak, United States	3.50m.	(11' 6")
1908	A. C. Gilbert, United States		
	Edward Cooke Jr., United States	3.71m.	(12' 2")
1912	Harry Babcock, United States	3.95m.	(12' 11½")
1920	Frank Foss, United States	4.09m.	(13' 5")
1924	Lee Barnes, United States	3.95m.	(12' 11½")
1928	Sabin W. Carr, United States	4.20m.	(13' 9¼")
1932	William Miller, United States	4.31m.	(14' 1¾")
1936	Earle Meadows, United States	4.35m.	(14' 3¼")
1948	Guinn Smith, United States	4.30m.	(14' 1¼")
1952	Robert Richards, United States	4.55m.	(14' 11¼")
1956	Robert Richards, United States	4.56m.	(14' 11½")
1960	Don Bragg, United States	4.70m.	(15' 5")
1964	Fred Hansen, United States	5.10m.	(16' 8¾")
1968	Bob Seagren, United States	5.40m.	(17' 8½")
1972	Wolfgang Nordwig, E. Germany	5.50m.	(18' ½")
1976	Tadeusz Slusarski, Poland	5.50m.	(18' ½")
1980	Wladyslaw Kozakiewicz, Poland	5.78m.	(18' 11½")
1984	Pierre Quinon, France	5.75m.	(18' 10¼")
1988	Sergei Bubka, USSR	5.90m.	(19' 4¼")
1992	Maksim Tarassov, Unified Team	5.80m.	(19' ¼")
1996	Jean Galfione, France	5.92m.	(19' 5")*
2000	Nick Hysong, United States	5.90m.	(19' 4¼")
2004	Timothy Mack, United States	5.95m.	(19' 6¼")

16-lb. Shot Put

1896	Robert Garrett, United States	11.22m.	(36' 9¾")
1900	Richard Sheldon, United States	14.10m.	(46' 3¼")
1904	Ralph Rose, United States	14.81m.	(48' 7")
1908	Ralph Rose, United States	14.21m.	(46' 7½")
1912	Pat McDonald, United States	15.34m.	(50' 4")
1920	Ville Pörhölä, Finland	14.81m.	(48' 7¼")
1924	L. Clarence Houser, United States	14.99m.	(49' 2¼")
1928	John Kuck, United States	15.87m.	(52' ¾")
1932	Leo Sexton, United States	16.00m.	(52' 6")
1936	Hans Woellke, Germany	16.20m.	(53' 1¾")
1948	Wilbur Thompson, United States	17.12m.	(56' 2")
1952	W. Parry O'Brien, United States	17.41m.	(57' 1½")
1956	W. Parry O'Brien, United States	18.57m.	(60' 11¼")
1960	William Nieder, United States	19.68m.	(64' 6¾")
1964	Dallas Long, United States	20.33m.	(66' 8½")
1968	Randy Matson, United States	20.54m.	(67' 4¾")
1972	Wladyslaw Komar, Poland	21.18m.	(69' 6")
1976	Udo Beyer, E. Germany	21.05m.	(69' ¾")
1980	Vladimir Kyselyov, USSR	21.35m.	(70' ½")
1984	Alessandro Andrei, Italy	21.26m.	(69' 9")
1988	Ulf Timmermann, E. Germany	22.47m.	(73' 8¾")*
1992	Michael Stulce, United States	21.70m.	(71' 2½")
1996	Randy Barnes, United States	21.62m.	(70' 11¼")
2000	Arsi Harju, Finland	21.29m.	(69' 10¼")
2004	Yuriy Bilonog, Ukraine	21.16m.	(69' 5¼")

Decathlon (not held 1908)

1904	Thomas Kiely, Ireland	6,036 pts.
1912	Hugo Wieslander, Sweden (a)	7,724.49 pts.
1920	Helge Lovland, Norway	6,804.35 pts.
1924	Harold Osborn, United States	7,710.77 pts.
1928	Paavo Yrjola, Finland	8,053.29 pts.
1932	James Bausch, United States	8,462.23 pts.
1936	Glenn Morris, United States	7,900 pts.
1948	Robert Mathias, United States	7,139 pts.
1952	Robert Mathias, United States	7,887 pts.
1956	Milton Campbell, United States	7,937 pts.
1960	Rafer Johnson, United States	8,392 pts.
1964	Willi Holdorf, Germany (b)	7,887 pts.
1968	Bill Toomey, United States	8,193 pts.
1972	Nikolai Avilov, USSR	8,454 pts.
1976	Bruce Jenner, United States	8,617 pts.
1980	Daley Thompson, Great Britain	8,495 pts.
1984	Daley Thompson, Great Britain (c)	8,798 pts.
1988	Christian Schenk, E. Germany	8,488 pts.
1992	Robert Zmelik, Czechoslovakia	8,611 pts.
1996	Dan O'Brien, United States	8,824 pts.
2000	Erki Nool, Estonia	8,641 pts.
2004	Roman Sebrle, Czech Republic	8,893 pts.*

(a) Jim Thorpe of the U.S. won the 1912 Decathlon with 8,413 pts. but was disqualified and had to return his medals because he had played pro baseball prior to the Olympics. The IOC in 1982 posthumously restored his decathlon and pentathlon golds. (b) Former point systems used prior to 1964. (c) Scoring change effective Apr. 1985; Thompson's readjusted score is 8,847 pts.

TRACK AND FIELD—Women

100-Meter Run

1928	Elizabeth Robinson, United States	12.2s
1932	Stella Walsh, Poland (a)	11.9s
1936	Helen Stephens, United States	11.5s
1948	Francina Blankers-Koen, Netherlands	11.9s
1952	Marjorie Jackson, Australia	11.5s
1956	Betty Cuthbert, Australia	11.5s
1960	Wilma Rudolph, United States	11.0s
1964	Wyomia Tyus, United States	11.4s
1968	Wyomia Tyus, United States	11.08s
1972	Renate Stecher, E. Germany	11.07s
1976	Annegret Richter, W. Germany	11.08s
1980	Lyudmila Kondratyeva, USSR	11.06s
1984	Evelyn Ashford, United States	10.97s
1988	Florence Griffith-Joyner, United States	10.54s (w)
1992	Gail Devers, United States	10.82s
1996	Gail Devers, United States	10.94s
2000	Marion Jones, United States	10.75s
2004	Yuliya Nesterenko, Belarus	10.93s

(a) A 1980 autopsy determined that Walsh was a man.

200-Meter Run

1948	Francina Blankers-Koen, Netherlands	24.4s
1952	Marjorie Jackson, Australia	23.7s
1956	Betty Cuthbert, Australia	23.4s
1960	Wilma Rudolph, United States	24.0s
1964	Edith McGuire, United States	23.0s
1968	Irena Szewinska, Poland	22.5s
1972	Renate Stecher, E. Germany	22.40s
1976	Barbel Eckert, E. Germany	22.37s
1980	Barbel Wockel, E. Germany	22.03s
1984	Valerie Brisco-Hooks, United States	21.81s
1988	Florence Griffith-Joyner, United States	21.34s*
1992	Gwen Torrence, United States	21.81s
1996	Marie-Jose Perec, France	22.12s
2000	Marion Jones, United States	21.84s
2004	Veronica Campbell, Jamaica	22.05s

400-Meter Run

1964	Betty Cuthbert, Australia	52.0s
1968	Colette Besson, France	52.0s
1972	Monika Zehrt, E. Germany	51.08s
1976	Irena Szewinska, Poland	49.29s
1980	Marita Koch, E. Germany	48.88s
1984	Valerie Brisco-Hooks, United States	48.83s
1988	Olga Bryzgina, USSR	48.65s
1992	Marie-Jose Perec, France	48.83s
1996	Marie-Jose Perec, France	48.25s*
2000	Cathy Freeman, Australia	49.11s
2004	Tonique Williams-Darling, Bahamas	49.41s

800-Meter Run

1928	Lina Radke, Germany	2m. 16.8s
1960	Ludmila Shevtsova, USSR	2m. 4.3s
1964	Ann Packer, Great Britain	2m. 1.1s
1968	Madeline Manning, United States	2m. 0.9s
1972	Hildegard Falck, W. Germany	1m. 58.6s
1976	Tatyana Kazankina, USSR	1m. 54.94s
1980	Nadezhda Olizarenko, USSR	1m. 53.43s*
1984	Doina Melinte, Romania	1m. 57.60s
1988	Sigrun Wodars, E. Germany	1m. 56.10s

800-Meter Run

1992	Ellen Van Langen, Netherlands	1m. 55.54s
1996	Svetlana Masterkova, Russia	1m. 57.73s
2000	Maria Mutola, Mozambique	1m. 56.15s
2004	Kelly Holmes, Great Britain	1m. 56.38s

1,500-Meter Run

1972	Lyudmila Bragina, USSR	4m. 01.4s
1976	Tatyana Kazankina, USSR	4m. 05.48s
1980	Tatyana Kazankina, USSR	3m. 56.6s
1984	Gabriella Dorio, Italy	4m. 03.25s
1988	Paula Ivan, Romania	3m. 53.96s*
1992	Hassiba Boulmerka, Algeria	3m. 55.30s
1996	Svetlana Masterkova, Russia	4m. 00.83s
2000	Nouria Benida Merah, Algeria	4m. 05.10s
2004	Kelly Holmes, Great Britain	3m. 57.90s

3,000-Meter Run

1984	Maricica Puica, Romania	8m. 35.96s
1988	Tatyana Samolenko, USSR	8m. 26.53s*
1992	Elena Romanova, Unified Team	8m. 46.04s

5,000-Meter Run

1996	Wang Junxia, China	14m. 59.88s
2000	Gabriela Szabo, Romania	14m. 40.79s*
2004	Meseret Defar, Ethiopa	14m. 45.65s

10,000-Meter Run

1988	Olga Boldarenko, USSR	31m. 44.69s
1992	Derartu Tulu, Ethiopia	31m. 06.02s
1996	Fernanda Ribeiro, Portugal	31m. 01.63s
2000	Derartu Tulu, Ethiopia	30m. 17.49s*
2004	Xing Huina, China	30m. 24.36s

100-Meter Hurdles

1972	Annelie Ehrhardt, E. Germany	12.59s
1976	Johanna Schaller, E. Germany	12.77s
1980	Vera Komisova, USSR	12.56s
1984	Benita Brown-Fitzgerald, United States	12.84s
1988	Jordanka Donkova, Bulgaria	12.38s
1992	Paraskevi Patoulidou, Greece	12.64s
1996	Ludmila Enquist, Sweden	12.58s
2000	Olga Shishigina, Kazakhstan	12.65s
2004	Joanna Hayes, United States	12.37s*

400-Meter Hurdles

1984	Nawal el Moutawakii, Morocco	54.61s
1988	Debra Flintoff-King, Australia	53.17s
1992	Sally Gunnell, Great Britain	53.23s
1996	Deon Hemmings, Jamaica	52.82s
2000	Irina Privalova, Russia	53.02s
2004	Fani Halkia, Greece	52.82s*

400-Meter Relay

1928	Canada	48.4s
1932	United States	46.9s
1936	United States	46.9s
1948	Netherlands	47.5s
1952	United States	45.9s
1956	Australia	44.5s
1960	United States	44.5s
1964	Poland	43.6s
1968	United States	42.88s
1972	West Germany	42.81s
1976	East Germany	42.55s
1980	East Germany	41.60s*
1984	United States	41.65s
1988	United States	41.98s
1992	United States	42.11s
1996	United States	41.95s
2000	Bahamas	41.95s
2004	Jamaica	41.73s

1,600-Meter Relay

1972	East Germany	3m. 23s
1976	East Germany	3m. 19.23s
1980	USSR	3m. 20.02s
1984	United States	3m. 18.29s
1988	USSR	3m. 15.17s*
1992	Unified Team	3m. 20.20s
1996	United States	3m. 20.91s
2000	United States	3m. 22.62s
2004	United States	3m. 19.01s

10 Kilometer Walk

1992	Chen Yueling, China	44m. 32s
1996	Elena Nikolayeva, Russia	41m. 49s*

20 Kilometer Walk

2000	Wang Liping, China	1m. 29.05s*
2004	Athanasia Tsoumeleka, Greece	1m. 29:12s

Marathon

1984	Joan Benoit, United States	2h. 24m. 52s
1988	Rosa Mota, Portugal	2h. 25m. 40s
1992	Valentina Yegorova, Unified Team	2h. 32m. 41s
1996	Fatuma Roba, Ethiopia	2h. 26m. 05s
2000	Naoko Takahashi, Japan	2h. 23m. 14s*
2004	Mizuki Noguchi, Japan	2h. 26m. 20s

High Jump

1928	Ethel Catherwood, Canada	1.59m.	(5' 2½")
1932	Jean Shiley, United States	1.65m.	(5' 5")
1936	Ibolya Csák, Hungary	1.60m.	(5' 3")
1948	Alice Coachman, U. S.	1.68m.	(5' 6")
1952	Esther Brand, South Africa	1.67m.	(5' 5¾")
1956	Mildred L. McDaniel, U. S.	1.76m.	(5' 9¼")
1960	Iolanda Balas, Romania	1.85m.	(6' ¾")
1964	Iolanda Balas, Romania	1.90m.	(6' 2¾ ")
1968	Miloslava Resková, Czech.	1.82m.	(5' 11½")
1972	Ulrike Meyfarth, W. Germany	1.92m.	(6' 3½")
1976	Rosemarie Ackermann, E. Ger.	1.93m.	(6' 4")
1980	Sara Simeoni, Italy	1.97m.	(6' 5½")
1984	Ulrike Meyfarth, W. Germany	2.02m.	(6' 7½")
1988	Louise Ritter, United States	2.03m.	(6' 8")
1992	Heike Henkel, Germany	2.02m.	(6' 7½")
1996	Stefka Kostadinova, Bulgaria	2.05m.	(6' 8¾")*
2000	Yelena Yelesina, Russia	2.01m.	(6' 7")
2004	Yelena Slesarenko, Russia	2.06m.	(6' 9")*

Long Jump

1948	Olga Gyarmati, Hungary	5.69m.	(18' 8")
1952	Yvette Williams, New Zealand	6.24m.	(20' 5¼")
1956	Elzbieta Krzeskinska, Poland	6.35m.	(20' 10")
1960	Vira Krepkina, USSR	6.37m.	(20' 10¾)
1964	Mary Rand, Great Britain	6.76m.	(22' 2¼")
1968	Viorica Viscopoleanu, Romania	6.82m.	(22' 4½")
1972	Heidemarie Rosendahl, W. Ger.	6.78m.	(22' 3")
1976	Angela Voigt, E. Germany	6.72m.	(22' ¾")
1980	Tatyana Kolpakova, USSR	7.06m.	(23' 2")
1984	Anisoara Cusmir-Stanciu, Rom.	6.96m.	(22' 10")
1988	Jackie Joyner-Kersee, United States	7.40m.	(24' 3½")*
1992	Heike Drechsler, Germany	7.14m.	(23' 5¼")
1996	Chioma Ajunwa, Nigeria	7.12m.	(23' 4½")
2000	Heike Drechsler, Germany	6.99m.	(22' 11¼")
2004	Tatyana Lebedeva, Russia	7.07m.	(23' 2½"')

Triple Jump

1996	Inessa Kravets, Ukraine	15.33m.	(50' 3½")*
2000	Tereza Marinova, Bulgaria	15.20m.	(49' 10½")
2004	Francoise Mbango Etone, Cameroon	15.30m.	(50' 2⅓")

Discus Throw

1928	Halina Konopacka, Poland	39.62m.	(130' 0")
1932	Lillian Copeland, United States	40.58m.	(133' 2")
1936	Gisela Mauermayer, Germany	47.62m.	(156' 3")
1948	Micheline Ostermeyer, France	41.92m.	(137' 6")
1952	Nina Ponomareva, USSR	51.42m.	(168' 8")
1956	Olga Fikotová, Czech.	53.68m.	(176' 1")
1960	Nina Ponomareva, USSR	55.10m.	(180' 9")
1964	Tamara Press, USSR	57.26m.	(187' 10")
1968	Lia Manoliu, Romania	58.28m.	(191' 2")
1972	Faina Melnik, USSR	66.62m.	(218' 7")
1976	Evelin Jahl, E. Germany	69.00m.	(226' 4")
1980	Evelin Jahl, E. Germany	69.96m.	(229' 6")
1984	Ria Stalman, Netherlands	65.36m.	(214' 5")
1988	Martina Hellmann, E. Germany	72.30m.	(237' 2")*
1992	Maritza Martén Garcia, Cuba	70.06m.	(229' 10")
1996	Ilke Wyludda, Germany	69.66m.	(228' 6")
2000	Ellina Zvereva, Belarus	68.40m.	(224' 5")
2004	Natalya Sadova	67.02m.	(219' 9")

Hammer Throw

2000	Kamila Skolimowska, Poland	71.16m.	(233' 5¾")*
2004	Olga Kuzenkova, Russia	75.02m.	(246' 1")

Pole Vault

2000	Stacy Dragila, United States	4.60m.	(15' 1")*
2004	Yelena Isinbayeva, Russia	4.91m.	(16' 1⅓")

Shot Put (8 lb., 13 oz.)

1948	Micheline Ostermeyer, France	13.75m.	(45' 1½")
1952	Galina Zybina, USSR	15.28m.	(50' 1½")
1956	Tamara Tyshkyevich, USSR	16.59m.	(54' 5¼")
1960	Tamara Press, USSR	17.32m.	(56' 10")
1964	Tamara Press, USSR	18.14m.	(59' 6¼")
1968	Margitta Gummel, E. Germany	19.61m.	(64' 4")
1972	Nadezhda Chizova, USSR	21.03m.	(69' 0")
1976	Ivanka Khristova, Bulgaria	21.16m.	(69' 5¼")
1980	Ilona Slupianek, E. Germany	22.41m.	(73' 6¼")*
1984	Claudia Losch, W. Germany	20.49m.	(67' 2¼")
1988	Natalya Lisovskaya, USSR	22.24m.	(72' 11¾")
1992	Svetlana Krivelyova, Unified Team	21.06m.	(69' 1¼")
1996	Astrid Kumbernuss, Germany	20.56m.	(67' 5½")
2000	Yanina Karolchik, Belarus	20.56m.	(67' 5½")
2004	Yumileidi Cumba Jay, Cuba	19.59m.	(64' 3¼")

Javelin Throw

1932	"Babe" Didrikson, United States	43.68m.	(143' 4")
1936	Tilly Fleischer, Germany	45.18m.	(148' 3")
1948	Herma Bauma, Austria	45.56m.	(149' 6")
1952	Dana Zátopková, Czech.	50.46m.	(165' 7")
1956	Inese Jaunzeme, USSR	53.86m.	(176' 8")
1960	Elvira Ozolina, USSR	55.98m.	(183' 8")
1964	Mihaela Penes, Romania	60.54m.	(198' 7")

Javelin Throw

1968	Angéla Németh, Hungary	60.36m.	(198' 0")
1972	Ruth Fuchs, E. Germany	63.88m.	(209' 7")
1976	Ruth Fuchs, E. Germany	65.94m.	(216' 4")
1980	Maria Colón Ruenes, Cuba	68.40m.	(224' 5")
1984	Tessa Sanderson, Great Britain	69.56m.	(228' 2")
1988	Petra Felke, E. Germany	74.68m.	(245' 0")
1992	Silke Renke, Germany	68.34m.	(224' 2")
1996	Heli Rantanen, Finland	67.94m.	(222' 11")
2000	Trine Hattestad, Norway (a)	68.91m.	(226' 1")
2004	Osleidys Menendez, Cuba	71.53m.	(234' 8")*

(v) New records were kept after javelin was modified in 1999.

Heptathlon

1984	Glynis Nunn, Australia	6,390 pts.
1988	Jackie Joyner-Kersee, United States	7,291 pts.*
1992	Jackie Joyner-Kersee, United States	7,044 pts.
1996	Ghada Shouaa, Syria	6,780 pts.
2000	Denise Lewis, Britain	6,584 pts.
2004	Carolina Kluft, Sweden	6,952 pts.

SWIMMING AND DIVING—Men

50-Meter Freestyle

1988	Matt Biondi, United States	22.14
1992	Aleksandr Popov, Unified Team	21.91*
1996	Aleksandr Popov, Russia	22.13
2000	Anthony Ervin, United States	21.98
2000	Gary Hall Jr., United States	21.98
2004	Gary Hall Jr., United States	21.93

100-Meter Freestyle

1896	Alfred Hajos, Hungary	1:22.2
1904	Zoltan de Halmay, Hungary (100 yards)	1:02.8
1908	Charles Daniels, United States	1:05.6
1912	Duke P. Kahanamoku, United States	1:03.4
1920	Duke P. Kahanamoku, United States	1:01.4
1924	John Weissmuller, United States	59.0
1928	John Weissmuller, United States	58.6
1932	Yasuji Miyazaki, Japan	58.2
1936	Ferenc Csik, Hungary	57.6
1948	Wally Ris, United States	57.3
1952	Clark Scholes, United States	57.4
1956	Jon Henricks, Australia	55.4
1960	John Devitt, Australia	55.2
1964	Don Schollander, United States	53.4
1968	Mike Wenden, Australia	52.2
1972	Mark Spitz, United States	51.22
1976	Jim Montgomery, United States	49.99
1980	Jorg Woithe, E. Germany	50.40
1984	Rowdy Gaines, United States	49.80
1988	Matt Biondi, United States	48.63
1992	Aleksandr Popov, Unified Team	49.02
1996	Aleksandr Popov, Russia	48.74
2000	Pieter van den Hoogenband, Netherlands	48.30
2004	Pieter van den Hoogenband, Netherlands	48.17

200-Meter Freestyle

1968	Mike Wenden, Australia	1:55.2
1972	Mark Spitz, United States	1:52.78
1976	Bruce Furniss, United States	1:50.29
1980	Sergei Kopliakov, USSR	1:49.81
1984	Michael Gross, W. Germany	1:47.44
1988	Duncan Armstrong, Australia	1:47.25
1992	Yevgeny Sadovyi, Unified Team	1:46.70
1996	Danyon Loader, New Zealand	1:47.63
2000	Pieter van den Hoogenband, Netherlands	1:45.35
2004	Ian Thorpe, Australia	1:44.71*

400-Meter Freestyle

1904	C. M. Daniels, United States (440 yards)	6:16.2
1908	Henry Taylor, Great Britain	5:36.8
1912	George Hodgson, Canada	5:24.4
1920	Norman Ross, United States	5:26.8
1924	John Weissmuller, United States	5:04.2
1928	Albert Zorilla, Argentina	5:01.6
1932	Clarence Crabbe, United States	4:48.4
1936	Jack Medica, United States	4:44.5
1948	William Smith, United States	4:41.0
1952	Jean Boiteux, France	4:30.7
1956	Murray Rose, Australia	4:27.3
1960	Murray Rose, Australia	4:18.3
1964	Don Schollander, United States	4:12.2
1968	Mike Burton, United States	4:09.0
1972	Brad Cooper, Australia	4:00.27
1976	Brian Goodell, United States	3:51.93
1980	Vladimir Salnikov, USSR	3:51.31
1984	George DiCarlo, United States	3:51.23
1988	Ewe Dassler, E. Germany	3:46.95
1992	Yevgeny Sadovyi, Unified Team	3:45.00
1996	Danyon Loader, New Zealand	3:47.97
2000	Ian Thorpe, Australia	3:40.59*
2004	Ian Thorpe, Australia	3:43.10

1,500-Meter Freestyle

1908	Henry Taylor, Great Britain	22:48.4
1912	George Hodgson, Canada	22:00.0
1920	Norman Ross, United States	22:23.2
1924	Andrew Charlton, Australia	20:06.6
1928	Arne Borg, Sweden	19:51.8
1932	Kusuo Kitamura, Japan	19:12.4
1936	Noboru Terada, Japan	19:13.7
1948	James McLane, United States	19:18.5
1952	Ford Konno, United States	18:30.3
1956	Murray Rose, Australia	17:58.9
1960	Jon Konrads, Australia	17:19.6
1964	Robert Windle, Australia	17:01.7
1968	Mike Burton, United States	16:38.9
1972	Mike Burton, United States	15:52.58
1976	Brian Goodell, United States	15:02.40
1980	Vladimir Salnikov, USSR	14:58.27
1984	Michael O'Brien, United States	15:05.20
1988	Vladimir Salnikov, USSR	15:00.40
1992	Kieren Perkins, Australia	14:43.48
1996	Kieren Perkins, Australia	14:56.40
2000	Grant Hackett, Australia	14:48.33
2004	Grant Hackett, Australia	14:43.40*

100-Meter Backstroke

1904	Walter Brack, Germany (100 yds.)	1:16.8
1908	Arno Bieberstein, Germany	1:24.6
1912	Harry Hebner, United States	1:21.2
1920	Warren Kealoha, United States	1:15.2
1924	Warren Kealoha, United States	1:13.2
1928	George Kojac, United States	1:08.2
1932	Masaji Kiyokawa, Japan	1:08.6
1936	Adolph Kiefer, United States	1:05.9
1948	Allen Stack, United States	1:06.4
1952	Yoshi Oyakawa, United States	1:05.4
1956	David Thiele, Australia	1:02.2
1960	David Thiele, Australia	1:01.9
1968	Roland Matthes, E. Germany	58.7
1972	Roland Matthes, E. Germany	56.58
1976	John Naber, United States	55.49
1980	Bengt Baron, Sweden	56.33
1984	Rick Carey, United States	55.79
1988	Daichi Suzuki, Japan	55.05
1992	Mark Tewksbury, Canada	53.98
1996	Jeff Rouse, United States	54.10
2000	Lenny Krayzelburg, United States	53.72
2004	Aaron Peirsol, United States	54.06

200-Meter Backstroke

1964	Jed Graef, United States	2:10.3
1968	Roland Matthes, E. Germany	2:09.6
1972	Roland Matthes, E. Germany	2:02.82
1976	John Naber, United States	1:59.19
1980	Sandor Wladar, Hungary	2:01.93
1984	Rick Carey, United States	2:00.23
1988	Igor Polianski, USSR	1:59.37
1992	Martin Lopez-Zubero, Spain	1:58.47
1996	Brad Bridgewater, United States	1:58.54
2000	Lenny Krayzelburg, United States	1:56.76
2004	Aaron Peirsol, United States	1:54.95*

100-Meter Breaststroke

1968	Don McKenzie, United States	1:07.79
1972	Nobutaka Taguchi, Japan	1:04.94
1976	John Hencken, United States	1:03.11
1980	Duncan Goodhew, Great Britain	1:03.44
1984	Steve Lundquist, United States	1:01.65
1988	Adrian Moorhouse, Great Britain	1:02.04
1992	Nelson Diebel, United States	1:01.50
1996	Fred Deburghgraeve, Belgium	1:00.60
2000	Domenico Fioravanti, Italy	1:00.46
2004	Kosuke Kitajima, Japan	1:00.08

200-Meter Breaststroke

1908	Frederick Holman, Great Britain	3:09.2
1912	Walter Bathe, Germany	3:01.8
1920	Haken Malmroth, Sweden	3:04.4
1924	Robert Skelton, United States	2:56.6
1928	Yoshiyuki Tsuruta, Japan	2:48.8
1932	Yoshiyuki Tsuruta, Japan	2:45.4
1936	Tetsuo Hamuro, Japan	2:41.5
1948	Joseph Verdeur, United States	2:39.3
1952	John Davies, Australia	2:34.4
1956	Masura Furukawa, Japan	2:34.7
1960	William Mulliken, United States	2:37.4
1964	Ian O'Brien, Australia	2:27.8
1968	Felipe Munoz, Mexico	2:28.7
1972	John Hencken, United States	2:21.55
1976	David Wilkie, Great Britain	2:15.11
1980	Robertas Zhulpa, USSR	2:15.85
1984	Victor Davis, Canada	2:13.34
1988	Jozsef Szabo, Hungary	2:13.52
1992	Mike Barrowman, United States	2:10.16

200-Meter Breaststroke

1996	Norbert Rozsa, Hungary	2:12.57
2000	Domenico Fioravanti, Italy	2:10.87
2004	Kosuke Kitajima, Japan	2:09.44*

100-Meter Butterfly

1968	Doug Russell, United States	55.9
1972	Mark Spitz, United States	54.27
1976	Matt Vogel, United States	54.35
1980	Par Arvidsson, Sweden	54.92
1984	Michael Gross, W. Germany	53.08
1988	Anthony Nesty, Suriname	53.00
1992	Pablo Morales, United States	53.32
1996	Denis Pankratov, Russia	52.27
2000	Lars Froelander, Sweden	52.00
2004	Michael Phelps, United States	51.25*

200-Meter Butterfly

1956	William Yorzyk, United States	2:19.3
1960	Michael Troy, United States	2:12.8
1964	Kevin J. Berry, Australia	2:06.6
1968	Carl Robie, United States	2:08.7
1972	Mark Spitz, United States	2:00.70
1976	Mike Bruner, United States	1:59.23
1980	Sergei Fesenko, USSR	1:59.76
1984	Jon Sieben, Australia	1:57.04
1988	Michael Gross, W. Germany	1:56.94
1992	Mel Stewart, United States	1:56.26
1996	Denis Pankratov, Russia	1:56.51
2000	Tom Malchow, United States	1:55.35
2004	Michael Phelps, United States	1:54.04*

200-Meter Individual Medley

1968	Charles Hickcox, United States	2:12.0
1972	Gunnar Larsson, Sweden	2:07.17
1984	Alex Baumann, Canada	2:01.42
1988	Tamas Darnyi, Hungary	2:00.17
1992	Tamas Darnyi, Hungary	2:00.76
1996	Attila Czene, Hungary	1:59.91
2000	Massimiliano Rosolino, Italy	1:58.98
2004	Michael Phelps, United States	1:57.14*

400-Meter Individual Medley

1964	Dick Roth, United States	4:45.4
1968	Charles Hickcox, United States	4:48.4
1972	Gunnar Larsson, Sweden	4:31.98
1976	Rod Strachan, United States	4:23.68
1980	Aleksandr Sidorenko, USSR	4:22.89
1984	Alex Baumann, Canada	4:17.41
1988	Tamas Darnyi, Hungary	4:14.75
1992	Tamas Darnyi, Hungary	4:14.23
1996	Tom Dolan, United States	4:14.90
2000	Tom Dolan, United States	4:11.76
2004	Michael Phelps, United States	4:08.26*

400-Meter Freestyle Relay

1964	United States	3:31.2
1968	United States	3:31.7
1972	United States	3:26.42
1984	United States	3:19.03
1988	United States	3:16.53
1992	United States	3:16.74
1996	United States	3:15.41
2000	Australia	3:13.67
2004	South Africa	3:13.17*

800-Meter Freestyle Relay

1908	Great Britain	10:55.6
1912	Australia	10:11.6
1920	United States	10:04.4
1924	United States	9:53.4
1928	United States	9:36.2
1932	Japan	8:58.4
1936	Japan	8:51.5
1948	United States	8:46.0
1952	United States	8:31.1
1956	Australia	8:23.6
1960	United States	8:10.2
1964	United States	7:52.1
1968	United States	7:52.33
1972	United States	7:35.78
1976	United States	7:23.22
1980	USSR	7:23.50
1984	United States	7:15.69
1988	United States	7:12.51
1992	Unified Team	7:11.95
1996	United States	7:14.84
2000	Australia	7:07.05*
2004	United States	7:07.33

400-Meter Medley Relay

1960	United States	4:05.4
1964	United States	3:58.4
1968	United States	3:54.9
1972	United States	3:48.16
1976	United States	3:42.22

400-Meter Medley Relay

1980	Australia	3:45.70
1984	United States	3:39.30
1988	United States	3:36.93
1992	United States	3:36.93
1996	United States	3:34.84
2000	United States	3:33.73
2004	United States	3:30.68*

Springboard Diving — Points

1908	Albert Zurner, Germany	85.50
1912	Paul Guenther, Germany	79.23
1920	Louis Kuehn, U.S	675.40
1924	Albert White, United States	97.46
1928	Pete Desjardins, United States	185.04
1932	Michael Galitzen, United States	161.38
1936	Richard Degener, United States	163.57
1948	Bruce Harlan, United States	163.64
1952	David Browning, United States	205.29
1956	Robert Clotworthy, United States	159.56
1960	Gary Tobian, United States	170.00
1964	Kenneth Sitzberger, United States	159.90
1968	Bernie Wrightson, United States	170.15
1972	Vladimir Vasin, USSR	594.09
1976	Phil Boggs, United States	619.52
1980	Aleksandr Portnov, USSR	905.02
1984	Greg Louganis, United States	754.41
1988	Greg Louganis, United States	730.80
1992	Mark Lenzi, United States	676.53
1996	Xiong Ni, China	701.46
2000	Xiong Ni, China	708.72
2004	Peng Bo, China	787.30

Platform Diving — Points

1904	Dr. G.E. Sheldon, United States	112.75
1908	Hjalmar Johansson, Sweden	183.75
1912	Erik Adlerz, Sweden	73.94
1920	Clarence Pinkston, United States	100.67
1924	Albert White, United States	97.46
1928	Pete Desjardins, United States	98.74
1932	Harold Smith, United States	124.80
1936	Marshall Wayne, United States	113.58
1948	Sammy Lee, United States	130.05
1952	Sammy Lee, United States	156.28
1956	Joaquin Capilla, Mexico	152.44
1960	Robert Webster, United States	165.56
1964	Robert Webster, United States	148.58
1968	Klaus Dibiasi, Italy	164.18
1972	Klaus Dibiasi, Italy	504.12
1976	Klaus Dibiasi, Italy	600.51
1980	Falk Hoffmann, E. Germany	835.65
1984	Greg Louganis, United States	710.91
1988	Greg Louganis, United States	638.61
1992	Sun Shuwei, China	677.31
1996	Dmitri Sautin, Russia	692.34
2000	Tian Liang, China	724.53
2004	Hu Jia, China	748.08

Synchronized Platform

2004	Tian Liang and Yang Jinghui, China	383.88

Synchronized Springboard

2004	Nikolaos Siranidis and Thomas Bimis, Greece	353.34

SWIMMING AND DIVING—Women

50-Meter Freestyle

1988	Kristin Otto, E. Germany	25.49
1992	Yang Wenyi, China	24.76
1996	Amy Van Dyken, United States	24.87
2000	Inge de Bruijn, Netherlands	24.32
2004	Inge de Bruijn, Netherlands	24.58

100-Meter Freestyle

1912	Fanny Durack, Australia	1:22.2
1920	Ethelda Bleibtrey, United States	1:13.6
1924	Ethel Lackie, United States	1:12.4
1928	Albina Osipowich, United States	1:11.0
1932	Helene Madison, United States	1:06.8
1936	Hendrika Mastenbroek, Holland	1:05.9
1948	Greta Andersen, Denmark	1:06.3
1952	Katalin Szoke, Hungary	1:06.8
1956	Dawn Fraser, Australia	1:02.0
1960	Dawn Fraser, Australia	1:01.2
1964	Dawn Fraser, Australia	59.5
1968	Jan Henne, United States	1:00.0
1972	Sandra Neilson, United States	58.59
1976	Kornelia Ender, E. Germany	55.65
1980	Barbara Krause, E. Germany	54.79
1984	(tie) Carrie Steinseifer, United States	55.92
	Nancy Hogshead, United States	55.92
1988	Kristin Otto, E. Germany	54.93
1992	Zhuang Yong, China	54.64
1996	Li Jingyi, China	54.50
2000	Inge de Bruijn, Netherlands	53.83
2004	Jodie Henry, Australia	53.84

200-Meter Freestyle

1968	Debbie Meyer, United States	2:10.5
1972	Shane Gould, Australia	2:03.56
1976	Kornelia Ender, E. Germany	1:59.26
1980	Barbara Krause, E. Germany	1:58.33
1984	Mary Wayte, United States	1:59.23
1988	Heike Friedrich, E. Germany	1:57.65*
1992	Nicole Haislett, United States	1:57.90
1996	Claudia Poll, Costa Rica	1:58.16
2000	Susie O'Neill, Australia	1:58.24
2004	Camelia Potec, Romania	1:58.03

400-Meter Freestyle

1924	Martha Norelius, United States	6:02.2
1928	Martha Norelius, United States	5:42.8
1932	Helene Madison, United States	5:28.5
1936	Hendrika Mastenbroek, Netherlands	5:26.4
1948	Ann Curtis, United States	5:17.8
1952	Valerie Gyenge, Hungary	5:12.1
1956	Lorraine Crapp, Australia	4:54.6
1960	Susan Chris von Saltza, United States	4:50.6
1964	Virginia Duenkel, United States	4:43.3
1968	Debbie Meyer, United States	4:31.8
1972	Shane Gould, Australia	4:19.44
1976	Petra Thuemer, E. Germany	4:09.89
1980	Ines Diers, E. Germany	4:08.76
1984	Tiffany Cohen, United States	4:07.10
1988	Janet Evans, United States	4:03.85*
1992	Dagmar Hase, Germany	4:07.18
1996	Michelle Smith, Ireland	4:07.25
2000	Brooke Bennett, United States	4:05.80
2004	Laure Manaudou, France	4:05.34

800-Meter Freestyle

1968	Debbie Meyer, United States	9:24.0
1972	Keena Rothhammer, United States	8:53.68
1976	Petra Thuemer, E. Germany	8:37.14
1980	Michelle Ford, Australia	8:28.90
1984	Tiffany Cohen, United States	8:24.95
1988	Janet Evans, United States	8:20.20
1992	Janet Evans, United States	8:25.52
1996	Brooke Bennett, United States	8:27.89
2000	Brooke Bennett, United States	8:19.67*
2004	Ai Shibata, Japan	8:24.54

100-Meter Backstroke

1924	Sybil Bauer, United States	1:23.2
1928	Marie Braun, Netherlands	1:22.0
1932	Eleanor Holm, United States	1:19.4
1936	Dina Senff, Netherlands	1:18.9
1948	Karen Harup, Denmark	1:14.4
1952	Joan Harrison, South Africa	1:14.3
1956	Judy Grinham, Great Britain	1:12.9
1960	Lynn Burke, United States	1:09.3
1964	Cathy Ferguson, United States	1:07.7
1968	Kaye Hall, United States	1:06.2
1972	Melissa Belote, United States	1:05.78
1976	Ulrike Richter, E. Germany	1:01.83
1980	Rica Reinisch, E. Germany	1:00.86
1984	Theresa Andrews, United States	1:02.55
1988	Kristin Otto, E. Germany	1:00.89
1992	Krisztina Egerszegi, Hungary	1:00.68
1996	Beth Botsford, United States	1:01.19
2000	Diana Mocanu, Romania	1:00.21
2004	Natalie Coughlin, United States	1:00.37

200-Meter Backstroke

1968	Pokey Watson, United States	2:24.8
1972	Melissa Belote, United States	2:19.19
1976	Ulrike Richter, E. Germany	2:13.43
1980	Rica Reinisch, E. Germany	2:11.77
1984	Jolanda De Rover, Netherlands	2:12.38
1988	Krisztina Egerszegi, Hungary	2:09.29
1992	Krisztina Egerszegi, Hungary	2:07.06*
1996	Krisztina Egerszegi, Hungary	2:07.83
2000	Diana Mocanu, Romania	2:08.16
2004	Kirsty Coventry, Zimbabwe	2:09.19

100-Meter Breaststroke

1968	Djurdjica Bjedov, Yugoslavia	1:15.8
1972	Cathy Carr, United States	1:13.58
1976	Hannelore Anke, E. Germany	1:11.16
1980	Ute Geweniger, E. Germany	1:10.22
1984	Petra Van Staveren, Netherlands	1:09.88
1988	Tania Dangalakova, Bulgaria	1:07.95
1992	Elena Roudkovskaia, Unified Team	1:08.00
1996	Penny Heyns, South Africa	1:07.73
2000	Megan Quann, United States	1:07.05
2004	Luo Xuejuan, China	1:06.64*

200-Meter Breaststroke

1924	Lucy Morton, Great Britain	3:33.2
1928	Hilde Schrader, Germany	3:12.6
1932	Clare Dennis, Australia	3:06.3
1936	Hideko Maehata, Japan	3:03.6

200-Meter Breaststroke
1948	Nelly Van Vliet, Netherlands	2:57.2
1952	Eva Szekely, Hungary	2:51.7
1956	Ursula Happe, Germany	2:53.1
1960	Anita Lonsbrough, Great Britain	2:49.5
1964	Galina Prozumenschikova, USSR	2:46.4
1968	Sharon Wichman, United States	2:44.4
1972	Beverly Whitfield, Australia	2:41.71
1976	Marina Koshevaia, USSR	2:33.35
1980	Lina Kachushite, USSR	2:29.54
1984	Anne Ottenbrite, Canada	2:30.38
1988	Silke Hoerner, E. Germany	2:26.71
1992	Kyoko Iwasaki, Japan	2:26.65
1996	Penny Heyns, South Africa	2:25.41
2000	Agnes Kovacs, Hungary	2:24.35
2004	Amanda Beard, United States	2:23.37*

100-Meter Butterfly
1956	Shelley Mann, United States	1:11.0
1960	Carolyn Schuler, United States	1:09.5
1964	Sharon Stouder, United States	1:04.7
1968	Lynn McClements, Australia	1:05.5
1972	Mayumi Aoki, Japan	1:03.34
1976	Kornelia Ender, E. Germany	1:00.13
1980	Caren Metschuck, E. Germany	1:00.42
1984	Mary T. Meagher, United States	59.26
1988	Kristin Otto, E. Germany	59.00
1992	Qian Hong, China	58.62
1996	Amy Van Dyken, United States	59.13
2000	Inge de Bruijn, Netherlands	56.61*
2004	Petria Thomas, Australia	57.72

200-Meter Butterfly
1968	Ada Kok, Netherlands	2:24.7
1972	Karen Moe, United States	2:15.57
1976	Andrea Pollack, E. Germany	2:11.41
1980	Ines Geissler, E. Germany	2:10.44
1984	Mary T. Meagher, United States	2:06.90
1988	Kathleen Nord, E. Germany	2:09.51
1992	Summer Sanders, United States	2:08.67
1996	Susan O'Neill, Australia	2:07.76
2000	Misty Hyman, United States	2:05.88*
2004	Otylia Jedrzejczak, Poland	2:06.05

200-Meter Individual Medley
1968	Claudia Kolb, United States	2:24.7
1972	Shane Gould, Australia	2:23.07
1984	Tracy Caulkins, United States	2:12.64
1988	Daniela Hunger, E. Germany	2:12.59
1992	Lin Li, China	2:11.65
1996	Michelle Smith, Ireland	2:13.93
2000	Yana Klochkova, Ukraine	2:10.68*
2004	Yana Klochkova, Ukraine	2:11.14

400-Meter Individual Medley
1964	Donna de Varona, United States	5:18.7
1968	Claudia Kolb, United States	5:08.5
1972	Gail Neall, Australia	5:02.97
1976	Ulrike Tauber, E. Germany	4:42.77
1980	Petra Schneider, E. Germany	4:36.29
1984	Tracy Caulkins, United States	4:39.24
1988	Janet Evans, United States	4:37.76
1992	Krisztina Egerszegi, Hungary	4:36.54
1996	Michelle Smith, Ireland	4:39.18
2000	Yana Klochkova, Ukraine	4:33.59*
2004	Yana Klochkova, Ukraine	4:34.83

400-Meter Freestyle Relay
1912	Great Britain	5:52.8
1920	United States	5:11.6
1924	United States	4:58.8
1928	United States	4:47.6
1932	United States	4:38.0
1936	Netherlands	4:36.0
1948	United States	4:29.2
1952	Hungary	4:24.4
1956	Australia	4:17.1
1960	United States	4:08.9
1964	United States	4:03.8
1968	United States	4:02.5

400-Meter Freestyle Relay
1972	United States	3:55.19
1976	United States	3:44.82
1980	East Germany	3:42.71
1984	United States	3:43.43
1988	East Germany	3:40.63
1992	United States	3:39.46
1996	United States	3:39.29
2000	United States	3:36.61
2004	Australia	3:35.94*

800-Meter Freestyle Relay
1996	United States	7:59.87
2000	United States	7:57.80
2004	United States	7:53.42*

400-Meter Medley Relay
1960	United States	4:41.1
1964	United States	4:33.9
1968	United States	4:28.3
1972	United States	4:20.75
1976	East Germany	4:07.95
1980	East Germany	4:06.67
1984	United States	4:08.34
1988	East Germany	4:03.74
1992	United States	4:02.54
1996	United States	4:02.88
2000	United States	3:58.30
2004	Australia	3:57.32*

Springboard Diving
		Points
1920	Aileen Riggin, United States	539.90
1924	Elizabeth Becker, United States	474.50
1928	Helen Meany, United States	78.62
1932	Georgia Coleman United States	87.52
1936	Marjorie Gestring, United States	89.27
1948	Victoria M. Draves, United States	108.74
1952	Patricia McCormick, United States	147.30
1956	Patricia McCormick, United States	142.36
1960	Ingrid Kramer, Germany	155.81
1964	Ingrid Engel-Kramer, Germany	145.00
1968	Sue Gossick, United States	150.77
1972	Micki King, United States	450.03
1976	Jenni Chandler, United States	506.19
1980	Irina Kalinina, USSR	725.91
1984	Sylvie Bernier, Canada	530.70
1988	Gao Min, China	580.23
1992	Gao Min, China	572.40
1996	Fu Mingxia, China	547.68
2000	Fu Mingxia, China	609.42
2004	Guo Jingjing, China	633.15

Platform Diving
		Points
1912	Greta Johansson, Sweden	39.90
1920	Stefani Fryland-Clausen, Denmark	34.60
1924	Caroline Smith, United States	33.20
1928	Elizabeth B. Pinkston, United States	31.60
1932	Dorothy Poynton, United States	40.26
1936	Dorothy Poynton Hill, United States	33.93
1948	Victoria M. Draves, United States	8.87
1952	Patricia McCormick, United States	79.37
1956	Patricia McCormick, United States	84.85
1960	Ingrid Kramer, Germany	91.28
1964	Lesley Bush, United States	99.80
1968	Milena Duchkova, Czech.	109.59
1972	Ulrika Knape, Sweden	390.00
1976	Elena Vaytsekhouskaya, USSR	406.59
1980	Martina Jaschke, E. Germany	596.25
1984	Zhou Jihong, China	435.51
1988	Xu Yanmei, China	445.20
1992	Fu Mingxia, China	461.43
1996	Fu Mingxia, China	521.58
2000	Laura Wilkinson, United States	543.75
2004	Chantelle Newbery, Australia	590.31

Synchronized Platform
2004	Lao Lishi and Li Ting, China	352.14

Synchronized Springboard
2004	Wu Minxia and Guo Jingjing, China	336.90

BOXING

Lt. Flyweight (48 kg/106 lbs)
1968	Francisco Rodriguez, Venezuela
1972	Gyorgy Gedo, Hungary
1976	Jorge Hernandez, Cuba
1980	Shamil Sabyrov, USSR
1984	Paul Gonzalez, United States
1988	Ivailo Hristov, Bulgaria
1992	Rogelio Marcelo, Cuba
1996	Daniel Petrov, Bulgaria
2000	Brahim Asloum, France
2004	Yan Bhartelemy Varela, Cuba

Flyweight (51 kg/112 lbs)
1904	George Finnegan, United States
1920	William Di Gennara, United States
1924	Fidel LaBarba, United States
1928	Antal Kocsis, Hungary
1932	Istvan Enekes, Hungary
1936	Willi Kaiser, Germany
1948	Pascual Perez, Argentina
1952	Nathan Brooks, United States
1956	Terence Spinks, Great Britain
1960	GyulaTorok, Hungary
1964	Fernando Atzori, Italy
1968	Ricardo Delgado, Mexico
1972	Georgi Kostadinov, Bulgaria
1976	Leo Randolph, United States
1980	Peter Lessov, Bulgaria
1984	Steve McCrory, United States
1988	Kim Kwang Sun, S. Korea
1992	Su Choi Choi, N. Korea
1996	Maikro Romero, Cuba
2000	Wijan Ponlid, Thailand
2004	Yuriorkis Gamboa Toledano, Cuba

Bantamweight (54 kg /119 lbs)

1904	Oliver Kirk, United States
1908	A. Henry Thomas, Great Britain
1920	Clarence Walker, South Africa
1924	William Smith, South Africa
1928	Vittorio Tamagnini, Italy
1932	Horace Gwynne, Canada
1936	Ulderico Sergo, Italy
1948	Tibor Csik, Hungary
1952	Pentti Hamalainen, Finland
1956	Wolfgang Behrendt, E. Germany
1960	Oleg Grigoryev, USSR
1964	Takao Sakurai, Japan
1968	Valery Sokolov, USSR
1972	Orlando Martinez, Cuba
1976	Yong-Jo Gu, N. Korea
1980	Juan Hernandez, Cuba
1984	Maurizio Stecca, Italy
1988	Kennedy McKinney, United States
1992	Joel Casamayor, Cuba
1996	Istvan Kovacs, Hungary
2000	Guillermo Rigondeaux, Cuba
2004	Guillermo Rigondeaux Cuba

Featherweight (57 kg/125 lbs)

1904	Oliver Kirk, United States
1908	Richard Gunn, Great Britain
1920	Paul Fritsch, France
1924	John Fields, United States
1928	Lambertus van Klaveren, Netherlands
1932	Carmelo Robledo, Argentina
1936	Oscar Casanovas, Argentina
1948	Ernesto Formenti, Italy
1952	Jan Zachara, Czechoslovakia
1956	Vladimir Safronov, USSR
1960	Francesco Musso, Italy
1964	Stanislav Stephashkin, USSR
1968	Antonin Roldan, Mexico
1972	Boris Kousnetsov, USSR
1976	Angel Herrera, Cuba
1980	Rudi Fink, E. Germany
1984	Meldrick Taylor, United States
1988	Giovanni Parisi, Italy
1992	Andreas Tews, Germany
1996	Somluck Kamsing, Thailand
2000	Bekzat Sattarkhanov, Kazakhstan
2004	Alexei Tichtchenko, Russia

Lightweight (60 kg/132 lbs)

1904	Harry Spanger, United States
1908	Frederick Grace, Great Britain
1920	Samuel Mosberg, United States
1924	Hans Nielsen, Denmark
1928	Carlo Orlandi, Italy
1932	Lawrence Stevens, South Africa
1936	Imre Harangi, Hungary
1948	Gerald Dreyer, South Africa
1952	Aureliano Bolognesi, Italy
1956	Richard McTaggart, Great Britain
1960	Kazimierz Pazdzior, Poland
1964	Jozef Grudzien, Poland
1968	Ronald Harris, United States
1972	Jan Szczepanski, Poland
1976	Howard Davis, United States
1980	Angel Herrera, Cuba
1984	Pernell Whitaker, United States
1988	Andreas Zuelow, E. Germany
1992	Oscar De La Hoya, United States
1996	Hocine Soltani, Algeria

2000	Mario Kindelan, Cuba
2004	Mario Kindelan, Cuba

Lt. Welterweight (63.5 kg/139 lbs)

1952	Charles Adkins, United States
1956	Vladimir Yengibaryan, USSR
1960	Bohumil Nemecek, Czechoslovazkia
1964	Jerzy Kulej, Poland
1968	Jerzy Kulej, Poland
1972	Ray Seales, United States
1976	Ray Leonard, United States
1980	Patrizio Oliva, Italy
1984	Jerry Page, United States
1988	Viatcheslav Janovski, USSR
1992	Hector Vinent, Cuba
1996	Hector Vinent, Cuba
2000	Mahamadkadyz Abdullaev, Uzbekistan
2004	Manus Boonjumnong, Thailand

Welterweight (67 kg/147 lbs)

1904	Albert Young, United States
1920	Albert Schneider, Canada
1924	Jean Delarge, Belgium
1928	Edward Morgan, New Zealand
1932	Edward Flynn, United States
1936	Sten Suvio, Finland
1948	Julius Torma, Czechoslovakia
1952	Zygmunt Chychla, Poland
1956	Nicolae Linca, Romania
1960	Giovanni Benvenuti, Italy
1964	Marian Kasprzyk, Poland
1968	Manfred Wolke, E. Germany
1972	Emilio Correa, Cuba
1976	Jochen Bachfeld, E. Germany
1980	Andres Aldama, Cuba
1984	Mark Breland, United States
1988	Robert Wangila, Kenya
1992	Michael Carruth, Ireland
1996	Oleg Saitov, Russia
2000	Oleg Saitov, Russia
2004	Artayev Bakhtiyar, Kazakhstan

Lt. Middleweight (71 kg/156 lbs)

1952	Laszlo Papp, Hungary
1956	Laszlo Papp, Hungary
1960	Wilbert McClure, United States
1964	Boris Lagutin, USSR
1968	Boris Lagutin, USSR
1972	Dieter Kottysch, W. Germany
1976	Jerzy Rybicki, Poland
1980	Armando Martinez, Cuba
1984	Frank Tate, United States
1988	Park Si Hun, S. Korea
1992	Juan Lemus, Cuba
1996	David Reid, United States
2000	Yermakhan Ibraimov, Kazakhstan

Middleweight (75 kg/165 lbs)

1904	Charles Mayer, United States
1908	John Douglas, Great Britain
1920	Harry Mallin, Great Britain
1924	Harry Mallin, Great Britain
1928	Piero Toscani, Italy
1932	Carmen Barth, United States
1936	Jean Despeaux, France
1948	Laszlo Papp, Hungary
1952	Floyd Patterson, United States
1956	Gennady Schatkov, USSR
1960	Edward Crook, United States

1964	Valery Popenchenko, USSR
1968	Christopher Finnegan, Great Britain
1972	Vyacheslav Lemechev, USSR
1976	Michael Spinks, United States
1980	Jose Gomez, Cuba
1984	Joon-Sup Shin, S. Korea
1988	Henry Maske, E. Germany
1992	Ariel Hernandez, Cuba
1996	Ariel Hernandez, Cuba
2000	Jorge Gutierrez, Cuba
2004	Gaydarbek Gaydarbekov, Russia

Lt. Heavyweight (81 kg/178 lbs)

1920	Edward Eagan, United States
1924	Harry Mitchell, Great Britain
1928	Victor Avendano, Argentina
1932	David Carstens, South Africa
1936	Roger Michelot, France
1948	George Hunter, South Africa
1952	Norvel Lee, United States
1956	James Boyd, United States
1960	Cassius Clay, United States
1964	Cosimo Pinto, Italy
1968	Dan Poznyak, USSR
1972	Mate Parlov, Yugoslavia
1976	Leon Spinks, United States
1980	Slobodan Kacar, Yugoslavia
1984	Anton Josipovic, Yugoslavia
1988	Andrew Maynard, United States
1992	Torsten May, Germany
1996	Vassili Jirov, Kazakhstan
2000	Alexander Lebziak, Russia
2004	Andre Ward, United States

Heavyweight (91 kg/201 lbs)

1984	Henry Tillman, United States
1988	Ray Mercer, United States
1992	Felix Savon, Cuba
1996	Felix Savon, Cuba
2000	Felix Savon, Cuba
2004	Odlanier Solis Fonte, Cuba

Super Heavyweight (91+ kg/201+ lbs)

(known as heavyweight, 1904-80)

1904	Samuel Berger, United States
1908	Albert Oldham, Great Britain
1920	Ronald Rawson, Great Britain
1924	Otto von Porat, Norway
1928	Arturo Rodriguez Jurado, Argentina
1932	Santiago Lovell, Argentina
1936	Herbert Runge, Germany
1948	Rafael Iglesias, Argentina
1952	H. Edward Sanders, United States
1956	T. Peter Rademacher, United States
1960	Franco De Piccoli, Italy
1964	Joe Frazier, United States
1968	George Foreman, United States
1972	Teofilo Stevenson, Cuba
1976	Teofilo Stevenson, Cuba
1980	Teofilo Stevenson, Cuba
1984	Tyrell Biggs, United States
1988	Lennox Lewis, Canada
1992	Roberto Balado, Cuba
1996	Vladimir Klitchko, Ukraine
2000	Audley Harrison, Britain
2004	Alexander Povetkin, Russia

Winter Olympic Games Champions, 1924-2002

In 1992, the Unified Team represented the former Soviet republics of Russia, Ukraine, Belarus, Kazakhstan, and Uzbekistan.

Alpine Skiing

Men's Downhill

		Time
1948	Henri Oreiller, France	2:55.0
1952	Zeno Colo, Italy	2:30.8
1956	Toni Sailer, Austria	2:52.2
1960	Jean Vuarnet, France	2:06.0
1964	Egon Zimmermann, Austria	2:18.16
1968	Jean-Claude Killy, France	1:59.85
1972	Bernhard Russi, Switzerland	1:51.43
1976	Franz Klammer, Austria	1:45.73
1980	Leonhard Stock, Austria	1:45.50
1984	Bill Johnson, United States	1:45.49
1988	Pirmin Zurbriggen, Switzerland	1:59.63
1992	Patrick Ortlieb, Austria	1:50.37
1994	Tommy Moe, United States	1:45.75
1998	Jean-Luc Cretier, France	1:50.11
2002	Fritz Strobl, Austria	1:39.13

Men's Super Giant Slalom

		Time
1988	Franck Piccard, France	1:39.66
1992	Kjetil-Andre Aamodt, Norway	1:13.04
1994	Markus Wasmeier, Germany	1:32.53
1998	Hermann Maier, Austria	1:34.82
2002	Kjetil Andre Aamodt, Norway	1:21.58

Men's Giant Slalom

		Time
1952	Stein Eriksen, Norway	2:25.0
1956	Toni Sailer, Austria	3:00.1
1960	Roger Staub, Switzerland	1:48.3
1964	Francois Bonlieu, France	1:46.71
1968	Jean-Claude Killy, France	3:29.28
1972	Gustavo Thoeni, Italy	3:09.62
1976	Heini Hemmi, Switzerland	3:26.97
1980	Ingemar Stenmark, Sweden	2:40.74
1984	Max Julen, Switzerland	2:41.18
1988	Alberto Tomba, Italy	2:06.37

Men's Giant Slalom

Year	Champion	Time
1992	Alberto Tomba, Italy	2:06.98
1994	Markus Wasmeier, Germany	2:52.46
1998	Hermann Maier, Austria	2:38.51
2002	Stephan Eberharter, Austria	2:23.28

Men's Slalom

Year	Champion	Time
1948	Edi Reinalter, Switzerland	2:10.3
1952	Othmar Schneider, Austria	2:00.0
1956	Toni Sailer, Austria	3:14.7
1960	Ernst Hinterseer, Austria	2:08.9
1964	Josef Stiegler, Austria	2:11.13
1968	Jean-Claude Killy, France	1:39.73
1972	Francisco Fernandez-Ochoa, Spain	1:49.27
1976	Piero Gros, Italy	2:03.29
1980	Ingemar Stenmark, Sweden	1:44.26
1984	Phil Mahre, United States	1:39.41
1988	Alberto Tomba, Italy	1:39.47
1992	Finn Christian Jagge, Norway	1:44.39
1994	Thomas Stangassinger, Austria	2:02.02
1998	Hans-Petter Buraas, Norway	1:49.31
2002	Jean-Pierre Vidal, France	1:41.06

Men's Combined

Year	Champion	Time
1936	Franz-Pfnuer, Germany	99.25 (pts.)
1948	Henri Oreiller, France	3.27 (pts.)
1988	Hubert Strolz, Austria	36.55 (pts.)
1992	Josef Polig, Italy	14.58 (pts.)
1994	Lasse Kjus, Norway	3:17.53
1998	Mario Reiter, Austria	3:08.06
2002	Kjetil Andre Aamodt, Norway	3:17.56

Women's Downhill

Year	Champion	Time
1948	Hedi Schlunegger, Switzerland	2:28.3
1952	Trude Jochum-Beiser, Austria	1:47.1
1956	Madeleine Berthod, Switzerland	1:40.7
1960	Heidi Biebl, Germany	1:37.6
1964	Christl Haas, Austria	1:55.39
1968	Olga Pall, Austria	1:40.87
1972	Marie-Theres Nadig, Switzerland	1:36.68
1976	Rosi Mittermaier, W. Germany	1:46.16
1980	Annemarie Moser-Proell , Austria	1:37.52
1984	Michela Figini, Switzerland	1:13.36
1988	Marina Kiehl, W. Germany	1:25.86
1992	Kerrin Lee-Gartner, Canada	1:52.55
1994	Katja Seizinger, Germany	1:35.93
1998	Katja Seizinger, Germany	1:28.89
2002	Carole Montillet, France	1:39.56

Women's Super Giant Slalom

Year	Champion	Time
1988	Sigrid Wolf, Austria	1:19.03
1992	Deborah Compagnoni, Italy	1:21.22
1994	Diann Roffe (Steinrotter), United States	1:22.15
1998	Picabo Street, United States	1:18.02
2002	Daniela Ceccarelli, Italy	1:13.59

Women's Giant Slalom

Year	Champion	Time
1952	Andrea Mead Lawrence, United States	2:06.8
1956	Ossi Reichert, Germany	1:56.5
1960	Yvonne Ruegg, Switzerland	1:39.9
1964	Marielle Goitschel, France	1:52.24
1968	Nancy Greene, Canada	1:51.97
1972	Marie-Theres Nadig, Switzerland	1:29.90
1976	Kathy Kreiner, Canada	1:29.13
1980	Hanni Wenzel, Liechtenstein (2 runs)	2:41.66
1984	Debbie Armstrong, United States	2:20.98
1988	Vreni Schneider, Switzerland	2:06.49
1992	Pernilla Wiberg, Sweden	2:12.74
1994	Deborah Compagnoni, Italy	2:30.97
1998	Deborah Compagnoni, Italy	2:50.59
2002	Janica Kostelic, Croatia	2:30.01

Women's Slalom

Year	Champion	Time
1948	Gretchen Fraser, United States	1:57.2
1952	Andrea Mead Lawrence, United States	2:10.6
1956	Renee Colliard, Switzerland	1:52.3
1960	Anne Heggtveit, Canada	1:49.6
1964	Christine Goitschel, France	1:29.86
1968	Marielle Goitschel, France	1:25.86
1972	Barbara Ann Cochran, United States	1:31.24
1976	Rosi Mittermaier, W. Germany	1:30.54
1980	Hanni Wenzel, Liechtenstein	1:25.09
1984	Paoletta Magoni, Italy	1:36.47
1988	Vreni Schneider, Switzerland	1:36.69
1992	Petra Kronberger, Austria	1:32.68
1994	Vreni Schneider, Switzerland	1:56.01
1998	Hilde Gerg, Germany	1:32.40
2002	Janica Kostelic, Croatia	1:46.10

Women's Combined

Year	Champion	Time
1936	Christl Cranz, Germany	97.06 (pts.)
1948	Trude Beiser-Jochum, Austria	6.58 (pts.)
1988	Anita Wachter, Austria	29.25 (pts.)
1992	Petra Kronberger, Austria	2.55 (pts.)
1994	Pernilla Wiberg, Sweden	3:05.16
1998	Katja Seizinger, Germany	2:40.74
2002	Janica Kostelic, Croatia	2:43.28

Biathlon

Men's 10 Kilometers

Year	Champion	Time
1980	Frank Ullrich, E. Germany	32:10.69
1984	Eirik Kvalfoss, Norway	30:53.80
1988	Frank-Peter Roetsch, E. Germany	25:08.10
1992	Mark Kirchner, Germany	26:02.30
1994	Serguei Tchepikov, Russia	28:07.00
1998	Ole Einar Bjoerndalen, Norway	27:16.20
2002	Ole Einar Bjoerndalen, Norway	24:51.30

Men's 12.5 Kilometers

Year	Champion	Time
2002	Ole Einar Bjoerndalen, Norway	32:34.6

Men's 20 Kilometers

Year	Champion	Time
1960	Klas Lestander, Sweden (40 km)	1:33:21.6
1964	Vladimir Melanin, USSR	1:20:26.8
1968	Magnar Solberg, Norway	1:13:45.9
1972	Magnar Solberg, Norway	1:15:55.50
1976	Nikolai Kruglov, USSR	1:14:12.26
1980	Anatoly Aljabiev, USSR	1:08:16.31
1984	Peter Angerer, W. Germany	1:11:52.7
1988	Frank-Peter Roetsch, E. Germany	0:56:33.33
1992	Yevgeny Redkine, Unified Team	0:57:34.4
1994	Serguei Tarasov, Russia	0:57:25.3
1998	Halvard Hanevold, Norway	0:56:16.4
2002	Ole Einar Bjoerndalen, Norway	0:51:03.03

Men's 30-Kilometer Relay

Year	Champion	Time
1968	USSR, Norway, Sweden (40 km)	2:13:02.4
1972	USSR, Finland, E. Germany (40 km)	1:51:44.92
1976	USSR, Finland, E. Germany (40 km)	1:57:55.64
1980	USSR, E. Germany, W. Germany	1:34:03.27
1984	USSR, Norway, W. Germany	1:38:51.70
1988	USSR, W. Germany, Italy	1:22:30.00
1992	Germany, Unified Team, Sweden	1:24:43.50
1994	Germany, Russia, France	1:30:22.1
1998	Germany, Norway, Russia	1:19:43.3
2002	Norway, Germany, France	1:23:42.3

Women's 7.5 Kilometers

Year	Champion	Time
1992	Anfissa Restsova, Unified Team	24:29.2
1994	Myriam Bedard, Canada	26:08.8
1998	Galina Koukleva, Russia	23:08.0
2002	Kati Wilhelm, Germany	20:41.4

Women's 10 Kilometers

Year	Champion	Time
2002	Olga Pyleva, Russia	31:07.7

Women's 15 Kilometers

Year	Champion	Time
1992	Antje Misersky, Germany	51:47.2
1994	Myriam Bedard, Canada	52:06.6
1998	Ekaterina Dafovska, Bulgaria	54:52.0
2002	Andrea Henkel, Germany	47:30.0

Women's 22.5-Kilometer Relay

Year	Champion	Time
1992	France, Germany, Unified Team	1:15:55.6

Women's 30-Kilometer Relay

Year	Champion	Time
1994	Russia, Germany, France	1:47:19.5
1998	Germany, Russia, Norway	1:40:13.6
2002	Germany, Norway, Russia	1:27:55.0

Bobsledding

(Driver in parentheses)

4-Man Bob

Year	Champion	Time
1924	Switzerland (Eduard Scherrer)	5:45.54
1928	United States (William Fiske) (5-man)	3:20.50
1932	United States (William Fiske)	7:53.68
1936	Switzerland (Pierre Musy)	5:19.85
1948	United States (Francis Tyler)	5:20.10
1952	Germany (Andreas Ostler)	5:07.84
1956	Switzerland (Franz Kapus)	5:10.44
1964	Canada (Victor Emery)	4:14.46
1968	Italy (Eugenio Monti) (2 races)	2:17.39
1972	Switzerland (Jean Wicki)	4:43.07
1976	E. Germany (Meinhard Nehmer)	3:40.43
1980	E. Germany (Meinhard Nehmer)	3:59.92
1984	E. Germany (Wolfgang Hoppe)	3:20.22
1988	Switzerland (Ekkehard Fasser)	3:47.51
1992	Austria (Ingo Appelt)	3:53.90
1994	Germany (Wolfgang Hoppe)	3:27.28
1998	Germany II (Christoph Langen)	2:39.41
2002	Germany II (Andre Lange)	3:07.51

2-Man Bob

Year	Champion	Time
1932	United States (Hubert Stevens)	8:14.74
1936	United States (Ivan Brown)	5:29.29
1948	Switzerland (F. Endrich)	5:29.20
1952	Germany (Andreas Ostler)	5:24.54
1956	Italy (Dalla Costa)	5:30.14
1964	Great Britain (Anthony Nash)	4:21.90
1968	Italy (Eugenio Monti)	4:41.54
1972	W. Germany (Wolfgang Zimmerer)	4:57.07
1976	E. Germany (Meinhard Nehmer)	3:44.42
1980	Switzerland (Erich Schaerer)	4:09.36
1984	E. Germany (Wolfgang Hoppe)	3:25.56
1988	USSR (Janis Kipours)	3:54.19
1992	Switzerland (Gustav Weber)	4:03.26
1994	Switzerland (Gustav Weber)	3:30.81

2-Man Bob	Time
1998 Canada (Pierre Lueders),	
Italy (Guenther Huber) (tie)............3:37.24	
2002 Germany II (Christoph Langen) 3:10.11	

2-Woman Bob	Time
2002 United States II (Jill Bakken).............1:37.76	

Curling
Men
1998 Switzerland, Canada, Norway
2002 Norway, Canada, Switzerland

Women
1998 Canada, Denmark, Sweden
2002 Britain, Switzerland, Canada

Figure Skating
Men's Singles
1908 Ulrich Salchow, Sweden
1920 Gillis Grafstrom, Sweden
1924 Gillis Grafstrom, Sweden
1928 Gillis Grafstrom, Sweden
1932 Karl Schaefer, Austria
1936 Karl Schaefer, Austria
1948 Richard Button, United States
1952 Richard Button, United States
1956 Hayes Alan Jenkins, United States
1960 David W. Jenkins, United States
1964 Manfred Schnelldorfer, Germany
1968 Wolfgang Schwartz, Austria
1972 Ondrej Nepela, Czechoslovakia
1976 John Curry, Great Britain
1980 Robin Cousins, Great Britain
1984 Scott Hamilton, United States
1988 Brian Boitano, United States
1992 Viktor Petrenko, Unified Team
1994 Aleksei Urmanov, Russia
1998 Ilya Kulik, Russia
2002 Alexei Yagudin, Russia

Women's Singles
1908 Madge Syers, Great Britain
1920 Magda Julin-Mauroy, Sweden
1924 Herma von Szabo-Planck, Austria
1928 Sonja Henie, Norway
1932 Sonja Henie, Norway
1936 Sonja Henie, Norway
1948 Barbara Ann Scott, Canada
1952 Jeanette Altwegg, Great Britan
1956 Tenley Albright, United States
1960 Carol Heiss, United States
1964 Sjoukje Dijkstra, Netherlands
1968 Peggy Fleming, United States
1972 Beatrix Schuba, Austria
1976 Dorothy Hamill, United States
1980 Anett Poetzsch, E. Germany
1984 Katarina Witt, E. Germany
1988 Katarina Witt, E. Germany
1992 Kristi Yamaguchi, United States
1994 Oksana Baiul, Ukraine
1998 Tara Lipinski, United States
2002 Sarah Hughes, United States

Pairs
1908 Anna Hubler & Heinrich Burger, Germany
1920 Ludovika & Walter Jakobsson, Finland
1924 Helene Engelman & Alfred Berger, Austria
1928 Andree Joly & Pierre Brunet, France
1932 Andree Joly & Pierre Brunet, France
1936 Maxi Herber & Ernst Baier, Germany
1948 Micheline Lannoy & Pierre Baugniet, Belgium
1952 Ria and Paul Falk, Germany
1956 Elisabeth Schwartz & Kurt Oppelt, Austria
1964 Ludmila Beloussova & Oleg Protopopov, USSR
1968 Ludmila Beloussova & Oleg Protopopov, USSR
1972 Irina Rodnina & Alexei Ulanov, USSR
1976 Irina Rodnina & Aleksandr Zaitzev, USSR
1980 Irina Rodnina & Aleksandr Zaitzev, USSR
1984 Elena Valova & Oleg Vassiliev, USSR
1988 Ekaterina Gordeeva & Sergei Grinkov, USSR
1992 Natalia Mishkutienok & Artur Dimitriev, Unified Team
1994 Ekaterina Gordeeva & Sergei Grinkov, Russia
1998 Oksana Kazakova & Artur Dmitriev, Russia
2002 Elena Berezhnaya & Anton Sikharulidze, Russia;
     Jamie Sale & David Pelletier, Canada (tie)

Ice Dancing
1976 Ludmila Pakhomova & Aleksandr Gorshkov, USSR
1980 Natalya Linichuk & Gennadi Karponosov, USSR
1984 Jayne Torvill & Christopher Dean, Great Britain
1988 Natalia Bestemianova & Andrei Bukin, USSR
1992 Marina Klimova & Sergei Ponomarenko, Unified Team
1994 Pasha Grishuk & Evgeny Platov, Russia
1998 Pasha Grishuk & Evgeny Platov, Russia
2002 Marina Anissina & Gwendal Peizerat, France

Freestyle Skiing
Men's Moguls

		Points
1992	Edgar Grospiron, France	25.81
1994	Jean-Luc Brassard, Canada	27.24
1998	Jonny Moseley, United States	26.93
2002	Janne Lahtela, Finland................	27.97

Men's Aerials

		Points
1994	Andreas Schoenbaechler, Switzerland	234.67
1998	Eric Bergoust, United States	255.64
2002	Ales Valenta, Czech Republic	257.02

Women's Moguls

		Points
1992	Donna Weinbrecht, United States	23.69
1994	Stine Lise Hattestad, Norway..........	25.97
1998	Tae Satoya, Japan.................	25.06
2002	Kari Traa, Norway	25.94

Women's Aerials

		Points
1994	Lina Tcherjazova, Uzbekistan	166.84
1998	Nikki Stone, United States	193.00
2002	Alisa Camplin, Australia................	193.47

Ice Hockey
MEN
1920# Canada, United States, Czechoslovakia
1924 Canada, United States, Great Britain
1928 Canada, Sweden, Switzerland
1932 Canada, United States, Germany
1936 Great Britain, Canada, United States
1948 Canada, Czechoslovakia, Switzerland
1952 Canada, United States, Sweden
1956 USSR, United States, Canada
1960 United States, Canada, USSR
1964 USSR, Sweden, Czechoslovakia
1968 USSR, Czechoslovakia, Canada
1972 USSR, United States, Czechoslovakia
1976 USSR, Czechoslovakia, W. Germany
1980 United States, USSR, Sweden
1984 USSR, Czechoslovakia, Sweden
1988 USSR, Finland, Sweden
1992 Unified Team, Canada, Czechoslovakia
1994 Sweden, Canada, Finland
1998 Czech Republic, Russia, Finland
2002 Canada, United States, Russia

WOMEN
1998 United States, Canada, Finland
2002 Canada, United States, Sweden

Luge
Men's Singles

		Time
1964	Thomas Keohler, E. Germany	3:26.77
1968	Manfred Schmid, Austria	2:52.48
1972	Wolfgang Scheidel, E. Germany	3:27.58
1976	Detlef Guenther, E. Germany...........	3:27.688
1980	Bernhard Glass, E. Germany............	2:54.796
1984	Paul Hildgartner, Italy................	3:04.258
1988	Jens Mueller, E. Germany	3:05.548
1992	Georg Hackl, Germany	3:02.363
1994	Georg Hackl, Germany	3:21.571
1998	Georg Hackl, Germany	3:18.436
2002	Armin Zoeggeler, Italy	2:57.941

Women's Singles

		Time
1964	Ortun Enderlein, Germany..............	3:24.67
1968	Erica Lechner, Italy	2:28.66
1972	Anna M. Muller, E. Germany	2:59.18
1976	Margit Schumann, E. Germany	2:50.621
1980	Vera Zozulya, USSR	2:36.537
1984	Steffi Martin, E. Germany............	2:46.570
1988	Steffi Walter, E. Germany	3:03.973
1992	Doris Neuner, Austria...............	3:06.696
1994	Gerda Weissensteiner, Italy	3:15.517
1998	Silke Kraushaar, Germany............	3:23.779
2002	Sylke Otto, Germany	2:52.464

Men's Doubles

		Time
1964	Austria	1:41.62
1968	E. Germany	1:35.85
1972	Italy, E. Germany (tie)	1:28.35
1976	E. Germany	1:25.604
1980	E. Germany	1:19.331
1984	W. Germany....................	1:23.620
1988	E. Germany	1:31.940
1992	Germany	1:32.053
1994	Italy..........................	1:36.720
1998	Germany	1:41.105
2002	Germany	1:26.082

Skeleton
Men

		Time
1928	Jennison Heaton, United States........	3:01.8
1948	Nino Bibbia, Italy	5:23.2
2002	Jim Shea, United States..............	1:41.96

Women

		Time
2002	Tristan Gale, United States	1:45.11

Nordic Skiing
Cross-Country Events

Men's 1.5 Kilometers (0.93 miles)   Time
2002   Tor Arne Hetland, Norway 2:56.9

Men's 10 Kilometers (6.2 miles)   Time
1992   Vegard Ulvang, Norway 27:36.0
1994   Bjoern Daehlie, Norway 24:20.1
1998   Bjoern Daehlie, Norway 27:24.5
2002   (tie) Thomas Alsgaard, Norway; Frode Estil,
      Norway (a) 49:48.9
(a) Awarded gold after Johann Muehlegg of Spain was stripped of gold for a drug offense.

Men's 15 Kilometers (9.3 miles)   Time
1924   Thorleif Haug, Norway 1:14:31
1928   Johan Grottumsbraaten, Norway 1:37:01
1932   Sven Utterstrom, Sweden 1:23:07
1936   Erik-August Larsson, Sweden 1:14:38
1948   Martin Lundstrom, Sweden 1:13:50
1952   Hallgeir Brenden, Norway 1:01:34
1956   Hallgeir Brenden, Norway 0:49:39.0
1960   Haakon Brusveen, Norway 0:51:55.5
1964   Eero Maentyranta, Finland 0:50:54.1
1968   Harald Groenningen, Norway 0:47:54.2
1972   Sven-Ake Lundback, Sweden 0:45:28.24
1976   Nikolai Balukov, USSR 0:43:58.47
1980   Thomas Wassberg, Sweden 0:41:57.63
1984   Gunde Svan, Sweden 0:41:25.6
1988   Mikhail Deviatiarov, USSR 0:41:18.9
1992   Bjoern Daehlie, Norway 0:38:01.9
1994   Bjoern Daehlie, Norway 0:35:48.8
1998   Thomas Alsgaard, Norway 1:07:01.7
2002   Andrus Veerpalu, Estonia 0:37:07.4
(Note: approx. 18-km course 1924-1952)

Men's 30 Kilometers (18.6 miles)   Time
1956   Veikko Hakulinen, Finland 1:44:06.0
1956   Veikko Hakulinen, Finland 1:44:06.0
1960   Sixten Jernberg, Sweden 1:51:03.9
1964   Eero Maentyranta, Finland 1:30:50.7
1968   Franco Nones, Italy 1:35:39.2
1972   Vyacheslav Vedenine, USSR 1:36:31.15
1976   Sergei Saveliev, USSR 1:30:29.38
1980   Nikolai Zimyatov, USSR 1:27:02.80
1984   Nikolai Zimyatov, USSR 1:28:56.3
1988   Aleksei Prokourorov, USSR 1:24:26.3
1992   Vegard Ulvang, Norway 1:22:27.8
1994   Thomas Alsgaard, Norway 1:12:26.4
1998   Mika Myllylae, Finland 1:33:55.8
2002   Christian Hoffmann, Austria (a) 1:11:31.0
(a) Awarded gold after Johann Muehlegg of Spain was stripped of gold for a drug offense.

Men's 50 Kilometers (31.2 miles)   Time
1924   Thorleif Haug, Norway 3:44:32.0
1928   Per Erik Hedlund, Sweden 4:52:03.0
1932   Veli Saarinen, Finland 4:28:00.0
1936   Elis Wiklund, Sweden 3:30:11.0
1948   Nils Karlsson, Sweden 3:47:48.0
1952   Veikko Hakulinen, Finland 3:33:33.0
1956   Sixten Jernberg, Sweden 2:50:27.0
1960   Kalevi Hamalainen, Finland 2:59:06.3
1964   Sixten Jernberg, Sweden 2:43:52.6
1968   Ole Ellefsaeter, Norway 2:28:45.8
1972   Paal Tyldum, Norway 2:43:14.75
1976   Ivar Formo, Norway 2:37:30.05
1980   Nikolai Zimyatov, USSR 2:27:24.60
1984   Thomas Wassberg, Sweden 2:15:55.8
1988   Gunde Svan, Sweden 2:04:30.9
1992   Bjoern Daehlie, Norway 2:03:41.5
1994   Vladimir Smirnov, Kazakhstan 2:07:20.3
1998   Bjoern Daehlie, Norway 2:05:08.2
2002   Mikhail Ivanov, Russia 2:06:20.8

Men's 40-Kilometer Relay   Time
1936   Finland, Norway, Sweden   2:41:33.0
1948   Sweden, Finland, Norway 2:32:08.0
1952   Finland, Norway, Sweden 2:20:16.0
1956   USSR, Finland, Sweden 2:15:30.0
1960   Finland, Norway, USSR 2:18:45.6
1964   Sweden, Finland, USSR 2:18:34.6
1968   Norway, Sweden, Finland 2:08:33.5
1972   USSR, Norway, Switzerland 2:04:47.94
1976   Finland, Norway, USSR 2:07:59.72
1980   USSR, Norway, Finland 1:57:03.46
1984   Sweden, USSR, Finland 1:55:06.30
1988   Sweden, USSR, Czechoslovakia 1:43:58.60
1992   Norway, Italy, Finland 1:39:26.00
1994   Italy, Norway, Finland 1:41:15.00
1998   Norway, Italy, Finland 1:40:55.70
2002   Norway, Italy, Germany 1:32:45.5

Women's 1.5 Kilometers (0.93 miles)   Time
2002   Julia Tchepalova, Russia 3:10.6

Women's 5 Kilometers (3.1 miles)   Time
1964   Claudia Boyarskikh, USSR 17:50.5
1968   Toini Gustafsson, Sweden 16:45.2
1972   Galina Koulacova, USSR 17:00.50
1976   Helena Takalo, Finland 15:48.69
1980   Raisa Smetanina, USSR 15:06.92
1984   Marja-Liisa Haemaelainen, Finland 17:04.0
1988   Marjo Matikainen, Finland 15:04.0
1992   Marjut Lukkarinen, Finland 14:13.8
1994   Ljubov Egorova, Russia 14:08.8
1998   Larissa Lazutina, Russia 17:37.9
2002   Beckie Scott, Canada (a) 25:09.9
(a) Awarded gold after Olga Danilova of Russia was stripped of gold and Larissa Lazutina of Russia was stripped of silver for drug offenses.

Women's 10 Kilometers (6.2 miles)   Time
1952   Lydia Wideman, Finland 41:40.0
1956   Lyubov Kosyreva, USSR 38:11.0
1960   Maria Gusakova, USSR 39:46.6
1964   Claudia Boyarskikh, USSR 40:24.3
1968   Toini Gustafsson, Sweden 36:46.5
1972   Galina Koulacova, USSR 34:17.82
1976   Raisa Smetanina, USSR 30:13.41
1980   Barbara Petzold, E. Germany 30:31.54
1984   Marja-Liisa Haemaelainen, Finland 31:44.2
1988   Vida Ventsene, USSR 30:08.3
1992   Lyubov Egorova, Unified Team 25:53.7
1994   Lyubov Egorova, Russia 27:30.1
1998   Larissa Lazutina, Russia 46.06.9
2002   Bente Skari, Norway 28:05.6

Women's 15 Kilometers (9.3 miles)   Time
1992   Lyubov Egorova, Unified Team 42:20.8
1994   Manuela Di Centa, Italy 39:44.5
1998   Olga Danilova, Russia 46:55.4
2002   Stefania Belmondo, Italy 39:54.4

Women's 30 Kilometers (18.6 miles)   Time
1992   Stefania Belmondo, Italy 1:22:30.1
1994   Manuela Di Centa, Italy 1:25:41.6
1998   Julija Tchepalova, Russia 1:22:01.5
2002   Gabriella Paruzzi, Italy 1:30:57.1

Women's 20-Kilometer Relay   Time
1956   Finland, USSR, Sweden (15 km) 1:09:01.0
1960   Sweden, USSR, Finland (15 km) 1:04:21.4
1964   USSR, Sweden, Finland (15 km) 0:59:20.2
1968   Norway, Sweden, USSR (15 km) 0:57:30.0
1972   USSR, Finland, Norway (15 km) 0:48:46.15
1976   USSR, Finland, E. Germany 1:07:49.75
1980   E. Germany, USSR, Norway 1:02:11.1
1984   Norway, Czechoslovakia, Finland 1:06:49.7
1988   USSR, Norway, Finland 0:59:51.1
1992   United Team, Norway, Italy 0:59:34.8
1994   Russia, Norway, Italy 0:57:12.5
1998   Russia, Norway, Italy 0:55:13.5
2002   Germany, Norway, Switzerland 0:49:30.6

Combined Cross-Country & Jumping (Men)

7.5 Kilometer Nordic Combined
2002   Samppa Lajunen, FInland

15 Kilometer Nordic Combined
1924   Thorleif Haug, Norway
1928   Johan Grottumsbraaten, Norway
1932   Johan Grottumsbraaten, Norway
1936   Oddbjorn Hagen, Norway
1948   Heikki Hasu, Finland
1952   Simon Slattvik, Norway
1956   Sverre Stenersen, Norway
1960   Georg Thoma, W. Germany
1964   Tormod Knutsen, Norway
1968   Franz Keller, W. Germany
1972   Ulrich Wehling, E. Germany
1976   Ulrich Wehling, E. Germany
1980   Ulrich Wehling, E. Germany
1984   Tom Sandberg, Norway
1988   Hippolyt Kempf, Switzerland
1992   Fabrice Guy, France
1994   Fred Barre Lundberg, Norway
1998   Bjarte Engen Vik, Norway
2002   Samppa Lajunen, Finland

Team Nordic Combined
1988   W. Germany, Switzerland, Austria
1992   Japan, Norway, Austria
1994   Japan, Norway, Switzerland
1998   Norway, Finland, France
2002   Finland, Germany, Austria
Medals based on combination of points for jumping events and time for cross-country events.

Ski Jumping (Men)

Normal Hill

		Points
1964	Veikko Kankkonen, Finland	229.9
1968	Jiri Raska, Czechoslovakia	216.5
1972	Yukio Kasaya, Japan	244.2
1976	Hans-Georg Aschenbach, E. Germany	252.0
1980	Toni Innauer, Austria	266.3
1984	Jens Weissflog, E. Germany	215.2
1988	Matti Nykaenen, Finland	230.5
1992	Ernst Vettori, Austria	222.8
1994	Espen Bredesen, Norway	282.0
1998	Jani Soininen, Finland	234.5
2002	Simon Ammann, Switzerland	269.0

Large Hill

		Points
1924	Jacob Tullin Thams, Norway	18.960
1928	Alfred Andersen, Norway	19.208
1932	Birger Ruud, Norway	228.1
1936	Birger Ruud, Norway	232.0
1948	Petter Hugsted, Norway	228.1
1952	Arnfinn Bergmann, Norway	226.0
1956	Antti Hyvarinen, Finland	227.0
1960	Helmut Recknagel, E. Germany	227.2
1964	Toralf Engan, Norway	230.7
1968	Vladimir Beloussov, USSR	231.3
1972	Wojciech Fortuna, Poland	219.9
1976	Karl Schnabl, Austria	234.8
1980	Jouko Tormanen, Finland	271.0
1984	Matti Nykaenen, Finland	231.2
1988	Matti Nykaenen, Finland	224.0
1992	Toni Nieminen, Finland	239.5
1994	Jens Weissflog, Germany	274.5
1998	Kazuyoshi Funaki, Japan	272.3
2002	Simon Ammann, Switzerland	281.4

Team Large Hill

		Points
1988	Finland, Yugoslavia, Norway	634.4
1992	Finland, Austria, Czechoslovakia	644.4
1994	Germany, Japan, Austria	970.1
1998	Japan, Germany, Austria	933.0
2002	Germany, Finland, Slovenia	974.1

Snowboarding

Men's Giant Slalom

		Time
1998	Ross Rebagliati, Canada	2:03.96
2002	Philipp Schoch, Switzerland	

Men's Halfpipe

		Points
1998	Gian Simmen, Switzerland	85.2
2002	Ross Powers	46.1

Women's Giant Slalom

		Time
1998	Karine Ruby, France	2:17.34
2002	Isabelle Blanc, France	

Women's Halfpipe

		Points
1998	Nicola Thost, Germany	74.6
2002	Kelly Clark, United States	47.9

Speed Skating

*indicates Olympic record

Men's 500 Meters

		Time[1]
1924	Charles Jewtraw, United States	0:44.0
1928	Thunberg, Finland & Evensen, Norway (tie)	0:43.4
1932	John A. Shea, United States	0:43.4
1936	Ivar Ballangrud, Norway	0:43.4
1948	Finn Helgesen, Norway	0:43.1
1952	Kenneth Henry, United States	0:43.2
1956	Evgeniy Grishin, USSR	0:40.2
1960	Evgeniy Grishin, USSR	0:40.2
1964	Terry McDermott, United States	0:40.1
1968	Erhard Keller, W. Germany	0:40.3
1972	Erhard Keller, W. Germany	0:39.44
1976	Evgeny Kulikov, USSR	0:39.17
1980	Eric Heiden, United States	0:38.03
1984	Sergei Fokichev, USSR	0:38.19
1988	Uwe-Jens Mey, E. Germany	0:36.45
1992	Uwe-Jens Mey, Germany	0:37.14
1994	Aleksandr Golubev, Russia	0:36.33
1998	Hiroyasu Shimizu, Japan	0:35.59
2002	Casey FitzRandolph, United States	0:34.42*

Men's 1,000 Meters

		Time
1976	Peter Mueller, U.S	1:19.32
1980	Eric Heiden, United States	1:15.18
1984	Gaetan Boucher, Canada	1:15.80
1988	Nikolai Guiliaev, USSR	1:13.03
1992	Olaf Zinke, Germany	1:14.85
1994	Dan Jansen, United States	1:12.43
1998	Ids Postma, Netherlands	1:10.64
2002	Gerard van Velde, Netherlands	1:07.18*

Men's 1,500 Meters

		Time
1924	Clas Thunberg, Finland	2:20.8
1928	Clas Thunberg, Finland	2:21.1
1932	John A. Shea, United States	2:57.5
1936	Charles Mathiesen, Norway	2:19.2
1948	Sverre Farstad, Norway	2:17.6
1952	Hjalmar Andersen, Norway	2:20.4
1956	Grishin, & Mikhailov, both USSR (tie)	2:08.6
1960	Aas, Norway & Grishin, USSR (tie)	2:10.4
1964	Ants Anston, USSR	2:10.3
1968	Cornetis Verkerk, Netherlands	2:03.4
1972	Ard Schenk, Netherlands	2:02.96
1976	Jan Egil Storholt, Norway	1:59.38
1980	Eric Heiden, United States	1:55.44
1984	Gaetan Boucher, Canada	1:58.36
1988	Andre Hoffmann, E. Germany	1:52.06
1992	Johann Koss, Norway	1:54.81
1994	Johann Koss, Norway	1:51.29
1998	Aadne Sondral, Norway	1:47.87
2002	Derek Parra, United States	1:43.95*

Men's 5,000 Meters

		Time
1924	Clas Thunberg, Finland	8:39.0
1928	Ivar Ballangrud, Norway	8:50.5
1932	Irving Jaffee, United States	9:40.8
1936	Ivar Ballangrud, Norway	8:19.6
1948	Reidar Liaklev, Norway	8:29.4
1952	Hjalmar Andersen, Norway	8:10.6
1956	Boris Shilkov, USSR	7:48.7
1960	Viktor Kosichkin, USSR	7:51.3
1964	Knut Johannesen, Norway	7:38.4
1968	F. Anton Maier, Norway	7:22.4
1972	Ard Schenk, Netherlands	7:23.61
1976	Sten Stensen, Norway	7:24.48
1980	Eric Heiden, United States	7:02.29
1984	Sven Tomas Gustafson, Sweden	7:12.28
1988	Tomas Gustafson, Sweden	6:44.63
1992	Geir Karlstad, Norway	6:59.97
1994	Johann Koss, Norway	6:34.96
1998	Gianni Romme, Netherlands	6:22.20
2002	Jochem Uytdehaage, Netherlands	6:14.66*

Men's 10,000 Meters

		Time
1924	Julius Skutnabb, Finland	18:04.8
1928	Event not held because of thawing of ice	
1932	Irving Jaffee, United States	19:13.6
1936	Ivar Ballangrud, Norway	17:24.3
1948	Ake Seyffarth, Sweden	17:26.3
1952	Hjalmar Andersen, Norway	16:45.8
1956	Sigvard Ericsson, Sweden	16:35.9
1960	Knut Johannesen, Norway	15:46.6
1964	Jonny Nilsson, Sweden	15:50.1
1968	Jonny Hoeglin, Sweden	15:23.6
1972	Ard Schenk, Netherlands	15:01.35
1976	Piet Kleine, Netherlands	14:50.59
1980	Eric Heiden, United States	14:28.13
1984	Igor Malkov, USSR	14:39.90
1988	Tomas Gustafson, Sweden	13:48.20
1992	Bart Veldkamp, Netherlands	14:12.12
1994	Johann Koss, Norway	13:30.55
1998	Gianni Romme, Netherlands	13:15.33
2002	Jochem Uytdehaage, Netherlands	12:58.92*

Women's 500 Meters

		Time
1960	Helga Haase, Germany	0:45.9
1964	Lydia Skoblikova, USSR	0:45.0
1968	Ludmila Titova, USSR	0:46.1
1972	Anne Henning, United States	0:43.33
1976	Sheila Young, United States	0:42.76
1980	Karin Enke, E. Germany	0:41.78
1984	Christa Rothenburger, E. Germany	0:41.02
1988	Bonnie Blair, United States	0:39.10
1992	Bonnie Blair, United States	0:40.33
1994	Bonnie Blair, United States	0:39.25
1998	Catriona Le May-Doan, Canada	0:38.21
2002	Catriona Le May Doan, Canada	0:37.30

Women's 1,000 Meters

		Time
1960	Klara Guseva, USSR	1:34.1
1964	Lydia Skoblikova, USSR	1:33.2
1968	Carolina Geijssen, Netherlands	1:32.6
1972	Monika Pflug, W. Germany	1:31.40
1976	Tatiana Averina, USSR	1:28.43
1980	Natalya Petruseva, USSR	1:24.10
1984	Karin Enke, E. Germany	1:21.61
1988	Christa Rothenburger, E. Germany	1:17.65
1992	Bonnie Blair, United States	1:21.90
1994	Bonnie Blair, United States	1:18.74
1998	Marianne Timmer, Netherlands	1:16.51
2002	Chris Witty, United States	1:13.83*

Women's 1,500 Meters	Time
1960 Lydia Skoblikova, USSR	2:52.2
1964 Lydia Skoblikova, USSR	2:22.6
1968 Kaija Mustonen, Finland	2:22.4
1972 Dianne Holum, United States	2:20.85
1976 Galina Stepanskaya, USSR	2:16.58
1980 Anne Borckink, Netherlands	2:10.95
1984 Karin Enke, E. Germany	2:03.42
1988 Yvonne van Gennip, Netherlands	2:00.68
1992 Jacqueline Boerner, Germany	2:05.87
1994 Emese Hunyady, Austria	2:02.19
1998 Marianne Timmer, Netherlands	1:57.58
2002 Anni Friesinger, Germany,	1:54.02*

Women's 3,000 Meters	Time
1960 Lydia Skoblikova, USSR	5:14.3
1964 Lydia Skoblikova, USSR	5:14.9
1968 Johanna Schut, Netherlands	4:56.2
1972 Christina Baas-Kaiser, Netherlands	4:52.14
1976 Tatiana Averina, USSR	4:45.19
1980 Bjoerg Eva Jensen, Norway	4:32.13
1984 Andrea Schoene, E. Germany	4:24.79
1988 Yvonne van Gennip, Netherlands	4:11.94
1992 Gunda Niemann, Germany	4:19.90
1994 Svetlana Bazhanova, Russia	4:17.43
1998 Gunda Niemann-Stirnemann, Germany	4:07.29
2002 Claudia Pechstein, Germany,	3:57.70*

Women's 5,000 Meters	Time
1988 Yvonne van Gennip, Netherlands	7:14.13
1992 Gunda Niemann, Germany	7:31.57
1994 Claudia Pechstein, Germany	7:14.37
1998 Claudia Pechstein, Germany	6:59.61
2002 Claudia Pechstein, Germany	6:46.91*

Short-Track Speed Skating
indicates Olympic record

Men's 500 Meters	Time
1998 Takafumi Nishitani, Japan	42.862
2002 Marc Gagnon, Canada	41.802*

Men's 1,000 Meters	Time
1992 Kim Ki-Hoon, S. Korea	1:30.76
1994 Kim Ki-Hoon, S. Korea	1:34.57
1998 Dong-Sung Kim, S. Korea	1:32.375
2002 Steven Bradbury, Australia	1:29.109

Men's 1,500 Meters	Time
2002 Apolo Anton Ohno, United States	2:18.541

Men's 5,000-Meter Relay	Time
1992 S. Korea, Canada, Japan	7:14.02
1994 Italy, United States, Australia	7:11.74
1998 Canada, S. Korea, China	7:06.075
2002 Canada, Italy, China	6:51.579

Women's 500 Meters	Time
1992 Cathy Turner, United States	47.04
1994 Cathy Turner, United States	45.98
1998 Annie Perreault, Canada	46.568
2002 Yang Yang (a)	44.187

Women's 1,000 Meters	Time
1998 Chun Lee-Kyung, S. Korea	1:42.776
2002 Yang Yang (a) China	1:36.391

Women's 1,500 Meters	Time
2002 Gi-Hyun Ko, S. Korea	2:31.581

Women's 3,000 Meter Relay	Time
1992 Canada, United States, Unified Team	4:36.62
1994 S. Korea, Canada, United States	4:26.64
1998 S. Korea, China, Canada	4:16.26
2002 S. Korea, China, Canada	4:12.793*

Olympic Information

The modern Olympic Games, first held in Athens, Greece, in 1896, were the result of efforts by Baron Pierre de Coubertin, a French educator, to promote interest in education and culture and to foster better international understanding through love of athletics. His inspiration was the ancient Greek Olympic Games, most notable of the 4 Panhellenic celebrations. The games were combined patriotic, religious, and athletic festivals held every 4 years. The first such recorded festival was held in 776 BC, which the Greeks began to keep their calendar by "Olympiads," or 4-year spans between the games.

Baron de Coubertin enlisted 13 nations to send athletes to the first modern Olympics in 1896; now athletes from nearly 200 nations and territories compete in the Summer Olympics. The Winter Olympic Games were started in 1924.

Symbol: Five rings or circles, linked together to represent the sporting friendship of all peoples. They also symbolize 5 geographic areas—Europe, Asia, Africa, Australia, and America. Each ring is a different color—blue, yellow, black, green, or red.
Flag: The symbol of the 5 rings on a plain white background.
Creed: "The most important thing in the Olympic Games is not to win but to take part, just as the most important thing in life is not the triumph but the struggle. The essential thing is not to have conquered but to have fought well."

Motto: "Citius, Altius, Fortius." Latin meaning "swifter, higher, stronger."
Oath: "In the name of all competitors I promise that we will take part in these Olympic Games, respecting and abiding by the rules which govern them, in the true spirit of sportsmanship for the glory of sport and the honor of our teams."
Flame: The modern version of the flame was adopted in 1936. The torch used to kindle it is first lit by the sun's rays at Olympia, Greece, then carried to the site of the Games by relays of runners. Ships and planes are used when necessary.

Sites of Winter Olympic Games

1924 Chamonix, France	1952 Oslo, Norway	1976 Innsbruck, Austria	1998 Nagano, Japan
1928 St. Moritz, Switzerland	1956 Cortina d'Ampezzo, Italy	1980 Lake Placid, NY	2002 Salt Lake City, UT
1932 Lake Placid, NY	1960 Squaw Valley, CA	1984 Sarajevo, Yugoslavia	2006 Turin, Italy
1952 Garmisch-Partenkirchen, Germany	1964 Innsbruck, Austria	1988 Calgary, Canada	2010 Vancouver, B.C., Canada
1948 St. Moritz, Switzerland	1968 Grenoble, France	1992 Albertville, France	
	1972 Sapporo, Japan	1994 Lillehammer, Norway	

Sites of Summer Olympic Games

1896 Athens, Greece	1924 Paris, France	1960 Rome, Italy	1988 Seoul, South Korea
1900 Paris, France	1928 Amsterdam, Netherlands	1964 Tokyo, Japan	1992 Barcelona, Spain
1904 St. Louis, MO	1932 Los Angeles, CA	1968 Mexico City, Mexico	1996 Atlanta, GA
1906 Athens, Greece*	1936 Berlin, Germany	1972 Munich, W. Germany	2000 Sydney, Australia
1908 London, England	1948 London, England	1976 Montreal, Canada	2004 Athens, Greece
1912 Stockholm, Sweden	1952 Helsinki, Finland	1980 Moscow, USSR	2008 Beijing, China
1920 Antwerp, Belgium	1956 Melbourne, Australia	1984 Los Angeles, CA	

*Games not recognized by International Olympic Committee. Games VI (1916), XII (1940), and XIII (1944) were not celebrated.

Paralympics

The first Olympic games for the disabled were held in Rome after the 1960 Summer Olympics; use of the name "paralympic" began with the 1964 games in Tokyo. The Paralympics are held by the Olympic host country in the same year and usually the same city or venue. A goal of the Paralympics is to provide elite competition to athletes with functional disabilities that prevent their involvement in the Olympics. In 1976 the first Winter Paralympics were held, in Ornskoldsvik, Sweden.

The XII Paralympic Summer Games were held Sept. 17-28, 2004, in Athens, Greece. A record 3,969 athletes from a record 136 nations competed in 19 sports. China won the most medals, with 141, and the most golds, with 63. Australia was 2nd, with a total of 100 medals, and Great Britain was 3rd, with 94. Japanese swimmer Mayumi Narita won the most individual medals, with 7 golds and 1 bronze. A total of 304 world and 448 Paralympic records were set in Athens.

The IX Paralympic Winter Games were to be held Mar. 10-19, 2006, in Torino, Italy, where wheelchair curling will be contested for the first time.

Special Olympics

Special Olympics is an international program of year-round sports training and athletic competition dedicated to "empowering individuals with mental retardation." All 50 U.S. states, Washington, DC, and Guam have chapter offices. In addition, there are accredited Special Olympics programs in nearly 150 countries. Persons wishing to volunteer or find out more can contact Special Olympics International Headquarters, 1325 G St. NW, Suite 500, Washington, DC 20005, or access the Special Olympics website at www.specialolympics.org

The 11th Special Olympics World Summer Games were held June 21-29, 2003, in Dublin, Ireland. More than 7,000 athletes, 3,000 coaches and delegates, and 28,000 others attended the first Special Olympic World Games outside the U.S. Competition included aquatics, athletics, badminton, bocce, bowling, cycling, equestrian sports, golf, gymnastics (artistic and rhythmic), power lifting, rollerskating, table tennis, and tennis. Scheduled team sports were basketball, handball, sailing, soccer, and volleyball. Kayaking and pitch-and-putt (a form of golf) were included as demonstration sports.

The 8th Special Olympics World Winter Games were scheduled to be held Feb. 26 through Mar. 5, 2005, in Nagano, Japan. About 2,500 athletes from 80 countries are to compete. The competition will include alpine skiing, cross-country skiing, floor hockey, figure skating, speed skating, snowsheeing, and snowboarding, all to be held in the same venues used at the 1998 Olympic Games.

TRACK AND FIELD
World Track and Field Outdoor Records
As of Oct. 1, 2004

The International Amateur Athletic Federation, the world body of track and field, recognizes only records in metric distances, except for the mile. *Pending ratification.

Men's Records
Running

Event	Record	Holder	Country	Date	Where made
100 meters	9.78 s.	Tim Montgomery	U.S.	Sept. 14, 2002	Paris, France
200 meters	19.32 s.	Michael Johnson	U.S.	Aug. 1, 1996	Atlanta, GA
400 meters	43.18 s.	Michael Johnson	U.S.	Aug. 26, 1999	Seville, Spain
800 meters	1 m., 41.11 s.	Wilson Kipketer	Denmark	Aug. 24, 1997	Cologne, Germany
1,000 meters	2 m., 11.96 s.	Noah Ngeny	Kenya	Sept. 5, 1999	Rieti, Italy
1,500 meters	3 m., 26.00 s.	Hicham El Guerrouj	Morocco	July 14, 1998	Rome, Italy
1 mile	3 m., 43.13 s.	Hicham El Guerrouj	Morocco	July 7, 1999	Rome, Italy
2,000 meters	4 m., 44.79 s.	Hicham El Guerrouj	Morocco	Sept. 7, 1999	Berlin, Germany
3,000 meters	7 m., 20.67 s.	Daniel Komen	Kenya	Sept. 1, 1996	Rieti, Italy
5,000 meters	12 m., 37.35 s.	Kenenisa Bekele	Ethiopia	May 31, 2004	Hengelo, Netherlands
10,000 meters	26 m., 20.31 s.	Kenenisa Bekele	Ethiopia	June 8, 2004	Ostrava, Czech Republic
20,000 meters	56 m., 55.6 s.	Arturo Barrios	Mexico	Mar. 30, 1991	La Fléche, France
25,000 meters	1 hr., 13 m., 55.8 s.	Toshihiko Seko	Japan	Mar. 22, 1981	Christchurch, NZ
3,000 meter stpl.	7 m., 53.63 s.*	Saif Saaeed Shaheen	Qatar	Sept. 3, 2004	Brussels, Belgium
Marathon	2 hr., 4 m., 55 s.	Paul Tergat	Kenya	Sept. 28, 2003	Berlin, Germany

Hurdles

Event	Record	Holder	Country	Date	Where made
110 meters	12.91 s.	Colin Jackson	Gr. Britain	Aug. 20, 1993	Stuttgart, Germany
		Liu Xiang*	China	Aug. 27, 2004	Athens, Greece
400 meters	46.78 s.	Kevin Young	U.S.	Aug. 6, 1992	Barcelona, Spain

Relay Races

Event	Record	Holder	Country	Date	Where made
400 mtrs. (4x100)	37.40 s.	(Marsh, Burrell, Mitchell, Lewis)	U.S.	Aug. 8, 1992	Barcelona, Spain
		(Drummond, Cason, Mitchell, Burrell)	U.S.	Aug. 21, 1993	Stuttgart, Germany
800 mtrs. (4x200)	1 m., 18.68 s.	(Marsh, Burrell, Heard, Lewis)	U.S.	Apr. 17, 1994	Walnut, CA
1,600 mtrs. (4x400)	2 m., 54.20 s.	(Young, Pettigrew, Washington, Johnson)	U.S.	July 22, 1998	Long Island, NY
3,200 mtrs. (4x800)	7 m., 03.89 s.	(Elliott, Cook, Cram, Coe)	Gr. Britain	Aug. 30, 1982	London, England

Field Events

Event	Record	Holder	Country	Date	Where made
High jump	2.45m (8' ½")	Javier Sotomayor	Cuba	July 27, 1993	Salamanca, Spain
Long jump	8.95m (29' 4½")	Mike Powell	U.S.	Aug. 30, 1991	Tokyo, Japan
Triple jump	18.29m (60' ¼")	Jonathan Edwards	Gr. Britain	Aug. 7, 1995	Göteborg, Sweden
Pole vault	6.14m (20' 1¾")	Sergei Bubka	Ukraine	July 31, 1994	Sestriere, Italy
16-lb. shot put	23.12m (75' 10¼")	Randy Barnes	U.S.	May 20, 1990	Los Angeles, CA
Discus	74.08m (243' 0")	Juergen Schult	E. Germany	June 6, 1986	Neubrandenburg, Germany
Javelin	98.48m (323' 1")	Jan Zelezny	Czech Rep.	May 25, 1996	Jena, Germany
16-lb. hammer	86.74m (284' 7")	Yuri Sedykh	USSR	Aug. 30, 1986	Stuttgart, W. Germany
Decathlon	9,026 pts.	Roman Sebrle	Czech Rep.	May 27, 2001	Götzis, Austria

Women's Records
Running

Event	Record	Holder	Country	Date	Where made
100 meters	10.49 s.	Florence Griffith Joyner	U.S.	July 16, 1988	Indianapolis, IN
200 meters	21.34 s.	Florence Griffith Joyner	U.S.	Sept. 29, 1988	Seoul, S. Korea
400 meters	47.60 s.	Marita Koch	E. Germany	Oct. 6, 1985	Canberra, Australia
800 meters	1 m., 53.28 s.	Jarmila Kratochvilova	Czech Rep.	July 26, 1983	Munich, Germany
1,000 meters	2 m., 28.98 s.	Svetlana Masterkova	Russia	Aug. 23, 1996	Brussels, Belgium
1,500 meters	3 m., 50.46 s.	Qu Yunxia	China	Sept. 11, 1993	Beijing, China
1 mile	4 m., 12.56 s.	Svetlana Masterkova	Russia	Aug. 14, 1996	Zurich, Switzerland
2,000 meters	5 m., 25.36 s.	Sonia O'Sullivan	Ireland	July 8, 1994	Edinburgh, Scotland
3,000 meters	8 m., 06.11 s.	Wang Junxia	China	Sept. 13, 1993	Beijing, China
3,000 meter stpl.	9 m., 1.59 s.	Gulnara Samitova	Russia	July 4, 2004	Iraklio, Greece
5,000 meters	14 m., 24.68 s.	Elvan Abeylegesse	Turkey	June 11, 2004	Bergen, Norway

Event	Record	Holder	Country	Date	Where made
10,000 meters	29 m., 31.78 s.	Wang Junxia	China	Sept. 8, 1993	Beijing, China
20,000 meters	1 h., 05m. 26.6 s.	Tegla Loroupe	Kenya	Sept. 3, 2000	Borgholzhausen, Germany
30,000 meters	1 h., 45 m., 50 s.	Tegla Loroupe	Kenya	June 6, 2003	Warstein, Germany
Marathon	2 h., 15 m., 25	Paula Radcliffe	Gr. Britain	April 13, 2003	London, England

Hurdles

Event	Record	Holder	Country	Date	Where made
100 meters	12.21 s.	Yordanka Donkova	Bulgaria	Aug. 20, 1988	Stara Zagora, Bulgaria
400 meters	52.34 s.	Yuliya Pechonkina	Russia	Aug. 10, 2003	Tula, Russia

Relay Races

Event	Record	Holder	Country	Date	Where made
400 mtrs. (4×100)	.41.37 s.	(Gladisch, Rieger, Auerswald, Goehr)	E. Germany	Oct. 6, 1985	Canberra, Australia
800 mtrs. (4×200)	.1 m., 27.46 s.	U.S. "Blue" (Jenkins, Clarke, Richardson, Jamieson)	U.S.	Sept. 28, 2000	Philadelphia, PA
1,600 mtrs. (4×400)	3 m., 15.17 s.	(Ledovskaya, Nazarova, Pinigina, Bryzgina)	USSR	Oct. 1, 1988	Seoul, S. Korea
3,200 mtrs. (4×800)	7 m., 50.17 s.	(Olizarenko, Gurina, Borisova, Podyalovskaya)	USSR	Aug. 5, 1984	Moscow, USSR

Field Events

Event	Record	Holder	Country	Date	Where made
High jump	2.09m (6' 10¼")	Stefka Kostadinova	Bulgaria	Aug. 30, 1987	Rome, Italy
Long jump	7.52m (24' 8¼")	Galina Chistyakova	USSR	June 11, 1988	Leningrad
Triple jump	15.50m (50' 10¼")	Inessa Kravets	Ukraine	Aug. 10, 1995	Göteborg, Sweden
Pole vault	4.92m (16' 1¾")*	Yelena Isinbayeva	Russia	Sept. 3, 2004	Brussels, Belgium
Shot put	22.63m (74' 3")	Natalya Lisovskaya	USSR	June 7, 1987	Moscow, Russia
Discus	76.80m (252' 0")	Gabriele Reinsch	E. Germany	July 9, 1988	Neubrandenburg, Germany
Hammer	76.07m (249' 7")	Mihaela Melinte	Romania	Aug. 29, 1999	Rüdlingen, Switzerland
Javelin	71.54m (234' 8")	Osleidys Menéndez	Cuba	July 1, 2001	Réthymno, Greece
Heptathlon	7,291 pts.	Jackie Joyner-Kersee	U.S.	Sept. 23-24, 1988	Seoul, S. Korea

World Track and Field Indoor Records

As of Oct. 1, 2004

The International Amateur Athletic Federation first recognized world indoor track and field records on Jan. 1, 1987. World indoor bests set prior to Jan. 1, 1987, are subject to approval as world records providing they meet the IAAF world records criteria, including drug testing. Criteria for indoor and outdoor records are the same, except that a track performance cannot be set on an indoor track larger than 200 meters. (a)=altitude.

Men's Records

Event	Record	Holder	Country	Date	Where made
50 meters	5.56 (a)	Donovan Bailey	Canada	Feb. 9, 1996	Reno, NV
	5.56	Maurice Greene	U.S	Feb. 13, 1999	Los Angeles, CA
60 meters	6.39	Maurice Greene	U.S.	Mar. 3, 2001	Atlanta, GA
	6.39	Maurice Greene	U.S.	Feb. 3, 1998	Madrid, Spain
200 meters	19.92	Frankie Fredericks	Namibia	Feb. 18, 1996	Lievin, France
400 meters	44.63	Michael Johnson	U.S.	Mar. 4, 1995	Atlanta, GA
800 meters	1:42.67	Wilson Kipketer	Denmark	Mar. 9, 1997	Paris, France
1,000 meters	2:14.96	Wilson Kipketer	Denmark	Feb. 20, 2000	Birmingham, England
1,500 meters	3:31.18	Hicham El Guerrouj	Morocco	Feb. 2, 1997	Stuttgart, Germany
1 mile	3:48.45	Hicham El Guerrouj	Morocco	Feb. 12, 1997	Ghent, Belgium
3,000 meters	7:24.90	Daniel Komen	Kenya	Feb. 6, 1998	Budapest, Hungary
5,000 meters	12:49.60	Kenenisa Bekele	Ethiopia	Feb. 20, 2004	Birmingham, England
50-meter hurdles	6.25	Mark McKoy	Canada	Mar. 5, 1986	Kobe, Japan
60-meter hurdles	7.30	Colin Jackson	Gr. Britain	Mar. 6, 1994	Sindelfingen, Germany
High jump	2.43m (7' 11½")	Javier Sotomayor	Cuba	Mar. 4, 1989	Budapest, Hungary
Pole vault	6.15m (20' 2")	Sergei Bubka	Ukraine	Feb. 21, 1993	Donyetsk, Ukraine
Long jump	8.79m (28' 10¼")	Carl Lewis	U.S.	Jan. 27, 1984	New York, NY
Triple jump	17.83 (58' 6")	Aliecer Urrutia	Cuba	Mar. 1, 1997	Sindelfingen, Germany
		Christian Olsson	Sweden	Mar. 7, 2004	Budapest, Hungary
Shot put	22.66m (74' 4¼")	Randy Barnes	U.S.	Jan. 20, 1989	Los Angeles, CA

Women's Records

Event	Record	Holder	Country	Date	Where made
50 meters	5.96	Irina Privalova	Russia	Feb. 9, 1995	Madrid, Spain
60 meters	6.92	Irina Privalova	Russia	Feb. 9, 1995	Madrid, Spain
		Irina Privalova	Russia	Feb. 11, 1993	Madrid, Spain
200 meters	21.87	Merlene Ottey	Jamaica	Feb. 13, 1993	Lievin, France
400 meters	49.59	Jarmila Kratochvilova	Czechoslovakia	Mar. 7, 1982	Milan, Italy
800 meters	1:55.82	Jolanda Ceplak	Slovenia	Mar. 3, 2002	Vienna, Austria
1,000 meters	2:30.94	Maria Mutola	Mozambique	Feb. 25, 1999	Stockholm, Sweden
1,500 meters	3:59.98	Regina Jacobs	U.S.	Feb. 1, 2003	Boston, MA
1 mile	4:17.14	Doina Melinte	Romania	Feb. 9, 1990	E. Rutherford, NJ
3,000 meters	8:29.15	Berhane Adere	Ethiopia	Mar. 3, 2002	Stuttgart, Germany
5,000 meters	14:39.29	Berhane Adere	Ethiopia	Jan. 31, 2004	Stuttgart, Germany
50-meter hurdles	6.58	Cornelia Oschkenat	E. Germany	Feb. 20, 1988	Berlin, Germany
60-meter hurdles	7.69	Lyudmila Engquist	USSR	Feb. 4, 1990	Chelyabinsk, USSR
High jump	2.07m (6' 9½")	Heike Henkel	Germany	Feb. 8, 1992	Karlsruhe, Germany
Pole vault	4.86m (15' 11¼")	Yelena Isinbayeva	Russia	Mar. 6, 2004	Budapest, Hungary
Long jump	7.37m (24' 2¼")	Heike Drechsler	E. Germany	Feb. 13, 1988	Vienna, Austria
Triple jump	15.36m (50' 4¾")	Tatyana Lebedeva	Russia	Mar. 3, 2004	Budapest, Hungary
Shot put	22.50m (73' 10")	Helena Fibingerova	Czechoslovakia	Feb. 19, 1977	Jablonec, Czechoslovakia

> **IT'S A FACT:** Russia's Yelena Isinbayeva set eight world records in the pole vault in the first nine months of 2004. She set her eighth record—4.92 meters (16 feet, 1¾ inches)—on Sept. 3, just 10 days after winning an Olympic gold medal with another record vault.

BASEBALL

Major League Baseball 2004:
Bonds Passes 700 HR; Suzuki Collects 262 Hits; Expos Set Move to D.C.

San Francisco left fielder Barry Bonds continued his assault on the record books in 2004, becoming only the 3rd player in MLB history to hit 700 home runs. He hit 45 homers on the season to finish with a career total of 703, trailing only Babe Ruth (714) and Hank Aaron (755). Bonds hit .362 to win the NL batting title, and his .609 on-base percentage broke the record of .582 that he set in 2002. Seattle right fielder Ichiro Suzuki finished the season with 262 hits, eclipsing George Sisler's 1920 mark of 257, and led MLB with a .372 batting average. Chicago pitcher Greg Maddux became the 22nd pitcher to win 300 games, finishing the season with 305. Arizona's Randy Johnson, 40, pitched a perfect game on May 18.

Atlanta extended its record for consecutive division titles, winning the NL East for the 13th straight year. St. Louis ran away with the NL Central, posting the best record (105-57) in the majors, and Los Angeles edged San Francisco for the NL West title. Houston began a 36-10 run Aug. 15 that included 18 straight home wins, and clinched the NL wild-card on Oct. 3, the final day of the season. In the AL, the Yankees won the East, with longtime rival Boston taking the wild-card. The AL West came down to a series between Anaheim and Oakland on the season's final weekend, with Anaheim winning Friday and Saturday to clinch the division. Minnesota won the AL Central title for the 3rd straight year.

MLB commissioner Bud Selig announced Sept. 29 that the long-struggling Montreal Expos franchise would be moved to D.C. in 2005. MLB also broke its 2000 overall attendance record. The new mark was 73,022,969, about 30,000 per game.

Major League Pennant Winners, 1901–1968

	National League						American League			
Year	Winner	Won	Lost	Pct	Manager	Year	Winner	Won	Lost	Pct	Manager
---	---	---	---	---	---	---	---	---	---	---	---
1901	Pittsburgh	90	49	.647	Clarke	1901	Chicago	83	53	.610	Griffith
1902	Pittsburgh	103	36	.741	Clarke	1902	Philadelphia	83	53	.610	Mack
1903	Pittsburgh	91	49	.650	Clarke	1903	Boston	91	47	.659	Collins
1904	New York	106	47	.693	McGraw	1904	Boston	95	59	.617	Collins
1905	New York	105	48	.686	McGraw	1905	Philadelphia	92	56	.622	Mack
1906	Chicago	116	36	.763	Chance	1906	Chicago	93	58	.616	Jones
1907	Chicago	107	45	.704	Chance	1907	Detroit	92	58	.613	Jennings
1908	Chicago	99	55	.643	Chance	1908	Detroit	90	63	.588	Jennings
1909	Pittsburgh	110	42	.724	Clarke	1909	Detroit	98	54	.645	Jennings
1910	Chicago	104	50	.675	Chance	1910	Philadelphia	102	48	.680	Mack
1911	New York	99	54	.647	McGraw	1911	Philadelphia	101	50	.669	Mack
1912	New York	103	48	.682	McGraw	1912	Boston	105	47	.691	Stahl
1913	New York	101	51	.664	McGraw	1913	Philadelphia	96	57	.627	Mack
1914	Boston	94	59	.614	Stallings	1914	Philadelphia	99	53	.651	Mack
1915	Philadelphia	90	62	.592	Moran	1915	Boston	101	50	.669	Carrigan
1916	Brooklyn	94	60	.610	Robinson	1916	Boston	91	63	.591	Carrigan
1917	New York	98	56	.636	McGraw	1917	Chicago	100	54	.649	Rowland
1918	Chicago	84	45	.651	Mitchell	1918	Boston	75	51	.595	Barrow
1919	Cincinnati	96	44	.686	Moran	1919	Chicago	88	52	.629	Gleason
1920	Brooklyn	93	60	.604	Robinson	1920	Cleveland	98	56	.636	Speaker
1921	New York	94	56	.614	McGraw	1921	New York	98	55	.641	Huggins
1922	New York	93	61	.604	McGraw	1922	New York	94	60	.610	Huggins
1923	New York	95	58	.621	McGraw	1923	New York	98	54	.645	Huggins
1924	New York	93	60	.608	McGraw	1924	Washington	92	62	.597	Harris
1925	Pittsburgh	95	58	.621	McKechnie	1925	Washington	96	55	.636	Harris
1926	St. Louis	89	65	.578	Hornsby	1926	New York	91	63	.591	Huggins
1927	Pittsburgh	94	60	.610	Bush	1927	New York	110	44	.714	Huggins
1928	St. Louis	95	59	.617	McKechnie	1928	New York	101	53	.656	Huggins
1929	Chicago	98	54	.645	McCarthy	1929	Philadelphia	104	46	.693	Mack
1930	St. Louis	92	62	.597	Street	1930	Philadelphia	102	52	.662	Mack
1931	St. Louis	101	53	.656	Street	1931	Philadelphia	107	45	.704	Mack
1932	Chicago	90	64	.584	Grimm	1932	New York	107	47	.695	McCarthy
1933	New York	91	61	.599	Terry	1933	Washington	99	53	.651	Cronin
1934	St. Louis	95	58	.621	Frisch	1934	Detroit	101	53	.656	Cochrane
1935	Chicago	100	54	.649	Grimm	1935	Detroit	93	58	.616	Cochrane
1936	New York	91	62	.597	Terry	1936	New York	102	51	.667	McCarthy
1937	New York	95	57	.625	Terry	1937	New York	102	52	.662	McCarthy
1938	Chicago	89	63	.586	Hartnett	1938	New York	99	53	.651	McCarthy
1939	Cincinnati	97	57	.630	McKechnie	1939	New York	106	45	.702	McCarthy
1940	Cincinnati	100	53	.654	McKechnie	1940	Detroit	90	64	.584	Baker
1941	Brooklyn	100	54	.649	Durocher	1941	New York	101	53	.656	McCarthy
1942	St. Louis	106	48	.688	Southworth	1942	New York	103	51	.669	McCarthy
1943	St. Louis	105	49	.682	Southworth	1943	New York	98	56	.636	McCarthy
1944	St. Louis	105	49	.682	Southworth	1944	St. Louis	89	65	.578	Sewell
1945	Chicago	98	56	.636	Grimm	1945	Detroit	88	65	.575	O'Neill
1946	St. Louis	98	58	.628	Dyer	1946	Boston	104	50	.675	Cronin
1947	Brooklyn	94	60	.610	Shotton	1947	New York	97	57	.630	Harris
1948	Boston	91	62	.595	Southworth	1948	Cleveland	97	58	.626	Boudreau
1949	Brooklyn	97	57	.630	Shotton	1949	New York	97	57	.630	Stengel
1950	Philadelphia	91	63	.591	Sawyer	1950	New York	98	56	.636	Stengel
1951	New York	98	59	.624	Durocher	1951	New York	98	56	.636	Stengel
1952	Brooklyn	96	57	.627	Dressen	1952	New York	95	59	.617	Stengel
1953	Brooklyn	105	49	.682	Dressen	1953	New York	99	52	.656	Stengel
1954	New York	97	57	.630	Durocher	1954	Cleveland	111	43	.721	Lopez
1955	Brooklyn	98	55	.641	Alston	1955	New York	96	58	.623	Stengel
1956	Brooklyn	93	61	.604	Alston	1956	New York	97	57	.630	Stengel
1957	Milwaukee	95	59	.617	Haney	1957	New York	98	56	.636	Stengel
1958	Milwaukee	92	62	.597	Haney	1958	New York	92	62	.597	Stengel
1959	Los Angeles	88	68	.564	Alston	1959	Chicago	94	60	.610	Lopez
1960	Pittsburgh	95	59	.617	Murtaugh	1960	New York	97	57	.630	Stengel
1961	Cincinnati	93	61	.604	Hutchinson	1961	New York	109	53	.673	Houk
1962	San Francisco	103	62	.624	Dark	1962	New York	96	66	.593	Houk
1963	Los Angeles	99	63	.611	Alston	1963	New York	104	57	.646	Houk

	National League						American League				
Year	Winner	Won	Lost	Pct	Manager	Year	Winner	Won	Lost	Pct	Manager
1964	St. Louis	93	69	.574	Keane	1964	New York	99	63	.611	Berra
1965	Los Angeles	97	65	.599	Alston	1965	Minnesota	102	60	.630	Mele
1966	Los Angeles	95	67	.586	Alston	1966	Baltimore	97	63	.606	Bauer
1967	St. Louis	101	60	.627	Schoendienst	1967	Boston	92	70	.568	Williams
1968	St. Louis	97	65	.599	Schoendienst	1968	Detroit	103	59	.636	Smith

Major League Pennant Winners, 1969-2003
National League

		East				West					Pennant
Year	Winner	W	L	Pct	Manager	Winner	W	L	Pct	Manager	Winner
1969	N.Y. Mets	100	62	.617	Hodges	Atlanta	93	69	.574	Harris	New York
1970	Pittsburgh	89	73	.549	Murtaugh	Cincinnati	102	60	.630	Anderson	Cincinnati
1971	Pittsburgh	97	65	.599	Murtaugh	San Francisco	90	72	.556	Fox	Pittsburgh
1972	Pittsburgh	96	59	.619	Virdon	Cincinnati	95	59	.617	Anderson	Cincinnati
1973	N.Y. Mets	82	79	.509	Berra	Cincinnati	99	63	.611	Anderson	New York
1974	Pittsburgh	88	74	.543	Murtaugh	Los Angeles	102	60	.630	Alston	Los Angeles
1975	Pittsburgh	92	69	.571	Murtaugh	Cincinnati	108	54	.667	Anderson	Cincinnati
1976	Philadelphia	101	61	.623	Ozark	Cincinnati	102	60	.630	Anderson	Cincinnati
1977	Philadelphia	101	61	.623	Ozark	Los Angeles	98	64	.605	Lasorda	Los Angeles
1978	Philadelphia	90	72	.556	Ozark	Los Angeles	95	67	.586	Lasorda	Los Angeles
1979	Pittsburgh	98	64	.605	Tanner	Cincinnati	90	71	.559	McNamara	Pittsburgh
1980	Philadelphia	91	71	.562	Green	Houston	93	70	.571	Virdon	Philadelphia
1981(a)	Philadelphia	34	21	.618	Green	Los Angeles	36	21	.632	Lasorda	(c)
1981(b)	Montreal	30	23	.566	Williams, Fanning	Houston	33	20	.623	Virdon	Los Angeles
1982	St. Louis	92	70	.568	Herzog	Atlanta	89	73	.549	Torre	St. Louis
1983	Philadelphia	90	72	.556	Corrales, Owens	Los Angeles	91	71	.562	Lasorda	Philadelphia
1984	Chicago	96	65	.596	Frey	San Diego	92	70	.568	Williams	San Diego
1985	St. Louis	101	61	.623	Herzog	Los Angeles	95	67	.586	Lasorda	St. Louis
1986	N.Y. Mets	108	54	.667	Johnson	Houston	96	66	.593	Lanier	New York
1987	St. Louis	95	67	.586	Herzog	San Francisco	90	72	.556	Craig	St. Louis
1988	N.Y. Mets	100	60	.625	Johnson	Los Angeles	94	67	.584	Lasorda	Los Angeles
1989	Chicago	93	69	.571	Zimmer	San Francisco	92	70	.568	Craig	San Francisco
1990	Pittsburgh	95	67	.586	Leyland	Cincinnati	91	71	.562	Piniella	Cincinnati
1991	Pittsburgh	98	64	.605	Leyland	Atlanta	94	68	.580	Cox	Atlanta
1992	Pittsburgh	96	66	.593	Leyland	Atlanta	98	64	.605	Cox	Atlanta
1993	Philadelphia	97	65	.599	Fregosi	Atlanta	104	58	.642	Cox	Philadelphia

Year	Division	Winner	W	L	Pct	Manager	Playoffs	Pennant Winner
1994(d)	East	Montreal	74	40	.649	Alou	—	—
	Central	Cincinnati	66	48	.579	Johnson		
	West	Los Angeles	58	56	.509	Lasorda		
1995	East	Atlanta	90	54	.625	Cox	Atlanta 3, Colorado* 1	Atlanta
	Central	Cincinnati	85	59	.590	Johnson	Cincinnati 3, Los Angeles 0	
	West	Los Angeles	78	66	.542	Lasorda	Atlanta 4, Cincinnati 0	
1996	East	Atlanta	96	66	.593	Cox	Atlanta 3, Los Angeles* 0	Atlanta
	Central	St. Louis	88	74	.543	La Russa	St. Louis 3, San Diego 0	
	West	San Diego	91	71	.562	Bochy	Atlanta 4, St. Louis 3	
1997	East	Atlanta	101	61	.623	Cox	Atlanta 3, Houston 0	Florida* (e)
	Central	Houston	84	78	.519	Dierker	Florida* 3, San Francisco 0	
	West	San Francisco	90	72	.556	Baker	Florida* 4, Atlanta 2	
1998	East	Atlanta	106	56	.654	Cox	Atlanta 3, Chicago* 0	San Diego
	Central	Houston	102	60	.630	Dierker	San Diego 3, Houston 1	
	West	San Diego	97	64	.602	Bochy	San Diego 4, Atlanta 2	
1999	East	Atlanta	103	59	.636	Cox	Atlanta 3, Houston 1	Atlanta
	Central	Houston	97	65	.599	Dierker	New York* 3, Arizona 1	
	West	Arizona	100	62	.617	Showalter	Atlanta 4, New York 2	
2000	East	Atlanta	95	67	.586	Cox	St. Louis 3, Atlanta 0	New York* (f)
	Central	St. Louis	95	67	.586	La Russa	New York* 3, San Francisco 1	
	West	San Francisco	97	65	.599	Baker	New York* 4, St. Louis 1	
2001	East	Atlanta	88	74	.543	Cox	Atlanta 3, Houston 0	Arizona
	Central	Houston	93	69	.574	Dierker	Arizona 3, St. Louis* 2	
	West	Arizona	92	70	.568	Brenly	Arizona 4, Atlanta 1	
2002	East	Atlanta	101	59	.631	Cox	St. Louis 3, Arizona 0	San Francisco* (g)
	Central	St. Louis	97	65	.599	La Russa	San Francisco* 3, Atlanta 2	
	West	Arizona	98	64	.605	Brenly	San Francisco 4, St. Louis 1	
2003	East	Atlanta	101	61	.623	Cox	Chicago 3, Atlanta 2	Florida*(i)
	Central	Chicago	88	74	.543	Baker	Florida* 3, San Francisco 2	
	West	San Francisco	100	61	.621	Alou	Florida* 4, Chicago 3	
2004	East	Atlanta	96	66	.593	Cox	Houston* 3, Atlanta 2	(j)
	Central	St. Louis	105	57	.648	La Russa	St. Louis 3, Dodgers 1	
	West	Los Angeles	93	69	.594	Tracy	(j)	

American League

		East				West					Pennant
Year	Winner	W	L	Pct	Manager	Winner	W	L	Pct	Manager	Winner
1969	Baltimore	109	53	.673	Weaver	Minnesota	97	65	.599	Martin	Baltimore
1970	Baltimore	108	54	.667	Weaver	Minnesota	98	64	.605	Rigney	Baltimore
1971	Baltimore	101	57	.639	Weaver	Oakland	101	60	.627	Williams	Baltimore
1972	Detroit	86	70	.551	Martin	Oakland	93	62	.600	Williams	Oakland
1973	Baltimore	97	65	.599	Weaver	Oakland	94	68	.580	Williams	Oakland
1974	Baltimore	91	71	.562	Weaver	Oakland	90	72	.556	Dark	Oakland
1975	Boston	95	65	.594	Johnson	Oakland	98	64	.605	Dark	Boston
1976	New York	97	62	.610	Martin	Kansas City	90	72	.556	Herzog	New York

Year	Winner (East)	W	L	Pct	Manager	Winner (West)	W	L	Pct	Manager	Pennant Winner
1977	New York	100	62	.617	Martin	Kansas City	102	60	.630	Herzog	New York
1978	New York	100	63	.613	Martin, Lemon	Kansas City	92	70	.568	Herzog	New York
1979	Baltimore	102	57	.642	Weaver	California	88	74	.543	Fregosi	Baltimore
1980	New York	103	59	.636	Howser	Kansas City	97	65	.599	Frey	Kansas City
1981(a)	New York	34	22	.607	Michael	Oakland	37	23	.617	Martin	(c)
1981(b)	Milwaukee	31	22	.585	Rodgers	Kansas City	30	23	.566	Frey, Howser	New York
1982	Milwaukee	95	67	.586	Rodgers, Kuenn	California	93	69	.574	Mauch	Milwaukee
1983	Baltimore	98	64	.605	Altobelli	Chicago	99	63	.611	La Russa	Baltimore
1984	Detroit	104	58	.642	Anderson	Kansas City	84	78	.519	Howser	Detroit
1985	Toronto	99	62	.615	Cox	Kansas City	91	71	.562	Howser	Kansas City
1986	Boston	95	66	.590	McNamara	California	92	70	.568	Mauch	Boston
1987	Detroit	98	64	.605	Anderson	Minnesota	85	77	.525	Kelly	Minnesota
1988	Boston	89	73	.549	McNamara, Morgan	Oakland	104	58	.642	La Russa	Oakland
1989	Toronto	89	73	.549	Williams, Gaston	Oakland	99	63	.611	La Russa	Oakland
1990	Boston	88	74	.543	Morgan	Oakland	103	59	.636	La Russa	Oakland
1991	Toronto	91	71	.562	Gaston	Minnesota	95	67	.586	Kelly	Minnesota
1992	Toronto	96	66	.593	Gaston	Oakland	96	66	.593	La Russa	Toronto
1993	Toronto	95	67	.586	Gaston	Chicago	94	68	.580	Lamont	Toronto

Year	Division	Winner	W	L	Pct	Manager	Playoffs	Pennant Winner
1994(d)	East	New York	70	43	.619	Showalter	—	—
	Central	Chicago	67	46	.593	Lamont		
	West	Texas	52	62	.456	Kennedy		
1995	East	Boston	86	58	.597	Kennedy	Cleveland 3, Boston 0	Cleveland
	Central	Cleveland	100	44	.694	Hargrove	Seattle 3, New York* 2	
	West	Seattle	79	66	.545	Piniella	Cleveland 4, Seattle 2	
1996	East	New York	92	70	.568	Torre	Baltimore* 3, Cleveland 1	New York
	Central	Cleveland	99	62	.615	Hargrove	New York 3, Texas 1	
	West	Texas	90	72	.556	Oates	New York 4, Baltimore* 1	
1997	East	Baltimore	98	64	.605	Johnson	Baltimore 3, Seattle 1	Cleveland
	Central	Cleveland	86	75	.534	Hargrove	Cleveland 3, New York* 2	
	West	Seattle	90	72	.556	Piniella	Cleveland 4, Baltimore 2	
1998	East	New York	114	48	.704	Torre	New York 3, Texas 0	New York
	Central	Cleveland	89	73	.549	Hargrove	Cleveland 3, Boston* 1	
	West	Texas	88	74	.543	Oates	New York 4, Cleveland 2	
1999	East	New York	98	64	.605	Torre	New York 3, Texas 0	New York
	Central	Cleveland	97	65	.599	Hargrove	Boston* 3, Cleveland 2	
	West	Texas	95	67	.586	Oates	New York 4, Boston* 1	
2000	East	New York	87	74	.540	Torre	New York 3, Oakland 2	New York
	Central	Chicago	95	67	.586	Manuel	Seattle* 3, Chicago 0	
	West	Oakland	91	70	.565	Howe	New York 4, Seattle* 2	
2001	East	New York	95	65	.594	Torre	Seattle 3, Cleveland 2	New York
	Central	Cleveland	91	71	.562	Manuel	New York 3, Oakland 2	
	West	Seattle	116	46	.716	Piniella	New York 4, Seattle* 1	
2002	East	New York	103	58	.640	Torre	Anaheim* 3, New York 1	Anaheim* (h)
	Central	Minnesota	94	67	.584	Gardenhire	Minnesota 3, Oakland 2	
	West	Oakland	103	59	.636	Howe	Anaheim* 4, Minnesota 1	
2003	East	New York	101	61	.623	Torre	New York 3, Minnesota 1	New York
	Central	Minnesota	90	72	.556	Gardenhire	Boston* 3, Oakland 2	
	West	Oakland	96	66	.593	Macha	New York 4, Boston* 3	
2004	East	New York	101	61	.623	Torre	New York 3, Minnesota 1	(j)
	Central	Minnesota	92	70	.568	Gardenhire	Boston* 3, Anaheim 0	
	West	Anaheim	92	70	.568	Scioscia	(j)	

*Wild card team. (a) First half. (b) Second half. (c) Montreal, L.A., N.Y. Yankees, and Oakland won the divisional playoffs. (d) In Aug. 1994, a players' strike began that caused the cancellation of the remainder of the season, the playoffs, and the World Series. Teams listed as division "winners" for 1994 were leading their divisions at the time of the strike. (e) Florida manager: Jim Leyland. (f) New York manager Bobby Valentine. (g) San Francisco manager: Dusty Baker. (h) Anaheim manager: Mike Scioscia. (i) Florida manager: Jack McKeon. (j) Not decided at press time.

Home Run Leaders

Note: Asterisk (*) indicates the all-time single-season record for each league.

National League

Year	Player, Team	HR
1901	Sam Crawford, Cincinnati	16
1902	Thomas Leach, Pittsburgh	6
1903	James Sheckard, Brooklyn	9
1904	Harry Lumley, Brooklyn	9
1905	Fred Odwell, Cincinnati	9
1906	Timothy Jordan, Brooklyn	12
1907	David Brain, Boston	10
1908	Timothy Jordan, Brooklyn	12
1909	Red Murray, New York	7
1910	Fred Beck, Boston; Frank Schulte, Chicago	10
1911	Frank Schulte, Chicago	21
1912	Henry Zimmerman, Chicago	14
1913	Gavvy Cravath, Philadelphia	19
1914	Gavvy Cravath, Philadelphia	19
1915	Gavvy Cravath, Philadelphia	24
1916	Dave Robertson, N.Y.; Fred (Cy) Williams, Chi.	12
1917	Dave Robertson, N.Y.; Gavvy Cravath, Phi.	12
1918	Gavvy Cravath, Philadelphia	8
1919	Gavvy Cravath, Philadelphia	12
1920	Cy Williams, Philadelphia	15
1921	George Kelly, New York	23
1922	Rogers Hornsby, St. Louis	42
1923	Cy Williams, Philadelphia	41

American League

Year	Player, Team	HR
1901	Napoleon Lajoie, Philadelphia	13
1902	Socks Seybold, Philadelphia	16
1903	Buck Freeman, Boston	13
1904	Harry Davis, Philadelphia	10
1905	Harry Davis, Philadelphia	8
1906	Harry Davis, Philadelphia	12
1907	Harry Davis, Philadelphia	8
1908	Sam Crawford, Detroit	7
1909	Ty Cobb, Detroit	9
1910	Jake Stahl, Boston	10
1911	J. Franklin Baker, Philadelphia	9
1912	J. Franklin Baker, Philadelphia; Tris Speaker, Boston	10
1913	J. Franklin Baker, Philadelphia	13
1914	J. Franklin Baker, Philadelphia	9
1915	Robert Roth, Chicago-Cleveland	7
1916	Wally Pipp, New York	12
1917	Wally Pipp, New York	9
1918	Babe Ruth, Boston; Tilly Walker, Philadelphia	11
1919	Babe Ruth, Boston	29
1920	Babe Ruth, New York	54
1921	Babe Ruth, New York	59
1922	Ken Williams, St. Louis	39
1923	Babe Ruth, New York	41

National League			American League		
Year	Player, Team	HR	Year	Player, Team	HR
1924	Jacques Fournier, Brooklyn	27	1924	Babe Ruth, New York	46
1925	Rogers Hornsby, St. Louis	39	1925	Bob Meusel, New York	33
1926	Hack Wilson, Chicago	21	1926	Babe Ruth, New York	47
1927	Hack Wilson, Chicago; Cy Williams, Philadelphia	30	1927	Babe Ruth, New York	60
1928	Hack Wilson, Chicago; Jim Bottomley, St. Louis	31	1928	Babe Ruth, New York	54
1929	Chuck Klein, Philadelphia	43	1929	Babe Ruth, New York	46
1930	Hack Wilson, Chicago	56	1930	Babe Ruth, New York	49
1931	Chuck Klein, Philadelphia	31	1931	Babe Ruth, Lou Gehrig, both New York	46
1932	Chuck Klein, Philadelphia; Mel Ott, New York	38	1932	Jimmie Foxx, Philadelphia	58
1933	Chuck Klein, Philadelphia	28	1933	Jimmie Foxx, Philadelphia	48
1934	Rip Collins, St. Louis; Mel Ott, New York	35	1934	Lou Gehrig, New York	49
1935	Walter Berger, Boston	34	1935	Jimmie Foxx, Philadelphia; Hank Greenberg, Detroit	36
1936	Mel Ott, New York	33	1936	Lou Gehrig, New York	49
1937	Mel Ott, New York; Joe Medwick, St. Louis	31	1937	Joe DiMaggio, New York	46
1938	Mel Ott, New York	36	1938	Hank Greenberg, Detroit	58
1939	John Mize, St. Louis	28	1939	Jimmie Foxx, Boston	35
1940	John Mize, St. Louis	43	1940	Hank Greenberg, Detroit	41
1941	Dolph Camilli, Brooklyn	34	1941	Ted Williams, Boston	37
1942	Mel Ott, New York	30	1942	Ted Williams, Boston	36
1943	Bill Nicholson, Chicago	29	1943	Rudy York, Detroit	34
1944	Bill Nicholson, Chicago	33	1944	Nick Etten, New York	22
1945	Tommy Holmes, Boston	28	1945	Vern Stephens, St. Louis	24
1946	Ralph Kiner, Pittsburgh	23	1946	Hank Greenberg, Detroit	44
1947	Ralph Kiner, Pittsburgh; John Mize, New York	51	1947	Ted Williams, Boston	32
1948	Ralph Kiner, Pittsburgh; John Mize, New York	40	1948	Joe DiMaggio, New York	39
1949	Ralph Kiner, Pittsburgh	54	1949	Ted Williams, Boston	43
1950	Ralph Kiner, Pittsburgh	47	1950	Al Rosen, Cleveland	37
1951	Ralph Kiner, Pittsburgh	42	1951	Gus Zernial, Chicago-Philadelphia	33
1952	Ralph Kiner, Pittsburgh; Hank Sauer, Chicago	37	1952	Larry Doby, Cleveland	32
1953	Ed Mathews, Milwaukee	47	1953	Al Rosen, Cleveland	43
1954	Ted Kluszewski, Cincinnati	49	1954	Larry Doby, Cleveland	32
1955	Willie Mays, New York	51	1955	Mickey Mantle, New York	37
1956	Duke Snider, Brooklyn	43	1956	Mickey Mantle, New York	52
1957	Hank Aaron, Milwaukee	44	1957	Roy Sievers, Washington	42
1958	Ernie Banks, Chicago	47	1958	Mickey Mantle, New York	42
1959	Ed Mathews, Milwaukee	46	1959	Rocky Colavito, Cleve.; Harmon Killebrew, Wash.	42
1960	Ernie Banks, Chicago	41	1960	Mickey Mantle, New York	40
1961	Orlando Cepeda, San Francisco	46	1961	Roger Maris, New York	*61
1962	Willie Mays, San Francisco	49	1962	Harmon Killebrew, Minnesota	48
1963	Hank Aaron, Milwaukee; Willie McCovey, S.F.	44	1963	Harmon Killebrew, Minnesota	45
1964	Willie Mays, San Francisco	47	1964	Harmon Killebrew, Minnesota	49
1965	Willie Mays, San Francisco	52	1965	Tony Conigliaro, Boston	32
1966	Hank Aaron, Atlanta	44	1966	Frank Robinson, Baltimore	49
1967	Hank Aaron, Atlanta	39	1967	Carl Yastrzemski, Boston; Harmon Killebrew, Minn.	44
1968	Willie McCovey, San Francisco	36	1968	Frank Howard, Washington	44
1969	Willie McCovey, San Francisco	45	1969	Harmon Killebrew, Minnesota	49
1970	Johnny Bench, Cincinnati	45	1970	Frank Howard, Washington	44
1971	Willie Stargell, Pittsburgh	48	1971	Bill Melton, Chicago	33
1972	Johnny Bench, Cincinnati	40	1972	Dick Allen, Chicago	37
1973	Willie Stargell, Pittsburgh	44	1973	Reggie Jackson, Oakland	32
1974	Mike Schmidt, Philadelphia	36	1974	Dick Allen, Chicago	32
1975	Mike Schmidt, Philadelphia	38	1975	George Scott, Milwaukee; Reggie Jackson, Oakland	36
1976	Mike Schmidt, Philadelphia	38	1976	Graig Nettles, New York	32
1977	George Foster, Cincinnati	52	1977	Jim Rice, Boston	39
1978	George Foster, Cincinnati	40	1978	Jim Rice, Boston	46
1979	Dave Kingman, Chicago	48	1979	Gorman Thomas, Milwaukee	45
1980	Mike Schmidt, Philadelphia	48	1980	Reggie Jackson, New York; Ben Oglivie, Milwaukee	41
1981	Mike Schmidt, Philadelphia	31	1981	Bobby Grich, California; Tony Armas, Oakland; Dwight Evans, Boston; Eddie Murray, Baltimore	22
1982	Dave Kingman, New York	37	1982	Gorman Thomas, Milwaukee; Reggie Jackson, Cal.	39
1983	Mike Schmidt, Philadelphia	40	1983	Jim Rice, Boston	39
1984	Mike Schmidt, Phi.; Dale Murphy, Atlanta	36	1984	Tony Armas, Boston	43
1985	Dale Murphy, Atlanta	37	1985	Darrell Evans, Detroit	40
1986	Mike Schmidt, Philadelphia	37	1986	Jesse Barfield, Toronto	40
1987	Andre Dawson, Chicago	49	1987	Mark McGwire, Oakland	49
1988	Darryl Strawberry, New York	39	1988	Jose Canseco, Oakland	42
1989	Kevin Mitchell, San Francisco	47	1989	Fred McGriff, Toronto	36
1990	Ryne Sandberg, Chicago	40	1990	Cecil Fielder, Detroit	51
1991	Howard Johnson, New York	38	1991	Cecil Fielder, Detroit; Jose Canseco, Oakland	44
1992	Fred McGriff, San Diego	35	1992	Juan Gonzalez, Texas	43
1993	Barry Bonds, San Francisco	46	1993	Juan Gonzalez, Texas	46
1994	Matt Williams, San Francisco	43	1994	Ken Griffey Jr., Seattle	40
1995	Dante Bichette, Colorado	40	1995	Albert Belle, Cleveland	50
1996	Andres Galarraga, Colorado	47	1996	Mark McGwire, Oakland	52
1997[1]	Larry Walker, Colorado	49	1997[1]	Ken Griffey Jr., Seattle	56
1998	Mark McGwire, St. Louis	70	1998	Ken Griffey Jr., Seattle	56
1999	Mark McGwire, St. Louis	65	1999	Ken Griffey Jr., Seattle	48
2000	Sammy Sosa, Chicago	50	2000	Troy Glaus, Anaheim	47
2001	Barry Bonds, San Francisco	*73	2001	Alex Rodriguez, Texas	52
2002	Sammy Sosa, Chicago	49	2002	Alex Rodriguez, Texas	57
2003	Jim Thome, Philadelphia	47	2003	Alex Rodriguez, Texas	47
2004	Adrian Beltre, Los Angeles	48	2004	Manny Ramirez, Boston	43

(1) In 1997, Mark McGwire hit 58 home runs; 34 with the Oakland Athletics (AL) and 24 with the St. Louis Cardinals (NL).

Runs Batted In Leaders

Note: Asterisk (*) indicates the all-time single-season record for each league since beginning of "modern" era in 1901.

National League Year	Player, Team	RBI	American League Year	Player, Team	RBI
1907	Sherwood Magee, Philadelphia	85	1907	Ty Cobb, Detroit	116
1908	Honus Wagner, Pittsburgh	109	1908	Ty Cobb, Detroit	108
1909	Honus Wagner, Pittsburgh	100	1909	Ty Cobb, Detroit	107
1910	Sherwood Magee, Philadelphia	123	1910	Sam Crawford, Detroit	120
1911	Frank Schulte, Chicago	121	1911	Ty Cobb, Detroit	144
1912	Henry Zimmerman, Chicago	103	1912	J. Franklin Baker, Philadelphia	133
1913	Gavvy Cravath, Philadelphia	128	1913	J. Franklin Baker, Philadelphia	126
1914	Sherwood Magee, Philadelphia	103	1914	Sam Crawford, Detroit	104
1915	Gavvy Cravath, Philadelphia	115	1915	Sam Crawford, Detroit; Robert Veach, Detroit	112
1916	Henry Zimmerman, Chicago-New York	83	1916	Del Pratt, St. Louis	103
1917	Henry Zimmerman, New York	102	1917	Robert Veach, Detroit	103
1918	Sherwood Magee, Philadelphia	76	1918	Robert Veach, Detroit	78
1919	Hi Myers, Boston	73	1919	Babe Ruth, Boston	114
1920	George Kelly, N.Y.; Rogers Hornsby, St. Louis	94	1920	Babe Ruth, New York	137
1921	Rogers Hornsby, St. Louis	126	1921	Babe Ruth, New York	171
1922	Rogers Hornsby, St. Louis	152	1922	Ken Williams, St. Louis	155
1923	Emil Meusel, New York	125	1923	Babe Ruth, New York	131
1924	George Kelly, New York	136	1924	Goose Goslin, Washington	129
1925	Rogers Hornsby, St. Louis	143	1925	Bob Meusel, New York	138
1926	Jim Bottomley, St. Louis	120	1926	Babe Ruth, New York	145
1927	Paul Waner, Pittsburgh	131	1927	Lou Gehrig, New York	175
1928	Jim Bottomley, St. Louis	136	1928	Babe Ruth, New York; Lou Gehrig, New York	142
1929	Hack Wilson, Chicago	159	1929	Al Simmons, Philadelphia	157
1930	Hack Wilson, Chicago	*191	1930	Lou Gehrig, New York	174
1931	Chuck Klein, Philadelphia	121	1931	Lou Gehrig, New York	*184
1932	Don Hurst, Philadelphia	143	1932	Jimmie Foxx, Philadelphia	169
1933	Chuck Klein, Philadelphia	120	1933	Jimmie Foxx, Philadelphia	163
1934	Mel Ott, New York	135	1934	Lou Gehrig, New York	165
1935	Walter Berger, Boston	130	1935	Hank Greenberg, Detroit	170
1936	Joe Medwick, St. Louis	138	1936	Hal Trosky, Cleveland	162
1937	Joe Medwick, St. Louis	154	1937	Hank Greenberg, Detroit	183
1938	Joe Medwick, St. Louis	122	1938	Jimmie Foxx, Boston	175
1939	Frank McCormick, Cincinnati	128	1939	Ted Williams, Boston	145
1940	John Mize, St. Louis	137	1940	Hank Greenberg, Detroit	150
1941	Adolph Camilli, Brooklyn	120	1941	Joe DiMaggio, New York	125
1942	John Mize, New York	110	1942	Ted Williams, Boston	137
1943	Bill Nicholson, Chicago	128	1943	Rudy York, Detroit	118
1944	Bill Nicholson, Chicago	122	1944	Vern Stephens, St. Louis	109
1945	Dixie Walker, Brooklyn	124	1945	Nick Etten, New York	111
1946	Enos Slaughter, St. Louis	130	1946	Hank Greenberg, Detroit	127
1947	John Mize, New York	138	1947	Ted Williams, Boston	114
1948	Stan Musial, St. Louis	131	1948	Joe DiMaggio, New York	155
1949	Ralph Kiner, Pittsburgh	127	1949	Ted Williams, Bos.; Vern Stephens, Bos.	159
1950	Del Ennis, Philadelphia	126	1950	Walt Dropo, Bos.; Vern Stephens, Bos.	144
1951	Monte Irvin, New York	121	1951	Gus Zernial, Chicago-Philadelphia	129
1952	Hank Sauer, Chicago	121	1952	Al Rosen, Cleveland	105
1953	Roy Campanella, Brooklyn	142	1953	Al Rosen, Cleveland	145
1954	Ted Kluszewski, Cincinnati	141	1954	Larry Doby, Cleveland	126
1955	Duke Snider, Brooklyn	136	1955	Ray Boone, Detroit; Jackie Jensen, Boston	116
1956	Stan Musial, St. Louis	109	1956	Mickey Mantle, New York	130
1957	Hank Aaron, Milwaukee	132	1957	Roy Sievers, Washington	114
1958	Ernie Banks, Chicago	129	1958	Jackie Jensen, Boston	122
1959	Ernie Banks, Chicago	143	1959	Jackie Jensen, Boston	112
1960	Hank Aaron, Milwaukee	126	1960	Roger Maris, New York	112
1961	Orlando Cepeda, San Francisco	142	1961	Roger Maris, New York	142
1962	Tommy Davis, Los Angeles	153	1962	Harmon Killebrew, Minnesota	126
1963	Hank Aaron, Milwaukee	130	1963	Dick Stuart, Boston	118
1964	Ken Boyer, St. Louis	119	1964	Brooks Robinson, Baltimore	118
1965	Deron Johnson, Cincinnati	130	1965	Rocky Colavito, Cleveland	108
1966	Hank Aaron, Atlanta	127	1966	Frank Robinson, Baltimore	122
1967	Orlando Cepeda, St. Louis	111	1967	Carl Yastrzemski, Boston	121
1968	Willie McCovey, San Francisco	105	1968	Ken Harrelson, Boston	109
1969	Willie McCovey, San Francisco	126	1969	Harmon Killebrew, Minnesota	140
1970	Johnny Bench, Cincinnati	148	1970	Frank Howard, Washington	126
1971	Joe Torre, St. Louis	137	1971	Harmon Killebrew, Minnesota	119
1972	Johnny Bench, Cincinnati	125	1972	Dick Allen, Chicago	113
1973	Willie Stargell, Pittsburgh	119	1973	Reggie Jackson, Oakland	117
1974	Johnny Bench, Cincinnati	129	1974	Jeff Burroughs, Texas	118
1975	Greg Luzinski, Philadelphia	120	1975	George Scott, Milwaukee	109
1976	George Foster, Cincinnati	121	1976	Lee May, Baltimore	109
1977	George Foster, Cincinnati	149	1977	Larry Hisle, Minnesota	119
1978	George Foster, Cincinnati	120	1978	Jim Rice, Boston	139
1979	Dave Winfield, San Diego	118	1979	Don Baylor, California	139
1980	Mike Schmidt, Philadelphia	121	1980	Cecil Cooper, Milwaukee	122
1981	Mike Schmidt, Philadelphia	91	1981	Eddie Murray, Baltimore	78
1982	Dale Murphy, Atlanta; Al Oliver, Montreal	109	1982	Hal McRae, Kansas City	133
1983	Dale Murphy, Atlanta	121	1983	Cecil Cooper, Milwaukee; Jim Rice, Boston	126
1984	Gary Carter, Montreal; Mike Schmidt, Phi.	106	1984	Tony Armas, Boston	123
1985	Dave Parker, Cincinnati	125	1985	Don Mattingly, New York	145
1986	Mike Schmidt, Philadelphia	119	1986	Joe Carter, Cleveland	121
1987	Andre Dawson, Chicago	137	1987	George Bell, Toronto	134
1988	Will Clark, San Francisco	109	1988	Jose Canseco, Oakland	124
1989	Kevin Mitchell, San Francisco	125	1989	Ruben Sierra, Texas	119
1990	Matt Williams, San Francisco	122	1990	Cecil Fielder, Detroit	132
1991	Howard Johnson, New York	117	1991	Cecil Fielder, Detroit	133

National League		American League	
Year Player, Team	RBI	Year Player, Team	RBI
1992 Darren Daulton, Philadelphia	109	1992 Cecil Fielder, Detroit	124
1993 Barry Bonds, San Francisco	123	1993 Albert Belle, Cleveland	129
1994 Jeff Bagwell, Houston	116	1994 Kirby Puckett, Minnesota	112
1995 Dante Bichette, Colorado	128	1995 Albert Belle, Cleveland; Mo Vaughn, Boston	126
1996 Andres Galarraga, Colorado	150	1996 Albert Belle, Cleveland	148
1997 Andres Galarraga, Colorado	140	1997 Ken Griffey Jr., Seattle	147
1998 Sammy Sosa, Chicago	158	1998 Juan Gonzalez, Texas	157
1999 Mark McGwire, St. Louis	147	1999 Manny Ramirez, Cleveland	165
2000 Todd Helton, Colorado	147	2000 Edgar Martinez, Seattle	145
2001 Sammy Sosa, Chicago	160	2001 Bret Boone, Seattle	141
2002 Lance Berkman, Houston	128	2002 Alex Rodriguez, Texas	142
2003 Preston Wilson, Colorado	141	2003 Carlos Delgado, Toronto	145
2004 Vinny Castilla, Colorado	131	2004 Miguel Tejada, Baltimore	150

Batting Champions

Note: Asterisk (*) indicates the all-time single-season record for each league since the beginning of the "modern" era in 1901.

National League				American League			
Year	Player	Team	Avg.	Year	Player	Team	Avg.
1901	Jesse C. Burkett	St. Louis	.382	1901	Napoleon Lajoie	Philadelphia	*.426
1902	Clarence Beaumont	Pittsburgh	.357	1902	Ed Delahanty	Washington	.376
1903	Honus Wagner	Pittsburgh	.355	1903	Napoleon Lajoie	Cleveland	.355
1904	Honus Wagner	Pittsburgh	.349	1904	Napoleon Lajoie	Cleveland	.381
1905	James Seymour	Cincinnati	.377	1905	Elmer Flick	Cleveland	.306
1906	Honus Wagner	Pittsburgh	.339	1906	George Stone	St. Louis	.358
1907	Honus Wagner	Pittsburgh	.350	1907	Ty Cobb	Detroit	.350
1908	Honus Wagner	Pittsburgh	.354	1908	Ty Cobb	Detroit	.324
1909	Honus Wagner	Pittsburgh	.339	1909	Ty Cobb	Detroit	.377
1910	Sherwood Magee	Philadelphia	.331	1910¹	Ty Cobb	Detroit	.385
1911	Honus Wagner	Pittsburgh	.334	1911	Ty Cobb	Detroit	.420
1912	Henry Zimmerman	Chicago	.372	1912	Ty Cobb	Detroit	.410
1913	Jacob Daubert	Brooklyn	.350	1913	Ty Cobb	Detroit	.390
1914	Jacob Daubert	Brooklyn	.329	1914	Ty Cobb	Detroit	.368
1915	Larry Doyle	New York	.320	1915	Ty Cobb	Detroit	.369
1916	Hal Chase	Cincinnati	.339	1916	Tris Speaker	Cleveland	.386
1917	Edd Roush	Cincinnati	.341	1917	Ty Cobb	Detroit	.383
1918	Zach Wheat	Brooklyn	.335	1918	Ty Cobb	Detroit	.382
1919	Edd Roush	Cincinnati	.321	1919	Ty Cobb	Detroit	.384
1920	Rogers Hornsby	St. Louis	.370	1920	George Sisler	St. Louis	.407
1921	Rogers Hornsby	St. Louis	.397	1921	Harry Heilmann	Detroit	.394
1922	Rogers Hornsby	St. Louis	.401	1922	George Sisler	St. Louis	.420
1923	Rogers Hornsby	St. Louis	.384	1923	Harry Heilmann	Detroit	.403
1924	Rogers Hornsby	St. Louis	*.424	1924	Babe Ruth	New York	.378
1925	Rogers Hornsby	St. Louis	.403	1925	Harry Heilmann	Detroit	.393
1926	Eugene Hargrave	Cincinnati	.353	1926	Henry Manush	Detroit	.378
1927	Paul Waner	Pittsburgh	.380	1927	Harry Heilmann	Detroit	.398
1928	Rogers Hornsby	Boston	.387	1928	Goose Goslin	Washington	.379
1929	Lefty O'Doul	Philadelphia	.398	1929	Lew Fonseca	Cleveland	.369
1930	Bill Terry	New York	.401	1930	Al Simmons	Philadelphia	.381
1931	Chick Hafey	St. Louis	.349	1931	Al Simmons	Philadelphia	.390
1932	Lefty O'Doul	Brooklyn	.368	1932	Dale Alexander	Detroit-Boston	.367
1933	Chuck Klein	Philadelphia	.368	1933	Jimmie Foxx	Philadelphia	.356
1934	Paul Waner	Pittsburgh	.362	1934	Lou Gehrig	New York	.363
1935	Arky Vaughan	Pittsburgh	.385	1935	Buddy Myer	Washington	.349
1936	Paul Waner	Pittsburgh	.373	1936	Luke Appling	Chicago	.388
1937	Joe Medwick	St. Louis	.374	1937	Charlie Gehringer	Detroit	.371
1938	Ernie Lombardi	Cincinnati	.342	1938	Jimmie Foxx	Boston	.349
1939	John Mize	St. Louis	.349	1939	Joe DiMaggio	New York	.381
1940	Debs Garms	Pittsburgh	.355	1940	Joe DiMaggio	New York	.352
1941	Pete Reiser	Brooklyn	.343	1941	Ted Williams	Boston	.406
1942	Ernie Lombardi	Boston	.330	1942	Ted Williams	Boston	.356
1943	Stan Musial	St. Louis	.357	1943	Luke Appling	Chicago	.328
1944	Dixie Walker	Brooklyn	.357	1944	Lou Boudreau	Cleveland	.327
1945	Phil Cavarretta	Chicago	.355	1945	George Stirnweiss	New York	.309
1946	Stan Musial	St. Louis	.365	1946	Mickey Vernon	Washington	.353
1947	Harry Walker	St.L.-Phi.	.363	1947	Ted Williams	Boston	.343
1948	Stan Musial	St. Louis	.376	1948	Ted Williams	Boston	.369
1949	Jackie Robinson	Brooklyn	.342	1949	George Kell	Detroit	.343
1950	Stan Musial	St. Louis	.346	1950	Billy Goodman	Boston	.354
1951	Stan Musial	St. Louis	.355	1951	Ferris Fain	Philadelphia	.344
1952	Stan Musial	St. Louis	.336	1952	Ferris Fain	Philadelphia	.327
1953	Carl Furillo	Brooklyn	.344	1953	Mickey Vernon	Washington	.337
1954	Willie Mays	New York	.345	1954	Roberto Avila	Cleveland	.341
1955	Richie Ashburn	Philadelphia	.338	1955	Al Kaline	Detroit	.340
1956	Hank Aaron	Milwaukee	.328	1956	Mickey Mantle	New York	.353
1957	Stan Musial	St. Louis	.351	1957	Ted Williams	Boston	.388
1958	Richie Ashburn	Philadelphia	.350	1958	Ted Williams	Boston	.328
1959	Hank Aaron	Milwaukee	.355	1959	Harvey Kuenn	Detroit	.353
1960	Dick Groat	Pittsburgh	.325	1960	Pete Runnels	Boston	.320
1961	Roberto Clemente	Pittsburgh	.351	1961	Norm Cash	Detroit	.361
1962	Tommy Davis	Los Angeles	.346	1962	Pete Runnels	Boston	.326
1963	Tommy Davis	Los Angeles	.326	1963	Carl Yastrzemski	Boston	.321
1964	Roberto Clemente	Pittsburgh	.339	1964	Tony Oliva	Minnesota	.323
1965	Roberto Clemente	Pittsburgh	.329	1965	Tony Oliva	Minnesota	.321
1966	Matty Alou	Pittsburgh	.342	1966	Frank Robinson	Baltimore	.316
1967	Roberto Clemente	Pittsburgh	.357	1967	Carl Yastrzemski	Boston	.326
1968	Pete Rose	Cincinnati	.335	1968	Carl Yastrzemski	Boston	.301
1969	Pete Rose	Cincinnati	.348	1969	Rod Carew	Minnesota	.332

National League				American League		
Year	Player	Team	Avg.	Year	Player	Team	Avg.
1970	Rico Carty	Atlanta	.366	1970	Alex Johnson	California	.329
1971	Joe Torre	St. Louis	.363	1971	Tony Oliva	Minnesota	.337
1972	Billy Williams	Chicago	.333	1972	Rod Carew	Minnesota	.318
1973	Pete Rose	Cincinnati	.338	1973	Rod Carew	Minnesota	.350
1974	Ralph Garr	Atlanta	.353	1974	Rod Carew	Minnesota	.364
1975	Bill Madlock	Chicago	.354	1975	Rod Carew	Minnesota	.359
1976	Bill Madlock	Chicago	.339	1976	George Brett	Kansas City	.333
1977	Dave Parker	Pittsburgh	.338	1977	Rod Carew	Minnesota	.388
1978	Dave Parker	Pittsburgh	.334	1978	Rod Carew	Minnesota	.333
1979	Keith Hernandez	St. Louis	.344	1979	Fred Lynn	Boston	.333
1980	Bill Buckner	Chicago	.324	1980	George Brett	Kansas City	.390
1981	Bill Madlock	Pittsburgh	.341	1981	Carney Lansford	Boston	.336
1982	Al Oliver	Montreal	.331	1982	Willie Wilson	Kansas City	.332
1983	Bill Madlock	Pittsburgh	.323	1983	Wade Boggs	Boston	.361
1984	Tony Gwynn	San Diego	.351	1984	Don Mattingly	New York	.343
1985	Willie McGee	St. Louis	.353	1985	Wade Boggs	Boston	.368
1986	Tim Raines	Montreal	.334	1986	Wade Boggs	Boston	.357
1987	Tony Gwynn	San Diego	.370	1987	Wade Boggs	Boston	.363
1988	Tony Gwynn	San Diego	.313	1988	Wade Boggs	Boston	.366
1989	Tony Gwynn	San Diego	.336	1989	Kirby Puckett	Minnesota	.339
1990	Willie McGee	St. Louis	.335	1990	George Brett	Kansas City	.329
1991	Terry Pendleton	Atlanta	.319	1991	Julio Franco	Texas	.341
1992	Gary Sheffield	San Diego	.330	1992	Edgar Martinez	Seattle	.343
1993	Andres Galarraga	Colorado	.370	1993	John Olerud	Toronto	.363
1994	Tony Gwynn	San Diego	.394	1994	Paul O'Neill	New York	.359
1995	Tony Gwynn	San Diego	.368	1995	Edgar Martinez	Seattle	.356
1996	Tony Gwynn	San Diego	.353	1996	Alex Rodriguez	Seattle	.358
1997	Tony Gwynn	San Diego	.372	1997	Frank Thomas	Chicago	.347
1998	Larry Walker	Colorado	.363	1998	Bernie Williams	New York	.339
1999	Larry Walker	Colorado	.379	1999	Nomar Garciaparra	Boston	.357
2000	Todd Helton	Colorado	.372	2000	Nomar Garciaparra	Boston	.372
2001	Larry Walker	Colorado	.350	2001	Ichiro Suzuki	Seattle	.350
2002	Barry Bonds	San Francisco	.370	2002	Manny Ramirez	Boston	.349
2003	Albert Pujols	St. Louis	.359	2003	Bill Mueller	Boston	.326
2004	Barry Bonds	San Francisco	.362	2004	Ichiro Suzuki	Seattle	.372

(1) Some baseball researchers have concluded that Ty Cobb actually hit .382 in 1910 while Napoleon Lajoie, Cleveland, hit .383.

Cy Young Award Winners

Year	Player, Team	Year	Player, Team	Year	Player, Team
1956	Don Newcombe, Dodgers	1977	(NL) Steve Carlton, Phillies	1992	(NL) Greg Maddux, Cubs
1957	Warren Spahn, Braves		(AL) Sparky Lyle, Yankees		(AL) Dennis Eckersley, A's
1958	Bob Turley, Yankees	1978	(NL) Gaylord Perry, Padres	1993	(NL) Greg Maddux, Braves
1959	Early Wynn, White Sox		(AL) Ron Guidry, Yankees		(AL) Jack McDowell, White Sox
1960	Vernon Law, Pirates	1979	(NL) Bruce Sutter, Cubs	1994	(NL) Greg Maddux, Braves
1961	Whitey Ford, Yankees		(AL) Mike Flanagan, Orioles		(AL) David Cone, Royals
1962	Don Drysdale, Dodgers	1980	(NL) Steve Carlton, Phillies	1995	(NL) Greg Maddux, Braves
1963	Sandy Koufax, Dodgers		(AL) Steve Stone, Orioles		(AL) Randy Johnson, Mariners
1964	Dean Chance, Angels	1981	(NL) Fernando Valenzuela,	1996	(NL) John Smoltz, Braves
1965	Sandy Koufax, Dodgers		Dodgers		(AL) Pat Hentgen, Blue Jays
1966	Sandy Koufax, Dodgers		(AL) Rollie Fingers, Brewers	1997	(NL) Pedro Martinez, Expos
1967	(NL) Mike McCormick, Giants	1982	(NL) Steve Carlton, Phillies		(AL) Roger Clemens, Blue Jays
	(AL) Jim Lonborg, Red Sox		(AL) Pete Vuckovich, Brewers	1998	(NL) Tom Glavine, Braves
1968	(NL) Bob Gibson, Cardinals	1983	(NL) John Denny, Phillies		(AL) Roger Clemens, Blue Jays
	(AL) Dennis McLain, Tigers		(AL) LaMarr Hoyt, White Sox	1999	(NL) Randy Johnson,
1969	(NL) Tom Seaver, Mets	1984	(NL) Rick Sutcliffe, Cubs		Diamondbacks
	(AL) (tie) Dennis McLain, Tigers		(AL) Willie Hernandez, Tigers		(AL) Pedro Martinez, Red Sox
	Mike Cuellar, Orioles	1985	(NL) Dwight Gooden, Mets	2000	(NL) Randy Johnson,
1970	(NL) Bob Gibson, Cardinals		(AL) Bret Saberhagen, Royals		Diamondbacks
	(AL) Jim Perry, Twins	1986	(NL) Mike Scott, Astros		(AL) Pedro Martinez, Red Sox
1971	(NL) Ferguson Jenkins, Cubs		(AL) Roger Clemens, Red Sox	2001	(NL) Randy Johnson,
	(AL) Vida Blue, A's	1987	(NL) Steve Bedrosian, Phillies		Diamondbacks
1972	(NL) Steve Carlton, Phillies		(AL) Roger Clemens, Red Sox		(AL) Roger Clemens, Yankees
	(AL) Gaylord Perry, Indians	1988	(NL) Orel Hershiser, Dodgers	2002	(NL) Randy Johnson,
1973	(NL) Tom Seaver, Mets		(AL) Frank Viola, Twins		Diamondbacks
	(AL) Jim Palmer, Orioles	1989	(NL) Mark Davis, Padres		(AL) Barry Zito, A's
1974	(NL) Mike Marshall, Dodgers		(AL) Bret Saberhagen, Royals	2003	(NL) Eric Gagne, Dodgers
	(AL) Jim (Catfish) Hunter, A's	1990	(NL) Doug Drabek, Pirates		(AL) Roy Halladay, Blue Jays
1975	(NL) Tom Seaver, Mets		(AL) Bob Welch, A's		
	(AL) Jim Palmer, Orioles	1991	(NL) Tom Glavine, Braves		
1976	(NL) Randy Jones, Padres		(AL) Roger Clemens, Red Sox		
	(AL) Jim Palmer, Orioles				

Most Valuable Player

(As selected by the Baseball Writers' Assoc. of America. Prior to 1931, MVP honors were named by various sources.)

National League

Year	Player, team	Year	Player, team	Year	Player, team
1931	Frank Frisch, St. Louis	1942	Mort Cooper, St. Louis	1953	Roy Campanella, Brooklyn
1932	Chuck Klein, Philadelphia	1943	Stan Musial, St. Louis	1954	Willie Mays, N.Y.
1933	Carl Hubbell, New York	1944	Martin Marion, St. Louis	1955	Roy Campanella, Brooklyn
1934	Dizzy Dean, St. Louis	1945	Phil Cavarretta, Chicago	1956	Don Newcombe, Brooklyn
1935	Gabby Hartnett, Chicago	1946	Stan Musial, St. Louis	1957	Hank Aaron, Milwaukee
1936	Carl Hubbell, N.Y.	1947	Bob Elliott, Boston	1958	Ernie Banks, Chicago
1937	Joe Medwick, St. Louis	1948	Stan Musial, St. Louis	1959	Ernie Banks, Chicago
1938	Ernie Lombardi, Cincinnati	1949	Jackie Robinson, Brooklyn	1960	Dick Groat, Pittsburgh
1939	Bucky Walters, Cincinnati	1950	Jim Konstanty, Philadelphia	1961	Frank Robinson, Cincinnati
1940	Frank McCormick, Cincinnati	1951	Roy Campanella, Brooklyn	1962	Maury Wills, L.A.
1941	Dolph Camilli, Brooklyn	1952	Hank Sauer, Chicago	1963	Sandy Koufax, L.A.

Year	Player, team
1964	Ken Boyer, St. Louis
1965	Willie Mays, San Francisco
1966	Roberto Clemente, Pittsburgh
1967	Orlando Cepeda, St. Louis
1968	Bob Gibson, St. Louis
1969	Willie McCovey, San Francisco
1970	Johnny Bench, Cincinnati
1971	Joe Torre, St. Louis
1972	Johnny Bench, Cincinnati
1973	Pete Rose, Cincinnati
1974	Steve Garvey, L.A.
1975	Joe Morgan, Cincinnati
1976	Joe Morgan, Cincinnati

Year	Player, team
1977	George Foster, Cincinnati
1978	Dave Parker, Pittsburgh
(tie)	Keith Hernandez, St. Louis
1980	Mike Schmidt, Philadelphia
1981	Mike Schmidt, Philadelphia
1982	Dale Murphy, Atlanta
1983	Dale Murphy, Atlanta
1984	Ryne Sandberg, Chicago
1985	Willie McGee, St. Louis
1986	Mike Schmidt, Philadelphia
1987	Andre Dawson, Chicago
1988	Kirk Gibson, L.A.
1989	Kevin Mitchell, San Francisco

Year	Player, team
1990	Barry Bonds, Pittsburgh
1991	Terry Pendleton, Atlanta
1992	Barry Bonds, Pittsburgh
1993	Barry Bonds, San Francisco
1994	Jeff Bagwell, Houston
1995	Barry Larkin, Cincinnati
1996	Ken Caminiti, San Diego
1997	Larry Walker, Colorado
1998	Sammy Sosa, Chicago
1999	Chipper Jones, Atlanta
2000	Jeff Kent, San Francisco
2001	Barry Bonds, San Francisco
2002	Barry Bonds, San Francisco
2003	Barry Bonds, San Francisco

American League

Year	Player, team
1931	Lefty Grove, Philadelphia
1932	Jimmie Foxx, Philadelphia
1933	Jimmie Foxx, Philadelphia
1934	Mickey Cochrane, Detroit
1935	Hank Greenberg, Detroit
1936	Lou Gehrig, N.Y.
1937	Charley Gehringer, Detroit
1938	Jimmie Foxx, Boston
1939	Joe DiMaggio, N.Y.
1940	Hank Greenberg, Detroit
1941	Joe DiMaggio, N.Y.
1942	Joe Gordon, N.Y.
1943	Spurgeon Chandler, N.Y.
1944	Hal Newhouser, Detroit
1945	Hal Newhouser, Detroit
1946	Ted Williams, Boston
1947	Joe DiMaggio, N.Y.
1948	Lou Boudreau, Cleveland
1949	Ted Williams, Boston
1950	Phil Rizzuto, N.Y.
1951	Yogi Berra, N.Y.
1952	Bobby Shantz, Philadelphia
1953	Al Rosen, Cleveland
1954	Yogi Berra, N.Y.
1955	Yogi Berra, N.Y.

Year	Player, team
1956	Mickey Mantle, N.Y.
1957	Mickey Mantle, N.Y.
1958	Jackie Jensen, Boston
1959	Nellie Fox, Chicago
1960	Roger Maris, N.Y.
1961	Roger Maris, N.Y.
1962	Mickey Mantle, N.Y.
1963	Elston Howard, N.Y.
1964	Brooks Robinson, Baltimore
1965	Zoilo Versalles, Minnesota
1966	Frank Robinson, Baltimore
1967	Carl Yastrzemski, Boston
1968	Denny McLain, Detroit
1969	Harmon Killebrew, Minnesota
1970	John (Boog) Powell, Baltimore
1971	Vida Blue, Oakland
1972	Dick Allen, Chicago
1973	Reggie Jackson, Oakland
1974	Jeff Burroughs, Texas
1975	Fred Lynn, Boston
1976	Thurman Munson, N.Y.
1977	Rod Carew, Minnesota
1978	Jim Rice, Boston
1979	Don Baylor, California

Year	Player, team
1980	George Brett, Kansas City
1981	Rollie Fingers, Milwaukee
1982	Robin Yount, Milwaukee
1983	Cal Ripken, Jr., Baltimore
1984	Willie Hernandez, Detroit
1985	Don Mattingly, N.Y.
1986	Roger Clemens, Boston
1987	George Bell, Toronto
1988	Jose Canseco, Oakland
1989	Robin Yount, Milwaukee
1990	Rickey Henderson, Oakland
1991	Cal Ripken, Jr., Baltimore
1992	Dennis Eckersley, Oakland
1993	Frank Thomas, Chicago
1994	Frank Thomas, Chicago
1995	Mo Vaughn, Boston
1996	Juan Gonzalez, Texas
1997	Ken Griffey Jr., Seattle
1998	Juan Gonzalez, Texas
1999	Ivan Rodriguez, Texas
2000	Jason Giambi, Oakland
2001	Ichiro Suzuki, Seattle
2002	Miguel Tejada, Oakland
2003	Alex Rodriguez, Texas

Rookie of the Year

(As selected by the Baseball Writers' Assoc. of America)

1947—Combined selection—Jackie Robinson, Brooklyn, 1b; 1948—Combined selection—Alvin Dark, Boston, N.L., ss

National League

Year	Player, team
1949	Don Newcombe, Brooklyn, p
1950	Sam Jethroe, Boston, of
1951	Willie Mays, N.Y., of
1952	Joe Black, Brooklyn, p
1953	Jim Gilliam, Brooklyn, 2b
1954	Wally Moon, St. Louis, of
1955	Bill Virdon, St. Louis, of
1956	Frank Robinson, Cincinnati, of
1957	Jack Sanford, Philadelphia, p
1958	Orlando Cepeda, S.F., 1b
1959	Willie McCovey, S.F., 1b
1960	Frank Howard, L.A., of
1961	Billy Williams, Chicago, of
1962	Ken Hubbs, Chicago, 2b
1963	Pete Rose, Cincinnati, 2b
1964	Richie Allen, Philadelphia, 3b
1965	Jim Lefebvre, L.A., 2b
1966	Tommy Helms, Cincinnati, 2b
1967	Tom Seaver, N.Y., p

Year	Player, team
1968	Johnny Bench, Cincinnati, c
1969	Ted Sizemore, L.A., 2b
1970	Carl Morton, Montreal, p
1971	Earl Williams, Atlanta, c
1972	Jon Matlack, N.Y., p
1973	Gary Matthews, S.F., of
1974	Bake McBride, St. Louis, of
1975	John Montefusco, S.F., p
1976	Butch Metzger, San Diego, p
(tie)	Pat Zachry, Cincinnati, p
1977	Andre Dawson, Montreal, of
1978	Bob Horner, Atlanta, 3b
1979	Rick Sutcliffe, L.A., p
1980	Steve Howe, L.A., p
1981	Fernando Valenzuela, L.A., p
1982	Steve Sax, L.A., 2b
1983	Darryl Strawberry, N.Y., of
1984	Dwight Gooden, N.Y., p

Year	Player, team
1985	Vince Coleman, St. Louis, of
1986	Todd Worrell, St. Louis, p
1987	Benito Santiago, San Diego, c
1988	Chris Sabo, Cincinnati, 3b
1989	Jerome Walton, Chicago, of
1990	Dave Justice, Atlanta, 1b
1991	Jeff Bagwell, Houston, 1b
1992	Eric Karros, L.A., 1b
1993	Mike Piazza, L.A., c
1994	Raul Mondesi, L.A., of
1995	Hideo Nomo, L.A., p
1996	Todd Hollandsworth, L.A., of
1997	Scott Rolen, Philadelphia, 3b
1998	Kerry Wood, Chicago, p
1999	Scott Williamson, Cincinnati, p
2000	Rafael Furcal, Atlanta, ss
2001	Albert Pujols, St. Louis, of
2002	Jason Jennings, Colorado, p
2003	Dontrelle Willis, Florida, p

American League

Year	Player, team
1949	Roy Sievers, St. Louis, of
1950	Walt Dropo, Boston, 1b
1951	Gil McDougald, N.Y., 3b
1952	Harry Byrd, Philadelphia, p
1953	Harvey Kuenn, Detroit, ss
1954	Bob Grim, N.Y., p
1955	Herb Score, Cleveland, p
1956	Luis Aparicio, Chicago, ss
1957	Tony Kubek, N.Y., if-of
1958	Albie Pearson, Washington, of
1959	Bob Allison, Washington, of
1960	Ron Hansen, Baltimore, ss
1961	Don Schwall, Boston, p
1962	Tom Tresh, N.Y., if-of
1963	Gary Peters, Chicago, p
1964	Tony Oliva, Minnesota, of
1965	Curt Blefary, Baltimore, of
1966	Tommie Agee, Chicago, of
1967	Rod Carew, Minnesota, 2b

Year	Player, team
1968	Stan Bahnsen, N.Y., p
1969	Lou Piniella, Kansas City, of
1970	Thurman Munson, N.Y., c
1971	Chris Chambliss, Cleveland, 1b
1972	Carlton Fisk, Boston, c
1973	Al Bumbry, Baltimore, of
1974	Mike Hargrove, Texas, 1b
1975	Fred Lynn, Boston, of
1976	Mark Fidrych, Detroit, p
1977	Eddie Murray, Baltimore, dh
1978	Lou Whitaker, Detroit, 2b
1979	John Castino, Minnesota, 3b
(tie)	Alfredo Griffin, Toronto, ss
1980	Joe Charboneau, Cleveland, of
1981	Dave Righetti, N.Y., p
1982	Cal Ripken, Jr., Baltimore, ss
1983	Ron Kittle, Chicago, of
1984	Alvin Davis, Seattle, 1b
1985	Ozzie Guillen, Chicago, ss

Year	Player, team
1986	Jose Canseco, Oakland, of
1987	Mark McGwire, Oakland, 1b
1988	Walt Weiss, Oakland, ss
1989	Gregg Olson, Baltimore, p
1990	Sandy Alomar, Jr., Cleveland, c
1991	Chuck Knoblauch, Minnesota, 2b
1992	Pat Listach, Milwaukee, ss
1993	Tim Salmon, California, of
1994	Bob Hamelin, Kansas City, dh
1995	Marty Cordova, Minnesota, of
1996	Derek Jeter, N.Y., ss
1997	Nomar Garciaparra, Boston, ss
1998	Ben Grieve, Oakland, of
1999	Carlos Beltran, Kansas City, of
2000	Kazuhiro Sasaki, Seattle, p
2001	Ichiro Suzuki, Seattle, of
2002	Eric Hinske, Toronto, 3b
2003	Angel Berroa, Kansas City, ss

WORLD ALMANAC EDITORS' PICKS
2004 All-World Baseball Team

The editors of *The World Almanac* have chosen the following as the best players at each position based on 2004 regular season performance.

Position	World Almanac 2004 Best	Position	World Almanac 2004 Best
1st base	Albert Pujols (St. Louis Cardinals)	Catcher	Ivan Rodriguez (Detroit Tigers)
2nd base	Mark Loretta (San Diego Padres)	Designated hitter	David Ortiz (Boston Red Sox)
3rd base	Adrian Beltre (Los Angeles Dodgers)	Right-handed starting pitcher	Curt Schilling (Boston Red Sox)
Shortstop	Miguel Tejada (Baltimore Orioles)	Left-handed starting pitcher	Johan Santana (Minnesota Twins)
Left field	Barry Bonds (San Fransciso Giants)	Right-handed relief pitcher	Eric Gagne (Los Angeles Dodgers)
Center field	Jim Edmonds (St. Louis Cardinals)	Left-handed relief pitcher	Billy Wagner (Philadelphia Phillies)
Right field	Vladimir Guerrero (Anaheim Angels)		

Manager of the Year

1983 (NL) Tommy Lasorda, L.A.
(AL) Tony La Russa, Chicago
1984 (NL) Jim Frey, Chicago
(AL) Sparky Anderson, Detroit
1985 (NL) Whitey Herzog, St. Louis
(AL) Bobby Cox, Toronto
1986 (NL) Hal Lanier, Houston
(AL) John McNamara, Boston
1987 (NL) Buck Rodgers, Montreal
(AL) Sparky Anderson, Detroit
1988 (NL) Tommy Lasorda, L.A.
(AL) Tony La Russa, Oakland
1989 (NL) Don Zimmer, Chicago
(AL) Frank Robinson, Baltimore
1990 (NL) Jim Leyland, Pittsburgh
(AL) Jeff Torborg, Chicago

1991 (NL) Bobby Cox, Atlanta
(AL) Tom Kelly, Minnesota
1992 (NL) Jim Leyland, Pittsburgh
(AL) Tony La Russa, Oakland
1993 (NL) Dusty Baker, San Francisco
(AL) Gene Lamont, Chicago
1994 (NL) Felipe Alou, Montreal
(AL) Buck Showalter, N.Y.
1995 (NL) Don Baylor, Colorado
(AL) Lou Piniella, Seattle
1996 (NL) Bruce Bochy, San Diego
(AL) (tie) Joe Torre, N.Y.,
Johnny Oates, Texas
1997 (NL) Dusty Baker, San Francisco
(AL) Davey Johnson, Baltimore

1998 (NL) Larry Dierker, Houston
(AL) Joe Torre, N.Y.
1999 (NL) Jack McKeon, Cincinnati
(AL) Jimy Williams, Boston
2000 (NL) Dusty Baker, San Francisco
(AL) Jerry Manuel, Chicago
2001 (NL) Larry Bowa, Philadelphia
(AL) Lou Piniella, Seattle
2002 (NL) Tony La Russa, St. Louis
(AL) Mike Scioscia, Anaheim
2003 (NL) Jack McKeon, Florida
(AL) Tony Pena, Kansas City

The Rawlings Gold Glove Awards: 2003 and All-Time Leaders

American League

Mike Mussina, New York, p
Bengie Molina, Anaheim, c
John Olerud, Seattle, 1b
Bret Boone, Seattle, 2b
Eric Chavez, Oakland, 3b

Alex Rodriguez, Texas, ss
Mike Cameron, Seattle, of
Torii Hunter, Minnesota, of
Ichiro Suzuki, Seattle, of

National League

Mike Hampton, Atlanta, p
Mike Matheny, St. Louis, c
Derrek Lee, Florida, 1b
Luis Castillo, Florida, 2b
Scott Rolen, St. Louis, 3b

Edgar Renteria, St. Louis, ss
Jim Edmonds, St. Louis, of
Andruw Jones, Atlanta, of
Jose Cruz Jr., San Francisco, of

The following are the players at each position who have won the most Gold Gloves since the award was instituted in 1957.

Pitcher: Jim Kaat 16
Greg Maddux 13
Catcher: Johnny Bench 10
Ivan Rodriguez 10
First base: Keith Hernandez 11
Don Mattingly 9

Second base: Roberto Alomar 10
Ryne Sandberg 9
Bill Mazeroski 8
Frank White 8
Third base: Brooks Robinson 16
Mike Schmidt 10

Shortstop: Ozzie Smith 13
Luis Aparicio 9
Outfield: Roberto Clemente . . . 12
Willie Mays 12
Al Kaline 10
Ken Griffey Jr 10

National League Final Standings, 2004

Eastern Division

	W	L	Pct.	GB	Home	Road	vs. East	vs. Central	vs. West	vs. AL
Atlanta	96	66	.593	–	49-32	47-34	51-25	18-18	19-13	8-10
Philadelphia	86	76	.531	10.0	42-39	44-37	39-37	18-18	20-12	9-9
Florida	83	79	.512	13.0	42-38	41-41	43-33	15-21	18-14	7-11
New York	71	91	.438	25.0	38-43	33-48	29-47	15-21	17-15	10-8
Montreal	67	95	.414	29.0	35-45	32-50	28-48	17-19	15-17	7-11

Central Division

	W	L	Pct.	GB	Home	Road	vs. East	vs. Central	vs. West	vs. AL
St. Louis	105	57	.648	–	53-28	52-29	19-11	54-36	21-9	11-1
Houston*	92	70	.568	13.0	48-33	44-37	16-14	55-35	14-16	7-5
Chicago	89	73	.549	16.0	45-37	44-36	16-14	50-40	15-15	8-4
Cincinnati	76	86	.469	29.0	40-41	36-45	18-12	38-52	15-15	5-7
Pittsburgh	72	89	.447	32.5	39-41	33-48	17-13	37-52	16-14	2-10
Milwaukee	67	94	.416	37.5	36-45	31-49	11-19	35-54	13-17	8-4

Western Division

	W	L	Pct.	GB	Home	Road	vs. East	vs. Central	vs. West	vs. AL
Los Angeles	93	69	.574	–	49-32	44-37	14-18	22-14	47-29	10-8
San Francisco	91	71	.562	2.0	47-35	44-36	19-13	20-16	41-35	11-7
San Diego	87	75	.537	6.0	42-39	45-36	18-14	19-17	42-34	8-10
Colorado	68	94	.420	25.0	38-43	30-51	11-21	10-26	39-37	8-10
Arizona	51	111	.315	42.0	29-52	22-59	9-23	15-21	21-55	6-12

*Wild card team.

National League Statistics, 2004

(Individual Statistics: Batting—at least 150 at-bats; Pitching—at least 70 innings or 10 saves; *changed teams within NL during season; entry includes statistics for more than 1 team; # changed teams to or from AL during season; entry includes only NL stats)

TEAM BATTING

Team	BA	AB	R	H	HR	RBI
St. Louis	.278	5555	855	1544	214	817
Colorado	.275	5577	833	1531	202	795
San Diego	.273	5573	768	1521	139	722
Atlanta	.270	5570	803	1503	178	767
San Francisco	.270	5546	850	1500	183	805
Chicago	.268	5628	789	1508	235	755
Houston	.267	5468	803	1458	187	756
Philadelphia	.267	5643	840	1505	215	802
Florida	.264	5486	718	1447	148	677
Los Angeles	.262	5542	761	1450	203	731
Pittsburgh	.260	5483	680	1428	142	648
Arizona	.253	5544	615	1401	135	582
Cincinnati	.250	5518	750	1380	194	713
Montreal	.249	5474	635	1361	151	605
New York	.249	5532	684	1376	185	658
Milwaukee	.248	5483	634	1358	135	601

TEAM PITCHING

Team	ERA	IP	H	SO	BB	SV
Atlanta	3.74	1450.0	1475	1025	523	48
St. Louis	3.75	1453.2	1378	1041	440	57
Chicago	3.81	1465.1	1363	1346	545	42
Los Angeles	4.01	1453.1	1386	1066	521	51
San Diego	4.03	1441.0	1460	1079	422	44
Houston	4.05	1443.0	1416	1282	525	47
New York	4.09	1449.0	1452	977	592	31
Florida	4.10	1439.0	1395	1116	513	53
Milwaukee	4.24	1442.0	1440	1098	476	42
Pittsburgh	4.29	1428.0	1451	1079	576	46
San Francisco	4.29	1457.0	1481	1020	548	46
Montreal	4.33	1447.0	1477	1032	582	31
Philadelphia	4.45	1462.2	1488	1070	502	43
Arizona	4.98	1436.0	1480	1153	668	33
Cincinnati	5.19	1443.2	1595	992	572	47
Colorado	5.54	1435.1	1634	947	697	36

Arizona Diamondbacks

BATTERS	BA	AB	R	H	HR	RBI	SO	SB
S. Hillenbrand	.310	562	68	174	15	80	49	2
Q. McCracken	.288	156	20	45	2	13	23	2
D. Bautista	.286	539	64	154	11	65	66	6
C. Tracy	.285	481	45	137	8	53	60	2
A. Cintron	.262	564	56	148	4	49	59	3
L. Gonzalez	.259	379	69	98	17	48	58	2
S. Hairston	.248	339	39	84	13	29	88	3
M. Kata	.247	162	17	40	2	13	29	4
L. Terrero	.245	229	21	56	4	14	78	10
R. Hammock	.241	195	22	47	4	18	39	3
J. Brito	.205	171	17	35	3	12	41	1

PITCHERS	W-L	ERA	IP	H	BB	SO	SV
R. Johnson	16-14	2.60	245.2	177	44	290	0
G. Aquino	0-2	3.06	35.1	24	17	26	16
B. Webb	7-16	3.59	208.0	194	119	164	0
M. Koplove	4-4	4.05	86.2	86	37	55	2
J. Fassero	3-8	5.46	112.0	136	44	60	0
S. Randolph	2-5	5.51	81.2	73	76	62	0
S. Sparks	3-7	6.04	120.2	139	45	57	0
C. Fossum	4-15	6.65	142.0	171	63	117	0

Manager-Bob Brenly, Al Pedrique

Atlanta Braves

BATTERS	BA	AB	R	H	HR	RBI	SO	SB
E. Marrero	.320	250	37	80	10	40	50	4
J. Estrada	.314	462	56	145	9	76	66	0
M. Giles	.311	379	61	118	8	48	70	17
J. Franco	.309	320	37	99	6	57	68	4
J. Drew	.305	518	118	158	31	93	116	12
C. Thomas	.288	236	35	68	7	31	45	3
R. Furcal	.279	563	103	157	14	59	71	29
A. LaRoche	.278	324	45	90	13	45	78	0
N. Green	.273	264	40	72	3	26	63	1
A. Jones	.261	570	85	149	29	91	147	6
C. Jones	.248	472	69	117	30	96	96	2
M. DeRosa	.239	309	33	74	3	31	53	1
E. Perez	.229	170	14	39	3	13	29	0
D. Wise	.228	162	24	37	6	17	28	6

PITCHERS	W-L	ERA	IP	H	BB	SO	SV
A. Alfonseca	6-4	2.57	73.2	71	28	45	0
J. Cruz	6-2	2.75	72.0	59	30	70	0
J. Smoltz	0-1	2.76	81.2	75	13	85	44
J. Wright	15-8	3.28	186.1	168	70	159	0
J. Thomson	14-8	3.72	198.1	210	52	133	0
P. Byrd	8-7	3.94	114.1	123	19	79	0
C. Reitsma	6-4	4.07	79.2	89	20	60	2

PITCHERS	W-L	ERA	IP	H	BB	SO	SV
R. Ortiz	15-9	4.13	204.2	197	112	143	0
M. Hampton	13-9	4.28	172.1	198	65	87	0

Manager-Bobby Cox

Chicago Cubs

BATTERS	BA	AB	R	H	HR	RBI	SO	SB
A. Ramirez	.318	547	99	174	36	103	62	0
M. Grudzielanek	.307	257	32	79	6	23	32	1
N. Garciaparra#	.297	165	28	49	4	20	14	2
M. Alou	.293	601	106	176	39	106	80	3
M. Barrett	.287	456	55	131	16	65	64	1
D. Lee	.278	605	90	168	32	98	128	12
T. Walker	.274	372	60	102	15	50	52	0
J. Macias	.268	194	23	52	3	22	38	4
C. Patterson	.266	631	91	168	24	72	168	32
B. Grieve*	.260	250	30	65	8	35	70	0
N. Perez	.255	381	40	97	4	39	41	1
S. Sosa	.253	478	69	121	35	80	133	0
R. Martinez	.246	260	22	64	3	30	40	1

PITCHERS	W-L	ERA	IP	H	BB	SO	SV
L. Hawkins	5-4	2.63	82.0	72	14	69	25
C. Zambrano	16-8	2.75	209.2	174	81	188	0
G. Rusch	6-2	3.47	129.2	127	33	90	2
M. Clement	9-13	3.68	181.0	155	77	190	0
K. Wood	8-9	3.72	140.1	127	51	144	0
G. Maddux	16-11	4.02	212.2	218	33	151	0
M. Prior	6-4	4.02	118.2	112	48	139	0

Manager-Dusty Baker

Cincinnati Reds

BATTERS	BA	AB	R	H	HR	RBI	SO	SB
S. Casey	.324	571	101	185	24	99	36	2
B. Larkin	.289	346	55	100	8	44	39	2
R. Freel	.277	505	74	140	3	28	88	37
D. Jimenez	.270	563	76	152	12	67	99	13
A. Dunn	.266	568	105	151	46	102	195	6
W. Pena	.259	336	45	87	26	66	108	5
K. Griffey	.253	300	49	76	20	60	67	1
J. LaRue	.251	390	46	98	14	55	108	0
J. Castro	.244	299	36	73	5	26	51	1
F. Lopez	.242	264	35	64	7	31	81	1
J. Valentin	.233	202	18	47	6	20	36	0
A. Kearns	.230	217	28	50	9	32	71	2

PITCHERS	W-L	ERA	IP	H	BB	SO	SV
D. Graves	1-6	3.95	68.1	77	13	40	41
P. Wilson	11-6	4.36	183.2	192	63	117	0
A. Harang	10-9	4.86	161.0	177	53	125	0
J. Riedling	5-3	5.10	77.2	90	40	46	0
J. Acevedo	5-12	5.94	157.2	188	45	117	0
T. Van Poppel	4-6	6.09	115.1	136	32	72	0

Manager-Dave Miley

Colorado Rockies

BATTERS	BA	AB	R	H	HR	RBI	SO	SB
T. Helton	.347	547	115	190	32	96	72	3
A. Miles	.293	522	75	153	6	47	53	12
L. Gonzalez	.292	322	42	94	12	40	67	1
M. Holliday	.290	400	65	116	14	57	86	3
J. Burnitz	.283	540	94	153	37	110	124	5
T. Greene	.282	195	23	55	10	35	38	0
R. Clayton	.279	574	95	160	8	54	125	10
V. Castilla	.271	583	93	158	35	131	113	0
M. Sweeney	.266	177	25	47	9	40	51	1
P. Wilson	.248	202	24	50	6	29	49	2
C. Johnson	.236	305	42	72	13	47	91	2

PITCHERS	W-L	ERA	IP	H	BB	SO	SV
J. Kennedy	9-7	3.66	162.1	163	67	117	0
J. Wright	2-3	4.12	78.2	82	45	41	0
A. Cook	6-4	4.28	96.2	112	39	40	0
J. Jennings	11-12	5.51	201.0	241	101	133	0
S. Estes	15-8	5.84	202.0	223	105	117	0
S. Chacon	1-9	7.11	63.1	71	52	52	35

Manager-Clint Hurdle

Florida Marlins

BATTERS	BA	AB	R	H	HR	RBI	SO	SB
J. Pierre	.326	678	100	221	3	49	35	45
M. Cabrera	.294	603	101	177	33	112	148	5
M. Lowell	.293	598	87	175	27	85	77	5
L. Castillo	.291	564	91	164	2	47	68	21
P. Lo Duca*	.286	535	68	153	13	80	49	4
J. Conine	.280	521	55	146	14	83	78	5
M. Redmond	.256	246	19	63	2	25	28	1
D. Easley	.238	223	26	53	9	43	36	4
J. Encarnacion*	.236	484	63	114	16	62	86	5
A. Gonzalez	.232	561	67	130	23	79	126	3

PITCHERS	W-L	ERA	IP	H	BB	SO	SV
A. Benitez	2-2	1.29	69.2	36	21	62	47
C. Pavano	18-8	3.00	222.1	212	49	139	0
G. Mota*	9-8	3.07	96.2	75	37	85	4
A. Burnett	7-6	3.68	120.0	102	38	113	0
J. Beckett	9-9	3.79	156.2	137	54	152	0
D. Willis	10-11	4.02	197.0	210	61	139	0
D. Weathers*	7-7	4.15	82.1	85	35	61	0
N. Bump	2-4	5.01	73.2	86	32	44	1
I. Valdez*	14-9	5.19	170.0	202	49	67	0

Manager-Jack McKeon

Houston Astros

BATTERS	BA	AB	R	H	HR	RBI	SO	SB
L. Berkman	.316	544	104	172	30	106	101	9
J. Kent	.289	540	96	156	27	107	96	7
M. Lamb	.288	278	38	80	14	58	63	1
C. Biggio	.281	633	100	178	24	63	94	7
M. Ensberg	.275	411	51	113	10	66	46	6
J. Vizcaino	.274	358	34	98	3	33	39	1
A. Everett	.273	384	66	105	8	31	56	13
J. Bagwell	.266	572	104	152	27	89	131	6
C. Beltran#	.258	333	70	86	23	53	57	28
B. Ausmus	.248	403	38	100	5	31	56	2
R. Chavez	.210	162	9	34	0	23	38	0

PITCHERS	W-L	ERA	IP	H	BB	SO	SV
B. Lidge	6-5	1.90	94.2	57	30	157	29
R. Clemens	18-4	2.98	214.1	169	79	218	0
O. Dotel#	0-4	3.12	34.2	27	15	50	14
W. Miller	7-7	3.35	88.2	76	44	74	0
R. Oswalt	20-10	3.49	237.0	233	62	206	0
D. Miceli	6-6	3.59	77.2	74	27	83	2
A. Pettitte	6-4	3.90	83.0	71	31	79	0
P. Munro	4-7	5.15	99.2	120	26	63	0
T. Redding	5-7	5.72	100.2	125	43	56	0
D. Oliver*	3-3	5.94	72.2	87	21	40	0

Manager-Jimy Williams, Phil Garner

Los Angeles Dodgers

BATTERS	BA	AB	R	H	HR	RBI	SO	SB
A. Beltre	.334	598	104	200	48	121	87	7
J. Hernandez	.289	211	32	61	13	29	61	3
C. Izturis	.288	670	90	193	4	62	70	25
S. Finley*	.271	628	92	170	36	94	82	9
M. Bradley	.267	516	72	138	19	67	123	15
S. Green	.266	590	92	157	28	86	114	5
A. Cora	.264	405	47	107	10	47	41	3
J. Werth	.262	290	56	76	16	47	85	4
D. Roberts	.253	233	45	59	2	21	31	33
H. Choi*	.251	343	53	86	15	46	96	1
R. Ventura	.243	152	19	37	5	28	31	0
B. Mayne*	.221	190	14	42	0	15	41	1
J. Grabowski	.220	173	18	38	7	20	50	0
D. Ross	.170	165	13	28	5	15	62	0

PITCHERS	W-L	ERA	IP	H	BB	SO	SV
E. Gagne	7-3	2.19	82.1	53	22	114	45
B. Penny*	9-10	3.15	143.0	130	45	111	0
O. Perez	7-6	3.25	196.1	180	44	128	0
D. Sanchez	3-1	3.38	80.0	81	27	44	0
J. Weaver	13-13	4.01	220.0	219	67	153	0
W. Alvarez	7-6	4.03	120.2	109	31	102	1
J. Lima	13-5	4.07	170.1	178	34	93	0
E. Dessens*	2-6	4.46	105.0	123	31	73	2
K. Ishii	13-8	4.71	172.0	155	98	99	0
H. Nomo	4-11	8.25	84.0	105	42	54	0

Manager-Jim Tracy

Milwaukee Brewers

BATTERS	BA	AB	R	H	HR	RBI	SO	SB
L. Overbay	.301	579	83	174	16	87	128	2
B. Clark	.280	353	41	99	7	46	48	15
J. Spivey	.272	228	33	62	7	28	48	5
G. Jenkins	.264	617	88	163	27	93	152	3
W. Helms	.263	274	24	72	4	28	60	0
K. Ginter	.262	386	47	101	19	60	100	8
S. Podsednik	.244	640	85	156	12	39	105	70
C. Counsell	.241	473	59	114	2	23	88	17
B. Hall	.238	390	43	93	9	53	119	12
R. Branyan	.234	158	21	37	11	27	68	1
G. Bennett	.224	219	18	49	3	20	32	1
C. Moeller	.208	317	25	66	5	27	74	0

PITCHERS	W-L	ERA	IP	H	BB	SO	SV
B. Sheets	12-14	2.70	237.0	201	32	264	0
D. Kolb	0-4	2.98	57.1	50	15	21	39
D. Davis	12-12	3.39	207.1	192	79	166	0
L. Vizcaino	4-4	3.75	72.0	61	24	63	1
J. Bennett	1-5	4.79	71.1	78	26	45	0
V. Santos	11-12	4.97	154.0	169	57	115	0
C. Capuano	6-8	4.99	88.1	91	37	80	0
W. Obermueller	6-8	5.80	118.0	138	42	59	0

Manager-Ned Yost

Montreal Expos

BATTERS	BA	AB	R	H	HR	RBI	SO	SB
J. Rivera	.307	391	48	120	12	49	45	6
J. Vidro	.294	412	51	121	14	60	43	3
J. Carroll	.289	218	36	63	0	16	21	5
E. Chavez	.277	502	65	139	5	34	40	32
T. Sledge	.269	398	45	107	15	62	66	3
B. Schneider	.257	436	40	112	12	49	63	0
B. Wilkerson	.255	572	112	146	32	67	152	13
N. Johnson	.251	251	35	63	7	33	58	6
O. Cabrera#	.246	390	41	96	4	31	31	12
T. Batista	.241	606	76	146	32	110	78	14

PITCHERS	W-L	ERA	IP	H	BB	SO	SV
L. Ayala	6-12	2.69	90.1	92	15	63	2
C. Cordero	7-3	2.94	82.2	68	43	83	14
T. Ohka	3-7	3.40	84.2	98	20	38	0
L. Hernandez	11-15	3.60	255.0	234	83	186	0
Z. Day	5-10	3.93	116.2	117	45	61	0
S. Kim	4-6	4.58	135.2	145	55	87	0
T. Armas	2-4	4.88	72.0	66	45	54	0
J. Patterson	4-7	5.03	98.1	100	46	99	0
C. Vargas	5-5	5.25	118.1	120	64	89	0
R. Biddle	4-8	6.92	78.0	98	31	51	11

Manager-Frank Robinson

New York Mets

BATTERS	BA	AB	R	H	HR	RBI	SO	SB
D. Wright	.293	263	41	77	14	40	40	6
S. Spencer#	.281	185	21	52	4	26	37	6
V. Wilson	.274	157	18	43	4	21	24	1
K. Matsui	.272	460	65	125	7	44	97	14
E. Valent	.267	270	39	72	13	34	61	0
M. Piazza	.266	455	47	121	20	54	78	0
C. Floyd	.260	396	55	103	18	63	103	11
J. Reyes	.255	220	33	56	2	14	31	19
R. Hidalgo*	.239	523	67	125	25	82	129	4
K. Garcia#	.234	192	24	45	7	22	35	3
T. Zeile	.233	348	30	81	9	35	83	0
M. Cameron	.231	493	76	114	30	76	143	22
J. Phillips	.218	362	34	79	7	34	42	0

PITCHERS	W-L	ERA	IP	H	BB	SO	SV
B. Looper	2-5	2.70	83.1	86	16	60	29
M. Stanton	2-6	3.16	77.0	70	33	58	0
A. Leiter	10-8	3.21	173.2	138	97	117	0
T. Glavine	11-14	3.60	212.1	204	70	109	0
S. Trachsel	12-13	4.00	202.2	203	83	117	0
K. Benson*	12-12	4.31	200.1	202	61	134	0
J. Seo	5-10	4.90	117.2	133	50	54	0

Manager-Art Howe

Philadelphia Phillies

BATTERS	BA	AB	R	H	HR	RBI	SO	SB
B. Abreu	.301	574	118	173	30	105	116	40
P. Polanco	.298	503	74	150	17	55	39	7
D. Bell	.291	533	67	155	18	77	75	1
J. Rollins	.289	657	119	190	14	73	73	30
J. Thome	.274	508	97	139	42	105	144	0
J. Michaels	.274	299	44	82	10	40	80	2
M. Lieberthal	.271	446	58	129	17	61	69	1
C. Utley	.266	267	36	71	13	57	40	4
P. Burrell	.257	448	66	115	24	84	130	2
M. Byrd	.228	346	48	79	5	33	68	2
T. Perez	.216	176	22	38	6	21	44	0
D. Glanville	.210	162	21	34	2	14	21	8

PITCHERS	W-L	ERA	IP	H	BB	SO	SV
R. Madson	9-3	2.34	77.0	68	19	55	1
B. Wagner	4-0	2.42	48.1	31	6	59	21
R. Cormier	4-5	3.56	81.0	70	26	46	0
T. Worrell	5-6	3.68	78.1	75	21	64	19
T. Jones*	11-5	4.15	82.1	84	33	59	2
R. Wolf	5-8	4.28	136.2	145	36	89	0
V. Padilla	7-7	4.53	115.1	119	36	82	0
E. Milton	14-6	4.75	201.0	196	75	161	0
K. Millwood	9-6	4.85	141.0	155	51	125	0
C. Lidle*	12-12	4.90	211.1	224	61	126	0
B. Myers	11-11	5.52	176.0	196	62	116	0

Manager-Larry Bowa

Pittsburgh Pirates

BATTERS	BA	AB	R	H	HR	RBI	SO	SB
J. Kendall	.319	574	86	183	3	51	41	11
J. Wilson	.308	652	82	201	11	59	71	8
J. Bay	.282	411	61	116	26	82	129	4
T. Redman	.280	546	65	153	8	51	52	18
B. Hill	.266	233	28	62	2	27	39	0
C. Wilson	.264	561	97	148	29	82	169	2
T. Wigginton*	.261	494	63	129	17	66	82	7
J. Castillo	.256	383	44	98	8	39	92	3
D. Ward	.249	293	39	73	15	57	45	0
R. Mackowiak	.246	491	65	121	17	75	114	13
A. Nunez	.236	182	17	43	2	13	36	1

BATTERS	BA	AB	R	H	HR	RBI	SO	SB
C. Stynes	.216	162	16	35	1	16	23	0
R. Simon#	.194	175	14	34	3	14	17	0

PITCHERS	W-L	ERA	IP	H	BB	SO	SV
S. Torres	7-7	2.64	92.0	87	22	62	0
O. Perez	12-10	2.98	196.0	145	81	239	0
J. Mesa	5-2	3.25	69.1	78	20	37	43
B. Meadows	2-4	3.58	78.0	76	19	46	1
K. Wells	5-7	4.55	138.1	145	66	116	0
J. Fogg	11-10	4.64	178.1	193	66	82	0
S. Burnett	5-5	5.02	71.2	86	28	30	0
R. Vogelsong	6-13	6.50	133.0	148	67	92	0

Manager-Lloyd McClendon

St. Louis Cardinals

BATTERS	BA	AB	R	H	HR	RBI	SO	SB
A. Pujols	.331	592	133	196	46	123	52	5
S. Rolen	.314	500	109	157	34	124	92	4
T. Womack	.307	553	91	170	5	38	60	26
J. Edmonds	.301	498	102	150	42	111	150	8
L. Walker*	.298	258	51	77	17	47	57	6
J. Mabry	.296	240	32	71	13	40	63	0
S. Taguchi	.291	179	26	52	3	25	23	6
E. Renteria	.287	586	84	168	10	72	78	17
R. Cedeno	.265	200	22	53	3	23	41	5
R. Sanders	.260	446	64	116	22	67	118	21
R. Lankford	.255	200	36	51	6	22	55	2
H. Luna	.249	173	25	43	3	22	37	6
M. Matheny	.247	385	28	95	5	50	83	0
M. Anderson	.237	253	31	60	8	28	38	6

PITCHERS	W-L	ERA	IP	H	BB	SO	SV
J. Isringhausen	4-2	2.87	75.1	55	23	71	47
C. Carpenter	15-5	3.46	182.0	169	38	152	0
J. Marquis	15-7	3.71	201.1	215	70	138	0
J. Suppan	16-9	4.16	188.0	192	65	110	0
W. Williams	11-8	4.18	189.2	193	58	131	0
M. Morris	15-10	4.72	202.0	205	56	131	0

Manager-Tony La Russa

San Diego Padres

BATTERS	BA	AB	R	H	HR	RBI	SO	SB
M. Loretta	.335	620	108	208	16	76	45	5
S. Burroughs	.298	523	76	156	2	47	52	5
T. Long	.295	288	31	85	3	28	51	3
R. Klesko	.291	402	58	117	9	66	67	3
P. Nevin	.289	547	78	158	26	105	121	0
B. Giles	.284	609	97	173	23	94	80	10
R. Hernandez	.276	384	45	106	18	63	45	1
K. Greene	.273	484	67	132	15	65	94	4
J. Payton	.260	458	57	119	8	55	56	2
M. Ojeda	.256	156	23	40	8	26	34	0
A. Gonzalez*	.225	285	36	64	7	27	64	2

PITCHERS	W-L	ERA	IP	H	BB	SO	SV
A. Otsuka	7-2	1.75	77.1	56	26	87	2
S. Linebrink	7-3	2.14	84.0	61	26	83	0
J. Peavy	15-6	2.27	166.1	146	53	173	0
T. Hoffman	3-3	2.30	54.2	42	8	53	41
D. Wells	12-8	3.73	195.2	203	20	101	0
B. Lawrence	15-14	4.12	203.0	226	55	121	0
A. Eaton	11-14	4.61	199.1	204	52	153	0

Manager-Bruce Bochy

San Francisco Giants

BATTERS	BA	AB	R	H	HR	RBI	SO	SB
B. Bonds	.362	373	129	135	45	101	41	6
J. Snow	.327	346	62	113	12	60	61	4
D. Cruz	.292	397	46	116	7	55	32	1
E. Alfonzo	.289	519	66	150	11	77	40	1
R. Durham	.282	471	95	133	17	65	60	10
M. Grissom	.279	562	78	157	22	90	83	3
P. Feliz	.276	503	72	139	22	84	85	5
D. Mohr	.274	263	52	72	7	28	64	0
A. Pierzynski	.272	471	45	128	11	77	27	0
M. Tucker	.256	464	77	119	13	62	106	5
R. Ledee*	.233	176	25	41	7	30	47	3
Y. Torrealba	.227	172	19	39	6	23	31	2

PITCHERS	W-L	ERA	IP	H	BB	SO	SV
J. Schmidt	18-7	3.20	225.0	165	77	251	0
J. Brower	7-7	3.29	93.0	90	36	63	1
N. Lowry	6-0	3.82	92.0	91	28	72	0
B. Tomko	11-7	4.04	194.0	196	64	108	0
D. Burba*	4-1	4.21	77.0	70	26	50	2
J. Williams	10-7	4.24	129.1	123	44	80	0
D. Hermanson	6-9	4.53	131.0	132	46	102	17
K. Rueter	9-12	4.73	190.1	225	66	56	0
M. Herges	4-5	5.23	65.1	90	21	39	23

Manager-Felipe Alou

American League Final Standings, 2004

Eastern Division

	W	L	Pct.	GB	Home	Road	vs. East	vs. Central	vs. West	vs. NL
New York	101	61	.623	–	57-24	44-37	49-27	20-12	22-14	10-8
Boston*	98	64	.605	3.0	55-26	43-38	48-28	19-13	22-14	9-9
Baltimore	78	84	.481	23.0	38-43	40-41	37-39	21-15	15-17	5-13
Tampa Bay	70	91	.435	30.5	41-39	29-52	26-49	19-17	10-22	15-3
Toronto	67	94	.416	33.5	40-41	27-53	29-46	13-19	17-19	8-10

Central Division

	W	L	Pct.	GB	Home	Road	vs. East	vs. Central	vs. West	vs. NL
Minnesota	92	70	.568	–	49-32	43-38	19-17	46-30	16-16	11-7
Chicago	83	79	.512	9.0	46-35	37-44	16-16	40-36	19-17	8-10
Cleveland	80	82	.494	12.0	44-37	36-45	17-15	36-40	17-19	10-8
Detroit	72	90	.444	20.0	38-43	34-47	12-20	36-40	15-21	9-9
Kansas City	58	104	.358	34.0	33-47	25-57	12-24	32-44	8-24	6-12

Western Division

	W	L	Pct.	GB	Home	Road	vs. East	vs. Central	vs. West	vs. NL
Anaheim	92	70	.568	–	45-36	47-34	25-18	28-15	32-26	7-11
Oakland	91	71	.562	1.0	52-29	39-42	23-20	27-16	31-27	10-8
Seattle	89	73	.549	3.0	51-30	38-43	25-18	23-20	31-27	10-8
Texas	63	99	.389	29.0	38-44	25-55	13-30	19-17	22-36	9-9

*Wild card team.

American League Team Statistics, 2004

(Individual Statistics: Batting—at least 150 at-bats; Pitching—at least 70 innings or 10 saves; *changed teams within AL during season, entry includes statistics for more than one team; # changed teams to or from NL during season, entry includes only AL stats)

TEAM BATTING

Team	BA	AB	R	H	HR	RBI
Anaheim	.282	5675	836	1603	162	783
Boston	.282	5720	949	1613	222	912
Baltimore	.281	5736	842	1614	169	803
Cleveland	.276	5676	858	1565	184	820
Detroit	.272	5623	827	1531	201	800
Oakland	.270	5728	793	1545	189	752
Seattle	.270	5722	698	1544	136	658
Chicago	.268	5534	865	1481	242	823
New York	.268	5527	897	1483	242	863
Minnesota	.266	5623	780	1494	191	735
Texas	.266	5615	860	1492	227	825
Toronto	.260	5531	719	1438	145	680
Kansas City	.259	5538	720	1432	150	675
Tampa Bay	.258	5483	714	1416	145	685

TEAM PITCHING

Team	ERA	IP	H	SO	BB	SV
Minnesota	4.03	1476.0	1523	1123	431	48
Oakland	4.17	1471.1	1466	1034	544	35
Boston	4.18	1451.1	1430	1132	447	36
Anaheim	4.28	1454.1	1476	1164	502	50
Texas	4.53	1439.2	1536	979	547	52
New York	4.69	1443.2	1532	1058	445	59
Baltimore	4.70	1455.1	1488	1090	687	27
Seattle	4.76	1459.1	1498	1036	575	28
Cleveland	4.81	1466.2	1553	1115	579	32
Tampa Bay	4.81	1417.0	1459	923	580	35
Chicago	4.91	1432.1	1505	1013	527	34
Toronto	4.91	1421.0	1505	956	608	37
Detroit	4.93	1439.2	1542	995	530	35
Kansas City	5.15	1420.1	1638	887	518	47

Anaheim Angels

BATTERS	BA	AB	R	H	HR	RBI	SO	SB
R. Quinlan	.344	160	23	55	5	23	26	3
V. Guerrero	.337	612	124	206	39	126	74	15
G. Anderson	.301	442	57	133	14	75	75	2
C. Figgins	.296	577	83	171	5	60	94	34
D. Erstad	.295	495	79	146	7	69	74	16
J. Guillen	.294	565	88	166	27	104	92	5
A. Kennedy	.278	468	70	130	10	48	92	15
J. DaVanon	.277	285	41	79	7	34	54	18
D. Eckstein	.276	566	92	156	2	35	49	16
B. Molina	.276	337	36	93	10	54	35	0
J. Molina	.261	203	26	53	3	25	52	4
T. Salmon	.253	186	15	47	2	23	41	1
T. Glaus	.251	207	47	52	18	42	52	2

PITCHERS	W-L	ERA	IP	H	BB	SO	SV
F. Rodriguez	4-1	1.82	84.0	51	33	123	12
T. Percival	2-3	2.90	49.2	43	19	33	33
S. Shields	8-2	3.33	105.1	97	40	109	4
K. Escobar	11-12	3.93	208.1	192	76	191	0
K. Gregg	5-2	4.21	87.2	86	28	84	1
R. Ortiz	5-7	4.43	128.0	139	38	82	0
J. Washburn	11-8	4.64	149.1	159	40	86	0
J. Lackey	14-13	4.67	198.1	215	60	144	0
B. Colon	18-12	5.01	208.1	215	71	158	0
A. Sele	9-4	5.05	132.0	163	51	51	0

Manager-Mike Scioscia

Baltimore Orioles

BATTERS	BA	AB	R	H	HR	RBI	SO	SB
M. Mora	.340	550	111	187	27	104	95	11
J. Lopez	.316	579	83	183	23	86	97	0
M. Tejada	.311	653	107	203	34	150	73	4
D. Newhan	.311	373	66	116	8	54	72	11
B. Surhoff	.309	343	49	106	8	50	46	2
J. Hairston	.303	287	43	87	2	24	29	13
L. Bigbie	.280	478	76	134	15	68	113	8
B. Roberts	.273	641	107	175	4	53	95	29
R. Palmeiro	.258	550	68	142	23	88	61	2
J. Gibbons	.246	346	36	85	10	47	64	1
L. Matos	.224	330	36	74	6	28	60	12

PITCHERS	W-L	ERA	IP	H	BB	SO	SV
B. Ryan	4-6	2.28	87.0	64	35	122	3
J. Parrish	6-3	3.46	78.0	68	55	71	1
R. Lopez	14-9	3.59	170.2	164	54	121	0
J. Julio	2-5	4.57	69.0	59	39	70	22
E. Bedard	6-10	4.59	137.1	149	71	121	0
D. Cabrera	12-8	5.00	147.2	145	89	76	1
S. Ponson	11-15	5.30	215.2	265	69	115	0
E. DuBose	4-6	6.39	74.2	76	44	48	0

Manager-Lee Mazzilli

Boston Red Sox

BATTERS	BA	AB	R	H	HR	RBI	SO	SB
N. Garciaparra#	.321	156	24	50	5	21	16	2
M. Ramirez	.308	568	108	175	43	130	124	2
J. Damon	.304	621	123	189	20	94	71	19
D. Ortiz	.301	582	94	175	41	139	133	0
K. Millar	.297	508	74	151	18	74	91	1
J. Varitek	.296	463	67	137	18	73	126	10
O. Cabrera#	.294	228	33	67	6	31	23	4
B. Mueller	.283	399	75	113	12	57	56	2
D. Mirabelli	.281	160	27	45	9	32	46	0
G. Kapler	.272	290	51	79	6	33	49	5
M. Bellhorn	.264	523	93	138	17	82	177	6
K. Youkilis	.260	208	38	54	7	35	45	0
D. McCarty	.258	151	24	39	4	17	40	1
D. Mientkiewicz*	.238	391	47	93	6	35	56	2
P. Reese	.221	244	32	54	3	29	60	6

PITCHERS	W-L	ERA	IP	H	BB	SO	SV
K. Foulke	5-3	2.17	83.0	63	15	79	32
C. Schilling	21-6	3.26	226.2	206	35	203	0
P. Martinez	16-9	3.90	217.0	193	61	227	0
B. Arroyo	10-9	4.03	178.2	171	47	142	0
M. Timlin	5-4	4.13	76.1	75	19	56	1
T. Adams*	6-4	4.76	70.0	84	28	56	3
T. Wakefield	12-10	4.87	188.1	197	63	116	0
D. Lowe	14-12	5.42	182.2	224	71	105	0

Manager-Terry Francona

Chicago White Sox

BATTERS	BA	AB	R	H	HR	RBI	SO	SB
R. Gload	.321	234	28	75	7	44	37	0
A. Rowand	.310	487	94	151	24	69	91	17
C. Lee	.305	591	103	180	31	99	86	11
M. Ordonez	.292	202	32	59	9	37	22	0
J. Uribe	.283	502	82	142	23	74	96	9
P. Konerko	.277	563	84	156	41	117	107	1
F. Thomas	.271	240	53	65	18	49	57	0
C. Everett#	.266	154	21	41	5	21	26	1
W. Harris	.262	409	68	107	2	27	79	19
T. Perez	.246	293	38	72	5	40	29	3

BATTERS	BA	AB	R	H	HR	RBI	SO	SB
J. Crede	.239	490	67	117	21	69	81	1
J. Valentin	.216	450	73	97	30	70	139	8
B. Davis*	.207	193	22	40	6	18	49	1
J. Borchard	.174	201	26	35	9	20	57	1

PITCHERS	W-L	ERA	IP	H	BB	SO	SV
S. Takatsu	6-4	2.31	62.1	40	21	50	19
D. Marte	6-5	3.42	73.2	56	34	68	6
F. Garcia*	13-11	3.81	210.0	192	64	184	0
M. Buehrle	16-10	3.89	245.1	257	51	165	0
J. Garland	12-11	4.89	217.0	223	76	113	0
J. Contreras*	13-9	5.50	170.1	166	84	150	0
S. Schoeneweis	6-9	5.59	112.2	129	49	69	0

Manager-Ozzie Guillen

Cleveland Indians

BATTERS	BA	AB	R	H	HR	RBI	SO	SB
T. Hafner	.311	482	96	150	28	109	111	3
C. Crisp	.297	491	78	146	15	71	69	20
O. Vizquel	.291	567	82	165	7	59	62	19
L. Merloni	.289	190	25	55	4	28	41	1
V. Martinez	.283	520	77	147	23	108	69	0
R. Belliard	.282	599	78	169	12	70	98	3
M. Lawton	.277	591	109	164	20	70	84	23
B. Broussard	.275	418	57	115	17	82	95	4
C. Blake	.271	587	93	159	28	88	139	5
J. Gerut	.252	481	72	121	11	51	59	13
J. Phelps*	.251	371	51	93	17	61	93	0
A. Escobar	.211	152	20	32	1	12	42	1

PITCHERS	W-L	ERA	IP	H	BB	SO	SV
J. Westbrook	14-9	3.38	215.2	208	61	116	0
D. Riske	7-3	3.72	77.1	69	41	78	5
C. Sabathia	11-10	4.12	188.0	176	72	139	0
B. Wickman	0-2	4.25	29.2	33	10	26	13
S. Elarton	3-5	4.53	117.1	107	42	80	0
R. White	5-5	5.29	78.1	88	29	44	1
C. Lee	14-8	5.43	179.0	188	81	161	0
J. Davis	2-7	5.51	114.1	148	51	72	0

Manager-Eric Wedge

Detroit Tigers

BATTERS	BA	AB	R	H	HR	RBI	SO	SB
I. Rodriguez	.334	527	72	176	19	86	91	7
A. Sanchez	.322	332	41	107	2	26	50	19
C. Guillen	.318	522	97	166	20	97	87	12
C. Monroe	.293	447	65	131	18	72	79	3
B. Inge	.287	408	43	117	13	64	72	5
D. Young	.272	389	72	106	18	60	71	0
R. White	.270	448	76	121	19	67	77	1
O. Infante	.264	503	69	133	16	55	112	13
M. Thames	.255	165	24	42	10	33	42	0
B. Higginson	.246	448	63	110	12	64	84	5
C. Pena	.241	481	89	116	27	82	146	7
J. Smith	.239	155	20	37	5	19	37	1
E. Munson	.212	321	36	68	19	49	90	1

PITCHERS	W-L	ERA	IP	H	BB	SO	SV
E. Yan	3-6	3.83	87.0	92	32	69	7
M. Maroth	11-13	4.31	217.0	244	59	108	0
U. Urbina	4-6	4.50	54.0	38	32	56	21
A. Levine	3-4	4.58	70.2	83	24	32	0
J. Bonderman	11-13	4.89	184.0	168	73	168	0
N. Robertson	12-10	4.90	196.2	210	66	155	1
J. Johnson	8-15	5.13	196.2	222	60	125	0
G. Knotts	7-6	5.25	135.1	142	58	81	2

Manager-Alan Trammell

Kansas City Royals

BATTERS	BA	AB	R	H	HR	RBI	SO	SB
J. Randa	.287	485	65	139	8	56	77	0
K. Harvey	.287	456	47	131	13	55	89	1
M. Sweeney	.287	411	56	118	22	79	44	3
D. DeJesus	.287	363	58	104	7	39	53	8
C. Beltran#	.278	266	51	74	15	51	44	14
B. Santiago	.274	175	15	48	6	23	32	1
R. Gotay	.270	152	17	41	1	16	36	0
M. Stairs	.267	439	46	117	18	66	92	1
T. Graffanino	.263	278	37	73	3	26	38	10
A. Berroa	.262	512	72	134	8	43	87	14
D. Brown	.251	195	19	49	4	24	50	2
J. Buck#	.235	238	36	56	12	30	79	1
A. Nunez#	.226	221	31	50	5	29	48	0
D. Relaford	.221	380	45	84	6	34	56	5

PITCHERS	W-L	ERA	IP	H	BB	SO	SV
Z. Greinke	8-11	3.97	145.0	143	26	100	0
D. Reyes	4-8	4.75	108.0	114	50	91	0
J. Affeldt	3-4	4.95	76.1	91	32	49	13
J. Gobble	9-8	5.35	148.0	157	43	49	0
D. May	9-19	5.61	186.0	234	55	120	0
B. Anderson	6-12	5.64	166.0	217	53	70	0
M. Wood*	3-8	5.94	100.0	112	28	54	0

Manager-Tony Pena

Minnesota Twins

BATTERS	BA	AB	R	H	HR	RBI	SO	SB
S. Stewart	.304	378	46	115	11	47	44	6
L. Ford	.299	569	89	170	15	72	75	20
C. Guzman	.274	576	84	158	8	46	64	10
T. Hunter	.271	520	79	141	23	81	101	21
J. Morneau	.271	280	39	76	19	58	54	0
M. LeCroy	.269	264	25	71	9	39	60	0
M. Cuddyer	.263	339	49	89	12	45	74	5
L. Rivas	.256	336	44	86	10	34	53	15
J. Offerman	.256	172	22	44	2	22	31	1
J. Jones	.254	555	69	141	24	80	117	13
C. Koskie	.251	422	68	106	25	71	103	9
H. Blanco	.206	315	36	65	10	37	56	0

PITCHERS	W-L	ERA	IP	H	BB	SO	SV
J. Nathan	1-2	1.62	72.1	48	23	89	44
J. Santana	20-6	2.61	228.0	156	54	265	0
J. Rincon	11-6	2.63	82.0	52	32	106	2
B. Radke	11-8	3.48	219.2	229	26	143	0
J. Romero	7-4	3.51	74.1	61	38	69	1
C. Silva	14-8	4.21	203.0	255	35	76	0
J. Roa	2-3	4.50	70.0	84	24	47	0
T. Mulholland	5-9	5.18	123.1	163	33	60	0
K. Lohse	9-13	5.34	194.0	240	76	111	0

Manager-Ron Gardenhire

New York Yankees

BATTERS	BA	AB	R	H	HR	RBI	SO	SB
H. Matsui	.298	584	109	174	31	108	103	3
D. Jeter	.292	643	111	188	23	78	99	23
M. Cairo	.292	360	48	105	6	42	49	11
G. Sheffield	.290	573	117	166	36	121	83	5
A. Rodriguez	.286	601	112	172	36	106	131	28
K. Lofton	.275	276	51	76	3	18	27	7
J. Posada	.272	449	72	122	21	81	92	1
B. Williams	.262	561	105	147	22	70	96	1
J. Olerud*	.259	425	45	110	9	48	61	0
R. Sierra	.244	307	40	75	17	65	55	1
T. Clark	.221	253	37	56	16	49	92	0
E. Wilson	.213	240	19	51	6	31	20	1
J. Giambi	.208	264	33	55	12	40	62	0

PITCHERS	W-L	ERA	IP	H	BB	SO	SV
M. Rivera	4-2	1.94	78.2	65	20	66	53
T. Gordon	9-4	2.21	89.2	56	23	96	4
O. Hernandez	8-2	3.30	84.2	73	36	84	0
K. Brown	10-6	4.09	132.0	132	35	83	0
J. Lieber	14-8	4.33	176.2	216	18	102	0
M. Mussina	12-9	4.59	164.2	178	40	132	0
P. Quantrill	7-3	4.72	95.1	124	20	37	1
J. Vazquez	14-10	4.91	198.0	195	60	150	0
T. Sturtze	6-2	5.47	77.1	75	33	56	1
E. Loaiza*	10-7	5.70	183.0	217	71	117	0

Manager-Joe Torre

Oakland Athletics

BATTERS	BA	AB	R	H	HR	RBI	SO	SB
E. Durazo	.321	511	80	164	22	88	104	3
M. Kotsay	.314	606	78	190	15	63	70	8
S. Hatteberg	.284	550	87	156	15	82	48	0
E. Byrnes	.283	569	91	161	20	73	111	17
E. Chavez	.276	475	87	131	29	77	99	6
M. Scutaro	.273	455	50	124	7	43	58	0
D. Miller	.272	397	39	108	9	58	87	0
J. Dye	.265	532	87	141	23	80	128	4
A. Melhuse	.257	214	23	55	11	31	47	0
M. McLemore	.248	250	29	62	2	21	33	0
B. Crosby	.239	545	70	130	22	64	141	7
B. Kielty	.214	238	29	51	7	31	47	1

PITCHERS	W-L	ERA	IP	H	BB	SO	SV
J. Duchscherer	7-6	3.27	96.1	85	32	59	0
T. Hudson	12-6	3.53	188.2	194	44	103	0
R. Harden	11-7	3.99	189.2	171	81	167	0
O. Dotel#	6-2	4.09	50.2	41	18	72	22
M. Mulder	17-8	4.43	225.2	223	83	140	0
B. Zito	11-11	4.48	213.0	216	81	163	0
M. Redman	11-12	4.71	191.0	218	68	102	0

Manager-Ken Macha

Seattle Mariners

BATTERS	BA	AB	R	H	HR	RBI	SO	SB
I. Suzuki	.372	704	101	262	8	60	63	36
R. Ibanez	.304	481	67	146	16	62	72	1
R. Winn	.286	626	84	179	14	81	98	21
B. Jacobsen	.275	160	17	44	9	28	47	0
J. Cabrera	.270	359	38	97	6	47	70	10
E. Martinez	.263	486	45	128	12	63	107	1
B. Boone	.251	593	74	149	24	83	135	10
D. Wilson	.251	319	23	80	2	33	57	0
W. Bloomquist	.245	188	27	46	2	18	48	13
R. Aurilia#	.241	261	27	63	4	28	43	1
M. Olivo*	.233	301	46	70	13	40	84	7
J. Lopez	.232	207	28	48	5	22	31	0
S. Spiezio	.215	367	38	79	10	41	60	4

PITCHERS	W-L	ERA	IP	H	BB	SO	SV
E. Guardado	2-2	2.78	45.1	31	14	45	18
B. Madritsch	6-3	3.27	88.0	74	33	60	0
R. Villone	8-6	4.08	117.0	102	64	86	0
J. Pineiro	6-11	4.67	140.2	144	43	111	0
R. Franklin	4-16	4.90	200.1	224	61	104	0
G. Meche	7-7	5.01	127.2	139	47	99	0
J. Moyer	7-13	5.21	202.0	217	63	125	0

Manager-Bob Melvin

Tampa Bay Devil Rays

BATTERS	BA	AB	R	H	HR	RBI	SO	SB
J. Cantu	.301	173	25	52	2	17	44	0
A. Huff	.297	600	92	178	29	104	74	5
C. Crawford	.296	626	104	185	11	55	81	59
R. Baldelli	.280	518	79	145	16	74	88	17
J. Lugo	.275	581	83	160	7	75	106	21
T. Martinez	.262	458	63	120	23	76	72	3
B. Upton	.258	159	19	41	4	12	46	4
T. Hall	.255	404	35	103	8	60	41	0
R. Sanchez	.246	285	23	70	2	26	28	0
J. Cruz	.242	545	76	132	21	78	117	11
G. Blum	.215	339	38	73	8	35	58	2
B. Fordyce	.205	151	14	31	2	9	34	0
R. Fick	.201	214	12	43	6	26	32	0

PITCHERS	W-L	ERA	IP	H	BB	SO	SV
L. Carter	3-3	3.47	80.1	77	23	36	0
D. Baez	4-4	3.57	68.0	60	29	52	30
T. Harper	6-2	3.89	78.2	69	23	59	0
V. Zambrano#	9-7	4.43	128.0	107	96	109	0
R. Bell	8-8	4.46	123.0	121	41	57	0
J. Halama	7-6	4.70	118.2	134	27	59	0
D. Brazelton	6-8	4.77	120.2	121	53	64	0
M. Hendrickson	10-15	4.81	183.1	211	46	87	0
J. Sosa	4-7	5.53	99.1	100	54	94	1
D. Waechter	5-7	6.01	70.1	68	33	36	0

Manager-Lou Piniella

Texas Rangers

BATTERS	BA	AB	R	H	HR	RBI	SO	SB
M. Young	.313	690	114	216	22	99	89	12
E. Young	.288	344	55	99	1	27	28	14
M. Teixeira	.281	545	101	153	38	112	117	4
A. Soriano	.280	608	77	170	28	91	121	18
K. Mench	.279	438	69	122	26	71	63	0
H. Blalock	.276	624	107	172	32	110	149	2
G. Matthews	.275	280	37	77	11	36	64	5
R. Barajas	.249	358	50	89	15	58	63	0
L. Nix	.248	371	58	92	14	46	113	1
D. Dellucci	.242	331	59	80	17	61	88	9
B. Fullmer	.233	258	41	60	11	33	30	1
B. Jordan	.222	212	27	47	5	23	35	2

PITCHERS	W-L	ERA	IP	H	BB	SO	SV
F. Cordero	3-4	2.13	71.2	60	32	79	49
C. Almanzar	7-3	3.72	72.2	66	19	44	0
R. Drese	14-10	4.20	207.2	233	58	98	0
K. Rogers	18-9	4.76	211.2	248	66	126	0
C. Park	4-7	5.46	95.2	105	33	63	0
R. Dickey	6-7	5.61	104.1	136	33	57	1
J. Benoit	3-5	5.68	103.0	113	31	95	0

Manager-Buck Showalter

Toronto Blue Jays

BATTERS	BA	AB	R	H	HR	RBI	SO	SB
F. Catalanotto	.293	249	27	73	1	26	33	1
A. Rios	.286	426	55	122	1	28	84	15
C. Gomez	.282	341	41	96	3	37	41	3
F. Menechino	.275	269	40	74	9	26	52	0
V. Wells	.272	536	82	146	23	67	83	9
R. Johnson	.270	537	68	145	10	61	98	6
O. Hudson	.270	489	73	132	12	58	98	7
C. Delgado	.269	458	74	123	32	99	115	0
G. Zaun	.269	338	46	91	6	36	61	0
D. Berg	.253	154	13	39	3	23	27	0
E. Hinske	.246	570	66	140	15	69	109	12
C. Woodward	.235	213	21	50	1	24	46	1
K. Cash	.193	181	18	35	4	21	59	0

PITCHERS	W-L	ERA	IP	H	BB	SO	SV
D. Bush	5-4	3.69	97.2	95	25	64	0
T. Lilly	12-10	4.06	197.1	171	89	168	0
J. Frasor	4-6	4.08	68.1	64	36	54	17
R. Halladay	8-8	4.20	133.0	140	39	95	0
M. Batista	10-13	4.80	198.2	206	96	104	5
J. Towers	9-9	5.11	116.1	148	26	51	0
J. Miller	3-4	6.06	81.2	101	42	47	0

Manager-Carlos Tosca, John Gibbons

National Baseball Hall of Fame and Museum, Cooperstown, NY[1]

#Aaron, Hank	Clarke, Fred	Foster, Bill	Keefe, Timothy	*#Molitor, Paul	Snider, Duke
Alexander, Grover	Clarkson, John	Fox, Nellie	Keeler, William	#Morgan, Joe	#Spahn, Warren
Cleveland	#Clemente, Roberto	Foxx, Jimmie	Kell, George	#Murray, Eddie	Spalding, Albert
Alston, Walt	Cobb, Ty[2]	Frick, Ford	Kelley, Joe	#Musial, Stan	Speaker, Tris
Anderson, Sparky	Cochrane, Mickey	Frisch, Frank	Kelly, George	Newhouser, Hal	#Stargell, Willie
Anson, Cap	Collins, Eddie	Galvin, Pud	Kelly, King	Nichols, Kid	Stearnes, Norman
Aparicio, Luis	Collins, James	#Gehrig, Lou	Killebrew, Harmon	Niekro, Phil	"Turkey"
Appling, Luke	Combs, Earle	Gehringer, Charles	Kiner, Ralph	O'Rourke, James	Stengel, Casey
Ashburn, Richie	Comiskey,	#Gibson, Bob	Klein, Chuck	Ott, Mel	Sutton, Don
Averill, Earl	Charles A.	Gibson, Josh	Klem, Bill	Paige, Satchel	Terry, Bill
Baker, Home Run	Conlan, Jocko	Giles, Warren	#Koufax, Sandy	#Palmer, Jim	Thompson, Sam
Bancroft, Dave	Connolly, Thomas H.	Gomez, Lefty	Lajoie, Napoleon	Pennock, Herb	Tinker, Joe
#Banks, Ernie	Connor, Roger	Goslin, Goose	Landis, Kenesaw M.	Perez, Tony	Traynor, Pie
Barlick, Al	Coveleski, Stan	Greenberg, Hank	Lasorda, Tom	Perry, Gaylord	Vance, Dazzy
Barrow, Edward G.	Crawford, Sam	Griffith, Clark	Lazzeri, Tony	Plank, Ed	Vaughan, Arky
Beckley, Jake	Cronin, Joe	Grimes, Burleigh	Lemon, Bob	#Puckett, Kirby	Veeck, Bill
Bell, Cool Papa	Cummings, Candy	Grove, Lefty	Leonard, Buck	Radbourn, Charlie	Waddell, Rube
#Bench, Johnny	Cuyler, Kiki	Hafey, Chick	Lindstrom, Fred	Reese, Pee Wee	Wagner, Honus[2]
Bender, Chief	Dandridge, Ray	Haines, Jesee	Lloyd, Pop	Rice, Sam	Wallace, Roderick
Berra, Yogi	Davis, George	Hamilton, Bill	Lombardi, Ernie	Rickey, Branch	Walsh, Ed
Bottomley, Jim	"Gorgeous"	Hanlon, Ned	Lopez, Al	Rixey, Eppa	Waner, Lloyd
Boudreau, Lou	Day, Leon	Harridge, Will	Lyons, Ted	Rizzuto, Phil	Waner, Paul
Bresnahan, Roger	Dean, Dizzy	Harris, Bucky	Mack, Connie	(Scooter)	Ward, John
#Brett, George	Delahanty, Ed	Hartnett, Gabby	MacPhail, Larry	Roberts, Robin	Weaver, Earl
#Brock, Lou	Dickey, Bill	Heilmann, Harry	MacPhail, Lee	#Robinson, Brooks	Weiss, George
Brouthers, Dan	DiHigo, Martin	Herman, Billy	#Mantle, Mickey	#Robinson, Frank	Welch, Mickey
Brown, Mordecai	DiMaggio, Joe	Hooper, Harry	Manush, Henry	#Robinson, Jackie	Wells, Willie
(Three Finger)	#Doby, Larry	Hornsby, Rogers	Maranville, Rabbit	Robinson, Wilbert	Wheat, Zach
Bulkeley, Morgan C.	Doerr, Bobby	Hoyt, Waite	Marichal, Juan	Rogan, Joe "Bullet"	Wilhelm, Hoyt
Bunning, Jim	Drysdale, Don	Hubbard, Cal	Marquard, Rube	Roush, Edd	Williams, Billy
Burkett, Jesse C.	Duffy, Hugh	Hubbell, Carl	Mathews, Eddie	Ruffing, Red	Williams, Smokey
Campanella, Roy	Durocher, Leo	Huggins, Miller	Mathewson,	Rusie, Amos	Joe
#Carew, Rod	*#Eckersly, Dennis	Hulbert, William	Christy[2]	#Ruth, Babe[2]	#Williams, Ted
Carey, Max	Evans, Billy	Hunter, Catfish	#Mays, Willie	#Ryan, Nolan	Williams, Vic
#Carlton, Steve	Evers, John	Irvin, Monte	Mazeroski, Bill	Schalk, Ray	Wilson, Hack
Carter, Gary	Ewing, Buck	#Jackson, Reggie	McCarthy, Joe	#Schmidt, Mike	#Winfield, Dave
Cartwright,	Faber, Urban	Jackson, Travis	McCarthy, Thomas	Schoendienst, Red	Wright, George
Alexander	#Feller, Bob	Jenkins, Ferguson	#McCovey, Willie	#Seaver, Tom	Wright, Harry
Cepeda, Orlando	Ferrell, Rick	Jennings, Hugh	McGinnity, Joe	Selee, Frank	Wynn, Early
Chadwick, Henry	Fingers, Rollie	Johnson, Byron	McGowan, Bill	Sewell, Joe	#Yastrzemski, Carl
Chance, Frank	Fisk, Carlton	Johnson, William	McGraw, John	Simmons, Al	Yawkey, Tom
Chandler, Happy	Flick, Elmer H.	(Judy)	McKechnie, Bill	Sisler, George	Young, Cy
Charleston, Oscar	Ford, Whitey	Johnson, Walter[2]	McPhee, John "Bid"	Slaughter, Enos	Youngs, Ross
Chesbro, John	Foster, Andrew	Joss, Addie	Medwick, Joe	Smith, Hilton	#Yount, Robin
Chylak, Nestor	(Rube)	#Kaline, Al	Mize, Johnny	#Smith, Ozzie	

(1) Player must generally be retired for five complete seasons before being eligible for induction. (2) Players inducted in 1936 (the year the Hall of Fame began). # Denotes players chosen in first year of Hall of Fame eligibility or under special circumstances earlier. *Denotes 2004 inductees. **NOTE:** Four players, Babe Ruth (1936), Lou Gehrig (1939), Joe DiMaggio (1955), and Roberto Clemente (1973), were inducted less than five years after retirement or, in Clemente's case, death.

Major League Leaders in 2004

American League

Batting: Ichiro Suzuki, Seattle, .372; Melvin Mora, Baltimore, .340; Vladimir Guerrero, Anaheim, .337; Ivan Rodriguez, Detroit, .334; Erubiel Durazo, Oakland, .321.

Runs: Vladimir Guerrero, Anaheim, 124; Johnny Damon, Boston, 123; Gary Sheffield, New York, 117; Michael Young, Texas, 114; Alex Rodriguez, New York, 112.

Runs Batted In: Miguel Tejada, Baltimore, 150; David Ortiz, Boston, 139; Manny Ramirez, Boston, 130; Vladimir Guerrero, Anaheim, 126; Gary Sheffield, New York, 121.

Hits: Ichiro Suzuki, Seattle, 262*; Michael Young, Texas, 216; Vladimir Guerrero, Anaheim, 206; Miguel Tejada, Baltimore, 203; Mark Kotsay, Oakland, 190.

Doubles: Brian Roberts, Baltimore, 50; Ronnie Belliard, Cleveland, 48; David Ortiz, Boston, 47; Derek Jeter, New York, 44; Manny Ramirez, Boston, 44.

Triples: Carl Crawford, Tampa Bay, 19; Chone Figgins, Anaheim, 17; Carlos Guillen, Detroit, 10; Omar Infante, Detroit, 9; Michael Young, Texas, 9.

* MLB Record.

Home Runs: Manny Ramírez, Boston, 43; Paul Konerko, Chicago, 41; David Ortiz, Boston, 41; Vladimir Guerrero, Anaheim, 39; Mark Teixeira, Texas, 38.

Stolen Bases: Carl Crawford, Tampa Bay, 59; Ichiro Suzuki, Seattle, 36; Chone Figgins, Anaheim, 34; Brian Roberts, Baltimore, 29; Alex Rodriguez, New York, 28.

Pitching Wins: Curt Schilling, Boston, 21-6; Johan Santana, Minnesota, 20-6; Bartolo Colon, Anaheim, 18-12; Kenny Rogers, Texas, 18-9; Mark Mulder, Oakland, 17-8.

Earned Run Average: Johan Santana, Minnesota, 2.61; Curt Schilling, Boston, 3.26; Jake Westbrook, Cleveland, 3.38; Brad Radke, Minnesota, 3.48; Tim Hudson, Oakland, 3.53.

Strikeouts: Johan Santana, Minnesota, 265; Pedro Martínez, Boston, 227; Curt Schilling, Boston, 203; Kelvim Escobar, Anaheim, 191; Freddy Garcia, Chicago, 184.

Saves: Mariano Rivera, New York, 53; Francisco Cordero, Texas, 49; Joe Nathan, Minnesota, 44; Troy Percival, Anaheim, 33; Keith Foulke, Boston, 32.

National League

Batting: Barry Bonds, San Francisco, .362; Todd Helton, Colorado, .347; Mark Loretta, San Diego, .335; Adrian Beltre, Los Angeles, .334; Albert Pujols, St. Louis, .331.

Runs: Albert Pujols, St. Louis, 133; Barry Bonds, San Francisco, 129; Jimmy Rollins, Philadelphia, 119; Bobby Abreu, Philadelphia, 118; J.D. Drew, Atlanta, 118.

Runs Batted In: Vinny Castilla, Colorado, 131; Scott Rolen, St. Louis, 124; Albert Pujols, St. Louis, 123; Adrian Beltre, Los Angeles, 121; Miguel Cabrera, Florida, 112.

Hits: Juan Pierre, Florida, 221; Mark Loretta, San Diego, 208; J Wilson, Pittsburgh, 201; Adrian Beltre, Los Angeles, 200; Albert Pujols, St. Louis, 196.

Doubles: Lyle Overbay, Milwaukee, 53; Albert Pujols, St. Louis, 51; Todd Helton, Colorado, 49; Bobby Abreu, Philadelphia, 47; Craig Biggio, Houston, 47; Mark Loretta, San Diego, 47.

Triples: Juan Pierre, Florida, 12; Jimmy Rollins, Philadelphia, 12; Jack Wilson, Pittsburgh, 12; Cesar Izturis, Los Angeles, 9; 4 players tied with 8.

Home Runs: Adrian Beltre, Los Angeles, 48; Adam Dunn, Cincinnati, 46; Albert Pujols, St. Louis, 46; Barry Bonds, San Francisco, 45; Jim Edmonds, St. Louis, 42; Jim Thome, Philadelphia, 42.

Stolen Bases: Scott Podsednik, Milwaukee, 70; Juan Pierre, Florida, 45; Bobby Abreu, Philadelphia, 40; Ryan Freel, Cincinnati, 37; Dave Roberts, Los Angeles, 33.

Pitching Wins: Roy Oswalt, Houston, 20-10; Roger Clemens, Houston, 18-4; Jason Schmidt, San Francisco, 18-7; Carl Pavano, Florida, 18-8; Carlos Zambrano, Chicago, 16-8; Jeff Suppan, St. Louis, 16-9; Greg Maddux, Chicago, 16-11; Randy Johnson, Arizona, 16-14.
Earned Run Average: Jake Peavy, San Diego, 2.27; Randy Johnson, Arizona, 2.60; Ben Sheets, Milwaukee, 2.70; Carlos Zambrano, Chicago, 2.75; Roger Clemens, Houston, 2.98; Oliver Perez, Pittsburgh, 2.98.
Strikeouts: Randy Johnson, Arizona, 290; Ben Sheets, Milwaukee, 264; Jason Schmidt, San Francisco, 251; Oliver Perez, Pittsburgh, 239; Roger Clemens, Houston, 218.
Saves: Armando Benitez, Florida, 47; Jason Isringhausen, St. Louis, 47; Eric Gagne, Los Angeles, 45; John Smoltz, Atlanta, 44; Jose Mesa, Pittsburgh, 43.

50 Home Run Club

Only Mark McGwire and Barry Bonds have ever hit 70 or more home runs in a season. Five players—including Babe Ruth and Roger Maris—have hit 60 or more, a feat Sammy Sosa accomplished for the 3rd time in 2001. These 5 are at the pinnacle of a select group of players to have hit 50 or more homers in a season. The following list shows each time a player achieved this mark.

HR	Player, team	Year	HR	Player, team	Year
73	Barry Bonds, San Francisco Giants	2001	54	Babe Ruth, N.Y. Yankees	1928
70	Mark McGwire, St. Louis Cardinals	1998	54	Ralph Kiner, Pittsburgh Pirates	1949
66	Sammy Sosa, Chicago Cubs	1998	54	Mickey Mantle, N.Y. Yankees	1961
65	Mark McGwire, St. Louis Cardinals	1999	52	Mickey Mantle, N.Y. Yankees	1956
64	Sammy Sosa, Chicago Cubs	2001	52	Willie Mays, San Francisco Giants	1965
63	Sammy Sosa, Chicago Cubs	1999	52	George Foster, Cincinnati Reds	1977
61	Roger Maris, N.Y. Yankees	1961	52	Mark McGwire, Oakland A's	1996
60	Babe Ruth, N.Y. Yankees	1927	52	Alex Rodriguez, Texas Rangers	2001
59	Babe Ruth, N.Y. Yankees	1921	52	Jim Thome, Cleveland Indians	2002
58	Jimmie Foxx, Philadelphia Athletics	1932	51	Ralph Kiner, Pittsburgh Pirates	1947
58	Hank Greenberg, Detroit Tigers	1938	51	Johnny Mize, N.Y. Giants	1947
58	Mark McGwire, Oakland A's/St. Louis Cardinals	1997	51	Willie Mays, N.Y. Giants	1955
57	Luis Gonzalez, Arizona Diamondbacks	2001	51	Cecil Fielder, Detroit Tigers	1990
57	Alex Rodriguez, Texas Rangers	2002	50	Jimmie Foxx, Boston Red Sox	1938
56	Hack Wilson, Chicago Cubs	1930	50	Albert Belle, Cleveland Indians	1995
56	Ken Griffey Jr., Seattle Mariners	1997	50	Brady Anderson, Baltimore Orioles	1996
56	Ken Griffey Jr., Seattle Mariners	1998	50	Greg Vaughn, San Diego Padres	1998
54	Babe Ruth, N.Y. Yankees	1920	50	Sammy Sosa, Chicago Cubs	2000

Earned Run Average Leaders

	National League					American League			
Year	Player, team	G	IP	ERA	Year	Player, team	G	IP	ERA
1977	John Candelaria, Pittsburgh	33	231	2.34	1977	Frank Tanana, California	31	241	2.54
1978	Craig Swan, New York	29	207	2.43	1978	Ron Guidry, New York	35	274	1.74
1979	J. R. Richard, Houston	38	292	2.71	1979	Ron Guidry, New York	33	236	2.78
1980	Don Sutton, Los Angeles	32	212	2.21	1980	Rudy May, New York	41	175	2.47
1981	Nolan Ryan, Houston	21	149	1.69	1981	Steve McCatty, Oakland	22	186	2.32
1982	Steve Rogers, Montreal	35	277	2.40	1982	Rick Sutcliffe, Cleveland	34	216	2.96
1983	Atlee Hammaker, San Francisco	23	172	2.25	1983	Rick Honeycutt, Texas	25	174	2.42
1984	Alejandro Pena, Los Angeles	28	199	2.48	1984	Mike Boddicker, Baltimore	34	261	2.79
1985	Dwight Gooden, New York	35	276	1.53	1985	Dave Stieb, Toronto	36	265	2.48
1986	Mike Scott, Houston	37	275	2.22	1986	Roger Clemens, Boston	33	254	2.48
1987	Nolan Ryan, Houston	34	211	2.76	1987	Jimmy Key, Toronto	36	261	2.76
1988	Joe Magrane, St. Louis	24	165	2.18	1988	Allan Anderson, Minnesota	30	202	2.45
1989	Scott Garrelts, San Francisco	30	193	2.28	1989	Bret Saberhagen, Kansas City	36	262	2.16
1990	Danny Darwin, Houston	48	162	2.21	1990	Roger Clemens, Boston	31	228	1.93
1991	Dennis Martinez, Montreal	31	222	2.39	1991	Roger Clemens, Boston	35	271	2.62
1992	Bill Swift, San Francisco	30	164	2.08	1992	Roger Clemens, Boston	32	246	2.41
1993	Greg Maddux, Atlanta	36	267	2.36	1993	Kevin Appier, Kansas City	34	238	2.56
1994	Greg Maddux, Atlanta	25	202	1.56	1994	Steve Ontiveros, Oakland	27	115	2.65
1995	Greg Maddux, Atlanta	28	209	1.63	1995	Randy Johnson, Seattle	30	214	2.48
1996	Kevin Brown, Florida	32	233	1.89	1996	Juan Guzman, Toronto	27	187	2.93
1997	Pedro Martinez, Montrea	31	241	1.90	1997	Roger Clemens, Toronto	34	264	2.05
1998	Greg Maddux, Atlanta	34	251	2.22	1998	Roger Clemens, Toronto	33	234	2.65
1999	Randy Johnson, Arizona	35	271	2.48	1999	Pedro Martinez, Boston	31	213	2.07
2000	Kevin K. Brown, Los Angeles	33	230	2.58	2000	Pedro Martinez, Boston	29	217	1.74
2001	Randy Johnson, Arizona	35	249	2.49	2001	Freddy Garcia, Seattle	34	238	3.05
2002	Randy Johnson, Arizona	35	260	2.32	2002	Pedro Martinez, Boston	30	199	2.26
2003	Jason Schmidt, San Francisco	29	207	2.34	2003	Pedro Martinez, Boston	29	186	2.22
2004	Jake Peavy, San Diego	27	166.1	2.27	2004	Johan Santana, Minnesota	34	228	2.61

ERA is computed by multiplying earned runs allowed by 9, then dividing by innings pitched.

Strikeout Leaders

Note: Asterisk (*) indicates the all-time single-season record for each league.

	National League			American League	
Year	Pitcher, Team	SO	Year	Pitcher, Team	SO
1901	Noodles Hahn, Cincinnati	239	1901	Cy Young, Boston	158
1902	Vic Willis, Boston	225	1902	Rube Waddell, Philadelphia	210
1903	Christy Mathewson, New York	267	1903	Rube Waddell, Philadelphia	302
1904	Christy Mathewson, New York	212	1904	Rube Waddell, Philadelphia	349
1905	Christy Mathewson, New York	206	1905	Rube Waddell, Philadelphia	287
1906	Fred Beebe, Chicago-St. Louis	171	1906	Rube Waddell, Philadelphia	196
1907	Christy Mathewson, New York	178	1907	Rube Waddell, Philadelphia	232
1908	Christy Mathewson, New York	259	1908	Ed Walsh, Chicago	269
1909	Orval Overall, Chicago	205	1909	Frank Smith, Chicago	177
1910	Earl Moore, Philadelphia	185	1910	Walter Johnson, Washington	313
1911	Rube Marquard, New York	237	1911	Ed Walsh, Chicago	255
1912	Grover Alexander, Philadelphia	195	1912	Walter Johnson, Washington	303
1913	Tom Seaton, Philadelphia	168	1913	Walter Johnson, Washington	243
1914	Grover Alexander, Philadelphia	214	1914	Walter Johnson, Washington	225
1915	Grover Alexander, Philadelphia	241	1915	Walter Johnson, Washington	203

National League			American League		
Year	Pitcher, Team	SO	Year	Pitcher, Team	SO
1916	Grover Alexander, Philadelphia	167	1916	Walter Johnson, Washington	228
1917	Grover Alexander, Philadelphia	201	1917	Walter Johnson, Washington	188
1918	Hippo Vaughn, Chicago	148	1918	Walter Johnson, Washington	162
1919	Hippo Vaughn, Chicago	141	1919	Walter Johnson, Washington	147
1920	Grover Alexander, Chicago	173	1920	Stan Coveleski, Cleveland	133
1921	Burleigh Grimes, Brooklyn	136	1921	Walter Johnson, Washington	143
1922	Dazzy Vance, Brooklyn	134	1922	Urban Shocker, St. Louis	149
1923	Dazzy Vance, Brooklyn	197	1923	Walter Johnson, Washington	130
1924	Dazzy Vance, Brooklyn	262	1924	Walter Johnson, Washington	158
1925	Dazzy Vance, Brooklyn	221	1925	Lefty Grove, Philadelphia	116
1926	Dazzy Vance, Brooklyn	140	1926	Lefty Grove, Philadelphia	194
1927	Dazzy Vance, Brooklyn	184	1927	Lefty Grove, Philadelphia	174
1928	Dazzy Vance, Brooklyn	200	1928	Lefty Grove, Philadelphia	183
1929	Pat Malone, Chicago	166	1929	Lefty Grove, Philadelphia	170
1930	Bill Hallahan, St. Louis	177	1930	Lefty Grove, Philadelphia	209
1931	Bill Hallahan, St. Louis	159	1931	Lefty Grove, Philadelphia	175
1932	Dizzy Dean, St. Louis	191	1932	Red Ruffing, New York	190
1933	Dizzy Dean, St. Louis	199	1933	Lefty Gomez, New York	163
1934	Dizzy Dean, St. Louis	195	1934	Lefty Gomez, New York	158
1935	Dizzy Dean, St. Louis	190	1935	Tommy Bridges, Detroit	163
1936	Van Lingle Mungo, Brooklyn	238	1936	Tommy Bridges, Detroit	175
1937	Carl Hubbell, New York	159	1937	Lefty Gomez, New York	194
1938	Clay Bryant, Chicago	135	1938	Bob Feller, Cleveland	240
1939	Claude Passeau, Philadelphia-Chicago Bucky Walters, Cincinnati	137	1939	Bob Feller, Cleveland	246
1940	Kirby Higbe, Philadelphia	137	1940	Bob Feller, Cleveland	261
1941	John Vander Meer, Cincinnati	202	1941	Bob Feller, Cleveland	260
1942	John Vander Meer, Cincinnati	186	1942	Tex Hughson, Boston Bobo Newsom, Washington	113
1943	John Vander Meer, Cincinnati	174	1943	Allie Reynolds, Cleveland	151
1944	Bill Voiselle, New York	161	1944	Hal Newhouser, Detroit	187
1945	Preacher Roe, Pittsburgh	148	1945	Hal Newhouser, Detroit	212
1946	Johnny Schmitz, Cincinnati	135	1946	Bob Feller, Cleveland	348
1947	Ewell Blackwell, Cincinnati	193	1947	Bob Feller, Cleveland	196
1948	Harry Brecheen, St. Louis	149	1948	Bob Feller, Cleveland	164
1949	Warren Spahn, Boston	151	1949	Virgil Trucks, Detroit	153
1950	Warren Spahn, Boston	191	1950	Bob Lemon, Cleveland	170
1951	Warren Spahn, Boston Don Newcombe, Brooklyn	164	1951	Vic Raschi, New York	164
1952	Warren Spahn, Boston	183	1952	Allie Reynolds, New York	160
1953	Robin Roberts, Philadelphia	198	1953	Billy Pierce, Chicago	186
1954	Robin Roberts, Philadelphia	185	1954	Bob Turley, Baltimore	185
1955	Sam Jones, Chicago	198	1955	Herb Score, Cleveland	245
1956	Sam Jones, Chicago	176	1956	Herb Score, Cleveland	263
1957	Jack Sanford, Philadelphia	188	1957	Early Wynn, Cleveland	184
1958	Sam Jones, St. Louis	225	1958	Early Wynn, Chicago	179
1959	Don Drysdale, Los Angeles	242	1959	Jim Bunning, Detroit	201
1960	Don Drysdale, Los Angeles	246	1960	Jim Bunning, Detroit	201
1961	Sandy Koufax, Los Angeles	269	1961	Camilo Pacual, Minnesota	221
1962	Don Drysdale, Los Angeles	232	1962	Camilo Pacual, Minnesota	206
1963	Sandy Koufax, Los Angeles	306	1963	Camilo Pacual, Minnesota	202
1964	Bob Veale, Pittsburgh	250	1964	Al Downing, New York	217
1965	Sandy Koufax, Los Angeles	*382	1965	Sam McDowell, Cleveland	325
1966	Sandy Koufax, Los Angeles	317	1966	Sam McDowell, Cleveland	225
1967	Jim Bunning, Philadelphia	253	1967	Jim Lonborg, Boston	246
1968	Bob Gibson, St. Louis	268	1968	Sam McDowell, Cleveland	283
1969	Ferguson Jenkins, Chicago	273	1969	Sam McDowell, Cleveland	279
1970	Tom Seaver, New York	283	1970	Sam McDowell, Cleveland	304
1971	Tom Seaver, New York	289	1971	Mickey Lolich, Detroit	308
1972	Steve Carlton, Philadelphia	310	1972	Nolan Ryan, California	329
1973	Tom Seaver, New York	251	1973	Nolan Ryan, California	*383
1974	Steve Carlton, Philadelphia	240	1974	Nolan Ryan, California	367
1975	Tom Seaver, New York	243	1975	Frank Tanana, California	269
1976	Tom Seaver, New York	235	1976	Nolan Ryan, California	327
1977	Phil Niekro, Atlanta	262	1977	Nolan Ryan, California	341
1978	J.R. Richard, Houston	303	1978	Nolan Ryan, California	260
1979	J.R. Richard, Houston	313	1979	Nolan Ryan, California	223
1980	Steve Carlton, Philadelphia	286	1980	Len Barker, Cleveland	187
1981	Fernando Valenzuela, Los Angeles	180	1981	Len Barker, Cleveland	127
1982	Steve Carlton, Philadelphia	286	1982	Floyd Bannister, Seattle	209
1983	Steve Carlton, Philadelphia	275	1983	Jack Morris, Detroit	232
1984	Dwight Gooden, New York	276	1984	Mark Langston, Seattle	204
1985	Dwight Gooden, New York	268	1985	Bert Blyleven, Cleveland-Minnesota	206
1986	Mike Scott, Houston	306	1986	Mark Langston, Seattle	245
1987	Nolan Ryan, Houston	270	1987	Mark Langston, Seattle	262
1988	Nolan Ryan, Houston	228	1988	Roger Clemens, Boston	291
1989	Jose DeLeon, St. Louis	201	1989	Nolan Ryan, Texas	301
1990	David Cone, New York	233	1990	Nolan Ryan, Texas	232
1991	David Cone, New York	241	1991	Roger Clemens, Boston	241
1992	John Smoltz, Atlanta	215	1992	Randy Johnson, Seattle	241
1993	Jose Rijo, Cincinnati	227	1993	Randy Johnson, Seattle	308
1994	Andy Benes, San Diego	189	1994	Randy Johnson, Seattle	204
1995	Hideo Nomo, Los Angeles	236	1995	Randy Johnson, Seattle	294
1996	John Smoltz, Atlanta	276	1996	Roger Clemens, Boston	257
1997	Curt Schilling, Philadelphia	319	1997	Roger Clemens, Toronto	292
1998	Curt Schilling, Philadelphia	300	1998	Roger Clemens, Toronto	271

National League			American League		
Year	Pitcher, Team	SO	Year	Pitcher, Team	SO
1999	Randy Johnson, Arizona	364	1999	Pedro Martinez, Boston	313
2000	Randy Johnson, Arizona	347	2000	Pedro Martinez, Boston	284
2001	Randy Johnson, Arizona	372	2001	Hideo Nomo, Boston	220
2002	Randy Johnson, Arizona	334	2002	Pedro Martinez, Boston	239
2003	Kerry Wood, Chicago	266	2003	Esteban Loaiza, Chicago	207
2004	Randy Johnson, Arizona	290	2004	Johan Santana, Minnesota	265

Victory Leaders

Note: Asterisk (*) indicates the all-time single-season record for each league in the "modern" era beginning in 1901.

National League			American League		
Year	Pitcher, Team	Wins	Year	Pitcher, Team	Wins
1901	Bill Donavan, Brooklyn	25	1901	Cy Young, Boston	33
1902	Jack Chesbro, Pittsburgh	28	1902	Cy Young, Boston	32
1903	Joe McGinnity, New York	31	1903	Cy Young, Boston	28
1904	Joe McGinnity, New York	35	1904	Jack Chesbro, New York	*41
1905	Christy Mathewson, New York	31	1905	Rube Waddell, Philadelphia	27
1906	Joe McGinnity, New York	27	1906	Al Orth, New York	27
1907	Christy Mathewson, New York	24	1907	Doc White, Chicago	27
1908	Christy Mathewson, New York	*37	1908	Ed Walsh, Chicago	40
1909	Mordecai Brown, Chicago	27	1909	George Mullin, Detroit	29
1910	Christy Mathewson, New York	27	1910	Jack Coombs, Philadelphia	31
1911	Grover Alexander, Chicago	28	1911	Jack Coombs, Philadelphia	28
1912	Rube Marquard, New York	26	1912	Joe Wood, Boston	34
1913	Tom Seaton, Philadelphia	27	1913	Walter Johnson, Washington	36
1914	Grover Alexander, Philadelphia	27	1914	Walter Johnson, Washington	28
1915	Grover Alexander, Philadelphia	31	1915	Walter Johnson, Washington	27
1916	Grover Alexander, Philadelphia	33	1916	Walter Johnson, Washington	25
1917	Grover Alexander, Philadelphia	30	1917	Eddie Cicotte, Chicago	28
1918	Hippo Vaughn, Chicago	22	1918	Walter Johnson, Washington	23
1919	Jesse Barnes, New York	25	1919	Eddie Cicotte, Chicago	29
1920	Grover Alexander, Philadelphia	27	1920	Jim Bagby, Cleveland	31
1921	Burleigh Grimes, Brooklyn	22	1921	Urban Shocker, St. Louis	27
1922	Eppa Rixey, Cincinnati	25	1922	Eddie Rommel, Philadelphia	27
1923	Dolf Luque, Cincinnati	27	1923	George Uhle, Cleveland	26
1924	Dazzy Vance, Brooklyn	28	1924	Walter Johnson, Washington	23
1925	Dazzy Vance, Brooklyn	22	1925	Eddie Rommel, Philadelphia	21
1926	Flint Rhem, St. Louis	20	1926	George Uhle, Cleveland	27
1927	Charlie Root, Chicago	26	1927	Ted Lyons, Chicago	22
1928	Burleigh Grimes, Pittsburgh	25	1928	George Pipgras, New York	24
1929	Pat Malone, Chicago	22	1929	George Earnshaw, Philadelphia	24
1930	Pat Malone, Chicago	20	1930	Lefty Grove, Philadelphia	28
1931	Heine Meine, Pittsburgh	19	1931	Lefty Grove, Philadelphia	31
1932	Lon Warneke, Chicago	22	1932	Alvin Crowder, Washington	26
1933	Carl Hubbell, New York	23	1933	Lefty Grove, Philadelphia	24
1934	Dizzy Dean, St. Louis	30	1934	Lefty Gomez, New York	26
1935	Dizzy Dean, St. Louis	28	1935	Wes Ferrell, Boston	25
1936	Carl Hubbell, New York	26	1936	Tommy Bridges, Detroit	23
1937	Carl Hubbell, New York	22	1937	Lefty Gomez, New York	21
1938	Bill Lee, Chicago	22	1938	Red Ruffing, New York	21
1939	Bucky Walters, Cincinnati	27	1939	Bob Feller, Cleveland	24
1940	Bucky Walters, Cincinnati	22	1940	Bob Feller, Cleveland	27
1941	Whit Wyatt, Brooklyn	22	1941	Bob Feller, Cleveland	25
1942	Mort Cooper, St. Louis	22	1942	Tex Hughson, Boston	22
1943	Rip Sewell, Pittsburgh	21	1943	Dizzy Trout, Detroit	20
1944	Bucky Walters, Cincinnati	23	1944	Hal Newhouser, Detroit	29
1945	Red Barrett, Boston-St. Louis	23	1945	Hal Newhouser, Detroit	25
1946	Howie Pollet, St. Louis	21	1946	Hal Newhouser, Detroit	26
1947	Ewell Blackwell, Cincinnati	22	1947	Bob Feller, Cleveland	20
1948	Johnny Sain, Boston	24	1948	Hal Newhouser, Detroit	21
1949	Warren Spahn, Boston	21	1949	Mel Parnell, Boston	25
1950	Warren Spahn, Boston	21	1950	Bob Lemon, Cleveland	23
1951	Sal Maglie, New York	23	1951	Bob Feller, Cleveland	22
1952	Robin Roberts, Philadelphia	28	1952	Bobby Shantz, Philadelphia	24
1953	Warren Spahn, Milwaukee	23	1953	Bob Porterfield, Washington	22
1954	Robin Roberts, Philadelphia	23	1954	Early Wynn, Cleveland	23
1955	Robin Roberts, Philadelphia	23	1955	Frank Sullivan, Boston	18
1956	Don Newcombe, Brooklyn	27	1956	Frank Lary, Detroit	21
1957	Warren Spahn, Milwaukee	21	1957	Billy Pierce, Chicago	20
1958	Warren Spahn, Milwaukee	22	1958	Bob Turley, New York	21
1959	Warren Spahn, Milwaukee	21	1959	Early Wynn, Chicago	22
1960	Warren Spahn, Milwaukee	21	1960	Jim Perry, Cleveland	18
1961	Warren Spahn, Milwaukee	21	1961	Whitey Ford, New York	25
1962	Don Drysdale, Los Angeles	25	1962	Ralph Terry, New York	23
1963	Juan Marichal, San Francisco	25	1963	Whitey Ford, New York	24
1964	Larry Jackson, Chicago	24	1964	Gary Peters, Chicago	20
1965	Sandy Koufax, Los Angeles	26	1965	Mudcat (Jim) Grant, Minnesota	21
1966	Sandy Koufax, Los Angeles	27	1966	Jim Kaat, Minnesota	25
1967	Mike McCormick, San Francisco	22	1967	Earl Wilson, Detroit	22
1968	Juan Marichal, San Francisco	26	1968	Denny McLain, Detroit	31
1969	Tom Seaver, New York	25	1969	Denny McLain, Detroit	24
1970	Gaylord Perry, San Francisco	23	1970	Jim Perry, Minnesota	24
1971	Fergie Jenkins, Chicago	24	1971	Mickey Lolich, Detroit	25
1972	Steve Carlton, Philadelphia	27	1972	Wilbur Wood, Chicago	24
1973	Ron Bryant, San Francisco	24	1973	Wilbur Wood, Chicago	24
1974	Phil Niekro, Atlanta	20	1974	Fergie Jenkins, Texas	25

National League			American League		
Year	Pitcher, Team	Wins	Year	Pitcher, Team	Wins
1975	Tom Seaver, New York	22	1975	Jim Palmer, Baltimore	23
1976	Randy Jones, San Diego	22	1976	Jim Palmer, Baltimore	22
1977	Steve Carlton, Philadelphia	23	1977	Jim Palmer, Baltimore	20
1978	Gaylord Perry, San Diego	21	1978	Ron Guidry, New York	25
1979	Phil Niekro, Atlanta	21	1979	Mike Flanagan, Baltimore	23
1980	Steve Carlton, Philadelphia	24	1980	Steve Stone, Baltimore	25
1981	Tom Seaver, Cincinnati	14	1981	Pete Vuckovich, Milwaukee	14
1982	Steve Carlton, Philadelphia	23	1982	La Marr Hoyt, Chicago	19
1983	John Denny, Philadelphia	19	1983	La Marr Hoyt, Chicago	24
1984	Joaquin Andujar, St. Louis	20	1984	Mike Boddicker, Baltimore	20
1985	Dwight Gooden, New York	24	1985	Ron Guidry, New York	22
1986	Fernando Valenzuela, Los Angeles	21	1986	Roger Clemens, Boston	24
1987	Rick Sutcliffe, Chicago	18	1987	Dave Stewart, Oakland; Roger Clemens, Boston	20
1988	Danny Jackson, Cincinnati	23	1988	Frank Viola, Minnesota	24
1989	Mike Scott, Houston	20	1989	Bret Saberhagen, Kansas City	23
1990	Doug Drabek, Pittsburgh	22	1990	Bob Welch, Oakland	27
1991	John Smiley, Pittsburgh	20	1991	Bill Gullickson, Detroit	20
1992	Greg Maddux, Chicago	20	1992	Jack Morris, Toronto	21
1993	Tom Glavine, Atlanta	22	1993	Jack McDowell, Chicago	22
1994	Greg Maddux, Atlanta	16	1994	Jimmy Key, New York	17
1995	Greg Maddux, Atlanta	19	1995	Mike Mussina, Baltimore	19
1996	John Smoltz, Atlanta	24	1996	Andy Pettitte, New York	21
1997	Denny Neagle, Atlanta	20	1997	Roger Clemens, Toronto	21
1998	Tom Glavine, Atlanta	20	1998	Rick Helling, Texas; Roger Clemens, Toronto	20
1999	Mike Hampton, Houston	22	1999	Pedro Martinez, Boston	23
2000	Tom Glavine, Atlanta	21	2000	David Wells, Toronto	20
2001	Matt Morris, St. Louis; Curt Schilling, Arizona	22	2001	Mark Mulder, Oakland	21
2002	Randy Johnson, Arizona	24	2002	Barry Zito, Oakland	23
2003	Russ Ortiz, Atlanta	21	2003	Roy Halladay, Toronto	22
2004	Roy Oswalt, Houston	20	2004	Curt Schilling, Boston	21

All-Time World Series Career Leaders

(Through 2003. * Player active in 2003.)

Batting Leaders

Batter	Hits	AB	Avg.	Batter	Hits	AB	Avg.
1. Bobby Brown	18	41	.439	6. Lou Brock	34	87	.391
2. Paul Molitor	23	55	.418	7. Marquis Grissom*	30	77	.390
3. Pepper Martin	23	55	.418	8. Troy Glaus*	10	26	.385
4. J.T. Snow*	11	27	.407	9. George Brett	19	51	.373
5. Hal McRae	18	45	.400	10. Thurman Munson	25	67	.373

Games Played

Yogi Berra	75
Mickey Mantle	65
Elston Howard	54
Hank Bauer	53
Gil McDougald	53
Phil Rizzuto	52
Joe DiMaggio	51
Frankie Frisch	50
Pee Wee Reese	44
Roger Maris	41
Babe Ruth	41

Hits

Yogi Berra	71
Mickey Mantle	59
Frankie Frisch	58
Joe DiMaggio	54
Hank Bauer	46
PeeWee Reese	46
Phil Rizzuto	45
Gil McDougald	45
Lou Gehrig	43
Elston Howard	42
Babe Ruth	42
Eddie Collins	42

Runs

Mickey Mantle	42
Yogi Berra	41
Babe Ruth	37
Lou Gehrig	30
Joe DiMaggio	27
Derek Jeter*	27
Roger Maris	26
Elston Howard	25
Gil McDougald	23
Jackie Robinson	22

Runs Batted In

Mickey Mantle	40
Yogi Berra	39
Lou Gehrig	35
Babe Ruth	33
Joe DiMaggio	30
Bill Skowron	29
Duke Snider	26
Reggie Jackson	24
Hank Bauer	24
Bill Dickey	24
Gil McDougald	24

Home Runs

Mickey Mantle	18
Babe Ruth	15
Yogi Berra	12
Duke Snider	11
Reggie Jackson	10
Lou Gehrig	10
Joe DiMaggio	8
Bill Skowron	8
Frank Robinson	8
Hank Bauer	7
Gil McDougald	7
Goose Goslin	7

Stolen Bases

Lou Brock	14
Eddie Collins	14
Frank Chance	10
Dave Lopes	10
Phil Rizzuto	10
Frank Frisch	9
Honus Wagner	9
Johnny Evers	8
Roberto Alomar*	7
Rickey Henderson	7
Pepper Martin	7
Joe Morgan	7
Joe Tinker	7

Pitching Leaders

Games Pitched

Whitey Ford	22
Mariano Rivera*	20
Rollie Fingers	16
Jeff Nelson*	16
Allie Reynolds	15
Mike Stanton*	15
Bob Turley	15
Clay Carroll	14
Clem Labine	13
Mark Wohlers	13
Waite Hoyt	12
Catfish Hunter	12
Art Nehf	12

Wins

Whitey Ford	10
Bob Gibson	7
Allie Reynolds	7
Red Ruffing	7
Chief Bender	6
Lefty Gomez	6
Waite Hoyt	6
Three Finger Brown	5
Jack Coombs	5
Catfish Hunter	5
Herb Pennock	5
Vic Raschi	5
Christy Mathewson	5

Strikeouts

Whitey Ford	94
Bob Gibson	92
Allie Reynolds	62
Sandy Koufax	61
Red Ruffing	61
Chief Bender	59
George Earnshaw	56
John Smoltz*	52
Waite Hoyt	49
Christy Mathewson	48

Saves

Mariano Rivera*	9
Rollie Fingers	6
Johnny Murphy	4
Allie Reynolds	4
John Wetteland	4
Robb Nen	4

World Series Results, 1903-2003

1903	Boston AL 5, Pittsburgh NL 3	1937	New York AL 4, New York NL 1	1971	Pittsburgh NL 4, Baltimore AL 3
1904	No series	1938	New York AL 4, Chicago NL 0	1972	Oakland AL 4, Cincinnati NL 3
1905	New York NL 4, Philadelphia AL 1	1939	New York AL 4, Cincinnati NL 0	1973	Oakland AL 4, New York NL 3
1906	Chicago AL 4, Chicago NL 2	1940	Cincinnati NL 4, Detroit AL 3	1974	Oakland AL 4, Los Angeles NL 1
1907	Chicago NL 4, Detroit AL 0, 1 tie	1941	New York AL 4, Brooklyn NL 1	1975	Cincinnati NL 4, Boston AL 3
1908	Chicago NL 4, Detroit AL 1	1942	St. Louis NL 4, New York AL 1	1976	Cincinnati NL 4, New York AL 0
1909	Pittsburgh NL 4, Detroit AL 3	1943	New York AL 4, St. Louis NL 1	1977	New York AL 4, Los Angeles NL 2
1910	Philadelphia AL 4, Chicago NL 1	1944	St. Louis NL 4, St. Louis AL 2	1978	New York AL 4, Los Angeles NL 2
1911	Philadelphia AL 4, New York NL 2	1945	Detroit AL 4, Chicago NL 3	1979	Pittsburgh NL 4, Baltimore AL 3
1912	Boston AL 4, New York NL 3, 1 tie	1946	St. Louis NL 4, Boston AL 3	1980	Philadelphia NL 4, Kansas City AL 2
1913	Philadelphia AL 4, New York NL 1	1947	New York AL 4, Brooklyn NL 3	1981	Los Angeles NL 4, New York AL 2
1914	Boston NL 4, Philadelphia AL 0	1948	Cleveland AL 4, Boston NL 2	1982	St. Louis NL 4, Milwaukee AL 3
1915	Boston AL 4, Philadelphia NL 1	1949	New York AL 4, Brooklyn NL 1	1983	Baltimore AL 4, Philadelphia NL 1
1916	Boston AL 4, Brooklyn NL 1	1950	New York AL 4, Philadelphia NL 0	1984	Detroit AL 4, San Diego NL 1
1917	Chicago AL 4, New York NL 2	1951	New York AL 4, New York NL 2	1985	Kansas City AL 4, St. Louis NL 3
1918	Boston AL 4, Chicago NL 2	1952	New York AL 4, Brooklyn NL 3	1986	New York NL 4, Boston AL 3
1919	Cincinnati NL 5, Chicago AL 3	1953	New York AL 4, Brooklyn NL 2	1987	Minnesota AL 4, St. Louis NL 3
1920	Cleveland AL 5, Brooklyn NL 2	1954	New York NL 4, Cleveland AL 0	1988	Los Angeles NL 4, Oakland AL 1
1921	New York NL 5, New York AL 3	1955	Brooklyn NL 4, New York AL 3	1989	Oakland AL 4, San Francisco NL 0
1922	New York NL 4, New York AL 0, 1 tie	1956	New York AL 4, Brooklyn NL 3	1990	Cincinnati NL 4, Oakland AL 0
1923	New York AL 4, New York NL 2	1957	Milwaukee NL 4, New York AL 3	1991	Minnesota AL 4, Atlanta NL 3
1924	Washington AL 4, New York NL 3	1958	New York AL 4, Milwaukee NL 3	1992	Toronto AL 4, Atlanta NL 2
1925	Pittsburgh NL 4, Washington AL 3	1959	Los Angeles NL 4, Chicago AL 2	1993	Toronto AL 4, Philadelphia NL 2
1926	St. Louis NL 4, New York AL 3	1960	Pittsburgh NL 4, New York AL 3	1994	No series
1927	New York AL 4, Pittsburgh NL 0	1961	New York AL 4, Cincinnati NL 1	1995	Atlanta NL 4, Cleveland AL 2
1928	New York AL 4, St. Louis NL 0	1962	New York AL 4, San Francisco NL 3	1996	New York AL 4, Atlanta NL 2
1929	Philadelphia AL 4, Chicago NL 1	1963	Los Angeles NL 4, New York AL 0	1997	Florida NL 4, Cleveland AL 3
1930	Philadelphia AL 4, St. Louis NL 2	1964	St. Louis NL 4, New York AL 3	1998	New York AL 4, San Diego NL 0
1931	St. Louis NL 4, Philadelphia AL 3	1965	Los Angeles NL 4, Minnesota AL 3	1999	New York AL 4, Atlanta NL 0
1932	New York AL 4, Chicago NL 0	1966	Baltimore AL 4, Los Angeles NL 0	2000	New York AL 4, New York NL 1
1933	New York NL 4, Washington AL 1	1967	St. Louis NL 4, Boston AL 3	2001	Arizona NL 4, New York AL 3
1934	St. Louis NL 4, Detroit AL 3	1968	Detroit AL 4, St. Louis NL 3	2002	Anaheim AL 4, San Francisco NL 3
1935	Detroit AL 4, Chicago NL 2	1969	New York NL 4, Baltimore AL 1	2003	Florida NL 4, New York AL 2
1936	New York AL 4, New York NL 2	1970	Baltimore AL 4, Cincinnati NL 1		

World Series MVP

Year	Player, Position, Team	Year	Player, Position, Team	Year	Player, Position, Team
1955	Johnny Podres, p, Brooklyn	1973	Reggie Jackson, of, Oakland	1988	Orel Hershiser, p, LA
1956	Don Larsen, p, New York, AL	1974	Rollie Fingers, p, Oakland	1989	Dave Stewart, p, Oakland
1957	Lew Burdette, p, Milwaukee, NL	1975	Pete Rose, 3b, Cincinnati	1990	Jose Rijo, p, Cincinnati
1958	Bob Turley, p, NY AL	1976	Johnny Bench, c, Cincinnati	1991	Jack Morris, p, Minnesota
1959	Larry Sherry, p, LA	1977	Reggie Jackson, of, NY, AL	1992	Pat Borders, c, Toronto
1960[1]	Bobby Richardson, 2b, NY, AL	1978	Bucky Dent, ss, NY, AL	1993	Paul Molitor, dh, Toronto
1961	Whitey Ford, p, NY, AL	1979	Willie Stargell, 1b, Pittsburgh	1994	no series
1962	Ralph Terry, p, NY, AL	1980	Mike Schmidt, 3b, Philadelphia	1995	Tom Glavine, p, Atlanta
1963	Sandy Koufax, p, Los Angeles, NL	1981	Ron Cey, 3b, LA	1996	John Wetteland, p, NY, AL
1964	Bob Gibson, p, St. Louis		Pedro Guerrero, of, LA	1997	Livan Hernandez, p, Florida
1965	Sandy Koufax, p, Los Angeles, NL		Steve Yeager, c, LA	1998	Scott Brosius, 3b, NY, AL
1966	Frank Robinson, of, Baltimore	1982	Darrell Porter, c, St. Louis	1999	Mariano Rivera, p, NY, AL
1967	Bob Gibson, p, St. Louis	1983	Rick Dempsey, c, Baltimore	2000	Derek Jeter, ss, NY, AL
1968	Mickey Lolich, p, Detroit	1984	Alan Trammell, ss, Detroit	2001	Curt Schilling, p, Arizona
1969	Donn Clendenon, 1b, NY, NL	1985	Bret Saberhagen, p, Kansas City		Randy Johnson, p, Arizona
1970	Brooks Robinson, 3b, Baltimore	1986	Ray Knight, 3b, NY, NL	2002	Troy Glaus, 3b, Anaheim
1971	Roberto Clemente, of, Pittsburgh	1987	Frank Viola, p, Minnesota	2003	Josh Beckett, p, Florida
1972	Gene Tenace, c, Oakland				

(1) Bobby Richardson won the MVP although Pittsburgh beat New York.

World Series Won-Lost Records, by Franchise[1]

Team	Wins	Losses	Team	Wins	Losses
New York Yankees	26	13	Florida Marlins	2	0
Philadelphia/Kansas City/Oakland A's	9	5	Toronto Blue Jays	2	0
St. Louis Cardinals	9	6	New York Mets	2	2
Brooklyn/Los Angeles Dodgers	6	12	Chicago White Sox	2	2
Pittsburgh Pirates	5	2	Cleveland Indians	2	3
Boston Red Sox	5	4	Chicago Cubs	2	8
Cincinnati Reds	5	4	LA/California/Anaheim Angels	1	0
New York/San Francisco Giants	5	12	Arizona Diamondbacks	1	0
Detroit Tigers	4	5	Kansas City Royals	1	1
Washington Senators/Minnesota Twins	3	3	Philadelphia Phillies	1	4
St. Louis Browns/Baltimore Orioles	3	4	Seattle Pilots/Milwaukee Brewers	0	1
Boston/Milwaukee/Atlanta Braves	3	6	San Diego Padres	0	2

(1) Through 2003.

All-Time Major League Leaders

(Source: www.mlb.com; *player active in 2004 season)

Games		At Bats		Runs Batted In		Runs	
Pete Rose	3,562	Pete Rose	14,053	Hank Aaron	2,297	Rickey Henderson	2,295
Carl Yastrzemski	3,308	Hank Aaron	12,364	Babe Ruth	2,213	Ty Cobb	2,245
Hank Aaron	3,298	Carl Yastrzemski	11,988	Cap Anson	2,076	Hank Aaron	2,174
Rickey Henderson	3,081	Cal Ripken Jr.	11,551	Lou Gehrig	1,995	Babe Ruth	2,174
Ty Cobb	3,035	Ty Cobb	11,429	Stan Musial	1,951	Pete Rose	2,165
Eddie Murray	3,026	Eddie Murray	11,336	Ty Cobb	1,938	Barry Bonds*	2,070
Stan Musial	3,026	Robin Yount	11,008	Jimmie Foxx	1,922	Willie Mays	2,062
Cal Ripken Jr.	3,001	Dave Winfield	11,003	Eddie Murray	1,917	Cap Anson	1,996
Willie Mays	2,992	Stan Musial	10,972	Willie Mays	1,903	Stan Musial	1,949
Dave Winfield	2,973	Rickey Henderson	10,961	Mel Ott	1,860	Lou Gehrig	1,888

Stolen Bases

Rickey Henderson	1,406
Lou Brock	938
Billy Hamilton	912
Ty Cobb	892
Tim Raines	808
Vince Coleman	752
Eddie Collins	745
Arlie Latham	739
Max Carey	738
Honus Wagner	722

Triples

Sam Crawford	309
Ty Cobb	297
Honus Wagner	252
Jake Beckley	243
Roger Connor	233
Tris Speaker	222
Fred Clarke	220
Dan Brouthers	205
Joe Kelley	194
Paul Waner	191

Batting Average

Ty Cobb	.367
Rogers Hornsby	.358
Ed Delahanty	.346
Tris Speaker	.345
Billy Hamilton	.344
Ted Williams	.344
Dan Brouthers	.342
Harry Heilmann	.342
Babe Ruth	.342
Willie Keeler	.341
Bill Terry	.341

Walks

Barry Bonds*	2,302
Rickey Henderson	2,190
Babe Ruth	2,062
Ted Williams	2,019
Joe Morgan	1,865
Carl Yastrzemski	1,845
Mickey Mantle	1,733
Mel Ott	1,708
Eddie Yost	1,614
Darrell Evans	1,605

Strikeouts

Nolan Ryan	5,714
Roger Clemens*	4,317
Randy Johnson*	4,161
Steve Carlton	4,136
Bert Blyleven	3,701
Tom Seaver	3,640
Don Sutton	3,574
Gaylord Perry	3,534
Walter Johnson	3,508
Phil Niekro	3,342

Saves

Lee Smith	478
John Franco*	424
Trevor Hoffman*	393
Dennis Eckersley	390
Jeff Reardon	367
Randy Myers	347
Rollie Fingers	341
Mariano Rivera*	336
John Wetteland	330
Roberto Hernandez*	320

Shutouts

Walter Johnson	110
Grover Alexander	90
Christy Mathewson	79
Cy Young	76
Eddie Plank	69
Warren Spahn	63
Nolan Ryan	61
Tom Seaver	61
Bert Blyleven	60
Don Sutton	58

Losses

Cy Young	316
Jim Galvin	310
Nolan Ryan	292
Walter Johnson	279
Phil Niekro	274
Gaylord Perry	265
Don Sutton	256
Jack Powell	254
Eppa Rixey	251
Bert Blyleven	250

All-Time Home Run Leaders

(Source: www.mlb.com; *player active in 2004 season)

Hank Aaron	755	Willie McCovey	521	Carl Yastrzemski	452
Babe Ruth	714	Ted Williams	521	Jeff Bagwell*	446
Barry Bonds*	703	Ernie Banks	512	Dave Kingman	442
Willie Mays	660	Ed Mathews	512	Andre Dawson*	438
Frank Robinson	586	Mel Ott	511	Frank Thomas*	436
Mark McGwire	583	Eddie Murray	504	Juan Gonzalez*	434
Sammy Sosa*	574	Ken Griffey Jr.*	501	Cal Ripken Jr.	431
Harmon Killebrew	573	Lou Gehrig	493	Billy Williams	426
Reggie Jackson	563	Fred McGriff*	493	Jim Thome*	423
Rafael Palmeiro*	551	Stan Musial	475	Gary Sheffield*	415
Mike Schmidt	548	Willie Stargell	475	Darrell Evans	414
Mickey Mantle	536	Dave Winfield	465	Duke Snider	407
Jimmie Foxx	534	Jose Canseco	462	Andres Galarraga*	399

Al Kaline	399
Dale Murphy	398
Joe Carter	396
Graig Nettles	390
Manny Ramirez*	390
Johnny Bench	389
Dwight Evans	385
Harold Baines	384
Frank Howard	382
Jim Rice	382
Albert Belle	381
Alex Rodriguez*	381

Players With 3,000 Major League Hits

(Source: www.mlb.com; *player active in 2004 season)

Pete Rose	4,256	Honus Wagner	3,415	Cal Ripken Jr.	3,184	Rickey Henderson	3,055
Ty Cobb	4,189	Paul Molitor	3,319	George Brett	3,154	Rod Carew	3,053
Hank Aaron	3,771	Eddie Collins	3,315	Paul Waner	3,152	Lou Brock	3,023
Stan Musial	3,630	Willie Mays	3,283	Robin Yount	3,142	Wade Boggs	3,010
Tris Speaker	3,514	Eddie Murray	3,255	Tony Gwynn	3,141	Al Kaline	3,007
Carl Yastrzemski	3,419	Nap Lajoie	3,242	Dave Winfield	3,110	Roberto Clemente	3,000
Cap Anson	3,418						

Pitchers With 300 Major League Wins

(Source: www.mlb.com; *player active in 2004 season)

Cy Young	511	Kid Nichols	361	Nolan Ryan	324	Charley Radbourn	309
Walter Johnson	417	Tim Keefe	342	Don Sutton	324	Mickey Welch	307
Grover Alexander	373	Steve Carlton	329	Phil Niekro	318	Greg Maddux*	305
Christy Mathewson	373	John Clarkson	328	Gaylord Perry	314	Lefty Grove	300
Jim Galvin	365	Roger Clemens*	328	Tom Seaver	311	Early Wynn	300
Warren Spahn	363	Eddie Plank	326				

All-Time Major League Single-Season Leaders

(Source: www.mlb.com; *player active in 2004 season; records for "modern" era beginning 1901)

Home Runs

Barry Bonds* (2001)	73
Mark McGwire (1998)	70
Sammy Sosa* (1998)	66
Mark McGwire (1999)	65
Sammy Sosa* (2001)	64

Batting Average

Nap Lajoie (1901)	.426
Rogers Hornsby (1924)	.424
George Sisler (1922)	.420
Ty Cobb (1911)	.420
Ty Cobb (1912)	.410

Earned Run Average

Dutch Leonard (1914)	0.96
Mordecai Brown (1906)	1.04
Bob Gibson (1968)	1.12
Walter Johnson (1913)	1.14
Christy Mathewson (1909)	1.14

Runs

Babe Ruth (1921)	177
Lou Gehrig (1936)	167
Lou Gehrig (1931)	163
Babe Ruth (1928)	163
Chuck Klein (1930)	158
Babe Ruth (1920, 1927)	158

Stolen Bases

Rickey Henderson (1982)	130
Lou Brock (1974)	118
Vince Coleman (1985)	110
Vince Coleman (1987)	109
Rickey Henderson (1983)	108

Wins

Jack Chesbro (1904)	41
Ed Walsh (1908)	40
Christy Mathewson (1908)	37
Walter Johnson (1913)	36
Joe McGinnity (1904)	35

Hits

Ichiro Suzuki* (2004)	262
George Sisler (1920)	257
Lefty O'Doul (1929)	254
Bill Terry (1930)	254
Al Simmons (1925)	253

Walks (Batter)

Barry Bonds* (2004)	232
Barry Bonds* (2002)	198
Barry Bonds* (2001)	177
Babe Ruth (1923)	170
Mark McGwire (1998)	162
Ted Williams (1947, 1949)	162

Strikeouts

Nolan Ryan (1973)	383
Sandy Koufax (1965)	382
Randy Johnson* (2001)	372
Nolan Ryan (1974)	367
Randy Johnson* (1999)	364

Runs Batted In

Hack Wilson (1930)	191
Lou Gehrig (1931)	184
Hank Greenberg (1937)	183
Jimmie Foxx (1938)	175
Lou Gehrig (1927)	175

Strikeouts (Batter)

Adam Dunn* (2004)	195
Bobby Bonds (1970)	189
Jose Hernandez* (2002)	188
Bobby Bonds (1969)	187
Preston Wilson* (2000)	187
Rob Deer (1987)	186

Saves

Bobby Thigpen (1990)	57
Eric Gagne* (2003)	55
John Smoltz* (2002)	55
Trevor Hoffman* (1998)	53
Randy Myers (1993)	53
Mariano Rivera* (2004)	53

Official Major League Perfect Games Since 1900

Date	Pitcher	Teams	Date	Pitcher	Teams
5/5/04	Cy Young	Boston 3 vs. Phil. 0 (AL)	5/15/81	Len Barker	Clev. 3 vs. Toronto 0 (AL)
10/2/08	Addie Joss	Clev. 1 vs. Chicago 0 (AL)	9/30/84	Mike Witt	Calif.1 at Texas 0 (AL)
4/30/22	Charlie Robertson	Chicago 2 at Detroit 0 (AL)	9/16/88	Tom Browning	Cincinnati 1 vs. L.A. 0 (NL)
10/8/56	Don Larsen	N.Y. 2 vs. Brooklyn 0 (AL)*	7/28/91	Dennis Martinez	Montreal 2 vs. L.A. 0 (NL)
6/21/64	Jim Bunning	Phil. 6 at N.Y. 0 (NL)	7/28/94	Kenny Rogers	Texas 4 vs. California 0 (AL)
9/9/65	Sandy Koufax	L.A. 1 vs. Chicago 0 (NL)	5/17/98	David Wells	N.Y. 4 vs. Minn. 0 (AL)
5/8/68	Catfish Hunter	Oakland 4 vs. Minn.0 (AL)	7/18/99	David Cone	N.Y. 6 vs. Montreal 0 (AL)
*World Series Game			5/18/04	Randy Johnson	Ariz. 2 vs. Atlanta 0 (NL)

Most Career Major League No-Hitters

No.	Pitcher
7	Nolan Ryan
4	Sandy Koufax
3	Larry Corcoran, Bob Feller, Cy Young
2	Jim Bunning, Steve Busby, Carl Erskine, Bob Forsch, Pud Galvin, Ken Holtzman, Randy Johnson, Addie Joss, Dutch Leonard, Jim Maloney, Christy Mathewson, Hideo Nomo, Allie Reynolds, Frank Smith, Warren Spahn, Bill Stoneman, Virgil Trucks, Johnny Vander Meer, Ed Walsh, Don Wilson

All-Star Baseball Games, 1933-2004

Year	Winner, Score	Host team	Year	Winner, Score	Host team	Year	Winner, Score	Host team
1933*	American, 4-2	Chicago (AL)	1959*	National, 5-4	Pittsburgh	1980	National, 4-2	Los Angeles
1934*	American, 9-7	New York (NL)	1959*	American, 5-3	Los Angeles	1981	National, 5-4	Cleveland
1935*	American, 4-1	Cleveland	1960*	National, 5-3	Kansas City	1982	National, 4-1	Montreal
1936*	National, 4-3	Boston (NL)	1960*	National, 6-0	New York (AL)	1983	American, 13-3	Chicago (AL)
1937*	American, 8-3	Washington	1961*	National, 5-4[3]	San Francisco	1984	National, 3-1	San Francisco
1938*	National, 4-1	Cincinnati	1961*	Called–rain, 1-1	Boston	1985	National, 6-1	Minnesota
1939*	American, 3-1	New York (AL)	1962*	National, 3-1[3]	Washington	1986	American, 3-2	Houston
1940*	National, 4-0	St. Louis (NL)	1962*	American, 9-4	Chicago (NL)	1987	National, 2-0[5]	Oakland
1941*	American, 7-5	Detroit	1963*	National, 5-3	Cleveland	1988	American, 2-1	Cincinnati
1942	American, 3-1	New York (NL)	1964*	National, 7-4	New York (NL)	1989	American, 5-3	California
1943	American, 5-3	Philadelphia (AL)	1965*	National, 6-5	Minnesota	1990	American, 2-0	Chicago (NL)
1944	National, 7-1	Pittsburgh	1966*	National, 2-1[3]	St. Louis	1991	American, 4-2	Toronto
1945	(Not played)		1967*	National, 2-1[4]	California	1992	American, 13-6	San Diego
1946*	American, 12-0	Boston (AL)	1968	National, 1-0	Houston	1993	American, 9-3	Baltimore
1947*	American, 2-1	Chicago (NL)	1969*	National, 9-3	Washington	1994	National, 8-7[3]	Pittsburgh
1948*	American, 5-2	St. Louis (AL)	1970	National, 5-4[2]	Cincinnati	1995	National, 3-2	Texas
1949*	American, 11-7	Brooklyn	1971	American, 6-4	Detroit	1996	National, 6-0	Philadelphia
1950*	National, 4-3[1]	Chicago (AL)	1972	National, 4-3[3]	Atlanta	1997	American, 3-1	Cleveland
1951*	National, 8-3	Detroit	1973	National, 7-1	Kansas City	1998	American, 13-8	Colorado
1952*	National, 3-2	Philadelphia (NL)	1974	National, 7-2	Pittsburgh	1999	American, 4-1	Boston
1953*	National, 5-1	Cincinnati	1975	National, 6-3	Milwaukee	2000	American, 6-3	Atlanta
1954*	American, 11-9	Cleveland	1976	National, 7-1	Philadelphia	2001	American, 4-1	Seattle
1955*	National, 6-5[2]	Milwaukee	1977	National, 7-5	New York (AL)	2002	Called—Comm decision[6]	
1956*	National, 7-3	Washington	1978	National, 7-3	San Diego	2003	American, 7-6[7]	Chicago (AL)
1957*	American, 6-5	St. Louis	1979	National, 7-6	Seattle	2004	American, 9-4	Houston
1958*	American, 4-3	Baltimore						

*Denotes day game. (1) 14 innings. (2) 12 innings. (3) 10 innings. (4) 15 innings. (5) 13 innings. (6) Game called in the 11th inning when both teams ran out of pitchers. (7) Under rule change beginning in 2003, league winning All-Star games earned World Series home-field advantage.

Major League Franchise Shifts and Additions

1953—Boston Braves (NL) became Milwaukee Braves.
1954—St. Louis Browns (AL) became Baltimore Orioles.
1955—Philadelphia Athletics (AL) became Kansas City Athletics.
1958—New York Giants (NL) became San Francisco Giants.
1958—Brooklyn Dodgers (NL) became L.A. Dodgers.
1961—Washington Senators (AL) became Minnesota Twins.
1961—L.A. Angels (renamed California Angels in 1965 and Anaheim Angels in 1997) enfranchised by the American League.
1961—Washington Senators enfranchised by the American League (a new team, replacing the former Washington club, whose franchise was moved to Minneapolis-St. Paul).
1962—Houston Colt .45's (renamed the Houston Astros in 1965) enfranchised by the National League.
1962—New York Mets enfranchised by the National League.

1966—Milwaukee Braves (NL) became Atlanta Braves.
1968—Kansas City Athletics (AL) became Oakland Athletics.
1969—Kansas City Royals and Seattle Pilots enfranchised by the American League; Montreal Expos and San Diego Padres enfranchised by the National League.
1970—Seattle Pilots became Milwaukee Brewers.
1971—Washington Senators became Texas Rangers (Dallas-Fort Worth area).
1977—Toronto Blue Jays and Seattle Mariners enfranchised by the American League.
1993—Colorado Rockies (Denver) and Florida Marlins (Miami) enfranchised by the National League.
1998—Tampa Bay Devil Rays began play in the American League; Arizona Diamondbacks (Phoenix) began play in the National League (both teams enfranchised in 1995). Milwaukee Brewers moved from the AL to the NL.

Baseball Stadiums[1]

National League

Team	Stadium (year opened)	Surface	Home run distances (ft.)			Seating capacity
			LF	Center	RF	
Arizona Diamondbacks	Bank One Ballpark (1998)	Grass	330	407	334	49,033
Atlanta Braves	Turner Field (1997)	Grass	335	401	330	50,096
Chicago Cubs	Wrigley Field (1914)	Grass	355	400	353	38,902
Cincinnati Reds	Great American Ballpark (2003)	Grass	328	404	325	42,059
Colorado Rockies	Coors Field (1995)	Grass	347	415	350	50,445
Florida Marlins	Pro Player Stadium (1987)	Grass	330	434	345	47,662
Houston Astros	Minute Maid Park (2000)	Grass	315	435	326	40,950
Los Angeles Dodgers	Dodger Stadium (1962)	Grass	330	395	330	56,000

National League

Team	Stadium (year opened)	Surface	Home run distances (ft.)			Seating capacity
			LF	Center	RF	
Milwaukee Brewers	Miller Park (2001)	Grass	344	400	345	42,400
Montreal Expos	Olympic Stadium (1976)	Artificial	325	404	325	46,500
New York Mets	Shea Stadium (1964)	Grass	338	410	338	55,601
Philadelphia Phillies	Citizens Bank Park (2004)	Grass	329	401	330	43,500
Pittsburgh Pirates	PNC Park (2001)	Grass	325	399	320	38,365
St. Louis Cardinals	Busch Stadium (1966)	Grass	330	402	330	50,345
San Diego Padres	PETCO Park (2004)	Grass	334	396	322	42,500
San Francisco Giants	SBC Park (2000)	Grass	335	404	307	41,584

American League

Team	Stadium (year opened)	Surface	LF	Center	RF	Seating capacity
Anaheim Angels	Angel Stadium of Anaheim (1966)	Grass	330	406	330	45,050
Baltimore Orioles	Oriole Park at Camden Yards (1992)	Grass	333	400	318	48,876
Boston Red Sox	Fenway Park (1912)	Grass	310	420	302	33,871
Chicago White Sox	U.S. Cellular Field (1991)	Grass	330	400	335	47,098
Cleveland Indians	Jacobs Field (1994)	Grass	325	405	325	43,368
Detroit Tigers	Comerica Park (2000)	Grass	345	420	330	40,000
Kansas City Royals	Kauffman Stadium (1973)	Grass	330	410	330	40,793
Minnesota Twins	Hubert H. Humphrey Metrodome (1982)	Artificial	343	408	327	48,678
New York Yankees	Yankee Stadium (1923)	Grass	318	408	314	57,478
Oakland A's	Network Associates Coliseum (1968)	Grass	330	400	330	43,662
Seattle Mariners	Safeco Field (1999)	Grass	331	405	327	47,116
Tampa Bay Devil Rays	Tropicana Field (1990)	Artificial	315	404	322	45,000
Texas Rangers	Ameriquest Field in Arlington (1994)	Grass	332	400	325	49,200
Toronto Blue Jays	SkyDome (1989)	Artificial	328	400	328	50,516

(1) As of 2004 season.

Little League World Series

The Little League World Series is played annually in Williamsport, PA. Pitcher Yuutaro Tanaka hit a home run and struck out 14 batters to lead Japan's Tokyo Musashi-Fuchu team to a 10-1 win over East Boynton Beach (FL) in the 2003 Little League World Series final, Aug. 25. Florida teams have been to the LLWS a record 8 times without a championship.

Year	Winning / Losing Team	Score	Year	Winning / Losing Team	Score
1947	Williamsport, PA; Lock Haven, PA	16-7	1976	Tokyo, Japan; Campbell, CA	10-3
1948	Lock Haven, PA; St. Petersburg, FL	6-5	1977	Taiwan; El Cajon, CA	7-2
1949	Hammonton, NJ; Pensacola, FL	5-0	1978	Taiwan; Danville, CA	11-1
1950	Houston, TX; Bridgeport, CT	2-1	1979	Taiwan; Campbell, CA	2-1
1951	Stamford, CT; Austin, TX	3-0	1980	Taiwan; Tampa, FL	4-3
1952	Norwalk, CT; Monongahela, PA	4-3	1981	Taiwan; Tampa, FL	4-2
1953	Birmingham, AL; Schenectady, NY	1-0	1982	Kirkland, WA; Taiwan	6-0
1954	Schenectady, NY; Colton, CA	7-5	1983	Marietta, GA; Dominican Rep.	3-1
1955	Morrisville, PA; Merchantville, NJ	4-3	1984	South Korea; Altamonte Springs, FL	6-2
1956	Roswell, NM; Delaware, NJ	3-1	1985	South Korea; Mexico	7-1
1957	Mexico; La Mesa, CA	4-0	1986	Taiwan; Tucson, AZ	12-0
1958	Mexico; Kankakee, IL	10-1	1987	Chinese Taipei; Irvine, CA	21-1
1959	Hamtramck, MI; Auburn, CA	12-0	1988	Chinese Taipei; Pearl City, HI	10-0
1960	Levittown, PA; Ft. Worth, TX	5-0	1989	Trumbull, CT; Chinese Taipei	5-2
1961	El Cajon, CA; El Campo, TX	4-2	1990	Chinese Taipei; Shippensburg, PA	9-0
1962	San Jose, CA; Kankakee, IL	3-0	1991	Chinese Taipei; Danville, CA	11-0
1963	Granada Hills, CA; Stratford, CT	2-1	1992	Long Beach, CA; Philippines*	6-0
1964	Staten Island, NY; Mexico	4-0	1993	Long Beach, CA; Panama	3-2
1965	Windsor Locks, CT; Ontario, Canada	3-1	1994	Venezuela; Northridge, CA	4-3
1966	Houston, TX; W. New York, NJ	8-2	1995	Taiwan; Spring, TX	17-3
1967	Tokyo, Japan; Chicago, IL	4-1	1996	Taiwan; Cranston, RI	13-3
1968	Osaka, Japan; Richmond, VA	1-0	1997	Mexico; Mission Viejo, CA	5-4
1969	Taiwan; Santa Clara, CA	5-0	1998	Toms River, NJ; Japan	12-9
1970	Wayne, NJ; Campbell, CA	2-0	1999	Japan; Phenix City, AL	5-0
1971	Taiwan; Gary, IN	12-3	2000	Venezuela; Bellaire, TX	3-2
1972	Taiwan; Hammond, IN	6-0	2001	Japan; Apopka, FL	2-1
1973	Taiwan; Tucson, AZ	12-0	2002	Louisville, KY; Japan	1-0
1974	Taiwan; Red Bluff, CA	12-1	2003	Japan; East Boynton Beach, FL	10-1
1975	Lakewood, NJ; Tampa, FL	4-3	2004	Curacao; Conejo Valley of Thousand Oaks, CA	5-2

*Philippines won 15-4, but was disqualified for using ineligible players. Long Beach was awarded title by forfeit 6-0 (1 run per inning).

NCAA Baseball Division I Champions

1947	California	1958	USC	1970	USC	1982	Miami (FL)	1994	Oklahoma
1948	Southern California	1959	Oklahoma St.	1971	USC	1983	Texas	1995	Cal. St.-Fullerton
		1960	Minnesota	1972	USC	1984	Cal. St.-Fullerton	1996	LSU
1949	Texas	1961	USC	1973	USC	1985	Miami (FL)	1997	LSU
1950	Texas	1962	Michigan	1974	USC	1986	Arizona	1998	USC
1951	Oklahoma	1963	USC	1975	Texas	1987	Stanford	1999	Miami (FL)
1952	Holy Cross	1964	Minnesota	1976	Arizona	1988	Stanford	2000	LSU
1953	Michigan	1965	Arizona St.	1977	Arizona St.	1989	Wichita St.	2001	Miami (FL)
1954	Missouri	1966	Ohio St.	1978	USC	1990	Georgia	2002	Texas
1955	Wake Forest	1967	Arizona St.	1979	Cal. St.-Fullerton	1991	LSU	2003	Rice
1956	Minnesota	1968	USC	1980	Arizona	1992	Pepperdine	2004	Cal. St.-Fullerton
1957	California	1969	Arizona St.	1981	Arizona St.	1993	LSU		

NCAA Women's Softball Division I Champions

1982	UCLA	1987	Texas A&M	1992	UCLA	1997	Arizona	2002	California
1983	Texas A&M	1988	UCLA	1993	Arizona	1998	Fresno St.	2003	UCLA
1984	UCLA	1989	UCLA	1994	Arizona	1999	UCLA	2004	UCLA
1985	UCLA	1990	UCLA	1995	UCLA	2000	Oklahoma		
1986	Cal St. Fullerton	1991	Arizona	1996	Arizona	2001	Arizona		

NATIONAL BASKETBALL ASSOCIATION

2003-2004 Season: Pistons Upset Lakers in Finals; Jackson Quits Lakers, O'Neal Traded

The Detroit Pistons defeated the Los Angeles Lakers, 4 games to 1, in the 2004 NBA Finals, in one of the biggest upsets in league history. Pistons guard Chauncey Billups was named MVP of the Finals. Pistons coach Larry Brown won the first title of his 21-year NBA career, and became the first coach to win both an NBA and NCAA championship. Three days after the Finals, Lakers coach Phil Jackson said he would not return for the 2004-05 season; Rudy Tomjanovich was hired as his replacement July 10. The Lakers traded star center Shaquille O'Neal to the Miami Heat July 14 for Lamar Odom, Caron Butler, Brian Grant, and future draft picks. Minnesota Timberwolves forward Kevin Garnett was named the MVP of the NBA regular season. Orlando Magic guard Tracy McGrady led the league in scoring, averaging 28 points per game.

On June 24, Dwight Howard (Orlando) became the 3rd high school player picked 1st in the NBA Draft. The Charlotte Bobcats, an expansion team that would begin play in the 2004-05 season, selected 19 players in an expansion draft held June 22. The Bobcats, with the 2nd selection in the June 24 draft, picked University of Connecticut star Emeka Okafor.

Final Standings, 2003-2004 Season

(playoff seedings in parentheses; in each conference the 2 division winners automatically get the number 1 and 2 seeds)

Eastern Conference
Atlantic Division

	W	L	Pct	GB
New Jersey (2)	47	35	.573	—
Miami (4)	42	40	.512	5
New York (7)	39	43	.476	8
Boston (8)	36	46	.439	11
Philadelphia	33	49	.402	14
Washington	25	57	.305	22
Orlando	21	61	.256	26

Central Division

	W	L	Pct	GB
Indiana (1)	61	21	.744	—
Detroit (3)	54	28	.659	7
New Orleans (5)	41	41	.500	20
Milwaukee (6)	41	41	.500	20
Cleveland	35	47	.427	26
Toronto	33	49	.402	28
Atlanta	28	54	.341	33
Chicago	23	59	.280	38

Western Conference
Midwest Division

	W	L	Pct	GB
Minnesota (1)	58	24	.707	—
San Antonio (3)	57	25	.695	1
Dallas (5)	52	30	.634	6
Memphis (6)	50	32	.610	8
Houston (7)	45	37	.549	13
Denver (8)	43	39	.524	15
Utah	42	40	.512	16

Pacific Division

	W	L	Pct	GB
L.A. Lakers (2)	56	26	.683	—
Sacramento (4)	55	27	.671	1
Portland	41	41	.500	15
Golden State	37	45	.451	19
Seattle	37	45	.451	19
Phoenix	29	53	.354	27
L.A. Clippers	28	54	.341	28

NBA Regular Season Individual Highs in 2003-2004

Minutes, game: 59, Cuttino Mobley, Houston v. Atlanta, Feb. 22.

Points, game: 62, Tracy McGrady, Orlando v. Wash, Mar. 10.

Field goals, game: 20, Tracy McGrady, Orlando v. Wash., March 10; Allen Iverson, Philadelphia v. Atlanta, Nov. 29; Tracy McGrady, Orlando at Denver, Nov. 14.

FG attempts, game: 37, Tracy McGrady, Orlando v. Wash., March 10.

3-pointers, game: 8, 4 players tied (Gilbert Arenas, Tracy McGrady, Dirk Nowitzki, Quentin Richardson).

3-pt. attempts, game: 15, Tracy McGrady, Orlando v. Milwaukee, March 3.

Free throws, game: 18, Allen Iverson, Philadelphia v. Toronto, Dec. 2; Corey Maggette, L.A. Clippers v. Houston, Nov. 24.

FT attempts, game: 26, Tracy McGrady, Orlando v. Wash., March 10.

Rebounds, game: 26, Shaquille O'Neal, L.A. Lakers v. Milwaukee, March 21.

Assists, game: 19, Steve Nash, Dallas v. Sacramento, April 1.

Steals, game: 9, Dirk Nowitzki, Dallas at Houston, March 7.

Blocks, game: 10, 3 players tied (Amare Stoudemire, Calvin Booth, Dikembe Mutombo).

Minutes, season: 3,331; Joe Johnson, Phoenix.

Off. rebounds, season: 344, Erick Dampier, Golden State.

Def. rebounds, season: 894, Kevin Garnett, Minnesota.

Personal fouls, season: 300, Theo Ratliff*, Atlanta/Portland.

* Ratliff played 85 games in 2003-04—53 for Atlanta and 32 for Portland, after being traded midseason. NBA teams play 82 games in a season.

2004 NBA Playoff Results

Eastern Conference
Indiana defeated Boston 4 games to 0
New Jersey defeated New York 4 games to 0
Detroit defeated Milwaukee 4 games to 1
Miami defeated New Orleans 4 games to 3
Detroit defeated New Jersey 4 games to 3
Indiana defeated Miami 4 games to 2
Detroit defeated Indiana 4 games to 2

Western Conference
Minnesota defeated Denver 4 games to 1
L.A. Lakers defeated Houston 4 games to 1
San Antonio defeated Memphis 4 games to 0
Sacramento defeated Dallas 4 games to 1
Minnesota defeated Sacramento 4 games to 3
L.A. Lakers defeated San Antonio 4 games to 2
L.A. Lakers defeated Minnesota 4 games to 2

Championship
Detroit defeated L.A. Lakers 4 games to 1 [87-75, 91-99 (OT), 88-68, 88-80, 100-87].

Pistons Defense Reigns in 2004

The Detroit Pistons won the NBA Championship, upsetting the Los Angeles Lakers, 100-87, in the 5th and deciding game at the Palace in Auburn Hills, MI, on June 15. The Pistons, coached by Larry Brown, used superb defense and teamwork to overcome the Lakers, who featured stars such as Shaquille O'Neal, Kobe Bryant, Karl Malone, and Gary Payton. Pistons guard Chauncey Billups, who averaged 21 points and 5.2 assists per game in the series, was named the MVP of the Finals.

NBA Finals Composite Box Scores

Los Angeles	FG M-A	FT M-A	Reb O-T	Ast	Avg
Shaquille O'Neal	53-84	27-55	15-54	8	26.6
Kobe Bryant	43-113	23-25	2-14	22	22.6
Derek Fisher	11-36	4-7	5-15	9	6.4
Devean George	11-28	2-4	3-14	3	5.8
Karl Malone	8-24	4-6	8-29	9	5.0
Gary Payton	9-28	1-2	6-15	22	4.2
S. Medvedenko	6-17	6-8	6-18	3	3.6
Kareem Rush	7-22	0-0	0-5	2	3.6
Luke Walton	5-13	2-2	3-12	18	3.3
Rick Fox	4-7	0-0	0-3	7	2.7
Brian Cook	1-6	2-2	3-8	0	1.3
Bryon Russell	0-2	0-0	1-1	0	0.0

Detroit	FG M-A	FT M-A	Reb O-T	Ast	Avg
Richard Hamilton	37-92	29-34	12-26	20	21.4
Chauncey Billups	29-57	39-42	3-16	26	21.0
Rasheed Wallace	24-53	14-18	7-39	7	13.0
Ben Wallace	22-46	10-34	19-68	7	10.8
Tayshaun Prince	21-54	5-11	15-34	10	10.0
Corliss Williamson	6-15	9-10	4-12	1	4.2
Lindsey Hunter	5-17	6-6	1-7	4	3.6
Elden Campbell	6-16	5-10	6-13	8	3.4
Mehmet Okur	4-9	2-4	1-6	2	2.8
Mike James	2-4	0-0	2-4	4	0.8
Darvin Ham	1-1	0-0	1-1	0	0.5
Darko Milicic	0-2	0-2	1-2	0	0.0

NBA Finals MVP

1969	Jerry West, Los Angeles	1981	Cedric Maxwell, Boston	1993	Michael Jordan, Chicago
1970	Willis Reed, New York	1982	Magic Johnson, Los Angeles	1994	Hakeem Olajuwon, Houston
1971	Lew Alcindor (Kareem Abdul-Jabbar), Milwaukee	1983	Moses Malone, Philadelphia	1995	Hakeem Olajuwon, Houston
		1984	Larry Bird, Boston	1996	Michael Jordan, Chicago
1972	Wilt Chamberlain, Los Angeles	1985	Kareem Abdul-Jabbar, L.A. Lakers	1997	Michael Jordan, Chicago
1973	Willis Reed, New York			1998	Michael Jordan, Chicago
1974	John Havlicek, Boston	1986	Larry Bird, Boston	1999	Tim Duncan, San Antonio
1975	Rick Barry, Golden State	1987	Magic Johnson, L.A. Lakers	2000	Shaquille O'Neal, L.A. Lakers
1976	Jo Jo White, Boston	1988	James Worthy, L.A. Lakers	2001	Shaquille O'Neal, L.A. Lakers
1977	Bill Walton, Portland	1989	Joe Dumars, Detroit	2002	Shaquille O'Neal, L.A. Lakers
1978	Wes Unseld, Washington	1990	Isiah Thomas, Detroit	2003	Tim Duncan, San Antonio
1979	Dennis Johnson, Seattle	1991	Michael Jordan, Chicago	2004	Chauncey Billups, Detroit
1980	Magic Johnson, Los Angeles	1992	Michael Jordan, Chicago		

NBA Finals All-Time Statistical Leaders

(at the end of the 2004 NBA season finals; *denotes active in 2003-2004)

Scoring Average (Minimum 10 games)

	G	FG	FT	Pts.	Avg
Rick Barry	10	138	87	363	36.3
Michael Jordan	35	438	258	1,176	33.6
*Shaquille O'Neal	24	306	171	783	32.6
Jerry West	55	612	455	1,679	30.5
Bob Pettit	25	241	227	709	28.4

Scoring Average (Minimum 10 games)

	G	FG	FT	Pts.	Avg
Hakeem Olajuwon	17	187	91	467	27.5
Elgin Baylor	44	442	277	1,161	26.4
*Tim Duncan	11	105	72	282	25.6
Julius Erving	22	216	128	561	25.5
Joe Fulks	11	84	104	272	24.7

Games Played

Bill Russell	70
Sam Jones	64
Kareem Abdul-Jabbar	56
Jerry West	55
Tom Heinsohn	52

Rebounds

Bill Russell	1,718
Wilt Chamberlain	862
Elgin Baylor	593
Kareem Abdul-Jabbar	507
Tom Heinsohn	473

Assists

Magic Johnson	584
Bob Cousy	400
Bill Russell	315
Jerry West	306
Dennis Johnson	228

NBA Scoring Leaders

Year	Scoring champion	Pts	Avg	Year	Scoring champion	Pts	Avg
1947	Joe Fulks, Philadelphia	1,389	23.2	1976	Bob McAdoo, Buffalo	2,427	31.1
1948	Max Zaslofsky, Chicago	1,007	21.0	1977	Pete Maravich, New Orleans	2,273	31.1
1949	George Mikan, Minneapolis	1,698	28.3	1978	George Gervin, San Antonio	2,232	27.2
1950	George Mikan, Minneapolis	1,865	27.4	1979	George Gervin, San Antonio	2,365	29.6
1951	George Mikan, Minneapolis	1,932	28.4	1980	George Gervin, San Antonio	2,585	33.1
1952	Paul Arizin, Philadelphia	1,674	25.4	1981	Adrian Dantley, Utah	2,452	30.7
1953	Neil Johnston, Philadelphia	1,564	22.3	1982	George Gervin, San Antonio	2,551	32.3
1954	Neil Johnston, Philadelphia	1,759	24.4	1983	Alex English, Denver	2,326	28.4
1955	Neil Johnston, Philadelphia	1,631	22.7	1984	Adrian Dantley, Utah	2,418	30.6
1956	Bob Pettit, St. Louis	1,849	25.7	1985	Bernard King, New York	1,809	32.9
1957	Paul Arizin, Philadelphia	1,817	25.6	1986	Dominique Wilkins, Atlanta	2,366	30.3
1958	George Yardley, Detroit	2,001	27.8	1987	Michael Jordan, Chicago	3,041	37.1
1959	Bob Pettit, St. Louis	2,105	29.2	1988	Michael Jordan, Chicago	2,868	35.0
1960	Wilt Chamberlain, Philadelphia	2,707	37.9	1989	Michael Jordan, Chicago	2,633	32.5
1961	Wilt Chamberlain, Philadelphia	3,033	38.4	1990	Michael Jordan, Chicago	2,753	33.6
1962	Wilt Chamberlain, Philadelphia	4,029	50.4	1991	Michael Jordan, Chicago	2,580	31.5
1963	Wilt Chamberlain, San Francisco	3,586	44.8	1992	Michael Jordan, Chicago	2,404	30.1
1964	Wilt Chamberlain, San Francisco	2,948	36.5	1993	Michael Jordan, Chicago	2,541	32.6
1965	Wilt Chamberlain, San Francisco, Phil.	2,534	34.7	1994	David Robinson, San Antonio	2,383	29.8
1966	Wilt Chamberlain, Philadelphia	2,649	33.5	1995	Shaquille O'Neal, Orlando	2,315	29.3
1967	Rick Barry, San Francisco	2,775	35.6	1996	Michael Jordan, Chicago	2,465	30.4
1968	Dave Bing, Detroit	2,142	27.1	1997	Michael Jordan, Chicago	2,431	29.6
1969	Elvin Hayes, San Diego	2,327	28.4	1998	Michael Jordan, Chicago	2,357	28.7
1970	Jerry West, Los Angeles	2,309	31.2	1999	Allen Iverson, Philadelphia	1,284	26.8
1971	Lew Alcindor (Kareem Abdul-Jabbar), Milwaukee	2,596	31.7	2000	Shaquille O'Neal, L.A. Lakers	2,344	29.7
1972	Kareem Abdul-Jabbar, Milwaukee	2,822	34.8	2001	Allen Iverson, Philadelphia	2,207	31.1
1973	Nate Archibald, Kans. City-Omaha	2,719	34.0	2002	Allen Iverson, Philadelphia	1,883	31.4
1974	Bob McAdoo, Buffalo	2,261	30.6	2003	Tracy McGrady, Orlando	2,407	32.1
1975	Bob McAdoo, Buffalo	2,831	34.5	2004	Tracy McGrady, Orlando	1,878	28.0

NBA Most Valuable Player

1956	Bob Pettit, St. Louis	1972	Kareem Abdul-Jabbar, Milwaukee	1989	Magic Johnson, L.A. Lakers
1957	Bob Cousy, Boston	1973	Dave Cowens, Boston	1990	Magic Johnson, L.A. Lakers
1958	Bill Russell, Boston	1974	Kareem Abdul-Jabbar, Milwaukee	1991	Michael Jordan, Chicago
1959	Bob Pettit, St. Louis	1975	Bob McAdoo, Buffalo	1992	Michael Jordan, Chicago
1960	Wilt Chamberlain, Philadelphia	1976	Kareem Abdul-Jabbar, L.A. Lakers	1993	Charles Barkley, Phoenix
1961	Bill Russell, Boston	1977	Kareem Abdul-Jabbar, L.A. Lakers	1994	Hakeem Olajuwon, Houston
1962	Bill Russell, Boston	1978	Bill Walton, Portland	1995	David Robinson, San Antonio
1963	Bill Russell, Boston	1979	Moses Malone, Houston	1996	Michael Jordan, Chicago
1964	Oscar Robertson, Cincinnati	1980	Kareem Abdul-Jabbar, L.A. Lakers	1997	Karl Malone, Utah
1965	Bill Russell, Boston	1981	Julius Erving, Philadelphia	1998	Michael Jordan, Chicago
1966	Wilt Chamberlain, Philadelphia	1982	Moses Malone, Houston	1999	Karl Malone, Utah
1967	Wilt Chamberlain, Philadelphia	1983	Moses Malone, Philadelphia	2000	Shaquille O'Neal, L.A. Lakers
1968	Wilt Chamberlain, Philadelphia	1984	Larry Bird, Boston	2001	Allen Iverson, Philadelphia
1969	Wes Unseld, Baltimore	1985	Larry Bird, Boston	2002	Tim Duncan, San Antonio
1970	Willis Reed, New York	1986	Larry Bird, Boston	2003	Tim Duncan, San Antonio
1971	Lew Alcindor (Kareem Abdul-Jabbar), Milwaukee	1987	Magic Johnson, L.A. Lakers	2004	Kevin Garnett, Minnesota
		1988	Michael Jordan, Chicago		

NBA Champions, 1947-2004

Year	Eastern Conference	Western Conference	Champion	Coach	Runner-up
	Regular season			**Playoffs**	
1947	Washington Capitols	Chicago Stags	Philadelphia	Ed Gottlieb	Chicago
1948	Philadelphia Warriors	St. Louis Bombers	Baltimore	Buddy Jeannette	Philadelphia
1949	Washington Capitols	Rochester	Minneapolis	John Kundla	Washington
1950	Syracuse	Minneapolis	Minneapolis	John Kundla	Syracuse
1951	Philadelphia Warriors	Minneapolis	Rochester	Lester Harrison	New York
1952	Syracuse	Rochester	Minneapolis	John Kundla	New York
1953	New York	Minneapolis	Minneapolis	John Kundla	New York
1954	New York	Minneapolis	Minneapolis	John Kundla	Syracuse
1955	Syracuse	Ft. Wayne	Syracuse	Al Cervi	Ft. Wayne
1956	Philadelphia Warriors	Ft. Wayne	Philadelphia	George Senesky	Ft. Wayne
1957	Boston	St. Louis	Boston	Red Auerbach	St. Louis
1958	Boston	St. Louis	St. Louis	Alex Hannum	Boston
1959	Boston	St. Louis	Boston	Red Auerbach	Minneapolis
1960	Boston	St. Louis	Boston	Red Auerbach	St. Louis
1961	Boston	St. Louis	Boston	Red Auerbach	St. Louis
1962	Boston	Los Angeles	Boston	Red Auerbach	Los Angeles
1963	Boston	Los Angeles	Boston	Red Auerbach	Los Angeles
1964	Boston	San Francisco	Boston	Red Auerbach	San Francisco
1965	Boston	Los Angeles	Boston	Red Auerbach	Los Angeles
1966	Philadelphia	Los Angeles	Boston	Red Auerbach	Los Angeles
1967	Philadelphia	San Francisco	Philadelphia	Alex Hannum	San Francisco
1968	Philadelphia	St. Louis	Boston	Bill Russell	Los Angeles
1969	Baltimore	Los Angeles	Boston	Bill Russell	Los Angeles
1970	New York	Atlanta	New York	Red Holzman	Los Angeles

Year	Atlantic	Central	Midwest	Pacific	Champion	Coach	Runner-up
1971	New York	Baltimore	Milwaukee	Los Angeles	Milwaukee	Larry Costello	Baltimore
1972	Boston	Baltimore	Milwaukee	Los Angeles	Los Angeles	Bill Sharman	New York
1973	Boston	Baltimore	Milwaukee	Los Angeles	New York	Red Holzman	Los Angeles
1974	Boston	Capital	Milwaukee	Los Angeles	Boston	Tom Heinsohn	Milwaukee
1975	Boston	Washington	Chicago	Golden State	Golden State	Al Attles	Washington
1976	Boston	Cleveland	Milwaukee	Golden State	Boston	Tom Heinsohn	Phoenix
1977	Philadelphia	Houston	Denver	Los Angeles	Portland	Jack Ramsay	Philadelphia
1978	Philadelphia	San Antonio	Denver	Portland	Washington	Dick Motta	Seattle
1979	Washington	San Antonio	Kansas City	Seattle	Seattle	Len Wilkens	Washington
1980	Boston	Atlanta	Milwaukee	Los Angeles	Los Angeles	Paul Westhead	Philadelphia
1981	Boston	Milwaukee	San Antonio	Phoenix	Boston	Bill Fitch	Houston
1982	Boston	Milwaukee	San Antonio	Los Angeles	Los Angeles	Pat Riley	Philadelphia
1983	Philadelphia	Milwaukee	San Antonio	Los Angeles	Philadelphia	Billy Cunningham	Los Angeles
1984	Boston	Milwaukee	Utah	Los Angeles	Boston	K.C. Jones	Los Angeles
1985	Boston	Milwaukee	Denver	L.A. Lakers	L.A. Lakers	Pat Riley	Boston
1986	Boston	Milwaukee	Houston	L.A. Lakers	Boston	K.C. Jones	Houston
1987	Boston	Atlanta	Dallas	L.A. Lakers	L.A. Lakers	Pat Riley	Boston
1988	Boston	Detroit	Denver	L.A. Lakers	L.A. Lakers	Pat Riley	Detroit
1989	New York	Detroit	Utah	L.A. Lakers	Detroit	Chuck Daly	L.A. Lakers
1990	Philadelphia	Detroit	San Antonio	L.A. Lakers	Detroit	Chuck Daly	Portland
1991	Boston	Chicago	San Antonio	Portland	Chicago	Phil Jackson	L.A. Lakers
1992	Boston	Chicago	Utah	Portland	Chicago	Phil Jackson	Portland
1993	New York	Chicago	Houston	Phoenix	Chicago	Phil Jackson	Phoenix
1994	New York	Atlanta	Houston	Seattle	Houston	Rudy Tomjanovich	New York
1995	Orlando	Indiana	San Antonio	Phoenix	Houston	Rudy Tomjanovich	Orlando
1996	Orlando	Chicago	San Antonio	Seattle	Chicago	Phil Jackson	Seattle
1997	Miami	Chicago	Utah	Seattle	Chicago	Phil Jackson	Utah
1998	Miami	Chicago	Utah	L.A. Lakers	Chicago	Phil Jackson	Utah
1999	Miami	Indiana	San Antonio	Portland	San Antonio	Gregg Popovich	New York
2000	Miami	Indiana	Utah	L.A. Lakers	L.A. Lakers	Phil Jackson	Indiana
2001	Philadelphia	Milwaukee	San Antonio	L.A. Lakers	L.A. Lakers	Phil Jackson	Philadelphia
2002	New Jersey	Detroit	San Antonio	Sacramento	L.A. Lakers	Phil Jackson	New Jersey
2003	New Jersey	Detroit	San Antonio	Sacramento	San Antonio	Gregg Popovich	New Jersey
2004	New Jersey	Indiana	Minnesota	L.A. Lakers	Detroit	Larry Brown	L.A. Lakers

NBA Coach of the Year, 1963-2004

1963 Harry Gallatin, St. Louis Hawks
1964 Alex Hannum, San Francisco Warriors
1965 Red Auerbach, Boston Celtics
1966 Dolph Schayes, Philadelphia 76ers
1967 Johnny Kerr, Chicago Bulls
1968 Richie Guerin, St. Louis Hawks
1969 Gene Shue, Baltimore Bullets
1970 Red Holzman, New York Knicks
1971 Dick Motta, Chicago Bulls
1972 Bill Sharman, Los Angeles Lakers
1973 Tom Heinsohn, Boston Celtics
1974 Ray Scott, Detroit Pistons
1975 Phil Johnson, Kansas City-Omaha Kings
1976 Bill Fitch, Cleveland Cavaliers

1977 Tom Nissalke, Houston Rockets
1978 Hubie Brown, Atlanta Hawks
1979 Cotton Fitzsimmons, Kansas City Kings
1980 Bill Fitch, Boston Celtics
1981 Jack McKinney, Indiana Pacers
1982 Gene Shue, Washington Bullets
1983 Don Nelson, Milwaukee Bucks
1984 Frank Layden, Utah Jazz
1985 Don Nelson, Milwaukee Bucks
1986 Mike Fratello, Atlanta Hawks
1987 Mike Schuler, Portland Trail Blazers
1988 Doug Moe, Denver Nuggets
1989 Cotton Fitzsimmons, Phoenix Suns
1990 Pat Riley, Los Angeles Lakers
1991 Don Chaney, Houston Rockets

1992 Don Nelson, Golden State Warriors
1993 Pat Riley, New York Knicks
1994 Lenny Wilkens, Atlanta Hawks
1995 Del Harris, Los Angeles Lakers
1996 Phil Jackson, Chicago Bulls
1997 Pat Riley, Miami Heat
1998 Larry Bird, Indiana Pacers
1999 Mike Dunleavy, Portland Trail Blazers
2000 Glenn "Doc" Rivers, Orlando Magic
2001 Larry Brown, Philadelphia 76ers
2002 Rick Carlisle, Detroit Pistons
2003 Gregg Popovich, San Antonio
2004 Hubie Brown, Memphis

NBA All-League and All-Defensive Teams, 2003-2004

All-League Team

First team	Second team	Position
Tim Duncan, San Antonio	Jermaine O'Neal, Indiana	Forward
Kevin Garnett, Minnesota	Peja Stojakovic, Sacramento	Forward
Shaquille O'Neal, L.A. Lakers	Ben Wallace, Detroit	Center
Kobe Bryant, L.A. Lakers	Sam Cassell, Minnesota	Guard
Jason Kidd, New Jersey	Tracy McGrady, Orlando	Guard

All-Defensive Team

First team	Second team
Ron Artest, Indiana	Andrei Kirilenko, Utah
Kevin Garnett, Minnesota	Tim Duncan, San Antonio
Ben Wallace, Detroit	Theo Ratliff, Portland
Bruce Bowen, San Antonio	Doug Christie, Sacramento
Kobe Bryant, L.A. Lakers	Jason Kidd, New Jersey

NBA Statistical Leaders, 2003-2004

Scoring Average
(Minimum 70 games or 1,400 pts)

	G	FG	FT	Pts	Avg
Tracy McGrady, Orlando	67	653	398	1,878	28.0
Peja Stojakovic, Sacramento	81	665	394	1,964	24.2
Kevin Garnett, Minnesota	82	804	368	1,987	24.2
Kobe Bryant, L.A. Lakers	65	516	454	1,557	24.0
Paul Pierce, Boston	80	602	517	1,836	23.0
Baron Davis, New Orleans	67	554	237	1,532	22.9
Vince Carter, Toronto	73	608	336	1,645	22.5
Tim Duncan, San Antonio	69	592	352	1,538	22.3
Dirk Nowitzki, Dallas	77	605	371	1,680	21.8
Michael Redd, Milwaukee	82	633	383	1,776	21.7

3-Point Field Goal Percentage
(Minimum 55 3-point field goals made)

	FG	FGA	Pct
Anthony Peeler, Sacramento	68	141	.482
Brent Barry, Seattle	114	252	.452
Brian Cardinal, Golden State	55	124	.444
Fred Hoiberg, Minnesota	76	172	.442
Aaron McKie, Philadelphia	75	172	.436
Predrag (Peja) Stojakovic, Sacramento	240	554	.433
Allan Houston, New York	87	202	.431
Hidayet Turkoglu, San Antonio	101	241	.419
Casey Jacobson, Phoenix	75	180	.417
Charlie Ward, San Antonio	84	206	.408

Rebounds per Game
(Minimum 70 games or 800 rebounds)

	G	Off	Def	Tot	Avg
Kevin Garnett, Minnesota	82	245	894	1,139	13.9
Tim Duncan, San Antonio	69	227	632	859	12.4
Ben Wallace, Detroit	81	324	682	1,006	12.4
Erick Dampier, Golden State	74	344	543	887	12.0
Carlos Boozer, Cleveland	75	230	627	857	11.4
Zach Randolph, Portland	81	242	609	851	10.5
Jamaal Magloire, New Orleans	82	268	579	847	10.3
Brad Miller, Sacramento	72	191	552	743	10.3
Kenny Thomas, Philadelphia	74	261	489	750	10.1
Marcus Camby, Denver	72	211	516	727	10.1

Assists per Game
(Minimum 70 games or 400 assists)

	G	No	Avg
Jason Kidd, New Jersey	67	618	9.2
Stephon Marbury, New York	81	719	8.9
Steve Nash, Dallas	78	687	8.8
Baron Davis, New Orleans	67	501	7.5
Sam Cassell, Minnesota	81	592	7.3
Eric Snow, Philadelphia	82	563	6.9
Jason Williams, Memphis	72	492	6.8
Kirk Hinrich, Chicago	76	517	6.8
Steve Francis, Houston	79	493	6.2
Jeff McInnis, Cleveland	70	430	6.1
Andre Miller, Denver	82	501	6.1
Damon Stoudamire, Portland	82	500	6.1

Field Goal Percentage
(Minimum 300 field goals made)

	FGM	FGA	Pct
Shaquille O'Neal, L.A. Lakers	554	948	.584
Mark Blount, Boston	342	604	.566
Erick Dampier, Golden State	348	650	.535
Antawn Jamison, Dallas	488	913	.530
Nene Hilario, Denver	334	630	.523
Carlos Boozer, Cleveland	471	900	.522
Yao Ming, Houston	535	1,025	.522
Brad Miller, Sacramento	373	731	.510
Corliss Williamson, Detroit	304	602	.505
Tim Duncan, San Antonio	592	1,181	.501

Steals per Game
(Minimum 70 games or 125 steals)

	G	No	Avg
Baron Davis, New Orleans	67	158	2.36
Shawn Marion, Phoenix	79	167	2.11
Ron Artest, Indiana	73	152	2.08
Andrei Kirilenko, Utah	78	150	1.92
Doug Christie, Sacramento	82	151	1.84
Stephen Jackson, Atlanta	80	142	1.78
Emanuel Ginobili, San Antonio	77	136	1.77
Ben Wallace, Detroit	81	143	1.77
Steve Francis, Houston	79	139	1.76
Andre Miller, Denver	82	142	1.73

Free Throw Percentage
(Minimum 125 free throws made)

	FTM	FTA	Pct
Predrag (Peja) Stojakovic, Sacramento	394	425	.927
Steve Nash, Dallas	230	251	.916
Allan Houston, New York	157	172	.913
Ray Allen, Seattle	245	271	.904
Reggie Miller, Indiana	146	165	.885
Chauncey Billups, Detroit	404	460	.878
Brian Cardinal, Golden State	238	271	.878
Dirk Nowitzki, Dallas	371	423	.877
Earl Boykins, Denver	142	162	.877
Damon Stoudamire, Portland	127	145	.876

Blocked Shots per Game
(Minimum 70 games or 100 blocked shots)

	G	Blk	Avg
Theo Ratliff, Atlanta/Portland*	85	307	3.61
Ben Wallace, Detroit	81	246	3.04
Andrei Kirilenko, Utah	78	215	2.76
Tim Duncan, San Antonio	69	185	2.68
Marcus Camby, Denver	72	187	2.60
Jermaine O'Neal, Indiana	78	199	2.55
Zydrunas Ilgauskas, Cleveland	81	201	2.48
Shaquille O'Neal, L.A. Lakers	67	166	2.48
Samuel Dalembert, Philadelphia	82	189	2.30
Elton Brand, L.A. Clippers	69	154	2.23

*Ratliff played 85 games in 2003-04—53 for Atlanta and 32 for Portland, after being traded midseason. NBA teams play 82 games in a season.

NBA Defensive Player of the Year

1983 Sidney Moncrief, Milwaukee	1991 Dennis Rodman, Detroit	1998 Dikembe Mutombo, Atlanta
1984 Sidney Moncrief, Milwaukee	1992 David Robinson, San Antonio	1999 Alonzo Mourning, Miami
1985 Mark Eaton, Utah	1993 Hakeem Olajuwon, Houston	2000 Alonzo Mourning, Miami
1986 Alvin Robertson, San Antonio	1994 Hakeem Olajuwon, Houston	2001 Dikembe Mutombo, Philadelphia
1987 Michael Cooper, L.A. Lakers	1995 Dikembe Mutombo, Denver	2002 Ben Wallace, Detroit
1988 Michael Jordan, Chicago	1996 Gary Payton, Seattle	2003 Ben Wallace, Detroit
1989 Mark Eaton, Utah	1997 Dikembe Mutombo, Atlanta	2004 Ron Artest, Indiana
1990 Dennis Rodman, Detroit		

NBA Rookie of the Year

Year	Player	Year	Player	Year	Player
1953	Don Meineke, Ft. Wayne	1971	Dave Cowens, Boston;	1989	Mitch Richmond, Golden State
1954	Ray Felix, Baltimore		Geoff Petrie, Portland (tie)	1990	David Robinson, San Antonio
1955	Bob Pettit, Milwaukee	1972	Sidney Wicks, Portland	1991	Derrick Coleman, New Jersey
1956	Maurice Stokes, Rochester	1973	Bob McAdoo, Buffalo	1992	Larry Johnson, Charlotte
1957	Tom Heinsohn, Boston	1974	Ernie DiGregorio, Buffalo	1993	Shaquille O'Neal, Orlando
1958	Woody Sauldsberry,	1975	Keith Wilkes, Golden State	1994	Chris Webber, Golden State
	Philadelphia	1976	Alvan Adams, Phoenix	1995	Grant Hill, Detroit;
1959	Elgin Baylor, Minneapolis	1977	Adrian Dantley, Buffalo		Jason Kidd, Dallas (tie)
1960	Wilt Chamberlain, Philadelphia	1978	Walter Davis, Phoenix	1996	Damon Stoudamire, Toronto
1961	Oscar Robertson, Cincinnati	1979	Phil Ford, Kansas City	1997	Allen Iverson, Philadelphia
1962	Walt Bellamy, Chicago	1980	Larry Bird, Boston	1998	Tim Duncan, San Antonio
1963	Terry Dischinger, Chicago	1981	Darrell Griffith, Utah	1999	Vince Carter, Toronto
1964	Jerry Lucas, Cincinnati	1982	Buck Williams, New Jersey	2000	Elton Brand, Chicago;
1965	Willis Reed, New York	1983	Terry Cummings, San Diego		Steve Francis, Houston (tie)
1966	Rick Barry, San Francisco	1984	Ralph Sampson, Houston	2001	Mike Miller, Orlando
1967	Dave Bing, Detroit	1985	Michael Jordan, Chicago	2002	Pau Gasol, Memphis
1968	Earl Monroe, Baltimore	1986	Patrick Ewing, New York	2003	Amaré Stoudemire, Phoenix
1969	Wes Unseld, Baltimore	1987	Chuck Person, Indiana	2004	LeBron James, Cleveland
1970	Lew Alcindor, Milwaukee	1988	Mark Jackson, New York		

NBA Sixth Man Award

Year	Player	Year	Player	Year	Player
1983	Bobby Jones, Philadelphia	1991	Detlef Schrempf, Seattle	1998	Danny Manning, Phoenix
1984	Kevin McHale, Boston	1992	Detlef Schrempf, Seattle	1999	Darrell Armstrong, Orlando
1985	Kevin McHale, Boston	1993	Clifford Robinson, Portland	2000	Rodney Rogers, Phoenix
1986	Bill Walton, Boston	1994	Dell Curry, Charlotte	2001	Aaron McKie, Philadelphia
1987	Ricky Pierce, Milwaukee	1995	Anthony Mason, New York	2002	Corliss Williamson, Detroit
1988	Roy Tarpley, Dallas	1996	Toni Kukoc, Chicago	2003	Bobby Jackson, Sacramento
1989	Eddie Johnson, Phoenix	1997	John Starks, New York	2004	Antawn Jamison, Dallas
1990	Ricky Pierce, Milwaukee				

2004 NBA Player Draft, First-Round Picks

(held June 24, 2004)

Team	Player, College/Team	Team	Player, College/Team
Orlando 1.	Dwight Howard, F, Southwest Atlanta Christian Academy (GA)	15. Boston	Al Jefferson, F, Prentiss HS (MI)
2. Charlotte[1]	Emeka Okafor, F/C, Connecticut	16. Utah[5]	Kirk Snyder, G, Nevada
3. Chicago	Ben Gordon, G, Connecticut	17. Atlanta[6]	Josh Smith, F, Oak Hill Academy (VA)
4. L.A. Clippers[2]	Shaun Livingston, G, Peoria Central HS (IL)	18. New Orleans	J.R. Smith, G, St. Benedict's Prep (NJ)
5. Washington[3]	Devin Harris[11], G, Wisconsin	19. Miami	Dorell Wright, F, Leuzinger HS (CA)
6. Atlanta	Josh Childress, F, Stanford	20. Denver	Jameer Nelson[12], G, St. Joseph's
7. Phoenix	Luol Deng[4], F, Duke	21. Utah[7]	Pavel Podkolzine[13], C, Varese (Italy)
8. Toronto	Rafael Araujo, C, Brigham Young	22. New Jersey	Viktor Khryapa[14], F, CSKA Moscow (Russia)
9. Philadelphia	Andre Iguodala, F, Arizona	23. Portland[8]	Sergey Monia, F, CSKA Moscow
10. Cleveland	Luke Jackson, F, Oregon	24. Boston	Delonte West, G, St. Joseph's
11. Golden State	Andris Biedrins, F, BK Skonto Riga (Latvia)	25. Boston[10]	Tony Allen, G, Oklahoma State
12. Seattle	Robert Swift, C, Bakersfield HS (CA)	26. Sacramento	Kevin Martin, F, Western Carolina
13. Portland	Sebastian Telfair, G, Abraham Lincoln HS (NY)	27. L.A. Lakers	Sasha Vujacic, G, Snaidero Udine (Slovenia)
14. Utah	Kris Humphries, F, Minnesota	28. San Antonio	Beno Udrih, G, Breil Milano (Slovenia)
		29. Indiana	David Harrison, C, Colorado

(1) From L.A. Clippers. (2) From Charlotte. (3) From Dallas. (4) Rights traded to Chicago. (5) From New York via Phoenix. (6) From Milwaukee via Denver and Detroit. (7) From Houston. (8) From Memphis. (9) From Dallas. (10) From Detroit. (11) Rights traded to Dallas. (12) Rights traded to Orlando. (13) Rights traded to Dallas. (14) Rights traded to Portland.

Number-One First-Round NBA Draft Picks, 1966-2004

Year	Team	Player, college	Year	Team	Player, college
1966	New York	Cazzie Russell, Michigan	1986	Cleveland	Brad Daugherty, North Carolina
1967	Detroit	Jimmy Walker, Providence	1987	San Antonio	David Robinson, Navy
1968	Houston	Elvin Hayes, Houston	1988	L.A. Clippers	Danny Manning, Kansas
1969	Milwaukee	Lew Alcindor[1], UCLA	1989	Sacramento	Pervis Ellison, Louisville
1970	Detroit	Bob Lanier, St. Bonaventure	1990	New Jersey	Derrick Coleman, Syracuse
1971	Cleveland	Austin Carr, Notre Dame	1991	Charlotte	Larry Johnson, UNLV
1972	Portland	LaRue Martin, Loyola-Chicago	1992	Orlando	Shaquille O'Neal, LSU
1973	Philadelphia	Doug Collins, Illinois St.	1993	Orlando	Chris Webber[3], Michigan
1974	Portland	Bill Walton, UCLA	1994	Milwaukee	Glenn Robinson, Purdue
1975	Atlanta	David Thompson[2], N.C. State	1995	Golden State	Joe Smith, Maryland
1976	Houston	John Lucas, Maryland	1996	Philadelphia	Allen Iverson, Georgetown
1977	Milwaukee	Kent Benson, Indiana	1997	San Antonio	Tim Duncan, Wake Forest
1978	Portland	Mychal Thompson, Minnesota	1998	L.A. Clippers	Michael Olowokandi, Pacific
1979	L.A. Lakers	Magic Johnson, Michigan St.	1999	Chicago Bulls	Elton Brand, Duke
1980	Golden State	Joe Barry Carroll, Purdue	2000	New Jersey	Kenyon Martin, Cincinnati
1981	Dallas	Mark Aguirre, DePaul	2001	Washington	Kwame Brown, Glynn Academy (HS)
1982	L.A. Lakers	James Worthy, North Carolina	2002	Houston	Yao Ming, Shanghai Sharks (China)
1983	Houston	Ralph Sampson, Virginia	2003	Cleveland	LeBron James, St. Vincent-St. Mary (HS)
1984	Houston	Akeem Olajuwon, Houston	2004	Orlando	Dwight Howard, Southwest Atlanta Christian Academy (HS)
1985	New York	Patrick Ewing, Georgetown			

(1) Later Kareem Abdul-Jabbar. (2) Signed with Denver of the ABA. (3) Traded to Golden State.

All-Time NBA Statistical Leaders

(At the end of the 2003-2004 season. *Player active in 2003-2004 season.)

Scoring Average
(Minimum 400 games or 10,000 points)

	G	Pts.	Avg
Michael Jordan	1,072	32,292	30.1
Wilt Chamberlain	1,045	31,419	30.1
Elgin Baylor	846	23,149	27.4
*Shaquille O'Neal	809	21,914	27.1
Jerry West	932	25,192	27.0
*Allen Iverson	535	14,436	27.0
Bob Pettit	792	20,880	26.4
George Gervin	791	20,708	26.2
Oscar Robertson	1,040	26,710	25.7
*Karl Malone	1,476	36,928	25.0

Field Goal Percentage
(Minimum 2,000 field goals made)

	FGA	FGM	Pct.
Artis Gilmore	9,570	5,732	.599
Mark West	4,356	2,528	.580
*Shaquille O'Neal	15,020	8,670	.577
Steve Johnson	4,965	2,841	.572
Darryl Dawkins	6,079	3,477	.572
James Donaldson	5,442	3,105	.571
Jeff Ruland	3,734	2,105	.564
Kareem Abdul-Jabbar	28,307	15,837	.559
Kevin McHale	12,334	6,830	.554
Bobby Jones	6,199	3,412	.550

Free Throw Percentage
(Minimum 1,200 free throws made)

	FTA	FTM	Pct.
Mark Price	2,362	2,135	.904
Rick Barry	4,243	3,818	.900
*Steve Nash	1,409	1,258	.893
Calvin Murphy	3,864	3,445	.892
Scott Skiles	1,741	1,548	.889
*Reggie Miller	6,758	5,987	.886
Larry Bird	4,471	3,960	.886
*Predrag Stojakovic	1,373	1,551	.885
*Ray Allen	2,486	2,199	.885
*Darrell Armstrong	1,446	1,279	.885

3-Point Field Goal Percentage
(Minimum 250 3-point field goals made)

	3-FGA	3-FGM	Pct.
Steve Kerr	1,599	726	.454
*Hubert Davis	1,651	728	.441
Drazen Petrovic	583	255	.437
Tim Legler	603	260	.431
B.J. Armstrong	1,026	436	.425
*Wesley Person	2,665	1,109	.416
*Steve Nash	1,618	673	.416
*Pat Garrity	1,242	513	.413
*Dana Barros	2,652	1,090	.411
Trent Tucker	1,410	575	.408

Games Played

Robert Parish	1,611
Kareem Abdul-Jabbar	1,560
John Stockton	1,504
*Karl Malone	1,476
*Kevin Willis	1,390
Moses Malone	1,329
Buck Williams	1,307
Elvin Hayes	1,303
Sam Perkins	1,286
*Charles Oakley	1,282

Field Goals Attempted

Kareem Abdul-Jabbar	28,307
*Karl Malone	26,210
Michael Jordan	24,537
Elvin Hayes	24,272
John Havlicek	23,930
Wilt Chamberlain	23,497
Dominique Wilkins	21,589
Alex English	21,036
Hakeem Olajuwon	20,991
Elgin Baylor	20,171

Points

Kareem Abdul-Jabbar	38,387
*Karl Malone	36,928
Michael Jordan	32,292
Wilt Chamberlain	31,419
Moses Malone	27,409
Elvin Hayes	27,313
Hakeem Olajuwon	26,946
Oscar Robertson	26,710
Dominique Wilkins	26,668
John Havlicek	26,395

Minutes Played

Kareem Abdul-Jabbar	57,446
*Karl Malone	54,852
Elvin Hayes	50,000
Wilt Chamberlain	47,859
John Stockton	47,764
John Havlicek	46,471
Robert Parish	45,704
*Reggie Miller	45,514
Moses Malone	45,071
Hakeem Olajuwon	44,222

Field Goals Made

Kareem Abdul-Jabbar	15,837
*Karl Malone	13,528
Wilt Chamberlain	12,681
Michael Jordan	12,192
Elvin Hayes	10,976
Hakeem Olajuwon	10,749
Alex English	10,659
John Havlicek	10,513
Dominique Wilkins	9,963
Patrick Ewing	9,702

Rebounds

Wilt Chamberlain	23,924
Bill Russell	21,620
Kareem Abdul-Jabbar	17,440
Elvin Hayes	16,279
Moses Malone	16,212
*Karl Malone	14,968
Robert Parish	14,715
Nate Thurmond	14,464
Walt Bellamy	14,241
Wes Unseld	13,769

Personal Fouls

Kareem Abdul-Jabbar	4,657
*Karl Malone	4,578
Robert Parish	4,443
*Charles Oakley	4,421
Hakeem Olajuwon	4,383
Buck Williams	4,267
Elvin Hayes	4,193
Otis Thorpe	4,146
*Kevin Willis	4,108
James Edwards	4,042

3- Point Field Goals Attempted

*Reggie Miller	6,188
Tim Hardaway	4,345
Dale Ellis	4,269
Vernon Maxwell	3,931
*Glen Rice	3,896
*Nick Van Exel	3,867
Mookie Blaylock	3,816
Dan Majerle	3,798
John Starks	3,591
Mitch Richmond	3,417

Assists

John Stockton	15,806
*Mark Jackson	10,334
Magic Johnson	10,141
Oscar Robertson	9,887
Isiah Thomas	9,061
*Gary Payton	8,039
*Rod Strickland	7,948
Maurice Cheeks	7,392
Lenny Wilkens	7,211
Terry Porter	7,160

Blocked Shots

Hakeem Olajuwon	3,830
Kareem Abdul-Jabbar	3,189
Mark Eaton	3,064
*Dikembe Mutombo	2,996
David Robinson	2,954
Patrick Ewing	2,894
Tree Rollins	2,542
Robert Parish	2,361
*Shaquille O'Neal	2,102
Manute Bol	2,086

3- Point Field Goals Made

*Reggie Miller	2,464
Dale Ellis	1,719
*Glen Rice	1,559
Tim Hardaway	1,542
*Nick Van Exel	1,373
Dan Majerle	1,360
Mitch Richmond	1,326
Terry Porter	1,297
Mookie Blaylock	1,283
*Ray Allen	1,277

Steals

John Stockton	3,265
Michael Jordan	2,514
Maurice Cheeks	2,310
*Scottie Pippen	2,307
*Gary Payton	2,243
Clyde Drexler	2,207
Hakeem Olajuwon	2,162
Alvin Robertson	2,112
*Karl Malone	2,085
Mookie Blaylock	2,075

All-Time NBA Coaching Victories

(At the end of the 2003-2004 season. *Active through 2003-2004 season.)

Coach	W-L	Pct.	Coach	W-L	Pct.	Coach	W-L	Pct.
Lenny Wilkens*	1,315-1,133	.537	Jerry Sloan*	917-561	.620	Red Holzman	696-604	.535
Don Nelson*	1,148-858	.572	Jack Ramsay	864-783	.525	Rick Adelman*	658-411	.616
Pat Riley	1,110-569	.661	Phil Jackson*	832-316	.725	Chuck Daly	638-437	.593
Bill Fitch	944-1,106	.460	Cotton Fitzsimmons	832-775	.518	Doug Moe	628-529	.543
Red Auerbach	938-479	.662	Gene Shue	784-861	.477	Mike Fratello	572-465	.552
Dick Motta	935-1,017	.479	George Karl	708-499	.587	Alvin Attles	557-518	.518
Larry Brown*	933-713	.567	John MacLeod	707-657	.518			

Basketball Hall of Fame, Springfield, MA

(2004 inductees have an asterisk*)

PLAYERS

Abdul-Jabbar, Kareem
Archibald, Nate
Arizin, Paul
Barlow, Thomas
Barry, Rick
Baylor, Elgin
Beckman, John
Bellamy, Walt
Belov, Sergei
Bing, Dave
Bird, Larry
Blazejowski, Carol
Borgmann, Bennie
Bradley, Bill
Brennan, Joseph
Cervi, Al
Chamberlain, Wilt
Cooper, Charles
Cosic, Kresimir
Cousy, Bob
Cowens, Dave
Crawford, Joan
Cunningham, Billy
Curry, Denise
*Dalipagic, Drazen
Davies, Bob
DeBernardi, Forrest
DeBusschere, Dave
Denhart, Dutch
Donovan, Anne
*Drexler, Clyde
Endacott, Paul
English, Alex
Erving, Julius (Dr. J)
Foster, Bud
Frazier, Walt
Friedman, Max
Fulks, Joe
Gale, Lauren
Gallatin, Harry
Gates, Pop
Gervin, George
Gola, Tom
Goodrich, Gail
Greer, Hal
Gruenig, Ace
Hagan, Cliff
Hanson, Victor
Harris-Stewart, Luisa
Havlicek, John
Hawkins, Connie
Hayes, Elvin
Haynes, Marques
Heinsohn, Tom

Holman, Nat
Houbregs, Bob
Howell, Bailey
Hyatt, Chuck
Issel, Dan
Jeannette, Buddy
Johnson, Earvin "Magic"
Johnson, William
Johnston, Neil
Jones, K.C.
Jones, Sam
Krause, Moose
Kurland, Bob
Lanier, Bob
Lapchick, Joe
Lemon, Meadowlark
Lieberman-Cline, Nancy
Lloyd, Earl
Lovellette, Clyde
Lucas, Jerry
Luisetti, Hank
Macauley, Ed
Malone, Moses
Maravich, Pete
Martin, Slater
McAdoo, Bob
McCracken, Branch
McCracken, Jack
McDermott, Bobby
McGuire, Dick
McHale, Kevin
Meneghin, Dino
Meyers, Ann
Mikan, George
Mikkelsen, Vern
Miller, Cheryl
Monroe, Earl
Murphy, Calvin
Murphy, Stretch
Page, Pat
Parish, Robert
Petrovic, Drazen
Pettit, Bob
Phillip, Andy
Pollard, Jim
Ramsey, Frank
Reed, Willis
Risen, Arnie
Robertson, Oscar
Roosma, John S.
Russell, Bill
Russell, Honey
Schayes, Adolph
Schmidt, Ernest
Schommer, John

Sedran, Barney
Semjonova, Uljana
Sharman, Bill
Steinmetz, Christian
*Stokes, Maurice
Thomas, Isiah
Thompson, Cat
Thompson, David
Thurmond, Nate
Twyman, Jack
Unseld, Wes
Vandivier, Fuzzy
Wachter, Edward
Walton, Bill
Wanzer, Bobby
West, Jerry
White, Nera
Wilkens, Lenny
*Woodard, Lynette
Wooden, John
Worthy, James
Yardley, George

COACHES

Allen, Forrest (Phog)
Anderson, Harold
Auerbach, Red
Barmore, Leon
Barry, Sam
Blood, Ernest
Brown, Larry
Cann, Howard
Carlson, Dr. H. C.
Carnesecca, Lou
Carnevale, Ben
Carril, Pete
Case, Everett
Chaney, John
Conradt, Jody
Crum, Denny
Daly, Chuck
Dean, Everett
Diaz-Miguel, Antonio
Diddle, Edgar
Drake, Bruce
Gaines, Clarence
Gardner, Jack
Gill, Slats
Gomelsky, Aleksandr
Hannum, Alex
Harshman, Marv
Haskins, Don
Hickey, Edgar
Hobson, Howard
Holzman, Red

Iba, Hank
Julian, Alvin
Keaney, Frank
Keogan, George
Knight, Bob
Krzyzewski, Mike
Kundla, John
Lambert, Ward
Litwack, Harry
Loeffler, Kenneth
Lonborg, Dutch
McCutchan, Arad
McGuire, Al
McGuire, Frank
McLendon, John
Meanwell, Dr. W. E.
Meyer, Ray
Miller, Ralph
Moore, Billie
Newell, Pete
Nikolic, Aleksandar
Olson, Lute
Ramsay, Jack
Rubini, Cesare
Rupp, Adolph
Sachs, Leonard
*Sharman, Bill
Shelton, Everett
Smith, Dean
Summitt, Pat
Taylor, Fred
Thompson, John
Wade, Margaret
Watts, Stan
Wilkens, Lenny
Wooden, John
Woolpert, Phil
Wootten, Morgan
Yow, Kay

TEAMS

First Team
Original Celtics
Buffalo Germans
NY Renaissance
Harlem Globetrotters

REFEREES

Enright, James
Hepbron, George
Hoyt, George
Kennedy, Matthew
Leith, Lloyd
Mihalik, Red
Nucatola, John

Quigley, Ernest
Shirley, J. Dallas
Strom, Earl
Tobey, David
Walsh, David

CONTRIBUTORS

Abbott, Senda B.
Bee, Clair
Biasone, Danny
Brown, Walter
Bunn, John
*Colangelo, Jerry
Douglas, Bob
Duer, Al O.
Embry, Wayne
Fagan, Cliff
Fisher, Harry
Fleisher, Larry
Gottlieb, Edward
Gulick, Dr. L. H.
Harrison, Lester
Hearn, Francis "Chick"
Hepp, Dr. Ferenc
Hickox, Edward
Hinkle, Tony
Irish, Ned
Jones, R. W.
Kennedy, Walter
Liston, Emil
Mokray, Bill
Morgan, Ralph
Morgenweck, Frank
Naismith, Dr. James
Newton, C. M.
O'Brien, John
O'Brien, Larry
Olsen, Harold
Podoloff, Maurice
Porter, H. V.
Reid, William
Ripley, Elmer
St. John, Lynn
Saperstein, Abe
Schabinger, Arthur
Stagg, Amos Alonzo
Stankovich, Boris
Steitz, Edward
Taylor, Chuck
Teague, Bertha
Tower, Oswald
Trester, Arthur
Wells, Clifford
Wilke, Lou
Zollner, Fred

NBA Home Courts[1]

Team	Name (built)	Capacity
Atlanta	Philips Arena (1999)	20,000
Boston	FleetCenter (1995)	18,624
Chicago	United Center (1994)	21,500
Cleveland	Gund Arena (1994)	20,562
Dallas	American Airlines Center (2001)	19,200
Denver	Pepsi Center (1999)	19,099
Detroit	The Palace of Auburn Hills (1988)	22,076
Golden State	Arena in Oakland[2] (1966)	19,596
Houston	Toyota Center (2003)	18,300
Indiana	Conseco Fieldhouse (1999)	18,345
L.A. Clippers	Staples Center (1999)	19,060
L.A. Lakers	Staples Center (1999)	18,997
Memphis	The Pyramid (1991)	20,142
Miami	American Airlines Arena (1999)	19,600
Milwaukee	Bradley Center (1988)	18,600
Minnesota	Target Center (1990)	19,006
New Jersey	Continental Airlines Arena[3] (1981)	20,049
New Orleans	New Orleans Arena (1999)	18,500
New York	Madison Square Garden (1968)	19,763
Orlando	TD Waterhouse Centre[4] (1989)	17,248
Philadelphia	Wachovia Center[5] (1996)	20,444
Phoenix	America West Arena (1992)	19,023
Portland	The Rose Garden (1995)	19,980
Sacramento	ARCO Arena (1988)	17,317
San Antonio	SBC Center (2002)	18,500
Seattle	KeyArena at Seattle Center[6] (1962)	17,072
Toronto	Air Canada Centre (1999)	19,800
Utah	Delta Center (1991)	19,911
Washington	MCI Center (1997)	20,674

(1) At the end of the 2003-2004 season. (2) Oakland Coliseum Arena, 1966-96; renovated and renamed in 1997. (3) Brendan Byrne/Meadowlands Arena, 1981-96. (4) Orlando Arena, 1989-2000. (5) CoreStates Center, 1996-98; First Union Center, 1998-2003. (6) Seattle Center Coliseum, 1962-94; renovated, expanded, and renamed in 1995.

WOMEN'S PROFESSIONAL BASKETBALL

WNBA 2004: Seattle Beats Connecticut for First Title

The Seattle Storm defeated the Connecticut Sun, 74-60, in Seattle, WA on Oct. 12 to take the third and deciding game of the WNBA Finals. Seattle guard Betty Lennox scored 16 of her 23 points in the second half of Game 3 to lead the Storm to victory. Lennox, who averaged 22.3 points per game in the Finals, was named the most valuable player of the series. The Storm—led by regular-season leading scorer Lauren Jackson and guard Sue Bird—overcame the Minnesota Lynx and the Sacramento Monarchs on their march to the Finals. Seattle coach Ann Donovan became the first woman to lead a team to the WNBA title. The Sun, in only their second year of existence as a franchise, had the best record in the Eastern Conference in the regular season, and earned a spot in the Finals after defeating the Washington Mystics and the New York Liberty.

The WNBA took a month-long break during the 2004 season in order for many of its players to participate in the Summer Olympic Games in Athens, Greece. The U.S. Olympic team, consisting entirely of WNBA players, took the gold medal.

WNBA Final Standings, 2004 Season

x-clinched playoff berth; y-clinched top seed

Eastern Conference	W	L	Pct	G B	Western Conference	W	L	Pct	GB
y-Connecticut	18	16	0.529	—	y-Los Angeles	25	9	0.735	—
x-New York	18	16	0.529	—	x-Seattle	20	14	0.588	5.0
x-Detroit	17	17	0.500	1.0	x-Minnesota	18	16	0.529	7.0
x-Washington	17	17	0.500	1.0	x-Sacramento	18	16	0.529	7.0
Charlotte	16	18	0.471	2.0	Phoenix	17	17	0.500	8.0
Indiana	15	19	0.441	3.0	Houston	13	21	0.382	12.0
					San Antonio	9	25	0.265	16.0

2004 WNBA Playoffs

(Playoff seeding in parentheses; Conference winner automatically gets top seed)

Eastern Conference
Connecticut (1) defeated Washington (4), 2 games to 1
New York (2) defeated Detroit (3), 2 games to 1
Connecticut defeated New York, 2 games to 0

Western Conference
Sacramento (4) defeated Los Angeles (1), 2 games to 1
Seattle (2) defeated Minnesota (3), 2 games to 0
Seattle defeated Sacramento, 2 games to 1

WNBA Championship (Best of 3)

Seattle defeated Connecticut, 2 games to 1 [64-68, 67-65, 74-60]

2004 All-WNBA Teams

First Team	Position	Second Team
Lisa Leslie, Los Angeles	Center	Yolanda Griffith, Sacramento
Lauren Jackson, Seattle	Forward	Tamika Catchings, Indiana
Tina Thompson, Houston	Forward	Swin Cash, Detroit
Diana Taurasi, Phoenix	Guard	Nikki Teasley, Los Angeles
Sue Bird, Seattle	Guard	Nykesha Sales, Connecticut

WNBA Statistical Leaders and Awards in 2004

Minutes played — 1,152, Anna DeForge, Phoenix
Total points — 634, Lauren Jackson, Seattle
Points per game — 20.5, Lauren Jackson, Seattle
Highest field goal % — .540, Tamika Williams, Minnesota
Highest 3-pt. field goal % — .500, Charlotte Smith-Taylor, Charlotte
Highest free throw % — .899, Katie Smith, Minnesota
Total rebounds — 336, Lisa Leslie, Los Angeles
Rebounds per game — 9.9, Lisa Leslie, Los Angeles

Total assists — 207, Nikki Teasley, Los Angeles
Assists per game — 6.1, Nikki Teasley, Los Angeles
Total steals — 75, Yolanda Griffith, Sacramento
Steals per game — 2.21, Yolanda Griffith, Sacramento
Total blocked shots — 98, Lisa Leslie, Los Angeles
Coach of the year — Suzie McConnell Serio, Minnesota
Defensive player of year — Lisa Leslie, Los Angeles
Most improved player — (tie) Wendy Palmer, Connecticut, Kelly Miller, Indiana

WNBA Champions

	Regular season		Playoffs		
Year	Eastern Conference	Western Conference	Champion	Coach	Runner-up
1997	Houston Comets	Phoenix Mercury	Houston	Van Chancellor	New York
1998	Cleveland Rockers	Houston Comets	Houston	Van Chancellor	Phoenix
1999	New York Liberty	Houston Comets	Houston	Van Chancellor	New York
2000	New York Liberty	Los Angeles Sparks	Houston	Van Chancellor	New York
2001	Cleveland Rockers	Los Angeles Sparks	Los Angeles	Michael Cooper	Charlotte
2002	New York Liberty	Los Angeles Sparks	Los Angeles	Michael Cooper	New York
2003	Detroit Shock	Los Angeles Sparks	Detroit	Bill Laimbeer	Los Angeles
2004	Connecticut Sun	Los Angeles Sparks	Seattle	Ann Donovan	Connecticut

WNBA Scoring Leaders

Year	Scoring champion	Pts	Avg	Year	Scoring champion	Pts	Avg
1997	Cynthia Cooper, Houston	621	22.2	2001	Katie Smith, Minnesota	739	23.1
1998	Cynthia Cooper, Houston	680	22.7	2002	Chamique Holdsclaw, Washington	397	19.9
1999	Cynthia Cooper, Houston	686	22.1	2003	Lauren Jackson, Seattle	698	21.2
2000	Sheryl Swoopes, Houston	643	20.7	2004	Lauren Jackson, Seattle	634	20.5

WNBA Finals MVP

1997	Cynthia Cooper, Houston
1998	Cynthia Cooper, Houston
1999	Cynthia Cooper, Houston
2000	Cynthia Cooper, Houston
2001	Lisa Leslie, Los Angeles
2002	Lisa Leslie, Los Angeles
2003	Ruth Riley, Detroit
2004	Betty Lennox, Seattle

WNBA Most Valuable Player

1997	Cynthia Cooper, Houston
1998	Cynthia Cooper, Houston
1999	Yolanda Griffith, Sacramento
2000	Sheryl Swoopes, Houston
2001	Lisa Leslie, Los Angeles
2002	Sheryl Swoopes, Houston
2003	Lauren Jackson, Seattle
2004	Lisa Leslie, Los Angeles

WNBA Rookie of the Year

1997	no award
1998	Tracy Reid, Charlotte
1999	Chamique Holdsclaw, Washington
2000	Betty Lennox, Minnesota
2001	Jackie Stiles, Portland
2002	Tamika Catchings, Indiana
2003	Cheryl Ford, Detroit
2004	Diana Taurasi, Phoenix

COLLEGE BASKETBALL

Men's Final NCAA Division I Conference Standings, 2003-2004

(*conference tournament champion)

America East

	Conf. W	Conf. L	All W	All L
Boston U.	17	1	23	6
Vermont*	15	3	22	9
Northeastern	13	5	19	11
Maine	12	6	20	10
Binghamton	10	8	14	15
Hartford	6	12	12	17
New Hampshire	5	13	10	20
Stony Brook	5	13	10	20
MD Baltimore Co.	4	14	7	21
Albany	3	15	5	23

Atlantic Coast

	Conf. W	Conf. L	All W	All L
Duke	13	3	31	6
North Carolina St.	11	5	21	10
Georgia Tech	9	7	28	10
Wake Forest	9	7	21	10
North Carolina	8	8	19	11
Maryland*	7	9	20	12
Florida St.	6	10	19	14
Virginia	6	10	18	13
Clemson	3	13	10	18

Atlantic Sun

	Conf. W	Conf. L	All W	All L
Troy St.	18	2	23	7
Central Florida*	17	3	25	6
Belmont	15	5	21	9
Georgia St.	14	6	20	9
Stetson	10	10	12	15
Mercer	9	11	12	18
Jacksonville	8	12	13	15
Florida Atlantic	6	14	9	19
Gardner-Webb	6	14	9	20
Lipscomb	4	16	7	21
Campbell	3	17	3	24

Atlantic 10
East Division

	Conf. W	Conf. L	All W	All L
Saint Joseph's	16	0	30	2
Temple	9	7	15	14
Rhode Island	7	9	20	14
Massachusetts	4	12	10	19
St. Bonaventure	3	13	7	21
Fordham	3	13	6	22

West Division

	Conf. W	Conf. L	All W	All L
Dayton	12	4	24	9
George Washington	11	5	18	12
Xavier*	10	6	26	11
Richmond	10	6	20	13
Duquesne	6	10	12	17
La Salle	5	11	10	20

Big East

	Conf. W	Conf. L	All W	All L
Pittsburgh	13	3	31	5
Connecticut*	12	4	33	6
Syracuse	11	5	23	8
Providence	11	5	20	9
Boston College	10	6	24	10
Seton Hall	10	6	21	10
Notre Dame	9	7	19	13
Rutgers	7	9	20	13
West Virginia	7	9	17	14
Virginia Tech	7	9	15	14
Villanova	6	10	18	17
Georgetown	4	12	13	15
Miami (FL)	4	12	14	16
St. John's	1	15	6	21

Big Sky

	Conf. W	Conf. L	All W	All L
Eastern Wash.*	11	3	17	13
Northern Arizona	7	7	15	14
Weber St.	7	7	15	14
Sacramento St.	7	7	13	15
Idaho St.	7	7	11	19
Montana St.	6	8	14	13
Montana	6	8	10	18
Portland St.	5	9	11	16

Big South

	Conf. W	Conf. L	All W	All L
Birmingham-Southern	12	4	19	7
Liberty*	12	4	18	15
High Point	10	6	19	11
Winthrop	10	6	16	12

	Conf. W	Conf. L	All W	All L
Coastal Carolina	8	8	14	15
Radford	7	9	12	16
UNC Asheville	6	10	9	20
Va. Military Inst.	4	12	6	22
Charleston Southern	3	13	6	22

Big 10

	Conf. W	Conf. L	All W	All L
Illinois	13	3	26	7
Wisconsin*	12	4	25	7
Michigan St.	12	4	18	12
Iowa	9	7	16	13
Michigan	8	8	23	11
Northwestern	8	8	14	15
Purdue	7	9	17	14
Indiana	7	9	14	15
Ohio St.	6	10	14	16
Minnesota	3	13	12	18
Penn St.	3	13	9	19

Big 12

	Conf. W	Conf. L	All W	All L
Oklahoma St.*	14	2	31	4
Texas	12	4	25	8
Kansas	12	4	24	9
Colorado	10	6	18	11
Texas Tech	9	7	23	11
Missouri	9	7	16	14
Oklahoma	8	8	20	11
Iowa St.	7	9	20	13
Nebraska	6	10	18	13
Kansas St.	6	10	14	14
Baylor	3	13	8	21
Texas A&M	0	16	7	21

Big West

	Conf. W	Conf. L	All W	All L
Utah St.	17	1	25	4
Pacific*	17	1	25	8
UC Santa Barbara	10	8	16	12
Idaho	9	9	14	16
Cal St. Northridge	7	11	14	16
UC Riverside	7	11	11	17
Cal St. Fullerton	7	11	11	17
Cal Poly	6	12	11	16
UC Irvine	6	12	11	17
Long Beach St.	4	14	6	21

Colonial Athletic Association

	Conf. W	Conf. L	All W	All L
Va. Commonwealth*	14	4	23	8
Drexel	13	5	18	11
George Mason	12	6	23	10
Old Dominion	11	7	17	12
Delaware	10	8	16	12
Hofstra	10	8	14	15
UNC Wilmington	9	9	15	15
Towson	4	14	8	21
William & Mary	4	14	7	21
James Madison	3	15	7	21

Conference USA

	Conf. W	Conf. L	All W	All L
Cincinnati*	12	4	25	7
Memphis	12	4	22	8
DePaul	12	4	22	10
UAB	12	4	22	10
Charlotte	12	4	20	9
Louisville	9	7	20	10
Saint Louis	9	7	19	13
Marquette	8	8	19	12
TCU	7	9	12	17
Southern Miss	6	10	13	15
East Carolina	5	11	13	14
Tulane	4	12	11	17
Houston	3	13	9	18
S. Fla.	1	15	7	20

Horizon

	Conf. W	Conf. L	All W	All L
Wisc.-Milwaukee	13	3	20	11
Illinois-Chicago*	12	4	24	8
Wisc.-Green Bay	11	5	17	11
Detroit	10	6	19	11
Wright St.	10	6	14	14
Butler	8	8	16	14
Loyola (Chicago)	4	12	9	20
Youngstown St.	4	12	8	20
Cleveland St.	0	16	4	25

Ivy League[1]

	Conf. W	Conf. L	All W	All L
Princeton	13	1	20	8
Penn	10	4	17	10
Brown	10	4	14	13
Yale	7	7	12	15
Cornell	6	8	11	16
Columbia	6	8	10	17
Harvard	3	11	4	23
Dartmouth	1	13	3	25

Metro Atlantic Athletic

	Conf. W	Conf. L	All W	All L
Manhattan*	16	2	25	6
Niagara	13	5	22	10
Fairfield	12	6	19	11
St. Peter's	12	6	17	12
Rider	10	8	17	14
Siena	9	9	14	16
Iona	8	10	11	18
Canisius	5	13	10	20
Marist	4	14	6	22
Loyola (MD)	1	17	1	27

Mid-American
East Division

	Conf. W	Conf. L	All W	All L
Kent St.	13	5	22	9
Miami (OH)	12	6	18	11
Buffalo	11	7	17	12
Marshall	8	10	12	17
Akron	7	11	13	15
Ohio	7	11	10	20

West Division

	Conf. W	Conf. L	All W	All L
Western Mich.*	15	3	26	5
Toledo	12	6	20	11
Ball St.	10	8	14	15
Bowling Green	8	10	14	17
Eastern Mich.	7	11	13	15
No. Illinois	5	13	10	20
Central Mich.	2	16	6	24

Mid Continent

	Conf. W	Conf. L	All W	All L
Valparaiso*	11	5	18	13
Indiana-Purdue	10	6	21	11
Oral Roberts	10	6	17	11
Centenary	10	6	16	12
Missouri-KC	9	7	15	14
Chicago St.	9	7	12	20
Oakland	6	10	13	17
So. Utah	6	10	10	18
W. Illinois	1	15	3	25

Mid-Eastern Athletic

	Conf. W	Conf. L	All W	All L
South Carolina St.	14	4	18	11
Coppin St.	14	4	18	14
Delaware St.	11	7	13	15
Hampton	11	7	13	17
Florida A&M*	10	8	15	17
Norfolk St.	10	8	12	17
Morgan St.	9	9	11	16
Bethune-Cookman	7	11	8	21
MD-Eastern Shore	6	12	8	21
Howard	4	14	6	22
N.Carolina A&T	3	15	3	25

Missouri Valley

	Conf. W	Conf. L	All W	All L
Southern IL	17	1	25	5
Creighton	12	6	20	9
Northern Iowa*	12	6	21	10
Wichita St.	12	6	21	11
SMS	9	9	19	14
Bradley	7	11	15	16
Drake	7	11	12	16
Indiana St.	5	13	9	19
Evansville	5	13	7	22
Illinois St.	4	14	10	19

Mountain West

	Conf. W	Conf. L	All W	All L
Air Force	12	2	22	7
Brigham Young	10	4	21	9
Utah*	9	5	24	9
UNLV	7	7	18	13
New Mexico	5	9	14	14
San Diego St.	5	9	14	16
Colorado St.	4	10	13	16
Wyoming	4	10	11	17

Northeast

Team	Conf. W	Conf. L	All W	All L
Monmouth*	12	6	21	12
St. Francis (NY)	12	6	15	13
Fairleigh Dickinson	11	7	17	12
Robert Morris	10	8	14	15
St. Francis (PA)	10	8	13	15
Wagner	10	8	13	16
Central Conn. St.	9	9	14	14
Sacred Heart	8	10	12	15
Mt. St. Mary's	8	10	10	19
Quinnipiac	5	13	9	20
Long Island	4	14	8	19

Ohio Valley

Team	Conf. W	Conf. L	All W	All L
Austin Peay	16	0	22	10
Murray St.*	14	2	28	6
Morehead St.	10	6	16	13
Eastern Kentucky	8	8	14	15
Jacksonville St.	7	9	14	14
Tenn. Tech	7	9	13	15
Samford	7	9	12	16
Tenn. St.	6	10	7	21
Tenn. Martin	5	11	10	18
SE Missouri	4	12	11	16
Eastern Illinois	4	12	6	21

Pacific-10

Team	Conf. W	Conf. L	All W	All L
Stanford*	17	1	30	2
Washington	12	6	19	12
Arizona	11	7	20	10
Oregon	9	9	18	13
California	9	9	13	15
USC	8	10	13	15
Washington St.	7	11	13	16
UCLA	7	11	11	17
Oregon St.	6	12	12	16
Arizona St.	4	14	10	17

Patriot

Team	Conf. W	Conf. L	All W	All L
Lehigh*	10	4	20	11
American	10	4	18	13
Lafayette	9	5	18	10
Bucknell	9	5	14	15
Holy Cross	7	7	13	15
Colgate	6	8	15	14
Army	3	11	6	21
Navy	2	12	5	23

Southeastern

East Division

Team	Conf. W	Conf. L	All W	All L
Kentucky*	13	3	27	5
Florida	9	7	20	11
S. Carolina	8	8	23	11
Vanderbilt	8	8	23	10
Georgia	7	9	16	14
Tennessee	7	9	15	14

West Division

Team	Conf. W	Conf. L	All W	All L
Miss. St.	14	2	26	4
Alabama	8	8	20	13
LSU	8	8	18	11
Auburn	5	11	14	14
Ole Miss	5	11	13	15
Arkansas	4	12	12	16

Southern

North Division

Team	Conf. W	Conf. L	All W	All L
E.Tenn. St.*	15	1	27	6
Chattanooga	10	6	19	11
Elon	7	9	12	18
NC Greensboro	7	9	11	17
W. Carolina	6	10	13	15
Appalachian St.	4	12	9	21

South Division

Team	Conf. W	Conf. L	All W	All L
Georgia Southern	11	5	21	8
Coll. of Charleston	11	5	20	9
Davidson	11	5	17	12
Furman	8	8	17	12
Wofford	4	12	9	20
The Citadel	2	14	6	22

Southland

Team	Conf. W	Conf. L	All W	All L
SE Louisiana	11	5	20	9
TX-San Antonio*	11	5	20	13
TX-Arlington	11	5	17	12
Stephen F. Austin	10	6	21	9
Sam Houston St.	8	8	13	15
Texas St.	8	8	13	15
Louisiana-Monroe	8	8	12	19
Northwestern St.	8	8	11	17
McNeese St.	7	9	11	16
Lamar	5	11	11	18
Nicholls St.	1	15	6	21

Southwest Athletic

Team	Conf. W	Conf. L	All W	All L
Miss. Valley St.	16	2	22	7
Tex. Southern	11	7	15	14
Alabama St.*	11	7	16	15
Alabama A&M	9	9	13	17
Jackson St.	9	9	12	17
Grambling St.	9	9	11	18
Alcorn St.	9	9	11	18
Southern	8	10	11	17
Prairie View A&M	7	11	7	20
Ark. Pine Bluff	1	17	1	26

Sun Belt

East Division

Team	Conf. W	Conf. L	All W	All L
Ark.-Little Rock	9	5	17	12
Western Kentucky	8	6	15	13
Middle Tenn.	8	6	17	12
Arkansas St.	7	7	17	11
Florida Int'l.	1	13	5	22

West Division

Team	Conf. W	Conf. L	All W	All L
La.-Lafayette*	12	3	20	9
New Orleans	9	6	17	14
North Texas	8	7	13	15
Denver	6	9	14	13
New Mexico St.	6	9	13	14
South Alabama	6	9	12	16

West Coast

Team	Conf. W	Conf. L	All W	All L
Gonzaga*	14	0	28	3
St. Mary's (CA)	9	5	19	12
Pepperdine	9	5	15	16
San Francisco	7	7	17	14
Santa Clara	6	8	16	16
Loyola Marymount	5	9	15	14
Portland	5	9	11	17
San Diego	1	13	4	26

Western Athletic Conference

Team	Conf. W	Conf. L	All W	All L
Nevada*	13	5	25	9
UTEP	13	5	24	8
Boise St.	12	6	23	10
Rice	12	6	22	11
Hawaii	11	7	21	12
Fresno St.	10	8	14	15
La. Tech	8	10	15	15
SMU	5	13	12	18
Tulsa	5	13	9	20
San Jose St.	1	17	6	23

Independents

Team	Conf. W	Conf. L	All W	All L
Tex. A&M Corp. Chris.	—	—	14	11
Tex. Pan American	—	—	13	14
Savannah St.	—	—	5	23
I-P Fort Wayne	—	—	3	25

(1) Conference does not hold a tournament. (2) Trans America Athletic Conference, 1979-2001.

All-Time Winningest Division I College Teams by Percentage

(through 2003-2004 season)

TEAM	Yrs	Won	Lost	Pct.
Kentucky	101	1,876	577	0.765
N. Carolina	94	1,827	677	0.730
UNLV	46	946	376	0.716
Kansas	106	1,825	762	0.705
Duke	99	1,737	781	0.690
UCLA	85	1,530	690	0.689
Syracuse	103	1,630	752	0.684
St. John's-NY	97	1,668	784	0.680
W. Kentucky	85	1,481	736	0.668
Utah	96	1,541	793	0.660
Indiana	104	1,555	839	0.650
Illinois	99	1,483	803	0.649
Louisville	90	1,451	788	0.648
Arkansas	81	1,389	758	0.647
Temple	108	1,623	888	0.646
Arizona	99	1,458	798	0.646
Notre Dame	99	1,548	851	0.645
Weber State	42	771	427	0.644
Pennsylvania	104	1,572	886	0.639
DePaul	81	1,280	726	0.638

Major College Basketball Tournaments

The National Invitation Tournament (NIT), first played in 1938, is the nation's oldest basketball tournament. The first National Collegiate Athletic Association (NCAA) national championship tournament was played one year later. Selections for both tournaments are made in March, with the NCAA selecting first from among the top Division I teams.

National Invitation Tournament Champions

Year	Champion	Year	Champion	Year	Champion	Year	Champion	Year	Champion
1938	Temple	1952	LaSalle	1966	Brigham Young	1979	Indiana	1992	Virginia
1939	Long Island Univ.	1953	Seton Hall	1967	Southern Illinois	1980	Virginia	1993	Minnesota
1940	Colorado	1954	Holy Cross	1968	Dayton	1981	Tulsa	1994	Villanova
1941	Long Island Univ.	1955	Duquesne	1969	Temple	1982	Bradley	1995	Virginia Tech
1942	West Virginia	1956	Louisville	1970	Marquette	1983	Fresno State	1996	Nebraska
1943	St. John's	1957	Bradley	1971	North Carolina	1984	Michigan	1997	Michigan
1944	St. John's	1958	Xavier (Ohio)	1972	Maryland	1985	UCLA	1998	Minnesota
1945	De Paul	1959	St. John's	1973	Virginia Tech	1986	Ohio State	1999	California
1946	Kentucky	1960	Bradley	1974	Purdue	1987	So. Mississippi	2000	Wake Forest
1947	Utah	1961	Providence	1975	Princeton	1988	Connecticut	2001	Tulsa
1948	St. Louis	1962	Dayton	1976	Kentucky	1989	St. John's	2002	Memphis
1949	San Francisco	1963	Providence	1977	St. Bonaventure	1990	Vanderbilt	2003	St. John's
1950	CCNY	1964	Bradley	1978	Texas	1991	Stanford	2004	Michigan
1951	Brigham Young	1965	St. John's						

2004 MEN'S NCAA BASKETBALL TOURNAMENT

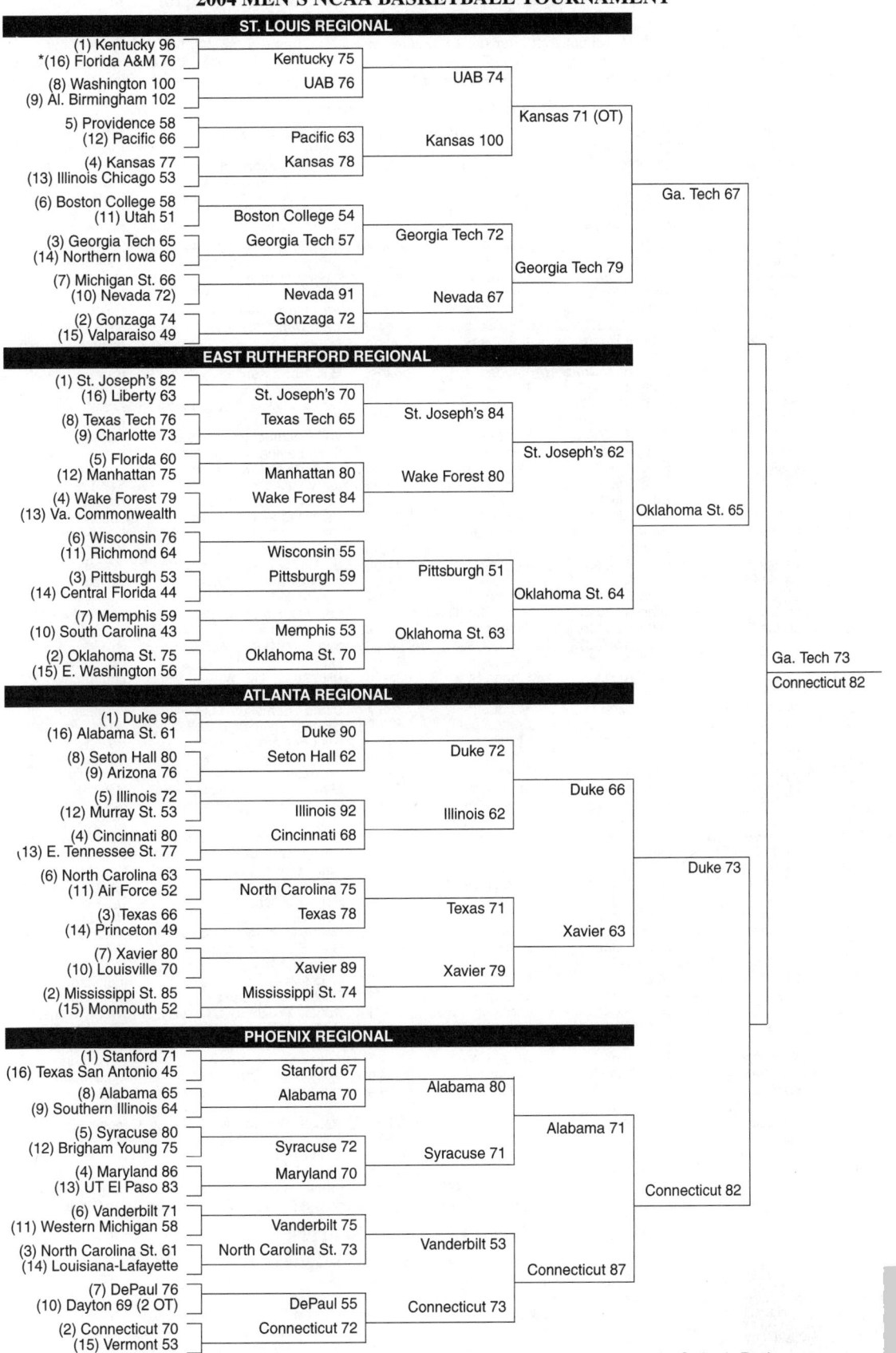

ST. LOUIS REGIONAL

(1) Kentucky 96
*(16) Florida A&M 76
   Kentucky 75
   UAB 76
(8) Washington 100
(9) Al. Birmingham 102

UAB 74

Kansas 71 (OT)

(5) Providence 58
(12) Pacific 66
   Pacific 63
   Kansas 78
(4) Kansas 77
(13) Illinois Chicago 53

Kansas 100

Ga. Tech 67

(6) Boston College 58
(11) Utah 51
   Boston College 54
   Georgia Tech 57
(3) Georgia Tech 65
(14) Northern Iowa 60

Georgia Tech 72

Georgia Tech 79

(7) Michigan St. 66
(10) Nevada 72)
   Nevada 91
   Gonzaga 72
(2) Gonzaga 74
(15) Valparaiso 49

Nevada 67

EAST RUTHERFORD REGIONAL

(1) St. Joseph's 82
(16) Liberty 63
   St. Joseph's 70
   Texas Tech 65
(8) Texas Tech 76
(9) Charlotte 73

St. Joseph's 84

St. Joseph's 62

(5) Florida 60
(12) Manhattan 75
   Manhattan 80
   Wake Forest 84
(4) Wake Forest 79
(13) Va. Commonwealth

Wake Forest 80

Oklahoma St. 65

(6) Wisconsin 76
(11) Richmond 64
   Wisconsin 55
   Pittsburgh 59
(3) Pittsburgh 53
(14) Central Florida 44

Pittsburgh 51

Oklahoma St. 64

(7) Memphis 59
(10) South Carolina 43
   Memphis 53
   Oklahoma St. 70
(2) Oklahoma St. 75
(15) E. Washington 56

Oklahoma St. 63

Ga. Tech 73
Connecticut 82

ATLANTA REGIONAL

(1) Duke 96
(16) Alabama St. 61
   Duke 90
   Seton Hall 62
(8) Seton Hall 80
(9) Arizona 76

Duke 72

Duke 66

(5) Illinois 72
(12) Murray St. 53
   Illinois 92
   Cincinnati 68
(4) Cincinnati 80
(13) E. Tennessee St. 77

Illinois 62

Duke 73

(6) North Carolina 63
(11) Air Force 52
   North Carolina 75
   Texas 78
(3) Texas 66
(14) Princeton 49

Texas 71

Xavier 63

(7) Xavier 80
(10) Louisville 70
   Xavier 89
   Mississippi St. 74
(2) Mississippi St. 85
(15) Monmouth 52

Xavier 79

PHOENIX REGIONAL

(1) Stanford 71
(16) Texas San Antonio 45
   Stanford 67
   Alabama 70
(8) Alabama 65
(9) Southern Illinois 64

Alabama 80

Alabama 71

(5) Syracuse 80
(12) Brigham Young 75
   Syracuse 72
   Maryland 70
(4) Maryland 86
(13) UT El Paso 83

Syracuse 71

Connecticut 82

(6) Vanderbilt 71
(11) Western Michigan 58
   Vanderbilt 75
   North Carolina St. 73
(3) North Carolina St. 61
(14) Louisiana-Lafayette

Vanderbilt 53

Connecticut 87

(7) DePaul 76
(10) Dayton 69 (2 OT)
   DePaul 55
   Connecticut 72
(2) Connecticut 70
(15) Vermont 53

Connecticut 73

*Florida A&M defeated Lehigh, 72-57, in a special play-in game on Mar. 16 to earn the 16th seed in the St. Louis Region.

2004 Men's NCAA Tournament: UConn Dominates Georgia Tech for Title

The Connecticut Huskies (31-6) defeated the Georgia Tech Yellow Jackets (27-9), 82-73, to win the national title in San Antonio, TX, April 5. The Huskies did not trail after the 1st minute, and at one point in the 2nd half led by as many as 25 points. Georgia Tech hit four 3-pointers in the final 44 seconds of the game to make the final score closer. Huskies center Emeka Okafor scored 24 points and had 15 rebounds, and was named the Most Outstanding Player of the Final Four.

NCAA Division I Champions

Year	Champion	Coach	Final opponent	Score	Outstanding player	Site
1939	Oregon	Howard Hobson	Ohio St.	46-33	None	Evanston, IL
1940	Indiana	Branch McCracken	Kansas	60-42	Marvin Huffman, Indiana	Kansas City, MO
1941	Wisconsin	Harold Foster	Washington St.	39-34	John Kotz, Wisconsin	Kansas City, MO
1942	Stanford	Everett Dean	Dartmouth	53-38	Howard Dallmar, Stanford	Kansas City, MO
1943	Wyoming	Everett Shelton	Georgetown	46-34	Ken Sailors, Wyoming	New York, NY
1944	Utah	Vadal Peterson	Dartmouth	42-40[1]	Arnold Ferrin, Utah	New York, NY
1945	Oklahoma St.[2]	Henry Iba	NYU	49-45	Bob Kurland, Oklahoma St.	New York, NY
1946	Oklahoma St.[2]	Henry Iba	North Carolina	43-40	Bob Kurland, Oklahoma St.	New York, NY
1947	Holy Cross	Alvin Julian	Oklahoma	58-47	George Kaftan, Holy Cross	New York, NY
1948	Kentucky	Adolph Rupp	Baylor	58-42	Alex Groza, Kentucky	New York, NY
1949	Kentucky	Adolph Rupp	Oklahoma St.	46-36	Alex Groza, Kentucky	Seattle, WA
1950	CCNY	Nat Holman	Bradley	71-68	Irwin Dambrot, CCNY	New York, NY
1951	Kentucky	Adolph Rupp	Kansas St.	68-58	None	Minneapolis, MN
1952	Kansas	Forrest Allen	St. John's	80-63	Clyde Lovellette, Kansas	Seattle, WA
1953	Indiana	Branch McCracken	Kansas	69-68	B.H. Born, Kansas	Kansas City, MO
1954	La Salle	Kenneth Loeffler	Bradley	92-76	Tom Gola, La Salle	Kansas City, MO
1955	San Francisco	Phil Woolpert	LaSalle	77-63	Bill Russell, San Francisco	Kansas City, MO
1956	San Francisco	Phil Woolpert	Iowa	83-71	Hal Lear, Temple	Evanston, IL
1957	North Carolina	Frank McGuire	Kansas	54-53[1]	Wilt Chamberlain, Kansas	Kansas City, MO
1958	Kentucky	Adolph Rupp	Seattle	84-72	Elgin Baylor, Seattle	Louisville, KY
1959	California	Pete Newell	West Virginia	71-70	Jerry West, West Virginia	Louisville, KY
1960	Ohio St.	Fred Taylor	California	75-55	Jerry Lucas, Ohio St.	San Francisco, CA
1961	Cincinnati	Edwin Jucker	Ohio St.	70-65[1]	Jerry Lucas, Ohio St.	Kansas City, MO
1962	Cincinnati	Edwin Jucker	Ohio St.	71-59	Paul Hogue, Cincinnati	Louisville, KY
1963	Loyola (IL)	George Ireland	Cincinnati	60-58[1]	Art Heyman, Duke	Louisville, KY
1964	UCLA	John Wooden	Duke	98-83	Walt Hazzard, UCLA	Kansas City, MO
1965	UCLA	John Wooden	Michigan	91-80	Bill Bradley, Princeton	Portland, OR
1966	Texas-El Paso[3]	Don Haskins	Kentucky	72-65	Jerry Chambers, Utah	College Park, MD
1967	UCLA	John Wooden	Dayton	79-64	Lew Alcindor, UCLA	Louisville, KY
1968	UCLA	John Wooden	North Carolina	78-55	Lew Alcindor, UCLA	Los Angeles, CA
1969	UCLA	John Wooden	Purdue	92-72	Lew Alcindor, UCLA	Louisville, KY
1970	UCLA	John Wooden	Jacksonville	80-69	Sidney Wicks, UCLA	College Park, MD
1971	UCLA	John Wooden	Villanova*	68-62	Howard Porter, Villanova*	Houston, TX
1972	UCLA	John Wooden	Florida St.	81-76	Bill Walton, UCLA	Los Angeles, CA
1973	UCLA	John Wooden	Memphis St.	87-66	Bill Walton, UCLA	St. Louis, MO
1974	North Carolina St.	Norm Sloan	Marquette	76-64	David Thompson, N.C. St.	Greensboro, NC
1975	UCLA	John Wooden	Kentucky	92-85	Richard Washington, UCLA	San Diego, CA
1976	Indiana	Bob Knight	Michigan	86-68	Kent Benson, Indiana	Philadelphia, PA
1977	Marquette	Al McGuire	North Carolina	67-59	Butch Lee, Marquette	Atlanta, GA
1978	Kentucky	Joe Hall	Duke	94-88	Jack Givens, Kentucky	St. Louis, MO
1979	Michigan St.	Jud Heathcote	Indiana St.	75-64	Magic Johnson, Michigan St.	Salt Lake City, UT
1980	Louisville	Denny Crum	UCLA*	59-54	Darrell Griffith, Louisville	Indianapolis, IN
1981	Indiana	Bob Knight	North Carolina	63-50	Isiah Thomas, Indiana	Philadelphia, PA
1982	North Carolina	Dean Smith	Georgetown	63-62	James Worthy, N. Carolina	New Orleans, LA
1983	North Carolina St.	Jim Valvano	Houston	54-52	Hakeem Olajuwon, Houston	Albuquerque, NM
1984	Georgetown	John Thompson	Houston	84-75	Patrick Ewing, Georgetown	Seattle, WA
1985	Villanova	Rollie Massimino	Georgetown	66-64	Ed Pinckney, Villanova	Lexington, KY
1986	Louisville	Denny Crum	Duke	72-69	Pervis Ellison, Louisville	Dallas, TX
1987	Indiana	Bob Knight	Syracuse	74-73	Keith Smart, Indiana	New Orleans, LA
1988	Kansas	Larry Brown	Oklahoma	83-79	Danny Manning, Kansas	Kansas City, MO
1989	Michigan	Steve Fisher	Seton Hall	80-79[1]	Glen Rice, Michigan	Seattle, WA
1990	UNLV	Jerry Tarkanian	Duke	103-73	Anderson Hunt, UNLV	Denver, CO
1991	Duke	Mike Krzyzewski	Kansas	72-65	Christian Laettner, Duke	Indianapolis, IN
1992	Duke	Mike Krzyzewski	Michigan	71-51	Bobby Hurley, Duke	Minneapolis, MN
1993	North Carolina	Dean Smith	Michigan	77-71	Donald Williams, N. Carolina	New Orleans, LA
1994	Arkansas	Nolan Richardson	Duke	76-72	Corliss Williamson, Arkansas	Charlotte, NC
1995	UCLA	Jim Harrick	Arkansas	89-78	Ed O'Bannon, UCLA	Seattle, WA
1996	Kentucky	Rick Pitino	Syracuse	76-67	Tony Delk, Kentucky	E. Rutherford, NJ
1997	Arizona	Lute Olson	Kentucky	84-79[1]	Miles Simon, Arizona	Indianapolis, IN
1998	Kentucky	Tubby Smith	Utah	78-69	Jeff Sheppard, Kentucky	San Antonio, TX
1999	Connecticut	Jim Calhoun	Duke	77-74	Richard Hamilton, Connecticut	St. Petersburg, FL
2000	Michigan St.	Tom Izzo	Florida	89-76	Mateen Cleaves, Michigan St.	Indianapolis, IN
2001	Duke	Mike Krzyzewski	Arizona	82-72	Shane Battier, Duke	Minneapolis, MN
2002	Maryland	Gary Williams	Indiana	64-52	Juan Dixon, Maryland	Atlanta, GA
2003	Syracuse	Jim Boeheim	Kansas	81-78	Carmelo Anthony, Syracuse	New Orleans, LA
2004	Connecticut	Jim Calhoun	Georgia Tech	82-73	Emeka Okafor, Connecticut	San Antonio, TX

*Declared ineligible after the tournament. (1) Overtime. (2) Then known as Oklahoma A&M. (3) Then known as Texas Western.

Top Division I Career Scorers

(minimum 1,500 points; ranked by average)

Player, school	Years	Points	Avg	Player, school	Years	Points	Avg
Pete Maravich, LSU	1968-70	3,667	44.2	Frank Selvy, Furman	1952-54	2,538	32.5
Austin Carr, Notre Dame	1969-71	2,560	34.6	Rick Mount, Purdue	1968-70	2,323	32.3
Oscar Robertson, Cincinnati	1958-60	2,973	33.8	Darrell Floyd, Furman	1954-56	2,281	32.1
Calvin Murphy, Niagara	1968-70	2,548	33.1	Nick Werkman, Seton Hall	1962-64	2,273	32.0
Dwight Lamar, SW Louisiana	1972-73	1,862	32.7	Willie Humes, Idaho State	1970-71	1,510	31.5

John R. Wooden Award

Awarded to the nation's outstanding college basketball player by the Los Angeles Athletic Club.

1977	Marques Johnson, UCLA	1987	David Robinson, Navy	1996	Marcus Camby, Massachusetts
1978	Phil Ford, North Carolina	1988	Danny Manning, Kansas	1997	Tim Duncan, Wake Forest
1979	Larry Bird, Indiana State	1989	Sean Elliott, Arizona	1998	Antawn Jamison, North Carolina
1980	Darrell Griffith, Louisville	1990	Lionel Simmons, La Salle	1999	Elton Brand, Duke
1981	Danny Ainge, Brigham Young	1991	Larry Johnson, UNLV	2000	Kenyon Martin, Cincinnati
1982	Ralph Sampson, Virginia	1992	Christian Laettner, Duke	2001	Shane Battier, Duke
1983	Ralph Sampson, Virginia	1993	Calbert Cheaney, Indiana	2002	Jay Williams, Duke
1984	Michael Jordan, North Carolina	1994	Glenn Robinson, Purdue	2003	T.J. Ford, Texas
1985	Chris Mullin, St. John's	1995	Ed O'Bannon, UCLA	2004	Jameer Nelson, St. Joseph's
1986	Walter Berry, St. John's				

Most Coaching Victories in the NCAA Tournament Through 2004

(Coaches active in 2003-2004 season in bold)

Coach, School(s), First/Last appearance	Wins	Tourns.	Coach, School(s), First/Last appearance	Wins	Tourns.
Dean Smith, North Carolina, 1967/1997	65	27	**Roy Williams**, Kansas, N. Carolina, 1990/2004	35	15
Mike Krzyzewski, Duke, 1984/2004	64	20	**Eddie Sutton**, Creighton, Arkansas, Kentucky,		
John Wooden, UCLA, 1950/1975	47	16	Oklahoma St., 1974/2004	35	24
Bob Knight, Indiana, Texas Tech, 1973/2004	43	26	**Jim Calhoun**, Northeastern, Connecticut,		
Denny Crum, Louisville, 1972/2000	42	23	1981/2004	34	16
Lute Olson, Iowa, Arizona, 1979/2004	42	24	John Thompson, Georgetown, 1975/1997	34	20
Jim Boeheim, Syracuse, 1977/2004	40	23			

WOMEN'S COLLEGE BASKETBALL

2004 Women's NCAA Tournament: UConn Wins 3rd Straight Title

The two-time defending champion Connecticut Huskies (30-4) beat the Tennessee Lady Vols (31-3), 70-61, in New Orleans, LA, on April 6 to win the women's national title. Connecticut guard Diana Taurasi was named the Most Outstanding Player of the Final Four for the 2nd year in a row. The title was the 5th for Connecticut and its coach, Geno Auriemma. Auriemma's 5 titles were second only to the 6 won by Tennessee's Pat Summitt. The only other women's team to have won 3 straight titles was Tennessee (1996-1998).

NCAA Division I Women's Champions

Year	Champion	Coach	Final opponent	Score	Outstanding player	Site
1982	Louisiana Tech	Sonja Hogg	Cheyney	76-62	Janice Lawrence, La. Tech	Norfolk, VA
1983	USC	Linda Sharp	Louisiana Tech	69-67	Cheryl Miller, USC	Norfolk, VA
1984	USC	Linda Sharp	Tennessee	72-61	Cheryl Miller, USC	Los Angeles, CA
1985	Old Dominion	Marianne Stanley	Georgia	70-65	Tracy Claxton, Old Dominion	Austin, TX
1986	Texas	Jody Conradt	USC	97-81	Clarissa Davis, Texas	Lexington, KY
1987	Tennessee	Pat Summitt	Louisiana Tech	67-44	Tonya Edwards, Tennessee	Austin, TX
1988	Louisiana Tech	Leon Barmore	Auburn	56-54	Erica Westbrooks, La. Tech	Tacoma, WA
1989	Tennessee	Pat Summitt	Auburn	76-60	Bridgette Gordon, Tennessee	Tacoma, WA
1990	Stanford	Tara VanDerveer	Auburn	88-81	Jennifer Azzi, Stanford	Knoxville, TN
1991	Tennessee	Pat Summitt	Virginia	70-67*	Dawn Staley, Virginia	New Orleans, LA
1992	Stanford	Tara VanDerveer	W. Kentucky	78-62	Molly Goodenbour, Stanford	Los Angeles, CA
1993	Texas Tech	Marsha Sharp	Ohio St.	84-82	Sheryl Swoopes, Texas Tech	Atlanta, GA
1994	North Carolina	Sylvia Hatchell	Louisiana Tech	60-59	Charlotte Smith, North Carolina	Richmond, VA
1995	Connecticut	Geno Auriemma	Tennessee	70-64	Rebecca Lobo, Connecticut	Minneapolis, MN
1996	Tennessee	Pat Summitt	Georgia	83-65	Michelle Marciniak, Tennessee	Charlotte, NC
1997	Tennessee	Pat Summitt	Old Dominion	68-59	Chamique Holdsclaw, Tennessee	Cincinnati, OH
1998	Tennessee	Pat Summitt	Louisiana Tech	93-75	Chamique Holdsclaw, Tennessee	Kansas City, MO
1999	Purdue	Carolyn Peck	Duke	62-45	Ukari Figgs, Purdue	San Jose, CA
2000	Connecticut	Geno Auriemma	Tennessee	71-52	Shea Ralph, Connecticut	Philadelphia, PA
2001	Notre Dame	Muffet McGraw	Purdue	68-66	Ruth Riley, Notre Dame	St. Louis, MO
2002	Connecticut	Geno Auriemma	Oklahoma	82-70	Swin Cash, Connecticut	San Antonio, TX
2003	Connecticut	Geno Auriemma	Tennessee	73-68	Diana Taurasi, Connecticut	Atlanta, GA
2004	Connecticut	Geno Auriemma	Tennessee	70-61	Diana Taurasi, Connecticut	New Orleans, LA

* Overtime.

Wade Trophy

Awarded by National Assn. for Girls and Women in Sport for academics, community service, and player performance.

Year	Player, school	Year	Player, school	Year	Player, school
1978	Carol Blazejowski, Montclair St.	1988	Teresa Weatherspoon,	1997	DeLisha Milton, Florida
1979	Nancy Lieberman, Old Dominion		Louisiana Tech	1998	Chamique Holdsclaw,
1980	Nancy Lieberman, Old Dominion	1989	Clarissa Davis, Texas		Tennessee
1981	Lynette Woodard, Kansas	1990	Jennifer Azzi, Stanford	1999	Stephanie White-McCarty,
1982	Pam Kelly, Louisiana Tech	1991	Daedra Charles, Tennessee		Purdue
1983	LaTaunya Pollard, Long Beach St.	1992	Susan Robinson, Penn St.	2000	Edwina Brown, Texas
1984	Janice Lawrence, Louisiana Tech	1993	Karen Jennings, Nebraska	2001	Jackie Stiles, SW Missouri St.
1985	Cheryl Miller, USC	1994	Carol Ann Shudlick, Minnesota	2002	Sue Bird, Connecticut
1986	Kamie Ethridge, Texas	1995	Rebecca Lobo, Connecticut	2003	Diana Taurasi, Connecticut
1987	Shelly Pennefeather, Villanova	1996	Jennifer Rizzotti, Connecticut	2004	Alana Beard, Duke

Top Division I Women's Career Scorers

(Minimum 1,500 points; ranked by average)

Player, school	Years	Points	Avg	Player, school	Years	Points	Avg
Patricia Hoskins, Miss. Valley St.	1985-89	3,122	28.4	Valorie Whiteside, Appalachian St.	1984-88	2,944	25.4
Sandra Hodge, New Orleans	1981-84	2,860	26.7	Joyce Walker, LSU	1981-84	2,906	24.8
Jackie Stiles, SW Missouri St.	1997-2001	3,393	26.3	Tarcha Hollis, Grambling	1988-91	2,058	24.2
Lorri Bauman, Drake	1981-84	3,115	26.0	Korie Hlede, Duquesne	1994-98	2,631	24.1
Andrea Congreaves, Mercer	1989-93	2,796	25.9	Erma Jones, Bethune-Cookman	1982-84	2,095	24.1
Cindy Blodgett, Maine	1994-98	3,005	25.5	Karen Pelphrey, Marshall	1983-86	2,746	24.1

2004 WOMEN'S NCAA BASKETBALL TOURNAMENT

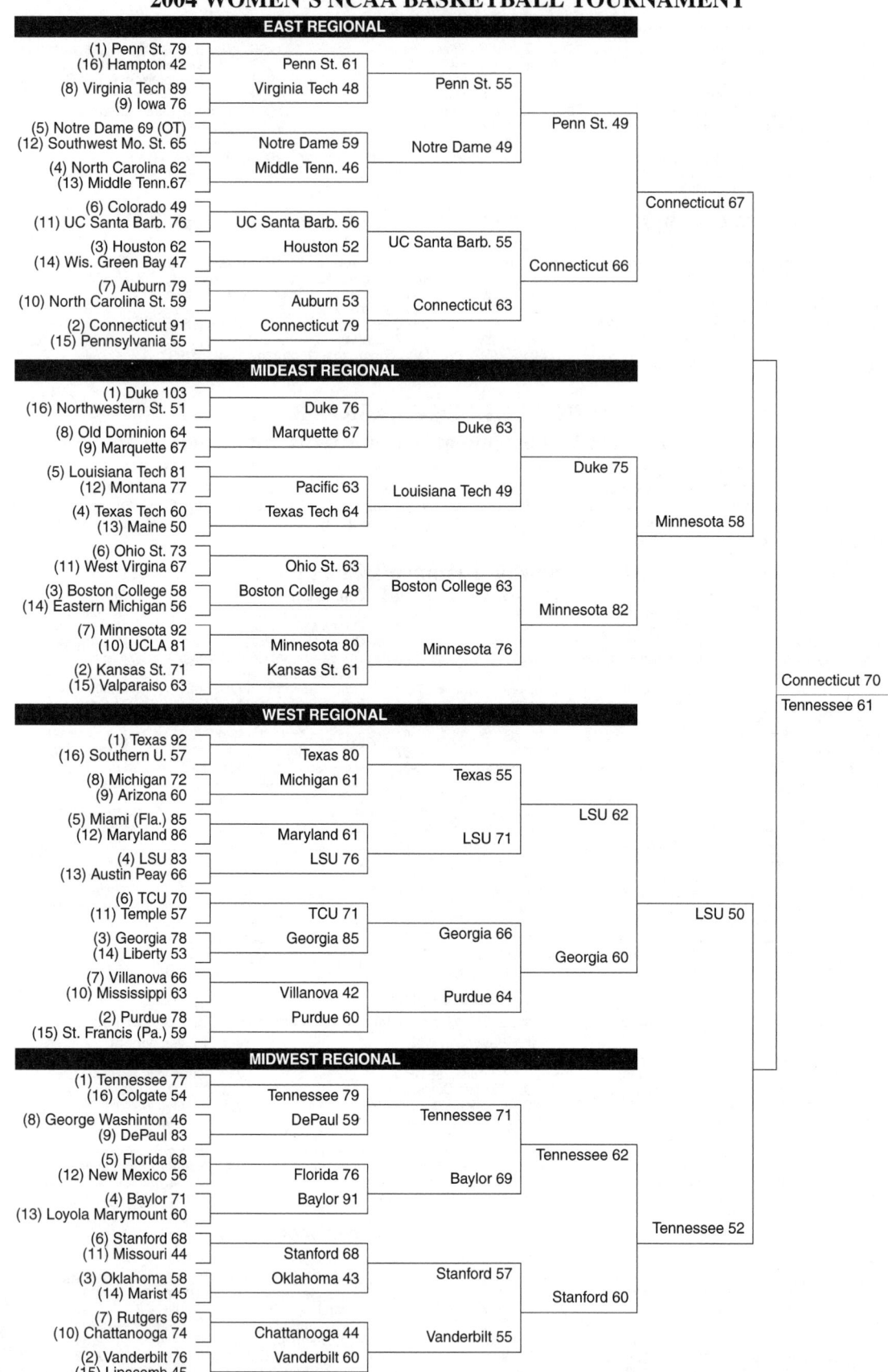

EAST REGIONAL

(1) Penn St. 79
(16) Hampton 42
    Penn St. 61

(8) Virginia Tech 89
(9) Iowa 76
    Virginia Tech 48
       Penn St. 55

          Penn St. 49

(5) Notre Dame 69 (OT)
(12) Southwest Mo. St. 65
    Notre Dame 59

(4) North Carolina 62
(13) Middle Tenn. 67
    Middle Tenn. 46
       Notre Dame 49

             Penn St. 49

Connecticut 67

(6) Colorado 49
(11) UC Santa Barb. 76
    UC Santa Barb. 56

(3) Houston 62
(14) Wis. Green Bay 47
    Houston 52
       UC Santa Barb. 55

          Connecticut 66

(7) Auburn 79
(10) North Carolina St. 59
    Auburn 53

(2) Connecticut 91
(15) Pennsylvania 55
    Connecticut 79
       Connecticut 63

MIDEAST REGIONAL

(1) Duke 103
(16) Northwestern St. 51
    Duke 76

(8) Old Dominion 64
(9) Marquette 67
    Marquette 67
       Duke 63

          Duke 75

(5) Louisiana Tech 81
(12) Montana 77
    Pacific 63

(4) Texas Tech 60
(13) Maine 50
    Texas Tech 64
       Louisiana Tech 49

             Minnesota 58

(6) Ohio St. 73
(11) West Virgina 67
    Ohio St. 63

(3) Boston College 58
(14) Eastern Michigan 56
    Boston College 48
       Boston College 63

          Minnesota 82

(7) Minnesota 92
(10) UCLA 81
    Minnesota 80

(2) Kansas St. 71
(15) Valparaiso 63
    Kansas St. 61
       Minnesota 76

Connecticut 70

Tennessee 61

WEST REGIONAL

(1) Texas 92
(16) Southern U. 57
    Texas 80

(8) Michigan 72
(9) Arizona 60
    Michigan 61
       Texas 55

          LSU 62

(5) Miami (Fla.) 85
(12) Maryland 86
    Maryland 61

(4) LSU 83
(13) Austin Peay 66
    LSU 76
       LSU 71

             LSU 50

(6) TCU 70
(11) Temple 57
    TCU 71

(3) Georgia 78
(14) Liberty 53
    Georgia 85
       Georgia 66

          Georgia 60

(7) Villanova 66
(10) Mississippi 63
    Villanova 42

(2) Purdue 78
(15) St. Francis (Pa.) 59
    Purdue 60
       Purdue 64

MIDWEST REGIONAL

(1) Tennessee 77
(16) Colgate 54
    Tennessee 79

(8) George Washinton 46
(9) DePaul 83
    DePaul 59
       Tennessee 71

          Tennessee 62

(5) Florida 68
(12) New Mexico 56
    Florida 76

(4) Baylor 71
(13) Loyola Marymount 60
    Baylor 91
       Baylor 69

             Tennessee 52

(6) Stanford 68
(11) Missouri 44
    Stanford 68

(3) Oklahoma 58
(14) Marist 45
    Oklahoma 43
       Stanford 57

          Stanford 60

(7) Rutgers 69
(10) Chattanooga 74
    Chattanooga 44

(2) Vanderbilt 76
(15) Lipscomb 45
    Vanderbilt 60
       Vanderbilt 55

NATIONAL FOOTBALL LEAGUE

NFL 2003-2004: Pats Super, Manning; McNair MVPs; Milestone for J. Lewis; Records for Holmes, Vanderjagt, & B. Smith

In what was called one of the most exciting Super Bowls ever, the New England Patriots defeated the upstart Carolina Panthers, 32-29, in Super Bowl XXXVIII in Houston Feb. 1, 2004. The Patriots, as in their 2002 Super Bowl triumph, were led by game MVP quarterback Tom Brady, and won on a last-minute field goal by Adam Vinatieri. The Patriots, under NFL coach of the year Bill Belichick, posted a 14-2 regular-season record, and won 15 straight games, including the Super Bowl.

Two quarterbacks, Indianapolis's Peyton Manning and Tennessee's Steve McNair, were named co-MVPs of the NFL season. Baltimore running back Jamal Lewis rushed for 2,066 yards, the second-most ever in a season, behind Eric Dickerson's 2,105 yards in 1984. Kansas City running back Priest Holmes rushed for 27 touchdowns, breaking Emmitt Smith's record of 25 rushing touchdowns in a season (1995) and Marshall Faulk's record of 26 overall touchdowns in a season (2000). Indianapolis's Mike Vanderjagt kicked his 41st straight successful field goal dating back to Dec. 2002, besting Gary Anderson's record of 40, set in 1998. Vanderjagt did not miss a field goal or extra point all season. Washington defensive end Bruce Smith ended the season with 200 career sacks, breaking Reggie White's NFL record of 198, set in 2000.

Final 2003 Standings

American Football Conference

East Division

	W	L	T	Pct.	Pts.	Opp.	Div.
New England	14	2	0	.875	348	238	5-1
Miami	10	6	0	.625	311	261	4-2
Buffalo	6	10	0	.375	243	279	2-4
NY Jets	6	10	0	.375	283	299	1-5

North Division

	W	L	T	Pct.	Pts.	Opp.	Div.
Baltimore	10	6	0	.625	391	281	4-2
Cincinnati	8	8	0	.500	346	384	3-3
Pittsburgh	6	10	0	.375	300	327	3-3
Cleveland	5	11	0	.312	254	322	2-4

South Division

	W	L	T	Pct.	Pts.	Opp.	Div.
Indianapolis	12	4	0	.750	447	336	5-1
Tennessee*	12	4	0	.750	435	324	4-2
Jacksonville	5	11	0	.312	276	331	2-4
Houston	5	11	0	.312	255	380	1-5

West Division

	W	L	T	Pct.	Pts.	Opp.	Div.
Kansas City	13	3	0	.812	484	332	5-1
Denver*	10	6	0	.625	381	301	5-1
Oakland	4	12	0	.250	270	379	1-5
San Diego	4	12	0	.250	313	441	1-5

* Wild card team.

National Football Conference

East Division

	W	L	T	Pct.	Pts.	Opp.	Div.
Philadelphia	12	4	0	.750	374	287	5-1
Dallas	10	6	0	.625	289	260	5-1
Washington	5	11	0	.312	287	372	1-5
NY Giants	4	12	0	.250	243	387	1-5

North Division

	W	L	T	Pct.	Pts.	Opp.	Div.
Green Bay	10	6	0	.625	442	307	4-2
Minnesota	9	7	0	.562	416	353	4-2
Chicago	7	9	0	.438	283	346	2-4
Detroit	5	11	0	.312	270	379	2-4

South Division

	W	L	T	Pct.	Pts.	Opp.	Div.
Carolina	11	5	0	.688	325	304	5-1
New Orleans	8	8	0	.500	340	326	3-3
Tampa Bay	7	9	0	.438	301	264	2-4
Atlanta	5	11	0	.312	299	422	2-4

West Division

	W	L	T	Pct.	Pts.	Opp.	Div.
St. Louis	12	4	0	.750	447	328	4-2
Seattle*	10	6	0	.625	404	327	5-1
San Francisco	7	9	0	.438	384	337	2-4
Arizona	4	12	0	.250	225	452	1-5

AFC Playoffs—Tennessee 20, Baltimore17; Indianapolis 41, Denver 10; Indianapolis 38, Kansas City 31; New England 17, Tennessee 14; Championship: New England 24, Indianapolis 14.

NFC Playoffs—Green Bay 33, Seattle 27 (OT); Carolina 29, Dallas 10; Carolina 29, St. Louis 23 (2OT); Philadelphia 20, Green Bay 17 (OT); Championship: Carolina 14, Philadelphia 3. **Super Bowl**—New England 32, Carolina 29.

National Football League Champions

Year	East Winner (W-L-T)	West Winner (W-L-T)	Playoff
1933	New York Giants (11-3-0)	Chicago Bears (10-2-1)	Chicago Bears 23, New York 21
1934	New York Giants (8-5-0)	Chicago Bears (13-0-0)	New York 30, Chicago Bears 13
1935	New York Giants (9-3-0)	Detroit Lions (7-3-2)	Detroit 26, New York 7
1936	Boston Redskins (7-5-0)	Green Bay Packers (10-1-1)	Green Bay 21, Boston 6
1937	Washington Redskins (8-3-0)	Chicago Bears (9-1-1)	Washington 28, Chicago Bears 21
1938	New York Giants (8-2-1)	Green Bay Packers (8-3-0)	New York 23, Green Bay 17
1939	New York Giants (9-1-1)	Green Bay Packers (9-2-0)	Green Bay 27, New York 0
1940	Washington Redskins (9-2-0)	Chicago Bears (8-3-0)	Chicago Bears 73, Washington 0
1941	New York Giants (8-3-0)	Chicago Bears (10-1-1)(a)	Chicago Bears 37, New York 9
1942	Washington Redskins (10-1-1)	Chicago Bears (11-0-0)	Washington 14, Chicago Bears 6
1943	Washington Redskins (6-3-1)	Chicago Bears (8-1-1)	Chicago Bears, 41, Washington 21
1944	New York Giants (8-1-1)	Green Bay Packers (8-2-0)	Green Bay 14, New York 7
1945	Washington Redskins (8-2-0)	Cleveland Rams (9-1-0)	Cleveland 15, Washington 14
1946	New York Giants (7-3-1)	Chicago Bears (8-2-1)	Chicago Bears 24, New York 14
1947	Philadelphia Eagles (8-4-0)(a)	Chicago Cardinals (9-3-0)	Chicago Cardinals 28, Philadelphia 21
1948	Philadelphia Eagles (9-2-1)	Chicago Cardinals (11-1-0)	Philadelphia 7, Chicago Cardinals 0
1949	Philadelphia Eagles (11-1-0)	Los Angeles Rams (8-2-2)	Philadelphia 14, Los Angeles 0
1950	Cleveland Browns (10-2-0)(a)	Los Angeles Rams (9-3-0)(a)	Cleveland 30, Los Angeles 28
1951	Cleveland Browns (11-1-0)	Los Angeles Rams (8-4-0)	Los Angeles 24, Cleveland 17
1952	Cleveland Browns (8-4-0)	Detroit Lions (9-3-0)(a)	Detroit 17, Cleveland 7
1953	Cleveland Browns (11-1-0)	Detroit Lions (10-2-0)	Detroit 17, Cleveland 16
1954	Cleveland Browns (9-3-0)	Detroit Lions (9-2-1)	Cleveland 56, Detroit 10
1955	Cleveland Browns (9-2-1)	Los Angeles Rams (8-3-1)	Cleveland 38, Los Angeles 14
1956	New York Giants (8-3-1)	Chicago Bears (9-2-1)	New York 47, Chicago Bears 7
1957	Cleveland Browns (9-2-1)	Detroit Lions (8-4-0)(a)	Detroit 59, Cleveland 14
1958	New York Giants (9-3-0)(a)	Baltimore Colts (9-3-0)	Baltimore 23, New York 17(b)
1959	New York Giants (10-2-0)	Baltimore Colts (9-3-0)	Baltimore 31, New York 16
1960	Philadelphia Eagles (10-2-0)	Green Bay Packers (8-4-0)	Philadelphia 17, Green Bay 13
1961	New York Giants (10-3-1)	Green Bay Packers (11-3-0)	Green Bay 37, New York 0
1962	New York Giants (12-2-0)	Green Bay Packers (13-1-0)	Green Bay 16, New York 7
1963	New York Giants (11-3-0)	Chicago Bears (11-1-2)	Chicago 14, New York 10
1964	Cleveland Browns (10-3-1)	Baltimore Colts (12-2-0)	Cleveland 27, Baltimore 0
1965	Cleveland Browns (11-3-0)	Green Bay Packers (10-3-1)(a)	Green Bay 23, Cleveland 12
1966	Dallas Cowboys (10-3-1)	Green Bay Packers (12-2-0)	Green Bay 34, Dallas 27

(a) Won divisional playoff. (b) Won at 8:15 of sudden death overtime period.

Year	Conference	Division	Winner (W-L-T)	Playoffs(c)	Year
1967	East	Century	Cleveland Browns (9-5-0)	Dallas 52, Cleveland 14	1967
		Capitol	Dallas Cowboys (9-5-0)		
	West	Central	Green Bay Packers (9-4-1)	Green Bay 28, Los Angeles 7	
		Coastal	Los Angeles Rams (11-1-2)(a)	Green Bay 21, Dallas 17	
1968	East	Century	Cleveland Browns (10-4-0)	Cleveland 31, Dallas 20	1968
		Capitol	Dallas Cowboys (12-2-0)		
	West	Central	Minnesota Vikings (8-6-0)	Baltimore 24, Minnesota 14	
		Coastal	Baltimore Colts (13-1-0)	Baltimore 34, Cleveland 0	
1969	East	Century	Cleveland Browns (10-3-1)	Cleveland 38, Dallas 14	1969
		Capitol	Dallas Cowboys (11-2-1)		
	West	Central	Minnesota Vikings (12-2-0)	Minnesota 23, Los Angeles 20	
		Coastal	Los Angeles Rams (11-3-0)	Minnesota 27, Cleveland 7	
1970	American	Eastern	Baltimore Colts (11-2-1)	Baltimore 17, Cincinnati 0	1970
		Central	Cincinnati Bengals (8-6-0)	Oakland 21, Miami* 14	
		Western	Oakland Raiders (8-4-2)	Baltimore 27, Oakland 17	
	National	Eastern	Dallas Cowboys (10-4-0)	Dallas 5, Detroit* 0	
		Central	Minnesota Vikings (12-2-0)	San Francisco 17, Minnesota 14	
		Western	San Francisco 49ers (10-3-1)	Dallas 17, San Francisco 10	
1971	American	Eastern	Miami Dolphins (10-3-1)	Miami 27, Kansas City* 24	1971
		Central	Cleveland Browns (9-5-0)	Baltimore 20, Cleveland 3	
		Western	Kansas City Chiefs (10-3-1)	Miami 21, Baltimore 0	
	National	Eastern	Dallas Cowboys (11-3-0)	Dallas 20, Minnesota 12	
		Central	Minnesota Vikings (11-3-0)	San Francisco 24, Washington* 20	
		Western	San Francisco 49ers (9-5-0)	Dallas 14, San Francisco 3	
1972	American	Eastern	Miami Dolphins (14-0-0)	Miami 20, Cleveland* 14	1972
		Central	Pittsburgh Steelers (11-3-0)	Pittsburgh 13, Oakland 7	
		Western	Oakland Raiders (10-3-1)	Miami 21, Pittsburgh 17	
	National	Eastern	Washington Redskins (11-3-0)	Washington 16, Green Bay 3	
		Central	Green Bay Packers (10-4-0)	Dallas* 30, San Francisco 28	
		Western	San Francisco 49ers (8-5-1)	Washington 26, Dallas* 3	
1973	American	Eastern	Miami Dolphins (12-2-0)	Miami 34, Cincinnati 16	1973
		Central	Cincinnati Bengals (10-4-0)	Oakland 33, Pittsburgh* 14	
		Western	Oakland Raiders (9-4-1)	Miami 27, Oakland 10	
	National	Eastern	Dallas Cowboys (10-4-0)	Dallas 27, Los Angeles 16	
		Central	Minnesota Vikings (12-2-0)	Minnesota 27, Washington* 20	
		Western	Los Angeles Rams (12-2-0)	Minnesota 27, Dallas 10	
1974	American	Eastern	Miami Dolphins (11-3-0)	Oakland 28, Miami 26	1974
		Central	Pittsburgh Steelers (10-3-1)	Pittsburgh 32, Buffalo* 14	
		Western	Oakland Raiders (12-2-0)	Pittsburgh 24, Oakland 13	
	National	Eastern	St. Louis Cardinals (10-4-0)	Minnesota 30, St. Louis 14	
		Central	Minnesota Vikings (10-4-0)	Los Angeles 19, Washington* 10	
		Western	Los Angeles Rams (10-4-0)	Minnesota 14, Los Angeles 10	
1975	American	Eastern	Baltimore Colts (10-4-0)	Pittsburgh 28, Baltimore 10	1975
		Central	Pittsburgh Steelers (12-2-0)	Oakland 31, Cincinnati* 28	
		Western	Oakland Raiders (11-3-0)	Pittsburgh 16, Oakland 10	
	National	Eastern	St. Louis Cardinals (11-3-0)	Dallas* 17, Minnesota 14	
		Central	Minnesota Vikings (12-2-0)	Los Angeles 35, St. Louis 23	
		Western	Los Angeles Rams (12-2-0)	Dallas* 37, Los Angeles 7	
1976	American	Eastern	Baltimore Colts (11-3-0)	Pittsburgh 40, Baltimore 14	1976
		Central	Pittsburgh Steelers (10-4-0)	Oakland 24, New England* 21	
		Western	Oakland Raiders (13-1-0)	Oakland 24, Pittsburgh 7	
	National	Eastern	Dallas Cowboys (11-3-0)	Minnesota 35, Washington* 20	
		Central	Minnesota Vikings (11-2-1)	Los Angeles 14, Dallas 12	
		Western	Los Angeles Rams (10-3-1)	Minnesota 24, Los Angeles 13	
1977	American	Eastern	Baltimore Colts (10-4-0)	Oakland* 37, Baltimore 31	1977
		Central	Pittsburgh Steelers (9-5-0)	Denver 34, Pittsburgh 21	
		Western	Denver Broncos (12-2-0)	Denver 20, Oakland* 17	
	National	Eastern	Dallas Cowboys (12-2-0)	Dallas 37, Chicago* 7	
		Central	Minnesota Vikings (9-5-0)	Minnesota 14, Los Angeles 7	
		Western	Los Angeles Rams (10-4-0)	Dallas 23, Minnesota 6	
1978	American	Eastern	New England Patriots (11-5-0)	Pittsburgh 33, Denver 10	1978
		Central	Pittsburgh Steelers (14-2-0)	Houston* 31, New England 14	
		Western	Denver Broncos (10-6-0)	Pittsburgh 34, Houston* 5	
	National	Eastern	Dallas Cowboys (12-4-0)	Dallas 27, Atlanta* 20	
		Central	Minnesota Vikings (8-7-1)	Los Angeles 34, Minnesota 10	
		Western	Los Angeles Rams (12-4-0)	Dallas 28, Los Angeles 0	
1979	American	Eastern	Miami Dolphins (10-6-0)	Houston* 17, San Diego 14	1979
		Central	Pittsburgh Steelers (12-4-0)	Pittsburgh 34, Miami 14	
		Western	San Diego Chargers (12-4-0)	Pittsburgh 27, Houston* 13	
	National	Eastern	Dallas Cowboys (11-5-0)	Tampa Bay 24, Philadelphia* 17	
		Central	Tampa Bay Buccaneers (10-6-0)	Los Angeles 21, Dallas 19	
		Western	Los Angeles Rams (9-7-0)	Los Angeles 9, Tampa Bay 0	
1980	American	Eastern	Buffalo Bills (11-5-0)	San Diego 20, Buffalo 14	1980
		Central	Cleveland Browns (11-5-0)	Oakland* 14, Cleveland 12	
		Western	San Diego Chargers (11-5-0)	Oakland* 34, San Diego 27	
	National	Eastern	Philadelphia Eagles (12-4-0)	Philadelphia 31, Minnesota 16	
		Central	Minnesota Vikings (9-7-0)	Dallas* 30, Atlanta 27	
		Western	Atlanta Falcons (12-4-0)	Philadelphia 20, Dallas* 7	
1981	American	Eastern	Miami Dolphins (11-4-1)	San Diego 41, Miami 38	1981
		Central	Cincinnati Bengals (12-4-0)	Cincinnati 28, Buffalo* 21	
		Western	San Diego Chargers (10-6-0)	Cincinnati 27, San Diego 7	
	National	Eastern	Dallas Cowboys (12-4-0)	Dallas 38, Tampa Bay 0	
		Central	Tampa Bay Buccaneers (9-7-0)	San Francisco 38, N.Y. Giants* 24	
		Western	San Francisco 49ers (13-3-0)	San Francisco 28, Dallas 27	
1982 (d)	American		Los Angeles Raiders (8-1-0)	Strike-shortened season (see	1982 (d)
	National		Washington Redskins (8-1-0)	playoff results after footnote)	
1983	American	Eastern	Miami Dolphins (12-4-0)	Seattle* 27, Miami 20	1983
		Central	Pittsburgh Steelers (10-6-0)	L.A. Raiders 38, Pittsburgh 10	
		Western	Los Angeles Raiders (12-4-0)	L.A. Raiders 30, Seattle* 14	
	National	Eastern	Washington Redskins (14-2-0)	Washington 51, L.A. Rams* 7	
		Central	Detroit Lions (9-7-0)	San Francisco 24, Detroit 23	
		Western	San Francisico 49ers (10-6-0)	Washington 24, San Francisco 21	

Year	Conference	Division	Winner (W-L-T)	Playoffs(c)	Year
1984	American	Eastern	Miami Dolphins (14-2-0)	Miami 31, Seattle* 10	1984
		Central	Pittsburgh Steelers (9-7-0)	Pittsburgh 24, Denver 17	
		Western	Denver Broncos (13-3-0)	Miami 45, Pittsburgh 28	
	National	Eastern	Washington Redskins (11-5-0)	Chicago 23, Washington 19	
		Central	Chicago Bears (10-6-0)	San Francisco 21, N.Y. Giants* 10	
		Western	San Francisco 49ers (15-1-0)	San Francisco 23, Chicago 0	
1985	American	Eastern	Miami Dolphins (12-4-0)	New England* 27, L.A. Raiders 20	1985
		Central	Cleveland Browns (8-8-0)	Miami 24, Cleveland 21	
		Western	Los Angeles Raiders (12-4-0)	New England* 31, Miami 14	
	National	Eastern	Dallas Cowboys (10-6-0)	Chicago 21, N.Y. Giants* 0	
		Central	Chicago Bears (15-1-0)	L.A. Rams 20, Dallas 0	
		Western	Los Angeles Rams (11-5-0)	Chicago 24, L.A. Rams 0	
1986	American	Eastern	New England Patriots (11-5-0)	Denver 22, New England 17	1986
		Central	Cleveland Browns (12-4-0)	Cleveland 23, N.Y. Jets* 20	
		Western	Denver Broncos (11-5-0)	Denver 23, Cleveland 20	
	National	Eastern	New York Giants (14-2-0)	N.Y. Giants 49, San Francisco 3	
		Central	Chicago Bears (14-2-0)	Washington* 27, Chicago 13	
		Western	San Francisco 49ers (10-5-1)	N.Y. Giants 17, Washington* 0	
1987	American	Eastern	Indianapolis Colts (9-6-0)	Cleveland 38, Indianapolis 21	1987
		Central	Cleveland Browns (10-5-0)	Denver 34, Houston* 10	
		Western	Denver Broncos (10-4-1)	Denver 38, Cleveland 33	
	National	Eastern	Washington Redskins (11-4-0)	Washington 21, Chicago 17	
		Central	Chicago Bears (11-4-0)	Minnesota* 36, San Francisco 24	
		Western	San Francisco 49ers (13-2-0)	Washington 17, Minnesota* 10	
1988	American	Eastern	Buffalo Bills (12-4-0)	Buffalo 17, Houston* 10	1988
		Central	Cincinnati Bengals (12-4-0)	Cincinnati 21, Seattle 13	
		Western	Seattle Seahawks (9-7-0)	Cincinnati 21, Buffalo 10	
	National	Eastern	Philadelphia Eagles (10-6-0)	Chicago 20, Philadelphia 12	
		Central	Chicago Bears (12-4-0)	San Francisco 34, Minnesota* 9	
		Western	San Francisco 49ers (10-6-0)	San Francisco 28, Chicago 3	
1989	American	Eastern	Buffalo Bills (9-7-0)	Cleveland 34, Buffalo 30	1989
		Central	Cleveland Browns (9-6-1)	Denver 24, Pittsburgh* 23	
		Western	Denver Broncos (11-5-0)	Denver 37, Cleveland 21	
	National	Eastern	New York Giants (12-4-0)	San Francisco 41, Minnesota 13	
		Central	Minnesota Vikings (10-6-0)	L.A. Rams* 19, N.Y. Giants 13	
		Western	San Francisco 49ers (14-2-0)	San Francisco 30, L.A. Rams* 3	
1990	American	Eastern	Buffalo Bills (13-3-0)	L.A. Raiders 20, Cincinnati 10	1990
		Central	Cincinnati Bengals (9-7-0)	Buffalo 44, Miami* 34	
		Western	Los Angeles Raiders (12-4-0)	Buffalo 51, L.A. Raiders 3	
	National	Eastern	New York Giants (13-3-0)	San Francisco 28, Washington* 10	
		Central	Chicago Bears (11-5-0)	N.Y. Giants 31, Chicago 3	
		Western	San Francisco 49ers (14-2-0)	N.Y. Giants 15, San Francisco 13	
1991	American	Eastern	Buffalo Bills (13-3-0)	Denver 26, Houston 24	1991
		Central	Houston Oilers (11-5-0)	Buffalo 37, Kansas City* 14	
		Western	Denver Broncos (12-4-0)	Buffalo 10, Denver 7	
	National	Eastern	Washington Redskins (14-2-0)	Washington 24, Atlanta* 7	
		Central	Detroit Lions (12-4-0)	Detroit 38, Dallas* 6	
		Western	New Orleans Saints (11-5-0)	Washington 41, Detroit 10	
1992	American	Eastern	Miami Dolphins (11-5-0)	Miami 31, San Diego 0	1992
		Central	Pittsburgh Steelers (11-5-0)	Buffalo* 24, Pittsburgh 3	
		Western	San Diego Chargers (11-5-0)	Buffalo* 29, Miami 10	
	National	Eastern	Dallas Cowboys (13-3-0)	Dallas 34, Philadelphia* 10	
		Central	Minnesota Vikings (11-5-0)	San Francisco 20, Washington* 13	
		Western	San Francisco 49ers (14-2-0)	Dallas 30, San Francisco 20	
1993	American	Eastern	Buffalo Bills (12-4-0)	Buffalo 29, L.A. Raiders* 23	1993
		Central	Houston Oilers (12-4-0)	Kansas City 28, Houston 20	
		Western	Kansas City Chiefs (11-5-0)	Buffalo 30, Kansas City 13	
	National	Eastern	Dallas Cowboys (12-4-0)	Dallas 27, Green Bay* 17	
		Central	Detroit Lions (10-6-0)	San Francisco 44, N.Y. Giants* 3	
		Western	San Francisco 49ers (10-6-0)	Dallas 38, San Francisco 21	
1994	American	Eastern	Miami Dolphins (10-6-0)	Pittsburgh 29, Cleveland* 9	1994
		Central	Pittsburgh Steelers (12-4-0)	San Diego 22, Miami 21	
		Western	San Diego Chargers (11-5-0)	San Diego 17, Pittsburgh 13	
	National	Eastern	Dallas Cowboys (12-4-0)	San Francisco 44, Chicago* 15	
		Central	Minnesota Vikings (10-6-0)	Dallas 35, Green Bay* 9	
		Western	San Francisco 49ers (13-3-0)	San Francisco 38, Dallas 28	
1995	American	Eastern	Buffalo Bills (10-6-0)	Indianapolis* 10, Kansas City 7	1995
		Central	Pittsburgh Steelers (11-5-0)	Pittsburgh 40, Buffalo 21	
		Western	Kansas City Chiefs (13-3-0)	Pittsburgh 20, Indianapolis* 16	
	National	Eastern	Dallas Cowboys (12-4-0)	Dallas 30, Philadelphia* 11	
		Central	Green Bay Packers (11-5-0)	Green Bay 27, San Francisco 17	
		Western	San Francisco 49ers (11-5-0)	Dallas 38, Green Bay 27	
1996	American	Eastern	New England Patriots (11-5-0)	Jacksonville* 30, Denver 27	1996
		Central	Pittsburgh Steelers (10-6-0)	New England 28, Pittsburgh 3	
		Western	Denver Broncos (13-3-0)	New England 20, Jacksonville* 6	
	National	Eastern	Dallas Cowboys (10-6-0)	Green Bay 35, San Francisco* 14	
		Central	Green Bay Packers (13-3-0)	Carolina 26, Dallas 17	
		Western	Carolina Panthers (12-4-0)	Green Bay 30, Carolina 13	
1997	American	Eastern	New England Patriots (10-6-0)	Pittsburgh 7, New England 6	1997
		Central	Pittsburgh Steelers (11-5-0)	Denver* 14, Kansas City 10	
		Western	Kansas City Chiefs (13-3-0)	Denver* 24, Pittsburgh 21	
	National	Eastern	New York Giants (10-5-1)	San Francisco 38, Minnesota* 22	
		Central	Green Bay Packers (13-3-0)	Green Bay 21, Tampa Bay* 7	
		Western	San Francisco 49ers (13-3-0)	Green Bay 23, San Francisco 10	
1998	American	Eastern	N.Y. Jets (12-4-0)	Denver 38, Miami* 3	1998
		Central	Jacksonville Jaguars (11-5-0)	N.Y. Jets 34, Jacksonville 24	
		Western	Denver Broncos (14-2-0)	Denver 23, N.Y. Jets 10	
	National	Eastern	Dallas Cowboys (10-6-0)	Atlanta 20, San Francisco* 18	
		Central	Minnesota Vikings (15-1-0)	Minnesota 41, Arizona* 21	
		Western	Atlanta Falcons (14-2-0)	Atlanta 30, Minnesota 27 (OT)	

Year	Conference	Division	Winner (W-L-T)	Playoffs(c)	Year
1999	American	Eastern	Indianapolis Colts (13-3-0)	Jacksonville 62, Miami* 7	1999
		Central	Jacksonville Jaguars (14-2-0)	Tennessee* 19, Indianapolis 16	
		Western	Seattle Seahawks (9-7-0)	Tennessee* 33, Jacksonville 14	
	National	Eastern	Washington Redskins (10-6-0)	Tampa Bay 14, Washington 13	
		Central	Tampa Bay Buccaneers (11-5-0)	St. Louis 49, Minnesota* 37	
		Western	St. Louis Rams (13-3-0)	St. Louis 11, Tampa Bay 6	
2000	American	Eastern	Miami Dolphins (11-5-0)	Oakland 27, Miami 0	2000
		Central	Tennessee Titans (13-3-0)	Baltimore* 24, Tennessee 10	
		Western	Oakland Raiders (12-4-0)	Baltimore* 16, Oakland 3	
	National	Eastern	N.Y. Giants (12-4-0)	Minnesota 34, New Orleans 16	
		Central	Minnesota Vikings (11-5-0)	N.Y. Giants 20, Philadelphia* 10	
		Western	New Orleans Saints (10-6-0)	N.Y. Giants 41, Minnesota 0	
2001	American	Eastern	New England Patriots (11-5-0)	New England 16, Oakland 13	2001
		Central	Pittsburgh Steelers (13-3-0)	Pittsburgh 27, Baltimore* 10	
		Western	Oakland Raiders (10-6-0)	New England 24, Pittsburgh 17	
	National	Eastern	Philadelphia Eagles (11-5-0)	Philadelphia 33, Chicago 19	
		Central	Chicago Bears (13-3-0)	St. Louis 45, Green Bay* 17	
		Western	St. Louis Rams (14-2-0)	St. Louis 29, Philadelphia 24	
2002	American	East	N.Y. Jets (9-7-0)	Oakland 30, N.Y. Jets 10	2002
		North	Pittsburgh Steelers (10-5-1)	Tennessee 34, Pittsburgh 31	
		South	Tennessee Titans (11-5-0)	Oakland 41, Tennessee 24	
		West	Oakland Raiders (11-5-0)		
	National	East	Philadelphia Eagles (12-4-0)	Philadelphia 20, Atlanta* 6	
		North	Green Bay Packers (12-4-0)	Tampa Bay 31, San Francisco 6	
		South	Tampa Bay Buccaneers (12-4-0)	Tampa Bay 27, Philadelphia 10	
		West	San Francisco 49ers (10-6-0)		
2003	American	East	New England Patriots (14-2-0)	Indianapolis 38, Kansas City 31	2003
		North	Baltimore Ravens (10-6-0)	New England 17, Tennessee* 14	
		South	Indianapolis Colts (12-4-0)	New England 24, Indianapolis 14	
		West	Kansas City Chiefs (13-3-0)		
	National	East	Philadelphia Eagles (12-4-0)	Carolina 29, St. Louis 23	
		North	Green Bay Packers (10-6-0)	Philadelphia 20, Green Bay 17	
		South	Carolina Panthers (11-5-0)	Carolina 14, Philadelphia 3	
		West	St. Louis Rams (12-4-0)		

*Wild card team. (c) From 1978 on, only the final 2 conference playoff rounds are shown. (d) A strike shortened the 1982 season from 16 to 9 games. The top 8 teams in each conference played in a tournament to determine the conference champion. See below. **AFC playoffs**—Miami 28, New England 13; L.A. Raiders 27, Cleveland 10; N.Y. Jets 44, Cincinnati 17; San Diego 31, Pittsburgh 28; N.Y. Jets 17, L.A. Raiders 14; Miami 34, San Diego 13; Miami 14, N.Y. Jets 0. **NFC playoffs**—Washington 31, Detroit 7; Green Bay 41, St. Louis 16; Dallas 30, Tampa Bay 17; Minnesota 30, Atlanta 24; Washington 21, Minnesota 7; Dallas 37, Green Bay 26; Washington 31, Dallas 17. **AFC Champion**—Miami Dolphins. **NFC Champion**—Washington Redskins.

Super Bowl XXXVIII: New England 32, Carolina 29

On Feb. 1, 2004, the favored New England Patriots edged out the Carolina Panthers, 32-29, in Super Bowl XXXVIII in Houston, TX. In what was described as one of the most dramatic Super Bowls ever, the two defense-oriented teams stood at a 0-0 stalemate until late in the 2nd quarter, before scoring 24 total points in 3 minutes. After a scoreless 3rd quarter, the two teams combined for 37 points and 3 lead changes in the 4th quarter, with both defenses uncharacteristically giving up long plays. Carolina tied the score at 29 with just over 1 minute left in the game, after an 80-yard drive. Patriots quarterback Tom Brady, the game's MVP, then drove the Patriots to within field-goal range, and Adam Vinatieri kicked the decisive 3-pointer with just seconds remaining. During a controversial halftime show by pop stars Janet Jackson and Justin Timberlake, Jackson's breast was exposed to a live TV audience, in what Timberlake later called a "wardrobe malfunction."

Score by Quarters

Carolina	0	10	0	19	29
N. England	0	14	0	18	32

Scoring

New England—Branch 5 yd. pass from Brady (Vinatieri kick)
Carolina—S. Smith 39 yd. pass from Delhomme (Kasay kick)
New England—Givens 5 yd. pass from Brady (Vinatieri kick)
Carolina—Kasay 50 yd. field goal
New England—A. Smith 2 yd. run (Vinatieri kick)
Carolina—Foster 33 yd. run (pass failed)
Carolina—Muhammad 85 yd. pass from Delhomme (pass failed)
New England—Vrabel 1 yd. pass from Brady (Faulk run for 2-pt. conversion)
Carolina—Proehl 12 yd. pass from Delhomme (Kasay kick)
New England—Vinatieri 41 yd. field goal

Individual Statistics

Rushing–Carolina: Davis 13-49, Foster 3-43. New England: A. Smith 26-83, Faulk 6-42, Brady 2-12, Brown 1-(–10).
Passing–Carolina: Delhomme 16-33, 323 yds, 3 TD, 0 Int. New England: Brady 32-48, 354 yds, 3 TD, 1 Int.

Receiving–Carolina: Muhammad 4-140, S. Smith 4-80, Proehl 4-71, Wiggins 2-21, Foster 1-9, Mangum 1-2. New England: Branch 10-143, Brown 8-76, Givens 5-69, Graham 4-46, Faulk 4-19, Vrabel 1-1.

Team Statistics	Car	NE
First downs	17	29
Total net yards	387	481
Rushes-yards	16-92	35-127
Passing yards, net	295	354
Punt returns-yards	1-2	5-42
Kickoff returns-yards	6-116	4-78
Interception returns-yards	1-12	0-0
Att.-comp.-int.	33-16-0	48-32-1
Field goals made-attempts	1-1	1-3
Sacked-yards lost	4-28	0-0
Punts-average	7-44.3	5-34.6
Fumbles-lost	1-1	1-0
Penalties-yards	12-73	8-60
Time of possession	21:02	38:58

Attendance—71,525. **Time**—4:05.

Super Bowl Results

	Year	Winner	Loser	Winning coach	Site
I	1967	Green Bay Packers, 35	Kansas City Chiefs, 10	Vince Lombardi	Los Angeles Coliseum, CA
II	1968	Green Bay Packers, 33	Oakland Raiders, 14	Vince Lombardi	Orange Bowl, Miami, FL
III	1969	New York Jets, 16	Baltimore Colts, 7	Weeb Ewbank	Orange Bowl, Miami, FL
IV	1970	Kansas City Chiefs, 23	Minnesota Vikings, 7	Hank Stram	Tulane Stadium, New Orleans, LA
V	1971	Baltimore Colts, 16	Dallas Cowboys, 13	Don McCafferty	Orange Bowl, Miami, FL
VI	1972	Dallas Cowboys, 24	Miami Dolphins, 3	Tom Landry	Tulane Stadium, New Orleans, LA
VII	1973	Miami Dolphins, 14	Washington Redskins, 7	Don Shula	Los Angeles Coliseum, CA
VIII	1974	Miami Dolphins, 24	Minnesota Vikings, 7	Don Shula	Rice Stadium, Houston, TX
IX	1975	Pittsburgh Steelers, 16	Minnesota Vikings, 6	Chuck Noll	Tulane Stadium, New Orleans, LA
X	1976	Pittsburgh Steelers, 21	Dallas Cowboys, 17	Chuck Noll	Orange Bowl, Miami, FL
XI	1977	Oakland Raiders, 32	Minnesota Vikings, 14	John Madden	Rose Bowl, Pasadena, CA
XII	1978	Dallas Cowboys, 27	Denver Broncos, 10	Tom Landry	Superdome, New Orleans, LA
XIII	1979	Pittsburgh Steelers, 35	Dallas Cowboys, 31	Chuck Noll	Orange Bowl, Miami, FL

	Year	Winner	Loser	Winning coach	Site
XIV	1980	Pittsburgh Steelers, 31	Los Angeles Rams, 19	Chuck Noll	Rose Bowl, Pasadena, CA
XV	1981	Oakland Raiders, 27	Philadelphia Eagles, 10	Tom Flores	Superdome, New Orleans, LA
XVI	1982	San Francisco 49ers, 26	Cincinnati Bengals, 21	Bill Walsh	Silverdome, Pontiac, MI
XVII	1983	Washington Redskins, 27	Miami Dolphins, 17	Joe Gibbs	Rose Bowl, Pasadena, CA
XVIII	1984	Los Angeles Raiders, 38	Washington Redskins, 9	Tom Flores	Tampa Stadium, FL
XIX	1985	San Francisco 49ers, 38	Miami Dolphins, 16	Bill Walsh	Stanford Stadium, Palo Alto, CA
XX	1986	Chicago Bears, 46	New England Patriots, 10	Mike Ditka	Superdome, New Orleans, LA
XXI	1987	New York Giants, 39	Denver Broncos, 20	Bill Parcells	Rose Bowl, Pasadena, CA
XXII	1988	Washington Redskins, 42	Denver Broncos, 10	Joe Gibbs	San Diego Stadium, CA
XXIII	1989	San Francisco 49ers, 20	Cincinnati Bengals, 16	Bill Walsh	Joe Robbie Stadium, Miami, FL
XXIV	1990	San Francisco 49ers, 55	Denver Broncos, 10	George Seifert	Superdome, New Orleans, LA
XXV	1991	New York Giants, 20	Buffalo Bills, 19	Bill Parcells	Tampa Stadium, FL
XXVI	1992	Washington Redskins, 37	Buffalo Bills, 24	Joe Gibbs	Metrodome, Minneapolis, MN
XXVII	1993	Dallas Cowboys, 52	Buffalo Bills, 17	Jimmy Johnson	Rose Bowl, Pasadena, CA
XXVIII	1994	Dallas Cowboys, 30	Buffalo Bills, 13	Jimmy Johnson	Georgia Dome, Atlanta, GA
XXIX	1995	San Francisco 49ers, 49	San Diego Chargers, 26	George Seifert	Joe Robbie Stadium, Miami, FL
XXX	1996	Dallas Cowboys, 27	Pittsburgh Steelers, 17	Barry Switzer	Sun Devil Stadium, Tempe, AZ
XXXI	1997	Green Bay Packers, 35	New England Patriots, 21	Mike Holmgren	Superdome, New Orleans, LA
XXXII	1998	Denver Broncos, 31	Green Bay Packers, 24	Mike Shanahan	Qualcomm Stadium, San Diego, CA
XXXIII	1999	Denver Broncos, 34	Atlanta Falcons, 19	Mike Shanahan	Pro Player Stadium, Miami, FL
XXXIV	2000	St. Louis Rams, 23	Tennessee Titans, 16	Dick Vermeil	Georgia Dome, Atlanta, GA
XXXV	2001	Baltimore Ravens, 34	New York Giants, 7	Brian Billick	Raymond James Stad., Tampa, FL
XXXVI	2002	New England Patriots, 20	St. Louis Rams, 17	Bill Belichick	Superdome, New Orleans, LA
XXXVII	2003	Tampa Bay Buccaneers, 48	Oakland Raiders, 21	Jon Gruden	Qualcomm Stadium, San Diego, CA
XXXVIII	2004	New England Patriots, 32	Carolina Panthers, 29	Bill Belichick	Reliant Stadium, Houston, TX

Super Bowl Single-Game Statistical Leaders

Passing Yards

	Year	Att/Comp	Yds	TDs
Kurt Warner, Rams	2000	45/24	414	2
Kurt Warner, Rams	2002	44/28	365	1
Joe Montana, 49ers	1989	36/23	357	2

Receiving Yards

	Year	Recept.	Yds	TDs
Jerry Rice, 49ers	1989	11	215	1
Ricky Sanders, Redskins ..	1988	9	193	2
Isaac Bruce, Rams.......	2000	6	162	1

Rushing Yards

	Year	Attempts	Yds	TDs
Timmy Smith, Redskins ...	1988	22	204	2
Marcus Allen, Raiders	1984	20	191	2
John Riggins, Redskins ...	1983	38	166	1

Passing Touchdowns

	Year	Att/Comp	Yds	TDs
Steve Young, 49ers......	1995	36/24	325	6
Joe Montana, 49ers......	1990	29/22	297	5
Troy Aikman, Cowboys ...	1993	30/22	273	4
Doug Williams, Redskins..	1988	29/18	340	4
Terry Bradshaw, Steelers .	1979	30/17	318	4

Scoring

	Year	Points	
Terrell Davis, Broncos........	1998	18	3 TDs
Jerry Rice, 49ers............	1995	18	3 TDs
Ricky Watters, 49ers.........	1995	18	3 TDs
Jerry Rice, 49ers............	1990	18	3 TDs
Roger Craig, 49ers	1985	18	3 TDs
Don Chandler, Packers	1968	15	4 FG, 3PATs

Super Bowl MVPs

1967	Bart Starr, Green Bay	1980	Terry Bradshaw, Pittsburgh	1993	Troy Aikman, Dallas
1968	Bart Starr, Green Bay	1981	Jim Plunkett, Oakland	1994	Emmitt Smith, Dallas
1969	Joe Namath, N.Y. Jets	1982	Joe Montana, San Francisco	1995	Steve Young, San Francisco
1970	Len Dawson, Kansas City	1983	John Riggins, Washington	1996	Larry Brown, Dallas
1971	Chuck Howley, Dallas	1984	Marcus Allen, L.A. Raiders	1997	Desmond Howard, Green Bay
1972	Roger Staubach, Dallas	1985	Joe Montana, San Francisco	1998	Terrell Davis, Denver
1973	Jake Scott, Miami	1986	Richard Dent, Chicago	1999	John Elway, Denver
1974	Larry Csonka, Miami	1987	Phil Simms, N.Y. Giants	2000	Kurt Warner, St. Louis
1975	Franco Harris, Pittsburgh	1988	Doug Williams, Washington	2001	Ray Lewis, Baltimore
1976	Lynn Swann, Pittsburgh	1989	Jerry Rice, San Francisco	2002	Tom Brady, New England
1977	Fred Biletnikoff, Oakland	1990	Joe Montana, San Francisco	2003	Dexter Jackson, Tampa Bay
1978	Randy White, Harvey Martin, Dallas	1991	Ottis Anderson, N.Y. Giants	2004	Tom Brady, New England
1979	Terry Bradshaw, Pittsburgh	1992	Mark Rypien, Washington		

American Football Conference Leaders

(American Football League, 1960-69)

Player, team	Passing[1] Att	Com	YG	TD	Year	Player, team	Receiving Rec.	YG	TD
Jack Kemp, L.A. Chargers	406	211	3,018	20	1960	Lionel Taylor, Denver	92	1,235	12
George Blanda, Houston	362	187	3,330	36	1961	Lionel Taylor, Denver	100	1,176	4
Len Dawson, Dallas Texans	310	189	2,759	29	1962	Lionel Taylor, Denver	77	908	4
Tobin Rote, San Diego	286	170	2,510	20	1963	Lionel Taylor, Denver	78	1,101	10
Len Dawson, Kansas City	354	199	2,879	30	1964	Charley Hennigan, Houston	101	1,546	8
John Hadl, San Diego	348	174	2,798	20	1965	Lionel Taylor, Denver	85	1,131	6
Len Dawson, Kansas City	284	159	2,527	26	1966	Lance Alworth, San Diego	73	1,383	13
Daryle Lamonica, Oakland	425	220	3,228	30	1967	George Sauer, N.Y. Jets	75	1,189	6
Len Dawson, Kansas City	224	131	2,109	17	1968	Lance Alworth, San Diego	68	1,312	10
Greg Cook, Cincinnati	197	106	1,854	15	1969	Lance Alworth, San Diego	64	1,003	4
Daryle Lamonica, Oakland	356	179	2,516	22	1970	Marlin Briscoe, Buffalo	57	1,036	8
Bob Griese, Miami	263	145	2,089	19	1971	Fred Biletnikoff, Oakland	61	929	9
Earl Morrall, Miami	150	83	1,360	11	1972	Fred Biletnikoff, Oakland	58	802	7
Ken Stabler, Oakland	260	163	1,997	14	1973	Fred Willis, Houston	57	371	1
Ken Anderson, Cincinnati	328	213	2,667	18	1974	Lydell Mitchell, Baltimore Colts	72	544	2
Ken Anderson, Cincinnati	377	228	3,169	21	1975	Reggie Rucker, Cleveland	60	770	3
						Lydell Mitchell, Baltimore Colts	60	554	4
Ken Stabler, Oakland	291	194	2,737	27	1976	MacArthur Lane, Kansas City	66	686	1
Bob Griese, Miami	307	180	2,252	22	1977	Lydell Mitchell, Baltimore Colts	71	620	4
Terry Bradshaw, Pittsburgh	368	207	2,915	28	1978	Steve Largent, Seattle	71	1,168	8
Dan Fouts, San Diego	530	332	4,082	24	1979	Joe Washington, Baltimore Colts	82	750	3
Brian Sipe, Cleveland	554	337	4,132	30	1980	Kellen Winslow, San Diego	89	1,290	9

Passing[1] / Receiving

Player, team	Att	Com	YG	TD	Year	Player, team	Rec.	YG	TD
Ken Anderson, Cincinnati	479	300	3,754	29	1981	Kellen Winslow, San Diego	88	1,075	10
Ken Anderson, Cincinnati	309	218	2,495	12	1982	Kellen Winslow, San Diego	54	721	6
Dan Marino, Miami	296	173	2,210	20	1983	Todd Christensen, L.A. Raiders	92	1,247	12
Dan Marino, Miami	564	362	5,084	48	1984	Ozzie Newsome, Cleveland	89	1,001	5
Ken O'Brien, N.Y. Jets	488	297	3,888	25	1985	Lionel James, San Diego	86	1,027	6
Dan Marino, Miami	623	378	4,746	44	1986	Todd Christensen, L.A. Raiders	95	1,153	8
Bernie Kosar, Cleveland	389	241	3,033	22	1987	Al Toon, N.Y. Jets	68	976	5
Boomer Esiason, Cincinnati	388	223	3,572	28	1988	Al Toon, N.Y. Jets	93	1,067	5
Boomer Esiason, Cincinnati	455	258	3,525	28	1989	Andre Reed, Buffalo	88	1,312	9
Jim Kelly, Buffalo	346	219	2,829	24	1990	Haywood Jeffires, Houston	74	1,048	8
						Drew Hill, Houston	74	1,019	5
Jim Kelly, Buffalo	474	304	3,844	33	1991	Haywood Jeffires, Houston	100	1,181	7
Warren Moon, Houston	346	224	2,521	18	1992	Haywood Jeffires, Houston	90	913	9
John Elway, Denver	551	348	4,030	25	1993	Reggie Langhorne, Indianapolis	85	1,038	3
Dan Marino, Miami	615	385	4,453	30	1994	Ben Coates, New England	96	1,174	7
Jim Harbaugh, Indianapolis	314	200	2,575	17	1995	Carl Pickens, Cincinnati	99	1,234	17
John Elway, Denver	466	287	3,328	26	1996	Carl Pickens, Cincinnati	100	1,180	12
Mark Brunell, Jacksonville	435	264	3,281	18	1997	Tim Brown, Oakland	104	1,408	5
Vinny Testaverde, N.Y. Jets	421	259	3,256	29	1998	O.J. McDuffie, Miami	90	1,050	7
Peyton Manning, Indianapolis	533	331	4,135	26	1999	Jimmy Smith, Jacksonville	116	1,636	6
Brian Griese, Denver	336	216	2,688	19	2000	Marvin Harrison, Indianapolis	102	1,413	14
Rich Gannon, Oakland	549	361	3,828	27	2001	Marvin Harrison, Indianapolis	109	1,524	15
Chad Pennington, N.Y. Jets	399	275	3,120	22	2002	Marvin Harrison, Indianapolis	143	1,722	11
Steve McNair, Tennessee	400	250	3,215	24	2003	Chad Johnson, Cincinnati	90	1,355	10

Scoring / Rushing

Player, team	TD	PAT	FG	Pts	Year	Player, team	Yds	Att	TD
Gene Mingo, Denver	6	33	18	123	1960	Abner Haynes, Dallas Texans	875	156	9
Gino Cappelletti, Boston	8	48	17	147	1961	Billy Cannon, Houston	948	200	6
Gene Mingo, Denver	4	32	27	137	1962	Cookie Gilchrist, Buffalo	1,096	214	13
Gino Cappelletti, Boston	2	35	22	113	1963	Clem Daniels, Oakland	1,099	215	3
Gino Cappelletti, Boston	7	36	25	155	1964	Cookie Gilchrist, Buffalo	981	230	6
Gino Cappelletti, Boston	9	27	17	132	1965	Paul Lowe, San Diego	1,121	222	7
Gino Cappelletti, Boston	6	35	16	119	1966	Jim Nance, Boston	1,458	299	11
George Blanda, Oakland	0	56	20	116	1967	Jim Nance, Boston	1,216	269	7
Jim Turner, N.Y. Jets	0	43	34	145	1968	Paul Robinson, Cincinnati	1,023	238	8
Jim Turner, N.Y. Jets	0	33	32	129	1969	Dick Post, San Diego	873	182	6
Jan Stenerud, Kansas City	0	26	30	116	1970	Floyd Little, Denver	901	209	3
Garo Yepremian, Miami	0	33	28	117	1971	Floyd Little, Denver	1,133	284	6
Bobby Howfield, N.Y. Jets	0	40	27	121	1972	O.J. Simpson, Buffalo	1,251	292	6
Roy Gerela, Pittsburgh	0	36	29	123	1973	O.J. Simpson, Buffalo	2,003	332	12
Roy Gerela, Pittsburgh	0	33	20	93	1974	Otis Armstrong, Denver	1,407	263	9
O.J. Simpson, Buffalo	23	0	0	138	1975	O.J. Simpson, Buffalo	1,817	329	16
Toni Linhart, Baltimore Colts	0	49	20	109	1976	O.J. Simpson, Buffalo	1,503	290	8
Errol Mann, Oakland	0	39	20	99	1977	Mark van Eeghen, Oakland	1,273	324	7
Pat Leahy, N.Y. Jets	0	41	22	107	1978	Earl Campbell, Houston	1,450	302	13
John Smith, New England	0	46	23	115	1979	Earl Campbell, Houston	1,697	368	19
John Smith, New England	0	51	26	129	1980	Earl Campbell, Houston	1,934	373	13
Jim Breech, Cincinnati	0	49	22	115	1981	Earl Campbell, Houston	1,376	361	10
Nick Lowery, Kansas City	0	37	26	115					
Marcus Allen, L.A. Raiders	14	0	0	84	1982	Freeman McNeil, N.Y. Jets	786	151	6
Gary Anderson, Pittsburgh	0	38	27	119	1983	Curt Warner, Seattle	1,446	335	13
Gary Anderson, Pittsburgh	0	45	24	117	1984	Earnest Jackson, San Diego	1,179	296	8
Gary Anderson, Pittsburgh	0	40	33	139	1985	Marcus Allen, L.A. Raiders	1,759	380	11
Tony Franklin, New England	0	44	32	140	1986	Curt Warner, Seattle	1,481	319	13
Jim Breech, Cincinnati	0	25	24	97	1987	Eric Dickerson, L.A. Rams-Ind.	1,288*	283	6
Scott Norwood, Buffalo	0	33	32	129	1988	Eric Dickerson, Indianapolis	1,659	388	14
David Treadwell, Denver	0	39	27	120	1989	Christian Okoye, Kansas City	1,480	370	12
Nick Lowery, Kansas City	0	37	34	139	1990	Thurman Thomas, Buffalo	1,297	271	11
Pete Stoyanovich, Miami	0	28	31	121	1991	Thurman Thomas, Buffalo	1,407	288	7
Pete Stoyanovich, Miami	0	34	30	124	1992	Barry Foster, Pittsburgh	1,690	390	11
Jeff Jaeger, L.A. Raiders	0	27	35	132	1993	Thurman Thomas, Buffalo	1,315	355	6
John Carney, San Diego	0	33	34	135	1994	Chris Warren, Seattle	1,545	333	9
Norm Johnson, Pittsburgh	0	39	34	141	1995	Curtis Martin, New England	1,487	368	14
Cary Blanchard, Indianapolis	0	27	36	135	1996	Terrell Davis, Denver	1,538	345	13
Mike Hollis, Jacksonville	0	41	31	134	1997	Terrell Davis, Denver	1,750	369	15
Steve Christie, Buffalo	0	41	33	140	1998	Terrell Davis, Denver	2,008	392	21
Mike Vanderjagt, Indianapolis	0	43	34	145	1999	Edgerrin James, Indianapolis	1,553	369	13
Matt Stover, Baltimore	0	30	35	135	2000	Edgerrin James, Indianapolis	1,709	387	13
Mike Vanderjagt, Indianapolis	0	41	28	125	2001	Priest Holmes, Kansas City	1,555	325	8
Priest Holmes, Kansas City	24	0	0	144	2002	Ricky Williams, Miami	1,853	383	16
Priest Holmes, Kansas City	27	0	0	162	2003	Jamal Lewis, Baltimore	2,066	387	14

*Includes 277 yards after being traded to NFC; 1,011 yards led AFC. (1) Based on quarterback rating points.

National Football Conference Leaders

(National Football League, 1960-69)

Passing[1] / Receiving

Player, team	Att	Com	YG	TD	Year	Player, team	Rec.	YG	TD
Milt Plum, Cleveland	250	151	2,297	21	1960	Raymond Berry, Baltimore Colts	74	1,298	10
Milt Plum, Cleveland	302	177	2,416	18	1961	Jim Phillips, L.A. Rams	78	1,092	5
Bart Starr, Green Bay	285	178	2,438	12	1962	Bobby Mitchell, Washington	72	1,384	11
Y.A. Tittle, N.Y. Giants	367	221	3,145	36	1963	Bobby Joe Conrad, St. Louis Cardinals	73	967	10
Bart Starr, Green Bay	272	163	2,144	15	1964	Johnny Morris, Chicago	93	1,200	10
Rudy Bukich, Chicago	312	176	2,641	20	1965	Dave Parks, San Francisco	80	1,344	12
Bart Starr, Green Bay	251	156	2,257	14	1966	Charley Taylor, Washington	72	1,119	12
Sonny Jurgensen, Washington	508	288	3,747	31	1967	Charley Taylor, Washington	70	990	9
Earl Morrall, Baltimore Colts	317	182	2,909	26	1968	Clifton McNeil, San Francisco	71	994	7
Sonny Jurgensen, Washington	442	274	3,102	22	1969	Dan Abramowicz, New Orleans	73	1,015	7

Passing[1]

Player, team	Att	Com	YG	TD	Year
John Brodie, San Francisco	378	223	2,941	24	1970
Roger Staubach, Dallas	211	126	1,882	15	1971
Norm Snead, N.Y. Giants	325	196	2,307	17	1972
Roger Staubach, Dallas	286	179	2,428	23	1973
Sonny Jurgensen, Washington	167	107	1,185	11	1974
Fran Tarkenton, Minnesota	425	273	2,994	25	1975
James Harris, L.A. Rams	158	91	1,460	8	1976
Roger Staubach, Dallas	361	210	2,620	18	1977
Roger Staubach, Dallas	413	231	3,190	25	1978
Roger Staubach, Dallas	461	267	3,586	27	1979
Ron Jaworski, Philadelphia	451	257	3,529	27	1980
Joe Montana, San Francisco	488	311	3,565	19	1981
Joe Thiesmann, Washington	252	161	2,033	13	1982
Steve Bartkowski, Atlanta	432	274	3,167	22	1983
Joe Montana, San Francisco	432	279	3,630	28	1984
Joe Montana, San Francisco	494	303	3,653	27	1985
Tommy Kramer, Minnesota	372	208	3,000	24	1986
Joe Montana, San Francisco	398	266	3,054	31	1987
Wade Wilson, Minnesota	332	204	2,746	15	1988
Joe Montana, San Francisco	386	271	3,521	26	1989
Phil Simms, N.Y. Giants	311	184	2,284	15	1990
Steve Young, San Francisco	279	180	2,517	17	1991
Steve Young, San Francisco	402	268	3,465	25	1992
Steve Young, San Francisco	462	314	4,023	29	1993
Steve Young, San Francisco	461	324	3,969	35	1994
Brett Favre, Green Bay	570	359	4,413	38	1995
Steve Young, San Francisco	316	214	2,410	14	1996
Steve Young, San Francisco	356	241	3,029	19	1997
Randall Cunningham, Minnesota	425	259	3,704	34	1998
Kurt Warner, St. Louis	499	325	4,353	41	1999
Trent Green, St. Louis	240	145	2,063	16	2000
Kurt Warner, St. Louis	546	375	4,830	36	2001
Brad Johnson, Tampa Bay	451	281	3,049	22	2002
Daunte Culpepper, Minnesota	454	295	3,479	25	2003

Receiving

Year	Player, team	Rec.	YG	TD
1970	Dick Gordon, Chicago	71	1,026	13
1971	Bob Tucker, N.Y. Giants	59	791	4
1972	Harold Jackson, Philadelphia	62	1,048	4
1973	Harold Carmichael, Philadelphia	67	1,116	9
1974	Charles Young, Philadelphia	63	696	3
1975	Chuck Foreman, Minnesota	73	691	9
1976	Drew Pearson, Dallas	58	806	6
1977	Ahmad Rashad, Minnesota	51	681	2
1978	Rickey Young, Minnesota	88	704	5
1979	Ahmad Rashad, Minnesota	80	1,156	9
1980	Earl Cooper, San Francisco	83	567	4
1981	Dwight Clark, San Francisco	85	1,105	4
1982	Dwight Clark, San Francisco	60	913	5
1983	Roy Green, St. Louis Cardinals	78	1,227	14
	Charlie Brown, Washington	78	1,225	8
	Earnest Gray, N.Y. Giants	78	1,139	5
1984	Art Monk, Washington	106	1,372	7
1985	Roger Craig, San Francisco	92	1,016	6
1986	Jerry Rice, San Francisco	86	1,570	15
1987	J.T. Smith, St. Louis Cardinals	91	1,117	8
1988	Henry Ellard, L.A. Rams	86	1,414	10
1989	Sterling Sharpe, Green Bay	90	1,423	12
1990	Jerry Rice, San Francisco	100	1,502	13
1991	Michael Irvin, Dallas	93	1,523	8
1992	Sterling Sharpe, Green Bay	108	1,461	13
1993	Sterling Sharpe, Green Bay	112	1,274	11
1994	Cris Carter, Minnesota	122	1,256	7
1995	Herman Moore, Detroit	123	1,686	14
1996	Jerry Rice, San Francisco	108	1,254	8
1997	Herman Moore, Detroit	104	1,293	8
1998	Frank Sanders, Arizona	89	1,145	3
1999	Muhsin Muhammad, Carolina	96	1,253	8
2000	Muhsin Muhammad, Carolina	102	1,183	6
2001	David Boston, Arizona	98	1,598	8
2002	Randy Moss, Minnesota	106	1,347	7
2003	Torry Holt, St. Louis	117	1,696	12

Scoring

Player, team	TD	PAT	FG	Pts	Year
Paul Hornung, Green Bay	15	41	15	176	1960
Paul Hornung, Green Bay	10	41	15	146	1961
Jim Taylor, Green Bay	19	0	0	114	1962
Don Chandler, N.Y. Giants	0	52	18	106	1963
Lenny Moore, Baltimore Colts	20	0	0	120	1964
Gale Sayers, Chicago	22	0	0	132	1965
Bruce Gossett, L.A. Rams	0	29	28	113	1966
Jim Bakken, St. Louis Cardinals	0	36	27	117	1967
Leroy Kelly, Cleveland	20	0	0	120	1968
Fred Cox, Minnesota	0	43	26	121	1969
Fred Cox, Minnesota	0	35	30	125	1970
Curt Knight, Washington	0	27	29	114	1971
Chester Marcol, Green Bay	0	29	33	128	1972
David Ray, L.A. Rams	0	40	30	130	1973
Chester Marcol, Green Bay	0	19	25	94	1974
Chuck Foreman, Minnesota	22	0	0	132	1975
Mark Moseley, Washington	0	31	22	97	1976
Walter Payton, Chicago	16	0	0	96	1977
Frank Corral, L.A. Rams	0	31	29	118	1978
Mark Moseley, Washington	0	39	25	114	1979
Ed Murray, Detroit	0	35	27	116	1980
Ed Murray, Detroit	0	46	25	121	1981
Rafael Septien, Dallas	0	40	27	121	
Wendell Tyler, L.A. Rams	13	0	0	78	1982
Mark Moseley, Washington	0	62	33	161	1983
Ray Wersching, San Francisco	0	56	25	131	1984
Kevin Butler, Chicago	0	51	31	144	1985
Kevin Butler, Chicago	0	36	28	120	1986
Jerry Rice, San Francisco	23	0	0	138	1987
Mike Cofer, San Francisco	0	40	27	121	1988
Mike Cofer, San Francisco	0	49	29	136	1989
Chip Lohmiller, Washington	0	41	30	131	1990
Chip Lohmiller, Washington	0	56	31	149	1991
Morten Andersen, New Orleans	0	33	29	120	1992
Chip Lohmiller, Washington	0	30	30	120	
Jason Hanson, Detroit	0	28	34	130	1993
Fuad Reveiz, Minnesota	0	30	34	132	1994
Emmitt Smith, Dallas	22	0	0	132	
Emmitt Smith, Dallas	25	0	0	150	1995
John Kasay, Carolina	0	34	37	145	1996
Richie Cunningham, Dallas	0	24	34	126	1997
Gary Anderson, Minnesota	0	59	35	164	1998
Jeff Wilkins, St. Louis	0	64	20	124	1999
Marshall Faulk, St. Louis	26	0	0	156	2000
Marshall Faulk, St. Louis	21	0	0	128	2001
Jay Feely, Atlanta	0	42	32	138	2002
Jeff Wilkins, St. Louis	0	46	39	163	2003

Rushing

Year	Player, team	Yds	Att	TD
1960	Jim Brown, Cleveland	1,257	215	9
1961	Jim Brown, Cleveland	1,408	305	8
1962	Jim Taylor, Green Bay	1,474	272	19
1963	Jim Brown, Cleveland	1,863	291	12
1964	Jim Brown, Cleveland	1,446	280	7
1965	Jim Brown, Cleveland	1,544	289	17
1966	Gale Sayers, Chicago	1,231	229	8
1967	Leroy Kelly, Cleveland	1,205	235	11
1968	Leroy Kelly, Cleveland	1,239	248	16
1969	Gale Sayers, Chicago	1,032	236	8
1970	Larry Brown, Washington	1,125	237	5
1971	John Brockington, Green Bay	1,105	216	4
1972	Larry Brown, Washington	1,216	285	8
1973	John Brockington, Green Bay	1,144	265	3
1974	Lawrence McCutcheon, L.A. Rams	1,109	236	3
1975	Jim Otis, St. Louis Cardinals	1,076	269	5
1976	Walter Payton, Chicago	1,390	311	13
1977	Walter Payton, Chicago	1,852	339	14
1978	Walter Payton, Chicago	1,395	333	11
1979	Walter Payton, Chicago	1,610	369	14
1980	Walter Payton, Chicago	1,460	317	6
1981	George Rogers, New Orleans	1,674	378	13
1982	Tony Dorsett, Dallas	745	177	5
1983	Eric Dickerson, L.A. Rams	1,808	390	18
1984	Eric Dickerson, L.A. Rams	2,105	379	14
1985	Gerald Riggs, Atlanta	1,719	397	10
1986	Eric Dickerson, L.A. Rams	1,821	404	11
1987	Charles White, L.A. Rams	1,374	324	11
1988	Herschel Walker, Dallas	1,514	361	5
1989	Barry Sanders, Detroit	1,470	280	14
1990	Barry Sanders, Detroit	1,304	255	13
1991	Emmitt Smith, Dallas	1,563	365	12
1992	Emmitt Smith, Dallas	1,713	373	18
1993	Emmitt Smith, Dallas	1,486	283	9
1994	Barry Sanders, Detroit	1,883	331	7
1995	Emmitt Smith, Dallas	1,773	377	25
1996	Barry Sanders, Detroit	1,553	307	11
1997	Barry Sanders, Detroit	2,053	335	11
1998	Jamal Anderson, Atlanta	1,846	410	14
1999	Stephen Davis, Washington	1,405	290	17
2000	Robert Smith, Minnesota	1,521	295	7
2001	Stephen Davis, Washington	1,432	356	5
2002	Deuce McAllister, New Orleans	1,388	325	13
2003	Ahman Green, Green Bay	1,883	355	15

(1) Based on quarterback rating points.

2003 NFL Individual Leaders

American Football Conference

PASSING	Att	Comp	Pct Comp	Yds	Yds/Att.	Long	TD	Pct TD	Int	Rating Points
Steve McNair, Tennessee	400	250	62.5	3,215	8.04	73	24	6.0	7	100.4
Peyton Manning, Indianapolis	566	379	67.0	4,267	7.54	79	29	5.1	10	99.0
Trent Green, Kansas City	523	330	63.1	4,039	7.72	67	24	4.6	12	92.6
Jake Plummer, Denver	302	189	62.6	2,182	7.23	60	15	5.0	7	91.2
Jon Kitna, Cincinnati	520	324	62.3	3,591	6.91	82	26	5.0	15	87.4
Tom Brady, New England	527	317	60.2	3,620	6.87	82	23	4.4	12	85.9
Chad Pennington, N.Y. Jets	297	189	63.6	2,139	7.20	65	13	4.4	12	82.9
Tommy Maddox, Pittsburgh	519	298	57.4	3,414	6.58	53	18	3.5	17	75.3

RUSHING	Att	Yds	Avg	Long	TD
Jamal Lewis, Baltimore	387	2,066	5.3	82	14
LaDainian Tomlinson, San Diego	313	1,645	5.3	73	13
Clinton Portis, Denver	290	1,591	5.5	65	14
Fred Taylor, Jacksonville	345	1,572	4.6	62	6
Priest Holmes, Kansas City	320	1,420	4.4	31	27*
Ricky Williams, Miami	392	1,372	3.5	45	9
Travis Henry, Buffalo	331	1,356	4.1	64	10
Curtis Martin, N.Y. Jets	323	1,308	4.0	56	2
Edgerrin James, Indianapolis	310	1,259	4.1	43	11
Eddie George, Tennessee	312	1,031	3.3	27	5
Domanick Davis, Houston	238	1,031	4.3	51	8

RECEIVING	Catches	Yds	Avg	Long	TD
LaDainian Tomlinson, San Diego	100	725	7.3	73	4
Derrick Mason, Tennessee	95	1,303	13.7	50	8
Hines Ward, Pittsburgh	95	1,163	12.2	50	10
Marvin Harrison, Indiana	94	1,272	13.5	79	10
Chad Johnson, Cincinnati	90	1,355	15.1	82	10
Peter Warrick, Cincinnati	79	819	10.4	77	7
Santana Moss, N.Y. Jets	74	1,105	14.9	65	10
Rod Smith, Denver	74	845	11.4	38	3
Priest Holmes, Kansas City	74	690	9.3	36	0

SCORING—KICKERS	PAT	FG	Long	Pts
Mike Vanderjagt, Indianapolis	46/46	37/37	50	157
Matt Stover, Baltimore	35/35	33/38	49	134
Gary Anderson, Tennessee	42/42	27/31	43	123
Jason Elam, Denver	39/39	27/31	51	120
Adam Vinatieri, New England	37/38	25/34	48	112

*NFL Record

SCORING—NON-KICKERS	TD	Rush	Rec.	2 Pt	Pts
Priest Holmes, Kansas City	27*	27*	0	0	162
LaDainian Tomlinson, S. Diego	17	13	4	0	102
Clinton Portis, Denver	14	14	0	1	86
Jamal Lewis, Baltimore	14	14	0	0	84

INTERCEPTIONS	No.	Yds	Avg	Long	TD
Ed Reed, Baltimore	7	132	18.9	54	1
Marcus Coleman, Houston	7	95	13.6	41	0
Patrick Surtain, Miami	7	59	8.4	32	0

KICKOFF RETURNS	No.	Yds	Avg	Long	TD
Bethel Johnson, New England	30	847	28.2	92	1
Michael Bates, N.Y. Jets	22	596	27.1	48	0
Dante Hall, Kansas City	57	1,478	25.9	100	2

PUNT RETURNS	No.	Yds	Avg	Long	TD
Dante Hall, Kansas City	29	427	16.3	93	2
Phillip Buchanon, Oakland	36	491	13.6	80	2
Antwaan Randle El, Pittsburgh	45	542	12.0	84	2
David Allen, Jacksonville	27	324	12.0	52	0

PUNTING	No.	Yds	Long	Avg
Shane Lechler, Oakland	96	4,503	73	46.9
Brian Moorman, Buffalo	85	3,788	71	44.6
Craig Hentrich, Tennessee	71	3,117	58	43.9
Micah Knorr, Denver	68	2,937	62	43.2
Hunter Smith, Indianapolis	62	2,617	55	42.2

SACKS: Adewale Ogunleye, Miami, 15.0; Jason Taylor, Miami, 13.0; Shaun Ellis, N.Y. Jets, 12.5; Terrell Suggs, Baltimore, 12.0; Aaron Schobel, Buffalo, 11.5; Bertrand Berry, Denver, 11.5

National Football Conference

PASSING	Att	Comp	Pct Comp	Yds	Yds/Att.	Long	TD	Pct TD	Int	Rating points
Daunte Culpepper, Minnesota	454	295	65.0	3,479	7.66	59	25	5.5	11	96.4
Brett Favre, Green Bay	471	308	65.4	3,361	7.14	66	32	6.8	21	90.4
Aaron Brooks, New Orleans	518	306	59.1	3,546	6.85	76	24	4.6	8	88.8
Matt Hasselbeck, Seattle	513	313	61.0	3,841	7.49	80	26	5.1	15	88.8
Brad Johnson, Tampa Bay	570	354	62.1	3,811	6.69	76	26	4.6	21	81.5
Marc Bulger, St. Louis	532	336	63.2	3,845	7.23	48	22	4.1	22	81.4
Jake Delhomme, Carolina	449	266	59.2	3,219	7.17	67	19	4.2	16	80.6
Jeff Garcia, San Francisco	392	225	57.4	2,704	6.90	75	18	4.6	13	80.1

RUSHING	Att	Yds	Avg	Long	TD
Ahman Green, Green Bay	355	1,883	5.3	98	15
Deuce McAllister, New Orleans	351	1,641	4.7	76	8
Stephen Davis, Carolina	318	1,444	4.5	40	8
Shaun Alexander, Seattle	326	1,435	4.4	55	14
Tiki Barber, N.Y. Giants	278	1,216	4.4	27	2
Anthony Thomas, Chicago	244	1,024	4.2	67	6
Kevan Barlow, San Francisco	201	1,024	5.1	78	6
Troy Hambrick, Dallas	275	972	3.5	42	5
Marcel Shipp, Arizona	228	830	3.6	36	0
Marshall Faulk, St. Louis	209	818	3.9	52	10

RECEIVING	Catches	Yds	Avg	Long	TD
Torry Holt, St. Louis	117	1,696	14.5	48	12
Randy Moss, Minnesota	111	1,632	14.7	72	17
Anquan Boldin, Arizona	101	1,377	13.6	71	8
Steve Smith, Carolina	88	1,110	12.6	67	7
Keenan McCardell, Tampa Bay	84	1,174	14.0	76	8
Laveranues Coles, Washington	82	1,204	14.7	64	6
Terrell Owens, San Francisco	80	1,102	13.8	75	9
Joe Horn, New Orleans	78	973	12.5	50	10
Michael Pittman, Tampa Bay	75	597	8.0	68	2

SCORING—KICKERS	PAT	FG	Long	Pts
Jeff Wilkins, St. Louis	46/46	39/42	53	163
John Kasay, Carolina	29/30	32/38	53	125
Ryan Longwell, Green Bay	51/51	23/26	50	120
David Akers, Philadelphia	42/42	24/29	57	114
Josh Brown, Seattle	48/48	22/30	58	114

SCORING—NON-KICKERS	TD	Rush	Rec.	Ret.	Pts.
Ahman Green, Green Bay	20	15	5	0	120
Randy Moss, Minnesota	17	0	17	0	102
Shaun Alexander, Seattle	16	14	2	0	96
Brian Westbrook, Philadelphia	13	7	4	2	78

INTERCEPTIONS	No.	Yds	Avg	Long	TD
Tony Parrish, San Francisco	9	202	49	49	0
Brian Russell, Minnesota	9	185	50	50	0
Corey Chavous, Minnesota	8	143	39	39	1

KICKOFF RETURNS	No.	Yds	Avg	Long	TD
Jerry Azumah, Chicago	41	1,191	29.0	89	2
James Thrash, Philadelphia	34	815	24.0	54	0
Reggie Swinton, Dallas/Detroit	43	1,029	23.9	96	1

PUNT RETURNS	No.	Yds	Avg	Long	TD
Brian Westbrook, Philadelphia	20	306	15.3	84	2
Allen Rossum, Atlanta	39	545	14.0	72	1
Reggie Swinton, Dallas/Detroit	24	318	13.3	89	1
R.W. McQuarters, Chicago	37	452	12.2	60	1

PUNTING	No.	Yds	Long	Avg
Todd Sauerbrun, Carolina	77	3,433	64	44.6
Mitch Berger, New Orleans	71	3,144	59	44.3
Tom Tupa, Tampa Bay	83	3,590	60	43.3
Scott Player, Arizona	82	3,511	64	42.8
Sean Landeta, St. Louis	59	2,525	57	42.8

SACKS: Michael Strahan, N.Y. Giants, 18; Simeon Rice, Tampa Bay, 15.0; Leonard Little, St. Louis, 12.5; Mike Rucker, Carolina, 12.0; Kevin Williams, Minnnesota, 10.5

First-Round Selections in the 2004 NFL Draft

Team	Player	Pos	College	Team	Player	Pos	College
1. San Diego[1]	Eli Manning	QB	Mississippi	17. Denver[6]	D.J. Williams	OLB	Miami (FL)
2. Oakland	Robert Gallery	OT	Iowa	18. New Orleans	Will Smith	DE	Ohio St.
3. Arizona	Larry Fitzgerald	WR	Pittsburgh	19. Miami[7]	Vernon Carey	G	Miami (FL)
4. N.Y. Giants[2]	Philip Rivers	QB	North Carolina St.	20. Minnesota[8]	Kenechi Udeze	DE	USC
5. Washington	Sean Taylor	FS	Miami (FL)	21. New England[9]	Vince Wilfork	DT	Miami (FL)
6. Cleveland[3]	Kellen Winslow	TE	Miami (FL)	22. Buffalo[10]	J.P. Losman	QB	Tulane
7. Detroit[4]	Roy Williams	WR	Texas	23. Seattle	Marcus Tubbs	DT	Texas
8. Atlanta	DeAngelo Hall	CB	Virginia Tech	24. St. Louis[11]	Steven Jackson	RB	Oregon St.
9. Jacksonville	Reggie Williams	WR	Washington	25. Green Bay	Ahmad Carroll	CB	Arkansas
10. Houston	Dunta Robinson	CB	South Carolina	26. Cincinnati[12]	Chris Perry	RB	Michigan
11. Pittsburgh	Ben Roethlisberger	QB	Miami (OH)	27. Houston[13]	Jason Babin	DE	Western Michigan
12. N.Y. Jets	Jonathan Vilma	ILB	Miami (FL)	28. Carolina[14]	Chris Gamble	CB	Ohio St.
13. Buffalo	Lee Evans	WR	Wisconsin	29. Atlanta[15]	Michael Jenkins	WR	Ohio St.
14. Chicago	Tommie Harris	DT	Oklahoma	30. Detroit[16]	Kevin Jones	RB	Virginia Tech
15. Tampa Bay	Michael Clayton	WR	Louisiana St.	31. San Francisco[17]	Rashaun Woods	WR	Oklahoma St.
16. Philadelphia[5]	Shawn Andrews	OT	Arkansas	32. New England	Ben Watson	TE	Georgia

(1) Rights traded to N.Y. Giants. (2) Rights traded to San Diego. (3) From Detroit. (4) From Cleveland. (5) From San Francisco. (6) From Cincinnati. (7) From Minnesota. (8) From Miami. (9) From Baltimore. (10) From Dallas. (11) From Denver through Cincinnati. (12) From St. Louis. (13) From Tennessee. (14) From Philadelphia through San Francisco. (15) From Indianapolis. (16) From Kansas City. (17) From Carolina.

Number One NFL Draft Choices, 1936-2004

Year	Team	Player, Pos., College	Year	Team	Player, Pos., College
1936	Philadelphia	Jay Berwanger, HB, Chicago	1971	New England	Jim Plunkett, QB, Stanford
1937	Philadelphia	Sam Francis, FB, Nebraska	1972	Buffalo	Walt Patulski, DE, Notre Dame
1938	Cleveland Rams	Corbett Davis, FB, Indiana	1973	Houston	John Matuszak, DE, Tampa
1939	Chicago Cards	Ki Aldrich, C, TCU	1974	Dallas	Ed "Too Tall" Jones, DE, Tenn. St.
1940	Chicago Cards	George Cafego, HB, Tennessee	1975	Atlanta	Steve Bartkowski, QB, Cal.
1941	Chicago Bears	Tom Harmon, HB, Michigan	1976	Tampa Bay	Lee Roy Selmon, DE, Oklahoma
1942	Pittsburgh	Bill Dudley, HB, Virginia	1977	Tampa Bay	Ricky Bell, RB, USC
1943	Detroit	Frank Sinkwich, HB, Georgia	1978	Houston	Earl Campbell, RB, Texas
1944	Boston Yanks	Angelo Bertelli, QB, Notre Dame	1979	Buffalo	Tom Cousineau, LB, Ohio St.
1945	Chicago Cards	Charley Trippi, HB, Georgia	1980	Detroit	Billy Sims, RB, Oklahoma
1946	Boston Yanks	Frank Dancewicz, QB, Notre Dame	1981	New Orleans	George Rogers, RB, S.Carolina
1947	Chicago Bears	Bob Fenimore, HB, Okla. A&M	1982	New England	Kenneth Sims, DT, Texas
1948	Washington	Harry Gilmer, QB, Alabama	1983	Baltimore Colts	John Elway, QB, Stanford
1949	Philadelphia	Chuck Bednarik, C, Penn	1984	New England	Irving Fryar, WR, Nebraska
1950	Detroit	Leon Hart, E, Notre Dame	1985	Buffalo	Bruce Smith, DE, Va.Tech
1951	N.Y. Giants	Kyle Rote, HB, SMU	1986	Tampa Bay	Bo Jackson, RB, Auburn
1952	L.A. Rams	Bill Wade, QB, Vanderbilt	1987	Tampa Bay	Vinny Testaverde, QB, Miami (FL)
1953	San Francisco	Harry Babcock, E, Georgia	1988	Atlanta	Aundray Bruce, LB, Auburn
1954	Cleveland	Bobby Garrett, QB, Stanford	1989	Dallas	Troy Aikman, QB, UCLA
1955	Baltimore Colts	George Shaw, QB, Oregon	1990	Indianapolis	Jeff George, QB, Illinois
1956	Pittsburgh	Gary Glick, DB, Col. A&M	1991	Dallas	Russell Maryland, DL, Miami (FL)
1957	Green Bay	Paul Hornung, QB, Notre Dame	1992	Indianapolis	Steve Emtman, DL, Washington
1958	Chicago Cards	King Hill, QB, Rice	1993	New England	Drew Bledsoe, QB, Washington St.
1959	Green Bay	Randy Duncan, QB, Iowa	1994	Cincinnati	Dan Wilkinson, DT, Ohio St.
1960	L.A. Rams	Billy Cannon, HB, LSU	1995	Cincinnati	Ki-Jana Carter, RB, Penn State
1961	Minnesota	Tommy Mason, HB, Tulane	1996	N.Y. Jets	Keyshawn Johnson, WR, USC
1962	Washington	Ernie Davis, HB, Syracuse	1997	St. Louis	Orlando Pace, T, Ohio St.
1963	L.A. Rams	Terry Baker, QB, Oregon St.	1998	Indianapolis	Peyton Manning, QB, Tennessee
1964	San Francisco	Dave Parks, E, Texas Tech	1999	Cleveland	Tim Couch, QB, Kentucky
1965	N.Y. Giants	Tucker Frederickson, HB, Auburn	2000	Cleveland	Courtney Brown, DE, Penn State
1966	Atlanta	Tommy Nobis, LB, Texas	2001	Atlanta	Michael Vick, QB, Virginia Tech
1967	Baltimore Colts	Bubba Smith, DT, Michigan St.	2002	Houston	David Carr, QB, Fresno St.
1968	Minnesota	Ron Yary, T, USC	2003	Cincinnati	Carson Palmer, QB, USC
1969	Buffalo	O.J. Simpson, RB, USC	2004	San Diego	Eli Manning, QB, Mississippi
1970	Pittsburgh	Terry Bradshaw, QB, La.Tech			

NFL MVP, Defensive Player of the Year, and Rookie of the Year

The Most Valuable Player and Defensive Player of the Year are two of many awards given out annually by the Associated Press. Rookie of the Year is one of many awards given out annually by *The Sporting News*. Many other organizations give out annual awards honoring the NFL's best players.

Most Valuable Player

Year	Player	Year	Player	Year	Player
1957	Jim Brown, Cleveland	1973	O.J. Simpson, Buffalo	1990	Joe Montana, San Francisco
1958	Gino Marchetti, Baltimore Colts	1974	Ken Stabler, Oakland	1991	Thurman Thomas, Buffalo
1959	Charley Conerly, N.Y. Giants	1975	Fran Tarkenton, Minnesota	1992	Steve Young, San Francisco
1960	Norm Van Brocklin, Philadelphia; Joe Schmidt, Detroit	1976	Bert Jones, Baltimore	1993	Emmitt Smith, Dallas
		1977	Walter Payton, Chicago	1994	Steve Young, San Francisco
1961	Paul Hornung, Green Bay	1978	Terry Bradshaw, Pittsburgh	1995	Brett Favre, Green Bay
1962	Jim Taylor, Green Bay	1979	Earl Campbell, Houston	1996	Brett Favre, Green Bay
1963	Y.A. Tittle, N.Y. Giants	1980	Brian Sipe, Cleveland	1997	(tie) Brett Favre, Green Bay
1964	John Unitas, Baltimore Colts	1981	Ken Anderson, Cincinnati		Barry Sanders, Detroit
1965	Jim Brown, Cleveland	1982	Mark Moseley, Washington	1998	Terrell Davis, Denver
1966	Bart Starr, Green Bay	1983	Joe Theismann, Washington	1999	Kurt Warner, St. Louis
1967	John Unitas, Baltimore Colts	1984	Dan Marino, Miami	2000	Marshall Faulk, St. Louis
1968	Earl Morrall, Baltimore Colts	1985	Marcus Allen, L.A. Raiders	2001	Kurt Warner, St. Louis
1969	Roman Gabriel, L.A. Rams	1986	Lawrence Taylor, N.Y. Giants	2002	Rich Gannon, Oakland
1970	John Brodie, San Francisco	1987	John Elway, Denver	2003	(tie) Peyton Manning, Indianapolis
1971	Alan Page, Minnesota	1988	Boomer Esiason, Cincinnati		Steve McNair, Tennessee
1972	Larry Brown, Washington	1989	Joe Montana, San Francisco		

Defensive Player of the Year

1966 Larry Wilson, St. Louis	1979 Lee Roy Selmon, Tampa Bay	1991 Pat Swilling, New Orleans
1967 Deacon Jones, Los Angeles	1980 Lester Hayes, Oakland	1992 Junior Seau, San Diego
1968 Deacon Jones, Los Angeles	1981 Joe Klecko, N.Y. Jets	1993 Bruce Smith, Buffalo
1969 Dick Butkus, Chicago	1982 Mark Gastineau, N.Y. Jets	1994 Deion Sanders, San Francisco
1970 Dick Butkus, Chicago	1983 Jack Lambert, Pittsburgh	1995 Bryce Paup, Buffalo
1971 Carl Eller, Minnesota	1984 Mike Haynes, L.A. Raiders	1996 Bruce Smith, Buffalo
1972 Joe Greene, Pittsburgh	1985 Howie Long, L.A. Raiders; Andre	1997 Dana Stubblefield, San Francisco
1973 Alan Page, Minnesota	Tippett, New England	1998 Reggie White, Green Bay
1974 Joe Greene, Pittsburgh	1986 Lawrence Taylor, N.Y. Giants	1999 Warren Sapp, Tampa Bay
1975 Curley Culp, Houston	1987 Reggie White, Philadelphia	2000 Ray Lewis, Baltimore
1976 Jerry Sherk, Cleveland	1988 Mike Singletary, Chicago	2001 Michael Strahan, NY Giants
1977 Harvey Martin, Dallas	1989 Tim Harris, Green Bay	2002 Derrick Brooks, Tampa Bay
1978 Randy Gradishar, Denver	1990 Bruce Smith, Buffalo	2003 Ray Lewis, Baltimore

Rookie of the Year

1964 Charley Taylor, Washington	1975 NFC: Steve Bartkowski, Atlanta	1987 Robert Awalt, St. Louis
1965 Gale Sayers, Chicago	AFC: Robert Brazile, Houston	1988 Keith Jackson, Philadelphia
1966 Tommy Nobis, Atlanta	1976 NFC: Sammy White, Minnesota	1989 Barry Sanders, Detroit
1967 Mel Farr, Detroit	AFC: Mike Haynes, New England	1990 Richmond Webb, Miami
1968 Earl McCullouch, Detroit	1977 NFC: Tony Dorsett, Dallas	1991 Mike Croel, Denver
1969 Calvin Hill, Dallas	AFC: A. J. Duhe, Miami	1992 Santana Dotson, Tampa Bay
1970 NFC: Bruce Taylor, San Francisco	1978 NFC: Al Baker, Detroit	1993 Jerome Bettis, L.A. Rams
AFC: Dennis Shaw, Buffalo	AFC: Earl Campbell, Houston	1994 Marshall Faulk, Indianapolis
1971 NFC: John Brockington, Green Bay	1979 NFC: Ottis Anderson, St. Louis	1995 Curtis Martin, New England
AFC: Jim Plunkett, New England	AFC: Jerry Butler, Buffalo	1996 Eddie George, Houston
1972 NFC: Chester Marcol, Green Bay	1980 Billy Sims, Detroit	1997 Warrick Dunn, Tampa Bay
AFC: Franco Harris, Pittsburgh	1981 George Rogers, New Orleans	1998 Randy Moss, Minnesota
1973 NFC: Chuck Foreman, Minnesota	1982 Marcus Allen, L.A. Raiders	1999 Edgerrin James, Indianapolis
AFC: Boobie Clark, Cincinnati	1983 Dan Marino, Miami	2000 Brian Urlacher, Chicago
1974 NFC: Wilbur Jackson, San Francisco	1984 Louis Lipps, Pittsburgh	2001 Kendrell Bell, Pittsburgh
AFC: Don Woods, San Diego	1985 Eddie Brown, Cincinnati	2002 Clinton Portis, Denver
	1986 Rueben Mayes, New Orleans	2003 Anquan Boldin, Arizona

The Sporting News 2003 NFL All-Pro Team

Offense—Quarterback: Peyton Manning, Indianapolis. Running Backs: Priest Holmes, Kansas City; Jamal Lewis, Baltimore. Wide Receivers: Marvin Harrison, Indianapolis; Torry Holt, St. Louis. Tight End: Tony Gonzalez, Kansas City. Tackles: Jonathan Ogden, Baltimore; Orlando Pace, St. Louis. Guards: Steve Hutchinson, Seattle; Will Shields, Kansas City. Center: Matt Birk, Minnesota.

Defense—Linebackers: Derrick Brooks, Tampa Bay; Ray Lewis, Baltimore; Julian Peterson, San Francisco. Defensive Ends: Simeon Rice, Tampa Bay; Michael Strahan, NY Giants. Defensive Tackles: Kris Jenkins, Carolina; Richard Seymour, New England. Cornerbacks: Champ Bailey, Washington; Patrick Surtain, Miami. Safeties: Ed Reed, Baltimore; Roy Williams, Dallas.

Special Teams—Kicker: Mike Vanderjagt, Indianapolis. Punter: Todd Sauerbrun, Carolina. Punt Returner: Dante Hall, Kansas City. Kick Returner: Jerry Azumah, Chicago.

All-Time NFL Coaching Victories

(at end of 2003 season; ranked by career wins; *active in 2003)

			Regular Season				Career			
Coach	Years	Teams	W	L	T	Pct	W	L	T	Pct
Don Shula	33	Colts, Dolphins...................	328	156	6	.676	347	173	6	.665
George Halas.............	40	Bears	318	148	31	.671	324	151	31	.671
Tom Landry	29	Cowboys	250	162	6	.605	270	178	6	.601
Curly Lambeau............	33	Packers, Cardinals, Redskins.......	226	132	22	.624	229	134	22	.623
Chuck Noll	23	Steelers	193	148	1	.566	209	156	1	.572
Dan Reeves*	23	Broncos, Giants, Falcons	190	165	2	.535	201	174	2	.536
Chuck Knox	22	Rams, Bills, Seahawks...........	186	147	1	.558	193	158	1	.550
Paul Brown..............	21	Browns, Bengals	166	100	6	.621	170	109	6	.607
Marty Schottenheimer*	18	Browns, Chiefs, Redskins, Chargers ..	165	113	1	.593	170	124	1	.578
Bud Grant................	18	Vikings	158	96	5	.620	168	108	5	.607
Bill Parcells*	16	Giants, Patriots, Jets, Cowboys	148	106	1	.582	159	113	1	.584
Steve Owen	23	Giants........................	153	100	17	.598	155	108	17	.584
Marv Levy	17	Chiefs, Bills	143	112	0	.561	154	120	0	.562
Joe Gibbs	12	Redskins	124	60	0	.674	140	65	0	.683
Hank Stram	17	Chiefs, Saints..................	131	97	10	.571	136	100	10	.573
Weeb Ewbank	20	Colts, Jets	130	129	7	.502	134	130	7	.507
Mike Ditka	14	Bears, Saints	121	95	0	.560	127	101	0	.557
Jim Mora	15	Saints, Colts...................	125	106	0	.541	125	112	0	.527
Mike Holmgren*	12	Packers, Seahawks	116	76	0	.604	125	83	0	.601
George Seifert	11	49ers, Panthers	114	62	0	.648	124	67	0	.649

All-Time Professional (NFL and AFL) Football Records

(at end of 2003 season; *active in 2003; (a) includes AFL statistics)

Leading Lifetime Scorers

Player	Yrs	TD	PAT	FG	Total	Player	Yrs	TD	PAT	FG	Total
Gary Anderson*	22	0	783	521	2,346	John Carney*.............	16	0	404	343	1,433
Morten Andersen*	22	0	753	502	2,259	Matt Bahr................	17	0	522	300	1,422
George Blanda (a)	26	9	943	335	2,002	Mark Moseley	16	0	482	300	1,382
Norm Johnson	18	0	638	366	1,736	Jim Bakken	17	0	534	282	1,380
Nick Lowery	18	0	562	383	1,711	Steve Christie*...........	14	0	435	314	1,377
Jan Stenerud (a)	19	0	580	373	1,699	Fred Cox	15	0	519	282	1,365
Eddie Murray	19	0	538	352	1,594	Matt Stover*..............	13	0	401	321	1,364
Al Del Greco.............	17	0	543	347	1,584	Lou Groza	17	1	641	234	1,349
Pat Leahy	18	0	558	304	1,470	Jason Elam*	11	0	449	288	1,313
Jim Turner (a)	16	1	521	304	1,439	Jim Breech	14	0	517	243	1,246

Leading Lifetime Touchdown Scorers

Player	Yrs	Rush	Rec	Ret	Total	Player	Yrs	Rush	Rec	Ret	Total
Jerry Rice*	19	10	194	1	205	Tim Brown*	16	1	99	4	104
Emmitt Smith*	14	155	11	0	166	Steve Largent	14	1	100	0	101
Marcus Allen	16	123	21	1	145	Franco Harris	13	91	9	0	100
Marshall Faulk*	10	97	34	0	131	Eric Dickerson	11	90	6	0	96
Cris Carter	16	0	130	1	131	Jim Taylor	10	83	10	0	93
Jim Brown	9	106	20	0	126	Tony Dorsett	12	77	13	1	91
Walter Payton	13	110	15	0	125	Bobby Mitchell	11	18	65	8	91
John Riggins	14	104	12	0	116	Ricky Watters	10	78	13	0	91
Lenny Moore	12	63	48	2	113	Leroy Kelly	10	74	13	3	90
Barry Sanders	10	99	10	0	109	Charley Taylor	13	11	79	0	90
Don Hutson	11	3	99	3	105						

Most Points, Season — 176, Paul Hornung, Green Bay Packers, 1960 (15 TDs, 41 PATs, 15 FGs).
Most Points, Game — 40, Ernie Nevers, Chicago Cardinals vs. Chicago Bears, Nov. 28, 1929 (6 TDs, 4 PATs).
Most Touchdowns, Season — 27, Priest Holmes, Kansas City Chiefs, 2003 (27 rushing, 0 receiving).
Most Touchdowns, Game — 6, Ernie Nevers, Chicago Cardinals vs. Chicago Bears, Nov. 28, 1929 (6 rushing); Dub Jones, Cleveland Browns vs. Chicago Bears, Nov. 25, 1951 (4 rushing, 2 pass receptions); Gale Sayers, Chicago Bears vs. San Francisco 49ers, Dec. 12, 1965 (4 rushing, 1 pass reception, 1 punt return).
Most Points After TD, Season — 66, Uwe von Schamann, Miami Dolphins, 1984.
Most Consecutive Points After TD — 371, Jason Elam, Denver Broncos, 1993-2002.
Most Field Goals, Season — 39, Olindo Mare, Miami Dolphins, 1999; Jeff Wilkins, St. Louis Rams, 2003.
Most Field Goals, Game — 7, Jim Bakken, St. Louis Cardinals vs. Pittsburgh Steelers, Sept. 24, 1967; Rich Karlis, Minnesota Vikings vs. L.A. Rams, Nov. 5, 1989 (OT); Chris Boniol, Dallas Cowboys vs. Green Bay Packers, Nov. 18, 1996; Billy Cundiff, Dallas Cowboys vs. N.Y. Giants, Sept. 15, 2003 (OT).
Most Field Goals, Career — 521, Gary Anderson, Pitts. Steelers-Phil. Eagles-SF 49ers-Minn. Vikings-Tenn. Titans, 1982-2003.
Longest Field Goal — 63 yds., Tom Dempsey, New Orleans Saints vs. Detroit Lions, Nov. 8, 1970; Jason Elam, Denver Broncos vs. Jacksonville Jaguars, Oct. 25, 1998.

Defensive Records

(at end of 2003 season)

Most Interceptions, Career — 81, Paul Krause, Washington Redskins-Minnesota Vikings, 1964-79.
Most Interceptions, Season — 14, Dick "Night Train" Lane, L. A. Rams, 1952.
Most Touchdowns, Career — 12, Rod Woodson, Pittsburgh Steelers-San Francisco 49ers-Baltimore Ravens-Oakland Raiders, 1987-2002.
Most Touchdowns, Season — 4, Ken Houston, Houston Oilers, 1971; Jim Kearney, Kansas City Chiefs, 1972; Eric Allen, Philadelphia Eagles, 1993.
Most Sacks, Career (Since 1982) — 200, Bruce Smith, Buffalo Bills-Washington Redskins, 1985-2003.
Most Sacks, Season (Since 1982) — 22.5, Michael Strahan, N.Y. Giants, 2002.
Most Sacks, Game (Since 1982) — 7, Derrick Thomas, Kansas City Chiefs vs. Seattle Seahawks, Nov. 11, 1990.

Leading Lifetime Rushers

(ranked by rushing yards)

Player	Yrs	Att	Yards	Avg	Long	TD	Player	Yrs	Att	Yards	Avg	Long	TD
Emmitt Smith*	14	4,142	17,418	4.2	75	155	Curtis Martin*	9	2,927	11,669	4.0	70	73
Walter Payton	13	3,838	16,726	4.4	76	110	John Riggins	14	2,916	11,352	3.9	66	104
Barry Sanders	10	3,062	15,269	5.0	85	99	O.J. Simpson (a)	11	2,404	11,236	4.7	94	61
Eric Dickerson	11	2,996	13,259	4.4	85	90	Marshall Faulk*	10	2,576	11,213	4.4	71	97
Tony Dorsett	12	2,936	12,739	4.3	99	77	Ricky Watters*	10	2,622	10,643	4.1	57	78
Jerome Bettis*	11	3,119	12,353	4.0	71	69	Ottis Anderson	14	2,562	10,273	4.0	76	81
Jim Brown	9	2,359	12,312	5.2	80	106	Eddie George*	8	2,733	10,009	3.7	76	64
Marcus Allen	16	3,022	12,243	4.1	61	123	Earl Campbell	8	2,187	9,407	4.3	81	74
Franco Harris	13	2,949	12,120	4.1	75	91	Terry Allen	10	2,152	8,614	4.0	55	73
Thurman Thomas	13	2,877	12,074	4.2	80	65	Jim Taylor	10	1,941	18,597	4.4	84	83

Most Yards Gained, Season — 2,105, Eric Dickerson, L.A. Rams, 1984.
Most Yards Gained, Game — 295, Jamal Lewis, Baltimore Ravens vs. Cleveland Browns, Sept. 14, 2003.
Most Touchdowns Rushing, Career — 155, Emmitt Smith, Dallas Cowboys-Ariz. Cardinals, 1990-2003.
Most Touchdowns Rushing, Season — 27, Priest Holmes, Kansas City Chiefs, 2003.
Most Touchdowns Rushing, Game — 6, Ernie Nevers, Chicago Cardinals vs. Chicago Bears, Nov. 28, 1929.
Most Rushing Attempts, Game — 45, Jamie Morris, Washington Redskins vs. Cincinnati Bengals, Dec. 17, 1988 (overtime).
Longest Run From Scrimmage — 99 yds., Tony Dorsett, Dallas Cowboys vs. Minnesota Vikings, Jan. 3, 1983 (touchdown).

Leading Lifetime Receivers

(ranked by number of receptions)

Player	Yrs	No.	Yards	Avg	Long	TD	Player	Yrs	No.	Yards	Avg	Long	TD
Jerry Rice*	19	1,519	22,466	14.8	96	194	James Lofton	16	764	14,004	18.3	80	75
Cris Carter	16	1,101	13,899	12.6	80	130	Marvin Harrison*	8	759	10,072	13.3	79	83
Tim Brown*	16	1,070	14,734	13.8	80	99	Michael Irvin	12	750	11,904	15.9	87	65
Andre Reed	16	951	13,198	13.9	83	87	Charlie Joiner (a)	18	750	12,146	16.2	87	65
Art Monk	16	940	12,721	13.5	79	68	Andre Rison	12	743	10,205	13.7	80	84
Irving Fryar	17	851	12,785	15.0	80	84	Keenan McCardell*	12	724	9,370	12.9	76	52
Larry Centers*	14	827	6,797	8.2	54	28	Jimmy Smith	10	718	10,092	14.1	75	55
Steve Largent	14	819	13,089	16.0	74	100	Gary Clark	11	699	10,856	15.5	84	65
Shannon Sharpe*	14	815	10,060	12.3	82	62	Terance Mathis	13	689	8,809	12.8	81	63
Henry Ellard	16	814	13,777	16.9	81	65	Isaac Bruce*	10	688	10,461	15.2	80	68

Most Yards Gained, Career — 22,466, Jerry Rice, San Francisco 49ers, Oakland Raiders, 1985-2003.
Most Yards Gained, Season — 1,848, Jerry Rice, San Francisco 49ers, 1995.
Most Yards Gained, Game — 336, Willie "Flipper" Anderson, L. A. Rams vs. New Orleans, Nov. 26, 1989 (overtime).
Most Pass Receptions, Season — 143, Marvin Harrison, Indianapolis Colts, 2002.
Most Pass Receptions, Game — 20, Terrell Owens, San Francisco 49ers vs. Chicago Bears, Dec. 17, 2000 (283 yards).
Most Touchdown Receptions, Career — 194, Jerry Rice, San Francisco 49ers, Oakland Raiders, 1985-2003.
Most Touchdown Receptions, Season — 22, Jerry Rice, San Francisco 49ers, 1987.
Most Touchdown Receptions, Game — 5, Bob Shaw, Chicago Cardinals vs. Baltimore Colts, Oct. 2, 1950; Kellen Winslow, San Diego Chargers vs. Oakland Raiders, Nov. 22, 1981; Jerry Rice, San Francisco 49ers vs. Atlanta Falcons, Oct. 14, 1990.

Leading Lifetime Passers

(minimum 1,500 attempts; ranked by quarterback rating points)

Player	Yrs	Att	Comp	Yds	TD	Int	Pts[1]	Player	Yrs	Att	Comp	Yds	TD	Int	Pts[1]
Kurt Warner*	6	1,688	1,121	14,447	102	65	97.2	Mark Brunell*....	10	3,643	2,196	25,793	144	86	85.2
Steve Young.....	15	4,149	2,667	33,124	232	107	96.8	Rich Gannon* ...	15	4,138	2,492	28,219	177	102	84.7
Joe Montana	15	5,391	3,409	40,551	273	139	92.3	Jim Kelly	11	4,779	2,874	35,467	237	175	84.4
Jeff Garcia*	5	2,360	1,449	16,408	113	56	88.3	Brad Johnson*...	10	3,401	2,101	23,239	140	95	84.12
Peyton Manning* .	6	3,383	2,128	24,885	167	110	88.1	Steve McNair* ...	9	3,180	1,884	22,637	132	83	84.08
Daunte Culpepper*	5	1,843	1,160	13,881	90	63	88.0	Roger Staubach .	11	2,958	1,685	22,700	153	109	83.4
Brett Favre*	13	6,464	3,960	45,646	346	209	86.9	Brian Griese*....	6	1,808	1,118	12,576	76	59	83.0
Dan Marino......	17	8,358	4,967	61,361	420	252	86.4	Neil Lomax	8	3,153	1,817	22,771	136	90	82.7
Trent Green*	6	2,266	1,336	17,016	106	65	86.1	Sonny Jurgensen	18	4,262	2,433	32,224	255	189	82.63
Tom Brady*	4	1,544	955	10,233	69	38	85.9	Len Dawson (a)..	19	3,741	2,136	28,711	239	183	82.56

(1) Rating points based on performances in the following categories: Percentage of completions, percentage of touchdown passes, percentage of interceptions, and average gain per pass attempt.

Most Yards Gained, Career — 61,361, Dan Marino, Miami Dolphins, 1983-99.
Most Yards Gained, Season — 5,084, Dan Marino, Miami Dolphins, 1984.
Most Yards Gained, Game — 554, Norm Van Brocklin, L. A. Rams vs. N.Y. Yanks, Sept. 28, 1951 (27 completions in 41 attempts).
Most Touchdowns Passing, Career — 420, Dan Marino, Miami Dolphins, 1983-99.
Most Touchdowns Passing, Season — 48, Dan Marino, Miami Dolphins, 1984.
Most Touchdowns Passing, Game — 7, Sid Luckman, Chicago Bears vs. N.Y. Giants, Nov. 14, 1943; Adrian Burk, Phil. Eagles vs. Washington Redskins, Oct. 17, 1954; George Blanda, Houston Oilers vs. N.Y. Titans, Nov. 19, 1961; Y.A. Tittle, N.Y. Giants vs. Washington Redskins, Oct. 28, 1962; Joe Kapp, Minnesota Vikings vs. Baltimore Colts, Sept. 28, 1969.
Most Passes Completed, Career — 4,967, Dan Marino, Miami Dolphins, 1983-99.
Most Passes Completed, Season — 418, Rich Gannon, Oakland Raiders, 2002.
Most Passes Completed, Game — 45, Drew Bledsoe, New England Patriots vs. Minnesota Vikings, Nov. 13, 1994 (OT).

National Football League Franchise Origins

(founding year, league; home stadium location; subsequent history)

Arizona Cardinals—1920, American Professional Football Association (APFA)[1]. Chicago, 1920-59; St. Louis, 1960-87; Tempe, AZ, 1988-present.
Atlanta Falcons—1996, NFL. Atlanta, 1966-present.
Baltimore Ravens—1996, NFL. Baltimore, 1996-present.
Buffalo Bills—1969, American Football League (AFL)[2]. Buffalo, 1960-72; Orchard Park, NY, 1972-present.
Carolina Panthers—1995, NFL. Clemson, SC, 1995; Charlotte, NC, 1996-present.
Chicago Bears—1920 APFA. Decatur, IL, 1920; Chicago, 1921-present.
Cincinnati Bengals—1968, AFL. Cincinnati, 1968-present.
Cleveland Browns—1946, All-America Football Conference (AAFC)[3]. Cleveland, 1946-95; 1999-present.
Dallas Cowboys—1960, NFL. Dallas, 1960-70; Irving, TX, 1971-present.
Denver Broncos—1960, AFL. Denver, 1960-present.
Detroit Lions—1930, NFL. Portsmouth, OH, 1930-33; Detroit, 1934-74; Pontiac, MI, 1975-present.
Green Bay Packers—1921, APFA. Green Bay, WI, 1921-present.
Houston Texans—2002, NFL. Houston 2002-present.
Indianapolis Colts—1953, NFL. Baltimore, 1953-83; Indianapolis, 1984-present.
Jacksonville Jaguars—1995, NFL. Jacksonville, FL, 1995-present.
Kansas City Chiefs—1960, AFL. Dallas, 1960-62; Kansas City, 1963-present.
Miami Dolphins—1966, AFL. Miami, 1966-present.
Minnesota Vikings—1961, NFL. Bloomington, MN, 1961-81; Minneapolis, 1982-present.
New England Patriots—1960, AFL. Boston, 1960-70; Foxboro, MA, 1971-present.
New Orleans Saints—1967, NFL. New Orleans, 1967-present.
New York Giants—1925, NFL. New York, 1925-73, 1975; New Haven, CT, 1973-74; E. Rutherford, NJ, 1976-present.
New York Jets—1960, AFL. New York, 1960-83; E. Rutherford, NJ, 1984-present.
Oakland Raiders—1960, AFL. Oakland, CA, 1960-81, 1995-present; Los Angeles, 1982-94.
Philadelphia Eagles—1933, NFL. Piladelphia, 1933-present.
Pittsburgh Steelers—1933, NFL. Pittsburgh, 1933-present.
St. Louis Rams—1937, NFL. Cleveland, 1936-45; Los Angeles, 1946-79; Anaheim, 1980-94; St. Louis, 1995-present.
San Diego Chargers—1960, AFL. Los Angeles, 1960; San Diego, 1961-present.
Seattle Seahawks—1976, NFL. Seattle, 1976-present.
San Francisco 49ers—1946, AAFC. San Francisco, 1946-present.
Tampa Bay Buccaneers—1976, NFL. Tampa, 1976-present.
Tennessee Titans—1960, AFL. Houston, 1969-96; Memphis, 1997; Nashville, 1998-present.
Washington Redskins—1932, NFL. Boston, 1932-36, Washington, DC, 1937-96; Landover, MD, 1997-present.

(1) The American Professional Football Association (APFA) was formed in 1920 to standardize the rules of professional football. In 1922, the name was changed to the National Football League. (2) The most successful of 4 separate leagues called the "American Football League" (1926; 1936-37; 1940-41, 1960-69). Congress approved an NFL/AFL merger in 1966. Baltimore, Cleveland, and Pittsburgh agreed to join the 10 incoming AFL teams to form the American Football Conference. The NFL began play in 1970 with 26 teams. (3) The All-America Football Conference, 1946-49. In 1950, 3 of its teams joined the NFL (Baltimore, Cleveland, and San Francisco). The Baltimore franchise failed, but the NFL awarded the city a 2nd one, also called the Colts, in 1953.

American Football League Champions

Year	Eastern Division	Western Division	Championship
1960	Houston Oilers (10-4-0)...............	Los Angeles Chargers (10-4-0)........	Houston 24, Los Angeles 16
1961	Houston Oilers (10-3-1)...............	San Diego Chargers (12-2-0)	Houston 10, San Diego 3
1962	Houston Oilers (11-3-0)...............	Dallas Texans (11-3-0)	Dallas 20, Houston 17 (2 overtimes)
1963	Boston Patriots (7-6-1)(a)	San Diego Chargers (11-3-0)	San Diego 51, Boston 10
1964	Buffalo Bills (12-2-0)	San Diego Chargers (8-5-1)	Buffalo 20, San Diego 7
1965	Buffalo Bills (10-3-1)	San Diego Chargers (9-2-3)	Buffalo 23, San Diego 0
1966	Buffalo Bills (9-4-1)	Kansas City Chiefs (11-2-1)	Kansas City 31, Buffalo 7
1967	Houston Oilers (9-4-1)................	Oakland Raiders (13-1-0)	Oakland 40, Houston 7
1968	New York Jets (11-3-0)	Oakland Raiders (12-2-0)(b)..........	New York 27, Oakland 23
1969	New York Jets (10-4-0)	Oakland Raiders (12-1-1)	Kansas City 17, Oakland 7 (c)

(a) Defeated Buffalo Bills in divisional playoff. (b) Defeated Kansas City Chiefs in divisional playoff. (c) Kansas City Chiefs defeated N.Y. Jets and Oakland Raiders defeated Houston Oilers in divisional playoffs.

Pro Football Hall of Fame, Canton, Ohio

(Asterisks indicate 2004 inductees.)

Herb Adderley
George Allen
Marcus Allen
Lance Alworth
Doug Atkins
Morris "Red" Badgro
Lem Barney
Cliff Battles
Sammy Baugh
Chuck Bednarik
Bert Bell
Bobby Bell
Raymond Berry
Elvin Bethea
Charles Bidwill
Fred Biletnikoff
George Blanda
Mel Blount
Terry Bradshaw
*Bob Brown
Jim Brown
Paul Brown
Roosevelt Brown
Willie Brown
Buck Buchanan
Nick Buoniconti
Dick Butkus
Earl Campbell
Tony Canadeo
Joe Carr
Dave Casper
Guy Chamberlin
Jack Christiansen
Earl "Dutch" Clark
George Connor
Jim Conzelman
Lou Creekmur
Larry Csonka
Al Davis
Willie Davis
Len Dawson
Joe DeLamielleure
Eric Dickerson
Dan Dierdorf
Mike Ditka
Art Donovan

Tony Dorsett
John "Paddy" Driscoll
Bill Dudley
Glen "Turk" Edwards
*Carl Eller
*John Elway
Weeb Ewbank
Tom Fears
Jim Finks
Ray Flaherty
Len Ford
Dr. Daniel Fortmann
Dan Fouts
Frank Gatski
Bill George
Joe Gibbs
Frank Gifford
Sid Gillman
Otto Graham
Red Grange
Bud Grant
Joe Greene
Forrest Gregg
Bob Griese
Lou Groza
Joe Guyon
George Halas
Jack Ham
Dan Hampton
John Hannah
Franco Harris
Mike Haynes
Ed Healey
Mel Hein
Ted Hendricks
Wilbur "Pete" Henry
Arnold Herber
Bill Hewitt
Clarke Hinkle
Elroy "Crazylegs"
  Hirsch
Paul Hornung
Ken Houston
Cal Hubbard
Sam Huff

Lamar Hunt
Don Hutson
Jimmy Johnson
John Henry Johnson
Charlie Joiner
David "Deacon" Jones
Stan Jones
Henry Jordan
Sonny Jurgensen
Jim Kelly
Leroy Kelly
Walt Kiesling
Frank "Bruiser" Kinard
Paul Krause
Earl "Curly" Lambeau
Jack Lambert
Tom Landry
Dick "Night Train" Lane
Jim Langer
Willie Lanier
Steve Largent
Yale Lary
Dante Lavelli
Bobby Layne
Alphonse "Tuffy"
  Leemans
Marv Levy
Bob Lilly
Larry Little
James Lofton
Vince Lombardi
Howie Long
Ronnie Lott
Sid Luckman
Roy "Link" Lyman
Tom Mack
John Mackey
Tim Mara
Wellington Mara
Gino Marchetti
George Preston
  Marshall
Ollie Matson
Don Maynard
George McAfee
Mike McCormack

Tommy McDonald
Hugh McElhenny
Johnny "Blood" McNally
Mike Michalske
Wayne Millner
Bobby Mitchell
Ron Mix
Joe Montana
Lenny Moore
Marion Motley
Mike Munchak
Anthony Munoz
George Musso
Bronko Nagurski
Joe Namath
Earle "Greasy" Neale
Ernie Nevers
Ozzie Newsome
Ray Nitschke
Chuck Noll
Leo Nomellini
Merlin Olsen
Jim Otto
Steve Owen
Alan Page
Clarence "Ace" Parker
Jim Parker
Walter Payton
Joe Perry
Pete Pihos
Hugh "Shorty" Ray
Dan Reeves
Mel Renfro
John Riggins
Jim Ringo
Andy Robustelli
Art Rooney
Dan Rooney
Pete Rozelle
Bob St. Clair
*Barry Sanders
Gale Sayers
Joe Schmidt
Tex Schramm
Lee Roy Selmon
Billy Shaw

Art Shell
Don Shula
O.J. Simpson
Mike Singletary
Jackie Slater
Jackie Smith
John Stallworth
Bart Starr
Roger Staubach
Ernie Stautner
Jan Stenerud
Dwight Stephenson
Hank Stram
Ken Strong
Joe Stydahar
Lynn Swann
Fran Tarkenton
Charley Taylor
Jim Taylor
Lawrence "LT" Taylor
Jim Thorpe
Y.A. Tittle
George Trafton
Charley Trippi
Emlen Tunnell
Clyde "Bulldog" Turner
Johnny Unitas
Gene Upshaw
Norm Van Brocklin
Steve Van Buren
Doak Walker
Bill Walsh
Paul Warfield
Bob Waterfield
Mike Webster
Arnie Weinmeister
Randy White
Dave Wilcox
Bill Willis
Larry Wilson
Kellen Winslow
Alex Wojciechowicz
Willie Wood
Ron Yary
Jack Youngblood

NFL Stadiums[1]

Team—Stadium, Location, Turf (Year Built)	Capacity
Bears—New Soldier Field[2], Chicago, IL, G (1924)	61,500
Bengals—Paul Brown Stad., Cincinnati, OH, G (2000)	65,600
Bills—Ralph Wilson Stad., Orchard Park, NY, A (1973)	73,967
Broncos—Invesco Field at Mile High, Denver, CO, G (2001)	76,125
Browns—Cleveland Browns Stad., Cleveland, OH, G (1999)	73,300
Buccaneers—Raymond James Stad., Tampa, FL, G (1998)	65,657
Cardinals—Sun Devil Stad., Tempe, AZ, G (1958)	73,014
Chargers—Qualcomm Stad.[3], San Diego, CA, G (1967)	71,500
Chiefs—Arrowhead Stad., Kansas City, MO, G (1972)	79,451
Colts—RCA Dome[4], Indianapolis, IN, A (1983)	56,127
Cowboys—Texas Stad., Irving, TX, A (1971)	65,675
Dolphins—Pro Player Stad.[5], Miami, FL, G (1987)	75,192
Eagles—Lincoln Financial Field, Philadelphia, PA, G (2003)	65,352
Falcons—Georgia Dome, Atlanta, GA, A (1992)	71,228
49ers—3Com Park[6], San Francisco, CA, G (1960)	69,734
Giants—Giants Stad., E. Rutherford, NJ, G (1976)	79,466
Jaguars—ALLTEL Stad.[7], Jacksonville, FL, G (1946)	73,000
Jets—Giants Stad., E. Rutherford, NJ, G (1976)	79,466
Lions—Ford Field, Detroit, MI, A (2002)	65,000
Packers—Lambeau Field[8], Green Bay, WI, G (1957)	72,515
Panthers—Bank of America Stad.[9], Charlotte, NC, G (1996)	73,258
Patriots—Gillette Stad., Foxboro, MA, G (2002)	68,000
Raiders—Network Associates Coliseum[10], Oakland, CA, G (1966)	63,132
Rams—Edward Jones Dome[11], St. Louis, MO, A (1995)	66,000
Ravens—M & T Bank Stad.[12], Baltimore, MD, SG (1998)	69,354
Redskins—FedEx Field[13], Landover, MD, G (1997)	80,116
Saints—Louisiana Superdome, New Orleans, LA (1975)	69,703
Seahawks—Qwest Field[14], Seattle, WA, A (2002)	67,000
Steelers—Heinz Field, Pittsburgh, PA, A (2001)	64,450
Texans—Reliant Stadium, Houston, TX, G (2002)	69,500
Titans—The Coliseum[15], Nashville, TN, G (1999)	67,000
Vikings—Hubert H. Humphrey Metrodome, Minn., MN, A (1982)	64,121

G=Grass. A=Artificial turf. SG=Sport Grass (hybrid of artificial and natural turf). (1) As of the start of the 2004 season. (2) Renovation in 2002 replaced interior of stadium (3) Formerly San Diego Stadium (1967-80), San Diego Jack Murphy Stadium (1981-97). (4) Formerly the Hoosier Dome (1983-94). (5) Formerly Joe Robbie Stadium (1987-96). (6) Formerly Candlestick Park; full name: 3Com Park at Candlestick Point. (7) Formerly Jacksonville Municipal Stadium (1946-97). (8) Formerly City Stadium (1957-65). (9) Formerly Ericsson Stadium (1996-2003). (10) Formerly Oakland/Alameda County Coliseum. (11) Formerly Trans World Dome (1995-2001); full name: Edward Jones Dome at America's Center. (12) Formerly PSINet Stadium (1998-2002); Ravens Stadium (2002-2003). (13) Formerly Jack Kent Cooke Stadium (1997-99). (14) Formerly Seahawks Stadium (2002-04). (15) Formerly Adelphia Col. (1999-2002).

Future Sites of the Super Bowl

(Information subject to change.)

No.	Site	Date	No.	Site	Date
XXXIX	ALLTEL Stadium, Jacksonville, FL	Feb. 6, 2005	XLI	Pro Player Stadium, Miami, FL	Feb. 4, 2007
XL	Ford Field, Detroit, MI	Feb. 5, 2006	XLII	Stadium, Glendale, AZ	2008; date not set

COLLEGE FOOTBALL

LSU, USC Split National Title

The Louisiana State University Tigers and the University of Southern California Trojans split the NCAA football national title Jan. 5, 2004. LSU had defeated the Oklahoma Sooners, 21-14, in New Orleans, LA, Jan. 4 to win the Sugar Bowl, which had been designated as the national title game by the Bowl Championship Series. USC, which had been ranked atop both final regular-season polls—the Associated Press poll of media members and the USA Today/ESPN coaches' poll—had beaten the Michigan Wolverines, 28-14, on Jan. 1 in Pasadena, CA, to win the Rose Bowl. With its Sugar Bowl win, LSU (13-1) was automatically ranked number 1 in the final coaches' poll, under BCS rules. USC (12-1) topped the final AP poll.

National College Football Champions, 1936-2003

The unofficial champion as selected by the AP poll of writers and USA Today/ESPN (until 1991, UPI; 1991-1996 USA Today/CNN) poll of coaches. Where the polls disagreed, both teams are listed (AP winner first). The AP poll started in 1936; the UPI poll in 1950.

1936 Minnesota	1951 Tennessee	1966 Notre Dame	1979 Alabama	1992 Alabama
1937 Pittsburgh	1952 Michigan St.	1967 USC	1980 Georgia	1993 Florida St.
1938 Texas Christian	1953 Maryland	1968 Ohio St.	1981 Clemson	1994 Nebraska
1939 Texas A&M	1954 Ohio St., UCLA	1969 Texas	1982 Penn St.	1995 Nebraska
1940 Minnesota	1955 Oklahoma	1970 Nebraska, Texas	1983 Miami (FL)	1996 Florida
1941 Minnesota	1956 Oklahoma	1971 Nebraska	1984 Brigham Young	1997 Michigan,
1942 Ohio St.	1957 Auburn, Ohio St.	1972 USC	1985 Oklahoma	Nebraska
1943 Notre Dame	1958 Louisiana St.	1973 Notre Dame,	1986 Penn St.	1998 Tennessee
1944 Army	1959 Syracuse	Alabama	1987 Miami (FL)	1999 Florida St.
1945 Army	1960 Minnesota	1974 Oklahoma, USC	1988 Notre Dame	2000 Oklahoma
1946 Notre Dame	1961 Alabama	1975 Oklahoma	1989 Miami (FL)	2001 Miami (FL)
1947 Notre Dame	1962 USC	1976 Pittsburgh	1990 Colorado, GA Tech	2002 Ohio State
1948 Michigan	1963 Texas	1977 Notre Dame	1991 Miami (FL),	2003 LSU, USC
1949 Notre Dame	1964 Alabama	1978 Alabama, USC	Washington	
1950 Oklahoma	1965 Alabama, Mich. St.			

2003 Final AP and USA Today/ESPN Rankings

Associated Press Poll

1. USC......... 12-1	6. Michigan 10-3	11. Florida State ... 10-3	16. Boise State ... 13-1	21. Utah......... 10-2
2. LSU 13-1	7. Georgia...... 11-3	12. Texas........ 10-3	17. Maryland..... 10-3	22. Clemson 9-4
3. Oklahoma ... 12-2	8. Iowa......... 10-3	13. Mississippi ... 10-3	18. Purdue....... 9-4	23. Bowling Green. 11-3
4. Ohio State ... 11-2	9. Washington State 10-3	14. Kansas State .. 11-4	19. Nebraska..... 10-3	24. Florida....... 8-5
5. Miami (FL) 11-2	10. Miami (OH) ... 13-1	15. Tennessee 10-3	20. Minnesota.... 10-3	25. Texas Christian 11-2

USA Today/ESPN Coaches' Poll

1. LSU 13-1	6. Georgia...... 11-3	11. Texas.........10-3	16. Tennessee.... 10-3	21. Utah......... 10-2
2. USC......... 12-1	7. Michigan 10-3	12. Miami (OH)....13-1	17. Minnesota.... 10-3	22. Clemson 9-4
3. Oklahoma 12-2	8. Iowa......... 10-3	13. Kansas State .. 11-4	18. Nebraska..... 10-3	23. Bowling Green. 11-3
4. Ohio State 11-2	9. Washington State 10-3	14. Mississippi 10-3	19. Purdue....... 9-4	24. Texas Christian 11-2
5. Miami (FL) 11-2	10. Florida State .. 10-3	15. Boise State 13-1	20. Maryland..... 10-3	25. Florida....... 8-5

Note: Team records include bowl games. The American Football Coaches Assoc. prohibits coaches from voting for schools on major NCAA probation. The NCAA placed the Univ. of Alabama on 5-year probation Feb. 1, 2002, for recruiting violations.

Annual Results of Major Bowl Games

(Dates indicate year the game was played; bowl games are generally played in late December or early January.)

Rose Bowl, Pasadena, CA

1902	(Jan.) Michigan 49, Stanford 0	1946	Alabama 34, USC 14	1976	UCLA 23, Ohio St. 10
1916	Washington St. 14, Brown 0	1947	Illinois 45, UCLA 14	1977	USC 14, Michigan 6
1917	Oregon 14, Pennsylvania 0	1948	Michigan 49, USC 0	1978	Washington 27, Michigan 20
1918-19	Service teams	1949	Northwestern 20, California 14	1979	USC 17, Michigan 10
1920	Harvard 7, Oregon 6	1950	Ohio St. 17, California 14	1980	USC 17, Ohio St. 16
1921	California 28, Ohio St. 0	1951	Michigan 14, California 6	1981	Michigan 23, Washington 6
1922	Wash. & Jeff. 0, California 0	1952	Illinois 40, Stanford 7	1982	Washington 28, Iowa 0
1923	USC 14, Penn St. 3	1953	USC 7, Wisconsin 0	1983	UCLA 24, Michigan 14
1924	Navy 14, Washington 14	1954	Mich. St. 28, UCLA 20	1984	UCLA 45, Illinois 9
1925	Notre Dame 27, Stanford 10	1955	Ohio St. 20, USC 7	1985	USC 20, Ohio St. 17
1926	Alabama 20, Washington 19	1956	Mich. St. 17, UCLA 14	1986	UCLA 45, Iowa 28
1927	Alabama 7, Stanford 7	1957	Iowa 35, Oregon St. 19	1987	Arizona St. 22, Michigan 15
1928	Stanford 7, Pittsburgh 6	1958	Ohio St. 10, Oregon 7	1988	Mich. St. 20, USC 17
1929	Georgia Tech 8, California 7	1959	Iowa 38, California 12	1989	Michigan 22, USC 14
1930	USC 47, Pittsburgh 14	1960	Washington 44, Wisconsin 8	1990	USC 17, Michigan 10
1931	Alabama 24, Wash. St. 0	1961	Washington 17, Minnesota 7	1991	Washington 46, Iowa 34
1932	USC 21, Tulane 12	1962	Minnesota 21, UCLA 3	1992	Washington 34, Michigan 14
1933	USC 35, Pittsburgh 0	1963	USC 42, Wisconsin 37	1993	Michigan 38, Washington 31
1934	Columbia 7, Stanford 0	1964	Illinois 17, Washington 7	1994	Wisconsin 21, UCLA 16
1935	Alabama 29, Stanford 13	1965	Michigan 34, Oregon St. 7	1995	Penn St. 38, Oregon 20
1936	Stanford 7, SMU 0	1966	UCLA 14, Mich. St. 12	1996	USC 41, Northwestern 32
1937	Pittsburgh 21, Washington 0	1967	Purdue 14, USC 13	1997	Ohio St. 20, Arizona St. 17
1938	California 13, Alabama 0	1968	USC 14, Indiana 3	1998	Michigan 21, Wash. St. 16
1939	USC 7, Duke 3	1969	Ohio St. 27, USC 16	1999	Wisconsin 38, UCLA 31
1940	USC 14, Tennessee 0	1970	USC 10, Michigan 3	2000	Wisconsin 17, Stanford 9
1941	Stanford 21, Nebraska 13	1971	Stanford 27, Ohio St. 17	2001	Washington 34, Purdue 24
1942*	Oregon St. 20, Duke 16	1972	Stanford 13, Michigan 12	2002	Miami (FL) 37, Nebraska 14
1943	Georgia 9, UCLA 0	1973	USC 42, Ohio St. 17	2003	Oklahoma, 34, Washington St. 14
1944	USC 29, Washington 0	1974	Ohio St. 42, USC 21	2004	USC 28, Michigan 14
1945	USC 25, Tennessee 0	1975	USC 18, Ohio St. 17		

*Played at Durham, NC.

Orange Bowl, Miami, FL

1935	(Jan.) Bucknell 26, Miami (FL) 0	1943	Alabama 37, Boston Coll. 21	1951	Clemson 15, Miami (FL) 14
1936	Catholic U. 20, Mississippi 19	1944	LSU 19, Texas A&M 14	1952	Georgia Tech 17, Baylor 14
1937	Duquesne 13, Mississippi St. 12	1945	Tulsa 26, Georgia Tech 12	1953	Alabama 61, Syracuse 6
1938	Auburn 6, Michigan St. 0	1946	Miami (FL) 13, Holy Cross 6	1954	Oklahoma 7, Maryland 0
1939	Tennessee 17, Oklahoma 0	1947	Rice 8, Tennessee 0	1955	Duke 34, Nebraska 7
1940	Georgia Tech 21, Missouri 7	1948	Georgia Tech 20, Kansas 14	1956	Oklahoma 20, Maryland 6
1941	Mississippi St. 14, Georgetown 7	1949	Texas 41, Georgia 28	1957	Colorado 27, Clemson 21
1942	Georgia 40, TCU 26	1950	Santa Clara 21, Kentucky 13	1958	Oklahoma 48, Duke 21

1959 Oklahoma 21, Syracuse 6	1975 Notre Dame 13, Alabama 11	1990 Notre Dame 21, Colorado 6
1960 Georgia 14, Missouri 0	1976 Oklahoma 14, Michigan 6	1991 Colorado 10, Notre Dame 9
1961 Missouri 21, Navy 14	1977 Ohio St. 27, Colorado 10	1992 Miami (FL) 22, Nebraska 0
1962 LSU 25, Colorado 7	1978 Arkansas 31, Oklahoma 6	1993 Florida St. 27, Nebraska 14
1963 Alabama 17, Oklahoma 0	1979 Oklahoma 31, Nebraska 24	1994 Florida St. 18, Nebraska 16
1964 Nebraska 13, Auburn 7	1980 Oklahoma 24, Florida St. 7	1995 Nebraska 24, Miami (FL) 17
1965 Texas 21, Alabama 17	1981 Oklahoma 18, Florida St. 17	1996 Florida St. 31, Notre Dame 26
1966 Alabama 39, Nebraska 28	1982 Clemson 22, Nebraska 15	1996 (Dec.) Nebraska 41, Virginia Tech 21
1967 Florida 27, Georgia Tech 12	1983 Nebraska 21, LSU 20	1998 (Jan.) Nebraska 42, Tennessee 17
1968 Oklahoma 26, Tennessee 24	1984 Miami (FL) 31, Nebraska 30	1999 Florida 31, Syracuse 10
1969 Penn St. 15, Kansas 14	1985 Washington 28, Oklahoma 17	2000 Michigan 35, Alabama 34 (OT)
1970 Penn St. 10, Missouri 3	1986 Oklahoma 25, Penn St. 10	2001 Oklahoma 13, Florida St. 2
1971 Nebraska 17, LSU 12	1987 Oklahoma 42, Arkansas 8	2002 Florida 56, Maryland 23
1972 Nebraska 38, Alabama 6	1988 Miami (FL) 20, Oklahoma 14	2003 USC 38, Iowa 17
1973 Nebraska 40, Notre Dame 6	1989 Miami (FL) 23, Nebraska 3	2004 Miami 16, Florida State 14
1974 Penn St. 16, LSU 9		

Sugar Bowl, New Orleans, LA

1935 (Jan.) Tulane 20, Temple 14	1959 LSU 7, Clemson 0	1982 Pittsburgh 24, Georgia 20
1936 TCU 3, LSU 2	1960 Mississippi 21, LSU 0	1983 Penn St. 27, Georgia 23
1937 Santa Clara 21, LSU 14	1961 Mississippi 14, Rice 6	1984 Auburn 9, Michigan 7
1938 Santa Clara 6, LSU 0	1962 Alabama 10, Arkansas 3	1985 Nebraska 28, LSU 10
1939 TCU 15, Carnegie Tech 7	1963 Mississippi 17, Arkansas 13	1986 Tennessee 35, Miami (FL) 7
1940 Texas A&M 14, Tulane 13	1964 Alabama 12, Mississippi 7	1987 Nebraska 30, LSU 15
1941 Boston Col. 19, Tennessee 13	1965 LSU 13, Syracuse 10	1988 Syracuse 16, Auburn 16
1942 Fordham 2, Missouri 0	1966 Missouri 20, Florida 18	1989 Florida St. 13, Auburn 7
1943 Tennessee 14, Tulsa 7	1967 Alabama 34, Nebraska 7	1990 Miami (FL) 33, Alabama 25
1944 Georgia Tech 20, Tulsa 18	1968 LSU 20, Wyoming 13	1991 Tennessee 23, Virginia 22
1945 Duke 29, Alabama 26	1969 Arkansas 16, Georgia 2	1992 Notre Dame 39, Florida 28
1946 Oklahoma A&M 33, St. Mary's 13	1970 Mississippi 27, Arkansas 22	1993 Alabama 34, Miami (FL) 13
1947 Georgia 20, N. Carolina 10	1971 Tennessee 34, Air Force 13	1994 Florida 41, West Virginia 7
1948 Texas 27, Alabama 7	1972 Oklahoma 40, Auburn 22	1995 Florida St. 23, Florida 17
1949 Oklahoma 14, N. Carolina 6	1972 (Dec.) Oklahoma 14, Penn St. 0	1995 (Dec.) Virginia Tech 28, Texas 10
1950 Oklahoma 35, LSU 0	1973 Notre Dame 24, Alabama 23	1997 (Jan.) Florida 52, Florida St. 20
1951 Kentucky 13, Oklahoma 7	1974 Nebraska 13, Florida 10	1998 Florida St. 31, Ohio St. 14
1952 Maryland 28, Tennessee 13	1975 Alabama 13, Penn St. 6	1999 Ohio St. 24, Texas A&M 14
1953 Georgia Tech 24, Mississippi 7	1977 (Jan.) Pittsburgh 27, Georgia 3	2000 Florida St. 46, Virginia Tech 29
1954 Georgia Tech 42, West Virginia 19	1978 Alabama 35, Ohio St. 6	2001 Miami (FL) 37, Florida 20
1955 Navy 21, Mississippi 0	1979 Alabama 14, Penn St. 7	2002 LSU 47, Illinois 34
1956 Georgia Tech 7, Pittsburgh 0	1980 Alabama 24, Arkansas 9	2003 Georgia 26, Florida St. 13
1957 Baylor 13, Tennessee 7	1981 Georgia 17, Notre Dame 10	2004 LSU 21, Oklahoma 14
1958 Mississippi 39, Texas 7		

Cotton Bowl, Dallas, TX

1937 (Jan.) TCU 16, Marquette 6	1960 Syracuse 23, Texas 14	1983 SMU 7, Pittsburgh 3
1938 Rice 28, Colorado 14	1961 Duke 7, Arkansas 6	1984 Georgia 10, Texas 9
1939 St. Mary's 20, Texas Tech 13	1962 Texas 12, Mississippi 7	1985 Boston Coll. 45, Houston 28
1940 Clemson 6, Boston Coll. 3	1963 LSU 13, Texas 0	1986 Texas A&M 36, Auburn 16
1941 Texas A&M 13, Fordham 12	1964 Texas 28, Navy 6	1987 Ohio St. 28, Texas A&M 12
1942 Alabama 29, Texas A&M 21	1965 Arkansas 10, Nebraska 7	1988 Texas A&M 35, Notre Dame 10
1943 Texas 14, Georgia Tech 7	1966 LSU 14, Arkansas 7	1989 UCLA 17, Arkansas 3
1944 Randolph Field 7, Texas 7	1966 (Dec.) Georgia 24, SMU 9	1990 Tennessee 31, Arkansas 27
1945 Oklahoma A&M 34, TCU 0	1968 (Jan.) Texas A&M 20, Alabama 16	1991 Miami (FL) 46, Texas 3
1946 Texas 40, Missouri 27	1969 Texas 36, Tennessee 13	1992 Florida St. 10, Texas A&M 2
1947 Arkansas 0, LSU 0	1970 Texas 21, Notre Dame 17	1993 Notre Dame 28, Texas A&M 3
1948 SMU 13, Penn St. 13	1971 Notre Dame 24, Texas 11	1994 Notre Dame 24, Texas A&M 21
1949 SMU 21, Oregon 13	1972 Penn St. 30, Texas 6	1995 USC. 55, Texas Tech 14
1950 Rice 27, North Carolina 13	1973 Texas 17, Alabama 13	1996 Colorado 38, Oregon 6
1951 Tennessee 20, Texas 14	1974 Nebraska 19, Texas 3	1997 Brigham Young 19, Kansas St. 15
1952 Kentucky 20, TCU 7	1975 Penn St. 41, Baylor 20	1998 UCLA 29, Texas A&M 23
1953 Texas 16, Tennessee 0	1976 Arkansas 31, Georgia 10	1999 Texas 38, Mississippi St. 11
1954 Rice 28, Alabama 6	1977 Houston 30, Maryland 21	2000 Arkansas 27, Texas 6
1955 Georgia Tech 14, Arkansas 6	1978 Notre Dame 38, Texas 10	2001 Kansas St. 35, Tennessee 21
1956 Mississippi 14, TCU 13	1979 Notre Dame 35, Houston 34	2002 Oklahoma 10, Arkansas 3
1957 TCU 28, Syracuse 27	1980 Houston 17, Nebraska 14	2003 Texas 35, LSU 20
1958 Navy 20, Rice 7	1981 Alabama 30, Baylor 2	2004 Mississippi 31, Oklahoma St. 28
1959 TCU 0, Air Force 0	1982 Texas 14, Alabama 12	

Sun Bowl, El Paso, TX (John Hancock Bowl, 1989-93)

1936 (Jan.) Hardin-Simmons 14, New Mexico St. 14	1958 (Dec.) Wyoming 14, Hardin-Simmons 6	1980 Nebraska 31, Mississippi St. 17
1937 Hardin-Simmons 34, Texas Mines 6	1959 New Mexico St. 28, N. Texas St. 8	1981 Oklahoma 40, Houston 14
1938 West Virginia 7, Texas Tech 6	1960 New Mexico St. 20, Utah St. 13	1982 North Carolina 26, Texas 10
1939 Utah 26, New Mexico 0	1961 Villanova 17, Wichita 9	1983 Alabama 28, SMU 7
1940 Catholic U. 0, Arizona St. 0	1962 West Texas St. 15, Ohio U. 14	1984 Maryland 28, Tennessee 27
1941 Western Reserve 26, Arizona St. 13	1963 Oregon 21, SMU 14	1985 Georgia 13, Arizona 13
1942 Tulsa 6, Texas Tech 0	1964 Georgia 7, Texas Tech 0	1986 Alabama 28, Washington 6
1943 2d Air Force 13, Hardin-Simmons 7	1965 Texas Western 13, TCU 12	1987 Oklahoma St. 35, West Virginia 33
1944 Southwestern (TX) 7, New Mexico 0	1966 Wyoming 28, Florida St. 20	1988 Alabama 29, Army 28
1945 Southwestern (TX) 35, Univ. of Mexico 0	1967 UTEP 14, Mississippi 7	1989 Pittsburgh 31, Texas A&M 28
1946 New Mexico 34, Denver 24	1968 Auburn 34, Arizona 10	1990 Michigan St. 17, USC 16
1947 Cincinnati 18, Virginia Tech 6	1969 Nebraska 45, Georgia 6	1991 UCLA 6, Illinois 3
1948 Miami (OH) 13, Texas Tech 12	1970 Georgia Tech. 17, Texas Tech 9	1992 Baylor 20, Arizona 15
1949 West Virginia 21, Texas Mines 12	1971 LSU 33, Iowa St. 15	1993 Oklahoma 41, Texas Tech 10
1950 Texas Western 33, Georgetown 20	1972 North Carolina 32, Texas Tech 28	1994 Texas 35, North Carolina 31
1951 West Texas St. 14, Cincinnati 13	1973 Missouri 34, Auburn 17	1995 Iowa 38, Washington 18
1952 Texas Tech 25, Pacific (CA) 14	1974 Mississippi St. 26, North Carolina 24	1996 Stanford 38, Michigan St. 0
1953 Pacific (CA) 26, S. Mississippi 7	1975 Pittsburgh 33, Kansas 19	1997 Arizona St. 17, Iowa 7
1954 Texas Western 37, S. Miss. 14	1977 (Jan.) Texas A&M 37, Florida 14	1998 TCU 28, USC 19
1955 Texas Western 47, Florida St. 20	1977 (Dec.) Stanford 24, LSU 14	1999 Oregon 24, Minnesota 20
1956 Wyoming 21, Texas Tech 14	1978 Texas 42, Maryland 0	2000 Wisconsin 21, UCLA 20
1957 Geo. Washington 13, TX Western 0	1979 Washington 14, Texas 7	2001 Washington St. 33, Purdue 27
1958 Louisville 34, Drake 20		2002 Purdue 34, Washington 24
		2003 Minnesota 31, Oregon 30

Fiesta Bowl, Tempe, AZ

1971 (Dec.) Arizona St. 45, Florida St. 38	1983 Arizona St. 32, Oklahoma 21	1994 Arizona 29, Miami (FL) 0
1972 Arizona St. 49, Missouri 35	1984 Ohio St. 28, Pittsburgh 23	1995 Colorado 41, Notre Dame 24
1973 Arizona St. 28, Pittsburgh 7	1985 UCLA 39, Miami (FL) 37	1996 Nebraska 62, Florida 24
1974 Okla. St. 16, Brigham Young 6	1986 Michigan 27, Nebraska 23	1997 Penn St. 38, Texas 15
1975 Arizona St. 17, Nebraska 14	1987 Penn St. 14, Miami (FL) 10	1997 (Dec.) Kansas St. 35, Syracuse 18
1976 Oklahoma 41, Wyoming 7	1988 Florida St. 31, Nebraska 28	1999 (Jan.) Tennessee 23, Florida St. 16
1977 Penn St. 42, Arizona St. 30	1989 Notre Dame 34, W. Virginia 21	2000 Nebraska 31, Tennessee 21
1978 UCLA 10, Arkansas 10	1990 Florida St. 41, Nebraska 17	2001 Oregon St. 41, Notre Dame 9
1979 Pittsburgh 16, Arizona 10	1991 Louisville 34, Alabama 7	2002 Oregon 38, Colorado 16
1980 Penn St. 31, Ohio St. 19	1992 Penn St. 42, Tennessee 17	2003 Ohio St. 31, Miami 24 (2 OT)
1982 (Jan.) Penn St. 26, USC 10	1993 Syracuse 26, Colorado 22	2004 Ohio St. 35, Kansas St. 28

Gator Bowl, Jacksonville, FL

1946 (Jan.) Wake Forest 26, S. Carolina 14	1965 (Dec.) GA Tech 31, Texas Tech 21	1985 Florida St. 34, Oklahoma St. 23
1947 Oklahoma 34, N. Carolina St. 13	1966 Tennessee 18, Syracuse 12	1986 Clemson 27, Stanford 21
1948 Maryland 20, Georgia 20	1967 Penn St. 17, Florida St. 17	1987 LSU 30, S. Carolina 13
1949 Clemson 24, Missouri 23	1968 Missouri 35, Alabama 10	1989 (Jan.) Georgia 34, Michigan St. 27
1950 Maryland 20, Missouri 7	1969 Florida 14, Tennessee 13	1989 (Dec.) Clemson 27, W. Virginia 7
1951 Wyoming 20, Washington & Lee 7	1971 (Jan.) Auburn 35, Mississippi 28	1991 (Jan.) Michigan 35, Mississippi 3
1952 Miami (FL) 14, Clemson 0	1971 (Dec.) Georgia 7, N. Carolina 3	1991 (Dec.) Oklahoma 48, Virginia 14
1953 Florida 14, Tulsa 13	1972 Auburn 24, Colorado 3	1992 Florida 27, N. Carolina St. 10
1954 Texas Tech 35, Auburn 13	1973 Texas Tech 28, Tennessee 19	1993 Alabama 24, N. Carolina 10
1954 (Dec.) Auburn 33, Baylor 13	1974 Auburn 27, Texas 3	1994 Tennessee 45, Virginia Tech 23
1955 Vanderbilt 25, Auburn 13	1975 Maryland 13, Florida 0	1996 (Jan.) Syracuse 41, Clemson 0
1956 Georgia Tech 21, Pittsburgh 14	1976 Notre Dame 20, Penn St. 9	1997 N. Carolina 20, W. Virginia 13
1957 Tennessee 3, Texas A&M 0	1977 Pittsburgh 34, Clemson 3	1998 N. Carolina 42, Virginia Tech 3
1958 Mississippi 7, Florida 3	1978 Clemson 17, Ohio St. 15	1999 Georgia Tech 35, Notre Dame 28
1960 (Jan.) Arkansas 14, Georgia Tech 7	1979 N. Carolina 17, Michigan 15	2000 Miami (FL) 28, Georgia Tech 13
1960 (Dec.) Florida 13, Baylor 12	1980 Pittsburgh 37, S. Carolina 9	2001 Virginia Tech 41, Clemson 20
1961 Penn St. 30, Georgia Tech 15	1981 N. Carolina 31, Arkansas 27	2002 Florida St. 30, Virginia Tech 17
1962 Florida 17, Penn St. 7	1982 Florida St. 31, West Virginia 12	2003 N. Carolina St. 28, Notre Dame 6
1963 N. Carolina 35, Air Force 0	1983 Florida 14, Iowa 6	2004 Maryland 41, West Virginia 7
1965 (Jan.) Florida St. 36, Okla.19	1984 Oklahoma St. 21, S. Carolina 14	

Liberty Bowl, Memphis, TN

1959 (Dec.) Penn St. 7, Alabama 0	1974 Tennessee 7, Maryland 3	1989 Mississippi 42, Air Force 29
1960 Penn St. 41, Oregon 12	1975 USC 20, Texas A&M 0	1990 Air Force 23, Ohio St. 11
1961 Syracuse 15, Miami (FL) 14	1976 Alabama 36, UCLA 6	1991 Air Force 38, Mississippi St. 15
1962 Oregon St. 6, Villanova 0	1977 Nebraska 21, N. Carolina 17	1992 Mississippi 13, Air Force 0
1963 Mississippi St. 16, N. Carolina St. 12	1978 Missouri 20, LSU 15	1993 Louisville 18, Michigan St. 7
1964 Utah 32, West Virginia 6	1979 Penn St. 9, Tulane 6	1994 Illinois 30, East Carolina 0
1965 Mississippi 13, Auburn 7	1980 Purdue 28, Missouri 25	1995 East Carolina 19, Stanford 13
1966 Miami (FL) 14, Virginia Tech 7	1981 Ohio St. 31, Navy 28	1996 Syracuse 30, Houston 17
1967 N. Carolina St. 14, Georgia 7	1982 Alabama 21, Illinois 15	1997 So. Mississippi 41, Pittsburgh 7
1968 Mississippi 34, Virginia Tech 17	1983 Notre Dame 19, Boston Coll. 18	1998 Tulane 41, Brigham Young 27
1969 Colorado 47, Alabama 33	1984 Auburn 21, Arkansas 15	1999 So. Mississippi 23, Colorado St. 17
1970 Tulane 17, Colorado 3	1985 Baylor 21, LSU 7	2000 Colorado St. 22, Louisville 17
1971 Tennessee 14, Arkansas 13	1986 Tennessee 21, Minnesota 14	2001 Louisville 28, BYU 10
1972 Georgia Tech 31, Iowa St. 30	1987 Georgia 20, Arkansas 17	2002 TCU 17, Colorado St. 3
1973 N. Carolina St. 31, Kansas 18	1988 Indiana 34, S. Carolina 10	2003 Utah 17, So. Mississippi 0

Capital One Bowl, Orlando, FL
(Florida Citrus Bowl 1984-2002, Tangerine Bowl, 1947-1983)

1947 (Jan.) Catawba 31, Maryville 6	1964 E. Carolina 14, Massachusetts 13	1984 Georgia 17, Florida St. 17
1948 Catawba 7, Marshall 0	1965 E. Carolina 31, Maine 0	1985 Ohio St. 10, Brigham Young 7
1949 Murray St. 21, Sul Ross St. 21	1966 Morgan St. 14, West Chester 6	1987 (Jan.) Auburn 16, USC 7
1950 St. Vincent 7, Emory & Henry 6	1967 Tenn.-Martin 25, West Chester 8	1988 Clemson 35, Penn St. 10
1951 Morris Harvey 35, Emory & Henry 14	1968 Richmond 49, Ohio U. 42	1989 Clemson 13, Oklahoma 6
1952 Stetson 35, Arkansas St. 20	1969 Toledo 56, Davidson 33	1990 Illinois 31, Virginia 21
1953 East Texas St. 33, Tenn. Tech 0	1970 Toledo 40, William & Mary 12	1991 Georgia Tech 45, Nebraska 21
1954 East Texas St. 7, Arkansas St. 7	1971 Toledo 28, Richmond 3	1992 California 37, Clemson 13
1955 Neb.-Omaha 7, E. Kentucky 6	1972 Tampa 21, Kent St. 18	1993 Georgia 21, Ohio St. 14
1956 Juniata 6, Missouri Valley 6	1973 Miami (OH) 16, Florida 7	1994 Penn St. 31, Tennessee 13
1957 West Texas St. 20, So. Miss. 13	1974 Miami (OH) 21, Georgia 10	1995 Alabama 24, Ohio St. 17
1958 East Texas St. 10, So. Miss. 9	1975 Miami (OH) 20, S. Carolina 7	1996 Tennessee 20, Ohio St. 14
1958 (Dec.) East Texas St. 26,	1976 Okla. St. 49, Brigham Young 21	1997 Tennessee 48, Northwestern 28
Missouri Valley 7	1977 Florida St. 40, Texas Tech 17	1998 Florida 21, Penn St. 6
1960 (Jan.) Middle Tennessee 21,	1978 N. Carolina St. 30, Pittsburgh 17	1999 Michigan 45, Arkansas 31
Presbyterian 12	1979 LSU 34, Wake Forest 10	2000 Michigan St. 37, Florida 34
1960 (Dec.) Citadel 27, Tenn. Tech 0	1980 Florida 35, Maryland 20	2001 Michigan 31, Auburn 28
1961 Lamar 21, Middle Tennessee 14	1981 Missouri 19, So. Mississippi 17	2002 Tennessee 45, Michigan 17
1962 Houston 49, Miami (OH) 21	1982 Auburn 33, Boston College 26	2003 Auburn 13, Penn St. 9
1963 Western Ky. 27, Coast Guard 0	1983 Tennessee 30, Maryland 23	2004 Georgia 34, Purdue 27 (OT)

Peach Bowl, Atlanta, GA

1968 (Dec.) LSU 31, Florida St. 27	1981 (Jan.) Miami (FL) 20, Virginia Tech 10	1993 N. Carolina 21, Mississippi St. 17
1969 W. Virginia 14, S. Carolina 3	1981 (Dec.) W. Virginia 26, Florida 6	1993 (Dec.) Clemson 14, Kentucky 13
1970 Arizona St. 48, N. Carolina 26	1982 Iowa 28, Tennessee 22	1995 (Jan.) N. Carolina St. 28, Miss. St. 24
1971 Mississippi 41, Georgia Tech 18	1983 Florida St. 28, N. Carolina 3	1995 (Dec.) Virginia 34, Georgia 27
1972 N. Carolina St. 49, W. Virginia 13	1984 Virginia 27, Purdue 22	1996 LSU 10, Clemson 7
1973 Georgia 17, Maryland 16	1985 Army 31, Illinois 29	1998 (Jan.) Auburn 21, Clemson 17
1974 Vanderbilt 6, Texas Tech 6	1986 Va. Tech 25, N. Carolina St. 24	1998 (Dec.) Georgia 35, Virginia 33
1975 W. Virginia 13, N. Carolina St. 10	1988 (Jan.) Tennessee 28, Indiana 22	1999 Mississippi St. 27, Clemson 7
1976 Kentucky 21, N. Carolina 0	1988 (Dec.) N. Carolina St. 28, Iowa 23	2000 LSU 28, Georgia Tech 14
1977 N. Carolina St. 24, Iowa St. 14	1989 Syracuse 19, Georgia 18	2001 North Carolina 16, Auburn 10
1978 Purdue 41, Georgia Tech. 21	1990 Auburn 27, Indiana 23	2002 Maryland 30, Tennessee 3
1979 Baylor 24, Clemson 18	1992 (Jan.) E. Carolina 37, NC St. 34	2003 Clemson 27, Tennessee 14

Other Bowl Results, Late 2003 - Early 2004

Alamo Bowl, San Antonio, TX: Nebraska 17, Michigan St. 3
Continental Tire Bowl, Charlotte, NC: Virginia 23, Pittsburgh 16
Fort Worth (Texas) Bowl, Ft. Worth, TX: Boise St. 34, TCU 31
GMAC Bowl, Mobile, AL: Miami (OH) 49, Louisville 28
Hawaii Bowl, Honolulu, HI: Hawaii 54, Houston 48 (3 OT)
Holiday Bowl, San Diego, CA: Washington St. 28, Texas 20
Houston Bowl, Houston, TX: Texas Tech 38, Navy 14
Humanitarian Bowl, Boise, ID: Georgia Tech 52, Tulsa 10
Independence Bowl, Shreveport, LA: Arkansas 27, Missouri 14
Insight.com Bowl, Phoenix, AZ.: California 52, Virginia Tech 49

Las Vegas Bowl, Las Vegas, NV: Oregon St. 55, New Mexico 14
Motor City Bowl, Pontiac, MI: Bowling Green 28, Northwestern 24
Music City Bowl, Nashville, TN: Auburn 28, Wisconsin 14
New Orleans Bowl, New Orleans, LA: Memphis 27, North Texas 17
Outback Bowl, Tampa, FL: Iowa 37, Florida 17
San Francisco Bowl, San Francisco, CA: Boston College 35, Colorado St. 21
Silicon Valley Classic, San Jose, CA: Fresno St. 17, UCLA 9
Tangerine Bowl, Orlando, FL: NC State 56, Kansas 26

All-Time NCAA Division I-A Statistical Leaders

(At end of 2003 season. Prior to 2002, postseason games were not included in NCAA final football statistics or records. Beginning with the 2002 season, all postseason games were included.)

Career Rushing Yards

Player, team	Yrs	Carries	Yds	Avg
Ron Dayne, Wisconsin	1996-99	1,115	6,397	5.74
Ricky Williams, Texas	1995-98	1,011	6,279	6.21
Tony Dorsett, Pittsburgh	1973-76	1,074	6,082	5.66
Charles White, USC	1976-79	1,023	5,598	5.47
Travis Prentice, Miami (OH)	1996-99	1,138	5,596	4.92

Career Passing Yards

Player, team	Yrs	Comp/Att	Yds
Ty Detmer, BYU	1988-91	958/1,530	15,031
Tim Rattay, Louisiana Tech	1997-99	1,015/1,552	12,746
Chris Redman, Louisville	1996-99	1,031/1,679	12,541
Kliff Kingsbury, Texas Tech	1999-02	1,231/1,883	12,429
Todd Santos, San Diego St.	1984-87	910/1,484	11,425

Career Rushing Yard/Game (min. 2,500 yds.)

Player, team	Yrs	Carries	Yds	Avg/Game
Ed Marinaro, Cornell	1969-71	918	4,715	174.6
O.J. Simpson, USC	1967-68	621	3,124	164.4
Herschel Walker, Georgia	1980-82	994	5,259	159.4
LeShon Johnson, N. Illinois	1992-93	592	3,314	150.6
Ron Dayne, Wisconsin	1996-99	1,115	6,397	148.8

Career Receiving Yards

Player, team	Yrs	Rec	Yds	Avg
Trevor Insley, Nevada	1996-99	298	5,005	16.8
Marcus Harris, Wyoming	1993-96	259	4,518	17.4
Ryan Yarborough, Wyoming	1990-93	229	4,357	19.0
Troy Edwards, Louisiana Tech	1996-98	280	4,352	15.5
Aaron Turner, Pacific (CA)	1989-92	266	4,345	16.3

Selected College Division I Football Teams in 2003

(W-L records in last column are for 2003 season and records include bowl games and Division I-AA playoff games; coaches listed are as of the start of 2004 season)

Team	Nickname	Team colors	Conference	Coach	(W-L)
Air Force	Falcons	Blue & silver	Mountain West	Fisher DeBerry	7-5
Akron	Zips	Blue & gold	Mid-American	J.D. Brookhart	7-5
Alabama	Crimson Tide	Crimson & white	Southeastern	Mike Shula	4-9
Arizona	Wildcats	Cardinal & navy	Pacific Ten	Mike Stoops	2-10
Arizona State	Sun Devils	Maroon & gold	Pacific Ten	Dirk Koetter	5-7
Arkansas	Razorbacks	Cardinal & white	Southeastern	Houston Nutt	9-4
Arkansas State	Indians	Scarlet & black	Sun Belt	Steve Roberts	5-7
Army	Cadets, Black Knights	Black, gold, gray	Conference USA	Bobby Ross	0-13
Auburn	Tigers	Burnt orange & navy	Southeastern	Tommy Tuberville	8-5
Ball State	Cardinals	Cardinal & white	Mid-American	Brady Hoke	4-8
Baylor	Bears	Green & gold	Big Twelve	Guy Morriss	3-9
Boise State	Broncos	Blue & orange	Western Athletic	Dan Hawkins	13-1
Boston College	Eagles	Maroon & gold	Big East	Tom O'Brien	8-5
Bowling Green	Falcons	Orange & brown	Mid-American	Gregg Brandon	11-3
Brigham Young (BYU)	Cougars	Royal blue, white, tan	Mountain West	Gary Crowton	4-8
Brown	Bears	Brown, cardinal, white	Ivy League	Phil Estes	5-5
California	Golden Bears	Blue & gold	Pacific Ten	Jeff Tedford	8-6
Central Michigan	Chippewas	Maroon & gold	Mid-American	Brian Kelly	3-9
Cincinnati	Bearcats	Red & black	Conference USA	Mike Dantonio	5-7
Citadel	Bulldogs	Blue & white	Southern	John Zernhelt	6-6
Clemson	Tigers	Purple & orange	Atlantic Coast	Tommy Bowden	9-4
Colgate	Red Raiders	Maroon, gray, & white	Patriot League	Dick Biddle	15-1
Colorado	Buffaloes	Silver, gold, & black	Big Twelve	Gary Barnett	5-7
Colorado State	Rams	Green & gold	Mountain West	Sonny Lubick	7-6
Columbia	Lions	Columbia blue & white	Ivy League	Bob Shoop	4-6
Connecticut	Huskies	Blue & white	Independent	Randy Edsall	9-3
Cornell	Big Red	Carnelian & white	Ivy League	Jim Knowles	1-9
Dartmouth	Big Green	Dartmouth green & white	Ivy League	John Lyons	5-5
Delaware	Fightin' Blue Hens	Blue & gold	Atlantic Ten	K.C. Keeler	15-1
Delaware State	Hornets	Red & blue	Mid-Eastern Athletic	Alton Lavan	1-10
Duke	Blue Devils	Royal blue & white	Atlantic Coast	Ted Roof	4-8
East Carolina	Pirates	Purple & gold	Conference USA	John Thompson	1-11
Eastern Illinois	Panthers	Blue & gray	Ohio Valley	Bob Spoo	4-8
Eastern Kentucky	Colonels	Maroon & white	Ohio Valley	Danny Hope	7-5
Eastern Michigan	Eagles	Dark green & white	Mid-American	Jeff Genyk	3-9
Eastern Washington	Eagles	Red & white	Big Sky	Paul Wulff	6-5
Florida	Gators	Orange & blue	Southeastern	Ron Zook	8-5
Florida A&M	Rattlers	Orange & green	Mid-Eastern Athletic	Billy Joe	6-6
Florida State	Seminoles	Garnet & gold	Atlantic Coast	Bobby Bowden	10-3
Fresno State	Bulldogs	Cardinal & blue	Western Athletic	Pat Hill	9-5
Furman	Paladins	Purple & white	Southern	Bobby Lamb	6-5
Georgia	Bulldogs	Red & black	Southeastern	Mark Richt	11-3
Georgia Southern	Eagles	Blue & white	Southern	Mike Sewak	7-4
Georgia Tech	Yellow Jackets	Old gold & white	Atlantic Coast	Chan Gailey	7-6
Grambling State	Tigers	Black & gold	Southwestern Athletic	Melvin Spears	9-3
Harvard	Crimson	Crimson, black, white	Ivy League	Tim Murphy	7-3
Hawaii	Warriors	Green, black, white, silver	Western Athletic	June Jones	9-5
Holy Cross	Crusaders	Royal purple	Patriot League	Tom Gilmore	1-11
Houston	Cougars	Scarlet & white	Conference USA	Art Brilesl	7-6
Howard	Bison	Blue, white & red	Mid-Eastern Athletic	Rayford Petty	4-7
Idaho	Vandals	Silver & gold	Sun Belt	Nick Holt	3-9
Idaho State	Bengals	Orange & black	Big Sky	Larry Lewis	8-4

Team	Nickname	Team colors	Conference	Coach	(W-L)
Illinois	Fighting Illini	Orange & blue	Big Ten	Ron Turner	1-11
Illinois State	Redbirds	Red & white	Gateway	Denver Johnson	6-6
Indiana	Hoosiers	Cream & crimson	Big Ten	Gerry DiNardo	2-10
Indiana State	Sycamores	Blue & white	Gateway	Tim McGuire	3-9
Iowa	Hawkeyes	Old gold & black	Big Ten	Kirk Ferentz	10-3
Iowa State	Cyclones	Cardinal & gold	Big Twelve	Dan McCarney	2-10
Jackson State	Tigers	Blue & white	Southwestern Athletic	James Bell	2-10
James Madison	Dukes	Purple & gold	Atlantic Ten	Mickey Matthews	6-6
Kansas	Jayhawks	Crimson & blue	Big Twelve	Mark Mangino	6-7
Kansas State	Wildcats	Purple & white	Big Twelve	Bill Snyder	11-4
Kent State	Golden Flashes	Navy blue & gold	Mid-American	Doug Martin	5-7
Kentucky	Wildcats	Blue & white	Southeastern	Rich Brooks	4-8
Lafayette	Leopards	Maroon & white	Patriot League	Frank Tavani	5-6
Lehigh	Mountain Hawks	Brown & white	Patriot League	Pete Lembo	8-3
Liberty	Flames	Red, white, blue	Big South	Ken Karcher	6-6
Louisiana-Lafayette	Ragin' Cajuns	Vermilion & white	Sun Belt	Rickey Bustle	4-8
Louisiana-Monroe	Indians	Maroon & gold	Sun Belt	Charlie Weatherbie	1-11
Louisiana State (LSU)	Fighting Tigers	Purple & gold	Southeastern	Nick Saban	13-1
Louisiana Tech	Bulldogs	Red & blue	Western Athletic	Jack Bicknell III	5-7
Louisville	Cardinals	Red, black, white	Conference USA	Bobby Petrino	9-4
Maine	Black Bears	Blue & white	Atlantic Ten	Jack Cosgrove	6-5
Marshall	Thundering Herd	Green & white	Mid-American	Bob Pruett	8-4
Maryland	Terrapins	Red, white, black, gold	Atlantic Coast	Ralph Friedgen	10-3
Massachusetts	Minutemen	Maroon & white	Atlantic Ten	Don Brown	10-3
McNeese State	Cowboys	Blue & gold	Southland	Tommy Tate	10-2
Memphis	Tigers	Blue & gray	Conference USA	Tommy West	9-4
Miami (Florida)	Hurricanes	Orange, green, white	Big East	Larry Coker	11-2
Miami (Ohio)	RedHawks	Red & white	Mid-American	Terry Hoeppner	13-1
Michigan	Wolverines	Maize & blue	Big Ten	Lloyd Carr	10-3
Michigan State	Spartans	Green & white	Big Ten	John L. Smith	8-5
Middle Tennessee State	Blue Raiders	Blue & white	Sun Belt	Andy McCollum	4-8
Minnesota	Golden Gophers	Maroon & gold	Big Ten	Glen Mason	10-3
Mississippi	Rebels	Cardinal red & navy	Southeastern	David Cutcliffe	10-3
Mississippi State	Bulldogs	Maroon & white	Southeastern	Sylvester Croom	2-10
Mississippi Valley State	Delta Devils	Green & white	Southwestern Athletic	Willie Totten	2-9
Missouri	Tigers	Old gold & black	Big Twelve	Gary Pinkel	8-5
Montana	Grizzlies	Copper, silver, gold	Big Sky	Bobby Hauck	9-4
Montana State	Bobcats	Blue & gold	Big Sky	Mike Kramer	7-6
Morehead State	Eagles	Blue & gold	Pioneer	Matt Ballard	8-3
Morgan State	Bears	Blue & orange	Mid-Eastern Athletic	Donald Hill-Eleyl	6-5
Murray State	Racers	Blue & gold	Ohio Valley	Joe Pannunzio	4-8
Navy	Midshipmen	Navy blue & gold	Independent	Paul Johnson	8-5
Nebraska	Cornhuskers	Scarlet & cream	Big Twelve	Bill Callahan	10-3
Nevada	Wolf Pack	Silver & blue	Western Athletic	Chris Ault	6-6
Nev.-Las Vegas (UNLV)	Runnin' Rebels	Scarlet & gray	Mountain West	John Robinson	6-6
New Hampshire	Wildcats	Blue & white	Atlantic Ten	Sean McDonnell	5-7
New Mexico	Lobos	Cherry & silver	Mountain West	Rocky Long	8-5
New Mexico State	Aggies	Crimson & white	Sun Belt	Tony Samuel	3-9
Nicholls State	Colonels	Red & gray	Southland	Jay Thomas	5-6
North Carolina	Tar Heels	Carolina blue & white	Atlantic Coast	John Bunting	2-10
North Carolina A & T	Aggies	Blue & gold	Mid-Eastern Athletic	George Small	10-3
North Carolina State	Wolfpack	Red & white	Atlantic Coast	Chuck Amato	8-5
North Texas	Mean Green	Green & white	Sun Belt	Darrell Dickey	9-4
Northeastern	Huskies	Red & black	Atlantic Ten	Rocky Hager	8-4
Northern Arizona	Lumberjacks	Blue & gold	Big Sky	Jerome Souers	9-4
Northern Illinois	Huskies	Cardinal & black	Mid-American	Joe Novak	10-2
Northern Iowa	Panthers	Purple & old gold	Gateway	Mark Farley	10-3
Northwestern	Wildcats	Purple & white	Big Ten	Randy Walker	6-7
Northwestern State	Demons	Purple, white, & orange	Southland	Scott Stoker	6-6
Notre Dame	Fighting Irish	Gold & blue	Independent	Tyrone Willingham	5-7
Ohio	Bobcats	Hunter green & white	Mid-American	Brian Knorr	2-10
Ohio State	Buckeyes	Scarlet & gray	Big Ten	Jim Tressel	11-2
Oklahoma	Sooners	Crimson & cream	Big Twelve	Bob Stoops	12-2
Oklahoma State	Cowboys	Orange & black	Big Twelve	Les Miles	9-4
Oregon	Ducks	Green & yellow	Pacific Ten	Mike Bellotti	8-5
Oregon State	Beavers	Orange & black	Pacific Ten	Mike Riley	8-5
Penn State	Nittany Lions	Blue & white	Big Ten	Joe Paterno	3-9
Pennsylvania	Quakers	Red & blue	Ivy League	Al Bagnoli	10-0
Pittsburgh	Panthers	Blue & gold	Big East	Walt Harris	8-5
Princeton	Tigers	Orange & black	Ivy League	Roger Hughes	2-8
Purdue	Boilermakers	Old gold & black	Big Ten	Joe Tiller	9-4
Rhode Island	Rams	Light & dark blue, white	Atlantic Ten	Tim Stowers	4-8
Rice	Owls	Blue & gray	Western Athletic	Ken Hatfield	5-7
Richmond	Spiders	Red & white	Atlantic Ten	Dave Clawson	2-9
Rutgers	Scarlet Knights	Scarlet	Big East	Greg Schiano	5-7
Sam Houston State	Bearkats	Orange & white	Southland	Ron Randleman	2-9
Samford	Bulldogs	Crimson & blue	Ohio Valley	Bill Gray	7-4
San Diego State	Aztecs	Scarlet & black	Mountain West	Tom Craft	6-6
San Jose State	Spartans	Gold, white, blue	Western Athletic	Fitz Hill	3-8
South Carolina	Gamecocks	Garnet & black	Southeastern	Lou Holtz	5-7
South Carolina State	Bulldogs	Garnet & blue	Mid-Eastern Athletic	Oliver Pough	8-4
SE Missouri State	Indians	Red & white	Ohio Valley	Tim Billings	5-7
Southern California (USC)	Trojans	Cardinal & gold	Pacific Ten	Pete Carroll	12-1
Southern Illinois	Salukis	Maroon & white	Gateway	Jerry Kill	10-2
Southern Methodist (SMU)	Mustangs	Red & blue	Western Athletic	Phil Bennett	0-12
Southern Mississippi	Golden Eagles	Black & gold	Conference USA	Jeff Bower	9-4
SW Missouri State	Bears	Maroon & white	Gateway	Randy Ball	4-7
Stanford	Cardinal	Cardinal & white	Pacific Ten	Buddy Teevens	4-7
Stephen F. Austin	Lumberjacks	Purple & white	Southland	Mike Santiago	7-4
Syracuse	Orange	Orange	Big East	Paul Pasqualoni	6-6
Temple	Owls	Cherry & white	Big East	Bobby Wallace	1-11

Team	Nickname	Team colors	Conference	Coach	(W-L)
Tennessee	Volunteers	Orange & white	Southeastern	Phillip Fulmer	10-3
Tennessee-Chattanooga	Mocs	Navy blue & gold	Southern	Rodney Allison	3-9
Tennessee-Martin	Skyhawks	Orange, white, blue	Ohio Valley	Matt Griffin	2-10
Tennessee State	Tigers	Royal blue & white	Ohio Valley	James Reese III	7-5
Tennessee Tech	Golden Eagles	Purple & gold	Ohio Valley	Mike Hennigan	2-9
Texas	Longhorns	Burnt orange & white	Big Twelve	Mack Brown	10-3
Texas A & M	Aggies	Maroon & white	Big Twelve	Dennis Franchione	4-8
Texas Christian (TCU)	Horned Frogs	Purple & white	Western Athletic	Gary Patterson	11-2
Texas Southern	Tigers	Maroon & gray	Southwestern Athletic	Steve Wilson	5-6
Texas State	Bobcats	Maroon & gold	Southland	David Bailiff	4-8
Texas Tech	Red Raiders	Scarlet & black	Big Twelve	Mike Leach	8-5
Toledo	Rockets	Blue & gold	Mid-American	Tom Amstutz	8-4
Troy State	Trojans	Cardinal & black	Independent	Larry Blakeney	6-6
Tulane	Green Wave	Olive green & sky blue	Conference USA	Chris Scelfo	5-7
Tulsa	Golden Hurricane	Blue, gold, crimson	Western Athletic	Steve Kragthorpe	8-5
UCLA	Bruins	Blue & gold	Pacific Ten	Karl Dorrell	6-7
Utah	Utes	Crimson & white	Mountain West	Urban Meyer	10-2
Utah State	Aggies	Navy blue & white	Sun Belt	Mick Dennehy	3-9
UTEP (Texas-El Paso)	Miners	Orange, blue, silver	Western Athletic	Mike Price	2-11
Vanderbilt	Commodores	Black & gold	Southeastern	Bobby Johnson	2-10
Villanova	Wildcats	Blue & white	Atlantic Ten	Andy Talley	7-4
Virginia	Cavaliers	Burnt orange & blue	Atlantic Coast	Al Groh	8-5
Virginia Military Inst. (VMI)	Keydets	Red, white, yellow	Big South	Cal McCombs	6-6
Virginia Tech	Hokies	Burnt orange & maroon	Big East	Frank Beamer	8-5
Wake Forest	Demon Deacons	Old gold & black	Atlantic Coast	Jim Grobe	5-7
Washington	Huskies	Purple & gold	Pacific Ten	Keith Gilbertson	6-6
Washington State	Cougars	Crimson & gray	Pacific Ten	Bill Doba	10-3
Weber State	Wildcats	Royal purple & white	Big Sky	Jerry Graybeal	8-4
West Virginia	Mountaineers	Old gold & blue	Big East	Rich Rodriquez	8-5
Western Carolina	Catamounts	Purple & gold	Southern	Kent Briggs	5-7
Western Illinois	Leathernecks	Purple & gold	Gateway	Don Patterson	9-4
Western Kentucky	Hilltoppers	Red & white	Gateway	David Elson	9-4
Western Michigan	Broncos	Brown & gold	Mid-American	Gary Darnell	5-7
William & Mary	Tribe	Green, gold, silver	Atlantic Ten	Jimmye Laycock	5-5
Wisconsin	Badgers	Cardinal & white	Big Ten	Barry Alvarez	7-6
Wyoming	Cowboys	Brown & gold	Mountain West	Joe Glenn	4-8
Yale	Bulldogs, Elis	Yale blue & white	Ivy League	Jack Siedlecki	6-4
Youngstown State	Penguins	Red & white	Gateway	Jon Heacock	5-7

Heisman Trophy Winners

Awarded annually to the nation's outstanding college football player by the Downtown Athletic Club.

> **Note:** To read more about Heisman Trophy winners in later life, see page 978.

1935 Jay Berwanger, Chicago, HB	1958 Pete Dawkins, Army, HB	1981 Marcus Allen, USC, RB
1936 Larry Kelley, Yale, E	1959 Billy Cannon, LSU, HB	1982 Herschel Walker, Georgia, RB
1937 Clinton Frank, Yale, HB	1960 Joe Bellino, Navy, HB	1983 Mike Rozier, Nebraska, RB
1938 David O'Brien, Texas Christian, QB	1961 Ernest Davis, Syracuse, HB	1984 Doug Flutie, Boston College, QB
1939 Nile Kinnick, Iowa, HB	1962 Terry Baker, Oregon St., QB	1985 Bo Jackson, Auburn, RB
1940 Tom Harmon, Michigan, HB	1963 Roger Staubach, Navy, QB	1986 Vinny Testaverde, Miami, QB
1941 Bruce Smith, Minnesota, HB	1964 John Huarte, Notre Dame, QB	1987 Tim Brown, Notre Dame, WR
1942 Frank Sinkwich, Georgia, HB	1965 Mike Garrett, USC, HB	1988 Barry Sanders, Oklahoma St., RB
1943 Angelo Bertelli, Notre Dame, QB	1966 Steve Spurrier, Florida, QB	1989 Andre Ware, Houston, QB
1944 Leslie Horvath, Ohio St., QB	1967 Gary Beban, UCLA, QB	1990 Ty Detmer, BYU, QB
1945 Felix Blanchard, Army, FB	1968 O. J. Simpson, USC, RB	1991 Desmond Howard, Michigan, WR
1946 Glenn Davis, Army, HB	1969 Steve Owens, Oklahoma, RB	1992 Gino Torretta, Miami, QB
1947 John Lujack, Notre Dame, QB	1970 Jim Plunkett, Stanford, QB	1993 Charlie Ward, Florida St., QB
1948 Doak Walker, SMU, HB	1971 Pat Sullivan, Auburn, QB	1994 Rashaan Salaam, Colorado, RB
1949 Leon Hart, Notre Dame, E	1972 Johnny Rodgers, Nebraska, RB-WR	1995 Eddie George, Ohio St., RB
1950 Vic Janowicz, Ohio St., HB	1973 John Cappelletti, Penn St., RB	1996 Danny Wuerffel, Florida, QB
1951 Richard Kazmaier, Princeton, HB	1974 Archie Griffin, Ohio St., RB	1997 Charles Woodson, Michigan, CB
1952 Billy Vessels, Oklahoma, HB	1975 Archie Griffin, Ohio St., RB	1998 Ricky Williams, Texas, RB
1953 John Lattner, Notre Dame, HB	1976 Tony Dorsett, Pittsburgh, RB	1999 Ron Dayne, Wisconsin, RB
1954 Alan Ameche, Wisconsin, FB	1977 Earl Campbell, Texas, RB	2000 Chris Weinke, Florida St., QB
1955 Howard Cassady, Ohio St., HB	1978 Billy Sims, Oklahoma, RB	2001 Eric Crouch, Nebraska, QB
1956 Paul Hornung, Notre Dame, QB	1979 Charles White, USC, RB	2002 Carson Palmer, USC, QB
1957 John Crow, Texas A & M, HB	1980 George Rogers, S. Carolina, RB	2003 Jason White, Oklahoma, QB

Outland Award Winners

Honoring the outstanding interior lineman selected by the Football Writers Association of America.

1946 George Connor, Notre Dame, T	1966 Loyd Phillips, Arkansas, T	1985 Mike Ruth, Boston College, NG
1947 Joe Steffy, Army, G	1967 Ron Yary, Southern Cal, T	1986 Jason Buck, BYU, DT
1948 Bill Fischer, Notre Dame, G	1968 Bill Stanfill, Georgia, T	1987 Chad Hennings, Air Force, DT
1949 Ed Bagdon, Michigan St., G	1969 Mike Reid, Penn St., DT	1988 Tracy Rocker, Auburn, DT
1950 Bob Gain, Kentucky, T	1970 Jim Stillwagon, Ohio St., MG	1989 Mohammed Elewonibi, BYU, G
1951 Jim Weatherall, Oklahoma, T	1971 Larry Jacobson, Nebraska, DT	1990 Russell Maryland, Miami (FL), DT
1952 Dick Modzelewski, Maryland, T	1972 Rich Glover, Nebraska, MG	1991 Steve Emtman, Washington, DT
1953 J. D. Roberts, Oklahoma, G	1973 John Hicks, Ohio St., OT	1992 Will Shields, Nebraska, G
1954 Bill Brooks, Arkansas, G	1974 Randy White, Maryland, DE	1993 Rob Waldrop, Arizona, NG
1955 Calvin Jones, Iowa, G	1975 Lee Roy Selmon, Oklahoma, DT	1994 Zach Wiegert, Nebraska, OT
1956 Jim Parker, Ohio St., G	1976 Ross Browner, Notre Dame, DE	1995 Jonathan Ogden, UCLA, OT
1957 Alex Karras, Iowa, T	1977 Brad Shearer, Texas, DT	1996 Orlando Pace, Ohio St., OT
1958 Zeke Smith, Auburn, G	1978 Greg Roberts, Oklahoma, G	1997 Aaron Taylor, Nebraska, OT
1959 Mike McGee, Duke, T	1979 Jim Ritcher, North Carolina St., C	1998 Kris Farris, UCLA, OT
1960 Tom Brown, Minnesota, G	1980 Mark May, Pittsburgh, OT	1999 Chris Samuels, Alabama, OT
1961 Merlin Olsen, Utah St., T	1981 Dave Rimington, Nebraska, C	2000 John Henderson, Tennessee, DT
1962 Bobby Bell, Minnesota, T	1982 Dave Rimington, Nebraska, C	2001 Bryant McKinnie, Miami (FL), OT
1963 Scott Appleton, Texas, T	1983 Dean Steinkuhler, Nebraska, G	2002 Rien Long, Washington St., DT
1964 Steve Delong, Tennessee, T	1984 Bruce Smith, Virginia Tech, DT	2003 Robert Gallery, Iowa (OT)
1965 Tommy Nobis, Texas, G		

All-Time Team Won-Lost Records*

	Years	Won	Lost	Tied	Pct.	Total		Years	Won	Lost	Tied	Pct.	Total
Notre Dame	115	796	257	42	.746	1,095	South Fla (2000)	7	51	26	0	.662	77
Michigan	124	833	272	36	.746	1,141	Miami (Ohio)	115	624	343	44	.639	1,011
Alabama	109	758	293	43	.713	1,094	Georgia	110	673	370	54	.638	1,097
Oklahoma	109	737	284	53	.711	1,074	Washington	114	638	353	50	.637	1,041
Ohio St.	114	756	294	53	.709	1,103	Miami (Fla)	77	507	285	19	.637	811
Texas	111	776	309	33	.709	1,118	LSU	110	649	369	47	.631	1,065
Nebraska	114	781	311	40	.708	1,132	Auburn	111	634	379	47	.620	1,060
Tennessee	107	736	303	53	.698	1,092	Arizona St.	91	507	310	24	.617	841
Southern California	111	707	297	54	.694	1,058	Florida	97	590	359	40	.617	989
Penn St.	117	756	331	41	.688	1,128	Colorado	114	635	391	36	.615	1,062
Boise St (1996)	36	284	135	2	.677	421	Central Michigan	103	522	326	36	.611	884
Florida St.	57	419	197	17	.675	633	Texas A&M	109	627	404	48	.603	1,079
							Syracuse	114	658	428	49	.601	1,135

*Includes records as senior college only. Bowl and playoff games are included, and each tie game is computed as half won and half lost. Teams listed with years in parentheses indicates reclassification to Division I-A. The year in parentheses is the first year of Division I-A membership. Tiebreaker rule began with 1996 season.

College Football Coach of the Year

The Division I-A Coach of the Year has been selected by the American Football Coaches Assn. since 1935 and selected by the Football Writers Assn. of America since 1957. When polls disagree, both winners are indicated.

1935 Lynn Waldorf, Northwestern
1936 Dick Harlow, Harvard
1937 Edward Mylin, Lafayette
1938 Bill Kern, Carnegie Tech
1939 Eddie Anderson, Iowa
1940 Clark Shaughnessy, Stanford
1941 Frank Leahy, Notre Dame
1942 Bill Alexander, Georgia Tech
1943 Amos Alonzo Stagg, Pacific
1944 Carroll Widdoes, Ohio St.
1945 Bo McMillin, Indiana
1946 Earl "Red" Blaik, Army
1947 Fritz Crisler, Michigan
1948 Bennie Oosterbaan, Michigan
1949 Bud Wilkinson, Oklahoma
1950 Charlie Caldwell, Princeton
1951 Chuck Taylor, Stanford
1952 Biggie Munn, Michigan St.
1953 Jim Tatum, Maryland
1954 Henry "Red" Sanders, UCLA
1955 Duffy Daugherty, Michigan St.
1956 Bowden Wyatt, Tennessee
1957 Woody Hayes, Ohio St.
1958 Paul Dietzel, LSU
1959 Ben Schwartzwalder, Syracuse
1960 Murray Warmath, Minnesota
1961 Paul "Bear" Bryant, Ala. (AFCA); Darrell Royal, Texas (FWAA)
1962 John McKay, USC
1963 Darrell Royal, Texas

1964 Ara Parseghian, Notre Dame, & Frank Broyles, Arkansas (AFCA); Ara Parseghian (FWAA)
1965 Tommy Prothro, UCLA (AFCA); Duffy Daugherty, Mich. St. (FWAA)
1966 Tom Cahill, Army
1967 John Pont, Indiana
1968 Joe Paterno, Penn St. (AFCA); Woody Hayes, Ohio St. (FWAA)
1969 Bo Schembechler, Michigan
1970 Charles McClendon, LSU, & Darrell Royal, Texas (AFCA); Alex Agase, Northwestern (FWAA)
1971 Paul "Bear" Bryant, Alabama (AFCA); Bob Devaney, Nebraska (FWAA)
1972 John McKay, USC
1973 Paul "Bear" Bryant, Alabama (AFCA); Johnny Majors, Pittsburgh (FWAA)
1974 Grant Teaff, Baylor
1975 Frank Kush, Arizona St. (AFCA); Woody Hayes, Ohio St. (FWAA)
1976 Johnny Majors, Pittsburgh
1977 Don James, Washington (AFCA); Lou Holtz, Arkansas (FWAA)
1978 Joe Paterno, Penn St.
1979 Earle Bruce, Ohio St.
1980 Vince Dooley, Georgia
1981 Danny Ford, Clemson
1982 Joe Paterno, Penn St.

1983 Ken Hatfield, Air Force (AFCA); Howard Schnellenberger, Miami (FL) (FWAA)
1984 LaVell Edwards, Brigham Young
1985 Fisher De Berry, Air Force
1986 Joe Paterno, Penn St.
1987 Dick MacPherson, Syracuse
1988 Don Nehlen, W. Virginia (AFCA); Lou Holtz, Notre Dame (FWAA)
1989 Bill McCartney, Colorado
1990 Bobby Ross, Georgia Tech
1991 Don James, Washington
1992 Gene Stallings, Alabama
1993 Barry Alvarez, Wisconsin (AFCA); Terry Bowden, Auburn (FWAA)
1994 Tom Osborne, Nebraska (AFCA); Rich Brooks, Oregon (FWAA)
1995 Gary Barnett, Northwestern
1996 Bruce Snyder, Arizona St.
1997 Mike Price, Washington St.
1998 Phillip Fulmer, Tennessee
1999 Frank Beamer, Virginia Tech
2000 Bob Stoops, Oklahoma
2001 Larry Coker, Miami (FL) & Ralph Friedgen, Maryland (AFCA); Ralph Friedgen, Maryland (FWAA)
2002 Jim Tressel, Ohio St.
2003 Pete Carroll, USC (AFCA); Nick Saban, LSU (FWAA)

All-Time Division I-A Coaching Victories (Including Bowl Games)

*Bobby Bowden	342	Bo Schembechler	234	Dan McGugin	197	Gil Dobie	180
*Joe Paterno	339	Hayden Fry	232	Fielding Yost	196	*Jackie Sherrill	180
Paul "Bear" Bryant	323	Jess Neely	207	Howard Jones	194	Carl Snavely	180
Glenn "Pop" Warner	319	Warren Woodson	203	John Cooper	192	Jerry Claiborne	179
Amos Alonzo Stagg	314	Don Nehlen	202	John Vaught	190	Ben Schwartzwalder	178
LaVell Edwards	257	Eddie Anderson	201	George Welsh	189	Frank Kush	176
Tom Osborne	255	Vince Dooley	201	John Heisman	185	Don James	176
*Lou Holtz	243	Jim Sweeney	200	Johnny Majors	185	Ralph Jordan	176
Woody Hayes	238	Dana X. Bible	198	Darrell Royal	184		

Coaches active in 2003 are denoted by an asterisk(*). Eddie Robinson of Grambling State Univ. (Div. I-AA), who retired after the 1997 season, holds the record for most college football victories, with 408.

NCAA Div. I-A Football Conference Champions (1980-2003)

Atlantic Coast	
1980	North Carolina
1981	Clemson
1982	Clemson
1983	Maryland
1984	Maryland
1985	Maryland
1986	Clemson
1987	Clemson
1988	Clemson
1989	Virginia, Duke
1990	Georgia Tech
1991	Clemson
1992	Florida St.
1993	Florida St.
1994	Florida St.
1995	Virginia, Florida St.
1996	Florida St.
1997	Florida St.
1998	Florida St., Georgia Tech
1999	Florida St.
2000	Florida St.
2001	Maryland
2002	Florida St.
2003	Florida St.

Big 12*	
1996	Texas
1997	Nebraska
1998	Texas A&M
1999	Nebraska
2000	Oklahoma
2001	Colorado
2002	Oklahoma
2003	Oklahoma

Big East	
1991	Miami (FL), Syracuse
1992	Miami (FL)
1993	West Virginia
1994	Miami (FL)
1995	Virginia Tech, Miami (FL)
1996	Virginia Tech, Miami (FL), Syracuse
1997	Syracuse
1998	Syracuse
1999	Virginia Tech
2000	Miami (FL)
2001	Miami (FL)
2002	Miami (FL)
2003	Miami (FL)

Big Ten	
1980	Michigan
1981	Iowa, Ohio St.
1982	Michigan
1983	Illinois
1984	Ohio St.
1985	Iowa
1986	Michigan, Ohio St.
1987	Michigan St.
1988	Michigan
1989	Michigan
1990	Iowa, Ill., Mich., Mich. St.
1991	Michigan
1992	Michigan
1993	Ohio St., Wisconsin
1994	Penn St.
1995	Northwestern
1996	Ohio St., Northwestern
1997	Michigan
1998	Ohio St., Wisconsin, Michigan
1999	Wisconsin
2000	Michigan, Northwestern, Purdue
2001	Illinois
2002	Iowa, Ohio St.
2003	Michigan

Big West**
1980	Long Beach St.
1981	San Jose St.
1982	Fresno St.
1983	Cal St.-Fullerton
1984	Cal St.-Fullerton
1985	Fresno St.
1986	San Jose St.
1987	San Jose St.
1988	Fresno St.
1989	Fresno St.
1990	San Jose St.
1991	San Jose St., Fresno St.
1992	Nevada
1993	SW Louisiana, Utah St.
1994	Nevada, SW Louisiana, UNLV
1995	Nevada
1996	Nevada, Utah St.
1997	Nevada, Utah St.
1998	Idaho
1999	Boise St.
2000	Boise St.

Conference USA
1996	So. Mississippi, Houston
1997	So. Mississippi
1998	Tulane
1999	So. Mississippi
2000	Louisville
2001	Louisville
2002	Cincinnati, TCU
2003	So. Mississippi

Mid-American Athletic
1980	Central Michigan
1981	Toledo
1982	Bowling Green
1983	Northern Illinois
1984	Toledo
1985	Bowling Green
1986	Miami (OH)
1987	E. Michigan
1988	W. Michigan
1989	Ball St.
1990	Central Michigan
1991	Bowling Green
1992	Bowling Green
1993	Ball St.
1994	Central Michigan
1995	Toledo
1996	Ball St.
1997	Marshall
1998	Marshall
1999	Marshall
2000	Marshall
2001	Toledo
2002	Marshall
2003	Miami (OH)

Mountain West***
1999	BYU, Colorado St., Utah
2000	Colorado St.
2001	BYU
2002	Colorado St.
2003	Utah

Pacific Ten
1980	Washington
1981	Washington
1982	UCLA
1983	UCLA
1984	USC
1985	UCLA
1986	Arizona St.
1987	UCLA, USC
1988	USC
1989	USC
1990	Washington
1991	Washington
1992	Washington, Stanford
1993	UCLA, Arizona, USC
1994	Oregon
1995	USC, Washington
1996	Arizona St.
1997	Washington St., UCLA
1998	UCLA
1999	Stanford
2000	Washington, Oregon St., Oregon
2001	Oregon
2002	USC, Washington St.
2003	USC

Southeastern
1980	Georgia
1981	Georgia, Alabama
1982	Georgia
1983	Auburn
1984	Florida (title vacated)
1985	Tennessee
1986	LSU
1987	Auburn
1988	Auburn, LSU
1989	Ala., Tenn., Auburn
1990	Tennessee
1991	Florida
1992	Alabama
1993	Florida
1994	Florida
1995	Florida
1996	Florida
1997	Tennessee
1998	Tennessee
1999	Alabama
2000	Florida
2001	LSU
2002	Georgia
2003	LSU

Sun Belt**
2001	LSU
2002	North Texas
2003	North Texas

Western Athletic
1980	Brigham Young (BYU)
1981	Brigham Young
1982	Brigham Young
1983	Brigham Young
1984	Brigham Young
1985	BYU, Air Force
1986	San Diego St.
1987	Wyoming
1988	Wyoming
1989	Brigham Young
1990	Brigham Young
1991	Brigham Young
1992	Hawaii, BYU, Fresno St.
1993	Wyoming, Fresno St., BYU
1994	Colorado St.
1995	Colorado St., Air Force, Utah, BYU
1996	Brigham Young
1997	Colorado St.
1998	Air Force
1999	Fresno St., Hawaii, TCU
2000	Texas Christian, UTEP
2001	Louisiana Tech
2002	Boise St.
2003	Boise St.

(*) In 1996 all former Big Eight teams joined with 4 of the 8 Southwest Conf. teams to form the Big 12. (**) In 2001, former Big West teams Ark. St., Idaho, New Mexico St., and N. Texas joined La.-Lafayette, La.-Monroe (Southland), and Middle Tenn. (Ohio Valley) to form the Sun Belt Conf. Boise St. moved to the WAC, and Utah St. became an independent. (***) In 1999, 8 Western Athletic teams formed the Mountain West Conf.

NCAA Div. I-AA Football Conference Champions (1990-2003)

Atlantic 10
1990	Massachusetts
1991	Delaware, Villanova
1992	Delaware
1993	Boston U.
1994	New Hampshire
1995	Delaware
1996	William & Mary
1997	Villanova
1998	Richmond
1999	J. Madison, Mass.
2000	Delaware, Richmond
2001	Hofstra, Maine, Villanova, Will. & Mary
2002	Maine, Northeastern
2003	Delaware, Mass.

Big Sky
1990	Nevada
1991	Nevada
1992	Idaho, Eastern Wash.
1993	Montana
1994	Boise St.
1995	Montana
1996	Montana
1997	Eastern Wash.
1998	Montana
1999	Montana
2000	Montana
2001	Montana
2002	Idaho St., Montana, Montana St.
2003	Montana St., Montana, No. Arizona

Big South
2002	Gardner-Webb
2003	Gardner-Webb

Gateway
1990	Northern Iowa
1991	Northern Iowa
1992	Northern Iowa
1993	Northern Iowa
1994	Northern Iowa
1995	N. Iowa, Eastern Ill.
1996	Northern Iowa
1997	Western Illinois
1998	Western Illinois
1999	Illinois St.
2000	Western Illinois
2001	Northern Iowa
2002	W. Illinois, W. Kentucky
2003	No. Iowa, So. Illinois

Ivy Group
1990	Cornell, Dartmouth
1991	Dartmouth
1992	Dartmouth, Princeton
1993	Penn
1994	Penn
1995	Princeton
1996	Dartmouth
1997	Harvard
1998	Penn
1999	Brown, Yale
2000	Penn
2001	Harvard
2002	Pennsylvania
2003	Pennsylvania

Metro Atlantic
1993	Iona
1994	Marist, St. John's (NY)
1995	Duquesne
1996	Duquesne
1997	Georgetown
1998	Fairfield, Georgetown
1999	Duquesne
2000	Duquesne
2001	Duquesne
2002	Duquesne
2003	Duquesne

Mid-East Athletic
1990	Florida A&M
1991	North Carolina A&T
1992	North Carolina A&T
1993	Howard
1994	South Carolina St.
1995	Florida A&M
1996	Florida A&M
1997	Hampton
1998	Florida A&M, Hampton
1999	North Carolina A&T
2000	Florida A&M
2001	Florida A&M
2002	Bethune-Cookman
2003	North Carolina A&T

Northeast
1996	R. Morris, Monmouth
1997	Robert Morris
1998	R.Morris, Monmouth
1999	Robert Morris
2000	Robert Morris
2001	Sacred Heart
2002	Albany (NY)
2003	Albany, Monmouth

Ohio Valley
1990	E. Ky., Middle Tenn.
1991	Eastern Kentucky
1992	Middle Tennessee
1993	Eastern Kentucky
1994	Eastern Kentucky
1995	Murray St.
1996	Murray St.
1997	Eastern Kentucky
1998	Tennessee St.
1999	Tennessee St.
2000	Western Kentucky
2001	Eastern Illinois
2002	Eastern Illinois
2003	Jacksonville St.

Patriot
1990	Holy Cross
1991	Holy Cross
1992	Lafayette
1993	Lehigh
1994	Lafayette
1995	Lehigh
1996	Bucknell
1997	Colgate
1998	Lehigh
1999	Colgate, Lehigh
2000	Lehigh
2001	Lehigh
2002	Colgate, Fordham
2003	Colgate

Pioneer
1993	Dayton
1994	Dayton, Butler
1995	Drake
1996	Dayton
1997	Dayton
1998	Drake
1999	Dayton
2000	Dayton, Drake, Valparaiso
2001	Dayton
2002	Dayton
2003	Valparaiso

Southern
1990	Furman
1991	Appalachian St.
1992	Citadel
1993	Georgia Southern
1994	Marshall
1995	Appalachian St.
1996	Marshall
1997	Georgia Southern
1998	Georgia Southern
1999	Appalachian St., GA Southern, Furman
2000	Georgia Southern
2001	Georgia Southern
2002	Georgia Southern
2003	Wofford

Southland
1990	La.-Monroe
1991	McNeese St.
1992	La.-Monroe
1993	McNeese St.
1994	North Texas
1995	McNeese St.
1996	Troy St.
1997	McNeese St., Northwestern St.
1998	Northwestern St.
1999	Troy St., S. F. Austin
2000	Troy St.
2001	Sam Houston St., McNeese St.
2002	McNeese St.
2003	McNeese St.

Southwestern Athletic
1990	Jackson St.
1991	Alabama St.
1992	Alcorn St.
1993	Southern U.
1994	Grambling, Alcorn St.
1995	Jackson St.
1996	Jackson St.
1997	Southern U.
1998	Southern U.
1999	Southern U.
2000	Grambling
2001	Grambling
2002	Grambling
2003	Southern U.

NATIONAL HOCKEY LEAGUE

2003-2004: Tampa Bay Wins 1st Stanley Cup; Owners Lock Out Players

The Tampa Bay Lightning won the first NHL title in their 12-year history, defeating the Calgary Flames, 2-1, in Game 7 of the Stanley Cup Finals in Tampa, FL, on June 7. The Lightning, coached by John Tortorella, came back from a 3-games-to-2 deficit to win the championship. Lightning center Brad Richards, who scored a record 7 game-winning goals in the playoffs and led all playoff scorers with 26 points, won the Conn Smythe Trophy as MVP of the NHL postseason. Lightning forward Martin St. Louis, the NHL's regular-season points leader, later won the Hart Trophy as MVP of the 2003-2004 season.

The NHL season was blighted by a vicious hit by Vancouver's Todd Bertuzzi that left Colorado's Steve Moore with serious neck and head injuries during a game in Vancouver, BC, March 8. The NHL suspended Bertuzzi for the rest of the regular season (13 games) and the playoffs for the incident. BC prosecutors filed assault charges against Bertuzzi June 24.

The NHL locked out its players beginning Sept. 16, one day after the league's collective bargaining agreement expired. The NHL and the players' union were at an impasse over the league's desire to impose a salary cap. The NHL claimed that its teams all together lost $224 million in the 2003-2004 season and $273 million the season before, and blamed skyrocketing player salaries that had outpaced revenue. The players' union was against any proposals involving a salary cap. Both sides were firmly entrenched and it was possible that the lockout could wipe out much or all of the 2004-2005 season.

Final Standings 2003-2004

(playoff seeding in parentheses; division winners automatically seeded 1, 2, or 3; overtime losses [OTL] worth 1 point.)

Eastern Conference

Atlantic Division	W	L	T	OTL	GF	GA	Pts
Philadelphia (3)	40	21	15	6	229	186	101
New Jersey (6)	43	25	12	2	213	164	100
N.Y. Islanders (8)	38	29	11	4	237	210	91
N.Y. Rangers	27	40	7	8	206	250	69
Pittsburgh	23	47	8	4	190	303	58

Northeast Division	W	L	T	OTL	GF	GA	Pts
Boston (2)	41	19	15	7	209	188	104
Toronto (4)	45	24	10	3	242	204	103
Ottawa (5)	43	23	10	6	262	189	102
Montreal (7)	41	30	7	4	208	192	93
Buffalo	37	34	7	4	220	221	85

Southeast Division	W	L	T	OTL	GF	GA	Pts
Tampa Bay (1)	46	22	8	6	245	192	106
Atlanta	33	37	8	4	214	243	78
Carolina	28	34	14	6	172	209	76
Florida	28	35	15	4	188	221	75
Washington	23	46	10	3	186	253	59

Western Conference

Central Division	W	L	T	OTL	GF	GA	Pts
Detroit (1)	48	21	11	2	255	189	109
St. Louis (7)	39	30	11	2	191	198	91
Nashville (8)	38	29	11	4	216	217	91
Columbus	25	45	8	4	177	238	62
Chicago	20	43	11	8	188	259	59

Northwest Division	W	L	T	OTL	GF	GA	Pts
Vancouver (3)	43	24	10	5	235	194	101
Colorado (4)	40	22	13	7	236	198	100
Calgary (6)	42	30	7	3	200	176	94
Edmonton	36	29	12	5	221	208	89
Minnesota	30	29	20	3	188	183	83

Pacific Division	W	L	T	OTL	GF	GA	Pts
San Jose (2)	43	21	12	6	219	183	104
Dallas (5)	41	26	13	2	194	175	97
Los Angeles	28	29	16	9	205	217	81
Anaheim	29	35	10	8	184	213	76
Phoenix	22	36	18	6	188	245	68

2004 Stanley Cup Playoff Results

Eastern Conference
Tampa Bay defeated N.Y. Islanders 4 games to 1
Montreal defeated Boston 4 games to 3
Philadelphia defeated New Jersey 4 games to 1
Toronto defeated Ottawa 4 games to 3
Tampa Bay defeated Montreal 4 games to 0
Philadelphia defeated Toronto 4 games to 2
Tampa Bay defeated Philadelphia 4 games to 3

Western Conference
Detroit defeated Nashville 4 games to 2
San Jose defeated St. Louis 4 games to 1
Calgary defeated Vancouver 4 games to 3
Colorado defeated Dallas 4 games to 1
Calgary defeated Detroit 4 games to 2
San Jose defeated Colorado 4 games to 2
Calgary defeated San Jose 4 games to 2

Finals
Tampa Bay defeated Calgary 4 games to 3 [1-4, 4-1, 0-3, 1-0, 2-3 (OT), 3-2 (2 OT), 2-1].

Stanley Cup Champions Since 1927

Year	Champion	Coach	Final opponent	Year	Champion	Coach	Final opponent
1927	Ottawa	Dave Gill	Boston	1959	Montreal	Toe Blake	Toronto
1928	N.Y. Rangers	Lester Patrick	Montreal	1960	Montreal	Toe Blake	Toronto
1929	Boston	Cy Denneny	N.Y. Rangers	1961	Chicago	Rudy Pilous	Detroit
1930	Montreal	Cecil Hart	Boston	1962	Toronto	Punch Imlach	Chicago
1931	Montreal	Cecil Hart	Chicago	1963	Toronto	Punch Imlach	Detroit
1932	Toronto	Dick Irvin	N.Y. Rangers	1964	Toronto	Punch Imlach	Detroit
1933	N.Y. Rangers	Lester Patrick	Toronto	1965	Montreal	Toe Blake	Chicago
1934	Chicago	Tommy Gorman	Detroit	1966	Montreal	Toe Blake	Detroit
1935	Montreal Maroons	Tommy Gorman	Toronto	1967	Toronto	Punch Imlach	Montreal
1936	Detroit	Jack Adams	Toronto	1968	Montreal	Toe Blake	St. Louis
1937	Detroit	Jack Adams	N.Y. Rangers	1969	Montreal	Claude Ruel	St. Louis
1938	Chicago	Bill Stewart	Toronto	1970	Boston	Harry Sinden	St. Louis
1939	Boston	Art Ross	Toronto	1971	Montreal	Al MacNeil	Chicago
1940	N.Y. Rangers	Frank Boucher	Toronto	1972	Boston	Tom Johnson	N.Y. Rangers
1941	Boston	Cooney Weiland	Detroit	1973	Montreal	Scotty Bowman	Chicago
1942	Toronto	Hap Day	Detroit	1974	Philadelphia	Fred Shero	Boston
1943	Detroit	Jack Adams	Boston	1975	Philadelphia	Fred Shero	Buffalo
1944	Montreal	Dick Irvin	Chicago	1976	Montreal	Scotty Bowman	Philadelphia
1945	Toronto	Hap Day	Detroit	1977	Montreal	Scotty Bowman	Boston
1946	Montreal	Dick Irvin	Boston	1978	Montreal	Scotty Bowman	Boston
1947	Toronto	Hap Day	Montreal	1979	Montreal	Scotty Bowman	N.Y. Rangers
1948	Toronto	Hap Day	Detroit	1980	N.Y. Islanders	Al Arbour	Philadelphia
1949	Toronto	Hap Day	Detroit	1981	N.Y. Islanders	Al Arbour	Minnesota
1950	Detroit	Tommy Ivan	N.Y. Rangers	1982	N.Y. Islanders	Al Arbour	Vancouver
1951	Toronto	Joe Primeau	Montreal	1983	N.Y. Islanders	Al Arbour	Edmonton
1952	Detroit	Tommy Ivan	Montreal	1984	Edmonton	Glen Sather	N.Y. Islanders
1953	Montreal	Dick Irvin	Boston	1985	Edmonton	Glen Sather	Philadelphia
1954	Detroit	Tommy Ivan	Montreal	1986	Montreal	Jean Perron	Calgary
1955	Detroit	Jimmy Skinner	Montreal	1987	Edmonton	Glen Sather	Philadelphia
1956	Montreal	Toe Blake	Detroit	1988	Edmonton	Glen Sather	Boston
1957	Montreal	Toe Blake	Boston	1989	Calgary	Terry Crisp	Montreal
1958	Montreal	Toe Blake	Boston	1990	Edmonton	John Muckler	Boston

Year	Champion	Coach	Final opponent	Year	Champion	Coach	Final opponent
1991	Pittsburgh	Bob Johnson	Minnesota	1998	Detroit	Scotty Bowman	Washington
1992	Pittsburgh	Scotty Bowman	Chicago	1999	Dallas	Ken Hitchcock	Buffalo
1993	Montreal	Jacques Demers	Los Angeles	2000	New Jersey	Larry Robinson	Dallas
1994	N.Y. Rangers	Mike Keenan	Vancouver	2001	Colorado	Bob Hartley	New Jersey
1995	New Jersey	Jacques Lemaire	Detroit	2002	Detroit	Scotty Bowman	Carolina
1996	Colorado	Marc Crawford	Florida	2003	New Jersey	Pat Burns	Anaheim
1997	Detroit	Scotty Bowman	Philadelphia	2004	Tampa Bay	John Tortorella	Calgary

Individual Leaders, 2003-2004

Points

Martin St. Louis, Tampa Bay, 94; Ilya Kovalchuk, Atlanta, 87; Joe Sakic, Colorado, 87; Markus Naslund, Vancouver, 84; Marian Hossa, Ottawa, 82; Patrik Elias, New Jersey, 81.

Goals

Jarome Iginla, Calgary, 41; Ilya Kovalchuk, Atlanta, 41; Rick Nash, Columbus, 41; Martin St. Louis, Tampa Bay, 38; Patrik Elias, New Jersey, 38; Marian Hossa, Ottawa, 36.

Assists

Martin St. Louis, Tampa Bay, 56; Scott Gomez, New Jersey, 56; Cory Stillman, Tampa Bay, 55; Joe Sakic, Colorado, 54; Alex Tanguay, Colorado, 54; Brad Richards, Tampa Bay, 53.

Power-play goals

Rick Nash, Columbus, 19; Keith Tkachuk, St. Louis, 18; Ilya Kovalchuk, Atlanta, 16; Milan Hejduk, Colorado, 16; Marian Hossa, Ottawa, 14; Mark Recchi, Philadelphia, 14; Peter Bondra, Ottawa, 14.

Shorthanded goals

Martin St. Louis, Tampa Bay, 8; Kris Draper, Detroit, 5; Kevyn Adams, Carolina, 5; Six players tied with 4.

Shooting percentage
(minimum 82 shots)

Mark Parrish, N.Y. Islanders, 22.9; Gary Roberts, Toronto, 22.6; Pavel Datsyuk, Detroit, 22.1; Alex Tanguay, Colorado, 21.4; Peter Forsberg, Colorado, 21.2.

Plus/Minus

Marek Malik, Vancouver, 35; Martin St. Louis, Tampa Bay, 35; Zdeno Chara, Ottawa, 33; Fredrik Modin, Tampa Bay, 31; Nils Ekman, San Jose, 30; Alex Tanguay, Colorado, 30.

Penalty minutes

Sean Avery, Los Angeles, 261; Chris Simon, Calgary, 250; Krzysztof Oliwa, Calgary, 247; Jody Shelley, Columbus, 228; Donald Brashear, Philadelphia, 212.

Goaltending Leaders
(minimum 25 games)
Goals against average

Miikka Kiprusoff, Calgary, 1.69; Dwayne Roloson, Minnesota, 1.88; Marty Turco, Dallas, 1.98; Martin Brodeur, New Jersey, 2.03; Robert Esche, Philadelphia, 2.04.

Wins

Martin Brodeur, New Jersey, 38; Marty Turco, Dallas, 37; Ed Belfour, Toronto, 34; Tomas Vokoun, Nashville, 34; Dan Cloutier, Vancouver, 33; Jose Theodore, Montreal, 33.

Save percentage

Miikka Kiprusoff, Calgary, .933; Dwayne Roloson, Minnesota, .933; Roberto Luongo, Florida, .931; Vesa Toskala, San Jose, .930; Andrew Raycroft, Boston, .924.

Shutouts

Martin Brodeur, New Jersey, 11; Ed Belfour, Toronto, 10; Marty Turco, Dallas, 9; Evgeni Nabokov, San Jose, 9; Roberto Luongo, Florida, 7; Jose Theodore, Montreal, 6; Kevin Weekes, Carolina, 6.

All-Time Leading Scorers

Player	Goals	Assists	Points	Player	Goals	Assists	Points	Player	Goals	Assists	Points
Wayne Gretzky .	894	1,963	2,857	Phil Esposito . . .	717	873	1,590	Dale Hawerchuk	518	891	1,409
Mark Messier* . .	694	1,193	1,887	Ray Bourque . . .	410	1,169	1,579	Joe Sakic*	542	860	1,402
Gordie Howe . . .	801	1,049	1,850	Paul Coffey . . .	396	1,135	1,531	Jari Kurri	601	797	1,398
Ron Francis* . . .	549	1,249	1,798	Stan Mikita	541	926	1,467	Brett Hull*	741	649	1,390
Marcel Dionne . .	731	1,040	1,771	Bryan Trottier . .	524	901	1,425	Luc Robitaille* . .	653	717	1,370
Steve Yzerman*	678	1,043	1,721	Adam Oates* . .	341	1,079	1,420	John Bucyk	556	813	1,369
Mario Lemieux* .	683	1,018	1,701	Doug Gilmour . .	450	964	1,414				

Note: Through end of 2003-2004 season. *Active in the 2003-2004 season.

Most NHL Goals in a Season

Player	Team	Season	Goals	Player	Team	Season	Goals
Wayne Gretzky	Edmonton	1981-82	92	Jari Kurri	Edmonton	1984-85	71
Wayne Gretzky	Edmonton	1983-84	87	Brett Hull	St. Louis	1991-92	70
Brett Hull	St. Louis	1990-91	86	Mario Lemieux	Pittsburgh	1987-88	70
Mario Lemieux	Pittsburgh	1988-89	85	Bernie Nicholls	Los Angeles	1988-89	70
Phil Esposito	Boston	1971-72	76	Mike Bossy	N.Y. Islanders	1978-79	69
Alexander Mogilny	Buffalo	1992-93	76	Mario Lemieux	Pittsburgh	1992-93	69
Teemu Selanne	Winnipeg	1992-93	76	Mario Lemieux	Pittsburgh	1995-96	69
Wayne Gretzky	Edmonton	1984-85	73	Mike Bossy	N.Y. Islanders	1980-81	68
Brett Hull	St. Louis	1989-90	72	Phil Esposito	Boston	1973-74	68
Wayne Gretzky	Edmonton	1982-83	71	Jari Kurri	Edmonton	1985-86	68

Hart Memorial Trophy (MVP)

1927	Herb Gardiner, Montreal	1953	Gordie Howe, Detroit	1979	Bryan Trottier, N.Y. Islanders
1928	Howie Morenz, Montreal	1954	Al Rollins, Chicago	1980	Wayne Gretzky, Edmonton
1929	Roy Worters, N.Y. Americans	1955	Ted Kennedy, Toronto	1981	Wayne Gretzky, Edmonton
1930	Nels Stewart, Montreal Maroons	1956	Jean Beliveau, Montreal	1982	Wayne Gretzky, Edmonton
1931	Howie Morenz, Montreal	1957	Gordie Howe, Detroit	1983	Wayne Gretzky, Edmonton
1932	Howie Morenz, Montreal	1958	Gordie Howe, Detroit	1984	Wayne Gretzky, Edmonton
1933	Eddie Shore, Boston	1959	Andy Bathgate, N.Y. Rangers	1985	Wayne Gretzky, Edmonton
1934	Aurel Joliat, Montreal	1960	Gordie Howe, Detroit	1986	Wayne Gretzky, Edmonton
1935	Eddie Shore, Boston	1961	Bernie Geoffrion, Montreal	1987	Wayne Gretzky, Edmonton
1936	Eddie Shore, Boston	1962	Jacques Plante, Montreal	1988	Mario Lemieux, Pittsburgh
1937	Babe Siebert, Montreal	1963	Gordie Howe, Detroit	1989	Wayne Gretzky, Los Angeles
1938	Eddie Shore, Boston	1964	Jean Beliveau, Montreal	1990	Mark Messier, Edmonton
1939	Toe Blake, Montreal	1965	Bobby Hull, Chicago	1991	Brett Hull, St. Louis
1940	Ebbie Goodfellow, Detroit	1966	Bobby Hull, Chicago	1992	Mark Messier, N.Y. Rangers
1941	Bill Cowley, Boston	1967	Stan Mikita, Chicago	1993	Mario Lemieux, Pittsburgh
1942	Tom Anderson, N.Y. Americans	1968	Stan Mikita, Chicago	1994	Sergei Fedorov, Detroit
1943	Bill Cowley, Boston	1969	Phil Esposito, Boston	1995	Eric Lindros, Philadelphia
1944	Babe Pratt, Toronto	1970	Bobby Orr, Boston	1996	Mario Lemieux, Pittsburgh
1945	Elmer Lach, Montreal	1971	Bobby Orr, Boston	1997	Dominik Hasek, Buffalo
1946	Max Bentley, Chicago	1972	Bobby Orr, Boston	1998	Dominik Hasek, Buffalo
1947	Maurice Richard, Montreal	1973	Bobby Clarke, Philadelphia	1999	Jaromir Jagr, Pittsburgh
1948	Buddy O'Connor, N.Y. Rangers	1974	Phil Esposito, Boston	2000	Chris Pronger, St. Louis
1949	Sid Abel, Detroit	1975	Bobby Clarke, Philadelphia	2001	Joe Sakic, Colorado
1950	Chuck Rayner, N.Y. Rangers	1976	Bobby Clarke, Philadelphia	2002	Jose Theodore, Montreal
1951	Milt Schmidt, Boston	1977	Guy Lafleur, Montreal	2003	Peter Forsberg, Colorado
1952	Gordie Howe, Detroit	1978	Guy Lafleur, Montreal	2004	Martin St. Louis, Tampa Bay

Calder Memorial Trophy (Rookie of the Year)

Year	Winner	Year	Winner	Year	Winner
1933	Carl Voss, Detroit	1957	Larry Regan, Boston	1981	Peter Stastny, Quebec
1934	Russ Blinco, Montreal Maroons	1958	Frank Mahovlich, Toronto	1982	Dale Hawerchuk, Winnipeg
1935	Dave Schriner, N.Y. Americans	1959	Ralph Backstrom, Montreal	1983	Steve Larmer, Chicago
1936	Mike Karakas, Chicago	1960	Bill Hay, Chicago	1984	Tom Barrasso, Buffalo
1937	Syl Apps, Toronto	1961	Dave Keon, Toronto	1985	Mario Lemieux, Pittsburgh
1938	Cully Dahlstrom, Chicago	1962	Bobby Rousseau, Montreal	1986	Gary Suter, Calgary
1939	Frank Brimsek, Boston	1963	Kent Douglas, Toronto	1987	Luc Robitaille, Los Angeles
1940	Kilby Macdonald, N.Y. Rangers	1964	Jacques Laperriere, Montreal	1988	Joe Nieuwendyk, Calgary
1941	John Quilty, Montreal	1965	Roger Crozier, Detroit	1989	Brian Leetch, N.Y. Rangers
1942	Grant Warwick, N.Y. Rangers	1966	Brit Selby, Toronto	1990	Sergei Makarov, Calgary
1943	Gaye Stewart, Toronto	1967	Bobby Orr, Boston	1991	Ed Belfour, Chicago
1944	Gus Bodnar, Toronto	1968	Derek Sanderson, Boston	1992	Pavel Bure, Vancouver
1945	Frank McCool, Toronto	1969	Danny Grant, Minnesota	1993	Teemu Selanne, Winnipeg
1946	Edgar Laprade, N.Y. Rangers	1970	Tony Esposito, Chicago	1994	Martin Brodeur, New Jersey
1947	Howie Meeker, Toronto	1971	Gilbert Perreault, Buffalo	1995	Peter Forsberg, Quebec
1948	Jim McFadden, Detroit	1972	Ken Dryden, Montreal	1996	Daniel Alfredsson, Ottawa
1949	Pentti Lund, N.Y. Rangers	1973	Steve Vickers, N.Y. Rangers	1997	Bryan Berard, N.Y. Islanders
1950	Jack Gelineau, Boston	1974	Denis Potvin, N.Y. Islanders	1998	Sergei Samsonov, Boston
1951	Terry Sawchuk, Detroit	1975	Eric Vail, Atlanta	1999	Chris Drury, Colorado
1952	Bernie Geoffrion, Montreal	1976	Bryan Trottier, N.Y. Islanders	2000	Scott Gomez, New Jersey
1953	Gump Worsley, N.Y. Rangers	1977	Willi Plett, Atlanta	2001	Evgeni Nabokov, San Jose
1954	Camille Henry, N.Y. Rangers	1978	Mike Bossy, N.Y. Islanders	2002	Dany Heatley, Atlanta
1955	Ed Litzenberger, Chicago	1979	Bobby Smith, Minnesota	2003	Barret Jackman, St. Louis
1956	Glenn Hall, Detroit	1980	Ray Bourque, Boston	2004	Andrew Raycroft, Boston

Conn Smythe Trophy (MVP in Playoffs)

Year	Winner	Year	Winner	Year	Winner
1965	Jean Beliveau, Montreal	1979	Bob Gainey, Montreal	1992	Mario Lemieux, Pittsburgh
1966	Roger Crozier, Detroit	1980	Bryan Trottier, N.Y. Islanders	1993	Patrick Roy, Montreal
1967	Dave Keon, Toronto	1981	Butch Goring, N.Y. Islanders	1994	Brian Leetch, N.Y. Rangers
1968	Glenn Hall, St. Louis	1982	Mike Bossy, N.Y. Islanders	1995	Claude Lemieux, New Jersey
1969	Serge Savard, Montreal	1983	Billy Smith, N.Y. Islanders	1996	Joe Sakic, Colorado
1970	Bobby Orr, Boston	1984	Mark Messier, Edmonton	1997	Mike Vernon, Detroit
1971	Ken Dryden, Montreal	1985	Wayne Gretzky, Edmonton	1998	Steve Yzerman, Detroit
1972	Bobby Orr, Boston	1986	Patrick Roy, Montreal	1999	Joe Nieuwendyk, Dallas
1973	Yvan Cournoyer, Montreal	1987	Ron Hextall, Philadelphia	2000	Scott Stevens, New Jersey
1974	Bernie Parent, Philadelphia	1988	Wayne Gretzky, Edmonton	2001	Patrick Roy, Colorado
1975	Bernie Parent, Philadelphia	1989	Al MacInnis, Calgary	2002	Nicklas Lidstrom, Detroit
1976	Reg Leach, Philadelphia	1990	Bill Ranford, Edmonton	2003	Jean-Sebastien Giguere, Anaheim
1977	Guy Lafleur, Montreal	1991	Mario Lemieux, Pittsburgh	2004	Brad Richards, Tampa Bay
1978	Larry Robinson, Montreal				

Lady Byng Memorial Trophy (Most Gentlemanly Player)

Year	Winner	Year	Winner	Year	Winner
1925	Frank Nighbor, Ottawa	1952	Sid Smith, Toronto	1979	Bob MacMillan, Atlanta
1926	Frank Nighbor, Ottawa	1953	Red Kelly, Detroit	1980	Wayne Gretzky, Edmonton
1927	Billy Burch, N.Y. Americans	1954	Red Kelly, Detroit	1981	Rick Kehoe, Pittsburgh
1928	Frank Boucher, N.Y. Rangers	1955	Sid Smith, Toronto	1982	Rick Middleton, Boston
1929	Frank Boucher, N.Y. Rangers	1956	Earl Reibel, Detroit	1983	Mike Bossy, N.Y. Islanders
1930	Frank Boucher, N.Y. Rangers	1957	Andy Hebenton, N.Y. Rangers	1984	Mike Bossy, N.Y. Islanders
1931	Frank Boucher, N.Y. Rangers	1958	Camille Henry, N.Y. Rangers	1985	Jari Kurri, Edmonton
1932	Joe Primeau, Toronto	1959	Alex Delvecchio, Detroit	1986	Mike Bossy, N.Y. Islanders
1933	Frank Boucher, N.Y. Rangers	1960	Don McKenney, Boston	1987	Joe Mullen, Calgary
1934	Frank Boucher, N.Y. Rangers	1961	Red Kelly, Toronto	1988	Mats Naslund, Montreal
1935	Frank Boucher, N.Y. Rangers	1962	Dave Keon, Toronto	1989	Joe Mullen, Calgary
1936	Doc Romnes, Chicago	1963	Dave Keon, Toronto	1990	Brett Hull, St. Louis
1937	Marty Barry, Detroit	1964	Ken Wharram, Chicago	1991	Wayne Gretzky, Los Angeles
1938	Gordie Drillon, Toronto	1965	Bobby Hull, Chicago	1992	Wayne Gretzky, Los Angeles
1939	Clint Smith, N.Y. Rangers	1966	Alex Delvecchio, Detroit	1993	Pierre Turgeon, N.Y. Islanders
1940	Bobby Bauer, Boston	1967	Stan Mikita, Chicago	1994	Wayne Gretzky, Los Angeles
1941	Bobby Bauer, Boston	1968	Stan Mikita, Chicago	1995	Ron Francis, Pittsburgh
1942	Syl Apps, Toronto	1969	Alex Delvecchio, Detroit	1996	Paul Kariya, Anaheim
1943	Max Bentley, Chicago	1970	Phil Goyette, St. Louis	1997	Paul Kariya, Anaheim
1944	Clint Smith, Chicago	1971	John Bucyk, Boston	1998	Ron Francis, Pittsburgh
1945	Bill Mosienko, Chicago	1972	Jean Ratelle, N.Y. Rangers	1999	Wayne Gretzky, N.Y. Rangers
1946	Toe Blake, Montreal	1973	Gil Perreault, Buffalo	2000	Pavol Demitra, St. Louis
1947	Bobby Bauer, Boston	1974	John Bucyk, Boston	2001	Joe Sakic, Colorado
1948	Buddy O'Connor, N.Y. Rangers	1975	Marcel Dionne, Detroit	2002	Ron Francis, Carolina
1949	Bill Quackenbush, Detroit	1976	Jean Ratelle, N.Y.R.-Boston	2003	Alexander Mogilny, Toronto
1950	Edgar Laprade, N.Y. Rangers	1977	Marcel Dionne, Los Angeles	2004	Brad Richards, Tampa Bay
1951	Red Kelly, Detroit	1978	Butch Goring, Los Angeles		

James Norris Memorial Trophy (Outstanding Defenseman)

Year	Winner	Year	Winner	Year	Winner
1954	Red Kelly, Detroit	1971	Bobby Orr, Boston	1988	Ray Bourque, Boston
1955	Doug Harvey, Montreal	1972	Bobby Orr, Boston	1989	Chris Chelios, Montreal
1956	Doug Harvey, Montreal	1973	Bobby Orr, Boston	1990	Ray Bourque, Boston
1957	Doug Harvey, Montreal	1974	Bobby Orr, Boston	1991	Ray Bourque, Boston
1958	Doug Harvey, Montreal	1975	Bobby Orr, Boston	1992	Brian Leetch, N.Y. Rangers
1959	Tom Johnson, Montreal	1976	Denis Potvin, N.Y. Islanders	1993	Chris Chelios, Chicago
1960	Doug Harvey, Montreal	1977	Larry Robinson, Montreal	1994	Ray Bourque, Boston
1961	Doug Harvey, Montreal	1978	Denis Potvin, N.Y. Islanders	1995	Paul Coffey, Detroit
1962	Doug Harvey, N.Y. Rangers	1979	Denis Potvin, N.Y. Islanders	1996	Chris Chelios, Chicago
1963	Pierre Pilote, Chicago	1980	Larry Robinson, Montreal	1997	Brian Leetch, N.Y. Rangers
1964	Pierre Pilote, Chicago	1981	Randy Carlyle, Pittsburgh	1998	Rob Blake, Los Angeles
1965	Pierre Pilote, Chicago	1982	Doug Wilson, Chicago	1999	Al MacInnis, St. Louis
1966	Jacques Laperriere, Montreal	1983	Rod Langway, Washington	2000	Chris Pronger, St. Louis
1967	Harry Howell, N.Y. Rangers	1984	Rod Langway, Washington	2001	Nicklas Lidstrom, Detroit
1968	Bobby Orr, Boston	1985	Paul Coffey, Edmonton	2002	Nicklas Lidstrom, Detroit
1969	Bobby Orr, Boston	1986	Paul Coffey, Edmonton	2003	Nicklas Lidstrom, Detroit
1970	Bobby Orr, Boston	1987	Ray Bourque, Boston	2004	Scott Niedermayer, New Jersey

Maurice "Rocket" Richard Trophy (Most Goals)

1999 Teemu Selanne, Anaheim	2002 Jarome Iginla, Calgary	2004 Jarome Iginla, Calgary; Ilya
2000 Pavel Bure, Florida	2003 Milan Hejduk, Colorado	Kovalchuk, Atlanta; Rick Nash
2001 Pavel Bure, Florida		Columbus

Art Ross Trophy (Leading Points Scorer)

1927 Bill Cook, N.Y. Rangers	1953 Gordie Howe, Detroit	1979 Bryan Trottier, N.Y. Islanders
1928 Howie Morenz, Montreal	1954 Gordie Howe, Detroit	1980 Marcel Dionne, Los Angeles
1929 Ace Bailey, Toronto	1955 Bernie Geoffrion, Montreal	1981 Wayne Gretzky, Edmonton
1930 Cooney Weiland, Boston	1956 Jean Beliveau, Montreal	1982 Wayne Gretzky, Edmonton
1931 Howie Morenz, Montreal	1957 Gordie Howe, Detroit	1983 Wayne Gretzky, Edmonton
1932 Harvey Jackson, Toronto	1958 Dickie Moore, Montreal	1984 Wayne Gretzky, Edmonton
1933 Bill Cook, N.Y. Rangers	1959 Dickie Moore, Montreal	1985 Wayne Gretzky, Edmonton
1934 Charlie Conacher, Toronto	1960 Bobby Hull, Chicago	1986 Wayne Gretzky, Edmonton
1935 Charlie Conacher, Toronto	1961 Bernie Geoffrion, Montreal	1987 Wayne Gretzky, Edmonton
1936 Dave Schriner, N.Y. Americans	1962 Bobby Hull, Chicago	1988 Mario Lemieux, Pittsburgh
1937 Dave Schriner, N.Y. Americans	1963 Gordie Howe, Detroit	1989 Mario Lemieux, Pittsburgh
1938 Gordie Drillon, Toronto	1964 Stan Mikita, Chicago	1990 Wayne Gretzky, Los Angeles
1939 Toe Blake, Montreal	1965 Stan Mikita, Chicago	1991 Wayne Gretzky, Los Angeles
1940 Milt Schmidt, Boston	1966 Bobby Hull, Chicago	1992 Mario Lemieux, Pittsburgh
1941 Bill Cowley, Boston	1967 Stan Mikita, Chicago	1993 Mario Lemieux, Pittsburgh
1942 Bryan Hextall, N.Y. Rangers	1968 Stan Mikita, Chicago	1994 Wayne Gretzky, Los Angeles
1943 Doug Bentley, Chicago	1969 Phil Esposito, Boston	1995 Jaromir Jagr, Pittsburgh
1944 Herbie Cain, Boston	1970 Bobby Orr, Boston	1996 Mario Lemieux, Pittsburgh
1945 Elmer Lach, Montreal	1971 Phil Esposito, Boston	1997 Mario Lemieux, Pittsburgh
1946 Max Bentley, Chicago	1972 Phil Esposito, Boston	1998 Jaromir Jagr, Pittsburgh
1947 Max Bentley, Chicago	1973 Phil Esposito, Boston	1999 Jaromir Jagr, Pittsburgh
1948 Elmer Lach, Montreal	1974 Phil Esposito, Boston	2000 Jaromir Jagr, Pittsburgh
1949 Roy Conacher, Chicago	1975 Bobby Orr, Boston	2001 Jaromir Jagr, Pittsburgh
1950 Ted Lindsay, Detroit	1976 Guy Lafleur, Montreal	2002 Jarome Iginla, Calgary
1951 Gordie Howe, Detroit	1977 Guy Lafleur, Montreal	2003 Peter Forsberg, Colorado
1952 Gordie Howe, Detroit	1978 Guy Lafleur, Montreal	2004 Martin St. Louis, Tampa Bay

Frank J. Selke Trophy (Best Defensive Forward)

1978 Bob Gainey, Montreal	1987 Dave Poulin, Philadelphia	1996 Sergei Federov, Detroit
1979 Bob Gainey, Montreal	1988 Guy Carbonneau, Montreal	1997 Michael Peca, Buffalo
1980 Bob Gainey, Montreal	1989 Guy Carbonneau, Montreal	1998 Jere Lehtinen, Dallas
1981 Bob Gainey, Montreal	1990 Rick Meagher, St. Louis	1999 Jere Lehtinen, Dallas
1982 Steve Kasper, Boston	1991 Dirk Graham, Chicago	2000 Steve Yzerman, Detroit
1983 Bobby Clarke, Philadelphia	1992 Guy Carbonneau, Montreal	2001 John Madden, New Jersey
1984 Doug Jarvis, Washington	1993 Doug Gilmour, Toronto	2002 Michael Peca, N.Y. Islanders
1985 Craig Ramsay, Buffalo	1994 Sergei Fedorov, Detroit	2003 Jere Lehtinen, Dallas
1986 Troy Murray, Chicago	1995 Ron Francis, Pittsburgh	2004 Kris Draper, Detroit

Vezina Trophy (Outstanding Goalie)*

1927 George Hainsworth, Montreal	1954 Harry Lumley, Toronto	1980 Sauve, Edwards, Buffalo
1928 George Hainsworth, Montreal	1955 Terry Sawchuk, Detroit	1981 Sevigny, Larocque, Herron,
1929 George Hainsworth, Montreal	1956 Jacques Plante, Montreal	Montreal
1930 Tiny Thompson, Boston	1957 Jacques Plante, Montreal	1982 Bill Smith, N.Y. Islanders
1931 Roy Worters, N.Y. Americans	1958 Jacques Plante, Montreal	1983 Pete Peeters, Boston
1932 Charlie Gardiner, Chicago	1959 Jacques Plante, Montreal	1984 Tom Barrasso, Buffalo
1933 Tiny Thompson, Boston	1960 Jacques Plante, Montreal	1985 Pelle Lindbergh, Philadelphia
1934 Charlie Gardiner, Chicago	1961 John Bower, Toronto	1986 John Vanbiesbrouck, N.Y. Rangers
1935 Lorne Chabot, Chicago	1962 Jacques Plante, Montreal	1987 Ron Hextall, Philadelphia
1936 Tiny Thompson, Boston	1963 Glenn Hall, Chicago	1988 Grant Fuhr, Edmonton
1937 Normie Smith, Detroit	1964 Charlie Hodge, Montreal	1989 Patrick Roy, Montreal
1938 Tiny Thompson, Boston	1965 Sawchuk, Bower, Toronto	1990 Patrick Roy, Montreal
1939 Frank Brimsek, Boston	1966 Worsley, Hodge, Montreal	1991 Ed Belfour, Chicago
1940 Dave Kerr, N.Y. Rangers	1967 Hall, DeJordy, Chicago	1992 Patrick Roy, Montreal
1941 Turk Broda, Toronto	1968 Worsley, Vachon, Montreal	1993 Ed Belfour, Chicago
1942 Frank Brimsek, Boston	1969 Hall, Plante, St. Louis	1994 Dominik Hasek, Buffalo
1943 Johnny Mowers, Detroit	1970 Tony Esposito, Chicago	1995 Dominik Hasek, Buffalo
1944 Bill Durnan, Montreal	1971 Giacomin, Villemure, N.Y. Rangers	1996 Jim Carey, Washington
1945 Bill Durnan, Montreal	1972 Esposito, Smith, Chicago	1997 Dominik Hasek, Buffalo
1946 Bill Durnan, Montreal	1973 Ken Dryden, Montreal	1998 Dominik Hasek, Buffalo
1947 Bill Durnan, Montreal	1974 Bernie Parent, Philadelphia;	1999 Dominik Hasek, Buffalo
1948 Turk Broda, Toronto	Tony Esposito, Chicago	2000 Olaf Kolzig, Washington
1949 Bill Durnan, Montreal	1975 Bernie Parent, Philadelphia	2001 Dominik Hasek, Buffalo
1950 Bill Durnan, Montreal	1976 Ken Dryden, Montreal	2002 Jose Theodore, Montreal
1951 Al Rollins, Toronto	1977 Dryden, Larocque, Montreal	2003 Martin Brodeur, New Jersey
1952 Terry Sawchuk, Detroit	1978 Dryden, Larocque, Montreal	2004 Martin Brodeur, New Jersey
1953 Terry Sawchuk, Detroit	1979 Dryden, Larocque, Montreal	

*Before 1982, awarded to the goalie or goalies who played a minimum of 25 games for the team that allowed the fewest goals; since 1982, awarded to the outstanding goalie, as determined by a vote of NHL general managers.

National Hockey Hall of Fame, Toronto, Ontario

(2004 inductees have an asterisk*)

PLAYERS	Bauer, Bobby	Boucher, George	Burch, Billy	Conacher, Roy	Delvecchio, Alex
Abel, Sid	Beliveau, Jean	*Bourque, Ray	Cameron, Harry	Connell, Alex	Denneny, Cy
Adams, Jack	Benedict, Clint	Bower, Johnny	Cheevers, Gerry	Cook, Bill	Dionne, Marcel
Apps, Syl	Bentley, Doug	Bowie, Dubbie	Clancy, King	Cook, Bun	Drillon, Gordie
Armstrong, George	Bentley, Max	Brimsek, Frank	Clapper, Dit	Coulter, Art	Drinkwater, Gra-
Bailey, Ace	Blake, Toe	Broadbent, Punch	Clarke, Bobby	Cournoyer, Yvan	ham
Bain, Dan	Boivin, Leo	Broda, Turk	Cleghorn, Sprague	Cowley, Bill	Dryden, Ken
Baker, Hobey	Boon, Dickie	Bucyk, John	*Coffey, Paul	Crawford, Rusty	Dumart, Woody
Barber, Bill	Bossy, Mike	Burch, Billy	Colville, Neil	Darragh, Jack	Dunderdale,
Barry, Marty	Bouchard, Butch	Cameron, Harry	Conacher, Charlie	Davidson, Scotty	Tommy
Bathgate, Andy	Boucher, Frank	Bucyk, John	Conacher, Lionel	Day, Hap	Durnan, Bill

Dutton, Red
Dye, Babe
Esposito, Phil
Esposito, Tony
Farrel, Arthur
Federko, Bernie
Fetisov, Viacheslav
Flaman, Fernie
Foyston, Frank
Fredrickson, Frank
Fuhr, Grant
Gadsby, Bill
Gainey, Bob
Gardiner, Chuck
Gardiner, Herb
Gardiner, Jimmy
Gartner, Mike
Geoffrion, Bernie
Gerard, Eddie
Giacomin, Eddie
Gilbert, Rod
Gillies, Clark
Gilmour, Billy
Goheen, Moose
Goodfellow, Ebbie
Goulet, Michel
Grant, Mike
Green, Shorty
Gretzky, Wayne
Griffis, Si
Hainsworth,
　George
Hall, Glenn
Hall, Joe
Harvey, Doug
Hawerchuk, Dale
Hay, George
Hern, Riley
Hextall, Bryan
Holmes, Hap
Hooper, Tom
Horner, Red
Horton, Tim
Howe, Gordie
Howe, Syd
Howell, Harry
Hull, Bobby
Hutton, Bouse
Hyland, Harry
Irvin, Dick

Jackson, Busher
Johnson, Ching
Johnson, Ernie
Johnson, Tom
Joliat, Aurel
Keats, Duke
Kelly, Red
Kennedy, Ted
Keon, Dave
Kurri, Jari
Lach, Elmer
Lafleur, Guy
LaFontaine, Pat
Lalonde, Newsy
Langway, Rod
Laperriere,
　Jacques
Lapointe, Guy
Laprade, Edgar
Laviolette, Jack
LeSueur, Percy
Lehman, Hughie
Lemaire, Jacques
Lemieux, Mario
Lewis, Herbie
Lindsay, Ted
Lumley, Harry
MacKay, Mickey
Mahovlich, Frank
Malone, Joe
Mantha, Sylvio
Marshall, Jack
Maxwell, Fred
McDonald, Lanny
McGee, Frank
McGimsie, Billy
McNamara, George
Mikita, Stan
Moore, Dickie
Moran, Paddy
Morenz, Howie
Mosienko, Bill
Mullen, Joe
*Murphy, Larry
Nighbor, Frank
Noble, Reg
O'Connor, Buddy
Oliver, Harry
Olmstead, Bert
Orr, Bobby

Parent, Bernie
Park, Brad
Patrick, Lester
Patrick, Lynn
Perreault, Gilbert
Phillips, Tom
Pilote, Pierre
Pitre, Didier
Plante, Jacques
Potvin, Denis
Pratt, Babe
Primeau, Joe
Pronovost, Marcel
Pulford, Bob
Pulford, Harvey
Quackenbush, Bill
Rankin, Frank
Ratelle, Jean
Rayner, Chuck
Reardon, Kenny
Richard, Henri
Richard, Maurice
Richardson,
　George
Roberts, Gordie
Robinson, Larry
Ross, Art
Russel, Blair
Russell, Ernie
Ruttan, Jack
Salming, Borje
Savard, Denis
Savard, Serge
Sawchuk, Terry
Scanlan, Fred
Schmidt, Milt
Schriner, Sweeney
Seibert, Earl
Seibert, Oliver
Shore, Eddie
Shutt, Steve
Siebert, Babe
Simpson, Joe
Sittler, Darryl
Smith, Alf
Smith, Billy
Smith, Clint
Smith, Hooley
Smith, Tommy
Stanley, Allan

Stanley, Barney
Stastny, Peter
Stewart, Jack
Stewart, Nels
Stuart, Bruce
Stuart, Hod
Taylor, Cyclone
Thompson, Tiny
Tretiak, Vladislav
Trihey, Harry
Trottier, Bryan
Ullman, Norm
Vezina, Georges
Walker, Jack
Walsh, Marty
Watson,
　Harry (Moose)
Watson, Harry
　Percival
Weiland, Cooney
Westwick, Harry
Whitcroft, Fred
Wilson, Phat
Worsley, Gump
Worters, Roy

BUILDERS
Adams, Charles
Adams, Weston
Ahearn, Bunny
Ahearn, Frank
Allan, Sir Montagu
Allen, Keith
Arbour, Al
Ballard, Harold
Bauer, Father David
Bickell, J.P.
Bowman, Scotty
Brown, George
Brown, Walter
Buckland, Frank
Bush, Walter, Jr.
Butterfield, Jack
Calder, Frank
Campbell, Angus
Campbell, Clarence
Cattarinich, Joseph
Dandurand, Leo
Dilio, Frank

Dudley, George
Dunn, James
*Fletcher, Cliff
Francis, Emile
Gibson, Jack
Gorman, Tommy
Griffiths, Frank
Hanley, Bill
Hay, Charles
Hendy, Jim
Hewitt, Foster
Hewitt, William
Hume, Fred
Ilitch, Mike
Imlach, Punch
Ivan, Tommy
Jennings, William
Johnson, Bob
Juckes, Gordon
Kilpatrick, John
Kilrea, Brian
Knox, Seymour
LeBel, Robert
Leader, Al
Lockhart, Thomas
Loicq, Paul
Mariucci, John
Mathers, Frank
McLaughlin,
　Frederic
Milford, Jake
Molson, Sen.
　Hartland
Morrison,
　Ian "Scotty"
Murray, Pere Athol
Neilson, Roger
Nelson, Francis
Norris, Bruce
Norris, James
Norris, James Sr.
Northey, William
O'Brien, J. Ambrose
O'Neill, Brian
Page, Frederick
Patrick, Craig
Patrick, Frank
Pickard, Allan

Pilous, Rudy
Poile, Bud
Pollock, Sam
Raymond,
　Sen. Donat
Robertson,
　John Ross
Robinson, Claude
Ross, Phillip
Sabetzki, Gunther
Sather, Glen
Selke, Frank
Sinden, Harry
Smith, Frank
Smythe, Conn
Snider, Ed
Stanley, Lord (of
　Preston)
Sutherland, Capt.
　James T.
Tarasov, Anatoli
Torrey, Bill
Turner, Lloyd
Tutt, William
Voss, Carl
Waghorne, Fred
Wirtz, Arthur
Wirtz, Bill
Ziegler, John A., Jr.

**REFEREES
AND
LINESMEN**
Armstrong, Neil
Ashley, John
Chadwick, Bill
D'Amico, John
Elliott, Chaucer
Hayes, George
Hewiston, Bobby
Ion, Mickey
Pavelich, Matt
Rodden, Mike
Smeaton, Cooper
Storey, Red
Udvari, Frank
Van Hellemond,
　Andy

NHL Home Ice[1]

Team	Name (built)	Capacity	Team	Name (built)	Capacity
Anaheim	The Arrowhead Pond of Anaheim (1993)	17,174	Montreal	Le Centre Bell[6] (1996)	21,273
Atlanta	Philips Arena (1999)	18,750	Nashville	Gaylord Entertainment Center[7] (1996)	17,500
Boston	FleetCenter (1995)	17,565	New Jersey	Continental Airlines Arena[8] (1981)	19,040
Buffalo	HSBC Arena[2] (1996)	18,690	N.Y. Islanders	Nassau Veterans Memorial Col. (1972)	16,297
Calgary	Pengrowth Saddledome (1983)	17,104	N.Y. Rangers	Madison Square Garden (1968)	18,200
Carolina	RBC Center[3] (1999)	18,730	Ottawa	Corel Centre (1996)	18,500
Chicago	United Center (1994)	20,500	Philadelphia	Wachovia Center[9] (1996)	19,519
Colorado	Pepsi Center (1999)	18,007	Phoenix	Glendale Arena (2003)	17,500
Columbus	Nationwide Arena (2000)	18,500	Pittsburgh	Mellon Arena[10] (1961)	17,537
Dallas	American Airlines Center (2001)	18,000	St. Louis	Savvis Center[11] (1994)	21,000
Detroit	Joe Louis Arena (1979)	19,983	San Jose	HP Pavilion[12] (1993)	17,483
Edmonton	Rexall Place[4] (1974)	17,100	Tampa Bay	St. Pete Times Forum[13] (1996)	19,758
Florida	Office Depot Center[5] (1998)	19,250	Toronto	Air Canada Centre (1999)	18,800
Los Angeles	Staples Center (1999)	18,118	Vancouver	GM Place (1995	18,422
Minnesota	Xcel Energy Arena (2000)	18,600	Washington	MCI Center (1997)	19,700

(1) At the end of the 2003-2004 season. (2) Marine Midland Arena, 1996-2000. (3) Entertainment & Sports Arena, 1996-2002. (4) Northlands Col., 1974-79; Edmonton Col., 1979-98; Skyreach Centre, 1998-2003. (5) National Car Rental Center, 1998-2002. (6) Le Centre Molson, 1996-2002. (7) Nashville Arena, 1997-1999. (8) Brendan Byrne/Meadowlands Arena, 1981-96. (9) First Union Center, 1996-2003. (10) Civic Arena, 1961-99. (11) Kiel Center, 1994-2000. (12) San Jose Arena, 1993-2000; Compaq Center, 2001. (13) Ice Palace, 1996-2002.

NCAA HOCKEY CHAMPIONS

1948	Michigan	1963	North Dakota	1977	Wisconsin	1991	N. Michigan
1949	Boston College	1964	Michigan	1978	Boston Univ.	1992	Lake Superior St.
1950	Colorado College	1965	Michigan Tech	1979	Minnesota	1993	Maine
1951	Michigan	1966	Michigan State	1980	North Dakota	1994	Lake Superior St.
1952	Michigan	1967	Cornell	1981	Wisconsin	1995	Boston Univ.
1953	Michigan	1968	Denver	1982	North Dakota	1996	Michigan
1954	RPI	1969	Denver	1983	Wisconsin	1997	North Dakota
1955	Michigan	1970	Cornell	1984	Bowling Green	1998	Michigan
1956	Michigan	1971	Boston Univ.	1985	RPI	1999	Maine
1957	Colorado College	1972	Boston Univ.	1986	Michigan State	2000	North Dakota
1958	Denver	1973	Wisconsin	1987	North Dakota	2001	Boston College
1959	North Dakota	1974	Minnesota	1988	Lake Superior St.	2002	Minnesota
1960	Denver	1975	Michigan Tech	1989	Harvard	2003	Minnesota
1961	Denver	1976	Minnesota	1990	Wisconsin	2004	Denver
1962	Michigan Tech						

SOCCER
2004 European Championships

Upstart Greece defeated Portugal, 1-0, in the final of the European Championships on July 4, 2004, at the Estadio da Luz in Lisbon, Portugal. Greek striker Angelos Charisteas scored the winning goal in the 57th minute. Greece's victory in Euro 2004 was hailed as one of the greatest upsets in soccer history. Led by German coach Otto Rehhagel, the Greeks used stifling defense and timely goals to beat their more heralded opponents, including Portugal, the Czech Republic and defending champion France—teams that featured some of soccer's biggest stars. Greek captain Theo Zagorakis, a midfielder, was named the top player of Euro 2004. Czech striker Milan Baros won the Golden Boot as the tournament's highest scorer, with 5 goals.

Euro 2004 First Round Standings

COUNTRY	Group A						COUNTRY	Group C					
	W	L	T	GF	GA	Pts		W	L	T	GF	GA	Pts
Portugal	2	1	0	4	2	6	Sweden	1	0	2	8	3	5
Greece	1	1	1	4	4	4	Denmark	1	0	2	4	2	5
Spain	1	1	1	2	2	4	Italy	1	0	2	3	2	5
Russia	1	2	0	2	4	3	Bulgaria	0	3	0	1	9	0

COUNTRY	Group B						COUNTRY	Group D					
	W	L	T	GF	GA	Pts		W	L	T	GF	GA	Pts
France	2	0	1	7	4	7	Czech Republic	3	0	0	7	4	9
England	2	1	0	8	4	6	Netherlands	1	1	1	6	4	4
Croatia	0	1	2	4	6	2	Germany	0	1	2	2	3	2
Switzerland	0	2	1	1	6	1	Latvia	0	2	1	1	5	1

Euro 2004 Elimination Round Results

Quarterfinals
Portugal 2, England 2 (Port. win 6-5 on pens.) (June 24)
Greece 1, France 0 (June 25)
Netherlands 0, Sweden 0 (Neth. won 5-4 on pens.) (June 26)
Czech Republic 3, Denmark 0 (June 27)

Semifinals
Portugal 2, Netherlands 1 (June 30)
Greece 1, Czech Rep. 0 (Greece won on silver goal) (July 1)

Final
Greece 1, Portugal 0 (July 4)

European Championships, 1960-2004

Year	Winner	Final opponent	Score	Site
1960	USSR	Yugoslavia	2-1 (extra time)	France
1964	Spain	USSR	2-1	Spain
1968	Italy	Yugoslavia	2-0	Italy
1972	W. Germany	USSR	3-0	Belgium
1976	Czechoslovakia	W. Germany	2-2 (Czech. won 5-3 on pens.)	Yugoslavia
1980	W. Germany	Belgium	2-1	Italy
1984	France	Spain	2-0	France
1988	Netherlands	USSR	2-0	W. Germany
1992	Denmark	Germany	2-0	Sweden
1996	Germany	Czech Rep.	2-1 (extra time)	England
2000	France	Italy	2-1 (extra time)	Belgium/Neth.
2004	Greece	Portugal	1-0	Portugal

2002 Men's World Cup

Soccer superpower Brazil won 7 straight matches, including a 2-0 win over Germany on June 30, 2002, to claim a record 5th World Cup. Favorites France, Argentina, and Portugal failed to advance to the 2nd round, while the U.S. had an unexpectedly strong showing, defeating Mexico, 2-0, before losing 1-0 to Germany in the quarterfinals. Co-host South Korea also played well, finishing 4th overall. A total of 198 teams vied for the 29 of 32 spots in the competition. (Co-hosts Japan and S. Korea, and 1998 winner France had automatic bids.) Brazilian forward Ronaldo won the Golden Boot for most goals, 8, including 2 in the final. Germany's Oliver Kahn became the 1st goalkeeper to win the Golden Ball as the tournament's best player.

The next World Cup was scheduled to be held in 12 German cities in 2006. Berlin was scheduled to host the finals. South Africa was awarded the 2010 World Cup on May 15, 2004, becoming the 1st African nation to win the rights to host the tournament.

Men's World Cup, 1930-2002

Year	Winner	Final opponent	Score	Site
1930	Uruguay	Argentina	4-2	Uruguay
1934	Italy	Czechoslovakia	2-1 (extra time)	Italy
1938	Italy	Hungary	4-2	France
1950	Uruguay	Brazil	2-1	Brazil
1954	W. Germany	Hungary	3-2	Switzerland
1958	Brazil	Sweden	5-2	Sweden
1962	Brazil	Czechoslovakia	3-1	Chile
1966	England	W. Germany	4-2 (extra time)	England
1970	Brazil	Italy	4-1	Mexico
1974	W. Germany	Netherlands	2-1	W. Germany
1978	Argentina	Netherlands	3-1 (extra time)	Argentina
1982	Italy	W. Germany	3-1	Spain
1986	Argentina	W. Germany	3-2	Mexico
1990	W. Germany	Argentina	1-0	Italy
1994	Brazil	Italy	0-0 (Braz. won 3-2 on pens.)	U.S.
1998	France	Brazil	3-0	France
2002	Brazil	Germany	2-0	Japan/S. Korea

► **IT'S A FACT:** Prior to its upset victory in the 2004 European Championships, Greece had qualified for only 2 other major soccer tournaments—the 1994 World Cup and the 1980 European Championships—and did not win a game in either event.

Major League Soccer

The San Jose Earthquakes won the Major League Soccer (MLS) Cup in Carson, CA, on Nov. 23, 2003, defeating the Chicago Fire, 4-2. Earthquakes forward Landon Donovan, who was also a star on the U.S. national team, scored 2 goals and was named the game's most valuable player. San Jose also won the MLS title in 2001. Kansas City Wizards midfielder Preki Radosavljevic was named the MVP of the MLS 2003 regular season. Radosavljevic, 40, was the league's leading scorer in 2003, with 12 goals and 17 assists. He also won the award in 1997, and is the first player to win it twice.

The 2004 MLS season opened April 3. On opening day, D.C. United beat the Earthquakes, 2-1, in Washington, D.C. In that game, 14-year-old United rookie forward Freddy Adu came on in the 61st minute, becoming the youngest player ever in MLS and one of the youngest people ever to play for a professional sports team in the U.S.

Salt Lake City, UT, was awarded an expansion franchise, to begin play in the 2005 season. The franchise was to be owned by a group led by Dave Checketts, a longtime sports executive. MLS awarded a second 2005 expansion franchise to Jorge Vergara, owner of the Guadalajara, Mexico-based club Chivas. That club would be based in Los Angeles, CA, and be named Club Deportivo Chivas USA. The expansion would bring the total number of MLS teams to 12 in 2005.

Major League Soccer (MLS) Cup Champions, 1996-2003

Year	Winner	Final opponent	Score	Site	MVP
1996	Washington, DC	Los Angeles	3-2 (OT)	Foxboro, MA	Marco Etcheverry
1997	Washington, DC	Colorado	2-1	Washington, DC	Jaime Moreno
1998	Chicago	Washington, DC	2-0	Pasadena, CA	Peter Nowak
1999	Washington, DC	Los Angeles	2-0	Foxboro, MA	Ben Olsen
2000	Kansas City	Chicago	1-0	Washington, DC	Tony Meola
2001	San Jose	Los Angeles	2-1 (OT)	Columbus, OH	Dwayne DeRosario
2002	Los Angeles	New England	1-0 (OT)	Foxboro, MA	Carlos Ruiz
2003	San Jose	Chicago	4-2	Carson, CA	Landon Donovan

2003 Women's World Cup

Germany defeated Sweden, 2-1, in extra time, in the final of the Women's World Cup Oct. 12, 2003, at the Home Depot Center in Carson, CA. The U.S. defeated Canada, 3-1, in the 3rd-place game Oct. 11. The next Women's World Cup was scheduled to be held in 2007 in China.

Women's World Cup, 1991-2003

Year	Winner	Final Opponent	Score	Site	Third Place
1991	U.S.	Norway	2-1	China	Germany
1995	Norway	Germany	2-0	Sweden	U.S.
1999	U.S.	China	0-0*	Pasadena, CA	Brazil
2003	Germany	Sweden	2-1 (extra time)	Carson, CA	U.S.

* U.S. 5-4, penalty kicks

Women's United Soccer Association

On Sept. 15, 2003, just 5 days before the start of the 2003 Women's World Cup, the Women's United Soccer Association announced that it would fold. Though some top players had taken pay cuts, the league reportedly had a deficit of about $16 million. Lack of TV ratings and sponsorship spelled doom for the league, which saw its average attendance fall from more than 8,000 per game in its inaugural year (2001) to 6,700 in 2003.

NCAA Soccer Champions, 1982-2003

Year[1]	Men	Women	Year[1]	Men	Women
1982	Indiana	North Carolina	1993	Virginia	North Carolina
1983	Indiana	North Carolina	1994	Virginia	North Carolina
1984	Clemson	North Carolina	1995	Wisconsin	Notre Dame
1985	UCLA	George Mason	1996	St. John's (NY)	North Carolina
1986	Duke	North Carolina	1997	UCLA	North Carolina
1987	Clemson	North Carolina	1998	Indiana	Florida
1988	Indiana	North Carolina	1999	Indiana	North Carolina
1989	Santa Clara (tie, 2 OT) Virginia	North Carolina	2000	Connecticut	North Carolina
1990	UCLA	North Carolina	2001	North Carolina	Santa Clara
1991	Virginia	North Carolina	2002	UCLA	Portland
1992	Virginia	North Carolina	2003	Indiana	North Carolina

(1) NCAA Championships began in 1959 for men, in 1982 for women.

RUGBY

2003 Rugby World Cup

England defeated defending champion Australia, 20-17, in extra time on Nov. 22, 2003, to win the Rugby World Cup, rugby union's premier tournament, before a crowd of 82,957 at Telstra Stadium in Sydney, Australia. England won the final in the last 30 seconds of the 20-minute extra-time period, when star fly-half Jonny Wilkinson slotted a drop goal from just outside the 22-meter line. Wilkinson, 24, tallied 113 points in the tournament, the most of any player. England became the 1st team from the Northern Hemisphere to win the quadrennial Rugby World Cup, which had first been played in 1987.

Rugby World Cup, 1987-2003

Year	Winner	Final Opponent	Score	Site
1987	New Zealand	France	29-9	Australia/New Zealand
1991	Australia	England	12-6	G. Britain/Ireland/France
1995	South Africa	New Zealand	15-12 (extra time)	South Africa
1999	Australia	France	35-12	G. Britain/Ireland/France
2003	England	Australia	20-17 extra time)	Australia

GOLF

Men's All-Time Major Professional Championship Leaders

(Through the 2004 season; *active PGA player; (a)=amateur.)

Player	Masters	U.S. Open	British Open	PGA	Total
Jack Nicklaus	1963, '65-66, '72, '75, '86	1962, '67, '72, '80	1966, '70, '78	1963, '71, '73, '75, '80	18
Walter Hagen	—	1914, '19	1922, '24, '28-29	1921, '24-27	11
Ben Hogan	1951, '53	1948, '50-51, '53	1953	1946, '48	9
Gary Player	1961, '74, '78	1965	1959, '68, '74	1962, '72	9
Tom Watson*	1977, '81	1982	1975, '77, '80, '82-83	—	8
Tiger Woods*	1997, 2001, 2002	2000, 2002	2000	1999, 2000	8
Bobby Jones (a)	—	1923, '26, '29-30	1926-27, '30	—	7
Arnold Palmer	1958, '60, '62, '64	1960	1961-62	—	7
Gene Sarazen	1935	1922, '32	1932	1922-23, '33	7
Sam Snead	1949, '52, '54	—	1946	1942, '49, '51	7
Harry Vardon	—	1900	1896, '98-99, 1903, '11, '14	—	7
Nick Faldo*	1989-90, '96	—	1987, '90, '92	—	6
Lee Trevino	—	1968, '71	1971-72	1974, '84	6

Professional Golfers' Association Leading Money Winners, by Year

Year	Player	Earnings	Year	Player	Earnings	Year	Player	Earnings
1946	Ben Hogan	$42,556	1966	Billy Casper	$121,944	1985	Curtis Strange	$542,321
1947	Jimmy Demaret	27,936	1967	Jack Nicklaus	188,988	1986	Greg Norman	653,296
1948	Ben Hogan	36,812	1968	Billy Casper	205,168	1987	Curtis Strange	925,941
1949	Sam Snead	31,593	1969	Frank Beard	175,223	1988	Curtis Strange	1,147,644
1950	Sam Snead	35,758	1970	Lee Trevino	157,037	1989	Tom Kite	1,395,278
1951	Lloyd Mangrum	26,088	1971	Jack Nicklaus	244,490	1990	Greg Norman	1,165,477
1952	Julius Boros	37,032	1972	Jack Nicklaus	320,542	1991	Corey Pavin	979,430
1953	Lew Worsham	34,002	1973	Jack Nicklaus	308,362	1992	Fred Couples	1,344,188
1954	Bob Toski	65,819	1974	Johnny Miller	353,201	1993	Nick Price	1,478,557
1955	Julius Boros	65,121	1975	Jack Nicklaus	323,149	1994	Nick Price	1,499,927
1956	Ted Kroll	72,835	1976	Jack Nicklaus	266,438	1995	Greg Norman	1,654,959
1957	Dick Mayer	65,835	1977	Tom Watson	310,653	1996	Tom Lehman	1,780,159
1958	Arnold Palmer	42,407	1978	Tom Watson	362,429	1997	Tiger Woods	2,066,833
1959	Art Wall, Jr.	53,167	1979	Tom Watson	462,636	1998	David Duval	2,591,031
1960	Arnold Palmer	75,262	1980	Tom Watson	530,808	1999	Tiger Woods	6,616,585
1961	Gary Player	64,540	1981	Tom Kite	375,699	2000	Tiger Woods	9,188,321
1962	Arnold Palmer	81,448	1982	Craig Stadler	446,462	2001	Tiger Woods	5,687,777
1963	Arnold Palmer	128,230	1983	Hal Sutton	426,668	2002	Tiger Woods	6,912,625
1964	Jack Nicklaus	113,284	1984	Tom Watson	476,260	2003	Vijay Singh	7,573,907
1965	Jack Nicklaus	140,752						

Masters Golf Tournament Winners

Year	Winner	Year	Winner	Year	Winner	Year	Winner
1934	Horton Smith	1954	Sam Snead	1971	Charles Coody	1988	Sandy Lyle
1935	Gene Sarazen	1955	Cary Middlecoff	1972	Jack Nicklaus	1989	Nick Faldo
1936	Horton Smith	1956	Jack Burke	1973	Tommy Aaron	1990	Nick Faldo
1937	Byron Nelson	1957	Doug Ford	1974	Gary Player	1991	Ian Woosnam
1938	Henry Picard	1958	Arnold Palmer	1975	Jack Nicklaus	1992	Fred Couples
1939	Ralph Guldahl	1959	Art Wall Jr.	1976	Ray Floyd	1993	Bernhard Langer
1940	Jimmy Demaret	1960	Arnold Palmer	1977	Tom Watson	1994	Jose Maria Olazabal
1941	Craig Wood	1961	Gary Player	1978	Gary Player	1995	Ben Crenshaw
1942	Byron Nelson	1962	Arnold Palmer	1979	Fuzzy Zoeller	1996	Nick Faldo
1943-45	not played	1963	Jack Nicklaus	1980	Seve Ballesteros	1997	Tiger Woods
1946	Herman Keiser	1964	Arnold Palmer	1981	Tom Watson	1998	Mark O'Meara
1947	Jimmy Demaret	1965	Jack Nicklaus	1982	Craig Stadler	1999	Jose Maria Olazabal
1948	Claude Harmon	1966	Jack Nicklaus	1983	Seve Ballesteros	2000	Vijay Singh
1949	Sam Snead	1967	Gay Brewer, Jr.	1984	Ben Crenshaw	2001	Tiger Woods
1950	Jimmy Demaret	1968	Bob Goalby	1985	Bernhard Langer	2002	Tiger Woods
1951	Ben Hogan	1969	George Archer	1986	Jack Nicklaus	2003	Mike Weir
1952	Sam Snead	1970	Billy Casper	1987	Larry Mize	2004	Phil Mickelson
1953	Ben Hogan						

United States Open Winners

(First contested in 1895)

Year	Winner	Year	Winner	Year	Winner	Year	Winner
1934	Olin Dutra	1954	Ed Furgol	1971	Lee Trevino	1988	Curtis Strange
1935	Sam Parks, Jr.	1955	Jack Fleck	1972	Jack Nicklaus	1989	Curtis Strange
1936	Tony Manero	1956	Cary Middlecoff	1973	Johnny Miller	1990	Hale Irwin
1937	Ralph Guldahl	1957	Dick Mayer	1974	Hale Irwin	1991	Payne Stewart
1938	Ralph Guldahl	1958	Tommy Bolt	1975	Lou Graham	1992	Tom Kite
1939	Byron Nelson	1959	Billy Casper	1976	Jerry Pate	1993	Lee Janzen
1940	Lawson Little	1960	Arnold Palmer	1977	Hubert Green	1994	Ernie Els
1941	Craig Wood	1961	Gene Littler	1978	Andy North	1995	Corey Pavin
1942-45	not played	1962	Jack Nicklaus	1979	Hale Irwin	1996	Steve Jones
1946	Lloyd Mangrum	1963	Julius Boros	1980	Jack Nicklaus	1997	Ernie Els
1947	L. Worsham	1964	Ken Venturi	1981	David Graham	1998	Lee Janzen
1948	Ben Hogan	1965	Gary Player	1982	Tom Watson	1999	Payne Stewart
1949	Cary Middlecoff	1966	Billy Casper	1983	Larry Nelson	2000	Tiger Woods
1950	Ben Hogan	1967	Jack Nicklaus	1984	Fuzzy Zoeller	2001	Retief Goosen
1951	Ben Hogan	1968	Lee Trevino	1985	Andy North	2002	Tiger Woods
1952	Julius Boros	1969	Orville Moody	1986	Ray Floyd	2003	Jim Furyk
1953	Ben Hogan	1970	Tony Jacklin	1987	Scott Simpson	2004	Retief Goosen

▶ **IT'S A FACT:** With his victory in the British Open in July 2004, American Todd Hamilton became the seventh first-time winner of a major in the last eight major tournaments in men's golf.

British Open Winners

(First contested in 1860)

Year	Winner	Year	Winner	Year	Winner	Year	Winner
1934	Henry Cotton	1956	Peter Thomson	1973	Tom Weiskopf	1989	Mark Calcavecchia
1935	Alf Perry	1957	Bobby Locke	1974	Gary Player	1990	Nick Faldo
1936	Alf Padgham	1958	Peter Thomson	1975	Tom Watson	1991	Ian Baker-Finch
1937	T.H. Cotton	1959	Gary Player	1976	Johnny Miller	1992	Nick Faldo
1938	R.A. Whitcombe	1960	Kel Nagle	1977	Tom Watson	1993	Greg Norman
1939	Richard Burton	1961	Arnold Palmer	1978	Jack Nicklaus	1994	Nick Price
1940-45	not played	1962	Arnold Palmer	1979	Seve Ballesteros	1995	John Daly
1946	Sam Snead	1963	Bob Charles	1980	Tom Watson	1996	Tom Lehman
1947	Fred Daly	1964	Tony Lema	1981	Bill Rogers	1997	Justin Leonard
1948	Henry Cotton	1965	Peter Thomson	1982	Tom Watson	1998	Mark O'Meara
1949	Bobby Locke	1966	Jack Nicklaus	1983	Tom Watson	1999	Paul Lawrie
1950	Bobby Locke	1967	Roberto de Vicenzo	1984	Seve Ballesteros	2000	Tiger Woods
1951	Max Faulkner	1968	Gary Player	1985	Sandy Lyle	2001	David Duval
1952	Bobby Locke	1969	Tony Jacklin	1986	Greg Norman	2002	Ernie Els
1953	Ben Hogan	1970	Jack Nicklaus	1987	Nick Faldo	2003	Ben Curtis
1954	Peter Thomson	1971	Lee Trevino	1988	Seve Ballesteros	2004	Todd Hamilton
1955	Peter Thomson	1972	Lee Trevino				

PGA Championship Winners

(First contested in 1916)

Year	Winner	Year	Winner	Year	Winner	Year	Winner
1934	Paul Runyan	1952	James Turnesa	1970	Dave Stockton	1988	Jeff Sluman
1935	Johnny Revolta	1953	Walter Burkemo	1971	Jack Nicklaus	1989	Payne Stewart
1936	Denny Shute	1954	Melvin Harbert	1972	Gary Player	1990	Wayne Grady
1937	Denny Shute	1955	Doug Ford	1973	Jack Nicklaus	1991	John Daly
1938	Paul Runyan	1956	Jack Burke	1974	Lee Trevino	1992	Nick Price
1939	Henry Picard	1957	Lionel Hebert	1975	Jack Nicklaus	1993	Paul Azinger
1940	Byron Nelson	1958	Dow Finsterwald	1976	Dave Stockton	1994	Nick Price
1941	Victor Ghezzi	1959	Bob Rosburg	1977	Lanny Wadkins	1995	Steve Elkington
1942	Sam Snead	1960	Jay Hebert	1978	John Mahaffey	1996	Mark Brooks
1943	not played	1961	Jerry Barber	1979	David Graham	1997	Davis Love III
1944	Bob Hamilton	1962	Gary Player	1980	Jack Nicklaus	1998	Vijay Singh
1945	Byron Nelson	1963	Jack Nicklaus	1981	Larry Nelson	1999	Tiger Woods
1946	Ben Hogan	1964	Bob Nichols	1982	Ray Floyd	2000	Tiger Woods
1947	Jim Ferrier	1965	Dave Marr	1983	Hal Sutton	2001	David Toms
1948	Ben Hogan	1966	Al Geiberger	1984	Lee Trevino	2002	Rich Beem
1949	Sam Snead	1967	Don January	1985	Hubert Green	2003	Shaun Micheel
1950	Chandler Harper	1968	Julius Boros	1986	Bob Tway	2004	Vijay Singh
1951	Sam Snead	1969	Ray Floyd	1987	Larry Nelson		

Women's All-Time Major Professional Championship Leaders

(Through the 2004 season; *active LPGA player.)

Player	Nabisco[1]	LPGA	U.S. Women's Open	du Maurier/ British Open[2]	Titleholders[3]	Western Open[4]	Total
Patty Berg	—	—	1946	—	1937-39, '48, '53, '55, '57	1941, '43, '48, '51, '55, '57-58	15
Mickey Wright. . . .	—	1958, '60-61, '63	1958-59, '61, '64	—	1961-62	1962-63, '66	13
Louise Suggs	—	1957	1949, '52	—	1946, '54, '56, '59	1946-47, '49, '53	11
Babe Zaharias . . .	—	—	1948, '50, '54	—	1947, '50, '52	1940, '44-45, '50	10
Betsy Rawls	—	1959, '69	1951, '53, '57, '60	—	—	1952, '59	8
Juli Inkster*.	1984, '89	1999, 2000	1999, 2002	1984	—	—	7
Annika Sorenstam*	2001-02	2003, 2004	1995-96	2003	—	—	7
Pat Bradley*.	1986	1986	1981	1980, '85-86	—	—	6
Betsy King*.	1987, '90, '97	1992	1989-90	—	—	—	6
Patty Sheehan* . .	1996	1983-84, '93	1992, '94	—	—	—	6
Kathy Whitworth. .	—	1967, '71, '75	—	—	1965-66	1967	6
Karrie Webb*	2000	2001	2000-2001	1999, 2002	—	—	6

(1) Nabisco Championship, formerly Nabisco Dinah Shore (1982-1999), designated major in 1983. (2) In 2001, the British Open replaced the du Maurier Classic as the LPGA's 4th major. (3) Titleholders Championship was major from 1930 to 1972. (4) Western Open was major from 1937 to 1967.

Ladies Professional Golf Association Leading Money Winners

Year	Player	Earnings	Year	Player	Earnings	Year	Player	Earnings
1954	Patty Berg.	$16,011	1971	Kathy Whitworth. . . .	$41,181	1988	Sherri Turner	$347,255
1955	Patty Berg.	16,492	1972	Kathy Whitworth. . . .	65,063	1989	Betsy King	654,132
1956	Marlene Hagge.	20,235	1973	Kathy Whitworth. . . .	82,854	1990	Beth Daniel	863,578
1957	Patty Berg.	16,272	1974	JoAnne Carner.	87,094	1991	Pat Bradley	763,118
1958	Beverly Hanson	12,629	1975	Sandra Palmer	94,805	1992	Dottie Mochrie	693,335
1959	Betsy Rawls	26,774	1976	Judy Rankin	150,734	1993	Betsy King	595,992
1960	Louise Suggs	16,892	1977	Judy Rankin	122,890	1994	Laura Davies	687,201
1961	Mickey Wright.	22,236	1978	Nancy Lopez	189,813	1995	Annika Sorenstam . .	666,533
1962	Mickey Wright.	21,641	1979	Nancy Lopez	215,987	1996	Karrie Webb.	1,002,000
1963	Mickey Wright.	31,269	1980	Beth Daniel.	231,000	1997	Annika Sorenstam . .	1,236,789
1964	Mickey Wright.	29,800	1981	Beth Daniel.	206,977	1998	Annika Sorenstam . .	1,092,748
1965	Kathy Whitworth	28,658	1982	JoAnne Carner.	310,399	1999	Karrie Webb.	1,591,959
1966	Kathy Whitworth	33,517	1983	JoAnne Carner.	291,404	2000	Karrie Webb.	1,876,853
1967	Kathy Whitworth	32,937	1984	Betsy King	266,771	2001	Annika Sorenstam . .	2,105,868
1968	Kathy Whitworth	48,379	1985	Nancy Lopez	416,472	2002	Annika Sorenstam . .	2,863,904
1969	Carol Mann.	49,152	1986	Pat Bradley.	492,021	2003	Annika Sorenstam . .	2,029,506
1970	Kathy Whitworth	30,235	1987	Ayako Okamoto	466,034			

Nabisco Championship Winners[1]

Year	Winner	Year	Winner	Year	Winner	Year	Winner
1983	Amy Alcott	1989	Juli Inkster	1995	Nanci Bowen	2000	Karrie Webb
1984	Juli Inkster	1990	Betsy King	1996	Patty Sheehan	2001	Annika Sorenstam
1985	Alice Miller	1991	Amy Alcott	1997	Betsy King	2002	Annika Sorenstam
1986	Pat Bradley	1992	Dottie Pepper	1998	Pat Hurst	2003	Patricia Meunier-Lebouc
1987	Betsy King	1993	Helen Alfredsson	1999	Dottie Pepper	2004	Grace Park
1988	Amy Alcott	1994	Donna Andrews				

(1) Formerly the Colgate Dinah Shore (1972-81), the Nabisco Dinah Shore (1982-99). Designated as a major championship in 1983.

LPGA Championship Winners

Year	Winner	Year	Winner	Year	Winner	Year	Winner
1955	Beverly Hanson	1968	Sandra Post	1981	Donna Caponi	1993	Patty Sheehan
1956	Marlene Hagge	1969	Betsy Rawls	1982	Jan Stephenson	1994	Laura Davies
1957	Louise Suggs	1970	Shirley Englehorn	1983	Patty Sheehan	1995	Kelly Robbins
1958	Mickey Wright	1971	Kathy Whitworth	1984	Patty Sheehan	1996	Laura Davies
1959	Betsy Rawls	1972	Kathy Ahern	1985	Nancy Lopez	1997	Chris Johnson
1960	Mickey Wright	1973	Mary Mills	1986	Pat Bradley	1998	Se Ri Pak
1961	Mickey Wright	1974	Sandra Haynie	1987	Jane Geddes	1999	Juli Inkster
1962	Judy Kimball	1975	Kathy Whitworth	1988	Sherri Turner	2000	Juli Inkster
1963	Mickey Wright	1976	Betty Burfeindt	1989	Nancy Lopez	2001	Karrie Webb
1964	Mary Mills	1977	Chako Higuchi	1990	Beth Daniel	2002	Se Ri Pak
1965	Sandra Haynie	1978	Nancy Lopez	1991	Meg Mallon	2003	Annika Sorenstam
1966	Gloria Ehret	1979	Donna Caponi	1992	Betsy King	2004	Annika Sorenstam
1967	Kathy Whitworth	1980	Sally Little				

U.S. Women's Open Winners

Year	Winner	Year	Winner	Year	Winner	Year	Winner
1946	Patty Berg	1961	Mickey Wright	1975	Sandra Palmer	1990	Betsy King
1947	Betty Jameson	1962	Murle Lindstrom	1976	JoAnne Carner	1991	Meg Mallon
1948	Babe Zaharias	1963	Mary Mills	1977	Hollis Stacy	1992	Patty Sheehan
1949	Louise Suggs	1964	Mickey Wright	1978	Hollis Stacy	1993	Lauri Merten
1950	Babe Zaharias	1965	Carol Mann	1979	Jerilyn Britz	1994	Patty Sheehan
1951	Betsy Rawls	1966	Sandra Spuzich	1980	Amy Alcott	1995	Annika Sorenstam
1952	Louise Suggs	1967	Catherine Lacoste	1981	Pat Bradley	1996	Annika Sorenstam
1953	Betsy Rawls		(amateur)	1982	Janet Alex	1997	Alison Nicholas
1954	Babe Zaharias	1968	Susie Maxwell Berning	1983	Jan Stephenson	1998	Se Ri Pak
1955	Fay Crocker	1969	Donna Caponi	1984	Hollis Stacy	1999	Juli Inkster
1956	Mrs. K. Cornelius	1970	Donna Caponi	1985	Kathy Baker	2000	Karrie Webb
1957	Betsy Rawls	1971	JoAnne Carner	1986	Jane Geddes	2001	Karrie Webb
1958	Mickey Wright	1972	Susie Maxwell Berning	1987	Laura Davies	2002	Juli Inkster
1959	Mickey Wright	1973	Susie Maxwell Berning	1988	Liselotte Neumann	2003	Hilary Lunke
1960	Betsy Rawls	1974	Sandra Haynie	1989	Betsy King	2004	Meg Mallon

Women's British Open Winners[1]

Year	Winner	Year	Winner	Year	Winner	Year	Winner
2001	Se Ri Pak	2002	Karrie Webb	2003	Annika Sorenstam	2004	Karen Stupples

(1) First held as the Ladies' British Open in 1976; became the LPGA's 4th major championship in 2001, replacing the du Maurier Classic.

du Maurier Classic Winners[1]

Year	Winner	Year	Winner	Year	Winner	Year	Winner
1979	Amy Alcott	1985	Pat Bradley	1991	Nancy Scranton	1996	Laura Davies
1980	Pat Bradley	1986	Pat Bradley	1992	Sherri Steinhauer	1997	Colleen Walker
1981	Jan Stephenson	1987	Jody Rosenthal	1993	Brandie Burton	1998	Brandie Burton
1982	Sandra Haynie	1988	Sally Little	1994	Martha Nause	1999	Karrie Webb
1983	Hollis Stacy	1989	Tammie Green	1995	Jenny Lidback	2000	Meg Mallon
1984	Juli Inkster	1990	Cathy Johnston				

(1) Formerly the Peter Jackson Classic (1974-82). Designated a major championship, 1979-2000.

International Golf

Ryder Cup

Began as a biennial team competition between pro golfers from the U.S. and Great Britain. The British team was expanded in 1973 to include players from Ireland and in 1979 from the rest of Europe. Europe routed the Americans in the 2004 Ryder Cup, held Sept. 17-19 at Oakland Hills CC, Bloomfield Township, MI. Led by captain Bernhard Langer, Europe won 18½-9½, the biggest margin of victory ever for a European team.

Year	Winner	Year	Winner	Year	Winner	Year	Winner
1927	U.S., 9½-2½	1951	U.S., 9½-2½	1969	Draw, 16-16	1987	Europe, 15-13
1929	Britain-Ireland, 7-5	1953	U.S., 6½-5½	1971	U.S., 18½-13½	1989	Draw, 14-14
1931	U.S., 9-3	1955	U.S., 8-4	1973	U.S., 19-13	1991	U.S., 14½-13½
1933	Britain, 6½-5½	1957	Britain-Ireland, 7½-4½	1975	U.S., 21-11	1993	U.S., 15-13
1935	U.S., 9-3	1959	U.S., 8½-3½	1977	U.S., 12½-7½	1995	Europe, 14½-13½
1937	U.S., 8-4	1961	U.S., 14½-9½	1979	U.S., 17-11	1997	Europe, 14½-13½
1939-45	Not played	1963	U.S., 23-9	1981	U.S., 18½-9½	1999	U.S., 14½-13½
1947	U.S., 11-1	1965	U.S., 19½-12½	1983	U.S., 14½-13½	2002	Europe, 15½-12½
1949	U.S., 7-5	1967	U.S., 23½-8½	1985	Europe, 16½-11½	2004	Europe, 18½-9½

Solheim Cup

Began in 1990 as a biennial team competition between pro women golfers from Europe and the U.S. In the Sept. 14 final round of the 2003 Cup in Sweden, Europe reached the 14½ points needed to win with 5 matches in progress. In an unprecedented move, the trailing players conceded, and all the golfers walked off the course. Competition moved to odd years in 2003 to alternate with the Ryder Cup, which was postponed and moved permanently to even years after the Sept. 2001 terrorist attacks. The 2005 Cup was scheduled to be held Sept. 9-11, at Crooked Stick Golf Club in Carmel, IN.

Year	Winner	Year	Winner	Year	Winner	Year	Winner
1990	U.S., 11½-4½	1994	U.S., 13-7	1998	U.S., 16-12	2002	U.S., 15½-12½
1992	Europe, 11½-6½	1996	U.S., 17-11	2000	Europe, 14½-11½	2003	Europe, 17½-10½

TENNIS

Australian Open Singles Champions, 1969-2004

(First contested 1905 for men, 1922 for women. Became an Open Championship in 1969.)

*2 tournaments held in 1977 (Jan. & Dec.). **In 1986 tournament moved to Jan. 1987; no championship in 1986.

Men's Singles

Year	Champion	Final Opponent
1969	Rod Laver	Andres Gimeno
1970	Arthur Ashe	Dick Crealy
1971	Ken Rosewall	Arthur Ashe
1972	Ken Rosewall	Mal Anderson
1973	John Newcombe	Onny Parun
1974	Jimmy Connors	Phil Dent
1975	John Newcombe	Jimmy Connors
1976	Mark Edmondson	John Newcombe
1977*	Roscoe Tanner	Guillermo Vilas
	Vitas Gerulaitis	John Lloyd
1978	Guillermo Vilas	John Marks
1979	Guillermo Vilas	John Sadri
1980	Brian Teacher	Kim Warwick
1981	Johan Kriek	Steve Denton
1982	Johan Kriek	Steve Denton
1983	Mats Wilander	Ivan Lendl
1984	Mats Wilander	Kevin Curren
1985**	Stefan Edberg	Mats Wilander
1987	Stefan Edberg	Pat Cash
1988	Mats Wilander	Pat Cash
1989	Ivan Lendl	Miloslav Mecir
1990	Ivan Lendl	Stefan Edberg
1991	Boris Becker	Ivan Lendl
1992	Jim Courier	Stefan Edberg
1993	Jim Courier	Stefan Edberg
1994	Pete Sampras	Todd Martin
1995	Andre Agassi	Pete Sampras
1996	Boris Becker	Michael Chang
1997	Pete Sampras	Carlos Moya
1998	Petr Korda	Marcelo Rios
1999	Yevgeny Kafelnikov	Thomas Enqvist
2000	Andre Agassi	Yevgeny Kafelnikov
2001	Andre Agassi	Arnaud Clement
2002	Thomas Johansson	Marat Safin
2003	Andre Agassi	Rainer Schuettler
2004	Roger Federer	Marat Safin

Women's Singles

Year	Champion	Final Opponent
1969	Margaret Smith Court	Billie Jean King
1970	Margaret Smith Court	Kerry Melville Reid
1971	Margaret Smith Court	Evonne Goolagong
1972	Virginia Wade	Evonne Goolagong
1973	Margaret Smith Court	Evonne Goolagong
1974	Evonne Goolagong	Chris Evert
1975	Evonne Goolagong	Martina Navratilova
1976	Evonne Goolagong	Renata Tomanova
1977*	Kerry Reid	Dianne Balestrat
	Evonne Goolagong	Helen Gourlay
1978	Chris O'Neill	Betsy Nagelsen
1979	Barbara Jordan	Sharon Walsh
1980	Hana Mandlikova	Wendy Turnbull
1981	Martina Navratilova	Chris Evert Lloyd
1982	Chris Evert Lloyd	Martina Navratilova
1983	Martina Navratilova	Kathy Jordan
1984	Chris Evert Lloyd	Helena Sukova
1985**	Martina Navratilova	Chris Evert Lloyd
1987	Hana Mandlikova	Martina Navratilova
1988	Steffi Graf	Chris Evert
1989	Steffi Graf	Helena Sukova
1990	Steffi Graf	Mary Joe Fernandez
1991	Monica Seles	Jana Novotna
1992	Monica Seles	Mary Joe Fernandez
1993	Monica Seles	Steffi Graf
1994	Steffi Graf	Arantxa Sánchez Vicario
1995	Mary Pierce	Arantxa Sánchez Vicario
1996	Monica Seles	Anke Huber
1997	Martina Hingis	Mary Pierce
1998	Martina Hingis	Conchita Martínez
1999	Martina Hingis	Amelie Mauresmo
2000	Lindsay Davenport	Martina Hingis
2001	Jennifer Capriati	Martina Hingis
2002	Jennifer Capriati	Martina Hingis
2003	Serena Williams	Venus Williams
2004	Justine Henin-Hardenne	Kim Clijsters

French Open Singles Champions, 1968-2004

(First contested 1891 for men, 1897 for women. Became an Open Championship in 1968.)

Men's Singles

Year	Champion	Final Opponent
1968	Ken Rosewall	Rod Laver
1969	Rod Laver	Ken Rosewall
1970	Jan Kodes	Zeljko Franulovic
1971	Jan Kodes	Ilie Nastase
1972	Andres Gimeno	Patrick Proisy
1973	Ilie Nastase	Nikki Pilic
1974	Bjorn Borg	Manuel Orantes
1975	Bjorn Borg	Guillermo Vilas
1976	Adriano Panatta	Harold Solomon
1977	Guillermo Vilas	Brian Gottfried
1978	Bjorn Borg	Guillermo Vilas
1979	Bjorn Borg	Victor Pecci
1980	Bjorn Borg	Vitas Gerulaitis
1981	Bjorn Borg	Ivan Lendl
1982	Mats Wilander	Guillermo Vilas
1983	Yannick Noah	Mats Wilander
1984	Ivan Lendl	John McEnroe
1985	Mats Wilander	Ivan Lendl
1986	Ivan Lendl	Mikael Pernfors
1987	Ivan Lendl	Mats Wilander
1988	Mats Wilander	Henri Leconte
1989	Michael Chang	Stefan Edberg
1990	Andres Gomez	Andre Agassi
1991	Jim Courier	Andre Agassi
1992	Jim Courier	Petr Korda
1993	Sergi Bruguera	Jim Courier
1994	Sergi Bruguera	Alberto Berasategui
1995	Thomas Muster	Michael Chang
1996	Yevgeny Kafelnikov	Michael Stich
1997	Gustavo Kuerten	Sergei Bruguera
1998	Carlos Moya	Alex Corretja
1999	Andre Agassi	Andrei Medvedev
2000	Gustavo Kuerten	Magnus Norman
2001	Gustavo Kuerten	Alex Corretja
2002	Albert Costa	Juan Carlos Ferrero
2003	Juan Carlos Ferrero	Martin Verkerk
2004	Gaston Gaudio	Guillermo Coria

Women's Singles

Year	Champion	Final Opponent
1968	Nancy Richey	Ann Jones
1969	Margaret Smith Court	Ann Jones
1970	Margaret Smith Court	Helga Niessen
1971	Evonne Goolagong	Helen Gourlay
1972	Billie Jean King	Evonne Goolagong
1973	Margaret Smith Court	Chris Evert
1974	Chris Evert	Olga Morozova
1975	Chris Evert	Martina Navratilova
1976	Sue Barker	Renata Tomanova
1977	Mima Jausovec	Florenza Mihai
1978	Virginia Ruzici	Mima Jausovec
1979	Chris Evert Lloyd	Wendy Turnbull
1980	Chris Evert Lloyd	Virginia Ruzici
1981	Hana Mandlikova	Sylvia Hanika
1982	Martina Navratilova	Andrea Jaeger
1983	Chris Evert Lloyd	Mima Jausovec
1984	Martina Navratilova	Chris Evert Lloyd
1985	Chris Evert Lloyd	Martina Navratilova
1986	Chris Evert Lloyd	Martina Navratilova
1987	Steffi Graf	Martina Navratilova
1988	Steffi Graf	Natalia Zvereva
1989	Arantxa Sánchez Vicario	Steffi Graf
1990	Monica Seles	Steffi Graf
1991	Monica Seles	Arantxa Sánchez Vicario
1992	Monica Seles	Steffi Graf
1993	Steffi Graf	Mary Joe Fernandez
1994	Arantxa Sánchez Vicario	Mary Pierce
1995	Steffi Graf	Arantxa Sánchez Vicario
1996	Steffi Graf	Arantxa Sánchez Vicario
1997	Iva Majoli	Martina Hingis
1998	Arantxa Sánchez Vicario	Monica Seles
1999	Steffi Graf	Martina Hingis
2000	Mary Pierce	Conchita Martinez
2001	Jennifer Capriati	Kim Clijsters
2002	Serena Williams	Venus Williams
2003	Justine Henin-Hardenne	Kim Clijsters
2004	Anastasia Myskina	Elena Dementieva

U.S. Open Champions, 1925-2004
(Became an Open Championship in 1970.)

Men's Singles			Women's Singles		
(First contested 1881)			(First contested 1887)		
Year	Champion	Final Opponent	Year	Champion	Final Opponent
1925	Bill Tilden	William Johnston	1925	Helen Willis	Kathleen McKane
1926	Rene Lacoste	Jean Borotra	1926	Molla B. Mallory	Elizabeth Ryan
1927	Rene Lacoste	Bill Tilden	1927	Helen Wills	Betty Nuthall
1928	Henri Cochet	Francis Hunter	1928	Helen Wills	Helen Jacobs
1929	Bill Tilden	Francis Hunter	1929	Helen Wills	M. Watson
1930	John Doeg	Francis Shields	1930	Betty Nuthall	L. A. Harper
1931	H. Ellsworth Vines	George Lott	1931	Helen Wills Moody	E. B. Whittingstall
1932	H. Ellsworth Vines	Henri Cochet	1932	Helen Jacobs	Carolin A. Babcock
1933	Fred Perry	John Crawford	1933	Helen Jacobs	Helen Wills Moody
1934	Fred Perry	Wilmer Allison	1934	Helen Jacobs	Sarah H. Palfrey
1935	Wilmer Allison	Sidney Wood	1935	Helen Jacobs	Sarah Palfrey Fabyan
1936	Fred Perry	Don Budge	1936	Alice Marble	Helen Jacobs
1937	Don Budge	Baron G. von Cramm	1937	Anita Lizana	Jadwiga Jedrzejowska
1938	Don Budge	C. Gene Mako	1938	Alice Marble	Nancye Wynne
1939	Robert Riggs	S. Welby Van Horn	1939	Alice Marble	Helen Jacobs
1940	Don McNeill	Robert Riggs	1940	Alice Marble	Helen Jacobs
1941	Robert Riggs	F. L. Kovacs	1941	Sarah Palfrey Cooke	Pauline Betz
1942	F. R. Schroeder Jr.	Frank Parker	1942	Pauline Betz	Louise Brough
1943	Joseph Hunt	Jack Kramer	1943	Pauline Betz	Louise Brough
1944	Frank Parker	William Talbert	1944	Pauline Betz	Margaret Osborne
1945	Frank Parker	William Talbert	1945	Sarah Palfrey Cooke	Pauline Betz
1946	Jack Kramer	Thomas Brown Jr.	1946	Pauline Betz	Doris Hart
1947	Jack Kramer	Frank Parker	1947	Louise Brough	Margaret Osborne
1948	Pancho Gonzales	Eric Sturgess	1948	Margaret Osborne duPont	Louise Brough
1949	Pancho Gonzales	F. R. Schroeder Jr.	1949	Margaret Osborne duPont	Doris Hart
1950	Arthur Larsen	Herbert Flam	1950	Margaret Osborne duPont	Doris Hart
1951	Frank Sedgman	E. Victor Seixas Jr.	1951	Maureen Connolly	Shirley Fry
1952	Frank Sedgman	Gardnar Mulloy	1952	Maureen Connolly	Doris Hart
1953	Tony Trabert	E. Victor Seixas Jr.	1953	Maureen Connolly	Doris Hart
1954	E. Victor Seixas Jr.	Rex Hartwig	1954	Doris Hart	Louise Brough
1955	Tony Trabert	Ken Rosewall	1955	Doris Hart	Patricia Ward
1956	Ken Rosewall	Lewis Hoad	1956	Shirley Fry	Althea Gibson
1957	Malcolm Anderson	Ashley Cooper	1957	Althea Gibson	Louise Brough
1958	Ashley Cooper	Malcolm Anderson	1958	Althea Gibson	Darlene Hard
1959	Neale A. Fraser	Alejandro Olmedo	1959	Maria Bueno	Christine Truman
1960	Neale A. Fraser	Rod Laver	1960	Darlene Hard	Maria Bueno
1961	Roy Emerson	Rod Laver	1961	Darlene Hard	Ann Haydon
1962	Rod Laver	Roy Emerson	1962	Margaret Smith	Darlene Hard
1963	Rafael Osuna	F. A. Froehling 3rd	1963	Maria Bueno	Margaret Smith
1964	Roy Emerson	Fred Stolle	1964	Maria Bueno	Carole Graebner
1965	Manuel Santana	Cliff Drysdale	1965	Margaret Smith	Billie Jean Moffitt
1966	Fred Stolle	John Newcombe	1966	Maria Bueno	Nancy Richey
1967	John Newcombe	Clark Graebner	1967	Billie Jean King	Ann Haydon Jones
1968	Arthur Ashe	Tom Okker	1968	Virginia Wade	Billie Jean King
1969	Rod Laver	Tony Roche	1969	Margaret Smith Court	Nancy Richey
1970	Ken Rosewall	Tony Roche	1970	Margaret Smith Court	Rosemary Casals
1971	Stan Smith	Jan Kodes	1971	Billie Jean King	Rosemary Casals
1972	Ilie Nastase	Arthur Ashe	1972	Billie Jean King	Kerry Melville
1973	John Newcombe	Jan Kodes	1973	Margaret Smith Court	Evonne Goolagong
1974	Jimmy Connors	Ken Rosewall	1974	Billie Jean King	Evonne Goolagong
1975	Manuel Orantes	Jimmy Connors	1975	Chris Evert	Evonne Goolagong
1976	Jimmy Connors	Bjorn Borg	1976	Chris Evert	Evonne Goolagong
1977	Guillermo Vilas	Jimmy Connors	1977	Chris Evert	Wendy Turnbull
1978	Jimmy Connors	Bjorn Borg	1978	Chris Evert	Pam Shriver
1979	John McEnroe	Vitas Gerulaitis	1979	Tracy Austin	Chris Evert Lloyd
1980	John McEnroe	Bjorn Borg	1980	Chris Evert Lloyd	Hana Mandlikova
1981	John McEnroe	Bjorn Borg	1981	Tracy Austin	Martina Navratilova
1982	Jimmy Connors	Ivan Lendl	1982	Chris Evert Lloyd	Hana Mandlikova
1983	Jimmy Connors	Ivan Lendl	1983	Martina Navratilova	Chris Evert Lloyd
1984	John McEnroe	Ivan Lendl	1984	Martina Navratilova	Chris Evert Lloyd
1985	Ivan Lendl	John McEnroe	1985	Hana Mandlikova	Martina Navratilova
1986	Ivan Lendl	Miloslav Mecir	1986	Martina Navratilova	Helena Sukova
1987	Ivan Lendl	Mats Wilander	1987	Martina Navratilova	Steffi Graf
1988	Mats Wilander	Ivan Lendl	1988	Steffi Graf	Gabriela Sabatini
1989	Boris Becker	Ivan Lendl	1989	Steffi Graf	Martina Navratilova
1990	Pete Sampras	Andre Agassi	1990	Gabriela Sabatini	Steffi Graf
1991	Stefan Edberg	Jim Courier	1991	Monica Seles	Martina Navratilova
1992	Stefan Edberg	Pete Sampras	1992	Monica Seles	Arantxa Sanchez Vicario
1993	Pete Sampras	Cedric Pioline	1993	Steffi Graf	Helena Sukova
1994	Andre Agassi	Michael Stich	1994	Arantxa Sanchez Vicario	Steffi Graf
1995	Pete Sampras	Andre Agassi	1995	Steffi Graf	Monica Seles
1996	Pete Sampras	Michael Chang	1996	Steffi Graf	Monica Seles
1997	Patrick Rafter	Greg Rusedski	1997	Martina Hingis	Venus Williams
1998	Patrick Rafter	Mark Philippoussis	1998	Lindsay Davenport	Martina Hingis
1999	Andre Agassi	Todd Martin	1999	Serena Williams	Martina Hingis
2000	Marat Safin	Pete Sampras	2000	Venus Williams	Lindsay Davenport
2001	Lleyton Hewitt	Pete Sampras	2001	Venus Williams	Serena Williams
2002	Pete Sampras	Andre Agassi	2002	Serena Williams	Venus Williams
2003	Andy Roddick	Juan Carlos Ferrero	2003	Justine Henin-Hardenne	Kim Clijsters
2004	Roger Federer	Lleyton Hewitt	2004	Svetlana Kuznetsova	Elena Dementieva

All-England Champions, Wimbledon, 1925-2004
(Became an Open Championship in 1968.)

Men's Singles
(First contested 1877)

Women's Singles
(First contested 1884)

Year	Champion	Final Opponent	Year	Champion	Final Opponent
1925	Rene Lacoste	Jean Borotra	1925	Suzanne Lenglen	Joan Fry
1926	Jean Borotra	Howard Kinsey	1926	Kathleen McKane Godfree	Lili de Alvarez
1927	Henri Cochet	Jean Borotra	1927	Helen Wills	Lili de Alvarez
1928	Rene Lacoste	Henri Cochet	1928	Helen Wills	Lili de Alvarez
1929	Henri Cochet	Jean Borotra	1929	Helen Wills	Helen Jacobs
1930	Bill Tilden	Wilmer Allison	1930	Helen Wills Moody	Elizabeth Ryan
1931	Sidney B. Wood	Francis X. Shields	1931	Cilly Aussem	Hilde Kranwinkel
1932	Ellsworth Vines	Henry Austin	1932	Helen Wills Moody	Helen Jacobs
1933	Jack Crawford	Ellsworth Vines	1933	Helen Wills Moody	Dorothy Round
1934	Fred Perry	Jack Crawford	1934	Dorothy Round	Helen Jacobs
1935	Fred Perry	Gottfried von Cramm	1935	Helen Wills Moody	Helen Jacobs
1936	Fred Perry	Gottfried von Cramm	1936	Helen Jacobs	Hilde Kranwinkel Sperling
1937	Donald Budge	Gottfried von Cramm	1937	Dorothy Round	Jadwiga Jedrzejowska
1938	Donald Budge	Henry Austin	1938	Helen Wills Moody	Helen Jacobs
1939	Bobby Riggs	Elwood Cooke	1939	Alice Marble	Kay Stammers
1940-45	Not held	Not held	1940-45	Not held	Not held
1946	Yvon Petra	Geoff E. Brown	1946	Pauline Betz	Louise Brough
1947	Jack Kramer	Tom P. Brown	1947	Margaret Osborne	Doris Hart
1948	Bob Falkenburg	John Bromwich	1948	Louise Brough	Doris Hart
1949	Ted Schroeder	Jaroslav Drobny	1949	Louise Brough	Margaret Osborne duPont
1950	Budge Patty	Frank Sedgman	1950	Louise Brough	Margaret Osborne duPont
1951	Dick Savitt	Ken McGregor	1951	Doris Hart	Shirley Fry
1952	Frank Sedgman	Jaroslav Drobny	1952	Maureen Connolly	Louise Brough
1953	Vic Seixas	Kurt Nielsen	1953	Maureen Connolly	Doris Hart
1954	Jaroslav Drobny	Ken Rosewall	1954	Maureen Connolly	Louise Brough
1955	Tony Trabert	Kurt Nielsen	1955	Louise Brough	Beverly Fleitz
1956	Lew Hoad	Ken Rosewall	1956	Shirley Fry	Angela Buxton
1957	Lew Hoad	Ashley Cooper	1957	Althea Gibson	Darlene Hard
1958	Ashley Cooper	Neale Fraser	1958	Althea Gibson	Angela Mortimer
1959	Alex Olmedo	Rod Laver	1959	Maria Bueno	Darlene Hard
1960	Neale Fraser	Rod Laver	1960	Maria Bueno	Sandra Reynolds
1961	Rod Laver	Chuck McKinley	1961	Angela Mortimer	Christine Truman
1962	Rod Laver	Martin Mulligan	1962	Karen Hantze-Susman	Vera Sukova
1963	Chuck McKinley	Fred Stolle	1963	Margaret Smith	Billie Jean Moffitt
1964	Roy Emerson	Fred Stolle	1964	Maria Bueno	Margaret Smith
1965	Roy Emerson	Fred Stolle	1965	Margaret Smith	Maria Bueno
1966	Manuel Santana	Dennis Ralston	1966	Billie Jean King	Maria Bueno
1967	John Newcombe	Wilhelm Bungert	1967	Billie Jean King	Ann Haydon Jones
1968	Rod Laver	Tony Roche	1968	Billie Jean King	Judy Tegart
1969	Rod Laver	John Newcombe	1969	Ann Haydon-Jones	Billie Jean King
1970	John Newcombe	Ken Rosewall	1970	Margaret Smith Court	Billie Jean King
1971	John Newcombe	Stan Smith	1971	Evonne Goolagong	Margaret Smith Court
1972	Stan Smith	Ilie Nastase	1972	Billie Jean King	Evonne Goolagong
1973	Jan Kodes	Alex Metreveli	1973	Billie Jean King	Chris Evert
1974	Jimmy Connors	Ken Rosewall	1974	Chris Evert	Olga Morozova
1975	Arthur Ashe	Jimmy Connors	1975	Billie Jean King	Evonne Goolagong Cawley
1976	Bjorn Borg	Ilie Nastase	1976	Chris Evert	Evonne Goolagong Cawley
1977	Bjorn Borg	Jimmy Connors	1977	Virginia Wade	Betty Stove
1978	Bjorn Borg	Jimmy Connors	1978	Martina Navratilova	Chris Evert
1979	Bjorn Borg	Roscoe Tanner	1979	Martina Navratilova	Chris Evert Lloyd
1980	Bjorn Borg	John McEnroe	1980	Evonne Goolagong	Chris Evert Lloyd
1981	John McEnroe	Bjorn Borg	1981	Chris Evert Lloyd	Hana Mandlikova
1982	Jimmy Connors	John McEnroe	1982	Martina Navratilova	Chris Evert Lloyd
1983	John McEnroe	Chris Lewis	1983	Martina Navratilova	Andrea Jaeger
1984	John McEnroe	Jimmy Connors	1984	Martina Navratilova	Chris Evert Lloyd
1985	Boris Becker	Kevin Curren	1985	Martina Navratilova	Chris Evert Lloyd
1986	Boris Becker	Ivan Lendl	1986	Martina Navratilova	Hana Mandlikova
1987	Pat Cash	Ivan Lendl	1987	Martina Navratilova	Steffi Graf
1988	Stefan Edberg	Boris Becker	1988	Steffi Graf	Martina Navratilova
1989	Boris Becker	Stefan Edberg	1989	Steffi Graf	Martina Navratilova
1990	Stefan Edberg	Boris Becker	1990	Martina Navratilova	Zina Garrison
1991	Michael Stich	Boris Becker	1991	Steffi Graf	Gabriela Sabatini
1992	Andre Agassi	Goran Ivanisevic	1992	Steffi Graf	Monica Seles
1993	Pete Sampras	Jim Courier	1993	Steffi Graf	Jana Novotna
1994	Pete Sampras	Goran Ivanisevic	1994	Conchita Martinez	Martina Navratilova
1995	Pete Sampras	Boris Becker	1995	Steffi Graf	Arantxa Sánchez Vicario
1996	Richard Krajicek	MaliVai Washington	1996	Steffi Graf	Arantxa Sánchez Vicario
1997	Pete Sampras	Cedric Pioline	1997	Martina Hingis	Jana Novotna
1998	Pete Sampras	Goran Ivanisevic	1998	Jana Novotna	Nathalie Tauziat
1999	Pete Sampras	Andre Agassi	1999	Lindsay Davenport	Steffi Graf
2000	Pete Sampras	Patrick Rafter	2000	Venus Williams	Lindsay Davenport
2001	Goran Ivanisevic	Patrick Rafter	2001	Venus Williams	Justine Henin
2002	Lleyton Hewitt	David Nalbandian	2002	Serena Williams	Venus Williams
2003	Roger Federer	Mark Philippoussis	2003	Serena Williams	Venus Williams
2004	Roger Federer	Andy Roddick	2004	Maria Sharapova	Serena Williams

WORLD ALMANAC QUICK QUIZ

Can you list these men's tennis champs by number of U.S. Open singles victories (from fewest to most)?

(a) Andre Agassi   (b) John McEnroe   (c) Pete Sampras   (d) Ivan Lendl

For the answer look in this chapter, or see page 1008.

Davis Cup, 1900-2003*

Year	Result	Year	Result	Year	Result
1900	United States 3, British Isles 0	1935	Great Britain 5, United States 0	1972	United States 3, Romania 2
1901	Not held	1936	Great Britain 3, Australia 2	1973	Australia 5, United States 0
1902	United States 3, British Isles 2	1937	United States 4, Great Britain 1	1974	South Africa (default by India)
1903	British Isles 4, United States 1	1938	United States 3, Australia 2	1975	Sweden 3, Czechoslovakia 2
1904	British Isles 5, Belgium 0	1939	Australia 3, United States 2	1976	Italy 4, Chile 1
1905	British Isles 5, United States 0	1940-45	Not held	1977	Australia 3, Italy 1
1906	British Isles 5, United States 0	1946	United States 5, Australia 0	1978	United States 4, Great Britain 1
1907	Australia 3, British Isles 2	1947	United States 4, Australia 1	1979	United States 5, Italy 0
1908	Australasia 3, United States 2	1948	United States 5, Australia 0	1980	Czechoslovakia 4, Italy 1
1909	Australasia 5, United States 0	1949	United States 4, Australia 1	1981	United States 3, Argentina 1
1910	Not held	1950	Australia 4, United States 1	1982	United States 4, France, 1
1911	Australasia 5, United States 0	1951	Australia 3, United States 2	1983	Australia 3, Sweden 2
1912	British Isles 3, Australasia 2	1952	Australia 4, United States 1	1984	Sweden 4, United States 1
1913	United States 3, British Isles 2	1953	Australia 3, United States 2	1985	Sweden 3, W. Germany 2
1914	Australasia 3, United States 2	1954	United States 3, Australia 2	1986	Australia 3, Sweden 2
1915-18	Not held	1955	Australia 5, United States 0	1987	Sweden 5, India 0
1919	Australasia 4, British Isles 1	1956	Australia 5, United States 0	1988	W. Germany 4, Sweden 1
1920	United States 5, Australasia 0	1957	Australia 3, United States 2	1989	W. Germany 3, Sweden 2
1921	United States 5, Japan 0	1958	United States 3, Australia 2	1990	United States 3, Australia 2
1922	United States 4, Australasia 1	1959	Australia 3, United States 2	1991	France 3, United States 1
1923	United States 4, Australasia 1	1960	Australia 4, Italy 1	1992	United States 3, Switzerland 1
1924	United States 5, Australasia 0	1961	Australia 5, Italy 0	1993	Germany 4, Australia 1
1925	United States 5, France 0	1962	Australia 5, Mexico 0	1994	Sweden 4, Russia 1
1926	United States 4, France 1	1963	United States 3, Australia 2	1995	United States 3, Russia 2
1927	France 3, United States 2	1964	Australia 3, United States 2	1996	France 3, Sweden 2
1928	France 4, United States 1	1965	Australia 4, Spain 1	1997	Sweden 5, United States 0
1929	France 3, United States 2	1966	Australia 4, India 1	1998	Sweden 4, Italy 1
1930	France 4, United States 1	1967	Australia 4, Spain 1	1999	Australia 3, France 2
1931	France 3, Great Britain 2	1968	United States 4, Australia	2000	Spain 3, Australia 1
1932	France 3, United States 2	1969	United States 5, Romania 0	2001	France 3, Australia 2
1933	Great Britain 3, France 2	1970	United States 5, W. Germany 0	2002	Russia 3, France 2
1934	Great Britain 4, United States 1	1971	United States 3, Romania 2	2003	Australia 3, Spain 1

*The challenge round format, which guaranteed the previous year's winner a spot in the finals at home, was eliminated in 1972.

All-Time Grand Slam Singles Titles Leaders

Men	Australian Open	French Open[2]	Wimbledon	U.S. Open	Total
Pete Sampras	1994, '97	—	1993-95, 1997-2000	1990, '93, '95-96, 2002	14
Roy Emerson	1961, '63-67	1963, '67	1964-65	1961, '64	12
Bjorn Borg	—	1974-75, 1978-81	1976-80	—	11
Rod Laver	1960, '62, '69	1962, '69	1961-62, '68-69	1962, '69	11
Bill Tilden	—	—	1920-21, '30	1920-25, '29	10
Andre Agassi[1]	1995, 2000, '01, '03	1999	1992	1994, '99	8
Jimmy Connors	1974	—	1974, '82	1974, '76, '78, '82-83	8
Ivan Lendl	1989-90	1984, '86-87	—	1985-87	8
Fred Perry	1934	1935	1934-36	1933-34, '36	8
Ken Rosewall	1953, '55, '71-72	1953, '68	—	1956, '70	8
Women					
Margaret Smith Court	1960-66, '69-71, '73	1962, '64, '69-70, '73	1963, '65, '70	1962, '65, '69-70, '73	24
Steffi Graf	1988-90, '94	1987-88, '93, '95-96, '99	1988-89, '91-93, '95-96	1988-89, '93, '95-96	22
Helen Wills Moody	—	1928-30, '32	1927-30, '32-33, '35, '38	1923-25, '27-29, '31	19
Chris Evert Lloyd	1982, '84	1974-75, '79-80, '83, '85-86	1974, '76, '81	1975-78, '80, '82	18
Martina Navratilova	1981, '83, '85	1982, '84	1978-79, '82-87, '90	1983-84, '86-87	18
Billie Jean King	1968	1972	1966-68, '72-73, '75	1967, '71-72, '74	12
Suzanne Lenglen	—	1920-23, '25-26	1919-23, '25	—	12
Maureen Connolly	1953	1953-54	1952-54	1951-53	9
Monica Seles[1]	1991-93, '96	1990-92	—	1991-92	9

(1) Active player in 2004. (2) Prior to 1925, French Open entry was limited to members of French clubs.

RIFLE AND PISTOL INDIVIDUAL CHAMPIONSHIPS

Source: National Rifle Association

National Outdoor Rifle and Pistol Championships in 2004

Pistol—GYSG Brian H. Zins, USMC, King George, VA, 2635-123x

Civilian Pistol—Steve F. Reiter, Sparks, NV, 2621-122x

Woman Pistol—Judy Tant, East Lansing, MI, 2558-75x

Smallbore Rifle Prone—Jamie L. Beyerle, Lebanon, PA, 5591-428x

Civilian Smallbore Rifle Prone—Jamie L. Beyerle, Lebanon, PA, 5591-428x

Woman Smallbore Rifle Prone—Jamie L. Beyerle, Lebanon, PA, 5591-428x

Smallbore Rifle NRA 3-Position—Jeffrey Doerschler, Wethersfield, CT, 2153-51x

Civilian Smallbore Rifle NRA 3-Position—Jeffrey Doerschler, Wethersfield, CT, 2153-51x

Woman Smallbore Rifle NRA 3-Position—Jamie L. Beyerle, Lebanon, PA, 2150-38x

High Power Rifle—Norman G. Houle, West Warwick, RI, 2381-105x

Woman High Power Rifle—Sherri J. Gallagher, Prescott, AZ, 2370-97x

High Power Rifle Long Range—David Tubb, Canadian, TX, 1450-101x

Woman High Power Rifle Long Range—Nancy H. Tomkins-Gallagher, Prescott, AZ, 1448-90x

National Indoor Rifle and Pistol Championships in 2004

Smallbore Rifle 4-Position—Jeffrey Doerschler, Wethersfield, CT, 797-69x

Woman Smallbore Rifle 4-Position—Michelle Bohren, Taylor, MI, 793-61x

Smallbore Rifle NRA 3-Position—Joseph Hein, Mason, MI, 1184-80x

Woman Smallbore Rifle NRA 3-Position—Michelle Bohren, Taylor, MI, 1170-74x

International Smallbore Rifle—Matthew Rawlings, Wharton, TX, 1186-84x

Woman International Smallbore Rifle—Danielle Langfield, Orlando, FL, 1174-70x

Air Rifle—Matthew Rawlings, Wharton, TX, 597

Woman Air Rifle—Casey Gabriel, Flemington, NJ, 586

Conventional Pistol—John Zurek, Phoenix, AZ, 888-38x

Woman Conventional Pistol—Kathy Chatterton, Glen Rock, NJ, 873-27x

International Free Pistol—Jason Turner, Colorado Springs, CO, 550

Woman International Free Pistol—Susan McConnell, Clifton Park, NY, 506

International Standard Pistol—John Zurek, Phoenix, AZ, 580

Woman International Standard Pistol—Rebecca Snyder, Colorado Springs, CO, 545

Air Pistol—John Zurek, Phoenix, AZ, 585

Woman Air Pistol—Rebecca Snyder, Colorado Springs, CO, 566

NRA Bianchi Cup National Action Pistol Championships in 2004

Action Pistol—Doug Koenig, Albertus, PA, 1920-177x

Woman Action Pistol—Vera Koo, Menlo Park, CA, 1886-136x

Junior Action Pistol—Jordan Dick, Hutchinson, KS, 1865-140x

AUTO RACING

Indianapolis 500 Winners, 1911-2004

(At Indianapolis Motor Speedway in Indianapolis, IN)

Year	Winner, Car (Chassis-Engine)	MPH[1]	Year	Winner, Car (Chassis-Engine)	MPH[1]
1911	Ray Harroun, Marmon	74.602	1960	Jim Rathmann, Watson-Offy	138.767
1912	Joe Dawson, National	78.719	1961	A.J. Foyt Jr., Trevis-Offy	139.130
1913	Jules Goux, Peugeot	75.933	1962	Rodger Ward, Watson-Offy	140.293
1914	Rene Thomas, Delage	82.474	1963	Parnelli Jones, Watson-Offy	143.137
1915	Ralph DePalma, Mercedes	89.840	1964	A.J. Foyt Jr., Watson-Offy	147.350
1916	Dario Resta, Peugeot	84.001	1965	Jim Clark, Lotus-Ford	150.686
1917-18—Not held			1966	Graham Hill, Lola-Ford	144.317
1919	Howdy Wilcox, Peugeot	88.050	1967	A.J. Foyt Jr., Coyote-Ford	151.207
1920	Gaston Chevrolet, Frontenac	88.618	1968	Bobby Unser, Eagle-Offy	152.882
1921	Tommy Milton, Frontenac	89.621	1969	Mario Andretti, Hawk-Ford	156.867
1922	Jimmy Murphy, Duesenberg-Miller	94.484	1970	Al Unser, P.J. Colt-Ford	155.749
1923	Tommy Milton, Miller	90.954	1971	Al Unser, P.J. Colt-Ford	157.735
1924	L.L. Corum-Joe Boyer, Duesenberg	98.234	1972	Mark Donohue, McLaren-Offy	162.962
1925	Peter DePaolo, Duesenberg	101.127	1973	Gordon Johncock, Eagle-Offy	159.036
1926	Frank Lockhart, Miller	95.904	1974	Johnny Rutherford, McLaren-Offy	158.589
1927	George Souders, Duesenberg	97.545	1975	Bobby Unser, Eagle-Offy	149.213
1928	Louie Meyer, Miller	99.482	1976	Johnny Rutherford, McLaren-Offy	148.725
1929	Ray Keech, Miller	97.585	1977	A.J. Foyt Jr., Coyote-Foyt	161.331
1930	Billy Arnold, Summers-Miller	100.448	1978	Al Unser, Lola-Cosworth	161.363
1931	Louis Schneider, Stevens-Miller	96.629	1979	Rick Mears, Penske-Cosworth	158.899
1932	Fred Frame, Wetteroth-Miller	104.144	1980	Johnny Rutherford, Chaparral-Cosworth	142.862
1933	Louie Meyer, Miller	104.162	1981	Bobby Unser, Penske-Cosworth	139.084
1934	Bill Cummings, Miller	104.863	1982	Gordon Johncock, Wildcat-Cosworth	162.029
1935	Kelly Petillo, Wetteroth-Offy	106.240	1983	Tom Sneva, March-Cosworth	162.117
1936	Louie Meyer, Stevens-Miller	109.069	1984	Rick Mears, March-Cosworth	163.612
1937	Wilbur Shaw, Shaw-Offy	113.580	1985	Danny Sullivan, March-Cosworth	152.982
1938	Floyd Roberts, Wetteroth-Miller	117.200	1986	Bobby Rahal, March-Cosworth	170.722
1939	Wilbur Shaw, Maserati	115.035	1987	Al Unser, March-Cosworth	162.175
1940	Wilbur Shaw, Maserati	114.277	1988	Rick Mears, Penske-Chevy Indy V8	144.809
1941	Floyd Davis-Mauri Rose, Wetteroth-Offy	115.117	1989	Emerson Fittipaldi, Penske-Chevy Indy V8	167.581
1942-45—Not held			1990	Arie Luyendyk, Lola-Chevy Indy V8	185.981*
1946	George Robson, Adams-Sparks	114.820	1991	Rick Mears, Penske-Chevy Indy V8	176.457
1947	Mauri Rose, Deidt-Offy	116.338	1992	Al Unser Jr., Galmer-Chevy Indy V8A	134.477
1948	Mauri Rose, Deidt-Offy	119.814	1993	Emerson Fittipaldi, Penske-Chevy Indy V8C	157.207
1949	Bill Holland, Deidt-Offy	121.327	1994	Al Unser Jr., Penske-Mercedes Benz	160.872
1950	Johnnie Parsons, Kurtis-Offy	124.002	1995	Jacques Villeneuve, Reynard-Ford Cosworth XB	153.616
1951	Lee Wallard, Kurtis-Offy	126.244	1996	Buddy Lazier, Reynard-Ford Cosworth	147.956
1952	Troy Ruttman, Kuzma-Offy	128.922	1997	Arie Luyendyk, G Force-Aurora	145.827
1953	Bill Vukovich, KK500A-Offy	128.740	1998	Eddie Cheever, Dallara-Aurora	145.155
1954	Bill Vukovich, KK500A-Offy	130.840	1999	Kenny Brack, Dallara-Aurora	153.176
1955	Bob Sweikert, KK500C-Offy	128.213	2000	Juan Montoya, G Force-Aurora	167.607
1956	Pat Flaherty, Watson-Offy	128.490	2001	Helio Castroneves, Reynard-Honda	131.294
1957	Sam Hanks, Salih-Offy	135.601	2002	Helio Castroneves, Reynard-Honda	166.499
1958	Jimmy Bryan, Salih-Offy	133.791	2003	Gil de Ferran, G Force-Toyota	156.291
1959	Rodger Ward, Watson-Offy	135.857	2004	Buddy Rice, G Force-Honda	138.518

(1) Average speed. *Race record. **Note:** The race was less than 500 mi in the following years: 1916 (300 mi), 1926 (400 mi), 1950 (345 mi), 1973 (332.5 mi), 1975 (435 mi), 1976 (255 mi), 2004 (450 mi).

CART Champ Car World Series PPG Cup Winners, 1959-2003

(U.S. Auto Club Champions prior to 1979; Championship Auto Racing Teams [CART] Champions, 1979-present)

Year	Driver	Year	Driver	Year	Driver	Year	Driver
1959	Roger Ward	1971	Joe Leonard	1982	Rick Mears	1993	Nigel Mansell
1960	A. J. Foyt	1972	Joe Leonard	1983	Al Unser	1994	Al Unser Jr.
1961	A. J. Foyt	1973	Roger McCluskey	1984	Mario Andretti	1995	Jacques Villeneuve
1962	Rodger Ward	1974	Bobby Unser	1985	Al Unser	1996	Jimmy Vasser
1963	A. J. Foyt	1975	A. J. Foyt	1986	Bobby Rahal	1997	Alex Zanardi
1964	A. J. Foyt	1976	Gordon Johncock	1987	Bobby Rahal	1998	Alex Zanardi
1965	Mario Andretti	1977	Tom Sneva	1988	Danny Sullivan	1999	Juan Montoya
1966	Mario Andretti	1978	Tom Sneva	1989	Emerson Fittipaldi	2000	Gil de Ferran
1967	A. J. Foyt	1979	Rick Mears	1990	Al Unser Jr.	2001	Gil de Ferran
1968	Bobby Unser	1980	Johnny Rutherford	1991	Michael Andretti	2002	Cristiano da Matta
1969	Mario Andretti	1981	Rick Mears	1992	Bobby Rahal	2003	Paul Tracy
1970	Al Unser						

Indy Racing League (IRL) Winners, 1996-2004

(The Indy Racing League was begun in 1994 by a break-away group of CART drivers; its first championship was awarded in 1996)

Year	Driver	Year	Driver	Year	Driver	Year	Driver	Year	Driver
1996	(tie) Scott Sharp,	1997	Tony Stewart	1999	Greg Ray	2001	Sam Hornish, Jr.	2003	Scott Dixon
	Buzz Calkins	1998	Kenny Brack	2000	Buddy Lazier	2002	Sam Hornish, Jr.	2004	Tony Kanaan

NASCAR Racing

Winston Cup Champions, 1949-2003

Year	Driver	Year	Driver	Year	Driver	Year	Driver	Year	Driver
1949	Red Byron	1960	Rex White	1971	Richard Petty	1982	Darrell Waltrip	1993	Dale Earnhardt
1950	Bill Rexford	1961	Ned Jarrett	1972	Richard Petty	1983	Bobby Allison	1994	Dale Earnhardt
1951	Herb Thomas	1962	Joe Weatherly	1973	Benny Parsons	1984	Terry Labonte	1995	Jeff Gordon
1952	Tim Flock	1963	Joe Weatherly	1974	Richard Petty	1985	Darrell Waltrip	1996	Terry Labonte
1953	Herb Thomas	1964	Richard Petty	1975	Richard Petty	1986	Dale Earnhardt	1997	Jeff Gordon
1954	Lee Petty	1965	Ned Jarrett	1976	Cale Yarborough	1987	Dale Earnhardt	1998	Jeff Gordon
1955	Tim Flock	1966	David Pearson	1977	Cale Yarborough	1988	Bill Elliott	1999	Dale Jarrett
1956	Buck Baker	1967	Richard Petty	1978	Cale Yarborough	1989	Rusty Wallace	2000	Bobby Labonte
1957	Buck Baker	1968	David Pearson	1979	Richard Petty	1990	Dale Earnhardt	2001	Jeff Gordon
1958	Lee Petty	1969	David Pearson	1980	Dale Earnhardt	1991	Dale Earnhardt	2002	Tony Stewart
1959	Lee Petty	1970	Bobby Isaac	1981	Darrell Waltrip	1992	Alan Kulwicki	2003	Matt Kenseth

NASCAR Rookie of the Year, 1958-2003

Year	Driver	Year	Driver	Year	Driver	Year	Driver	Year	Driver
1958	Shorty Rollins	1968	Pete Hamilton	1977	Ricky Rudd	1986	Alan Kulwicki	1995	Ricky Craven
1959	Richard Petty	1969	Dick Brooks	1978	Ronnie Thomas	1987	Davey Allison	1996	Johnny Benson
1960	David Pearson	1970	Bill Dennis	1979	Dale Earnhardt	1988	Ken Bouchard	1997	Mike Skinner
1961	Woodie Wilson	1971	Walter Ballard	1980	Jody Riley	1989	Dick Trickle	1998	Kenny Irwin
1962	Tom Cox	1972	Larry Smith	1981	Ron Bouchard	1990	Rob Moroso	1999	Tony Stewart
1963	Billy Wade	1973	Lennie Pond	1982	Geoff Bodine	1991	Bobby Hamilton	2000	Matt Kenseth
1964	Doug Cooper	1974	Earl Ross	1983	Sterling Martin	1992	Jimmy Hensley	2001	Kevin Harvick
1965	Sam McQuagg	1975	Bruce Hill	1984	Rusty Wallace	1993	Jeff Gordon	2002	Ryan Newman
1966	James Hylton	1976	Skip Manning	1985	Ken Schrader	1994	Jeff Burton	2003	Jamie McMurray
1967	Donnie Allison								

Daytona 500 Winners, 1959-2004

(At Daytona International Speedway in Daytona Beach, FL)

Year	Driver, car	Avg. MPH	Year	Driver, car	Avg. MPH	Year	Driver, car	Avg. MPH
1959	Lee Petty, Oldsmobile	135.521	1975	Benny Parsons, Chevrolet	153.649	1990	Derrike Cope, Chevrolet	165.761
1960	Junior Johnson, Chevrolet	124.740	1976	David Pearson, Mercury	152.181	1991	Ernie Irvan, Chevrolet	148.148
1961	Marvin Panch, Pontiac	149.601	1977	Cale Yarborough, Chevrolet	153.218	1992	Davey Allison, Ford	160.256
1962	Fireball Roberts, Pontiac	152.529	1978	Bobby Allison, Ford	159.730	1993	Dale Jarrett, Chevrolet	154.972
1963	Tiny Lund, Ford	151.566	1979	Richard Petty, Oldsmobile	143.977	1994	Sterling Marlin, Chevrolet	156.931
1964	Richard Petty, Plymouth	154.334	1980	Buddy Baker, Oldsmobile	177.602	1995	Sterling Marlin, Chevrolet	141.710
1965	Fred Lorenzen, Ford (a)	141.539	1981	Richard Petty, Buick	169.651	1996	Dale Jarrett, Ford	154.308
1966	Richard Petty, Plymouth (b)	160.627	1982	Bobby Allison, Buick	153.991	1997	Jeff Gordon, Chevrolet	148.295
1967	Mario Andretti, Ford	146.926	1983	Cale Yarborough, Pontiac	155.979	1998	Dale Earnhardt, Chevrolet	172.712
1968	Cale Yarborough, Mercury	143.251	1984	Cale Yarborough, Chevrolet	150.994	1999	Jeff Gordon, Chevrolet	161.551
1969	LeeRoy Yarbrough, Ford	160.875	1985	Bill Elliott, Ford	172.265	2000	Dale Jarrett, Ford	155.669
1970	Pete Hamilton, Plymouth	149.601	1986	Geoff Bodine, Chevrolet	148.124	2001	Michael Waltrip, Chevrolet	161.783
1971	Richard Petty, Plymouth	144.456	1987	Bill Elliott, Ford	176.263	2002	Ward Burton, Dodge	142.971
1972	A. J. Foyt, Mercury	161.550	1988	Bobby Allison, Buick	137.531	2003	Michael Waltrip, Chevrolet (d)	133.870
1973	Richard Petty, Dodge	157.205	1989	Darrell Waltrip, Chevrolet	148.466	2004	Dale Earnhardt Jr., Chevrolet	156.345
1974	Richard Petty, Dodge (c)	140.894						

(a) 322.5 mi. (b) 495 mi. (c) 450 mi. (d) 272.5 mi.

Coca-Cola 600 Winners, 1960-2004

(At Lowe's Motor Speedway in Concord, NH. Known as World 600, 1960-85. *=rain-shortened.)

Year	Driver, car	Avg. MPH	Year	Driver, car	Avg. MPH	Year	Driver, car	Avg. MPH
1960	Joe Lee Johnson, Chevrolet	107.735	1974	David Pearson, Mercury	135.720	1990	Rusty Wallace, Pontiac	137.650
1961	David Pearson, Pontiac	111.633	1975	Richard Petty, Dodge	145.327	1991	Davey Allison, Ford	138.951
1962	Nelson Stacy, Ford	125.552	1976	David Pearson, Mercury	137.352	1992	Dale Earnhardt, Chevrolet	132.980
1963	Fred Lorenzen, Ford	132.418	1977	Richard Petty, Dodge	137.676	1993	Dale Earnhardt, Chevrolet	145.504
1964	Jim Paschal, Plymouth	125.772	1978	Darrell Waltrip, Chevrolet	138.355	1994	Jeff Gordon, Chevrolet	139.445
1965	Fred Lorenzen, Ford	121.772	1979	Darrell Waltrip, Chevrolet	136.674	1995	Bobby Labonte, Chevrolet	151.952
1966	Marvin Panch, Plymouth	135.042	1980	Benny Parsons, Chevrolet	119.265	1996	Dale Jarrett, Ford	147.581
1967	Jim Paschal, Plymouth	135.832	1981	Bobby Allison, Buick	129.326	1997	Jeff Gordon, Chevrolet*	136.745
1968	Buddy Baker, Dodge*	104.207	1982	Neil Bonnett, Ford	130.058	1998	Jeff Gordon, Chevrolet	136.424
1969	LeeRoy Yarborough, Mercury	134.361	1983	Neil Bonnett, Chevrolet	140.707	1999	Jeff Burton, Ford	151.367
1970	Donnie Allison, Ford	129.680	1984	Bobby Allison, Buick	129.233	2000	Matt Kenseth, Ford	142.640
1971	Bobby Allison, Mercury	140.422	1985	Darrell Waltrip, Chevrolet	141.807	2001	Jeff Burton, Ford	138.107
1972	Buddy Baker, Dodge	142.255	1986	Dale Earnhardt, Chevrolet	140.406	2002	Mark Martin, Ford	137.729
1973	Buddy Baker, Dodge	134.890	1987	Kyle Petty, Ford	131.483	2003	Jimmie Johnson, Chevrolet*	126.198
			1988	Darrell Waltrip, Chevrolet	124.460	2004	Jimmie Johnson, Chevrolet	142.763
			1989	Darrell Waltrip, Chevrolet	144.077			

Brickyard 400 Winners, 1994-2004

(At Indianapolis Motor Speedway in Indianapolis, IN)

Year	Driver, car	Avg. MPH	Year	Driver, car	Avg. MPH	Year	Driver, car	Avg. MPH
1994	Jeff Gordon, Chevrolet	131.977	1998	Jeff Gordon, Chevrolet	126.772	2002	Bill Elliott, Dodge	125.033
1995	Dale Earnhardt, Chevrolet	155.206	1999	Dale Jarrett, Ford	148.194	2003	Kevin Harvick, Chevrolet	134.554
1996	Dale Jarrett, Ford	139.508	2000	Bobby Labonte, Pontiac	155.912	2004	Jeff Gordon, Chevrolet	115.037
1997	Ricky Rudd, Ford	130.814	2001	Jeff Gordon, Chevrolet	130.790			

IT'S A FACT: German driver Michael Schumacher clinched the 2004 Formula One championship on Aug. 29, 2004, becoming the first driver to win 5 titles in a row (and a record 7 in all). Argentina's Juan Manuel Fangio had set a record of 4 titles in a row (1954-57).

Southern 500 Winners, 1950-2003

(At Darlington International Raceway in Darlington, SC. *=rain-shortened.)

Year	Driver, car	Avg. MPH	Year	Driver, car	Avg. MPH	Year	Driver, car	Avg. MPH
1950	Johnny Mantz, Plymouth	76.260	1968	Cale Yarborough, Mercury	126.132	1986	Tim Richmond, Chevrolet	121.068
1951	Herb Thomas, Hudson	76.900	1969	LeeRoy Yarbrough, Ford*	105.612	1987	Dale Earnhardt, Chevrolet*	115.520
1952	Fonty Flock, Oldsmobile	74.510	1970	Buddy Baker, Dodge	128.817	1988	Bill Elliott, Ford	128.297
1953	Buck Baker, Oldsmobile	92.780	1971	Bobby Allison, Mercury	131.398	1989	Dale Earnhardt, Chevrolet	135.462
1954	Herb Thomas, Hudson	94.930	1972	Bobby Allison, Chevrolet	128.124	1990	Dale Earnhardt, Chevrolet	123.141
1955	Herb Thomas, Chevrolet	93.281	1973	Cale Yarborough, Oldsmobile	134.033	1991	Harry Gant, Oldsmobile	133.508
1956	Curtis Turner, Ford	95.067	1974	Cale Yarborough, Chevrolet	111.075	1992	Darrell Waltrip, Chevrolet*	129.114
1957	Speedy Thompson, Chevrolet	100.094	1975	Bobby Allison, Matador	116.825	1993	Mark Martin, Ford*	137.932
1958	Fireball Roberts, Chevrolet	102.590	1976	David Pearson, Mercury	120.534	1994	Bill Elliott, Ford	127.952
1959	Jim Reed, Chevrolet	111.840	1977	David Pearson, Mercury	106.797	1995	Jeff Gordon, Chevrolet	121.231
1960	Buck Baker, Pontiac	105.901	1978	Cale Yarborough, Oldsmobile	116.828	1996	Jeff Gordon, Chevrolet	135.757
1961	Nelson Stacy, Ford	117.787	1979	David Pearson, Chevrolet	126.259	1997	Jeff Gordon, Chevrolet*	121.149
1962	Larry Frank, Ford	117.965	1980	Terry Labonte, Chevrolet	115.210	1998	Jeff Gordon, Chevrolet	139.031
1963	Fireball Roberts, Ford	129.784	1981	Neil Bonnett, Ford	126.410	1999	Jeff Burton, Ford*	107.816
1964	Buck Baker, Dodge	117.757	1982	Cale Yarborough, Buick	115.224	2000	Bobby Labonte, Pontiac*	108.273
1965	Ned Jarrett, Ford	115.924	1983	Bobby Allison, Buick	123.343	2001	Ward Burton, Dodge	'122.773
1966	Darel Dieringer, Mercury	114.830	1984	Harry Gant, Chevrolet	128.270	2002	Jeff Gordon, Chevrolet	118.617
1967	Richard Petty, Plymouth	130.423	1985	Bill Elliott, Ford	121.254	2003	Terry Labonte, Chevrolet	120.744

Formula One Racing

World Grand Prix Champions, 1950-2004

Year	Driver	Year	Driver	Year	Driver
1950	Nino Farini, Italy	1969	Jackie Stewart, Scotland	1987	Nelson Piquet, Brazil
1951	Juan Manuel Fangio, Argentina	1970	Jochen Rindt, Austria	1988	Ayrton Senna, Brazil
1952	Alberto Ascari, Italy	1971	Jackie Stewart, Scotland	1989	Alain Prost, France
1953	Alberto Ascari, Italy	1972	Emerson Fittipaldi, Brazil	1990	Ayrton Senna, Brazil
1954	Juan Manuel Fangio, Argentina	1973	Jackie Stewart, Scotland	1991	Ayrton Senna, Brazil
1955	Juan Manuel Fangio, Argentina	1974	Emerson Fittipaldi, Brazil	1992	Nigel Mansell, Britain
1956	Juan Manuel Fangio, Argentina	1975	Niki Lauda, Austria	1993	Alain Prost, France
1957	Juan Manuel Fangio, Argentina	1976	James Hunt, England	1994	Michael Schumacher, Germany
1958	Mike Hawthorne, England	1977	Niki Lauda, Austria	1995	Michael Schumacher, Germany
1959	Jack Brabham, Australia	1978	Mario Andretti, United States	1996	Damon Hill, England
1960	Jack Brabham, Australia	1979	Jody Scheckter, South Africa	1997	Jacques Villeneuve, Canada
1961	Phil Hill, United States	1980	Alan Jones, Australia	1998	Mika Hakkinen, Finland
1962	Graham Hill, England	1981	Nelson Piquet, Brazil	1999	Mika Hakkinen, Finland
1963	Jim Clark, Scotland	1982	Keke Rosberg, Finland	2000	Michael Schumacher, Germany
1964	John Surtees, England	1983	Nelson Piquet, Brazil	2001	Michael Schumacher, Germany
1965	Jim Clark, Scotland	1984	Niki Lauda, Austria	2002	Michael Schumacher, Germany
1966	Jack Brabham, Australia	1985	Alain Prost, France	2003	Michael Schumacher, Germany
1967	Denis Hulme, New Zealand	1986	Alain Prost, France	2004	Michael Schumacher, Germany
1968	Graham Hill, England				

2004 Le Mans 24 Hours Race

Danish driver Tom Kristensen was part of a 3-man team, driving the No. 5 Audi Sport Japan Team Goh car, that won the "24 Hours of Le Mans" race held June 13, 2004. It was the 6th career victory for Kristensen, tying Jacky Ickx's record for the most wins in the race's history. Kristensen also became the 1st driver to win the race 5 straight years. Kristensen, Seiji Ara (Japan) and Rinaldo Capello (Italy) completed a record 379 laps, breaking the record of 377 laps set in 2003.

Notable One-Mile Land Speed Records

Andy Green, a Royal Air Force pilot, broke the sound barrier and set the first supersonic world speed record on land, Oct. 15, 1997, in Black Rock Desert, NV. Green, driving a car built by Richard Noble, had 2 runs at an average speed of 763.035 mph, as calculated according to the rules of the Federation Internationale Automobiliste (FIA). This record and speed exceeded the speed of sound, calculated at 751.251 mph for that place and time.

Date	Driver	Car	MPH	Date	Driver	Car	MPH
1/26/06	Marriott	Stanley (Steam)	127.659	11/19/37	Eyston	Thunderbolt 1	311.42
3/16/10	Oldfield	Benz	131.724	9/16/38	Eyston	Thunderbolt 1	357.5
4/23/11	Burman	Benz	141.732	8/23/39	Cobb	Railton	368.9
2/12/19	DePalma	Packard	149.875	9/16/47	Cobb	Railton-Mobil	394.2
4/27/20	Milton	Dusenberg	155.046	8/05/63	Breedlove	Spirit of America	407.45
4/28/26	Parry-Thomas	Thomas Spl.	170.624	10/27/64	Arfons	Green Monster	536.71
3/29/27	Seagrave	Sunbeam	203.790	11/15/65	Breedlove	Spirit of America	600.601
4/22/28	Keech	White Triplex	207.552	10/23/70	Gabelich	Blue Flame	622.407
3/11/29	Seagrave	Irving-Napier	231.446	10/09/79	Barrett	Budweiser Rocket	638.637*
2/05/31	Campbell	Napier-Campbell	246.086	10/04/83	Noble	Thrust 2	633.468
2/24/32	Campbell	Napier-Campbell	253.96	9/25/97	Green	Thrust SSC	714.144
2/22/33	Campbell	Napier-Campbell	272.109	10/15/97	Green	Thrust SSC	763.035
9/03/35	Campbell	Bluebird Special	301.13				

*Not recognized as official by sanctioning bodies.

BOXING
Champions by Classes

There are many boxing governing bodies, including the World Boxing Council, World Boxing Assn., International Boxing Fed., World Boxing Org., U.S. Boxing Assn., N. American Boxing Fed., and European Boxing Union. All have their own champions and divisions. The following are the recognized champions—as of Oct. 12, 2004—in the principal divisions of the WBA, WBC, and IBF.

Class, Weight limit	WBA	WBC	IBF
Heavyweight	John Ruiz, U.S.	Vitali Klitschko, Ukraine	Chris Byrd, U.S.
Cruiserweight (190 lb)	Jean-Marc Mormeck, France	Wayne Braithwaite, Guyana	Kelvin Davis, U.S.
Light Heavyweight (175 lb)	Fabrice Tiozzo, France	Antonio Tarver, U.S.	Glencoffe Johnson, U.S.
Super Middleweight (168 lb)	Manuel Siaca, U.S./P.R.	Markus Beyer, Germany	Jeff Lacy, U.S.
Middleweight (160 lb)	Bernard Hopkins, U.S.[1]	Bernard Hopkins, U.S.	Bernard Hopkins, U.S.
Jr. Middleweight (154 lb)	Ronald Wright, U.S.[2]	Ronald Wright, U.S.	Kassim Ouma, U.S.
Welterweight (147 lb)	Cory Spinks, U.S.[3]	Cory Spinks, U.S.	Cory Spinks, U.S.
Jr. Welterweight (140 lb)	Vivian Harris, Guyana	Kostya Tszyu, Australia[5]	Kostya Tszyu, Australia
Lightweight (135 lb)	Juan Diaz, U.S.	Floyd Mayweather, U.S.[6]	Julio Diaz, U.S.
Jr. Lightweight (130 lb)	Yodsanan Nanthachai, Thailand	Erik Morales, Mexico	Erik Morales, Mexico
Featherweight (126 lb)	Juan Manuel Marquez, Mexico[4]	Chi In-jin, Korea	Juan Manuel Marquez, Mexico
Jr. Featherweight (122 lb)	Mahyar Monshipor, France	Oscar Larios, Mexico	Israel Vazquez, Mexico
Bantamweight (118 lb)	Johnny Bredahl, Denmark	Veeraphol Sahaprom, Thailand	Rafael Marquez, Mexico
Jr. Bantamweight (115 lb)	Alexander Munoz, Venezuela	Katsushige Kawashima, Japan	Luis Perez, Nicaragua
Flyweight (112 lb)	Lorenzo Parra, Venezuela	Pongsaklek Wonjongkam, Thai.	Irene Pacheco, Colombia
Jr. Flyweight (108 lb)	Rosendo Alvarez, Nicaragua	Jorge Arce, Mexico	Jose Victor Burgos, Mexico
Strawweight (105 lb)	Yukata Niida, Japan	Eagle Akakura, Japan	Muhammad Rachman, Indo.

Note: The WBA and WBC designate certain title holders as "Super World Champs" and "Emeritus Champions of the World," respectively (listed above), and permit concurrent "World" champions. Following are the "World" champions: (1) Maselino Masoe, New Zealand. (2) Travis Simms, U.S. (3) Jose Rivera, U.S. (4) Chris John, Indonesia. (5) Arturo Gatti, U.S. (6) Jose Luis Castillo, Mexico.

Ring Champions by Years

(*abandoned the title or was stripped of it; IBF champions listed only for heavyweight division)

Heavyweights

1882-1892	John L. Sullivan (a)	1970-1973	Joe Frazier	1990-1992	Evander Holyfield (WBA, WBC, IBF)
1892-1897	James J. Corbett (b)	1973-1974	George Foreman		
1897-1899	Robert Fitzsimmons	1974-1978	Muhammad Ali	1992-1993	Riddick Bowe (WBA, IBF,WBC*)
1899-1905	James J. Jeffries* (c)	1978-1979	Muhammad Ali* (WBA)	1992-1994	Lennox Lewis (WBC)
1905-1906	Marvin Hart	1978	Leon Spinks (WBC*, WBA) (e);	1993-1994	Evander Holyfield (WBA, IBF)
1906-1908	Tommy Burns		Ken Norton (WBC)	1994	Michael Moorer (WBA, IBF)
1908-1915	Jack Johnson	1978-1983	Larry Holmes* (WBC) (f)	1994-1995	Oliver McCall (WBC);
1915-1919	Jess Willard	1979-1980	John Tate (WBA)		George Foreman (WBA*, IBF*)
1919-1926	Jack Dempsey	1980-1982	Mike Weaver (WBA)	1995	Frans Botha* (IBF)
1926-1928	Gene Tunney*	1982-1983	Michael Dokes (WBA)	1995-1996	Bruce Seldon (WBA);
1928-1930	Vacant	1983-1984	Gerrie Coetzee (WBA)		Frank Bruno (WBC)
1930-1932	Max Schmeling	1983-1985	Larry Holmes (IBF) (f)	1996	Mike Tyson (WBC*, WBA)
1932-1933	Jack Sharkey	1984	Tim Witherspoon (WBC)	1996-1997	Michael Moorer (IBF)
1933-1934	Primo Carnera	1984-1985	Greg Page (WBA)	1996-1999	Evander Holyfield (WBA, IBF)
1934-1935	Max Baer	1984-1986	Pinklon Thomas (WBC)	1997-2001	Lennox Lewis (WBC)
1935-1937	James J. Braddock	1985-1986	Tony Tubbs (WBA)	1999-2001	Lennox Lewis (WBA*, WBC, IBF)
1937-1949	Joe Louis*	1985-1987	Michael Spinks* (IBF)	2000-2001	Evander Holyfield (WBA)
1949-1951	Ezzard Charles	1986	Tim Witherspoon (WBA);	2001-2003	John Ruiz (WBA)
1951-1952	Joe Walcott		Trevor Berbick (WBC)	2001	Hasim Rahman (WBC, IBF)
1952-1956	Rocky Marciano*	1986-1987	Mike Tyson (WBC);	2001-2002	Lennox Lewis (IBF*)
1956-1959	Floyd Patterson		James "Bonecrusher" Smith (WBA)	2001-2004	Lennox Lewis (WBC)(g)
1959-1960	Ingemar Johansson	1987	Tony Tucker (IBF)	2002-2004	Chris Byrd (IBF)
1960-1962	Floyd Patterson	1987-1990	Mike Tyson (WBC, WBA, IBF)	2003	Roy Jones Jr. (WBA)
1962-1964	Sonny Liston	1990	"Buster" Douglas (WBA,	2004	Vitali Klitschko (WBC);
1964-1967	Cassius Clay (Muhammad Ali) (d)		WBC, IBF)		John Ruiz (WBA)

(a) London Prize Ring (bare knuckle champion). (b) First Marquis of Queensberry champion. (c) Jeffries vacated title (1905), designated Marvin Hart and Jack Root as logical contenders. Hart def. Root in 12 rounds (1905), in turn was def. by Tommy Burns (1906), who claimed the title. Jack Johnson def. Burns (1908) and was recognized as champ. Johnson won the title by defeating Jeffries in the latter's attempted comeback (1910). (d) Title declared vacant by the WBA and others in 1967 after Ali refused military induction. Joe Frazier recognized as champ by 6 states, Mexico, and South America. Jimmy Ellis declared champ by the WBA. Frazier KOd Ellis, Feb. 16, 1970. (e) After Spinks defeated Ali, the WBC recognized Ken Norton as champ. Ali def. Spinks in 1978 rematch for WBA title, retired in 1979. (f) Holmes relinquished WBC title in Dec. 1983, to fight as champ of the new IBF. (g) Lewis retired in Feb. 2004.

Light Heavyweights

1903	Jack Root, George Gardner	1963-1965	Willie Pastrano	1987-1991	Virgil Hill (WBA)
1903-1905	Bob Fitzsimmons	1965-1966	Jose Torres	1987	Thomas Hearns* (WBC)
1905-1912	Philadelphia Jack O'Brien*	1966-1968	Dick Tiger	1987-1988	Don Lalonde (WBC)
1912-1916	Jack Dillon	1968-1974	Bob Foster*	1988	Sugar Ray Leonard* (WBC)
1916-1920	Battling Levinsky	1974-1977	John Conteh (WBC)	1989	Dennis Andries (WBC)
1920-1922	George Carpentier	1974-1978	Victor Galindez (WBA)	1989-1990	Jeff Harding (WBC)
1922-1923	Battling Siki	1977-1978	Miguel Cuello (WBC)	1990-1991	Dennis Andries (WBC)
1923-1925	Mike McTigue	1978	Mate Parlov (WBC)	1991-1994	Jeff Harding (WBC)
1925-1926	Paul Berlenbach	1978-1979	Mike Rossman (WBA);	1991-1992	Thomas Hearns (WBA)
1926-1927	Jack Delaney*		Marvin Johnson (WBC)	1992	Iran Barkley* (WBA)
1927-1929	Tommy Loughran*	1979-1981	Matthew Saad Muhammad	1992-1997	Virgil Hill (WBA)
1930-1934	Maxey Rosenbloom		(WBC)	1994-1995	Mike McCallum (WBC)
1934-1935	Bob Olin	1979-1980	Marvin Johnson (WBA)	1995-1996	Fabrice Tiozzo* (WBC)
1935-1939	John Henry Lewis*	1980-1981	Eddie Mustafa Muhammad	1996-1997	Roy Jones Jr. (WBC)
1939	Melio Bettina		(WBA)	1997	Montell Griffin (WBC);
1939-1941	Billy Conn*	1981-1983	Michael Spinks (WBA);		Roy Jones Jr. (WBC);
1941	Anton Christoforidis (won NBA title)		Dwight Braxton (WBC)		Darius Michalczewski*(WBA)
		1983-1985	Michael Spinks*	1997-1998	Lou Del Valle (WBA)
1941-1948	Gus Lesnevich, Freddie Mills	1985-1986	J. B. Williamson (WBC)	1998-2003	Roy Jones Jr. (WBA*, WBC*)
1948-1950	Freddie Mills	1986-1987	Marvin Johnson (WBA);	2003	Mehdi Sahnoune (WBA)
1950-1952	Joey Maxim		Dennis Andries (WBC)	2003-2004	Antonio Tarver (WBC)
1952-1962	Archie Moore	1987	Leslie Stewart (WBA)	2004	Fabrice Tiozzo (WBA)
1962-1963	Harold Johnson				

Middleweights

Years	Champion
1884-1891	Jack "Nonpareil" Dempsey
1891-1897	Bob Fitzsimmons*
1897-1907	Tommy Ryan*
1907-1908	Stanley Ketchel; Billy Papke
1908-1910	Stanley Ketchel
1911-1913	vacant
1913	Frank Klaus; George Chip
1914-1917	Al McCoy
1917-1920	Mike O'Dowd
1920-1923	Johnny Wilson
1923-1926	Harry Greb
1926-1931	Tiger Flowers; Mickey Walker
1931-1932	Gorilla Jones (NBA)
1932-1937	Marcel Thil
1938	Al Hostak (NBA); Solly Krieger (NBA)
1939-1940	Al Hostak (NBA)
1941-1947	Tony Zale
1947-1948	Rocky Graziano
1948	Tony Zale; Marcel Cerdan
1949-1951	Jake LaMotta
1951	Ray Robinson; Randy Turpin; Ray Robinson*
1953-1955	Carl (Bobo) Olson
1955-1957	Ray Robinson
1957	Gene Fullmer; Ray Robinson
1957-1958	Carmen Basilio
1958	Ray Robinson
1959	Gene Fullmer (NBA); Ray Robinson (NY)
1960	Gene Fullmer (NBA); Paul Pender (NY and MA)
1961	Gene Fullmer (NBA); Terry Downes (NY, MA, Europe)
1962	Gene Fullmer; Dick Tiger (NBA); Paul Pender (NY and MA)*
1963	Dick Tiger (universal)
1963-1965	Joey Giardello
1965-1966	Dick Tiger
1966-1967	Emile Griffith
1967	Nino Benvenuti
1967-1968	Emile Griffith
1968-1970	Nino Benvenuti
1970-1977	Carlos Monzon*
1977-1978	Rodrigo Valdez
1978-1979	Hugo Corro
1979-1980	Vito Antuofermo
1980	Alan Minter
1980-1987	Marvin Hagler
1987	Sugar Ray Leonard* (WBC)
1987-1989	Sumbu Kalambay (WBA)
1987-1988	Thomas Hearns (WBC)
1988-1989	Iran Barkley (WBC)
1989-1990	Roberto Duran* (WBC)
1989-1991	Mike McCallum (WBA)
1990-1993	Julian Jackson (WBC)
1992-1993	Reggie Johnson (WBA)
1993-1995	Gerald McClellan* (WBC)
1993-1994	John David Jackson (WBA)
1994-1997	Jorge Castro (WBA)
1995	Julian Jackson (WBA)
1995-1996	Quincy Taylor (WBC); Shinji Takehara (WBA)
1996-1998	Keith Holmes (WBC)
1996-1997	William Joppy (WBA)
1997	Julio Cesar Green (WBA)
1998-2001	William Joppy (WBA)
1998-1999	Hassine Cherifi (WBC)
1999-2001	Keith Holmes (WBC)
2001	Felix Trinidad (WBA)
2001-2004	Bernard Hopkins (WBC, WBA)

Welterweights

Years	Champion
1892-1894	Mysterious Billy Smith
1894-1896	Tommy Ryan
1896	Kid McCoy*
1900	Rube Ferns; Matty Matthews
1901	Rube Ferns
1901-1904	Joe Walcott
1904-1906	Dixie Kid; Joe Walcott; Honey Mellody
1907-1911	Mike Sullivan
1911-1915	Vacant
1915-1919	Ted Lewis
1919-1922	Jack Britton
1922-1926	Mickey Walker
1926	Pete Latzo
1927-1929	Joe Dundee
1929	Jackie Fields
1930	Jack Thompson; Tommy Freeman
1931	Tommy Freeman; Jack Thompson; Lou Brouillard
1932	Jackie Fields
1933	Young Corbett; Jimmy McLarnin
1934	Barney Ross; Jimmy McLarnin
1935-1938	Barney Ross
1938-1940	Henry Armstrong
1940-1941	Fritzie Zivic
1941-1946	Fred Cochrane
1946	Marty Servo*
1946-1951	Ray Robinson* (a)
1951	Johnny Bratton (NBA)
1951-1954	Kid Gavilan
1954-1955	Johnny Saxton
1955	Tony De Marco
1955-1956	Carmen Basilio
1956	Johnny Saxton
1956-1957	Carmen Basilio*
1958	Virgil Akins
1958-1960	Don Jordan
1960-1961	Benny Paret
1961	Emile Griffith
1961-1962	Benny Paret
1962-1963	Emile Griffith
1963	Luis Rodriguez
1963-1966	Emile Griffith*
1966-1969	Curtis Cokes
1969-1970	Jose Napoles
1970-1971	Billy Backus
1971-1975	Jose Napoles
1975-1976	John Stracey (WBC); Angel Espada (WBA)
1976-1979	Carlos Palomino (WBC)
1976-1980	Jose Cuevas (WBA)
1979	Wilfredo Benitez (WBC)
1979-1980	Sugar Ray Leonard (WBC)
1980	Roberto Duran (WBC)
1980-1981	Thomas Hearns (WBA)
1980-1982	Sugar Ray Leonard*
1983-1985	Donald Curry (WBA); Milton McCrory (WBC)
1985-1986	Donald Curry
1986-1987	Lloyd Honeyghan (WBC)
1987	Mark Breland (WBA)
1987-1988	Marlon Starling (WBA); Jorge Vaca (WBC)
1988-1989	Tomas Molinares (WBA); Lloyd Honeyghan (WBC)
1989-1990	Marlon Starling (WBC); Mark Breland (WBA)
1990-1991	Maurice Blocker (WBC); Aaron Davis (WBA)
1991	Simon Brown (WBC)
1991-1992	Meldrick Taylor (WBA)
1991-1993	Buddy McGirt (WBC)
1992-1994	Crisanto Espana (WBA)
1993-1997	Pernell Whitaker (WBC)
1994-1998	Ike Quartey (WBA*)
1997-1999	Oscar De La Hoya (WBC*)
1998	James Page (WBA*)
1999-2000	Felix Trinidad (WBC*)
2000	Oscar De La Hoya (WBC*)
2000-2002	Shane Mosley (WBC)
2001-2002	Andrew Lewis (WBA)
2002	Ricardo Mayorga (WBA)
2002-2003	Vernon Forrest (WBC)
2003	Ricardo Mayorga (WBA, WBC)
2004	Cory Spinks (WBA, WBC)

(a) Robinson gained the title by defeating Tommy Bell in an elimination agreed to by the New York Commission and the National Boxing Association. Both claimed Robinson waived his title when he won the middleweight crown from LaMotta in 1951.

Lightweights

Years	Champion
1896-1899	Kid Lavigne
1899-1902	Frank Erne
1902-1908	Joe Gans
1908-1910	Battling Nelson
1910-1912	Ad Wolgast
1912-1914	Willie Ritchie
1914-1917	Freddie Welsh
1917-1925	Benny Leonard*
1925	Jimmy Goodrich; Rocky Kansas
1926-1930	Sammy Mandell
1930	Al Singer; Tony Canzoneri
1930-1933	Tony Canzoneri
1933-1935	Barney Ross*
1935-1936	Tony Canzoneri
1936-1938	Lou Ambers
1938	Henry Armstrong
1939	Lou Ambers
1940	Lew Jenkins
1941-1943	Sammy Angott
1944	S. Angott (NBA); J. Zurita (NBA)
1945-1951	Ike Williams (NBA: later universal)
1951-1952	James Carter
1952	Lauro Salas; James Carter
1953-1954	James Carter
1954	Paddy De Marco; James Carter
1955	James Carter; Bud Smith
1956	Bud Smith; Joe Brown
1956-1962	Joe Brown
1962-1965	Carlos Ortiz
1965	Ismael Laguna
1965-1968	Carlos Ortiz
1968-1969	Teo Cruz
1969-1970	Mando Ramos
1970	Ismael Laguna
1970-1972	Ken Buchanan (WBA)
1971-1972	Pedro Carrasco (WBC)
1972-1979	Roberto Duran* (WBA)
1972	Mando Ramos (WBC); Chango Carmona (WBC)
1972-1974	Rodolfo Gonzalez (WBC)
1974-1976	Ishimatsu Suzuki (WBC)
1976-1978	Esteban De Jesus (WBC)
1979-1981	Jim Watt (WBC)
1979-1980	Ernesto Espana (WBA)
1980-1981	Hilmer Kenty (WBA)
1981	Sean O'Grady (WBA); Claude Noel (WBA)
1981-1983	Alexis Arguello* (WBC)
1981-1982	Arturo Frias (WBA)
1982-1984	Ray Mancini (WBA)
1983-1984	Edwin Rosario (WBC)
1984-1986	Livingstone Bramble (WBA)
1984-1985	Jose Luis Ramirez (WBC)
1985-1986	Hector (Macho) Camacho (WBC)
1986-1987	Edwin Rosario (WBA)
1987-1988	Julio Cesar Chavez (WBA); Jose Luis Ramirez (WBC)
1988-1989	Julio Cesar Chavez (WBA, WBC)
1989-1990	Edwin Rosario (WBA); Pernell Whitaker (WBC)
1990	Juan Nazario (WBA)
1990-1992	Pernell Whitaker*
1992	Joey Gamache (WBA)
1992-1996	Miguel Angel Gonzalez* (WBC)
1992-1993	Tony Lopez (WBA)
1993	Dingaan Thobela (WBA)
1993-1998	Orzubek Nazarov (WBA)
1996-1997	Jean-Baptiste Mendy (WBC)
1997-1998	Steve Johnston (WBC)
1998-1999	Jean-Baptiste Mendy (WBA); Cesar Bazan (WBC)
1999	Julian Lorcy (WBA); Stefano Zoff (WBA)
1999-2000	Gilberto Serrano (WBA); Steve Johnston (WBC)
2000-2001	Takanori Hatakeyama (WBA);
2000-2002	Jose Luis Castillo (WBC)
2001	Julien Lorcy (WBA)
2001-2002	Raul Balbi (WBA)
2002-2003	Leonard Dorin (WBA)
2002-2004	Floyd Mayweather (WBC)
2004	Juan Diaz (WBA)

Featherweights

1892-1900	George Dixon (disputed)	1968	Paul Rojas (WBA)	1985-1986	Barry McGuigan (WBA)
1900-1901	Terry McGovern; Young Corbett*	1968-1969	Jose Legra (WBC)	1986-1987	Steve Cruz (WBA)
1901-1912	Abe Attell	1968-1971	Shozo Saijyo (WBA)	1987-1991	Antonio Esparragoza (WBA)
1912-1923	Johnny Kilbane	1969-1970	Johnny Famechon (WBC)	1988-1990	Jeff Fenech* (WBC)
1923	Eugene Criqui; Johnny Dundee	1970	Vicente Salvidar (WBC)	1990-1991	Marcos Villasana (WBC)
1923-1925	Johnny Dundee*	1970-1972	Kuniaki Shibata (WBC)	1991-1993	Park Yung Kyun (WBA);
1925-1927	Kid Kaplan*	1971-1972	Antonio Gomez (WBA)		Paul Hodkinson (WBC)
1927-1928	Benny Bass; Tony Canzoneri	1972	Clemente Sanchez* (WBC)	1993	Goyo Vargas (WBC)
1928-1929	Andre Routis	1972-1974	Ernesto Marcel* (WBA)	1993-1995	Kevin Kelley (WBC)
1929-1932	Battling Battalino*	1972-1973	Jose Legra (WBC)	1993-1996	Eloy Rojas (WBA)
1932-1934	Tommy Paul (NBA)	1973-1974	Eder Jofre* (WBC)	1995	Alejandro Gonzalez (WBC)
1933-1936	Freddie Miller	1974	Ruben Olivares (WBA)	1995-1996	Manuel Medina (WBC)
1936-1937	Petey Sarron	1974-1975	Bobby Chacon (WBC)	1995-1999	Luisito Espinosa (WBC)
1937-1938	Henry Armstrong*	1974-1976	Alexis Arguello* (WBA)	1996-1997	Wilfredo Vasquez* (WBA)
1938-1940	Joey Archibald (a)	1975	Ruben Olivares (WBC)	1998	Freddie Norwood (WBA)
1940-1941	Harry Jeffra	1975-1976	David Kotey (WBC)	1998-1999	Antonio Ceremeno (WBA)
1942-1948	Willie Pep	1976-1980	Danny Lopez (WBC)	1999	Cesar Soto (WBC);
1948-1949	Sandy Saddler	1977	Rafael Ortega (WBA)		Naseem Hamed* (WBC);
1949-1950	Willie Pep	1977-1978	Cecilio Lastra (WBA)		Freddie Norwood (WBA)
1950-1957	Sandy Saddler*	1978-1985	Eusebio Pedrosa (WBA)	2000-2001	Guty Espadas (WBC)
1957-1959	Hogan (Kid) Bassey	1980-1982	Salvador Sanchez (WBC)	2000-2003	Derrick Gainer (WBA)
1959-1963	Davey Moore	1982-1984	Juan LaPorte (WBC)	2001-2004	Erik Morales (WBC)(b)
1963-1964	Sugar Ramos	1984	Wilfredo Gomez (WBC)	2003-2004	Juan Manuel Marquez (WBA)
1964-1967	Vicente Saldivar*	1984-1988	Azumah Nelson (WBC)	2004	Chi In-jin (WBC)

(a) After Petey Scalzo knocked out Archibald in an overweight match and was refused a title bout, the NBA named Scalzo champion. NBA title succession: Scalzo, 1938-41; Richard Lemos, 1941; Jackie Wilson, 1941-43; Jackie Callura, 1943; Phil Terranova, 1943-44; Sal Bartolo, 1944-46. (b) Marco Antonio Barrera won unan. decision over Morales, June 22, 2002, but refused WBC title. Morales regained WBC title with unan. decision over Paulie Ayala, Nov. 16, 2002. Morales moved up to Junior Lightweight div. in 2004.

History of Heavyweight Championship Bouts
(bouts in which title changed hands)

1889—July 8, John L. Sullivan def. Jake Kilrain, 75, Richburg, MS. (Last championship bare knuckles bout.)

1892—Sept. 7, James J. Corbett def. John L. Sullivan, 21, New Orleans. (Big gloves used for first time.)

1897—Bob Fitzsimmons def. James J. Corbett, 14, Carson City, NV.

1899—June 9, James J. Jeffries def. Bob Fitzsimmons, 11, Coney Island, NY. (Jeffries retired as champion in 1905.)

1905—July 3, Marvin Hart KOd Jack Root, 12, Reno, NV. (Jeffries refereed, gave title to Hart. Jack O'Brien also claimed the title.)

1906—Feb. 23, Tommy Burns def. Marvin Hart, 20, Los Angeles.

1908—Dec. 26, Jack Johnson KOd Tommy Burns, 14, Sydney, Australia. (Police halted contest.)

1915—April 5, Jess Willard KOd Jack Johnson, 26, Havana.

1919—July 4, Jack Dempsey KOd Jess Willard, Toledo, OH. (Willard failed to answer bell for 4th round.)

1926—Sept. 23, Gene Tunney def. Jack Dempsey, 10, Philadelphia. (Tunney retired as champion in 1928.)

1930—June 12, Max Schmeling def. Jack Sharkey, 4, NY. (Sharkey fouled Schmeling in a bout generally considered to have resulted in the election of a successor to Tunney.)

1932—June 21, Jack Sharkey def. Max Schmeling, 15, NY.

1933—June 29, Primo Carnera KOd Jack Sharkey, 6, NY.

1934—June 14, Max Baer KOd Primo Carnera, 11, NY.

1935—June 13, James J. Braddock def. Max Baer, 15, NY.

1937—June 22, Joe Louis def James J. Braddock, 8, Chicago. (Louis retired as champion in 1949.)

1949—June 22, Ezzard Charles def. Joe Walcott, 15, Chicago; NBA recognition only.

1951—July 18, Joe Walcott KOd Ezzard Charles, 7, Pittsburgh.

1952—Sept. 23, Rocky Marciano KOd Joe Walcott, 13, Philadelphia. (Marciano retired as champion in 1956.)

1956—Nov. 30, Floyd Patterson KOd Archie Moore, 5, Chicago.

1959—June 26, Ingemar Johansson KOd Floyd Patterson, 3, NY.

1960—June 20, Floyd Patterson KOd Ingemar Johansson, 5, NY. (Patterson was 1st heavyweight to regain title.)

1962—Sept. 25, Sonny Liston KOd Floyd Patterson, 1, Chicago.

1964—Feb. 25, Cassius Clay (Muhammad Ali) KOd Sonny Liston, 7, Miami Beach, FL. (In 1967, Ali was stripped of his title by the WBA and others for refusing military service.)

1970—Feb. 16, Joe Frazier KOd Jimmy Ellis, 5, NY. (Frazier def. Ali in 15 rounds, Mar. 8, 1971, in NY.)

1973—Jan. 22, George Foreman KOd Joe Frazier, 2, Jamaica.

1974—Oct. 30, Muhammad Ali KOd George Foreman, 8, Kinshasa, Zaire.

1978—Feb. 15, Leon Spinks def. Muhammad Ali, 15, Las Vegas. (WBC recognized Ken Norton as champion after Spinks refused to fight him before his rematch with Ali.); June 9, (WBC) Larry Holmes def. Ken Norton, 15, Las Vegas. (Holmes gave up title in Dec. 1983.); Sept. 15, (WBA) Muhammad Ali def. Leon Spinks, 15, New Orleans. (Ali retired as champion in 1979.)

1979—Oct. 20, (WBA) John Tate def. Gerrie Coetzee, 15, Pretoria, South Africa.

1980—Mar. 31, (WBA) Mike Weaver KOd John Tate, 15, Knoxville.

1982—Dec. 10, (WBA) Michael Dokes KOd Mike Weaver, 1, Las Vegas.

1983—Sept. 23, (WBA) Gerrie Coetzee KOd Michael Dokes, 10, Richfield, OH; in Dec., Larry Holmes relinquished the WBC title and was named champion of the newly formed IBF.

1984—Mar. 9, (WBC) Tim Witherspoon def. Greg Page, 12, Las Vegas; Aug. 31, (WBC) Pinklon Thomas def. Tim Witherspoon, 12, Las Vegas; Dec. 2, (WBA) Greg Page KOd Gerrie Coetzee, 8, Sun City, Bophuthatswana.

1985—Apr. 29, (WBA) Tony Tubbs def. Greg Page, 15, Buffalo, NY; Sept. 21, (IBF) Michael Spinks def. Larry Holmes, 15, Las Vegas. (Spinks relinquished title in Feb. 1987.)

1986—Jan. 17, (WBA) Tim Witherspoon def. Tony Tubbs, 15, Atlanta, GA; Mar. 23, (WBC) Trevor Berbick def. Pinklon Thomas, 12, Miami; Nov. 22, (WBC) Mike Tyson KOd Trevor Berbick, 2, Las Vegas; Dec. 12, (WBA) James "Bonecrusher" Smith KOd Tim Witherspoon, 1, NY.

1987—Mar. 7, (WBA, WBC) Mike Tyson def. James "Bonecrusher" Smith, 12, Las Vegas; May 30, (IBF) Tony Tucker KO'd James "Buster" Douglas, 10, Las Vegas; Aug. 1, (WBA, WBC, IBF) Mike Tyson def. Tony Tucker, 12, Las Vegas. (Tyson became undisputed champion.)

1990—Feb. 11, (WBA, WBC, IBF) James "Buster" Douglas KOd Mike Tyson, 10, Tokyo; Oct. 25, (WBA, WBC, IBF) Evander Holyfield KOd James "Buster" Douglas, 3, Las Vegas.

1992—Nov. 13, (WBA, WBC, IBF) Riddick Bowe def. Evander Holyfield, 12, Las Vegas. (Lennox Lewis was later named WBC champion when Bowe refused to fight him.)

1993—Nov. 6, (WBA, IBF) Evander Holyfield def. Riddick Bowe, 12, Las Vegas.

1994—Apr. 22, (WBA, IBF) Michael Moorer def. Evander Holyfield, 12, Las Vegas; Sept. 24, (WBC) Oliver McCall KOd Lennox Lewis, 2, London; Nov. 5, (WBA, IBF) George Foreman KOd Michael Moorer, 10, Las Vegas. (In Mar. 1995, Foreman was stripped of the WBA title; he relinquished the IBF title in June.)

1995—Sept. 2, (WBC) Frank Bruno def. Oliver McCall, 12, London; Dec. 9, (IBF) Frans Botha def. Axel Schulz, 12, Las Vegas. (Botha was subsequently stripped of title.)

1996—Mar. 16, (WBC) Mike Tyson KOd Frank Bruno, 3, Las Vegas; June 22, (IBF) Michael Moorer def. Axel Schulz, 12, Dortmund, Germany; Sept. 7, (WBA, WBC) Mike Tyson KOd Bruce Seldon, 1, Las Vegas. (Tyson was subsequently stripped of WBC title.); Nov. 9, (WBA) Evander Holyfield KOd Mike Tyson, 11, Las Vegas.

1997—Feb. 7, (WBC) Lennox Lewis KOd Oliver McCall, 5, Las Vegas; Nov. 8, (IBF) Evander Holyfield def. Michael Moorer, 8, Las Vegas.

1999—Nov. 13, (WBA, WBC, IBF) Lennox Lewis def. Evander Holyfield, 12, Las Vegas. (Lewis became undisputed champion. In April 2000, Lewis was stripped of his WBA title.)

2000—Aug. 12, (WBA) Evander Holyfield def. John Ruiz, 12, Las Vegas.

2001—Mar. 3, (WBA) John Ruiz def. Evander Holyfield, 12, Las Vegas; Apr. 21, (WBC, IBF) Hasim Rahman KOd Lennox Lewis, 5, Brakpan, South Africa; Nov. 17, (WBC, IBF) Lennox Lewis KOd Hasim Rahman, 4, Las Vegas.

2002—Dec. 14, (IBF) Chris Byrd def. Evander Holyfield, 12, Atlantic City.

2003—Mar. 1, (WBA) Roy Jones Jr. def. John Ruiz, 12, Las Vegas. Dec. 13, (WBA) John Ruiz def. Hasim Rahman, 12, Atlantic City, NJ, to take "interim" title. (Ruiz gained full title when Jones Jr. relinquished it Feb. 20, 2004.)

2004—Apr. 24, (WBC) Vitali Klitschko TKOd Corrie Sanders, 8, Los Angeles, CA, to win title vacated when champ Lennox Lewis retired in Feb.

THOROUGHBRED RACING
Triple Crown Winners
Since 1920, colts have carried 126 lb. in triple crown events; fillies, 121 lb.
(Kentucky Derby, Preakness, and Belmont Stakes)

Year	Horse	Jockey	Trainer	Year	Horse	Jockey	Trainer
1919	Sir Barton	J. Loftus	H. G. Bedwell	1946	Assault	W. Mehrtens	M. Hirsch
1930	Gallant Fox	E. Sande	J. Fitzsimmons	1948	Citation	E. Arcaro	H. A. Jones
1935	Omaha	W. Sanders	J. Fitzsimmons	1973	Secretariat	R. Turcotte	L. Laurin
1937	War Admiral	C. Kurtsinger	G. Conway	1977	Seattle Slew	J. Cruguet	W. H. Turner Jr.
1941	Whirlaway	E. Arcaro	B. A. Jones	1978	Affirmed	S. Cauthen	L. S. Barrera
1943	Count Fleet	J. Longden	G. D. Cameron				

Kentucky Derby
Churchill Downs, Louisville, KY; inaug. 1875; distance 1-1/4 mi; 1-1/2 mi until 1896. 3-year-olds.
Best time: 1:59 2/5, by Secretariat, 1973; 2004 time: 2:04.06.

Year	Winner	Jockey	Year	Winner	Jockey	Year	Winner	Jockey
1875	Aristides	O. Lewis	1919	Sir Barton	J. Loftus	1962	Decidedly	W. Hartack
1876	Vagrant	R. Swim	1920	Paul Jones	T. Rice	1963	Chateaugay	B. Baeza
1877	Baden Baden	W. Walker	1921	Behave Yourself	C. Thompson	1964	Northern Dancer	W. Hartack
1878	Day Star	Carter	1922	Morvich	A. Johnson	1965	Lucky Debonair	W. Shoemaker
1879	Lord Murphy	C. Schauer	1923	Zev	E. Sande	1966	Kauai King	D. Brumfield
1880	Fonso	G. Lewis	1924	Black Gold	J. D. Mooney	1967	Proud Clarion	R. Ussery
1881	Hindoo	J. McLaughlin	1925	Flying Ebony	E. Sande	1968	Dancer's Image#	R. Ussery
1882	Apollo	B. Hurd	1926	Bubbling Over	A. Johnson	1969	Majestic Prince	W. Hartack
1883	Leonatus	W. Donohue	1927	Whiskery	L. McAtee	1970	Dust Commander	M. Manganello
1884	Buchanan	I. Murphy	1928	Reigh Count	C. Lang	1971	Canonero II	G. Avila
1885	Joe Cotton	E. Henderson	1929	Clyde Van Dusen	L. McAtee	1972	Riva Ridge	R. Turcotte
1886	Ben Ali	P. Duffy	1930	Gallant Fox	E. Sande	1973	Secretariat	R. Turcotte
1887	Montrose	I. Lewis	1931	Twenty Grand	C. Kurtsinger	1974	Cannonade	A. Cordero
1888	Macbeth II	G. Covington	1932	Burgoo King	E. James	1975	Foolish Pleasure	J. Vasquez
1889	Spokane	T. Kiley	1933	Brokers Tip	D. Meade	1976	Bold Forbes	A. Cordero
1890	Riley	I. Murphy	1934	Cavalcade	M. Garner	1977	Seattle Slew	J. Cruguet
1891	Kingman	I. Murphy	1935	Omaha	W. Saunders	1978	Affirmed	S. Cauthen
1892	Azra	A. Clayton	1936	Bold Venture	I. Hanford	1979	Spectacular Bid	R. Franklin
1893	Lookout	E. Kunze	1937	War Admiral	C. Kurtsinger	1980	Genuine Risk*	J. Vasquez
1894	Chant	F. Goodale	1938	Lawrin	E. Arcaro	1981	Pleasant Colony	J. Velasquez
1895	Halma	J. Perkins	1939	Johnstown	J. Stout	1982	Gato del Sol	E. Delahoussaye
1896	Ben Brush	W. Simms	1940	Gallahadion	C. Bierman	1983	Sunny's Halo	E. Delahoussaye
1897	Typhoon II	F. Garner	1941	Whirlaway	E. Arcaro	1984	Swale	L. Pincay
1898	Plaudit	W. Simms	1942	Shut Out	W. D. Wright	1985	Spend a Buck	A. Cordero
1899	Manuel	F. Taral	1943	Count Fleet	J. Longden	1986	Ferdinand	W. Shoemaker
1900	Lieut. Gibson	J. Boland	1944	Pensive	C. McCreary	1987	Alysheba	C. McCarron
1901	His Eminence	J. Winkfield	1945	Hoop, Jr.	E. Arcaro	1988	Winning Colors*	G. Stevens
1902	Alan-a-Dale	J. Winkfield	1946	Assault	W. Mehrtens	1989	Sunday Silence	P. Valenzuela
1903	Judge Himes	H. Booker	1947	Jet Pilot	E. Guerin	1990	Unbridled	C. Perret
1904	Elwood	F. Prior	1948	Citation	E. Arcaro	1991	Strike the Gold	C. Antley
1905	Agile	J. Martin	1949	Ponder	S. Brooks	1992	Lil E. Tee	P. Day
1906	Sir Huon	R. Troxler	1950	Middleground	W. Boland	1993	Sea Hero	J. Bailey
1907	Pink Star	A. Minder	1951	Count Turf	C. McCreary	1994	Go for Gin	C. McCarron
1908	Stone Street	A. Pickens	1952	Hill Gail	E. Arcaro	1995	Thunder Gulch	G. Stevens
1909	Wintergreen	V. Powers	1953	Dark Star	H. Moreno	1996	Grindstone	J. Bailey
1910	Donau	F. Herbert	1954	Determine	R. York	1997	Silver Charm	G. Stevens
1911	Meridian	G. Archibald	1955	Swaps	W. Shoemaker	1998	Real Quiet	K. Desormeaux
1912	Worth	C.H. Shilling	1956	Needles	D. Erb	1999	Charismatic	C. Antley
1913	Donerail	R. Goose	1957	Iron Liege	W. Hartack	2000	Fusaichi Pegasus	K. Desormeaux
1914	Old Rosebud	J. McCabe	1958	Tim Tam	I. Valenzuela	2001	Monarchos	J. Chavez
1915	Regret*	J. Notter	1959	Tomy Lee	W. Shoemaker	2002	War Emblem	V. Espinoza
1916	George Smith	J. Loftus	1960	Venetian Way	W. Hartack	2003	Funny Cide	J. Santos
1917	Omar Khayyam	C. Borel	1961	Carry Back	J. Sellers	2004	Smarty Jones	S. Elliot
1918	Exterminator	W. Knapp						

*Regret, Genuine Risk, and Winning Colors are the only fillies to have won the Derby. # Dancer's Image was disqualified from purse money after tests disclosed that he had run with a pain-killing drug, phenylbutazone, in his system. All wagers were paid on Dancer's Image. Forward Pass was awarded first place money. The Kentucky Derby has been won 5 times by 2 jockeys: Eddie Arcaro, 1938, 1941, 1945, 1948, and 1952; and Bill Hartack, 1957, 1960, 1962, 1964, and 1969. It was won 4 times by Willie Shoemaker, 1955, 1959, 1965, and 1986; and 3 times by each of 4 jockeys: Isaac Murphy, 1884, 1890, and 1891; Earle Sande, 1923, 1925, and 1930; Angel Cordero, 1974, 1976, and 1985; and Gary Stevens, 1988, 1995, and 1997.

Top 10 Fastest Winning Times for the Kentucky Derby
(Official Kentucky Derby times measured in fifths of a second.)

Time	Horse	Jockey	Year	Time	Horse	Jockey	Year
1m. 59 2/5 s.	Secretariat	Ron Turcotte	1973	2m. 1 1/5 s.	Thunder Gulch	Gary Stevens	1995
1m. 59 4/5 s.	Monarchos	Jorge Chavez	2001		Affirmed	Steve Cauthen	1978
2m.	Northern Dancer	Bill Hartack	1964		Lucky Debonair	Bill Shoemaker	1965
2m. 1/5 s.	Spend a Buck	Angel Cordero Jr.	1985	2m. 1 2/5 s.	Whirlaway	Eddie Arcaro	1941
2m. 2/5 s.	Decidedly	Bill Hartack	1962	2m. 1 3/5 s.	Bold Forbes	Angel Cordero Jr.	1976
2m. 3/5 s.	Proud Clarion	Robert Ussery	1967		Hill Gail	Eddie Arcaro	1952
2m. 1 s.	Funny Cide	Jose Santos	2003		Middleground	William Boland	1950
	War Emblem	Victor Espinoza	2002				
	Fusaichi Pegasus	Kent Desormeaux	2000				
	Grindstone	Jerry Bailey	1996				

Preakness Stakes

Pimlico Race Course, Baltimore, MD; inaug. 1873; distance 1-3/16 mi. 3-year-olds.
Best time: 1:53 2/5, by Tank's Prospect (1985) and Louis Quatorze (1996); 2004 time: 1:55.59.

Year	Winner	Jockey	Year	Winner	Jockey	Year	Winner	Jockey
1873	Survivor	G. Barbee	1919	Sir Barton	J. Loftus	1963	Candy Spots	W. Shoemaker
1874	Culpepper	M. Donohue	1920	Man o' War	C. Kummer	1964	Northern Dancer	W. Hartack
1875	Tom Ochiltree	L. Hughes	1921	Broomspun	F. Coltiletti	1965	Tom Rolfe	R. Turcotte
1876	Shirley	G. Barbee	1922	Pillory	L. Morris	1966	Kauai King	D. Brumfield
1877	Cloverbrook	C. Holloway	1923	Vigil	B. Marinelli	1967	Damascus	W. Shoemaker
1878	Duke of Magenta	C. Holloway	1924	Nellie Morse	J. Merimee	1968	Forward Pass	I. Valenzuela
1879	Harold	L. Hughes	1925	Coventry	C. Kummer	1969	Majestic Prince	W. Hartack
1880	Grenada	L. Hughes	1926	Display	J. Malben	1970	Personality	E. Belmonte
1881	Saunterer	W. Costello	1927	Bostonian	A. Abel	1971	Canonero II	G. Avila
1882	Vanguard	W. Costello	1928	Victorian	R. Workman	1972	Bee Bee Bee	E. Nelson
1883	Jacobus	G. Barbee	1929	Dr. Freeland	L. Schaefer	1973	Secretariat	R. Turcotte
1884	Knight of Ellerslie	S. H. Fisher	1930	Gallant Fox	E. Sande	1974	Little Current	M. Rivera
1885	Tecumseh	J. McLaughlin	1931	Mate	G. Ellis	1975	Master Derby	D. McHargue
1886	The Bard	S. H. Fisher	1932	Burgoo King	E. James	1976	Elocutionist	J. Lively
1887	Dunboyne	W. Donohue	1933	Head Play	C. Kurtsinger	1977	Seattle Slew	J. Cruguet
1888	Refund	F. Littlefield	1934	High Quest	R. Jones	1978	Affirmed	S. Cauthen
1889	Buddhist	G. Anderson	1935	Omaha	W. Saunders	1979	Spectacular Bid	R. Franklin
1890	Montague	W. Martin	1936	Bold Venture	G. Woolf	1980	Codex	A. Cordero
1894	Assignee	F. Taral	1937	War Admiral	C. Kurtsinger	1981	Pleasant Colony	J. Velasquez
1895	Belmar	F. Taral	1938	Dauber	M. Peters	1982	Aloma's Ruler	J. Kaenel
1896	Margrave	H. Griffin	1939	Challedon	G. Seabo	1983	Deputed	
1897	Paul Kauvar	C. Thorpe	1940	Bimelech	F.A. Smith		Testamony	D. Miller
1898	Sly Fox	W. Simms	1941	Whirlaway	E. Arcaro	1984	Gate Dancer	A. Cordero
1899	Half Time	R. Clawson	1942	Alsab	B. James	1985	Tank's Prospect	P. Day
1900	Hindus	H. Spencer	1943	Count Fleet	J. Longden	1986	Snow Chief	A. Solis
1901	The Parader	F. Landry	1944	Pensive	C. McCreary	1987	Alysheba	C. McCarron
1902	Old England	L. Jackson	1945	Polynesian	W.D. Wright	1988	Risen Star	E. Delahoussaye
1903	Flocarline	W. Gannon	1946	Assault	W. Mehrtens	1989	Sunday Silence	P. Valenzuela
1904	Bryn Mawr	E. Hildebrand	1947	Faultless	D. Dodson	1990	Summer Squall	P. Day
1905	Cairngorm	W. Davis	1948	Citation	E. Arcaro	1991	Hansel	J. Bailey
1906	Whimsical	W. Miller	1949	Capot	T. Atkinson	1992	Pine Bluff	C. McCarron
1907	Don Enrique	G. Mountain	1950	Hill Prince	E. Arcaro	1993	Prairie Bayou	M. Smith
1908	Royal Tourist	E. Dugan	1951	Bold	E. Arcaro	1994	Tabasco Cat	P. Day
1909	Effendi	W. Doyle	1952	Blue Man	C. McCreary	1995	Timber Country	P. Day
1910	Layminster	R. Estep	1953	Native Dancer	E. Guerin	1996	Louis Quatorze	P. Day
1911	Watervale	E. Dugan	1954	Hasty Road	J. Adams	1997	Silver Charm	G. Stevens
1912	Colonel Holloway	C. Turner	1955	Nashua	E. Arcaro	1998	Real Quiet	K. Desormeaux
1913	Buskin	J. Butwell	1956	Fabius	W. Hartack	1999	Charismatic	C. Antley
1914	Holiday	A. Schuttinger	1957	Bold Ruler	E. Arcaro	2000	Red Bullet	J. Bailey
1915	Rhine Maiden	D. Hoffman	1958	Tim Tam	I. Valenzuela	2001	Point Given	G. Stevens
1916	Damrosch	L. McAtee	1959	Royal Orbit	W. Harmatz	2002	War Emblem	V. Espinoza
1917	Kalitan	E. Haynes	1960	Bally Ache	R. Ussery	2003	Funny Cide	J. Santos
1918*	War Cloud	J. Loftus	1961	Carry Back	J. Sellers	2004	Smarty Jones	S. Elliot
	Jack Hare Jr.	C. Peak	1962	Greek Money	J.L. Rotz			

*Horses ran in 2 divisions.

Belmont Stakes

Belmont Park, Elmont, NY; inaug. 1867; distance 1-1/2 mi. 3-year-olds. Best time: 2:24, Secretariat, 1973; 2004 time: 2:27.50.

Year	Winner	Jockey	Year	Winner	Jockey	Year	Winner	Jockey
1867	Ruthless	J. Gilpatrick	1903	Africander	J. Bullman	1941	Whirlaway	E. Arcaro
1868	General Duke	R. Swim	1904	Delhi	G. Odom	1942	Shut Out	E. Arcaro
1869	Fenian	C. Miller	1905	Tanya	E. Hildebrand	1943	Count Fleet	J. Longden
1870	Kingfisher	W. Dick	1906	Burgomaster	L. Lyne	1944	Bounding Home	G. L. Smith
1871	Harry Bassett	W. Miller	1907	Peter Pan	G. Mountain	1945	Pavot	E. Arcaro
1872	Joe Daniels	J. Rowe	1908	Colin	J. Notter	1946	Assault	W. Mehrtens
1873	Springbok	J. Rowe	1909	Joe Madden	E. Dugan	1947	Phalanx	R. Donoso
1874	Saxon	G. Barbee	1910	Sweep	J. Butwell	1948	Citation	E. Arcaro
1875	Calvin	R. Swim	1913	Prince Eugene	R. Troxler	1949	Capot	T. Atkinson
1876	Algerine	W. Donohue	1914	Luke McLuke	M. Buxton	1950	Middleground	W. Boland
1877	Cloverbrook	C. Holloway	1915	The Finn	G. Byrne	1951	Counterpoint	D. Gorman
1878	Duke of Magenta	L. Hughes	1916	Friar Rock	E. Haynes	1952	One Count	E. Arcaro
1879	Spendthrift	S. Evans	1917	Hourless	J. Butwell	1953	Native Dancer	E. Guerin
1880	Grenada	L. Hughes	1918	Johren	F. Robinson	1954	High Gun	E. Guerin
1881	Saunterer	T. Costello	1919	Sir Barton	J. Loftus	1955	Nashua	E. Arcaro
1882	Forester	J. McLaughlin	1920	Man o' War	C. Kummer	1956	Needles	D. Erb
1883	George Kinney	J. McLaughlin	1921	Grey Lag	E. Sande	1957	Gallant Man	W. Shoemaker
1884	Panique	J. McLaughlin	1922	Pillory	C. H. Miller	1958	Cavan	P. Anderson
1885	Tyrant	P. Duffy	1923	Zev	E. Sande	1959	Sword Dancer	W. Shoemaker
1886	Inspector	B.J. McLaughlin	1924	Mad Play	E. Sande	1960	Celtic Ash	W. Hartack
1887	Hanover	J. McLaughlin	1925	American Flag	A. Johnson	1961	Sherluck	B. Baeza
1888	Sir Dixon	J. McLaughlin	1926	Crusader	A. Johnson	1962	Jaipur	W. Shoemaker
1889	Eric	W. Hayward	1927	Chance Shot	E. Sande	1963	Chateaugay	B. Baeza
1890	Burlington	S. Barnes	1928	Vito	C. Kummer	1964	Quadrangle	M. Ycaza
1891	Foxford	E. Garrison	1929	Blue Larkspur	M. Garner	1965	Hail to All	J. Sellers
1892	Patron	W. Hayward	1930	Gallant Fox	E. Sande	1966	Amberoid	W. Boland
1893	Comanche	W. Simms	1931	Twenty Grand	C. Kurtsinger	1967	Damascus	W. Shoemaker
1894	Henry of Navarre	W. Simms	1932	Faireno	T. Malley	1968	Stage Door Johnny	H. Gustines
1895	Belmar	F. Taral	1933	Hurryoff	M. Garner	1969	Arts and Letters	B. Baeza
1896	Hastings	H. Griffin	1934	Peace Chance	W. D. Wright	1970	High Echelon	J. L. Rotz
1897	Scottish Chieftain	J. Scherrer	1935	Omaha	W. Saunders	1971	Pass Catcher	W. Blum
1898	Bowling Brook	F. Littlefield	1936	Granville	J. Stout	1972	Riva Ridge	R. Turcotte
1899	Jean Bereaud	R. R. Clawson	1937	War Admiral	C. Kurtsinger	1973	Secretariat	R. Turcotte
1900	Ildrim	N. Turner	1938	Pasteurized	J. Stout	1974	Little Current	M. Rivera
1901	Commando	H. Spencer	1939	Johnstown	J. Stout	1975	Avatar	W. Shoemaker
1902	Masterman	J. Bullman	1940	Bimelech	F. A. Smith	1976	Bold Forbes	A. Cordero

Year	Winner	Jockey	Year	Winner	Jockey	Year	Winner	Jockey
1977	Seattle Slew	J. Cruguet	1987	Bet Twice	C. Perret	1996	Editor's Note	R. Douglas
1978	Affirmed	S. Cauthen	1988	Risen Star	E. Delahoussaye	1997	Touch Gold	C. McCarron
1979	Coastal	R. Hernandez	1989	Easy Goer	P. Day	1998	Victory Gallop	G. Stevens
1980	Temperence Hill	E. Maple	1990	Go and Go	M. Kinane	1999	Lemon Drop Kid	J. Santos
1981	Summing	G. Martens	1991	Hansel	J. Bailey	2000	Commendable	P. Day
1982	Conquistador Cielo	L. Pincay	1992	A.P. Indy	E. Delahoussaye	2001	Point Given	G. Stevens
1983	Caveat	L. Pincay	1993	Colonial Affair	J. Krone	2002	Sarava	E. Prado
1984	Swale	L. Pincay	1994	Tabasco Cat	P. Day	2003	Empire Maker	J. Bailey
1985	Creme Fraiche	E. Maple	1995	Thunder Gulch	G. Stevens	2004	Birdstone	E. Prado
1986	Danzig Connection	C. McCarron						

Annual Leading Jockey — Money Won[1]

Year	Jockey	Earnings	Year	Jockey	Earnings	Year	Jockey	Earnings
1957	Bill Hartack	$3,060,501	1973	Laffit Pincay, Jr.	$4,093,492	1989	Jose Santos	$13,838,389
1958	Willie Shoemaker	2,961,693	1974	Laffit Pincay, Jr.	4,251,060	1990	Gary Stevens	13,881,198
1959	Willie Shoemaker	2,843,133	1975	Braulio Baeza	3,695,198	1991	Chris McCarron	14,441,083
1960	Willie Shoemaker	2,123,961	1976	Angel Cordero, Jr.	4,709,500	1992	Kent Desormeaux	14,193,006
1961	Willie Shoemaker	2,690,819	1977	Steve Cauthen	6,151,750	1993	Mike Smith	14,024,815
1962	Willie Shoemaker	2,916,844	1978	Darrel McHargue	6,029,885	1994	Mike Smith	15,979,820
1963	Willie Shoemaker	2,526,925	1979	Laffit Pincay, Jr.	8,193,535	1995	Jerry Bailey	16,311,876
1964	Willie Shoemaker	2,649,553	1980	Chris McCarron	7,663,300	1996	Jerry Bailey	19,465,376
1965	Braulio Baeza	2,582,702	1981	Chris McCarron	8,397,604	1997	Jerry Bailey	18,320,743
1966	Braulio Baeza	2,951,022	1982	Angel Cordero, Jr.	9,483,590	1998	Gary Stevens	19,622,855
1967	Braulio Baeza	3,088,888	1983	Angel Cordero, Jr.	10,116,697	1999	Pat Day	18,092,845
1968	Braulio Baeza	2,835,108	1984	Chris McCarron	12,045,813	2000	Pat Day	17,479,838
1969	Jorge Velasquez	2,542,315	1985	Laffit Pincay, Jr.	13,353,299	2001	Jerry Bailey	22,597,720
1970	Laffit Pincay, Jr.	2,626,526	1986	Jose Santos	11,329,297	2002	Jerry Bailey	22,871,814
1971	Laffit Pincay, Jr.	3,784,377	1987	Jose Santos	12,375,433	2003	Jerry Bailey	22,829,570
1972	Laffit Pincay, Jr.	3,225,827	1988	Jose Santos	14,877,298			

(1) Total earnings for all horses that jockey raced in year listed; does not reflect jockey's earnings.

Breeders' Cup World Thoroughbred Championships

The Breeders' Cup was inaugurated in 1984 and consists of 7 races at one track on one day late in the year to determine Thoroughbred racing's champion contenders. It has been held at the following locations:

1984 Hollywood Park, CA	1991 Churchill Downs, KY	1998 Churchill Downs, KY
1985 Aqueduct Racetrack, NY	1992 Gulfstream Park, FL	1999 Gulfstream Park, FL
1986 Santa Anita Park, CA	1993 Santa Anita Park, CA	2000 Churchill Downs, KY
1987 Hollywood Park, CA	1994 Churchill Downs, KY	2001 Belmont Park, NY
1988 Churchill Downs, KY	1995 Belmont Park, NY	2002 Arlington Park, IL
1989 Gulfstream Park, FL	1996 Woodbine Racetrack, Ontario	2003 Santa Anita Park, CA
1990 Belmont Park, NY	1997 Hollywood Park, CA	

Juvenile
Distances: 1 mi 1984-85, 1987; 1-1/16 mi 1986 and since 1988

Year		Jockey	Year		Jockey	Year		Jockey
1984	Chief's Crown	D. MacBeth	1991	Arazi	P. Valenzuela	1998	Answer Lively	J. Bailey
1985	Tasso	L. Pincay, Jr.	1992	Gilded Time	C. McCarron	1999	Anees	G. Stevens
1986	Capote	L. Pincay, Jr.	1993	Brocco	G. Stevens	2000	Macho Uno	J. Bailey
1987	Success Express	J. Santos	1994	Timber Country	P. Day	2001	Johannesburg	M. Kinane
1988	Is It True	L. Pincay, Jr.	1995	Unbridled's Song	M. Smith	2002	Vindication	M. Smith
1989	Rhythm	C. Perret	1996	Boston Harbor	J. Bailey	2003	Action This Day	D. Flores
1990	Fly So Free	J. Santos	1997	Favorite Trick	P. Day			

Juvenile Fillies
Distances: 1 mi 1984-85, 1987; 1-1/16 mi 1986 and since 1988

Year		Jockey	Year		Jockey	Year		Jockey
1984	*Outstandingly	W. Guerra	1991	Pleasant Stage	E. Delahoussaye	1998	Silverbulletday	G. Stevens
1985	Twilight Ridge	J. Velasquez	1992	Eliza	P. Valenzuela	1999	Cash Run	J. Bailey
1986	Brave Raj	P. Valenzuela	1993	Phone Chatter	L. Pincay, Jr.	2000	Caressing	J. Velazquez
1987	Epitome	P. Day	1994	Flanders	P. Day	2001	Tempera	D. Flores
1988	Open Mind	A. Cordero, Jr.	1995	My Flag	J. Bailey	2002	Storm Flag Flying	J. Velazquez
1989	Go for Wand	R. Romero	1996	Storm Song	C. Perret	2003	Halfbridled	J. Krone
1990	Meadow Star	J. Santos	1997	Countess Diana	S. Sellers			

*By disqualification.

Sprint
Distance: 6 furlongs

Year		Jockey	Year		Jockey	Year		Jockey
1984	Eillo	C. Perret	1991	Sheikh Albadou	P. Eddery	1998	Reraise	C. Nakatani
1985	Precisionist	C. McCarron	1992	Thirty Slews	E. Delahoussaye	1999	Artax	J. Chaves
1986	Smile	J. Vasquez	1993	Cardmania	E. Delahoussaye	2000	Kona Gold	A. Solis
1987	Very Subtle	P. Valenzuela	1994	Cherokee Run	M. Smith	2001	Squirtle Squirt	J. Bailey
1988	Gulch	A. Cordero, Jr.	1995	Desert Stormer	K. Desormeaux	2002	Orientate	J. Bailey
1989	Dancing Spree	A. Cordero, Jr.	1996	Lit De Justice	C. Nakatani	2003	Cajun Beat	C. Velasquez
1990	Safely Kept	C. Perret	1997	Elmhurst	C. Nakatani			

Mile

Year		Jockey	Year		Jockey	Year		Jockey
1984	Royal Heroine	F. Toro	1991	Opening Verse	P. Valenzuela	1998	Da Hoss	J. Velazquez
1985	Cozzene	W. Guerra	1992	Lure	M. Smith	1999	Silic	C. Nakatani
1986	Last Tycoon	Y. St.-Martin	1993	Lure	M. Smith	2000	War Chant	G. Stevens
1987	Miesque	F. Head	1994	Barathea	L. Dettori	2001	Val Royal	J. Valdivia Jr.
1988	Miesque	F. Head	1995	Ridgewood Pearl	J. Murtagh	2002	Domedriver	T. Thulliez
1989	Steinlen	J. Santos	1996	Da Hoss	G. Stevens	2003	Six Perfections	J. Bailey
1990	Royal Academy	L. Piggott	1997	Spinning World	C. Asmussan			

Filly & Mare Turf
Distance: 1-3/8 mi 1999-2000, 1-1/4 mi 2002

Year		Jockey	Year		Jockey	Year		Jockey
1999	Soaring Softly	J. Bailey	2001	Banks Hill	O. Peslier	2003	Islington	K. Fallon
2000	Perfect Sting	J. Bailey	2002	Starine	J. Velazquez			

Distaff
Distances: 1-1/4 mi 1984-87; 1-1/8 mi since 1988

Year		Jockey	Year		Jockey	Year		Jockey
1984	Princess Rooney	E. Delahoussaye	1991	Dance Smartly	P. Day	1998	Escena	G. Stevens
1985	Life's Magic	A. Cordero, Jr.	1992	Paseana	C. McCarron	1999	Beautiful Pleasure	J. Chaves
1986	Lady's Secret	P. Day	1993	Hollywood Wildcat	E. Delahoussaye	2000	Spain	V. Espinoza
1987	Sacahuista	R. Romero	1994	One Dreamer	G. Stevens	2001	Unbridled Elaine	P. Day
1988	Personal Ensign	R. Romero	1995	Inside Information	M. Smith	2002	Azeri	M. Smith
1989	Bayakoa	L. Pincay, Jr.	1996	Jewel Princess	C. Nakatani	2003	Adoration	P. Valenzuela
1990	Bayakoa	L. Pincay, Jr.	1997	Ajina	M. Smith			

Turf
Distance: 1-1/2 mi

Year		Jockey	Year		Jockey	Year		Jockey
1984	Lashkari	Y. St.-Martin	1991	Miss Alleged	E. Legrix	1998	Buck's Boy	S. Sellers
1985	Pebbles	P. Eddery	1992	Fraise	P. Valenzuela	1999	Daylami	L. Dettori
1986	Manila	J. Santos	1993	Kotashaan	K. Desormeaux	2000	Kalanisi	J. Murtagh
1987	Theatrical	P. Day	1994	Tikkanen	M. Smith	2001	Fantastic Light	L. Dettori
1988	Great		1995	Northern Spur	C. McCarron	2002	High Chaparral	M. Kinane
	Communicator	R. Sibille	1996	Pilsudski	W. Swinburn	2003	tie-High Chaparral	M. Kinane
1989	Prized	E. Delahoussaye	1997	Chief Bearhart	J. Santos		Johar	A. Solis
1990	In The Wings	G. Stevens						

Classic
Distance: 1-1/4 mi

Year		Jockey	Year		Jockey	Year		Jockey
1984	Wild Again	P. Day	1991	Black Tie Affair	J. Bailey	1998	Awesome Again	P. Day
1985	Proud Truth	J. Velasquez	1992	A.P. Indy	E. Delahoussaye	1999	Cat Thief	P. Day
1986	Skywalker	L. Pincay, Jr.	1993	Arcangues	J. Bailey	2000	Tiznow	C. McCarron
1987	Ferdinand	W. Shoemaker	1994	Concern	J. Bailey	2001	Tiznow	C. McCarron
1988	Alysheba	C. McCarron	1995	Cigar	J. Bailey	2002	Volponi	P. Johnson
1989	Sunday Silence	C. McCarron	1996	Alphabet Soup	C. McCarron	2003	Pleasantly Perfect	A. Solis
1990	Unbridled	P. Day	1997	Skip Away	M. Smith			

Eclipse Awards

The Eclipse Awards, honoring the Horse of the Year and other champions of the sport, began in 1971 and are sponsored by the *Daily Racing Form,* the National Thoroughbred Racing Association, and the National Turf Writers Assn. Prior to 1971, the *DRF* (1936-70) and the TRA (1950-70) issued separate selections for Horse of the Year.

Eclipse Awards for 2003

Horse of the Year—Mineshaft
2-year-old colt or gelding—Action This Day
2-year-old filly—Halfbridled
3-year-old colt or gelding—Funny Cide
3-year-old filly—Bird Town

Older male (4-year-olds & up)—Mineshaft
Older female (4-year-olds & up)—Azeri
Male turf horse—High Chaparral
Turf filly or mare—Islington
Sprinter—Aldebaran

Steeplechase horse—McDynamo
Trainer—Robert Frankel
Jockey—Jerry Bailey
Apprentice jockey—Eddie Castro
Breeder—Juddmonte Farms
Owner—Juddmonte Farms

Horse of the Year

1936	Granville	1953	Tom Fool	1969	Arts and Letters	1986	Lady's Secret
1937	War Admiral	1954	Native Dancer	1970	Fort Marcy (DRF)	1987	Ferdinand
1938	Seabiscuit	1955	Nashua		Personality (TRA)	1988	Alysheba
1939	Challedon	1956	Swaps	1971	Ack Ack	1989	Sunday Silence
1940	Challedon	1957	Bold Ruler (DRF)	1972	Secretariat	1990	Criminal Type
1941	Whirlaway		Dedicate (TRA)	1973	Secretariat	1991	Black Tie Affair
1942	Whirlaway	1958	Round Table	1974	Forego	1992	A.P. Indy
1943	Count Fleet	1959	Sword Dancer	1975	Forego	1993	Kotashaan
1944	Twilight Tear	1960	Kelso	1976	Forego	1994	Holy Bull
1945	Busher	1961	Kelso	1977	Seattle Slew	1995	Cigar
1946	Assault	1962	Kelso	1978	Affirmed	1996	Cigar
1947	Armed	1963	Kelso	1979	Affirmed	1997	Favorite Trick
1948	Citation	1964	Kelso	1980	Spectacular Bid	1998	Skip Away
1949	Capot	1965	Roman Brother (DRF)	1981	John Henry	1999	Charismatic
1950	Hill Prince		Moccasin (TRA)	1982	Conquistador Cielo	2000	Tiznow
1951	Counterpoint	1966	Buckpasser	1983	All Along	2001	Point Given
1952	One Count (DRF)	1967	Damascus	1984	John Henry	2002	Azeri
	Native Dancer (TRA)	1968	Dr. Fager	1985	Spend A Buck	2003	Mineshaft

HARNESS RACING
Harness Horse of the Year
(Chosen by the U.S. Trotting Assn. and the U.S. Harness Writers Assn.)

1947	Victory Song	1962	Su Mac Lad	1976	Keystone Ore	1990	Beach Towel
1948	Rodney	1963	Speedy Scot	1977	Green Speed	1991	Precious Bunny
1949	Good Time	1964	Bret Hanover	1978	Abercrombie	1992	Artsplace
1950	Proximity	1965	Bret Hanover	1979	Niatross	1993	Staying Together
1951	Pronto Don	1966	Bret Hanover	1980	Niatross	1994	Cam's Card Shark
1952	Good Time	1967	Nevele Pride	1981	Fan Hanover	1995	CR Kay Suzie
1953	Hi Lo's Forbes	1968	Nevele Pride	1982	Cam Fella	1996	Continentalvictory
1954	Stenographer	1969	Nevele Pride	1983	Cam Fella	1997	Malabar Man
1955	Scott Frost	1970	Fresh Yankee	1984	Fancy Crown	1998	Moni Maker
1956	Scott Frost	1971	Albatross	1985	Nihilator	1999	Moni Maker
1957	Torpid	1972	Albatross	1986	Forrest Skipper	2000	Gallo Blue Chip
1958	Emily's Pride	1973	Sir Dalrae	1987	Mack Lobell	2001	Bunny Lake
1959	Bye Bye Byrd	1974	Delmonica Hanover	1988	Mack Lobell	2002	Real Desire
1960	Adios Butler	1975	Savoir	1989	Matt's Scooter	2003	No Pan Intended
1961	Adios Butler						

The Hambletonian (3-year-old trotters)

Year	Winner	Driver	Year	Winner	Driver
1965	Egyptian Candor	Del Cameron	1985	Prakas	Bill O'Donnell
1966	Kerry Way	Frank Ervin	1986	Nuclear Kosmos	Ulf Thoresen
1967	Speedy Streak	Del Cameron	1987	Mack Lobell	John Campbell
1968	Nevele Pride	Stanley Dancer	1988	Armbro Goal	John Campbell
1969	Lindy's Pride	Howard Beissinger	1989	Park Avenue Joe	Ron Waples
1970	Timothy T.	John Simpson, Sr.	1990	Harmonious	John Campbell
1971	Speedy Crown	Howard Beissinger	1991	Giant Victory	Jack Moiseyev
1972	Super Bowl	Stanley Dancer	1992	Alf Palema	Mickey McNicholl
1973	Flirth	Ralph Baldwin	1993	American Winner	Ron Pierce
1974	Christopher T.	Bill Haughton	1994	Victory Dream	Michel Lachance
1975	Bonefish	Stanley Dancer	1995	Tagliabue	John Campbell
1976	Steve Lobell	Bill Haughton	1996	Continental-victory	Michel Lachance
1977	Green Speed	Bill Haughton	1997	Malabar Man	Malvern Burroughs
1978	Speedy Somolli	Howard Beissinger	1998	Muscles Yankee	John Campbell
1979	Legend Hanover	George Sholty	1999	Self Possessed	Mike Lachance
1980	Burgomeister	Bill Haughton	2000	Yankee Paco	Trevor Ritchie
1981	Shiaway St. Pat	Ray Remmen	2001	Scarlet Knight	Stefan Melander
1982	Speed Bowl	Tommy Haughton	2002	Chip Chip Hooray	Eric Ledford
1983	Duenna	Stanley Dancer	2003	Amigo Hall	Mike Lachance
1984	Historic Freight	Ben Webster	2004	Windsong's Legacy	Trond Smedshammer

NCAA WRESTLING CHAMPIONS

Year	Champion	Year	Champion	Year	Champion	Year	Champion
1964	Oklahoma State	1975	Iowa	1985	Iowa	1995	Iowa
1965	Iowa State	1976	Iowa	1986	Iowa	1996	Iowa
1966	Oklahoma State	1977	Iowa State	1987	Iowa State	1997	Iowa
1967	Michigan State	1978	Iowa	1988	Arizona State	1998	Iowa
1968	Oklahoma State	1979	Iowa	1989	Oklahoma State	1999	Iowa
1969	Iowa State	1980	Iowa	1990	Oklahoma State	2000	Iowa
1970	Iowa State	1981	Iowa	1991	Iowa	2001	Minnesota
1971	Oklahoma State	1982	Iowa	1992	Iowa	2002	Minnesota
1972	Iowa State	1983	Iowa	1993	Iowa	2003	Oklahoma State
1973	Iowa State	1984	Iowa	1994	Oklahoma State	2004	Oklahoma State
1974	Oklahoma						

CHESS
World Chess Champions

Sources: U.S. Chess Federation; International Chess Federation (FIDE)
Official world champions since the title was first used are as follows:

1866-1894	Wilhelm Steinitz, Austria	**1963-1969**	Tigran Petrosian, USSR
1894-1921	Emanuel Lasker, Germany	**1969-1972**	Boris Spassky, USSR
1921-1927	Jose R. Capablanca, Cuba	**1972-1975**	Bobby Fischer, U.S. (b)
1927-1935	Alexander A. Alekhine, France	**1975-1985**	Anatoly Karpov, USSR
1935-1937	Max Euwe, Netherlands	**1985-1993**	Garry Kasparov, USSR/Russia (c)
1937-1946	Alexander A. Alekhine, France (a)	**1993-1995**	Garry Kasparov, Russia (PCA) (d)
1948-1957	Mikhail Botvinnik, USSR	**1993-1999**	Anatoly Karpov, Russia (FIDE)
1957-1958	Vassily Smyslov, USSR	**1999**	Aleksandr Khalifman, Russia (FIDE)
1958-1959	Mikhail Botvinnik, USSR	**2000**	Viswanathan Anand, India (FIDE) (e)
1960-1961	Mikhail Tal, USSR	**2002-2004**	Ruslan Ponomariov, Ukraine (FIDE)
1961-1963	Mikhail Botvinnik, USSR	**2004**	Rustam Kasimdzhanov, Uzbekistan (FIDE)

(a) After Alekhine died in 1946, the title was vacant until 1948, when Botvinnik won the 1st championship match sanctioned by the International Chess Federation (FIDE). (b) Defaulted championship after refusal to accept FIDE rules for a championship match, Apr. 1975. (c) Kasparov broke with FIDE, Feb. 26, 1993. FIDE stripped Kasparov of his title Mar. 23. Kasparov defeated Nigel Short of Great Britain in a world championship match played Sept.-Oct. 1993 under the auspices of a new organization the two had founded, the Professional Chess Association (PCA). FIDE held a championship match between Anatoly Karpov (Russia) and Jan Timman (the Netherlands), which Karpov won in Nov. 1993. (d) The PCA folded in 1995. (e) In Nov. 2000, Vladimir Kramnik (Russia) defeated Garry Kasparov (Russia), widely recognized as the unofficial world champion, 8½-6½, at the Braingames World Chess Championships in London. **Recent/Upcoming matches:** Rustam Kasimdzhanov (Uzbekistan) beat Michael Adams (England) to win FIDE's World Championship on July 13, 2004. FIDE announced on Oct. 13, 2004, that Kasimdzhanov would play Garry Kasparov (Russia), the world's top-ranked player, in Jan. 2005. The winner of that match would play the winner of a world chess championship match between defending champion Vladimir Kramnik (Russia) and challenger Peter Leko (Hungary), which was held Sept. 25-Oct. 18, 2004. **Further information:** More information on chess and chess champions may be accessed on FIDE's Internet site, www.fide.org; or www.worldchesschampionship.com

BOWLING
Professional Bowlers Association
Hall of Fame

PERFORMANCE			MERITORIOUS SERVICE		
Bill Allen	Buzz Fazio	Mark Roth	Glenn Allison	Lou Frantz	Keijiro Nakano
Glenn Allison	Dave Ferraro	Carmen Salvino	Joe Antenora	Harry Golden	Chuck Pezzano
Earl Anthony	Jim Godman	Ernie Schlegel	John Archibald	John Guenther	Jack Reichert
Mike Aulby	Billy Hardwick	Harry Smith	Barry Asher	Ted Hoffman Jr.	Joe Richards
Joe Berardi	Marshall Hollman	Dave Soutar	Tom Baker	Joe Joseph	Jim St. John
Ray Bluth	Tommy Hudson	Jim Stefanich	Chuck Clemens	John Jowdy	Chris Schenkel
Parker Bohn III	Dave Husted	Brian Voss	Eddie Elias	Joe Kelley	Ernie Schlegel
Roy Buckley	Don Johnson	Wayne Webb	Frank Esposito	Larry Lichstein	Teata Semiz
Nelson Burton Jr.	Joe Joseph	Dick Weber	Dick Evans	Mike Limongello	Lorraine Stilzlein
Don Carter	Larry Laub	Pete Weber	Raymond Firestone	Andy Marzich	Bob Strampe
Pat Colwell	Amleto Monacelli	Billy Welu	E. A. "Bud" Fisher	Don McCune	Al Thompson
Steve Cook	David Ozio	Mark Williams	Jim Fitzgerald	Mike McGrath	Roger Zeller
Dave Davis	George Pappas	Walter Ray Williams	Skee Foremsky	Steve Nagy	
Gary Dickinson	Johnny Petraglia	Jr.			
Mike Durbin	Dick Ritger	Wayne Zahn			

Tournament of Champions

Year	Winner	Year	Winner	Year	Winner	Year	Winner
1965	Billy Hardwick	1975	Dave Davis	1985	Mark Williams	1994	Norm Duke
1966	Wayne Zahn	1976	Marshall Holman	1986	Marshall Holman	1996	Dave D'Entremont
1967	Jim Stefanich	1977	Mike Berlin	1987	Pete Weber	1997	John Gant
1968	Dave Davis	1978	Earl Anthony	1988	Mark Williams	1998	Bryan Goebel
1969	Jim Godman	1979	George Pappas	1989	Del Ballard, Jr.	1999	Jason Couch
1970	Don Johnson	1980	Wayne Webb	1990	Dave Ferraro	2000	Jason Couch
1971	Johnny Petraglia	1981	Steve Cook	1991	David Ozio	2001	Walter Ray Williams Jr.
1972	Mike Durbin	1982	Mike Durbin	1992	Marc McDowell	2002	Jason Couch
1973	Jim Godman	1983	Joe Berardi	1993	George Branham, 3rd	2003	Patrick Healey Jr.
1974	Earl Anthony	1984	Mike Durbin				

PBA Leading Money Winners

Total winnings are from PBA, ABC Masters, and BPAA All-Star tournaments only and do not include numerous other tournaments or earnings from special television shows and matches. In 2001, the PBA began an Oct.-Mar. season schedule. After 2000, year shown is year the season ended.

Year	Bowler	Amount	Year	Bowler	Amount	Year	Bowler	Amount
1962	Don Carter	$49,972	1976	Earl Anthony	$110,833	1990	Amleto Monacelli	$204,775
1963	Dick Weber	46,333	1977	Mark Roth	105,583	1991	David Ozio	225,585
1964	Bob Strampe	33,592	1978	Mark Roth	134,500	1992	Marc McDowell	174,215
1965	Dick Weber	47,674	1979	Mark Roth	124,517	1993	Walter Ray Williams Jr.	296,370
1966	Wayne Zahn	54,720	1980	Wayne Webb	116,700	1994	Norm Duke	273,753
1967	Dave Davis	54,165	1981	Earl Anthony	164,735	1995	Mike Aulby	219,792
1968	Jim Stefanich	67,377	1982	Earl Anthony	134,760	1996	Walter Ray Williams Jr.	241,330
1969	Billy Hardwick	64,160	1983	Earl Anthony	135,605	1997	Walter Ray Williams Jr.	240,544
1970	Mike McGrath	52,049	1984	Mark Roth	158,712	1998	Walter Ray Williams Jr.	238,225
1971	Johnny Petraglia	85,065	1985	Mike Aulby	201,200	1999	Parker Bohn III	240,912
1972	Don Johnson	56,648	1986	Walter Ray Williams Jr.	145,550	2000	Norm Duke	143,325
1973	Don McCune	69,000	1987	Pete Weber	175,491	2002	Parker Bohn III	245,200
1974	Earl Anthony	99,585	1988	Brian Voss	225,485	2003	Walter Ray Williams Jr.	419,700
1975	Earl Anthony	107,585	1989	Mike Aulby	298,237	2004	Mika Koivuniemi	238,590

Leading PBA Averages by Year

Year	Bowler	Average	Year	Bowler	Average	Year	Bowler	Average
1962	Don Carter	212.84	1976	Mark Roth	215.97	1990	Amleto Monacelli	218.15
1963	Billy Hardwick	210.34	1977	Mark Roth	218.17	1991	Norm Duke	218.20
1964	Ray Bluth	210.51	1978	Mark Roth	219.83	1992	Dave Ferraro	219.70
1965	Dick Weber	211.89	1979	Mark Roth	221.66	1993	Walter Ray Williams Jr.	222.98
1966	Wayne Zahn	208.66	1980	Earl Anthony	218.53	1994	Norm Duke	222.83
1967	Wayne Zahn	212.34	1981	Mark Roth	216.69	1995	Mike Aulby	225.49
1968	Jim Stefanich	211.89	1982	Marshall Holman	212.84	1996	Walter Ray Williams Jr.	225.37
1969	Bill Hardwick	212.95	1983	Earl Anthony	216.64	1997	Walter Ray Williams Jr.	222.00
1970	Nelson Burton Jr.	214.90	1984	Marshall Holman	213.91	1998	Walter Ray Williams Jr.	226.13
1971	Don Johnson	213.97	1985	Mark Baker	213.71	1999	Parker Bohn III	228.04
1972	Don Johnson	215.29	1986	John Gant	214.37	2000	Chris Barnes	220.93
1973	Earl Anthony	215.79	1987	Marshall Holman	216.80	2002	Parker Bohn III	221.54
1974	Earl Anthony	219.39	1988	Mark Roth	218.03	2003	Walter Ray Williams Jr.	224.94
1975	Earl Anthony	219.06	1989	Pete Weber	215.43	2004	Mika Koivuniemi	222.73

American Bowling Congress
ABC Masters Tournament Champions

Year	Winner	Year	Winner	Year	Winner
1980	Neil Burton, St. Louis, MO	1989	Mike Aulby, Indianapolis, IN	1997	Jason Queen, Decatur, IL
1981	Randy Lightfoot, St. Charles, MO	1990	Chris Warren, Dallas, TX	1998	Mike Aulby, Indianapolis, IN
1982	Joe Berardi, Brooklyn, NY	1991	Doug Kent, Canandaigua, NY	1999	Brian Boghosian, Middletown, CT
1983	Mike Lastowski, Havre de Grace, MD	1992	Ken Johnson, N. Richmond Hills, TX	2000	Mika Koivuniemi, Finland
1984	Earl Anthony, Dublin, CA	1993	Norm Duke, Oklahoma City, OK	2001	Parker Bohn III, Jackson, NJ
1985	Steve Wunderlich, St. Louis, MO	1994	Steve Fehr, Cincinnati, OH	2002	Brett Wolfe, Reno, NV
1986	Mark Fahy, Chicago, IL	1995	Mike Aulby, Indianapolis, IN	2003	Bryon Smith, Roseburg, OR
1987	Rick Steelsmith, Wichita, KS	1996	Ernie Schlegel, Vancouver, WA	2004	Walter Ray Williams Jr., FL
1988	Del Ballard, Jr., Richardson, TX				

Champions in 2004

Regular Singles: John Janawicz, Winter Haven, FL
Regular Doubles: Joseph Crocco Jr. & Mike P. Vasey, Racine, WI
Regular All Events: John Janawicz, Winter Haven, FL
Regular Team: S&B Pro Shop #1, Clinton Twp. MI
Classified Singles: Ryan Downs, Pflugerville, TX

Classified Doubles: Kent S. Smallcomb, Kearney, NE, & Larry Harrington, Whitehall, MT
Classified All Events: Lou Ortiz, Vallejo, CA
Classified Team: Connections #3, Vallejo, CA

Most Sanctioned 300 Games

Jeff Carter, Springfield, IL 79	Robert Faragon, Albany, NY 61	John Chacko Jr., Larksville, PA ... 56
Joe Jimenez, Saginaw, MI 72	Jeff Jensen, Wichita, KS 60	Jim Johnson Jr., Tampa, FL 54
Jerry Kessler, Dayton, OH 70	Bob Learn Jr., Erie, PA 60	Ralph Burley Jr., Dayton, OH 54
Chris Hayward, Toledo, OH 69	Randy Choat, Granite City, IL 59	Gordon Childers, Benton, AR 54
Jeff Ripic, Endicott, NY 66	John Delp III, West Lawn, PA 59	Mike Whalin, Cincinnati, OH 53
Frank Massengale Jr., Hixon, TN. .. 66	Jim Tomek Jr., Camp Hill, PA 58	John Wilcox Jr., Lewisburg, PA. ... 53
Dean Wolf, Reading, PA 65	Bob Buckery, McAdoo, PA 57	Randy Lightfoot, St. Charles, MO .. 53

Women's International Bowling Congress
Champions in 2004

Queens Tournament: Marianne DiRupo, Succasunna, NJ
Classic Singles: Sharon Smith, Bowling Green, KY
Classic Doubles: Lynda Barnes, Flower Mound, TX & Carolyn Dorin-Ballard, N. Richland Hills, TX
Classic All Events: Kim Adler, Merritt Island, FL

Classic Team: High Roller, Henderson, NV
Div. I Singles: Darlene Anderson, Elizabethtown, PA
Div. I Doubles: Deb Jacobs & Julia Halve, Waco, TX
Div. I All Events: Jenni Ferguson, Anderson, IN
Div. I Team: Chi-Town, Lyons, IL

Most Sanctioned 300 Games

Tish Johnson, Panorama City, CA . . . 35
Jodi Musto, Schenectady, NY 32
Aleta Sill, Dearborn, MI 27
Altramese Webb, Detroit, MI 27
Debbie McMullen, Denver, CO 26
Dede Davidson, Woodland Hills, CA   25
Leanne Barrette, Yukon, OK 25
Jeanne Naccarato, Tacoma, WA 23

Vicki Fischel, Wheat Ridge, CO 23
Anne-Marie Duggan, Edmond, OK . . .22
Marianne DiRupo, Succasunna, NJ . .22
Jodi Hughes, Greenville, SC 21
Cheryl Daniels, Detroit, MI. 21
Carolyn Dorin-Ballard, N. Richland
  Hills, TX. 21
Kim Terrell, San Francisco, CA 21

Shannon Duplantis, New Orleans,
  LA 20
Mandy Wilson, Dayton, OH. 19
Kim Adler, Palm City, FL. 18
Cindy Coburn-Carroll, Tonawanda,
  NY. 17
Tiffany Stanbrough, Oklahoma City,
  OK. 17

FIGURE SKATING
U.S. and World Individual Champions, 1952-2004

	U.S. Champions			World Champions	
MEN	WOMEN	YEAR	MEN		WOMEN
Dick Button	Tenley Albright	1952	Dick Button, U.S.		Jacqueline du Bief, France
Hayes Jenkins	Tenley Albright	1953	Hayes Jenkins, U.S.		Tenley Albright, U.S.
Hayes Jenkins	Tenley Albright	1954	Hayes Jenkins, U.S.		Gundi Busch, W. Germany
Hayes Jenkins	Tenley Albright	1955	Hayes Jenkins, U.S.		Tenley Albright, U.S.
Hayes Jenkins	Tenley Albright	1956	Hayes Jenkins, U.S.		Carol Heiss, U.S.
Dave Jenkins	Carol Heiss	1957	Dave Jenkins, U.S.		Carol Heiss, U.S.
Dave Jenkins	Carol Heiss	1958	Dave Jenkins, U.S.		Carol Heiss, U.S.
Dave Jenkins	Carol Heiss	1959	Dave Jenkins, U.S.		Carol Heiss, U.S.
Dave Jenkins	Carol Heiss	1960	Alain Giletti, France		Carol Heiss, U.S.
Bradley Lord	Laurence Owen	1961	none		none
Monty Hoyt	Barbara Roles Pursley	1962	Don Jackson, Canada		Sjoukje Dijkstra, Netherlands
Tommy Litz	Lorraine Hanlon	1963	Don McPherson, Canada		Sjoukje Dijkstra, Netherlands
Scott Allen	Peggy Fleming	1964	Manfred Schnelldorfer, W. Germany		Sjoukje Dijkstra, Netherlands
Gary Visconti	Peggy Fleming	1965	Alain Calmat, France		Petra Burka, Canada
Scott Allen	Peggy Fleming	1966	Emmerich Danzer, Austria		Peggy Fleming, U.S.
Gary Visconti	Peggy Fleming	1967	Emmerich Danzer, Austria		Peggy Fleming, U.S.
Tim Wood	Peggy Fleming	1968	Emmerich Danzer, Austria		Peggy Fleming, U.S.
Tim Wood	Janet Lynn	1969	Tim Wood, U.S.		Gabriele Seyfert, E. Germany
Tim Wood	Janet Lynn	1970	Tim Wood, U.S.		Gabriele Seyfert, E. Germany
John Misha Petkevich	Janet Lynn	1971	Ondrej Nepela, Czechoslovakia		Beatrix Schuba, Austria
Ken Shelley	Janet Lynn	1972	Ondrej Nepela, Czechoslovakia		Beatrix Schuba, Austria
Gordon McKellen, Jr.	Janet Lynn	1973	Ondrej Nepela, Czechoslovakia		Karen Magnussen, Canada
Gordon McKellen, Jr.	Dorothy Hamill	1974	Jan Hoffmann, E. Germany		Christine Errath, E. Germany
Gordon McKellen, Jr.	Dorothy Hamill	1975	Sergei Volkov, USSR		Dianne de Leeuw, Neth.-U.S.
Terry Kubicka	Dorothy Hamill	1976	John Curry, Gr. Britain		Dorothy Hamill, U.S.
Charles Tickner	Linda Fratianne	1977	Vladimir Kovalev, USSR		Linda Fratianne, U.S.
Charles Tickner	Linda Fratianne	1978	Charles Tickner, U.S.		Anett Poetzsch, E. Germany
Charles Tickner	Linda Fratianne	1979	Vladimir Kovalev, USSR		Linda Fratianne, U.S.
Charles Tickner	Linda Fratianne	1980	Jan Hoffmann, E. Germany		Anett Poetzsch, E. Germany
Scott Hamilton	Elaine Zayak	1981	Scott Hamilton, U.S.		Denise Biellmann, Switzerland
Scott Hamilton	Rosalynn Sumners	1982	Scott Hamilton, U.S.		Elaine Zayak, U.S.
Scott Hamilton	Rosalynn Sumners	1983	Scott Hamilton, U.S.		Rosalynn Sumners, U.S.
Scott Hamilton	Rosalynn Sumners	1984	Scott Hamilton, U.S.		Katarina Witt, E. Germany
Brian Boitano	Tiffany Chin	1985	Aleksandr Fadeev, USSR		Katarina Witt, E. Germany
Brian Boitano	Debi Thomas	1986	Brian Boitano, U.S.		Debi Thomas, U.S.
Brian Boitano	Jill Trenary	1987	Brian Orser, Canada		Katarina Witt, E. Germany
Brian Boitano	Debi Thomas	1988	Brian Boitano, U.S.		Katarina Witt, E. Germany
Christopher Bowman	Jill Trenary	1989	Kurt Browning, Canada		Midori Ito, Japan
Todd Eldredge	Jill Trenary	1990	Kurt Browning, Canada		Jill Trenary, U.S.
Todd Eldredge	Tonya Harding	1991	Kurt Browning, Canada		Kristi Yamaguchi, U.S.
Christopher Bowman	Kristi Yamaguchi	1992	Viktor Petrenko, Ukraine		Kristi Yamaguchi, U.S.
Scott Davis	Nancy Kerrigan	1993	Kurt Browning, Canada		Oksana Baiul, Ukraine
Scott Davis	vacant[1]	1994	Elvis Stojko, Canada		Yuka Sato, Japan
Todd Eldredge	Nicole Bobek	1995	Elvis Stojko, Canada		Chen Lu, China
Rudy Galindo	Michelle Kwan	1996	Todd Eldredge, U.S.		Michelle Kwan, U.S.
Todd Eldredge	Tara Lipinski	1997	Elvis Stojko, Canada		Tara Lipinski, U.S.
Todd Eldredge	Michelle Kwan	1998	Alexei Yagudin, Russia		Michelle Kwan, U.S.
Michael Weiss	Michelle Kwan	1999	Alexei Yagudin, Russia		Maria Butyrskaya, Russia
Michael Weiss	Michelle Kwan	2000	Alexei Yagudin, Russia		Michelle Kwan, U.S.
Timothy Goebel	Michelle Kwan	2001	Yevgeny Plushchenko, Russia		Michelle Kwan, U.S.
Todd Eldredge	Michelle Kwan	2002	Alexei Yagudin, Russia		Irina Slutskaya, Russia
Michael Weiss	Michelle Kwan	2003	Yevgeny Plushchenko, Russia		Michelle Kwan, U.S.
Johnny Weir	Michelle Kwan	2004	Yevgeny Plushchenko, Russia		Shizuka Arakawa, Japan

(1) Tonya Harding was stripped of title.

SKIING
World Cup Alpine Champions, 1967-2004

Men

	Men			
1967	Jean Claude Killy, France	1979	Peter Luescher, Switzerland	1992 Paul Accola, Switzerland
1968	Jean Claude Killy, France	1980	Andreas Wenzel, Liechtenstein	1993 Marc Girardelli, Luxembourg
1969	Karl Schranz, Austria	1981	Phil Mahre, U.S.	1994 Kjetil Andre Aamodt, Norway
1970	Karl Schranz, Austria	1982	Phil Mahre, U.S.	1995 Alberto Tomba, Italy
1971	Gustavo Thoeni, Italy	1983	Phil Mahre, U.S.	1996 Lasse Kjus, Norway
1972	Gustavo Thoeni, Italy	1984	Pirmin Zurbriggen, Switzerland	1997 Luc Alphand, France
1973	Gustavo Thoeni, Italy	1985	Marc Girardelli, Luxembourg	1998 Hermann Maier, Austria
1974	Piero Gros, Italy	1986	Marc Girardelli, Luxembourg	1999 Lasse Kjus, Norway
1975	Gustavo Thoeni, Italy	1987	Pirmin Zurbriggen, Switzerland	2000 Hermann Maier, Austria
1976	Ingemar Stenmark, Sweden	1988	Pirmin Zurbriggen, Switzerland	2001 Hermann Maier, Austria
1977	Ingemar Stenmark, Sweden	1989	Marc Girardelli, Luxembourg	2002 Stephan Eberharter, Austria
1978	Ingemar Stenmark, Sweden	1990	Pirmin Zurbriggen, Switzerland	2003 Stephan Eberharter, Austria
		1991	Marc Girardelli, Luxembourg	2004 Hermann Maier, Austria

Women

1967	Nancy Greene, Canada
1968	Nancy Greene, Canada
1969	Gertrud Gabl, Austria
1970	Michele Jacot, France
1971	Annemarie Proell, Austria
1972	Annemarie Proell, Austria
1973	Annemarie Proell, Austria
1974	Annemarie Proell, Austria
1975	Annemarie Proell, Austria
1976	Rose Mittermaier, W. Germany
1977	Lise-Marie Morerod, Switzerland
1978	Hanni Wenzel, Liechtenstein
1979	Annemarie Proell Moser, Austria
1980	Hanni Wenzel, Liechtenstein
1981	Marie-Theres Nadig, Switzerland
1982	Erika Hess, Switzerland
1983	Tamara McKinney, U.S.
1984	Erika Hess, Switzerland
1985	Michela Figini, Switzerland
1986	Maria Walliser, Switzerland
1987	Maria Walliser, Switzerland
1988	Michela Figini, Switzerland
1989	Vreni Schneider, Switzerland
1990	Petra Kronberger, Austria
1991	Petra Kronberger, Austria
1992	Petra Kronberger, Austria
1993	Anita Wachter, Austria
1994	Vreni Schneider, Switzerland
1995	Vreni Schneider, Switzerland
1996	Katja Seizinger, Germany
1997	Pernilla Wiberg, Sweden
1998	Katja Seizinger, Germany
1999	Alexandra Meissnitzer, Austria
2000	Renate Goetschl, Austria
2001	Janica Kostelic, Croatia
2002	Michaela Dorfmeister, Austria
2003	Janica Kostelic, Croatia
2004	Anja Paerson, Sweden

LACROSSE

Lacrosse Champions in 2004

Major League Lacrosse—Boston, MA, Aug. 22: Philadelphia Barrage 13, Boston Cannons 11.

U.S. Club Lacrosse Association Championship—Malvern, PA, June 13: Single Source Solutions 13, New York Althletic Club 11.

National Lacrosse League Championship—Calgary, AB, May 7: Calgary Roughnecks 14, Buffalo Bandits 11.

NCAA Men's Division I Championship—Baltimore, MD, May 31: Syracuse 14, Navy 13.

NCAA Women's Division I Championship—Princeton, NJ, May 23: Virginia 10, Princeton 4.

2004 Men's NCAA Division I All-America Team

Attack: Ryan Boyle, Princeton; Mike Powell, Syracuse; Jed Prossner, North Carolina; Joe Walters, Maryland.
Midfield: Walid Hajj, Georgetown; Kyle Harrison, Johns Hopkins; Sean Lindsay, Syracuse; Brodie Merrill, Georgetown.

Defense: Chris Passavia, Maryland; Ronnie Staines, North Carolina; Lee Zink, Maryland.
Goal: Matt Russell, Navy.

2004 Women's NCAA Division I All-America Team

Attack: Michelle Allen, Vanderbilt; Amy Appelt, Virginia; Lindsay Biles, Princeton; Meredith Simon, Notre Dame; Lana Smith, Dartmouth; Leigh-Ann Zimmer, Syracuse.
Midfield: Kelly Coppedge, Maryland; Gail Decker, James Madison; Heidi Pearce, Johns Hopkins; Elizabeth Pillion, Princeton; Theresa Sherry, Princeton; Miles Whitman, Yale.

Defense: Michi Ellers, Georgetown; Nikki Lieb, Virginia; Katie Norbury, Princeton.
Goal: Elizabeth Tortorelli, Penn State.

NCAA Division I Lacrosse Champions 1982-2004

Year[1]	Men	Women	Year[1]	Men	Women	Year[1]	Men	Women
1982	North Carolina	Massachusetts	1990	vacated	Harvard	1998	Princeton	Maryland
1983	Syracuse	Delaware	1991	North Carolina	Virginia	1999	Virginia	Maryland
1984	Johns Hopkins	Temple	1992	Princeton	Maryland	2000	Syracuse	Maryland
1985	Johns Hopkins	New Hampshire	1993	Syracuse	Virginia	2001	Princeton	Maryland
1986	North Carolina	Maryland	1994	Princeton	Princeton	2002	Syracuse	Princeton
1987	Johns Hopkins	Penn St.	1995	Syracuse	Maryland	2003	Virginia	Princeton
1988	Syracuse	Temple	1996	Princeton	Maryland	2004	Syracuse	Virginia
1989	Syracuse	Penn St.	1997	Princeton	Maryland			

(1) NCAA Championships began in 1971 for men, in 1982 for women.

SWIMMING

World Swimming Records

(Long course, as of Oct. 12, 2004)

Men's Records

Freestyle

Distance	Time	Holder	Country	Where made	Date
50 meters	0:21.64	Alexander Popov	Russia	Moscow, Russia	June 16, 2000
100 meters	0:47.84	Pieter van den Hoogenband	Netherlands	Sydney, Australia	Sept. 19, 2000
200 meters	1:44.06	Ian Thorpe	Australia	Fukuoka, Japan	July 25, 2001
400 meters	3:40.08	Ian Thorpe	Australia	Manchester, England	July 30, 2002
800 meters	7:39.16	Ian Thorpe	Australia	Fukuoka, Japan	July 24, 2001
1,500 meters	14:34.56	Grant Hackett	Australia	Fukuoka, Japan	July 29, 2001

Breaststroke

50 meters	0:27.18	Oleg Lisogor	Ukraine	Berlin, Germany	Aug. 2, 2002
100 meters	0:59.30	Brendan Hansen	U.S.	Long Beach, CA	July 8, 2004
200 meters	2:09.04	Brendan Hansen	U.S.	Long Beach, CA	July 11, 2004

Butterfly

50 meters	0:23.30	Ian Crocker	U.S.	Austin, TX	Feb. 29, 2004
100 meters	0:50.76	Ian Crocker	U.S.	Long Beach, CA	July 13, 2004
200 meters	1:53.93	Michael Phelps	U.S.	Barcelona, Spain	July 22, 2003

Backstroke

50 meters	0:24.80	Thomas Rupprath	Germany	Barcelona, Spain	July 27, 2003
100 meters	0:53.45	Aaron Peirsol (relay lead-off)	U.S.	Athens, Greece	Aug. 21, 2004
200 meters	1:54.74	Aaron Peirsol	U.S.	Long Beach, CA	July 12, 2004

Individual Medley

200 meters	1:55.94	Michael Phelps	U.S.	College Park, MD	Aug. 9, 2003
400 meters	4.08.26	Michael Phelps	U.S.	Athens, Greece	Aug. 14, 2004

Medley Relay

400 m. (4×100)	3:30.68	(Peirsol, Hansen, Crocker, Phelps)	U.S.	Athens, Greece	Aug. 21, 2004

Freestyle Relays

400 m. (4×100)	3:13.17	(Schoeman, Ferns, Townsend, Neethling)	South Africa	Athens, Greece	Aug. 15, 2004
800 m. (4×200)	7:04.66	(Hackett, Klim, Kirby, Thorpe)	Australia	Fukuoka, Japan	July 27, 2001

Women's Records

Freestyle

Distance	Time	Holder	Country	Where made	Date
50 meters	0:24.13	Inge de Bruijn	Netherlands	Sydney, Australia	Sept. 22, 2000
100 meters	0:53.52	Jodie Henry	Australia	Athens, Greece	Aug. 18, 2004
200 meters	1:56.64	Franziska Van Almsick	Germany	Berlin, Germany	Aug. 3, 2002
400 meters	4:03.85	Janet Evans	U.S.	Seoul, South Korea	Sept. 22, 1988
800 meters	8:16.22	Janet Evans	U.S.	Tokyo, Japan	Aug. 20, 1989
1,500 meters	15:52.10	Janet Evans	U.S.	Orlando, FL	Mar. 26, 1988

Breaststroke

Distance	Time	Holder	Country	Where made	Date
50 meters	0:30.57	Zoe Baker	U.K.	Manchester, England	July 30, 2002
100 meters	1:06.37	Jones Leisel	Australia	Barcelona, Spain	July 21, 2003
200 meters	2:22.44	Amanda Beard	U.S.	Long Beach, CA	July 12, 2004

Butterfly

Distance	Time	Holder	Country	Where made	Date
50 meters	0:25.57	Anna-Karin Kammerling	Sweden	Berlin, Germany	July 30, 2000
100 meters	0:56.61	Inge de Bruijn	Netherlands	Sydney, Australia	Sept. 17, 2000
200 meters	2:05.78	Otylia Jedrzejczak	Poland	Berlin, Germany	Aug. 4, 2002

Backstroke

Distance	Time	Holder	Country	Where made	Date
50 meters	0:28.25	Sandra Voelker	Germany	Berlin, Germany	June 17, 2000
100 meters	0:59.58	Natalie Coughlin	U.S.	Ft. Lauderdale, FL	Aug. 13, 2002
200 meters	2:06.62	Kristina Egerszegi	Hungary	Athens, Greece	Aug. 25, 1991

Individual Medley

Distance	Time	Holder	Country	Where made	Date
200 meters	2:09.72	Yanyan Wu	China	Shanghai, China	Oct. 17, 1997
400 meters	4:33.59	Yana Klochkova	Ukraine	Sydney, Australia	Sept. 16, 2000

Freestyle Relays

Distance	Time	Holder	Country	Where made	Date
400 m. (4×100)	3:35.94	(Mills, Lenton, Thomas, Henry)	Australia	Athens, Greece	Aug. 14, 2004
800 m. (4×200)	7:53.42	(Coughlin, Piper, Vollmer, Sandeno)	U.S.	Athens, Greece	Aug. 18, 2004

Medley Relay

Distance	Time	Holder	Country	Where made	Date
400 m. (4×100)	3:57.32	(Rooney, Jones, Thomas, Henry)	Australia	Athens, Greece	Aug. 21, 2004

YACHTING
The America's Cup

In the 31st America's Cup, the Swiss boat *Alinghi* swept 2-time defending champion *Team New Zealand,* 5-0, in the best-of-nine series, held in the Hauraki Gulf off the coast of Auckland, New Zealand in Feb. and Mar. 2003. *Alinghi* was skippered by New Zealander Russell Coutts, who had helped guide New Zealand to victory in 1995 and 2000. For the 1st time in its 152-year history, the Cup resides on the European continent, in landlocked Switzerland.

The *Alinghi* team announced on Nov. 26, 2003, that the next America's Cup would be held in Valencia, on Spain's Mediterranean coast, in 2007. However, Coutts would not be involved in *Alinghi*'s title defense—he was fired on July 26, 2004, after reportedly clashing with syndicate owner Ernesto Bertarelli.

Competition for the America's Cup grew out of the first contest to establish a world yachting championship, one of the carnival features of the London Exposition of 1851. The race covered a 60-mile course around the Isle of Wight; the prize was a cup worth about $500, donated by the Royal Yacht Squadron of England, known as the "America's Cup" because it was first won by the U.S. yacht *America.*

Winners of the America's Cup

1851 America
1870 Magic defeated Cambria, England, (1-0)
1871 Columbia (first three races) and Sappho (last two races) defeated Livonia, England, (4-1)
1876 Madeline defeated Countess of Dufferin, Canada, (2-0)
1881 Mischief defeated Atalanta, Canada, (2-0)
1885 Puritan defeated Genesta, England, (2-0)
1886 Mayflower defeated Galatea, England, (2-0)
1887 Volunteer defeated Thistle, Scotland, (2-0)
1893 Vigilant defeated Valkyrie II, England, (3-0)
1895 Defender defeated Valkyrie III, England, (3-0)
1899 Columbia defeated Shamrock, England, (3-0)
1901 Columbia defeated Shamrock II, England, (3-0)
1903 Reliance defeated Shamrock III, England, (3-0)
1920 Resolute defeated Shamrock IV, England, (3-2)
1930 Enterprise defeated Shamrock V, England, (4-0)
1934 Rainbow defeated Endeavour, England, (4-2)
1937 Ranger defeated Endeavour II, England, (4-0)

1958 Columbia defeated Sceptre, England, (4-0)
1962 Weatherly defeated Gretel, Australia, (4-1)
1964 Constellation defeated Sovereign, England, (4-0)
1967 Intrepid defeated Dame Pattie, Australia, (4-0)
1970 Intrepid defeated Gretel II, Australia, (4-1)
1974 Courageous defeated Southern Cross, Australia, (4-0)
1977 Courageous defeated Australia, Australia, (4-0)
1980 Freedom defeated Australia, Australia, (4-1)
1983 Australia II, Australia, defeated Liberty, (4-3)
1987 Stars & Stripes defeated Kookaburra III, Australia, (4-0)
1988 Stars & Stripes defeated New Zealand, New Zealand, (2-0)
1992 America[3] defeated Il Moro di Venezia, Italy, (4-1)
1995 Black Magic 1, New Zealand, defeated Young America, (5-0)
2000 New Zealand, NZ, defeated Luna Rossa, Italy, (5-0)
2003 Alinghi, Switzerland, defeated Team New Zealand, NZ, (5-0)

POWER BOATING
American Power Boat Assn. Gold Cup Champions, 1978-2004

Year	Boat	Driver	Year	Boat	Driver
1978	Atlas Van Lines	Bill Muncey	1991	Winston Eagle	Mark Tate
1979	Atlas Van Lines	Bill Muncey	1992	Miss Budweiser	Chip Hanauer
1980	Miss Budweiser	Dean Chenoweth	1993	Miss Budweiser	Chip Hanauer
1981	Miss Budweiser	Dean Chenoweth	1994	Smokin' Joe's	Mark Tate
1982	Atlas Van Lines	Chip Hanauer	1995	Miss Budweiser	Chip Hanauer
1983	Atlas Van Lines	Chip Hanauer	1996	Pico American Dream	Dave Villwock
1984	Atlas Van Lines	Chip Hanauer	1997	Miss Budweiser	Dave Villwock
1985	Miller American	Chip Hanauer	1998	Miss Budweiser	Dave Villwock
1986	Miller American	Chip Hanauer	1999	Miss PICO	Chip Hanauer
1987	Miller American	Chip Hanauer	2000	Miss Budweiser	Dave Villwock
1988	Circus Circus	Chip Hanauer	2001	Miss Tubby's Subs	Mike Hanson
1989	Miss Budweiser	Tom D'Eath	2002	Miss Budweiser	Dave Villwock
1990	Miss Budweiser	Tom D'Eath	2003	Miss Fox Hills	Mitch Evans
			2004	Miss Detroit Yacht Club	Nate Brown

RODEO
Pro Rodeo Cowboy All-Around Champions, 1977-2003

Year	Winner	Money won	Year	Winner	Money won
1977	Tom Ferguson, Miami, OK	$76,730	1991	Ty Murray, Stephenville, TX	$244,230
1978	Tom Ferguson, Miami, OK	103,734	1992	Ty Murray, Stephenville, TX	225,992
1979	Tom Ferguson, Miami, OK	96,272	1993	Ty Murray, Stephenville, TX	297,896
1980	Paul Tierney, Rapid City, SD	105,568	1994	Ty Murray, Stephenville, TX	246,170
1981	Jimmie Cooper, Monument, NM	105,862	1995	Joe Beaver, Huntsville, TX	141,753
1982	Chris Lybbert, Coyote, CA	123,709	1996	Joe Beaver, Huntsville, TX	166,103
1983	Roy Cooper, Durant, OK	153,391	1997	Dan Mortensen, Manhattan, MT	184,559
1984	Dee Pickett, Caldwell, ID	122,618	1998	Ty Murray, Stephenville, TX	264,673
1985	Lewis Feild, Elk Ridge, UT	130,347	1999	Fred Whitfield, Hockley, TX	217,819
1986	Lewis Feild, Elk Ridge, UT	166,042	2000	Joe Beaver, Huntsville, TX	225,396
1987	Lewis Feild, Elk Ridge, UT	144,335	2001	Cody Ohl, Stephensville, TX	296,419
1988	Dave Appleton, Arlington, TX	121,546	2002	Trevor Brazile, Anson, TX	273,997
1989	Ty Murray, Odessa, TX	134,806	2003	Trevor Brazile, Anson, TX	294,839
1990	Ty Murray, Stephenville, TX	213,772			

DOGS
Westminster Kennel Club, 1989-2004

Year	Best-in-show	Breed	Owner(s)
1989	Ch. Royal Tudor's Wild As The Wind	Doberman	Sue & Art Kemp, Richard & Carolyn Vida, Beth Wilhite
1990	Ch. Wendessa Crown Prince	Pekingese	Ed Jenner
1991	Ch. Whisperwind on a Carousel	Poodle	Joan & Frederick Hartsock
1992	Ch. Registry's Lonesome Dove	Fox Terrier	Marion & Sam Lawrence
1993	Ch. Salilyn's Condor	English Springer Spaniel	Donna & Roger Herzig
1994	Ch. Chidley Willum	Norwich Terrier	Ruth Cooper & Patricia Lussier
1995	Ch. Gaelforce Post Script	Scottish Terrier	Dr. Vandra Huber & Dr. Joe Kinnarney
1996	Ch. Clussexx Country Sunrise	Clumber Spaniel	Judith & Richard Zaleski
1997	Ch. Parsifal Di Casa Netzer	Standard Schnauzer	Rita Holloway & Gabrio Del Torre
1998	Ch. Fairewood Frolic	Norwich Terrier	Sandina Kennels
1999	Ch. Loteki Supernatural Being	Papillon	John Oulton
2000	Ch. Salilyn 'N Erin's Shameless	English Springer Spaniel	Carl Blain, Fran Sunseri, & Julia Gasow
2001	Ch. Special Times Just Right	Bichons Frises	Cecilia Ruggles, E. McDonald, & F. Werneck
2002	Ch. Surrey Spice Girl	Poodle (Miniature)	Ron L. & Barbara Scott
2003	Ch. Torum's Scarf Michael	Kerry Blue Terrier	Marilu Hanson
2004	Ch. Darbydale's All Rise Pouchcove	Newfoundland	Peggy Helming & Carol A. Bernard Bergmann

2004 Iditarod Trail Sled Dog Race

Mitch Seavey won the 32nd annual Iditarod Trail Sled Dog Race from Anchorage to Nome, Alaska, on Mar. 16, 2004. Seavey, a 43-year-old native of Alaska, finished the 1,100-mile course in 9 days, 12 hours, 20 minutes and 22 seconds. A record 87 mushers started the race on Mar. 6.

MARATHONS
Boston Marathon, 2004

Catherine Nderéba of Kenya won the women's race in the 108th Boston Marathon for the 3rd time in her career Apr. 19, finishing in two hours, 24 minutes, and 27 seconds. Elfenesh Alemu of Ethiopia was 2nd, followed by Olivera Jevtic of Serbia and Montenegro. Kenyans swept the top 3 places in the men's race; Timothy Cherigat won with a time of 2:10:37, Robert Cheboror was 2nd and Martin Lel was 3rd. For the 1st time in the Boston Marathon, the elite women runners started separately from the rest of the field, with 34 top women starting 29 minutes before the rest of the participants.

Boston Marathon Winners, 1972-2004
All times in hour:minute:second format. *Course records.

Men's Winner	Time	Year	Women's Winner	Time
Olavi Suomalainen, Finland	2:15:39	1972	Nina Kuscsik, U.S.	3:10:26
Jon Anderson, U.S.	2:16:03	1973	Jacqueline Hansen, U.S.	3:05:59
Neil Cusack, Ir.	2:13:39	1974	Michiko Gorman, U.S.	2:47:11
Bill Rodgers, U.S.	2:09:55	1975	Liane Winter, West Ger.	2:42:24
Jack Fultz, U.S.	2:20:19	1976	Kim Merritt, U.S.	2:47:10
Jerome Drayton, Can.	2:14:46	1977	Michiko Gorman, U.S.	2:48:33
Bill Rodgers, U.S.	2:10:13	1978	Gayle S. Barron, U.S.	2:44:52
Bill Rodgers, U.S.	2:09:27	1979	Joan Benoit, U.S.	2:35:15
Bill Rodgers, U.S.	2:12:11	1980	Jacqueline Gareau, Can.	2:34:28
Toshihiko Seko, Japan	2:09:26	1981	Allison Roe, N. Zealand	2:26:46
Alberto Salazar, U.S.	2:08:52	1982	Charlotte Teske, West Ger.	2:29:33
Greg Myer, U.S.	2:09:00	1983	Joan Benoit, U.S.	2:22:43
Geoff Smith, G.B.	2:10:34	1984	Lorraine Moller, N. Zealand	2:29:28
Geoff Smith, G.B.	2:14:05	1985	Lisa Larsen Weidenbach, U.S.	2:34:06
Robert de Castella, Australia	2:07:51	1986	Ingrid Kristiansen, Nor.	2:24:55
Toshihiko Seko, Japan	2:11:50	1987	Rosa Mota, Portugal	2:25:21
Ibrahim Hussein, Ken.	2:08:43	1988	Rosa Mota, Portugal	2:24:30
Abebe Mekonnen, Eth.	2:09:06	1989	Ingrid Kristiansen, Nor.	2:24:33
Gelindo Bordin, Italy	2:08:19	1990	Rosa Mota, Portugal	2:25:24
Ibrahim Hussein, Kenya	2:11:06	1991	Wanda Panfil, Poland	2:24:18
Ibrahim Hussein, Kenya	2:08:14	1992	Olga Markova, CIS	2:23:43
Cosmas Ndeti, Kenya	2:09:33	1993	Olga Markova, CIS	2:25:27
Cosmas Ndeti, Kenya	2:07:15*	1994	Uta Pippig, Germany	2:21:45*
Cosmas Ndeti, Kenya	2:09:22	1995	Uta Pippig, Germany	2:25:11
Moses Tanui, Kenya	2:09:15	1996	Uta Pippig, Germany	2:27:12
Lameck Aguta, Kenya	2:10:34	1997	Fatuma Roba, Ethiopia	2:26:23
Moses Tanui, Kenya	2:07:34	1998	Fatuma Roba, Ethiopia	2:23:21

Men's Winner	Time	Year	Women's Winner	Time
Joseh Chebet, Kenya	2:09:52	1999	Fatuma Roba, Ethiopia	2:23:25
Elijah Lagat, Kenya	2:09:47	2000	Catherine Ndereba, Kenya	2:26:11
Lee Bong-ju, S. Korea	2:09:43	2001	Catherine Ndereba, Kenya	2:23:53
Rodgers Rop, Kenya	2:09:02	2002	Margaret Okayo, Kenya	2:20:43
Robert K. Cheruiyot, Kenya	2:10:11	2003	Svetlana Zakharova, Russia	2:25:20
Timothy Cherigat, Kenya	2:10:37	2004	Catherine Ndereba, Kenya	2:24:27

Boston Marathon Winners, 1897-1971

The 1st Boston Marathon was held in 1897. Women were officially accepted into the race in 1972.

Year	Winner	Time	Year	Winner	Time
1897	John J. McDermott, New York	2:55:10	1935	John A. Kelley, Massachusetts	2:32:07
1898	Ronald J. MacDonald, Canada	2:42:00	1936	Ellison M. Brown, Rhode Island	2:33:40
1899	Lawrence Brignolia, Massachusetts	2:54:38	1937	Walter Young, Canada	2:33:20
1900	John Caffery, Canada	2:39:44	1938	Leslie S. Pawson, Rhode Island	2:35:34
1901	John Caffery, Canada	2:29:23	1939	Ellison M. Brown, Rhode Island	2:28:51
1902	Sammy Mellor, New York	2:43:12	1940	Gerard Cote, Canada	2:28:28
1903	John Lorden , Massachusetts	2:41:29	1941	Leslie S. Pawson, Rhode Island	2:30:38
1904	Michael Spring, New York	2:38:04	1942	Joe Smith, Massachusetts	2:26:51
1905	Frederick Lorz, New York	2:38:25	1943	Gerard Cote, Canada	2:28:25
1906	Tim Ford, Massachusetts	2:45:45	1944	Gerard Cote, Canada	2:31:50
1907	Thomas Longboat, Canada	2:24:24	1945	John A. Kelley, Massachusetts	2:30:40
1908	Thomas Morrissey, New York	2:25:43	1946	Stylianos Kyriakides, Greece	2:29:27
1909	Henri Renaud, New Hampshire	2:53:36	1947	Yun Bok Suh, Korea	2:25:39
1910	Fred Cameron, Canada	2:28:52	1948	Gerard Cote, Canada	2:31:02
1911	Clarence DeMar, Massachusetts	2:21:39	1949	Karl Leandersson, Sweden	2:31:50
1912	Michael Ryan, New York	2:21:18	1950	Kee Yong Ham, Korea	2:32:39
1913	Fritz Carlson, Minnesota	2:25:14	1951	Shigeki Tanaka, Japan	2:27:45
1914	James Duffy, Canada	2:25:14	1952	Doroteo Flores, Guatemala	2:31:53
1915	Edouard Fabre, Canada	2:31:41	1953	Keizo Yamada, Japan	2:18:51
1916	Arthur Roth, Massachusetts	2:27:16	1954	Veikko Karvonen, Finland	2:20:39
1917	Bill Kennedy, New York	2:28:37	1955	Hideo Hamamura, Japan	2:18:22
1918	Military Relay, Camp Devens	2:29:53	1956	Antti Viskari, Finland	2:14:14
1919	Carl Linder, Massachusetts	2:29:13	1957	John J. Kelley, Connecticut	2:20:05
1920	Peter Trivoulides, New York	2:29:31	1958	Franjo Mihalic, Yugoslavia	2:25:54
1921	Frank Zuna, New York	2:18:57	1959	Eino Oksanen, Finland	2:22:42
1922	Clarence DeMar, Massachusetts	2:18:10	1960	Paavo Kotila, Finland	2:20:54
1923	Clarence DeMar, Massachusetts	2:23:47	1961	Eino Oksanen, Finland	2:23:39
1924	Clarence DeMar, Massachusetts	2:29:40	1962	Eino Oksanen, Finland	2:23:48
1925	Charles Mellor, Illinois	2:33:00	1963	Aurele Vandendriessche, Belgium	2:18:58
1926	John C. Miles, Canada	2:25:40	1964	Aurele Vandendriessche, Belgium	2:19:59
1927	Clarence DeMar, Massachusetts	2:40:22	1965	Morio Shigematsu, Japan	2:16:33
1928	Clarence DeMar, Massachusetts	2:37:07	1966	Kenji Kemihara, Japan	2:17:11
1929	John C. Miles, Canada	2:33:08	1967	David McKenzie, New Zealand	2:15:45
1930	Clarence DeMar, Massachusetts	2:34:48	1968	Amby Burfoot, Connecticut	2:22:17
1931	James P. Henigan, Massachusetts	2:46:45	1969	Yoshiaki Unetani, Japan	2:13:49
1932	Paul DeBruyn, Germany	2:33:36	1970	Ron Hill, Great Britain	2:10:30
1933	Leslie S. Pawson, Rhode Island	2:31:01	1971	Alvaro Mejia, Colombia	2:18:45
1934	Dave Komonen, Canada	2:32:53			

New York City Marathon

All time in hour:minute:second format; *Course record.

Men's Winner	Time	Year	Women's Winner	Time
Gary Muhrcke, U.S.	2:31:38	1970	no finisher	—
Norman Higgins, U.S.	2:22:54	1971	Beth Bonner, U.S.	2:55:22
Sheldon Karlin, U.S.	2:27:52	1972	Nina Kuscsik, U.S.	3:08:41
Tom Fleming, U.S.	2:19:25	1973	Nina Kuscsik, U.S.	2:57:07
Norbert Sander, U.S.	2:26:30	1974	Katherine Switzer, U.S.	3:07:29
Tom Fleming, U.S.	2:19:27	1975	Kim Merritt, U.S.	2:46:14
Bill Rodgers, U.S.	2:10:10	1976	Miki Gorman, U.S.	2:39:11
Bill Rodgers, U.S.	2:11:28	1977	Miki Gorman, U.S.	2:43:10
Bill Rodgers, U.S.	2:12:12	1978	Grete Waitz, Norway	2:32:30
Bill Rodgers, U.S.	2:11:42	1979	Grete Waitz, Norway	2:27:33
Alberto Salazar, U.S.	2:09:41	1980	Grete Waitz, Norway	2:25:42
Alberto Salazar, U.S.	2:08:13	1981	Allison Roe, N. Zealand	2:25:29
Alberto Salazar, U.S.	2:09:29	1982	Grete Waitz, Norway	2:27:14
Rod Dixon, N.Z.	2:08:59	1983	Grete Waitz, Norway	2:27:00
Orlando Pizzolato, Italy	2:14:53	1984	Grete Waitz, Norway	2:29:30
Orlando Pizzolato, Italy	2:11:34	1985	Grete Waitz, Norway	2:28:34
Gianni Poli, Italy	2:11:06	1986	Grete Waitz, Norway	2:28:06
Ibrahim Hussein, Kenya	2:11:01	1987	Priscilla Welch, G.B.	2:30:17
Steve Jones, G.B.	2:08:20	1988	Grete Waitz, Norway	2:28:07
Juma Ikangaa, Tanz.	2:08:01	1989	Ingrid Kristiansen, Norway	2:25:30
Douglas Wakiihuri, Ken.	2:12:39	1990	Wanda Panfil, Poland	2:30:45
Salvador Garcia, Mexico	2:09:28	1991	Liz McColgan, G.B.	2:27:32
Willie Mtolo, S. Afr.	2:09:29	1992	Lisa Ondieki, Australia	2:24:40*
Andres Espinosa, Mex.	2:10:04	1993	Uta Pippig, Germany	2:26:24
German Silva, Mexico	2:11:21	1994	Tegla Loroupe, Kenya	2:27:37
German Silva, Mexico	2:11:00	1995	Tegla Loroupe, Kenya	2:28:06
Giacomo Leone, Italy	2:09:54	1996	Anuta Catuna, Romania	2:28:43
John Kagwe, Kenya	2:08:12	1997	F. Rochat-Moser, Switzerland	2:28:43
John Kagwe, Kenya	2:08:45	1998	Franca Fiacconi, Italy	2:25:17
Joseph Chebet, Kenya	2:09:14	1999	Adriana Fernandez, Mex.	2:25:06
Abdelkhader El Mouaziz, Morocco	2:10:09	2000	Ludmila Petrova, Russia	2:25:45
Tesfaye Jifar, Ethiopia	2:07:43*	2001	Margaret Okayo, Kenya	2:24:21
Rodgers Rop, Kenya	2:08:07	2002	Joyce Chepchumba, Kenya	2:25:56
Martin Lel, Kenya	2:10:30	2003	Margaret Okayo, Kenya	2:22:31*

Other Marathon Results in 2004

Los Angeles Marathon—Mar. 7. Men: David Kirui, Kenya, 2:13:40. Women: Tatyana Pozdnyakora, Ukraine, 2:30:16.

Paris Marathon—Apr. 4. Men: Ambesa Tolosa, 2:08:56. Women: Salina Kosgei, Kenya, 2:24:32.

Rotterdam Marathon—Apr. 4. Men: Felix Limo, Kenya, 2:06:14. Women: Zhor El Kamch, Morocco, 2:26:10.

London Marathon—Apr. 18. Men: Evans Rutto, Kenya, 2:06:18. Women: Margaret Okayo, Kenya, 2:22:35.

Berlin Marathon—Sept. 26. Men: Felix Limo, Kenya, 2:06:44. Women: Yoko Shibui, Japan, 2:19:41.

Chicago Marathon—Oct. 10. Men: Evans Rutto, Kenya, 2:06:16. Women: Constantina Tomescu-Dita, Romania, 2:23:44.

Ironman Triathlon World Championships

The Ironman Triathlon World Championships—a 2.4-mile ocean swim, 112-mile bike ride and 26.2-mile run—are held annually at Kailua-Kona, Hawaii. On Oct. 18, 2003, the men's race was won by Canada's Peter Reid in 8:22:35. Canada's Lori Bowden won the women's race in 9:11:55. All times in hour:minute:second format. *Course records.

Men's Winner	Time	Year	Women's Winner	Time
Gordon Haller, U.S.	11:46:58	1978	no finisher	—
Tom Warren, U.S.	11:15:56	1979	Lyn Lemaire, U.S.	12:55:00
Dave Scott, U.S.	9:24:33	1980	Robin Beck, U.S.	11:21:24
John Howard, U.S.	9:38:29	1981	Linda Sweeney, U.S.	12:00:32
Dave Scott, U.S.	9:08:23	1982	Julie Leach, U.S.	10:54:08
Dave Scott, U.S.	9:05:57	1983	Sylviane Puntous, Canada	10:43:36
Dave Scott, U.S.	8:54:20	1984	Sylvanie Puntous, Canada	10:25:13
Scott Tinley, U.S.	8:50:54	1985	Joanne Ernst, U.S.	10:25:22
Dave Scott, U.S.	8:28:37	1986	Paula Newby-Fraser, Zimbabwe	9:49:14
Dave Scott, U.S.	8:34:13	1987	Erin Baker, New Zealand	9:35:25
Scott Molina, U.S.	8:31:00	1988	Paula Newby-Fraser, Zimbabwe	9:01:01
Mark Allen, U.S.	8:09:15	1989	Paula Newby-Fraser, Zimbabwe	9:00:56
Mark Allen, U.S.	8:28:17	1990	Erin Baker, New Zealand	9:13:42
Mark Allen, U.S.	8:18:32	1991	Paula Newby-Fraser, Zimbabwe	9:07:52
Mark Allen, U.S.	8:09:08	1992	Paula Newby-Fraser, Zimbabwe	8:55:28*
Mark Allen, U.S.	8:07:45	1993	Paula Newby-Fraser, Zimbabwe	8:58:23
Greg Welch, Australia	8:20:27	1994	Paula Newby-Fraser, Zimbabwe	9:20:14
Mark Allen, U.S.	8:20:34	1995	Karen Smyers, U.S.	9:16:46
Luc Van Lierde, Belgium	8:04:08*	1996	Paula Newby-Fraser, Zimbabwe	9:06:49
Thomas Hellriegel, Germany	8:33:01	1997	Heather Fuhr, Canada	9:31:43
Peter Reid, Canada	8:24:20	1998	Natascha Badmann, Switz.	9:24:16
Luc Van Lierde, Belgium	8:17:17	1999	Lori Bowden, U.S.	9:13:02
Peter Reid, Canada	8:21:01	2000	Natascha Badmann, Switz.	9:26:16
Timothy Deboom, U.S.	8:31:18	2001	Natascha Badmann, Switz.	9:28:37
Timothy Deboom, U.S.	8:29:56	2002	Natascha Badmann, Switz.	9:07:54
Peter Reid, Canada	8:22:35	2003	Lori Bowden, Canada	9:11:55

CYCLING

2004 Tour de France

On July 25, 2004, America's Lance Armstrong won the 101st Tour de France, cycling's premier event, for a record 6th straight year. Armstrong, riding for the U.S. Postal Service team, prior to the 2004 Tour was tied with 4 other riders—France's Jacques Anquetil and Bernard Hinault, Belgium's Eddy Merckx and Spain's Miguel Indurain—for the most victories in the race's history, with 5. Indurain was the only other rider to win 5 times in a row. Armstrong finished the 2,107-mile race in 83 hours, 36 minutes and two seconds. Germany's Andreas Kloeden was 2nd, 6:19 behind Armstrong, and Italy's Ivan Basso was 3rd, 6:40 behind the winner.

Tour de France Winners, 1980-2004

Year	Winner	Year	Winner	Year	Winner
1980	Zoop Zoetemelk, The Netherlands	1989	Greg LeMond, U.S.	1997	Jan Ullrich, Germany
1981	Bernard Hinault, France	1990	Greg LeMond, U.S.	1998	Marco Pantani, Italy
1982	Bernard Hinault, France	1991	Miguel Indurain, Spain	1999	Lance Armstrong, U.S.
1983	Laurent Fignon, France	1992	Miguel Indurain, Spain	2000	Lance Armstrong, U.S.
1984	Laurent Fignon, France	1993	Miguel Indurain, Spain	2001	Lance Armstrong, U.S.
1985	Bernard Hinault, France	1994	Miguel Indurain, Spain	2002	Lance Armstrong, U.S.
1986	Greg LeMond, U.S.	1995	Miguel Indurain, Spain	2003	Lance Armstrong, U.S.
1987	Stephen Roche, Ireland	1996	Bjarne Riis, Denmark	2004	Lance Armstrong, U.S.
1988	Pedro Delgado, Spain				

SULLIVAN AWARD

James E. Sullivan Memorial Trophy Winners

The James E. Sullivan Memorial Trophy, named after the former president of the Amateur Athletic Union (AAU) and inaugurated in 1930, is awarded annually by the AAU to the athlete who "by his or her performance, example and influence as an amateur, has done the most during the year to advance the cause of sportsmanship."

Year	Winner	Sport	Year	Winner	Sport	Year	Winner	Sport
1930	Bobby Jones	Golf	1942	Cornelius Warmerdam	Track	1953	Dr. Sammy Lee	Diving
1931	Barney Berlinger	Track	1943	Gilbert Dodds	Track	1954	Mal Whitfield	Track
1932	Jim Bausch	Track	1944	Ann Curtis	Swimming	1955	Harrison Dillard	Track
1933	Glenn Cunningham	Track	1945	Doc Blanchard	Football	1956	Patricia McCormick	Diving
1934	Bill Bonthron	Track	1946	Arnold Tucker	Football	1957	Bobby Joe Morrow	Track
1935	Lawson Little	Golf	1947	John Kelly, Jr.	Rowing	1958	Glenn Davis	Track
1936	Glenn Morris	Track	1948	Robert Mathias	Track	1959	Parry O'Brien	Track
1937	Don Budge	Tennis	1949	Dick Button	Skating	1960	Rafer Johnson	Track
1938	Don Lash	Track	1950	Fred Wilt	Track	1961	Wilma Rudolph Ward	Track
1939	Joe Burk	Rowing	1951	Rev. Robert Richards	Track	1962	James Beatty	Track
1940	Greg Rice	Track	1952	Horace Ashenfelter	Track	1963	John Pennel	Track
1941	Leslie MacMitchell	Track				1964	Don Schollander	Swimming

Year	Winner	Sport
1965	Bill Bradley	Basketball
1966	Jim Ryun	Track
1967	Randy Matson	Track
1968	Debbie Meyer	Swimming
1969	Bill Toomey	Track
1970	John Kinsella	Swimming
1971	Mark Spitz	Swimming
1972	Frank Shorter	Track
1973	Bill Walton	Basketball
1974	Rick Wohlhutter	Track
1975	Tim Shaw	Swimming
1976	Bruce Jenner	Track
1977	John Naber	Swimming
1978	Tracy Caulkins	Swimming
1979	Kurt Thomas	Gymnastics

Year	Winner	Sport
1980	Eric Heiden	Speed Skating
1981	Carl Lewis	Track
1982	Mary Decker	Track
1983	Edwin Moses	Track
1984	Greg Louganis	Diving
1985	Joan Benoit Samuelson	Marathon
1986	Jackie Joyner-Kersee	Track
1987	Jim Abbott	Baseball
1988	Florence Griffith Joyner	Track
1989	Janet Evans	Swimming
1990	John Smith	Wrestling
1991	Mike Powell	Track

Year	Winner	Sport
1992	Bonnie Blair	Speed Skating
1993	Charlie Ward	Football, Basketball
1994	Dan Jansen	Speed Skating
1995	Bruce Baumgartner	Wrestling
1996	Michael Johnson	Track
1997	Peyton Manning	Football
1998	Chamique Holdsclaw	Basketball
1999	Coco Miller and Kelly Miller	Basketball
2000	Rulon Gardner	Wrestling
2001	Michelle Kwan	Figure Skating
2002	Sarah Hughes	Figure Skating
2003	Michael Phelps	Swimming

FISHING

Selected IGFA Saltwater & Freshwater All-Tackle World Records

Source: International Game Fish Association; records confirmed to Sept. 1, 2004

Saltwater Fish Records

Species	Weight	Where caught	Date	Angler
Albacore	88 lbs. 2 oz.	Canary Islands, Spain	Nov. 19, 1977	Siegfried Dickemann
Amberjack, greater	155 lbs. 12 oz.	Bermuda	Aug. 16, 1992	Larry Trott
Barracuda, great	85 lbs.	Christmas Island, Kiribati	Apr. 11, 1992	John W. Helfrich
Barracuda, Mexican	21 lbs.	Phantom Isle, Costa Rica	Mar. 27, 1987	E. Greg Kent
Barracuda, Pacific	26 lbs. 8 oz.	Playa Matapalo, Costa Rica	Jan. 3, 1999	Doug Hettinger
Bass, barred sand	13 lbs. 3 oz.	Huntington Beach, CA	Aug. 29, 1988	Robert Halal
Bass, black sea	10 lbs. 4 oz.	Virginia Beach, VA	Jan. 1, 2000	Allan P. Paschall
Bass, giant sea	563 lbs. 8 oz.	Anacapa Island, CA	Aug. 20, 1968	James D. McAdam Jr.
Bass, striped	78 lbs. 8 oz.	Atlantic City, NJ	Sept. 21, 1982	Albert R. McReynolds
Bluefish	31 lbs. 12 oz.	Hatteras Inlet, NC	Jan. 30, 1972	James M. Hussey
Bonefish	19 lbs.	Zululand, South Africa	May 26, 1962	Brian W. Batchelor
Bonito, Atlantic	18 lbs. 4 oz.	Faial Island, Azores	July 8, 1953	D. Gama Higgs
Bonito, Pacific	21 lbs. 3 oz.	Malibu, CA	July 30, 1978	Gino M. Picciolo
Cabezon	23 lbs.	Juan De Fuca Strait, WA	Aug. 4, 1990	Wesley S. Hunter
Cobia	135 lbs. 9 oz.	Shark Bay, Australia	July 9, 1985	Peter W. Goulding
Cod, Atlantic	98 lbs. 12 oz.	Isle of Shoals, NH	June 8, 1969	Alphonse J. Bielevich
Cod, Pacific	35 lbs.	Unalaska Bay, AK	June 16, 1999	Jim Johnson
Conger	133 lbs. 4 oz.	Berry Head, S. Devon, England	June 5, 1995	Vic Evans
Dolphin	88 lbs.	Exuma, Bahamas	May 5, 1998	Richard D. Evans
Drum, black	113 lbs. 1 oz.	Lewes, DE	Sept. 15, 1975	Gerald M. Townsend
Drum, red	94 lbs. 2 oz.	Avon, NC	Nov. 7, 1984	David G. Deuel
Eel, American	9 lbs. 4 oz.	Cape May, NJ	Nov. 9, 1995	Jeff Pennick
Eel, marbled	36 lbs. 1 oz.	Hazelmere Dam, South Africa	June 10, 1984	Ferdie Van Nooten
Flounder, southern	20 lbs. 9 oz.	Nassau Sound, FL	Dec. 23, 1983	Larenza W. Mungin
Flounder, summer	22 lbs. 7 oz.	Montauk, NY	Sept. 15, 1975	Charles Nappi
Grouper, Goliath	680 lbs.	Fernandina Beach, FL	May 20, 1961	Lynn Joyner
Grouper, Warsaw	436 lbs. 12 oz.	Gulf of Mexico, Destin, FL	Dec. 22, 1985	Steve Haeusler
Halibut, Atlantic	355 lbs. 6 oz.	Valevag, Norway	Oct. 20, 1997	Odd Arve Gunderstad
Halibut, California	58 lbs. 9 oz.	Santa Rosa Island, CA	June 26, 1999	Roger W. Borrell
Halibut, Pacific	459 lbs.	Dutch Harbor, AK	June 11, 1996	Jack Tragis
Jack, crevalle	58 lbs. 6 oz.	Barra do Kwanza, Angola	Dec. 10, 2000	Nuno Abohbot Po da Silva
Jack, horse-eye	29 lbs. 8 oz.	Ascencion Island, South Atlantic	May 28, 1993	Mike Hanson
Jack, Pacific crevalle	39 lbs.	Playa Zancudo, Costa Rica	Mar. 3, 1997	Ingrid Callaghan
Kawakawa	29 lbs.	Clarion Island, Mexico	Dec. 17, 1986	Ronald Nakamura
Lingcod	76 lbs. 9 oz.	Gulf of Alaska, AK	Aug. 11, 2001	Antwan D. Tinsley
Mackerel, cero	17 lbs. 2 oz.	Islamorada, FL	Apr. 5, 1986	G. Michael Mills
Mackerel, king	93 lbs.	San Juan, PR	Apr. 18, 1999	Steve Perez Graulau
Mackerel, Spanish	13 lbs.	Ocracoke Inlet, NC	Nov. 4, 1987	Robert Cranton
Marlin, Atlantic blue	1,402 lbs. 2 oz.	Vitoria, Brazil	Feb. 29, 1992	Paulo Roberto A. Amorim
Marlin, black	1,560 lbs.	Cabo Blanco, Peru	Aug. 4, 1953	Alfred C. Glassell Jr.
Marlin, Pacific blue	1,376 lbs.	Kaaiwi Pt., Kona, HI	May 31, 1982	Jay W. deBeaubien
Marlin, striped	494 lbs.	Tutukaka, New Zealand	Jan. 16, 1986	Bill Boniface
Marlin, white	181 lbs. 14 oz.	Vitoria, Brazil	Dec. 8, 1979	Evandro Luiz Coser
Permit	60 lbs. 0 oz.	Ilha do Mel, Paranagua, Brazil	Dec. 14, 2002	Renato P. Fiedler
Pollack, European	27 lbs. 6 oz.	Salcombe, Devon, England	Jan. 16, 1986	Robert Samuel Milkins
Pollock	50 lbs.	Salstraumen, Norway	Nov. 30, 1995	Thor-Magnus Lekang
Pompano, African	50 lbs. 8 oz.	Daytona Beach, FL	Apr. 21, 1990	Tom Sargent
Roosterfish	114 lbs.	La Paz, Baja Cal., Mexico	June 1, 1960	Abe Sackheim
Runner, blue	11 lbs. 2 oz.	Dauphin Isl., AL	June 28, 1997	Stacey Michelle Moiren
Runner, rainbow	37 lbs. 9 oz.	Clarion Island, Mexico	Nov. 21, 1991	Tom Pfleger
Sailfish, Atlantic	141 lbs. 1 oz.	Luanda, Angola	Feb. 19, 1994	Alfredo de Sousa Neves
Sailfish, Pacific	221 lbs.	Santa Cruz Island, Ecuador	Feb. 12, 1947	C. W. Stewart
Seabass, white	83 lbs. 12 oz.	San Felipe, Mexico	Mar. 31, 1953	L. C. Baumgardner
Seatrout, spotted	17 lbs. 7 oz.	Ft. Pierce, FL	May 11, 1995	Craig F. Carson
Shark, bigeye thresher	802 lbs.	Tutukaka, New Zealand	Feb. 8, 1981	Dianne North
Shark, bignose	369 lbs. 14 oz.	Markham R., Papua New Guinea	Oct. 23, 1993	Lester J. Rohrlach
Shark, blue	528 lbs.	Montauk Point, NY	Aug. 9, 2001	Joe Seidel
Shark, great hammerhead	991 lbs.	Sarasota, FL	May 30, 1982	Allen Ogle
Shark, Greenland	1,708 lbs. 9 oz.	Trondheimsfjord, Norway	Oct. 18, 1987	Terje Nordtvedt
Shark, porbeagle	507 lbs.	Caithness, Scotland	Mar. 9, 1993	Christopher Bennett
Shark, shortfin mako	1,221 lbs.	Chatham, MA	July 21, 2001	Luke Sweeney
Shark, tiger	1,780 lbs.	Cherry Grove, SC	June 14, 1964	Walter Maxwell

Species	Weight	Where caught	Date	Angler
Shark, white	2,664 lbs.	Ceduna, S.A., Australia	Apr. 21, 1959	Alfred Dean
Sheepshead	21 lbs. 4 oz.	New Orleans, LA	Apr. 16, 1982	Wayne Desselle
Skipjack, black	26 lbs.	Thetis Bank, Baja Cal., Mexico	Oct. 23, 1991	Clifford Hamaishi
Snapper, cubera	121 lbs. 8 oz.	Cameron, LA	July 5, 1982	Mike Hebert
Snapper, red	50 lbs. 4 oz.	Gulf of Mexico, LA	June 23, 1996	Capt. Doc Kennedy
Snook, common	53 lbs. 10 oz.	Parismina Ranch, Costa Rica	Oct. 18, 1978	Gilbert Ponzi
Spearfish, Mediterranean	90 lbs. 13 oz.	Madeira Island, Portugal	June 2, 1980	Joseph Larkin
Swordfish	1,182 lbs.	Iquique, Chile	May 7, 1953	L. B. Marron
Tarpon	286 lbs. 9 oz.	Rubane, Guinea-Bissau	Mar. 20, 2003	Max Domecq
Tautog	25 lbs.	Ocean City, NJ	Jan. 20, 1998	Anthony R. Monica
Trevally, bigeye	31 lbs. 8 oz.	Poivre Isl., Seychelles	Apr. 23, 1997	Les Sampson
Trevally, giant	145 lbs. 8 oz.	Makena, Maui, HI	Mar. 28, 1991	Russell Mori
Tuna, Atlantic bigeye	392 lbs. 6 oz.	Canary Islands, Spain	July 15, 1996	Dieter Vogel
Tuna, blackfin	45 lbs. 8 oz.	Key West, FL	May 4, 1996	Sam J. Burnett
Tuna, bluefin	1,496 lbs.	Aulds Cove, Nova Scotia	Oct. 26, 1979	Ken Fraser
Tuna, longtail	79 lbs. 2 oz.	Montague Isl., N.S.W., Australia	Apr. 12, 1982	Tim Simpson
Tuna, Pacific bigeye	435 lbs.	Cabo Blanco, Peru	Apr. 17, 1957	Dr. Russel V. A. Lee
Tuna, skipjack	45 lbs. 4 oz.	Flathead Bank, Baja Cal., Mexico	Nov. 16, 1996	Brian Evans
Tuna, southern bluefin	348 lbs. 5 oz.	Whakatane, New Zealand	Jan. 16, 1981	Rex Wood
Tuna, yellowfin	388 lbs. 12 oz.	San Benedicto Island, Mexico	Apr. 1, 1977	Curt Wiesenhutter
Tunny, little	35 lbs. 2 oz.	Cap de Garde, Algeria	Dec. 14, 1988	Jean Yves Chatard
Wahoo	158 lbs. 8 oz.	Loreto, Baja Cal., Mexico	June 10, 1996	Keith Winter
Weakfish	19 lbs. 2 oz.	Jones Beach Inlet, NY	Oct. 11, 1984	Dennis Roger Rooney
		Delaware Bay, DE	May 20, 1989	William E. Thomas
Yellowtail, California	88 lbs. 3 oz.	Alijos Rocks, Baja Cal., Mexico	June 21, 2000	Ronald Tadashi Fujii
Yellowtail, southern	114 lbs. 10 oz.	Tauranga, New Zealand	Feb. 5, 1984	Mike Godfrey
		White Island, New Zealand	Jan. 9, 1987	David Lugton

Freshwater Fish Records

Species	Weight	Where caught	Date	Angler
Barramundi	83 lbs. 7 oz.	Lake Tinaroo, N. Queensland, Australia	Sept. 23, 1999	David Powell
Bass, largemouth	22 lbs. 4 oz.	Montgomery Lake, GA	June 2, 1932	George W. Perry
Bass, rock	3 lbs.	York River, Ontario	Aug. 1, 1974	Peter Gulgin
	3 lbs.	Lake Erie, PA	June 18, 1998	Herbert G. Ratner, Jr.
Bass, shoal	8 lbs. 12 oz.	Apalachicola River, FL	Jan. 28, 1995	Carl W. Davis
Bass, smallmouth	10 lbs. 14 oz.	Dale Hollow Lake, TN	Apr. 24, 1969	John T. Gorman
Bass, white	6 lbs. 13 oz.	Lake Orange, VA	July 31, 1989	Ronald L. Sprouse
Bass, whiterock	27 lbs. 5 oz.	Greers Ferry Lake, AR	April 24, 1997	Jerald C. Shaum
Bass, yellow	2 lbs. 9 oz.	Waverly, TN	Feb. 27, 1998	John T. Chappell
Bluegill	4 lbs. 12 oz.	Ketona Lake, AL	Apr. 9, 1950	T. S. Hudson
Bowfin	21 lbs. 8 oz.	Florence, SC	Jan. 29, 1980	Robert L. Harmon
Bream	13 lbs. 3 oz.	Hagbyan Creek, Sweden	May 11, 1984	Luis Kilian Rasmussen
Buffalo, bigmouth	70 lbs. 5 oz.	Bastrop, LA	Apr. 21, 1980	Delbert Sisk
Buffalo, black	63 lbs. 6 oz.	Mississippi River, IA	Aug. 14, 1999	Jim Winters
Buffalo, smallmouth	82 lbs. 3 oz.	Athens Lake, AR	June 6, 1993	Randy Collins
Bullhead, brown	6 lbs. 5 oz.	Lake Mahopac, NY	Sept. 8, 2002	Ray Lawrence
Bullhead, yellow	4 lbs. 4 oz.	Mormon Lake, AZ	May 11, 1984	Emily Williams
Burbot	18 lbs. 11 oz.	Angenmanalren, Sweden	Oct. 22, 1996	Margit Agren
Carp, common	75 lbs. 11 oz.	Lac de St. Cassien, France	May 21, 1987	Leo van der Gugten
Catfish, blue	116 lbs. 12 oz.	Mississippi R., AR	Aug 3, 2001	Charles Ashley Jr.
Catfish, channel	58 lbs.	Santee-Cooper Res., SC	July 7, 1964	W. B. Whaley
Catfish, flathead	123 lbs. 9 oz.	Independence, KS	May 14, 1998	Ken Paulie
Catfish, white	21 lbs. 8 oz.	Gorton Pond, CT	Apr. 22, 2001	Thomas Urguhart
Char, Arctic	32 lbs. 9 oz.	Tree River, Canada	July 30, 1981	Jeffrey L. Ward
Crappie, white	5 lbs. 3 oz.	Enid Dam, MS	July 31, 1957	Fred L. Bright
Dolly Varden	20 lbs. 14oz.	Wulik R., AK	July 7, 2001	Raz Reid
Dorado	51 lbs. 5 oz.	Toledo (Corrientes), Argentina	Sept. 27, 1984	Armando Giudice
Drum, freshwater	54 lbs. 8 oz.	Nickajack Lake, TN	Apr. 20, 1972	Benny E. Hull
Gar, alligator	279 lbs.	Rio Grande, TX	Dec. 2, 1951	Bill Valverde
Gar, Florida	10 lbs.	Everglades, FL	Jan. 28, 2002	Herbert G. Ratner Jr.
Gar, longnose	50 lbs. 5 oz.	Trinity River, TX	July 30, 1954	Townsend Miller
Gar, shortnose	5 lbs. 12 oz.	Ren Lake, IL	July 16, 1995	Donna K. Willmert
Gar, spotted	9 lbs. 12 oz.	Lake Mexia, TX	Apr. 7, 1994	Rick Rivard
Grayling, Arctic	5 lbs. 15 oz.	Katseyedie River, N.W.T.	Aug. 16, 1967	Jeanne P. Branson
Inconnu	53 lbs.	Pah River, AK	Aug. 20, 1986	Lawrence E. Hudnall
Kokanee	9 lbs. 6 oz.	Okanagan Lake, Vernon, B.C.	June 18, 1988	Norm Kuhn
Muskellunge	67 lbs. 8 oz.	Lake Court Oreilles, WI	July 24, 1949	Cal Johnson
Muskellunge, tiger	51 lbs. 3 oz.	Lac Vieux-Desert, MI	July 16, 1919	John Knobla
Perch, Nile	230 lbs.	Lake Nasser, Egypt	Dec. 20, 2000	William Toth
Perch, white	3 lbs. 1 oz.	Forest Hill Park, NJ	May 6, 1989	Edward Tango
Perch, yellow	4 lbs. 3 oz.	Bordentown, NJ	May, 1865	Dr. C. C. Abbot
Pickerel, chain	9 lbs. 6 oz.	Homerville, GA	Feb. 17, 1961	Baxley McQuaig Jr.
Pike, northern	55 lbs. 1 oz.	Lake of Grefeern, W. Germany	Oct. 16, 1986	Lothar Louis
Redhorse, greater	9 lbs. 3 oz.	Salmon River, Pulaski, NY	May 11, 1985	Jason Wilson
Redhorse, silver	11 lbs. 7 oz.	Plum Creek, WI	May 29, 1985	Neal Long
Salmon, Atlantic	79 lbs. 2 oz.	Tana River, Norway	1928	Henrik Henriksen
Salmon, chinook	97 lbs. 4 oz.	Kenai River, AK	May 17, 1985	Les Anderson
Salmon, chum	35 lbs.	Edye Pass, BC	July 11, 1995	Todd A. Johansson
Salmon, coho	33 lbs. 4 oz.	Salmon River, Pulaski, NY	Sept. 27, 1989	Jerry Lifton
Salmon, pink	14 lbs. 13 oz.	Monroe, WA	Sept. 30, 2001	Alexander Minerich
Salmon, sockeye	15 lbs. 3 oz.	Kenai River, AK	Aug. 9, 1987	Stan Roach
Sauger	8 lbs. 12 oz.	Lake Sakakawea, ND	Oct. 6, 1971	Mike Fischer
Shad, American	11 lbs. 4 oz.	Connecticut River, MA	May 19, 1986	Bob Thibodo
Sturgeon, beluga	224 lbs. 13 oz.	Guryev, Kazakhstan	May 3, 1993	Merete Lehne
Sturgeon, white	468 lbs.	Benicia, CA	July 9, 1983	Joey Pallotta 3d
Sunfish, green	2 lbs. 2 oz.	Stockton Lake, MO	June 18, 1971	Paul M. Dilley
Sunfish, redbreast	1 lb. 12 oz.	Suwannee River, FL	May 29, 1984	Alvin Buchanan

Species	Weight	Where caught	Date	Angler
Sunfish, redear	5 lbs. 7oz.	Diverson Canal, GA	Nov. 6, 1998	Amos M. Gay
Tigerfish, giant	97 lbs.	Zaire River, Kinshasa, Zaire	July 9, 1988	Raymond Houtmans
Tilapia, Nile	13 lbs. 3 oz.	Antelope Isl., Karibe, Zimbabwe	July 5, 2002	Sorel van Rooyen
Trout, Apache	5 lb. 3 oz.	Apache Res., AZ	May 29, 1991	John Baldwin
Trout, brook	14 lbs. 8 oz.	Nipigon River, Ontario	July, 1916	Dr. W. J. Cook
Trout, bull	32 lbs.	Lake Pend Oreille, ID	Oct. 27, 1949	N. L. Higgins
Trout, cutthroat	41 lbs.	Pyramid Lake, NV	Dec., 1925	John Skimmerhorn
Trout, golden	11 lbs.	Cooks Lake, WY	Aug. 5, 1948	Charles S. Reed
Trout, lake	72 lbs.	Great Bear Lake, N.W.T.	Aug. 9, 1995	Lloyd E. Bull
Trout, rainbow	42 lbs. 2 oz.	Bell Island, AK	June 22, 1970	David Robert White
Trout, tiger	20 lbs. 13 oz.	Lake Michigan, WI	Aug. 12, 1978	Pete M. Friedland
Walleye	25 lbs.	Old Hickory Lake, TN	Aug. 2, 1960	Mabry Harper
Warmouth	2 lbs. 7 oz.	Yellow River, Holt, FL	Oct. 19, 1985	Tony D. Dempsey
Whitefish, lake	14 lbs. 6 oz.	Meaford, Ontario	May 21, 1984	Dennis M. Laycock
Whitefish, mountain	5 lbs. 8 oz.	Elbow River, Calgary, AB	Aug. 1, 1995	Randy G. Woo
Whitefish, round	6 lbs.	Putahow R., Manitoba, Can.	June 14, 1984	Allan J. Ristori
Zander	25 lbs. 2 oz.	Trosa, Sweden	June 12, 1986	Harry Lee Tennison

DIRECTORY OF SPORTS ORGANIZATIONS

Major League Baseball

Commissioner's Office, 245 Park Ave., 31st Fl., New York, NY 10167
Website: www.mlb.com

American League

Anaheim Angels
2000 Gene Autry Way
Anaheim, CA 92806

Baltimore Orioles
333 W. Camden St.
Baltimore, MD 21201

Boston Red Sox
4 Yawkey Way
Boston, MA 02215

Chicago White Sox
333 W. 35th St.
Chicago, IL 60616

Cleveland Indians
2401 Ontario St.
Cleveland, OH 44115

Detroit Tigers
2100 Woodward Ave.
Detroit, MI 48201

Kansas City Royals
1 Royal Way
Kansas City, MO 64141

Minnesota Twins
34 Kirby Puckett Place
Minneapolis, MN 55415

New York Yankees
161st St. and River Ave.
Bronx, NY 10451

Oakland Athletics
7000 Coliseum Way
Oakland, CA 94621

Seattle Mariners
83 King St.
Seattle, WA 98104

Tampa Bay Devil Rays
One Tropicana Dr.
St. Petersburg, FL 33705

Texas Rangers
1000 Ballpark Way
Arlington, TX 76011

Toronto Blue Jays
1 Blue Jays Way, Ste 3200
Toronto, ON M5V 1J1

National League

Arizona Diamondbacks
401 E. Jefferson St.
Phoenix, AZ 85001

Atlanta Braves
755 Hank Aaron Drive
Atlanta, GA 30302

Chicago Cubs
1060 W. Addison St.
Chicago, IL 60613

Cincinnati Reds
100 Cinergy Field
Cincinnati, OH 45202

Colorado Rockies
2001 Blake St.
Denver, CO 80205

Florida Marlins
2269 Dan Marino Blvd.
Miami, FL 33056

Houston Astros
501 Crawford St.
Houston, TX 77002

Los Angeles Dodgers
1000 Elysian Park Ave.
Los Angeles, CA 90012

Milwaukee Brewers
One Brewers Way
Milwaukee, WI 53214

Montreal Expos
4549 Ave. Pierre de
Coubertin
Montreal, QC H1V 3N7

New York Mets
123-01 Roosevelt Ave.
Flushing, NY 11368

Philadelphia Phillies
3501 S. Broad St.
Philadelphia, PA 19148

Pittsburgh Pirates
115 Federal St.
Pittsburgh, PA 15212

St. Louis Cardinals
250 Stadium Plaza
St. Louis, MO 63102

San Diego Padres
8880 Rio San Diego Dr.,
Ste. 400
San Diego, CA 92112

San Francisco Giants
24 Willie Mays Plaza
San Francisco, CA 94107

National Basketball Association

League Office, Olympic Tower, 645 5th Ave., New York, NY 10022
Website: www.nba.com

Atlanta Hawks
One CNN Center, Ste. 405,
South Tower
Atlanta, GA 30303

Boston Celtics
151 Merrimac St.
Boston, MA 02114

Chicago Bulls
1901 W. Madison St.
Chicago, IL 60612

Cleveland Cavaliers
1 Center Court
Cleveland, OH 44115

Dallas Mavericks
2909 Taylor St.
Dallas, TX 75226

Denver Nuggets
1000 Chopper Cr.
Denver, CO 80204

Detroit Pistons
Two Championship Dr.
Auburn Hills, MI 48326

Golden State Warriors
1011 Broadway
Oakland, CA 94607

Houston Rockets
Two Greenway Plaza,
Ste. 400
Houston, TX 77046

Indiana Pacers
125 S. Pennsylvania St.
Indianapolis, IN 46204

Los Angeles Clippers
1111 S. Figueroa St.,
Ste. 1100
Los Angeles, CA 90015

Los Angeles Lakers
555 Nash St.
El Segundo, CA 90245

Memphis Grizzlies
One Auction Ave.
Memphis, TN 38105

Miami Heat
601 Biscayne Blvd.
Miami, FL 33132

Milwaukee Bucks
1001 N. 4th St.
Milwaukee, WI 53203

Minnesota Timberwolves
600 1st Ave. North
Minneapolis, MN 55403

New Jersey Nets
390 Murray Hill Parkway
E. Rutherford, NJ 07073

New Orleans Hornets
1501 Girod St.
New Orleans, LA 70113

New York Knickerbockers
Two Pennsylvania Plaza
New York, NY 10121

Orlando Magic
Two Magic Place
8701 Maitland Summit Blvd.
Orlando, FL 32810

Philadelphia 76ers
3601 S. Broad St.
Philadelphia, PA 19148

Phoenix Suns
201 E. Jefferson
Phoenix, AZ 85004

Portland Trail Blazers
One Center Ct.
Portland, OR 97227

Sacramento Kings
One Sports Parkway
Sacramento, CA 95834

San Antonio Spurs
100 Montana St.
San Antonio, TX 78203

Seattle SuperSonics
351 Elliott Ave., West
Suite 500
Seattle, WA 98119

Toronto Raptors
40 Bay St., Ste. 400
Toronto, ON M5J 2X2

Utah Jazz
301 W. South Temple
Salt Lake City, UT 84101

Washington Wizards
601 F St., NW
Washington, DC 20004

National Hockey League

League Headquarters, 1251 Ave. of the Americas, 47th Fl., New York, NY 10020
Website: www.nhl.com

Mighty Ducks of Anaheim
2695 E. Katella Ave.
Anaheim, CA 92806

Atlanta Thrashers
1 CNN Ctr.,
12th Fl., S. Tower
Atlanta, GA 30348

Boston Bruins
One FleetCenter,
Ste. 250
Boston, MA 02114

Buffalo Sabres
HSBC Arena
One Seymour H. Knox III
Plaza
Buffalo, NY 14203

Calgary Flames
PO Box 1540, Station M
Calgary, AB T2P 3B9

Carolina Hurricanes
1400 Edwards Mill Rd.
Raleigh, NC 27607

Chicago Blackhawks
1901 W. Madison St.
Chicago, IL 60612

Colorado Avalanche
1000 Chopper Cr.
Denver, CO 80204

Columbus Blue Jackets
200 W. Nationwide Blvd.
Columbus, OH 43215

Dallas Stars
211 Cowboys Parkway
Irving, TX 75063

Detroit Red Wings
600 Civic Center Dr.
Detroit, MI 48226

Edmonton Oilers
11230 110 St.
Edmonton, AB T5G 3H7

Florida Panthers
One Panther Parkway
Sunrise, FL 33323

Los Angeles Kings
1111 S. Figueroa St.
Los Angeles, CA 90015

Minnesota Wild
317 Washington St.
St. Paul, MN 55102

Montreal Canadiens
1260 rue de La Gauchetière
St. W
Montreal, QC H3B 5E8

Nashville Predators
501 Broadway
Nashville, TN 37203

New Jersey Devils
50 Rte. 120 N. PO Box 504
E. Rutherford, NJ 07073

New York Islanders
Nassau Veterans Memorial
Coliseum
1255 Hempstead Tpke.
Uniondale, NY 11553

New York Rangers
Two Pennsylvania Plaza,
14th Fl.
New York, NY 10121

Ottawa Senators
1000 Palladium Dr.
Kanata, ON K2V 1A5

Philadelphia Flyers
First Union Center
3601 South Broad St.
Philadelphia, PA 19148

Phoenix Coyotes
5800 W. Glenn Dr., Ste. 350
Glendale, AZ 85301

Pittsburgh Penguins
66 Mario Lemieux Place
Pittsburgh, PA 15219

St. Louis Blues
1401 Clark Ave.
St. Louis, MO 63103

San Jose Sharks
525 W. Santa Clara St.
San Jose, CA 95113

Tampa Bay Lightning
401 Channelside Dr.
Tampa, FL 33602

Toronto Maple Leafs
40 Bay St., Ste. 400
Toronto, ON M5J 2X2

Vancouver Canucks
800 Griffiths Way
Vancouver, BC V6B 6G1

Washington Capitals
401 9th St. NW Ste. 750
Washington, DC 20004

National Football League

League Office, 280 Park Ave., New York, NY 10017
Website: www.nfl.com

Arizona Cardinals
8701 S. Hardy Dr.
Tempe, AZ 85284

Atlanta Falcons
4400 Falcon Parkway
Flowery Branch, GA 30542

Baltimore Ravens
200 St. Paul Pl., Ste. 2400
Baltimore, MD 21202

Buffalo Bills
One Bills Drive
Orchard Park, NY 14127

Carolina Panthers
800 S. Mint St.
Charlotte, NC 28202

Chicago Bears
1000 Football Dr.
Lake Forest, IL 60045

Cincinnati Bengals
One Paul Brown Stadium Dr.
Cincinnati, OH 45202

Cleveland Browns
76 Lou Groza Blvd.
Berea, OH 44017

Dallas Cowboys
One Cowboys Parkway
Irving, TX 75063

Denver Broncos
13655 Broncos Parkway
Englewood, CO 80112

Detroit Lions
1200 Featherstone Rd.
Pontiac, MI 48342

Green Bay Packers
1265 Lombardi Ave.
Green Bay, WI 54307

Houston Texans
One Reliant Park
Houston, TX 77054

Indianapolis Colts
7001 W. 56th St.
Indianapolis, IN 46254

Jacksonville Jaguars
One ALLTELL Stadium
Place
Jacksonville, FL 32202

Kansas City Chiefs
One Arrowhead Drive
Kansas City, MO 64129

Miami Dolphins
7500 SW 30th St.
Davie, FL 33329

Minnesota Vikings
9520 Viking Dr.
Eden Prairie, MN 55344

New England Patriots
60 Washington St.
Foxboro, MA 02035

New Orleans Saints
1500 Podras St.
New Orleans, LA 70112

New York Giants
Giants Stadium
E. Rutherford, NJ 07073

New York Jets
1000 Fulton Ave.
Hempstead, NY 11550

Oakland Raiders
1220 Harbor Bay Parkway
Alameda, CA 94502

Philadelphia Eagles
3501 S. Broad St.
Philadelphia, PA 19148

Pittsburgh Steelers
3400 S. Water St.
Pittsburgh, PA 15203

St. Louis Rams
One Rams Way
St. Louis, MO 63045

San Diego Chargers
4020 Murphy Rd.
PO Box 609609
San Diego, CA 92160

San Francisco 49ers
4949 Centennial Blvd.
Santa Clara, CA 95054

Seattle Seahawks
11220 NE 53d St.
Kirkland, WA 98033

Tampa Bay Buccaneers
One Buccaneer Place
Tampa, FL 33607

Tennessee Titans
460 Great Circle Rd.
Nashville, TN 37228

Washington Redskins
21300 Redskin Park Dr.
Ashburn, VA 20147

Other North American Sports Organizations

Amateur Athletic Union,
PO Box 22409,
Lake Buena Vista, FL 32830
www.aausports.org

Amateur Softball Assn.
2801 NE 50th St.
Oklahoma City, OK 73111
www.softball.org

American Kennel Club
260 Madison Ave., 4th Fl.
New York, NY 10016
www.akc.org

Canadian Football League
50 Wellington St. E, 3rd Fl.
Toronto, Ont. M5E 1C8
www.cfl.ca

CART (Championship Auto
Racing Teams)
5350 Lakeview Pkwy.
South Dr., Building 36
Indianapolis, IN 46268
www.cart.com

Intl. Game Fish Assn.
300 Gulf Stream Way
Dania Beach, FL 33004
www.igfa.org

LPGA
100 International Golf Dr.
Daytona Beach, FL 32124
www.lpga.com

Little League Baseball
PO Box 3485
Williamsport, PA 17701
www.littleleague.org

Major League Soccer
110 E. 42d St., 10th Fl.
New York, NY 10017
www.mlsnet.com

NASCAR
P.O. Box 2875
Daytona Beach, FL 32120
www.nascar.com

NCAA (National Collegiate
Athletic Association)
700 W. Washington St.
PO Box 6222
Indianapolis, IN 46206
www.ncaa.org

National Rifle Assn.
11250 Waples Mill Rd.
Fairfax, VA 22030
www.nra.org

Pro Bowlers Assn.
719 Second Ave., Ste. 701
Seattle, WA 98104
www.pbatour.com

PGA
100 Ave. of the Champions
Box 109601
Palm Beach Gardens, FL
33410
www.pga.com

Pro Rodeo Cowboys Assn.
101 Pro Rodeo Dr.
Colorado Springs, CO 80919
www.prorodeo.com

Special Olympics
1325 G St., NW, Ste. 500
Washington, DC 20005
www.specialolympics.org

Thoroughbred Racing Assn.
420 Fair Hill Dr.
Elkton, MD 21921
www.tra-online.com

USA Equestrian
4047 Iron Works Pkwy.
Lexington, KY 40511
www.equestrian.org

USA Rugby
1033 Walnut St., Suite 200
Boulder, CO 80302
www.usarugby.org

USA Swimming
One Olympic Plaza
Colorado Springs, CO 80909
www.usa-swimming.org

USA Track & Field
1 RCA Dome, Ste. 140
Indianapolis, IN 46225
www.usatf.org

U.S. Auto Club
4910 W. 16th St.
Speedway, IN 46224
www.usacracing.com

U.S. Figure Skating Assn.
20 First St.
Colorado Springs, CO 80906
www.usfsa.org

U.S. Olympic Committee
One Olympic Plaza
Colorado Springs, CO 80909
www.usoc.org

U.S. Skiing Assn.
1500 Kearns Blvd.
PO Box 100
Park City, UT 84060
www.usskiteam.com

U.S. Soccer Federation
1801 S. Prairie Ave.
Chicago, IL 60616
www.ussoccer.com

U.S. Tennis Assn.
70 W. Red Oak Lane
West Harrison, NY 10604
www.usta.com

U.S. Trotting Assn.
750 Michigan Ave.
Columbus, OH 43215
www.ustrotting.com

WNBA
Olympic Tower
645 5th Ave.
New York, NY 10022
www.wnba.com

NOTABLE SPORTS PERSONALITIES

Henry (Hank) Aaron, b. 1934: Milwaukee-Atlanta outfielder; hit record 755 home runs, led NL 4 times; record 2,297 RBI.

Kareem Abdul-Jabbar, b. 1947: Milwaukee, L.A. Lakers center; MVP 6 times; all-time leading NBA scorer, 38,387 points.

Andre Agassi, b. 1970: won: Wimbledon, '92; U.S. Open, '94, '99, '99; Aust. Open, '95, 2000-01, 2003; French Open, '99.

Troy Aikman, b. 1966: quarterback; led Dallas Cowboys to Super Bowl wins in 1993-94, 1996; Super Bowl MVP, 1993.

Amy Alcott, b. 1956: golfer; 29 career wins (5 majors), inducted into World Golf Hall of Fame in 1999.

Grover Cleveland "Pete" Alexander (1887-1950): pitcher; won 373 NL games; pitched 16 shutouts, 1916.

Muhammad Ali, b. 1942: 3-time heavyweight champion.

Gary Anderson, b. 1959: kicker; NFL's career points leader, with 2,346 through the end of the 2003 season.

Sparky Anderson, b. 1934: only manager to win World Series in the NL (Cincinnati, 1975-76) and the AL (Detroit, 1984).

Mario Andretti (1938-2001): race-car driver; won Daytona 500 (1967), Indy 500 (1969); Formula 1 world title (1978).

Earl Anthony (1938-2001): bowler; won record 6 PBA Championships (1973-75, 1981-83), 41 career PBA tournaments.

Eddie Arcaro (1916-97): only jockey to win racing's Triple Crown twice, 1941,1948; rode to 4,779 wins in his career.

Henry Armstrong (1912-88): boxer; held feather-, welter-, light-weight titles simultaneously, 1937-38.

Lance Armstrong, b. 1971: cyclist; record 6-time winner of the Tour de France (1999-2004).

Arthur Ashe (1943-93): tennis player; won U.S. Open (1968); Wimbledon (1975); died of AIDS.

Evelyn Ashford, b. 1957: sprinter; won 100m gold (1984) and silver (1988); member of 5 U.S. Olympic teams (1976-1992).

Red Auerbach, b. 1917: coached Boston to 9 NBA titles.

Tracy Austin, b. 1962: youngest player to win U.S. Open tennis title (age 16 in 1979), 2-time AP Female Athlete of the Year.

Ernie Banks, b. 1931: Chicago Cubs slugger; hit 512 NL homers; twice MVP; never played in World Series.

Roger Bannister, b. 1929: British physician; ran first sub 4-minute mile, May 6, 1954 (3 min. 59.4 sec.).

Charles Barkley, b. 1963: NBA MVP, 1993; 4th player ever to surpass 20,000 pts, 10,000 rebounds, and 4,000 assists.

Rick Barry, b. 1944: NBA scoring leader, 1967; ABA, 1969.

Sammy Baugh, b. 1914: Washington Redskins quarterback; held numerous records upon retirement after 16 seasons.

Elgin Baylor, b. 1934: L.A. Lakers forward; 10-time all-star.

Bob Beamon, b. 1946: Olympic long jump gold medalist in 1968; world record jump of 29' 2½" stood until 1991.

Boris Becker, b. 1967: German tennis star; won U.S. Open 1989; Wimbledon champ 3 times.

David Beckham, b. 1975: English soccer star; captain of 2002 World Cup team.

Jean Beliveau, b. 1931: Montreal Canadiens center; scored 507 goals; twice MVP.

Johnny Bench, b. 1947: Cincinnati Reds catcher; MVP twice; led league in home runs twice, RBIs 3 times.

Patty Berg, b. 1918: won more than 80 golf tournaments; AP Woman Athlete-of-the-Year 3 times.

Yogi Berra, b. 1925: Yankee catcher (1946-63); 3-time MVP.

Abebe Bikila (1932-73): Ethiopian runner; won consecutive Olympic marathon gold medals in 1960 (barefoot), 1964.

Matt Biondi, b. 1965: swimmer; won 5 golds, 1988 Olympics.

Larry Bird, b. 1956: Boston Celtics forward; NBA MVP, 1984-86; 1998 coach of the year with Indiana Pacers.

Bonnie Blair, b. 1964: speed skater; won 5 individual gold medals in 3 Olympics (1988, '92, '94).

George Blanda, b. 1927: quarterback, kicker; 26 years as active player, scored 2,002 career points.

Fanny Blankers-Koen (1918-2004): track; won 4 golds in 1948 Olympics.

Wade Boggs, b. 1958: AL batting champ, 1983, 1985-88; reached 3,000 career hits, 1999 (3,010).

Barry Bonds, b. 1964: outfielder; hit record 73 homers in 2001; NL MVP 1990, 1992-93, 2001-03; 3rd all-time in HRs (703).

Bjorn Borg, b. 1956: led Sweden to first Davis Cup, 1975; Wimbledon champion 5 times.

Mike Bossy, b. 1957: N.Y. Islanders right wing; scored more than 50 goals in a season 9 times.

Ray Bourque, b. 1960: Boston defenseman,1979-2000; 5-time Norris Trophy winner; won Stanley Cup with Colorado, 2001.

Bill Bradley, b. 1943: All-America at Princeton; led N.Y. Knicks to 2 NBA titles (1970, '73); U.S. senator, 1979-97.

Donald Bradman (1908-2001): Australian; widely regarded as the greatest cricketer ever; set several scoring records.

Terry Bradshaw, b. 1948: quarterback; led Pittsburgh to 4 Super Bowl wins (1975-76, 1978-80); NFL MVP, 1978.

George Brett, b. 1953: Kansas City Royals infielder; led AL in batting, 1976, 1980, 1990; MVP, 1980.

Lou Brock, b. 1939: St. Louis Cardinals outfielder; stole NL record 118 bases, 1974; led NL 8 times.

Jim Brown, b. 1936: Clev. fullback; 12,312 career yds.; 2-time Associated Press MVP.

Paul Brown (1908-91): football owner, coach; led eponymous Cleveland Browns to 3 NFL championships.

Kobe Bryant, b. 1978: guard; won 3 straight titles with Lakers (2000-02); charged with rape in 2003, charges dropped 2004.

Paul "Bear" Bryant (1913-83): college football coach with 323 wins; led Alabama to 5 national titles (1961, '64, '65, '78, '79).

Sergei Bubka, b. 1963: Ukrainian pole vaulter; first to clear 20 feet; gold medal, 1988 Olympics.

Don Budge (1915-2000): won numerous amateur and pro tennis titles; Grand Slam, 1938.

Maria Bueno, b. 1939: Brazilian tennis player; 4 U.S., 3 Wimbledon titles.

Dick Butkus, b. 1942: Chicago Bears linebacker; twice chosen best NFL defensive player.

Dick Button, b. 1929: figure skater; won 1948, 1952 Olympic gold medals; world titlist, 1948-52.

Walter Camp (1859-1925): Yale football player, coach, athletic director; established many rules.

Roy Campanella (1921-93): Hall of Fame catcher for the Brooklyn Dodgers (1948-57); 3-time NL MVP.

Earl Campbell, b. 1955: NFL running back; MVP 1978-79.

Jennifer Capriati, b. 1976: won Aust. (2001-02) and French Opens (2001), at 14 in 1990 was youngest top-10 player.

Rod Carew, b. 1945: AL infielder; 7 batting titles, 1977 MVP.

Steve Carlton, b. 1944: NL pitcher; won 20 games 6 times, Cy Young award 4 times; 4,136 career strikeouts.

Billy Casper, b. 1931: PGA Player-of-the-Year 3 times; U.S. Open champ twice.

Tracy Caulkins, b. 1963: swimmer; won 3 Olympic golds, 1984; set 63 U.S. and 5 world records; won 48 individual U.S. titles.

Wilt Chamberlain (1936-99): center; was NBA leading scorer 7 times, MVP 4 times; scored 100 pts. in a game, 1962.

Bobby Clarke, b. 1949: Philadelphia Flyers center; led team to 2 Stanley Cup championships; MVP 3 times.

Roger Clemens, b. 1962: pitcher; 1986 AL MVP; only 6-time Cy Young winner (1986-87, '91, '97-98, 2001); twice recorded record 20 Ks in a game; 328 wins, 4,317 Ks (2nd all-time).

Roberto Clemente (1934-72): Pittsburgh Pirates outfielder; won 4 batting titles; MVP, 1966; killed in plane crash.

Ty Cobb (1886-1961): Detroit Tigers outfielder; had record .367 lifetime batting average, 12 batting titles.

Sebastian Coe, b. 1956: British runner; won Olympic 1,500m gold medal and 800m silver medal in 1980 and 1984.

Nadia Comaneci, b. 1961: Romanian gymnast, won 3 gold medals, achieved 7 perfect scores, 1976 Olympics.

Maureen Connolly (1934-69): won tennis Grand Slam, 1953; AP Woman-Athlete-of-the-Year 3 times.

Jimmy Connors, b. 1952: tennis; 5 U.S. titles, 2 Wimbledon.

Cynthia Cooper, b. 1963: basketball; 4-time MVP of the WNBA finals and 2-time league MVP for the Houston Comets.

James J. Corbett (1866-1933): heavyweight champion, 1892-97; credited with being the first "scientific" boxer.

Angel Cordero Jr., b. 1942: jockey; leading money winner, 1976, 1982-83; rode 3 Kentucky Derby winners.

Howard Cosell (1920-95): commentator for ABC's *Monday Night Football* and *Wide World of Sports*.

Margaret Smith Court, b. 1942: Australian tennis great; won 24 Grand Slam events.

Bob Cousy, b. 1928: Boston guard; 6 NBA titles; 1957 MVP.

Bjoern Daehlie, b. 1967: Norwegian cross-country skier; won record 8 Winter Olympic gold medals.

Lindsay Davenport, b. 1976: tennis; won Olympic gold (1996), U.S. Open (1998), Wimbledon (1999), Aust. Open (2000).

Dizzy Dean (1910-74): colorful pitcher for St. Louis Cardinals' "Gashouse Gang" in the 30s; MVP, 1934.

Mary Decker Slaney, b. 1958: runner; has held 7 separate American records from the 800m to 10,000m.

Oscar De La Hoya, b. 1972: won IBF lightweight (1995); WBC super lightweight (1996) and welterweight (1997, 2000) titles.

Donna de Varona, b. 1947: 2 Olympic swimming golds,1964; 1st female sportscaster at a major network (ABC), 1965.

Jack Dempsey (1895-1983): heavyweight champ, 1919-26.

Gail Devers, b. 1966: Olympic 100m gold medalist, 1992, '96.

Eric Dickerson, b. 1960: NFL record 2,105 rushing yds.,1984.

Joe DiMaggio (1914-99): N.Y. Yankees outfielder; hit safely in record 56 consecutive games, 1941; AL MVP 3 times.

Tony Dorsett, b. 1954: Heisman winner who led the Dallas Cowboys to an NFL title in his rookie year (1977).

Tim Duncan, b. 1976: San Antonio center; 2-time NBA Finals MVP (1999, 2003); NBA MVP, 2002-03.

Roberto Duran, b. 1951: Panamanian boxer, held titles at 3 weights; lost 1980 "no mas" fight to Sugar Ray Leonard.

Leo Durocher (1905-91): manager; won 3 NL pennants (Brooklyn-1941, N.Y. Giants-1951, '54) and 1954 World Series.

Dale Earnhardt (1951-2001): 7-time NASCAR Winston Cup champ; died in a last-lap crash at 2001 Daytona 500.

Stefan Edberg, b. 1966: Swedish tennis player; U.S. Open champ, 1991, 1992; Wimbledon champ, 1988, 1990.

Gertrude Ederle (1906-2003): first woman to swim English Channel, broke existing men's record, 1926.

Teresa Edwards, b. 1964: basketball; 5-time Olympian; gold medalist in 1984, '88, '96, 2000 and bronze medal in 1992.

Hicham El Guerrouj, b. 1974: Moroccan runner; holds world records in mile (3:43.13) and 1,500m (3:26); won gold medals in 1,500m and 5,000m in 2004 Olympics.

John Elway, b. 1960: quarterback; led Denver Broncos to 2 Super Bowl wins, 1998, 1999; regular-season MVP, 1987.

Julius Erving, b. 1950: 3-time ABA MVP, 1981 NBA MVP.

Phil Esposito, b. 1942: NHL scoring leader 5 times.

Janet Evans, b. 1971: 4 Olympic swimming golds, 1988-92.

Lee Evans, b. 1947: Olympic 400m gold medalist in 1968 with a 43.86 sec. world record not broken until 1988.

Chris Evert, b. 1954: U.S. Open tennis champ 6 times, Wimbledon champ 3 times.

Ray Ewry (1873-1937): track-and-field star; won 8 gold medals, 1900, 1904, and 1908 Olympics.

Nick Faldo, b. 1957: British golfer; won Masters, British Open 3 times each.

Juan Manuel Fangio (1911-95): Argentinian; 5-time World Grand Prix driving champ (1951, 1954-57).

Marshall Faulk, b. 1973: 2000 NFL MVP; scored then-record 26 TDs in 2001; 3-time Off. Player of the Year (1999-2001).

Brett Favre, b. 1969: quarterback; led Green Bay to Super Bowl win, 1997; NFL MVP, 1995, 1996; co-MVP, 1997.

Bob Feller, b. 1918: Cleveland Indians pitcher; won 266 games; pitched 3 no-hitters, 12 one-hitters.

Rollie Fingers, b. 1946: pitcher; 341 career saves; AL MVP, Cy Young Award, 1981; World Series MVP, 1974.

Peggy Fleming, b. 1948: world figure skating champion, 1966-68; gold medalist, 1968 Olympics.

Whitey Ford, b. 1928: N.Y. Yankees pitcher; won record 10 World Series games.

George Foreman, b. 1949: heavyweight champion, 1973-74, 1994-95; at 45, the oldest to win a heavyweight title.

Dick Fosbury, b. 1947: high jumper; won 1968 Olympic gold medal; developed the "Fosbury Flop."

Jimmie Foxx (1907-67): Red Sox, Athletics slugger; MVP 3 times; triple crown, 1933.

A.J. Foyt, b. 1935: won Indy 500 4 times; U.S. Auto Club champ 7 times.

Joe Frazier, b. 1944: heavyweight champion, 1970-73.

Walt Frazier, b. 1945: Hall of Fame guard for N.Y. Knicks' NBA championship teams (1970, '73).

Haile Gebrselassie, b. 1973: Ethiopian runner; 10,000m gold medalist in 1996, 2000 Olympics.

Lou Gehrig (1903-41): N.Y. Yankees 1st baseman; MVP, 1927, 1936; triple crown, 1934; AL record 184 RBIs, 1931; played in 2,130 straight games (1925-39), a record that stood untl 1995.

George Gervin, b. 1952: top NBA scorer, 1978-80, 1982.

Althea Gibson (1927-2003): 2-time U.S. and Wimbledon champ.

Bob Gibson, b. 1935: St. Louis Cardinals pitcher; won Cy Young award twice; struck out 3,117 batters.

Josh Gibson (1911-47): Hall of Fame catcher; known as "Babe Ruth of the Negro Leagues"; credited with as many as 84 homers in 1 season and about 800 in his career.

Marc Girardelli, b. 1963: skier (Lux.); won 5 World Cup titles.

Jeff Gordon, b. 1971: race car driver; youngest to win NASCAR title 4 times (1995, 1997-98, 2001).

Steffi Graf, b. 1969: German; won tennis Grand Slam, 1988; U.S. champ 5 times; Wimbledon champ 7 times.

Otto Graham, b. (1921-2003): Cleveland quarterback; 4-time all-pro.

Red Grange (1903-91): All-America at Univ. of Illinois, 1923-25; played for Chicago Bears, 1925-35.

Joe Greene, b. 1946: Pittsburgh Steelers lineman; twice NFL outstanding defensive player.

Wayne Gretzky, b. 1961: top scorer in NHL history with record 894 goals, 1,963 assists, 2,857 points; MVP, 1980-87, 1989.

Bob Griese, b. 1945: All-Pro quarterback; led Miami Dolphins to 17-0 season (1972) and 2 Super Bowl titles (1973-74).

Ken Griffey Jr., b. 1969: outfielder; led AL in homers 1994, 1997-1999; 1997 AL MVP; 10 gold gloves.

Archie Griffin, b. 1954: Ohio State running back; only 2-time winner of the Heisman Trophy (1974-75).

Florence Griffith Joyner (1959-98): sprinter; won 3 gold medals at 1988 Olympics; world and Olympic record for 100m.

Lefty Grove (1900-75): pitcher; won 300 AL games.

Janet Guthrie, b. 1938: 1st woman driver in Indy 500 (1977).

Tony Gwynn, b. 1960: 8-time NL batting champ, 1984, 1987-89, 1994-97; 3,141 career hits.

Walter Hagen (1892-1969): golfer; 5 PGA, 4 British Open titles.

George Halas (1895-1983): founder-coach of Chicago Bears; won 5 NFL championships.

Dorothy Hamill, b. 1956: figure skater; gold medalist at Olympics and World championships in 1976.

Scott Hamilton, b. 1958: U.S. and world figure skating champion, 1981-84; Olympic gold medalist, 1984.

Mia Hamm, b. 1972: led U.S. to World Cup (1991, '99) and Olympic ('96, 2004) titles; most career goals in women's soccer.

Franco Harris, b. 1950: running back; led Steelers to 4 Super Bowls (1975-76, 1979-80); 1,000+ yds. in a season 8 times.

Bill Hartack, b. 1932: jockey; rode 5 Kentucky Derby winners.

Dominik Hasek, b. 1965: NHL goaltender; won Vezina Trophy, 1994-95, 1997-99, 2001; NHL MVP, 1997-98.

John Havlicek, b. 1940: Boston forward; scored 26,395 NBA pts.

Eric Heiden, b. 1958: speed skater; won 5 Olympic golds, 1980.

Rickey Henderson, b. 1958: outfielder; 1990 AL MVP; record 130 stolen bases, 1982; all-time leader in steals, runs.

Sonja Henie (1912-69): Norwegian world champion figure skater, 1927-36; Olympic gold medalist, 1928, 1932, 1936.

Martina Hingis, b. 1980: Swiss; won Aust. and U.S. Opens, Wimbledon; youngest No. 1 player (16 yrs., 6 m.), 1997.

Ben Hogan (1912-97): golfer; won 4 U.S. Open titles, 2 PGA Championships, 2 Masters.

Chamique Holdsclaw, b. 1977: basketball; 2-time national player of the year, led Tennessee to 3 NCAA titles (1996-98).

Evander Holyfield, b. 1962: 4-time heavyweight champion.

Rogers Hornsby (1896-1963): NL 2nd baseman; batted record .424 in 1924; twice won triple crown.

Paul Hornung, b. 1935: Green Bay Packers runner, placekicker; scored record 176 points, 1960.

Gordie Howe, b. 1928: hockey forward; NHL MVP 6 times; scored 801 goals in 26 NHL seasons.

Carl Hubbell (1903-88): N.Y. Giants pitcher; 20-game winner 5 consecutive years, 1933-37.

Bobby Hull, b. 1939: NHL all-star 10 times; MVP, 1965-66.

Brett Hull, b. 1964: St. Louis Blues forward; led NHL in goals, 1990-92; MVP, 1991.

Catfish Hunter (1946-99): pitched perfect game, 1968; 20-game winner 5 times.

Don Hutson (1913-97): Packers receiver; caught 99 TD passes; 2-time NFL MVP.

Juli Inkster, b. 1960: Hall of Fame golfer; 2nd to win all 4 of LPGA's modern majors; won 7 career major titles.

Phil Jackson, b. 1945: won 9 NBA titles as coach of Bulls and Lakers; 1973 title as a N.Y. Knick.

Reggie Jackson, b. 1946: slugger; led AL in home runs 4 times; MVP, 1973; hit 5 World Series home runs, 1977.

"Shoeless" Joe Jackson (1889-1951): outfielder; 3rd highest career batting average (.356); one of the "Black Sox" banned for allegedly throwing 1919 World Series.

Jaromir Jagr, b. 1972: Czech hockey player; NHL MVP in 1999; Art Ross Trophy (leading scorer) 1995, 1998-2001.

Bruce Jenner, b. 1949: Olympic decathlon gold medalist, 1976.

Lynn Jennings, b. 1960: runner; 3-time World and 9-time U.S. cross country champ; bronze at 1992 Olympics (10,000m).

Earvin (Magic) Johnson, b. 1959: NBA MVP, 1987, 1989, 1990; Playoff MVP, 1980, 1982, 1987; 2nd in career assists.

Jack Johnson (1878-1946): heavyweight champion, 1908-15.

Michael Johnson, b. 1967: 5-time Olympic gold medalist (1996, 2000); world and Olympic record, 200m and 400m.

Randy Johnson, b. 1963: 5-time Cy Young winner; strikeout leader: 1992-95, 1999-2004; 4,161 strikeouts (3rd all-time); pitched perfect game, 2004.

Walter Johnson (1887-1946): Washington Senators pitcher; won 416 games; record 110 shutouts.

Bobby Jones (1902-71): won golf's Grand Slam, 1930; U.S. Amateur champ 5 times, U.S. Open champ 4 times.

David "Deacon" Jones, b. 1938: 5-time All-Pro with L.A. Rams (1965-69); "sack" specialist credited with inventing the term.

Marion Jones, b. 1975: 2000 Olympic 100m, 200m, 1,600m relay gold medalist, bronze in long jump and 400m relay.

Roy Jones Jr., b. 1969: undisputed light heavyweight champ, 1999-2004.

Michael Jordan, b. 1963: guard; leading NBA scorer, 1987-93, 1996-98; MVP, 1988, 1991-92, '96, '98; playoff MVP, 1991-93, 1996-98; ESPN Athlete of the Century.

Dorothy Kamenshek, b. 1925: led Rockford (IL) Peaches to 4 All-American Girls Baseball League titles in the 1940s.

Jackie Joyner-Kersee, b. 1962: Olympic gold medalist in heptathlon (1988,'92) and long jump (1988).

Harmon Killebrew, b. 1936: Minnesota Twins slugger; led AL in home runs 6 times; 573 lifetime.

Jean-Claude Killy, b. 1943: French skier; 3 1968 Olympic golds.

Ralph Kiner, b. 1922: Pittsburgh Pirates slugger; led NL in home runs 7 consecutive years, 1946-52.

Billie Jean King, b. 1943: U.S. singles champ 4 times, Wimbledon champ 6 times; beat Bobby Riggs, 1973.

Bob Knight, b. 1940: basketball coach; led Indiana U. to NCAA title in 1976, '81, '87.

Olga Korbut, b. 1955: Soviet gymnast; 3 1972 Olympic golds.

Sandy Koufax, b. 1935: 3-time Cy Young winner; lowest ERA in NL, 1962-66; pitched 4 no-hitters, one a perfect game.

Ingrid Kristiansen, b. 1956: Norwegian; only runner to hold world records in 5,000m, 10,000m, and marathon.

Julie Krone, b. 1963: winningest female jockey; only woman to ride a winner in a Triple Crown race (Belmont, 1993).

Michelle Kwan, b.1980: figure skater; 8 U.S. and 5 World titles; silver medalist at 1998 Olympics, bronze in 2002.

Guy Lafleur, b. 1951: 3-time NHL scoring leader; 1977-78 MVP.

Kennesaw Mountain Landis (1866-1944): 1st commissioner of baseball (1920-44); banned the 8 "Black Sox" involved in fixing 1919 World Series.

Tom Landry (1924-2000): Dallas Cowboys head coach, 1960-88; won 2 Super Bowls (1972, '78); 3rd in career wins (270).

Dick "Night Train" Lane (1928-2002): Hall of Fame defensive back, intercepted an NFL season record 14 passes (1952).

Don Larsen, b. 1929: As N.Y. Yankee, pitched only World Series perfect game, Oct. 8, 1956—a 2-0 win over Brooklyn.

Rod Laver, b. 1938: Australian; won tennis Grand Slam twice, 1962, 1969; Wimbledon champ 4 times.

Mario Lemieux, b. 1965: 6-time NHL leading scorer; MVP, 1988, 1993, 1996; playoff MVP, 1991-92.

Greg Lemond, b. 1961: cyclist; 3-time Tour de France winner (1986, '89-90); first American to win the event.

Ivan Lendl, b. 1960: Czech; U.S. Open tennis champ, 1985-87.

Sugar Ray Leonard, b. 1956: boxer; held titles in 5 different weight classes.

Carl Lewis, b. 1961: track-and-field star; won 9 Olympic gold medals in sprinting and the long jump.

Lennox Lewis, b. 1965: Brit.; heavyweight champ, 1997-2004.

Tara Lipinski, b. 1982: youngest figure skater to win U.S. and world championships, 1997, and Winter Olympic gold, 1998.

Vince Lombardi (1913-70): Green Bay Packers coach; led team to 5 NFL championships and 2 Super Bowl victories.

Nancy Lopez, b. 1957: Hall of Fame golfer; 4-time LPGA Player of the Year, 3-time winner of the LPGA Championship.

Greg Louganis, b. 1960: won Olympic gold medals in both springboard and platform diving, 1984, 1988.

Joe Louis (1914-81): heavyweight champion, 1937-49.

Sid Luckman (1916-98): Chicago Bears quarterback; led team to 4 NFL championships; MVP, 1943.

Connie Mack (1862-1956): Philadelphia Athletics manager, 1901-50; won 9 pennants, 5 championships.

John Madden, b. 1936: won Super Bowl as coach of the Oakland Raiders (1977); NFL TV analyst since 1982.

Greg Maddux, b. 1966: NL pitcher, won 4 consecutive Cy Young awards, 1992-95; 305 career wins.

Karl Malone, b. 1963: Utah Jazz, L.A. Laker forward; MVP, 1997, 1999; 14-time All-Star; 36,928 career points (2nd all-time).

Moses Malone, b. 1955: NBA center; MVP, 1979, 1982-83.

Mickey Mantle (1931-95): N.Y. Yankees outfielder; triple crown, 1956; 18 World Series home runs; MVP 3 times.

Pete Maravich (1948-88): guard; scored NCAA record 44.2 ppg during collegiate career; led NBA in scoring, 1977.

Rocky Marciano (1923-69): heavyweight champion, 1952-56; retired undefeated.

Dan Marino, b. 1961: Miami quarterback; NFL record 5,084 yds passing and 48 TDs, 1984; career leader, TDs, yds passing.

Roger Maris (1934-85): N.Y. Yankees outfielder; hit AL record 61 home runs, 1961; MVP, 1960 and 1961.

Eddie Mathews (1931-2000): Milwaukee-Atlanta 3rd baseman; hit 512 career home runs.

Christy Mathewson (1880-1925): pitcher; won 373 games.

Bob Mathias, b. 1930: decathlon gold, 1948, 1952 Olympics.

Willie Mays, b. 1931: N.Y.-S.F. Giants center fielder; hit 660 home runs, led NL 4 times; had 3,283 hits; twice MVP.

Willie McCovey, b. 1938: S.F. Giants slugger; hit 521 home runs; led NL 3 times; MVP, 1969.

John McEnroe, b. 1959: U.S. Open tennis champ, 1979-81, 1984; Wimbledon champ, 1981, 1983-84.

John McGraw (1873-1934): N.Y. Giants manager; led team to 10 pennants, 3 championships.

Mark McGwire, b. 1963: hit then-record 70 home runs in 1998; 583 career home runs (6th).

Tamara McKinney, b. 1962: 1st U.S. skier to win overall Alpine World Cup championship (1983).

Mary T. Meagher, b. 1964: swimmer; "Madame Butterfly" won 3 Olympic gold medals in 1984.

Mark Messier, b. 1961: center; NHL MVP, 1990, 1992; Conn Smythe Trophy, 1984.

Debbie Meyer, b. 1952: 1st swimmer to win 3 individual Olympic golds (1968).

George Mikan, b. 1924: Minn. Lakers center; considered the best basketball player of the first half of the 20th century.

Stan Mikita, b. 1940: Chicago Blackhawks center; led NHL in scoring 4 times; MVP twice.

Billy Mills, b. 1938: runner; upset winner of the 1964 Olympic 10,000m; only American man ever to win the event.

Joe Montana, b. 1956: S.F. 49ers quarterback; Super Bowl MVP, 1982, 1985, 1990.

Archie Moore (1913-98): light-heavyweight champ, 1952-62.

Howie Morenz (1902-37): Montreal Canadiens forward; considered best hockey player of first half of the 20th century.

Edwin Moses, b. 1955: undefeated in 122 consecutive 400m hurdles races, 1977-87; Olympic gold medalist, 1976, '84.

Shirley Muldowney, b. 1940: 1st woman to race National Hot Rod Assoc. Top Fuel dragsters; 3-time NHRA points champ.

Eddie Murray, b. 1956: durable slugger; 3rd player to combine 3,000+ hits with 500+ home runs.

Stan Musial, b. 1920: St. Louis Cardinals star; won 7 NL batting titles; MVP 3 times.

Bronko Nagurski (1908-90): Chicago Bears fullback and tackle; gained more than 4,000 yds. rushing.

Joe Namath, b. 1943: Jets quarterback; 1969 Super Bowl MVP.

Martina Navratilova, b. 1956: tennis; Wimbledon champ 9 times, U.S. Open champ 1983-84, 1986-87.

Byron Nelson, b. 1912: won 11 consecutive golf tournaments in 1945; twice Masters and PGA titlist.

Ernie Nevers (1903-76): Stanford football star; selected as best college fullback to play between 1919-69.

Paula Newby-Fraser, b. 1972: 8-time Ironman Triathlon World Champ; holds women's course record.

John Newcombe, b. 1943: Australian; twice U.S. Open tennis champ; Wimbledon titlist 3 times.

Jack Nicklaus, b. 1940: PGA Player-of-the-Year, 1967, 1972; leading money winner 8 times; won 18 majors (6 Masters).

Chuck Noll, b. 1931: Pittsburgh coach; won 4 Super Bowls.

Paavo Nurmi (1897-1973): Finnish distance runner; won 6 Olympic gold medals, 1920, 1924, 1928.

Al Oerter, b. 1936: discus thrower; won gold medal at 4 consecutive Olympics, 1956-68.

Hakeem Olajuwon, b. 1963: Houston center; NBA MVP, 1994, playoffs MVP, 1994-95; career blocked shots leader.

Barney Oldfield (1878-1946): pioneer auto racer; was first to drive a car 60 mph (1903).

Shaquille O'Neal, b. 1972: center; led L.A. Lakers to NBA titles, 2000-2002; 2000, 2002 Finals MVP; 2000 NBA MVP.

Bobby Orr, b. 1948: Boston Bruins defenseman; 8-time Norris Trophy winner; led NHL in scoring twice, assists 5 times.

Mel Ott (1909-1958): N.Y. Giants outfielder; hit 511 home runs; led NL 6 times.

Jesse Owens (1913-80): track and field; 4 1936 Olympic golds.

Satchel Paige (1906-82): pitcher; starred in Negro leagues, 1924-48; entered major leagues at age 42.

Arnold Palmer, b. 1929: golf's first $1 million winner; won 4 Masters, 2 British Opens.

Jim Palmer, b. 1945: Baltimore Orioles pitcher; won Cy Young award 3 times; 20-game winner 8 times.

Joe Paterno, b. 1926: football coach; 2nd-most wins in NCAA Div. I-A (339 through 2003); led Penn St. to titles, 1982, 1986.

Floyd Patterson, b. 1935: 2-time heavyweight champion.

Walter Payton (1954-1999): Chicago Bears running back; most rushing yards in NFL history; top NFC rusher, 1976-80.

Pelé (Edson Arantes do Nascimento), b. 1940: soccer; led Brazil to 3 World Cups (1958, '62, '70); scored 1,281 goals.

Bob Pettit, b. 1932: first NBA player to score 20,000 points; twice NBA scoring leader.

Richard Petty, b. 1937: NASCAR national champ 7 times; 7-time Daytona 500 winner.

Michael Phelps, b. 1985: swimmer; won 8 medals (6 gold, 2 bronze) at 2004 Olympics; set numerous world records.

Laffit Pincay Jr., b. 1946: jockey; leading money-winner, 1970-74, 1979, 1985.

Jacques Plante (1929-86): NHL goaltender; 7 Vezina trophies; first goalie to wear a mask in a game.

Gary Player, b. 1936: South African golfer; won 3 Masters, 3 British Opens, 2 PGA Championships, and the U.S. Open.

Steve Prefontaine (1951-75): runner; 1st to win 4 NCAA titles in same event (5,000m, 1970-73); died in auto accident.

Paula Radcliffe, b. 1973: British runner; set marathon world record of 2:15:25 in London, 2003.

Willis Reed, b. 1942: N.Y. Knicks center; MVP, 1970; playoff MVP, 1970, 1973.

Mary Lou Retton, b. 1968: gymnast; won all-around gold medal at 1984 Olympics; also won 2 silvers and 2 bronzes.

Jerry Rice, b. 1962: receiver; 1989 Super Bowl MVP; NFL record for career touchdowns (205) and receptions (1,519).

Maurice Richard (1921-2000): Montreal Canadiens forward; scored 544 regular season goals, 82 playoff goals.

Branch Rickey (1881-1965): MLB executive; helped break baseball's color barrier, 1947; initiated farm system, 1919.

Cal Ripken Jr., b. 1960: Baltimore shortstop; AL MVP 1983, 1991; most consecutive games played (2,632).

Oscar Robertson, b. 1938: NBA guard; averaged career 25.7 points per game; 4th in career assists (9,887); MVP, 1964.

Brooks Robinson, b. 1937: Baltimore Orioles 3rd baseman; played in 4 World Series; MVP, 1964; 16 gold gloves.

Frank Robinson, b. 1935: MVP in both NL and AL; triple crown, 1966; 586 career home runs; first black manager in majors.

Jackie Robinson (1919-72): broke baseball's color barrier with Brooklyn Dodgers, 1947; MVP, 1949.

Sugar Ray Robinson (1920-89): boxer; middleweight champion 5 times, welterweight champion.

Knute Rockne (1888-1931): Notre Dame football coach, 1918-31; revolutionized game by stressing forward pass.

Bill Rodgers, b. 1947: runner; won Boston and New York City marathons 4 time each, 1975-80.

Ronaldo (Ronaldo Luiz Nazario de Lima), b. 1976: soccer player; led Brazil to 2002 World Cup; 3-time FIFA world player of the year (1996-97, 2002).

Pete Rose, b. 1941: won 3 NL batting titles; hit in 44 consecutive games, 1978; most career hits, 4,256; banned for gambling, 1989; admitted betting on his team, 2004.

Ken Rosewall, b. 1934: Australian tennis player; 2-time U.S. champ, 8 Grand Slam singles titles.

Patrick Roy, b. 1965: Montreal-Colorado goalie; only 3-time NHL Playoffs MVP (Conn Smythe Trophy), 1986, '93, 2001.

Wilma Rudolph (1940-94): sprinter; won 3 1960 Olympic golds.

Adolph Rupp (1901-77): NCAA basketball coach; led Kentucky to 4 national titles, 1948-49, 1951, 1958.

Bill Russell, b. 1934: Boston Celtics center; led team to 11 NBA titles; MVP 5 times; first black coach of major pro sports team.

Babe Ruth (1895-1948): N.Y. Yankees outfielder; hit 60 home runs, 1927; 714 lifetime (2nd all-time); led AL 12 times.

Johnny Rutherford, b. 1938: auto racer; won 3 Indy 500s.

Nolan Ryan, b. 1947: pitcher; holds season (383), career (5,714) strikeout records; won 324 games (7 no-hitters).

Pete Sampras, b. 1971: tennis star; 1st man in Open era to win 7 Wimbledons; most career Grand Slam wins (14).

Joan Benoit Samuelson, b. 1968: won 1st Olympic women's marathon (1984), Boston Marathon (1979, '83).

Barry Sanders, b. 1968: rushed for 2,053 yards in 1997; led NFL in rushing, 1990, 1994, 1996, 1997.

Gene Sarazen (1902-99): golfer; won PGA championship 3 times, U.S. Open twice; developed the sand wedge.

Gale Sayers, b. 1943: Chicago back; twice led NFL in rushing.

Mike Schmidt, b. 1949: Phillies 3rd baseman; led NL in home runs 8 times; 548 lifetime; NL MVP, 1980, 1981, 1986.

Michael Schumacher, b. 1969: German race-car driver; 7-time Formula 1 world champ (1994-95, 2000-2004).

Tom Seaver, b. 1944: pitcher; won NL Cy Young award 3 times; won 311 major league games.

Monica Seles, b. 1973: tennis; won U.S. ('91-92), Aust. ('91-93, '96), French ('90-92) Opens; stabbed on court by fan, 1993.

Patty Sheehan, b. 1956: Hall of Fame golfer; 3 LPGA Championships (1983-84, '93).

Willie Shoemaker (1931-2003): jockey; rode 4 Kentucky Derby and 5 Belmont Stakes winners; leading career money winner.

Eddie Shore (1902-85): Boston Bruins defenseman; MVP 4 times, first-team all-star 7 times.

Frank Shorter, b. 1947: runner, only American to win men's Olympic marathon (1972) since 1908; silver medalist in 1976.

Don Shula, b. 1930: all-time winningest NFL coach (347 games).

Al Simmons (1902-56): AL outfielder; lifetime .334 batting avg.

O.J. Simpson, b. 1947: running back; rushed for 2,003 yds., 1973; AFC leading rusher 4 times; acquitted of murder, 1995.

George Sisler (1893-1973): St. Louis Browns 1st baseman; had then-record 257 hits, 1920; batted .340 lifetime.

Dean Smith, b. 1931: basketball coach; most career Division I wins (879); led North Carolina to 2 NCAA titles (1982, '93).

Emmitt Smith, b. 1969: running back; NFL and Super Bowl MVP, 1993.

Lee Smith, b. 1957: relief pitcher; all-time saves leader (478).

Conn Smythe (1895-1980): won 7 Stanley Cups as Toronto GM (1929-1961); playoff MVP award named in his honor.

Sam Snead (1912-2002): PGA and Masters champ 3 times each, record 82 PGA tournament victories.

Annika Sorenstam, b. 1970: Swedish golfer; set LPGA 18-hole record of 59 (−13) and 72-hole record of 27-under-par, 2001; won 7 LPGA majors, including career Grand Slam.

Sammy Sosa, b. 1968: Cubs outfielder; 66 homers, NL MVP, 1998; 1st to hit 60+ homers 3 times (63 in 1999, 64 in 2001).

Warren Spahn, b. 1921: pitcher; won 363 NL games; 20-game winner 13 times; Cy Young award, 1957.

Tris Speaker (1885-1958): AL outfielder; batted .345 over 22 seasons; hit record 792 career doubles.

Mark Spitz, b. 1950: swimmer; won 7 golds at 1972 Olympics.

Amos Alonzo Stagg (1862-1965): football innovator; Univ. of Chicago football coach for 41 years, 5 undefeated seasons.

Bart Starr, b. 1934: Green Bay Packers quarterback; led team to 5 NFL titles and 2 Super Bowl victories.

Roger Staubach, b. 1942: Dallas Cowboys quarterback; leading NFC passer 5 times.

Casey Stengel (1890-1975): managed Yankees to 10 pennants, 7 championships, 1949-60.

Jackie Stewart, b. 1939: Scot auto racer; 27 Grand Prix wins.

John Stockton, b. 1962: Utah Jazz guard; NBA career leader in assists, steals; NBA assists leader, 1988-96.

Picabo Street, b. 1971: skier; 2-time World Cup downhill champion (1995-96); Olympic super G gold medalist, 1998.

Louise Suggs, b. 1923: golfer; U.S. Women's Open champ., 1949, '52; 11 major victories, ranks 3rd all-time.

John L. Sullivan (1858-1918): last bareknuckle heavyweight champion, 1882-1892.

Pat Summit, b. 1952: women's basketball coach; led Tennessee Lady Vols to 6 NCAA titles (1987, '89, '91, '96-98).

Fran Tarkenton, b. 1940: Minnesota, N.Y. Giants quarterback; 3rd in career TD passes (342); 1975 Player of the Year.

Lawrence Taylor, b. 1959: linebacker; led N.Y. Giants to 2 Super Bowl titles; played in 10 Pro Bowls.

Jenny Thompson, b. 1973: swimmer; most decorated U.S. female Olympian with 12 medals (8 gold) in 1992, '96, 2000, '04.

Daley Thompson, b. 1958: British decathlete; Olympic gold medalist in 1980, '84.

Jim Thorpe (1888-1953): football All-America, 1911, 1912; won pentathlon and decathlon, 1912 Olympics.

Bill Tilden (1893-1953): won 7 U.S. tennis titles, 3 Wimbledon.

Y. A. Tittle, b. 1926: N.Y. Giants quarterback; MVP, 1961, 1963.

Alberto Tomba, b. 1966: Italian skier; 5 Olympic alpine medals (3 golds, 2 silver) in 1988, 1992.

Lee Trevino, b. 1939: golfer; won U.S., British Open twice.

Bryan Trottier, b. 1956: Islanders, Penguins center for 6 Stanley Cup champs.

Gene Tunney, (1897-1978): heavyweight champion, 1926-28.

Mike Tyson, b. 1966: Undisputed heavyweight champ, 1987-1990; at 19, youngest to win a heavyweight title (WBC, 1986).

Wyomia Tyus, b. 1945: Olympic 100m gold medalist, 1964, '68.

Johnny Unitas, (1933-2002): Baltimore Colts quarterback; passed for more than 40,000 yds; MVP, 1957, 1967.

Al Unser, b. 1939: Indy 500 winner 4 times.

Bobby Unser, b. 1934: Indy 500 winner 3 times.

Norm Van Brocklin (1926-83): quarterback; passed for game record 554 yds., 1951; MVP, 1960.

Amy Van Dyken, b. 1973: swimmer, first American woman to win 4 gold medals in one Olympics (1996).

Lasse Viren, b. 1949: Finnish runner; Olympic 5,000m and 10,000m gold medalist in 1972 and 1976.

Honus Wagner (1874-1955): Pirates shortstop; 8 NL batting titles.

Grete Waitz, b. 1953: Norwegian; 9-time winner of the New York City Marathon (1978-80, 1982-86, '88).

"Jersey" Joe Walcott (1914-94): boxer; became heavyweight champion at age 37, 1951-52.

Bill Walton, b. 1952: center; led Portland Trail Blazers to 1977 NBA title; MVP, 1978; NBA TV commentator.

Kurt Warner, b. 1971: Rams, Giants quarterback; NFL MVP 1999, 2001; Super Bowl MVP, 2000.

Tom Watson, b. 1949: golfer; 6-time PGA Player of the Year, won 5 British Opens, 2 Masters, U.S. Open.

Karrie Webb, b. 1974: Australian golfer; youngest woman (26 yrs. 6 mos.) to win career Grand Slam, 1999-2001.

Johnny Weissmuller (1903-84): swimmer; won 52 national championships, 5 Olympic gold medals; set 67 world records.

Jerry West, b. 1938: L.A. Lakers guard; had career average 27 points per game; first team all-star 10 times.

Byron "Whizzer" White (1917-2002): running back; led NCAA in scoring and rushing at Colorado (1937); led NFL in rushing twice (1938, '40); Supreme Court justice, 1962-93.

Kathy Whitworth, b. 1939: 7-time LPGA Player of the Year (1966-69, 1971-73); 88 tour wins most on LPGA or PGA tour.

Lenny Wilkens, b. 1937: winningest coach in NBA history; in Hall of Fame as player and coach.

Serena Williams, b. 1981: tennis; 2-time Wimbledon, U.S. Open champ; Australian Open (2003); French Open (2002).

Ted Williams (1918-2002): Boston Red Sox outfielder; won 6 batting titles, 2 triple crowns; hit .406 in 1941.

Venus Williams, b. 1980: tennis; Wimbledon, U.S. Open, Olympic champ (2000); Wimbledon, U.S. Open champ (2001).

Helen Willis Moody (1905-98): tennis star; won U.S. Open 7 times, Wimbledon 8 times.

Katarina Witt, b. 1965: German figure skater; won Olympic gold medal, 1984, 1988; world champ, 1984-84, 1987-88.

John Wooden, b. 1910: UCLA basketball coach; 10 NCAA titles.

Tiger Woods, b. 1975: golfer; youngest to win career Grand Slam, at age 24 (1997-2000); 8 major titles.

Mickey Wright, b. 1935: golfer; won LPGA and U.S. Open championship 4 times; 82 career wins, including 13 majors.

Kristi Yamaguchi, b. 1971: figure skater; won national, world, and Olympic titles in 1992.

Carl Yastrzemski, b. 1939: Boston Red Sox slugger; won 3 batting titles; triple crown, 1967.

Cy Young (1867-1955): pitcher; won record 511 games.

Steve Young, b. 1961: 49ers quarterback; led NFL in passing, 1991-94, 1996, 1997; Super Bowl MVP, 1995.

Babe Didrikson Zaharias (1911-56): all-around athlete; 3 track & field medals (2 golds), 1932 Olympics; won 10 golf majors; also played baseball; 6-time AP Female Athlete of the Year.

Emil Zátopek (1922-2000): Czech runner; won 3 gold medals at 1952 Olympics (5,000m, 10,000m, and marathon).

Zinedine Zidane, b. 1972: soccer; led France to 1998 World Cup (named top player); 3-time FIFA world player of the year (1998, 2000, '03).

Spotlight: 70 Years of Heisman Winners

The avidly sought Heisman Trophy, which recognizes "the Outstanding College Football Player of the United States," has been given out annually since 1935 by the Downtown Athletic Club in New York City. It is named for coach John W. Heisman, who served in his later years as DAC athletic director; in 1916 his Georgia Tech team whomped Cumberland, 222-0, in what is still the biggest blowout in U.S. college football history. Eight Heisman Trophy winners have earned membership in the Pro Football Hall of Fame. Others have won renown off the gridiron. For several winners, the Heisman was no protection from life's misfortunes.

All records below are through the 2003 season unless otherwise indicated. Numbers in parentheses after career totals show all-time rank. For list of all Heisman Trophy winners, see page 935. (*Player was active in 2004 NFL season.)

10 Who Became Pro Football Stars

Doak Walker (Southern Methodist U./RB, 1948): all-round runner, passer, receiver, kicker, kick returner, and defensive back; NFL scoring leader, 1950, 1955; Pro Football Hall of Fame, 1986.

Paul Hornung (Notre Dame/QB, 1956): versatile ball carrier, receiver, and kicker; NFL MVP, 1961; NFL scoring leader, 1959-61; most points, season, 176 in 1960 (1st); NFL Hall of Fame, 1986. Known as the "Golden Boy," Hornung is the only player who won the Heisman while a member of a losing team (2-8-0).

Roger Staubach (Navy/QB, 1963): Super Bowl MVP, 1972; NFC passing leader, 1971, 1973, 1977-79; Pro Football Hall of Fame, 1985.

Jim Plunkett (Stanford/QB, 1970): AFC Rookie of the Year, 1971; Super Bowl MVP, 1981.

Tony Dorsett (U. Pittsburgh/RB, 1976): NFC Rookie of the Year, 1977; NFC rushing yds leader, 1982; rushing yds, career, 12,739 (5th); longest run from scrimmage, 99 yds in 1983 (1st); Pro Football Hall of Fame, 1994.

Earl Campbell (U. Texas/RB, 1977): AFC Rookie of the Year, 1978; NFL MVP, 1979; AFC rushing yds leader, 1978-81; most games 200+ yds rushing in a season, 4 in 1980 (1st); Pro Football Hall of Fame, 1991.

Marcus Allen (U. Southern California/RB, 1981): NFL Rookie of the Year, 1982; Super Bowl MVP, 1984; AFC rushing yds leader, 1985; rushing TDs, career, 123 (2nd); rushing yds, career, 12,243 (8th); Pro Football Hall of Fame, 2003.

Doug Flutie* (Boston Coll./QB, 1984): in 8 seasons (1990-97) with the Canadian Football League, CFL Outstanding Player Award 1991-94, 96-97; Grey Cup MVP, 1992, 1996-97; CFL passing yds leader, 1991, 1993-94, 1996-97.

Tim Brown* (Notre Dame/WR, 1987): pass receptions, career, 1,070 (3rd); pass receiving yds, career, 14,734 (2nd); most seasons, 1,000+ yds pass receiving, 9 (2nd).

Barry Sanders (Oklahoma St./RB, 1988): NFL Rookie of the Year, 1989; NFL MVP, 1997 (tied with Brett Favre); NFC rushing yds leader, 1989-90, 1994, 1996-97; rushing yds, career, 15,269 (3rd); rushing yds, season, 2,053 in 1997 (3rd); most games, 100+ yds, season, 14 in 1997 (1st); Pro Football Hall of Fame, 2004.

5 Who Achieved Success in Other Fields

Pete Dawkins (Army/HB, 1958): Rhodes Scholar, Oxford, 1959-62; Ph.D., Princeton, 1979; career military officer (Vietnam, 1965-66), retiring in 1983 with the rank of brigadier general; became a millionaire as an investment banker and financial executive.

Tom Harmon (Michigan/HB, 1940): awarded Silver Star and Purple Heart as a bomber and fighter pilot in World War II; became nationally known as a network sports broadcaster, 1947-88.

Bo Jackson (Auburn/RB, 1985): played major league baseball for 8 seasons (1986-91, 1993-94), with 141 career HRs and 415 RBIs.

Steve Spurrier (Florida/QB, 1966): coached Florida Gators to national college football championship in 1996 and had a record of 122-27-1 in 12 seasons (1990-2001).

Charlie Ward (Florida St./QB, 1993): Natl. Basketball Assn. guard (1994-present) primarily with the New York Knicks.

3 Whose Lives Were Touched by Tragedy

Ernie Davis (Syracuse/HB, 1961): 1st African-American to win the Heisman; died of leukemia in 1963.

Vic Janowicz (Ohio St./HB, 1950): finished 2nd in NFL scoring with 88 pts in 1955; pro sports career ended when he suffered a brain injury in a near-fatal auto accident in 1956.

Nile Kinnick (Iowa/HB, 1939): fighter pilot in World War II; missing and presumed dead after his plane crashed on a training mission, June 1943.

1 Who Became Notorious

O.J. Simpson (U. Southern California/RB, 1968): won Heisman by largest margin ever; NFL MVP, 1973; 1st pro player to rush for 2,000+ yds in a season, 1973; AFC rushing yds leader, 1972-73, 1975-76; Pro Football Hall of Fame, 1985. Simpson, a sports broadcaster and media celebrity, was accused in 1994 of murdering his ex-wife, Nicole Brown Simpson, and her friend Ronald Goldman; he was acquitted in a criminal trial in 1995, but a civil jury in 1997 found him liable for the 2 deaths and required him to pay $33.5 million in damages to the victims' families. His Heisman Trophy, surrendered to the court, brought $230,000 at auction 2 years later.

Some Who Never Got a Heisman

1935-60: For the first 26 years of Heisman balloting, no African-American won the trophy. Among those passed over was **Jim Brown** (Syracuse/HB), who led the NFL in rushing 8 years (1957-61, 1963-65) and entered the Pro Football Hall of Fame in 1971. Brown's highest Heisman ranking was 5th in 1956, the year Hornung won.

1964: John Huarte (Notre Dame/QB) had an unexceptional pro career, after which he founded a tile, marble, and granite countertop distributing company. Passed over that year were seniors **Dick Butkus** (Illinois, C-LB), **Gale Sayers** (Kansas/RB), and **Joe Namath** (Alabama/QB)—all now in the Pro Football Hall of Fame.

1967: Gary Beban (UCLA/QB) threw 1 pass in 3 seasons in the NFL before launching a career as a property and investment specialist. **Simpson**, who took 2nd place as a junior in 1967, won the award the following year. Finishing 4th in 1967 was senior **Larry Csonka** (Syracuse/FB), who propelled the Miami Dolphins to two Super Bowl championships (1973-74) and entered the Pro Football Hall of Fame in 1987.

1989: Andre Ware (U. Houston/QB) won the Heisman as a junior; finishing 7th that year was another junior, **Emmitt Smith** (Florida/RB). Ware flopped in both the NFL and the CFL; after retiring from pro football in 1999, he became a computer consultant and sports broadcaster. After 14 seasons in the NFL, Smith ranked 1st in career yds rushing (17,418) and rushing TDs (155).

1992: Gino Torretta (U. Miami, FL/QB) was picked 192nd in the NFL draft and played in just 2 games as a pro; he has pursued a career in financial asset management. The 1992 runner-up, sophomore **Marshall Faulk*** (San Diego St./RB), came in 4th behind **Ward** in 1993. Faulk was NFL Rookie of the Year in 1994 and MVP in 2000.

Other Heisman Facts

Seven Heisman winners have been picked 1st in the NFL draft: **Carson Palmer*** (U. Southern California/QB, 2002), by the Cincinnati Bengals, 2003; **Vinny Testaverde*** (U. Miami, FL/QB, 1986), by Tampa Bay, 1987; **Bo Jackson**, by Tampa Bay, 1986; **George Rogers** (South Carolina/RB, 1980), by New Orleans, 1981; **Billy Sims** (Oklahoma/RB, 1978), by Detroit, 1980; **Earl Campbell**, by Houston, 1978; and **Jim Plunkett**, by New England, 1971.

More players from Notre Dame (7) have won the Heisman than from any other school. Ohio St. has produced 6 different winners, U. Southern California 5, and Oklahoma 4. Two of the first three winners were from Yale; no Ivy Leaguer has won the award since **Dick Kazmaier** (Princeton/RB, 1951).

The oldest player ever to win the Heisman was **Chris Weinke*** (Florida St./QB, 2000), who was 28 when selected. He played minor league baseball for 6 years in the Toronto Blue Jays organization before enrolling in college in 1997.

Archie Griffin (Ohio St./RB) was the only player to win the Heisman Trophy twice; he finished 5th in the balloting in 1973 before coming in 1st in 1974 and 1975. Three others players placed in the top 5 for 3 consecutive years: **Doc Blanchard** (Army/FB), who was 3rd in 1944, 1st in 1945, and 4th in 1946; **Doak Walker**, 3rd in 1947, 1st in 1948, and 3rd in 1949; and **Herschel Walker** (Georgia/RB), 3rd as a freshman in 1980, 2nd in 1981, and 1st in 1982.

Running backs (41) and quarterbacks (23) predominated among the first 69 winners; one trophy holder, **Les Horvath** (Ohio St./1944) was listed as both. The 1st defensive specialist to win the Heisman was cornerback **Charles Woodson*** (Michigan, 1997).

Yvonne Ameche Davis is the only woman known to have married 2 Heisman winners. The widow of **Alan Ameche** (Wisconsin/FB, 1954), she married **Glenn Davis** (Army/HB, 1946) in 1996; the couple became acquainted at Heisman ceremonies.

GENERAL INDEX

Note: Page numbers in **boldface** indicate key reference. Page numbers in *italics* indicate photos.

CROSSWORD PUZZLE ANSWERS

ACROSS: 1. Zinc, 5 Saki, 9 Raid, 13 A Lee, 14 Egan, 15 Nancy, 16 Hit record, 18 Elton, 19 Nestle, 20 Lifeline, 22 Aida, 24 Audi, 25 Chisels, 28 Eleven, 32 Rain, 33 Double date, 35 Ant, 36 NNE, 37 Pat, 38 Good figure, 43 Both, 44 Senora, 45 Peppers, 47 Gems, 49 Tile, 50 End table, 54 Tut tut, 58 Derek, 59 Autograph, 61 Nanas, 62 Cram, 63 Erte, 64 Atom, 65 Kobe, 66 Doom

DOWN: 1 Zahn, 2 Ilie, 3 Nets, 4 Certain, 5 Seceded, 6 Ago, 7 Karl, 8 India, 9 Rallied, 10 Anti, 11 Icon, 12 Dyne, 15 Needle, 17 Elis, 21 Fuel, 23 Along, 25 Canoe, 26 Hit on, 27 Sunup, 29 Vapor, 30 Etats, 31 Neth, 32 Rags, 34 Beret, 39 Dog team, 40 Freaks, 41 I am b, 42 Epitome, 43 Beet red, 46 Plug, 48 Slack, 50 Edna, 51 Neat, 52 Dr No, 53 Euro, 55 Taro, 56 Up to, 57 Them, 60 Tab

SPORTS QUICK REFERENCE INDEX

FOR COMPLETE INDEX, SEE PAGES 979-1007.

WORLD ALMANAC QUICK QUIZ ANSWERS

73–d; **88**–c; **99**–a, c, d, b; **104**–b, a, c, d; **145**–a, c, b, d; **148**–b; **153**–c, b, d, a; **154**–d, a, c, b; **178**–c, b, a, d; **201**–d, b, a, c; **218**–b; **231**–a, b, c, d; **239**–d, a, b, c; **247**–a; **265**–a, b, c, d; **324**–c; **341**–c, a, d, b; **343**–b; **383**–b; **387**–b, d, a, c; **388**–a; **407**–b, a, d, c; **411**–c, a, d, b; **413**–a; **442**–b; **455**–b, d, a, c; **480**–a; **510**–d; **515**–b, c, a, d; **520**–a; **530**–b; **544**–c, b, a, d; **552**–d, b, a, c; **572**–d; **575**–d; **586**–d; **587**–d; **610**–a; **613**–d; **633**–a; **691**–d; **698**–d, c; **705**–d; **723**–d, c, a, b; **725**–b; **734**–b; **775**–a, c, d; **847**–a; **950**–a, d, b, c